S0-ADO-621

Headquarters USA®

Directory of Contact Information for Headquarters and Other Central Offices of Major Businesses & Organizations in the United States and in Canada

2012

34th EDITION

Volume 2:
Classification by Subject

Mailing Address, Telephone Numbers, Toll-Free Phone Numbers, Fax Numbers, and World Wide Web Addreses for:

- AssociationsFoundations, and Similar Orgnization
- Busiesses, Idustries, and Professions of All Type
- Collges, Uniersities, Vocational & Techical Schols, and Other Educational Institutions
- Electonic Resurces, including Internet Compnies, Organizations, and Web Sites
- Embasies, Consulates, and UN Missions & Agencs
- Goverment Agencies & Offices at All Levels– City, County, State, Federal
- Libraries, Museums & Galleries, Zoos & Botanical Gardens, Performing Arts Organizations & Facilities, and Other Cultural Institutions
- Media Newspapers, Magazines, Newsletters; and Radio & Television Companies, Networks, Stations and Syndicators
- Research Centers & Organizations, including Scientific, Public Policy, and Market Research
- Professional Sports Teams, Other Sports Organizations, and Sports Facilities

And also iluding an Area/Zip Code Guide Covering more than 10,000 US Cities and Towns, as well as Area Code ables in State & Numerical Order; and a detailed Index to Classified Headings under which listings arerganized in the Directory's Classified Section

Rich's Business Directories Inc

Rich's Business Directories Inc.

Julia Leeper, *Editor*

* * *

Yeshwant Sai, *Research Manager*

ISBN 978-1-934228-52-4

ISSN 1531-2909

Printed in the United States of America

RICH'S BUSINESS DIRECTORIES INC.
General Correspondence: 1820 Gateway Drive, Suite 170, San Mateo CA 94404
Phone Orders: 800-234-1340 • Fax Orders: 800-875-1340
Mail Orders: P.O. Box 8002 • Ashton, PA 19014-8002
Internet Orders: www.omnigraphics.com

Table of Contents

Volume 1:
Alphabetical by Organization Name

Volume 2:
Classified by Subject

Classified Headings Table

Listed here are all of the headings under which listings are categorized in the Classified Section of this directory. The headings are numbered sequentially, and these numbers correspond to those printed in the "Class' column that accompanies listings in the Alphabetical Section. Just match the number in the "Class" column to the corresponding number printed in this table in order to identify the type of business or organization of any white pages listing. Use this table, too, to locate the page on which that subject category appears in the classified section.

For a more detailed list of classified headings, including "See" and "See also" references, please see the Index to Classified Headings at the back of this book.

A

B

Still can't find what you're looking for? *For a more detailed subject selection, see the Index to Classified Headings at the back of this directory.*

C

Still can't find what you're looking for? *For a more detailed subject selection, see the Index to Classified Headings at the back of this directory.*

Still can't find what you're looking for? *For a more detailed subject selection, see the Index to Classified Headings at the back of this directory.*

Still can't find what you're looking for? *For a more detailed subject selection, see the Index to Classified Headings at the back of this directory.*

Still can't find what you're looking for? *For a more detailed subject selection, see the Index to Classified Headings at the back of this directory.*

Still can't find what you're looking for? *For a more detailed subject selection, see the Index to Classified Headings at the back of this directory.*

S

T

Still can't find what you're looking for? *For a more detailed subject selection, see the Index to Classified Headings at the back of this directory.*

U

V

W

Z

Still can't find what you're looking for? *For a more detailed subject selection, see the Index to Classified Headings at the back of this directory.*

Classified Section

Listings in the Classified Section are organized alphabetically (or, where noted, by city or state names) under subject headings denoting a business or organization type. Alphabetizing is on a word-by-word rather than letter-by-letter basis.

For a detailed explanation of the scope and arrangement of listings, please refer to “"How to Use This Directory' at the beginning of this book. Page elements and listing formats are illustrated on the sample pages with accompanying explanatory notes found just inside the back cover.

1 ABRASIVE PRODUCTS

Company	City	State	Zip	Phone	Fax
3M Abrasive Systems Div 3M Ctr Bldg 0223-06-N-01 *TF:* 800-742-9546 ■ *Web:* www.3m.com/product/business-units/abrasive-systems.html	Saint Paul	MN	55144	651-737-6501	737-7117
3M Mfg & Industry Solutions 3M Ctr. *TF:* 888-364-3577 ■ *Web:* solutions.3m.com/wps/portal/3M/en_US/Products/ProdServ/Dir/Mfg-Ind	Saint Paul	MN	55144	651-733-1110	733-9973
Acme Holding Co 24200 Marmon Ave *Web:* www.acmeabrasive.com	Warren	MI	48089	586-759-6555	759-3334
Asw Holding Corp 1540 E Dundee Rd Suite 210 *Web:* www.gmt-inc.com	Palatine	IL	60074	847-202-7000	215-4838
Avery Abrasives Inc 2225 Reservoir Ave **Fax:* Cust Svc ■ *Web:* www.averyabrasives.com	Trumbull	CT	06611	203-372-3513	372-3714*
Basic Carbide Corp 900 Main St *TF:* 800-426-4291 ■ *Web:* www.basiccarbide.com	Lowber	PA	15660	724-446-1630	446-1656
Bullard Abrasives Inc 6 Carol Dr *TF:* 800-227-4469 ■ *Web:* www.bullardabrasives.com	Lincoln	RI	02865	401-333-3000	333-3077
Camel Grinding Wheels 7525 N Oak Pk Ave *TF:* 800-447-4248 ■ *Web:* www.cgwheels.com	Niles	IL	60714	847-647-5994	647-1861
Comco Inc 2151 N Lincoln St *TF:* 800-796-6626 ■ *Web:* www.comcoinc.com	Burbank	CA	91504	818-841-5500	955-8365
Composition Materials Co Inc 249 Pepes Farm Rd *TF:* 800-262-7763 ■ *Web:* www.compomat.com	Milford	CT	06460	203-874-6500	874-6505
Diagrind Inc 10491 164th Pl *TF:* 800-790-4333 ■ *Web:* www.diagrind.com	Orland Park	IL	60467	708-460-4333	460-8842
Diamond Innovations 6325 Huntley Rd *TF Cust Svc:* 800-443-1955 ■ *Web:* www.abrasivesnet.com	Columbus	OH	43229	614-438-2000	438-2931
Eagle Grinding Wheel Corp 2519 W Fulton St *Web:* www.eaglegrindingwheel.com	Chicago	IL	60612	312-733-1770	733-5949
Ervin Industries Inc 3893 Research Pk Dr *TF:* 800-748-0055 ■ *Web:* www.ervinindustries.com	Ann Arbor	MI	48108	734-769-4600	663-0136
Formax Mfg Corp 168 Wealthy St SW *TF:* 800-242-2833 ■ *Web:* www.formaxmfg.com	Grand Rapids	MI	49503	616-456-5458	456-7507
Garfield Industries 62 Clinton Rd *Web:* www.polishingbuffs.com	Fairfield	NJ	07004	973-575-8800	575-6840
Gemtex Abrasives 60 Belfield Rd **Fax Area Code:* 416 ■ *TF:* 800-387-5100 ■ *Web:* www.gemtexabrasives.com	Toronto	ON	M9W1G1	800-873-1811	245-3723*
Glit/Microtron 809 Broad St PO Box 709 **Fax Area Code:* 706 ■ *TF:* 800-325-1051 ■ *Web:* www.glit-microtron.com	Wrens	GA	30833	314-739-8585	547-6367*
Hermes Abrasives Ltd PO Box 2389 *Web:* www.hermesabrasives.com	Virginia Beach	VA	23450	757-486-6623	431-2372
JacksonLea 1715 Conover Blvd E PO Box 699 *TF:* 800-438-6880 ■ *Web:* www.jacksonlea.com	Conover	NC	28613	828-464-1376	464-7094
Kennametal Inc 2879 Aero Pk Dr **Fax:* Sales ■ *TF:* 800-662-2131 ■ *Web:* www.kennametal.com	Traverse City	MI	49686	231-946-2100	946-3025*
Marvel Abrasive Products Inc 6230 S Oak Pk Ave *TF:* 800-621-0673 ■ *Web:* www.marvelabrasives.com	Chicago	IL	60638	773-586-8700	586-0187
Modern Abrasive Corp PO Box 219 *Web:* www.modernabrasive.com	Spring Grove	IL	60081	815-675-2352	675-2822
Mosher Co 15 Exchange St *Web:* www.mocomfg.com	Chicopee	MA	01014	413-598-8341	594-7647
Moyco Technologies Inc 200 Commerce Dr *TF:* 800-331-8837	Montgomeryville	PA	18936	215-855-4300	362-3809
Pacific Grinding Wheel Co 13120 State Ave **Fax Area Code:* 800 ■ *TF:* 800-688-9328 ■ *Web:* www.pacificgrindingwheel.com	Marysville	WA	98271	360-659-6201	659-6654*
Precision H2O Inc 6328 E Utah Ave *TF:* 800-425-2098 ■ *Web:* www.precisionh2o.com	Spokane	WA	99212	509-536-9214	536-9205
Radiac Abrasives Inc 1015 S College Ave **Fax:* Cust Svc ■ *TF:* 800-851-1095 ■ *Web:* www.radiac.com	Salem	IL	62881	618-548-4200	548-4207*
Raytech Industries 475 Smith St *TF Cust Svc:* 800-243-7163 ■ *Web:* www.raytech-ind.com	Middletown	CT	06457	860-632-2020	632-1699
Red Hill Grinding Wheel Corp PO Box 150	Pennsburg	PA	18073	215-679-7964	679-3715
Saint-Gobain Abrasives Inc 2770 W Washington St *Web:* www.nortonconstructionproducts.com	Stephenville	TX	76401	254-918-2310	918-2312
Sancap Abrasives 16123 Armour St NE *TF:* 800-433-6663 ■ *Web:* www.sancapabrasives.com	Alliance	OH	44601	330-821-3510	821-3516
Sandusky-Chicago Abrasive Wheel Co 1100 W Barker Ave *TF:* 800-843-4980 ■ *Web:* www.sanduskychicago.com	Michigan City	IN	46360	219-879-6601	872-8139
Schaffner Mfg Co Inc 21 Herron Ave Schaffner Ctr *TF:* 800-292-9903 ■ *Web:* www.schaffnermfg.com	Pittsburgh	PA	15202	412-761-9902	761-8998
Spedecut Abrasives 10042 Rancho Rd *Web:* www.spedecut.com	Adelanto	CA	92301	760-246-6850	246-6889
Stan Sax Corp 101 S Waterman St *Web:* www.stansaxcorp.com	Detroit	MI	48209	313-841-7170	841-7235
Superior Abrasives Inc 4800 Wadsworth Rd *TF:* 800-235-9123 ■ *Web:* www.superiorabrasives.com	Dayton	OH	45414	937-278-9123	278-7581
Trumbull Industries Inc 400 Dietz Rd NE *TF:* 800-477-1799 ■ *Web:* www.trumbull.com	Warren	OH	44482	330-393-6624	399-4421
TYROLIT Wickman Inc 10325 Capital Ave *TF:* 800-366-4431 ■ *Web:* www.wickmancorp.com	Oak Park	MI	48237	248-548-3822	548-3831
United Abrasives Inc 185 Boston Post Rd *Web:* www.unitedabrasives.com	North Windham	CT	06256	860-456-7131	456-8341
VSM Abrasives 1012 E Wabash St *TF Cust Svc:* 800-737-0176 ■ *Web:* www.vsmabrasives.com	O'Fallon	MO	63366	636-272-7432	272-7434
Washington Mills Electro Minerals Co 20 N Main St *Web:* www.washingtonmills.com	North Grafton	MA	01536	508-839-6511	839-7675

2 ACCOUNTING FIRMS

Company	City	State	Zip	Phone	Fax
Anchin Block & Anchin LLP 1375 Broadway 18th Fl *Web:* www.anchin.com	New York	NY	10018	212-840-3456	840-7066
Argy Wiltse & Robinson PC 8405 Greensboro Dr Suite 700 *Web:* www.argy.com	McLean	VA	22102	703-893-0600	893-2766
Arledge & Assoc Inc 309 N Bryant Ave *Web:* www.jmacpas.com	Edmond	OK	73034	405-348-0615	348-0931
Armanino McKenna LLP 12667 Alcosta Blvd Suite 500 *Web:* www.amllp.com	San Ramon	CA	94583	925-790-2600	790-2601
Aronson & Co 700 King Farm Blvd 3rd Fl *Web:* www.aronsoncompany.com	Rockville	MD	20850	301-231-6200	231-7630
Baker Spindler Holtz 161 Ottawa Ave NW Suite 409-A *Web:* www.bakerspindlerholtz.com	Grand Rapids	MI	49503	616-458-1835	458-1895
Baker Tilly Virchow Krause LLP 205 N Michigan Ave **Fax Area Code:* 608 ■ *Web:* www.bakertilly.com	Chicago	IL	60601	312-729-8000	249-8532*
BDO Seidman LLP 1 Prudential Plaza 130 E Randolph St Suite 2800 *Web:* www.bdo.com	Chicago	IL	60601	312-240-1236	240-3311
Beers & Cutler PLLC 8219 Leesburg Pike Suite 800 *TF Cust Svc:* 877-214-2443 ■ *Web:* www.bakertilly.net	Vienna	VA	22182	703-923-8300	923-8330
Berdon LLP 360 Madison Ave 8th Fl *Web:* www.berdonllp.com	New York	NY	10017	212-832-0400	371-1159
Berkowitz Dick Pollack & Brant LLP 200 S Biscayne Blvd 6th Fl *TF:* 800-999-1272 ■ *Web:* www.bdpb.com	Miami	FL	33131	305-379-7000	379-8200
BKD LLP 901 E St Louis St Suite 1800 *Web:* www.bkd.com	Springfield	MO	65806	417-831-7283	831-4763
Blackman Kallick 10 S Riverside Plaza Suite 900 *Web:* www.blackmankallick.com	Chicago	IL	60606	312-207-1040	207-1066
Blue & Co 12800 N Meridian St Suite 400 *TF:* 800-717-2568 ■ *Web:* www.blueandco.com	Carmel	IN	46032	317-848-8920	573-2458
Blum Shapiro 29 S Main St 4th Fl *TF:* 800-561-6889 ■ *Web:* www.bshapiro.com	West Hartford	CT	06107	860-561-4000	521-9241
Bonadio Group The 171 Sully's Trail Suite 201 *Web:* www.bonadio.com	Pittsford	NY	14534	585-381-1000	381-3131
Burr Pilger & Mayer LLP (BPMLLP) 600 California St Suite 1300 *Web:* www.bpmllp.com	San Francisco	CA	94108	415-421-5757	288-6288
C J Schlosser & Co LLC 233 E Ctr Dr PO Box 416 *Web:* www.cjsco.com	Alton	IL	62002	618-465-7717	465-7710
Carlin Charron & Rosen LLP (CCRLLP) 1400 Computer Dr *TF:* 800-888-2102 ■ *Web:* www.ccrllp.com	Westborough	MA	01581	508-926-2200	616-2972
Carr Riggs & Ingram LLC 1117 Boll Weevil Cir PO Box 311070 *Web:* www.cricpa.com	Enterprise	AL	36331	334-347-0088	347-7650
CBIZ Inc 6050 Oak Tree Blvd S Suite 500 *NASDAQ:* CBIZ ■ *Web:* www.cbizinc.com	Cleveland	OH	44131	216-447-9000	447-9007
CBIZ Tofias PC 350 Massachusetts Ave *TF:* 888-761-8835 ■ *Web:* www.cbiz.com	Cambridge	MA	02139	617-761-0600	761-0601
Certipay 199 Ave B NW Suite 270 *TF:* 800-422-3782 ■ *Web:* www.certipay.com	Winter Haven	FL	33881	863-299-2400	299-2131
Cherry Bekaert & Holland LLP 1700 Bayberry Ct Suite 300 *TF:* 800-849-8281 ■ *Web:* www.cbh.com	Richmond	VA	23226	804-673-4224	673-4290

	City	State	Zip	Phone	Fax
Citrin Cooperman & Co LLP 529 5th Ave 2nd Fl *Web:* www.citrincooperman.com	New York	NY	10017	212-697-1000	697-1004
Clark Nuber PS 10900 NE 4th St Suite 1700 *TF:* 800-504-8747 ■ *Web:* www.clarknuber.com	Bellevue	WA	98004	425-454-4919	454-4620
Clark Schaefer Hackett & Co 160 N Breiel Blvd *Web:* www.cshco.com	Middletown	OH	45042	513-424-5000	422-7882
Clayton & Mckervey PC 2000 Town Ctr Suite 1800 *Web:* www.claytonmckervey.com	Southfield	MI	48075	248-208-8860	208-9115
Clifton Gunderson LLP 301 SW Adams St Suite 900 *Web:* www.cliftoncpa.com	Peoria	IL	61602	309-671-4500	671-4508
CompuPay Inc 3450 Lakeside Dr Suite 400 *Fax Area Code: 866 ■ *TF:* 877-729-6299 ■ *Web:* www.compupay.com	Miramar	FL	33027	954-874-4800	821-1535*
Deloitte & Touche USA LLP 1633 Broadway *Web:* www.deloitte.com	New York	NY	10019	212-489-1600	489-1687
Deloitte Touche Tohmatsu 1633 Broadway *Web:* www.deloitte.com	New York	NY	10019	212-489-1600	492-4154
Dixon Hughes PLLC 500 Ridgefield Ct *TF:* 800-425-7182 ■ *Web:* www.dhgllp.com	Asheville	NC	28806	828-254-2254	254-6859
Doeren Mayhew 755 W Big Beaver Rd Suite 2300 *Web:* www.doeren.com	Troy	MI	48084	248-244-3000	244-3090
Ehrhardt Keefe Steiner & Hottman PC 7979 E Tufts Ave Suite 400 *TF:* 888-740-9400 ■ *Web:* www.eksh.com	Denver	CO	80237	303-740-9400	740-9009
Eide Bailly LLP 3203 32nd Ave *TF:* 888-777-9552 ■ *Web:* www.eidebailly.com	Fargo	ND	58103	701-239-8500	239-8600
Eisner LLP 750 3rd Ave *Web:* www.eisnerllp.com	New York	NY	10017	212-949-8700	891-4100
Elliott Davis LLC 200 E Broad St PO Box 6286 *TF:* 800-503-4721 ■ *Web:* www.elliottdavis.com	Greenville	SC	29606	864-242-3370	232-7161
Ennis Pellum & Assoc Cpas 5150 Belfort Rd S Bldg 600 *Web:* www.jaxcpa.com	Jacksonville	FL	32256	904-396-5965	399-4094
Ernst & Young Ernst & Young Tower 222 Bay St PO Box 251 *TF:* 800-291-3380 ■ *Web:* www.ey.com	Toronto	ON	M5K1J7	416-864-1234	864-1174
Ernst & Young 5 Times Sq *Fax: Mail Rm ■ *Web:* www.ey.com	New York	NY	10036	212-773-3000	773-6350*
Federal Management Systems Inc 462 K St NW *Web:* www.fmshq.com	Washington	DC	20001	202-842-3003	829-4470
Fiducial 1370 Avenue of the Americas 31st Fl *TF:* 866-343-8242 ■ *Web:* www.fiducial.com	New York	NY	10019	212-207-4700	308-2613
Frank Rimerman & Co LLP 1801 Page Mill Rd *Web:* www.frankrimerman.com	Palo Alto	CA	94304	650-845-8100	494-1975
Friedman LLP 1700 Broadway *Web:* www.friedmanllp.com	New York	NY	10019	212-842-7000	842-7001
Gallagher Flynn & Co LLP 55 Community Dr *Web:* www.gfc.com	South Burlington	VT	05403	802-863-1331	651-7305
Gillispie & Ogilbee Pc 4400 N Meridian Ave *Web:* www.gocpas.com	Oklahoma City	OK	73112	405-947-3030	942-0017
Grant Thornton International Ltd 175 W Jackson Blvd 20th Fl *Web:* www.gti.org	Chicago	IL	60604	312-856-0200	602-8099
Grant Thornton LLP 175 W Jackson Blvd 20th Fl *Web:* www.grantthornton.com	Chicago	IL	60604	312-856-0001	602-8099
Habif Arogeti & Wynne LLP 5 Concourse Pkwy NE *TF:* 800-792-9651 ■ *Web:* www.hawcpa.com	Atlanta	GA	30342	404-892-9651	
Hartman Blitch & Gartside 4929 Atlantic Blvd *Web:* www.hbgcpa.com	Jacksonville	FL	32207	904-396-9802	396-1528
Hein & Assoc LLP 717 17th St Suite 1600 *Web:* www.heincpa.com	Denver	CO	80202	303-298-9600	298-8118
Hill Barth & King LLC 7680 Market St *TF:* 800-733-8613 ■ *Web:* www.hbkcpa.com	Boardman	OH	44512	330-758-8613	758-0357
Holthouse Carlin & Van Trigt LLP 1601 Cloverfield Blvd Suite 300-S *Web:* www.hcvt.com	Santa Monica	CA	90404	310-566-1900	566-1901
Holtz Rubenstein Reminick LLP 125 Baylis Rd *Web:* www.hrcpa.com	Melville	NY	11747	631-752-7400	752-1742
Honkamp Krueger & Co PC 2345 JFK Rd PO Box 699 *TF:* 888-556-0123 ■ *Web:* www.honkamp.com	Dubuque	IA	52004	563-556-0123	556-8762
Horne LLP 200 E Capitol St Suite 1400 *Web:* www.horne-llp.com	Jackson	MS	39201	601-948-0940	355-6521
House Park & Dobratz Pc 605 W 47th St Suite 301 *Web:* www.hpdco.com	Kansas City	MO	64112	816-931-3393	931-9636
JH Cohn LLP 4 Becker Farm Rd *TF:* 800-879-2571 ■ *Web:* www.jhcohn.com	Roseland	NJ	07068	973-228-3500	228-0330
John Gerlach & Co LLP 37 W Broad St Suite 530 *Web:* www.johngerlach.com	Columbus	OH	43215	614-224-2164	224-1391
Johnson & Mackowiak 70 E Main St *Web:* www.chaut-cpas.com	Fredonia	NY	14063	716-672-4770	679-1512
Johnson Lambert & Co. LLP 700 Spring Forest Rd *Web:* www.jlco.com	Raleigh	NC	27609	919-719-6400	
Joseph Decosimo & Co PLLC 2 Union Sq Tallan Bldg Suite 1100 *TF:* 800-782-8382 ■ *Web:* www.decosimo.com	Chattanooga	TN	37402	423-756-7100	756-2939
JPMS Cox PLLC 11300 Cantrell Rd Suite 301 *Web:* www.jpmscpa.com	Little Rock	AR	72212	501-227-5800	227-5851
Katz Sapper & Miller 800 E 96th St Suite 500 *Web:* www.ksmcpa.com	Indianapolis	IN	46240	317-580-2000	580-2117
Kaufman Rossin & Co PA 2699 S Bayshore Dr Suite 300 *Web:* www.krco-cpa.com	Miami	FL	33133	305-858-5600	856-3284
Keefe McCullough & Co LLP Certified Public Accountants 6550 N Federal Hwy Suite 410 *Web:* www.kmccpa.com	Fort Lauderdale	FL	33308	954-771-0896	938-9353
Kennedy & Coe LLC 3030 Cortland Cir PO Box 1100 *TF:* 800-967-0098 ■ *Web:* www.kcoe.com	Salina	KS	67402	785-825-1561	825-5371
KPMG LLP US 3 Chestnut Ridge Rd *Web:* www.kpmg.com	Montvale	NJ	07645	201-307-7000	307-7575
Lane Gorman Trubitt LLP 2626 Howell St Suite 700 *Web:* www.lgt-cpa.com	Dallas	TX	75204	214-871-7500	871-0011
LarsonAllen LLP 220 S 6th St Suite 300 *TF:* 888-335-6080 ■ *Web:* www.larsonallen.com	Minneapolis	MN	55402	612-376-4500	376-4850
Lattimore Black Morgan & Cain PC 5250 Virginia Way *Web:* www.lbmc.com	Brentwood	TN	37027	615-377-4600	309-2500
LeMaster Daniels PLLC 601 W Riverside Ave Suite 700 *TF:* 866-622-5553 ■ *Web:* www.lemasterdaniels.com	Spokane	WA	99201	509-624-4315	624-8874
Lipsey Youngren Means Ogren & Sandberg LLP 525 B St Suite 1400 *Web:* www.lymscpa.com	San Diego	CA	92101	619-234-0877	234-9319
Lumsden & McCormick LLP 403 Main St Suite 430 *TF:* 888-586-7336 ■ *Web:* www.lumsdencpa.com	Buffalo	NY	14203	716-856-3300	856-2524
Lurie Besikof Lapidus & Co LLP 2501 Wayzata Blvd *Web:* www.lblco.com	Minneapolis	MN	55405	612-377-4404	377-1325
Margolin Winer & Evens LLP 400 Garden City Plaza 5th Fl *Web:* www.mwellp.com	Garden City	NY	11530	516-747-2000	747-6707
Marks Paneth & Shron LLP 622 3rd Ave 7th Fl *Web:* www.markspaneth.com	New York	NY	10017	212-503-8800	212-3759
Mauldin & Jenkins Certified Public Accountants LLC 200 Galleria Pkwy SE *Fax Area Code: 229 ■ *Web:* www.mjcpa.com	Atlanta	GA	30339	770-955-8600	446-3664*
McCrory & Mcdowell LLC 20 Stanwix St 9th FL *Web:* www.mccmcd.com	Pittsburgh	PA	15222	412-281-9690	281-5925
McKonly & Asbury LLP 415 Fallowfield Rd *Web:* www.macpas.com	Camp Hill	PA	17011	717-761-7910	761-7944
Moore Stephens Lovelace PA 1201 S Orlando Ave Suite 400 *TF:* 800-683-5401 ■ *Web:* www.mslcpa.com	Winter Park	FL	32789	407-740-5400	740-0012
Morrison Brown Argiz & Farra LLP 1001 Brickell Bay Dr 9th Fl *TF:* 800-239-3843 ■ *Web:* www.mbafcpa.com	Miami	FL	33131	305-373-5500	373-0056
Moss Adams LLP 999 3rd Ave Suite 2800 *Web:* www.mossadams.com	Seattle	WA	98104	206-302-6500	622-9975
Novogradac & Co LLP 246 1st St 5th Fl *Web:* www.novoco.com	San Francisco	CA	94105	415-356-8000	356-8001
Null - Lairson PC 3411 Richmond Ave Suite 500 *Web:* www.null-lairson.com	Houston	TX	77046	713-621-1515	621-1570
O'Connor Davies Munns & Dobbins LLP 60 E 42nd St 36th Fl *Web:* www.odmd.com	New York	NY	10165	212-286-2600	286-4080
Ostrow Reisin Berk & Abrams Ltd 455 N Cityfront Plaza Dr *Web:* www.orba.com	Chicago	IL	60611	312-670-7444	670-8301
Padgett Business Services 160 Hawthorne Pk *TF:* 800-723-4388 ■ *Web:* www.smallbizpros.com	Athens	GA	30606	706-548-1040	543-8537
Pannell Kerr Forster Of Texas Pc 5847 San Felipe St *Web:* www.pkftexas.com	Houston	TX	77057	713-860-1400	355-3909
Parente Randolph LLC 1650 Market St 1 Liberty Pl *Web:* www.parentenet.com	Philadelphia	PA	19103	215-972-0701	563-4925
PAYCOR INC 644 Linn St Suite 200 *Web:* www.paycor.com	Cincinnati	OH	45203	513-381-0505	381-4219
Peachin Schwartz & Weingardt Pc 9449 Priority Way W Dr Suite 150 *Web:* www.psw-cpa.com	Indianapolis	IN	46240	317-574-4280	574-4286
Pearce Bevill Leesburg & Moore Pc 110 Office Pk Dr *Web:* www.pearcebevill.com	Birmingham	AL	35223	205-323-5440	328-8523
Plante & Moran PLLC 27400 Northwestern Hwy *TF:* 800-827-1280 ■ *Web:* www.plantemoran.com	Southfield	MI	48034	248-352-2500	352-0018
PRG-Schultz International Inc 600 Galleria Pkwy Suite 100 *NASDAQ: PRGX* ■ *TF:* 800-752-5894 ■ *Web:* www.prgx.com	Atlanta	GA	30339	770-779-3900	779-3133
PricewaterhouseCoopers LLP 300 Madison Ave *Fax Area Code: 813 ■ *Web:* www.pwc.com	New York	NY	10017	646-471-4000	286-6000*
REA & Assoc Inc 419 W High Ave PO Box 1020 *Web:* www.reacpa.com	New Philadelphia	OH	44663	330-339-6651	308-9506
Rehmann Group 5800 Gratiot St Suite 201 *TF:* 866-799-9580 ■ *Web:* www.rehmann.com	Saginaw	MI	48638	989-799-9580	799-0227
Reznick Group PC 7700 Old Georgetown Rd Suite 400 *Web:* www.rfs.com	Bethesda	MD	20814	301-652-9100	652-1848
RGL Forensic 5619 DTC Pkwy Suite 1010 *Web:* www.rgl.com	Englewood	CO	80111	303-721-8898	721-8936
Rosen Seymour Shapss Martin & Co LLP 757 3rd Ave 6th Fl *Web:* www.rssmcpa.com	New York	NY	10017	212-303-1800	755-5600
Ross Buehler Falk & Co LLP (RBF) 1500 Lititz Pike *Web:* www.rbfco.com	Lancaster	PA	17601	717-393-2700	393-1743

Company	City	State	Zip	Phone	Fax
Rothstein Kass 4 Becker Farm Rd *Web:* www.rkco.com	Roseland	NJ	07068	973-994-6666	994-0337
RSM/McGladrey & Pullen LLP 3600 American Blvd W 3rd Fl *Web:* www.rsmmcgladrey.com	Bloomington	MN	55431	952-921-7700	921-7702
RubinBrown LLP 1 N Brentwood Blvd Suite 1100 *TF:* 800-678-3134 ■ *Web:* www.rubinbrown.com	Saint Louis	MO	63105	314-290-3300	290-3400
S R Snodgrass AC 2100 Corporate Dr Suite 400 *Web:* www.srsnodgrass.com	Wexford	PA	15090	724-934-0344	934-0345
Santa Monica Partners 1865 Palmer Ave Suite 108 *Web:* www.smplp.com	Larchmont	NY	10538	914-833-0875	
SC&H Group LLC 910 Ridgebrook Rd *TF:* 800-832-3008 ■ *Web:* www.scandh.com	Sparks	MD	21152	410-403-1500	403-1570
Schenck Business Solutions 200 E Washington St *TF:* 800-236-2246 ■ *Web:* www.schencksolutions.com	Appleton	WI	54911	920-731-8111	731-8037
Schneider Downs & Co Inc 1133 Penn Ave *Web:* www.schneiderdowns.com	Pittsburgh	PA	15222	412-261-3644	261-4876
Seiler LLP 3 Lagoon Dr Suite 400 *Web:* www.seiler.com	Redwood City	CA	94065	650-365-4646	368-4055
Siegfried Group LLP The 1201 N Market St Suite 700 *TF:* 800-999-1695 ■ *Web:* www.siegfriedgroup.com	Wilmington	DE	19801	302-984-1800	
Sikich LLP 998 Corporate Blvd *TF:* 877-279-1900 ■ *Web:* www.sikich.com/sg	Aurora	IL	60502	630-566-8400	566-8401
Singer Lewak Greenbaum & Goldstein LLP 10960 Wilshire Blvd Suite 1100 *Web:* www.slgg.com	Los Angeles	CA	90024	310-477-3924	478-6070
Squar Milner Peterson Miranda & Williamson LLP 4100 Newport Pl Dr Suite 300 *Web:* www.squarmilner.com	Newport Beach	CA	92660	949-222-2999	222-2989
SS&G Financial Services Inc 32125 Solon Rd *Web:* www.ssandg.com	Solon	OH	44139	440-248-8787	248-0841
Steakley & Gilbert PC 110 N Robinson Ave *Web:* www.cpaokc.net	Oklahoma City	OK	73102	405-235-4400	236-2207
Steudle Spears & Co PSC 2821 S Hurstbourne Pkwy *Web:* www.ssfcpas.com	Louisville	KY	40220	502-491-5253	491-5270
Suby Von Haden & Assoc SC 1221 John Q Hammons Dr *TF:* 800-279-2616 ■ *Web:* www.sva.com	Madison	WI	53717	608-831-8181	831-4243
Talbot Korvola & Warwick LLP 4800 SW Macadam Ave Suite 400 PO Box 69422 *Web:* www.tkw.com	Portland	OR	97239	503-274-2849	274-2853
Teal Becker & Chiramonte (TBC) 7 Washington Sq *Web:* www.tbccpa.com	Albany	NY	12205	518-456-6663	456-3975
Thompson Cobb Bazilio & Assoc Pc 1101 15th St NW Suite 400 *Web:* www.tcba.com	Washington	DC	20005	202-778-3421	737-2684
Tice Brunell & Baker Cpa Pc 14 Corporate Woods Blvd *Web:* www.tbbcpas.com	Albany	NY	12211	518-482-1887	
Timmins Kroll & Jacobson LLP 10550 New York Ave Suite 200 *Web:* www.tkjcpa.com	Des Moines	IA	50322	515-270-8080	276-8329
Toski Schaefer & Co 555 International Dr Suite 100 *Web:* www.toskischaefer.com	Williamsville	NY	14221	716-634-0700	634-0764
UHY Advisors Inc 30 S Wacker Dr Suite 2850 *Web:* www.uhyadvisors-us.com	Chicago	IL	60606	312-578-9600	346-6500
Vavrinek Trine Day & Co LLP 8270 Aspen St *Web:* www.vtdcpa.com	Rancho Cucamonga	CA	91730	909-466-4410	466-4431
Warren Averett Kimbrough & Marino LLC 2500 Acton Rd *Web:* www.wakm.com	Birmingham	AL	35243	205-979-4100	979-6313
Watkins Meegan Drury & Co LLC 7700 Wisconsin Ave Suite 500 *Web:* www.wmdco.com	Bethesda	MD	20814	301-654-7555	656-9115
Weiser LLP 135 W 50th St *Web:* www.mrweiser.com	New York	NY	10020	212-812-7000	375-6888
Williams Benator & Libby LLP 1040 Crown Pinte Pkwy NE Suite 400 *Web:* www.wblcpa.com	Atlanta	GA	30338	770-512-0500	512-0200
Wipfli LLP 10000 Innovation Dr Suite 250 *Web:* www.wipfli.com	Milwaukee	WI	53226	414-431-9300	431-9303
WithumSmith+Brown 5 Vaughn Dr *Web:* www.withum.com	Princeton	NJ	08540	609-520-1188	520-9882

3 ADHESIVES & SEALANTS

Company	City	State	Zip	Phone	Fax
Adco Global Inc 100 Tri State International Suite 135 *Web:* www.adcoglobal.com	Lincolnshire	IL	60069	847-282-3485	282-3481
Adhesives Research Inc 400 Seaks Run Rd PO Box 100 *TF:* 800-445-6240 ■ *Web:* www.adhesivesresearch.com	Glen Rock	PA	17327	717-235-7979	235-8320
Advanced Chemistry & Technology Inc 7341 Anaconda Ave *TF:* 800-284-2551 ■ *Web:* www.actechaero.com	Garden Grove	CA	92841	714-373-2837	677-0043
Arclin 5865 McLaughlin Rd Suite 3 *Web:* www.dynea.com	Mississauga	ON	L5R1B8	905-712-0900	712-0901
Arlon Adhesives & Films 2811 S Harbor Blvd *TF:* 800-540-2811 ■ *Web:* www.arlon.com	Santa Ana	CA	92704	714-540-2811	431-4305
Atlas Minerals & Chemicals Inc 1227 Valley Rd *TF Cust Svc:* 800-523-8269 ■ *Web:* www.atlasmin.com	Mertztown	PA	19539	610-682-7171	682-9200
Avery Dennison Corp 150 N Orange Grove Blvd *NYSE: AVY* ■ *TF Cust Svc:* 800-252-8379 ■ *Web:* www.averydennison.com	Pasadena	CA	91103	626-304-2000	304-2192
Axson North America Inc 1611 Hults Dr *Web:* www.axson-na.com	Eaton Rapids	MI	48827	517-663-8191	663-0523
BASF Corp/Bldg Systems 889 Valley Pk Dr **Fax:* Cust Svc ■ *TF Cust Svc:* 800-433-9517 ■ *Web:* www.buildingsystems.basf.com	Shakopee	MN	55379	952-496-6000	496-6062*
Bemis Assoc Inc 1 Bemis Way *TF:* 800-543-1324 ■ *Web:* www.bemisworldwide.com	Shirley	MA	01464	978-425-6761	425-2278
Bostik Inc 11320 Watertown Plank Rd *TF:* 800-558-4302 ■ *Web:* www.bostik-us.com	Wauwatosa	WI	53226	414-774-2250	774-8075
Br 111 Imports & Exports Inc 12800 NW 107th Ct **Fax Area Code:* 800 ■ *TF:* 800-525-2711 ■ *Web:* www.br111.com	Medley	FL	33178	757-761-4300	577-2711*
Brady Coated Products 6555 W Good Hope Rd **Fax Area Code:* 800 ■ *TF:* 800-635-7557 ■ *Web:* www.coatedproducts.com	Milwaukee	WI	53223	414-358-6600	541-1686*
BW Holdings LLC 180 E Broad St	Columbus	OH	43215	614-225-4000	
CFC International Inc 500 State St *Web:* www.cfcintl.com	Chicago Heights	IL	60411	708-891-3456	758-5989
Chase Corp 26 Summer St *AMEX: CCF* ■ *Web:* www.chasecorp.com	Bridgewater	MA	02324	508-279-1789	697-6419
Chemence Inc 185 Bluegrass Valley Pkwy *Web:* www.chemence.com	Alpharetta	GA	30005	770-664-6624	664-6620
Colloid Environmental Technologies Co (CETCO) 1500 W Shure Dr *TF:* 800-527-9948 ■ *Web:* www.cetco.com	Arlington Heights	IL	60004	847-392-5800	577-6150
Custom Bldg Products 13001 Seal Beach Blvd *TF:* 800-272-8786 ■ *Web:* www.custombuildingproducts.com	Seal Beach	CA	90740	562-598-8808	598-4008
DAP Inc 2400 Boston St Suite 200 **Fax:* Cust Svc ■ *TF Cust Svc:* 800-584-3840 ■ *Web:* www.dap.com	Baltimore	MD	21224	410-675-2100	558-1068*
Devcon Inc 30 Endicott St *TF:* 800-626-7226 ■ *Web:* www.devcon.com	Danvers	MA	01923	978-777-1100	774-0516
Dymax Corp 318 Industrial Ln Suite 2 *TF:* 877-396-2963 ■ *Web:* www.dymax.com	Torrington	CT	06790	860-482-1010	496-0608
Eclectic Products Inc 1075 Arrowsmith St 2nd Fl Suite B *TF:* 800-693-4667 ■ *Web:* www.eclecticproducts.com	Eugene	OR	97402	541-284-4667	746-1983
EFTEC North America LLC 2710 Bellingham Dr Suite 100 *TF:* 800-633-7789 ■ *Web:* www.eftec.com	Troy	MI	48083	248-585-2200	585-3699
Elmer's Products Inc 1 Easton Oval **Fax Area Code:* 614 ■ *TF:* 888-435-6377 ■ *Web:* www.elmers.com	Columbus	OH	43219	888-435-6377	985-2605*
Engineered Materials Systems Inc (EMS) 132 Johnson Dr *Web:* www.emsadhesives.com	Delaware	OH	43015	740-362-4444	362-4433
Euclid Chemical Co 19218 Redwood Rd *TF:* 800-321-7628 ■ *Web:* www.euclidchemical.com	Cleveland	OH	44110	216-531-9222	531-9596
Foster Construction Products Inc 1105 S Frontenac St *TF:* 800-231-9541 ■ *Web:* www.fosterproducts.com	Aurora	IL	60504	800-231-9541	942-6856
Fox Industries Inc 3100 Falls Cliff Rd *TF:* 888-760-0369 ■ *Web:* www.fox-ind.com	Baltimore	MD	21211	410-243-8856	243-2701
Franklin International 2020 Bruck St *TF:* 800-877-4583 ■ *Web:* www.franklini.com	Columbus	OH	43207	614-443-0241	445-1493
Geocel Corp PO Box 398 **Fax Area Code:* 800 ■ *TF:* 800-348-7615 ■ *Web:* www.geocelusa.com	Elkhart	IN	46515	574-264-0645	348-7009*
Grace Darex Packaging Technologies 62 Whittemore Ave *Web:* www.gracedarex.com	Cambridge	MA	02140	617-498-4987	498-4433
HB Fuller Co 1200 Willow Lake Blvd PO Box 64683 *NYSE: FUL* ■ *TF:* 888-423-8553 ■ *Web:* www.hbfuller.com	Saint Paul	MN	55164	651-236-5900	236-5898
Henkel Corp 1 Henkel Way *TF:* 800-842-0041 ■ *Web:* www.henkel.com	Rocky Hill	CT	06067	860-571-5100	571-5465
Hercules Chemical Co Inc 111 S St *TF:* 800-221-9330 ■ *Web:* www.herchem.com	Passaic	NJ	07055	973-778-5000	777-4115
Hexion Specialty Chemicals Inc 180 E Broad St *Web:* www.hexionchem.com	Columbus	OH	43215	614-225-4000	
Houghton International Inc 945 Madison Ave PO Box 930 *TF:* 888-459-9844 ■ *Web:* www.houghtonintl.com	Valley Forge	PA	19482	610-666-4000	666-0174
Illinois Tool Works Inc TACC Div 56 Air Stn Industrial Pk **Fax Area Code:* 800 ■ **Fax:* Cust Svc ■ *TF:* 800-503-6991 ■ *Web:* www.taccint.com	Rockland	MA	02370	781-878-7015	231-8222*
Inovex Industries Inc 45681 Oakbrook Ct Suite 102 *TF:* 888-374-3366 ■ *Web:* www.ride-on.com	Sterling	VA	20166	703-421-9778	421-1967
IPS Corp 455 W Victoria St *TF:* 800-888-8312 ■ *Web:* www.ipscorp.com	Compton	CA	90220	310-898-3300	898-3367
ITW Insulcast Inc 565 Eagle Rock Ave *TF:* 800-645-7546 ■ *Web:* www.insulcast.com	Roseland	NJ	07068	973-403-0603	403-0046
Key Polymer Corp 17 Shepherd St *TF:* 888-539-7659 ■ *Web:* www.keypolymer.com	Lawrence	MA	01843	978-683-9411	686-7729
Kindt-Collins Co LLC 12651 Elmwood Ave **Fax:* Cust Svc ■ *TF:* 800-321-3170 ■ *Web:* www.kindt-collins.com	Cleveland	OH	44111	216-252-4122	252-5639*
L & L Products Inc 160 McLean Dr PO Box 308 *Web:* www.llproducts.com	Romeo	MI	48065	586-336-1700	336-1699
LaPolla Industries Inc 15402 Vantage Pkwy E Suite 322 *OTC: LPAD* ■ *Web:* www.lapollaindustries.com	Houston	TX	77032	281-219-4700	219-4102
Laticrete International Inc 91 Amity Rd *TF:* 800-243-4788 ■ *Web:* www.laticrete.com	Bethany	CT	06524	203-393-0010	393-1684
Light Fabrications Inc 40 Hytec Cir *TF:* 800-836-6920 ■ *Web:* www.lightfab.com	Rochester	NY	14606	585-426-5330	426-5239
Lord Corp 111 Lord Dr *TF:* 800-524-2885 ■ *Web:* www.lord.com	Cary	NC	27511	919-468-5979	
Manus Products Of Minnesota Inc 866 Industrial Blvd *Web:* www.manus.net	Waconia	MN	55387	952-442-3323	442-3327
MAPEI Corp 1144 E Newport Ctr Dr *TF:* 800-426-2734 ■ *Web:* www.mapei.com	Deerfield Beach	FL	33442	954-246-8888	246-8830

				Phone	Fax
Mask-Off Co Inc 345 W Maple Ave	Monrovia	CA	91016	626-359-3261	359-7160
Web: www.mask-off.com					
Morgan Adhesives Co 4560 Darrow Rd	Stow	OH	44224	330-688-1111	688-2540
TF: 800-762-2822 ■ *Web:* www.mactac.com					
Multiseal Inc 4320 Hitch Peters Rd	Evansville	IN	47711	812-428-3422	428-3432
Web: www.multiseal-usa.com					
National Casein Co 601 W 80th St	Chicago	IL	60620	773-846-7300	487-5709
Web: www.nationalcasein.com					
Newport Adhesives & Composites Inc					
1822 Reynolds Ave	Irvine	CA	92614	949-253-5680	253-5692
Web: www.newportad.com					
Nylok Corp 15260 Hallmark Dr	Macomb	MI	48042	586-786-0100	786-0598
TF: 800-826-5161 ■ *Web:* www.nylok.com					
Ohio Sealants Inc 7405 Production Dr	Mentor	OH	44060	440-624-7767	974-8358
TF: 800-321-3578 ■ *Web:* www.osipro.com					
Para-Chem Southern Inc					
863 SE Main St PO Box 127	Simpsonville	SC	29681	864-967-7691	963-1241
TF: 800-763-7272 ■ *Web:* www.parabond.com					
Pecora Corp 165 Wambold Rd	Harleysville	PA	19438	215-723-6051	799-2518
TF: 800-523-6688 ■ *Web:* www.pecora.com					
PrescoTech Industries 1001 W Oak St	Louisville	KY	40210	502-585-5866	587-1175
Web: www.prescotech.com					
Ptc Fastening Inc 16 Celina Ave Unit 13	Nashua	NH	03063	603-880-5051	
Rectorseal Corp The 2601 Spenwick Dr	Houston	TX	77055	713-263-8001	263-7577
TF: 800-231-3345 ■ *Web:* www.rectorseal.com					
Red Devil Inc					
1437 S Boulder Suite 750, Boulder Towers	Tulsa	OK	74119	918-585-8111	585-8120
TF: 800-423-3845 ■ *Web:* www.reddevil.com					
Ritrama 800 Kasota Ave SE	Minneapolis	MN	55414	612-378-2277	378-9327
TF: 800-328-5071 ■ *Web:* www.ritrama.com					
Solar Compounds Corp 1201 W Blancke St	Linden	NJ	07036	908-862-2813	862-8061
Web: www.solarcompounds.com					
Southern Grouts & Mortars Inc					
1502 SW 2nd Pl	Pompano Beach	FL	33069	954-943-2288	943-2402
TF: 800-641-9247 ■ *Web:* www.sgm.cc					
Super Glue Corp					
9420 Santa Anita Ave	Rancho Cucamonga	CA	91730	909-987-0550	987-0490
TF: 800-538-3091 ■ *Web:* www.supergluecorp.com					
Surteco USA Inc 7104 Cessna Dr	Greensboro	NC	27409	336-668-9555	668-7795
Web: www.canplast.com					
Tailored Chemical Products Inc					
3719 1st Ave SW	Hickory	NC	28602	828-322-6512	322-7688
TF: 800-627-1687 ■ *Web:* www.tailoredchemical.com					
TEC Specialty Products Inc					
1105 S Frontenac Rd	Aurora	IL	60504	800-832-9002	776-4452*
**Fax Area Code:* 847 ■ *TF:* 800-832-9002 ■ *Web:* www.tecspecialty.com					
Tremco Inc Roofing Div 3735 Green Rd	Beachwood	OH	44122	216-292-5000	760-3070*
**Fax Area Code:* 800 ■ **Fax:* Cust Svc ■ *TF:* 800-852-6013 ■ *Web:* www.tremcoroofing.com					
Uniseal Inc 1800 W Maryland St	Evansville	IN	47712	812-436-4840	429-1831
TF: 800-443-9081 ■ *Web:* www.uniseal.com					
Valspar Corp Packaging Coatings Div					
2001 Tracy St	Pittsburgh	PA	15233	412-766-9300	732-3131
TF: 800-873-5575					
W.f. Taylor Co Inc 11545 Pacific Ave	Fontana	CA	92337	951-360-6677	360-1177
TF: 800-397-4583 ■ *Web:* www.wftaylor.com					
Western American National Bank					
1518 Taney St	Kansas City	MO	64116	816-421-3000	421-3122
Web: www.westernadhesives.com					
Worthen Industries Inc 3 E Spit Brook Rd	Nashua	NH	03060	603-888-5443	888-7945
TF: 800-967-8436 ■ *Web:* www.worthenindustries.com					

4 ADVERTISING AGENCIES

SEE ALSO Public Relations Firms p. 2460

				Phone	Fax
22 Squared 1170 Peachtree St NE Suite 1500	Atlanta	GA	30309	404-347-8700	347-8800
Web: www.22squared.com					
A Web That Works 2733 Concession Rd 7	Bowmanville	ON	L1C3K6	905-263-2666	263-8989
TF: 800-579-9253 ■ *Web:* www.awebthatworks.com					
Abelson-Taylor Inc 33 W Monroe Suite 6004	Chicago	IL	60603	312-781-1700	894-5526
Web: www.abelson-taylor.com					
Acento Adv Inc 2254 S Sepulveda Blvd	Los Angeles	CA	90064	310-943-8300	943-8310
Web: www.acento.com					
Ackerman McQueen Inc					
1601 NW Expy Suite 1100	Oklahoma City	OK	73118	405-843-7777	848-8034
Web: www.am.com					
Adair-Greene McCann Healthcare Communications					
1575 Northside Dr NW					
200 Atlanta Technology Ctr	Atlanta	GA	30318	404-351-8424	351-1495
AdMasters 16901 Dallas Pkwy Suite 204	Addison	TX	75001	972-866-9300	866-9292
TF: 877-236-2783 ■ *Web:* www.admasters.com					
AdPlex Inc 650 Century Plaza Dr Suite 120	Houston	TX	77073	281-443-4301	443-1040
Web: www.adplex.com					
Adwest Direct Inc 2939 16th St Suite 100	Santa Monica	CA	90405	310-396-5015	312-1359
TF: 877-239-3781 ■ *Web:* www.adwestworldwide.com					
Agent 16 79 5th Ave 16th Fl	New York	NY	10003	212-367-3800	367-3880
Web: www.agent16.com					
AKQA Inc 118 King St 6th Fl	San Francisco	CA	94107	415-645-9400	645-9420
Web: www.akqa.com					
Al Paul Lefton Co Inc					
100 S Independence Mall W # 1	Philadelphia	PA	19106	215-923-9600	351-4298
Web: www.lefton.com					
All-Ways Adv Co 1442 Broad St	Bloomfield	NJ	07003	973-338-0700	338-1410
TF: 800-255-9291 ■ *Web:* www.awadv.com					
Allen & Gerritsen (A&G) 311 Arsenal St Suite 4	Watertown	MA	02472	617-926-4005	926-0133
Web: www.a-g.com					
Alloy Marketing & Promotions LLC					
77 N Washington St	Boston	MA	02114	617-723-8929	723-2188
Web: www.ampagency.com					
American Telecast Corp					
1230 American Blvd	West Chester	PA	19380	610-430-7800	
Web: www.americantelecast.com					
AMPM Inc 1380 E Wackerly Rd	Midland	MI	48642	989-837-8800	832-0781
TF: 800-530-9100 ■ *Web:* www.ampminc.com					
Anderson Communications					
1691 Phoenix Blvd # 390	Atlanta	GA	30349	404-766-8000	767-5264
Web: www.andercom.com					
Archer/Malmo Adv Inc 65 Union Ave Suite 500	Memphis	TN	38103	901-523-2000	523-7654
Web: www.archermalmo.com					
Arnold Worldwide 110 5th Ave	New York	NY	10011	212-463-1000	463-1490
Web: www.arn.com					
Arnold Worldwide 101 Huntington Ave	Boston	MA	02199	617-587-8000	587-8004
TF: 800-782-4893 ■ *Web:* www.arnoldworldwide.com					
Aspen Marketing Services 1240 N Ave	West Chicago	IL	60185	630-293-9600	293-9600
TF: 800-848-0212 ■ *Web:* www.aspenms.com					
Avrett Free Ginsberg					
1 Dag Hammarskjold Plaza	New York	NY	10017	212-832-3800	
Web: www.afg1.com					
Bader Rutter & Assoc Inc 13845 Bishops Dr	Brookfield	WI	53005	262-784-7200	938-5595
Web: www.baderrutter.com					
Bailey Lauerman & Assoc Inc					
1248 O St Suite 900	Lincoln	NE	68508	402-475-2800	475-5115
TF: 800-869-0411 ■ *Web:* www.baileylauerman.com					
Barkley 1740 Main St	Kansas City	MO	64108	816-842-1500	
Web: www.beap.com					
BBDO Worldwide Inc					
1285 Avenue of the Americas	New York	NY	10019	212-459-5000	459-6645
Web: www.bbdo.com					
Berenter Greenhouse & Webster Inc					
300 Pk Ave S 4th Fl	New York	NY	10010	212-727-5687	727-5601
Web: www.bgwad.com					
Bernard Hodes Group 220 E 42 St	New York	NY	10017	212-999-9000	999-9484
TF: 888-438-9911 ■ *Web:* www.hodes.com					
Bernstein-Rein					
4600 Madison Ave Suite 1500	Kansas City	MO	64112	816-756-0640	756-1753
TF: 800-571-6246 ■ *Web:* www.bernstein-rein.com					
Brand Pharm 79 Madison Ave 3rd Fl	New York	NY	10010	212-684-0909	213-4694
Web: www.brandpharmusa.com					
Bromley Communications LLC					
401 E Houston St	San Antonio	TX	78205	210-244-2000	244-2116
Web: www.bromleyville.com					
Brouillard Communications Inc					
466 Lexington Ave 6th Fl	New York	NY	10017	212-210-8563	210-8511
Web: www.brouillard.com					
Buntin Adv Inc 1001 Hawkins St	Nashville	TN	37203	615-244-5720	256-5539
Web: www.buntingroup.com					
Burrell 233 N Michigan Ave 29th Fl	Chicago	IL	60601	312-297-9600	297-9601
Web: www.burrell.com					
Campbell Mithun 222 S 9th St	Minneapolis	MN	55402	612-347-1000	347-1000
Web: www.campbell-mithun.com					
Campbell-Ewald 30400 Van Dyke Ave	Warren	MI	48093	586-574-3400	558-5891*
**Fax:* Hum Res ■ *Web:* www.c-e.com					
Carmichael Lynch 800 Hennepin Ave	Minneapolis	MN	55403	612-334-6000	334-6126
Web: www.carmichaellynch.com					
Carol H Williams Adv 555 12th St Suite 1700	Oakland	CA	94607	510-763-5200	763-9266
Web: www.carolhwilliams.com					
Carrafiello Diehl & Assoc 90 N Broadway	Irvington	NY	10533	914-674-3900	674-3989
Web: www.carrafiellodiehl.com					
Chicago Creative Partnership					
314 W Superior St 5th Fl	Chicago	IL	60654	312-335-4330	335-8339
Web: www.chicagocp.com					
Clarity Coverdale Fury (CCF)					
120 S 6th St					
1 Financial Plaza Suite 1300	Minneapolis	MN	55402	612-339-3902	359-4392
Web: www.claritycoverdalefury.com					
Clear Ink 741 Alston Way	Berkeley	CA	94710	510-549-4200	549-4205
Cline Davis & Mann Inc 220 E 42nd St	New York	NY	10017	212-907-4300	907-4300
Web: www.clinedavis.com					
CMD 1631 NW Thurman St	Portland	OR	97209	503-223-6794	223-2430
Web: www.cmdpdx.com					
Cole & Weber United 221 Yale Ave N Suite 600	Seattle	WA	98109	206-447-9595	233-0178
TF: 800-262-8515 ■ *Web:* www.coleweber.com					
Colle & McVoy Inc 400 1st Ave N Suite 700	Minneapolis	MN	55401	612-305-6000	305-6500
Web: www.collemcvoy.com					
CommonHealth 400 Interpace Pkwy	Parsippany	NJ	07054	973-352-1000	352-2251
Web: www.commonhealth.com					
Compas Inc 4300 Haddonfield Rd Suite 200	Pennsauken	NJ	08109	856-667-8577	667-6112
Web: www.compasonline.com					
Corbett Accel Healthcare Group					
211 E Chicago Ave	Chicago	IL	60611	312-475-2500	475-2500
Web: www.corbett.com					
Cossette Communications					
415 Madison Ave 3rd Fl	New York	NY	10017	212-753-4700	840-4222*
**Fax Area Code:* 646 ■ *Web:* www.cossette.com					
Cramer 425 University Ave	Norwood	MA	02062	781-278-2300	278-8464
Web: www.crameronline.com					
Cramer-Krasselt 246 E Chicago St	Milwaukee	WI	53202	414-227-3500	
Web: www.c-k.com					
Cranford Johnson Robinson Woods					
303 W Capitol Ave	Little Rock	AR	72201	501-975-6251	975-4241
TF: 888-383-2579 ■ *Web:* www.cjrw.com					
Creative Alliance Inc 437 W Jefferson St	Louisville	KY	40202	502-584-8787	589-9900
TF: 800-525-0294 ■ *Web:* www.cre8.com					
Creative Marketing Alliance Inc					
191 Clarksville Rd	Princeton Junction	NJ	08550	609-799-6000	799-7032
Web: www.cmasolutions.com					
Dailey & Assoc 8687 Melrose Ave	West Hollywood	CA	90069	310-360-3100	360-3100*
**Fax:* Acctg ■ *Web:* www.daileyideas.com					
Dalton Agency Inc The					
140 W Monroe St Suite 200	Jacksonville	FL	32202	904-398-5222	398-5220
Web: www.daltonagency.com					

Name / Address	City	State	Zip	Phone	Fax
Dana Communications Inc 2 E Broad St *Web:* www.danacommunications.com	Hopewell	NJ	08525	609-466-9187	466-0285
Davis Elen Adv 865 S Figueroa St 12th Fl *TF:* 800-729-4322 ■ *Web:* www.daviselen.com	Los Angeles	CA	90017	213-688-7000	688-7288
DDB Worldwide 437 Madison Ave *TF:* 800-332-3336 ■ *Web:* www.ddb.com	New York	NY	10022	212-415-2000	415-3414
Della Femina/Rothschild/Jeary & Partners 902 Broadway 15th Fl *Web:* www.dfjp.com	New York	NY	10010	212-506-0700	506-0751
Dentsu America Inc 32 Avenue of the Americas 16th Fl *Web:* www.dentsuamerica.com	New York	NY	10013	212-397-3333	397-3322
Deutsch Inc 111 8th Ave 14th Fl *TF:* 800-287-3457 ■ *Web:* www.deutschinc.com	New York	NY	10011	212-981-7600	981-7525
Dieste 1999 Bryan St Suite 2700 *Web:* www.dieste.com	Dallas	TX	75201	214-259-8000	259-8040
Diversified Agency Services 437 Madison Ave *Web:* www.dasglobal.com	New York	NY	10022	212-415-3049	415-3530
Doner Adv 25900 Northwestern Hwy	Southfield	MI	48075	248-354-9700	827-0880*
Doremus & Co 200 Varick St 11th Fl *Web:* www.doremus.com	New York	NY	10014	212-366-3000	366-3660
Dudnyk 5 Walnut Grove Dr Suite 280 **Fax Area Code: 267* ■ *TF:* 800-438-3695 ■ *Web:* www.dudnyk.com	Horsham	PA	19044	215-443-9406	532-1021*
Dudnyk Exchange 5 Walnut Grove Suite 280 **Fax Area Code: 215* ■ *Web:* www.dudnykexchange.com	Horsham	PA	19044	267-532-1384	443-0207*
Duffy & Shanley Inc 10 Charles St *Web:* www.duffyshanley.com	Providence	RI	02904	401-274-0001	274-3535
E Morris Communications Inc 820 N Orleans *Web:* www.emorris.com	Chicago	IL	60610	312-943-2900	943-5856
Educationdynamics LLC 5 Marine View Plaza Suite 212 *Web:* www.educationdynamics.com	Hoboken	NJ	07030	201-377-3000	222-0848
Engauge 420 Fort Duquesne Blvd Suite 1900 1Gateway Ctr *TF:* 800-937-3657 ■ *Web:* www.engauge.com	Pittsburgh	PA	15222	412-471-5300	471-3308
Engauge 375 N Front St Suite 400 *TF:* 866-415-1010 ■ *Web:* www.engauge.com	Columbus	OH	43215	614-573-1010	573-1011
Eric Mower & Assoc 211 W Jefferson St *Web:* www.mower.com	Syracuse	NY	13202	315-466-1000	466-2000
Ernst-Van Praag Inc 4800 N Federal Hwy Suite E 207 *Web:* www.evpconsulting.com	Boca Raton	FL	33431	561-447-0557	447-0527
Euro RSCG Life 200 Madison Ave 2nd Fl *Web:* www.eurorscglife.com	New York	NY	10016	212-251-8800	251-8819
Euro RSCG Life Chelsea 75 9th Ave *Web:* www.eurorscg.com	New York	NY	10011	212-299-5000	299-5050
Euro RSCG Worldwide 350 Hudson St 6th Fl *TF:* 800-263-7590 ■ *Web:* www.eurorscg.com	New York	NY	10014	212-886-2000	886-5013
Exposed Brick 1 Astor Pl Suite 7-T *Web:* www.exposedbrick.com	New York	NY	10003	646-454-0880	
Fahlgren Inc 414 Walnut St Suite 1006 *TF:* 800-543-2663 ■ *Web:* www.fahlgren.com	Cincinnati	OH	45202	513-241-9200	241-5982
Fallon 901 Marquette Ave Suite 2400 *TF:* 888-758-2345 ■ *Web:* www.fallon.com	Minneapolis	MN	55402	612-758-2345	758-2346
FCB HealthCare 100 W 33rd St 7th Fl *Web:* www.draftfcbhealthcare.com	New York	NY	10001	212-672-2300	885-3300
Finelight Inc 1801 S Liberty Dr Suite 300 *Web:* www.finelight.com	Bloomington	IN	47403	812-339-6700	
Fitzgerald & Co 3333 Piedmont Rd 11th Fl *Web:* www.fitzco.com	Atlanta	GA	30305	404-504-6900	239-0548
Fkq Adv Inc 15351 Roosevelt Blvd **Fax Area Code: 866* ■ *Web:* www.fkq.com	Clearwater	FL	33760	727-539-8800	707-6648*
Fogarty Klein Monroe 1845 W 1st St Suite 100 *TF:* 866-228-3252 ■ *Web:* www.fkmagency.com	Houston	TX	77024	713-862-5100	869-6560
Frogdesign Inc 660 3rd St 4th Fl *Web:* www.frogdesign.com	San Francisco	CA	94107	415-442-4804	442-4803
Fry Hammond Barr 600 E Washington St *Web:* www.fhbnet.com	Orlando	FL	32801	407-849-0100	849-0817
FutureBrand 300 Pk Ave S 7th Fl *Web:* www.futurebrand.com	New York	NY	10010	212-931-6300	931-6310
G2 USA 200 5th Ave *Web:* www.g2directanddigital.com	New York	NY	10010	212-546-2222	537-3737
Gelia Wells & Mohr Inc 390 S Youngs Rd *Web:* www.gelia.com	Buffalo	NY	14221	716-759-0930	629-3299
GKV Adv Inc 1030 Hull St 4th Fl *Web:* www.gkv.com	Baltimore	MD	21230	410-539-5400	234-2441
Global Hue 4000 Town Ctr 16th Fl *Web:* www.globalhue.com	Southfield	MI	48075	248-223-8900	304-5960
GlobalWorks Group LLC 220 5th Ave *Web:* www.globalworks.com	New York	NY	10001	212-252-8800	252-0002
Goodby Silverstein & Partners 720 California St *Web:* www.goodbysilverstein.com	San Francisco	CA	94108	415-392-0669	788-4303
Gotham Inc 150 E 42nd St 12th Fl *Web:* www.gothaminc.com	New York	NY	10017	212-414-7000	414-7095
Grafica Inc 525 Main St *Web:* www.grafica.com	Chester	NJ	07930	908-879-2169	879-2569
Graham Group Inc The 2014 W Pinhook Rd Suite 210 *Web:* www.graham-group.com	Lafayette	LA	70508	337-232-8214	235-3787
Greer Margolis Mitchell Burns 1010 Wisconsin Ave NW Suite 800 *TF:* 800-283-7606 ■ *Web:* www.gmmb.com	Washington	DC	20007	202-338-8700	338-2334
Grey Healthcare Group Inc 114 5th Ave *Web:* www.ghgroup.com	New York	NY	10011	212-886-3000	
Grey Worldwide 200 5th Ave *Web:* www.grey.com	New York	NY	10010	212-546-2000	546-1495
GSD & M Idea City 828 W 6th St *Web:* www.gsdm.com	Austin	TX	78703	512-242-4736	242-4700
GSW Worldwide 500 Old Worthington Rd *Web:* www.gsw-w.com	Westerville	OH	43082	614-848-4848	848-3477
Hal Lewis Group 1700 Market St 6th Fl *TF:* 888-778-6115 ■ *Web:* www.hlg.com	Philadelphia	PA	19103	215-563-4461	563-1148
Hamilton Communications Group 20 N Wacker St Suite 1960 *Web:* www.hamiltongrp.com	Chicago	IL	60606	312-321-5000	321-5005
Hanft Raboy & Partners 205 Hudson St 7th Fl *Web:* www.hanftraboy.com	New York	NY	10013	646-256-6213	
Harrison & Star 16 W 22nd St 8th Fl *Web:* www.hs-ideas.com	New York	NY	10010	212-727-1330	822-6590
HEILBrice Inc 9840 Irvine Ctr Dr *Web:* www.heilbrice.com	Irvine	CA	92618	949-336-8800	336-8819
Hill Holliday 622 3rd Ave 14th Fl *Web:* www.hhcc.com	New York	NY	10017	212-905-7200	905-7100
Hill Holliday 53 State St *Web:* www.hillholliday.com	Boston	MA	02109	617-366-4000	
Howard Merrell & Partners Inc 8521 Six Forks Rd Suite 400 *Web:* www.merrellgroup.com	Raleigh	NC	27615	919-848-2400	848-2420
Hunter Hamersmith & Assoc Inc 725 NE 125th St *Web:* www.hhadvertising.net	North Miami	FL	33161	305-895-8430	892-9611
Hyphen 711 3rd Ave 17th Fl *Web:* www.hyphenhealth.com	New York	NY	10017	212-856-8700	856-8602
ICC Loew Pace Inc 35 Waterview Blvd Suite 3 *Web:* www.paceconnect.com	Parsippany	NJ	07054	973-658-1206	
Innis Maggiore Group Inc 4715 Whipple Ave NW *TF:* 800-460-4111 ■ *Web:* www.innismaggiore.com	Canton	OH	44718	330-492-5500	492-5568
Integer Group LLC The 7245 W Alaska Dr *Web:* www.integer.com	Lakewood	CO	80226	303-393-3500	393-3717
Intermark Group Inc 101 25th St N *TF:* 877-527-3479 ■ *Web:* www.intermarkgroup.com	Birmingham	AL	35203	205-326-0200	870-3843
Interpublic Group 1114 Avenue of the Americas *NYSE: IPG* ■ *Web:* www.interpublic.com	New York	NY	10036	212-704-1200	704-2101
Inuvo Inc 15550 Lightwave Dr Suite 300 *AMEX: INUV* ■ *Web:* www.inuvo.com	Clearwater	FL	33760	727-324-0211	
J Walter Thompson 466 Lexington Ave *Web:* www.jwt.com	New York	NY	10017	212-210-7000	
K&L Adv 285 Madison Ave 23rd Fl *Web:* www.kanglee.com	New York	NY	10017	212-375-8111	375-8255
Kane & Finkel LLC 534 4th St *Web:* www.kaneandfinkel.com	San Francisco	CA	94107	415-777-4990	
Kaplan Thaler Group Ltd 1675 Broadway *Web:* www.kaplanthaler.com	New York	NY	10019	212-474-5000	474-5400
Keiler & Co 304 Main St *Web:* www.keiler.com	Farmington	CT	06032	860-677-8821	676-8164
Keller Crescent Co Inc 1100 E Louisiana St **Fax: Cust Svc* ■ *TF:* 800-457-3837 ■ *Web:* www.kellercrescent.com	Evansville	IN	47711	812-464-2461	426-7601*
Kilgannon Inc 1360 Peachtree St 1 Midtown Plaza Suite 700 *Web:* www.kilgannon.com	Atlanta	GA	30309	404-876-2800	876-2830
King Group Inc 1801 N Hampton Rd Suite 410	DeSoto	TX	75115	214-720-9046	720-1435
Kleber & Assoc 1215 Hightower Trial Bldg C *Web:* www.kleberandassociates.com	Atlanta	GA	30350	770-518-1000	518-2700
Korey Kay & Partners 130 5th Ave 8th Fl *Web:* www.koreykay.com	New York	NY	10011	212-620-4300	620-7149
Kovel/Fuller LLC 9925 Jefferson Blvd *Web:* www.kovelfuller.com	Culver City	CA	90232	310-841-4444	841-4599
Kraus-Anderson Communications Group 523 S 8th St *Web:* www.kacommunications.com	Minneapolis	MN	55404	612-375-1080	342-2239
Krome Communications Inc 307 4th Ave Suite 1500 *Web:* www.krome.com	Pittsburgh	PA	15222	412-471-0840	471-0246
Laird Partners LLC 475 10th Ave 7th Fl *Web:* www.lairdandpartners.com	New York	NY	10018	212-478-8181	478-8210
Latorra Paul & Mccann Inc 120 E Washington St University Bldg 10th Fl *Web:* www.lpm-adv.com	Syracuse	NY	13202	315-476-1646	476-1611
Laughlin/Constable Inc 207 E Michigan St *Web:* www.laughlin.com	Milwaukee	WI	53202	414-272-2400	272-3056
Lawrence & Schiller Inc 3932 S Willow Ave *TF:* 800-356-9377 ■ *Web:* www.l-s.com	Sioux Falls	SD	57105	605-338-8000	338-8892
Lehman Millet Inc 2 Atlantic Ave *TF:* 800-634-5315 ■ *Web:* www.lehmanmillet.com	Boston	MA	02110	617-624-9500	722-6099
Leo Burnett Co Inc 35 W Wacker Dr *Web:* www.leoburnett.com	Chicago	IL	60601	312-220-5959	220-3299
Lewis Communications Inc 600 Meadow Brook Corp 2 *Web:* www.lewiscommunications.com	Birmingham	AL	35242	205-980-0774	437-0250
Liggett-Stashower Inc 1422 Euclid Ave Suite 400 *TF:* 800-877-4573 ■ *Web:* www.liggett.com	Cleveland	OH	44115	216-348-8500	861-1284
Lindsay Stone & Briggs Inc 100 State St Suite 400 *Web:* www.lsb.com	Madison	WI	53703	608-251-7070	251-8989
Lopez Negrete Communications Inc 3336 Richmond Ave Suite 200 *Web:* www.lopeznegrete.com	Houston	TX	77098	713-877-8777	877-8796
Lou Beres & Assoc Inc 175 Delaware Pl Suite 5812 *Web:* www.louberes.com	Chicago	IL	60611	312-720-7347	670-2586
LOVE ADV INC 770 S Post Oak Ln Suite 101 *Web:* www.loveadv.com	Houston	TX	77056	713-552-1055	552-9155
Luckie & Co 600 Luckie Dr PO Box 530584 *Web:* www.luckie.com	Birmingham	AL	35223	205-879-2121	877-9713
Luquire George Andrews Inc 4201 Congress St Suite 400 *Web:* www.lgaadv.com	Charlotte	NC	28209	704-552-6565	552-1972

Agency	City	State	ZIP	Phone	Fax
LyonHeart 220 E 42nd St 3rd Fl *TF:* 800-599-0188	New York	NY	10017	212-771-3000	771-3000
Mangan Holcomb Partners 2300 Cottondale Ln *Web:* www.manganholcomb.com	Little Rock	AR	72202	501-376-0321	376-6127
MARC USA 225 W Station Sq Dr Suite 500 *Web:* www.marcusa.com	Pittsburgh	PA	15219	412-562-2000	562-2022
Marcus Thomas LLC Highlands Business Pk, 24865 Emery Rd *TF:* 888-482-4455 ■ *Web:* www.marcusthomasad.com	Cleveland	OH	44128	216-292-4700	378-0396
Marketing Support Inc 200 E Randolph Dr Suite 5000 *Web:* www.msinet.com	Chicago	IL	60601	312-565-0044	946-6100
Mars Adv Co Inc 25200 Telegraph Rd *TF:* 800-521-9317 ■ *Web:* www.marsusa.com	Southfield	MI	48034	248-936-2200	936-2501
Marshad Technology Group 12 Desbrosses St *Web:* www.marshad.com	New York	NY	10013	212-292-8910	292-8912
Martin Agency Inc 1 Shockoe Plaza *Web:* www.martinagency.com	Richmond	VA	23219	804-698-8000	698-8001
Martin Thomas Inc 42 Riverside Dr **Fax Area Code:* 866 ■ *Web:* www.martinthomas.com	Barrington	RI	02806	401-245-8500	899-2710*
Martin-Williams Adv 60 S 6th St Suite 2800 *TF:* 800-632-1388 ■ *Web:* www.martinwilliams.com	Minneapolis	MN	55402	612-340-0800	342-9700
MARTZ & Assoc INC 7077 E Marilyn Bldg 2 Suite 110 *Web:* www.martzagency.com	Scottsdale	AZ	85254	480-998-3154	998-7985
Matlock Adv & Public Relations 107 Luckie St *Web:* www.matlock-adpr.com	Atlanta	GA	30303	404-872-3200	876-4929
McKee Wallwork Cleveland LLC 1030 18th St NW *Web:* www.mckeewallworkcleveland.com	Albuquerque	NM	87104	505-821-2999	821-0006
McKinney 318 Blackwell St *Web:* www.mckinney.com	Durham	NC	27701	919-313-0802	313-0805
Media Logic USA LLC 1 Pk Pl *TF:* 866-353-3011 ■ *Web:* www.mlinc.com	Albany	NY	12205	518-456-3015	456-4279
Media Storm LLC 99 Washington St *Web:* www.mediastorm.biz	South Norwalk	CT	06854	203-852-8001	852-0746
Mediamind Technologies Inc 135 W 18th St 5th Fl *NASDAQ: MDMD* ■ **Fax Area Code:* 212 ■ *Web:* www.mediamind.com	New York	NY	10011	646-202-1320	686-9208*
Medicus Life Brands 1675 Broadway *Web:* www.medicusny.com	New York	NY	10019	212-468-3100	468-3208
MedPoint Digital Inc 909 Davis St Suite 500 *Web:* www.medpt.com	Evanston	IL	60201	847-869-4700	
Mendelsohn/Zien Adv 11111 Santa Monica Blvd Suite 2150 *Web:* www.mzad.com	Los Angeles	CA	90025	310-444-1990	444-9888
Merkley & Partners 200 Varick St 12th Fl *Web:* www.merkleyandpartners.com	New York	NY	10014	212-366-3500	366-3637
Meyer & Wallis Inc 731 N Jackson St 7th Fl *Web:* www.meyerwallis.com	Milwaukee	WI	53202	414-224-0212	224-0420
Mgh Adv Inc 100 Painters Mill Rd Suite 600 *Web:* www.mghus.com	Owings Mills	MD	21117	410-902-5000	902-8712
MindShare 498 7th Ave *Web:* www.mindshareworld.com	New York	NY	10018	212-297-7000	297-8888
MKTG Inc 75 9th Ave 3rd Fl *TF:* 800-680-9998 ■ *Web:* www.mktg.com	New York	NY	10011	212-366-3400	
MMG Worldwide 4601 Madison Ave *Web:* www.mmgworldwide.com	Kansas City	MO	64112	816-472-5988	471-5395
Molecular Inc 343 Arsenal St *Web:* www.molecular.com	Watertown	MA	02472	617-218-6500	218-6700
Momentum Worldwide 161 6th Ave 8th Fl **Fax Area Code:* 646 ■ *Web:* www.momentumww.com	New York	NY	10013	212-367-4500	638-5401*
Moroch Partners 3625 N Hall St Suite 1100 *TF:* 800-916-4327 ■ *Web:* www.moroch.com	Dallas	TX	75219	214-520-9700	520-5611
MRM Partners Worldwide 622 3rd Ave *Web:* www.mrmworldwide.com	New York	NY	10017	646-865-2000	487-9610
Mullen 40 Broad St *TF:* 800-363-6010 ■ *Web:* www.mullen.com	Boston	MA	02109	617-226-9000	226-9100
Muse Communications Inc 5358 Melrose Ave W Bldg Ground Fl *Web:* www.museusa.com	Hollywood	CA	90038	323-960-4080	960-4081
NAS Recruitment Communications 1 Infinity Corporate Ctr Dr *TF:* 866-627-7327 ■ *Web:* www.nasrecruitment.com	Cleveland	OH	44125	216-478-0300	468-8280
Noble 2155 W Chesterfield Blvd *Web:* www.noble.net	Springfield	MO	65807	417-875-5000	875-5051
Northlich 720 E Pete Rose Way Suite 120 *Web:* www.northlich.com	Cincinnati	OH	45202	513-421-8840	287-1858
NOWAK Assoc INC 6075 E Molloy Rd Suite 13 *Web:* www.nowakagency.com	Syracuse	NY	13211	315-463-1001	463-7933
Nurun 75 5th St NW Suite 600 *Web:* www.nurun.com	Atlanta	GA	30308	404-591-1600	876-7226
O'Leary & Partners 5000 Birch St Suite 1000 *Web:* www.olearyandpartners.com	Newport Beach	CA	92660	949-833-8006	833-9155
O2 Ideas Inc 600 University Pk Pl *Web:* www.o2ideas.com	Birmingham	AL	35209	205-949-9569	949-9449
Ogilvy & Mather Worldwide 636 11th Ave *Web:* www.ogilvy.com	New York	NY	10036	212-237-4000	237-5123
Ogilvy Interactive 309 W 49th St Worldwide Plaza *Web:* www.ogilvy.com/o_interactive	New York	NY	10036	212-237-4000	237-5123
Ogilvy One Worldwide 636 11th Ave *Web:* www.ogilvy.com	New York	NY	10036	212-237-6000	237-5123
Olson Co Inc 1625 Hennepin Ave *Web:* www.oco.com	Minneapolis	MN	55403	612-215-9800	215-9801
Osborn & Barr Cupples Stn 9 914 Spruce St *Web:* www.osborn-barr.com	St. Louis	MO	63102	314-726-5511	726-6350
Pacific Communications 575 Anton Blvd Suite 900 *Web:* www.pacific-com.com	Costa Mesa	CA	92626	714-427-1900	
Pacifico Inc 3880 S Bascom Ave Suite 215 *Web:* www.pacifico.com	San Jose	CA	91524	408-559-8880	
Pedone & Partners 49 W 27th St *Web:* www.pedonepartners.com	New York	NY	10001	212-627-3300	627-3966
Penny Ohlmann Neiman Inc 1605 N Main St *Web:* www.ponweb.com	Dayton	OH	45405	937-278-0681	277-1723
Periscope 921 Washington Ave S *TF:* 800-339-2103 ■ *Web:* www.periscope.com	Minneapolis	MN	55415	612-339-2100	399-0600
Peterson Milla Hooks 1315 Harmon Pl *Web:* www.pmhadv.com	Minneapolis	MN	55403	612-349-9116	349-9141
Phelps Group The 901 Wilshire Blvd *Web:* www.thephelpsgroup.com	Santa Monica	CA	90401	310-752-4400	752-4444
PKA Marketing 1009 W Glen Oaks Ln Suite 107 *Web:* www.pkamar.com	Mequon	WI	53092	262-241-9414	241-9454
Posner Adv 30 Broad St *Web:* www.posneradv.com	New York	NY	10004	212-867-3900	480-3440
Prime Access Inc 345 7th Ave *Web:* www.primeaccess.net	New York	NY	10001	212-868-6800	868-9495
Princeton Partners Inc 205 Rockingham Row *Web:* www.princetonpartners.com	Princeton	NJ	08540	609-452-8500	452-7212
Publicis & Hal Riney 2001 Embarcadero *Web:* www.hrp.com	San Francisco	CA	94133	415-293-2001	293-2628
Publicis USA 4 Herald Sq 950 6th Ave *Web:* www.publicis-usa.com	New York	NY	10001	212-279-5550	279-5560
R2c Group Inc 207 NW Pk Ave *Web:* www.r2cgroup.com	Portland	OR	97209	503-222-0025	276-4096
Rare Method 1812 4th St SW Suite 500 *Web:* www.raremethod.com	Calgary	AB	T2S1W1	403-543-4500	532-3004
Rdw Group Inc 125 Holden St *Web:* www.rdwgroup.com	Providence	RI	02908	401-521-2700	521-0014
ReachLocal Inc 21700 Oxnard St Suite 1600 *NASDAQ: RLOC* ■ *Web:* www.reachlocal.com	Woodland Hills	CA	91367	818-274-0260	
RealTime Solutions 12925 Prosperity Ave *Web:* www.realtime-solutions.net	Becker	MN	55308	763-262-3150	262-3150
Redstone Communications Group Inc 10031 Maple St *Web:* www.redstonespark.com	Omaha	NE	68134	402-393-5435	
Register Tapes Unlimited Inc 17015 Pk Row *TF:* 800-247-4793 ■ *Web:* www.rtui.com	Houston	TX	77084	281-206-2500	492-6390
Reply Inc 12667 Alcosta Blvd Suite 200 *TF:* 888-466-8677 ■ *Web:* www.reply.com	San Ramon	CA	94583	925-983-3400	
Resource Interactive 343 N Front St *TF:* 800-550-5815 ■ *Web:* www.resource.com	Columbus	OH	43215	614-621-2888	621-2873
Rhea & Kaiser 400 E Diehl Rd Suite 500 *Web:* www.rkconnect.com	Naperville	IL	60563	630-505-1100	505-1109
Richards Group 8750 N Central Expy Suite 1200 *Web:* www.richards.com	Dallas	TX	75231	214-891-5700	
Risdall Adv Agency 550 Main St *TF:* 888-747-3255 ■ *Web:* www.risdall.com	New Brighton	MN	55112	651-631-1098	631-2561
Rives/Carlberg 1900 W Loop S Suite 1100 *Web:* www.richardscarlberg.com	Houston	TX	77027	713-965-0764	965-0135
RJ Dale Adv & Public Relations 211 E Ontario St Suite 200 *Web:* www.rjdale.com	Chicago	IL	60611	312-644-2316	644-2688
RJC Inc 1120 Pennsylvania NE PO Box 4770 *Web:* www.rjc.com	Albuquerque	NM	87110	505-266-1100	262-0525
Roberts Communications Inc 64 Commercial St *Web:* www.robertscomm.com	Rochester	NY	14614	585-325-6000	325-6001
Ron Foth Adv 8100 N High St *TF:* 888-766-3684 ■ *Web:* www.ronfoth.com	Columbus	OH	43235	614-888-7771	888-5933
Rosen Inc 1631 NE Broadway Suite 615 *Web:* www.rgrosen.com	Portland	OR	97232	503-224-9811	224-9761
Rubin Postaer & Assoc 2525 Colorado Ave *Web:* www.rpa.com	Santa Monica	CA	90404	310-394-4000	
Runyon Saltzman & Einhorn Inc 1 Capitol Mall 4th Fl *Web:* www.rs-e.com	Sacramento	CA	95814	916-446-9900	446-3619
Saatchi & Saatchi 375 Hudson St *Web:* www.saatchiny.com	New York	NY	10014	212-463-2000	463-9856
Saint John & Partners Adv & Public Relations 5220 Belfort Rd Suite 400 *TF:* 800-642-2828 ■ *Web:* www.sjp.com	Jacksonville	FL	32256	904-281-2500	281-0030
Sanders/Wingo Adv Inc 221 N Kansas Suite 900 *Web:* www.sanderswingo.com	El Paso	TX	79901	915-533-9583	533-3601
Sawtooth Group 100 Woodbridge Ctr Dr Suite 102 *Web:* www.sawtoothgroup.com	Woodbridge	NJ	07095	732-636-6600	602-4212
Sbc Adv Ltd 333 W Nationwide Blvd *Web:* www.sbcadvertising.com	Columbus	OH	43215	614-255-2333	255-2600
Scott Howell & Co Inc 3900 Willow St Suite 200 *Web:* www.scott-howell.com	Dallas	TX	75226	214-951-9494	688-0555
Seiden Group 708 3rd Ave 13th Fl *Web:* www.seidenadvertising.com	New York	NY	10017	212-223-8700	223-1188
Serino Coyne Inc 1515 Broadway 36th Fl *Web:* www.serinocoyne.com	New York	NY	10036	212-626-2700	626-2799
Shaker Recruitment Adv & Communications 1100 Lake St 3rd Fl *TF:* 800-323-5170 ■ *Web:* www.shaker.com	Oak Park	IL	60301	708-383-5320	383-7670
Shepherd Inc 500 Bishopgate Ln *Web:* www.trsg.net	Jacksonville	FL	32204	904-359-0981	359-0808
Sherry Matthews Inc 200 S Congress Ave *Web:* www.sherrymatthews.com	Austin	TX	78704	512-478-4397	478-4978
Shumsky Enterprises Inc 811 E 4th St *TF:* 800-223-2203 ■ *Web:* www.shumsky.com	Dayton	OH	45402	937-223-2203	223-2252
SicolaMartin 206 E 9th St Suite 1800 *Web:* www.sicolamartin.com	Austin	TX	78701	512-343-0264	343-0659
SIDES & Assoc Inc 222 Jefferson St Suite B PO Box 3267 *Web:* www.sides.com	Lafayette	LA	70501	337-233-6473	233-6485

	City	State	ZIP	Phone	Fax
Siegel & Gale 625 Avenue of the Americas 4th Fl *Web:* www.siegelgale.com	New York	NY	10011	212-453-0400	453-0401
Sky Adv Inc 14 E 33rd St APT 7s *Web:* www.skyad.com	New York	NY	10016	212-677-2500	
Slingshot LLC 208 N Market St Suite 500 *Web:* www.davidandgoliath.com	DALLAS	TX	75202	214-634-4411	634-5511
Source Communications Inc 433 Hackensack Ave 8th Fl *Web:* www.sourcead.com	Hackensack	NJ	07601	201-343-5222	343-5710
SPAR Group Inc 560 White Plains Rd 6th Fl *NASDAQ: SGRP* ■ *Web:* www.sparinc.com	Tarrytown	NY	10591	914-332-4100	332-0741
Stephan & Brady Inc 1850 Hoffman St PO Box 1588 *Web:* www.stephanbrady.com	Madison	WI	53704	608-241-4141	241-4246
Sterling-Rice Group The (SRG) 1801 13th St Suite 400 *Web:* www.srg.com	Boulder	CO	80302	303-381-6400	444-6637
Stern Adv Inc 29125 Chagrin Blvd 3rd Fl *Web:* www.sternadvertising.com	Pepper Pike	OH	44122	216-464-4850	464-7859
Stone & Ward Inc 225 E Markham St *Web:* www.stoneward.com	Little Rock	AR	72201	501-375-3003	375-8314
Sudler & Hennessey 230 Pk Ave S **Fax:* Hum Res ■ *Web:* www.sudler.com	New York	NY	10003	212-614-4100	598-6930*
Sullivan Higdon & Sink Inc 255 N Mead *Web:* www.wehatesheep.com	Wichita	KS	67202	316-263-0124	263-7017
Swanson Russell 1222 P St *Web:* www.swansonrussell.com	Lincoln	NE	68508	402-437-6400	437-6401
TBWA Chiat/Day Inc 488 Madison Ave 7th Fl *TF:* 877-666-2347 ■ *Web:* www.tbwachiat.com	New York	NY	10022	212-804-1000	804-1200
Team One 1960 E Grand Ave Suite 700 *Web:* www.teamone-usa.com	El Segundo	CA	90245	310-615-2000	322-7565
Thomasarts Inc PO Box 70 *Web:* www.thomasarts.com	Farmington	UT	84025	801-451-5365	
Thompson Marketing 70 NE Loop 410 Suite 1050 *Web:* www.thompsonmarketing.us	San Antonio	TX	78216	210-349-9925	349-8558
Three Marketeers Adv Inc 785 The Almeda *Web:* www.3marketeers.com	San Jose	CA	95126	408-293-3233	293-2433
Tinsley Adv 2000 S Dixie Hwy *Web:* www.tinsley.com	Miami	FL	33133	305-856-6060	858-3877
TM Adv LP 1717 Main St Suite 2000 *Web:* tm.com	Dallas	TX	75201	972-556-1100	830-2619
Torre Lazur-McCann HealthCare Worldwide 20 Waterview Blvd Waterview Corp Ctr *Web:* www.torrelazur.com	Parsippany	NJ	07054	973-263-9100	263-4113
Trahan Burden & Charles Inc (TBC) 900 S Wolfe St *Web:* www.tbc.us	Baltimore	MD	21231	410-347-7500	986-1299
Tribal DDB Worldwide 437 Madison Ave 8th Fl *Web:* www.tribalddb.com	New York	NY	10022	212-515-8600	515-8660
Trone 4035 Piedmont Pkwy *TF:* 877-493-3043 ■ *Web:* www.trone.com	High Point	NC	27265	336-886-1622	886-4242
UniWorld Group Inc 1 Metro Ctr N 11th Fl *TF:* 800-900-2958 ■ *Web:* www.uniworldgroup.com	Brooklyn	NY	11201	212-219-1600	219-6395
Vantage Media LLC 2101 Rosecrans Ave *Web:* www.vantagemedia.com	El Segundo	CA	90245	310-482-3737	640-9960
VIA Agency 619 Congress St *Web:* www.vianow.com	Portland	ME	04101	207-221-3000	761-9422
VML Inc 250 NW Richards Rd *TF:* 800-990-2468 ■ *Web:* www.vml.com	Kansas City	MO	64116	816-283-0700	283-0954
Vox Medica Inc 601 Walnut St Suite 250-S *TF:* 800-842-6482 ■ *Web:* www.voxmedica.com	Philadelphia	PA	19106	215-238-8500	238-0881
Wasserman Media Group LLC 10960 Wilshire Blvd Suite 2200 *Web:* www.wmgllc.com	Los Angeles	CA	90024	310-407-0200	407-0300
Weintraub Adv Inc 7745 Carondelet Ave *Web:* www.weintraubadv.com	Saint Louis	MO	63105	314-721-5050	721-6850
White & Partners Inc 13665 Dulles Tech Dr Suite 150 *Web:* www.whiteandpartners.com	Herndon	VA	20171	703-793-3000	793-1495
Wieden & Kennedy 224 NW 13th Ave *Web:* www.wk.com	Portland	OR	97209	503-937-7000	937-8000
Williams Whittle Assoc Inc 711 Princess St *Web:* www.williamswhittle.com	Alexandria	VA	22314	703-836-9222	684-3285
Winner Communications Inc 37 Union Sq W 5th Fl *Web:* www.winnercommunications.com	New York	NY	10003	212-206-0111	627-9874
WKP & Spier New York 2 Pk Ave *Web:* www.wkpadv.com	New York	NY	10016	212-686-2914	686-5652
WPP Group USA Inc 125 Pk Ave 4th Fl *Web:* www.wpp.com	New York	NY	10017	212-632-2200	632-2222
Wyse Adv 668 Euclid Ave # 100 *Web:* www.wyseadv.com	Cleveland	OH	44114	216-696-2424	736-4440
Zimmerman Adv 2200 W Commercial Blvd Suite 300 *TF:* 800-248-8522 ■ *Web:* www.zadv.com	Fort Lauderdale	FL	33309	954-644-4000	644-6000
Zubi Adv Services Inc 355 Alhambra Cir FL 10 *Web:* www.zubiad.com	Miami	FL	33134	305-448-9824	460-7011

ADVERTISING DISPLAYS

SEE Displays - Exhibit & Trade Show p. 1785; Displays - Point-of-Purchase p. 1785; Signs p. 2657

5 ADVERTISING SERVICES - DIRECT MAIL

	City	State	ZIP	Phone	Fax
Access Direct Systems Inc 91 Executive Blvd *Web:* www.accessresponsesite.com	Farmingdale	NY	11735	631-420-0770	420-1647
Accurate Mailings Inc 215 O'Neill Ave *TF:* 800-732-3290 ■ *Web:* www.accuratemailings.com	Belmont	CA	94002	650-508-8885	594-8428
Acxiom Direct 620 Airpark Ctr Dr *TF:* 888-816-0925 ■ *Web:* www.acxiom.com	Nashville	TN	37217	615-850-3000	399-9867
Adtron Inc 1700 Morrissey Dr	Bloomington	IL	61704	309-662-1221	663-6691
Advanced Technology Marketing 400 N Continental Blvd Suite 200 *Web:* www.advancedtechmktg.com	El Segundo	CA	90245	310-642-1881	414-9436
American List Counsel Inc 4300 US Hwy 1 *Web:* www.alc.com	Princeton	NJ	08543	609-580-2800	580-2888
American Mailers - Illinois Inc 820 Frontenac Rd *Web:* www.anetorder.com	Naperville	IL	60563	630-579-8800	
American Student List LLC 330 Old Country Rd *TF:* 888-462-5600 ■ *Web:* www.studentlist.com	Mineola	NY	11501	516-248-6100	248-6364
Americomm 804 Greenbrier Cir *TF:* 800-527-6757 ■ *Web:* www.americomm.net	Chesapeake	VA	23320	757-622-2724	624-5713
Arista Information Systems Inc 1105 Fairchild Rd *Web:* www.aristainfo.com	Winston-Salem	NC	27105	336-776-1105	776-1104
Bancroft & Sons Transportation Inc 3390 High Prairie Rd *Web:* www.bancroftandsons.com	Grand Prairie	TX	75050	972-790-3777	986-0347
Bennett Kuhn Varner Inc 3390 Peachtree Rd NE # 1000 *Web:* www.bkv.com	Atlanta	GA	30326	404-233-0332	233-0302
Brierley & Partners 8401 N Central Expy Suite 1000 *Web:* www.brierley.com	Dallas	TX	75225	214-760-8700	743-5511
Carl Bloom Assoc Inc 81 Main St Suite 126 *Web:* www.carlbloom.com	White Plains	NY	10601	914-761-2800	761-2744
Catalina Marketing Corp 200 Carillon Pkwy *NYSE: POS* ■ *TF:* 888-322-3814 ■ *Web:* www.catmktg.com	Saint Petersburg	FL	33716	727-579-5000	579-5248
CBIZ the Leifer Group 6050 Oak Tree Blvd S Suite 500 *Web:* www.cbiz.com/leifer	Cleveland	OH	44131	216-447-9000	447-9007
Centron Data Services Inc 1175 Devin Dr *TF Cust Svc:* 800-732-8787 ■ *Web:* www.centrondata.com	Norton Shores	MI	49441	231-798-1221	799-0092
Century Direct LLC 30-00 47th Ave 3rd Fl **Fax Area Code:* 718 ■ *Web:* www.centurydirect.net	Long Island City	NY	11101	212-763-0600	349-9528*
Cenveo Inc 201 Broad St 1 Canterberry Green *NYSE: CVO* ■ *Web:* www.cenveo.com	Stamford	CT	06901	203-595-3000	595-3070
City Directories 5711 S 86th Cir *TF:* 888-508-0866 ■ *Web:* www.infousacity.com	Omaha	NE	68127	402-593-4500	596-7677
Creative Automation Co 220 Fencl Ln *TF:* 800-773-1588 ■ *Web:* www.cauto.com	Hillside	IL	60162	708-449-2800	
CTRAC Computer Services Inc 16855 Foltz Pkwy *Web:* www.ctrac.com	Strongsville	OH	44149	440-572-1000	572-3330
Denison Direct 9601 Newton Ave S *Web:* www.denisonmailing.com	Minneapolis	MN	55431	952-888-1460	888-9641
Direct Media Inc 200 Pemberwick Rd *Web:* www.dmminfo.com	Greenwich	CT	06830	402-836-5700	
DL Blair Inc 1051 Franklin Ave *Web:* www.dlblair.com	Garden City	NY	11530	516-746-3700	746-3889
DMW Worldwide LLC 701 Lee Rd Suite 103 *Web:* www.dmwdirect.com	Chesterbrook	PA	19087	610-407-0407	407-0410
Draftfcb 101 E Erie St *Web:* www.draftfcb.com	Chicago	IL	60611	312-425-5000	425-5010
Edith Roman Holdings Inc 1 Blue Hill Plaza, 16th Fl PO Box 1556 *TF:* 800-223-2194 ■ *Web:* www.edithroman.com	Pearl River	NY	10965	845-620-9000	620-9035
Focus Direct LLC 9707 Broadway *TF:* 800-299-9185 ■ *Web:* www.focusdirect.com	San Antonio	TX	78217	210-805-9185	
G2 USA 200 5th Ave *Web:* www.g2directanddigital.com	New York	NY	10010	212-546-2222	537-3737
Gannett Direct Marketing Services Inc 3400 Robards Ct **Fax:* Hum Res ■ *TF:* 800-345-5654 ■ *Web:* www.gdms.com	Louisville	KY	40218	502-454-6660	452-8518*
Haines & Co Inc 8050 Freedom Ave *TF:* 800-843-8452 ■ *Web:* www.haines.com	North Canton	OH	44720	330-494-9111	494-3862
Hallmark Data Systems 7300 Linder Ave *Web:* www.halldata.com	Skokie	IL	60077	847-983-2000	763-9542
Harte-Hanks Inc 9601 McAllister Fwy Suite 610 *NYSE: HHS* ■ *TF:* 800-456-9748 ■ *Web:* www.harte-hanks.com	San Antonio	TX	78216	210-829-9000	829-9403
Hawkeye 325 Arlington Ave Suite 700 *Web:* www.hawkeyeww.com	Charlotte	NC	28203	704-344-7900	344-7920
Haynes & Partners Communications 5745 Lee Rd	Indianapolis	IN	46216	317-860-3000	860-3001
Hecks Direct Mail & Printing Service Inc 202 W Florence Ave *TF:* 800-997-4325 ■ *Web:* www.hecksprinting.com	Toledo	OH	43605	419-661-6000	661-6036
Heritage Publishing Co 2402 Wildwood Ave **Fax:* Hum Res ■ *TF:* 800-643-8822 ■ *Web:* www.theheritagecompany.com	Sherwood	AR	72120	501-835-5000	835-5834*
Hibbert Group 400 Pennington Ave *TF:* 888-442-2378 ■ *Web:* www.hibbertco.com	Trenton	NJ	08650	609-394-7500	
Hkm Direct Market Communications Inc 5501 Cass Ave *TF:* 800-860-4456 ■ *Web:* www.hkmdirectmarket.com	Cleveland	OH	44102	216-651-9500	216-6330
iDirect Marketing 9880 Research Dr Suite 100 *TF:* 877-339-3737 ■ *Web:* www.idirectmarketing.com	Irvine	CA	92618	949-753-7300	753-7523
Jacobs & Clevenger Inc 303 E Wacker Dr Suite 2350 *Web:* www.jacobsclevenger.com	Chicago	IL	60601	312-894-3000	894-3005
Johnson & Quin Inc 7460 N Lehigh Ave *Web:* www.j-quin.com	Niles	IL	60714	847-588-4800	647-6949

Company	City	State	Zip	Phone	Fax
JS & A Group Inc 3350 Palms Centre Dr	Las Vegas	NV	89103	702-798-9000	597-2002
TF: 800-323-6400					
King Organization 245 S 4th Ave	Mount Vernon	NY	10550	914-667-4200	667-5281
Web: www.kinglitho.com					
Lake Group Media Inc					
411 Theodore Fremd Ave Suite 2-N	Rye	NY	10580	914-925-2400	925-2499
Web: www.lakegroupmedia.com					
Lewis Direct Marketing 325 E Oliver St	Baltimore	MD	21202	410-539-5100	685-5144
TF: 800-533-5394 ■ *Web:* www.lewisdirect.com					
Lortz Direct Marketing Inc (LDMI) 13936 Gold Cir	Omaha	NE	68144	402-334-9446	334-9622
TF: 800-366-7686 ■ *Web:* www.ldmiomaha.com					
Market Data Retrieval 6 Armstrong Rd	Shelton	CT	06484	203-926-4800	926-0784
TF: 800-333-8802 ■ *Web:* www.schooldata.com					
Marketing Drive LLC					
800 Connecticut Ave 3rd Fl East	Norwalk	CT	06854	203-857-6100	857-6176
Web: www.marketingdrive.com					
Marketing Resource Group Inc (MRG)					
225 S Washington Sq	Lansing	MI	48933	517-372-4400	372-4045
Web: www.mrgmi.com					
McCann WorldGroup 600 Battery St	San Francisco	CA	94111	646-865-2000	646-9610
Web: www.mccannworldgroup.com					
Modern Printing & Mailing					
3535 Enterprise St	San Diego	CA	92110	619-222-0535	222-0657
Web: www.home.pacbell.net/modprint/homepage.html					
Money Mailer LLC 12131 Western Ave	Garden Grove	CA	92841	714-889-3800	889-4618
TF: 800-234-2771 ■ *Web:* www.moneymailer.com					
News America Marketing					
1185 Avenue of the Americas 27	New York	NY	10036	212-782-8000	575-5847
TF: 800-462-0852 ■ *Web:* www.newsamerica.com					
O'Halloran Adv Inc 270 Saugatuck Ave	Westport	CT	06880	203-571-6203	341-9422
TF: 800-759-3556 ■ *Web:* www.ohalloranagency.com					
Odell Simms & Lynch Inc					
7704 Leesburg Pike	Falls Church	VA	22043	703-903-9797	903-8850
Web: www.odellsimms.com					
Ogilvy Action 350 W Mart Ctr Dr Suite 1150	Chicago	IL	60654	312-527-3900	527-3327
TF: 888-414-1410 ■ *Web:* www.ogilvyaction.com					
Ogilvy One Worldwide 636 11th Ave	New York	NY	10036	212-237-6000	237-5123
Web: www.ogilvy.com					
Priority Integrated Marketing					
6700 France Ave S Suite 300	Edina	MN	55435	800-727-6397	920-9930*
**Fax Area Code:* 952 ■ *TF:* 800-727-6397 ■ *Web:* www.prioritypub.com					
Promotions Unlimited PO Box 087601	Racine	WI	53408	262-681-7000	681-7001
TF: 800-992-9307 ■ *Web:* www.promot.com					
Publi-Sac Group 523 boul Lebeau	Saint-Laurent	QC	H4N3M7	514-337-6920	832-5083
Web: www.publisac.com					
Publishers Mailing Service 230 Aurora Ave N	Seattle	WA	98109	206-448-0411	441-4564
Rauxa Direct LLC 275 McCormick Ave A	Costa Mesa	CA	92626	714-427-1271	427-0661
Web: www.rauxa.com					
RDI Marketing Services					
4350 Glendale Milford Rd Suite 250	Cincinnati	OH	45242	513-984-5927	984-6126
TF: 800-388-7636 ■ *Web:* www.rdimarketing.com					
RR Donnelley Logistics 1000 Windham Pkwy	Bolingbrook	IL	60490	630-226-6100	226-6555
TF: 888-744-7773 ■ *Web:* www.rrdonnelley.com					
RR Donnelley Response Marketing Services					
3075 Highland Pkwy	Downers Grove	IL	60515	630-963-9494	
TF: 800-745-0780					
RSVP Publications					
6730 W Linebaugh Ave Suite 201	Tampa	FL	33625	813-960-7787	725-0621*
**Fax Area Code:* 877 ■ *TF:* 800-360-7787 ■ *Web:* www.rsvppublications.com					
RTC Relationship Marketing					
1055 Thomas Jefferson St NW Suite 200	Washington	DC	20007	202-625-2111	424-7900
Web: www.rtcdirect.com					
Russ Reid Co Inc 2 N Lake Ave Suite 600	Pasadena	CA	91101	626-449-6100	449-6190
Web: www.russreid.com					
Sherman & Assoc 333 Harmon Ave NW	Warren	OH	44483	330-399-4500	399-6747
Web: www.shermanexperience.com					
Simon Marketing Inc					
5200 W Century Blvd Suite 420	Los Angeles	CA	90045	310-417-4660	417-4670
Sitel Operating Corp					
3102 W End Ave Suite 1000	Nashville	TN	37203	615-301-7100	301-7150
TF: 866-957-4835 ■ *Web:* www.sitel.com					
SourceLink Inc 500 Pk Blvd Suite 415	Itasca	IL	60143	866-947-6872	438-5016*
**Fax Area Code:* 847 ■ *TF:* 866-947-6872 ■ *Web:* www.sourcelink.com					
Step Saver Inc 213 Spring St	Southington	CT	06489	860-628-9645	621-1841
Web: www.stepsaver.com					
Summit Marketing 8515 Bluejacket St	Lenexa	KS	66214	913-888-6222	888-2493
TF: 800-843-7347 ■ *Web:* www.summitmarketing.com					
SuperCoups 350 Revolutionary Dr	East Taunton	MA	02718	508-977-2000	977-0644
TF: 800-626-2620 ■ *Web:* www.supercoups.com					
Tension Envelope Corp 819 E 19th St	Kansas City	MO	64108	816-471-3800	283-1498
TF: 800-388-5122 ■ *Web:* www.tension.com					
United Letter Service Inc					
2200 Estes Ave	Elk Grove Village	IL	60007	312-427-3537	435-1192
Web: www.unitedgmg.com					
United Marketing Solutions					
7644 Dynatech Ct	Springfield	VA	22153	703-644-0200	455-8519
TF: 800-368-3501					
Valassis 1 Targeting Ctr	Windsor	CT	06095	860-285-6100	
TF: 800-238-6462 ■ *Web:* www.valassis.com					
Valpak Direct Marketing Systems Inc					
8605 Largo Lakes Dr	Largo	FL	33773	727-393-1270	393-8060
TF: 800-237-6266 ■ *Web:* www.valpak.com					
Vertis Media & Marketing Services					
21 Corporate Dr	Clifton Park	NY	12065	518-373-0419	373-5890
Web: www.vertisinc.com					
WA Wilde Co 201 Summer St PO Box 5838	Holliston	MA	01746	508-429-5515	893-0399
TF: 866-825-5515 ■ *Web:* www.wilde.com					
World Marketing 7950 Joliet Rd Suite 200	McCook	IL	60525	708-871-6000	871-6245
Web: www.worldmarkinc.com					
Wright Casino Marketing 10325 E 47th Ave	Denver	CO	80238	303-393-4530	393-5320
TF: 800-824-5886 ■ *Web:* www.wrightcasinomarketing.com					
Yeck Bros Co 2222 Arbor Blvd	Dayton	OH	45439	937-294-4000	294-6985
TF: 800-417-2767 ■ *Web:* www.yeck.com					

6 ADVERTISING SERVICES - MEDIA BUYERS

Company	City	State	Zip	Phone	Fax
Allan Hackel Organization Inc					
1330 Ctr St	Newton Center	MA	02459	617-965-4400	527-6005
Web: www.hackelbarter.com					
Arnold Romedy & Sullivan Adv Inc					
1001 Reads Lake Rd	Chattanooga	TN	37415	423-875-3743	875-5346
Beachbody LLC 3301 Exposition Blvd	Santa Monica	CA	90404	310-883-9000	
TF: 800-987-3677 ■ *Web:* www.beachbody.com					
Believe La 1040 N Las Palmas Bldg 10	Los Angeles	CA	90038	323-645-1000	645-1001
Web: www.believemedia.com					
Cablevision Media Sales 530 5th Ave 6th Fl	New York	NY	10036	212-382-6100	382-6128
Web: www.rainbow-media.com/adsales/index.html					
Corinthian Communications Inc					
500 8th Ave 5th Fl	New York	NY	10018	212-279-5700	279-5700
Web: www.mediabuying.com					
Ektron Inc 542 Amherst St (Rt 101A)	Nashua	NH	03063	603-594-0249	594-0258
TF: 888-987-6667 ■ *Web:* www.ektron.com					
J B Dollar Stretcher Magazine					
3105 Farnham Rd	Richfield	OH	44286	330-659-3590	659-6741
TF: 800-673-2531 ■ *Web:* www.jbdollar.com					
Katz Media Group Inc 125 W 55th St	New York	NY	10019	212-424-6000	424-6110*
**Fax:* Hum Res ■ *Web:* www.katz-media.com					
Lopito Ileana & Howie Inc PO Box 11856	San Juan	PR	00922	787-783-1160	783-8063
MAGNA Global USA					
1 Dag Hammarskjold Plaza 7th Fl	New York	NY	10017	917-542-7000	542-7001
Web: www.magnaglobal.com					
Media Networks Inc (MNI) 1 Stn Pl 5th Fl	Stamford	CT	06902	203-967-3100	967-6472
TF: 877-275-4664 ■ *Web:* www.mni.com					
Media Space Inc					
101 Merritt 7 Corporate Pk 3rd Fl	Norwalk	CT	06851	203-849-8855	849-5946
TF: 888-672-2100 ■ *Web:* www.mediaspacesolutions.com					
Omni Media Group Inc PO Box 14928	Cincinnati	OH	45250	513-381-5000	684-9276
Web: www.omnimediagroup.com					
Petry Media 3 E 54th St	New York	NY	10022	212-230-5900	230-5843
Web: www.petrymedia.com					
PGR Media 34 Farnsworth St 2nd Fl	Boston	MA	02210	617-502-8400	451-0451
Web: www.pgrmedia.com					
TaigMarks Inc 223 S Main St Suite 100	Elkhart	IN	46516	574-294-8844	294-8855
Web: www.taigmarks.com					
Telerep Inc 1 Dag Hammarskjold Plaza	New York	NY	10017	212-759-8787	486-8746
Web: www.telerepinc.com					
Transvideo Studios 990 Villa St	Mountain View	CA	94041	650-965-4898	962-1753
Web: www.transvideo.com					
Universal McCann 100 W 33rd St	New York	NY	10001	212-883-4700	
Web: www.umww.com					
Winstar Interactive Media 100 Pk Ave 5th Fl	New York	NY	10017	212-916-0700	896-8321
TF Cust Svc: 888-961-8800 ■ *Web:* www.winstarinteractive.com					
Working Mother Media Inc 60 E 42nd St 27th	New York	NY	10165	212-351-6400	351-6487
TF: 800-627-0690 ■ *Web:* www.workingmother.com					
Worldata 3000 N Military Trail	Boca Raton	FL	33431	561-393-8200	368-8345
TF: 800-331-8102 ■ *Web:* www.worldata.com					

7 ADVERTISING SERVICES - ONLINE

Company	City	State	Zip	Phone	Fax
ACSYS Inc 6 Executive Dr Suite 106	Farmington	CT	06032	860-679-9332	679-9344
TF: 866-497-3725 ■ *Web:* www.acsysinteractive.com					
Active Network 10182 Telesis Ct Suite 100	San Diego	CA	92121	858-964-3800	551-7619
TF: 888-543-7223 ■ *Web:* www.info.activenetwork.com					
Acxiom Digital					
1051 E Hillsdale Blvd Suite 400	Foster City	CA	94404	650-356-3400	356-3410
TF: 800-491-9320 ■ *Web:* www.acxiomdigital.com					
Advance Internet Inc 30 Journal Sq	Jersey City	NJ	07306	201-459-2899	
TF: 888-275-0257 ■ *Web:* www.advanceinternet.com					
Advertising.com Inc 1020 Hull St Suite 100	Baltimore	MD	21230	410-244-1370	244-1699
TF: 877-835-6699 ■ *Web:* www.advertising.com					
Agency.com Ltd 488 Madison Ave 4th Fl	New York	NY	10022	212-358-2600	358-2604
TF: 800-736-4644 ■ *Web:* www.agency.com					
Arc Worldwide 35 W Wacker Dr 15th Fl	Chicago	IL	60601	312-220-3200	220-1995
Web: www.arcww.com					
AspenMedia Inc 27031 Vista Terr	Lake Forest	CA	92630	949-412-9281	
Web: www.aspenmedia.com					
Beyond Interaction Inc					
2301 Platt Rd Suite 400	Ann Arbor	MI	48108	734-327-4763	677-8001
BigBad Inc 321 Summer St	Boston	MA	02210	617-338-7770	338-7787
Biggs/Gilmore Communications					
261 E Kalamazoo Ave Suite 300	Kalamazoo	MI	49007	269-349-7711	349-3051
Web: www.biggs-gilmore.com					
Blue Cat Design 4753 Mast Woods Rd	Port Hope	ON	L1A3V5	905-753-1017	753-2777
TF: 888-258-3228 ■ *Web:* www.bluecatdesign.com					
Blue Diesel 500 Olde Worthington Rd	Westerville	OH	43082	614-540-4226	540-3155
Web: www.bluediesel.com					
Brunner Inc 11 Stanwix St 5th Fl	Pittsburgh	PA	15222	412-995-9500	995-9501
TF: 800-545-5372 ■ *Web:* www.brunnerworks.com					
Burst Media 8 New England Executive Pk	Burlington	MA	01803	781-272-5544	272-0897
Web: www.burstmedia.com					
Butler Shine Stern & Partners					
20 Liberty Ship Way	Sausalito	CA	94965	415-331-6049	331-3524
Web: www.sfinteractive.com					
Carve Media Inc 35 Miller Rd Suite 192	Mill Valley	CA	94941	800-280-7863	
TF: 800-280-7863 ■ *Web:* www.carve.com					
CityGrid Media 8833 Sunset Blvd	West Hollywood	CA	90069	310-360-4500	
TF: 800-611-4827 ■ *Web:* www.citygridmedia.com					
Commission Junction Inc					
530 E Montecito St	Santa Barbara	CA	93103	805-730-8000	730-8001
TF: 800-761-1072 ■ *Web:* www.cj.com					

				Phone	Fax
Consona Corp 450 E 96th St Suite 300 *TF:* 866-662-3847 ■ *Web:* www.consona.com	Indianapolis	IN	46240	317-249-1200	249-1999
D2 Creative 28 World's Fair Dr. *Web:* www.nyd2.com	Somerset	NJ	08873	732-805-9297	805-0637
Digital Pulp Inc 220 E 23rd St Suite 900 *Web:* www.digitalpulp.com	New York	NY	10010	212-679-0676	679-6217
DigitalDay 122 Broad Blvd. *Web:* www.digitaldaycreative.com	Cuyahoga Falls	OH	44221	330-940-2565	940-2560
e21 corp 47787 Fremont Blvd *Web:* www.e21mm.com	Fremont	CA	94538	510-226-6780	226-0679
Epsilon Interactive 16 W 20th St 9th Fl. **Fax Area Code:* 646 ■ *Web:* www.epsiloninteractive.com	New York	NY	10011	212-457-7000	619-4431*
Euro RSCG 4D 350 Hudson St *Web:* www.eurorscg4d.com	New York	NY	10014	212-886-2000	886-2016
Focalex Inc 450 Sansome St Suite 200 **Fax Area Code:* 415 ■ *TF:* 877-362-2539 ■ *Web:* www.focalex.com	San Francisco	CA	94111	877-362-2539	295-4880*
Fusionary Media 820 Monroe Ave NW Suite 212 *Web:* www.fusionary.com	Grand Rapids	MI	49503	616-454-2357	454-6827
GSI Commerce Inc 935 1st Ave *NASDAQ:* GSIC ■ *TF:* 877-708-4305 ■ *Web:* www.gsicommerce.com	King of Prussia	PA	19406	610-491-7000	265-2866
Hacker Group Inc 1215 4th Ave Suite 2100 *Web:* www.hackergroup.com	Seattle	WA	98161	206-805-1500	805-1599
Interact Multimedia Corp 115 Highland Ave Suite 5 *Web:* www.interactmedical.com	Jersey City	NJ	07306	201-209-1569	
Inuvo Inc 15550 Lightwave Dr 3rd Fl Suite 300 *Web:* inuvo.com	Clearwater	FL	33760	727-324-0211	
iProspect 311 Arsenal St *TF:* 800-522-1152 ■ *Web:* www.iprospect.com	Watertown	MA	02472	617-923-7000	923-7004
LinkShare Corp 215 Pk Ave S 9th Fl *TF:* 800-875-5465 ■ *Web:* www.linkshare.com	New York	NY	10003	646-943-8200	943-8204
LiveWorld Inc 4340 Stevens Creek Blvd Suite 101 *Web:* www.liveworld.com	San Jose	CA	95129	408-871-5200	871-5300
LSF Network Inc 395 Oyster Pt Blvd Suite 110 *TF:* 877-616-8226 ■ *Web:* www.lsfnetwork.com	South San Francisco	CA	94080	650-616-8226	624-5412
Macquarium Intelligent Communications 1800 Peachtree St NW Suite 250 *Web:* www.macquarium.com	Atlanta	GA	30309	404-554-4000	554-4001
Marchex Inc 520 Pike St Suite 2000 *NASDAQ:* MCHX ■ *TF:* 800-840-1012 ■ *Web:* www.marchex.com	Seattle	WA	98101	206-331-3300	331-3695
Market Leader Inc 11332 NE 122nd Way Suite 200 *NASDAQ:* LEDR ■ *TF:* 877-450-0088 ■ *Web:* www.marketleader.com	Kirkland	WA	98034	425-852-5500	952-5691
mediSpecialty Inc 170a schmar *Web:* www.medispecialty.com	Del Valle	TX	78617	512-247-7964	514-1355
MetaDesign North America 615 Battery St 6th Fl *Web:* www.metadesign.com	San Francisco	CA	94111	415-627-0790	627-0795
MyPoints.com Inc 50 california 3rd Fl *TF:* 888-262-4528 ■ *Web:* www.mypoints.com	San Francisco	CA	94111	415-829-6100	829-6122
NetGain Technology Inc 720 W St Germain St Suite 200 *Web:* www.netgaintechnology.com	Saint Cloud	MN	56301	320-251-4700	251-5030
non-linear creations Inc 987 Wellington St Suite 201 *TF:* 866-915-2997 ■ *Web:* www.nonlinear.ca	Ottawa	ON	K1Y2Y1	613-241-2067	241-3086
Organic Inc 555 Market St 4th Fl *Web:* www.organic.com	San Francisco	CA	94105	415-581-5300	581-5400
Pacifico Inc 3880 S Bascom Ave Suite 215 *Web:* www.pacifico.com	San Jose	CA	91524	408-559-8880	
Q Interactive Inc 1 N Dearborn St Suite 12 *TF:* 888-729-6465 ■ *Web:* www.qinteractive.com	Chicago	IL	60602	312-224-5000	224-5001
R/GA 350 W 39th St *Web:* www.rga.com	New York	NY	10018	212-946-4000	946-4010
Renegade LLC 41 E 11th St Fl 3 *Web:* www.renegade.com	New York	NY	10003	646-486-7702	486-7800
Return Path Inc 304 Pk Ave S 7th Fl *Web:* www.returnpath.net	New York	NY	10010	212-905-5500	905-5501
ShopLocal LLC 225 N Michigan Ave Suite 1600 *Web:* www.aboutshoplocal.com	Chicago	IL	60601	312-616-5800	
Siegel & Gale 625 Avenue of the Americas 4th Fl *Web:* www.siegelgale.com	New York	NY	10011	212-453-0400	453-0401
Stein + Partners Brand Activation (SPBA) 432 Pk Ave S *Web:* steinbrand.com	New York	NY	10016	212-213-1112	779-7305
Topica Inc 685 Market St Suite 300 *Web:* www.topica.com	San Francisco	CA	94105	415-344-0800	344-0900
Transcontinental Inc 1100 Rene-Levesque Blvd W 24th Fl *TF:* 800-361-5479 ■ *Web:* www.transcontinentalmedia.com	Montreal	QC	H3B4X9	514-392-9000	
ValueClick Inc 30699 Russell Ranch Rd Suite 250 *NASDAQ:* VCLK ■ *TF:* 877-825-8323 ■ *Web:* www.valueclick.com	Westlake Village	CA	91361	818-575-4500	575-4501
ValueClick Media 530 E Montecito St *Web:* www.valueclickmedia.com	Santa Barbara	CA	93103	805-879-1600	456-6611
Vermont Media Publishing Co LTD Rt 100 PO Box 310 *Web:* www.dvalnews.com	West Dover	VT	05356	802-464-3388	464-7255
Yahoo! Search Marketing 74 N Pasadena Ave 3rd Fl *TF:* 888-811-4686	Pasadena	CA	91103	626-685-5600	685-5601
yesmail inc 959 Skyway Rd Suite 150 *TF:* 877-937-6245 ■ *Web:* www.yesmail.com	San Carlos	CA	94070	650-620-1200	620-1273

8 ADVERTISING SERVICES - OUTDOOR ADVERTISING

				Phone	Fax
Adams Outdoor Adv Co 911 SW Adams St *Web:* www.adamsoutdoor.com	Peoria	IL	61602	309-692-2482	692-8452
Bowlin Travel Centers Inc 150 Louisiana Blvd NE *TF:* 800-334-2236 ■ *Web:* www.bowlintc.com	Albuquerque	NM	87108	505-266-5985	266-7821
CBS Outdoor 405 Lexington Ave 14th Fl *TF:* 800-926-8834 ■ *Web:* www.cbsoutdoor.com	New York	NY	10174	212-297-6400	370-1817
Clear Ch Outdoor Inc 2201 E Camelback Rd Suite 500 *Web:* www.clearchanneloutdoor.com	Phoenix	AZ	85016	602-381-5700	381-5782
Colby Poster Printing Co Inc 1332 W 12th Pl *Web:* www.colbyposter.com	Los Angeles	CA	90015	213-747-5108	747-3209
Diamond Outdoor Adv 1200 E Golf Rd *Web:* www.diamondoutdoor.com	Des Plaines	IL	60016	847-827-1771	827-6551
Fairway Outdoor Adv 713 Broad St *Web:* www.fairwayoutdoor.com	Augusta	GA	30901	706-724-8987	724-6308
Kubin-Nicholson Corp 8440 N 87th St *TF:* 800-858-9557 ■ *Web:* www.kubin.com	Milwaukee	WI	53224	414-586-4300	586-6802
Lamar Adv Co 5321 Corporate Blvd *NASDAQ:* LAMR ■ *TF:* 800-235-2627 ■ *Web:* www.lamar.com	Baton Rouge	LA	70808	225-926-1000	923-0658
Lamar Outdoor Adv 5953 Susquehanna Plaza Dr *TF:* 800-632-9014 ■ *Web:* www.lamaroutdoor.com	York	PA	17406	717-252-1528	252-4832
May Adv International Ltd 1200 Forum Way S **Fax Area Code:* 800 ■ *TF:* 800-800-4629 ■ *Web:* www.mayadvertising.com	Fort Worth	TX	76140	817-336-5671	800-3299*
National Print Group Inc National Posters Div 1001 Latta St *TF:* 800-624-0408 ■ *Web:* www.nationalposters.com	Chattanooga	TN	37406	423-622-1106	624-4289
NextMedia Group Inc 6312 S Fiddlers Green Cir Suite 205 *Web:* www.nextmediagroup.net	Greenwood Village	CO	80111	303-694-9118	694-4940
Peachtree Packaging Inc 770 Marathon Pkwy *Web:* www.peachtreepackaging.com	Lawrenceville	GA	30045	770-822-1304	995-8447
Witt Sign Co Inc 306 McCowan Dr	Lebanon	TN	37087	615-444-3898	444-3980

9 ADVERTISING SPECIALTIES

SEE ALSO Signs p. 2657; Smart Cards p. 2658; Trophies, Plaques, Awards p. 2734

				Phone	Fax
Adco Litho Line Inc 2700 W Roosevelt Rd *TF:* 800-875-2326 ■ *Web:* www.adcolitholine.com	Broadview	IL	60155	708-345-8200	345-8297
Adimage Promotional Group 2300 Main St *TF:* 800-344-8809 ■ *Web:* www.adgpromo.com	Hugo	MN	55038	800-344-8809	896-9228
Adventures in Adv (AIA) 800 Winneconne Ave *TF:* 800-460-7836 ■ *Web:* www.aiagearedforgrowth.com	Neenah	WI	54956	920-886-3700	886-3701
Airmate Co Inc 16280 County Rd D *TF:* 800-544-3614 ■ *Web:* www.airmatecompany.com	Bryan	OH	43506	419-636-3184	636-4210
Alexander Mfg Co 12978 Tesson Ferry Rd **Fax Area Code:* 800 ■ *TF Cust Svc:* 800-467-5343 ■ *Web:* www.alexandermc.com	Saint Louis	MO	63128	314-842-3344	391-2539*
Allen Co 712 E Main St *TF:* 800-329-2491 ■ *Web:* www.allenmugs.com	Blanchester	OH	45107	937-783-2491	783-4831
Americanna Co 29 Aldrin Rd *TF Cust Svc:* 888-747-5550 ■ *Web:* www.americanna.com	Plymouth	MA	02360	508-747-5550	747-5578
AmPro Inc 1511 S Garfield Pl *TF:* 800-325-3895	Mason City	IA	50401	641-422-9950	422-0244
Amsterdam Printing & Litho Corp 166 County Hwy 15 *TF:* 800-833-6231 ■ *Web:* www.amsterdamprinting.com	Amsterdam	NY	12010	518-842-6000	843-5204
Arnold Pen Co 15 N Union St **Fax Area Code:* 800 ■ *TF:* 800-296-6612 ■ *Web:* www.arnoldpen.com	Petersburg	VA	23803	804-733-6612	658-4623*
Arthur Blank & Co Inc 225 Rivermoor St *TF:* 800-776-7333 ■ *Web:* www.arthurblank.com	Boston	MA	02132	617-325-9600	327-1235
Atlas Match LLC 1801 S Airport Cir *TF:* 800-628-2426 ■ *Web:* www.atlasmatch.com	Euless	TX	76040	817-267-1500	354-7478
Atlas Pen & Pencil Corp 408 Madison St Suite 126 *TF:* 800-327-3232 ■ *Web:* www.atlaspen.com	San Diego	CA	92131	800-327-3232	342-8889
Barton Nelson Inc 13700 Wyandotte *TF:* 800-821-6697 ■ *Web:* www.bebco.com	Kansas City	MO	64145	816-942-3100	942-6995
Bastian Co PO Box 250 *TF:* 800-609-0097 ■ *Web:* www.bastiancompany.com	Phelps	NY	14532	315-548-2300	548-2310
Belaire Products Inc 763 S Broadway St *TF:* 800-886-3224 ■ *Web:* www.belaireproducts.com	Akron	OH	44311	330-253-3116	376-7790
Bergamot Inc 820 E Wisconsin St **Fax:* Sales ■ *TF Cust Svc:* 800-922-6733 ■ *Web:* www.bergamot.net	Delavan	WI	53115	262-728-5572	728-3750*
Brown & Bigelow Inc 345 Plato Blvd E **Fax:* Hum Res ■ *TF Cust Svc:* 800-628-1755 ■ *Web:* www.brownandbigelow.com	Saint Paul	MN	55107	651-293-7000	293-7025*
Churchwell Co 814 S Edgewood Ave *TF:* 800-245-0075 ■ *Web:* www.churchwellcompany.com	Jacksonville	FL	32205	904-356-5721	354-2436
Clear Ch Merchandising 1 Noyes Ave *Web:* www.clearchannel.com/Merchandising	Rumford	RI	02916	954-423-1909	424-0193
Crown Products LLC 3107 Halls Mill Rd *TF:* 800-367-2769 ■ *Web:* www.crownprod.com	Mobile	AL	36606	251-476-7777	471-2095
Dard Products Inc 912 Custer Ave *TF:* 800-323-2925 ■ *Web:* www.tagmaster.net	Evanston	IL	60202	847-328-5000	328-7835
Dunn Mfg Inc 1400 Goldmine Rd *TF:* 800-868-7111	Monroe	NC	28110	704-283-2147	289-6857
EBSCO Creative Concepts 825 5th Ave S *TF:* 800-756-7023 ■ *Web:* www.ebscocreativeconcepts.com	Birmingham	AL	35233	205-323-4618	226-8429
Elliott Sales 2502 S 12th St *TF:* 800-576-3945 ■ *Web:* www.elliottsales.com	Tacoma	WA	98405	253-383-3883	383-3130

				Phone	Fax
Ever-Lite Co Inc 1717 N Bayshore Dr Unit 1632 *TF:* 800-891-4670 ■ *Web:* www.ever-lite.com	Miami	FL	33132	305-577-0819	577-0819
Evigna Brand Insight 800 Tech Row *Web:* www.evigna.com	Madison Heights	MI	48071	248-458-5000	
Flair Communications Agency Inc 214 W Erie St *TF:* 800-621-8317 ■ *Web:* www.flairagency.com	Chicago	IL	60654	312-943-5959	943-5316
Francis & Lusky LLC 1450 Elm Hill Pike *TF:* 800-251-3711 ■ *Web:* www.promoville.com	Nashville	TN	37210	615-242-0501	256-0862
Geiger 70 Mt Hope Ave *Web:* www.geiger.com	Lewiston	ME	04240	207-755-2000	755-2423
Geiger Bros Promotional Marketing 2010 Oakgrove Rd *TF Cust Svc:* 800-264-9291	Hattiesburg	MS	39402	601-264-1991	268-1175
Gigunda Group Inc 540 N Commercial St 3rd Fl *Web:* www.gigundagroup.com	Manchester	NH	03101	603-314-5000	314-5001
Gold Bond Inc 5485 Hixson Pike **Fax Area Code:* 800 ■ *Web:* www.goldbondinc.com	Hixson	TN	37343	423-842-5844	729-4852*
HALO Branded Solutions 1980 Industrial Dr *TF:* 866-840-6401 ■ *Web:* www.leewayne.com	Sterling	IL	61081	815-625-0980	548-9193
Hit Promotional Products Inc 7150 Bryan Dairy Rd *TF:* 800-237-6305 ■ *Web:* www.hitpromo.net	Largo	FL	33777	727-541-5561	541-5130
Imageworks Mfg Inc 49 S St *TF:* 800-950-1122 ■ *Web:* www.imageworksmfg.com	Park Forest	IL	60466	708-503-1122	503-1133
Instant Imprints 5897 Oberlin Dr # 200 *TF:* 800-542-3437 ■ *Web:* www.instantimprints.com	San Diego	CA	92121	858-642-4848	453-6513
Jordan Industries Inc Specialty Printing & Labeling Group 1751 Lake Cook Rd Suite 550 ArborLake Ctr *Web:* www.jordanindustries.com	Deerfield	IL	60015	847-945-5591	945-5698
Lewtan Industries Corp 30 High St *TF:* 800-539-8268	Hartford	CT	06103	860-278-9800	278-9019
Marco Promotional Products 2640 Commerce Dr **Fax Area Code:* 866 ■ *TF:* 877-545-9322 ■ *Web:* www.marcopromotionalproducts.com	Harrisburg	PA	17110	877-545-9322	545-5672*
Marietta Corp 37 Huntington St PO Box 5250 **Fax Area Code:* 800 ■ **Fax:* Cust Svc ■ *TF:* 800-950-7772 ■ *Web:* www.mariettacorp.com	Cortland	NY	13045	607-753-6746	756-0658*
Maryland Match Corp 605 Alluvion St *TF:* 800-423-0013 ■ *Web:* www.marylandmatch.com	Baltimore	MD	21230	410-752-8164	752-3441
Mid-America Merchandising Inc 204 W 3rd St *TF:* 800-333-6737 ■ *Web:* www.mmipromo.com	Kansas City	MO	64105	816-471-5600	842-0952
MMG Works/Status Promotions 4601 Madison Ave *TF:* 800-945-4044 ■ *Web:* www.mmgworks.com	Kansas City	MO	64112	816-472-5988	472-7107
Morco Inc 125 High St *TF:* 800-247-4093 ■ *Web:* www.morcoline.com	Cochranton	PA	16314	814-425-7476	425-7119
Myron Corp 205 Maywood Ave *TF:* 800-526-9766 ■ *Web:* www.myron.com	Maywood	NJ	07607	201-843-6464	
National Pen Corp 12121 Scripps Summit Dr # 200 *TF:* 800-854-1000 ■ *Web:* www.pens.com	San Diego	CA	92131	858-675-3000	675-0890
Nationwide Adv Specialty Inc 2025 S Cooper St *Web:* www.nationwideadvertising.net	Arlington	TX	76010	817-275-2678	274-4301
Neely Mfg Inc 2178 Hwy 2 *TF:* 800-247-1785 ■ *Web:* www.neelymfg.com	Corydon	IA	50060	641-872-1100	872-2039
Newton Mfg Co 1123 1st Ave E *TF:* 800-500-7227 ■ *Web:* www.newtonmfg.com	Newton	IA	50208	641-792-4121	792-6261
Norscot Group Inc 1000 W Donges Bay Rd PO Box 998 *TF:* 800-653-3313 ■ *Web:* www.norscot.com	Mequon	WI	53092	262-241-3313	241-4904
Norwood Promotional Products Inc 10 W Market St Suite 1400 *TF:* 800-959-9138 ■ *Web:* www.norwood.com	Indianapolis	IN	46204	317-275-2500	
Numo Mfg Co 1072 E Hwy 175 *TF:* 800-253-0434 ■ *Web:* www.numomfg.com	Kaufman	TX	75142	972-962-5400	962-5436
Perrygraf Co 25 W 550 Geneva Rd *TF:* 800-423-5329 ■ *Web:* www.perrygraf.com	Carol Stream	IL	60188	630-784-0100	784-6690
Pilgrim Plastic Products Co 1200 W Chestnut St *TF:* 877-343-7810 ■ *Web:* www.pilgrimplastics.com	Brockton	MA	02301	508-436-6300	580-3542
Prime Resources Corp 1100 Boston Ave **Fax Area Code:* 800 ■ *TF:* 800-873-7746 ■ *Web:* www.primeline.com	Bridgeport	CT	06610	203-331-9100	314-3812*
Quick Point Inc 1717 Fenpark Dr *Web:* www.quickpoint.com	Fenton	MO	63026	636-343-9400	343-3587
Quikey Mfg Co 1500 Industrial Pkwy *TF:* 877-901-1200 ■ *Web:* www.quikey.com	Akron	OH	44310	330-633-8106	633-6670
RM Crow Co 200 Factory Dr	Waco	TX	76710	254-772-5280	772-0941
Sanders Mfg Co 1422 Lebanon Rd *TF:* 866-254-6611 ■ *Web:* www.samcoline.com	Nashville	TN	37210	615-254-6611	242-3732
Slack & Co Inc 233 N Michigan Ave Suite 3050 *Web:* www.slackandcompany.com	Chicago	IL	60601	312-970-5800	970-5850
Sport It Inc PO Box 50777 *TF:* 888-233-2659 ■ *Web:* www.sport-it.com	San Diego	CA	92150	760-597-9700	752-8681
Staples Promotional Products 7500 W 110th St *TF:* 800-848-8028 ■ *Web:* www.staplespromotionalproducts.com	Overland Park	KS	66210	913-319-3100	319-4960
Universal Creative Concepts Corp 10143 Royalton Rd Suite E *Web:* www.uccadv.com	North Royalton	OH	44133	440-230-1366	230-1919
Vanguard East 1172 Azalea Garden Rd *TF:* 800-221-1264 ■ *Web:* www.vanguardmil.com	Norfolk	VA	23502	757-857-3600	857-0222
VATEX America 2395 Hermitage Rd *Web:* www.vatex.com	Richmond	VA	23220	804-353-9010	353-8939
Vernon Co 1 Promotion Pl PO Box 600 *Web:* www.vernoncompany.com	Newton	IA	50208	641-792-9000	792-6901
Vitronic/Four Seasons 4680 Pkwy Dr Suite 200 **Fax Area Code:* 513 ■ *TF:* 877-844-5032 ■ *Web:* www.vitronicpromotional.com	Mason	OH	45040	877-844-5032	398-7165*
Western Plastic Products Inc 1556 W Esther St *TF:* 800-453-1881 ■ *Web:* www.wbadges.com	Long Beach	CA	90813	562-435-4881	495-2232
Zebra Marketing 7306 Coldwater Canyon Unit 11 *TF:* 800-348-2422 ■ *Web:* www.zebramerchandise.blogspot.com	North Hollywood	CA	91605	818-765-6442	765-3996

AGRICULTURAL CHEMICALS

SEE Fertilizers & Pesticides p. 1843

AGRICULTURAL MACHINERY & EQUIPMENT

SEE Farm Machinery & Equipment - Mfr p. 1838; Farm Machinery & Equipment - Whol p. 1839

10 AGRICULTURAL PRODUCTS

SEE ALSO Fruit Growers p. 1890; Horse Breeders p. 2026; Horticultural Products Growers p. 2026; Seed Companies p. 2650

				Phone	Fax
Border Valley Trading Ltd 604 E Mead Rd *Web:* www.bordervalley.com	Brawley	CA	92227	760-344-6700	344-4305
United Farmers Co-op (UFC) 705 E 4th St PO Box 461 *TF:* 866-998-3266 ■ *Web:* www.ufcmn.com	Winthrop	MN	55396	507-647-6600	647-6620

10-1 Cattle Ranches, Farms, Feedlots (Beef Cattle)

				Phone	Fax
A Duda & Sons Inc 1200 Duda Trail *Web:* www.duda.com	Oviedo	FL	32765	407-365-2111	365-2147
Agri Beef Co 1555 Shoreline Dr Suite 320 *TF:* 800-657-6305 ■ *Web:* www.agribeef.com	Boise	ID	83702	208-338-2500	338-2605
Agri Beef Co Boise Valley Feeders Div 2201 Ridgeway Rd *Web:* www.agribeef.com	Parma	ID	83660	208-722-8090	722-8093
Agri Beef Co El Oro Cattle Feeders Div 18857 Rd 2.7 SE *Web:* www.agribeef.com	Moses Lake	WA	98837	509-349-2321	349-2272
Ainsworth Feed Yards Co PO Box 267 *TF:* 800-438-3148	Ainsworth	NE	69210	402-387-2455	387-0105
Ashland Feeders 2590 CRL *Web:* www.ashlandfeeders.com	Ashland	KS	67831	620-635-2213	635-2291
AzTx Cattle Co PO Box 390 *TF:* 800-999-5065 ■ *Web:* www.aztx.com	Hereford	TX	79045	806-364-8871	364-3842
Bar G Feedyard PO Box 1797 *Web:* www.bar-g.com	Hereford	TX	79045	806-357-2241	357-2245
Barton County Feeders Inc 1164 SE 40th Rd	Ellinwood	KS	67526	620-564-2200	564-2253
Beef Belt Feeders Inc 1350 E Rd 70	Scott City	KS	67871	620-872-3059	872-7060
Beef Northwest Feeders Inc 3455 Victorio Rd *Web:* www.beefnw.com	Nyssa	OR	97913	541-372-2101	372-5661
Beef Tech Cattle Feeders Inc 3476 Country Rd 9	Hereford	TX	79045	806-363-6080	363-6078
Bledsoe Cattle Co PO Box 406	Wray	CO	80758	970-332-4955	332-4837
Bracht Feedyards Inc 1931 'I' Rd	West Point	NE	68788	402-372-3662	372-3669
Brookover Feed Yards Inc 3013 N US Hwy 83 *Web:* www.brookover.com	Garden City	KS	67846	620-276-6662	276-4447
Buffalo Feeders LLC PO Box 409 *Web:* www.buffalofeeders.com	Buffalo	OK	73834	580-735-2511	735-6035
Cactus Feeders Inc 2209 W 7th Ave *TF:* 877-698-7355 ■ *Web:* www.cactusfeeders.com	Amarillo	TX	79106	806-373-2333	371-4775
Canadian Feedyards Inc PO Box 866	Canadian	TX	79014	806-323-5333	323-8422
Cattlco PO Box 1271	Sterling	CO	80751	970-522-8260	522-8269
Cedar Bluff Cattle Feeders Inc RR 2 PO Box 7171	Ellis	KS	67637	785-726-3100	726-3690
Christensen Cattle Co Inc 2967 Hwy 14	Fullerton	NE	68638	308-536-2405	536-2562
Coleman Natural Foods 1667 Cole Blvd Bldg 19 Suite 300 *TF:* 800-442-8666 ■ *Web:* www.colemannatural.com	Lakewood	CO	80401	303-468-2500	277-9263
Coyote Lake Feedyard Inc 1287 FM 1731 *TF:* 800-299-3321 ■ *Web:* www.coyotelakefeedyard.com	Muleshoe	TX	79347	806-946-3321	946-3329
CRI Feeders Inc Rt 2 PO Box 114	Guymon	OK	73942	580-545-3344	545-3642
Darr Feedlot Inc 42826 Rd 759 *Web:* www.darrfeedlot.com	Cozad	NE	69130	308-324-2363	324-2365
Dean Cluck Cattle Co Ltd 105 Dean Cluck Ave	Gruver	TX	79040	806-733-5021	733-2244
Dinklage Feedyards PO Box 274 *TF:* 888-343-5940 ■ *Web:* www.dinklagefeedyards.com	Sidney	NE	69162	308-254-5940	254-6260
Fall River Feedyard LLC PO Box 892	Hot Springs	SD	57747	605-745-4109	745-3352
Ford County Feed Yard Inc 12466 US Hwy 400 *TF:* 800-783-2739	Ford	KS	67842	620-369-2252	369-2250
Friona Feedyard 2370 FM 3140 *TF:* 800-658-6086 ■ *Web:* www.frionaind.com	Friona	TX	79035	806-265-3574	265-3577
Friona Industries LP 500 S Taylor St Suite 601 PO Box 15568 *TF:* 800-658-6014 ■ *Web:* www.frionaind.com	Amarillo	TX	79105	806-374-1811	374-1324
Garden City Feed Yard 1805 W Annie Scheer Rd *TF:* 800-272-4191	Garden City	KS	67846	620-275-4191	
Gottsch Feeding Corp 20507 Nicholas Cir Suite 100	Elkhorn	NE	68022	402-289-4421	289-4202
Gray County Feed Yard Inc 23405 SR 23	Cimarron	KS	67835	620-855-3486	855-7739
Great Bend Feeding Inc 355 NW 30 Ave *Web:* www.ilsbeef.com	Great Bend	KS	67530	620-792-2508	792-5047
Hansford County Feeders LP 13800 County Rd 19	Spearman	TX	79081	806-733-5025	477-1910
Hays Feeders LLC 1174 Feedlot Rd *Web:* www.prattfeeders.com	Hays	KS	67601	785-625-3415	625-0074
Henry C Hitch Feedyards PO Box 1559 *TF:* 800-951-2533 ■ *Web:* www.hitchok.com	Guymon	OK	73942	580-338-2533	338-2718

	City	State	Zip	Phone	Fax
High Choice Feeders LLC 553 W Rd 40	Scott City	KS	67871	620-872-7271	872-5763
Hurd Co 83973 489th Ave	Bartlett	NE	68622	402-482-5931	482-5971
Ingalls Feed Yard 10505 US Hwy 50	Ingalls	KS	67853	620-335-5174	335-5232
TF: 800-477-6907 ■ *Web:* www.irsikanddoll.com					
Irsik & Doll Co PO Box 847	Cimarron	KS	67835	620-855-3111	855-3748
Web: www.irsikanddoll.com					
JR Simplot Co 999 W Main St # 1300	Boise	ID	83702	208-336-2110	389-7515
TF: 800-635-5008 ■ *Web:* www.simplot.com					
King Ranch Inc Three Riverway Suite 1600	Houston	TX	77056	832-681-5700	
Web: www.king-ranch.com					
Knight Feedlot Inc 1768 Ave J	Lyons	KS	67554	620-257-5106	257-3347
Littlefield Feedyard RR 1 PO Box 26	Amherst	TX	79312	806-385-5141	385-3485
TF: 800-687-5141 ■ *Web:* www.frionaind.com/feedyard/little_field.htm					
McLean Feedyard Ltd 13948 County Rd A	McLean	TX	79057	806-779-2405	779-2319
Web: www.ranches.org					
Midwest Feeders Inc 5013 13 Rd	Ingalls	KS	67853	620-335-5790	
Web: www.midwest-feeders.com					
Morrison Enterprises PO Box 609	Hastings	NE	68902	402-463-3191	462-8542
North Platte Livestock Feeders Inc 1831 E S St	Hastings	NE	68901	402-463-6215	463-6715
Web: www.gottschcattlecompany.com					
Oshkosh Feed Yard PO Box 440	Oshkosh	NE	69154	308-772-3237	
Perryton Feeders Inc 13210 Hwy 70 S	Perryton	TX	79070	806-435-5466	435-3197
Pinneo Feed Lot Ltd Liability Co PO Box 384	Brush	CO	80723	970-842-0701	842-0720
PM Beef Group LLC 2850 Hwy 60 E	Windom	MN	56101	507-831-2761	831-6216
TF: 800-622-5213 ■ *Web:* www.pmbeef.com					
Pratt Feeders LLC PO Box 945	Pratt	KS	67124	620-672-6448	672-7797
Web: www.prattfeeders.com					
Premium Feeders Inc PO Box 230	Scandia	KS	66966	785-335-2222	335-2558
Web: www.premiumfeeders.com					
Quality Beef Producers 5000 IH- 40	Wildorado	TX	79098	806-426-3325	426-3582
Web: www.qualitybeefproducers.com					
Rafter 3 Feedyard Inc PO Box 1127	Dimmitt	TX	79027	806-647-5103	
Randall County Feedyard 15000 FM 2219	Amarillo	TX	79119	806-499-3701	499-3439
TF: 800-658-6063 ■ *Web:* www.frionaind.com					
Red Rock Feeding Co PO Box 1039	Red Rock	AZ	85145	520-682-3448	682-3830
Royal Beef Feed Yard 11060 N Falcon Rd	Scott City	KS	67871	620-872-5371	872-3380
Web: www.irsikanddoll.com					
Runnells Peters Cattle Co Inc 9505 Mines Rd Suite 116 PMB 152	Laredo	TX	78045	956-724-3637	724-5269
Snake River Cattle Feeders 2394 Feed Lot Rd	American Falls	ID	83211	208-226-5126	226-5128
Sparrowk Livestock 18780 E Hwy 88	Clements	CA	95227	209-759-3530	759-3831
Web: www.sparrowk.com					
Sublette Feeders PO Box 917	Sublette	KS	67877	620-668-5501	
Swisher County Cattle Co PO Box 129	Tulia	TX	79088	806-627-4231	627-4254
TF: 800-658-6064 ■ *Web:* www.frionaind.com					
Taylor/Herring Co PO Box 2805	Amarillo	TX	79105	806-376-6347	376-6340
Tejas Feeders Ltd PO Box 1782	Pampa	TX	79066	806-665-2303	669-0210
Tejon Ranch Co 4436 Lebec Rd PO Box 1000	Lebec	CA	93243	661-248-3000	248-3100
NYSE: TRC ■ *Web:* www.tejonranch.com					
Texas County Feed Yard E Hwy 54 PO Box 1029	Guymon	OK	73942	580-338-7714	338-0782
Tri-State Feeders Inc PO Box 7	Turpin	OK	73950	580-778-3600	778-3750
Van de Graaf Ranches Inc 1691 Midvale Rd	Sunnyside	WA	98944	509-837-3151	837-7414
Walter Lasley & Sons Inc PO Box 168	Stratford	TX	79084	806-753-4411	753-4435
Web: www.walterlasleyandsons.com					
Weborg Cattle Inc 1737 V Rd	Pender	NE	68047	402-385-3441	385-2441
Western Feed Yard Inc 548 S Rd I	Johnson	KS	67855	620-492-6256	492-6239

10-2 Cotton Farms

	City	State	Zip	Phone	Fax
Circle C Farms 1393 Yates Spring Rd	Brinson	GA	39825	229-246-7090	246-0605
E Ritter & Co Inc 106 Frisco St	Marked Tree	AR	72365	870-358-2200	358-4160
TF: 800-323-0355 ■ *Web:* www.ritterag.com					
JG Boswell Co 101 W Walnut St	Pasadena	CA	91103	626-583-3000	583-3090
JR Norton Co 3200 E Camelback Rd Suite 389	Phoenix	AZ	85018	602-954-8812	954-8908
McCleskey Cotton Co LLC Hwy 118 PO Box 171	Bronwood	GA	39826	229-995-2616	995-5702
Salyer American 210 Oregon Ave PO Box 488	Corcoran	CA	93212	559-992-2131	992-5403
Wesson Farms Inc 25 Victoria Rd	Victoria	AR	72370	870-563-2674	563-6927
Westlake Farms Inc 23311 Newton Ave	Stratford	CA	93266	559-947-3328	947-3590

10-3 Dairy Farms

	City	State	Zip	Phone	Fax
Big D Ranch 7590 S 10 Mile Rd	Meridian	ID	83642	208-888-1710	888-0075
Web: www.bigdranch.com					
Fred Rau Dairy 10255 W Manning Ave	Fresno	CA	93706	559-237-3393	237-3879
G & R Foods Inc PO Box 610	Reedsburg	WI	53959	608-524-3776	524-1752
Web: www.grfoodsinc.com					
Hollandia Dairy Inc 622 E Mission Rd	San Marcos	CA	92069	760-744-3222	744-2789
TF: 800-794-0978 ■ *Web:* www.hollandiadairy.com					
Kreider Farms 1461 Lancaster Rd	Manheim	PA	17545	717-665-4415	665-9614
TF: 888-665-4415 ■ *Web:* www.kreiderfarms.com					
Marburger Farm Dairy Inc 1506 Mars Evans City Rd	Evans City	PA	16033	724-538-4800	538-3250
TF: 800-331-1295 ■ *Web:* www.marburgerdairy.com					
Maytag Dairy Farms Inc PO Box 806	Newton	IA	50208	641-792-1133	792-1567
TF: 800-247-2458					
Meadow Gold Dairy 55 S Wakea Ave	Kahului	HI	96732	808-877-5541	871-6224
TF Cust Svc: 800-362-8531 ■ *Web:* www.lanimoo.com					
Price's Producers Inc 201 E Main Dr Suite 1521	El Paso	TX	79901	915-532-2296	532-1727
Shamrock Farms Co 40034 W Clayton Rd	Stanfield	AZ	85272	480-988-1452	988-1634
Web: www.shamrockfarms.net					

10-4 General Farms

	City	State	Zip	Phone	Fax
ABF Farm Services Inc 7761 W Undine Rd	Stockton	CA	95206	209-462-0208	462-9429
Agrex Inc 10975 Grandview Dr St Suite 200	Overland Park	KS	66210	913-851-6300	851-6210
TF: 800-334-6788 ■ *Web:* www.agrexinc.com					
Amana Colonies 622 46th Ave PO Box 189	Amana	IA	52203	319-622-7622	622-3090
TF: 800-579-2294 ■ *Web:* www.amanasociety.com					
Aunt Mid Produce Co 7939 W Lafayette Blvd	Detroit	MI	48209	313-841-7911	
TF: 877-286-8643 ■ *Web:* www.auntmids.com					
Belk Farms PO Box 24	Coachella	CA	92236	760-399-5951	399-1223
Bunge North America Inc 11720 Borman Dr	St. Louis	MO	63146	314-292-2000	292-2110
Web: www.bungenorthamerica.com					
Burford Ranch 1443 W Sample Ave	Fresno	CA	93711	559-431-0902	431-1625
DM Camp & Sons PO Box 80007	Bakersfield	CA	93380	661-399-5511	393-5113
Web: www.dmcampandsons.com					
Dubois County Farm Bureau Co-op Assn Inc PO Box 420	Huntingburg	IN	47542	812-683-2809	683-2811
Web: www.superiorag.com					
FarmTek 1440 Field of Dreams Way	Dyersville	IA	52040	563-875-2288	
TF: 800-327-6835 ■ *Web:* www.farmtek.com					
Fisher Ranch Corp 10600 Ice Plant Rd	Blythe	CA	92225	760-922-6171	922-3080
Fredericksburg Farmers Coop (FFC) 110 N Jefferson PO Box 261	Fredericksburg	IA	50630	563-237-5324	237-6123
TF: 800-562-8389 ■ *Web:* www.fburgcoop.com					
Gilkey Enterprises 241 Whitley Ave PO Box 426	Corcoran	CA	93212	559-992-2136	992-8266
Gold-eagle Co-op 515 N Locust PO Box 280	Goldfield	IA	50542	800-825-3331	825-3732*
**Fax Area Code:* 515 ■ *TF:* 800-825-3331 ■ *Web:* www.goldeaglecoop.com					
Great American Farms Inc 1255 W Atlantic Blvd Suite 218	Pompano Beach	FL	33069	954-785-9400	941-2977
Mercer Canyons Inc 46 Sonova Rd	Prosser	WA	99350	509-894-4773	894-4965
Web: www.mercercanyons.com					
Mid Valley Agricultural Services Inc 16401 E Hwy 26 PO Box 593	Linden	CA	95236	209-931-7600	931-0747
Web: www.midvalleyag.com					
Millhaven Co Inc 1705 Millhaven Rd	Sylvania	GA	30467	912-829-4742	829-4745
TF: 800-421-8043					
Morrison Enterprises PO Box 609	Hastings	NE	68902	402-463-3191	462-8542
Nevada Nile Ranch Inc PO Box 1150	Lovelock	NV	89419	775-273-2646	273-7208
Nickel Family LLC 15701 Hwy 178	Bakersfield	CA	93306	661-872-5050	872-7141
Oji Bros Farms Inc 8547 Sawtelle Ave	Yuba City	CA	95991	530-673-0845	673-8742
OPC Farms Inc 22300 Railroad Ave PO Box 817	San Joaquin	CA	93660	559-693-2701	
Plains Grain & Agronomy LLC 109 3rd Ave PO Box 6	Enderlin	ND	58027	701-437-2400	437-2406
TF: 800-950-2219 ■ *Web:* www.plainsgrain.com					
River Garden Farms Co 41758 County Rd 112	Knights Landing	CA	95645	530-735-6274	735-6734
Star of the West Milling Co 121 E Tuscola St	Frankenmuth	MI	48734	989-652-9971	652-6358
Web: www.starofthewest.com					
Stone Land Co 28521 Nevada Ave	Stratford	CA	93266	559-945-2205	945-9442
Sumner Peck Ranch Inc 14354 Rd 204	Madera	CA	93636	559-822-2525	
Tarter Gate Cy LLC PO Box 10	Dunnville	KY	42528	606-787-7455	
TF: 800-733-4283 ■ *Web:* www.tartergate.com					
Tosh Farms 1586 Atlantic Ave	Henry	TN	38231	731-243-4861	243-4860
TF: 888-243-4885					

10-5 Grain Farms

	City	State	Zip	Phone	Fax
AgriNorthwest 7404 W Hood Pl Suite B	Kennewick	WA	99336	509-734-1195	734-1092
TF: 800-333-8175					
Alger Farms 950 NW 8th St	Homestead	FL	33030	305-247-4334	247-4157
Big River Resources West Burlington LLC 15210 103rd St	West Burlington	IA	52655	319-753-1100	753-1103
TF: 800-463-9850 ■ *Web:* www.bigriverresources.com					
Busch Agricultural Resources Inc 2101 26th St S	Moorhead	MN	56560	218-233-8531	233-6082
Web: www.anheuser-busch.com					
Colusa Elevator Co PO Box 26	Colusa	IL	62329	217-755-4221	755-4202
Web: www.colusaelevator.com					
Country Pride Co-op (CPC) 648 W 2nd St PO Box 529	Winner	SD	57580	605-842-2711	842-2715
TF: 888-325-7743 ■ *Web:* www.countrypridecoop.com					
Erwin-Keith Inc 1529 Hwy 193	Wynne	AR	72396	870-238-2079	238-8621
Garst Seed Co Inc 2369 330th St	Slater	IA	50244	515-685-5000	685-5080
TF: 888-464-2778 ■ *Web:* www.garstseed.com					
Golden Grain Energy LLC 1822 43rd St SW	Mason City	IA	50401	641-423-8525	421-8457
TF: 888-443-2676 ■ *Web:* www.goldengrainenergy.com					
Golden Harvest Seeds Inc 100 JC Robinson Blvd	Waterloo	NE	68069	402-289-0230	779-3317
TF: 800-228-9906 ■ *Web:* www.syngenta.com					
Hoegemeyer Hybrids Inc 1755 Hoegemeyer Rd	Hooper	NE	68031	402-654-3399	654-3342
TF: 800-245-4631 ■ *Web:* www.therightseed.com					
Illinois Foundation Seeds Inc (IFSI) 1083 County Rd 900 N	Tolono	IL	61880	217-485-6260	485-3687
Web: www.ifsi.com					
Joe Heidrick Enterprises Inc 36826 CR 24	Woodland	CA	95695	530-662-3046	662-1715
Knight Management Inc 205 SW 1st St	Belle Glade	FL	33430	561-996-6262	992-8995
MFA Inc 201 Ray Young Dr	Columbia	MO	65201	573-874-5111	876-5430
Web: www.mfaincorporated.com					
Midwest Coop PO Box 787	Pierre	SD	57501	605-224-5935	224-9550
Web: www.midwestcooperatives.com					
Minn-Dak Growers Ltd 4034 40th Ave N	Grand Forks	ND	58203	701-746-7453	780-9050
Web: www.minndak.com					
Moews Seed Co Inc 9821 IL Hwy 89	Granville	IL	61326	815-339-2201	
TF: 800-663-9795 ■ *Web:* www.moews.com					
Morrow County Grain Growers Inc (MCGG) 305 Main	Lexington	OR	97839	541-989-8221	989-8229
TF: 800-452-7396 ■ *Web:* www.mcgg.net					

Company	City	State	ZIP	Phone	Fax
Pioneer Hi-Bred International Inc PO Box 1000	Johnston	IA	50131	515-535-3200	535-4415
TF: 800-247-6803 ■ *Web:* www.pioneer.com					
Remington Seeds 15691 W 600 S	Francesville	IN	47946	219-567-9141	567-2645
Richard Gumz Farms 8905 S Gumz Rd	North Judson	IN	46366	574-896-5441	896-5443
Stonington Co-op grain 402 Walnut St PO Box 350	Stonington	IL	62567	217-325-3211	
TF: 800-252-3219 ■ *Web:* www.stoncoop.com					
Sunray Coop 201 N Main PO Box 430	Sunray	TX	79086	806-948-4121	948-1991
Web: www.sunraycoop.com					
Twomey Co PO Box 158	Smithshire	IL	61478	309-325-7100	325-7109
TF: 800-896-6397 ■ *Web:* www.twomeyco.com					
Wesson Farms Inc 25 Victoria Rd	Victoria	AR	72370	870-563-2674	563-6927
Westlake Farms Inc 23311 Newton Ave	Stratford	CA	93266	559-947-3328	947-3590
William F Renk & Sons Inc 6809 Wilburn Rd	Sun Prairie	WI	53590	608-837-7351	825-6143
TF: 800-289-7365 ■ *Web:* www.renkseed.com					
Wyffels Hybrids Inc 13344 US Hwy 6	Geneseo	IL	61254	309-944-8334	944-8338
TF: 800-369-7833 ■ *Web:* www.wyffels.com					

10-6 Hog Farms

Company	City	State	ZIP	Phone	Fax
Black River Farms PO Box 1	Harrells	NC	28444	910-532-2814	532-2898
Cargill Inc 15407 McGinty Rd W	Wayzata	MN	55391	952-742-7575	742-7209*
**Fax:* Cust Svc ■ *TF:* 800-227-4455 ■ *Web:* www.cargill.com					
Christensen Farms 23971 County Rd 10	Sleepy Eye	MN	56085	507-794-5310	794-2471
Web: www.christensenfarms.com					
Garland Farm Supply 250 Belgrade Ave PO Box 741	Garland	NC	28441	910-529-9731	529-1844
Hanor Co E 4614 Hwy 14-60	Spring Green	WI	53588	608-588-9170	588-2308
Hastings Pork PO Box 67	Hastings	NE	68902	402-463-0551	463-1349
Hog Slat 206 Fayetteville St	Newton Grove	NC	28366	910-594-0219	594-1392
TF: 800-949-4647 ■ *Web:* www.hogslat.com					
Iowa Select Farms LP 811 S Oak St PO Box 400	Iowa Falls	IA	50126	641-648-4479	648-4251
Web: www.iowaselect.com					
LL Murphrey Co 39 Vandiford-Thomas Rd	Farmville	NC	27828	252-753-5361	753-8759
Murphy Brown LLC 2822 Hwy 24 W	Warsaw	NC	28398	910-293-3434	293-6957
TF: 800-311-9458 ■ *Web:* www.murphybrownllc.com					
Murphy-Brown LLC 2822 Hwy 24 W	Warsaw	NC	28398	910-293-3434	293-6957
Web: www.murphybrownllc.com					
NG Purvis Farms Inc 2504 Spies Rd	Robbins	NC	27325	910-948-2297	948-3213
PIC USA 100 Bluegrass Commons Blvd Suite 2200	Hendersonville	TN	37075	615-265-2700	265-2849
TF: 800-325-3398 ■ *Web:* www.pic.com/usa					
Pilgrims Pride 244 Perimeter Ctr Pkwy NE	Atlanta	GA	30346	770-393-5000	393-5262
Web: www.pilgrimspride.com					
Prestage Farms 4651 Taylors Bridge Hwy	Clinton	NC	28329	910-592-5771	592-9552
Web: www.prestagefarms.com					
Seaboard Foods 9000 W 67th St Suite 200	Shawnee Mission	KS	66202	913-261-2600	261-2626
TF: 800-262-7907 ■ *Web:* www.seaboardfoods.com					
Smithfield Foods Inc 200 Commerce St	Smithfield	VA	23430	757-365-3000	365-3017
NYSE: SFD ■ *TF:* 800-276-6158 ■ *Web:* www.smithfieldfoods.com					
Swine Graphics Enterprises LP 1620 Superior St PO BOX 668	Webster City	IA	50595	515-832-5481	832-2237
Web: www.97.64.202.66/Extranet/home.htm					
Texas Farm LLC 4200 S Main St	Perryton	TX	79070	806-435-5935	435-3656
Web: www.texasfarmpork.com					
Tyson Foods Inc 2210 W Oaklawn Dr PO Box 2020	Springdale	AR	72762	479-290-4000	290-4217*
NYSE: TSN ■ **Fax:* Hum Res ■ *TF:* 800-643-3410 ■ *Web:* www.tyson.com					
Wakefield Pork Inc 410 Main Ave E	Gaylord	MN	55334	507-237-5581	237-5584
Web: www.wakefieldpork.com					

10-7 Mushroom Growers

Company	City	State	ZIP	Phone	Fax
Modern Mushroom Farms Inc PO Box 340	Avondale	PA	19311	610-268-3535	268-3099
Web: www.modernmush.com					
Monterey Mushrooms Inc 260 Westgate Dr	Watsonville	CA	95076	831-763-5300	763-0700
TF: 800-333-6874 ■ *Web:* www.montereymushrooms.com					
Ostrom Mushroom Farms 8323 Steilacoom Rd SE	Olympia	WA	98513	360-491-1410	438-2594
TF: 800-640-7408 ■ *Web:* www.ostrommushrooms.com					
Phillips Mushroom Farms Inc 1011 Kaolin Rd	Kennett Square	PA	19348	610-925-0520	925-0527
TF: 800-722-8818 ■ *Web:* www.phillipsmushroomfarms.com					
Sylvan Inc 199 Nolte Dr	Kittanning	PA	16201	724-543-2242	545-9113
TF: 866-352-7520 ■ *Web:* www.sylvaninc.com					

10-8 Poultry & Eggs Production

Company	City	State	ZIP	Phone	Fax
Allen's Hatchery Inc 126 N Shipley St	Seaford	DE	19973	302-629-9163	629-0514
TF: 800-777-8966 ■ *Web:* www.allenfamilyfoods.com					
Amick Farms Inc PO Box 2309	Batesburg-Leesville	SC	29070	803-532-1400	532-1492*
**Fax:* Sales ■ *TF:* 800-926-4257 ■ *Web:* www.amickfarms.com					
Aviagen Group 5015 Bradford Dr	Huntsville	AL	35805	256-890-3800	890-3919
TF: 800-826-9685 ■ *Web:* www.en.aviagen.com					
Cagle's Farms Inc 1513 S Dixie Hwy	Dalton	GA	30720	706-278-2372	226-6169
Web: www.cagles.net					
Cal-Maine Foods Inc 3320 Woodrow Wilson Dr PO Box 2960	Jackson	MS	39209	601-948-6813	969-0905
NASDAQ: CALM ■ *Web:* www.calmainefoods.com					
Cobb-Vantress Inc 4703 Hwy 412 E	Siloam Springs	AR	72761	479-524-3166	524-3043
TF: 800-748-9719 ■ *Web:* www.cobb-vantress.com					
Coleman Natural Foods 1667 Cole Blvd Bldg 19 Suite 300	Lakewood	CO	80401	303-468-2500	277-9263
TF: 800-442-8666 ■ *Web:* www.colemannatural.com					
Cooper Farms 22348 County Rd 140 PO Box 547	Oakwood	OH	45873	419-594-3325	594-3372
TF: 888-594-8759 ■ *Web:* www.cooperfarms.com					
Creighton Bros LP PO Box 220	Atwood	IN	46502	574-267-3101	267-6446
TF: 800-847-3447 ■ *Web:* www.cb-cl.com					
Cuddy Farms Inc A-I Crew Locker Rm	Wadesboro	NC	28119	704-694-9929	
Culver Duck Farms Inc PO Box 910	Middlebury	IN	46540	574-825-9537	825-2613
TF: 800-825-9225 ■ *Web:* www.culverduck.com					
CWT Farms International Inc PO Box 1396	Gainesville	GA	30503	770-532-3181	531-0555
Demler Egg Ranch 1455 N Warren Rd	San Jacinto	CA	92582	951-654-8166	487-9766
Diestel Turkey Ranch 22200 Lyons Bald Mountain Rd	Sonora	CA	95370	209-532-4950	532-5059
Web: www.diestelturkey.com					
Dorothy Egg Farms LLC 271 Turkey Ln	Winthrop	ME	04364	207-377-9927	
Echo Lake Farm Produce Co 33102 S Honey Lake Rd PO Box 279	Burlington	WI	53105	262-763-9551	763-4593
TF: 800-888-3447 ■ *Web:* www.echolakefoods.com					
Esbenshade Farms 220 Eby Chiques Rd	Mount Joy	PA	17552	717-653-8061	653-6922
Feather Crest Farms Inc PO Box 129	Kurten	TX	77862	979-589-2576	589-3052
Foster Farms Inc 1000 Davis St PO Box 457	Livingston	CA	95334	209-394-7901	394-6342
Web: www.fosterfarms.com					
Glenwood Foods LLC 20850 Jackson Ln	Jetersville	VA	23083	804-561-3447	561-3228
Harrison Poultry Inc Star St PO Box 550	Bethlehem	GA	30620	770-867-7511	867-0999
Hickman's Egg Ranch Inc 6515 S Jackrabbit Trail	Buckeye	AZ	85236	623-872-1120	872-9220
TF: 800-224-2123 ■ *Web:* www.hickmanseggs.com					
Hillandale Farms Inc PO Box 2109	Lake City	FL	32056	386-397-1300	397-1130
Hubbard ISA 195 Main St	Walpole	NH	03608	603-756-3311	756-9034
TF: 800-482-2442 ■ *Web:* www.hubbardbreeders.com					
Hy-Line International 1755 W Lakes Pkwy	West Des Moines	IA	50266	515-225-6030	225-6425
Web: www.hy-line.com					
JFC Inc PO Box 1106	Saint Cloud	MN	56302	320-251-3570	240-6250
TF: 800-328-8236					
Kofkoff Egg Farm LLC 17 Schwartz Rd	Bozrah	CT	06334	860-886-2445	886-1138
Maple Leaf Farms Inc PO Box 308	Milford	IN	46542	574-658-4121	658-2208
Web: www.mapleleaffarms.com					
Mar-Jac Poultry Inc 1020 Aviation Blvd PO Box 1017	Gainesville	GA	30501	770-531-5007	531-5049
Web: www.marjacpoultry.com					
McClain Enterprises Inc 801 S College St Suite 2	Mountain Home	AR	72653	870-425-5700	
Michael Foods Inc 301 Carlson Pkwy Suite 400	Minnetonka	MN	55305	952-258-4000	258-4940
TF: 800-325-4270 ■ *Web:* www.michaelfoods.com					
Murphy-Brown LLC 2822 Hwy 24 W	Warsaw	NC	28398	910-293-3434	293-6957
Web: www.murphybrownllc.com					
Nebraska Turkey Growers Co-op Assoc 12 Lawn Ave	Gibbon	NE	68840	308-468-5711	468-5715
Norco Ranch Inc 1811 Mountain Ave	Norco	CA	92860	951-737-6735	737-9405
Oakdell Egg Farms Inc 7401 N Glade Rd	Pasco	WA	99301	509-547-8665	547-9656
PECO Foods Inc 3701 Kauloosa Ave	Tuscaloosa	AL	35403	205-345-3955	343-2401
Web: www.pecofoods.com					
Perdue Farms Inc 31149 Old Ocean City Rd	Salisbury	MD	21804	410-543-3000	543-3212
TF: 800-457-3738 ■ *Web:* www.perdue.com					
Peterson Farms Inc 250 S Main St	Decatur	AR	72722	479-752-5400	752-5650
Pilgrim's Corp 1770 Promontory Cir	Greeley	CO	80634	800-727-5366	
NYSE: PPC ■ *TF:* 800-727-5366 ■ *Web:* www.pilgrimspride.com					
Plainville Farms Inc 304 S Water St PO Box 38	New Oxford	PA	17350	717-624-2191	701-1354*
**Fax Area Code:* 315 ■ *Web:* www.plainvillefarms.com					
Primera Foods Corp 612 S 8th St PO Box 373	Cameron	WI	54822	715-458-4075	458-4078
TF: 800-365-2409 ■ *Web:* www.primerafoods.com					
Puglisi Egg Farms Inc 75 Easy St	Howell	NJ	07731	732-938-2373	938-2232
Ritewood Inc 3643 S 4000 E PO Box 120	Franklin	ID	83237	208-646-2213	646-2217
Rose Acre Farms Inc RR 5 PO Box 1250	Seymour	IN	47274	812-497-2557	497-3311
Web: www.roseacre.com					
Sanderson Farms Inc PO Box 988	Laurel	MS	39441	601-426-1454	425-0704
NASDAQ: SAFM ■ *TF:* 800-844-4030 ■ *Web:* www.sandersonfarms.com					
Shinn Turkeys Inc 41121 Sandhills Rd	Dunning	NE	68833	308-533-2272	
Simpson's Eggs Inc 5015 E Hwy 218	Monroe	NC	28110	704-753-1478	753-4762
Sleepy Creek Farms Inc 938 Millers Chapel Rd PO Box 10009	Goldsboro	NC	27534	919-778-3130	778-8111
Tampa Farm Service Inc 14425 Haynes Rd	Dover	FL	33527	813-659-0605	659-0197
TF: 800-441-3447 ■ *Web:* www.4grain.com					
Tarheel Turkey Hatchery Inc Hwy 401 N Raeford PO Box 150	Raeford	NC	28376	910-875-8711	875-8712
Tyson Foods Inc 2210 W Oaklawn Dr PO Box 2020	Springdale	AR	72762	479-290-4000	290-4217*
NYSE: TSN ■ **Fax:* Hum Res ■ *TF:* 800-643-3410 ■ *Web:* www.tyson.com					
Ward Egg Ranch Inc 2900 Harmony Grove Rd	Escondido	CA	92029	760-745-5689	745-5865
Wayne Farms LLC 4110 Continental Dr	Oakwood	GA	30566	678-450-3100	531-0858*
**Fax Area Code:* 770 ■ *TF:* 800-392-0844 ■ *Web:* www.waynefarmsllc.com					
Weiss Lake Egg Co Inc Hwy 411	Centre	AL	35960	256-927-5546	927-2596
Wilcox Farms Inc 40400 Harts Lake Valley Rd	Roy	WA	98580	360-458-7774	458-6950
TF: 800-568-6456 ■ *Web:* www.wilcoxfarms.com					
Willmar Poultry Co 3735 County Rd 5 SW PO Box 753	Willmar	MN	56201	320-235-8850	235-8869
TF: 800-328-8842 ■ *Web:* www.willmarpoultry.com/wpc.htm					
Zacky Farms Inc 2020 S East Ave	Fresno	CA	93721	562-641-2020	641-2040
TF: 800-888-0235 ■ *Web:* www.zacky.com					
Zephyr Egg Co Inc 4622 Gall Blvd	Zephyrhills	FL	33542	813-782-1521	782-7070
TF: 800-488-6543					

10-9 Sugarcane & Sugarbeets Growers

Company	City	State	ZIP	Phone	Fax
A Duda & Sons Inc 1200 Duda Trail	Oviedo	FL	32765	407-365-2111	365-2147
Web: www.duda.com					

	City	State	ZIP	Phone	Fax
Alico Inc PO Box 338 *NASDAQ: ALCO* ■ *Web:* www.alicoinc.com	La Belle	FL	33975	863-675-2966	675-6928
Florida Crystals Corp 1 N Clematis St Suite 200 *Web:* www.floridacrystals.com	West Palm Beach	FL	33401	561-655-6303	659-3206
Gay & Robinson Inc 1 Kaumakani Ave PO Box 156	Kaumakani	HI	96747	808-335-3133	335-6424
Joe Heidrick Enterprises Inc 36826 CR 24	Woodland	CA	95695	530-662-3046	662-1715
Knight Management Inc 205 SW 1st St	Belle Glade	FL	33430	561-996-6262	992-8995
Sugar Cane Growers Co-op of Florida PO Box 666 *Web:* www.scgc.org	Belle Glade	FL	33430	561-996-5556	996-4747
US Sugar Corp 111 Ponce de Leon Ave *Web:* www.ussugar.com	Clewiston	FL	33440	863-983-8121	983-9827
Wedgworth Farms Inc 651 NW 9th St PO Box 2076 *TF:* 800-477-2077	Belle Glade	FL	33430	561-996-2076	996-0613

10-10 Tree Nuts Growers

	City	State	ZIP	Phone	Fax
Agri-World Co-op 31545 Donald Ave	Madera	CA	93636	559-673-1306	673-1318
Baker Farming Co 45499 W Panoche Rd	Firebaugh	CA	93622	559-659-3942	659-7114
Blue Diamond Growers 1802 C St *Web:* www.bluediamond.com	Sacramento	CA	95811	916-442-0771	446-8620
Braden Farms Inc PO Box 1022	Hughson	CA	95326	209-883-4061	883-4862
Columbia Empire Farms 31461 NE Bell Rd *Web:* www.columbiaempirefarms.com	Sherwood	OR	97140	503-554-9060	537-9693
Cummings Violich Inc 1750 Dayton Rd	Chico	CA	95928	530-894-5494	891-4946
Diamond Walnut Growers Inc PO Box 1727 *Web:* www.diamondnuts.com	Stockton	CA	95201	209-467-6000	467-6257
Farmland Management Services 301 E Main St	Turlock	CA	95380	209-669-0742	669-0811
Green Valley Pecan Co 1625 E Sahuarita Rd *TF:* 800-533-5269	Sahuarita	AZ	85629	520-625-8809	791-2853
Hammons Products Co 105 Hammons Dr PO Box 140 *TF:* 888-429-6887 ■ *Web:* www.hammonsproducts.com	Stockton	MO	65785	417-276-5181	276-5187
Lassen Land Co 320 E S St PO Box 607	Orland	CA	95963	530-865-7676	865-8085
MacFarms of Hawaii LLC 89-406 Mamalahoa Hwy *Web:* www.macfarms.com	Captain Cook	HI	96704	808-328-2435	328-8081
Mauna Loa Macadamia Nut Corp 16-701 Macadamia Rd **Fax:* Cust Svc ■ *TF Cust Svc:* 888-628-6256 ■ *Web:* www.maunaloa.com	Keaau	HI	96749	808-966-8618	966-8410*
ML Macadamia Orchards LP 26-238 Hawaii Belt Rd *NYSE: NUT* ■ *Web:* www.mlmacadamia.com	Hilo	HI	96720	808-969-8057	969-8123
Paramount Farming Co 33141 Lerdo Hwy	Bakersfield	CA	93308	661-399-4456	399-1735
Spycher Bros Farms 14827 W Harding Rd *Web:* www.spycherbros.com	Turlock	CA	95380	209-668-2471	668-4988
Stahmann Farms Inc 22500 S Hwy 28 *TF:* 800-654-6887 ■ *Web:* www.stahmanns.com	La Mesa	NM	88044	575-526-2453	526-5760
Sunnyland Farms Inc 2314 Willson Rd *TF:* 800-999-2488 ■ *Web:* www.sunnylandfarms.com	Albany	GA	31705	229-436-5654	888-8332
Tejon Ranch Co 4436 Lebec Rd PO Box 1000 *NYSE: TRC* ■ *Web:* www.tejonranch.com	Lebec	CA	93243	661-248-3000	248-3100

10-11 Vegetable Farms

	City	State	ZIP	Phone	Fax
A Duda & Sons Inc 1200 Duda Trail *Web:* www.duda.com	Oviedo	FL	32765	407-365-2111	365-2147
Abe-El Produce 42143 Rd 120	Orosi	CA	93647	559-528-3030	528-6772
Agri-Empire Corp PO Box 490 *Web:* www.agri-empire.com	San Jacinto	CA	92581	951-654-7311	654-7639
Amigo Farms Inc 4245 E Hwy 80 *Web:* www.amigofarms.com	Yuma	AZ	85365	928-726-3738	726-3744
Anderson Farms Inc 4600 2nd St	Davis	CA	95616	530-753-5695	753-5764
Barkley Co PO Box 2706 *Web:* www.barkleyag.com	Yuma	AZ	85366	928-343-2918	343-2940
Barnes Farming Corp 7840 Old Bailey Hwy *TF:* 800-367-2799 ■ *Web:* www.farmpak.com	Spring Hope	NC	27882	252-459-3101	459-9020
Betteravia Farms 1850 W Stowell Rd *TF:* 800-328-8816 ■ *Web:* www.bonipak.com	Santa Maria	CA	93458	805-925-2417	922-7982
Black Gold 4575 32nd Ave S Suite 2A *Web:* www.blackgoldpotato.com	Grand Forks	ND	58201	701-792-3414	772-0749
Bo-Jac Seed Co 245 County Rd 1500 E *TF:* 800-397-2069 ■ *Web:* www.bo-jac.com	Mount Pulaski	IL	62548	217-792-5001	792-5006
Borzynski Bros Distributing Inc PO Box 133 *TF:* 800-248-0420	Franksville	WI	53126	262-886-1623	886-2111
Boskovich Farms Inc 711 Diaz Ave *Web:* www.boskovichfarms.com	Oxnard	CA	93030	805-487-2299	487-5189
Boutonnet Farms 10855 Ocean Mist Pkwy Suite B	Castroville	CA	95012	831-633-4977	633-4577
Buurma Farms Inc 3909 Kok Rd *TF:* 888-428-8762 ■ *Web:* www.buurmafarms.com	Willard	OH	44890	419-935-6411	935-1918
Byrd Foods Inc 20305 Greenbush Rd PO Box 318 *TF:* 800-777-2973	Parksley	VA	23421	757-665-5194	665-6425
Cargil Produce Co PO Box 1146	Uvalde	TX	78802	830-278-5616	278-4935
Charles H West Farms Inc 2953 Tub Mill Pond Rd	Milford	DE	19963	302-335-3936	335-0438
Christopher Ranch 305 Bloomfield Ave *TF:* 800-321-9333 ■ *Web:* www.christopherranch.com	Gilroy	CA	95020	408-847-1100	847-5488
Circle C Farms 1393 Yates Spring Rd	Brinson	GA	39825	229-246-7090	246-0605
CROPP Co-op 1 Organic Way **Fax Area Code:* 608 ■ *TF:* 888-444-6455 ■ *Web:* www.organicvalley.coop	LaFarge	WI	54639	888-444-6455	625-3025*
D'Arrigo Bros Co of California Inc PO Box 850 *TF Cust Svc:* 800-995-5939 ■ *Web:* www.andyboy.com	Salinas	CA	93902	831-455-4500	455-4445
Dean Kincaid Inc N 2028 Hwy 106	Palmyra	WI	53156	262-495-3000	
Dole Fresh Vegetables Co PO Box 2018 *TF Sales:* 800-333-5454 ■ *Web:* www.dole.com	Monterey	CA	93942	831-754-3519	757-0973
Doug Mellon Farms Inc 2197 S 4th Ave Suite 206	Yuma	AZ	85364	928-782-4482	782-0688
Dresick Farms Inc PO Box 1260	Huron	CA	93234	559-945-2513	945-9627
Earthbound Farm 1721 San Juan Hwy *TF:* 800-690-3200 ■ *Web:* www.ebfarm.com	San Juan Bautista	CA	95045	831-623-7880	623-4988
Elmore & Stahl Inc 4012 E Goodwin Rd	Mission	TX	78574	956-205-7300	585-5825
Everkrisp Vegetables Inc 9202 W Harrison St	Tolleson	AZ	85353	623-936-3321	936-1008
Farming Technology Corp 6950 Neuhaus St *TF:* 800-395-2004	Houston	TX	77061	713-923-5807	928-2437
Frank Capurro & Son LLC 2250 Hwy 1 PO Box 410	Moss Landing	CA	95039	831-786-0731	728-0241
Fresh Express Inc 950 E Blanco Rd *TF Cust Svc:* 800-242-5472 ■ *Web:* www.freshexpress.com	Salinas	CA	93901	831-422-5917	775-2331
George Wood Farms Inc PO Box 159 *Web:* www.georgewoodfarms	Camden	NC	27921	252-335-4357	335-4075
Grant Family Farms 1020 W County Rd 72 *Web:* www.grantfarms.com	Wellington	CO	80549	970-568-7654	568-7655
Greenheart Farms Inc 902 Zenon Way PO Box 1510 *TF:* 800-549-5531 ■ *Web:* www.greenheartfarms.com	Arroyo Grande	CA	93420	805-481-2234	481-7374
Griffin Ranches Inc 9490 W County 19th St	Somerton	AZ	85350	928-627-8809	627-8909
Grimmway Farms Inc PO Box 81498 **Fax Area Code:* 661 ■ *TF:* 800-301-3101 ■ *Web:* www.grimmway.com	Bakersfield	CA	93380	800-301-3101	845-9750*
Harris Farms Inc 23304 W Oakland Ave *TF:* 800-691-1199 ■ *Web:* www.harrisfarms.com	Coalinga	CA	93210	559-884-2477	884-2267
Hartung Bros Inc 708 Heartland Trail # 2000 *TF:* 800-362-2522 ■ *Web:* www.hartungbrothers.com	Madison	WI	53717	608-829-6000	829-6001
Heartland Farms Inc 907 3rd Ave	Hancock	WI	54943	715-249-5555	249-5265
Hundley Farms Inc PO Box H	Loxahatchee	FL	33470	561-996-6855	996-1158
Jack Bros Co PO Box 116	Brawley	CA	92227	760-344-3781	344-2373
Leach Farms Inc W1102 Buttercup Ct *Web:* www.leachfarms.com	Berlin	WI	54923	920-361-1880	361-4474
Long Farms Inc 2849 Lust Rd	Apopka	FL	32703	407-889-4141	889-5069
Major Farms Inc PO Box 719	Salinas	CA	93902	831-422-9616	422-9618
Martori Farms 7332 E Butherus Dr *TF:* 800-627-8674 ■ *Web:* www.martorifarms.com	Scottsdale	AZ	85260	480-998-1444	483-6723
McClure Farms/West Coast Tomato Inc 502 6th Ave W	Palmetto	FL	34221	941-722-4545	729-6778
Mecca Farms Inc PO Box 541779	Lake Worth	FL	33454	561-968-3605	968-3740
Merrill Farms LLC 1067 Merrill St PO Box 659 *Web:* www.merrillfarms.com	Salinas	CA	93902	831-424-7365	424-0447
Mount Dora Farms 16398 Jacinto Fort Blvd *Web:* www.mountdorafarms.com	Houston	TX	77015	713-821-7400	821-7342
My-T Acres Inc 8127 Lewiston Rd	Batavia	NY	14020	585-343-1026	343-2051
Nash Produce Co 6160 S N Carolina 58 *TF:* 800-334-3032 ■ *Web:* www.nashproduce.com	Nashville	NC	27856	252-443-6011	443-6746
Navajo Agricultural Products Industry PO Drawer 1318 *Web:* www.navajopride.com	Farmington	NM	87499	505-566-2600	324-9458
Nunes Vegetables Inc PO Box 50956	Oxnard	CA	93031	805-487-7472	487-8274
Ocean Mist Farms 10855 Ocean Mist Pkwy Suite A *Web:* www.oceanmist.com	Castroville	CA	95012	831-633-2144	633-0561
Pacific Tomato Growers 503 10th St W *Web:* www.sunripeproduce.com	Palmetto	FL	34221	941-722-0778	729-4707
Papen Farms Inc 847 Papen Ln	Dover	DE	19904	302-697-3291	697-2380
Paramount Farms Inc PO Box 188 *Web:* www.paramountfarmsinc.com	Bancroft	WI	54921	715-335-6357	335-6091
Pasquinelli Produce Co PO Box 2949	Yuma	AZ	85366	928-783-7813	343-4093
Peri & Sons Farms Inc PO Box 35 *Web:* www.periandsons.com	Yerington	NV	89447	775-463-3640	463-4028
Pero Family Farms Inc 14095 US Hwy 441 *Web:* www.peroveg.com	Delray Beach	FL	33446	561-498-4533	496-4009
Petrocco Farms 14110 Brighton Rd *TF:* 888-876-2207 ■ *Web:* www.petroccofarms.com	Brighton	CO	80601	303-659-6498	659-7645
RD Offutt Co PO Box 7160 *TF:* 877-444-7363 ■ *Web:* www.rdoequipment.com	Fargo	ND	58106	701-237-6062	239-8787
Rio Farms 1051 S Pacific Ave *Web:* www.riofarms.com	Oxnard	CA	93030	805-240-1979	240-1953
Roth Farms Inc 27502 County Rd 880 *Web:* www.rothfarms.com	Belle Glade	FL	33430	561-996-2991	996-8501
Rousseau Farming Co 9601 W Harrison Ave	Tolleson	AZ	85353	623-936-7100	936-7386
Russo Farms Inc 1962 S E Ave	Vineland	NJ	08360	856-692-5942	692-8534
Sackett Ranch Inc 2939 Neff Rd NE	Stanton	MI	48888	989-762-5049	762-5500
Sakata Farms Inc PO Box 508	Brighton	CO	80601	303-659-1559	
Sam S Accursio & Sons Farms PO Box 901767 *TF:* 800-233-6826	Homestead	FL	33090	305-246-3455	242-8815
San Miguel Produce Inc 4444 Naval Air Rd *TF:* 888-347-3367 ■ *Web:* www.cutncleangreens.com	Oxnard	CA	93033	805-488-0981	488-2103
Sea Mist Farms 10855 Ocean Mist Pkwy Suite C *Web:* www.oceanmist.com	Castroville	CA	95012	831-633-2144	633-8163
Six L's Packing Co Inc 315 E New Market Rd *Web:* www.sixls.com	Immokalee	FL	34142	239-657-3117	657-6951
SMT Farms PO Box 170	Yuma	AZ	85366	928-341-9616	341-9644
Sun & Sands Enterprises LLC 86-705 Ave 54 Suite A *Web:* www.primetimeproduce.com	Coachella	CA	92236	760-399-4278	399-4281
Sun World International Inc 16350 Driver Rd *Web:* www.sun-world.com	Bakersfield	CA	93308	661-392-5000	392-4678
Suwannee Farms 19620 N County Rd 349	O"Brien	FL	32071	386-776-1025	776-1089
Tanimura & Antle Inc PO Box 4070 *TF:* 800-772-4542 ■ *Web:* www.taproduce.com	Salinas	CA	93912	831-455-2950	455-4112
Taylor & Fulton Inc 932 5th Ave W *TF:* 800-457-5577 ■ *Web:* www.taylorfulton.com	Palmetto	FL	34221	941-729-3883	723-2969
Teixeira Farms Inc 2600 Bonita Lateral Rd *Web:* www.teixeirafarms.com	Santa Maria	CA	93458	805-928-3801	928-9405
Thomas Produce Co 9905 Clint Moore Rd *Web:* www.thomasproduce.com	Boca Raton	FL	33496	561-482-1111	852-0018

	City	State	Zip	Phone	Fax
Tom Bengard Ranch Inc PO Box 80090 *TF:* 800-546-3517	Salinas	CA	93912	831-422-9021	422-7782
Torrey Farms Inc Maltby Rd PO Box 187	Elba	NY	14058	585-757-9941	757-2528
Tri-Campbell Farms 15111 Hwy 17 *TF:* 800-222-7783 ■ *Web:* www.tricampbellfarms.com	Grafton	ND	58237	701-520-2727	352-2008
Triple E Produce Corp PO Box 239 *Web:* www.sunriteproduce.com	Tracy	CA	95378	209-835-5123	836-1164
Turek Farms 8558 SR 90 *Web:* www.turekfarms.com	King Ferry	NY	13081	315-364-8735	364-5257
Twin Garden Farms 23017 Illinois 173 *Web:* www.twingardenfarms.com	Harvard	IL	60033	815-943-7448	943-8024
Village Farms LP 7 Christopher Way *TF:* 877-777-7718 ■ *Web:* www.villagefarms.com	Eatontown	NJ	07724	732-676-3000	676-3032
Wada Farms Potatoes Inc 326 S 1400 W *Web:* www.wadafarms.com	Pingree	ID	83262	208-684-9801	684-4157
Walker Farms PO Box 129	Menan	ID	83434	208-754-4696	754-4961
Waymon Farms Inc 9700 W Hwy 95	Somerton	AZ	85350	928-627-8836	627-2988
Weber Farms 3559 Rd 'K' NW	Quincy	WA	98848	509-787-4578	787-4465
Wiers Farm Inc PO Box 385 *TF:* 800-825-6525	Willard	OH	44890	419-935-0131	933-2017
William Bolthouse Farms Inc 7200 E Brundage Ln **Fax:* Sales ■ *TF:* 800-350-7205 ■ *Web:* www.bolthouse.com	Bakersfield	CA	93307	661-366-7207	366-2834*
Wilson Farm Inc 10 Pleasant St *Web:* www.wilsonfarm.com	Lexington	MA	02421	781-862-3900	863-0469
Wolfsen Inc 1269 W 'I' St *Web:* www.wolfseninc.com	Los Banos	CA	93635	209-827-7700	827-7785
Worzella & Sons Inc 2801 Hoover Ave	Plover	WI	54467	715-344-4098	344-4803
WP Hearne Produce Co Inc PO Box 1975	Salisbury	MD	21802	410-742-7363	749-6107
Wysocki Produce Farm Inc 6320 3rd Ave	Plainfield	WI	54966	715-366-7175	366-7177

11 AGRICULTURAL SERVICES

11-1 Crop Preparation Services

	City	State	Zip	Phone	Fax
AG Plus Inc 401 N Main PO Box 306 *Web:* www.agplusinc.com	South Whitley	IN	46787	260-723-5141	273-5143
Agricor Inc PO Box 807 *Web:* www.agricor.org	Marion	IN	46952	765-662-0606	662-7189
American Raisin Packers Inc 2335 Chandler St PO Box 30 *Web:* www.americanraisin.com	Selma	CA	93662	559-896-4760	896-8942
Andrews Distribution Co 13650 Copus Rd *Web:* www.andrewsag.com	Bakersfield	CA	93313	661-858-2266	858-2965
Baird-Neece Packing Corp 60 S E St PO Box 791	Porterville	CA	93258	559-784-3393	784-7773
Ballantine Produce 10550 S Buttonwillow Ave *Web:* www.ballantineproduce.com	Reedley	CA	93654	559-638-9277	638-6050
Borg Produce Co 1601 E Olympic Blvd Bldg 100 *Web:* www.borgproduce.com	Los Angeles	CA	90021	213-688-9388	688-9381
Calberi Inc 3605 W Pendleton Ave	Santa Ana	CA	92704	714-979-5221	641-7542
California Family Foods LLC 6050 Struckmeyer Ave	Arbuckle	CA	95912	530-476-3326	476-3524
Cecelia Packing Corp 24780 E S Ave	Orange Cove	CA	93646	559-626-5000	626-7561
Central Valley Processing Inc 4315 E Chiles Ave	Merced	CA	95340	209-723-2950	723-4931
Chooljian Bros Packing Co Inc 3192 S Indianola St *Web:* www.chooljianbrothers.com	Sanger	CA	93657	559-875-5501	875-1582
Cummins Family Produce Inc 2570 Eldridge Ave *Web:* www.firstprizepotatoes.com	Twin Falls	ID	83303	208-733-5371	734-2754
Deardorff-Jackson Co Inc PO Box 1188 *Web:* www.deardorfffamilyfarms.com	Oxnard	CA	93032	805-487-7801	483-1286
Delta Packing Co 6021 E Kettleman Ln *Web:* www.deltapacking.com	Lodi	CA	95240	209-334-1023	334-0811
Diamond Fruit Growers Inc 3515 Chevron Dr *Web:* www.diamondfruit.com	Hood River	OR	97031	541-354-5300	354-5394
DiMare Bros/New England Farms Packing Co 84 New England Produce Ctr *Web:* www.dimareinc.com	Chelsea	MA	02150	617-889-3800	889-2067
Dundee Citrus Growers Assn 111 1st St N *TF:* 800-447-1574 ■ *Web:* www.dun-d.com	Dundee	FL	33838	863-439-1574	439-1574
Emerald Packing Co Inc 2823 N Orange Blossom Trail *TF:* 800-985-8839	Orlando	FL	32804	407-423-0531	423-6426
Erwin-Keith Inc 1529 Hwy 193	Wynne	AR	72396	870-238-2079	238-8621
Farmers Co-operative Union The 225 SO BROADWAY PO Box 159 *TF:* 800-585-3839 ■ *Web:* www.coopunion.com	Sterling	KS	67579	620-278-2141	278-2147
Federal Dryer & Storage Co Hwy 165	England	AR	72046	501-842-2301	842-2877
Fillmore-Piru Citrus Assn (FPCA) 355 N Main St PO Box 350 *TF:* 800-524-8787 ■ *Web:* www.fillmorepirucitrus.com	Piru	CA	93040	805-521-1781	521-0990
Food Technology Service Inc 502 Prairie Mine Rd *NASDAQ:* VIFL ■ *Web:* www.foodtechservice.com	Mulberry	FL	33860	863-425-0039	425-5526
Fresh Express Inc 950 E Blanco Rd *TF Cust Svc:* 800-242-5472 ■ *Web:* www.freshexpress.com	Salinas	CA	93901	831-422-5917	775-2331
Golden Peanut Co LLC 100 N Pt Ctr E Suite 400 *Web:* www.goldenpeanut.com	Alpharetta	GA	30022	770-752-8160	752-8308
Great Lakes Packers Inc 400 Great Lakes Pkwy PO Box 366 *TF:* 800-624-8464	Bellevue	OH	44811	419-483-2956	483-6922
Gruma Corp 1159 Cottonwood L Suite 200 *TF:* 800-627-3221 ■ *Web:* www.gruma.com	Irving	TX	75038	972-232-5000	232-5176
GTC-GTC LLC 14574 Weld County Rd 64	Greeley	CO	80631	970-351-6000	351-6003
Haines City Citrus Growers Assn (HCCGA) 8 Railroad Ave PO Box 337 *TF Sales:* 800-327-6676 ■ *Web:* www.hilltopcitrus.com	Haines City	FL	33844	863-422-1174	422-3938
Harllee Packing Inc 2308 US Hwy 301	Palmetto	FL	34221	941-722-7747	723-3027
Harris Woolf Almonds 26060 Colusa Rd	Coalinga	CA	93210	559-884-2147	884-2746
Hazelnut Growers of Oregon 401 N 26th Ave *TF:* 800-273-4676 ■ *Web:* www.westnut.com	Cornelius	OR	97113	503-648-4176	648-9515
Hunt Bros Co-op Inc 2404 Hunt Brothers Rd SE	Lake Wales	FL	33898	863-676-9471	676-8362
Index Fresh Inc 18184 Slover Ave *TF:* 800-352-6931 ■ *Web:* www.indexfresh.com	Bloomington	CA	92316	909-877-0999	877-1999
Indian River Exchange Packers Inc 7355 9th St SW	Vero Beach	FL	32968	772-562-2252	569-7484
Inland Joseph Fruit Co 300 N Frontage Rd	Wapato	WA	98951	509-877-2126	877-2012
JLG Harvesting Inc 1450 S Atlantic Ave	Yuma	AZ	85365	928-329-7548	329-7551
Kingsburg Apple Packers Inc 10363 E Davis Ave PO Box 456	Kingsburg	CA	93631	559-897-5132	897-4532
Kingston Cos 477 Shoup Ave Suite 207	Idaho Falls	ID	83402	208-522-2365	522-7488
Klink Citrus Assn Inc 32921 Rd 159 PO Box 188	Ivanhoe	CA	93235	559-798-1881	798-2226
LA Hearne Co Inc 512 Metz Rd *TF:* 800-253-7346 ■ *Web:* www.hearneco.com	King City	CA	93930	831-385-5441	385-4377
Lake Region Packing Assn Inc 1293 S Duncan Dr	Tavares	FL	32778	352-343-3111	343-1616
Larson Fruit Co 109 N Wenas Rd PO Box 70	Selah	WA	98942	509-697-7208	697-5281
Mann Packing Co Inc PO Box 690 *TF:* 800-285-1002 ■ *Web:* www.broccoli.com	Salinas	CA	93902	831-422-7405	422-1131
Mariani Nut Co 709 Dutton St *Web:* www.marianinut.com	Winters	CA	95694	530-662-3311	795-2681
Mariani Packing Co Inc 500 Crocker Dr *TF:* 800-231-1287 ■ *Web:* www.marianifruit.com	Vacaville	CA	95688	707-452-2800	452-2973
Mesa Citrus Growers Assn 254 W Broadway Rd	Mesa	AZ	85210	480-964-8615	834-0764
Mooney Farms 1220 Fortress St *Web:* www.mooneyfarms.com	Chico	CA	95973	530-899-2661	899-7746
Northern Fruit Co PO Box 1986 *Web:* www.northernfruit.com	East Wenatchee	WA	98807	509-884-3575	884-1990
Packers of Indian River Ltd 5700 W Midway Rd	Fort Pierce	FL	34979	772-468-8835	466-0108
Phelan & Taylor Produce Co Inc PO Box 458	Oceano	CA	93475	805-489-2413	489-0191
Pleasant Valley Potato Inc PO Box 538 *Web:* www.pleasantvalleypotato.com	Aberdeen	ID	83210	208-397-4194	397-4841
River Ranch Fresh Foods 1156 Abbott St *TF:* 800-538-5868 ■ *Web:* www.riverranchfreshfoods.com	Salinas	CA	93901	831-758-1390	755-8281
Rivermaid Travelling Co PO Box 350 *Web:* www.rivermaid.com	Lodi	CA	95241	209-369-3586	369-5465
RPAC LLC 21490 S Ortigalita Rd *Web:* www.rpacalmonds.com	Los Banos	CA	93635	209-826-0272	826-3882
Sun Pacific Packers Inc 1250 E Myer Rd *Web:* www.sunpacific.com	Exeter	CA	93221	559-592-5168	592-3852
Taylor Fresh Foods Inc 911 Blanco Cir Suite B *TF:* 800-731-7388 ■ *Web:* www.taylorfarms.com	Salinas	CA	93901	831-754-1715	754-0473
Tracy-Luckey Co Inc 110 N Hicks St PO Box 880 *TF:* 800-476-4796 ■ *Web:* www.tracy-luckey.com	Harlem	GA	30814	706-556-6216	556-6210
Trout-Blue Chelan Inc 8 Houser Rd PO Box 669	Chelan	WA	98816	509-682-2591	682-4620
Uni-Kool Partners 395 W Market St	Salinas	CA	93901	831-424-6613	
Veg-Pro Inc 11800 Gordon Ave PO Box 635	Grant	MI	49327	231-834-5657	834-5662
Wilco Peanut Co 3391 US Hwy 281 N PO Box B *Web:* www.wilcopeanut.com	Pleasanton	TX	78064	830-569-3808	569-2743

11-2 Livestock Improvement Services

	City	State	Zip	Phone	Fax
ABS Global Inc 1525 River Rd PO Box 459 *TF Cust Svc:* 800-356-5331 ■ *Web:* www.absglobal.com	DeForest	WI	53532	608-846-3721	846-6442
Accelerated Genetics E 10890 Penny Ln *TF:* 800-451-9275 ■ *Web:* www.accelgen.com	Baraboo	WI	53913	608-356-8357	356-4387
Alta California PO Box 437 *Web:* www.altagenetics.com	Watertown	WI	53094	920-261-5065	262-8022
Alta Genetics Inc RR 2 *TF:* 800-932-2855 ■ *Web:* www.altagenetics.com	Balzac	AB	T0M0E0	403-226-0666	226-4259
AMS Genetics Inc 400 Bottom Rd PO Box 207 *Web:* www.amsgenetics.com	Milleville	PA	17846	570-458-5185	458-5529
Certified Semen Services 401 Bernadette Dr PO Box 1033 *Web:* www.naab-css.org	Columbia	MO	65203	573-445-4406	446-2279
COBA/Select Sires Inc 1224 Alton Darby Creek Rd *TF:* 800-837-2621 ■ *Web:* www.cobaselect.com	Columbus	OH	43228	614-878-5333	870-2622
Cobb-Vantress Inc 4703 Hwy 412 E *TF:* 800-748-9719 ■ *Web:* www.cobb-vantress.com	Siloam Springs	AR	72761	479-524-3166	524-3043
Dairy One 730 Warren Rd *TF:* 800-344-2697 ■ *Web:* www.dairyone.com	Ithaca	NY	14850	607-257-1272	257-6808
Equine Embryos Inc 26 Burnside Dr *Web:* www.equineembryos.com	Ayr	ON	N0B1E0	519-277-0627	624-2097
Flatness International Inc 104 Stony Mountain Rd *Web:* www.flatnessintl.com	Tunkhannock	PA	18657	570-836-3527	836-1549
Genex Co-op Inc/CRI 117 E Green Bay St *TF:* 888-333-1783 ■ *Web:* www.genex.crinet.com	Shawano	WI	54166	715-526-2141	526-4511
Hagyard-Davidson-McGee Assoc PSC 4250 Iron Works Pike *Web:* www.hagyard.com	Lexington	KY	40511	859-255-8741	253-0196
NA of Animal Breeders (NAAB) 401 Bernadette Dr *Web:* www.naab-css.org	Columbia	MO	65203	573-445-4406	446-2279
National Dairy Herd Improvement Assn Inc 421 S 9 Mound Rd PO Box 930399 *Web:* www.dhia.org	Verona	WI	53593	608-848-6455	848-7675

Company	City	State	Zip	Phone	Fax
Newsham Choice Genetics LC 5058 Grand Ridge Dr Suite 200 *TF:* 800-622-2627 ■ *Web:* www.newsham.com	West Des Moines	IA	50265	515-225-9420	225-9560
Reproduction Enterprises Inc 908 N Prairie Rd *TF:* 866-734-2855 ■ *Web:* www.reproductionenterprises.com	Stillwater	OK	74075	405-377-8037	377-4541
SEK Genetics 9525 70th Rd *TF:* 800-443-6389 ■ *Web:* www.sekgenetics.com	Galesburg	KS	66740	620-763-2211	763-2231
Select Sires Inc 11740 US Hwy 42 N *Web:* www.selectsires.com	Plain City	OH	43064	614-873-4683	873-5751
Simonsen Laboratories Inc 1180-C Day Rd *Web:* www.simlab.com	Gilroy	CA	95020	408-847-2002	847-4176
Taurus Service Inc PO Box 164 Grift Flat Rd *TF:* 800-836-5123 ■ *Web:* www.taurus-service.com	Mehoopany	PA	18629	570-833-5123	833-2690

12 AIR CARGO CARRIERS

Company	City	State	Zip	Phone	Fax
ABX Air Inc 145 Hunter Dr *TF:* 800-736-3973 ■ *Web:* www.abxair.com	Wilmington	OH	45177	937-382-5591	383-1233
Aeronet Worldwide 42 Corporate Pk *TF:* 800-552-3869 ■ *Web:* www.aeronet.com	Irvine	CA	92606	949-474-3000	474-1477
Air Canada Cargo LaGuardia International Airport Hangar 5B *TF:* 800-688-2274 ■ *Web:* www.aircanada.com/cargo/en/index.html	Flushing	NY	11371	718-899-9128	651-5467
Air-Sea Forwarders Inc PO Box 90637 *Web:* www.airseainc.com	Los Angeles	CA	90009	310-216-1616	216-2625
Alaska Airlines Cargo Services 2600 S 165th St **Fax:* Hum Res ■ *TF:* 800-426-0333 ■ *Web:* www.alaskaair.com	Seattle	WA	98158	206-392-6585	392-6512*
Alex Nichols Agency 3800 Hampton Rd *Web:* www.anaht.com	Oceanside	NY	11572	516-678-9100	678-1344
Alpine Air Express 1177 Alpine Air Way *TF:* 888-808-0073 ■ *Web:* www.alpine-air.com	Provo	UT	84601	801-373-1508	377-3781
Ameriflight Inc 4700 Empire Ave Hangar 1 **Fax:* Cust Svc ■ *TF:* 800-800-4538 ■ *Web:* www.ameriflight.com	Burbank	CA	91505	818-847-0000	847-0305*
Amerijet International Inc 2800 S Andrews Ave *TF:* 800-927-6059 ■ *Web:* www.amerijet.com	Fort Lauderdale	FL	33316	954-320-5300	765-3521
Arrow Air Inc 1701 NW 63rd Ave Bldg 712 *Web:* www.arrowcargo.com	Miami	FL	33126	305-876-6600	876-6693
Atlas Air Worldwide Holdings Inc 2000 Westchester Ave *Web:* www.atlasair.com	Purchase	NY	10577	914-701-8000	701-8001
ATM Freight Services 1924 Rankin Rd PO Box 60092 *TF:* 800-231-0221 ■ *Web:* www.atmairfrt.com	Houston	TX	77073	800-231-0221	
British Airways World Cargo 4200 S Cargo Dr PO Box 45368 *Web:* www.baworldcargo.com	Atlanta	GA	30320	404-921-0690	684-9752
Capital Cargo International Airlines 7100 TPC Dr Suite 200 *TF:* 800-593-9119 ■ *Web:* www.capitalcargo.com	Orlando	FL	32822	407-855-2004	855-6620
Cargo Services Inc 1601 NW 70th Ave *TF:* 800-597-6010 ■ *Web:* www.cargo-services.com	Miami	FL	33126	305-599-9333	599-6262
Cargolux Airlines International 710 N McDonnell Rd *TF:* 800-722-2023 ■ *Web:* www.cargolux.com	San Francisco	CA	94128	650-877-0820	
Cathay Pacific Cargo 6040 Avion Dr Suite 338 *TF:* 800-628-6960 ■ *Web:* www.cathaypacific.com/cgo	Los Angeles	CA	90045	310-417-0052	348-9789
Cayman Airways Cargo Services 6101 NW 72nd Ave *TF:* 800-422-9626 ■ *Web:* www.caymanairways.com	Miami	FL	33166	305-526-3190	871-7971
Central Airlines Inc 411 NW Lou Holland Dr *Web:* www.centralairsouthwest.com	Kansas City	MO	64116	816-472-7711	472-1682
Centurion Cargo 1851 NW 68th Ave Bldg 706 Suite 225 *Web:* www.centurioncargo.com	Miami	FL	33126	305-871-0130	871-0118
China Airlines Cargo Sales & Service 11201 Aviation Blvd *TF:* 800-421-1289 ■ *Web:* www.china-airlines.com	Los Angeles	CA	90045	310-646-4293	846-4525
Continental Airlines Inc Cargo Div 1600 Smith St *TF:* 800-421-2456 ■ *Web:* www.cargo.cocargo.com/cargo	Houston	TX	77002	713-324-5000	
Delta Air Cargo 1600 Charles W Grant Pkwy PO Box 20706 *TF:* 800-352-2746 ■ *Web:* www.delta-air.com/business_programs_services/delta_cargo/index.jsp	Atlanta	GA	30320	404-715-2600	715-1400
East Coast Air Charter Inc PO Box 7137 *TF:* 888-277-7434 ■ *Web:* www.eastcoastaircharter.com	Statesville	NC	28687	704-838-1991	838-1982
Empire Airlines Inc 11559 N Atlas Rd *Web:* www.empireairlines.com	Hayden	ID	83835	208-292-3850	292-3851
Evergreen International Airlines Inc 3850 Three-Mile Ln *TF:* 800-383-5338 ■ *Web:* www.evergreenairlines.com	McMinnville	OR	97128	503-472-9361	472-1048
Evergreen International Aviation Inc 3850 Three Mile Ln *TF:* 800-472-9361 ■ *Web:* www.evergreenaviation.com	McMinnville	OR	97128	503-472-9361	472-1048
Iberia Air Cargo 1651 NW 68th Cargo Bldg 706 Suite 207 *TF:* 800-221-6002 ■ *Web:* www.iberia-cargo.com	Miami	FL	33126	305-526-5877	871-6228
ICL Express 2307 Coney Island Ave *Web:* www.icl-express.com	Brooklyn	NY	11223	718-376-1023	376-1073
Japan Airlines International Co Ltd 944 N Field Rd *Web:* www.jal.co.jp/en/jalcargo/ar	San Francisco	CA	94128	650-737-5130	737-0227
Kalitta Flying Service 2669 IH- 94 Service Dr *TF:* 800-521-1590 ■ *Web:* www.kalittaair.com	Ypsilanti	MI	48198	734-484-0088	484-7178
Lan Cargo 6500 NW 22nd St **Fax Area Code:* 305 ■ *Web:* www.en.lancargo.com	Miami	FL	33122	786-265-6000	871-4981*
LOT Polish Airlines Cargo JFK International Airport Cargo Bldg 21-B *Web:* www.lot.com	Jamaica	NY	11430	718-656-2674	656-6063
Lynden Air Cargo LLC 6441 S Airpark Pl *TF:* 888-243-7248 ■ *Web:* www.lac.lynden.com	Anchorage	AK	99502	907-243-6150	243-2143
MartinAire Aviation LLC 4745 Frank Luke Dr *TF:* 866-557-1861 ■ *Web:* www.martinaire.com	Addison	TX	75001	972-349-5700	349-5750
Northern Air Cargo Inc 3900 Old International Airport Rd *TF:* 800-727-2141 ■ *Web:* www.northernaircargo.com	Anchorage	AK	99502	907-243-3331	249-5193
Polar Air Cargo 2000 Westchester Ave *Web:* www.polaraircargo.com	Purchase	NY	10577	914-701-8000	701-8001
Qantas Airways Cargo 6555 W Imperial Hwy *TF General:* 800-227-0290 ■ *Web:* www.qantas.com	Los Angeles	CA	90045	310-665-2280	665-2201
Rhoades Aviation Inc 4770 Ray Boll Blvd *Web:* www.rhoadesaviation.com	Columbus	IN	47203	812-372-1819	378-2708
Ryan International Airlines Inc 4949 Harrison Ave *TF:* 800-727-0457 ■ *Web:* www.flyryan.com	Rockford	IL	61108	815-316-5420	398-0192
Service by Air Inc 222 Crossways Pk Dr *TF:* 800-243-5545 ■ *Web:* www.servicebyair.com	Woodbury	NY	11797	516-921-4101	921-4304
Singapore Airlines Cargo PO Box 280746 *Web:* www.siacargo.com	San Francisco	CA	94128	650-876-7350	875-0678
Southwest Airlines Air Cargo 2702 Love Field Dr *TF:* 800-533-1222 ■ *Web:* www.swacargo.com	Dallas	TX	75235	214-792-5534	792-5594
Tampa Airlines Cargo 1850 NW 66th Ave Bldg 708	Miami	FL	33122	305-526-6720	871-6913
Thai Airways International Cargo 6501 W Imperial Hwy *TF:* 800-426-8678 ■ *Web:* www.thaicargo.com	Los Angeles	CA	90045	310-670-8591	670-1057
United Airlines Cargo PO Box 66100 *TF:* 800-822-2746 ■ *Web:* www.unitedcargo.com	Chicago	IL	60666	800-822-2746	
Virgin Atlantic Cargo JFK International Airport Bldg 15 *TF:* 800-828-6822 ■ *Web:* www.virgin-atlantic.com	Jamaica	NY	11430	516-775-2600	354-3760

13 AIR CHARTER SERVICES

SEE ALSO Aviation - Fixed-Base Operations p. 1502; Helicopter Transport Services p. 2011

Company	City	State	Zip	Phone	Fax
Active Aero Group 2068 E St **Fax:* Hum Res ■ *TF Cust Svc:* 800-872-5387 ■ *Web:* www.activeaero.com	Belleville	MI	48111	734-547-7200	547-7222*
Actus Aviation LLC 2030 Airport Rd	Napa	CA	94558	707-252-8152	254-3733
Aero Air LLC 2050 NE 25th Ave *TF:* 800-448-2376 ■ *Web:* www.aeroair.com	Hillsboro	OR	97124	503-640-3711	681-6514
Air America Jet Charter Inc 2323 S Voss Rd Suite 525 *TF:* 888-423-9110 ■ *Web:* www.airamericajetcharter.com	Houston	TX	77057	713-640-2900	640-2193
Air Charter Team 10015 NW Ambassador Dr Suite 202 *TF:* 800-205-6610 ■ *Web:* www.aircharterteam.com	Kansas City	MO	64153	816-283-3280	283-3185
Air Orlando Aviation Inc 319 N Crystal Lake Dr *Web:* www.flyairorlando.com	Orlando	FL	32803	407-896-0721	896-7551
Air Palm Springs 145 S Gene Autry Trail Suite 14 *TF:* 800-760-7774 ■ *Web:* www.airps.com	Palm Springs	CA	92262	760-322-1104	322-1204
Air Royale International Inc 9100 Wilshire Blvd Suite 420 *TF:* 800-776-9253 ■ *Web:* www.airroyale.com	Beverly Hills	CA	90212	310-289-9800	289-9804
AirFlite Inc 3250 AirFlite Way *TF:* 800-241-3548 ■ *Web:* www.airflight.com	Long Beach	CA	90807	562-490-6200	490-6290
American Air Charter Network PO Box 32146 **Fax Area Code:* 323 ■ *TF:* 800-393-2884 ■ *Web:* www.privateaircharterjets.com	Palm Beach Gardens	FL	33420	516-768-3202	883-0071*
American Jet Charter 5901 Philip J Rhoads Hanger 14 Wiley Post Airport *TF:* 800-495-5453 ■ *Web:* www.american-jet.com	Bethany	OK	73008	405-495-5453	495-5472
Atkin Air 1420 Flightline Dr Suite B *TF:* 800-924-2471	Lincoln	CA	95648	916-645-6242	645-7132
Aviation Charter Services 6551 Pierson Dr *TF:* 800-522-2296 ■ *Web:* www.avcharter.com	Indianapolis	IN	46241	317-244-7200	241-8091
Avstar Aviation 12 N Haven Ln *TF:* 800-575-2359 ■ *Web:* www.avstaraviation.com	East Northport	NY	11731	631-499-0048	499-0051
Berkshire Aviation Enterprises Inc 70 Egremont Plain Rd *Web:* www.greatbarringtonairport.com	Great Barrington	MA	01230	413-528-1010	528-2030
Berry Aviation Inc 1807 Airport Dr *TF:* 800-229-2379	San Marcos	TX	78666	512-353-2379	353-2593
Bighorn Airways Inc 912 W Brundage Ln *Web:* www.bighornairways.com	Sheridan	WY	82801	307-672-3421	672-8580
Bluffton Flying Service Co 1080 Navajo Dr *TF:* 800-468-6359 ■ *Web:* www.blufftonflyingservice.com	Bluffton	OH	45817	419-358-7045	358-6851
Bridgeford Flying Services 2030 Airport Rd Napa County Airport *TF:* 800-229-6272 ■ *Web:* www.bfsnapa.com	Napa	CA	94558	707-224-0887	257-7770
Charter Flight Inc 1928 S Blvd Suite 3103 *TF:* 800-521-3148 ■ *Web:* www.charterflightinc.com	Charlotte	NC	28203	704-359-9124	359-9128
Charter Services Inc PO Box 88043 *TF:* 800-657-1555 ■ *Web:* www.csijets.com	Mobile	AL	36608	251-633-6090	633-6850
Chrysler Aviation Inc (CAI) 7120 Hayvenhurst Ave Suite 309 *TF:* 800-995-0825 ■ *Web:* www.chrysleraviation.com	Van Nuys	CA	91406	818-989-7900	
Clay Lacy Aviation 7435 Valjean Ave *TF:* 800-423-2904 ■ *Web:* www.claylacy.com	Van Nuys	CA	91406	818-989-2900	904-3450

Company / Address	City	State	Zip	Phone	Fax
Clintondale Aviation Inc 652 SR 299 # 201	Highland	NY	12528	845-883-5277	883-5293
Web: www.clintondale.com					
Corporate Flight Inc 6150 Highland Rd	Waterford	MI	48327	248-666-8800	666-8804
TF: 800-767-2473 ■ *Web:* www.corporateflight.com					
Corporate Flight International 5220 Haven St Suite 104	Las Vegas	NV	89119	702-736-0077	736-6258
TF: 800-869-8591 ■ *Web:* www.cfi-inc.com					
CSI Aviation Services Inc 3700 Rio Grand Blvd NW Suite 1	Albuquerque	NM	87107	505-761-9000	342-7377
TF: 800-765-9464 ■ *Web:* www.airchartertravel.com					
East Coast Flight Services Inc 29111 Newman Rd Easton Municipal Airport	Easton	MD	21601	410-820-6633	763-7404
TF Sales: 800-554-0550 ■ *Web:* www.eastcoastflight.com					
Elite Aviation LLC 7501 Hayvenhurst Pl	Van Nuys	CA	91406	818-988-5387	988-2111
TF: 888-334-7777 ■ *Web:* www.eliteaviation.com					
Era Helicopters LLC 600 Airport Service Rd PO Box 6550	Lake Charles	LA	70606	337-478-6131	474-3918
TF: 800-256-2372 ■ *Web:* www.erahelicopters.com					
Exec Air Montana Inc 2430 Airport Rd	Helena	MT	59601	406-442-2190	442-2199
TF: 800-513-2190 ■ *Web:* www.execairmontana.com					
Executive Fliteways 1 Clark Dr	Ronkonkoma	NY	11779	631-588-5454	588-5527
TF: 800-533-3363 ■ *Web:* www.fly-efi.com					
Executive Jet 4556 Airport Rd	Cincinnati	OH	45226	513-979-6600	979-6600
TF: 877-356-5387 ■ *Web:* www.executivejetmanagement.com					
Fairwind Air Charter 2525 SE Witham Field Dr Hanger 7	Stuart	FL	34996	772-288-4130	288-4230
TF: 800-989-9665 ■ *Web:* www.fairwindaircharter.com					
Flight Options 26180 Curtiss Wright Pkwy	Richmond Heights	OH	44143	216-261-3500	261-3595
TF: 800-433-1285 ■ *Web:* www.flightoptions.com					
Flightstar Corp 7 Airport Rd Willard Airport	Savoy	IL	61874	217-351-7700	351-9843
TF: 800-747-4777 ■ *Web:* www.flightstar.com					
Hop-A-Jet Inc 5525 NW 15th Ave Suite 150	Fort Lauderdale	FL	33309	954-771-5779	772-6981
TF: 800-556-6633 ■ *Web:* www.hopajetworldwide.com					
International Charter Inc of Oregon (ICI) 17080 Butler Hill Rd	Dallas	OR	97338	503-623-4426	623-7665
Web: www.icioregon.com					
International Jet Aviation Services 8511 Aviator Ln	Centennial	CO	80112	303-790-0414	790-4144
TF: 800-858-5891 ■ *Web:* www.internationaljet.com					
Jet Aviation Business Jets Inc 112 Charles A Lindbergh Dr	Teterboro	NJ	07608	201-462-4100	462-4136
TF: 800-736-8538 ■ *Web:* www.jetaviation.com					
Jet Resource Inc 455 Wilmer Ave Lunken Airport Hangar 27	Cincinnati	OH	45226	513-762-6909	871-4181
TF: 800-404-5387 ■ *Web:* www.jetresource.com					
JetCorp 657 N Bell Ave	Chesterfield	MO	63005	636-530-7000	530-7001
TF: 877-728-6255 ■ *Web:* www.jetcorp.com					
KaiserAir Inc 8433 Earhart Rd PO Box 2626	Oakland	CA	94614	510-569-9622	569-9670
TF: 800-538-2625 ■ *Web:* www.kaiserair.com					
Key Air LLC 3 Juliano Dr Suite 201	Oxford	CT	06478	203-264-0605	264-0218
TF: 800-258-6975 ■ *Web:* www.keyair.com					
Life Flight Network LLC 22285 Yellow Gate Ln Ne	Aurora	OR	97002	503-678-4364	
TF: 800-232-0911 ■ *Web:* www.lifeflight.org					
LR Services 600 Hayden Cir	Allentown	PA	18109	610-266-2500	266-3100
TF: 888-675-9650 ■ *Web:* www.lrservices.com					
Maguire Aviation Group 7155 Valjean Ave	Van Nuys	CA	91406	818-989-2300	909-0604
TF: 800-451-7270 ■ *Web:* www.maguireaviation.com					
Maine Aviation Corp 1001 Westbrook St	Portland	ME	04102	207-780-1811	775-3359
TF: 888-359-7600 ■ *Web:* www.maineaviation.com					
Mayo Aviation Inc 7735 S Peoria St	Englewood	CO	80112	303-792-4020	790-4909
TF: 800-525-0194 ■ *Web:* www.mayoaviation.com					
Miami Air International Inc 5000 NW 36 St Suite 307	Miami	FL	33122	305-876-3600	871-4222
Web: www.miamiair.com					
Million Air Interlink Inc 8501 Telephone Rd	Houston	TX	77061	713-640-4000	283-8274*
**Fax Area Code:* 866 ■ *TF:* 888-589-9059 ■ *Web:* www.millionair.com					
Nashville Jet 635 Hangar Ln	Nashville	TN	37217	615-350-8400	350-8408
TF: 800-824-4778 ■ *Web:* www.nashvillejetcharters.com					
New England Life Flight Inc 1727 Robins St Hangar	Bedford	MA	01730	781-863-2213	
TF: 800-233-8998 ■ *Web:* www.bostonmedflight.org					
New York Aviation Corp LaGuardia Airport PO Box 438	Flushing	NY	11371	718-279-4000	279-3814
Web: www.privatejetcharters.com					
Ohio Medical Transportation Inc 2827 W Dblin Granville Rd	Columbus	OH	43235	614-734-8001	
TF: 877-633-3598 ■ *Web:* www.medflight.com					
Pacific Coast Jet Charter Inc 10600 White Rock Rd # 100	Rancho Cordova	CA	95670	916-631-6507	631-6687
TF: 800-655-3599 ■ *Web:* www.pacificjet.com					
Paragon Air PO Box 575	Kahului	HI	96733	808-244-3356	573-8218
Pentastar Aviation 7310 Highland Rd	Waterford	MI	48327	248-666-3630	666-9668*
**Fax:* Mktg ■ *TF:* 800-662-9612 ■ *Web:* www.pentastaraviation.com					
Personal Jet Charter Inc 5401 E Perimeter Rd	Fort Lauderdale	FL	33309	954-776-4515	491-5771
TF: 800-432-1538 ■ *Web:* www.personaljet.com					
Planemasters Ltd 32 W 611 Tower Rd DuPage Airport	West Chicago	IL	60185	630-513-2100	377-3283
TF: 800-994-6400 ■ *Web:* www.planemasters.com					
Premier Jets 2146 NE 25th Ave	Hillsboro	OR	97124	503-640-2927	681-3064
TF: 800-635-8583 ■ *Web:* www.premierjets.com					
Presidential Aviation 1725 NW 51st Pl Fort Lauderdale Executive Airport Hangar 71	Fort Lauderdale	FL	33309	954-772-8622	771-2622
TF: 888-772-8622 ■ *Web:* www.presidential-aviation.com					
Priester Aviation 1061 S Wolf Rd	Wheeling	IL	60090	847-537-1133	459-0778
TF: 888-323-7887 ■ *Web:* www.priesterav.com					
PrivatAir Inc 611 Access Rd	Stratford	CT	06615	203-337-4600	380-4017
TF: 800-380-4009 ■ *Web:* www.privatair.com					
Ryan International Airlines Inc 4949 Harrison Ave	Rockford	IL	61108	815-316-5420	398-0192
TF: 800-727-0457 ■ *Web:* www.flyryan.com					
S Jet 1251 W Blee Rd	Springfield	OH	45502	937-323-5804	323-8168
Web: www.spectrajetinc.com					
Salmon Air 29 Hamner Dr	Salmon	ID	83467	208-756-6211	756-6219
TF: 800-448-3413 ■ *Web:* www.salmonair.com					
San Juan Airlines Co 4000 Airport Rd Suite A	Anacortes	WA	98221	360-293-4691	299-0981
TF: 800-874-4434 ■ *Web:* www.sanjuanairlines.com					
Seneca Flight Operations 2262 Airport Dr	Penn Yan	NY	14527	315-536-4471	536-4558
Web: www.senecaflight.com					
Sentient Jet LLC 97 Libbey Pkwy 4th Fl Suite 400	Weymouth	MA	02189	781-763-0200	871-8002
TF: 866-307-3684 ■ *Web:* www.sentient.com					
Skyservice Airlines Inc 31 Fasken Dr	Etobicoke	ON	M9W1K6	416-679-5700	679-5703
TF: 800-701-9448 ■ *Web:* www.skyservicebas.com					
Sunset Aviation 351 Airport Rd	Novato	CA	94945	415-897-4522	898-9672
TF: 800-359-7861 ■ *Web:* www.sunsetaviation.com					
Superior Air Charter Inc 2040 Milligan Way Suite 100	Medford	OR	97504	541-842-2260	842-2261
TF: 888-842-0550					
Tavaero Jet Charter 7930 Airport Blvd	Houston	TX	77061	713-644-6431	643-5398
TF: 800-343-3771 ■ *Web:* www.tavaero.com					
TDM Inc 2709 Fanta Reed Rd	La Crosse	WI	54603	608-783-8359	783-8050
TF: 800-658-9498 ■ *Web:* www.colgan-air.com					
Trans-Exec Air Service Inc 7240 Hayvenhurst Pl Suite 200	Van Nuys	CA	91406	818-904-6900	904-6909
Web: www.transexec.com					
Tulip City Air Service Inc 1581 S Washington Ave	Holland	MI	49423	616-392-7831	392-1841
TF: 800-748-0515 ■ *Web:* www.tulipcityair.com					
Twin Cities Air Service 81 Airport Dr	Auburn	ME	04210	800-564-3882	784-5326*
**Fax Area Code:* 207 ■ *TF:* 800-564-3882 ■ *Web:* www.twincitiesairservice.com					
West Coast Aviation Services 19711 Campus Dr Suite 150	Santa Ana	CA	92707	949-852-8340	260-3999
Web: www.westcoastaviationservices.net					
World Airways Inc 101 World Dr HLH Bldg	Peachtree City	GA	30269	770-632-8000	
TF: 800-274-3601 ■ *Web:* www.worldairways.com					

AIR CONDITIONING EQUIPMENT - AUTOMOTIVE

SEE Air Conditioning & Heating Equipment - Residential p. 1384

AIR CONDITIONING EQUIPMENT - WHOL

SEE Plumbing, Heating, Air Conditioning Equipment & Supplies - Whol p. 2434

14 AIR CONDITIONING & HEATING EQUIPMENT - COMMERCIAL/INDUSTRIAL

SEE ALSO Air Conditioning & Heating Equipment - Residential p. 1384; Refrigeration Equipment - Mfr p. 2532

Company / Address	City	State	Zip	Phone	Fax
AAON Inc 2425 S Yukon Ave	Tulsa	OK	74107	918-583-2266	583-6094
NASDAQ: AAON ■ *Web:* www.aaon.com					
Absolut Aire Inc 5496 N Riverview Dr	Kalamazoo	MI	49004	269-382-1875	382-5291
TF: 800-804-4000 ■ *Web:* www.absolutaire.com					
Advantage Engineering Inc 525 E S- 18 Rd	Greenwood	IN	46143	317-887-0729	881-1277
Web: www.advantageengineering.com					
AEC Inc 1100 E Woodfield Rd Suite 588	Schaumburg	IL	60173	847-273-7700	273-7804
TF: 800-783-7835 ■ *Web:* www.aecinternet.com					
Airco Mechanical Inc 8210 Demetre Ave	Sacramento	CA	95828	916-381-4523	386-0350
Web: www.aircomech.com					
Aitken Products Inc 566 N Eagle St PO Box 151	Geneva	OH	44041	440-466-5711	466-5716
TF: 800-569-9341 ■ *Web:* www.aitkenproducts.com					
American Coolair Corp 3604 Mayflower St	Jacksonville	FL	32205	904-389-3646	387-3449
Web: www.coolair.com					
American Industrial Heat Transfer Inc 3905 SR- 173	Zion	IL	60099	847-731-1000	731-1010
Web: www.aihti.com					
Anderson-Snow Corp 9225 Ivanhoe St	Schiller Park	IL	60176	847-678-3823	678-0413
TF: 800-346-2645 ■ *Web:* www.anscorcoils.com					
Arctic Industries Inc 9731 NW 114th Way	Miami	FL	33178	305-883-5581	883-4651
Web: www.arcticwalk-ins.com					
Armstrong International Inc 2081 SE Ocean Blvd 4th Fl	Stuart	FL	34996	772-286-7175	286-1001
Web: www.armstronginternational.com					
Auer Steel & Heating Supply Co 2935 W Silver Spring Dr	Milwaukee	WI	53209	414-463-1234	463-0303
TF: 800-242-0406 ■ *Web:* www.auersteel.com					
Bally Refrigerated Boxes Inc 135 Little Nine Rd	Morehead City	NC	28557	252-240-2829	240-0384
Web: www.ballyrefboxes.com					
Baltimore Aircoil Co 7600 Dorsey Run Rd	Baltimore	MD	20794	410-799-6200	799-6416
Web: www.baltaircoil.com					
Birdwell Co 3708 Greenhouse Rd	Houston	TX	77084	281-492-1786	492-1036
TF: 800-237-2095 ■ *Web:* www.birdwellco.com					
Blissfield Mfg Co 626 Depot St	Blissfield	MI	49228	517-486-2121	486-2128
TF Cust Svc: 800-626-1772 ■ *Web:* www.blissfield.com					
Bristol Compressors Inc 15185 County Rd 1717	Bristol	VA	24202	276-466-4121	645-2423
Web: www.bristolcompressors.com					
Brooks Automation Inc Polycold Systems 3800 Lakeville Hwy	Petaluma	CA	94954	707-769-7000	769-1380
TF: 888-476-5926 ■ *Web:* www.brooks.com					
Bruner Corp 3637 Lacon Rd	Hilliard	OH	43026	614-334-9000	334-9001
Web: www.brunercorp.com					
Bry-Air Inc 10793 SR 37 W	Sunbury	OH	43074	740-965-2974	965-5470
TF: 877-379-2479 ■ *Web:* www.bry-air.com					
Carnes Co 448 S Main St	Verona	WI	53593	608-845-6411	845-6470
Web: www.carnes.com					

Company	City	State	Zip	Phone	Fax
Carrier Corp 1 Carrier Pl *Fax: Hum Res ■ TF: 800-227-7437 ■ Web: www.corp.carrier.com	Farmington	CT	06034	860-674-3000	674-3125*
CEI Enterprises Inc 245 Woodward Rd SE *Fax Area Code: 505 ■ TF: 800-545-4034 ■ Web: www.ceienterprises.com	Albuquerque	NM	87102	800-545-4034	243-1422*
Champion Energy Corp 1 Radisson Plaza Suite 801 Web: www.championenergy.com	New Rochelle	NY	10801	914-576-6190	576-6126
ClimateMaster Inc 7300 SW 44th St *Fax: Cust Svc ■ TF: 800-299-9747 ■ Web: www.climatemaster.com	Oklahoma City	OK	73179	405-745-6000	745-2006*
Colmac Coil Mfg Inc 370 N Lincoln St PO Box 571 TF: 800-845-6778 ■ Web: www.colmaccoil.com	Colville	WA	99114	509-684-2595	684-8331
Colonial Commercial Corp 275 Wagaraw Rd PINK: CCOM ■ Web: www.colonialcomm.com	Hawthorne	NJ	07506	973-427-8224	427-6981
Combustion Service & Equipment Co 2016 Babcock Blvd Web: www.combustionservice.com	Pittsburgh	PA	15209	412-821-8900	821-2644
Danfoss Inc 7941 Corporate Dr TF: 800-236-3677 ■ Web: www.danfoss.com	Baltimore	MD	21236	410-931-8250	931-8256
Dectron Inc 4300 Poirier Blvd TF: 888-332-8766 ■ Web: www.dry-o-tron.com	Montreal	QC	H4R2C5	514-334-9609	334-9184
DiversiTech Inc 6650 Sugarloaf Pkwy Suite 100 TF: 800-995-2222 ■ Web: www.diversitech.com	Duluth	GA	30097	678-542-3600	542-3700
Dometic Corp 2320 Industrial Pkwy PO Box 490 TF: 800-544-4881 ■ Web: www.dometic.com	Elkhart	IN	46516	574-294-2511	293-9686
Doucette Industries Inc 20 Leigh Dr TF: 800-445-7511 ■ Web: www.doucetteindustries.com	York	PA	17406	717-845-8746	845-2864
DRISTEEM Corp 14949 Technology Dr TF: 800-328-4447 ■ Web: www.dristeem.com	Eden Prairie	MN	55344	952-949-2415	229-3200
DRS Sustainment Systems Inc 7375 Industrial Rd Web: www.drs.com	Florence	KY	41042	859-525-2102	795-1475
Duro Dyne Corp 81 Spence St TF: 800-899-3876 ■ Web: www.durodyne.com	Bay Shore	NY	11706	631-249-9000	249-9000
EGS Electrical Group LLC EasyHeat Div 2 Connecticut S Dr TF: 800-537-4732 ■ Web: www.easyheat.com	East Granby	CT	06026	860-653-1600	653-4938
Electro Impulse Laboratory Inc 1805 State Hwy 33 Web: www.electroimpulse.com	Neptune	NJ	07753	732-776-5800	776-6793
Electrofilm Mfg Corp 25395 Rye Canyon Rd Web: www.hartzellaerospace.com	Valencia	CA	91385	661-257-2242	257-2242
Elliott-lewis Corp 2900 Black Lake Pl Web: www.elliottlewis.com	Philadelphia	PA	19154	215-698-4400	698-4436
Ellis & Watts Inc 4400 Glen Willow Lake Ln Web: www.elliswatts.com	Batavia	OH	45103	513-752-9000	752-4983
Emerson Climate Technologies 1675 Campbell Rd Web: www.emersonclimate.com	Sidney	OH	45365	937-498-3011	498-3887
Environmental Air Systems Inc 521 Banner Ave Web: www.easinc.net	Greensboro	NC	27401	336-273-1975	273-1975
Evapco Inc 5151 Allendale Ln Web: www.evapco.com	Taneytown	MD	21787	410-756-2600	756-6450
Factory Air Conditioning Corp 421 Fredericksburg Rd TF: 800-487-1037 ■ Web: www.facair.com	San Antonio	TX	78201	210-732-9984	732-9666
Fidelity Engineering Corp 25 Loveton Cir PO Box 2500 TF: 800-787-6000 ■ Web: www.fidelityengineering.com	Sparks	MD	21152	410-771-9400	771-9412
Fieldhouse Refrigeration 9905 Express Dr TF: 800-451-2377	Highland	IN	46322	219-924-5000	924-5000
First Operations LP 8273 Moberly Ln Web: www.firstco.com	Dallas	TX	75227	214-388-5751	388-2255
Friedrich 10001 Reunion Pl Suite 500 TF: 800-541-6645 ■ Web: www.friedrich.com	San Antonio	TX	78216	210-546-0500	357-4480
Governair Corp 4841 N Sewell Ave Web: www.governair.com	Oklahoma City	OK	73118	405-525-6546	528-4724
Great Lakes Plumbing and Heating Co Inc 4521 W Diversey Ave Web: www.glph.com	Chicago	IL	60639	773-489-0400	489-1492
Hankison International 1000 Philadelphia St Web: www.hankisonintl.com	Canonsburg	PA	15317	724-745-1555	745-6040
Hastings HVAC Inc 3606 Yost Ave PO Box 669 TF Cust Svc: 800-228-4243 ■ Web: www.hastingshvac.com	Hastings	NE	68902	402-463-9821	463-6273
Heat Controller Inc 1900 Wellworth Ave Web: www.heatcontroller.com	Jackson	MI	49203	517-787-2100	787-9341
Heat Pipe Technology Inc 4340 NE 49th Ave Web: www.heatpipe.com	Gainesville	FL	32609	352-367-0999	367-1688
Henry Technologies 701 S Main St TF: 800-964-3679 ■ Web: www.henrytech.com	Chatham	IL	62629	217-483-2406	483-2408
Howden Buffalo Inc 2029 W Dekalb St Web: www.howden.com	Camden	SC	29020	803-713-2200	713-2222
Huntair Inc 11555 SW Myslony St Web: www.huntair.com	Tualatin	OR	97062	503-639-0113	639-1269
Hunton Group The 10555 Westpark Dr Web: www.huntongroup.com	Houston	TX	77042	713-266-3900	267-5753
International Environmental Corp (IEC) PO Box 2598 TF: 800-226-5406 ■ Web: www.iec-okc.com	Oklahoma City	OK	73101	405-605-5000	605-5001
IPAC Inc 155 Pineview Dr TF: 800-388-3211 ■ Web: www.ipacinc.com	Amhurst	NY	14228	716-204-9580	204-9593
ITT Corp 1133 Westchester Ave *Fax: Mktg ■ Web: www.bellgossett.com	White Plains	NY	10604	914-641-2000	696-2950*
ITW Vortec 10125 Carver Rd TF: 800-441-7475 ■ Web: www.itw-air.com	Cincinnati	OH	45242	513-891-7485	891-4092
J & D Mfg Inc 6200 Hwy 12 TF Cust Svc: 800-848-7998 ■ Web: www.jdmfg.com	Eau Claire	WI	54701	715-834-1439	834-3812
Kobelco Compressors (America) Inc 3000 Hammond Ave Web: www.kobelcocompressors.com	Elkhart	IN	46516	574-295-3145	293-1641
Kooltronic Inc 30 Pennington-Hopewell Rd TF: 800-321-5665 ■ Web: www.kooltronic.com	Pennington	NJ	08534	609-466-3400	466-1114
Krack Corp 1300 N Arlington Heights Rd Suite 1305 Web: www.krack.com	Itasca	IL	60143	630-629-7500	629-0535
Lawler Mfg Corp 7 Kilmer Ct Web: www.lawlercorp.com	Edison	NJ	08817	732-777-2040	777-4828
Layton Mfg Corp 825 Remsen Ave TF: 800-545-8002 ■ Web: www.laytonmfg.com	Brooklyn	NY	11236	718-498-6000	498-6003
Lintern Corp 8685 Stn St TF: 800-321-3638 ■ Web: www.lintern.com	Mentor	OH	44060	440-255-9333	255-6427
Lomanco Inc 2101 W Main St TF: 800-643-5596 ■ Web: www.lomanco.com	Jacksonville	AR	72076	501-982-6511	982-1258
Mammoth Inc 13200 Pioneer Trail Suite 150 TF: 800-328-3321 ■ Web: www.mammoth-inc.com	Chaska	MN	55318	952-358-6600	358-6700
Maradyne Corp 4540 W 160th St TF: 800-537-7444	Cleveland	OH	44135	216-362-0755	362-0799
Marc Climatic Controls Inc 13415 Emmett Rd TF: 800-397-0131 ■ Web: www.marcclimatic.com	Houston	TX	77041	713-464-8587	468-8810
Master-Bilt Products 908 Hwy 15 N TF: 800-647-1284 ■ Web: www.master-bilt.com	New Albany	MS	38652	662-534-9061	534-6049
Mobile Climate Control Corp 17103 State Rd 4 E PO Box 150 *Fax Area Code: 913 ■ Web: www.mcc-hvac.com	Goshen	IN	46528	574-534-1516	371-4452*
Munters Corp 210 6th St PO Box 6428 *Fax: Cust Svc ■ TF: 800-446-6868 ■ Web: www.munters.com	Fort Myers	FL	33907	239-936-1555	278-8790*
Munters Corp DHI 79 Monroe St TF Sales: 800-843-5360 ■ Web: www.munters.com	Amesbury	MA	01913	978-388-0600	241-1215
Niagara Blower Co Inc 673 Ontario St TF: 800-426-5169 ■ Web: www.niagarablower.com	Buffalo	NY	14207	716-875-2000	875-1077
Nordyne Inc 8000 Phoenix Pkwy *Fax: Sales ■ TF: 800-422-4328 ■ Web: www.nordyne.com	O'Fallon	MO	63368	636-561-7300	561-7323*
Pacific Rim Mechanical 7655 Convoy Ct Web: www.prmech.com	San Diego	CA	92111	858-974-6500	974-6501
Packless Metal Hose Inc PO Box 20668 TF: 800-347-4859 ■ Web: www.packless.com	Waco	TX	76702	254-666-7700	666-7893
Peerless of America Inc 1201 Wabash Ave Web: www.peerlessofamerica.com	Effingham	IL	62401	217-342-0400	342-0412
Penn Refrigeration Service Corp PO Box 1261 Web: www.pennrefrig.com	Wilkes Barre	PA	18703	570-825-5666	825-5705
Petro 2187 Atlantic St TF: 800-645-4328 ■ Web: www.petrohp.com	Stamford	CT	06902	203-325-5400	328-7422
Phelps Fan LLC 10701 I-30 TF: 800-742-6899 ■ Web: www.phelpsfan.com	Little Rock	AR	72209	501-568-5550	568-3363
Phoenix Mfg Inc 3655 E Roeser Rd TF Cust Svc: 800-325-6952 ■ Web: www.evapcool.com	Phoenix	AZ	85040	602-437-1034	437-4833
Pittsburgh Plumbing Heating & Industrial (PPHI) 434 Melwood Ave Web: www.pphind.com	Pittsburgh	PA	15213	412-622-8100	622-8145
Powercold Corp 115 Canfield Rd PO Box 1239 PINK: PWCL ■ Web: www.powercold.com	La Vernia	TX	78121	830-779-5213	253-8181
Proair LLC 28731 County Rd 6 TF: 800-338-8544 ■ Web: www.proairllc.com	Elkhart	IN	46514	574-264-5494	264-2194
RAE Corp Technical Systems Div 4492 Hunt St TF: 888-498-8922 ■ Web: www.rae-corp.com/tech_sys.htm	Pryor	OK	74361	918-825-7222	825-0723
Rama Corp 600 W Esplanade Ave TF: 800-472-5670 ■ Web: www.ramacorporation.com	San Jacinto	CA	92583	951-654-7351	654-3748
Refrigeration Research Inc 525 N 5th St Web: www.refresearch.com	Brighton	MI	48116	810-227-1151	227-3700
Rheem Mfg Co 1100 Abernathy Rd Suite 1400 Web: www.rheem.com	Atlanta	GA	30328	770-351-3000	351-3003
Rheem Mfg Co Air Conditioning Div 5600 Old Greenwood Rd Web: www.rheem.com	Fort Smith	AR	72903	479-646-4311	
Rink Systems Inc 1103 Hershey St TF: 800-944-7930 ■ Web: www.rinksystems.com	Albert Lea	MN	56007	507-373-9175	377-1060
Russell Div HTP Group 221 S Berry St TF: 800-356-8367 ■ Web: www.russellcoil.com	Brea	CA	92821	714-529-1935	529-7203
Sealed Unit Parts Co Inc 2230 Landmark Pl TF: 800-333-9125 ■ Web: www.supco.com	Allenwood	NJ	08720	732-223-6644	223-1617
Seasons-4 Inc 4500 Industrial Access Rd Web: www.seasons4.net	Douglasville	GA	30134	770-489-0716	489-2938
Skuttle Mfg Co 101 Margaret St TF: 800-848-9786 ■ Web: www.skuttle.com	Marietta	OH	45750	740-373-9169	373-9565
Slant Fin Corp 100 Forest Dr TF: 800-775-4552 ■ Web: www.slantfin.com	Greenvale	NY	11548	516-484-2600	484-2600
SmartEnergy Water Heating Services Inc 77 Grove St *Fax Area Code: 802 ■ TF: 800-762-7861 ■ Web: www.smarthotwater.com	Rutland	VT	05701	800-762-7861	747-2191*
Snyder Capital Corp 8409 Pickwick Ln Suite 379	Dallas	TX	75225	214-754-0500	754-0350
Standard Refrigeration Co 2050 N Ruby St Web: www.stanref.com	Melrose Park	IL	60160	708-345-5400	345-3513
T Rad North America Inc 210 Bill Bryan Blvd PO Box 2300 Web: www.copar.net	Hopkinsville	KY	42240	270-885-9116	885-9518
Tecumseh Products Co Paris Div 2700 W Wood St	Paris	TN	38242	731-642-6394	644-8181
Temp-Control Mechanical Corp (TCM) 4800 N Ch Ave TF: 877-826-3828 ■ Web: www.tcmcorp.com	Portland	OR	97217	503-285-9851	285-9978
Temtrol LLC 106 N Industrial Blvd Web: www.temtrol.com	Okarche	OK	73762	405-263-7286	263-4924
Thermal Care Inc 7720 N Lehigh Ave TF: 888-828-7387 ■ Web: www.thermalcare.com	Niles	IL	60714	847-966-2260	966-9358
Thermo King Corp 314 W 90th St Web: www.thermoking.com	Minneapolis	MN	55420	952-887-2200	887-2615
ThermoElectric Cooling America Corp 4048 W Schubert Ave TF: 888-832-2872 ■ Web: www.thermoelectric.com	Chicago	IL	60639	773-342-4900	342-0191
Tom Barrow Co (TBC) 2800 Plant Atkinson Rd TF: 800-229-8226 ■ Web: www.tombarrow.com	Smyrna	GA	30080	404-351-1010	350-9121

Phone | Fax

Traulsen & Co Inc 4401 Blue Mound Rd — Fort Worth TX 76106 800-825-8220 624-4302*
*Fax Area Code: 817 ■ *Fax: Cust Svc ■ TF: 888-446-2278 ■ Web: www.traulsen.com

Tulsa Heaters Inc 1350 S Boulder Suite 800 — Tulsa OK 74119 918-582-9918 582-9916
Web: www.tulsaheaters.com

Tutco Inc 500 Gould Dr — Cookeville TN 38506 931-432-4141 432-4140
TF: 877-262-4533 ■ Web: www.tutco.com

United CoolAir Corp 491 E Princess St — York PA 17403 717-843-4311 854-4462
TF: 877-905-1111 ■ Web: www.unitedcoolair.com

United Electric Co LP 501 Galveston St — Wichita Falls TX 76301 940-397-2100 397-2166
Web: www.magicaire.com

Watsco Inc 2665 S Bayshore Dr Suite 901 — Coconut Grove FL 33133 305-714-4100 858-4492
NYSE: WSO ■ TF: 800-492-8726 ■ Web: www.watsco.com

Watts Radiant Inc 4500 E Progress Pl — Springfield MO 65803 417-864-6108 864-8161
TF: 800-276-2419 ■ Web: www.wattsradiant.com

Whalen Co The PO Box 1390 — Easton MD 21601 410-822-9200 822-8926
Web: www.whalencompany.com

WSA Engineered Systems 2018 S 1st St — Milwaukee WI 53207 414-481-4120 481-4121
Web: www.wsaes.com

York Airside Service 1237 Penn Ave — Hollsopple PA 15935 814-479-4023 479-7113

York International Corp Engineered Systems Group
5005 York Dr — Norman OK 73069 405-364-4040 419-6214
TF: 877-874-7378 ■ Web: www.york.com

York International Corp Unitary Products Group
5005 York Dr — Norman OK 73069 405-364-4040 419-6214*
*Fax: Hum Res ■ TF: 877-874-7378 ■ Web: www.york.com

15 AIR CONDITIONING & HEATING EQUIPMENT - RESIDENTIAL

SEE ALSO Air Conditioning & Heating Equipment - Commercial/Industrial p. 1382

Phone | Fax

Airefco Inc 18755 SW Teton Ave PO Box 1349 — Tualatin OR 97062 503-692-3210 691-2392
TF: 800-869-1349 ■ Web: www.airefco.com

Allied Air Enterprises
215 Metropolitan Dr — West Columbia SC 29170 803-738-4000 738-4001
Web: www.alliedair.com

Amana Appliances Inc 2800 220th Trail — Amana IA 52204 319-622-5511 622-2180
TF Cust Svc: 800-843-0304 ■ Web: www.amana.com

Bard Mfg Co Inc 1914 Randolph Dr — Bryan OH 43506 419-636-1194 636-2640
Web: www.bardhvac.com

Behr Climate Systems 5020 Augusta Dr — Fort Worth TX 76106 817-624-7273 624-3328
TF: 800-247-6558 ■ Web: www.behrgroup.com

Bergstrom Mfg Co 2390 Blackhawk Rd — Rockford IL 61125 815-874-7821 874-2144
Web: www.bergstrominc.com

Butler Vent-A-Matic Corp
100 Washington Rd — Mineral Wells TX 76067 940-325-7887 325-9311
TF: 800-433-1626 ■ Web: www.bvc.com

CalsonicKansei North America Inc
1 Calsonic Way — Shelbyville TN 37160 931-684-4490 684-2724
Web: www.calsonic.com

Carrier Corp Carrier Transicold Div
6304 Thompson Rd Bldg TR-20 — East Syracuse NY 13057 315-432-6000 432-6207
TF: 800-255-7382 ■ Web: www.carrier.transicold.com

Delphi Harrison Thermal Systems
200 Upper Mountain Rd — Lockport NY 14094 716-439-2011 439-2885

Evans Tempcon Inc 701 Ann St NW — Grand Rapids MI 49504 616-361-2681 361-9646
Web: www.evanstempcon.com

Friedrich 10001 Reunion Pl Suite 500 — San Antonio TX 78216 210-546-0500 357-4480
TF: 800-541-6645 ■ Web: www.friedrich.com

Goodman Mfg Co LP
5151 San Felipe St Suite 500 — Houston TX 77056 713-861-2500 861-7972
Web: www.goodmanmfg.com

Hunter Mfg Co 30500 Aurora Rd Suite 100 — Solon OH 44139 440-248-6111 248-1691
Web: www.hdtglobal.com

International Comfort Products Corp (ICP)
650 Heil Quaker Ave PO Box 128 — Lewisburg TN 37091 931-359-3511 270-3312
TF: 800-458-6650 ■ Web: www.icpusa.com

Johnson Controls Inc - YORK
5757 N Green Bay Ave — Milwaukee WI 53202 414-524-1200 771-7440*
*Fax Area Code: 717 ■ Web: www.johnsoncontrols.com

Kim Hotstart Mfg Co 5723 E Alki Ave — Spokane WA 99212 509-536-8660 563-4216
TF: 800-224-5550 ■ Web: www.hotstart.com

Lennox Industries Inc 2100 Lake Pk Blvd — Richardson TX 75080 972-497-5000 497-5299
TF Cust Svc: 800-953-6669 ■ Web: www.lennox.com

Lennox International Inc
2140 Lake Pk Blvd — Richardson TX 75080 972-497-5000 497-5299*
NYSE: LII ■ *Fax: Mail Rm ■ TF: 800-453-6669 ■ Web: www.lennoxinternational.com

Modine Mfg Co 1500 De Koven Ave — Racine WI 53403 262-636-1200 636-1424
NYSE: MOD ■ Web: www.modine.com

National System of Garage Ventilation Inc
714 N Church St PO Box 1186 — Decatur IL 62525 217-423-7314 422-5387
TF: 800-728-8368 ■ Web: www.nsgv.com

Nortek Inc 50 Kennedy Plaza — Providence RI 02903 401-751-1600 751-4610
Web: www.nortek-inc.com

Rheem Mfg Co 1100 Abernathy Rd Suite 1400 — Atlanta GA 30328 770-351-3000 351-3003
Web: www.rheem.com

Simpson Mfg Co Inc
5956 W Las Positas Blvd — Pleasanton CA 94588 925-560-9000 847-3871
NYSE: SSD ■ TF: 800-925-5099 ■ Web: www.simpsonmfg.com

Takagi Industrial Co USA Inc 5 Whatney — Irvine CA 92618 949-770-7171 770-3171
TF: 888-882-5244 ■ Web: www.takagi.com

TPI Corp PO Box 4973 — Johnson City TN 37602 423-477-4131 477-0084
TF: 800-251-0382 ■ Web: www.tpicorp.com

Trane Co Unitary Products Group 6200 Troup Hwy — Tyler TX 75707 903-581-3200 581-3482
Web: www.trane.com

Van Natta Mechanical Corp 25 Whitney Rd — Mahwah NJ 07430 201-391-3700 930-0295
Web: www.vannattamechanical.com

Whirlpool Corp 2000 N M-63 — Benton Harbor MI 49022 269-923-5000 923-5443
NYSE: WHR ■ TF: 800-253-1301 ■ Web: www.whirlpoolcorp.com

Phone | Fax

York International Corp Unitary Products Group
5005 York Dr — Norman OK 73069 405-364-4040 419-6214*
*Fax: Hum Res ■ TF: 877-874-7378 ■ Web: www.york.com

Young Touchstone Inc 200 Smith Ln — Jackson TN 38301 731-424-5045 265-2302
TF Sales: 800-238-8230 ■ Web: www.youngtouchstone.com

16 AIR FARE CONSOLIDATORS

Phone | Fax

Airline Tariff Publishing Co (ATPCO)
45005 Aviation Dr Suite 400 — Dulles VA 20166 703-471-4717 471-6584
Web: www.atpco.net

BMD Travel Services Inc
7401 E Brainerd Rd Suite 100 — Chattanooga TN 37421 423-485-1291 485-1420
TF: 888-468-5385 ■ Web: www.airlineconsolidator.com

Brazilian Travel Service (BTS)
16 W 46th St 2nd Fl — New York NY 10036 212-764-6161 719-4142
TF: 800-342-5746 ■ Web: www.btstravelonline.com

C & H International
4751 Wilshire Blvd Suite 201 — Los Angeles CA 90010 323-933-2288 939-2286
TF: 800-833-8888 ■ Web: www.cnhintl.com

Centrav Inc
350 W Burnsville Pkwy Suite 250 — Burnsville MN 55337 952-886-7650 886-7640
TF: 800-874-2033 ■ Web: www.centrav.com

DER Travel Services
9501 W Devon Ave Suite 301 — Rosemont IL 60018 847-430-0000 268-3308*
*Fax Area Code: 877 ■ TF: 800-782-2424 ■ Web: www.der.com

Global Network Tours Inc
350 5th Ave Empire State Bldg Suite 6724 — New York NY 10118 212-695-1647 695-7756
TF: 800-671-9961 ■ Web: www.air-supply.com

GTT Global 4100 Spring Valley Rd Suite 202 — Dallas TX 75244 972-490-3394 387-5847
TF: 800-485-6828 ■ Web: www.gttglobal.com

International Travel Systems Inc
194 Blvd 2nd Fl — Hasbrouck Heights NJ 07604 201-727-0470 727-0473
TF: 800-258-0135

Mill-Run Inc 424 Madison Ave 12th Fl — New York NY 10017 212-486-9840 223-8129
TF: 800-645-5786 ■ Web: www5.millrun.com

Picasso Travel
11099 S La Cienega Blvd Suite 210 — Los Angeles CA 90045 310-645-4400 645-0412
TF: 800-742-2776 ■ Web: www.picassotravel.net

Premier Gateway Inc
320 SW Stark St Suite 315 — Portland OR 97204 503-294-6478 294-2199
TF: 800-759-7515 ■ Web: www.premiergateway.com

Sky Bird Travel & Tours Inc 24701 Swanson — Southfield MI 48033 248-372-4800 372-4810
TF: 888-759-2473 ■ Web: www.skybirdtravel.com

Skylink Travel 980 Avenue of the Americas — New York NY 10018 212-573-8980 573-8878
TF: 800-247-6659 ■ Web: www.skylinkus.com

Solar Tours 1629 K St NW Suite 604 — Washington DC 20006 202-861-5864 452-0905
TF: 800-388-7652 ■ Web: www.solartours.com

Trans Am Travel 4222 King St Suite 130 — Alexandria VA 22302 703-998-7676 824-8190
TF: 800-822-7600 ■ Web: www.transamtravel.com

17 AIR PURIFICATION EQUIPMENT - HOUSEHOLD

SEE ALSO Appliances - Small - Mfr p. 1397

Phone | Fax

Air Quality Engineering Inc
7140 Northland Dr N — Brooklyn Park MN 55428 763-531-9823 531-9900
TF: 800-328-0787 ■ Web: www.air-quality-eng.com

Airguard Industries Inc 3807 Bishop Ln — Louisville KY 40218 502-969-2304 995-3030*
*Fax: Cust Svc ■ TF: 800-999-3458 ■ Web: www.airguard.com

Dayton Reliable Air Filter Inc
2294 N Moraine Dr — Dayton OH 45439 937-293-4611 293-3975
TF Orders: 800-699-0747 ■ Web: www.reliablefilter.com

Electrocorp 595 Portal St Suite A — Cotati CA 94931 707-665-9616 665-9620
TF: 800-525-0711 ■ Web: www.electrocorp.net

Field Controls LLC 2630 Airport Rd — Kinston NC 28504 252-522-3031 522-0214
Web: www.fieldcontrols.com

Gaylord Industries Inc 10900 SW Avery St — Tualatin OR 97062 503-691-2010 692-6048
TF: 800-547-9696 ■ Web: www.gaylordusa.com

General Filters Inc 43800 Grand River Ave — Novi MI 48375 248-349-2481 349-2366
Web: www.generalfilters.com

HEPA Corp 3071 E Coronado St — Anaheim CA 92806 714-630-5700 630-2894
Web: www.hepa.com

Home Care Industries Inc ALFCO Div
1 Lisbon St — Clifton NJ 07013 973-365-1600 365-1770
TF Cust Svc: 800-240-7998 ■ Web: www.homecareind.com

Indoor Purification Systems Inc
334 N Marshall Way Suite C — Layton UT 84041 801-547-1162 991-4838
TF: 888-812-1516 ■ Web: www.indoorpurifiers.com

Kaz Home Environment 250 Tpke Rd — Southborough MA 01772 508-490-7000
Web: www.kaz.com

Koch Filter Corp 625 W Hill St — Louisville KY 40208 502-634-4796 637-2280
Web: www.kochfilter.com

Lau Industries 4509 Springfield St — Dayton OH 45431 937-476-6500 254-9519
Web: www.laufan.com

Lipidex Corp 411 Plain St — Marshfield MA 02050 781-834-1600 834-1601
Web: www.aircycler.com

Permatron Group 2020 Touhy Ave — Elk Grove Village IL 60007 847-434-1421 451-1811
TF: 800-882-8012 ■ Web: www.permatron.com

Praxair Trailigaz Ozone Co
8190 Beechmont Ave Suite 308 — Cincinnati OH 45255 513-233-0444 233-9555
Web: www.praxair.com

PuriTec 7251 W Lake Mead Blvd Suite 300 — Las Vegas NV 89128 702-562-8802 446-4841
TF: 888-491-4100 ■ Web: www.puritec.com

Purolator Products Air Filtration Co
880 Facet Rd — Henderson NC 27536 252-492-1141 356-2397*
*Fax Area Code: 800 ■ TF: 800-334-6659 ■ Web: www.purolatorair.com

Company	City	State	ZIP	Phone	Fax
Rena Ware International Inc 15885 NE 28th St *Web:* www.renaware.com	Bellevue	WA	98008	425-881-6171	882-7500
Research Products Corp 1015 E Washington Ave. *TF:* 800-334-6011 ■ *Web:* www.aprilaire.com	Madison	WI	53703	608-257-8801	257-4357
RPS Products Inc 281 Keyes Ave *TF:* 800-683-7030 ■ *Web:* www.rpsproducts.com	Hampshire	IL	60140	847-683-3400	683-3939
Spencer Turbine Co 600 Day Hill Rd *TF:* 800-232-4321 ■ *Web:* www.spencerturbine.com	Windsor	CT	06095	860-688-8361	688-0098
Sterilone LLC 2125 Biscayne Blvd Suite 580 **Fax Area Code:* 419 ■ *TF:* 877-271-1057 ■ *Web:* www.sterilone.com	Miami Beach	FL	33137	305-572-0660	831-2824*
Tjernlund Products Inc 1601 9th St *TF:* 800-255-4208 ■ *Web:* www.tjernlund.com	White Bear Lake	MN	55110	651-426-2993	426-9547
United Air Specialists Inc (UAS) 4440 Creek Rd *TF:* 800-252-4647 ■ *Web:* www.uasinc.com	Cincinnati	OH	45242	513-891-0400	891-4171
Vornado Air Circulation Systems Inc 415 E 13th St *TF:* 800-297-0883 ■ *Web:* www.vornado.com	Andover	KS	67002	316-733-0035	733-1544

18 AIR PURIFICATION EQUIPMENT - INDUSTRIAL

Company	City	State	ZIP	Phone	Fax
AAF International Corp 10300 Ormsby Pk Pl Suite 600 **Fax Area Code:* 888 ■ *TF:* 888-223-2003 ■ *Web:* www.aafintl.com	Louisville	KY	40223	502-637-0011	223-6500*
Acme Engineering & Mfg Corp 1820 N York *Web:* www.acmefan.com	Muskogee	OK	74403	918-682-7791	682-0134
Advantec MFS Inc 6723 Sierra Ct Suite A *TF:* 800-334-7132 ■ *Web:* www.advantecmfs.com	Dublin	CA	94568	925-479-0625	479-0630
Aerovent Inc 5959 Trenton Ln *Web:* www.aerovent.com	Plymouth	MN	55442	763-551-7500	551-7501
Aget Mfg Co 1408 E Church St *TF:* 800-832-2438 ■ *Web:* www.agetmfg.com	Adrian	MI	49221	517-263-5781	263-7154
Air Filter Sales & Service of Denver Inc 134 Yuma St *Web:* www.airfilters.com	Denver	CO	80223	303-777-2603	777-2619
Air Quality Engineering Inc 7140 Northland Dr N *TF:* 800-328-0787 ■ *Web:* www.air-quality-eng.com	Brooklyn Park	MN	55428	763-531-9823	531-9900
Aircon Filter Mfg Co 441 Green St. *TF:* 800-833-3019 ■ *Web:* www.filtersales.com	Philadelphia	PA	19123	215-922-5222	922-5316
Airflow Systems Inc 11221 Pagemill Rd *TF:* 800-818-6185 ■ *Web:* www.airflowsystems.com	Dallas	TX	75243	214-503-8008	503-9596
Airfoil Impellers Corp 2010 Fountain Ave *Web:* www.airfoil.com	Bryan	TX	77801	979-823-7556	775-5588
Airguard Industries Inc 3807 Bishop Ln **Fax:* Cust Svc ■ *TF:* 800-999-3458 ■ *Web:* www.airguard.com	Louisville	KY	40218	502-969-2304	995-3030*
Airmaster Fan Co 1300 Falahee Rd **Fax Area Code:* 800 ■ *Web:* www.airmasterfan.com	Jackson	MI	49203	517-764-2300	255-3084*
Airtech Corp 4260 Artesia Ave *TF:* 800-634-4453 ■ *Web:* www.airtechlaminarflow.com	Fullerton	CA	92833	714-562-9295	562-9273
Alanco Technologies Inc 15575 N 83rd Way Suite 3 *NASDAQ: ALAN* ■ *Web:* www.alanco.com	Scottsdale	AZ	85260	480-607-1010	607-1515
Amerex Industries Inc 119 VIP Dr Suite 204 *TF:* 800-359-2586 ■ *Web:* www.amerexind.com	Wexford	PA	15090	724-935-1300	935-1342
American Fan Co Inc 2933 Symmes Rd *TF:* 866-771-6266 ■ *Web:* www.americanfan.com	Fairfield	OH	45014	513-874-2400	870-6249
AMETEK Rotron Mil-Aero Products Div 55 Hasbrouck Ln *Web:* www.ametekaerodefense.com	Woodstock	NY	12498	845-679-1371	679-1371
AMETEK Technical & Industrial Products 627 Lake St. **Fax Area Code:* 330 ■ *Web:* www.ametektip.com	Kent	OH	44240	215-256-6601	677-3306*
Anguil Environmental Systems Inc 8855 N 55th St *TF:* 800-488-0230 ■ *Web:* www.anguil.com	Milwaukee	WI	53223	414-365-6400	365-6410
Arrow Pneumatics Inc 2111 W 21st St *Web:* www.arrowpneumatics.com	Broadview	IL	60155	708-343-9595	343-1907
Baghouse & Industrial Sheet Metal Services Inc 1731 Pomona Rd *TF:* 866-997-3784 ■ *Web:* www.1888baghouse.com	Corona	CA	92880	951-272-6610	272-1241
Beckett Air Inc 37850 Beckett Pkwy *TF:* 800-831-7839 ■ *Web:* www.beckettair.com	North Ridgeville	OH	44039	440-327-9999	327-3569
Beltran Assoc Inc 1133 E 35th St. *Web:* www.beltranassociates.com	Brooklyn	NY	11210	718-338-3311	253-9028
Bruning & Federle Mfg Co 2503 Northside Dr PO Box 5547 *Web:* www.bruning-federle.com	Statesville	NC	28687	704-873-7237	878-0647
Buffalo Air Handling Co 467 Zane Snead Dr *Web:* www.buffaloair.com	Amherst	VA	24521	434-946-7455	946-5486
Camfil Farr Co 2121 E Paulhan St *TF:* 800-310-3277 ■ *Web:* www.camfilfarr.com	Rancho Dominguez	CA	90220	310-668-6300	609-2164
CECO Environmental Corp 3120 Forrer St. *NASDAQ: CECE* ■ *TF:* 800-333-5475 ■ *Web:* www.cecoenviro.com	Cincinnati	OH	45209	513-458-2600	458-2647
Cincinnati Fan & Ventilator 7697 Snider Rd *Web:* www.cincinnatifan.com	Mason	OH	45040	513-573-0600	573-0640
Clarcor Inc 840 Crescent Ctr Dr Suite 600. *NYSE: CLC* ■ *TF:* 800-252-7267 ■ *Web:* www.clarcor.com	Franklin	TN	37067	615-771-3100	771-5616
Cleanroom Systems 7000 Performance Dr. *TF:* 800-825-3268 ■ *Web:* www.cleanroomsystems.com	North Syracuse	NY	13212	315-452-7400	452-7420
Clements National Co 6650 S Narragansett Ave *TF:* 800-966-0016 ■ *Web:* www.cadillacproducts.com	Chicago	IL	60638	708-594-5890	594-2481
CMI Schneible Co 209 Elm St. *TF:* 800-627-6508 ■ *Web:* www.cmischneible.com	Holly	MI	48442	248-634-8134	634-8135
Columbus Industries Inc 2938 SR-752 *TF:* 800-766-2552 ■ *Web:* www.colind.com	Ashville	OH	43103	740-983-2552	983-4622
Comair Rotron Inc 2675 Customhouse Ct Suite F *Web:* www.comairrotron.com	San Diego	CA	92154	619-661-6688	661-6057
Corning Environmental Technologies 1 Riverfront Plaza *Web:* www.corning.com/environmentaltechnologies	Corning	NY	14831	607-974-9000	974-8776
CSM Worldwide Inc 269 Sheffield St Suite 1 *TF:* 800-952-5227 ■ *Web:* www.csmworldwide.com	Mountainside	NJ	07092	908-233-2882	233-1064
CUNO Inc 400 Research Pkwy *TF:* 800-243-6894 ■ *Web:* www.cuno.com	Meriden	CT	06450	203-237-5541	238-8701
Daw Technologies Inc 1600 W 2200 S Suite 201 *Web:* www.dawtech.com	Salt Lake City	UT	84119	801-977-3100	973-6640
Dectron Inc 4300 Poirier Blvd *TF:* 888-332-8766 ■ *Web:* www.dry-o-tron.com	Montreal	QC	H4R2C5	514-334-9609	334-9184
Disa Systems Inc 150 Transit Ave *TF:* 800-532-0830 ■ *Web:* www.disagroup.com	Thomasville	NC	27360	336-889-5599	884-0017
Donaldson Co 115 E Steels Corners Rd *Web:* www.donaldson.com	Stow	OH	44224	330-928-4100	928-0122
Ducon Technologies Inc 19 Engineers Ln *Web:* www.ducon.com	Farmingdale	NY	11735	631-420-4900	420-4985
Dustex Corp 100 Chastain Ctr Blvd # 195 *Web:* www.dustex.com	Kennesaw	GA	30144	770-429-5575	429-5556
Dynamic Air Engineering Inc 620 E Dyer Rd *Web:* www.dynamic-air.com	Santa Ana	CA	92705	714-540-1000	545-9145
EBM Industries Inc *EBM-papst Inc* 100 & 110 Hyde Rd. *Web:* www.ebmpapst.us	Farmington	CT	06034	860-674-1515	674-8536
Electrocorp 595 Portal St Suite A *TF:* 800-525-0711 ■ *Web:* www.electrocorp.net	Cotati	CA	94931	707-665-9616	665-9620
Engineered Cooling Systems Inc 201 W Carmel Dr	Carmel	IN	46032	317-571-4750	
Epcon Industrial Systems Inc 17777 IH- 45 S. *TF:* 800-447-7872 ■ *Web:* www.epconind.com	Conroe	TX	77385	936-273-1774	273-1774
Filtertech Inc 113 Fairgrounds Dr PO Box 527 *Web:* www.filtertech.com	Manlius	NY	13104	315-682-8815	682-8825
Filtration Group Inc 912 E Washington St **Fax Area Code:* 800 ■ *TF:* 800-739-4600 ■ *Web:* www.filtrationgroup.com	Joliet	IL	60433	815-726-4600	518-1162*
Flanders Corp 531 Flanders Filters Rd *NASDAQ: FLDR* ■ *TF:* 800-637-2803 ■ *Web:* www.flanderscorp.com	Washington	NC	27889	252-946-8081	946-3425
Fuel Tech Inc 27601 Bella Vista Pkwy *NASDAQ: FTEK* ■ *TF:* 800-666-9688 ■ *Web:* www.ftek.com	Warrenville	IL	60555	630-845-4500	845-4502
Gardner Denver Blower Div 100 Gardner Pk. *TF:* 800-543-7736 ■ *Web:* www.gardnerdenver.com	Peachtree City	GA	30269	770-632-5000	632-5095
Gaylord Industries Inc 10900 SW Avery St *TF:* 800-547-9696 ■ *Web:* www.gaylordusa.com	Tualatin	OR	97062	503-691-2010	692-6048
General Filters Inc 43800 Grand River Ave *Web:* www.generalfilters.com	Novi	MI	48375	248-349-2481	349-2366
Glasfloss Industries Inc 400 S Hall St **Fax Area Code:* 800 ■ *Web:* www.glasfloss.com	Dallas	TX	75226	214-741-7056	435-8377*
Great Lakes Filters 301 Arch Ave *TF:* 800-521-8565 ■ *Web:* www.greatlakesfilters.com	Hillsdale	MI	49242	517-437-2635	437-8942
Greenheck Fan Corp 1100 Industrial Ave PO Box 410 *Web:* www.greenheck.com	Schofield	WI	54476	715-359-6171	355-2399
Griffin Environmental Co Inc 7066 I- Island Rd *TF:* 877-293-8789 ■ *Web:* www.griffinenviro.com	Syracuse	NY	13209	315-451-5300	451-2338
Hardie-Tynes Co Inc 800 28th St N *Web:* www.hardie-tynes.com	Birmingham	AL	35203	205-252-5191	252-3254
Hartzell Fan Inc 910 S Downing St. *TF:* 800-336-3267 ■ *Web:* www.hartzellfan.com	Piqua	OH	45356	937-773-7411	773-8994
HEPA Corp 3071 E Coronado St *Web:* www.hepa.com	Anaheim	CA	92806	714-630-5700	630-2894
Home Care Industries Inc ALFCO Div 1 Lisbon St. *TF Cust Svc:* 800-240-7998 ■ *Web:* www.homecareind.com	Clifton	NJ	07013	973-365-1600	365-1770
Honeyville Metal Inc 4200 S 900 W *Web:* www.honeyvillemetal.com	Topeka	IN	46571	260-593-2266	593-2486
Houston Service Industries Inc 7901 Hansen Rd *TF:* 800-725-2291 ■ *Web:* www.hsiblowers.com	Houston	TX	77061	713-947-1623	947-6409
Howden Buffalo Inc 2029 W Dekalb St *Web:* www.howden.com	Camden	SC	29020	803-713-2200	713-2222
Ion Systems Inc 1750 N Loop Rd *TF:* 800-367-2452 ■ *Web:* www.ion.com	Alameda	CA	94502	510-217-0600	217-0484
King Engineering Corp 3201 S State St. *TF Cust Svc:* 800-959-0128 ■ *Web:* www.king-gage.com	Ann Arbor	MI	48106	734-662-5691	662-6652
Koch Filter Corp 625 W Hill St *Web:* www.kochfilter.com	Louisville	KY	40208	502-634-4796	637-2280
La Calhene Inc 1325 Field Ave S *TF:* 800-322-7604 ■ *Web:* www.getinge-lacalhene.com	Rush City	MN	55069	320-358-4713	358-4713
Lau Industries 4509 Springfield St *Web:* www.laufan.com	Dayton	OH	45431	937-476-6500	254-9519
Loren Cook Co 2015 E Dale St. *Web:* www.lorencook.com	Springfield	MO	65803	417-869-6474	862-3820
Lydall Inc 1 Colonial Rd *NYSE: LDL* ■ *TF:* 800-365-9325 ■ *Web:* www.lydall.com	Manchester	CT	06042	860-646-1233	646-4917
Mafi-Trench Corp 3037 Industrial Pkwy *Web:* www.mafi-trench.com	Santa Maria	CA	93455	805-928-5757	925-3861
Marsulex Environmental Technology 200 N 7th St *Web:* www.met-apc.com	Lebanon	PA	17046	717-274-7000	274-7103
McIntire Co 745 Clark Ave. *TF:* 800-437-9247 ■ *Web:* www.mcintireco.com	Bristol	CT	06010	860-585-0050	314-4500
Met-Pro Corp Duall Div 1550 Industrial Dr *Web:* www.dualldiv.com	Owosso	MI	48867	989-725-8184	725-8188
Met-Pro Corp Flex-Kleen Div 955 Hawthorn Dr *TF:* 800-621-0734 ■ *Web:* www.flex-kleen.com	Itasca	IL	60143	630-775-0707	875-3212

Phone Fax

Met-Pro Corp Systems Div
160 Cassell Rd PO Box 144 ...... Harleysville PA 19438 215-732-9300 723-8501
Web: www.met-prosystems.com
Midwesco Filter Resources Inc
385 Battaile Dr ...... Winchester VA 22601 540-667-8500 667-9074
TF: 800-336-7300 ■ *Web:* www.midwescofilter.com
Midwest International Standard Products Inc
105 Stover Rd ...... Charlevoix MI 49720 231-547-4000 547-9453
Web: www.midwestmagic.com
NAO Inc 1284 E Sedgley Ave ...... Philadelphia PA 19134 215-743-5300 743-3018
TF Cust Svc: 800-523-3495 ■ *Web:* www.nao.com
National Filter Media Corp
691 N 400 W ...... Salt Lake City UT 84103 801-363-6736 531-1293
TF: 800-777-4248 ■ *Web:* www.nfm-filter.com
New York Blower Co 7660 Quincy St ...... Willowbrook IL 60527 630-794-5700 794-5776
Web: www.nyb.com
Parker Hannifin Corp Finite Filtratio & Separation Div
500 Glaspie St ...... Oxford MI 48371 248-628-6400 628-1850
TF: 800-521-4357 ■ *Web:* www.parker.com
Pneumech Systems Mfg LLC
201 Pneu Mech Dr ...... Statesville NC 28625 704-873-2475 871-2780
TF: 800-358-7374 ■ *Web:* www.pneu-mech.com
Praxair Trailigaz Ozone Co
8190 Beechmont Ave Suite 308 ...... Cincinnati OH 45255 513-233-0444 233-9555
Web: www.praxair.com
Precipitator Services Group Inc
1625 Broad St ...... Elizabethton TN 37643 423-543-7331 543-8737
TF: 800-345-0484 ■ *Web:* www.psgtn.net
Process Equipment Inc
2770 Welborn St PO Box 1607 ...... Pelham AL 35124 205-663-5330 663-6037
TF: 888-663-2028 ■ *Web:* www.processbarron.com
PSP Industries 300 Montague Expy Suite 200 ...... Milpitas CA 95035 408-942-1155 262-5388
Web: www.pspindustries.com
Purafil Inc 2654 Weaver Way ...... Doraville GA 30340 770-662-8545 263-6922
TF: 800-222-6367 ■ *Web:* www.purafil.com
Purolator Products Air Filtration Co
880 Facet Rd ...... Henderson NC 27536 252-492-1141 356-2397*
**Fax Area Code:* 800 ■ *TF:* 800-334-6659 ■ *Web:* www.purolatorair.com
Revcor Inc 251 E Edwards Ave ...... Carpentersville IL 60110 847-428-4411 426-4630
TF: 800-323-8261 ■ *Web:* www.revcor.com
Robinson Industries Inc 400 Robinson Dr ...... Zelienople PA 16063 724-452-6121 452-0388
Web: www.robinsonfans.com
RP Fedder Corp 740 Driving Pk Ave ...... Rochester NY 14613 585-288-1600 288-2481
TF: 800-288-1660 ■ *Web:* www.rpfedder.com
RPS Products Inc 281 Keyes Ave ...... Hampshire IL 60140 847-683-3400 683-3939
TF: 800-683-7030 ■ *Web:* www.rpsproducts.com
Seneca Environmental Products Inc
1685 S Seneca County Rd Airport Industrial Pk ...... Tiffin OH 44883 419-447-1282 448-4048
Web: www.senecaenvironmental.com
Sly Inc 8300 Dow Cir ...... Strongsville OH 44136 440-891-3200 891-3210
TF: 800-334-2957 ■ *Web:* www.slyinc.com
Sonic Air Systems Inc 1050 Beacon St ...... Brea CA 92821 714-255-0124 255-8366
TF: 800-827-6642 ■ *Web:* www.sonicairsystems.com
Spencer Turbine Co 600 Day Hill Rd ...... Windsor CT 06095 860-688-8361 688-0098
TF: 800-232-4321 ■ *Web:* www.spencerturbine.com
Standard Filter Corp 5928 Balfour Ct ...... Carlsbad CA 92008 760-929-8559 929-1901
TF: 800-634-5837 ■ *Web:* www.standardfilter.com
Sterling Blower Co 135 Vista Ctr Dr ...... Forest VA 24551 434-316-5310 316-5910
Web: www.sterlingblower.com
Strobic Air Corp
160 Cassell Rd PO Box 144 ...... Harleysville PA 19438 215-723-4700 723-6758
Web: www.strobicair.com
Tek Air Systems Inc 41 Eagle Rd ...... Danbury CT 06810 203-791-1400 798-6534
Web: www.tek-air.com
Terra Universal Inc 800 S Ramon Ave ...... Fullerton CA 92831 714-526-0100 992-2179
TF: 800-767-0100 ■ *Web:* www.terrauni.com
Tjernlund Products Inc 1601 9th St ...... White Bear Lake MN 55110 651-426-2993 426-9547
TF: 800-255-4208 ■ *Web:* www.tjernlund.com
Tri-Dim Filter Corp 93 Industrial Dr Bldg 2 ...... Louisa VA 23093 540-967-2600 967-9670
TF: 800-458-9835 ■ *Web:* www.tridim.com
Tri-Mer Corp 1400 Monroe St PO Box 730 ...... Owosso MI 48867 989-723-7838 723-7844
TF: 800-688-7838 ■ *Web:* www.tri-mer.com
Trion Inc 101 McNeill Rd ...... Sanford NC 27330 919-775-2201 774-8771
TF: 866-829-2440 ■ *Web:* www.trioniaq.com
Turbosonic Technologies Inc
239 New Rd Bldg B-205 ...... Parsippany NJ 07054 973-244-9544 244-9545
Web: www.turbosonic.com
Tuthill Corp M-D Pneumatics Div
4840 W Kearney St ...... Springfield MO 65803 417-865-8715 865-2950
TF: 800-825-6937 ■ *Web:* www.tuthill.com
Twin City Fan Cos Ltd 5959 Trenton Ln N ...... Minneapolis MN 55442 763-551-7600 551-7601
Web: www.tcf.com
United Air Specialists Inc (UAS)
4440 Creek Rd ...... Cincinnati OH 45242 513-891-0400 891-4171
TF: 800-252-4647 ■ *Web:* www.uasinc.com
Venturedyne Ltd 600 College Ave ...... Pewaukee WI 53072 262-691-9900 691-9901
Web: www.venturedyne.com
Waco 2546 Gen Armistead Ave ...... Norristown PA 19403 610-630-4800 630-4904
TF: 800-928-7159 ■ *Web:* www.wacofilters.com
Walton Enterprises Inc 125 W Central Ave ...... Bentonville AR 72712 479-273-5743 464-1500

19 AIR TRAFFIC CONTROL SERVICES

The Federal Aviation Administration (A Us Government Agency) And Nav Canada (A Private, Not-For-Profit Canadian Firm) Provide Air Traffic Services Nationwide In The Us And Canada, Respectively. The Types Of Services Provided Include Aircraft Routing, Approach And Departure Instruction, And Weather Information.

Phone Fax

Federal Aviation Administration (FAA)
800 Independence Ave SW ...... Washington DC 20591 866-835-5322
TF: 866-835-5322 ■ *Web:* www.faa.gov
Air Traffic Organization
800 Independence Ave SW Rm 1002 ...... Washington DC 20591 202-267-3666 267-5456
Web: www.faa.gov/about/office_org/headquarters_offices/ato
Great Lakes Region 2300 E Devon Ave ...... Des Plaines IL 60018 847-294-7272 294-7036
Web: www.faa.gov
Federal Aviation Administration Northwest Mountain Region
1601 Lind Ave SW ...... Renton WA 98057 425-227-2001 227-1006
TF: 800-220-5715 ■ *Web:* www.faa.gov
Federal Aviation Administration Regional Offices (FAA)
Alaskan Region 222 W 7th Ave ...... Anchorage AK 99513 907-271-5296
Web: www.alaska.faa.gov
Central Region Federal Bldg 901 Locust St ...... Kansas City MO 64106 816-329-3050 329-3055
Web: www.faa.gov/cen
Eastern Region
1 Aviation Plaza 159-30 Rockaway Blvd ...... Jamaica NY 11434 718-553-3001
Web: www.aea.faa.gov
New England Region
12 New England Executive Pk ...... Burlington MA 01803 781-238-7020 238-7608
Web: www.faa.gov/airports/new_england
Western Pacific Region 15000 Aviation Blvd ...... Lawndale CA 90261 310-725-7800 725-6811
Web: www.faa.gov/airports/western_pacific
Federal Aviation Administration Southern Region
1701 Columbia Ave ...... College Park GA 30337 404-305-5000 305-5010
Web: www.faa.gov
NAV CANADA 77 Metcalfe St PO Box 3411 Sta D ...... Ottawa ON K1P5L6 613-563-5588 563-3426
TF: 800-876-4693 ■ *Web:* www.navcanada.ca

20 AIRCRAFT

SEE ALSO Airships p. 1394

Phone Fax

AeroVironment Inc
181 W Huntington Dr Suite 202 ...... Monrovia CA 91016 626-357-9983 359-9628
NASDAQ: AVAV ■ *Web:* www.avinc.com
Air Tractor Inc 1524 Lelind Snow Way ...... Olney TX 76374 940-564-5616 564-5625
Web: www.airtractor.com
American Champion Aircraft Corp
32032 Washington Ave ...... Rochester WI 53167 262-534-6317 534-2395
Web: www.amerchampionaircraft.com
American Eurocopter Corp 2701 Forum Dr ...... Grand Prairie TX 75052 972-641-0000 641-3550
TF: 800-873-0001 ■ *Web:* www.eurocopterusa.com
Bell Helicopter Textron Inc
600 E Hurst Blvd (State Hwy 10) ...... Fort Worth TX 76053 817-280-2011 280-2321
TF: 800-359-2355 ■ *Web:* www.bellhelicopter.textron.com
Boeing Business Jets PO Box 3707 MS 1E-77 ...... Seattle WA 98124 206-662-4300 662-4330
Web: www.boeing.com/commercial/bbj
Boeing Co Commercial Airplane Group
PO Box 3707 ...... Seattle WA 98124 206-655-2121
Web: www.boeing.com/commercial
Boeing Co The 100 N Riverside Plaza ...... Chicago IL 60606 312-544-2000 544-2082
NYSE: BA ■ *Web:* www.boeing.com
Bombardier Aerospace 400 Cote-Vertu Rd W ...... Dorval QC H4S1Y9 514-855-5000 855-7401
TF: 866-855-5001 ■ *Web:* www.aerospace.bombardier.com
Bombardier Aerospace Learjet 1 Learjet Way ...... Wichita KS 67209 316-946-2000 946-2220
TF: 800-289-5327 ■ *Web:* www.learjet.com
Bombardier Inc 800 RenT-LTvesque Blvd W ...... Montreal QC H3B1Y8 514-861-9481 861-7769
TSE: BBD.A ■ *Web:* www.bombardier.com
Cessna Aircraft Co 1 Cessna Blvd ...... Wichita KS 67215 316-517-6000 517-7250
Web: www.cessna.com
Dassault Falcon Jet Corp
PO Box 2000 ...... South Hackensack NJ 07606 201-440-6700 541-4401*
**Fax: Hum Res* ■ *TF:* 800-526-7071 ■ *Web:* www.dassaultfalcon.com
Embraer Aircraft Corp 276 SW 34th St ...... Fort Lauderdale FL 33315 954-359-3700 359-3701
TF: 800-362-7237 ■ *Web:* www.embraer.com
Enstrom Helicopter Corp USA
2209 22nd St PO Box 490 ...... Menominee MI 49858 906-863-1200 863-6821
Web: www.enstromhelicopter.com
Erickson Air-Crane Co
3100 Willow Springs Rd PO Box 3247 ...... Central Point OR 97502 541-664-5544 664-2312
TF: 800-424-2413 ■ *Web:* www.erickson-aircrane.com
Groen Bros Aviation Inc
2640 W California Ave Suite A ...... Salt Lake City UT 84104 801-973-0177 973-4027
Web: www.groenbros.com
Gulfstream Aerospace Corp 500 Gulfstream Rd ...... Savannah GA 31408 912-965-3000 965-3775
Web: www.gulfstream.com
Hawker Beechcraft Corp PO Box 85 ...... Wichita KS 67201 316-676-5034 676-6614
Web: www.hawkerbeechcraft.com
Kaman Aerospace Corp
Old Windsor Rd PO Box 2 ...... Bloomfield CT 06002 860-242-4461 243-7514
Web: www.kamanaero.com
Kaman Aerospace International Corp
PO Box 2 ...... Bloomfield CT 06002 860-242-4461 243-7514
Web: www.kamanaero.com
Lockheed Martin Aeronautics Co
1 Lockheed Blvd ...... Fort Worth TX 76108 817-777-2000 777-2115
Web: www.lockheedmartin.com
Lockheed Martin Corp 6801 Rockledge Dr ...... Bethesda MD 20817 301-897-6000 897-6083
NYSE: LMT ■ *TF:* 866-562-2363 ■ *Web:* www.lockheedmartin.com
M7 Aerospace 10823 NE Entrance Rd ...... San Antonio TX 78216 210-824-9421 824-9476
Web: www.m7aerospace.com
Maule Air Inc 2099 GA Hwy 133 S ...... Moultrie GA 31788 229-985-2045 890-2402
Web: www.mauleairinc.com
Mooney Aircraft Corp 165 Al Mooney Rd ...... Kerrville TX 78028 830-896-6000 896-3133
TF: 800-456-3033 ■ *Web:* www.mooney.com
New Piper Aircraft Inc 2926 Piper Dr ...... Vero Beach FL 32960 772-567-4361 978-6592
Web: www.piper.com
Northrop Grumman Corp 1840 Century Pk E ...... Los Angeles CA 90067 310-553-6262 201-3023
NYSE: NOC ■ *Web:* www.northropgrumman.com

Company	City	State	Zip	Phone	Fax
Northrop Grumman Corp Military Aircraft Systems Div 1 Hornet Way	El Segundo	CA	90245	310-332-1000	553-2076
Robinson Helicopter Co 2901 Airport Dr. *Web:* www.robinsonheli.com	Torrance	CA	90505	310-539-0508	539-5198
Ryan Aerospace Corp PO Box 500261 *Web:* www.ryanaerospace.com	Austin	TX	78750	512-576-0427	219-6881
Sabreliner Corp 3551 Doniphan Dr. **Fax:* Cust Svc ■ *TF:* 800-325-4663 ■ *Web:* www.sabreliner.com	Neosho	MO	64850	417-451-1810	455-7728*
Scaled Composites Inc 1624 Flight Line Rd *Web:* www.scaled.com	Mojave	CA	93501	661-824-4541	824-4174
Sikorsky Aircraft Corp 6900 Main St PO Box 9729 *Web:* www.sikorsky.com	Stratford	CT	06615	203-386-4000	
Snow Aviation International Inc 7201 Paul Tibbets St.	Columbus	OH	43217	614-492-7669	492-7679
Thrush Aircraft Inc 300 Old Pretoria Rd. *Web:* www.thrushaircraft.com	Albany	GA	31706	229-883-1440	439-9790

21 AIRCRAFT ENGINES & ENGINE PARTS

Company	City	State	Zip	Phone	Fax
A & B Aerospace Inc 612 Ayon Ave *TF:* 888-999-9397	Azusa	CA	91702	626-334-2976	334-6539
AAR Corp 1100 N Wood Dale Rd 1 AAR Pl *NYSE:* AIR ■ *TF:* 800-422-2213 ■ *Web:* www.aarcorp.com	Wood Dale	IL	60191	630-227-2000	227-2019
Alpha Q Inc 87 Upton Rd	Colchester	CT	06415	860-537-4681	537-4332
Barnes Aerospace 169 Kennedy Rd *Web:* www.barnesaerospace.com	Windsor	CT	06095	860-298-7740	298-7738
Beacon Industries Inc 12300 Old Tesson Rd *TF:* 800-454-7159 ■ *Web:* www.beacontechnology.com	St. Louis	MO	63128	314-487-7600	487-0100
BH Aircraft Co Inc 2230 Smithtown Ave. *Web:* www.bhaircraft.com	Ronkonkoma	NY	11779	631-981-4200	981-0221
Budney Industries Inc PO Box 8316 *Web:* www.budney.com	Berlin	CT	06037	860-828-1950	828-7528
Cbol Corp 8944 Mason Ave *Web:* www.cbol.com	Chatsworth	CA	91311	818-704-8200	704-4336
Cbs Mfg Co The 35 Kripes Rd *Web:* www.cbsmfg.com	East Granby	CT	06026	860-653-8100	688-8872
Chromalloy Gas Turbine LLC 330 Blaisdell Rd *Web:* www.chromalloy.com	Orangeburg	NY	10962	845-359-4700	
Continental Motors Inc 2039 Broad St *TF:* 800-718-3411 ■ *Web:* www.tcmlink.com	Mobile	AL	36615	251-438-3411	432-7352
Delta Industries 39 Bradley Pk Rd *Web:* www.delta-industries-ct.com	East Granby	CT	06026	860-653-5041	653-5792
Engine Components Inc 9503 Middlex Dr. *TF:* 800-324-2359 ■ *Web:* www.eci2fly.com	San Antonio	TX	78217	210-820-8100	820-8103
GA Telesis LLC 1850 NW 49th St. *Web:* www.gatelesis.com	Fort Lauderdale	FL	33309	954-676-3111	676-9998
Garsite LLC 539 S 10th St *TF:* 888-427-7483 ■ *Web:* www.garsite.com	Kansas City	KS	66105	913-342-5600	342-0638
GE Aircraft Engines 1 Neumann Way **Fax:* Sales ■ *Web:* www.geae.com	Cincinnati	OH	45215	513-243-2000	552-2177*
GE Aviation 1 Neumann Way *Web:* www.geaviation.com	Cincinnati	OH	45215	513-243-2000	
Gentz Industries Inc 25250 Easy St *Web:* www.gentz.net	Warren	MI	48089	586-772-2500	772-2913
Goodrich Corp Pump & Engine Control Systems Div Charter Oak Blvd.	West Hartford	CT	06133	860-236-0651	236-1062
Goodrich Corp Turbo Machinery Products Div 323 S Bracken Ln *Web:* www.goodrich.com	Chandler	AZ	85224	480-857-5700	899-9094
Gros-Ite Industries 1790 New Britain Ave *TF:* 800-242-1790 ■ *Web:* www.edactechnologies.com	Farmington	CT	06032	860-677-2603	677-6316
Hamilton Sundstrand Power Systems 4400 Ruffin Rd PO Box 85757 *Web:* www.hsapps.utc.com	San Diego	CA	92186	858-627-6000	627-6601
HEICO Corp 3000 Taft St *NYSE:* HEI ■ *Web:* www.heico.com	Hollywood	FL	33021	954-987-4000	987-8228
Heroux-Devtek Inc 1111 St Charles St W Suite 658 E Tower *TSX:* HRX ■ *Web:* www.herouxdevtek.com	Longueuil	QC	J4K5G4	450-679-3330	679-3666
Hitchcock Industries Inc 8701 Harriet Ave S *Web:* www.hitchcock-ind.com	Bloomington	MN	55420	952-881-1000	887-7858
Kreisler Industrial Corp 180 Van Riper Ave *Web:* www.kreislermfg.com	Elmwood Park	NJ	07407	201-791-0700	791-8015
Kreisler Mfg Corp 180 Van Riper Ave *OTC:* KRSL ■ *Web:* www.kreislermfg.com	Elmwood Park	NJ	07407	201-791-0700	791-8015
Lear Romec Crane Corp 241 S Abbe Rd PO Box 4014 *Web:* www.craneae.com	Elyria	OH	44036	440-323-3211	322-3378
Meco Inc 2121 S Main St.	Paris	IL	61944	217-465-7575	465-5230
Middleton Aerospace Corp 206 S Main St.	Middleton	MA	01949	978-774-6000	777-5640
Moeller Mfg Co Inc Aircraft Div 30100 Beck Rd. *Web:* www.moelleraircraft.com	Wixom	MI	48393	248-960-3999	960-1593
MTU Aero Engines North America Inc 795 Brook St Bldg 5 *Web:* www.mtu.de	Rocky Hill	CT	06067	860-258-9700	258-9797
Niles Precision Co PO Box 548 *Web:* www.nilesprecision.com	Niles	MI	49120	269-683-0585	683-7762
Northstar Aerospace Inc 6006 W 73rd St. *TSE:* NAS ■ *Web:* www.nsaero.com	Bedford Park	IL	60638	708-728-2000	728-2009
Parker Gas Turbine Fuel Systems Div 8940 Tyler Blvd. *Web:* www.parker.com/gasturbine	Mentor	OH	44060	440-266-2300	266-2311
Parker Hannifin Corp 6035 Parkland Blvd *NYSE:* PH ■ *TF Cust Svc:* 800-272-7537 ■ *Web:* www.parker.com	Cleveland	OH	44124	216-896-3000	896-4000
Parker Hannifin Corp Nichols Airborne Div 14 Robbins Pond Rd. *Web:* www.parker.com/ag/NAD	Devens	MA	01434	978-784-1200	784-1400
Pratt & Whitney 400 Main St **Fax:* Sales ■ *Web:* www.pratt-whitney.com	East Hartford	CT	06108	860-565-4321	565-6609*
Pratt & Whitney Canada Inc 1000 Marie-Victorin Blvd *TF:* 800-268-8000 ■ *Web:* www.pwc.ca	Longueuil	QC	J4G1A1	450-677-9411	647-3620
Pratt & Whitney Government Engines & Space Propulsion Div PO Box 109600 **Fax:* Sales ■ *TF:* 800-327-3246	West Palm Beach	FL	33410	561-796-2000	796-5876*
Rolls-Royce North America 14850 Conference Ctr Dr Suite 200 *TF:* 800-274-5387 ■ *Web:* www.rolls-royce.com/northamerica/na	Chantilly	VA	20190	703-834-1700	709-6086
Senior Aerospace Ketema Div 790 Greenfield Dr *Web:* www.sfketema.com	El Cajon	CA	92021	619-442-3451	440-1456
Sifco Industries Inc 970 E 64th St *AMEX:* SIF ■ *Web:* www.sifco.com	Cleveland	OH	44103	216-881-8600	432-6281
Teledyne Technologies Inc 1049 Camino Dos Rios *NYSE:* TDY ■ *TF:* 877-666-6968 ■ *Web:* www.teledynetechnologies.com	Thousand Oaks	CA	91360	805-373-4545	
Teleflex Aerospace Mfg Group 280 Adams St. *Web:* www.teleflexaerospace.com	Manchester	CT	06040	860-643-2473	643-2477
Twigg Aerospace Components 659 E York St *Web:* www.twiggcorp.com	Martinsville	IN	46151	765-342-7126	342-1553
Unison Industries Inc 7575 Baymeadows Way *Web:* www.unisonindustries.com	Jacksonville	FL	32256	904-739-4000	739-4006
Wall Colmonoy Corp 101 W Girard Ave *TF:* 800-521-2412 ■ *Web:* www.wallcolmonoy.com	Madison Heights	MI	48071	248-585-6400	585-7960
Williams International 2280 E W Maple Rd PO Box 200 *Web:* www.williams-int.com	Walled Lake	MI	48390	248-624-5200	669-1577

22 AIRCRAFT PARTS & AUXILIARY EQUIPMENT

SEE ALSO Precision Machined Products p. 2443

Company	City	State	Zip	Phone	Fax
AAR Cargo Systems 12633 Inkster Rd *TF:* 800-247-1273 ■ *Web:* www.aarcorp.com	Livonia	MI	48150	734-522-2000	522-2240
AAR Composites 14201 Myerlake Cir *TF:* 888-227-3597 ■ *Web:* www.aarcorp.com/manufact/composites.html	Clearwater	FL	33760	727-539-8585	539-0316
AAR Corp 1100 N Wood Dale Rd 1 AAR Pl *NYSE:* AIR ■ *TF:* 800-422-2213 ■ *Web:* www.aarcorp.com	Wood Dale	IL	60191	630-227-2000	227-2019
Ace Clearwater Enterprises 19815 Magellan Dr *Web:* www.aceclearwater.com	Torrance	CA	90502	310-538-5380	323-2137
Acromil Corp 18421 Railroad St *Web:* www.acromil.com	City of Industry	CA	91748	626-964-2522	810-6100
Advanced Machine & Stretchform International Inc 18620 S Broadway St *Web:* www.amsicom.com	Gardena	CA	90248	310-538-3857	538-0723
Advanced Technology Co WII 2858 E Walnut St *Web:* www.at-co.com	Pasadena	CA	91107	626-449-2696	793-9442
Aero Gear Inc 1050 Day Hill Rd. *Web:* www.aerogear.com	Windsor	CT	06095	860-688-0888	285-8514
Aero Parts Mfg & Repair Inc 431 Rio Rancho Blvd NE *Web:* www.aeroparts.aero	Rio Rancho	NM	87124	505-891-6600	891-6650
Aeronca Inc 2320 Wedekind Dr. *Web:* www.aeroncainc.com	Middletown	OH	45042	513-422-2751	422-0812
Aerospace Products International (API) 3778 Distriplex Dr N **Fax Area Code:* 800 ■ *TF:* 888-274-2497 ■ *Web:* www.apiworldwide.com	Memphis	TN	38118	901-365-3470	950-1411*
Apex Engineering International LLC 1234 Wellington Pl *Web:* www.aeillc.com	Wichita	KS	67203	316-262-1494	262-8659
Arden Engineering Inc 1878 N Main St. *Web:* www.arden-engr.com	Orange	CA	92865	714-998-6410	998-0956
Arkwin Industries Inc 686 Main St **Fax:* Sales ■ *Web:* www.arkwin.com	Westbury	NY	11590	516-333-2640	334-6786*
Arrow Gear Co Inc 2301 Curtiss St. *Web:* www.arrowgear.com	Downers Grove	IL	60515	630-969-7640	969-0253
Arrowhead Products Corp 4411 Katella Ave *Web:* www.arrowheadproducts.net	Los Alamitos	CA	90720	714-828-7770	220-6487
Arvan Inc 14083 S Normandie Ave *Web:* www.arvaninc.com	Gardena	CA	90249	310-327-1818	324-6634
Aurora Flight Sciences Corp 9950 Wakeman Dr *Web:* www.aurora.aero	Manassas	VA	20110	703-369-3633	369-4514
Avox Systems Inc 225 Erie St *TF:* 866-278-3237 ■ *Web:* www.avoxsys.com	Lancaster	NY	14086	716-683-5100	686-1597
B/E Aerospace Inc 1400 Corporate Ctr Way *NASDAQ:* BEAV ■ *TF:* 888-223-2376 ■ *Web:* www.beaerospace.com	Wellington	FL	33414	561-791-5000	791-7900
Boeing Co Commercial Airplane Group PO Box 3707 *Web:* www.boeing.com/commercial	Seattle	WA	98124	206-655-2121	
Carleton Life Support Systems Inc 2734 Hickory Grove Rd. *Web:* www.cobham.com	Davenport	IA	52804	563-383-6000	383-6430
CEF Industries Inc 320 S Church St. *TF:* 800-888-6419 ■ *Web:* www.cefind.com	Addison	IL	60101	630-628-2593	628-1386
Cfan Co 1000 Technology Way *Web:* www.c-fan.com	San Marcos	TX	78666	512-353-2832	353-2838
Chem-Fab Corp 1923 Central Ave *Web:* www.chem-fab.com	Hot Springs	AR	71901	501-321-9325	321-2859
Cox & Co Inc 200 Varick St *Web:* www.coxandco.com	New York	NY	10014	212-366-0200	366-0222
CRS Jet Spares Inc 6701 NW 12th Ave *Web:* www.crsjetspares.com	Fort Lauderdale	FL	33309	954-972-2807	972-2708

	City	State	Zip	Phone	Fax
CTL Aerospace Inc 5616 Spellmire Dr *Web:* www.ctlaerospace.com	Cincinnati	OH	45246	513-874-7900	874-2499
Curtiss-Wright Corp 10 Waterview Blvd 2nd Fl *NYSE: CW* ■ *Web:* www.curtisswright.com	Parsippany	NJ	07054	973-541-3700	541-3699
Curtiss-Wright Flight Systems 201 Old Boiling Springs Rd **Fax:* Cust Svc ■ *Web:* www.curtisswright.com	Shelby	NC	28152	704-481-1150	482-1903*
Dukes Aerospace 9060 Winnetka Ave *Web:* www.dukesaerospace.com	Northridge	CA	91324	818-998-9811	998-9811
Engineered Arresting Systems Corp 2550 Market St *Web:* www.esco-usa.com	Aston	PA	19014	610-494-8000	494-8989
Enviro Systems Inc 12037 N Hwy 99 *Web:* www.enviro-ok.com	Seminole	OK	74868	405-382-0731	382-0737
Essex Cryogenic of Missouri Inc 8007 Chivvis Dr *Web:* www.essexind.com	Saint Louis	MO	63123	314-832-8077	832-8208
Esterline -Advanced Input Devices Inc 600 W Wilbur Ave *TF:* 800-444-5923 ■ *Web:* www.advanced-input.com	Coeur D'Alene	ID	83815	208-765-8000	292-2275
Exotic Metals Forming Co LLC 5411 S 226th St *Web:* www.exoticmetals.com	Kent	WA	98032	253-395-3710	872-8033
Fairchild Controls Corp 540 Highland St *Web:* www.fairchildcontrols.com	Frederick	MD	21701	301-228-3400	682-6885
FDC/aerofilter Inc 8 Digital Dr Suite 104 *Web:* www.fdc-aerofilter.com	Novato	CA	94949	415-884-0555	884-0505
Fenn Technologies 300 Fenn Rd *Web:* www.spxprecision.com	Newington	CT	06111	860-666-2471	666-2471
FletchAir Inc 103 Turkey Run Ln *TF:* 800-329-4647 ■ *Web:* www.fletchair.com	Comfort	TX	78013	830-995-5900	995-5903
Flight Safety Technologies Inc 655 Engineering Dr Suite 300 *AMEX: FLT* ■ *TF:* 800-877-9019 ■ *Web:* www.fleetcor.com	Norcross	GA	30092	770-449-0479	449-3471
GE Aviation Systems Div 3290 Patterson Ave SE *Web:* www.geaviationsystems.com	Grand Rapids	MI	49512	616-241-7000	241-7533
GKN Aerospace Chem-tronics Inc 1150 W Bradley Ave *Web:* www.chem-tronics.com	El Cajon	CA	92020	619-448-2320	258-5270
Global Ground Support LLC 540 E Hwy 56 *TF:* 888-780-0303 ■ *Web:* www.global-llc.com	Olathe	KS	66061	913-780-0300	780-0829
Globe Engineering Co Inc PO Box 12407 *Web:* www.globeeng.com	Wichita	KS	67277	316-943-1266	943-3089
Goodrich Corp Aircraft Interior Products Div 3414 S 5th St *TF:* 888-419-4344 ■ *Web:* www.goodrich.com/Goodrich/Businesses/Interiors	Phoenix	AZ	85040	602-243-2200	243-2300
Goodrich Corp De-Icing & Specialty Systems Div 1555 Corporate Woods Pkwy *Web:* www.goodrich.com	Uniontown	OH	44685	330-374-2020	374-2290
Goodrich Corp Landing Gear Div 8000 Marble Ave *Web:* www.lgd.goodrich.com	Cleveland	OH	44105	216-341-1700	429-4800
Goodrich Corp Sensor Systems Div 14300 Judicial Rd *Web:* www.goodrich.com/Goodrich/Businesses/Sensors-and-Integrated-Systems	Burnsville	MN	55306	952-892-4000	892-4800
Goodrich Corp Wheels & Brakes Div 101 Waco St PO Box 340 *TF:* 800-448-2102 ■ *Web:* www.goodrich.com/Goodrich/Businesses/Aircraft-Wheels-and-Brakes	Troy	OH	45373	937-339-3811	440-3286
Growth Industries Inc 12523 3rd St PO Box 900 *Web:* www.growthind.com	Grandview	MO	64030	816-763-7676	765-4925
Hamilton Sundstrand Aerospace 4747 Harrison Ave PO Box 7002 *Web:* www.hamiltonsundstrand.com	Rockford	IL	61125	815-226-6000	394-2414
Hartwell Corp 900 Richfield Rd *Web:* www.hartwellcorp.com	Placentia	CA	92870	714-993-4200	579-4419
Hartzell Propeller Inc 1 Propeller Pl *Web:* www.hartzellprop.com	Piqua	OH	45356	937-778-4200	778-4271
Heizer Aerospace Inc 8750 Pevely Industrial Dr *Web:* www.haiusa.com	Pevely	MO	63070	636-475-6300	464-4206
Honeywell Aerospace 1944 E Sky Harbor Cir **Fax Area Code:* 602 ■ *TF:* 800-601-3099 ■ *Web:* www.honeywell.com	Phoenix	AZ	85034	800-601-3099	365-3343*
Honeywell Inc Aircraft Landing Systems 3520 Westmoor St *TF:* 800-707-4555	South Bend	IN	46628	574-231-2000	231-2020
Hydro-Aire Inc 3000 Winona Ave *Web:* www.craneae.com	Burbank	CA	91504	818-526-2600	526-2284
Jamco America Inc 1018 80th St SW *Web:* www.jamcoamerica.com	Everett	WA	98203	425-347-4735	355-0237
Kaman Aerospace Corp Old Windsor Rd PO Box 2 *Web:* www.kamanaero.com	Bloomfield	CT	06002	860-242-4461	243-7514
L-3 Communications Integrated Systems 10001 Jack Finney Blvd *Web:* www.l-3com.com	Greenville	TX	75402	903-455-3450	457-4413
LMI Aerospace Inc (LMIA) 411 Fountain Lakes Blvd *NASDAQ: LMIA* ■ *Web:* www.lmiaerospace.com	Saint Charles	MO	63301	636-946-6525	949-1576
Magellan Aerospace Corp 3160 Derry Rd E *Web:* www.magellan.aero	Mississauga	ON	L4T1A9	905-677-1889	677-5658
Mayday Mfg Co 1500 I- 35 W *Web:* www.maydaymfg.com	Denton	TX	76207	940-898-8301	898-8305
MC Gill Corp 4056 Easy St *Web:* www.mcgillcorp.com	El Monte	CA	91731	626-443-6094	350-5880
Middle River Aircraft Systems (MRAS) 103 Chesapeake Pk Plaza *TF:* 800-880-9975 ■ *Web:* www.mras-usa.com	Baltimore	MD	21220	410-682-1500	682-1230
Mnemonics Inc 3900 Dow Rd *TF:* 800-842-5333 ■ *Web:* www.mnemonics-esd.com	Melbourne	FL	32934	321-254-7300	242-0862
Nasco Aircraft Brake Inc 13300 Estrella Ave *Web:* www.nascoaircraft.com	Gardena	CA	90248	310-532-4430	532-6014
National Machine Co 4880 Hudson Dr *Web:* www.nationalmachinecompany.com	Stow	OH	44224	330-688-6494	688-6952
Neill Aircraft Co 1260 W 15th St *Web:* www.neillaircraft.com	Long Beach	CA	90813	562-432-7981	491-0483
NORDAM Group 6911 N Whirlpool Dr PO Box 3365 **Fax:* Sales ■ *Web:* www.nordam.com	Tulsa	OK	74101	918-587-4105	878-4808*
Northrop Grumman Corp 1840 Century Pk E *NYSE: NOC* ■ *Web:* www.northropgrumman.com	Los Angeles	CA	90067	310-553-6262	201-3023
Paramount Panels Inc 1531 E Cedar St *Web:* www.paramountpanels.com	Ontario	CA	91761	909-947-5168	947-8012
Parker Aerospace Group 14300 Alton Pkwy *Web:* www.parker.com/ag	Irvine	CA	92618	949-833-3000	851-3277
Precision Pattern Inc 1643 S Maize Rd *TF:* 800-448-5127	Wichita	KS	67209	316-721-3100	721-2053
Shimadzu Precision Instruments inc 3111 Lomita Blvd *Web:* www.shimadzu.com	Torrance	CA	90505	310-517-9910	517-9180
Stellex Bandy Machining Inc 3420 N San Fernando Blvd *Web:* www.bandy-machining.com	Burbank	CA	91510	818-846-9020	846-0621
Symbolic Displays Inc 1917 E St Andrew Pl *Web:* www.symbolicdisplays.com	Santa Ana	CA	92705	714-258-2811	258-2810
TransDigm Group Inc 1301 E 9th St Suite 3000 *NYSE: TDG* ■ *Web:* www.transdigm.com	Cleveland	OH	44114	216-706-2690	
Triumph Thermal Systems Inc 200 Railroad St *Web:* www.triumphgroup.com	Forest	OH	45843	419-273-2511	273-3285
Tronair Inc 1740 Eber Rd Suite E *TF:* 800-426-6301 ■ *Web:* www.tronair.com	Holland	OH	43528	419-866-6301	867-0634
Vibro-Meter Inc 144 Harvey Rd *TF:* 800-842-4291 ■ *Web:* www.vibro-meter.com	Londonderry	NH	03053	603-669-0940	669-0931
Vought Aircraft Div 9314 W Jefferson Blvd *Web:* www.triumphgroup.com/companies/triumph-aerostructures-vought-aircraft-division	Dallas	TX	75211	972-946-2011	

23 AIRCRAFT RENTAL

SEE ALSO Aviation - Fixed-Base Operations p. 1502

	City	State	Zip	Phone	Fax
AeroCentury Corp 1440 Chapin Ave Suite 310 *AMEX: ACY* ■ *Web:* www.aerocentury.com	Burlingame	CA	94010	650-340-1888	696-3929
AeroTurbine Inc 2323 NW 82nd Ave **Fax:* Cust Svc ■ *TF Cust Svc:* 877-747-2370 ■ *Web:* www.aeroturbine.com	Miami	FL	33122	305-590-2600	717-3568*
Aircastle Ltd 300 First Stamford Pl 5th Fl *NYSE: AYR* ■ *Web:* www.aircastle.com	Stamford	CT	06902	203-504-1020	504-1021
Aviation Capital Group Corp 610 Newport Ctr Dr Suite 1400 *Web:* www.aviationcapitalgroup.com	Newport Beach	CA	92660	949-219-4600	759-5675
Aviation Leasing Group 8080 Ward Pkwy Suite 407 *Web:* www.algkc.com	Kansas City	MO	64114	816-931-7300	931-8200
GE Aviation Services 201 High Ridge Rd *Web:* www.gecas.com	Stamford	CT	06927	203-357-3776	316-7865
International Lease Finance Corp (ILFC) 10250 Constellation Blvd Suite 3400 *Web:* www.ilfc.com	Los Angeles	CA	90067	310-788-1999	788-1990
Jetscape Inc 10 S New River Dr E Suite 200 *TF:* 800-355-5387 ■ *Web:* www.jetscape.aero	Fort Lauderdale	FL	33301	954-763-4737	763-4757
Jones Aviation Service Inc 1234 Clyde Jones Rd *TF:* 800-945-6637 ■ *Web:* www.jonesav.com	Sarasota	FL	34243	941-355-8100	351-9700
Wright Air Service Inc 3842 University Ave S PO Box 60142 *Web:* www.wrightairservice.com	Fairbanks	AK	99706	907-474-0502	474-0375

24 AIRCRAFT SERVICE & REPAIR

	City	State	Zip	Phone	Fax
AAR Aircraft Component Services 747 Zeckendorf Blvd *Web:* www.aarcorp.com	Garden City	NY	11530	516-222-9000	222-0987
AAR Aircraft Services 6611 S Meridian Ave *Web:* www.aarcorp.com	Oklahoma City	OK	73159	405-218-3000	218-3610
AAR Corp 1100 N Wood Dale Rd 1 AAR Pl *NYSE: AIR* ■ *TF:* 800-422-2213 ■ *Web:* www.aarcorp.com	Wood Dale	IL	60191	630-227-2000	227-2019
AAR Landing Gear Services 9371 NW 100th St *Web:* www.aarcorp.com	Miami	FL	33178	305-887-4027	887-9437
AAR Power Services 148 Industrial Pk Dr *Web:* www.aarcorp.com	Frankfort	NY	13340	315-731-3700	731-3737
Aero Twin Inc 2403 Merrill Field Dr *Web:* www.aerotwin.com	Anchorage	AK	99501	907-274-6166	274-4285
AeroThrust Corp 5300 NW 36th St PO Box 522236 *TF:* 800-228-0665 ■ *Web:* www.aerothrust.com	Miami	FL	33152	305-871-1790	526-7388
American Avionics 7023 Perimeter Rd S *TF Sales:* 800-518-5858 ■ *Web:* www.americanavionics.com	Seattle	WA	98108	206-763-8530	763-2036
Barfield Inc 4101 NW 29th St *TF:* 800-321-1039 ■ *Web:* www.barfieldinc.com	Miami	FL	33142	305-894-5300	871-5629
Basler Turbo Conversions LLC 255 W 35th St PO Box 2305 *Web:* www.baslerturbo.com	Oshkosh	WI	54903	920-236-7820	235-0381
Bridgestone Aircraft Tire USA Inc 802 S Ayersville Rd	Mayodan	NC	27027	336-548-8100	548-7441
Byerly Aviation 6100 EM Dirkson Pkwy *Web:* www.byerlyaviation.com	Peoria	IL	61607	309-697-6300	697-2779

	City	State	Zip	Phone	Fax
Christiansen Aviation Inc PO Box 702412	Tulsa	OK	74170	918-299-2687	299-0694
TF: 800-331-5550 ■ *Web:* www.christiansenaviation.com					
Curtiss-Wright Controls Inc					
15800 John J Delaney Dr Suite 200	Charlotte	NC	28277	704-869-4600	869-4601
TF: 877-319-8468 ■ *Web:* www.cwcontrols.com					
Cutter Aviation 2802 E Old Tower Rd	Phoenix	AZ	85034	602-273-1237	275-4010
TF: 800-234-5382 ■ *Web:* www.cutteraviation.com					
Duncan Aviation Inc					
3701 Aviation Rd PO Box 81887	Lincoln	NE	68501	402-475-2611	475-5541
TF: 800-228-4277 ■ *Web:* www.duncanaviation.com					
Elbit Systems of America					
4700 Marine Creek Pkwy	Fort Worth	TX	76179	817-234-6799	
Web: www.elbitsystems-us.com					
Elliott Aviation Inc 6601 74th Ave PO Box 100	Milan	IL	61264	309-799-3183	799-2014
TF: 800-447-6711 ■ *Web:* www.elliottaviation.com					
Emteq Inc 5349 S Emmer Dr	New Berlin	WI	53151	262-679-6170	679-6175
Web: www.emteq.com					
Evergreen Maintenance Center Inc					
24641 E Pinal Air Pk Rd # 3	Marana	AZ	85653	520-682-4181	682-2056
TF: 800-624-6838 ■ *Web:* www.evergreenaviation.com					
GKN Aerospace Chem-tronics Inc					
1150 W Bradley Ave	El Cajon	CA	92020	619-448-2320	258-5270
Web: www.chem-tronics.com					
Hawker Pacific Aerospace					
11240 Sherman Way	Sun Valley	CA	91352	818-765-6201	765-8073
Web: www.hawker.com					
Helicomb International Inc 1402 S 69th E Ave	Tulsa	OK	74112	918-835-3999	834-4451
Web: www.helicomb.com					
Honeywell Inc Aircraft Landing Systems					
3520 Westmoor St	South Bend	IN	46628	574-231-2000	231-2020
TF: 800-707-4555					
Jet Aviation 112 Charles A Lindbergh Dr	Teterboro	NJ	07608	201-288-8400	462-4005
TF: 800-538-0832 ■ *Web:* www.jetaviation.com					
Kfs Inc PO Box 612584	Dallas	TX	75261	817-488-4115	488-4350
TF: 888-820-4565 ■ *Web:* www.kfsinc.com					
L-3 Communications Flight International Aviation LLC					
1 Lear Dr	Newport News	VA	23602	757-886-5500	874-7481
TF: 800-358-4685 ■ *Web:* www.l-3com.com/fi					
Martin Aviation 19300 Ike Jones Rd	Santa Ana	CA	92707	714-210-2945	557-0637
McKinley Air Transport Inc PO Box 2406	North Canton	OH	44720	330-499-3316	499-0444
TF: 800-225-6446					
Mercury Air Group Inc 5456 McConnell Ave	Los Angeles	CA	90066	310-827-2737	827-8921
Web: www.mercuryairgroup.com					
Million Air Interlink Inc 8501 Telephone Rd	Houston	TX	77061	713-640-4000	283-8274*
**Fax Area Code:* 866 ■ *TF:* 888-589-9059 ■ *Web:* www.millionair.com					
NORDAM Group 6911 N Whirlpool Dr PO Box 3365	Tulsa	OK	74101	918-587-4105	878-4808*
**Fax:* Sales ■ *Web:* www.nordam.com					
Northern Air Inc					
5500 44th St SE Bldg 403	Grand Rapids	MI	49512	616-336-4700	336-4777
TF: 800-262-4953 ■ *Web:* www.northernair.net					
Pemco Aviation Group Inc 1943 50th St N	Birmingham	AL	35212	205-592-0011	592-0195
NASDAQ: PAGI					
Pemco World Air Services 100 Pemco Dr	Dothan	AL	36303	334-983-4571	983-7046*
**Fax:* Hum Res ■ *Web:* www.pemcoair.com					
Precision Airmotive LLC 14800 40th Ave NE	Marysville	WA	98271	360-651-8282	651-8080*
**Fax:* Sales ■ *Web:* www.precisionairmotive.com					
Priester Aviation 1061 S Wolf Rd	Wheeling	IL	60090	847-537-1133	459-0778
TF: 888-323-7887 ■ *Web:* www.priesterav.com					
Rolls-Royce Engine Services Inc					
7200 Earhart Rd	Oakland	CA	94621	510-613-1000	635-3221
TF: 800-622-2677 ■ *Web:* www.rolls-royce.com					
Sabreliner Corp 7733 Forsyth Blvd Suite 1500	Clayton	MO	63105	314-863-6880	863-6887
TF: 800-325-4663 ■ *Web:* www.sabreliner.com					
Serco Inc 1818 Library St Suite 1000	Reston	VA	20190	703-939-6000	939-6000
TF: 877-427-9414 ■ *Web:* www.serco-na.com					
Servisair 151 Northpoint Dr	Houston	TX	77060	516-487-8610	487-4855
Web: www.servisair.com					
SGT Inc 7701 Greenbelt Rd Suite 400	Greenbelt	MD	20770	301-614-8600	614-8601
Web: www.sgt-inc.com					
Sierra Industries Ltd 122 Howard Langford Dr	Uvalde	TX	78801	830-278-4481	278-7649
TF: 888-835-9377 ■ *Web:* www.sijet.com					
Sifco Industries Inc 970 E 64th St	Cleveland	OH	44103	216-881-8600	432-6281
AMEX: SIF ■ *Web:* www.sifco.com					
Southern California Aviation Inc					
18438 Readiness St	Victorville	CA	92394	760-530-2400	246-1186
Web: www.scaviation.com					
ST Mobile Aerospace Engineering Inc					
2100 9th St Brookley Complex	Mobile	AL	36615	251-438-8888	438-8892
Summit Aviation Inc					
4200 Summit Bridge Rd PO Box 258	Middletown	DE	19709	302-834-5400	378-7035
TF: 800-441-9343 ■ *Web:* www.summit-aviation.com					
TAG Aviation Inc 6855 34th Ave S	Minneapolis	MN	55450	612-726-1673	726-9532
TF: 800-726-1673 ■ *Web:* www.tagaviation.com					
TIMCO Aviation Services Inc 623 Radar Rd	Greensboro	NC	27410	336-668-4410	665-0134*
**Fax:* Hum Res ■ *Web:* www.timco.aero					
Triumph Accessory Services 411 N W Rd	Wellington	KS	67152	620-326-2235	326-3761
Web: www.triumphgroup.com					
Triumph Group Inc					
1550 Liberty Ridge Dr Suite 100	Wayne	PA	19087	610-251-1000	251-1555
NYSE: TGI ■ *Web:* www.triumphgroup.com					
Tulsair Beechcraft Inc 3207 N Sheridan Rd	Tulsa	OK	74115	918-835-7651	835-7413
TF: 800-331-4071 ■ *Web:* www.tulsair.com					
Twin Air Inc 498 SW 34th St	Fort Lauderdale	FL	33315	954-359-8266	359-8271
Web: www.flytwinair.com					
West Star Aviation Inc					
796 Heritage Way	Grand Junction	CO	81506	970-243-7500	248-5243
TF: 800-255-4193 ■ *Web:* www.weststaraviation.com					
Windsor Airmotive 7 Connecticut S Dr	East Granby	CT	06026	860-653-5531	653-0397
Web: www.windsorairmotive.com					
Wood Group Turbo Power LLC					
14820 NW 60th Ave	Miami Lakes	FL	33014	305-820-3225	820-0404
TF: 800-403-6737 ■ *Web:* www.woodgroupturbopower.com					

25 AIRLINES - COMMERCIAL

SEE ALSO Air Cargo Carriers p. 1381; Air Charter Services p. 1381; Airlines - Frequent Flyer Programs p. 1390

	City	State	Zip	Phone	Fax
Aer Lingus 300 Jericho Quadrangle Suite 130	Jericho	NY	11753	516-622-4000	622-4281
TF: 800-474-7424 ■ *Web:* www.aerlingus.com					
Aeroflot Russian International Airlines					
10 Rockefeller Plaza Suite 1015	New York	NY	10020	212-944-2300	944-5200
TF: 888-340-6400 ■ *Web:* www.aeroflot.com					
Aerolineas Argentinas					
6205 Blue Lagoon Dr Suite 350	Miami	FL	33126	305-648-4100	
TF: 800-333-0276 ■ *Web:* www.aerolineas.com.ar					
AeroMexico					
George Bush International Airport Terminal D					
PO Box 60216	Houston	TX	77032	281-233-3400	
TF: 800-237-6639 ■ *Web:* www.aeromexico.com					
Air Canada 7373 Cote-Vertu W	Saint-Laurent	QC	H4S1Z3	514-393-3333	237-3563*
**Fax Area Code:* 800 ■ *TF:* 888-247-2262 ■ *Web:* www.aircanada.ca					
Air Canada Jazz 310 Goudey Dr	Enfield	NS	B2T1E4	902-873-5000	873-2098
TF Cust Svc: 877-942-2274 ■ *Web:* www.flyjazz.ca					
Air China 150 E 52 St Fl 31	New York	NY	10022	212-371-9898	935-7951
TF: 800-982-8802 ■ *Web:* www.airchina.com					
Air Evac Leasing Corp					
306 Davis Dr PO Box 768	West Plains	MO	65775	417-256-0010	256-0846
Web: www.lifeteam.net					
Air France 125 W 55th St	New York	NY	10019	212-830-4000	
TF Resv: 800-237-2747 ■ *Web:* www.airfrance.us					
Air India 570 Lexington Ave 15th Fl	New York	NY	10022	212-407-1368	407-1416
TF: 800-223-7776 ■ *Web:* www.airindia.com					
Air Jamaica 95-25 Queens Blvd 7th FL	Rego Park	NY	11374	718-830-0622	275-8717
TF: 800-523-5585 ■ *Web:* www.airjamaica.com					
Air Midwest Inc 2299 Airport Rd	Wichita	KS	67209	316-946-4901	945-0947
TF: 800-428-4322 ■ *Web:* www.usair.com					
Air New Zealand Ltd					
1960 E Grand Ave Suite 300	El Segundo	CA	90245	310-648-7000	272-9494*
**Fax Area Code:* 800 ■ *TF:* 800-262-1234 ■ *Web:* www.airnz.com/default.htm					
Air Sunshine Inc 300 Terminal Dr	Fort Lauderdale	FL	33315	954-434-8900	359-8211
TF: 800-327-8900 ■ *Web:* www.airsunshine.com					
Air Tahiti Nui 1990 E Grand Ave	El Segundo	CA	90245	310-662-1860	640-3683
TF Cust Svc: 877-824-4846 ■ *Web:* www.airtahitinui-usa.com					
Air Wisconsin Airlines Corp					
W6390 Challenger Dr Suite 203	Appleton	WI	54914	920-739-5123	749-4233
Web: www.airwis.com					
AirTran Airways 9955 AirTran Blvd	Orlando	FL	32827	800-965-2107	251-5727*
**Fax Area Code:* 407 ■ *TF:* 800-247-8726 ■ *Web:* www.airtran.com					
Alaska Airlines Inc PO Box 68900	Seattle	WA	98168	206-433-3200	392-5366*
**Fax:* Mktg ■ *TF Resv:* 800-252-7522 ■ *Web:* www.alaskaair.com					
Alitalia Airlines 350 5th Ave 37th Fl	New York	NY	10118	212-903-3300	903-3541*
**Fax:* Mktg ■ *TF:* 800-223-5730 ■ *Web:* www.alitaliausa.com					
All Nippon Airways Co Ltd					
2050 W 190th St Suite 100	Torrance	CA	90504	800-235-9262	840-5858*
**Fax Area Code:* 212 ■ *TF:* 800-235-9262 ■ *Web:* www.ana.co.jp/eng/index.html					
Allegiant Air 8360 S Durango Dr	Las Vegas	NV	89113	702-851-7300	851-7301
NASDAQ: ALGT ■ *Web:* www.allegiantair.com					
American Airlines Inc PO Box 619616	DFW Airport	TX	75261	817-963-1234	967-4162*
**Fax:* Cust Svc ■ *TF:* 800-433-7300 ■ *Web:* www.aa.com					
Atlantic Southeast Airlines Inc					
990 Toffie Terr	Atlanta	GA	30354	404-856-1000	
Web: www.flyasa.com					
Austrian Airlines					
1720 Whitestone Expy Suite 500	Whitestone	NY	11357	718-670-8600	670-8619
TF: 800-843-0002					
Avianca Airlines 8350 NW 52nd Terr Suite 100	Miami	FL	33166	800-284-2622	599-7282*
**Fax Area Code:* 305 ■ *TF:* 800-284-2622 ■ *Web:* www.preferenciacorporativo.com					
Bearskin Airlines 1475 W Walsh St	Thunder Bay	ON	P7E4X6	807-577-1141	474-2609
TF: 800-465-2327 ■ *Web:* www.bearskinairlines.com					
Bering Air 1470 Sepalla Dr PO Box 1650	Nome	AK	99762	907-443-5464	443-5919
TF: 800-478-5422 ■ *Web:* www.beringair.com					
British Airways (BA) 75-20 Astoria Blvd	Jackson Heights	NY	11370	347-418-4000	418-4395
TF: 800-247-9297 ■ *Web:* www.britishairways.com					
CanJet Airlines PO Box 980	Enfield	NS	B2T1R6	902-873-7800	973-6580
TF Resv: 800-809-7777 ■ *Web:* www.canjet.com					
Cape Air 660 Barnstable Rd	Hyannis	MA	02601	508-771-6944	775-8815
TF: 866-227-3247 ■ *Web:* www.flycapeair.com					
Cathay Pacific Airways Canada					
550 W 6th Ave Suite 500	Vancouver	BC	V5Z4P2	604-606-8888	606-2938
TF: 800-268-6868 ■ *Web:* www.cathaypacific.com					
Cayman Airways Ltd 8400 NW 52nd St	Miami	FL	33166	305-266-4141	267-2925
TF: 800-422-9626 ■ *Web:* www.caymanairways.com					
Chautauqua Airlines Inc					
8909 Purdue Rd Suite 300	Indianapolis	IN	46268	317-484-6000	484-6040
Web: www.flychautauqua.com					
Commutair Inc 240 Valley Rd	South Burlington	VT	05403	802-951-2500	
Web: www.commutair.com					
Continental Airlines Inc 1600 Smith St	Houston	TX	77002	713-324-5000	214-0506*
NYSE: CAL ■ **Fax Area Code:* 800 ■ *TF:* 800-525-0280 ■ *Web:* www.continental.com					
Czech Airlines					
1350 Avenue of the Americas Suite 601	New York	NY	10019	212-765-6545	765-6588
TF: 800-223-2365 ■ *Web:* www.csa.cz					
Delta Air Lines Inc 1030 Delta Blvd	Atlanta	GA	30354	404-715-2600	715-1400
TF: 800-221-1212 ■ *Web:* www.delta.com					
EgyptAir 19 W 44th St Suite 170	New York	NY	10036	212-581-5600	586-6599
TF: 800-334-6787 ■ *Web:* www.egyptair.com.eg					
El Al Israel Airlines Ltd					
15 E 26th St 6th Fl	New York	NY	10010	212-852-0600	768-9440
TF: 800-223-6700 ■ *Web:* www.elal.co.il					

Phone | Fax

Era Alaska 5245 Airport Industrial Rd .... Fairbanks AK 99709 907-450-7250 450-7274
TF Resv: 800-478-6779 ■ *Web:* www.frontierflying.com

Era Alaska
4700 Old International Airport Rd .... Anchorage AK 99502 907-248-4422 266-8384
TF: 800-866-8394 ■ *Web:* www.flyera.com

Ethiopian Airlines
277 S Washington St Suite 120 .... Alexandria VA 22314 703-682-0569 682-0573
TF: 800-445-2733 ■ *Web:* www.flyethiopian.com

EVA Airways
200 N Sepulveda Blvd Suite 1600 .... El Segundo CA 90245 310-362-6600 362-6660
TF: 800-695-1188 ■ *Web:* www.evaair.com

Finnair 228 E 45th St .... New York NY 10017 212-499-9000 499-9040
TF: 800-950-5000 ■ *Web:* www.finnair.fi

Frontier Airlines 7001 Tower Rd .... Denver CO 80249 720-374-4200 374-4622
TF: 800-265-5505 ■ *Web:* www.frontierairlines.com

Great Lakes Aviation Ltd 1022 Airport Pkwy .... Cheyenne WY 82001 307-432-7000 432-7071*
**Fax:* Hum Res ■ *TF:* 800-554-5111 ■ *Web:* www.greatlakesav.com

Gulfstream International Airlines
3201 Griffin Rd 4th Fl .... Fort Lauderdale FL 33312 954-985-1500 985-5245
TF: 800-457-4853 ■ *Web:* www.gulfstreamair.com

Hawaiian Airlines Inc
3375 Koapaka St Suite G350 .... Honolulu HI 96819 808-835-3700 835-3690
AMEX: HA ■ *TF:* 800-367-5320 ■ *Web:* www.hawaiianair.com

Horizon Air Industries Inc
19300 International Blvd PO Box 68977 .... Seattle WA 98188 206-241-6757 431-4624
Web: www.alaskaair.com

Iberia Airlines of Spain
5835 Blue Lagoon Dr Suite 350 .... Miami FL 33126 305-267-7747 262-8763
TF: 800-772-4642 ■ *Web:* www.iberia.com

Icelandair 5950 Symphony Woods Rd Suite 410 .... Columbia MD 21044 410-715-1600 715-3547
TF: 800-223-5500 ■ *Web:* www.icelandair.com

Japan Airlines (JAL) 461 5th Ave 6th Fl .... New York NY 10017 212-810-1200
TF: 800-525-3663

Jat Airways 274 Madison Ave Suite 1500 .... New York NY 10016 212-689-1677 689-2583
Web: www.jat.com

JetBlue Airways 29 Queens Blvd Suite 118 .... Forest Hills NY 11375 718-286-7900 709-3621
NASDAQ: JBLU ■ *TF:* 800-538-2583 ■ *Web:* www.jetblue.com

Kenmore Air Harbor Inc 6321 NE 175th St .... Kenmore WA 98028 425-486-1257 485-4774
TF: 800-543-9595 ■ *Web:* www.kenmoreair.com

KLM Royal Dutch Airlines 2700 Lone Oak Pkwy .... Eagan MN 55121 612-727-0688
TF: 800-618-0104 ■ *Web:* www.klm.com

Korean Air 6101 W Imperial Hwy .... Los Angeles CA 90045 310-417-5200 417-3051
TF: 800-438-5000

LACSA 3600 Wilshire Blvd Suite 100P .... Los Angeles CA 90010 213-385-9424 385-5880
TF Sales: 800-225-2272 ■ *Web:* www.taca.com

LanChile Airlines 6500 NW 22nd St .... Miami FL 33122 305-670-9999
TF: 866-435-9526 ■
Web: www.lan.com/en_us/sitio_personas/contactenos/index.html

LanPeru Airlines 6500 NW 22nd St .... Miami FL 33122 786-265-6050

Lloyd Aereo Boliviano 1651 NW 68th Ave .... Miami FL 33126 305-374-4600 871-5760*
**Fax:* Sales ■ *Web:* www.labairlines.com

Malaysia Airlines
100 N Sepulveda Blvd Suite 400 .... El Segundo CA 90245 310-535-9288 535-9088
TF: 800-552-9264 ■ *Web:* www.malaysiaairlines.com

Malev-Hungarian Airlines Canada
175 Bloor St E Suite 909 .... Toronto ON M4W3R8 416-944-0093 944-0095

Martinair 8750 NW 36th St Suite 300 .... Doral FL 33178 305-704-9800 704-9960
TF: 800-627-8462 ■ *Web:* www.martinairusa.com

Mesaba Airlines 1000 Blue Gentian Rd Suite 200 .... Eagan MN 55121 651-367-5000 367-5394
Web: www.mesaba.com

New England Airlines Inc 56 Airport Rd .... Westerly RI 02891 401-596-2460 596-7366
TF: 800-243-2460 ■ *Web:* www.block-island.com/nea

Olympic Airways 7000 Austin St .... Forest Hills NY 11375 718-269-2200 269-2212
TF: 800-736-5717 ■ *Web:* www.olympicairlines.com

Pacific Wings 1 Kahului Airport Rd # 30 .... Kahului HI 96732 808-873-0877 873-7920
TF: 888-575-4547 ■ *Web:* www.pacificwings.com

Pakistan International Airlines Corp
505 8th Ave 14th Fl .... New York NY 10018 212-760-8484 971-5434
TF: 800-221-2552 ■ *Web:* www.piac.com.pk

Peninsula Airways Inc 6100 Boeing Ave .... Anchorage AK 99502 907-771-2500 771-2661
TF: 800-448-4226 ■ *Web:* www.penair.com

Phoenix Air Group Inc
100 Phoenix Air Dr SW .... Cartersville GA 30120 770-387-2000 387-4545
Web: www.phoenixair.com

Piedmont Airlines Inc
5443 Airport Terminal Rd .... Salisbury MD 21804 410-742-2996 742-4478
TF: 800-354-3394 ■ *Web:* www.piedmont-airlines.com

Pinnacle Airlines Inc
1689 Nonconnah Blvd Suite 111 .... Memphis TN 38132 901-348-4100 348-4130
NASDAQ: PNCL ■ *TF:* 800-603-4594 ■ *Web:* www.nwairlink.com

PSA Airlines Inc 3400 Terminal Dr .... Vandalia OH 45377 937-454-1116 264-3911
TF: 800-235-0986 ■ *Web:* www.psaairlines.net

Qantas Airways Ltd 6080 Ctr Dr Suite 400 .... Los Angeles CA 90045 310-726-1400 726-1485
TF: 800-227-4500 ■ *Web:* www.qantas.com

Royal Nepal Airlines North America
16250 Ventura Blvd Suite 115 .... Encino CA 91436 800-266-3725 501-2098*
**Fax Area Code:* 818 ■ *TF:* 800-266-3725

Saudi Arabian Airlines 12555 N Burrough Dr .... Houston TX 77067 281-872-5212
Web: www.saudiairlines.com

Scandinavian Airlines System (SAS)
9 Polito Ave .... Lyndhurst NJ 07071 800-221-2350 896-3735*
**Fax Area Code:* 201 ■ *TF:* 800-221-2350 ■ *Web:* www.scandinavian.net

Singapore Airlines Ltd
222 N Sepulveda Blvd Suite 1600 .... El Segundo CA 90245 310-647-1922
TF: 800-742-3333 ■ *Web:* www.singaporeair.com

Skyservice Airlines Inc 31 Fasken Dr .... Etobicoke ON M9W1K6 416-679-5700 679-5703
TF: 800-701-9448 ■ *Web:* www.skyservicebas.com

SkyWest Airlines 444 S River Rd .... Saint George UT 84790 435-634-3000 634-3105
Web: www.skywest.com

South African Airways
515 E Las Olas Blvd 16th Fl .... Fort Lauderdale FL 33301 954-769-5000 769-5079*
**Fax:* Sales ■ *TF:* 800-722-9675 ■ *Web:* www.flysaa.com

Southwest Airlines Co
2702 Love Field Dr PO Box 36611 .... Dallas TX 75235 214-792-4000 792-5015
NYSE: LUV ■ *TF:* 800-435-9792 ■ *Web:* www.southwest.com

Spirit Airlines Inc 2800 Executive Way .... Miramar FL 33025 800-772-7117
TF: 800-772-7117 ■ *Web:* www.spirit.com

SriLankan Airlines 379 Thornall St 6th Fl .... Edison NJ 08837 732-205-0017 205-0299
TF: 877-915-2652 ■ *Web:* www.srilankanusa.com

Sun Country Airlines Inc
1300 Mendota Heights Rd .... Mendota Heights MN 55120 651-681-3900 681-3970
TF: 800-359-6786 ■ *Web:* www.suncountry.com

Surinam Airways Ltd 7270 NW 12th St Suite 255 .... Miami FL 33126 305-599-1196 591-3466
TF: 800-327-6864 ■ *Web:* www.surinamairways.net

Swiss International Airlines Ltd
1640 Hempstead Tpke .... East Meadow NY 11554 800-429-5413
TF: 800-429-5413 ■ *Web:* www.swiss.com

TAP Air Portugal 399 Market St .... Newark NJ 07105 973-854-6800 344-7344
TF: 800-221-7370

Thai Airways International Ltd
222 N Sepulveda Blvd Suite 100 .... El Segundo CA 90245 310-640-0097 322-8728*
**Fax:* Sales ■ *TF:* 800-426-5204 ■ *Web:* www.thaiairwaysusa.com

Turkish Airlines
1400 Old Country Rd Suite 304 .... Westbury NY 11590 516-247-5402 247-5425
Web: www.turkishairlines.com

Ukraine International Airlines
1643 W Henderson Suite A .... Cleburne TX 76033 800-876-0114 641-4477*
**Fax Area Code:* 817 ■ *TF:* 800-876-0114 ■
Web: www.flyuia.com/eng/company/ukraine-international-airlines

United Airlines Inc PO Box 66100 .... Chicago IL 60666 847-700-4000 700-2214
TF: 800-241-6522 ■ *Web:* www.united.com

US Airways Express 111 Rio Salado Pkwy .... Tempe AZ 85284 480-693-0800
TF: 800-428-4322 ■ *Web:* www.usairways.com

US Airways Inc 111 W Rio Salado Pkwy .... Tempe AZ 85281 480-693-0800
TF: 800-428-4322 ■ *Web:* www.usairways.com

US Airways Shuttle Inc
La Guardia Airport LaGuardia Rd .... Flushing NY 11371 718-397-6281
TF: 800-428-4322 ■ *Web:* www.usairways.com

USA 3000 Airlines
335 Bishop Hollow Rd Suite 100 .... Newtown Square PA 19073 610-325-1280 325-1285
TF: 877-872-3000 ■ *Web:* www.usa3000.com

Virgin Atlantic Airways Ltd 747 Belden Ave .... Norwalk CT 06850 203-750-2000 750-6430*
**Fax:* Mktg ■ *TF:* 800-862-8621 ■ *Web:* www.virgin-atlantic.com

WestJet Airlines Ltd 22 Aerial Pl NE .... Calgary AB T2E3J1 403-539-7070 648-8715
TSX: WJA ■ *TF:* 888-293-7853 ■ *Web:* www.westjet.com

Xojet Inc 959 Skyway Rd .... San Carlos CA 94070 650-594-6300 594-6301
TF: 877-599-6538 ■ *Web:* www.xojet.com

26 AIRLINES - FREQUENT FLYER PROGRAMS

Phone | Fax

Aer Lingus Airlines Gold Circle Club
300 Jericho Quad Suite 130 .... Jericho NY 11753 800-474-7424 622-4287*
**Fax Area Code:* 516 ■ *TF:* 800-474-7424 ■ *Web:* www.aerlingus.com

Air Canada Aeroplan 50 Bay St 8th Fl .... Toronto ON M5J3A5 416-352-3728
TF: 866-689-8080 ■ *Web:* www1.aeroplan.com

Air China Companion Club 150 E 52nd St .... New York NY 10022 212-371-9898 935-7951
Web: www.ffp.airchina.com.cn/EN

Air Jamaica 7th Heaven 9200 S Dadeland Blvd .... Miami FL 33156 305-670-3222 669-6631
TF: 800-523-5585 ■ *Web:* www.airjamaica.com

Air New Zealand Airpoints
1960 E Grand Ave Suite 300 .... El Segundo CA 90245 800-223-9494 272-9494
TF: 800-223-9494 ■ *Web:* www.airnewzealand.com

AirßTahitißNui 1990 E Grand Ave Suite 320 .... El Segundo CA 90245 310-662-1860 640-3683
TF: 877-824-4846 ■ *Web:* www.airtahitinui-usa.com

AirTran Airways A-Plus Rewards
1224 Bob Harman Rd .... Savannah GA 31408 888-327-5878 966-6376*
**Fax Area Code:* 912 ■ *TF:* 888-327-5878 ■ *Web:* www.airtran.com/programs/aplus

Alaska Airlines Mileage Plan
Customer Service Ctr PO Box 24948 .... Seattle WA 98124 800-654-5669 433-3477*
**Fax Area Code:* 206 ■ *TF:* 800-654-5669 ■ *Web:* www.alaskaair.com/mileageplan/MPtoc.asp

Alitalia Airlines 51 Madison Ave Suite 3700 .... New York NY 10010 800-223-5730
TF: 800-223-5730 ■ *Web:* www.alitalia.com

All Nippon Airways Mileage Club (ANA)
2050 W 190th St Suite 100 .... Torrance CA 90504 310-782-3000
TF: 800-235-9262 ■ *Web:* www.ana.co.jp

Asiana Airlines Asiana Club
3530 Wilshire Blvd Suite 1700 .... Los Angeles CA 90010 213-365-4500 380-1688
TF Resv: 800-227-4262 ■ *Web:* www.us.flyasiana.com

British Airways Executive Club PO Box 300743 .... Jamaica NY 11430 800-452-1201 251-6767*
**Fax Area Code:* 212 ■ *TF:* 800-452-1201 ■ *Web:* www.britishairways.com

Continental Airlines Inc 900 Grand Plaza Dr .... Houston TX 77067 713-952-1630
TF: 800-621-7467 ■ *Web:* www.continental.com

Czech Airlines OK Plus
1350 Avenue of the Americas Suite 601 .... New York NY 10019 212-765-6545 765-6588
TF: 800-223-2365 ■ *Web:* www.csa.cz

Delta Air Lines SkyMiles
SkyMiles Service Ctr Dept 654 PO Box 20532 .... Atlanta GA 30320 800-323-2323 773-1945*
**Fax Area Code:* 404 ■ *TF:* 800-323-2323 ■ *Web:* www.delta.com/skymiles

EgyptAir Plus 19 W 44th St Suite 1701 .... New York NY 10036 212-581-5600 586-6599
TF Cust Svc: 800-334-6787 ■ *Web:* www.egyptair.com.eg/docs/frequent.htm

Frontier Airlines EarlyReturns
7001 Tower Rd PO Box 17304 .... Denver CO 80217 866-263-2759
TF: 800-432-1359 ■ *Web:* www.frontierairlines.com

GlobalPass 6355 NW 36th St Suite 600 .... Miami FL 33166 305-870-7500 870-7555
TF: 877-946-4537 ■ *Web:* www.globalpass.com

Hawaiian Airlines HawaiianMiles
PO Box 30008 .... Honolulu HI 96820 877-426-4537 838-6777*
**Fax Area Code:* 808 ■ *TF:* 877-426-4537 ■ *Web:* www.hawaiianair.com/hawaiianmiles

Icelandair North America 1900 Crown Colony Dr .... Quincy MA 02169 800-223-5500
TF: 800-223-5500 ■ *Web:* www.icelandair.com

	City	State	ZIP	Phone	Fax
Jat Airways One Flight More 274 Madison Ave Suite 1500 *Web:* www.jat.com	New York	NY	10016	212-689-1677	689-2583
Korean Air Skypass 1813 Wilshire Blvd Suite 300 **Fax Area Code:* 310 ■ *TF:* 800-438-5000 ■ *Web:* www.koreanair.com	Los Angeles	CA	90057	213-484-1900	417-5678*
Kuwait Airways Oasis Club 400 Kelby St *TF:* 800-458-9248 ■ *Web:* www.oasisclub-ku.com	Fort Lee	NJ	07024	201-582-9222	947-8113
Mediplane Inc 451 Aviation Blvd Suite 201 *Web:* www.mediplane.com	Santa Rosa	CA	95403	707-324-2400	324-2478
Miles & More PO Box 946 **Fax Area Code:* 661 ■ *TF:* 866-846-4283 ■ *Web:* www.miles-and-more.com	Santa Clarita	CA	91380	800-581-6400	244-4950*
Qantas Airways Frequent Flyer Program 6080 Ctr Dr **Fax Area Code:* 310 ■ *TF:* 800-227-4220 ■ *Web:* www.qantas.com.au	Los Angeles	CA	90045	800-227-4220	726-1401*
Saudi Arabian Airlines Alfursan Program 12555 N Burrough Dr **Fax Area Code:* 281 ■ *TF:* 800-472-8342 ■ *Web:* www.saudiairlines.com	Houston	TX	77067	718-551-3027	873-1069*
Scandinavian Airlines System EuroBonus (SAS) 9 Polito Ave **Fax Area Code:* 201 ■ *TF:* 800-437-5807 ■ *Web:* www.scandinavian.net	Lyndhurst	NJ	07071	800-437-5807	896-3729*
Singapore Airlines KrisFlyer 5670 Wilshire Blvd Suite 1900 *TF:* 800-742-3333 ■ *Web:* www.singaporeair.com	Los Angeles	CA	90036	800-742-3333	
Southwest Airlines Rapid Rewards PO Box 36647-1CR *TF:* 800-135-9792 ■ *Web:* www.southwest.com/rapidrewards/overview	Dallas	TX	75235	214-792-4223	
SriLankan Travel Inc 379 Thornall St 6th Fl *TF:* 877-915-2652 ■ *Web:* www.srilankanusa.com	Edison	NJ	08837	732-205-0017	205-0299
United Mileage Plus PO Box 6124 *TF:* 800-421-4655 ■ *Web:* www.united.com	Rapid City	SD	57709	800-421-4655	
US Airways Dividend Miles Program 4000 E Sky Harbor *Web:* www.usairways.com/dividendmiles	Phoenix	AZ	85034	480-693-5729	693-5546
Virgin Atlantic Flying Club 747 Belden Ave **Fax Area Code:* 203 ■ *TF:* 800-365-9500 ■ *Web:* www.virgin-atlantic.com/en/us/frequentflyer/index.jsp	Norwalk	CT	06850	800-365-9500	750-6450*

27 AIRPORTS

SEE ALSO Ports & Port Authorities p. 2440

Listings For Airports In The Us And Canada Are Organized By States And Provinces, And Then By City Names Within Those Groupings.

	City	State	ZIP	Phone	Fax
Birmingham International Airport 5900 Messer Airport Hwy	Birmingham	AL	35212	205-595-0533	599-0538
Huntsville International Airport 1000 Glenn Hearn Blvd PO Box 20008 *Web:* www.hsvairport.org	Huntsville	AL	35824	256-772-9395	772-0305
Mobile Regional Airport 8400 Airport Blvd *TF:* 800-357-5373 ■ *Web:* www.mobairport.com	Mobile	AL	36608	251-633-4510	639-7437
Montgomery Regional Airport 4445 Selma Hwy *Web:* www.iflymontgomery.com	Montgomery	AL	36108	334-281-5040	281-5041
Ted Stevens Anchorage International Airport 5000 W International Airport Rd PO Box 196960 *Web:* www.anchorageairport.com	Anchorage	AK	99502	907-266-2526	266-2458
Fairbanks International Airport 6450 Airport Way *Web:* www.dot.state.ak.us/faiiap	Fairbanks	AK	99709	907-474-2500	474-2513
Juneau International Airport 1873 Shell Simmons Dr Suite 200 *Web:* www.juneau.org/airport	Juneau	AK	99801	907-789-7821	789-1227
Calgary International Airport 2000 Airport Rd NE NULL *TF:* 877-254-7427 ■ *Web:* www.calgaryairport.com	Calgary	AB	T2E6W5	403-735-1200	735-1281
Edmonton International Airport PO Box 9860 *TF:* 800-268-7134 ■ *Web:* www.edmontonairports.com	Edmonton	AB	T5J2T2	780-890-8900	890-8329
Flagstaff Pulliam Airport 6200 S Pulliam Dr *Web:* www.flagstaff.az.gov	Flagstaff	AZ	86001	928-556-1234	556-1288
Phoenix Sky Harbor International Airport 3400 E Sky Harbor Blvd Suite 3300 *Web:* skyharbor.com	Phoenix	AZ	85034	602-273-3300	683-4887
Tucson International Airport 7250 S Tucson Blvd *TF:* 800-758-1874 ■ *Web:* www.flytucsonairport.com	Tucson	AZ	85706	520-573-8100	573-8008
Northwest Arkansas Regional Airport One Airport Blvd Suite 100 *Web:* www.flyxna.com	Bentonville	AR	72712	479-205-1000	205-1001
Fort Smith Regional Airport 6700 McKennon Blvd Suite 200 *Web:* www.fortsmithairport.com	Fort Smith	AR	72903	479-452-7000	452-7008
Hot Springs Memorial Field 525 Airport Rd *Web:* www.hotspringsairport.net	Hot Springs	AR	71913	501-321-6750	321-6754
Little Rock National Airport/Adams Field One Airport Dr *Web:* www.fly-lit.com	Little Rock	AR	72202	501-372-3439	372-0612
Vancouver International Airport Airport Postal Outlet PO Box 23750 *Web:* www.yvr.ca	Richmond	BC	V7B1Y7	604-207-7077	
Meadows Field Airport 3701 Wings wy Suite 300 *Web:* www.meadowsfield.com	Bakersfield	CA	93308	661-391-1800	391-1801
Bob Hope Airport 2627 N Hollywood Way *Web:* www.bobhopeairport.com	Burbank	CA	91505	818-840-8840	848-1173
Fresno Yosemite International Airport 5175 E Clinton Way *TF:* 800-244-2359 ■ *Web:* www.fresno.gov	Fresno	CA	93727	559-621-4500	251-4825
Long Beach Airport LGB 4100 Donald Douglas Dr *Web:* www.lgb.org	Long Beach	CA	90808	562-570-2600	570-2601
Modesto City Airport 617 Airport Way *Web:* www.modestogov.com	Modesto	CA	95354	209-577-5319	576-1985
Monterey Peninsula Airport 200 Fred Kane Dr Suite 200 *Web:* www.montereyairport.com	Monterey	CA	93940	831-648-7000	373-2625
Oakland International Airport 1 Airport Dr *TF:* 888-247-6255 ■ *Web:* www.flyoakland.com	Oakland	CA	94621	510-563-3300	430-9392
Ontario International Airport 1923 E Avion St *Web:* www.lawa.org/welcomeONT.aspx	Ontario	CA	91761	909-937-2700	937-2743
Oxnard Airport 2889 W Fifth St *Web:* www.iflyoxnard.com	Oxnard	CA	93030	805-382-3024	382-9845
Palm Springs International Airport 3200 E Tahquitz Canyon Way *Web:* www.palmspringsairport.com	Palm Springs	CA	92262	760-318-3800	318-3815
Palo Alto Airport 1925 Embarcadero Rd *Web:* www.countyairports.org	Palo Alto	CA	94303	408-918-7700	
Sacramento International Airport 6900 Airport Blvd *Web:* www.sacairports.org	Sacramento	CA	95837	916-929-5411	648-0636
San Diego International Airport - Lindbergh Field 3225 N Harbor Dr San Diego County Regional Airport Authority 3rd Fl *Web:* www.san.org	San Diego	CA	92101	619-400-2404	400-2866
San Francisco International Airport PO Box 8097 *TF:* 800-435-9736 ■ *Web:* www.sfoairport.com	San Francisco	CA	94128	650-821-8211	821-5005
Norman Y Mineta San Jose International Airport 1701 Airport Blvd Suite B-1130 *Web:* www.sjc.org	San Jose	CA	95110	408-501-7600	573-1675
John Wayne Airport 18601 Airport Way *Web:* www.ocair.com	Santa Ana	CA	92707	949-252-5200	252-5290
Colorado Springs Municipal Airport 7770 Milton E Proby Pkwy *Web:* www.springsgov.com	Colorado Springs	CO	80916	719-550-1900	550-1901
Denver International Airport 8500 Pena Blvd *TF:* 800-247-2336 ■ *Web:* www.flydenver.com	Denver	CO	80249	303-342-2000	342-2215
Fort Collins/Loveland Municipal Airport 4900 Earhart Rd *Web:* www.fortloveair.com	Loveland	CO	80538	970-962-2850	962-2855
Tweed New Haven Regional Airport 155 Burr St *Web:* www.flytweed.com	New Haven	CT	06512	203-466-8833	466-1199
Bradley International Airport 11 Schoephoester Rd *TF:* 888-624-1533 ■ *Web:* www.bradleyairport.com	Windsor Locks	CT	06096	860-292-2000	627-3594
Ronald Reagan Washington National Airport 1 Aviation Cir **Fax:* PR ■ *Web:* www.mwaa.com	Washington	DC	20001	703-417-8000	417-8371*
Washington Dulles International Airport Dulles Airport Access Rd *Web:* www.metwashairports.com/Dulles	Washington	DC	20041	703-572-2700	572-5718
Saint Petersburg-Clearwater International Airport 1400 Terminal Blvd *Web:* www.fly2pie.com	Clearwater	FL	33762	727-453-7800	453-7846
Daytona Beach International Airport 700 Catalina Dr Suite 300 *Web:* www.flydaytonafirst.com	Daytona Beach	FL	32114	386-248-8030	248-8038
Fort Lauderdale Executive Airport 6000 NW 21st Ave *Web:* www.ci.ftlaud.fl.us	Fort Lauderdale	FL	33309	954-828-4955	938-4974
Fort Lauderdale/Hollywood International Airport 100 Aviation Blvd *TF:* 866-135-9355 ■ *Web:* www.fll.net	Fort Lauderdale	FL	33315	954-359-1200	359-0027
Southwest Florida International Airport 11000 Terminal Access Rd Suite 8671 *Web:* www.flylcpa.com	Fort Myers	FL	33913	239-590-4800	590-4511
Jacksonville International Airport 2400 Yankee Clipper Dr *Web:* www.flyjacksonville.com	Jacksonville	FL	32218	904-741-4902	741-2224
Key West International Airport 3491 S Roosevelt Blvd	Key West	FL	33040	305-809-5200	292-3578
Miami International Airport 2261 NW 66TH Ave Bldg 702 Suite 217 *Web:* www.miami-airport.com	Miami	FL	33122	305-876-7000	876-8077
Naples Municipal Airport 160 Aviation Dr N *Web:* www.flynaples.com	Naples	FL	34104	239-643-0733	643-4084
Orlando International Airport 1 Jeff Fuqua Blvd *Web:* www.orlandoairports.net	Orlando	FL	32827	407-825-2001	825-2202
Pensacola Gulf Coast Regional Airport 2430 Airport Blvd Suite 225 *Web:* www.flypensacola.com	Pensacola	FL	32504	850-436-5000	436-5006
Sarasota-Bradenton International Airport 6000 Airport Cir *Web:* www.srq-airport.com	Sarasota	FL	34243	941-359-5200	359-5054
Tallahassee Regional Airport 3300 Capital Cir SW	Tallahassee	FL	32310	850-891-7800	891-7837
Tampa International Airport 4100 George J Bean Pkwy PO Box 22287 *TF:* 800-767-8882 ■ *Web:* www.tampaairport.com	Tampa	FL	33607	813-870-8700	875-6670
Palm Beach International Airport 1000 Turnage Blvd *Web:* www.pbia.org	West Palm Beach	FL	33406	561-471-7420	471-7427
Hartsfield-Jackson Atlanta International Airport 6000 N Terminal Pkwy Suite 4000 *TF:* 800-897-1910 ■ *Web:* www.atlanta-airport.com	Atlanta	GA	30320	404-530-6600	530-6803
Augusta Regional Airport - Bush Field (AGS) 1501 Aviation Way *Web:* www.ags.skyharbors.com	Augusta	GA	30906	706-798-3236	798-1551

Phone Fax

Columbus Metropolitan Airport
3250 W Britt David Rd . . . . . Columbus GA 31909 706-324-2449 324-1016
Web: www.flycolumbusga.com

Middle Georgia Regional Airport
1000 Airport Dr. . . . . . Macon GA 31297 478-788-3760 784-9338

Savannah/Hilton Head International Airport
400 Airways Ave . . . . . Savannah GA 31408 912-964-0514 964-0877
TF: 877-359-2728 ■ *Web:* www.savannahairport.com

Honolulu International Airport
300 Rodgers Blvd . . . . . Honolulu HI 96819 808-831-3600 838-8734
Web: www.honoluluairport.com

Kahului Airport 1 Kahului Airport Rd. . . . . . Kahului HI 96732 808-872-3830 872-3829
Web: www.hawaii.gov/ogg

Kona International Airport
73-200 Kupipi Str. . . . . . Kailua-Kona HI 96740 808-327-9520 838-8067
Web: www.hawaii.gov/koa

Boise Airport 3201 Airport Way. . . . . . Boise ID 83705 208-383-3110 343-9667
Web: www.cityofboise.org

Pocatello Regional Airport
1950 Airport Way PO Box 4169 . . . . . Pocatello ID 83205 208-234-6154 233-8418
Web: www.pocatello.us

Chicago Midway Airport 5700 S Cicero Ave. . . . . . Chicago IL 60638 773-838-0600 838-0587
TF: 800-832-6352 ■ *Web:* www.flychicago.com

O'Hare International Airport
Dept of Aviation PO Box 66142 . . . . . Chicago IL 60666 773-686-3700 686-3573
TF: 800-832-6352 ■ *Web:* www.ohare.com

Prospect Airport Services Inc
2130 S Wolf Rd. . . . . . Des Plaines IL 60018 847-299-3636 299-3638
Web: www.prospectair.com

Peoria Regional Airport
6100 W Everett McKinley Dirksen Pkwy . . . . . Peoria IL 61607 309-697-8272 697-8132
Web: www.flypia.com

Greater Rockford Airport 60 Airport Dr . . . . . Rockford IL 61109 815-969-4000 969-4001
Web: www.flyrfd.com

Willard Airport 11 Airport Rd . . . . . Savoy IL 61874 217-244-8618 244-8644
Web: www.flycmi.com

Abraham Lincoln Capital Airport
1200 Capital Airport Dr. . . . . . Springfield IL 62707 217-788-1060 788-8056
Web: www.flyspi.com

Du Page Airport Authority
2700 Intl Dr Suite 200 . . . . . West Chicago IL 60185 630-584-2211 584-3022
TF: 800-208-5690 ■ *Web:* www.dupageairport.com

Evansville Regional Airport
7801 Bussing Dr. . . . . . Evansville IN 47725 812-421-4401 421-4412
Web: www.evvairport.com

Fort Wayne International Airport
3801 W Ferguson Rd Suite 209 . . . . . Fort Wayne IN 46809 260-747-4146 747-1762
Web: www.fwairport.com

South Bend Regional Airport
4477 Progress Dr . . . . . South Bend IN 46628 574-233-2185 239-2585
Web: www.flysbn.com

Eastern Iowa Airport The
2515 Arthur Collins PkwySW . . . . . Cedar Rapids IA 52404 319-362-8336 362-1670
Web: www.eiairport.org

Des Moines International Airport
5800 Fleur Dr . . . . . Des Moines IA 50321 515-256-5050 256-5025
Web: www.dsmairport.com

Dubuque Regional Airport 11000 Airport Rd . . . . . Dubuque IA 52003 563-589-4127 589-4108
Web: www.flydbq.com

Midcontinent Airport 2173 Air Cargo Rd. . . . . . Wichita KS 67209 316-946-4700 946-4793
Web: www.flywichita.com

Blue Grass Airport 4000 Terminal Dr . . . . . Lexington KY 40510 859-425-3114 233-1822
Web: www.bluegrassairport.com

Louisville International Airport
600 Administration Dr PO Box 9129. . . . . . Louisville KY 40209 502-368-6524 367-0199
Web: www.flylouisville.com

Baton Rouge Metropolitan Airport
9430 Jackie Cochran Dr Suite 300 . . . . . Baton Rouge LA 70807 225-355-0333 355-2334
Web: www.flybtr.com

Louis Armstrong New Orleans International Airport
900 Airline D PO Box 20007. . . . . . Kenner LA 70062 504-464-0831 465-1264
Web: www.flymsy.com

Lafayette Regional Airport 222 Tower Dr. . . . . . Lafayette LA 70508 337-266-4400
Web: www.lftairport.com

Shreveport Regional Airport
5103 Hollywood Ave. . . . . . Shreveport LA 71109 318-673-5370 673-5377
Web: www.shreveportla.gov

Augusta State Airport 75 Airport Rd . . . . . Augusta ME 04330 207-626-2306 626-2309
Web: www.augustame.govoffice3.com

Bangor International Airport 287 Godfrey Blvd. . . . . . Bangor ME 04401 207-992-4600 945-3607
TF: 866-359-2264 ■ *Web:* www.flybangor.com

Portland International Jetport
1001 Westbrook St . . . . . Portland ME 04102 207-874-8877 774-7740
Web: www.portlandjetport.org

Hancock County-Bar Harbor Airport
115 Caruso Dr . . . . . Trenton ME 04605 207-667-7329 667-0218
Web: www.bhbairport.com

Winnipeg James Armstrong Richardson International Airport
2000 Wellington Ave
Rm 249, Administration Bldg . . . . . Winnipeg MB R3H1C2 204-987-9400 987-9401
Web: www.waa.ca

Baltimore/Washington International Thurgood Marshall Airport (BWI)
PO Box 8766 . . . . . Baltimore MD 21240 410-859-7111 859-4729
TF: 800-435-9294 ■ *Web:* www.bwiairport.com

Salisbury Ocean City-Wicomico County Regional Airport
5485 Airport Terminal Rd . . . . . Salisbury MD 21804 410-548-4827 548-4945

Worcester Regional Airport 375 Airport Dr . . . . . Worcester MA 01602 508-799-1350 799-1866
Web: www.worcesterma.gov

Alpena County Regional Airport
1617 Airport Rd . . . . . Alpena MI 49707 989-354-2907 358-9988
Web: www.alpenaairport.com

Coleman A Young International Airport
11499 Conner. . . . . . Detroit MI 48213 313-628-2146 372-2448
Web: www.detroitmi.gov

Detroit Metropolitan Airport
Smith Terminal - Mezzanine Level . . . . . Detroit MI 48242 734-942-3550 942-3793
Web: www.metroairport.com

Bishop International Airport
G-3425 W Bristol Rd . . . . . Flint MI 48507 810-235-6560 233-3065
Web: www.bishopairport.org

Gerald R Ford International Airport
5500 44th St SE . . . . . Grand Rapids MI 49512 616-233-6000 233-6025
Web: www.grr.org

Capital Region International Airport
4100 Capital City Blvd . . . . . Lansing MI 48906 517-321-6121 321-6197
TF: 888-387-3536 ■ *Web:* www.flylansing.com

Duluth International Airport 4701 Grinden Dr. . . . . . Duluth MN 55811 218-727-2968 727-2960
Web: www.duluthairport.com

Rochester International Airport (RST)
7600 Helgerson Dr SW. . . . . . Rochester MN 55902 507-282-2328 282-2346
Web: www.rochesterintlairport.com

Minneapolis-Saint Paul International Airport
4300 Glumack Dr . . . . . Saint Paul MN 55111 612-726-5555 726-5527
Web: www.mspairport.com

Gulfport/Biloxi International Airport
14035 - L Airport Rd. . . . . . Gulfport MS 39503 228-863-5951 863-5953
TF: 866-447-8259 ■ *Web:* www.flygpt.com

Jackson International Airport
100 International Dr Suite 300 . . . . . Jackson MS 39208 601-939-5631 939-3713
Web: www.jmaa.com

Hattiesburg-Laurel Regional Airport
1002 Terminal Dr . . . . . Moselle MS 39459 601-649-2444 545-3155
Web: www.flypib.com

Tupelo Regional Airport 105 Lemons Dr. . . . . . Tupelo MS 38801 662-823-4359 823-8329
Web: www.flytupelo.com

Columbia Regional Airport
11300 S Airport Dr . . . . . Columbia MO 65201 573-874-7508 874-0105
Web: www.gocolumbiamo.com/PublicWorks/Airport

Kansas City International Airport
601 Brasilia Ave PO Box 20047 . . . . . Kansas City MO 64153 816-243-5237 243-3170
Web: www.flykci.com

Lambert Saint Louis International Airport
10701 Lambert International Blvd
PO Box 10212 . . . . . Saint Louis MO 63145 314-426-8000 426-1221
Web: www.lambert-stlouis.com

Springfield-Branson National Airport
2300 N Airport Blvd . . . . . Springfield MO 65802 417-868-0500 869-1031
Web: www.flyspringfield.com

Billings Logan International Airport
1901 Terminal Cir. . . . . . Billings MT 59105 406-657-8495 657-8438
Web: www.ci.billings.mt.us

Great Falls International Airport
2800 Terminal Dr . . . . . Great Falls MT 59404 406-727-3404 727-6929
Web: www.gtfairport.com

Helena Regional Airport 2850 Skyway Dr. . . . . . Helena MT 59602 406-442-2821 449-2340
Web: www.helenaairport.com

Lincoln Airport 2400 W Adams St. . . . . . Lincoln NE 68524 402-458-2480 458-2490
Web: www.lincolnairport.com

Eppley Airfield
4501 ABBOTT Dr Suite 2300, EPPLEY AIRFIELD . . . . . Omaha NE 68110 402-661-8000 661-8000
Web: www.flyoma.com

McCarran International Airport
5757 Wayne Newton Blvd PO Box 11005. . . . . . Las Vegas NV 89119 702-261-5211 597-9553
Web: www.mccarran.com

Reno-Tahoe International Airport
2001 E Plumb Ln . . . . . Reno NV 89502 775-328-6400 328-6510
Web: www.renoairport.com

Manchester-Boston Municipal Airport
1 Airport Rd . . . . . Manchester NH 03103 603-624-6556 666-4101
Web: www.flymanchester.com

Atlantic City International Airport (ACY)
101 Atlantic City Intl Airport
Suite 106 . . . . . Egg Harbor Township NJ 08234 609-645-7895 641-4348
Web: www.sjta.com

Newark Liberty International Airport
1 Hotel Rd. . . . . . Newark NJ 07114 973-961-6007 961-6259
TF: 888-397-4636 ■ *Web:* www.panynj.gov

Albuquerque International Sunport
2200 Sunport Blvd . . . . . Albuquerque NM 87106 505-244-7700 842-4278
Web: www.cabq.gov/airport

Las Cruces International Airport
8990 Zia Blvd . . . . . Las Cruces NM 88007 575-541-2471 527-6470
Web: www.las-cruces.org

Santa Fe Municipal Airport (SAF)
121 Aviation Dr PO Box 909. . . . . . Santa Fe NM 87504 505-955-2900 955-2905
Web: www.santafenm.gov/index.asp?NID=171

Albany International Airport
737 Albany-Shaker Rd . . . . . Albany NY 12211 518-242-2200 242-2641
Web: www.albanyairport.com

Buffalo Niagara International Airport
4200 Genesee St. . . . . . Cheektowaga NY 14225 716-630-6000 630-6070
Web: www.buffaloairport.com

John F Kennedy International Airport (JFK)
Van Wyck Expy . . . . . Queens NY 11422 718-244-4444 244-3505
Web: www.panynj.gov/aviation/jfkframe.HTM

Greater Rochester International Airport
1200 Brooks Ave. . . . . . Rochester NY 14624 585-753-7020 753-7008
Web: www.monroecounty.gov

Long Island MacArthur Airport
100 Arrival Ave Suite 100. . . . . . Ronkonkoma NY 11779 631-467-3300 467-3348
Web: www.macarthurairport.com

Syracuse Hancock International Airport
1000 Colonel Eileen Collins Blvd. . . . . . Syracuse NY 13212 315-454-4330 454-8757
Web: www.syrairport.org

			Phone	Fax
Westchester County Airport 240 Airport Rd Suite 202 .... White Plains *Web:* www.co.westchester.ny.us/airport	NY	10604	914-995-4860	995-3980
Charlotte/Douglas International Airport 5501 Josh Birmingham Pkwy PO Box 19066 .... Charlotte *Web:* www.charmeck.org/Departments/Airport/Home.htm	NC	28208	704-359-4000	359-4030
Asheville Regional Airport 61 Terminal Dr Suite 1 .... Fletcher *Web:* www.flyavl.com	NC	28732	828-684-2226	684-3404
Piedmont Triad International Airport 6415 Bryan Blvd .... Greensboro *Web:* www.flyfrompti.com	NC	27409	336-665-5600	665-1425
Raleigh-Durham International Airport PO Box 80001 .... Raleigh *Web:* www.rdu.com	NC	27623	919-840-2123	840-0175
Smith Reynolds Airport 3801 N Liberty St .... Winston-Salem *Web:* www.smithreynolds.org	NC	27105	336-767-6361	767-8556
Bismarck Municipal Airport 2301 University Dr Bldg 17 PO Box 991 .... Bismarck *TF:* 800-453-4244 ■ *Web:* www.bismarckairport.com	ND	58502	701-355-1800	221-6886
Hector International Airport 2801 32nd Ave NW .... Fargo *Web:* www.fargoairport.com	ND	58102	701-241-1501	241-1538
Grand Forks International Airport 2787 Airport Dr .... Grand Forks *Web:* www.gfkairport.com	ND	58203	701-795-6981	795-6979
Halifax Stanfield International Airport (HIAA) 1 Bell Blvd .... Enfield *Web:* www.hiaa.ca	NS	B2T1K2	902-873-4422	873-4750
Cincinnati-Northern Kentucky International Airport PO Box 752000 .... Cincinnati *Web:* www.cvgairport.com	OH	45275	859-767-3151	767-3080
Cleveland Hopkins International Airport 5300 Riverside Dr .... Cleveland *Web:* www.clevelandairport.com	OH	44135	216-265-6000	265-6021
Port Columbus International Airport 4600 International Gateway .... Columbus *Web:* www.columbusairports.com	OH	43219	614-239-4000	239-2219
Akron-Canton Airport 5400 Lauby Rd NW .... North Canton *TF:* 888-434-2359 ■ *Web:* www.akroncantonairport.com	OH	44720	330-499-4221	499-5176
Toledo Express Airport 11013 Airport Hwy .... Swanton *TF:* 866-888-7678 ■ *Web:* www.toledoexpress.com	OH	43558	419-865-2351	867-8245
Dayton International Airport 3600 Terminal Dr Suite 300 .... Vandalia *TF:* 877-359-3291 ■ *Web:* www.flydayton.com	OH	45377	937-454-8200	454-8284
Youngstown-Warren Regional Airport 1453 Youngstown-Kingsville Rd NE .... Vienna *Web:* www.yngwrnair.com	OH	44473	330-856-1537	609-5371
Will Rogers World Airport 7100 Terminal Dr PO Box 937 .... Oklahoma City *Web:* www.flyokc.com	OK	73159	405-680-3200	680-3319
Tulsa International Airport 7777 E Apache PO Box 581838 .... Tulsa *Web:* www.tulsaairports.com	OK	74115	918-838-5000	838-5199
Ottawa Macdonald-Cartier International Airport 1000 Airport PkwyPrivate Suite 2500 .... Ottawa *Web:* www.ottawa-airport.ca	ON	K1V9B4	613-248-2000	248-2003
Eugene Airport 28801 Douglas Dr .... Eugene *Web:* www.flyeug.com	OR	97402	541-682-5430	682-6838
Portland International Airport 7000 NE Airport Way .... Portland *TF:* 877-739-4636 ■ *Web:* www.portofportland.com	OR	97218	503-460-4040	460-4124
Lehigh Valley International Airport 3311 Airport Rd .... Allentown *TF:* 888-359-5842 ■ *Web:* www.lvia.org	PA	18109	610-266-6000	264-0115
Wilkes-Barre/Scranton International Airport 100 Terminal Dr Suite 1 .... Avoca *Web:* www.flyavp.com	PA	18641	570-602-2000	602-2010
Erie International Airport 4411 W 12th St .... Erie *Web:* www.erieairport.org	PA	16505	814-833-4258	833-0393
Harrisburg International Airport 1 Terminal Dr Suite 300 .... Middletown *TF:* 888-235-9442 ■ *Web:* www.flyhia.com	PA	17057	717-948-3900	948-4636
Philadelphia International Airport 8000 Essington Ave .... Philadelphia *TF:* 800-514-0301 ■ *Web:* www.phl.org	PA	19153	215-937-6937	937-6497
Pittsburgh International Airport Landside Terminal 4th Fl Mezz PO Box 12370 .... Pittsburgh *Web:* www.pitairport.com	PA	15231	412-472-3525	472-3636
Montreal-Pierre Elliott Trudeau International Airport 975 Romeo-Vachon N .... Dorval *TF:* 800-465-1213 ■ *Web:* www.admtl.com	QC	H4Y1H1	514-394-7377	394-7356
Quebec City Jean Lesage International Airport 505 Rue principale 4th Fl .... Quebec City *TF:* 877-769-2700 ■ *Web:* www.aeroportdequebec.com	QC	G2G0J4	418-640-2700	640-2656
Rhode Island Airport Corp 2000 Post Rd Warwick .... Warwick *TF:* 888-268-7222 ■ *Web:* www.pvdairport.com	RI	02886	401-691-2000	732-3034
Charleston International Airport 5500 International Blvd Suite 101 .... Charleston *Web:* www.chs-airport.com	SC	29418	843-767-7007	760-3020
Columbia Metropolitan Airport 3000 Aviation Way W PO Box 280037 .... Columbia *TF:* 888-562-5002 ■ *Web:* www.columbiaairport.com	SC	29170	803-822-5010	822-5140
Greenville-Spartanburg Airport (GSP) 2000 GSP Dr Suite 1 .... Greer *Web:* www.gspairport.com	SC	29651	864-877-7426	848-6225
Hilton Head Island Airport 120 Beach City Rd .... Hilton Head Island	SC	29926	843-255-2950	689-5411

			Phone	Fax
Myrtle Beach International Airport 1100 Jetport Rd .... Myrtle Beach *Web:* www.flymyrtlebeach.com	SC	29577	843-448-1589	626-9096
Pierre Regional Airport 4001 Airport Rd .... Pierre *TF Resv:* 800-221-1212 ■ *Web:* www.ci.pierre.sd.us	SD	57501	605-773-7447	773-7561
Rapid City Regional Airport 4550 Terminal Rd Suite 102 .... Rapid City *Web:* www.rcgov.org/Airport	SD	57703	605-393-9924	394-6190
Sioux Falls Regional Airport 2801 Jaycee Ln .... Sioux Falls *Web:* www.sfairport.com	SD	57104	605-336-0762	367-7374
McGhee Tyson Airport 2055 Alcoa Hwy .... Alcoa *Web:* www.tys.org	TN	37701	865-342-3000	342-3050
Tri-Cities Regional Airport 2525 Hwy 75 PO Box 1055 .... Blountville *Web:* www.triflight.com	TN	37617	423-325-6000	325-6060
Chattanooga Metropolitan Airport 1001 Airport Rd Suite 14 .... Chattanooga *Web:* www.chattairport.com	TN	37421	423-855-2202	855-2212
Memphis International Airport 2491 Winchester Rd Suite 113 .... Memphis *Web:* www.memphisairport.org	TN	38116	901-922-8000	922-8099
Metropolitan Nashville Airport Authority 1 Terminal Dr Suite 501 .... Nashville **Fax:* Hum Res ■ *Web:* www.flynashville.com	TN	37214	615-275-1675	275-1784*
Abilene Regional Airport 2933 Airport Blvd .... Abilene *Web:* www.abilenetx.com/airport	TX	79602	325-676-6367	676-6317
Rick Husband Amarillo International Airport 10801 Airport Blvd .... Amarillo *Web:* www.ci.amarillo.tx.us/departments/airport.html	TX	79111	806-335-1671	335-1672
Austin-Bergstrom International Airport (ABIA) 3600 Presidential Blvd .... Austin *Web:* www.ci.austin.tx.us	TX	78719	512-530-2242	530-7686
Corpus Christi International Airport 1000 International Dr .... Corpus Christi *Web:* www.corpuschristiairport.com	TX	78406	361-289-0171	289-0251
Dallas Love Field 8008 Cedar Springs Rd LB 16 .... Dallas *Web:* www.dallas-lovefield.com	TX	75235	214-670-6080	670-6051
Dallas-Fort Worth International Airport (DFW) 3200 E Airfield Dr PO Box 619428 .... Dallas *TF:* 800-762-0238 ■ *Web:* www.dfwairport.com	TX	75261	972-973-8888	574-5509
El Paso International Airport 6701 Convair Rd .... El Paso *Web:* www.elpasointernationalairport.com	TX	79925	915-780-4749	
Bush Intercontinental Airport 2800 N Terminal Rd .... Houston *Web:* www.fly2houston.com/iah	TX	77032	281-233-3100	233-3108
William P Hobby Airport 7800 Airport Blvd .... Houston *Web:* fly2houston.com/hobbyHome	TX	77061	713-640-3000	641-7779
Lubbock Preston Smith International Airport 5401 N Martin Luther King Blvd .... Lubbock *Web:* www.flylia.com	TX	79403	806-775-2044	775-3133
Midland International Airport 9506 Laforce Blvd PO BOX 60305 .... Midland *Web:* www.midlandinternational.com	TX	79711	432-560-2200	560-2237
San Antonio International Airport (Sat) 9800 Airport Blvd Rm 2041 .... San Antonio **Fax:* PR ■ *TF:* 800-237-6639 ■ *Web:* www.sanantonio.gov/aviation	TX	78216	210-207-3411	207-3500*
Ogden-Hinckley Airport 3909 Airport Rd .... Ogden *Web:* www.ogdencity.com	UT	84405	801-629-8251	627-8104
Salt Lake City International Airport 776 N Terminal Dr PO Box 145550 .... Salt Lake City *TF:* 800-595-2442 ■ *Web:* www.slcairport.com	UT	84116	801-575-2400	575-2499
Burlington International Airport 1200 Airport Dr .... South Burlington *Web:* www.burlingtonintlairport.com	VT	05403	802-863-1889	863-7947
Newport News/Williamsburg International Airport 900 Bland Blvd Suite G .... Newport News *Web:* www.nnwairport.com	VA	23602	757-877-0221	877-6369
Norfolk International Airport 2200 Norview Ave .... Norfolk *Web:* www.norfolkairport.com	VA	23518	757-857-3351	857-3265
Richmond International Airport 1 Richard E Byrd Terminal D Suite C .... Richmond **Fax:* Mail Rm ■ *Web:* www.flyrichmond.com	VA	23250	804-226-3052	652-2606*
Roanoke Regional Airport 5202 Aviation Dr NW .... Roanoke *Web:* www.roanokeairport.com	VA	24012	540-362-1999	563-4838
Seattle-Tacoma International Airport 17801 Pacific Hwy S Rm MT-353-3F .... Seattle *Web:* www.portseattle.org/seatac	WA	98158	206-433-5388	433-4641
Spokane International Airport 9000 W Airport Dr .... Spokane *Web:* www.spokaneairports.net	WA	99224	509-455-6455	624-6633
Yeager Airport 100 Airport Rd Suite 175 .... Charleston *Web:* www.yeagerairport.com	WV	25311	304-344-8033	344-8034
Morgantown Municipal Airport 100 Hartfield Rd .... Morgantown *Web:* www.morgantownairport.com	WV	26505	304-291-7461	291-7463
Austin Straubel International Airport 2077 Airport Dr Suite 18 .... Green Bay *Web:* www.co.brown.wi.us	WI	54313	920-498-4800	498-8799
Dane County Regional Airport 4000 International Ln .... Madison *Web:* www.msnairport.com	WI	53704	608-246-3380	246-3385
General Mitchell International Airport 5300 S Howell Ave .... Milwaukee *Web:* www.mitchellairport.com	WI	53207	414-747-5300	747-4525
Natrona County International Airport 8500 Airport Pkwy .... Casper *Web:* www.iflycasper.com	WY	82604	307-472-6688	472-1805
Cheyenne Regional Airport 4000 Airport Pkwy PO Box 2210 .... Cheyenne *Web:* www.cheyenneairport.com	WY	82001	307-634-7071	632-1206

Phone | Fax

Jackson Hole Airport
1250 E Airport Rd PO Box 159 ... Jackson WY 83001 307-733-7682 733-9270
Web: www.jacksonholeairport.com

28 AIRSHIPS

SEE ALSO Aircraft p. 1386

Phone | Fax

21st Century Airships Team Inc
Main Stn PO Box 177 ... Newmarket ON L3Y4X1 905-898-6274 898-7245
Web: www.21stcenturyairships.com
Advanced Hybrid Aircraft PO Box 144 ... Eugene OR 97440 604-541-8652
Web: www.ahausa.com
American Blimp Corp
1900 NE 25th Ave Suite 5 ... Hillsboro OR 97124 503-693-1611 681-0906
Web: www.americanblimp.com
Boland Balloon
Post Mills Airport PO Box 51 ... Post Mills VT 05058 802-333-9254 333-9254
Web: www.myairship.com
Cameron Balloons US PO Box 3672 ... Ann Arbor MI 48106 734-426-5525 426-5026
TF: 866-423-6178 ■ *Web:* www.cameronballoons.com
FireFly Balloons 850 Meacham Rd ... Statesville NC 28677 704-878-9501 878-9505
Web: www.fireflyballoons.net
ILC Dover Inc 1 Moonwalker Rd ... Frederica DE 19946 302-335-3911 335-0762
TF: 800-631-9567 ■ *Web:* www.ilcdover.com
ISL Information Systems Labs
10070 Barnes Canyon Rd ... San Diego CA 92121 858-535-9680 535-9848
Web: www.islinc.com
Lindstrand Balloons USA 11440 Dandar St ... Galena IL 61036 815-777-6006 777-6004
Web: www.lindstrand.com
Millennium Airship Inc
Bremerton National Airport PO Box 1972 ... Belfair WA 98528 360-674-2488 674-2494
Web: www.millenniumairship.com
TCOM LP 7115 Thomas Edison Dr ... Columbia MD 21046 410-312-2400 312-2455
TF: 800-767-8266 ■ *Web:* www.tcomlp.com
Worldwide Aeros Corp 1734 Gage Rd ... Montebello CA 90640 818-344-3999 201-8383*
**Fax Area Code:* 323 ■ *Web:* www.aerosml.com

29 ALL-TERRAIN VEHICLES

Phone | Fax

American Honda Motor Co Inc
1919 Torrance Blvd ... Torrance CA 90501 310-783-2000
TF: 800-999-1009 ■ *Web:* www.honda.com
American Suzuki Motor Corp 3251 Imperial Hwy ... Brea CA 92821 714-996-7040 524-2512
Web: www.suzuki.com
Berrien Buggy Inc 10644 US Hwy 31 ... Berrien Springs MI 49103 269-471-1411
Web: www.berrienbuggy.com
Cycle Country Accessories Corp
1701 38th Ave W ... Milford IA 51301 712-262-4191 262-0248
AMEX: ATC ■ *TF:* 800-841-2222 ■ *Web:* www.cyclecountry.com
Force Protection Inc 1520 Old Trolley Rd ... Summerville SC 29485 843-574-7001 329-0380
NASDAQ: FRPT ■ *Web:* www.forceprotection.net
Kawasaki Motors Corp USA PO Box 25252 ... Santa Ana CA 92799 949-770-0400 460-5600
Web: www.kawasaki.com
Ontario Drive & Gear Ltd (ODG)
220 Bergey Ct ... New Hamburg ON N3A2J5 519-662-2840
TF: 877-274-6288 ■ *Web:* www.argoatv.com
Polaris Industries Inc 2100 Hwy 55 ... Medina MN 55340 763-542-0500 542-0599
NYSE: PII ■ *Web:* www.polarisindustries.com
Recreatives Industries Inc 60 Depot St ... Buffalo NY 14206 716-855-2226 855-1094
TF: 800-255-2511 ■ *Web:* www.maxatvs.com
Yamaha Motor Corp USA 6555 Katella Ave ... Cypress CA 90630 714-761-7300
TF Cust Svc: 800-962-7926 ■ *Web:* www.yamaha-motor.com

30 AMBULANCE SERVICES

Phone | Fax

Abbott Ambulance Inc 2500 Abbott Pl ... Saint Louis MO 63143 314-768-1000 768-2105
TF: 888-281-1212 ■ *Web:* www.abbottems.org
Acadian Ambulance Service Inc
302 Hopkins St ... Lafayette LA 70501 337-291-3333 291-3326
TF: 800-259-3333 ■ *Web:* www.acadian.com
Air Methods Corp 7301 S Peoria St ... Englewood CO 80112 303-792-7400 790-0499
NASDAQ: AIRM
AirEvac Services Inc 2800 N 44th St Suite 800 ... Phoenix AZ 85008 602-244-9327 224-1689
TF: 800-421-6111 ■ *Web:* www.phiairmedical.com
American Medical Response (AMR)
6200 S Syracuse Way Suite 200 ... Greenwood Village CO 80111 303-495-1200 495-1649
TF: 800-244-4890 ■ *Web:* www.amr.net
Global Air Response 5919 Approach Rd ... Sarasota F FL 34238 941-926-2490 631-6565*
**Fax Area Code:* 888 ■ *TF:* 800-631-6565 ■ *Web:* www.usairambulance.com
MedjetAssist
3500 Colonnade Pkwy Suite 500
PO Box 43099 ... Birmingham AL 35243 205-595-6626 595-6658
TF: 800-527-7478 ■ *Web:* www.medjetassist.com
Metro Aviation Inc
1214 Hawn Ave PO Box 7008 ... Shreveport LA 71137 318-222-5529 222-0503
Web: www.metroaviation.com
Omniflight Helicopters Inc
16415 Addison Rd Suite 400 ... Addison TX 75001 972-776-0130
TF: 800-727-4644 ■ *Web:* www.omniflight.com
Rural/Metro Corp 9221 E Via de Ventura ... Scottsdale AZ 85258 480-994-3886 606-3268*
NASDAQ: RURL ■ **Fax:* Hum Res ■ *TF:* 800-352-2309 ■ *Web:* www.ruralmetro.com

Phone | Fax

Shock Trauma Air Rescue Society (STARS)
1441 Aviation Pk NE ... Calgary AB T2E7E2 403-295-1811 275-4891
Web: www.stars.ca
Skyservice Airlines Inc 31 Fasken Dr ... Etobicoke ON M9W1K6 416-679-5700 679-5703
TF: 800-701-9448 ■ *Web:* www.skyservicebas.com
Transcare Pennsylvania 400 Seco Rd ... Monroeville PA 15146 412-373-6300 373-8263
Web: www.transcarepa.com

31 AMUSEMENT PARK COMPANIES

SEE ALSO Circus, Carnival, Festival Operators p. 1604

Phone | Fax

Cedar Fair LP 1 Cedar Pt Dr ... Sandusky OH 44870 419-627-2233 627-2260
NYSE: FUN ■ *Web:* www.cedarfair.com
Herschend Family Entertainment Corp
399 Indian Pt Rd ... Branson MO 65616 417-338-2611 338-8080*
**Fax:* Mktg ■ *TF:* 800-952-6626
Hershey Entertainment & Resorts Co
100 W Hersheypark Dr ... Hershey PA 17033 717-534-3090 534-8991
TF: 800-437-7439 ■ *Web:* www.hersheypa.com
Kennywood Entertainment Corp
4800 Kennywood Blvd ... West Mifflin PA 15122 412-461-0500 464-0719
Web: www.kennywoodentertainment.com
Palace Entertainment Inc
4950 MacArthur Rd Suite 400 ... Newport Beach CA 92660 949-261-0404 261-1414
Web: www.palaceentertainment.com
Paramount Parks Inc
8720 Red Oak Blvd Suite 315 ... Charlotte NC 28217 704-525-5250 525-2960
Web: www.paramountparks.com
Ripley Entertainment Inc
7576 Kingspointe Pkwy Suite 188 ... Orlando FL 32819 407-345-8010 345-0801
Web: www.ripleys.com
Santa Cruz Seaside Co 400 Beach St ... Santa Cruz CA 95060 831-423-5590 423-2438
Web: www.beachboardwalk.com
Six Flags Entertainment Corp
230 Pk Ave 16th Fl ... New York NY 10169 405-475-2500 475-2555
NYSE: SIX ■ *TF:* 800-370-7488 ■ *Web:* www.sixflags.com
Universal Parks & Resorts
100 Universal City Plaza ... Universal City CA 91608 818-777-1000
Web: www.themeparks.universalstudios.com
Walt Disney Parks & Resorts
500 S Buena Vista St ... Burbank CA 91521 818-560-1000 560-1930

32 AMUSEMENT PARKS

Phone | Fax

Adventure Landing 1944 Beach Blvd ... Jacksonville Beach FL 32250 904-246-4386 249-1018
Web: www.adventurelanding.com
Adventure Landing 3311 Capital Blvd ... Raleigh NC 27604 919-872-1688 872-3408
Web: www.adventurelanding.com
Adventuredome 2880 Las Vegas Blvd S ... Las Vegas NV 89119 702-794-3912 792-2846
TF: 800-634-3450 ■ *Web:* www.adventuredome.com
Adventureland Park 3200 Adventureland Dr ... Altoona IA 50009 515-266-2121 266-9831
TF: 800-532-1286 ■ *Web:* www.adventureland-usa.com
Alabama Adventure
4599 Alabama Adventure Pkwy ... Bessemer AL 35022 205-481-4750 481-4758
Web: www.alabamaadventure.com
Astroland Amusement Park
1000 Surf Ave Coney Island ... Brooklyn NY 11224 718-265-2100 265-2155
Web: www.astroland.com
Busch Gardens Tampa Bay 10001 N McKinley Dr ... Tampa FL 33612 813-987-5082 987-5111
TF: 888-800-5447 ■ *Web:* www.buschgardens.com
Busch Gardens Williamsburg
1 Busch Gardens Blvd ... Williamsburg VA 23187 800-343-7946 253-3399*
**Fax Area Code:* 757 ■ **Fax:* Mktg ■ *TF:* 800-343-7946 ■ *Web:* www.buschgardens.com
California's Great America
4701 Great America Pkwy ... Santa Clara CA 95054 408-988-1776 986-5855*
**Fax:* Sales ■ *Web:* www.cagreatamerica.com
Camelbeach Mountain Waterpark
1 Camelback Rd PO Box 168 ... Tannersville PA 18372 570-629-1661 629-0942
Web: www.camelbeach.com
Casino Pier & Water Works
800 Ocean Terr ... Seaside Heights NJ 08751 732-793-6488 793-0461
Web: www.casinopiernj.com
Castle Park 3500 Polk St ... Riverside CA 92505 951-785-3000 785-3075
Web: www.castlepark.com
Cedar Point Amusement Park 1 Cedar Pt Dr ... Sandusky OH 44870 419-626-0830 627-2200*
**Fax:* Mktg ■ *Web:* www.cedarpoint.com
Children's Fairyland Theme Park
699 Bellevue Ave ... Oakland CA 94610 510-452-2259 452-2261
Web: www.fairyland.org
Coney Island Park 6201 Kellogg Ave ... Cincinnati OH 45228 513-232-8230 231-1352
Web: www.coneyislandpark.com
Darien Lake Theme Park Resort
9993 Allegheny Rd PO Box 91 ... Darien Center NY 14040 585-599-4641 599-4053
Web: www.godarienlake.com
Disney's Animal Kingdom
2901 Osceola Pkwy ... Lake Buena Vista FL 32830 407-938-3000 938-4799
Web: disneyworld.disney.go.com/parks/animal-kingdom
Disney's Blizzard Beach
1500 W Buena Vista Dr ... Lake Buena Vista FL 32830 407-824-4321
Web: www.disneyworld.com
Disney's California Adventure
1313 S Harbor Blvd ... Anaheim CA 92803 714-781-7290
Web: www.disneyland.com
Disney's Hollywood Studios
1675 N Buena Vista Dr ... Lake Buena Vista FL 32830 407-939-6244
Web: disneyworld.disney.go.com/parks/hollywood-studios

				Phone	Fax
Disney's Typhoon Lagoon 1145 E Buena Vista Dr *Web:* www.disneyworld.com	Lake Buena Vista	FL	32830	407-560-7223	560-7405
Disney's Wide World of Sports 700 Victory Way *Web:* www.disneysports.com	Kissimmee	FL	34747	407-939-1500	
Disneyland 1313 S Harbor Blvd *Web:* www.disneyland.disney.go.com	Anaheim	CA	92802	714-781-7290	
DisneyQuest 1486 E Lake Buena Vista Dr *Web:* www.disneyquest.com	Lake Buena Vista	FL	32830	407-828-4600	938-6202
Dollywood 1020 Dollywood Ln **Fax:* Mktg ■ *TF:* 800-365-5996 ■ *Web:* www.dollywood.com	Pigeon Forge	TN	37863	865-428-9400	428-9494*
Dorney Park & Wildwater Kingdom 3830 Dorney Pk Rd *TF:* 800-386-8463 ■ *Web:* www.dorneypark.com	Allentown	PA	18104	610-395-3724	391-7650
Dutch Wonderland Family Amusement Park 2249 Lincoln Hwy E *TF:* 866-386-2839 ■ *Web:* www.dutchwonderland.com	Lancaster	PA	17602	717-291-1888	291-1595
Elitch Gardens 2000 Elitch Cir *Web:* www.elitchgardens.com	Denver	CO	80204	303-595-4386	534-2221
EPCOT 1200 Epcot Resort Blvd *Web:* disneyworld.disney.go.com/parks/epcot	Lake Buena Vista	FL	32830	407-824-4321	
Family Kingdom Amusement Park & Oceanfront Water Park 300 S Ocean Blvd *Web:* www.familykingdomfun.com	Myrtle Beach	SC	29577	843-626-3447	448-4548
Frontier City Theme Park 11501 NE Expy *Web:* www.frontiercity.com	Oklahoma City	OK	73131	405-478-2412	478-3104
Fun Town Splash Town USA Inc PO Box 29 *Web:* www.funtownsplashtownusa.com	Saco	ME	04072	207-284-5139	283-4716
Geauga Lake Wildwater Kingdom 1100 Squires Rd *Web:* www.geaugalake.com	Aurora	OH	44202	330-562-8303	
Great Escape & Splashwater Kingdom 1172 SR 9 *Web:* www.sixflags.com	Queensbury	NY	12084	518-792-3500	792-3404
Hersheypark 100 Hershey Pk Dr *TF:* 800-437-7439 ■ *Web:* www.hersheypark.com	Hershey	PA	17033	717-534-3900	534-3165
Holiday World & Splashin' Safari 452 E Christmas Blvd *TF:* 877-463-2645 ■ *Web:* www.holidayworld.com	Santa Claus	IN	47579	812-937-4401	937-4405
Holy Land Experience 4655 Vineland Rd *TF:* 800-447-7235 ■ *Web:* www.theholylandexperience.com	Orlando	FL	32811	407-872-2272	872-3393
Idlewild & Soak Zone 2582 US 30 *Web:* www.idlewild.com	Ligonier	PA	15658	724-238-3666	238-6544
Indiana Beach 5224 E Indiana Beach Rd *TF:* 800-583-4306 ■ *Web:* www.indianabeach.com	Monticello	IN	47960	574-583-4141	583-4125
Kennywood Park 4800 Kennywood Blvd *Web:* www.kennywood.com	West Mifflin	PA	15122	412-461-0500	464-0719
Knight's Action Park & Caribbean Water Adventure 1700 Recreation Dr *Web:* www.knightsactionpark.com	Springfield	IL	62711	217-546-8881	546-8995
Knoebels Amusement Resort 391 Knoebels Blvd *TF:* 800-487-4386 ■ *Web:* www.knoebels.com	Elysburg	PA	17824	570-672-2572	672-3293
Knott's Berry Farm 8039 Beach Blvd *Web:* www.knotts.com	Buena Park	CA	90620	714-220-5220	220-5124
Knott's Soak City Orange County 8039 Beach Blvd *Web:* www.knotts.com/public/park/soakcity/orange_county	Buena Park	CA	90620	714-220-5200	220-5028
Knott's Soak City Palm Spring 1500 S Gene Autry Trail *Web:* www.soakcityusa.com	Palm Springs	CA	92264	760-327-0499	322-4191
Knott's Soak City San Diego 2052 Entertainment Cir *Web:* www.knotts.com	Chula Vista	CA	91911	619-661-7373	661-7393
La Ronde Theme Park 22 ch Macdonald *Web:* www.laronde.com	Montreal	QC	H3C6A3	514-397-2000	
Lagoon & Pioneer Village 375 N Lagoon Dr *TF:* 800-748-5246 ■ *Web:* www.lagoonpark.com	Farmington	UT	84025	801-451-8000	451-8015
Lake Compounce Theme Park 271 Enterprise Dr *Web:* www.lakecompounce.com	Bristol	CT	06010	860-583-3300	589-7974
Lake Winnepesaukah Amusement Park 1730 Lakeview Dr *TF:* 877-525-3946 ■ *Web:* www.lakewinnie.com	Rossville	GA	30741	706-866-5681	858-0497
LEGOLAND California 1 Legoland Dr *TF:* 877-534-6526 ■ *Web:* www.legoland.com	Carlsbad	CA	92008	760-438-5346	918-5459
Magic Kingdom Park 3111 World Dr *Web:* disneyworld.disney.go.com/parks/magic-kingdom	Lake Buena Vista	FL	32830	407-939-6244	
Magic Springs Theme Park & Crystal Falls Water Park 1701 E Grand Ave *Web:* www.magicsprings.com	Hot Springs	AR	71901	501-624-0100	318-5367
Marineland 7657 Portage Rd *Web:* www.marinelandcanada.com	Niagara Falls	ON	L2E6X8	905-356-9565	374-6652
Morey's Piers & Raging Waters Waterparks 3501 Boardwalk *Web:* www.moreyspiers.com	Wildwood	NJ	08260	609-522-3900	522-0788
Myrtle Waves Water Park 3000 10th Ave N Ext *Web:* www.myrtlewaves.com	Myrtle Beach	SC	29577	843-913-9260	
NASCAR SpeedPark 1 Bass Pro Mills Dr Vaughan Mills Mall Space E-2 *Web:* www.nascarspeedpark.com	Vaughan	ON	L4K5W4	905-669-7370	669-7371
Oaks Amusement Park 1 SE Spokane St *Web:* www.oakspark.com	Portland	OR	97202	503-233-5777	236-9143
Paramount Canada's Wonderland 9580 Jane St *Web:* www.canadaswonderland.com	Vaughan	ON	L6A1S6	905-832-7000	832-7519
Paramount's Carowinds 14523 Carowinds Blvd *TF:* 800-888-4386 ■ *Web:* www.carowinds.com	Charlotte	NC	28273	704-588-2600	587-9034
Paramount's Kings Dominion 16000 Theme Pkwy *TF:* 800-553-7277 ■ *Web:* www.kingsdominion.com	Doswell	VA	23047	804-876-5400	876-5864
Paramount's Kings Island 6300 Kings Island Dr PO Box 901 *TF:* 800-288-0808 ■ *Web:* www.pki.com	Kings Island	OH	45034	513-754-5700	754-5710

				Phone	Fax
Park at Mall of America 5000 Ctr Ct *Web:* www.info.theparkatmoa.com	Bloomington	MN	55425	952-883-8500	883-8683
Pharaoh's Theme & Water Park 1101 N California St	Redlands	CA	92374	909-335-7275	307-2622
Raging Waters 2333 S White Rd *Web:* www.rwsplash.com	San Jose	CA	95148	408-238-9900	270-2022
Raging Waters Sacramento 1600 Exposition Blvd *Web:* www.rwsac.com	Sacramento	CA	95815	916-924-3747	924-1314
Sandcastle Water Park 1000 Sandcastle Dr *Web:* www.sandcastlewaterpark.com	Pittsburgh	PA	15120	412-462-6666	462-0827
Santa Cruz Beach Boardwalk 400 Beach St *Web:* www.beachboardwalk.com	Santa Cruz	CA	95060	831-423-5590	460-3335
Schlitterbahn Beach Waterpark 33261 State Pk Rd Hwy 100 *Web:* www.schlitterbahn.com	South Padre Island	TX	78597	956-772-7873	761-3960
Schlitterbahn Waterpark Resort 381 E Austin St *Web:* www.schlitterbahn.com	New Braunfels	TX	78130	830-625-2351	625-3515
SeaWorld Orlando 7007 Sea World Dr **Fax:* Cust Svc ■ *TF:* 800-327-2424 ■ *Web:* www.seaworldorlando.com	Orlando	FL	32821	407-351-3600	363-2409*
SeaWorld San Antonio 10500 SeaWorld Dr **Fax:* Mktg ■ *TF:* 800-700-7786 ■ *Web:* www.seaworld.com	San Antonio	TX	78251	210-523-3000	523-3199*
SeaWorld San Diego 500 SeaWorld Dr *TF:* 800-257-4268 ■ *Web:* www.seaworld.com	San Diego	CA	92109	619-226-3901	
Sesame Place 100 Sesame Rd *Web:* www.sesameplace.com	Langhorne	PA	19047	215-752-7070	741-5307
Seven Peaks Water Park 1330 E 300 N *Web:* www.sevenpeaks.com	Provo	UT	84606	801-373-8777	373-8791
Silver Springs 5656 E Silver Springs Blvd *Web:* www.silversprings.com	Silver Springs	FL	34488	352-236-2121	236-1732
Six Flags America 13710 Central Ave *Web:* www.sixflags.com/parks/america	Mitchellville	MD	20721	301-249-1500	249-8853
Six Flags Discovery Kingdom 1001 Fairgrounds Dr *Web:* www.sixflags.com	Vallejo	CA	94589	707-644-4000	644-0241
Six Flags Fiesta Texas 17000 IH-10 W *TF:* 800-473-4378 ■ *Web:* www.sixflags.com	San Antonio	TX	78257	210-697-5000	697-5415
Six Flags Great Adventure 1 Six Flags Blvd *TF:* 800-772-2287 ■ *Web:* www.sixflags.com/parks/greatadventure	Jackson	NJ	08527	732-928-1821	928-2775
Six Flags Great America 542 N Rt 21 *Web:* www.sixflags.com	Gurnee	IL	60031	847-249-2133	249-2390
Six Flags Hurricane Harbor Dallas 1800 E Lamar Blvd *Web:* www.sixflags.com/parks/hurricaneharbordallas	Arlington	TX	76006	817-265-3356	607-6184
Six Flags Hurricane Harbor Los Angeles 26101 Magic Mountain Pkwy *Web:* www.sixflags.com/parks/hurricaneharborla	Valencia	CA	91355	661-255-4527	255-4170
Six Flags Hurricane Harbor New Jersey Rt 537 PO Box 120 *TF:* 800-772-2287 ■ *Web:* www.sixflags.com/parks/hurricaneharbornj	Jackson	NJ	08527	732-928-1821	928-2775
Six Flags Magic Mountain 26101 Magic Mountain Pkwy *Web:* www.sixflags.com	Valencia	CA	91355	661-255-4100	255-4170
Six Flags New England Rt 159 1623 Main St **Fax:* Mktg ■ *TF:* 800-370-7488 ■ *Web:* www.sixflags.com	Agawam	MA	01001	413-786-9300	821-2402*
Six Flags Over Georgia 275 Riverside PkwySW *Web:* www.sixflags.com	Austell	GA	30168	770-948-9290	948-4378
Six Flags Over Texas 2201 Rd to Six Flags *Web:* www.sixflags.com/parks/overtexas	Arlington	TX	76011	817-640-8900	607-6140
Six Flags Saint Louis 4900 Six Flags Rd PO Box 60 *Web:* www.sixflags.com/parks/stlouis	Eureka	MO	63025	636-938-5300	587-3617
Six Flags White Water Park 250 Cobb Pkwy N *Web:* www.sixflags.com/parks/whitewater	Marietta	GA	30062	770-424-9283	424-7565
Six Flags Wild Safari 1 Six Flags Blvd *TF:* 800-772-2287 ■ *Web:* www.sixflags.com/parks/wildsafari	Jackson	NJ	08527	732-928-1821	928-2775
Soak City 1 Cedar Pt Dr **Fax:* Mktg ■ *Web:* www.experiencethepoint.com	Sandusky	OH	44870	419-627-2350	627-2200*
Splashtown Water Park 21300 IH-45 N *Web:* www.splashtownpark.com	Spring	TX	77373	281-355-3300	353-7946
Splish Splash 2549 Splish Splash Dr *Web:* www.splishsplashlongisland.com	Riverhead	NY	11901	631-727-3600	
Universal Orlando 6000 Universal Blvd *TF:* 877-801-9720 ■ *Web:* www.themeparks.universalstudios.com	Orlando	FL	32819	407-363-8000	363-8006
Universal Studios Hollywood 100 Universal City Plaza **Fax:* Hum Res ■ *TF:* 800-864-8377 ■ *Web:* www.universalstudioshollywood.com	Universal City	CA	91608	818-622-3801	866-1516*
Universal's Islands of Adventure 6000 Universal Studios Plaza *TF:* 877-801-9720 ■ *Web:* www.themeparks.universalstudios.com	Orlando	FL	32819	407-363-8000	224-6942
Valleyfair 1 Valleyfair Dr *TF:* 800-386-7433 ■ *Web:* www.valleyfair.com	Shakopee	MN	55379	952-445-7600	445-1539
Village Vacances Valcartier 1860 Valcartier Blvd *TF:* 888-384-5524 ■ *Web:* www.valcartier.com	Valcartier	QC	G0A4S0	418-844-2200	844-1239
Water Country USA 176 Water Country Pkwy *TF:* 800-343-7946 ■ *Web:* www.watercountryusa.com	Williamsburg	VA	23185	757-229-9300	220-2816
Waterworld California 1950 Waterworld Pkwy *Web:* www.waterworldcalifornia.com	Concord	CA	94520	925-609-1364	609-1360
Weeki Wachee Springs 6131 Commercial Way *Web:* www.weekiwachee.com	Spring Hill	FL	34606	352-596-2062	597-1388
Western Playland Amusement Park 1249 Futurity Dr *Web:* www.westernplayland.com	Sunland Park	NM	88063	575-589-3410	589-0877
Wet 'n Wild Emerald Pointe 3910 S Holden Rd *TF:* 800-555-5900 ■ *Web:* www.emeraldpointe.com	Greensboro	NC	27406	336-852-9721	852-2391
Wet 'n Wild Orlando 6200 International Dr *TF:* 800-992-9453 ■ *Web:* www.wetnwild.com	Orlando	FL	32819	407-351-1800	363-1147

	City	State	Zip	Phone	Fax
White Water 3505 W Hwy 76	Branson	MO	65616	800-475-9370	336-7791*
*Fax Area Code: 417 ■ TF: 800-475-9370 ■ Web: www.whitewater.silverdollarcity.com					
White Water Bay 3908 W Reno Ave	Oklahoma City	OK	73107	405-943-0392	
Web: www.whitewaterbay.com					
Wild Waters 5656 E Silver Springs Blvd	Silver Springs	FL	34488	352-236-2121	236-1732
Web: www.wildwaterspark.com					
Wild Waves/Enchanted Village 36201 Enchanted Pkwy S	Federal Way	WA	98003	253-661-8000	925-1332*
*Fax: Hum Res ■ Web: wildwaves.com					
Wonderland Amusement Park 2601 Dumas Dr	Amarillo	TX	79107	806-383-0832	383-8737
TF: 800-383-4712 ■ Web: www.wonderlandpark.com					
Worlds of Fun & Oceans of Fun 4545 NE Worlds of Fun Dr	Kansas City	MO	64161	816-454-4545	454-4655
Web: www.worldsoffun.com					
Grand Harbor Resort & Waterpark 350 Bell St	Dubuque	IA	52001	563-690-4000	690-0558
TF: 866-690-4006 ■ Web: www.grandharborresort.com					

33 ANIMATION COMPANIES

SEE ALSO Motion Picture Production - Special Interest p. 2256; Motion Picture & Television Production p. 2257

	City	State	Zip	Phone	Fax
Advanced Animations PO Box 34	Stockbridge	VT	05772	802-746-8974	746-8971
Web: www.advancedanimations.com					
Atomic Cartoons Inc 112 W 6th Sve	Vancouver	BC	V5Y1K6	604-734-2866	734-2869
Web: www.atomiccartoons.com					
Big Idea Inc 230 Franklin Rd Bldg 2A	Franklin	TN	37064	615-224-2200	224-2250
Web: www.bigidea.com					
Bix Pix Entertainment Inc 1917 W Belmont	Chicago	IL	60657	773-248-5430	248-5480
Web: www.bixpix.com					
Blue Sky Studios Inc 1 American Ln	Greenwich	NY	06831	203-992-6000	992-6001
Web: www.blueskystudios.com					
Blur Studio 589 Venice Blvd	Venice	CA	90291	310-581-8848	581-8850
Web: www.blur.com					
Brilliant Digital Entertainment Inc 14011 Ventura Blvd Suite 501	Sherman Oaks	CA	91423	818-386-2180	615-0995
Web: www.brilliantdigital.com					
CineGroupe 1151 Rue Alexandre-DeSeve 5th Fl	Montreal	QC	H2L2T7	514-524-7567	849-9846
Web: www.cinegroupe.com					
Cookie Jar Co The 266 King St W 2nd Fl	Toronto	ON	M5V1H8	416-977-3238	977-4526
Web: www.thecookiejarcompany.com					
Cuppa Coffee Animation 53 Ontario St	Toronto	ON	M5A2V1	416-340-8869	340-9819
Web: www.cuppacoffee.com					
DNA Productions 2201 W Royal Ln Suite 275	Irving	TX	75063	214-352-4694	496-9333
Web: www.dnahelix.com					
Dreamworks Animation LLC 1000 Flower St	Glendale	CA	91201	818-695-5000	695-7574
NYSE: DWA ■ Web: www.dreamworks.com					
DUCK 2205 Stoner Ave	Los Angeles	CA	90064	310-478-0771	478-0773
Web: www.duckstudios.com					
Film Roman Inc 2950 N Hollywood Way 3rd Fl	Burbank	CA	91505	818-748-4000	748-4619
Web: www.filmroman.com					
Hash Inc 10411 NE 110th Cir	Vancouver	WA	98662	360-750-0042	750-0451
Web: www.hash.com					
iNTELEFILM Inc Curious Pictures Div 440 Lafayette St 6th Fl	New York	NY	10003	212-674-1400	674-0081
Web: www.curiouspictures.com					
Itoons 6348 N Milwaukee Ave Suite 345	Chicago	IL	60646	773-594-1272	
Jim Henson's Creature Shop 1416 N LaBrea Ave	Hollywood	CA	90028	323-802-1525	802-1891
Web: www.creatureshop.com					
Klasky Csupo Inc 1238 N Highland Ave	Los Angeles	CA	90028	323-468-2600	468-2675
Web: www.klaskycsupo.com					
Krislin Co 23901 Calabasas Rd Suite 2090	Calabasas	CA	91302	818-222-2660	222-2661
Web: www.krislincompany.com					
Laika 1400 NW 22nd Ave	Portland	OR	97210	503-225-1130	226-3746
Web: www.laika.com					
Loop Filmworks Inc 45 Main St 5th Fl Suite 504	Brooklyn	NY	11201	718-522-5667	522-5668
Lucasfilm Ltd Animation 1110 Gorgas St PO Box 29901	San Francisco	CA	94129	415-662-1800	
Web: www.lucasfilm.com					
Mercury Filmworks 740 Nicola St	Vancouver	BC	V6G2Z1	604-684-9117	684-8339
Web: www.mercuryfilmworks.com					
Nelvana Ltd 135 Liberty Suite 101	Toronto	ON	M6K1A7	416-535-0935	530-2832
Web: www.nelvana.com					
NestFamily 1461 S Beltline Rd Suite 500	Coppell	TX	75019	972-402-7100	629-7181
TF: 800-447-5958 ■ Web: www.nestfamily.com					
Pixar Animation Studios 1200 Pk Ave	Emeryville	CA	94608	510-752-3000	752-3151
TF: 800-888-9856 ■ Web: www.pixar.com					
Pixel Factory Inc PO Box 618413	Orlando	FL	32861	407-835-1220	
Web: www.pixfactory.com					
Renegade Animation Inc 116 N Maryland Ave Lower Level	Glendale	CA	91206	818-551-2351	551-2350
Web: www.renegadeanimation.com					
Rhythm & Hues Inc 5404 Jandy Pl	Los Angeles	CA	90066	310-448-7500	448-7600
Web: www.rhythm.com					
Sony Pictures Animation 9050 W Washington Blvd	Culver City	CA	90232	323-857-7801	
Web: www.sonypictures.com/tv/kids					
Topix 35 McCaul St Suite 200	Toronto	ON	M5T1V7	416-971-7711	971-9277
Web: www.topix.com					
Universal Animation Studios 100 Universal City Plaza	Universal City	CA	91608	818-777-1000	
Walt Disney Feature Animation 500 S Buena Vista St MC 91521-4876	Burbank	CA	91521	818-560-1000	
Warner Bros Classic Animation 15301 Ventura Blvd Unit E	Sherman Oaks	CA	91403	818-977-8700	977-0125
Warner Bros Feature Animation 15301 Ventura Blvd Unit E	Sherman Oaks	CA	91403	818-977-8700	977-0125

34 APPAREL FINDINGS

	City	State	Zip	Phone	Fax
Copen Assoc Inc 1 W 37th St 10th Fl	New York	NY	10018	212-819-0008	819-0008
Web: www.copen.org					
Cushman & Marden Inc 56 Pulaski St PO Box 3001	Peabody	MA	01960	978-532-1670	532-1670
Web: www.cushmanandmarden.com					
Dallas Bias Fabrics Inc 1401 N Carroll Ave	Dallas	TX	75204	214-824-2036	824-2036
Web: www.dallasbias.com					
International Molders Inc 3578 Hayden Ave	Culver City	CA	90230	310-559-8300	559-0452
Web: www.internationalmoldersinc.com					
Metric Products Inc 4671 Leahy St	Culver City	CA	90232	310-815-9000	838-0241
TF: 800-763-8742 ■ Web: www.metric-products.com					
Modern Quilters Inc 62038 Minnesota Hwy 24 PO Box 570	Litchfield	MN	55355	320-693-7987	693-2288
QST Industries Inc 550 W Adams St Suite 200	Chicago	IL	60661	312-930-9400	648-0312
Web: www.qst.com					

35 APPLIANCE & HOME ELECTRONICS STORES

SEE ALSO Computer Stores p. 1694; Department Stores p. 1783; Furniture Stores p. 1899; Home Improvement Centers p. 2024

	City	State	Zip	Phone	Fax
ABC Appliance Inc 1 W Silverdome Industrial Pk	Pontiac	MI	48342	248-335-4222	335-2853*
*Fax: Hum Res ■ TF: 800-981-3866 ■ Web: www.abcwarehouse.com					
Adray Appliance Photo & Sound Ctr 20219 Carlysle St	Dearborn	MI	48124	313-274-9500	274-6875
TF: 800-652-3729 ■ Web: www.adray.com					
American TV & Appliance of Madison Inc 2404 W Beltline Hwy	Madison	WI	53713	608-271-1000	275-7439
Web: www.americantv.com					
Arthur F Schultz Co 939 W 26th St	Erie	PA	16508	814-454-8171	454-3052
Web: www.arthurfschultz.com					
Audio Direct 460 W Roger Rd Suite 105	Tucson	AZ	85705	888-628-3467	292-6101*
*Fax Area Code: 520 ■ TF Cust Svc: 888-628-3467 ■ Web: www.audio-direct.com					
Audio King Corp 321 W 84th Ave Suite A	Thornton	CO	80260	303-412-2500	412-2501
TF: 800-260-2660 ■ Web: www.ultimateelectronics.com					
Best Buy Co Inc 7601 Penn Ave S	Richfield	MN	55423	612-291-1000	238-3160*
NYSE: BBY ■ *Fax Area Code: 952 ■ *Fax: Cust Svc ■ TF: 888-237-8289 ■ Web: www.bestbuy.com					
BrandsMart USA Corp 3200 SW 42nd St	Hollywood	FL	33312	954-797-4000	797-4061
TF: 800-432-8579 ■ Web: www.brandsmartusa.com					
Conn's Inc 3295 College St	Beaumont	TX	77701	409-832-1696	832-4344
NASDAQ: CONN ■ TF Cust Svc: 800-511-5750 ■ Web: www.conns.com					
eCOST.com Inc 2555 W 190th St Suite 106	Torrance	CA	90504	310-225-4044	225-4030
TF: 800-555-3613 ■ Web: www.ecost.com					
Eklund's Appliance & TV Co 1007 Central Ave W	Great Falls	MT	59404	406-761-3430	453-6942
Web: www.eklundsappliance.com					
Filco Inc 1433 Fulton Ave	Sacramento	CA	95825	916-483-4526	978-3455
Fry's Electronics 600 E Brokaw Rd	San Jose	CA	95112	408-487-4500	487-4700*
*Fax: PR ■ Web: www.frys.com					
GNP Audio Video Inc 1254 E Colorado Blvd	Pasadena	CA	91106	626-577-7767	584-6994
Web: www.gnpaudiovideo.com					
Gregg Appliances Inc 4151 E 96th St	Indianapolis	IN	46240	317-848-8710	848-8723
NYSE: HGG ■ TF: 800-284-7344 ■ Web: www.hhgregg.com					
HBI Office Interiors LLC 3600 136th Pl SE Suite 4	Bellevue	WA	98006	425-274-7500	274-7400
Henshaw's Electronics Co 7622 Wornall Rd	Kansas City	MO	64114	816-444-3434	363-4466
TF: 888-445-3434 ■ Web: www.henshaws.com					
Howard's Appliance & Big Screen Superstores 901 E Imperial Hwy	La Habra	CA	90631	714-871-2700	871-2719
Web: www.howards.com					
IbuyDigital.com Inc 252 Conover St	Brooklyn	NY	11231	646-218-2200	254-9393*
*Fax Area Code: 718 ■ TF: 866-243-4289 ■ Web: www.ibuydigital.com					
Interbond Corp of America 3200 SW 42nd St	Hollywood	FL	33312	954-797-4000	797-4061*
*Fax: Hum Res ■ TF: 800-432-8579 ■ Web: www.brandsmartusa.com					
LetsTalk.com Inc 6341 Blvd 26 Suite 500	North Richland Hills	TX	76180	866-825-5460	
TF: 866-825-5460 ■ Web: www5.letstalk.com					
Midland Radio Corp 5900 Parretta Dr	Kansas City	MO	64120	816-241-8500	241-5713
Web: www.midlandradio.com					
National Auto Sound Inc 11001 E Hwy 40	Independence	MO	64055	816-356-8700	356-7230
Web: www.nationalautosound.com					
Niederauer Inc 1976 W San Carlos St	San Jose	CA	95128	408-297-2440	286-9436
Onecall 229 N Ella Rd PO Box 13069	Spokane	WA	99212	509-838-1018	838-4387
TF: 800-663-5255 ■ Web: www.onecall.com					
PC Richard & Son Inc 150 Price Pkwy	Farmingdale	NY	11735	631-843-4300	843-4309
TF: 800-696-2000 ■ Web: www.pcrichard.com					
Pieratt's Inc 110 S Mt Tabor Rd	Lexington	KY	40517	859-268-6000	268-9065
Web: www.pieratts.net					
Presentation Technologies Inc 3373 Towerwood Dr	Dallas	TX	75234	972-241-5444	247-2590
TF: 800-852-8771 ■ Web: www.jsav.com					
Queen City TV & Appliance Co Inc 2430 I-85 S	Charlotte	NC	28208	704-391-6000	391-6038
TF: 800-365-6665 ■ Web: www.queencitytv.com					
RadioShack 320 Trinity Campus Cir	Fort Worth	TX	76102	817-415-3011	415-3240
TF: 800-843-7422 ■ Web: www.radioshack.com					
RadioShack Corp 300 RadioShack Cir	Fort Worth	TX	76102	817-415-3011	415-3240
NYSE: RSH ■ TF: 800-843-7422 ■ Web: www.radioshackcorporation.com					
REX American Resources Corp 2875 Needmore Rd	Dayton	OH	45414	937-276-3931	276-8643
NYSE: REX ■ TF: 800-528-9739 ■ Web: www.rexstores.com					

Company	City	State	ZIP	Phone	Fax
Simutek Inc 3136 E Fort Lowell Rd *Web:* www.simutek.com	Tucson	AZ	85716	520-321-9077	321-9078
Sound Advice Inc 2501 SW 32nd Terr *TF Cust Svc:* 800-749-1897	Pembroke Park	FL	33023	954-922-4434	
Star Cellular 1371 S Bascom Ave *TF:* 800-969-0023	San Jose	CA	95128	408-288-8500	288-8556
Starsound Audio Inc 2679 Oddie Blvd *Web:* www.starsound.com	Reno	NV	89512	775-331-1010	331-1030
Valu Home Centers Inc 45 S Rossler Ave *Web:* www.valuhomecenters.com	Buffalo	NY	14206	716-825-7377	
Videoland Inc 6808 Hornwood Dr *TF:* 800-877-2900 ■ *Web:* www.hometheaterstore.com	Houston	TX	77074	713-772-6200	772-0500
Wireless Zone 34 Industrial Pk Pl *TF:* 800-411-2355 ■ *Web:* www.wirelesszone.com	Middletown	CT	06457	860-632-9494	632-9343
Yale Appliance 296 Freeport St *TF:* 800-289-9253 ■ *Web:* www.yaleappliance.com	Dorchester	MA	02122	617-825-9253	825-6541

36 APPLIANCES - MAJOR - MFR

SEE ALSO Air Conditioning & Heating Equipment - Residential p. 1384

Company	City	State	ZIP	Phone	Fax
Anaheim Mfg Co 4240 E La Palma Ave PO Box 4146 *TF Cust Svc:* 800-854-3229 ■ *Web:* www.anaheimmfg.com	Anaheim	CA	92807	714-524-7770	996-7073
AO Smith Corp 11270 W Pk Pl Suite 170 PO Box 245008 *NYSE: AOS* ■ *TF:* 800-359-4065 ■ *Web:* www.aosmith.com	Milwaukee	WI	53224	414-359-4000	359-4180
AO Smith Water Products Co 500 Tennessee Waltz Pkwy **Fax Area Code:* 615 ■ *TF:* 800-527-1953 ■ *Web:* www.hotwater.com	Ashland City	TN	37015	800-527-1953	792-2163*
ASKO Appliances Inc PO Box 940609 **Fax Area Code:* 800 ■ *TF:* 866-223-5549 ■ *Web:* www.askousa.com	Plano	TX	75094	866-223-5549	260-0631*
Atlanta Attachment Co Inc 362 Industrial Pk Dr *Web:* www.atlatt.com	Lawrenceville	GA	30045	770-963-7369	963-7641
Bradford White Corp 725 Talamore Dr *TF:* 800-523-2931 ■ *Web:* www.bradfordwhite.com	Ambler	PA	19002	215-641-9400	641-1612
Bradley Direct 7100 Jamesson Rd **Fax Area Code:* 706 ■ *TF:* 800-252-8248 ■ *Web:* www.grilllovers.com	Midland	GA	31820	800-252-8248	565-2121*
Brown Stove Works Inc 1422 Carolina Ave NE *TF:* 800-251-7485 ■ *Web:* www.fivestarrange.com	Cleveland	TN	37311	423-476-6544	476-6599
Cemline Corp PO Box 55 *TF:* 800-245-6268 ■ *Web:* www.cemline.com	Cheswick	PA	15024	724-274-5430	274-5448
Cervitor Kitchens Inc 10775 Lower Azusa Rd *TF:* 800-523-2666 ■ *Web:* www.cervitor.com	El Monte	CA	91731	626-443-0184	443-0400
Char-Broil 1442 Belfast Ave **Fax:* Cust Svc ■ *TF Cust Svc:* 800-352-4111 ■ *Web:* www.charbroil.com	Columbus	GA	31904	706-324-0421	576-6355*
CookTek LLC 156 N Jefferson St Suite 300 *TF:* 888-266-5835 ■ *Web:* www.cooktek.com	Chicago	IL	60661	312-563-9600	432-6220
Crosley Corp 675 N Main St *TF:* 800-849-1112 ■ *Web:* www.crosley.com	Winston-Salem	NC	27101	336-722-1112	721-0685
Dwyer Products Corp 1226 Michael Dr Suite S *TF:* 800-348-8508 ■ *Web:* www.dwyerkitchens.com	Wood Dale	IL	60191	630-741-7970	741-7974
Electric Heater Co 45 Seymour St *TF:* 800-647-3165 ■ *Web:* www.hubbellheaters.com	Stratford	CT	06615	203-378-2659	378-3593
Electrolux 20445 Emerald Pkwy Suite 250	Cleveland	OH	44135	216-898-1800	
Emerson Radio Corp 85 Oxford Dr *AMEX: MSN* ■ *TF:* 800-909-1240 ■ *Web:* www.emersonradio.com	Moonachie	NJ	07074	973-884-5800	428-2067
Fisher & Paykel Appliances Inc 5900 Skylab Rd **Fax Area Code:* 800 ■ *TF:* 888-936-7872 ■ *Web:* www.fisherpaykel.com	Huntington Beach	CA	92647	888-936-7872	547-1971*
Frigidaire Home Products Co 250 Bobby Jones Expy *TF Sales:* 800-288-4924 ■ *Web:* www.frigidaire.com	Augusta	GA	30907	706-651-1751	651-7754
In-Sink-Erator 4700 21st St *TF:* 800-558-5712 ■ *Web:* www.insinkerator.com	Racine	WI	53406	262-554-5432	554-3546
Jenn-Air Co 403 W 4th St N *TF:* 800-688-9900 ■ *Web:* www.jennair.com	Newton	IA	50208	641-792-7000	787-8395
LG Electronics USA Inc 1000 Sylvan Ave *TF Tech Supp:* 800-243-0000 ■ *Web:* www.us.lge.com	Englewood Cliffs	NJ	07632	201-816-2000	816-0636
Lochinvar Corp 300 Maddox Simpson Pkwy *Web:* www.lochinvar.com	Lebanon	TN	37090	615-889-8900	547-1000
Maytag Appliances 403 W 4th St N **Fax:* Mail Rm ■ *TF Cust Svc:* 800-688-9900 ■ *Web:* www.maytag.com	Newton	IA	50208	641-792-7000	787-8395*
Miele Inc 9 Independence Way *TF:* 800-843-7231 ■ *Web:* www.miele.com	Princeton	NJ	08540	609-419-9898	419-4298
Multi-Pak Corp 180 Atlantic St *TF:* 800-234-7441 ■ *Web:* www.multipakcorp.com	Hackensack	NJ	07601	201-342-7474	342-6525
Northland Corp 1260 E Van Deinse St *TF:* 800-223-3900 ■ *Web:* www.northlandnka.com	Greenville	MI	48838	616-754-5601	754-0970
Peerless Premier Appliance Co 119 S 14th St *TF:* 800-858-5844 ■ *Web:* www.premierrange.com	Belleville	IL	62222	618-233-0475	235-1771
Roper Corp 1507 Broomtown Rd	La Fayette	GA	30728	706-638-5100	638-5767
Sanyo Fisher Co 21605 Plummer St *Web:* us.sanyo.com	Chatsworth	CA	91311	818-998-7322	701-4194
Sharp Electronics Corp 1 Sharp Plaza *TF:* 800-237-4277 ■ *Web:* www.sharpusa.com	Mahwah	NJ	07430	201-529-8200	529-8413
Siemens Home Appliances 5551 McFadden Ave *TF:* 888-474-3636 ■ *Web:* www.siemens-home.com	Huntington Beach	CA	92649	714-901-6600	901-5360
Thermador 5551 McFadden Ave *TF:* 800-735-4328 ■ *Web:* www.thermador.com	Huntington Beach	CA	92649	714-901-6600	901-5980
Vaughn Mfg Corp 26 Old Elm St PO Box 5431 *TF:* 800-282-8446 ■ *Web:* www.vaughncorp.com	Salisbury	MA	01952	978-462-6683	462-6497
Weber-Stephen Products Co 200 E Daniels Rd *TF Cust Svc:* 800-446-1071 ■ *Web:* www.weberbbq.com	Palatine	IL	60067	847-934-5700	934-3153
Whirlpool Corp 2000 N M-63 *NYSE: WHR* ■ *TF:* 800-253-1301 ■ *Web:* www.whirlpoolcorp.com	Benton Harbor	MI	49022	269-923-5000	923-5443
Whirlpool Corp North American Region 2000 N M-63 **Fax:* Hum Res ■ *TF:* 800-253-1301 ■ *Web:* www.whirlpoolcorp.com	Benton Harbor	MI	49022	269-923-5000	923-5443*
Wisco Industries Inc 736 Janesville St *TF:* 800-999-4726 ■ *Web:* www.wiscoind.com	Oregon	WI	53575	608-835-3106	835-7399

37 APPLIANCES - SMALL - MFR

SEE ALSO Air Purification Equipment - Household p. 1384; Vacuum Cleaners - Household p. 2752

Company	City	State	ZIP	Phone	Fax
Abatement Technologies 605 Satellite Blvd Suite 300 **Fax Area Code:* 800 ■ *TF:* 800-634-9091 ■ *Web:* www.abatement.com	Suwanee	GA	30024	678-889-4200	358-2394*
Adams Mfg Co Inc 9790 Midwest Ave *Web:* www.adamsmanufacturing.com	Cleveland	OH	44125	216-587-6801	587-6807
Aisin Holdings of America Inc 1665 E Fourth St *Web:* www.aisinworld.com	Seymour	IN	47274	812-524-8144	524-8146
Andis Co 1800 County Rd H *TF:* 800-558-9441 ■ *Web:* www.andis.com	Sturtevant	WI	53177	262-884-2600	884-1100
Applica Consumer Products Inc 3633 Flamingo Rd *TF Cust Svc:* 800-231-9786 ■ *Web:* www.applicainc.com	Miramar	FL	33027	954-883-1000	883-1070
Bernina of America Inc 3702 Prairie Lake Ct *Web:* www.berninausa.com	Aurora	IL	60504	630-978-2500	978-8214
Braun North America 1 Gillette Pk **Fax Area Code:* 800 ■ *TF Cust Svc:* 800-272-8611 ■ *Web:* www.braun.com/na	Boston	MA	02127	617-463-3000	796-4565*
Broan-NuTone LLC 926 W State St PO Box 140 *TF Cust Svc:* 800-558-1711 ■ *Web:* www.broan.com	Hartford	WI	53027	262-673-4340	673-8709
Bunn-O-Matic Corp 1400 Adlai Stevenson Dr *TF:* 800-637-8606 ■ *Web:* www.bunnomatic.com	Springfield	IL	62703	217-529-6601	529-6622
Cadet Mfg Co Inc 2500 W 4th Plain Blvd *TF:* 800-442-2338 ■ *Web:* www.cadetco.com	Vancouver	WA	98660	360-693-2505	694-6939
Casablanca Fan Co 761 Corporate Ctr Dr *TF:* 888-227-2178 ■ *Web:* www.casablancafanco.com	Pomona	CA	91768	909-629-1477	629-3243
Conair Corp 1 Cummings Pt Rd *TF:* 800-726-6247 ■ *Web:* www.conair.com	Stamford	CT	06902	203-351-9000	351-9180
Craftmade International Inc 650 S Royal Ln *NASDAQ: CRFT* ■ *TF:* 800-527-2578 ■ *Web:* www.craftmade.com	Coppell	TX	75019	972-393-3800	304-3750
Cuisinart 1 Cummings Pt Rd *TF:* 800-726-0190 ■ *Web:* www.cuisinart.com	Stamford	CT	06902	203-975-4600	975-4660
El Electronics LLC 1800 Shames Dr *TF:* 877-346-3837 ■ *Web:* www.electroind.com	Westbury	NY	11590	516-334-0870	338-4741
Electrolux 20445 Emerald Pkwy Suite 250	Cleveland	OH	44135	216-898-1800	
Fan-Tastic Vent Corp 2083 S Almont Ave *TF:* 800-521-0298 ■ *Web:* www.fantasticvent.com	Imlay City	MI	48444	810-724-3818	724-3460
Hamilton Beach/Proctor-Silex Inc 4421 Waterfront Dr *TF Cust Svc:* 800-851-8900 ■ *Web:* www.hambeach.com	Glen Allen	VA	23060	804-273-9777	527-7142
Hitachi Home Electronics Inc 900 Hitachi Way *TF:* 800-981-2588	Chula Vista	CA	91914	619-591-5200	591-5201
Holmes Group Inc 1 Holmes Way *TF:* 800-546-5637 ■ *Web:* www.holmesproducts.com	Milford	MA	01757	508-634-8050	634-1211
Hotronic USA Inc 25 Omega Dr *Web:* www.hotronic.com	Williston	VT	05495	802-862-7403	863-6519
Hunter Fan Co 7130 Goodlett Farms Pkwy Suite 400 *TF:* 888-830-1326 ■ *Web:* www.hunterfan.com	Memphis	TN	38116	901-743-1360	
Kaz Home Environment 250 Tpke Rd *Web:* www.kaz.com	Southborough	MA	01772	508-490-7000	
Kaz Inc 250 Tpke Rd *TF:* 800-477-0457 ■ *Web:* www.kaz.com	Southborough	MA	01772	800-477-0457	
King Electrical Mfg Co 9131 10th Ave S *TF:* 800-603-5464 ■ *Web:* www.king-electric.com	Seattle	WA	98108	206-762-0400	763-7738
Krups North America 196 Boston Ave **Fax Area Code:* 781 ■ *TF:* 800-526-5377 ■ *Web:* www.krupsusa.com	Medford	MA	02155	800-526-5377	396-1313*
Lasko Metal Products Inc 820 Lincoln Ave *TF:* 800-394-3267 ■ *Web:* www.laskoproducts.com	West Chester	PA	19380	610-692-7400	696-4648
LG Electronics USA Inc 1000 Sylvan Ave *TF Tech Supp:* 800-243-0000 ■ *Web:* www.us.lge.com	Englewood Cliffs	NJ	07632	201-816-2000	816-0636
Lifetime Brands Inc Farberware Div 1000 Stewart Ave *TF:* 800-252-3390 ■ *Web:* www.farberware.com	Garden City	NY	11530	516-683-6000	683-6161
Marley Engineered Products 470 Beauty Spot Rd E *TF:* 800-452-4179 ■ *Web:* www.marleymeh.com	Bennettsville	SC	29512	843-479-4006	479-8912
National Presto Industries Inc 3925 N Hastings Way *NYSE: NPK* ■ *TF:* 800-877-0441 ■ *Web:* www.gopresto.com	Eau Claire	WI	54703	715-839-2121	839-2148
Nesco/American Harvest 1700 Monroe St PO Box 237 *TF Cust Svc:* 800-288-4545 ■ *Web:* www.nesco.com	Two Rivers	WI	54241	920-793-1368	793-1086
Rowenta Inc 2199 Eden Rd *TF:* 800-769-3682 ■ *Web:* www.rowentausa.com	Millville	NJ	08332	781-396-0600	396-1313
Schawbel Corp 100 Crosby Dr Suite 102 *TF:* 866-753-3837 ■ *Web:* www.thermacell.net	Bedford	MA	01730	781-541-6900	541-6007
Sharp Electronics Corp 1 Sharp Plaza *TF:* 800-237-4277 ■ *Web:* www.sharpusa.com	Mahwah	NJ	07430	201-529-8200	529-8413
Singer Sewing Co 1224 Hill Quaker Blvd PO Box 7017 *TF:* 877-738-9869 ■ *Web:* www.singerco.com	La Vergne	TN	37086	615-213-0880	213-0894

	City	State	ZIP	Phone	Fax
Sunbeam Products Inc					
2381 Executive Ctr Dr	Boca Raton	FL	33431	561-912-4100	912-4567
Web: www.sunbeam.com					
T-Fal Corp 1 Boland Dr Suite 101	West Orange	NJ	07052	973-736-0300	736-9078
TF: 800-395-8325 ■ *Web:* www.t-falusa.com					
Vita-Mix Corp 8615 Usher Rd	Cleveland	OH	44138	440-235-4840	235-3726
TF: 800-848-2649 ■ *Web:* www.vitamix.com					
Waring Products Inc 314 Ella T Grasso Ave	Torrington	CT	06790	860-496-3100	496-9017
TF: 800-269-6640 ■ *Web:* www.waringproducts.com					
West Bend Housewares LLC					
2845 Wingate St PO Box 2780	West Bend	WI	53095	800-290-1851	513-2498*
**Fax Area Code:* 224 ■ *TF:* 800-688-1989 ■ *Web:* www.westbend.com					
Whirlpool Corp KitchenAid Div					
553 Benson Rd	Benton Harbor	MI	49022	269-923-5000	923-5443
TF: 800-422-1230 ■ *Web:* www.kitchenaid.com					
World Dryer Corp 5700 McDermott Dr	Berkeley	IL	60163	708-449-6950	449-6958
TF: 800-323-0701 ■ *Web:* www.worlddryer.com					

38 APPLIANCES - WHOL

	City	State	ZIP	Phone	Fax
All Inc 185 Plato Blvd W	Saint Paul	MN	55107	651-227-6331	292-0541
TF: 800-829-2127 ■ *Web:* www.allinc.com					
Allison-Erwin Co					
2920 N Tyron St PO Box 32308	Charlotte	NC	28232	704-334-8621	334-8381
TF Sales: 800-253-0370					
Almo Corp 2709 Commerce Way	Philadelphia	PA	19154	215-698-4000	698-4080*
**Fax:* Hum Res ■ *TF:* 800-345-2566 ■ *Web:* www.almo.com					
Amco McLean Corp 561 S 4th Ave	Mount Vernon	NY	10550	914-237-4000	237-4341
TF: 800-431-2010					
Ard Distributors Inc 1600 NW 159th St	Miami	FL	33169	305-624-0106	621-2901
TF: 800-654-7721 ■ *Web:* www.ardonline.com					
Autco Distributing Inc					
10900 Midwest Industrial Blvd	Saint Louis	MO	63132	314-426-6524	426-7378
TF Cust Svc: 800-443-0044 ■ *Web:* www.autco.com					
Aves Audio Visual Systems Inc PO Box 500	Sugar Land	TX	77487	281-295-1300	295-1310
TF: 800-365-2837 ■ *Web:* www.avesav.com					
Blodgett Supply Co Inc 100 Ave D PO Box 759	Williston	VT	05495	802-864-9831	864-3645
TF: 800-223-6911 ■ *Web:* www.blodgettsupply.com					
Brady Marketing Co 80 Berry Dr Suite A	Pacheco	CA	94553	925-676-1300	676-3082
TF: 800-326-6080 ■ *Web:* www.bradymarketing.com					
Brooke Distributors Inc 16250 NW 52nd Ave	Miami	FL	33014	305-624-9752	620-3988
TF: 800-275-8792 ■ *Web:* www.brooke.com					
Bursma Electronic Distributing Inc					
2851 Buchanan Ave SW	Grand Rapids	MI	49548	616-831-0080	831-9400
Web: www.bursma.com					
C & L Supply Co PO Box 578	Vinita	OK	74301	918-256-6411	256-3836
TF: 800-256-6411 ■ *Web:* www.clsupplyinc.com					
Carl Schaedel & Co Inc 4 Sperry Rd	Fairfield	NJ	07004	973-244-1311	244-0822
TF: 800-783-6008 ■ *Web:* www.carlschaedel.com					
Ceavco Audio-visual Co 6240 W 54th Ave	Arvada	CO	80002	303-539-3400	539-3401
Web: www.ceavco.com					
Collins Appliance Parts Inc					
1533 Metropolitan St	Pittsburgh	PA	15233	412-321-3700	323-1232
TF: 800-366-9969 ■ *Web:* www.appliancepartscollins.com					
Cowboy Maloney's Electric City					
1313 Harding St	Jackson	MS	39202	601-948-5600	948-5617
Web: www.cowboymaloney.com					
Cunningham Distributing Inc 2015 Mills Ave	El Paso	TX	79901	915-533-6993	545-1320
D.A.S. Inc 724 Lawn Rd	Palmyra	PA	17078	717-964-3642	437-3659*
**Fax Area Code:* 800 ■ *TF:* 866-622-7979 ■ *Web:* www.das-roadpro.com					
Electrical Distributing Inc					
4600 NW St Helens Rd	Portland	OR	97210	503-226-4044	226-4040
TF: 800-932-3774 ■ *Web:* www.edinw.com					
Factory Direct Appliance Inc					
14105 Marshall Dr	Shawnee Mission	KS	66215	913-888-8028	888-7570
Web: www.kcfda.com					
Fretz Corp 2001 Woodhaven Rd	Philadelphia	PA	19116	866-987-2122	987-2125
TF: 866-987-2122 ■ *Web:* www.fretz.com					
Gamla Enterprises North America Inc					
875 Avenue of The Americas Suite 205	New York	NY	10001	212-947-3790	947-3559
TF: 800-442-6526 ■ *Web:* www.gamlaphoto.com					
Gerhard's Appliances 290 N Keswick Ave	Glenside	PA	19038	215-884-8650	884-0349
TF: 888-248-2806 ■ *Web:* www.gerhardsappliance.com					
Glindmeyer Distributing Co Inc					
2910 Lausat St	Metairie	LA	70001	504-832-2223	832-2228
TF: 800-466-1754					
Goldberg Co Inc 2423-A Grenoble Rd	Richmond	VA	23294	804-228-5700	228-5701
TF: 800-365-6533					
Gotham Sales Co 302 Main St	Millburn	NJ	07041	973-912-8412	912-0814
Web: www.gothamsales.com					
GPX Inc 900 N 23rd St	Saint Louis	MO	63106	314-621-3314	621-0869
Web: www.gpx.com					
H Schultz & Sons Inc 777 Lehigh Ave	Union	NJ	07083	908-687-5400	687-1788
Web: www.housewaresandthings.com					
Hall Electric Supply Co Inc 263 main St	Stoneham	MA	02180	781-438-3800	438-3833
TF: 800-444-3726 ■ *Web:* www.hescoapplianceparts.com					
Hamburg Bros Inc 40 24th St	Pittsburgh	PA	15222	412-227-6200	227-6258
TF: 800-568-4824 ■ *Web:* www.hamburgbrothers.com					
Hb Communications Inc 60 Dodge Ave	North Haven	CT	06473	203-234-9246	234-2013
TF: 800-243-4414 ■ *Web:* www.hbcommunications.com					
Helen of Troy Ltd 1 Helen of Troy Plaza	El Paso	TX	79912	915-225-8000	225-8004
NASDAQ: HELE ■ *TF:* 800-487-8432 ■ *Web:* www.hotus.com					
Home Entertainment Distributors Inc					
120 Shawmut Rd	Canton	MA	02021	781-821-0087	821-6408
TF: 800-343-9619 ■ *Web:* www.insurersworld.com					
Klaus Radio Inc 8400 N Allen Rd	Peoria	IL	61615	309-691-4840	693-1724
TF: 800-545-5287 ■ *Web:* www.klausco.com					
M.d.m. Commercial Enterprises Inc					
1102 A1a N Suite 205	Ponte Vedra	FL	32082	904-241-2340	241-3133
TF: 800-359-6741 ■ *Web:* www.mdmcommercial.com					
Midwest Sales & Service Inc					
917 S Chapin St	South Bend	IN	46601	574-287-3365	287-3429
TF: 800-772-7262					
Mirama Enterprises Inc 6469 Flanders Dr	San Diego	CA	92121	858-558-6688	558-7300
TF: 800-276-6286 ■ *Web:* www.aroma-housewares.com					
Nelson & Small Inc 212 Canco Rd	Portland	ME	04103	207-775-5666	775-4303
TF: 800-341-0780 ■ *Web:* www.nelsonsmall.com					
O'Rourke Sales Co 3885 Elmore Ave Suite 100	Davenport	IA	52807	563-823-1501	823-1534
TF: 800-523-4730 ■ *Web:* www.orourkesales.com					
Oakton Distributors Inc 125 E Oakton St	Des Plaines	IL	60018	847-294-5858	294-6816
TF: 800-262-5866					
Oregon Scientific Inc 19861 SW 95th Pl	Tualatin	OR	97062	503-783-5100	691-6208
Web: www.oregonscientific.com					
Peirce-Phelps Inc 2000 N 59th St	Philadelphia	PA	19131	215-879-7000	879-5141
TF: 800-222-2742 ■ *Web:* www.peirce.com					
Potter Distributing Inc					
4037 Roger B Chaffee Blvd	Grand Rapids	MI	49548	616-531-6860	531-9578
TF: 800-748-0568 ■ *Web:* www.potterdistributing.com					
Precision Trading Corp 1430 NW 88th Ave	Miami	FL	33172	305-592-4500	593-6169
Web: www.precisiontrading.com					
Prudential Distributors Inc					
3304 E Ferry PO Box 3088	Spokane	WA	99220	509-535-2401	534-9145
TF: 800-767-5567					
R & B Wholesale Distributors Inc					
2350 S Milliken Ave	Ontario	CA	91761	909-230-5400	230-5405
Web: www.rbdist.com					
Radio Distributing Co Inc					
27015 Trolley Industrial Dr	Taylor	MI	48180	313-295-4500	295-3710
TF General: 800-462-1544 ■ *Web:* www.radiodistributing.com					
Roth Distributing Co 11300 W 47th St	Minnetonka	MN	55343	952-933-4428	935-8795
TF: 800-642-3227 ■ *Web:* www.rothdistributing.com					
Rott-Keller Supply Co Inc					
6520 8th St PO Box 390	Fargo	ND	58107	701-235-0563	232-7900
TF: 800-342-4709 ■ *Web:* www.rottkeller.com					
Servall Co 6761 E Ten Mile Rd	Center Line	MI	48015	586-754-1818	754-2260
TF: 800-989-7378					
Siano Appliance Distributors Inc					
5372 Pleasant View Rd	Memphis	TN	38134	901-382-5833	372-3621
Web: www.sianoappliances.net					
Speco Technologies 200 New Hwy	Amityville	NY	11701	631-957-8700	957-9142
TF: 800-645-5516 ■ *Web:* www.specotech.com					
Tacony Corp 1760 Gilsinn Ln	Fenton	MO	63026	636-349-3000	349-2333
TF: 800-482-2669 ■ *Web:* www.tacony.com					
Telerent Leasing Corp PO Box 26627	Raleigh	NC	27611	919-772-8604	662-7070
Web: www.telerent.com					
Tri-State Video Services Inc					
1379 Pittsburgh Rd	Valencia	PA	16059	724-898-1630	898-2330
TF: 888-382-7768 ■ *Web:* www.tristatevideo.com					
W. N. L. Inc PO Box 427	Clackamas	OR	97015	503-655-2563	656-8829
Web: www.splendide.com					
Web Service Co Inc					
3690 Redondo Beach Ave	Redondo Beach	CA	90278	323-772-5131	643-6958*
**Fax Area Code:* 310 ■ *TF:* 800-421-6897 ■ *Web:* www.weblaundry.com					
Westye Group					
2615 E Beltline Rd PO Box 111400	Carrollton	TX	75011	972-416-6677	416-0661
TF: 800-441-9260 ■ *Web:* www.westye.com					
Whirlpool Canada 1901 Minnesota Ct	Mississauga	ON	L5N3A7	905-821-6400	821-4151
TF: 800-807-6777 ■ *Web:* www.whirlpoolcanada.com					
Williams Distributing & Kitchen & Bath					
658 Richmond St NW	Grand Rapids	MI	49504	616-771-0505	771-0429
TF: 800-968-3718 ■ *Web:* www.williamskitchen.com					
Woodson & Bozeman Inc 3870 New Getwell Rd	Memphis	TN	38118	901-362-1500	362-1509
TF: 800-876-4243 ■ *Web:* www.woodsonbozeman.com					

39 APPLICATION SERVICE PROVIDERS (ASPS)

Application Service Providers Rent, Deliver, License, Manage, And/Or Host Proprietary And/Or Third-Party Business Software ("Applications") And/Or Computer Services To Multiple Users (Customers). Included Here Are Companies That Host Software Applications As Well As Companies That Provide The Equipment Necessary To Do So.

	City	State	ZIP	Phone	Fax
5 by 5 Networks 1455 McCarthy Blvd	Milpitas	CA	95053	408-433-5295	433-5298
Access Data Corp 2 Chatham Ctr 11th Fl	Pittsburgh	PA	15219	412-201-6000	201-6060
TF: 888-799-1744 ■ *Web:* www.accessdc.com					
Alliance Commerce Inc					
2141 N University Drt Suite 302	Coral Springs	FL	33071	954-575-2300	
TF: 877-638-2777 ■ *Web:* www.alliancecommerce.net					
AllMeds Inc 151 Lafayette Dr Suite 401	Oak Ridge	TN	37830	865-482-1999	481-0921
TF: 888-343-6337 ■ *Web:* www.allmeds.com					
American Data Ctr Inc 25 W Palatine Rd	Palatine	IL	60067	847-358-7111	358-7635
Web: www.hgcaonline.com					
Application Consulting Group					
121 Headquarters Plaza N Tower 2nd Fl	Morristown	NJ	07960	973-898-0012	898-6647
Web: www.acgi.com					
Ariba Inc 807 11th Ave	Sunnyvale	CA	94089	650-390-1000	390-1100
NASDAQ: ARBA ■ *TF:* 888-237-3131 ■ *Web:* www.ariba.com					
Atomz Corp 1111 Bayhill Dr Suite 285	San Bruno	CA	94066	650-244-1400	244-1401
Web: www.atomz.com					
Avanade Inc 818 Stewart St	Seattle	WA	98101	206-239-5600	239-5605
Web: www.avanade.com					
Avazpour Networking Services Inc					
10895 Grandview Dr Suite 250	Overland Park	KS	66210	913-498-8777	498-8778
Web: www.avazpour.com					
Baillio's Inc 5301 Menaul Blvd Ne	Albuquerque	NM	87110	505-883-7511	338-3377
TF: 800-540-7511 ■ *Web:* baillios.com					
BizLand Inc 70 Blanchard Rd	Burlington	MA	01803	781-272-5585	272-2915
TF: 866-599-9964 ■ *Web:* www.bizland.com					
BluePoint Data Storage Inc					
1200 N Federal Hwy Suite 200	Boca Raton	FL	33432	561-417-0324	417-0347
TF: 866-786-7390 ■ *Web:* www.bluepointdata.com					

			Phone	Fax
BroadVision Inc				
1600 Seaport Blvd Suite 550 . . . . Redwood City	CA	94063	650-295-0716	364-3425
NASDAQ: BVSN ■ *Web:* www.broadvision.com				
CaseCentral Inc 50 California St. . . . . San Francisco	CA	94111	415-989-2300	989-2373
TF: 800-714-2727 ■ *Web:* www.casecentral.com				
Cayenta Canada Corp				
4200 N Fraser Way Suite 201 . . . . .Burnaby	BC	V5J5K7	604-570-4300	291-0742
TF: 866-229-3682 ■ *Web:* www.cayenta.com				
CenterBeam Inc 30 Rio Robles Dr . . . . San Jose	CA	95134	408-750-0500	750-0555
Web: www.centerbeam.com				
Centric Software Inc 50 Las Colinas Ln . . . . San Jose	CA	95119	408-574-7802	574-7809
TF: 888-537-2639 ■ *Web:* www.centricsoftware.com				
Chemical Safety Corp				
5901 Christie Ave Suite 502. . . . . Emeryville	CA	94608	510-594-1000	594-1100
TF: 888-594-1100 ■ *Web:* www.chemicalsafety.com				
CliniComp International 9655 Towne Ctr Dr. . . . . San Diego	CA	92121	858-546-8202	546-1801
TF: 800-350-8202 ■ *Web:* www.clinicomp.com				
Cogency Software Inc				
500 Airport Blvd Suite 200. . . . . Burlingame	CA	94010	650-685-2500	685-2515
Web: www.cogencysoftware.com				
College Central Network Inc				
245 8th Ave Suite 892 . . . . .New York	NY	10011	800-442-3614	
TF: 800-442-3614 ■ *Web:* www.collegecentralnetwork.com				
Computer Programs & Systems Inc (CPSI)				
6600 Wall St. . . . . .Mobile	AL	36695	251-639-8100	639-8214
NASDAQ: CPSI ■ *TF:* 800-711-2774 ■ *Web:* www.cpsinet.com				
Concur Technologies Inc				
18400 NE Union Hill Rd . . . . .Redmond	WA	98052	425-702-8808	702-8828
NASDAQ: CNQR ■ *TF:* 800-358-0610 ■ *Web:* www.concur.com				
Connectria Corp				
10845 Olive Blvd Suite 300 . . . . Saint Louis	MO	63141	314-587-7000	587-7090
TF: 800-781-7820 ■ *Web:* www.connectria.com				
Crexendo Inc 1615 S 52nd St . . . . Tempe	AZ	85281	801-431-4695	
AMEX: IIG ■ *Web:* www.crexendoinc.com				
Critical Path Inc 1215 Bordeaux Dr . . . . Sunnyvale	CA	94085	415-541-2500	520-5737
TF: 877-441-7284 ■ *Web:* www.criticalpath.net				
CyberData Inc 20 Max Ave . . . . .Hicksville	NY	11801	516-942-8000	942-0800
Cyveillance Inc 2677 Prosperity Ave Suite 400 . . . . Fairfax	VA	22031	703-351-1000	560-2506
TF: 888-243-0097 ■ *Web:* www.cyveillance.com				
Daptiv 1008 Western Ave Suite 500 . . . . Seattle	WA	98104	206-341-9117	341-9123
TF: 888-621-8361 ■ *Web:* www.daptiv.com				
DataServ LLC 1630 Des Peres Rd Suite 301 . . . . Saint Louis	MO	63131	314-842-1155	842-6161
TF: 877-700-3282 ■ *Web:* www.dataserv.us				
Digital River Inc				
9625 W 76th St Suite 150. . . . . .Eden Prairie	MN	55344	952-253-1234	253-8497
NASDAQ: DRIV ■ *Web:* www.digitalriver.com				
DigitalWork.com Inc				
130 S Jefferson St Suite 100 . . . . .Chicago	IL	60661	312-379-5950	379-5952
TF: 877-496-7571 ■ *Web:* www.digitalwork.com				
DocMan Technologies 31300 Bainbridge Rd. . . . . Cleveland	OH	44139	440-542-9660	542-9668
TF: 888-636-2626 ■ *Web:* www.docmantech.com				
E-Builder Inc 1800 NW 69 Ave Suite 201 . . . . Plantation	FL	33313	954-556-6701	792-5949
TF: 800-580-9322 ■ *Web:* www.e-builder.net				
E-Markets Inc 1606 Golden Aspen Dr Suite 108. . . . . .Ames	IA	50010	515-233-8720	956-9388
TF: 877-674-7419 ■ *Web:* www.e-markets.com				
eGain Communications Corp				
345 E Middlefield Rd . . . . Mountain View	CA	94043	650-230-7500	230-7600
TF: 888-603-4246 ■ *Web:* www.egain.com				
Electric Mail Co Inc				
3999 Henning Dr Suite 300 . . . . .Burnaby	BC	V5C6P9	604-482-1111	482-1110
TF: 800-419-7463 ■ *Web:* www.electricmail.com				
Emdeon Business Services LLC				
3055 Lebanon Pike. . . . . .Nashville	TN	37214	615-932-3000	
Web: www.emdeon.com				
Employease Inc				
3295 River Exchange Dr Suite 500 . . . . Norcross	GA	30092	770-325-7700	325-7702
TF: 888-327-3638 ■ *Web:* www.employease.com				
ePlus Inc 13595 Dulles Technology Dr. . . . . Herndon	VA	20171	703-984-8400	984-8600
NASDAQ: PLUS ■ *TF:* 800-827-5711 ■ *Web:* www.eplus.com				
eWork Exchange Inc				
717 Market St Suite 600. . . . . San Francisco	CA	94103	415-546-4800	546-4889
Exenet Technologies Inc 85 10th Ave. . . . . .New York	NY	10011	646-230-7558	
FinancialCAD Corp 13450 102nd Ave Suite 1750 . . . . Surrey	BC	V3T5X3	604-957-1200	957-1201
TF: 800-304-0702 ■ *Web:* www.fincad.com				
Flying Aces Technology LLC				
305 N Westgate Rd Suite 100. . . . . .Mount Prospect	IL	60056	847-299-7815	
Web: www.flying-aces.com				
HealthMEDX 5100 N Towne Ctr Dr. . . . . .Ozark	MO	65721	417-582-1816	582-0296
TF: 877-875-1200 ■ *Web:* www.healthmedx.com				
I-Business Network LLC 2256 NW Pkwy Suite E. . . . . .Marietta	GA	30067	678-627-0646	627-0688
TF: 877-336-4426 ■ *Web:* www.i-bn.net				
IE Discovery Inc 13640 Briarwick Dr Suite 250 . . . . Austin	TX	78729	512-498-7400	498-7444
TF: 800-656-8444 ■ *Web:* www.iediscovery.com				
Incentivecity 7370 Bramalea Rd Suite 3 . . . . Mississauga	ON	L5S1N6	905-362-0951	362-0957
TF: 877-387-2529 ■ *Web:* www.incentivecity.com				
Infogain Corp 485 Alberto Way . . . . Los Gatos	CA	95032	408-355-6000	355-7000
Web: www.infogain.com				
InsynQ Inc 1127 Broadway Plaza Suite 202 . . . . Tacoma	WA	98402	253-284-2000	722-5605
TF: 866-796-9925 ■ *Web:* www.insynq.com				
Intacct Corp 125 S Market St Suite 600 . . . . San Jose	CA	95113	408-878-0900	878-9010
TF: 877-968-0600 ■ *Web:* www.us.intacct.com				
Integrity eLearning Inc				
751 S Weir Canyon Rd Suite 157451 . . . . Anaheim Hills	CA	92808	714-637-9480	
Web: www.ielearning.com				
Internap Network Services Corp				
250 Williams St Suite E-100. . . . . .Atlanta	GA	30303	404-302-9700	475-0520
NASDAQ: INAP ■ *TF:* 877-843-7627 ■ *Web:* www.internap.com				
IntraLinks Inc 150 E 42nd St # 8. .New York	NY	10017	212-543-7700	543-7978
TF: 888-546-5383 ■ *Web:* www.intralinks.com				
Jamcracker Inc				
4677 Old Ironsides Dr Suite 450 . . . . Santa Clara	CA	95054	408-496-5500	456-9944
TF: 866-559-0035 ■ *Web:* www.jamcracker.com				

			Phone	Fax
Journyx Inc 9011 Mountain Ridge Suite 200. . . . . Austin	TX	78759	512-834-8888	834-8858
TF: 800-755-9878 ■ *Web:* www.journyx.com				
Kleinschmidt Inc 450 Lake Cook Rd. . . . . Deerfield	IL	60015	847-945-1000	945-4619
Web: www.kleinschmidt.com				
Learningstation.com Inc				
4651 Charlotte Pk Dr . . . . Charlotte	NC	28217	704-926-5400	926-5401
TF: 888-679-7058 ■ *Web:* www.learningstation.com				
Legal Systems Holding Co				
155 108 Ave NE Suite 650 . . . . .Bellevue	WA	98004	425-732-5555	732-5554
Web: www.serengetilaw.com				
LivePerson Inc 462 7th Ave 2nd & 3rd Fl . . . . .New York	NY	10018	212-609-4200	609-4201
NASDAQ: LPSN ■ *Web:* www.liveperson.com				
Management Dynamics Inc				
1 Meadowlands Plaza. . . . . East Rutherford	NJ	07073	201-935-8588	935-5187
Web: www.managementdynamics.com				
MetraTech Corp 200 W St. . . . . Waltham	MA	02451	781-839-8300	839-8301
Web: www.metratech.com				
NeoMedia Technologies Inc				
2201 2nd St Suite 402 . . . . .Fort Myers	FL	33901	239-337-3434	337-3668
Web: www.neom.com				
NetBase Corp				
4443 Brookfield Corporate Dr Suite 200. . . . . Chantilly	VA	20151	703-814-4040	814-4074
TF: 888-456-6528				
NetSuite Inc 2955 Campus Dr Suite 100. . . . . .San Mateo	CA	94403	650-627-1000	627-1001
TF: 800-762-5524 ■ *Web:* www.netsuite.com				
OneMind Connect Inc				
2 Corporate Plaza Suite 100. . . . . Newport Beach	CA	92660	949-640-0701	640-0711
TF: 877-658-5022 ■ *Web:* www.onemindconnect.com				
onProject Inc 3 Wing Dr Suite 225 . . . . Cedar Knolls	NJ	07927	973-971-9970	971-9971
TF: 877-936-6776 ■ *Web:* www.onproject.com				
Open Solutions Inc 799 Market St 4th Fl . . . . San Francisco	CA	94103	415-344-4200	267-0944
NASDAQ: OPEN ■ *Web:* www.opentable.com				
OpenAir Inc 268 Summer St 4th Fl .Boston	MA	02210	617-351-0230	351-0220
TF Sales: 888-367-1715 ■ *Web:* www.openair.com				
Oracle Corp 500 Oracle Pkwy. . . . . .Redwood Shores	CA	94065	650-506-7000	506-7200
NASDAQ: ORCL ■ *TF Sales:* 800-392-2999 ■ *Web:* www.oracle.com				
Outstart Inc 745 Atlantic Ave 4th Fl. .Boston	MA	02111	617-897-6800	897-6801
Web: www.outstart.com				
Paramount Technologies Inc				
2075 E W Maple Rd Suite B-203 . . . . .Commerce Township	MI	48390	248-960-0909	960-1919
TF: 800-725-4408 ■ *Web:* www.paramountusa.com				
Passkey International				
180 Old Colony Ave 3rd Fl . . . . .Quincy	MA	02170	866-649-1539	328-1461*
**Fax Area Code:* 617 ■ *TF:* 866-649-1539 ■ *Web:* www.passkey.com				
PBM Corp 20600 Chagrin Blvd Suite 450. . . . . Cleveland	OH	44122	216-283-7999	283-7931
TF: 800-341-5809 ■ *Web:* www.pbmcorp.com				
Perfect Commerce Inc				
2713 Magruder Blvd Suite A. . . . . Hampton	VA	23666	757-766-8211	865-3452
TF Sales: 877-871-3788 ■ *Web:* www.perfect.com				
PhDx Systems Inc				
1001 University Blvd SE Suite 103. . . . . Albuquerque	NM	87106	505-764-0174	764-0120
TF: 888-999-7439 ■ *Web:* www.phdx.com				
PicoSearch LLC 10 Fawcett St. . . . . .Cambridge	MA	02138	617-547-4020	576-7227
Web: www.picosearch.com				
Pointivity 5355 Mira Sorrento Pl # 600 . . . . San Diego	CA	92121	858-777-6900	777-6915
Web: www.pointivity.com				
Premiere Global Services Inc (PGI)				
3280 Peachtree Rd NE				
Suite 1000 the Terminus Bldg. . . . . .Atlanta	GA	30305	719-457-6901	
NYSE: PGI ■ *TF:* 866-548-3203 ■ *Web:* www.pgi.com				
Prodata Systems Inc				
3855 Monte Villa Pkwy Suite 105. . . . . .Bothell	WA	98021	425-487-8300	487-8355
TF: 866-487-8346 ■ *Web:* www.prodata.com				
Prosum technology services				
2321 Rosecrans Ave Suite 4225. El Segundo	CA	90245	310-426-0600	426-0690
Web: www.prosum.com				
PureWorks Inc				
1321 Murfreesboro Rd Suite 200 .Nashville	TN	37217	615-367-4404	367-3887
TF: 888-202-3016 ■ *Web:* www.puresafety.com				
QuickArrow Inc 11675 Jollyville Rd Suite 200 . . . . Austin	TX	78759	512-381-0600	381-0660
Web: www.quickarrow.com				
Quovera 800 W El Camino Real Suite 100 . . . . Mountain View	CA	94040	650-962-6300	
Web: www.quovera.com				
Radware Inc 575 Corporate Dr Lbby 2. . . . . .Mahwah	NJ	07430	201-512-9771	512-9774
TF: 888-234-5763 ■ *Web:* www.radware.com				
Realm Business Solutions Inc				
13727 Noel Rd Suite 800 . . . . Dallas	TX	75240	469-791-1000	791-1810
TF: 866-697-3256 ■ *Web:* www.realm.com				
Resource Development Corp				
280 Daines St Suite 200. . . . . .Birmingham	MI	48009	248-646-2300	646-0789
TF: 800-360-7222 ■ *Web:* www.resourcedev.com				
Responsys Inc 3 Lagwood Dr Suite 300 . . . . Redwood City	CA	94065	650-801-7400	801-7401
TF: 800-624-5356 ■ *Web:* www.responsys.com				
RightNow Technologies Inc				
136 Enterprise Blvd PO Box 9300. Bozeman	MT	59718	406-522-4200	522-4227
NASDAQ: RNOW ■ *TF:* 877-363-5678 ■ *Web:* www.rightnowtech.com				
Salesforce.com Inc				
1 Market St The Landmark Suite 300 . . . . San Francisco	CA	94105	415-901-7000	901-7040
NYSE: CRM ■ *TF:* 800-667-6389 ■ *Web:* www.salesforce.com				
Salesnet Inc 268 Summer St 4th Fl. .Boston	MA	02210	617-979-6100	979-6188
TF: 877-350-0160 ■ *Web:* www.salesnet.com				
Shareholder.com 12 Clock Tower Pl Suite 300. . . . . Maynard	MA	01754	978-461-3111	897-3739
TF: 800-990-6397 ■ *Web:* www.shareholder.com				
Siemens Medical Solutions Health Services Corp				
51 Valley Stream Pkwy . . . . .Malvern	PA	19355	610-219-6300	219-3124
TF: 888-767-8326 ■ *Web:* www.smed.com				
SiteLite Corp 111 Theory 2nd Fl . . . . .Irvine	CA	92612	949-265-6200	265-6399
Web: www.sitelite.com				
Smart Online Inc PO Box 12794. . . . . Research Triangle Park	NC	27709	919-765-5000	765-5020
TF: 800-578-9000 ■ *Web:* www.smartonline.com				
Spyre Infostructure Inc				
25 Imperial St Suite 210. . . . . Toronto	ON	M5P1B9	416-487-7797	487-7706
TF: 888-467-7973 ■ *Web:* www.spyre.com				

				Phone	Fax
StorageASP Inc 515 Consumers Rd Suite 405 . . . . Toronto *Web:* www.storageasp.com	ON	M2J4Z2	416-750-4002	750-8802
Strategic Systems Consulting Inc 3150 Holcomb Bridge Rd . . . . Norcross *Web:* www.eapps.com	GA	30071	770-448-2100	416-1570
Streamline Health Solutions Inc 10200 Alliance Rd Suite 200 . . . . Cincinnati *NASDAQ: STRM* ■ *TF:* 800-878-5269 ■ *Web:* www.heat.streamlinehealth.net	OH	45242	513-794-7100	794-9770
Syntrio 33 New Montgomery St Suite 1280 . . . . San Francisco *TF:* 888-858-2887 ■ *Web:* www.syntrio.com	CA	94105	415-951-7913	951-7915
Talisma Corp 3015 112th Ave NE # 100 . . . . Bellevue *TF:* 877-934-3276 ■ *Web:* www.talisma.com	WA	98004	425-688-3800	688-3899
TALX Corp 11432 Lackland Dr . . . . Saint Louis *TF:* 800-888-8277 ■ *Web:* www.talx.com	MO	63146	314-214-7000	214-7588
Thoughtworks Inc 200 E Randolph St 25th Fl . . . . Chicago *Web:* www.thoughtworks.com	IL	60601	312-373-1000	373-1001
Toolwire Inc 6120 Stoneridge Mall Rd Suite 110 . . . . Pleasanton *TF:* 866-935-8665 ■ *Web:* www.toolwire.com	CA	94588	925-227-8500	227-8501
TriZetto Group Inc 6061 S Willow Dr Suite 310 . . . . Greenwood Village *NASDAQ: TZIX* ■ *TF:* 800-569-1222 ■ *Web:* www.trizetto.com	CO	80111	949-719-2200	219-2197
UnicornHRO 25 Hanover Rd # B . . . . Florham Park *TF:* 800-343-6844 ■ *Web:* www.unicornhro.com	NJ	07932	973-360-0688	360-0699
USA.NET Inc 1155 Kelly Johnson Blvd Suite 400 . . . . Colorado Springs *TF:* 800-653-0179 ■ *Web:* www.usa.net	CO	80920	719-265-2930	265-2922
Vocus Inc 4296 Forbes Blvd. . . . . Lanham *NASDAQ: VOCS* ■ *TF:* 800-345-5572 ■ *Web:* www.vocus.com	MD	20706	301-459-2590	459-2827
Voxeo Corp 189 S Orange Ave Suite 2050 . . . . Orlando *Web:* www.voxeo.com	FL	32801	407-418-1800	264-8530
Webauthor.com LLC 2737 Misty Oakes Cir . . . . Royal Palm Beach *Web:* www.webauthor.com	FL	33411	561-282-3300	
Webhire Inc 91 Hartwell Ave . . . . Lexington *TF:* 877-932-4473 ■ *Web:* www.webhire.com	MA	02421	781-869-5000	869-5050
WebMD Health Holdings Inc 111 8th Ave 7th Fl. . . . . New York *NASDAQ: WBMD* ■ *Web:* www.webmd.com	NY	10011	212-624-3700	624-3800
Wizmo Inc 7646 Golden Triangle Dr. . . . . Eden Prairie *Web:* www.wizmo.com	MN	55344	952-983-3300	983-3600
Workscape Inc 123 Selton St . . . . Marlborough *TF:* 888-605-9620 ■ *Web:* www.workscape.com	MA	01752	508-861-5500	573-9500
WTS Inc 1100 Olive Way Suite 1100. . . . . Seattle *TF:* 877-987-7253 ■ *Web:* www.wts.com	WA	98101	206-436-3300	436-3305
Zantaz Inc 5671 Gibraltar Dr . . . . Pleasanton *TF:* 800-636-0095 ■ *Web:* www.zantaz.com	CA	94588	925-598-3000	598-3145

40 AQUARIUMS - PUBLIC

SEE ALSO Botanical Gardens & Arboreta p. 1537; Zoos & Wildlife Parks p. 2780

			Phone	Fax
Adventure Aquarium 1 Aquarium Dr . . . . Camden *TF:* 800-616-5297 ■ *Web:* www.adventureaquarium.com	NJ	08103	856-365-3300	365-3311
Albuquerque Aquarium 2601 Central Ave NW. . . . . . . Albuquerque *Web:* www.cabq.gov/biopark/aquarium	NM	87104	505-764-6200	848-7192
Aquarium et Centre Marin de Shippagan 100 Aquarium St. . . . . Shippagan *Web:* www.aquariumnb.ca/home.html	NB	E8S1H9	506-336-3013	336-3057
Aquarium of the Bay The Embarcadero at Beach St Pier 39. . . . . San Francisco *TF:* 888-732-3483 ■ *Web:* www.aquariumofthebay.com	CA	94133	415-623-5300	623-5324
Aquarium of the Pacific 100 Aquarium Way. . . . . Long Beach *Web:* www.aquariumofpacific.org	CA	90802	562-590-3100	950-3109
Audubon Aquarium of the Americas 6500 Magazine St. . . . . New Orleans *TF:* 800-774-7394 ■ *Web:* www.auduboninstitute.org	LA	70118	504-581-4629	565-3871
Birch Aquarium at Scripps 2300 Expedition Way . . . . La Jolla *Web:* www.aquarium.ucsd.edu	CA	92037	858-534-3474	534-7114
Cabrillo Marine Aquarium 3720 Stephen M White Dr . . . . San Pedro *Web:* www.cabrillomarineaquarium.org	CA	90731	310-548-7562	548-2649
Clearwater Marine Aquarium 249 Windward Passage . . . . Clearwater *TF:* 888-239-9414 ■ *Web:* www.cmaquarium.org	FL	33767	727-441-1790	447-4922
Dallas Aquarium at Fair Park 1462 1st Ave & ML King Blvd. . . . . Dallas *Web:* www.dallas-zoo.org	TX	75210	214-670-8443	670-8452
Dallas World Aquarium 1801 N Griffin St . . . . Dallas *TF:* 800-732-7957 ■ *Web:* www.dwazoo.com	TX	75202	214-720-2224	720-2242
Dauphin Island Sea Lab Estuarium 101 Bienville Blvd. . . . . Dauphin Island *TF:* 866-403-4400 ■ *Web:* www.disl.org	AL	36528	251-861-2141	861-4646
Downtown Aquarium 410 Bagby St & Memorial Dr . . . . Houston *Web:* www.downtownaquarium.com	TX	77002	713-223-3474	
Downtown Aquarium - Denver 700 Water St . . . . Denver *Web:* www.aquariumrestaurants.com	CO	80211	303-561-4450	561-4650
Florida Aquarium 701 Channelside Dr. . . . . Tampa *TF:* 800-353-4741 ■ *Web:* www.flaquarium.org	FL	33602	813-273-4000	273-4160
Fluvarium The 5 Nagle's Pl . . . . Saint John's *Web:* fluvarium.ca	NL	A1B2Z2	709-754-3474	754-5947
Georgia Aquarium 225 Baker St . . . . Atlanta *Web:* www.georgiaaquarium.org	GA	30313	404-581-4000	
Great Lakes Aquarium 353 Harbor Dr. . . . . Duluth *TF:* 877-866-3474 ■ *Web:* www.glaquarium.org	MN	55802	218-740-3474	740-2020
JL Scott Marine Education Center & Aquarium 703 E Beach Dr. . . . . Ocean Springs *Web:* www.usm.edu/aquarium	MS	39564	228-818-8890	818-8894
John G Shedd Aquarium 1200 S Lake Shore Dr. . . . . Chicago *Web:* www.sheddaquarium.org	IL	60605	312-939-2438	939-3793
Key West Aquarium 1 Whitehead St. . . . . Key West *TF:* 800-868-7482 ■ *Web:* www.keywestaquarium.com	FL	33040	305-296-2051	293-7094
Maria Mitchell Assn Aquarium 4 Vestal St . . . . Nantucket *Web:* www.mmo.org/marine-science/mma-aquarium.html	MA	02554	508-228-5387	228-1031
Marineland of Florida 9600 Ocean Shore Blvd . . . . Saint Augustine *TF:* 888-279-9194 ■ *Web:* www.marineland.net	FL	32080	904-460-1275	471-1111
Marinelife Center of Juno Beach 14200 US Hwy 1 Loggerhead Pk . . . . Juno Beach *Web:* www.marinelife.org	FL	33408	561-627-8280	627-8305
Maritime Aquarium at Norwalk 10 N Water St . . . . Norwalk *Web:* www.maritimeaquarium.org	CT	06854	203-852-0700	838-5416
Maui Ocean Ctr 192 Maalaea Rd. . . . . Wailuku *TF:* 800-350-5634 ■ *Web:* www.mauioceancenter.com	HI	96793	808-270-7000	270-7070
Miami Seaquarium 4400 Rickenbacker Cswy. . . . . Miami *Web:* www.miamiseaquarium.com	FL	33149	305-361-5705	361-6077
Monterey Bay Aquarium 886 Cannery Row. . . . . Monterey *TF:* 800-555-3656 ■ *Web:* www.montereybayaquarium.org	CA	93940	831-648-4800	648-4810
Moody Gardens 1 Hope Blvd. . . . . Galveston *TF:* 800-582-4673 ■ *Web:* www.moodygardens.com	TX	77554	409-744-4673	683-4926
Mystic Aquarium & Institute for Exploration 55 Coogan Blvd . . . . Mystic *Web:* www.mysticaquarium.org	CT	06355	860-572-5955	572-5969
National Aquarium 14th & Constitution Ave NW Dept of Commerce Bld Rm B-077. . . . . Washington *Web:* www.nationalaquarium.com	DC	20230	202-482-2825	482-4946
National Aquarium in Baltimore 501 E Pratt St Pier 3. . . . . Baltimore *Web:* www.aqua.org	MD	21202	410-576-3800	576-8238
National Park Aquarium 209 Central Ave . . . . Hot Springs	AR	71901	501-624-3474	
New England Aquarium 1 Central Wharf . . . . Boston *Web:* www.neaq.org	MA	02110	617-973-5200	720-5098
New York Aquarium W 8th St & Surf Ave. . . . . Brooklyn *Web:* www.nyaquarium.com	NY	11224	718-265-3474	265-3385
Newport Aquarium One Aquarium Way . . . . Newport *TF:* 800-406-3474 ■ *Web:* www.newportaquarium.com	KY	41071	859-261-7444	261-5888
North Carolina Aquarium at Fort Fisher 900 Loggerhead Rd . . . . Kure Beach *TF:* 866-301-3476 ■ *Web:* www.ncaquariums.com	NC	28449	910-458-8257	458-6812
North Carolina Aquarium on Roanoke Island 374 Airport Rd PO Box 967 . . . . Manteo *TF:* 866-332-3475 ■ *Web:* www.ncaquariums.com	NC	27954	252-473-3493	473-1980
Ocean Life Center Aquarium 800 N New Hampshire Ave . . . . Atlantic City *Web:* www.oceanlifecenter.com	NJ	08401	609-348-2880	
Oklahoma Aquarium 300 S Aquarium Dr . . . . Jenks *Web:* www.okaquarium.org	OK	74037	918-296-3474	296-3467
Oregon Coast Aquarium 2820 SE Ferry Slip Rd . . . . Newport *Web:* www.aquarium.org	OR	97365	541-867-3474	867-6846
Pacific Undersea Gardens 490 Belleville St . . . . Victoria *Web:* www.pacificunderseagardens.com	BC	V8V1W9	250-382-5717	382-5210
Parc Aquarium du Quebec 1675 des Hotels Ave. . . . . Quebec *TF:* 866-659-5264 ■ *Web:* www.sepaq.com	QC	G1W4S3	418-659-5264	646-9238
Pier Aquarium 800 2nd Ave NE 2nd Fl . . . . Saint Petersburg *Web:* www.stpete-pier.com/pieraquarium.php?LID=3	FL	33701	727-895-7437	894-1212
Pittsburgh Zoo & PPG Aquarium 1 Wild Pl . . . . Pittsburgh *TF:* 800-474-4966 ■ *Web:* www.pittsburghzoo.com	PA	15206	412-665-3639	665-3661
Point Defiance Zoo & Aquarium 5400 N Pearl St . . . . Tacoma *Web:* www.pdza.org	WA	98407	253-591-5337	591-5448
Ripley's Aquarium 1110 Celebrity Cir. . . . . Myrtle Beach *TF:* 800-734-8888 ■ *Web:* www.myrtlebeach.ripleyaquariums.com	SC	29577	843-916-0888	916-0752
Sea Life Park 41-202 Kalanianaole Hwy Suite 7. . . . . Waimanalo *TF:* 866-365-7446 ■ *Web:* www.sealifeparkhawaii.com	HI	96795	808-259-2500	259-7373
Seattle Aquarium 1483 Alaskan Way Pier 59. . . . . Seattle *Web:* www.seattleaquarium.org	WA	98101	206-386-4300	386-4328
SeaWorld Orlando 7007 Sea World Dr . . . . Orlando **Fax:* Cust Svc ■ *TF:* 800-327-2424 ■ *Web:* www.seaworldorlando.com	FL	32821	407-351-3600	363-2409*
SeaWorld San Antonio 10500 SeaWorld Dr. . . . . San Antonio **Fax:* Mktg ■ *TF:* 800-700-7786 ■ *Web:* www.seaworld.com	TX	78251	210-523-3000	523-3199*
South Carolina Aquarium 100 Aquarium Wharf. . . . . Charleston *TF:* 800-722-6455 ■ *Web:* www.scaquarium.org	SC	29401	843-720-1990	579-8511
Steinhart Aquarium *California Academy of Sciences* 55 Music Concourse Dr. . . . . San Francisco *Web:* www.calacademy.org/aquarium	CA	94118	415-321-8000	321-8610
Tennessee Aquarium 1 Broad St . . . . Chattanooga *TF:* 800-262-0695 ■ *Web:* www.tennis.org	TN	37401	423-265-0695	267-3561
Texas State Aquarium 2710 N Shoreline Blvd . . . . Corpus Christi *TF:* 800-477-4853 ■ *Web:* www.texasstateaquarium.org	TX	78402	361-881-1200	881-1257
University of Georgia Aquarium 30 Ocean Science Cir . . . . Savannah *Web:* www.marex.uga.edu/aquarium	GA	31411	912-598-2496	598-2302
Vancouver Aquarium Marine Science Ctr 845 Avison Way . . . . Vancouver *TF:* 800-931-1186 ■ *Web:* www.vanaqua.org	BC	V6G3E2	604-659-3474	659-3515
Waikiki Aquarium 2777 Kalakaua Ave . . . . Honolulu *Web:* www.waquarium.org	HI	96815	808-923-9741	923-1771
ZooQuarium 674 Rt 28 . . . . West Yarmouth *Web:* www.zooquariumcapecod.net	MA	02673	508-775-8883	

41 ARBITRATION SERVICES - LEGAL

	City	State	ZIP	Phone	Fax
American Arbitration Assn Inc (AAA) 1633 Broadway 10th Fl *TF:* 800-778-7879 ■ *Web:* www.adr.org	New York	NY	10019	212-716-5800	716-5905
Arbitration Forums Inc 3350 Buschwood Pk Dr Suite 295 *TF Cust Svc:* 800-967-8889 ■ *Web:* www.arbfile.org	Tampa	FL	33618	813-931-4004	931-4618
Council of Better Business Bureaus Inc *Dispute Resolution Services & Mediation Training* 4200 Wilson Blvd Suite 800 *TF:* 800-537-4600 ■ *Web:* www.dr.bbb.org	Arlington	VA	22203	703-276-0100	525-8277
CPR Institute for Dispute Resolution 575 Lexington Ave 21st Fl *Web:* www.cpradr.org	New York	NY	10022	212-949-6490	949-8859
Federal Mediation & Conciliation Service 2100 K St NW *Web:* www.fmcs.gov	Washington	DC	20427	202-606-8100	606-4251
Inland Valley Arbitration & Mediation Service (IVAMS) 8287 White Oak Ave *TF:* 800-944-8267 ■ *Web:* www.ivams.com	Rancho Cucamonga	CA	91730	909-466-1665	466-1796
JAMS/Endispute 500 N State College Blvd Suite 600 *TF:* 800-352-5267 ■ *Web:* www.jamsadr.com	Orange	CA	92868	714-939-1300	939-1787
Judicate West 1851 E 1st St Suite 1450 *TF:* 800-488-8805 ■ *Web:* www.adjudicateinc.com	Santa Ana	CA	92705	714-834-1340	834-1344
National Arbitration & Mediation 990 Stewart Ave *TF:* 800-358-2550 ■ *Web:* www.namadr.com	Garden City	NY	11530	516-794-8950	794-8518
Resolute Systems Inc 1550 N Prospect Ave *TF:* 800-776-6060 ■ *Web:* www.resolutesystems.com	Milwaukee	WI	53202	414-276-4774	270-0932

ARCHITECTS

SEE Engineering & Design p. 1823

ART - COMMERCIAL

SEE Graphic Design p. 1999

42 ART DEALERS & GALLERIES

	City	State	ZIP	Phone	Fax
Abbozzo Gallery 179 Lakeshore Rd E *TF:* 866-844-4481 ■ *Web:* www.abbozzogallery.com	Oakville	ON	L6J1H5	905-844-4481	844-2036
ACA Galleries 529 W 20th St 5th Fl *Web:* www.acagalleries.com	New York	NY	10011	212-206-8080	206-8498
Acquavella Galleries Inc 18 E 79th St *Web:* www.acquavellagalleries.com	New York	NY	10075	212-734-6300	794-9394
Adams Davidson Galleries 2727 29th St NW Suite 504 *Web:* www.adgal.com	Washington	DC	20008	202-965-3800	265-3395
Albert White Gallery 80 Spadina Ave Suite 208	Toronto	ON	M5V2J4	416-703-1021	703-1675
Aldis Browne Fine Arts 1614 Crescent Pl	Venice	CA	90291	310-301-6976	301-0698
Alexander & Bonin LLC 132 10th Ave *Web:* www.alexanderandbonin.com	New York	NY	10011	212-367-7474	367-7337
Allan Stone Gallery 113 E 90th St *Web:* www.allanstonegallery.com	New York	NY	10128	212-987-4997	987-1655
Alpha Gallery 38 Newbury St *Web:* www.alphagallery.com	Boston	MA	02116	617-536-4465	536-5695
Angles Gallery 2754 S La Cienega Blvd *Web:* www.anglesgallery.com	Los Angeles	CA	90034	310-396-5019	202-6330
Anna Kustera Gallery 520 W 21st St *Web:* www.annakustera.com	New York	NY	10011	212-989-0082	989-0456
Art Emporium 2928 Granville St *Web:* www.theartemporium.ca	Vancouver	BC	V6H3J7	604-738-3510	733-5427
Art Placement Inc 228 3rd Ave S Suite 228 *Web:* www.artplacement.com	Saskatoon	SK	S7K1L9	306-664-3385	933-2521
Atelier Gallery 2421 Granville St	Vancouver	BC	V6H3G5	604-732-3021	
Babcock Galleries 724 5th Ave 11th Fl *Web:* www.artnet.com	New York	NY	10019	212-767-1852	767-1857
Barbara Gladstone Gallery 515 W 24th St *Web:* www.gladstonegallery.com	New York	NY	10011	212-206-9300	206-9301
Barbara Krakow Gallery 10 Newbury St 5th Fl *Web:* www.barbarakrakowgallery.com	Boston	MA	02116	617-262-4490	262-8971
Barbara Mathes Gallery 22 E 80th St *Web:* www.bmathesgallery.com	New York	NY	10075	212-570-4190	570-4191
Bau-Xi Gallery 3045 Granville St *Web:* www.bau-xi.com	Vancouver	BC	V6H3J9	604-733-7011	733-3211
Beckett Fine Art Ltd 33 Hazelton Ave Suite 212 *Web:* www.beckettfineart.com	Toronto	ON	M5R2E3	416-922-5582	922-9869
Berry-Hill Galleries Inc 11 E 70th St *Web:* www.berry-hill.com	New York	NY	10021	212-744-2300	744-2838
Brooke Alexander Editions 59 Wooster St *Web:* www.baeditions.com	New York	NY	10012	212-925-4338	941-9565
Buschlen Mowatt Fine Arts Ltd 1445 W Georgia St *TF:* 800-663-8071 ■ *Web:* www.buschlenmowatt.com	Vancouver	BC	V6G2T3	604-682-1234	682-6004
Catriona Jeffries Gallery 274 E 1st Ave *Web:* www.catrionajeffries.com	Vancouver	BC	V5T1A6	604-736-1554	736-1054
Charles Cowles Gallery Inc 537 W 24th St *Web:* www.cowlesgallery.com	New York	NY	10011	212-741-8999	741-6222
Cheim & Read 547 W 25th St *Web:* www.cheimread.com	New York	NY	10001	212-242-7727	242-7737
Christopher Cutts Gallery 21 Morrow Ave *Web:* www.cuttsgallery.com	Toronto	ON	M6R2H9	416-532-5566	532-7272
Conner Rosenkranz LLC 19 E 74th St *Web:* www.crsculpture.com	New York	NY	10021	212-517-3710	734-7678
Corkin Shopland Gallery 55 Mill St Bldg 61 *Web:* www.corkingallery.com	Toronto	ON	M5A3C4	416-979-1980	979-7018
CRG Gallery 548 W 22nd St *Web:* www.crggallery.com	New York	NY	10011	212-229-2766	229-2788
D'Amelio Terras 525 W 22nd St *Web:* www.damelioterras.com	New York	NY	10011	212-352-9460	352-9464
Danese 535 W 24th St 6th Fl *Web:* www.danese.com	New York	NY	10011	212-223-2227	605-1016
David Findlay Galleries Inc 984 Madison Ave *Web:* www.davidfindlaygalleries.com	New York	NY	10075	212-249-2909	249-2912
David Findlay Jr Fine Art 41 E 57th St Suite 1120 *Web:* www.davidfindlayjr.com	New York	NY	10022	212-486-7660	486-6377
David Nolan Gallery 527 W 29th St *Web:* www.davidnolangallery.com	New York	NY	10001	212-925-6190	334-9139
David Tunick Inc 19 E 66th St *Web:* www.tunickart.com	New York	NY	10065	212-570-0090	744-8931
David Zwirner Gallery 525 W 19th St *Web:* www.davidzwirner.com	New York	NY	10011	212-727-2070	727-2072
Davis & Langdale Co Inc 231 E 60th St	New York	NY	10022	212-838-0333	752-7764
Dickinson Roundell Inc 19 E 66th St *Web:* www.simondickinson.com	New York	NY	10065	212-772-8083	772-8186
Didier Aaron Inc 32 E 67th St *Web:* www.didieraaron.com	New York	NY	10021	212-988-5248	737-3513
Donald Young Gallery 224 S Michigan Ave Suite 266 *Web:* www.donaldyoung.com	Chicago	IL	60604	312-322-3600	322-3033
Douglas Udell Gallery 10332 124th St *Web:* www.douglasudellgallery.com	Edmonton	AB	T5N1R2	780-488-4445	488-8335
Drabinsky Gallery 114 Yorkville Ave *Web:* www.drabinskygallery.com	Toronto	ON	M5R1B9	416-324-5766	324-5770
Edward Day Gallery Inc 952 Queen St W *Web:* www.edwarddaygallery.com	Toronto	ON	M6J1G8	416-921-6540	
Edwynn Houk Gallery 745 5th Ave 4th Fl *Web:* www.houkgallery.com	New York	NY	10151	212-750-7070	688-4848
Elkon Gallery Inc 18 E 81st St Suite 2-A	New York	NY	10028	212-535-3940	737-8479
Equinox Gallery 2321 Granville St *Web:* www.equinoxgallery.com	Vancouver	BC	V6H3G4	604-736-2405	736-0464
EV Thaw & Co Inc 726 Pk Ave	New York	NY	10021	212-535-6333	535-1465
Feheley Fine Arts 14 Hazelton Ave *Web:* www.feheleyfinearts.com	Toronto	ON	M5R2E2	416-323-1373	323-0121
Fischbach Gallery 210 11th Ave *Web:* www.fischbachgallery.com	New York	NY	10001	212-759-2345	366-1783
Forum Gallery 730 5th Ave *Web:* www.forumgallery.com	New York	NY	10019	212-355-4545	355-4547
Fraenkel Gallery 49 Geary St *Web:* www.artnet.com	San Francisco	CA	94108	415-981-2661	981-4014
Friedrich Petzel Gallery 535 W 22nd St *Web:* www.petzel.com	New York	NY	10011	212-680-9467	680-9473
Galerie Lelong 528 W 26th St *Web:* www.galerie-lelong.com	New York	NY	10001	212-315-0470	262-0624
Galerie Saint Etienne 24 W 57th St *Web:* www.gseart.com	New York	NY	10019	212-245-6734	765-8493
Galerie Valentin 1490 Sherbrooke Quest Suite 200 *Web:* www.galerievalentin.com	Montreal	QC	H3G1L3	514-939-0500	939-0413
Galerie Walter Klinkhoff Inc 1200 Sherbrooke St W *Web:* www.klinkhoff.com	Montreal	QC	H3A1H6	514-288-7306	288-5972
Gallery 78 Inc 796 Queen St *TF:* 888-883-8322 ■ *Web:* www.gallery78.com	Fredericton	NB	E3B1C6	506-454-5192	443-0199
Gallery Moos Ltd 622 Richmond St W *Web:* www.gallerymoos.com	Toronto	ON	M5V1Y9	416-504-5445	504-5446
Gallery One 121 Scollard St *Web:* www.artgalleryone.com	Toronto	ON	M5R1G4	416-929-3103	929-0278
Gallery Paule Anglim 14 Geary St *Web:* www.gallerypauleanglim.com	San Francisco	CA	94108	415-433-2710	433-1501
George Adams Gallery 525 W 26th St *Web:* www.artnet.com	New York	NY	10001	212-564-8480	564-8485
Greenberg Van Doren Gallery 3540 Washington Ave *Web:* www.greenbergvandoren.com	Saint Louis	MO	63103	314-361-7600	361-7743
Greenberg Van Doren Gallery 730 5th Ave 7th Fl *Web:* www.agvdgallery.com	New York	NY	10019	212-445-0444	445-0442
Hans P Kraus Jr Inc 962 Pk Ave	New York	NY	10028	212-794-2064	744-2770
Heffel Gallery Ltd 2247 Granville St *TF:* 800-528-9608 ■ *Web:* www.heffel.com/gallery	Vancouver	BC	V6H3G1	604-732-6505	732-4245
Hirschl & Adler Galleries Inc 730 5th Ave *Web:* www.hirschlandadler.com	New York	NY	10019	212-535-8810	772-7237
Houston North Gallery 110 Montague St PO Box 1055 *TF:* 866-634-8869 ■ *Web:* www.houston-north-gallery.ns.ca	Lunenburg	NS	B0J2C0	902-634-8869	634-8332
Inuit Gallery of Vancouver Ltd 206 Cambie St Gastown *TF:* 888-615-8399 ■ *Web:* www.inuit.com	Vancouver	BC	V6B2M9	604-688-7323	
Jack Kilgore & Co Inc 154 E 71st St 3rd Fl	New York	NY	10021	212-650-1149	650-1389
Jack Tilton Gallery 8 E 76th St *Web:* www.jacktiltongallery.com	New York	NY	10021	212-737-2221	396-1725
James Goodman Gallery 41 E 57th St Suite 802 *Web:* www.jamesgoodmangallery.com	New York	NY	10022	212-593-3737	980-0195
James Graham & Sons Inc 32 E 67th St *Web:* www.jamesgrahamandsons.com	New York	NY	10065	212-535-5767	794-2454
Jason McCoy Inc 595 Madison Ave # 1100 *Web:* www.jasonmccoyinc.com	New York	NY	10022	212-319-1996	319-4799
Jill Newhouse Gallery 4 E 81st St *Web:* www.jillnewhouse.com	New York	NY	10028	212-249-9216	734-4098
John Berggruen Gallery 228 Grant Ave *Web:* www.berggruen.com	San Francisco	CA	94108	415-781-4629	781-0126
June Kelly Gallery 166 Mercer St # 3C *Web:* www.junekellygallery.com	New York	NY	10012	212-226-1660	226-2433
Kinsman Robinson Galleries 108 Cumberland St *Web:* www.kinsmanrobinson.com	Toronto	ON	M5R1A6	416-964-2374	964-9042
Kinz & Tillou Fine Art 20 Beekman Pl Suite 8-A *Web:* www.ktfineart.com	New York	NY	10022	212-929-0500	929-0065

				Phone	Fax
Knoedler & Co 19 E 70th St	New York	NY	10021	212-794-0550	772-6932
Web: www.knoedlergallery.com					
Kraushaar Galleries Inc 74 E 79th St Suite 9B	New York	NY	10021	212-288-2558	288-2557
Web: www.kraushaargalleries.com					
L & M Arts 45 E 78th St	New York	NY	10075	212-861-0020	861-7858
Web: www.lmgallery.com					
LA Louver Inc 45 N Venice Blvd	Venice	CA	90291	310-822-4955	821-7529
Web: www.lalouver.com					
Laurence Miller Gallery 20 W 57th St 3rd Fl	New York	NY	10019	212-246-5360	397-3932
Lennon Weinberg Inc 514 W 25th St	New York	NY	10001	212-941-0012	929-3265
Web: www.lennonweinberg.com					
Leo Castelli Gallery 18 E 77th St	New York	NY	10021	212-249-4470	249-5220
Web: www.castelligallery.com					
Leo Kamen Gallery 80 Spadina Ave Suite 406	Toronto	ON	M5V2J4	416-504-9515	504-3194
Web: www.leokamengallery.com					
Leonard Hutton Galleries 41 E 57th St	New York	NY	10022	212-751-7373	832-2261
Web: www.leonardhuttongalleries.com					
Leslie Tonkonow Artworks & Projects 535 W 22nd St 6th Fl	New York	NY	10011	212-255-8450	414-8744
Web: www.tonkonow.com					
Lillian Heidenberg Fine Art 45 E 66th St	New York	NY	10021	212-628-6110	628-4958
Locks Gallery 600 Washington Sq S	Philadelphia	PA	19106	215-629-1000	629-3868
Web: www.locksgallery.com					
Luhring Augustine Gallery 531 W 24th St	New York	NY	10011	212-206-9100	206-9055
Web: www.luhringaugustine.com					
Manny Silverman Gallery 619 N Almont Dr	Los Angeles	CA	90069	310-659-8256	659-1001
Margo Leavin Gallery 812 N Robertson Blvd	Los Angeles	CA	90069	310-273-0603	273-9131
Web: www.margoleavingallery.com					
Marian Goodman Gallery 24 W 57th St	New York	NY	10019	212-977-7160	581-5187
Web: www.mariangoodman.com					
Mary Boone Gallery 541 W 24th St	New York	NY	10001	212-752-2929	752-3939
Web: www.maryboonegallery.com					
Mary Ryan Gallery 527 W 26th St 2nd Fl	New York	NY	10001	212-397-0669	397-0766
Web: www.maryryangallery.com					
Mary-Anne Martin Fine Art 23 E 73rd St 4th Fl	New York	NY	10021	212-288-2213	861-7656
Web: www.mamfa.com					
Masters Gallery Ltd 2115 4th St SW	Calgary	AB	T2S1W8	403-245-2064	244-1636
TF: 866-245-0616 ■ *Web:* www.mastersgalleryltd.com					
Matthew Marks Gallery 523 W 24th St	New York	NY	10011	212-243-0200	243-0047
Web: www.matthewmarks.com					
Maxwell Davidson Gallery 724 5th Ave 4th Fl	New York	NY	10019	212-759-7555	759-5824
Web: www.davidsongallery.com					
McKee Gallery 745 5th Ave 4th Fl	New York	NY	10151	212-688-5951	752-5638
Web: www.mckeegallery.com					
Meredith Long & Co 2323 San Felipe Blvd	Houston	TX	77019	713-523-6671	523-2355
Web: www.meredithlonggallery.com					
Metro Pictures Gallery 519 W 24th St	New York	NY	10011	212-206-7100	337-0070
Web: www.artnet.com/metropictures.html					
Meyer East Gallery 225 Canyon Rd	Santa Fe	NM	87501	505-983-1657	988-9867
Web: www.meyereastgallery.com					
Michael Gibson Gallery 157 Carling St	London	ON	N6A1H5	519-439-0451	439-2842
TF: 866-644-2766 ■ *Web:* www.gibsongallery.com					
Michael Rosenfeld Gallery 24 W 57th St 7th Fl	New York	NY	10019	212-247-0082	247-0402
Web: www.michaelrosenfeldart.com					
Michael Werner Gallery 4 E 77th St 2nd Fl	New York	NY	10075	212-988-1623	988-1774
Web: www.michaelwerner.com					
Mira Godard Gallery 22 Hazelton Ave	Toronto	ON	M5R2E2	416-964-8197	964-5912
Web: www.godardgallery.com					
Miriam Shiell Fine Art Ltd 16-A Hazelton Ave	Toronto	ON	M5R2E2	416-925-2461	925-2471
Web: www.miriamshiell.com					
Mitchell-Iness & Nash Gallery 1018 Madison Ave	New York	NY	10075	212-744-7400	744-7401
Web: www.miandn.com					
Modernism Inc 685 Market St Suite 290	San Francisco	CA	94105	415-541-0461	541-0425
Web: www.modernisminc.com					
Moeller Fine Art Ltd 36 E 64th St	New York	NY	10065	212-644-2133	644-2134
Web: www.moellerart.com					
Montgomery Gallery 406 Jackson St	San Francisco	CA	94111	415-788-8300	788-5469
Web: www.montgomerygallery.com					
Nancy Hoffman Gallery 520 W 27th St	New York	NY	10001	212-966-6676	334-5078
Web: www.nancyhoffmangallery.com					
Newzones Gallery of Contemporary Art 730 11th Ave SW	Calgary	AB	T2R0E4	403-266-1972	266-1987
Web: www.newzones.com					
Nohra Haime Gallery 41 E 57th St 6th Fl	New York	NY	10022	212-888-3550	888-7869
Nouveau Gallery 2146 Albert St	Regina	SK	S4P2T9	306-569-9279	352-2453
Web: www.nouveaugallery.com					
O'Hara Gallery 41 E 57th St Suite 1302	New York	NY	10022	212-355-3330	355-3361
Odon Wagner Gallery 196 Davenport Rd	Toronto	ON	M5R1J2	416-962-0438	962-1581
TF: 800-551-2465 ■ *Web:* www.odonwagnergallery.com					
Olga Korper Gallery 17 Morrow Ave	Toronto	ON	M6R2H9	416-538-8220	538-8772
Web: www.olgakorpergallery.com					
Otto Naumann Ltd 22 E 80th St 2nd Fl	New York	NY	10075	212-734-4443	535-0617
Web: www.dutchpaintings.com					
Pace Prints 32 E 57th St 3rd Fl	New York	NY	10022	212-421-3237	832-5162
TF: 877-440-7223 ■ *Web:* www.paceprints.com					
Pace Wildenstein 32 E 57th St 4th Fl	New York	NY	10022	212-421-3292	421-0835
Web: www.pacewildenstein.com					
Paul Kuhn Gallery 724 11th Ave SW	Calgary	AB	T2R0E4	403-263-1162	262-9426
Web: www.paulkuhngallery.com					
Paula Cooper Gallery 534 W 21st St	New York	NY	10011	212-255-1105	255-5156
Web: www.paulacoopergallery.com					
Peter Findlay Gallery 16 E 79th St	New York	NY	10075	212-644-4433	644-1675
Web: www.findlay.com					
Phyllis Kind Gallery 236 W 26th St Suite 503	New York	NY	10011	212-925-1200	941-7841
Web: www.phylliskindgallery.com					
Pilkington-Olsoff Fine Arts Inc 555 W 25th St	New York	NY	10001	212-647-1044	647-1043
Prime Gallery 52 McCaul St	Toronto	ON	M5T1V9	416-593-5750	593-0942
Rachel Adler Fine Art 24 E 71st St	New York	NY	10021	212-308-0511	308-0516
Web: www.racheladlerfineart.com					
Rena Bransten Gallery 77 Geary St	San Francisco	CA	94108	415-982-3292	982-1807
Web: www.renabranstengallery.com					
Rhona Hoffman Gallery 118 N Peoria St	Chicago	IL	60607	312-455-1990	455-1727
Web: www.artnet.com					
Richard Gray Gallery 875 N Michigan Ave Suite 2503	Chicago	IL	60611	312-642-8877	642-8488
Web: www.richardgraygallery.com					
Richard L Feigen & Co 34 E 69th St	New York	NY	10065	212-628-0700	249-4574
Web: www.rlfeigen.com					
Riva Yares Gallery 123 Grant Ave	Santa Fe	NM	07501	505-984-0330	986-8661
Web: www.rivayaresgallery.com					
Robert Miller Gallery 524 W 26th St	New York	NY	10001	212-366-4774	366-4454
Web: www.robertmillergallery.com					
Roberts Gallery Ltd 641 Yonge St	Toronto	ON	M4Y1Z9	416-924-8731	
Web: www.robertsgallery.net					
Ronald Feldman Fine Arts Inc 31 Mercer St	New York	NY	10013	212-226-3232	941-1536
Web: www.feldmangallery.com					
Russell Gallery of Fine Art 165 King St	Peterborough	ON	K9J2R8	705-743-0151	
Web: www.russellgallery.com					
S2 Art Group Ltd 1 W Superior St Suite 3102	Chicago	IL	60654	312-943-8500	943-8587
TF: 877-252-2122 ■ *Web:* www.jackgallery.com					
Schwarz Gallery 1806 Chestnut St	Philadelphia	PA	19103	215-563-4887	561-5621
Web: www.schwarzgallery.com					
Sikkema Jenkins & Co 530 W 22nd St	New York	NY	10011	212-929-2262	929-2340
Web: www.sikkemajenkinsco.com					
Sperone Westwater 257 Bowery	New York	NY	10002	212-999-7337	999-7338
Web: www.speronewestwater.com					
Stair Sainty Matthiesen Inc 22 E 80th St	New York	NY	10021	212-288-1088	628-2449
Web: www.europeanpaintings.com					
Stephen Bulger Gallery 1026 Queen St W	Toronto	ON	M6J1H6	416-504-0575	504-8929
Web: www.bulgergallery.com					
Stephen Mazoh & Co Inc 19 Pink Ln	Rhinebeck	NY	12572	845-876-2723	876-5838
Susan Hobbs Gallery Inc 137 Tecumseth St	Toronto	ON	M6J2H2	416-504-3699	504-8064
Web: www.susanhobbs.com					
Susan Sheehan Gallery 136 E 16th St	New York	NY	10003	212-489-3331	489-4009
Web: www.susansheehangallery.com					
Tasende Gallery 820 Prospect St	La Jolla	CA	92037	858-454-3691	454-0589
Web: www.tasendegallery.com					
Tatar Gallery 527 King St W Suite 300	Toronto	ON	M5V1K4	416-360-3822	362-3843
Web: www.tatargallery.com					
Thielsen Gallery 1038 Adelaide St N	London	ON	N5Y2M9	519-434-7681	434-8814
Web: www.thielsengallery.com					
Tibor de Nagy Gallery 724 5th Ave 12th Fl	New York	NY	10019	212-262-5050	262-1841
Web: www.tibordenagy.com					
TrepanierBaer Gallery 999 8th St SW Suite 105	Calgary	AB	T2R1J5	403-244-2066	244-2094
Web: www.trepanierbaer.com					
Ubu Gallery 416 E 59th St	New York	NY	10022	212-753-4444	753-4470
Web: www.ubugallery.com					
Uno Langmann Ltd 2117 Granville St	Vancouver	BC	V6H3E9	604-736-8825	
TF: 800-730-8825 ■ *Web:* www.langmann.com					
Valley House Gallery Inc 6616 Spring Valley Rd	Dallas	TX	75254	972-239-2441	239-1462
Web: www.valleyhouse.com					
Virginia Christopher Galleries Ltd 816 11th Ave SW	Calgary	AB	T2R0E5	403-263-4346	
Web: www.virginiachristopherfineart.com					
Vivian Horan Fine Art 35 E 67th St 2nd Fl	New York	NY	10021	212-517-9410	772-6107
Waddington & Gorce Inc 7 Jackes Ave Suite 1707	Toronto	ON	M4T1E3	416-929-5591	
Web: www.waddingtongorce.com					
Wallace Galleries Ltd 500 5th Ave SW	Calgary	AB	T2P3L5	403-262-8050	264-7112
Web: www.wallacegalleries.com					
West End Gallery Ltd 12308 Jasper Ave	Edmonton	AB	T5N3K5	780-488-4892	488-4893
Web: www.westendgalleryltd.com					
Winchester Galleries Ltd 2260 Oak Bay Ave	Victoria	BC	V8R1G7	250-595-2777	595-2310
Web: www.winchestergalleriesltd.com					
WM Brady & Co Inc 22 E 80th St 4th Fl	New York	NY	10075	212-249-7212	628-6587
Wynick Tuck Gallery 401 Richmond St W Unit 128	Toronto	ON	M5V3A8	416-504-8716	504-8699
Web: www.wynicktuckgallery.ca					
Zabriskie Gallery 41 E 57th St 4th Fl	New York	NY	10022	212-752-1223	752-1224
Web: www.zabriskiegallery.com					
Zolla Lieberman Gallery 325 W Huron St	Chicago	IL	60654	312-944-1990	944-8967
Web: www.zollaliebermangallery.com					
Zwickers Gallery 5415 Doyle St	Halifax	NS	B3J1H9	902-423-7662	422-3870
Web: www.zwickersgallery.ca					

43 ART MATERIALS & SUPPLIES - MFR

SEE ALSO Pens, Pencils, Parts p. 2391

				Phone	Fax
Adco Inc 12029 Denton Dr	Dallas	TX	75234	972-484-6177	484-1726
TF: 800-486-4583 ■ *Web:* www.gluestick.com					
Alvin & Co Inc 1335 Blue Hills Ave	Bloomfield	CT	06002	860-243-8991	777-2896*
**Fax Area Code: 800* ■ *TF:* 800-444-2584 ■ *Web:* www.alvinco.com					
American Art Clay Co (AMACO) 6060 Guion Rd	Indianapolis	IN	46254	317-244-6871	248-9300
TF: 800-374-1600 ■ *Web:* www.amaco.com					
American Mat & Frame Co 760 E Lambert Suite F	La Habra	CA	90631	562-697-4700	694-3875
TF: 800-537-0984					
American Metalcraft Inc 2074 George St	Melrose Park	IL	60160	708-345-1177	345-5758
TF: 800-333-9133 ■ *Web:* www.amnow.com					
Ampersand Art Supply 1500 E 4th St	Austin	TX	78702	512-322-0278	322-9928
TF: 800-822-1939 ■ *Web:* www.ampersandart.com					
ART Studio Clay Co 9320 Michigan Ave	Sturtevant	WI	53177	262-884-4278	884-4343
TF: 800-323-0212 ■ *Web:* www.artclay.com					

				Phone	Fax
Artist Brand Canvas 2448 Loma Ave	South El Monte	CA	91733	626-579-2740	686-2658*
*Fax Area Code: 323 ■ TF Orders: 888-579-2704 ■ Web: www.artistbrandcanvas.com					
Badger Air Brush Co 9128 Belmont Ave	Franklin Park	IL	60131	847-678-3104	671-4352
TF: 800-222-7553 ■ Web: www.badgerairbrush.com					
Binney & Smith Inc 1100 Church Ln	Easton	PA	18044	610-253-6271	250-5768
TF: 800-272-9652 ■ Web: www.binney-smith.com					
Canson Inc 21 Industrial Dr	South Hadley	MA	01075	413-538-9250	533-6554
TF: 800-628-9283 ■ Web: www.canson-us.com					
Chartpak Inc 1 River Rd	Leeds	MA	01053	413-584-5446	584-6781
TF: 800-628-1910 ■ Web: www.chartpak.com					
Daler-Rowney USA Ltd 2 Corporate Dr	Cranbury	NJ	08512	609-655-5252	655-5852
Web: www.daler-rowney.com					
DecoArt Inc 49 Cotton Ave	Stanford	KY	40484	606-365-3193	365-9739
TF: 800-367-3047 ■ Web: www.decoart.com					
Delta Creative Inc 2690 Pellissier Pl	City of Industry	CA	90601	562-695-7969	695-4227
TF: 800-423-4135 ■ Web: www.deltacreative.com					
Duncan Enterprises 5673 E Shields Ave	Fresno	CA	93727	559-291-4444	291-4444
TF: 800-438-6226 ■ Web: www.ilovetocreate.com					
Duro Art Industries Inc 1832 Juneway Terr	Chicago	IL	60626	773-743-3430	743-3882
TF Cust Svc: 800-621-5144 ■ Web: www.duroart.com					
Gare Inc 165 Rosemont St	Haverhill	MA	01832	978-373-9131	292-0885*
*Fax Area Code: 800 ■ TF: 888-511-4273 ■ Web: www.gare.com					
General Pencil Co Inc 3160 Bay Rd	Redwood City	CA	94063	650-369-4889	369-7169
Web: www.generalpencil.com					
Georgie's Ceramic & Clay Co Inc 756 NE Lombard St	Portland	OR	97211	503-283-1353	283-1387
TF: 800-999-2529 ■ Web: www.georgies.com					
Golden Artists Colors Inc 188 Bell Rd	New Berlin	NY	13411	607-847-6154	847-6767
TF: 800-959-6543 ■ Web: www.goldenpaints.com					
Houston Art 10770 Moss Ridge Rd	Houston	TX	77043	713-462-1086	462-1783
TF Cust Svc: 800-272-3804 ■ Web: www.houstonart.com					
Jack Richeson & Co Inc 557 Marcella Dr	Kimberly	WI	54136	920-738-0744	738-9156
TF: 800-233-2404 ■ Web: www.richesonart.com					
Martin/F Weber Co 2727 Southampton Rd	Philadelphia	PA	19154	215-677-5600	677-3336
Web: www.weberart.com					
National Artcraft Supply Co 7996 Darrow Rd	Twinsburg	OH	44087	330-963-6011	963-6711
TF Orders: 800-526-7419					
Paasche Airbrush Co 4311 N Normandy	Chicago	IL	60634	773-867-9191	867-9198
TF Sales: 800-621-1907 ■ Web: www.paascheairbrush.com					
Plaid Enterprises Inc 3225 Westech Dr	Norcross	GA	30092	678-291-8100	291-8368*
*Fax: Mktg ■ TF: 800-842-4197 ■ Web: www.plaidonline.com					
Royal Brush Mfg Inc 6707 Broadway	Merrillville	IN	46321	219-660-4170	660-4181
TF: 800-247-2211 ■ Web: www.royalbrush.com					
Sargent Art Inc 100 E Diamond Ave	Hazleton	PA	18201	570-454-3596	459-1752
TF: 800-424-3596 ■ Web: www.sargentart.com					
Sinopia Inc 3385 22nd St	San Francisco	CA	94110	415-824-3180	824-3280
Web: www.sinopia.com					
Smooth-On Inc 2000 St John St	Easton	PA	18042	610-252-5800	252-6200
TF: 800-766-6841 ■ Web: www.smooth-on.com					
Spraylat Corp One Shot LLC 1701 E 122nd St	Chicago	Il	60633	773-646-2778	646-3743
Web: www.1shot.com					
Tara Materials Inc 111 Fredrix Alley PO Box 646	Lawrenceville	GA	30046	800-241-8129	963-1044*
*Fax Area Code: 770 ■ TF: 800-241-8129 ■ Web: www.taramaterials.com					
Testor Corp 440 Blackhawk Pk Ave	Rockford	IL	61104	815-962-6654	962-7401
TF: 800-837-8677 ■ Web: www.testors.com					
Tri-Chem 681 Main St Bldg 24	Belleville	NJ	07109	973-751-9200	450-1260
Web: www.trichem.com					
Utrecht 6 Corporate Dr	Cranbury	NJ	08512	609-409-8001	409-8002
TF: 800-223-9132					

44 ART MATERIALS & SUPPLIES - WHOL

				Phone	Fax
American Hobby Craft Distributors Inc 2040 W N Ln	Phoenix	AZ	85021	602-861-1239	944-7124
Crafts Etc Ltd 7717 SW 44th St	Oklahoma City	OK	73179	405-745-1200	745-1225
TF: 800-888-0321					
Creative Hobbies Inc 900 Creek Rd	Bellmawr	NJ	08031	856-933-2540	992-7675*
*Fax Area Code: 800 ■ TF: 800-843-5456 ■ Web: www.creative-hobbies.com					
CWI Gifts & Crafts 77 Cypress St SW	Reynoldsburg	OH	43068	740-964-6210	964-6212
TF: 800-666-5858 ■ Web: www.shopcwi.com					
D & L Stained Glass Supply Inc 4939 N Broadway	Boulder	CO	80304	303-449-8737	442-3429
TF: 800-525-0940 ■ Web: www.dlstainedglass.com					
Darice Inc 13000 Darice Pkwy	Strongsville	OH	44149	440-238-9150	238-1680
TF: 800-321-1494 ■ Web: www.darice.com					
Decorator & Craft Corp (DC & C) 428 S Zelta St	Wichita	KS	67207	316-685-6265	685-7606
TF: 800-835-3013 ■ Web: www.dcccrafts.com					
Dumouchelle Art Galleries Co 409 E Jefferson Ave	Detroit	MI	48226	313-963-6255	963-8199
Web: www.dumouchelles.com					
Howell's Craftand Imports 6030 NE 112th Ave	Portland	OR	97220	503-255-2002	255-6878
TF: 800-547-0368 ■ Web: www.howells-craftland.com					
King Craft Co 142 N Main St PO Box 671	Herkimer	NY	13350	315-866-5500	866-8062
Web: www.kingcraftco.com					
MacPherson's-Artcraft 1351 Ocean Ave	Emeryville	CA	94608	510-428-9011	768-6630
TF Cust Svc: 800-289-9800 ■ Web: www.macphersonart.com					
Pioneer Wholesale Co 500 W Bagley Rd	Berea	OH	44017	440-234-5400	234-5403
TF: 888-234-5400 ■ Web: www.pioneerwholesaleco.com					
Sax Arts & Crafts Inc 2725 S Moorland Rd Suite 101	New Berlin	WI	53151	262-784-6880	328-4729*
*Fax Area Code: 800 ■ TF Cust Svc: 800-558-6696 ■ Web: www.schoolspecialty.com					
Sbar's Inc 14 Sbar Blvd	Moorestown	NJ	08057	856-234-8220	234-9159
TF: 800-989-7227 ■ Web: www.sbarsonline.com					
Sepp Leaf Products Inc 381 Pk Ave S Suite 1301	New York	NY	10016	212-683-2840	725-0308
TF: 800-971-7377 ■ Web: www.seppleaf.com					
Wholesale Art & Hobby Distributors Inc 7207 114th Ave N Suite CF	Largo	FL	33773	727-548-1999	548-7676
TF: 800-227-2520					
Zweigart-Joan Toggitt Ltd 262 Old New Brunswick Rd Suite E	Piscataway	NJ	08854	732-562-8888	562-8866
Web: www.zweigart.com					

45 ART SUPPLY STORES

				Phone	Fax
A & S Poliquin Inc 5401 6th Ave	Tacoma	WA	98406	253-759-9585	759-9713
Web: www.artcocrafts.com					
Aaron Bros Inc 1221 S Beltline Rd Suite 500	Coppell	TX	75019	214-492-6200	
TF: 888-372-6464 ■ Web: www.aaronbrothers.com					
AC Moore Arts & Crafts Inc 130 AC Moore Dr	Berlin	NJ	08009	856-768-4930	753-4723
NASDAQ: ACMR ■ Web: www.acmoore.com					
Al Friedman Co Inc 44 W 18th St 4th Fl	New York	NY	10011	212-243-9000	929-7320
TF: 800-204-6352 ■ Web: www.aifriedman.com					
Alabama Art Supply Inc 1006 23rd St S	Birmingham	AL	35205	205-322-4741	254-3116
TF Cust Svc: 800-749-4741 ■ Web: www.alabamaart.com					
All Media Art Supply 417 E Main St	Kent	OH	44240	330-678-8078	678-0794
Arizona Art Supply 118 W Indian School Rd	Phoenix	AZ	85013	602-264-9514	264-1009
Web: www.arizonaartsupply.com					
Art & Drafting Connection 2353 Schoenersville Rd	Bethlehem	PA	18017	610-882-0533	882-0566
Web: www.artanddrafting.com					
Art & Woodcrafters Supply 671 Hwy 165	Branson	MO	65616	417-335-8382	335-8367
TF Orders: 800-786-4818					
Art Corner 264 Washington St	Salem	MA	01970	978-745-9524	
Art Ctr 3101 E Yandell Dr	El Paso	TX	79903	915-566-2410	566-5628
Art Essentials 32 E Victoria St	Santa Barbara	CA	93101	805-965-5456	965-3347
TF: 877-965-5456 ■ Web: www.sbartessentials.com					
Art Hardware 402 S Nevada Ave	Colorado Springs	CO	80903	719-635-2348	635-4857
TF: 800-355-4229 ■ Web: www.arthardware.com					
Art Supply Headquarters Inc 707 Monroe St	Jackson	MS	39202	601-948-4141	353-7973
Art Supply Warehouse 6672 Westminster Blvd	Westminster	CA	92683	714-891-3626	895-6701
TF: 800-854-6467 ■ Web: www.artsupplywarehouse.com					
Artmart 2325 S Hanley Rd	Saint Louis	MO	63144	314-781-9999	781-3121
Web: www.artmartstl.com					
Asel Art Supply 2701 Cedar Springs	Dallas	TX	75201	214-871-2425	871-0007
TF: 888-273-5278 ■ Web: www.aselart.com					
Ben Franklin Stores Promotions Unlimited Corp 7601	Racine	WI	53408	262-681-7000	
TF: 800-992-9307 ■ Web: www.benfranklinstores.com					
Blaine's Art Supply 1025 photo Ave	Anchorage	AK	99503	907-561-5344	562-5988
Web: www.blainesart.com					
Brudno Art Supply 29 E Balbo Ave	Chicago	IL	60605	312-787-0030	341-1345
Web: www.brudnoartsupply.com					
Champion's Craft & Decorating 9750 Regency Sq Blvd	Jacksonville	FL	32225	904-725-3020	725-5489
Commercial Art Supply 935 Erie Blvd E	Syracuse	NY	13210	315-474-1000	474-5311
TF: 800-669-2787					
Continental Art Supplies 7041 Reseda Blvd	Reseda	CA	91335	818-345-1044	345-5004
TF: 800-499-5146 ■ Web: www.continentalart.com					
Crafts Frames & Things 108 Owen Dr	Fayetteville	NC	28304	910-485-4833	
Web: www.craftsframesandthings.com					
Deck The Walls Inc 221 First Executive Ave Suite 1280	Saint Peters	MO	63376	866-719-8200	
TF: 866-719-8200 ■ Web: www.deckthewalls.com					
Dick Blick Co 864 Enterprise Ave	Galesburg	IL	61401	309-343-6181	343-5785
TF: 800-447-8192 ■ Web: www.dickblick.com					
Douglas & Sturgess Inc 730 Bryant St	San Francisco	CA	94107	415-896-6283	896-6379
TF: 888-278-7883 ■ Web: www.artstuf.com					
Evergreen Art Works 3280 Middle Rd	Bettendorf	IA	52722	563-359-8324	359-8901
TF: 800-468-7280 ■ Web: www.bettoffice.com					
Fastframe USA Inc 1200 Lawrence Dr Suite 300	Newbury Park	CA	91320	805-498-4463	498-8983
TF: 888-863-7263 ■ Web: www.fastframe.com					
Flax Art & Design 240 Valley Dr	Brisbane	CA	94005	800-343-3529	352-9123
TF: 800-343-3529 ■ Web: www.flaxart.com					
Framing & Art Centre 1800 Appleby Line Rd	Burlington	ON	L7L6A1	800-563-7263	565-5755
TF: 800-563-7263 ■ Web: www.framingartcentre.com					
G & H Art Co 4300 Hamilton Rd	Columbus	GA	31904	706-576-5551	
Georgie's Ceramic & Clay Co Inc 756 NE Lombard St	Portland	OR	97211	503-283-1353	283-1387
TF: 800-999-2529 ■ Web: www.georgies.com					
Great Frame Up The 101 S Hanley Rd Suite 1280	Saint Louis	MO	63105	314-719-8200	
TF: 866-719-8200 ■ Web: www.greatframeup.com					
Herweck's Art & Drafting Supplies 300 Broadway St	San Antonio	TX	78205	210-227-1349	227-8533
TF: 800-725-1349 ■ Web: www.herwecks.com					
Hobby Lobby Creative Centers 7707 SW 44th St	Oklahoma City	OK	73179	405-745-1100	745-1547
Web: www.hobbylobby.com					
Hobbytown USA 1233 Libra Dr	Lincoln	NE	68512	402-434-5385	
TF Cust Svc: 800-869-0424 ■ Web: www.hobbytown.com					
Hungates Inc 102 Hungate Dr	Greenville	NC	27858	252-756-9565	756-2397
Jerry's Artarama 5325 Departure Dr	Raleigh	NC	27616	919-878-6782	873-9575
TF Cust Svc: 800-827-8478 ■ Web: www.jerrysartarama.com					
Lee's Art Shop Inc 220 W 57th St	New York	NY	10019	212-247-0110	247-0507
Web: www.leesartshop.com					
Michaels Stores Inc 8000 Bent Branch Dr	Irving	TX	75063	972-409-1300	409-7570*
*Fax: Hum Res ■ TF Cust Svc: 800-642-4235 ■ Web: www.michaels.com					
Millers Artist Supplies Co 33332 W 12 Mile Rd	Farmington Hills	MI	48334	248-489-8070	489-8643
Web: www.millersart.com					
National Art Shop 509 S National Ave	Springfield	MO	65802	417-866-3743	866-3748
New York Central Art Supply 62 3rd Ave	New York	NY	10003	212-473-7705	475-2513
TF: 800-950-6111 ■ Web: www.nycentralart.com					

	City	State	ZIP	Phone	Fax
Pat Catan's Craft Centers 21160 Drake Rd *TF:* 800-321-1494 ■ *Web:* www.patcatans.com	Strongsville	OH	44149	440-238-9150	238-8320
Plaza Art 633 Middleton St *Web:* www.plazaart.com	Nashville	TN	37203	615-254-3368	254-1814
Plaza Artists Materials of the MidAtlantic Inc 173 Madison Ave *TF:* 800-327-3200	New York	NY	10016	212-689-2870	689-3386
Rex Artist Supplies 3160 SW 22 St *TF:* 800-739-2782 ■ *Web:* www.rexart.com	Miami	FL	33145	305-445-1413	445-1412
Richards Art & Crafts 4502 Las Positas Rd *Web:* www.richardsartsandcrafts.com	Livermore	CA	94551	925-447-0471	447-0999
RISD Store Art Supplies 30 N Main St	Providence	RI	02903	401-454-6465	454-6453
Riverside Art Shop 1600 Grand Army Hwy *TF:* 800-354-9899 ■ *Web:* www.riversideart.com	Somerset	MA	02726	508-672-6735	672-6797
Spokane Art Supply Inc 1303 N Monroe St *TF:* 800-556-5568 ■ *Web:* www.spokaneartsupply.com	Spokane	WA	99201	509-327-6622	327-6629
Starvin' Artist Supplies 651 Graceland Ave *TF:* 800-427-8478 ■ *Web:* www.starvinartistsupply.com	Des Plaines	IL	60016	847-294-1300	795-8760
Suder's Art $tore 1309 Vine St	Cincinnati	OH	45202	513-241-0800	
Texas Art Supply 2001 Montrose Blvd *TF:* 800-888-9278 ■ *Web:* www.texasart.com	Houston	TX	77006	713-526-5221	524-7474
Thomson's Art Store 184 Mamaroneck Ave *TF:* 800-287-4885	White Plains	NY	10601	914-949-4885	949-4978
Top Notch Art Ctr 411 S Craig St	Pittsburgh	PA	15213	412-683-4444	683-2831
Trinity Ceramic Supply Inc 9016 Diplomacy Row *Web:* www.trinityceramic.com	Dallas	TX	75247	214-631-0540	637-6463
Village Art Supply 715 Hahman Dr *Web:* www.villageartsupply.com	Santa Rosa	CA	95405	707-575-4501	568-2112
Wet Paint Inc 1684 W Grand Ave *Web:* www.wetpaintart.com	Saint Paul	MN	55105	651-698-6431	698-8041
Woodcraft Supply LLC 1177 Rosemar Rd PO Box 1686 **Fax Area Code:* 304 ■ *TF:* 800-535-4482 ■ *Web:* www.woodcraft.com	Parkersburg	WV	26105	800-535-4482	428-8271*

46 ASPHALT PAVING & ROOFING MATERIALS

	City	State	ZIP	Phone	Fax
AE Stone Inc 1435 Doughty Rd *Web:* www.aestone.com	Egg Harbor Township	NJ	08234	609-641-2781	641-0374
American Asphalt Paving Co 500 Chase Rd *TF:* 800-326-9362 ■ *Web:* www.amerasphalt.com	Shavertown	PA	18708	570-696-1181	696-3486
Antioch Bldg Materials Co PO Box 870	Antioch	CA	94509	925-432-0171	432-9441
Asphalt Materials Inc PO Box 5 *Web:* asphaltmaterials.net	West Jordan	UT	84084	801-561-4231	561-7795
Atlas Roofing Corp 2322 Valley Rd *TF Cust Svc:* 800-478-0258 ■ *Web:* www.atlasroofing.com	Meridian	MS	39307	601-483-7111	483-7344
Baker Rock Resources 21880 SW Farmington Rd *TF:* 800-340-7621 ■ *Web:* www.baker-rock.com	Beaverton	OR	97007	503-642-2531	642-2534
Brannan Sand & Gravel Co 2500 Brannan Way *Web:* www.brannan1.com	Denver	CO	80229	303-534-1231	534-1231
Brewer Co 1354 US Hwy 50 *TF:* 800-394-0017 ■ *Web:* www.brewercote.com	Milford	OH	45150	513-576-6300	576-1414
Brox Industries Inc 1471 Methuen St *Web:* www.broxindustries.com	Dracut	MA	01826	978-454-9105	805-9720
Burkholder Paving 621 Martindale Rd **Fax Area Code:* 888 ■ *TF:* 866-839-3426 ■ *Web:* www.burkholderpaving.com	Ephrata	PA	17522	717-354-1340	428-7469*
Capitol Aggregates Ltd 12625 Wetmore Rd Suite 301 *TF:* 800-292-5315 ■ *Web:* www.capaggltd.com	San Antonio	TX	78247	210-871-6100	599-0560
CertainTeed Corp 750 E Swedesford Rd *TF Prod Info:* 800-782-8777 ■ *Web:* www.certainteed.com	Valley Forge	PA	19482	610-341-7000	341-7797
Coastal Bridge Co Llc 4825 Jamestown Ave PO Box 14715 *Web:* www.coastalbridge.com	Baton Rouge	LA	70898	225-766-0244	766-0423
Community Asphalt Corp 9725 NW 117 Ave Suite 110 *TF:* 800-741-0806 ■ *Web:* www.cacorp.net	Miami	FL	33178	305-884-9444	
Consolidated Fiberglass Products Co 3801 Standard St *Web:* www.conglas.com	Bakersfield	CA	93308	661-323-6026	324-2635
Coopers Creek Chemical Corp 884 River Rd *Web:* www.cooperscreekchemical.com	West Conshohocken	PA	19428	610-828-0375	828-9720
Crafco Inc 420 N Roosevelt Ave **Fax Area Code:* 480 ■ *TF:* 800-528-8242 ■ *Web:* www.crafco.com	Chandler	AZ	85226	602-276-0406	961-0513*
Dalrymple Gravel & Contracting Co Inc 2105 S Broadway *Web:* www.dalrymplecompanies.com	Pine City	NY	14871	607-737-6200	737-1056
Dalton Enterprises Inc 131 Willow St *TF:* 800-851-5606 ■ *Web:* www.latexite.com	Cheshire	CT	06410	203-272-3221	271-3396
Dewitt Products Co 5860 Plumer Ave *TF Cust Svc:* 800-962-8599 ■ *Web:* www.dewittproducts.com	Detroit	MI	48209	313-554-0575	554-2171
Fields Co LLC 2240 Taylor Way *TF:* 800-627-4098 ■ *Web:* www.fieldscorp.com	Tacoma	WA	98421	253-627-4098	383-2181
GAF Materials Corp 1361 Alps Rd **Fax:* Hum Res ■ *TF:* 800-365-7353 ■ *Web:* www.gaf.com	Wayne	NJ	07470	973-628-3000	628-3577*
Gardner Asphalt Corp PO Box 5449 *TF:* 800-237-1155	Tampa	FL	33675	813-248-2101	248-6768
Garland Co Inc 3800 E 91st St *TF:* 800-321-9336 ■ *Web:* www.garlandco.com	Cleveland	OH	44105	216-641-7500	641-0633
General Asphalt Co Inc 4850 NW 72nd Ave	Miami	FL	33166	305-592-3480	477-4675
Glenn O Hawbaker Inc 1952 Waddle Rd # 203 *TF:* 800-221-1355 ■ *Web:* www.goh-inc.com	State College	PA	16803	814-237-1444	
Granite Construction Inc 585 W Beach St *NYSE:* GVA ■ *Web:* www.graniteconstruction.com	Watsonville	CA	95076	831-724-1011	722-9657
Heely-Brown Co Inc 1280 Chattahoochee Ave *TF:* 800-241-4628 ■ *Web:* www.heelybrown.com	Atlanta	GA	30318	404-352-0022	350-2693
Hempt Bros Inc 205 Creek Rd	Camp Hill	PA	17011	717-737-3411	761-5019
Henry Co 909 N Sepulveda Blvd Suite 650 **Fax Area Code:* 866 ■ **Fax:* Cust Svc ■ *TF:* 800-598-7663 ■ *Web:* www.henry.com	El Segundo	CA	90245	310-955-9200	223-1285*
HRI Inc 1750 W College Ave *Web:* www.hrico.com	State College	PA	16801	814-238-5071	238-0131
Innovative Metals Co Inc (IMETCO) 2070 Steel Dr *TF:* 800-646-3826 ■ *Web:* www.imetco.com	Tucker	GA	30084	770-908-1030	908-2264
Jax Asphalt Inc PO Box 1725	Mount Vernon	IL	62864	618-244-0500	244-0833
Jd Ramming Paving Co Inc 16409 Bratton Ln *TF:* 877-251-3713 ■ *Web:* www.rammingpaving.com	Austin	TX	78728	512-251-3713	251-3709
Karnak Corp The 330 Central Ave *TF:* 800-526-4236 ■ *Web:* www.karnakcorp.com	Clark	NJ	07066	732-388-0300	388-9422
Kool Seal Inc 101 Prospect Ave NW **Fax Area Code:* 888 ■ *TF:* 888-321-5665 ■ *Web:* www.koolseal.com	Cleveland	OH	44115	330-425-4717	296-5665*
Koppers Inc 436 7th Ave *NYSE:* KOP ■ *TF:* 800-321-9876 ■ *Web:* www.koppers.com	Pittsburgh	PA	15219	412-227-2001	227-2333
Lunday-Thagard Co PO Box 1519	South Gate	CA	90280	562-928-7000	806-4032
Malarkey Roofing Products PO Box 17217 *TF:* 800-545-1191 ■ *Web:* www.malarkeyroofing.com	Portland	OR	97217	503-283-1191	289-7644
Marathon Petroleum LLC PO Box 1 *Web:* www.marathonpetroleum.com	Findlay	OH	45839	419-422-2121	425-7040
Martin Asphalt Co 3 Riverway Suite 400 *TF:* 800-662-0987 ■ *Web:* www.martinasphalt.com	South Houston	TX	77056	713-350-6800	350-6801
Midland Asphalt Materials Inc 640 Young St *TF:* 800-573-0400 ■ *Web:* www.midlandasphalt.com	Tonawanda	NY	14150	716-692-0730	692-0613
Mt. Carmel Stabilization Group Inc PO Box 458 *Web:* www.mtcsg.com	Mount Carmel	IL	62863	618-262-5118	263-4084
Neyra Industries 10700 Evendale Dr *TF:* 800-543-7077 ■ *Web:* www.neyra.com	Cincinnati	OH	45241	513-733-1000	733-3989
Oldcastle Materials Inc 900 Ashwood Pkwy Suite 700 *TF:* 800-241-7074 ■ *Web:* www.apac.com	Atlanta	GA	30338	770-552-5600	522-5008
Owatonna Construction Co 900 30th Pl PO Box 246	Owatonna	MN	55060	507-451-8950	451-8950
Pace Products Inc 4510 W 89th St Suite 110 *TF:* 888-389-8203 ■ *Web:* www.paceproducts.com	Prairie Village	KS	66207	913-469-5588	469-4067
Package Pavement Co Inc PO Box 408 *TF:* 800-724-8193 ■ *Web:* www.packagepavement.com	Stormville	NY	12582	845-221-2224	221-0433
Palmer Asphalt Co 196 W 5th St PO Box 58 *TF:* 800-352-9898 ■ *Web:* www.palmerasphalt.com	Bayonne	NJ	07002	201-339-0855	339-8320
Peckham Industries Inc 20 Haarlem Ave *Web:* www.peckham.com	White Plains	NY	10603	914-949-2000	949-2075
Pike Industries Inc 3 Eastgate Pk Rd *TF:* 800-283-7453 ■ *Web:* www.pikeindustries.com	Belmont	NH	03220	603-527-5100	527-5101
Rason Asphalt Inc PO Box 530	Old Bethpage	NY	11804	631-293-6210	293-6849
Russell Standard Corp 2 Prestley Rd *TF:* 800-323-3053 ■ *Web:* www.russellstandard.com	Bridgeville	PA	15017	412-221-7300	221-3811
Saint Gobain Technical Fabrics 1795 Baseline Rd *TF:* 800-762-6694 ■ *Web:* www.sgtf.com	Grand Island	NY	14072	716-775-3900	775-3901
Seaboard Asphalt Products Co 3601 Fairfield Rd *TF:* 800-536-0332 ■ *Web:* www.seaboardasphalt.com	Baltimore	MD	21226	410-355-0330	355-5864
Sika Sarnafil Inc 100 Dan Rd *TF:* 800-451-2504 ■ *Web:* usa.sarnafil.sika.com	Canton	MA	02021	781-828-5400	828-5365
Simon Roofing & Sheet Metal Corp 70 Karago Ave *TF:* 800-523-7714 ■ *Web:* www.simonroofing.com	Youngstown	OH	44512	330-629-7663	629-7399
South State Inc 202 Reeves Rd	Bridgeton	NJ	08302	856-451-5300	455-3461
Stavola Contracting PO Box 482 *Web:* www.stavola.com	Red Bank	NJ	07701	732-542-2328	389-6083
Suit-Kote Corp 1911 Lorings Crossing Rd *TF:* 800-622-5636 ■ *Web:* www.suit-kote.com	Cortland	NY	13045	607-753-1100	756-8611
Tilcon Connecticut Inc PO Box 1357 *Web:* www.tilconct.com	New Britain	CT	06050	860-224-6005	225-1865
Vaca Valley Roofing Inc 707 Aldridge Rd Suite A	Vacaville	CA	95688	707-469-7470	469-6248
Vance Bros Inc 5201 Brighton PO Box 300107 *TF:* 800-821-8549 ■ *Web:* www.vancebrothers.com	Kansas City	MO	64130	816-923-4325	923-6472
Vulcan Materials Co 1200 Urban Ctr Dr PO Box 385014 *NYSE:* VMC ■ *TF:* 800-615-4331 ■ *Web:* www.vulcanmaterials.com	Birmingham	AL	35238	205-298-3000	298-2942
Weldon Materials 141 Central Ave *Web:* www.weldonmat.com	Westfield	NJ	07090	908-233-4444	233-9440

47 ASSOCIATION MANAGEMENT COMPANIES

	City	State	ZIP	Phone	Fax
Able Management Solutions Inc 5310 E Main St Suite 104 *Web:* www.ablemgt.com	Columbus	OH	43213	614-868-1144	868-1177
Administrative Systems Inc 5204 Fairmount Ave Suite 208 *Web:* www.asihq.com	Downers Grove	IL	60515	630-655-0112	493-0798
Advanced Management Concepts 136 S Keowee St *Web:* www.advmgtconcepts.com	Dayton	OH	45402	937-222-1024	222-5794
Allen Marketing & Management 810 E 10th St PO Box 1897 *TF:* 800-627-0932	Lawrence	KS	66044	785-843-1235	843-1274
Alliance Management Group 1707 L St NW # 570 *Web:* www.alliancemg.com	Washington	DC	20036	202-293-7642	293-0495
Amber Assn Partners LLC 801 N Fairfax St Suite 211	Alexandria	VA	22314	703-299-0000	299-9233
AMR Management Services 201 E Main St Suite 1405 *Web:* www.amrms.com	Lexington	KY	40507	859-514-9150	514-9207

Company / Address	City	State	Zip	Phone	Fax
Applied Measurement Professionals Inc (AMP) 18000 W 105th St *Web:* www.goamp.com	Olathe	KS	66061	913-895-4600	895-4650
APT Inc 2900 E Broadway Suite 5 *Web:* www.aptnd.com	Bismarck	ND	58501	701-224-1815	224-9824
ARDEL Group PO Box 16377 **Fax Area Code:* 952 ■ *Web:* www.ardel.com	Minneapolis	MN	55416	763-765-2300	303-4060*
Assn & Society Management International Inc 201 Pk Washington Ct *Web:* www.asmii.com	Falls Church	VA	22046	703-533-0251	241-5603
Assn Assoc Inc Mercerville Rd Bldg B Suite 514 *Web:* www.hq4u.com	Trenton	NJ	08691	609-890-9207	581-8244
Assn Enterprise Inc (AE) 1601 N Bond St Suite 303 *Web:* www.associationenterprise.org	Naperville	IL	60563	630-369-3772	369-3773
Assn Headquarters Inc 15000 Commerce Pkwy Suite C *Web:* www.associationheadquarters.com	Mount Laurel	NJ	08054	856-439-0500	439-0525
Assn Insight 1255 SW Prairie Trail Pkwy *Web:* www.associationinsight.com	Ankeny	IA	50023	515-727-0648	251-8657
Assn Management & Communications 349 Granada Rd *Web:* www.association-management.net	West Palm Beach	FL	33401	561-802-4310	659-1824
Assn Management Centre PO Box 4143 *Web:* www.assocworldwide.com	Calgary	AB	T2T5M9	403-244-7831	244-4627
Assn Management Consultants Inc (AMC) 409 Granville St Suite 315 *TF:* 866-668-5344 ■ *Web:* www.amcdirectory.com	Vancouver	BC	V6C1T2	604-669-5344	669-5343
Assn Management Ctr 4700 W Lake Ave **Fax Area Code:* 866 ■ *Web:* www.connect2amc.com	Glenview	IL	60025	847-375-4700	586-7616*
Assn Management Group Inc (AMG) 8400 Westpark Dr 2nd Fl *Web:* www.amg-inc.com	McLean	VA	22102	703-610-9000	610-9005
Assn Management Ltd 100 E Grand Ave Suite 330 *Web:* www.aml.org	Des Moines	IA	50309	515-243-1558	243-2049
Assn Management Resources 2810 Industrial Plaza Dr Bldg C *Web:* www.mgmtresources.org	Tallahassee	FL	32301	850-656-8848	656-3038
Assn Management Solutions LLC (AMSL) 48377 Freemont Blvd Suite 117 *Web:* www.amsl.com	Fremont	CA	94538	510-492-4000	492-4001
Assn Management Specialists 275 E Hillcrest Dr Suite 215 *Web:* www.assoc-mgmt.net	Thousand Oaks	CA	91360	805-557-1111	557-1133
Assn Management Systems Inc 214 N Hale St *Web:* www.association-mgmt.com	Wheaton	IL	60187	630-510-4500	510-4501
Assn Managers Inc 12427 Hedges Run Dr Suite 104 *TF:* 800-403-3374 ■ *Web:* www.assnmgrs.com	Lake Ridge	VA	22192	703-426-8100	426-8400
Assn Resource Ctr 785 Orchard Dr *Web:* www.4arc.com	Folsom	CA	95630	916-932-2200	932-2209
Assn Resources Inc 342 N Main St *Web:* www.associationresources.com	West Hartford	CT	06117	860-586-7500	586-7550
Assn Solutions Ltd 1111 Burlington Ave Suite 102 *Web:* www.associationsolutions.com	Lisle	IL	60532	630-241-3100	241-0142
Assn Xpertise Inc 105-150 Crowfoot Crescent NW *Web:* www.axi.ca	Calgary	AB	T3G3T2	403-374-1822	374-1823
AssociationsFirst Ltd 39 River St *Web:* www.associationsfirst.com	Toronto	ON	M5A3P1	416-646-1600	646-9460
Bannister & Assoc Inc 34 N High St *Web:* www.bannister.com	New Albany	OH	43054	614-895-1355	895-3466
BB & C Assn Management Services 2233 Argentia Rd Suite 100 *Web:* www.bbandc.com	Mississauga	ON	L5N2X7	905-826-6665	826-4873
Bostrom Corp 230 E Ohio St Suite 400 *Web:* www.bostrom.com	Chicago	IL	60611	312-644-0828	644-8557
BTF Enterprises Inc 3540 Soquel Ave Suite A *Web:* www.btfenterprises.com	Santa Cruz	CA	95062	831-464-4880	464-4881
Calabrese Management 4305 N 6th St Suite A-2 *Web:* www.calabresemgt.com	Harrisburg	PA	17110	717-238-9989	238-9985
Capitol Consulting LLC 2302 N 3rd St PO Box 13116 *Web:* www.capitolconsultingaz.com	Phoenix	AZ	85004	602-712-1121	252-5265
Center for Assn Growth 1926 Waukegan Rd Suite 1 *TF:* 800-492-6462 ■ *Web:* www.tcag.com	Glenview	IL	60025	847-657-6700	657-6819
Center for Assn Resources Inc 1901 N Roselle Rd *TF:* 888-705-1434	Schaumburg	IL	60195	847-885-5680	885-5681
Challenge Management Inc (CMI) 4230 LBJ Fwy Suite 414 *Web:* www.challenge-management.com	Dallas	TX	75244	972-755-2560	755-2561
Clemons & Assoc Inc 5024 Campbell Blvd Suite R *Web:* www.clemonsmgmt.com	Baltimore	MD	21236	410-931-8100	931-8111
CM Services Inc 800 Roosevelt Rd Bldg C Suite 312 *TF:* 800-613-6672 ■ *Web:* www.cmservices.com	Glen Ellyn	IL	60137	630-858-7337	790-3095
Coulter Cos 1760 Old Meadow Rd Suite 500 *Web:* www.coultercos.com	McLean	VA	22102	703-506-3260	506-3266
Crow-Segal Management Co 341 N Maitland Ave Suite 130 *Web:* www.crowsegal.com	Maitland	FL	32751	407-647-8839	629-2502
Custom Management Group LLC 154 Hansen Rd *Web:* www.custommanagement.com	Charlottesville	VA	22911	434-971-4788	977-1856
Degnon Assoc Inc 6728 Old McLean Village Dr *Web:* www.degnon.org	McLean	VA	22101	703-556-9222	556-8729
DeSantis Management Group 1950 Old Tustin Ave *Web:* www.desantisgroup.com	Santa Ana	CA	92705	714-550-9155	550-9234
Diversified Management Services 525 SW 5th St Suite A *Web:* www.assoc-mgmt.com	Des Moines	IA	50309	515-282-8192	282-9117
Drake & Co 16020 Swingley Ridge Rd Suite 300 *Web:* www.drakeco.com	Chesterfield	MO	63017	636-449-5050	449-5051
Drohan Management Group (DMG) 12100 Sunset Hills Rd Suite 130 *Web:* www.drohanmgmt.com	Reston	VA	20190	703-437-4377	435-4390
Droz Group LLC 511 San Nicholas Ct *Web:* www.thedrozgroup.com	Laguna Beach	CA	92651	949-715-6932	715-6931
Ewald Consulting Group Inc 26 Exchange St E *Web:* www.ewald.com	Saint Paul	MN	55101	651-290-6260	290-2266
Executive Administration Inc 85 W Algonquin Rd Suite 550 *Web:* www.execadmin.com	Arlington Heights	IL	60005	847-427-9600	427-9656
Executive Director Inc 555 E Wells St Suite 1100 *Web:* www.execinc.com	Milwaukee	WI	53202	414-276-6445	276-3349
Executive Management Assoc 210 N Glenoaks Blvd Suite C *Web:* www.emaoffice.com	Burbank	CA	91502	818-843-5660	843-7423
Fanning Group Inc 1280 Main St 2nd Fl PO Box 479 *Web:* www.fanningnet.com	Hanson	MA	02341	781-293-4100	294-0808
Fernley & Fernley Inc 100 N 20th St 4th Fl *Web:* www.fernley.com	Philadelphia	PA	19103	215-564-3484	564-2175
Giuffrida Assoc Inc 204 E St NE *Web:* www.giuffrida.org	Washington	DC	20002	202-547-6340	547-6348
Grassley Group 409 Washington St Suite A **Fax Area Code:* 703 ■ *TF:* 866-619-5580	XwsE dlla	IA	50613	866-619-5580	342-0411*
Guild Assoc Inc 389 Main St Suite 202	Malden	MA	02148	781-397-8870	397-8887
Harrington Co 4248 Pk Glen Rd *Web:* www.harringtoncompany.com	Minneapolis	MN	55416	952-928-4666	929-1318
Hauck & Assoc Inc 1255 23rd St NW Suite 200 *Web:* www.hauck.com	Washington	DC	20037	202-452-8100	833-3636
IMI Assn Executives Inc 2501 Aerial Ctr Pkwy Suite 103 *Web:* www.imiae.com	Morrisville	NC	27560	919-459-2070	459-2075
Interactive Management Inc 3030 W 81st Ave *TF:* 800-243-1233 ■ *Web:* www.imigroup.org	Westminster	CO	80031	303-433-4446	458-0002
J Edgar Eubanks & Assoc 1 Windsor Cove Suite 305 *TF:* 800-445-8629 ■ *Web:* www.jee.com	Columbia	SC	29223	803-252-5646	765-0860
Kellen Co 1156 15th St NW Suite 900 *Web:* www.kellencompany.com	Washington	DC	20005	202-785-3232	331-2714
King Stringfellow Group 2105 Laurel Bush Rd Suite 200 *Web:* www.ksgroup.org	Bel Air	MD	21015	443-640-1030	640-1031
Lagniappe Assoc Inc 1016 Rosser St *Web:* www.lagniappeassociates.com	Conyers	GA	30012	770-388-7979	388-7722
Leading Associations 2640 W 26th Ave Suite 245-C *Web:* www.leadingassociations.com	Denver	CO	80211	720-259-3432	221-7242
LoBue & Majdalany Management Group 572B Ruger St PO Box 29920 *Web:* www.lm-mgmt.com	San Francisco	CA	94129	415-561-6110	561-6120
Madeleine Crouch & Co Inc 14070 Proton Rd Suite 100 *Web:* www.madcrouch.com	Dallas	TX	75244	972-233-9107	490-4219
Management Solutions Plus Inc 9707 Key W Ave Suite 100 *Web:* www.mgmtsol.com	Rockville	MD	20850	301-258-9210	990-9771
McBride & Assoc Inc 1633 Normandy Ct Suite A-200 *Web:* www.mcbridemanagement.com	Lincoln	NE	68512	402-476-3852	476-6547
Melby Cameron & Hull Co 23607 Hwy 99 Suite 2C PO Box 2016 *Web:* www.melbycameronhull.com	Edmonds	WA	98026	425-774-7479	771-9588
Milde Rollins & Assoc LLC 1712 Devonshire Rd **Fax Area Code:* 866	Sacramento	CA	95864	916-270-2023	746-3815*
Multiservice Management Co 994 Old Eagle School Rd Suite 1019 *Web:* www.mmco1.com	Wayne	PA	19087	610-971-4850	971-4859
National Administration Co 16476 Wild Horse Creek *TF:* 800-992-8044 ■ *Web:* www.egroupmanager.com	Chesterfield	MO	63017	636-530-7200	530-7777
NeuStar Secretariat Services 21575 Ridgetop Cir *Web:* www.foretec.com	Sterling	VA	20166	571-434-5729	434-5786
Offinger Management Co 1100-H Brandywine Blvd *Web:* www.offinger.com	Zanesville	OH	43701	740-452-4541	452-2552
Organization Management Group 638 Independence Pkwy Suite 100 *Web:* www.managegroup.com	Chesapeake	VA	23320	757-473-8701	473-9897
PAI Management Corp 5272 River Rd Suite 630 *Web:* www.paimgmt.com	Bethesda	MD	20816	301-656-4224	656-0989
Pathfinder Group 6009 Quinpool Rd Suite 700 *Web:* www.pathfinder-group.com	Halifax	NS	B3K5J7	902-425-2445	425-2441
Prime Management Services 3416 Primm Ln *Web:* www.primemanagement.net	Birmingham	AL	35216	205-823-6106	823-2760
Professional Management Assoc 390 Meanwell Rd Suite 402	Hillsbrough	NJ	08844	908-359-1184	359-7619

	City	State	Zip	Phone	Fax
Professional Management Assoc LLC 203 Towne Centre Dr *Web:* www.profmgmt.com	Hillsborough	NJ	08844	908-359-1184	359-7619
Queen Communications LLC 1215 Anthony Ave. *Web:* www.queencommunicationsllc.com	Columbia	SC	29201	803-779-0340	254-3773
R W Armstrong 300 S Meridian St. *TF:* 800-321-6959 ■ *Web:* www.rwa.com	Indianapolis	IN	46225	317-786-0461	788-0957
Raybourn Group International Inc 7150 Winton Dr Suite 300 *TF:* 800-362-2546 ■ *Web:* www.raybourn.com	Indianapolis	IN	46268	317-328-4421	280-8527
Rees Group Inc 2810 Crossroads Dr Suite 3800 *Web:* www.reesgroupinc.com	Madison	WI	53718	608-443-2468	443-2478
REM Assn Services 2001 Jefferson Davis Hwy Suite 1004 *Web:* www.remservices.biz	Arlington	VA	22202	703-416-0010	416-0014
Resource Center for Associations 10200 W 44th Ave Suite 304 *TF:* 877-382-7823 ■ *Web:* www.resourcenter.com	Wheat Ridge	CO	80033	303-422-2615	422-8894
Resource Management Plus Inc 100 N 20th St 4th Fl *TF:* 800-408-8951	Philadelphia	PA	19103	215-545-1985	545-8107
Robstan Group Inc 400 Admiral Blvd *Web:* www.robstan.com	Kansas City	MO	64106	816-472-8870	472-7765
Ruggles Service Corp 2209 Dickens Rd *Web:* www.societyhq.com	Richmond	VA	23230	804-282-0062	282-0090
S & S Management Services Inc 1 Regency Dr *Web:* www.ssmgt.com	Bloomfield	CT	06002	860-243-3977	286-0787
Sanford Organization Inc The (TSO) 1000 N Rand Rd Suite 214 *Web:* www.tso.net	Wauconda	IL	60084	847-526-2010	526-3993
Sherwood Group Inc 111 Deer Lake Rd Suite 100 *Web:* www.sherwood-group.com	Deerfield	IL	60015	847-480-9080	480-9282
SmithBucklin Corp 401 N Michigan Ave Suite 2200 *TF:* 800-539-9740 ■ *Web:* www.smithbucklin.com	Chicago	IL	60611	312-644-6610	245-1080
Solutions for Associations Inc 140 N Bloomingdale Rd *Web:* www.solutions-for-assoc.com	Bloomingdale	IL	60108	630-351-8669	351-8490
STAT Assn Marketing & Management Inc 11240 Waples Mill Rd Suite 200 *Web:* www.statmarketing.com	Fairfax	VA	22030	703-934-0160	359-7562
Synergy Resource Group Inc 491 3rd St SW **Fax Area Code:* 763 ■ *Web:* www.synergy-resource.com	Delano	MN	55328	612-619-4110	566-5780*
Talley Management Group Inc 19 Mantua Rd *TF:* 888-423-4233 ■ *Web:* www.talley.com	Mount Royal	NJ	08061	856-423-7222	423-3420
Technical Enterprises Inc 7044 S 13th St *Web:* www.techenterprises.net	Oak Creek	WI	53154	414-768-8000	768-8001
TH Management Inc 212 S Tryon St Suite 1150 *Web:* www.associationoffices.com	Charlotte	NC	28281	704-365-3622	365-3678
Thomas Assoc Inc 1300 Sumner Ave *Web:* www.taol.com	Cleveland	OH	44115	216-241-7333	241-0105
Total Management Solutions Inc 55 Harristown Rd *TF:* 866-544-0707 ■ *Web:* www.totmgtsol.com	Glen Rock	NJ	07452	201-447-0707	447-3831
Trade Assn Management Inc 25 N Broadway *Web:* www.taminc.com	Tarrytown	NY	10591	914-332-0040	332-1541
Verto Solutions 1620 'I' St NW Suite 925 *Web:* www.vertosolutions.net	Washington	DC	20006	202-293-5800	463-8998
Virtual Inc 401 Edgewater Pl Suite 600 *Web:* www.virtualmgmt.com	Wakefield	MA	01880	781-246-0500	224-1239
Wanner Assoc Inc 908 N 2nd St *Web:* www.wannerassoc.com	Harrisburg	PA	17102	717-236-2050	236-2046
Ward Management Group Inc 10293 N Meridian St Suite 175 *Web:* www.wardmanage.com	Indianapolis	IN	46290	317-816-1619	816-1633
Wherry Assoc Inc 30200 Detroit Rd *Web:* www.wherryassoc.com	Cleveland	OH	44145	440-899-0010	892-1404
Williams Management Resources Inc 1755 Pk St Suite 260 *Web:* www.wmrhq.com	Naperville	IL	60563	630-416-1166	416-9798
Willow Group 1485 Laperriere Ave. *Web:* www.thewillowgroup.com	Ottawa	ON	K1Z7S8	613-722-8796	729-6206
XMi Assn Management 618 Church St Suite 220 *Web:* www.xmi-amc.com	Nashville	TN	37219	615-254-3687	254-7047

48 ASSOCIATIONS & ORGANIZATIONS - GENERAL

SEE ALSO Performing Arts Organizations p. 2401; Political Action Committees p. 2436; Political Parties (Major) p. 2438

48-1 Accreditation & Certification Organizations

	City	State	Zip	Phone	Fax
AACSB International - Assn to Advance Collegiate Schools of Business 777 S Harbour Island Blvd Suite 750 *Web:* www.aacsb.edu	Tampa	FL	33602	813-769-6500	769-6559
ABET Inc 111 Market Pl Suite 1050 *Web:* www.abet.org	Baltimore	MD	21202	410-347-7700	625-2238
Accreditation Assn for Ambulatory Health Care (AAAHC) 5250 Old Orchard Rd Suite 200 *Web:* www.aaahc.org	Skokie	IL	60077	847-853-6060	853-9028
Accreditation Commission for Acupuncture & Oriental Medicine (ACAOM) 7501 Greenway Ctr Dr Suite 760 *Web:* www.acaom.org	Greenbelt	MD	20770	301-313-0855	313-0912
Accreditation Council for Accountancy & Taxation (ACAT) 1010 N Fairfax St *TF:* 888-289-7763 ■ *Web:* www.acatcredentials.org	Alexandria	VA	22314	703-549-2228	549-2984
Accreditation Council for Continuing Medical Education (ACCME) 515 N State St Suite 1801 *TF:* 800-475-2761 ■ *Web:* www.accme.org	Chicago	IL	60610	312-527-9200	410-9026
Accreditation Council for Graduate Medical Education (ACGME) 515 N State St Suite 2000 *Web:* www.acgme.org	Chicago	IL	60610	312-755-5000	755-7498
Accreditation Council for Pharmacy Education 20 N Clark St Suite 2500 *Web:* www.acpe-accredit.org	Chicago	IL	60602	312-664-3575	664-4652
Accreditation Council on Optometric Education (ACOE) 243 N Lindbergh Blvd *TF:* 800-365-2219 ■ *Web:* www.aoa.org	Saint Louis	MO	63141	314-991-4100	991-4101
Accreditation Review Commission on Education for the Physician Assistant Inc (ARC-PA) 12000 Findley Rd Suite 240 *Web:* www.arc-pa.org	Duluth	GA	30097	770-476-1224	476-1738
Accrediting Bureau of Health Education Schools (ABHES) 7777 Leesburg Pike Suite 314 N *Web:* www.abhes.org	Falls Church	VA	22043	703-917-9503	917-4109
Accrediting Commission of Career Schools & Colleges of Technology (ACCSCT) 2101 Wilson Blvd Suite 302 *Web:* www.accsct.org	Arlington	VA	22201	703-247-4212	247-4533
Accrediting Council for Continuing Education & Training (ACCET) 1722 N St NW *Web:* www.accet.org	Washington	DC	20036	202-955-1113	955-1118
Accrediting Council for Independent Colleges & Schools (ACICS) 750 1st St NE Suite 980 *Web:* www.acics.org	Washington	DC	20002	202-336-6780	842-2593
Accrediting Council on Education in Journalism & Mass Communications (ACEJMC) *Univ of Kansas School of Journalism Stauffer-Flint Hall* 1435 Jayhawk Blvd *Web:* www2.ku.edu	Lawrence	KS	66045	785-864-3973	864-5225
American Academy for Liberal Education (AALE) 1050 17th St NW Suite 400 *Web:* www.aale.org	Washington	DC	20036	202-452-8611	452-8620
American Assn for Accreditation of Ambulatory Surgery Facilities Inc (AAAASF) 5101 Washington St Suite 2F PO Box 9500 *TF:* 888-545-5222 ■ *Web:* www.aaaasf.org	Gurnee	IL	60031	847-775-1985	775-1985
American Assn for Laboratory Accreditation (A2LA) 5301 Buckeystown Pike Suite 350 *Web:* www.a2la.org	Frederick	MD	21704	301-644-3248	662-2974
American Board of Funeral Service Education (ABFSE) 3432 Ashland Ave Suite U *Web:* www.abfse.org	Saint Joseph	MO	64506	816-233-3747	233-3703
American Board of Internal Medicine (ABIM) 510 Walnut St Suite 1700 *TF:* 800-441-2246 ■ *Web:* www.abim.org	Philadelphia	PA	19106	215-446-3500	446-3590
American Board of Medical Specialties (ABMS) 1007 Church St Suite 404 *Web:* www.abms.org	Evanston	IL	60201	847-491-9091	328-3596
American College of Nurse-Midwives Div of Accreditation 8403 Colesville Rd Suite 1550 *Web:* www.midwife.org	Silver Spring	MD	20910	240-485-1800	485-1818
American Council for Construction Education (ACCE) 1717 FM 1044 Es *Web:* www.acce-hq.org	San Antonio	TX	78259	210-495-6161	495-6168
American Culinary Federation Inc (ACF) 180 Ctr Pl Way *TF:* 800-624-9458 ■ *Web:* www.acfchefs.org	Saint Augustine	FL	32095	904-824-4468	825-4758
American Library Assn Committee on Accreditation 50 E Huron St *TF:* 800-545-2433 ■ *Web:* www.ala.org/ala/accreditation	Chicago	IL	60611	312-944-6780	280-2433
American National Standards Institute (ANSI) 11 W 42nd St # 13 *Web:* www.ansi.org	New York	NY	10036	212-642-4900	398-0023
American Osteopathic Assn (AOA) 142 E Ontario St *TF:* 800-621-1773 ■ *Web:* www.osteopathic.org	Chicago	IL	60611	312-202-8000	202-8200
American Podiatric Medical Assn Inc (APMA) 9312 Old Georgetown Rd *TF:* 800-275-2762 ■ *Web:* www.apma.org	Bethesda	MD	20814	301-581-9200	571-4903
American Psychological Assn Committee on Accreditation 750 1st St NE *Web:* www.apa.org/ed	Washington	DC	20002	202-336-5979	336-5978
American Veterinary Medical Assn Council on Education 1931 N Meacham Rd Suite 100 *TF:* 800-248-2862 ■ *Web:* www.avma.org	Schaumburg	IL	60173	847-925-8070	925-1329
Assn for Assessment & Accreditation of Laboratory Animal Care International 5283 Corporate Dr Suite 203 *TF:* 800-926-0066 ■ *Web:* www.aaalac.org	Frederick	MD	21703	301-696-9626	696-9627
Assn for Biblical Higher Education (AABC) 5850 T G Lee Blvd # 130 *Web:* www.abhe.org	Orlando	FL	32822	407-207-0808	207-0840
Assn for Clinical Pastoral Education (ACPE) 1549 Clairmont Rd Suite 103 *Web:* www.acpe.edu	Decatur	GA	30033	404-320-1472	320-0849
Assn of Advanced Rabbinical & Talmudic Schools (AARTS) 11 Broadway	New York	NY	10004	212-363-1991	533-5335
Assn of Collegiate Business Schools & Programs (ACBSP) 7007 College Blvd Suite 420 *Web:* www.acbsp.org	Overland Park	KS	66211	913-339-9356	339-6226
Assn of Specialized & Professional Accreditors (ASPA) 3304 N Broadway St Suite 214 *Web:* www.aspa-usa.org	Chicago	IL	60657	773-857-7900	857-7901
Canadian Architectural Certification Board 1 Nicholas St Suite 710 *Web:* www.cacb-ccca.ca	Ottawa	ON	K1N7B7	613-241-8399	241-7991
Canadian Assn of Occupational Therapists (CAOT) 1125 Colonel By Dr *TF:* 800-434-2268 ■ *Web:* www.caot.ca	Ottawa	ON	K1S5R1	613-523-2268	523-2552

Phone Fax

Canadian Assn of Speech-Language Pathologists & Audiologists (CASLPA)
1 Nicholas St Suite 1000 .... Ottawa ON K1N7B7 613-567-9968 567-2859
TF: 800-259-8519 ■ *Web:* www.caslpa.ca/english
Canadian Council for Accreditation of Pharmacy Programs (CCAPP)
1765 W 8th Ave Suite 200 .... Vancouver BC V6J5C6 604-676-4230 676-4231
Web: www.ccapp-accredit.ca
Canadian Forestry Accreditation Board
18 Pommel Crescent .... Kanata ON K2M1A2 613-599-7259 599-8107
Web: www.cfab.ca
Canadian Information Processing Society (CIPS)
5090 Explorer Dr Suite 801 .... Mississauga ON L4W4T9 905-602-1370 602-7884
TF: 877-275-2477 ■ *Web:* www.cips.ca
Certified Financial Planner Board of Standards Inc
1425 K St NW Suite 500 .... Washington DC 20005 202-379-2200 379-2299
TF: 800-487-1497 ■ *Web:* www.cfp.net
CoAEMSP
4101 W Green Oaks Blvd Suite 305-599 .... Arlington TX 76016 817-330-0080 330-0089
Web: www.coaemsp.org
COLA 9881 Broken Land Pkwy Suite 200 .... Columbia MD 21046 410-381-6581 381-8611*
**Fax:* Hum Res ■ *TF:* 800-981-9883 ■ *Web:* www.cola.org
Commission on Accreditation for Dietetics Education (CADE)
120 S Riverside Plaza Suite 2000 .... Chicago IL 60606 312-899-0040 899-4758
TF: 800-877-1600 ■ *Web:* www.eatright.org
Commission on Accreditation for Law Enforcement Agencies (CALEA)
13575 Heathcote Blvd Suite 320 .... Fairfax VA 20155 703-352-4225 890-3126
TF: 800-368-3757 ■ *Web:* www.calea.org
Commission on Accreditation in Physical Therapy Education (CAPTE)
1111 N Fairfax St .... Alexandria VA 22314 703-706-3245 838-8910
TF: 800-999-2782 ■ *Web:* www.capteonline.org/home.aspx
Commission on Accreditation of Allied Health Education Programs (CAAHEP)
1361 Pk St .... Clearwater FL 33756 727-210-2350 210-2354
Web: www.caahep.org
Commission on Accreditation of Healthcare Management Education
2000 14th St N Suite 790 .... Arlington VA 22201 703-894-0960 894-0941
Commission on Accreditation of Rehabilitation Facilities International (CARF)
6951 E Southpoint Rd .... Tucson AZ 85756 520-325-1044 318-1129
TF: 888-281-6531 ■ *Web:* www.carf.org
Commission on Collegiate Nursing Education
1 Dupont Cir NW Suite 530 .... Washington DC 20036 202-887-6791 887-8476
Web: www.aacn.nche.edu
Commission on Dental Accreditation
211 E Chicago Ave 18th Fl .... Chicago IL 60611 312-440-2500 440-2800
TF: 800-621-8099 ■ *Web:* www.ada.org/prof/ed
Commission on Dental Accreditation of Canada
1815 Alta Vista Dr .... Ottawa ON K1G3Y6 613-523-7114 523-7736
TF: 866-521-2322 ■ *Web:* www.cda-adc.ca
Commission on English Language Program Accreditation (CEA)
801 N Fairfax St Suite 402A .... Alexandria VA 22314 703-519-2070 519-2071
Web: www.cea-accredit.org
Commission on Massage Therapy Accreditation
1007 Church St Suite 302 .... Evanston IL 60201 847-869-5039 869-6739
Web: www.comta.org
Commission on Opticianry Accreditation
PO Box 208 .... Hillsborough NC 27278 703-468-0566
Web: www.coaccreditation.com
Community Health Accreditation Program Inc (CHAP)
1275 K St NW # 800 .... Washington DC 20005 202-862-3413 862-3419
TF: 800-656-9656 ■ *Web:* www.chapinc.org
Continuing Care Accreditation Commission (CARF-CCAC)
1730 Rhode Island Ave NW Suite 209 .... Washington DC 20036 202-587-5001 587-5009
TF: 866-888-1122 ■ *Web:* www.carf.org
Council for Higher Education Accreditation (CHEA)
1 Dupont Cir NW Suite 510 .... Washington DC 20036 202-955-6126 955-6129
Web: www.chea.org
Council for Interior Design Accreditation
146 Monroe Ctr NW Suite 1318 .... Grand Rapids MI 49503 616-458-0400 458-0460
Web: www.accredit-id.org
Council of the Section of Legal Education & Admissions to the Bar
321 N Clark St 21st Fl .... Chicago IL 60654 312-988-6738 988-5681
Web: www.americanbar.org
Council on Academic Accreditation in Audiology & Speech-Language Pathology
2200 Research Blvd .... Rockville MD 20850 301-296-5700
TF: 800-498-2071 ■ *Web:* www.asha.org
Council on Accreditation (COA)
120 Wall St 11th Fl .... New York NY 10005 212-797-3000 797-1428
TF: 866-262-8088 ■ *Web:* www.coanet.org
Council on Accreditation of Nurse Anesthesia Educational Programs
222 S Prospect Ave .... Park Ridge IL 60068 847-692-7050 692-6968
Web: www.aana.com
Council on Aviation Accreditation (CAA)
Aviation Accreditation Board International
3410 Skyway Dr .... Auburn AL 36830 334-844-2431 844-2432
Web: www.aabi.aero
Council on Chiropractic Education Commission on Accreditation
8049 N 85th Way .... Scottsdale AZ 85258 480-443-8877 483-7333
Web: www.cce-usa.org
Council on Education for Public Health
800 I St NW Suite 202 .... Washington DC 20001 202-789-1050 789-1895
Web: www.ceph.org
Council on Naturopathic Medical Education
342 Main St .... Great Barrington MA 01230 413-528-8877 528-8880
Web: www.cnme.org
Council on Occupational Education
7840 Roswell Rd # 300-325 .... Atlanta GA 30350 770-396-3898 396-3790
TF: 800-917-2081 ■ *Web:* www.council.org
Council on Quality & Leadership The (CQL)
100 W Rd Suite 300-A .... Towson MD 21204 410-583-0060 583-0063
Web: www.thecouncil.org
Council on Rehabilitation Education Commission
1699 Woodfield Rd Suite 300 .... Schaumburg IL 60173 847-944-1345 944-1346
Web: www.core-rehab.org

Phone Fax

Distance Education & Training Council (DETC)
1601 18th St NW Suite 2 .... Washington DC 20009 202-234-5100 332-1386
Web: www.detc.org
Emergency Management Accreditation Program Inc (EMAP)
PO Box 11910 .... Lexington KY 40578 859-244-8222 244-8239
Web: www.emaponline.org
Engineers Canada 180 Elgin St Suite 1100 .... Ottawa ON K2P2K3 613-232-2474 230-5759
TF: 877-408-9273 ■ *Web:* www.engineerscanada.ca
Intersocietal Commission for the Accreditation of Vascular Laboratories (ICAVL)
8830 Stanford Blvd Suite 306 .... Columbia MD 21045 410-872-0100 872-0030
TF: 800-838-2110 ■ *Web:* www.icavl.org
Joint Commission on Accreditation of Healthcare Organizations (JCAHO)
1 Renaissance Blvd .... Oakbrook Terrace IL 60181 630-792-5000 792-5005
Web: www.jointcommission.org
Joint Review Committee on Education in Radiologic Technology (JRCERT)
20 N Wacker Dr Suite 2850 .... Chicago IL 60606 312-704-5300 704-5304
Web: www.jrcert.org
Joint Review Committee on Educational Programs in Nuclear Medicine Technology (JRCNMT)
2000 W Danforth Rd Suite 130 203 .... Edmond OK 73003 405-285-0546 285-0579
Web: www.jrcnmt.org
Landscape Architectural Accreditation Board (LAAB)
636 'I' St NW .... Washington DC 20001 202-898-2444 898-1185
Web: www.asla.org/nonmembers/education.cfm
Liaison Committee on Medical Education (LCME)
American Medical Assn 515 N State St .... Chicago IL 60610 312-464-4933 464-5830
TF: 800-621-8335 ■ *Web:* www.lcme.org
Middle States Commission on Higher Education
3624 Market St .... Philadelphia PA 19104 267-284-5000 662-5501*
**Fax Area Code:* 215 ■ *Web:* www.msche.org
Montessori Accreditation Council for Teacher Education (MACTE)
313 Second St SE Suite 112 .... Charlottesville VA 22902 434-202-7793 525-8838*
**Fax Area Code:* 888 ■ *Web:* www.macte.org
NA for the Education of Young Children (NAEYC)
1313 L St NW Suite 500 .... Washington DC 20005 202-232-8777 328-1846
TF: 800-424-2460 ■ *Web:* www.naeyc.org
NA of Industrial Technology (NAIT)
Assn of Technology Management & Applied Engineering
1390 Eisenhower Pl .... Ann Arbor MI 48108 734-677-0720 677-0046
Web: www.atmae.org
NA of Nurse Practitioners in Women's Health Council on Accreditation
505 C St NE .... Washington DC 20002 202-543-9693 543-9858
Web: www.npwh.org
NA of Schools of Art & Design (NASAD)
11250 Roger Bacon Dr Suite 21 .... Reston VA 20190 703-437-0700 437-6312
Web: www.nasad.arts-accredit.org
NA of Schools of Public Affairs & Administration Commission on Peer Review & Accreditation
1029 Vermont Ave NW Suit 1100 .... Washington DC 20005 202-628-8965 626-4978
Web: www.naspaa.org
National Accreditation Council for Agencies Serving People with Blindness or Visual Impairment (NA-CASB)
21475 Lorain Rd Suite 300 .... Fairview Park OH 44126 440-409-0340 409-0173
Web: www.nacasb.org
National Accrediting Agency for Clinical Laboratory Sciences (NAACLS)
8410 W Bryn Mawr Ave Suite 670 .... Chicago IL 60631 773-714-8880 714-8886
Web: www.naacls.org
National Accrediting Commission of Cosmetology Arts & Sciences (NACCAS)
4401 Ford Ave Suite 1300 .... Alexandria VA 22302 703-600-7600 379-2200
Web: www.naccas.org
National Architectural Accrediting Board (NAAB)
1735 New York Ave NW .... Washington DC 20006 202-783-2007 783-2822
Web: www.naab.org
National Board of Trial Advocacy (NBTA)
200 Stonewall Blvd Suite 1 .... Wrentham MA 02093 508-384-6565 384-8223
TF: 866-384-6565
National Certification Commission for Acupuncture & Oriental Medicine (NCCAOM)
76 S Laura St Suite 1290 .... Jacksonville FL 32202 904-598-1005 598-5001
Web: www.nccaom.org
National Commission on Certification of Physician Assistants
12000 Findley Rd Suite 200 .... Duluth GA 30097 678-417-8100 417-8135
Web: www.nccpa.net
National Council for Accreditation of Teacher Education (NCATE)
2010 Massachusetts Ave NW Suite 500 .... Washington DC 20036 202-466-7496 296-6620
Web: www.ncate.org
National Federation of Nonpublic School State Accrediting Associations
6300 Father Tribou St .... Little Rock AR 72205 501-664-0340 664-9075
Web: www.nfnssaa.com
National League for Nursing Accrediting Commission Inc (NLNAC)
61 Broadway 33rd Fl .... New York NY 10006 212-363-5555 812-0390
TF: 800-669-1656 ■ *Web:* www.nlnac.org
National Recreation & Park Assn
22377 Belmont Ridge Rd .... Ashburn VA 20148 703-858-0784 858-0794
Web: www.nrpa.org
New England Assn of Schools & Colleges (NEASC)
209 Burlington Rd .... Bedford MA 01730 781-271-0022 541-5400
Web: www.neasc.org
North Central Assn Commission on Accreditation & School Improvement (NCA CASI)
9115 Westside Pkwy .... Alpharetta GA 30009 888-413-3669
TF: 888-413-3669 ■ *Web:* www.ncacasi.org
North Central Assn Higher Learning Commission
230 S LaSalle St .... Chicago IL 60604 312-263-0456 263-7462
TF: 800-621-7440 ■ *Web:* www.ncacihe.org
Northwest Assn of Accredited Schools (NAAS)
1510 Robert St Suite 103 .... Boise ID 83705 208-493-5077 334-3228
Web: www.northwestaccreditation.org
Northwest Commission on Colleges & Universities (NWCCU)
8060 165th Ave NE Suite 100 .... Redmond WA 98052 425-558-4224 376-0596
Web: www.nwccu.org
Office of Social Work Accreditation & Education Excellence
1725 Duke St Suite 500 .... Alexandria VA 22314 703-683-8080 683-8099
Web: www.cswe.org
Society of Accredited Marine Surveyors Inc (SAMS)
4605 Cardinal Blvd .... Jacksonville FL 32210 904-384-1494 388-3958
TF: 800-344-9077 ■ *Web:* www.marinesurvey.org

			Phone	Fax
Society of American Foresters (SAF) 5400 Grosvenor Ln. Bethesda *Web:* www.safnet.org	MD	20814	301-897-8720	897-3690
Southern Assn of Colleges & Schools 1866 Southern Ln. Decatur *TF:* 800-248-7701 ■ *Web:* www.sacs.org	GA	30033	404-679-4500	679-4556
Teacher Education Accreditation Council (TEAC) 1 Dupont Cir Suite 320. Washington *Web:* www.teac.org	DC	20036	202-466-7236	466-7238
TransNational Assn of Christian Colleges & Schools (TRACS) 15935 Forest Rd PO Box 328. Forest *Web:* www.tracs.org	VA	24551	434-525-9539	525-9538
URAC 1220 L St NW Suite 400. Washington *Web:* www.urac.org	DC	20005	202-216-9010	216-9006
Western Assn of Schools & Colleges (WASC) 985 Atlantic Ave Suite 100. Alameda *Web:* www.wascweb.org	CA	94501	510-748-9001	748-9797

48-2 Agricultural Organizations

			Phone	Fax
Agricultural Retailers Assn (ARA) 1156 15th St NW Suite 500. Washington *Web:* www.aradc.org	DC	20005	202-457-0825	457-0864
Agriculture Council of America (ACA) 11020 King St Suite 205. Overland Park *TF:* 888-982-4329 ■ *Web:* www.agday.org	KS	66210	913-491-1895	491-6502
American Agricultural Economics Assn (AAEA) 555 E Wells St Suite 1100. Milwaukee *Web:* www.aaea.org	WI	53202	414-918-3190	272-6070
American Angus Assn (AAA) 3201 Frederick Ave. Saint Joseph *TF:* 800-821-5478 ■ *Web:* www.angus.org	MO	64506	816-383-5100	233-9703
American Assn of Bovine Practitioners (AABP) 3320 Skyway Dr Suite 802 PO Box 3610. Auburn *TF:* 800-269-2227 ■ *Web:* www.aabp.org	AL	36831	334-821-0442	821-9532
American Dairy Goat Assn (ADGA) 209 W Main St PO Box 865. Spindale *Web:* www.adga.org	NC	28160	828-286-3801	287-0476
American Dairy Science Assn (ADSA) 1111 N Dunlap Ave. Savoy *Web:* www.adsa.org	IL	61874	217-356-5146	398-4119
American Egg Board (AEB) 1460 Renaissance Dr Suite 301. Park Ridge *Web:* www.aeb.org	IL	60068	847-296-7043	296-7007
American Farm Bureau Federation 600 Maryland Ave SW Suite 1000-W. Washington *Web:* www.fb.org	DC	20024	202-406-3600	406-3606
American Farmland Trust (AFT) 1200 18th St. Washington *TF:* 800-431-1499 ■ *Web:* www.farmland.org	DC	20036	202-331-7300	659-8339
American Feed Industry Assn (AFIA) 2101 Wilson Blvd Suite 916. Arlington *Web:* www.afia.org	VA	22201	703-524-0810	524-1921
American Fisheries Society (AFS) 5410 Grosvenor Ln Suite 110. Bethesda *Web:* www.fisheries.org	MD	20814	301-897-8616	897-8096
American Forest & Paper Assn (AF&PA) 1111 19th St NW Suite 800. Washington *TF:* 800-878-8878 ■ *Web:* www.afandpa.org	DC	20036	202-463-2700	463-2785
American Forest Foundation (AFF) 1111 19th St NW Suite 780. Washington *TF:* 888-889-4466 ■ *Web:* www.affoundation.org	DC	20036	202-463-2462	463-2461
American Gelbvieh Assn 10900 Dover St. Westminster *Web:* www.gelbvieh.org	CO	80021	303-465-2333	465-2339
American Hereford Assn 1501 Wyandotte St. Kansas City *Web:* www.hereford.org	MO	64108	816-842-3757	842-6931
American Jersey Cattle Assn 6486 E Main St. Reynoldsburg *Web:* www.usjersey.com	OH	43068	614-861-3636	861-8040
American Land Rights Assn (ALRA) 30218 NE 82nd Ave PO Box 400. Battle Ground *Web:* www.landrights.org	WA	98604	360-687-3087	687-2973
American National CattleWomen Inc (ANCW) PO Box 3881. Englewood *Web:* www.ancw.org	CO	80155	303-694-0313	694-2390
American Nursery & Landscape Assn (ANLA) 1000 Vermont Ave NW Suite 300. Washington *Web:* www.anla.org	DC	20005	202-789-2900	789-1893
American Poultry International Ltd 5420 I 55 N # B. Jackson *Web:* www.apipoultry.com	MS	39211	601-956-1715	956-1755
American Royal Assn 1701 American Royal Ct. Kansas City *TF:* 800-821-5857 ■ *Web:* www.americanroyal.com	MO	64102	816-221-9800	221-8189
American Seed Trade Assn (ASTA) 225 Reinekers Ln Suite 650. Alexandria *TF:* 888-890-7333 ■ *Web:* www.amseed.com	VA	22314	703-837-8140	837-9365
American Sheep Industry Assn (ASI) 9785 Maroon Cir Suite 360. Englewood *Web:* www.sheepusa.org	CO	80112	303-771-3500	771-8200
American Simmental Assn (ASA) 1 Simmental Way. Bozeman *Web:* www.simmental.org	MT	59715	406-587-4531	587-9301
American Society for Horticultural Science (ASHS) 1018 Duke St. Alexandria *Web:* www.ashs.org	VA	22314	703-836-4606	836-2024
American Society of Agricultural & Biological Engineers (ASABE) 2950 Niles Rd. Saint Joseph *TF Orders:* 800-695-2723 ■ *Web:* www.asabe.org	MI	49085	269-429-0300	429-3852
American Society of Agricultural Consultants (ASAC) N78W14573 Appleton Ave Suite 287. Menomonee Falls *Web:* www.agconsultants.org	WI	53051	262-253-6902	253-6903
American Society of Agronomy (ASA) 5585 Guilford Rd. Madison *Web:* www.agronomy.org	WI	53711	608-273-8080	273-2021
American Society of Animal Science (ASAS) 1111 N Dunlap Ave. Savoy *Web:* www.asas.org	IL	61874	217-356-9050	398-4119
American Society of Farm Managers & Rural Appraisers (ASFMRA) 950 S Cherry St Suite 508. Denver *Web:* www.asfmra.org	CO	80246	303-758-3513	758-0190
American Society of Landscape Architects (ASLA) 636 'I' St NW. Washington *TF:* 888-999-2752 ■ *Web:* www.asla.org	DC	20001	202-898-2444	898-1185
American Soybean Assn (ASA) 12125 Woodcrest Executive Dr Suite 100. Saint Louis *TF:* 800-688-7692 ■ *Web:* www.soygrowers.com	MO	63141	314-576-1770	576-2786
American Sugar Cane League 206 E Bayou Rd. Thibodaux *Web:* www.amscl.org	LA	70301	985-448-3707	448-3722
American-International Charolais Assn (AICA) 11700 NW Plaza Cir. Kansas City *Web:* www.charolaisusa.com	MO	64153	816-464-5977	464-5759
Assn of Consulting Foresters of America (ACF) 312 Montgomery St Suite 208. Alexandria *TF:* 888-540-8733 ■ *Web:* www.acf-foresters.org	VA	22314	703-548-0990	548-6395
Assn of Farmworker Opportunity Programs (AFOP) 1726 M St NW Suite 602. Washington *Web:* afop.org	DC	20036	202-828-6006	828-6005
Assn of Water Technologies (AWT) 15245 Shady Grove Rd Suite 130. Rockville *TF:* 800-858-6683 ■ *Web:* www.awt.org	MD	20850	301-790-1421	990-9771
Beattie Farmers Union Co-op Assn PO Box 79. Beattie *Web:* www.beattiecoop.com	KS	66406	785-353-2237	353-2236
Beefmaster Breeders United (BBU) 6800 Pk Ten Blvd Suite 290-W. San Antonio *Web:* www.beefmasters.org	TX	78213	210-732-3132	732-7711
Beet Sugar Development Foundation 800 Grant St Suite 300. Denver *Web:* www.bsdf-assbt.org	CO	80203	303-832-4460	832-4468
Breg Inc 2611 Commerce Way Suite C. Vista **Fax Area Code:* 800 ■ *TF:* 800-897-2734 ■ *Web:* www.breg.com	CA	92081	760-599-3000	329-2734*
Brown Swiss Cattle Breeders Assn of the USA 800 Pleasant St. Beloit *Web:* www.brownswissusa.com	WI	53511	608-365-4474	365-5577
Burley Tobacco Growers Co-op Assn 620 S Broadway. Lexington *Web:* www.burleytobacco.com	KY	40508	859-252-3561	231-9804
California Redwood Assn (CRA) 818 Grayson Rd Suite 201. Pleasant Hill *TF:* 888-225-7339 ■ *Web:* www.calredwood.org	CA	94523	925-935-1499	935-1496
Corn Refiners Assn Inc (CRA) 1701 Pennsylvania Ave. Washington *Web:* www.corn.org	DC	20006	202-331-1634	331-2054
Cotton Council International 1521 New Hampshire Ave NW. Washington *Web:* www.cottonusa.org	DC	20036	202-745-7805	483-4040
Cotton Inc 6399 Weston Pkwy. Cary *TF:* 800-334-5868 ■ *Web:* www.cottoninc.com	NC	27513	919-678-2220	678-2230
Crop Science Society of America (CSSA) 677 S Segoe Rd. Madison *Web:* www.crops.org	WI	53711	608-273-8080	273-2021
CropLife America 1156 15th St NW Suite 400. Washington *TF:* 888-295-1588 ■ *Web:* www.croplifeamerica.org	DC	20005	202-296-1585	463-0474
Dairy Management Inc (DMI) 10255 W Higgins Rd Suite 900. Rosemont *TF:* 800-853-2479 ■ *Web:* www.dairyinfo.com	IL	60018	847-803-2000	803-2077
Decatur Co-op Assn 305 S York Ave PO Box 68. Oberlin *TF:* 800-886-2293 ■ *Web:* www.decaturcoop.net	KS	67749	785-475-2234	475-3469
Farm Aid 501 Cambridge St 3rd Fl. Cambridge *TF:* 800-327-6243 ■ *Web:* www.farmaid.org	MA	02141	617-354-2922	354-6992
Farm Equipment Manufacturers Assn (FEMA) 1000 Executive Pkwy Suite 100. Saint Louis *Web:* www.farmequip.org	MO	63141	314-878-2304	732-1480
Farmer's Co-op Assn 110 S Keokuk Wash Rd. Keota *Web:* www.keotafarmerscoop.com	IA	52248	641-636-3748	636-2460
Farmers Co-op PO Box 1640. Van Buren *Web:* www.farmercoop.com	AR	72957	479-474-6622	474-4787
Farmers Co-op Society 317 3rd St NW. Sioux Center *Web:* www.farmerscoopsociety.com	IA	51250	712-722-2671	722-2674
Farmers Educational & Co-op Union of America 20 F St NW Suite 300. Washington *Web:* www.nfu.org	DC	20001	202-554-1600	554-1654
Fertilizer Institute The (TFI) 425 3rd St SW Suite 950. Washington *Web:* www.tfi.org	DC	20024	202-962-0490	962-0577
Forest Products Society 2801 Marshall Ct. Madison *TF:* 800-354-7164 ■ *Web:* www.forestprod.org	WI	53705	608-231-1361	231-2152
Georgia Peanut Commission 110 4th St E. Tifton *Web:* www.gapeanuts.com	GA	31794	229-386-3470	386-3501
Golf Course Superintendents Assn of America (GCSAA) 1421 Research Pk Dr. Lawrence *TF:* 800-472-7878 ■ *Web:* www.gcsaa.org	KS	66049	785-841-2240	832-4455
Herb Growing & Marketing Network (HGMN) PO Box 245. Silver Spring *Web:* www.herbworld.com	PA	17575	717-393-3295	393-9261
Hohman Assoc Inc (HAI) 6951 W Little York. Houston *TF:* 800-324-0978 ■ *Web:* www.hohmanassociates.com	TX	77040	713-896-0978	896-9419
Holstein Assn USA Inc 1 Holstein Pl. Brattleboro *TF Orders:* 800-952-5200 ■ *Web:* www.holsteinusa.com	VT	05302	802-254-4551	254-8251
Hoo-Hoo International PO Box 118. Gurdon *TF:* 800-979-9950	AR	71743	870-353-4997	353-4151
Humane Farming Assn (HFA) PO Box 3577. San Rafael *Web:* www.hfa.org	CA	94912	415-485-1495	485-0106
International Banana Assn 1901 Pennsylvania Ave NW Suite 1100. Washington	DC	20006	202-303-3400	303-3433

				Phone	Fax
International Brangus Breeders Assn (IBBA) 5750 Epsilon Dr PO Box 696020 *Web:* www.gobrangus.com	San Antonio	TX	78269	210-696-8231	696-8718
International Fertilizer Development Ctr (IFDC) PO Box 2040 *Web:* www.ifdc.org	Muscle Shoals	AL	35662	256-381-6600	381-7408
International Plant Nutrition Institute (IPNI) 3500 PkwyLn Suite 550 *Web:* www.ipni.net	Norcross	GA	30092	770-447-0335	448-0439
International Society of Arboriculture (ISA) 1400 W Anthony Dr PO Box 3129 *TF:* 888-472-8733 ■ *Web:* www.isa-arbor.com	Champaign	IL	61826	217-355-9411	355-9516
Irrigation Assn (IA) 6540 Arlington Blvd *Web:* www.irrigation.org	Falls Church	VA	22042	703-536-7080	536-7019
Landscape Nursery Council 1611 Creekview Dr.	Florence	KY	41042	859-525-1809	525-9114
Livestock Marketing Assn (LMA) 10510 N Ambassador Dr *TF:* 800-821-2048 ■ *Web:* www.lmaweb.com	Kansas City	MO	64153	816-891-0502	891-7926
Mid-Kansas Co-op Assn (MKC) 307 W Cole St PO Box D *TF:* 800-864-4428 ■ *Web:* www.mkcoop.com	Moundridge	KS	67107	620-345-6328	345-6330
Milk Industry Foundation (MIF) 1250 H St NW Suite 900 *Web:* www.idfa.org	Washington	DC	20005	202-737-4332	331-7820
Mohair Council of America 233 W Twohig Rd PO Box 5337 *TF:* 800-583-3161 ■ *Web:* www.mohairusa.com	San Angelo	TX	76902	325-655-3161	655-4761
NA of Wheat Growers (NAWG) 415 2nd St NE Suite 300 *Web:* www.wheatworld.org	Washington	DC	20002	202-547-7800	546-2638
National Agri-Marketing Assn (NAMA) 11020 King St Suite 205 *TF:* 800-530-5646 ■ *Web:* www.nama.org	Overland Park	KS	66210	913-491-6500	491-6502
National Agricultural Aviation Assn (NAAA) 1005 E St SE *Web:* www.agaviation.org	Washington	DC	20003	202-546-5722	546-5726
National Alliance of Independent Crop Consultants (NAICC) 349 E Nolley Dr *Web:* www.naicc.org	Collierville	TN	38017	901-861-0511	861-0512
National Cattlemen's Beef Assn (NCBA) 9110 E Nichols Ave Suite 300 *Web:* www.beefusa.org	Centennial	CO	80112	303-694-0305	694-2851
National Chicken Council 1015 15th St NW Suite 930 *Web:* www.eatchicken.com	Washington	DC	20005	202-296-2622	293-4005
National Christmas Tree Assn (NCTA) 16020 Swingley Ridge Rd Suite 300 *Web:* www.realchristmastrees.org	Chesterfield	MO	63017	636-449-5070	449-5051
National Corn Growers Assn (NCGA) 632 Cepi Dr *Web:* www.ncga.com	Chesterfield	MO	63005	636-733-9004	733-9005
National Cotton Council of America 7193 Goodlett Farms Pkwy *TF:* 800-377-9030 ■ *Web:* www.cotton.org	Memphis	TN	38016	901-274-9030	725-0510
National Cottonseed Products Assn (NCPA) 866 Willow Tree Cir Suite 200 *Web:* www.cottonseed.com	Cordova	TN	38108	901-682-0800	682-2856
National Council of Agricultural Employers (NCAE) 1112 16th St NW Suite 920 *Web:* www.ncaeonline.org	Washington	DC	20036	202-728-0300	728-0303
National Council of Farmer Co-ops (NCFC) 50 F St NW Suite 900 *Web:* www.ncfc.org	Washington	DC	20001	202-626-8700	626-8722
National Crop Insurance Services (NCIS) 8900 Indian Creek Pkwy Suite 600 *TF:* 800-951-6247 ■ *Web:* www.ag-risk.org	Overland Park	KS	66210	913-685-2767	685-3080
National Dairy Council (NDC) 10255 W Higgins Rd Suite 900 *Web:* www.nationaldairycouncil.org	Rosemont	IL	60018	847-803-2000	803-2077
National Endangered Species Act Reform Coalition (NESARC) 1050 Thomas Jefferson St NW 6th Fl *Web:* www.nesarc.org	Washington	DC	20007	202-333-7481	338-2416
National Family Farm Coalition (NFFC) 110 Maryland Ave NE Suite 307 *Web:* www.nffc.net	Washington	DC	20002	202-543-5675	543-0978
National Farmers Organization (NFO) 528 Billy Sunday Rd Suite 100 PO Box 2508 *TF:* 800-247-2110 ■ *Web:* www.nfo.org	Ames	IA	50010	515-292-2000	292-7106
National FFA Organization 6060 FFA Dr. *TF:* 800-772-0939 ■ *Web:* www.ffa.org	Indianapolis	IN	46268	317-802-6060	802-6061
National Fisheries Institute Inc 7918 Jones Branch Dr Suite 700 *Web:* www.aboutseafood.com	McLean	VA	22102	703-752-8880	752-7583
National Grain & Feed Assn (NGFA) 1250 'I' St NW Suite 1003 *TF:* 800-680-9223 ■ *Web:* www.ngfa.org	Washington	DC	20005	202-289-0873	289-5388
National Grange 1616 H St NW *TF:* 888-447-2643 ■ *Web:* www.nationalgrange.org	Washington	DC	20006	202-628-3507	347-1091
National Oilseed Processors Assn 1300 L St NW Suite 1020 *Web:* www.nopa.org	Washington	DC	20005	202-842-0463	842-9126
National Onion Assn (NOA) 822 7th St Suite 510 *Web:* www.onions-usa.org	Greeley	CO	80631	970-353-5895	353-5897
National Renderers Assn (NRA) 801 N Fairfax St Suite 205 *Web:* www.nationalrenderers.org	Alexandria	VA	22314	703-683-0155	683-2626
National Turkey Federation (NTF) 1225 New York Ave NW Suite 400 *Web:* www.eatturkey.com	Washington	DC	20005	202-898-0100	898-0203
National Woodland Owners Assn (NWOA) 374 Maple Ave E Suite 310 *TF:* 800-476-8733 ■ *Web:* www.woodlandowners.org	Vienna	VA	22180	703-255-2700	281-9200
North American Blueberry Council (NABC) 80 Iron Pt Cir Dr *Web:* www.blueberry.org	Folsom	CA	95630	916-983-0111	983-9370
North American Limousin Foundation (NALF) 7383 S Alton Way Suite 100 *Web:* www.nalf.org	Englewood	CO	80112	303-220-1693	220-1884
Organic Trade Assn (OTA) 60 Wells St PO Box 547 *Web:* www.ota.com	Greenfield	MA	01302	413-774-7511	774-6432
Professional Landcare Network (PLANET) 950 Herndon Pkwy Suite 450 *TF:* 800-395-2522 ■ *Web:* www.landcarenetwork.org	Herndon	VA	20170	703-736-9666	736-9668
Red Angus Assn of America 4201 N IH- 35 *Web:* www.redangus.org	Denton	TX	76207	940-387-3502	383-4036
River Country Co-op 425 Clinton Ave *Web:* www.rivercountry.coop	South Saint Paul	MN	55075	651-451-1151	451-8582
Rural Coalition 1012 14th St NW Suite 1100 *Web:* www.ruralco.org	Washington	DC	20005	202-628-7160	393-1816
Santa Gertrudis Breeders International PO Box 1257 *Web:* www.santagertrudis.com	Kingsville	TX	78364	361-592-9357	592-8572
Shelburne Farms 1611 Harbor Rd. *Web:* www.shelburnefarms.org	Shelburne	VT	05482	802-985-8686	985-8123
Skagit Farmers Supply 1833 Pk Ln PO Box 266 *Web:* www.skagitfarmers.com	Burlington	WA	98233	360-757-6053	757-4143
Society of American Foresters (SAF) 5400 Grosvenor Ln. *Web:* www.safnet.org	Bethesda	MD	20814	301-897-8720	897-3690
Soil Science Society of America (SSSA) 677 S Segoe Rd *Web:* www.soils.org	Madison	WI	53711	608-273-8080	273-2021
Southern Forest Products Assn (SFPA) 2900 Indiana Ave *Web:* www.sfpa.org	Kenner	LA	70065	504-443-4464	443-6612
Sugar Assn 1300 L St NW Suite 1001 *Web:* www.sugar.org	Washington	DC	20005	202-785-1122	785-5019
Supima 4141 E Broadway Rd *Web:* www.supima.com	Phoenix	AZ	85040	602-792-6002	792-6004
Texas Longhorn Breeders Assn of America (TLBAA) 2315 N Main St Suite 402 *Web:* www.tlbaa.org	Fort Worth	TX	76164	817-625-6241	625-1388
Tobacco Assoc Inc 1306 Annapolis Dr Suite 102 *Web:* www.tobaccoassociatesinc.org	Raleigh	NC	27605	919-821-7670	821-7674
Tobacco Merchants Assn (TMA) PO Box 8019 *Web:* www.tma.org	Princeton	NJ	08543	609-275-4900	275-8379
United Fresh Produce Assn 1901 Pennsylvania Ave NW Suite 1100 *Web:* www.unitedfresh.org	Washington	DC	20006	202-303-3400	303-3433
United Producers Inc 5909 Cleveland Ave *TF:* 800-456-3276 ■ *Web:* www.uproducers.com	Columbus	OH	43229	614-890-6666	890-4776
United Soybean Board (USB) 16305 Swingley Ridge Rd # 150 *TF:* 800-989-8721 ■ *Web:* www.unitedsoybean.org	Chesterfield	MO	63017	636-530-1777	530-1560
US Apple Assn 8233 Old Courthouse Rd Suite 200 *TF:* 800-781-4443 ■ *Web:* www.usapple.org	Vienna	VA	22182	703-442-8850	790-0845
US Grains Council 1400 K St NW Suite 1200 *Web:* www.grains.org	Washington	DC	20005	202-789-0789	898-0522
US Potato Board (USPB) 7555 E Hampden Ave Suite 412 *Web:* www.uspotatoes.com	Denver	CO	80231	303-369-7783	369-7718
US Poultry & Egg Assn 1530 Cooledge Rd *Web:* www.poultryegg.org	Tucker	GA	30084	770-493-9401	493-9257
US Wheat Assoc (USW) 3103 10th St N Suite 300 **Fax Area Code:* 703 ■ *Web:* www.uswheat.org	Arlington	VA	22201	202-463-0999	524-4399*
USA Rice Federation 4301 N Fairfax Dr Suite 425 *TF:* 800-888-7423 ■ *Web:* www.usarice.com	Arlington	VA	22203	703-236-2300	236-2301
Western Wood Products Assn (WWPA) 522 SW 5th Ave Suite 500 *Web:* www2.wwpa.org	Portland	OR	97204	503-224-3930	224-3934
Wheat Quality Council 29067 Blue Grama *Web:* www.wheatqualitycouncil.org	Pierre	SD	57501	605-224-5187	224-0517
Wild Blueberry Assn of North America (WBANA) PO Box 100 *Web:* www.wildblueberries.com	Old Town	ME	04468	207-570-3535	581-3499

48-3 Animals & Animal Welfare Organizations

				Phone	Fax
African Wildlife Foundation (AWF) 1400 16th St NW Suite 120 *TF:* 888-494-5354 ■ *Web:* www.awf.org	Washington	DC	20036	202-939-3333	939-3332
Alaska Wildlife Alliance 308 G St #308 *Web:* www.akwildlife.org	Anchorage	AK	99501	907-277-0897	277-7423
American Animal Hospital Assn (AAHA) 12575 W Bayaud Ave *TF:* 800-252-2242 ■ *Web:* www.aahanet.org	Lakewood	CO	80228	303-986-2800	986-1700
American Assn of Equine Practitioners (AAEP) 4075 Iron Works Pkwy *TF:* 800-443-0177 ■ *Web:* www.aaep.org	Lexington	KY	40511	859-233-0147	233-1968
American Buckskin Registry Assn Inc (ABRA) 1141 Hartnell Ave PO Box 493850 *Web:* www.americanbuckskin.org	Redding	CA	96049	530-223-1420	
American Cetacean Society (ACS) 745 W Paseo Del Mar *Web:* www.acsonline.org	San Pedro	CA	90731	310-548-6279	548-6950
American Donkey & Mule Society (ADMS) 1346 Morningside Ave *Web:* www.lovelongears.com	Lewisville	TX	75057	972-219-0781	420-9980

Organization	City	State	Zip	Phone	Fax
American Horse Council (AHC) 1616 H St NW 7th Fl. *Web:* www.horsecouncil.org	Washington	DC	20006	202-296-4031	296-1970
American Humane Assn (AHA) 63 Inverness Dr E *TF:* 800-227-4645 ■ *Web:* www.americanhumane.org	Englewood	CO	80112	303-792-9900	792-5333
American Miniature Horse Assn (AMHA) 5601 S IH- 35 W *Web:* www.amha.org	Alvarado	TX	76009	817-783-5600	783-6403
American Morgan Horse Assn (AMHA) 4066 Shelburne Rd Suite 5 *Web:* www.morganhorse.com	Shelburne	VT	05482	802-985-4944	985-8897
American Ornithologists' Union (AOU) 1313 Dolley Madison Blvd Suite 402 *Web:* www.aou.org	McLean	VA	22101	703-790-1745	790-2672
American Paint Horse Assn (APHA) 2800 Meacham Blvd *Web:* www.apha.com	Fort Worth	TX	76137	817-834-2742	834-3152
American Quarter Horse Assn (AQHA) 1600 Quarter Horse Dr *TF:* 800-414-7433 ■ *Web:* www.aqha.com	Amarillo	TX	79104	806-376-4811	349-6404
American Rabbit Breeders Assn (ARBA) 8 Westport Ct *Web:* www.arba.net	Bloomington	IL	61704	309-664-7500	664-0941
American Saddlebred Horse Assn (ASHA) 4093 Iron Works Pkwy *Web:* www.saddlebred.com	Lexington	KY	40511	859-259-2742	259-1628
American Shetland Pony Club (ASPC) 81B E Queenwood Rd # 2 *Web:* www.shetlandminiature.com	Morton	IL	61550	309-263-4044	263-5113
American Shorthorn Assn 8288 Hascall St *Web:* www.shorthorn.org	Omaha	NE	68124	402-393-7200	393-7203
American Society for the Prevention of Cruelty to Animals (ASPCA) 424 E 92nd St **Fax:* Hum Res ■ *Web:* www.aspca.org	New York	NY	10128	212-876-7700	876-0014*
American Warmblood Registry (AWR) PO Box 197 **Fax Area Code:* 775 ■ *Web:* www.americanwarmblood.com	Carter	MT	54920	406-734-5499	667-0516*
Animal Alliance of Canada 221 Broadview Ave *Web:* www.animalalliance.ca	Toronto	ON	M4M2G3	416-462-9541	462-9647
Animal Health Institute (AHI) 1325 G St NW Suite 700 *Web:* www.ahi.org	Washington	DC	20005	202-637-2440	393-1667
Appaloosa Horse Club (ApHC) 2720 W Pullman Rd *Web:* www.appaloosa.com	Moscow	ID	83843	208-882-5578	882-8150
Arabian Horse Assn (AHA) 10805 E Bethany Dr *Web:* www.arabianhorses.org	Aurora	CO	80014	303-696-4500	696-4599
ASPCA Animal Poison Control Ctr 424 E 92nd St *TF:* 888-426-4435 ■ *Web:* www.aspca.org	New York	NY	10128	217-337-5030	337-0599
Assn of Zoos & Aquariums (AZA) 8403 Colesville Rd Suite 710 *Web:* www.aza.org	Silver Spring	MD	20910	301-562-0777	562-0888
Atlantic Salmon Federation (ASF) PO Box 5200 *TF:* 800-565-5666 ■ *Web:* www.asf.ca	Saint Andrews	NB	E5B3S8	506-529-1033	529-4438
Bat Conservation International (BCI) 500 N Capital of Texas Hwy *TF:* 800-538-2287 ■ *Web:* www.batcon.org	Austin	TX	78746	512-327-9721	327-9724
Belgian Draft Horse Corp of America 125 Southwood Dr *Web:* www.belgiancorp.com	Wabash	IN	46992	260-563-3205	
Bird Studies Canada 115 Front St PO Box 160 *TF:* 888-448-2473 ■ *Web:* www.bsc-eoc.org	Port Rowan	ON	N0E1M0	519-586-3531	586-3532
Born Free USA United with Animal Protection Institute 1122 S St *TF:* 800-348-7387 ■ *Web:* www.bornfreeusa.org	Sacramento	CA	95814	916-447-3085	447-3070
Canadian Federation of Humane Societies (CFHS) 30 Concourse Gate Suite 102 *TF:* 888-678-2347 ■ *Web:* cfhs.ca	Ottawa	ON	K2E7V7	613-224-8072	723-0252
Canadian Kennel Club (CKC) 200 Ronson Dr Suite 400 *TF:* 800-250-8040 ■ *Web:* www.ckc.ca	Etobicoke	ON	M9W5Z9	416-675-5511	675-6506
Canadian Peregrine Foundation 1450 O'Connor Dr Bldg B Suite 214 *TF:* 888-709-3944 ■ *Web:* www.peregrine-foundation.ca	Toronto	ON	M4B2T8	416-481-1233	481-7158
Certified Horsemanship Assn (CHA) 4037 Iron Works Pkwy Suite 180 *TF:* 800-399-0138 ■ *Web:* www.cha-ahse.org	Lexington	KY	40511	859-259-3399	255-0726
Defenders of Wildlife 1130 17th St NW *TF:* 800-385-9712 ■ *Web:* www.defenders.org	Washington	DC	20036	202-682-9400	682-1331
Delta Waterfowl Foundation PO Box 3128 *TF:* 888-987-3695 ■ *Web:* www.deltawaterfowl.org	Bismarck	ND	58502	701-222-8857	224-1924
Dian Fossey Gorilla Fund International 800 Cherokee Ave SE *TF:* 800-851-0203 ■ *Web:* www.gorillafund.org	Atlanta	GA	30315	404-624-5881	624-5999
Ducks Unlimited Inc 1 Waterfowl Way *TF:* 800-453-8257 ■ *Web:* www.ducks.org	Memphis	TN	38120	901-758-3825	758-3850
Friends of Animals Inc (FoA) 777 Post Rd Suite 205 *TF:* 800-321-7387 ■ *Web:* www.friendsofanimals.org	Darien	CT	06820	203-656-1522	656-0267
Fund for Animals The 200 W 57th St *TF:* 888-405-3863 ■ *Web:* www.fundforanimals.org	New York	NY	10019	212-246-2096	246-2633
Great Bear Foundation 802 E Front St *Web:* www.greatbear.org	Missoula	MT	59802	406-829-9378	829-9379
Greyhound Friends Inc 167 Saddle Hill Rd *Web:* www.greyhound.org	Hopkinton	MA	01748	508-435-5969	435-0547
Hawk Mountain Sanctuary (HMS) 1700 Hawk Mountain Rd *Web:* www.hawkmountain.org	Kempton	PA	19529	610-756-6961	756-4468
Humane Farming Assn (HFA) PO Box 3577 *Web:* www.hfa.org	San Rafael	CA	94912	415-485-1495	485-0106
Humane Society of the US (HSUS) 2100 L St NW *Web:* www.humanesociety.org	Washington	DC	20037	202-452-1100	778-6132
In Defense of Animals (IDA) 3010 Kerner Blvd *Web:* www.idausa.org	San Rafael	CA	94901	415-448-0048	454-1031
International Fund for Animal Welfare (IFAW) 290 Summer St *TF:* 800-932-4329 ■ *Web:* www.ifaw.org	Yarmouth Port	MA	02675	508-744-2000	744-2009
International Primate Protection League (IPPL) 120 Primate Ln *Web:* www.ippl.org	Summerville	SC	29483	843-871-2280	871-7988
International Society for Animal Rights (ISAR) PO Box F *TF:* 800-543-4727 ■ *Web:* www.isaronline.org	Clarks Summit	PA	18411	570-586-2200	586-9580
International Society for the Protection of Mustangs & Burros (ISPMB) PO Box 55 *Web:* www.ispmb.org	Lantry	SD	57636	605-964-6866	
International Veterinary Acupuncture Society (IVAS) 1730 S College Ave Suite 301 *Web:* www.ivas.org	Fort Collins	CO	80525	970-266-0666	266-0777
Jane Goodall Institute for Wildlife Research Education & Conservation (JGI) 4245 N Fairfax Dr Suite 600 *TF:* 800-592-5263 ■ *Web:* www.janegoodall.org	Arlington	VA	22203	703-682-9220	682-9312
Missouri Fox Trotting Horse Breed Assn Inc PO Box 1027 *Web:* www.mfthba.com	Ava	MO	65608	417-683-2468	683-6144
Mountain Lion Foundation 1107 9th St # 340 *TF:* 800-319-7621 ■ *Web:* www.mountainlion.org	Sacramento	CA	95814	916-442-2666	442-2871
NA of Animal Breeders (NAAB) 401 Bernadette Dr *Web:* www.naab-css.org	Columbia	MO	65203	573-445-4406	446-2279
National Animal Control Assn 101 N Church St Suite C *Web:* www.nacanet.org	Olathe	KS	66061	913-768-1319	768-1378
National Anti-Vivisection Society (NAVS) 53 W Jackson Blvd Suite 1552 *TF:* 800-888-6287 ■ *Web:* www.navs.org	Chicago	IL	60604	312-427-6065	427-6524
National Cutting Horse Assn (NCHA) 260 Bailey Ave *Web:* www.nchacutting.com	Fort Worth	TX	76107	817-244-6188	244-2015
National Disaster Search Dog Foundation 501 E Ojai Ave *TF:* 888-459-4376 ■ *Web:* www.searchdogfoundation.org	Ojai	CA	93023	805-646-1015	640-1848
National Dog Registry (NDR) PO Box 51105 *TF:* 800-637-3647 ■ *Web:* www.nationaldogregistry.com	Mesa	AZ	85208	480-350-7786	
National Reining Horse Assn (NRHA) 3000 NW 10th St *Web:* www.nrha.com	Oklahoma City	OK	73107	405-946-7400	946-8425
National Wild Turkey Federation (NWTF) 770 Augusta Rd PO Box 530 *TF Cust Svc:* 800-843-6983 ■ *Web:* www.nwtf.com	Edgefield	SC	29824	803-637-3106	637-0034
National Wildlife Federation (NWF) 11100 Wildlife Ctr Dr *TF:* 800-822-9919 ■ *Web:* www.nwf.org	Reston	VA	20190	703-438-6000	438-3570
Paso Fino Horse Assn 101 N Collins St *Web:* www.pfha.org	Plant City	FL	33566	813-719-7777	719-7872
People for the Ethical Treatment of Animals (PETA) 501 Front St *TF:* 800-483-4366 ■ *Web:* www.peta.org	Norfolk	VA	23510	757-622-7382	622-0457
Performing Animal Welfare Society (PAWS) 11435 Simmerhorn Rd *Web:* www.pawsweb.org	Galt	CA	95632	209-745-2606	745-1809
Pet Care Services Assn (PCSA) 1702 E Pikes Peak Ave *TF:* 877-570-7788	Colorado Springs	CO	80909	719-667-1600	667-0116
Pet Sitters International (PSI) 201 E King St *Web:* www.petsit.com	King	NC	27021	336-983-9222	983-5266
Pinto Horse Assn of America 7330 NW 23rd St *Web:* www.pinto.org	Bethany	OK	73008	405-491-0111	787-0773
Racking Horse Breeders Assn of America (RHBAA) 67 Horse Ctr Rd *Web:* www.rackinghorse.com	Decatur	AL	35603	256-353-7225	353-7266
Ruffed Grouse Society (RGS) 451 McCormick Rd *TF:* 888-564-6747 ■ *Web:* www.ruffedgrousesociety.org	Coraopolis	PA	15108	412-262-4044	262-9207
Save the Manatee Club (SMC) 500 N Maitland Ave Suite 210 *TF:* 800-432-5646 ■ *Web:* www.savethemanatee.org	Maitland	FL	32751	407-539-0990	539-0871
Tennessee Walking Horse Breeders' & Exhibitors' Assn (TWHBEA) 250 N Ellington Pkwy PO Box 286 *Web:* www.twhbea.com	Lewisburg	TN	37091	931-359-1574	359-7530
Thoroughbred Owners & Breeders Assn (TOBA) PO Box 910668 *TF:* 888-606-8622 ■ *Web:* www.toba.org	Lexington	KY	40591	859-276-2291	276-2462
Trout Unlimited (TU) 1300 N 17th St Suite 500 *TF:* 800-834-2419 ■ *Web:* www.tu.org	Arlington	VA	22209	703-522-0200	284-9400
Wildlife Conservation Society (WCS) 2300 Southern Blvd *TF:* 800-234-5128 ■ *Web:* www.wcs.org	Bronx	NY	10460	718-220-5100	
Wildlife Forever 2700 Fwy Blvd Suite 1000 *Web:* www.wildlifeforever.org	Brooklyn Center	MN	55430	763-253-0222	560-9961
Wildlife Management Institute (WMI) 1101 14th St NW *Web:* www.wildlifemanagementinstitute.org	Washington	DC	20005	202-371-1808	408-5059
Wildlife Society 5410 Grosvenor Ln Suite 200 *Web:* www.joomla.wildlife.org	Bethesda	MD	20814	301-897-9770	530-2471
World Society for the Protection of Animals (WSPA) 89 S St Suite 201 Lincoln Plaza *TF:* 800-883-9772 ■ *Web:* www.wspa-usa.org	Boston	MA	02111	617-896-9214	737-4404
World Wildlife Fund (WWF) 1250 24th St NW PO Box 97180 *TF:* 800-225-5993 ■ *Web:* www.worldwildlife.org	Washington	DC	20090	202-293-4800	293-9211
World Wildlife Fund Canada (WWF) 245 Eglinton Ave E Suite 410 *TF:* 800-267-2632 ■ *Web:* www.wwf.ca	Toronto	ON	M4P3J1	416-489-8800	489-3611

	City	State	ZIP	Phone	Fax
Zoocheck Canada 788 1/2 O'Connor Dr. *TF:* 888-801-3222 ■ *Web:* www.zoocheck.com	Toronto	ON	M4B2S6	416-285-1744	285-4670

48-4 Arts & Artists Organizations

	City	State	ZIP	Phone	Fax
Academy of Motion Picture Arts & Sciences 8949 Wilshire Blvd *Web:* www.oscars.org	Beverly Hills	CA	90211	310-247-3000	859-9619
Actors' Equity Assn 1560 Broadway *Web:* www.actorsequity.org	New York	NY	10036	212-869-8530	719-9815
Alliance of Motion Picture & Television Producers (AMPTP) 15301 Ventura Blvd Bldg E *Web:* www.amptp.org	Sherman Oaks	CA	91403	818-995-3600	
American Academy of Arts & Letters 633 W 155th St *Web:* www.artsandletters.org	New York	NY	10032	212-368-5900	212-4615
American Academy of Arts & Sciences 136 Irving St *Web:* www.amacad.org	Cambridge	MA	02138	617-576-5000	576-5050
American Accordionists Assn (AAA) 152 Homefair Dr *Web:* www.ameraccord.com	Fairfield	CT	06825	203-335-2045	335-2048
American Antiquarian Society (AAS) 185 Salisbury St *Web:* www.americanantiquarian.org	Worcester	MA	01609	508-755-5221	753-3311
American Arts Alliance *Performing Arts Alliance* 1211 Connecticut Ave NW Suite 200 *Web:* www.theperformingartsalliance.org	Washington	DC	20036	202-207-3850	833-1543
American Assn for State & Local History (AASLH) 1717 Church St *Web:* www.aaslh.org	Nashville	TN	37203	615-320-3203	327-9013
American Assn of Museums (AAM) 1575 Eye St NW # 400 *TF:* 866-266-2150 ■ *Web:* www.aam-us.org	Washington	DC	20005	202-289-1818	289-6578
American Ceramic Society (ACerS) 600 N Cleveland Ave # 210 *Web:* www.ceramics.org	Westerville	OH	43082	614-890-4700	899-6109
American Choral Directors Assn (ACDA) 545 Couch Dr *Web:* www.acda.org	Oklahoma City	OK	73102	405-232-8161	232-8162
American College of Musicians 808 Rio Grande St *Web:* www.pianoguild.com	Austin	TX	78701	512-478-5775	478-5843
American Composers Alliance (ACA) 73 Spring St *Web:* www.composers.com	New York	NY	10012	212-925-0458	925-6798
American Craft Council 72 Spring St 6th Fl *TF:* 800-836-3470 ■ *Web:* www.craftcouncil.org	New York	NY	10012	212-274-0630	274-0650
American Design Drafting Assn (ADDA) 105 E Main St *Web:* www.adda.org	Newbern	TN	38059	731-627-0802	627-9321
American Federation of Arts (AFA) 305 E 47th St 10th Fl *Web:* www.afaweb.org	New York	NY	10017	212-988-7700	861-2487
American Federation of Musicians of the US & Canada (AFM) 1501 Broadway Suite 600 *TF:* 800-762-3444 ■ *Web:* www.afm.org	New York	NY	10036	212-869-1330	764-6134
American Film Institute (AFI) 2021 N Western Ave *Web:* www.afi.com	Los Angeles	CA	90027	323-856-7600	467-4578
American Guild of Musical Artists (AGMA) 1430 Broadway 14th Fl *TF:* 800-543-2462 ■ *Web:* www.musicalartists.org	New York	NY	10018	212-265-3687	262-9088
American Guild of Organists (AGO) 475 Riverside Dr Suite 1260 *TF:* 800-246-5115 ■ *Web:* www.agohq.org	New York	NY	10115	212-870-2310	870-2163
American Guild of Variety Artists (AGVA) 363 7th Ave 17th Fl	New York	NY	10001	212-675-1003	633-0097
American Institute for Conservation of Historic & Artistic Works (AIC) 1156 15th St NW Suite 320 *Web:* www.conservation-us.org	Washington	DC	20005	202-452-9545	452-9328
American Institute of Architects (AIA) 1735 New York Ave NW *TF Orders:* 800-242-3837 ■ *Web:* www.aia.org	Washington	DC	20006	202-626-7300	626-7547
American Institute of Graphic Arts (AIGA) 164 5th Ave *TF:* 800-548-1634 ■ *Web:* www.aiga.org	New York	NY	10010	212-807-1990	807-1799
American Music Ctr (AMC) 30 W 26th St Suite 1001 *Web:* www.amc.net	New York	NY	10010	212-366-5260	366-5265
American Musicological Society (AMS) 6010 College Stn *TF:* 888-679-7648 ■ *Web:* www.ams-net.org	Brunswick	ME	04011	207-798-4243	798-4254
American Society of Artists PO Box 1326 *Web:* www.community-2.webtv.net	Palatine	IL	60078	312-751-2500	
American Society of Cinematographers (ASC) 1782 N Orange Dr *TF:* 800-448-0145 ■ *Web:* www.theasc.com	Hollywood	CA	90028	323-969-4333	882-6391
American Society of Interior Designers (ASID) 608 Massachusetts Ave *Web:* www.asid.org	Washington	DC	20002	202-546-3480	546-3240
Americans for the Arts 1000 Vermont Ave NW 6th Fl *Web:* www.ww3.artsusa.org	Washington	DC	20005	202-371-2830	371-0424
Archives of American Art 750 9th St NW Suite 2200 *Web:* www.artarchives.si.edu	Washington	DC	20001	202-633-7940	633-7994
Art Dealers Assn of America (ADAA) 205 Lexington Ave Suite 901 **Fax Area Code:* 646 ■ *Web:* www.artdealers.org	New York	NY	10016	212-488-5550	688-6809*
Art Dealers Assn of Canada (ADAC) 111 Peter St Suite 501 *Web:* www.ad-ac.ca	Toronto	ON	M5V2H1	416-934-1583	934-1584
Art Directors Guild (ADG) 11969 Ventura Blvd Suite 200 *Web:* www.adg.org	Studio City	CA	91604	818-762-9995	762-9997
Arts & Business Council of Americans for the Arts 1 E 53rd St 2nd Fl *Web:* www.artsandbusiness.org	New York	NY	10022	212-223-2787	980-4857
Assn for Information Media & Equipment (AIME) PO Box 9844 *Web:* www.aime.org	Cedar Rapids	IA	52409	319-654-0608	654-0609
Assn for Recorded Sound Collections (ARSC) PO Box 543 *Web:* www.arsc-audio.org	Annapolis	MD	21404	410-757-0488	349-0175
Assn of Children's Museums (ACM) 1300 L St NW Suite 975 *Web:* www.childrensmuseums.org	Washington	DC	20005	202-898-1080	898-1086
Assn of Film Commissioners International (AFCI) 109 E 17th St **Fax Area Code:* 413 ■ *Web:* www.afci.org	Cheyenne	WY	82001	307-637-4422	375-2903*
Assn of Performing Arts Presenters 1211 Connecticut Ave NW Suite 200 *TF:* 888-820-2787 ■ *Web:* www.apap365.org	Washington	DC	20036	202-833-2787	833-1543
Assn of Talent Agents 9255 Sunset Blvd Suite 930 *Web:* www.agentassociation.com	Los Angeles	CA	90069	310-274-0628	274-5063
Associated Actors & Artistes of America 165 W 46th St	New York	NY	10036	212-869-0358	869-1746
Authors Guild 31 E 32nd St 7th Fl *Web:* www.authorsguild.org	New York	NY	10016	212-563-5904	564-5363
Ballet Theatre Foundation American Ballet Theatre 890 Broadway 3rd Fl *Web:* www.abt.org	New York	NY	10003	212-477-3030	254-5938
Bix Beiderbecke Memorial Society 102 S Harrison St # 201 *TF:* 888-249-5487 ■ *Web:* www.bixsociety.org	Davenport	IA	52801	563-324-7170	326-1732
Broadcast Music Inc (BMI) 250 Greenwich St 7 World Trade Ctr *Web:* www.bmi.com	New York	NY	10007	212-220-3000	220-4474
Broadway League The 729 7th Ave 5th Fl *Web:* www.broadwayleague.com	New York	NY	10019	212-764-1122	944-2136
Business Committee for the Arts Inc (BCA) 29-27 Queens Plaza N 8th Fl	Long Island City	NY	11101	718-482-9900	482-9911
Chamber Music America (CMA) 305 7th Ave 5th Fl *Web:* www.chamber-music.org	New York	NY	10001	212-242-2022	242-7955
Choristers Guild 2834 W Kingsley Rd *TF:* 800-246-7478 ■ *Web:* www.choristersguild.org	Garland	TX	75041	972-271-1521	840-3113
Chorus America 1156 15th St NW Suite 310 *Web:* www.chorusamerica.org	Washington	DC	20005	202-331-7577	331-7599
Clowns of America International (COAI) PO Box C *TF:* 888-522-5696 ■ *Web:* www.coai.org	Richeyville	PA	15358	888-522-5696	
College Art Assn (CAA) 275 7th Ave *Web:* www.collegeart.org	New York	NY	10001	212-691-1051	627-2381
Conductors Guild 719 Twinridge Ln *Web:* www.conductorsguild.org	Richmond	VA	23235	804-553-1378	553-1876
Country Music Assn (CMA) 1 Music Cir S *TF:* 800-788-3045 ■ *Web:* www.cmaworld.com	Nashville	TN	37203	615-244-2840	726-0314
Dance/USA 1111 16 St NW Suite 300 *Web:* www.danceusa.org	Washington	DC	20036	202-833-1717	833-2686
Design Management Institute (DMI) 101 Fremont St Suite 300 *Web:* www.dmi.org	Boston	MA	02108	617-338-6380	338-6570
Dramatists Guild of America Inc 1501 Broadway Suite 701 *Web:* www.dramatistsguild.com	New York	NY	10036	212-398-9366	944-0420
Drum Corps International (DCI) PO Box 3129 *TF Orders:* 800-495-7469 ■ *Web:* www.dci.org	Indianapolis	IN	46206	317-275-1212	713-0690
Earshot Jazz 3429 Fremont Pl Suite 309 *Web:* www.earshot.org	Seattle	WA	98103	206-547-6763	547-6286
Educational Theatre Assn 2343 Auburn Ave *Web:* www.schooltheatre.org	Cincinnati	OH	45219	513-421-3900	421-3900
Folk Alliance International 510 S Main St 1st Fl *Web:* www.folkalliance.org	Memphis	TN	38103	901-522-1170	522-1172
Frank Lloyd Wright Foundation Taliesin West 12621 N Frank Lloyd Wright Blvd PO Box 4430 *Web:* www.franklloydwright.org	Scottsdale	AZ	85259	480-860-2700	391-4009
Glass Art Society (GAS) 6512 23rd Ave NW Suite 329 *Web:* www.glassart.org	Seattle	WA	98121	206-382-1305	382-2630
Gold Coast Jazz Society 1350 E Sunrise Blvd *Web:* www.goldcoastjazz.org	Fort Lauderdale	FL	33304	954-524-0805	525-7880
Gospel Music Assn (GMA) 1205 Division St *Web:* www.gospelmusic.org	Nashville	TN	37203	615-242-0303	254-9755
Graphic Artists Guild Inc 32 Broadway Suite 1114 *Web:* www.graphicartistsguild.org	New York	NY	10004	212-791-3400	791-0333
Guild of American Luthiers 8222 S Pk Ave *Web:* www.luth.org	Tacoma	WA	98408	253-472-7853	
Hollywood Foreign Press Assn (HFPA) 646 N Robertson Blvd *Web:* www.goldenglobes.org	West Hollywood	CA	90069	310-657-1731	657-5576
Independent Feature Project (IFP) 104 W 29th St 12th Fl *Web:* www.ifp.org	New York	NY	10001	212-465-8200	465-8525

Organization	City	State	Zip	Phone	Fax
Independent Film & Television Alliance (IFTA) 10850 Wilshire Blvd 9th Fl *Web:* www.ifta-online.org	Los Angeles	CA	90024	310-446-1047	446-1600
Indian Arts & Crafts Assn (IACA) 4010 Carlisle Blvd NE Suite C *Web:* www.iaca.com	Albuquerque	NM	87107	505-265-9149	265-8251
International Brotherhood of Magicians (IBM) 11155 S Towne Sq Suite C *Web:* www.magician.org	Saint Louis	MO	63123	314-845-9200	845-9220
International Center of Medieval Art (ICMA) 799 Fort Washington Ave The Cloisters Fort Tryon Pk *Web:* www.medievalart.org	New York	NY	10040	212-928-1146	928-9946
International Federation for Choral Music (IFCM) *Univ of Illinois at Chicago Dept of Performing Arts* 1040 W Harrison St Suite L018 *Web:* www.ifcm.net	Chicago	IL	60607	312-996-8744	996-0954
International Interior Design Assn (IIDA) 222 Merchandise Mart Plaza Suite 567 *TF:* 888-799-4432 ■ *Web:* www.iida.org	Chicago	IL	60654	312-467-1950	467-0779
International Society for the Performing Arts Foundation (ISPA) 305 7th Ave 5th Fl **Fax Area Code: 212* ■ *Web:* www.ispa.org	New York	NY	10001	914-921-1550	206-8603*
International Society of Bassists (ISB) 14070 Proton Rd Suite 100 LBG *Web:* www.isbworldoffice.com	Dallas	TX	75244	972-233-9107	490-4219
International Ticketing Assn (INTIX) 1 College Pk 8910 Purdue Rd Suite 480 *Web:* www.intix.org	Indianapolis	IN	46268	212-629-4036	629-8532
Kansas City Jazz Ambassadors (KCJA) PO Box 36181 *Web:* www.kcjazzambassadors.com	Kansas City	MO	64171	913-967-6767	
League of American Orchestras 33 W 60th St 5th Fl *Web:* www.americanorchestras.org	New York	NY	10023	212-262-5161	262-5198
League of Resident Theatres (LORT) 1501 Broadway Suite 2401 *Web:* www.lort.org	New York	NY	10036	212-944-1501	768-0785
Motion Picture & Television Fund 23388 Mulholland Dr *Web:* www.mptvfund.org	Woodland Hills	CA	91364	818-876-1888	
Motion Picture Assn (MPA) 15503 Ventura Blvd *TF:* 800-662-6797 ■ *Web:* www.mpaa.org	Encino	CA	91436	818-995-6600	285-4403
Motion Picture Assn of America 15503 Ventura Blvd Bldg E *Web:* www.mpaa.org	Encino	CA	91436	818-995-6600	285-4403
Mystery Writers of America Inc (MWA) 17 E 47th St 6th Fl *Web:* www.mysterywriters.org	New York	NY	10017	212-888-8171	888-8107
NA of Pastoral Musicians (NPM) 962 Wayne Ave Suite 210 *Web:* www.npm.org	Silver Spring	MD	20910	240-247-3000	247-3001
NA of Science Writers (NASW) PO Box 890 *Web:* www.nasw.org	Hedgesville	WV	25427	304-754-5077	754-5076
NA of Theatre Owners (NATO) 750 1st St NE Suite 1130 *TF:* 800-282-6286 ■ *Web:* www.natoonline.org	Washington	DC	20002	202-962-0054	962-0370
National Academy of Recording Arts & Sciences 3030 Olympic Blvd *TF:* 800-423-2017 ■ *Web:* www.grammy.com	Santa Monica	CA	90404	310-392-3777	392-2306
National Academy of Television Arts & Sciences 111 W 57th St Suite 600 *Web:* www.emmyonline.org	New York	NY	10019	212-586-8424	246-8129
National Council for the Traditional Arts (NCTA) 1320 Fenwick Ln Suite 200 *Web:* www.ncta.net	Silver Spring	MD	20910	301-565-0654	565-0472
National Guild of Piano Teachers PO Box 1807 *Web:* pianoguild.com	Austin	TX	78767	512-478-5775	478-5843
National Humanities Alliance (NHA) 21 Dupont Cir NW Suite 604 *Web:* www.nhalliance.org	Washington	DC	20036	202-296-4994	872-0884
National League of American Pen Women Inc 1300 17th St NW *Web:* www.americanpenwomen.org	Washington	DC	20036	202-785-1997	452-8868
National Music Publishers' Assn (NMPA) 101 Constitution Ave NW Suite 705 Et *Web:* www.nmpa.org	Washington	DC	20001	202-742-4375	742-4377
National Speakers Assn (NSA) 1500 S Priest Dr *Web:* www.nsaspeaker.org	Tempe	AZ	85281	480-968-2552	968-0911
Percussive Arts Society (PAS) 110 W Washington St *Web:* www.pas.org	Indianapolis	IN	46204	317-974-4488	974-4499
PLASA North America 630 9th Ave Suite 609 *Web:* www.plasa.org	New York	NY	10036	212-244-1505	244-1502
Professional Photographers of America Inc (PPA) 229 Peachtree St NE Suite 2200 *TF:* 800-786-6277 ■ *Web:* www.ppa.com	Atlanta	GA	30303	404-522-8600	614-6400
Professional Picture Framers Assn (PPFA) 3000 Picture Pl *TF:* 800-762-9287 ■ *Web:* www.pmai.org/ppfa	Jackson	MI	49201	517-788-8100	788-8371
Recording Industry Assn of America Inc (RIAA) 1025 F St NW 10th Fl *Web:* www.riaa.com	Washington	DC	20004	202-775-0101	775-7253
Sacramento Traditional Jazz Society (STJS) 2787 Del Monte St *Web:* www.sacjazz.com	West Sacramento	CA	95691	916-372-5277	372-3479
Screen Actors Guild (SAG) 5757 Wilshire Blvd *TF:* 800-724-0767 ■ *Web:* www.sag.org	Los Angeles	CA	90036	323-954-1600	549-6775
SESAC Inc 55 Music Sq E *TF:* 800-826-9996 ■ *Web:* www.sesac.com	Nashville	TN	37203	615-320-0055	963-3527
SITE Santa Fe 1606 Paseo de Peralta *Web:* www.sitesantafe.org	Santa Fe	NM	87501	505-989-1199	989-1188
Society for Ethnomusicology (SEM) Indiana University 1165 E 3rd St Morrison Hall 005 *Web:* www.ethnomusicology.org	Bloomington	IN	47405	812-855-6672	855-6673
Society of American Archivists (SAA) 17 N State St Suite 1425 *TF:* 866-722-7858 ■ *Web:* www2.archivists.org	Chicago	IL	60602	312-606-0722	606-0728
Society of Animal Artists Inc 47 5th Ave *Web:* www.societyofanimalartists.com	New York	NY	10003	212-741-2880	741-2262
Society of Glass & Ceramic Decorators (SGCD) 47 N 4th St *Web:* www.sgcd.org	Zanesville	OH	43701	740-588-9882	588-0245
Society of Motion Picture & Television Engineers (SMPTE) 3 Barker Ave *Web:* www.smpte.org	White Plains	NY	10601	914-761-1100	761-3115
Songwriters Guild of America 209 10th Ave S Suite 321 *Web:* www.songwritersguild.com	Nashville	TN	37203	615-742-9945	742-9948
Stuntwomen's Assn of Motion Pictures 3760 Cahuenga Blvd Suite 104 *Web:* www.stuntwomen.com	Studio City	CA	91604	818-762-0907	762-9534
Tucson Jazz Society (TJS) 6061 E Broadway Blvd # 121 *Web:* www.tucsonjazz.org	Tucson	AZ	85711	520-903-1265	903-1266
Visual Artists & Galleries Assn 350 5th Ave Suite 2820	New York	NY	10118	212-736-6666	736-6767
Women in Film (WIF) 6100 Wilshire Blvd Suite 710 *Web:* www.wif.org	Los Angeles	CA	90048	323-935-2211	935-2212
World Monuments Fund (WMF) 95 Madison Ave 9th Fl *TF:* 800-547-9171 ■ *Web:* www.wmf.org	New York	NY	10016	646-424-9594	424-9593
Young Audiences Inc 115 E 92nd St *Web:* www.youngaudiences.org	New York	NY	10128	212-831-8110	289-1202

48-5 Charitable & Humanitarian Organizations

Organization	City	State	Zip	Phone	Fax
ACDI/VOCA 50 F St NW # 1075 *TF:* 800-929-8622 ■ *Web:* www.acdivoca.org	Washington	DC	20001	202-638-4661	626-8726
Action Against Hunger 247 W 37th St 10th Fl *TF:* 877-777-1420 ■ *Web:* www.actionagainsthunger.org	New York	NY	10018	212-967-7800	967-5480
Adventist Community Services 12501 Old Columbia Pike *TF:* 877-227-2702 ■ *Web:* www.communityservices.org	Silver Spring	MD	20904	301-680-6438	680-6125
Adventist Development & Relief Agency International (ADRA) 12501 Old Columbia Pike *TF:* 800-424-2372 ■ *Web:* www.adra.org	Silver Spring	MD	20904	301-680-6380	680-6370
African Medical & Research Foundation (AMREF) 4 W 43rd St *Web:* www.amref.org	New York	NY	10036	212-768-2440	768-4230
Africare Inc 440 R St NW *Web:* www.africare.org	Washington	DC	20001	202-462-3614	387-1034
Aga Khan Foundation USA (AKF) 1825 K St NW Suite 901 *Web:* www.akdn.org/agency/akf.html	Washington	DC	20006	202-293-2537	785-1752
Aid to Artisans Inc (ATA) 1030 New Britain Ave Suite 102 *Web:* www.aidtoartisans.org	Hartford	CT	06110	860-756-5550	756-5558
Air Serv International 410 Rosedale Ct Suite 100 *Web:* www.airserv.org	Warrenton	VA	20186	540-428-2323	428-2326
Alan Guttmacher Institute (AGI) 125 Maiden Ln 7th Fl *TF:* 800-355-0244 ■ *Web:* www.guttmacher.org	New York	NY	10038	212-248-1111	248-1951
America's Development Foundation (ADF) 101 N Union St Suite 200 *Web:* www.adfusa.org	Alexandria	VA	22314	703-836-2717	836-3379
America's Second Harvest 35 E Wacker Dr Suite 2000 *TF:* 800-771-2303 ■ *Web:* www.feedingamerica.org	Chicago	IL	60601	312-263-2303	263-5626
American Anti-Slavery Group The 198 Tremont St Suite 421 *TF:* 800-884-0719 ■ *Web:* www.iabolish.org	Boston	MA	02116	617-426-8161	507-8257
American Council for Voluntary International Action 1400 16th St NW Suite 210 *Web:* www.interaction.org	Washington	DC	20036	202-667-8227	667-8236
American Friends Service Committee (AFSC) 1501 Cherry St *Web:* www.afsc.org	Philadelphia	PA	19102	215-241-7000	241-7275
American Institute of Philanthropy (AIP) 3450 N Lake Shore Dr *Web:* www.charitywatch.org	Chicago	IL	60657	773-529-2300	529-0024
American Jewish Joint Distribution Committee (JDC) 711 3rd Ave 10th Fl *Web:* www.jdc.org	New York	NY	10017	212-687-6200	370-5467
American Jewish World Service (AJWS) 45 W 36th St *TF:* 800-889-7146 ■ *Web:* www.ajws.org	New York	NY	10018	212-792-2900	792-2930
American Lebanese Syrian Associated Charities (ALSAC) 501 St Jude Pl *TF:* 800-822-6344 ■ *Web:* www.stjude.org	Memphis	TN	38105	901-578-2000	578-2805
American Leprosy Missions (ALM) 120 Broadus Ave *TF:* 800-543-3135 ■ *Web:* www.leprosy.org	Greenville	SC	29601	864-271-7040	271-7062
American Near East Refugee Aid (ANERA) 1111 14th St NW # 400 *Web:* www.anera.org	Washington	DC	20005	202-842-2766	842-4064
American Red Cross 2025 E St NW *Web:* www.redcross.org	Washington	DC	20006	202-303-4498	303-0044

Organization	State	ZIP	Phone	Fax
American Refugee Committee (ARC) 430 Oak Grove St Suite 204 ... Minneapolis *TF:* 800-875-7060 ■ *Web:* www.arcrelief.org	MN	55403	612-872-7060	607-6499
AmeriCares Foundation 88 Hamilton Ave ... Stamford *TF:* 800-486-4357 ■ *Web:* www.americares.org	CT	06902	203-658-9500	327-5200
Amigos de las Americas 5618 Star Ln ... Houston *TF:* 800-231-7796 ■ *Web:* www.amigoslink.org	TX	77057	713-782-5290	782-9267
Amnesty International USA (AIUSA) 5 Penn Plaza 14th Fl ... New York *TF:* 866-273-4466 ■ *Web:* www.amnestyusa.org	NY	10001	212-807-8400	627-1451
Arms Control Assn 1313 L St NW Suite 130 ... Washington *Web:* www.armscontrol.org	DC	20005	202-463-8270	463-8273
Assn of Fundraising Professionals (AFP) 4300 Wilson Blvd Suite 300 ... Arlington *TF:* 800-666-3863 ■ *Web:* www.afpnet.org	VA	22203	703-684-0410	684-0540
Bread for the World 50 F St NW Suite 500 ... Washington *TF Cust Svc:* 800-822-7323 ■ *Web:* www.bread.org	DC	20001	202-639-9400	639-9401
Brother's Brother Foundation (BBF) 1200 Galveston Ave ... Pittsburgh *Web:* www.brothersbrother.org	PA	15233	412-321-3160	321-3325
Canadian Council for International Cooperation (CCIC) 450 Rideau St Suite 200 ... Ottawa *Web:* www.ccic.ca	ON	K1N5Z4	613-241-7007	241-5302
CARE USA 151 Ellis St NE ... Atlanta **Fax:* Hum Res ■ *TF:* 800-521-2273 ■ *Web:* www.care.org	GA	30303	404-681-2552	577-5977*
Catholic Charities USA 66 Canal Ctr Plaza Suite 600 ... Alexandria *Web:* www.catholiccharitiesusa.org	VA	22314	703-549-1390	549-1656
Catholic Medical Mission Board (CMMB) 10 W 17th St ... New York *TF:* 800-678-5659 ■ *Web:* www.cmmb.org	NY	10011	212-242-7757	645-1485
Catholic Relief Services (CRS) 228 W Lexington St ... Baltimore *TF:* 800-235-2772 ■ *Web:* www.crs.org	MD	21201	410-625-2220	685-1635
Center for Community Change (CCC) 1536 U St NW ... Washington *TF:* 877-777-1536 ■ *Web:* www.communitychange.org	DC	20009	202-339-9300	387-4891
Center for Human Services 7200 Wisconsin Ave Suite 600 ... Bethesda *TF:* 800-444-2969 ■ *Web:* www.chs-urc.org	MD	20814	301-654-8338	941-8427
Centre for Development & Population Activities (CEDPA) 1133 21st St NW Suite 800 ... Washington *Web:* www.cedpa.org	DC	20036	202-667-1142	332-4496
Child Health Foundation 10630 Little Patuxent Pkwy Century Plaza Suite 126 ... Columbia *Web:* www.childhealthfoundation.org	MD	21044	410-992-5512	992-5641
Children International 2000 E Red Bridge Rd ... Kansas City *TF:* 800-888-3089 ■ *Web:* www.children.org	MO	64131	816-942-2000	942-3714
Children's Miracle Network 4220 Steeles Ave W Suite C18 ... Woodbridge *Web:* www.childrensmiraclenetwork.ca	ON	L4L3S8	905-265-9750	265-9749
Children's Miracle Network Hospitals 4525 S 2300 E ... Salt Lake City *Web:* www.childrensmiraclenetwork.org	UT	84117	801-278-8900	277-8787
Christian Appalachian Project PO Box 55911 ... Lexington **Fax Area Code:* 859 ■ *TF:* 866-270-4227 ■ *Web:* www.chrisapp.org	KY	40555	866-270-4227	269-0617*
Christian Blind Mission (CBM) 450 E Pk Ave ... Greenville *TF:* 800-937-2264 ■ *Web:* www.cbmus.org	SC	29601	864-239-0065	239-0069
Christian Disaster Response International PO Box 3339 ... Winter Haven *Web:* www.cdresponse.org	FL	33885	863-967-4357	662-5745
Christian Reformed World Relief Committee (CRWRC) 2850 Kalamazoo Ave SE ... Grand Rapids *TF:* 800-552-7972 ■ *Web:* www.crwrc.org	MI	49560	616-241-1691	224-0806
Christian Relief Services 2550 Huntington Ave Suite 200 ... Alexandria *TF:* 800-337-3543 ■ *Web:* www.christianrelief.org	VA	22303	703-317-9086	317-9690
Church World Service 28606 Phillips St PO Box 968 ... Elkhart *TF:* 800-297-1516 ■ *Web:* www.churchworldservice.org	IN	46515	574-264-3102	262-0966
Church World Service Emergency Response Program 475 Riverside Dr Suite 700 ... New York *TF:* 800-297-1516 ■ *Web:* www.cwserp.org	NY	10115	212-870-3151	870-2236
Citizens Network for Foreign Affairs (CNFA) 1828 L St NW Suite 710 ... Washington *TF:* 888-872-2632 ■ *Web:* www.cnfa.org	DC	20036	202-296-3920	296-3948
Coalition on Human Needs (CHN) 1120 Connecticut Ave NW Suite 910 ... Washington *Web:* www.chn.org	DC	20036	202-223-2532	223-2538
Community Action Partnership 1140 Connecticut Ave NW Suite 1210 ... Washington *Web:* www.communityactionpartnership.com	DC	20036	202-265-7546	265-5048
Community Food Bank of New Jersey Inc 31 Evans Terminal ... Hillside *Web:* www.njfoodbank.org	NJ	07205	908-355-3663	355-0270
Community Health Charities 200 N Glebe Rd Suite 801 ... Arlington *TF:* 800-654-0845 ■ *Web:* www.healthcharities.org	VA	22203	703-528-1007	528-1365
Community Renewal Team Inc 555 Windsor St ... Hartford *Web:* www.crtct.org	CT	06120	860-560-5600	
Compassion International 12290 Voyager Pkwy ... Colorado Springs **Fax:* Hum Res ■ *TF:* 800-336-7676 ■ *Web:* www.compassion.com	CO	80921	719-487-7000	623-0620*
Concern America 2015 N Broadway ... Santa Ana *TF:* 800-266-2376 ■ *Web:* www.concernamerica.org	CA	92706	714-953-8575	953-1242
Concern Worldwide US Inc 104 E 40th St Suite 903 ... New York *Web:* www.concernusa.org	NY	10016	212-557-8000	557-8004
Congressional Hunger Ctr 400 N Capitol St NW Suite G-100 ... Washington *Web:* www.hungercenter.org	DC	20001	202-547-7022	547-7575

Organization	State	ZIP	Phone	Fax
Council on Foundations 2121 Crystal Dr Suite 700 ... Arlington *TF:* 800-673-9036 ■ *Web:* www.cof.org	VA	22202	703-879-0600	879-0800
CRISTA Ministries 19303 Fremont Ave N ... Seattle *TF:* 800-442-4003 ■ *Web:* www.crista.org	WA	98133	206-546-7200	546-7214
Direct Relief International 27 S La Patera Ln ... Santa Barbara *TF:* 800-676-1638 ■ *Web:* www.directrelief.org	CA	93117	805-964-4767	681-4838
Doctors Without Borders USA Inc 333 7th Ave 2nd Fl ... New York *TF:* 888-392-0392 ■ *Web:* www.doctorswithoutborders.org	NY	10001	212-679-6800	679-7016
Dress for Success Worldwide 32 E 31st St 7th Fl ... New York *Web:* www.dressforsuccess.org	NY	10016	212-532-1922	684-9563
Elton John AIDS Foundation PO Box 17139 ... Beverly Hills *Web:* www.ejaf.org	CA	90209	310-535-1775	
Enterprise Community Partners Inc 10227 Wincopin Cir ... Columbia *TF:* 800-624-4298 ■ *Web:* www.enterprisefoundation.org	MD	21044	410-964-1230	964-1918
EnterpriseWorks/VITA 1100 H StNW Suite 1200 ... Washington *Web:* www.enterpriseworks.org	DC	20005	202-639-8660	639-8664
Episcopal Migration Ministries (EMM) 815 2nd Ave ... New York *TF:* 800-334-7626 ■ *Web:* www.episcopalchurch.org/emm	NY	10017	212-716-6258	972-0860
Episcopal Relief & Development 815 2nd Ave ... New York **Fax Area Code:* 212 ■ *TF:* 800-334-7626 ■ *Web:* www.er-d.org	NY	10017	800-334-7626	687-5302*
Ethiopian Community Development Council Inc (ECDC) 901 S Highland St ... Arlington *Web:* www.ecdcinternational.org	VA	22204	703-685-0510	685-0529
Evangelical Council for Financial Accountability (ECFA) 440 W Jubal Early Dr Suite 130 ... Winchester *TF:* 800-323-9473 ■ *Web:* www.ecfa.org	VA	22601	540-535-0103	535-0533
Fair Labor Assn (FLA) 1111 19th St NW Suite 401 ... Washington *Web:* www.fairlabor.org	DC	20036	202-898-1000	898-9050
Family Health International (FHI) PO Box 13950 ... Research Triangle Park *Web:* www.fhi.org	NC	27709	919-544-7040	544-7261
Farm Aid 501 Cambridge St 3rd Fl ... Cambridge *TF:* 800-327-6243 ■ *Web:* www.farmaid.org	MA	02141	617-354-2922	354-6992
Feed the Children (FTC) PO Box 36 ... Oklahoma City *TF:* 800-627-4556 ■ *Web:* www.feedthechildren.org	OK	73101	405-942-0228	945-4177
First Book 1319 F St NW Suite 1000 ... Washington *Web:* www.firstbook.org	DC	20004	202-393-1222	628-1258
First Voice International (FVI) 8515 Georgia Ave 9th Fl ... Silver Spring	MD	20910	301-960-1273	960-1157
Food for All 201 Pk Washington Ct ... Falls Church *TF:* 800-896-5101 ■ *Web:* www.foodforall.org	VA	22046	703-237-3677	237-4163
Food for the Hungry Inc 1224 E Washington St ... Phoenix *Web:* www.fh.org	AZ	85034	480-998-3100	889-5401
Food for the Poor Inc (FFP) 6401 Lyons Rd ... Coconut Creek *TF:* 800-427-9104 ■ *Web:* www.foodforthepoor.org	FL	33073	954-427-2222	570-7654
Foundation for International Community Assistance (FINCA) 1101 14th St NW 11th Fl ... Washington *Web:* www.finca.org	DC	20005	202-682-1510	682-1535
Freedom from Hunger 1644 DaVinci Ct ... Davis *TF:* 800-708-2555 ■ *Web:* www.freedomfromhunger.org	CA	95618	530-758-6200	758-6241
Friends of the World Food Programme (WFP) 1819 L St NW Suite 900 ... Washington *Web:* www.usa.wfp.org	DC	20036	202-530-1694	530-1698
Fund for Peace The 1701 K St NW 7th Fl ... Washington *Web:* www.fundforpeace.org	DC	20006	202-223-7940	223-7947
Gifts In Kind International 333 N Fairfax St Suite 100 ... Alexandria **Fax Area Code:* 877 ■ *Web:* www.giftsinkind.org	VA	22314	703-836-2121	798-3192*
Giving Institute 4700 W Lake Ave ... Glenview *TF:* 800-462-2372 ■ *Web:* www.givinginstitute.org	IL	60025	847-375-4709	375-6487
Global Children's Organization 3580 Wilshire Blvd # 1800 ... Los Angeles **Fax Area Code:* 213 ■ *Web:* www.globalchild.org	CA	90010	310-581-2234	389-1237*
Global Health Council 1111 19th St NW Suite 1120 ... Washington *Web:* www.globalhealth.org	DC	20036	202-833-5900	833-0075
Goodwill Industries International Inc 15810 Indianola Dr ... Rockville *TF:* 800-741-0197 ■ *Web:* www.goodwill.org	MD	20855	301-530-6500	530-1516
Grantmakers in Health (GIH) 1100 Connecticut Ave NW Suite 1200 ... Washington *Web:* www.gih.org	DC	20036	202-452-8331	452-8340
Habitat for Humanity International Inc 121 Habitat St ... Americus *TF:* 800-422-4828 ■ *Web:* www.habitat.org	GA	31709	229-924-6935	924-6541
Healing the Children (HTC) 2624 W Beacon Ave ... Spokane *TF:* 800-992-0324 ■ *Web:* www.healingthechildren.org	WA	99208	509-327-4281	327-4284
HealthRight International 80 Maiden Ln ... New York *Web:* www.healthright.org	NY	10038	212-226-9890	226-7026
Heart to Heart International 401 S Clairborne Rd Suite 302 ... Olathe *Web:* www.hearttoheart.org	KS	66062	913-764-5200	764-0809
Hebrew Immigrant Aid Society (HIAS) 333 7th Ave 16th Fl ... New York *TF:* 800-442-7714 ■ *Web:* www.hias.org	NY	10001	212-967-4100	967-4483
Heifer International 1 World Ave ... Little Rock *TF:* 800-422-0474 ■ *Web:* www.heifer.org	AR	72202	501-907-2600	907-2902
Helen Keller International 352 Pk Ave S Suite 1200 ... New York *TF:* 877-535-5374 ■ *Web:* www.hki.org	NY	10010	212-532-0544	532-6014
HELP USA 5 Hanover Sq ... New York *Web:* www.helpusa.org	NY	10004	212-400-7000	400-7005

Organization	City	State	Zip	Phone	Fax
Hole in the Wall Gang Camps Inc 265 Church St Suite 503 *Web:* www.holeinthewallcamps.org	New Haven	CT	06510	203-562-1203	562-1207
Hope Enterprises Inc 2401 Reach Rd PO Box 1837 *Web:* www.heionline.org	Williamsport	PA	17703	570-326-3745	326-1258
HOPE Worldwide 353 W Lancaster Ave Suite 200 *Web:* www.hopeww.org	Wayne	PA	19087	610-254-8800	254-8989
Housing Assistance Council (HAC) 1025 Vermont Ave NW Suite 606 *TF:* 800-989-4422 ■ *Web:* www.ruralhome.org	Washington	DC	20005	202-842-8600	347-3441
Hunger Project The 5 Union Sq W *TF:* 800-228-6691 ■ *Web:* www.thp.org	New York	NY	10003	212-251-9100	532-9785
I Have a Dream Foundation (IHAD) 330 7th Ave 20th Fl *Web:* www.ihaveadreamfoundation.org	New York	NY	10001	212-293-5480	293-5478
Independent Charities of America (ICA) 1100 Larkspur Landing Cir Suite 340 *TF:* 800-477-0733 ■ *Web:* www.independentcharities.org	Larkspur	CA	94939	415-925-2600	925-2650
Independent Order of Foresters (IOF) 789 Don Mills Rd *TF:* 800-828-1540 ■ *Web:* www.foresters.com	Toronto	ON	M3C1T9	416-429-3000	429-3896
Independent Sector 1602 L St NW # 900 *TF:* 888-860-8118 ■ *Web:* www.independentsector.org	Washington	DC	20036	202-467-6100	467-6101
INMED Partnerships for Children 20110 Ashbrook Pl Suite 260 *Web:* www.inmed.org	Ashburn	VA	20147	703-729-4951	858-7253
Institute for Food & Development Policy 398 60th St *Web:* www.foodfirst.org	Oakland	CA	94618	510-654-4400	654-4551
Interchurch Medical Assistance Inc (IMA) 500 Main St PO Box 429 *Web:* www.interchurch.org	New Windsor	MD	21776	410-635-8720	635-8726
International Aid Inc 17011 W Hickory St *TF:* 800-968-7490 ■ *Web:* www.internationalaid.org	Spring Lake	MI	49456	616-846-7490	846-3842
International Catholic Migration Commission (ICMC) c/o MRS/US Conference of Catholic Bishops 3211 4th St NE *Web:* www.icmc.net	Washington	DC	20017	202-541-3389	541-3222
International Eye Foundation (IEF) 10801 Connecticut Ave *Web:* www.iefusa.org	Kensington	MD	20895	240-290-0263	290-0269
International Institute of Rural Reconstruction (IIRR) 40 Exchange Pl Suite 1111 *Web:* www.iirr.org	New York	NY	10005	212-880-9147	880-9148
International Medical Corps (IMC) 1919 Santa Monica Blvd Suite 400 *TF:* 800-481-4462 ■ *Web:* www.internationalmedicalcorps.org	Santa Monica	CA	90404	310-826-7800	442-6622
International Orthodox Christian Charities (IOCC) 110 W Rd Suite 360 *TF:* 877-803-4622 ■ *Web:* www.iocc.org	Baltimore	MD	21204	410-243-9820	243-9824
International Planned Parenthood Federation - Western Hemisphere Region (IPPF/WHR) 120 Wall St 9th Fl *Web:* www.ippfwhr.org	New York	NY	10005	212-248-6400	248-4221
International Rescue Committee (IRC) 122 E 42nd St 12th Fl *Web:* www.rescue.org	New York	NY	10168	212-551-3000	551-3179
Jesuit Refugee Service - North America (JRS) 1016 16th St NW Suite 500 *Web:* www.jesref.org	Washington	DC	20036	202-462-0400	328-9212
Katalysis Bootstrap Fund 3601 Pacific Ave **Fax Area Code: 866*	Stockton	CA	95211	209-644-6245	403-6571*
Lutheran Disaster Response 8765 W Higgins Rd **Fax Area Code: 773* ■ *TF:* 800-638-3522 ■ *Web:* www.ldr.org	Chicago	IL	60631	800-638-3522	380-2707*
Lutheran Immigration & Refugee Service (LIRS) 700 Light St *Web:* www.lirs.org	Baltimore	MD	21230	410-230-2700	230-2890
Lutheran World Relief (LWR) 700 Light St *TF:* 800-597-5972 ■ *Web:* www.lwr.org	Baltimore	MD	21230	410-230-2700	230-2882
Make-A-Wish Foundation of America 4742 N 24th St # 400 *TF:* 800-722-9474 ■ *Web:* www.wish.org	Phoenix	AZ	85016	602-279-9474	279-0855
MAP International 4700 Glynco Pkwy *TF:* 800-225-8550 ■ *Web:* www.map.org	Brunswick	GA	31525	912-265-6010	265-6170
Marine Toys for Tots Foundation 18251 Quantico Gateway Dr *Web:* www.toysfortots.org	Triangle	VA	22172	703-640-9433	649-2054
Meals on Wheels Assn of America (MOWAA) 203 S Union St *Web:* www.mowaa.org	Alexandria	VA	22314	703-548-5558	548-8024
Medical Care Development International (MCDI) 8401 Colesville Rd Suite 425 *Web:* www.mcdi.mcd.org	Silver Spring	MD	20910	301-562-1920	562-1921
Medical Teams International (MTI) PO Box 10 *TF:* 800-959-4325 ■ *Web:* www.medicalteams.org	Portland	OR	97207	503-624-1000	624-1001
Mennonite Central Committee (MCC) 21 S 12th St PO Box 500 *TF:* 888-563-4676 ■ *Web:* www.mcc.org	Akron	PA	17501	717-859-1151	859-2171
Mennonite Disaster Service (MDS) 1018 Main St *TF:* 800-241-8111 ■ *Web:* www.mds.mennonite.net	Akron	PA	17501	717-859-2210	859-4910
MENTOR/National Mentoring Partnership 1600 Duke St Suite 300 *Web:* www.mentoring.org	Alexandria	VA	22314	703-224-2200	226-2581
Mercy Corps 3015 SW 1st Ave *TF:* 800-292-3355 ■ *Web:* www.mercycorps.org	Portland	OR	97201	503-796-6800	796-6844
Mercy-USA for Aid & Development Inc (M-USA) 44450 Pinetree Dr Suite 201 *TF:* 800-556-3729 ■ *Web:* www.mercyusa.org	Plymouth	MI	48170	734-454-0011	454-0303
Michigan Municipal League 1675 Green Rd PO Box 1487 *TF:* 800-653-2483 ■ *Web:* www.mml.org	Ann Arbor	MI	48105	734-662-3246	662-8083
Migration & Refugee Services US Conference of Catholic Bishops 3211 4th St NE *Web:* www.nccbuscc.org/mrs	Washington	DC	20017	202-541-3000	722-8755
NA for the Exchange of Industrial Resources (NAEIR) 560 McClure St *TF:* 800-562-0955 ■ *Web:* www.naeir.org	Galesburg	IL	61401	309-343-0704	343-7316
National Alliance to End Homelessness 1518 K St NW Suite 410 *Web:* www.endhomelessness.org	Washington	DC	20005	202-638-1526	638-4664
National AMBUCS Inc (AMBUCS) 4285 Regency Ct PO Box 5127 *TF:* 800-838-1845 ■ *Web:* www.ambucs.org	High Point	NC	27265	336-852-0052	852-6830
National Benevolent Assn (NBA) 149 Weldon Pkwy Suite 115 *Web:* www.nbacares.org	Maryland Heights	MO	63043	314-993-9000	993-9018
National Children's Advocacy Ctr (NCAC) 210 Pratt Ave *Web:* www.nationalcac.org	Huntsville	AL	35801	256-533-5437	534-6883
National Coalition for the Homeless (NCH) 2201 P St NW *Web:* www.nationalhomeless.org	Washington	DC	20037	202-462-4822	462-4823
National Committee for Responsive Philanthropy (NCRP) 2001 S St NW Suite 620 *Web:* www.ncrp.org	Washington	DC	20009	202-387-9177	332-5084
National Peace Corps Assn (NPCA) 1900 L St NW Suite 404 *TF:* 800-424-8580 ■ *Web:* www.peacecorpsconnect.org	Washington	DC	20036	202-293-7728	293-7554
National Peace Foundation (NPF) 666 11th St NW Suite 202 *TF:* 800-237-3223 ■ *Web:* www.nationalpeace.org	Washington	DC	20001	202-783-7030	783-7040
National Student Campaign Against Hunger & Homelessness (NSCAHH) 328 S Jefferson St Suite 620 *TF:* 800-664-8647 ■ *Web:* www.nscahh.org	Chicago	IL	60661	312-544-4436	275-7150
Near East Foundation 430-432 Crouse Hinds Hall 900 S Crouse Ave *Web:* www.neareast.org	Syracuse	NY	13244	212-710-5588	425-2350
Neighborhood Service Organization Inc 220 Bagley St Suite 1200 *Web:* www.nso-mi.org	Detroit	MI	48226	313-961-4890	961-5120
North American Mission Board SBC 4200 N Pt Pkwy *TF:* 800-634-2462 ■ *Web:* www.namb.net/site/c.9qKILUOzEpH/b.224451/k.A400/Disaster_Relief.htm	Alpharetta	GA	30022	770-410-6000	410-6133
Nuclear Age Peace Foundation (NAPF) 1187 Coast Village Rd Suite 1 PMB 121 *Web:* www.wagingpeace.org	Santa Barbara	CA	93108	805-965-3443	568-0466
OIC International 1500 Walnut St Suite 1304 *Web:* www.oicinternational.org	Philadelphia	PA	19102	215-842-0220	842-2276
Operation USA 3617 Hayden Ave Suite A *TF:* 800-678-7255 ■ *Web:* www.opusa.org	Culver City	CA	90232	310-838-3455	838-3477
ORBIS International Inc 520 8th Ave 11th Fl *TF:* 800-672-4787 ■ *Web:* www.orbis.org	New York	NY	10018	646-674-5500	674-5599
Oregon Food Bank Inc PO Box 55370 *Web:* www.oregonfoodbank.org	Portland	OR	97238	503-282-0555	282-0922
ORT American Inc 75 Maiden Ln 10th Fl *TF:* 800-364-9678 ■ *Web:* www.aort.org	New York	NY	10038	212-505-7700	674-3057
Outreach International 129 W Lexington PO Box 210 *TF:* 888-833-1235 ■ *Web:* www.outreach-international.org	Independence	MO	64050	816-833-0883	833-0103
Oxfam America 226 Cswy St 5th Fl *TF:* 800-776-9326 ■ *Web:* www.oxfamamerica.org	Boston	MA	02114	617-482-1211	728-2594
Pan American Development Foundation (PADF) 1889 F St NW 2nd Fl *Web:* www.padf.org	Washington	DC	20006	202-458-3969	458-6316
Partners of the Americas 1424 K St NW Suite 700 *TF:* 800-322-7844 ■ *Web:* www.partners.net	Washington	DC	20005	202-628-3300	628-3306
Partnership for Philanthropic Planning (NCPG) 233 McCrea St Suite 400 *Web:* www.pppnet.org	Indianapolis	IN	46225	317-269-6274	269-6276
Pathfinder International 9 Galen St Suite 217 *TF:* 888-603-6500 ■ *Web:* www.pathfind.org	Watertown	MA	02472	617-924-7200	924-3833
Peace Action 8630 Fenton St *Web:* www.peace-action.org	Silver Spring	MD	20910	301-565-4050	565-0850
People-to-People Health Foundation 255 Carter Hall Ln *TF:* 800-544-4673 ■ *Web:* www.projecthope.org	Millwood	VA	22646	540-837-2100	837-1813
Physicians for Human Rights (PHR) 2 Arrow St Suite 301 *Web:* www.phrusa.org	Cambridge	MA	02138	617-301-4200	301-4250
Physicians for Social Responsibility (PSR) 1875 Connecticut Ave NW Suite 1012 *Web:* www.psr.org	Washington	DC	20009	202-667-4260	667-4201
Points of Light Foundation & Volunteer Center National Network 1400 'I' St NW Suite 800 *TF:* 800-750-7653 ■ *Web:* www.pointsoflight.org	Washington	DC	20005	202-729-8000	729-8100
Population Action International (PAI) 1300 19th St NW 2nd Fl *Web:* www.populationaction.org	Washington	DC	20036	202-557-3400	728-4177
Population Communication 1250 E Walnut St Suite 220	Pasadena	CA	91106	626-793-4750	793-4791
Population Connection 2120 L St NW Suite 5001 *TF:* 800-767-1956 ■ *Web:* www.populationconnection.org	Washington	DC	20037	202-332-2200	332-2302
Population Resource Ctr (PRC) 1725 K St NW *Web:* www.prcdc.org	Washington	DC	20006	202-467-5030	467-5034
Presbyterian Disaster Assistance (PDA) 100 Witherspoon St *TF:* 888-728-7228 ■ *Web:* www.pcusa.org/pda	Louisville	KY	40202	502-569-5839	569-8039
Private Agencies Collaborating Together (PACT) 1200 18th St NW Suite 350 *Web:* www.pactworld.org	Washington	DC	20036	202-466-5666	466-5669

Organization	City	State	ZIP	Phone	Fax
Project Concern International (PCI) 5151 Murphy Canyon Rd Suite 320 *TF:* 877-724-4673 ■ *Web:* www.pciglobal.org	San Diego	CA	92123	858-279-9690	694-0294
ProLiteracy Worldwide 1320 Jamesville Ave *TF:* 800-448-8878 ■ *Web:* www.proliteracy.org	Syracuse	NY	13210	315-422-9121	422-6369
Public Responsibility in Medicine Research (PRIM&R) 126 Brookline Ave Suite 202 PO Box 845203 *Web:* www.primr.org/membership/overview.html	Boston	MA	02215	617-423-4112	423-1185
Rainbow/PUSH Coalition Inc 930 E 50th St *Web:* www.rainbowpush.org	Chicago	IL	60615	773-373-3366	373-3571
Random Acts of Kindness Foundation 1727 Tremont Pl *TF:* 800-660-2811 ■ *Web:* www.randomactsofkindness.org	Denver	CO	80202	303-297-1964	297-2919
REACT International Inc 5210 Auth Rd Suite 403 *Web:* www.reactintl.org	Suitland	MD	20746	301-316-2900	316-2903
Rebuilding Together Inc 1899 L St NW Suite 1000 *TF:* 800-473-4229 ■ *Web:* www.rebuildingtogether.org	Washington	DC	20036	202-483-9083	483-9081
Refugees International (RI) 2001 S St NW Suite 700-K *TF:* 800-733-8433 ■ *Web:* www.refugeesinternational.org	Washington	DC	20009	202-828-0110	828-0819
Research!America 1101 King St Suite 520 *TF:* 800-366-2873 ■ *Web:* www.researchamerica.org	Alexandria	VA	22314	703-739-2577	739-2372
Resource Foundation The 237 W 35th St Suite 1203 *Web:* www.resourcefnd.org	New York	NY	10001	212-675-6170	268-5325
Resource Inc 1900 Chicago Ave S *Web:* www.resource-mn.org	Minneapolis	MN	55404	612-752-8000	752-8001
RESULTS 750 1st St NE # 1040 *Web:* www.results.org	Washington	DC	20002	202-783-7100	783-2818
Ronald McDonald House Charities (RMHC) 1 Kroc Dr Dept 014 *Web:* www.rmhc.org	Oak Brook	IL	60523	630-623-7048	623-7488
Rotary Foundation The 1560 Sherman Ave *Web:* www.rotary.org	Evanston	IL	60201	847-866-3000	328-8554
Salvation Army 6528 Little River Tpke *TF:* 800-725-2769 ■ *Web:* www.salvationarmyusa.org	Alexandria	VA	22312	703-642-9270	642-3556
Save the Children Federation Inc 54 Wilton Rd *TF:* 800-728-3843 ■ *Web:* www.savethechildren.org	Westport	CT	06880	203-221-4000	
Second Harvest Food Bank of Central Florida 2008 Brengle Ave *Web:* www.foodbankcentralflorida.org	Orlando	FL	32808	407-295-1066	292-4758
Senior Gleaners Inc 1951 Bell Ave *TF:* 800-585-1530 ■ *Web:* www.seniorgleaners.org	Sacramento	CA	95838	916-925-3240	568-1528
Sertoma International 1912 E Meyer Blvd *TF:* 800-593-5646 ■ *Web:* www.sertoma.org	Kansas City	MO	64132	816-333-8300	333-4320
SHARE El Salvador 2425 College Ave *Web:* www.share-elsalvador.org	Berkeley	CA	94704	510-848-8487	
Share Our Strength 1730 M St NW Suite 700 *TF:* 800-969-4767 ■ *Web:* www.strength.org	Washington	DC	20036	202-393-2925	347-5868
Smile Train Inc 41 Madison Ave # 28 *TF:* 877-543-7645 ■ *Web:* www.smiletrain.org	New York	NY	10010	212-689-9199	689-9299
Society of Saint Andrew (SoSA) 3383 Sweet Hollow Rd *TF:* 800-333-4597 ■ *Web:* www.endhunger.org	Big Island	VA	24526	434-299-5956	299-5949
Soroptimist International of the Americas 1709 Spruce St *Web:* www.soroptimist.org	Philadelphia	PA	19103	215-893-9000	893-5200
Southeast Asia Resource Action Ctr (SEARAC) 1628 16th St NW 3rd Fl *TF:* 800-600-9188 ■ *Web:* www.searac.org	Washington	DC	20009	202-667-4690	667-6449
Special Wish Foundation Inc 1250 Memory Ln Suite B-1 *TF:* 800-486-9474 ■ *Web:* www.spwish.org	Columbus	OH	43209	614-258-3186	258-3518
Survivor Corps 2100 M St NW Suite 170-342 *Web:* www.survivorcorps.org	Washington	DC	20037	202-464-0007	464-0011
Synergos Institute Inc 51 Madison Ave 21st Fl *Web:* www.synergos.org	New York	NY	10010	212-447-8111	447-8119
TechnoServe 49 Day St *TF:* 800-999-6757 ■ *Web:* www.technoserve.org	Norwalk	CT	06854	203-852-0377	838-6717
Trickle Up Program Inc 104 W 27th St 12th Fl *TF:* 866-246-9980 ■ *Web:* www.trickleup.org	New York	NY	10001	212-255-9980	255-9974
Turning Point Community Programs 3440 Viking Dr Suite 114 *Web:* www.tpcp.org	Sacramento	CA	95827	916-364-8395	
Unitarian Universalist Service Committee (UUSC) 689 Massachusetts Ave *TF:* 800-388-3920 ■ *Web:* www.uusc.org	Cambridge	MA	02139	617-868-6600	868-7102
United Methodist Committee on Relief (UMCOR) 475 Riverside Dr Rm 1520 *TF:* 800-554-8583 ■ *Web:* www.gbgm-umc.org/umcor	New York	NY	10115	212-870-3951	870-3624
United Nations Children's Fund (UNICEF) 3 United Nations Plaza *TF:* 800-553-1200 ■ *Web:* www.unicef.org	New York	NY	10017	212-326-7000	888-7465
United Nations Foundation (UNF) 1800 Massachusetts Ave NW Suite 400 *Web:* www.unfoundation.org	Washington	DC	20036	202-887-9040	887-9021
United Way International 701 N Fairfax St *Web:* www.worldwide.unitedway.org	Alexandria	VA	22314	703-894-4955	519-0097
United Way of America 701 N Fairfax St *TF:* 800-892-2757 ■ *Web:* www.liveunited.org	Alexandria	VA	22314	703-836-7100	683-7840
US Committee for Refugees & Immigrants (USCRI) 2231 Crystal Dr Suite 350 *Web:* www.refugees.org	Arlington	VA	22202	703-310-1130	769-4241
US Fund for UNICEF 125 Maiden Ln *Web:* www.unicefusa.org	New York	NY	10016	212-922-2649	779-1679
USA for UNHCR 1775 K St NW Suite 290 *TF:* 800-770-1100 ■ *Web:* www.unrefugees.org	Washington	DC	20006	202-296-1115	296-1081
Veterans for Peace Inc (VFP) 216 S Meramec Ave *Web:* www.veteransforpeace.org	Saint Louis	MO	63105	314-725-6005	725-7103
Voices of September 11th 161 Cherry St *TF:* 866-505-3911 ■ *Web:* www.voicesofsept11.org	New Canaan	CT	06840	203-966-3911	966-5701
Volunteers of America 1660 Duke St *TF:* 800-899-0089 ■ *Web:* www.voa.org	Alexandria	VA	22314	703-341-5000	341-7000
War Resisters League 339 Lafayette St *Web:* www.warresisters.org	New York	NY	10012	212-228-0450	228-6193
Women's Action for New Directions (WAND) 691 Massachusetts Ave *Web:* www.wand.org	Arlington	MA	02476	781-643-6740	643-6744
World Concern 19303 Fremont Ave N *TF:* 800-755-5022 ■ *Web:* www.worldconcern.org	Seattle	WA	98133	206-546-7201	546-7269
World Education Inc 44 Farnsworth St *Web:* www.worlded.org	Boston	MA	02210	617-482-9485	482-0617
World Hunger Year Inc (WHY) 505 8th Ave Suite 2100 *TF:* 800-548-6479 ■ *Web:* www.whyhunger.org	New York	NY	10018	212-629-8850	465-9274
World Learning 1015 18th St NW Suite 1000 *TF:* 800-826-0196 ■ *Web:* www.worldlearning.org	Washington	DC	20036	202-898-0950	842-0885
World Neighbors Inc (WN) 4127 NW 122nd St *TF:* 800-242-6387 ■ *Web:* www.wn.org	Oklahoma City	OK	73120	405-752-9700	752-9393
World Peace Prayer Society 26 Benton Rd *Web:* www.worldpeace.org	Wassaic	NY	12592	845-877-6093	877-6862
World Relief 7 E Baltimore St *TF:* 800-535-5433 ■ *Web:* www.worldrelief.org	Baltimore	MD	21202	443-451-1900	451-1995
World Vision Inc PO Box 9716 **Fax: Cust Svc* ■ *TF:* 888-511-6443 ■ *Web:* www.donate.worldvision.org	Federal Way	WA	98063	253-815-1000	815-5951*

48-6 Children & Family Advocacy Organizations

Organization	City	State	ZIP	Phone	Fax
AARP 601 E St NW *TF:* 888-687-2277 ■ *Web:* www.aarp.org	Washington	DC	20049	202-434-2277	434-7597
AARP Grandparent Information Ctr 601 E St NW *TF:* 888-687-2277 ■ *Web:* www.aarp.org/grandparents	Washington	DC	20049	202-434-3525	434-6474
ABA Center on Children & the Law 740 15th St NW 9th Fl *TF:* 800-285-2221 ■ *Web:* www.americanbar.org	Washington	DC	20005	202-662-1720	662-1755
Adoption ARC Inc 4701 Pine St Suite J-7 *TF:* 800-884-4004 ■ *Web:* www.adoptionarc.com	Philadelphia	PA	19143	215-748-1441	842-9881
Adoptive Families of America 39 W 37th St 15th Fl *Web:* www.adoptivefamilies.com	New York	NY	10018	646-366-0830	366-0842
Alliance for Aging Research (AAR) 750 17th St NW Suite 1100 *TF:* 800-639-2421 ■ *Web:* www.agingresearch.org	Washington	DC	20006	202-293-2856	255-8394
Alliance for Children & Families Inc 11700 W Lake Pk Dr *TF:* 800-221-3726 ■ *Web:* www.alliance1.org	Milwaukee	WI	53224	414-359-1040	359-1074
Alliance for Retired Americans 815 16th St NW 4th Fl *TF:* 888-373-6497 ■ *Web:* www.retiredamericans.org	Washington	DC	20006	202-637-5399	637-5398
America's Promise - the Alliance for Youth 909 N Washington St Suite 400 *TF:* 800-365-0153 ■ *Web:* www.americaspromise.org	Alexandria	VA	22314	703-684-4500	535-3900
American Academy of Pediatrics (AAP) 141 NW Pt Blvd *TF:* 800-433-9016 ■ *Web:* www.aap.org	Elk Grove Village	IL	60007	847-434-4000	434-8000
American Adoption Congress (AAC) PO Box 42730 *Web:* www.americanadoptioncongress.org	Washington	DC	20015	202-483-3399	
American Assn for Marriage & Family Therapy (AAMFT) 112 S Alfred St *Web:* www.aamft.org	Alexandria	VA	22314	703-838-9808	838-9805
American Coalition for Fathers & Children (ACFC) 1420 Spring Hill Rd **Fax Area Code: 703* ■ *TF:* 800-978-3237 ■ *Web:* www.acfc.org	McLean	VA	22102	800-978-3237	442-5313*
American Culinary Federation Chef & Child Foundation 180 Ctr Pl Way *TF:* 800-624-9458 ■ *Web:* www.acfchefs.org/Content/ACFPrograms/ChefandChild	Saint Augustine	FL	32095	904-824-4468	825-4758
American Humane Assn (AHA) 63 Inverness Dr E *TF:* 800-227-4645 ■ *Web:* www.americanhumane.org	Englewood	CO	80112	303-792-9900	792-5333
American Senior Fitness Assn (SFA) PO Box 2575 *TF:* 888-689-6791 ■ *Web:* www.seniorfitness.org	New Smyrna Beach	FL	32170	386-423-6634	427-0613
American Seniors Housing Assn (ASHA) 5225 Wisconsin Ave NW # 502 *Web:* www.seniorshousing.org	Washington	DC	20015	202-237-0900	237-1616
American SIDS Institute 528 Raven Way *TF:* 800-232-7437 ■ *Web:* www.sids.org	Naples	FL	34110	239-431-5425	431-5536
American Society on Aging (ASA) 71 Stevenson St # 1450 *TF:* 800-537-9728 ■ *Web:* www.asaging.org	San Francisco	CA	94105	415-974-9600	974-0300
Assn for Couples in Marriage Enrichment (ACME) PO Box 21374 *TF:* 800-634-8325 ■ *Web:* www.bettermarriages.org	Winston-Salem	NC	27120	336-724-1526	721-4746
Assn of Jewish Aging Services (AJAS) 316 Pennsylvania Ave SE Suite 402 *Web:* www.ajas.org	Washington	DC	20003	202-543-7500	543-4090
Athletes & Entertainers for Kids (AEFK) 14340 Bolsa Chica Rd Unit C	Westminster	CA	92683	714-894-5450	
Believe In Tomorrow National Children's Foundation 6601 Frederick Rd *TF:* 800-933-5470 ■ *Web:* www.believeintomorrow.org	Baltimore	MD	21228	410-744-1032	744-1984
Big Bros Big Sisters of America (BBBSA) 230 N 13th St *Web:* www.bbbs.org	Philadelphia	PA	19107	215-567-7000	567-0394

Organization	City	State	Zip	Phone	Fax
Blue Grass Regional Mental Health-Mental Retardation Board Inc 1351 Newtown Pike Bldg 1 *Web:* www.bluegrass.org	Lexington	KY	40511	859-253-1686	255-4866
Boys Town 14100 Crawford St *TF:* 800-448-3000 ■ *Web:* www.boystown.org	Boys Town	NE	68010	402-498-1300	498-1348
Buckner International 600 N Pearl St Suite 2000, 20th Fl *TF:* 800-442-4800 ■ *Web:* www.buckner.org	Dallas	TX	75201	214-758-8000	758-8159
Cal Farley's Boys Ranch 600 W 11th St PO Box 1890 *TF:* 800-687-3722 ■ *Web:* www.calfarley.org	Amarillo	TX	79174	806-372-2341	372-6638
Camelot Community Care Inc 4910 D Creekside Dr *Web:* www.camelotcommunitycare.org	Clearwater	FL	33760	727-593-0003	595-0735
Campaign for a Commercial-Free Childhood (CCFC) Judge Baker Children's Ctr 3 Parker Hill Ave *Web:* www.commercialexploitation.org	Boston	MA	02120	617-278-4172	232-7343
CARP: Canada's Assn for the Fifty-Plus 1304-27 Queen St E *TF:* 800-363-9736 ■ *Web:* www.50plus.com	Toronto	ON	M5C2M6	416-363-8748	363-8747
Center For Community & Family Services (CCFS) 2555 E Colorado Blvd Suite 200 *Web:* www.ccafs.org	Pasadena	CA	91107	626-795-7990	795-7897
Child Alert Foundation (CAF) Rt 87 S PO Box 357 *Web:* www.childalert.org	Dushore	PA	18614	570-928-8422	928-8110
Child Find Canada 212-2211 McPhillips St *TF:* 800-387-7962 ■ *Web:* www.childfind.ca	Winnipeg	MB	R2V0M5	204-339-5584	339-5587
Child Lures Prevention 5166 Shelburne Rd *TF:* 800-552-2197 ■ *Web:* www.childluresprevention.com	Shelburne	VT	05482	802-985-8458	985-8418
Child Quest International 1060 N 4th St Suite 200 *TF:* 888-818-4673 ■ *Web:* www.childquest.org	San Jose	CA	95112	408-287-4673	287-4676
Child Trends 4301 Connecticut Ave NW Suite 100 *Web:* www.childtrends.org	Washington	DC	20008	202-572-6000	362-8420
Child Welfare League of America (CWLA) 2345 Crystal Dr Suite 250 *Web:* www.cwla.org	Arlington	VA	22202	703-412-2430	412-2401
Childhelp USA 15757 N 78th St Suite B *TF:* 800-422-4453 ■ *Web:* www.childhelpusa.org	Scottsdale	AZ	85260	480-922-8212	922-7061
Children Awaiting Parents Inc (CAP) 595 Blossom Rd Suite 306 *TF:* 888-835-8802 ■ *Web:* www.capbook.org	Rochester	NY	14610	585-232-5110	232-2634
Children Inc 4205 Dover Rd *TF:* 800-538-5381 ■ *Web:* www.children-inc.org	Richmond	VA	23221	804-359-4562	
Children of Aging Parents PO Box 167 **Fax Area Code:* 215 ■ *TF:* 800-227-7294 ■ *Web:* www.caps4caregivers.org	Richboro	PA	18954	800-227-7294	945-8720*
Children of Deaf Adults International Inc (CODA) 3131 Calle Mariposa *Web:* www.coda-international.org	Santa Barbara	CA	93105	805-682-0997	
Children of the Night 14530 Sylvan St *TF:* 800-551-1300 ■ *Web:* www.childrenofthenight.org	Van Nuys	CA	91411	818-908-4474	908-1468
Children's Defense Fund (CDF) 25 E St NW *TF:* 800-233-1200 ■ *Web:* www.childrensdefense.org	Washington	DC	20001	202-628-8787	662-3510
Children's Rights Council (CRC) 8181 Professional Pl Suite 240 *TF:* 800-787-5437 ■ *Web:* www.crckids.org	Landover	MD	20785	301-459-1220	459-1227
Christian Children's Fund Inc (CCF) 2821 Emerywood Pkwy *TF:* 800-776-6767 ■ *Web:* www.christianchildrensfund.org	Richmond	VA	23294	804-756-2700	756-2718
Christian Foundation for Children & Aging (CFCA) 1 Elmwood Ave *TF:* 800-875-6564 ■ *Web:* www.cfcausa.org	Kansas City	KS	66103	913-384-6500	384-2211
CityKids Foundation 57 Leonard St *Web:* www.citykids.com	New York	NY	10013	212-925-3320	925-0128
Common Sense About Kids & Guns 1225 I St NW Suite 1100 *TF:* 877-955-5437 ■ *Web:* www.kidsandguns.org	Washington	DC	20005	202-546-0200	371-9615
Communities in Schools Inc (CIS) 277 S Washington St Suite 210 *TF:* 800-247-4543 ■ *Web:* www.cisnet.org	Alexandria	VA	22314	703-519-8999	519-7537
Community Options Inc 16 Farber Rd *Web:* www.comop.org	Princeton	NJ	08540	609-951-9900	951-9112
Connecting Generations 100 W 10th St Suite 1115 *TF:* 877-202-9050 ■ *Web:* www.connecting-generations.org	Wilmington	DE	19801	302-656-2122	656-2123
Consortium for Citizens with Disabilities (CCD) 1660 L St NW Suite 701 *Web:* www.c-c-d.org	Washington	DC	20036	202-783-2229	783-8250
Corps Network The 666 11th St NW Suite 1000 *TF:* 800-666-2722 ■ *Web:* www.corpsnetwork.org	Washington	DC	20001	202-737-6272	737-6277
Council for Equal Rights in Adoption 444 E 76th St *Web:* www.adoptionhealing.com	New York	NY	10021	212-988-0110	988-0291
Covenant House 5 Penn Plaza 3rd Fl **Fax:* Hum Res ■ *TF:* 800-999-9999 ■ *Web:* www.covenanthouse.org	New York	NY	10001	212-727-4000	727-6516*
Crossroads For Youth 930 E Drahner PO Box 9 *Web:* www.crossroadsforyouth.org	Oxford	MI	48371	248-628-2561	628-3080
DePelchin Children's Ctr 4950 Memorial Dr *Web:* www.depelchin.org	Houston	TX	77007	713-730-2335	802-3801
Eden Alternative 14500 RR 12 Suite 2 *Web:* www.edenalt.com	Wimberley	TX	78676	512-847-6061	847-6191
Envision Inc 610 N Main St *Web:* www.envisionus.com	Wichita	KS	67203	316-440-1500	440-1540
Evan B Donaldson Adoption Institute 120 E 38th St **Fax Area Code:* 775 ■ *Web:* www.adoptioninstitute.org	New York	NY	10016	212-925-4089	796-6592*
Experience Works Inc 2200 Clarendon Blvd Suite 1000 *TF:* 866-397-9757 ■ *Web:* www.experienceworks.org	Arlington	VA	22203	703-522-7272	522-0141
Family Research Council (FRC) 801 G St NW *TF:* 800-225-4008 ■ *Web:* www.frc.org	Washington	DC	20001	202-393-2100	393-2134
Family Violence Prevention Fund (FVPF) 383 Rhode Island St Suite 304 *Web:* www.futureswithoutviolence.org	San Francisco	CA	94103	415-252-8900	252-8991
Federation of Families for Children's Mental Health (FFCMH) 9605 Medical Ctr Dr Suite 280 *Web:* www.ffcmh.org	Rockville	MD	28050	240-403-1901	403-1909
Find the Children 2656 29th St Suite 203 *TF:* 888-477-6721 ■ *Web:* www.findthechildren.com	Santa Monica	CA	90405	310-314-3213	314-3169
First Candle 1314 Bedford Ave Suite 210 *TF:* 800-221-7437 ■ *Web:* www.firstcandle.org	Baltimore	MD	21208	410-653-8226	653-8709
Focus on the Family 8605 Explorer Dr *TF Sales:* 800-232-6459 ■ *Web:* www.focusonthefamily.com	Colorado Springs	CO	80920	719-531-3400	548-4670
Food Research & Action Ctr (FRAC) 1875 Connecticut Ave NW Suite 540 *Web:* www.frac.org	Washington	DC	20009	202-986-2200	986-2525
Generations United (GU) 1333 H St NW Suite 500-W *Web:* www.gu.org	Washington	DC	20005	202-289-3979	289-3952
Gill Foundation Inc The 2215 Market St *TF:* 888-530-4455 ■ *Web:* www.gillfoundation.org	Denver	CO	80205	303-292-4455	292-2155
Girls Inc 120 Wall St 3rd Fl *TF:* 800-374-4475 ■ *Web:* www.girlsinc.org	New York	NY	10005	212-509-2000	509-8708
Grandparents Rights Organization (GRO) 100 W Long Lake Rd Suite 250 *Web:* www.grandparentsrights.org	Bloomfield Hills	MI	48304	248-646-7177	646-9722
Gray Panthers 1612 K St NW Suite 3000 *TF:* 800-280-5362 ■ *Web:* www.graypanthers.org	Washington	DC	20006	202-737-6637	737-1160
Head Start Child Development Council Inc 2451 Country Club Blvd *Web:* www.hscdc.org	Stockton	CA	95204	209-466-5541	466-7300
Healthy Teen Network 1501 St Paul St Suite 124 *Web:* www.healthyteennetwork.org	Baltimore	MD	21202	410-685-0410	685-0481
Human Life International (HLI) 4 Family Life Ln *TF Orders:* 800-549-5433 ■ *Web:* www.hli.org	Front Royal	VA	22630	540-635-7884	622-6247
Ignitus Worldwide 9200 S Dadeland Blvd Suite 417 *Web:* www.ignitusworldwide.org	Miami	FL	33156	305-670-2409	670-3805
International MOMS Club 1464 Madera Rd Suite N-191 *Web:* www.momsclub.org	Simi Valley	CA	93065	805-526-2725	
International Soundex Reunion Registry PO Box 2312 *Web:* www.isrr.net	Carson City	NV	89702	775-882-7755	
Jewish Assn for Services for the Aged (JASA) 132 W 31st St *Web:* www.jasa.org	New York	NY	10001	212-273-5272	695-9070
Jewish Board of Family & Children Services (JBFCS) 120 W 57th St *TF:* 888-523-2769 ■ *Web:* www.jbfcs.org	New York	NY	10019	212-582-9100	956-5676
Kansas Children's Service League (KCSL) 3545 SW 5th *TF:* 877-530-5275 ■ *Web:* www.kcsl.org	Topeka	KS	66606	785-274-3100	
Kempe Children's Ctr 1825 Marion St *Web:* www.kempe.org	Denver	CO	80218	303-864-5300	864-5302
KlaasKids Foundation 19 Cypress Pl *Web:* www.klaaskids.org	Sausalito	CA	94965	415-331-6867	331-5633
Leading Age 2519 Connecticut Ave NW *Web:* www.leadingage.org	Washington	DC	20008	202-783-2242	783-2255
Little Flower Children & Family Services of New York 2450 N Wading River Rd *Web:* www.littleflowerny.org	Wading River	NY	11792	631-929-6200	929-6121
Margaret Sanger Center International (MSCI) 26 Bleecker St *Web:* www.plannedparenthood.org	New York	NY	10012	212-965-7000	274-7299
May Institute Inc 41 Pacella Pk Dr *TF:* 800-778-7601 ■ *Web:* www.mayinstitute.org	Randolph	MA	02368	781-440-0400	
Men Against Destruction Defending Against Drugs & Social Disorder Inc (MAD DADS) 555 Stockton St *Web:* www.maddads.com	Jacksonville	FL	32204	904-388-8171	
MENTOR/National Mentoring Partnership 1600 Duke St Suite 300 *Web:* www.mentoring.org	Alexandria	VA	22314	703-224-2200	226-2581
Mentoring USA 5 Hanover Sq *Web:* www.helpusa.org	New York	NY	10004	212-400-8294	400-8278
MOPS International 2370 S Trenton Way *TF:* 800-691-8061 ■ *Web:* www.mops.org	Denver	CO	80231	303-733-5353	733-5770
Mothers & More 101 N Addison Ave # 204 *Web:* www.mothersandmore.org	Elmhurst	IL	60126	630-941-3553	941-3551
Mothers Against Drunk Driving (MADD) 511 E John Carpenter Fwy Suite 700 **Fax Area Code:* 972 ■ *TF:* 877-275-6233 ■ *Web:* www.madd.org	Irving	TX	75062	214-744-6233	869-2207*
Mothers of Supertwins (MOST) 116 Yuma Ln *Web:* www.mostonline.org	East Islip	NY	11730	631-859-1110	
NA for Hispanic Elderly 1452 W Temple St Suite 100	Los Angeles	CA	90026	213-202-5900	202-5905
NA for Home Care & Hospice (NAHC) 228 7th St SE *Web:* www.nahc.org	Washington	DC	20003	202-547-7424	547-3540
NA of Child Care Professionals (NACCP) 7608 W Hwy 71 # E *TF:* 800-537-1118 ■ *Web:* www.naccp.org	Austin	TX	78735	512-301-5557	301-5080
NA of Child Care Resource & Referral Agencies (NACCRRA) 3101 Wilson Blvd Suite 350 *TF:* 800-424-2246 ■ *Web:* www.naccrra.org	Arlington	VA	22201	703-341-4100	341-4101
NAMES Project Foundation/AIDS Memorial Quilt 101 Krog St *Web:* www.aidsquilt.org	Atlanta	GA	30307	404-688-5500	688-5552

				Phone	Fax
National Adoption Ctr 1500 Walnut St Suite 701 .... Philadelphia *Web:* www.adopt.org	PA	19102	215-735-9988	735-9410
National Adult Day Services Assn (NADSA) 1421 E Broad St Suite 425 .... Fuquay Varina *TF:* 877-745-1440 ■ *Web:* www.nadsa.org	NC	27526	919-552-0254	552-0254
National Alliance for Caregiving 4720 Montgomery Ln 5th Fl .... Bethesda *Web:* www.caregiving.org	MD	20814	301-718-8444	652-7711
National Caregiving Foundation 801 N Pitt St Suite 116 .... Alexandria *TF:* 800-930-1357 ■ *Web:* www.caregivingfoundation.org	VA	22314	703-299-9300	299-9304
National Caucus & Center on Black Aged Inc (NCBA) 1220 L St NW Suite 800 .... Washington *Web:* www.ncba-aged.org	DC	20005	202-637-8400	347-0895
National Center for Children in Poverty (NCCP) 215 W 125th St 3rd Fl .... New York *Web:* www.nccp.org	NY	10027	646-284-9600	284-9623
National Center for Family Literacy (NCFL) 325 W Main St Suite 300 .... Louisville *TF:* 877-326-5481 ■ *Web:* www.famlit.org	KY	40202	502-584-1133	584-0172
National Center for Missing & Exploited Children (NCMEC) 699 Prince St .... Alexandria *TF:* 800-843-5678 ■ *Web:* www.missingkids.com	VA	22314	703-274-3900	274-2200
National Center on Elder Abuse (NCEA) 297 Graham Hall .... Newark *Web:* www.ncea.aoa.gov	DE	19716	302-831-3525	831-4225
National Child Care Assn (NCCA) 1325 G St NW Suite 500 .... Washington *TF:* 800-543-7161 ■ *Web:* www.nccanet.org	DC	20005	202-367-1133	
National Child Safety Council (NCSC) 4065 Page Ave .... Jackson *TF:* 800-327-5107	MI	49204	517-764-6070	764-3068
National Child Support Enforcement Assn (NCSEA) 1760 Old Meadow Rd Suite 500 .... McLean *Web:* www.ncsea.org	VA	22102	703-506-2880	506-3266
National Coalition Against Domestic Violence (NCADV) One Broadway Suite B210 .... Denver *TF:* 800-799-7233 ■ *Web:* www.ncadv.org	CO	80203	303-839-1852	831-9251
National Coalition for the Protection of Children & Families (NCPCF) 800 Compton Rd Suite 9224 .... Cincinnati *Web:* www.eos.net	OH	45231	513-521-6227	521-6337
National Council for Adoption (NCFA) 225 N Washington St .... Alexandria *Web:* www.adoptioncouncil.org	VA	22314	703-299-6633	299-6004
National Council on Family Relations (NCFR) 3989 Central Ave NE Suite 550 .... Minneapolis *TF:* 888-781-9331 ■ *Web:* www.ncfr.com	MN	55421	763-781-9331	781-9348
National Council on the Aging (NCOA) 1901 L St NW 4th Fl .... Washington *TF:* 800-424-9046 ■ *Web:* www.ncoa.org	DC	20036	202-479-1200	479-0735
National Court Appointed Special Advocate Assn (CASA) 100 W Harrison St N Tower Suite 500 .... Seattle *TF:* 800-628-3233 ■ *Web:* www.casaforchildren.org	WA	98119	206-270-0072	270-0078
National Domestic Violence Hotline (NDVH) PO Box 161810 .... Austin *TF:* 800-799-7233 ■ *Web:* www.thehotline.org	TX	78716	512-794-1133	453-8541
National Family Caregivers Assn (NFCA) 10400 Connecticut Ave Suite 500 .... Kensington *TF:* 800-896-3650 ■ *Web:* www.nfcacares.org	MD	20895	301-942-6430	942-2302
National Healthy Mothers Healthy Babies Coalition (HMHB) 2000 N Beauregard St 6th Fl .... Alexandria *Web:* www.hmhb.org	VA	22311	703-837-4792	634-5968
National Hispanic Council on Aging (NHCOA) 734 15th St NW Suite 1050 .... Washington *Web:* www.nhcoa.org	DC	20005	202-347-9733	347-9735
National Independent Living Assn (NILA) 4203 Southpoint Blvd .... Jacksonville *Web:* www.nilausa.org	FL	32216	904-296-1038	296-1953
National Indian Council on Aging (NICOA) 10501 Montgomery Blvd NE Suite 210 .... Albuquerque *Web:* www.nicoa.org	NM	87111	505-292-2001	292-1922
National Interfaith Coalition on Aging (NICA) 1901 L St NW 4th Fl .... Washington *TF:* 800-424-9046 ■ *Web:* www.ncoa.org	DC	20036	202-479-1200	479-0735
National Network for Youth The 741 8th St SE .... Washington *Web:* www.nn4youth.org	DC	20003	202-783-7949	783-7955
National Organization of Mothers of Twins Clubs Inc (NOMOTC) PO Box 700860 .... Plymouth *Web:* www.nomotc.org	MI	48170	248-231-4480	
National Organization of Single Mothers PO Box 68 .... Midland *Web:* www.singlemothers.org	NC	28107	704-888-5437	
National Program on Women & Aging Brandeis University Institute on Assets & Social Policy MS 035 .... Waltham *Web:* iasp.brandeis.edu/womenandaging	MA	02454	781-736-8685	
National Resource Center on Domestic Violence (NRCDV) 6400 Flank Dr Suite 1300 .... Harrisburg *TF:* 800-537-2238 ■ *Web:* www.nrcdv.org	PA	17112	717-545-6400	545-9456
National Resource Center on Native American Aging (NRCNAA) 501 N Columbia Rd Rm 4535 .... Grand Forks *TF:* 800-896-7628 ■ *Web:* www.med.und.nodak.edu/depts/rural//nrcnaa	ND	58202	701-777-3437	777-6779
National Resource Center on Nutrition Physical Activity & Aging Florida International Univ 11200 SW 8th St Bldg OE200 .... Miami *Web:* nutritionandaging.fiu.edu	FL	33199	305-348-1517	348-1518
National Runaway Switchboard (NRS) 3080 N Lincoln Ave .... Chicago *TF:* 800-621-4000 ■ *Web:* www.nrscrisisline.org	IL	60657	773-880-9860	929-5150
National SAFE KIDS Campaign 1301 Pennsylvania Ave NW Suite 1000 .... Washington *Web:* www.safekids.org	DC	20004	202-662-0600	393-2072
National Senior Citizens Law Ctr (NSCLC) 1444 'I' St Suite 1100 .... Washington *Web:* www.nsclc.org	DC	20005	202-289-6976	289-7224
National Urban Technology Ctr 80 Maiden Ln Suite 606 .... New York *TF:* 800-998-3212 ■ *Web:* www.urbantech.org	NY	10038	212-528-7350	528-7355
National WIC Assn (NWA) 2001 S St NW Suite 580 .... Washington *Web:* www.nwica.org	DC	20009	202-232-5492	387-5281
National Youth Advocacy Coalition (NYAC) 1638 R St NW Suite 300 .... Washington *TF:* 800-541-6922 ■ *Web:* www.nyacyouth.org	DC	20009	202-319-7596	319-7365
North America Missing Children Assn Inc (NAMCA) 202 Brownlow Ave Bldg F, Unit L .... Dartmouth *TF:* 800-260-0753 ■ *Web:* www.chebucto.ns.ca	NS	B3B1T5	902-468-2524	468-2803
North American Council on Adoptable Children (NACAC) 970 Raymond Ave Suite 106 .... Saint Paul *Web:* www.nacac.org	MN	55114	651-644-3036	644-9848
Orphan Foundation of America (OFA) 12020 N Shore Dr .... Reston *TF:* 800-950-4673 ■ *Web:* www.orphan.org	VA	20190	571-203-0270	203-0273
Parents Helping Parents (PHP) 1400 Parkmoor Ave Suite 100 .... San jose *TF:* 855-727-5775 ■ *Web:* www.php.com	CA	95126	408-727-5775	286-1116
Parents of Murdered Children (POMC) 100 E 8th St Suite B-41 .... Cincinnati *TF:* 888-818-7662 ■ *Web:* www.pomc.com	OH	45202	513-721-5683	345-4489
Parsons Child & Family Ctr 60 Academy Rd .... Albany *Web:* www.parsonscenter.org	NY	12208	518-426-2600	447-5234
Pension Rights Ctr 1350 Connecticut Ave NW Suite 206 .... Washington *Web:* www.pensionrights.org	DC	20036	202-296-3776	833-2472
Plan USA 155 Plan Way .... Warwick *TF:* 800-556-7918 ■ *Web:* www.planusa.org	RI	02886	401-738-5600	738-5608
Planned Parenthood Federation of America 434 W 33rd St .... New York *TF:* 800-829-7732 ■ *Web:* www.plannedparenthood.org	NY	10001	212-541-7800	245-1845
Pressley Ridge 5500 Corporate Dr Suite 400 .... Pittsburgh *Web:* www.pressleyridge.org	PA	15237	412-872-9400	872-9478
Prevent Child Abuse America 200 S Michigan Ave 17th Fl .... Chicago *TF:* 800-244-5373 ■ *Web:* www.preventchildabuse.org	IL	60604	312-663-3520	939-8962
Promise Keepers (PK) PO Box 11798 .... Denver *TF:* 866-776-6473 ■ *Web:* www.promisekeepers.org	CO	80211	303-964-7600	433-1036
Rainbows 1360 hamilton Pkwy .... Itasca *TF:* 800-266-3206 ■ *Web:* www.rainbows.org	IL	60143	847-952-1770	952-1774
Rape Abuse & Incest National Network (RAINN) 635 Pennsylvania Ave SE # B .... Washington *TF:* 800-656-4673 ■ *Web:* www.rainn.org	DC	20003	202-544-1034	544-3556
Safer Foundation 571 W Jackson Blvd .... Chicago *Web:* www.saferfoundation.org	IL	60661	312-922-2200	922-0839
SOS Children's Villages-USA 1317 F St NW1200 6th St NW Suite 550 .... Washington **Fax:* Hum Res ■ *TF:* 800-886-5767 ■ *Web:* www.sos-childrensvillages.org	DC	20005	202-347-7920	347-7334*
Spaulding for Children 16250 Northland Dr Suite 120 .... Southfield *TF Cust Svc:* 877-767-5437 ■ *Web:* www.spaulding.org	MI	48075	248-443-7080	443-7099
Stand For Children 516 SE Morrison St Suite 206 .... Portland *TF:* 800-663-4032 ■ *Web:* www.stand.org	OR	97214	503-235-2305	963-9517
Stars of David International Inc 3175 Commercial Ave Suite 100 .... Northbrook **Fax Area Code:* 773 ■ *TF:* 800-782-7349 ■ *Web:* www.starsofdavid.org	IL	60062	800-782-7349	274-1527*
Stepfamily Foundation 310 W 85th St .... New York **Fax Area Code:* 646 ■ *Web:* www.stepfamily.org	NY	10024	212-877-3244	863-3166*
Students Against Destructive Decisions (SADD) 255 Main St .... Marlborough *TF:* 877-723-3462 ■ *Web:* www.sadd.org	MA	01752	508-481-3568	481-5759
Triplet Connection PO Box 429 .... Spring City *Web:* www.tripletconnection.org	UT	84662	435-851-1105	462-7466
United Cerebral Palsy of New York City 80 Maiden Ln Fl 8 .... New York *TF:* 877-827-2666 ■ *Web:* www.ucpnyc.org	NY	10038	212-683-6700	
United Way of Greater Cincinnati 2400 Reading Rd .... Cincinnati *Web:* www.uwgc.org	OH	45202	513-762-7100	762-7146
Vanished Children's Alliance (VCA) 991 W Hedding St Suite 101 .... San Jose *TF:* 800-826-4743 ■ *Web:* www.vca.org	CA	95126	408-296-1113	296-1117
Voices for America's Children 1000 Vermont Ave NW Suite 700 .... Washington *Web:* www.voicesforamericaschildren.org	DC	20005	202-289-0777	289-0776
Well Spouse Assn 63 W Main St Suite H .... Freehold *TF:* 800-838-0879 ■ *Web:* www.wellspouse.org	NJ	07728	732-577-8899	577-8644
YMCA of the USA (YMCA) 101 N Wacker Dr 14th Fl .... Chicago *TF:* 800-872-9622 ■ *Web:* www.ymca.net	IL	60606	312-977-0031	977-9063
YWCA USA (YWCA) 2025 M Stree NW Suite 550 .... Washington *TF:* 800-992-2871 ■ *Web:* www.ywca.org	DC	20036	202-467-0801	467-0802

48-7 Civic & Political Organizations

			Phone	Fax
Advocates for Self-Government 1010 N Tennessee St # 215 .... Cartersville *TF:* 800-932-1776 ■ *Web:* www.theadvocates.org	GA	30120	770-386-8372	386-8372
AIDS Action 1424 K St NW # 200 .... Washington *Web:* www.aidsaction.org	DC	20005	202-530-8030	530-8031
Alliance for Justice (AFJ) 11 Dupont Cir NW 2nd Fl .... Washington *Web:* www.afj.org	DC	20036	202-822-6070	822-6068

Organization / Address	City	State	Zip	Phone	Fax
Alliance of Nonprofit Mailers (ANM)					
1211 Connecticut Ave NW Suite 620	Washington	DC	20036	202-462-5132	462-0423
Web: www.nonprofitmailers.org					
American Assn of Political Consultants (AAPC)					
600 Pennsylvania Ave SE Suite 330	Washington	DC	20003	202-544-9815	544-9816
Web: www.theaapc.org					
American Cause The 501 Church St Suite 315	Vienna	VA	22180	703-255-2632	255-2219
Web: www.theamericancause.org					
American Conservative Union The (ACU)					
1007 Cameron St	Alexandria	VA	22314	703-836-8602	836-8606
TF: 800-228-7345 ■ *Web:* www.conservative.org					
American Council for an Energy-Efficient Economy (ACEEE)					
529 14th St NW Suite 600	Washington	DC	20045	202-507-4000	429-2248
Web: www.aceee.org					
American Israel Public Affairs Committee (AIPAC)					
251 H St	Washington	DC	20001	202-639-5200	347-4918
Web: www.aipac.org					
American Jewish Congress					
825 3rd Ave Suite 1800	New York	NY	10022	212-879-4500	758-1633
Web: www.ajcongress.org					
American Legislative Exchange Council (ALEC)					
1101 Vermont Ave NW 11th Fl	Washington	DC	20005	202-466-3800	466-3801
Web: www.alec.org					
Americans for Democratic Action (ADA)					
1625 K St NW Suite 210	Washington	DC	20006	202-785-5980	785-5969
TF: 800-787-2734 ■ *Web:* www.adaction.org					
Americans for Fair Taxation					
3100 Timmons Ln # 120	Houston	TX	77027	713-963-9023	963-8403
TF: 800-324-7829 ■ *Web:* www.fairtax.org					
Americans for Peace Now (APN)					
1101 14th St NW 6th Fl	Washington	DC	20005	202-728-1893	728-1895
Web: www.peacenow.org					
Americans United for Separation of Church & State					
518 C St NE	Washington	DC	20002	202-466-3234	466-2587
TF: 800-875-3707 ■ *Web:* www.au.org					
Assn of Community Organizations for Reform Now (ACORN)					
739 8th St SE	Washington	DC	20003	202-547-2500	546-2483
TF: 877-552-2676 ■ *Web:* www.acorn.org					
Brady Campaign to Prevent Gun Violence					
1225 'I' St NW Suite 1100	Washington	DC	20005	202-898-0792	371-9615
Web: www.bradycampaign.org					
Brady Center to Prevent Gun Violence					
1225 'I' St NW Suite 1100	Washington	DC	20005	202-289-7319	408-1851
Web: www.bradycenter.org					
Campaign Legal Ctr					
Media Policy Program Campaign Legal Ctr					
1640 Rhode Island Ave NW Suite 650	Washington	DC	20036	202-736-2200	736-2222
Web: www.campaignlegalcenter.org					
CapitolWatch PO Box 650911	Potomac Falls	VA	20165	202-544-2600	430-6623*
**Fax Area Code: 703* ■ *TF:* 888-468-9282 ■ *Web:* www.capitolwatch.org					
Center for Democracy & Technology (CDT)					
1634 'I' St NW 11th Fl	Washington	DC	20006	202-637-9800	637-0968
Web: www.cdt.org					
Center for Third World Organizing (CTWO)					
1218 E 21st St	Oakland	CA	94606	510-533-7583	533-0923
Web: www.ctwo.org					
Christian Coalition of America					
PO Box 37030	Washington	DC	20013	202-479-6900	479-4260
TF: 888-440-2262 ■ *Web:* www.cc.org					
Citizens Against Government Waste (CAGW)					
1301 Pennsylvania Ave NW # 1075	Washington	DC	20004	202-467-5300	467-4253
TF: 800-232-6479 ■ *Web:* www.cagw.org					
Citizens Committee for the Right to Keep & Bear Arms (CCRKBA)					
12500 NE 10th Pl	Bellevue	WA	98005	425-454-4911	451-3959
TF: 800-426-4302 ■ *Web:* www.ccrkba.org					
Citizens for Tax Justice (CTJ)					
1616 P St NW Suite 200-B	Washington	DC	20036	202-299-1066	299-1065
TF: 888-626-2622 ■ *Web:* www.ctj.org					
Close Up Foundation Inc					
1330 Braddock Pl # 400	Alexandria	VA	22314	703-706-3300	706-0000
TF: 800-256-7387 ■ *Web:* www.closeup.org					
Coalition to Stop Gun Violence					
1023 15th St NW Suite 301	Washington	DC	20005	202-408-0061	408-0062
Web: www.csgv.org					
Common Cause 1133 19th St NW 9th Fl	Washington	DC	20036	202-833-1200	659-3716
TF: 800-926-1064 ■ *Web:* www.commoncause.org					
Community Associations Institute (CAI)					
6402 Arlington Blvd Suite 500	Falls Church	VA	22042	703-970-9220	970-9558
TF: 888-224-4321 ■ *Web:* www.caionline.org					
Concord Coalition					
1011 Arlington Blvd Suite 300	Arlington	VA	22209	703-894-6222	894-6231
TF: 888-333-4248 ■ *Web:* www.concordcoalition.org					
Congress Watch 215 Pennsylvania Ave SE	Washington	DC	20003	202-546-4996	547-7392
TF: 800-289-3787 ■ *Web:* www.citizen.org/congress					
Constitutional Rights Foundation					
601 S Kingsley Dr	Los Angeles	CA	90005	213-487-5590	386-0459
TF: 800-488-4273 ■ *Web:* www.crf-usa.org					
Council of Canadians					
170 Laurier Ave W Suite 700	Ottawa	ON	K1P5V5	613-233-2773	233-6776
Web: www.canadians.org					
Council of the Americas 680 Pk Ave	New York	NY	10065	212-628-3200	249-5868
TF: 800-733-2342					
Council on American-Islamic Relations (CAIR)					
453 New Jersey Ave SE	Washington	DC	20003	202-488-8787	488-0833
Web: www.kair.com					
Democracy 21 1825 I St NW	Washington	DC	20006	202-429-2008	429-9574
Web: www.democracy21.org					
Democratic Congressional Campaign Committee (DCCC)					
430 S Capitol St SE	Washington	DC	20003	202-863-1500	485-3536
Web: www.dccc.org					
Democratic Governors Assn (DGA)					
1401 K St NW Suite 200	Washington	DC	20005	202-772-5600	772-5602
Web: www.democraticgovernors.org					
Democratic Senatorial Campaign Committee (DSCC)					
120 Maryland Ave NE	Washington	DC	20002	202-224-2447	969-0354
Web: www.dscc.org					
Do Something 32 Union Sq E # 4L	New York	NY	10003	212-254-2390	254-2391
Web: www.dosomething.org					
EMILY's List					
1120 Connecticut Ave NW Suite 1100	Washington	DC	20036	202-326-1400	326-1415
TF: 800-683-6459 ■ *Web:* www.emilyslist.org					
Evangelicals for Social Action (ESA)					
6 E Lancaster Ave	Wynnewood	PA	19096	484-384-2990	493-1528
TF: 800-650-6600 ■ *Web:* www.esa-online.org					
Families USA					
1201 New York Ave NW Suite 1100	Washington	DC	20005	202-628-3030	347-2417
TF: 800-593-5041 ■ *Web:* www.familiesusa.org					
Federation for American Immigration Reform (FAIR)					
25 Massachusetts Ave NW Suite 330	Washington	DC	20009	202-328-7004	387-3447
TF: 877-627-3247 ■ *Web:* www.fairus.org					
Foreign Policy Assn (FPA) 470 Pk Ave S	New York	NY	10016	212-481-8100	481-9275
TF: 800-628-5754 ■ *Web:* www.fpa.org					
Foundation for Moral Law PO Box 4086	Montgomery	AL	36103	334-262-1245	262-1708
Web: www.morallaw.org					
Freedom Forum 555 Pennsylvania Ave NW	Washington	DC	20001	202-292-6100	
Web: www.freedomforum.org					
FreedomWorks					
601 Pennsylvania Ave NW Suite 700-N	Washington	DC	20004	202-783-3870	942-7649
TF: 888-564-6273 ■ *Web:* www.freedomworks.org					
Girls Nation					
American Legion Auxiliary					
8945 N Meridian St	Indianapolis	IN	46260	317-569-4500	569-4502
Web: www.alaforveterans.org					
Global Exchange					
2017 Mission St Suite 303	San Francisco	CA	94110	415-255-7296	255-7498
TF: 800-497-1994 ■ *Web:* www.globalexchange.org					
HALT - An Organization of Americans for Legal Reform					
1612 K St NW Suite 510	Washington	DC	20006	202-887-8255	887-9699
TF: 888-367-4258 ■ *Web:* www.halt.org					
Interfaith Alliance					
1212 New York Ave NW Suite 1250	Washington	DC	20005	202-238-3300	238-3301
TF: 800-510-0969 ■ *Web:* www.interfaithalliance.org					
International Society of Political Psychology (ISPP)					
Syracuse Univ Moynihan Institute of Global Affairs					
346 Eggers Hall	Syracuse	NY	13244	315-443-4470	443-9085
Web: www.ispp.org					
Interreligious Foundation for Community Organization (IFCO)					
418 W 145th St	New York	NY	10031	212-926-5757	926-5842
Web: www.ifconews.org					
Judicial Watch Inc 425 3rd St SW Suite 800	Washington	DC	20024	202-646-5172	646-5199
TF: 888-593-8442 ■ *Web:* www.judicialwatch.org					
Junior Chamber International (JCI)					
15645 Olive Blvd	Chesterfield	MO	63017	636-449-3100	449-3107
TF: 800-905-5499 ■ *Web:* www.jci.cc					
Keep America Beautiful Inc					
1010 Washington Blvd	Stamford	CT	06901	203-323-8987	325-9199
Web: www.kab.org					
Landmark Volunteers 800 N Main St	Sheffield	MA	01257	413-229-0255	229-2050
Web: www.volunteers.com					
League of Conservation Voters					
1920 L St NW Suite 800	Washington	DC	20036	202-785-8683	835-0491
Web: www.lcv.org					
League of Women Voters (LWV)					
1730 M St NW Suite 1000	Washington	DC	20036	202-429-1965	429-0854
TF: 800-249-8683 ■ *Web:* www.lwv.org					
NA of Neighborhoods (NAN)					
1300 Pennsylvania Ave NW Suite 700	Washington	DC	20004	202-332-7766	332-2314
Web: www.nanworld.org					
NA of Town Watch (NATW)					
1 E Wynnewood Rd Suite 102	Wynnewood	PA	19096	610-649-7055	649-5456
TF: 800-648-3688 ■ *Web:* www.nationaltownwatch.org					
National Center for Neighborhood Enterprise (NCNE)					
1625 K St Suite 1200	Washington	DC	20006	202-518-6500	588-0314
TF: 866-518-1263 ■ *Web:* www.cneonline.org					
National Civic League (NCL) 1889 York St	Denver	CO	80206	303-571-4343	571-4404
Web: www.ncl.org					
National Coalition on Black Civic Participation Inc (NCBCP)					
1900 L St NW Suite 700	Washington	DC	20036	202-659-4929	659-5025
National Committee to Preserve Social Security & Medicare (NCPSSM)					
10 G St NE Suite 600	Washington	DC	20002	202-216-0420	216-0451
TF: 800-966-1935 ■ *Web:* www.ncpssm.org					
National Community Action Foundation (NCAF)					
1 Massachusetts Ave NW # 310	Washington	DC	20001	202-842-2092	842-2095
Web: www.ncaf.org					
National Conference of Black Mayors (NCBM)					
1151 Cleveland Ave Suite D	East Point	GA	30344	404-765-6444	765-6430
Web: www.ncbm.org					
National Council of Women of the US Inc (NCWO)					
777 UN Plaza	New York	NY	10017	212-697-1278	972-0164
National Council on Public History (NCPH)					
425 University Blvd 327 Cavanaugh Hall	Indianapolis	IN	46202	317-274-2716	278-5230
Web: www.ncph.org					
National Endowment for Democracy (NED)					
1025 F St NW Suite 800	Washington	DC	20004	202-378-9700	
Web: www.ned.org					
National Federation of Democratic Women (NFDW)					
7211 E Lincoln	Wichita	KS	67207	316-612-9709	
Web: www.nfdw.com					
National Federation of Republican Women (NFRW)					
124 N Alfred St	Alexandria	VA	22314	703-548-9688	548-9836
TF: 800-373-9688 ■ *Web:* www.nfrw.org					
National Taxpayers Union (NTU)					
108 N Alfred St	Alexandria	VA	22314	703-683-5700	683-5722
TF: 800-829-4258 ■ *Web:* www.ntu.org					

Organization	City	State	Zip	Phone	Fax
National Women's Political Caucus (NWPC) PO Box 50476 *Web:* www.nwpc.org	Washington	DC	20091	202-785-1100	370-6306
Native American Community Board (NACB) PO Box 572 *Web:* www.nativeshop.org	Lake Andes	SD	57356	605-487-7072	487-7964
OMB Watch 1742 Connecticut Ave NW *Web:* www.ombwatch.org	Washington	DC	20009	202-234-8494	234-8584
Organization of American States (OAS) 1889 F St NW *Web:* www.oas.org	Washington	DC	20006	202-458-3000	458-3967
People for the American Way (PFAW) 2000 M St NW Suite 400 *TF:* 800-326-7329 ■ *Web:* www.pfaw.org	Washington	DC	20036	202-467-4999	293-2672
Population Reference Bureau (PRB) 1875 Connecticut Ave NW Suite 520 *TF:* 800-877-9881 ■ *Web:* www.prb.org	Washington	DC	20009	202-483-1100	328-3937
Population-Environment Balance Inc 2000 P St NW Suite 600 *TF:* 800-866-6269 ■ *Web:* www.balance.org	Washington	DC	20036	202-955-5700	955-6161
Preservation Action 401 F St NW Suite 324 *Web:* www.preservationaction.org	Washington	DC	20001	202-637-7873	637-7874
Project Vote 739 8th St SE Suite 202 *TF:* 800-546-8683 ■ *Web:* www.projectvote.org	Washington	DC	20003	202-546-4173	546-2483
Project Vote Smart 1 Common Ground *TF:* 888-868-3762 ■ *Web:* www.votesmart.org	Philipsburg	MT	59858	406-859-8683	859-8680
Public Affairs Council (PAC) 2033 K St NW Suite 700 *Web:* www.pac.org	Washington	DC	20006	202-872-1790	835-8343
Public Citizen 1600 20th St NW *Web:* www.citizen.org	Washington	DC	20009	202-588-1000	588-7796
Public Forum Institute The 2300 M St NW Suite 900 *Web:* www.publicforuminstitute.org	Washington	DC	20037	202-973-2872	293-5717
Public Service Research Foundation 320-D Maple Ave E *Web:* www.psrf.org	Vienna	VA	22180	703-242-3575	242-3579
Republican Governors Assn (RGA) 1747 Pennsylvania Ave NW Suite 250 *Web:* www.rga.org	Washington	DC	20006	202-662-4140	662-4925
Ripon Society 1300 L St NW Suite 900 *Web:* www.riponsoc.org	Washington	DC	20005	202-216-1008	216-0036
Rock the Vote (RTV) 1001 Connecticut Ave NW Suite 640 *Web:* www.rockthevote.com	Washington	DC	20036	202-719-9910	
Secure America's Future Economy (SAFE) 214 N Spring Valley Rd *Web:* www.s-a-f-e.org	Wilmington	DE	19807	302-478-0676	
Sister Cities International (SCI) 1301 Pennsylvania Ave NW Suite 850 *Web:* www.sister-cities.org	Washington	DC	20004	202-347-8630	393-6524
US Junior Chamber of Commerce 7447 S Lewis Ave *TF:* 800-529-2337 ■ *Web:* www.usjaycees.org	Tulsa	OK	74136	918-584-2481	584-4422
US Term Limits (USTL) 9900 Main St Suite 303 *TF:* 800-733-6440 ■ *Web:* www.ustl.org	Fairfax	VA	22031	703-383-0907	383-5288
Violence Policy Ctr (VPC) 1730 Rhode Island Ave NW Suite 1014 *Web:* www.vpc.org	Washington	DC	20036	202-822-8200	
WISH List 333 N Fairfax St Suite 302 *Web:* www.thewishlist.org	Alexandria	VA	22314	703-778-5550	778-5554
Women's Campaign Fund (WCF) 1900 L St NW Suite 500 *TF:* 800-446-8170 ■ *Web:* www.wcfonline.org	Washington	DC	20005	202-393-8164	393-0649
Young America's Foundation 110 Elden St *TF:* 800-292-9231 ■ *Web:* www.yaf.org	Herndon	VA	20170	703-318-9608	318-9122
Young Democrats of America (YDA) PO Box 77496 *Web:* www.yda.org	Washington	DC	20013	202-639-8585	318-3221

48-8 Civil & Human Rights Organizations

Organization	City	State	Zip	Phone	Fax
ACT UP 12 Wooster St *Web:* www.actupny.org	New York	NY	10013	212-966-4873	
Alliance of Guardian Angels 717 5th Ave Suite 401 *Web:* www.guardianangels.org	New York	NY	10022	212-860-5575	223-8180
American Civil Liberties Union (ACLU) 125 Broad St 18th Fl *Web:* www.aclu.org	New York	NY	10004	212-549-2500	549-2580
American Jewish Committee (AJC) 165 E 56th St *Web:* www.ajc.org	New York	NY	10022	212-751-4000	750-0326
American Society of Access Professionals (ASAP) 1444 'I' St NW Suite 700 *Web:* www.accesspro.org	Washington	DC	20005	202-712-9054	216-9646
American-Arab Anti Discrimination Committee (ADC) 1732 Wisconsin Ave *Web:* www.adc.org	Washington	DC	20007	202-244-2990	244-3196
Americans for Effective Law Enforcement (AELE) 841 W Touhy Ave *TF:* 800-763-2802 ■ *Web:* www.aele.org	Park Ridge	IL	60068	847-685-0700	685-9700
Americans for Tax Reform (ATR) 722 12th St NW # 4 *Web:* www.atr.org	Washington	DC	20005	202-785-0266	785-0261
Anti-Defamation League (ADL) 605 3rd Ave *Web:* www.adl.org	New York	NY	10158	212-885-7700	867-0779
Arab American Institute (AAI) 1600 K St NW Suite 601 *Web:* www.aaiusa.org	Washington	DC	20006	202-429-9210	429-9214
Asian American Legal Defense & Education Fund (AALDEF) 99 Hudson St 12th Fl *TF:* 800-966-5946 ■ *Web:* www.aaldef.org	New York	NY	10013	212-966-5932	966-4303

Organization	City	State	Zip	Phone	Fax
Assn for Women's Rights in Development (AWID) 215 Spadina Ave Suite 150 *Web:* www.awid.org	Toronto	ON	M5T2C7	416-594-3773	594-0330
Becket Fund for Religious Liberty 1350 Connecticut Ave NW Suite 605 *TF:* 800-232-5385 ■ *Web:* www.becketfund.org	Washington	DC	20036	202-955-0095	955-0090
Center for Individual Rights (CIR) 1233 20th St NW Suite 300 *TF:* 877-426-2665 ■ *Web:* www.cir-usa.org	Washington	DC	20036	202-833-8400	833-8410
Center for Reproductive Rights 120 Wall St 14th Fl *Web:* www.reproductiverights.org	New York	NY	10005	917-637-3600	637-3666
Children's Rights Council (CRC) 8181 Professional Pl Suite 240 *TF:* 800-787-5437 ■ *Web:* www.crckids.org	Landover	MD	20785	301-459-1220	459-1227
Congress of Racial Equality (CORE) 817 Broadway 3rd Fl *Web:* www.core-online.org	New York	NY	10003	212-598-4000	529-3568
Corporate Accountability International 10 milk St Suite 610 *TF:* 800-688-8797 ■ *Web:* www.stopcorporateabuse.org	Boston	MA	02108	617-695-2525	695-2626
Crime Stoppers International PO Box 1219 **Fax Area Code:* 905 ■ *TF:* 800-850-7574 ■ *Web:* www.c-s-i.org	Keewatin	ON	P0X1C0	800-850-7574	951-2416*
Cultural Survival Inc 215 Prospect St *Web:* www.culturalsurvival.org	Cambridge	MA	02139	617-441-5400	441-5417
Digital Freedom Network (DFN) 520 Broad St 3rd FL **Fax Area Code:* 202 ■ *Web:* www.dfn.org	Newark	NJ	07102	973-438-7345	969-9900*
Disability Rights Center Inc 18 Low Ave *TF:* 800-834-1721 ■ *Web:* www.drcnh.org	Concord	NH	03301	603-228-0432	225-2077
Drug Policy Alliance 70 W 36th St 16th Fl *Web:* www.drugpolicy.org	New York	NY	10018	212-613-8020	613-8021
Ethics Resource Ctr 2345 Crystal Dr Suite 201 *Web:* www.ethics.org	Arlington	VA	22202	703-647-2185	647-2180
Families Against Mandatory Minimums (FAMM) 1612 K St NW Suite 700 *Web:* www.famm.org	Washington	DC	20006	202-822-6700	822-6704
Gay & Lesbian Alliance Against Defamation (GLAAD) 104 W 29th St 4th Fl *Web:* www.glaad.org	New York	NY	10001	212-629-3322	629-3225
Grandparents Rights Organization (GRO) 100 W Long Lake Rd Suite 250 *Web:* www.grandparentsrights.org	Bloomfield Hills	MI	48304	248-646-7177	646-9722
Human Rights Campaign 1640 Rhode Island Ave NW *TF:* 800-777-4723 ■ *Web:* www.hrc.org	Washington	DC	20036	202-628-4160	347-5323
Human Rights Watch 350 5th Ave 34th Fl *Web:* www.hrw.org	New York	NY	10118	212-290-4700	736-1300
Institute for Health Freedom 1875 'I' St NW Suite 500 *TF:* 888-616-1976 ■ *Web:* www.forhealthfreedom.org	Washington	DC	20006	202-429-6610	861-1973
Integrative Strategies Forum Inc (ISF) 8715 First Ave Suite 710-D *Web:* www.isforum.org	Silver Spring	MD	20910	301-558-5550	770-6377
International Gay & Lesbian Human Rights Commission (IGLHRC) 80 Maiden Ln Suite 1505 *Web:* www.iglhrc.org	New York	NY	10038	212-268-8040	430-6060
International Organization for Migration 1752 N St NW Suite 700 *Web:* www.iom.int	Washington	DC	20036	202-862-1826	862-1879
King Ctr The 449 Auburn Ave NE *Web:* www.thekingcenter.org	Atlanta	GA	30312	404-526-8962	
La Causa Inc PO Box 4188 *Web:* www.lacausa.org	Milwaukee	WI	53204	414-647-8750	647-8797
Lambda Legal Defense & Education Fund 120 Wall St Suite 1500 *Web:* www.lambdalegal.org	New York	NY	10005	212-809-8585	809-0055
Leadership Conference on Civil Rights (LCCR) 1629 K St NW Suite 1000 *Web:* www.civilrights.org	Washington	DC	20006	202-466-3311	466-3435
Legal Counsel for the Elderly 601 E St NW Bldg A 4th Fl *Web:* www.aarp.org	Washington	DC	20049	202-434-2170	434-6464
Media Watch 501 Mission St # 6 *TF:* 800-631-6355 ■ *Web:* www.mediawatch.com	Santa Cruz	CA	95060	831-423-6355	
Medicare Rights Ctr (MRC) 520 8th Ave N Wing 3rd Fl *TF hotline:* 800-333-4114 ■ *Web:* www.medicarerights.org	New York	NY	10018	212-869-3850	869-3532
Migrant Legal Action Program (MLAP) 1001 Connecticut Ave NW Suite 915 *Web:* www.mlap.org	Washington	DC	20036	202-775-7780	775-7784
NA for the Advancement of Colored People (NAACP) 4805 Mt Hope Dr *TF:* 877-622-2798 ■ *Web:* www.naacp.org	Baltimore	MD	21215	410-580-5777	486-9255
NA to Advance Fat Acceptance (NAAFA) PO Box 22510 *Web:* www.naafa.org	Oakland	CA	94609	916-558-6880	558-6881
NARAL Pro-Choice America 1156 15th St NW Suite 700 *Web:* www.naral.org	Washington	DC	20005	202-973-3000	973-3096
National Abortion Federation (NAF) 1755 Massachusetts Ave NW *TF:* 800-772-9100 ■ *Web:* www.prochoice.org	Washington	DC	20036	202-667-5881	667-5890
National Center for Juvenile Justice (NCJJ) 3700 S Water St Suite 200 *Web:* www.ncjjservehttp.org	Pittsburgh	PA	15203	412-227-6950	227-6955
National Center for Victims of Crime The 2000 M St NW Suite 480 *TF:* 800-394-2255 ■ *Web:* www.ncvc.org	Washington	DC	20036	202-467-8700	467-8701
National Coalition Against Censorship (NCAC) 275 7th Ave 9th Fl *Web:* www.ncac.org	New York	NY	10001	212-807-6222	807-6245

Organization	City	State	ZIP	Phone	Fax
National Coalition Against Domestic Violence (NCADV) One Broadway Suite B210 *TF:* 800-799-7233 ■ *Web:* www.ncadv.org	Denver	CO	80203	303-839-1852	831-9251
National Coalition to Abolish the Death Penalty (NCADP) 1705 DeSales St NW 5th Fl *TF:* 888-286-2237 ■ *Web:* www.ncadp.org	Washington	DC	20033	202-331-4090	331-4099
National Conference on Citizenship (NCOC) 1875 K St NW 5th Fl *Web:* www.ncoc.net	Washington	DC	20006	202-729-8038	449-8276
National Consumer Law Ctr (NCLC) 7 Winthrop Sq *Web:* www.nclc.org	Boston	MA	02110	617-542-8010	542-8028
National Council on Crime & Delinquency (NCCD) 1970 Broadway Suite 500 *Web:* www.nccd-crc.org	Oakland	CA	94612	510-208-0500	208-0511
National Crime Prevention Council (NCPC) 2345 Crystal Dr Suite 500 *Web:* www.ncpc.org	Arlington	VA	22202	202-466-6272	296-1356
National Freedom of Information Coalition Univ of Missouri 101 A Reynolds Journalism Institute *Web:* www.nfoic.org	Columbia	MO	65211	573-882-4856	884-6204
National Gay & Lesbian Task Force (NGLTF) 1325 Massachusetts Ave NW Suite 600 *Web:* www.thetaskforce.org	Washington	DC	20005	202-393-5177	393-2241
National Immigration Forum 50 F St NW Suite 300 *Web:* www.immigrationforum.org	Washington	DC	20001	202-347-0040	347-0058
National Organization for the Reform of Marijuana Laws (NORML) 1600 K St NW Suite 501 *TF:* 888-676-6765 ■ *Web:* www.norml.org	Washington	DC	20006	202-483-5500	483-0057
National Organization for Victim Assistance (NOVA) 510 King St Suite 424 *TF:* 800-879-6682 ■ *Web:* www.trynova.org	Alexandria	VA	22314	703-535-6682	535-5500
National Right to Life Committee Inc (NRLC) 512 10th St NW *Web:* www.nrlc.org	Washington	DC	20004	202-626-8800	737-9189
National Urban League Inc 120 Wall St 8th Fl *Web:* www.nul.org	New York	NY	10005	212-558-5300	344-5332
No Peace Without Justice (NPWJ) 866 UN Plaza Suite 408 *Web:* www.npwj.org	New York	NY	10017	212-980-2558	980-1072
Nuclear Information & Resource Service (NIRS) 6930 Carroll Ave Suite 340 *Web:* www.nirs.org	Takoma Park	MD	20912	301-270-6477	270-4291
Osborne Assn 809 Westchester Ave *Web:* www.osborneny.org	Bronx	NY	10455	718-707-2600	707-3103
Parents Families & Friends of Lesbians & Gays (PFLAG) 1828 L St NW Suite 660 *Web:* community.pflag.org/Page.aspx?pid=194&srcid=-2	Washington	DC	20036	202-467-8180	349-0788
Patients Rights Council (PRC) PO Box 760 *TF:* 800-958-5678 ■ *Web:* www.patientsrightscouncil.org	Steubenville	OH	43952	740-282-3810	
PEN American Ctr 588 Broadway *Web:* www.pen.org	New York	NY	10012	212-334-1660	334-2181
Pro-Life Action League 6160 N Cicero Ave Suite 600 *Web:* www.prolifeaction.org	Chicago	IL	60646	773-777-2900	777-3061
Rutherford Institute PO Box 7482 *TF:* 800-225-1791 ■ *Web:* www.rutherford.org	Charlottesville	VA	22906	434-978-3888	978-1789
Second Amendment Foundation 12500 NE 10th Pl *TF:* 800-426-4302 ■ *Web:* www.saf.org	Bellevue	WA	98005	425-454-7012	451-3959
Sentencing Project 1705 DeSales St NW 8th Fl	Washington	DC	20036	202-628-0871	628-1091
Simon Wiesenthal Ctr 1399 Roxbury Dr # 100 *TF:* 800-900-9036 ■ *Web:* www.wiesenthal.com	Los Angeles	CA	90035	310-553-9036	772-7655
Southern Poverty Law Ctr (SPLC) 400 Washington Ave *Web:* www.splcenter.org	Montgomery	AL	36104	334-956-8200	956-8483
Thomas Jefferson Center for the Protection of Free Expression 400 Worrell Dr *Web:* www.tjcenter.org	Charlottesville	VA	22911	434-295-4784	296-3621
Urban Land Institute (ULI) 1025 Thomas Jefferson St NW Suite 500W *TF Orders:* 800-321-5011 ■ *Web:* www.uli.org	Washington	DC	20007	202-624-7000	624-7140
US Privacy Council PO Box 302	Cabin John	MD	20818	301-229-7002	229-8011
WeTip Inc PO Box 1296 *TF:* 800-782-7463 ■ *Web:* www.wetip.com	Rancho Cucamonga	CA	91729	909-987-5005	987-2477

48-9 Computer & Internet Organizations

Organization	City	State	ZIP	Phone	Fax
1394 Trade Assn 315 Lincoln Suite E *Web:* www.1394ta.org	Mukilteo	WA	76092	425-870-6574	320-3897
Advanced Network & Services Inc 2600 S Rd Suite 44-193 *Web:* www.advanced.org	Poughkeepsie	NY	12601	845-795-2090	795-2180
American Registry for Internet Numbers (ARIN) 3635 Concorde Pkwy Suite 200 PO Box 79010 *Web:* www.arin.net	Chantilly	VA	20151	703-227-9840	227-0671
American Society for Information Science & Technology (ASIS&T) 1320 Fenwick Ln Suite 510 *Web:* www.asis.org	Silver Spring	MD	20910	301-495-0900	495-0810
Apache Software Foundation (ASF) 1901 Munsey Dr *Web:* www.apache.org	Forest Hill	MD	21050	410-420-0140	803-2258
Assn for Computing Machinery (ACM) 2 Penn Plaza Suite 701 *TF:* 800-342-6626 ■ *Web:* www.acm.org	New York	NY	10121	212-626-0500	944-1318
Assn For Data Center Management Professionals (AFCOM) 742 E Chapman Ave *Web:* www.afcom.com	Orange	CA	92866	714-997-7966	997-9743
Assn for the Advancement of Artificial Intelligence (AAAI) 445 Burgess Dr Suite 100 *Web:* www.aaai.org	Menlo Park	CA	94025	650-328-3123	321-4457
Assn for Women in Computing (AWC) PO Box 2768 *Web:* www.awc-hq.org	Oakland	CA	94602	415-905-4663	358-4667
Assn of Service & Computer Dealers International (ASCDI) 131 NW 1st Ave *Web:* www.ascdi.com	Delray Beach	FL	33444	561-266-9016	431-6302
Assn of Shareware Professionals (ASP) PO Box 1522 **Fax Area Code:* 815 ■ *Web:* www.asp-shareware.org	Martinsville	IN	46151	765-349-4740	301-3756*
Assn of Support Professionals The 122 Barnard Ave *Web:* www.asponline.com	Watertown	MA	02472	617-924-3944	924-7288
Broadband Forum 48377 Fremont Blvd Suite 117 *Web:* www.broadband-forum.org	Fremont	CA	94538	510-492-4020	
Business Software Alliance (BSA) 1150 18th St NW Suite 700 *TF:* 888-667-4722 ■ *Web:* www.bsa.org	Washington	DC	20036	202-872-5500	872-5501
CANARIE 110 O'Connor St 4th Fl *Web:* www.canarie.ca	Ottawa	ON	K1P5M9	613-943-5454	943-5443
Coalition for Networked Information 21 Dupont Cir NW Euram Bldg Suite 800 *Web:* www.cni.org	Washington	DC	20036	202-296-5098	872-0884
CommerceNet 169 University Ave *Web:* www.commerce.net	Palo Alto	CA	94301	650-289-4040	289-4041
Computer Assisted Language Instruction Consortium (CALICO) 601 University Dr 214 Centennial Hall *Web:* www.calico.org	San Marcos	TX	78666	512-245-2360	245-8298
Computer Measurement Group (CMG) 151 Fries Mill Rd Suite 104 *TF:* 800-436-7264 ■ *Web:* www.cmg.org	Turnersville	NJ	08012	856-401-1700	401-1708
Computer Professionals for Social Responsibility (CPSR) PO Box 20046 *Web:* www.cpsr.org	Sanford	CA	94309	650-989-1294	322-4748
Computer Security Institute (CSI) 350 Hudson St Suite 300 **Fax Area Code:* 347 ■ *TF:* 888-234-9476 ■ *Web:* www.gocsi.com	New York	NY	10014	215-989-4901	962-3931*
Computing Research Assn 1828 L St NW *Web:* www.cra.org	Washington	DC	20036	202-234-2111	667-1066
Computing Technology Industry Assn (CompTIA) 3500 Lacey Rd Suite 100 *Web:* www.comptia.org	Downers Grove	IL	60515	630-678-8300	678-8384
Consortium for School Networking (CoSN) 1025 Vermont Ave NW Suite 1010 *TF:* 866-267-8747 ■ *Web:* www.cosn.org	Washington	DC	20005	202-861-2676	393-2011
Corp for National Research Initiatives (CNRI) 1895 Preston White Dr Suite 100 *Web:* www.cnri.reston.va.us	Reston	VA	20191	703-620-8990	620-0913
Data Interchange Standards Assn (DISA) 7600 Leesburg Pike Suite 430 *Web:* www.disa.org	Falls Church	VA	22043	703-970-4480	970-4488
EDUCAUSE 1150 18th St NW Suite 1010 *Web:* www.educause.edu	Washington	DC	20036	202-872-4200	872-4318
Electronic Frontier Foundation Inc (EFF) 454 Shotwell St *Web:* www.eff.org	San Francisco	CA	94110	415-436-9333	436-9993
Electronic Privacy Information Ctr (EPIC) 1718 Connecticut Ave NW Suite 200 *Web:* www.epic.org	Washington	DC	20009	202-483-1140	483-1248
Entertainment Software Assn (ESA) 575 7th St NW Suite 300 *Web:* www.theesa.com	Washington	DC	20004	202-223-2400	223-2401
Independent Computer Consultants Assn (ICCA) 11131 S Towne Sq Suite F *TF:* 800-774-4222	Saint Louis	MO	63123	314-892-1675	487-1345
Information Systems Audit & Control Assn (ISACA) 3701 Algonquin Rd Suite 1010 *Web:* www.isaca.org	Rolling Meadows	IL	60008	847-253-1545	253-1443
Information Technology Industry Council (ITI) 1101 K St NW # 610 *Web:* www.itic.org	Washington	DC	20005	202-737-8888	638-4922
Institute for Certification of Computing Professionals (ICCP) 2400 E Devon Ave # 281 *TF:* 800-843-8227 ■ *Web:* www.iccp.org	Des Plaines	IL	60018	847-299-4227	299-4280
Institute for Women & Technology (IWT) 1501 Page Mill Rd MS 1105 *Web:* www.iwt.org	Palo Alto	CA	94304	650-236-4756	852-8172
International Academy of Digital Arts & Sciences (IADAS) 19 W 21st St Suite 602 **Fax Area Code:* 415 ■ *Web:* www.iadas.net	New York	NY	10010	212-675-4890	826-9111*
International Disk Drive Equipment & Materials Assn (IDEMA) 1226 Lincoln Ave Suite 100 *Web:* www.idema.org	San Jose	CA	95125	408-719-0082	719-0087
International Webmasters Assn (IWA) 119 E Union St Suite F *Web:* www.iwanet.org	Pasadena	CA	91103	626-449-3709	449-8308
Internet Assigned Numbers Authority (IANA) 4676 Admiralty Way Suite 330 *Web:* www.iana.org	Marina del Rey	CA	90292	310-823-9358	823-8649
Internet Corp for Assigned Names & Numbers (ICANN) 4676 Admiralty Way Suite 330 *Web:* www.icann.org	Marina del Rey	CA	90292	310-823-9358	823-8649
Internet Scambusters 197 New Market Ctr Suite 115 *Web:* www.scambusters.com	Boone	NC	28607	815-642-0460	
Internet Society (ISOC) 1775 Wiehle Ave Suite 102 *Web:* www.isoc.org	Reston	VA	20190	703-439-2120	326-9881
Internet2 1000 Oakbrook Dr Suite 300 *Web:* www.internet2.edu	Ann Arbor	MI	48108	734-913-4250	913-4255

Organization	City	State	ZIP	Phone	Fax
ITechLaw Assn 401 Edgewater Pl Suite 600 *Web:* www.itechlaw.org	Wakefield	MA	01880	781-876-8877	224-1239
National Urban Technology Ctr 80 Maiden Ln Suite 606 *TF:* 800-998-3212 ■ *Web:* www.urbantech.org	New York	NY	10038	212-528-7350	528-7355
Network & Systems Professionals Assn Inc (NaSPA) 7044 S 13th St *Web:* www.naspa.com	Oak Creek	WI	53154	414-768-8000	768-8001
Object Management Group (OMG) 140 Kendrick St Suite 300 *Web:* www.omg.org	Needham	MA	02494	781-444-0404	444-0320
Online Privacy Alliance (OPA) c/o Hogan & Hartson LLP 555 13th St NW *Web:* www.privacyalliance.org	Washington	DC	20004	202-637-5600	637-5710
Open Group 44 Montgomery St Suite 960 *Web:* www.opengroup.org	San Francisco	CA	94104	415-374-8280	374-8293
Personal Computer Memory Card International Assn (PCMCIA) 2635 N 1st St Suite 218	San Jose	CA	95134	408-433-2273	433-9558
Portable Computer & Communications Assn (PCCA) PO Box 680 **Fax Area Code:* 413 ■ *Web:* www.pcca.org	Hood River	OR	97031	541-490-5140	410-8447*
Print Services & Distribution Assn (PSDA) 433 E Monroe Ave *TF:* 800-336-4641 ■ *Web:* www.psda.org	Alexandria	VA	22301	703-836-6232	836-2241
Society for Information Display (SID) 1475 S Bascom Ave Suite 114 *Web:* www.sid.org	Campbell	CA	95008	408-879-3901	879-3833
Society for Information Management (SIM) 401 N Michigan Ave Suite 2400 *TF:* 800-527-6734 ■ *Web:* www.simnet.org	Chicago	IL	60611	312-527-6734	644-6363
Society for Modeling & Simulation International (SCS) 4838 Ronson Ct Suite L PO Box 17900 *Web:* www.scs.org	San Diego	CA	92111	858-277-3888	277-3930
Software & Information Industry Assn (SIIA) 1090 Vermont Ave NW 6th Fl *Web:* www.siia.net	Washington	DC	20005	202-289-7442	289-7097
Software Productivity Consortium 2214 Rock Hill Rd Suite 1 SPC Bldg	Herndon	VA	20170	703-742-8877	742-7347
TechNet 1625 'I' St NW Suite 620 *Web:* www.technet.org	Washington	DC	20006	202-877-8897	777-2060
TechServe Alliance 1420 King St Suite 610 *Web:* www.techservealliance.org	Alexandria	VA	22314	703-838-2050	838-3610
TeleManagement Forum 240 Headquarters Plaza E Twr 10th Fl *Web:* www.tmforum.org	Morristown	NJ	07960	973-944-5100	944-5110
Transaction Processing Performance Council (TPC) 572 Ruger St *Web:* www.tpc.org	San Francisco	CA	94129	415-561-6272	561-6120
TRUSTe 55 2nd St 2nd Fl *Web:* www.truste.org	San Francisco	CA	94105	415-618-3400	618-3420
Urban & Regional Information Systems Assn (URISA) 1460 Renaissance Dr Suite 305 *Web:* www.urisa.org	Park Ridge	IL	60068	847-824-6300	824-6363
US Internet Industry Assn (USIIA) 1800 Diagonal Rd Suite 600 *Web:* www.usiia.org	Alexandria	VA	22314	703-647-7440	647-6009
USENIX Assn 2560 9th St Suite 215 *Web:* www.usenix.org	Berkeley	CA	94710	510-528-8649	548-5738
Video Electronics Standards Assn (VESA) 39899 Balentine Dr Suite 125 *Web:* www.vesa.org	Newark	CA	94560	510-651-5122	651-5127
Webby Awards 19 W 21st St Suite 602 *Web:* www.webbyawards.com	New York	NY	10010	212-675-4890	
World Wide Web Consortium (W3C) 32 Vassar St Rm 32-G515 *Web:* www.w3.org	Cambridge	MA	02139	617-253-2613	258-5999

48-10 Consumer Interest Organizations

Organization	City	State	ZIP	Phone	Fax
Accuracy in Media Inc (AIM) 4455 Connecticut Ave NW Suite 330 *TF:* 800-787-4567 ■ *Web:* www.aim.org	Washington	DC	20008	202-364-4401	364-4098
Advocates for Highway & Auto Safety 750 1st St NE Suite 901 *TF:* 800-659-2247 ■ *Web:* www.saferoads.org	Washington	DC	20002	202-408-1711	408-1699
Alliance Against Fraud in Telemarketing & Electronic Commerce (AAFT) 1701 K St NW Suite 1200 *Web:* www.fraud.org/aaft/aaftinfo.htm	Washington	DC	20006	202-835-3323	835-0747
American Council on Consumer Interests (ACCI) 555 E Wells St Suite 1100 *Web:* www.consumerinterests.org	Milwaukee	WI	53202	414-918-3189	276-3349
American Council on Science & Health (ACSH) 1995 Broadway 2nd Fl *TF:* 866-905-2694 ■ *Web:* www.acsh.org	New York	NY	10023	212-362-7044	362-4919
American Homeowners Assn (AHA) 1 Stamford Plaza 9th Fl *TF Cust Svc:* 800-470-2242 ■ *Web:* www.ahahome.com	Stamford	CT	06901	203-323-7715	323-4558
Auriton Solutions 1700 W Hwy 36 Suite 301 *TF:* 877-332-8700 ■ *Web:* www.auritonnew.org	Roseville	MN	55113	651-631-8000	
Call for Action 11820 Parklawn Dr Suite 340 *Web:* www.callforaction.org	Rockville	MD	20852	240-747-0225	
Carpet & Rug Institute (CRI) 730 College Dr *Web:* www.carpet-rug.com	Dalton	GA	30720	706-278-3176	278-8835
Center for Auto Safety (CAS) 1825 Connecticut Ave NW Suite 330 *Web:* www.autosafety.org	Washington	DC	20009	202-328-7700	387-0140
Center for Science in the Public Interest (CSPI) 1875 Connecticut Ave NW Suite 300 *Web:* www.cspinet.org	Washington	DC	20009	202-332-9110	265-4954
Consumer Federation of America (CFA) 1620 I St NW Suite 200 *Web:* www.consumerfed.org	Washington	DC	20006	202-387-6121	265-7989
Consumers' Research Council of America (CRCA) 2020 Pennsylvania Ave NW Suite 300-A *Web:* www.consumersresearchcncl.org	Washington	DC	20006	202-835-9698	835-9739
Council of Better Business Bureaus (CBBB) 4200 Wilson Blvd Suite 800 *Web:* www.bbb.org	Arlington	VA	22203	703-276-0100	525-8277
Council of Better Business Bureaus Inc Wise Giving Alliance 4200 Wilson Blvd Suite 800 *Web:* www.bbb.org	Arlington	VA	22203	703-276-0100	525-8277
Essential Information PO Box 19405 *Web:* www.essential.org	Washington	DC	20036	202-387-8030	234-5176
Funeral Consumers Alliance 33 Patchen Rd *TF:* 800-765-0107 ■ *Web:* www.funerals.org	South Burlington	VT	05403	802-865-8300	865-2626
Funeral Service Help Line 13625 Bishops Dr *TF:* 800-662-7666	Brookfield	WI	53005	262-789-1880	
Green Seal 1001 Connecticut Ave NW Suite 827 *Web:* www.greenseal.org	Washington	DC	20036	202-872-6400	872-4324
Insurance Information Institute (III) 110 William St 24th Fl *TF:* 800-331-9146 ■ *Web:* www.iii.org	New York	NY	10038	212-346-5500	732-1916
Internet Alliance (IA) 1615 L St NW Suite 1100 *Web:* www.internetalliance.org	Washington	DC	20036	202-861-2407	
Internet Fraud Watch c/o National Fraud Information Ctr 1701 K St NW Suite 1200 *Web:* www.fraud.org/internet/intinfo.htm	Washington	DC	20006	202-835-3323	835-0747
Investor Responsibility Research Ctr (IRRC) 1350 Connecticut Ave NW Suite 1101 *Web:* www.irrc.org	Washington	DC	20036	202-833-0700	833-3555
NA of Child Care Resource & Referral Agencies (NACCRRA) 3101 Wilson Blvd Suite 350 *TF:* 800-424-2246 ■ *Web:* www.naccrra.org	Arlington	VA	22201	703-341-4100	341-4101
National Center for Employee Ownership (NCEO) 1736 Franklin St 8th Fl *Web:* www.nceo.org	Oakland	CA	94612	510-208-1300	272-9510
National Committee for Quality Assurance (NCQA) 1100 13th St *TF:* 800-275-7585 ■ *Web:* www.ncqa.org	Washington	DC	20005	202-955-3500	955-3599
National Consumers League (NCL) 1701 K St NW Suite 1200 *TF:* 800-876-7060 ■ *Web:* www.natlconsumersleague.org	Washington	DC	20006	202-835-3323	835-0747
National Endowment for Financial Education (NEFE) 5299 DTC Blvd Suite 1300 *Web:* www.nefe.org	Greenwood Village	CO	80111	303-741-6333	220-0838
National Fireworks Assn (NFA) 8224 NW Bradford Ct *Web:* www.nationalfireworks.org	Kansas City	MO	64151	816-505-3589	741-1348
National Fraud Information Ctr (NFIC) 1701 K St NW Suite 1200 *TF:* 800-876-7060 ■ *Web:* www.fraud.org	Washington	DC	20006	202-835-3323	835-0747
NeighborWorks America 1325 G St NW Suite 800 *Web:* www.nw.org	Washington	DC	20005	202-220-2300	376-2600
Philanthropic Research Inc 4801 Courthouse St Suite 220 *TF:* 800-784-9378	Williamsburg	VA	23188	757-229-4631	229-8912
Privacy Rights Clearinghouse 3100 5th Ave Suite B *Web:* www.privacyrights.org	San Diego	CA	92103	619-298-3396	298-5681
Private Citizen Inc PO Box 233 *TF:* 800-288-5865 ■ *Web:* www.privatecitizen.com	Naperville	IL	60566	630-393-1555	
Public Citizen 1600 20th St NW *Web:* www.citizen.org	Washington	DC	20009	202-588-1000	588-7796
Public Citizen Health Research Group 1600 20th St NW *Web:* www.citizen.org/hrg	Washington	DC	20009	202-588-1000	588-7796
SOCAP International 675 N Washington St Suite 200 *Web:* www.socap.org	Alexandria	VA	22314	703-519-3700	549-4886
US Metric Assn Inc (USMA) 10245 Andasol Ave *Web:* www.lamar.colostate.edu	Northridge	CA	91325	818-363-5606	

48-11 Educational Associations & Organizations

Organization	City	State	ZIP	Phone	Fax
A Better Chance 240 W 35th St 9th Fl *TF:* 800-543-7181 ■ *Web:* www.abetterchance.org	New York	NY	10001	646-346-1310	346-1311
AACSB International - Assn to Advance Collegiate Schools of Business 777 S Harbour Island Blvd Suite 750 *Web:* www.aacsb.edu	Tampa	FL	33602	813-769-6500	769-6559
Academy for Educational Development (AED) 1825 Connecticut Ave NW Suite 800 *Web:* www.aed.org	Washington	DC	20009	202-884-8000	884-8400
Academy of Political Science 475 Riverside Dr Suite 1274 *Web:* www.psqonline.org	New York	NY	10115	212-870-2500	870-2202
Advanced Network & Services Inc 2600 S Rd Suite 44-193 *Web:* www.advanced.org	Poughkeepsie	NY	12601	845-795-2090	795-2180
AFS International Inc 71 W 23rd St 17th Fl *Web:* www.afs.org	New York	NY	10010	212-807-8686	807-1001
Alliance for Excellent Education 1201 Connecticut Ave Suite 901 *Web:* www.all4ed.org	Washington	DC	20036	202-828-0828	828-0821

Organization	City	State	ZIP	Phone	Fax
Alliance for International Educational & Cultural Exchange 1776 Massachusetts Ave NW Suite 620 *Web:* www.alliance-exchange.org	Washington	DC	20036	202-293-6141	293-6144
American Academy of Political & Social Science 3814 Walnut St *Web:* www.aapss.org	Philadelphia	PA	19104	215-746-6500	573-3003
American Indian College Fund 8333 Greenwood Blvd *TF:* 800-776-3863 ■ *Web:* www.collegefund.org	Denver	CO	80221	303-426-8900	426-1200
American Institute for Foreign Study (AIFS) 9 W Broad St *TF:* 800-727-2437 ■ *Web:* www.aifs.org	Stamford	CT	06902	203-399-5000	399-5590
American Montessori Society (AMS) 281 Pk Ave S 6th Fl *Web:* www.amshq.org	New York	NY	10010	212-358-1250	358-1256
American Philosophical Society (APS) 104 S 5th St *Web:* www.amphilsoc.org	Philadelphia	PA	19106	215-440-3400	440-3436
Americas Society 680 Pk Ave 68th St *Web:* www.americas-society.org	New York	NY	10065	212-628-3200	628-3200
Archaeological Institute of America (AIA) 656 Beacon St 4th Fl *Web:* www.archaeological.org	Boston	MA	02215	617-353-9361	353-6550
Assn for Asian Studies (AAS) 1021 E Huron St *Web:* www.aasianst.org	Ann Arbor	MI	48104	734-665-2490	665-3801
Assn for Humanistic Psychology (AHP) 1516 Oak St Suite 320A *Web:* www.ahpweb.org	Alameda	CA	94501	510-769-6495	769-6433
Assn of Boarding Schools (TABS) 1 N Pack Sq Suite 301 *Web:* www.boardingschools.com	Asheville	NC	28801	828-258-5354	258-6428
Assn of Jesuit Colleges & Universities (AJCU) 1 Dupont Cir NW Suite 405 *Web:* www.ajcunet.edu	Washington	DC	20036	202-862-9893	862-8523
Assn of Writers & Writing Programs (AWP) George Mason Univ MS 1E3 *Web:* awpwriter.org	Fairfax	VA	22030	703-993-4301	993-4302
Associated Collegiate Press (ACP) 2221 University Ave SE Suite 121 *Web:* www.studentpress.org	Minneapolis	MN	55414	612-625-8335	626-0720
Astronomical Society of the Pacific 390 Ashton Ave *Web:* www.astrosociety.org	San Francisco	CA	94112	415-337-1100	337-5205
Braille Institute of America Inc 741 N Vermont Ave *TF:* 800-272-4553 ■ *Web:* www.brailleinstitute.org	Los Angeles	CA	90029	323-663-1111	663-0867
Breakthrough Collaborative 545 Sansome St Suite 700 *Web:* www.breakthroughcollaborative.org	San Francisco	CA	94111	415-442-0600	442-0609
Bryan City School District 1350 Fountain Grove Dr *Web:* www.bryan.k12.oh.us	Bryan	OH	43506	419-636-6973	636-0313
Center for Education Reform 910 17th St NW Suite 1120 *TF:* 800-521-2118 ■ *Web:* www.edreform.com	Washington	DC	20006	202-822-9000	822-5077
Challenger Center for Space Science Education 300 N Lee St # 301 *TF:* 800-987-8277 ■ *Web:* www.challenger.org	Alexandria	VA	22314	703-683-9740	683-7546
Chickasaw Nation The 520 Arlington St PO Box 1548 *TF:* 866-466-1481 ■ *Web:* www.chickasaw.net	Ada	OK	74821	580-436-2603	436-7297
College Board 45 Columbus Ave **Fax:* PR ■ *TF:* 800-927-4302 ■ *Web:* www.collegeboard.com	New York	NY	10023	212-713-8000	713-8184*
College Parents of America (CPA) 2020 Pennsylvania Ave N W Suite 020 **Fax Area Code:* 703 ■ *TF:* 888-761-6702 ■ *Web:* www.collegeparents.org	Washington	DC	20006	888-761-6702	875-2199*
Columbia Scholastic Press Assn (CSPA) Columbia University MC 5711 *Web:* www.columbia.edu/cu/cspa	New York	NY	10027	212-854-9400	854-9401
Committee for Education Funding (CEF) 1640 Rhode Island Ave NW # 600 *Web:* www.cef.org	Washington	DC	20036	202-383-0083	383-0097
Communities in Schools Inc (CIS) 277 S Washington St Suite 210 *TF:* 800-247-4543 ■ *Web:* www.cisnet.org	Alexandria	VA	22314	703-519-8999	519-7537
Comstar Enterprises Inc 224 Industrial Cir PO Box 6698 *TF:* 800-533-2343 ■ *Web:* www.comstar-inc.com	Springdale	AR	72762	479-361-2111	361-1069
Council For Economic Opportunities In Greater Cleveland 1228 Euclid Ave Suite 700 *Web:* www.ceogc.org	Cleveland	OH	44115	216-696-9077	696-0770
Council for Opportunity in Education 1025 Vermont Ave NW Suite 900 *Web:* www.coenet.us	Washington	DC	20005	202-347-7430	347-0786
Education Development Center Inc (EDC) 55 Chapel St *Web:* www.edc.org	Newton	MA	02458	617-969-7100	969-5979
Education Trust 1250 H St NW Suite 700 *Web:* www.edtrust.org	Washington	DC	20005	202-293-1217	293-2605
Facing History & Ourselves 16 Hurd Rd *TF:* 800-856-9039 ■ *Web:* www.facing.org	Brookline	MA	02445	617-232-1595	232-0281
Family Career & Community Leaders of America (FCCLA) 1910 Assn Dr *TF:* 800-234-4425 ■ *Web:* www.fcclainc.org	Reston	VA	20191	703-476-4900	860-2713
FIRST 200 Bedford St *TF:* 800-871-8326 ■ *Web:* www.usfirst.org	Manchester	NH	03101	603-666-3906	666-3907
Foundation Ctr 79 5th Ave 2nd Fl *TF:* 800-424-9836 ■ *Web:* www.foundationcenter.org	New York	NY	10003	212-620-4230	807-3691
Future Business Leaders of America-Phi Beta Lambda Inc (FBLA-PBL) 1912 Assn Dr **Fax Area Code:* 866 ■ *TF:* 800-325-2946 ■ *Web:* www.fbla-pbl.org	Reston	VA	20191	800-325-2946	500-5610*
German Academic Exchange Service (DAAD) 871 United Nations Plaza *Web:* www.daad.org	New York	NY	10017	212-758-3223	755-5780
Graduate Management Admission Council (GMAC) 11921 Freedom Dr Suite 300 *Web:* www.gmac.com	Reston	VA	20190	703-668-9600	668-9601
Great Books Foundation 35 E Wacker Dr Suite 400 *TF:* 800-222-5870 ■ *Web:* www.greatbooks.org	Chicago	IL	60601	312-332-5870	407-0334
Health Occupations Students of America (HOSA) 6021 Morriss Rd Suite 111 *TF:* 800-321-4672 ■ *Web:* www.hosa.org	Flower Mound	TX	75028	972-874-0062	874-0063
Institute for Education & the Arts 1156 15th St NW Suite 600 *Web:* www.edartsinstitute.org	Washington	DC	20005	202-223-9721	223-4720
Institute of Consumer Financial Education PO Box 34070 *Web:* www.financial-education-icfe.org	San Diego	CA	92163	619-232-8811	923-3284
Institute of General Semantics (IGS) 72-11 Austin St Suite 233 **Fax Area Code:* 718 ■ *Web:* www.generalsemantics.org	Forest Hills	NY	11375	212-729-7973	793-2527*
Institute of International Education (IIE) 809 United Nations Plaza # 1 *Web:* www.iie.org	New York	NY	10017	212-883-8200	984-5452
Intercollegiate Studies Institute (ISI) 3901 Centerville Rd *TF:* 800-526-7022 ■ *Web:* www.isi.org	Wilmington	DE	19807	302-652-4600	652-1760
Intercultural Development Research Assn (IDRA) 5815 Callaghan Rd Suite 101 *Web:* www.idra.org	San Antonio	TX	78228	210-444-1710	444-1714
International Montessori Council & The Montessori Foundation 2400 Miguel Bay Dr PO Box 130 *TF:* 800-655-5843 ■ *Web:* www.montessori.org	Terra Ceia Island	FL	34250	941-729-9565	729-9594
International Studies Assn (ISA) 324 Social Sciences Univ of Arizona *Web:* www.isanet.org	Tucson	AZ	85721	520-621-7715	621-5780
JA Worldwide 1130 Via Belcanto *Web:* www.ja.org	San Antonio	TX	78258	210-651-3366	
Jewish Education Service of North America (JESNA) 111 8th Ave Suite 11-E *Web:* www.jesna.org	New York	NY	10011	212-284-6950	284-6951
Junior Achievement of Canada (JACAN) 1 Eva Rd Suite 218 *TF:* 800-265-0699 ■ *Web:* www.jacan.org	Toronto	ON	M9C4Z5	416-622-4602	622-6861
Junior State of America (JSA) 400 S El Camino Real Suite 300 *TF:* 800-334-5353 ■ *Web:* www.jsa.org	San Mateo	CA	94402	650-347-1600	347-7200
League for Innovation in the Community College 4505 E Chandler Blvd Suite 250 *Web:* www.league.org	Phoenix	AZ	85048	480-705-8200	705-8201
Linguistic Society of America (LSA) 1325 18th St NW Suite 211 *Web:* www.lsadc.org	Washington	DC	20036	202-835-1714	835-1717
Medieval Academy of America The 104 Mt Auburn St 5th Fl *Web:* www.medievalacademy.org	Cambridge	MA	02138	617-491-1622	492-3303
Minnesota Medical Foundation Inc 300 McNamara Alumni Ctr 200 Oak St SE *TF:* 800-922-1663 ■ *Web:* www.mmf.umn.edu	Minneapolis	MN	55455	612-625-1440	625-5673
Music for All 39 Jackson Pl # 150 *TF:* 800-848-2263 ■ *Web:* www.musicforall.org	Indianapolis	IN	46225	317-636-2263	524-6200
NA for Year-Round Education (NAYRE) PO Box 711386 **Fax Area Code:* 858 ■ *Web:* www.nayre.org	San Diego	CA	92171	619-276-5296	571-5754*
National Alliance of Blind Students Inc The 1155 15th St NW Suite 1004 *TF:* 800-424-8666 ■ *Web:* www.blindstudents.org	Washington	DC	20005	202-467-5081	467-5085
National Center for Education Information (NCEI) 4401-A Connecticut Ave NW Suite 212 *Web:* www.ncei.com	Washington	DC	20008	202-822-8280	822-8284
National Center for Family Literacy (NCFL) 325 W Main St Suite 300 *TF:* 877-326-5481 ■ *Web:* www.famlit.org	Louisville	KY	40202	502-584-1133	584-0172
National Forensic League (NFL) 125 Watson St PO Box 38 *Web:* www.nflonline.org	Ripon	WI	54971	920-748-6206	748-9478
National Head Start Assn (NHSA) 1651 Prince St *TF:* 800-355-6472 ■ *Web:* www.nhsa.org	Alexandria	VA	22314	703-739-0875	739-0878
National Honor Society (NHS) 1904 Assn Dr *TF:* 800-253-7746 ■ *Web:* www.nhs.us	Reston	VA	20191	703-860-0200	476-5432
National Research Council (NRC) 500 5th St NW *Web:* www.nationalacademies.org/nrc	Washington	DC	20001	202-334-2000	
National Scholastic Press Assn (NSPA) 2221 University Ave SE Suite 121 *Web:* www.studentpress.org/nspa	Minneapolis	MN	55414	612-625-8335	626-0720
National Society for Experiential Education (NSEE) 19 Mantua Rd *Web:* www.nsee.org	Mount Royal	NJ	08061	856-423-3427	423-3420
North-American Interfraternity Conference (NIC) 3901 W 86th St Suite 390 *Web:* www.nicindy.org	Indianapolis	IN	46268	317-872-1112	872-1134
Northwestern Illinois Assn 245 W Exchange St Suite 4 *Web:* www.thenia.org	Sycamore	IL	60178	815-895-9227	895-2971
Panhandle-Plains Higher Education Authority Inc (PPHEA) 1303 23rd St PO Box 839 *TF:* 877-629-3669 ■ *Web:* www.pphea.org	Canyon	TX	79015	806-324-4100	655-3669
Public Education Network (PEN) 601 13th St NW Suite 710-S *Web:* www.publiceducation.org	Washington	DC	20005	202-628-7460	628-1893
Reading Is Fundamental Inc (RIF) 1825 Connecticut Ave NW Suite 400 *TF:* 877-743-7323 ■ *Web:* www.rif.org	Washington	DC	20009	202-536-3400	287-3196

Organization	City	State	Zip	Phone	Fax
Rolling Readers USA 2515 Camino del Rio S Suite 330 *Web:* www.rollingreaders.org	San Diego	CA	92108	619-516-4095	516-4096
Scholarship America 1 Scholarship Way PO Box 297 *TF:* 800-537-4180 ■ *Web:* www.scholarshipamerica.org	Saint Peter	MN	56082	507-931-1682	931-9168
SkillsUSA 14001 James Monroe Hwy *TF:* 800-321-8422 ■ *Web:* www.skillsusa.org	Leesburg	VA	20176	703-777-8810	777-8999
United Negro College Fund Inc (UNCF) 8260 Willow Oaks Corporate Dr Suite 400 *TF:* 800-331-2244	Fairfax	VA	22031	703-205-3400	205-3507
US Student Assn (USSA) 1211 Connecticut Ave NW Suite 406 *Web:* www.usstudents.org	Washington	DC	20036	202-640-6570	233-4005
White House Historical Assn 740 Jackson Pl NW *Web:* www.whitehousehistory.org	Washington	DC	20506	202-737-8292	789-0440
Woodrow Wilson National Fellowship Foundation 5 Vaughn Dr # 300 *Web:* www.woodrow.org	Princeton	NJ	08540	609-452-7007	452-0066
World Assn of International Studies (WAIS) Hoover Institution 766 Santa Ynez St *Web:* wais.stanford.edu	Stanford	CA	94305	650-322-2026	723-1687
World Learning International Development Programs 1015 15th St NW Suite 750 *Web:* www.worldlearning.org	Washington	DC	20005	202-408-5420	408-5397
Young Astronaut Council 5200 27th St NW	Washington	DC	20015	301-617-0923	776-0858
Youth For Understanding USA 6400 Goldsboro Rd Suite 100 *TF:* 800-424-3691 ■ *Web:* www.yfuusa.org	Bethesda	MD	20817	240-235-2100	235-2104

48-12 Energy & Natural Resources Organizations

Organization	City	State	Zip	Phone	Fax
Air & Waste Management Assn (A&WMA) 420 Fort Duquesne Blvd 1 Gateway Ctr 3rd Fl *TF:* 800-270-3444 ■ *Web:* www.awma.org	Pittsburgh	PA	15122	412-232-3444	232-3450
Alliance to Save Energy (ASE) 1850 M St NW Suite 600 *Web:* www.ase.org	Washington	DC	20036	202-857-0666	331-9588
American Academy of Environmental Engineers 130 Holiday Ct Suite 100 *Web:* www.aaee.net	Annapolis	MD	21401	410-266-3311	266-7653
American Assn of Petroleum Geologists (AAPG) 1444 S Boulder Ave PO Box 979 *TF:* 800-364-2274 ■ *Web:* www.aapg.org	Tulsa	OK	74119	918-584-2555	560-2665
American Assn of Professional Landmen (AAPL) 4100 Fossil Creek Blvd *TF:* 888-566-2275 ■ *Web:* www.landman.org	Fort Worth	TX	76137	817-847-7700	847-7704
American Coal Ash Assn (ACAA) 15200 E Girard Ave Suite 3050 *Web:* www.acaa-usa.org	Aurora	CO	80014	720-870-7897	870-7889
American Coalition for Clean Coal Electricity (ACCCE) 333 John Carlyle St Suite 530 *Web:* www.cleancoalusa.org	Alexandria	VA	22314	703-684-6292	684-6297
American Coke & Coal Chemicals Institute (ACCCI) 1140 Connecticut Ave NW Suite 705 *Web:* www.accci.org	Washington	DC	20036	202-452-7198	463-6573
American Gas Assn (AGA) 400 N Capitol St NW 4th Fl *Web:* www.aga.org	Washington	DC	20001	202-824-7000	824-7115
American Hydrogen Assn (AHA) 2350 W Shangri La *Web:* www.clean-air.org	Phoenix	AZ	85029	602-328-4238	
American Institute of Mining Metallurgical & Petroleum Engineers (AIME) 8307 Shaffer Pkwy PO Box 270728 *Web:* www.aimehq.org	Littleton	CO	80127	303-948-4255	948-4260
American Oil Chemists Society (AOCS) 2710 S Boulder PO Box 17190 *TF:* 800-336-2627 ■ *Web:* www.aocs.org	Urbana	IL	61802	217-359-2344	351-8091
American Petroleum Institute (API) 1220 L St NW 9th Fl *Web:* www.api-ec.api.org	Washington	DC	20005	202-682-8000	682-8029
American Public Gas Assn (APGA) 201 Massachusetts Ave NE Suite C-4 *TF:* 800-927-4204 ■ *Web:* www.apga.org	Washington	DC	20002	202-464-2742	464-0246
American Public Power Assn (APPA) 1875 Connecticut Ave Suite 1200 *TF:* 800-515-2772 ■ *Web:* www.appanet.org	Washington	DC	20009	202-467-2900	467-2910
American Solar Energy Society (ASES) 2400 Central Ave Suite A *Web:* www.ases.org	Boulder	CO	80301	303-443-3130	443-3212
American Water Works Assn (AWWA) 6666 W Quincy Ave *TF:* 800-926-7337 ■ *Web:* www.awwa.org	Denver	CO	80235	303-794-7711	347-0804
American Wind Energy Assn (AWEA) 1501 M St NW Suite 1000 *Web:* www.awea.org	Washington	DC	20005	202-383-2500	383-2505
Assn of Energy Engineers (AEE) 4025 Pleasantdale Rd Suite 420 *Web:* www.aeecenter.org	Atlanta	GA	30340	770-447-5083	446-3969
Assn of Energy Service Cos (AESC) three wellman 14531 fm 529 Suite 250 *TF:* 800-692-0771 ■ *Web:* www.aesc.net	Houston	TX	77095	713-781-0758	781-7542
Automatic Meter Reading Assn (AMRA) 111 Deerlake Rd Suite 100 *Web:* www.amra-intl.org	Deerfield	IL	60015	847-480-9628	480-9282
Bituminous Coal Operators Assn 1776 I St NW	Washington	DC	20006	202-783-3195	783-4862
Coalition for Fair Lumber Imports (CFLI) 975 F St NW *Web:* www.fairlumbercoalition.org	Washington	DC	20004	202-862-3686	862-1093
Cooling Technology Institute (CTI) 2611 FM 1960 Rd W Suite A-101 *Web:* www.cti.org	Houston	TX	77068	281-583-4087	537-1721
Edison Electric Institute (EEI) 701 Pennsylvania Ave NW *TF:* 800-334-4688 ■ *Web:* www.eei.org	Washington	DC	20004	202-508-5000	508-5051
Electric Power Supply Assn (EPSA) 1401 New York Ave NW 11th Fl *Web:* www.epsa.org	Washington	DC	20005	202-628-8200	628-8260
Electricity Consumers Resource Council (ELCON) 1333 H St NW W Tower 8th Fl *Web:* www.elcon.org	Washington	DC	20005	202-682-1390	289-6370
Energy Recovery Council (IWSA) 1730 Rhode Island Ave NW Suite 700 *Web:* www.wte.org	Washington	DC	20036	202-467-6240	467-6225
Environmental Industry Associations 4301 Connecticut Ave NW Suite 300 *TF:* 800-424-2869 ■ *Web:* www.environmentalistseveryday.org	Washington	DC	20008	202-244-4700	966-4824
Environmental Technology Council (ETC) 734 15th St NW Suite 720	Washington	DC	20005	202-783-0870	737-2038
Gas Processors Assn (GPA) 6526 E 60th St *Web:* www.gasprocessors.com	Tulsa	OK	74145	918-493-3872	493-3875
Gas Processors Suppliers Assn (GPSA) 6526 E 60th St *Web:* www.gpsa.gpaglobal.org	Tulsa	OK	74145	918-493-3872	493-3875
Independent Petroleum Assn of America (IPAA) 1201 15th St NW Suite 300 *TF:* 800-433-2851 ■ *Web:* www.ipaa.org	Washington	DC	20005	202-857-4722	857-4799
Institute of Clean Air Cos (ICAC) 1730 M St NW Suite 206 *Web:* www.icac.com	Washington	DC	20036	202-457-0911	331-1388
Institute of Hazardous Materials Management (IHMM) 11900 Parklawn Dr Suite 450 *Web:* www.ihmm.org	Rockville	MD	20852	301-984-8969	984-1516
Institute of Nuclear Power Operations 700 Galleria Pkwy SE Suite 100 *Web:* www.inpo.info	Atlanta	GA	30339	770-644-8000	644-8549
Institute of Scrap Recycling Industries Inc (ISRI) 1615 L St NW Suite 600 *Web:* www.isri.org/iMIS15_PROD/ISRI/Default.aspx	Washington	DC	20036	202-662-8500	626-0900
International Institute for Energy Conservation (IIEC) 10005 Leamoore Ln Suite 100 *Web:* www.iiec.org	Vienna	VA	22181	703-281-7263	938-5153
Interstate Oil & Gas Compact Commission (IOGCC) 900 NE 23rd St PO Box 53127 *TF:* 800-822-4015 ■ *Web:* www.iogcc.state.ok.us	Oklahoma City	OK	73152	405-525-3556	525-3592
Methanol Institute (MI) 4100 Fairfax Dr # 740 *TF:* 888-275-0768 ■ *Web:* www.methanol.org	Arlington	VA	22203	703-248-3636	248-3997
NA of Regulatory Utility Commissioners (NARUC) 1101 Vermont Ave NW Suite 200 *Web:* www.naruc.org	Washington	DC	20005	202-898-2200	898-2213
NA of State Utility Consumer Advocates (NASUCA) 8380 Colesville Rd Suite 101 *Web:* www.nasuca.org	Silver Spring	MD	20910	301-589-6313	589-6380
NA of Water Cos (NAWC) 2001 L St NW Suite 850 *Web:* www.nawc.com	Washington	DC	20036	202-833-8383	331-7442
National Energy Services Assn (NESA) 6430 FM 1960 W Suite 213 *Web:* www.nesanet.org	Houston	TX	77069	713-856-6525	856-6199
National Ground Water Assn (NGWA) 601 Dempsey Rd *TF:* 800-551-7379 ■ *Web:* www.ngwa.org	Westerville	OH	43081	614-898-7791	898-7786
National Mining Assn (NMA) 101 Constitution Ave NW Suite 500-E *Web:* www.nma.org	Washington	DC	20001	202-463-2600	463-2666
National Ocean Industries Assn (NOIA) 1120 G St NW Suite 900 *Web:* www.noia.org	Washington	DC	20005	202-347-6900	347-8650
National Petrochemical & Refiners Assn (NPRA) 1667 K St NW Suite 700 *Web:* www.npradc.org	Washington	DC	20036	202-457-0480	457-0486
National Propane Gas Assn (NPGA) 1899 L St NW # 350 *Web:* www.npga.org	Washington	DC	20036	202-466-7200	466-7205
National Rural Electric Co-op Assn (NRECA) 4301 Wilson Blvd *TF:* 866-673-2299 ■ *Web:* www.nreca.org	Arlington	VA	22203	703-907-5500	907-5528
National Rural Water Assn (NRWA) 2915 S 13th St *Web:* www.nrwa.org	Duncan	OK	73533	580-252-0629	255-4476
National Water Resources Assn (NWRA) 3800 Fairfax Dr # 4 *Web:* www.nwra.org	Arlington	VA	22203	703-524-1544	524-1548
Natural Gas Supply Assn (NGSA) 805 15th St NW Suite 510 *Web:* www.ngsa.org	Washington	DC	20005	202-326-9300	326-9330
North American Electric Reliability Council (NERC) 116-390 Village Blvd *TF:* 800-726-8060 ■ *Web:* www.nerc.com	Princeton	NJ	08540	609-452-8060	452-9550
Nuclear Energy Institute (NEI) 1776 'I' St NW Suite 400 *Web:* www.nei.org	Washington	DC	20006	202-739-8000	785-4019
Petroleum Technology Transfer Council (PTTC) 125 W 15th St PO Box 979 *TF:* 888-843-7882 ■ *Web:* www.pttc.org	Tulsa	OK	74101	918-560-2649	560-2632
Renewable Fuels Assn (RFA) 425 3rd St SW *Web:* www.ethanolrfa.org	Washington	DC	20024	202-289-3835	289-7519
Society of Exploration Geophysicists (SEG) 8801 S Yale Ave Suite 500 PO Box 702740 *Web:* www.seg.org	Tulsa	OK	74137	918-497-5500	497-5557
Society of Petroleum Engineers (SPE) 222 Palisades Creek Dr *TF:* 800-456-6863 ■ *Web:* www.spe.org	Richardson	TX	75080	972-952-9393	952-9435

Organization	City	State	Zip	Phone	Fax
Society of Petrophysicists & Well Log Analysts (SPWLA) 8866 Gulf Fwy Suite 320 *Web:* www.spwla.org	Houston	TX	77017	713-947-8727	947-7181
Solar Energy Industries Assn (SEIA) 805 15th St NW Suite 510 *Web:* www.seia.org	Washington	DC	20005	202-682-0556	628-7779
US Energy Assn (USEA) 1300 Pennsylvania Ave NW Suite 550 *Web:* www.usea.org	Washington	DC	20004	202-312-1230	682-1826
Water Quality Assn (WQA) 4151 Naperville Rd *Web:* www.wqa.org	Lisle	IL	60532	630-505-0160	505-9637
Western Forestry & Conservation Assn 4033 SW Canyon Rd *TF:* 888-722-9416 ■ *Web:* www.westernforestry.org	Portland	OR	97221	503-226-4562	226-2515

48-13 Environmental Organizations

Organization	City	State	Zip	Phone	Fax
Adirondack Council 103 Hand Ave Suite 3 PO Box 2 *TF:* 877-873-2240 ■ *Web:* www.adirondackcouncil.org	Elizabethtown	NY	12932	518-873-2240	873-6675
Alaska Wilderness League 122 C St NW Suite 240 *Web:* www.alaskawild.org	Washington	DC	20001	202-544-5205	544-5197
Alliance for Responsible Atmospheric Policy 2111 Wilson Blvd 8th Fl *Web:* www.arap.org	Arlington	VA	22201	703-243-0344	243-2874
America the Beautiful Fund 725 15th St NW Suite 605 *TF:* 800-522-3557 ■ *Web:* www.america-the-beautiful.org	Washington	DC	20006	202-638-1649	638-2175
American Cave Conservation Assn 119 E Main St PO Box 409 *Web:* www.cavern.org	Horse Cave	KY	42749	270-786-1466	786-1467
American Farmland Trust (AFT) 1200 18th St *TF:* 800-431-1499 ■ *Web:* www.farmland.org	Washington	DC	20036	202-331-7300	659-8339
American Forests 734 15th St NW *TF:* 800-368-5748 ■ *Web:* www.americanforests.org	Washington	DC	20005	202-737-1944	737-2457
American Lands Alliance 726 7th St SE	Washington	DC	20002	202-547-9400	547-9213
American Littoral Society (ALS) 18 S Hartshorne Dr *Web:* www.littoralsociety.org	Highlands	NJ	07732	732-291-0055	291-3551
American Public Information on the Environment 316 Oak St PO Box 676 *TF:* 800-320-2743 ■ *Web:* www.americanpie.org	Northfield	MN	55057	507-645-5613	645-5724
American Rivers 1101 14th St NW Suite 1400 *TF:* 877-347-7550 ■ *Web:* www.americanrivers.org	Washington	DC	20005	202-347-7550	347-9240
American Shore & Beach Preservation Assn (ASBPA) 5460 Beaujolais Ln *Web:* www.asbpa.org	Fort Myers	FL	33919	239-489-2616	489-9917
American Wildlands 321 E Main St Suite 418	Bozeman	MT	59715	406-586-8175	586-8242
Appalachian Mountain Club (AMC) 5 Joy St *TF Orders:* 800-262-4455 ■ *Web:* www.outdoors.org	Boston	MA	02108	617-523-0655	523-0722
APVA Preservation Virginia 204 W Franklin St *Web:* www.devel.preservationvirginia.org	Richmond	VA	23220	804-648-1889	775-0802
Archaeological Conservancy 5301 Central Ave NE Suite 902 *Web:* www.americanarchaeology.org	Albuquerque	NM	87108	505-266-1540	266-0311
Audubon Naturalist Society 8940 Jones Mill Rd *Web:* www.audubonnaturalist.org	Chevy Chase	MD	20815	301-652-9188	951-7179
Beyond Pesticides 701 E St SE Suite 200 *Web:* www.beyondpesticides.org	Washington	DC	20003	202-543-5450	543-4791
Big Bend Natural History Assn PO Box 196 *Web:* www.bigbendbookstore.org	Big Bend National Park	TX	79834	432-477-2236	477-2234
Canadian Parks & Wilderness Society (CPAWS) 250 City Ctr Ave Suite 506 *TF:* 800-333-9453 ■ *Web:* www.cpaws.org	Ottawa	ON	K1R6K7	613-569-7226	569-7098
Canadian Water Resources Assn (CWRA) 9 Corvus Ct *Web:* www.cwra.org	Ottawa	ON	K1P5G8	613-237-9363	594-5190
Canadian Wildlife Federation (CWF) 350 Michael Cowpland Dr *TF:* 800-563-9453 ■ *Web:* www.cwf-fcf.org	Kanata	ON	K2M2W1	613-599-9594	599-4428
Center for Plant Conservation (CPC) PO Box 299 *Web:* www.centerforplantconservation.org	Saint Louis	MO	63166	314-577-9450	577-9465
Charles A & Anne Morrow Lindbergh Foundation 2150 3rd Ave N Suite 310 *Web:* www.lindberghfoundation.org	Anoka	MN	55303	763-576-1596	576-1664
Circumpolar Conservation Union (CCU) 1730 Rhode Island Ave NW Suite 707	Washington	DC	20036	202-775-5671	775-2179
Citizens Network for Sustainable Development (CitNet) PO Box 7458 *Web:* www.citnet.org	Silver Spring	MD	20907	301-588-5550	
Civil War Preservation Trust (CWPT) 1331 H St NW Suite 1001 *TF:* 888-606-1400 ■ *Web:* www.civilwar.org	Washington	DC	20005	202-367-1861	367-1865
Clean Water Action 4455 Connecticut Ave NW *TF:* 800-709-2837 ■ *Web:* www.cleanwateraction.org	Washington	DC	20008	202-895-0420	895-0438
Clean Water Fund (CWF) 4455 Connecticut Ave NW Suite A300-16 *TF:* 800-709-2837 ■ *Web:* www.cleanwaterfund.org	Washington	DC	20008	202-895-0432	895-0438
Co-op America 1612 K St NW Suite 600 *TF:* 800-584-7336 ■ *Web:* www.greenamerica.org	Washington	DC	20006	202-872-5307	331-8166
Coalition for Responsible Waste Incineration (CRWI) 1615 L St NW Suite 1350 *Web:* www.crwi.org	Washington	DC	20036	202-452-1241	887-8044
Coastal Conservation Assn (CCA) 6919 Portwest Dr Suite 100 *TF:* 800-201-3474 ■ *Web:* www.joincca.org	Houston	TX	77024	713-626-4234	626-5852
Conservation Fund 1655 N Fort Myer Dr Suite 1300 *Web:* www.conservationfund.org	Arlington	VA	22209	703-525-6300	525-4610
Conservation International (CI) 2011 Crystal Dr Suite 500 *TF:* 800-406-2306 ■ *Web:* www.conservation.org	Arlington	VA	22202	703-341-2400	553-0654
Conservation Treaty Support Fund (CTSF) 3705 Cardiff Rd *TF:* 800-654-3150	Chevy Chase	MD	20815	301-654-3150	652-6390
Consortium for Ocean Leadership 1201 New York Ave NW Suite 420 *Web:* www.coreocean.org	Washington	DC	20005	202-232-3900	462-8754
Corp for Jefferson's Poplar Forest The PO Box 419 *Web:* www.poplarforest.org	Forest	VA	24551	434-525-1806	525-7252
Earth Day Network (EDN) 1616 P St NW Suite 340 *Web:* www.earthday.net	Washington	DC	20036	202-518-0044	518-8794
Earth Island Institute 300 Broadway Suite 28 *Web:* www.earthisland.org	San Francisco	CA	94704	415-788-3666	788-7324
Earth Share 7735 Old Georgetown Rd Suite 900 *TF:* 800-875-3863 ■ *Web:* www.earthshare.org	Bethesda	MD	20814	240-333-0300	333-0301
Earthjustice 426 17th St 6th Fl *TF:* 800-584-6460 ■ *Web:* www.earthjustice.org	Oakland	CA	94612	510-550-6700	550-6740
EarthRights International 1612 K St NW Suite 401 *Web:* www.earthrights.org	Washington	DC	20006	202-466-5188	466-5189
Earthwatch Institute 114 Western Ave *TF:* 800-776-0188 ■ *Web:* www.earthwatch.org	Boston	MA	02134	978-461-0081	461-2332
Ecojustice Canada 131 Water St Suite 214 *TF:* 800-926-7744 ■ *Web:* www.ecojustice.ca	Vancouver	BC	V6B4M3	604-685-5618	685-7813
Educational Communications Inc PO Box 351419 *Web:* www.ecoprojects.org	Los Angeles	CA	90035	310-559-9160	559-9160
Environmental Defense 257 Pk Ave S *TF:* 800-505-0703 ■ *Web:* www.edf.org	New York	NY	10010	212-505-2100	505-2100
Environmental Information Assn (EIA) 6935 Wisconsin Ave Suite 306 *TF:* 888-343-4342 ■ *Web:* www.eia-usa.org	Chevy Chase	MD	20815	301-961-4999	961-3094
Environmental Law Institute (ELI) 2000 L St NW Suite 620 *TF:* 800-433-5120 ■ *Web:* www.eli.org	Washington	DC	20036	202-939-3800	939-3868
Environmental Protection Information Ctr (EPIC) PO Box 397 *Web:* www.wildcalifornia.org	Garberville	CA	95542	707-923-2931	923-4210
Forest Guild 80 E San Francisco PO Box 519 *Web:* forestguild.org	Santa Fe	NM	87504	505-983-8992	986-0798
Forest History Society 701 William Vickers Ave *Web:* www.foresthistory.org	Durham	NC	27701	919-682-9319	682-2349
Forest Landowners Assn (FLA) 900 Cir 75 Pkwy Suite 205 *TF:* 800-325-2954 ■ *Web:* www.forestlandowners.com	Atlanta	GA	30339	404-325-2954	325-2955
Freshwater Society 2500 Shadywood Rd *TF:* 888-471-9773 ■ *Web:* www.freshwater.org	Excelsior	MN	55331	952-471-9773	471-7685
Friends of the Earth 1717 Massachusetts Ave NW Suite 600 *TF:* 877-843-8687 ■ *Web:* www.foe.org	Washington	DC	20036	202-783-7400	783-0444
Friends of the Earth Canada 260 St Patrick St Suite 300 *TF:* 888-385-4444 ■ *Web:* www.foecanada.org	Ottawa	ON	K1N5K5	613-241-0085	241-7998
Friends of the Everglades 7800 Red Rd Suite 215K *Web:* www.everglades.org	South Miami	FL	33143	305-669-0858	669-4108
Friends of the River 1418 20th St Suite 100 *TF:* 888-464-2477 ■ *Web:* www.friendsoftheriver.org	Sacramento	CA	95811	916-442-3155	442-3396
Grand Canyon Trust 2601 N Fort Valley Rd *TF:* 888-428-5550 ■ *Web:* www.grandcanyontrust.org	Flagstaff	AZ	86001	928-774-7488	774-7570
Great Lakes United (GLU) Buffalo State College Cassety Hall 1300 Elmwood Ave *TF:* 800-846-0142 ■ *Web:* www.glu.org	Buffalo	NY	14222	716-886-0142	886-0303
Greater Yellowstone Coalition (GYC) 13 S Willson Ave Suite 2 *TF:* 800-775-1834 ■ *Web:* www.greateryellowstone.org	Bozeman	MT	59715	406-586-1593	556-2839
Greenpeace Canada 33 Cecil St *TF:* 800-320-7183 ■ *Web:* www.greenpeace.org	Toronto	ON	M5T1N1	416-597-8408	597-8422
Greenpeace USA 702 H St NW Suite 300 *TF:* 800-326-0959 ■ *Web:* www.greenpeace.org	Washington	DC	20001	202-462-1177	462-4507
Ground Water Protection Council (GWPC) 13308 N MacArthur Blvd *Web:* www.gwpc.org	Oklahoma City	OK	73142	405-516-4972	516-4973
Hells Canyon Preservation Council 105 Fir St Suite 327 PO Box 2768 *Web:* www.hellscanyon.org	La Grande	OR	97850	541-963-3950	963-0584
Heritage Canada Foundation 5 Blackburn Ave *TF:* 866-964-1066 ■ *Web:* www.heritagecanada.org	Ottawa	ON	K1N8A2	613-237-1066	237-5987
Historic New England 141 Cambridge St *Web:* www.historicnewengland.org	Boston	MA	02114	617-227-3956	227-9204
International Assn of Wildland Fire (IAWF) 3416 Primm Ln *Web:* www.iawfonline.org	Birmingham	AL	35216	205-824-7614	
International Society of Tropical Foresters (ISTF) 5400 Grosvenor Ln **Fax Area Code: 877* ■ *TF:* 866-897-8720 ■ *Web:* www.istf-bethesda.org	Bethesda	MD	20814	301-530-4514	665-6473*
Island Nature Trust PO Box 265 *Web:* www.islandnaturetrust.ca	Charlottetown	PE	C1A7K4	902-566-9150	628-6331

Organization	City	State	ZIP	Phone	Fax
Izaak Walton League of America (IWLA) 707 Conservation Ln *TF:* 800-453-5463 ■ *Web:* www.iwla.org	Gaithersburg	MD	20878	301-548-0150	548-0146
Land Trust Alliance (LTA) 1660 L St NW Suite 1100 *Web:* www.landtrustalliance.org	Washington	DC	20036	202-638-4725	638-4730
League to Save Lake Tahoe 2608 Lake Tahoe Blvd *Web:* www.keeptahoeblue.org	South Lake Tahoe	CA	96150	530-541-5388	541-5454
Montana Wilderness Assn (MWA) 30 S Ewing St *Web:* www.wildmontana.org	Helena	MT	59601	406-443-7350	443-0750
Mount Rushmore Society 711 N Creek Dr *Web:* www.mountrushmoresociety.com	Rapid City	SD	57703	605-341-8883	341-0433
NA for Olmsted Parks 1111 16th St NW Suite 310 *TF:* 866-666-6905 ■ *Web:* www.olmsted.org	Washington	DC	20036	202-223-9113	223-9112
NA for PET Container Resources (NAPCOR) 17474 Sonoma Hwy PO Box 1327 *Web:* www.napcor.com	Sonoma	CA	95476	707-996-4207	935-1998
National Alliance of Preservation Commissions 325 S Lumpkin St Founders Garden House *Web:* www.uga.edu/sed/pso/programs/napc/napc.htm	Athens	GA	30602	706-542-4731	204-9521
National Arbor Day Foundation 100 Arbor Ave *TF:* 888-448-7337 ■ *Web:* www.arborday.org	Nebraska City	NE	68410	402-474-5655	474-0820
National Audubon Society (NAS) 225 Varick St *Web:* www.audubon.org	New York	NY	10014	212-979-3000	979-3188
National Council for Air & Stream Improvement Inc (NCASI) PO Box 13318 *Web:* www.ncasi.org	Research Triangle Park	NC	27709	919-941-6400	941-6401
National Fish & Wildlife Foundation 1120 Connecticut Ave NW Suite 900 *Web:* www.nfwf.org	Washington	DC	20036	202-857-0166	857-0162
National Forest Foundation 27 Fort Missoula Rd Bldg 27 Suite 3 *TF:* 866-733-4633 ■ *Web:* www.natlforests.org	Missoula	MT	59804	406-542-2805	542-2810
National Marine Sanctuary Foundation 8601 Georgia Ave Suite 501 *Web:* www.nmsfocean.org	Silver Spring	MD	20910	301-608-3040	608-3044
National Park Foundation (NPF) 1201 'I' St NW Suite 550-B *Web:* www.nationalparks.org	Washington	DC	20005	202-354-6460	371-2066
National Park Trust (NPT) 401 E Jefferson St Suite 102 *Web:* www.parktrust.org	Rockville	MD	20850	301-279-7275	279-7211
National Parks Conservation Assn (NPCA) 1300 19th St NW Suite 300 *TF:* 800-628-7275 ■ *Web:* www.npca.org	Washington	DC	20036	202-223-6722	
National Trust for Historic Preservation 1785 Massachusetts Ave NW *TF:* 800-944-6847 ■ *Web:* www.preservationnation.org	Washington	DC	20036	202-588-6000	588-6038
National Wildlife Refuge Assn (NWRA) 1250 Connecticut Ave NW Suite 600 *Web:* www.refugeassociation.org	Washington	DC	20036	202-292-2402	292-2435
Natural Areas Assn (NAA) 115 NW Oregon Ave # 24 *Web:* www.naturalarea.org	Bend	OR	97701	541-317-0199	
Natural Resources Council of America (NRCA) 1616 P St NW Suite 340	Washington	DC	20036	202-232-6531	518-8794
Natural Resources Defense Council (NRDC) 40 W 20th St *Web:* www.nrdc.org	New York	NY	10011	212-727-2700	727-1773
Nature Canada 75 Albert St Suite 300 *TF:* 800-267-4088 ■ *Web:* www.naturecanada.ca	Ottawa	ON	K1P6A4	613-562-3447	562-3371
Nature Conservancy 4245 N Fairfax Dr Suite 100 *TF Cust Svc:* 800-628-6860 ■ *Web:* www.nature.org	Arlington	VA	22203	703-841-5300	841-1283
Nature Conservancy of Canada 36 Eglinton Ave W Suite 400 *TF:* 800-465-8005 ■ *Web:* www.natureconservancy.ca	Toronto	ON	M4R1A1	416-932-3202	932-3208
Negative Population Growth (NPG) 2861 Duke St Suite 36 *Web:* www.npg.org	Alexandria	VA	22314	703-370-9510	370-9514
New England Wild Flower Society 180 Hemenway Rd *Web:* www.newfs.org	Framingham	MA	01701	508-877-7630	877-3658
Ocean Conservancy 1300 19th St NW 8th Fl *TF:* 800-519-1541 ■ *Web:* www.oceanconservancy.org	Washington	DC	20036	202-429-5609	872-0619
Ocean Futures Society 325 Chapala St *Web:* www.oceanfutures.org	Santa Barbara	CA	93101	805-899-8899	899-8898
Open Space Institute (OSI) 1350 Broadway Suite 201 *Web:* www.osiny.org	New York	NY	10018	212-290-8200	244-3441
Pacific Rivers Council (PRC) 1326 SW 16th Ave *Web:* www.pacificrivers.org	Portland	OR	97201	503-228-3555	228-3556
Pew Charitable Trust 1200 18th St NW 5th Fl *Web:* www.pewtrusts.org	Washington	DC	20036	202-887-8800	887-8877
Pollution Probe 150 Ferrand Dr Suite 208 *Web:* www.pollutionprobe.org	Toronto	ON	M3C3E5	416-926-1907	926-1601
Project for Public Spaces 700 Broadway 4th Fl *Web:* www.pps.org	New York	NY	10003	212-620-5660	620-3821
Public Lands Foundation (PLF) PO Box 7226 *Web:* www.publicland.org	Arlington	VA	22207	703-790-1988	821-3490
Rails-to-Trails Conservancy (RTC) 2121 Ward Ct NW 5th Fl *Web:* www.railtrails.org	Washington	DC	20033	202-331-9696	223-9257
Rainforest Action Network (RAN) 221 Pine St Fifth Fl *TF:* 800-989-7246 ■ *Web:* www.ran.org	San Francisco	CA	94104	415-398-4404	398-2732
Renewable Natural Resources Foundation (RNRF) 5430 Grosvenor Ln *Web:* www.rnrf.org	Bethesda	MD	20814	301-493-9101	493-6148
Royal Oak Foundation The 35 W 35th St Suite 1200 *TF:* 800-913-6565 ■ *Web:* www.royal-oak.org	New York	NY	10001	212-480-2889	785-7234
Save America's Forests 4 Library Ct SE *Web:* www.saveamericasforests.org	Washington	DC	20003	202-544-9219	544-7462
Save-the-Redwoods League 114 Sansome St Rm 1200 *TF:* 888-836-0005 ■ *Web:* www.savetheredwoods.org	San Francisco	CA	94104	415-362-2352	362-7017
Scenic America 1250 'I' St NW Suite 750 *Web:* www.scenic.org	Washington	DC	20005	202-638-0550	638-3171
Sea Grant Assn (SGA) 5784 York Complex University of Maine *Web:* www.sga.seagrant.org	Orono	ME	04469	207-581-1435	581-1426
Shelburne Farms 1611 Harbor Rd *Web:* www.shelburnefarms.org	Shelburne	VT	05482	802-985-8686	985-8123
Sierra Club 85 2nd St 2nd Fl *Web:* www.sierraclub.org	San Francisco	CA	94105	415-977-5500	977-5799
Sierra Club Canada 412-1 Nicholas St *TF:* 888-810-4204 ■ *Web:* www.sierraclub.ca	Ottawa	ON	K1N7B7	613-241-4611	241-2292
Sierra Club Foundation 85 2nd St Suite 750 *TF:* 800-216-2110 ■ *Web:* www.sierraclub.org	San Francisco	CA	94105	415-995-1780	995-1791
Society for Ecological Restoration International (SERI) 1017 O St NW **Fax Area Code: 270* ■ *Web:* www.ser.org	Washington	DC	20001	202-299-9518	626-5485*
Society of Architectural Historians (SAH) 1365 N Astor St *Web:* www.sah.org	Chicago	IL	60610	312-573-1365	573-1141
Society Promoting Environmental Conservation (SPEC) 2060 B Pine St *Web:* www.spec.bc.ca	Vancouver	BC	V6J4P8	604-736-7732	736-7115
Soil & Water Conservation Society (SWCS) 945 SW Ankeny Rd *TF:* 800-843-7645 ■ *Web:* www.swcs.org	Ankeny	IA	50023	515-289-2331	289-1227
Southern Utah Wilderness Alliance (SUWA) 425 E 100 S *Web:* www.suwa.org	Salt Lake City	UT	84111	801-486-3161	
Student Conservation Assn (SCA) 689 River Rd PO Box 550 *TF:* 888-722-9675 ■ *Web:* www.thesca.org	Charlestown	NH	03603	603-543-1700	543-1828
Tall Timbers 13093 Henry Beadel Dr *Web:* www.talltimbers.org	Tallahassee	FL	32312	850-893-4153	893-6470
Thornton W Burgess Society 6 Discovery Hill Rd *Web:* www.thorntonburgess.org	East Sandwich	MA	02537	508-888-6870	888-1919
Tongass Conservation Society (TCS) 308 Grant St PO Box 23377 *Web:* www.tongassconservation.org	Ketchikan	AK	99901	907-225-3275	
Tree Care Industry Assn (TCIA) 136 Harvey Rd Suite 101 *TF:* 800-733-2622 ■ *Web:* www.treecareindustry.org	Londonderry	NH	03053	603-314-5380	314-5386
Trust for Public Land (TPL) 116 New Montgomery St 4th Fl *TF:* 800-714-5263 ■ *Web:* www.tpl.org	San Francisco	CA	94105	415-495-4014	495-4103
Union of Concerned Scientists (UCS) 2 Brattle Sq 6th Fl *TF:* 800-666-8276 ■ *Web:* www.ucsusa.org	Cambridge	MA	02238	617-547-5552	864-9405
Upper Mississippi River Conservation Committee (UMRCC) 555 Lester Ave *Web:* www.umrcc.org	Onalaska	WI	54650	608-783-8432	783-8450
US Committee of the International Council on Monuments & Sites (US/ICOMOS) 401 F St NW # 331 *Web:* www.icomos.org	Washington	DC	20001	202-842-1866	842-1866
Walden Woods Project The 44 Baker Farm Rd *TF:* 800-554-3569 ■ *Web:* www.walden.org	Lincoln	MA	01773	781-259-4700	259-4710
Water Environment Federation (WEF) 601 Wythe St *TF:* 800-666-0206 ■ *Web:* www.wef.org	Alexandria	VA	22314	703-684-2400	684-2492
Western Canada Wilderness Committee (WCWC) 227 Abbott St *TF:* 800-661-9453 ■ *Web:* www.wildernesscommittee.org	Vancouver	BC	V6B2K7	604-683-8220	683-8229
Wilderness Society 1615 M St NW *Web:* www.wilderness.org	Washington	DC	20036	202-833-2300	429-3958
Wildlife Habitat Council (WHC) 8737 Colesville Rd Suite 800 *Web:* www.wildlifehc.org	Silver Spring	MD	20910	301-588-8994	588-4629
World Forestry Ctr 4033 SW Canyon Rd *Web:* www.worldforestry.org	Portland	OR	97221	503-228-1367	228-4608
World Resources Institute (WRI) 10 G St NE Suite 800 *Web:* www.wri.org	Washington	DC	20002	202-729-7600	729-7610
Yosemite Assn *Yosemite Conservancy* 5020 El Portal Rd PO Box 230 *Web:* www.yosemiteconservancy.org	El Portal	CA	95318	209-379-2317	379-2486

48-14 Ethnic & Nationality Organizations

Organization	City	State	ZIP	Phone	Fax
Africa-America Institute (AAI) 420 Lexington Ave Suite 1706 *Web:* www.aaionline.org	New York	NY	10170	212-949-5666	682-6174
American Folklore Society (AFS) Ohio State Univ Mershon Ctr 1501 Neil Ave *Web:* www.afsnet.org	Columbus	OH	43201	614-292-4715	292-2407
American Hellenic Educational Progressive Assn (AHEPA) 1909 Q St NW Suite 500 *Web:* www.ahepa.org	Washington	DC	20009	202-232-6300	232-2140
American Historical Society of Germans from Russia 631 D St *Web:* www.ahsgr.org	Lincoln	NE	68502	402-474-3363	474-7229

Organization	City	State	Zip	Phone	Fax
American Latvian Assn Inc 400 Hurley Ave *Web:* www.alausa.org	Rockville	MD	20850	301-340-1914	340-8732
Arab American Institute (AAI) 1600 K St NW Suite 601 *Web:* www.aaiusa.org	Washington	DC	20006	202-429-9210	429-9214
Armenian Assembly of America 1334 G8St NW *Web:* www.aaainc.org	Washington	DC	20005	202-393-3434	638-4904
Armenian General Benevolent Union (AGBU) 55 E 59th St 7th Fl *Web:* www.agbu.org	New York	NY	10022	212-319-6383	319-6507
ASPIRA Assn Inc 1444 'I' St NW Suite 800 *Web:* www.aspira.org	Washington	DC	20005	202-835-3600	835-3613
Assembly of Turkish American Associations (ATAA) 1526 18th St NW *Web:* www.ataa.org	Washington	DC	20036	202-483-9090	483-9092
Assn of Jewish Aging Services (AJAS) 316 Pennsylvania Ave SE Suite 402 *Web:* www.ajas.org	Washington	DC	20003	202-543-7500	543-4090
Center for Cuban Studies 231 W 29th St # 401 *Web:* www.cubaupdate.org	New York	NY	10001	212-242-0559	242-1937
China Institute in America 125 E 65th St *Web:* www.chinainstitute.org	New York	NY	10065	212-744-8181	628-4159
Colombian-American Assn 30 Vesey St Suite 506 *Web:* www.colombianamerican.org	New York	NY	10007	212-233-7776	233-7779
Congress of Russian-Americans 2460 Sutter St *Web:* www.russian-americans.org	San Francisco	CA	94115	415-928-5841	928-5831
Croatian Fraternal Union of America (CFU) 100 Delaney Dr *Web:* www.croatianfraternalunion.org	Pittsburgh	PA	15235	412-843-0380	823-1594
Cuban American National Council 1223 SW 4th St *Web:* www.cnc.org	Miami	FL	33135	305-642-3484	642-9122
Cuban American National Foundation 1312 SW 27th Ave Suite 301 *Web:* www.canfnet.org	Miami	FL	33145	305-642-2220	592-7889
Ecuadorian-American Assn Inc 150 Nassau St Suite 2015	New York	NY	10038	212-233-7776	233-7779
First Nations Development Institute 2217 Princess Anne St Suite 111-1 **Fax Area Code:* 888 ■ *Web:* www.firstnations.org	Fredericksburg	VA	22408	540-371-5615	371-3686*
Foundation for Jewish Culture 330 7th Ave 21st Fl PO Box 489 *Web:* jewishculture.org	New York	NY	10001	212-629-0500	629-0508
French Institute Alliance Francaise (FIAF) 22 E 60th St *Web:* www.fiaf.org	New York	NY	10022	212-355-6100	935-4119
German-American National Congress (DANK) 4740 N Western Ave Suite 206 *TF:* 888-872-3265 ■ *Web:* www.dank.org	Chicago	IL	60625	773-275-1100	275-4010
Hispanic Society of America 613 W 155th St *Web:* www.hispanicsociety.org	New York	NY	10032	212-926-2234	690-0743
Ibero-American Action League Inc 817 E Main St *Web:* www.iaal.org	Rochester	NY	14605	585-256-8900	256-0120
Japan Society 333 E 47th St *Web:* www.japansociety.org	New York	NY	10017	212-832-1155	755-6752
Japanese American Citizens League (JACL) 1765 Sutter St *Web:* www.jacl.org	San Francisco	CA	94115	415-921-5225	931-4671
Korean American Coalition (KAC) 3727 W 6th St Suite 515 *Web:* www.kacla.org	Los Angeles	CA	90020	213-365-5999	380-7990
Kurdish Heritage Foundation of America 345 Pk Pl *Web:* www.kurdishlibrarymuseum.com	Brooklyn	NY	11238	718-783-7930	398-4365
Latin American Studies Assn (LASA) *Univ of Pittsburgh* 416 Bellefield Hall *Web:* www.lasa.international.pitt.edu	Pittsburgh	PA	15260	412-648-7929	624-7145
Lithuanian-American Community Inc 2715 E Allegheny Ave **Fax Area Code:* 815 ■ *TF:* 800-625-1170 ■ *Web:* www.lietuviu-bendruomene.org	Philadelphia	PA	19134	800-625-1170	327-8881*
Mexican American Legal Defense & Educational Fund (MALDEF) 634 S Spring St *Web:* www.maldef.org	Los Angeles	CA	90014	213-629-2512	629-0266
Mexican-American Opportunity Foundation (MAOF) 401 N Garfield Ave *Web:* www.maof.org	Montebello	CA	90640	323-890-9600	890-9637
National Congress of American Indians (NCAI) 1516 P St NW *Web:* www.ncai.org	Washington	DC	20005	202-466-7767	466-7797
National Council of La Raza (NCLR) 1126 16th St NW 6th Fl *Web:* www.nclr.org	Washington	DC	20036	202-785-1670	776-1792
National Hispanic Institute (NHI) 472 FM 1966 Rd *Web:* www.nhi-net.org	Maxwell	TX	78656	512-357-6137	357-2206
National Indian Council on Aging (NICOA) 10501 Montgomery Blvd NE Suite 210 *Web:* www.nicoa.org	Albuquerque	NM	87111	505-292-2001	292-1922
National Puerto Rican Coalition Inc (NPRC) 1444 I St NW Suite 800 *Web:* www.bateylink.org	Washington	DC	20005	202-223-3915	429-2223
National Slovak Society of the USA (NSS) 351 Valley Brook Rd *TF:* 800-488-1890 ■ *Web:* www.nsslife.com	McMurray	PA	15317	724-731-0094	731-0145
Order Sons of Italy in America (OSIA) 219 E St NE *Web:* www.osia.org	Washington	DC	20002	202-547-2900	546-8168
Organization of Chinese Americans (OCA) 1322 18th St NW *Web:* www.ocanational.org	Washington	DC	20036	202-223-5500	296-0540
Polish American Congress 5711 N Milwaukee Ave *Web:* www.pac1944.org	Chicago	IL	60646	773-763-9944	763-7114
Scottish Heritage USA 315 Page Rd # 10 *Web:* www.scottishheritageusa.org	Pinehurst	NC	28374	910-295-4448	295-3147
Sons of Norway 1455 W Lake St 2nd Fl *TF:* 800-945-8851 ■ *Web:* www.sofn.com	Minneapolis	MN	55408	612-827-3611	827-0658
Swedish Council of America 2600 Pk Ave *Web:* www.swedishcouncil.org	Minneapolis	MN	55407	612-871-0593	871-0687
Tolstoy Foundation Inc 104 Lake Rd PO Box 578 *Web:* www.tolstoyfoundation.org	Valley Cottage	NY	10989	845-268-6722	268-6937
Ukrainian NA Inc (UNA) 2200 Rt 10 PO Box 280 *TF:* 800-253-9862 ■ *Web:* www.ukrainiannationalassociation.org	Parsippany	NJ	07054	973-292-9800	292-0900
US Hispanic Chamber of Commerce 2175 K St NW Suite 100 *TF:* 800-874-2286 ■ *Web:* www.ushcc.com	Washington	DC	20037	202-842-1212	842-3221
US Pan Asian American Chamber of Commerce (USPAACC) 1329 18th St NW *TF:* 800-696-7818 ■ *Web:* www.uspaacc.com	Washington	DC	20036	202-296-5221	296-5225
Venezuelan-American Assn of the US 30 Vesey St Suite 506 *Web:* www.venezuelanamerican.org	New York	NY	10007	212-233-7776	233-7779

48-15 Fraternal & Social Organizations

Organization	City	State	Zip	Phone	Fax
American Mensa Ltd 1229 Corporate Dr W *TF:* 800-666-3672 ■ *Web:* www.us.mensa.org	Arlington	TX	76006	817-607-0060	649-5232
Assn of Junior Leagues International Inc (AJLI) 80 Maiden Ln Suite 305 *TF:* 800-955-3248 ■ *Web:* www.ajli.org	New York	NY	10038	212-683-1515	481-7196
Astor Home For Children The 6339 Mill St PO Box 5005 *Web:* www.astorservices.org	Rhinebeck	NY	12572	845-871-1000	
Athletes in Action 651 Taylor Dr *Web:* www.aia.com	Xenia	OH	45385	937-352-1000	352-1001
Benevolent & Protective Order of Elks of the USA 2750 N Lakeview Ave *Web:* www.elks.org	Chicago	IL	60614	773-755-4700	755-4790
Boy Scouts of America (BSA) 1325 W Walnut Hill Ln PO Box 152079 *Web:* www.scouting.org	Irving	TX	75015	972-580-2000	580-2502
Boys & Girls Clubs of America 1230 W Peachtree St NW *TF:* 800-854-2582 ■ *Web:* www.bgca.org	Atlanta	GA	30309	404-487-5700	487-5757
Camp Fire USA 1100 Walnut St Suite 1900 *TF:* 800-669-6884 ■ *Web:* www.campfireusa.org	Kansas City	MO	64106	816-285-2010	285-9444
Citizens For Citizens Inc 264 Griffin St *Web:* www.cfcinc.org	Fall River	MA	02724	508-679-0041	324-7503
Civitan International PO Box 130744 *TF:* 800-248-4826 ■ *Web:* www.civitan.org	Birmingham	AL	35213	205-591-8910	591-8910
Community Counseling & Correctional Service (CCCS) 471 E Mercury St *Web:* www.cccscorp.com	Butte	MT	59701	406-782-0417	782-6964
Cosmopolitan International 7341 W 80th St PO Box 4588 *TF:* 800-648-4331 ■ *Web:* www.cosmopolitan.org	Overland Park	KS	66204	913-648-4330	648-4330
DeMolay International 10200 NW Ambassabor Dr *TF Orders:* 800-336-6529 ■ *Web:* www.demolay.org	Kansas City	MO	64153	816-891-8333	891-9062
English-Speaking Union of the US 144 E 39th St *Web:* www.esuus.org	New York	NY	10016	212-818-1200	818-1200
Fraternal Order of Police (FOP) 701 Marriott Dr *TF:* 800-451-2711 ■ *Web:* www.fop.net	Nashville	TN	37214	615-399-0900	399-0400
Friars Club 57 E 55th St *Web:* www.friarsclub.com	New York	NY	10022	212-751-7272	355-0217
General Grand Chapter Order of the Eastern Star 1618 New Hampshire Ave NW *TF:* 800-648-1182 ■ *Web:* www.easternstar.org	Washington	DC	20009	202-667-4737	462-5162
Girl Scouts of the USA 420 5th Ave *TF:* 800-223-0624 ■ *Web:* www.girlscouts.org	New York	NY	10018	212-852-8000	852-6517
Goodwill Industries of Central Texas 1015 Norwood Pk Blvd *TF:* 877-464-4660 ■ *Web:* www.austingoodwill.org	Austin	TX	78753	512-637-7100	637-7400
Grand Aerie Fraternal Order of Eagles 1623 Gateway Cir S *Web:* www.foe.com	Grove City	OH	43123	614-883-2200	883-2201
House of The Good Shepherd The 1550 Champlin Ave *Web:* www.hgs-utica.com	Utica	NY	13502	315-235-7600	235-7609
Independent Order of Odd Fellows 422 N Trade St *TF:* 800-235-8358 ■ *Web:* www.ioof.org	Winston-Salem	NC	27101	336-725-5955	722-7317
International Assn of Lions Clubs 300 W 22nd St *Web:* www.lionsclubs.org	Oak Brook	IL	60523	630-571-5466	571-8890
KenCrest Services Inc 502 W Germantown Pike Suite 200 *Web:* www.kencrest.org	Plymouth Meeting	PA	19462	610-825-9360	
Key Club International 3636 Woodview Trace *TF:* 800-549-2647 ■ *Web:* www.keyclub.org	Indianapolis	IN	46268	317-875-8755	879-0204
Klingberg Family Centers Inc 370 Linwood St *Web:* www.klingberg.org	New Britain	CT	06052	860-224-9113	832-8221
Knights of Columbus 1 Columbus Plaza *TF Cust Svc:* 800-380-9995 ■ *Web:* www.kofc.org	New Haven	CT	06510	203-752-4000	752-4100

Organization	City	State	Zip	Phone	Fax
Life Inc 2609 Royall Ave *Web:* www.lifeincorporated.com	Goldsboro	NC	27534	919-778-1900	778-1911
Life's WORC 1501 Franklin Ave PO Box 8165 *Web:* www.lifesworc.org	Garden City	NY	11530	516-741-9000	741-5560
Lifestream Inc PO Box 50487 *Web:* www.lifestreaminc.com	New Bedford	MA	02745	508-993-1991	991-5228
Louisiana Baptist Children's Home Inc (LBCH) 7200 DeSiard St *Web:* www.lbch.org	Monroe	LA	71203	318-343-2244	
Lutheran Homes Society Inc 2021 N McCord Rd *Web:* www.lutheranhomessociety.org	Toledo	OH	43615	419-861-4990	861-4949
Lutheran Social Services of Illinois 1001 E Touhy Ave Suite 50 *TF:* 888-671-0300 ■ *Web:* www.lssi.org	Des Plaines	IL	60018	847-635-4600	
Masonic Service Assn of North America (MSANA) 8120 Fenton St Suite 203 *Web:* www.msana.com	Silver Spring	MD	20910	301-588-4010	608-3457
Mennonite Home 1520 Harrisburg Pike *Web:* www.mennonitehome.org	Lancaster	PA	17601	717-393-1301	393-1389
Mesa Developmental Services 950 Grand Ave *Web:* www.mesadev.org	Grand Junction	CO	81501	970-243-3702	243-7751
Mile High United Way Inc 2505 18th St *Web:* www.unitedwaydenver.org	Denver	CO	80211	303-433-8383	455-6462
Moose International Inc 155 S International Dr *Web:* www.mooseintl.org	Mooseheart	IL	60539	630-859-2000	859-6616
National Exchange Club 3050 W Central Ave *TF:* 800-924-2643 ■ *Web:* www.nationalexchangeclub.org	Toledo	OH	43606	419-535-3232	535-1989
Neighbor To Family Inc 220 S Ridgewood Ave Suite 260 *Web:* www.neighbortofamily.org	Daytona Beach	FL	32114	386-523-1440	523-1459
Optimist International 4494 Lindell Blvd *TF:* 800-500-8130 ■ *Web:* www.optimist.org	Saint Louis	MO	63108	314-371-6000	371-6006
Oswego County Opportunities Inc 239 Oneida St *Web:* www.oco.org	Fulton	NY	13069	315-598-4717	592-7533
Partnerships In Community Living Inc 480 Main St East PO Box 129 *Web:* www.pclpartnership.org	Monmouth	OR	97361	503-838-2403	838-5815
Presbyterian Homes Inc The PO Box 2127 *Web:* www.presbyhomesinc.org	Jamestown	NC	27282	336-886-6553	886-4102
Procrastinators Club America PO Box 712	Bryn Athyn	PA	19009	215-947-9020	947-7210
Professional Bull Riders Inc (PBR) 101 W Riverwalk *Web:* www.pbrnow.com	Pueblo	CO	81003	719-242-2800	242-2855
Quota International 1420 21st St NW *Web:* www.quota.org	Washington	DC	20036	202-331-9694	331-4395
Rotary International 1560 Sherman Ave 1 Rotary Ctr *Web:* www.rotary.org	Evanston	IL	60201	847-866-3000	328-8554
Ruritan National PO Box 487 *TF:* 877-787-8727 ■ *Web:* www.ruritan.org	Dublin	VA	24084	540-674-5431	674-2304
Shrine of North America 2900 N Rocky Pt Dr **Fax:* Acctg ■ *Web:* www.shrinershq.org	Tampa	FL	33607	813-281-0300	281-2519*
Skill Creations Inc PO Box 1664 *Web:* www.skillcreations.com	Goldsboro	NC	27533	919-734-7398	735-5064
Spectrum Health Systems Inc 10 Mechanic St Suite 302 *TF:* 800-464-9555 ■ *Web:* www.spectrumhealthsystems.org	Worcester	MA	01608	508-792-5400	
Starr Commonwealth 13725 Starr Commonwealth Rd *TF:* 800-837-5591 ■ *Web:* www.starr.org	Albion	MI	49224	517-629-5591	630-2400
Sunnyvale Lumber Inc 870 W Evelyn Ave *Web:* www.sunnyvalelumber.com	Sunnyvale	CA	94086	408-736-5411	736-6738
TelecomPioneers 1801 California St 44th Fl *TF:* 800-872-5995 ■ *Web:* www.telecompioneers.org	Denver	CO	80202	303-571-1200	572-0520
TERI Inc 251 Airport Rd *Web:* www.teriinc.org	Oceanside	CA	92058	760-721-1706	
Toastmasters International 23182 Arroyo Vista *Web:* www.toastmasters.org	Rancho Santa Margarita	CA	92688	949-858-8255	858-1207
Uhlich Children's Advantage Network (UCAN) 3737 N Mozart St *Web:* www.ucanchicago.org	Chicago	IL	60618	773-588-0180	588-7762
Up With People 6830 Broadway *TF:* 877-264-8856 ■ *Web:* www.upwithpeople.org	Denver	CO	80221	303-460-7100	225-4649
Wabash Center Inc 2000 Greenbush St *Web:* www.wabashcenter.com	Lafayette	IN	47904	765-423-5531	
Way Station Inc 230 W Patrick St PO Box 3826 *Web:* www.waystationinc.org	Frederick	MD	21705	301-662-0099	662-1837

48-16 Greek Letter Societies

Organization	City	State	Zip	Phone	Fax
Alpha Beta Gamma International Business Honor Society 75 Grasslands Rd *Web:* www.abg.org	Valhalla	NY	10595	914-606-6877	606-6331
Alpha Chi National College Honor Scholarship Society 915 E Market Ave *TF:* 800-477-4225 ■ *Web:* www.harding.edu	Searcy	AR	72149	501-279-4443	279-4589
Alpha Chi Omega 5939 Castle Creek Pkwy N Dr *Web:* www.alphachiomega.org	Indianapolis	IN	46250	317-579-5050	579-5051
Alpha Chi Rho Fraternity Inc 109 Oxford Way *Web:* www.alphachirho.org	Neptune	NJ	07753	732-869-1895	988-5357
Alpha Chi Sigma 2141 N Franklin Rd *TF:* 800-252-4369 ■ *Web:* www.alphachisigma.org	Indianapolis	IN	46219	317-357-5944	351-9702
Alpha Delta Phi International Fraternity 6126 Lincoln Ave *Web:* www.alphadeltaphi.org	Morton Grove	IL	60053	847-965-1832	965-1871
Alpha Delta Pi 1386 Ponce de Leon Ave NE *Web:* www.alphadeltapi.org	Atlanta	GA	30306	404-378-3164	373-0084
Alpha Epsilon Delta (AED) Texas Christian University PO Box BOX 298810 *Web:* www.nationalaed.org	Fort Worth	TX	76129	817-257-4550	257-0201
Alpha Epsilon Phi Sorority (AEPhi) 11 Lake Ave Ext Suite 1-A *Web:* www.aephi.org	Danbury	CT	06811	203-748-0029	748-0039
Alpha Epsilon Pi Fraternity Inc 8815 Wesleyan Rd *TF:* 800-223-2374 ■ *Web:* www.aepi.org	Indianapolis	IN	46268	317-876-1913	876-1057
Alpha Gamma Delta 8701 Founders Rd *Web:* www.alphagammadelta.org	Indianapolis	IN	46268	317-872-2655	875-5824
Alpha Gamma Rho 10101 N Ambassador Dr *Web:* www.agrs.org	Kansas City	MO	64153	816-891-9200	891-9401
Alpha Kappa Alpha Sorority Inc 5656 S Stony Island Ave *Web:* www.aka1908.com	Chicago	IL	60637	773-684-1282	288-8251
Alpha Kappa Psi (AKPsi) 7801 E 88th St *Web:* www.akpsi.com	Indianapolis	IN	46256	317-872-1553	872-1567
Alpha Omega International Dental Fraternity 55 Harristown Rd **Fax Area Code:* 201 ■ *TF:* 800-677-8468 ■ *Web:* www.ao.org	Glen Rock	NJ	07452	877-677-8468	447-3831*
Alpha Omicron Pi International 5390 Virginia Way *Web:* www.alphaomicronpi.org	Brentwood	TN	37027	615-370-0920	371-9736
Alpha Phi Alpha Fraternity Inc 2313 St Paul St *Web:* www.alpha-phi-alpha.com	Baltimore	MD	21218	410-554-0040	554-0054
Alpha Phi Delta Fraternity Inc 71 Terr St Suite 204 *Web:* www.apd.org	Struthers	OH	44471	330-755-1891	
Alpha Phi International Fraternity 1930 Sherman Ave *Web:* www.alphaphi.org	Evanston	IL	60201	847-475-0663	475-6820
Alpha Phi Omega (APO) 14901 E 42nd St *Web:* www.apo.org	Independence	MO	64055	816-373-8667	373-5975
Alpha Sigma Alpha (ASA) 9002 Vincennes Cir *Web:* www.alphasigmaalpha.org	Indianapolis	IN	46268	317-871-2920	871-2924
Alpha Sigma Phi National Fraternity 710 Adams St *TF:* 800-800-1845 ■ *Web:* www.alphasigmaphi.org	Carmel	IN	46032	317-843-1911	843-2966
Alpha Tau Omega Fraternity (ATO) 1 N Pennsylvania St 12th Fl *TF:* 800-798-9286 ■ *Web:* www.ato.org	Indianapolis	IN	46204	317-684-1865	684-1862
Alpha Xi Delta Women's Fraternity 8702 Founders Rd *Web:* www.alphaxidelta.org	Indianapolis	IN	46268	317-872-3500	872-2947
Beta Alpha Psi Palladian I 220 Leigh Farm Rd *Web:* www.bap.org	Durham	NC	27707	919-402-4044	402-4040
Beta Beta Beta National Biological Honor Society Univ of N Alabama PO Box 5079 *Web:* www.tri-beta.org	Florence	AL	35632	256-765-6220	765-6221
Beta Gamma Sigma Inc (BGS) 125 Weldon Pkwy *TF:* 800-337-4677 ■ *Web:* www.betagammasigma.org	Maryland Heights	MO	63043	314-432-5650	432-7083
Beta Phi Mu Florida State Univ College of Information 142 Collegiate Loop Rm 101 LSB *Web:* www.beta-phi-mu.org	Tallahassee	FL	32306	850-644-3907	644-9763
Beta Theta Pi 5134 Bonham Rd PO Box 6277 *TF:* 800-800-2382 ■ *Web:* www.betathetapi.org	Oxford	OH	45056	513-523-7591	523-2381
Chi Alpha Campus Ministries USA 1445 Booneville Ave *Web:* www.chialpha.com	Springfield	MO	65802	417-862-2781	865-9947
Chi Omega Fraternity 3395 Players Club Pkwy *Web:* www.chiomega.com	Memphis	TN	38125	901-748-8600	748-8686
Chi Phi Fraternity 1160 Satellite Blvd **Fax Area Code:* 678 ■ *TF:* 800-849-1824 ■ *Web:* www.chiphi.org	Suwanee	GA	30024	404-231-1824	389-4457*
Chi Psi Fraternity 45 Rutledge St *Web:* www.chipsi.org	Nashville	TN	37210	615-736-2520	736-2366
Delta Chi Fraternity Inc 314 Church St *Web:* www.deltachi.com	Iowa City	IA	52245	319-337-4811	337-5529
Delta Delta Delta Fraternity 2331 Brookhollow Plaza Dr *Web:* www.tridelta.org	Arlington	TX	76006	817-633-8001	652-0212
Delta Gamma 3250 Riverside Dr PO Box 21397 *Web:* www.deltagamma.org	Columbus	OH	43221	614-481-8169	481-0133
Delta Kappa Epsilon Fraternity (DKE) 611 1/2 E William St **Fax Area Code:* 202 ■ *Web:* www.dke.org	Ann Arbor	MI	48104	734-302-4210	478-0374*
Delta Nu Alpha Transportation Fraternity (DNA) 435 Pennsylvania Ave Suite 102 *Web:* www.deltanualpha.org	Glen Ellyn	IL	60137	630-653-3622	653-3632
Delta Phi Epsilon International Sorority 251 S Camac St *Web:* www.dphie.org	Philadelphia	PA	19107	215-732-5901	732-5906
Delta Phi Fraternity Inc PO Box 4633 *Web:* www.deltaphi.org	Chapel Hill	NC	27515	919-294-9385	381-6059
Delta Pi Epsilon (DPE) 1200 John Barrow Rd # 408 *Web:* www.dpe.org	Little Rock	AR	72205	501-219-1866	219-1876
Delta Sigma Phi Fraternity 1331 N Delaware St *Web:* www.deltasig.org	Indianapolis	IN	46202	317-634-1899	634-1410
Delta Sigma Pi 330 S Campus Ave *Web:* www.dspnet.org	Oxford	OH	45056	513-523-1907	523-7292
Delta Sigma Theta Sorority Inc 1707 New Hampshire Ave NW *Web:* www.deltasigmatheta.org	Washington	DC	20009	202-986-2400	986-2513

Organization	City	State	ZIP	Phone	Fax
Delta Tau Delta Fraternity 10000 Allisonville Rd *TF:* 800-335-8795 ■ *Web:* www.delts.org	Fishers	IN	46038	317-284-0203	284-0214
Delta Theta Phi 38640 Butternut Ridge Rd **Fax Area Code:* 888 ■ *TF:* 800-783-2600 ■ *Web:* www.deltathetaphi.org	Elyria	OH	44035	440-323-1900	833-1687*
Delta Upsilon International Fraternity 8705 Founders Rd PO Box 68942 *Web:* www.deltau.org	Indianapolis	IN	46268	317-875-8900	876-1629
Delta Zeta Sorority 202 E Church St *Web:* www.deltazeta.org	Oxford	OH	45056	513-523-7597	523-1921
Epsilon Sigma Phi PO Box 357340 *Web:* www.espnational.org	Gainesville	FL	32635	352-378-6665	375-0722
Eta Sigma Gamma 2000 University Ave *TF:* 800-715-2559 ■ *Web:* www.etasigmagamma.org	Muncie	IN	47306	765-285-2258	285-3210
Fraternity of Alpha Kappa Lambda 4735 Statesmen Dr Suite F **Fax Area Code:* 866 ■ *Web:* www.akl.org	Indianapolis	IN	46250	317-585-4911	556-8719*
Gamma Beta Phi Society 78 Mitchell Rd # A *TF:* 800-628-9920 ■ *Web:* www.gammabetaphi.org	Oak Ridge	TN	37830	865-483-6212	483-9801
Gamma Phi Beta International Sorority (GPB) 12737 E Euclid Dr *Web:* www.gammaphibeta.org	Centennial	CO	80111	303-799-1874	799-1876
International Fraternity of Phi Gamma Delta 1201 Red Mile Rd PO Box 4599 *Web:* www.phigam.org	Lexington	KY	40544	859-255-1848	253-0779
Kappa Alpha Order 115 Liberty Hall Rd *Web:* www.kappaalphaorder.org	Lexington	VA	24450	540-463-1865	463-2140
Kappa Alpha Psi Fraternity Inc 2322 N Broad St *Web:* www.kappaalphapsi.com	Philadelphia	PA	19132	215-228-7184	228-7181
Kappa Alpha Theta Fraternity 8740 Founders Rd *TF:* 800-526-1870 ■ *Web:* www.kappaalphatheta.org	Indianapolis	IN	46268	317-876-1870	876-1925
Kappa Delta Epsilon (KDE) 119 Ridge View Dr *Web:* www.kappadeltaepsilon.org	Ball Ground	GA	30107	770-393-1766	755-1974
Kappa Delta Pi 3707 Woodview Trace *TF:* 800-284-3167 ■ *Web:* www.kdp.org	Indianapolis	IN	46268	317-871-4900	704-2323
Kappa Delta Sorority 3205 Players Ln *TF:* 800-536-1897 ■ *Web:* www.kappadelta.org	Memphis	TN	38125	901-748-1897	748-0949
Kappa Kappa Gamma PO Box 38 *TF:* 866-554-1870 ■ *Web:* www.kappakappagamma.org	Columbus	OH	43216	614-228-6515	228-7809
Kappa Kappa Iota 1875 E 15th St *TF:* 800-678-0389 ■ *Web:* www.kappakappaiota.org	Tulsa	OK	74104	918-744-0389	744-0578
Kappa Kappa Psi National Honorary Band Fraternity 401 E 9th Ave *TF:* 800-543-6505 ■ *Web:* www.kkpsi.org	Stillwater	OK	74074	405-372-2333	372-2363
Kappa Sigma Fraternity 1610 Scottsville Rd *Web:* www.kappasigma.org	Charlottesville	VA	22902	434-295-3193	296-9557
Lambda Chi Alpha International Fraternity 8741 Founders Rd *TF:* 800-209-6837 ■ *Web:* www.lambdachi.org	Indianapolis	IN	46268	317-872-8000	875-3828
Mu Phi Epsilon International Music Fraternity 4705 N Sonora Ave Suite 114 *TF:* 888-259-1471 ■ *Web:* www.home.muphiepsilon.org	Fresno	CA	93722	559-277-1898	277-2825
National Alpha Lambda Delta 328 Orange St *Web:* www.nationalald.org	Macon	GA	31201	478-744-9595	744-9924
National Fraternity of Kappa Delta Rho (KDR) 331 S Main St *TF:* 800-536-5371 ■ *Web:* www.kdr.com	Greensburg	PA	15601	724-838-7100	838-7101
Omega Psi Phi Fraternity Inc 3951 Snapfinger Pkwy *Web:* www.oppf.org	Decatur	GA	30035	404-284-5533	284-0333
Omicron Delta Epsilon (ODE) PO Box 1486 *TF:* 800-584-5514 ■ *Web:* www.omicrondeltaepsilon.org	Hattiesburg	MS	39403	601-264-3115	264-3669
Phi Alpha Delta Law Fraternity International 345 N Charles St 3rd Fl *Web:* www.padcommunity.org	Baltimore	MD	21201	410-347-3118	347-3119
Phi Alpha Theta *Univ of South Florida* 4202 E Fowler Ave SOC 107 **Fax Area Code:* 813 ■ *TF:* 800-394-8195 ■ *Web:* www.phialphatheta.org	Tampa	FL	33620	800-394-8195	974-8215*
Phi Beta Kappa Society 1606 New Hampshire Ave NW *Web:* www.pbk.org/home/index.aspx	Washington	DC	20009	202-265-3808	986-1601
Phi Beta Sigma Fraternity Inc 145 Kennedy St NW *Web:* www.pbs1914.org	Washington	DC	20011	202-726-5434	882-1681
Phi Chi Theta 1508 E Beltline Rd Suite 104 *Web:* www.phichitheta.org	Carrollton	TX	75006	972-245-7202	
Phi Delta Kappa International (PDK) 408 N Union St *TF:* 800-766-1156 ■ *Web:* www.pdkintl.org	Bloomington	IN	47405	812-339-1156	339-0018
Phi Delta Phi International Legal Fraternity 1426 21st St NW *TF:* 800-368-5606 ■ *Web:* www.phideltaphi.org	Washington	DC	20036	202-223-6801	223-6808
Phi Delta Theta 2 S Campus Ave *Web:* www.phideltatheta.org	Oxford	OH	45056	513-523-6345	523-9200
Phi Eta Sigma National Honor Society 1 Big Red Way *Web:* www.phietasigma.org	Bowling Green	KY	42101	270-745-6540	745-3893
Phi Kappa Psi 5395 Emerson Way *TF:* 800-486-1852 ■ *Web:* www.phikappapsi.com	Indianapolis	IN	46226	317-632-1852	
Phi Kappa Sigma International Fraternity Inc 2 Timber Dr *Web:* www.pks.org	Chester Springs	PA	19425	610-469-3282	469-3286
Phi Kappa Tau 5221 Morning Sun Rd *TF:* 800-758-1906 ■ *Web:* www.phikappatau.org	Oxford	OH	45056	513-523-4193	523-9325
Phi Kappa Theta National Fraternity 9640 N Augusta Dr Suite 420 *Web:* www.phikaps.org	Carmel	IN	46032	317-872-9934	879-1889
Phi Mu Alpha Sinfonia Fraternity of America Inc 10600 Old State Rd *TF:* 800-473-2649 ■ *Web:* www.sinfonia.org	Evansville	IN	47711	812-867-2433	867-0633
Phi Mu Fraternity 400 Westpark Dr *TF:* 888-744-6836 ■ *Web:* www.phimu.org	Peachtree City	GA	30269	770-632-2090	632-2136
Phi Sigma Kappa International 2925 E 96th St *TF:* 888-846-6851 ■ *Web:* www.phisigmakappa.org	Indianapolis	IN	46240	317-573-5420	573-5430
Phi Sigma Pi National Honor Fraternity Inc 2119 Ambassador Cir *TF:* 800-366-1916 ■ *Web:* www.phisigmapi.org	Lancaster	PA	17603	717-299-4710	390-3054
Phi Sigma Sigma Fraternity Inc 8178 Lark Brown Rd Suite 202 *Web:* www.phisigmasigma.org	Elkridge	MD	21075	410-799-1224	799-9186
Phi Theta Kappa International Honor Society 1625 Eastover Dr *TF:* 800-946-9995 ■ *Web:* www.ptk.org	Jackson	MS	39211	601-984-3504	984-3550
Pi Beta Phi Fraternity for Women 1154 Town & Country Commons Dr *Web:* www.pibetaphi.org	Town and Country	MO	63017	636-256-0680	256-8095
Pi Kappa Alpha Fraternity 8347 W Range Cove *Web:* www.pka.com	Memphis	TN	38125	901-748-1868	748-3100
Pi Kappa Phi Fraternity 2015 Ayrsley Town Blvd # 200 *Web:* www.pikapp.org	Charlotte	NC	28273	704-504-0888	504-0880
Pi Lambda Phi Fraternity Inc 60 Newtown Rd # 118 *TF:* 800-394-7573 ■ *Web:* www.pilambdaphi.org	Danbury	CT	06810	203-740-1044	740-1644
Pi Lambda Theta 408 N Union St PO Box 7888 **Fax Area Code:* 800 ■ *Web:* www.pilambda.org	Bloomington	IN	47407	812-339-1156	766-1156*
Pi Sigma Alpha 1527 New Hampshire Ave NW *Web:* www.apsanet.org/~psa	Washington	DC	20036	202-483-2512	483-2657
Pi Sigma Epsilon (PSE) 3747 S Howell Ave *TF:* 800-761-9350 ■ *Web:* www.pse.org	Milwaukee	WI	53207	414-328-1952	328-1953
Psi Chi National Honor Society in Psychology 825 Vine St **Fax Area Code:* 877 ■ *Web:* www.psichi.org	Chattanooga	TN	37403	423-756-2044	774-2443*
Psi Upsilon Fraternity 3003 E 96th St *TF:* 800-394-1833 ■ *Web:* www.psiu.org	Indianapolis	IN	46240	317-571-1833	844-5170
Sigma Alpha Epsilon Fraternity (SAE) 1856 Sheridan Rd *TF:* 800-233-1856 ■ *Web:* www.sae.net	Evanston	IL	60201	847-475-1856	475-2250
Sigma Alpha Iota (SAI) 1 Tunnel Rd *Web:* www.sai-national.org	Asheville	NC	28805	828-251-0606	251-0644
Sigma Alpha Mu Fraternity 9245 N Meridian St Suite 105 *TF:* 888-369-9361 ■ *Web:* www.sam.org	Indianapolis	IN	46260	317-846-0600	846-9462
Sigma Chi Fraternity 1714 Hinman Ave *Web:* www.sigmachi.org	Evanston	IL	60201	847-869-3655	869-4906
Sigma Delta Tau 714 Adams St *Web:* www.sigmadeltatau.com	Carmel	IN	46032	317-846-7747	575-5562
Sigma Gamma Rho Sorority Inc 1000 Southhill Dr Suite 200 *TF:* 888-747-1922 ■ *Web:* www.sgrho1922.org	Cary	NC	27513	919-678-9720	678-9721
Sigma Kappa Sorority 8733 Founders Rd *Web:* www.sigmakappa.org	Indianapolis	IN	46268	317-872-3275	872-0716
Sigma Nu Fraternity Inc 9 Lewis St PO Box 1869 *Web:* www.sigmanu.org	Lexington	VA	24450	540-463-1869	463-1669
Sigma Phi Epsilon Fraternity 310 S Blvd *TF:* 800-313-1901 ■ *Web:* www.sigep.org	Richmond	VA	23220	804-353-1901	359-8160
Sigma Pi Fraternity PO Box 1897 *TF:* 800-332-1897 ■ *Web:* www.sigmapi2.org	Brentwood	TN	37024	615-373-5728	373-8949
Sigma Tau Gamma 101 Ming St PO Box 54 *Web:* www.sigmataugamma.org	Warrensburg	MO	64093	660-747-2222	
Sigma Theta Tau International 550 W N St *TF:* 888-634-7575 ■ *Web:* www.nursingsociety.org	Indianapolis	IN	46202	317-634-8171	634-8188
Sigma Xi Scientific Research Society 3106 E NC Hwy 54 PO Box 13975 *TF:* 800-243-6534 ■ *Web:* www.sigmaxi.org	Research Triangle Park	NC	27709	919-549-4691	549-0090
Tau Alpha Chi 82 Thompson St	Alpharetta	GA	30009	770-475-4253	475-4408
Tau Beta Pi Assn 1512 Middle Dr *Web:* www.tbp.org	Knoxville	TN	37996	865-546-4578	546-4579
Tau Beta Sigma National Honorary Band Sorority PO Box 849 *TF Cust Svc:* 800-543-6505 ■ *Web:* www.tbsigma.org	Stillwater	OK	74076	405-372-2333	372-2363
Tau Kappa Epsilon (TKE) 8645 Founders Rd *Web:* www.tke.org	Indianapolis	IN	46268	317-872-6533	875-8353
Theta Delta Chi Inc 214 Lewis Wharf *TF:* 800-999-1847 ■ *Web:* www.thetadeltachi.net	Boston	MA	02110	617-742-8886	742-8868
Theta Phi Alpha Fraternity Inc 27025 Knickerbocker Rd *TF:* 877-843-8274 ■ *Web:* www.thetaphialpha.org	Bay Village	OH	44140	440-899-9282	899-9293
Theta Tau Professional Engineering Fraternity 1011 San Jacinto Suite 205 *TF:* 800-264-1904 ■ *Web:* www.thetatau.org	Austin	TX	78701	512-472-1904	472-4820
Theta Xi Fraternity PO Box 411134 *TF:* 800-783-6294 ■ *Web:* www.thetaxi.org	Saint Louis	MO	63141	314-993-6294	993-8760
Zeta Beta Tau Fraternity Inc (ZBT) 3905 Vincennes Rd Suite 300 *Web:* www.zbt.org	Indianapolis	IN	46268	317-334-1898	334-1899
Zeta Phi Beta Sorority Inc 1734 New Hampshire Ave NW *TF:* 800-368-5772 ■ *Web:* www.zphib1920.org	Washington	DC	20009	202-387-3103	232-4593
Zeta Psi Fraternity of North America 15 S Henry St *TF:* 800-477-1847 ■ *Web:* www.zetapsi.org	Pearl River	NY	10965	845-735-1847	735-1989
Zeta Tau Alpha Fraternity (ZTA) 3450 Founders Rd *Web:* www.zetataualpha.org	Indianapolis	IN	46268	317-872-0540	876-3948

48-17 Health & Health-Related Organizations

Organization	City	State	Zip	Phone	Fax
Acoustic Neuroma Assn (ANA) 600 Peachtree Pkwy Suite 108 *TF:* 877-200-8211 ■ *Web:* www.anausa.org	Cumming	GA	30041	770-205-8211	205-0239
AIDS Treatment Data Network (ATDN) 611 Broadway Suite 613 *TF:* 800-734-7104 ■ *Web:* www.atdn.org	New York	NY	10012	212-260-8868	260-8869
Alexander Graham Bell Assn for the Deaf & Hard of Hearing (AGBell) 3417 Volta Pl NW *Web:* www.nc.agbell.org	Washington	DC	20007	202-337-5220	337-8314
Alliance for Aging Research (AAR) 750 17th St NW Suite 1100 *TF:* 800-639-2421 ■ *Web:* www.agingresearch.org	Washington	DC	20006	202-293-2856	255-8394
Alliance for Lupus Research (ALA) 28 W 44th St Suite 501 *TF:* 800-867-1743 ■ *Web:* www.lupusresearch.org	New York	NY	10036	212-218-2840	218-2848
ALS Assn 27001 Agoura Rd Suite 150 *TF:* 800-782-4747 ■ *Web:* www.alsa.org	Calabasas Hills	CA	91301	818-880-9007	880-9006
Alzheimer's Assn 225 N Michigan Ave Suite 1700 **Fax Area Code: 866* ■ *TF:* 800-272-3900 ■ *Web:* www.alz.org	Chicago	IL	60601	312-335-8700	699-1246*
American Academy for Cerebral Palsy & Developmental Medicine (AACPDM) 555 E Wells St Suite 1100 *Web:* www.aacpdm.org	Milwaukee	WI	53202	414-918-3014	276-2146
American Academy of Medical Acupuncture (AAMA) 1970 E Grand Ave Suite 330 **Fax Area Code: 323* ■ *Web:* www.medicalacupuncture.org	El Segundo	CA	90245	310-364-0193	937-0959*
American Academy of Sleep Medicine (AASM) 1 Westbrook Corporate Ctr Suite 920 *Web:* www.aasmnet.org	Westchester	IL	60154	708-492-0930	492-0943
American Amputee Foundation (AAF) PO Box 94227 *Web:* www.americanamputee.org	North Little Rock	AR	72190	501-835-9290	835-9292
American Assn of Acupunture & Oriental Medicine (AAAOM) PO Box 162340 *TF:* 866-455-7999 ■ *Web:* www.aaaomonline.org	Sacramento	CA	95816	916-443-4770	443-4766
American Assn of Drugless Practitioners (AADP) 2200 Market St Suite 329 *TF:* 888-764-2237 ■ *Web:* www.aadp.net	Galveston	TX	77550	409-621-2600	
American Assn of Naturopathic Physicians (AANP) 4000 Albemarle St NW # 403 *TF:* 866-538-2267 ■ *Web:* www.naturopathic.org	Washington	DC	20016	202-237-8150	237-8152
American Assn of Suicidology (AAS) 5221 Wisconsin Ave NW 2nd Fl *Web:* www.suicidology.org	Washington	DC	20015	202-237-2280	237-2282
American Assn on Intellectual & Developmental Disabilities (AAIDD) 444 N Capitol St NW Suite 846 *TF:* 800-424-3688 ■ *Web:* www.aaidd.org	Washington	DC	20001	202-387-1968	387-2193
American Autoimmune Related Disease Assn (AARDA) 22100 Gratiot Ave *TF:* 800-598-4668 ■ *Web:* www.aarda.org	Eastpointe	MI	48021	586-776-3900	776-3903
American Bone Marrow Donor Registry 2733 N St *TF:* 800-745-2452 ■ *Web:* www.abmdr.org	Mandeville	LA	70448	985-626-1749	626-7414
American Botanical Council 6200 Manor Rd PO Box 144345 *TF:* 800-373-7105 ■ *Web:* www.abc.herbalgram.org	Austin	TX	78714	512-926-4900	926-2345
American Brain Tumor Assn (ABTA) 2720 River Rd *TF:* 800-886-2282 ■ *Web:* www.hope.abta.org	Des Plaines	IL	60018	847-827-9910	827-9918
American Cancer Society (ACS) 250 William St NW Suite 6001 *TF:* 800-227-2345 ■ *Web:* www.cancer.org	Atlanta	GA	30303	404-320-3333	325-9341
American Chronic Pain Assn (ACPA) PO Box 850 *TF:* 800-533-3231 ■ *Web:* www.theacpa.org	Rocklin	CA	95677	916-632-0922	632-3208
American Council for Drug Education (ACDE) c/o Phoenix House 164 W 74th St *TF:* 800-378-4435 ■ *Web:* www.acde.org	New York	NY	10023	212-595-5810	721-7384
American Council for Headache Education (ACHE) 19 Mantua Rd *TF:* 800-255-2243 ■ *Web:* www.achenet.org	Mount Royal	NJ	08061	856-423-0043	423-0082
American Council of the Blind (ACB) 1155 15th St NW Suite 1004 *TF:* 800-424-8666 ■ *Web:* www.acb.org	Washington	DC	20005	202-467-5081	467-5085
American Council on Alcoholism (ACA) 1000 E Indian School Rd *TF:* 800-527-5344	Phoenix	AZ	85014	602-264-7403	
American Council on Exercise (ACE) 4851 Paramount Dr *TF:* 800-825-3636 ■ *Web:* www.acefitness.org	San Diego	CA	92123	858-576-6500	576-6564
American Diabetes Assn (ADA) 1701 N Beauregard St *TF:* 800-232-3472 ■ *Web:* www.diabetes.org	Alexandria	VA	22311	703-549-1500	836-2464
American Dietetic Assn (ADA) 120 S Riverside Plaza Suite 2000 *TF:* 800-877-1600 ■ *Web:* www.eatright.org	Chicago	IL	60606	312-899-0040	899-4899
American Epilepsy Society (AES) 342 N Main St *Web:* www.aesnet.org	West Hartford	CT	06117	860-586-7505	586-7550
American Foundation for AIDS Research (amfAR) 120 Wall St 13th Fl *Web:* www.amfar.org	New York	NY	10005	212-806-1600	806-1601
American Foundation for Suicide Prevention (AFSP) 120 Wall St 22nd Fl *TF:* 888-333-2377 ■ *Web:* www.afsp.org	New York	NY	10005	212-363-3500	363-6237
American Foundation for the Blind (AFB) 2 Penn Plaza *TF:* 800-232-5463 ■ *Web:* www.afb.org	New York	NY	10001	212-502-7600	502-7777
American Hair Loss Council (AHLC) 1606 S 28th Ave *Web:* www.ahlc.org	Hattiesburg	MS	39402	601-296-6003	296-6006
American Hearing Research Foundation 8 S Michigan Ave Suite 814 *Web:* www.american-hearing.org	Chicago	IL	60603	312-726-9670	726-9695
American Heart Assn (AHA) 7272 Greenville Ave *TF:* 800-242-8721 ■ *Web:* www.americanheart.org	Dallas	TX	75231	214-373-6300	706-1191
American Holistic Health Assn (AHHA) PO Box 17400 *Web:* www.ahha.org	Anaheim	CA	92817	714-779-6152	
American Holistic Nurses' Assn (AHNA) 323 N San Francisco St Suite 201 *TF:* 800-278-2462 ■ *Web:* www.ahna.org	Flagstaff	AZ	86001	928-526-2196	526-2752
American Institute of Stress The (AIS) 124 Pk Ave *Web:* www.stress.org	Yonkers	NY	10703	914-963-1200	965-6267
American Juvenile Arthritis Organization (AJAO) 1330 W Peachtree St Suite 100 *TF:* 800-283-7800 ■ *Web:* www.arthritis.org/communities	Atlanta	GA	30309	404-965-7538	872-9559
American Kidney Fund (AKF) 6110 Executive Blvd Suite 1010 *TF:* 800-638-8299 ■ *Web:* www.akfinc.org	Rockville	MD	20852	301-881-3052	881-0898
American Leprosy Missions (ALM) 120 Broadus Ave *TF:* 800-543-3135 ■ *Web:* www.leprosy.org	Greenville	SC	29601	864-271-7040	271-7062
American Liver Foundation (ALF) 39 Broadway *TF:* 800-465-4837 ■ *Web:* www.liverfoundation.org	New York	NY	10006	212-668-1000	483-8179
American Lung Assn (ALA) 14 Wall St *TF:* 800-586-4872 ■ *Web:* www.lungusa.org	New York	NY	10005	212-315-8700	315-8872
American Massage Therapy Assn (AMTA) 500 Davis St Suite 900 *TF:* 877-905-2700 ■ *Web:* www.amtamassage.org	Evanston	IL	60201	847-864-0123	864-1178
American Menopause Foundation Inc 350 5th Ave Suite 2822	New York	NY	10118	212-714-2398	
American Music Therapy Assn Inc (AMTA) 8455 Colesville Rd Suite 1000 *Web:* www.musictherapy.org	Silver Spring	MD	20910	301-589-3300	589-5175
American Naturopathic Medical Assn (ANMA) 3163 S Eastern Ave *Web:* www.anma.com	Las Vegas	NV	89169	702-897-7053	897-7140
American Organization for Bodywork Therapies of Asia (AOBTA) 1010 Haddonfield-Berlin Rd Suite 408 *Web:* www.aobta.org	Voorhees	NJ	08043	856-782-1616	782-1653
American Orthotic & Prosthetic Assn (AOPA) 330 John Carlyle St Suite 200 *Web:* www.aopanet.org	Alexandria	VA	22314	571-431-0876	431-0899
American Pain Society (APS) 4700 W Lake Ave *Web:* www.ampainsoc.org	Glenview	IL	60025	847-375-4715	375-6479
American Parkinson Disease Assn (APDA) 135 Parkinson Ave *TF:* 800-223-2732 ■ *Web:* www.apdaparkinson.org	Staten Island	NY	10305	718-981-8001	981-4399
American Polarity Therapy Assn (APTA) 122 N Elm St Suite 512 *Web:* www.polaritytherapy.org	Greensboro	NC	27401	336-574-1121	574-1151
American Prostate Society 7188 Ridge Rd PO Box 870 *TF:* 800-308-1106 ■ *Web:* www.americanprostatesociety.com	Hanover	MD	21076	410-859-3735	850-0818
American SIDS Institute 528 Raven Way *TF:* 800-232-7437 ■ *Web:* www.sids.org	Naples	FL	34110	239-431-5425	431-5536
American Sleep Apnea Assn (ASAA) 6856 Eastern Ave NW #203 *Web:* www.sleepapnea.org	Washington	DC	20012	202-293-3650	293-3656
American Social Health Assn (ASHA) PO Box 13827 *Web:* www.ashastd.org	Research Triangle Park	NC	27709	919-361-8400	361-8425
American Society of Alternative Therapists (ASAT) PO Box 703 *Web:* www.asat.org	Rockport	MA	01966	978-281-4400	282-1144
American Therapeutic Recreation Assn (ATRA) 629 N Main St *Web:* www.atra-online.com	Hattiesburg	MS	39401	601-450-2872	582-3354
American Tinnitus Assn (ATA) 522 SW 5th Ave # 825 *TF:* 800-634-8978 ■ *Web:* www.ata.org	Portland	OR	97204	503-248-9985	248-0024
American Urological Assn Foundation 1000 Corporate Blvd *TF:* 800-828-7866 ■ *Web:* www.auafoundation.org	Linthicum	MD	21090	410-689-3990	689-3998
Americans for Better Care of the Dying (ABCD) 1700 Diagonal Rd Suite 635 *Web:* www.abcd-caring.org	Alexandria	VA	22314	703-647-8505	837-1233
Americans for Nonsmokers' Rights (ANR) 2530 San Pablo Ave Suite J *Web:* www.no-smoke.org	Berkeley	CA	94702	510-841-3032	841-3071
Anxiety Disorders Assn of America (ADAA) 8730 Georgia Ave Suite 600 *Web:* www.adaa.org	Silver Spring	MD	20910	240-485-1001	485-1035
Arc of the US 1010 Wayne Ave Suite 650 *TF:* 800-433-5255 ■ *Web:* www.thearc.org	Silver Spring	MD	20910	301-565-3842	565-3843
Arthritis Foundation 1330 W Peachtree St Suite 100 *TF:* 800-283-7800 ■ *Web:* www.arthritis.org	Atlanta	GA	30309	404-872-7100	872-0457
Assn for Applied & Therapeutic Humor (AATH) 65 Enterprise *TF:* 888-747-2284 ■ *Web:* www.aath.org	Aliso Viejo	CA	92656	949-715-4681	715-6931
Assn for Children with Down Syndrome Inc (ACDS) 4 Fern Pl *Web:* www.acds.org	Plainview	NY	11803	516-933-4700	933-9524

Organization	City	State	ZIP	Phone	Fax
Assn for Macular Diseases Inc 210 E 64th St 8th Fl *Web:* www.macula.org	New York	NY	10021	212-605-3719	605-3795
Assn for Research & Enlightenment (ARE) 215 67th St *TF:* 800-333-4499 ■ *Web:* www.edgarcayce.org	Virginia Beach	VA	23451	757-428-3588	422-6921
Assn for the Advancement of the Blind & Retarded (AABR) 1508 College Pt Blvd *Web:* www.aabr.org	College Point	NY	11356	718-321-3800	321-8688
Associated Bodywork & Massage Professionals (ABMP) 25188 Genesee Trail Rd Suite 200 **Fax Area Code:* 800 ■ *TF:* 800-458-2267 ■ *Web:* www.abmp.com	Golden	CO	80401	303-674-8478	667-8260*
Asthma & Allergy Foundation of America (AAFA) 8201 Corporate Dr Suite 1000 *TF:* 800-727-8462 ■ *Web:* www.aafa.org	Landover	MD	20785	202-466-7643	466-8940
Attention Deficit Disorder Assn 15000 Commerce Pkwy Suite C *Web:* www.add.org	Mount Laurel	NJ	08054	856-439-9099	439-0525
Autism Research Institute (ARI) 4182 Adams Ave *Web:* www.autism.com	San Diego	CA	92116	619-281-7165	563-6840
Autism Society of America (ASA) 7910 Woodmont Ave Suite 300 *TF:* 800-328-8476 ■ *Web:* www.autism-society.org	Bethesda	MD	20814	301-657-0881	657-0869
BACCHUS Network The PO Box 100430 *Web:* www.bacchusgamma.org	Denver	CO	80250	303-871-0901	871-0907
BEGINNINGS for Parents of Children Who Are Deaf or Hard of Hearing Inc 302 Jefferson St Suite 110 *TF:* 800-541-4327 ■ *Web:* www.ncbegin.org	Raleigh	NC	27605	919-715-4092	715-4093
Better Hearing Institute (BHI) 1444 I St NW Suite 700 *Web:* www.betterhearing.org	Washington	DC	20005	202-449-1100	
Better Sleep Council 501 Wythe St *Web:* www.bettersleep.org	Alexandria	VA	22314	703-683-8371	683-4503
Better Vision Institute The (BVI) *The Vision Council* 225 Reinekers Ln Suite 700 *TF:* 866-826-0290 ■ *Web:* www.thevisioncouncil.org/bvi	Alexandria	VA	22314	703-548-4560	548-4580
Brain Injury Assn of America 1608 Spring Hill Rd Suite 110 *TF:* 800-444-6443 ■ *Web:* www.biausa.org	Vienna	VA	22182	703-761-0750	761-0755
Breast Cancer Network of Strength 135 S LaSalle St Suite 2000 *TF:* 800-221-2141 ■ *Web:* www.networkofstrength.org	Chicago	IL	60603	312-986-8338	294-8597
Campaign for Tobacco-Free Kids 1400 'I' St NW Suite 1200 *TF:* 800-284-5437 ■ *Web:* www.tobaccofreekids.org	Washington	DC	20005	202-296-5469	296-5427
Cancer Care Inc 275 7th Ave 22nd Fl *TF:* 800-813-4673 ■ *Web:* www.cancercare.org	New York	NY	10001	212-712-8400	712-8495
Candlelighters Childhood Cancer Foundation 10920 Connecticut Ave Suuite A PO Box 498 *TF:* 800-366-2223 ■ *Web:* www.acco.org	Kensington	MD	20895	301-962-3520	962-3521
Canine Companions for Independence Inc (CCI) 2965 Dutton Ave PO Box 446 *TF:* 800-572-2275 ■ *Web:* www.caninecompanions.org	Santa Rosa	CA	95402	707-577-1700	
Carcinoid Cancer Foundation Inc 333 Mamaroneck Ave Suite 492 *TF:* 888-722-3132 ■ *Web:* www.carcinoid.org	White Plains	NY	10605	212-722-3132	
Center for Jewish Genetic Diseases Mt Sinai School of Medicine One Gustave L Levy Pl PO Box 1497 *Web:* www.nfjgd.org	New York	NY	10029	212-659-6774	
Center for Practical Bioethics 1111 Main St Suite 500 *TF:* 800-344-3829 ■ *Web:* www.practicalbioethics.org	Kansas City	MO	64105	816-221-1100	221-2002
Center on Human Policy 805 S Crouse Ave *TF:* 800-894-0826 ■ *Web:* www.thechp.syr.edu	Syracuse	NY	13244	315-443-3851	443-4338
CFIDS Assn of America Inc 6827 Fairview Rd PO Box 220398 *Web:* www.cfids.org	Charlotte	NC	28222	704-365-2343	365-9755
Children & Adults with Attention-Deficit/Hyperactivity Disorder (CHADD) 8181 Professional Pl Suite 150 *TF:* 800-233-4050 ■ *Web:* www.chadd.org	Landover	MD	20785	301-306-7070	306-7090
Children's Eye Foundation 1527 W State Hwy 114 Suite 500 *Web:* www.childrenseyefoundation.org	Grapevine	TX	76051	817-891-1144	329-5532
Children's Leukemia Research Assn 585 Stewart Ave Suite 18 *Web:* www.childrensleukemia.org	Garden City	NY	11530	516-222-1944	222-0457
Children's Organ Transplant Assn (COTA) 2501 W Cota Dr *TF:* 800-366-2682 ■ *Web:* www.cota.org	Bloomington	IN	47403	812-336-8872	336-8885
Children's Tumor Foundation 95 Pine St 16th Fl *TF:* 800-323-7938 ■ *Web:* www.ctf.org	New York	NY	10005	212-344-6633	747-0004
Children's Wish Foundation International 8615 Roswell Rd *TF:* 800-323-9474 ■ *Web:* www.childrenswish.org	Atlanta	GA	30350	770-393-9474	393-0683
Christopher Reeve Foundation 636 Morris Tpke Suite 3A *TF:* 800-225-0292 ■ *Web:* www.christopherreeve.org	Short Hills	NJ	07078	973-379-2690	912-9433
Cje Seniorlife 3003 W Touhy Ave *Web:* www.cje.net	Chicago	IL	60645	773-508-1000	508-1028
Cleft Palate Foundation (CPF) 1504 E Franklin St Suite 102 *TF:* 800-242-5338 ■ *Web:* www.cleftline.org	Chapel Hill	NC	27514	919-933-9044	933-9604
Compassion & Choices PO Box 101810 **Fax Area Code:* 866 ■ *TF:* 800-247-7421 ■ *Web:* www.compassionandchoices.org	Denver	CO	80250	303-639-1202	312-2690*
Cornelia de Lange Syndrome Foundation Inc (CdLS) 302 W Main St Suite 100 *TF:* 800-753-2357 ■ *Web:* www.cdlsusa.org	Avon	CT	06001	860-676-8166	676-8337
Council for Affordable Health Insurance (CAHI) 127 S Peyton St Suite 210 *Web:* www.cahi.org	Alexandria	VA	22314	703-836-6200	836-6550
Council on Size & Weight Discrimination (CSWD) PO Box 305 *Web:* www.cswd.org	Mount Marion	NY	12456	845-679-1209	679-1206
Creutzfeldt-Jakob Disease Foundation Inc 3632 W Market St PO Box 5312 *TF:* 800-659-1991 ■ *Web:* www.cjdfoundation.org	Akron	OH	44334	330-665-5590	668-2474
Crohn's & Colitis Foundation of America (CCFA) 386 Pk Ave S 17th Fl *TF:* 800-932-2423 ■ *Web:* www.ccfa.org	New York	NY	10016	212-685-3440	779-4098
Cystic Fibrosis Foundation 6931 Arlington Rd Suite 200 *TF:* 800-344-4823 ■ *Web:* www.cff.org	Bethesda	MD	20814	301-951-4422	951-6378
Deafness Research Foundation (DRF) 641 Lexington Ave 15th Fl *Web:* www.drf.org	New York	NY	10022	212-328-9480	
Delta Society 875 124th Ave NE Suite 101 *Web:* www.deltasociety.org	Bellevue	WA	98005	425-679-5500	679-5539
Dental Lifeline Network 1800 15th St Unit 100 *TF:* 888-471-6334 ■ *Web:* www.nfdh.org	Denver	CO	80202	303-534-5360	534-5290
Depression & Bipolar Support Alliance (DBSA) 730 N Franklin St Suite 501 *TF:* 800-826-3632 ■ *Web:* www.dbsalliance.org	Chicago	IL	60610	312-642-0049	642-7243
Diabetes Exercise & Sports Assn (DESA) 310 W Liberty Suite 604 *TF:* 800-898-4322 ■ *Web:* www.diabetes-exercise.org	Louisville	KY	40202	502-581-0207	581-0206
Disability Rights Center Inc 18 Low Ave *TF:* 800-834-1721 ■ *Web:* www.drcnh.org	Concord	NH	03301	603-228-0432	225-2077
Disabled & Alone/Life Services for the Handicapped 61 Broadway Suite 510 *TF:* 800-995-0066 ■ *Web:* www.disabledandalone.org	New York	NY	10006	212-532-6740	532-3588
Dystonia Medical Research Foundation 1 E Wacker Dr Suite 2810 *TF:* 800-863-4863 ■ *Web:* www.dystonia-foundation.org	Chicago	IL	60601	312-755-0198	803-0138
Easter Seals 230 W Monroe St Suite 1800 *TF:* 800-221-6827 ■ *Web:* www.easterseals.com	Chicago	IL	60606	312-726-6200	726-1494
ECRI Institute 5200 Butler Pike *Web:* www.ecri.org	Plymouth Meeting	PA	19462	610-825-6000	834-1275
Eden Alternative 14500 RR 12 Suite 2 *Web:* www.edenalt.com	Wimberley	TX	78676	512-847-6061	847-6191
El Paso First Health Plans Inc 1145 Westmoreland Dr *TF:* 877-532-3778 ■ *Web:* www.epfirst.com	El Paso	TX	79925	915-532-3778	532-2877
Elder Service Plan of The North Shore Inc 37 Friend St Suite 3 *Web:* www.pacenorthshore.org	Lynn	MA	01902	781-715-6608	715-6699
Elizabeth Glaser Pediatric AIDS Foundation 1140 Connecticut Ave NW Suite 200 *TF:* 888-499-4673 ■ *Web:* www.pedaids.org	Washington	DC	20036	202-296-9165	296-9185
Endometriosis Assn 8585 N 76th Pl *TF:* 800-992-3636 ■ *Web:* www.endometriosisassn.org	Milwaukee	WI	53223	414-355-2200	355-6065
EngenderHealth 440 9th Ave 13th Fl *TF:* 800-564-2872 ■ *Web:* www.engenderhealth.org	New York	NY	10001	212-561-8000	561-8067
Epilepsy Foundation 8301 Professional Pl E *TF:* 800-332-1000 ■ *Web:* www.epilepsyfoundation.org	Landover	MD	20785	301-459-3700	577-2684
Euthanasia Research & Guidance Organization (ERGO) 24829 Norris Ln *Web:* www.finalexit.org	Junction City	OR	97448	541-998-1873	
FaithTrust Institute 2400 N 45th St Suite 101 *TF:* 877-860-2255 ■ *Web:* www.faithtrustinstitute.org	Seattle	WA	98103	206-634-1903	634-0115
Families of Spinal Muscular Atrophy 925 Busse Rd PO Box 196 *TF:* 800-886-1762 ■ *Web:* www.fsma.org	Libertyville	IL	60048	847-367-7620	367-7623
Family Caregiver Alliance (FCA) 180 Montgomery St Suite 900 *TF:* 800-445-8106 ■ *Web:* www.caregiver.org	San Francisco	CA	94104	415-434-3388	434-3508
Family of the Americas Foundation PO Box 1170 *TF:* 800-443-3395 ■ *Web:* www.familyplanning.net	Dunkirk	MD	20754	301-627-3346	627-0847
Feingold Assn of the US 37 Shell Rd 2nd Fl *TF:* 800-321-3287 ■ *Web:* www.feingold.org	Rocky Point	NY	11778	631-369-9340	369-2988
First Candle 1314 Bedford Ave Suite 210 *TF:* 800-221-7437 ■ *Web:* www.firstcandle.org	Baltimore	MD	21208	410-653-8226	653-8709
Food Allergy & Anaphylaxis Network (FAAN) 11781 Lee Jackson Hwy Suite 160 *TF:* 800-929-4040 ■ *Web:* www.foodallergy.org	Fairfax	VA	22033	703-691-3179	691-2713
Foundation Fighting Blindness 11435 Cron Hill Dr *TF:* 800-683-5555 ■ *Web:* www.blindness.org	Owings Mills	MD	21117	410-568-0150	363-2393
Freedom From Fear (FFF) 308 Seaview Ave *Web:* www.freedomfromfear.org	Staten Island	NY	10305	718-351-1717	980-5022
Gay Men's Health Crisis (GMHC) 119 W 24th St *TF:* 800-243-7692 ■ *Web:* www.gmhc.org	New York	NY	10011	212-367-1000	367-1220
GBS/CIDP Foundation International 104 1/2 Forrest Ave Holly Bldg. *TF:* 866-224-3301 ■ *Web:* www.gbs-cidp.org	Narberth	PA	19072	610-667-0131	667-7036
Genetic Alliance Inc 4301 Connecticut Ave NW Suite 404 *TF:* 800-336-4363 ■ *Web:* www.geneticalliance.org	Washington	DC	20008	202-966-5557	966-8553
Gift of Life Bone Marrow Foundation 800 Yamato Rd Suite 101 *TF:* 800-962-7769 ■ *Web:* www.giftoflife.org	Boca Raton	FL	33431	561-982-2900	982-2902
Gilda Radner Familial Ovarian Cancer Registry Roswell Pk Cancer Institute Elm & Carlton Sts *TF:* 800-682-7426 ■ *Web:* www.ovariancancer.com	Buffalo	NY	14263	716-845-4503	845-8266

Phone Fax

Glaucoma Foundation (TGF)
80 Maiden Ln Suite 700 New York NY 10038 212-285-0080 651-1888
Web: www.glaucomafoundation.org

Glaucoma Research Foundation
251 Post St Suite 600 San Francisco CA 94108 415-986-3162 986-3763
TF: 800-826-6693 ■ *Web:* www.glaucoma.org

Gluten Intolerance Group (GIG)
31214 124th Ave SE Auburn WA 98092 253-833-6655 833-6675
Web: www.gluten.net

Guide Dog Foundation for the Blind Inc
371 E Jericho Tkpe Smithtown NY 11787 631-265-2121 930-9009
TF: 800-548-4337 ■ *Web:* www.guidedog.org

Guide Dogs for the Blind
350 Los Ranchitos Rd San Rafael CA 94903 415-499-4000 499-4035
TF: 800-295-4050 ■ *Web:* www.guidedogs.com

Guide Dogs of America 13445 Glenoaks Blvd Sylmar CA 91342 818-362-5834 362-6870
TF: 800-459-4843 ■ *Web:* www.guidedogsofamerica.org

Head Injury Hotline 212 Pioneer Bldg Seattle WA 98104 206-621-8558 329-4355
Web: www.headinjury.com

Health Physics Society
1313 Dolley Madison Blvd Suite 402 McLean VA 22101 703-790-1745 790-2672
Web: www.hps.org

Healthcare Leadership Council (HLC)
750 9th St NW Suite 500 Washington DC 20004 202-452-8700 296-9561
Web: hlc.org

Hearing Loss Assn of America
7910 Woodmont Ave Suite 1200 Bethesda MD 20814 301-657-2248 913-9413
Web: www.hearingloss.org

HEATH Resource Ctr 2134 G St NW Washington DC 20052 202-973-0904 994-3365
TF: 800-544-3284 ■ *Web:* www.heath.gwu.edu

Hepatitis Foundation International (HFI)
504 Blick Dr Silver Spring MD 20904 301-622-4200 622-4702
TF: 800-891-0707 ■ *Web:* www.hepfi.org

Herb Research Foundation (HRF) 4140 15th St Boulder CO 80304 303-449-2265 449-7849
TF: 800-748-2617 ■ *Web:* www.herbs.org

Hereditary Disease Foundation (HDF)
3960 Broadway 6th Fl New York NY 10032 212-928-2121 928-2172
Web: www.hdfoundation.org

Hospice Education Institute
3 Unity Sq PO Box 98 Machiasport ME 04655 207-255-8800 255-8008
TF: 800-331-1620 ■ *Web:* www.hospiceworld.org

Human Factors & Ergonomics Society (HFES)
1124 Montana Ave Suite B PO Box 1369 Santa Monica CA 90406 310-394-1811 394-2410
Web: www.hfes.org

Human Growth Foundation
997 Glen Cove Ave Suite 5 Glen Head NY 11545 516-671-4041 671-4055
TF: 800-451-6434 ■ *Web:* www.hgfound.org

Huntington's Disease Society of America (HDSA)
505 8th Ave Suite 902 New York NY 10018 212-242-1968 239-3430
TF: 800-345-4372 ■ *Web:* www.hdsa.org

Hysterectomy Educational Resources & Services Foundation (HERS)
422 Bryn Mawr Ave Bala Cynwyd PA 19004 610-667-7757 667-8096
TF: 888-750-4377 ■ *Web:* www.hersfoundation.com

Immune Deficiency Foundation (IDF)
40 W Chesapeake Ave Suite 308 Towson MD 21204 410-321-6647 321-9165
TF: 800-296-4433 ■ *Web:* www.primaryimmune.org

International Assn for the Study of Pain (IASP)
111 Queen Anne Ave N Suite 501 Seattle WA 98109 206-283-0311 283-9403
Web: www.iasp-pain.org

International Center for the Disabled (ICD)
340 E 24th St New York NY 10010 212-585-6000 585-6262
Web: www.icdnyc.org

International Cesarean Awareness Network Inc (ICAN)
1304 Kingsdale Ave Redondo Beach CA 90278 785-608-4678 608-4678
TF: 800-686-4226

International Dyslexia Assná The (IDA)
40 York Rd 4th Fl Baltimore MD 21204 410-296-0232 321-5069
TF: 800-222-3123 ■ *Web:* www.interdys.org

International Hearing Society (IHS)
16880 Middlebelt Rd Suite 4 Livonia MI 48154 734-522-7200 522-0200
TF: 800-521-5247 ■ *Web:* www.ihsinfo.org

International OCD Foundation (OCF) PO Box 961029 Boston MA 02196 617-973-5801 973-5803
Web: www.ocfoundation.org

Iron Overload Diseases Assn (IOD)
525 Mayflower Rd West Palm Beach FL 33405 561-586-8246
TF: 866-768-8629 ■ *Web:* www.ironoverload.org

Juvenile Diabetes Research Foundation International (JDRF)
120 Wall St New York NY 10005 212-785-9500 785-9595
TF: 800-533-2873 ■ *Web:* www.jdrf.org

Kristin Brooks Hope Ctr (KBHC) 615 7th St NE Washington DC 20002 202-536-3200 536-3206
TF: 800-784-2433 ■ *Web:* www.hopeline.com

La Leche League International Inc (LLLI)
957 N Plum Grove Rd Schaumburg IL 60173 847-519-7730 969-0460
TF: 800-525-3243 ■ *Web:* www.lalecheleague.org

Lamaze International
2025 M St NW Suite 800 Washington DC 20036 202-367-1128 367-2128
TF: 800-368-4404 ■ *Web:* www.lamaze.org

Laurent Clerc National Deaf Education Ctr
800 Florida Ave NE Washington DC 20002 202-651-5050 651-5708
TF: 866-637-0102 ■ *Web:* clerccenter.gallaudet.edu

Learning Disabilities Assn of America (LDA)
4156 Library Rd Pittsburgh PA 15234 412-341-1515 344-0224
TF: 888-300-6710 ■ *Web:* www.ldanatl.org

Lifespire 350 5th Ave Suite 301 New York NY 10118 212-741-0100 242-0696
Web: www.lifespire.org

Light for Life Foundation International
PO Box 644 Westminster CO 80036 303-429-3530 426-4496
Web: www.yellowribbon.org

Lighthouse International 111 E 59th St New York NY 10022 212-821-9200 821-9707*
**Fax:* Hum Res ■ *TF:* 800-829-0500 ■ *Web:* www.lighthouse.org

Phone Fax

Living Bank PO Box 6725 Houston TX 77625 713-961-9431 961-0979
TF: 800-528-2971 ■ *Web:* www.livingbank.org

Lupus Foundation of America Inc (LFA)
2000 L St NW Suite 710 Washington DC 20036 202-349-1155 349-1156
TF: 800-558-0121 ■ *Web:* www.lupus.org

Lyme Disease Foundation Inc (LDF) PO Box 332 Tolland CT 06084 860-870-0070 870-0080
TF: 800-886-5963 ■ *Web:* www.lyme.org

Lymphoma Research Foundation (LRF)
115 Broadway Suite 1301 New York NY 10006 212-349-2910 349-2886
TF: 800-500-9976 ■ *Web:* www.lymphoma.org

Macula Foundation Inc 210 E 64th St 8th Fl New York NY 10021 212-605-3777 605-3795
Web: www.macula.org

Male Survivor
5505 Connecticut Ave NW PMB 103 Washington DC 20015 800-738-4181
TF: 800-738-4181 ■ *Web:* www.malesurvivor.org

March of Dimes Birth Defects Foundation
1275 Mamaroneck Ave White Plains NY 10605 914-428-7100 428-8203
Web: www.marchofdimes.com

Match Foundation
National Marrow Donor Program
3001 Broadway St NE Suite 100 Minneapolis MN 55413 612-627-5800 638-0641*
**Fax Area Code:* 202 ■ *Web:* www.marrow-donor.org

MCS Referral & Resources Inc
6101 Gentry Ln Baltimore MD 21210 410-889-6666 889-4944
Web: www.mcsrr.org

MedicAlert Foundation International
2323 Colorado Ave Turlock CA 95382 209-668-3333 669-2495
TF Cust Svc: 800-432-5378 ■ *Web:* www.medicalert.org

Medicare Rights Ctr (MRC)
520 8th Ave N Wing 3rd Fl New York NY 10018 212-869-3850 869-3532
TF hotline: 800-333-4114 ■ *Web:* www.medicarerights.org

Mended Hearts Inc The
8150 N Central Expy M2075 Dallas TX 75206 214-296-9252 295-9552
TF: 888-432-7899 ■ *Web:* www.mendedhearts.org

Mental Health America (MHA)
2000 N Beauregard St 6th Fl Alexandria VA 22311 703-684-7722 684-5968
TF Help Line: 800-969-6642 ■ *Web:* www.nmha.org

Migraine Awareness Group: A National Understanding for Migraineurs (MAGNUM)
100 N Union St Suite B Alexandria VA 22314 703-349-1929 884-1300*
**Fax Area Code:* 800 ■ *Web:* www.migraines.org

Mothers Supporting Daughters with Breast Cancer (MSDBC)
25235 Fox Chase Dr Chestertown MD 21620 410-778-1982 778-1411
Web: www.mothersdaughters.org

Mountain States Group Inc (MSG)
1607 W Jefferson St Boise ID 83702 208-336-5533 336-0880
Web: www.mtnstatesgroup.org

Multiple Sclerosis Foundation (MSF)
6350 N Andrews Ave Fort Lauderdale FL 33309 954-776-6805 938-8708
TF: 800-225-6495 ■ *Web:* www.msfocus.org

Muscular Dystrophy Assn (MDA) 3300 E Sunrise Dr Tucson AZ 85718 520-529-2000 529-5300
TF: 800-572-1717 ■ *Web:* www.mda.org

Myasthenia Gravis Foundation of America (MGFA)
1821 University Ave W Suite S256 Saint Paul MN 55104 651-917-6256 917-1835
TF: 800-541-5454 ■ *Web:* www.myasthenia.org

NA for Biomedical Research (NABR)
818 Connecticut Ave NW Suite 200 Washington DC 20006 202-857-0540 659-1902
Web: www.nabr.org

NA for Continence (NAFC) PO Box 1019 Charleston SC 29402 843-377-0900 377-0905
TF: 800-252-3337 ■ *Web:* www.nafc.org

NA for Parents of Children with Visual Impairments (NAPVI)
PO Box 317 Watertown MA 02471 617-972-7441 972-7444
TF: 800-562-6265 ■ *Web:* www.spedex.com/napvi

NA of Anorexia Nervosa & Associated Disorders (ANAD)
PO Box 7 Highland Park IL 60035 847-831-3438 433-4632
Web: www.anad.org

NA of Certified Natural Health Professionals (CNHP)
220 Parker St Warsaw IN 46580 800-321-1005 268-5393*
**Fax Area Code:* 574 ■ *TF:* 800-321-1005 ■ *Web:* www.cnhp.org

NA of People with AIDS (NAPWA)
8401 Colesville Rd Suite 750 Silver Spring MD 20910 240-247-0880 247-0574
Web: www.napwa.org

NA of Protection & Advocacy Systems (NAPAS)
900 2nd St NE Suite 211 Washington DC 20002 202-408-9514 408-9520
Web: www.napas.org

NA of the Deaf (NAD)
8630 Fenton St Suite 820 Silver Spring MD 20910 301-587-1788 587-1791
Web: www.nad.org

NA on Drug Abuse Problems Inc (NADAP)
355 Lexington Ave 2nd Fl New York NY 10017 212-986-1170 697-2939
Web: www.nadap.org

Narcolepsy Network Inc PO Box 294 Pleasantville NY 10570 401-667-2523 633-6567
Web: www.narcolepsynetwork.org

National Adrenal Diseases Foundation (NADF)
505 Northern Blvd Great Neck NY 11021 516-487-4992
Web: www.medhelp.org/nadf

National Allergy Bureau (NAB)
555 E Wells St 11th Fl Milwaukee WI 53202 414-272-6071 272-6070
Web: www.aaaai.org/nab

National Alliance for Hispanic Health
1501 16th St NW Washington DC 20036 202-387-5000 797-4353
Web: www.hispanichealth.org

National Alliance on Mental Illness (NAMI)
3803 N Fairfax Dr Suite 100 Arlington VA 22203 703-524-7600 524-9094
TF: 800-950-6264 ■ *Web:* www.nami.org

National Alopecia Areata Foundation (NAAF)
14 Mitchell Blvd San Rafael CA 94903 415-472-3780 472-5343
Web: www.naaf.org

National Amputation Foundation 40 Church St Malverne NY 11565 516-887-3600 887-3667
Web: www.nationalamputation.org

Organization	City	State	Zip	Phone	Fax
National Breast Cancer Coalition (NBCC) 1101 17th St NW Suite 1300 *TF:* 800-622-2838 ■ *Web:* www.breastcancerdeadline2020.org	Washington	DC	20036	202-296-7477	265-6854
National Cancer Registrars Assn (NCRA) 1340 Braddock Pl Suite 203 *Web:* www.ncra-usa.org	Alexandria	VA	22314	703-299-6640	299-6620
National Center for Homeopathy (NCH) 101 S Whiting St *TF:* 877-624-0613 ■ *Web:* www.homeopathic.org	Alexandria	VA	22304	703-548-7790	548-7792
National Center for Stuttering (NCS) 200 E 33rd St *TF:* 800-221-2483 ■ *Web:* www.stuttering.com	New York	NY	10016	212-532-1460	683-1372
National Children's Cancer Society (NCCS) 1 S Memorial Dr Suite 800 *TF:* 800-532-6459 ■ *Web:* www.nationalchildrenscancersociety.com	Saint Louis	MO	63102	314-241-1600	241-1996
National Citizens' Coalition for Nursing Home Reform (NCCNHR) *The National Consumer Voice for Quality Long-Term Care* 1828 L St NW Suite 801 *Web:* www.theconsumervoice.org	Washington	DC	20036	202-332-2275	332-2949
National Coalition for Cancer Survivorship (NCCS) 1010 Wayne Ave Suite 770 *TF:* 888-650-9127 ■ *Web:* www.canceradvocacy.org	Silver Spring	MD	20910	301-650-9127	565-9670
National Coalition on Health Care 1120 G St NW # 810 *Web:* www.nchc.org	Washington	DC	20005	202-638-7151	638-7166
National Committee for Quality Assurance (NCQA) 1100 13th St *TF:* 800-275-7585 ■ *Web:* www.ncqa.org	Washington	DC	20005	202-955-3500	955-3599
National Council on Alcoholism & Drug Dependence Inc (NCADD) 244 E 58th St 4th Fl *TF:* 800-622-2255 ■ *Web:* www.ncadd.org	New York	NY	10022	212-269-7797	269-7510
National Dissemination Center for Children with Disabilities 1825 Connecticut Ave *TF:* 800-695-0285 ■ *Web:* www.nichcy.org	Washington	DC	20009	202-884-8200	884-8441
National Down Syndrome Congress (NDSC) 1370 Ctr Dr Suite 102 *TF:* 800-232-6372 ■ *Web:* www.ndsccenter.org	Atlanta	GA	30338	770-604-9500	604-9898
National Down Syndrome Society (NDSS) 666 Broadway 8th Fl *TF:* 800-221-4602 ■ *Web:* www.ndss.org	New York	NY	10012	212-460-9330	979-2873
National Eating Disorders Assn 603 Stewart St Suite 803 *TF:* 800-931-2237 ■ *Web:* www.nationaleatingdisorders.org	Seattle	WA	98101	206-382-3587	829-8501
National Federation of the Blind (NFB) 1800 Johnson St *Web:* www.nfb.org	Baltimore	MD	21230	410-659-9314	685-5653
National Fibromyalgia Partnership Inc (NFP) 140 Zinn Way PO Box 160 *TF:* 866-725-4404 ■ *Web:* www.fmpartnership.org	Linden	VA	22642	866-725-4404	666-2727
National Fire Protection Assn (NFPA) 1 Batterymarch Pk *TF:* 800-344-3555 ■ *Web:* www.nfpa.org	Quincy	MA	02169	617-770-3000	770-0700
National Gaucher Foundation (NGF) 2227 Idlewood Rd Suite 6 *TF:* 800-504-3189 ■ *Web:* www.gaucherdisease.org	Tucker	GA	30084	770-934-2910	934-2911
National Headache Foundation (NHF) 820 N Orleans St Suite 217 **Fax Area Code:* 312 ■ *TF:* 888-643-5552 ■ *Web:* www.headaches.org	Chicago	IL	60610	888-643-5552	640-9049*
National Health Assn (NHA) PO Box 30630 *Web:* www.healthscience.org	Tampa	FL	33630	813-855-6607	855-8052
National Health Council (NHC) 1730 M St NW Suite 500 *TF:* 800-684-6814 ■ *Web:* www.nhcouncil.org	Washington	DC	20036	202-785-3910	785-5923
National Healthy Mothers Healthy Babies Coalition (HMHB) 2000 N Beauregard St 6th Fl *Web:* www.hmhb.org	Alexandria	VA	22311	703-837-4792	634-5968
National Hearing Conservation Assn (NHCA) 7995 E Prentice Ave Suite 100 *Web:* www.hearingconservation.org	Greenwood Village	CO	80111	303-224-9022	770-1614
National Hemophilia Foundation (NHF) 116 W 32nd St 11th Fl *TF:* 800-424-2634 ■ *Web:* www.hemophilia.org	New York	NY	10001	212-328-3700	328-3777
National Herpes Resource Ctr (HRC) PO Box 13827 *Web:* www.ashastd.org/hrc	Research Triangle Park	NC	27709	919-361-8488	361-8425
National HPV & Cervical Cancer Prevention Resource Ctr PO Box 13827 *Web:* www.ashastd.org/hpvccrc	Research Triangle Park	NC	27709	919-361-8400	361-8425
National Industries for the Blind (NIB) 1310 Braddock Pl *TF Cust Svc:* 800-433-2304 ■ *Web:* www.nib.org	Alexandria	VA	22314	703-310-0500	
National Inhalant Prevention Coalition (NIPC) 322-A Thompson St *TF:* 800-269-4237 ■ *Web:* www.inhalants.org	Chattanooga	TN	37405	423-265-4662	265-4889
National Kidney Foundation (NKF) 30 E 33rd St 8th Fl *TF:* 800-622-9010 ■ *Web:* www.kidney.org	New York	NY	10016	212-889-2210	779-8056
National Marfan Foundation (NMF) 382 Main St *TF:* 800-862-7326 ■ *Web:* www.marfan.org	Port Washington	NY	11050	516-883-8712	883-8040
National Marrow Donor Program (NMDP) 3001 Broadway St NE Suite 100 *TF:* 800-526-7809 ■ *Web:* www.marrow.org	Minneapolis	MN	55413	612-627-5800	627-5877
National Minority AIDS Council (NMAC) 1931 13th St NW *Web:* www.nmac.org	Washington	DC	20009	202-483-6622	483-1135
National Multiple Sclerosis Society 733 3rd Ave 3rd Fl *TF:* 800-344-4867 ■ *Web:* www.nationalmssociety.org	New York	NY	10017	212-986-3240	986-7981
National Native American AIDS Prevention Ctr (NNAAPC) 720 S Colorado Blvd Suite 650-S *Web:* www.nnaapc.org	Denver	CO	80246	720-382-2244	382-2248
National Niemann-Pick Disease Foundation Inc (NNPDF) 401 Madison Ave Suite B PO Box 49 *TF:* 877-287-3672 ■ *Web:* www.nnpdf.org	Fort Atkinson	WI	53538	920-563-0930	563-0931
National Odd Shoe Exchange 3200 N Delaware St *Web:* www.oddshoe.org	Chandler	AZ	85225	480-892-3484	892-3568
National Oral Health Information Clearinghouse (NOHIC) 1 NOHIC Way *TF:* 866-232-4528 ■ *Web:* www.healthfinder.gov/orgs/HR2457.htm	Bethesda	MD	20892	301-496-4261	480-4098
National Organization for Albinism & Hypopigmentation (NOAH) PO Box 959 *TF:* 800-648-2310 ■ *Web:* www.albinism.org	East Hampstead	NH	03826	603-887-2310	887-6049
National Organization for Rare Disorders (NORD) 55 Kenosia Ave PO Box 1968 *TF:* 800-999-6673 ■ *Web:* www.rarediseases.org	Danbury	CT	06813	203-744-0100	798-2291
National Organization of Circumcision Information Resource Centers (NOCIRC) PO Box 2512 *Web:* www.nocirc.org	San Anselmo	CA	94979	415-488-9883	488-9660
National Organization of Restoring Men (NORM) 3205 Northwood Dr Suite 209 *Web:* www.norm.org	Concord	CA	94520	925-827-4077	827-4119
National Organization on Disability (NOD) 910 16th St NW Suite 600 *Web:* www.nod.org	Washington	DC	20006	202-293-5960	293-7999
National Osteoporosis Foundation (NOF) 1232 22nd St NW *TF:* 800-221-4222 ■ *Web:* www.nof.org	Washington	DC	20037	202-223-2226	223-2237
National Ovarian Cancer Coalition (NOCC) 2501 Oak Lawn Ave Suite 435 **Fax Area Code:* 214 ■ *TF:* 888-682-7426 ■ *Web:* www.ovarian.org	Dalls	TX	75219	888-682-7426	273-4201*
National Parkinson Foundation (NPF) 1501 NW 9th Ave *TF:* 800-327-4545 ■ *Web:* www.parkinson.org	Miami	FL	33136	305-547-6666	243-5595
National Pesticide Information Ctr (NPIC) 333 Weniger Hall **Fax Area Code:* 541 ■ *TF:* 800-858-7378 ■ *Web:* www.npic.orst.edu	Corvallis	OR	97331	800-858-7378	737-0761*
National Psoriasis Foundation (NPF) 6600 SW 92nd Ave Suite 300 *TF:* 800-723-9166 ■ *Web:* www.psoriasis.org	Portland	OR	97223	503-244-7404	245-0626
National Rehabilitation Assn (NRA) 633 S Washington St *Web:* www.nationalrehab.org	Alexandria	VA	22314	703-836-0850	836-0848
National Rehabilitation Information Ctr (NARIC) 8201 Corporate Dr Suite 600 *TF:* 800-346-2742 ■ *Web:* www.naric.com	Landover	MD	20785	301-459-5900	459-4263
National Reye's Syndrome Foundation (NRSF) 426 N Lewis St *TF:* 800-233-7393 ■ *Web:* www.reyessyndrome.org	Bryan	OH	43506	419-924-9000	924-9999
National Rosacea Society 800 S NW Hwy Suite 200 *TF:* 888-662-5874 ■ *Web:* www.rosacea.org	Barrington	IL	60010	847-382-8971	382-5567
National SAFE KIDS Campaign 1301 Pennsylvania Ave NW Suite 1000 *Web:* www.safekids.org	Washington	DC	20004	202-662-0600	393-2072
National Safety Council (NSC) 1121 Spring Lake Dr *TF:* 800-621-7615 ■ *Web:* www.nsc.org	Itasca	IL	60143	630-285-1121	285-1315
National Self-Help Clearinghouse 365 5th Ave Suite 3300	New York	NY	10016	212-817-1822	817-1561
National Sleep Foundation (NSF) 1522 K St NW Suite 500 *Web:* www.sleepfoundation.org	Washington	DC	20005	202-347-3471	347-3472
National Society of Genetic Counselors (NSGC) 401 N Michigan Ave *Web:* www.nsgc.org	Chicago	IL	60611	312-321-6834	673-6972
National Spinal Cord Injury Assn (NSCIA) 75-20 Astoria Blvd Suite 120 **Fax Area Code:* 866 ■ *TF:* 800-962-9629 ■ *Web:* www.spinalcord.org	Jackson Heights	NY	11370	718-512-0010	387-2197*
National Stroke Assn (NSA) 9707 E Easter Ln *TF Cust Svc:* 800-787-6537 ■ *Web:* www.stroke.org	Englewood	CO	80112	303-649-9299	649-1328
National Stuttering Assn (NSA) 119 W 40th St 14th Fl *TF:* 800-937-8888 ■ *Web:* www.nsastutter.org	New York	NY	10018	212-944-4050	944-8244
National Tay-Sachs & Allied Diseases Assn (NTSAD) 2001 Beacon St Suite 204 *TF:* 800-906-8723 ■ *Web:* www.ntsad.org	Brighton	MA	02135	617-277-4463	277-0134
National Vaccine Information Ctr (NVIC) 407 Church St Suite H *TF:* 800-909-7468 ■ *Web:* www.nvic.org	Vienna	VA	22180	703-938-0342	938-5768
National Wellness Institute (NWI) 1300 College Ct PO Box 827 *TF:* 800-243-8694 ■ *Web:* www.nationalwellness.org	Stevens Point	WI	54481	715-342-2969	342-2979
New West Health Services 130 Neill Ave *TF:* 888-500-3355 ■ *Web:* www.newwesthealth.com	Helena	MT	59601	406-457-2200	457-2299
NISH 8401 Old Courthouse Rd *Web:* www.nish.org	Vienna	VA	22182	703-560-6800	849-8916
North American Menopause Society The (NAMS) 5900 Landerbrook Dr Suite 390 *Web:* www.menopause.org	Mayfield Heights	OH	44124	440-442-7550	442-2660
Obesity Society 8630 Fenton St *TF:* 800-986-2373 ■ *Web:* www.obesity.org	Silver Spring	MD	20910	301-563-6526	563-6595
Oley Foundation 214 Hun Memorial MC-28 Albany Medical Ctr *TF:* 800-776-6539 ■ *Web:* www.oley.org	Albany	NY	12208	518-262-5079	262-5528
Oral Health America 410 N Michigan Ave Suite 352 *TF:* 800-523-3438 ■ *Web:* www.oralhealthamerica.org	Chicago	IL	60611	312-836-9900	836-9986

Phone | Fax

Paget Foundation for Paget's Disease of Bone & Related Disorders
120 Wall St Suite 1602 . . . New York NY 10005 212-509-5335 509-8492
TF: 800-237-2438 ■ *Web:* www.paget.org

Parkinson's Disease Foundation (PDF)
1359 Broadway . . . New York NY 10018 212-923-4700 923-4778
TF: 800-457-6676 ■ *Web:* www.pdf.org

Partnership for a Drug-Free America
405 Lexington Ave Suite 1601 . . . New York NY 10174 212-922-1560 922-1570
TF: 888-575-3115 ■ *Web:* www.drugfree.org

Pedorthic Footwear Assn (PFA)
2025 M St NW Suite 800 . . . Washington DC 20036 202-367-1145 367-2145
TF: 800-673-8447 ■ *Web:* www.pedorthics.org

Phoenix Society for Burn Survivors Inc
1835 RW Berends Dr SW . . . Grand Rapids MI 49519 616-458-2773 458-2831
TF: 800-888-2876 ■ *Web:* www.phoenix-society.org

Population Services International (PSI)
1120 19th St NW Suite 600 . . . Washington DC 20036 202-785-0072 785-0120
Web: www.psi.org

Postpartum Support International
PO Box 60931 . . . Santa Barbara CA 93160 800-944-4773 204-0635*
**Fax Area Code:* 323 ■ *TF:* 800-944-4773 ■ *Web:* www.postpartum.net

Prader-Willi Syndrome Assn (USA)
8588 Potter Pk Dr Suite 500 . . . Sarasota FL 34238 941-312-0400 312-0142
TF: 800-926-4797 ■ *Web:* www.pwsausa.org

Prevent Blindness America
211 W Wacker Dr Suite 1700 . . . Chicago IL 60606 312-363-6001 363-6052
TF: 800-331-2020 ■ *Web:* www.preventblindness.org

Prevent Cancer Foundation (PCF)
1600 Duke St Suite 500 . . . Alexandria VA 22314 703-836-4412 836-4413
TF: 800-227-2732 ■ *Web:* preventcancer.org

Program for Appropriate Technology in Health (PATH)
1455 NW Leary Way . . . Seattle WA 98107 206-285-3500 285-6619
Web: www.path.org

Project Inform 1375 Mission St . . . San Francisco CA 94103 415-558-8669 558-0684
Web: www.projinf.org

Public Health Institute 555 12th St 10th Fl . . . Oakland CA 94607 510-285-5500 285-5501
Web: www.phi.org

RA Bloch Cancer Foundation
1 H&R Block Way . . . Kansas City MO 64105 816-854-5050 854-8024
TF: 800-433-0464 ■ *Web:* www.blochcancer.org

Recording for the Blind & Dyslexic (RFB&D)
20 Roszel Rd . . . Princeton NJ 08540 609-452-0606 987-8116
TF: 800-221-4792 ■ *Web:* www.rfbd.org

Registry of Interpreters for the Deaf Inc (RID)
333 Commerce St . . . Alexandria VA 22314 703-838-0030 838-0454
Web: www.rid.org

Rehabilitation Engineering & Assistive Technology Society of North America (RESNA)
1700 N Moore St Suite 1540 . . . Arlington VA 22209 703-524-6686 524-6630
Web: www.resna.org

Research to Prevent Blindness Inc (RPB)
645 Madison Ave 21st Fl . . . New York NY 10022 212-752-4333 688-6231
TF: 800-621-0026 ■ *Web:* www.rpbusa.org

RESOLVE: National Infertility Assn
1760 Old Meadow Rd Suite 500 . . . McLean VA 22102 703-556-7172 506-3266
Web: www.resolve.org

Restless Legs Syndrome Foundation Inc
1610 14th St NW Suite 300 . . . Rochester MN 55901 507-287-6465 287-6312
TF: 877-463-6757 ■ *Web:* www.rls.org

Rocky Mountain Health Foundation
2775 Crossroads Blvd . . . Grand Junction CO 81506 970-248-5027 244-7880
Web: www.rmhp.org

Rolf Institute of Structural Integration
5055 Chaparral Ct Suite 103 . . . Boulder CO 80301 303-449-5903 449-5978
TF: 800-530-8875 ■ *Web:* www.rolf.org

RP International PO Box 900 . . . Woodland Hills CA 91365 818-992-0500 992-3265
Web: www.rpinternational.org

Scleroderma Foundation
300 Rosewood Dr Suite 105 . . . Danvers MA 01923 978-463-5843 463-5809
TF: 800-722-4673 ■ *Web:* www.scleroderma.org

Scoliosis Assn Inc 2500 N Military Trail . . . Boca Raton FL 33431 561-994-4435 994-2455
TF: 800-800-0669 ■ *Web:* www.scoliosis-assoc.org

Seventh-day Adventist Dietetic Assn (SDADA)
6100 Leoni Rd . . . Grizzly Flats CA 95636 530-626-3610 626-8524
Web: www.leonimeadowf.org

Sickle Cell Disease Assn of America (SCDAA)
231 E Baltimore St Suite 800 . . . Baltimore MD 21202 410-528-1555 528-1495
TF: 800-421-8453 ■ *Web:* www.sicklecelldisease.org

Simon Foundation for Incontinence
PO Box 815 . . . Wilmette IL 60091 847-864-3913 864-9758
TF: 800-237-4666 ■ *Web:* www.simonfoundation.org

Skin Cancer Foundation
149 Madison Ave Suite 901 . . . New York NY 10016 212-725-5176 725-5751
TF: 800-754-6490 ■ *Web:* www.skincancer.org

Society for Women's Health Research
1025 Connecticut Ave NW Suite 701 . . . Washington DC 20036 202-223-8224 833-3472
Web: www.womenshealthresearch.org

Spina Bifida Assn (SBAA)
4590 MacArthur Blvd NW Suite 250 . . . Washington DC 20007 202-944-3285 944-3295
TF: 800-621-3141 ■ *Web:* www.spinabifidaassociation.org

Starlight Starbright Children's Foundation
5757 Wilshire Blvd Suite M-100 . . . Los Angeles CA 90036 310-479-1212 479-1235
TF: 800-315-2580 ■ *Web:* www.starlight.org

Stuttering Foundation of America
3100 Walnut Grove Rd Suite 603 . . . Memphis TN 38111 901-452-7343 452-3931
TF: 800-992-9392 ■ *Web:* www.stuttersfa.org

Support Dogs Inc 11645 Lilburn Pk Rd . . . Saint Louis MO 63146 314-997-2325 997-7202
Web: www.supportdogs.org

Susan G Komen for the Cure
5005 LBJ Fwy Suite 250 . . . Dallas TX 75244 972-855-1600 855-4372
TF: 877-465-6636 ■ *Web:* www.ww5.komen.org

Phone | Fax

TASH 1001 Connecticut Ave NW Suite 235 . . . Washington DC 20005 202-540-9020 540-9019
Web: www.tash.org

TOPS Club Inc 4575 S 5th St . . . Milwaukee WI 53207 414-482-4620 482-1655
TF: 800-932-8677 ■ *Web:* www.tops.org

Touch for Health Kinesiology Assn
7121 New Light Trail . . . Chapel Hill NC 27516 919-969-0027
TF: 800-466-8342 ■ *Web:* www.tfhka.org

Tourette Syndrome Assn Inc
42-40 Bell Blvd Suite 205 . . . Bayside NY 11361 718-224-2999 279-9596
TF: 888-486-8738 ■ *Web:* www.tsa-usa.org

Trichotillomania Learning Center Inc (TLC)
207 McPherson St Suite H . . . Santa Cruz CA 95060 831-457-1004 426-4383
Web: www.trich.org

UCare Minnesota
500 Stinson Blvd NE PO Box 52 . . . Minneapolis MN 55413 612-676-6500 676-6501
TF: 866-457-7144 ■ *Web:* www.ucare.org

Undersea & Hyperbaric Medical Society (UHMS)
21 W Colony Pl Suite 280 . . . Durham NC 27705 919-490-5140 490-5140
TF: 877-533-8467 ■ *Web:* www.uhms.org

United Cerebral Palsy (UCP)
1660 L St NW Suite 700 . . . Washington DC 20036 202-776-0406 776-0414
TF: 800-872-5827 ■ *Web:* www.ucp.org

United Network for Organ Sharing (UNOS)
700 N 4th St . . . Richmond VA 23219 804-782-4800 782-4817
TF: 888-894-6361 ■ *Web:* www.unos.org

Vegan Action PO Box 4288 . . . Richmond VA 23220 804-502-8736
Web: www.vegan.org

Vegetarian Resource Group The (VRG)
PO Box 1463 . . . Baltimore MD 21203 410-366-8343 366-8804
Web: www.vrg.org

Virginia Hospital & Healthcare Assn (VHHA)
4200 Innslake Dr . . . Glen Allen VA 23060 804-965-1216 965-0475
Web: www.vhha.com

Vocational Evaluation & Career Assessment Professionals (VECAP)
5500 University Pkwy Rm CE-120 . . . San Bernardino CA 67402 909-537-3696 922-7580
Web: www.vecap.org

Voice of the Retarded (VOR)
836 S Arlington Heights Rd
Suite 351 . . . Elk Grove Village IL 60007 605-399-1624 399-1631
TF: 877-399-4867 ■ *Web:* www.vor.net

Washington Business Group on Health (WBGH)
50 F St NW Suite 600 . . . Washington DC 20001 202-628-9320 628-9244
Web: www.wbgh.org

Well Spouse Assn 63 W Main St Suite H . . . Freehold NJ 07728 732-577-8899 577-8644
TF: 800-838-0879 ■ *Web:* www.wellspouse.org

Women Alive 1566 Burnside Ave . . . Los Angeles CA 90019 323-965-1564 965-9886
TF: 800-554-4876 ■ *Web:* www.women-alive.org

Xeroderma Pigmentosum Society Inc (XPS)
437 Snydertown Rd . . . Craryville NY 12521 518-851-9490
Web: www.xps.org

48-18 Hobby Organizations

Phone | Fax

Academy of Model Aeronautics (AMA)
5161 E Memorial Dr . . . Muncie IN 47302 765-287-1256 289-4248
TF: 800-435-9262 ■ *Web:* www.modelaircraft.org

American Bonanza Society (ABS) 1922 Midfield Rd . . . Wichita KS 67206 316-945-1700 945-1710
Web: www.bonanza.org

American Contract Bridge League (ACBL)
6575 Windchase Blvd . . . Horn Lake MS 38637 662-253-3100 253-3187
TF Sales: 800-264-2743 ■ *Web:* www.acbl.org

American Craft Council 72 Spring St 6th Fl . . . New York NY 10012 212-274-0630 274-0650
TF: 800-836-3470 ■ *Web:* www.craftcouncil.org

American Federation of Astrologers (AFA)
6535 S Rural Rd . . . Tempe AZ 85283 480-838-1751 838-8293
TF: 888-301-7630 ■ *Web:* www.astrologers.com

American Horticultural Society (AHS)
7931 E Blvd Dr . . . Alexandria VA 22308 703-768-5700 768-8700
TF: 800-777-7931 ■ *Web:* www.ahs.org

American Kennel Club (AKC)
260 Madison Ave 4th Fl . . . New York NY 10016 212-696-8200 696-8299
Web: www.akc.org

American Philatelic Society (APS)
100 Match Factory Pl . . . Bellefonte PA 16823 814-933-3803 933-6128
Web: www.stamps.org

American Radio Relay League (ARRL)
225 Main St . . . Newington CT 06111 860-594-0200 594-0259
Web: www.arrl.org

American Rose Society (ARS)
8877 Jefferson Paige Rd . . . Shreveport LA 71119 318-938-5402 938-5405
TF: 800-637-6534 ■ *Web:* www.ars.org

American Stamp Dealers Assn Inc (ASDA)
217-14 Northern Blvd Suite 205 . . . Bayside NY 11361 718-224-2500 224-2501
Web: www.americanstampdealer.com

Antique Automobile Club of America (AACA)
501 W Governor Rd PO Box 417 . . . Hershey PA 17033 717-534-1910 534-9101
Web: www.aaca.org

Art & Creative Materials Institute Inc (ACMI)
1280 Main St PO Box 479 . . . Hanson MA 02341 781-293-4100 294-0808
Web: www.acminet.org

Barbershop Harmony Society 110 7th Ave N . . . Nashville TN 37203 615-823-3993 313-7619
TF: 800-876-7464 ■ *Web:* www.barbershop.org

BMW Motorcycle Owners of America
PO Box 3982 . . . Ellisville MO 63022 636-394-7277 391-1811
Web: www.bmwmoa.org

Craft & Hobby Assn (CHA) 319 E 54th St . . . Elmwood Park NJ 07407 201-835-1200 797-0657
TF: 800-822-0494 ■ *Web:* www.craftandhobby.org

	City	State	Zip	Phone	Fax
Embroiderers Guild of America (EGA) 426 W Jefferson St *Web:* www.egausa.org	Louisville	KY	40202	502-589-6956	584-7900
Experimental Aircraft Assn (EAA) 3000 Poberezny Rd *TF:* 800-236-4800 ■ *Web:* www.eaa.org	Oshkosh	WI	54902	920-426-4800	426-4828
Handweavers Guild of America (HGA) 1255 Hwy 23 NW # 211 *Web:* www.weavespindye.org	Suwanee	GA	30024	678-730-0010	730-0836
Knitting Guild of America The (TKGA) 1100-H Brandywine Blvd *Web:* www.tkga.com	Zanesville	OH	43701	740-452-4541	452-2552
National Craft Assn (NCA) 2012 Ridge Rd E Suite 120 *TF:* 800-715-9594 ■ *Web:* www.craftassoc.com	Rochester	NY	14622	585-266-5472	785-3231
National Garden Clubs Inc (NGC) 4401 Magnolia Ave *TF:* 800-550-6007 ■ *Web:* www.gardenclub.org	Saint Louis	MO	63110	314-776-7574	776-5108
National Gardening Assn (NGA) 1100 Dorset St *TF:* 800-538-7476 ■ *Web:* www.garden.org	South Burlington	VT	05403	802-863-5251	864-6889
National Genealogical Society (NGS) 3108 Columbia Pike Suite 300 *TF:* 800-473-0060 ■ *Web:* www.ngsgenealogy.org	Arlington	VA	22204	703-525-0050	525-0052
National Model Railroad Assn (NMRA) 4121 Cromwell Rd *Web:* www.nmra.org	Chattanooga	TN	37421	423-892-2846	899-4869
National NeedleArts Assn (TNNA) 1100-H Brandywine Blvd *TF:* 800-889-8662 ■ *Web:* www.netforum.avectra.com	Zanesville	OH	43701	740-455-6773	452-2552
National Scrabble Assn 403 Front St PO Box 700 *Web:* www2.scrabble-assoc.com	Greenport	NY	11944	631-477-0033	
National Wood Carvers Assn (NWCA) 7424 Miami Ave	Cincinnati	OH	45243	513-561-9051	
Philatelic Foundation 70 W 40th St 15th Fl *Web:* www.philatelicfoundation.org	New York	NY	10018	212-221-6555	221-6208
Society of Decorative Painters 393 N McLean Blvd *Web:* www.decorativepainters.org	Wichita	KS	67203	316-269-9300	269-9191
Sports Car Club of America (SCCA) 6700 SW Topeka Blvd # 300 *TF:* 800-770-2055 ■ *Web:* www.scca.com	Topeka	KS	66619	785-357-7222	232-7228
Sweet Adelines International 9110 S Toledo Ave *TF:* 800-992-7464 ■ *Web:* www.sweetadelineintl.org	Tulsa	OK	74137	918-622-1444	665-0894
US Chess Federation (USCF) PO Box 3967 *TF:* 800-903-8723 ■ *Web:* www.uschess.org	Crossville	TN	38557	931-787-1234	787-1200
World Pen Pals PO Box 337 *Web:* www.world-pen-pals.com	Saugerties	NY	12477	845-246-7828	246-7828

48-19 Military, Veterans, Patriotic Organizations

	City	State	Zip	Phone	Fax
Air Force Assn (AFA) 1501 Lee Hwy 4th Fl *TF:* 800-727-3337 ■ *Web:* www.afa.org	Arlington	VA	22209	703-247-5800	247-5853
Air Force Sergeants Assn (AFSA) 5211 Auth Rd *TF:* 800-638-0594 ■ *Web:* www.afsahq.org	Suitland	MD	20746	301-899-3500	899-8136
Alpha-66 2250 SW 8th St *Web:* www.alpha66.org	Miami	FL	33135	305-541-5433	541-2252
American Legion Auxiliary 8945 N Meridian St 2nd Fl *Web:* www.alaforveterans.org	Indianapolis	IN	46260	317-569-4500	569-4502
American Legion The 700 N Pennsylvania St *TF Cust Svc:* 800-433-3318 ■ *Web:* www.legion.org	Indianapolis	IN	46204	317-630-1200	630-1223
American Logistics Assn (ALA) 1133 15th St NW Suite 640 *Web:* www.ala-national.org	Washington	DC	20005	202-466-2520	296-4419
American Society of Military Comptrollers (ASMC) 415 N Alfred St *TF:* 800-462-5637 ■ *Web:* www.asmconline.org	Alexandria	VA	22314	703-549-0360	549-3181
AMVETS 4647 Forbes Blvd *TF:* 877-726-8387 ■ *Web:* www.amvets.org	Lanham	MD	20706	301-459-9600	459-7924
Armed Forces Communications & Electronics Assn (AFCEA) 4400 Fair Lakes Ct *TF:* 800-336-4583 ■ *Web:* www.afcea.org	Fairfax	VA	22033	703-631-6100	631-4693
Armed Services Mutual Benefit Assn (ASMBA) PO Box 160384 *TF:* 800-251-8434 ■ *Web:* www.asmba.com	Nashville	TN	37216	615-851-0800	851-9484
Army Aviation Assn of America (AAAA) 755 Main St Suite 4D *Web:* www.quad-a.org	Monroe	CT	06468	203-268-2450	268-5870
Army Distaff Foundation 6200 Oregon Ave NW *TF:* 800-541-4255 ■ *Web:* www.armydistaff.org	Washington	DC	20015	202-541-0105	541-0128
Assn of Civilian Technicians (ACT) 12620 Lake Ridge Dr *Web:* www.actnat.com	Woodbridge	VA	22192	703-494-4845	494-0961
Assn of Old Crows (AOC) 1000 N Payne St Suite 300 *TF:* 888-653-2769 ■ *Web:* www.crows.org	Alexandria	VA	22314	703-549-1600	549-2589
Assn of the US Army (AUSA) 2425 Wilson Blvd *TF:* 800-336-4570 ■ *Web:* www.ausa.org	Arlington	VA	22201	703-841-4300	525-9039
Delta Phi Epsilon Professional Foreign Service Fraternity Inc PO Box 25401 *Web:* www.deltaphiepsilon.net/National_Fraternity.html	Washington	DC	20027	202-337-7116	
Disabled American Veterans (DAV) 3725 Alexandria Pike *TF:* 877-426-2838 ■ *Web:* www.dav.org	Cold Spring	KY	41076	859-441-7300	441-1416
Enlisted Assn of the National Guard of the US (EANGUS) 3133 Mt Vernon Ave *TF:* 800-234-3264 ■ *Web:* www.memberconnections.com	Alexandria	VA	22305	703-519-3846	519-3849
Fleet Reserve Assn (FRA) 125 N W St *TF:* 800-372-1924 ■ *Web:* www.fra.org	Alexandria	VA	22314	703-683-1400	549-6610
Marine Corps Assn (MCA) PO Box 1775 *TF:* 800-336-0291 ■ *Web:* www.mca-marines.org	Quantico	VA	22134	703-640-6161	640-0823
Marine Corps League (MCL) PO Box 3070 *TF:* 800-625-1775 ■ *Web:* www.mcleague.org	Merrifield	VA	22116	703-207-9588	207-0047
Marine Corps Reserve Assn (MCRA) 8626 Lee Hwy Suite 205 *Web:* www.usmcra.org	Fairfax	VA	22031	703-289-1204	289-1206
Military Benefit Assn (MBA) 14605 Avion Pkwy PO Box 221110 *TF:* 800-336-0100 ■ *Web:* www.militarybenefit.org	Chantilly	VA	20153	703-968-6200	968-6423
Military Officers Assn of America (MOAA) 201 N Washington St *TF:* 800-234-6622 ■ *Web:* www.moaa.org	Alexandria	VA	22314	703-549-2311	838-8173
NA for Uniformed Services (NAUS) 5535 Hempstead Way *TF:* 800-842-3451 ■ *Web:* www.naus.org	Springfield	VA	22151	703-750-1342	354-4380
National Committee for Employer Support of the Guard & Reserve (ESGR) 1555 Wilson Blvd Suite 200 *TF:* 800-336-4590 ■ *Web:* www.esgr.org	Arlington	VA	22209	703-696-1386	696-1411
National Defense Industrial Assn (NDIA) 2111 Wilson Blvd Suite 400 *Web:* www.ndia.org	Arlington	VA	22201	703-522-1820	522-1885
National Fallen Firefighters Foundation PO Box 498 *Web:* www.firehero.org	Emmitsburg	MD	21727	301-447-1365	447-1645
National Guard Assn of the US (NGAUS) 1 Massachusetts Ave NW Suite 200 *TF:* 888-226-4287 ■ *Web:* www.ngaus.org	Washington	DC	20001	202-789-0031	682-9358
National League of Families of American Prisoners & Missing in Southeast Asia 1005 N Glebe Rd Suite 170 *Web:* www.pow-miafamilies.org	Arlington	VA	22201	703-465-7432	465-7433
National Society Daughters of the American Revolution (DAR) 1776 D St NW *Web:* www.dar.org	Washington	DC	20006	202-628-1776	879-3252
National Society of the Sons of the American Revolution (NSSAR) 1000 S 4th St *Web:* www.sar.org	Louisville	KY	40203	502-589-1776	589-1671
Naval Enlisted Reserve Assn (NERA) 6703 Farragut Ave *TF:* 800-776-9020 ■ *Web:* www.nera.org	Falls Church	VA	22042	703-534-1329	534-3617
Naval Reserve Assn (NRA) 1619 King St **Fax Area Code:* 866 ■ *TF:* 866-628-9411 ■ *Web:* www.navy-reserve.org	Alexandria	VA	22314	703-548-5800	683-3647*
Navy League of the US 2300 Wilson Blvd *TF:* 800-356-5760 ■ *Web:* www.navyleague.org	Arlington	VA	22201	703-528-1775	528-2333
Navy-Marine Corps Relief Society (NMCRS) 875 N Randolph St Suite 225 *TF:* 800-654-8364 ■ *Web:* www.nmcrs.org	Arlington	VA	22203	703-696-4904	696-0144
Non Commissioned Officers Assn (NCOA) 9330 Corporate Dr Suite 701 *TF:* 800-662-2620 ■ *Web:* www.ncoausa.org	Selma	TX	78154	210-653-6161	637-3337
Paralyzed Veterans of America (PVA) 801 18th St NW **Fax:* PR ■ *TF:* 800-424-8200 ■ *Web:* www.pva.org	Washington	DC	20006	202-872-1300	416-7641*
Reserve Officers Assn of the US (ROA) 1 Constitution Ave NE *TF:* 800-809-9448 ■ *Web:* www.roa.org	Washington	DC	20002	202-479-2200	547-1641
Retired Enlisted Assn (TREA) 15821 E Centre Tech Cir *Web:* www.trea.org	Aurora	CO	80011	303-340-3939	340-4516
Society of American Military Engineers (SAME) 607 Prince St *TF:* 800-336-3097 ■ *Web:* www.same.org	Alexandria	VA	22314	703-549-3800	684-0231
Society of Military Widows (SMW) 5535 Hempstead Way *TF:* 800-842-3451 ■ *Web:* www.militarywidows.org	Springfield	VA	22151	703-750-1342	354-4380
Tailhook Assn 9696 Businesspark Ave *TF:* 800-322-4665 ■ *Web:* www.tailhook.org	San Diego	CA	92131	858-689-9223	578-8839
United Service Organizations (USO) 2111 Wilson Blvd Suite 1200 *Web:* www.uso.org	Arlington	VA	22201	703-908-6400	908-6401
US Coast Guard Chief Petty Officers Assn 5520-G Hempstead Way *Web:* www.uscgcpoa.org	Springfield	VA	22151	703-941-0395	941-0397
US Naval Institute 291 Wood Rd *TF:* 800-233-8764 ■ *Web:* www.usni.org	Annapolis	MD	21402	410-268-6110	295-1084
Veterans for Peace Inc (VFP) 216 S Meramec Ave *Web:* www.veteransforpeace.org	Saint Louis	MO	63105	314-725-6005	725-7103
Veterans of Foreign Wars of the US (VFW) 406 W 34th St *TF:* 800-963-3180 ■ *Web:* www.vfw.org	Kansas City	MO	64111	816-756-3390	968-1149
Vietnam Veterans of America (VVA) 8605 Cameron St Suite 400 *TF:* 800-882-1316 ■ *Web:* www.vva.org	Silver Spring	MD	20910	301-585-4000	585-0519
Women in Military Service for America Memorial Foundation Inc Dept 560 *TF:* 800-222-2294 ■ *Web:* www.womensmemorial.org	Washington	DC	20042	703-533-1155	931-4208

48-20 Religious Organizations

Organization	City	State	Zip	Phone	Fax
92nd St Young Men's & Young Women's Hebrew Assn 1395 Lexington Ave; *Web:* www.92y.org	New York	NY	10128	212-415-5500	415-5788
American Academy of Religion (AAR) 825 Houston Mill Rd NE Suite 300; *Web:* www.aarweb.org	Atlanta	GA	30329	404-727-3049	727-7959
American Baptist Assn (ABA) 4605 N State Line Ave.; *TF:* 800-264-2482 ■ *Web:* www.abaptist.org	Texarkana	TX	75503	903-792-2783	792-8128
American Baptist Churches USA PO Box 851; *TF:* 800-222-3872 ■ *Web:* www.abc-usa.org	Valley Forge	PA	19482	610-768-2000	768-2275
American Council of Christian Churches (ACCC) PO Box 5455; *Web:* www.amcouncilcc.org	Bethlehem	PA	18015	610-865-3009	865-3033
American Theological Library Assn (ATLA) 300 S Wacker Dr Suite 2100; *TF:* 888-665-2852 ■ *Web:* www.atla.com	Chicago	IL	60606	312-454-5100	454-5505
American Tract Society (ATS) 325 Gold St Suite 104; *TF:* 800-548-7228 ■ *Web:* www.atstracts.org	Garland	TX	75040	972-276-9408	272-9642
Antiochian Orthodox Christian Archdiocese of North America 358 Mountain Rd; *Web:* www.antiochian.org	Englewood	NJ	07631	201-871-1355	871-7954
Apostolic Assembly of The Faith In Christ Jesus 10807 Laurel St; *Web:* www.apostolicassembly.org	Rancho Cucamonga	CA	91730	909-987-3013	481-5691
Armenian Church of America 630 2nd Ave; *Web:* www.armenianchurch.org	New York	NY	10016	212-686-0710	779-3558
Assemblies of God (A/G) 1445 N Boonville Ave; *TF:* 800-641-4310 ■ *Web:* www.ag.org	Springfield	MO	65802	417-862-2781	862-8558
Assn of Professional Chaplains (APC) 1701 E Woodfield Rd Suite 400; *Web:* www.professionalchaplains.org	Schaumburg	IL	60173	847-240-1014	240-1015
Avant Ministries 10000 N Oak Trafficway; *TF:* 800-468-1892 ■ *Web:* www.avantministries.org	Kansas City	MO	64155	816-734-8500	734-4601
B'nai B'rith International 2020 K St NW 7th Fl; *TF:* 888-388-4224 ■ *Web:* www.bnaibrith.org	Washington	DC	20006	202-857-6600	857-6609
B'nai B'rith Youth Organization (BBYO) 2020 K St NW; *Web:* www.bbyo.org	Washington	DC	20006	202-857-6633	857-6568
Baptist Bible Fellowship International (BBFI) 720 E Kearney St; *Web:* www.bbfi.org	Springfield	MO	65803	417-862-5001	865-0794
Baptist Mid-Missions 7749 Webster Rd; *Web:* www.bmm.org	Cleveland	OH	44130	440-826-3930	826-4457
Baptist Missionary Assn of America (BMA) 9219 Sibley Hole Rd PO Box 30910; *Web:* www.bmaamissions.org	Little Rock	AR	72209	501-455-4977	455-3636
Baptist World Alliance 405 N Washington St; *Web:* www.bwanet.org	Falls Church	VA	22046	703-790-8980	790-5719
Bible League PO Box 28000; *TF:* 866-825-4636 ■ *Web:* www.bibleleague.org	Chicago	IL	60628	708-367-8500	367-8600
Billy Graham Evangelistic Assn 1 Billy Graham Pkwy PO Box 1270; *TF:* 877-247-2426 ■ *Web:* www.billygraham.org	Charlotte	NC	28201	704-401-2432	401-2140
Buddhist Churches of America (BCA) 1710 Octavia St; *Web:* www.bcahq.org	San Francisco	CA	94109	415-776-5600	771-6293
California Southern Baptist Convention 678 E Shaw Ave; *TF:* 888-462-7729 ■ *Web:* www.csbc.com	Fresno	CA	93710	559-229-9533	229-2824
California-Pacific Annual Conference of the United Methodist Church PO Box 6006; *TF:* 800-244-8622 ■ *Web:* www.cal-pac.org	Pasadena	CA	91102	626-568-7300	796-7297
Calvary Chapel of Costa Mesa Inc 3800 S Fairview St; *Web:* www.calvarychapelcostamesa.com	Santa Ana	CA	92704	714-979-4422	
Campus Crusade for Christ International 100 Lake Hart Dr.; *TF:* 877-924-7478 ■ *Web:* www.ccci.org	Orlando	FL	32832	407-826-2000	
Canon Law Society of America (CLSA) 3025 4th St NE Suite 111; *Web:* www.clsa.org	Washington	DC	20017	202-832-2350	832-2331
Catholic Biblical Assn of America 433 Caldwell Hall; *Web:* www.studentorg.cua.edu/cbib	Washington	DC	20064	202-319-5519	319-4799
Catholic Church Extension Society of the USA 150 S Wacker Dr 20th Fl; *TF:* 800-842-7804 ■ *Web:* www.catholicextension.org	Chicago	IL	60606	312-236-7240	236-5276
Central Conference of American Rabbis (CCAR) 355 Lexington Ave 18th Fl; *TF:* 800-935-2227 ■ *Web:* www.ccarnet.org	New York	NY	10017	212-972-3636	692-0819
Christian & Missionary Alliance 8595 Explorer Dr; *TF:* 877-248-3762 ■ *Web:* www.cmalliance.org	Colorado Springs	CO	80920	719-599-5999	
Christian Aid Ministries PO Box 360	Berlin	OH	44610	330-893-2428	893-2305
Christian Church (Disciples of Christ) 130 E Washington St; *Web:* www.disciples.org	Indianapolis	IN	46204	317-635-3100	635-3700
Christian Reformed Church in North America (CRC) 2850 Kalamazoo Ave SE; *TF:* 800-272-5125 ■ *Web:* www.crcna.org	Grand Rapids	MI	49560	616-241-1691	224-0834
Christophers The 5 Hanover Sq 11th Fl; *TF:* 888-298-4050 ■ *Web:* www.christophers.org	New York	NY	10004	212-759-4050	838-5073
Church of God in Christ Inc 930 Mason St.; *Web:* www.cogic.org	Memphis	TN	38126	901-947-9300	947-9359
Church of God Ministries 1201 E 5th St; *TF:* 800-848-2464 ■ *Web:* www.chog.org	Anderson	IN	46012	765-642-0256	642-5652
Church of God World Missions (COGWM) 2490 Keith St PO Box 8016; *TF:* 800-345-7492 ■ *Web:* www.cogwm.org	Cleveland	TN	37320	423-478-7190	478-7155
Church of Jesus Christ of Latter-Day Saints 50 E N Temple St; *Web:* www.lds.org	Salt Lake City	UT	84150	801-240-1000	240-2033
Church of the Brethren 1451 Dundee Ave.; *TF:* 800-323-8039 ■ *Web:* www.brethren.org	Elgin	IL	60120	847-742-5100	742-1407
Church of the Nazarene 17001 Prairie Star Pkwy; *Web:* www.nazarene.org	Lenexa	KS	66220	913-577-0500	
Church Women United (CWU) 475 Riverside Dr Rm 1626; *TF:* 800-298-5551 ■ *Web:* www.churchwomen.org	New York	NY	10115	212-870-2347	870-2338
Community of Christ 1001 W Walnut St; **Fax:* Hum Res ■ *TF:* 800-825-2806 ■ *Web:* www.cofchrist.org	Independence	MO	64050	816-833-1000	521-3085*
Connecting Businessmen to Christ (CBMC) 5746 Marlin Rd Suite 602 Osborne Ctr.; *TF:* 800-575-2262 ■ *Web:* www.cbmc.com	Chattanooga	TN	37411	423-698-4444	629-4434
Coral Ridge Presbyterian Church Inc 5555 N Federal Hwy; *Web:* www.crpc.org	Fort Lauderdale	FL	33308	954-771-8840	
Diocese of Greensburg 723 E Pittsburgh St; *TF:* 866-409-6455 ■ *Web:* www.dioceseofgreensburg.org	Greensburg	PA	15601	724-837-0901	
Diocese of Metuchen PO Box 191; *Web:* www.diometuchen.org	Metuchen	NJ	08840	732-562-1990	
Diocese of St. Augustine Inc 11625 Old St Augustine; *TF:* 800-775-4659 ■ *Web:* www.dosafl.com	Jacksonville	FL	32258	904-262-3200	
Episcopal Church USA 815 2nd Ave; *TF:* 800-334-7626 ■ *Web:* www.episcopalchurch.org	New York	NY	10017	212-716-6000	867-0395
Evangelical Church Alliance (ECA) 205 W Broadway St PO Box 9; *TF:* 888-855-6060 ■ *Web:* www.ecainternational.org	Bradley	IL	60915	815-937-0720	937-0720
Evangelical Covenant Church Inc The 5101 N Francisco Ave.; *TF:* 888-373-7888 ■ *Web:* www.covchurch.org	Chicago	IL	60625	773-784-3000	
Evangelical Fellowship of Canada (EFC) 600 Alden Rd Suite 300, Markham Industrial Pk PO Box 3745; *TF:* 866-302-3362 ■ *Web:* www.evangelicalfellowship.ca	Markham	ON	L3R0Y4	905-479-5885	479-4742
Evangelical Lutheran Church in America (ELCA) 8765 W Higgins Rd; *TF:* 800-638-3522 ■ *Web:* www.elca.org	Chicago	IL	60631	773-380-2700	380-1465
Evangelical Training Assn (ETA) PO Box 237; *TF:* 800-369-8291 ■ *Web:* www.etaworld.org	Wheaton	IL	60187	630-384-6920	384-6927
First Baptist Church Dallas 1707 San Jacinto St; *Web:* www.firstdallas.org	Dallas	TX	75201	214-969-0111	
First Baptist Church of Orlando Inc The 3000 S John Young Pkwy.; *TF:* 800-356-8904 ■ *Web:* www.firstorlando.com	Orlando	FL	32805	407-425-2555	425-2954
First Church of Christ Scientist 210 Massachusetts Ave; *Web:* www.christianscience.com	Boston	MA	02115	617-450-2000	
Franciscan Sisters of Chicago Inc 1055 175th St Suite 202; *TF:* 800-524-6126 ■ *Web:* www.franciscancommunities.com	Homewood	IL	60430	708-647-6500	
General Assn of Regular Baptist Churches (GARBC) 1300 N Meacham Rd; *TF:* 888-588-1600 ■ *Web:* www.garbcinternational.org	Schaumburg	IL	60173	847-585-0816	843-3757
Greek Orthodox Archdiocese of America 8 E 79th St; *Web:* www.goarch.org	New York	NY	10021	212-570-3500	570-3569
Hadassah Women's Zionist Organization of America Inc 50 W 58th St.; *TF:* 888-303-3640 ■ *Web:* www.hadassah.org	New York	NY	10019	212-355-7900	303-8282
IFCA International 3520 Fairlane Ave SW; *TF:* 800-347-1840 ■ *Web:* www.ifca.org	Grandville	MI	49418	616-531-1840	531-1814
International Bible Society (IBS) *Biblica* 1820 Jet Stream Dr; *TF Cust Svc:* 800-524-1588 ■ *Web:* www.biblica.com	Colorado Springs	CO	80921	719-488-9200	867-2870
International Centers for Spiritual Living 901 E 2nd Ave Suite 301; *TF:* 800-662-1348 ■ *Web:* www.rsintl.org	Spokane	WA	99202	509-624-7000	624-9322
International Church of the Foursquare Gospel (ICFG) 1910 W Sunset Blvd PO Box 26902; *TF:* 888-635-4234 ■ *Web:* www.foursquare.org	Los Angeles	CA	90026	213-989-4234	989-4590
International Pentecostal Holiness Church (IPHC) PO Box 12609; *Web:* www.iphc.org	Oklahoma City	OK	73157	405-787-7110	789-3957

Organization	City	State	Zip	Phone	Fax
InterVarsity Christian Fellowship/USA 6400 Schroeder Rd *TF:* 866-734-4823 ■ *Web:* www.intervarsity.org	Madison	WI	53711	608-274-9001	274-7882
Jewish Community Centers Assn of North America 520 8th Ave *Web:* www.jcca.org	New York	NY	10018	212-532-4949	481-4174
Jewish National Fund (JNF) 42 E 69th St *TF:* 800-542-8733 ■ *Web:* www.jnf.org	New York	NY	10021	212-879-9300	
Jewish Reconstructionist Federation (JRF) 101 Greenwood Ave Suite 430 *Web:* www.jrf.org	Jenkintown	PA	19046	215-885-5601	885-5603
Jewish United Fund/Jewish Federation of Metropolitan Chicago (JUF) 30 S Wells St *TF:* 888-346-6700 ■ *Web:* www.juf.org	Chicago	IL	60606	312-346-6700	444-2086
Jews for Jesus 60 Haight St *TF:* 800-366-5521 ■ *Web:* www.jewsforjesus.org	San Francisco	CA	94102	415-864-2600	552-8325
Jimmy Swaggart Ministries (JSM) 8919 World Ministry Blvd PO Box 262550 *TF Orders:* 800-288-8350 ■ *Web:* www.jsm.org	Baton Rouge	LA	70810	225-768-8300	769-2244
King Benevolent Fund Inc 1119 Commonwealth Ave *TF:* 800-321-9234 ■ *Web:* www.kingswaycharities.org	Bristol	VA	24201	276-466-3014	466-0955
Lutheran Church Missouri Synod (LCMS) 1333 S Kirkwood Rd *TF:* 888-843-5267 ■ *Web:* www.lcms.org	Saint Louis	MO	63122	314-965-9000	996-1016
Lutheran Hour Ministries 660 Mason Ridge Ctr **Fax:* Hum Res ■ *TF:* 800-876-9880 ■ *Web:* www.lhm.org	Saint Louis	MO	63141	314-317-4100	317-4291*
Lutheran Social Services of The South Inc (LSS) 8305 Cross Pk Dr PO Box 140767 *TF:* 800-938-5777 ■ *Web:* www.lsss.org	Austin	TX	78754	512-459-1000	467-2746
Mission Aviation Fellowship (MAF) 112 N Pilatus Ln *TF:* 800-359-7623 ■ *Web:* www.maf.org	Nampa	ID	83687	208-498-0800	498-0801
NA of Congregational Christian Churches (NACCC) 8473 S Howell Ave *TF:* 800-262-1620 ■ *Web:* www.naccc.org	Oak Creek	WI	53154	414-764-1620	764-0319
NA of Evangelicals (NAE) 701 G St SW *Web:* www.nae.net	Washington	DC	20024	202-789-1011	842-0392
NA of Free Will Baptists (NAFWB) 5233 Mt View Rd *TF:* 877-767-7659 ■ *Web:* www.nafwb.org	Antioch	TN	37013	615-731-6812	731-0771
Nation of Islam 7351 S Stony Island *Web:* www.noi.org	Chicago	IL	60649	773-324-6000	324-6309
National Baptist Convention of America Inc 777 SRL Thornton Fwy *Web:* www.nbcainc.com	Dallas	TX	75203	214-942-3311	942-4696
National Baptist Convention USA Inc 1700 Baptist World Ctr Dr *TF:* 866-531-3054 ■ *Web:* www.nationalbaptist.com	Nashville	TN	37207	615-228-6292	262-3917
National Conference on Ministry to the Armed Forces (NCMAF) 7724 Silver Sage Ct *Web:* www.ncmaf.org	Springfield	VA	22153	703-608-2100	
National Council of the Churches of Christ in the USA (NCCCUSA) 475 Riverside Dr Suite 880 *Web:* www.ncccusa.org	New York	NY	10115	212-870-2227	870-2030
National Spiritual Assembly of the Baha'is of the US 1233 Central St *Web:* www.bahai.us	Evanston	IL	60201	847-869-9039	869-0247
Navigators The PO Box 6000 *TF:* 866-568-7827 ■ *Web:* www.navigators.org	Colorado Springs	CO	80934	719-598-1212	260-0479
New Hampshire Catholic Charities Inc 215 Myrtle St PO Box 686 *TF:* 800-562-5249 ■ *Web:* www.nh-cc.org	Manchester	NH	03104	603-669-3030	626-1252
New Life Christian Fellowship 2701 Hodges Blvd *Web:* www.televisiontrucks.com	Jacksonville	FL	32224	904-223-6000	223-8400
New Tribes Mission (NTM) 1000 E 1st St *TF:* 800-321-5375 ■ *Web:* www.usa.ntm.org	Sanford	FL	32771	407-323-3430	
North American Christian Convention (NACC) 110 Boggs Ln Suite 330 *Web:* www.2011.gotonacc.org	Cincinnati	OH	45246	513-772-9970	772-9980
Orthodox Union (OU) 11 Broadway *Web:* www.ou.org	New York	NY	10004	212-563-4000	564-9058
Pioneers 10123 William Carey Dr *Web:* www.pioneers.org	Orlando	FL	32832	407-382-6000	382-1008
Potomac Conference Corp of Seventh Day Adventists 606 Greenville Ave *TF:* 800-732-1844 ■ *Web:* www.pcsda.org	Staunton	VA	24401	540-886-0771	886-5734
Presbyterian Church (USA) 100 Witherspoon St *TF:* 888-728-7228 ■ *Web:* www.pcusa.org	Louisville	KY	40202	502-569-5000	569-5018
Presbyterian Church in America (PCA) 1700 N Brown Rd Suite 105 *Web:* www.pcanet.org	Lawrenceville	GA	30043	678-825-1000	825-1001
Progressive National Baptist Convention Inc (PNBC) 601 50th St NE *TF:* 800-876-7622 ■ *Web:* www.pnbc.org	Washington	DC	20019	202-396-0558	398-4998
Promise Keepers (PK) PO Box 11798 *TF:* 866-776-6473 ■ *Web:* www.promisekeepers.org	Denver	CO	80211	303-964-7600	433-1036
Rabbinical Assembly 3080 Broadway *Web:* www.rabbinicalassembly.org	New York	NY	10027	212-280-6000	
Reconstructionist Rabbinical Assn (RRA) 1299 Church Rd *Web:* www.therra.org	Wyncote	PA	19095	215-576-5210	576-8051
Reformed Church in America 475 Riverside Dr 18th Fl *TF:* 800-722-9977 ■ *Web:* www.rca.org	New York	NY	10115	212-870-3071	870-2499
Salvation Army 6528 Little River Tpke *TF:* 800-725-2769 ■ *Web:* www.salvationarmyusa.org	Alexandria	VA	22312	703-642-9270	642-3556
Seat of the Soul Foundation PO Box 3310 *TF:* 888-440-7685 ■ *Web:* www.seatofthesoul.org	Ashland	OR	97520	541-482-1515	482-9176
Seventh-day Adventist World Church 12501 Old Columbia Pike *Web:* www.adventist.org	Silver Spring	MD	20904	301-680-6000	680-6090
Sim USA Inc PO Box 7900 *TF:* 800-521-6449 ■ *Web:* www.simusa.org	Charlotte	NC	28241	704-588-4300	587-1518
Society of Biblical Literature (SBL) The Luce Ctr 825 Houston Mill Rd *TF:* 866-727-9955 ■ *Web:* www.sbl-site.org	Atlanta	GA	30329	404-727-3100	727-3101
Southern Baptist Convention (SBC) 901 Commerce St *Web:* www.sbc.net	Nashville	TN	37203	615-244-2355	742-8919
Standing Conference of Canonical Orthodox Bishops in the Americas 8 E 79th St **Fax Area Code:* 325 ■ *Web:* www.scoba.us	New York	NY	10021	212-774-0506	646-6804*
Traditional Values Coalition (TVC) 139 C St SE *Web:* www.traditionalvalues.org	Washington	DC	20003	202-547-8570	546-6403
Union for Reformed Judaism 633 3rd Ave *Web:* www.urj.org	New York	NY	10017	212-650-4000	650-4159
Union of Orthodox Rabbis of the US & Canada 235 E Broadway	New York	NY	10002	212-964-6337	
Unitarian Universalist Assn (UUA) 25 Beacon St *Web:* www.uua.org	Boston	MA	02108	617-742-2100	367-3237
United Church of Christ (UCC) 700 Prospect Ave *TF:* 866-822-8224 ■ *Web:* www.ucc.org	Cleveland	OH	44115	216-736-2100	736-2103
United Pentecostal Church International (UPCI) 8855 Dunn Rd *Web:* www.upci.org	Hazelwood	MO	63042	314-837-7300	837-4503
United Synagogue of Conservative Judaism (USCJ) 155 5th Ave	New York	NY	10010	212-533-7800	353-9439
Urban Alternative PO Box 4000 *TF:* 800-800-3222 ■ *Web:* www.tonyevans.org	Dallas	TX	75208	214-943-3868	943-2632
US Conference of Catholic Bishops (USCCB) 3211 4th St NE *Web:* www.usccb.org	Washington	DC	20017	202-541-3000	541-3322
US National Committee to the International Dairy Federation PO Box 930398 *Web:* www.usnac.org	Verona	WI	53593	608-848-6455	848-7675
Watchtower Bible & Tract Society 25 Columbia Heights *Web:* www.watchtower.org	Brooklyn	NY	11201	718-560-5000	560-7300
Wheat Ridge Ministries 1 Pierce Pl Suite 250E *TF:* 800-762-6748 ■ *Web:* www.wheatridge.org	Itasca	IL	60143	630-766-9066	766-9622
Wider Church Ministries 700 Prospect Ave 7th Fl *TF:* 866-822-8224 ■ *Web:* www.ucc.org	Cleveland	OH	44115	216-736-3200	736-3203
Wisconsin Evangelical Lutheran Synod (WELS) 2929 N Mayfair Rd *Web:* www.wels.net	Milwaukee	WI	53222	414-256-3888	256-3899
Woman's Missionary Union (WMU) 100 Missionary Ridge *TF:* 800-968-7301 ■ *Web:* www.wmu.com	Birmingham	AL	35242	205-991-8100	991-4990
World Gospel Mission (WGM) 3783 E State Rd 18 PO Box 948 *TF:* 888-214-2651 ■ *Web:* www.wgm.org	Marion	IN	46952	765-664-7331	671-7230
World Methodist Council PO Box 518 *Web:* www.worldmethodistcouncil.org	Lake Junaluska	NC	28745	828-456-9432	456-9433
WorldVenture 1501 W Mineral Ave *TF:* 800-487-4224 ■ *Web:* www.worldventure.com	Littleton	CO	80120	720-283-2000	283-9383
Wycliffe Bible Translators 11221 John Wycliffe Blvd *TF:* 800-992-5433 ■ *Web:* www.wycliffe.org	Orlando	FL	32832	407-852-3600	852-3601
Youth for Christ/USA 7670 S Vaughn Ct *TF:* 800-735-3252	Englewood	CO	80112	303-843-9000	843-9002

48-21 Self-Help Organizations

Organization	City	State	Zip	Phone	Fax
Adult Children of Alcoholics World Service Organization Inc (ACAWSO) PO Box 3216 *Web:* www.adultchildren.org	Torrance	CA	90510	562-595-7831	
Agoraphobics Bldg Independent Lives Inc 3212 Cutshaw Ave Suite 315 *Web:* www.anxietysupport.org	Richmond	VA	23230	804-257-5591	353-3687
Al-Anon Family Group Inc 1600 Corporate Landing Pkwy *TF:* 888-425-2666 ■ *Web:* www.al-anon.org	Virginia Beach	VA	23454	757-563-1600	563-1655

Organization	City	State	ZIP	Phone	Fax
Alateen 1600 Corporate Landing Pkwy *TF:* 888-425-2666 ■ *Web:* www.alateen.org	Virginia Beach	VA	23454	757-563-1600	563-1655
Alcoholics Anonymous (AA) 475 Riverside Dr 11th Fl *Web:* www.aa.org	New York	NY	10115	212-870-3400	870-3003
Alcoholics Victorious (AV) 4509 Troost St *Web:* www.kcfootprints.org	Kansas City	MO	64130	816-561-7791	
ARTS Anonymous 133 W 72nd St *Web:* www.artsanonymous.org	New York	NY	10023	212-873-7075	
Bereaved Parents of the USA PO Box 95 *Web:* www.bereavedparentsusa.org	Park Forest	IL	60466	708-748-7866	
Burns United Support Group PO Box 36416	Detroit	MI	48236	313-881-5577	881-5577
Calix Society The 3881 Highland Ave Suite 201 *TF:* 800-398-0524 ■ *Web:* www.calixsociety.org	White Bear Lake	MN	55110	651-773-3117	777-3069
Candlelighters Childhood Cancer Foundation 10920 Connecticut Ave Suuite A PO Box 498 *TF:* 800-366-2223 ■ *Web:* www.acco.org	Kensington	MD	20895	301-962-3520	962-3521
Chemically Dependent Anonymous (CDA) PO Box 423 *TF:* 888-232-4673 ■ *Web:* www.cdaweb.org	Severna Park	MD	21146	888-232-4673	
Children of Lesbians & Gays Everywhere (COLAGE) 1550 Bryant St Suite 830 *Web:* www.colage.org	San Francisco	CA	94103	415-861-5437	255-8345
Cleptomaniacs & Shoplifters Anonymous Inc (CASA) PO Box 250008 *Web:* www.kleptomaniacsanonymous.com	Franklin	MI	48205	248-358-8508	
Clutterers Anonymous World Service Organization (CLA) PO Box 91413 *Web:* www.sites.google.com/site/clutterersanonymous	Los Angeles	CA	90009	310-281-6064	
Co-Anon Family Groups PO Box 12722 *TF:* 800-898-9985 ■ *Web:* www.co-anon.org	Tucson	AZ	85732	520-513-5028	
Co-Dependents Anonymous Inc (CODA) PO Box 33577 *Web:* www.codependents.org	Phoenix	AZ	85067	602-277-7991	
Cocaine Anonymous World Services Inc (CA) 3740 Overland Ave Suite C *TF:* 800-347-8998 ■ *Web:* www.ca.org	Los Angeles	CA	90034	310-559-5833	559-2554
Community Teamwork Inc 155 Merrimack St *Web:* www.comteam.org	Lowell	MA	01852	978-459-0551	
Compassionate Friends PO Box 3696 *TF:* 877-969-0010 ■ *Web:* www.compassionatefriends.org	Oak Brook	IL	60522	630-990-0010	990-0246
Compulsive Eaters Anonymous - HOW (CEA-HOW) 5500 E Atherton St Suite 227B *Web:* www.ceahow.org	Long Beach	CA	90815	562-342-9344	
Concerned United Birthparents Inc (CUB) PO Box 503475 **Fax Area Code:* 858 ■ *TF:* 800-822-2777 ■ *Web:* www.cubirthparents.org	San Diego	CA	92150	800-822-2777	712-3317*
Concerns of Police Survivors Inc (COPS) 3096 S State Hwy 5 PO Box 3199 *TF:* 800-784-2677 ■ *Web:* www.nationalcops.org	Camdenton	MO	65020	573-346-4911	346-1414
Crystal Meth Anonymous General Service Organization 8205 Santa Monica Blvd PMB 1-114 *Web:* www.crystalmeth.org	West Hollywood	CA	90046	213-488-4455	
Debtors Anonymous (DA) PO Box 920888 *TF:* 800-421-2383 ■ *Web:* www.debtorsanonymous.org	Needham	MA	02492	781-453-2743	453-2745
Depressed Anonymous PO Box 17414 *Web:* www.depressedanon.com	Louisville	KY	40217	502-569-1989	
DignityUSA Inc PO Box 376 **Fax Area Code:* 781 ■ *TF:* 800-877-8797 ■ *Web:* www.dignityusa.org	Medford	MA	02155	202-861-0017	397-0584*
Double Trouble in Recovery Inc PO Box 245055	Brooklyn	NY	11224	718-373-2684	
Emotions Anonymous International (EA) PO Box 4245 *Web:* www.emotionsanonymous.org	Saint Paul	MN	55104	651-647-9712	647-1593
Families Anonymous Inc (FA) PO Box 3475 *TF:* 800-736-9805 ■ *Web:* www.familiesanonymous.org	Culver City	CA	90231	310-815-8010	815-9682
Food Addicts Anonymous (FAA) 529 N W Prima Vista Blvd Suite 301 A *Web:* www.foodaddictsanonymous.org	Port St. Lucie	FL	34983	561-967-3871	967-9815
Food Addicts In Recovery Anonymous (FA) 400 W Cummings Pk Suite 1700 *Web:* www.foodaddicts.org	Woburn	MA	01801	781-932-6300	932-6322
Gam-Anon International Service Office Inc PO Box 157 *Web:* www.gam-anon.org	Whitestone	NY	11357	718-352-1671	746-2571
Gamblers Anonymous (GA) 3255 Wilshire Blvd # 1804 *TF:* 888-424-3577 ■ *Web:* www.gamblersanonymous.org	Los Angeles	CA	90010	213-386-8789	386-0030
GROW Inc 2403 W Springfield Ave PO Box 3667 *Web:* www.growinamerica.org	Champaign	IL	61826	217-352-6989	352-8530
HEARTBEAT/Survivors After Suicide Inc 2015 Devon St *Web:* www.heartbeatsurvivorsaftersuicide.org	Colorado Springs	CO	80909	719-596-2575	
Incest Survivors Anonymous (ISA) PO Box 17245 *Web:* www.lafn.org/medical/isa	Long Beach	CA	90807	562-428-5599	
International Lawyers in Alcoholics Anonymous (ILAA) 316 - 2800 E 1st Ave *Web:* www.ilaa.org	Vancouver	BC	V5M4P3	604-253-4525	253-1080
Jewish Alcoholics Chemically Dependent Persons & Significant Others 135 W 50th St 6th Fl *Web:* www.jacsweb.org	New York	NY	10020	212-632-4600	399-3525
LifeRing Secular Recovery 1440 Broadway Suite 312 *TF:* 800-811-4142 ■ *Web:* www.lifering.org	Oakland	CA	94612	510-763-0779	763-1513
Lightning Strike & Electric Shock Survivors International Inc (LSESSI) PO Box 1156	Jacksonville	NC	28541	910-346-4708	
Marijuana Anonymous World Services (MAWS) PO Box 7807 *TF:* 800-766-6779 ■ *Web:* www.marijuana-anonymous.org	Torrance	CA	90504	800-766-6779	
MISS Foundation PO Box 5333 *TF:* 888-455-6477 ■ *Web:* www.missfoundation.org	Peoria	AZ	85385	623-979-1000	979-1001
Moderation Management Network Inc (MM) 22 W 27th St 5th Fl *Web:* www.moderation.org	New York	NY	10001	212-871-0974	213-6582
Nar-Anon Family Groups Headquarters Inc 22527 Crenshaw Blvd Suite 200B *TF:* 800-477-6291 ■ *Web:* www.naranon.com	Torrance	CA	90505	310-534-8188	534-8688
Narcotics Anonymous World Services Inc (NA) PO Box 9999 *Web:* www.na.org	Van Nuys	CA	91409	818-773-9999	700-0700
Native American Indian General Service Office of Alcoholics Anonymous (NAIGSO-AA) PO Box 1253 *Web:* www.naigso-aa.org	Lakeside	CA	92040	951-927-2626	
Nicotine Anonymous World Services 419 Main St PMB 370 *Web:* www.nicotine-anonymous.org	Huntington Beach	CA	92648	415-750-0328	
Overcomers in Christ PO Box 34460 *TF:* 866-573-0966 ■ *Web:* www.overcomersinchrist.org	Omaha	NE	68134	402-573-0966	573-0960
Overcomers Outreach PO Box 922950 *TF:* 800-310-3001 ■ *Web:* www.overcomersoutreach.org	Sylmar	CA	91392	818-833-1803	833-1546
Overeaters Anonymous Inc (OA) PO Box 44020 *Web:* www.oa.org	Rio Rancho	NM	87174	505-891-2664	891-4320
Parents Anonymous Inc 675 W Foothill Blvd Suite 220 *Web:* www.parentsanonymous.org	Claremont	CA	91711	909-621-6184	625-6304
Pathways to Peace Inc PO Box 259 *TF:* 800-775-4212 ■ *Web:* www.pathwaystopeaceinc.com	Cassadaga	NY	14718	716-595-3884	595-3886
Rational Recovery PO Box 800 *Web:* www.rational.org	Lotus	CA	95651	530-621-2667	622-4296
Recovering Couples Anonymous (RCA) PO Box 11029 *Web:* www.recovering-couples.org	Oakland	CA	94611	510-663-2312	
reFocus Inc PO Box 2180 *Web:* www.refocus.org	Flagler Beach	FL	32136	386-439-7541	439-7537
Rest Ministries Inc PO Box 502928 **Fax Area Code:* 800 ■ *TF:* 888-751-7378 ■ *Web:* www.restministries.com	San Diego	CA	92150	858-486-4685	933-1078*
S-Anon International Family Groups Inc PO Box 111242 *TF:* 800-210-8141 ■ *Web:* www.sanon.org	Nashville	TN	37222	615-833-3152	
Secular Organizations for Sobriety (SOS) 4773 Hollywood Blvd *Web:* www.cfiwest.org/sos	Hollywood	CA	90027	323-666-4295	666-4271
Seiu United Healthcare Workers West 560 Thomas L Berkley Way *Web:* www.seiu-uhw.org	Oakland	CA	94612	510-251-1250	763-2680
Sex & Love Addicts Anonymous (SLAA) 1550 NE Loop 410 Suite 118 *Web:* www.slaafws.org	San Antonio	TX	78209	210-828-7900	828-7922
Sex Addicts Anonymous (SAA) PO Box 70949 *TF:* 800-477-8191 ■ *Web:* www.saa-recovery.org	Houston	TX	77270	713-869-4902	692-0105
Sexaholics Anonymous (SA) PO Box 3565 *TF:* 866-424-8777 ■ *Web:* www.sa.org	Brentwood	TN	37024	615-370-6062	370-0882
SHARE Pregnancy & Infant Loss Support Inc 402 Jackson St *TF:* 800-821-6819 ■ *Web:* www.nationalshareoffice.com	Saint Charles	MO	63301	636-947-6164	947-7486
Single Mothers by Choice Inc (SMC) Gracie Sq Stn PO Box 1642 *Web:* www.mattes.home.pipeline.com	New York	NY	10028	212-988-0993	
Sisters Network Inc 2922 Rosedale St *TF:* 866-781-1808 ■ *Web:* www.sistersnetworkinc.org	Houston	TX	77004	713-781-0255	780-8998
SMART Recovery 7304 Mentor Ave Suite F *TF:* 866-951-5357 ■ *Web:* www.smartrecovery.org	Mentor	OH	44060	440-951-5357	951-5358
Straight Spouse Network (SSN) PO Box 507 *Web:* www.straightspouse.org	Mahwah	NJ	07430	201-825-7763	
Survivors Network of Those Abused by Priests (SNAP) PO Box 6416 *TF:* 877-762-7432 ■ *Web:* www.snapnetwork.org	Chicago	IL	60680	312-455-1499	
Survivors of Incest Anonymous (SIA) PO Box 190 *Web:* www.siawso.org	Benson	MD	21018	410-893-3322	
Take Root PO Box 930 *TF:* 800-777-8774 ■ *Web:* www.takeroot.org	Kalama	WA	98625	360-673-3720	673-3732
TOPS Club Inc 4575 S 5th St *TF:* 800-932-8677 ■ *Web:* www.tops.org	Milwaukee	WI	53207	414-482-4620	482-1655
Twinless Twins Support Group International (TTSG) PO Box 980481 *TF:* 888-205-8962 ■ *Web:* www.twinlesstwins.org	Ypsilanti	MI	48198	888-205-8962	
Valley of the Sun United Way 1515 E Osborn Rd *Web:* www.vsuw.org	Phoenix	AZ	85014	602-631-4800	631-4809
White Bison Inc 701 N 20th St *TF:* 877-871-1495 ■ *Web:* www.whitebison.org	Colorado Springs	CO	80904	719-548-1000	548-9407
Wings Foundation 8725 W 14th Ave Suite 150 *TF:* 800-373-8671 ■ *Web:* www.wingsfound.org	Lakewood	CO	80215	303-238-8660	
Wings of Light Inc PO Box 1097 *Web:* www.wingsoflight.org	Sun City	AZ	85372	623-516-1115	
Women for Sobriety Inc (WFS) PO Box 618 *Web:* www.womenforsobriety.org	Quakertown	PA	18951	215-536-8026	538-9026
Workaholics Anonymous World Service Organization PO Box 289 *Web:* www.workaholics-anonymous.org	Menlo Park	CA	94026	510-273-9253	

48-22 Sports Organizations

Organization / Address	City	State	ZIP	Phone	Fax
Adventure Cycling Assn 150 E Pine St PO Box 8308 *TF:* 800-755-2453 ■ *Web:* www.adventurecycling.org	Missoula	MT	59807	406-721-1776	721-8754
Aerobics & Fitness Assn of America (AFAA) 15250 Ventura Blvd Suite 200 *TF:* 877-968-7263 ■ *Web:* www.afaa.com	Sherman Oaks	CA	91403	818-905-0040	990-5468
Amateur Athletic Union of the US (AAU) 1910 Hotel Plaza Blvd. *Web:* www.aausports.org	Lake Buena Vista	FL	32830	407-934-7200	934-7242
Amateur Softball Assn of America Inc (ASA) 2801 NE 50th St *TF:* 800-654-8337 ■ *Web:* www.softball.org	Oklahoma City	OK	73111	405-424-5266	424-3855
Amateur Trapshooting Assn (ATA) 601 W National Rd *Web:* www.shootata.com	Vandalia	OH	45377	937-898-4638	898-5472
American Alliance for Health Physical Education Recreation & Dance (AAHPERD) 1900 Assn Dr *TF:* 800-213-7193 ■ *Web:* www.aahperd.org	Reston	VA	20191	703-476-3400	476-9527
American Amateur Baseball Congress (AABC) 100 W Broadway *TF:* 866-557-3120 ■ *Web:* www.aabc.us	Farmington	NM	87401	505-327-3120	327-3132
American Baseball Coaches Assn (ABCA) 108 S University Ave Suite 3 *Web:* www.abca.org	Mount Pleasant	MI	48858	989-775-3300	775-3600
American Bicycle Assn (ABA) 1645 W Sunrise Blvd *TF:* 800-886-1269 ■ *Web:* www.ababmx.com	Gilbert	AZ	85233	480-961-1903	961-1842
American Canoe Assn (ACA) 1340 Central Pk Blvd Suite 210 *Fax Area Code: 703 ■ *Web:* www.americancanoe.org	Fredericksburg	VA	22401	540-907-4460	636-0296*
American Council on Exercise (ACE) 4851 Paramount Dr *TF:* 800-825-3636 ■ *Web:* www.acefitness.org	San Diego	CA	92123	858-576-6500	576-6564
American Football Coaches Assn (AFCA) 100 Legends Ln *Web:* www.afca.com	Waco	TX	76706	254-754-9900	754-7373
American Motorcyclist Assn (AMA) 13515 Yarmouth Dr *TF:* 800-262-5646 ■ *Web:* www.ama-cycle.org	Pickerington	OH	43147	614-856-1900	856-1920
American Poolplayers Assn Inc (APA) 1000 Lake St Louis Blvd Suite 325 *TF:* 800-372-2536 ■ *Web:* www.poolplayers.com	Lake Saint Louis	MO	63367	636-625-8611	625-2975
American Running Assn 4405 E W Hwy # 405 *TF:* 800-776-2732 ■ *Web:* www.americanrunning.org	Bethesda	MD	20814	301-913-9517	913-9520
American Society of Golf Course Architects (ASGCA) 125 N Executive Dr Suite 106 *Web:* www.asgca.org	Brookfield	WI	53005	262-786-5960	786-5919
American Sportfishing Assn (ASA) 225 Reinekers Ln Suite 420 *Web:* www.asafishing.org	Alexandria	VA	22314	703-519-9691	519-1872
American Sports Institute (ASI) 116 E Blithedale Ave *Web:* www.amersports.org	Mill Valley	CA	94941	415-383-5750	
American Volksport Assn (AVA) 1001 Pat Booker Rd Suite 101 *TF:* 800-830-9255 ■ *Web:* www.ava.org	Universal City	TX	78148	210-659-2112	659-1212
American Watercraft Assn PO Box 1993 *Fax Area Code: 703 ■ *TF:* 800-913-2921	Ashburn	VA	20147	800-913-2921	421-9889*
American Youth Soccer Organization (AYSO) 19750 S Vermont Ave Suite 200 *TF Cust Svc:* 800-872-2976 ■ *Web:* soccer.org	Torrance	CA	90502	310-643-6455	525-1155
Aquatic Exercise Assn (AEA) 201 S Tamiami Trail Suite 3 PO Box 1609 *TF:* 888-232-9283 ■ *Web:* www.aeawave.com	Nokomis	FL	34275	941-486-8600	486-8820
Assn of Professional Ball Players of America 101 S Kraemer Ave Suite 112 *Web:* www.apbpa.org	Placentia	CA	92870	714-528-2012	528-2037
Assn of Surfing Professionals (ASP) 300 Pacific Coast Hwy # 308 *Web:* www.aspworldtour.com	Huntington Beach	CA	92648	714-536-3500	536-4482
ATP Tour Inc 201 ATP Tour Blvd *Web:* www.atpworldtour.com	Ponte Vedra Beach	FL	32082	904-285-8000	285-5966
Babe Ruth League Inc 1770 Brunswick Pike PO Box 5000 *TF:* 800-880-3142 ■ *Web:* www.baberuthleague.org	Trenton	NJ	08638	609-695-1434	695-2505
Billiard Congress of America 12303 Airport Way Suite 140 *Web:* www.bca-pool.com	Broomfield	CO	80021	303-243-5070	243-5075
Boat Owners Assn of the US 880 S Pickett St *TF:* 800-395-2628 ■ *Web:* www.boatus.com	Alexandria	VA	22304	703-823-9550	461-2847
Continental Basketball Assn (CBA) 195 Washington Ave. *Web:* www.cbahoopsonline.com	Albany	NY	12210	518-694-0100	694-0101
Cross Country Ski Areas Assn (CCSAA) 259 Bolton Rd. *TF:* 877-779-2754 ■ *Web:* www.xcski.org	Winchester	NH	03470	603-239-4341	239-6387
Disabled Sports USA (DS/USA) 451 Hungerford Dr Suite 100 *Web:* www.dsusa.org	Rockville	MD	20850	301-217-0960	217-0968
Fellowship of Christian Athletes (FCA) 8701 Leeds Rd *TF:* 800-289-0909 ■ *Web:* www.fca.org	Kansas City	MO	64129	816-921-0909	921-8755
Hockey North America (HNA) PO Box 78 *TF:* 800-446-2539 ■ *Web:* www.hna.com	Sterling	VA	20167	703-430-8100	421-9205
Ice Skating Institute (ISI) 6000 Custer Rd Bldg 9 *Web:* www.skateisi.com	Plano	TX	75023	972-735-8800	735-8815
IDEA Inc 10455 Pacific Ctr Ct *TF:* 800-999-4332 ■ *Web:* www.ideafit.com	San Diego	CA	92121	858-535-8979	535-8234
Indy Racing League 4565 W 16th St *Web:* www.indycar.com	Indianapolis	IN	46222	317-492-6526	492-6525
International Assn of Approved Basketball Officials (IAABO) PO Box 355 *Web:* www.iaabo.org	Carlisle	PA	17013	717-713-8129	718-6164
International Collegiate Licensing Assn (ICLA) 24651 Detroit Rd *TF:* 800-996-2232 ■ *Web:* www.nacda.com/icla/nacda-icla.html	Westlake	OH	44145	440-892-4000	892-4007
International Health Racquet & Sportsclub Assn (IHRSA) 263 Summer St 8th Fl. *TF:* 800-228-4772 ■ *Web:* www.ihrsa.org	Boston	MA	02210	617-951-0055	951-0056
International Hot Rod Assn (IHRA) 9 1/2 E Main St. *Web:* www.ihra.com	Norwalk	OH	44857	419-663-6666	663-4472
International Motor Sports Assn (IMSA) 1394 Broadway Ave *Web:* www.imsaracing.net	Braselton	GA	30517	706-658-2120	658-2130
International Professional Rodeo Assn (IPRA) PO Box 83377 *Web:* www.iprarodeo.com	Oklahoma City	OK	73148	405-235-6540	235-6577
International Shooting Coaches Assn 17446 SW Granada Dr	Beaverton	OR	97007	503-642-5873	
International Sports Sciences Assn (ISSA) 1015 Mark Ave *TF:* 800-892-4772 ■ *Web:* www.issaonline.com	Carpinteria	CA	93013	805-884-8111	884-8119
Jockey Club 40 E 52nd St 15th Fl *Web:* www.jockeyclub.com	New York	NY	10022	212-371-5970	371-6123
Jockeys' Guild Inc 103 Wind Haven Dr Suite 200 *TF:* 866-465-6257 ■ *Web:* www.jockeysguild.com	Nicholasville	KY	40356	859-305-0606	219-9892
Ladies Professional Golf Assn (LPGA) 100 International Golf Dr *Web:* www.lpga.com	Daytona Beach	FL	32124	386-274-6200	274-1099
League of American Bicyclists 1612 K St NW Suite 800 *Web:* www.bikeleague.org	Washington	DC	20006	202-822-1333	822-1334
Little League Baseball Inc 539 US Rt 15 Hwy PO Box 3485 *Web:* www.littleleague.org	Williamsport	PA	17701	570-326-1921	326-1074
Maccabi USA/Sports for Israel 1926 Arch St Suite 4R *Web:* www.maccabiusa.com	Philadelphia	PA	19103	215-561-6900	561-5470
Major Indoor Soccer League (MISL) 1175 Post Rd E Suite 2 *TF:* 866-647-5638 ■ *Web:* www.misl.net	Westport	CT	06880	203-222-4900	221-7300
Major League Baseball Players Assn 12 E 49th St 24th Fl *Web:* mlbplayers.mlb.com/NASApp/mlb/pa/index.jsp	New York	NY	10017	212-826-0808	752-4378
NA for Girls & Women in Sport (NAGWS) 1900 Assn Dr *TF:* 800-213-7193 ■ *Web:* www.aahperd.org	Reston	VA	20191	703-476-3400	476-4566
NA for Stock Car Auto Racing (NASCAR) 1801 W International Speedway Blvd *Fax: Mktg ■ *Web:* www.nascar.com	Daytona Beach	FL	32114	386-253-0611	947-6712*
NA of Basketball Coaches (NABC) 1111 Main St Suite 1000 *Web:* www.nabc.ocsn.com	Kansas City	MO	64105	816-878-6222	878-6223
NA of Collegiate Directors of Athletics (NACDA) 24651 Detroit Rd *TF:* 800-996-2232 ■ *Web:* www.nacda.com	Westlake	OH	44145	440-892-4000	892-4007
NA of Intercollegiate Athletics (NAIA) 1200 Grand Blvd. *Web:* www.naia.org	Kansas City	KS	64106	816-595-8000	595-8200
NA of Police Athletic Leagues (PAL) 658 W Indiantown Rd # 201 *TF:* 800-725-7743 ■ *Web:* www.nationalpal.org	Jupiter	FL	33458	561-745-5535	745-3147
NA of Professional Baseball Leagues 201 Bayshore Dr SE *Web:* www.minorleaguebaseball.com	Saint Petersburg	FL	33701	727-822-6937	821-5819
NA of Sports Officials (NASO) 2017 Lathrop Ave *TF:* 800-733-6100 ■ *Web:* www.naso.org	Racine	WI	53405	262-632-5448	632-5460
NA of Underwater Instructors (NAUI) 1232 Tech Blvd. *TF:* 800-553-6284 ■ *Web:* www.naui.org	Tampa	FL	33619	813-628-6284	628-8253
National Aeronautic Assn (NAA) 1 Reagan National Airport Hangar 7 Suite 202 *TF:* 800-644-9777	Washington	DC	20001	703-416-4888	416-4877
National Alliance for Youth Sports 2050 Vista Pkwy *TF:* 800-729-2057 ■ *Web:* www.nays.org	West Palm Beach	FL	33411	561-684-1141	684-2546
National Athletic Trainers Assn (NATA) 2952 N Stemmons Fwy # 200 *TF:* 800-879-6282 ■ *Web:* www.nata.org	Dallas	TX	75247	214-637-6282	637-2206
National Basketball Players Assn (NBPA) 310 Malcolm X Blvd *Web:* www.nbpa.com	New York	NY	10027	212-655-0880	655-0881
National Baton Twirling Assn PO Box 266	Janesville	WI	53547	608-754-2238	754-1986
National Center for Bicycling & Walking (NCBW) 8120 Woodmont Ave Suite 520 *Web:* www.bikewalk.org	Bethesda	MD	20814	301-656-4220	656-4225

Organization	City	State	ZIP	Phone	Fax
National Collegiate Athletic Assn (NCAA) 700 W Washington St PO Box 6222 *Web:* www.ncaa.org	Indianapolis	IN	46206	317-917-6222	917-6888
National Congress of State Games 1631 Mesa Ave Suite E *Web:* www.stategames.org	Colorado Springs	CO	80906	719-634-7333	634-5198
National Dart Assn (NDA) 7150 Winton Dr Suite 300-S *TF:* 800-808-9884 ■ *Web:* www.ndadarts.com	Indianapolis	IN	46268	317-387-1299	387-0999
National Disability Sports Alliance (NDSA) 25 W Independence Way	Kingston	RI	02881	401-792-7130	792-7132
National Federation of State High School Associations (NFHS) PO Box 690 *TF Cust Svc:* 800-776-3462 ■ *Web:* www.nfhs.org	Indianapolis	IN	46206	317-972-6900	822-5700
National Football League Players Assn (NFLPA) 1133 20th St NW *TF:* 800-372-2000	Washington	DC	20036	202-463-2200	756-9320
National Golf Foundation (NGF) 1150 S US Hwy 1 Suite 401 *TF:* 800-733-6006 ■ *Web:* www.ngf.org	Jupiter	FL	33477	561-744-6006	744-6107
National Greyhound Assn (NGA) 729 Old 40 *Web:* www.ngagreyhounds.com	Abilene	KS	67410	785-263-4660	263-4689
National Hockey League Players Assn (NHLPA) 20 Bay St Suite 1700 *TF:* 800-363-4625 ■ *Web:* www.nhlpa.com	Toronto	ON	M5J2N8	416-313-2300	313-2301
National Intramural-Recreational Sports Assn (NIRSA) 4185 SW Research Way *Web:* www.nirsa.org	Corvallis	OR	97333	541-766-8211	766-8284
National Junior College Athletic Assn (NJCAA) 1755 Telstar Dr Suite 103 *Web:* www.njcaa.org	Colorado Springs	CO	80920	719-590-9788	590-7324
National Little Britches Rodeo Assn (NLBRA) 5050 Edison Ave Suite 105 *TF:* 800-763-3694 ■ *Web:* www.nlbra.org	Colorado Springs	CO	80915	719-389-0333	578-1367
National Rifle Assn of America (NRA) 11250 Waples Mill Rd *TF Cust Svc:* 800-672-3888 ■ *Web:* www.nrahq.org	Fairfax	VA	22030	703-267-1000	267-3957
National Senior Golf Assn (NSGA) 200 Perrine Rd Suite 201 *TF:* 800-282-6772 ■ *Web:* www.nsgatour.com	Old Bridge	NJ	08857	732-525-1871	525-9590
National Shooting Sports Foundation (NSSF) 11 Mile Hill Rd *Web:* www.nssf.org	Newtown	CT	06470	203-426-1320	426-1087
National Soccer Coaches Assn of America (NSCAA) 800 Ann Ave *TF:* 800-458-0678 ■ *Web:* www.nscaa.com	Kansas City	KS	66101	913-362-1747	362-3439
National Strength & Conditioning Assn (NSCA) 1885 Bob Johnson Dr *TF:* 800-815-6826 ■ *Web:* www.nsca-lift.org	Colorado Springs	CO	80906	719-632-6722	632-6367
National Thoroughbred Racing Assn (NTRA) 2525 Harrodsburg Rd Suite 500 *TF:* 800-792-6872 ■ *Web:* www.ntra.com	Lexington	KY	40504	859-223-5444	223-3945
National Tractor Pullers Assn (NTPA) 6155-B Huntley Rd *Web:* www.ntpapull.com	Columbus	OH	43229	614-436-1761	436-0964
National Youth Sports Coaches Assn (NYSCA) 2050 Vista Pkwy *TF:* 800-729-2057 ■ *Web:* www.nays.org	West Palm Beach	FL	33411	561-684-1141	684-2546
National Youth Sports Safety Foundation (NYSSF) 1 Beacon St Suite 3333 *Web:* www.healthfinder.gov/orgs/hr2693.htm	Boston	MA	02108	617-367-6677	722-9999
New York Arm Wrestling Assn (NYAWA) PO Box 670952 *Web:* www.nycarms.com	Flushing	NY	11367	718-544-4592	261-8111
North American Youth Sport Institute (NAYSI) PO Box 140 **Fax Area Code:* 877 ■ *TF:* 800-767-4916 ■ *Web:* www.naysi.com	Huddleston	VA	24104	336-784-4926	297-9052*
PGA of America 100 Avenue of the Champions *TF:* 800-477-6465 ■ *Web:* www.pga.com	Palm Beach Gardens	FL	33418	561-624-8400	624-8439
PGA Tour Inc 112 PGA Tour Blvd *Web:* www.pgatour.com	Ponte Vedra Beach	FL	32082	904-285-3700	
PONY Baseball/Softball Inc 1951 Pony Pl PO Box 225 *Web:* www.pony.org	Washington	PA	15301	724-225-1060	225-9852
Pop Warner Little Scholars Inc 586 Middletown Blvd Suite C-100 *Web:* www.popwarner.com	Langhorne	PA	19047	215-752-2691	752-2879
Professional Assn of Diving Instructors International (PADI) 30151 Tomas St *TF Sales:* 800-729-7234 ■ *Web:* www.padi.com	Rancho Santa Margarita	CA	92688	949-858-7234	267-1267
Professional Bowlers Assn (PBA) 719 2nd Ave Suite 701 *Web:* www.pba.com	Seattle	WA	98104	206-332-9688	654-6030
Professional Rodeo Cowboys Assn (PRCA) 101 Pro Rodeo Dr *Web:* www.prorodeo.com	Colorado Springs	CO	80919	719-593-8840	548-4876
Professional Tennis Registry PO Box 4739 *TF:* 800-421-6289 ■ *Web:* www.ptrtennis.org	Hilton Head Island	SC	29938	843-785-7244	686-2033
Roller Skating Assn International (RSAI) 6905 Corporate Dr *Web:* www.rollerskating.org	Indianapolis	IN	46278	317-347-2626	347-2636
Senior Softball USA 2701 K St Suite 101A *Web:* www.seniorsoftball.com	Sacramento	CA	95816	916-326-5303	326-5304
Special Olympics Inc 1133 19th St NW 11th Fl *TF:* 800-700-8585 ■ *Web:* www.specialolympics.org	Washington	DC	20036	202-628-3630	824-0200
Sports Turf Managers Assn 805 New Hampshire St Suite E *TF:* 800-323-3875 ■ *Web:* www.sportsturfmanager.com	Lawrence	KS	66044	785-843-2549	843-2977
Thoroughbred Racing Associations (TRA) 420 Fair Hill Dr Suite 1 *Web:* www.tra-online.com	Elkton	MD	21921	410-392-9200	398-1366
United States Bowling Congress (USBC) 5301 S 76th St **Fax Area Code:* 414 ■ *TF:* 800-514-2695 ■ *Web:* www.bowl.com	Greendale	WI	53129	800-514-2695	421-8560*
US Assn of Blind Athletes (USABA) 33 N Institute St *Web:* www.usaba.org	Colorado Springs	CO	80903	719-630-0422	630-0616
US Auto Club (USAC) 4910 W 16th St *Web:* www.usacracing.com	Speedway	IN	46224	317-247-5151	247-0123
US Biathlon Assn 49 Pineland Dr Suite 301-A *TF:* 800-242-8456 ■ *Web:* www.biathlon.teamusa.org	New Gloucester	ME	04260	207-688-6500	688-6505
US Bobsled & Skeleton Federation (USBSF) 196 Old Military Rd PO Box 828 *TF:* 800-262-7533 ■ *Web:* www.bobsled.teamusa.org	Lake Placid	NY	12946	518-523-1842	523-9491
US Curling Assn (USCA) PO Box 866 *TF:* 888-287-5377 ■ *Web:* www.curlingrocks.net	Stevens Point	WI	54482	715-344-1199	344-2279
US Equestrian Federation Inc 4047 Iron Works Pkwy *Web:* www.usef.org	Lexington	KY	40511	859-258-2472	231-6662
US Equestrian Team Foundation Inc (USET) 1040 Pottersville Rd PO Box 355 *Web:* www.uset.org	Gladstone	NJ	07934	908-234-1251	234-0670
US Fencing Assn (USFA) 1 Olympic Plaza *Web:* www.usfencing.org	Colorado Springs	CO	80909	719-866-4511	632-5737
US Field Hockey Assn 1 Olympic Plaza *Web:* www.usafieldhockey.com	Colorado Springs	CO	80909	719-866-4567	632-0979
US Figure Skating Assn (USFSA) 20 1st St *Web:* www.usfsa.org	Colorado Springs	CO	80906	719-635-5200	635-9548
US Golf Assn (USGA) 77 Liberty Corner Rd *TF Orders:* 800-336-4446 ■ *Web:* www.usga.org	Far Hills	NJ	07931	908-234-2300	234-9687
US Luge Assn 57 Church St *Web:* www.usaluge.org	Lake Placid	NY	12946	518-523-2071	523-4106
US Olympic Committee (USOC) 1 Olympic Plaza *Web:* www.teamusa.org	Colorado Springs	CO	80909	719-632-5551	866-4677
US Parachute Assn (USPA) 5401 Southpoint Ctr Blvd *TF:* 800-371-8772 ■ *Web:* www.uspa.org	Fredericksburg	VA	22407	540-604-9740	604-9741
US Power Squadrons (USPS) PO Box 30423 *TF:* 888-367-8777 ■ *Web:* www.usps.org	Raleigh	NC	27622	888-367-8777	304-0813
US Professional Tennis Assn (USPTA) 3535 Briarpark Dr Suite 1 *TF:* 800-877-8248 ■ *Web:* www.uspta.org	Houston	TX	77042	713-978-7782	978-7780
US Racquet Stringers Assn (USRSA) 330 Main St *TF:* 888-900-3545 ■ *Web:* www.racquettech.com	Vista	CA	92084	760-536-1177	536-1171
US Racquetball Assn (USRA) 1685 W Uintah St *TF:* 800-234-5396 ■ *Web:* www.usra.org	Colorado Springs	CO	80904	719-635-5396	635-0685
US Rowing Assn 2 Wall St *TF:* 800-314-4769 ■ *Web:* www.usrowing.org	Princeton	NJ	08540	609-751-0700	924-1578
US Sailing Assn 15 Maritime Dr PO Box 1260 *TF:* 800-877-2451 ■ *Web:* www.home.ussailing.org	Portsmouth	RI	02871	401-683-0800	683-0840
US Ski & Snowboard Assn 1 Victory Ln PO Box 100 *Web:* www.ussa.org	Park City	UT	84060	435-649-9090	649-3613
US Soccer Federation 1801 S Prairie Ave *TF:* 800-759-9636 ■ *Web:* www.ussoccer.com	Chicago	IL	60616	312-808-1300	808-1301
US Squash Racquets Assn (USSRA) 555 8th Ave Suite 1102 *Web:* www.ussquash.com	New York	NY	10018	212-268-4090	268-4091
US Synchronized Swimming 132 E Washington St # 800 *Web:* www.usasynchro.org	Indianapolis	IN	46204	317-237-5700	237-5705
US Taekwondo Union 1 Olympic Plaza Suite 104C *Web:* www.usa-taekwondo.us	Colorado Springs	CO	80909	719-866-4632	866-4642
US Tennis Assn (USTA) 70 W Red Oak Ln *TF:* 800-990-8782 ■ *Web:* www.usta.com	White Plains	NY	10604	914-696-7000	696-7167
US Trotting Assn (USTA) 750 Michigan Ave *TF:* 800-887-8782 ■ *Web:* www.ustrotting.com	Columbus	OH	43215	614-224-2291	224-4575
USA Archery (NAA) 1 Olympic Plaza *Web:* www.usarchery.org	Colorado Springs	CO	80909	719-866-4576	632-4733
USA Baseball 403 Blackwell St *Web:* www.web.usabaseball.com	Durham	NC	27701	919-474-8721	474-8822
USA Basketball 5645 Mark Dabling *Web:* www.usabasketball.com	Colorado Springs	CO	80918	719-590-4800	590-4811
USA Boxing Inc 1 Olympic Plaza *Web:* www.usaboxing.org	Colorado Springs	CO	80909	719-866-4506	632-3426
USA Canoe/Kayak (USACK) 301 S Tryon St Suite 1750 *Web:* www.usack.org	Charlotte	NC	28282	704-348-4330	348-4418
USA Cycling Inc 1 Olympic Plaza *Web:* www.usacycling.org	Colorado Springs	CO	80909	719-866-4581	866-4628
USA Deaf Sports Federation 102 N Krohn Pl *Web:* www.usadsf.org	Sioux Falls	SD	57103	605-367-5760	367-5958
USA Diving Inc 201 S Capitol Ave Suite 430 *Web:* www.usadiving.org	Indianapolis	IN	46225	317-237-5252	237-5257
USA Gymnastics 201 S Capitol Ave Suite 300 *TF:* 800-345-4719 ■ *Web:* www.usa-gymnastics.org	Indianapolis	IN	46225	317-237-5050	237-5069
USA Hockey 1775 Bob Johnson Dr *Web:* www.usahockey.com	Colorado Springs	CO	80906	719-576-8724	538-1160
USA Judo Inc 1 Olympic Plaza Suite 505 *Web:* www.usjudo.org	Colorado Springs	CO	80909	719-866-4730	866-4733

	City	State	Zip	Phone	Fax
USA Roller Sports 4730 S St.	Lincoln	NE	68506	402-483-7551	483-1465
Web: www.usarollersports.org					
USA Swimming 1 Olympic Plaza	Colorado Springs	CO	80909	719-866-4578	866-4669
Web: www.usaswimming.org					
USA Table Tennis 1 Olympic Plaza	Colorado Springs	CO	80909	719-866-4583	632-6071
Web: www.usatt.org					
USA Team Handball 1 Olympic Plaza	Colorado Springs	CO	80909	719-866-4036	866-4055
Web: www.usateamhandball.org					
USA Track & Field (USATF)					
132 E Washington St Suite 800	Indianapolis	IN	46204	317-261-0500	261-0481
Web: www.usatf.org					
USA Triathlon 5825 Delmonico Dr.	Colorado Springs	CO	80919	719-597-9090	597-2121
Web: www.usatriathlon.org					
USA Water Polo					
2124 Main St Suite 210	Huntington Beach	CA	92648	714-500-5445	960-2431
Web: www.usawaterpolo.com					
USA Water Ski 1251 Holy Cow Rd.	Polk City	FL	33868	863-324-4341	325-8259
TF: 800-533-2972 ■ *Web:* www.usawaterski.org					
USA Weightlifting (USAW)					
1 Olympic Plaza	Colorado Springs	CO	80909	719-866-4508	866-4741
Web: www.usaweightlifting.org					
USA Wrestling 6155 Lehman Dr	Colorado Springs	CO	80918	719-598-8181	598-9440
TF: 800-999-8531 ■ *Web:* www.themat.com/usawrestling.org					
Western Golf Assn (WGA) 1 Briar Rd.	Golf	IL	60029	847-724-4600	724-7133
Web: www.wgaesf.org					
Wheelchair & Ambulatory Sports USA					
PO Box 5266	Kendall Park	NJ	08824	732-266-2634	355-6500
Web: www.wsusa.org					
Women's Sports Foundation					
1899 Hempstead Tpke					
Suite 400 Eisenhower Pk	East Meadow	NY	11554	516-542-4700	542-4716
TF: 800-227-3988 ■ *Web:* www.womenssportsfoundation.org					
WTA Tour Inc					
1 Progress Plaza Suite 1500	Saint Petersburg	FL	33701	727-895-5000	894-1982
TF: 800-764-8579 ■ *Web:* www.wtatennis.com					

48-23 Travel & Recreation Organizations

	City	State	Zip	Phone	Fax
Access Fund PO Box 17010	Boulder	CO	80308	303-545-6772	545-6774
TF: 888-863-6237 ■ *Web:* www.accessfund.org					
Adirondack Mountain Club 814 Goggins Rd	Lake George	NY	12845	518-668-4447	668-3746
TF Orders: 800-395-8080 ■ *Web:* www.adk.org					
Alberta Hotel & Lodging Assn (AHLA)					
2707 Ellwood Dr.	Edmonton	AB	T6X0P7	780-436-6112	436-5404
TF: 888-436-6112 ■ *Web:* www.ahla.ca					
America Outdoors 5816 Kingston Pike.	Knoxville	TN	37919	865-558-3595	558-3598
TF: 800-524-4814 ■ *Web:* www.americaoutdoors.org					
American Amusement Machine Assn (AAMA)					
450 E Higgins Rd Suite 201	Elk Grove Village	IL	60007	847-290-9088	290-9121
TF: 866-372-5190 ■ *Web:* www.coin-op.org					
American Assn for Physical Activity & Recreation (AAPAR)					
1900 Assn Dr	Reston	VA	20191	703-476-3400	476-9527
TF: 800-213-7193 ■ *Web:* www.aahperd.org/aapar					
American Automobile Assn Inc (AAA) 1000 AAA Dr	Heathrow	FL	32746	407-444-4240	444-4247
Web: www.aaa.com					
American Camp Assn (ACA)					
5000 State Rd 67 N.	Martinsville	IN	46151	765-342-8456	342-2065
TF: 800-428-2267 ■ *Web:* www.acacamps.org					
American Gaming Assn (AGA)					
1299 Pennsylvania Ave NW Suite 1175	Washington	DC	20004	202-552-2675	552-2676
Web: www.americangaming.org					
American Hiking Society (AHS)					
1422 Fenwick Ln	Silver Spring	MD	20910	301-565-6704	565-6714
Web: www.americanhiking.org					
American Hotel & Lodging Assn (AH&LA)					
1201 New York Ave NW Suite 600	Washington	DC	20005	202-289-3100	289-3185
Web: www.ahla.com					
American Park & Recreation Society (APRS)					
22377 Belmont Ridge Rd	Ashburn	VA	20148	703-858-0784	858-0794
TF: 800-626-6772 ■ *Web:* www.arcat.com					
American Recreation Coalition (ARC)					
1225 New York Ave NW Suite 450	Washington	DC	20005	202-682-9530	682-9529
Web: www.funoutdoors.com					
American Society of Travel Agents (ASTA)					
1101 King St Suite 200.	Alexandria	VA	22314	703-739-2782	684-8319
TF: 800-440-2782 ■ *Web:* www.asta.org					
American Trails PO Box 491797.	Redding	CA	96049	530-547-2060	547-2035
Web: www.americantrails.org					
American Whitewater (AW) PO Box 1540	Cullowhee	NC	28723	828-586-1930	586-2840
TF: 866-262-8429 ■ *Web:* www.americanwhitewater.org					
Amusement & Music Operators Assn (AMOA)					
600 Spring Hill Ring Rd Suite 111	West Dundee	IL	60118	847-428-7699	428-7719
TF: 800-937-2662 ■ *Web:* www.amoa.com					
Appalachian Mountain Club (AMC) 5 Joy St	Boston	MA	02108	617-523-0655	523-0722
TF Orders: 800-262-4455 ■ *Web:* www.outdoors.org					
Appalachian Trail Conservancy (ATC)					
799 Washington St PO Box 807	Harpers Ferry	WV	25425	304-535-6331	535-2667
TF Sales: 888-287-8673 ■ *Web:* www.appalachiantrail.org					
Assn of Corporate Travel Executives (ACTE)					
515 King St Suite 440.	Alexandria	VA	22314	703-683-5322	683-2720
TF: 800-228-3669 ■ *Web:* www.acte.org					
Assn of Destination Management Executives (ADME)					
11 W Monument Ave	Dayton	OH	45402	937-586-3727	586-3699
Web: www.adme.org					
Back Country Horsemen of America (BCHA)					
PO Box 1367	Graham	WA	98338	360-832-2461	832-2471
TF: 888-893-5161 ■ *Web:* www.backcountryhorse.com					
Bowling Proprietors' Assn of America (BPAA)					
621 Six Flags Dr PO Box 5802	Arlington	TX	76011	817-649-5105	633-2940
TF: 800-343-1329 ■ *Web:* www.bpaa.com					
Canadian Automobile Assn (CAA)					
1145 Hunt Club Rd Suite 200.	Ottawa	ON	K1V0Y3	613-247-0117	247-0118
Web: www.caa.ca					
Canadian Parks & Recreation Assn (CPRA)					
1180 Walkley Rd PO Box 83069	Ottawa	ON	K1V2M5	613-523-5315	523-1182
Web: www.cpra.ca					
Colorado Dude & Guest Ranch Assn (CDGRA)					
PO Box D	Shawnee	CO	80475	866-942-3472	
TF: 866-942-3472 ■ *Web:* www.coloradoranch.com					
Continental Divide Trail Society (CDT)					
3704 N Charles St Suite 601	Baltimore	MD	21218	410-235-9610	243-1960
Web: www.cdtsociety.org					
Cruise Lines International Assn (CLIA)					
910 SE 17th St Suite 400	Fort Lauderdale	FL	33316	754-224-2200	224-2250
Web: www.cruising.org					
Destination Marketing Assn International					
2025 M St NW Suite 500	Washington	DC	20036	202-296-7888	296-7889
TF: 888-275-3140 ■ *Web:* www.destinationmarketing.org					
Dude Ranchers' Assn 1122 12th St PO Box 2307	Cody	WY	82414	307-587-2339	587-2776
TF: 866-399-2339 ■ *Web:* www.duderanch.org					
Elderhostel Inc 11 Ave de Lafayette	Boston	MA	02111	617-426-7788	426-2166*
**Fax Area Code:* 877 ■ *TF:* 800-454-5768 ■ *Web:* www.roadscholar.org					
Environmental Traveling Companions (ETC)					
Fort Mason Ctr Bldg C	San Francisco	CA	94123	415-474-7662	474-3919
Web: www.etctrips.org					
Escapees RV Club 100 Rainbow Dr	Livingston	TX	77399	936-327-8873	327-4388
TF: 800-231-9896 ■ *Web:* www.escapees.com					
Family Campers & RVers (FCRV)					
4804 Transit Rd Bldg 2	Depew	NY	14043	716-668-6242	
TF: 800-245-9755 ■ *Web:* www.fcrv.org					
Family Motor Coach Assn (FMCA)					
8291 Clough Pike	Cincinnati	OH	45244	513-474-3622	474-2332
TF: 800-543-3622 ■ *Web:* www.fmca.com					
Global Business Travel Assn The (GBTA)					
123 N Pitt St	Alexandria	VA	22314	703-684-0836	684-0263
Web: www.gbta.org					
Good Sam Club PO Box 6888	Englewood	CO	80155	800-234-3450	728-7306*
**Fax Area Code:* 303 ■ *TF:* 800-234-3450 ■ *Web:* www.goodsamclub.com					
Hostelling International USA - American Youth Hostels (HI-AYH)					
8401 Colesville Rd Suite 600	Silver Spring	MD	20910	301-495-1240	495-6697
Web: www.hiusa.org					
International Airline Passengers Assn (IAPA)					
5204 Tennyson Pkwy	Plano	TX	75024	972-404-9980	233-5348
TF: 800-821-4272 ■ *Web:* www.iapa.com					
International Assn for Medical Assistance to Travellers (IAMAT)					
2162 Gordon St	Guelph	ON	N1L1G6	519-836-0102	836-3412
Web: www.iamat.org/index.cfm					
International Assn of Amusement Parks & Attractions (IAAPA)					
1448 Duke St	Alexandria	VA	22314	703-836-4800	836-6742
Web: www.iaapa.org					
International Assn of Fairs & Expositions The (IAFE)					
3043 E Cairo	Springfield	MO	65802	417-862-5771	862-0156
TF: 800-516-0313 ■ *Web:* www.fairsandexpos.com					
International Ecotourism Society The (TIES)					
Ste 34145 PO Box 96503	Washington	DC	20005	202-506-5033	789-7279
Web: www.ecotourism.org					
International Festivals & Events Assn (IFEA)					
2603 W Eastover Terr	Boise	ID	83706	208-433-0950	433-9812
Web: www.ifea.com					
International Gay & Lesbian Travel Assn (IGLTA)					
1201 NE 26th St Suite 103	Fort Lauderdale	FL	33305	954-630-1637	630-1652
TF: 800-448-8550 ■ *Web:* www.iglta.org					
International Mountain Bicycling Assn (IMBA)					
207 Canyon Blvd Suite 301 PO Box 7578	Boulder	CO	80306	303-545-9011	545-9026
TF: 888-442-4622 ■ *Web:* www.imba.com					
Leave No Trace Center for Outdoor Ethics Inc					
1830 17th St.	Boulder	CO	80302	303-442-8222	442-8217
TF: 800-332-4100 ■ *Web:* www.lnt.org					
Lewis & Clark Trail Heritage Foundation					
4201 Giant springs Rd	Great Falls	MT	59405	406-454-1234	771-9237
TF: 888-701-3434 ■ *Web:* www.lewisandclark.org					
Lincoln Highway Assn 136 N Elm St	Franklin Grove	IL	61031	815-456-3030	
Web: www.lincolnhighwayassoc.org					
Loners on Wheels (LoW) 1795 O'Kelley Rd SE	Deming	NM	88030	575-544-7303	546-1350
TF: 866-569-2582 ■ *Web:* www.lonersonwheels.com					
Mountaineers The 7700 Sand Pt Way NE.	Seattle	WA	98115	206-521-6000	523-6763
Web: www.mountaineers.org					
NA of Commissioned Travel Agents					
1101 King St Suite 200.	Alexandria	VA	22314	703-739-6826	739-6861
TF: 877-226-2282 ■ *Web:* www.nacta.org					
National Caves Assn 1900 Mammoth Cave Pkwy	Park City	KY	42160	270-749-2228	749-2428
Web: www.cavern.com					
National Club Assn (NCA)					
1201 15th St NW Suite 450	Washington	DC	20005	202-822-9822	822-9808
TF: 800-625-6221 ■ *Web:* www.natlclub.org					
National Forest Recreation Assn (NFRA)					
PO Box 488	Woodlake	CA	93286	559-564-2365	564-2048
Web: www.nfra.org					
National Golf Course Owners Assn (NGCOA)					
291 Seven Farms Dr 2nd Fl	Charleston	SC	29492	843-881-9956	881-9958
TF: 800-933-4262 ■ *Web:* www.ngcoa.org					
National Indian Gaming Assn (NIGA)					
224 2nd St SE.	Washington	DC	20003	202-546-7711	546-1755
TF: 800-286-6442 ■ *Web:* www.indiangaming.org					
National Ski Areas Assn (NSAA)					
133 S Van Gordon St Suite 300	Lakewood	CO	80228	303-987-1111	986-2345
Web: www.nsaa.org					
National Society for Park Resources (NSPR)					
c/o National Recreation & Pk Assn					
22377 Belmont Ridge Rd	Ashburn	VA	20148	703-858-0784	858-0794
TF: 800-626-6772 ■ *Web:* www.nrpa.org					

			Phone	Fax
National Tour Assn (NTA) 546 E Main St . . . . Lexington *TF:* 800-682-8886 ■ *Web:* www.ntaonline.com	KY	40508	859-226-4444	226-4404
North Country Trail Assn 229 E Main St . . . . Lowell *TF:* 866-445-3628 ■ *Web:* www.northcountrytrail.org	MI	49331	616-897-5987	897-6605
Oregon-California Trails Assn 524 S Osage St PO Box 1019 . . . . Independence *TF:* 888-811-6282 ■ *Web:* www.octa-trails.org	MO	64051	816-252-2276	836-0989
Pacific Crest Trail Assn (PCTA) 1331 Garden Hwy . . . . .Sacramento *TF:* 888-728-7245 ■ *Web:* www.pcta.org	CA	95833	916-285-1846	285-1865
Pennsylvania AAA Federation 600 N 3rd St . . . . Harrisburg *Web:* www.aaapa.org	PA	17105	717-238-7192	238-6574
Relais & Chateaux Assn 10 E 53rd St . . . . New York *TF:* 800-735-2478 ■ *Web:* www.relaischateaux.com	NY	10022	212-319-4880	319-4666
RVing Women 879 N Plaza Dr # B103 . . . . Apache Junction *TF:* 888-557-8464 ■ *Web:* www.rvingwomen.org	AZ	85120	480-671-6226	671-6230
Santa Fe Trail Assn 1349 K-156 Hwy. . . . . Larned *Web:* www.santafetrail.org	KS	67550	620-285-2054	
Society of Incentive & Travel Executives (SITE) 401 N Michigan Ave . . . . .Chicago *Web:* www.siteglobal.com	IL	60611	312-321-5148	527-6783
Society of Park & Recreation Educators (SPRE) c/o National Recreation & Pk Assn 22377 Belmont Ridge Rd . . . . .Ashburn *TF:* 800-626-6772 ■ *Web:* www.nrpa.org	VA	20148	703-858-0784	858-0794
Special Military Active Retired Travel Club (SMART) 600 University Office Blvd Suite 1A . . . . Pensacola *TF:* 800-354-7681 ■ *Web:* www.smartrving.net	FL	32504	850-478-1986	
Statue of Liberty-Ellis Island Foundation Inc The 17 Battery Pl Suite 210. . . . . .New York *Web:* www.statueofliberty.org	NY	10004	212-561-4500	779-1990
Travel Institute 148 Linden St Suite 305 . . . . .Wellesley *TF:* 800-542-4282 ■ *Web:* www.thetravelinstitute.com	MA	02482	781-237-0280	237-3860
US Tour Operators Assn (USTOA) 275 Madison Ave Suite 2014 . . . . .New York *Web:* www.ustoa.com	NY	10016	212-599-6599	599-6744
Washington Trails Assn (WTA) 705 2nd Ave Suite 300 . . . . .Seattle *Web:* www.wta.org	WA	98121	206-625-1367	625-9249
Western National Parks Assn (WNPA) 12880 N Vistoso Village Dr . . . . .Tucson *Web:* www.wnpa.org	AZ	85755	520-622-1999	623-9519
Wilderness Inquiry (WI) 808 14th Ave SE . . . . Minneapolis *TF:* 800-728-0719 ■ *Web:* www.wildernessinquiry.org	MN	55414	612-676-9400	676-9401

48-24 Women's Organizations

			Phone	Fax
9to5 NA of Working Women (NAWW) 207 E Buffalo St Suite 211 . . . . .Milwaukee *TF:* 800-522-0925 ■ *Web:* www.9to5.org	WI	53202	414-274-0925	272-2870
Assn for Women's Rights in Development (AWID) 215 Spadina Ave Suite 150. . . . . Toronto *Web:* www.awid.org	ON	M5T2C7	416-594-3773	594-0330
Center for Women Policy Studies 1776 Masachusetts Ave NW Suite 450. . . . . .Washington *Web:* www.centerwomenpolicy.org	DC	20036	202-872-1770	296-8962
Coalition of Labor Union Women (CLUW) 815 16th St NW 2nd Fl. . . . . .Washington *Web:* www.cluw.org	DC	20006	202-508-6969	508-6968
Equal Rights Advocates (ERA) 1663 Mission St Suite 250. . . . . San Francisco *TF:* 800-839-4372 ■ *Web:* www.equalrights.org	CA	94103	415-621-0672	621-6744
Feminist Majority Foundation-East Coast (FMF) 1600 Wilson Blvd Suite 801. . . . . .Arlington *Web:* www.feminist.org	VA	22209	703-522-2214	522-2219
General Federation of Women's Clubs (GFWC) 1734 N St NW. . . . . .Washington *Web:* www.gfwc.org	DC	20036	202-347-3168	835-0246
Girls Inc 120 Wall St 3rd Fl. . . . . .New York *TF:* 800-374-4475 ■ *Web:* www.girlsinc.org	NY	10005	212-509-2000	509-8708
Inter-American Commission of Women 1889 F St NW Rm 350 . . . . .Washington *Web:* www.oas.org/CIM	DC	20006	202-458-6084	458-6094
International Alliance for Women (TIAW) 8405 Greensboro Dr Suite 800. . . . . .McLean **Fax Area Code:* 905 ■ *TF:* 866-533-8429 ■ *Web:* www.tiaw.org	VA	22102	703-506-3284	305-1548*
International Center for Research on Women (ICRW) 1120 20th St NW Suite 500-N . . . . .Washington *Web:* www.icrw.org	DC	20036	202-797-0007	797-0020
Ms Foundation for Women 120 Wall St 33rd Fl . . . . .New York *Web:* www.ms.foundation.org	NY	10005	212-742-2300	742-1653
National Congress of Neighborhood Women 249 Manhattan Ave. . . . . Brooklyn	NY	11211	718-388-8915	388-0285
National Council of Jewish Women (NCJW) 475 Riverside Dr Suite 520. . . . . .New York *TF:* 800-829-6259 ■ *Web:* www.ncjw.org	NY	10115	212-645-4048	645-7466
National Council of Negro Women Inc (NCNW) 633 Pennsylvania Ave NW . . . . .Washington *Web:* www.ncnw.org	DC	20004	202-737-0120	737-0476
National Organization for Women (NOW) 1100 H St NW 3rd Fl . . . . .Washington *Web:* www.now.org	DC	20005	202-628-8669	785-8576
National Partnership for Women & Families 1875 Connecticut Ave NW Suite 650 . . . . .Washington *Web:* www.nationalpartnership.org	DC	20009	202-986-2600	986-2539
National Woman's Party 144 Constitution Ave NE. . . . . .Washington *Web:* www.sewallbelmont.org	DC	20002	202-546-1210	546-3997
National Women's Law Ctr (NWLC) 11 Dupont Cir NW Suite 800 . . . . .Washington *Web:* www.nwlc.org	DC	20036	202-588-5180	588-5185
New Ways to Work Inc 103 Morris St Suite A . . . . Sebastopol *Web:* www.nww.org	CA	95472	707-824-4000	824-4410
Ninety-Nines Inc 4300 Amelia Earhart Rd . . . . .Oklahoma City *Web:* www.ninety-nines.org	OK	73159	405-685-7969	685-7985
Pennsylvania Women 411 7th Ave Suite 925. . . . . Pittsburgh *TF:* 866-729-9279 ■ *Web:* pawomenwork.org	PA	15219	412-281-9240	281-9279
Wider Opportunities for Women (WOW) 1001 Connecticut Ave NW Suite 930 . . . . .Washington *Web:* www.wowonline.org	DC	20036	202-464-1596	464-1660
Women Employed 65 E Wacker Pl .Chicago *Web:* www.womenemployed.org	IL	60601	312-782-3902	782-5249
Women's Economic Agenda Project (WEAP) 449 15th St 2nd Fl . . . . .Oakland *Web:* www.weap.org	CA	94612	510-986-8620	986-8628
Women's Research & Education Institute (WREI) 714 G Str S E Suite 200 . . . . .Washington *Web:* www.wrei.org	DC	20003	703-812-7990	812-0687
Women's Sports Foundation 1899 Hempstead Tpke Suite 400 Eisenhower Pk . . . . .East Meadow *TF:* 800-227-3988 ■ *Web:* www.womenssportsfoundation.org	NY	11554	516-542-4700	542-4716
Zonta International 1211 W 22nd St Suite 900 . . . . Oak Brook *Web:* www.zonta.org	IL	60523	630-928-1400	928-1559

49 ASSOCIATIONS & ORGANIZATIONS - PROFESSIONAL & TRADE

SEE ALSO Bar Associations - State p. 1515; Dental Associations - State p. 1782; Labor Unions p. 2139; Library Associations - State & Province p. 2176; Medical Associations - State p. 2226; Nurses Associations - State p. 2320; Pharmacy Associations - State p. 2418; Realtor Associations - State p. 2528; Veterinary Medical Associations - State p. 2761

49-1 Accountants Associations

			Phone	Fax
AACE International - Assn for the Advancement of Cost Engineering 209 Prairie Ave Suite 100. . . . . Morgantown *TF:* 800-858-2678 ■ *Web:* www.aacei.org	WV	26501	304-296-8444	291-5728
AGN International-North America 2851 S Parker Rd Suite 850 . . . . Aurora *TF:* 800-782-2272 ■ *Web:* www.agn-na.org	CO	80014	303-743-7880	743-7660
American Accounting Assn 5717 Bessie Dr. . . . . Sarasota *Web:* www.aaahq.org	FL	34233	941-921-7747	923-4093
American Institute of Certified Public Accountants (AICPA) 1211 Avenue of the Americas . . . . .New York *TF:* 888-777-7077 ■ *Web:* www.aicpa.org	NY	10036	212-596-6200	596-6213
American Institute of Professional Bookkeepers (AIPB) 6001 Montrose Rd Suite 500 . . . . Rockville *TF:* 800-622-0121 ■ *Web:* www.aipb.org	MD	20852	800-622-0121	541-0066
American Society of Women Accountants (ASWA) 1760 Old Meadows Rd Suite 500 . . . . McLean *Web:* www.aswa.org	VA	22102	703-506-3265	506-3266
American Woman's Society of Certified Public Accountants (AWSCPA) 136 S Keowee St. . . . . .Dayton *TF:* 800-297-2721 ■ *Web:* www.awscpa.org	OH	45402	937-222-1872	222-5794
Assn for Accounting Administration (AAA) 136 S Keowee St. . . . . .Dayton *Web:* www.cpaadmin.org	OH	45402	937-222-0030	222-5794
Assn of Certified Fraud Examiners (ACFE) 716 W Ave . . . . Austin *TF:* 800-245-3321 ■ *Web:* www.acfe.com	TX	78701	512-478-9000	478-9297
Assn of Chartered Accountants in the US (ACAUS) 341 Lafayette St Suite 4246 . . . . .New York *Web:* www.acaus.org	NY	10012	212-334-2078	431-5786
Assn of Government Accountants (AGA) 2208 Mt Vernon Ave. . . . . .Alexandria *TF:* 800-242-7211 ■ *Web:* www.agacgfm.org	VA	22301	703-684-6931	548-9367
Assn of Healthcare Internal Auditors (AHIA) 10200 W 44th Ave Suite 304 . . . . Wheat Ridge *TF:* 888-275-2442 ■ *Web:* www.ahia.org	CO	80063	303-327-7546	422-8894
BKR International 19 Fulton St Suite 306 . . . . .New York *TF:* 800-257-4685 ■ *Web:* www.bkr.com	NY	10038	212-964-2115	964-2133
Construction Financial Management Assn (CFMA) 29 Emmons Dr Suite F-50 . . . . .Princeton *Web:* www.cfma.org	NJ	08540	609-452-8000	452-0474
CPA Assoc International Inc 301 Rt 17 N . . . . .Rutherford *Web:* www.cpaai.com	NJ	07070	201-804-8686	804-9222
CPA Auto Dealer Consultants Assn (CADCA) 624 Grassmere Pk Dr Suite 15 . . . . Nashville *TF:* 888-231-2524 ■ *Web:* www.autodealercpas.net	TN	37211	615-377-3392	377-7092
CPA Mfg Services Assn 624 Grassmere Pk Suite 15 . . . . Nashville *TF:* 888-475-4476 ■ *Web:* www.manufacturingcpas.com	TN	37211	615-373-9880	377-7092
CPAmerica International 11801 Research Dr. . . . . Alachua *TF:* 800-992-2324 ■ *Web:* www.cpamerica.org	FL	32615	386-418-4001	418-4002
Financial Accounting Foundation (FAF) 401 Merritt 7 PO Box 5116. . . . . .Norwalk	CT	06856	203-847-0700	849-9714

Organization	City	State	ZIP	Phone	Fax
Financial Accounting Standards Board (FASB) 401 Merritt 7 PO Box 5116 *TF:* 800-748-0659 ■ *Web:* www.fasb.org	Norwalk	CT	06856	203-847-0700	849-9714
Foundation for Accounting Education (FAE) 3 Pk Ave 18th Fl *TF:* 800-537-3635 ■ *Web:* www.nysscpa.org/page/continuing-education/fae-conferences	New York	NY	10016	212-719-8300	719-3365
Hospitality Financial & Technology Professionals (HFTP) 11709 Boulder Ln Suite 110 *TF:* 800-856-4242 ■ *Web:* www.hftp.org	Austin	TX	78726	512-249-5333	249-1533
IGAF Worldwide 3235 Satellite Blvd Bldg 400 Suite 300 *TF:* 800-272-4423 ■ *Web:* www.igafworldwide.org	Duluth	GA	30096	678-417-7730	999-3959
Institute of Internal Auditors (IIA) 247 Maitland Ave *Web:* www.theiia.org	Altamonte Springs	FL	32701	407-937-1100	937-1101
Institute of Management Accountants Inc (IMA) 10 Paragon Dr *TF:* 800-638-4427 ■ *Web:* www.imanet.org	Montvale	NJ	07645	201-573-9000	474-1600
International Federation of Accountants 545 5th Ave 14th Fl *Web:* www.ifac.org	New York	NY	10017	212-286-9344	286-9570
NA of Black Accountants (NABA) 7249-A Hanover Pkwy *Web:* www.nabainc.org	Greenbelt	MD	20770	301-474-6222	474-3114
NA of State Boards of Accountancy (NASBA) 150 4th Ave N Suite 700 *TF:* 800-272-3926 ■ *Web:* www.nasba.org	Nashville	TN	37219	615-880-4200	880-4290
NA of Tax Professionals (NATP) 720 Assn Dr **Fax Area Code:* 800 ■ *TF:* 800-558-3402 ■ *Web:* www.natptax.com	Appleton	WI	54914	920-749-1040	747-0001*
National Accounting & Finance Council (NAFC) American Trucking Associations 950 N Glebe Rd *Web:* www.truckline.com	Arlington	VA	22307	703-838-1915	836-0751
National CPA Health Care Advisors Assn (HCAA) 624 Grassmere Pk Suite 15 *TF:* 888-475-4476 ■ *Web:* www.hcaa.com	Nashville	TN	37211	615-373-9880	377-7092
National Society of Accountants (NSA) 1010 N Fairfax St *TF:* 800-966-6679 ■ *Web:* www.nsacct.org	Alexandria	VA	22314	703-549-6400	549-2984
Not-for-Profit Services Assn (NSA) 624 Grassmere Pk Suite 15 *TF:* 888-475-4476 ■ *Web:* www.nonprofitcpas.com	Nashville	TN	37211	615-373-9880	377-7092
Polaris International 9200 S Dadeland Blvd Suite 510 *Web:* www.accountants.org	Miami	FL	33156	305-670-0580	670-3818
Tax Executives Institute (TEI) 1200 G St NW Suite 300 *Web:* www.tei.org	Washington	DC	20005	202-638-5601	638-5607

49-2 Banking & Finance Professionals Associations

Organization	City	State	ZIP	Phone	Fax
ABA Marketing Network 1120 Connecticut Ave NW *TF:* 800-226-5377 ■ *Web:* www.aba.com/MarketingNetwork	Washington	DC	20036	202-663-5000	828-5053
ACA International - Assn of Credit & Collection Professionals 4040 W 70th St PO Box 390106 *Web:* www.acainternational.org	Minneapolis	MN	55439	952-926-6547	926-1624
America's Community Bankers (ACB) 1120 Connecticut Ave NW *TF:* 800-226-5377 ■ *Web:* www.aba.com	Washington	DC	20036	202-857-3100	296-8716
American Assn of Daily Money Managers (AADMM) 174 Crestview Dr **Fax Area Code:* 814 ■ *TF:* 877-326-5991 ■ *Web:* www.aadmm.com	Bellefonte	PA	16823	877-326-5991	355-2452*
American Assn of Individual Investors (AAII) 625 N Michigan Ave Suite 1900 *TF:* 800-428-2244 ■ *Web:* www.aaii.com	Chicago	IL	60611	312-280-0170	280-9883
American Bankers Assn (ABA) 1120 Connecticut Ave NW **Fax:* Hum Res ■ *TF Cust Svc:* 800-226-5377 ■ *Web:* www.aba.com	Washington	DC	20036	202-663-5000	828-5045*
American Benefits Council 1501 M St NW # 600 *Web:* www.americanbenefitscouncil.org	Washington	DC	20005	202-289-6700	289-4582
American Council for Capital Formation (ACCF) 1750 K St NW Suite 400 *Web:* www.accf.org	Washington	DC	20006	202-293-5811	785-8165
American Economic Assn (AEA) 2014 Broadway Suite 305 *Web:* www.aeaweb.org	Nashville	TN	37203	615-322-2595	343-7590
American Finance Assn (AFA) Blackwell Publishing 350 Main St *TF:* 800-835-6770 ■ *Web:* www.afajof.org	Malden	MA	02148	781-388-8599	388-8232
American Financial Services Assn (AFSA) 919 18th St NW Suite 300 *Web:* www.afsaonline.org	Washington	DC	20006	202-296-5544	223-0321
American Institute of Certified Planners (AICP) 1776 Massachusetts Ave NW Suite 400 *Web:* www.planning.org/aicp	Washington	DC	20036	202-872-0611	872-0643
Assn for Financial Professionals (AFP) 4520 E W Hwy Suite 750 *Web:* www.afponline.org	Bethesda	MD	20814	301-907-2862	907-2864
Bank Administration Institute (BAI) 1 N Franklin St Suite 1000 **Fax:* Cust Svc ■ *TF Cust Svc:* 800-224-9889 ■ *Web:* www.bai.org	Chicago	IL	60606	312-553-4600	683-2321*
Better Investing PO Box 220 *TF:* 877-275-6242 ■ *Web:* www.betterinvesting.org	Royal Oak	MI	48068	248-583-6242	583-4880
Certified Financial Planner Board of Standards Inc 1425 K St NW Suite 500 *TF:* 800-487-1497 ■ *Web:* www.cfp.net	Washington	DC	20005	202-379-2200	379-2299
CFA Institute 560 Ray C Hunt Dr PO Box 3668 *TF:* 800-247-8132 ■ *Web:* www.cfainstitute.org	Charlottesville	VA	22903	434-951-5499	951-5262
Community Banking Advisory Network (CBAN) 624 Grassmere Pk Dr Suite 15 *TF:* 888-475-4476 ■ *Web:* www.bankingcpas.com	Nashville	TN	37211	615-377-3392	377-7092
Consumer Bankers Assn (CBA) 1000 Wilson Blvd Suite 2500 *Web:* www.cbanet.org	Arlington	VA	22209	703-276-1750	528-1290
Consumer Data Industry Assn (CDIA) 1090 Vermont Ave NW Suite 200 *Web:* www.cdiaonline.org	Washington	DC	20005	202-371-0910	371-0134
Council of Institutional Investors 888 17th St NW Suite 500 *Web:* www.cii.org	Washington	DC	20006	202-822-0800	822-0801
Credit Professionals International 525B N Laclede Stn Rd *Web:* www.creditprofessionals.org	Saint Louis	MO	63119	314-961-0031	961-0040
Credit Research Foundation (CRF) 8840 Columbia 100 Pkwy *TF:* 866-557-3242 ■ *Web:* www.crfonline.org	Columbia	MD	21045	410-740-5499	740-4620
Credit Union Executives Society (CUES) 5510 Research Pk Dr *TF:* 800-252-2664 ■ *Web:* www.cues.org	Madison	WI	53711	608-271-2664	271-2303
Electronic Funds Transfer Assn (EFTA) 11350 Random Hills Rd Suite 800 *Web:* www.efta.org	Fairfax	VA	22030	703-934-6052	934-6058
Emerging Markets Traders Assn (EMTA) 360 Madison Ave 18th Fl *Web:* www.emta.org	New York	NY	10017	212-313-1100	313-1016
Farm Credit Council 50 F St NW Suite 900 *Web:* www.fccouncil.com	Washington	DC	20001	202-626-8710	626-8718
Financial Executives International (FEI) 200 Campus Dr PO Box 674 *Web:* www.financialexecutives.org	Florham Park	NJ	07932	973-765-1000	765-1018
Financial Industry Regulatory Authority (FINRA) 9509 Key W Ave *Web:* www.finra.org	Rockville	MD	20850	301-590-6500	
Financial Management Assn International (FMA) 4202 E Fowler Ave *Web:* www.fma.org	Tampa	FL	33620	813-974-2084	974-3318
Financial Managers Society (FMS) 100 W Monroe St Suite 810 *TF Cust Svc:* 800-275-4367 ■ *Web:* www.fmsinc.org	Chicago	IL	60603	312-578-1300	578-1308
Financial Planning Assn (FPA) 4100 E Mississippi Ave Suite 400 *TF:* 800-945-4237 ■ *Web:* www.fpanet.org	Denver	CO	80246	303-759-4900	759-0749
Financial Service Centers of America Inc (FiSCA) 21 Main St 1st Fl *Web:* www.fisca.org	Hackensack	NJ	07602	201-487-0412	487-3954
Financial Services Roundtable 1001 Pennsylvania Ave NW Suite 500 *Web:* www.fsround.org	Washington	DC	20005	202-289-4322	628-2507
Financial Women International (FWI) 1027 W Roselawn Ave *TF:* 866-236-2007 ■ *Web:* www.fwi.org	Roseville	MN	55113	651-487-7632	489-1322
FINRA 1735 K St NW *TF:* 800-289-9999 ■ *Web:* www.finra.org	Washington	DC	20006	202-728-8000	
Futures Industry Assn (FIA) 2001 Pennsylvania Ave NW Suite 600 *Web:* www.fiafii.org	Washington	DC	20006	202-466-5460	296-3184
Independent Community Bankers of America (ICBA) 1615 L St NW Suite 900 *TF:* 800-422-8439 ■ *Web:* www.icba.org	Washington	DC	20036	202-659-8111	861-5503
Industry Council for Tangible Assets (ICTA) PO Box 1365 *Web:* www.ictaonline.org	Severna Park	MD	21146	410-626-7005	626-7007
Institute of International Bankers (IIB) 299 Pk Ave 17th Fl *Web:* www.iib.org	New York	NY	10171	212-421-1611	421-1119
Institute of International Finance (IIF) 1333 H St NW Suite 800-E *Web:* www.iif.com	Washington	DC	20005	202-857-3600	775-1430
International Financial Services Assn (IFSA) 9 Sylvan Way 1st Fl *Web:* www.ifsa.org	Parsippany	NJ	07054	973-656-1900	656-1915
International Swaps & Derivatives Assn (ISDA) 360 Madison Ave 16th Fl *Web:* www2.isda.org	New York	NY	10017	212-901-6000	901-6001
Investment Co Institute (ICI) 1401 H St NW Suite 1200 *Web:* www.ici.org	Washington	DC	20005	202-326-5800	326-5985
Investment Management Consultants Assn (IMCA) 5619 DTC Pkwy Suite 500 *Web:* www.imca.org	Greenwood Village	CO	80111	303-770-3377	770-1812
Investment Program Assn 1140 Connecticut Ave NW Suite 1040 *Web:* www.theipaonline.org	Washington	DC	20036	202-775-9750	331-8446
Investor Protection Trust 919 18th St NW Suite 300 *Web:* www.investorprotection.org	Washington	DC	20006	202-775-2111	
Life Insurance Settlement Assn (LISA) 1011 E Colonial Dr Suite 500 *Web:* www.lisassociation.org	Orlando	FL	32803	407-894-3797	897-1325

Organization	City	State	ZIP	Phone	Fax
Mortgage Bankers Assn (MBA) 1919 Pennsylvania Ave NW *Fax: Cust Svc ■ *TF:* 800-793-6222 ■ *Web:* www.mortgagebankers.org	Washington	DC	20006	202-557-2700	721-0247*
Municipal Securities Rulemaking Board (MSRB) 1900 Duke St Suite 600 *Web:* www.msrb.org	Alexandria	VA	22314	703-797-6600	797-6700
Mutual Fund Education Alliance (MFEA) 100 NW Englewood Rd Suite 130 *Web:* www.mfea.com	Kansas City	MO	64118	816-454-9422	454-9322
NA of Credit Management (NACM) 8840 Columbia 100 Pkwy *TF:* 800-955-8815 ■ *Web:* www.nacm.org	Columbia	MD	21045	410-740-5560	740-5574
NA of Development Organizations (NADO) 400 N Capitol St NW Suite 390 *Web:* www.nado.org	Washington	DC	20001	202-624-7806	624-8813
NA of Federal Credit Unions (NAFCU) 3138 10th St N *TF:* 800-336-4644 ■ *Web:* www.nafcu.org	Arlington	VA	22201	703-522-4770	524-1082
NA of Financial & Estate Planning (NAFEP) 545 E 4500 S Suite E-220 *Web:* www.nafep.com	Salt Lake City	UT	84107	801-266-9900	266-1019
NA of Government Guaranteed Lenders (NAGGL) 215 E 9th Ave *Web:* www.naggl.org	Stillwater	OK	74074	405-377-4022	377-3931
NA of Mortgage Brokers (NAMB) 7900 Westpark Dr Suite T309 *Web:* www.namb.org	McLean	VA	22102	703-342-5900	342-5905
NA of Personal Financial Advisors (NAPFA) 3250 N Arlington Heights Rd Suite 109 *TF:* 800-366-2732 ■ *Web:* www.napfa.org	Arlington Heights	IL	60004	847-483-5400	483-5415
NA of Professional Surplus Lines Offices (NAPSLO) 200 NE 54th St Suite 2000 *Web:* www.napslo.org	Kansas City	MO	64118	816-741-3910	741-5409
NA of Small Business Investment Cos (NASBIC) 1100 H St NW Suite 610 *Web:* www.nasbic.org	Washington	DC	20005	202-628-5055	628-5080
NA of Stock Plan Professionals (NASPP) PO Box 21639 *Web:* www.naspp.com	Concord	CA	94521	925-685-9271	685-5402
NACHA - Electronic Payments Assn 13665 Dulles Technology Dr Suite 300 *TF:* 800-487-9180 ■ *Web:* www.nacha.org	Herndon	VA	20171	703-561-1100	787-0996
National Federation of Community Development Credit Unions (NFCDCU) 39 Broadway 21st Fl *TF:* 800-437-8711 ■ *Web:* www.natfed.org	New York	NY	10006	212-809-1850	809-3274
National Futures Assn (NFA) 300 S Riverside Plaza Suite 1800 *TF:* 800-366-6321 ■ *Web:* www.nfa.futures.org	Chicago	IL	60606	312-781-1300	781-1467
National Investment Co Service Assn (NICSA) 8400 Westpark Dr 2nd Fl *Web:* www.nicsa.org	McLean	VA	22102	508-485-1500	485-1560
National Investor Relations Institute (NIRI) 8020 Towers Crescent Dr Suite 250 *Web:* www.niri.org	Vienna	VA	22182	703-506-3570	506-3571
North American Securities Administrators Assn (NASAA) 750 1st St NE Suite 1140 *TF:* 888-846-2722 ■ *Web:* www.nasaa.org	Washington	DC	20002	202-737-0900	783-3571
Pension Real Estate Assn (PREA) 100 Pearl St 13th Fl *Web:* www.prea.org	Hartford	CT	06103	860-692-6341	692-6351
Risk Management Assn (RMA) 1801 Market St Suite 300 *TF Cust Svc:* 800-677-7621 ■ *Web:* www.rmahq.org	Philadelphia	PA	19103	215-446-4000	446-4101
Savings Coalition of America 1050 17th St NW Suite 1000 *Web:* www.savingscoalition.org	Washington	DC	20036	202-223-2632	223-2634
Securities Industry & Financial Markets Assn (SIFMAA) 120 Broadway 35th Fl *Web:* www.sifma.org	New York	NY	10271	212-313-1200	313-1301
Security Traders Assn 420 Lexington Ave Suite 2334 *Web:* www.securitytraders.org	New York	NY	10170	212-867-7002	867-7030
Smart Card Alliance Inc 191 Clarkville Rd *TF:* 800-556-6828 ■ *Web:* www.smartcardalliance.org	Princeton Junction	NJ	08550	609-799-5654	799-7032
Western Economic Assn International (WEAI) 18837 Brookhurst St Suite 304 *Web:* www.weai.org	Fountain Valley	CA	92708	714-965-8800	965-8829
Winter Kloman Moter & Repp SC (WKMR) 235 N Executive Dr Suite 160 *Web:* www.wkmr.com	Brookfield	WI	53005	262-797-9050	797-8251
World Council of Credit Unions Inc (WOCCU) 5710 Minerial Pt Rd *Web:* www.woccu.org	Madison	WI	53705	608-395-2000	395-2001

49-3 Construction Industry Associations

Organization	City	State	ZIP	Phone	Fax
Air Conditioning Contractors of America (ACCA) 2800 S Shirlington Rd # 300 *Web:* www.acca.org	Arlington	VA	22206	703-575-4477	575-8107
Air Movement & Control Assn International Inc (AMCA) 30 W University Dr *Web:* www.amca.org	Arlington Heights	IL	60004	847-394-0150	253-0088
American Architectural Manufacturers Assn (AAMA) 1827 Walden Office Sq Suite 550 *Web:* www.aamanet.org	Schaumburg	IL	60173	847-303-5664	303-5774
American Concrete Institute International (ACI) 38800 Country Club Dr PO Box 9094 *Web:* www.concrete.org	Farmington Hills	MI	48331	248-848-3700	848-3701
American Concrete Pavement Assn (ACPA) 5420 Old Orchard Rd Suite A-100 *Web:* www.pavement.com	Skokie	IL	60077	847-966-2272	966-9970
American Concrete Pipe Assn 8445 Freeport Pkwy Suite 350 *Web:* www.concrete-pipe.org	Irving	TX	75063	972-506-7216	506-7682
American Congress on Surveying & Mapping (ACSM) 6 Montgomery Village Ave Suite 403 *Web:* www.acsm.net	Gaithersburg	MD	20879	240-632-9716	632-1321
American Fence Assn (AFA) 800 Roosevelt Rd Bldg C-312 *TF:* 800-822-4342 ■ *Web:* www.americanfenceassociation.com	Glen Ellyn	IL	60137	630-942-6598	790-3095
American Fire Sprinkler Assn (AFSA) 12750 Merit Dr Suite 350 *Web:* www.firesprinkler.org	Dallas	TX	75251	214-349-5965	343-8898
American Institute of Constructors (AIC) 700 N Fairfax St Suite 510 *Fax Area Code: 571 ■ *Web:* www.professionalconstructor.org	Alexandria	VA	22314	703-683-4999	527-3105*
American Institute of Steel Construction (AISC) 1 E Wacker Dr Suite 3100 *Web:* www.aisc.org	Chicago	IL	60601	312-670-2400	670-5403
American Institute of Timber Construction (AITC) 7012 S Revere Pkwy Suite 140 *Web:* www.aitc-glulam.org	Centennial	CO	80112	303-792-9559	792-0669
American Lumber Standard Committee Inc (ALSC) 19715 Waters Rd *Web:* www.alsc.org	Germantown	MD	20874	301-972-1700	540-8004
American Road & Transportation Builders Assn (ARTBA) 1219 28th St NW *Web:* www.artba.org	Washington	DC	20007	202-289-4434	289-4435
American Society of Heating Refrigerating & Air-Conditioning Engineers Inc (ASHRAE) 1791 Tullie Cir NE *TF Cust Svc:* 800-527-4723 ■ *Web:* www.ashrae.org	Atlanta	GA	30329	404-636-8400	321-5478
American Society of Home Inspectors (ASHI) 932 Lee St Suite 101 *TF:* 800-743-2744 ■ *Web:* www.ashi.org	Des Plaines	IL	60016	847-759-2820	759-1620
American Society of Professional Estimators (ASPE) 2525 Perimeter Pl Dr Suite 103 *Web:* www.aspenational.com	Nashville	TN	37214	615-316-9200	316-9800
American Subcontractors Assn Inc (ASA) 1004 Duke St *Web:* www.asaonline.com	Alexandria	VA	22314	703-684-3450	836-3482
American Welding Society (AWS) 550 NW 42nd Ave *TF:* 800-443-9353 ■ *Web:* www.aws.org	Miami	FL	33126	305-443-9353	443-7559
APA - Engineered Wood Assn 7011 S 19th St *Web:* www.apawood.org	Tacoma	WA	98466	253-565-6600	565-7265
Architectural Precast Assn (APA) 6710 Winkler Rd Suite 8 *Web:* www.archprecast.org	Fort Myers	FL	33919	239-454-6989	454-6787
Architectural Woodwork Institute (AWI) 46179 Westlake Dr Suite 120 *Web:* www.awinet.org	Potomac Falls	VA	20165	571-323-3636	323-3630
Asphalt Institute 2696 Research Pk Dr *Web:* www.asphaltinstitute.org	Lexington	KY	40511	859-288-4960	288-4999
Asphalt Recycling & Reclaiming Assn (ARRA) 3 Church Cir PMB 250 *Web:* www.arra.org	Annapolis	MD	21401	410-267-0023	267-7546
Asphalt Roofing Manufacturers Assn (ARMA) 529 14th St NW # 750 *TF:* 800-785-3255 ■ *Web:* www.asphaltroofing.org	Washington	DC	20045	202-207-0917	223-9741
Assn for Retail Environment (ARE) 4651 Sheridan St Suite 470 *Web:* www.retailenvironments.org	Hollywood	FL	33021	954-893-7300	893-7500
Assn of Millwork Distributors (AMD) 10047 Robert Trent Jones Pkwy *TF:* 800-786-7274 ■ *Web:* www.amdweb.com	New Port Richey	FL	34655	727-372-3665	372-2879
Assn of the Wall & Ceiling Industries International (AWCI) 513 W Broad St Suite 210 *Web:* www.awci.org	Falls Church	VA	22046	703-534-8300	534-8307
Associated Builders & Contractors Inc (ABC) 4250 Fairfax Dr *Web:* www.abc.org	Arlington	VA	22203	703-812-2000	812-8203
Associated General Contractors of America (AGC) 2300 Wilson Blvd Suite 400 *TF:* 800-242-1766 ■ *Web:* www.agc.org	Arlington	VA	22201	703-548-3118	548-3119
Associated Locksmiths of America (ALOA) 3500 Easy St *TF:* 800-532-2562 ■ *Web:* www.aloa.org	Dallas	TX	75254	214-819-9733	819-9736
Brick Industry Assn (BIA) 1850 Centennial Pk Dr Suite 301 *Web:* www.gobrick.com	Reston	VA	20191	703-620-0010	620-3928
Building & Construction Trades Dept AFL-CIO 815 16th St NW Suite 600 *Web:* www.buildingtrades.org	Washington	DC	20006	202-347-1461	628-0724
Building Material Dealers Assn (BMDA) 12540 SW Main St Suite 200 *TF:* 800-666-2632 ■ *Web:* www.bmda.com	Tigard	OR	97223	503-624-0561	620-1016
Cedar Shake & Shingle Bureau 7101 Horne St Suite 2 *Web:* www.cedarbureau.org	Mission	BC	V2V7A2	604-820-7700	820-0266

	City	State	Zip	Phone	Fax
Ceilings & Interior Systems Construction Assn (CISCA) 405 Illinois Ave Unit 2-B *Web:* cisca.org	Saint Charles	IL	60174	630-584-1919	584-2003
Cement Assn of Canada (CAC) 502-350 Sparks St *Web:* www.cement.ca	Ottawa	ON	K1R7S8	613-236-9471	563-4498
Cement Kiln Recycling Coalition (CKRC) PO Box 7553 **Fax Area Code:* 202 ■ *Web:* www.ckrc.org	Arlington	VA	22207	703-869-4718	466-5009*
Central Station Alarm Assn (CSAA) 8150 Leesburg Pike Suite 700 *Web:* www.csaaul.org	Vienna	VA	22180	703-242-4670	242-4675
Composite Panel Assn 19465 Deerfield Ave Suite 306 *TF:* 866-426-6767 ■ *Web:* www.pbmdf.com	Leesburg	VA	20176	703-724-1128	274-1588
Concrete Reinforcing Steel Institute (CRSI) 933 N Plum Grove Rd *Web:* www.crsi.org	Schaumburg	IL	60173	847-517-1200	517-1206
Construction Financial Management Assn (CFMA) 29 Emmons Dr Suite F-50 *Web:* www.cfma.org	Princeton	NJ	08540	609-452-8000	452-0474
Construction Specifications Institute (CSI) 99 Canal Ctr Plaza Suite 300 *TF:* 800-689-2900 ■ *Web:* www.csinet.org	Alexandria	VA	22314	703-684-0300	684-0465
Distribution Contractors Assn (DCA) 101 W Renner Rd Suite 460 *Web:* www.dca-online.org	Richardson	TX	75082	972-680-0261	680-0461
Door & Hardware Institute (DHI) 14150 Newbrook Dr Suite 200 *Web:* www.dhi.org	Chantilly	VA	20151	703-222-2010	222-2410
Electronic Security Assn Inc (ESA) 2300 Valley View Ln Suite 230 *TF:* 888-447-1689 ■ *Web:* www.esaweb.org	Irving	TX	75062	214-260-5970	260-5979
Forest Resources Assn Inc 600 Jefferson Plaza Suite 350 *Web:* www.forestresources.org	Rockville	MD	20852	301-838-9385	838-9481
Hardwood Plywood & Veneer Assn (HPVA) 1825 Michael Faraday Dr *Web:* www.hpva.org	Reston	VA	20195	703-435-2900	435-2537
Interlocking Concrete Pavement Institute (ICPI) 1444 'I' St NW Suite 700 *TF:* 800-241-3652 ■ *Web:* www.icpi.org	Washington	DC	20005	202-712-9036	408-0285
International Assn of Drilling Contractors (IADC) 10370 Richmond Ave Suite 760 *Web:* www.iadc.org	Houston	TX	77042	713-292-1945	292-1946
International Assn of Electrical Inspectors (IAEI) 901 Waterfall Way Suite 602 *TF:* 800-786-4234 ■ *Web:* www.iaei.org	Richardson	TX	75080	972-235-1455	235-6858
International Code Council (ICC) 500 New Jersey Ave NW 6th Fl **Fax Area Code:* 292 ■ *TF:* 888-422-7233 ■ *Web:* www.iccsafe.org	Washington	DC	20001	202-370-1800	783-2348*
International Council of Employers of Bricklayers & Allied Craftworkers (ICEBAC) PO Box 21462 *Web:* www.icebac.org	Washington	DC	20009	202-457-9040	457-9051
International Council of Shopping Centers (ICSC) 1221 Avenue of the Americas 41st Fl **Fax Area Code:* 212 ■ *Web:* www.icsc.org	New York	NY	10020	646-728-3800	589-5555*
International District Energy Assn (IDEA) 24 Lyman St Suite 230 *Web:* www.districtenergy.org	Westborough	MA	01581	508-366-9339	366-0019
International Institute of Ammonia Refrigeration 1001 N Fairfax St Suite 503 *Web:* www.iiar.org	Alexandria	VA	22314	703-312-4200	312-0065
International Masonry Institute (IMI) 42 E St **Fax Area Code:* 301 ■ *TF:* 800-803-0295 ■ *Web:* www.imiweb.org	Annapolis	MD	21401	410-280-1305	261-2855*
International Road Federation (IRF) 500 Mongomery St 5th Fl *Web:* www.irfnet.org	Alexandria	VA	22314	703-535-1001	535-1007
International Union of Elevator Constructors (IUEC) 7154 Columbia Gateway Dr *Web:* www.iuec.org	Columbia	MD	21046	410-953-6150	953-6169
International Wood Products Assn (IWPA) 4214 King St *Web:* www.iwpawood.org	Alexandria	VA	22302	703-820-6696	820-8550
Log Home Builder's Assn of North America 22203 State Rt 203 *Web:* www.loghomebuilders.org	Monroe	WA	98272	360-794-4469	
Manufactured Housing Institute (MHI) 2101 Wilson Blvd Suite 610 *TF:* 800-505-5500 ■ *Web:* www.manufacturedhousing.org	Arlington	VA	22201	703-558-0400	558-0401
Marble Institute of America (MIA) 28901 Clemens Rd Suite 100 *Web:* www.marble-institute.com	Westlake	OH	44145	440-250-9222	250-9223
Mason Contractors Assn of America (MCAA) 33 S Roselle Rd *TF:* 800-536-2225 ■ *Web:* www.masoncontractors.org	Schaumburg	IL	60193	847-301-0001	301-1110
Mechanical Contractors Assn of America (MCAA) 1385 Piccard Dr *TF:* 800-556-3653 ■ *Web:* www.mcaa.org	Rockville	MD	20850	301-869-5800	990-9690
Metal Bldg Manufacturers Assn (MBMA) 1300 Sumner Ave *Web:* www.mbma.com	Cleveland	OH	44115	216-241-7333	241-0105
Monument Builders of North America (MBNA) 136 S Keowee St **Fax Area Code:* 937 ■ *TF:* 800-233-4472 ■ *Web:* www.monumentbuilders.org	Dayton	OH	45402	800-233-4472	222-5794*
NA of Home Builders (NAHB) 1201 15th St NW *TF:* 800-368-5242 ■ *Web:* www.nahb.org	Washington	DC	20005	202-266-8200	266-8586
NA of Home Inspectors Inc (NAHI) 4248 Pk Glen Rd *TF:* 800-448-3942 ■ *Web:* www.nahi.org	Minneapolis	MN	55416	952-928-4641	929-1318
NA of Minority Contractors (NAMC) 1300 Pennsylvania Ave Suite 700 *TF:* 866-688-6262 ■ *Web:* www.namconline.org	Washington	DC	20004	202-204-3093	789-7349
NA of the Remodeling Industry (NARI) 780 Lee St Suite 200 *TF:* 800-611-6274 ■ *Web:* www.nari.org	Des Plaines	IL	60016	847-298-9200	298-9225
NA of Women in Construction (NAWIC) 327 S Adams St *TF:* 800-552-3506 ■ *Web:* www.nawic.org	Fort Worth	TX	76104	817-877-5551	877-0324
National Associatoin of Tower Erectors (NATE) 8 2nd St SE *TF:* 888-882-5865 ■ *Web:* www.natehome.com	Watertown	SD	57201	605-882-5865	886-5184
National Community Renaissance of California 9065 Haven Ave Suite 100 *Web:* www.nationalcore.org	Rancho Cucamonga	CA	91730	909-483-2444	438-2448
National Concrete Masonry Assn 13750 Sunrise Valley Dr *Web:* www.ncma.org	Herndon	VA	20171	703-713-1900	713-1910
National Conference of States on Bldg Codes & Standards (NCSBCS) 505 Huntmar Pk Dr Suite 210 *TF:* 800-362-2633 ■ *Web:* www.ncsbcs.org	Herndon	VA	20170	703-437-0100	481-3596
National Corrugated Steel Pipe Assn (NCSPA) 14070 Proton Rd Suite 100 *Web:* www.ncspa.org	Dallas	TX	75244	972-850-1907	490-4219
National Council of Examiners for Engineering & Surveying (NCEES) 280 Seneca Creek Rd *TF:* 800-250-3196 ■ *Web:* www.ncees.org	Seneca	SC	29678	864-654-6824	654-6033
National Electrical Contractors Assn (NECA) 3 Bethesda Metro Ctr Suite 1100 *Web:* www.necanet.org	Bethesda	MD	20814	301-657-3110	215-4500
National Elevator Industry Inc 1677 County Rd 64 PO Box 838 *Web:* www.neii.org	Salem	NY	12865	518-854-3100	854-3257
National Fire Sprinkler Assn (NFSA) 40 Jon Barrett Rd *Web:* www.nfsa.org	Patterson	NY	12563	845-878-4200	878-4215
National Frame Builders Assn (NFBA) 4700 W Lake Ave **Fax Area Code:* 847 ■ *TF:* 800-557-6957 ■ *Web:* www.nfba.org	Glenview	IL	60025	785-843-2444	375-6495*
National Hardwood Lumber Assn (NHLA) 6830 Raleigh-LaGrange Rd *TF:* 800-933-0318 ■ *Web:* www.nhla.com	Memphis	TN	38134	901-377-1818	382-6419
National Housing Conference (NHC) 1801 K St NW Suite M-100 *Web:* www.nhc.org	Washington	DC	20006	202-466-2121	466-2122
National Institute of Bldg Sciences (NIBS) 1090 Vermont Ave NW Suite 700 *Web:* www.nibs.org	Washington	DC	20005	202-289-7800	289-1092
National Insulation Assn (NIA) 99 Canal Ctr Plaza Suite 222 *TF:* 877-968-7642 ■ *Web:* www.insulation.org	Alexandria	VA	22314	703-683-6422	549-4838
National Kitchen & Bath Assn (NKBA) 687 Willow Grove St *TF:* 800-843-6522 ■ *Web:* www.nkba.org	Hackettstown	NJ	07840	908-852-0033	852-1695
National Parking Assn (NPA) 1112 16th St NW Suite 840 *TF:* 800-647-7275 ■ *Web:* www.npapark.org	Washington	DC	20036	202-296-4336	396-3102
National Precast Concrete Assn (NPCA) 10333 N Meridian St Suite 272 *TF:* 800-366-7731 ■ *Web:* www.precast.org	Indianapolis	IN	46290	317-571-9500	571-0041
National Ready Mixed Concrete Assn (NRMCA) 900 Spring St *TF:* 888-846-7622 ■ *Web:* www.nrmca.org	Silver Spring	MD	20910	301-587-1400	585-4219
National Roofing Contractors Assn (NRCA) 10255 W Higgins Rd Suite 600 *TF Cust Svc:* 800-323-9545 ■ *Web:* www.nrca.net	Rosemont	IL	60018	847-299-9070	299-1183
National Stone Sand & Gravel Assn (NSSGA) 1605 King St *TF:* 800-342-1415 ■ *Web:* www.nssga.org	Alexandria	VA	22314	703-525-8788	525-7782
National Wood Flooring Assn (NWFA) 111 Chesterfield Industrial Blvd *TF:* 800-422-4556 ■ *Web:* www.woodfloors.org	Chesterfield	MO	63005	636-519-9663	519-9664
North American Bldg Material Distribution Assn (NBMDA) 401 N Michigan Ave Suite 2400 *TF:* 888-747-7862 ■ *Web:* www.nbmda.org	Chicago	IL	60611	312-644-6610	321-6869
North American Insulation Manufacturers Assn (NAIMA) 44 Canal Ctr Plaza Suite 310 *Web:* www.naima.org	Alexandria	VA	22314	703-684-0084	684-0427
North American Wholesale Lumber Assn (NAWLA) 3601 Algonquin Rd Suite 400 *TF:* 800-527-8258 ■ *Web:* www.lumber.org	Rolling Meadows	IL	60008	847-870-7470	870-0201
Operative Plasterers' & Cement Masons' International Assn of the US & Canada (OPCMIA) 11720 Beltsville Dr Suite 700 *Web:* www.opcmia.org	Beltsville	MD	20705	301-623-1000	623-1032
Painting & Decorating Contractors of America (PDCA) 1801 Pk 270th Dr Suite 220 *TF Cust Svc:* 800-332-7322 ■ *Web:* www.pdca.org	Saint Louis	MO	63146	314-514-7322	514-9417
Partnership for Air-Conditioning Heating Refrigeration Accreditation 4100 N Fairfax Dr Suite 200 *Web:* www.ari.org	Arlington	VA	22203	703-524-8800	528-3816
Plumbing Manufacturers Institute (PMI) 1921 Rohlwing Rd Unit G *Web:* www.pmihome.org	Rolling Meadows	IL	60008	847-481-5500	481-5501
Plumbing-Heating-Cooling Contractors NA (PHCC) 180 S Washington St *TF:* 800-533-7694 ■ *Web:* www.phccweb.org	Falls Church	VA	22040	703-237-8100	237-7442

			Phone	Fax
Portland Cement Assn (PCA) 5420 Old Orchard Rd....... Skokie	IL	60077	847-966-6200	966-9781
Web: www.cement.org				
Precast/Prestressed Concrete Institute (PCI)				
200 W Adams St # 2100.......... Chicago	IL	60606	312-786-0300	786-0353
Web: www.pci.org				
Precision Metalforming Assn (PMA)				
6363 Oak Tree Blvd.......... Independence	OH	44131	216-901-8800	901-9190
Web: www.pma.org/home				
Refrigeration Service Engineers Society (RSES)				
1666 Rand Rd.......... Des Plaines	IL	60016	847-297-6464	297-5038
TF: 800-297-5660 ■ *Web:* www.rses.org				
Sheet Metal & Air Conditioning Contractors' NA (SMACNA)				
4201 Lafayette Ctr Dr.......... Chantilly	VA	20151	703-803-2980	803-3732
Web: www.smacna.org				
Sheet Metal Workers International Assn (SMWIA)				
1750 New York Ave NW 6th Fl.......... Washington	DC	20006	202-783-5880	662-0894
TF: 800-457-7694 ■ *Web:* www.smwia.org				
Single Ply Roofing Institute (SPRI)				
411 Waverly Oaks Rd Suite 331-B.......... Waltham	MA	02452	781-647-7026	647-7222
Web: www.spri.org				
Steel Framing Alliance				
1140 Connecticut Ave N W Suite 705.......... Washington	DC	20036	202-785-2022	785-3856
Web: www.steelframing.org				
Tile Council of America Inc (TCA)				
100 Clemson Research Blvd.......... Anderson	SC	29625	864-646-8453	646-2821
Web: www.tileusa.com				
Tilt-up Concrete Assn (TCA) 113 1st St NW....... Mount Vernon	IA	52314	319-895-6911	213-5555*
**Fax Area Code:* 320 ■ *Web:* www.tilt-up.org				
US Society on Dams (USSD) 1616 17th St Suite 483....... Denver	CO	80202	303-628-5430	628-5431
Web: www.ussdams.org				
Window & Door Manufacturers Assn (WDMA)				
401 N Michigan Ave 24th Fl.......... Chicago	IL	60611	847-299-5200	299-1286
TF: 800-223-2301 ■ *Web:* www.wdma.com				
Wood Moulding & Millwork Producers Assn (WMMPA)				
507 First St.......... Woodland	CA	95695	530-661-9591	661-9586
TF: 800-550-7889 ■ *Web:* www.wmmpa.com				
Wood Products Manufacturers Assn (WPMA)				
18 Elliott St.......... Westminster	MA	01473	978-874-5445	874-9946
Web: www.wpma.org				
Wood Truss Council of America (WTCA)				
6300 Enterprise Ln.......... Madison	WI	53719	608-274-4849	274-3329
Web: www.sbcindustry.com				

49-4 Consumer Sales & Service Professionals Associations

			Phone	Fax
Advanced Medical Technology Assn				
701 Pennsylvania Ave NW Suite 800.......... Washington	DC	20004	202-783-8700	783-8750
Web: www.advamed.org				
AeA: Advancing the Business of Technology				
400 Great America Pkwy Suite 400.......... Santa Clara	CA	95054	408-987-4200	987-4298
TF: 800-284-4232 ■ *Web:* www.aeanet.org				
AHRI - Air-Conditioning Heating & Refrigeration Institute				
4100 N Fairfax Dr Suite 200.......... Arlington	VA	22203	703-524-8800	528-3816
Web: www.ahrinet.org				
American Apparel & Footwear Assn (AAFA)				
1601 N Kent St Suite 1200.......... Arlington	VA	22209	703-524-1864	522-6741
TF: 800-520-2262 ■ *Web:* www.apparelandfootwear.org				
American Bio-Recovery Assn (ABRA)				
45-06 Queens Blvd Suite 144.......... Sunnyside	NY	11104	888-979-2272	356-4606*
**Fax Area Code:* 987 ■ *TF:* 888-979-2272 ■ *Web:* americanbiorecovery.com				
American Boat & Yacht Council Inc (ABYC)				
613 3rd St Suite 10.......... Annapolis	MD	21403	410-990-4460	990-4466
Web: www.abycinc.org				
American Gem Society (AGS) 8881 W Sahara Ave..... Las Vegas	NV	89117	702-255-6500	255-7420
TF: 866-805-6500 ■ *Web:* www.americangemsociety.org				
American Gem Trade Assn (AGTA)				
3030 LBJ Fwy Suite 840.......... Dallas	TX	75234	214-742-4367	742-7334
TF: 800-972-1162 ■ *Web:* www.agta.org				
American Hardware Manufacturers Assn (AHMA)				
801 N Plaza Dr.......... Schaumburg	IL	60173	847-605-1025	605-1030
Web: www.ahma.org				
American Health & Beauty Aids Institute (AHBAI)				
PO Box 19510.......... Chicago	IL	60619	708-633-6328	633-6329
Web: www.ahbai.org				
American Home Furnishings Alliance (AHFA)				
317 W High Ave 10th Fl.......... High Point	NC	27260	336-884-5000	884-5303
Web: www.ahfa.us				
American Institute of Floral Designers (AIFD)				
720 Light St.......... Baltimore	MD	21230	410-752-3318	752-8295
Web: www.aifd.org				
American Lighting Assn (ALA)				
2050 Stemmons Fwy Suite 10046.......... Dallas	TX	75207	214-698-9898	
TF: 800-605-4448 ■ *Web:* www.americanlightingassoc.com				
American Pet Products Manufacturers Assn (APPMA)				
255 Glenville Rd.......... Greenwich	CT	06831	203-532-0000	532-0551
TF: 800-452-1225 ■ *Web:* www.americanpetproducts.org				
American Rental Assn (ARA) 1900 19th St.......... Moline	IL	61265	309-764-2475	764-1533
TF: 800-334-2177 ■ *Web:* www.ararental.org				
American Sportfishing Assn (ASA)				
225 Reinekers Ln Suite 420.......... Alexandria	VA	22314	703-519-9691	519-1872
Web: www.asafishing.org				
American Watchmakers-Clockmakers Institute (AWI)				
701 Enterprise Dr.......... Harrison	OH	45030	513-367-9800	367-1414
TF: 866-367-2924 ■ *Web:* www.awci.com				

			Phone	Fax
Aspirin Foundation of America				
1299 Pennsylvania Ave 10th Fl.......... Washington	DC	20045	202-508-9523	508-9700
Web: www.aspirin-foundation.com				
Assn for Linen Management				
2161 Lexington Rd Suite 2.......... Richmond	KY	40475	859-624-0177	624-3580
TF: 800-669-0863 ■ *Web:* www.almnet.org				
Assn of Home Appliance Manufacturers (AHAM)				
1111 19th St NW Suite 402.......... Washington	DC	20036	202-872-5955	872-9354
Web: www.aham.org				
Assn of Pool & Spa Professionals (APSP)				
2111 Eisenhower Ave Suite 500.......... Alexandria	VA	22314	703-838-0083	549-0493
TF: 800-323-3996 ■ *Web:* www.apsp.org				
Automotive Recyclers Assn (ARA)				
3975 Fair Ridge Dr Suite 20N.......... Fairfax	VA	22033	703-385-1001	385-1494
TF: 888-385-1005 ■ *Web:* www.a-r-a.org				
Awards & Recognition Assn (ARA)				
4700 W Lake Ave.......... Glenview	IL	60025	847-375-4800	375-6480
TF: 800-344-2148 ■ *Web:* www.ara.org				
Carpet & Rug Institute (CRI) 730 College Dr.......... Dalton	GA	30720	706-278-3176	278-8835
Web: www.carpet-rug.com				
Cigar Assn of America Inc				
818 Donnecticut Ave NW Suite 200.......... Washington	DC	20006	202-223-8204	833-0379
TF: 866-482-3570				
Clothing Manufacturers Assn of the USA				
730 Broadway 10th Fl.......... New York	NY	10003	212-529-0823	
Coin Laundry Assn (CLA)				
1315 Butterfield Rd Suite 212.......... Downers Grove	IL	60515	630-963-5547	963-5864
TF: 800-570-5629 ■ *Web:* www.coinlaundry.org				
Consumer Healthcare Products Assn (CHPA)				
1150 Connecticut Ave NW # 700.......... Washington	DC	20036	202-429-9260	223-6835
Web: www.chpa-info.org				
Contact Lens Manufacturers Assn PO Box 29398...... Lincoln	NE	68529	402-465-4122	465-4187
TF: 800-344-9060 ■ *Web:* www.clma.net				
Cosmetic Toiletry & Fragrance Assn (CTFA)				
1101 17th St NW Suite 300.......... Washington	DC	20036	202-331-1770	331-1969
Web: www.ctfa.org				
Cremation Assn of North America (CANA)				
401 N Michigan Ave Suite 2400.......... Chicago	IL	60611	312-644-6610	321-4098
Web: www.cremationassociation.org				
Dental Trade Alliance (DTA)				
2300 Clarendon Blvd Suite 1003.......... arlington	VA	22201	703-379-7755	931-9429
Web: www.dentaltradealliance.org				
Diamond Council of America (DCA)				
3212 W End Ave Suite 202.......... Nashville	TN	37203	615-385-5301	385-4955
TF: 877-283-5669 ■ *Web:* www.diamondcouncil.org				
Diving Equipment & Marketing Assn (DEMA)				
3750 Convoy St Suite 310.......... San Diego	CA	92111	858-616-6408	616-6495
TF: 800-862-3483 ■ *Web:* www.dema.org				
Drycleaning & Laundry Institute				
14700 Sweitzer Ln.......... Laurel	MD	20707	301-622-1900	295-0685*
**Fax Area Code:* 240 ■ *TF:* 800-638-2627 ■ *Web:* www.ifi.org				
ENKWSA (WSA) 15821 Ventura Blvd Suite 415.......... Encino	CA	91436	818-379-9400	379-9410
Web: www.wsashow.com				
Envelope Manufacturers Assn (EMA)				
500 Montgomery St Suite 550.......... Alexandria	VA	22314	703-739-2200	739-2209
Web: www.envelope.org				
Fashion Group International Inc (FGI)				
8 W 40th St 7th Fl.......... New York	NY	10018	212-302-5511	302-5533
Web: www.fgi.org				
Footwear Distributors & Retailers of America (FDRA)				
1319 F St NW Suite 700.......... Washington	DC	20004	202-737-5660	638-2615
Web: www.fdra.org				
Fragrance Foundation 145 E 32nd St.......... New York	NY	10016	212-725-2755	779-9058
Web: www.fragrance.org				
Gemological Institute of America (GIA)				
5345 Armada Dr.......... Carlsbad	CA	92008	760-603-4000	603-4003
TF: 800-421-7250 ■ *Web:* www.gia.edu				
Hearth Patio & Barbecue Assn (HPBA)				
1901 N Moore St Suite 600.......... Arlington	VA	22209	703-522-0086	522-0548
Web: www.hpba.org				
Home Furnishings Independents Assn (HFIA)				
2050 Stemmons World Trade Ctr Suite 170				
PO Box 420807.......... Dallas	TX	75342	214-741-7632	742-9103
TF: 800-942-4663 ■ *Web:* www.hfia.com				
Hosiery Assn				
7421 Carmel Executive Pk Suite 200-B.......... Charlotte	NC	28226	704-365-0913	362-2056
Web: www.hosieryassociation.com				
Independent Jewelers Organization (IJO)				
25 Seir Hill Rd.......... Norwalk	CT	06850	203-846-4215	846-8571
TF: 800-624-9252 ■ *Web:* www.independentjewelers.com				
Independent Office Products & Furniture Dealers Assn (IOPFDA)				
301 N Fairfax St Suite 200.......... Alexandria	VA	22314	703-549-9040	683-7552
TF: 800-542-6672 ■ *Web:* www.iopfda.org				
Institute of Inspection Cleaning & Restoration Certification (IICRC)				
2715 E Mill Plain Blvd.......... Vancouver	WA	98661	360-693-5675	693-4858
Web: www.iicrc.org				
International Assn of Lighting Designers (IALD)				
200 World Trade Ctr				
Merchandise Mart Suite 9-104.......... Chicago	IL	60654	312-527-3677	527-3680
Web: www.iald.org				
International Card Manufacturers Assn (ICMA)				
191 Clarksville Rd.......... Princeton Junction	NJ	08550	609-799-4900	799-7032
Web: www.icma.com				
International Cemetery Cremation & Funeral Assn (ICCFA)				
107 Carpenter Dr Suite 100.......... Sterling	VA	20164	703-391-8400	391-8416
TF: 800-645-7700 ■ *Web:* www.iccfa.com				
International Engraved Graphics Assn				
305 Plus Pk Blvd.......... Nashville	TN	37217	615-366-1094	366-4192
TF: 800-821-3138 ■ *Web:* www.iega.org				

Organization / Address	City	State	ZIP	Phone	Fax
International Executive Housekeepers Assn (IEHA) 1001 Eastwind Dr Suite 301	Westerville	OH	43081	614-895-7166	895-1248
TF: 800-200-6342 ■ *Web:* www.ieha.org					
International Furniture Rental Assn (IFRA) 5229 College Hill Rd	Woodstock	VT	05091	802-457-1658	
Web: www.ifra.org					
International Housewares Assn (IHA) 6400 Shafer Ct Suite 650	Rosemont	IL	60018	847-292-4200	292-4211
Web: www.housewares.org					
International Order of the Golden Rule (OGR) 3520 Executive Ctr Dr Suite 300	Austin	TX	78731	512-334-5504	334-5514
TF: 800-637-8030 ■ *Web:* www.ogr.org					
International Precious Metals Institute (IPMI) 5101 N 12th Ave Suite C216	Pensacola	FL	32504	850-476-1156	476-1548
Web: www.ipmi.org					
International Sign Assn (ISA) 1001 N Fairfax St Suite 301	Alexandria	VA	22314	703-836-4012	836-8353
TF: 888-472-7446 ■ *Web:* www.signs.org					
International Sleep Products Assn (ISPA) 501 Wythe St	Alexandria	VA	22314	703-683-8371	683-4503
Web: www.sleepproducts.org					
Jewelers Board of Trade (JBT) 95 Jefferson Blvd	Warwick	RI	02888	401-467-0055	467-1199
Web: www.jewelersboard.com					
Jewelers of America (JA) 52 Vanderbilt Ave 19th Fl	New York	NY	10017	646-658-0246	658-0256
TF: 800-223-0673 ■ *Web:* www.jewelers.org					
Jewish Funeral Directors of America (JFDA) 150 Lynnway Suite 506	Lynn	MA	01902	781-477-9300	477-9393
Web: www.jfda.org					
Juvenile Products Manufacturers Assn 15000 Commerce Pkwy Suite C	Mount Laurel	NJ	08054	856-638-0420	439-0525
Web: www.jpma.org					
Leather Industries of America (LIA) 3050 K St NW Suite 400	Washington	DC	20007	202-342-8497	342-8583
Web: www.leatherusa.com					
Manufacturing Jewelers & Suppliers of America Inc (MJSA) 57 John L Dietsch Sq	Attleboro Falls	MA	02763	401-274-3840	274-0265
TF: 800-444-6572 ■ *Web:* www.mjsa.org					
NA of Professional Band Instrument Repair Technicians Inc (NAPBIRT) 2026 Eagle Rd PO Box 51	Normal	IL	61761	309-452-4257	452-4825
Web: www.napbirt.org					
NA of Professional Organizers (NAPO) 15000 Commerce Pkwy Suite C	Mount Laurel	NJ	08054	856-380-6828	439-0525
Web: www.napo.net					
National Beauty Culturists' League Inc (NBCL) 25 Logan Cir NW	Washington	DC	20005	202-332-2695	332-0940
Web: www.nbcl.org					
National Bicycle Dealers Assn (NBDA) 777 W 19th St Suite O	Costa Mesa	CA	92627	949-722-6909	722-1747
Web: www.nbda.com					
National Cleaners Assn 252 W 29th St 2nd Fl	New York	NY	10001	212-967-3002	967-2240
TF: 800-888-1622 ■ *Web:* www.nca-i.com					
National Funeral Directors & Morticians Assn (NFDMA) 6290 Shannon Pkwy	Union City	GA	30291	404-286-6680	286-6573
TF: 800-434-0958 ■ *Web:* www.nfdma.com					
National Funeral Directors Assn (NFDA) 13625 Bishop's Dr	Brookfield	WI	53005	262-789-1880	789-6977
TF: 800-228-6332 ■ *Web:* www.nfda.org					
National Home Furnishings Assn (NHFA) 3910 Tinsley Dr Suite 101	High Point	NC	27265	336-886-6100	801-6102
TF: 800-888-9590 ■ *Web:* www.nhfa.org					
National Pest Management Assn Inc (NPMA) 10460 N St	Fairfax	VA	22030	703-573-8330	352-3031
Web: www.pestworld.org					
National Shoe Retailers Assn (NSRA) 7150 Columbia Gateway Dr Suite G	Columbia	MD	21046	410-381-8282	381-1167
TF: 800-673-8446 ■ *Web:* www.nsra.org					
National Sporting Goods Assn (NSGA) 1601 Feehanville Dr Suite 300	Mount Prospect	IL	60056	847-296-6742	391-9827
TF: 800-815-5422 ■ *Web:* www.nsga.org					
National Volunteer Fire Council (NVFC) 7582 Walker Dr Suite 450	Greenbelt	MD	20770	202-887-5700	887-5291
TF: 888-275-6832 ■ *Web:* www.nvfc.org					
Outdoor Industry Assn (OIA) 4909 Pearl E Cir Suite 200	Boulder	CO	80301	303-444-3353	444-3284
Web: www.outdoorindustry.org					
Outdoor Power Equipment Institute Inc (OPEI) 341 S Patrick St	Alexandria	VA	22314	703-549-7600	549-7604
Web: www.opei.org					
Pet Food Institute (PFI) 2025 M St NW Suite 800	Washington	DC	20036	202-367-1120	367-2120
Web: www.petfoodinstitute.org					
Pet Industry Joint Advisory Council (PIJAC) 1220 19th St NW Suite 400	Washington	DC	20036	202-452-1525	293-4377
TF: 800-553-7387 ■ *Web:* www.pijac.org					
Piano Technicians Guild 4444 Forest Ave	Kansas City	KS	66106	913-432-9975	432-9986
Web: www.ptg.org					
Professional Assn of Innkeepers International (PAII) 207 White Horse Pike	Haddon Heights	NJ	08035	856-310-1102	895-0432
TF: 800-468-7244 ■ *Web:* www.innkeeping.org					
Real Diaper Industry Assn (RDIA) 1017 L St Suite 338	Sacramento	CA	95814	310-400-6985	244-0609*
**Fax Area Code:* 916 ■ *Web:* www.realdiaperindustry.org					
Recreation Vehicle Industry Assn (RVIA) 1896 Preston White Dr	Reston	VA	20191	703-620-6003	620-5071
TF: 800-336-0154 ■ *Web:* www.rvia.org					
Salon Assn (TSA) 15825 N 71st St Suite 100	Scottsdale	AZ	85254	480-281-0424	905-0708
TF: 800-211-4872 ■ *Web:* www.probeauty.org/salonspa					
Security Industry Assn (SIA) 635 Slaters Ln Suite 110	Alexandria	VA	22314	703-683-2075	683-2469
TF: 866-817-8888 ■ *Web:* www.siaonline.org					
Selected Independent Funeral Homes 500 Lake Cook Rd Suite 205	Deerfield	IL	60015	847-236-9401	236-9968
TF: 800-323-4219 ■ *Web:* www.selectedfuneralhomes.org					
SGMA International 1150 17th St NW Suite 850	Washington	DC	20036	202-775-1762	296-7462
Web: www.sgma.com					
Shoe Service Institute of America (SSIA) 18 School St	North Brookfield	MA	01535	508-867-7731	867-4600
Web: www.ssia.info					
Silver Institute 888 16th St NW Suite 303	Washington	DC	20006	202-835-0185	835-0155
Web: www.silverinstitute.org					
SnowSports Industries America (SIA) 8377 Greensboro Dr # B	McLean	VA	22102	703-556-9020	821-8276
Web: www.snowsports.org					
Society of American Florists (SAF) 1601 Duke St	Alexandria	VA	22314	703-836-8700	836-8705
TF: 800-336-4743 ■ *Web:* www.safnow.org					
Specialty Sleep Assn (SSA) 46639 Jones Ranch Rd	Friant	CA	93626	559-868-4187	868-4185
Web: www.sleepinformation.org					
Textile Rental Services Assn (TRSA) 1800 Diagonal Rd Suite 200	Alexandria	VA	22314	703-519-0029	519-0026
TF: 800-868-8772 ■ *Web:* www.trsa.org					
Tire Industry Assn (TIA) 1532 Pointer Ridge Pl Suite E	Bowie	MD	20716	301-430-7280	430-7283
TF: 800-876-8372 ■ *Web:* www.tireindustry.org					
Toy Industry Assn 1115 Broadway Suite 400	New York	NY	10010	212-675-1141	633-1429
Web: www.toyassociation.org					
Uniform & Textile Service Assn (UTSA) 1501 Lee Hwy Suite 304	Arlington	VA	22209	703-247-2600	841-4750
TF: 800-486-6745					
Vision Council The 225 Reinekers Ln Suite 700	Alexandria	VA	22314	703-548-4560	548-4580
TF: 866-826-0290 ■ *Web:* www.thevisioncouncil.org					
Wallcoverings Assn 401 N Michigan Ave Suite 2200	Chicago	IL	60611	312-644-6610	527-6705
Web: www.wallcoverings.org					
World Floor Covering Assn (WFCA) 2211 Howell Ave	Anaheim	CA	92806	714-978-6440	978-6066
TF: 800-624-6880 ■ *Web:* www.wfca.org					
World Gold Council 444 Madison Ave Suite 301	New York	NY	10022	212-317-3800	688-0410
Web: www.gold.org					

49-5 Education Professionals Associations

Organization / Address	City	State	ZIP	Phone	Fax
American Anthropological Assn (AAA) 2200 Wilson Blvd Suite 600	Arlington	VA	22201	703-528-1902	528-3546
Web: www.aaanet.org					
American Assn for Adult & Continuing Education (AAACE) 10111 ML King Jr Hwy Suite 200-C	Bowie	MD	20720	301-459-6261	459-6241
Web: www.aaace.org					
American Assn of Colleges for Teacher Education (AACTE) 1307 New York Ave NW Suite 300	Washington	DC	20005	202-293-2450	457-8095
Web: www.aacte.org					
American Assn of Colleges of Nursing (AACN) 1 Dupont Cir NW Suite 530	Washington	DC	20036	202-463-6930	785-8320
Web: www.aacn.nche.edu					
American Assn of Colleges of Pharmacy (AACP) 1426 Prince St	Alexandria	VA	22314	703-739-2330	836-8982
Web: www.aacp.org					
American Assn of Collegiate Registrars & Admissions Officers (AACRAO) 1 Dupont Cir NW Suite 520	Washington	DC	20036	202-293-9161	872-8857
Web: www.aacrao.org					
American Assn of Community Colleges (AACC) 1 Dupont Cir NW Suite 410	Washington	DC	20036	202-728-0200	833-2467
Web: www.aacc.nche.edu					
American Assn of Family & Consumer Sciences (AAFCS) 400 N Columbus St Suite 202	Alexandria	VA	22314	703-706-4600	706-4663
TF: 800-424-8080 ■ *Web:* www.aafcs.org					
American Assn of Physics Teachers (AAPT) 1 Physics Ellipse	College Park	MD	20740	301-209-3300	209-0845
Web: www.aapt.org					
American Assn of School Administrators (AASA) 801 N Quincy St Suite 700	Arlington	VA	22203	703-528-0700	841-1543
TF: 800-771-1162 ■ *Web:* www.aasa.org					
American Assn of State Colleges & Universities (AASCU) 1307 New York Ave NW 5th Fl	Washington	DC	20005	202-293-7070	296-5819
TF: 800-542-2062 ■ *Web:* www.aascu.org					
American Assn of Teachers of Arabic The (AATA) 3416 Primm Ln	Birmingham	AL	35216	205-822-6800	823-2760
Web: aataweb.org					
American Assn of Teachers of French (AATF) Southern Illinois Univ MC 4510	Carbondale	IL	62901	618-453-5731	453-5733
Web: www.frenchteachers.org					
American Assn of Teachers of German (AATG) 112 Haddontowne Ct Suite 104	Cherry Hill	NJ	08034	856-795-5553	795-9398
Web: www.aatg.org					
American Assn of Teachers of Spanish & Portuguese (AATSP) 900 Ladd Rd	Walled Lake	MI	48390	248-960-2180	960-9570
Web: www.aatsp.org					
American Assn of University Professors (AAUP) 1133 Nineteenth St Suite 200	Washington	DC	20036	202-737-5900	737-5526
TF: 800-424-2973 ■ *Web:* www.aaup.org					

Phone Fax

American Assn of University Women (AAUW)
1111 16th St NW .... Washington DC 20036 202-785-7700 872-1425
TF: 800-326-2289 ■ *Web:* www.aauw.org
American College Personnel Assn (ACPA)
1 Dupont Cir NW Suite 300 .... Washington DC 20036 202-835-2272 296-3286
Web: www2.myacpa.org
American Council on Education (ACE)
1 Dupont Cir NW Suite 800 .... Washington DC 20036 202-939-9300 833-4760
Web: www.acenet.edu
American Council on the Teaching of Foreign Languages (ACTFL)
1001 N Fairfax St Suite 200 .... Alexandria VA 22314 703-894-2900 894-2905
Web: www.actfl.org
American Councils for International Education
1776 Massachusetts Ave NW Suite 700 .... Washington DC 20036 202-833-7522 833-7523
Web: www.americancouncils.org
American Dental Education Assn (ADEA)
1400 K St NW Suite 1100 .... Washington DC 20005 202-289-7201 289-7204
TF: 800-353-2237 ■ *Web:* www.adea.org
American Educational Research Assn (AERA)
1430 K St NW Suite 1200 .... Washington DC 20005 202-238-3200 238-3250
Web: www.aera.net
American Federation of School Administrators (AFSA)
1101 17th St NW Suite 408 .... Washington DC 20036 202-986-4209 986-4211
TF: 800-354-2372 ■ *Web:* www.admin.org
American Historical Assn (AHA) 400 A St SE .... Washington DC 20003 202-544-2422 544-8307
Web: www.historians.org
American Library Assn (ALA) 50 E Huron St .... Chicago IL 60611 312-944-6780 944-2641
TF: 800-545-2433 ■ *Web:* www.ala.org
American Medical Student Assn (AMSA)
1902 Assn Dr .... Reston VA 20191 703-620-6600 620-5873
TF: 800-767-2266 ■ *Web:* www.amsa.org
American Philological Assn (APA)
Univ of Pennsylvania
220 S 40th St Suite 201E .... Philadelphia PA 19104 215-898-4975 573-7874
Web: www.apaclassics.org
American Political Science Assn (APSA)
1527 New Hampshire Ave NW .... Washington DC 20036 202-483-2512 483-2657
Web: www.apsanet.org
American School Counselor Assn (ASCA)
1101 King St Suite 625 .... Alexandria VA 22314 703-683-2722 683-1619
TF: 800-306-4722 ■ *Web:* www.schoolcounselor.org
American School Health Assn (ASHA)
7263 State Rt 43 PO Box 708 .... Kent OH 44240 330-678-1601 678-4526
TF: 800-445-2742 ■ *Web:* www.ashaweb.org
American Society for Engineering Education (ASEE)
1818 N St NW Suite 600 .... Washington DC 20036 202-331-3500 265-8504
Web: www.asee.org
American Society for Training & Development (ASTD)
1640 King St 3rd Fl PO Box 1443 .... Alexandria VA 22313 703-683-8100 683-1523
TF: 800-628-2783 ■ *Web:* www.astd.org
American Sociological Assn (ASA)
1307 New York Ave .... Washington DC 20005 202-383-9005 638-0882
Web: www.asanet.org
American String Teachers Assn (ASTA)
4155 Chain Bridge Rd .... Fairfax VA 22030 703-279-2113 279-2114
Web: www.astaweb.com
American Studies Assn (ASA)
1120 19th St NW Suite 301 .... Washington DC 20036 202-467-4783 467-4786
Web: www.theasa.net
American Translators Assn (ATA)
225 Reinekers Ln Suite 590 .... Alexandria VA 22314 703-683-6100 683-6122
Web: www.atanet.org
Assn for Advanced Training in the Behavioral Sciences (AATBS)
5126 Ralston St .... Ventura CA 93003 805-676-3030 676-3033
TF: 800-472-1931
Assn for Career & Technical Education (ACTE)
1410 King St .... Alexandria VA 22314 703-683-3111 683-7424
TF: 800-826-9972 ■ *Web:* www.acteonline.org
Assn for Childhood Education International (ACEI)
17904 Georgia Ave Suite 215 .... Olney MD 20832 301-570-2111 570-2212
TF: 800-423-3563 ■ *Web:* www.acei.org
Assn for Communications Technology Professionals in Higher Education (ACUTA)
152 W Zandale Dr Suite 200 .... Lexington KY 40503 859-278-3338 278-3268
Web: www.acuta.org
Assn for Continuing Higher Education (ACHE)
PO Box 118067 .... Charleston SC 29423 800-807-2243 574-6470*
**Fax Area Code:* 843 ■ *TF:* 800-807-2243 ■ *Web:* www.acheinc.org
Assn for Educational Communications & Technology (AECT)
1800 N Stonelake Dr Suite 2 PO Box 2447 .... Bloomington IN 47404 812-335-7675 335-7678
TF: 877-677-2328 ■ *Web:* www.aect.org
Assn for Gerontology in Higher Education (AGHE)
1220 L St NW Suite 901 .... Washington DC 20005 202-289-9806 289-9824
Web: www.aghe.org
Assn for Practical & Professional Ethics
618 E 3rd St .... Bloomington IN 47405 812-855-6450 856-4969
Web: www.indiana.edu/appe
Assn for Supervision & Curriculum Development (ASCD)
1703 N Beauregard St .... Alexandria VA 22311 703-578-9600 575-5400
TF: 800-933-2723 ■ *Web:* www.ascd.org
Assn for the Advancement of Computing in Education (AACE)
PO Box 1545 .... Chesapeake VA 23327 757-366-5606 997-8760*
**Fax Area Code:* 703 ■ *Web:* www.aace.org
Assn of Advanced Rabbinical & Talmudic Schools (AARTS)
11 Broadway .... New York NY 10004 212-363-1991 533-5335
Assn of American Colleges & Universities (AAC&U)
1818 R St NW .... Washington DC 20009 202-387-3760 265-9532
Web: www.aacu.org

Phone Fax

Assn of American Law Schools (AALS)
1201 Connecticut Ave NW Suite 800 .... Washington DC 20036 202-296-8851 296-8869
Web: www.aals.org
Assn of American Medical Colleges (AAMC)
2450 N St NW .... Washington DC 20037 202-828-0400 828-1125
Web: www.aamc.org
Assn of American Universities (AAU)
1200 New York Ave NW Suite 550 .... Washington DC 20005 202-408-7500 408-8184
Web: www.aau.edu
Assn of Christian Schools International (ACSI)
731 Chapel Hills Dr .... Colorado Springs CO 80920 719-528-6906 531-0631
TF Cust Svc: 800-367-0798 ■ *Web:* www.acsi.org
Assn of College & University Housing Officers International (ACUHO-I)
941 Chatham Ln Suite 318 .... Columbus OH 43221 614-292-0099 292-3205
Web: www.acuho-i.org
Assn of College Unions International (ACUI)
120 W 7th St 1 City Ctr Suite 200 .... Bloomington IN 47404 812-245-2284 245-6710
Web: www.acui.org
Assn of Collegiate Schools of Architecture (ACSA)
1735 New York Ave NW 3rd Fl .... Washington DC 20006 202-785-2324 628-0448
Web: www.acsa-arch.org
Assn of Community College Trustees (ACCT)
1233 20th St NW Suite 605 .... Washington DC 20036 202-775-4667 223-1297
Web: www.acct.org
Assn of Fraternity Advisors (AFA)
9640 N Augusta Dr Suite 433 .... Carmel IN 46032 317-876-1632 876-3981
Web: www.fraternityadvisors.org
Assn of Governing Boards of Universities & Colleges (AGB)
1133 20th St NW Suite 300 .... Washington DC 20036 202-296-8400 223-7053
TF: 800-356-6317 ■ *Web:* www.agb.org
Assn of Higher Education Facilities Officers (APPA)
1643 Prince St .... Alexandria VA 22314 703-684-1446 549-2772
Web: www.appa.org
Assn of Program Directors in Internal Medicine (APDIM)
2501 M St NW Suite 550 .... Washington DC 20037 202-861-9351 861-9731
Web: www.im.org/APDIM
Assn of Public & Land-grant Universities (APLU)
1307 New York Ave NW Suite 400 .... Washington DC 20005 202-478-6040 478-6046
Web: www.aplu.org
Assn of Research Libraries (ARL)
21 Dupont Cir NW Suite 800 .... Washington DC 20036 202-296-2296 872-0884
Web: www.arl.org
Assn of School Business Officials International (ASBO)
11401 N Shore Dr .... Reston VA 20190 703-478-0405 478-0205
TF: 866-682-2729 ■ *Web:* asbointl.org
Assn of Schools of Public Health (ASPH)
1900 M St NW # 710 #710 .... Washington DC 20036 202-296-1099 296-1252
Web: www.asph.org
Assn of Test Publishers
601 Pennsylvania Ave NW Suite 900 .... Washington DC 20004 866-240-7909
TF: 866-240-7909 ■ *Web:* www.testpublishers.org
Assn of Theological Schools in the US & Canada (ATS)
10 Summit Pk Dr .... Pittsburgh PA 15275 412-788-6505 788-6510
Web: www.ats.edu
Assn of Universities for Research in Astronomy (AURA)
1200 New York Ave NW Suite 350 .... Washington DC 20005 202-483-2101 483-2106
Web: www.aura-astronomy.org
Assn of University Centers on Disabilities (AUCD)
1010 Wayne Ave Suite 920 .... Silver Spring MD 20910 301-588-8252 588-2842
Web: www.aucd.org
Broadcast Education Assn (BEA) 1771 N St NW .... Washington DC 20036 202-243-2339 775-2981
TF: 888-380-7222 ■ *Web:* www.beaweb.org
Business Professionals of America
5454 Cleveland Ave .... Columbus OH 43231 614-895-7277 895-1165
TF: 800-334-2007 ■ *Web:* www.bpa.org
Business-Higher Education Forum
2025 M St NW Suite 800 .... Washington DC 20036 202-367-1189 367-2269
Web: www.bhef.com
Career College Assn (CCA)
1101 Connecticut Ave NW Suite 900 .... Washington DC 20036 202-336-6700 336-6828
Web: www.career.org
Christian Schools International (CSI)
3350 E Paris Ave SE .... Grand Rapids MI 49512 616-957-1070 957-5022
TF: 800-635-8288 ■ *Web:* www.csionline.org
College & University Professional Assn for Human Resources (CUPA-HR)
1811 Commons Pt Dr .... Knoxville TN 37932 865-637-7673 637-7674
TF: 877-287-2474 ■ *Web:* www.cupahr.org
College Music Society (CMS) 312 E Pine St .... Missoula MT 59802 406-721-9616 721-9419
TF: 800-729-0235 ■ *Web:* www.music.org
Conference on College Composition & Communication (CCCC)
1111 W Kenyon Rd .... Urbana IL 61801 217-328-3870 278-3763
TF: 877-369-6283 ■ *Web:* www.ncte.org/cccc
Council for Advancement & Support of Education (CASE)
1307 New York Ave NW Suite 1000 .... Washington DC 20005 202-328-5900 387-4973
TF Orders: 800-554-8536 ■ *Web:* www.case.org
Council for Christian Colleges & Universities (CCCU)
321 8th St NE .... Washington DC 20002 202-546-8713 546-8913
Web: www.cccu.org
Council for Exceptional Children (CEC)
2900 Crystal Dr Suite 1000 .... Arlington VA 22202 800-232-7733 264-9494*
**Fax Area Code:* 703 ■ *TF:* 800-232-7733 ■ *Web:* www.cec.sped.org
Council for International Exchange of Scholars (CIES)
3007 Tilden St NW Suite 5L .... Washington DC 20008 202-686-4000 362-3442
Web: www.cies.org
Council for Professional Recognition
2460 16th St NW .... Washington DC 20009 202-265-9090 265-9161
TF: 800-424-4310 ■ *Web:* www.cdacouncil.org

Organization	City	State	ZIP	Phone	Fax
Council of Administrators of Special Education (CASE) Osigian Office Centre 101 Katelyn Cir Suite E *TF:* 800-585-1753 ■ *Web:* www.casecec.org	Warner Robins	GA	31088	478-333-6892	333-2453
Council of Chief State School Officers (CCSSO) 1 Massachusetts Ave NW Suite 700 *Web:* www.ccsso.org	Washington	DC	20001	202-408-5505	408-8072
Council of Graduate Schools (CGS) 1 Dupont Cir NW Suite 230 *Web:* www.cgsnet.org	Washington	DC	20036	202-223-3791	331-7157
Council of Independent Colleges (CIC) 1 Dupont Cir NW Suite 320 *Web:* www.cic.edu	Washington	DC	20036	202-466-7230	466-7238
Council of the Great City Schools 1301 Pennsylvania Ave NW Suite 702 *Web:* www.cgcs.org	Washington	DC	20004	202-393-2427	393-2400
Council on International Educational Exchange (CIEE) 300 Fore St 2nd Fl *TF Cust Svc:* 888-268-6245 ■ *Web:* www.ciee.org	Portland	ME	04101	207-553-4000	553-5272
Council on Social Work Education (CSWE) 1701 Duke St *Web:* www.cswe.org	Alexandria	VA	22314	703-683-8080	683-8099
Distance Education & Training Council (DETC) 1601 18th St NW Suite 2 *Web:* www.detc.org	Washington	DC	20009	202-234-5100	332-1386
Distributive Education Clubs of America (DECA) 1908 Assn Dr *Web:* www.deca.org	Reston	VA	20191	703-860-5000	860-4013
Econometric Society New York Univ Dept of Economics 19 W 4th St 6th Fl. *Web:* www.econometricsociety.org	New York	NY	10012	212-998-3820	995-4487
Economic History Assn (EHA) *Santa Clara University Dept of Economics* 500 El Camino Real *Web:* www.eh.net/EHA	Santa Clara	CA	95053	408-554-4348	554-2331
Education Commission of the States (ECS) 700 Broadway Suite 810 *Web:* www.ecs.org	Denver	CO	80203	303-299-3600	296-8332
Educational Housing Services Inc 31 Lexington Ave *TF:* 800-385-1689 ■ *Web:* www.studenthousing.org	New York	NY	10010	212-977-7622	307-0701
Foundation for Independent Higher Education 1920 N St NW Suite 210 *Web:* www.fihe.org	Washington	DC	20036	202-367-0333	367-0334
Hispanic Assn of Colleges & Universities (HACU) 8415 Datapoint Dr Suite 400 *TF:* 800-780-4228 ■ *Web:* www.hacu.net	San Antonio	TX	78229	210-692-3805	692-0823
Independent Educational Consultants Assn (IECA) 3251 Old Lee Hwy Suite 510 *TF:* 800-808-4322 ■ *Web:* www.educationalconsulting.org	Fairfax	VA	22030	703-591-4850	591-4860
International Council on Hotel Restaurant & Institutional Education (CHRIE) 2810 N Parham Rd Suite 230 *Web:* www.chrie.org	Richmond	VA	23294	804-346-4800	346-5009
International Reading Assn (IRA) 800 Barksdale Rd PO Box 6021 *TF:* 800-336-7323 ■ *Web:* www.reading.org	Newark	DE	19714	302-731-1600	737-0878
International Society for Technology in Education (ISTE) 1710 Rhode Island Ave NW Suite 900 *TF:* 866-654-4777 ■ *Web:* www.iste.org	Washington	DC	20036	202-861-7777	861-0888
International Technology Education Assn (ITEA) 1914 Assn Dr Suite 201 *Web:* www.iteaconnect.org	Reston	VA	20191	703-860-2100	860-0353
Languages Canada 5886 169 A St **Fax Area Code:* 888 ■ *Web:* www.languagescanada.ca	Surrey	BC	V3S6Z8	604-574-1532	277-0522*
Law School Admission Council Inc (LSAC) PO Box 40 *Web:* www.lsac.org	Newtown	PA	18940	215-968-1101	968-1169
MENC: NA for Music Education 1806 Robert Fulton Dr *TF:* 800-336-3768 ■ *Web:* www.menc.org	Reston	VA	20191	703-860-4000	860-1531
Middle States Commission on Higher Education 3624 Market St **Fax Area Code:* 215 ■ *Web:* www.msche.org	Philadelphia	PA	19104	267-284-5000	662-5501*
Modern Language Assn (MLA) 26 Broadway 3rd Fl *Web:* www.mla.org	New York	NY	10004	646-576-5000	458-0030
Music Teachers NA (MTNA) 441 Vine St Suite 3100 *TF:* 888-512-5278 ■ *Web:* www.mtna.org	Cincinnati	OH	45202	513-421-1420	421-2503
NA for Bilingual Education (NABE) 1313 L St NW Suite 210 *Web:* www.nabe.org	Washington	DC	20005	202-898-1829	789-2866
NA for Campus Activities (NACA) 13 Harbison Way *TF:* 800-845-2338 ■ *Web:* www.naca.org	Columbia	SC	29212	803-732-6222	749-1047
NA for College Admission Counseling (NACAC) 1631 Prince St *TF:* 800-822-6285 ■ *Web:* www.nacacnet.org	Alexandria	VA	22314	703-836-2222	243-9375
NA for the Education of Young Children (NAEYC) 1313 L St NW Suite 500 *TF:* 800-424-2460 ■ *Web:* www.naeyc.org	Washington	DC	20005	202-232-8777	328-1846
NA of Biology Teachers (NABT) 12030 Sunrise Valley Dr Suite 110 *TF:* 800-406-0775 ■ *Web:* www.nabt.org	Reston	VA	20191	703-264-9696	264-7778
NA of Catholic School Teachers (NACST) 1700 Sansom St Suite 903 *TF:* 800-996-2278 ■ *Web:* www.nacst.com	Philadelphia	PA	19103	215-665-0993	568-8270
NA of College & University Business Officers (NACUBO) 1110 Vermont Ave NW Suite 800 *TF:* 800-462-4916 ■ *Web:* www.nacubo.org	Washington	DC	20005	202-861-2500	861-2583
NA of College Auxiliary Services (NACAS) 7 Boars Head Ln *Web:* www.nacas.org	Charlottesville	VA	22903	434-245-8425	245-8453
NA of Colleges & Employers (NACE) 62 Highland Ave *TF:* 800-544-5272 ■ *Web:* www.naceweb.org	Bethlehem	PA	18017	610-868-1421	868-1421
NA of Elementary School Principals (NAESP) 1615 Duke St *TF:* 800-386-2377 ■ *Web:* www.naesp.org	Alexandria	VA	22314	703-684-3345	548-6021
NA of Independent Colleges & Universities (NAICU) 1025 Connecticut Ave NW Suite 700 *Web:* www.naicu.edu	Washington	DC	20036	202-785-8866	835-0003
NA of Independent Schools (NAIS) 1620 L St NW Suite 1100 *Web:* www.nais.org	Washington	DC	20036	202-973-9700	973-9790
NA of Schools of Art & Design (NASAD) 11250 Roger Bacon Dr Suite 21 *Web:* www.nasad.arts-accredit.org	Reston	VA	20190	703-437-0700	437-6312
NA of Schools of Dance (NASD) 11250 Roger Bacon Dr Suite 21 *Web:* www.nasd.arts-accredit.org	Reston	VA	20190	703-437-0700	437-6312
NA of Schools of Music (NASM) 11250 Roger Bacon Dr Suite 21 *Web:* www.nasm.arts-accredit.org	Reston	VA	20190	703-437-0700	437-6312
NA of Secondary School Principals (NASSP) 1904 Assn Dr *TF:* 800-253-7746 ■ *Web:* www.nassp.org	Reston	VA	20191	703-860-0200	476-5432
NA of State Boards of Education (NASBE) 277 S Washington St Suite 100 *TF:* 800-368-5023	Alexandria	VA	22314	703-684-4000	836-2313
NA of Student Activity Advisors 1904 Assn Dr *Web:* www.nasc.us	Reston	VA	20191	703-860-0200	476-5432
NA of Student Financial Aid Administrators (NASFAA) 1101 Connecticut Ave Suite 1100 *Web:* www.nasfaa.org	Washington	DC	20036	202-785-0453	785-1487
NA of Student Personnel Administrators (NASPA) 1875 Connecticut Ave NW Suite 418 *Web:* www.naspa.org	Washington	DC	20009	202-265-7500	797-1157
NAFSA: Assn of International Educators 1307 New York Ave NW 8th Fl *Web:* www.nafsa.org	Washington	DC	20005	202-737-3699	737-3657
National Academy of Education 500 5th St NW Suite 333 *Web:* www.naeducation.org	Washington	DC	20001	202-334-2341	334-2350
National Art Education Assn (NAEA) 1806 Robert Fulton Dr *TF:* 800-299-8321 ■ *Web:* www.arteducators.org	Reston	VA	20191	703-860-8000	860-2960
National Business Education Assn (NBEA) 1914 Assn Dr *Web:* www.nbea.org	Reston	VA	20191	703-860-8300	620-4483
National Catholic Educational Assn (NCEA) 1077 30th St NW Suite 100 *Web:* www.ncea.org	Washington	DC	20007	202-337-6232	333-6706
National Coalition of Girls' Schools (NCGS) 50 Leonard St Suite 2C *Web:* www.ncgs.org	Belmont	MA	02478	617-489-0013	489-0024
National Communication Assn (NCA) 1765 N St NW *Web:* www.natcom.org	Washington	DC	20036	202-464-4622	464-4600
National Community Education Assn (NCEA) 3929 Old Lee Hwy Suite 91-A *Web:* www.ncea.com	Fairfax	VA	22030	703-359-8973	359-0972
National Council for the Social Studies (NCSS) 8555 16th St Suite 500 *TF Orders:* 800-683-0812 ■ *Web:* www.ncss.org	Silver Spring	MD	20910	301-588-1800	588-2049
National Council of Supervisors of Mathematics (NCSM) 6000 E Evans Ave Suite 3-205 *Web:* www.ncsmonline.org	Denver	CO	80222	303-758-9611	758-9616
National Council of Teachers of English (NCTE) 1111 W Kenyon Rd *TF:* 877-369-6283 ■ *Web:* www.ncte.org	Urbana	IL	61801	217-328-3870	328-0977
National Council of Teachers of Mathematics (NCTM) 1906 Assn Dr *TF Orders:* 800-235-7566 ■ *Web:* www.nctm.org	Reston	VA	20191	703-620-9840	476-2970
National Council on Economic Education (NCEE) 122 E 42nd St Suite 2600 *TF:* 800-338-1192 ■ *Web:* www.councilforeconed.org	New York	NY	10168	212-730-7007	730-1793
National Education Assn (NEA) 1201 16th St NW *Web:* www.nea.org	Washington	DC	20036	202-833-4000	822-7974
National Environmental Safety & Health Training Assn (NESHTA) 2700 N Central Ave Suite 900 *Web:* www.neshta.org	Phoenix	AZ	85004	602-956-6099	234-1867
National Guild of Community Schools of the Arts 520 8th Ave Suite 302 *Web:* www.nationalguild.org	New York	NY	10018	212-268-3337	268-3995
National Middle School Assn (NMSA) 4151 Executive Pkwy Suite 300 *TF:* 800-528-6672 ■ *Web:* www.nmsa.org	Westerville	OH	43081	614-895-4730	895-4750
National School Boards Assn (NSBA) 1680 Duke St *Web:* www.nsba.org	Alexandria	VA	22314	703-838-6722	683-7590

Organization	City	State	Zip	Phone	Fax
National School Public Relations Assn (NSPRA) 15948 Derwood Rd *Web:* www.nspra.org	Rockville	MD	20855	301-519-0496	519-0494
National Science Teachers Assn (NSTA) 1840 Wilson Blvd *TF Sales:* 800-722-6782 ■ *Web:* www.nsta.org	Arlington	VA	22201	703-243-7100	243-7177
National Staff Development Council (NSDC) 504 S Locust St *TF:* 800-727-7288 ■ *Web:* www.learningforward.org	Oxford	OH	45056	513-523-6029	523-0638
North Central Assn Higher Learning Commission 230 S LaSalle St *TF:* 800-621-7440 ■ *Web:* www.ncacihe.org	Chicago	IL	60604	312-263-0456	263-7462
Oak Ridge Associated Universities (ORAU) 130 Badger Ave PO Box 117 *Web:* www.orau.org	Oak Ridge	TN	37831	865-576-3000	576-3643
Organization for Tropical Studies (OTS) 410 Swift Ave PO Box 90630 *Web:* www.ots.ac.cr	Durham	NC	27705	919-684-5774	684-5661
Organization of American Historians (OAH) 112 N Bryan Ave PO Box 5457 *Web:* www.oah.org	Bloomington	IN	47408	812-855-7311	855-0696
Registry of Interpreters for the Deaf Inc (RID) 333 Commerce St *Web:* www.rid.org	Alexandria	VA	22314	703-838-0030	838-0454
Society for American Archaeology (SAA) 900 2nd St NE Suite 12 *Web:* www.saa.org	Washington	DC	20002	202-789-8200	789-0284
Society for College & University Planning (SCUP) 339 E Liberty St Suite 300 *Web:* www.scup.org	Ann Arbor	MI	48104	734-998-7832	998-6532
Society for Research in Child Development (SRCD) 2950 S State St Suite 401 *Web:* www.srcd.org	Ann Arbor	MI	48104	734-926-0600	926-0601
Society of Park & Recreation Educators (SPRE) c/o National Recreation & Pk Assn 22377 Belmont Ridge Rd *TF:* 800-626-6772 ■ *Web:* www.nrpa.org	Ashburn	VA	20148	703-858-0784	858-0794
Southern Assn of Colleges & Schools 1866 Southern Ln *TF:* 800-248-7701 ■ *Web:* www.sacs.org	Decatur	GA	30033	404-679-4500	679-4556
Surratt Society 9118 Brandywine Rd *Web:* www.surratt.org	Clinton	MD	20735	301-868-1121	868-8177
Teach For America 315 W 36th St 7th Fl *TF:* 800-832-1230 ■ *Web:* www.teachforamerica.org	New York	NY	10018	212-279-2080	279-2081
Teachers of English to Speakers of Other Languages (TESOL) 700 S Washington St Suite 200 *TF:* 888-547-3369 ■ *Web:* www.tesol.org	Alexandria	VA	22314	703-836-0774	836-7864
Teaching & Mentoring Communities (TMC) PO Box 2579 *TF:* 888-836-5151 ■ *Web:* www.tmccentral.org	Laredo	TX	78044	956-722-5174	725-0907
Torah Umesorah-National Society for Hebrew Day Schools 1090 Coney Island Ave	Brooklyn	NY	11230	212-227-1000	406-6934
Trees for Tomorrow (TFT) 519 Sheridan St E PO Box 609 *TF:* 800-838-9472 ■ *Web:* www.treesfortomorrow.com	Eagle River	WI	54521	715-479-6456	479-2318
Washington Education Assn Inc 32032 Weyerhaeuser Way S PO Box 9100 *TF:* 800-622-3393 ■ *Web:* www.washingtonea.org	Federal Way	WA	98001	253-941-6700	
Western Assn of Schools & Colleges (WASC) 985 Atlantic Ave Suite 100 *Web:* www.wascweb.org	Alameda	CA	94501	510-748-9001	748-9797
Women's College Coalition (WCC) 1678 Asylum Ave W PO Box 1952 *Web:* www.womenscolleges.org	Hartford	CT	06117	860-231-5247	

49-6 Food & Beverage Industries Professional Associations

Organization	City	State	Zip	Phone	Fax
American Assn of Cereal Chemists Inc (AACC) 3340 Pilot Knob Rd *Web:* www.aaccnet.org/default.aspx	Saint Paul	MN	55121	651-454-7250	454-0766
American Beverage Assn 1101 16th St NW *Web:* www.ameribev.org	Washington	DC	20036	202-463-6732	659-5349
American Beverage Licensees (ABL) 5101 River Rd Suite 108 *TF:* 800-656-3241 ■ *Web:* www.ablusa.org	Bethesda	MD	20816	301-656-1494	656-7539
American Culinary Federation Inc (ACF) 180 Ctr Pl Way *TF:* 800-624-9458 ■ *Web:* www.acfchefs.org	Saint Augustine	FL	32095	904-824-4468	825-4758
American Dairy Products Institute (ADPI) 116 N York St Suite 200 *Web:* www.adpi.org	Elmhurst	IL	60126	630-530-8700	530-8707
American Malting Barley Assn (AMBA) 740 N Plankinton Ave Suite 830 *Web:* www.ambainc.org	Milwaukee	WI	53203	414-272-4640	
American Meat Institute (AMI) 1150 Connecticut Ave NW Suite 1200 *Web:* www.meatami.com	Washington	DC	20036	202-587-4200	587-4300
American Peanut Shellers Assn 2336 Lake Pk Dr *Web:* www.peanut-shellers.org	Albany	GA	31707	229-888-2508	888-5150
American Seafood Distributors Assn 7918 Jones Branch Dr Suite 700 *TF:* 877-206-2732 ■ *Web:* www.freetradeinseafood.org	McLean	VA	22102	703-752-8880	752-7583
American Society for Nutrition (ASNS) 9650 Rockville Pike Suite L3503A *TF:* 800-433-2732 ■ *Web:* www.nutrition.org	Bethesda	MD	20814	301-634-7029	634-7099
American Spice Trade Assn (ASTA) 2025 M St NW Suite 800 *Web:* www.astaspice.org	Washington	DC	20036	202-367-1127	367-2127
Assn of Food Industries Inc (AFI) 3301 Rt 66 Bldg C Suite 205 *Web:* www.afi.mytradeassociation.org	Neptune	NJ	07753	732-922-3008	922-3590
At-sea Processors Assn (APA) 4039 21st Ave W Suite 400 *Web:* www.atsea.org	Seattle	WA	98199	206-285-5139	285-1841
Beer Institute 122 C St NW Suite 350 *TF:* 800-379-2739 ■ *Web:* www.beerinstitute.org	Washington	DC	20001	202-737-2337	737-7004
Biscuit & Cracker Manufacturers Assn (B&CMA) 6325 Woodside Ct Suite 125 **Fax Area Code:* 410 ■ *Web:* www.thebcma.org	Columbia	MD	21046	443-545-1645	290-8585*
CIES - Food Business Forum 8455 Colesville Rd Suite 705 *Web:* www.ciesnet.com	Silver Spring	MD	20910	301-563-3383	563-3386
Confrerie de la Chaine des Rotisseurs 285 Madison Ave *Web:* www.chaineus.org	Madison	NJ	07940	973-360-9200	360-9330
Council for Responsible Nutrition (CRN) 1828 L St NW Suite 900 *Web:* www.crnusa.org	Washington	DC	20036	202-776-7929	204-7980
Distilled Spirits Council of the US Inc 1250 'I' St NW Suite 400 *TF:* 888-862-7597 ■ *Web:* www.discus.org	Washington	DC	20005	202-628-3544	682-8888
Flavor & Extract Manufacturers Assn of the US (FEMA) 1620 'I' St NW Suite 925 *Web:* www.femaflavor.org	Washington	DC	20006	202-293-5800	463-8998
Food Institute 1 Broadway *Web:* www.foodinstitute.com	Elmwood Park	NJ	07407	201-791-5570	791-5222
Food Marketing Institute (FMI) 2345 Crystal Dr Suite 800 *Web:* www.fmi.org	Arlington	VA	22202	202-220-0600	429-4519
Foodservice Group Inc The PO Box 681864 *Web:* www.fsgroup.com	Marietta	GA	30068	770-971-8116	971-1094
Institute of Food Technologists (IFT) 525 W Van Buren St Suite 1000 *TF:* 800-438-3663 ■ *Web:* www.ift.org	Chicago	IL	60607	312-782-8424	782-8348
International Assn for Food Protection (IAFP) 6200 Aurora Ave Suite 200W *TF:* 800-369-6337 ■ *Web:* www.foodprotection.org	Des Moines	IA	50322	515-276-3344	276-8655
International Assn of Culinary Professionals (IACP) 455 S 4th St Suite 650 *TF:* 800-928-4227 ■ *Web:* www.iacp.com	Louisville	KY	40202	502-583-3783	589-3602
International Bottled Water Assn (IBWA) 1700 Diagonal Rd Suite 650 *TF:* 800-928-3711 ■ *Web:* www.bottledwater.org	Alexandria	VA	22314	703-683-5213	683-4074
International Dairy Foods Assn (IDFA) 1250 H St NW Suite 900 *Web:* www.idfa.org	Washington	DC	20005	202-737-4332	331-7820
International Dairy-Deli-Bakery Assn (IDDBA) 313 Price Pl *Web:* www.iddba.org	Madison	WI	53705	608-238-7908	238-6330
International Food Information Council Foundation (IFIC) 1100 Connecticut Ave NW Suite 430 *Web:* www.foodinsight.org	Washington	DC	20036	202-296-6540	296-6547
International Foodservice Distributors Assn (IFDA) 1410 Spring Hill Rd Suite 210 *Web:* www.ifdaonline.org	McLean	VA	22102	703-532-9400	538-4673
International Foodservice Manufacturers Assn (IFMA) 180 N Stetson Ave 2 Prudential Plaza Suite 4400 *Web:* www.ifmaworld.com	Chicago	IL	60601	312-540-4400	540-4401
International Ice Cream Assn 1250 H St NW Suite 900 *Web:* www.idfa.org	Washington	DC	20005	202-737-4332	331-7820
Master Brewers Assn of the Americas (MBAA) 3340 Pilot Knob Rd *Web:* www.mbaa.com	Saint Paul	MN	55121	651-454-7250	454-0766
NA for the Specialty Food Trade Inc (NASFT) 120 Wall St 27th Fl *TF:* 800-627-3869 ■ *Web:* www.specialtyfoodmarket.com	New York	NY	10005	212-482-6440	482-6459
NA of Catering Executives (NACE) 9881 Broken Land Pkwy Suite 101 *Web:* www.nace.net	Columbia	MD	21046	410-290-5410	290-5460
NA of Pizzeria Operators 908 S 8th St Suite 200 *TF:* 800-489-8324 ■ *Web:* www.napo.com	Louisville	KY	40203	502-736-9500	736-9501
National Beer Wholesalers Assn (NBWA) 1101 King St Suite 600 *TF:* 800-300-6417 ■ *Web:* www.nbwa.org	Alexandria	VA	22314	703-683-4300	683-8965
National Cheese Institute 1250 H St NW Suite 900 *Web:* www.idsa.org	Washington	DC	20005	202-737-4332	331-7820
National Coffee Assn of USA Inc (NCA) 45 Broadway Suite 1140 *Web:* www.ncausa.org	New York	NY	10006	212-766-4007	766-5815
National Confectioners Assn (NCA) 8320 Old Courthouse Rd Suite 300 *TF:* 800-433-1200 ■ *Web:* www.candyusa.org	Vienna	VA	22182	703-790-5750	790-5752
National Frozen & Refrigerated Foods Assn (NFRA) 4755 Linglestown Rd Suite 300 PO Box 6069 *Web:* www.nfraweb.org	Harrisburg	PA	17112	717-657-8601	657-9862
National Grocers Assn (NGA) 1005 N Glebe Rd Suite 250 *Web:* www.nationalgrocers.org	Arlington	VA	22201	703-516-0700	516-0115
National Meat Assn (NMA) 1970 Broadway Suite 825 *Web:* www.nmaonline.org	Oakland	CA	94612	510-763-1533	763-6186

				Phone	Fax
National Milk Producers Federation (NMPF) 2101 Wilson Blvd Suite 400 *Web:* www.nmpf.org	Arlington	VA	22201	703-243-6111	841-9328
National Pork Producers Council (NPPC) 122 C St NW Suite 875 *Web:* www.nppc.org	Washington	DC	20001	202-347-3600	347-5265
National Restaurant Assn (NRA) 1200 17th St NW *TF:* 800-424-5156 ■ *Web:* www.restaurant.org	Washington	DC	20036	202-331-5900	331-2429
North American Meat Processors Assn (NAMP) 1910 Assn Dr *Web:* www.namp.com	Reston	VA	20191	703-758-1900	758-8001
North American Millers Assn (NAMA) 600 Maryland Ave SW Suite 825-W *Web:* www.namamillers.org	Washington	DC	20024	202-484-2200	488-7416
Popcorn Board 401 N Michigan Ave *TF:* 877-767-2568 ■ *Web:* www.popcorn.org	Chicago	IL	60611	312-644-6610	527-6658
Produce Marketing Assn (PMA) 1500 Casho Mill Rd *Web:* www.pma.com	Newark	DE	19711	302-738-7100	731-2409
Retail Confectioners International (RCI) 2053 S Waverly Suite C *TF:* 800-545-5381 ■ *Web:* www.retailconfectioners.org	Springfield	MO	65804	417-883-2775	883-1108
Salt Institute 700 N Fairfax St Suite 600 *Web:* www.saltinstitute.org	Alexandria	VA	22314	703-549-4648	548-2194
School Nutrition Assn (SNA) 700 S Washington St Suite 300 *TF:* 800-877-8822 ■ *Web:* www.schoolnutrition.org	Alexandria	VA	22314	703-739-3900	739-3915
Snack Food Assn 1600 Wilson Blvd Suite 650 *TF:* 800-628-1334 ■ *Web:* www.sfa.org	Arlington	VA	22209	703-836-4500	836-8262
Specialty Coffee Assn of America (SCAA) 330 Golden Shore Ave Suite 50 *Web:* www.scaa.org	Long Beach	CA	90802	562-624-4100	624-4101
Tea Assn of the USA Inc 362 5th Ave Suite 801 *Web:* www.teausa.com	New York	NY	10001	212-986-9415	697-8658
Tea Council of the USA Inc 362 5th Ave Suite 801 *Web:* www.teausa.com	New York	NY	10001	212-986-6998	697-8658
US Dairy Export Council 2101 Wilson Blvd Suite 400 *Web:* www.usdec.org	Arlington	VA	22201	703-528-3049	528-3705
US Meat Export Federation Inc (USMEF) 1050 17th St Suite 2200 *Web:* www.usmef.org	Denver	CO	80265	303-623-6328	623-0297
USA Poultry & Egg Export Council (USAPEEC) 2300 W Pk Pl Blvd Suite 100 *Web:* www.usapeec.org	Stone Mountain	GA	30087	770-413-0006	413-0007
Wheat Foods Council 10841 S Crossroads Dr Suite 105 *Web:* www.wheatfoods.org	Parker	CO	80134	303-840-8787	840-6877
Wine & Spirits Shippers Assn Inc (WSSA) 11800 Sunrise Valley Dr Suite 425 *TF:* 800-368-3167 ■ *Web:* www.wssa.com	Reston	VA	22091	703-860-2300	860-2422
Wine & Spirits Wholesalers of America Inc (WSWA) 805 15th St NW Suite 430 *Web:* www.wswa.org	Washington	DC	20005	202-371-9792	789-2405
Wine Institute 425 Market St Suite 1000 *Web:* www.wineinstitute.org	San Francisco	CA	94105	415-512-0151	442-0742
WineAmerica 1015 18th St NW # 500 *TF:* 800-879-4637 ■ *Web:* www.wineamerica.org	Washington	DC	20036	202-783-2756	347-6341
World Cocoa Foundation (WCF) 1411 K St NW Suite 1300 *Web:* www.worldcocoafoundation.org	Washington	DC	20005	202-737-7870	737-7832

49-7 Government & Public Administration Professional Associations

				Phone	Fax
American Assn of Motor Vehicle Administrators (AAMVA) 4301 Wilson Blvd Suite 400 *TF:* 800-515-8881 ■ *Web:* www.aamva.org	Arlington	VA	22203	703-522-4200	522-1553
American Assn of State Highway & Transportation Officials (AASHTO) 444 N Capitol St NW Suite 249 *Web:* www.transportation.org	Washington	DC	20001	202-624-5800	624-5806
American Conference of Governmental Industrial Hygienists (ACGIH) 1330 Kemper Meadows Dr *Web:* www.acgih.org	Cincinnati	OH	45240	513-742-2020	742-3355
American Correctional Assn (ACA) 206 N Washington St Suite 200 *TF:* 800-222-5646 ■ *Web:* www.aca.org	Alexandria	VA	22314	703-224-0000	224-0010
American Federation of Police & Concerned Citizens 6350 Horizon Dr *Web:* www.afp-cc.org	Titusville	FL	32780	321-264-0911	264-0033
American Foreign Service Assn (AFSA) 2101 E St NW *TF:* 800-704-2372 ■ *Web:* www.afsa.org	Washington	DC	20037	202-338-4045	338-6820
American Foreign Service Protective Assn 1716 N St NW *Web:* www.afspa.org	Washington	DC	20036	202-833-4910	833-4918
American Jail Assn (AJA) 1135 Professional Ct *Web:* www.aja.org	Hagerstown	MD	21740	301-790-3930	790-2941
American Public Human Services Assn (APHSA) 810 1st St NE Suite 500 *Web:* www.aphsa.org	Washington	DC	20002	202-682-0100	289-6555
American Public Works Assn (APWA) 2345 Grand Blvd Suite 700 *TF:* 800-848-2792 ■ *Web:* www.apwa.net	Kansas City	MO	64108	816-472-6100	472-1610
American Society for Public Administration (ASPA) 1301 Pennsylvania Ave NW Suite 840 *Web:* www.aspanet.org	Washington	DC	20004	202-393-7878	638-4952
Assn of Conservation Engineers (ACE) Missouri Dept of Conservation PO Box 180 *Web:* www.conservationengineers.org	Jefferson City	MO	65102	573-522-4115	522-2324
Assn of Maternal & Child Health Programs (AMCHP) 1220 19th St NW Suite 801 *Web:* www.amchp.org	Washington	DC	20036	202-775-0436	466-5471
Assn of Public Health Laboratories (APHL) 8515 Georgia Ave Suite 700 *Web:* www.aphl.org	Silver Spring	MD	20910	240-485-2745	485-2700
Assn of Public-Safety Communications Officials International Inc 351 N Williamson Blvd *TF:* 888-272-6911 ■ *Web:* www.apcointl.org	Daytona Beach	FL	32114	386-322-2500	322-2501
Assn of Racing Commissioners International (ARCI) 1510 Newtown Pike # 210 *Web:* www.arci.com	Lexington	KY	40511	859-224-7070	224-7071
Assn of Social Work Boards (ASWB) 400 S Ridge Pkwy Suite B *TF:* 800-225-6880 ■ *Web:* www.aswb.org	Culpeper	VA	22701	540-829-6880	829-0142
Assn of State & Interstate Water Pollution Control Administrators (ASIWPCA) 1221 Connecticut Ave NW 2nd Fl *Web:* www.asiwpca.org	Washington	DC	20036	202-756-0600	898-0929
Assn of State & Territorial Health Officials (ASTHO) 2231 Crystal Dr Suite 450 **Fax Area Code: 571* ■ *Web:* www.astho.org	Arlington	VA	22203	202-371-9090	527-3189*
Assn of State & Territorial Solid Waste Management Officials (ASTSWMO) 444 N Capitol St NW Suite 315 *Web:* www.astswmo.org	Washington	DC	20001	202-624-5828	624-7875
Assn of State Wetland Managers 2 Basin Rd *Web:* www.aswm.org	Windham	ME	04062	207-892-3399	892-3089
Commission on Accreditation for Law Enforcement Agencies (CALEA) 13575 Heathcote Blvd Suite 320 *TF:* 800-368-3757 ■ *Web:* www.calea.org	Fairfax	VA	20155	703-352-4225	890-3126
Conference of Radiation Control Program Directors (CRCPD) 1030 Burlington Ln # 4B *Web:* www.crcpd.org	Frankfort	KY	40601	502-227-4543	227-7862
Conference of State Bank Supervisors (CSBS) 1155 Connecticut Ave NW 5th Fl *TF:* 800-886-2727 ■ *Web:* www.csbs.org	Washington	DC	20036	202-296-2840	296-1928
Council of State & Territorial Epidemiologists (CSTE) 2872 Woodcock Blvd Suite 303 *Web:* www.cste.org	Atlanta	GA	30341	770-458-3811	458-8516
Council of State Governments (CSG) 2760 Research Pk Dr *TF Sales:* 800-800-1910 ■ *Web:* www.csg.org	Lexington	KY	40511	859-244-8000	244-8001
Council on Licensure Enforcement & Regulation (CLEAR) 403 Marquis Ave Suite 200 *Web:* www.clearhq.org	Lexington	KY	40502	859-269-1289	231-1943
Federal Bureau of Investigation Agents Assn (FBIAA) PO Box 12650 *Web:* www.fbiaa.org	Arlington	VA	22219	703-247-2173	247-2175
Federal Law Enforcement Officers Assn (FLEOA) 1100 Connecticut Ave NW Suite 900 **Fax Area Code: 717* ■ *Web:* www.fleoa.org	Washington	DC	20036	202-293-1550	932-2262*
Federal Managers Assn (FMA) 1641 Prince St *Web:* www.fedmanagers.org	Alexandria	VA	22314	703-683-8700	683-8707
Federally Employed Women (FEW) 700 N Fairfax St Suite 510 **Fax Area Code: 703* ■ *Web:* www.few.org	Alexandria	DC	22314	202-898-0994	299-9233*
Federation of State Medical Boards of the US Inc (FSMB) 400 Fuller Wiser Rd Suite 300 *TF:* 800-876-5396 ■ *Web:* www.fsmb.org	Euless	TX	76039	817-868-4000	868-4098
Federation of Tax Administrators (FTA) 444 N Capitol St NW Suite 348 *Web:* www.taxadmin.org	Washington	DC	20001	202-624-5890	624-7888
Forest Service Employees for Environmental Ethics (FSEEE) PO Box 11615 *Web:* www.fseee.org	Eugene	OR	97440	541-484-2692	484-3004
Government Finance Officers Assn (GFOA) 203 N LaSalle St Suite 2700 *Web:* www.gfoa.org	Chicago	IL	60601	312-977-9700	977-4806
International Assn of Arson Investigators (IAAI) 2111 Baldwin Ave # 203 *Web:* www.firearson.com	Crofton	MD	21114	410-451-3473	451-9049
International Assn of Assessing Officers (IAAO) 314 W 10th St *TF:* 800-616-4226 ■ *Web:* www.iaao.org	Kansas City	MO	64105	816-701-8100	701-8149
International Assn of Auto Theft Investigators (IAATI) PO Box 223 *Web:* www.iaati.org	Clinton	NY	13323	315-853-1913	793-0048
International Assn of Chiefs of Police (IACP) 515 N Washington St *TF:* 800-843-4227 ■ *Web:* www.theiacp.org	Alexandria	VA	22314	703-836-6767	836-4543
International Assn of Fire Chiefs (IAFC) 4025 Fair Ridge Dr Suite 300 *TF:* 866-385-9110 ■ *Web:* www.iafc.org	Fairfax	VA	22033	703-273-0911	273-9363
International Assn of Fish & Wildlife Agencies (IAFWA) 444 N Capitol St NW Suite 725 *Web:* www.fishwildlife.org	Washington	DC	20001	202-624-7890	624-7891
International Assn of Plumbing & Mechanical Officials (IAPMO) 4755 E Philadelphia St *Web:* www.iapmo.org	Ontario	CA	91761	909-472-4100	472-4150

				Phone	Fax
International Bridge Tunnel & Turnpike Assn (IBTTA)					
1146 19th St NW Suite 600	Washington	DC	20036	202-659-4620	659-0500
Web: www.ibtta.org					
International City/County Management Assn (ICMA)					
777 N Capitol St NE Suite 500	Washington	DC	20002	202-289-4262	962-3500
TF: 800-745-8780 ■ *Web:* www.icma.org					
International Conference of Funeral Service Examining Boards Inc					
1885 Shelby Ln	Fayetteville	AR	72704	479-442-7076	442-7090
Web: www.theconferenceonline.org					
International Institute of Municipal Clerks (IIMC)					
8331 Utica Ave Suite 200	Rancho Cucamonga	CA	91730	909-944-4162	944-8545
TF: 800-251-1639 ■ *Web:* www.iimc.com					
International Municipal Signal Assn (IMSA)					
165 E Union St PO Box 539	Newark	NY	14513	315-331-2182	331-8205
TF: 800-723-4672 ■ *Web:* www.imsasafety.org					
International Narcotic Enforcement Officers Assn (INEOA)					
112 State St Suite 1200	Albany	NY	12207	518-463-6232	432-3378
Web: www.ineoa.org					
International Society of Fire Service Instructors (ISFSI)					
14001C St Germain Dr	Suite 128	VA	20121	800-435-0005	435-0005
TF: 800-435-0005 ■ *Web:* www.isfsi.org					
Kansas Assn of Counties (KAC)					
300 SW 8th St 3rd Fl	Topeka	KS	66603	785-272-2585	272-3585
Web: www.kansascounties.org					
Maryland Assn of Counties (MACo)					
169 Conduit St	Annapolis	MD	21401	410-269-0043	268-1775
Web: www.mdcounties.org					
NA for Search & Rescue (NASAR)					
4500 Southgate Pl Suite 100	Chantilly	VA	20151	703-222-6277	222-6283
TF: 877-893-0702 ■ *Web:* www.nasar.org					
NA of Area Agencies on Aging (N4A)					
1730 Rhode Island Ave NW Suite 1200	Washington	DC	20036	202-872-0888	872-0057
Web: www.n4a.org					
NA of Attorneys General (NAAG)					
2030 M St NW 8th Fl	Washington	DC	20036	202-326-6000	331-1427
TF: 888-245-6224 ■ *Web:* www.naag.org					
NA of Boards of Examiners of Long Term Care Administrators (NAB)					
1444 'I' St NW Suite 700	Washington	DC	20005	202-712-9040	216-9646
Web: www.nabweb.org					
NA of Boards of Pharmacy (NABP)					
1600 Feehanville Dr	Mount Prospect	IL	60056	847-391-4406	391-4502
Web: www.nabp.net					
NA of Chiefs of Police (NACOP)					
6350 Horizon Dr	Titusville	FL	32780	321-264-0911	264-0033
Web: www.aphf.org/nacop.html					
NA of Clean Air Agencies The (NACAA)					
444 N Capitol St NW Suite 307	Washington	DC	20001	202-624-7864	624-7863
Web: www.cleanairworld.org					
NA of Clean Water Agencies (NACWA)					
1816 Jefferson Pl NW	Washington	DC	20036	202-833-2672	833-4657
Web: www.nacwa.org					
NA of Conservation Districts (NACD)					
509 Capitol Ct NE	Washington	DC	20002	202-547-6223	547-6450
TF: 888-695-2433 ■ *Web:* www.nacdnet.org					
NA of County & City Health Officials (NACCHO)					
1100 17th St 2nd Fl	Washington	DC	20036	202-783-5550	783-1583
Web: www.naccho.org					
NA of Government Archives & Records Administrators (NAGARA)					
90 State St Suite 1009	Albany	NY	12207	518-463-8644	463-8656
Web: www.nagara.org					
NA of Government Employees (NAGE)					
159 Thomas Burgin Pkwy	Quincy	MA	02169	617-376-0220	376-0285
Web: www.nage.org					
NA of Housing & Redevelopment Officials (NAHRO)					
630 'I' St NW	Washington	DC	20001	202-289-3500	289-8181
TF: 877-866-2476 ■ *Web:* www.nahro.org					
NA of Insurance Commissioners (NAIC)					
2301 McGee St Suite 800	Kansas City	MO	64108	816-842-3600	783-8175
Web: www.naic.org					
NA of Latino Elected & Appointed Officials (NALEO)					
1122 W Washington Blvd 3rd Fl	Los Angeles	CA	90015	213-747-7606	747-7664
Web: www.naleo.org					
NA of Local Housing Finance Agencies (NALHFA)					
2025 M St NW Suite 800	Washington	DC	20036	202-367-1197	367-2197
Web: www.nalhfa.org					
NA of Postal Supervisors (NAPS)					
1727 King St Suite 400	Alexandria	VA	22314	703-836-9660	836-9665
Web: www.naps.org					
NA of Postmasters of the US (NAPUS)					
8 Herbert St	Alexandria	VA	22305	703-683-9027	683-6820
Web: www.napus.org					
NA of Regional Councils (NARC)					
1666 Connecticut Ave NW Suite 300	Washington	DC	20009	202-986-1032	986-1038
Web: www.narc.org					
NA of Regulatory Utility Commissioners (NARUC)					
1101 Vermont Ave NW Suite 200	Washington	DC	20005	202-898-2200	898-2213
Web: www.naruc.org					
NA of Rehabilitation Providers & Agencies (NARA)					
701 8th St NW Suite 500	Washington	DC	20001	866-839-7710	716-1847*
**Fax Area Code:* 800 ■ *TF:* 866-839-7710 ■ *Web:* www.naranet.org					
NA of Social Workers (NASW)					
750 1st St NE Suite 700	Washington	DC	20002	202-408-8600	336-8311
TF: 800-638-8799 ■ *Web:* www.naswdc.org					
NA of State Alcohol & Drug Abuse Directors (NASADAD)					
808 17th St NW Suite 410	Washington	DC	20006	202-293-0090	293-1250
Web: www.nasadad.org					
NA of State Auditors Comptrollers & Treasurers (NASACT)					
449 Lewis Hargett Cir Suite 290	Lexington	KY	40503	859-276-1147	278-0507
Web: www.nasact.org					
NA of State Aviation Officials (NASAO)					
Washington National Airport					
Hangar 7 Suite 218	Washington	DC	20001	703-417-1880	417-1885
Web: www.nasao.org					
NA of State Budget Officers (NASBO)					
444 N Capitol St NW Suite 642	Washington	DC	20001	202-624-5382	624-7745
Web: www.nasbo.org					
NA of State Chief Information Officers					
201 E Main St Suite 1405	Lexington	KY	40507	859-514-9156	514-9166
Web: www.nascio.org					
NA of State Depts of Agriculture (NASDA)					
1156 15th St NW Suite 1020	Washington	DC	20005	202-296-9680	296-9686
Web: www.nasda.org					
NA of State Fire Marshals (NASFM)					
1319 F St NW Suite 301	Washington	DC	20004	202-737-1226	393-1296
TF: 877-996-2736 ■ *Web:* www.firemarshals.org					
NA of State Foresters (NASF)					
444 N Capitol St NW Suite 540	Washington	DC	20001	202-624-5415	624-5407
Web: www.stateforesters.org					
NA of State Mental Health Program Directors (NASMHPD)					
66 Canal Ctr Plaza Suite 302	Alexandria	VA	22314	703-739-9333	548-9517
Web: www.nasmhpd.org					
NA of State Procurement Officials (NASPO)					
201 E Main St Suite 1405	Lexington	KY	40507	859-514-9159	
Web: www.naspo.org					
NA of State Units on Aging					
1201 15th St NW Suite 350	Washington	DC	20005	202-898-2578	898-2583
Web: www.nasua.org					
NA of State Workforce Agencies					
444 N Capitol St NW Suite 142	Washington	DC	20001	202-434-8020	434-8033
Web: www.naswa.org					
NA of Towns & Townships (NATaT)					
1130 Connecticut Ave NW Suite 300	Washington	DC	20036	202-454-3954	331-1598
TF: 866-830-0008 ■ *Web:* www.natat.org					
NA of Unclaimed Property Administrators (NAUPA)					
2760 Research Pk Dr PO Box 11910	Lexington	KY	40511	859-244-8150	244-8053
Web: www.unclaimed.org					
National Academy of Public Administration					
900 7th St NW Suite 600	Washington	DC	20001	202-347-3190	393-0993
TF: 800-883-3190 ■ *Web:* www.napawash.org					
National Alcohol Beverage Control Assn (NABCA)					
4401 Ford Ave Suite 700	Alexandria	VA	22302	703-578-4200	820-3551
Web: www.nabca.org					
National American Indian Housing Council (NAIHC)					
50 F St NW Suite 3300	Washington	DC	20001	202-789-1754	789-1758
TF: 800-284-9165 ■ *Web:* www.naihc.net					
National Assembly of State Arts Agencies (NASAA)					
1029 Vermont Ave NW 2nd Fl	Washington	DC	20005	202-347-6352	737-0526
Web: www.nasaa-arts.org					
National Board of Boiler & Pressure Vessel Inspectors					
1055 Crupper Ave	Columbus	OH	43229	614-888-8320	847-1147*
**Fax:* Cust Svc ■ *Web:* www.nationalboard.org					
National Center for State Courts (NCSC)					
300 Newport Ave	Williamsburg	VA	23185	757-259-1525	220-0449
TF: 800-616-6164 ■ *Web:* www.ncsconline.org					
National Conference of State Historic Preservation Officers					
444 N Capitol St NW Suite 342	Washington	DC	20001	202-624-5465	624-5419
Web: www.ncshpo.org					
National Conference of State Legislatures					
7700 E 1st Pl	Denver	CO	80230	303-364-7700	364-7800
Web: www.ncsl.org					
National Conference of States on Bldg Codes & Standards (NCSBCS)					
505 Huntmar Pk Dr Suite 210	Herndon	VA	20170	703-437-0100	481-3596
TF: 800-362-2633 ■ *Web:* www.ncsbcs.org					
National Council of Architectural Registration Boards (NCARB)					
1801 K St NW Suite 700-K	Washington	DC	20006	202-783-6500	783-0290
Web: www.ncarb.org					
National Council of State Housing Agencies (NCSHA)					
444 N Capitol St NW Suite 438	Washington	DC	20001	202-624-7710	624-5899
Web: www.ncsha.org					
National District Attorneys Assn (NDAA)					
99 Canal Ctr Plaza Suite 510	Alexandria	VA	22314	703-549-9222	836-3195
Web: www.ndaa.org					
National Emergency Management Assn (NEMA)					
PO Box 11910	Lexington	KY	40578	859-244-8000	244-8002
Web: www.nemaweb.org					
National Environmental Health Assn (NEHA)					
720 S Colorado Blvd 100 N Tower	Denver	CO	80246	303-756-9090	691-9490
Web: www.neha.org					
National Fire Protection Assn (NFPA)					
1 Batterymarch Pk	Quincy	MA	02169	617-770-3000	770-0700
TF: 800-344-3555 ■ *Web:* www.nfpa.org					
National Forum for Black Public Administrators (NFBPA)					
777 N Capitol St NE Suite 807	Washington	DC	20002	202-408-9300	408-8558
Web: www.nfbpa.org					
National Governors Assn (NGA)					
444 N Capitol St NW Suite 267	Washington	DC	20001	202-624-5300	624-5313
Web: www.nga.org					
National Institute of Governmental Purchasing (NIGP)					
151 Spring St	Herndon	VA	20170	703-736-8900	736-9644
TF: 800-367-6447 ■ *Web:* www.nigp.org					

Organization / Address	City	State	Zip	Phone	Fax
National League of Cities (NLC) 1301 Pennsylvania Ave NW Suite 550 *Web:* www.nlc.org	Washington	DC	20004	202-626-3000	626-3043
National Organization of Black Law Enforcement Executives (NOBLE) 4609 Pinecrest Office Pk Dr Suite F *Web:* www.noblenatl.org	Alexandria	VA	22312	703-658-1529	658-9479
National Sheriffs' Assn (NSA) 1450 Duke St *TF:* 800-424-7827 ■ *Web:* www.sheriffs.org	Alexandria	VA	22314	703-836-7827	683-6541
National Ski Patrol System Inc (NSP) 133 S Van Gordon St Suite 100 *Web:* www.nsp.org	Lakewood	CO	80228	303-988-1111	988-3005
National Volunteer Fire Council (NVFC) 7582 Walker Dr Suite 450 *TF:* 888-275-6832 ■ *Web:* www.nvfc.org	Greenbelt	MD	20770	202-887-5700	887-5291
North American Assn of State & Provincial Lotteries (NASPL) 6 N Broadway *Web:* www.naspl.org	Geneva	OH	44041	440-466-5630	466-5649
Opportunity Finance Network 620 Chestnut St Suite 572 *Web:* www.opportunityfinance.net	Philadelphia	PA	19106	215-923-4754	923-4755
Police Executive Research Forum (PERF) 1120 Connecticut Ave NW Suite 930 *TF:* 888-202-4563 ■ *Web:* www.policeforum.org	Washington	DC	20036	202-466-7820	466-7826
Public Employees Roundtable (PER) PO Box 75248 *Web:* www.theroundtable.org	Washington	DC	20013	202-927-4926	927-4920
Public Risk Management Assn (PRIMA) 700 S Washington St Suite 218 *Web:* www.primacentral.org	Alexandria	VA	22314	703-528-7701	739-0200
Public Technology Inc 1301 Pennsylvania Ave NW Suite 830 *Web:* www.pti.org	Washington	DC	20004	202-626-2400	626-2498
United Federation of Police Officers Inc 540 N State Rd *TF:* 800-227-4291 ■ *Web:* www.policefederation.com	Briarcliff Manor	NY	10510	914-941-4103	941-4472
US Conference of Mayors 1620 'I' St NW Suite 400 *Web:* www.usmayors.org	Washington	DC	20006	202-293-7330	293-2352
US Ombudsman Assn (USOA) 5619 NW 86th St Suite 600 *Web:* www.usombudsman.org	Johnston	IA	50131	515-225-2323	327-5050
US Travel Assn 1100 New York Ave NW Suite 450 *Web:* www.ustravel.org	Washington	DC	20005	202-408-8422	408-1255
West Virginia Assn of Counties (WVACO) 2211 Washington St *Web:* www.wvaco.org	Charleston	WV	25311	304-346-0591	346-0592

49-8 Health & Medical Professionals Associations

Organization / Address	City	State	Zip	Phone	Fax
Academy of General Dentistry (AGD) 211 E Chicago Ave Suite 900 *TF:* 888-243-3368 ■ *Web:* www.agd.org	Chicago	IL	60611	312-440-4300	440-0559
Academy of Managed Care Pharmacy (AMCP) 100 N Pitt St Suite 400 *TF:* 800-827-2627 ■ *Web:* www.amcp.org	Alexandria	VA	22314	703-683-8416	683-8417
Academy of Osseointegration 85 W Algonquin Rd Suite 550 *TF:* 800-656-7736 ■ *Web:* www.osseo.org	Arlington Heights	IL	60005	847-439-1919	439-1569
Academy of Pharmacy Practice & Management American Pharmacists Assn 1100 15th St NW Suite 400 *TF:* 800-237-2742 ■ *Web:* www.pharmacist.com	Washington	DC	20005	202-628-4410	783-2351
Academy of Students of Pharmacy American Pharmacists Assn 1100 15th St NW Suite 400 *TF:* 800-237-2742 ■ *Web:* www.pharmacist.com	Washington	DC	20005	202-628-4410	783-2351
AcademyHealth 1801 K St NW # 701 *Web:* www.academyhealth.org	Washington	DC	20006	202-292-6700	292-6800
Advancing Transfusion & Cellular Therapies Worldwide (AABB) 8101 Glenbrook Rd *TF:* 866-222-2498 ■ *Web:* www.aabb.org	Bethesda	MD	20814	301-907-6977	907-6895
Aerospace Medical Assn (AMA) 320 S Henry St *Web:* www.asma.org	Alexandria	VA	22314	703-739-2240	739-9652
America's Blood Centers (ABC) 725 15th St NW Suite 700 *TF:* 888-872-5663 ■ *Web:* www.americasblood.org	Washington	DC	20005	202-393-5725	393-1282
American Academy of Allergy Asthma & Immunology (AAAAI) 555 E Wells St Suite 1100 *TF:* 800-822-2762 ■ *Web:* www.aaaai.org	Milwaukee	WI	53202	414-272-6071	272-6070
American Academy of Ambulatory Care Nursing (AAACN) E Holly Ave PO Box 56 *TF:* 800-262-6877 ■ *Web:* www.aaacn.org	Pitman	NJ	08071	856-256-2350	589-7463
American Academy of Audiology (AAA) 11730 Plaza America Dr Suite 300 *TF:* 800-222-2336 ■ *Web:* www.audiology.org	Reston	VA	20190	703-790-8466	790-8631
American Academy of Cosmetic Dentistry (AACD) 402 W Wilson St *TF:* 800-543-9220 ■ *Web:* www.aacd.com	Madison	WI	53703	608-222-8583	222-9540
American Academy of Cosmetic Surgery (AACS) 737 N Michigan Ave Suite 2100 *Web:* www.cosmeticsurgery.org	Chicago	IL	60611	312-981-6760	981-6787
American Academy of Dental Group Practice (AADGP) 2525 E Arizona Biltmore Cir Suite 127 *Web:* www.aadgp.org	Phoenix	AZ	85016	602-381-1185	381-1093
American Academy of Dermatology (AAD) 930 E Woodfield Rd *Web:* www.aad.org	Schaumburg	IL	60173	847-330-0230	330-0050
American Academy of Disability Evaluating Physicians (AADEP) 223 W Jackson Blvd Suite 1104 *TF:* 800-456-6095 ■ *Web:* www.aadep.org	Chicago	IL	60606	312-663-1171	663-1175
American Academy of Facial Plastic & Reconstructive Surgery (AAFPRS) 310 S Henry St *Web:* www.aafprs.org	Alexandria	VA	22314	703-299-9291	299-8898
American Academy of Family Physicians (AAFP) 11400 Tomahawk Creek Pkwy *TF:* 800-274-2237 ■ *Web:* www.aafp.org	Leawood	KS	66211	913-906-6000	906-6075
American Academy of Home Care Physicians (AAHCP) 612 Rivershore Ct *Web:* www.aahcp.org	Edgewood	MD	21040	410-676-7966	
American Academy of Hospice & Palliative Medicine (AAHPM) 4700 W Lake Ave **Fax Area Code: 877* ■ *Web:* www.aahpm.org	Glenview	IL	60025	847-375-4712	734-8671*
American Academy of Neurology (AAN) 1080 Montreal Ave *TF:* 800-879-1960 ■ *Web:* www.aan.com	Saint Paul	MN	55116	651-695-1940	695-2791
American Academy of Nurse Practitioners (AANP) PO Box 12846 *Web:* www.aanp.org	Austin	TX	78711	512-442-4262	442-6469
American Academy of Ophthalmology 655 Beach St *TF:* 866-561-8558 ■ *Web:* www.aao.org	San Francisco	CA	94109	415-561-8500	561-8575
American Academy of Optometry (AAO) 6110 Executive Blvd Suite 506 *Web:* www.aaopt.org	Rockville	MD	20852	301-984-1441	984-4737
American Academy of Orthopaedic Surgeons (AAOS) 6300 N River Rd *TF:* 800-346-2267 ■ *Web:* www.aaos.org	Rosemont	IL	60018	847-823-7186	823-8125
American Academy of Orthotists & Prosthetists (AAOP) 526 King St Suite 201 *Web:* www.oandp.org	Alexandria	VA	22314	703-836-0788	836-0737
American Academy of Otolaryngology-Head & Neck Surgery (AAO-HNS) 1650 Diagonal Rd *TF:* 877-722-6467 ■ *Web:* www.entnet.org	Alexandria	VA	22314	703-836-4444	683-5100
American Academy of Pain Management (AAPM) 13947 Mono Way Suite A *Web:* www.aapainmanage.org	Sonora	CA	95370	209-533-9744	533-9750
American Academy of Pediatric Dentistry (AAPD) 211 E Chicago Ave Suite 1700 *Web:* www.aapd.org	Chicago	IL	60611	312-337-2169	337-6329
American Academy of Pediatrics (AAP) 141 NW Pt Blvd *TF:* 800-433-9016 ■ *Web:* www.aap.org	Elk Grove Village	IL	60007	847-434-4000	434-8000
American Academy of Periodontology (AAP) 737 N Michigan Ave Suite 800 *TF:* 800-282-4867 ■ *Web:* www.perio.org	Chicago	IL	60611	312-787-5518	787-3670
American Academy of Physical Medicine & Rehabilitation (AAPM&R) 9700 W Bryn Mawr Ave Suite 200 *Web:* www.aapmr.org	Rosemont	IL	60018	847-737-6000	737-6001
American Academy of Physician Assistants (AAPA) 950 N Washington St *Web:* www.aapa.org	Alexandria	VA	22314	703-836-2272	684-1924
American Assn for Cancer Research (AACR) 615 Chestnut St 17th Fl *TF:* 866-423-3965 ■ *Web:* www.aacr.org	Philadelphia	PA	19106	215-440-9300	440-7228
American Assn for Homecare 2011 Crystal Dr Suite 725 *Web:* www.aahomecare.org	Arlington	VA	22202	703-836-6263	836-6730
American Assn for Respiratory Care (AARC) 9425 N MacArthur Blvd Suite 100 *Web:* www.aarc.org	Irving	TX	75063	972-243-2272	484-2720
American Assn for the Study of Liver Diseases (AASLD) 1001 N Fairfax St Suite 400 *Web:* www.aasld.org	Alexandria	VA	22314	703-299-9766	299-9622
American Assn for Thoracic Surgery (AATS) 900 Cummings Ctr Suite 221-U *Web:* www.aats.org	Beverly	MA	01915	978-927-8330	524-8890
American Assn of Bioanalysts (AAB) 906 Olive St Suite 1200 *Web:* www.aab.org	Saint Louis	MO	63101	314-241-1445	241-1449
American Assn of Clinical Endocrinologists (AACE) 245 Riverside Ave Suite 2000 *Web:* www.aace.com	Jacksonville	FL	32202	904-353-7878	353-8185
American Assn of Colleges of Osteopathic Medicine (AACOM) 5550 Friendship Blvd Suite 310 *Web:* www.aacom.org	Chevy Chase	MD	20815	301-968-4100	968-4101
American Assn of Colleges of Podiatric Medicine (AACPM) 15850 Crabbs Branch Way Suite 320 *TF:* 800-922-9266 ■ *Web:* www.aacpm.org	Rockville	MD	20855	301-948-9760	948-1928
American Assn of Critical-Care Nurses (AACN) 101 Columbia *TF:* 800-809-2273 ■ *Web:* www.aacn.org	Aliso Viejo	CA	92656	949-362-2000	362-2020
American Assn of Diabetes Educators (AADE) 100 W Monroe St *TF:* 800-338-3633 ■ *Web:* www.diabeteseducator.org	Chicago	IL	60603	312-424-2426	424-2427
American Assn of Endodontists (AAE) 211 E Chicago Ave Suite 1100 *TF:* 800-872-3636 ■ *Web:* www.aae.org	Chicago	IL	60611	312-266-7255	266-9867
American Assn of Gynecological Laparoscopists (AAGL) 6757 Katella Ave *TF:* 800-554-2245 ■ *Web:* www.aagl.org	Cypress	CA	90630	714-503-6200	503-6201
American Assn of Healthcare Consultants (AAHC) 1205 Johnson Ferry Rd Suite 136-420 *Web:* www.aahc.net	Marietta	GA	30068	770-635-8758	874-4401

	City	State	ZIP	Phone	Fax
American Assn of Immunologists (AAI)					
9650 Rockville Pike	Bethesda	MD	20814	301-634-7178	634-7887
Web: www.aai.org					
American Assn of Integrated Healthcare Delivery Systems Inc (AAIHDS)					
4435 Waterfront Dr Suite 101	Glen Allen	VA	23060	804-747-5823	747-5316
Web: www.aaihds.org					
American Assn of Managed Care Nurses (AAMCN)					
4435 Waterfront Dr Suite 101	Glen Allen	VA	23060	804-527-1905	747-5316
TF: 800-722-0376 ■ *Web:* www.namcp.com					
American Assn of Medical Assistants (AAMA)					
20 N Wacker Dr Suite 1575	Chicago	IL	60606	312-899-1500	899-1259
TF: 800-228-2262 ■ *Web:* www.aama-ntl.org					
American Assn of Medical Review Officers (AAMRO)					
PO Box 12873	Research Triangle Park	NC	27709	919-489-5407	490-1010
TF: 800-489-1839 ■ *Web:* www.aamro.com					
American Assn of Medical Society Executives (AAMSE)					
555 E Wells St Suite 1100	Milwaukee	WI	53202	414-221-9275	276-3349
Web: www.aamse.org					
American Assn of Neurological Surgeons (AANS)					
5550 Meadowbrook Dr	Rolling Meadows	IL	60008	847-378-0500	378-0600
TF: 888-566-2267 ■ *Web:* www.aans.org					
American Assn of Neuromuscular & Electrodiagnostic Medicine (AANEM)					
2621 Superior Dr NW	Rochester	MN	55901	507-288-0100	288-1225
Web: www.aanem.org					
American Assn of Neuroscience Nurses (AANN)					
4700 W Lake Ave	Glenview	IL	60025	847-375-4733	375-6430
TF: 888-557-2266 ■ *Web:* www.aann.org					
American Assn of Nurse Anesthetists (AANA)					
222 S Prospect Ave	Park Ridge	IL	60068	847-692-7050	692-6968
Web: www.aana.com					
American Assn of Nutritional Consultants (AANC)					
400 Oakhill Dr	Winona Lake	IN	46590	574-269-6165	268-2120
TF: 888-828-2262 ■ *Web:* www.aanc.net					
American Assn of Oral & Maxillofacial Surgeons (AAOMS)					
9700 W Bryn Mawr Ave	Rosemont	IL	60018	847-678-6200	678-6286
TF: 800-822-6637 ■ *Web:* www.aaoms.org					
American Assn of Orthodontists (AAO)					
401 N Lindbergh Blvd	Saint Louis	MO	63141	314-993-1700	997-1745
TF: 800-424-2841 ■ *Web:* www.braces.org					
American Assn of Physician Specialists Inc (AAPS)					
5550 W Executive Dr Suite 400	Tampa	FL	33609	813-433-2277	830-6599
TF: 800-447-9397 ■ *Web:* www.aapsus.org					
American Assn of Poison Control Centers (AAPCC)					
3201 New Mexico Ave Suite 330	Washington	DC	20016	202-362-7217	362-3240
TF: 800-222-1222 ■ *Web:* www.aapcc.org					
American Assn of Preferred Provider Organizations (AAPPO)					
222 S 1st St Suite 303	Louisville	KY	40202	502-403-1122	403-1129
Web: www.aappo.org					
American Assn of Tissue Banks (AATB)					
1320 Old Chain Bridge Rd Suite 450	McLean	VA	22101	703-827-9582	356-2198
TF: 800-635-2282 ■ *Web:* www.aatb.org					
American Auditory Society 19 Mantua Rd	Mount Royal	NJ	08061	856-423-3118	423-3420
Web: www.amauditorysoc.org					
American Autoimmune Related Disease Assn (AARDA)					
22100 Gratiot Ave	Eastpointe	MI	48021	586-776-3900	776-3903
TF: 800-598-4668 ■ *Web:* www.aarda.org					
American Board of Physician Nutrition Specialists (ABPNS)					
The University of Alabama at Birmingham					
933 19th St S	Birmingham	AL	35294	205-966-2513	934-7438
Web: www.main.uab.edu/Sites/abpns					
American Burn Assn (ABA)					
625 N Michigan Ave Suite 2550	Chicago	IL	60611	312-642-9260	642-9130
Web: www.ameriburn.org					
American Cancer Society (ACS)					
250 William St NW Suite 6001	Atlanta	GA	30303	404-320-3333	325-9341
TF: 800-227-2345 ■ *Web:* www.cancer.org					
American Chiropractic Assn (ACA)					
1701 Clarendon Blvd 2nd Fl	Arlington	VA	22209	703-276-8800	243-2593
TF: 800-986-4636 ■ *Web:* www.acatoday.org					
American Cleft Palate-Craniofacial Assn					
1504 E Franklin St Suite 102	Chapel Hill	NC	27514	919-933-9044	933-9604
Web: www.acpa-cpf.org					
American College Health Assn (ACHA)					
PO Box 28937	Baltimore	MD	21240	410-859-1500	859-1510
Web: www.acha.org					
American College of Allergy Asthma & Immunology (ACAAI)					
85 W Algonquin Rd Suite 550	Arlington Heights	IL	60005	847-427-1200	427-1294
Web: www.acaai.org					
American College of Cardiology (ACC)					
2400 N St NW	Washington	DC	20037	202-375-6000	375-7000
TF Cust Svc: 800-253-4636 ■ *Web:* www.cardiosource.org/acc					
American College of Chest Physicians (ACCP)					
3300 Dundee Rd	Northbrook	IL	60062	847-498-1400	498-5460
TF: 800-343-2227 ■ *Web:* www.chestnet.org					
American College of Clinical Pharmacy (ACCP)					
13000 W 87th St Pkwy	Lenexa	KS	66215	913-492-3311	492-0088
Web: www.accp.com					
American College of Dentists (ACD)					
839 Quince Orchard Blvd Suite J	Gaithersburg	MD	20878	301-977-3223	977-3330
TF: 888-223-1920 ■ *Web:* www.acd.org					
American College of Emergency Physicians (ACEP)					
1125 Executive Cir PO Box 619911	Dallas	TX	75261	972-550-0911	580-2816
TF: 800-798-1822 ■ *Web:* www.acep.org					
American College of Eye Surgeons/American Board of Eye Surgery (ACES)					
334 E Lake Rd Suite 135	Palm Lake Harbor	FL	34685	727-366-1487	836-9783
Web: www.aces-abes.org					

	City	State	ZIP	Phone	Fax
American College of Foot & Ankle Surgeons (ACFAS)					
8725 W Higgins Rd Suite 555	Chicago	IL	60631	773-693-9300	693-9304
TF: 800-421-2237 ■ *Web:* www.acfas.org					
American College of Forensic Examiners International (ACFEI)					
2750 E Sunshine St	Springfield	MO	65804	417-881-3818	881-4702
TF: 800-423-9737 ■ *Web:* www.acfei.com					
American College of Gastroenterology (ACG)					
6400 Goldsboro Rd Suite 450	Bethesda	MD	20817	301-263-9000	263-9025
Web: www.acg.gi.org					
American College of Health Care Administrators (ACHCA)					
12100 Sunset hillds Rd Suite 130	Reston	VA	20190	703-739-7900	435-4390
TF: 888-882-2422 ■ *Web:* www.achca.org					
American College of Healthcare Executives (ACHE)					
1 N Franklin St Suite 1700	Chicago	IL	60606	312-424-2800	424-0023
Web: www.ache.org					
American College of Managed Care Medicine (ACMCM)					
4435 Waterfront Dr Suite 101	Glen Allen	VA	23060	804-527-1906	747-5316
Web: www.acmcm.org					
American College of Nurse-Midwives (ACNM)					
8403 Colesville Rd Suite 1550	Silver Spring	MD	20910	240-485-1800	485-1818
Web: www.midwife.org					
American College of Nutrition					
300 S Duncan Ave Suite 225	Clearwater	FL	33755	727-446-6086	446-6202
American College of Obstetricians & Gynecologists (ACOG)					
409 12th St SW PO Box 96920	Washington	DC	20090	202-638-5577	863-4284
Web: www.acog.com					
American College of Occupational & Environmental Medicine (ACOEM)					
25 NW Pt Blvd Suite 700	Elk Grove Village	IL	60007	847-818-1800	818-9266
Web: www.acoem.org					
American College of Osteopathic Family Physicians (ACOFP)					
330 E Algonquin Rd Suite 1	Arlington Heights	IL	60005	847-952-5100	228-9755
TF: 800-323-0794 ■ *Web:* www.acofp.org					
American College of Physician Executives (ACPE)					
400 N Ashley Dr Suite 4001	Tampa	FL	33602	813-287-2000	287-8993
TF: 800-562-8088 ■ *Web:* www.acpe.org					
American College of Physicians (ACP)					
190 N Independence Mall W	Philadelphia	PA	19106	215-351-2400	351-2594
TF: 800-523-1546 ■ *Web:* www.acponline.org					
American College of Preventive Medicine (ACPM)					
455 Massachusetts Ave NW	Washington	DC	20001	202-466-2044	466-2662
Web: www.acpm.org					
American College of Radiology (ACR)					
1892 Preston White Dr	Reston	VA	20191	703-648-8900	295-6772
TF: 800-227-5463 ■ *Web:* www.acr.org					
American College of Rheumatology (ACR)					
2200 Lake Blvd NE	Atlanta	GA	30319	404-633-3777	633-1870
Web: www.rheumatology.org					
American College of Sports Medicine (ACSM)					
401 W Michigan St PO Box 1440	Indianapolis	IN	46202	317-637-9200	634-7817
Web: www.acsm.org					
American College of Surgeons (ACS)					
633 N St Clair St	Chicago	IL	60611	312-202-5000	202-5001
TF: 800-621-4111 ■ *Web:* www.facs.org					
American College of Toxicology					
9650 Rockville Pike	Bethesda	MD	20814	301-634-7840	634-7852
Web: www.actox.org					
American Congress of Community Supports & Employment Services (ACCSES)					
1501 M St NW 7th Fl	Washington	DC	20005	202-466-3355	466-7571
Web: www.accses.org					
American Dental Assistants Assn (ADAA)					
35 E Wacker Dr Suite 1730	Chicago	IL	60601	312-541-1550	541-1496
TF: 877-874-3785 ■ *Web:* www.dentalassistant.org					
American Dental Assn (ADA) 211 E Chicago Ave	Chicago	IL	60611	312-440-2500	440-2395*
**Fax:* Hum Res ■ *Web:* www.ada.org					
American Dental Hygienists' Assn (ADHA)					
444 N Michigan Ave Suite 3400	Chicago	IL	60611	312-440-8900	467-1806
TF: 800-243-2342 ■ *Web:* www.adha.org					
American Diabetes Assn (ADA)					
1701 N Beauregard St	Alexandria	VA	22311	703-549-1500	836-2464
TF: 800-232-3472 ■ *Web:* www.diabetes.org					
American Dietetic Assn (ADA)					
120 S Riverside Plaza Suite 2000	Chicago	IL	60606	312-899-0040	899-4899
TF: 800-877-1600 ■ *Web:* www.eatright.org					
American Embryo Transfer Assn (AETA)					
1111 N Dunlap Ave	Savoy	IL	61847	217-398-2217	398-4119
Web: www.aeta.org					
American Endodontic Society 265 N Main St	Glen Ellyn	IL	60137	773-519-4879	858-0525*
**Fax Area Code:* 630 ■ *Web:* www.aesoc.com					
American Epilepsy Society (AES)					
342 N Main St	West Hartford	CT	06117	860-586-7505	586-7550
Web: www.aesnet.org					
American Federation for Aging Research (AFAR)					
55 W 39th St 16th Fl	New York	NY	10018	212-703-9977	997-0330
TF: 888-582-2327 ■ *Web:* www.afar.org					
American Federation for Medical Research (AFMR)					
900 Cummings Ctr Suite 221-U	Beverly	MA	01915	978-927-8330	524-8890
Web: www.afmr.org					
American Gastroenterological Assn (AGA)					
7910 Woodmont Ave	Bethesda	MD	20814	301-654-2055	654-5920
Web: www.gastro.org					
American Geriatrics Society (AGS)					
350 5th Ave Empire State Bldg Suite 801	New York	NY	10018	212-308-1414	832-8646
Web: www.americangeriatrics.org					
American Headache Society (AHS)					
19 Mantua Rd	Mount Royal	NJ	08061	856-423-0043	423-0082
Web: www.americanheadachesociety.org					

Organization / Address	City	State	ZIP	Phone	Fax
American Health Care Assn (AHCA) 1201 L St NW	Washington	DC	20005	202-842-4444	842-3860
TF: 800-321-0343 ■ *Web:* www.ahca.org					
American Health Information Management Assn (AHIMA) 233 N Michigan Ave Suite 2100	Chicago	IL	60601	312-233-1100	233-1090
TF: 800-335-5535 ■ *Web:* www.ahima.org					
American Health Quality Assn (AHQA) 1776 I St NW # 9	Washington	DC	20006	202-331-5790	331-9334
Web: www.ahqa.org					
American Healthcare Radiology Administrators (AHRA) 490-B Boston Post Rd Suite 200	Sudbury	MA	01776	978-443-7591	443-8046
TF: 800-334-2472 ■ *Web:* www.ahraonline.org					
American Herbal Products Assn (AHPA) 8630 Fenton St Suite 918	Silver Spring	MD	20910	301-588-1171	588-1174
Web: www.ahpa.org					
American Hospital Assn (AHA) 1 N Franklin St	Chicago	IL	60606	312-422-3000	422-4796
TF: 800-424-4301 ■ *Web:* www.aha.org					
American Institute of Ultrasound in Medicine (AIUM) 14750 Sweitzer Ln Suite 100	Laurel	MD	20707	301-498-4100	498-4450
TF: 800-638-5352 ■ *Web:* www.aium.org					
American Lung Assn (ALA) 14 Wall St	New York	NY	10005	212-315-8700	315-8872
TF: 800-586-4872 ■ *Web:* www.lungusa.org					
American Medical Assn (AMA) 515 N State St	Chicago	IL	60610	312-464-5000	464-4184
TF: 800-621-8335 ■ *Web:* www.ama-assn.org					
American Medical Directors Assn (AMDA) 11000 Broken Land Pkwy Suite 400	Columbia	MD	21044	410-740-9743	740-4572
TF: 800-876-2632 ■ *Web:* www.amda.com					
American Medical Group Assn (AMGA) 1422 Duke St	Alexandria	VA	22314	703-838-0033	548-1890
Web: www.amga.org					
American Medical Informatics Assn (AMIA) 4720 Montgomery Ln Suite 500	Bethesda	MD	20814	301-657-1291	657-1296
Web: www.amia.org					
American Medical Rehabilitation Providers Assn (AMRPA) 1710 N St NW	Washington	DC	20036	202-223-1920	223-1925
TF: 888-346-4624					
American Medical Technologists (AMT) 10700 W Higgins Rd Suite 150	Rosemont	IL	60018	847-823-5169	823-0458
TF: 800-275-1268 ■ *Web:* www.amt1.com					
American Medical Women's Assn (AMWA) 100 N 20th St 4th Fl	Philadelphia	PA	19103	215-320-3716	564-2175
Web: www.amwa-doc.org					
American Nephrology Nurses Assn (ANNA) 200 E Holly Ave	Sewell	NJ	08080	856-256-2320	589-7463
TF: 888-600-2662 ■ *Web:* www.annanurse.org					
American Neurological Assn (ANA) 5841 Cedar Lake Rd Suite 204	Minneapolis	MN	55416	952-545-6284	545-6073
Web: www.aneuroa.org					
American Nurses Assn (ANA) 8515 Georgia Ave Suite 400	Silver Spring	MD	20910	301-628-5000	628-5001
TF: 800-274-4262 ■ *Web:* nursingworld.org					
American Occupational Therapy Assn Inc (AOTA) 4720 Montgomery Ln PO Box 31220	Bethesda	MD	20824	301-652-2682	652-7711
Web: www.aota.org					
American Optometric Assn (AOA) 243 N Lindbergh Blvd	Saint Louis	MO	63141	314-991-4100	991-4101
TF: 800-365-2219 ■ *Web:* www.aoa.org					
American Organization of Nurse Executives (AONE) 1 N Franklin St 32nd Fl	Chicago	IL	60606	312-422-2800	422-4503
Web: www.aone.org					
American Orthopaedic Assn (AOA) 6300 N River Rd Suite 505	Rosemont	IL	60018	847-318-7330	318-7339
Web: www.aoassn.org					
American Orthopaedic Society for Sports Medicine (AOSSM) 6300 N River Rd Suite 500	Rosemont	IL	60018	847-292-4900	292-4905
TF: 877-321-3500 ■ *Web:* www.sportsmed.org					
American Osteopathic Assn (AOA) 142 E Ontario St	Chicago	IL	60611	312-202-8000	202-8200
TF: 800-621-1773 ■ *Web:* www.osteopathic.org					
American Pain Society (APS) 4700 W Lake Ave	Glenview	IL	60025	847-375-4715	375-6479
Web: www.ampainsoc.org					
American Physical Therapy Assn (APTA) 1111 N Fairfax St	Alexandria	VA	22314	703-684-2782	684-6748
TF: 800-999-2782 ■ *Web:* www.apta.org					
American Physiological Society (APS) 9650 Rockville Pike	Bethesda	MD	20814	301-634-7164	634-7241
Web: www.the-aps.org					
American Podiatric Medical Assn (APMA) 9312 Old Georgetown Rd	Bethesda	MD	20814	301-581-9200	530-2752
TF: 800-275-2762 ■ *Web:* www.apma.org					
American Professional Practice Assn (APPA) 350 Fairway Dr Suite 200	Deerfield Beach	FL	33441	954-571-1877	571-8582
TF: 800-221-2168 ■ *Web:* www.appa-assn.com					
American Psychiatric Nurses Assn (APNA) 1555 Wilson Blvd Suite 530	Arlington	VA	22209	703-243-2443	243-3390
TF: 866-243-2443 ■ *Web:* www.apna.org					
American Public Health Assn (APHA) 800 'I' St NW	Washington	DC	20001	202-777-2742	777-2533
Web: www.apha.org					
American Registry of Diagnostic Medical Sonographers (ARDMS) 51 Monroe St Plaza E 1	Rockville	MD	20850	301-738-8401	738-0312
TF: 800-541-9754 ■ *Web:* www.ardms.org					
American Roentgen Ray Society (ARRS) 44211 Slatestone Ct	Leesburg	VA	20176	703-729-3353	729-4839
TF: 800-438-2777 ■ *Web:* www.arrs.org					
American Society for Aesthetic Plastic Surgery (ASAPS) 11081 Winners Cir	Los Alamitos	CA	90720	562-799-2356	799-1098
TF: 800-364-2147 ■ *Web:* www.surgery.org					
American Society for Bone & Mineral Research (ASBMR) 2025 M St NW Suite 800	Washington	DC	20036	202-367-1161	367-2161
Web: www.asbmr.org					
American Society for Clinical Laboratory Science (ASCLS) 6701 Democracy Blvd Suite 300	Bethesda	MD	20817	301-657-2768	657-2909
Web: www.ascls.org					
American Society for Clinical Pathology (ASCP) 33 W Monroe St Suite 1600	Chicago	IL	60603	312-541-4999	541-4998
TF Cust Svc: 800-621-4142 ■ *Web:* www.ascp.org					
American Society for Colposcopy & Cervical Pathology (ASCCP) 152 W Washington St	Hagerstown	MD	21740	301-733-3640	733-5775
TF: 800-787-7227 ■ *Web:* www.asccp.org					
American Society for Dermatologic Surgery (ASDS) 5550 Meadowbrook Dr Suite 120	Rolling Meadows	IL	60008	847-956-0900	956-0999
Web: www.asds.net					
American Society for Gastrointestinal Endoscopy (ASGE) 1520 Kensington Rd Suite 202	Oak Brook	IL	60523	630-573-0600	573-0691
TF: 866-353-2743 ■ *Web:* www.asge.org					
American Society for Healthcare Engineering (ASHE) 1 N Franklin St 28th Fl	Chicago	IL	60606	312-422-3800	422-4571
Web: www.ashe.org					
American Society for Histocompatibility & Immunogenetics (ASHI) 15000 Commerce Pkwy Suite C	Mount Laurel	NJ	08054	856-638-0428	439-0525
Web: www.ashi-hla.org					
American Society for Laser Medicine & Surgery Inc (ASLMS) 2100 Stewart Ave Suite 240	Wausau	WI	54401	715-845-9283	848-2493
TF: 877-258-6028 ■ *Web:* www.aslms.org					
American Society for Microbiology (ASM) 1752 N St NW	Washington	DC	20036	202-737-3600	
Web: www.asm.org					
American Society for Parenteral & Enteral Nutrition (ASPEN) 8630 Fenton St Suite 412	Silver Spring	MD	20910	301-587-6315	587-2365
TF: 800-727-4567 ■ *Web:* www.nutritioncare.org					
American Society for Pharmacology & Experimental Therapeutics (ASPET) 9650 Rockville Pike	Bethesda	MD	20814	301-634-7060	634-7061
Web: www.aspet.org					
American Society for Reproductive Medicine (ASRM) 1209 Montgomery Hwy	Birmingham	AL	35216	205-978-5000	978-5005
Web: www.asrm.org					
American Society for Surgery of the Hand (ASSH) 6300 N River Rd Suite 600	Rosemont	IL	60018	847-384-8300	384-1435
TF: 888-576-2774 ■ *Web:* www.assh.org					
American Society for Therapeutic Radiology & Oncology (ASTRO) 8280 Willow Oaks Corporate Dr Suite 500	Fairfax	VA	22031	703-502-1550	502-7852
TF: 800-962-7876 ■ *Web:* www.astro.org					
American Society of Abdominal Surgeons (ASAS) 824 Main St 2nd Fl Suite 1	Melrose	MA	02176	781-665-6102	665-4127
Web: www.abdominalsurg.org					
American Society of Addiction Medicine (ASAM) 4601 N Pk Ave Upper Arcade Suite 101	Chevy Chase	MD	20815	301-656-3920	656-3815
Web: www.asam.org					
American Society of Andrology (ASA) 1100 E Woodfield St Suite 520	Schaumburg	IL	60173	847-619-4909	517-7229
Web: www.andrologysociety.com					
American Society of Anesthesiologists (ASA) 520 N NW Hwy	Park Ridge	IL	60068	847-825-5586	825-1692
TF: 800-562-8666 ■ *Web:* www.asahq.org					
American Society of Bariatric Physicians (ASBP) 2821 S Parker Rd Suite 625	Aurora	CO	80014	303-770-2526	779-4834
Web: www.asbp.org					
American Society of Cataract & Refractive Surgery (ASCRS) 4000 Legato Rd Suite 700	Fairfax	VA	22033	703-591-2220	591-0614
TF: 800-451-1339 ■ *Web:* www.ascrs.org					
American Society of Clinical Hypnosis (ASCH) 140 N Bloomingdale Rd	Bloomingdale	IL	60108	630-980-4740	351-8490
Web: www.asch.net					
American Society of Clinical Oncology (ASCO) 1900 Duke St Suite 200	Alexandria	VA	22314	703-299-0158	299-0255
TF: 888-282-2552 ■ *Web:* www.asco.org					
American Society of Consultant Pharmacists (ASCP) 1321 Duke St	Alexandria	VA	22314	703-739-1300	739-1321
TF: 800-355-2727 ■ *Web:* www.ascp.com					
American Society of Dermatopathology The 111 Deer Lake Rd Suite 100	Northbrook	IL	60015	847-400-5820	480-9282
Web: www.asdp.org					
American Society of Echocardiography (ASE) 2100 Gateway Centre Blvd Suite 310	Morrisville	NC	27560	919-861-5574	882-9900
Web: www.asecho.org					
American Society of Health-System Pharmacists (ASHP) 7272 Wisconsin Ave	Bethesda	MD	20814	301-664-8700	664-8877
TF: 866-279-0681 ■ *Web:* www.ashp.org					
American Society of Hematology (ASH) 1900 M St NW Suite 200	Washington	DC	20036	202-776-0544	776-0545
Web: www.hematology.org					
American Society of Hypertension (ASH) 148 Madison Ave 5th Fl	New York	NY	10016	212-696-9099	696-0711
Web: www.ash-us.org					
American Society of Nephrology (ASN) 1725 'I' St NW Suite 510	Washington	DC	20006	202-659-0599	659-0709
Web: www.asn-online.com					
American Society of Neuroradiology (ASNR) 2210 Midwest Rd Suite 207	Oak Brook	IL	60523	630-574-0220	574-0661
Web: www.asnr.org					
American Society of Nuclear Cardiology (ASNC) 4550 Montgomery Ave Suite 780-N	Bethesda	MD	20814	301-215-7575	215-7113
Web: www.asnc.org					
American Society of PeriAnesthesia Nurses (ASPAN) 90 Frontage Rd	Cherry Hill	NJ	08034	856-616-9600	616-9601
TF: 877-737-9696 ■ *Web:* www.aspan.org					

Organization / Address	City	State	Zip	Phone	Fax
American Society of Plastic Surgeons (ASPS) 444 E Algonquin Rd	Arlington Heights	IL	60005	847-228-9900	228-9131
TF: 888-475-2784 ■ *Web:* www.plasticsurgery.org					
American Society of Radiologic Technologists (ASRT) 15000 Central Ave SE	Albuquerque	NM	87123	505-298-4500	298-5063
TF: 800-444-2778 ■ *Web:* www.asrt.org					
American Society of Regional Anesthesia & Pain Medicine (ASRA) 520 N NW Hwy	Park Ridge	IL	60068	847-825-7246	825-1692
TF: 800-562-8666 ■ *Web:* www.asra.com					
American Society of Transplantation (AST) 15000 Commerce Pkwy Suite C	Mount Laurel	NJ	08054	856-439-9986	439-0525
Web: www.a-s-t.org					
American Society of Tropical Medicine & Hygiene 111 Deer Lake Rd Suite 100	Deerfield	IL	60015	847-480-9592	480-9282
Web: www.astmh.org					
American Speech-Language-Hearing Assn (ASHA) 2200 Research Blvd	Rockville	MD	20850	301-296-5700	296-8580
TF: 800-498-2071 ■ *Web:* www.asha.org					
American Thoracic Society (ATS) 61 Broadway 4th Fl	New York	NY	10006	212-315-8600	315-6498
Web: www.thoracic.org					
American Trauma Society 7611 S Osborne Rd Suite 202	Upper Marlboro	MD	20772	301-574-4300	574-4301
TF: 800-556-7890 ■ *Web:* www.amtrauma.org					
American Urological Assn (AUA) 1000 Corporate Blvd	Linthicum	MD	21090	410-689-3700	689-3800
TF: 866-746-4282 ■ *Web:* www.auanet.org					
American Veterinary Medical Assn (AVMA) 1931 N Meacham Rd Suite 100	Schaumburg	IL	60173	847-925-8070	925-1329
TF: 800-925-8070 ■ *Web:* www.avma.org					
AORN Inc 2170 S Parker Rd Suite 300	Denver	CO	80231	303-755-6300	750-3212*
**Fax:* Cust Svc ■ *TF:* 800-755-2676 ■ *Web:* www.aorn.org					
Arthroscopy Assn of North America (AANA) 6300 N River Rd Suite 104	Rosemont	IL	60018	847-292-2262	292-2268
Web: www.aana.org					
Assisted Living Federation of America (ALFA) 1650 King St Suite 602	Alexandria	VA	22314	703-894-1805	894-1831
Web: www.alfa.org					
Assn for Applied Psychophysiology & Biofeedback (AAPB) 10200 W 44th Ave Suite 304	Wheat Ridge	CO	80033	303-422-8436	422-8894
TF: 800-477-8892 ■ *Web:* www.aapb.org					
Assn for Death Education & Counseling (ADEC) 60 Revere Dr Suite 500	Northbrook	IL	60062	847-509-0403	480-9282
Web: www.adec.org					
Assn for Healthcare Documentation Integrity (AHDI) 4230 Kiernan Ave Suite 130	Modesto	CA	95356	209-527-9620	527-9633
TF: 800-982-2182 ■ *Web:* www.ahdionline.org					
Assn for Healthcare Philanthropy (AHP) 313 Pk Ave Suite 400	Falls Church	VA	22046	703-532-6243	532-7170
Web: www.ahp.org					
Assn for Professionals in Infection Control & Epidemiology Inc (APIC) 1275 K St NW Suite 1000	Washington	DC	20005	202-789-1890	789-1899
Web: www.apic.org					
Assn for Research in Vision & Ophthalmology (ARVO) 12300 Twinbrook Pkwy Suite 250	Rockville	MD	20852	240-221-2900	221-0370
Web: www.arvo.org					
Assn for the Advancement of Medical Instrumentation (AAMI) 4301 N Fairfax Dr Suite 301	Arlington	VA	22203	703-525-4890	276-0793
TF: 800-332-2264 ■ *Web:* www.aami.org					
Assn for Vascular Access (AVA) 5526 W 13400 S Suite 229	Herriman	UT	84096	801-792-9079	601-8012
TF: 888-576-2826 ■ *Web:* www.avainfo.org					
Assn of Academic Health Centers (AHC) 1400 16th St NW Suite 720	Washington	DC	20036	202-265-9600	265-7514
TF: 800-925-4755 ■ *Web:* www.aahcdc.org					
Assn of Air Medical Services (AAMS) 526 King St Suite 415	Alexandria	VA	22314	703-836-8732	836-8920
Web: www.aams.org					
Assn of American Indian Physicians (AAIP) 1225 Sovereign Row Suite 103	Oklahoma City	OK	73108	405-946-7072	946-7651
Web: www.aaip.org					
Assn of Clinical Research Professionals (ACRP) 500 Montgomery St Suite 800	Alexandria	VA	22314	703-254-8100	254-8101
Web: www.acrpnet.org					
Assn of Community Cancer Centers (ACCC) 11600 Nebel St Suite 201	Rockville	MD	20852	301-984-9496	770-1949
Web: www.accc-cancer.org					
Assn of Emergency Physicians (AEP) 911 Whitewater Dr	Mars	PA	16046	724-772-1818	422-7794*
**Fax Area Code:* 866 ■ *TF:* 866-772-1818 ■ *Web:* www.aep.org					
Assn of Military Surgeons of the United States (AMSUS) 9320 Old Georgetown Rd	Bethesda	MD	20814	301-897-8800	530-5446
TF: 800-761-9320 ■ *Web:* www.amsus.org					
Assn of Nurses in AIDS Care (ANAC) 3538 Ridgewood Rd	Akron	OH	44333	330-670-0101	670-0109
TF: 800-260-6780 ■ *Web:* www.nursesinaidscare.org					
Assn of Osteopathic Directors & Medical Educators (AODME) 142 E Ontario St	Chicago	IL	60611	312-202-8211	202-8224
TF: 800-621-1773 ■ *Web:* www.aodme.org					
Assn of Program Directors in Internal Medicine (APDIM) 2501 M St NW Suite 550	Washington	DC	20037	202-861-9351	861-9731
Web: www.im.org/APDIM					
Assn of Rehabilitation Nurses (ARN) 4700 W Lake Ave	Glenview	IL	60025	847-375-4710	375-6481
TF: 800-229-7530 ■ *Web:* www.rehabnurse.org					
Assn of Reproductive Health Professionals (ARHP) 1901 L St NW # 300	Washington	DC	20036	202-466-3825	466-3826
Web: www.arhp.org					
Assn of Schools & Colleges of Optometry (ASCO) 6110 Executive Blvd Suite 420	Rockville	MD	20852	301-231-5944	770-1828
Web: www.opted.org					
Assn of Schools of Allied Health Professions (ASAHP) 4400 Jenifer St NW Suite 333	Washington	DC	20015	202-237-6481	237-6485
TF: 800-497-8080 ■ *Web:* www.asahp.org					
Assn of Staff Physician Recruiters (ASPR) 1000 Westgate Dr Suite 252	St. Paul	MN	55114	800-830-2777	
TF: 800-830-2777 ■ *Web:* www.aspr.org					
Assn of Surgical Technologists (AST) 6 W Dry Creek Cir Suite 200	Littleton	CO	80120	303-694-9130	694-9169
TF: 800-637-7433 ■ *Web:* www.ast.org					
Assn of University Programs in Health Administration (AUPHA) 2000 N 14th St Suite 780	Arlington	VA	22201	703-894-0940	894-0941
Web: www.aupha.org					
Assn of Women's Health Obstetric & Neonatal Nurses (AWHONN) 2000 L St NW Suite 740	Washington	DC	20036	202-261-2400	728-0575
TF: 800-673-8499 ■ *Web:* www.awhonn.org					
Asthma & Allergy Foundation of America (AAFA) 8201 Corporate Dr Suite 1000	Landover	MD	20785	202-466-7643	466-8940
TF: 800-727-8462 ■ *Web:* www.aafa.org					
Canada's Research-Based Pharmaceutical Cos (Rx&D) 55 Metcalfe St Suite 1220	Ottawa	ON	K1P6L5	613-236-0455	236-6756
TF: 800-363-0203 ■ *Web:* www.canadapharma.org					
Canadian Academy of Sport Medicine (CASM) 5330 Canotek Rd Unit 4	Ottawa	ON	K1T9C1	613-748-5851	748-5792
TF: 877-585-2394 ■ *Web:* www.casm-acms.org					
Canadian Assn of Emergency Physicians (CAEP) 1785 Alta Vista Dr Suite 104	Ottawa	ON	K1G3Y6	613-523-3343	523-0190
TF: 800-463-1158 ■ *Web:* www.caep.ca					
Canadian Medical Assn (CMA) 1867 Alta Vista Dr	Ottawa	ON	K1G5W8	613-731-9331	731-7314
TF: 800-663-7336 ■ *Web:* www.cma.ca					
Canadian Veterinary Medical Assn (CVMA) 339 Booth St	Ottawa	ON	K1R7K1	613-236-1162	236-9681
Web: canadianveterinarians.net					
Case Management Society of America (CMSA) 6301 Ranch Dr	Little Rock	AR	72223	501-225-2229	221-9068
TF: 800-216-2672 ■ *Web:* www.cmsa.org					
Catholic Health Assn of the US (CHA) 4455 Woodson Rd	Saint Louis	MO	63134	314-427-2500	427-0029
Web: www.chausa.org					
Certification Board for Nutrition Specialists (CBNS) 1350 Connecticut Ave NW 5th Fl	Washington	DC	20036	202-903-0267	
Web: www.cbns.org					
Children's Hospice International (CHI) 1101 King St Suite 360	Alexandria	VA	22314	703-684-0330	684-0226
TF: 800-242-4453 ■ *Web:* www.chionline.org					
Christian Medical & Dental Assn (CMDA) 2604 Hwy 421 PO Box 7500	Bristol	TN	37620	423-844-1000	844-1005
TF: 888-231-2637 ■ *Web:* www.cmda.org					
Clinical & Laboratory Standards Institute (CLSI) 940 W Valley Rd Suite 1400	Wayne	PA	19087	610-688-0100	688-0700
TF: 877-447-1888 ■ *Web:* www.clsi.org					
Clinical Immunology Society (CIS) 611 E Wells St # 1100	Milwaukee	WI	53202	414-224-8095	272-6070
Web: www.clinimmsoc.org					
COLA 9881 Broken Land Pkwy Suite 200	Columbia	MD	21046	410-381-6581	381-8611*
**Fax:* Hum Res ■ *TF:* 800-981-9883 ■ *Web:* www.cola.org					
College of American Pathologists (CAP) 325 Waukegan Rd	Northfield	IL	60093	847-832-7000	832-8168
TF: 800-323-4040 ■ *Web:* www.cap.org					
Dietary Managers Assn (DMA) 406 Surrey Woods Dr	Saint Charles	IL	60174	630-587-6336	587-6308
TF: 800-323-1908 ■ *Web:* www.dmaonline.org					
Emergency Nurses Assn (ENA) 915 Lee St	Des Plaines	IL	60016	847-460-4000	460-4001
TF: 800-900-9659 ■ *Web:* www.ena.org					
Endocrine Society 8401 Connecticut Ave Suite 900	Chevy Chase	MD	20815	301-941-0200	941-0259
TF: 888-363-6274 ■ *Web:* www.endo-society.org					
Eye Bank Assn of America (EBAA) 1015 18th St NW Suite 1010	Washington	DC	20036	202-775-4999	429-6036
Web: www.restoresight.org					
Federal Nurses Assn (FedNA) 8515 Georgia Ave Suite 400	Silver Spring	MD	20910	301-628-5333	628-5001
Web: www.nursingworld.org/Fedna					
Federation of American Hospitals 750 9th St NW Suite 600	Washington	DC	20004	202-624-1500	624-1500
TF: 877-219-6800 ■ *Web:* www.fah.org					
Federation of State Medical Boards of the US Inc (FSMB) 400 Fuller Wiser Rd Suite 300	Euless	TX	76039	817-868-4000	868-4098
TF: 800-876-5396 ■ *Web:* www.fsmb.org					
Gerontological Society of America The 1220 L St NW Suite 901	Washington	DC	20005	202-842-1275	842-1150
Web: www.geron.org					
Gynecologic Oncology Group (GOG) 1600 JFK Blvd Suite 1020	Philadelphia	PA	19103	215-854-0770	854-0716
TF: 800-225-3053 ■ *Web:* www.gog.org					
Health Industry Business Communications Council (HIBCC) 2525 E Arizona Biltmore Cir Suite 127	Phoenix	AZ	85016	602-381-1091	381-1093
Web: www.hibcc.org					
Healthcare Financial Management Assn (HFMA) 2 Westbrook Corporate Ctr Suite 700	Westchester	IL	60154	708-531-9600	531-0032
TF: 800-252-4362 ■ *Web:* www.hfma.org					
Healthcare Information & Management Systems Society (HIMSS) 230 E Ohio St Suite 500	Chicago	IL	60610	312-664-4467	664-6143
Web: www.himss.org					
Heart Rhythm Society 1400 K St NW Suite 500	Washington	DC	20005	202-464-3400	464-3401
Web: www.hrsonline.org					

Phone | Fax

Hospice & Palliative Nurses Assn (HPNA)
1 Penn Ctr W # 229 Pittsburgh PA 15276 412-787-9301 787-9305
Web: www.hpna.org

Hospice Foundation of America (HFA)
1710 Rhode Island Ave NW Suite 400 Washington DC 20036 202-457-5811 457-5815
TF: 800-854-3402 ■ *Web:* www.hospicefoundation.org

Infectious Diseases Society of America (IDSA)
1300 Wilson Blvd Suite 300 Arlington VA 22209 703-299-0200 299-0204
Web: www.idsociety.org

Infusion Nurses Society (INS) 315 Norwood Pk S Norwood MA 02062 781-440-9408 440-9409
TF: 800-694-0298 ■ *Web:* www.ins1.org

Institute for Healthcare Improvement (IHI)
20 University Rd 7th Fl Cambridge MA 02138 617-301-4800 301-4848
TF: 866-787-0831 ■ *Web:* www.ihi.org

Institute for the Advancement of Human Behavior (IAHB)
4370 Alpine Rd Suite 209 Portola Valley CA 94028 650-851-8411 851-0406
TF: 800-258-8411 ■ *Web:* www.iahb.org

Institute of Medicine 500 5th St NW Washington DC 20001 202-334-2352 334-1412
Web: www.iom.edu

Interamerican College of Physicians & Surgeons (ICPS)
233 Broadway Suite 806 New York NY 10279 212-777-3642 267-5394
Web: www.icps.org

International Academy of Compounding Pharmacists (IACP)
4638 Riverstone Blvd Missouri City TX 77459 281-933-8400 495-0602
TF: 800-927-4227 ■ *Web:* www.iacprx.org

International Assn for Dental Research (IADR)
1619 Duke St Alexandria VA 22314 703-548-0066 548-1883
Web: www.iadr.com

International Assn of Physicians in AIDS Care (IAPAC)
123 Madison St Suite 1400 Chicago IL 60602 312-795-4933 795-4938
TF: 866-474-2722 ■ *Web:* www.iapac.org

International Chiropractors Assn (ICA)
1110 N Glebe Rd Suite 650 Arlington VA 22201 703-528-5000 528-5023
TF: 800-423-4690 ■ *Web:* www.chiropractic.org

International College of Dentists (ICD)
51 Monroe St Suite 1400 Rockville MD 20850 301-251-8861 738-9143
Web: www.icd.org

International College of Surgeons (ICS)
1516 N Lake Shore Dr Chicago IL 60610 312-642-3555 787-1624
Web: www.icsglobal.org

International Congress of Oral Implantologists (ICOI)
248 Lorraine Ave 3rd Fl Upper Montclair NJ 07043 973-783-6300 295-8509*
**Fax Area Code:* 267 ■ *TF:* 800-442-0525 ■ *Web:* www.icoi.org

International Nurses Society on Addictions (IntNSA)
PO Box 163635 Columbus OH 43216 614-221-9989 221-2335
Web: www.intnsa.org

International Society for Heart & Lung Transplantation (ISHLT)
14673 Midway Rd Suite 200 Addison TX 75001 972-490-9495 490-9499
Web: www.ishlt.org

International Society for Magnetic Resonance in Medicine (ISMRM)
2030 Addison St Suite 700 Berkeley CA 94704 510-841-1899 841-2340
Web: www.ismrm.org

International Society for Peritoneal Dialysis (ISPD)
66 Martin St Milton ON L9T2R2 905-875-2456 875-2864
TF: 888-834-1001 ■ *Web:* www.ispd.org

International Society for Pharmacoeconomics & Outcomes Research (ISPOR)
3100 Princeton Pike Bldg 3 Suite E Lawrenceville NJ 08648 609-219-0773 219-0774
TF: 800-992-0643 ■ *Web:* www.ispor.org

International Society for Pharmacoepidemiology (ISPE)
5272 River Rd Suite 630 Bethesda MD 20816 301-718-6500 656-0989
Web: www.pharmacoepi.org

International Society of Refractive Surgery (ISRS)
655 Beach St PO Box 7424 San Francisco CA 94109 415-561-8581 561-8575
Web: www.isrs.org

International Society of Travel Medicine (ISTM)
315 W Ponce de Leon Ave Suite 245 Decatur GA 30030 404-373-8282 373-8283
Web: www.istm.org

International Transplant Nurses Society (ITNS)
1739 E Carson St PO Box 351 Pittsburgh PA 15203 412-343-4867 343-3959
Web: www.itns.org

Islamic Medical Assn of North America (IMANA)
101 W 22nd St Suite 106 Lombard IL 60148 630-932-0000 932-0005
Web: www.imana.org

Journal of Clinical Investigation (JCI)
15 Research Dr Ann Arbor MI 48107 734-222-6050 222-6058
Web: www.jci.org

Lamaze International
2025 M St NW Suite 800 Washington DC 20036 202-367-1128 367-2128
TF: 800-368-4404 ■ *Web:* www.lamaze.org

Medical Group Management Assn (MGMA)
104 Inverness Terr E Englewood CO 80112 303-799-1111 784-6105
TF: 877-275-6462 ■ *Web:* www.mgma.com

NA for Healthcare Quality (NAHQ)
4700 W Lake Ave Glenview IL 60025 847-375-4720 375-6320
TF: 800-966-9392 ■ *Web:* www.nahq.org

NA for Home Care & Hospice (NAHC)
228 7th St SE Washington DC 20003 202-547-7424 547-3540
Web: www.nahc.org

NA for the Support of Long Term Care (NASL)
1321 Duke St Suite 304 Alexandria VA 22314 703-549-8500 549-8342
Web: www.netforum.avectra.com

NA Medical Staff Services (NAMSS)
2025 M St NW Suite 800 Washington DC 20036 202-367-1196 367-2196
Web: www.namss.org

NA of Addiction Treatment Providers (NAATP)
313 W Liberty St Suite 129 Lancaster PA 17603 717-392-8480 392-8481
Web: www.naatp.org

NA of Children's Hospitals & Related Institutions (NACHRI)
401 Wythe St Alexandria VA 22314 703-684-1355 684-1589
Web: www.childrenshospitals.net

NA of Community Health Centers (NACHC)
7200 Wisconsin Ave Suite 210 Bethesda MD 20814 301-347-0400 347-0459
Web: www.nachc.com

NA of Dental Laboratories (NADL)
325 John Knox Rd Suite L-103 Tallahassee FL 32303 850-205-5626 222-0053
TF: 800-950-1150 ■ *Web:* www.nadl.org

NA of Directors of Nursing Administration in Long Term Care
11353 Reed Hartman Hwy Suite 210 Cincinnati OH 45241 513-791-3679 791-3699
TF: 800-222-0539 ■ *Web:* www.nadona.org

NA of Health Data Organizations (NAHDO)
448 E 400 S Suite 301 Salt Lake City UT 84111 801-532-2299 532-2228
Web: www.nahdo.org

NA of Neonatal Nurses (NANN) 4700 W Lake Ave Glenview IL 60025 847-375-3660 375-6491
TF: 800-451-3795 ■ *Web:* www.nann.org

NA of Nurse Practitioners in Women's Health
505 C St NE Washington DC 20002 202-543-9693 543-9858
Web: www.npwh.org

NA of Orthopaedic Nurses (NAON)
401 N Michigan Ave Suite 2200 Chicago IL 60611 800-289-6266 527-6658*
**Fax Area Code:* 312 ■ *TF:* 800-289-6266 ■ *Web:* www.orthonurse.org

NA of Physician Recruiters (NAPR)
222 S Westmonte Dr Suite 101 Altamonte Springs FL 32714 407-774-7880 774-6440
TF: 800-726-5613 ■ *Web:* www.napr.org

NA of Professional Geriatric Care Managers (GCM)
3275 W Ina Rd # 130 Tucson AZ 85741 520-881-8008 325-7925
Web: www.caremanager.org

NA of Public Hospitals & Health Systems (NAPH)
1301 Pennsylvania Ave NW Suite 950 Washington DC 20004 202-585-0100 585-0101
Web: www.naph.org

NA of School Nurses (NASN)
8484 Georgia Ave Suite 420 Silver Spring MD 20910 240-821-1130 585-1791*
**Fax Area Code:* 301 ■ *TF:* 877-627-6476 ■ *Web:* www.nasn.org

National Abortion Federation (NAF)
1755 Massachusetts Ave NW Washington DC 20036 202-667-5881 667-5890
TF: 800-772-9100 ■ *Web:* www.prochoice.org

National Board of Medical Examiners (NBME)
3750 Market St Philadelphia PA 19104 215-590-9500
Web: www.nbme.org

National Community Pharmacists Assn (NCPA)
100 Daingerfield Rd Alexandria VA 22314 703-683-8200 683-3619
TF: 800-544-7447 ■ *Web:* www.ncpanet.org

National Council of State Boards of Nursing (NCSBN)
111 E Wacker Dr Suite 2900 Chicago IL 60601 312-525-3600 279-1032
Web: www.ncsbn.org

National Council on Problem Gambling Inc
730 11th St NW Suite 601 Washington DC 20001 202-547-9204 547-9206
TF: 800-522-4700 ■ *Web:* www.ncpgambling.org

National Foundation for Infectious Diseases (NFID)
4733 Bethesda Ave Suite 750 Bethesda MD 20814 301-656-0003 907-0878
Web: www.nfid.org

National Home Infusion Assn (NHIA)
100 Daingerfield Rd Alexandria VA 22314 703-549-3740 683-1484
TF: 800-544-7447 ■ *Web:* www.nhia.org

National Hospice & Palliative Care Organization (NHPCO)
1700 Diagonal Rd Suite 625 Alexandria VA 22314 703-837-1500 837-1233
TF Help Line: 800-658-8898 ■ *Web:* www.nhpco.org

National League for Nursing (NLN)
61 Broadway 33rd Fl New York NY 10006 212-363-5555 812-0391
TF: 800-669-1656 ■ *Web:* www.nln.org

National Medical Assn (NMA)
8403 Colesville Rd Suite 920 Silver Spring MD 20910 202-347-1895 347-0722
TF: 800-662-0554 ■ *Web:* www.nmanet.org

National Nursing Staff Development Organization (NNSDO)
7794 Grow Dr Pensacola FL 32514 850-474-0995 484-8762
TF: 800-489-1995 ■ *Web:* www.nnsdo.org

National Nutrition Alliance
300 S Duncan Ave Suite 225 Clearwater FL 33755 727-446-6086 446-6202

National Organization for Rare Disorders (NORD)
55 Kenosia Ave PO Box 1968 Danbury CT 06813 203-744-0100 798-2291
TF: 800-999-6673 ■ *Web:* www.rarediseases.org

National Pharmaceutical Council (NPC)
1894 Preston White Dr Reston VA 20191 703-620-6390 476-0904
Web: www.npcnow.org

National Pharmacy Technicians Assn (NPTA)
15832 W Hardy Rd Suite 640 Houston TX 77060 281-999-2111 999-5230
TF: 888-247-8700 ■ *Web:* www.pharmacytechnician.org

National Renal Administrators Assn (NRAA)
100 N 20th St Suite 400 Philadelphia PA 19103 215-320-4655 564-2175
Web: www.nraa.org

National Student Nurses Assn (NSNA)
45 Main St Suite 606 Brooklyn NY 11201 718-210-0705 210-0710
Web: www.nsna.org

North American Menopause Society The (NAMS)
5900 Landerbrook Dr Suite 390 Mayfield Heights OH 44124 440-442-7550 442-2660
Web: www.menopause.org

North American Spine Society (NASS)
7075 Veterans Blvd Burr Ridge IL 60527 630-230-3600
TF: 877-774-6337 ■ *Web:* www.spine.org

Oncology Nursing Society (ONS)
125 Enterprise Dr Pittsburgh PA 15275 412-859-6100 369-5497*
**Fax Area Code:* 877 ■ *TF:* 866-257-4667 ■ *Web:* www.ons.org

Optical Laboratories Assn (OLA)
225 Reinekers Ln Suite 700 Alexandria VA 22314 703-548-6619 548-4580
TF: 800-477-5652 ■ *Web:* www.ola-labs.org

Organization / Address	City	State	Zip	Phone	Fax
Optical Society of America (OSA) 2010 Massachusetts Ave NW	Washington	DC	20036	202-223-8130	223-1096
TF: 800-762-6960 ■ *Web:* www.osa.org					
Opticians Assn of America (OAA) 4064 E Fir Hill Dr	Lakeland	TN	38002	901-388-2423	388-2348
TF: 800-433-8997 ■ *Web:* www.oaa.org					
Parental Drug Assn (PDA) 4350 East-West Hwy	Bethesda	MD	20814	301-656-5900	986-1093
Web: www.pda.org					
Pharmaceutical Care Management Assn (PCMA) 601 Pennsylvania Ave NW Suite 740	Washington	DC	20004	202-207-3610	207-3623
Web: www.pcmanet.org					
Pharmaceutical Research & Manufacturers of America (PhRMA) 950 F St NW Suite 3000	Washington	DC	20004	202-835-3400	835-3414
Web: www.phrma.org					
Physicians Committee for Responsible Medicine (PCRM) 5100 Wisconsin Ave NW Suite 400	Washington	DC	20016	202-686-2210	686-2216
TF: 866-416-7276 ■ *Web:* www.pcrm.org					
Physicians for Social Responsibility (PSR) 1875 Connecticut Ave NW Suite 1012	Washington	DC	20009	202-667-4260	667-4201
Web: www.psr.org					
Plasma Protein Therapeutics Assn (PPTA) 147 Old Solomon's Island Rd Suite 100	Annapolis	MD	21401	202-789-3100	263-2298*
**Fax Area Code:* 410 ■ *Web:* www.pptaglobal.org					
Radiological Society of North America (RSNA) 820 Jorie Blvd	Oak Brook	IL	60523	630-571-2670	571-7837
TF: 800-381-6660 ■ *Web:* www.rsna.org					
Radiology Business Management Assn (RBMA) 10300 Eaton Pl Suite 460	Fairfax	VA	22030	703-621-3355	621-3356
TF: 888-224-7262 ■ *Web:* www.rbma.org					
Regulatory Affairs Professionals Society (RAPS) 5635 Fishers Ln Suite 550	Rockville	MD	20852	301-770-2920	770-2924
Web: www.raps.org					
Renal Physicians Assn (RPA) 1700 Rockville Pike Suite 220	Rockville	MD	20852	301-468-3515	468-3511
Web: www.renalmd.org					
Society for Academic Emergency Medicine (SAEM) 2340 S River Rd Suite 200	Des Plaines	IL	60018	847-813-9823	813-5450
Web: www.saem.org					
Society for Healthcare Epidemiology of America 1300 Wilson Blvd Suite 300	Arlington	VA	22209	703-684-1006	684-1009
Web: www.shea-online.org					
Society for Healthcare Strategy & Market Development (SHSMD) 155 N Wacker Dr Suite 400	Chicago	IL	60606	312-422-3888	278-0883
TF: 800-242-2626 ■ *Web:* www.shsmd.org					
Society for Investigative Dermatology Inc (SID) 526 Superior Ave E Suite 540	Cleveland	OH	44114	216-579-9300	579-9333
Web: www.sidnet.org					
Society for Medical Decision Making 100 N 20th St 4th Fl	Philadelphia	PA	19103	215-545-7697	564-2175
Web: www.smdm.org					
Society for Neuroscience (SFN) 1121 14th St NW Suite 1010	Washington	DC	20005	202-962-4000	962-4941
Web: www.web.sfn.org					
Society for Surgery of the Alimentary Tract (SSAT) 900 Cummings Ctr Suite 221-U	Beverly	MA	01915	978-927-8330	524-8890
Web: www.ssat.com					
Society for Vascular Surgery (SVS) 633 N St Clair St 22nd Fl	Chicago	IL	60611	312-334-2300	334-2320
TF: 800-258-7188 ■ *Web:* www.vascularweb.org					
Society of American Gastrointestinal & Endoscopic Surgeons (SAGES) 11300 W Olympic Blvd Suite 600	Los Angeles	CA	90064	310-437-0544	437-0585
Web: www.sages.org					
Society of Cardiovascular Anesthesiologists (SCA) 2209 Dickens Rd	Richmond	VA	23230	804-282-0084	282-0090
Web: www.scahq.org					
Society of Critical Care Medicine (SCCM) 500 Midway Dr Suite 200	Mount Prospect	IL	60056	847-827-6869	827-6886
Web: www.sccm.org					
Society of Diagnostic Medical Sonography (SDMS) 2745 Dallas Pkwy	Plano	TX	75093	214-473-8057	473-8563
TF: 800-229-9506 ■ *Web:* www.sdms.org					
Society of Gastroenterology Nurses & Assoc Inc (SGNA) 401 N Michigan Ave	Chicago	IL	60611	312-321-5165	673-6694
TF: 800-245-7462 ■ *Web:* www.sgna.org					
Society of Interventional Radiology (SIR) 3975 Fair Rdige Dr Suite 400 N	Fairfax	VA	22033	703-691-1805	691-1855
TF: 800-488-7284 ■ *Web:* www.sirweb.org					
Society of Laparoendoscopic Surgeons (SLS) 7330 SW 62nd Pl Suite 410	South Miami	FL	33143	305-665-9959	667-4123
TF: 800-446-2659 ■ *Web:* www.sls.org					
Society of Nuclear Medicine (SNM) 1850 Samuel Morse Dr	Reston	VA	20190	703-708-9000	708-9015
TF: 800-487-5620 ■ *Web:* www.snm.org					
Society of Teachers of Family Medicine (STFM) 11400 Tomahawk Creek Pkwy Suite 540	Leawood	KS	66211	913-906-6000	906-6096
TF: 800-274-7928 ■ *Web:* www.stfm.org					
Society of Thoracic Surgeons (STS) 633 N St Clair St Suite 2320	Chicago	IL	60611	312-202-5800	202-5801
Web: www.sts.org					
Society of Toxicology (SOT) 1767 Business Ctr Dr	Reston	VA	20190	703-438-3115	438-3113
Web: www.toxicology.org					
Southern Medical Assn (SMA) 35 W Lakeshore Dr	Birmingham	AL	35209	205-945-1840	945-1548
TF: 800-423-4992 ■ *Web:* www.sma.org					
Special Care Dentistry Assn 401 N Michigan Ave Suite 2200	Chicago	IL	60611	312-527-6764	673-6663
Web: www.scdonline.org					
Sports Cardiovascular & Wellness Nutritionists (SCAN) 902 Ash St	Winnetka	IL	60093	847-441-7200	556-0352
TF: 800-249-2875 ■ *Web:* www.scandpg.org					
Therapeutic Communities of America (TCA) 1601 Connecticut Ave NW Suite 803	Washington	DC	20009	202-296-3503	518-5475
Web: www.therapeuticcommunitiesofamerica.org					
US Pharmacopeia (USP) 12601 Twinbrook Pkwy	Rockville	MD	20852	301-881-0666	816-8525*
**Fax:* Hum Res ■ *TF:* 800-227-8772 ■ *Web:* www.usp.org					
Visiting Nurse Associations of America (VNAA) 900 19th St NW Suite 200	Washington	DC	20006	202-384-1420	384-1444
TF: 800-426-2547 ■ *Web:* www.vnaa.org					
World Allergy Organization (WAO) 555 E Wells St Suite 1100	Milwaukee	WI	53202	414-276-1791	276-3349
Web: www.worldallergy.org					
World Foundation for Medical Studies in Female Health (WFFH) 39 Marlin Ln	Port Washington	NY	11050	516-944-3192	944-8663
Web: www.wffh.org					
Wound Ostomy & Continence Nurses Society (WOCN) 15000 Commerce Pkwy Suite C	Mount Laurel	NJ	08054	888-224-9626	615-8560*
**Fax Area Code:* 866 ■ *TF:* 888-224-9626 ■ *Web:* www.wocn.org					

49-9 Insurance Industry Associations

Organization / Address	City	State	Zip	Phone	Fax
America's Health Insurance Plans (AHIP) 601 Pennsylvania Ave NW Suite 500	Washington	DC	20004	202-778-3200	331-7487
TF Cust Svc: 877-291-2247 ■ *Web:* www.ahip.org					
American Academy of Actuaries 1100 17th St NW 7th Fl	Washington	DC	20036	202-223-8196	872-1948
Web: www.actuary.org					
American Assn of Crop Insurers (AACI) 1 Massachusetts Ave NW Suite 800	Washington	DC	20001	202-789-4100	408-7763
Web: www.cropinsurers.com					
American Assn of Insurance Services (AAIS) 1745 S Naperville Rd	Wheaton	IL	60189	630-681-8347	681-8356
TF: 800-564-2247 ■ *Web:* www.aaisonline.com					
American Assn of Managing General Agents (AAMGA) 150 S Warner Rd Suite 156	King of Prussia	PA	19406	610-225-1999	225-1996
Web: www.aamga.org					
American Council of Life Insurers (ACLI) 101 Constitution Ave NW Suite 700 W	Washington	DC	20001	202-624-2000	624-2319
Web: www.acli.com					
American Institute for CPCU & Insurance Institute of America (AICPCU/IIA) 720 Providence Rd Suite 100	Malvern	PA	19355	610-644-2100	640-9576
TF: 800-644-2101 ■ *Web:* www.aicpcu.org					
American Institute of Marine Underwriters (AIMU) 14 Wall St 8th Fl	New York	NY	10005	212-233-0550	227-5102
Web: www.aimu.org					
American Insurance Assn (AIA) 2101 L St	Washington	DC	20037	202-828-7100	293-1219
Web: www.aiadc.org					
American Nuclear Insurers (ANI) 95 Glastonbury Blvd Suite 300	Glastonbury	CT	06033	860-682-1301	659-0002
TF: 866-301-1301 ■ *Web:* www.amnucins.com					
American Society for Healthcare Risk Management (ASHRM) 1 N Franklin St	Chicago	IL	60606	312-422-3980	422-4580
Web: www.ashrm.org					
Assn for Advanced Life Underwriting (AALU) 2901 Telestar Ct Suite 400	Falls Church	VA	22042	703-641-9400	641-9885
TF: 888-275-0092 ■ *Web:* www.aalu.org					
Assn for Co-op Operations Research & Development (ACORD) 2 Blue Hill Plaza 3rd Fl PO Box 1529	Pearl River	NY	10965	845-620-1700	620-3600
TF: 800-444-3341 ■ *Web:* www.acord.org					
Assn of Health Insurance Advisors (AHIA) 2901 Telestar Ct	Falls Church	VA	22042	703-770-8200	770-8201
Web: www.ahia.net					
Associated Risk Managers (ARM) 2 Pierce Pl	Itasca	IL	60143	630-285-4324	285-3590
Web: www.armiweb.com					
Blue Cross & Blue Shield Assn 225 N Michigan Ave	Chicago	IL	60601	312-297-6000	297-6609
TF: 888-663-2583 ■ *Web:* www.bluecares.com					
Casualty Actuarial Society (CAS) 4350 Fairfax Dr # 250	Arlington	VA	22203	703-276-3100	276-3108
Web: www.casact.org					
Coalition Against Insurance Fraud 1012 14th St NW Suite 200	Washington	DC	20005	202-393-7330	318-9189
Web: www.insurancefraud.org					
Consumer Credit Industry Assn (CCIA) 6300 Powers Ferry Rd Suite 600-286	Atlanta	GA	30339	678-858-4001	939-8287*
**Fax Area Code:* 312 ■ *Web:* www.cciaonline.com					
Council for Affordable Health Insurance (CAHI) 127 S Peyton St Suite 210	Alexandria	VA	22314	703-836-6200	836-6550
Web: www.cahi.org					
Council of Insurance Agents & Brokers 701 Pennsylvania Ave NW Suite 750	Washington	DC	20004	202-783-4400	783-4410
TF: 888-919-4400 ■ *Web:* www.ciab.com					
CPCU Society 720 Providence Rd	Malvern	PA	19355	800-932-2728	251-2780*
**Fax Area Code:* 610 ■ *TF:* 800-932-2728 ■ *Web:* www.cpcusociety.org					
GAMA International 2901 Telestar Ct Suite 140	Falls Church	VA	22042	703-770-8184	770-8182
TF Cust Svc: 800-345-2687 ■ *Web:* www.gamaweb.com					
Independent Insurance Agents & Brokers of America Inc (IIABA) 127 S Peyton St	Alexandria	VA	22314	703-683-4422	683-7556
TF: 800-221-7917 ■ *Web:* www.iiaba.org					

	City	State	Zip	Phone	Fax
Institute for Business & Home Safety (IBHS) 4775 E Fowler Ave *TF:* 866-657-4247 ■ *Web:* www.disastersafety.org	Tampa	FL	33617	813-286-3400	286-9960
Insurance Information Institute (III) 110 William St 24th Fl *TF:* 800-331-9146 ■ *Web:* www.iii.org	New York	NY	10038	212-346-5500	732-1916
Insurance Institute for Highway Safety 1005 N Glebe Rd Suite 800 *Web:* www.iihs.org	Arlington	VA	22201	703-247-1500	247-1588
Insurance Marketing Communications Assn (IMCA) 4916 Pt Fosdick Dr NW Suite 180 *Web:* www.imcanet.com	Gig Harbor	WA	98335	206-219-9811	210-2481
Insurance Research Council (IRC) 720 Providence Rd *TF:* 800-644-2101 ■ *Web:* www.ircweb.org	Malvern	PA	19355	610-644-2212	644-5388
Insured Retirement Institute (IRI) 1101 NY Ave Suite 825 *Web:* www.irionline.org	Reston	VA	20190	202-469-3000	469-3030
Life Insurance Settlement Assn (LISA) 1011 E Colonial Dr Suite 500 *Web:* www.lisassociation.org	Orlando	FL	32803	407-894-3797	897-1325
LIMRA International Inc 300 Day Hill Rd *Web:* www.limra.com	Windsor	CT	06095	860-688-3358	298-9555
LOMA 2300 Windy Ridge Pkwy Suite 600 *TF:* 800-275-5662 ■ *Web:* www.loma.org	Atlanta	GA	30339	770-951-1770	984-0441
Million Dollar Round Table (MDRT) 325 W Touhy Ave *TF:* 800-879-6378 ■ *Web:* www.mdrt.org	Park Ridge	IL	60068	847-692-6378	518-8921
Mortgage Insurance Cos of America (MICA) 1425 K St NW Suite 210 *Web:* www.privatemi.com	Washington	DC	20005	202-682-2683	842-9252
NA of Dental Plans (NADP) 12700 Pk Central Dr *Web:* www.nadp.org	Dallas	TX	75251	972-458-6998	458-2258
NA of Health Underwriters (NAHU) 2000 N 14th St Suite 450 *Web:* www.nahu.org	Arlington	VA	22201	703-276-0220	841-7797
NA of Insurance & Financial Advisors (NAIFA) 2901 Telestar Ct *TF Sales:* 877-866-2432 ■ *Web:* www.naifa.org	Falls Church	VA	22042	703-770-8100	770-8224
NA of Insurance Commissioners (NAIC) 2301 McGee St Suite 800 *Web:* www.naic.org	Kansas City	MO	64108	816-842-3600	783-8175
NA of Mutual Insurance Cos (NAMIC) 3601 Vincennes Rd PO Box 68700 *TF:* 800-336-2642 ■ *Web:* www.namic.org	Indianapolis	IN	46268	317-875-5250	879-8408
NA of Professional Insurance Agents (PIA) 400 N Washington St *TF:* 800-742-6900 ■ *Web:* www.pianet.com	Alexandria	VA	22314	703-836-9340	836-1279
NA of Surety Bond Producers (NASBP) 1140 19th St NW #800 *Web:* www.nasbp.org	Washington	DC	20036	202-686-3700	686-3656
National Council for Prescription Drug Programs (NCPDP) 9240 E Raintree Dr *Web:* www.ncpdp.org	Scottsdale	AZ	85260	480-477-1000	767-1042
National Crop Insurance Services (NCIS) 8900 Indian Creek Pkwy Suite 600 *TF:* 800-951-6247 ■ *Web:* www.ag-risk.org	Overland Park	KS	66210	913-685-2767	685-3080
National Insurance Crime Bureau (NICB) 1111 E Touhy Ave Suite 400 **Fax:* Hum Res ■ *TF:* 800-447-6282 ■ *Web:* www.nicb.org	Des Plaines	IL	60018	847-544-7000	544-7102*
National Organization of Life & Health Insurance Guaranty Associations (NOLHGA) 13873 Pk Ctr Rd Suite 329 *Web:* www.nolhga.com	Herndon	VA	20171	703-481-5206	481-5209
Physician Insurers Assn of America 2275 Research Blvd Suite 250 *Web:* www.piaa.us	Rockville	MD	20850	301-947-9000	947-9090
Professional Insurance Marketing Assn (PIMA) 230 E Ohio St Suite 400 *Web:* www.pima-assn.org	Chicago	IL	60611	817-569-7462	569-7461
Professional Liability Underwriting Society 5353 Wayzata Blvd Suite 600 *TF:* 800-845-0778 ■ *Web:* www.plusweb.org	Minneapolis	MN	55416	952-746-2580	746-2599
Property Casualty Insurers Assn of America 2600 S River Rd *Web:* www.pciaa.net	Des Plaines	IL	60018	847-297-7800	297-5064
Property Loss Research Bureau (PLRB) 3025 Highland Pkwy Suite 800 *TF:* 888-711-7572 ■ *Web:* www.plrb.org	Downers Grove	IL	60515	630-724-2200	724-2260
Reinsurance Assn of America (RAA) 1301 Pennsylvania Ave NW Suite 900 *TF:* 800-638-3651 ■ *Web:* www.reinsurance.org	Washington	DC	20004	202-638-3690	638-0936
Risk & Insurance Management Society Inc (RIMS) 1065 Avenue of the Americas 13th Fl *TF:* 800-711-0317 ■ *Web:* www.rims.org	New York	NY	10018	212-286-9292	986-9716
Self-Insurance Institute of America Inc (SIIA) PO Box 1237 *TF:* 800-851-7789 ■ *Web:* www.siia.org	Simpsonville	SC	29681	864-962-2208	962-2483
Society of Actuaries (SOA) 475 N Martingale Rd Suite 600 *Web:* www.soa.org	Schaumburg	IL	60173	847-706-3500	706-3599
Society of Certified Insurance Counselors PO Box 27027 *TF:* 800-633-2165	Austin	TX	78755	512-345-7932	349-6194
Society of Financial Service Professionals (SFSP) 19 Campus Blvd # 100 *TF:* 800-392-6900 ■ *Web:* www.financialpro.org	Newtown Square	PA	19073	610-526-2500	527-4010
Surety & Fidelity Assn of America (SFAA) 1101 Connecticut Ave NW Suite 800 *Web:* www.surety.org	Washington	DC	20036	202-463-0600	463-0606
Workmen's Circle/Arbeter Ring Inc 247 W 37th St 5th Fl *TF:* 800-922-2558 ■ *Web:* www.circle.org	New York	NY	10018	212-889-6800	532-7518

49-10 Legal Professionals Associations

	City	State	Zip	Phone	Fax
ABA Commission on Domestic Violence 740 15th St NW 9th Fl *TF:* 800-799-7233 ■ *Web:* www.americanbar.org/groups/domestic_violence.html	Washington	DC	20005	202-662-1744	662-1594
ABA Commission on Law & Aging (COLA) 740 15th St NW 8th Fl *Web:* www.americanbar.org/groups/law_aging.html	Washington	DC	20005	202-662-1000	662-8698
American Academy of Psychiatry & the Law (AAPL) 1 Regency Dr PO Box 30 *TF:* 800-331-1389 ■ *Web:* www.aapl.org	Bloomfield	CT	06002	860-242-5450	286-0787
American Arbitration Assn Inc (AAA) 1633 Broadway 10th Fl *TF:* 800-778-7879 ■ *Web:* www.adr.org	New York	NY	10019	212-716-5800	716-5905
American Assn for Justice (AAJ) 777 6th St NW # 200 *TF:* 800-424-2725 ■ *Web:* www.justice.org	Washington	DC	20001	202-965-3500	625-7313
American Bankruptcy Institute (ABI) 44 Canal Ctr Plaza Suite 400 *Web:* www.abiworld.org	Alexandria	VA	22314	703-739-0800	739-1060
American Bar Assn (ABA) 321 N Clark St *TF:* 800-285-2221 ■ *Web:* www.abanet.org	Chicago	IL	60610	312-988-5522	988-6281
American College of Trust & Estate Counsel (ACTEC) 901 15th St NW Suite 525 *Web:* www.actec.org	Washington	DC	20005	202-684-8460	684-8459
American Health Lawyers Assn (AHLA) 1025 Connecticut Ave *Web:* www.healthlawyers.org	Washington	DC	20036	202-833-1100	833-1105
American Immigration Lawyers Assn (AILA) 918 F St NW *Web:* www.aila.org	Washington	DC	20004	202-216-2400	783-7853
American Intellectual Property Law Assn (AIPLA) 241 18th St S Suite 700 *Web:* www.aipla.org	Arlington	VA	22202	703-415-0780	415-0786
American Judicature Society (AJS) 2700 University Ave *TF:* 800-626-4089 ■ *Web:* www.ajs.org	Des Moines	IA	50311	515-271-2281	279-3090
American Land Title Assn (ALTA) 1828 L St NW Suite 705 *TF:* 800-787-2582 ■ *Web:* www.alta.org	Washington	DC	20036	202-296-3671	223-5843
American Law Institute (ALI) 4025 Chestnut St *TF:* 800-253-6397 ■ *Web:* www.ali.org	Philadelphia	PA	19104	215-243-1600	243-1636
American Society of International Law The (ASIL) 2223 Massachusetts Ave NW *Web:* www.asil.org	Washington	DC	20008	202-939-6000	797-7133
American Tort Reform Assn (ATRA) 1101 Connecticut Ave NW Suite 400 *Web:* www.atra.org	Washington	DC	20036	202-682-1163	682-1022
Assn for Conflict Resolution (ACR) 12100 Sunset Hills Rd Suite 130 *Web:* www.acrnet.org	Reston	VA	20190	703-234-4141	435-4390
Assn of American Law Schools (AALS) 1201 Connecticut Ave NW Suite 800 *Web:* www.aals.org	Washington	DC	20036	202-296-8851	296-8869
Assn of Corporate Counsel (ACC) 1025 Connecticut Ave NW Suite 200 *Web:* www.acc.com	Washington	DC	20036	202-293-4103	293-4701
Assn of Legal Administrators (ALA) 75 Tri-State International Suite 222 *Web:* www.alanet.org	Lincolnshire	IL	60069	847-267-1252	267-1329
Battered Women's Justice Project 1801 Nicollet Ave S Suite 102 *TF:* 800-903-0111 ■ *Web:* www.bwjp.org	Minneapolis	MN	55403	612-824-8768	824-8965
Christian Legal Society (CLS) 8001 Braddock Rd Suite 300 *Web:* www.clsnet.org	Springfield	VA	22151	703-642-1070	642-1075
Commercial Law League of America (CLLA) 70 E Lake St Suite 630 *TF:* 800-978-2552 ■ *Web:* www.clla.org	Chicago	IL	60601	312-781-2000	781-2010
Defense Research Institute (DRI) 55 W Monroe St # 20 *TF:* 800-667-8108 ■ *Web:* www.dri.org	Chicago	IL	60603	312-795-1101	795-0749
Environmental Law Institute (ELI) 2000 L St NW Suite 620 *TF:* 800-433-5120 ■ *Web:* www.eli.org	Washington	DC	20036	202-939-3800	939-3868
Federalist Society for Law & Public Policy Studies 1015 18th St NW Suite 425 *Web:* www.fed-soc.org	Washington	DC	20036	202-822-8138	296-8061
Food & Drug Law Institute (FDLI) 1155 15th St NW Suite 800 *TF:* 800-956-6293 ■ *Web:* www.fdli.org	Washington	DC	20005	202-371-1420	371-0649
Hispanic National Bar Assn (HNBA) 1111 Pennsylvania Ave NW 3rd Fl *Web:* www.hnba.com	Washington	DC	20004	202-223-4777	223-2324

Phone Fax

Institute for Professionals in Taxation (IPT)
600 N Pk Town Ctr
1200 Abernathy Rd Suite L-2 . . . . Atlanta GA 30328 404-240-2300 240-2315
Web: www.ipt.org
Institute of Judicial Administration
NYU School of Law
40 Washington Sq S Vanderbilt Hall. . . . . New York NY 10012 212-998-6196 995-4036
International Assn of Defense Counsel (IADC)
303 W Madison St # 925 . . . . Chicago IL 60606 312-368-1494 368-1854
Web: www.iadclaw.org
International Intellectual Property Alliance (IIPA)
2101 L St NW Suite 1000. . . . . Washington DC 20037 202-833-4198 261-0151
Web: www.iipa.com
International Law Institute (ILI)
1055 Thomas Jefferson St NW Suite M-100. . . . . Washington DC 20007 202-247-6006 247-6010
Web: www.ili.org
International Municipal Lawyers Assn (IMLA)
7910 Woodmont Ave Suite 1440 . . . . Bethesda MD 20814 202-466-5424 785-0152
Web: www.imla.org
Justice Research & Statistics Assn (JRSA)
777 N Capitol St NE Suite 801 . . . . Washington DC 20002 202-842-9330 842-9329
Web: www.jrsainfo.org
Lawyers for Civil Justice (LCJ)
1140 Connecticut Ave NW Suite 503 . . . . Washington DC 20036 202-429-0045 429-6982
Web: www.lfcj.com
Lawyers' Committee for Civil Rights Under Law
1401 New York Ave NW Suite 400 . . . . Washington DC 20005 202-662-8600 783-0857
Web: www.lawyerscommittee.org
Media Law Resource Ctr (MLRC)
266 W 37th St # 20. . . . . New York NY 10018 212-337-0200 337-9893
Web: www.medialaw.org
NA for Court Management (NACM)
National Ctr for State Cts
300 Newport Ave. . . . . Williamsburg VA 23185 757-259-1841 259-1520
TF: 800-616-6165 ■ *Web:* www.nacmnet.org
NA for Law Placement (NALP)
1025 Connecticut Ave NW Suite 1110 . . . . Washington DC 20036 202-835-1001 835-1112
Web: www.nalp.org
NA of Bond Lawyers (NABL)
230 W Monroe St Suite 320. . . . . Chicago IL 60606 312-648-9590 648-9588
Web: www.nabl.org
NA of College & University Attorneys (NACUA)
1 Dupont Cir NW Suite 620 . . . . Washington DC 20036 202-833-8390 296-8379
Web: www.nacua.org
NA of Criminal Defense Lawyers (NACDL)
1150 18th St NW Suite 950 . . . . Washington DC 20036 202-872-8600 872-8690
Web: www.nacdl.org
NA of Enrolled Agents (NAEA)
1120 Connecticut Ave NW Suite 460 . . . . Washington DC 20036 202-822-6232 822-6270
Web: www.naea.org
NA of Estate Planners & Councils (NAEPC)
1120 Chester Ave Suite 470. . . . . Cleveland OH 44114 866-226-2224 696-2582*
**Fax Area Code:* 216 ■ *TF:* 866-226-2224 ■ *Web:* www.naepc.org
NA of Legal Assistants (NALA)
1516 S Boston Ave Suite 200. . . . . Tulsa OK 74119 918-587-6828 582-6772
Web: www.nala.org
NA of Professional Process Servers (NAPPS)
1020 SW Taylor St # 240 . . . . Portland OR 97205 503-222-4180 222-3950
TF: 800-477-8211 ■ *Web:* www.napps.org
NALS - Assn for Legal Professionals
8159 E 41st St . . . . Tulsa OK 74145 918-582-5188 582-5907
Web: www.nals.org
National Bar Assn (NBA) 1225 11th St NW. . . . . Washington DC 20001 202-842-3900 289-6170
Web: www.nationalbar.net
National Council of Juvenile & Family Court Judges (NCJFCJ)
Univ of Nevada PO Box 8970. . . . . Reno NV 89507 775-784-6012 784-6628
Web: www.ncjfcj.org
National Court Reporters Assn (NCRA)
8224 Old Courthouse Rd . . . . Vienna VA 22182 703-556-6272 556-6291
TF: 800-272-6272 ■ *Web:* www.ncraonline.org
National Employment Lawyers Assn (NELA)
44 Montgomery St Suite 2080 . . . . San Francisco CA 94104 415-296-7629 677-9445
Web: www.nela.org
National Federation of Paralegal Associations (NFPA)
23607 Hwy 99 Suite 2-C . . . . Edmonds WA 98020 425-967-0045 771-9588
Web: www.paralegals.org
National Legal Aid & Defender Assn (NLADA)
1140 Connecticut Ave NW Suite 900 . . . . Washington DC 20036 202-452-0620 872-1031
Web: www.nlada.org
National Network of Estate Planning Attorneys Inc (NNEPA)
3500 DePauw Blvd Suite 2090. . . . . Indianapolis IN 46268 800-638-8681 964-3800*
**Fax Area Code:* 402 ■ *TF:* 800-638-8681 ■ *Web:* www.nnepa.com
National Partnership for Women & Families
1875 Connecticut Ave NW Suite 650 . . . . Washington DC 20009 202-986-2600 986-2539
Web: www.nationalpartnership.org
National Senior Citizens Law Ctr (NSCLC)
1444 'I' St Suite 1100. . . . . Washington DC 20005 202-289-6976 289-7224
Web: www.nsclc.org
Native American Rights Fund (NARF)
1506 Broadway. . . . . Boulder CO 80302 303-447-8760 443-7776
Web: www.narf.org
Pension Rights Ctr
1350 Connecticut Ave NW Suite 206 . . . . Washington DC 20036 202-296-3776 833-2472
Web: www.pensionrights.org
Practising Law Institute (PLI)
810 7th Ave 26th Fl . . . . New York NY 10019 212-824-5700 477-0300*
**Fax Area Code:* 800 ■ **Fax:* Cust Svc ■ *TF:* 800-260-4754 ■ *Web:* www.pli.edu

Phone Fax

Taxpayers Against Fraud Education Fund (TAF)
1220 19th St NW Suite 501. . . . . Washington DC 20036 202-296-4826 296-4838
TF: 800-873-2573 ■ *Web:* www.taf.org
Vera Institute of Justice
233 Broadway 12th Fl. . . . . New York NY 10279 212-334-1300 941-9407
Web: www.vera.org
World Jurist Assn (WJA)
7910 Woodmont Ave Suite 1440 . . . . Bethesda MD 20814 202-466-5428 452-8540
Web: www.worldjurist.org

49-11 Library & Information Science Associations

Phone Fax

American Assn of Law Libraries (AALL)
53 W Jackson Blvd Suite 940. . . . . Chicago IL 60604 312-939-4764 431-1097
Web: www.aallnet.org
American Assn of School Librarians (AASL)
50 E Huron St. . . . . Chicago IL 60611 312-280-4386 664-7459
TF: 800-545-2433 ■ *Web:* www.ala.org/aasl
American Library Assn (ALA) 50 E Huron St . . . . Chicago IL 60611 312-944-6780 944-2641
TF: 800-545-2433 ■ *Web:* www.ala.org
American Theological Library Assn (ATLA)
300 S Wacker Dr Suite 2100. . . . . Chicago IL 60606 312-454-5100 454-5505
TF: 888-665-2852 ■ *Web:* www.atla.com
Assn for Library & Information Science Education (ALISE)
65 E Wacker Pl Suite 1900. . . . . Chicago IL 60601 312-795-0996 419-8950
Web: www.alise.org
Assn for Library Collections & Technical Services (ALCTS)
50 E Huron St. . . . . Chicago IL 60611 312-280-5038 280-5033
TF: 800-545-2433 ■ *Web:* www.ala.org/alcts
Assn for Library Service to Children (ALSC)
50 E Huron St. . . . . Chicago IL 60611 312-280-2163 944-7671
TF: 800-545-2433 ■ *Web:* www.ala.org/alsc
Assn for Library Trustees & Advocates (ALTA)
50 E Huron St. . . . . Chicago IL 60611 312-280-2161 280-3256
Web: www.ala.org/alta
Assn of College & Research Libraries (ACRL)
50 E Huron St. . . . . Chicago IL 60611 312-280-2519 280-2520
TF: 800-545-2433 ■ *Web:* www.ala.org/acrl.html
Assn of Jewish Libraries PO Box 1118. . . . . Teaneck NY 07666 212-725-5359
Web: www.jewishlibraries.org
Assn of Specialized & Co-op Library Agencies (ASCLA)
50 E Huron St. . . . . Chicago IL 60611 312-280-4395 944-8085
TF: 800-545-2433 ■ *Web:* www.ala.org/ascla
Cal Poly Pomona Foundation Inc
3801 W Temple Ave Bldg 55. . . . . Pomona CA 91768 909-869-2950 869-3716
Web: www.foundation.csupomona.edu
Canadian Assn for School Libraries (CSLA)
1150 Morrison Dr Suite 400. . . . . Ottawa ON K2H8S9 613-232-9625 563-9895
Web: www.cla.ca/divisions/csla
Canadian Assn of Law Libraries (CALL)
4 Cataraqui St Suite 310 PO Box 1570. . . . . Kingston ON K7L5C8 613-531-9338 303-0626*
**Fax Area Code:* 866 ■ *Web:* www.callacbd.ca
Canadian Assn of Special Libraries & Information Services (CASLIS)
1150 Morrison Dr Suite 400. . . . . Ottawa ON K2H8S9 613-232-9625 563-9895
Web: www.cla.ca/caslis/index.htm
Canadian Health Libraries Assn (CHLA)
39 River St . . . . Toronto ON M5A3P1 416-646-1600 646-9460
Web: www.chla-absc.ca
Canadian Library Assn (CLA) 328 Frank St. . . . . Ottawa ON K2P0X8 613-232-9625 563-9895
Web: www.cla.ca
Canadian Library Assn (CLA)
1150 Morrison Dr Suite 400. . . . . Ottawa ON K2H8S9 613-232-9625 563-9895
Web: www.cla.ca/divisions/capl/index.htm
Canadian Library Assn (CLTA)
1150 Morrison Dr Suite 400. . . . . Ottawa ON K2H8S9 613-232-9625 563-9895
Web: www.cla.ca/divisions/clta/clta.htm
Library & Information Technology Assn (LITA)
50 E Huron St. . . . . Chicago IL 60611 312-280-4270 280-3257
TF: 800-545-2433 ■ *Web:* www.lita.org
Library Administration & Management Assn (LAMA)
50 E Huron St. . . . . Chicago IL 60611 312-280-5036 280-5033
TF: 800-545-2433 ■ *Web:* www.ala.org/lama
Medical Library Assn (MLA)
65 E Wacker Pl Suite 1900. . . . . Chicago IL 60601 312-419-9094 419-8950
Web: www.mlanet.org
Music Library Assn (MLA)
8551 Research Way Suite 180 . . . . Middleton WI 53562 608-836-5825 831-8200
Web: www.musiclibraryassoc.org
New England Library Assn (NELA) 31 Connor Ln . . . . Wilton NH 03031 603-654-3533 654-3526
Web: www.nelib.org
Online Computer Library Center Inc (OCLC)
6565 Kilgour Pl . . . . Dublin OH 43017 614-764-6000 764-6096
TF: 800-848-5878 ■ *Web:* www.oclc.org
Public Library Assn (PLA) 50 E Huron St . . . . Chicago IL 60611 312-280-5752 280-5029
TF: 800-545-2433 ■ *Web:* www.pla.org
Reference & User Services Assn (RUSA)
50 E Huron St. . . . . Chicago IL 60611 312-280-4398 944-8085
TF: 800-545-2433 ■ *Web:* www.ala.org/rusa
Special Libraries Assn (SLA)
331 S Patrick St . . . . Alexandria VA 22314 703-647-4900 647-4901
Web: www.sla.org
Urban Libraries Council (ULC)
125 S Wacker Dr Suite 1050. . . . . Chicago IL 60606 847-866-9999 866-9989
Web: www.urbanlibraries.org

	City	State	Zip	Phone	Fax
Young Adult Library Services Assn (YALSA) 50 E Huron St *TF:* 800-545-2433 ■ *Web:* www.ala.org/yalsa	Chicago	IL	60611	312-280-4390	664-7459

49-12 Management & Business Professional Associations

	City	State	Zip	Phone	Fax
Academy of Management (AOM) 235 Elm Rd PO Box 3020 *Web:* www.aomonline.org	Briarcliff Manor	NY	10510	914-923-2607	923-2615
AMC Institute 100 N 20th St 4th Fl *Web:* www.member.amcinstitute.org	Philadelphia	PA	19103	215-564-3484	963-9785
American Business Conference (ABC) 1828 L St NW Suite 908 *Web:* www.americanbusinessconference.org	Washington	DC	20036	202-822-9300	467-4070
American Business Women's Assn (ABWA) 11050 Roe Ave Suite 200 **Fax Area Code:* 913 ■ *TF:* 800-228-0007 ■ *Web:* www.abwa.org	Overland Park	KS	66211	800-228-0007	660-0101*
American Businesspersons Assn (ABA) 350 Fairway Dr Suite 200 *TF:* 800-221-2168 ■ *Web:* www.aba-assn.com	Deerfield Beach	FL	33441	954-571-1877	571-8582
American Cash Flow Assn (ACFA) 255 S Orange Ave Suite 600 *TF:* 800-253-1294	Orlando	FL	32801	407-843-2032	206-6507
American Chamber of Commerce Executives (ACCE) 4875 Eisenhower Ave Suite 250 *TF:* 800-394-2223 ■ *Web:* www.acce.org	Alexandria	VA	22304	703-998-0072	212-9512
American Management Assn (AMA) 1601 Broadway *TF:* 800-262-9699 ■ *Web:* www.amanet.org	New York	NY	10019	212-586-8100	903-8168
American Payroll Assn (APA) 660 N Main Ave Suite 100 *Web:* www.americanpayroll.org	San Antonio	TX	78205	210-226-4600	226-4027
American Seminar Leaders Assn (ASLA) 2405 E Washington Blvd. *TF:* 800-735-0511 ■ *Web:* www.asla.com	Pasadena	CA	91104	626-791-1211	798-0701
American Society of Assn Executives (ASAE) 1575 'I' St NW *TF:* 888-950-2723 ■ *Web:* www.asaecenter.org	Washington	DC	20005	202-626-2723	371-8825
American Society of Notaries (ASN) PO Box 5707 *Web:* www.notaries.org	Tallahassee	FL	32314	850-671-5164	671-5165
American Society of Pension Professionals & Actuaries (ASPPA) 4245 N Fairfax Dr Suite 750 *Web:* www.asppa.org	Arlington	VA	22203	703-516-9300	516-9308
American Staffing Assn (ASA) 277 S Washington St Suite 200 *Web:* www.americanstaffing.net	Alexandria	VA	22314	703-253-2020	253-2053
Appraisers Assn of America (AAA) 386 Pk Ave S Suite 2000 *Web:* www.appraisersassoc.org	New York	NY	10016	212-889-5404	889-5503
APQC 123 N Post Oak Ln Suite 300 *TF:* 800-776-9676 ■ *Web:* www.apqc.org	Houston	TX	77024	713-681-4020	681-8578
ARMA International 11880 College Blvd Suite 450 *TF:* 800-422-2762 ■ *Web:* www.arma.org	Overland Park	KS	66210	913-341-3808	341-3742
ASIS International 1625 Prince St *Web:* www.asisonline.org	Alexandria	VA	22314	703-519-6200	519-6299
Assn for Business Communication PO Box 6143 *Web:* www.businesscommunication.org	Nacogdoches	TX	75962	936-468-6280	468-6281
Assn for Corporate Growth (ACG) 71 S Wacker Dr Suite 2760 *TF:* 877-358-2220 ■ *Web:* www.acg.org	Chicago	IL	60606	312-957-4260	
Assn for Mfg Excellence (AME) 3115 N Wilke Rd Suite G *Web:* www.ame.org	Arlington Heights	IL	60004	224-232-5980	232-5981
Assn for Mfg Technology (AMT) 7901 Westpark Dr *TF:* 800-524-0475 ■ *Web:* www.amtonline.org	McLean	VA	22102	703-893-2900	893-1151
Assn of Executive Search Consultants (AESC) 12 E 41st St 17th Fl *TF:* 877-843-2372 ■ *Web:* www.aesc.org	New York	NY	10017	212-398-9556	398-9560
Assn of Fundraising Professionals (AFP) 4300 Wilson Blvd Suite 300 *TF:* 800-666-3863 ■ *Web:* www.afpnet.org	Arlington	VA	22203	703-684-0410	684-0540
Assn of Management (AoM) 920 S Battlefield Blvd Suite 100	Chesapeake	VA	23322	757-482-2273	482-0325
Assn of Management Consulting Firms (AMCF) 380 Lexington Ave Suite 1700 *Web:* www.amcf.org	New York	NY	10168	212-551-7887	551-7934
Assn of Proposal Management Professionals (APMP) PO Box 668 *Web:* www.apmp.org	Dana Point	CA	92629	949-493-9398	
Business Council for International Understanding (BCIU) 1212 Avenue of the Americas 10th Fl *Web:* www.bciu.org	New York	NY	10036	212-490-0460	697-8526
Business Executives for National Security (BENS) 1030 15th St NW # 200 *TF:* 800-296-2125 ■ *Web:* www.bens.org	Washington	DC	20005	202-296-2125	296-2490
Business Forms Management Assn (BFMA) 3800 Old Cheney Rd Suite 101-285 **Fax Area Code:* 877 ■ *TF:* 888-367-3078 ■ *Web:* www.bfma.org	Lincoln	NE	68516	402-216-0479	204-5979*
Business Roundtable (BR) 1717 Rhode Island Ave NW Suite 800 *Web:* businessroundtable.org	Washington	DC	20036	202-872-1260	466-3509
Chief Executives Organization 7920 Norfolk Ave Suite 400 *TF:* 800-634-2655 ■ *Web:* www.ceo.org	Bethesda	MD	20814	301-656-9220	656-9221
Christian Leadership Alliance 635 Camino De Los Mares Suite 205 *TF:* 800-727-4262 ■ *Web:* www.christianleadershipalliance.com	San Clemente	CA	92673	949-487-0900	487-0927
Club Managers Assn of America (CMAA) 1733 King St *Web:* www.cmaa.org	Alexandria	VA	22314	703-739-9500	739-0124
Coalition of Service Industries (CSI) 805 15th St NW *Web:* www.uscsi.org	Washington	DC	20005	202-289-7460	775-1726
Conference Board Inc 845 3rd Ave *Web:* www.conference-board.org	New York	NY	10022	212-759-0900	980-7014
Council for Community & Economic Research (C2ER) 3330 N Washington Blvd 2nd Fl *Web:* www.c2er.org	Arlington	VA	22201	703-522-4980	522-4985
Council on State Taxation (COST) 122 C St NW Suite 330 *Web:* www.cost.org	Washington	DC	20001	202-484-5222	484-5229
Cre Partnership LP 1000 Main St Suite 3200	Houston	TX	77002	713-621-9500	621-1441
Employee Assistance Professionals Assn Inc (EAPA) 4350 N Fairfax Dr Suite 410 *Web:* www.eapassn.org	Arlington	VA	22203	703-387-1000	522-4585
Employee Involvement Assn (EIA) 11 W Monument Ave Suite 510 *Web:* www.eianet.org	Dayton	OH	45402	937-586-3724	586-3699
Employee Relocation Council (ERC) 4401 Wilson Blvd Suite 510 *TF:* 888-372-2255 ■ *Web:* www.worldwideerc.org	Arlington	VA	22203	703-842-3400	842-3400
Employers Council on Flexible Compensation (ECFC) 927 15th St NW Suite 100 *Web:* www.ecfc.org	Washington	DC	20005	202-659-4300	371-1467
ESOP Assn 1726 M St NW Suite 501 *TF:* 866-366-3832 ■ *Web:* www.esopassociation.org	Washington	DC	20036	202-293-2971	293-7568
Executive Women International (EWI) 7414 S State St *TF:* 877-439-4669 ■ *Web:* www.executivewomen.org	Midvale	UT	84047	801-355-2800	355-2852
Family Firm Institute (FFI) 200 Lincoln St Suite 201 *Web:* www.ffi.org	Boston	MA	02111	617-482-3045	482-3049
Foundation on Economic Trends 4520 E W Hwy Suite 600 *Web:* www.foet.org	Bethesda	MD	20814	301-656-6272	654-0208
Human Resource Planning Society (HRPS) 317 Madison Ave Suite 1509	New York	NY	10017	212-490-6387	682-6851
Institute for a Drug-Free Workplace 8614 Westwood Ctr Dr Suite 950 *Web:* www.drugfreeworkplace.org	Vienna	VA	22182	703-288-4300	
Institute for Alternative Futures (IAF) 100 N Pitt St Suite 235 *Web:* www.altfutures.com	Alexandria	VA	22314	703-684-5880	684-0640
Institute for Supply Management (ISM) 2055 Centennial Cir *TF Cust Svc:* 800-888-6276 ■ *Web:* www.ism.ws	Tempe	AZ	85284	480-752-6276	752-7890
Institute of Business Appraisers (IBA) 7500 NW 5th St # 116 *TF:* 800-299-4130 ■ *Web:* www.go-iba.org	Plantation	FL	33317	954-584-1144	584-1184
Institute of Certified Professional Managers (ICPM) James Madison University MSC 5504 *TF:* 800-568-4120 ■ *Web:* www.icpm.biz	Harrisonburg	VA	22807	540-568-3247	801-8650
Institute of Management Consultants USA Inc (IMC USA) 2025 M St NW Suite 800 *TF:* 800-221-2557 ■ *Web:* www.imcusa.org	Washington	DC	20036	202-367-1134	367-2134
International Assn for Human Resource Information Management Inc (IHRIM) PO Box 1086 **Fax Area Code:* 781 ■ *TF:* 800-804-3983 ■ *Web:* www.ihrim.org	Burlington	MA	01803	800-804-3983	998-8011*
International Assn for Impact Assessment (IAIA) 1330 23rd St S Suite C *Web:* www.iaia.org	Fargo	ND	58103	701-297-7908	297-7917
International Assn of Administrative Professionals (IAAP) 10502 NW Ambassador Dr PO Box 20404 *Web:* www.iaap-hq.org	Kansas City	MO	64153	816-891-6600	891-9118
International Assn of Business Communicators (IABC) 601 Montgomery St # 1900 *TF:* 800-766-4222 ■ *Web:* www.iabc.com	San Francisco	CA	94111	415-544-4700	544-4747
International Assn of Conference Centers (IACC) 243 N Lindbergh Blvd. *Web:* www.iacconline.org	Saint Louis	MO	63141	314-993-8575	993-8919
International Assn of Venue Managers Inc (IAVM) 635 Fritz Dr Suite 100 *TF:* 800-935-4226 ■ *Web:* www.iavm.org	Coppell	TX	75019	972-906-7441	906-7418
International Assn of Workforce Professionals (IAPES) 1801 Louisville Rd *TF:* 888-898-9960 ■ *Web:* www.iawponline.org	Frankfort	KY	40601	502-223-4459	223-4127
International Council of Shopping Centers (ICSC) 1221 Avenue of the Americas 41st Fl **Fax Area Code:* 212 ■ *Web:* www.icsc.org	New York	NY	10020	646-728-3800	589-5555*
International Economic Development Council (IEDC) 734 15th St NW Suite 900 *Web:* www.iedconline.org	Washington	DC	20005	202-223-7800	223-4745
International Facility Management Assn (IFMA) 1 Greenway Plaza # 1100 *Web:* www.ifma.org	Houston	TX	77046	713-623-4362	623-6124
International Graphoanalysis Society (IGAS) 842 5th Ave. **Fax Area Code:* 509 ■ *Web:* www.igas.com	New Kensington	PA	15068	724-472-9701	271-1149*
International Network of M&A Partners 1707 High St *Web:* www.imap.com	Des Moines	IA	50309	515-282-8019	282-0325
International Public Management Assn for Human Resources (IPMA-HR) 1617 Duke St *TF:* 800-220-4762 ■ *Web:* www.ipma-hr.org	Alexandria	VA	22314	703-549-7100	684-0948
International Society for Performance Improvement (ISPI) 1400 Spring St Suite 260 *Web:* www.ispi.org	Silver Spring	MD	20910	301-587-8570	587-8573
International Society of Certified Employee Benefit Specialists (ISCEBS) 18700 W Bluemond Rd PO Box 209 *TF:* 888-334-3327 ■ *Web:* www.iscebs.org	Brookfield	WI	53008	262-786-8771	786-8650
International Trademark Assn (INTA) 655 3rd Ave 10th Fl *Web:* www.inta.org	New York	NY	10017	212-768-9887	768-7796
Labor & Employment Relations Assn (LERA)					

Phone | Fax

121 Labor & Employment Relations Bldg
504 E Armory Ave — Champaign IL 61820 — 217-333-0072 — 265-5130
Web: www.leraweb.org

Latin Business Assn (LBA)
120 S San Pedro St Suite 530 — Los Angeles CA 90012 — 213-628-8510 — 628-8519
Web: www.lbausa.com

Manufacturers Alliance/MAPI Inc
1600 Wilson Blvd Suite 1100 — Arlington VA 22209 — 703-841-9000 — 841-9514
Web: www.mapi.net

Meeting Professionals International (MPI)
3030 LBJ Fwy Suite 1700 — Dallas TX 75234 — 972-702-3000 — 702-3070
Web: www.mpiweb.org

NA for Business Economics (NABE)
1233 20th St NW Suite 505 — Washington DC 20036 — 202-463-6223 — 463-6239
Web: www.nabe.com

NA for the Self-Employed (NASE)
PO Box 241 — Annapolis Junction MD 20701 — 800-649-6273
TF: 800-649-6273 ■ *Web:* www.nase.org

NA of Certified Valuation Analysts (NACVA)
1111 E Brickyard Rd Suite 200 — Salt Lake City UT 84106 — 801-486-0600 — 486-7500
TF: 800-677-2009 ■ *Web:* www.nacva.com

NA of Corporate Directors (NACD)
1133 21st St NW Suite 700 — Washington DC 20036 — 202-775-0509 — 775-4857
Web: www.nacdonline.org

NA of Ecumenical & Interreligious Staff (NAEIS)
PO Box 95949 — Seattle WA 98145 — 206-625-9790 — 625-9791
Web: www.naeis.org

NA of Manufacturers (NAM)
1331 Pennsylvania Ave NW Suite 600 — Washington DC 20004 — 202-637-3000 — 637-3182
TF: 800-814-8468 ■ *Web:* www.nam.org

NA of Parliamentarians (NAP) 213 S Main St — Independence MO 64050 — 816-833-3892 — 833-3893
TF: 888-627-2929 ■ *Web:* www.parliamentarians.org

NA of Personnel Services (NAPS)
131 Prominence Ln Suite 130 — Dawsonville GA 30534 — 706-531-0060 — 739-4750*
**Fax Area Code:* 866 ■ *Web:* www.recruitinglife.com

NA of Professional Employer Organizations (NAPEO)
707 N St Asaph St — Alexandria VA 22314 — 703-836-0466 — 836-0976
Web: www.napeo.org

NA of Publicly Traded Partnerships
1940 Duke St Suite 200 — Alexandria VA 22314 — 703-518-4185 — 842-8333
Web: naptp.org

NA of Service Managers (NASM) PO Box 250796 — Milwaukee WI 53225 — 414-466-6060 — 466-0840
Web: www.nasm.com

NA of Women Business Owners (NAWBO)
8405 Greensboro Dr Suite 800 — McLean VA 22102 — 703-506-3268 — 506-3266
TF: 800-556-2926 ■ *Web:* www.nawbo.org

NA of Workforce Development Professionals (NAWDP)
810 1st St NE Suite 525 — Washington DC 20002 — 202-589-1790 — 589-1799
Web: www.nawdp.org

National Black MBA Assn (NBMBAA)
180 N Michigan Ave Suite 1400 — Chicago IL 60601 — 312-236-2622 — 236-0390
Web: www.nbmbaa.org

National Business Assn (NBA)
5151 Beltline Rd Suite 1150 — Dallas TX 75254 — 972-458-0900 — 960-9149
Web: www.nationalbusiness.org

National Business Coalition on Health (NBCH)
1015 18th St NW Suite 730 — Washington DC 20036 — 202-775-9300 — 775-1569
TF: 877-775-6224 ■ *Web:* www.nbch.org

National Business Incubation Assn (NBIA)
20 E Cir Dr PO Box 37198 — Athens OH 45701 — 740-593-4331 — 593-1996
Web: www.nbia.org

National Co-op Business Assn (NCBA)
1401 New York Ave NW Suite 1100 — Washington DC 20005 — 202-638-6222 — 638-1374
Web: www.ncba.coop

National Coalition of Black Meeting Planners (NCBMP)
8630 Fenton St Suite 126 — Silver Spring MD 20910 — 202-628-3952 — 588-0011*
**Fax Area Code:* 301 ■ *Web:* www.ncbmp.com

National Contract Management Assn (NCMA)
21740 Beaumeade Cir Suite 125 — Ashburn VA 20147 — 571-382-0082 — 448-0939*
**Fax Area Code:* 703 ■ *TF:* 800-344-8096 ■ *Web:* www.ncmahq.org

National Council for Advanced Mfg (NACFAM)
2025 M St NW Suite 800 — Washington DC 20036 — 202-429-2220 — 429-2422
Web: www.nacfam.org

National Institute for Work & Learning (NIWL)
1825 Connecticut Ave NW 7th Fl — Washington DC 20009 — 202-884-8186 — 884-8422
Web: www.niwl.org

National Management Assn (NMA) 2210 Arbor Blvd — Dayton OH 45439 — 937-294-0421 — 294-2374
Web: www.nma1.org

National Minority Business Council Inc (NMBC)
120 Broadway 19th Fl — New York NY 10271 — 212-693-5050 — 693-5048
Web: www.nmbc.org

National Notary Assn (NNA) 9350 DeSoto Ave — Chatsworth CA 91313 — 818-739-4000 — 700-1830
TF: 800-876-6827 ■ *Web:* www.nationalnotary.org

National Right to Work Committee (NRTWC)
8001 Braddock Rd Suite 500 — Springfield VA 22160 — 703-321-8510 — 321-7342
TF: 800-325-7892 ■ *Web:* www.right-to-work.org

National Small Business Assn (NSBA)
1156 15th St NW Suite 1100 — Washington DC 20005 — 202-293-8830 — 872-8543
TF: 800-345-6728 ■ *Web:* www.nsba.biz

National Society of Compliance Professionals (NSCP)
22 Kent Rd — Cornwall Bridge CT 06754 — 860-672-0843 — 672-3005
Web: www.nscp.org

New York Celebrity Assistants
459 Columbus Ave Suite 216 — New York NY 10024 — 212-803-5444
Web: www.nycelebrityassistants.org

Organization for International Investment (OFII)
1225 19th St NW Suite 501 — Washington DC 20033 — 202-659-1903 — 659-2293
Web: www.ofii.org

Product Development & Management Assn (PDMA)
15000 Commerce Pkwy Suite C — Mount Laurel NJ 08054 — 856-439-0500 — 439-0525
TF: 800-232-5241 ■ *Web:* www.pdma.org

Professional Convention Management Assn (PCMA)
2301 S Lake Shore Dr Suite 1001 — Chicago IL 60616 — 312-423-7262 — 423-7222
TF: 877-827-7262 ■ *Web:* www.pcma.org

Professional Records & Information Services Management International
1418 Aversboro Rd Suite 201 — Garner NC 27529 — 919-771-0657 — 771-0457
TF: 800-336-9793 ■ *Web:* www.prismintl.org

Professional Services Council (PSC)
4401 Wilson Blvd Suite 1110 — Arlington VA 22203 — 703-875-8059 — 875-8922
Web: www.pscouncil.org

Profit Sharing/401(k) Council of America (PSCA)
20 N Wacker Dr Suite 3700 — Chicago IL 60606 — 312-419-1863 — 419-1864
Web: www.psca.org

Project Management Institute (PMI)
14 Campus Blvd — Newtown Square PA 19073 — 610-356-4600 — 356-4647
TF: 866-276-4764 ■ *Web:* www.pmi.org

Religious Conference Management Assn Inc (RCMA)
7702 Woodland Dr Suite 120 — Indianapolis IN 46278 — 317-632-1888 — 632-7909
Web: www.rcmaweb.org

Relocation Directors Council Inc (RDC)
8 S Michigan Ave Suite 1000 — Chicago IL 60603 — 312-726-7410 — 580-0165
Web: www.relocationdirectorscouncil.org

SCORE Assn 1175 Herndon Pkwy Suite 900 — Herndon VA 20170 — 800-634-0245 — 487-3066*
**Fax Area Code:* 703 ■ *TF:* 800-634-0245 ■ *Web:* www.score.org

Service Industry Assn (SIA)
2164 Historic Decatur Rd Villa 19 — San Diego CA 92106 — 619-221-9200 — 221-8201
Web: www.servicenetwork.org

Small Business & Entrepreneurship Council
2944 Hunter Mill Rd Suite 204 — Oakton VA 22124 — 703-242-5840 — 242-5841
Web: www.sbsc.org

Small Business Legislative Council (SBLC)
1100 H St NW Suite 540 — Washington DC 20005 — 202-639-8500 — 296-5333
Web: www.sblc.org

Society for Advancement of Management (SAM)
6300 Ocean Dr - OCNR 330 — Corpus Christi TX 78412 — 361-825-6045 — 825-2725
TF: 888-827-6077 ■ *Web:* www.cob.tamucc.edu/sam

Society for Human Resource Management (SHRM)
1800 Duke St — Alexandria VA 22314 — 703-548-3440 — 836-0367
TF: 800-283-7476 ■ *Web:* www.shrm.org

Society of Competitive Intelligence Professionals (SCIP)
1700 Diagonal Rd Suite 600 — Alexandria VA 22314 — 703-739-0696 — 739-2524
Web: www.scip.org

Society of Corporate Secretaries & Governance Professionals Inc
521 5th Ave 32nd Fl — New York NY 10175 — 212-681-2000 — 681-2005
Web: www.governanceprofessionals.org

Society of Professional Benefit Administrators (SPBA)
2 Wisconsin Cir Suite 670 — Chevy Chase MD 20815 — 301-718-7722 — 718-9440
Web: www.spbatpa.org

SOLE - International Society of Logistics
8100 Professional Pl Suite 111 — Hyattsville MD 20785 — 301-459-8446 — 459-1522
Web: www.sole.org

US Business & Industry Council
910 16th St NW Suite 300 — Washington DC 20006 — 202-728-1980 — 728-1981
Web: www.usbusiness.org

US Council for International Business (USCIB)
1212 Avenue of the Americas 18th Fl — New York NY 10036 — 212-354-4480 — 575-0327
Web: www.uscib.org

US-ASEAN Business Council
1101 17th St NW Suite 411 — Washington DC 20036 — 202-289-1911 — 289-0519
Web: www.us-asean.org

US-China Business Council The
1818 N St NW Suite 200 — Washington DC 20036 — 202-429-0340 — 775-2476
Web: www.uschina.org

US-Japan Business Council 1020 19th St NW — Washington DC 20036 — 202-728-0068 — 728-0073
Web: www.usjbc.org

US-Russia Business Council
1110 Vermont Ave NW # 330 — Washington DC 20005 — 202-739-9180 — 659-5920
Web: www.usrbc.org

US-Saudi Arabian Business Council
8081 Wolftrap Rd Suite 300 — Vienna VA 22182 — 703-962-9300 — 204-0332
Web: www.us-sabc.org

Vistage International
11452 El Camino Real Suite 400 — San Diego CA 92130 — 858-532-6800 — 532-6802
TF: 800-589-0531 ■ *Web:* www.vistage.com

World Trade Centers Assn (WTCA)
420 Lexington Ave Suite 518 — New York NY 10170 — 212-432-2626 — 488-0064
Web: www.world.wtca.org

WorldatWork 14040 N Northsight Blvd — Scottsdale AZ 85260 — 202-315-5500 — 315-5550
TF: 877-951-9191 ■ *Web:* www.worldatwork.org

Worldwide Employee Benefits Network Inc (WEB)
1700 Pennsylvania Ave Suite 400 — Washington DC 20006 — 202-349-2049 — 318-8778
Web: www.webnetwork.org

Young Presidents' Organization (YPO)
600 E Las Colinas Blvd Suite 1000 — Irving TX 75039 — 972-587-1500 — 587-1611
TF: 800-773-7976 ■ *Web:* www.ypo.org

YPO-WPO 600 E Las Colinas Blvd Suite 1000 — Irving TX 75039 — 972-587-1500 — 587-1600
Web: www.wpo.org

49-13 Manufacturing Industry Professional & Trade Associations

Phone | Fax

Adhesive & Sealant Council Inc (ASC)
7101 Wisconsin Ave # 990 — Bethesda MD 20814 — 301-986-9700 — 986-9795
Web: www.ascouncil.org

Alliance for the Polyurethanes Industry (API)
1300 Wilson Blvd — Arlington VA 22209 — 703-741-5656 — 741-5655
Web: www.polyurethane.org

Aluminum Assn 1528 Wilson Blvd Suite 600 — Arlington VA 22209 — 703-358-2960 — 358-2961
Web: www.aluminum.org

Aluminum Extruders Council (AEC)
1000 N Rand Rd Suite 214 — Wauconda IL 60084 — 847-526-2010 — 526-3993
Web: www.aec.org

American Assn of Textile Chemists & Colorists (AATCC)
1 Davis Dr PO Box 12215 — Research Triangle Park NC 27709 — 919-549-8141 — 549-8933
Web: www.aatcc.org

American Boiler Manufacturers Assn (ABMA)
8221 Old Courthouse Rd Suite 207 — Vienna VA 22182 — 703-356-7172 — 356-4543
Web: www.abma.com

American Chemistry Council (ACC)
700 Second St NE — Washington DC 20002 — 202-249-7000 — 249-6100
Web: www.americanchemistry.com

American Composites Manufacturers Assn (ACMA)
1010 N Glebe Rd Suite 450 — Arlington VA 22201 — 703-525-0511 — 525-0743
Web: www.acmanet.org

American Fiber Manufacturers Assn Inc (AFMA)
1530 Wilson Blvd Suite 690 — Arlington VA 22209 — 703-875-0432 — 875-0907

Organization / Address	City	State	Zip	Phone	Fax
Web: www.afma.org					
American Foundry Society (AFS)					
1695 E Penny Ln	Schaumburg	IL	60173	847-824-0181	824-7848
TF: 800-537-4237 ■ *Web:* www.afsinc.org					
American Galvanizers Assn (AGA)					
6881 S Holly Cir Suite 108	Centennial	CO	80112	720-554-0900	554-0909
TF: 800-468-7732 ■ *Web:* www.galvanizeit.org					
American Gear Manufacturers Assn (AGMA)					
500 Montgomery St Suite 350	Alexandria	VA	22314	703-684-0211	684-0242
Web: www.agma.org					
American Industrial Hygiene Assn (AIHA)					
2700 Prosperity Ave Suite 250	Fairfax	VA	22031	703-849-8888	207-3561
Web: www.aiha.org					
American Iron & Steel Institute (AISI)					
1101 17th St NW	Washington	DC	20036	202-452-7100	463-6573
Web: www.steel.org					
American Society for Quality (ASQ)					
600 N Plankinton Ave	Milwaukee	WI	53203	414-272-8575	272-1734
TF: 800-248-1946 ■ *Web:* www.asq.org					
American Textile Machinery Assn (ATMA)					
201 Pk Washington Ct	Falls Church	VA	22046	703-538-1789	241-5603
Web: www.atmanet.org					
American Wire Producers Assn (AWPA)					
801 N Fairfax St Suite 211	Alexandria	VA	22314	703-299-4434	299-9233
Web: www.awpa.org					
APICS - Assn for Operations Management					
8430 W Bryn Mawr Ave Suite 1000	Chicago	IL	60631	773-867-1778	409-7020
TF: 800-444-2742 ■ *Web:* www.apics.org					
Asia America MultiTechnology Assn (AAMA)					
PO Box 7522	Menlo Park	CA	94026	650-738-1480	738-1486
Web: www.aamasv.com					
ASM International 9639 Kinsman Rd	Materials Park	OH	44073	440-338-5151	338-4634
TF: 800-336-5152 ■ *Web:* www.asminternational.org					
Assn for Facilities Engineering (AFE)					
12801 Worldgate Dr Suite 500	Herndon	VA	20170	571-203-7171	766-2142
Web: www.afe.org					
Assn for Iron & Steel Technology (AIST)					
186 Thorn Hill Rd	Warrendale	PA	15086	724-814-3000	814-3001
Web: www.aist.org					
Assn of Equipment Manufacturers (AEM)					
6737 W Washington St Suite 2400	Milwaukee	WI	53214	414-272-0943	272-1170
TF: 866-236-0442 ■ *Web:* www.aem.org					
Assn of Industrial Metallizers Coaters & Laminators (AIMCAL)					
201 Springs St	Fort Mill	SC	29715	803-802-7820	802-7821
Web: www.aimcal.org					
Assn of Rotational Molders International (ARM)					
800 Roosevelt Rd Suite C-312	Glen Ellyn	IL	60127	630-942-6589	790-3095
Web: www.rotomolding.org					
Assn of Vacuum Equipment Manufacturers (AVEM)					
201 Pk Washington Ct	Falls Church	VA	22046	703-538-3543	241-5603
Web: www.avem.org					
Basic Acrylic Monomer Manufacturers Inc (BAMM)					
17260 Vannes Ct	Hamilton	VA	20158	540-751-2093	751-2094
Web: www.bamm.net					
Building Service Contractors Assn International (BSCAI)					
401 N Michigan Ave Suite 2200	Chicago	IL	60611	312-321-5167	673-6735
TF: 800-368-3414 ■ *Web:* www.bscai.org					
Business & Institutional Furniture Manufacturers Assn (BIFMA)					
678 Front Ave NW Suite 150	Grand Rapids	MI	49504	616-285-3963	285-3765
Web: www.bifma.com					
Can Manufacturers Institute (CMI)					
1730 Rhode Island Ave NW Suite 1000	Washington	DC	20036	202-232-4677	232-5756
Web: www.cancentral.com					
Chlorine Institute Inc 1300 Wilson Blvd	Arlington	VA	22209	703-894-4140	894-4130
Web: www.chlorineinstitute.org					
Color Pigments Manufacturers Assn Inc					
300 N Washington St Suite 105	Alexandria	VA	22314	703-684-4044	684-1795
Web: www.pigments.org					
Composite Can & Tube Institute (CCTI)					
50 S Pickett St Suite 110	Alexandria	VA	22310	703-823-7234	823-7237
Web: www.cctiwdc.org					
Compressed Gas Assn (CGA)					
4221 Walney Rd 5th Fl	Chantilly	VA	20151	703-788-2700	961-1831
Web: www.cganet.com					
Consortium for Advanced Mfg - International (CAM-I)					
911 Benjamin Dr	Burleson	TX	76028	817-426-5744	426-5799
Web: www.cam-i.org					
Consumer Health Products Canada (CHP)					
1111 Prince of Wales Dr Suite 406	Ottawa	ON	K2C3T2	613-723-0777	723-0779
Web: www.chpcanada.ca/index.cfm?fuseaction=main.dspWelcome					
Consumer Specialty Products Assn (CSPA)					
900 17th St NW Suite 300	Washington	DC	20006	202-872-8110	872-8114
Web: www.cspa.org					
Copper Development Assn Inc					
260 Madison Ave 16th Fl	New York	NY	10016	212-251-7200	251-7234
TF: 800-232-3282 ■ *Web:* www.copper.org					
Cordage Institute					
994 Old Eagle School Rd Suite 1019	Wayne	PA	19087	610-971-4854	971-4859
Web: www.ropecord.com					
Council of Industrial Boiler Owners (CIBO)					
6035 Burke Ctr Pkwy Suite 360	Burke	VA	22015	703-250-9042	239-9042
TF: 800-570-2426 ■ *Web:* www.cibo.org					
Crane Manufacturers Assn of America (CMAA)					
8720 Red Oak Blvd Suite 201	Charlotte	NC	28217	704-676-1190	676-1199
TF: 800-345-1815 ■ *Web:* www.mhia.org/psc					
Ductile Iron Pipe Research Assn (DIPRA)					
245 Riverchase Pkwy E Suite 'O'	Birmingham	AL	35244	205-402-8700	402-8730
Web: www.dipra.org					
Edison Welding Institute (EWI)					
1250 Arthur E Adams Dr	Columbus	OH	43221	614-688-5000	688-5001
Web: www.ewi.org					
Engine Manufacturers Assn (EMA)					
333 W Wacker Dr Suite 810	Chicago	IL	60606	312-929-1970	929-1975
Web: www.enginemanufacturers.org					
Equipment & Tool Institute (ETI)					
134 W University Dr Suite 205	Rochester	MI	48307	248-656-5080	971-2375*
**Fax Area Code:* 603 ■ *Web:* www.etools.org					
Expandable Polystyrene Resin Suppliers Council (ERSC)					
1300 Wilson Blvd	Arlington	VA	22209	703-741-5000	741-6000
Fabricators & Manufacturers Assn International (FMA)					
833 Featherstone Rd	Rockford	IL	61107	815-399-8700	484-7700
TF: 800-432-2832 ■ *Web:* www.fmanet.org					
Federation of Societies for Coatings Technology (FSCT)					
492 Norristown Rd	Blue Bell	PA	19422	610-940-0777	940-0777
Fibre Box Assn (FBA) 25 NW Pt Blvd Suite 510	Elk Grove Village	IL	60007	847-364-9600	364-9639
Web: www.fibrebox.org					
Flexible Packaging Assn (FPA)					
971 Corporate Blvd Suite 403	Linthicum	MD	21090	410-694-0800	694-0900
Web: www.flexpack.org					
Fluid Controls Institute 1300 Sumner Ave	Cleveland	OH	44115	216-241-7333	241-0105
Web: www.fluidcontrolsinstitute.org					
Fluid Power Distributors Assn (FPDA)					
PO Box 1420	Cherry Hill	NJ	08034	856-424-8998	424-9248
Web: www.fpda.org					
Food Processing Machinery Assn (FPMA)					
1451 Dolley Madison Blvd Suite 200	McLean	VA	22101	703-761-2600	
TF: 800-833-4337 ■ *Web:* www.foodprocessingmachinery.com					
Foodservice & Packaging Institute (FPI)					
201 Pk Washington Ct	Falls Church	VA	22046	703-538-3551	241-5603
Web: www.fpi.org					
Forging Industry Assn (FIA)					
1111 Superior Ave Suite 615	Cleveland	OH	44114	216-781-6260	781-0102
Web: www.forging.org					
Glass Assn of North America (GANA)					
800 SW Jackson St Suite 1500	Topeka	KS	66612	785-271-0208	271-0166
Web: www.glasswebsite.com					
Glass Packaging Institute (GPI)					
700 N Fairfax St # 510	Alexandria	VA	22314	703-684-6359	299-1543
Web: www.gpi.org					
Gypsum Assn 810 1st St NE Suite 510	Washington	DC	20002	202-289-5440	289-3707
Web: www.gypsum.org					
Homeland Security Industries Assn					
666 11th St NW Suite 315	Washington	DC	20001	202-331-3096	331-8191
Illuminating Engineering Society of North America (IESNA)					
120 Wall St 17th Fl	New York	NY	10005	212-248-5000	248-5017
Web: www.iesna.org					
INDA: Assn of the Nonwoven Fabrics Industry					
1100 Crescent Green Suite 115	Cary	NC	27518	919-233-1210	233-1282
Web: www.inda.org					
Independent Lubricant Manufacturers Assn (ILMA)					
400 N Columbus St Suite 201	Alexandria	VA	22314	703-684-5574	836-8503
Web: www.ilma.org					
Industrial Designers Society of America (IDSA)					
45195 Business Ct Suite 250	Dulles	VA	20166	703-707-6000	787-8501
Web: www.idsa.org					
Industrial Diamond Assn of America (IDA)					
6081 Central Pk Dr	Columbus	OH	43231	614-797-2265	797-2264
Web: www.superabrasives.org					
Industrial Fabrics Assn International (IFAI)					
1801 County Rd 'B' W	Roseville	MN	55113	651-222-2508	631-9334
TF: 800-225-4324 ■ *Web:* www.ifai.com					
Institute of Caster & Wheel Manufacturers (ICWM)					
8720 Red Oak Blvd Suite 201	Charlotte	NC	28217	704-676-1190	676-1199
Web: www.mhia.org/psc					
Institute of Industrial Engineers (IIE)					
3577 PkwyLn Suite 200	Norcross	GA	30092	770-449-0460	441-3295
TF Cust Svc: 800-494-0460 ■ *Web:* www.iienet2.org					
Institute of Makers of Explosives (IME)					
1120 19th St NW Suite 310	Washington	DC	20036	202-429-9280	293-2420
Web: www.ime.org					
Institute of Packaging Professionals (IoPP)					
1601 Bond St Suite 101	Naperville	IL	60563	630-544-5050	544-5055
TF: 800-432-4085 ■ *Web:* www.iopp.org					
Institute of Paper Science & Technology (IPST)					
500 10th St NW	Atlanta	GA	30332	404-894-5700	894-4778
TF: 800-558-6611 ■ *Web:* www.ipst.gatech.edu					
International AntiCounterfeiting Coalition (IACC)					
1730 M St NW Suite 1020	Washington	DC	20006	202-223-6667	223-6668
Web: www.iacc.org					
International Copper Assn					
260 Madison Ave 16th Fl	New York	NY	10016	212-251-7240	251-7245
Web: www.copperinfo.com					
International Ground Source Heat Pump Assn (IGSHPA)					
Oklahoma State University 374 Cordell S	Stillwater	OK	74078	405-744-5175	744-5283
TF: 800-626-4747 ■ *Web:* www.igshpa.okstate.edu					

Organization	City	State	ZIP	Phone	Fax
International Institute of Synthetic Rubber Producers Inc (IISRP) 2077 S Gessner Rd Suite 133 *Web:* www.iisrp.com	Houston	TX	77063	713-783-7511	783-7253
International Magnesium Assn (IMA) 1000 N Rand Rd Suite 214 *Web:* www.intlmag.org	Wauconda	IL	60084	847-526-2010	526-3993
Investment Casting Institute (ICI) 136 Summit Ave *Web:* www.investmentcasting.org	Montvale	NJ	07645	201-573-9770	573-9771
Material Handling Equipment Distributors Assn (MHEDA) 201 US Hwy 45 *Web:* www.mheda.org	Vernon Hills	IL	60061	847-680-3500	362-6989
Material Handling Industry of America (MHIA) 8720 Red Oak Blvd Suite 201 *TF:* 800-345-1815 ■ *Web:* www.mhia.org	Charlotte	NC	28217	704-676-1190	676-1199
Metal Powder Industries Federation (MPIF) 105 College Rd E *Web:* www.mpif.org	Princeton	NJ	08540	609-452-7700	987-8523
Metals Service Center Institute (MSCI) 4201 Euclid Ave *Web:* www.msci.org	Rolling Meadows	IL	60008	847-485-3000	485-3001
Minerals Metals & Materials Society (TMS) 184 Thorn Hill Rd *TF:* 800-759-4867 ■ *Web:* www.tms.org	Warrendale	PA	15086	724-776-9000	776-3770
NA for Surface Finishing (NASF) 1155 15th St NW Suite 500 *Web:* www.nasf.org	Washington	DC	20005	202-457-8404	530-0659
NA of Steel Pipe Distributors (NASPD) 1501 E Mockingbird Ln Suite 307 **Fax Area Code:* 832 ■ *Web:* www.naspd.com	Victoria	TX	77904	361-574-7878	201-9479*
NACE International: Corrosion Society 1440 S Creek Dr *TF:* 800-797-6223 ■ *Web:* www.nace.org	Houston	TX	77084	281-228-6200	228-6300
National Coil Coating Assn (NCCA) 1300 Sumner Ave *Web:* www.coilcoating.org	Cleveland	OH	44115	216-241-7333	241-0105
National Council of Textile Organizations (NCTO) 910 17th St NW Suite 1020 *Web:* www.ncto.org	Washington	DC	20006	202-822-8028	822-8029
National Electrical Manufacturers Assn (NEMA) 1300 N 17th St Suite 1752 *Web:* www.nema.org	Rosslyn	VA	22209	703-841-3200	841-5900
National Fluid Power Assn (NFPA) 3333 N Mayfair Rd Suite 211 *Web:* www.nfpa.com	Milwaukee	WI	53222	414-778-3344	778-3361
National Glass Assn (NGA) 8200 Greensboro Dr Suite 302 *TF:* 866-342-5642 ■ *Web:* www.glass.org	McLean	VA	22102	703-442-4890	442-0630
National Marine Electronics Assn (NMEA) 7 Riggs Ave *TF:* 800-808-6632 ■ *Web:* www.nmea.org	Severna Park	MD	21146	410-975-9425	975-9450
National Paint & Coatings Assn (NPCA) 1500 Rhode Island Ave NW *Web:* www.paint.org	Washington	DC	20005	202-462-6272	462-8549
National Textile Assn (NTA) 6 Beacon St Suite 1125 *Web:* www.nationaltextile.org	Boston	MA	02108	617-542-8220	542-2199
National Tooling & Machining Assn (NTMA) 6363 Oak Tree Blvd **Fax Area Code:* 301 ■ *TF:* 800-248-6862 ■ *Web:* www.ntma.org	Independence	OH	44131	800-248-6862	248-7104*
National Wooden Pallet & Container Assn (NWPCA) 1421 Prince St Suite 340 *Web:* www.palletcentral.com	Alexandria	VA	22314	703-519-6104	519-4720
North American Assn of Food Equipment Manufacturers (NAFEM) 161 N Clark St Suite 2020 *Web:* www.nafem.org	Chicago	IL	60601	312-821-0201	821-0202
North American Die Casting Assn (NADCA) 241 Holbrook Dr *Web:* www.diecasting.org	Wheeling	IL	60090	847-279-0001	279-0002
Open Applications Group Inc (OAGI) PO Box 4897 **Fax Area Code:* 801 ■ *Web:* www.oagi.org	Marietta	GA	30061	404-402-1962	740-0100*
Packaging Machinery Manufacturers Institute (PMMI) 4350 N Fairfax Dr Suite 600 *TF:* 888-275-7664 ■ *Web:* www.pmmi.org	Arlington	VA	22203	703-243-8555	243-8556
Paper Industry Management Assn (PIMA) 15 Technology Pkwy S *Web:* www.pima-online.org	Norcross	GA	30092	770-209-7230	209-7359
Plastics Institute of America (PIA) Univ MA-Lowell Campus Wannalancit Ctr 600 Suffolk St CVIP 2nd Fl S *Web:* www.plasticsinstitute.org	Lowell	MA	01854	978-934-3130	458-4141
Polystyrene Packaging Council (PSPC) 1300 Wilson Blvd *Web:* www.polystyrene.org	Arlington	VA	22209	703-253-0649	253-0651
Polyurethane Manufacturers Assn (PMA) 6737 W Washington St Suite 1420 *Web:* www.pmahome.org	Milwaukee	WI	53214	414-431-3094	
Portable Rechargeable Battery Assn (PRBA) 1776 K St NW 4th Fl *Web:* www.prba.org	Washington	DC	20006	202-719-4978	
Precision Machined Products Assn (PMPA) 6700 W Snowville Rd *Web:* www.pmpa.org	Brecksville	OH	44141	440-526-0300	526-5803
Process Equipment Manufacturers' Assn (PEMA) 201 Pk Washington Ct *Web:* www.pemanet.org	Falls Church	VA	22046	703-538-1796	241-5603
Recycled Paperboard Technical Assn 920 Davis Rd Suite 306 *Web:* www.rpta.org	Elgin	IL	60123	847-622-2544	622-2546
Reusable Industrial Packaging Assn (RIPA) 8401 Corporate Dr Suite 450 *TF:* 800-533-3786 ■ *Web:* www.reusablepackaging.org	Landover	MD	20785	301-577-3786	577-6476
Rubber Manufacturers Assn (RMA) 1400 K St NW Suite 900 *TF:* 800-220-7622 ■ *Web:* www.rma.org	Washington	DC	20005	202-682-4800	682-4854
Sewn Products Equipment Suppliers Assn (SPESA) 9650 Strickland Rd Suite 103-324 *Web:* www.spesa.org	Raleigh	NC	27615	919-872-8909	872-1915
Society for Mining Metallurgy & Exploration Inc (SME) 8307 Shaffer Pkwy *TF:* 800-763-3132 ■ *Web:* www.smenet.org	Littleton	CO	80127	303-973-9550	973-3845
Society for Protective Coatings (SSPC) 40 24th St 6th Fl *TF:* 877-281-7772 ■ *Web:* www.sspc.org	Pittsburgh	PA	15222	412-281-2331	281-9995
Society of Mfg Engineers (SME) 1 SME Dr *TF Cust Svc:* 800-733-4763 ■ *Web:* www.sme.org	Dearborn	MI	48128	313-425-3000	425-3400
Society of Plastics Engineers (SPE) 14 Fairfield Dr *Web:* www.4spe.org	Brookfield	CT	06804	203-775-0471	775-8490
Society of the Plastics Industry Inc (SPI) 1801 K St NW *Web:* www.plasticsindustry.org	Washington	DC	20006	202-974-5200	296-7005
Society of Tribologists & Lubrication Engineers (STLE) 840 Busse Hwy *Web:* www.stle.org	Park Ridge	IL	60068	847-825-5536	825-1456
Society of Vacuum Coaters (SVC) 71 Pinon Hill Pl NE *Web:* www.svc.org	Albuquerque	NM	87122	505-856-7188	856-6716
Spring Manufacturers Institute (SMI) 2001 Midwest Rd Suite 106 *Web:* www.smihq.org	Oak Brook	IL	60523	630-495-8588	495-8595
Steel Founders' Society of America (SFSA) 780 McArdle Dr Suite G *Web:* www.sfsa.org	Crystal Lake	IL	60014	815-455-8240	455-8241
Steel Manufacturers Assn (SMA) 1150 Connecticut Ave NW Suite 715 *Web:* www.steelnet.org	Washington	DC	20036	202-296-1515	296-2506
Steel Plate Fabricators Assn (SPFA) 944 Donata Ct *Web:* www.steeltank.com	Lake Zurich	IL	60047	847-438-8265	438-8766
Steel Tank Institute (STI) 944 Donata Ct *TF:* 800-275-1300 ■ *Web:* www.steeltank.com	Lake Zurich	IL	60047	847-438-8265	438-8766
Sulphur Institute (TSI) 1140 Connecticut Ave NW Suite 612 *Web:* www.sulphurinstitute.org	Washington	DC	20036	202-331-9660	293-2940
Technical Assn of the Pulp & Paper Industry (TAPPI) 15 Technology Pkwy S *TF Sales:* 800-332-8686 ■ *Web:* www.tappi.org	Norcross	GA	30092	770-446-1400	446-6947
TRI/Princeton 601 Prospect Ave PO Box 625 *Web:* www.triprinceton.org	Princeton	NJ	08542	609-430-4820	
Valve Manufacturers Assn of America (VMA) 1050 17th St NW Suite 280 *Web:* www.vma.org	Washington	DC	20036	202-331-8105	296-0378
Vinyl Siding Institute (VSI) 1201 15th St NW Suite 220 *TF:* 888-367-8741 ■ *Web:* www.vinylsiding.org	Washington	DC	20005	202-587-5100	
Wire Assn International Inc (WAI) 1570 Boston Post Rd PO Box 578 *Web:* www.wirenet.org	Guilford	CT	06437	203-453-2777	453-8384
Wiring Harness Manufacturers Assn (WHMA) 7500 Flying Cloud Dr Suite 900 *Web:* www.whma.org	Eden Prairie	MN	55344	952-253-6225	835-4774
Wood Machinery Manufacturers of America (WMMA) 500 Citadel Dr Suite 200 *Web:* www.wmma.org	Commerce	CA	90040	323-215-0330	215-0331

49-14 Media Professionals Associations

Organization	City	State	ZIP	Phone	Fax
Academy of Television Arts & Sciences 5220 Lankershim Blvd *Web:* www.emmys.tv	North Hollywood	CA	91601	818-754-2800	761-2827
Accuracy in Media Inc (AIM) 4455 Connecticut Ave NW Suite 330 *TF:* 800-787-4567 ■ *Web:* www.aim.org	Washington	DC	20008	202-364-4401	364-4098
American Medical Writers Assn (AMWA) 30 W Gude Dr Suite 525 *Web:* www.amwa.org	Rockville	MD	20850	301-294-5303	294-9006
American Radio Relay League (ARRL) 225 Main St *Web:* www.arrl.org	Newington	CT	06111	860-594-0200	594-0259
American Society of Journalists & Authors (ASJA) 1501 Broadway Suite 302 *Web:* www.asja.org	New York	NY	10036	212-997-0947	937-2315
American Society of Media Photographers (ASMP) 150 N 2nd St *Web:* www.asmp.org	Philadelphia	PA	19106	215-451-2767	451-0880
American Society of News Editors (ASNE) 11690-B Sunrise Valley Dr *Web:* www.asne.org	Reston	VA	20191	703-453-1122	453-1133
American Women in Radio & Television (AWRT) 8405 Greensboro Dr Suite 800 *Web:* www.awrtnyc.org	McLean	VA	22102	703-506-3290	506-3266
Assn for Maximum Service Television (MSTV) 4100 Wisconsin Ave NW 1st Fl *Web:* www.mstv.org	Washington	DC	20016	202-966-1956	966-9617
Assn for Women in Communications (AWC) 3337 Duke St *Web:* www.womcom.org	Alexandria	VA	22314	703-370-7436	370-7437
Assn of Alternative Newsweeklies (AAN) 115615th St NW Suite 905 *Web:* www.altweeklies.com	Washington	DC	20005	202-289-8484	289-2004
Assn of Independents in Radio (AIR) 42 Charles St 2nd Fl *Web:* www.airmedia.org	Dorchester	MA	02125	617-825-4400	
Assn of Public Television Stations (APTS) 2100 Crystal Dr Suite 700 *Web:* www.apts.org	Arlington	VA	22202	202-654-4200	654-4236
Cable & Telecommunications Assn for Marketing (CTAM) 201 N Union St Suite 440 *Web:* www.ctam.com	Alexandria	VA	22314	703-549-4200	684-1167

Organization / Address	City	State	ZIP	Phone	Fax
Cable Television Laboratories Inc					
858 Coal Creek Cir	Louisville	CO	80027	303-661-9100	661-9199
Web: www.cablelabs.com					
Catholic Press Assn (CPA)					
205 W Monroe St Suite 470	Chicago	IL	60606	312-380-6789	361-0256
Web: www.catholicpress.org					
Center for Media Literacy					
23852 Pacific Coast Hwy Suite 472	Malibu	CA	90265	310-456-1225	456-0020
Web: www.medialit.org					
Content Delivery & Storage Assn (CDSA)					
39 N Bayles Ave	Port Washington	NY	11050	516-767-6720	883-5793
Web: www.cdsaonline.org					
Country Radio Broadcasters Inc (CRB)					
819 18th Ave S	Nashville	TN	37203	615-327-4487	329-4492
Web: www.crb.org					
Essential Information PO Box 19405	Washington	DC	20036	202-387-8030	234-5176
Web: www.essential.org					
Foundation for American Communications (FACS)					
85 S Grand Ave	Pasadena	CA	91105	626-584-0010	584-0627
Inter American Press Assn (IAPA)					
1801 SW 3rd Ave 8th Fl	Miami	FL	33129	305-634-2465	635-2272
Web: www.sipiapa.org/v4/index.php					
Intercollegiate Broadcasting System Inc (IBS)					
367 Windsor Hwy	New Windsor	NY	12553	845-565-0003	565-7446
Web: www.ibsradio.org					
International Communication Assn (ICA)					
1500 21st St NW	Washington	DC	20036	202-955-1444	955-1448
Web: www.icahdq.org					
International Newspaper Marketing Assn (INMA)					
10300 N Central Expy Suite 467	Dallas	TX	75231	214-373-9111	373-9112
Web: www.inma.org					
International Radio & Television Society Foundation Inc (IRTS)					
420 Lexington Ave Suite 1601	New York	NY	10170	212-867-6650	867-6653
Web: www.irts.org					
Media Coalition Inc 275 7th Ave Suite 1504	New York	NY	10001	212-587-4025	587-2436
Web: www.mediacoalition.org					
Media Communications Assn International (MCA-I)					
2810 Crossroads Dr Suite 3800	Madison	WI	53718	608-443-2464	443-2478
Web: www.mca-i.org					
Media Financial Management Assn (MFM)					
550 W Frontage Rd Suite 3600	Northfield	IL	60093	847-716-7000	716-7004
Web: www.bcfm.com					
NA of Broadcasters (NAB) 1771 N St NW	Washington	DC	20036	202-429-5300	
Web: www.nab.org					
NA of Hispanic Journalists (NAHJ)					
529 14th St NW					
National Press Bldg Suite 1000	Washington	DC	20045	202-662-7145	662-7144
Web: www.nahj.org					
NA of Television Program Executives (NATPE)					
5757 Wilshire Blvd PH-10	Los Angeles	CA	90036	310-453-4440	453-5258
Web: www.natpe.org					
National Cable & Telecommunications Assn (NCTA)					
25 Massachusetts Ave NW Suite 100	Washington	DC	20001	202-222-2300	
Web: www.ncta.com					
National Cable Television Co-op Inc (NCTC)					
11200 Corporate Ave	Lenexa	KS	66219	913-599-5900	599-5903
TF: 800-888-6282 ■ Web: www.ncta.com					
National Federation of Community Broadcasters (NFCB)					
1970 Broadway Suite 1000	Oakland	CA	94612	510-451-8200	451-8208
TF: 888-280-6322 ■ Web: www.nfcb.org					
National Newspaper Assn (NNA)					
127 Neff Annex PO Box 7540	Columbia	MO	65205	573-882-5800	884-5490
TF: 800-829-4662 ■ Web: www.nna.org					
National Newspaper Publishers Assn (NNPA)					
3200 13th St NW	Washington	DC	20010	202-588-8764	588-8960
Web: www.nnpa.org					
National Press Club (NPC) 529 14th St NW	Washington	DC	20045	202-662-7500	662-7569
Web: www.press.org					
National Press Photographers Assn (NPPA)					
3200 Croasdaile Dr Suite 306	Durham	NC	27705	919-383-7246	383-7261
Web: www.nppa.org					
National Religious Broadcasters (NRB)					
9510 Technology Dr	Manassas	VA	20110	703-330-7000	330-7100
Web: www.nrb.org					
Newspaper Assn of America (NAA)					
4401 Wilson Blvd Suite 900	Arlington	VA	22203	571-366-1000	366-1195
Web: www.naa.org					
Overseas Press Club of America (OPC)					
40 W 45th St	New York	NY	10036	212-626-9220	626-9210
Web: www.opcofamerica.org					
Parents Television Council (PTC)					
707 Wilshire Blvd Suite 2075	Los Angeles	CA	90017	213-629-9255	629-9254
Web: www.parentstv.org					
Radio-Television News Directors Assn (RTNDA)					
1600 K St NW Suite 700	Washington	DC	20006	202-659-6510	223-4007
TF: 800-807-8632 ■ Web: www.rtnda.org					
Satellite Broadcasting & Communications Assn (SBCA)					
1730 M St NW Suite 600	Washington	DC	20036	202-349-3620	349-3621
TF: 800-541-5981 ■ Web: www.sbca.com					
Society for News Design (SND)					
424 E Central Blvd Suite 406	Orlando	FL	32801	401-420-7748	420-7697*
*Fax Area Code: 407 ■ Web: www.snd.org					
Society for Technical Communication (STC)					
901 N Stuart St Suite 904	Arlington	VA	22203	703-522-4114	522-2075
Web: www.stc.org					
Society of Broadcast Engineers Inc (SBE)					
9102 N Meridian St Suite 150	Indianapolis	IN	46260	317-846-9000	846-9120
Web: www.sbe.org					
Society of Environmental Journalists (SEJ)					
115 W Ave	Jenkintown	PA	19046	215-884-8174	884-8175
Web: www.sej.org					
Society of Professional Journalists (SPJ)					
3909 N Meridian St	Indianapolis	IN	46208	317-927-8000	920-4789
Web: www.spj.org					
Specialized Information Publishers Assn (SIPA)					
8229 Boone Blvd Suite 260	Vienna	VA	22182	703-992-9339	992-7512
TF: 800-356-9302 ■ Web: sipaonline.com					
White House News Photographers' Assn (WHNPA)					
Ben Franklin Stn PO Box 7119	Washington	DC	20044	202-785-5230	
Web: www.whnpa.org					
Women in Cable Telecommunications (WICT)					
14555 Avion Pkwy Suite 250	Chantilly	VA	20151	703-234-9810	817-1595
Web: www.wict.org					

49-15 Mental Health Professionals Associations

Organization / Address	City	State	ZIP	Phone	Fax
Administrators in Academic Psychiatry (AAP)					
Univ of Michigan Dept of Psychiatry					
UH9C 9151	Ann Arbor	MI	48109	734-936-4860	936-6880
Web: www.adminpsych.org					
American Academy of Addiction Psychiatry (AAAP)					
400 Massasoit Ave 2nd Fl Suite 307	East Providence	RI	02914	401-524-3076	272-0922
Web: www.aaap.org					
American Academy of Child & Adolescent Psychiatry (AACAP)					
3615 Wisconsin Ave NW	Washington	DC	20016	202-966-7300	966-2891
TF: 800-333-7636 ■ Web: www.aacap.org					
American Academy of Psychiatry & the Law (AAPL)					
1 Regency Dr PO Box 30	Bloomfield	CT	06002	860-242-5450	286-0787
TF: 800-331-1389 ■ Web: www.aapl.org					
American Assn for Geriatric Psychiatry (AAGP)					
7910 Woodmont Ave Suite 1050	Bethesda	MD	20814	301-654-7850	654-4137
Web: www.aagpgpa.org					
American College of Psychiatrists					
122 S Michigan Ave # 1360	Chicago	IL	60603	312-662-1020	662-1025
Web: www.acpsych.org					
American Council of Hypnotist Examiners					
700 S Central Ave	Glendale	CA	91204	818-242-1159	247-9379
TF: 800-894-9766 ■ Web: www.hypnotistexaminers.org					
American Counseling Assn (ACA)					
5999 Stevenson Ave	Alexandria	VA	22304	703-823-9800	823-0252
TF: 800-347-6647 ■ Web: www.counseling.org					
American Group Psychotherapy Assn (AGPA)					
25 E 21st St 6th Fl	New York	NY	10010	212-477-2677	979-6627
TF: 877-668-2472 ■ Web: www.agpa.org					
American Mental Health Counselors Assn (AMHCA)					
801 N Fairfax St Suite 304	Alexandria	VA	22314	703-548-6002	548-4775
TF: 800-326-2642 ■ Web: www.amhca.org					
American Orthopsychiatric Assn					
Dept of Psychology					
Arizona State University PO Box 1104	Tempe	AZ	85287	480-727-7518	
Web: www.aoatoday.com					
American Psychiatric Assn (APA)					
1000 Wilson Blvd Suite 1825	Arlington	VA	22209	703-907-7300	907-1085
TF: 888-357-7924 ■ Web: www.psych.org					
American Psychiatric Nurses Assn (APNA)					
1555 Wilson Blvd Suite 530	Arlington	VA	22209	703-243-2443	243-3390
TF: 866-243-2443 ■ Web: www.apna.org					
American Psychoanalytic Assn (APsaA)					
309 E 49th St	New York	NY	10017	212-752-0450	593-0571
Web: www.apsa.org					
American Psychological Assn (APA)					
750 1st St NE	Washington	DC	20002	202-336-5500	336-5962
TF: 800-374-2721 ■ Web: www.apa.org					
American Society for Adolescent Psychiatry (ASAP)					
PO Box 570218	Dallas	TX	75357	972-613-0985	613-5532
Web: www.adolpsych.org					
Arc Baltimore Inc The 7215 York Rd	Baltimore	MD	21212	410-296-2272	296-2394
Web: www.arcofbaltimore.org					
Arc Of Stanly County The					
350 Pee Dee Ave Suite A	Albemarle	NC	28001	704-986-1500	
Web: www.monarchnc.org					
Assn for Behavioral & Cognitive Therapies (ABCT)					
305 7th Ave 16th Fl	New York	NY	10001	212-647-1890	647-1865
TF: 800-685-2228 ■ Web: www.abct.org/Home					
Assn for Play Therapy (APT)					
3198 Willow Ave Suite 110	Clovis	CA	93612	559-294-2128	294-2129
Web: www.a4pt.org					
Assn for Psychological Science (APS)					
1133 15th St NW Suite 1000	Washington	DC	20005	202-293-9300	293-9350
Web: www.psychologicalscience.org					
Assn for Psychological Type (APT)					
9650 Rockville Pike	Bethesda	MD	20814	301-634-7450	634-7099
TF: 800-847-9943 ■ Web: www.aptcentral.org					
Catholic Charities of Buffalo New York Inc					
741 Delaware Ave	Buffalo	NY	14209	716-218-1400	856-2005
Web: www.ccwny.org					
Depression & Related Affective Disorders Assn (DRADA)					
8201 Greensboro Dr Suite 300	McLean	VA	22102	703-610-9026	
Web: www.drada.org					
Edinburg Center Inc The 1040 Waltham St	Lexington	MA	02421	781-862-3600	863-5903
Web: www.edinburgcenter.org					
Federation of Families for Children's Mental Health (FFCMH)					
9605 Medical Ctr Dr Suite 280	Rockville	MD	28050	240-403-1901	403-1909
Web: www.ffcmh.org					
International Assn of Marriage & Family Counselors (IAMFC)					
c/o American Counseling Assn					
5999 Stevenson Ave	Alexandria	VA	22304	703-823-9800	823-0252
TF: 800-545-2223 ■ Web: www.iamfc.com					

Organization	City	State	ZIP	Phone	Fax
International Neuropsychological Society (INS) 700 Ackerman Rd Suite 625 *Web:* www.the-ins.org	Columbus	OH	43202	614-263-4200	263-4366
International Society for Traumatic Stress Studies (ISTSS) 111 Deer Lake Rd Suite 100 *Web:* www.istss.org	Deerfield	IL	60015	847-480-9028	480-9282
International Transactional Analysis Assn (ITAA) 2186 Rheem Dr Suite B-1 *Web:* www.itaa-net.org	Pleasanton	CA	94588	925-600-8110	600-8112
Lifespring Inc 460 Spring St *TF:* 800-456-2117 ■ *Web:* www.lifespr.com	Jeffersonville	IN	47130	812-280-2080	
NA of Psychiatric Health Systems (NAPHS) 701 13th St NW Suite 950 *Web:* www.naphs.org	Washington	DC	20005	202-393-6700	783-6041
NA of School Psychologists (NASP) 4340 E W Hwy Suite 402 *TF:* 866-331-6277 ■ *Web:* www.nasponline.org	Bethesda	MD	20814	301-657-0270	657-0275
NAADAC - Assn for Addiction Professionals 1001 N Fairfax St Suite 201 **Fax Area Code:* 800 ■ *TF:* 800-548-0497 ■ *Web:* www.naadac.org	Alexandria	VA	22314	703-741-7686	377-1136*
National Council for Therapeutic Recreation Certification Inc (NCTRC) 7 Elmwood Dr *Web:* www.nctrc.org	New City	NY	10956	845-639-1439	639-1471
National Psychological Assn for Psychoanalysis (NPAP) 40 W 13th St # 1 *Web:* www.npap.org	New York	NY	10011	212-924-7440	989-7543
National Resource Center on Homelessness & Mental Illness (NRCHMI) 189 Wells Ave Suite 200 *TF:* 800-444-7415 ■ *Web:* www.nrchmi.samhsa.gov	Newton Centre	MA	02459	617-467-6014	467-6015
New Center Community Mental Health Services 2051 W Grand Blvd *Web:* www.newcentercmhs.org	Detroit	MI	48208	313-961-3200	
Northern Arizona Regional Behavioral Health Authority Inc (NARBHA) 1300 S Yale St *TF:* 877-923-1400 ■ *Web:* www.narbha.org	Flagstaff	AZ	86001	928-774-7128	774-5665
Northwestern Counseling Support & Services Inc 107 Fisher Pond Rd *TF:* 800-834-7793 ■ *Web:* www.ncssinc.org	Saint Albans	VT	05478	802-524-6554	527-7801
SAVE - Suicide Awareness Voices of Education 8120 Penn Ave S Suite 470 *TF:* 888-511-7283 ■ *Web:* www.save.org	Bloomington	MN	55431	952-946-7998	829-0841
Scranton Counseling Center Inc 326 Adams Ave *Web:* www.scrantonscc.org	Scranton	PA	18503	570-348-6100	
Society for Social Work Leadership in Health Care 100 N 20th St 4th Fl *TF:* 866-237-9542 ■ *Web:* www.sswlhc.org	Philadelphia	PA	19103	215-599-6134	564-2175
Society of Behavioral Medicine (SBM) 555 E Wells St Suite 1100 *Web:* www.sbm.org	Milwaukee	WI	53202	414-918-3156	276-3349
Suncoast Center Inc PO Box 10970 *Web:* www.suncoastcenter.com	Saint Petersbu	FL	33733	727-327-7656	323-8978
Valeo Behavioral Health Care Inc 5401 SW 7th St *Web:* www.valeotopeka.org	Topeka	KS	66606	785-233-1730	
West Oakland Health Council Inc (WOHC) 700 Adeline St *Web:* www.wohc.org	Oakland	CA	94607	510-835-9610	272-0209
Yakima Neighborhood Health Services (YNHS) 12 S 8 th St PO Box 2605 *Web:* www.ynhs.org	Yakima	WA	98907	509-454-4143	454-3651

49-16 Publishing & Printing Professional Associations

Organization	City	State	ZIP	Phone	Fax
American Book Producers Assn (ABPA) 381 Pk Ave S *TF:* 800-209-4575 ■ *Web:* www.abpaonline.org	New York	NY	10016	212-645-2368	802-2893
American Business Media (ABM) 201 E 42nd St # 7 *Web:* www.americanbusinessmedia.com	New York	NY	10017	212-661-6360	370-0736
American Society of Business Publication Editors (ASBPE) 214 N Hale St *Web:* www.asbpe.org	Wheaton	IL	60187	630-510-4588	510-4501
American Society of Indexers (ASI) 10200 W 44th Ave Suite 304 *Web:* www.asindexing.org	Wheat Ridge	CO	80033	303-463-2887	422-8894
Assn of American Publishers Inc (AAP) 71 5th Ave *Web:* www.publishers.org	New York	NY	10003	212-255-0200	255-7007
Assn of American University Presses 28 West 36th St Suite 602 *Web:* www.aaupnet.org	New York	NY	10018	212-989-1010	989-0975
Assn of Directory Publishers (ADP) 116 Cass St **Fax Area Code:* 231 ■ *TF:* 800-267-9002 ■ *Web:* www.adp.org	Traverse City	MI	49684	800-267-9002	486-2182*
Associated Church Press (ACP) PO Box 621001 *Web:* www.theacp.org	Oviedo	FL	32762	407-341-6615	386-3236
Book Industry Study Group Inc (BISG) 370 Lexington Ave Suite 900 *Web:* www.bisg.org	New York	NY	10017	646-336-7141	336-6214
Book Manufacturers Institute Inc (BMI) 2 Armand Beach Dr Suite 1-B *Web:* www.bmibook.org	Palm Coast	FL	32137	386-986-4552	986-4553
Canadian Newspaper Assn 890 Yonge St Suite 200 *TF:* 877-305-2262 ■ *Web:* www.newspaperscanada.ca	Toronto	ON	M4W3P4	416-923-3567	923-7206
Children's Book Council (CBC) 54 W 39th St 14th Fl *TF Orders:* 800-999-2160 ■ *Web:* www.cbcbooks.org	New York	NY	10018	212-966-1990	966-2073
Copyright Clearance Center Inc (CCC) 222 Rosewood Dr *Web:* www.copyright.com	Danvers	MA	01923	978-750-8400	646-8600
Copyright Society of the USA 1133 Avenue of the Americas *Web:* www.csusa.org	New York	NY	10036	212-354-6401	354-2847
Editorial Freelancers Assn (EFA) 71 W 23rd St 4th Fl *TF:* 866-929-5400 ■ *Web:* www.the-efa.org	New York	NY	10010	212-929-5400	929-5439
Evangelical Christian Publishers Assn (ECPA) 9633 S 48th St Suite 140 *Web:* www.ecpa.org	Phoenix	AZ	85044	480-966-3998	966-1944
Flexographic Technical Assn (FTA) 900 Marconi Ave *Web:* www.flexography.org	Ronkonkoma	NY	11779	631-737-6020	737-6813
Greeting Card Assn (GCA) 1133 Westchester Ave Suite N136 *Web:* www.greetingcard.org	White Plain	NY	10604	914-421-3331	948-1484
Independent Book Publishers Assn The (IBPA) 627 Aviation Way *Web:* www.pma-online.org	Manhattan Beach	CA	90266	310-372-2732	374-3342
International Assn of Printing House Craftsmen (IAPHC) PO Box 2549 **Fax Area Code:* 763 ■ *TF:* 800-466-4274 ■ *Web:* www.iaphc.org	Maple Grove	MN	55311	612-508-6212	560-1350*
International Digital Enterprise Alliance 1421 Prince St Suite 230 *Web:* www.idealliance.org	Alexandria	VA	22314	703-837-1070	837-1072
International Publishing Management Assn (IPMA) 710 Regency Dr Suite 6 *Web:* www.ipma.org	Kearney	MO	64060	816-902-4762	902-4766
International Reprographic Assn (IRgA) 401 N Michigan Ave Suite 2200 *TF:* 800-833-4742 ■ *Web:* www.irga.com	Chicago	IL	60611	312-245-1026	673-6724
IPA - the Assn of Graphic Solutions Providers 7200 France Ave S Suite 223 *TF:* 800-255-8141 ■ *Web:* www.ipa.org	Edina	MN	55435	952-896-1908	
Magazine Publishers of America (MPA) 810 7th Ave 24th Fl *TF:* 888-567-3228 ■ *Web:* www.magazine.org	New York	NY	10019	212-872-3700	888-4217
NA for Printing Leadership (NAPL) 75 W Century Rd *TF Cust Svc:* 800-642-6275 ■ *Web:* www.napl.org	Paramus	NJ	07652	201-634-9600	634-0324
NA of Printing Ink Manufacturers (NAPIM) 581 Main St 5th Fl *Web:* www.napim.org	Woodbridge	NJ	07095	732-855-1525	855-1838
NA Printing Leadership (NAPL) 1 Meadowlands Plaza Suite 1511 *TF:* 800-642-6275 ■ *Web:* www.napl.org	East Rutherford	NJ	07073	201-634-9600	634-0324
National Information Standards Organization (NISO) 1 N Charles St Suite 1905 **Fax Area Code:* 410 ■ *Web:* www.niso.org	Baltimore	MD	21201	301-654-2512	685-5278*
National Press Foundation (NPF) 1211 Connecticut Ave NW Suite 310 *Web:* www.nationalpress.org	Washington	DC	20036	202-663-7280	530-2855
NPES: Assn for Suppliers of Printing Publishing & Converting Technologies 1899 Preston White Dr *TF:* 866-381-9839 ■ *Web:* www.npes.org	Reston	VA	20191	703-264-7200	620-0994
Online Publishers Assn (OPA) 249 W 17th St 14th Fl *Web:* www.online-publishers.org	New York	NY	10011	212-204-1488	204-1514
Printing Industries of America/Graphic Arts Technical Foundation (PIA/GATF) 200 Deer Run Rd *TF:* 800-910-4283 ■ *Web:* www.printing.org	Sewickley	PA	15143	412-741-6860	741-2311
Society for Imaging Science & Technology (IS&T) 7003 Kilworth Ln *Web:* www.imaging.org	Springfield	VA	22151	703-642-9090	642-9094
Society for Scholarly Publishing (SSP) 10200 W 44th Ave Suite 304 *Web:* www.sspnet.org	Wheat Ridge	CO	80033	303-422-3914	422-8894
Society of Publication Designers Inc (SPD) 17E 47th St 6th Fl *Web:* www.spd.org	New York	NY	10017	212-223-3332	223-5880
Specialty Graphic Imaging Assn (SGIA) 10015 Main St *TF:* 888-385-3588 ■ *Web:* www.sgia.org	Fairfax	VA	22031	703-385-1335	273-0456

49-17 Real Estate Professionals Associations

Organization	City	State	ZIP	Phone	Fax
AIR Commercial Real Estate Assn 800 W 6th St Suite 800 *Web:* www.airea.com	Los Angeles	CA	90017	213-687-8777	687-8616
American Homeowners Foundation (AHF) 6776 Little Falls Rd *TF:* 800-489-7776 ■ *Web:* www.americanhomeowners.org	Arlington	VA	22213	703-536-7776	536-7079
American Planning Assn (APA) 1030 15th St NW *Web:* www.planning.org	Washington	DC	20005	202-872-0611	872-0643
American Resort Development Assn (ARDA) 1201 15th St NW Suite 400 *Web:* www.arda.org	Washington	DC	20005	202-371-6700	289-8544
American Society of Appraisers (ASA) 555 Herndon Pkwy Suite 125 *TF:* 800-272-8258 ■ *Web:* www.appraisers.org	Herndon	VA	20170	703-478-2228	742-8471
Appraisal Institute 550 W Van Buren St Suite 1000 *Web:* www.appraisalinstitute.org	Chicago	IL	60607	312-335-4100	335-4400
Building Owners & Managers Assn International (BOMA) 1101 15th St NW Suite 800 *TF:* 800-426-6292 ■ *Web:* www.boma.org	Washington	DC	20005	202-408-2662	326-6377
Building Owners & Managers Institute 1 Pk Pl Suite 475 *TF:* 800-235-2664 ■ *Web:* www.igreenbuild.com	Annapolis	MD	21401	410-974-1410	974-0544
CCIM Institute 430 N Michigan Ave Suite 800 *TF:* 800-621-7027 ■ *Web:* www.ccim.com	Chicago	IL	60611	312-321-4460	321-4530
CoreNet Global Inc 260 Peachtree St NW Suite 1500 *TF:* 800-726-8111 ■ *Web:* www.corenetglobal.org	Atlanta	GA	30303	404-589-3200	589-3201
Council of Real Estate Brokerage Managers (CRB) 430 N Michigan Ave Suite 300 **Fax Area Code:* 312 ■ *TF:* 800-621-8738 ■ *Web:* www.crb.com	Chicago	IL	60611	800-621-8738	329-8882*
Council of Residential Specialists 430 N Michigan Ave Suite 300 *TF:* 800-462-8841 ■ *Web:* www.crs.com	Chicago	IL	60611	312-321-4400	329-8882
Counselors of Real Estate (CRE) 430 N Michigan Ave 2nd Fl *Web:* www.cre.org	Chicago	IL	60611	312-329-8427	329-8881
Institute of Business Appraisers (IBA)					

Phone | Fax

7500 NW 5th St # 116 Plantation FL 33317 954-584-1144 584-1184
TF: 800-299-4130 ■ Web: www.go-iba.org

Institute of Real Estate Management (IREM)
430 N Michigan Ave Chicago IL 60611 312-329-6000 338-4736*
*Fax Area Code: 800 ■ TF: 800-837-0706 ■ Web: www.irem.org

International Downtown Assn (IDA)
1250 Thomas Jefferson St NW Suite 500 W Washington DC 20007 202-393-6801 393-6869
Web: www.ida-downtown.org/eweb

NA of Exclusive Buyer Agents (NAEBA)
1481 N Eliseo C Felix Jr Way Suite 223 Avondale AZ 85323 623-932-0098 932-0212
TF: 888-623-2299 ■ Web: www.naeba.org

NA of Housing Co-ops (NAHC)
1444 'I' St NW Suite 700 Washington DC 20005 202-737-0797 216-9646
Web: www.coophousing.org

NA of Independent Fee Appraisers (NAIFA)
401 N Michigan Ave Suite 2200 Chicago IL 60611 312-321-6830 673-6652
Web: www.naifa.com

NA of Industrial & Office Properties (NAIOP)
2201 Co-op Way 3rd Fl Herndon VA 20171 703-904-7100 904-7942
TF: 800-666-6780 ■ Web: www.naiop.org

NA of Master Appraisers 303 W Cypress St San Antonio TX 78212 210-271-0781 271-0791
TF: 800-229-6262

NA of Real Estate Cos (NAREC)
216 W Jackson Blvd Suite 625 Chicago IL 60606 312-263-1755 750-1203
Web: www.narec.org

NA of Real Estate Investment Trusts (NAREIT)
1875 'I' St NW Suite 600 Washington DC 20006 202-739-9400 739-9401
TF: 800-362-7348 ■ Web: www.reit.com

NA of REALTORS 430 N Michigan Ave Chicago IL 60611 312-329-8200 329-8390*
*Fax: Mktg ■ TF: 800-874-6500 ■ Web: www.realtor.org

NA of Residential Property Managers (NARPM)
638 Independence Pkwy Suite 100 Chesapeake VA 23320 757-473-9700 473-9897
TF: 800-782-3452 ■ Web: www.narpm.org

NA of Royalty Owners (NARO) 15 W 6th St Suite 2626 Tulsa OK 74119 918-794-1660 794-1662
TF: 800-558-0557 ■ Web: www.naro-us.org

NA of Screening Agencies (NASA) 3337 Duke St Alexandria VA 22314 703-370-7436
Web: www.n-a-s-a.com

National Apartment Assn (NAA)
4300 Wilson Blvd Suite 400 Arlington VA 22203 703-518-6141 248-9440
Web: www.naahq.org

National Council of Exchangors (NCE)
630 Quintana Rd # 150 Morro Bay CA 93442 805-772-4662 332-3004*
*Fax Area Code: 866 ■ TF: 800-324-1031 ■ Web: www.infoville.com

National Housing & Rehabilitation Assn (NH&RA)
1400 16th St NW Suite 420 Washington DC 20036 202-939-1750 265-4435
Web: www.housingonline.com

National Multi Housing Council (NMHC)
1850 M St NW Suite 540 Washington DC 20036 202-974-2300 775-0112
Web: www.nmhc.org

Real Estate Buyer's Agent Council (REBAC)
430 N Michigan Ave Chicago IL 60611 312-329-8656 329-8632
TF: 800-648-6224 ■ Web: www.rebac.net

Real Estate Educators Assn (REEA)
2000 I- Pk Dr Suite 306 Montgomery AL 36109 334-625-8650 260-2903
Web: www.reea.org

Real Estate Roundtable
801 Pennsylvania Ave NW Suite 720 Washington DC 20004 202-639-8400 639-8442
Web: www.rer.org

Realtors Land Institute 430 N Michigan Ave Chicago IL 60611 312-329-8446 329-8633
TF: 800-441-5263 ■ Web: www.rliland.com

Society Of Industrial & Office Realtors (SIOR)
1201 New York Ave NW Suite 350 Washington DC 20005 202-449-8200 216-9325
Web: www.sior.com

Vacation Rental Managers Assn (VRMA)
9100 Purdue Rd Suite 200 Indianapolis IN 46268 317-454-8315 458-3637*
*Fax Area Code: 831 ■ TF: 800-871-8762 ■ Web: www.vrma.com

Women's Council of REALTORS (WCR)
430 N Michigan Ave Chicago IL 60611 312-329-8483 329-3290
TF: 800-245-8512 ■ Web: www.wcr.org

49-18 Sales & Marketing Professional Associations

Phone | Fax

Advertising Council Inc
261 Madison Ave 11th Fl New York NY 10016 212-922-1500 922-1676
Web: www.adcouncil.org

Advertising Research Foundation (ARF)
432 Pk Ave S 6th Fl New York NY 10016 212-751-5656 319-5265

American Adv Federation (AAF)
1101 Vermont Ave NW Suite 500 Washington DC 20005 202-898-0089 898-0159
TF: 800-999-2231 ■ Web: www.aaf.org

American Assn of Adv Agencies (AAAA)
405 Lexington Ave 18th Fl New York NY 10174 212-682-2500 682-8391
Web: www.aaaa.org

American Assn of Exporters & Importers (AAEI)
1050 17th St NW Suite 810 Washington DC 20036 202-857-8009 857-7843
Web: www.aaei.org

American Assn of Franchisees & Dealers (AAFD)
3500 5th Ave Suite 103 San Diego CA 92103 619-209-3775 209-3777
TF: 800-733-9858 ■ Web: www.aafd.org

American Booksellers Assn (ABA)
200 White Plains Rd Suite 600 Tarrytown NY 10591 914-591-2665 591-2720
TF: 800-637-0037 ■ Web: www.bookweb.org

AMERICAN FIREARMS 2620 Alamanda Ct Fort Lauderdale FL 33311 954-467-9994 463-2501
Web: www.amfire.com

American Hardwood Export Council (AHEC)
1111 19th St NW Suite 800 Washington DC 20036 202-463-2720 463-2787
Web: www.ahec.org

American International Automobile Dealers Assn (AIADA)
211 N Union St Suite 300 Alexandria VA 22314 703-519-7800 519-7810
TF: 800-462-4232 ■ Web: www.aiada.org

American Machine Tool Distributors' Assn (AMTDA)
1445 Research Blvd Suite 450 Rockville MD 20850 301-738-1200 738-9499
TF: 800-878-2683 ■ Web: www.amtda.org

American Marketing Assn (AMA)
311 S Wacker Dr Suite 5800 Chicago IL 60606 312-542-9000 542-9001
TF: 800-262-1150 ■ Web: www.marketingpower.com

American Supply Assn (ASA)
222 Merchandise Mart Plaza Suite 1400 Chicago IL 60654 312-464-0090 464-0091
Web: www.asa.net

American Wholesale Marketers Assn (AWMA)
2750 Prosperity Ave Suite 530 Fairfax VA 22031 703-208-3358 573-5738
TF: 800-482-2962 ■ Web: www.awmanet.org

Assn for Postal Commerce 1901 Fort Myer Dr Arlington VA 22209 703-524-0096 524-1871
Web: www.postcom.org

Assn of National Advertisers (ANA)
708 3rd Ave 33rd Fl New York NY 10017 212-697-5950 687-7310
Web: www.ana.net

Assn of Progressive Rental Organizations (APRO)
1504 Robin Hood Trail Austin TX 78703 512-794-0095 794-0097
TF: 800-204-2776 ■ Web: www.rtohq.org

Associated Equipment Distributors (AED)
615 W 22nd St Oak Brook IL 60523 630-574-0650 574-0132
TF: 800-388-0650 ■ Web: www.aednet.org

Audit Bureau of Circulations (ABC)
900 N Meacham Rd Schaumburg IL 60173 847-605-0909 605-0483
Web: www.accessabc.com

Automotive Distribution Network
3985 Fountainside Dr Suite 210 Germantown TN 38138 901-682-9090 682-9098
TF Cust Svc: 800-727-8112 ■ Web: www.partsplus.com

BPA Worldwide 100 Beard Sawmill Rd 6th Fl Shelton CT 06484 203-447-2800 447-2900
Web: www.bpaww.com

Brick Industry Assn (BIA)
1850 Centennial Pk Dr Suite 301 Reston VA 20191 703-620-0010 620-3928
Web: www.gobrick.com

Business Marketing Assn (BMA)
1601 Bond St Suite 101 Naperville IL 60563 630-544-5054 544-5055
TF: 800-664-4262 ■ Web: www.marketing.org

Business Technology Assn (BTA)
12411 Wornall Rd Kansas City MO 64145 816-941-3100 941-2829
TF: 800-316-9721 ■ Web: www.bta.org

Cabletelevision Adv Bureau (CAB)
830 3rd Ave 2nd Fl New York NY 10022 212-508-1200 832-3268
Web: www.cabletvadbureau.com

Canadian Assn of Chemical Distributors (CACD)
627 Lyons Ln Suite 301 Oakville ON L6J5Z7 905-844-9140 844-5706
Web: www.cacd.ca

CBA International
9240 Explorer Dr Suite 200 Colorado Springs CO 80920 719-265-9895 272-3510
TF: 800-252-1950 ■ Web: www.cbaonline.org

Center for Exhibition Industry Research (CEIR)
8111 LBJ Fwy Suite 750 Dallas TX 75251 972-687-9242 692-6020
Web: www.ceir.org

Chain Drug Marketing Assn (CDMA)
43157 W Nine-Mile Rd PO Box 995 Novi MI 48376 248-449-9300 449-9396
TF: 800-935-2362 ■ Web: www.chaindrug.com

Clio Awards Inc 770 Broadway 6th Fl New York NY 10003 212-683-4300 683-4796
TF: 800-946-2546 ■ Web: www.clioawards.com

Coalition for Employment Through Exports (CEE)
1625 K St NW # 200 Washington DC 20006 202-296-6107 296-9709
Web: www.usaexport.org

Coalition for Government Procurement
1990 M St NW Suite 450 Washington DC 20036 202-331-0975 822-9788
Web: www.netforum.avectra.com

Color Marketing Group (CMG)
5845 Richmond Hwy Suite 410 Alexandria VA 22303 703-329-8500 329-0155
Web: www.colormarketing.org

Council of Supply Chain Management Professionals
377 E Butterfield Rd Lombard IL 60148 630-574-0985 574-0989
Web: www.cscmp.org

Dairyamerica Inc
4974 E Clinton Way Suite C-121 Fresno CA 93727 559-251-0992 251-1078
TF: 800-722-3110 ■ Web: www.dairyamerica.com

Direct Marketing Assn Inc (DMA)
1120 Avenue of the Americas New York NY 10036 212-768-7277 302-6714
Web: www.the-dma.org

Direct Selling Assn (DSA)
1667 K St NW Suite 1100 Washington DC 20006 202-452-8866 452-9010
Web: www.dsa.org

Electronic Retailing Assn (ERA)
2000 N 14th St Suite 300 Arlington VA 22201 703-841-1751 841-8290
TF: 800-987-6462 ■ Web: www.retailing.org

Electronics Representatives Assn (ERA)
300 W Adams St Suite 617 Chicago IL 60606 312-527-3050 527-3783
TF: 800-776-7377 ■ Web: www.era.org

Equipment Leasing & Finance Assn (ELFA)
1825 K St NW Suite 900 Washington DC 20006 202-238-3400 238-3401
Web: www.elfaonline.org

Exhibit Designers & Producers Assn (EDPA)
10 Norden Pl Norwalk CT 06855 203-852-5698 854-6735
Web: www.edpa.com

Food Marketing Institute (FMI)
2345 Crystal Dr Suite 800 Arlington VA 22202 202-220-0600 429-4519
Web: www.fmi.org

Gases & Welding Distributors Assn (GAWDA)
550 NW LeJeune Rd Miami FL 33126 877-382-6440 442-7451*
*Fax Area Code: 305 ■ TF: 877-382-6440 ■ Web: www.gawda.org

Global Market Development Ctr (GMDC)
1275 Lake Plaza Dr Colorado Springs CO 80906 719-576-4260 576-2661
Web: www.gmdc.com

Global Offset & Countertrade Assn (GOCA)
818 Connecticut Ave NW 12th Fl Washington DC 20006 202-887-9011 872-8324
Web: www.globaloffset.org

HARDI Hydronic Heating & Cooling Council
1389 Dublin Rd Columbus OH 43215 614-488-1835 488-0482
TF: 888-253-2128 ■ Web: www.hardinet.org

Health Industry Distributors Assn (HIDA)
310 Montgomery St Alexandria VA 22314 703-549-4432 549-6495
TF: 800-549-4432 ■ Web: www.hida.org

Healthcare Communications & Marketing Assn (HCMA)
19 Matua Rd Mount Royal NJ 08061 856-423-2896 423-3420
TF: 800-551-2173 ■ Web: www.hcmathefamily.com

Healthcare Convention & Exhibitors Assn (HCEA)
1100 Johnson Ferry Rd Suite 300 Atlanta GA 30342 404-252-3663 252-0774
Web: www.hcea.org

Healthcare Distribution Management Assn (HDMA)
901 N Glebe Rd Suite 1000 Arlington VA 22203 703-787-0000 935-3200
Web: www.healthcaredistribution.org

Hospitality Sales & Marketing Assn International (HSMAI)

	City	State	Zip	Phone	Fax
8201 Greensboro Dr Suite 300	McLean	VA	22102	703-610-9024	610-9005
Web: www.hsmai.org					
International Adv Assn (IAA)					
275 Madison Ave Suite 2102	New York	NY	10016	212-557-1133	983-0455
International Assn of Exhibitions & Events (IAEE)					
8111 Lyndon B Johnson # 1150	Dallas	TX	75251	972-458-8002	458-8119
Web: www.iaee.com					
International Assn of Plastics Distribution (IAPD)					
6734 W 121 St	Overland Park	KS	66209	913-345-1005	345-1006
Web: www.iapd.org					
International Federation of Pharmaceutical Wholesalers (IFPW)					
10569 Crestwood Dr.	Manassas	VA	20109	703-331-3714	331-3715
Web: www.ifpw.com					
International Foodservice Distributors Assn (IFDA)					
1410 Spring Hill Rd Suite 210	McLean	VA	22102	703-532-9400	538-4673
Web: www.ifdaonline.org					
International Franchise Assn (IFA)					
1501 K St NW Suite 350	Washington	DC	20005	202-628-8000	628-0812
TF: 800-543-1038 ■ *Web:* www.franchise.org					
International Home Furnishings Representatives Assn (IHFRA)					
209 S Main St PO Box 670	High Point	NC	27261	336-889-3920	802-1959
TF: 866-528-8634 ■ *Web:* www.ihfra.org					
International Sanitary Supply Assn (ISSA)					
7373 N Lincoln Ave	Lincolnwood	IL	60712	847-982-0800	982-1012
TF: 800-225-4772 ■ *Web:* www.issa.com					
Licensing Executives Society (LES)					
1800 Diagonal Rd Suite 280	Alexandria	VA	22314	703-836-3106	836-3107
Web: www.lesi.org					
Machinery Dealers NA (MDNA) 315 S Patrick St	Alexandria	VA	22314	703-836-9300	836-9303
TF: 800-872-7807 ■ *Web:* www.mdna.org					
Mailing & Fulfillment Service Assn (MFSA)					
1421 Prince St Suite 410	Alexandria	VA	22314	703-836-9200	548-8204
TF: 800-333-6272 ■ *Web:* www.mfsanet.org					
Manufacturers' Agents NA (MANA)					
16-A Journey Suite 200	Aliso Viejo	CA	92656	949-859-4040	855-2973
TF: 877-626-2776 ■ *Web:* www.manaonline.org					
Marketing Research Assn Inc (MRA)					
110 National Dr	Glastonbury	CT	06033	860-682-1000	512-1050*
**Fax Area Code:* 888 ■ *Web:* www.mra-net.org					
Metals Service Center Institute (MSCI)					
4201 Euclid Ave	Rolling Meadows	IL	60008	847-485-3000	485-3001
Web: www.msci.org					
Multi-Level Marketing International Assn (MLMIA)					
119 Stanford Ct	Irvine	CA	92612	949-854-0484	854-7687
Web: www.mlmia.com					
NA for Retail Marketing Services (NARMS)					
2417 A Post Rd.	Stevens Point	WI	54481	715-342-0948	342-1943
TF: 888-526-2767 ■ *Web:* www.narms.com					
NA of Chain Drug Stores (NACDS) 413 N Lee St	Alexandria	VA	22314	703-549-3001	836-4869
TF: 800-678-6223 ■ *Web:* www.nacds.org					
NA of Chemical Distributors (NACD)					
1555 Wilson Blvd Suite 700	Arlington	VA	22209	703-527-6223	527-7747
Web: www.nacd.com					
NA of College Stores (NACS) 500 E Lorain St.	Oberlin	OH	44074	440-775-7777	775-4769
TF: 800-622-7498 ■ *Web:* www.nacs.org					
NA of Convenience Stores (NACS) 1600 Duke St	Alexandria	VA	22314	703-684-3600	836-4564
TF Cust Svc: 800-966-6227 ■ *Web:* www.nacsonline.com					
NA of Educational Procurement (NAEB)					
5523 Research Pk Dr Suite 340	Baltimore	MD	21228	443-543-5540	543-5550
Web: www.naepnet.org					
NA of Electrical Distributors Inc (NAED)					
1100 Corporate Sq Dr.	Saint Louis	MO	63132	314-991-9000	991-3060
TF: 888-791-2512 ■ *Web:* www.naed.org					
NA of Fire Equipment Distributors (NAFED)					
122 S Michigan Ave Suite 1040	Chicago	IL	60603	312-461-9600	461-0777
Web: www.nafed.org					
NA of Recording Merchandisers (NARM)					
9 Eves Dr Suite 120	Marlton	NJ	08053	856-596-2221	596-3268
Web: www.narm.com					
NA of Steel Pipe Distributors (NASPD)					
1501 E Mockingbird Ln Suite 307	Victoria	TX	77904	361-574-7878	201-9479*
**Fax Area Code:* 832 ■ *Web:* www.naspd.com					
NA of Wholesaler-Distributors (NAWD)					
1325 G St NW Suite 1000	Washington	DC	20005	202-872-0885	785-0586
Web: www.naw.org					
NAMM - International Music Products Assn					
5790 Armada Dr	Carlsbad	CA	92008	760-438-8001	438-7327
TF: 800-767-6266 ■ *Web:* www.namm.org					
National Agri-Marketing Assn (NAMA)					
11020 King St Suite 205	Overland Park	KS	66210	913-491-6500	491-6502
TF: 800-530-5646 ■ *Web:* www.nama.org					
National Art Materials Trade Assn					
15806 Brookway Dr Suite 300	Huntersville	NC	28078	704-892-6244	892-6247
Web: www.namta.org					
National Assn of General Merchandise Representatives					
16A Journey Suite 200	Aliso Viejo	CA	92656	949-859-4040	855-2973
Web: www.nagmr.com					
National Auctioneers Assn (NAA)					
8880 Ballentine St	Overland Park	KS	66214	913-541-8084	894-5281
TF: 888-541-8084 ■ *Web:* www.auctioneers.org					
National Auto Auction Assn (NAAA)					
5320 Spectrum Dr Suite D	Frederick	MD	21703	301-696-0400	631-1359
Web: www.naaa.com					
National Automatic Merchandising Assn (NAMA)					
20 N Wacker Dr Suite 3500	Chicago	IL	60606	312-346-0370	704-4140
Web: www.vending.org					
National Automobile Dealers Assn (NADA)					
8400 Westpark Dr.	McLean	VA	22102	703-821-7000	821-7075
TF: 800-252-6232 ■ *Web:* www.nada.org					
National Cotton Council of America					
7193 Goodlett Farms Pkwy	Memphis	TN	38016	901-274-9030	725-0510
TF: 800-377-9030 ■ *Web:* www.cotton.org					
National Electrical Manufacturers Representatives Assn (NEMRA)					
28 Deer St Suite 302	Portsmouth	NH	03801	914-524-8650	319-1667*
**Fax Area Code:* 603 ■ *TF:* 800-446-3672 ■ *Web:* www.nemra.org					
National Electronic Distributors Assn (NEDA)					
1111 Alderman Dr Suite 400	Alpharetta	GA	30005	678-393-9990	393-9998
TF: 800-347-6332 ■ *Web:* www.nedassoc.org					
National Electronics Service Dealers Assn (NESDA)					
3608 Pershing Ave	Fort Worth	TX	76107	817-921-9061	921-3741
TF: 800-946-0201 ■ *Web:* www.nesda.com					
National Foreign Trade Council (NFTC)					
1625 K St NW Suite 200	Washington	DC	20006	202-887-0278	452-8160
Web: www.nftc.org					
National Independent Automobile Dealers Assn (NIADA)					
2521 Brown Blvd	Arlington	TX	76006	817-640-3838	649-5866
TF: 800-682-3837 ■ *Web:* www.niada.com					
National Independent Flag Dealers Assn (NIFDA)					
214 N Hale St	Wheaton	IL	60187	630-510-4500	510-4501
TF: 877-544-3524 ■ *Web:* www.nifda.org					
National Luggage Dealers Assn (NLDA)					
1817 Elmdale Ave	Glenview	IL	60026	847-998-6869	998-6884
TF: 866-998-6869 ■ *Web:* www.nlda.com					
National Lumber & Bldg Material Dealers Assn (NLBMDA)					
2025 M St NW	Washington	DC	20036	202-367-1159	367-2169
TF: 800-634-8645 ■ *Web:* www.dealer.org					
National Mail Order Assn LLC (NMOA)					
2807 Polk St NE	Minneapolis	MN	55418	612-788-1673	788-1147
Web: www.nmoa.org					
National Marine Representatives Assn (NMRA)					
1333 Delany Rd Suite 500	Gurnee	IL	60031	847-662-3167	336-7146
Web: www.nmraonline.org					
National Minority Supplier Development Council (NMSDC)					
1359 Broadway 10th Fl	New York	NY	10018	212-944-2430	719-9611
TF: 888-396-1110 ■ *Web:* www.nmsdc.org					
National Retail Federation (NRF)					
325 7th St NW Suite 1100	Washington	DC	20004	202-783-7971	737-2849
TF: 800-673-4692 ■ *Web:* www.nrf.com					
National Retail Hardware Assn (NRHA)					
5822 W 74th St.	Indianapolis	IN	46278	317-290-0338	328-4354
TF Cust Svc: 800-772-4424 ■ *Web:* www.nrha.org					
National School Supply & Equipment Assn (NSSEA)					
8380 Colesville Rd Suite 250	Silver Spring	MD	20910	301-495-0240	495-3330
TF: 800-395-5550 ■ *Web:* www.nssea.org					
National Shoe Retailers Assn (NSRA)					
7150 Columbia Gateway Dr Suite G	Columbia	MD	21046	410-381-8282	381-1167
TF: 800-673-8446 ■ *Web:* www.nsra.org					
Network of Ingredient Marketing Specialists Inc (NIMS)					
630 Village Trace NE Bldg 15 Suite A	Marietta	GA	30067	770-989-0049	770-7498
Web: www.nimsgroup.com					
North American Bldg Material Distribution Assn (NBMDA)					
401 N Michigan Ave Suite 2400	Chicago	IL	60611	312-644-6610	321-6869
TF: 888-747-7862 ■ *Web:* www.nbmda.org					
North American Equipment Dealers Assn (NAEDA)					
1195 Smizer Mill Rd	Fenton	MO	63026	636-349-5000	349-5443
Web: www.naeda.com					
North American Wholesale Lumber Assn (NAWLA)					
3601 Algonquin Rd Suite 400	Rolling Meadows	IL	60008	847-870-7470	870-0201
TF: 800-527-8258 ■ *Web:* www.lumber.org					
NPTA Alliance 401 N Michigan Ave Suite 2200	Chicago	IL	60611	312-321-4092	673-6736
TF: 800-355-6782 ■ *Web:* www.gonpta.com					
Office Products Wholesalers Assn					
5024 Campbell Blvd Suite R	Baltimore	MD	21236	410-931-8100	931-8111
Web: www.opwa.org					
Paint & Decorating Retailers Assn (PDRA)					
1401 Triad Ctr Dr	St. Peters	MO	63376	636-326-2636	326-1823
TF: 800-737-0107 ■ *Web:* www.pdra.org					
Pet Industry Distributors Assn (PIDA)					
2105 Laurel Bush Rd Suite 200	Bel Air	MD	21015	443-640-1060	640-1031
Web: www.pida.org					
Petroleum Marketers Assn of America (PMAA)					
1901 N Fort Myer Dr Suite 500	Arlington	VA	22209	703-351-8000	351-9160
TF: 800-300-7622 ■ *Web:* www.pmaa.org					
Photo Marketing Assn International (PMA)					
3000 Picture Pl	Jackson	MI	49201	517-788-8100	788-8371
TF: 800-762-9287 ■ *Web:* www.pmai.org					
Point-of-Purchase Adv International (POPAI)					
1600 Duke St Suite 400	Alexandria	VA	22314	703-373-8800	373-8801
TF: 888-407-6724 ■ *Web:* www.popai.com					
Power Transmission Distributors Assn (PTDA)					
230 W Monroe St Suite 1410	Chicago	IL	60606	312-516-2100	516-2101
Web: www.ptda.org					
Private Label Manufacturers Assn (PLMA)					
630 3rd Ave 4th Fl	New York	NY	10017	212-972-3131	212-1382
Web: plma.com					

	City	State	Zip	Phone	Fax
Professional Beauty Assn (PBA) 15825 N 71st St Suite 100 *TF:* 800-468-2274 ■ *Web:* www.probeauty.org	Scottsdale	AZ	85254	480-281-0424	905-0708
Promotion Marketing Assn Inc (PMA) 650 1st Ave Suite 2-SW *Web:* www.pmalink.org	New York	NY	10016	212-420-1100	533-7622
Promotional Products Assn International (PPAI) 3125 Skyway Cir N *TF:* 888-426-7724 ■ *Web:* www.ppai.org	Irving	TX	75038	972-252-0404	258-3004
Public Relations Society of America (PRSA) 33 Maiden Ln 11th Fl *TF:* 800-937-7772 ■ *Web:* www.prsa.org	New York	NY	10038	212-460-1400	995-0757
Qualitative Research Consultants Assn Inc (QRCA) 1000 Westgate Dr Suite 252 *TF:* 888-674-7722 ■ *Web:* www.qrca.org	Saint Paul	MN	55114	651-290-7491	290-2260
Radio Adv Bureau (RAB) 125 W 55th St 21st Fl *TF:* 800-252-7234 ■ *Web:* www.rab.com	New York	NY	10019	212-681-7200	681-7223
Recreation Vehicle Dealers Assn (RVDA) 3930 University Dr 3rd Fl *TF:* 800-336-0355 ■ *Web:* www.rvda.org	Fairfax	VA	22030	703-591-7130	591-0734
Retail Adv & Marketing Assn (RAMA) 325 7th St NW Suite 1100 *TF:* 800-673-4692 ■ *Web:* www.rama-nrf.org	Washington	DC	20004	202-661-3052	737-2849
Retail Industry Leaders Assn (RILA) 1700 N Moore St Suite 2250 *Web:* www.rila.org	Arlington	VA	22209	703-841-2300	841-1184
Retail Solutions Providers Assn (RSPA) 415 Taggart Creek Rd **Fax Area Code:* 800 ■ *Web:* www.gorspa.org	Charlotte	NC	28208	704-357-3124	982-4043*
Society for Marketing Professional Services (SMPS) 99 Canal Ctr Plaza *TF:* 800-292-7677 ■ *Web:* www.smps.org	Alexandria	VA	22314	703-549-6117	549-2498
Society of Independent Gasoline Marketers of America (SIGMA) 11495 Sunset Hills Rd Suite 215 *Web:* www.sigma.org	Reston	VA	20190	703-709-7000	709-7007
Souvenirs Gifts & Novelties Trade Assn 10 E Athens Ave Suite 208 *TF:* 800-284-5451	Ardmore	PA	19003	610-645-6940	645-6943
Specialty Tools & Fasteners Distributors Assn (STAFDA) 500 Elm Grove Rd Suite 210 PO Box 44 *TF:* 800-352-2981 ■ *Web:* www.stafda.org	Elm Grove	WI	53122	262-784-4774	784-5059
Television Bureau of Adv (TVB) 3 E 54th St 10th Fl *Web:* www.tvb.org	New York	NY	10022	212-486-1111	935-5631
Trade Show Exhibitors Assn (TSEA) 2301 S Lake Shore Dr Suite 1005 *Web:* www.tsea.org	Chicago	IL	60616	312-842-8732	842-8744
Traffic Audit Bureau for Media Measurement (TAB) 271 Madison Ave Suite 1504 *Web:* www.tabonline.com	New York	NY	10016	212-972-8075	
Video Software Dealers Assn (VSDA) 16530 Ventura Blvd Suite 400 *TF:* 800-955-8732 ■ *Web:* www.idealink.org/Resource.phx/public/aboutvsda.htx	Encino	CA	91436	818-385-1500	385-0567
Wholesale Florist & Florist Supplier Assn (WF&FSA) 105 Eastern Ave Suite 104 *TF:* 888-289-3372 ■ *Web:* www.wffsa.org	Annapolis	MD	21403	410-940-6580	263-1659

49-19 Technology, Science, Engineering Professionals Associations

	City	State	Zip	Phone	Fax
ABET Inc 111 Market Pl Suite 1050 *Web:* www.abet.org	Baltimore	MD	21202	410-347-7700	625-2238
Acoustical Society of America (ASA) 2 Huntington Quadrangle Suite 1NO1 *Web:* www.acousticalsociety.org	Melville	NY	11747	516-576-2360	576-2377
AIIM - Enterprise Content Management Assn 1100 Wayne Ave Suite 1100 *TF:* 800-477-2446 ■ *Web:* www.aiim.org	Silver Spring	MD	20910	301-587-8202	587-2711
AIM Global - Assn for Automatic Identification & Mobility 125 Warrendale-Bayne Rd Suite 100 *TF:* 800-338-0206 ■ *Web:* www.aimglobal.org	Warrendale	PA	15086	724-934-4470	934-4495
American Assn for Clinical Chemistry Inc (AACC) 1850 K St NW Suite 625 *TF Cust Svc:* 800-892-1400 ■ *Web:* www.aacc.org	Washington	DC	20006	202-857-0717	887-5093
American Assn for Laboratory Accreditation (A2LA) 5301 Buckeystown Pike Suite 350 *Web:* www.a2la.org	Frederick	MD	21704	301-644-3248	662-2974
American Assn for Laboratory Animal Science (AALAS) 9190 Crestwyn Hills Dr *Web:* www.aalas.org	Memphis	TN	38125	901-754-8620	753-0046
American Assn for the Advancement of Science (AAAS) 1200 New York Ave NW *TF:* 800-731-4939 ■ *Web:* www.aaas.org	Washington	DC	20005	202-326-6400	682-0816
American Assn of Engineering Societies (AAES) 1620 'I' St NW Suite 210 *TF Orders:* 888-400-2237 ■ *Web:* www.aaes.org	Washington	DC	20006	202-296-2237	296-1151
American Assn of Pharmaceutical Scientists (AAPS) 2107 Wilson Blvd Suite 700 *TF:* 877-998-2277 ■ *Web:* www.aaps.org	Arlington	VA	22201	703-243-2800	243-9650
American Assn of Physicists in Medicine (AAPM) 1 Physics Ellipse *Web:* www.aapm.org	College Park	MD	20740	301-209-3350	209-0862
American Assn of Variable Star Observers (AAVSO) 49 Bay State Rd *Web:* www.aavso.org	Cambridge	MA	02138	617-354-0484	354-0665
American Astronomical Society (AAS) 2000 Florida Ave NW Suite 400 *Web:* www.aas.org	Washington	DC	20009	202-328-2010	234-2560
American Chemical Society (ACS) 1155 16th St NW *TF:* 800-227-5558 ■ *Web:* www.acs.org	Washington	DC	20036	202-872-4600	872-4615
American Council of Engineering Cos (ACEC) 1015 15th St NW 8th Fl *Web:* www.acec.org	Washington	DC	20005	202-347-7474	898-0068
American Council of Independent Laboratories (ACIL) 1875 I&St NW Suite 500 *Web:* www.acil.org	Washington	DC	20006	202-887-5872	887-0021
American Council on Science & Health (ACSH) 1995 Broadway 2nd Fl *TF:* 866-905-2694 ■ *Web:* www.acsh.org	New York	NY	10023	212-362-7044	362-4919
American Electrophoresis Society The 1202 Ann St *TF:* 800-462-3417 ■ *Web:* www.aesociety.org	Madison	WI	53713	608-258-1565	258-1569
American Geological Institute (AGI) 4220 King St *Web:* www.agiweb.org	Alexandria	VA	22302	703-379-2480	379-7563
American Geophysical Union (AGU) 2000 Florida Ave NW *TF:* 800-966-2481 ■ *Web:* www.agu.org	Washington	DC	20009	202-462-6900	328-0566
American Indian Science & Engineering Society (AISES) 2305 Renard SE Suite 200 *Web:* www.aises.org	Albuquerque	NM	87106	505-765-1052	765-5608
American Institute of Aeronautics & Astronautics Inc (AIAA) 1801 Alexander Bell Dr Suite 500 *TF:* 800-639-2422 ■ *Web:* www.aiaa.org	Reston	VA	20191	703-264-7500	264-7551
American Institute of Biological Sciences (AIBS) 1444 'I' St NW Suite 200 *TF:* 800-992-2427 ■ *Web:* www.aibs.org	Washington	DC	20005	202-628-1500	628-1509
American Institute of Chemical Engineers (AIChE) 3 Pk Ave 19th Fl *TF Cust Svc:* 800-242-4363 ■ *Web:* www.aiche.org	New York	NY	10016	203-702-7660	775-5177
American Institute of Chemists (AIC) 315 Chestnut St *Web:* www.theaic.org	Philadelphia	PA	19106	215-873-8224	925-1954
American Institute of Engineers Inc (AIE) 4630 Appian Way Suite 206 *Web:* www.aieonline.org	El Sobrante	CA	94803	510-758-6240	
American Institute of Physics 1 Physics Ellipse *Web:* www.aip.org	College Park	MD	20740	301-209-3100	209-0843
American Institute of Professional Geologists (AIPG) 1400 W 122nd Ave Suite 250 *Web:* www.aipg.org	Westminster	CO	80234	303-412-6205	253-9220
American Mathematical Society (AMS) 201 Charles St PO Box 6248 *TF Cust Svc:* 800-321-4267 ■ *Web:* www.ams.org	Providence	RI	02940	401-455-4000	331-3842
American Meteorological Society (AMS) 45 Beacon St *Web:* www.ametsoc.org	Boston	MA	02108	617-227-2425	742-8718
American Nuclear Society (ANS) 555 N Kensington Ave *TF:* 800-323-3044 ■ *Web:* www.ans.org	La Grange Park	IL	60526	708-352-6611	352-0499
American Physical Society (APS) 1 Physics Ellipse *Web:* www.aps.org	College Park	MD	20740	301-209-3200	209-0865
American Phytopathological Society The (APS) 3340 Pilot Knob Rd *Web:* www.apsnet.org/Pages/default.aspx	Saint Paul	MN	55121	651-454-7250	454-0766
American Rock Mechanics Assn (ARMA) 600 Woodland Terr *Web:* www.armarocks.org	Alexandria	VA	22302	703-683-1808	683-1815
American Society for Biochemistry & Molecular Biology (ASBMB) 9650 Rockville Pike *Web:* www.asbmb.org	Bethesda	MD	20814	301-634-7145	634-7126
American Society for Cell Biology (ASCB) 8120 Woodmont Ave Suite 750 *Web:* www.ascb.org	Bethesda	MD	20814	301-347-9300	347-9310
American Society for Engineering Education (ASEE) 1818 N St NW Suite 600 *Web:* www.asee.org	Washington	DC	20036	202-331-3500	265-8504
American Society for Nondestructive Testing Inc (ASNT) 1711 Arlingate Ln PO Box 28518 *TF Orders:* 800-222-2768 ■ *Web:* www.asnt.org	Columbus	OH	43228	614-274-6003	274-6899
American Society for Photobiology (ASP) 810 E 10th St *TF:* 800-627-0629 ■ *Web:* www.photobiology.org	Lawrence	KS	66044	785-843-1234	843-1274
American Society for Photogrammetry & Remote Sensing The (ASPRS) 5410 Grosvenor Ln Suite 210 *Web:* www.asprs.org	Bethesda	MD	20814	301-493-0290	493-0208

Organization	City	State	ZIP	Phone	Fax
American Society of Human Genetics (ASHG) 9650 Rockville Pike *TF:* 866-486-4363 ■ *Web:* www.ashg.org	Bethesda	MD	20814	301-634-7300	634-7079
American Society of Ichthyologists & Herpetologists Florida International Univ Biology Dept 11200 SW 8th St *Web:* www.asih.org	Miami	FL	33199	305-348-1235	348-1986
American Society of Limnology & Oceanography (ASLO) 5400 Bosque Blvd Suite 680 *TF:* 800-929-2756 ■ *Web:* www.aslo.org	Waco	TX	76710	254-399-9635	776-3767
American Society of Mechanical Engineers (ASME) 3 Pk Ave *TF Cust Svc:* 800-843-2763 ■ *Web:* www.asme.org	New York	NY	10016	212-591-7722	591-7739
American Society of Plant Biologists (ASPB) 15501 Monona Dr *Web:* www.aspb.org	Rockville	MD	20855	301-251-0560	279-2996
American Society of Safety Engineers (ASSE) 1800 E Oakton St *Web:* www.asse.org	Des Plaines	IL	60018	847-699-2929	768-3434
American Statistical Assn (ASA) 732 N Washington St *TF:* 888-231-3473 ■ *Web:* www.amstat.org	Alexandria	VA	22314	703-684-1221	684-2037
AOAC International 481 N Frederick Ave Suite 500 *TF:* 800-379-2622 ■ *Web:* www.aoac.org	Gaithersburg	MD	20877	301-924-7077	924-7089
ASFE 8811 Colesville Rd Suite G106 *Web:* www.asfe.org	Silver Spring	MD	20910	301-565-2733	589-2017
ASME International Gas Turbine Institute (IGTI) 6525 the Corners Pkwy *Web:* www.igti.asme.org	Norcross	GA	30092	404-847-0072	847-0151
Assn for Women in Science Inc (AWIS) 1321 Duke St Suite 210 *TF:* 800-886-2947 ■ *Web:* www.awis.org	Alexandria	VA	22314	703-894-4490	894-4489
Assn of American Geographers (AAG) 1710 16th St NW *Web:* www.aag.org	Washington	DC	20009	202-234-1450	234-2744
Assn of Consulting Chemists & Chemical Engineers (ACC&CE) PO Box 297 *Web:* www.chemconsult.org	Sparta	NJ	07871	973-729-6671	729-7088
Assn of Science-Technology Centers Inc (ASTC) 1025 Vermont Ave NW Suite 500 *Web:* www.astc.org	Washington	DC	20005	202-783-7200	783-7207
Assn of University Technology Managers (AUTM) 111 Deer Lake Rd SDuite 100 *Web:* www.autm.net	Deerfield	IL	60062	847-559-0846	480-9282
ASTM International 100 Barr Harbor Dr PO Box C700 *Web:* www.astm.org	West Conshohocken	PA	19428	610-832-9500	832-9555
Audio Engineering Society 60 E 42nd St Rm 2520 *TF:* 800-541-7299 ■ *Web:* www.aes.org	New York	NY	10165	212-661-8528	682-0477
AVS Science & Technology Society 120 Wall St 32nd Fl *Web:* www.avs.org	New York	NY	10005	212-248-0200	248-0245
Biophysical Society (BPS) 9650 Rockville Pike *Web:* www.biophysics.org	Bethesda	MD	20814	301-634-7114	634-7133
Biotechnology Industry Organization 1201 Maryland Ave SW Suite 900 *TF:* 800-255-3304 ■ *Web:* www.bio.org	Washington	DC	20024	202-962-9200	488-6301
Center for Chemical Process Safety (CCPS) 3 Pk Ave *Web:* www.aiche.org/CCPS/index.aspx	New York	NY	10016	646-495-1371	495-1504
Center for Science in the Public Interest (CSPI) 1875 Connecticut Ave NW Suite 300 *Web:* www.cspinet.org	Washington	DC	20009	202-332-9110	265-4954
Clinical Laboratory Management Assn (CLMA) 401 N Michigan Ave Suite 2200 *Web:* www.clma.org	Chicago	IL	60611	312-321-5111	673-6927
Clinical Ligand Assay Society (CLAS) 3139 S Wayne Rd *Web:* www.clas.org	Wayne	MI	48184	734-722-6290	722-7006
Commission on Professionals in Science & Technology (CPST) 1200 New York Ave NW Suite 113 *Web:* www.cpst.org	Washington	DC	20005	202-326-7080	842-1603
Committee of Concerned Scientists 145 W 79th St Suite 4D **Fax Area Code:* 917 ■ *Web:* www.libertynet.org/ccs	New York	NY	10024	212-362-4441	441-1759*
Controlled Release Society The (CRS) 3340 Pilot Knob Rd *Web:* www.controlledreleasesociety.org	Saint Paul	MN	55121	651-454-7250	454-0766
Coordinating Research Council Inc (CRC) 3650 Mansell Rd Suite 140 *Web:* www.crcao.com	Alpharetta	GA	30022	678-795-0506	795-0509
Council for Chemical Research Inc (CCR) 1730 Rhode Island Ave NW Suite 302 *Web:* www.ccrhq.org	Washington	DC	20036	202-429-3971	429-3976
Council for Responsible Genetics (CRG) 5 Upland Rd Suite 3 *Web:* www.councilforresponsiblegenetics.org	Cambridge	MA	02140	617-868-0870	491-5344
Cryogenic Society of America Inc (CSA) 218 Lake St *Web:* www.cryogenicsociety.org	Oak Park	IL	60302	708-383-6220	383-9337
Custom Electronic Design & Installation Assn (CEDIA) 7150 Winton Dr Suite 300 *TF:* 800-669-5329 ■ *Web:* www.cedia.net	Indianapolis	IN	46268	317-328-4336	735-4012
Drug Chemical & Associated Technologies Assn (DCAT) 1 Washington Blvd Suite 7 *TF:* 800-640-3228 ■ *Web:* www.dcat.org	Robbinsville	NJ	08691	609-448-1000	448-1944
Earthquake Engineering Research Institute (EERI) 499 14th St Suite 320 *Web:* www.eeri.org	Oakland	CA	94612	510-451-0905	451-5411
Ecological Society of America (ESA) 1990 M St Suite 700 *Web:* www.esa.org	Washington	DC	20036	202-833-8773	833-8775
Electrical Apparatus Service Assn (EASA) 1331 Baur Blvd *Web:* www.easa.com	Saint Louis	MO	63132	314-993-2220	993-1269
Electrochemical Society 65 S Main St Bldg D *Web:* www.electrochem.org	Pennington	NJ	08534	609-737-1902	737-2743
Electronics Technicians Assn International (ETA) 5 Depot St *TF:* 800-288-3824 ■ *Web:* www.eta-i.org	Greencastle	IN	46135	765-653-8262	653-4287
Engineering Contractors' Assn (ECA) 8310 Florence Ave *TF:* 800-293-2240 ■ *Web:* www.ecaonline.net	Downey	CA	90240	562-861-0929	923-6179
Entomological Society of America 10001 Derekwood Ln Suite 100 *Web:* www.entsoc.org	Lanham	MD	20706	301-731-4535	731-4538
Federation of American Scientists (FAS) 1725 DeSales St NW 6th Fl *Web:* www.fas.org	Washington	DC	20036	202-546-3300	315-5847
Federation of American Societies for Experimental Biology (FASEB) 9650 Rockville Pike *TF:* 800-433-2732 ■ *Web:* www.faseb.org	Bethesda	MD	20814	301-634-7000	634-7001
Foundation for Advanced Education in the Sciences (FAES) 1 Cloister Ct Suite 230 *Web:* www.faes.org	Bethesda	MD	20814	301-496-7976	402-0174
Generic Pharmaceutical Assn (GPhA) 2300 Clarendon Blvd Suite 400 *Web:* www.gphaonline.org	Arlington	VA	22201	703-647-2480	647-2481
Genetics Society of America (GSA) 9650 Rockville Pike *TF:* 866-486-4363 ■ *Web:* www.genetics-gsa.org	Bethesda	MD	20814	301-634-7300	634-7079
Geological Society of America The (GSA) 3300 Penrose Pl PO Box 9140 *TF:* 800-472-1988 ■ *Web:* www.geosociety.org	Boulder	CO	80301	303-357-1000	357-1070
Geospatial Information & Technology Assn (GITA) 14456 E Evans Ave *Web:* www.gita.org	Aurora	CO	80014	303-337-0513	337-1001
IEEE Aerospace & Electronics Systems Society IEEE Operations Ctr 445 Hoes Ln *TF:* 800-678-4333 ■ *Web:* www.ewh.ieee.org/soc/aes	Piscataway	NJ	08854	732-981-0060	562-6380
IEEE Antennas & Propagation Society (APS) IEEE Operations Ctr 445 Hoes Ln *TF:* 800-678-4333 ■ *Web:* www.ieeeaps.org	Piscataway	NJ	08854	732-981-0060	562-6380
IEEE Broadcast Technology Society (BTS) IEEE Operations Ctr 445 Hoes Ln *TF:* 800-678-4333 ■ *Web:* www.ieee.org/organizations/society/bt	Piscataway	NJ	08854	732-981-0060	562-6380
IEEE Circuits & Systems Society (CAS) IEEE Operations Ctr 445 Hoes Ln *TF:* 800-678-4333 ■ *Web:* www.ieee-cas.org	Piscataway	NJ	08854	732-981-0060	562-6380
IEEE Communications Society (COMSOC) 3 Pk Ave 17th Fl *Web:* www.comsoc.org	New York	NY	10016	212-705-8910	705-8999
IEEE Components Packaging & Mfg Technology Society 445 Hoes Ln PO Box 1331 *TF:* 800-678-4333 ■ *Web:* www.cpmt.org	Piscataway	NJ	08855	732-562-5529	981-1769
IEEE Computational Intelligence Society (CIS) 9330 Scranton Rd Suite 150 *Web:* www.ieee-cis.org	San Diego	CA	92121	858-455-6449	455-1560
IEEE Computer Society 2001 L St NW Suite 200 *TF:* 800-272-6657 ■ *Web:* www.computer.org	Washington	DC	20036	202-371-0101	728-9614
IEEE Consumer Electronics Society (CES) IEEE Operations Ctr 445 Hoes Ln *TF:* 800-678-4333 ■ *Web:* www.ewh.ieee.org/soc/ces	Piscataway	NJ	08854	732-981-0060	562-6380
IEEE Control Systems Society (CSS) IEEE Operations Ctr 445 Hoes Ln *TF:* 800-678-4333 ■ *Web:* www.ieeecss.org	Piscataway	NJ	08854	732-981-0060	562-6380
IEEE Dielectrics & Electrical Insulation Society IEEE Operations Ctr 445 Hoes Ln *Web:* www.tdei.sju.edu/deis	Piscataway	NJ	08854	732-981-0060	
IEEE Education Society (ES) IEEE Operations Ctr 445 Hoes Ln *TF:* 800-678-4333 ■ *Web:* www.ewh.ieee.org/soc/es	Piscataway	NJ	08854	732-981-0060	562-6380
IEEE Electromagnetic Compatibility Society (EMC) IEEE Operations Ctr 445 Hoes Ln *TF:* 800-678-4333 ■ *Web:* www.ewh.ieee.org/soc/emcs	Piscataway	NJ	08854	732-981-0060	562-6380
IEEE Electron Devices Society (EDS) IEEE Operations Ctr 445 Hoes Ln *TF:* 800-678-4333 ■ *Web:* www.eds.ieee.org	Piscataway	NJ	08854	732-981-0060	562-6380
IEEE Engineering in Medicine & Biology Society (EMB) *IEEE Operations Ctr* 445 Hoes Ln *TF:* 800-678-4333 ■ *Web:* www.embs.org	Piscataway	NJ	08855	732-981-3433	465-6435
IEEE Engineering Management Society (EMS) IEEE Operations Ctr 445 Hoes Ln *TF:* 800-678-4333 ■ *Web:* www.ewh.ieee.org/soc/ems	Piscataway	NJ	08854	732-981-0060	562-6380
IEEE Geoscience & Remote Sensing Society (GRSS) IEEE Operations Ctr 445 Hoes Ln *TF:* 800-678-4333 ■ *Web:* www.ewh.ieee.org/soc/grss	Piscataway	NJ	08854	732-981-0060	562-6380
IEEE Industrial Electronics Society (IES) IEEE Operations Ctr 445 Hoes Ln *TF:* 800-678-4333 ■ *Web:* www.ewh.ieee.org/soc/ies	Piscataway	NJ	08854	732-981-0060	562-6380
IEEE Industry Applications Society IEEE Operations Ctr 445 Hoes Ln *Web:* www.ias.ieee.org	Piscataway	NJ	08854	732-465-6627	
IEEE Instrumentation & Measurement Society (IM) IEEE Operations Ctr 445 Hoes Ln *TF:* 800-678-4333 ■ *Web:* www.ieee-ims.org	Piscataway	NJ	08854	732-981-0060	562-6380
IEEE Magnetics Society IEEE Operations Ctr 445 Hoes Ln *TF:* 800-678-4333 ■ *Web:* www.ieeemagnetics.org	Piscataway	NJ	08854	732-981-0060	562-6380
IEEE Microwave Theory & Techniques Society (MTT-S) IEEE Operations Ctr 445 Hoes Ln *TF:* 800-678-4333 ■ *Web:* www.mtt.org	Piscataway	NJ	08854	732-981-0060	562-6380

Phone | Fax

IEEE Nuclear & Plasma Sciences Society (NPSS)
IEEE Operations Ctr 445 Hoes Ln ... Piscataway NJ 08854 732-981-0060 562-6380
TF: 800-678-4333 ■ *Web:* www.ewh.ieee.org/soc/nps

IEEE Oceanic Engineering Society (OES)
IEEE Operations Ctr 445 Hoes Ln ... Piscataway NJ 08854 732-981-0060 562-6380
TF: 800-678-4333 ■ *Web:* www.oceanicengineering.org

IEEE Photonics Society
IEEE Operations Ctr 445 Hoes Ln ... Piscataway NJ 08854 732-981-0060 562-6380
TF: 800-678-4333 ■ *Web:* www.photonicssociety.org

IEEE Power Engineering Society (PES)
IEEE Operations Ctr 445 Hoes Ln ... Piscataway NJ 08854 732-562-3883 562-3881
TF: 800-678-4333 ■ *Web:* www.ieee.org/portal/index.jsp?pageID=pes_home

IEEE Product Safety Engineering Society
IEEE Operations Ctr 445 Hoes Ln ... Piscataway NJ 08854 732-981-0060 562-6380
TF: 800-678-4333 ■ *Web:* www.ewh.ieee.org/soc/pses

IEEE Reliability Society (RS)
IEEE Operations Ctr 445 Hoes Ln ... Piscataway NJ 08854 732-981-0060 562-6380
TF: 800-678-4333 ■ *Web:* www.ieee.org/portal/site

IEEE Robotics & Automation Society (RAS)
IEEE Operations Ctr 445 Hoes Ln ... Piscataway NJ 08854 732-981-0060 562-6380
TF: 800-678-4333 ■ *Web:* www.ieee-ras.org

IEEE Signal Processing Society
IEEE Operations Ctr 445 Hoes Ln ... Piscataway NJ 08854 732-981-0060 562-6380
TF: 800-678-4333 ■ *Web:* www.signalprocessingsociety.org

IEEE Society on Social Implications of Technology (SSIT)
IEEE Operations Ctr 445 Hoes Ln ... Piscataway NJ 08854 732-981-0060 562-6380
TF: 800-678-4333 ■ *Web:* www.ieeessit.org

IEEE Solid State Circuits Society (SSCS)
IEEE Operations Ctr 445 Hoes Ln ... Piscataway NJ 08854 732-981-0060 562-6380
TF: 800-678-4333 ■ *Web:* www.sscs.org

IEEE Systems Man & Cybernetics Society (SMC)
3 Pk Ave 17th Fl ... New York NY 10016 212-419-7900 752-4929
TF: 800-678-4333 ■ *Web:* www.ieeesmc.org

IEEE Ultrasonics Ferroelectrics & Frequency Control Society
IEEE Operations Ctr 445 Hoes Ln ... Piscataway NJ 08854 732-981-0060 562-6380
TF: 800-678-4333 ■ *Web:* www.ieee-uffc.org

IEEE Vehicular Technology Society (VTS)
IEEE Operations Ctr 445 Hoes Ln ... Piscataway NJ 08854 732-981-0060 562-6380
TF: 800-678-4333 ■ *Web:* www.vtsociety.org

Industrial Research Institute Inc (IRI)
2200 Clarendon Blvd Suite 1102 ... Arlington VA 22201 703-647-2580 647-2581
Web: www.iriweb.org

Institute for Operations Research & the Management Sciences (INFORMS)
7240 Pkwy Dr Suite 300 ... Hanover MD 21076 443-757-3500 757-3515
TF: 800-446-3676 ■ *Web:* www.informs.org

Institute of Electrical & Electronics Engineers (IEEE)
3 Pk Ave 17th Fl ... New York NY 10016 212-419-7900 752-4929
TF: 800-678-4333 ■ *Web:* www.ieee.org

Institute of Environmental Sciences & Technology (IEST)
2340 S Arlington Heights Rd
Suite 100 ... Arlington Heights IL 60005 847-981-0100 981-4130
Web: www.iest.org

International Assn for Radio Telecommunications & Electromagnetics (iNARTE)
840 Queen St ... New Bern NC 28560 252-672-0200 672-0111
TF: 800-896-2783 ■ *Web:* www.narte.org

International Biometric Society (IBS)
1444 'I' St NW Suite 700 ... Washington DC 20005 202-712-9049 216-9646
Web: www.tibs.org

International Center for Technology Assessment (ICTA)
660 Pennsylvania Ave SE Suite 302 ... Washington DC 20003 202-547-9359 547-9429
TF: 800-600-6664 ■ *Web:* www.icta.org

International Engineering Consortium (IEC)
300 W Adams St Suite 1210 ... Chicago IL 60606 312-559-4100 559-4111
Web: www.iec.org

International Fragrance Assn North America (IFRA)
1620 'I' St NW Suite 925 ... Washington DC 20006 202-293-5800 463-8998
Web: www.fmafragrance.org

International Microelectronics & Packaging Society (IMAPS)
611 2nd St NE ... Washington DC 20002 202-548-4001 548-6115
Web: www.imaps.org

International Society for Pharmaceutical Engineering (ISPE)
3109 W Dr ML King Jr Blvd Suite 250 ... Tampa FL 33607 813-960-2105 264-2816
Web: www.ispe.org

International Society of Certified Electronics Technicians (ISCET)
3608 Pershing Ave ... Fort Worth TX 76107 817-921-9101 921-3741
TF: 800-946-0201 ■ *Web:* www.iscet.org

International Titanium Assn (ITA)
2655 W Midway Blvd Suite 300 ... Broomfield CO 80020 303-404-2221 404-9111
Web: www.titanium.org

IPC - Assn Connecting Electronics Industries
3000 Lakeside Dr Suite 309 ... Bannockburn IL 60015 847-615-7100 615-7105
Web: www.ipc.org

ISA - Instrumentation Systems & Automation Society
67 Alexander Dr PO Box 12277 ... Research Triangle Park NC 27709 919-549-8411 549-8288
Web: www.isa.org

Laser Institute of America (LIA)
13501 Ingenuity Dr Suite 128 ... Orlando FL 32826 407-380-1553 380-5588
TF: 800-345-2737 ■ *Web:* www.lia.org

Materials Properties Council (MPC)
PO Box 201547 ... Shaker Heights OH 44120 216-658-3847 658-3854
Web: www.forengineers.org/mpc/index.html

Materials Research Society (MRS)
506 Keystone Dr ... Warrendale PA 15086 724-779-3003 779-8313
Web: www.mrs.org

Mathematical Assn of America (MAA)
1529 18th St NW ... Washington DC 20036 202-387-5200 265-2384
TF: 800-331-1622 ■ *Web:* www.maa.org

Microscopy Society of America (MSA)
230 E Ohio St Suite 400 ... Chicago IL 60611 312-644-1527 644-8557
TF: 800-538-3672 ■ *Web:* www.msa.microscopy.org

Phone | Fax

MTM Assn for Standards & Research
1111 E Touhy Ave Suite 280 ... Des Plaines IL 60018 847-299-1111 299-3509
Web: www.mtm.org

National Academies 500 5th St NW ... Washington DC 20001 202-334-2138 334-2229
TF: 800-624-6242 ■ *Web:* www.nas.edu

National Academy of Engineering
500 5th Ave ... Washington DC 20001 202-334-3200 334-2290
Web: www.nae.edu

National Council on Radiation Protection & Measurements (NCRP)
7910 Woodmont Ave Suite 400 ... Bethesda MD 20814 301-657-2652 907-8768
TF: 800-229-2652 ■ *Web:* www.ncrponline.org

National Environmental Balancing Bureau (NEBB)
8575 Grovemont Cir ... Gaithersburg MD 20877 301-977-3698 977-9589
Web: www.nebb.org

National Geographic Society
1145 17th St NW ... Washington DC 20036 202-857-7000
TF: 800-647-5463 ■ *Web:* www.nationalgeographic.com

National Institute for Women in Trades Technology & Science (IWITTS)
1150 Ballena Blvd Suite 102 ... Alameda CA 94501 510-749-0200 749-0500
Web: www.iwitts.org

National Society of Black Physicists (NSBP)
1100 N Glebe Rd # 1010 ... Arlington VA 22201 703-536-4207 536-4203
Web: www.nsbp.org

National Society of Professional Engineers (NSPE)
1420 King St ... Alexandria VA 22314 703-684-2800 836-4875
TF: 888-285-6773 ■ *Web:* www.nspe.org

National Space Society (NSS)
1620 'I' St NW Suite 615 ... Washington DC 20006 202-429-1600 463-8497
Web: www.nss.org

New York Academy of Medicine (NYAM)
1216 5th Ave ... New York NY 10029 212-822-7200 423-0275
Web: www.nyam.org

New York Academy of Sciences
250 Greenwich St 40th Fl ... New York NY 10007 212-298-8600 298-3610
TF: 800-843-6927 ■ *Web:* www.nyas.org

Plasma Protein Therapeutics Assn (PPTA)
147 Old Solomon's Island Rd Suite 100 ... Annapolis MD 21401 202-789-3100 263-2298*
**Fax Area Code: 410* ■ *Web:* www.pptaglobal.org

Robotic Industries Assn (RIA)
900 Victors Way Suite 140 ... Ann Arbor MI 48108 734-994-6088 994-3338
Web: www.robotics.org

Scientific Equipment & Furniture Assn (SEFA)
1205 Franklin Ave Suite 320 ... Garden City NY 11530 516-294-5424 294-2758
Web: www.sefalabs.com

Semiconductor Environmental Safety & Health Assn (SESHA)
1313 Dolley Madison Blvd Suite 402 ... McLean VA 22101 703-790-1745 790-2672
Web: www.seshaonline.org

Semiconductor Equipment & Materials International
3081 Zenker Rd ... San Jose CA 95134 408-943-6900 428-9600
TF: 800-974-7364 ■ *Web:* www.semi.org

Semiconductor Industry Assn (SIA)
181 Metro Dr Suite 450 ... San Jose CA 95110 408-436-6600 436-6646
Web: www.sia-online.org

Silicones Environmental Health & Safety Council of North America
11921 Freedom Dr Suite 550 ... Reston VA 20190 703-904-4322 925-5955
Web: www.sehsc.com

Silver Research Consortium (SRC)
2525 Meridian Pkwy Suite 100 ... Durham NC 27713 919-361-4647 361-1957
Web: www.ilzro.org

Society for Biomaterials
15000 Commerce Pkwy Suite C ... Mount Laurel NJ 08054 856-439-0826 439-0525
Web: www.biomaterials.org

Society for Experimental Mechanics Inc (SEM)
7 School St ... Bethel CT 06801 203-790-6373 790-4472
Web: www.sem.org

Society for Industrial & Applied Mathematics (SIAM)
3600 Market St 6th Fl ... Philadelphia PA 19104 215-382-9800 386-7999
TF: 800-447-7426 ■ *Web:* www.siam.org

Society for Integrative & Comparative Biology (SICB)
1313 Dolley Madison Blvd Suite 402 ... McLean VA 22101 703-790-1745 790-2672
Web: www.sicb.org

Society for Risk Analysis (SRA)
1313 Dolley Madison Blvd Suite 402 ... McLean VA 22101 703-790-1745 790-2672
Web: www.sra.org

Society for Sedimentary Geology (SEPM)
4111 S Darlington Suite 100 ... Tulsa OK 74135 918-610-3361 621-1685
TF: 800-865-9765 ■ *Web:* www.sepm.org

Society for the Advancement of Material & Process Engineering (SAMPE)
1161 Pk View Dr Suite 200 ... Covina CA 91724 626-331-0616 332-8929
TF: 800-562-7360 ■ *Web:* www.sampe.org

Society of Cable Telecommunications Engineers (SCTE)
140 Philips Rd ... Exton PA 19341 610-363-6888 363-5898
TF: 800-542-5040 ■ *Web:* www.scte.org

Society of Cosmetic Chemists (SCC)
120 Wall St Suite 2400 ... New York NY 10005 212-668-1500 668-1504
Web: www.scconline.org

Society of Environmental Toxicology & Chemistry (SETAC)
1010 N 12th Ave ... Pensacola FL 32501 850-469-1500 469-9778
Web: www.setac.org

Society of Hispanic Professional Engineers (SHPE)
5400 E Olympic Blvd Suite 210 ... Los Angeles CA 90022 323-725-3970 725-0316
Web: www.oneshpe.shpe.org

Society of Women Engineers (SWE)
120 S La Salle St # 1515 ... Chicago IL 60603 312-596-5223 596-5252
Web: www.societyofwomenengineers.org

SPIE - International Society for Optical Engineering
1000 20th St ... Bellingham WA 98225 360-676-3290 647-1445
Web: www.spie.org

Synthetic Organic Chemical Manufacturers Assn (SOCMA)
1850 M St NW Suite 700 ... Washington DC 20036 202-721-4100 296-8120
TF: 888-377-0778 ■ *Web:* www.socma.com

Universities Research Assn Inc (URA)
1111 19th St NW Suite 400 ... Washington DC 20036 202-293-1382 293-5012
Web: www.ura-hq.org

Phone | Fax

Universities Space Research Assn (USRA)
10211 Wincopin Cir Suite 500 .... Columbia MD 21044 410-730-2656 730-3496
Web: www.usra.edu

Vibration Institute
6262 Kingery Hwy # 212 .... Willowbrook IL 60527 630-654-2254 654-2271
Web: www.vibinst.org

Women in Technology International (WITI)
13351-D Riverside Dr Suite 441 .... Sherman Oaks CA 91423 818-788-9484 788-9410
TF: 800-334-9484 ■ *Web:* www.witi.com

World Future Society
7910 Woodmont Ave Suite 450 .... Bethesda MD 20814 301-656-8274 951-0394
TF: 800-989-8274 ■ *Web:* www.wfs.org

49-20 Telecommunications Professionals Associations

Phone | Fax

Alliance for Telecommunications Industry Solutions (ATIS)
1200 G St NW Suite 500 .... Washington DC 20005 202-628-6380 393-5453
TF: 888-429-7517 ■ *Web:* www.atis.org

American Public Communications Council Inc (APCC)
625 Slaters Ln Suite 104 .... Alexandria VA 22314 703-739-1322 739-1324
TF: 800-868-2722 ■ *Web:* www.apcc.net

Communications Supply Service Assn (CSSA)
5700 Murray St .... Little Rock AR 72209 501-562-7666 562-7616
TF: 800-252-2772 ■ *Web:* www.cssa.net

COMPTEL 900 17th St NW Suite 400 .... Washington DC 20006 202-296-6650 296-7585
Web: www.comptel.org

Computer & Communications Industry Assn (CCIA)
666 11th St NW .... Washington DC 20001 202-783-0070 783-0534
Web: www.ccianet.org

CTIA - Wireless Assn
1400 16th St NW Suite 600 .... Washington DC 20036 202-785-0081 785-0721
Web: www.ctia.org

Enterprise Wireless Alliance (EWA)
8484 Westpark Dr Suite 630 .... McLean VA 22102 703-528-5115 524-1074
TF: 800-482-8282 ■ *Web:* www.enterprisewireless.org

Forest Industries Telecommunications (FIT)
1565 Oak St .... Eugene OR 97401 541-485-8441 485-7556
Web: www.landmobile.com

International Communications Industries Assn (ICIA)
11242 Waples Mill Rd Suite 200 .... Fairfax VA 22030 703-273-7200 278-8082
TF: 800-659-7469 ■ *Web:* www.infocomm.org

National Systems Contractors Assn (NSCA)
625 1st St SE Suite 420 .... Cedar Rapids IA 52401 319-366-6722 366-4164
TF: 800-446-6722 ■ *Web:* www.nsca.org

National Telecommunications Co-op Assn (NTCA)
4121 Wilson Blvd 10th Fl .... Arlington VA 22203 703-351-2000 351-2001
Web: www.ntca.org

Organization for the Promotion & Advancement of Small Telecommunications Cos (OPASTCO)
21 Dupont Cir NW Suite 700 .... Washington DC 20036 202-659-5990 659-4619
Web: www.opastco.org

PCIA - Wireless Infrastructure Assn
901 N Washington St Suite 600 .... Alexandria VA 22314 703-739-0300 836-1608
TF: 800-759-0300 ■ *Web:* www.pcia.com

Society of Telecommunications Consultants (STC)
13275 California 89 .... Old Station CA 96071 530-335-7313 335-7360
TF: 800-782-7670 ■ *Web:* www.stcconsultants.org

Telecommunications Industry Assn (TIA)
2500 Wilson Blvd Suite 300 .... Arlington VA 22201 703-907-7700 907-7727
Web: www.tiaonline.org

US Telecom Assn (USTA)
607-14th St NW Suite 400 .... Washington DC 20005 202-326-7300 315-3603
Web: www.ustelecom.org

Utilities Telecom Council (UTC)
1129 20th St NW Suite 350 .... Washington DC 20006 202-872-0030 872-1331
Web: www.utc.org

Wireless Communications Assn International (WCA)
1333 H St NW Suite 700W .... Washington DC 20005 202-452-7823 452-0041
Web: www.wcai.com

49-21 Transportation Industry Associations

Phone | Fax

Aerospace Industries Assn of America (AIA)
1000 Wilson Blvd Suite 1700 .... Arlington VA 22209 703-358-1000 358-1011
Web: www.aia-aerospace.org

Air Traffic Control Assn (ATCA)
1101 King St Suite 300 .... Alexandria VA 22314 703-299-2430 299-2437
Web: www.atca.org

Air Transport Assn of America (ATA)
1301 Pennsylvania Ave NW Suite 1100 .... Washington DC 20004 202-626-4000 626-4068
TF: 800-319-2463 ■ *Web:* www.air-transport.org

Aircraft Owners & Pilots Assn (AOPA)
421 Aviation Way .... Frederick MD 21701 301-695-2000 695-2375
TF: 800-872-2672 ■ *Web:* www.aopa.org

Airlines Reporting Corp (ARC)
4100 N Fairfax Dr Suite 600 .... Arlington VA 22203 703-816-8000 816-8104
Web: www.arccorp.com

Airports Council International of North America (ACI-NA)
1775 K St NW Suite 500 .... Washington DC 20006 202-293-8500 331-1362
Web: www.aci-na.org

American Ambulance Assn (AAA)
8201 Greensboro Dr Suite 300 .... McLean VA 22102 703-610-9018 610-9005
TF: 800-523-4447 ■ *Web:* www.the-aaa.org

American Assn of Airport Executives (AAAE)
601 Madison St Suite 400 .... Alexandria VA 22314 703-824-0500 820-1395
TF: 800-367-2223 ■ *Web:* www.aaae.org

Phone | Fax

American Assn of Port Authorities (AAPA)
1010 Duke St .... Alexandria VA 22314 703-684-5700 684-6321
Web: www.aapa-ports.org

American Assn of State Highway & Transportation Officials (AASHTO)
444 N Capitol St NW Suite 249 .... Washington DC 20001 202-624-5800 624-5806
Web: www.transportation.org

American Boat & Yacht Council Inc (ABYC)
613 3rd St Suite 10 .... Annapolis MD 21403 410-990-4460 990-4466
Web: www.abycinc.org

American Bureau of Shipping (ABS)
16855 Northchase Dr .... Houston TX 77060 281-877-5800 877-6001
Web: www.eagle.org

American Cotton Shippers Assn (ACSA)
88 Union Ave Suite 1204 .... Memphis TN 38103 901-525-2272 527-8803
Web: www.acsa-cotton.org

American Helicopter Society International (AHS)
217 N Washington St .... Alexandria VA 22314 703-684-6777 739-9279
Web: www.vtol.org

American Highway Users Alliance
1101 14th St NW Suite 750 .... Washington DC 20005 202-857-1200 857-1220
Web: www.highways.org

American International Automobile Dealers Assn (AIADA)
211 N Union St Suite 300 .... Alexandria VA 22314 703-519-7800 519-7810
TF: 800-462-4232 ■ *Web:* www.aiada.org

American Maritime Congress
444 N Capitol St NW Suite 800 .... Washington DC 20001 202-347-8020 347-1550
Web: www.americanmaritime.org

American Moving & Storage Assn (AMSA)
1611 Duke St .... Alexandria VA 22314 703-683-7410 683-7527
TF: 888-849-2672 ■ *Web:* www.promover.org

American Pilots' Assn
499 S Capitol St SW Suite 409 .... Washington DC 20003 202-484-0700 484-9320
TF: 800-527-4568 ■ *Web:* www.americanpilots.org

American Public Transportation Assn (APTA)
1666 K St NW Suite 1100 .... Washington DC 20006 202-496-4800 496-4321
Web: www.apta.com

American Railway Engineering & Maintenance-of-Way Assn (AREMA)
10003 Derekwood Ln Suite 210 .... Lanham MD 20706 301-459-3200 459-8077
Web: www.arema.org

American Shipbuilding Assn (ASA)
600 Pennsylvania Ave SE Suite 305 .... Washington DC 20003 202-544-8170 544-8252
Web: www.americanshipbuilding.com

American Short Line & Regional Railroad Assn (ASLRRA)
50 F St NW Suite 7020 .... Washington DC 20001 202-628-4500 628-6430
Web: www.aslrra.org

American Society of Naval Engineers (ASNE)
1452 Duke St .... Alexandria VA 22314 703-836-6727 836-7491
Web: www.navalengineers.org

American Society of Transportation & Logistics (ASTL)
1331 H St NW Suite 500 .... Washington DC 20005 202-580-7270 962-3939
Web: www.astl.org

American Traffic Safety Services Assn (ATSSA)
15 Riverside Pkwy Suite 100 .... Fredericksburg VA 22406 540-368-1701 368-1717
TF: 800-272-8772 ■ *Web:* www.atssa.com

American Trucking Associations (ATA)
950 N Glebe Rd Suite 210 .... Arlington VA 22203 703-838-1700 684-5751
TF: 800-282-5463 ■ *Web:* www.trucking.org

American Waterways Operators (AWO)
801 N Quincy St Suite 200 .... Arlington VA 22203 703-841-9300 841-0389
Web: www.americanwaterways.com

Assn of American Railroads (AAR)
425 3rd St SW .... Washington DC 20024 202-639-2100 639-2466
Web: www.aar.org

Assn of Diesel Specialists (ADS)
400 Admiral Blvd .... Kansas City MO 64106 816-255-0810 472-7765
Web: www.diesel.org

Assn of Retail Travel Agents (ARTA)
4320 N Miller Rd .... Scottsdale AZ 85251 800-969-6069 743-2087*
**Fax Area Code:* 866 ■ *TF:* 800-969-6069 ■ *Web:* www.arta.travel

Automatic Transmission Rebuilders Assn (ATRA)
2400 Latigo Ave .... Oxnard CA 93030 805-604-2000 604-2003
TF: 866-464-2872 ■ *Web:* www.atra.com

Automotive Aftermarket Industry Assn (AAIA)
7101 Wisconsin Ave .... Bethesda MD 20814 301-654-6664 654-3299
Web: www.aftermarket.org

Automotive Engine Rebuilders Assn (AERA)
500 Coventry Ln Suite 180 .... Crystal Lake IL 60014 847-541-6550 541-5808
TF: 888-326-2372 ■ *Web:* www.aera.org

Automotive Fleet & Leasing Assn
1000 Westgate Dr Suite 252 .... Saint Paul MN 55114 651-203-7247 290-2266
Web: www.aflaonline.org

Automotive Industry Action Group (AIAG)
26200 Lahser Rd Suite 200 .... Southfield MI 48033 248-358-3570 358-3253
Web: www.aiag.org

Automotive Oil Change Assn (AOCA)
12810 Hillcrest Rd Suite 221 .... Dallas TX 75230 972-458-9468 458-9539
TF: 800-331-0329 ■ *Web:* www.aoca.org

Automotive Parts Remanufacturers Assn (APRA)
4215 Lafayette Ctr Dr Suite 3 .... Chantilly VA 20151 703-968-2772 968-2878
Web: www.apra.org

Automotive Recyclers Assn (ARA)
3975 Fair Ridge Dr Suite 20N .... Fairfax VA 22033 703-385-1001 385-1494
TF: 888-385-1005 ■ *Web:* www.a-r-a.org

Automotive Service Assn (ASA) 1901 Airport Fwy .... Bedford TX 76021 817-283-6205 685-0225
TF Cust Svc: 800-272-7467 ■ *Web:* www.asashop.org

Brotherhood of Railroad Signalmen
917 Shenandoah Shores Rd .... Front Royal VA 22630 540-622-6522 622-6532
Web: www.brs.org

Car Care Council 7101 Wisconsin Ave .... Bethesda MD 20814 240-333-1088 614-3299*
**Fax Area Code:* 301 ■ *Web:* www.carcare.org

Cargo Airline Assn 1620 L St NW # 610 .... Washington DC 20036 202-293-1030 293-4377

Center for Auto Safety (CAS)
1825 Connecticut Ave NW Suite 330 .... Washington DC 20009 202-328-7700 387-0140
Web: www.autosafety.org

Organization / Address	City	State	ZIP	Phone	Fax
Coalition Against Bigger Trucks (CABT) 901 N Pitt St Suite 310 *TF:* 888-222-8123 ■ *Web:* www.cabt.org	Alexandria	VA	22314	703-535-3131	535-3322
Coalition for Auto Repair Equality (CARE) 105 Oronoco St # 115 *TF:* 800-229-5380 ■ *Web:* www.careauto.org	Alexandria	VA	22314	703-519-7555	519-7747
Community Transportation Assn of America (CTAA) 1341 G St NW 10th Fl *TF:* 800-891-0590 ■ *Web:* www.ctaa.org	Washington	DC	20005	202-628-1480	737-9197
Containerization & Intermodal Institute 960 Holmdel Rd Bldg 2 *TF:* 800-231-8244 ■ *Web:* www.containerization.org	Holmdel	NJ	07733	732-817-9131	817-9133
Dangerous Goods Advisory Council (DGAC) 1100 H St NW Suite 740 *TF:* 800-634-1598 ■ *Web:* www.dgac.org	Washington	DC	20005	202-289-4550	289-4074
Electric Drive Transportation Assn 1101 Vermont Ave NW Suite 401 *Web:* www.electricdrive.org	Washington	DC	20005	202-408-0774	408-7610
Flight Safety Foundation 801 N Fairfax St Suite 400 *Web:* www.flightsafety.org	Alexandria	VA	22314	703-739-6700	739-6708
General Aviation Manufacturers Assn (GAMA) 1400 K St NW Suite 801 *Web:* www.gama.aero	Washington	DC	20005	202-393-1500	842-4063
Helicopter Assn International (HAI) 1635 Prince St *TF:* 800-435-4976 ■ *Web:* www.rotor.com	Alexandria	VA	22314	703-683-4646	683-4745
Independent Liquid Terminals Assn (ILTA) 1444 'I' St NW Suite 400 *Web:* www.ilta.org	Washington	DC	20005	202-842-9200	326-8660
Institute of International Container Lessors (IICL) 1990 M St NW Suite 650 *Web:* www.iicl.org	Washington	DC	20036	202-223-9800	223-9810
Institute of Navigation Inc (ION) 8551 Rixlew Ln Suite 360 *Web:* www.ion.org	Manassas	VA	20109	703-366-2723	366-2724
Institute of Transportation Engineers (ITE) 1099 14th St NW Suite 300W *Web:* www.ite.org	Washington	DC	20005	202-289-0222	289-7722
Insurance Institute for Highway Safety 1005 N Glebe Rd Suite 800 *Web:* www.iihs.org	Arlington	VA	22201	703-247-1500	247-1588
Intelligent Transportation Society of America (ITS) 1100 17th St NW Suite 1200 *Web:* www.itsa.org	Washington	DC	20036	202-484-4847	484-3483
Intermodal Assn of North America (IANA) 11785 Beltsville Dr Suite 1100 *Web:* www.intermodal.org	Calverton	MD	20705	301-982-3400	982-4815
International Air Cargo Assn (TIACA) 5600 NW 36th St Suite 620 *Web:* www.tiaca.org	Miami	FL	33266	786-265-7011	265-7012
International Air Transport Assn 800 Pl Victoria PO Box 113 *Web:* www.iata.org	Montreal	QC	H4Z1M1	514-874-0202	874-9632
International Airlines Travel Agent Network (IATAN) 800 Pl Victoria Suite 800 *TF:* 877-734-2826 ■ *Web:* www.iatan.org	Montreal	QC	H4Z1M1	514-868-8800	868-8858
International Assn of Refrigerated Warehouses (IARW) 1500 King St Suite 201 *Web:* www.iarw.org	Alexandria	VA	22314	703-373-4300	373-4301
International Carwash Assn 401 N Michigan Ave *TF:* 888-422-8422 ■ *Web:* www.carwash.org	Chicago	IL	60611	312-321-5199	245-1085
International Motor Coach Group Inc (IMG) 8695 College Blvd Suite 260 *TF:* 888-447-3466 ■ *Web:* www.imgcoach.com	Overland Park	KS	66210	913-906-0111	906-0115
International Parking Institute (IPI) 701 Kenmore Ave Suite 200 *Web:* www.parking.org	Fredericksburg	VA	22401	540-371-7535	371-8022
International Safe Transit Assn (ISTA) 1400 Abbott Rd Suite 160 *Web:* www.ista.org	East Lansing	MI	48823	517-333-3437	333-3813
International Warehouse Logistics Assn (IWLA) 2800 S River Rd Suite 260 *TF:* 800-525-0165 ■ *Web:* www.iwla.com	Des Plaines	IL	60018	847-813-4699	813-0115
Interstate Natural Gas Assn of America (INGAA) 10 G St NE Suite 700 *Web:* www.ingaa.org	Washington	DC	20002	202-216-5900	216-0870
Japan Automobile Manufacturers Assn (JAMA) 1050 17th St NW Suite 410 *Web:* www.jama.org	Washington	DC	20036	202-296-8537	872-1212
Jewelers Shipping Assn (JSA) 125 Carlsbad St *TF:* 800-688-4572 ■ *Web:* www.jewelersshipping.com	Cranston	RI	02920	401-943-6020	943-1490
Mid-West Truckers Assn Inc 2727 N Dirksen Pkwy *Web:* www.mid-westtruckers.com	Springfield	IL	62704	217-525-0310	525-0342
Mobile Air Conditioning Society Worldwide (MACS) 225 S Broad St *Web:* www.macsw.org	Lansdale	PA	19446	215-631-7020	631-7017
Motor & Equipment Manufacturers Assn (MEMA) 10 Laboratory Dr PO Box 13966 *Web:* www.mema.org	Research Triangle Park	NC	27709	919-549-4800	549-4824
Motorcycle Industry Council (MIC) 2 Jenner St Suite 150 *Web:* www.mic.org	Irvine	CA	92618	949-727-4211	727-3313
NA of Cruise Oriented Agencies (NACOA) 7378 W Atlantic Blvd Suite 115 **Fax Area Code: 866* ■ *Web:* www.nacoaonline.com	Margate	FL	33063	305-663-5626	816-7143*
NA of Fleet Administrators (NAFA) 125 Village Blvd Suite 200 Princeton Forrestal Village *Web:* www.nafa.org	Princeton	NJ	08540	609-720-0882	452-8004
NA of Marine Surveyors Inc (NAMS) PO Box 9306 *TF:* 800-822-6267 ■ *Web:* www.namsglobal.org	Chesapeake	VA	23321	757-638-9638	638-9639
National Air Carrier Assn (NACA) 1000 Wilson Blvd Suite 1700 *Web:* www.naca.cc	Arlington	VA	22209	703-358-8060	358-8070
National Air Transportation Assn (NATA) 4226 King St *TF:* 800-808-6282 ■ *Web:* www.nata.aero	Alexandria	VA	22302	703-845-9000	845-8176
National Automobile Dealers Assn (NADA) 8400 Westpark Dr *TF:* 800-252-6232 ■ *Web:* www.nada.org	McLean	VA	22102	703-821-7000	821-7075
National Automotive Radiator Service Assn (NARSA) 15000 Commerce Pkwy Suite C *TF:* 800-551-3232 ■ *Web:* www.narsa.org	Mount Laurel	NJ	08054	856-439-1575	439-9596
National Business Aviation Assn (NBAA) 1200 18th St NW Suite 400 *Web:* www.nbaa.org	Washington	DC	20036	202-783-9000	331-8364
National Cargo Bureau Inc (NCB) 17 Battery Pl Suite 1232 *Web:* www.natcargo.org	New York	NY	10004	212-785-8300	785-8333
National Customs Brokers & Forwarders Assn of America Inc (NCBFAA) 1200 18th St NW Suite 901 *Web:* www.ncbfaa.org	Washington	DC	20036	202-466-0222	466-0226
National EMS Pilots Assn (NEMSPA) PO Box 2128 **Fax Area Code: 866* ■ *TF:* 877-668-0430 ■ *Web:* www.nemspa.org	Layton	UT	84041	877-668-0430	906-6023*
National Industrial Transportation League (NITL) 1700 N Moore St Suite 1900 *Web:* www.nitl.org	Arlington	VA	22209	703-524-5011	524-5017
National Marine Manufacturers Assn (NMMA) 200 E Randolph Dr Suite 5100 *TF:* 800-985-2401 ■ *Web:* www.nmma.org	Chicago	IL	60601	312-946-6200	946-0388
National Motor Freight Traffic Assn (NMFTA) 1001 N Fairfax St Suite 600 *Web:* www.nmfta.org	Alexandria	VA	22314	703-838-1810	683-6296
National Motorists Assn (NMA) 402 W 2nd St *TF:* 800-882-2785 ■ *Web:* www.motorists.org	Waunakee	WI	53597	608-849-6000	849-8697
National Private Truck Council (NPTC) 950 Glebe Rd Suite 530 *Web:* www.nptc.org	Arlington	VA	22203	703-683-1300	683-1217
National Tank Truck Carriers Inc 950 N Glebe Rd Suite 520 *Web:* www.tanktruck.org	Arlington	VA	22203	703-838-1960	684-5753
National Truck Equipment Assn (NTEA) 37400 Hills Tech Dr *TF:* 800-441-6832 ■ *Web:* www.ntea.com	Farmington Hills	MI	48331	248-489-7090	489-8590
National Waterways Conference Inc (NWC) 4650 Washington Blvd Suite 608 *TF:* 866-371-1390 ■ *Web:* www.waterways.org	Arlington	VA	22201	703-243-4090	243-4155
NATSO Inc 1737 King St Suite 200 *Web:* www.natso.com	Alexandria	VA	22314	703-549-2100	684-4525
Owner-Operator Independent Drivers Assn Inc (OOIDA) 1 NW OOIDA Dr *TF:* 800-444-5791 ■ *Web:* www.ooida.com	Grain Valley	MO	64029	816-229-5791	229-0518
Passenger Vessel Assn (PVA) 801 N Quincy St Suite 200 *TF:* 800-807-8360 ■ *Web:* www.passengervessel.com	Arlington	VA	22203	703-807-0100	807-0103
Professional Aviation Maintenance Assn (PAMA) 400 Commonwealth Dr *TF:* 866-865-7262 ■ *Web:* www.pama.org	Warrendale	PA	15096	724-772-4092	772-4064
Propeller Club of the US 3927 Old Lee Hwy Suite 101-A *Web:* www.propellerclubhq.com	Fairfax	VA	22030	703-691-2777	691-4173
Railway Supply Institute Inc (RSI) 425 3Rd St Suite 920 *Web:* www.rsiweb.org	Washington	DC	20024	202-347-4664	347-0047
Recreation Vehicle Dealers Assn (RVDA) 3930 University Dr 3rd Fl *TF:* 800-336-0355 ■ *Web:* www.rvda.org	Fairfax	VA	22030	703-591-7130	591-0734
Recreation Vehicle Industry Assn (RVIA) 1896 Preston White Dr *TF:* 800-336-0154 ■ *Web:* www.rvia.org	Reston	VA	20191	703-620-6003	620-5071
Regional Airline Assn (RAA) 2025 M St NW Suite 800 *Web:* www.raa.org	Washington	DC	20036	202-367-1100	367-2170
Self Storage Assn (SSA) 1900 N Beauregard St Suite 450 *TF:* 888-735-3784 ■ *Web:* www.selfstorage.org	Alexandria	VA	22311	703-575-8000	575-8901
Shipbuilders Council of America (SCA) 1455 F St NW Suite 225 *Web:* www.shipbuilders.org	Washington	DC	20005	202-347-5462	347-5464
Shipowners Claims Bureau (SCB) 1 Battery Pk Plaza 31st Fl *Web:* www.american-club.com	New York	NY	10004	212-847-4500	847-4599
Society of Automotive Engineers Inc (SAE) 400 Commonwealth Dr *TF:* 877-606-7323 ■ *Web:* www.sae.org	Warrendale	PA	15096	724-776-4841	776-0790
Society of Government Travel Professionals (SGTP) PO Box 158 *Web:* www.sgtp.org	Glyndon	MD	21071	202-341-7487	379-1775
Society of Naval Architects & Marine Engineers (SNAME) 601 Pavonia Ave 4th Fl *Web:* www.sname.org	Jersey City	NJ	07306	201-798-4800	798-4975
Specialized Carriers & Rigging Assn (SC&RA) 2750 Prosperity Ave Suite 620 *Web:* www.scranet.org	Fairfax	VA	22031	703-698-0291	698-0297
Specialty Equipment Market Assn (SEMA) 1575 S Valley Vista Dr *Web:* www.sema.org	Diamond Bar	CA	91765	909-396-0289	860-0184
Specialty Vehicle Institute of America (SVIA) 2 Jenner St Suite 150 *TF:* 800-887-2887 ■ *Web:* www.atvsafety.org	Irvine	CA	92618	949-727-3727	727-4216

	City	State	Zip	Phone	Fax
Technology & Maintenance Council (TMC) American Trucking Associations 950 N Glebe Rd *Web:* www.truckline.com/aboutata/councils/tmc	Arlington	VA	22203	703-838-1761	838-1701
Towing & Recovery Assn of America (TRAA) 2121 Eisenhower Ave Suite 200 *TF:* 800-728-0136 ■ *Web:* www.towserver.net	Alexandria	VA	22314	703-684-7734	684-6720
Transport Workers Union of America 501 3rd St NW 9th Fl *Web:* www.twu.org	Washington	DC	10023	202-719-3900	347-0454
Transportation Institute 5201 Auth Way *Web:* www.trans-inst.org	Camp Springs	MD	20746	301-423-3335	423-0634
Transportation Intermediaries Assn (TIA) 1625 Prince St Suite 200 *Web:* www.tianet.org	Alexandria	VA	22314	703-299-5700	836-0123
Transportation Research Board (TRB) 500 5th St NW *Web:* www.trb.org	Washington	DC	20001	202-334-2934	334-2519
Truck Renting & Leasing Assn (TRALA) 675 N Washington St Suite 410 *Web:* www.trala.org	Alexandria	VA	22314	703-299-9120	299-9115
Truckload Carriers Assn (TCA) 555 E Braddock Rd *Web:* www.truckload.org	Alexandria	VA	22314	703-838-1950	836-6610
United Motorcoach Assn (UMA) 113 SW St 4th Fl *TF:* 800-424-8262 ■ *Web:* www.uma.org	Alexandria	VA	22314	703-838-2929	838-2950
Warehousing Education & Research Council (WERC) 1100 Jorie Blvd Suite 170 *Web:* www.werc.org	Oak Brook	IL	60523	630-990-0001	990-0256

50 ATTRACTIONS

SEE ALSO Amusement Parks p. 1394; Aquariums - Public p. 1400; Art Dealers & Galleries p. 1401; Botanical Gardens & Arboreta p. 1537; Cemeteries - National p. 1561; Presidential Libraries p. 2152; Special Collections Libraries p. 2170; Museums p. 2265; Museums - Children's p. 2290; Museums & Halls of Fame - Sports p. 2292; Parks - National - Canada p. 2339; Parks - National - US p. 2340; Parks - State p. 2346; Performing Arts Facilities p. 2392; Planetariums p. 2423; Zoos & Wildlife Parks p. 2780

50-1 Churches, Cathedrals, Synagogues, Temples

	City	State	Zip	Phone	Fax
Antioch Baptist Church 1057 Texas Ave	Shreveport	LA	71101	318-222-7090	222-5738
Arch Street Meeting House 320 Arch St *Web:* www.archstreetfriends.org	Philadelphia	PA	19106	215-627-2667	627-3624
Basilica of Saint Mary of the Immaculate Conception 232 Chapel St *Web:* www.basilicaofstmary.org	Norfolk	VA	23504	757-622-4487	625-7969
Basilica of the Assumption 409 Cathedral St *Web:* www.baltimorebasilica.org	Baltimore	MD	21201	410-727-3565	539-0407
Basilica of the National Shrine of the Immaculate Conception 400 Michigan Ave NE *Web:* www.nationalshrine.com	Washington	DC	20017	202-526-8300	526-8313
Big Zion African Methodist Episcopal Zion Church 112 S Bayou St	Mobile	AL	36602	251-433-8431	
Black Madonna Shrine St Joseph's Hill Rd PO Box 181 *Web:* www.franciscancaring.org/blackmadonnaforward.html	Eureka	MO	63025	636-938-5361	587-2789
Boardman Park 375 Boardman-Poland Rd *Web:* www.boardmanpark.com	Boardman	OH	44512	330-726-8107	726-4562
Carmel Mission 3080 Rio Rd *Web:* www.carmelmission.org	Carmel	CA	93923	831-624-1271	624-8050
Cathedral Basilica of Notre-Dame 56 Guigues Ave	Ottawa	ON	K1N5H5	613-241-7496	241-1627
Cathedral Basilica of Saint Joseph 80 S Market St *Web:* www.stjosephcathedral.org	San Jose	CA	95113	408-283-8100	283-8110
Cathedral Basilica of Saint Louis (New Cathedral) 4431 Lindell Blvd *Web:* www.cathedralstl.org	Saint Louis	MO	63108	314-373-8200	373-8290
Cathedral Basilica of the Sacred Heart 89 Ridge St *Web:* www.cathedralbasilica.org	Newark	NJ	07104	973-484-4600	483-8253
Cathedral Church of All Saints Martello St & University Ave *Web:* www.cathedralchurchofallsaints.com	Halifax	NS	B3H1X3	902-423-6002	423-1437
Cathedral Church of Saint John the Divine 1047 Amsterdam Ave *Web:* www.stjohndivine.org	New York	NY	10025	212-316-7490	932-7347
Cathedral Church of Saint Mark 231 E 100 S *Web:* www.stmarkscathedral-ut.org	Salt Lake City	UT	84111	801-322-3400	322-3410
Cathedral of Christ the King 299 Colony Blvd *Web:* www.cathedral.cdlex.org	Lexington	KY	40502	859-268-2861	268-8061
Cathedral of Our Lady of the Angels 555 W Temple St *Web:* www.olacathedral.org	Los Angeles	CA	90012	213-680-5200	620-1982
Cathedral of Saint John 271 N Main St	Providence	RI	02903	401-331-4622	831-8425
Cathedral of Saint Paul 239 Selby Ave *Web:* www.cathedralsaintpaul.org	Saint Paul	MN	55102	651-228-1766	228-9942
Cathedral of Saints Peter & Paul 30 Fenner St	Providence	RI	02903	401-331-2434	273-0687
Cathedral of the Blessed Sacrament 1017 11th St *Web:* www.blessedsaccathedral.org	Sacramento	CA	95814	916-444-3071	443-2749
Cathedral of the Immaculate Conception 2 S Claiborne St *Web:* www.mobilecathedral.org	Mobile	AL	36602	251-434-1565	434-1588
Cathedral of the Immaculate Conception 125 Eagle St *Web:* www.cathedralic.com	Albany	NY	12202	518-463-4447	436-5177
Cathedral of the Madeleine 331 E S Temple St *Web:* www.saltlakecathedral.org	Salt Lake City	UT	84111	801-328-8941	364-6504
Catholic Diocese of Peoria The 607 NE Madison Ave *Web:* www.cdop.org	Peoria	IL	61603	309-682-5823	682-6030
Center Church 60 Gold St *Web:* www.centerchurchhartford.org	Hartford	CT	06103	860-249-5631	246-3915
Christ Church 118 N Washington St *Web:* www.historicchristchurch.org	Alexandria	VA	22314	703-549-1450	549-5883
Christ Church Cathedral 125 Monument Cir *Web:* www.cccindy.org	Indianapolis	IN	46204	317-636-4577	635-1040
Christ Church Cathedral 45 Church St *Web:* www.cccathedral.org	Hartford	CT	06103	860-527-7231	527-5313
Christ Church Cathedral 1444 Union Ave *Web:* www.montrealcathedral.ca	Montreal	QC	H3A2B8	514-843-6577	843-6344
Christ Church Cathedral 1210 Locust St *Web:* www.yourcathedral.org	Saint Louis	MO	63103	314-231-3454	231-3142
Christ Church Cathedral 690 Burrard St *Web:* www.cathedral.vancouver.bc.ca	Vancouver	BC	V6C2L1	604-682-3848	682-8377
Christ Church in Philadelphia 20 N American St *Web:* www.christchurchphila.org	Philadelphia	PA	19106	215-922-1695	922-3578
Christ Episcopal Church 10 N Church St *Web:* www.ccgsc.org	Greenville	SC	29601	864-271-8773	242-0879
Christ Episcopal Church S State & Water Sts *Web:* www.christchurchdover.org	Dover	DE	19901	302-734-5731	734-7702
Church of the Transfiguration 1 E 29th St *Web:* www.littlechurch.org	New York	NY	10016	212-684-6770	684-1662
Circular Congregational Church 150 Meeting St *Web:* www.circularchurch.org	Charleston	SC	29401	843-577-6400	958-0594
Congregation Beth Elohim 90 Hasell St *Web:* www.kkbe.org	Charleston	SC	29401	843-723-1090	723-0537
Congregation Mikveh Israel 44 N 4th St *Web:* www.mikvehisrael.org	Philadelphia	PA	19106	215-922-5446	922-1550
Crystal Cathedral 12141 Lewis St **Fax:* Hum Res ■ *TF:* 877-456-7900 ■ *Web:* www.crystalcathedral.org	Garden Grove	CA	92840	714-971-4000	971-4906*
Dagom Gaden Tensung-Ling Monastery 102 Clubhouse Dr *Web:* www.ganden.org	Bloomington	IN	47404	812-339-0857	323-8803
Dexter Avenue King Memorial Baptist Church 454 Dexter Ave *Web:* www.dexterkingmemorial.org	Montgomery	AL	36104	334-263-3970	263-5223
Duke Memorial United Methodist Church 504 W Chapel Hill St *Web:* www.dukememorial.org	Durham	NC	27701	919-683-3467	682-3349
Ebenezer Baptist Church 407 Auburn Ave NE *Web:* www.historicebenezer.org	Atlanta	GA	30312	404-688-7263	521-1129
Emanuel African Methodist Episcopal Church 110 Calhoun St *Web:* www.cr.nps.gov	Charleston	SC	29401	843-722-2561	722-1869
First Congregational Church 62 Centre St	Nantucket	MA	02554	508-228-0950	228-0095
First Unitarian Church of Philadelphia 2125 Chestnut St *Web:* www.firstuu-philly.org	Philadelphia	PA	19103	215-563-3980	563-4209
Franciscan Monastery of the Holly Land 1400 Quincy St NE *Web:* www.myfranciscan.org	Washington	DC	20017	202-526-6800	529-9889
Historic Trinity Lutheran Church 812 Soulard St *Web:* www.historictrinitystlouis.org	Saint Louis	MO	63104	314-231-4092	231-5430
Holy Trinity Catholic Church 315 Marshall St *Web:* www.holytrinity-shreveport.com	Shreveport	LA	71101	318-221-5990	221-3545
Jewish Heritage Center of the Southwest 564 S Stone Ave *Web:* www.jewishheritagecenter.net	Tucson	AZ	85701	520-670-9073	670-9078
King's Chapel 58 Tremont St	Boston	MA	02108	617-227-2155	227-4101
Landmark on the Park 160 Central Pk W *Web:* www.landmarkonthepark.org	New York	NY	10023	212-595-1658	595-0134
Ling Shen Ching Tze Temple 17012 NE 40th Ct	Redmond	WA	98052	425-882-0916	
Martha's Vineyard Preservation Trust 99 Main St PO Box 5277 *Web:* www.mvpreservation.org	Edgartown	MA	02539	508-627-4440	627-8088
Mesa Arizona Temple 101 S LeSueur *Web:* www.lds.org/church/temples	Mesa	AZ	85204	480-833-1211	827-2828
Mission Dolores 3321 16th St *Web:* www.missiondolores.org	San Francisco	CA	94114	415-621-8204	621-2294
Mission of Nombre de Dios & Shrine of Our Lady of La Leche 27 Ocean Ave *TF:* 800-342-6529 ■ *Web:* www.missionandshrine.org	Saint Augustine	FL	32084	904-824-2809	829-0819
Mission San Fernando Rey De Espana 15151 San Fernando Mission Blvd	Mission Hills	CA	93145	818-361-0186	
Mission San Jose 701 E Pyron Ave *Web:* www.nps.gov	San Antonio	TX	78214	210-922-0543	932-2271

Name / Address	City	State	ZIP	Phone	Fax
Mission San Luis Rey de Francia 4050 Mission Ave. *Web:* www.sanluisrey.org	Oceanside	CA	92057	760-757-3651	757-4613
Mother Bethel AME Church 419 S 6th St. *Web:* www.motherbethel.org	Philadelphia	PA	19147	215-925-0616	925-1402
National Shrine of Our Lady of Lebanon The 2759 N Lipkey Rd *Web:* www.ourladyoflebanonshrine.com	North Jackson	OH	44451	330-538-3351	538-0455
National Shrine of Our Lady of the Snows 442 S De Mazenod Dr. *TF:* 800-682-2879 ■ *Web:* www.snows.org	Belleville	IL	62223	618-397-6700	398-6549
New England Peace Pagoda 100 Cave Hill Rd.	Leverett	MA	01054	413-367-2202	367-9369
Oakland Mormon Temple 4770 Lincoln Ave *Web:* www.ldschurchtemples.com	Oakland	CA	94602	510-531-3200	531-7625
Old Dutch Church of Sleepy Hollow 430 N Broadway *Web:* www.sleepyhollowchamber.com	Sleepy Hollow	NY	10591	914-631-1123	
Old First Reformed Church of Christ 151 N 4th St *Web:* www.oldfirstucc.org	Philadelphia	PA	19106	215-922-4566	922-6366
Old Mission San Jose 43300 Mission Blvd *Web:* www.saintjosephmsj.org	Fremont	CA	94539	510-657-1797	651-8332
Old North Church 193 Salem St *Web:* www.oldnorth.com	Boston	MA	02113	617-523-6676	725-0559
Old Pine Street Presbyterian Church 412 Pine St. *Web:* www.oldpine.org	Philadelphia	PA	19106	215-925-8051	922-7120
Old Saint Ferdinand's Shrine 1 Rue St Francois	Florissant	MO	63031	314-839-3829	
Old Saint Joseph's Church 321 Willings Alley *Web:* www.oldstjoseph.org	Philadelphia	PA	19106	215-923-1733	574-8529
Old Saint Mary's Church 123 E 13th St. *Web:* www.oldstmarys.org	Cincinnati	OH	45202	513-721-2988	721-0436
Old Saint Patrick's Church 700 W Adams St *Web:* www.oldstpats.org	Chicago	IL	60661	312-648-1021	648-9025
Our Lady Queen of the Most Holy Rosary Cathedral 2535 Collingwood Blvd *Web:* www.rosarycathedral.org	Toledo	OH	43610	419-244-9575	242-1901
Queen of Angels Monastery 840 S Main St. *Web:* www.benedictine-srs.org	Mount Angel	OR	97362	503-845-6141	845-6585
Saint George's Anglican Church 1101 Stanley St *Web:* www.st-georges.org	Montreal	QC	H3B2S6	514-866-7113	866-6096
Saint George's Church 2222 Brunswick St *Web:* www.roundchurch.ca	Halifax	NS	B3K2Z3	902-423-1059	423-0897
Saint Joan of Arc Chapel Marquette University Ministry 1442 W Wisconsin Ave. *Web:* www.marquette.edu/chapel	Milwaukee	WI	53233	414-288-3685	288-3696
Saint Joseph Cathedral 521 N Duluth Ave	Sioux Falls	SD	57104	605-336-7390	
Saint Louis Cathedral 615 Pere Antoine Alley *Web:* www.stlouiscathedral.org	New Orleans	LA	70116	504-525-9585	525-9583
Saint Mary's Cathedral 203 E 10th St. *Web:* www.smcaustin.org	Austin	TX	78701	512-476-6182	476-8799
Saint Mary's Catholic Church 155 Market St.	Memphis	TN	38105	901-522-9420	522-8314
Saint Matthew's United Church 1479 Barrington St *Web:* www.stmatts.ns.ca	Halifax	NS	B3J1Z2	902-423-9209	423-2833
Saint Patrick's Cathedral 14 E 51st St *Web:* www.saintpatrickscathedral.org	New York	NY	10126	212-753-2261	750-6646
Saint Paul's Episcopal Church 1430 J St *Web:* www.stpaulssacramento.org	Sacramento	CA	95814	916-446-2620	
Saint Photios Greek Orthodox National Shrine 41 St George St PO Box 1960 *Web:* www.stphotios.com	Saint Augustine	FL	32085	904-829-8205	829-8707
Salt Lake Temple 50 E N Temple St *TF:* 800-537-9703 ■ *Web:* www.ldschurchtemples.com	Salt Lake City	UT	84150	801-240-3221	240-4886
San Gabriel Mission 428 S Mission Dr *Web:* www.sangabrielmission.org	San Gabriel	CA	91776	626-457-3035	282-5308
San Miguel Mission 401 Old Santa Fe Trail	Santa Fe	NM	87501	505-983-3974	
San Xavier Del Bac Mission 1950 W San Xavier Rd *Web:* www.sanxaviermission.org	Tucson	AZ	85746	520-294-2624	294-3438
Santuario de Guadalupe 100 S Guadalupe St.	Santa Fe	NM	87501	505-988-2027	
Scottish Rite Cathedral 160 S Scott Ave	Tucson	AZ	85701	520-622-8364	
Shrine of Saint John Neumann 1019 N 5th St *TF:* 888-315-1860 ■ *Web:* www.stjohnneumann.org	Philadelphia	PA	19123	215-627-3080	627-3296
Sixteenth Street Baptist Church 1530 6th Ave N.	Birmingham	AL	35203	205-251-9402	251-9811
Socorro Mission 328 S Nevarez St	El Paso	TX	79927	915-859-7718	859-9452
Southern Union Conference Assn of The Seventh Day Adventist Church 3978 Memorial Dr PO Box 849. *Web:* www.southernunion.com	Decatur	GA	30031	404-299-1832	299-9726
Touro Synagogue National Historic Site 85 Touro St. *Web:* www.tourosynagogue.org	Newport	RI	02840	401-847-4794	841-6790
Trinity Cathedral 2230 Euclid Ave *Web:* www.trinitycleveland.org	Cleveland	OH	44115	216-771-3630	771-3657
Union Chapel 55 Narragansett Ave. *Web:* www.mvpreservation.org	Oak Bluffs	MA	02557	508-627-4440	
Union Church of Pocantico Hills 555 Bedford Rd. *Web:* www.hudsonvalley.org	Sleepy Hollow	NY	10591	914-631-8200	631-0089
Wayfarers Chapel 5755 Palos Verdes Dr. *Web:* www.wayfarerschapel.org	Rancho Palos Verdes	CA	90275	310-377-1650	541-1435
White Church Christian Church 2200 N 85th St	Kansas City	KS	66109	913-299-4056	299-1066
Ysleta Mission 131 S Zaragosa Rd *Web:* www.ysletamission.org	El Paso	TX	79907	915-859-9848	860-9340

50-2 Cultural & Arts Centers

ARIZONA

Name / Address	City	State	ZIP	Phone	Fax
Deer Valley Rock Art Ctr 3711 W Deer Valley Rd *Web:* www.asu.edu	Glendale	AZ	85308	623-582-8007	582-8831
Mesa Arts Ctr 1 E Main St PO Box 1466 *Web:* www.mesaartscenter.com	Mesa	AZ	85201	480-644-6501	644-6503

ARKANSAS

Name / Address	City	State	ZIP	Phone	Fax
Arkansas Arts Ctr 501 E 9th St *TF:* 800-264-2787 ■ *Web:* www.arkarts.com	Little Rock	AR	72202	501-372-4000	375-8053
Center for Art & Education 104 N 13th St *Web:* www.art-ed.org	Van Buren	AR	72956	479-474-7767	474-4411

CALIFORNIA

Name / Address	City	State	ZIP	Phone	Fax
Aerie Art Garden 71-255 Aerie Rd *Web:* www.aerieartgarden.com	Palm Desert	CA	92260	760-568-6366	
African American Art & Culture Complex 762 Fulton St Suite 300 *Web:* www.aaacc.org	San Francisco	CA	94102	415-922-2049	922-5130
Huntington Beach Arts Ctr 538 Main St	Huntington Beach	CA	92648	714-374-1650	374-5304
Jurupa Mountains Discovery Ctr 7621 Granite Hill Dr *Web:* www.jmdc.org	Riverside	CA	92509	951-685-5818	685-1240
La Raza Galeria Posada 1022-1024 22nd St. *Web:* www.larazagaleriaposada.org	Sacramento	CA	95816	916-446-5133	446-1324
Mission Cultural Center for Latino Arts 2868 Mission St *Web:* www.missionculturalcenter.org	San Francisco	CA	94110	415-821-1155	648-0933
Oakland Asian Cultural Ctr 388 9th St Suite 290 *Web:* www.oacc.cc	Oakland	CA	94607	510-637-0455	637-0459
Roy & Edna Disney/CALARTS Theater (REDCAT) (REDCAT) 631 W 2nd St *Web:* www.redcat.org	Los Angeles	CA	90012	213-237-2800	237-2811
Skirball Cultural Ctr 2701 N Sepulveda Blvd *Web:* www.skirball.org	Los Angeles	CA	90049	310-440-4500	440-4595

COLORADO

Name / Address	City	State	ZIP	Phone	Fax
Anasazi Heritage Ctr 27501 Hwy 184 *Web:* www.blm.gov	Dolores	CO	81323	970-882-5600	882-7035
Anderson Ranch Arts Ctr 5263 Owl Creek Rd PO Box 5598 *Web:* www.andersonranch.org	Snowmass Village	CO	81615	970-923-3181	923-3871
Dairy Center for the Arts 2590 Walnut St. *Web:* www.thedairy.org	Boulder	CO	80302	303-440-7826	440-7104
Durango Arts Ctr 802 E 2nd Ave *Web:* www.durangoarts.org	Durango	CO	81301	970-259-2606	259-6571
Southern Ute Cultural Center & Museum 14826 Hwy 172 PO Box 737 *Web:* www.succm.org	Ignacio	CO	81137	970-563-9583	563-4641

CONNECTICUT

Name / Address	City	State	ZIP	Phone	Fax
Charter Oak Cultural Ctr 21 Charter Oak Ave *Web:* www.charteroakcenter.org	Hartford	CT	06106	860-249-1207	524-8014
Rowayton Arts Ctr 145 Rowayton Ave *Web:* www.rowaytonartscenter.org	Rowayton	CT	06853	203-866-2744	866-1123
Silvermine Arts Ctr 1037 Silvermine Rd. *Web:* www.silvermineart.org	New Canaan	CT	06840	203-966-9700	966-2763
Westport Arts Ctr 51 Riverside Ave *Web:* www.westportartscenter.org	Westport	CT	06880	203-222-7070	222-7999

DELAWARE

Name / Address	City	State	ZIP	Phone	Fax
Delaware Center for the Contemporary Arts 200 S Madison St. *Web:* www.thedcca.org	Wilmington	DE	19801	302-656-6466	656-6944

FLORIDA

Name / Address	City	State	ZIP	Phone	Fax
African-American Research Library & Cultural Ctr 2650 NW Sistrunk Blvd *Web:* www.broward.org/library/aarlcc.htm	Fort Lauderdale	FL	33311	954-625-2800	625-2803
Armory Art Ctr 1700 Parker Ave *Web:* www.armoryart.org	West Palm Beach	FL	33401	561-832-1776	832-0191
Art Center South Florida 924 Lincoln Rd Suite 205 *Web:* www.artcentersf.org	Miami Beach	FL	33139	305-674-8278	674-8772
ArtSouth 240 N Krome Ave. *Web:* www.artsouthhomestead.org	Homestead	FL	33030	305-247-9406	247-7308
Lighthouse Center for the Arts 373 Tequesta Dr Gallery Sq N. *Web:* www.lighthousearts.org	Tequesta	FL	33469	561-746-3101	746-3241

			Phone	Fax
Maitland Art Ctr 231 W Packwood Ave. Maitland	FL	32751	407-539-2181	316-5729*
**Fax Area Code: 888* ■ *Web:* www.artandhistory.org				

GEORGIA

			Phone	Fax
Atlanta Contemporary Art Ctr 535 Means St NW Atlanta	GA	30318	404-688-1970	577-5856
Web: www.thecontemporary.org				
Callanwolde Fine Arts Ctr 980 Briarcliff Rd NE Atlanta	GA	30306	404-872-5338	872-5175
Web: www.callanwolde.org				
Center for Puppetry Arts 1404 Spring St NW Atlanta	GA	30309	404-873-3089	873-9907
Web: www.puppet.org				
City Market Art Ctr 219 W Bryan St Suite 207 Savannah	GA	31401	912-232-4903	232-2142
Web: www.savannahcitymarket.com/art.html				

IDAHO

			Phone	Fax
Pocatello Art Ctr (PAC) 444 N Main St Pocatello	ID	83204	208-232-0970	
Web: www.pocatelloartctr.org				

ILLINOIS

			Phone	Fax
City of Chicago 121 N LaSalle St Chicago	IL	60602	312-744-5000	
Web: www.cityofchicago.org				
Illinois Mennonite Heritage Ctr 675 SR-116 Metamora	IL	61548	309-367-2551	
Web: www.imhgs.org				
Irish American Heritage Ctr 4626 N Knox Ave. Chicago	IL	60630	773-282-7035	282-0380
Web: www.irish-american.org				
North Lakeside Cultural Ctr 6219 N Sheridan Rd Chicago	IL	60660	773-743-4477	743-1483
South Shore Cultural Ctr 7059 S Shore Dr Chicago	IL	60649	773-256-0149	256-1163
Web: www.chicagoparkdistrict.com				

INDIANA

			Phone	Fax
Indianapolis Art Ctr 820 E 67th St Indianapolis	IN	46220	317-255-2464	254-0486
Web: www.indianapolisartcenter.org				
John Waldron Arts Ctr 122 S Walnut St. Bloomington	IN	47404	812-334-3100	323-2787
Web: www.artlives.org				
Tibetan Cultural Ctr 3655 Snoddy Rd Bloomington	IN	47401	812-331-0014	334-7046
Web: www.tibetancc.com				

KENTUCKY

			Phone	Fax
Capital Gallery of Contemporary Art 314 Lewis St. Frankfort	KY	40601	502-223-2649	
Kentucky Center for African American Heritage 315 Guthrie Green Suite 400 Louisville	KY	40202	502-583-4100	583-4112
Web: www.kcaah.org				
Kentucky Museum of Art & Craft 715 W Main St Louisville	KY	40202	502-589-0102	589-0154
Web: www.kentuckyarts.org				

LOUISIANA

			Phone	Fax
Acadiana Center for the Arts 101 W Vermilion St. Lafayette	LA	70501	337-233-7060	233-7062
Web: www.acadianacenterforthearts.org				
Barnwell Garden & Art Ctr 601 Clyde Fant Pkwy Shreveport	LA	71101	318-673-7703	673-7707
Web: www.barnwellcenter.com				
Cannes Brulee Native American Ctr 415 Williams Blvd Rivertown Kenner	LA	70062	504-468-7231	471-2159
Web: www.rivertownkenner.com				

MAINE

			Phone	Fax
Maine Folklife Ctr 5773 S Stevens Hall University of Maine Orono	ME	04469	207-581-1891	581-1823
Web: www.umaine.edu/folklife				

MANITOBA

			Phone	Fax
Jewish Heritage Center of Western Canada C116-123 Doncaster St Winnipeg	MB	R3N2B2	204-477-7460	477-7465
Web: www.jhcwc.org				
Saint Norbert Arts & Cultural Centre (SNAC) 100 Rue des Ruines du Monastere PO Box 1752 Winnipeg	MB	R3V1L6	204-269-0564	261-1927
Web: www.snac.mb.ca				

MARYLAND

			Phone	Fax
Elizabeth Myers Mitchell Art Gallery 60 College Ave Annapolis	MD	21401	410-626-2556	
Maryland Art Place (MAP) 8 Market Pl Suite 100 Baltimore	MD	21202	410-962-8565	244-8017
Web: www.mdartplace.org				
Maryland Federation of Art Circle Gallery 18 State Cir. Annapolis	MD	21401	410-268-4566	268-4570
Web: www.mdfedart.org				

MASSACHUSETTS

			Phone	Fax
Worcester Center for Crafts 25 Sagamore Rd Worcester	MA	01605	508-753-8183	797-5626
Web: www.worcester.edu				

MICHIGAN

			Phone	Fax
Ann Arbor Art Ctr 117 W Liberty St. Ann Arbor	MI	48104	734-994-8004	994-3610
Web: www.annarborartcenter.org				
Detroit Gallery of Contemporary Crafts 3011 W Grand Blvd Suite 104 Detroit	MI	48202	313-873-7888	
Flint Cultural Center Corp 1310 E Kearsley St Flint	MI	48503	810-237-7333	237-7340
TF: 888-823-6837 ■ *Web:* www.flintculturalcenter.com				
Lansing Art Gallery 119 N Washington Sq. Lansing	MI	48933	517-374-6400	374-6385
Web: www.lansingartgallery.org				
Nokomis Learning Ctr 5151 Marsh Rd. Okemos	MI	48864	517-349-5777	349-8560
Web: www.nokomis.org				
Oakland University Art Gallery Oakland University 208 Wilson Hall Rochester	MI	48309	248-370-3005	370-4208
Web: www.oakland.edu/ouag				

MINNESOTA

			Phone	Fax
Rochester Art Ctr 40 Civic Ctr Dr SE Rochester	MN	55904	507-282-8629	282-7737
Web: www.rochesterartcenter.org				

MISSISSIPPI

			Phone	Fax
Mississippi Arts Ctr 201 E Pascagoula St Jackson	MS	39201	601-960-1500	960-1352
Municipal Art Gallery 839 N State St. Jackson	MS	39202	601-960-1582	960-2066

MISSOURI

			Phone	Fax
Center of Contemporary Arts 524 Trinity Ave Saint Louis	MO	63130	314-725-6555	725-6222
Web: www.cocastl.org				
Portfolio Gallery & Educational Ctr 3514 Delmar Blvd. Saint Louis	MO	63103	314-533-3323	531-3401
Web: www.portfoliogallerystl.org				

NEBRASKA

			Phone	Fax
Bemis Center for Contemporary Arts 724 S 12th St Omaha	NE	68102	402-341-7130	341-9791
Web: www.bemiscenter.org				
Gerald R Ford Conservation Center 1326 S 32nd St. Omaha	NE	68105	402-595-1180	595-1178
Web: www.nebraskahistory.org				

NEW JERSEY

			Phone	Fax
Atlantic City Art Ctr Boardwalk & New Jersey Ave Atlantic City	NJ	08401	609-347-5837	347-5844
Web: www.acartcenter.org				
Great Falls Historic District Cultural Ctr 65 McBride Ave Ext. Paterson	NJ	07501	973-279-9587	279-0587
Web: www.patersonnj.gov				

NEW MEXICO

			Phone	Fax
Branigan Cultural Ctr 500 N Water St Las Cruces	NM	88001	575-541-2155	541-2152
National Hispanic Cultural Ctr 1701 4th St SW Albuquerque	NM	87102	505-246-2261	246-2613
Web: www.nhccnm.org				
South Broadway Cultural Ctr 1025 Broadway SE Albuquerque	NM	87102	505-848-1320	848-1329
Web: www.cabq.gov/sbcc				

NEW YORK

			Phone	Fax
African American Cultural Center of Buffalo Inc 350 Masten Ave Buffalo	NY	14209	716-884-2013	885-2590
Web: www.africancultural.org				
Burchfield-Penney Art Ctr *Buffalo State College* 1300 Elmwood Ave Buffalo	NY	14222	716-878-6011	878-6003
Web: www.burchfieldpenney.org				
Hallwalls Contemporary Arts Ctr 341 Delaware Ave Buffalo	NY	14202	716-854-1694	854-1696
Web: www.hallwalls.org				
Rochester Contemporary Art Ctr 137 E Ave Rochester	NY	14604	585-461-2222	461-2223
Web: www.rochestercontemporary.org				

NORTH CAROLINA

Name / Address	City	State	Zip	Phone	Fax
African American Cultural Complex 119 Sunnybrook Rd *Web:* www.aaccmuseum.org	Raleigh	NC	27610	919-231-0625	212-3598
Afro-American Cultural Ctr 551 S Tryon St *Web:* www.ganttcenter.org	Charlotte	NC	28202	704-547-3700	
Center for Visual Arts - Greensboro 200 N Davie St PO Box 13 *Web:* www.greensboroart.org	Greensboro	NC	27401	336-333-7475	333-7477
Delta Fine Arts Inc 2611 New Walkertown Rd *Web:* www.deltafinearts.org	Winston-Salem	NC	27101	336-722-2625	722-9449
Greensboro Cultural Center at Festival Park 200 N Davie St *Web:* www.greensboro-nc.gov/Departments/Executive/events/hosting/culturalcenter	Greensboro	NC	27401	336-373-2712	373-4187
Pack Place 2 S Pack Sq *Web:* www.packplace.org	Asheville	NC	28801	828-257-4500	251-5652
Page-Walker Arts & History Ctr 119 Ambassador Loop *Web:* www.townofcary.org	Cary	NC	27513	919-460-4963	388-1141
Sawtooth Center for Visual Arts 251 N Spruce St *Web:* www.sawtooth.org	Winston-Salem	NC	27101	336-723-7395	773-0132
Sertoma Arts Ctr 1400 W Millbrook Rd	Raleigh	NC	27612	919-420-2329	420-2330
Southeastern Center for Contemporary Art 750 Marguerite Dr *Web:* www.secca.org	Winston-Salem	NC	27106	336-725-1904	722-6059
Spirit Square Center for Arts & Education 345 N College St	Charlotte	NC	28202	704-348-5750	348-5828

OHIO

Name / Address	City	State	Zip	Phone	Fax
Contemporary Arts Ctr 44 E 6th St *Web:* www.contemporaryartscenter.org	Cincinnati	OH	45202	513-345-8400	721-7422
Dayton Cultural Ctr 40 S Edwin C Moses Blvd *Web:* www.daytonrecreationandyou.com	Dayton	OH	45402	937-333-2489	333-7072
Dayton Visual Arts Ctr 118 N Jefferson St *Web:* www.daytonvisualarts.org	Dayton	OH	45402	937-224-3822	
King Arts Complex The 867 Mt Vernon Ave *Web:* www.thekingartscomplex.com	Columbus	OH	43203	614-645-5464	645-0672
Riverbend Arts Ctr 1301 E Siebenthaler Ave	Dayton	OH	45414	937-333-7000	333-3158

OKLAHOMA

Name / Address	City	State	Zip	Phone	Fax
City Arts Ctr 3000 Pershing Blvd *Web:* www.cityartscenter.org	Oklahoma City	OK	73107	405-951-0000	951-0003
Greenwood Cultural Ctr 322 N Greenwood Ave *Web:* www.greenwoodculturalcenter.com	Tulsa	OK	74120	918-596-1020	596-1029
Red Earth Museum 2100 NE 52nd St *Web:* www.redearth.org	Oklahoma City	OK	73111	405-427-5228	427-8079

OREGON

Name / Address	City	State	Zip	Phone	Fax
Bush Barn Art Ctr 600 Mission St SE *Web:* www.salemart.org	Salem	OR	97302	503-581-2228	371-3342
Maude Kerns Art Ctr 1910 E 15th Ave *Web:* www.mkartcenter.org	Eugene	OR	97403	541-345-1571	345-6248
Portland Institute for Contemporary Art 224 NW 13th Ave Suite 305 *Web:* www.pica.org	Portland	OR	97209	503-242-1419	243-1167

PENNSYLVANIA

Name / Address	City	State	Zip	Phone	Fax
Painted Bride Art Ctr 230 Vine St *Web:* www.paintedbride.org	Philadelphia	PA	19106	215-925-9914	925-7402
Pittsburgh Center for the Arts (PCA) 6300 5th Ave *Web:* www.pittsburgharts.org	Pittsburgh	PA	15232	412-361-0873	361-8338
Silver Eye Center for Photography 1015 E Carson St *Web:* www.silvereye.org	Pittsburgh	PA	15203	412-431-1810	431-5777

QUEBEC

Name / Address	City	State	Zip	Phone	Fax
L'Eglise du Gesu 1200 de Bleury *Web:* www.legesu.com	Montreal	QC	H3B3J3	514-861-4378	866-4853

SOUTH DAKOTA

Name / Address	City	State	Zip	Phone	Fax
Dahl Arts Ctr 713 7th St *Web:* www.thedahl.org	Rapid City	SD	57701	605-394-4101	394-6121
Horse Barn Arts Ctr 309 E Falls Pk Dr	Sioux Falls	SD	57104	605-977-2002	
Multi-Cultural Center of Sioux Falls 515 N Main Ave *Web:* www.sfmcc.org	Sioux Falls	SD	57104	605-367-7401	367-7404

TENNESSEE

Name / Address	City	State	Zip	Phone	Fax
Beck Cultural Exchange Center Inc 1927 Dandridge Ave *Web:* www.beckcecenter.net	Knoxville	TN	37915	865-524-8461	524-8462

TEXAS

Name / Address	City	State	Zip	Phone	Fax
Art Center of Corpus Christi 100 N Shoreline Blvd *Web:* www.artcentercc.org	Corpus Christi	TX	78401	361-884-6406	884-8836
ArtCentre of Plano The 901 18th St *Web:* www.artcentreofplano.org	Plano	TX	75074	972-423-7809	424-0745
Bath House Cultural Ctr (BHCC) 521 E Lawther Dr *Web:* www.dallasculture.org/bathHouseCultureCenter	Dallas	TX	75218	214-670-8749	670-8751
Blue Star Contemporary Arts Ctr 116 Blue Star Rd *Web:* www.bluestarart.org	San Antonio	TX	78204	210-227-6960	229-9412
Carver Community Cultural Ctr 226 N Hackberry St *Web:* www.thecarver.org	San Antonio	TX	78202	210-207-7211	207-4412
Center for Contemporary Arts The 220 Cypress St *Web:* www.center-arts.com	Abilene	TX	79601	325-677-8389	677-1171
Dallas Center for Contemporary Art 161 Glass St *Web:* www.thecontemporary.net	Dallas	TX	75207	214-821-2522	821-9103
Dougherty Arts Ctr 1110 Barton Springs Rd *Web:* www.cityofaustin.org/dougherty	Austin	TX	78704	512-397-1468	397-1475
Guadalupe Cultural Arts Ctr 1300 Guadalupe St *Web:* www.guadalupeculturalarts.org	San Antonio	TX	78207	210-271-3151	271-3480
Ice House Cultural Ctr 1004 W Page St *Web:* www.dallasculture.org/iceHouseCulturalCenter.cfm	Dallas	TX	75208	214-670-7524	670-0550
La Villita Historic Arts Village 418 Villita St *Web:* www.lavillita.com	San Antonio	TX	78205	210-207-8610	207-4390
Latino Cultural Ctr 2600 Live Oak St *Web:* www.dallasculture.org/latinocc	Dallas	TX	75204	214-671-0045	670-0633
Louise Hopkins Underwood Center for the Arts (LHUCA) 511 Ave K *Web:* www.lhuca.org	Lubbock	TX	79401	806-762-8606	762-8622
McKinney Avenue Contemporary (The MAC) 3120 McKinney Ave *Web:* www.the-mac.org	Dallas	TX	75204	214-953-1212	953-1873
Nasher Sculpture Ctr 2001 Flora St *Web:* www.nashersculpturecenter.org	Dallas	TX	75201	214-242-5100	242-5155

UTAH

Name / Address	City	State	Zip	Phone	Fax
Eccles Community Art Ctr 2580 Jefferson Ave *Web:* www.ogden4arts.org	Ogden	UT	84401	801-392-6935	392-5295

VIRGINIA

Name / Address	City	State	Zip	Phone	Fax
Arlington Arts Ctr (AAC) 3550 Wilson Blvd *Web:* www.arlingtonartscenter.org	Arlington	VA	22201	703-248-6800	248-6849
Contemporary Art Center of Virginia (CAC) 2200 Parks Ave *Web:* www.cacv.org	Virginia Beach	VA	23451	757-425-0000	425-8186
Ellipse Arts Ctr 3700 S Four Mile Run Dr *Web:* www.arlingtonarts.org	Arlington	VA	22206	703-228-7710	516-4468
Peninsula Fine Arts Ctr 101 Museum Dr *Web:* www.pfac-va.org	Newport News	VA	23606	757-596-8175	596-0807

WASHINGTON

Name / Address	City	State	Zip	Phone	Fax
Art Concepts on Broadway 924 Broadway Plaza *TF:* 800-758-7459	Tacoma	WA	98402	253-272-2202	272-0899
Corbin Art Ctr 507 W 7th Ave *Web:* www.spokaneparks.org	Spokane	WA	99204	509-625-6677	625-6684
Daybreak Star Ctr 3801 W Government Way PO Box 99100 *Web:* www.unitedindians.org	Seattle	WA	98199	206-285-4425	282-3640

WEST VIRGINIA

Name / Address	City	State	Zip	Phone	Fax
Artisan Ctr 1400 Main St Heritage Sq *Web:* www.artisancenter.com	Wheeling	WV	26003	304-232-1810	232-1812
Artworks Around Town Gallery & Art Ctr 2200 Market St *Web:* www.artworksaroundtown.org	Wheeling	WV	26003	304-233-7540	
Monongalia Arts Ctr (MAC) 107 High St PO Box 239 *Web:* www.monartscenter.com	Morgantown	WV	26507	304-292-3325	292-3326
Oglebay Institute's Stifel Fine Arts Ctr 1330 National Rd *TF:* 888-696-4283 ■ *Web:* www.oionline.com	Wheeling	WV	26003	304-242-7700	242-7747

WISCONSIN

	City	State	Zip	Phone	Fax
Irish Cultural & Heritage Center of Wisconsin 2133 W Wisconsin Ave *Web:* www.ichc.net	Milwaukee	WI	53233	414-345-8800	345-8805

50-3 Historic Homes & Buildings

ALABAMA

	City	State	Zip	Phone	Fax
Battle-Friedman House & Gardens 1010 Greensboro Ave *Web:* www.historictuscaloosa.org	Tuscaloosa	AL	35401	205-758-6138	
Conde-Charlotte Museum House 104 Theatre St	Mobile	AL	36602	251-432-4722	
Fort Gaines Historic Site 51 Bienville Blvd *Web:* www.dauphinisland.org/fort.htm	Dauphin Island	AL	36528	251-861-6992	861-6993
Old Alabama Town 301 Columbus St *TF:* 888-240-1850 ■ *Web:* www.oldalabamatown.com	Montgomery	AL	36104	334-240-4500	240-4519
Tannehill Ironworks Historical State Park 12632 Confederate Pkwy *Web:* www.tannehill.org	McCalla	AL	35111	205-477-5711	477-9400

ALASKA

	City	State	Zip	Phone	Fax
Gold Dredge Number Eight 1755 Old Steese Hwy N *Web:* www.golddredgeno8.com	Fairbanks	AK	99712	907-457-6058	457-8888

ARIZONA

	City	State	Zip	Phone	Fax
Arcosanti 6433 Doubletree Ranch Rd *TF:* 800-752-3187 ■ *Web:* www.arcosanti.org/expCosanti	Paradise Valley	AZ	86333	480-948-6145	998-4312
Frank Lloyd Wright Foundation 12621 N Frank Lloyd Wright Blvd PO Box 4430 *Web:* www.franklloydwright.org	Scottsdale	AZ	85259	480-860-2700	391-4009
Goldfield Ghost Town & Mine 4650 N Mammouth Rd *Web:* www.goldfieldghosttown.com	Goldfield	AZ	85219	480-983-0333	834-7947
Historic Heritage Square 115 N 6th St *Web:* www.phoenix.gov	Phoenix	AZ	85004	602-262-5071	732-2624
OK Corral 326 E Allen St *TF:* 800-518-1566 ■ *Web:* www.ok-corral.com	Tombstone	AZ	85638	520-457-3456	457-3456
Wrigley Mansion 2501 E Telawa Trail *TF:* 888-879-7201 ■ *Web:* www.wrigleymansionclub.com	Phoenix	AZ	85016	602-955-4079	956-8439

ARKANSAS

	City	State	Zip	Phone	Fax
Arkansas Governor's Mansion 1800 Ctr St *Web:* www.arkansasgovernorsmansion.com	Little Rock	AR	72206	501-324-9805	324-9808
Belle Grove Historic District Bounded by N 5th N 'H' N 8th & N 'C' Sts *TF:* 800-637-1477 ■ *Web:* www.fortsmith.org	Fort Smith	AR	72901	479-783-8888	784-2421
Miss Laura's Visitor Ctr 2 N 'B' St *TF:* 800-637-1477 ■ *Web:* www.fortsmith.org	Fort Smith	AR	72901	479-783-8888	784-2421
Quapaw Quarter Curran Hall 615 E Capitol Ave *Web:* www.quapaw.com	Little Rock	AR	72202	501-371-0075	374-8142

CALIFORNIA

	City	State	Zip	Phone	Fax
Camron-Stanford House 1418 Lakeside Dr *Web:* www.cshouse.org	Oakland	CA	94612	510-874-7802	874-7803
Casa del Herrero 1387 E Valley Rd *Web:* www.casadelherrero.com	Santa Barbara	CA	93108	805-565-5653	969-2371
Cohen-Bray House 1440 29th Ave *Web:* www.cohenbrayhouse.info	Oakland	CA	94601	510-536-1703	
Coit Tower 1 Telegraph Hill Blvd	San Francisco	CA	94133	415-362-0808	421-7795
Dunsmuir Hellman Historic Estate 2960 Peralta Oaks Ct *Web:* www.dunsmuir-hellman.org	Oakland	CA	94605	510-615-5555	562-8294
Ennis-Brown House 2655 Glendower Ave *Web:* www.ennishouse.org	Los Angeles	CA	90027	323-660-0607	660-3646
Fallon House 175 W St John St *Web:* www.historysanjose.org	San Jose	CA	95110	408-993-8300	993-8088
George White & Anna Gunn Marston House 3525 7th Ave	San Diego	CA	92103	619-298-3142	
Kimberly Crest House & Gardens 1325 Prospect Dr PO Box 206 *Web:* www.kimberlycrest.org	Redlands	CA	92373	909-792-2111	798-1716
McCallum Adobe 221 S Palm Canyon Dr Village Green Heritage Ctr	Palm Springs	CA	92262	760-323-8297	320-2561
McHenry Mansion 906 15th St *Web:* www.mchenrymuseum.org	Modesto	CA	95354	209-577-5344	491-4407
Old Sacramento Business Assn Inc 980 9th St Suite 400 *Web:* www.oldsacramento.com	Sacramento	CA	95814	916-442-8575	442-2053
Old Sacramento Schoolhouse 1200 Front St *Web:* www.scoe.net/oldsacschoolhouse	Sacramento	CA	95814	916-483-8818	972-7041
Olivas Adobe Historical Park 4200 Olivas Pk Dr *Web:* www.olivasadobe.org	Ventura	CA	93001	805-644-4346	
Peralta Adobe 175 W St John St *Web:* www.historysanjose.org	San Jose	CA	95110	408-993-8300	993-8088
Robinson Jeffers Tor House Foundation 26304 Ocean View Ave *Web:* www.torhouse.org	Carmel	CA	93923	831-624-1813	624-3696
Village Green Heritage Ctr 221 S Palm Canyon Dr *Web:* www.palmcanyondrive.org	Palm Springs	CA	92262	760-323-8297	320-2561
Winchester Mystery House 525 S Winchester Blvd *Web:* www.winchestermysteryhouse.com	San Jose	CA	95128	408-247-2000	247-2090

COLORADO

	City	State	Zip	Phone	Fax
Centennial House 1671 Galena St	Aurora	CO	80010	303-739-6660	
Pearce-McAllister Cottage 1880 Gaylord St	Denver	CO	80206	303-322-1053	322-3704

CONNECTICUT

	City	State	Zip	Phone	Fax
Bates-Scofield Homestead 45 Old King's Hwy N	Darien	CT	06820	203-655-9233	656-3892
Bush-Holley House 39 Strickland Rd *Web:* www.hstg.org	Cos Cob	CT	06807	203-869-6899	861-9720
Captain David Judson House 967 Academy Hill *Web:* www.stratfordhistoricalsociety.com	Stratford	CT	06615	203-378-0630	378-2562
Harriet Beecher Stowe House & Library 77 Forest St *Web:* www.harrietbeecherstowecenter.org	Hartford	CT	06105	860-525-9258	522-9259
Hoyt-Barnum House 713 Bedford St	Stamford	CT	06905	203-329-1183	322-1607
Isham-Terry House 211 High St *Web:* www.hartnet.org/als	Hartford	CT	06103	860-247-8996	249-4907
Mill Hill Historic Park & Museum 2 E Wall St *Web:* www.norwalkhistoricalsociety.org	Norwalk	CT	06851	203-846-0525	
Ogden House & Gardens 1520 Bronson Rd *Web:* www.fairfieldhistoricalsociety.org	Fairfield	CT	06824	203-259-1598	255-2716
Old State House 800 Main St *Web:* www.ctosh.org	Hartford	CT	06103	860-522-6766	522-2812
Pardee-Morris House 325 Lighthouse Rd	New Haven	CT	06512	203-562-4183	562-2002
Sheffield Island Lighthouse Ferry Dock Washington & N Water St *Web:* www.seaport.org/sheffield_island.htm	South Norwalk	CT	06854	203-838-9444	855-1017
Wheeler House 25 Avery Pl *Web:* www.westporthistory.org	Westport	CT	06880	203-222-1424	221-0981

DELAWARE

	City	State	Zip	Phone	Fax
Amstel House 2 E 4th St *Web:* www.newcastlehistory.org	New Castle	DE	19720	302-322-2794	322-8923
Dutch House 32 E 3rd St *Web:* www.newcastlehistory.org/houses/dutch.html	New Castle	DE	19720	302-322-9168	322-8923
Greenbank Mill 500 Greenbank Rd *Web:* www.greenbankmill.org	Wilmington	DE	19808	302-999-9001	
John Dickinson Plantation 340 Kitts Hummock Rd *Web:* history.delaware.gov	Dover	DE	19901	302-739-3277	
Preservation Delaware Inc 1405 Greenhill Ave *Web:* www.preservationde.org	Wilmington	DE	19806	302-651-9617	651-9603
Read House & Gardens 42 The Strand *Web:* www.hsd.org/read.htm	New Castle	DE	19720	302-322-8411	322-8557

DISTRICT OF COLUMBIA

	City	State	Zip	Phone	Fax
Dumbarton House 2715 Q St NW *Web:* www.dumbartonhouse.org	Washington	DC	20007	202-337-2288	337-0348
Old Stone House 3051 M St NW *Web:* www.nps.gov	Washington	DC	20007	202-426-6851	426-0215
Tudor Place Historic House & Garden 1644 31st St NW *Web:* www.tudorplace.org	Washington	DC	20007	202-965-0400	965-0164

FLORIDA

	City	State	Zip	Phone	Fax
Ann Norton Sculpture Gardens 253 Barcelona Rd *Web:* www.ansg.org	West Palm Beach	FL	33401	561-832-5328	835-9305
Brokaw-McDougall House 329 N Meridian St *Web:* www.taltrust.org	Tallahassee	FL	32301	850-891-3900	891-3902
Ernest Hemingway Home & Museum 907 Whitehead St *Web:* www.hemingwayhome.com	Key West	FL	33040	305-294-1136	294-2755
Historic Pensacola Village Church & Tarragona Sts *Web:* www.historicpensacola.org	Pensacola	FL	32502	850-595-5985	595-5989
King-Cromartie House 229 SW 2nd Ave	Fort Lauderdale	FL	33301	954-463-4431	523-6228
Merrick House 907 Coral Way	Coral Gables	FL	33134	305-460-5361	
Mission San Luis de Apalachee 2020 W Mission Rd *Web:* dhr.dos.state.fl.us/archaeology/sanluis	Tallahassee	FL	32304	850-487-3711	488-8015

	City	State	Zip	Phone	Fax
Old Saint Augustine Village 246 St George St	Saint Augustine	FL	32084	904-823-9722	823-9938
Oldest House - The Gonzalez-Alvarez House 14 St Francis St *Web:* www.staugustinehistoricalsociety.org	Saint Augustine	FL	32084	904-824-2872	824-2569
Oldest Wooden School House 14 St George St *TF:* 888-653-7245	Saint Augustine	FL	32084	904-824-0192	808-0549
Pablo Historical Park 380 Pablo Ave.	Jacksonville Beach	FL	32250	904-241-5657	241-6243
Ponce de Leon's Fountain of Youth 11 Magnolia Ave. *TF:* 800-356-8222 ■ *Web:* www.fountainofyouthflorida.com	Saint Augustine	FL	32084	904-829-3168	826-1913
Ponce Inlet Lighthouse 4931 S Peninsula Dr. *Web:* www.ponceinlet.org	Ponce Inlet	FL	32127	386-761-1821	761-3121
Sugar Mill Ruins 600 Mission Rd.	New Smyrna Beach	FL	32168	386-736-5953	943-7012

GEORGIA

	City	State	Zip	Phone	Fax
Andrew Low House The 329 Abercorn St. *Web:* www.andrewlowhouse.com	Savannah	GA	31401	912-233-6854	233-1828
Boyhood Home of President Woodrow Wilson 419 7th St. *Web:* www.wilsonboyhoodhome.org	Augusta	GA	30901	706-722-9828	724-3083
Ezekiel Harris House 1822 Broad St *Web:* www.augustamuseum.org/eh.htm	Augusta	GA	30901	706-722-8454	737-2820
Georgia Trust The 1516 Peachtree St NW. *Web:* www.georgiatrust.org	Atlanta	GA	30309	404-881-9980	875-2205
Gordon-Lee Mansion 217 Cove Rd *Web:* www.gordon-leemansion.com	Chickamauga	GA	30707	706-375-4728	357-9499
Green-Meldrim House 14 W Macon St	Savannah	GA	31401	912-232-1251	232-5559
Hammonds House 503 Peeples St SW *Web:* www.hammondshouse.org	Atlanta	GA	30310	404-612-0500	752-8733
Herndon Home 587 University Pl NW	Atlanta	GA	30314	404-581-9813	
Historic Roswell District 617 Atlanta St. *TF:* 800-776-7935 ■ *Web:* www.cvb.roswell.ga.us/attractions.html	Roswell	GA	30075	770-640-3253	640-3252
Juliette Gordon Low Girl Scout National Ctr 10 E Oglethorpe Ave *Web:* www.popeleighey1940.org	Savannah	GA	31401	912-233-4501	233-4659
Ma Rainey House 805 5th Ave	Columbus	GA	31901	706-322-0756	
Margaret Mitchell House 990 Peachtree St NE *Web:* www.margaretmitchellhouse.com	Atlanta	GA	30309	404-249-7015	249-7118
Old Fort Jackson 1 Fort Jackson Rd. *Web:* www.chsgeorgia.org/jackson	Savannah	GA	31404	912-232-3945	236-5126
Owens-Thomas House 124 Abercorn St. *Web:* www.telfair.org	Savannah	GA	31401	912-233-9743	
Pebble Hill Plantation Hwy 319 *Web:* www.pebblehill.com	Thomasville	GA	31792	229-226-2344	226-0780
Sidney Lanier Cottage 935 High St. *Web:* www.cityofmacon.net	Macon	GA	31201	478-743-3851	
Smith Plantation Home 935 Alpharetta St. *Web:* www.archibaldsmithplantation.org	Roswell	GA	30075	770-641-3978	641-3974
Stately Oaks Plantation 100 Carriage Ln *Web:* www.ststelyoaks.com	Jonesboro	GA	30236	770-473-0197	473-9855
Swan House Atlanta History Ctr 130 W Paces Ferry Rd *Web:* www.atlantahistorycenter.com	Atlanta	GA	30305	404-814-4000	814-2041
Woodruff House 988 Bond St *TF:* 800-837-2911	Macon	GA	31201	478-301-2715	301-4124

HAWAII

	City	State	Zip	Phone	Fax
Queen Emma Summer Palace 2913 Pali Hwy *Web:* www.daughtersofhawaii.org	Honolulu	HI	96817	808-595-6291	595-4395

IDAHO

	City	State	Zip	Phone	Fax
Old Idaho Penitentiary State Historic Site 2445 Old Penitentiary Rd *Web:* history.idaho.gov	Boise	ID	83712	208-334-2844	334-3225

ILLINOIS

	City	State	Zip	Phone	Fax
Dana-Thomas House (DTH) 301 E Lawrence Ave. *Web:* www.dana-thomas.org	Springfield	IL	62703	217-782-6776	788-9450
Jane Addams Hull-House Museum 800 S Halsted St. *Web:* www.uic.edu	Chicago	IL	60607	312-413-5353	413-2092
John C Flanagan House 942 NE Glen Oak Ave	Peoria	IL	61603	309-674-0322	674-1882
Lewis & Clark State Historic Site 1 Lewis & Clark Trail. *Web:* www.campriverdubois.com	Hartford	IL	62048	618-251-5811	
Lincoln-Herndon Law Offices State Historic Site 6th & Adams. *Web:* www.illinoishistory.gov/hs/lincoln_herndon.htm	Springfield	IL	62701	217-785-7289	
Sears Tower 233 S Wacker Dr *TF:* 877-759-3325 ■ *Web:* www.theskydeck.com	Chicago	IL	60606	312-875-9449	906-8193
Stephen Mack Home & Whitman Trading Post 2221 Freeport Rd *Web:* www.macktownlivinghistory.com	Rockton	IL	61072	815-624-4200	

INDIANA

	City	State	Zip	Phone	Fax
Allen County Courthouse 715 S Calhoun St.	Fort Wayne	IN	46802	260-449-7211	449-7919*
Morris-Butler House 1204 N Pk Ave *TF:* 800-450-4534	Indianapolis	IN	46202	317-636-5409	636-2630
President Benjamin Harrison Home 1230 N Delaware St *Web:* www.presidentbenjaminharrison.org	Indianapolis	IN	46202	317-631-1898	632-5488
Swinney Homestead 1424 W Jefferson Blvd *Web:* www.settlersinc.org	Fort Wayne	IN	46802	260-424-7212	

IOWA

	City	State	Zip	Phone	Fax
Brucemore 2160 Linden Dr SE. *Web:* www.brucemore.org	Cedar Rapids	IA	52403	319-362-7375	362-9481
Mamie Doud Eisenhower Birthplace 709 Carroll St. *Web:* www.booneiowa.com	Boone	IA	50036	515-432-1896	
Mathias Ham House Historic Site 2241 Lincoln Ave *TF:* 800-226-3369 ■ *Web:* www.mississippirivermuseum.com/features_historicsites_ham.cfm	Dubuque	IA	52001	563-557-9545	583-1241
Seminole Valley Farm 1400 Seminole Valley Rd NE	Cedar Rapids	IA	52411	319-378-9240	
Sherman Hill National Historic District 1620 Pleasant Suite 204. *Web:* www.historicshermanhill.com	Des Moines	IA	50314	515-284-5717	
Wallace House 756 16th St. *Web:* www.wallace.org	Des Moines	IA	50314	515-243-7063	243-8927

KANSAS

	City	State	Zip	Phone	Fax
Cedar Crest Governor's Mansion 1 SW Cedar Crest Rd	Topeka	KS	66606	785-296-3636	272-9024

KENTUCKY

	City	State	Zip	Phone	Fax
Ashland-The Henry Clay Estate 120 Sycamore Rd *Web:* www.henryclay.org	Lexington	KY	40502	859-266-8581	268-7266
Berry Hill Mansion 700 Louisville Rd. *Web:* www.historicproperties.ky.gov	Frankfort	KY	40601	502-564-3000	564-6505
Brennan House Historic Home 631 S 5th St *Web:* www.thebrennanhouse.org	Louisville	KY	40202	502-540-5145	540-5165
Daniel Boone's Grave 215 E Main St.	Frankfort	KY	40601	502-227-2403	
Hopemont the Hunt-Morgan House 201 N Mill St *Web:* www.cr.nps.gov/nr/travel/lexington/hun.htm	Lexington	KY	40508	859-233-3290	259-9210
Liberty Hall Historic Site 202 Wilkinson St *TF:* 888-516-5101 ■ *Web:* www.libertyhall.org	Frankfort	KY	40601	502-227-2560	227-3348
Locust Grove Historic Home 561 Blankenbaker Ln *Web:* www.locustgrove.org	Louisville	KY	40207	502-897-9845	897-0103
Loudoun House 209 Castlewood Dr. *TF:* 800-914-7990 ■ *Web:* www.lexingtonartleague.org/loudounhousegallery.htm	Lexington	KY	40505	859-254-7024	254-7214
Mary Todd Lincoln House 578 W Main St. *Web:* www.mtlhouse.org	Lexington	KY	40507	859-233-9999	252-2269
Old Louisville Historic Preservation District 1340 S 4th St *Web:* www.oldlouisville.com	Louisville	KY	40208	502-635-5244	635-5245
Riverside Farnsley-Moremen Landing 7410 Moorman Rd *Web:* www.riverside-landing.org	Louisville	KY	40272	502-935-6809	935-6821

LOUISIANA

	City	State	Zip	Phone	Fax
Beauregard-Keyes House 1113 Chartres St	New Orleans	LA	70116	504-523-7257	523-7257
Destrehan Plantation 13034 River Rd. *TF:* 877-453-2095 ■ *Web:* www.destrehanplantation.org	Destrehan	LA	70047	985-764-9315	725-1929
Elms Mansion & Gardens 3029 St Charles Ave. *Web:* www.elmsmansion.com	New Orleans	LA	70115	504-895-9200	899-3231
Greenwood Plantation 6838 Highland Rd. *TF:* 800-259-4475 ■ *Web:* www.greenwoodplantation.com	Saint Francisville	LA	70775	225-655-4475	655-3292
Hermann-Grima House 820 St Louis St. *Web:* www.hgghh.org	New Orleans	LA	70112	504-525-5661	568-9735
Houmas House Plantation & Gardens 40136 Hwy 942 *TF:* 866-850-5654 ■ *Web:* www.houmashouse.com	Darrow	LA	70725	225-473-7841	473-7891
Rosedown Plantation State Historic Site 12501 Hwy 10 *TF:* 888-376-1867 ■ *Web:* www.crt.state.la.us/parks/irosedown.aspx	Saint Francisville	LA	70775	225-635-3332	784-1382

MAINE

	City	State	Zip	Phone	Fax
Blaine House 192 State St.	Augusta	ME	04330	207-287-2121	287-6420
Fort Knox Historical Site 711 Fort Knox Rd	Prospect	ME	04981	207-469-7719	469-7719
Isaac Farrar Mansion 17 2nd St	Bangor	ME	04401	207-941-2808	941-2812
Neal Dow Memorial 714 Congress St	Portland	ME	04102	207-773-7773	
Portland Head Light 1000 Shore Rd *Web:* www.portlandheadlight.com	Cape Elizabeth	ME	04107	207-799-2661	799-2800
Victoria Mansion 109 Danforth St *Web:* www.victoriamansion.org	Portland	ME	04101	207-772-4841	772-6290

				Phone	Fax
Wadsworth-Longfellow House 487 Congress St *Web:* www.mainehistory.org/house_overview.shtml	Portland	ME	04101	207-879-0427	775-4301

MARYLAND

				Phone	Fax
Barracks The 43 Pinkney St *TF:* 800-603-4020 ■ *Web:* www.annapolis.org	Annapolis	MD	21401	410-267-7619	267-6189
Charles Carroll House 107 Duke of Gloucester St *Web:* www.charlescarrollhouse.com	Annapolis	MD	21401	410-269-1737	
Chase-Lloyd House 22 Maryland Ave	Annapolis	MD	21401	410-263-2723	
Evergreen House 4545 N Charles St *Web:* www.jhu.edu/~evrgreen/evergreen.html	Baltimore	MD	21210	410-516-6060	516-4585
Waterfront Warehouse 4 Pinkney St *TF:* 800-603-4020 ■ *Web:* www.annapolis.org/tour-properties.html	Annapolis	MD	21401	410-267-7619	267-6189
William Paca House & Garden 186 Prince George St *TF:* 800-603-4020 ■ *Web:* www.annapolis.org/paca-house.html	Annapolis	MD	21401	410-263-5553	626-1030

MASSACHUSETTS

				Phone	Fax
Barnstable Court House 3195 Main St	Barnstable	MA	02630	508-375-6685	362-7754
Captain Bangs Hallett House 2 Strawberry Ln *Web:* www.hsoy.org	Yarmouth Port	MA	02675	508-362-3021	
Freedom Trail 99 Chauncy St Suite 401 *Web:* www.thefreedomtrail.org	Boston	MA	02111	617-357-8300	357-8303
Grange Hall State Rd *Web:* www.mvpreservation.org	West Tisbury	MA	02575	508-627-4440	627-8088
Hadwen House 96 Main St *Web:* www.nha.org	Nantucket	MA	02554	508-228-1894	228-5618
Historic Mitchell House 1 Vestal St *Web:* www.mariamitchell.org/maria-mitchell-2/historic-mitchell-house	Nantucket	MA	02554	508-228-2896	228-1031
House of the Seven Gables 54 Turner St *Web:* www.7gables.org	Salem	MA	01970	978-744-0991	741-4350
Hoxie House 18 Water St	Sandwich	MA	02563	508-888-1173	
Olde Colonial Courthouse Rendezvous Ln & Rt 6A	Barnstable	MA	02630	508-362-8927	
Salisbury Mansion 40 Highland St *Web:* www.worcesterhistory.org/mansion.html	Worcester	MA	01609	508-753-8278	753-9070
Wistariahurst Museum 238 Cabot St *Web:* www.wistariahurst.org	Holyoke	MA	01040	413-322-5660	534-2344

MICHIGAN

				Phone	Fax
Applewood - the CS Mott Estate 1400 E Kearsley St	Flint	MI	48503	810-233-3031	232-6937
Edsel & Eleanor Ford House 1100 Lake Shore Rd *Web:* www.fordhouse.org	Grosse Pointe Shores	MI	48236	313-884-4222	884-5977
Heritage Hill Historic District 126 College Ave SE *Web:* www.heritagehillweb.org	Grand Rapids	MI	49503	616-459-8950	459-2409
Meyer May House 450 Madison Ave SE	Grand Rapids	MI	49503	616-246-4821	
Turner-Dodge House & Heritage Ctr 100 E N St *Web:* www.parks.cityoflansingmi.com	Lansing	MI	48906	517-483-4220	483-6081
Whaley Historical House Museum 624 E Kearsley St *Web:* www.gfn.org/whaley	Flint	MI	48503	810-235-6841	235-6186

MINNESOTA

				Phone	Fax
Alexander Ramsey House (ARH) 265 S Exchange St *Web:* www.mnhs.org/places/sites/arh	Saint Paul	MN	55102	651-296-8760	296-0100
Ard Godfrey House 28 University Ave SE *Web:* www.ardgodfreyhouse.com	Minneapolis	MN	55414	612-870-8001	813-5336
Comstock Historic House 506 8th St S *Web:* www.mnhs.org/places/sites/ch/index.html	Moorhead	MN	56560	218-291-4211	
Glensheen Mansion 3300 London Rd *TF:* 888-454-4536 ■ *Web:* www.d.umn.edu	Duluth	MN	55804	218-726-8910	726-8911
Historic Fort Snelling Hwy 55 E of Airport *Web:* www.mnhs.org/places/sites/hfs/index.html	Saint Paul	MN	55111	612-726-1171	725-2429
History Center of Olmsted County 1195 W Cir Dr SW *Web:* www.olmstedhistory.com	Rochester	MN	55902	507-282-9447	289-5481
James J Hill House 240 Summit Ave *TF:* 888-727-8386 ■ *Web:* www.mnhs.org	Saint Paul	MN	55102	651-297-2555	297-5655
Plummer House 1091 SW Plummer Ln *Web:* www.ci.rochester.mn.us/park/Plummer/plummer.htm	Rochester	MN	55902	507-328-2525	328-2535
Purcell-Cutts House 2328 Lake Pl *Web:* www.artsmia.org/unified-vision/purcell-cutts-house	Minneapolis	MN	55405	612-870-3131	

MISSISSIPPI

				Phone	Fax
Isaac Carter Cabin 1701 Old Richton Rd	Petal	MS	39465	601-583-3306	

MISSOURI

				Phone	Fax
1859 Jail Marshal's Home & Museum 217 N Main St *Web:* www.jchs.org/jail/museum.html	Independence	MO	64050	816-252-1892	252-1510
Fort Osage National Historic Landmark 105 Osage St *Web:* www.historicfortosage.com	Sibley	MO	64088	816-650-5737	795-7938
Frank Lloyd Wright House in Ebbsworth Park 120 N Ballas Rd *Web:* www.ebsworthpark.org	Kirkwood	MO	63122	314-822-8359	
General Daniel Bissell House 10225 Bellefontaine Rd *Web:* www.co.st-louis.mo.us/parks/cg-bissellhouse.html	Saint Louis	MO	63137	314-544-5714	638-5009
Harris-Kearney House 4000 Baltimore St *Web:* www.westporthistorical.org/house.html	Kansas City	MO	64111	816-561-1821	
Historic Christopher Hawken House 1155 S Rock Hill Rd *Web:* www.historicwebster.org/hawken_house.shtml	Saint Louis	MO	63119	314-968-1857	968-1857
Historic Hanley House 7600 Westmoreland St	Clayton	MO	63105	314-226-9893	290-8517
Historic Samuel Cupples House 3673 W Pine Mall *Web:* www.slu.edu	Saint Louis	MO	63108	314-977-3575	977-3581
Oakland House 7801 Genesta St *Web:* www.afftonoaklandhouse.com	Saint Louis	MO	63123	314-352-5654	
Vaile Mansion 1500 N Liberty St *Web:* www.vailemansion.org	Independence	MO	64050	816-325-7430	

MONTANA

				Phone	Fax
Moss Mansion 914 Division St *Web:* www.mossmansion.com	Billings	MT	59101	406-256-5100	252-0091

NEBRASKA

				Phone	Fax
General Crook House Museum 5730 N 30th St Bldg 11B *Web:* www.omahahistory.org/museum.htm	Omaha	NE	68111	402-455-9990	453-9448
Joslyn Castle 3902 Davenport St *Web:* www.joslyncastle.com	Omaha	NE	68131	402-595-2199	
Thomas P Kennard House PO Box 82554 *Web:* www.nebraskahistory.org	Lincoln	NE	68501	402-471-4764	

NEVADA

				Phone	Fax
Bowers Mansion 4005 US 395 S	Carson City	NV	89701	775-828-6642	849-9568

NEW HAMPSHIRE

				Phone	Fax
Kimball-Jenkins Estate 266 N Main St *Web:* www.kimballjenkins.com	Concord	NH	03301	603-225-3932	225-9288

NEW JERSEY

				Phone	Fax
Absecon Lighthouse 31 S Rhode Island Ave *Web:* www.abseconlighthouse.org	Atlantic City	NJ	08401	609-449-1360	449-1919
Ballantine House 49 Washington St *Web:* www.newarkmuseum.org	Newark	NJ	07102	973-596-6550	642-0459
Batsto Historic Village 4110 Nesco Rd Wharton State Forest *Web:* www.batstovillage.org	Hammonton	NJ	08037	609-561-0024	567-8116
Dey Mansion 199 Totowa Rd	Wayne	NJ	07470	973-696-1776	696-1365
Durand Hedden House 523 Ridgewood Rd	Maplewood	NJ	07040	973-763-7712	
Israel Crane House c/o Montclair Historical Society 110 Orange Rd *Web:* www.montclairhistorical.org	Montclair	NJ	07042	973-783-1717	783-9419
Pennsylvania Station 1 Raymond Plaza W	Newark	NJ	07107	973-491-8757	
Van Riper-Hopper House 533 Berdan Ave	Wayne	NJ	07470	973-694-7192	694-9100
William Trent House 15 Market St *Web:* www.williamtrenthouse.org	Trenton	NJ	08611	609-989-3027	278-7890

NEW MEXICO

				Phone	Fax
Coronado State Monument 485 Kuaua Rd *Web:* www.nmmonuments.org	Bernalillo	NM	87004	505-867-5351	867-1733
Picuris Pueblo Hwy 75	Penasco	NM	87553	505-587-2519	587-1071
Santa Fe Southern Railway 410 S Guadalupe St *TF:* 888-989-8600 ■ *Web:* www.sfsr.com	Santa Fe	NM	87501	505-989-8600	983-7620
Taos Pueblo PO Box 1846 *Web:* www.taospueblo.com	Taos	NM	87571	505-758-1028	758-4604

NEW YORK

				Phone	Fax
Browns Race Historic District 60 Browns Race	Rochester	NY	14614	585-325-2030	325-2414
Campbell-Whittlesey House 123 S Fitzhugh St	Rochester	NY	14608	585-546-7028	586-4788
Edgar Allan Poe Cottage E Kingsbridge Rd Grand Concourse	Bronx	NY	10458	718-881-8900	881-4827
Frank Lloyd Wright's martin House Complex 125 Jewett Pkwy *TF:* 877-377-3858 ■ *Web:* www.darwinmartinhouse.org	Buffalo	NY	14214	716-856-3858	856-4009

				Phone	Fax
George Eastman House & Gardens 900 E Ave *Web:* www.eastmanhouse.org	Rochester	NY	14607	585-271-3361	271-3970
Glenview Mansion 511 Warburton Ave Hudson River Museum *Web:* www.hrm.org	Yonkers	NY	10701	914-963-4550	
Gracie Mansion 88th St & E End Ave *Web:* www.nyc.gov/html/om/html/gracie.html	New York	NY	10128	212-570-4751	570-4493
Jacob Purdy House 60 Pk Ave	White Plains	NY	10603	914-328-1776	
Kykuit - The Rockefeller Estate Rt 9 *Web:* www.hudsonvalley.org	Sleepy Hollow	NY	10591	914-631-9491	
Lighthouse at Sleepy Hollow Palmer Ave Kingsland Pt Pk	Sleepy Hollow	NY	10549	914-366-5109	
Lyndhurst 635 S Broadway *Web:* www.lyndhurst.org	Tarrytown	NY	10591	914-631-4481	
Philipsburg Manor Rt 9 *Web:* www.hudsonvalley.org	Sleepy Hollow	NY	10591	914-631-3992	
Philipse Manor Hall 29 Warburton Ave *Web:* www.philipsemanorhall.blogspot.com	Yonkers	NY	10701	914-965-4027	965-6485
Pruyn House 207 Old Niskayuna Rd PO Box 1254 *Web:* www.colonie.com/pruyn	Latham	NY	12110	518-783-1435	783-1437
Queens Historical Society The *Kingsland Homestead* 143-35 37th Ave *Web:* www.queenshistoricalsociety.org/kingsland.html	Flushing	NY	11354	718-939-0647	539-9885
Sleepy Hollow Cemetery 540 N Broadway *Web:* www.sleepyhollowcemetery.org	Sleepy Hollow	NY	10591	914-631-0081	631-0085
Washington Irving's Sunnyside W Sunnyside Ln *Web:* www.hudsonvalley.org	Tarrytown	NY	10591	914-591-8763	591-4436
Washington's Heaquarters/Miller House 140 Virginia Rd	White Plains	NY	10603	914-949-1236	
Wilcox Octagon House 5420 W Genesee St	Camillus	NY	13031	315-488-7800	
Woodside Mansion 485 E Ave	Rochester	NY	14607	585-271-2705	271-9089

NORTH CAROLINA

				Phone	Fax
Biltmore Estate 1 Approach Rd *TF Resv:* 800-411-3812 ■ *Web:* www.biltmore.com	Asheville	NC	28803	828-225-1333	225-1629
Blandwood Mansion 447 W Washington St *Web:* www.blandwood.org	Greensboro	NC	27401	336-272-5003	272-8049
Castle McCulloch 3925 Kivett Dr *Web:* www.castlemcculloch.com	Jamestown	NC	27282	336-887-5413	887-5429
Haywood Hall House & Gardens 211 New Bern Pl *Web:* www.haywoodhall.org	Raleigh	NC	27601	919-832-8357	
Historic Latta Plantation 5225 Sample Rd *Web:* www.lattaplantation.org	Huntersville	NC	28078	704-875-2312	875-1724
James K Polk Memorial State Historic Site 12031 Lancaster Hwy PO Box 475 *Web:* www.nchistoricsites.org	Pineville	NC	28134	704-889-7145	889-3057
Mendenhall Plantation 603 W Main St PO Box 512 *Web:* www.mendenhallplantation.org	Jamestown	NC	27282	336-454-3819	
Mordecai Historic Park 1 Mimosa St *Web:* www.raleighnc.gov/mordecai	Raleigh	NC	27604	919-857-4364	
Reed Gold Mine State Historic Site 9621 Reed Mine Rd *Web:* www.nchistoricsites.org	Midland	NC	28107	704-721-4653	721-4657
Tannenbaum Historic Park 2200 New Garden Rd *Web:* www.greensboro-nc.gov	Greensboro	NC	27410	336-545-5315	545-5314
Thomas Wolfe Memorial 52 N Market St *Web:* www.wolfememorial.com	Asheville	NC	28801	828-253-8304	252-8171
Vance Birthplace State Historic Site 911 Reems Creek Rd *Web:* www.nchistoricsites.org/vance/vance.htm	Weaverville	NC	28787	828-645-6706	645-0936

OHIO

				Phone	Fax
Fort Meigs State Memorial 29100 W River Rd *TF:* 800-283-8916 ■ *Web:* www.fortmeigs.org	Perrysburg	OH	43551	419-874-4121	874-9446
German Village 588 S 3rd St *Web:* www.germanvillage.org	Columbus	OH	43215	614-221-8888	222-4747
Loghurst Farm 3967 Boardman-Canfield Rd	Canfield	OH	44406	330-533-4330	
Paul Laurence Dunbar House 219 N Paul Laurence Dunbar St *TF:* 800-860-0148	Dayton	OH	45402	937-224-7061	224-4256
Perkins Stone Mansion 550 Copley Rd	Akron	OH	44320	330-535-1120	535-0250
SunWatch Indian Village/Archaeological Park 2301 W River Rd *Web:* www.sunwatch.org	Dayton	OH	45418	937-268-8199	268-1760

OKLAHOMA

				Phone	Fax
Oklahoma Heritage Ctr 1400 N Classen Dr *TF:* 888-501-2059 ■ *Web:* www.oklahomaheritage.com	Oklahoma City	OK	73106	405-235-4458	235-2714

ONTARIO

				Phone	Fax
Zion Schoolhouse 1091 Finch Ave E	Toronto	ON	M2J2X3	416-395-7435	395-1208

OREGON

				Phone	Fax
Brunk House 5705 Salem-Dallas Hwy NW	Salem	OR	97304	503-371-8586	
Deepwood Estate 1116 Mission St SE *Web:* www.oregonlink.com/deepwood	Salem	OR	97302	503-363-1825	363-3586
Mission Mill Museum 1313 Mill St SE *Web:* www.missionmill.org	Salem	OR	97301	503-585-7012	588-9902
Shelton-McMurphey-Johnson House 303 Willamette St *Web:* www.smjhouse.org	Eugene	OR	97401	541-484-0808	984-1413

PENNSYLVANIA

				Phone	Fax
Besty Ross House 239 Arch St *Web:* www.betsyrosshouse.org	Philadelphia	PA	19106	215-686-1252	686-1256
Bishop White House 309 Walnut St	Philadelphia	PA	19106	215-597-0068	
Carpenters' Hall 320 Chestnut St *Web:* www.ushistory.org/carpentershall	Philadelphia	PA	19106	215-925-0167	925-3880
Cashier's House 417 State St *Web:* www.eriecountyhistory.org	Erie	PA	16501	814-454-1813	454-6890
Declaration House 7th & Market Sts	Philadelphia	PA	19106	215-597-0068	597-2744
Eastern State Penitentiary Historic Site 22nd St & Fairmount Ave *Web:* www.easternstate.org	Philadelphia	PA	19130	215-236-3300	236-5289
Fallingwater 1491 Mill Run Rd *Web:* www.wpconline.org	Mill Run	PA	15464	724-329-8501	329-0553
Fort Hunter Mansion & Park 5300 N Front St *Web:* www.forthunter.org	Harrisburg	PA	17110	717-599-5751	599-5838
Franklin Court 314-321 Market St *Web:* www.nps.gov/inde/franklin-court.htm	Philadelphia	PA	19106	215-597-2761	
Glen Foerd on the Delaware 5001 Grant Ave *Web:* www.glenfoerd.org	Philadelphia	PA	19114	215-632-5330	632-2312
Hans Herr House & Museum 1849 Hans Herr Dr *Web:* www.hansherr.org	Willow Street	PA	17584	717-464-4438	
Hartwood Mansion 200 Hartwood Acres	Pittsburgh	PA	15238	412-767-9200	767-0171
Historic Rock Ford Plantation 881 Rockford Rd *Web:* www.rockfordplantation.org	Lancaster	PA	17602	717-392-7223	392-7283
Independence Hall & Congress Hall Chestnut St-between 5th & 6th Sts *Web:* www.nps.gov/inde	Philadelphia	PA	19106	215-597-0068	597-8976
John Chadds House 1719 Creek Rd	Chadds Ford	PA	19317	610-388-7376	388-7480
John Harris-Simon Cameron Mansion The 219 S Front St *Web:* www.dauphincountyhistory.org	Harrisburg	PA	17104	717-233-3462	233-6059
Lancaster County's Historical Society & President James Buchanan's Wheatland 230 N President Ave *Web:* www.lancasterhistory.org	Lancaster	PA	17603	717-392-4633	293-2739
Liberty Bell Shrine 622 W Hamilton St *Web:* www.libertybellmuseum.org	Allentown	PA	18101	610-435-4232	435-5061
Physick House 321 S 4th St *Web:* www.philalandmarks.org	Philadelphia	PA	19106	215-925-2251	925-7909
Powel House 244 S 3rd St *Web:* www.philalandmarks.org/powel.aspx	Philadelphia	PA	19106	215-627-0364	627-1733
Scranton Iron Furnace 159 Cedar Ave	Scranton	PA	18505	570-963-4804	963-4194
Todd House 4th & Walnut Sts	Philadelphia	PA	19106	215-965-2305	597-1548

QUEBEC

				Phone	Fax
Artillery Park Heritage Site 2 D'Auteuil St PO Box 10 Stn B *TF:* 888-773-8888 ■ *Web:* www.pc.gc.ca	Quebec	QC	G1K7A1	418-648-7016	648-2506
Fortifications of Quebec National Historic Site 100 St Louis St PO Box 10 Stn B *Web:* www.museocapitale.qc.ca	Quebec	QC	G1K7A1	418-648-7016	948-9068
Parliament Bldg (Hotel du Parlement) 1045 Rue des Parlementaires *TF:* 866-337-8837 ■ *Web:* www.assnat.qc.ca	Quebec	QC	G1A1A3	418-643-7239	646-4271

RHODE ISLAND

				Phone	Fax
Astors' Beechwood Mansion 580 Bellevue Ave *Web:* www.astorsbeechwood.com	Newport	RI	02840	401-846-3772	849-6998
Belcourt Castle 657 Bellevue Ave *Web:* www.belcourtcastle.com	Newport	RI	02840	401-846-0669	846-5345
Chateau-Sur-Mer 474 Bellevue Ave *Web:* www.newportmansions.org	Newport	RI	02840	401-847-1000	847-1361
Edward King House 35 King St *TF:* 866-878-6954 ■ *Web:* www.edwardkinghouse.com	Newport	RI	02840	401-846-7426	846-5308
Hunter House 54 Washington St *Web:* www.newportmansions.org	Newport	RI	02840	401-847-1000	847-1361
John Brown House Museum 52 Power St *Web:* www.rihs.org	Providence	RI	02906	401-273-7507	751-2307
Marble House 596 Bellevue Ave *Web:* www.newportmansions.org	Newport	RI	02840	401-847-1000	847-1361
Nightingale-Brown House 357 Benefit St *Web:* www.brown.edu/Research/JNBC	Providence	RI	02903	401-863-1177	
Rose Island Lighthouse Foundation 365 Thames St 2nd Fl PO Box 1419 *Web:* www.roseislandlighthouse.org	Newport	RI	02840	401-847-4242	847-7262
Samuel Whitehorne House 416 Thames St *Web:* www.newportrestoration.com	Newport	RI	02840	401-849-7300	849-0125

SOUTH CAROLINA

				Phone	Fax
Aiken-Rhett House 48 Elizabeth St *Web:* www.historiccharleston.org	Charleston	SC	29401	843-723-1159	

	City	State	Zip	Phone	Fax
Beattie House 8 Bennett St	Greenville	SC	29601	864-233-9977	
Boone Hall Plantation 1235 State Rd S-10-97 *Web:* www.boonehallplantation.com	Mount Pleasant	SC	29464	843-884-4371	884-0475
Fort Hill - the John C Calhoun House Clemson University Fort Hill St	Clemson	SC	29634	864-656-2475	656-1026
Gassaway Mansion 106 Dupont Dr *Web:* www.gassawaymansion.com	Greenville	SC	29607	864-271-0188	242-9935
Hampton-Preston Mansion & Garden 1615 Blanding St *Web:* www.historiccolumbia.org	Columbia	SC	29201	803-252-1770	929-7695
Heyward-Washington House 87 Church St	Charleston	SC	29401	843-722-0354	
Kilgore-Lewis House The 560 N Academy St *Web:* www.kilgore-lewis.org	Greenville	SC	29602	864-232-3020	
Mann-Simons Cottage 1403 Richland St	Columbia	SC	29201	803-252-7742	929-7695
Nathaniel Russell House 51 Meeting St *Web:* www.historiccharleston.org	Charleston	SC	29401	843-724-8481	805-6732
Old Exchange & Provost Dungeon 122 E Bay St *TF:* 888-763-0448 ■ *Web:* www.oldexchange.com	Charleston	SC	29401	843-727-2165	727-2163
Robert Mills House & Gardens 1616 Blanding St *Web:* www.historiccolumbia.org	Columbia	SC	29201	803-252-7742	929-7695
Seibels House 1601 Richland St *Web:* www.historiccolumbia.org/rentals/seibels.html	Columbia	SC	29201	803-252-7742	929-7695
South Carolina State House 1100 Gervais St	Columbia	SC	29201	803-734-2430	734-2439
Woodrow Wilson Family Home 1705 Hampton St *Web:* www.historiccolumbia.org/history/wilson.html	Columbia	SC	29201	803-252-7742	929-7695

SOUTH DAKOTA

	City	State	Zip	Phone	Fax
Corn Palace 604 N Main St *TF:* 800-257-2676 ■ *Web:* www.cornpalace.org	Mitchell	SD	57301	605-996-5031	996-8273

TENNESSEE

	City	State	Zip	Phone	Fax
Armstrong-Lockett House 2728 Kingston Pike	Knoxville	TN	37919	865-637-3163	637-1709
Belmont Mansion 1900 Belmont Blvd *Web:* www.belmontmansion.com	Nashville	TN	37212	615-460-5459	460-5688
Blount Mansion 200 W Hill Ave *TF:* 888-654-0016 ■ *Web:* www.blountmansion.org	Knoxville	TN	37901	865-525-2375	546-5315
Carnton Plantation 1345 Carnton Ln *Web:* www.carnton.org	Franklin	TN	37064	615-794-0903	794-6563
Carter House 1140 Columbia Ave	Franklin	TN	37064	615-791-1861	794-1327
Confederate Memorial Hall 3148 Kingston Pike *Web:* www.knoxvillecmh.org	Knoxville	TN	37919	865-522-2371	
Davies Manor House 9336 Davies Plantation Rd *Web:* www.daviesmanorplantation.org	Memphis	TN	38133	901-386-0715	388-4677
Hunt-Phelan Home 533 Beale St *Web:* www.huntphelan.com	Memphis	TN	38103	901-525-8225	527-9120
Lauderdale Courts-Former Home of Elvis Presley 185 Winchester Suite 328 *Web:* www.lauderdalecourts.com	Memphis	TN	38105	901-523-8662	523-8299
Ramsey House 2614 Thorngrove Pike *Web:* www.ramseyhouse.org	Knoxville	TN	37914	865-546-0745	546-1851
Tipton-Haynes State Historic Site 2620 S Roan St *Web:* www.tipton-haynes.org	Johnson City	TN	37601	423-926-3631	
Travellers Rest Plantation & Museum 636 Farrell Pkwy *TF:* 866-832-8197 ■ *Web:* www.travellersrestplantation.org	Nashville	TN	37220	615-832-8197	832-8169
Woodruff-Fontaine House 680 Adams Ave	Memphis	TN	38105	901-526-1469	755-6075

TEXAS

	City	State	Zip	Phone	Fax
French-Galvan House 1581 N Chaparral St *Web:* www.co.nueces.tx.us/histcomm/frenchgalvanhouse.asp	Corpus Christi	TX	78401	361-826-3410	826-4301
Fulton Mansion 317 N Fulton Beach Rd *Web:* www.tpwd.state.tx.us	Rockport	TX	78382	361-729-0386	729-6581
Guenther House 205 E Guenther St *TF:* 800-235-8186 ■ *Web:* www.guentherhouse.com	San Antonio	TX	78204	210-227-1061	351-6372
Jalufka-Govatos House 1513 N Chaparral St	Corpus Christi	TX	78401	361-826-3410	826-4301
King William Historic District 1032 S Alamo St	San Antonio	TX	78210	210-227-8786	227-8030
McCampbell House 1501 N Chaparral St	Corpus Christi	TX	78401	361-826-3410	826-4301
Neill-Cochran House Museum 2310 San Gabriel St	Austin	TX	78705	512-478-2335	478-1865
Old German Free School Bldg 507 E 10th St *TF:* 866-482-4847 ■ *Web:* www.gths.net/school.html	Austin	TX	78701	512-482-0927	482-0636
Sidbury House 1609 N Chaparral St	Corpus Christi	TX	78401	361-826-3410	826-4301
Thistle Hill 1509 Pennsylvania Ave *Web:* www.thistlehill.org	Fort Worth	TX	76104	817-336-1212	335-5338

UTAH

	City	State	Zip	Phone	Fax
This is the Place Heritage Park 2601 E Sunnyside Ave *Web:* www.thisistheplace.org	Salt Lake City	UT	84108	801-582-1847	583-1869

VERMONT

	City	State	Zip	Phone	Fax
Chimney Point State Historic Site 7305 Vermont Rt 125 *Web:* www.historicvermont.org	Addison	VT	05491	802-759-2412	759-2547
Ethan Allen Homestead 1 Ethan Allen Homestead *Web:* www.ethanallenhomestead.org	Burlington	VT	05408	802-865-4556	865-0661
President Chester A Arthur State Historic Site 4588 Chester Arthur Rd *Web:* www.historicvermont.org/html/arthur.html	Fairfield	VT	05455	802-828-3051	828-3206

VIRGINIA

	City	State	Zip	Phone	Fax
Adam Thoroughgood House 1636 Parish Rd *Web:* www.eteamz.active.com	Virginia Beach	VA	23455	757-460-7588	460-7644
Athenaeum The 201 Prince St *Web:* www.nvfaa.org	Alexandria	VA	22314	703-548-0035	
Capitol Square 9th St N & E Grace St	Richmond	VA	23219	804-698-1788	698-1906
Francis Land House 3131 Virginia Beach Blvd *Web:* www.vbgov.com/dept/arts/francis_land	Virginia Beach	VA	23452	757-431-4000	431-3733
Frank Lloyd Wright's Pope-Leighey House 9000 Richmond Hwy PO Box 15097 *Web:* www.popeleighey1940.org	Alexandria	VA	22309	703-780-4000	780-8509
George Washington's Mount Vernon Estate & Gardens George Washington Memorial Pkwy PO Box 110 *Web:* www.mountvernon.org	Mount Vernon	VA	22121	703-780-2000	
James Madison's Montpelier 11407 Constitution Hwy *Web:* www.montpelier.org	Montpelier Station	VA	22957	540-672-2728	672-0411
John Marshall House The 818 E Marshall St *Web:* www.apva.org/marshall	Richmond	VA	23219	804-648-7998	648-5880
Lynnhaven House 4401 Wishart Rd *Web:* www.virginiabeachhistory.org	Virginia Beach	VA	23455	757-431-4000	
Monticello 931 Thomas Jefferson Pkwy PO Box 316 *Web:* www.monticello.org	Charlottesville	VA	22902	434-984-9822	977-7757
Norfolk Historical Society PO Box 6367 *Web:* www.norfolkhistorical.org/fort	Norfolk	VA	23508	757-640-1720	
Old Cape Henry Lighthouse 583 Atlantic Ave	Fort Story	VA	23459	757-422-9421	
Pope-Leighey House 9000 Richmond Hwy *Web:* www.popeleighey1940.org	Alexandria	VA	22309	703-780-4000	780-8509
Shirley Plantation 501 Shirley Plantation Rd *TF:* 800-232-1613 ■ *Web:* www.shirleyplantation.com	Charles City	VA	23030	804-829-5121	829-6322
Sully Historic Site 3650 Historic Sully Way *Web:* www.fairfaxcounty.gov/parks/sully	Chantilly	VA	20151	703-437-1794	787-3314
Virginia House 4301 Sulgrave Rd *Web:* www.vahistorical.org	Richmond	VA	23221	804-353-4251	354-8247
Willoughby-Baylor House 601 E Freemason St	Norfolk	VA	23501	757-441-1526	
Woodlawn Plantation 9000 Richmond Hwy PO Box 15097 *Web:* www.woodlawn1805.org	Alexandria	VA	22309	703-780-4000	780-8509

WASHINGTON

	City	State	Zip	Phone	Fax
Covington House 4201 Main St	Vancouver	WA	98663	360-695-6750	

WEST VIRGINIA

	City	State	Zip	Phone	Fax
Eckhart House The 810 Main St Old Town *TF:* 888-700-0118 ■ *Web:* www.eckharthouse.com	Wheeling	WV	26003	304-232-5439	
Pearl S Buck Birthplace Rt 219 PO Box 126 *Web:* www.pearlsbuckbirthplace.com	Hillsboro	WV	24946	304-653-4430	

WISCONSIN

	City	State	Zip	Phone	Fax
Kilbourntown House 4400 N Estabrook Dr Estabrook Pk	Milwaukee	WI	53211	414-273-8288	
Pabst Mansion 2000 W Wisconsin Ave *Web:* www.pabstmansion.com	Milwaukee	WI	53233	414-931-0808	931-1005
Taliesin 5607 County Hwy C *Web:* www.taliesinpreservation.org	Spring Green	WI	53588	608-588-7090	588-7514

50-4 Monuments, Memorials, Landmarks

	City	State	Zip	Phone	Fax
Air Force Memorial The 1 Air Force Memorial Dr *TF:* 800-222-2294 ■ *Web:* www.womensmemorial.org	Arlington	VA	22211	703-533-1155	892-7202
Alcatraz Island C/o Alcatraz Cruises LLC Pier 33 Hornblower Alcatraz Landing *Web:* www.nps.gov/alcatraz	San Francisco	CA	94133	415-981-7625	
Amistad Memorial 165 Church St	New Haven	CT	06510	203-387-0370	397-2539
Armed Forces Memorial 232 E Main St Town Pt Pk	Norfolk	VA	23510	757-664-6620	
Buffalo & Erie County Naval & Military Park 1 Naval Pk Cove *Web:* www.buffalonavalpark.org	Buffalo	NY	14202	716-847-1773	847-6405

Name / Address	City	State	ZIP	Phone	Fax
Bunker Hill Monument Monument Sq *Web:* www.nps.gov	Charlestown	MA	02129	617-242-5641	242-6006
Crazy Horse Memorial Avenue of the Chiefs *Web:* www.crazyhorsememorial.org	Crazy Horse	SD	57730	605-673-4681	673-2185
Desert Holocaust Memorial PO Box 11915 *Web:* www.palmsprings.com/points/holocaust	Palm Desert	CA	92255	760-325-7281	324-3154
Empire State Bldg 350 5th Ave Suite 3210 *Web:* www.esbnyc.com	New York	NY	10118	212-736-3100	967-6167
Franklin Delano Roosevelt Memorial 1850 W Basin Dr SW Potomac Pk *Web:* www.nps.gov/fdrm	Washington	DC	20042	202-376-6700	376-6702
Gateway Arch 11 N 4th St *Web:* www.nps.gov/jeff	Saint Louis	MO	63102	314-655-1700	655-1641
George Washington Masonic National Memorial 101 Callahan Dr *Web:* www.gwmemorial.org	Alexandria	VA	22301	703-683-2007	519-9270
Golden Gate Bridge Golden Gate Bridge Toll Plaza Presidio Stn PO Box 9000 *TF:* 877-229-8655 ■ *Web:* www.goldengate.org	San Francisco	CA	94129	415-921-5858	956-1663
Henry J Kaiser Shipyard Memorial & Interpretive Ctr Columbia Way Marine Pk	Vancouver	WA	98661	360-619-1127	696-8009
Holocaust Memorial of the Greater Miami Jewish Federation 1933-1945 Meridian Ave *Web:* www.holocaustmmb.org	Miami Beach	FL	33139	305-538-1663	538-2423
Hoover Dam Hwy 93 *TF:* 866-730-9097 ■ *Web:* www.usbr.gov/lc/hooverdam	Boulder City	NV	89006	702-494-2517	494-2587
Idaho Human Rights Education Ctr 777 S 8th St *Web:* www.idaho-humanrights.org	Boise	ID	83702	208-345-0304	433-1221
Illinois Korean War Memorial 1441 Monument Ave *Web:* www.state.il.us/hpa/hs/korean_memorial.htm	Springfield	IL	62702	217-782-2717	
Illinois Vietnam Veterans Memorial Oak Ridge Cemetery *Web:* www2.illinois.gov	Springfield	IL	62702	217-782-2717	524-3738
Jefferson Memorial E Basin Dr SW *Web:* www.nps.gov/thje	Washington	DC	20242	202-426-6841	252-0051
John Brown Statue 27th St & Sewell Ave	Kansas City	KS	66104	913-321-5800	
John F Kennedy Memorial Ocean St	Hyannis	MA	02601	508-362-9484	
Korean-Vietnam War Memorial 91st & Leavenworth Rd	Kansas City	KS	66109	913-596-7077	
Lewis & Clark Monument Frontier Pk **Fax Area Code:* 636 ■ *TF:* 800-366-2427	Saint Charles	MO	63303	800-366-2427	949-3217*
Liberty Bell Ctr 6th & Market Sts *Web:* www.nps.gov	Philadelphia	PA	19106	215-965-2305	861-4950
Lincoln Memorial Shrine 125 W Vine St *Web:* www.lincolnshrine.org	Redlands	CA	92373	909-798-7632	798-7566
Lincoln Tomb Oak Ridge Cemetery 1500 Monument Ave *Web:* www.illinoishistory.gov/hs/lincoln_tomb.htm	Springfield	IL	62702	217-782-2717	524-3738
Littleton Coin Co LLC 1309 Mt Eustis Rd *TF:* 800-645-3122 ■ *Web:* www.littletoncoin.com	Littleton	NH	03561	603-444-5386	444-0121
Mann Theatres 16530 Ventura Blvd Suite 500 *Web:* www.manntheatres.com	Encino	CA	91436	818-784-6266	
Martin Luther King Jr Memorial at Battle Garden 800 S Stadium Blvd	Columbia	MO	65203	573-874-7460	874-7640
Mason-Dixon Historical Park 61 Buckeye Rd *Web:* www.vicoa.com/mason-dixon	Core	WV	26529	304-879-4101	
Minnesota Vietnam Veterans' Memorial State Capitol Grounds *Web:* www.mvvm.org	Saint Paul	MN	55082	651-777-0686	
Missouri Veterans Memorial NE Corner of Capitol Grounds	Jefferson City	MO	65102	573-751-4127	
Mormon Battalion Visitors Ctr 2510 Juan St	San Diego	CA	92110	619-298-3317	298-5866
Mormon Trail Center at Historic Winter Quarter 3215 State St	Omaha	NE	68112	402-453-9372	453-1538
National War Memorial & Tomb of the Unknown Soldier Elgin & Wellington Sts Confederation Sq *Web:* www.veterans.gc.ca	Ottawa	ON	K1P5A1	613-992-7468	
New Haven Crypt 250 Temple St *Web:* www.newhavencenterchurch.org/crypt.html	New Haven	CT	06511	203-787-0121	787-2187
New Mexico Veterans Memorial 1100 Louisiana Blvd SE	Albuquerque	NM	87108	505-256-2042	294-6617
Philadelphia Vietnam Veterans Memorial Columbus Blvd & Spruce St	Philadelphia	PA	19104	215-535-0643	
Pilgrim Monument & Provincetown Museum 1 High Pole Hill Rd *Web:* www.pilgrim-monument.org	Provincetown	MA	02657	508-487-1310	487-4702
Potomac Assn The 540 Water St Jack London Sq *Web:* www.usspotomac.org	Oakland	CA	94607	510-627-1215	839-4729
Rosedale Memorial Arch Springfield & Memorial Dr	Kansas City	KS	66103	913-596-7077	677-3437
Soldiers & Sailors Memorial Arch 88 Trinity St Bushnell Pk *Web:* www.bushnellpark.org/poi/smarch.html	Hartford	CT	06106	860-232-6710	
Space Needle LLC 203 6th Ave N *TF:* 800-937-9582 ■ *Web:* www.spaceneedle.com	Seattle	WA	98109	206-905-2200	905-2107
Texas State Cemetery 909 Navasota St *Web:* www.cemetery.state.tx.us	Austin	TX	78702	512-463-0605	463-8811
Trenton Battle Monument 348 N Warren St *Web:* www.njparksandforests.org	Trenton	NJ	08625	609-737-0623	
US Marine Corps War Memorial Iwo Jima Meade St & Marshall Dr *Web:* www.nps.gov/gwmp/usmc.htm	Arlington	VA	22211	703-289-2500	289-2598
US Navy Memorial & Naval Heritage Ctr 701 Pennsylvania Ave NW Suite 123 *TF:* 800-821-8892 ■ *Web:* www.lonesailor.org	Washington	DC	20004	202-737-2300	737-2308
USS Alabama Battleship Memorial Park 2703 Battleship Pkwy PO Box 65 *TF:* 800-426-4929 ■ *Web:* www.ussalabama.com	Mobile	AL	36602	251-433-2703	433-2777
USS Indianapolis Memorial Walnut & Senate Ave *Web:* www.ussindianapolis.org/memorial.htm	Indianapolis	IN	46204	317-232-7615	233-4258
USS Kidd Veterans Memorial & Museum 305 S River Rd *Web:* www.usskidd.com	Baton Rouge	LA	70802	225-342-1942	342-2039
USS Missouri Memorial Assn Inc 63 Cowpens St *TF:* 877-644-4896 ■ *Web:* www.ussmissouri.com	Honolulu	HI	96818	808-455-1600	455-1598
USS South Dakota Battleship Memorial 12th St & Kiwanis Ave Sherman Pk	Sioux Falls	SD	57104	605-367-7060	367-4326
Vietnam Veterans Memorial 3027 Walnut St	Kansas City	MO	64111	816-561-8387	
Vietnam Veterans' Memorial Arkansas State Capitol Woodlane Capitol Ave	Little Rock	AR	72201	501-682-5080	
Vietnam Women's Memorial 5 Constitution Ave SW *Web:* www.nps.gov/vive/memorial/women.htm	Washington	DC	20004	202-426-6841	724-0764
Arkansas Post National Memorial 1741 Old Post Rd *Web:* www.nps.gov	Gillett	AR	72055	870-548-2207	548-2431
African-American Civil War Memorial & Museum 1200 U St NW *Web:* www.afroamcivilwar.org	Washington	DC	20001	202-667-2667	667-6771
Korean War Veterans Memorial c/o National Capital Parks - Central 900 Ohio Dr SW *Web:* www.nps.gov/kowa	Washington	DC	20004	202-426-6841	
Lincoln Memorial c/o National Capitol Parks - Central 900 Ohio Dr SW *Web:* www.nps.gov/linc	Washington	DC	20024	202-426-6841	724-0764
Washington Monument c/o National Capitol Pk - Central 900 Ohio Dr SW *Web:* www.nps.gov/wamo	Washington	DC	20024	202-426-6841	
De Soto National Memorial 8300 Desoto Memorial Hwy *Web:* www.nps.gov	Bradenton	FL	34209	941-792-0458	792-5094
Fort Caroline National Memorial 12713 Fort Caroline Rd *Web:* www.nps.gov/foca	Jacksonville	FL	32225	904-641-7155	641-3798
USS Arizona Memorial 1 Arizona Memorial Pl *Web:* www.nps.gov/usar	Honolulu	HI	96818	808-422-0561	483-8608
Lincoln Boyhood National Memorial 2916 E S St PO Box 1816 *Web:* www.nps.gov/libo	Lincoln City	IN	47552	812-937-4541	937-9929
Federal Hall National Memorial 26 Wall St *Web:* www.nps.gov/feha	New York	NY	10005	212-825-6888	825-6874
General Grant National Memorial Riverside Dr & W 122nd St *Web:* www.nps.gov/gegr	New York	NY	10027	212-666-1640	932-9631
Statue of Liberty National Monument & Ellis Island Liberty Island *Web:* www.nps.gov/stli	New York	NY	10004	212-363-3200	
Wright Bros National Memorial 1401 National Pk Dr *Web:* www.nps.gov/wrbr	Manteo	NC	27954	252-473-2111	473-2595
Perry's Victory & International Peace Memorial 93 Delaware Ave PO Box 549 *Web:* www.nps.gov/pevi	Put-in-Bay	OH	43456	419-285-2184	285-2516
Flight 93 National Memorial *National Park Service* 109 W Main St Suite 104 *Web:* www.nps.gov/flni/index.htm	Somerset	PA	15501	814-443-4557	443-2180
Thaddeus Kosciuszko National Memorial c/o Independence National Historical Pk 143 S 3rd St *Web:* www.nps.gov/thko	Philadelphia	PA	19106	215-597-9618	861-4950
Roger Williams National Memorial 282 N Main St *Web:* www.nps.gov/rowi	Providence	RI	02903	401-521-7266	521-7239
Chamizal National Memorial 800 S San Marcial St *Web:* www.nps.gov	El Paso	TX	79905	915-532-7273	532-7240
Lyndon Baines Johnson Memorial Grove on the Potomac Turkey Run Pk George Washington Memorial Pkwy *Web:* www.nps.gov/lyba	McLean	VA	22101	703-289-2500	289-2598
Theodore Roosevelt Island Park c/o Turkey Run Pk George Washington Memorial Pkwy *Web:* www.nps.gov/this	McLean	VA	22101	703-289-2500	289-2598

50-5 Nature Centers, Parks, Other Natural Areas

Name / Address	City	State	ZIP	Phone	Fax
Anita Purves Nature Ctr 1505 N Broadway *Web:* www.urbanaparks.org	Urbana	IL	61801	217-384-4062	384-1052
Anne Kolb Nature Ctr 751 Sheridan St *Web:* www.floridanaturepictures.com/dadebrow/annkolb/ann.htm	Hollywood	FL	33019	954-926-2480	926-2491
Ansonia Nature & Recreation Ctr 10 Deerfield Rd *Web:* www.ansonianaturecenter.org	Ansonia	CT	06401	203-736-1053	
Aurora Reservoir 15151 E Alameda Pkwy 4th Fl *Web:* www.auroragov.org	Aurora	CO	80012	303-739-7160	690-1654
Balboa Park 1549 El Prado Suite 1 *Web:* www.balboapark.org	San Diego	CA	92101	619-239-0512	525-2254
Bear Creek Nature Ctr 245 Bear Creek Rd *Web:* adm.elpasoco.com/Parks	Colorado Springs	CO	80906	719-520-6387	636-8968

Name / Address	City	State	ZIP	Phone	Fax
Beaver Lake Nature Ctr 8477 E Mud Lake Rd *Web:* www.onondagacountyparks.com	Baldwinsville	NY	13027	315-638-2519	638-7488
Biscayne Nature Ctr 6767 Crandon Blvd *Web:* www.biscaynenaturecenter.org	Key Biscayne	FL	33149	305-361-6767	365-8434
Black Hills Caverns 2600 Cavern Rd *TF:* 800-837-9358 ■ *Web:* www.blackhillscaverns.com	Rapid City	SD	57702	605-343-0542	
Blandford Nature Ctr 1715 Hillburn Ave NW *Web:* www.mixedgreens.org	Grand Rapids	MI	49504	616-735-6240	735-6255
Boulder Reservoir 5100 N 51st St *Web:* www.bouldercolorado.gov	Boulder	CO	80301	303-441-3461	441-1807
Box Springs Mountain Park 9699 Box Springs Mountain Rd *Web:* www.riversidecountyparks.org	Moreno Valley	CA	92557	951-684-7032	
Boyden Caverns 74101 E Kings Canyon Rd *Web:* www.caverntours.com	Kings Canyon Natl Park	CA	93633	209-736-2708	736-0330
Butterfly House 11455 Obee Rd *Web:* www.butterfly-house.com	Whitehouse	OH	43571	419-877-2733	
Butterfly House - Faust Park The 15193 Olive Blvd *Web:* www.butterflyhouse.org	Chesterfield	MO	63017	636-530-0076	530-1516
Butterfly World 3600 W Sample Rd Tradewinds Pk S *Web:* www.butterflyworld.com	Coconut Creek	FL	33073	954-977-4400	977-4501
Camelback Mountain & Echo Canyon Recreation Area 5950 N Echo Canyon Pkwy	Phoenix	AZ	85018	602-261-8318	495-5561
Capen Hill Nature Sanctuary 56 Capen Rd PO Box 218 *Web:* www.capenhill.org	Charlton City	MA	01508	508-248-5516	248-5516
Carson Hot Springs 1500 Hot Springs Rd *TF:* 888-917-3711 ■ *Web:* www.carsonhotspringsresort.com	Carson City	NV	89706	775-885-8844	887-0617
Cascade Caverns Park 226 Cascade Caverns Rd *Web:* www.cascadecaverns.com	Boerne	TX	78006	830-755-8080	755-2422
Cave of the Mounds 2975 CAvenue of the Mounds Rd PO Box 148 *Web:* www.caveofthemounds.com	Blue Mounds	WI	53517	608-437-3038	437-4181
Cave of the Winds W Hwy 24 PO Box 826 *Web:* www.caveofthewinds.com	Manitou Springs	CO	80829	719-685-5444	685-1712
Centennial Olympic Park 265 Pk Ave W NW *Web:* www.centennialpark.com	Atlanta	GA	30313	404-222-7275	223-4499
Central Park 830 5th Ave *Web:* www.centralparknyc.org	New York	NY	10065	212-360-8111	360-1329
Chattahoochee Nature Ctr 9135 Willeo Rd *Web:* www.chattnaturecenter.com	Roswell	GA	30075	770-992-2055	552-0926
Cherry Springs Nature Area Caribou-Targhee National Forest 4350 Cliffs Dr	Pocatello	ID	83204	208-236-7500	236-7555
Connecticut Audubon Society Nature Ctr 2325 Burr St *Web:* www.ctaudubon.org	Fairfield	CT	06824	203-259-6305	254-7365
Cypress Gardens 3030 Cypress Gardens Rd *Web:* www.cypressgardens.info	Moncks Corner	SC	29461	843-553-0515	569-0644
Darien Nature Center Inc 120 Brookside Rd PO Box 1603 *Web:* www.dariennaturecenter.org	Darien	CT	06820	203-655-7459	655-3185
DeGraaf Nature Ctr 600 Graafschap Rd	Holland	MI	49423	616-355-1057	355-1069
Devil's Den Preserve 33 Pent Rd *Web:* www.nature.org	Weston	CT	06883	203-226-4991	226-4807
Dodge Nature Ctr 365 Marie Ave W *Web:* www.dodgenaturecenter.org	West Saint Paul	MN	55118	651-455-4531	455-2575
Domaine Maizerets 2000 Montmorency Blvd	Quebec	QC	G1J5E7	418-641-6117	660-6295
Eagle River Nature Ctr 32750 Eagle River Rd *Web:* www.ernc.org	Eagle River	AK	99577	907-694-2108	694-2119
Earthplace 10 Woodside Ln PO Box 165 *Web:* www.earthplace.org	Westport	CT	06881	203-227-7253	227-8909
El Dorado East Regional Park & Nature Ctr 7550 E Spring St	Long Beach	CA	90815	562-570-1745	570-8530
Everglades Holiday Park 21940 Griffin Rd *TF:* 800-226-2244 ■ *Web:* www.evergladesholidaypark.com	Southwest Ranches	FL	33332	954-434-8111	434-4252
Falls Park on the Reedy S Main St & Camperdown Way	Greenville	SC	29601	864-467-4350	467-4185
Fern Forest Nature Ctr 201 Lyons Rd S *Web:* www.broward.org/parks	Coconut Creek	FL	33063	954-970-0150	970-0111
Forest Park Nature Ctr 5809 Forest Pk Dr	Peoria Heights	IL	61616	309-686-3360	686-8820
Fort DeSoto Park 3500 Pinellas Bayway S *Web:* www.fortdesoto.com	Tierra Verde	FL	33715	727-582-2267	552-1863
Fuller State Park 1500 W Mitchell Rd *Web:* www.tennessee.gov	Memphis	TN	38109	901-543-7581	785-8485
Golden Gate Park 2533 Noriega St *Web:* www.nps.gov	San Francisco	CA	94122	415-831-2700	831-2096
Great Plains Nature Ctr 6232 E 29th St N *Web:* www.gpnc.org	Wichita	KS	67220	316-683-5499	688-9555
Green Mountain Audubon Ctr 255 Sherman Hollow Rd *Web:* www.vt.audubon.org/centers.html	Huntington	VT	05462	802-434-3068	434-4686
Gulf Branch Nature Ctr 3608 Military Rd	Arlington	VA	22207	703-228-3403	228-4401
Gumbo Limbo Nature Ctr 1801 N Ocean Blvd *Web:* www.gumbolimbo.org	Boca Raton	FL	33432	561-338-1473	338-1483
Hanauma Bay Nature Preserve 100 Hanauma Bay Rd *Web:* www.co.honolulu.hi.us	Honolulu	HI	96825	808-396-4229	395-0468
Harlem Hills Nature Preserve Nimtz Rd & Flora Dr	Loves Park	IL	61111	815-964-6666	964-6661
Hemlock Bluffs Nature Preserve 2616 Kildaire Farm Rd	Cary	NC	27518	919-387-5980	
Heritage Square 65 E Central Blvd	Orlando	FL	32801	407-836-8500	836-6748
Houston Arboretum & Nature Ctr 4501 Woodway Dr *TF:* 866-510-7219 ■ *Web:* www.houstonarboretum.org	Houston	TX	77024	713-681-8433	681-1191
Ijams Nature Ctr 2915 Island Home Ave *Web:* www.ijams.org	Knoxville	TN	37920	865-577-4717	577-1683
Indian Creek Nature Ctr 6665 Otis Rd SE *Web:* www.indiancreeknaturecenter.org	Cedar Rapids	IA	52403	319-362-0664	362-2876
Jefferson Barracks County Park 345 N Rd *Web:* www.stlouisco.com/parks/j-b.html	Saint Louis	MO	63125	314-544-5714	638-5009
Katharine Ordway Preserve 4245 N Fairfax Dr Suite 100 *Web:* www.nature.org	Arlington	VA	22203	203-226-4991	226-4807
Lava Hot Springs State Foundation 430 E Main St PO Box 669 *TF:* 800-423-8597 ■ *Web:* www.lavahotsprings.com	Lava Hot Springs	ID	83246	208-776-5221	776-5273
Lewis & Clark National Historic Trail c/o National Pk Service 601 Riverfront Dr *TF:* 888-237-3252 ■ *Web:* www.nps.gov/lecl	Omaha	NE	68102	402-661-1804	661-1805
Lewis & Clark National Historic Trail Interpretive Ctr 4201 Giant Springs Rd *Web:* www.fs.usda.gov/lcnf	Great Falls	MT	59405	406-727-8733	453-6157
Lincoln Memorial Garden & Nature Ctr 2301 E Lake Dr *Web:* www.lincolnmemorialgarden.org	Springfield	IL	62712	217-529-1111	529-0134
Linville Caverns 19921 US 221 N *TF:* 800-419-0540 ■ *Web:* www.linvillecaverns.com	Marion	NC	28752	828-756-4171	756-4171
Long Branch Nature Ctr 625 S Carlin Springs Rd	Arlington	VA	22204	703-228-6535	845-2654
Long Wharf Nature Preserve Long Wharf Dr	New Haven	CT	06511	203-946-5713	
Lost River Caverns 726 Durham St PO Box M *Web:* www.lostcave.com	Hellertown	PA	18055	610-838-8767	838-2961
Martin Park Nature Ctr 5000 W Memorial Rd *Web:* www.okc.gov/parks/martin_park	Oklahoma City	OK	73142	405-755-0676	749-3072
McKelligon Canyon 3 McKelligon Canyon Rd	El Paso	TX	79930	915-534-0609	
Minnehaha Falls 4825 Minnehaha Ave S	Minneapolis	MN	55417	612-230-6400	230-6513
Mississippi Petrified Forest 124 Forest Pk Rd *Web:* www.mspetrifiedforest.com	Flora	MS	39071	601-879-8189	879-8165
Morrison-Knudsen Nature Ctr 600 S Walnut St	Boise	ID	83706	208-334-2225	287-2905
Mount Airy Forest & Arboretum 5083 Colerain Ave	Cincinnati	OH	45223	513-352-4080	541-8176
Mount Saint Helens National Volcanic Monument 42218 NE Yale Bridge Rd *Web:* www.fs.usda.gov	Amboy	WA	98601	360-449-7800	449-7801
Natural Bridge Caverns 26495 Natural Bridge Caverns Rd *Web:* www.naturalbridgecaverns.com	Natural Bridge Caverns	TX	78266	210-651-6101	651-6144
New Canaan Nature Ctr 144 Oenoke Ridge *Web:* www.newcanaannature.org	New Canaan	CT	06840	203-966-9577	966-6536
New York State Office of Parks Recreation & Historic Preservation Empire State Plaza Agency Bldg 1 *Web:* www.nysparks.state.ny.us	Albany	NY	12238	518-474-0456	486-1899
Nisqually Reach Nature Ctr (NRNC) 4949 D'Milluhr Rd NE *Web:* www.nisquallyestuary.org	Olympia	WA	98516	360-459-0387	
Oahe Dam & Reservoir 6 Miles N on Hwy 1804	Pierre	SD	57501	605-224-5862	224-5945
Ogden Nature Ctr 966 W 12th St *Web:* www.ogdennaturecenter.org	Ogden	UT	84404	801-621-7595	621-1867
Olentangy Indian Caverns 1779 Home Rd *Web:* www.olentangyindiancaverns.com	Delaware	OH	43015	740-548-7917	548-4572
Oxbow Meadows Environmental Learning Ctr 3535 S Lumpkin Rd *Web:* oxbow.colstate.edu	Columbus	GA	31907	706-687-4090	687-3020
Parkersville Landing Historical Park 24 S 'A' St	Washougal	WA	98671	360-834-4792	835-2197
Pike National Forest 601 S Weber St *Web:* www.fs.usda.gov	Colorado Springs	CO	80903	719-636-1602	477-4233
Pine Jog Environmental Education Ctr 6301 Summit Blvd *Web:* www.pinejog.org	West Palm Beach	FL	33415	561-686-6600	687-4968
Plains Conservation Ctr 21901 E Hampden Ave *Web:* www.plainsconservationcenter.org	Aurora	CO	80013	303-693-3621	693-3379
Powder Valley Conservation Nature Ctr 11715 Cragwold Rd *Web:* www.mdc.mo.gov/areas/cnc/powder	Saint Louis	MO	63122	314-301-1500	301-1501
Prairie Wetlands Learning Ctr 602 State Hwy 210 E *Web:* www.midwest.fws.gov	Fergus Falls	MN	56537	218-736-0938	736-0941
Provo Canyon N Hwy 189	Provo	UT	84606	801-851-2100	851-2109
Quarry Hill Nature Ctr 701 Silver Creek Rd NE *Web:* www.qhnc.org	Rochester	MN	55906	507-281-6114	287-1345
Raccoon Mountain Caverns 319 W Hills Dr *TF:* 800-823-2267 ■ *Web:* www.raccoonmountain.com	Chattanooga	TN	37419	423-821-9403	825-1289
Randall Davey Audubon Ctr 1800 Upper Canyon Rd PO Box 9314 *Web:* www.audubon.org/chapter/nm/nm/rdac	Santa Fe	NM	87504	505-983-4609	983-2355
Red Rock Canyon National Conservation Area HCR 33 PO Box 5500	Las Vegas	NV	89161	702-515-5350	363-6779
Riveredge Nature Ctr 4458 W Hawthorne Dr PO Box 26 *TF:* 800-287-8098 ■ *Web:* www.riveredgenaturecenter.org	Newburg	WI	53060	262-375-2715	375-2714
Rock City Gardens 1400 Patten Rd *TF:* 800-854-0675 ■ *Web:* www.seerockcity.com	Lookout Mountain	GA	30750	706-820-2531	820-2533
Ruby Falls 1720 S Scenic Hwy *TF:* 800-755-7105 ■ *Web:* www.rubyfalls.com	Chattanooga	TN	37409	423-821-2544	821-6705
Runge Conservation Nature Ctr Hwy 179 PO Box 180 *Web:* www.mdc.mo.gov/areas/cnc/runge	Jefferson City	MO	65102	573-526-5544	526-4496
Rushmore Cave 13622 Hwy 40 *Web:* www.rushmorecave.com	Keystone	SD	57751	605-255-4384	

Name / Address	City	State	Zip	Phone	Fax
Saint Marks Historic Railroad State Trail W of 363 S of 319 (Capital Cir)	Tallahassee	FL	32301	850-245-2052	245-2083
TF: 877-822-5208					
Santa Catalina Ranger District 5700 N Sabino Canyon Rd	Tucson	AZ	85750	520-749-8700	749-7723
Web: www.fs.fed.us					
Saw Mill River Audubon Inc 275 Millwood Rd	Chappaqua	NY	10514	914-666-6503	666-7430
Web: www.sawmillriveraudubon.org/Pruyn.html					
Schilling Wildlife Management Area 17614 Schilling Refuge Rd	Plattsmouth	NE	68048	402-296-0041	
Web: www.outdoornebraska.ne.gov					
Schlitz Audubon Nature Ctr 1111 E Brown Deer Rd	Bayside	WI	53217	414-352-2880	352-6091
Web: www.schlitzauduboncenter.com					
Sea Lion Caves 91560 Hwy 101	Florence	OR	97439	541-547-3111	547-3545
Web: www.sealioncaves.com					
Seven Falls Co 2850 S Cheyenne Canyon Rd	Colorado Springs	CO	80906	719-632-0765	632-0781
Web: www.sevenfalls.com					
Severson Dells Nature Ctr 8786 Montague Rd	Rockford	IL	61102	815-335-2915	335-2471
Web: www.seversondells.org					
Sitting Bull Crystal Caverns 13745 S Hwy 16	Rapid City	SD	57701	605-342-2777	
Web: www.sittingbullcrystalcave.com					
Snake River Birds of Prey National Conservation Area PO Box 84	Kuna	ID	83634	208-861-9131	384-3326
Web: www.snakeriverbirdsofpreyfestival.com					
Springfield Conservation Nature Ctr 4600 S Chrisman Ave	Springfield	MO	65804	417-888-4237	888-4241
Web: www.mdc.mo.gov					
Stepping Stone Falls 5161 Branch Rd	Flint	MI	48506	810-736-7100	736-7220
TF: 800-648-7275					
Stone Mountain Memorial Assn (SMMA) PO Box 689	Stone Mountain	GA	30086	770-498-5658	
TF: 800-317-2006 ■ *Web:* www.stonemountainpark.org					
Tacoma Nature Ctr 1919 S Tyler St	Tacoma	WA	98405	253-591-6439	593-4152
Thunderhead Falls 23199 Thunderhead Falls Rd	Rapid City	SD	57702	605-343-0081	
Web: www.blackhillsbadlands.com/thfalls					
Tree Hill Nature Ctr 7152 Lone Star Rd	Jacksonville	FL	32211	904-724-4646	724-9132
Web: www.treehill.org					
Vickers Nature Preserve Rt 224	Ellsworth Township	OH	44416	330-702-3000	702-3010
Web: www.millcreekmetroparks.com/vickers.htm					
Vista House 40700 E Historic Columbia River Hwy	Corbett	OR	97019	503-695-2230	695-2250
Web: www.vistahouse.com					
Weedon Island Preserve Cultural & Natural History Ctr 1800 Weedon Dr NE	Saint Petersburg	FL	33702	727-453-6500	
Web: www.weedonislandcenter.org					
Wehr Nature Ctr 9701 W College Ave	Franklin	WI	53132	414-425-8550	425-6992
Web: www.countyparks.com/horticulture/wehr					
Western North Carolina Nature Ctr 75 Gashes Creek Rd	Asheville	NC	28805	828-298-5600	298-2644
Web: www.wildwnc.org					
Westwood Hills Nature Ctr 8300 W Franklin Ave	Saint Louis Park	MN	55426	952-924-2544	797-9691
Woldumar Nature Ctr 5739 Old Lansing Rd	Lansing	MI	48917	517-322-0030	322-9394
Web: www.woldumar.org					
Woodcock Nature Ctr 54 Deer Run Rd	Wilton	CT	06897	203-762-7280	834-0062
Web: www.woodcocknaturecenter.org					
World Bird Sanctuary 125 Bald Eagle Ridge Rd	Valley Park	MO	63088	636-861-3225	861-3240
Web: www.worldbirdsanctuary.org					
Morikami Museum & Japanese Gardens 4000 Morikami Pk Rd	Delray Beach	FL	33446	561-495-0233	499-2557
Web: www.morikami.org					

50-6 Shopping/Dining/Entertainment Districts

Name / Address	City	State	Zip	Phone	Fax
601 Lexington 601 Lexington Ave	New York	NY	10022	212-751-1007	751-1012
Aloha Tower Marketplace 1 Aloha Tower Dr	Honolulu	HI	96813	808-528-5700	524-8334
Web: www.alohatower.com					
Bannister's Wharf 1 Bannister's Wharf	Newport	RI	02840	401-846-4500	849-8750
Web: www.bannistersnewport.com					
Barefoot Landing 4898 Hwy 17 S	North Myrtle Beach	SC	29582	843-272-8349	272-1052
TF: 800-272-2320 ■ *Web:* www.bflanding.com					
Bayside Marketplace 401 Biscayne Blvd	Miami	FL	33132	305-577-3344	577-0306
Web: www.baysidemarketplace.com					
Bazaar del Mundo 4133 Taylor St	San Diego	CA	92110	619-296-3161	296-3113
Web: www.bazaardelmundo.com					
Beale Street Historic District Downtown Memphis	Memphis	TN	38103	901-526-0110	526-0125
Web: www.bealestreet.com					
Belmar 408 S Teller St	Lakewood	CO	80226	303-742-1520	742-1502
Web: www.belmarcolorado.com					
BOB the (Big Old Bldg) 20 Monroe Ave NW	Grand Rapids	MI	49503	616-356-2000	493-2011
Web: www.thebob.com					
Bricktown N of Reno Ave & W of Stiles Rd	Oklahoma City	OK	73104	405-236-8666	602-3800
Web: www.bricktownokc.org					
Brightleaf Square Gregson & Main Sts 905 w Main st	Durham	NC	27701	919-682-9229	688-1953
Web: www.historicbrightleaf.com					
Broadway at the Beach 1325 Celebrity Cir	Myrtle Beach	SC	29577	843-444-3200	444-3222
TF: 800-444-3200 ■ *Web:* www.broadwayatthebeach.com					
Cannery at Del Monte Square 2801 Leavenworth St Mezzanine Level	San Francisco	CA	94133	415-771-3112	771-2424
Web: www.delmontesquare.com					
Cannery Row 765 Wave St	Monterey	CA	93940	831-649-6690	373-4812
Web: www.canneryrow.com					
Captain's Cove Seaport 1 Bostwick Ave	Bridgeport	CT	06605	203-335-1433	335-6793
Web: www.captainscoveseaport.com					
Center in the Square 1 Market Sq SE 5th Fl	Roanoke	VA	24011	540-342-5700	224-1238
Web: www.centerinthesquare.org					
Centro Ybor 1600 E 8th Ave	Tampa	FL	33605	813-242-4660	242-4664
Web: www.centroybor.com					
Channelside 615 Channelside Dr Suite 117	Tampa	FL	33602	813-223-4250	221-2161
Web: www.channelsidebayplaza.com					
City Market 219 W Bryan St Suite 207	Savannah	GA	31401	912-232-4903	232-2142
Web: www.savannahcitymarket.com					
CityPlace 700 S Rosemary Ave	West Palm Beach	FL	33401	561-366-1000	366-1001
Web: www.cityplace.com					
CocoWalk 3015 Grand Ave	Coconut Grove	FL	33133	305-444-0777	441-8936
Web: www.cocowalk.net					
Cooper Young Business Assn 2120 Young Ave	Memphis	TN	38104	901-276-7222	276-2043
Web: www.cooperyoung.com					
Country Club Plaza 4745 Central St	Kansas City	MO	64112	816-753-0100	753-4625
Web: www.countryclubplaza.com					
Crocker Park 189 Crocker Pk Blvd	Westlake	OH	44145	440-871-6880	871-6889
Web: www.crockerpark.com					
Deep Ellum 2630 Commerce St	Dallas	TX	75226	214-748-4332	
Desert Ridge Marketplace 21001 N Tatum Blvd	Phoenix	AZ	85050	480-513-7586	563-1829
Web: www.shopdesertridge.com					
District The 11 S 10th St	Columbia	MO	65201	573-442-6816	499-0421
Web: www.discoverthedistrict.com					
Dole Cannery 680 Iwilei Rd	Honolulu	HI	96817	808-548-4811	548-4085
Web: www.dole-cannery.com					
Downtown at the Gardens 11701 Lake Victoria Gardens Ave Suite 2203	Palm Beach Gardens	FL	33410	561-340-1600	355-8817
Web: www.downtownatthegardens.com					
Downtown Disney 1770 E Buena Vista Dr	Lake Buena Vista	FL	32830	407-828-3150	
Web: disney.go.com					
Downtown Disney S Disneyland Dr	Anaheim	CA	92802	714-781-4565	
Web: disneyland.disney.go.com					
East Town 770 N Jefferson St	Milwaukee	WI	53202	414-271-1416	271-6401
Web: www.easttown.com					
Faneuil Hall Marketplace 4 S Market Bldg 5th Fl	Boston	MA	02109	617-523-1300	523-1779
Web: www.faneuilhallmarketplace.com					
Fifth Street Public Market 296 E 5th Ave	Eugene	OR	97401	541-484-0383	686-1220
Web: www.5stmarket.com					
Findlay Market PO Box 14727	Cincinnati	OH	45250	513-665-4839	665-3480
Web: www.findlaymarket.org					
FlatIron Crossing 1 W FlatIron Cir Suite 1083	Broomfield	CO	80021	720-887-9900	887-0707
Web: www.flatironcrossing.com					
Fort Worth Stockyards National Historic District PO Box 64203	Fort Worth	TX	76164	817-626-7921	740-8635
Web: www.fortworthstockyards.org					
Fourth Avenue 4th Ave-between University Blvd & 9th St	Tucson	AZ	85705	520-624-5004	624-5933
TF: 800-933-2477 ■ *Web:* www.fourthavenue.org					
Gaslamp Quarter Assn 614 5th Ave Suite E	San Diego	CA	92101	619-233-5227	233-4693
Web: www.gaslamp.org					
Gateway The 400 W 100 S	Salt Lake City	UT	84101	801-456-0000	456-0005
Web: www.shopthegateway.com					
Ghirardelli Square 900 N Pt St Suite E-100	San Francisco	CA	94109	415-775-5500	775-0912
Web: www.ghirardellisq.com					
Great Lakes Crossing Outlets 4000 Baldwin Rd	Auburn Hills	MI	48326	248-454-5000	
TF: 877-746-7452 ■ *Web:* www.greatlakescrossingoutlets.com					
Harborplace & the Gallery 200 E Pratt St	Baltimore	MD	21202	410-332-4191	547-7317
TF: 800-427-2671 ■ *Web:* www.harborplace.com					
Hillcrest Historic District Kavanaugh & Markham Sts	Little Rock	AR	72205	501-371-0075	374-8142
Hollywood & Highland 6801 Hollywood Blvd	Hollywood	CA	90028	323-817-0220	460-6003
Web: www.hollywoodandhighland.com					
Hyde Park Village 1621 W Snow Cir	Tampa	FL	33606	813-251-3500	251-4158
Web: www.hydeparkvillage.net					
International Plaza & Bay Street 2223 N W Shore Blvd	Tampa	FL	33607	813-342-3790	342-3788
Web: www.shopinternationalplaza.com					
Jacksonville Landing 2 Independent Dr	Jacksonville	FL	32202	904-353-1188	353-1558
Web: www.jacksonvillelanding.com					
John's Pass Village & Boardwalk 150 John's Pass Boardwalk Pl	Madeira Beach	FL	33708	727-398-6577	397-6818
TF: 800-755-0677 ■ *Web:* www.johnspass.com					
Jordan Commons 9400 S State St	Sandy	UT	84070	801-304-4577	304-4515
Web: www.jordancommons.com					
Laclede's Landing 710 N 3rd St Suite 310-N	Saint Louis	MO	63102	314-241-5875	588-7310
Web: www.lacledeslanding.org					
Larimer Square 1430 Larimer St Suite 200	Denver	CO	80202	303-534-2367	623-1041
Web: www.larimersquare.com					
Las Olas Riverfront 300 SW 1st Ave Suite 106	Fort Lauderdale	FL	33301	954-522-6556	522-1899
Main Gate Square University Blvd-between Pk & Euclid	Tucson	AZ	85719	520-622-8613	622-0124
Web: www.maingatesquare.com					
Market Street at Celebration 610 Sycamore St Suite 310	Kissimmee	FL	34747	407-566-2200	566-4705
Web: www.celebrationfl.com/market_street/home.html					
Mellwood Arts & Entertainment Ctr 1860 Mellwood Ave	Louisville	KY	40206	502-895-3650	895-3680
Web: www.mellwoodartcenter.com					
Metreon 101 4th St	San Francisco	CA	94103	415-369-6000	369-6025
Web: www.westfield.com					

	City	State	Zip	Phone	Fax
Miracle Mile Shops at Planet Hollywood 3663 Las Vegas Blvd S *TF:* 888-800-8284 ■ *Web:* www.miraclemileshopslv.com	Las Vegas	NV	89109	702-866-0703	866-0717
New Roc City 33 LeCount Pl *Web:* www.newroccity.com	New Rochelle	NY	10801	914-637-7575	637-1048
Newport on the Levee 1 Levee Way Suite 1113 *TF:* 866-538-3359 ■ *Web:* www.newportonthelevee.com	Newport	KY	41071	859-291-0550	291-7020
Ocean Walk Shoppes at the Village 250 N Atlantic Ave Suite 201 *Web:* www.oceanwalkshoppes.com	Daytona Beach	FL	32118	386-258-9544	238-3864
Old Town 303 Romero St	Albuquerque	NM	87104	505-243-3215	
Peabody Place 150 Peabody Pl *Web:* www.belz.com	Memphis	TN	38103	901-261-7529	259-5570
Penn's Landing 301 S Columbus Blvd *Web:* www.delawareriverwaterfrontcorp.com	Philadelphia	PA	19106	215-928-8801	923-2801
Pier 39 Beach & Embarcadero Sts *Web:* www.pier39.com	San Francisco	CA	94133	415-981-7437	
Pier The 800 2nd Ave NE *Web:* www.stpetepier.com	Saint Petersburg	FL	33701	727-821-6443	821-6451
Pike at Rainbow Harbor 95 S Pine Ave *Web:* www.thepikeatlongbeach.com	Long Beach	CA	90802	562-432-8325	432-8374
Pike Place Market 65 Pike St Rm 500 *Web:* www.pikeplacemarket.org	Seattle	WA	98101	206-682-7453	625-0646
Pioneer Square 202 Yesler Way *Web:* www.pioneersquare.org	Seattle	WA	98104	206-667-0687	667-9739
Pointe Orlando 9101 International Dr Suite 1040 *Web:* www.pointeorlandofl.com	Orlando	FL	32819	407-248-2838	248-0078
Ports O'Call Village Berth 75-79	San Pedro	CA	90731	310-548-8076	
Power Plant Live! 34 Market St *TF:* 800-733-5444 ■ *Web:* www.powerplantlive.com	Baltimore	MD	21202	410-752-5444	659-9491
Quincy Market between Chatham & Clinton Sts	Boston	MA	02109	617-523-1300	
Red River District Downtown Shreveport Riverfront	Shreveport	LA	71101	318-220-0711	
Renaissance Ctr Detroit River *Web:* www.marriott.com/property/propertypage/DTWDT	Detroit	MI	48243	313-568-5600	568-5606
River Walk 110 Broadway Suite 500 *Web:* www.thesanantonioriverwalk.com	San Antonio	TX	78204	210-227-4262	212-7602
Rivertown 405 Williams Blvd *Web:* www.rivertownkenner.com	Kenner	LA	70062	504-468-7231	471-2159
Saint Armands Circle 300 Madison Dr Suite 201 *Web:* www.starmandscircleassoc.com	Sarasota	FL	34236	941-388-1554	388-2855
Sakura Square 1255 19th St	Denver	CO	80202	303-295-0305	295-0304
Santana Row 3055 Olin Ave Suite 2100 *Web:* www.santanarow.com	San Jose	CA	95128	408-551-4600	551-4616
Seaport Village 849 W Harbor Dr Suite D *Web:* www.spvillage.com	San Diego	CA	92101	619-235-4014	696-0025
Shops at Columbus Circle 10 Columbus Cir Suite 310 *Web:* www.shopsatcolumbuscircle.com	New York	NY	10019	212-823-6300	823-6050
Shoreline Village 429 Shoreline Village Dr # 100 *Web:* www.shorelinevillage.com	Long Beach	CA	90802	562-435-2668	435-6445
South Street Seaport Fulton & S Sts Pier 17 *Web:* www.southstreetseaport.com	New York	NY	10038	212-732-7678	964-8056
SouthSide Works Sidney St-between 26th & Hot Metal Sts *TF:* 877-977-8800 ■ *Web:* www.southsideworks.com	Pittsburgh	PA	15235	412-481-1750	481-1786
Station Square 125 W Stn Sq Dr *TF:* 800-859-8959 ■ *Web:* www.stationsquare.com	Pittsburgh	PA	15219	412-261-2811	261-2825
Stockyards Station 130 E Exchange Ave *Web:* www.stockyardsstation.com	Fort Worth	TX	76106	817-625-9715	625-9744
Streets at Southpoint & Main Street 6910 Fayetteville Rd *Web:* www.streetsatsouthpoint.com	Durham	NC	27713	919-572-8800	572-8818
Sundance Square 201 Main St Suite 700 *Web:* www.sundancesquare.com	Fort Worth	TX	76102	817-255-5700	390-8709
Underground Atlanta 50 Upper Alabama St Suite 007 *Web:* www.underground-atlanta.com	Atlanta	GA	30303	404-523-2311	523-0507
Union Station 50 Massachusetts Ave *Web:* www.unionstationdc.com	Washington	DC	20002	202-289-1908	
Universal Studios CityWalk 1000 Universal Studios Plaza *Web:* www.universalorlando.com/citywalk.html	Orlando	FL	32819	407-363-8000	
Universal Studios CityWalk Hollywood Universal City Plaza *Web:* www.citywalkhollywood.com	Los Angeles	CA	91608	818-622-4455	
Water Tower Place 835 N Michigan Ave *Web:* www.shopwatertower.com	Chicago	IL	60611	312-440-3166	440-1259
Waterside Festival Marketplace 333 Waterside Dr *Web:* www.watersidemarketplace.com	Norfolk	VA	23510	757-627-3300	627-3981
West End MarketPlace 603 Munger Ave *Web:* www.westendmarketplacedallas.com	Dallas	TX	75202	214-748-4801	748-4803
West Port Plaza I-270 & Page Blvd *Web:* www.westportstl.com	Saint Louis	MO	63146	314-576-7100	542-4095
Westport Historical Society 4000 Baltimore St *Web:* www.westporthistorical.com	Kansas City	MO	64111	816-561-1821	

50-7 Wineries

The Wineries Listed In This Category Feature Wine-Tasting As An Attraction.

	City	State	Zip	Phone	Fax
A Nonini Winery 2640 N Dickenson Ave *Web:* www.noniniwinery.com	Fresno	CA	93722	559-275-1936	241-7119
Adams County Winery 251 Peach Tree Rd *Web:* www.adamscountywinery.com	Orrtanna	PA	17353	717-334-4631	334-4026
Arbor Crest Wine Cellars 4705 N Fruithill Rd *Web:* www.arborcrest.com	Spokane	WA	99217	509-927-9463	927-0574
Bogle Vineyards & Winery 37783 County Rd 144 *Web:* www.boglewinery.com	Clarksburg	CA	95612	916-744-1139	744-1187
Butler Winery 1022 N College Ave *Web:* www.butlerwinery.com	Bloomington	IN	47404	812-339-7233	
Cap*Rock Winery 408 E Woodrow Rd *Web:* www.caprockwinery.com	Lubbock	TX	79423	806-863-2704	863-2712
Casa Rondena Winery 733 Chavez Rd NW *TF:* 800-706-1699 ■ *Web:* www.casarondena.com	Albuquerque	NM	87107	505-344-5911	343-1823
Caterina Winery 905 N Washington St *Web:* www.caterinawinery.com	Spokane	WA	99201	509-328-5069	328-9694
Chaddsford Winery 632 Baltimore Pike *Web:* www.chaddsford.com	Chadds Ford	PA	19317	610-388-6221	388-0360
Chateau Elan Winery 100 Tour de France *TF:* 800-233-9463 ■ *Web:* www.chateauelan.com	Braselton	GA	30517	678-425-0900	425-6000
Chateau Julien Wine Estate 8940 Carmel Valley Rd *TF:* 800-966-2601 ■ *Web:* www.chateaujulien.com	Carmel	CA	93923	831-624-2600	624-6138
Chateau Morrisette Winery 287 Winery Rd SW *Web:* www.chateaumorrisette.com	Floyd	VA	24091	540-593-2865	593-2868
Chateau Saint Jean 8555 Sonoma Hwy PO Box 293 *Web:* www.chateaustjean.com	Kenwood	CA	95452	707-833-4134	833-4200
Chateau Ste Michelle Winery 14111 NE 145th St *TF:* 800-267-6793 ■ *Web:* www.ste-michelle.com	Woodinville	WA	98072	425-415-3300	415-3657
Cherry Hill Winery 7867 Crowley Rd PO Box 66 *Web:* www.cherryhillwinery.com	Rickreall	OR	97371	503-623-7867	623-7878
Columbia Winery 14030 NE 145th St PO Box 1248 *TF:* 800-488-2347 ■ *Web:* www.columbiawinery.com	Woodinville	WA	98072	425-488-2776	488-3460
Countryside Vineyards Winery 658 Henry Harr Rd	Blountville	TN	37617	423-323-1660	323-1660
Denali Winery 1301 E Dowling Rd Suite 107	Anchorage	AK	99518	907-563-9434	563-9501
Easley Winery 205 N College Ave *Web:* www.easleywine.com	Indianapolis	IN	46202	317-636-4516	974-0128
Eola Hills Wine Cellars 501 S Pacific Hwy 99 W *TF:* 800-291-6730 ■ *Web:* www.eolahillswinery.com	Rickreall	OR	97371	503-623-2405	623-0350
Forks of Cheat Winery 2811 Stewart Town Rd *TF:* 877-989-4637 ■ *Web:* www.wvwines.com	Morgantown	WV	26508	304-598-2019	
Georgia Winery The 6469 Battlefield Pkwy *Web:* www.georgiawines.com	Ringgold	GA	30736	706-937-9463	937-9860
Gruet Winery 8400 Pan American Fwy NE *TF:* 888-857-9463 ■ *Web:* www.gruetwinery.com	Albuquerque	NM	87113	505-821-0055	857-0066
Honeywood Winery 1350 Hines St SE *TF:* 800-726-4101 ■ *Web:* www.honeywoodwinery.com	Salem	OR	97302	503-362-4111	362-4112
Huber's Orchard & Winery 19816 Huber Rd *TF:* 800-345-9463 ■ *Web:* www.huberwineries.com	Starlight	IN	47106	812-923-9463	923-3013
J Lohr Vineyards & Wines 1000 Lenzen Ave *Web:* www.jlohr.com	San Jose	CA	95126	408-288-5057	993-2276
James Arthur Vineyards & Winery 2001 W Raymond Rd *Web:* www.jamesarthurvineyards.com	Raymond	NE	68428	402-783-5255	783-5256
King Estate Winery 80854 Territorial Rd *TF:* 800-884-4441 ■ *Web:* www.kingestate.com	Eugene	OR	97405	541-942-9874	942-9867
La Vina Winery 4201 S Hwy 28 *Web:* www.lavinawinery.com	La Union	NM	88021	575-882-7632	
Latah Creek Winery 13030 E Indiana Ave *TF:* 800-528-2427 ■ *Web:* www.latahcreek.com	Spokane	WA	99216	509-926-0164	926-0710
LaVelle Vineyards 89697 Sheffler Rd *TF:* 800-645-8463 ■ *Web:* www.lavellevineyards.com	Elmira	OR	97437	541-935-9406	935-7202
Llano Estacado Winery 3426 E FM 1585 PO Box 3487 *TF:* 800-634-3854 ■ *Web:* www.llanowine.com	Lubbock	TX	79404	806-745-2258	748-1674
Lone Canary Winery 109 S Scott St Suite B2 *TF:* 866-822-6279 ■ *Web:* www.lonecanary.com	Spokane	WA	99202	509-534-9062	534-9066
Mazza Vineyards 11815 E Lake Rd Rt 5 *TF:* 800-796-9463 ■ *Web:* www.mazzawines.com	North East	PA	16428	814-725-8695	725-3948
Michael-David Vineyards 4580 W Hwy 12 *TF:* 888-707-9463 ■ *Web:* www.lodivineyards.com	Lodi	CA	95242	209-368-7384	368-5801
Mount Hope Estate & Winery 2775 Lebanon Rd	Manheim	PA	17545	717-665-7021	664-3466
Mountain Dome Winery 16315 E Temple Rd *Web:* www.mountaindome.com	Spokane	WA	99217	509-928-2788	922-8078
Nassau Valley Vineyards 32165 Winery Way *Web:* www.nassauvalley.com	Lewes	DE	19958	302-645-9463	645-6666
Oak Ridge Winery 6100 E Victor Rd *Web:* www.oakridgewinery.com	Lodi	CA	95240	209-369-4758	369-0202
Oliver Winery 8024 N SR-37 *TF:* 800-258-2783 ■ *Web:* www.oliverwinery.com	Bloomington	IN	47404	812-876-5800	876-9309
Orfila Vineyards & Winery 13455 San Pasqual Rd *TF:* 800-868-9463 ■ *Web:* www.orfila.com	Escondido	CA	92025	760-738-6500	745-3773
Penn Shore Vineyards & Winery 10225 Lake Rd *Web:* www.pennshore.com	North East	PA	16428	814-725-8688	725-8689
Redhawk Vineyard & Winery 2995 Michigan City Ave NW *Web:* www.redhawkwine.com	Salem	OR	97304	503-362-1596	589-9189
Saint Innocent Winery 5657 Zena Rd NW *Web:* www.stinnocentwine.com	Salem	OR	97304	503-378-1526	378-1041
Sakonnet Vineyards 162 W Main Rd *TF:* 800-919-4637 ■ *Web:* www.sakonnetwine.com	Little Compton	RI	02837	401-635-8486	635-2101
San Sebastian Winery 157 King St *TF:* 888-352-9463 ■ *Web:* www.sansebastianwinery.com	Saint Augustine	FL	32084	904-826-1594	826-1595
Silvan Ridge/Hinman Vineyards 27012 Briggs Hill Rd *TF:* 866-574-5826 ■ *Web:* www.silvanridge.com	Eugene	OR	97405	541-345-1945	345-6174

				Phone	Fax
Talon Winery & Vineyards 7086 Tates Creek Rd. Web: www.talonwine.com	Lexington	KY	40515	859-971-3214	971-8787
Westbend Vineyards 5394 Williams Rd. TF: 866-901-5032 ■ Web: www.westbendvineyards.com	Lewisville	NC	27023	336-945-5032	945-5294
Williamsburg Winery Ltd 5800 Wessex Hundred Web: www.williamsburgwinery.com	Williamsburg	VA	23185	757-229-0999	229-0911
Winery at Wolf Creek 2637 Cleveland Massillon Rd. TF: 800-436-0426 ■ Web: www.wineryatwolfcreek.com	Norton	OH	44203	330-666-9285	665-1445

51 AUCTIONS

				Phone	Fax
Abidon Inc 5301 E State St Suite 215	Rockford	IL	61108	815-226-8700	226-8769
Ableauctions.com Inc 1963 Lougheed Hwy TF: 888-599-2253 ■ Web: www.ableauctions.com	Coquitlam	BC	V3K3T8	604-521-3369	520-6706
ADESA Inc 13085 Hamilton Crossing Blvd TF: 800-923-3725 ■ Web: www.adesa.com	Carmel	IN	46032	317-815-1100	249-4600
Akron Auto Auction Inc 2471 Ley Dr. TF: 800-773-0033 ■ Web: www.akronautoauction.com	Akron	OH	44319	330-773-8245	773-1641
Auction Systems Auctioneers & Appraisers Inc 2324 E University Dr. TF: 800-801-8880 ■ Web: www.auctionandappraise.com	Phoenix	AZ	85034	602-252-4842	275-8548
Bonhams & Butterfields 220 San Bruno Ave. TF: 800-223-2854 ■ Web: www.bonhams.com	San Francisco	CA	94103	415-861-7500	861-8951
Christie's Inc 20 Rockefeller Plaza. Web: www.christies.com	New York	NY	10020	212-636-2000	636-2399
Collectors Universe Inc PO Box 6280. NASDAQ: CLCT ■ TF: 800-325-1121 ■ Web: www.collectors.com	Newport Beach	CA	92658	949-567-1234	833-7955
Copart Inc 4665 Business Ctr Dr NASDAQ: CPRT ■ Web: www.copart.com	Fairfield	CA	94534	707-639-5000	639-5188
Earl's Auction Co 5199 Lafayette Rd. Web: www.earlsauction.com	Indianapolis	IN	46254	317-291-5843	291-5844
eBay Inc 2065 Hamilton Ave. NASDAQ: EBAY ■ TF: 800-322-9266 ■ Web: www.ebay.com	San Jose	CA	95125	408-376-7400	376-7401
Fasig-Tipton Co Inc 2400 Newtown Pike Web: www.fasigtipton.com	Lexington	KY	40511	859-255-1555	254-0794
Frank H Boos Gallery 2830 W Maple Rd	Troy	MI	48084	248-643-1900	
Freeman/Fine Arts of Philadelphia 1808 Chestnut St Web: www.freemansauction.com	Philadelphia	PA	19103	215-563-9275	563-8236
Gallery of History Inc 3601 W Sahara Ave Suite 207 TF: 800-425-5379 ■ Web: www.galleryofhistory.com	Las Vegas	NV	89102	702-364-1000	364-1285
Gordon Bros Group LLC 101 Huntington Ave 10th Fl TF: 888-424-1903 ■ Web: www.gordonbrothers.com	Boston	MA	02199	617-426-3233	422-6222
Greater Rockford Auto Auction Inc (GRAA) 5937 Sandy Hollow Rd TF: 800-830-4722 ■ Web: www.graa.net	Rockford	IL	61109	815-874-7800	874-4722
Harry Davis & Co 1725 Blvd of Allies TF: 800-775-2289 ■ Web: www.harrydavis.com	Pittsburgh	PA	15219	412-765-1170	765-1170
Henderson Auctions 13340 Florida Blvd PO Box 336 TF: 800-850-2252 ■ Web: www.hendersonauctions.com	Livingston	LA	70754	225-686-2252	686-0647
Heritage Place Inc 2829 S MacArthur Web: www.heritageplace.com	Oklahoma City	OK	73128	405-682-4551	686-1267
iCollector Technologies Inc 1750 Coast Meridian Rd Suite 114 TF: 866-313-0123 ■ Web: www.icollector.com	Port Coquitlam	BC	V3C6R8	604-941-2221	
Insurance Auto Auctions Inc 2 Westbrook Corporate Ctr Suite 500 TF: 800-872-1501 ■ Web: www.iaai.com	Westchester	IL	60154	708-492-7000	492-7979
Ironplanet Inc 4695 Chabot Dr Suite 102 *Fax: Cust Svc ■ TF Cust Svc: 888-433-5426 ■ Web: www.ironplanet.com	Pleasanton	CA	94588	925-225-8600	225-8610*
Kennedy-Wilson Inc 9701 Wilshire Blvd # 700 TF: 800-522-6664 ■ Web: www.kennedywilson.com	Beverly Hills	CA	90212	310-887-6400	887-6414
Liquidity Services Inc 1920 L St NW 6th Fl NASDAQ: LQDT ■ TF: 800-310-4604 ■ Web: www.liquidityservicesinc.com	Washington	DC	20036	202-467-6868	467-5475
Manheim Export 6205 Peachtree Dunwoody Rd TF: 877-941-7447 ■ Web: www.exporttrader.com	Atlanta	GA	30328	877-941-7447	
NexTag.com Inc 1300 S El Camino Real Suite 600 Web: www.nextag.com	San Mateo	CA	94402	650-645-4700	341-3779
Priceline.com Inc 800 Connecticut Ave NASDAQ: PCLN ■ *Fax: Mktg ■ TF: 800-774-2354 ■ Web: www.priceline.com	Norwalk	CT	06854	203-299-8000	299-8955*
Rene Bates Auctioneers Inc 4660 County Rd 1006 Web: www.renebates.com	McKinney	TX	75071	972-548-9636	542-5495
Rouse Asset Services 361 S Robertson Blvd TF: 800-421-0816 ■ Web: www.rouseservices.com	Beverly Hills	CA	90211	310-360-9200	855-7854
Skinner Inc 357 Main St Web: www.skinnerinc.com	Bolton	MA	01740	978-779-6241	779-5144
Sotheby's Inc 1334 York Ave Web: www.sothebys.com	New York	NY	10021	212-606-7000	606-7028
Spear Auctioneers Inc PO Box 1052 Web: www.spearauctioneers.com	Russellville	AR	72811	479-968-2028	967-0573
Stack's Bowers Galleries 18061 Fitch TF: 800-458-4646 ■ Web: www.bowersandmerena.com	Irvine	CA	92614	949-253-0916	253-4091
Swann Galleries Inc 104 E 25th St Web: www.swanngalleries.com	New York	NY	10010	212-254-4710	979-1017
Theriault's 2148 Renard Ct PO Box 151 TF: 800-966-3655 ■ Web: www.theriaults.com	Annapolis	MD	21404	410-224-3655	224-2515
uBid Inc 8725 W Higgins Rd 9th Fl TF: 866-946-8243 ■ Web: www.ubid.com	Chicago	IL	60631	773-272-5000	272-4000
Yahoo! Auctions 701 1st Ave TF: 866-562-7219	Sunnyvale	CA	94089	408-349-3300	616-3702
Doyle New York 175 E 87th St TF: 800-808-0902 ■ Web: www.doylenewyork.com	New York	NY	10128	212-427-2730	369-0892

52 AUDIO & VIDEO EQUIPMENT

				Phone	Fax
Alpine Electronics of America 19145 Gramercy Pl *Fax: Hum Res ■ TF: 800-257-4631 ■ Web: www.alpine-usa.com	Torrance	CA	90501	310-326-8000	212-0884*
Amplifier Technologies Inc 1749 Chapin Rd Web: www.bgw.com	Montebello	CA	90640	323-278-0001	278-0083
AmpliVox Sound Systems LLC 3995 Commercial Ave TF: 800-267-5486 ■ Web: www.ampli.com	Northbrook	IL	60062	847-498-9000	498-6691
Applied Research & Technology 215 Tremont St Web: www.artroch.com	Rochester	NY	14608	585-436-2720	436-3942
Atlas Sound 1601 Jack McKay Blvd *Fax Area Code: 800 ■ TF: 800-876-3333 ■ Web: www.atlassound.com	Ennis	TX	75119	972-875-8413	765-3435*
Audio Command Systems 694 Main St TF: 800-382-2939 ■ Web: www.audiocommand.com	Westbury	NY	11590	516-997-5800	997-2195
Audio Research Corp 3900 Annapolis Ln N Web: www.audioresearch.com	Plymouth	MN	55447	763-577-9700	577-0323
Audio-Video Corp 213 Broadway Web: www.audiovideocorp.com	Albany	NY	12204	518-449-7213	449-1205
Audiosears Corp 2 S St TF: 800-533-7863 ■ Web: www.audiosears.com	Stamford	NY	12167	607-652-7305	652-3653
Audiovox Corp 180 Marcus Blvd NASDAQ: VOXX ■ TF: 800-645-4994 ■ Web: www.audiovox.com	Hauppauge	NY	11788	631-231-7750	434-3995
Automated Voice Systems Inc (AVSI) 17059 El Cajon Ave TF: 888-505-2026 ■ Web: www.mastervoice.com	Yorba Linda	CA	92886	714-524-4488	996-1127
Biamp Systems Inc 10074 SW Arctic Dr TF: 800-826-1457 ■ Web: www.biamp.com	Beaverton	OR	97005	503-641-7287	626-0281
Bogen Communications International Inc 50 Spring St TF: 800-999-2809 ■ Web: www.bogen.com	Ramsey	NJ	07446	201-934-8500	934-6532
Bose Corp The Mountain TF Sales: 800-444-2673 ■ Web: www.bose.com	Framingham	MA	01701	508-879-7330	820-3465
Boston Acoustics Inc 300 Jubilee Dr TF: 800-288-6148 ■ Web: www.bostonacoustics.com	Peabody	MA	01960	978-538-5000	538-5199
Cambridge Soundworks Inc 120 Water St TF: 800-367-4434 ■ Web: www.cambridgesoundworks.com	Andover	MA	01845	978-623-4400	794-2903
Car Toys Inc 20 W Galer St TF: 800-997-3644 ■ Web: www.cartoys.com	Seattle	WA	98119	206-443-0980	443-2525
Cerwin-Vega Inc 3000 SW 42nd St Web: www.cerwinvega.com	Hollywood	FL	33312	954-316-1501	316-1590
Clarion Corp of America 6200 Gateway Dr TF: 800-347-8667 ■ Web: www.clarion.com	Cypress	CA	90630	310-327-9100	327-1999
Community Professional Loudspeakers 333 E 5th St TF: 800-523-4934 ■ Web: www.community.chester.pa.us	Chester	PA	19013	610-876-3400	874-0190
Cornet Technology Inc 6800 Versar Ctr Suite 216 Web: www.cornet.com	Springfield	VA	22151	703-658-3400	658-3440
Creative Labs Inc 1901 McCarthy Blvd TF Cust Svc: 800-998-1000 ■ Web: www.us.creative.com	Milpitas	CA	95035	408-428-6600	428-6611
Crest Electronics Inc 3706 Alliance Dr TF: 888-502-7378 ■ Web: www.crestelectronics.com	Greensboro	NC	27407	336-855-6422	855-6676
Crown Audio Inc 1718 W Mishawaka Rd Web: www.crownaudio.com	Elkhart	IN	46517	574-294-8000	294-8250
Dana Innovations 212 Avenida Fabricante TF: 800-582-7777 ■ Web: www.sonance.com	San Clemente	CA	92672	949-492-7777	369-4038
Denon Electronics Ltd 100 Corporate Dr TF: 877-386-3666 ■ Web: www.denon.com	Mahwah	NJ	07430	201-762-6500	762-6670
Digit Professional Inc 3926 Varsity Dr TF: 877-767-8862 ■ Web: www.digitprofessional.com	Ann Arbor	MI	48108	734-677-0840	677-3027
Digital Innovations 3436 N Kennicott Suite 200 TF: 888-762-7858 ■ Web: www.digitalinnovations.com	Arlington Heights	IL	60004	847-463-9000	463-9001
Digital Video Systems Inc (DVS) 357 Castro St Suite 5 Web: www.dvsystems.com	Mountain View	CA	94041	650-938-8815	938-8829
Directed Electronics Inc 1 Viper Way NASDAQ: DEIX ■ TF: 800-876-0800 ■ Web: www.deiholdings.com	Vista	CA	92081	760-598-6200	598-6400
Dolby Laboratories Inc 100 Potrero Ave NYSE: DLB ■ Web: www.dolby.com	San Francisco	CA	94103	415-558-0200	645-4000
Dreamgear LLC 20001 S Western Ave TF: 877-777-3732 ■ Web: www.dreamgear.net	Torrance	CA	90501	310-222-5522	222-5577
DTS Inc 5220 Las Virgenes Rd NASDAQ: DTSI ■ TF: 800-959-4109 ■ Web: www.dts.com	Calabasas	CA	91302	818-436-1000	706-1868
Dynamic Instruments Inc 3860 Calle Fortunada TF: 800-793-3358 ■ Web: www.dynamicinst.com	San Diego	CA	92123	858-278-4900	278-6700
Echo Corp 6450 Via Real Suite 1 Web: www.echoaudio.com	Carpinteria	CA	93013	805-684-4593	684-6628
Educational Technology Inc 300 Bedford Ave Suite 202 TF Cust Svc: 800-942-2136 ■ Web: www.educationaltechnology.com	Bellmore	NY	11710	516-221-8440	221-9404
Emergent Technologies Inc 2508 Ashley Worth Blvd Suite 200 Web: www.emergenttechnologies.com	Austin	TX	78738	512-263-3232	263-3236
Emerson Radio Corp 85 Oxford Dr AMEX: MSN ■ TF: 800-909-1240 ■ Web: www.emersonradio.com	Moonachie	NJ	07074	973-884-5800	428-2067
Eminence Speaker LLC 838 Mulberry Pike PO Box 360 Web: www.eminence.com	Eminence	KY	40019	502-845-5622	845-5622
Encore Productions Inc 5150 S Decatur Blvd Web: www.encoreproductions.net	Las Vegas	NV	89118	702-739-8803	739-8831

Company	City	State	ZIP	Phone	Fax
Extron Electronics 1230 S Lewis St *TF Tech Supp:* 800-633-9876 ■ *Web:* www.extron.com	Anaheim	CA	92805	714-491-1500	491-1517
Ford Audio-Video Systems Inc 4800 W I- 40 *TF:* 800-654-6744 ■ *Web:* www.fordav.com	Oklahoma City	OK	73128	405-946-9966	946-9991
Foster Electric America 1000 E State Pkwy Suite G	Schaumburg	IL	60173	847-310-8200	310-8212
Fujitsu Ten Corp of America 19600 S Vermont Ave *TF:* 800-233-2216 ■ *Web:* www.eclipse-web.com	Torrance	CA	90502	310-327-2151	767-4375
Funai Corp 201 Rt 17 N Suite 903 *Web:* www.funai.us	Rutherford	NJ	07070	201-727-4560	288-8019
Furman Sound LLC 1690 Corporate Cir *TF:* 877-486-4738 ■ *Web:* www.furmansound.com	Petaluma	CA	94954	707-763-1010	763-1310
Gemini Sound Products Corp 1 Mayfield Ave *Web:* www.geminidj.com	Edison	NJ	08837	732-738-9003	738-9006
GlobalMedia Group LLC 15020 N 74th St *Web:* www.globalmedia.com	Scottsdale	AZ	85260	480-922-0044	922-1090
Harman International Industries Inc 400 Atlantic St 15th Fl *NYSE: HAR* ■ *TF:* 800-336-4525 ■ *Web:* www.harman.com	Stamford	CT	06901	203-328-3500	328-3964
Harman Kardon Inc 250 Crossways Pk Dr *Web:* www.harmankardon.com	Woodbury	NY	11797	516-496-3400	682-3510
Harman Music Group 8760 S Sandy Pkwy *TF:* 800-931-1117 ■ *Web:* www.dbxpro.com	Sandy	UT	84070	801-566-8800	566-7005
Harman/Becker Automotive Systems 39001 W 12 Mile Rd *Web:* www.harman.com	Farmington Hills	MI	48331	248-994-2100	994-2900
Hb Group Inc 60 Dodge Ave *TF:* 800-331-1804 ■ *Web:* www.hbrentals.com	North Haven	CT	06473	203-234-8107	239-4882
Hitachi Home Electronics Inc 900 Hitachi Way *TF:* 800-981-2588	Chula Vista	CA	91914	619-591-5200	591-5201
Infinity Systems Inc 250 Crossways Pk Dr *Web:* www.infinitysystems.com	Woodbury	NY	11797	516-496-3400	682-3510
JBL Consumer 250 Crossways Pk Dr *Web:* www.jbl.com	Woodbury	NY	11797	516-496-3400	682-3521
JBL Professional 8500 Balboa Blvd *TF:* 800-852-5776 ■ *Web:* www.jblpro.com	Northridge	CA	91329	818-894-8850	830-1220
JVC Co of America 1700 Valley Rd **Fax Area Code:* 956 ■ **Fax:* Cust Svc ■ *TF:* 800-252-5722 ■ *Web:* www.jvc.com	Wayne	NJ	07470	800-526-5308	682-4360*
JVC Professional Products Co 1700 Valley Rd **Fax Area Code:* 956 ■ *TF:* 800-252-5722 ■ *Web:* www.pro.jvc.com/prof	Wayne	NJ	07470	800-252-5722	682-4360*
Kenwood USA Corp 2201 E Dominguez St *TF:* 800-536-9663 ■ *Web:* www.kenwoodusa.com	Long Beach	CA	90810	310-639-9000	604-4488
KLH Audio Systems 11131 Dora St *TF:* 800-854-4441 ■ *Web:* www.klhaudio.com	Sun Valley	CA	91352	818-767-2843	767-8246
Klipsch LLC 137 Hempstead 278 *TF:* 800-554-7724 ■ *Web:* www.klipsch.com	Hope	AR	71801	870-777-6751	777-6753
Koss Corp 4129 N Port Washington Ave *NASDAQ: KOSS* ■ *TF:* 800-872-5677 ■ *Web:* www.koss.com	Milwaukee	WI	53212	414-964-5000	964-8615
Krell Industries Inc 45 Connair Rd *Web:* www.krellonline.com	Orange	CT	06477	203-799-9954	799-9796
KSC Industries Inc 881 Kuhn Dr Suite 200 *Web:* www.kscind.com	Chula Vista	CA	91914	619-671-0110	671-0330
Law Enforcement Assoc Corp (LEA) 2609 Discovery Dr Suite 125 *PINK: LAWE* ■ *TF:* 800-354-9669 ■ *Web:* www.leacorp.com	Raleigh	NC	27616	919-872-6210	872-6431
Lectrosonics Inc PO Box 15900 *TF:* 800-821-1121 ■ *Web:* www.lectrosonics.com	Rio Rancho	NM	87174	505-892-4501	892-6243
Lenoxx Electronics Corp 35 Brunswick Ave **Fax Area Code:* 732 ■ *TF:* 800-315-5885 ■ *Web:* www.lenoxx.com	Edison	NJ	08817	800-315-5885	777-0889*
LifeSize Communications Inc 1601 S Mopac Expwy Suite 100 *TF:* 877-543-3749 ■ *Web:* www.lifesize.com	Austin	TX	78746	512-347-9300	347-9301
Line 6 26580 Agoura Rd *Web:* www.line6.com	Calabasas	CA	91302	818-575-3600	575-3601
LKG Industries Inc 3660 Publisher's Dr *TF:* 800-645-2262 ■ *Web:* www.crankinpower.com	Rockford	IL	61109	815-874-2301	874-2896
Logitech Inc 6505 Kaiser Dr *TF Sales:* 800-231-7717 ■ *Web:* www.logitech.com	Fremont	CA	94555	510-795-8500	792-8901
LOUD Technologies Inc 16220 Wood Red Rd NE *PINK: LTEC* ■ *TF:* 866-858-5832 ■ *Web:* www.loudtechinc.com	Woodinville	WA	98072	425-892-6500	487-4337
Loudspeaker Components Corp 7596 US Hwy 61 S	Lancaster	WI	53813	608-723-2127	723-7775
Lowell Mfg Co 100 Integram Dr *TF:* 800-325-9660 ■ *Web:* www.lowellmfg.com	Pacific	MO	63069	636-257-3400	257-6606
M2 America Corp 470 Riverside St	Portland	ME	04103	207-797-2600	797-2604
Magna-Tech Electronic Co Inc (MTE) 1998 NE 150th St *Web:* www.magna-tech.com	North Miami	FL	33181	305-573-7339	573-8101
Marantz America Inc 100 Corporate Dr *Web:* www.marantz.com	Mahwah	NJ	07430	201-762-6500	762-6670
MartinLogan Ltd 2101 Delaware St *Web:* www.martinlogan.com	Lawrence	KS	66046	785-749-0133	749-5320
Matsushita Electric Corp of America 1 Panasonic Way *TF:* 888-275-2595	Secaucus	NJ	07094	201-348-7000	392-6007
McIntosh Laboratory Inc 2 Chambers St *TF:* 800-538-6576 ■ *Web:* www.mcintoshlabs.com	Binghamton	NY	13903	607-723-3512	724-0549
Metra Electronics Corp 460 Walker St *TF Sales:* 800-221-0932 ■ *Web:* www.metraonline.com	Holly Hill	FL	32117	386-257-1186	255-3965
Meyer Sound Laboratories Inc 2832 San Pablo Ave *Web:* www.meyersound.com	Berkeley	CA	94702	510-486-1166	486-8356
Mitsubishi Digital Electronics America Inc 9351 Jeronimo Rd **Fax:* Sales ■ *TF:* 800-332-2119 ■ *Web:* www.mitsubishi-tv.com	Irvine	CA	92618	949-465-6000	465-6155*
Mitsubishi Electric & Electronics USA Inc *Elevator & Escalator Div* 5665 Plaza Dr *Web:* www.mitsubishi-elevator.com	Cypress	CA	90630	714-220-4822	220-4812
Monster Cable Products Inc 455 Valley Dr *TF:* 877-800-8989 ■ *Web:* www.monstercable.com	Brisbane	CA	94005	415-840-2000	
MTX Corp 4545 E Baseline Rd *TF:* 800-225-5689 ■ *Web:* www.mtx.com	Phoenix	AZ	85042	602-438-4545	438-8692
Mustek Inc 15271 Barranca Pkwy *TF:* 800-308-7226 ■ *Web:* www.mustek.com	Irvine	CA	92618	949-790-3800	788-3670
Nady Systems Inc 6701 Shellmound St *Web:* www.nady.com	Emeryville	CA	94608	510-652-2411	652-5075
Omnitronics LLC 6573 Cochran Rd *TF:* 800-762-9266 ■ *Web:* www.cadaudio.com	Solon	OH	44139	440-349-4900	349-4900
OSRAM Sylvania Inc 100 Endicott St *Web:* www.sylvania.com	Danvers	MA	01923	978-777-1900	750-2152
Otari USA Sales Inc 21110 Nordhoff St Suite G/H *Web:* www.otari.com	Chatsworth	CA	91311	818-734-1785	594-7208
Panasonic Avionics Corp 26200 Enterprise Way *TF:* 800-755-2684 ■ *Web:* www.mascorp.com	Lake Forest	CA	92630	949-672-2000	462-7100
Panasonic Consumer Electronics Co 1 Panasonic Way *TF:* 888-275-2595 ■ *Web:* www.panasonic.com/consumer_electronics/home	Secaucus	NJ	07094	201-348-7000	392-6168
Panasonic Corp of North America 1 Panasonic Way **Fax:* Hum Res ■ *TF Cust Svc:* 800-211-7262 ■ *Web:* www.panasonic.com	Secaucus	NJ	07094	201-348-7000	392-6007*
Peavey Electronics Corp 5022 Hartley Peavey Dr *TF:* 877-732-8391 ■ *Web:* www.peavey.com	Meridian	MS	39305	601-483-5365	486-1278
Phase Technology 6400 Youngerman Cir **Fax Area Code:* 913 ■ *TF:* 888-742-7385 ■ *Web:* www.phasetech.com	Jacksonville	FL	32244	904-777-0700	663-9790*
Pioneer Electronics (USA) Inc 1925 E Dominguez St *TF:* 800-421-1404 ■ *Web:* www.pioneerelectronics.com	Long Beach	CA	90810	310-952-2000	952-2402
Polk Audio Inc 5601 Metro Dr *TF:* 800-377-7655 ■ *Web:* www.polkaudio.com	Baltimore	MD	21215	410-358-3600	764-5266
Power Quality Systems Inc 1200 Lebanon Rd *Web:* www.amsc.com	West Mifflin	PA	15122	412-464-1295	464-1229
Primo Microphones Inc 1805 Couch Dr *TF:* 800-767-7466 ■ *Web:* www.primomic.com	McKinney	TX	75069	972-548-9807	548-1351
QSC Audio Products Inc 1675 MacArthur Blvd **Fax:* Mktg ■ *TF:* 800-854-4079 ■ *Web:* www.qscaudio.com	Costa Mesa	CA	92626	714-754-6175	754-6174*
Quam-Nichols Co Inc 234 E Marquette Rd *TF:* 800-633-3669 ■ *Web:* www.quamspeakers.com	Chicago	IL	60637	773-488-5800	488-6944
Rane Corp 10802 47th Ave W *Web:* www.rane.com	Mukilteo	WA	98275	425-355-6000	347-7757
Record Play Tek Inc 110 E Vistula St *Web:* www.recordplaytek.com	Bristol	IN	46507	574-848-5233	848-5333
Renkus-heinz Inc 19201 Cook St *TF:* 888-632-8855 ■ *Web:* www.renkus-heinz.com	Foothill Ranch	CA	92610	949-588-9997	588-9514
ReQuest Inc 100 Saratoga Village Blvd Suite 45 **Fax:* Sales ■ *TF Sales:* 800-236-2812 ■ *Web:* www.request.com	Ballston Spa	NY	12020	518-899-1254	899-1251*
Roanwell Corp 2564 Pk Ave *Web:* www.roanwellcorp.com	Bronx	NY	10451	718-401-0288	401-0663
Robert Bosch Corp Blaupunkt Div 2800 S 25th Ave **Fax:* Sales ■ *TF Sales:* 800-323-1943 ■ *Web:* www.blaupunktusa.com	Broadview	IL	60155	708-865-5200	865-5296*
Rockford Corp 600 S Rockford Dr *NASDAQ: ROFO* ■ *TF:* 800-669-9899 ■ *Web:* www.rockfordcorp.com	Tempe	AZ	85281	480-967-3565	966-3983
Samsung Electronics America Inc 85 Challenger Rd *TF:* 800-726-7864 ■ *Web:* www.samsungusa.com	Ridgefield Park	NJ	07660	201-229-4000	229-4029
Sanyo Fisher Co 21605 Plummer St *Web:* us.sanyo.com	Chatsworth	CA	91311	818-998-7322	701-4194
Sanyo Mfg Corp 3333 Sanyo Rd **Fax:* Hum Res ■ *TF:* 800-877-5036 ■ *Web:* www.sanyoctv.com	Forrest City	AR	72335	870-633-5030	633-3179*
SDI Technologies Inc 1299 Main St **Fax:* Hum Res ■ *TF Cust Svc:* 800-888-4491 ■ *Web:* www.sdidirect.com	Rahway	NJ	07065	732-574-9000	574-1716*
Sharp Electronics Corp 1 Sharp Plaza *TF:* 800-237-4277 ■ *Web:* www.sharpusa.com	Mahwah	NJ	07430	201-529-8200	529-8413
Sherwood America 13101 Moore St *TF:* 800-777-8755 ■ *Web:* www.sherwoodamerica.com	Cerritos	CA	90703	562-741-0960	741-0967
Shure Inc 5800 W Touhy Ave *TF:* 800-257-4873 ■ *Web:* www.shure.com	Niles	IL	60714	847-866-2200	600-1212
Sima Products Corp 120 Pennsylvania Ave *TF:* 800-345-7462 ■ *Web:* www.simacorp.com	Oakmont	PA	15139	412-828-3700	828-3775
SLS International Inc 1650 W Jackson St *AMEX: SLS* ■ *Web:* www.nczon.com	Ozark	MO	65721	417-883-4549	883-4549
Snell Acoustics 300 Jubilee Dr *Web:* www.snellacoustics.com	Peabody	MA	01960	978-538-6262	538-6266
Sony Corp of America 550 Madison Ave *TF:* 800-282-2848 ■ *Web:* www.sony.com	New York	NY	10022	212-833-6800	
Sony Electronics Inc 1 Sony Dr **Fax:* Hum Res ■ *TF Cust Svc:* 800-222-7669 ■ *Web:* www.sony.com	Park Ridge	NJ	07656	201-930-1000	358-4058*
Sony of Canada Ltd 115 Gordon Baker Rd *Web:* www.sony.ca	Toronto	ON	M2H3R6	416-499-1414	499-1774
Sound Com Corp 227 Depot St *TF:* 800-628-8739 ■ *Web:* www.soundcom.net	Berea	OH	44017	440-234-2604	234-2614
Southern Audio Services 14763 Florida Blvd *TF Cust Svc:* 800-843-8823 ■ *Web:* www.bazooka.com	Baton Rouge	LA	70819	225-272-7135	272-9844
Stancil Corp 2644 S Croddy Way *TF:* 800-782-6245 ■ *Web:* www.stancilcorp.com	Santa Ana	CA	92704	714-546-2002	546-2092
Sunfire Corp 1920 Bickford Ave *Web:* www.sunfire.com	Snohomish	WA	98290	425-335-4748	335-4746
TDK USA Corp 901 Franklin Ave PO Box 9302 **Fax:* Sales ■ *TF:* 800-835-8273 ■ *Web:* www.tdk.com	Garden City	NY	11530	516-535-2600	294-7751*
TEAC America Inc 7733 Telegraph Rd *Web:* www.teac.com	Montebello	CA	90640	323-726-0303	727-7656
Telex Communications Inc 12000 Portland Ave S *TF:* 877-863-4169 ■ *Web:* www.telex.com	Burnsville	MN	55337	952-884-4051	884-0043

	City	State	Zip	Phone	Fax
Toshiba America Inc 1251 Avenue of the Americas Suite 4100 *TF:* 800-457-7777 ■ *Web:* www.toshiba.com	New York	NY	10020	212-596-0600	593-3875
Universal Audio Inc 1700 Green Hills Rd *TF:* 877-698-2834 ■ *Web:* www.uaudio.com	Scotts Valley	CA	95066	831-440-1176	461-1550
Universal Electronics Inc 6101 Gateway Dr *NASDAQ: UEIC* ■ *Web:* www.uei.com	Cypress	CA	90630	714-820-1000	820-1010
Verrex Corp 1130 Rt 22 W *Web:* www.verrex.com	Mountainside	NJ	07092	908-232-7000	232-7991
Vrex Inc 3 Westchester Plaza *Web:* www.vrex.com	Elmsford	NY	10523	914-345-8877	345-8772
Washington Professional Systems 109áGaitheráDr Suite 301 *Web:* www.wpsworld.com	Mount Laurel	NJ	08054	856-273-8688	273-8558
Wisdom Audio Corp 1572 College Pkwy Suite 164 *Web:* www.wisdomaudio.com	Carson City	NV	89706	775-887-8850	887-8820
Xantech Corp 1969 Kellogg Ave **Fax Area Code:* 800 ■ *TF Sales:* 800-843-5465 ■ *Web:* www.xantech.com	Carlsbad	CA	92008	818-362-0353	492-6832*
Yamaha Electronics Corp 6660 Orangethorpe Ave **Fax Area Code:* 800 ■ *TF Cust Svc:* 800-292-2982 ■ *Web:* www.yamaha.com/yec	Buena Park	CA	90620	714-522-9888	634-0355*

53 AUTO CLUBS

	City	State	Zip	Phone	Fax
AAA Akron 111 W Ctr St *Web:* www.aaa.com	Akron	OH	44308	330-762-0631	762-5965
AAA Alliance Auto Club 2322 S Union Ave *Web:* www.aaa.com	Alliance	OH	44601	330-823-9820	
AAA Allied Group Inc 15 W Central Pkwy *TF:* 800-543-2345 ■ *Web:* www.discover.aaa.com	Cincinnati	OH	45202	513-762-3100	762-3282
AAA Ashland County 502 Claremont Ave *TF:* 800-222-4357 ■ *Web:* www.aaa.com	Ashland	OH	44805	419-289-8133	281-1326
AAA Auto Club South 1515 N Westshore Blvd *Web:* www.aaasouth.com	Tampa	FL	33607	813-289-5000	289-5015
AAA Blue Grass/Kentucky 155 N MLK Blvd *TF:* 800-568-5222 ■ *Web:* www.aaa.com	Lexington	KY	40507	859-233-1111	281-1410
AAA Carolinas 6600 AAA Dr *TF:* 800-477-4222 ■ *Web:* www.aaacarolinas.com	Charlotte	NC	28212	704-569-3600	532-5822
AAA Central Penn 2023 Market St *TF:* 877-848-9990 ■ *Web:* www.aaa.com	Harrisburg	PA	17103	717-236-4021	236-0468
AAA Chicago Motor Club 975 Meridian Lake Dr *TF:* 866-968-7222 ■ *Web:* www.aaa.com	Aurora	IL	60504	630-328-7000	499-8200
AAA Colorado 4100 E Arkansas Ave *TF:* 866-625-3601 ■ *Web:* www.aaacolo.com	Denver	CO	80222	866-625-3601	
AAA Columbiana County 216 Broadway St *TF:* 800-222-4357 ■ *Web:* www.aaa.com	East Liverpool	OH	43920	330-385-2020	385-9718
AAA East Central 5900 Baum Blvd *Web:* www.aaa.com	Pittsburgh	PA	15206	412-363-5100	362-8943
AAA East Penn 1020 W Hamilton St *TF:* 800-552-6679 ■ *Web:* www.aaa.com	Allentown	PA	18101	610-434-5141	778-3390
AAA Hawaii 1130 N Nimitz Hwy Suite A-170 *TF:* 800-736-2886 ■ *Web:* www.hawaii.aaa.com/en-hi/Pages/Home.aspx	Honolulu	HI	96817	808-593-2221	591-9359
AAA Hoosier Motor Club 3750 Guion Rd **Fax:* Cust Svc ■ *Web:* www.aaa.com	Indianapolis	IN	46222	317-923-1500	923-5991*
AAA Hudson Valley 618 Delaware Ave *Web:* www.aaa.com	Albany	NY	12209	518-426-1000	426-1595
AAA Kentucky 435 E Broadway *TF:* 800-727-2552 ■ *Web:* www.aaa.com	Louisville	KY	40202	502-582-3311	584-1455
AAA Massillon Auto Club 1972 Wales Rd NE *TF:* 800-222-4357 ■ *Web:* www.aaa.com	Massillon	OH	44646	330-833-1084	833-5542
AAA Merrimack Valley 49 Orchard Hill Rd *Web:* www.aaa.com	North Andover	MA	01845	978-681-9200	688-4891
AAA Miami Valley 825 S Ludlow St *TF:* 800-624-2321 ■ *Web:* www.aaa.com	Dayton	OH	45402	937-224-2801	224-2892
AAA Michigan 1 Auto Club Dr *TF:* 800-222-6424 ■ *Web:* www.aaa.com	Dearborn	MI	48126	313-336-1234	336-1809
AAA Mid-Atlantic 1 River Pl **Fax Area Code:* 215 ■ *TF:* 800-222-4357 ■ *Web:* www.midatlantic.aaa.com/Default.aspx	Wilmington	DE	19801	302-299-4000	864-5170*
AAA Minneapolis 5400 Auto Club Way *Web:* www.aaa.com	Minneapolis	MN	55416	952-927-2600	927-2559
AAA Minnesota/Iowa 600 W Travelers Trail *TF:* 800-222-1333 ■ *Web:* www.aaa.com/PPInternational/International.html	Burnsville	MN	55337	952-707-4500	707-4220
AAA Missouri 12901 N Forty Dr *TF:* 800-222-4357 ■ *Web:* www.ouraaa.com	Saint Louis	MO	63141	314-523-7350	523-7427
AAA MountainWest 2100 11th Ave *TF:* 800-332-6119 ■ *Web:* www.aaa.com	Helena	MT	59062	406-447-8100	442-5671
AAA Nebraska 910 N 96th St **Fax:* Cust Svc ■ *TF:* 800-222-6327 ■ *Web:* www.aaa.com/PPInternational/International.html	Omaha	NE	68114	402-390-1000	390-6023*
AAA Niagara-Orleans Auto Club 7135 Rochester Rd *Web:* www.aaa.com	Lockport	NY	14094	716-434-2865	434-3452
AAA North Penn 1035 N Washington Ave *Web:* www.aaa.com	Scranton	PA	18509	570-348-2511	348-2563
AAA Northampton County 3914 Hecktown Rd *Web:* www.aaa.com	Easton	PA	18045	610-258-2371	258-5256
AAA Northern New England 68 Marginal Way *TF:* 800-222-4357 ■ *Web:* www.aaanne.com	Portland	ME	04104	207-780-6800	780-6986
AAA Northway 112 Railroad St *TF:* 866-222-7283 ■ *Web:* www.aaaNORTHWAY.com	Schenectady	NY	12305	518-374-4575	374-3140
AAA Northwest Ohio 7150 W Central Ave *TF:* 800-428-0060 ■ *Web:* www.aaanwohio.com	Toledo	OH	43617	419-843-1200	843-1249
AAA Ohio Auto Club 90 E Wilson Bridge Rd *TF:* 800-282-0585 ■ *Web:* www.aaaohio.com	Worthington	OH	43085	614-431-7800	431-7918
AAA Oklahoma 2121 E 15th St *TF:* 800-222-2582 ■ *Web:* www.aaaoklahoma.com	Tulsa	OK	74104	918-748-1000	748-1111
AAA Oregon/Idaho 600 SW Market St *TF Cust Svc:* 800-452-1643 ■ *Web:* www.aaa.com/PPInternational/International.html	Portland	OR	97201	503-222-6785	219-6222
AAA Reading-Berks 920 Van Reed Rd *Web:* www.aaa.com	Wyomissing	PA	19610	610-374-4531	374-1325
AAA Schuylkill County 340 S Centre St *Web:* www.aaa.com	Pottsville	PA	17901	570-622-4991	622-8179
AAA Shelby County 920 Wapakoneta Ave *Web:* www.aaa.com	Sidney	OH	45365	937-492-3167	492-7297
AAA South Jersey 700 Laurel Oak Rd *Web:* www.aaa.com	Voorhees	NJ	08043	856-783-4222	627-9100
AAA Southern New England 110 Royal Little Dr *TF:* 800-222-7448 ■ *Web:* www.aaa.com	Providence	RI	02904	401-868-2000	868-2085
AAA Southern New York 21 Washington St *Web:* www.aaa.com	Binghamton	NY	13901	607-722-7255	724-6935
AAA Southern Pennsylvania 2840 Eastern Blvd *TF:* 800-222-1469 ■ *Web:* www.aaa.com	York	PA	17402	717-600-8700	755-2142
AAA Susquehanna Valley 1001 Market St *Web:* www.aaa.com	Sunbury	PA	17801	570-286-4507	286-1130
AAA Tidewater Virginia 5366 Virginia Beach Blvd *Web:* www.aaa.com	Virginia Beach	VA	32462	757-233-3800	233-3896
AAA Tri County Motor Club 195 Oneida St Suite A *Web:* www.aaa.com	Oneonta	NY	13820	607-432-4512	432-9123
AAA Tuscarawas County 1112 4th St NW *Web:* www.aaa.com	New Philadelphia	OH	44663	330-343-4481	364-1116
AAA Utica & Central New York 409 Ct St *Web:* www.aaa.com	Utica	NY	13502	315-797-5000	797-5005
AAA Washington-Inland 1745 114th Ave SE *TF:* 800-562-2582 ■ *Web:* www.aaanewsroom.net	Bellevue	WA	98004	425-646-2058	467-7729
AAA Western & Central New York 100 International Dr *TF:* 800-836-2582	Buffalo	NY	14221	716-633-9860	633-4439
AAA Wisconsin 8401 Excelsior Dr *TF:* 800-236-1300 ■ *Web:* www.aaanewsroom.net	Madison	WI	53717	608-828-2487	828-2530
AARP Motoring Plan 200 N Martingale Rd *TF:* 800-555-1121 ■ *Web:* www.aarpmotoring.com	Schaumburg	IL	60173	800-555-1121	
American Automobile Assn Inc Alabama (AAA) 2400 Acton Rd *TF:* 800-521-8124 ■ *Web:* www.aaa.com	Birmingham	AL	35243	205-978-7000	978-7026
American Automobile Assn Inc Arizona (AAA) 3144 N 7th Ave *TF:* 800-352-5382 ■ *Web:* www.aaa.com	Phoenix	AZ	85013	602-274-1116	234-1327
American Automobile Assn Inc South Dakota (AAA) 1300 Industrial Ave *TF:* 800-222-4545 ■ *Web:* www.aaasouthdakota.com	Sioux Falls	SD	57104	605-336-3690	332-4055
Auto Club Ltd 106 E 6th St Suite 900 **Fax Area Code:* 512 ■ *TF:* 866-247-3728 ■ *Web:* www.theautoclub.com	Austin	TX	78701	866-247-3728	697-0661*
Auto Club of America Corp (ACA) 9411 N Georgia St *TF:* 800-411-2007 ■ *Web:* www.autoclubofamerica.com	Oklahoma City	OK	73120	405-751-4430	751-4462
Auto Club of New York Inc 1415 Kellum Pl *Web:* www.aaa.com/PPInternational/Benefits_Intl_to_US.html	Garden City	NY	11530	516-746-7730	873-2320
Auto Club of Pioneer Valley 150 Capital Dr *TF Cust Svc:* 800-622-9211 ■ *Web:* www.aaa.com	West Springfield	MA	01089	413-785-1381	205-2350
Automobile Club of Southern California 2601 S Figueroa St *TF:* 800-400-4222 ■ *Web:* www.aaa.com	Los Angeles	CA	90007	213-741-3686	741-4151
BP MotorClub PO Box 4441 **Fax Area Code:* 847 ■ *TF:* 800-334-3300 ■ *Web:* www.bpmotorclub.com	Carol Stream	IL	60197	800-334-3300	605-4864*
Brickell Financial Services Motor Club Inc 7300 Corporate Ctr Dr Suite 601 *TF:* 800-262-7262 ■ *Web:* www.road-america.com	Miami	FL	33126	305-392-4300	302-4301
British Columbia Automobile Assn (BCAA) 4567 Canada Way *TF:* 800-222-4357 ■ *Web:* www.bcaa.com	Burnaby	BC	V5G4T1	604-268-5000	268-5569
CAA Central Ontario 60 Commerce Valley Dr E *TF:* 800-268-3750 ■ *Web:* www.caasco.com	Thornhill	ON	L3T7P9	905-771-3000	771-3101
CAA Manitoba 870 Empress St *TF:* 800-222-4357 ■ *Web:* www.caamanitoba.com	Winnipeg	MB	R3C2Z3	204-262-6166	774-9961
CAA Maritimes Ltd 378 Westmorland Rd *TF:* 800-471-1611 ■ *Web:* ww2.aaa.com	Saint John	NB	E2J2G4	506-634-1400	653-9500
CAA North & East Ontario PO Box 8350 *TF:* 800-267-8713 ■ *Web:* www.caaneo.on.ca	Ottawa	ON	K1G3T2	613-820-1890	820-4646
CAA Quebec 444 Bouvier St *TF:* 800-222-4357 ■ *Web:* www.caaquebec.com	Quebec	QC	G2J1E3	418-624-8222	623-7331
CAA Saskatchewan 200 Albert St N *TF:* 800-564-6222 ■ *Web:* www.caask.ca	Regina	SK	S4R5E2	306-791-4321	949-4461
CAA Stoney Creek 163 Centennial Pkwy N *TF:* 800-992-8143 ■ *Web:* www.caasco.com	Hamilton	ON	L8E1H8	905-664-8000	664-8080
California State Automobile Assn 150 Van Ness Ave **Fax:* Hum Res ■ *TF Cust Svc:* 800-922-8228 ■ *Web:* www.csaa.com	San Francisco	CA	94102	415-565-2012	431-7572*
Canadian Automobile Assn (CAA) 1145 Hunt Club Rd Suite 200 *Web:* www.caa.ca	Ottawa	ON	K1V0Y3	613-247-0117	247-0118
Cross Country Automotive Services (CCAS) 1 Cabot Rd *Web:* www.crosscountry-auto.com	Medford	MA	02155	781-393-9300	395-6706
Dallas Model A Ford Club PO Box 1028 *Web:* www.dmafc.com	Addison	TX	75001	972-279-4786	
Findlay Automobile Club 1550 Tiffin Ave *Web:* www.aaa.com	Findlay	OH	45840	419-422-4961	422-5620
GE Motor Club Inc 200 N Martingale Rd *TF:* 800-616-9286	Schaumburg	IL	60173	800-616-9286	
GM Motor Club PO Box 1049 *TF:* 800-705-0055 ■ *Web:* www.gmmotorclub.com	Winston-Salem	NC	27102	800-705-0055	
Gulf Motor Club 929 N Plum Grove Rd **Fax Area Code:* 847 ■ *TF:* 800-633-3224	Schaumburg	IL	60173	800-633-3224	240-2114*

	City	State	Zip	Phone	Fax
Motor Club of America Enterprises Inc					
3200 Wilshire Blvd	Oklahoma City	OK	73156	800-288-2889	
TF: 800-288-2889					
National Automobile Club (NAC)					
1151 E Hillsdale Blvd	Foster City	CA	94404	650-294-7000	294-7040
Web: www.nationalautoclub.com					
National Motor Club of America Inc					
6500 Beltline Rd Suite 200	Irving	TX	75063	972-999-4400	999-4405
TF: 800-523-4582 ■ *Web:* www.nmca.com					
New Jersey Auto Club 1 Hanover Rd	Florham Park	NJ	07932	973-377-7200	377-7204
Web: www.ww2.aaa.com					
Pennsylvania AAA Federation 600 N 3rd St	Harrisburg	PA	17105	717-238-7192	238-6574
Web: www.aaapa.org					
Pinnacle Motor Club 130 E John Carpenter Fwy	Irving	TX	75062	800-446-1289	
TF: 800-446-1289 ■ *Web:* www.pinnaclemotorclub.com					
Roadgard Motor Club 11222 Quail Roost Dr	Miami	FL	33157	800-432-8603	
TF: 800-432-8603					
Travelers Motor Club 720 NW 50th St	Oklahoma City	OK	73154	405-848-1711	
TF: 800-654-9208 ■ *Web:* www.travelersmotorclub.com					
Trilegiant Corp 6 High Ridge Pk	Stamford	CT	06905	800-876-7787	
TF: 800-999-4227 ■ *Web:* www.autovantage.com					
US Auto Club Motoring Div Inc PO Box 660460	Dallas	TX	75226	800-348-2761	692-7209*
*Fax Area Code: 972 ■ *TF:* 800-348-2761 ■ *Web:* www.usacmd.com					
Zipcar Inc 25 1st St FL 4	Cambridge	MA	02141	617-336-4400	995-4300
Web: www.zipcar.com					

54 AUTO SUPPLY STORES

	City	State	Zip	Phone	Fax
Advance Auto Parts Inc 5008 Airport Rd	Roanoke	VA	24012	541-561-8452	561-6930*
NYSE: AAP ■ *Fax Area Code: 540 ■ *Fax: Hum Res ■ *TF:* 877-238-2623 ■ *Web:* www.advance-auto.com					
Anderson Auto Parts Co 102 Brown Rd	Anderson	SC	29621	864-225-1475	231-9553
Auto Barn 13 Harbor Pk Dr	Port Washington	NY	11050	516-484-9500	484-4341
Web: www.autobarn.com					
AutoZone Inc 123 S Front St	Memphis	TN	38103	901-495-6500	495-8300
NYSE: AZO ■ *TF:* 800-288-6966 ■ *Web:* www.autozone.com					
Bennett Auto Supply Inc					
3141 SW 10th St	Pompano Beach	FL	33069	954-335-8700	335-8834*
*Fax: Hum Res ■ *TF:* 800-766-5913 ■ *Web:* www.bennettauto.com					
Benny's Inc 340 Waterman Ave	Smithfield	RI	02917	401-231-1000	231-1080
Web: www.hellobennys.com					
Blue Star Automobile Stores Inc					
2001 S State St	Chicago	IL	60616	312-225-7174	225-7474
Web: www.bluestarautoparts.com					
Bond Auto Parts 272 Morrison Rd PO Box 687	Barre	VT	05641	802-479-0571	476-1308
TF: 800-639-1982 ■ *Web:* www.bondauto.com					
Carquest Corp 2635 E Millbrook Rd	Raleigh	NC	27604	919-573-3000	573-3558*
*Fax: Mktg ■ *TF:* 800-876-1291 ■ *Web:* www.carquest.com					
Crow-Burlingame Co Inc					
190 E Roosevelt St	Little Rock	AR	72203	501-372-5275	376-2769
TF: 877-282-6591					
Discount Tire Co 20225 N Scottsdale Rd	Scottsdale	AZ	85255	480-606-6000	443-3162*
*Fax: Cust Svc ■ *TF:* 800-347-4348 ■ *Web:* www.discounttire.com					
Hedahls Inc 122 N 1st St	Bismarck	ND	58501	701-223-8393	221-4251
TF: 800-433-2457 ■ *Web:* www.hedahls.com					
Knecht's Auto Parts 3400 Main St	Springfield	OR	97478	541-746-4532	746-0884
Web: www.knechts.com					
KOI Warehouse Inc 2701 Spring Grove Ave	Cincinnati	OH	45225	513-357-2400	412-3554
TF: 800-354-0408 ■ *Web:* www.koiautoparts.com					
Maita Enterprises Inc 2500 Auburn Blvd	Sacramento	CA	95821	916-481-0855	483-2194
TF: 888-360-4999 ■ *Web:* www.maitatoyota.com					
Max Auto Supply Co 1101 Monroe St	Toledo	OH	43604	419-243-7281	243-1626
Web: www.katzmidas.com					
Merle's Automotive Supply Inc					
33 W University Blvd	Tucson	AZ	85705	520-622-3526	622-2760
TF: 800-447-7202 ■ *Web:* www.merlesauto.com					
Mike Gatto Inc 15 W Hibiscus Blvd	Melbourne	FL	32901	321-676-2710	952-1302
Web: www.gattos.com					
NAPA Auto Parts Stores 2999 Cir 75 Pkwy NW	Atlanta	GA	30339	770-956-2200	956-2212
Web: www.napaonline.com					
O'Reilly Automotive Inc 233 S Patterson	Springfield	MO	65802	417-862-6708	863-2242
NASDAQ: ORLY ■ *TF:* 888-327-7153 ■ *Web:* www.oreillyauto.com					
Original Parts Group Inc (OPGI)					
1770 Saturn Way	Seal Beach	CA	90740	562-594-1000	594-1050
TF: 800-243-8355 ■ *Web:* www.opgi.com					
Peerless Tyre Co 5000 Kingston St	Denver	CO	80239	303-371-4300	371-4749
TF: 800-999-7810 ■ *Web:* www.peerlesstyreco.com					
Pep Boys - Manny Moe & Jack					
3111 W Allegheny Ave	Philadelphia	PA	19132	215-227-9000	227-7513*
NYSE: PBY ■ *Fax: Hum Res ■ *TF:* 800-737-2697 ■ *Web:* www.pepboys.com					
Rent-A-Tire Rent-A-Wheel					
15350 Sherman Way Suite 260	Van Nuys	CA	91406	818-786-7906	786-7458
Web: www.rentawheel.com					
Robertson Tire Co Inc PO Box 472287	Tulsa	OK	74147	918-664-2211	622-7221
Web: www.robertson-tire.com					
Strauss Discount Auto					
7 - C Brick Plant Rd	South River	NJ	08882	732-390-9000	390-9073
TF: 800-947-2637 ■ *Web:* www.straussauto.com					
Tire Warehouse 200 Holleder Pkwy	Rochester	NY	14615	800-876-6676	
TF: 800-876-6676 ■ *Web:* www.tirewarehouse.net					
Tireman Auto Service Centers Ltd PO Box 3456	Toledo	OH	43607	419-724-8473	724-8474
Web: www.thetireman.com					
Town Fair Tire Co Inc 460 Coe Ave	East Haven	CT	06512	203-467-8600	467-1630
TF: 800-972-2245 ■ *Web:* www.townfair.com					
United Auto Supply Inc 625 3rd St S	La Crosse	WI	54601	608-784-9198	784-4760
Vanguard Trucks Centers 700 Ruskin Dr	Forest Park	GA	30297	866-216-7925	363-4659*
*Fax Area Code: 404 ■ *TF:* 866-216-7925 ■ *Web:* www.vanguardtrucks.com					
VIP Discount Auto Ctr 12 Lexington St	Lewiston	ME	04240	207-784-5423	784-9178
Web: www.vipauto.com					

	City	State	Zip	Phone	Fax
Westbay Auto Parts Inc					
2610 SE Mile Hill Dr	Port Orchard	WA	98366	360-876-8008	876-7999
Web: www.westbayautoparts.com					

55 AUTOMATIC MERCHANDISING EQUIPMENT & SYSTEMS

SEE ALSO Food Service p. 1875

	City	State	Zip	Phone	Fax
Affiliated Control Equipment Inc					
640 Wheat Ln	Wood Dale	IL	60191	630-595-4680	595-6151
Web: www.affiliatedcontrol.com					
AIR-serv Group LLC					
1370 Mendota Heights Rd	Mendota Heights	MN	55120	651-454-0518	454-9542
TF: 800-227-5336 ■ *Web:* www.air-serv.com					
American Coin Merchandising Inc					
397 S Taylor Ave	Louisville	CO	80027	303-444-2559	247-1728
American Vending Sales Inc					
750 Morse Ave	Elk Grove Village	IL	60007	847-439-9400	439-9405
TF: 800-441-0009 ■ *Web:* www.americanvending.com					
Automatic Products International Ltd					
75 Plato Blvd W	Saint Paul	MN	55107	615-288-2975	224-5559*
*Fax Area Code: 651 ■ *Fax: Sales ■ *TF:* 800-523-8363 ■ *Web:* www.automaticproducts.com					
Bastian Material Handling LLC (BMH)					
9820 Assn Ct	Indianapolis	IN	46280	317-575-9992	575-8596
TF: 800-772-0464 ■ *Web:* www.bastiansolutions.com					
Betson Enterprises Inc					
303 Patterson Plank Rd	Carlstadt	NJ	07072	201-438-1300	438-4837
TF: 800-524-2343 ■ *Web:* www.betson.com					
Birmingham Vending Co 540 2nd Ave N	Birmingham	AL	35204	205-324-7526	322-6639
TF: 800-288-7635 ■ *Web:* www.bhmvending.com					
Coin Acceptors Inc 300 Hunter Ave	Saint Louis	MO	63124	314-725-0100	725-2896
TF: 800-325-2646 ■ *Web:* www.coinco.com					
Coinstar Inc 1800 114th Ave SE	Bellevue	WA	98004	425-943-8000	943-8030*
NASDAQ: CSTR ■ *Fax: Mktg ■ *TF:* 800-928-2274 ■ *Web:* www.coinstar.com					
Crane Merchandising Systems					
12955 Enterprise Way	Bridgeton	MO	63044	314-298-3500	298-3505*
*Fax: Sales ■ *TF:* 800-325-8811 ■ *Web:* www.cranems.com					
Dixie-Narco Inc 3330 Dixie-Narco Blvd	Williston	SC	29853	803-266-5000	266-5000
TF: 800-688-9090 ■ *Web:* www.dixie-narco.com					
Fawn Vendors Inc 8040 University Blvd	Des Moines	IA	50325	515-274-3641	274-5180*
*Fax: Sales ■ *TF:* 800-247-1787 ■ *Web:* www.fawnvendors.com					
Federal Machine Corp 8040 University Blvd	Des Moines	IA	50325	515-274-1555	274-5180*
*Fax: Sales ■ *TF:* 800-247-2446 ■ *Web:* www.federalmachine.com					
Glacier Water Services Inc 1385 Pk Ctr Dr	Vista	CA	92081	760-560-1111	560-3333
TF: 800-452-2437 ■ *Web:* www.glacierwater.com					
Harcourt Outlines Inc 7765 S 175 W PO Box 128	Milroy	IN	46156	765-629-2625	278-5165*
*Fax Area Code: 800 ■ *TF:* 800-428-6584 ■ *Web:* www.harcourtoutlines.com					
Melo-Tone Vending Inc 130 Broadway	Somerville	MA	02145	617-666-4900	666-4906
TF: 800-322-7741 ■ *Web:* www.melotone.com					
Northwestern Corp 922 E Armstrong St	Morris	IL	60450	815-942-1300	942-4477
TF: 800-942-1316 ■ *Web:* www.nwcorp.com					

56 AUTOMATIC TELLER MACHINES (ATMS)

	City	State	Zip	Phone	Fax
Accu-time Systems Inc 420 Somers Rd	Ellington	CT	06029	860-870-5000	872-1511
TF: 800-355-4648 ■ *Web:* www.accu-time.com					
Cardtronics Inc 3250 briarpark Suite 400	Houston	TX	77042	281-596-9988	596-9984
TF: 888-533-8375 ■ *Web:* www.cardtronics.com					
Diebold Inc 5995 Mayfair Rd	North Canton	OH	44720	330-490-4000	
NYSE: DBD ■ *TF:* 800-999-3600 ■ *Web:* www.diebold.com					
Electronic Cash Systems Inc					
30052 Aventura Suite C	Rancho Santa Margarita	CA	92688	949-888-8580	888-8024
TF: 888-327-2864 ■ *Web:* www.ecspayments.com					
Global Cash Access Holdings Inc (GCA)					
3525 E Post Rd Suite 120	Las Vegas	NV	89120	702-855-3000	672-4371*
NYSE: GCA ■ *Fax Area Code: 866 ■ *TF:* 800-833-7110 ■ *Web:* www.globalcashaccess.com					
Tidel Engineering Inc					
2025 W Belt Line Rd # 114	Carrollton	TX	75006	972-484-3358	484-1014
TF: 800-678-7577 ■ *Web:* www.tidel.com					
#1 Cochran of Monroeville					
4520 William Penn Hwy	Monroeville	PA	15146	412-373-3333	373-8906
TF: 877-262-4726 ■ *Web:* www.cochran.com					

57 AUTOMOBILE DEALERS & GROUPS

SEE ALSO Automobile Sales & Related Services - Online p. 1496

	City	State	Zip	Phone	Fax
32 Ford Mercury Inc 610 W Main St	Batavia	OH	45103	513-732-2124	732-6277
A C Nelson Rv World 11818 L St	Omaha	NE	68137	402-333-1122	333-1054
TF: 888-655-2332 ■ *Web:* www.acnrv.com					
Acura 101 West 24650 Calabasas Rd	Calabasas	CA	91302	818-222-5555	222-6495
TF: 800-472-3173 ■ *Web:* www.acura101west.com					
Alberic Colon Auto Sales Inc PO Box 11311	San Juan	PR	00920	787-999-8888	
Web: www.albericcolon.com					
Alford Motors Inc Hwy 171	Leesville	LA	71446	337-239-3811	238-5003
Web: www.alfordmotors.com					
Allan Vigil Ford 6790 Mt Zion Blvd	Marrow	GA	30260	678-364-3673	364-3333
TF: 800-222-3597 ■ *Web:* www.apps.dealerconnection.com					
Allen Samuels Auto Group 1625 N Valley Mills Dr	Waco	TX	76710	254-227-6841	761-6899
TF: 800-762-8850 ■ *Web:* www.allensamuelschevroletwaco.com					
America's Car-Mart Inc					
802 SE Plaza Ave Suite 200	Bentonville	AR	72712	479-464-9944	273-7556
NASDAQ: CRMT ■ *Web:* www.car-mart.com					
American Augers Inc 135 US Rt 42	West Salem	OH	44287	419-869-7107	869-7653
TF: 800-324-4930 ■ *Web:* www.americanaugers.com					

Company	City	State	ZIP	Phone	Fax
Ancira Winton Chevrolet 6111 Bandera Rd *TF:* 866-342-9380 ■ *Web:* www.ancira.com	San Antonio	TX	78238	210-231-4413	681-9413
Armstrong Buick Volkswagen Inc 20000 McLoughlin Blvd *TF:* 866-308-0032 ■ *Web:* www.armstrongvw.com	Gladstone	OR	97027	503-656-2924	656-1449
Arrow Truck Sales Inc 3200 Manchester Trfy *TF:* 800-311-7144 ■ *Web:* www.arrowtruck.com	Kansas City	MO	64129	816-923-5000	923-4005
Asbury Automotive Group Inc 2905 Premiere Pkwy Suite 300 *NYSE: ABG* ■ **Fax Area Code:* 678 ■ *Web:* www.asburyauto.com	Duluth	GA	30097	770-418-8200	542-2701*
Asheville Chevrolet Inc 205 Smokey Pk Hwy *TF:* 866-921-1073 ■ *Web:* www.ashevillechevrolet.com	Asheville	NC	28806	828-665-4444	665-9848
Asian Pacific Industries Inc 5080 Stevens Creek Blvd *TF:* 800-536-8522 ■ *Web:* www.landroversj.com	San Jose	CA	95129	408-247-7600	261-6975
Astoria Ford 710 W Marine Dr *TF:* 888-760-9303 ■ *Web:* www.astoriaford.dealerconnection.com	Astoria	OR	97103	503-325-6411	325-1743
Aurora-Naperville Enterprises Inc 4173 Ogden Ave *Web:* www.valleyhonda.com	Aurora	IL	60504	630-851-5700	851-4939
Auto Mall The 800 Pytney Rd *Web:* www.brattautomall.com	Brattleboro	VT	05301	802-275-4510	257-9327
AutoFair Automotive Group 200 Keller St *Web:* www.autofair.com	Manchester	NH	03103	603-634-1000	622-4079
Autofocus Inc 5994 W Las Positas Blvd Suite 221	Pleasanton	CA	94588	925-924-1105	924-1420
Autoland 170 Rt 22 E *TF Sales:* 877-813-7239 ■ *Web:* www.1800autoland.com	Springfield	NJ	07081	973-467-2900	467-1824
AutoNation Inc 200 SW 1st Ave Suite 1600 *NYSE: AN* ■ **Fax:* PR ■ *TF:* 800-899-4911 ■ *Web:* www.corp.autonation.com	Fort Lauderdale	FL	33301	954-769-7000	769-6537*
B & B Foreign Car Ctr 2983 El Camino Real *Web:* www.bbsaab.com	Santa Clara	CA	95051	408-246-6388	985-6757
Bachman Auto Group Hurstbourne Ln *Web:* www.bachmanautogroup.com	Louisville	KY	40299	502-499-6161	493-0595
Badger Truck Center Inc 2326 W St Paul Ave *Web:* www.badgertruck.com	Milwaukee	WI	53233	414-344-9500	344-4323
Bale Chevrolet Co 13101 Chenal Pkwy *TF Sales:* 888-592-0941 ■ *Web:* www.balechevrolet.com	Little Rock	AR	72211	501-221-9191	227-5960
Balise Motor Sales Co 1102 Riverdale St *Web:* www.baliseauto.com	West Springfield	MA	01089	413-733-8604	739-6441
Barry Bunker Chevrolet Inc 1307 N Wabash Ave *TF Sales:* 866-603-8625 ■ *Web:* www.barrybunker.com	Marion	IN	46952	765-664-1275	662-2665
Baskin Auto Truck & Tractor Inc 1844 Hwy 51 S *TF:* 877-476-2626 ■ *Web:* www.baskintrandtr.com	Covington	TN	38019	901-476-2626	476-2658
Bayview Ford Lincoln Mercury Inc 27180 Hwy 98 *TF:* 877-255-2717 ■ *Web:* www.bayviewflm.com	Daphne	AL	36526	251-626-7777	621-3104
Becker Motors Inc PO Box 740 *Web:* www.beckermotors.com	Canandaigua	NY	14424	585-393-9500	
Bell Aviation Inc 2404 Edmund Hwy *Web:* www.bellaviation.com	West Columbia	SC	29170	803-822-4114	822-8970
Bergstrom Automotive 1 Neenah Ctr *Web:* www.bergstromauto.com	Neenah	WI	54956	920-725-4444	729-5145
Bergstrom of Kaukauna 2929 Lawe St *Web:* www.vdhchrysler.com	Kaukauna	WI	54130	866-939-0130	
Best Chevrolet Inc 128 Derby St *Web:* www.bestchevyusa.com	Hingham	MA	02043	781-749-1950	749-8153
Biggers Chevrolet 1385 E Chicago St *TF:* 866-431-1555 ■ *Web:* www.biggerschevy.com	Elgin	IL	60120	847-742-9000	742-0061
Bill Collins 4220 Bardstown Rd *TF:* 800-258-2455 ■ *Web:* www.billcollinsford.com	Louisville	KY	40218	502-459-9550	459-1966
Bill Hesser Enterprises Inc 2009 Milton Ave *Web:* www.hessertoyota.com	Janesville	WI	53545	608-754-7754	756-8894
Bill Penney Toyota 4808 University Dr NW *Web:* www.billpenneytoyota.com	Huntsville	AL	35816	256-837-1111	837-2077
Bill Snethkamp Lansing Dodge Inc 6131 S Pennsylvania Ave *TF:* 800-863-6343 ■ *Web:* www.snethkampdodge.com	Lansing	MI	48911	517-394-1200	394-1205
Blaise Alexander Chevrolet Inc 933 Broad St *TF:* 877-575-4256 ■ *Web:* www.blaisealexanderautogroup.com	Montoursville	PA	17754	570-368-8677	368-1010
Bob Davidson Ford Lincoln 1845 E Joppa Rd *TF:* 888-643-0263 ■ *Web:* www.bobdavidsonford.com	Baltimore	MD	21234	410-661-6400	668-4306
Bob Fisher Chevrolet Inc 4111 Pottsville Pike *Web:* www.bobfisherchev.com	Reading	PA	19605	610-921-0261	921-2202
Bob Montgomery Chevrolet Honda Inc 5340 Dixie Hwy *Web:* www.bobmontgomery.com	Louisville	KY	40216	502-448-2820	449-8553
Bob Rohrman Auto Group 701 Sagamore Pkwy S *TF:* 800-488-3534 ■ *Web:* www.rohrman.com	Lafayette	IN	47905	765-448-1000	449-2266
Bob-Boyd Lincoln-Mercury Inc 5711 Scarborough Blvd *TF:* 800-621-9569 ■ *Web:* www.bobboyd.com	Columbus	OH	43232	614-863-2800	863-3787
Bommarito Automotive Group 15736 Manchester Rd *TF:* 800-367-2289 ■ *Web:* www.bommarito.com	Ellisville	MO	63011	636-391-7200	394-3241
Bonander Pontiac Inc 231 S Ctr St *Web:* www.bonanderauto.com	Turlock	CA	95380	209-632-8871	667-6253
Bonner Chevrolet Co Inc 694 Wyoming Ave *Web:* www.bonnerchevrolet.com	Kingston	PA	18704	570-287-2118	288-0853
Boucher Group Inc 4141 S 108th St *Web:* www.boucher.com	Greenfield	WI	53228	414-427-4141	427-4140
Bozeman Motors CO 2900 N 19th St *TF:* 800-578-5460 ■ *Web:* www.bozemanford.com	Bozeman	MT	59718	406-587-1221	586-1400
Bradley Jim Pontiac-Cadillac Gmc Inc 500 Auto Mall Dr	Ann Arbor	MI	48103	734-769-1200	769-1273

Company	City	State	ZIP	Phone	Fax
Braley & Graham Inc 2163 Fulton Ave *Web:* www.braley-graham.com	Sacramento	CA	95825	916-481-2200	481-1448
Braman Management Assn 2060 Biscayne Blvd 2nd Fl	Miami	FL	33137	305-576-1889	576-9898
Brandon Dodge Inc 9207 Adamo Dr E	Tampa	FL	33619	813-620-4300	622-7258
Brasher Motor Co Of Weimar Inc 1700 I- 10 *TF:* 800-783-1746 ■ *Web:* www.brashermotors.com	Weimar	TX	78962	979-725-8515	725-8118
Broome Cadillac 11911 E US Hwy 40 *Web:* www.broomecars.com	Independence	MO	64055	816-358-2500	313-1988
Bryan Imports Inc 3100 Briarcrest Dr *Web:* www.garlynsheltonbryan.com	Bryan	TX	77802	979-776-7600	774-2646
Buchanan Automotive Group 50 Central Ave Suite 900 *TF:* 888-292-4883 ■ *Web:* www.buchananautomotivegroup.com	Sarasota	FL	34236	941-364-9500	
Buckeye Nissan Inc 3820 Pkwy Ln *Web:* www.buckeyenissan.com	Hilliard	OH	43026	614-771-2345	771-2363
Burr Truck & Trailer Sales Inc 2901 Vestal Rd *TF:* 866-230-2383 ■ *Web:* www.burrtruck.com	Vestal	NY	13850	607-729-2211	729-4375
Bush Inc 2581 Hickory Blvd SE *Web:* www.roosterbush.com	Lenoir	NC	28645	828-728-4222	728-7075
Butler County Ford 400 S Main St *TF:* 888-871-0687 ■ *Web:* apps.dealerconnection.com	Butler	PA	16001	724-287-2766	283-0372
Byerly Ford 4041 Dixie Hwy *TF:* 877-929-3759 ■ *Web:* www.byerlyford.com	Louisville	KY	40216	502-448-1661	448-0819
Cable-Dahmer Chevrolet Inc 1834 S Noland Rd *Web:* www.cabledahmer.com	Independence	MO	64055	816-254-3860	521-7638
Capistrano Scion 33395 Camino Capistrano *TF:* 888-493-0040 ■ *Web:* www.capistranoscion.com	San Juan Capistrano	CA	92675	949-493-4100	240-2445
Capital Automobile Co 2210 Cobb Pkwy SE *Web:* www.capitalcadillac.com	Smyrna	GA	30080	770-952-2277	989-8439
Capital Ford Inc 4900 Capital Blvd *TF:* 800-849-3166 ■ *Web:* www.capitalford.com	Raleigh	NC	27616	919-790-4700	790-4668
Capitol Chevrolet Montgomery 711 Eastern Blvd *TF Sales:* 800-410-1137 ■ *Web:* www.capitolchevrolet.com	Montgomery	AL	36117	334-272-8700	260-7179
Car City Motor Co Inc 3100 S US Hwy 169 *TF:* 800-525-7008 ■ *Web:* www.carcitymotors.com	Saint Joseph	MO	64503	816-233-9149	279-0639
Carlsbad Auto Co PO Box 1978	Lubbock	TX	79408	806-797-3441	795-3414
CarMax Inc 12800 Tuckahoe Creek Pkwy *NYSE: KMX* ■ *TF:* 888-922-7629 ■ *Web:* www.carmax.com	Richmond	VA	23238	804-747-0422	217-6819
Carr Enterprises Inc 2302 39th Ave *Web:* www.hilandtoyota.com	Moline	IL	61265	309-764-2481	
Carriage Enterprises Ltd 4040 Stevens Creek Blvd *TF:* 877-379-6716 ■ *Web:* www.sanjosebritishmotors.com	San Jose	CA	95129	408-246-7600	249-9136
Castriota Chevrolet 1701 W Liberty Ave *TF:* 866-750-3604 ■ *Web:* www.castriotachevys.com	Pittsburgh	PA	15226	412-343-2100	
Cavender Cadillac Co 801 Broadway St *TF:* 800-626-6859 ■ *Web:* www.cavendercadillac.com	San Antonio	TX	78215	210-226-7221	226-8646
Charles Gabus Ford Inc 4545 Merle Hay Rd *TF Sales:* 800-934-2287 ■ *Web:* charlesgabusford.dealerconnection.com	Des Moines	IA	50310	515-270-0707	270-2162
Chastang Enterprises Inc 6200 N Loop E *TF:* 866-512-0970 ■ *Web:* www.chastangford.com	Houston	TX	77026	713-671-0101	678-5001
Checkered Flag Motor Car Corp 5225 Virginia Beach Blvd *TF:* 866-414-7820 ■ *Web:* www.checkeredflag.com	Virginia Beach	VA	23462	757-687-3486	
Cherry Creek Dodge 2727 S Havana St *TF Sales:* 888-891-7522 ■ *Web:* www.cherrycreekdodge.net	Denver	CO	80014	303-751-1104	
Chino Hills Ford 4480 Chino Hills Pkwy *TF:* 855-444-5910 ■ *Web:* www.chinohillsford.com	Chino	CA	91710	909-393-9331	539-6072
Chuck Patterson Inc 200 E Ave *Web:* www.chuckpattersonautoworld.com	Chico	CA	95926	530-895-1771	230-2371
Clapp Auto Group Inc 125 W Lewis & Clark Pkw *TF:* 866-308-0592 ■ *Web:* www.clappauto.com	Clarksville	IN	47129	812-948-1541	948-1240
Cliff Findlay Auto Center Inc 3730 Stockton Hill Rd *TF:* 888-935-4041 ■ *Web:* www.findlayautocenter.com	Kingman	AZ	86409	928-757-4041	757-9701
Coffman Truck Sales 1149 W Lake S PO Box 151 *TF:* 800-255-7641 ■ *Web:* www.coffmantrucks.com	Aurora	IL	60507	630-892-7093	892-1080
Collection LLC The 200 Bird Rd *TF:* 800-252-4827 ■ *Web:* www.thecollection.com	Coral Gables	FL	33146	305-444-5555	
Collins Sorrentino Inc PO Box 14200 *TF:* 800-362-8206 ■ *Web:* www.wisconsinkenworth.com	Madison	WI	53708	608-241-5616	241-8170
Colonie Motors Inc 2242 Central Ave *TF:* 866-308-3218 ■ *Web:* www.langanauto.com	Schenectady	NY	12304	518-783-1951	783-5456
Colussy Chevrolet 3073 Washington Pike *Web:* www.colussy.com	Bridgeville	PA	15017	412-564-4132	221-1607
Conant Auto Retail Group 17720 Studebaker Rd *Web:* www.thecargroup.com	Cerritos	CA	90703	562-402-3844	402-0442
Cook Gm Super Store 1193 W Saginaw Rd *Web:* www.cookgm.com	Vassar	MI	48768	989-823-0054	823-7321
Cooley Motors Corp 401 N Greenbush Rd *TF:* 866-308-0724 ■ *Web:* www.cooley.vwdealer.com	Rensselaer	NY	12144	518-283-2902	283-0258
Coral Springs Auto Mall 9400 W Atlantic Blvd *TF:* 800-353-8660 ■ *Web:* www.coralspringsautomall.com	Coral Springs	FL	33071	954-755-7400	346-9969
Coulter Cadillac Inc 1188 E Camelback Rd *TF:* 800-843-4237 ■ *Web:* www.coultercadillac.com	Phoenix	AZ	85014	602-264-1188	264-9005
Courtesy Chevrolet 1233 E Camelback Rd *TF:* 800-555-9322 ■ *Web:* www.houseofcourtesy.com	Phoenix	AZ	85014	602-279-3232	604-3063
Courtesy Motors 301 Green Ave N *Web:* www.courtesycorner.com	Stevens Point	WI	54481	715-341-2440	341-5424
Crossroads Ford Truck Sales Inc 100 N Hill St PO Box 6548 *TF:* 800-593-3673 ■ *Web:* www.crossroadstrucks.com	Springfield	IL	62708	217-528-0770	528-2039
Crown Automobile Inc 1800 Montgomery Hwy *TF:* 800-476-0659 ■ *Web:* www.crownautomobile.com	Hoover	AL	35244	205-985-4200	402-2256

Company	City	State	ZIP	Phone	Fax
Crown Motors Ltd 196 Regent Blvd TF: 800-466-7000 ■ Web: www.crownmotors.com	Holland	MI	49423	616-396-5268	396-4850
Cumberland Chrysler Ctr 1550 I- Dr. TF: 888-277-4902 ■ Web: www.cumberlandchryslercenter.com	Cookeville	TN	38501	931-526-5600	528-5851
Dan Wolf Chevrolet of Naperville 1515 W Ogden Ave TF: 877-450-1080 ■ Web: www.chevroletofnaperville.com	Naperville	IL	60540	630-596-1189	579-1296
DarCars Ltd 12210 Cherry Hill Rd Web: www.darcars.com	Silver Spring	MD	20904	301-622-0300	622-4915
Dave Smith Auto Group 210 N Division St. TF: 800-635-8000 ■ Web: www.usautosales.com	Kellogg	ID	83837	208-784-1208	783-1226
Davis Automotive Group Inc 6135 Kruse Dr. Web: www.davisautomotive.com	Solon	OH	44139	440-542-0600	542-0700
Day Automotive Group 1600 Golden Mile Hwy	Monroeville	PA	15146	724-327-0900	327-0765*
Dearth Motors Inc 520 8th St. TF: 877-495-5321 ■ Web: www.dearthmotorsinc.com	Monroe	WI	53566	608-325-3181	325-1262
Del Montell Motors Ltd 1127 Santa Monica Blvd. Web: www.smbmw.com	Santa Monica	CA	90401	310-829-3535	449-9126
Delaney Automotive Group 626 Water St TF: 866-292-4525 ■ Web: www.delaneyauto.com	Indiana	PA	15701	724-349-3000	349-1188
Dellenbach Motors 3111 S College Ave. *Fax Area Code: 970 ■ TF: 866-963-5689 ■ Web: www.dellenbach.com	Fort Collins	CO	80525	866-963-5689	226-0233*
DeMontrond 888 I- 45 S *Fax Area Code: 936 ■ TF Sales: 888-843-6583 ■ Web: www.demontrond.com	Conroe	TX	77304	281-443-2500	442-7370*
Desert European Motorcars Ltd 71387 Hwy 111 TF: 888-484-0466 ■ Web: www.deserteuropean.com	Rancho Mirage	CA	92270	760-773-5000	773-4406
Desert Sun Motors Inc 2600 N White Sands Blvd. TF: 888-337-3298 ■ Web: www.desertsunmotors.com	Alamagordo	NM	88310	575-437-7530	434-2097
Dick Dean Economy Cars Inc 15121 Manchester Rd. Web: www.deanteam.com	Ballwin	MO	63011	636-227-0100	227-0776
Dick Greenfield Dodge Chrysler Jeep Ram 2700 Brunswick Ave TF: 888-697-1266 ■ Web: www.dickgreenfield.com	Lawrenceville	NJ	08648	609-882-1010	
Dick Masheter Ford Inc 1090 S Hamilton Rd Web: www.masheter.com	Columbus	OH	43227	614-861-7150	861-7303
Dillon Dennis Auto Park & Truck Center Inc 2777 S Orchard St Web: www.dennisdillon.com	Boise	ID	83707	208-336-6000	336-6116
Don Johnson Motors Inc 2101 Central Blvd TF: 800-443-2570 ■ Web: www.realdonjohnson.com	Brownsville	TX	78520	956-546-2288	546-2509
Don McGill Toyota Inc 11800 Katy Fwy TF: 877-259-6888 ■ Web: www.donmcgilltoyota.com	Houston	TX	77079	281-496-2000	977-3097
Dothan Chrysler-Dodge Inc 4074 Ross Clark Cir NW *Fax Area Code: 334 ■ TF: 877-674-9574 ■ Web: www.dothanchryslerdodge.net	Dothan	AL	36303	877-674-9574	794-2600*
DriveKelley.com 811 Avenue of Autos TF: 877-853-5539 ■ Web: www.drivekelley.com	Fort Wayne	IN	46804	877-853-5539	
DriveTime Corp 4020 E Indian School Rd TF: 888-418-1212 ■ Web: www.drivetime.com	Phoenix	AZ	85018	602-852-6600	852-6696
Durocher Auto Sales Inc 92 Elizabeth St. TF: 800-638-9338 ■ Web: www.durocherauto.com	Plattsburgh	NY	12901	518-563-3587	563-3901
Duval Motor Co 1616 Cassat Ave Web: www.duval-ford.com	Jacksonville	FL	32210	904-381-6599	381-6544
Earnhardt Auto Centers 1301 N Arizona Ave *Fax: Sales ■ TF: 800-497-8740 ■ Web: www.earnhardt.com	Gilbert	AZ	85233	480-926-4000	558-4050*
East Bay Ford Truck Sales Inc PO Box 24113 TF: 888-307-3234 ■ Web: www.eastbaytruckcenter.com	Oakland	CA	94623	510-272-4400	835-4408
Ed Morse Automotive Group Inc 6363 NW 6th Way Suite 400 *Fax: Mktg ■ TF: 800-336-6773 ■ Web: www.edmorse.com	Fort Lauderdale	FL	33309	954-351-0055	771-5980*
Ed Schmid Ford Inc 21600 Woodward Ave. TF: 888-532-5850 ■ Web: www.edschmidford.com	Ferndale	MI	48220	248-399-1000	399-3755
Effingham Truck Sales Inc 1701 W Fayette Rd PO Box 840 Web: www.effinghamtrucksales.com	Effingham	IL	62401	217-342-9761	347-7004
El Dorado Motors Inc 2300 N Central Expy PO Box 8002 TF: 888-231-4338 ■ Web: www.eldoradomotors.com	McKinney	TX	75070	972-569-0101	569-0199
El Paso Saturn 7750 Gateway Blvd E. Web: www.saturnofelpaso.com	El Paso	TX	79915	915-591-1900	594-4943
Elm Chevrolet Co Inc 301 E Church St TF: 888-734-1535 ■ Web: www.elmchevrolet.com	Elmira	NY	14901	607-734-4141	734-4621
Enterprise Leasing Co of Detroit 29301 Grand River Ave. TF: 888-588-5688 ■ Web: www.enterprisecarsales.com	Farmington Hills	MI	48336	888-588-5688	
Erhard Bmw Of Bloomfield Hills 4065 W Maple Rd. TF: 800-332-4269 ■ Web: www.erhardbmw.com	Bloomfield Hills	MI	48301	248-642-6565	
Ernst Auto Center Inc 615 E 23rd St TF: 800-456-4854 ■ Web: www.ernstauto.com	Columbus	NE	68601	402-564-2736	564-4566
F C Kerbeck & Sons 100 Rt 73 N TF: 888-455-5185 ■ Web: www.fckerbeck.com	Palmyra	NJ	08065	856-829-8200	829-0313
Fairway Chevrolet Co 3100 E Sahara Ave PO Box 42997 TF Sales: 877-427-1194 ■ Web: www.fairwaychevy.com	Las Vegas	NV	89116	702-641-1400	
Fairway Lincoln-Mercury Inc 10101 Abercorn St Web: www.fairwaylincolnmercury.com	Savannah	GA	31406	912-927-1000	
Faulkner Pontiac-Buick Inc 705 Autopark Blvd TF: 877-328-5563 ■ Web: www.faulknerauto.com	West Chester	PA	19382	610-436-5600	436-9399
Ferguson Buick Gmc 1015 N I- Dr. Web: www.fergusonchallenge.com	Norman	OK	73069	405-253-0923	360-8854
Ferman Automotive Group 1306 W Kennedy Blvd Web: www.fermanauto.com	Tampa	FL	33606	813-251-2765	254-4798
Findlay Automotive Group 310 N Gibson Rd Web: www.findlayauto.com	Henderson	NV	89014	702-558-8888	558-8812
Finish Line Ford Inc 2100 W Pioneer Pkwy TF: 888-841-4002 ■ Web: www.finishlineford.net	Peoria	IL	61615	309-693-2525	272-7201
Five Star Dodge 3068 Riverside Dr. TF: 888-206-6227 ■ Web: www.fivestaronline.com	Macon	GA	31210	478-474-3700	757-4000
Fletch's Inc 825 Charlevoix Ave PO Box 265 TF: 877-238-0816 ■ Web: www.fletchs.com	Petoskey	MI	49770	231-347-9651	487-9665
Fletcher Jones Imports 7300 W Sahara Ave. TF: 888-350-8850 ■ Web: www.fjimports.com	Las Vegas	NV	89117	702-364-2700	795-7154
Folsom Buick Gmc 12640 Auto Mall Cir Web: www.folsombpg.com	Folsom	CA	95630	916-358-8963	355-1230
Folsom Lake Ford 12755 Folsom Blvd. TF: 800-655-0555 ■ Web: www.folsomlakeford.com	Folsom	CA	95630	916-353-2000	353-2080
Ford Los Feliz Inc 900 S Brand Blvd. TF: 800-239-0755 ■ Web: www.starford.com	Glendale	CA	91204	818-956-0977	956-3860
Ford Maguire Inc 504 S Meadow St. TF: 888-453-6037 ■ Web: www.maguirecars.com	Ithaca	NY	14850	607-272-8000	257-4542
Ford of Montebello Inc 2747 Via Campo TF: 800-701-8281 ■ Web: www.fordofmontebello.com	Montebello	CA	90640	323-838-6920	
Ford Tom's Inc 200 Hwy 35. TF: 800-767-1249 ■ Web: www.gototomsford.com	Keyport	NJ	07735	732-264-1600	264-4993
Fordham Auto Sales Inc 236 W Fordham Rd Web: www.fordhamtoyota.com	Bronx	NY	10468	718-367-0400	367-0773
Frank W Diver Inc 2101 Pennsylvania Ave Web: www.diverchev.com	Wilmington	DE	19806	302-575-0161	658-4599
Freightliner of Hartford Inc 222 Roberts St TF: 800-453-6967 ■ Web: www.freightlinerofhartford.com	East Hartford	CT	06108	860-289-0201	610-6242
Friendship Automotive Inc 1855 Volunteer Pkwy Web: www.friendshipautos.com	Bristol	TN	37620	423-652-6200	652-6207
G & J Buick 421 Tunxis Hill Rd Web: www.scapauto.com	Fairfield	CT	06825	203-384-9300	
Galloway Family of Dealerships PO Box 70 Web: www.gallowayfamily.com	Fort Myers	FL	33902	239-936-2193	274-2310
Galpin Motors Inc 15505 Roscoe Blvd. *Fax: Acctg ■ TF: 800-256-7137 ■ Web: www.galpin.com	North Hills	CA	91343	818-787-3800	778-2211*
Gary Force Toyota 1860 Campbell Ln PO Box 90000 TF: 866-756-5651 ■ Web: www.garyforcetoyota.com	Bowling Green	KY	42104	270-843-4321	
Gault Chevrolet Co Inc 2507 N St. Web: www.gaultauto.com	Endicott	NY	13760	607-748-8244	748-1714
Geo Byers Sons Inc 427 S Hamilton Rd	Columbus	OH	43213	614-737-7613	461-6030
Germain Motor Co 4250 Morse Crossing. TF: 866-771-2178 ■ Web: www.germain.com	Columbus	OH	43219	614-416-3377	416-3381
Gettel Automotive Group 3500 Bee Ridge Rd. Web: www.gettel.com	Sarasota	FL	34239	941-921-2655	927-1532
Gilboy Ford-Mercury Inc PO Box 284. Web: www.gilboyvw.com	Whitehall	PA	18052	610-434-4211	820-4180
Gilliss & Gilliss Inc 5819 United States Hwy 19. Web: www.friendlykia.com	New Port Richey	FL	34652	727-815-9611	843-0881
Gillman Cos 10595 W Sam Houston Pkwy S *Fax: Acctg ■ TF: 800-933-7809 ■ Web: www.gillmanauto.com	Houston	TX	77099	713-776-7000	776-6361*
Gilroy Chevrolet Cadillac Inc 6720 Bear Cat Ct TF: 800-201-7241 ■ Web: www.gilroychevy.com	Gilroy	CA	95020	408-842-9301	846-0649
Giuffre Volvo 1030 S Dirksen Pkwy. TF: 877-448-3373 ■ Web: www.autogiuffre.com	Springfield	IL	62703	217-788-2400	788-8075
Gladstone Dodge 5610 N Oak Trafficway TF: 866-630-6177 ■ Web: www.gladstonedodge.com	Gladstone	MO	64118	816-455-3500	414-3546
Glendale Infiniti 812 S Brand Blvd. TF: 800-449-9375 ■ Web: www.glendaleinfiniti.com	Glendale	CA	91204	818-240-6000	543-1585
Globe Motor Car Co 1230 Bloomfield Ave Web: www.globemotorcar.com	Fairfield	NJ	07004	973-227-3600	575-7835
Godfrey Chevrolet-Buick Inc 1701 N Mitchell St Web: www.godfreychevroletbuick.com	Cadillac	MI	49601	231-775-4661	775-5120
Gonzales Automotive Group 5800 Firestone Blvd TF: 888-318-5337 ■ Web: www.casadegonzales.com	South Gate	CA	90280	562-776-2330	776-2331
Gorges Motor Co Inc 2660 S Oliver St. TF: 877-322-8228 ■ Web: www.carbuyingfun.com	Wichita	KS	67210	316-685-2201	681-3220
Graff Truck Centers Inc 1401 S Saginaw St TF: 888-870-4203 ■ Web: www.grafftruckcenter.com	Flint	MI	48503	810-239-8300	239-8561
Greenway Automotive Group 9001 E Colonial Dr TF: 800-909-8280 ■ Web: www.greenwayfordoforlando.com	Orlando	FL	32817	407-275-3200	515-6464
Griffith Motor Co 1300 W Harmony St Web: www.griffithmotor.com	Neosho	MO	64850	417-451-2626	451-3626
Group 1 Automotive Inc 800 Gessner Suite 500 NYSE: GPI ■ *Fax: Hum Res ■ TF: 888-203-1112 ■ Web: www.group1auto.com	Houston	TX	77024	713-647-5700	647-5868*
Grubbs Infiniti Ltd 1661 Airport Fwy TF: 800-685-1111 ■ Web: www.grubbsinfiniti.com	Euless	TX	76040	817-318-1200	359-4100
Gulf States Toyota Inc 1375 Enclave Pkwy TF: 800-331-4331 ■ Web: www.toyota.com	Houston	TX	77077	713-580-3300	580-3332
Gunn Automotive Group 227 Broadway. Web: www.gunnauto.com	San Antonio	TX	78205	210-472-2501	472-2514
Gurley Leep Automotive Group 5302 Grape Rd. TF Sales: 866-980-6733 ■ Web: www.gurleyleep.com	Mishawaka	IN	46545	574-272-0990	256-5427
Gus Machado Ford 1200 W 49th St TF: 888-864-6630 ■ Web: www.gusmachadoford.com	Hialeah	FL	33012	305-822-3211	827-2116
Gustman Chevrolet Sales Inc PO Box 800. TF: 800-236-6606 ■ Web: www.gustman.com	Kaukauna	WI	54130	920-766-3581	766-0520
Hamilton Chevrolet 5800 E 14 Mile Rd Web: www.hamiltonchevrolet.com	Warren	MI	48092	586-264-1400	276-1531
Harte Nissan Inc 165 W Service Rd TF: 866-687-8971 ■ Web: www.hartenissan.com	Hartford	CT	06120	860-549-2800	
Harvey Cadillac Co 2600 28th St SE TF Sales: 877-845-1557 ■ Web: www.harveycadillac.com	Grand Rapids	MI	49512	616-949-1140	954-1201
Headquarter Toyota 5895 NW 167th St. TF: 800-549-0947 ■ Web: www.headquartertoyota.com	Miami	FL	33015	305-964-9888	824-1298
Heflin Jerry Courtesy Chevrolet Inc 3161 Madison Rd. TF: 800-722-0302 ■ Web: www.gocourtesy.com	Cincinnati	OH	45209	513-871-3161	871-7334

	City	State	Zip	Phone	Fax
Hendrick Automotive Group 6000 Monroe Rd Suite 100 *Web:* www.hendrickauto.com	Charlotte	NC	28212	704-568-5550	566-3295
Hennessy River View Ford 2200 US Hwy 30 *Web:* www.riverviewford.com	Oswego	IL	60543	630-897-8900	897-3366
Herb Chambers 259 McGrath Hwy *Web:* www.herbchambers.com	Somerville	MA	02145	617-666-8333	666-8448
Herb Chambers I 95 Inc 107 Andover St *TF:* 877-560-4141 ■ *Web:* www.danverschevroletbuickpontiac.com	Danvers	MA	01923	978-774-8840	762-8937
Herb Easley Motors Inc 1125 Central Fwy *TF:* 800-632-0423 ■ *Web:* www.herbeasley.com	Wichita Falls	TX	76306	940-723-6631	767-3655
Herb Gordon Nissan 3131 Automobile Blvd *TF:* 877-212-7065 ■ *Web:* www.herbgordonnissan.com	Silver Spring	MD	20904	877-212-7065	
Heritage Nissan 1500 Veterans Memorial Hwy PO Box 182 *TF:* 866-693-0806 ■ *Web:* www.romenissan.com	Rome	GA	30165	706-291-1981	295-0528
Herring Dub Ford Inc 820 Memorial Blvd *TF:* 888-868-8914 ■ *Web:* www.dubherringfordlincoln.com	Picayune	MS	39466	601-798-8682	799-0627
Herson's Inc 15525 Frederick Rd *Web:* www.herson.com	Rockville	MD	20855	301-279-8600	517-8369
Hertrich Family of Automobile Dealerships 26905 Sussex Hwy *Web:* www.hertrich.com	Seaford	DE	19973	302-629-5100	629-8428
Hitchcock Automotive Resources 17110 Gale Ave	City of Industry	CA	91748	626-839-8401	964-5516
Holler Automotive Group 1011 N Wymore Rd *Web:* www.hollerclassic.com	Winter Park	FL	32789	407-645-4969	
Holman Cadillac Co 1200 Rt 73 S *TF:* 866-865-6973 ■ *Web:* www.holmancadillac.com	Mount Laurel	NJ	08054	856-778-1000	222-9136
Honda of Santa Monica 1726 Santa Monica Blvd *TF:* 800-269-2031 ■ *Web:* www.hondaofsantamonica.com	Santa Monica	CA	90404	310-264-4900	829-9660
Hood Management Group Inc 212 Hollywood Blvd SW *TF:* 877-240-5253 ■ *Web:* www.prestonhood.com	Fort Walton Beach	FL	32548	850-664-7000	664-5599
Hoover Toyota 2686 Hwy 150 *TF:* 866-980-8082 ■ *Web:* www.hoovertoyota.com	Hoover	AL	35244	205-978-2600	978-2594
Horwith Trucks Inc PO Box 7 *TF:* 800-220-8807 ■ *Web:* www.horwithfreightliner.com	NorthHampton	PA	18067	610-261-2220	261-2916
Hub Buick Co 19300 NW Fwy *TF:* 888-215-5769 ■ *Web:* www.hubhouston.com	Houston	TX	77065	281-894-5200	894-4914
Hudspeth Motors Inc 311 Hwy 62 65 N *TF:* 888-769-4059 ■ *Web:* www.hudspethmotors.com	Harrison	AR	72601	870-743-3200	743-6520
Hunter Chevrolet Co Inc 2520 Asheville Hwy *TF:* 888-457-1795 ■ *Web:* www.hunterchevrolet.com	Hendersonville	NC	28791	828-693-8661	693-8661
Huntington Beach Dodge Inc 16555 Beach Blvd *Web:* www.hbdodge.com	Huntington Beach	CA	92647	714-847-5515	842-7408
Import Auto World 21571 Mission Blvd *Web:* importautoworldinc.com	Hayward	CA	94541	510-581-1200	581-1228
Indy Honda 8455 US 31 S *TF:* 888-752-4589 ■ *Web:* www.indyhonda.com	Indianapolis	IN	46227	317-887-0800	885-5723
Island Lincoln-Mercury Inc 1850 E Merritt Island Cswy *TF:* 800-354-9732 ■ *Web:* www.islandlm.dealerconnection.com	Merritt Island	FL	32952	321-452-9220	453-3498
Jack Giambalvo Motor Co 1390 Eden Rd *Web:* www.jackgiambalvo.com	York	PA	17402	717-781-2154	854-5509
Jay Wolfe Automotive Group 1011 W 103rd St *Web:* www.jaywolfe.com	Kansas City	MO	64114	816-943-6060	942-5399
Jenkins & Wynne Inc 328 College St *Web:* www.jenkinsandwynne.com	Clarksville	TN	37040	931-647-3353	245-5288
Jerry Haag Motors Inc 1475 N High St *Web:* www.jerryhaagmotors.com	Hillsboro	OH	45133	937-393-1981	393-4860
Jim Ellis Auto Dealerships 5901 Peachtree Industrial Blvd S *Web:* www.jimellis.com	Atlanta	GA	30341	770-458-6811	234-8187
Jim McKay Chevrolet Inc 3509 University Dr *Web:* www.jimmckaychevrolet.com	Fairfax	VA	22030	703-591-4800	591-8021
Jim Reed Automotive Group 1512 Broadway *TF:* 888-754-5271 ■ *Web:* www.jimreed.com	Nashville	TN	37203	615-329-2929	341-2990
JM Family Enterprises Inc 100 Jim Moran Blvd *Web:* www.jmfamily.com	Deerfield Beach	FL	33442	954-429-2000	429-2300
Joe Van Horn Chevrolet Inc PO Box 238 *TF:* 800-236-1415 ■ *Web:* www.vanhornchev.com	Plymouth	WI	53073	920-893-6361	893-0953
John Hine Mazda Inc 1545 Camino Del Rio S *Web:* www.johnhine.com	San Diego	CA	92108	619-297-4251	682-3713
John Lance Ford Inc 23775 Ctr Ridge Rd *Web:* www.johnlanceford.com	Westlake	OH	44145	440-871-8600	
John Watson Chevrolet 3535 Wall Ave *TF:* 866-647-9930 ■ *Web:* www.johnwatsonchevrolet.com	Ogden	UT	84401	801-394-2611	393-5002
Johnny Londoff Chevrolet Inc 1375 Dunn Rd *TF:* 888-232-1403 ■ *Web:* www.londoff.com	Florissant	MO	63031	314-837-1800	837-2001
Johnson Motors Inc 1891 Blinker Pkwy *TF:* 877-816-0659 ■ *Web:* www.johnsonauto.com	Du Bois	PA	15801	814-371-4444	371-7762
Joyce Motors Corp 3166 SR- 10 *TF:* 800-570-5873 ■ *Web:* www.joycehonda.com	Denville	NJ	07834	973-361-3000	361-5836
Kahlig Enterprises 9207 San Pedro St *TF:* 800-880-6756 ■ *Web:* www.nplm.com	San Antonio	TX	78216	210-341-8841	340-2507
Keeler Motor Car Co 1111 Troy Schenectady Rd *TF:* 800-474-4197 ■ *Web:* www.keeler.com	Latham	NY	12110	518-785-4197	785-7315
Keldaneri Corp 1152 Marina Blvd *Web:* www.marinaauto.com	San Leandro	CA	94577	510-347-3474	297-0192
Kemcamel Vack Hyundai Kia 2223 W Camelback Rd	Phoenix	AZ	85015	602-249-1133	246-6131
Ken Fowler Motors 1265 Airport Pk Blvd *TF:* 800-287-0107 ■ *Web:* www.fowlerautocenter.com	Ukiah	CA	95482	707-468-0101	462-2475
Ken Garff Automotive Group 405 S Main St *TF:* 888-323-5869 ■ *Web:* www.kengarff.com	Salt Lake City	UT	84111	801-257-3400	
Ken Nelson Auto Group 1100 N Galena Ave *Web:* www.kennelsonauto.com	Dixon	IL	61021	866-607-2835	
Kenwood Dealer Group Inc 9435 Waterstone Blvd *Web:* www.cincyautos.com	Cincinnati	OH	45249	513-683-5484	683-3671
Kenworth Northwest Inc 20220 International Blvd S PO Box 98967 *TF:* 800-562-0060 ■ *Web:* www.kenworthnorthwest.com	SeaTac	WA	98198	206-433-5911	878-7676
Kenworth of Indianapolis Inc 2929 S Holt Rd *TF:* 800-827-8421 ■ *Web:* www.palmertrucks.com	Indianapolis	IN	46241	317-247-8421	241-5742
Key Cadillac Inc 6825 York Ave S *TF:* 800-235-3182 ■ *Web:* www.keycadillac.com	Edina	MN	55435	952-920-4300	920-4821
Keyes Toyota 5855 Van Nuys Blvd *Web:* www.keyestoyota.com	Van Nuys	CA	91401	818-782-0122	907-4128
Keyser & Miller Ford Inc 8 E Main St *Web:* www.keysermillerford.com	Collegeville	PA	19426	610-489-9366	489-4590
Keyser Bros Cadillac Inc 4130 Sheridan Dr *Web:* www.keysercadillac.com	Williamsville	NY	14221	716-634-4100	634-4326
Kilpatrick Chevrolet Inc 1134 Hwy 431 *Web:* www.kilpatrickchevrolet.com	Boaz	AL	35957	256-281-3770	
King-o'rourke Cadillac Inc 756 Smithtown Byp *Web:* www.kingorourke.com	Smithtown	NY	11787	631-724-4700	724-4784
Kirkwood Motors Inc 3807 Kirkwood Hwy *TF:* 888-872-9392 ■ *Web:* www.bcpchrysler.com	Wilmington	DE	19808	302-999-0541	998-7440
Kleine Equipment Inc I-74 & Rt 34 Interchange *TF:* 800-217-7002 ■ *Web:* www.kleine-eq.com	Galesburg	IL	61401	309-342-3188	342-1415
Kolosso Toyota 3000 W Wisconsin Ave *TF:* 888-565-6776 ■ *Web:* www.kolossotoyota.com	Appleton	WI	54914	920-738-3666	738-3661
Koons Ford of Annapolis Inc 2540 Riva Rd *TF:* 888-339-8452 ■ *Web:* www.koonsfordannapolis.dealerconnection.com	Annapolis	MD	21401	410-224-2100	
Krumland Auto Group 211 W 2nd St **Fax Area Code:* 575 ■ *Web:* www.roswelltoyota.com	Roswell	NM	88201	505-622-5860	622-5899*
Kuni Automotive Group 203 SE Pk Plaza Dr Suite 290 **Fax Area Code:* 360 ■ *Web:* www.kuniauto.com	Vancouver	WA	98684	503-372-7457	567-0970*
L & S Truck Center of Appleton Inc 330 N Bluemound Dr PO Box 1255 *TF:* 800-544-7658 ■ *Web:* www.lstruck.com	Appleton	WI	54914	920-749-1700	749-0818
La Beau Bros Inc 295 N Harrison Ave PO Box 246 *TF:* 800-747-9519 ■ *Web:* www.labeautrucks.com	Kankakee	IL	60901	815-933-5519	933-4366
La Belle Dodge Chrysler Jeep Inc 501 S Main St **Fax Area Code:* 941 ■ *TF:* 800-226-1193 ■ *Web:* www.labelledodgechryslerjeep.com	Labelle	FL	33935	863-675-2701	379-6125*
La Mesa Rv Center Inc 7430 Copley Pk Pl *TF Sales:* 888-509-4199 ■ *Web:* www.lamesarv.com	San Diego	CA	92111	858-874-8000	874-8021
Lafferty Chevrolet 829 W St Rd *Web:* www.laffertychevy.com	Warminster	PA	18974	215-259-5817	672-3594
Lafontaine Honda 2245 S Telegraph Rd *Web:* www.lafontainehonda.com	Dearborn	MI	48124	866-567-5088	
Lake Manawa Nissan Inc 920 32nd Ave *TF:* 888-298-2016 ■ *Web:* www.lakemanawanissan.com	Council Bluffs	IA	51501	712-366-9481	366-6703
Lakeside International LLC 11000 W Silver Spring Rd *TF:* 800-236-0444 ■ *Web:* www.lakesidetrucks.com	Milwaukee	WI	53225	414-353-4800	353-2743
Lakeside Toyota 3701 N Cswy Blvd *TF Sales:* 877-752-9160 ■ *Web:* www.lakesidetoyota.com	Metairie	LA	70002	504-833-3311	831-7310
Lancaster Toyota Inc 5270 Manheim Pike *Web:* www.lancastertoyota.com	East Petersburg	PA	17520	717-569-7373	569-6713
Landers Ford Inc PO Box 1810 *Web:* www.landersfordmemphis.com	Collierville	TN	38017	901-854-3600	
Landmark Lincoln-Mercury Inc 5000 S Broadway Unit A *Web:* www.landmarklincolnmercurybroadway.dealerconnection.com	Englewood	CO	80113	303-761-1560	761-0405
Larry H Miller Automotive Group 9350 S 150 E Suite 100 *Web:* www.lhmauto.com	Sandy	UT	84070	801-563-4100	563-4198
Lavery Chevrolet-Buick Inc 1096 W State St PO Box 3545 *Web:* www.laverychevy.com	Alliance	OH	44601	330-823-1100	823-8754
Lawrence Hall Chevrolet Inc 1385 S Danville Dr *TF:* 800-568-7158 ■ *Web:* www.lawrencehall.com	Abilene	TX	79605	325-695-8800	692-1657
Lca Acquisition Corp 16915 S Dixie Hwy *Web:* www.southinfiniti.com	Miami	FL	33157	305-256-2000	256-2018
Lee Pontiac-Oldsmobile-Gmc Truck Inc 235 Miracle Strip Pkwy SW *Web:* www.leepontiacgmc.com	Fort Walton Beach	FL	32548	850-243-3123	243-5679
Lee-Chrysler-Plymouth-dodge 541 Mary Esther Cutoff *TF:* 888-643-4065 ■ *Web:* www.leechryslerdodgejeepflorida.com	Fort Walton Beach	FL	32548	850-244-7611	244-7341
Lee-Smith Inc PO Box 72843 *Web:* www.lee-smith.com	Chattanooga	TN	37407	423-622-4161	629-9540
Lemay Buick-Pontiac-Gmc-cadillac Inc 7110 74th Pl *Web:* www.lemayautogroup.com	Kenosha	WI	53142	262-694-1500	694-6370
Les Stanford Chevrolet Inc 21730 Michigan Ave *TF:* 800-836-0972 ■ *Web:* www.lesstanfordchevrolet.com	Dearborn	MI	48124	313-457-0364	
Levis Robert Chevrolet Inc 316 Howze Beach Rd *Web:* www.levischevycadillac.com	Slidell	LA	70461	985-718-0055	646-2698
Lewis Ford Sales Inc 3373 N College Ave PO Box 8430 *Web:* lewiscars.dealerconnection.com	Fayetteville	AR	72703	479-442-5301	443-7293

Company	City	State	Zip	Phone	Fax
Lexus of Memphis Inc 2600 Ridgeway Rd *TF Sales:* 888-203-4049 ■ *Web:* www.lexusofmemphis.com	Memphis	TN	38119	888-219-2532	
Lia Auto Group The 1258 Central Ave PO Box 5789 *Web:* www.liacars.com	Albany	NY	12205	518-489-2111	489-2112
Liberty Chevrolet Inc 2541 E Tremont Ave *TF:* 800-605-6579 ■ *Web:* www.bronxhonda.com	Bronx	NY	10461	718-823-6000	822-0759
Lithia Motors Inc 360 E Jackson St *NYSE: LAD* ■ *TF:* 800-866-9213 ■ *Web:* www.lithia.com	Medford	OR	97501	541-776-6868	774-7617
Littleton Chevrolet Buick Oldsmobile Pontiac Inc 851 meadow St PO Box 601 *TF:* 800-595-7035 ■ *Web:* www.littletonchevrolet.com	Littleton	NH	03561	603-444-5678	444-2304
Lloyd A Wise Cos 10550 International Blvd *Web:* www.lloydawise.com	Oakland	CA	94603	510-638-4800	430-8869
Lockhart Cadillac Inc 5550 N Keystone Ave *Web:* www.lockhartcadillac.com	Indianapolis	IN	46220	317-644-2817	
Loeber Motors Inc 4255 W Touhy Ave *TF:* 888-211-4485 ■ *Web:* www.loebermotors.com	Lincolnwood	IL	60712	847-675-1000	
Lou Bachrodt Automotive Group 1801 W Atlantic Blvd *TF:* 800-894-0599 ■ *Web:* www.bachrodt.com	Pompano Beach	FL	33069	954-971-3000	977-3500
Lou Fusz Automotive Network Inc 925 N Lindbergh Blvd *TF:* 800-371-7819 ■ *Web:* www.fusz.com	Saint Louis	MO	63141	314-997-3400	993-8641
Lou Sobh Automotive 2473 Pleasant Hill Rd	Duluth	GA	30096	770-232-0099	232-2695
Lujack's Northpark Auto Plaza 3700 N Harrison St **Fax Area Code:* 800 ■ *TF:* 877-449-5511 ■ *Web:* www.lujack.com	Davenport	IA	52806	563-386-1511	397-6823*
Lupient Automotive Group 750 Pennsylvania Ave S *TF:* 800-328-0608 ■ *Web:* www.lupient.com	Minneapolis	MN	55426	763-544-6666	513-5517
Lyall Len Chevrolet 14500 E Colfax Ave *TF:* 888-553-0950 ■ *Web:* www.lenlyallchevrolet.com	Aurora	CO	80011	303-344-3100	344-1629
Lynch Ford - Mt Vernon Inc 410 Hwy 30 SW *Web:* www.lynchfordchevy.com	Mount Vernon	IA	52314	319-895-8500	895-8100
M & J Motors Inc 120 Orchard Pk Rd *TF:* 855-729-5257 ■ *Web:* www.raylaks.com	West Seneca	NY	14224	716-826-4200	826-2107
Mac Haik Auto Group 11711 Katy Fwy *TF:* 800-367-4245 ■ *Web:* www.machaik.com	Houston	TX	77079	281-596-6387	
Mac Haik Ford Inc 10333 Katy Fwy *Web:* www.machaikford.com	Houston	TX	77024	713-932-5000	932-5020
Magnussen Dealership Group 545 Middlefield Rd Suite 240	Menlo Park	CA	94025	650-327-4100	327-4647
Maplewood Imports 2780 N Hwy 61 *Web:* www.maplewoodimports.com	Maplewood	MN	55109	888-679-1698	
Mark Chevrolet Inc 33200 Michigan Ave *Web:* www.markchevrolet.com	Wayne	MI	48184	734-629-4964	
Mark Christopher Auto Ctr 2131 E Convention Ctr Way *Web:* www.markchristopher.com	Ontario	CA	91764	909-390-2900	974-0302
Mark Thomas Motors Inc 2315 Santiam Hwy PO Box 188 *Web:* www.markthomasmotors.com	Albany	OR	97321	541-967-9105	
Mark Zimmerman Ford Inc 4001 1st Ave *TF:* 800-325-1966 ■ *Web:* www.gozimmerman.com	Cedar Rapids	IA	52406	319-366-4000	364-6972
Markley Motors 3325 S College Ave *TF:* 888-480-5167 ■ *Web:* www.markleymotors.com	Fort Collins	CO	80525	970-226-2214	226-2237
Marquette Public Service Garage 919 W Baraga Ave *Web:* www.publicservicegarage.com	Marquette	MI	49855	906-226-3592	228-6014
Martin Automotive Group 12101 W Olympic Blvd *Web:* www.martinautogroup.com	Los Angeles	CA	90064	310-826-3611	622-9334
Martin Automotive Group Inc 1065 Ashley St Suite 100 *Web:* www.martingp.com	Bowling Green	KY	42103	270-783-8080	781-4792
Martin Car Financing Inc 2350 Browns Bridge Rd *Web:* www.miltonmartintoyota.com	Gainesville	GA	30504	770-532-4355	536-1385
Marty Franich Auto Ctr 550 Auto Ctr Dr	Watsonville	CA	95076	831-722-4181	724-1853
Marvin K. Brown Auto Center Inc 1441 Camino Del Rio S *TF:* 888-611-9117 ■ *Web:* www.mkb.com	San Diego	CA	92108	619-291-2040	294-9135
Mastria Automotive Group 1525 Rt 44th *TF:* 888-848-0303 ■ *Web:* www.mastria.com	Raynham	MA	02767	508-880-7000	880-3190
Mazda Knoxville 8814 Kingston Pike *Web:* www.mazdaknoxville.com	Knoxville	TN	37923	865-690-9395	690-0619
McCloskey Motors Inc 6710 N Academy Blvd *TF:* 877-389-6671 ■ *Web:* www.bigjoeauto.com	Colorado Springs	CO	80918	719-594-9400	535-8036
McDevitt Trucks Inc 1 Mack Ave PO Box 4640 *TF:* 800-370-6225 ■ *Web:* www.mctrucks.com	Manchester	NH	03108	603-668-1700	668-1865
McGrath Auto Group 4610 Ctr Pt Rd NE *Web:* www.mcgrathauto.com	Cedar Rapids	IA	52402	319-393-4610	393-2621
McKenna Motor Co Inc 10850 Firestone Blvd *TF:* 800-332-4269 ■ *Web:* www.mckennacars.com	Norwalk	CA	90650	562-868-3233	345-1776
Mclean Implement Inc RR 4 Box *TF:* 800-535-3653 ■ *Web:* www.mcleanimp.com	Albion	IL	62806	618-445-3676	445-2846
Melloy Nissan 7707 Lomas Blvd Ne *Web:* www.melloynissan.com	Albuquerque	NM	87110	505-265-8721	268-0124
Memering Motorplex Inc 1949 Hart St *Web:* www.memeringmotorplex.com	Vincennes	IN	47591	812-882-5367	886-4605
Mercedes-Benz of San Francisco 500 8th St *TF:* 877-554-6016 ■ *Web:* www.sfbenz.com	San Francisco	CA	94103	415-673-2000	673-6100
Mesa Imports Inc 1320 W Broadway Rd	Mesa	AZ	85202	480-833-5177	
Metro Ford Inc 9000 NW 7th Ave *TF:* 888-232-3841 ■ *Web:* www.metroford.com	Miami	FL	33150	888-232-3841	
Mike Reed Chevrolet 1559 E Oglethorpe **Fax Area Code:* 912 ■ *Web:* www.mikereedchevy.com	Hinesville	GA	31313	877-228-3943	368-2336*
Mike Savoie Chevrolet Inc PO Box 520 *Web:* www.mikesavoie.com	Troy	MI	48099	248-643-8000	649-3007
Mike Shaw Chevrolet Saab 1080 S Colorado Blvd *TF:* 800-223-1615 ■ *Web:* www.mikeshawauto.com	Denver	CO	80246	303-757-6161	757-7845
Miller Buick-Pontiac-Gmc Corp 920 Rt 1 N *TF:* 866-566-5714 ■ *Web:* www.autobymiller.com	Woodbridge	NJ	07095	732-596-1955	596-1779
Mission Valley Ford Truck Sales Inc 780 E Brokaw Rd PO Box 611150 *Web:* www.missionvalleyford.com	San Jose	CA	95112	408-933-2300	436-0313
Modern Chevrolet of Winston-Salem 5955 University Pkwy *TF Sales:* 877-701-9381 ■ *Web:* www.modernchevy.com	Winston Salem	NC	27105	336-722-4191	785-8455
Molle Toyota Inc 601 W 103rd St *TF:* 888-510-7705 ■ *Web:* www.molletoyota.com	Kansas City	MO	64114	816-942-5200	942-4796
Molye Chevrolet Buik Sales Corp 115 W Main St PO Box 112 **Fax Area Code:* 585 ■ *Web:* www.molye.com	Honeoye Falls	NY	14472	866-999-1548	624-1832*
Morrison Industrial Equipment Co 1825 Monroe NW PO Box 1803 *Web:* www.morrison-ind.com	Grand Rapids	MI	49501	616-447-3800	361-0885
Moss Motors 1407 1407 Surrey St *Web:* www.mossisboss.com	Lafayette	LA	70501	337-235-9086	237-2173
Mossy Motors Inc 1331 S Broad St *TF:* 877-251-6621 ■ *Web:* www.mossymotors.com	New Orleans	LA	70125	504-822-2050	826-5614
Motor Inn Co 2114 E Main St *Web:* www.motorinn.com	Albert Lea	MN	56007	507-369-2358	379-3130
Motorcars International 3015 E Cairo St *TF:* 866-970-6800 ■ *Web:* www.motorcars-intl.com	Springfield	MO	65802	417-831-9999	831-9995
Nalley Lexus Smyrna 2750 Cobb Pkwy SE **Fax Area Code:* 770 ■ *TF:* 877-454-4206 ■ *Web:* www.nalleylexus.com	Smyrna	GA	30080	888-828-6611	421-9638*
National Car Mart Inc 9255 Brookpark Rd *Web:* www.nationalcarmart.com	Cleveland	OH	44129	216-712-7949	398-7046
Nationwide Lift Trucks Inc 3900 N 28th Ter *TF:* 800-327-4431 ■ *Web:* www.toyotanlt.com	Hollywood	FL	33020	954-922-4645	922-8770
Neil Huffman Subaru 4926 Dixie Hwy *TF:* 800-448-1442 ■ *Web:* www.neilhuffman.com	Louisville	KY	40216	502-448-6666	
New Auto Toy Store Inc 804 SW 17th St *Web:* www.thenewautotoystore.com	Fort Lauderdale	FL	33315	954-463-1700	467-3416
New Country Motor Car Group 358 Broadway *Web:* www.newcountry.com	Saratoga Springs	NY	12866	518-584-7700	584-8611
New Country Volkswagen of Greenwich 200 W Putnam Ave *TF:* 866-584-6747 ■ *Web:* www.newcountryvw.com	Greenwich	CT	06830	203-869-4600	622-1001
Newins Bay Shore Ford Inc 219 W Main St *Web:* www.newinsbayshoreford.com	Bay Shore	NY	11706	631-665-1300	665-1311
Nick Crivelli Chevrolet Inc 294 State Ave *Web:* www.nickcrivelli.com	Beaver	PA	15009	724-987-5000	728-9730
Nissan Bondesen-Hardy Inc 1520 N Tomoka Farms Rd *TF:* 888-205-1937 ■ *Web:* www.daytonanissan.com	Daytona Beach	FL	32124	386-255-2441	253-1196
Noarus Auto Group 6701 Ctr Dr W Suite 925 *Web:* www.noarus.com	Los Angeles	CA	90045	310-258-0920	337-4860
Norman Frede Chevrolet Co 16801 Feather Craft Ln *TF:* 888-341-3000 ■ *Web:* www.fredechevrolet.com	Houston	TX	77058	281-486-2200	
Norris Ford 901 Merritt Blvd *TF Sales:* 866-460-5275 ■ *Web:* www.norrisford.com	Baltimore	MD	21222	410-285-0200	285-0872
North Bay Nissan Inc 1250 Auto Ctr Dr *TF:* 877-818-6866 ■ *Web:* www.northbaynissan.com	Petaluma	CA	94952	707-769-7700	
Northern Motor Co 1419 Ludington St *TF:* 888-256-6929 ■ *Web:* www.northernmotor.com	Escanaba	MI	49829	906-786-1130	786-7788
O Neill's Chevrolet & Buick Inc 5 W Main St PO Box A *Web:* www.oneillschevybuick.com	Avon	CT	06001	860-269-3279	
O'Gara Coach Co LLC 8833 W Olympic Blvd **Fax Area Code:* 310 ■ *TF:* 888-291-5533 ■ *Web:* www.ogaracoach.com	Beverly Hills	CA	90211	888-291-5533	652-9656*
O'rielly Chevrolet Inc 6100 E Broadway Blvd *Web:* www.orielly.com	Tucson	AZ	85711	520-747-8000	790-7356
Orange Buick - Gmc Truck 3883 W Colonial Dr *Web:* www.orangebuickgmc.com	Orlando	FL	32808	407-295-8100	299-0340
Orange Coast Chrysler Jeep Dodge 2929 Harbor Blvd *Web:* www.ocauto.com	Costa Mesa	CA	92626	714-549-8023	549-2558
Orange Motors Co Inc 799 Central Ave *Web:* www.orangemotors.com	Albany	NY	12206	518-489-5414	489-5501
Otsego Mitsubishi 55 Oneida St *Web:* www.otsegomitsubishi.com	Oneonta	NY	13820	607-432-2800	432-6353
Ourisman Automotive Group 4400 Branch Ave **Fax:* Acctg ■ *Web:* www.ourisman.com	Marlow Heights	MD	20748	301-423-4000	423-1845*
Outten Chevrolet Inc 1701 w Tilghman St *Web:* www.outtenchevyallentown.com	Allentown	PA	18104	610-628-3600	820-5774
Pacifico Group 6701 Essington Ave *TF:* 888-475-1384 ■ *Web:* www.pacificocars.com	Philadelphia	PA	19153	215-492-1700	492-0893
Paddock Chevrolet Inc 3232 Delaware Ave *Web:* www.paddockchevrolet.com	Kenmore	NY	14217	716-876-0945	876-4016
Palm Automotive Group 1801 tamiami Trail PO Box 512049 *TF:* 800-226-7256 ■ *Web:* www.palmautomall.com	Punta Gorda	FL	33951	941-639-1155	575-6718
Palmer Auto Group 4545 E 96th St *Web:* www.palmerauto.com	Indianapolis	IN	46240	317-846-5555	582-4746
Papastavros Assoc Medical Imaging Inc 1701 Augustine Cut Off Bldg 4 *Web:* www.papastavros.com	Wilmington	DE	19803	302-652-3016	652-2534
Paramount Auto Group 17805 N Fwy **Fax Area Code:* 832 ■ *TF:* 800-631-5590	Houston	TX	77090	281-569-2200	484-9567*
Parsons Buick Co The 151 E St *TF:* 877-274-2613 ■ *Web:* www.parsonsbuick.com	Plainville	CT	06062	860-747-1693	747-5734

Company / Address	City	State	ZIP	Phone	Fax
Patchett's Motors Inc 5200 N Golden State Blvd. *Web:* www.patchettsford.com	Turlock	CA	95382	209-571-2500	669-5230
Paul Heuring Motors Inc 720 N Hobart Rd *TF:* 888-851-9702 ■ *Web:* paulheuring.dealerconnection.com/?lang=en	Hobart	IN	46342	219-942-3673	942-9637
Paul Miller Auto Group LLC 1040 Rt 23 N *Web:* www.paulmiller.com	Wayne	NJ	07470	973-575-7750	
Paul Moak Automotive Inc 740 Larson St *TF:* 888-804-2964 ■ *Web:* www.paulmoak.com	Jackson	MS	39202	601-352-2700	853-5842
Peck Road Truck Ctr 2450 Kella Ave *TF:* 877-605-7623 ■ *Web:* www.peckroad.com	Whittier	CA	90601	562-692-7267	695-1737
Penske Auto Group Inc 2555 S Telegraph Rd. *Web:* www.penskeautomotive.com	Bloomfield Hills	MI	48302	248-648-2500	648-2035
Penske Automotive Group Inc 2555 Telegraph Rd *Web:* www.penskeautomotive.com	Bloomfield Hills	MI	48302	248-648-2500	648-2525
Pepe Motors Corp 50 Bank St *Web:* www.mbwhiteplains.com	White Plains	NY	10606	914-949-4000	949-4024
Performance Cos 153 Treeline Pk Suite 300	San Antonio	TX	78209	210-829-1800	829-5001
Performance Petroplex Inc 1636 Westgate Cir *Web:* www.nashvillelexus.com	Brentwood	TN	37027	615-221-5000	221-8200
Pete Baur Buick GMC Inc 14000 Pearl Rd *Web:* www.petebaur.com	Cleveland	OH	44136	440-580-4256	572-8639
Peterbilt of Louisiana Inc 16310 Commercial Ave. *Web:* www.truckpaper.com	Baton Rouge	LA	70816	225-273-8300	273-8333
Phil Long Dealerships 1212 Motor City Dr. *Fax: Sales ■ *TF:* 800-685-5664 ■ *Web:* www.phillong.com	Colorado Springs	CO	80906	719-575-7100	575-2807*
Phil Smart Inc 600 E Pike St *TF:* 877-241-4528 ■ *Web:* www.philsmart.com	Seattle	WA	98122	206-324-5959	328-4478
Phil Smith Automotive Group 4250 N Federal Hwy *Web:* www.philsmithauto.com	Lighthouse Point	FL	33064	954-867-1234	316-9469
Phillips Buick-Pontiac-Gmc Truck Inc 2160 US Hwy 441 *TF:* 888-664-7454 ■ *Web:* www.phillips-buick.com	Fruitland Park	FL	34731	352-728-1212	728-1540
Piercey Automotive Group 13600 Beach Blvd. *Web:* www.pierceyautogroup.com	Westminster	CA	92683	714-896-9777	896-9779
Pitts Toyota Inc 210 N Jeffreson St PO Box 4013 *TF:* 888-561-8030 ■ *Web:* www.pittstoyota.com	Dublin	GA	31021	478-272-3244	272-1524
Potamkin Automotive Group 6600 Cowpen Rd Suite 200 *Web:* www.planetautomotive.com	Miami Lakes	FL	33014	305-774-7690	774-7696
Powell Stuart Ford Inc 225 S Danville Bypass PO Box 1335 *TF:* 800-334-0005 ■ *Web:* stuartpowellford.dealerconnection.com/?lang=en	Danville	KY	40422	859-236-8917	238-1188
Power Nissan of South Bay Hawthorne 14610 Hindry Ave. *Web:* www.powerdirect.com	Hawthorne	CA	90250	310-536-4000	
Prebul Chrysler Jeep Dodge of Chattanooga 402 W Martin Luther King Blvd	Chattanooga	TN	37402	423-265-0505	267-4724
Premier Subaru LLC 150 N Main St PO Box 3366 *TF:* 800-411-4551 ■ *Web:* www.premiersubaru.com	Branford	CT	06405	203-481-0687	481-1861
Prestige Automotive Group 1830 W Grand River *TF:* 888-937-4685 ■ *Web:* www.prestigeautomotive.com	Okemos	MI	48864	734-481-0210	544-2273
Prestige Chrysler Dodge Inc 200 Alpine St *TF:* 877-322-8228 ■ *Web:* www.prestigedodge.com	Longmont	CO	80501	303-651-3000	651-3438
Priority Chevrolet of Chesapeake 1495 S Military Hwy *TF:* 888-698-1913 ■ *Web:* www.priorityauto.com	Chesapeake	VA	23320	888-698-1913	
Prostrollo Motor Sales Inc PO Box 1415 *Web:* www.prostrollo.com	Huron	SD	57350	605-352-6411	352-9286
Purvis Ford Inc 3660 Jefferson Davis Hwy Suite 1 PO Box 3489 *Web:* purvisford.dealerconnection.com	Fredericksburg	VA	22408	540-898-3000	710-1432
Quality Motor Cars of Stockton 2222 E Hammer Ln. *TF:* 888-211-0835 ■ *Web:* www.acuraofstockton.com	Stockton	CA	95210	209-476-1640	473-8023
R & J Automotive Enterprises Inc 5901 28th St SE *TF:* 800-328-2471 ■ *Web:* www.bettenimports.com	Grand Rapids	MI	49546	616-301-2100	301-2105
Ray Catena Motor Car Corp 910 US Hiwy Rt 1 *Web:* www.raycatena.com	Edison	NJ	08817	732-549-6600	549-6983
Reed Motors Inc 3776 W Colonial Dr. *Web:* www.reednissan.com	Orlando	FL	32808	407-297-7333	581-1968
Reichard Buick GMC 161 Salem Ave *Web:* www.reichardbuick.com	Dayton	OH	45406	937-401-2034	220-6746
Reliable Chevrolet Inc 800 N Central Expy *Web:* www.reliablechev.com	Richardson	TX	75080	972-952-1500	952-8171
Republic Ford Inc 1740 Us Hwy 60 PO Box 700 *Web:* www.mr-big-volume.dealerconnection.com	Republic	MO	65738	888-865-2576	
Rhoden Auto Center Inc 3400 S Expy St. *TF:* 866-309-4008 ■ *Web:* www.rhodenloancity.com	Council Bluffs	IA	51501	712-366-9400	366-9648
Ricart Automotive Group 4255 S Hamilton Rd *TF:* 800-332-5872 ■ *Web:* www.ricart.com	Columbus	OH	43125	614-836-5321	836-6635
Rick Case Automotive Group 875 N SR 7 *Web:* www.rickcase.com	Fort Lauderdale	FL	33317	954-587-1111	587-6381
Rickenbaugh Cadillac Co 777 Broadway	Denver	CO	80203	303-573-7773	573-5808
Riverside Ford Inc 2089 Riverside Dr PO Box 225 *TF Sales:* 888-258-9801 ■ *Web:* www.riversideford.net	Macon	GA	31204	478-464-2900	752-7873
RnR RV Center 23203 E Knox Ave *TF:* 800-873-9002 ■ *Web:* www.rnrrv.com	Liberty Lake	WA	99019	509-927-9000	921-9144
Roberson Motors Inc 3100 Ryan Dr SE *TF:* 800-228-9733 ■ *Web:* www.robersonmotors.com	Salem	OR	97301	503-363-4117	370-2584
Roger Dean Chevrolet Inc 2235 Okeechobee Blvd *TF:* 877-827-4705 ■ *Web:* www.rogerdeanchevrolet.com	West Palm Beach	FL	33409	561-683-8100	683-7332
Roland D Kelly Infiniti Inc 155 Andover St. *Web:* www.kellyauto.com	Danvers	MA	01923	978-774-1000	774-8788
Romero Mazda 1307 Kettering Dr *TF:* 888-317-2233 ■ *Web:* www.romeromazda.com	Ontario	CA	91761	909-390-8484	390-4595
Ron Carter Automotive Group 3205 FM 528 *TF:* 800-769-2886 ■ *Web:* www.roncarter.com	Alvin	TX	77511	281-331-3111	331-4569
Ron Tonkin Dealerships 122 NE 122nd Ave *TF:* 800-460-5328 ■ *Web:* www.tonkin.com	Portland	OR	97230	503-255-4100	252-4899
Rosatti Auto Group 2740 Nostrand Ave *TF:* 800-999-5901 ■ *Web:* www.plazaautomall.com	Brooklyn	NY	11210	718-253-8400	677-9087
Rosenthal Automotive Organization 1100 S Glebe Rd. *Web:* www.rosenthalauto.com	Arlington	VA	22204	703-553-4300	553-8435
Rosner Motors 3507 Jefferson Davis Hwy *TF Sales:* 888-369-0361 ■ *Web:* www.rosnerauto.com	Fredericksburg	VA	22408	540-898-7900	710-8580
Roundtree Automotive Group LLC 910 Pierremont Rd Suite 312 *Web:* www.roundtreeautomotivegroup.com	Shreveport	LA	71106	318-798-6500	798-5424
RV World Inc of Nokomis 2110 Tamiami Trail N *TF:* 800-262-2182 ■ *Web:* www.rvworldinc.com	Nokomis	FL	34275	941-966-2182	966-4356
Ryan Automotive LLC 200 Carter Dr	Edison	NJ	08817	732-650-1550	
Ryan Kia of Springfield 321 Baltimore Pike *Web:* www.ryanspringfield.com	Springfield	PA	19064	484-477-4493	
Salisbury Motor Co Inc 700 W Innes St PO Box 4137 *Web:* www.salisburymotorcompany.com	Salisbury	NC	28144	704-636-1341	636-7041
Salmon River Motors Inc PO Box Q *Fax Area Code: 208 ■ *Web:* www.salmonautodealer.com	Salmon	ID	83467	800-491-2564	756-8665*
Sam Swope Auto Group LLC 64 S Hurstbourne Pkwy Suite I *Web:* www.samswope.com	Louisville	KY	40299	502-499-5000	499-3894
Sandy Sansing Chevrolet Inc 6200 N Pensacola Blvd. *TF Sales:* 888-427-1521 ■ *Web:* www.sandysansingchevrolet.com	Pensacola	FL	32505	850-476-2480	476-1163
Sansone Auto Network 3401 Rt 66 *Web:* www.sansoneauto.com	Neptune	NJ	07753	732-815-0500	815-2395
Santa Maria Ford Lincoln 1035 E Battles Rd *TF:* 888-865-4685 ■ *Web:* santamariaford.dealerconnection.com/?lang=en	Santa Maria	CA	93454	805-925-2445	925-7165
Saratoga Honda 3402 S Broadway PO Box 797 *Web:* www.saratogahonda.com	Saratoga Springs	NY	12866	518-587-9300	587-0846
Schmit Ford-Mercury Corp 121 N Main St PO Box 8 *Web:* schmitfordmerc.dealerconnection.com/?lang=en	Thiensville	WI	53092	262-242-1100	242-7028
Schukei Chevrolet Inc 721 S Monroe PO Box 1525 *Web:* www.schukeichevy.com	Mason City	IA	50401	866-916-6497	
Schumacher European Ltd 18530 N Scottsdale Rd *Web:* www.schumacher.mercedesdealer.com	Phoenix	AZ	85054	480-991-1155	
Scott Family of Dealerships 3333 Lehigh St *Fax Area Code: 610 ■ *TF:* 800-274-1039 ■ *Web:* www.scottcars.com	Allentown	PA	18103	800-274-1039	965-6905*
Scott-McRae Group 701 Riverside Pk Pl *Web:* www.scottmcraegroup.com	Jacksonville	FL	32204	904-354-4000	354-5102
Sears Imported Autos Inc 13500 Wayzata Blvd *TF Sales:* 800-493-1720 ■ *Web:* www.searsimports.com	Hopkins	MN	55305	952-546-5301	546-2899
Security Auto Sales Inc 345 Merrick Rd *TF:* 800-861-2038 ■ *Web:* www.securitydodge.com	Amityville	NY	11701	631-691-1737	691-1440
Serra Automotive Inc 3118 E Hill Rd *Web:* www.serrausa.com	Grand Blanc	MI	48439	810-694-1720	694-6405
Servco Pacific Inc 2850 Pukoloa Suite 300 *Web:* www.servco.com	Honolulu	HI	96819	808-564-1300	523-3937
Shamaley Buick GMC 955 Crockett Way *Web:* www.shamaleygm.com	El Paso	TX	79922	915-317-5958	
Sheehy Auto Stores 12701 Fair Lakes Cir Suite 250 *Web:* www.sheehy.com	Fairfax	VA	22033	703-802-3480	802-3481
Shelly Automotive Group *Irvine BMW* 9881 Research Dr *TF:* 800-817-2032 ■ *Web:* www.shellygroup.com	Irvine	CA	92618	800-817-2032	
Shepard Chevrolet Inc 930 Carriage Pk Ln *Web:* www.shepardchevrolet.com	Lake Bluff	IL	60044	847-234-7900	234-3912
Sheppard Motors 2300 W 7th Ave *TF Sales:* 800-723-8842 ■ *Web:* www.sheppardmotors.com	Eugene	OR	97402	800-723-8842	
Showcase Honda 1333 E Camelback Rd *TF:* 866-956-6719 ■ *Web:* www.showcasehonda.com	Phoenix	AZ	85014	602-264-2481	285-4621
Sierra Volkswagen Inc 510 E Norris Dr PO Box 456 *Fax Area Code: 815 ■ *Web:* www.sierravw.com	Ottawa	IL	61350	866-308-5670	431-2519*
Silver Star Automotive Group *Lotus of Thousand Oaks* 3905 Auto Mall Dr *TF:* 800-450-1749 ■ *Web:* www.silverstarauto.com	Thousand Oaks	CA	91362	800-450-1749	
Sitton Buick GMC 2640 Laurens Rd PO Box 6108 *TF:* 877-799-4284 ■ *Web:* www.sittongm.com	Greenville	SC	29606	864-288-2400	288-4648
Smith Motors Inc of Hammond 6405 Indianapolis Blvd. *TF:* 877-392-2689 ■ *Web:* www.smithchevyusa.com	Hammond	IN	46320	219-845-4000	989-7233
Smoky Mountain Truck Center LLC 841 Eastern Star Rd PO Box 5729 *TF:* 800-451-1508 ■ *Web:* www.smtruckcenter.com	Kingsport	TN	37663	423-349-3000	349-0431
Smythe European Inc 4500 Stevens Creek Blvd *TF Sales:* 866-314-4430 ■ *Web:* www.smythe.com	San Jose	CA	95129	408-983-5200	983-0971
Snyder Chevrolet Olds Co 524 N Perry St PO Box 506 *Fax Area Code: 419 ■ *Web:* www.snyderchevrolet.com	Napoleon	OH	43545	800-811-9414	599-5232*

	City	State	Zip	Phone	Fax
Sommer's Automotive 7211 W Meq PO Box 37	Mequon	WI	53092	262-242-0100	
TF: 888-494-4193 ■ Web: www.sommerscars.com					
Sonic Automotive Inc 6415 Idlewild Rd Suite 109	Charlotte	NC	28212	704-566-2400	536-4665
NYSE: SAH ■ Web: www.sonicautomotive.com					
South Charlotte Nissan 9215 S Blvd	Charlotte	NC	28273	704-552-9191	236-2502*
*Fax Area Code: 256 ■ TF: 800-546-1581 ■ Web: www.southcharlottenissan.com					
South Tacoma Honda 7802 S Tacoma Way	Tacoma	WA	98409	253-472-2300	472-2390
TF: 888-497-2416 ■ Web: www.southtacomahonda.com					
Southfield Dodge Chrysler Jeep Ram 28100 Telegraph Rd	Southfield	MI	48034	248-354-2950	352-3776
TF Sales: 888-388-0451 ■ Web: www.southfieldchrysler.com					
Southgate Automotive Inc 16501 Fort St	Southgate	MI	48195	734-282-3636	
TF: 800-417-4552 ■ Web: www.southgateford.com					
Southwick Inc 2400 Shattuck Ave	Berkeley	CA	94704	510-845-2530	845-9084
TF: 888-300-0961 ■ Web: www.toyotaofberkeley.com					
Spartan Autos Inc 5701 S Pennsylvania Ave	Lansing	MI	48911	517-394-6000	394-8007
TF: 866-250-3777 ■ Web: www.spartanmotormall.com					
Specialty Hearse & Ambulance Sale Corp 180 Dupont St Unit A	Plainview	NY	11803	516-349-7700	349-0482
TF: 800-349-6102 ■ Web: www.specialtyhearse.com					
Spirit Auto Center 1945 Kings Hwy	Swedesboro	NJ	08085	856-467-2200	467-3224
TF: 800-650-5515 ■ Web: www.spiritautocenter.com					
Sport Chevrolet 3101 Automobile Blvd	Silver Spring	MD	20904	301-890-6000	890-5650
TF: 800-824-8884 ■ Web: www.sportchevrolet.com					
Staluppi Auto Group 2010 Ave B	Riviera Beach	FL	33404	561-844-7148	844-6473
Steele Truck Center Inc 2150 Rockfill Rd	Fort Myers	FL	33916	239-334-7300	334-4676
TF: 888-806-4839 ■ Web: www.steeletruck.com					
Steve Barry Buick Inc 16000 Detroit Ave	Lakewood	OH	44107	216-920-0866	221-7001
Web: www.stevebarrybuick.com					
Stillwater Motor Co 5900 Stillwater Blvd N	Stillwater	MN	55082	651-323-2245	439-4425
Web: www.stillwatermotors.com					
Stoddard Imported Cars Inc 190 Alpha Pk	Highland Heights	OH	44143	440-869-9890	946-9410
TF: 800-342-1414 ■ Web: www.stoddard.com					
Stuart Bowman Auto Center Inc 1709 E Dixie Dr PO Box 1127	Asheboro	NC	27204	336-625-6123	625-6697
Web: www.stuartbowmanautocentre.com					
Suburban Collection 1810 Maplelawn Dr	Troy	MI	48084	248-643-0070	519-9793
TF: 877-471-7100 ■ Web: www.suburbancollection.com					
Sud's Motor Car Co Inc 1430 Fort Jesse Rd	Normal	IL	61761	309-454-1101	452-1486
TF: 800-345-1679 ■ Web: www.sudsmotors.com					
Sullivan Automotive Group 2406 N Section St	Sullivan	IN	47882	812-268-4321	268-4323
Web: www.shopsullivanauto.com					
Sulphur Springs Ford Lincoln Inc 1040 Gilmer St	Sulphur Springs	TX	75482	903-885-0502	438-4166
Web: www.toliverford.com					
Sunnyside Motor Co Inc 944 Main St	Holden	MA	01520	508-829-4333	829-5362
Web: www.sunnysideford.com					
Sunset Auto Co Inc 11700 Gravois Rd	Saint Louis	MO	63127	314-472-7109	
Web: sunsetautoco.dealerconnection.com/?lang=en					
Superior Buick & Cadillac 1151 W 104th St	Kansas City	MO	64114	816-942-7100	942-6855
TF: 866-255-4588 ■ Web: www.superiorbuickcadillac.com					
Superior Hyundai 110 S Quintard Ave	Anniston	AL	36201	256-403-4991	
Web: www.superiorhyundaial.com					
Susan Schein Automotive 3171 Pelham Pkwy PO Box 215	Pelham	AL	35124	205-267-6410	620-2935
TF: 800-845-1578 ■ Web: www.susanschein.com					
Sutton Ford Inc 21321 Central Ave	Matteson	IL	60443	708-720-8095	720-4293
TF: 866-232-2966 ■ Web: www.suttonford.com					
T & T Motors Inc 4195 S Hwy 27	Somerset	KY	42501	606-679-1601	
TF: 800-859-8761 ■ Web: www.toyotaofsomerset.com					
Tamiami Automotive Group 8250 SW 8th St	Miami	FL	33144	305-266-5500	266-5604
Tank Sports Inc 9657 Rush St	South El Monte	CA	91733	626-350-4039	602-8410
OTC: TNSP ■ Web: www.tank-sports.com					
Team Volkswagen of Hayward Corp 25115 Mission Blvd	Hayward	CA	94544	866-308-2825	
Web: www.vwhayward.com					
Tennessee Tractor LLC 15 S Bells St Suite 4	Alamo	TN	38001	731-696-5598	696-4458
Web: www.tennesseetractor.com					
Todey Motor Co Inc 1521 Auto Ctr Dr	Oxnard	CA	93036	805-988-4545	
Tom Bensen Chevrolet Co Inc 9400 San Pedro	San Antonio	TX	78216	210-341-3311	
TF: 800-727-8706 ■ Web: www.tombensonchevy.com					
Tom Naquin Chevrolet Inc 2500 W Lexington Ave	Elkhart	IN	46514	574-293-8621	294-3995
Web: www.tomnaquin.com					
Toms Truck Center Inc 1008 E 4th St PO Box 88	Santa Ana	CA	92701	714-338-6060	836-6039
TF: 800-638-1015 ■ Web: www.ttruck.com					
Tracy Auto LP 2895 Naglee Rd	Tracy	CA	95304	209-834-1111	830-5062
TF: 866-718-4798 ■ Web: www.tracytoyota.com					
Transit LLC 5622 W Main St	Kalamazoo	MI	49009	269-342-6600	327-9883
Web: www.maplehillauto.com					
Transwest 7626 Brighton Rd	Commerce City	CO	80022	303-289-3161	288-2310
TF: 800-289-3161 ■ Web: www.transwest.com					
Trebol Motors Corp PO Box 11204	San Juan	PR	00910	787-793-2828	749-9025
Web: www.trebolmotors.com					
Tri County Ford Mercury Inc 5101 W Hwy 146 PO Box 425	Buckner	KY	40010	502-241-7333	
TF: 800-945-2520 ■ Web: www.tricountyford.com					
Tri-valley Buick Pontiac Gmc Inc 4400 John Monego Ct	Dublin	CA	94568	925-560-4400	560-4449
TF: 888-753-6511 ■ Web: www.dublingmc.com					
Triangle Auto Center Inc 1841 N State Rd 7	Hollywood	FL	33021	954-966-2150	985-1611
TF: 888-413-0119 ■ Web: www.toyotaofhollywood.com					
Tropical Ford 9900 S Orange Blossom Trial	Orlando	FL	32837	407-851-3800	857-7185
TF Sales: 800-790-7137 ■ Web: www.tropicalford.com					
Truck Center Inc 1007 International Dr PO Box 529	Tupelo	MS	38802	662-842-3401	842-0172
TF: 800-844-8820 ■ Web: www.truckcenterinc.com					
Truck Sales & Service Inc PO Box 262	Midvale	OH	44653	740-922-3412	922-7239
Web: www.trksls.com					
Trucks & Parts of Tampa Inc 1015 S 50th St	Tampa	FL	33619	813-247-6637	247-4465
TF: 888-881-8260 ■ Web: www.trucks.com					
Tustin Cars Inc 50 Auto Ctr Dr	Tustin	CA	92782	714-734-2400	731-6938
TF: 866-861-7452 ■ Web: www.tustincadillac.com					
Tustin Nissan 30 Auto Ctr Dr	Tustin	CA	92782	714-669-8282	
TF Sales: 888-468-1391 ■ Web: www.tustinnissan.com					
Usem Inc 703 17th Ave NW	Austin	MN	55912	507-396-4720	433-1876
Web: www.useminc.com					
Utility/Keystone Trailer Sales Inc 1976 Auction Rd	Manheim	PA	17545	717-653-9444	653-9443
Web: www.utilitykeystone.com					
Valley Ford Truck Inc 5715 Canal Rd	Cleveland	OH	44125	216-524-2400	524-8527
TF: 888-853-8620 ■ Web: apps.dealerconnection.com					
Valley Freightliner Inc 277 Stewart Rd SW	Pacific	WA	98047	253-863-7393	863-6473
TF: 800-523-8014 ■ Web: www.valleyfreightliner.com					
Van Bortel Subaru 6327 SR- 96	Victor	NY	14564	585-924-5230	924-5500
TF: 800-724-8872 ■ Web: www.vanbortelsubaru.com					
Varsity Ford Lincoln Mercury Inc 1351 Earl Rudder Fwy S	College Station	TX	77845	979-779-0664	693-1601
Web: www.varsityflm.com					
Vic Canever Chevrolet Inc 3000 Owen Rd	Fenton	MI	48430	810-519-5634	750-1307
Web: www.viccaneverchevy.com					
Victory Automotive Group 5496 W Andrew Johnson Hwy	Morristown	TN	37814	423-586-9657	587-8113
Web: www.victoryautomotivegroup.com					
Village Luxury Imports Inc 16100 Wayzata Blvd	Wayzata	MN	55391	952-476-6111	476-8037
TF: 888-242-0526 ■ Web: www.lexusofwayzata.com					
Village Motors Inc 75 N Beacon St	Boston	MA	02134	617-560-1700	560-1700
Web: www.villageautomotive.com					
Vin Devers Inc 5570 Monroe St	Sylvania	OH	43560	419-885-5111	824-8122
TF: 888-659-4011 ■ Web: www.vindevers.com					
Vision Ford Lincoln Mercury Inc 1500 S White Sands Blvd	Alamogordo	NM	88310	505-434-4800	443-2840
TF: 800-376-8474 ■ Web: www.visionfordlm.com					
Vista Auto 21501 Ventura Blvd	Woodland Hills	CA	91364	818-884-7600	883-2975
TF: 888-232-3114 ■ Web: www.vistaford.com					
Vogler Motor Co Inc 1170 E Main PO Box 2946	Carbondale	IL	62902	618-457-8135	529-3010
TF: 888-856-4774 ■ Web: www.voglerford.com					
Voss Village Bmw 650 MMSBRG Centerville Rd	Dayton	OH	45459	937-428-2300	428-2310
TF: 888-837-0742 ■ Web: www.vosscadillac.com					
VT Inc 8500 Shawnee Mission Pkwy Suite 200	Shawnee Mission	KS	66202	913-432-6400	789-1039
TF: 800-747-4400					
Wallingford Buick GMC 1122 Old N Colony Rd	Wallingford	CT	06492	203-269-8741	284-8275
TF: 877-534-5135 ■ Web: www.wallingfordbuickgmc.com					
Walt Ford Sweeney Inc 5400 Glenway Ave	Cincinnati	OH	45238	513-922-4500	922-0786
TF: 888-868-0604 ■ Web: www.waltsweeney.com					
Warnock Automotive Group 175 Rt 10	East Hanover	NJ	07936	973-884-2100	884-9590
Web: www.warnockauto.com					
Waters Truck & Tractor Co Inc PO Box 831	Columbus	MS	39703	662-328-1575	327-7945
TF: 800-844-1500 ■ Web: www.waterstruck.com					
West One Automotive Group Inc 2031 SW 4th Ave	Portland	OR	97201	503-222-1335	
West-Herr Automotive Group Inc 3448 McKinley Pkwy	Blasdell	NY	14219	716-932-4400	932-4491
TF: 800-933-5701 ■ Web: www.westherr.com					
Westbury Nissan LLC 939 Old Country Rd	Westbury	NY	11590	516-338-5600	338-5667
Web: www.westburynissan.com					
Western Bus Sales Inc 30355 SE Hwy 212	Boring	OR	97009	503-905-0002	905-0003
TF: 800-258-2473 ■ Web: www.westernbus.com					
Western Slope Auto Co 2264 Hwy 6 & 50	Grand Junction	CO	81505	970-243-0843	245-0428
TF: 888-281-9789 ■ Web: www.westernslopeauto.com					
Westgate Chevrolet Inc 7300 I 40 W	Amarillo	TX	79106	806-356-5600	356-5628
TF Sales: 877-896-5035 ■ Web: www.westgatechevy.com					
Westlie Motor Co 500 S Broadway	Minot	ND	58701	701-852-1354	857-1659
Web: apps.dealerconnection.com					
Westman Freightliner Inc 2200 4th Ave Mankato PO Box 699	Mankato	MN	56002	507-625-4118	625-4127
TF: 866-576-6914 ■ Web: www.westmanfreightliner.com					
Whitaker Buick Co 131 19th St SW	Forest Lake	MN	55025	651-464-3146	645-1702
Web: www.whitakerauto.com					
White Plains Honda 344 Central Ave	White Plains	NY	10606	914-428-0880	428-0990
TF: 877-553-9292 ■ Web: www.whiteplainshonda.com					
Whited Ford 207 Perry Rd	Bangor	ME	04401	207-947-3673	947-8013
Web: www.whitedford.com					
Whitman Ford Co 7555 Lewis Ave	Temperance	MI	48182	734-847-3673	847-1538
TF: 800-221-3612 ■ Web: www.whitmanford.com					
Willey Dale Pontiac Cadillac GMC Truck Inc 2840 Iowa St PO Box 803	Lawrence	KS	66046	785-727-1124	843-4903
Web: www.dalewilleyauto.com					
Willey Honda 2215 S 500 W	Bountiful	UT	84010	801-295-4477	295-6831
TF Sales: 888-202-1216 ■ Web: www.willeyhonda.com					
Wilson Automotive Group 1400 N Tustin St	Orange	CA	92867	714-516-3111	997-9200
Web: www.wilsonautomotivegroup.net					
Winner Chevrolet Inc PO Box 1867	Colfax	CA	95713	530-346-8313	346-8258
Web: www.winnerchevy.com					
Winslow BMW 730 N Cir Dr	Colorado Springs	CO	80909	719-473-1373	473-1975
TF: 866-258-0927 ■ Web: www.winslowbmw.com					
Witt Lincoln 588 Camino Del Rio N	San Diego	CA	92108	619-358-5000	358-5008
TF: 877-978-9494 ■ Web: www.wittlm.com					
Woodland Motors Corp 1680 E Main St	Woodland	CA	95776	530-661-6661	661-6627
TF: 800-896-0199 ■ Web: www.woodlandmotors.com					
World Auto Group 3057 Rt 10 E	Denville	NJ	07834	973-442-0500	
Web: www.denvillenissan.com					
World Class Automotive Group PO Box 590087	Houston	TX	77259	281-443-3443	464-6100
Web: www.starbasejet.com					

	City	State	Zip	Phone	Fax
Wray Ford Inc 2851 Benton Rd *Web:* www.wrayford.com	Bossier City	LA	71111	318-686-7300	688-2931
Yonkers Motors Corp 2000 Central Pk Ave *Web:* www.yonkershonda.com	Yonkers	NY	10710	888-517-2382	
York Ford Inc 1481 Bwy *TF:* 888-874-0636 ■ *Web:* www.yorkford.com	Saugus	MA	01906	781-231-1945	941-2212
Young Chevrolet Oldsmobile & Cadillac 1500 E Main St *Web:* www.youngautosales.com	Owosso	MI	48867	888-719-9158	
Ziems Ford Corners Inc 5700 E Main St *Web:* www.ziemsford.com	Farmington	NM	87402	505-325-1961	325-6592
Zimmerman Ford Inc 2525 E Main St *Web:* www.zimmermanford.com	Saint Charles	IL	60174	630-584-1800	584-3753

AUTOMOBILE LEASING

SEE Credit & Financing - Commercial p. 1773; Credit & Financing - Consumer p. 1775; Fleet Leasing & Management p. 1849

58 AUTOMOBILE SALES & RELATED SERVICES - ONLINE

SEE ALSO Automobile Dealers & Groups p. 1489

	City	State	Zip	Phone	Fax
Autobytel Inc 18872 MacArthur Blvd *NASDAQ: ABTL* ■ *TF:* 888-422-8999 ■ *Web:* www.autobytel.com	Irvine	CA	92612	949-225-4500	225-4541
Autofusion Corp 9605 Scranton Rd Suite 450 *TF:* 800-410-7354 ■ *Web:* www.autofusion.com	San Diego	CA	92121	858-270-9444	270-6116
Automobile Consumer Services Inc 6249 Stewart Rd *TF:* 800-223-4882 ■ *Web:* www.acscorp.com	Cincinnati	OH	45227	513-527-7700	527-7705
Automotive Information Ctr 18872 MacArthur Blvd *TF:* 888-422-8999 ■ *Web:* www.autosite.com	Irvine	CA	92612	949-862-1335	757-8920
AUTOPEDIA 5455 Production Dr *Web:* www.autopedia.com	Huntington Beach	CA	92649	714-892-0969	
AutoVIN Inc 50 Mansell Ct Suite 200 *TF:* 877-428-8684 ■ *Web:* www.autovin.com	Roswell	GA	30076	678-585-8000	585-8201
Carfax Inc 10304 Eaton Pl Suite 500 *TF:* 800-274-2277 ■ *Web:* www.carfax.com	Fairfax	VA	22030	703-934-2664	218-2853
CarPrices.com c/o AutoFusion Corp 9605 Scranton Rd Suite 450 *TF:* 800-410-7354 ■ *Web:* www.carprices.com	San Diego	CA	92121	858-270-9444	270-6116
Cars.com c/o Classified Ventures LLC 175 W Jackson Blvd Suite 800 *Web:* www.cars.com	Chicago	IL	60604	312-601-5000	
CarsDirect.com Inc 909 N Sepulveda Blvd 11th Fl *TF Cust Svc:* 800-431-2500 ■ *Web:* www.carsdirect.com	El Segundo	CA	90245	310-280-4000	
CarSmart 18872 MacArthur Blvd Suite 200 *Web:* www.carsmart.com	Irvine	CA	92612	949-225-4500	
DealerNet c/o Cobalt Group Inc 2200 1st Ave S Suite 400 *TF:* 800-909-8244 ■ *Web:* www.dealernet.com	Seattle	WA	98134	206-269-6363	269-6350
Edmunds.com Inc 2401 Colorado Ave *Web:* www.edmunds.com	Santa Monica	CA	90404	310-309-6300	309-6400
IntelliChoice Inc 1901 S Bascom Ave Suite 600 *Web:* www.intellichoice.com	Campbell	CA	95008	408-377-4300	377-4303
Kelley Blue Book Co Inc 195 Technology Dr *TF:* 800-258-3266 ■ *Web:* www.kbb.com	Irvine	CA	92623	949-770-7704	837-1904
MotorPlace.com 2200 1st Ave S *TF:* 800-909-8244 ■ *Web:* www2.motorplace.com	Seattle	WA	98134	206-269-6363	
Williamson Cadillac Co 7815 SW 104th St *Web:* www.williamsoncadillac.com	Miami	FL	33156	305-670-7100	670-7136

59 AUTOMOBILES - MFR

SEE ALSO All-Terrain Vehicles p. 1394; Motor Vehicles - Commercial & Special Purpose p. 2260; Motorcycles & Motorcycle Parts & Accessories p. 2263; Snowmobiles p. 2658

	City	State	Zip	Phone	Fax
4 Guys Inc 230 Industrial Pk Rd PO Box 90 *Web:* www.4guysfire.com	Meyersdale	PA	15552	814-634-8373	634-0076
AM General LLC 105 N Niles Ave PO Box 7025 *Web:* www.amgeneral.com	South Bend	IN	46617	574-237-6222	284-2814
American Honda Motor Co Inc 1919 Torrance Blvd *TF:* 800-999-1009 ■ *Web:* www.honda.com	Torrance	CA	90501	310-783-2000	
American Honda Motor Co Inc Acura Div 1919 Torrance Blvd **Fax:* Hum Res ■ *TF:* 800-382-2238 ■ *Web:* www.acura.com	Torrance	CA	90501	310-783-2000	783-3535*
American Suzuki Motor Corp 3251 Imperial Hwy *Web:* www.suzuki.com	Brea	CA	92821	714-996-7040	524-2512
Aston Martin Lagonda of North America Inc 553 MacArthur Blvd *TF:* 800-637-6837 ■ *Web:* www.astonmartin.com	Mahwah	NJ	07430	201-818-8351	818-8328
Audi of America 3800 Hamlin Rd **Fax:* Hum Res ■ *TF:* 800-367-2834 ■ *Web:* www.audiusa.com	Auburn Hills	MI	48326	248-340-5000	754-6521*
Bentley Motors Inc 3 Copley Pl Suite 3701 *Web:* www.bentleymotors.com	Boston	MA	02116	617-488-8500	
BMW of North America LLC 300 Chestnut Ridge Rd *TF:* 800-526-0818 ■ *Web:* www.bmwusa.com	Woodcliff Lake	NJ	07677	201-307-4000	307-4095
Collins Bus Corp PO Box 2946 *TF:* 800-354-9802 ■ *Web:* www.collinsbus.com	Hutchinson	KS	67504	620-662-9000	662-3838
DaimlerChrysler Canada Inc 2199 Chrysler Ctr **Fax:* Sales ■ *TF:* 800-265-6904 ■ *Web:* www.daimlerchrysler.ca	Windsor	ON	N9A4H6	519-973-2000	973-2799*
DaimlerChrysler Corp Dodge Div 1000 Chrysler Dr **Fax:* Cust Svc ■ *TF Cust Svc:* 800-992-1997 ■ *Web:* www.dodge.com	Auburn Hills	MI	48321	248-576-5741	512-8840*
DaimlerChrysler Corp Jeep Div PO Box 21-8004 *TF Cust Svc:* 800-992-1997 ■ *Web:* www.jeep.com	Auburn Hills	MI	48321	248-576-5741	
DaimlerChrysler Corp Plymouth Div 1000 chrysler Dr *TF Cust Svc:* 800-992-1997 ■ *Web:* www.chryslergroupllc.com	Auburn Hills	MI	48326	248-576-5741	512-3920
Eldorado National Inc 9670 Galena St *TF:* 800-338-3211 ■ *Web:* www.enconline.com	Riverside	CA	92509	909-591-9557	591-5285
Ferrara Fire Apparatus Inc PO Box 249 *TF:* 800-443-9006 ■ *Web:* www.ferrarafire.com	Holden	LA	70744	225-567-7100	567-5260
Ferrari North America Inc 250 Sylvan Ave *Web:* www.ferrari.com	Englewood Cliffs	NJ	07632	201-816-2600	816-2626
Fiat USA Inc 7 Times Sq Tower Suite 4306 *Web:* www.fiat.com	New York	NY	10036	212-355-2600	755-6152
Ford Motor Co 1 The American Rd Suite 1026 *NYSE: F* ■ *TF:* 800-392-3673 ■ *Web:* www.ford.com	Dearborn	MI	48126	313-322-3000	845-6073
Ford Motor Co of Canada Ltd PO Box 2000 **Fax:* Mail Rm ■ *Web:* www.ford.ca	Oakville	ON	L6J5E4	905-845-2511	845-7016*
Freightliner Specialty Vehicles Inc 2300 S 13th St *TF:* 800-358-7624 ■ *Web:* www.sportchassis.com	Clinton	OK	73601	580-323-4100	323-4111
General Motors Corp (GMC) 100 Renaissance Ctr *NYSE: GM* ■ **Fax Area Code:* 248 ■ *Web:* www.gm.com	Detroit	MI	48265	313-556-5000	696-7300*
General Motors Corp Buick Motor Div 300 Renaissance Ctr PO Box 33136 **Fax Area Code:* 248 ■ *TF Cust Svc:* 800-521-7300 ■ *Web:* www.buick.com	Detroit	MI	48265	313-556-5000	696-4984*
General Motors Corp Cadillac Motor Car Div 300 Renaissance Ctr PO Box 33169 **Fax Area Code:* 248 ■ *TF Cust Svc:* 800-458-8006 ■ *Web:* www.cadillac.com	Detroit	MI	48265	313-556-5000	696-4984*
General Motors Corp Chevrolet Motor Div 300 Renaissance Ctr PO Box 33170 **Fax Area Code:* 248 ■ *TF Cust Svc:* 800-222-1020 ■ *Web:* www.chevrolet.com	Detroit	MI	48265	313-556-5000	696-4984*
General Motors Corp Pontiac Div 300 Renaissance Ctr PO Box 33172 **Fax:* Mktg ■ *TF Cust Svc:* 800-762-2737 ■ *Web:* www.pontiac.com	Detroit	MI	48265	313-556-5000	667-4001*
General Motors Corp Pontiac-GMC Div 300 Renaissance Ctr PO Box 33172 **Fax Area Code:* 248 ■ *TF Cust Svc:* 888-988-7267 ■ *Web:* www.gmc.com	Detroit	MI	48265	313-556-5000	696-4984*
General Motors of Canada Ltd 1908 Colonel Sam Dr *TF:* 800-263-3777 ■ *Web:* www.gm.ca/gm	Oshawa	ON	L1H8P7	905-644-5000	
Glaval Bus 914 County Rd 1 *TF:* 800-445-2825 ■ *Web:* www.glavalbus.com	Elkhart	IN	46514	574-262-2212	264-9036
Honda Canada Inc 715 Milner Ave *Web:* www.honda.ca	Toronto	ON	M1B2K8	416-284-8110	286-1322
Honda Mfg of Alabama LLC 1800 Honda Dr *Web:* www.hondaalabama.com	Lincoln	AL	35096	205-355-5000	355-5020
Horton Emergency Vehicles 3800 McDowell Rd *Web:* www.hortonambulance.com	Grove City	OH	43123	614-539-8181	539-8165
Hyundai Motor America 10550 Talbert Ave **Fax:* Mktg ■ *TF Cust Svc:* 800-633-5151 ■ *Web:* www.hyundaiusa.com	Fountain Valley	CA	92708	714-965-3000	965-3843*
International Armoring Corp 2335 Lincoln Ave *Web:* www.armormax.com	Ogden	UT	84401	801-393-1075	393-1078
Isuzu Motors America Inc 13340 183rd St **Fax:* Hum Res ■ *TF Cust Svc:* 800-255-6727 ■ *Web:* www.isuzu.com	Cerritos	CA	90702	562-229-5000	229-5463*
Jaguar Cars North America 555 MacArthur Blvd *TF Cust Svc:* 800-452-4827 ■ *Web:* www.jaguar.com/us	Mahwah	NJ	07430	201-818-8500	818-9770
Jefferson Industries Corp SR- 29 NE	West Jefferson	OH	43162	614-879-5300	879-6806
Land Rover North America Inc 555 MacArthur Blvd *TF:* 800-637-6837 ■ *Web:* www.landrover.com	Mahwah	NJ	07430	201-818-8500	818-9770
Lincoln-Mercury Co 16800 Executive Plaza Dr PO Box 6248 *TF:* 800-521-4140 ■ *Web:* www.lincolnmercury.com	Dearborn	MI	48121	800-521-4140	
Lotus Cars USA Inc 2236 Northmont Pkwy *TF Cust Svc:* 800-245-6887 ■ *Web:* www.lotuscars.com	Duluth	GA	30096	770-476-6540	476-6541
Mazda North American Operations 7755 Irvine Ctr Dr PO Box 19734 *TF Cust Svc:* 800-222-5500 ■ *Web:* www.mazdausa.com	Irvine	CA	92618	949-727-1990	727-6101
Mercedes-Benz USA LLC 1 Mercedes Dr PO Box 350 *TF Cust Svc:* 800-367-6372 ■ *Web:* www.mbusa.com	Montvale	NJ	07645	201-573-0600	573-2337
Mitsubishi Canada Ltd 2800-200 Granville St Suite 2800 *Web:* www.mitsubishicorp.com	Vancouver	BC	V6C1G6	604-654-8000	654-8222
Mitsubishi Motors America Inc 6400 W Katella Ave *Web:* www.mitsubishi-motors.co.jp	Cypress	CA	90630	714-372-6000	
New United Motor Mfg Inc (NUMMI) 45500 Fremont Blvd *Web:* www.nummi.com	Fremont	CA	94538	510-498-5500	
Nissan Canada Inc (NCI) 5290 Orbitor Dr *TF:* 800-387-0122 ■ *Web:* www.nissan.ca	Mississauga	ON	L4W4Z5	905-629-2888	629-6553
Nissan Motor Corp USA Infiniti Div 1 Nissan Way PO Box 685003 *TF:* 800-662-6200 ■ *Web:* www.infinitiusa.com	Franklin	TN	37067	800-662-6200	
Nissan North America Inc 333 Commerce St *TF:* 800-647-7263 ■ *Web:* www.nissanusa.com	Nashville	TN	37201	615-725-1000	723-3343
Peugeot Motors of America Inc 150 Clove Rd Overlook at Great Notch *TF:* 800-223-0587 ■ *Web:* www.peugeot.com	Little Falls	NJ	07424	973-812-4444	812-2280
Porsche Cars North America Inc 980 Hammond Dr Suite 1000 *TF:* 800-545-8039 ■ *Web:* www.porsche.com	Atlanta	GA	30328	770-290-3500	290-3708
Saab Cars USA Inc 100 Renaissance Ctr *TF:* 800-722-2872 ■ *Web:* www.saabusa.com	Detroit	MI	48265	313-556-5000	665-0550

Company	City	State	ZIP	Phone	Fax
Subaru of America Inc 2235 Marlton Pike W *TF:* 800-782-2783 ■ *Web:* www.subaru.com	Cherry Hill	NJ	08002	856-488-8500	488-3274
Toyota Canada Inc 1 Toyota Pl *TF Cust Svc:* 888-869-6828 ■ *Web:* www.toyota.ca	Scarborough	ON	M1H1H9	416-438-6320	431-1867
Toyota Motor Sales USA Inc 19001 S Western Ave *TF Cust Svc:* 800-331-4331 ■ *Web:* www.toyota.com	Torrance	CA	90501	310-468-4000	468-7814
Toyota Motor Sales USA Inc Lexus Div 19001 S Western Ave *TF Cust Svc:* 800-331-4331 ■ *Web:* www.lexus.com	Torrance	CA	90501	310-468-4000	468-7800
Volkswagen Canada Inc 777 Bayly St W *TF:* 800-822-8987 ■ *Web:* www.vw.ca	Ajax	ON	L1S7G7	905-428-6700	428-5838
Volkswagen Group Of America Inc 2200 Ferdinand Porsche Dr **Fax Area Code: 248* ■ *Web:* www.volkswagengroupamerica.com	Herndon	VA	20171	703-364-7000	340-5140*
Volkswagen of America Inc 3800 Hamlin Rd *TF:* 800-822-8987 ■ *Web:* www.vw.com	Auburn Hills	MI	48326	248-754-5000	
Volvo Cars of North America 1 Volvo Dr *TF Cust Svc:* 800-458-1552 ■ *Web:* www.volvocars.com	Rockleigh	NJ	07647	201-768-7300	768-1385

60 AUTOMOTIVE PARTS & SUPPLIES - MFR

SEE ALSO Carburetors, Pistons, Piston Rings, Valves p. 1555; Electrical Equipment for Internal Combustion Engines p. 1808; Engines & Turbines p. 1831; Gaskets, Packing, Sealing Devices p. 1903; Hose & Belting - Rubber or Plastics p. 2027; Motors (Electric) & Generators p. 2263

Company	City	State	ZIP	Phone	Fax
Aamp of America Inc 13160 56th Ct Suite 508 *TF:* 800-477-2267 ■ *Web:* www.aampofamerica.com	Clearwater	FL	33760	727-572-9255	573-9326
Acadia Polymers Inc 5251 Concourse Dr *TF:* 800-444-6165 ■ *Web:* www.acadiapolymers.com	Roanoke	VA	24019	540-265-2700	265-2764
Accuride Corp 7140 Office Cir *NYSE: ACW* ■ *TF Cust Svc:* 800-626-7096 ■ *Web:* www.accuridecorp.com	Evansville	IN	47715	812-962-5000	962-5400
Aer Mfg Inc PO Box 979 *TF:* 800-621-0545 ■ *Web:* www.aermanufacturing.com	Carrollton	TX	75011	972-418-6499	417-3150
Affinia Group Inc 1101 Technology Dr *Web:* www.affiniagroup.com	Ann Arbor	MI	48108	734-827-5400	827-5407
Airtex Products 407 W Main St *TF:* 800-880-3056 ■ *Web:* www.airtexproducts.com	Fairfield	IL	62837	618-842-2111	842-4069
Aisin Holdings of America Inc 1665 E Fourth St *Web:* www.aisinworld.com	Seymour	IN	47274	812-524-8144	524-8146
Aisin USA Mfg Inc 1700 E 4th St *Web:* www.aisinusa.com	Seymour	IN	47274	812-523-1969	523-1984
Alcoa Automotive 36555 Corporate Dr Suite 185	Farmington Hills	MI	48331	248-489-4900	
Alma Products Co 2000 Michigan Ave **Fax Area Code: 800* ■ *TF:* 877-427-2624 ■ *Web:* www.almaproducts.com	Alma	MI	48801	989-463-1151	457-2719*
Alpha Technology Corp 251 Mason Rd PO Box 168 *Web:* www.altec-us.com	Howell	MI	48844	517-546-9700	546-5926
Aluminum Casting & Engineering Co Inc 2039 S Lenox St *Web:* www.alumcast.com	Milwaukee	WI	53207	414-744-3902	744-6411
AMBAC International Inc 910 Spears Creek Ct *TF:* 800-628-6894 ■ *Web:* www.ambac.net	Elgin	SC	29045	803-735-1400	735-2163
American Auto Accessories Inc 35-06 Leavitt St Suite C **Fax Area Code: 347* ■ *Web:* www.3aracing.com	Flushing	NY	11354	718-886-6600	625-8600*
American Axle & Mfg Inc (AAM) One Dauch Dr *NYSE: AXL* ■ *TF:* 800-299-2953 ■ *Web:* www.aam.com	Detroit	MI	48211	313-758-2000	974-3090
American Cable Co PO Box 46827 *Web:* www.americancableco.com	Philadelphia	PA	19160	215-456-0700	456-1605
Amerigon Inc 21680 Haggerty Rd Suite 101 *NASDAQ: ARGN* ■ *Web:* www.amerigon.com	Northville	MI	48167	248-504-0500	348-9735
AMSTED Industries Inc 180 N Stetson St Suite 1800 **Fax: Hum Res* ■ *Web:* www.amsted.com	Chicago	IL	60601	312-645-1700	819-8504*
Angstrom Precision Metals Inc 8229 Tyler Blvd *Web:* www.w-pm.com	Mentor	OH	44060	440-255-6700	255-4263
Ap Exhaust Technologies Inc 300 Dixie Trial *TF:* 800-277-2787 ■ *Web:* www.apexhaust.com	Goldsboro	NC	27530	919-580-2000	580-2025
ARC Automotive Inc 1601 Midpark Rd Suite 100 *Web:* www.arcautomotive.com	Knoxville	TN	37921	865-583-7711	583-7611
ArvinMeritor Inc 2135 W Maple Rd *NYSE: ARM* ■ *Web:* www.arvinmeritor.com	Troy	MI	48084	248-435-1000	435-1393
Atwood Mobile Products 1120 N Main St *TF:* 800-546-8759 ■ *Web:* www.atwoodmobile.com	Elkhart	IN	46514	574-264-2131	262-2194
Autocam Corp 4070 E Paris Ave *TF:* 800-747-6978 ■ *Web:* www.autocam.com	Kentwood	MI	49512	616-698-0707	698-6876
Avis Industrial Corp 1909 S Main St *Web:* www.avisindustrial.com	Upland	IN	46989	765-998-8100	998-8111
Aw Transmission Engineering USA Inc 14920 Keel St *Web:* www.awtec.com	Plymouth	MI	48170	734-454-1710	454-1091
Baldwin Filters 4400 Hwy 30 **Fax Area Code: 800* ■ *TF:* 800-822-5394 ■ *Web:* www.baldwinfilter.com	Kearney	NE	68847	308-234-1951	828-4453*
Beach Mfg Co PO Box 129 *TF:* 800-543-5942 ■ *Web:* www.beachmfgco.com	Donnelsville	OH	45319	937-882-6372	882-6248
Black River Mfg Inc 2625 20th St *Web:* www.blackrivermfg.biz	Port Huron	MI	48060	810-982-9812	982-2074
BLD Products Ltd 534 E 48th St *Web:* www.bldproducts.com	Holland	MI	49423	616-395-5600	395-5605
BorgWarner Automatic Transmission Systems 3800 Automation Ave *Web:* www.borgwarner.com	Auburn Hills	MI	48326	248-754-9600	
BorgWarner Inc 3850 Hamlin Rd *NYSE: BWA* ■ *Web:* www.bwauto.com	Auburn Hills	MI	48326	248-754-9200	
BorgWarner Morse TEC 800 Warren Rd *Web:* www.borgwarner.com	Ithaca	NY	14850	607-257-6700	257-3359
BorgWarner TorqTransfer Systems 3800 Automation Ave *Web:* www.borgwarner.com	Auburn Hills	MI	48326	248-754-9600	754-9356
Borla Performance Industries Inc 3000 Bill Garland Rd *TF:* 877-462-6752 ■ *Web:* www.borla.com	Johnson City	TN	37604	423-979-4000	979-4099
Bowles Fluidics Corp 6625 Dobbin Rd *PINK: BOWE* ■ *Web:* www.bowlesfluidics.com	Columbia	MD	21045	410-381-0400	381-2718
Bushwacker Inc 6710 N Catlin Ave *TF:* 800-234-8920 ■ *Web:* www.bushwacker.com	Portland	OR	97203	503-283-4335	283-3007
Capsonic Automotive Inc 460 S 2nd St *TF:* 888-981-1500 ■ *Web:* www.capsonic.com	Elgin	IL	60123	847-888-7300	888-7543
Car Parts Warehouse Inc 5200 W 130th St *Web:* www.carpartswarehouse.net	Akron	OH	44311	216-676-5100	676-5516
Cardone Industries Inc 5501 Whitaker Ave *TF Cust Svc:* 800-777-4780 ■ *Web:* www.cardone.com	Philadelphia	PA	19124	215-912-3000	912-3498
Carlisle Cos Inc 13925 Ballantyne Corporate Pl Suite 400 *NYSE: CSL* ■ *Web:* www.carlisle.com	Charlotte	NC	28277	704-501-1100	501-1190
Carlisle Industrial Brake 1031 E Hillside Dr *TF:* 800-873-6361 ■ *Web:* www.carlislebrake.com	Bloomington	IN	47401	812-336-3811	334-8775
Casco Products Corp 1 Waterview Dr *Web:* www.cascoglobal.com	Shelton	CT	06484	203-922-3200	922-3201
Champion Laboratories Inc 200 S 4th St *Web:* www.champlabs.com	Albion	IL	62806	618-445-6011	445-4040
Clarcor Inc 840 Crescent Ctr Dr Suite 600 *NYSE: CLC* ■ *TF:* 800-252-7267 ■ *Web:* www.clarcor.com	Franklin	TN	37067	615-771-3100	771-5616
Commercial Vehicle Group Inc 7800 Walton Pkwy *NASDAQ: CVGI* ■ *Web:* www.cvgrp.com	New Albany	OH	43054	614-289-5360	289-5361
Competition Cams Inc 3406 Democrat Rd *TF:* 800-999-0853 ■ *Web:* www.compcams.com	Memphis	TN	38118	901-795-2400	366-1807
Consolidated Metco Inc 13940 N Rivergate Blvd **Fax: Sales* ■ *TF Sales:* 800-547-9473 ■ *Web:* www.conmet.com	Portland	OR	97203	503-286-5741	240-5488*
Cooper-Standard Automotive Fluid Systems Div 2110 Executive Hills Ct *Web:* www.cooperstandard.com	Auburn Hills	MI	48326	248-836-9400	836-9116
Cooper-Standard Automotive Inc 39550 Orchard Hill Pl Dr **Fax: Hum Res* ■ *Web:* www.cooperstandard.com	Novi	MI	48375	248-596-5900	596-6540*
Crower Cams & Equipment 6180 Business Ctr Ct *Web:* www.crower.com	San Diego	CA	92154	619-661-6477	661-6466
Cummins Filtration 2931 Elm Hill Pike *TF:* 800-777-7064 ■ *Web:* www.cumminsfiltration.com	Nashville	TN	37214	615-367-0040	399-3650
Cummins Inc 500 Jackson St PO Box 3005 *NYSE: CMI* ■ *TF:* 800-343-7357 ■ *Web:* www.cummins.com	Columbus	IN	47201	812-377-5000	377-3334
CWC Textron 1085 W Sherman Blvd *TF:* 800-892-9871	Muskegon	MI	49441	231-733-1331	739-2649
Dacco Inc 741 Dacco Dr PO Box 2789 *TF:* 800-443-2226 ■ *Web:* www.daccoatparts.com	Cookeville	TN	38502	931-528-7581	528-9777
Dana Holding Corp 4500 Dorr St PO Box 1000 *NYSE: DAN* ■ *TF:* 800-733-3879 ■ *Web:* www.dana.com	Toledo	OH	43697	419-535-4500	535-4643
Danaher Corp 2200 Pennsylvania Ave NW Suite 800 *NYSE: DHR* ■ *TF:* 866-873-5600 ■ *Web:* www.danaher.com	Washington	DC	20037	202-828-0850	828-0860
Davco Technology LLC 1600 Woodland Dr PO Box 487 *TF:* 800-328-2611 ■ *Web:* www.davcotec.com	Saline	MI	48176	734-429-5665	429-0741
Dayton Parts LLC 3500 Industrial Rd PO Box 5795 *TF Cust Svc:* 800-225-2159	Harrisburg	PA	17110	717-255-8500	255-8500
Decoma International Inc *magna exteriors & interiors* 50 Casmir Ct *TF:* 800-461-3967 ■ *Web:* www.magna.com	Concord	ON	L4K4J5	905-669-2888	669-4992
Delphi Corp 5725 Delphi Dr *Web:* www.delphi.com	Troy	MI	48098	248-813-2000	813-6866
Delphi Energy & Chassis Systems 5725 Delphi Dr *Web:* www.delphi.com	Troy	MI	48098	248-813-2000	813-6866
Denso International America Inc 24777 Denso Dr *TF:* 866-874-3104 ■ *Web:* www.densocorp-na.com	Southfield	MI	48033	248-350-7500	213-2337
Detroit Steel Products Co Inc 511 N Rangeline Rd	Morristown	IN	46161	765-763-6089	763-6306
Dexter Axle 2900 Industrial Pkwy *Web:* www.dexteraxle.com	Elkhart	IN	46516	574-295-7888	295-8666
Dorman Products Inc 3400 E Walnut St *NASDAQ: DORM* ■ *TF:* 800-868-5777 ■ *Web:* www.rbinc.com	Colmar	PA	18915	215-997-1800	997-1741
Douglas Autotech Corp 300 Albers Rd *Web:* www.douglasautotech.com	Bronson	MI	49028	517-369-2315	369-7217
Dreison International Inc 4540 W 160th St *Web:* www.dreison.com	Cleveland	OH	44135	216-265-8400	362-0799
Dura Automotive Systems Inc 2791 Research Dr *NASDAQ: DRRA* ■ *TF:* 800-362-3872 ■ *Web:* www.duraauto.com	Rochester Hills	MI	48309	248-299-7500	299-7501
Durakon Industries Inc 2101 N Lapeer Rd **Fax: Cust Svc* ■ *TF Cust Svc:* 800-955-3993 ■ *Web:* www.durakon.com	Lapeer	MI	48446	810-664-0850	667-7735*
Eagle Wings Industries Inc 400 Shellhouse Dr *Web:* www.ewiusa.com	Rantoul	IL	61866	217-892-4322	

Company / Address	City	State	Zip	Phone	Fax
Eagle-Picher Industries Inc 2424 John Daly Rd *Web:* www.epcorp.com	Inkster	MI	48141	313-278-5956	278-5982
East Penn Mfg Co Inc PO Box 147 *Web:* www.dekabatteries.com	Lyon Station	PA	19536	610-682-6361	682-6361
Eaton Corp 1111 Superior Ave Eaton Ctr *NYSE:* ETN ■ *Web:* www.eaton.com	Cleveland	OH	44114	216-523-5000	523-4787
Edelbrock Corp 2700 California St *TF:* 800-739-3737 ■ *Web:* www.edelbrock.com	Torrance	CA	90503	310-781-2222	320-1187
Engine Power Components Inc PO Box 837 *Web:* www.engpwr.com	Grand Haven	MI	49417	616-846-0110	847-0500
EnPro Industries Inc 5605 Carnegie Blvd Suite 500 *NYSE:* NPO ■ *TF:* 866-663-6776 ■ *Web:* www.enproindustries.com	Charlotte	NC	28209	704-731-1500	731-1511
Evercoat 6600 Cornell Rd *TF:* 800-729-7600 ■ *Web:* www.evercoat.com	Cincinnati	OH	45242	513-489-7600	489-9229
Extang Corp 1901 E Ellsworth Rd *TF:* 800-877-2588 ■ *Web:* www.extang.com	Ann Arbor	MI	48108	734-677-0444	677-8409
Faurecia Exhaust Systems Inc 543 Matzinger Rd *Web:* www.faurecia.com	Toledo	OH	43612	419-727-5000	727-5025
Federal-Mogul Corp 26555 Northwestern Hwy *TF Cust Svc:* 800-560-1400 ■ *Web:* www.federalmogul.com	Southfield	MI	48034	248-354-7700	354-7700
Firestone Industrial Products Co 250 W 96th St *TF:* 800-888-0650 ■ *Web:* www.firestoneindustrial.com	Indianapolis	IN	46260	317-818-8600	818-8645
Fleetline Products 784 Bill Jones Industrial Dr *TF:* 800-332-6653 ■ *Web:* www.fontainefl.com	Springfield	TN	37172	615-384-4338	382-1430
Flex-N-Gate Corp 1306 E University Ave *Web:* www.flex-n-gate.com	Urbana	IL	61802	217-278-2600	278-2616
Fontaine Fifth Wheel 7574 Commerce Cir *TF:* 800-874-9780 ■ *Web:* www.fifthwheel.com	Trussville	AL	35173	205-661-4900	655-9982
Fontaine Truck Equipment Co 2490 Pinson Valley Pkwy *TF:* 800-824-3033 ■ *Web:* www.fontaine.com	Birmingham	AL	35217	205-841-8582	849-9615
Franklin Precision Industry Inc (FPI) 3220 Bowling Green Rd *Web:* www.fpik.com	Franklin	KY	42134	270-586-4450	586-0180
Freudenberg-NOK General Partnership 47690 E Anchor Ct *TF:* 800-533-5656 ■ *Web:* www.freudenberg-nok.com	Plymouth	MI	48170	734-451-0020	451-0125
GDX Automotive Inc 36600 Corporate Dr *Web:* www.gdxautomotive.com	Farmington Hills	MI	48331	248-553-5300	553-5105
General Motors Corp Allison Transmission Div 4700 W 10th St *Web:* www.allisontransmission.com	Indianapolis	IN	46206	317-242-5000	242-0262
GKN Driveline North America Inc *GKN PLC* 3300 University Dr *Web:* www.gkn.com	Auburn Hills	MI	48326	248-377-1200	377-1370
Glasstite Inc 600 N Hwy 4 *TF:* 800-533-0450 ■ *Web:* www.glasstite.com	Dunnell	MN	56127	507-695-2378	695-2980
Griffin Thermal Products 100 Hurricane Creek Rd *TF:* 800-722-3723 ■ *Web:* www.griffinrad.com	Piedmont	SC	29673	864-845-5000	845-5001
Grote Industries Inc 2600 Lanier Dr *TF:* 800-628-0809 ■ *Web:* www.grote.com	Madison	IN	47250	812-273-2121	265-8440
Gunite Corp 302 Peoples Ave *TF:* 800-677-3786 ■ *Web:* www.gunite.com	Rockford	IL	61104	815-490-6364	964-0775
Hastings Mfg Co 325 N Hanover St *TF:* 800-776-1088 ■ *Web:* www.hastingsmfg.com	Hastings	MI	49058	269-945-2491	945-4667
HAWK Corp 200 Public Sq Suite 1500 *Web:* www.hawkcorp.com	Cleveland	OH	44114	216-861-3553	861-4546
Hayden Automotive 1241 Old Temescal Rd Suite 101 **Fax:* Cust Svc ■ *TF:* 800-621-3233 ■ *Web:* www.haydenauto.com	Corona	CA	92881	951-736-2665	736-2608*
Hayes Lemmerz International Inc 15300 Centennial Dr *PINK:* HAYL ■ **Fax Area Code:* 800 ■ *TF:* 800-521-0515 ■ *Web:* www.hayes-lemmerz.com	Northville	MI	48168	734-737-5000	521-0515*
Heckethorn Manfacturing Cos Inc 2005 Forrest St *Web:* www.hecomfg.com	Dyersburg	TN	38024	731-285-3310	286-2739
Hendrickson International 800 S Frontage Rd *Web:* www.hendrickson-intl.com	Woodridge	IL	60517	630-910-2800	910-2899
Hennessy Industries Inc 1601 JP Hennesey Dr **Fax:* Mktg ■ *TF:* 800-688-6359 ■ *Web:* www.ammcoats.com	La Vergne	TN	37086	615-641-7533	641-6069*
Holley Performance Products Inc 1801 Russellville Rd **Fax:* Cust Svc ■ *TF Sales:* 800-638-0032 ■ *Web:* www.holley.com	Bowling Green	KY	42101	270-782-2900	781-9940*
Hopkins Mfg Corp 428 Peyton St *TF:* 800-524-1458 ■ *Web:* www.hopkinsmfg.com	Emporia	KS	66801	620-342-7320	340-8590
Hutchens Industries Inc 215 N Patterson Ave **Fax:* Cust Svc ■ *TF:* 800-654-8824 ■ *Web:* www.hutch-susp.com	Springfield	MO	65802	417-862-5012	862-2317*
Hwh Corp 2096 Moscow Rd *TF:* 800-321-3494 ■ *Web:* www.hwhcorp.com	Moscow	IA	52760	563-724-3396	724-3408
Ilmor Engineering Inc 43939 Plymouth Oaks Blvd *Web:* www.ilmor.com	Plymouth	MI	48170	734-456-3600	
Indian Head Industries Inc 8530 Cliff Cameron Dr *TF:* 800-527-1534 ■ *Web:* www.indianheadindustries.com	Charlotte	NC	28269	704-547-7411	547-9367
Indian Head Industries Inc MGM Brakes Div 8530 Cliff Cameron Dr *TF:* 800-527-1534 ■ *Web:* www.mgmbrakes.com	Charlotte	NC	28269	704-547-7411	547-9367
Injex Industries Inc 30559 San Antonio St *Web:* www.injexindustries.com	Hayward	CA	94544	510-487-4960	487-8886
Interparts International Inc 190 Express St *Web:* www.interparts.com	Plainview	NY	11803	516-576-2000	
Intier Automotive Inc 39600 Lewis Dr *Web:* www.intier.com	Novi	MI	48377	248-567-4000	
Irvin Automotive Products Inc 2600 Centerpoint Pkwy *Web:* www.irvinautomotive.com	Pontiac	MI	48341	248-451-4100	451-4101
ITW ChronoTherm 935 N Oaklawn Ave *Web:* www.itwaccutherm.com	Elmhurst	IL	60126	630-993-9990	993-9399
J B Poindexter & Co Inc 600 Travis St Suite 200 *Web:* www.jbpoindexter.com	Houston	TX	77002	713-655-9800	951-9038
Jacobs Vehicle Systems Inc 22 E Dudley Town Rd *Web:* www.jakebrake.com	Bloomfield	CT	06002	860-243-1441	243-7632
Jason Inc 411 E Wisconsin Ave Suite 2120 *Web:* www.jasoninc.com	Milwaukee	WI	53202	414-277-9300	277-9445
JASPER Engines & Transmissions 815 Wernsing Rd PO Box 650 *TF:* 800-827-7455 ■ *Web:* www.jasperengines.com	Jasper	IN	47547	812-482-1041	634-1820
JL French Corp 3101 S Taylor Dr *TF:* 800-236-1117 ■ *Web:* www.jlfrench.com	Sheboygan	WI	53081	920-458-7724	458-0140
John Bean Co 309 Exchange Ave *TF:* 800-362-8326 ■ *Web:* www.johnbean.com	Conway	AR	72032	501-450-1500	450-1585
Johnson Controls Inc 5757 N Green Bay Ave *NYSE:* JCI ■ *TF:* 800-972-8040 ■ *Web:* www.johnsoncontrols.com	Milwaukee	WI	53209	414-524-1200	524-3232
Johnson Controls Inc Automotive Systems Group 49200 Halyard Dr **Fax:* Hum Res ■ *Web:* www.johnsoncontrols.com	Plymouth	MI	48170	734-254-5000	254-5843*
JSJ Corp 700 Robbins Rd *Web:* www.jsjcorp.com	Grand Haven	MI	49417	616-842-6350	847-3112
KONI North America 1961-A International Way *Web:* www.koni-na.com	Hebron	KY	41048	859-586-4100	334-3340
Lear Corp 21557 Telegraph Rd *NYSE:* LEA ■ *Web:* www.lear.com	Southfield	MI	48034	248-447-1500	447-1722
Linamar Corp 287 Speedvale Ave W *Web:* www.linamar.com	Guelph	ON	N1H1C5	519-836-7550	824-8479
Lorain County Automotive Systems Inc 7470 Industrial Pkwy Dr *Web:* www.camacollc.com	Lorain	OH	44053	440-960-7470	960-1878
LuK USA LLC 3401 Old Airport Rd *Web:* www.lukusa.com	Wooster	OH	44691	330-264-4383	264-4333
Lund International Holdings Inc 300 Horizon Dr **Fax Area Code:* 800 ■ **Fax:* Cust Svc ■ *TF:* 800-377-5863 ■ *Web:* www.lundinternational.com	Suwanee	GA	30024	678-804-3767	438-3788*
Luverne Truck Equipment Inc 1200 Birch St *Web:* www.luvernetruck.com	Brandon	SD	57005	605-582-7200	582-7434
MacLean-Fogg Co 1000 Allanson Rd *TF:* 800-323-4536 ■ *Web:* www.maclean-fogg.com	Mundelein	IL	60060	847-566-0010	949-0285
Magna International Inc 337 Magna Dr *NYSE:* MGA ■ *Web:* www.magnaint.com	Aurora	ON	L4G7K1	905-726-2462	726-7164
Magna International of America 600 Wilshire Dr *Web:* www.magna.com	Troy	MI	48084	248-729-2400	729-2410
MAGNA Powertrain AG 1870 Technology Dr *Web:* www.magnapowertrain.com	Troy	MI	48083	248-680-4900	680-4924
Magneti Marelli Powertrain USA Inc 2101 Nash St **Fax:* Mktg ■ *Web:* www.magnetimarelli.com	Sanford	NC	27331	919-776-4111	775-6339*
MAHLE Clevite Inc 1240 Eisenhower Pl *TF:* 800-338-8786 ■ *Web:* www.clevite.com	Ann Arbor	MI	48108	734-975-4777	975-7820
MAHLE Engine Components USA Inc 2020 Sanford St *TF:* 800-717-5398 ■ *Web:* www.us.mahle.com	Muskegon	MI	49444	231-722-1300	724-1940
Marmon-Herrington Co 13001 Magisterial Dr *TF:* 800-227-0727 ■ *Web:* www.marmon-herrington.com	Louisville	KY	40223	502-253-0277	253-0317
Masterack-Crown Inc 7315 E Lincon Way *TF Cust Svc:* 800-321-4934 ■ *Web:* www.crown-na.com	Apple Creek	OH	44606	330-262-6010	262-4095
Mayco International LLC PO Box 180149 *Web:* www.mayco-mi.com	Utica	MI	48318	586-803-6000	254-1555
Melling Tool Co 2620 Saradan St PO Box 1188 *TF:* 800-777-8172 ■ *Web:* www.melling.com	Jackson	MI	49204	517-787-8172	787-5304
Meridian Automotive Systems Inc 999 Republic Dr	Allen Park	MI	48101	313-336-4182	336-4184
Metaldyne Corp 47603 Halyard Dr *Web:* www.metaldyne.com	Plymouth	MI	48170	734-207-6200	207-6500
Mikuni American Corp 8910 Mikuni Ave *Web:* www.mikuni.com	Northridge	CA	91324	818-885-1242	993-6877
Mitsuba Bardstown Inc 901 Withrow Ct *TF:* 800-307-8787 ■ *Web:* www.mitsuba.co.jp/english/corp	Bardstown	KY	40004	502-348-3100	348-3204
Neapco Inc 740 Queen St PO Box 399 *TF:* 800-821-2374 ■ *Web:* www.neapco.com	Pottstown	PA	19464	610-323-6000	327-2551
Newcor Inc 1771 Harmon Rd Suite 200 *Web:* www.newcor.com	Auburn Hills	MI	48326	248-409-1070	409-1076
Omni Gear 7502 Mesa Rd *Web:* www.omnigear.com	Houston	TX	77028	713-635-6331	635-6360
P. T. M. Corp 6560 Bethuy Rd *TF:* 800-486-2212 ■ *Web:* www.ptmcorporation.com	Fair Haven	MI	48023	586-725-2211	725-6753
Penda Corp PO Box 449 **Fax:* Hum Res ■ *TF:* 800-356-7704 ■ *Web:* www.penda.com	Portage	WI	53901	608-742-5301	742-9402*
Penntecq Inc 106 Kuder Dr *Web:* www.penntecq.com	Greenville	PA	16125	724-646-4250	646-4261
Perfection Clutch Co 100 Perfection Way **Fax:* Sales ■ *TF:* 800-258-8312 ■ *Web:* www.perfectionclutch.com	Timmonsville	SC	29161	843-326-5544	326-5656*
Phillips & Temro Industries 9700 W 74th St *Web:* www.phillipsandtemro.com	Eden Prairie	MN	55344	952-941-9700	941-2285
Powers & Sons LLC 1613 Magda Dr *Web:* www.powersandsonsllc.com	Montpelier	OH	43543	419-485-3151	485-5490
Prime Wheel Corp 17705 S Main St *Web:* www.primewheel.com	Gardena	CA	90248	310-516-9126	516-9676

				Phone	Fax
Raybestos Products Co 1204 Darlington Ave	Crawfordsville	IN	47933	765-362-3500	362-9574
TF: 800-428-0825					
Remy International Inc 600 Corp Dr	Pendleton	IN	46064	765-778-6499	
TF: 800-372-3555 ■ *Web:* www.remyinc.com					
Ridewell Corp PO Box 4586	Springfield	MO	65808	417-833-4565	
TF: 877-434-8088 ■ *Web:* www.ridewellcorp.com					
Rieter Automotive North America Inc 38555 Hills Tech Dr	Farmington Hills	MI	48331	248-848-0100	848-0130
TF: 888-743-8370 ■ *Web:* www.rieter.com					
Robert Bosch LLC 2800 S 25th Ave	Broadview	IL	60155	708-865-5200	865-6430
Web: www.bosch.us					
Roush Mfg Inc 12068 Market St	Livonia	MI	48150	734-779-7028	
TF: 800-215-9658 ■ *Web:* www.roush.com					
Ryobi Die Casting Inc 800 W Mausoleum Rd	Shelbyville	IN	46176	317-398-3398	421-3725
Web: www.ryobidiecasting.com					
SAF-Holland USA 1950 Industrial Blvd	Muskegon	MI	49442	231-773-3271	767-8843
TF: 800-356-3929 ■ *Web:* www.ww1.safholland.us/sites/usa/en-US/Pages/default.aspx					
Sauer-Danfoss Inc 2800 E 13th St	Ames	IA	50010	515-239-6364	956-5364
NYSE: SHS ■ *TF:* 888-507-5871 ■ *Web:* www.sauer-danfoss.com					
Sealco Commercial Vehicle Products Inc 215 E Watkins St	Phoenix	AZ	85004	602-253-1007	222-2334*
**Fax Area Code:* 800 ■ *Web:* www.sealcocvp.com					
Sintering Technologies Inc 1024 Barachel Ln	Greensburg	IN	47240	812-663-5058	663-8118
Web: www.sti-us.net					
SmarTire Systems Inc 13151 Vanier Pl Suite 150	Richmond	BC	V5V2J1	604-276-9884	276-2350
TF: 888-982-3001 ■ *Web:* www.smartire.com					
Spalding Automotive Inc 4529 Adams Cir	Bensalem	PA	19020	215-638-3334	638-0313
Web: www.spaldingautomotive.com					
SPX Corp Filtran Div 875 Seegers Rd	Des Plaines	IL	60016	847-635-3833	635-7724
Web: www.filtranllc.com					
Stanadyne Corp 92 Deerfield Rd	Windsor	CT	06095	860-525-0821	683-4500
TF: 800-929-0919 ■ *Web:* www.stanadyne.com					
Standard Motor Products Inc 37-18 Northern Blvd	Long Island City	NY	11101	718-392-0200	729-4549
NYSE: SMP ■ *Web:* www.smpcorp.com					
Stemco LP 300 Industrial Blvd PO Box 1989	Longview	TX	75606	903-758-9981	232-3508*
**Fax:* Sales ■ *TF:* 800-527-8492 ■ *Web:* www.stemco.com					
Stoneridge Inc 9400 E Market St	Warren	OH	44484	330-856-2443	856-3618
NYSE: SRI ■ *TF:* 800-461-9330 ■ *Web:* www.stoneridge.com					
Strattec Security Corp 3333 W Good Hope Rd	Milwaukee	WI	53209	414-247-3333	247-3329
NASDAQ: STRT ■ *TF:* 888-710-5770 ■ *Web:* www.strattec.com					
Summit Polymers Inc 6717 S Sprinkle Rd	Portage	MI	49002	269-324-9323	324-9322
Web: www.summitpolymers.com					
Superior Industries International Inc 7800 Woodley Ave	Van Nuys	CA	94106	818-781-4973	780-3500
NYSE: SUP ■ *Web:* www.supind.com					
Systrand Mfg Corp 19050 Allen Rd	Brownstown	MI	48183	734-479-8100	479-8107
Web: www.systrand.com					
TAG Holdings LLC 2075 W Big Beaver Rd Suite 500	Troy	MI	48084	248-822-8056	822-8012
Web: www.taghold.com					
Taylor Devices Inc 90 Taylor Dr PO Box 748	North Tonawanda	NY	14120	716-694-0800	695-6015
NASDAQ: TAYD ■ *Web:* www.taylordevices.com					
TBDN Tennessee Co 1410 Hwy 70 Bypass	Jackson	TN	38301	731-421-4800	421-4879
Web: www.tbdn.com					
Teleflex Automotive Group Inc 700 Stephenson Hwy	Troy	MI	48083	248-616-3800	616-3810
Teleflex Power Systems 3831 No 6 Rd	Richmond	BC	V6V1P6	604-270-6899	270-7172
Web: www.teleflexpower.com					
TeleflexGFI Control Systems LP 100 Hollinger Crescent	Kitchener	ON	N2K2Z3	519-576-4270	576-7045
TF: 800-667-4275 ■ *Web:* www.teleflexgfi.com					
Tenneco Inc 500 N Field Dr	Lake Forest	IL	60045	847-482-5000	843-4169
NYSE: TEN ■ *TF:* 800-777-9564 ■ *Web:* www.tenneco.com					
ThyssenKrupp Budd Co 3155 W Big Beaver Rd PO Box 2601	Troy	MI	48007	248-643-3500	643-3593
Web: www.buddcompany.com					
TI Automotive 12345 E Nine-Mile Rd	Warren	MI	48090	586-758-4511	755-8375*
**Fax:* Hum Res ■ *TF:* 800-521-2500 ■ *Web:* www.tiauto.com					
Titan International Inc 2701 Spruce St	Quincy	IL	62301	217-228-6011	228-9331*
NYSE: TWI ■ **Fax:* Cust Svc ■ *TF:* 800-872-2327 ■ *Web:* www.titan-intl.com					
Titan Wheel Corp 2701 Spruce St	Quincy	IL	62301	217-228-6011	228-9331*
**Fax:* Cust Svc ■ *TF:* 800-518-4826 ■ *Web:* www.titan-intl.com					
Transform Automotive LLC 7026 Sterling Ponds Ct	Sterling Heights	MI	48312	586-826-8500	826-3656
Web: www.transformauto.com					
Trelleborg Automotive Americas 400 Aylworth Ave	South Haven	MI	49090	269-637-2116	637-8315
TF: 800-456-0557 ■ *Web:* www.trelleborg.com					
Triangle Suspension Systems Inc Maloney Rd	Du Bois	PA	15801	814-375-7211	371-4495
TF: 800-458-6077 ■ *Web:* www.trianglegroup.com					
Trico Products Corp 3255 W Hamlin Rd	Rochester Hills	MI	48309	248-371-1700	371-8300
TF: 888-565-9632 ■ *Web:* www.tricoproducts.com					
TRW Automotive 12025 Tech Ctr Dr	Livonia	MI	48150	734-855-2600	855-5702
Web: www.trwauto.com					
TRW Automotive Holdings Corp 12001 Tech Ctr Dr	Livonia	MI	48150	734-855-2600	855-5702
NYSE: TRW ■ *Web:* www.trwauto.com					
TS Trim Industries Inc 59 Gender Rd	Canal Winchester	OH	43110	614-837-4114	837-4127
Web: www.tstrim.com					
United Components Inc 14601 N Us Rt 41	Evansville	IN	47725	812-867-4156	867-4157
Web: www.ucinc.com					
Universal Mfg Co 405 Diagonal St PO Box 190	Algona	IA	50511	515-295-3557	295-5537
TF: 800-545-9350 ■ *Web:* www.universalmanf.com					
US Chemical & Plastics 600 Nova Dr SE PO Box 709	Massillon	OH	44648	330-830-6000	830-6005
TF: 800-321-0672 ■ *Web:* www.uschem.com					
US Mfg Corp 28201 Van Dyke Ave	Warren	MI	48093	586-467-1600	467-1630
Web: www.usmfg.com					
Valeo Inc 3000 University Dr	Auburn Hills	MI	48326	248-340-3000	340-3190*
**Fax:* Hum Res ■ *Web:* www.valeo.com					
Velvac Inc 2405 S Calhoun Rd	New Berlin	WI	53151	262-786-0700	786-7323
TF: 800-783-8871 ■ *Web:* www.velvac.com					
Visteon Corp 1 Village Ctr Dr	Van Buren Township	MI	48111	734-710-2020	755-7983*
NYSE: VC ■ **Fax Area Code:* 313 ■ *TF:* 800-847-8366 ■ *Web:* www.visteon.com					
Voith Turbo Inc 25 Winship Rd	York	PA	17406	717-767-3200	767-3210
Web: www.usa.voithturbo.com					
Webasto Roof Systems Inc 1757 Northfield Dr	Rochester Hills	MI	48309	248-997-5100	997-5581
Web: www.webasto.us					
Webb Automotive Group Inc 3911 E Main St	Farmington	NM	87402	505-325-1911	326-0909
Webb Wheel Products Inc 2310 Industrial Dr SW	Cullman	AL	35055	256-739-6660	739-6246*
**Fax:* Sales ■ *TF:* 800-633-3256 ■ *Web:* www.webbwheel.com					
Wells Mfg LP 26 S Brooke St PO Box 70	Fond du Lac	WI	54936	920-922-5900	922-3585
TF: 800-558-9770 ■ *Web:* www.wellsve.com					
Wescast Industries Inc 100 Water St	Wingham	ON	N0G2W0	519-357-4447	357-4127
TF Cust Svc: 800-215-4412 ■ *Web:* www.wecast.com					
Westport Innovations Inc 1750 W 75th Ave Suite 101	Vancouver	BC	V6P6G2	604-718-2000	718-2001
TSE: WPT ■ *Web:* www.westport.com					
Williams Controls Inc 14100 SW 72nd Ave	Portland	OR	97224	503-684-8600	684-3879
TF Cust Svc: 800-547-1889 ■ *Web:* www.wmco.com					
Wix Filtration Products 1 Wix Way PO Box 1967	Gastonia	NC	28053	704-864-6711	864-1843*
**Fax:* Cust Svc ■ *Web:* www.wixfilters.com					

61 AUTOMOTIVE PARTS & SUPPLIES - WHOL

				Phone	Fax
Aa Wheel & Truck Supply Inc 717 E 16th Ave	Kansas City	MO	64116	816-221-9556	221-9558
TF: 800-486-4335 ■ *Web:* www.aawheel.com					
Aapco Automotive Warehouse 2997 E La Palma Ave	Anaheim	CA	92806	714-630-5600	666-2913
ABC Auto Parts LLC 920 W Marshall Ave	Longview	TX	75604	903-232-3060	232-3095
Web: www.abcauto.com					
ABM Equipment & Supply LLC 333 2nd St Ne	Hopkins	MN	55343	952-938-5451	938-0159
Web: www.abm-highway.com					
Ace Tool Co 7337 Bryan Dairy Rd	Largo	FL	33777	727-544-4331	544-6211
TF: 800-777-5910 ■ *Web:* www.acetoolco.com					
Advantage Truck Accessories Inc PO Box 1747	Elkhart	IN	46515	574-522-2853	
Web: www.advantagetruckaccessories.com					
Advantech International Inc PO Box 6739	Somerset	NJ	08875	732-805-1900	805-0122
TF: 800-322-6150 ■ *Web:* www.advantechinternational.com					
Afx Industries LLC 522 Michigan St Suite B	Port Huron	MI	48060	810-966-4650	966-9522
Web: www.afxindustries.com					
All Products Automotive Inc 4701 W Cortland St	Chicago	IL	60639	773-889-4500	889-6328
Web: www.allprodauto.com					
Arrow Speed Warehouse 686 S Adams St	Kansas City	KS	66105	913-321-1200	321-7729
TF: 800-255-4606 ■ *Web:* www.arrow-speed.com					
Atsco Remanufacturing Inc 4525 N 43rd Ave	Phoenix	AZ	85031	623-842-4047	842-0485
TF: 800-261-4861 ■ *Web:* www.atscoreman.com					
Auto Parts Warehouse Inc 1073 E Artesia Blvd	Carson	CA	90746	323-770-0751	604-5088*
**Fax Area Code:* 310 ■ *Web:* www.apwks.com					
Automotive Distributors Co Inc 2981 Morse Rd	Columbus	OH	43231	800-421-5556	476-9469*
**Fax Area Code:* 614 ■ *TF:* 800-421-5556 ■ *Web:* www.adw1.com					
Automotive Parts Headquarters 2959 Clearwater Rd	Saint Cloud	MN	56301	320-252-5411	252-4256
TF: 800-247-0339					
Balkamp Inc 2601 S Holt Rd	Indianapolis	IN	46241	317-244-7241	381-2200
Web: www.balkamp.com					
Barron Motor Inc 1850 McCloud Pl NE	Cedar Rapids	IA	52402	319-393-6220	393-4864
TF: 800-332-7953 ■ *Web:* www.barronmotorsupply.com					
Bell Industries Inc Recreational Products Group 580 Yankee Doodle Rd Suite 1200	Eagan	MN	55121	651-450-9020	450-0844
TF: 800-388-2355 ■ *Web:* www.bellrpg.com					
Bendix Commercial Vehicle Systems LLC 901 Cleveland St	Elyria	OH	44035	440-329-9000	329-9557
TF: 800-247-2725 ■ *Web:* www.bendix.com					
Brake & Wheel Parts Industries Inc 2415 W 21st St	Chicago	IL	60608	773-847-7000	847-5149
TF: 800-621-8836 ■ *Web:* www.bwpindustries.com					
Carolina Rim & Wheel Co 1308 Upper Asbury Ave	Charlotte	NC	28206	704-334-7276	334-7270
TF: 800-532-6219 ■ *Web:* www.carolinarim.com					
Carolinas Auto Supply House Inc 2135 Tipton Dr	Charlotte	NC	28206	704-334-4646	377-7016*
**Fax Area Code:* 800 ■ *TF:* 800-438-4070 ■ *Web:* www.autosupplyhouse.com					
Carquest Corp 2635 E Millbrook Rd	Raleigh	NC	27604	919-573-3000	573-3558*
**Fax:* Mktg ■ *TF:* 800-876-1291 ■ *Web:* www.carquest.com					
Charleston Auto Parts Inc 3108 Losee Rd	North Las Vegas	NV	89030	702-642-7801	642-9174
TF Cust Svc: 800-879-7901 ■ *Web:* www.charltonautoparts.com					
Coast Distribution System 350 Woodview Ave	Morgan Hill	CA	95037	408-782-6686	782-7790
AMEX: CRV ■ *TF:* 800-495-5858 ■ *Web:* www.coastdistribution.com					
Custom Chrome Inc 18225 Serene Dr	Morgan Hill	CA	95037	408-778-0500	359-5700
TF: 800-729-3332 ■ *Web:* www.customchrome.com					
Delcoline Inc 4919 Lawrence St	Hyattsville	MD	20781	301-864-4455	
Web: www.delcoline.com					
Distributors Warehouse Inc 1900 10th St	Paducah	KY	42001	270-442-8201	442-4914
TF: 800-892-9966					
Dorian Drake International Inc 2 Gannett Dr	White Plains	NY	10604	914-697-9800	697-9683
Web: www.doriandrake.com					
Dreyco Inc 263 Veterans Blvd	Carlstadt	NJ	07072	201-896-9000	896-1378
Web: www.dreycoinc.com					

	City	State	Zip	Phone	Fax
Drive Train Industries Inc 5555 Joliet St	Denver	CO	80239	303-292-5176	297-0473
TF: 800-525-6177 ■ *Web:* www.drivetrainindustries.com					
Eagle Parts & Products Inc					
1411 Marvin Griffin Rd	Augusta	GA	30906	706-790-6687	790-6066
TF: 888-972-9911 ■ *Web:* www.eagleproducts.us					
Fisher Auto Parts Inc					
512 Greenville Ave PO Box 2246	Staunton	VA	24401	540-885-8901	885-1808
Web: www.fisherautoparts.com					
Flowers Auto Parts Co 935 Hwy 70 SE	Hickory	NC	28601	828-322-5414	322-9070
TF Cust Svc: 800-395-6272					
Frank Edwards Co 3626 Pkwy Blvd	West Valley City	UT	84120	801-736-8000	736-8051
TF: 800-366-8851					
General Truck Parts & Equipment Co					
3835 W 42nd St	Chicago	IL	60632	773-247-6900	247-2632
TF: 800-621-3914 ■ *Web:* www.generaltruckparts.com					
Genuine Parts Co 2999 Cir 75 Pkwy	Atlanta	GA	30339	770-953-1700	956-2211
NYSE: GPC ■ *Web:* www.genpt.com					
Globe Motorists Supply Co Inc					
560 S 3rd Ave	Mount Vernon	NY	10550	914-668-6430	668-0376
TF: 888-884-7278 ■ *Web:* www.tviparts.com					
Gooch Brake & Equipment Co					
6451 Universal Ave	Kansas City	MO	64120	816-421-3085	421-7970
TF: 800-444-3216 ■ *Web:* www.goochbrake.com					
Greddy Performance Products Inc Mnmt					
9 Vanderbilt	Irvine	CA	92618	949-588-8300	588-6318
Web: www.greddy.com					
Grupo Antolin Kentucky Inc					
208 Commerce Ct	Hopkinsville	KY	42240	270-885-2703	889-5186
Web: www.grupoantolin.com					
Hahn Automotive Warehouse Inc					
415 W Main St	Rochester	NY	14608	585-235-1595	
Web: www.hahnauto.com					
Harada Industry of America Inc 22925 Venture Dr	Novi	MI	48375	248-374-9000	374-9100
Web: www.harada.com					
Harris Battery Co Inc					
10708 Industrial Pkwy NW	Bolivar	OH	44612	330-874-0205	874-9936
TF: 800-367-7670 ■ *Web:* www.harrisbattery.com					
Hebco Products Inc 1232 Whetstone St	Bucyrus	OH	44820	419-562-7987	562-8577
Web: www.hebcoproducts.com					
Hedahls Inc 122 N 1st St	Bismarck	ND	58501	701-223-8393	221-4251
TF: 800-433-2457 ■ *Web:* www.hedahls.com					
Henderson Wheel & Warehouse Supply					
1825 S 300 W	Salt Lake City	UT	84115	801-486-2073	486-0353
TF: 800-748-5111 ■ *Web:* www.hendersonwheel.com					
Hilite International Inc 127 Public Sq	Cleveland	OH	44114	216-771-6700	574-9956
Web: www.hilite.com					
Instrument Sales & Service Inc					
16427 NE Airport Way	Portland	OR	97230	503-232-3422	333-4678*
**Fax Area Code:* 800 ■ *TF:* 800-333-7976 ■ *Web:* www.instrumentsales.com					
InterAmerican Motor Corp (IMC)					
8901 Canoga Ave	Canoga Park	CA	91304	818-678-1200	678-1330*
**Fax:* Sales ■ *TF:* 800-874-8925 ■ *Web:* www.imcparts.com					
International Brake Industries Inc					
1840 McCullough St	Lima	OH	45801	419-227-4421	993-8177*
**Fax:* Cust Svc ■ *TF:* 800-537-2838 ■ *Web:* www.ibilima.com					
Interstate Batteries 12770 Merit Dr Suite 400	Dallas	TX	75251	972-991-1444	455-6533
TF: 800-541-8419 ■ *Web:* www.interstatebatteries.com					
Intraco Corp 530 Stephenson Hwy	Troy	MI	48083	248-585-6900	585-6920
TF: 800-595-6900 ■ *Web:* www.intracousa.com					
Jead Auto Supply Corp 1810 E Tremont Ave	Bronx	NY	10460	718-792-7113	824-2898
Web: www.jeadauto.com					
Johnson Industries 5944 Peachtree Corners E	Norcross	GA	30071	770-441-1128	248-2896
TF Orders: 800-922-8111 ■ *Web:* www.teamji.com					
Kansas City Peterbilt Inc					
8915 Woodend Rd	Kansas City	KS	66111	913-441-2888	422-5029
TF: 800-489-1122 ■ *Web:* www.kcpete.com					
Keystone Automotive Operations Inc					
44 Tunkhannock Ave	Exeter	PA	18643	570-655-4514	603-2003
TF: 800-521-9999 ■ *Web:* www.keystoneautomotive.com					
Knopf Automotive 93 Shrewsbury Ave	Red Bank	NJ	07701	732-212-0444	212-0443
Web: www.mmknopf.com					
Liberty Bell Equipment Corp					
3201 S 76th St	Philadelphia	PA	19153	215-492-6700	492-5096
TF: 866-787-1000 ■ *Web:* www.medcotool.com					
LKQ Corp 120 N LaSalle St Suite 3300	Chicago	IL	60602	312-621-1950	621-1969
NASDAQ: LKQX ■ *TF:* 877-557-2677 ■ *Web:* www.lkqcorp.com					
Maxzone Vehicle Lighting Corp					
15889 Slover Ave Suite A	Fontana	CA	92337	909-822-3288	822-3399
Web: www.maxzone.com					
McGard LLC 3875 California Rd	Orchard Park	NY	14127	716-662-8980	662-8985
Web: www.mcgard.com					
Mid America Motorworks					
17082 N Us Hwy 45 PO Box 1368	Effingham	IL	62401	217-540-4200	347-2952
TF: 866-350-4543 ■ *Web:* www.mamotorworks.com					
Midwest Action Cycle Inc 251 Host Dr	Lake Geneva	WI	53147	262-249-0600	249-0608
TF: 800-323-0078 ■ *Web:* www.midwestactioncycle.com					
Midwest Truck & Auto Parts 1001 W Exchange	Chicago	IL	60609	312-225-1550	526-4885*
**Fax Area Code:* 800 ■ *TF:* 800-934-2727 ■ *Web:* www.midwesttruck.com					
Mighty Distributing System of America Inc					
650 Engineering Dr	Norcross	GA	30092	770-448-3900	446-8627
TF: 800-829-3900 ■ *Web:* www.mightyautoparts.com					
Mutual Wheel Co Inc 2345 4th Ave	Moline	IL	61265	309-757-1200	757-1241
Web: www.mutualwheel.com					
N.b.c. Truck Equipment Inc					
28130 Groesbeck Hwy	Roseville	MI	48066	586-774-4900	772-1280
TF: 800-778-8207 ■ *Web:* www.nbctruckequip.com					
National Automotive Parts Assn (NAPA)					
2999 Cir 75 Pkwy NW	Atlanta	GA	30339	770-956-2200	956-2212
Web: www.napaonline.com					
Northeast Battery & Alternator Inc					
240 Washington St	Auburn	MA	01501	508-832-2700	832-2706
TF: 800-441-8824 ■ *Web:* www.northeastbattery.com					

	City	State	Zip	Phone	Fax
Northern Factory Sales Inc PO Box 660	Willmar	MN	56201	320-235-2288	235-2297
TF: 800-328-8900 ■ *Web:* www.northernfactory.com					
O.E.M. Systems LLC PO Box 473	Okarche	OK	73762	405-263-7488	
Web: www.oemsystems.net					
PACCAR Parts 750 Houser Way N	Renton	WA	98055	425-254-4400	254-6200
TF: 800-477-0251 ■ *Web:* www.paccar.com					
PAM Div US Oil Co Inc 200 S Petro Ave	Sioux Falls	SD	57107	605-336-1788	339-9909
TF: 800-456-2660 ■ *Web:* www.pam-companies.com					
Parts Central Inc 3243 Whitfield St	Macon	GA	31204	478-745-0878	746-1177
TF: 800-226-9396 ■ *Web:* www.partscentral.net					
Parts Distribution Services Inc					
991 Governor Dr Suite 101	El Dorado Hills	CA	95762	916-939-6767	933-6005
Web: www.pdsi.net					
Pioneer Inc 5184 Pioneer Rd	Meridian	MS	39301	601-483-5211	821-2303*
**Fax Area Code:* 800 ■ *TF:* 800-647-6272 ■ *Web:* www.pioneerautoind.com					
Plaza Fleet Parts Inc 1520 S Broadway	Saint Louis	MO	63104	314-231-5047	231-5109
TF: 800-325-7618					
Quaker City Motor Parts Co 680 N Broad St	Middletown	DE	19709	302-378-9834	378-0726
TF: 800-538-6272 ■ *Web:* www.qcmponline.com					
Regional International Corp					
1007 Lehigh Stn Rd	Henrietta	NY	14467	585-359-2011	359-2418
TF: 800-836-0409 ■ *Web:* www.regionalinternational.com					
Replacement Parts Inc					
1901 E Roosevelt Rd	Little Rock	AR	72206	501-375-1215	374-7929*
**Fax:* Cust Svc ■ *TF:* 877-282-6591 ■					
Web: www.rpiintranet.com/intranet/creategrid.asp?mypage=RPIhome					
Ridge Co Inc 1535 S Main St	South Bend	IN	46613	574-234-3143	234-4227
TF: 800-348-2409 ■ *Web:* www.ridgeautoparts.com					
Rim & Wheel Service Inc 1014 Gest St	Cincinnati	OH	45203	513-721-6940	721-4160
TF: 800-783-6940 ■ *Web:* www.rimwheel.com					
Six Robblees' Inc					
11010 Tukwila International Blvd	Tukwila	WA	98168	206-767-7970	763-7416
TF: 800-275-7499 ■ *Web:* www.sixrobblees.com					
Six States Distributors Inc					
247 W 1700 S	Salt Lake City	UT	84115	801-488-4666	488-4676
TF Cust Svc: 800-453-5703 ■ *Web:* www.sixstates.com					
SKD Automotive Group					
1450 W Long Lake Rd Suite 210	Troy	MI	48098	248-267-9670	267-9686
Web: www.skdautomotive.com					
Tucker Rocky Distributing Inc					
4900 Alliance Gateway Fwy	Fort Worth	TX	76177	817-258-9000	258-9095*
**Fax:* Cust Svc ■ *TF:* 800-283-8787 ■ *Web:* www.tuckerrocky.com					
Twinco Romax 4635 Willow Dr	Medina	MN	55340	763-478-2360	478-3411
TF: 800-682-3800 ■ *Web:* www.twincoromax.com					
U S Auto Parts Network Inc 17150 S Margay Ave	Carson	CA	90746	310-735-0085	632-1681
NASDAQ: PRTS ■ *Web:* www.usautoparts.net					
UAP Inc 7025 Rue Ontario E	Montreal	QC	H1N2B3	514-256-5031	256-8469
Web: www.napacanada.com					
Vander Haag's Inc 3809 4th Ave W	Spencer	IA	51301	712-262-7000	262-7421
TF: 888-940-5030 ■ *Web:* www.vanderhaags.com					
W. W. Tire Service Inc 204 Main St PO Box 22	Bryant	SD	57221	605-628-2501	628-2018
Web: www.wwtireservice.com					
WAIglobal 411 Eagleview Blvd Suite 100	Exton	PA	19341	484-875-6600	948-6121*
**Fax Area Code:* 800 ■ *TF:* 800-877-3340 ■ *Web:* www.wai-wetherill.com					
Western Truck Parts & Equip Co					
3801 Airport Way S	Seattle	WA	98108	916-441-6151	444-9932
TF: 800-255-7383 ■ *Web:* www.wtpe.com					

62 AUTOMOTIVE SERVICES

SEE ALSO Gas Stations p. 1902

	City	State	Zip	Phone	Fax
Kele Inc PO Box 34817	Memphis	TN	38184	901-382-4300	592-5756
Web: www.kele.com					

62-1 Appearance Care - Automotive

	City	State	Zip	Phone	Fax
American Auto Wash Inc 512 E King Rd	Malvern	PA	19355	610-296-4126	296-2854
Autobell Car Wash Inc 1521 E 3rd St	Charlotte	NC	28204	704-527-9274	333-0526
TF: 800-582-8096 ■ *Web:* www.autobell.com					
Blue Beacon International Inc 500 Graves Blvd	Salina	KS	67401	785-825-2221	825-0801
Web: www.bluebeacon.com					
Carnett's Car Washes					
631 Indian Trail Lilburn Rd NW	Lilburn	GA	30047	770-381-6900	717-5860
Web: www.carnetts.com					
Clean Machine Car Care Center Inc					
1181 Worcester Rd	Framingham	MA	01701	508-872-5830	
Color-Glo International 7111 Ohms Ln	Minneapolis	MN	55439	952-835-1338	835-1395
TF: 800-328-6347 ■ *Web:* www.colorglo.com					
Creative Colors International Inc					
19015 S Jodi Rd Suite E	Mokena	IL	60448	708-478-1437	478-1636
TF: 800-933-2656 ■ *Web:* www.creativecolorsintl.com					
Don's Car Washes Inc 1802 Main Ave Suite A	Fargo	ND	58103	701-237-0133	237-9552
Dr Vinyl & Assoc Ltd					
201 NW Victoria Dr	Lee's Summit	MO	64086	816-525-6060	525-6333
TF: 800-531-6600 ■ *Web:* www.drvinyl.com					
Flagstop Corp 11031 Ironbridge Rd	Chester	VA	23831	804-768-0090	768-0094
Web: www.flagstopcarwash.com					
Fleetwash Inc PO Box 1577	West Caldwell	NJ	07007	973-882-8314	882-0585
TF: 800-847-3735 ■ *Web:* www.fleetwash.com					
Hoffman Car Wash 1757 Central Ave	Albany	NY	12205	518-869-3218	869-3574
Web: www.hoffmancarwash.com					
Jax Car Wash Inc 28845 Telegraph Rd	Southfield	MI	48034	248-353-4700	353-8591
TF: 866-529-5273 ■ *Web:* www.jaxcarwash.net					
Kaady Car Washes 7400 SW Barbur Blvd	Portland	OR	97219	503-246-7735	245-0851
Web: www.kaady.com					

				Phone	Fax
Mike's Carwash Inc 10251 Hague Rd	Indianapolis	IN	46256	317-572-9250	572-9251
TF: 888-285-9274 ■ *Web:* www.mikescarwash.com					
Mister Car Wash 3561 E Sunrise Dr Suite 125	Tucson	AZ	85718	520-615-4000	615-4001
TF Cust Svc: 866-254-3229 ■ *Web:* www.mistercarwash.com					
Oasis Carwash LLC 3425 E Flamingo Rd	Las Vegas	NV	89121	702-433-3680	433-3682
Web: www.oasiscarwash.com					
Precision Auto Care Inc 748 Miller Dr SE	Leesburg	VA	20175	703-777-9095	771-7108
TF: 800-438-8863 ■ *Web:* www.precisiontune.com					
ScrubaDub Auto Wash Centers Inc					
172 Worcester Rd	Natick	MA	01760	508-650-1155	655-9261
Web: www.scrubadub.com					
Simoniz Car Wash 435 Eastern Ave	Malden	MA	02148	781-321-1900	339-2760*
**Fax Area Code:* 800 ■ *Web:* www.washdepot.com					
Triangle Car Wash Inc 973 E Main St	Palmyra	PA	17078	717-838-7130	838-7131
TF: 800-331-9274 ■ *Web:* www.trianglecarwashes.com					
Vizzawash Inc 2208 NW Loop 410	San Antonio	TX	78230	210-493-8822	493-7835
TF Cust Svc: 866-493-8822 ■ *Web:* www.washtub.net					
Wash Depot Holdings Inc 14 Summer St	Malden	MA	02148	781-324-2000	321-5483
TF: 800-339-3949 ■ *Web:* www.washdepot.com					
Wonder Wash/Wonder Lube Management Inc					
1601 Caledonia St Suite 1	La Crosse	WI	54603	608-783-5525	783-5709
TF: 800-261-9274 ■ *Web:* www.wonderwash-wonderlube.com					
Ziebart International Corp 1290 E Maple Rd	Troy	MI	48083	248-588-4100	588-2513*
**Fax:* Orders ■ *TF:* 800-877-1312 ■ *Web:* www.ziebart.com					

62-2 Glass Replacement - Automotive

				Phone	Fax
ABRA Auto Body & Glass					
6601 Shingle Creek Pkwy Suite 200	Brooklyn Center	MN	55430	763-561-7220	585-6455*
**Fax:* Hum Res ■ *TF:* 888-872-2272 ■ *Web:* www.abraauto.com					
All Star Glass Co Inc 1845 Morena Blvd	San Diego	CA	92110	619-275-3343	275-1546
TF: 800-225-4185 ■ *Web:* www.allstarglass.net					
Auto Glass National 1537 W Alameda	Denver	CO	80223	303-722-9200	722-9900
TF: 800-388-0104					
Auto Glass Specialists IncSafelight Auto Glass					
2400 Farmers Dr 2nd Fl	Columbus	OH	43235	614-210-9000	
TF: 800-558-1000					
Cindy Rowe Auto Glass 4750 Lindle Rd	Harrisburg	PA	17111	717-939-7551	939-8617
TF Cust Svc: 800-882-4639 ■ *Web:* www.cindyrowe.com					
City Auto Glass Inc					
116 S Concord Exchange	South Saint Paul	MN	55075	651-552-1000	552-1080
TF: 888-552-4272 ■ *Web:* www.cityautoglass.com					
Ding Doctor Windshield Repair PO Box 855	La Vernia	TX	78121	210-225-3464	
Glass Specialty System Inc					
1712 E Hamilton Rd Suite E	Bloomington	IL	61704	309-664-1087	662-1246
TF: 800-500-0500 ■ *Web:* www.glassspecialty.com					
Guardian Glass Co 23919 Fwy Pk Dr	Farmington Hills	MI	48335	248-471-0180	471-7247
TF: 800-621-8682 ■ *Web:* www.guardianautoglass.com					
Martin Glass Co 25 Ctr Plaza	Belleville	IL	62220	618-277-1946	551-4592*
**Fax Area Code:* 800 ■ *TF:* 800-325-1946 ■ *Web:* www.martinglass.net					
NOVUS Auto Glass					
Eagle Creek Commerce Ctr 12800 Hwy 13 S					
Suite 500	Minneapolis	MN	55378	952-944-8000	944-2542
TF: 800-328-1137 ■ *Web:* www.novusglass.com					
Royal Glass Co 9241 Hampton Overlook	Capital Heights	MD	20743	301-808-2855	333-6570
TF: 800-509-4495 ■ *Web:* www.royalglass.com					
Safelite Group Inc 2400 Farmers Dr	Columbus	OH	43235	614-210-9465	210-9451
TF: 800-835-2257 ■ *Web:* www.safelite.com					
Speedy Auto & Glass Inc					
9675 SE 36th St	Mercer Island	WA	98040	206-275-0514	
SuperGlass Windshield Repair Inc					
6101 Chancellor Dr Suite 200	Orlando	FL	32809	407-240-1920	240-3266
TF: 866-557-7497 ■ *Web:* www.superglass.com					
Synergistic International Inc					
1020 N University Parks Dr	Waco	TX	76707	877-838-4527	745-5073*
**Fax Area Code:* 254 ■ *TF:* 877-838-4527 ■ *Web:* www.glassdoctor.com					

62-3 Mufflers & Exhaust Systems Repair - Automotive

				Phone	Fax
Car-X Assoc Corp					
1375 E Woodfield Rd Suite 500	Schaumburg	IL	60173	847-273-8920	619-3310
TF: 800-359-2359 ■ *Web:* www.carx.com					
Midas Inc 1300 Arlington Heights Rd	Itasca	IL	60143	630-438-3004	438-3700
NYSE: MDS ■ *Web:* www.midasinc.com					
Midas International Corp					
1300 Arlington Heights Rd	Itasca	IL	60143	630-438-3000	438-3700
TF: 800-621-0144 ■ *Web:* www.midas.com					
Monro Muffler Brake Inc 200 Holleder Pkwy	Rochester	NY	14615	585-647-6400	647-0945
NASDAQ: MNRO ■ *TF:* 800-876-6676 ■ *Web:* www.monro.com					

62-4 Paint & Body Work - Automotive

				Phone	Fax
1-Day Paint & Body Centers Inc					
21801 S Western Ave	Torrance	CA	90501	310-328-0390	328-3995
TF: 800-448-1908 ■ *Web:* www.1daypaint.com					
Caliber Collision Centers					
17771 Cowan Ave Suite 100	Irvine	CA	92614	949-224-0300	224-0313
TF: 888-225-3237 ■ *Web:* www.calibercollision.com					
CARSTAR Quality Collision Service					
8400 W 110th St Suite 200	Overland Park	KS	66210	913-451-1294	451-4436
TF Cust Svc: 800-227-7827 ■ *Web:* www.carstar.com					
CK Technologies LLC 1701 Magda Dr	Montpelier	OH	43543	419-485-1110	485-1405
Web: www.cktech.biz					
Collex Collision Experts					
44700 Enterprise Dr	Clinton Township	MI	48038	586-954-3850	954-0912
TF: 888-426-5539 ■ *Web:* www.collex.com					
Colors on Parade 642 Century Cir	Conway	SC	29526	843-347-8818	347-0349
TF Cust Svc: 800-929-3363 ■ *Web:* www.colorsonparade.com					
Dent Clinic Canada Inc					
711 48th Ave SE Suite 6	Calgary	AB	T2G4X2	403-255-3111	258-3555
TF: 888-722-3368 ■ *Web:* www.dentclinic.com					
Dent Wizard International					
4710 Earth City Expwy	Bridgeton	MO	63044	314-592-1800	592-1951
TF: 800-267-9369 ■ *Web:* www.dentwizard.com					
Earl Scheib Inc					
15206 Ventura Blvd Suite 200	Sherman Oaks	CA	91403	818-981-9992	981-8863*
**Fax:* Sales ■ *TF:* 800-639-3275 ■ *Web:* www.earlscheib.com					
Fike Chevrolet Jeep 213 N Main St	Masontown	PA	15461	724-583-7738	583-8463
TF: 866-603-0617 ■ *Web:* www.fikechevrolet.com					
Gerber Auto Collision & Glass Centers Inc					
8250 Skokie Blvd	Skokie	IL	60077	847-679-0510	679-0549
TF: 800-479-1230 ■ *Web:* www.gerbercollision.com					
Holmes Body Shop Inc 1095 E Colorado Blvd	Pasadena	CA	91106	626-795-6447	795-2123
Web: www.holmesbodyshop.com					
MAACO LLC					
610 Freedom Business Ctr Suite 200	King of Prussia	PA	19406	610-265-6606	337-6113
TF: 800-523-1180 ■ *Web:* www.maaco.com					
Master Collision Group LLC 2980 Empire Ln	Plymouth	MN	55447	763-509-0900	509-9022
Web: www.mastercollisiongroup.com					
Mike Rose's Auto Body Inc					
2260 Via de Marcardos	Concord	CA	94520	925-689-1739	689-0991
Web: www.mautobody.com					
Miracle Auto Painting Inc 2343 Lincoln Ave	Hayward	CA	94545	510-887-2211	887-3092
New Kabi LLC 9350 SW Tigard St	Tigard	OR	97223	503-598-1159	968-8099*
**Fax Area Code:* 509 ■ *Web:* www.kadels.com					
Peach Auto Painting & Collision Inc					
506 Manchester Expwy Suite A-4	Columbus	GA	31904	706-324-0103	324-0105
Service King Collision Repair Centers					
808 S Central Expy	Richardson	TX	75080	972-960-7595	980-4266
Web: www.serviceking.com					

62-5 Repair Service (General) - Automotive

				Phone	Fax
All Tune & Lube Brakes & More Inc					
8334 Veteran's Hwy	Millersville	MD	21108	410-987-1011	987-9080
TF: 800-935-8863 ■ *Web:* www.alltuneandlube.com					
All Tune & Lube International Inc					
ATL International Inc 8334 Veterans Hwy	Millersville	MD	21108	410-987-1011	987-9080
TF Cust Svc: 800-935-8863 ■ *Web:* www.alltuneandlube.com					
Allied Tire & Service Inc 4857 Edgewater Dr	Orlando	FL	32804	407-290-3389	
Web: www.goodyear.com					
Basin Tire & Auto Inc 2700 E Main St	Farmington	NM	87402	505-326-2231	325-9105
TF: 800-589-2414					
Bauer Radiator Inc 3805 Walden Ave	Lancaster	NY	14086	716-685-4625	685-1863
TF: 800-462-1837					
Belle Tire Inc 1000 Enterprise Dr	Allen Park	MI	48101	313-271-9400	271-6793
TF: 888-462-3553 ■ *Web:* www.belletire.com					
Bergey's Inc 462 Harleysville Pike	Souderton	PA	18964	215-723-6071	721-3479
TF: 800-237-4397 ■ *Web:* www.bergeys.com					
Big 10 Tire Co Inc					
3938 Government Blvd Suite 102	Mobile	AL	36693	251-666-9938	666-9431
Web: www.big10tires.com					
Big O Tires Inc 823 Donalad Ross Rd	Florida	CA	33408	561-383-3000	
TF: 800-926-8473 ■ *Web:* www.bigotires.com					
Bob Sumerel Tires & Service Inc					
3646 E Broad St	Columbus	OH	43213	614-237-6325	237-6328
TF: 800-858-0421 ■ *Web:* www.bobsumereltire.com					
Bridgestone Americas Holding Inc					
535 Marriott Dr	Nashville	TN	37214	615-937-5000	937-3621
TF Cust Svc: 800-543-7522 ■ *Web:* www.bridgestone-firestone.com					
Clark Tire & Auto Supply Co Inc 220 S Ctr St	Hickory	NC	28602	828-322-2303	327-2783
TF: 800-968-3092 ■ *Web:* www.clarktire.com					
Cross-Midwest Tire Inc 3570 Gardener Ave	Kansas City	MO	64120	816-231-6511	231-6393
Web: www.crossmidwest.com					
Divine Corp 203 W 3rd Ave	Spokane	WA	99201	509-455-8622	455-4327
Econo Lube N' Tune Inc PO Box 2470	Newport Beach	CA	92658	949-851-2259	851-2259
TF: 800-478-3795					
Evans Tire & Service Centers Inc					
510 N Broadway	Escondido	CA	92025	760-746-0594	480-1089
TF: 877-338-2678 ■ *Web:* www.evanstire.com					
Express Oil Change 1880 S Pk Dr	Hoover	AL	35244	205-945-1771	940-6025
TF: 888-945-1771 ■ *Web:* www.expressoil.com					
Express Tire 1148 Industrial Ave	Escondido	CA	92029	760-741-4044	741-5667
Web: www.expresstire.com					
Fyda Freightliner Youngstown Inc					
5260 76th Dr	Youngstown	OH	44515	330-797-0224	797-0230
TF: 800-837-3932 ■ *Web:* www.fydafreightliner.com					
Grease Monkey International Inc					
7100 E Belleview Ave Suite 305	Greenwood Village	CO	80111	303-308-1660	308-5908
TF: 800-822-7706 ■ *Web:* www.greasemonkeyintl.com					
Hart & Vogt Inc 5624 Airport Fwy	Fort Worth	TX	76117	817-831-4222	831-8234
Web: www.vogtrv.com					
Hunter Engineering Co 11250 Hunter Dr	Bridgeton	MO	63044	314-731-3020	731-1776
TF: 800-448-6848 ■ *Web:* www.hunter.com					
Jack Williams Tire Co Inc PO Box 3655	Scranton	PA	18505	570-457-5000	457-2852
TF: 800-833-5051 ■ *Web:* www.jackwilliams.com					
Jensen Tire & Auto 10609 I St	Omaha	NE	68127	402-339-2917	339-8815
Web: www.jensentireandauto.com					
Jiffy Lube PO Box 4427	Houston	TX	77210	713-546-4000	
TF: 800-344-6933 ■ *Web:* www.jiffylube.com					

Phone Fax

Jubitz Corp 33 NE Middlefield Rd .... Portland OR 97211 503-283-1111 240-5834
TF: 800-399-5480 ■ *Web:* www.jubitz.com
Kansas City Peterbilt Inc
8915 Woodend Rd .... Kansas City KS 66111 913-441-2888 422-5029
TF: 800-489-1122 ■ *Web:* www.kcpete.com
Kolstad Co Inc 8501 Naples St NE .... Blaine MN 55449 763-792-1033 792-3799
Lamb Ventures LP 11675 Jollyville Rd .... Austin TX 78759 512-257-2350 257-1895
TF: 800-325-5262 ■ *Web:* www.lambstire.com
Les Schwab Tire Centers Inc
646 NW Madras Hwy PO Box 667 .... Prineville OR 97754 541-447-4136 416-5157*
*Fax: Cust Svc ■ *Web:* www.lesschwab.com
Lucor Inc 790 Pershing Rd .... Raleigh NC 27608 919-828-9511 828-2433
TF Cust Svc: 800-345-8237 ■ *Web:* www.jiffylube-lucor.com
McGriff Transportation Inc
563 County Rd PO Box 1148 .... Cullman AL 35056 256-737-9035 737-1813
TF: 800-950-0780 ■ *Web:* www.mcgriffindustries.com
Meineke Car Care Centers
128 S Tryon St Suite 900 .... Charlotte NC 28202 704-377-8855 377-1490
TF: 800-275-5200
Merchant's Tire & Auto Centers
823 Donald Ross Rd .... Juno Beach FL 33408 561-842-4290 368-1658*
*Fax Area Code: 703 ■ *TF:* 800-368-3130 ■ *Web:* www.merchantstire.com
Merlin Corp 1 N River Ln Suite 206 .... Geneva IL 60134 630-208-9900 208-8601
TF: 800-637-5467 ■ *Web:* www.merlins.com
Mr Tire Auto Service Centers Inc
200 Holleder Pkwy .... Rochester NY 14615 800-876-6676 647-0945*
*Fax Area Code: 585 ■ *TF:* 800-876-6676 ■ *Web:* www.mrtire.com
National Tire & Battery (NTB)
823 Donald Ross Rd .... Juno Beach FL 33408 561-842-4290
Web: www.ntb.com
Oil Butler International Corp 1599 Rt 22 .... Union NJ 07083 908-687-3283 687-7617
Web: www.oilbutlercorp.com
Parrish Tire Co Inc 5130 Indiana Ave .... Winston-Salem NC 27106 336-767-0202 744-2716
TF: 800-849-8473 ■ *Web:* www.parrishtire.com
Payne Trucking Co
10411 Hall Industrial Dr .... Fredericksburg VA 22408 540-286-2308
Web: www.paynetrucking.com
Perry Bros Tire Service Inc 610 Wicker St .... Sanford NC 27330 919-775-7225 774-4853
Web: www.perrybros.com
Plaza Tire Service
2075 Corporate Cr PO Box 2048 .... Cape Girardeau MO 63702 573-334-5036 334-0322
TF: 800-334-5036 ■ *Web:* www.plazatireservice.com
Precision Auto Care Inc 748 Miller Dr SE .... Leesburg VA 20175 703-777-9095 771-7108
TF: 800-438-8863 ■ *Web:* www.precisiontune.com
Somerset Tire Services Inc PO Box 5936 .... brirdgewater NJ 08807 732-356-8500 356-8821
TF: 800-445-1434 ■ *Web:* www.ststire.com
Sullivan Tire Co Inc 41 Accord Pk Dr .... Norwell MA 02061 781-982-1550 871-6250
TF: 800-892-1955 ■ *Web:* www.sullivantire.com
Sun Devil Auto Inc 1830 E Elliott Rd Suite 104 .... Tempe AZ 85284 480-491-4210 491-4204
Web: www.sundevilauto.com
Techni-Car Inc 450 Commerce Blvd .... Oldsmar FL 34677 813-855-0022 855-2101
TF: 800-886-0022 ■ *Web:* www.techni-car.com
Ted Wiens Tire & Auto Centers Inc
1701 Las Vegas Blvd S .... Las Vegas NV 89104 702-732-2382 735-4061
Web: www.tedwiens.com
Tire Kingdom Inc 823 Donald Ross Rd .... Juno Beach FL 33408 561-842-4290 842-6314
Web: www.tirekingdom.com
Tire-Rama Inc
1401 Industrial Ave PO Box 23509 .... Billings MT 59104 406-245-4006 245-0257
TF: 800-828-1642 ■ *Web:* www.tirerama.com
Tires Plus Total Car Care
2021 Sunnydale Blvd .... Clearwater FL 33765 727-441-3727 443-2401
TF: 800-269-4424 ■ *Web:* www.tiresplus.com
Tom Stinnett Rv's 520 Marriott Dr .... Clarksville IN 47129 812-282-7718 285-7578
Web: www.stinnettrv.com
Transtek Inc 4303 Lewis Rd PO Box 4174 .... Harrisburg PA 17111 717-564-6151 564-1118
TF Cust Svc: 800-871-1935 ■ *Web:* www.pennfreightliner.com
Tri-State Trailer Sales Inc PO Box 9322 .... Pittsburgh PA 15225 412-747-7777 777-4010
Web: www.tristatetrailer.com
Tuffy Assoc Corp 7150 Granite Cir .... Toledo OH 43617 419-865-6900 865-7343
TF: 800-228-8339 ■ *Web:* www.tuffy.com
VIP Parts Tires & Service 12 Lexington St .... Lewiston ME 04240 207-784-5423 784-9178
Web: www.vipauto.com
Warren Tire Service Center Inc
4 Highland Ave Suite 3 .... Queensbury NY 12804 518-792-0316 792-8982
Wingfoot Commercial Tire Systems LLC
1000 S 21st St .... Fort Smith AR 72901 479-788-6400 788-6486
TF: 800-643-7330 ■ *Web:* www.wingfootct.com
Ziegler Tire & Supply Co Inc
4150 Millennium Blvd SE .... Massillon OH 44646 330-834-3332 834-3342
Web: www.zieglertyre.com

62-6 Transmission Repair - Automotive

Phone Fax

AAMCO Transmissions Inc
1 Presidential Blvd .... Bala Cynwyd PA 19004 610-668-2900 664-1226
TF Cust Svc: 800-523-0401 ■ *Web:* www.aamcotransmissions.com
All Tune Transmissions
8334 Veteran's Hwy .... Millersville MD 21108 410-987-1011 987-9080
TF: 800-935-8863 ■ *Web:* www.alltuneandlube.com
Certified Transmission Rebuilders Inc
1801 S 54th St .... Omaha NE 68106 402-558-2117 558-2202
TF: 800-554-7520 ■ *Web:* www.certifiedtransmission.com
Cottman Transmission Systems LLC
201 Gibraltar Rd Suite 150 .... Horsham PA 19044 215-643-5885 643-2519
TF: 800-394-6116 ■ *Web:* www.cottman.com
Lee Myles Auto Group 847 Fern Ave .... Reading PA 19607 201-262-0555 262-5177
TF: 800-533-6953 ■ *Web:* www.leemyles.com
Mr Transmission 9675 Yonge St 2nd Fl .... Richmond Hill ON L4C1V7 905-884-1511 884-4727
TF: 800-373-8432 ■ *Web:* www.mistertransmission.com

62-7 Van Conversions

Phone Fax

Clock Mobility 6700 Clay Ave .... Grand Rapids MI 49548 616-698-9400 698-9495
TF: 800-732-5625 ■ *Web:* www.clockmobility.com
Foley Inc 855 Centennial Ave .... Piscataway NJ 08854 732-885-5555 885-6612
TF: 888-417-6464 ■ *Web:* www.foleyinc.com
Marathon Coach 91333 Coburg Industrial Way .... Coburg OR 97408 541-343-9991 343-2401
TF: 800-234-9991 ■ *Web:* www.marathoncoach.com
Monaco Coach Corp 91320 Coburg Industrial Way .... Coburg OR 97408 541-686-8011 681-8037*
*Fax: Hum Res ■ *TF:* 800-634-0855 ■ *Web:* www.monaco-online.com
Overland Inc 1450 Laurens Rd .... Greenville SC 29607 864-232-7493 232-3380
Web: www.landrovercarolinas.com
Rollx Vans 6591 Hwy 13 W .... Savage MN 55378 952-890-7851 890-1903
TF: 800-956-6668 ■ *Web:* www.rollxvans.com
Sherrod Vans Inc 3151 Industrial Blvd .... Wayross GA 31503 912-490-1210 490-1212
TF: 800-824-6333 ■ *Web:* www.sherrodvans.com
Sidewinder Conversions 44658 Yale Rd W .... Chilliwack BC V2R0G5 604-792-2082 792-8920
TF: 888-266-2299 ■ *Web:* www.sidewinder-conversions.com
Unique Conversions Inc 1502 Hwy 157 N # D .... Mansfield TX 76063 817-477-5251 477-2711
Van Conversions Inc 925 S Trooper Rd .... Norristown PA 19403 610-666-9100 666-9102
TF Cust Svc: 800-884-8267 ■ *Web:* www.vanconinc.com
Vantage Mobility International (VMI)
5202 S 28th Pl .... Phoenix AZ 85040 602-243-2700 304-3290
TF: 800-348-8267 ■ *Web:* www.vantagemobility.com
Waldoch Crafts Inc 13821 Lake Dr NE .... Forest Lake MN 55025 651-464-3215 464-1117
Web: www.waldoch.com

63 AVIATION - FIXED-BASE OPERATIONS

SEE ALSO Air Cargo Carriers p. 1381; Air Charter Services p. 1381; Aircraft Rental p. 1388; Aircraft Service & Repair p. 1388

Phone Fax

A & M Aviation Inc
130 S Clow International Pkwy Suite B .... Bolingbrook IL 60490 630-759-1555 759-2281
Web: www.aandmaviation.com
Abilene Aero 2850 Airport Blvd .... Abilene TX 79602 325-677-2601 671-8018
Web: www.abileneaero.com
ACM Aviation Inc 1475 Airport Blvd .... San Jose CA 95110 408-286-3832 286-1629
TF: 800-359-7538 ■ *Web:* www.acmaviation.com
Aero Industries Inc
5690 Clarkson Rd
Richmond International Airport .... Richmond VA 23250 804-222-7211 236-1670
TF: 800-845-1308 ■ *Web:* www.aeroind.com
Aerodynamics Inc 6544 Highland Rd .... Waterford MI 48327 248-666-3500 666-9041
TF: 800-235-9234 ■ *Web:* www.flyadi.com
Air America Fuel & Service Inc
Grant County International Airport
7810 Andrews St NE Suite 134 .... Moses Lake WA 98837 509-762-2626 762-2299
Aircraft Specialists Inc
6005 Propeller Ln .... Sellersburg IN 47172 812-246-4696 246-4365
Web: www.800projets.com
Aire Shannon Inc
3380 Shannon Airport Cir .... Fredericksburg VA 22408 540-373-4431 373-0035
American Aviation 2495 Broad St .... Brooksville FL 34604 352-796-5173 799-4681
Web: www.americanaviation.com
Anniston Aviation
Anniston Metropolitan Airport PO Box 2185 .... Anniston AL 36202 256-831-4410 831-4411
Arcadia Aviation 170 Aviation Way .... Martinsburg WV 25405 304-262-9633 262-4715
TF: 800-550-2507 ■ *Web:* www.arcadiaaviation.com
Arlins Aircraft Service Inc
36 Gallatin Field .... Belgrade MT 59714 406-388-1351 388-7417
Web: www.arlins.com
Atlantic Aviation
10510 Superfortress Ave
Sacramento Mather Airport .... Mather CA 95655 916-368-1455 368-5770
TF: 800-565-2647 ■ *Web:* www.atlanticaviation.com
Atlantic Aviation 17725 John F Kennedy Blvd .... Houston TX 77032 281-443-3434 821-9149
Web: www.atlanticaviation.com
Atlantic Aviation Services
19711 Campus Dr
Suite 100 John Wayne Airport .... Santa Ana CA 92707 949-851-5061 851-1450
TF: 800-500-5061 ■ *Web:* www.atlanticaviation.com
Aurora Aviation 22785 Airport Rd NE .... Aurora OR 97002 503-678-1217 678-1219
Web: www.auroraaviation.com
Banyan Air Service 5360 NW 20th Terr .... Fort Lauderdale FL 33309 954-491-3170 771-0281
TF: 800-200-2031 ■ *Web:* www.banyanair.com
Basler Flight Service
Wittman Regional Airport PO Box 2464 .... Oshkosh WI 54903 920-236-7827 236-7833
Web: www.baslerflightservice.com
BMG Aviation Inc 984 S Kirby Rd .... Bloomington IN 47403 812-825-7979 825-7978
TF: 888-457-3787 ■ *Web:* www.bmgaviation.com
Boca Aviation 3700 Airport Rd .... Boca Raton FL 33431 561-368-1110 392-7113
TF: 800-335-2622 ■ *Web:* www.bocaaviation.com
Central Flying Service Inc 1501 Bond St .... Little Rock AR 72202 501-375-3245 375-7274
TF: 800-888-5387 ■ *Web:* www.flycfs.com
Channel Islands Aviation
305 Durley Ave Camarillo Airport .... Camarillo CA 93010 805-987-1301 987-8301
Web: www.flycia.com
Co-Mar Aviation
1065 Ashley St Suite 100 .... Bowling Green KY 42103 270-783-8080 781-4792
Web: www.comaraviation.com
Colonial Air 1605 Airport Rd .... New Bedford MA 02746 508-997-0620 990-2582
Web: www.colonial-air.com
Columbia Air Services
175 Tower Ave Groton-New London Airport .... Groton CT 06340 860-449-1400 405-7269
TF: 800-787-5001 ■ *Web:* www.columbiaairservices.com

			Phone	Fax
Cook Aviation Inc 970 S Kirby Rd . . . . Bloomington *TF:* 800-880-3499 ■ *Web:* www.cookaviation.com	IN	47403	812-825-2392	825-3701
Corporate Air LLC 15 Allegheny County Airport. . . . . .West Mifflin *TF:* 888-429-5377 ■ *Web:* www.travelredefined.com	PA	15122	412-469-6800	466-1162
Corporate Wings 355 Richmond Rd . . . . Cleveland *TF:* 800-261-1115 ■ *Web:* www.corporatewings.com	OH	44143	216-261-1111	261-4260
Crow Executive Air Inc 28331 Lemoyne Rd Toledo Metcalf Airport. . . . . Millbury *TF:* 800-972-2769 ■ *Web:* www.crowair.com	OH	43447	419-838-6921	838-6911
Dassault Falcon 151 N Dupont Hwy Suite 11 New Castle Airport-Ilg . . . . New Castle *TF:* 800-441-9390 ■ *Web:* www.atlanticaviation.com	DE	19720	302-322-7000	322-7331
DB Aviation Inc 3550 N McAree Rd . . . . Waukegan *TF:* 800-638-4990 ■ *Web:* www.dbaviation.com	IL	60087	847-263-5600	263-6486
Deer Horn Aviation Ltd Co PO Box 60248 . . . . .Midland *TF:* 800-759-3359 ■ *Web:* www.avionflight.net	TX	79711	432-563-2033	563-5344
Dodgen Aircraft 740 Grand St. . . . . Allegan *Web:* www.dodgenaircraft.com	MI	49010	269-673-4157	673-4157
Dolphin Aviation Inc 8191 N Tamiami Tr Sarasota Bradenton International Airport . . . . Sarasota **Fax:* Cust Svc ■ *Web:* www.dolphinaviation.com	FL	34243	941-355-7715	351-7197*
Dulles Aviation Inc 10501 Observation Rd Manassas Regional Airport. . . . . Manassas *TF:* 888-835-9324 ■ *Web:* www.dullesaviation.com	VA	20110	703-361-2171	361-4478
Dunkirk Aviation Sales & Service Inc 3389 Middle Rd . . . . Dunkirk *Web:* www.dkk.com	NY	14048	716-366-6938	366-6986
Dyersburg Avionics of Caruthersville 2204 Airport Dr. . . . . Caruthersville *Web:* www.dyersburgavionics.com	MO	63830	573-333-4296	333-0674
Eagle Aviation 2861 Aviation Way Columbia Metropolitan Airport . . . . West Columbia *TF:* 800-848-6359 ■ *Web:* www.eagle-aviation.com	SC	29170	803-822-5555	822-5529
Edwards Jet Ctr 1691 Aviation Pl . . . . Billings *TF:* 800-755-9624 ■ *Web:* www.edwardsjetcenter.com	MT	59105	406-252-0508	245-9491
Encore FBO Sioux Falls 3501 Aviation Ave . . . . Sioux Falls *TF:* 800-888-1646 ■ *Web:* www.landmarkaviation.com	SD	57104	605-336-7791	336-8009
Epps Aviation Inc 1 Aviation Way DeKalb Peachtree Airport . . . . .Atlanta *TF:* 800-241-6807 ■ *Web:* www.eppsaviation.com	GA	30341	770-458-9851	458-0320
Executive Air 2131 Airport Dr Austin Straubel International Airport. . . . . Green Bay *Web:* www.executiveair.com	WI	54313	920-498-4880	498-4890
Felts Field Aviation Inc 5829 E Rutter Ave . . . . Spokane *TF:* 800-676-5538 ■ *Web:* www.feltsfield.com	WA	99212	509-535-9011	535-9014
Flightcraft Inc 90454 Boeing Dr. . . . . Eugene *TF:* 800-776-6312 ■ *Web:* www.flightcraft.com	OR	97402	541-688-9291	688-5749
Flightline Group Inc 3256 Capital Cir SW . . . . Tallahassee *Web:* www.flightlinegroup.com	FL	32310	850-574-4444	576-4210
Flightline of Dothan Inc 751 Flightline Dr . . . . .Dothan *TF:* 866-466-5903 ■ *Web:* www.flightlineofdothan.com	AL	36303	334-983-5555	983-6666
Galvin Flying Services 7149 Perimeter Rd . . . . Seattle *TF:* 800-341-4102 ■ *Web:* www.galvinflying.com	WA	98108	206-763-0350	767-9333
Gibbs Flying Service 8906 Aero Dr . . . . San Diego *Web:* gibbsflyingservice.com	CA	92123	858-277-0162	277-0854
Grand Aire Express Inc 11777 W Airport Service Rd . . . . Swanton *TF:* 800-704-7263 ■ *Web:* www.grandaire.com	OH	43558	419-865-1780	865-2965
Grand Strand Aviation 2800 Terminal St. . . . . North Myrtle Beach *TF:* 800-433-8918 ■ *Web:* www.ramp66.com	SC	29582	843-272-5337	272-5822
Hardesty Co Inc 4141 N Memorial Dr. Tulsa *TF:* 800-897-5387 ■ *Web:* www.unitedstatesaviation.com	OK	74115	918-585-3100	836-7804
Holman Aviation Co 1940 Airport Ct . . . . .Great Falls *TF:* 800-843-7613 ■ *Web:* www.holmanaviation.com	MT	59404	406-453-7613	453-7204
Hunt Pan Am Aviation Inc 505 Amelia Earhart Dr. . . . . Brownsville *TF:* 800-888-7524 ■ *Web:* www.huntpanam.com	TX	78521	956-542-9111	542-9133
Inter-State Aviation 4800 Airport Complex N Airport Rd . . . . .Pullman	WA	99163	509-332-6596	334-1751
Interstate Aviation 62 Johnson Ave. . . . . Plainville *TF:* 800-573-5519 ■ *Web:* www.interstateaviation.com	CT	06062	860-747-5519	589-1853
Jet Harbor Inc 1475 Airport Rd . . . . Gallatin *Web:* www.jetharbor.com	TN	37066	615-452-6699	230-0414
Kansas City Aviation Center Inc 15325 S Pflumm Rd. . . . . Olathe *TF:* 800-720-5222 ■ *Web:* www.kcac.com	KS	66062	913-782-0530	782-9462
Keystone Aviation Services Inc 288 Christian St . . . . .Oxford *TF:* 866-436-2177	CT	06478	203-264-6525	264-0295
Landmark Aviation 4360 Agar Dr . . . . Richmond *TF:* 888-298-7326 ■ *Web:* www.fbovancouver.com	BC	V7B1A3	604-279-9922	279-9942
Landmark Aviation 1500 CityWest Blvd Suite 600 . . . . .Houston *Web:* www.landmarkaviation.com	TX	77042	713-895-9243	690-9553
Lane Aviation Corp 4389 International Gateway. . . . . Columbus **Fax:* Cust Svc ■ *TF:* 800-848-6263 ■ *Web:* www.laneaviation.com	OH	43219	614-237-3747	237-2048*
Leading Edge Aviation Service Inc 6582 Eureka Springs Rd . . . . Tampa *Web:* www.leadingedgeaviation.com	FL	33610	813-626-1515	623-6483
Loyd's Aviation Services Inc 1601 Skyway Dr Suite 100 PO Box 80958 . . . . .Bakersfield *TF:* 800-284-1334 ■ *Web:* www.bakersfieldjetcenter.com	CA	93308	661-393-1334	393-0824
M7 Aerospace LP 10823 NE Entrance Rd. . . . . .San Antonio **Fax:* Hum Res ■ *TF:* 800-327-2313 ■ *Web:* www.m7aerospace.com	TX	78216	210-824-9421	824-9476*
Maine Instrument Flight 215 Winthrop St . . . . .Augusta *TF:* 888-643-3597 ■ *Web:* www.mif.aero	ME	04330	207-622-1211	622-7858
Malloy Air East Inc Gabreski Airport . . . . WestHampton Beach *TF:* 888-673-9888 ■ *Web:* www.malloyaireast.com	NY	11978	631-288-5410	288-1470
McCall Aviation 300 Deinhard Ln. . . . . .McCall *TF:* 800-992-6559 ■ *Web:* www.mccallaviation.com	ID	83638	208-634-7137	634-3917
Miami Executive Aviation Inc 15001 NW 42 Ave . . . . Miami *TF:* 800-861-1343 ■ *Web:* www.miamiexecutive.com	FL	33054	305-687-8410	769-5815
Mid-Ohio Aviation 6250 N Honeytown Rd . . . . Smithville *TF:* 800-669-4243 ■ *Web:* www.midohioaviation.com	OH	44677	330-669-2671	669-2402
Midwest Corporate Aviation 3512 N Webb Rd . . . . Wichita *TF:* 800-435-9622 ■ *Web:* www.midwestaviation.com	KS	67226	316-636-9700	636-9747
Millenium Aviation 2365 Bernville Rd Reading Regional Airport. . . . . .Reading *TF:* 800-366-9419 ■ *Web:* www.majets.com	PA	19605	610-374-0100	374-7580
Million Air 4300 Westgrove Dr. . . . . .Addison *TF:* 800-248-1602 ■ *Web:* www.millionair.com	TX	75001	972-248-1600	733-5803
Minuteman Aviation Inc 5225 W Broadway St # 16 . . . . .Missoula *Web:* www.minutemanaviation.com	MT	59808	406-728-9363	728-6981
Miracle Strip Aviation - Avitat Destin 1001 Airport Rd . . . . Destin *Web:* www.avitat.com	FL	32541	850-837-6135	654-0618
Mobile Air Ctr 8400 Airport Blvd. . . . . .Mobile *TF:* 800-566-9411 ■ *Web:* www.mobileaircenter.com	AL	36608	251-633-5000	633-2225
Monroe Air Ctr 5410 Operations Rd . . . . Monroe *TF:* 800-223-3895 ■ *Web:* www.monroeair.com	LA	71203	318-387-0222	325-1538
Monroeville Aviation PO Box 189. . . . . .Monroeville	AL	36460	251-575-4235	575-1907
Monterey Bay Aviation 514 Airport Way . . . . Monterey *TF:* 866-930-6226 ■ *Web:* www.montereybayaviation.com	CA	93940	831-373-3201	373-2352
Montgomery Aviation Corp 4525 Selma Hwy. . . . . . . Montgomery *TF:* 800-392-8044 ■ *Web:* www.montgomeryaviation.com	AL	36108	334-288-7334	288-7337
National Jets Air Ctr 3495 SW 9th Ave . . . . .Fort Lauderdale *TF:* 800-525-0166 ■ *Web:* www.nationaljets.com/natjet/jet/index.html	FL	33315	954-359-9400	359-0064
Newton Aviation *Lewistown Airport* 410 Skyline Dr . . . . Lewistown *Web:* www.lewistownairport.com	MT	59457	406-538-8150	538-8166
North Coast Air 1601 Asbury Rd. . . . . Erie *Web:* www.ncair.com	PA	16505	814-836-9220	836-9901
Northeast Airmotive Inc 1011 Westbrook St. . . . . .Portland *TF:* 877-354-7881 ■ *Web:* www.northeastair.com	ME	04102	207-774-6318	874-4714
Northside Aviation Inc 1723 McCollum PkwyNW. . . . . . Kennesaw *TF:* 800-754-4300 ■ *Web:* www.atlantanorthsideaviation.com	GA	30144	770-422-4300	422-4382
Ocean Aire PO Box 1245 . . . . .Toms River *Web:* www.oceanaire.net	NJ	08754	732-797-1077	797-1076
Panorama Flight Service Inc 67 Tower Rd. . . . . White Plains *TF:* 888-359-7266 ■ *Web:* www.flypfs.com	NY	10604	914-328-9800	328-9684
Paul Fournet Air Service Inc 118 John Glen Dr Lafayette Regional Airport. . . . . Lafayette *Web:* www.fournet.com	LA	70508	337-237-0520	232-1188
Pelican Aviation 1314 Hangar Dr. . . . . .New Iberia	LA	70560	337-367-1401	
Pensacola Aviation Center Inc 4145 Jerry L Maygarden Rd . . . . Pensacola *TF:* 800-874-6580 ■ *Web:* www.pensacolaaviation.com	FL	32504	850-434-0636	434-3984
Personal Jet Charter Inc 5401 E Perimeter Rd. . . . . .Fort Lauderdale *TF:* 800-432-1538 ■ *Web:* www.personaljet.com	FL	33309	954-776-4515	491-5771
Phoenix Aviation Inc 701 Wilson Pt Rd PO Box 37 . . . . Middle River *Web:* www.phoenixaviation.com	MD	21220	410-574-3897	574-3810
Premier Jet Ctr 3301 NE Cornell Rd # A. . . . . Hillsboro *Web:* www.premierjetcenter.com	OR	97124	503-693-1096	640-0167
Prior Aviation Service Inc 50 N Airport Dr. . . . . .Buffalo *TF:* 800-621-2923 ■ *Web:* www.prioraviation.com	NY	14225	716-633-1000	633-1543
Private Sky Aviation Services Inc 1 Private Skyway. . . . . .Fort Myers *Web:* www.privatesky.net	FL	33913	239-225-6100	225-0798
PS Air Inc 3411 Beech Way SW . . . . .Cedar Rapids *Web:* www.psair.com	IA	52404	319-846-3600	846-3605
Regional Jet Ctr 12344 Tower Dr . . . . Bentonville *TF:* 866-962-3835	AR	72712	479-205-1100	205-1101
Richmor Aviation Inc 1142 Rt 9 H Columbia County Airport . . . . Hudson *TF:* 800-331-6101 ■ *Web:* www.richmor.com	NY	12534	518-828-9461	828-1303
Robinson Aviation 50 Thompson Ave. . . . . .East Haven *Web:* www.robinsonaviation.com	CT	06512	203-467-9555	467-6346
Ronson Aviation Inc Trenton Mercer Airport . . . . Trenton **Fax:* Cust Svc ■ *TF:* 800-257-0416 ■ *Web:* www.ronsonaviation.com	NJ	08628	609-771-9500	771-0885*
Saint Paul Flight Ctr 270 Airport Rd . . . . Saint Paul *TF:* 800-368-0107 ■ *Web:* www.stpaulflight.com	MN	55107	651-227-8108	227-6195
Sanford Aircraft Services Inc 701 Rod Sullivan Rd. . . . . Sanford *TF:* 888-871-1947 ■ *Web:* www.sanford-aircraft.com	NC	27330	919-708-5549	774-9627
Santa Fe Air Center Inc 121 Aviation Dr Bldg 3005 . . . . Santa Fe *TF:* 800-263-7695 ■ *Web:* www.santafejet.biz	NM	87507	505-471-2525	438-0671
Servicecenter Inc 7301 NW 50th St Wiley Post Airport. . . . . .Oklahoma City *TF:* 800-299-8546 ■ *Web:* www.thescinc.com	OK	73132	405-789-5000	789-5995
SheltAir Aviation Services Fort Lauderdale 4860 NE 12th Ave. . . . . .Fort Lauderdale *TF:* 800-700-2210 ■ *Web:* www.sheltairaviation.com	FL	33334	954-771-2210	771-3745
Showalter Flying Service 400 Herndon Ave PO Box 140753 . . . . Orlando *TF:* 800-894-7331 ■ *Web:* www.showalter.com	FL	32803	407-894-7331	894-5094
Signature Flight Support 201 S Orange Ave Suite 1100-S. . . . . Orlando **Fax:* Hum Res ■ *Web:* www.signatureflight.com	FL	32801	407-648-7200	206-8428*
Silverhawk Aviation Inc 1751 W Kearney Ave. . . . . Lincoln *TF:* 800-479-5851 ■ *Web:* www.silverhawkaviation.com	NE	68524	402-475-8600	475-1422

				Phone	Fax
Sky Bright 65 Aviation Dr	Gilford	NH	03249	603-528-6818	528-1814
TF: 800-639-6012 ■ *Web:* www.skybright.com					
Skyservice Airlines Inc 31 Fasken Dr	Etobicoke	ON	M9W1K6	416-679-5700	679-5703
TF: 800-701-9448 ■ *Web:* www.skyservicebas.com					
SkyTech Inc 550 Airport Rd	Rock Hill	SC	29732	803-366-5108	366-1519
TF: 888-386-3596 ■ *Web:* www.skytechinc.com					
Smyrna Air Ctr 300 Doug Warpoole Rd	Smyrna	TN	37167	615-459-3337	625-7020
Web: www.smyrnaaircenter.com					
Snohomish Flying Service Inc					
9900 Airport Way	Snohomish	WA	98296	360-568-1541	568-6034
Web: www.snohomishflying.com					
Southwest Airport Services Inc					
11811 Brantly Ave # 500	Houston	TX	77034	281-484-6551	484-8184
TF: 800-426-5237 ■ *Web:* www.swjetops.com					
Space Coast Jet Ctr 7003 Challenger Ave	Titusville	FL	32780	321-267-8355	267-0129
TF: 800-559-5473 ■ *Web:* www.spacecoastjetcenter.com					
Spanaflight 16715 Meridian	Puyallup	WA	98375	253-848-2020	840-5843
Web: www.spanaflight.com					
Statesville Flying Service PO Box 5056	Statesville	NC	28687	704-873-1111	873-1113
Stetson Aviation 1 Airport Rd	Kenedy	TX	78119	830-583-9897	583-9749
TF: 877-520-8118 ■ *Web:* www.stetsonaviation.com					
Stevens Aviation Inc					
600 Delaware St Donaldson Industrial Pk	Greenville	SC	29605	864-879-6000	879-6195
TF: 800-359-7838 ■ *Web:* www.stevensaviation.com					
Stuart Jet Center LLC 2501 Aviation Way	Stuart	FL	34996	772-288-6700	288-3782
TF: 877-735-9538 ■ *Web:* www.stuartjet.com					
Sundance Aviation Inc					
13000 N Sara Rd Sundance Airpark	Yukon	OK	73099	405-373-3886	373-3893
Web: www.sundanceairpark.com					
Swift Aviation 2710 E Old Tower Rd	Phoenix	AZ	85034	602-273-3770	273-3773
Web: www.swiftaviation.com					
Top Gun Aviation Inc					
Hammond Municipal Airport PO Box 2032	Hammond	LA	70404	985-542-0719	542-2077
Truman Arnold Cos 701 S Robison Rd	Texarkana	TX	75504	903-794-3835	832-7226
TF: 800-235-5343 ■ *Web:* www.tacair.com					
Vee Neal Aviation Inc					
148 Aviation Ln Suite 109	Latrobe	PA	15650	724-539-4533	539-5501
TF: 800-278-2710 ■ *Web:* www.veeneal.com					
Western Aircraft Inc 4300 S Kennedy St	Boise	ID	83705	208-338-1800	338-1887
TF: 800-333-3442 ■ *Web:* www.westair.com					
Western Cardinal Inc 205 Durley Ave	Camarillo	CA	93010	805-482-2586	484-2713
TF: 800-882-3018 ■ *Web:* www.westerncardinal.com					
Wilson Air Ctr					
2930 Winchester Rd					
Memphis International Airport	Memphis	TN	38118	901-345-2992	345-1088
TF: 800-464-2992 ■ *Web:* www.wilsonair.com					
Wings Air Charter					
236 Airport Hanger Dr	Wisconsin Rapids	WI	54494	715-424-3737	424-3737
Web: www.wingsaircharter.com					
Wisconsin Aviation Inc 1741 River Dr	Watertown	WI	53094	920-261-4567	206-6386
TF: 800-657-0761 ■ *Web:* www.wisconsinaviation.com					
Woodland Aviation Inc 25170 Aviation Ave	Davis	CA	95616	530-662-9631	662-3035
TF: 800-442-1333 ■ *Web:* www.woodlandaviation.com					

64 BABY PRODUCTS

SEE ALSO Children's & Infants' Clothing p. 1608; Household Furniture p. 1896; Paper Products - Sanitary p. 2338; Toys, Games, Hobbies p. 2723

				Phone	Fax
Baby Jogger Co 8575 Magellan Pkwy Suite 1000	Richmond	VA	23227	800-241-1848	262-6277*
**Fax Area Code:* 804 ■ *TF:* 800-241-1848 ■ *Web:* www.babyjogger.com					
Baby Trend Inc 1567 S Campus Ave	Ontario	CA	91761	800-328-7363	773-0108*
**Fax Area Code:* 909 ■ *TF Cust Svc:* 800-328-7363 ■ *Web:* www.babytrend.com					
Baby's Dream Furniture Inc					
411 Industrial Blvd PO Box 579	Buena Vista	GA	31803	229-649-4404	649-2007
TF: 800-835-2742 ■ *Web:* www.babysdream.com					
BabySwede LLC					
5700 Lombardo Ctr Dr Rock Run N Suite 202	Cleveland	OH	44131	216-447-9140	
TF: 866-424-0200 ■ *Web:* www.babyswede.com					
Ball Bounce & Sport Inc/Hedstrom Plastics					
100 Hedstrom Dr	Ashland	OH	44805	419-289-9310	281-3371
TF: 800-765-9665 ■ *Web:* www.hedstrom.com					
Basic Comfort Inc 5151 Franklin St	Denver	CO	80216	303-778-7535	778-0143
TF: 800-456-8687 ■ *Web:* www.basiccomfort.com					
Britax Child Safety Inc 13501 S Ridge Dr	Charlotte	NC	28273	704-409-1700	246-1962*
**Fax Area Code:* 800 ■ **Fax:* Cust Svc ■ *TF:* 888-427-4829 ■ *Web:* www.britaxusa.com					
C.D.M. Over the Shoulder Baby Holder					
PO Box 5191	San Clemente	CA	92673	949-361-1089	361-1336
TF: 800-637-9426 ■ *Web:* www.babymain.com					
Cardinal Gates 79 Amlajack Way	Newnan	GA	30265	770-252-4200	252-4122
TF: 800-318-3380 ■ *Web:* www.cardinalgates.com					
Central Specialties Ltd 220 Exchange Dr	Crystal Lake	IL	60014	815-459-6000	459-6562
TF: 800-873-4370 ■ *Web:* www.csltd.com					
Chicco USA 1817 Colonial Village Ln	Lancaster	PA	17601	877-424-4226	735-0888*
**Fax Area Code:* 717 ■ *TF:* 877-424-4226 ■ *Web:* www.chiccousa.com					
Crown Crafts Infant Products Inc					
711 W Walnut St	Compton	CA	90220	310-763-8100	537-2272*
**Fax:* Cust Svc ■ *TF:* 800-421-0526 ■ *Web:* www.ccipinc.com					
Delta Enterprises 114 W 26th St 8th Fl	New York	NY	10001	212-736-7000	627-0352
TF: 800-377-3777 ■ *Web:* www.deltaenterprise.com					
Dolly Inc 320 N 4th St	Tipp City	OH	45371	937-667-5711	667-5328
TF: 888-463-6559					
Dorel Juvenile Group USA 2525 State St	Columbus	IN	47201	812-372-0141	372-0911
TF: 800-544-1108 ■ *Web:* www.djgusa.com					
Evenflo Co Inc 1801 Commerce Dr	Piqua	OH	45356	937-415-3300	415-3112*
**Fax:* Hum Res ■ *TF:* 800-233-5921 ■ *Web:* www.evenflo.com					
Fisher-Price Inc 636 Girard Ave	East Aurora	NY	14052	716-687-3000	687-3476
TF: 800-432-5437 ■ *Web:* www.fisher-price.com					
Gerber Products Co 445 State St	Fremont	MI	49413	231-928-2000	928-2723
TF: 800-443-7237 ■ *Web:* www.gerber.com					
GRACO Children's Products Inc					
150 Oaklands Blvd	Exton	PA	19341	610-884-8000	884-8700
TF: 800-345-4109 ■ *Web:* www.gracobaby.com					
Infantino LLC 9909 Huennekens St	San Diego	CA	92121	858-457-9797	457-0181
TF: 800-365-8182 ■ *Web:* www.infantino.com					
Kelty 6235 Lookout Rd	Boulder	CO	80301	303-262-3320	504-2745*
**Fax Area Code:* 800 ■ *TF:* 800-423-2320 ■ *Web:* www.kelty.com					
KidCo Inc 1013 Technology Way	Libertyville	IL	60048	847-549-8600	549-8660
TF: 800-553-5529 ■ *Web:* www.kidco.com					
Kids II 555 N Pt Ctr E Suite 600	Alpharetta	GA	30022	770-751-0442	751-0543
TF: 877-325-7056 ■ *Web:* www.kidsii.com					
Kolcraft Enterprises Inc 10832 NC Hwy 211 E	Aberdeen	NC	28315	910-944-9345	
TF Cust Svc: 800-453-7673 ■ *Web:* www.kolcraft.com					
Lan Enterprises LLC					
Zooper North America					
10140-10200 SW Allen Blvd	Beaverton	OR	97005	888-742-9899	248-9471*
**Fax Area Code:* 503 ■ *TF:* 888-742-9899 ■ *Web:* www.zooperstrollers.com					
Little Tikes Co The 2180 Barlow Rd	Hudson	OH	44236	330-650-3000	
TF Cust Svc: 800-321-0183 ■ *Web:* www.littletikes.com					
Manhattan Toy 430 1st Ave N Suite 500	Minneapolis	MN	55401	612-337-9600	341-4457
TF: 800-541-1345 ■ *Web:* www.manhattantoy.com					
Peg-Perego USA Inc 3625 Independence Dr	Fort Wayne	IN	46808	260-482-8191	484-2940
TF Cust Svc: 800-671-1701 ■ *Web:* www.us.pegperego.com					
Prince Lionheart Inc 2421 Westgate Rd	Santa Maria	CA	93455	805-922-2250	922-9442
TF: 800-544-1132 ■ *Web:* www.princelionheart.com					
RC2 Brands 100 Technology Ctr Dr	Stoughton	MA	02072	800-225-0382	583-9067*
**Fax Area Code:* 508 ■ *TF:* 800-225-0382 ■ *Web:* www.thefirstyears.com					
REI 1700 45th St E	Sumner	WA	98352	253-891-2500	891-2523
TF: 800-426-4840 ■ *Web:* www.rei.com					
Sassy Inc 2305 Breton Industrial Pk Dr	Kentwood	MI	49508	616-243-0767	243-1042
TF: 800-323-6336 ■ *Web:* www.sassybaby.com					
Step2 Co 10010 Aurora-Hudson Rd	Streetsboro	OH	44241	330-656-0440	655-9685
TF Cust Svc: 800-347-8372 ■ *Web:* www.step2.com					
Tough Traveler Ltd 1012 State St	Schenectady	NY	12307	518-377-8526	377-5434
TF Cust Svc: 800-468-6844 ■ *Web:* www.toughtraveler.com					
Triboro Quilt Mfg Inc 172 S Broadway	White Plains	NY	10605	914-428-7551	428-0610
TF: 800-227-2077 ■ *Web:* www.cuddletime.com					
Triple Play Products LLC					
904 Main St Suite 330	Hopkins	MN	55343	952-938-0531	935-4835
TF: 800-829-1625 ■ *Web:* www.lillygold.com					

65 BAGS - PAPER

				Phone	Fax
AJM Packaging Corp					
4111 Andover Rd # 100E	Bloomfield Hills	MI	48302	248-901-0040	901-0061
Web: www.ajmpack.com					
Ampac Corp 30 Coldenham Rd	Walden	NY	12586	845-778-5511	778-2369
TF: 800-472-2247 ■ *Web:* www.ampaconline.com					
Bancroft Bag Inc 425 Bancroft Blvd	West Monroe	LA	71292	318-387-2550	324-2316*
**Fax:* Cust Svc ■ *TF:* 800-551-4950 ■ *Web:* www.bancroftbag.com					
Bemis Co Inc 1 Neenah Ctr 4th Fl PO Box 669	Neenah	WI	54957	920-727-4100	
NYSE: BMS ■ *Web:* www.bemis.com					
Bemis Co Inc Paper Packaging Div					
2445 Deer Pk Blvd	Omaha	NE	68105	800-541-4303	938-2609*
**Fax Area Code:* 402 ■ *TF:* 800-541-4303 ■ *Web:* www.bemispaper.com					
Bonita Pioneer Packaging Products Inc					
7333 SW Bonita Rd	Portland	OR	97224	503-684-6542	323-6027*
**Fax Area Code:* 800 ■ *TF:* 800-677-7725 ■ *Web:* www.bonitapioneer.com					
Colonial Bag Co 1 Ocean Pond Ave PO Box 929	Lake Park	GA	31636	229-559-8484	559-0085
TF: 800-392-4875 ■ *Web:* www.colonial-bag.com					
Duro Bag Mfg Co 7600 Empire Dr	Florence	KY	41042	859-371-2150	
TF: 800-879-3876 ■ *Web:* www.durobag.com					
El Dorado Paper Bag Mfg Co Inc					
204 Prescolite Dr	El Dorado	AR	71730	870-862-4977	862-8520
Hood Packaging Corp 25 Woodgreen Pl	Madison	MS	39110	601-853-7260	853-7299
TF: 800-321-8115 ■ *Web:* www.hoodpkg.com					
KYD Inc 2949 Koapaka St	Honolulu	HI	96819	808-836-3221	833-8995
Web: www.kydinc.com					
Longview Fibre Paper & Packaging Inc					
300 Fibre Way PO Box 639	Longview	WA	98632	360-425-1550	230-5135
Web: www.longviewfibre.com					
Master Design Co 789 State Rt 94 E	Fulton	KY	42041	270-838-7060	838-7060
Web: www.masterdesign.org					
Pacific Bag Inc					
15300 Woodinville Redmond Rd NE Suite A	Woodinville	WA	98072	425-455-1128	990-8582
TF: 800-562-2247 ■ *Web:* www.pacificbag.com					
Portco Corp 3601 SE Columbia Way Suite 260	Vancouver	WA	98661	360-696-1641	695-4849
TF: 800-676-8666 ■ *Web:* www.portco.com					
Roses Southwest Papers Inc					
1701 2nd St SW	Albuquerque	NM	87102	505-842-0134	242-0342
Web: www.rosessouthwest.com					
Ross & Wallace Paper Products Inc					
204 Old Covington Hwy	Hammond	LA	70403	985-345-1321	345-1370
TF: 800-854-2300 ■ *Web:* www.rossandwallace.com					
Stewart Sutherland Inc 5411 E 'V' Ave	Vicksburg	MI	49097	269-649-0530	649-3961
TF: 800-253-1034 ■ *Web:* www.ssbags.com					
Werthan Packaging Inc 1515 5th Ave N	Nashville	TN	37208	615-259-9331	726-1093
TF: 800-467-0348 ■ *Web:* www.werthan.com					
Weyerhaeuser Co 33663 Weyerhaeuser Way S	Federal Way	WA	98003	253-924-2345	924-2685
NYSE: WY ■ *TF:* 800-525-5440 ■ *Web:* www.weyerhaeuser.com					
Wright Packaging Inc 4818 Kimmel Dr	Davenport	IA	52802	563-324-5727	324-5960
Zenith Specialty Bag Co Inc					
17625 E Railroad St PO Box 8445	City of Industry	CA	91748	800-962-2247	284-8493
TF: 800-962-2247 ■ *Web:* www.zsb.com					

66 BAGS - PLASTICS

Company	City	State	Zip	Phone	Fax
Aabaco Plastics Inc 9520 Midwest Ave **Fax:* Sales ■ *Web:* www.aabacoplastics.com	Garfield Heights	OH	44125	216-663-9494	663-9475*
Admiral Packaging inc 10 Admiral St *TF:* 800-556-6454 ■ *Web:* www.admiralpkg.com	Providence	RI	02908	401-274-7000	331-1910
American Transparent Plastics Corp 180 National Rd *TF Orders:* 800-942-8725	Edison	NJ	08817	732-287-3000	287-1421
Ampac Packaging LLC 12025 Tricon Rd **Fax:* Cust Svc ■ *TF:* 800-543-7030 ■ *Web:* www.ampaconline.com	Cincinnati	OH	45246	513-671-1777	671-2920*
Armand Mfg Inc 2399 Silver Wolf Dr *TF:* 800-343-7982 ■ *Web:* www.armandmfg.com	Henderson	NV	89015	702-565-7500	565-3838
Associated Bag Co 400 W Boden St **Fax Area Code:* 800 ■ *TF:* 800-926-6100 ■ *Web:* www.associatedbag.com	Milwaukee	WI	53207	414-769-1000	926-4610*
Bag Makers Inc 6606 S Union Rd *Web:* www.bagmakersinc.com	Union	IL	60180	815-923-2247	458-9023
Bema Film Systems Inc 744 N Oaklawn Ave *TF:* 800-833-6657	Elmhurst	IL	60126	630-279-7800	279-0284
Bemis Co Inc 1 Neenah Ctr 4th Fl PO Box 669 *NYSE:* BMS ■ *Web:* www.bemis.com	Neenah	WI	54957	920-727-4100	
Bemis Co Inc Milprint Div 3550 Moser St PO Box 2968 *Web:* www.milprint.com	Oshkosh	WI	54903	920-527-2300	527-2310
Buckeye Boxes Inc 601 N Hague Ave *Web:* www.buckeyeboxes.com	Columbus	OH	43204	614-274-8484	274-7381
Clear View Bag Co 7137 Prospect Church Rd *TF:* 800-670-6483 ■ *Web:* www.clearviewbag.com	Thomasville	NC	27361	336-885-8131	885-1044
Clorox Co 1221 Broadway *NYSE:* CLX ■ *TF Cust Svc:* 800-292-2808 ■ *Web:* www.thecloroxcompany.com	Oakland	CA	94612	510-271-7000	832-1463
Colonial Bag Corp 205 E Fullerton Ave *TF:* 800-445-7496 ■ *Web:* www.colonialbag.com	Carol Stream	IL	60188	630-690-3999	690-1571
CPI Plastics Group Ltd 151 Courtney Pk Dr W *TF:* 800-251-9566	Mississauga	ON	L5W1Y5	905-795-5505	795-5523
Crown Poly Inc 5700 Bickett St *Web:* www.crownpoly.com	Huntington Park	CA	90255	323-585-5522	
Duro Bag Mfg Co 7600 Empire Dr *TF:* 800-879-3876 ■ *Web:* www.durobag.com	Florence	KY	41042	859-371-2150	
Enviro-Tote Inc 4 Cote Ln *TF:* 800-868-3224 ■ *Web:* www.enviro-tote.com	Bedford	NH	03110	603-647-7171	647-0116
Fortune Plastics Inc 1 Williams Ln *TF:* 800-243-0306 ■ *Web:* www.fortuneplastics.com	Old Saybrook	CT	06475	860-388-3426	388-9930
GB Plastics & Papers Inc 9927 Honeywell St	Houston	TX	77074	713-772-0739	772-2289
Glad Products Co The 1221 Broadway *Web:* www.glad.com	Oakland	CA	94612	510-271-7000	832-1463
Grand Packaging Inc 3840 E 26th St *TF:* 866-705-2247 ■ *Web:* www.restaurantbags.com	Los Angeles	CA	90058	866-705-2247	
Heritage Bags 1648 Diplomat Dr *TF:* 800-527-2247 ■ *Web:* www.heritage-bag.com	Carrollton	TX	75006	972-241-5525	241-5543
Home Care Industries Inc 1 Lisbon St *TF:* 888-772-2100 ■ *Web:* www.homecareind.com	Clifton	NJ	07013	973-365-1600	365-1770
International Poly Bag Inc 990 Pk Ctr Dr Suite F *TF:* 800-976-5922 ■ *Web:* www.intlpolybag.com	Vista	CA	92081	760-598-2468	598-2469
KYD Inc 2949 Koapaka St *Web:* www.kydinc.com	Honolulu	HI	96819	808-836-3221	833-8995
Mercury Plastics Inc 123 Willamette Ln *TF:* 800-347-0338	Bowling Green	KY	42101	270-782-8026	782-7478
Mexico Plastics Co (inc) PO Box 760 *Web:* www.continentalproducts.com	Mexico	MO	65265	573-581-4128	581-4461
Pacific Bag Inc 15300 Woodinville Redmond Rd NE Suite A *TF:* 800-562-2247 ■ *Web:* www.pacificbag.com	Woodinville	WA	98072	425-455-1128	990-8582
Pactiv Corp 1900 W Field Ct *NYSE:* PTV ■ *TF:* 888-828-2850 ■ *Web:* www.pactiv.com	Lake Forest	IL	60045	847-482-2000	482-4738
Pitt Plastics Inc 1400 Atkinson Ave *TF:* 800-835-0366 ■ *Web:* www.pittplastics.com	Pittsburg	KS	66762	620-231-4030	231-7612
Plastic Packaging Inc 1246 Main Ave SE **Fax:* Sales ■ *Web:* www.ppi-hky.com	Hickory	NC	28602	828-328-2466	322-1830*
Poly-America Inc 2000 W Marshall Dr *TF:* 800-527-3322 ■ *Web:* www.poly-america.com	Grand Prairie	TX	75051	972-337-7107	337-7410
Poly-Pak Industries Inc 125 Spagnoli Rd *TF:* 800-969-1995 ■ *Web:* www.poly-pak.com	Melville	NY	11747	631-293-6767	454-6366
Portco Corp 3601 SE Columbia Way Suite 260 *TF:* 800-676-8666 ■ *Web:* www.portco.com	Vancouver	WA	98661	360-696-1641	695-4849
Presto Products Co 670 N Perkins St *NYSE:* NPK ■ *TF:* 800-558-3525 ■ *Web:* www.prestoproducts.com	Appleton	WI	54912	920-739-9471	738-1458
Ronpak Inc 4301 New Brunswick Ave *Web:* www.ronpak.com	South Plainfield	NJ	07080	732-968-8000	752-6097
Roplast Industries Inc 3155 S 5th Ave *TF:* 800-767-5278 ■ *Web:* www.roplast.com	Oroville	CA	95965	530-532-9500	532-9576
Shields Bag & Printing Co PO Box 9848 *TF:* 800-541-8630 ■ *Web:* www.host45.hrwebservices.net/~shields/index.htm	Yakima	WA	98909	509-248-7500	248-6304
Star Packaging Corp 453 85th Cir *TF:* 800-252-5414 ■ *Web:* www.starpackagingcorp.com	College Park	GA	30349	404-763-2800	763-1914
Superbag Corp 9291 Baythrone Dr *TF:* 888-842-1177 ■ *Web:* www.superbag.com	Houston	TX	77041	713-462-1173	
Tara Plastics Corp 175 Lake Mirror Rd *Web:* www.taraplastics.com	Forest Park	GA	30297	404-366-4464	366-3816
Uniflex Holdings 383 W John St *TF:* 800-223-0564 ■ *Web:* www.uniflexbags.com	Hicksville	NY	11802	516-932-2000	932-3129
Waverly Plastics Co Inc PO Box 801 *TF:* 800-454-6377 ■ *Web:* www.waverlyplastics.com	Waverly	IA	50677	319-352-3333	352-3338
Webster Industries Inc 58 Pulaski St *TF:* 800-225-0796 ■ *Web:* www.websterindustries.com	Peabody	MA	01960	978-532-2000	531-3354
Western Summit Mfg Corp 13290 Daum Dr	City of Industry	CA	91746	626-333-3333	961-2247
White Bag Co Inc 8027 Hwy 161 N *TF:* 800-527-1733 ■ *Web:* www.whitebag.com	North Little Rock	AR	72117	501-835-1444	835-2226
Wisconsin Film & Bag Inc 3100 E Richmond St *TF:* 800-765-9224 ■ *Web:* www.wifb.com	Shawano	WI	54166	715-524-2565	524-3527

67 BAGS - TEXTILE

SEE ALSO Handbags, Totes, Backpacks p. 2003; Luggage, Bags, Cases p. 2189

Company	City	State	Zip	Phone	Fax
A Rifkin Co 1400 Sans Souci Pkwy *TF Cust Svc:* 800-458-7300 ■ *Web:* www.arifkin.com	Wilkes-Barre	PA	18706	570-825-9551	825-5282
Aceco Industrial Packaging 166 Frelinghuysen Ave *TF Cust Svc:* 800-832-2247	Newark	NJ	07114	973-242-2200	242-1044
American Bag & Burlap Co 32 Arlington St *Web:* www.cormanbag.com	Chelsea	MA	02150	617-884-7600	437-7917
Bag Bazaar 1 E 33rd St	New York	NY	10016	212-689-3508	696-2098
Bearse Mfg Co 3815 W Cortland St *Web:* www.bearseusa.com	Chicago	IL	60647	773-235-8710	235-8716
Bulk Lift International Inc (BLI) 1013 Tamarac Dr *TF:* 800-879-2247 ■ *Web:* www.bulklift.com	Carpentersville	IL	60110	847-428-6059	428-7180
Central Bag Co 1323 W 13th St	Kansas City	MO	64102	816-471-0388	842-5501
Fox Packaging Co 2200 Fox Dr *TF:* 800-336-6369 ■ *Web:* www.foxbag.com	McAllen	TX	78504	956-682-6176	682-5768
Fulton-Denver Co 3500 Wynkoop St *TF:* 800-776-6715	Denver	CO	80216	303-294-9292	292-9470
GEM Group 9 International Way *TF:* 800-800-3200 ■ *Web:* www.gemlinebags.com	Lawrence	MA	01843	978-691-2000	691-2085
Halsted Corp 78 Halladay St *TF:* 800-843-5184	Jersey City	NJ	07304	201-433-3323	333-0670
HBD Inc 3901 Riverdale Rd *TF:* 800-403-2247 ■ *Web:* www.hbdinc.com	Greensboro	NC	27406	336-275-4800	275-7242
Indian Valley Industries Inc 60-100 Corliss Ave PO Box 810 *TF:* 800-659-5111 ■ *Web:* www.iviindustries.com	Johnson City	NY	13790	607-729-5111	729-5158
J & M Industries Inc 300 Ponchatoula Pkwy *TF:* 800-989-1002 ■ *Web:* www.jm-ind.com	Ponchatoula	LA	70454	985-386-6000	386-9066
Langston Cos Inc 1760 S 3rd St *TF Cust Svc:* 800-444-7046	Memphis	TN	38101	901-774-4440	942-5402
LBU Inc 217 Brook Ave *TF:* 800-678-4528 ■ *Web:* www.lbuinc.com	Passaic	NJ	07055	973-773-4800	773-6005
Menardi 1 Maxwell Dr *TF:* 800-321-3218 ■ *Web:* www.menardifilters.com	Trenton	SC	29847	803-663-6551	663-4029
NYP Corp 805 E Grand St *TF:* 800-524-1052 ■ *Web:* www.nyp-corp.com	Elizabeth	NJ	07201	908-351-6550	351-0108
Sacramento Bag Mfg Co 530 Q St *TF:* 800-287-2247 ■ *Web:* www.sacbag.com	Sacramento	CA	95814	916-441-6121	448-3141
Super Sack Mfg Corp 11510 Data Dr *TF:* 800-331-9200 ■ *Web:* www.bagcorp.com	Dallas	TX	75218	214-340-7060	340-4598
Tenba Quality Cases Ltd 8 Westchester Plaza *Web:* www.tenba.com	Elmsford	NY	10523	914-347-3300	347-3309

68 BAKERIES

Company	City	State	Zip	Phone	Fax
Ace Endico Corp 80 International Blvd *Web:* www.aceendico.com	Brewster	NY	10509	845-940-1501	940-1516
Andre Boudin Bakeries Inc 221 Main St Suite 1230 *Web:* www.boudinbakery.com	San Francisco	CA	94105	415-882-1849	913-1818
Atlanta Bread Co 1200 Wilson Wy Suite 100 *TF:* 800-398-3728 ■ *Web:* www.atlantabread.com	Smyrna	GA	30082	770-432-0933	444-1991
Au Bon Pain 19 Fid Kennedy Ave *TF:* 800-825-5227 ■ *Web:* www.aubonpain.com	Boston	MA	02210	617-423-2100	423-7879
Awrey Bakeries Inc 12301 Farmington Rd *TF:* 800-950-2253 ■ *Web:* www.awrey.com	Livonia	MI	48150	734-522-1100	522-1453
Big Apple Bagels 500 Lake Cook Rd Suite 475 *TF:* 800-251-6101 ■ *Web:* www.babcorp.com	Deerfield	IL	60015	847-948-7520	405-8140
Bruegger's Enterprises 159 Bank St *Web:* www.brueggers.com	Burlington	VT	05401	802-660-4020	652-9293
Busken Bakery Inc 2675 Madison Rd *Web:* www.busken.com	Cincinnati	OH	45208	513-871-5330	871-2662
C-Street Bakery 2930 W Maple St *TF:* 800-336-1320 ■ *Web:* www.hotstufffoods.com/OurBrands	Sioux Falls	SD	57107	605-336-6961	336-0141
Certified Oil Corp 949 King Ave *Web:* www.certifiedoil.com	Columbus	OH	43212	614-421-7500	
Cheryl & Co 646 McCorkle Blvd *TF:* 800-443-8124 ■ *Web:* www.cheryls.com	Westerville	OH	43082	614-891-8822	891-8699
Collin Street Bakery Inc 401 W 7th Ave *TF Sales:* 800-504-1896 ■ *Web:* www.collinstreet.com	Corsicana	TX	75151	903-872-8111	872-6879
Cookies By Design Inc 1865 Summit Ave Suite 605 *TF:* 800-945-2665 ■ *Web:* www.cookiesbydesign.com	Plano	TX	75074	972-398-9536	398-9542
Cookies in Bloom Inc 7208 La Casa Rd *TF:* 800-222-3104 ■ *Web:* www.cookiesinbloom.com	Dallas	TX	75248	972-490-8644	490-8646
Corner Bakery Cafe 12700 Pk Central Dr Suite 1300 *TF:* 800-309-4642 ■ *Web:* www.cornerbakerycafe.com	Dallas	TX	75251	972-619-4100	
Crest Foods Inc 101 W Renner Rd Suite 240 *Web:* www.nestlecafe.com	Richardson	TX	75802	214-495-9533	853-5347
Damascus Bakery Inc 56 Gold St *TF:* 800-367-7482 ■ *Web:* www.damascusbakery.com	Brooklyn	NY	11201	718-855-1457	403-0948
Daylight Donut Flour Co LLC 11707 E 11th St *TF:* 800-331-2245 ■ *Web:* www.daylightdonuts.com	Tulsa	OK	74128	918-438-0800	438-0804

Name / Address	City	State	ZIP	Phone	Fax
Dext Co of Maryland 2811 Wilshire Blvd Suite 410 *Web:* www.scopeproducts.com	Santa Monica	CA	90403	310-458-1574	
Dunkin' Donuts 130 Royall St *TF Cust Svc:* 800-859-5339 ■ *Web:* www.dunkindonuts.com	Canton	MA	02021	781-737-3000	737-4000
East Balt Inc 1801 W 31st Pl *TF:* 800-621-8555 ■ *Web:* www.eastbalt.com	Chicago	IL	60608	773-376-4444	376-8137
Einstein/Noah Bagel Corp 1687 Cole Blvd *Web:* www.einsteinbros.com	Golden	CO	80401	303-568-8000	568-8039
Eleni's 75 9th Ave **Fax Area Code:* 718 ■ *TF:* 888-435-3647 ■ *Web:* www.elenis.com	New York	NY	10011	888-435-3647	361-8272*
Gold Medal Bakery Inc 1397 Bay St *TF:* 800-642-7568 ■ *Web:* www.goldmedalbakery.com	Fall River	MA	02724	508-674-5766	674-6090
Gonnella Baking Co 1001 W Chicago Ave *TF:* 800-262-3442 ■ *Web:* www.gonnella.com	Chicago	IL	60642	312-733-2020	733-7056
Great American Cookie Co Inc 4685 Frederick Dr SW *TF:* 800-332-4856 ■ *Web:* www.greatamericancookies.com	Atlanta	GA	30336	404-696-1700	699-0887
Great Harvest Bread Co 28 S Montana St *TF:* 800-442-0424 ■ *Web:* www.greatharvest.com	Dillon	MT	59725	406-683-6842	683-5537
Haas Baking Co 9769 Reavis Pk Dr *TF:* 800-325-3171 ■ *Web:* www.haasbaking.com	Saint Louis	MO	63123	314-631-6100	631-3464
Honey Dew Assoc Inc 2 Taunton St *TF:* 800-946-6393 ■ *Web:* www.honeydewdonuts.com	Plainville	MA	02762	508-699-3900	699-3949
Just Desserts Inc 550 85th Ave *Web:* www.justdesserts.com	Oakland	CA	94621	510-567-2910	567-2911
King Arthur Flour Co Inc The 135 Rt 5 S *Web:* www.kingarthurflour.com	Norwich	VT	05055	802-649-3881	649-3365
Krispy Kreme Doughnuts Corp 370 Knollwood St Suite 500 *NYSE: KKD* ■ *TF:* 800-334-1243 ■ *Web:* www.krispykreme.com	Winston-Salem	NC	27103	336-725-2981	733-3796
Manhattan Bagel Co Inc 100 Horizon Ctr Blvd *TF:* 800-308-2457 ■ *Web:* www.manhattanbagel.com	Hamilton	NJ	08691	609-631-7000	631-7068
Maple Donuts Inc 3455 E Market St *TF:* 800-627-5348 ■ *Web:* www.mapledonutsinc.com	York	PA	17402	717-757-7826	755-8725
Middle East Bakery Inc 30 International Way	Lawrence	MA	01841	978-688-2221	683-7954
Mrs Fields Original Cookies Inc 2855 E Cottonwood Pkwy Suite 400 *TF:* 800-348-6311 ■ *Web:* www.mrsfields.com	Salt Lake City	UT	84121	801-736-5600	736-5970
Olde Tyme Pastries 2225 Geer Rd *Web:* www.otpastries.com	Turlock	CA	95382	209-668-0928	668-2741
Panera Bread Co 3630 S Geyer Rd *NASDAQ: PNRA* ■ *TF:* 800-301-5566 ■ *Web:* www.panerabread.com	St. Louis	MO	63127	314-984-1000	909-3300
Quality Naturally Foods 18830 E San Jose Ave *Web:* www.qnfoods.com	City of Industry	CA	91748	626-854-6363	965-0978
Rotella's Italian Bakery Inc 6949 S 108th St *TF:* 800-759-0360 ■ *Web:* www.rotellas-bakery.com	La Vista	NE	68128	402-592-6600	592-2989
Southern Maid Donut Flour Co 3615 Cavalier Dr *TF:* 800-936-6887 ■ *Web:* www.southernmaiddonuts.com	Garland	TX	75042	972-272-6425	276-3549
Tip Top Cafe & Bakery Corp 3173 Akahi St	Lihue	HI	96766	808-245-2333	246-8988
Treats International Franchise Corp 1550-A Laperriere Ave Suite 201 *TF:* 800-461-4003 ■ *Web:* www.treats.com	Ottawa	ON	K1Z7T2	613-563-4073	563-1982
Vie de France Yamazaki Inc 2070 Chain Bridge Rd Suite 500 *TF:* 800-446-4404 ■ *Web:* www.vdfy.com	Vienna	VA	22182	703-442-9205	821-2695
Wetzel's Pretzels LLC 35 Hugus Alley Suite 300 *Web:* www.wetzels.com	Pasadena	CA	91103	626-432-6900	432-6904
Zaro's Bread Basket Inc 138 Bruckner Blvd	Bronx	NY	10454	718-993-5600	292-9353

69 BANKING-RELATED SERVICES

Name / Address	City	State	ZIP	Phone	Fax
Austin Trust Co 336 S Congress Ave Suite 100 *Web:* www.austintrust.com	Austin	TX	78704	512-478-2121	478-2616
Automatic Funds Transfer Services 151 S Landers St Suite C *TF:* 800-275-2033 ■ *Web:* www.afts.com	Seattle	WA	98134	206-254-0975	254-0968
Bankserv 222 Kearny St Suite 400 *TF:* 888-877-7703 ■ *Web:* www.bankserv.com	San Francisco	CA	94108	415-217-4581	277-9904
Benchmark Community Bank 100 S Broad St PO Box 569 *OTC: BMBN* ■ **Fax Area Code:* 434 ■ *Web:* www.bcbonline.com	Kenbridge	VA	23944	804-676-8444	676-1875*
Blackhawk Bank PO Box 719 *TF:* 888-769-2600 ■ *Web:* www.blackhawkbank.com	Beloit	WI	53511	608-364-4534	364-8946
Bremer Financial Corp 2100 Bremer Tower 445 Minnesota St *TF:* 800-908-2265 ■ *Web:* www.bremer.com	St. Paul	MN	55101	651-227-7621	312-3550
Capital Farm Credit Aca 7000 Woodway Dr PO Box 20097 *Web:* www.capitalfarmcredit.com	Waco	TX	76702	254-776-7506	776-8112
Chemung Canal Trust Co 1 Chemung Canal Plaza PO Box 1522 *TF:* 800-836-3711 ■ *Web:* www.chemungcanal.com	Elmira	NY	14902	607-737-3711	737-3850
Citizens Banking Co 100 E Water St *TF:* 888-645-4121 ■ *Web:* www.citizensbankco.com	Sandusky	OH	44870	419-625-4121	627-3359
Citizens Federal Savings & Loan Assn 110 N Main St PO Box 9 *Web:* www.citizensfederalsl.com	Bellefontaine	OH	43311	937-593-0015	593-6577
Comdata Corp 5301 Maryland Way *TF:* 800-741-3939 ■ *Web:* www.comdata.com	Brentwood	TN	37027	615-370-7000	370-7828
Community Bank 790 E Colorado Blvd *TF:* 800-788-9999 ■ *Web:* www.cbank.com	Pasadena	CA	91101	626-577-1700	
Credit Union 24 Inc 2252 Killearn Ctr Blvd Suite 300 *TF:* 877-570-2824 ■ *Web:* www.cu24.com	Tallahassee	FL	32309	850-701-2824	701-2424
Emida Corp 27442 Portola Pkwy Suite 150 *Web:* www.emida.net	Foothill Ranch	CA	92610	949-699-1401	699-1420
Emprise Financial Corp 257 N Broadway St PO Box 2970 *TF Cust Svc:* 800-201-7118 ■ *Web:* www.emprisebank.com	Wichita	KS	67202	316-383-4301	383-4433
Eureka Homestead 1922 Veterans Memorial Blvd *Web:* www.eurekahomestead.com	Metairie	LA	70005	504-834-0242	834-6909
First FSB 2323 Ring Rd PO Box 5006 *NASDAQ: FFKY* ■ *TF:* 800-314-2265 ■ *Web:* www.ffsbky.com	Elizabethtown	KY	42701	270-765-2131	765-2135
FirstBank Holding Co of Colorado 12345 W Colfax Ave *Web:* www.efirstbank.com	Lakewood	CO	80215	303-232-2000	235-1044
Fiserv Inc 255 Fiserv Dr PO Box 979 *NASDAQ: FISV* ■ *TF Mktg:* 800-872-7882 ■ *Web:* www.fiserv.com	Brookfield	WI	53008	262-879-5000	879-5000
Florida Credit Union League Inc PO Box 3108 *TF:* 866-231-0545 ■ *Web:* www.lscu.coop	Tallahassee	FL	32315	850-576-8171	
Hawaii National Bank 45 N King St *TF:* 800-528-2273 ■ *Web:* www.hawaiinational.com	Honolulu	HI	96817	808-528-7711	528-7728
Hillcrest Bank 11111 W 95th St *TF:* 800-681-1776 ■ *Web:* www.hillcrestbank.com	Overland Park	KS	66214	913-324-6400	
Moelis & Co LLC 399 Pk Ave 5th Fl *Web:* www.moelis.com	New York	NY	10022	212-883-3800	880-4260
MoneyGram International Inc 2828 N Harwood Fl 15 *NYSE: MGI* ■ *TF:* 800-666-3947 ■ *Web:* www.moneygram.com	Dallas	TX	75201	800-666-3947	
Moneytree Inc 6720 Fort Dent Way *TF:* 866-251-2512 ■ *Web:* www.moneytreeinc.com	Seattle	WA	98188	206-246-3500	248-3400
NYCE Corp 400 Plaza Dr *TF:* 800-522-6923 ■ *Web:* www.nyce.net	Secaucus	NJ	07094	201-865-9000	330-3374
Oak Ridge Financial 701 Xenia Ave S Suite 100 *TF:* 800-231-8364 ■ *Web:* www.oakridgefinancial.com	Golden Valley	MN	55416	763-923-2200	923-2283
OANDA Corp 140 Broadway 46th Fl *Web:* www.oanda.com	New York	NY	10005	416-593-9436	593-0185
Orchard First Source 2850 Golf Rd Suite 250 *Web:* www.ofscapital.com	Rolling Meadows	IL	60008	847-734-2000	734-7910
Pershing LLC 95 Christopher Columbus Dr **Fax:* Hum Res ■ *TF:* 800-443-4342 ■ *Web:* www.pershing.com	Jersey City	NJ	07302	201-413-2000	413-3103*
PULSE 1301 McKinney St Suite 2500 *TF:* 800-420-2122 ■ *Web:* www.pulsenetwork.com	Houston	TX	77010	713-223-1400	223-1204
Rock Springs National Bank 200 Second St PO Box 880 *TF:* 800-469-8801 ■ *Web:* www.rsnb.com	Rock Springs	WY	82902	307-362-8801	362-9432
Sherman Financial Group LLC 335 Madison Ave Fl 19 *Web:* www.sfg.com	New York	NY	10017	212-922-1616	661-1316
Travelex Worldwide Money 29 Broadway *Web:* www.travelex.com	New York	NY	10006	212-363-6206	
United Bank & Trust 205 E Chicago Blvd PO Box 248 *Web:* www.ubat.com	Tecumseh	MI	49286	517-423-8373	423-5041
Universal Money Centers Inc 6800 Squibb Rd *TF:* 800-234-6860 ■ *Web:* www.universalmoney.com	Shawnee Mission	KS	66202	913-831-2055	831-0248
Western Union Holdings Inc 12500 E Belford Ave *NYSE: WU* ■ *TF Cust Svc:* 800-325-6000 ■ *Web:* www.india.westernunion.com	Englewood	CO	80112	720-332-1000	332-4753

70 BANKS - COMMERCIAL & SAVINGS

SEE ALSO Credit & Financing - Commercial p. 1773; Credit & Financing - Consumer p. 1775; Credit Unions p. 1776; Bank Holding Companies p. 2012

Name / Address	City	State	ZIP	Phone	Fax
1st Colonial Bancorp Inc 1040 Haddon Ave *OTC: FCOB* ■ *TF:* 800-500-1044 ■ *Web:* www.1stcolonial.com	Collingswood	NJ	08108	856-858-1100	858-9255
1st Community Bank 2911 N Westwood Blvd *TF:* 888-831-3620 ■ *Web:* www.1stcombank.com	Poplar Bluff	MO	63901	573-778-0101	778-9138
1st Source Bank 100 N Michigan St **Fax:* Mktg ■ *TF:* 800-513-2360 ■ *Web:* www.1stsource.com	South Bend	IN	46601	574-235-2254	235-2948*
1st United Bank 1 N Federal Hwy *NASDAQ: FUBC* ■ *TF:* 877-362-3411 ■ *Web:* www.1stunitedbankfl.com	Boca Raton	FL	33432	561-362-3400	362-3436
3rd Federal Bank 3 Penns Trail *TF:* 888-918-4473 ■ *Web:* www.thirdfedbank.com	Newtown	PA	18940	215-579-4600	579-4748
Acacia FSB 7600 Leesburg Pike E Bldg Suite 200 *TF:* 800-950-0270 ■ *Web:* www.acaciafederal.com	Falls Church	VA	22043	703-506-8100	506-8160
Alliance Bank 541 Lawrence Rd *NASDAQ: ALLB* ■ *TF:* 800-550-4387 ■ *Web:* www.alliancebk.com	Broomall	PA	19008	610-353-2900	359-6908
Alliance Bank of Arizona 1 E Washington St *Web:* www.alliancebankofarizona.com	Phoenix	AZ	85004	602-629-1776	850-7390
Allied Irish Banks 405 Pk Ave *Web:* www.aib.ie	New York	NY	10022	212-339-8080	339-3007
Alma Exchange Bank 501 W 12th St PO Box 1988 *Web:* www.aebalma.com	Alma	GA	31510	912-632-8631	632-5780
Amalgamated Bank of Chicago 1 W Monroe PO Box 800 *Web:* www.aboc.com	Chicago	IL	60603	312-822-3000	267-8767
Amalgamated Bank of New York 275 7th Ave **Fax Area Code:* 202 ■ *TF:* 800-662-0860 ■ *Web:* www.amalgamatedbank.com	New York	NY	10001	212-255-6200	895-4507*
Amarillo National Bank 410 S Taylor St Plaza One **Fax:* Cust Svc ■ *TF:* 800-262-3733 ■ *Web:* www.anb.com	Amarillo	TX	79101	806-378-8000	373-7505*
Amboy National Bank 3590 US Hwy 9 S *TF:* 800-942-6269 ■ *Web:* www.amboybank.com	Old Bridge	NJ	08857	732-591-8700	591-0726

	City	State	Zip	Phone	Fax
Amegy Bank of Texas 4400 Post Oak Pkwy	Houston	TX	77027	713-235-8800	232-5948
TF: 800-287-0301 ■ *Web:* www.amegybank.com					
American Bank 4029 W Tilghman St	Allentown	PA	18104	610-366-1800	366-1900
TF Cust Svc: 888-366-6622					
American Bank of Texas NA 200 N Austin St	Seguin	TX	78155	830-379-5236	379-7843
Web: www.abtexasna.com					
American Exchange Bank (AEB)					
510 W Main St PO Box 818	Henryetta	OK	74437	918-652-3321	652-7057
TF: 888-652-3321 ■ *Web:* www.aebbank.net					
American Express Centurion Bank					
4315 S 2700 W	Salt Lake City	UT	84184	801-945-3000	
Web: www.home.americanexpress.com					
American First National Bank					
9999 Bellaire Blvd	Houston	TX	77036	713-596-2888	596-2555
Web: www.afnb.com					
American Heritage Bank 2 S Main PO BOX 1408	Sapulpa	OK	74067	918-224-3210	224-7689
Web: www.ahb-ok.com					
American National Bank PO Box 2139	Omaha	NE	68103	402-399-5000	399-5009
TF Cust Svc: 800-279-0007 ■ *Web:* www.anbank.com					
American Savings Bank FSB					
1001 Bishop St PO Box 2300	Honolulu	HI	96813	808-531-6262	536-3141
TF: 800-272-2566 ■ *Web:* www.asbhawaii.com					
Ameriserv Financial					
216 Franklin St PO Box 520	Johnstown	PA	15907	814-533-5300	533-5283
TF: 800-837-2265 ■ *Web:* www.ameriservfinancial.com					
AmTrust Bank 1801 E 9th St	Cleveland	OH	44114	216-622-4100	987-8732
TF: 888-696-4444 ■ *Web:* www.amtrust.com					
Anchor Bank 1055 Wayzata Blvd E	Wayzata	MN	55391	952-473-4606	476-5219
Web: www.anchorlink.com					
AnchorBank 25 W Main St PO Box 7933	Madison	WI	53703	608-252-8827	252-8783
TF: 800-252-6246 ■ *Web:* www.anchorbank.com					
ANZ Securities INC					
1177 Avenue of the Americas 6th Fl	New York	NY	10036	212-801-9160	801-9163
Web: www.anz.com					
Apple Bank for Savings 122 E 42nd St 9th Fl	New York	NY	10168	914-902-2775	224-6592*
**Fax Area Code:* 212 ■ **Fax:* Hum Res ■ *TF:* 800-824-0710 ■ *Web:* www.theapplebank.com					
Apple Creek Banc Corp					
3 W Main St PO BOX 237	Apple Creek	OH	44606	330-698-2631	698-4770
Web: www.applecreekbank.com					
Applied Bank 50 Applied Card Way	Glen Mills	PA	19342	561-982-8970	
TF: 800-225-5030 ■ *Web:* www.appliedbank.com					
Archer Bank 4970 S Archer Ave	Chicago	IL	60632	773-838-3000	884-4355
Web: www.archerbank.com					
Arthur State Bank 100 E Main St PO BOX 769	Union	SC	29379	864-427-1213	429-8537
Web: www.arthurstatebank.com					
Artisan's Bank 2961 Centerville Rd	Wilmington	DE	19808	302-884-6563	654-0559
Web: www.artisansbank.com					
Arvest Bank PO Box 1229	Bentonville	AR	72712	479-271-1253	271-1315
TF: 888-271-1253 ■ *Web:* www.arvest.com					
Ascencia 2500 Eastpoint Pkwy	Louisville	KY	40223	502-499-4800	499-4811
TF: 877-369-2265 ■ *Web:* www.ascenciabank.com					
Asheville Savings Bank S S B PO Box 652	Asheville	NC	28802	828-254-7411	252-1512
Web: www.ashevillesavings.com					
Associated Bank 2870 Holmgren Way	Green Bay	WI	54304	262-879-0133	
TF: 800-728-3501 ■ *Web:* www.associatedbank.com					
Associated Bank Green Bay NA					
200 N Adams St	Green Bay	WI	54301	920-433-3200	433-3060
TF: 800-236-3479 ■ *Web:* www.associatedbank.com					
Associated Bank Illinois NA 612 N Main St	Rockford	IL	61103	815-987-3500	987-3536
TF: 800-236-8866 ■ *Web:* www.associatedbank.com					
Associated Bank Milwaukee					
401 E Kilbourn Ave	Milwaukee	WI	53202	414-271-1786	283-2204
TF: 800-236-8866 ■ *Web:* www.associatedbank.com					
Associated Bank North 303 S 1st Ave	Wausau	WI	54402	715-845-4301	848-2244
TF: 800-236-8866 ■ *Web:* www.associatedbank.com					
Atlantic Bank of New York					
960 Avenue of the Americas	New York	NY	10001	212-967-7425	563-2729
TF: 800-535-2269 ■ *Web:* www.abny.com					
Banca Sanpaolol 1 William St	New York	NY	10004	212-607-3500	809-9785
Web: www.bancaintesa.us					
BancFirst Corp 101 N Broadway Ave	Oklahoma City	OK	73102	405-270-1086	270-1089
NASDAQ: BANF ■ *TF:* 877-602-2262 ■ *Web:* www.bancfirst.com					
Banco Popular de Puerto Rico PO Box 362708	San Juan	PR	00936	787-723-0077	758-0710*
**Fax:* Cust Svc ■ *TF:* 888-724-3650 ■ *Web:* www.popular.com					
Banco Santander Puerto Rico					
207 Ponce De Leon Ave PO Box 362589	San Juan	PR	00917	787-274-7200	
Web: www.santandernet.com					
Bancorp Bank 409 Silverside Rd Suite 105	Wilmington	DE	19809	302-385-5000	385-5099
NASDAQ: TBBK ■ *TF Cust Svc:* 800-545-0289 ■ *Web:* www.thebancorp.mybankingservices.com					
BancorpSouth 1 Mississippi Plaza	Tupelo	MS	38804	662-680-2000	680-2271
TF: 888-797-7711 ■ *Web:* www.bancorpsouthonline.com					
Bangor Savings Bank 3 State St	Bangor	ME	04401	207-942-5211	941-2752
TF: 877-226-4671 ■ *Web:* www.bangor.com					
Bank Financial 6415 W 95th St	Chicago Ridge	IL	60415	708-747-2000	675-6421
TF: 800-894-6900 ■ *Web:* www.bankfinancial.com					
Bank First National PO Box 10	Manitowoc	WI	54221	920-684-6611	652-3180
Web: www.bankfirstnational.com					
Bank Leumi USA 579 5th Ave	New York	NY	10017	917-542-2343	542-2254
TF: 800-892-5430 ■ *Web:* www.leumiusa.com					
Bank Midwest NA 1111 Main St Suite 350	Kansas City	MO	64105	816-471-9800	842-6291
Web: www.bankmw.com					
Bank of America NA 101 S Tryon St	Charlotte	NC	28255	704-386-5478	386-9928
TF: 800-432-1000 ■ *Web:* www.bankofamerica.com					
Bank of Blue Valley PO Box 26128	Overland Park	KS	66225	913-338-1000	338-2801
Web: www.bankbv.com					
Bank of Delmar Inc 2245 Northwood Dr	Salisbury	MD	21801	410-548-1100	
Web: www.bankofdelmarvahb.com					
Bank of East Asia Ltd 202 Canal St	New York	NY	10013	212-233-8833	219-3378
Bank of Georgia The 100 Westpark Dr	Peachtree City	GA	30269	770-631-9488	487-4368
PINK: GABA ■ *TF:* 866-645-1139 ■ *Web:* www.bankofgeorgia.com					
Bank Of Gleason 203 Main St PO Box 231	Gleason	TN	38229	731-648-5506	648-5090
Web: www.gleasononline.com					
Bank of Glen Burnie The 101 Crain Hwy SE	Glen Burnie	MD	21061	410-766-3300	787-8886
Web: www.thebankofglenburnie.com					
Bank of Hazlehurst PO Box 628	Hazlehurst	GA	31539	912-375-4228	375-4210
Web: www.bankofhazlehurst.com					
Bank Of Holly Springs PO Box 250	Holly Springs	MS	38635	662-252-2511	252-1816
Web: www.bankofhollysprings.com					
Bank of Landisburg The					
100 N Carlisle St PO Box 179	Landisburg	PA	17040	717-789-3213	789-4702
Web: www.bankoflandisburg.com					
Bank Of Las Vegas					
622 Douglas Ave PO BOX 3210	Las Vegas	NM	87701	505-425-7565	425-8501
Web: www.bankonblv.com					
Bank of Marin 504 Tamalpais Dr	Corte Madera	CA	94925	415-927-2265	927-8920
NASDAQ: BMRC ■ *TF:* 800-654-5111 ■ *Web:* www.bankofmarin.com					
Bank of Mauston The					
503 State Rd 82 E PO BOX 226	Mauston	WI	53948	608-847-6200	847-5372
Web: www.bankofmauston.com					
Bank of McKenney 20718 1st St	McKenney	VA	23872	804-478-4434	478-4704
OTC: BOMK ■ *TF:* 800-478-4409 ■ *Web:* www.bankofmckenney.com					
Bank of Montreal (BMO)					
100 King St W 1 First Canadian Pl 19th Fl	Toronto	ON	M5X1A1	416-867-6785	867-6793
TSE: BMO ■ *Web:* www2.bmo.com					
Bank of Montreal 3 Times Sq	New York	NY	10036	212-221-9061	
Bank of Morton 366 S 4th St PO Box 229	Morton	MS	39117	601-732-8944	732-8599
Web: www.bankofmorton.com					
Bank of New York Mellon 1 Wall St	New York	NY	10286	212-495-1784	635-1200
TF: 866-269-1784 ■ *Web:* www.bnymellon.com					
Bank of North Dakota 1200 Memorial Hwy	Bismarck	ND	58504	701-328-5600	328-5632
TF: 800-472-2166 ■ *Web:* www.banknd.nd.gov					
Bank of Nova Scotia 44 King St W 19th Fl	Toronto	ON	M5H1H1	416-866-6161	866-3750
TSE: BNS ■ *TF:* 800-472-6842 ■ *Web:* www.scotiabank.ca					
Bank of Nova Scotia 1 Liberty Plaza 26th Fl	New York	NY	10006	212-225-5011	225-5480
TF: 800-472-6842 ■ *Web:* www.scotiabank.com					
Bank of Oak Ridge 2211 Oak Ridge Rd	Oak Ridge	NC	27310	336-644-9944	644-6644
NASDAQ: BKOR ■ *Web:* www.bankofoakridge.com					
Bank of Oklahoma NA PO Box 2300	Tulsa	OK	74192	918-588-6000	588-6962*
**Fax:* Cust Svc ■ *TF Cust Svc:* 800-234-6181 ■ *Web:* www.bankofoklahoma.com					
Bank of Old Monroe The					
2100 Hwy C PO Box 188	Old Monroe	MO	63369	636-665-5601	665-5998
TF: 800-264-5578 ■ *Web:* www.bankofoldmonroe.com					
Bank of Stanly PO Box 338	Albemarle	NC	28002	704-983-6181	983-5548
TF: 800-438-6864 ■ *Web:* www.bankofstanly.com					
Bank Of Stockton PO Box 1110	Stockton	CA	95201	209-929-1600	929-1434
TF: 800-941-1494 ■ *Web:* www.bankofstockton.com					
Bank of Sunset & Trust Co 863 Napoleon Ave	Sunset	LA	70584	337-662-5222	662-5705
Web: www.bankofsunset.com					
Bank of Tampa The 601 Bayshore Blvd	Tampa	FL	33606	813-872-1216	998-2647
Web: www.bankoftampa.com					
Bank of the Carolinas					
135 Boxwood Village Dr	Mocksville	NC	27028	336-751-5755	751-4222
NASDAQ: BCAR ■ *TF:* 877-751-5755 ■ *Web:* www.bankofthecarolinas.com					
Bank of the Sierra PO Box 1930	Porterville	CA	93258	559-782-4900	782-4994
TF Cust Svc: 888-454-2265 ■ *Web:* www.bankofthesierra.com					
Bank of the West 1450 Treat Blvd	Walnut Creek	CA	94597	925-942-8300	
TF: 888-389-8668 ■ *Web:* www.bankofthewest.com					
Bank of Tokyo-Mitsubishi Ltd					
1251 Avenue of the Americas	New York	NY	10020	212-782-4000	782-6570*
**Fax:* Hum Res ■ *Web:* www.bk.mufg.jp					
Bank of Tuscaloosa					
2200 Jack Warner Pkwy PO Box 2508	Tuscaloosa	AL	35403	205-345-6200	343-0550
Web: www.bankoftuscaloosa.com					
Bank Of Utica 222 Genesee St	Utica	NY	13502	315-797-2700	797-2707
Web: www.bankofutica.com					
Bank of Virginia 11730 Hull St Rd	Midlothian	VA	23112	804-744-7576	744-2306
NASDAQ: BOVA ■ *TF:* 800-500-1044 ■ *Web:* www.bankofva.com					
BankAtlantic 2100 W Cypress Creek Rd	Fort Lauderdale	FL	33309	954-760-5000	940-5840
TF: 800-741-1700 ■ *Web:* www.bankatlantic.com					
Bankeast 607 Market St PO Box 24	Knoxville	TN	37901	865-540-5800	268-3275*
**Fax Area Code:* 931 ■ *Web:* www.bankeast.com					
Bankwest Inc 420 S Pierre St PO Box 998	Pierre	SD	57501	605-224-7391	224-7393
TF: 800-253-0362 ■ *Web:* www.bankwest-sd.com					
Banner Bank 10 S First Ave PO Box 907	Walla Walla	WA	99362	509-527-3636	524-5980*
**Fax:* Hum Res ■ *TF:* 800-272-9933 ■ *Web:* www.bannerbank.com					
Banterra Corp 1404 US Rt 45 S PO Box 291	Eldorado	IL	62930	618-273-9346	273-2782
TF: 877-541-2265 ■ *Web:* www.banterrabank.com					
Barrington Bank & Trust Co Na					
201 S Hough St	Barrington	IL	60010	847-842-4500	304-6697
Web: www.barringtonbank.com					
Bay Bank & Trust Co					
509 Harrison Ave PO Box 59350	Panama City	FL	32412	850-769-3333	785-9553
Web: www.baybankandtrust.com					
Bay Banks of Virginia Inc					
100 S Main St PO Box 1869	Kilmarnock	VA	22482	804-435-1171	435-0543
Web: www.bankoflancaster.com					
Baylake Bank 217 N 4th Ave	Sturgeon Bay	WI	54235	920-743-5551	746-3984
OTC: BYLK ■ *TF:* 800-267-3610 ■ *Web:* www.baylake.com					
BB & T Corp 200 W 2nd St	Winston-Salem	NC	27101	336-733-2000	
NYSE: BBT ■ *TF:* 800-682-6902 ■ *Web:* www.bbandt.com					
BB&T Corp 200 S College St	Charlotte	NC	28202	704-954-1000	
TF: 888-385-3301 ■ *Web:* www.bbt.com					
Beal Bank SSB 6000 Legacy Dr	Plano	TX	75024	469-467-5000	241-9564
TF: 877-879-2325 ■ *Web:* www.bealbank.com					
Beneficial Mutual Savings Bank					
530 Walnut St	Philadelphia	PA	19106	215-864-6000	864-6198
TF: 800-784-8490 ■ *Web:* www.thebeneficial.com					
Berkshire Bank PO Box 1308	Pittsfield	MA	01202	413-443-5601	447-1799
TF: 800-773-5601 ■ *Web:* www.berkshirebank.com					
BNC National Bank 322 E Main Ave PO Box 4050	Bismarck	ND	58501	701-250-3000	250-3028
TF: 800-262-2265 ■ *Web:* www.bncbank.com					
Boiling Springs Savings Bank (BSSB)					
25 Orient Way	Rutherford	NJ	07070	201-939-5000	939-3957
TF: 866-395-5343 ■ *Web:* www.bssbank.com					

	City	State	ZIP	Phone	Fax
Boone County National Bank 720 E Broadway PO Box 678	Columbia	MO	65201	573-874-8535	817-8754
TF: 800-842-2262 ■ *Web:* www.boonebank.com					
Borel Private Bank & Trust Co 160 Bovet Rd.	San Mateo	CA	94402	650-378-3700	378-3774
Web: www.borel.com					
Branch Banking & Trust Co 200 W 2nd St	Winston-Salem	NC	27101	336-733-2500	
TF: 800-226-5228 ■ *Web:* www.bbt.com					
Branch Banking & Trust Co of South Carolina 301 College St	Greenville	SC	29601	864-242-8026	242-9500
TF: 800-226-5228 ■ *Web:* www.bbt.com					
Branch Banking & Trust Co of Virginia 500 E Main St.	Norfolk	VA	23510	757-823-7899	626-0405
TF: 800-226-5228 ■ *Web:* www.bbt.com					
Broadway Bank 1177 NE Loop 410.	San Antonio	TX	78209	210-283-4000	
Web: www.broadwaybank.com					
Brown Bros Harriman & Co 140 Broadway	New York	NY	10005	212-483-1818	493-7287*
**Fax:* Hum Res ■ *Web:* www.bbh.com					
Burke & Herbert Bank & Trust Co 100 S Fairfax St	Alexandria	VA	22314	703-751-7701	548-5759
TF: 877-440-0800 ■ *Web:* www.burkeandherbertbank.com					
California Bank & Trust 11622 El Camino Real Suite 200	San Diego	CA	92130	858-793-7400	793-7438
TF: 800-400-6080 ■ *Web:* www.calbanktrust.com					
Calyon 1301 Avenue of the Americas	New York	NY	10019	212-261-7000	459-3182
Web: www.ca-cib.com					
Cambridge Savings Bank 1374 Massachusetts Ave	Cambridge	MA	02138	617-441-4155	441-4316*
**Fax:* Cust Svc ■ *TF:* 800-864-2265 ■ *Web:* www.cambridgesavings.com					
Canadian Imperial Bank of Commerce (CIBC) 199 Bay St Commerce Ct W	Toronto	ON	M5L1G9	800-465-2422	
TSE: CM ■ *TF:* 800-465-2422 ■ *Web:* www.cibc.com					
Canadian Western Bank 10303 Jasper Ave Suite 3000	Edmonton	AB	T5J3X6	780-423-8888	423-8897
TSE: CWB ■ *TF:* 888-877-6262 ■ *Web:* www.cwbank.com					
Canandaigua National Corp 72 S Main St	Canandaigua	NY	14424	585-394-4260	394-4001
OTC: CNND ■ *Web:* www.cnbank.com					
Cape Bank 225 N Main St	Cape May Court House	NJ	08210	609-465-5600	
Web: www.capebankonline2.com					
Cape Cod Five Cents Savings Bank 19 W Rd PO Box 20	Orleans	MA	02653	508-240-0555	240-1895*
**Fax:* Mktg ■ *TF:* 800-678-1855 ■ *Web:* www.capecodfive.com					
Capital City Bank 2111 N Monroe St PO Box 900	Tallahassee	FL	32302*	850-402-7500	
TF: 888-671-0400 ■ *Web:* www.ccbg.com					
Capital One Auto Finance Inc PO Box 60511	City of Industry	CA	91716	800-946-0332	
TF: 800-946-0332 ■ *Web:* www.capitalone.com					
Capital One FSB *Capital One Bank* 15000 Capital One Dr	Richmond	VA	23238	804-273-1144	
Web: www.capitalone.com					
Capitol FSB 700 S Kansas Ave.	Topeka	KS	66603	785-235-1341	231-6329
TF: 800-432-2926 ■ *Web:* www.capfed.com					
Carolina First Bank 104 S Main St Poinsett Plaza 10th Fl	Greenville	SC	29601	864-255-7900	239-6401
TF: 800-476-6400 ■ *Web:* www.carolinafirst.com					
Carolina Trust Bank 901 E Main St	Lincolnton	NC	28092	704-735-1104	735-1104
NASDAQ: CART ■ *Web:* www.carolinatrust.com					
Carver FSB 75 W 125th St	New York	NY	10027	718-230-2900	
Web: www.carverbank.com					
Casey State Bank 305-307 N Central Ave	Casey	IL	62420	217-932-2136	932-4370
Web: www.caseystatebank.com					
CBC National Bank 1891 S 14th St	Fernandina Beach	FL	32034	904-321-0400	321-1511
Web: www.fnb-palm.com					
Central BanCo Inc 238 Madison St	Jefferson City	MO	65101	573-634-1155	634-1100
Web: www.centralbancompany.com					
Central Pacific Bank PO Box 3590	Honolulu	HI	96811	808-544-0500	
NYSE: CPF ■ *TF Cust Svc:* 800-342-8422 ■ *Web:* www.centralpacificbank.com					
Central Progressive Bank (CPB) 29092 Kretel Rd	Lacombe	LA	70445	985-882-2269	882-6701
Web: www.cpb.com					
Central Valley Bank 537 W 2nd Ave	Toppenish	WA	98948	509-865-2511	865-2086
TF: 800-422-1566 ■ *Web:* www.cvbankwa.com					
Century Bank 100 S Federal Pl PO Box 1507	Santa Fe	NM	87501	505-995-1200	
TF: 877-424-2828 ■ *Web:* www.centurynetbank.com					
Century National Bank 14 S 5th St	Zanesville	OH	43701	740-454-2521	455-7201
TF: 800-321-7061 ■ *Web:* www.centurynationalbank.com					
Charter One Financial Inc 1215 Superior Ave	Cleveland	OH	44114	216-566-5300	566-1453
TF: 800-553-8981 ■ *Web:* www.charteronebank.com					
CharterBank 1233 OG Skinner Dr	West Point	GA	31833	706-645-1391	645-1370
NASDAQ: CHFN ■ *TF:* 800-763-4444 ■ *Web:* www.charterbk.com					
Chase Bank 1 Chase Manhattan Plaza	New York	NY	10005	212-552-5000	552-2050*
**Fax:* PR ■ *TF:* 800-935-9935 ■ *Web:* www.chase.com					
Cherokee Bank 1275 Riverstone Pkwy PO Box 4250	Canton	GA	30114	770-479-3400	720-6923
PINK: CHKJ ■ *Web:* www.cherokeebank.com					
Chevy Chase Bank FSB 7501 Wisconsin Ave	Bethesda	MD	20814	240-497-4102	497-4110
TF: 800-987-2265 ■ *Web:* www.capitalone.com					
Chiba Bank Ltd 1133 Avenue of the Americas 15th Fl	New York	NY	10036	212-354-7777	354-8575
Chinatrust Bank USA 22939 Hawthorne Blvd.	Torrance	CA	90505	310-791-2828	791-2880
TF: 888-839-9000 ■ *Web:* www.chinatrustusa.com					
Citibank (Delaware) 1 Penns Way	New Castle	DE	19720	302-323-3600	827-3122*
**Fax Area Code:* 646 ■ *TF:* 800-627-3999 ■ *Web:* www.citi.com					
Citibank (South Dakota) NA 701 E 60th St N	Sioux Falls	SD	57117	605-331-2626	357-2073
TF: 800-950-5114 ■ *Web:* www.citi.com					
Citibank (West) FSB 590 Market St	San Francisco	CA	94104	866-248-4937	
TF: 866-248-4937 ■ *Web:* www.citibank.com					
Citibank FSB 245 Market St.	San Francisco	CA	94105	866-248-4937	
TF: 866-248-4937 ■ *Web:* www.citi.com					
Citibank NA 399 Pk Ave	New York	NY	10022	800-627-3999	559-7373*
**Fax Area Code:* 212 ■ *TF:* 800-285-3000 ■ *Web:* www.citibank.com					
Citizen National Bank Of Bluffton The 102 S Main St PO Box 88	Bluffton	OH	45817	419-358-8040	358-5227
Web: www.cnbohio.com					
Citizens Bank 328 S Saginaw St 1 Citizens Banking Ctr	Flint	MI	48502	800-676-6276	
TF: 800-676-6276 ■ *Web:* www.cbclientsfirst.com					
Citizens Bank New Hampshire 875 Elm St.	Manchester	NH	03101	800-862-5000	
TF: 800-862-5000 ■ *Web:* www.citizensbank.com					
Citizens Bank of Clovis 421 Pile St PO Box 1629	Clovis	NM	88101	575-769-1911	762-7259
Web: www.citizensbankofclovis.com					
Citizens Bank of Cochran PO Box 427	Cochran	GA	31014	478-934-6277	934-3962
Web: www.citizensbankcochran.com					
Citizens Bank of Las Cruces 505 S Main St.	Las Cruces	NM	88004	575-647-4100	526-3409*
**Fax Area Code:* 505 ■ *Web:* www.citizenslc.com					
Citizens Bank of Massachusetts 28 State St	Boston	MA	02109	617-725-5500	
TF: 800-922-9999 ■ *Web:* www.citizensbank.com					
Citizens Bank of Mukwonago 301 N Rochester St PO Box 223	Mukwonago	WI	53149	262-363-6500	363-6515
Web: www.citizenbank.com					
Citizens Bank of Rhode Island 1 Citizens Plaza	Providence	RI	02903	401-456-7000	455-5715
TF Cust Svc: 800-922-9999 ■ *Web:* www.citizensbank.com					
Citizens Business Bank (CBB) 701 N Haven Ave	Ontario	CA	91764	909-980-4030	481-2135
TF Cust Svc: 888-222-5432 ■ *Web:* www.citizensbusinessbank.com					
Citizens Financial Services 707 Ridge Rd.	Munster	IN	46321	219-836-5500	836-0265
TF: 888-226-5237 ■ *Web:* www.bankcfs.com					
City National Bank 400 N Roxbury Dr	Beverly Hills	CA	90210	310-888-6000	888-6045*
**Fax:* Mktg ■ *TF Cust Svc:* 800-773-7100 ■ *Web:* www.cnb.com					
City National Bank of Florida 450 E Las Olas Blvd Suite 160	Fort Lauderdale	FL	33301	954-467-6667	524-8247
TF: 800-762-2489 ■ *Web:* www.citynationalcm.com					
City National Bank of New Jersey (CNB) 900 Broad St.	Newark	NJ	07102	973-624-0865	624-5754
TF: 877-350-3524 ■ *Web:* www.citynatbank.com					
City National Bank of West Virginia 3601 McCorckle Ave PO Box 7520	Charleston	WV	25356	304-926-3300	925-8073
TF: 877-203-8700 ■ *Web:* www.cityholding.com					
Clearfield Bank & Trust Co 11 N 2nd St PO Box 171	Clearfield	PA	16830	814-765-7551	765-2943
TF: 888-765-7551 ■ *Web:* www.cbtfinancial.com					
Cnlbank 450 S Orange Ave Suite 400	Orlando	FL	32801	407-244-3100	992-3755
TF: 800-910-2187 ■ *Web:* www.cnlbank.com					
Coast Capital Savings 645 Tyee Rd Suite 400	Victoria	BC	V9A6X5	250-483-7000	
TF: 888-517-7000 ■ *Web:* www.coastcapitalsavings.com					
College Savings Bank 5 Vaughn Dr Suite 100	Princeton	NJ	08540	609-987-3700	987-3760
TF: 800-888-2723 ■ *Web:* www.collegesavings.com					
Colorado East Bank & Trust Inc 100 W Pearl St	Lamar	CO	81052	719-336-5200	336-5944
Web: www.coloeast.com					
Colorado Fsb 8400 E Prentice Ave Suite 545	Greenwood Village	CO	80111	303-793-3555	793-3560
TF: 877-484-2372 ■ *Web:* www.coloradofederalbank.com					
Colorado State Bank & Trust NA PO Box 2300	Tulsa	OK	74192	303-861-2111	
Web: www.csbt.com					
Columbia Bank The 7168 Columbia Gateway Dr	Columbia	MD	21046	410-730-5070	
TF: 888-822-2265 ■ *Web:* www.thecolumbiabank.com					
Columbia Savings Bank 19-01 Rt 208	Fair Lawn	NJ	07410	201-794-5706	794-5706
TF Cust Svc: 800-747-4428 ■ *Web:* www.columbiabankonline.com					
Columbia State Bank PO Box 2156	Tacoma	WA	98401	253-305-1900	396-6960*
**Fax:* Hum Res ■ *TF:* 800-305-1905 ■ *Web:* www.columbiabank.com					
Columbus Bank & Trust Co 1148 Broadway	Columbus	GA	31901	706-649-4900	649-2481*
**Fax:* Cust Svc ■ *TF:* 800-334-9007 ■ *Web:* www.columbusbankandtrust.com					
Comerica Bank 500 Woodward Ave	Detroit	MI	48226	248-371-5000	
TF: 800-643-4418 ■ *Web:* www.comerica.com					
Comerica Bank-California 333 W Santa Clara St	San Jose	CA	95113	408-556-5300	298-6449*
**Fax:* Hum Res ■ *TF:* 800-522-2265 ■ *Web:* www.comerica.com					
Comerica Bank-Texas 1717 Main St	Dallas	TX	75201	800-925-2160	
TF: 800-925-2160 ■ *Web:* www.comerica.com					
Commercewest Bank NA 2111 Business Ctr Dr	Irvine	CA	92612	949-251-6959	251-6957
Web: www.cwbk.com					
Commercial Bank 301 N State St PO Box 638	Alma	MI	48801	989-463-2185	463-5996
OTC: CEFC ■ *Web:* www.commercial-bank.com					
Commerzbank AG 2 World Financial Ctr	New York	NY	10281	212-266-7200	266-7235
Web: www.commerzbank.us					
Commonwealth Bank of Australia 599 Lexington Ave 17th Fl	New York	NY	10022	212-848-9200	336-7725
Web: www.commbank.com.au/ie.htm					
Community Bank of Florida 28801 SW 157th Ave	Homestead	FL	33033	305-245-2211	242-4639
TF: 866-820-1533 ■ *Web:* www.communitybankfl.com					
Community Bank Of Midwest 2220 Broadway Ave	Great Bend	KS	67530	620-792-5111	792-5168
Web: www.communitybankmidwest.com					
Community Bank of Raymore PO Box 200	Raymore	MO	64083	816-322-2100	322-5915
TF: 888-322-6772 ■ *Web:* www.cbronline.net					
Community First Bank 925 Wisconsin Ave	Boscobel	WI	53805	608-375-4117	375-4119
Web: www.cfbank.com					
Community National Bank PO Box 259	Derby	VT	05829	802-334-7915	334-3148
Web: www.communitynationalbank.com					
Community Trust Bank NA 346 N Mayo Trail PO Box 2947	Pikeville	KY	41501	606-432-1414	433-4749*
**Fax:* Cust Svc ■ *TF:* 800-422-1090 ■ *Web:* www.ctbi.com					
Conneaut Savings Bank 305 Main St PO Box 740	Conneaut	OH	44030	440-599-8121	593-6446
TF: 888-453-2311 ■ *Web:* www.conneautsavings.com					
Country Bank for Savings 75 Main St.	Ware	MA	01082	413-967-6221	967-3289
TF: 800-322-8233 ■ *Web:* www.countrybank.com					
Credit Union of Denver 9305 W Alameda Ave	Lakewood	CO	80226	303-234-1700	239-1108
TF: 800-951-9014 ■ *Web:* www.cudenver.com					
D L Evans Bank 397 N Overland PO Box 1188	Burley	ID	83318	208-678-9076	678-9093
TF: 888-873-9777 ■ *Web:* www.dlevans.com					
DBS Bank Ltd 725 N Figueroa St	Los Angeles	CA	90017	213-627-0222	627-0228
Web: www.dbs.com					

Name / Address	City	State	ZIP	Phone	Fax
Dedham Institution For Savings 55 Elm St PO Box 9107	Dedham	MA	02026	781-329-6700	320-4892
TF: 888-289-0342 ■ *Web:* www.dedhamsavings.com					
Desert Community Bank PO Box 1349	Victorville	CA	92393	760-243-2140	243-5048*
**Fax:* Cust Svc ■ *TF:* 888-895-5650 ■ *Web:* www.dcbk.org					
Deutsche Bank Canada (DB) 199 Bay St Suite 4700 Commerce Ct W PO Box 263	Toronto	ON	M5L1E9	416-682-8000	682-8383
Web: www.db.com					
Devon Bank 6445 N Western Ave	Chicago	IL	60645	866-683-3866	973-5647*
**Fax Area Code:* 773 ■ *TF:* 877-849-5533 ■ *Web:* www.devonbank.com					
Dexia Bank 445 Pk Ave 8th Fl	New York	NY	10022	212-705-0700	705-0701
Web: www.dexia.com					
Dime Bank The 820 Church St PO Box 509	Honesdale	PA	18431	570-253-1902	253-5845
TF: 888-469-3463 ■ *Web:* www.thedimebank.com					
Discover Bank PO Box 30416	Salt Lake City	UT	84130	302-323-7810	
TF: 800-347-7000 ■ *Web:* www.discoverbank.com					
E*Trade Bank 671 N Glebe Rd	Arlington	VA	22203	703-247-3700	236-7210
TF: 800-387-2331 ■ *Web:* www.bankus.etrade.com					
Eagle Bancorp Montana Inc 1400 Prospect Ave	Helena	MT	59601	406-442-3080	457-4035
NASDAQ: EBMT ■ *Web:* www.americanfederalsavingsbank.com					
East West Bank 135 N Los Robels Ave 7th Fl	Pasadena	CA	91101	626-768-6000	
TF: 888-895-5650 ■ *Web:* www.eastwestbank.com					
East-West Bank 135 N Los Robles Ave	Pasadena	CA	91101	626-768-6000	683-7134
TF: 800-888-3932 ■ *Web:* www.eastwestbank.com					
Eastern Bank 1 Eastern Pl	Lynn	MA	01901	781-599-2100	598-7697
TF: 800-327-8376 ■ *Web:* www.easternbank.com					
Eastern Bank PO Box 391	Lynn	MA	01903	800-327-8376	942-8194*
**Fax Area Code:* 781 ■ *TF:* 800-447-1052 ■ *Web:* www.easternbank.com					
El Dorado Savings Bank 4040 El Dorado Rd	Placerville	CA	95667	530-622-1492	621-1659
TF: 800-874-9779 ■ *Web:* www.eldoradosavingsbank.com					
Elmira Savings Bank 333 E Water St	Elmira	NY	14901	607-734-3374	732-4007
NASDAQ: ESBK ■ *TF:* 888-372-9299 ■ *Web:* www.elmirasavingsbank.com					
Encore Bank 9 Greenway Plaza Suite 1000	Houston	TX	77046	713-787-3100	267-7787
NASDAQ: EBTX ■ *TF:* 800-308-6709 ■ *Web:* www.encorebank.com					
Enterprise Bank of SC 13497 Broxton Bridge Rd PO BOX 8	Ehrhardt	SC	29081	803-267-3191	267-2316
Web: www.ebanksc.com					
ESB Bank 600 Lawrence Ave	Ellwood City	PA	16117	724-758-5584	758-0576
TF: 800-533-4193 ■ *Web:* www.esbbank.com					
Essex Savings Bank PO Box 950	Essex	CT	06426	860-767-4414	767-4411
TF: 877-377-3922 ■ *Web:* www.essexsavings.com					
Evangeline Bank & Trust Co The 497 W Main St PO Box 346	Ville Platte	LA	70586	337-363-5541	363-0678
Web: www.therealbank.com					
Exchange State Bank 3992 Chandler St PO Box 68	Carsonville	MI	48419	810-657-9333	657-9810
TF: 888-488-9300 ■ *Web:* www.exchangestatebank.com					
F&m Bank PO Box 1130	Clarksville	TN	37041	931-645-2400	553-2020
TF: 800-645-4199 ■ *Web:* www.myfmbank.com					
Farm Bureau Bank 2165 Green Vista Dr Suite 204	Sparks	NV	89431	775-673-4566	674-4004
TF: 800-492-3276 ■ *Web:* www.farmbureaubank.com					
Farmers & Merchants Bank of Long Beach 302 Pine Ave	Long Beach	CA	90802	562-437-0011	437-8672
Web: www.fmb.com					
Farmers Bank & Savings Co Inc 211 W Second St	Pomeroy	OH	45769	740-992-2136	992-7583
Web: www.fbsc.com					
Farmers Bank The 9 E Clinton St PO Box 129	Frankfort	IN	46041	765-654-8731	654-8738
Web: www.thefarmersbank.com					
Farmers Merchants Bank & Trust Co 100 S Main St PO BOX 910	Breaux Bridge	LA	70517	337-332-2115	332-5089
Web: www.fmbanking.com					
Farmers National Bank of Buhl 914 Main St PO Box 392	Buhl	ID	83316	208-543-4351	543-8323
Web: www.farmersnatlbank.com					
Farmers National Bank of Prophetstown The 114 W Third St	Prophetstown	IL	61277	815-772-3700	
Web: www.fnbptown.com					
Farmers State Bancshares Inc 100 W Main St PO BOX 9	Mountain City	TN	37683	423-727-8121	727-5382
Web: www.fsbankmctn.com					
Farmers State Bank & Trust Co The 200 W State St	Jacksonville	IL	62650	217-479-4000	479-4125
Web: www.fsbtco.com					
Fauquier Bank The (TFB) 10 Courthouse Sq PO Box 561	Warrenton	VA	20186	540-347-2700	
TF: 800-638-3798 ■ *Web:* www.fauquierbank.com					
Fidelity Bancshares Nc Inc PO Box 8	Fuquay Varina	NC	27526	919-552-2242	557-4563
TF: 800-816-9608 ■ *Web:* www.fidelitybanknc.com					
Fidelity Bank 100 E English St	Wichita	KS	67201	316-268-7270	268-7383
TF: 800-658-1637 ■ *Web:* www.fidelitybank.com					
Fifth Third Bank Central Ohio 21 E State St	Columbus	OH	43215	614-744-7661	744-7516
Web: www.53.com					
Fifth Third Bank Western Ohio 1 S Main St	Dayton	OH	45402	937-227-3064	449-2678*
**Fax:* Hum Res ■ *TF:* 800-972-3030 ■ *Web:* www.53.com					
Fireside Bank PO Box 9080	Pleasanton	CA	94566	866-612-1801	730-3505*
**Fax Area Code:* 925 ■ *TF:* 800-825-1862 ■ *Web:* www.firesidebank.com					
First American Bank 261 S Western Ave	Carpentersville	IL	60110	847-426-6300	426-6300
Web: www.firstambank.com					
First American Bank & Trust 2785 Hwy 20 W PO Box 550	Vacherie	LA	70090	225-265-2265	265-7339
TF: 800-738-2265 ■ *Web:* www.fabt.com					
First Bank 11901 Olive Blvd	Creve Coeur	MO	63141	314-995-8700	567-7341
TF: 800-760-2265 ■ *Web:* www.firstbanks.com					
First Bank Financial Centre (FBFC) 155 W Wisconsin Ave PO Box 1004	Oconomowoc	WI	53066	262-569-9900	
TF: 888-569-9909 ■ *Web:* www.fbfcwi.com					
First Bank Muleshoe 202 S 1st PO Box 565	Muleshoe	TX	79347	806-272-4515	272-4436
First Bankers Trust Co NA 1201 Broadway PO Box 3566	Quincy	IL	62305	217-228-8000	228-8001
Web: www.firstbankers.com					
First Business Financial Services Inc 401 Charmany Dr	Madison	WI	53719	608-238-8008	232-5994
Web: www.firstbusiness.com					
First Calgary Savings 510 16th Ave NE	Calgary	AB	T2E1K4	403-230-1451	276-5299
TF: 866-923-4778 ■ *Web:* www.firstcalgary.com					
First Century Bank NA 500 Federal St PO Box 1559	Bluefield	WV	24701	304-325-8181	325-8198
TF: 877-214-9426 ■ *Web:* www.firstcentury.com					
First Citizens Bank & Trust Co Inc 1230 Main St	Columbia	SC	29201	803-771-8700	733-2763
TF: 888-612-4444 ■ *Web:* www.firstcitizensonline.com					
First Clover Leaf Bank 6814 Goshen Rd PO Box 540	Edwardsville	IL	62025	618-656-6122	656-1712
Web: www.firstcloverleafbank.com					
First County Bank Inc The 117 Prospect St	Stamford	CT	06901	203-462-4200	462-4442
Web: www.firstcountybank.com					
First Federal Bank Fsb 6900 N Executive Dr	Kansas City	MO	64120	816-245-4173	245-4181
Web: www.firstfedbankkc.com					
First Federal Bank of Arkansas FA 200 W Stephenson Ave	Harrison	AR	72601	870-741-7641	365-8369
TF: 800-345-2539 ■ *Web:* www.ffbh.com					
First Federal Bank Of Ohio 140 N Columbus St PO BOX 957	Galion	OH	44833	419-468-1518	468-2973
Web: www.firstfederalbankofohio.com					
First Federal Bank of the Midwest 601 Clinton St PO Box 248	Defiance	OH	43512	419-782-5015	782-5145
TF: 800-472-6292 ■ *Web:* www.first-fed.com					
First Federal Lakewood 14806 Detroit Ave	Lakewood	OH	44107	216-529-2700	226-0622
TF: 800-966-7300 ■ *Web:* www.ffl.net					
First Financial Bank 1 First Financial Plaza	Terre Haute	IN	47807	812-238-6000	238-6000
TF: 800-511-0045 ■ *Web:* www.first-online.com					
First Financial Bank 300 High St	Hamilton	OH	45011	513-867-4744	867-3111*
**Fax:* Cust Svc ■ *TF Cust Svc:* 800-543-2265 ■ *Web:* www.bankatfirst.com					
First Financial Bank 301 W Beauregard	San Angelo	TX	76903	325-659-5900	659-5956
Web: www.sanb-tx.com					
First Financial Bankshares 212 E Third St PO Box 272	Hereford	TX	79045	806-363-8200	363-8295
Web: www.hsbhereford.com					
First Hawaiian Bank 999 Bishop St	Honolulu	HI	96813	808-525-6340	525-8708*
**Fax:* Mktg ■ *TF:* 888-844-4444 ■ *Web:* www.fhb.com					
First Independent Bank PO Box 8904	Vancouver	WA	98668	360-699-4242	
Web: www.firstindy.com					
First Internet Bank of Indiana 7820 Innovation Blvd Suite 210	Indianapolis	IN	46278	317-532-7900	644-8678*
**Fax Area Code:* 888 ■ **Fax:* Cust Svc ■ *TF:* 888-873-3424 ■ *Web:* www.firstib.com					
First Interstate Bank 401 N 31st St	Billings	MT	59101	406-255-5000	255-5213*
**Fax:* Hum Res ■ *TF:* 888-752-3336 ■ *Web:* www.firstinterstatebank.com					
First Metro Bank 406 Avalon Ave	Muscle Shoals	AL	35661	256-386-0600	386-0651
Web: www.firstmetro.com					
First Mid-Illinois Bank & Trust 1515 Charleston Ave	Mattoon	IL	61938	217-258-0653	258-0426
OTC: FMBH ■ *Web:* www.firstmid.com					
First National Bank 205 W Oak St PO Box 578	Fort Collins	CO	80521	970-482-4861	495-9450
Web: www.1stnationalbank.com					
First National Bank Alaska 101 W 36 Ave PO Box 100720	Anchorage	AK	99510	907-777-4362	777-3828
TF: 800-856-4362 ■ *Web:* www.fnbalaska.com					
First National Bank Creston PO Box 445	Creston	IA	50801	641-782-2195	782-3499
TF: 877-782-2195 ■ *Web:* www.fnbcreston.com					
First National Bank Florida 6512 Caroline St PO Box 3654	Milton	FL	32570	850-623-2822	626-8631
TF: 800-277-0995 ■ *Web:* www.fnbfl.com					
First National Bank Group 505 S McColl Rd PO Box 810	Edinburg	TX	78539	956-383-8151	380-8521
TF: 877-380-8573 ■ *Web:* www.webfnb.com					
First National Bank In Alamogordo 414 Tenth St PO Box 9	Alamogordo	NM	88311	575-437-4880	437-1631*
**Fax Area Code:* 505 ■ *Web:* www.fnbalamo.com					
First National Bank In Mena 600 Hwy 71 S PO Box 1049	Mena	AR	71953	479-394-3552	394-2903
Web: www.fnbmena.com					
First National Bank In Sioux Falls The 100 S Phillips Ave	Sioux Falls	SD	57117	605-335-5200	335-5274
TF: 800-339-1160 ■ *Web:* www.fnbsf.com					
First National Bank In Tremont 134 S Sampson St PO Box 23	Tremont	IL	61568	309-925-2121	925-5448
TF: 800-925-5335 ■ *Web:* www.tremontbank.com					
First National Bank of Illinois Inc 3256 Ridge Rd	Lansing	IL	60438	708-474-1300	474-1331
Web: www.fnbiweb.com					
First National Bank Of Jasper 200 W 18th St PO Box 31	Jasper	AL	35502	205-221-3121	221-2030
Web: www.firstbankofjasper.com					
First National Bank of Muscatine 300 E 2nd St	Muscatine	IA	52761	563-263-4221	262-4213
Web: www.fnbmusc.com					
First National Bank of Omaha 1620 Dodge St	Omaha	NE	68197	402-341-0500	341-0500
TF: 800-228-4411 ■ *Web:* www.fnbomaha.com					
First National Bank of Oneida The 18418 Alberta St PO Box 4699	Oneida	TN	37841	423-569-8586	569-9826
Web: www.fnboneida.com					
First National Bank of Palmerton The 4th St & Lafayette Ave	Palmerton	PA	18071	610-826-2239	824-2393
TF: 800-344-2274 ■ *Web:* www.fnbpalmerton.com					
First National Bank of Paragould 200 W Ct St	Paragould	AR	72450	870-239-8521	
Web: www.fnbank.net					

Name / Address	City	State	Zip	Phone	Fax
First National Bank of Polk County 967 N Main St *Web:* www.fnbpolk.com	Cedartown	GA	30125	770-748-1750	749-2713
First National Bank of Santa Fe PO Box 609 *TF:* 888-912-2265 ■ *Web:* www.fnb-sf.com	Santa Fe	NM	87504	505-992-2000	992-2188
First National Bank of South Miami 5750 Sunset Dr 877-823-6276 *PINK: FMIA* ■ *Web:* www.fnbsm.com	Miami	FL	33143	305-665-5511	662-5440
First National Bank of St Louis 7707 Forsyth Blvd *Web:* www.fnbstl.com	Saint Louis	MO	63105	314-862-8300	746-4655
First National Bank of Waverly 316 E Bremer Ave PO Box 837 *Web:* www.fnbwaverly.com	Waverly	IA	50677	319-352-1340	352-6323
First National Bankers Bankshares Inc (FNBB) 7813 Office Pk Blvd *TF:* 800-421-6182 ■ *Web:* www.bankers-bank.com	Baton Rouge	LA	70809	225-924-8015	952-0899
First National London Bnkshrs 202 S Main St PO Box 100 *Web:* www.fnblondonky.com	London	KY	40743	606-878-5405	878-0142
First Niagara Financial Group 726 Exchange St Suite 618 *TF:* 800-421-0004 ■ *Web:* www.fnfg.com	Buffalo	NY	14210	716-625-7500	434-0160
First Olathe Bancshares PO Box 1500 *Web:* www.fnbolathe.com	Olathe	KS	66051	913-782-3211	791-9277
First Palmetto Savings Bank Fsb PO Box 430 *TF:* 800-922-7411 ■ *Web:* www.firstpalmetto.com	Camden	SC	29021	803-432-2265	
First Place Bank 185 E Market St **Fax:* Cust Svc ■ *TF:* 800-995-2646	Warren	OH	44481	330-373-1221	373-1221*
First Republic Bank 111 Pine St 3rd Fl *NYSE: FRC* ■ *TF:* 800-392-1400 ■ *Web:* www.firstrepublic.com	San Francisco	CA	94111	415-392-1400	392-1413
First Security Bancorp PO Box 1009 *Web:* www.fsbank.com	Searcy	AR	72145	501-279-3400	279-3455
First Security Bank of Missoula 1704 Dearborn PO Box 4506 *Web:* www.fsbmsla.com	Missoula	MT	59801	406-728-3115	
First Security Bank of Sleepy Eye 100 E Main PO BOX 469 *Web:* www.firstsecuritybanks.com	Sleepy	MN	56085	507-794-3911	794-5140
First State Bank 708 Azalea Dr PO Box 506 **Fax Area Code:* 601 ■ *TF:* 866-408-3582 ■ *Web:* www.firststatebnk.com	Waynesboro	MS	39367	866-408-3582	735-0231*
First State Bank & Trust Co 1005 E 23rd St *Web:* www.firststatebankandtrust.com	Fremont	NE	68025	402-721-2500	727-0208
First State Bank of Kansas City 650 Kansas Ave *TF:* 800-883-1242 ■ *Web:* www.fsbkcks.com	Kansas City	KS	66105	913-371-1242	371-7516
First Tennessee Bank 165 Madison Ave **Fax:* Mktg ■ *TF:* 800-382-5465 ■ *Web:* www.firsttennessee.com	Memphis	TN	38103	901-523-4883	523-4145*
First Texas Bank 501 E 3rd St PO Box 671 *Web:* www.firstexbank.com	Lampasas	TX	76550	512-556-3691	556-6104
First Trade Union Bank 1 Harbor St PO Box 55063 *Web:* www.ftubhb.com	Boston	MA	02210	617-482-4000	330-5104
First Western Bank & Trust PO Box 1090 *TF:* 800-688-2584 ■ *Web:* www.bankfirstwestern.com	Minot	ND	58702	701-852-3711	857-7212
First-Knox National Bank The PO Box 1270 *Web:* www.firstknox.com	Mount Vernon	OH	43050	740-399-5141	399-5268
Firstrust Savings Bank 15 E Ridge Pike 4th Fl *TF:* 800-220-2265 ■ *Web:* www.firstrust.com	Conshohocken	PA	19428	610-941-9898	238-5061
Flagstar Bank FSB 5151 Corporate Dr **Fax:* Hum Res ■ *TF:* 800-945-7700 ■ *Web:* www.flagstar.com	Troy	MI	48098	248-312-2000	312-6842*
Florence Savings Bank 85 Main St PO Box 60700 *Web:* www.florencesavings.com	Florence	MA	01062	413-587-1758	585-5102
Florida Community Bank Inc 1400 N 15th St *Web:* www.floridacommunitybank.net	Immokalee	FL	34142	239-657-3171	657-8482
Flushing Savings Bank FSB 144-51 Northern Blvd *Web:* www.flushingsavings.com	Flushing	NY	11354	718-512-2929	
Forcht Bank Na 2404 Sir Barton Way *TF:* 866-523-1445 ■ *Web:* www.forchtbank.com	Lexington	KY	40509	859-264-4265	263-3233
Four Oaks Bank & Trust Co PO Box 309 *TF:* 877-963-6257 ■ *Web:* www.fouroaksbank.com	Four Oaks	NC	27524	919-963-2177	963-2768
Fowler State Bank 300 E 5th St PO Box 511 *TF:* 800-439-3951 ■ *Web:* www.fowlerstatebank.com	Fowler	IN	47944	765-884-1200	884-3239
Franklin FSB 4501 Cox Rd PO Box 5310 *Web:* www.franklinfederal.com	Glen Allen	VA	23060	804-967-7000	967-7050
Fremont Bank PO Box 5101 *TF:* 800-359-2265 ■ *Web:* www.fremontbank.com	Fremont	CA	94538	510-792-2300	795-5760
Frontenac Bank 3330 Rider Trail S *TF:* 877-205-5777 ■ *Web:* www.frontenacbank.com	Earth City	MO	63045	314-298-8200	
Fulton Bank 1 Penn Sq *TF:* 800-385-8664 ■ *Web:* www.fultonbank.com	Lancaster	PA	17602	717-581-3000	295-3280
Garden State Community Bank 36 Ferry St *Web:* www.pennfsb.com	Newark	NJ	07105	973-589-8616	
Garnett State Savings Bank 106 E 5th St PO BOX 329 *Web:* www.gssb.us.com	Garnett	KS	66032	785-448-3111	448-6613
Giantbank.com 6300 NE 1st Ave *TF:* 877-446-4200 ■ *Web:* www.giantbank.com	Fort Lauderdale	FL	33334	954-958-0001	958-0190
Glens Falls National Bank & Trust Co 250 Glen St *Web:* www.gfnational.com	Glens Falls	NY	12801	518-793-4121	798-6403
Glenwood State Bank 5 E Minnesota Ave PO Box 197 *TF:* 800-207-7333 ■ *Web:* www.glenwoodstate.com	Glenwood	MN	56334	320-634-5111	634-5114
Gorham Savings Bank 64 Main St *Web:* www.gorhamsavingsbank.com	Gorham	ME	04038	207-839-4450	839-4790
Grants State Bank 824 W Santa Fe Ave PO Box 1088 *TF:* 877-285-6611 ■ *Web:* www.grantsbank.com	Grants	NM	87020	505-285-6611	287-2260
Grayson National Bank (GNB) 113 W Main St *Web:* www.graysonnationalbank.com	Independence	VA	24348	276-773-2811	773-3890
Greenfield Savings Bank 400 Main St PO BOX 1537 *Web:* www.greenfieldsavings.com	Greenfield	MA	01302	413-774-3191	774-6755
Greenville First Bank 100 Verdae Blvd Suite 100 *TF:* 877-679-9646 ■ *Web:* www.greenvillefirst.com	Greenville	SC	29606	864-679-9000	679-9099
Guaranty Bank 4000 W Brown Deer Rd *TF:* 800-840-0770 ■ *Web:* www.guarantybanking.com	Brown Deer	WI	53209	414-362-4000	365-6779
Guaranty Bank & Trust Co PO Box 1807 *Web:* www.guaranty-bank.com	Cedar Rapids	IA	52406	319-286-6200	362-7894
Guilford Savings Bank (GSB) PO Box 369 *TF:* 866-878-1480 ■ *Web:* www.gsb-yourbank.com	Guilford	CT	06437	203-453-2015	458-3927
Hamler State Bank 210 Randolph St PO Box 358 *TF:* 888-508-3955 ■ *Web:* www.hamlerstatebank.com	Hamler	OH	43524	419-274-3955	
Hampden Bank PO Box 2048 *Web:* www.hampdenbank.com	Springfield	MA	01103	413-452-5223	746-1018
Hampton Roads Bankshares Inc 999 Waterside Dr *NASDAQ: HMPR* ■ *Web:* www.bankofhamptonroads.com	Norfolk	VA	23510	757-217-1000	217-3656
Hardin County Bank The (HCB) 235 Wayne Rd PO BOX 940 *Web:* www.hardincountybank.com	Savannah	TN	38372	731-925-9001	925-8106
Harris Trust & Savings Bank 111 W Monroe St *TF:* 888-340-2265 ■ *Web:* www4.harrisbank.com	Chicago	IL	60603	312-461-7447	461-5788
Hatboro Federal Savings 221 S York Rd *Web:* www.hatborofed.com	Hatboro	PA	19040	215-675-4000	672-6684
Heartland Bancshares Inc 420 N Morton St PO Box 469 *OTC: HRTB* ■ *Web:* www.hcb-in.com	Franklin	IN	46131	317-738-3915	736-5022
Hebron Savings Bank (HSB) 101 N Main St PO Box 59 *Web:* www.hebronsavingsbank.com	Hebron	MD	21830	410-749-1186	543-0703
Hickory Point Bank & Trust FSB PO Box 2548 *TF Cust Svc:* 800-872-0081 ■ *Web:* www.hickorypointbank.com	Decatur	IL	62525	217-875-3131	872-6250
Highland Community Bank 307 Thacker Ave PO Box 1059 *Web:* www.highlandscommunitybank.com	Covington	VA	24426	540-962-2265	962-1203
Hills Bank & Trust Co 131 Main St PO Box 70 *TF:* 800-445-5725 ■ *Web:* www.hillsbank.com	Hills	IA	52235	319-679-2291	679-2180
Hingham Institution for Savings 55 Main St *NASDAQ: HIFS* ■ *TF:* 877-447-2265 ■ *Web:* www.hinghamsavings.com	Hingham	MA	02043	781-749-2200	740-4889
Hocking Valley Bank 7 W Stimson Ave PO BOX 4847 *Web:* www.hvbonline.com	Athens	OH	45701	740-592-4441	594-3147
Home Federal Bank 225 S Main Ave *TF:* 800-244-2149 ■ *Web:* www.homefederal.com	Sioux Falls	SD	57104	605-336-2470	333-7591
Home Federal Bank of Tennessee FSB 515 Market St *Web:* www.homefederalbanktn.com	Knoxville	TN	37902	865-546-0150	
Home FSB 715 N Broadway *TF:* 888-422-4117 ■ *Web:* www.justcallhome.com	Spring Valley	MN	55975	507-346-7345	346-9711
Home Savings & Loan Co of Youngstown 275 W Federal St *TF:* 888-822-4751 ■ *Web:* www.homesavings.com	Youngstown	OH	44503	330-742-0500	742-0615
HomeStreet Bank 601 Union St 2 Union Sq Suite 2000 *TF:* 800-654-1075 ■ *Web:* www.homestreetbank.com	Seattle	WA	98101	206-623-3050	389-7701
Hometown Bank 245 N Peters Ave *TF:* 877-261-2220 ■ *Web:* www.hometownbancorp.com	Fond du Lac	WI	54935	920-907-2220	
Hometrust Bank The PO Box 10 *Web:* www.hometrustbanking.com	Asheville	NC	28802	828-350-3064	258-8503
Hopewell Valley Community Bank 4 Rt 31 S *Web:* www.hvcbonline.com	Pennington	NJ	08534	609-466-2900	731-9144
HSBC Bank Canada 885 W Georgia St Suite 300 *TSE: HSB.PR.A* ■ *TF:* 888-310-4722 ■ *Web:* www.hsbc.ca	Vancouver	BC	V6C3E9	604-685-1000	641-2945
Hudson City Savings Bank W 80 Century Rd *TF:* 800-222-0194 ■ *Web:* www.hudsoncitysavingsbank.com	Paramus	NJ	07652	201-967-1900	
Hudson Valley Bank 21 Scarsdale Rd *Web:* www.hudsonvalleybank.com	Yonkers	NY	10707	914-961-6100	779-7350
Huntington National Bank 41 S High St Huntington Ctr *TF:* 800-480-2265 ■ *Web:* www.huntington.com	Columbus	OH	43287	614-480-8300	480-3761
Hyden Citizens Bank 22023 Main St PO Box 948 *Web:* www.hydencitizensbank.com	Hyden	KY	41749	606-672-2344	672-3627
Illinois Service Federal S & L 4619 S King Dr *Web:* www.isfbank.com	Chicago	IL	60653	773-624-2000	624-5340
Independence FSB 1301 9th St NW *PINK: IFSB* ■ *TF:* 888-922-6537 ■ *Web:* www.ifsb.com	Washington	DC	20001	202-628-5500	626-7106
Indiana Bank & Trust Co 222 W 2nd St *Web:* www.myindianabank.com	Seymour	IN	47274	812-522-1592	522-9561
Industrial Bank NA 4812 Georgia Ave NW *Web:* www.industrial-bank.com	Washington	DC	20011	202-722-2000	722-2040
InsurBanc 10 Executive Dr *TF:* 866-467-2262 ■ *Web:* www.insurbanc.com	Farmington	CT	06032	860-677-9701	677-9793
Integra Bank NA 21 SE 3rd St PO Box 868 *TF Cust Svc:* 800-467-1928 ■ *Web:* www.integrabank.com	Evansville	IN	47705	812-464-9800	461-9133
Inter-County Bakers Inc 1110 Rt 109 Suite 1 *TF:* 800-696-1350 ■ *Web:* www.icbakers.com	New York	NY	11757	631-957-1350	957-1013
International Bank of Commerce (IBC) 1200 San Bernardo Ave *Web:* www.ibc.com	Laredo	TX	78042	956-726-6651	726-6618
INTRUST Bank NA 105 N Main St **Fax:* Hum Res ■ *TF:* 800-895-2265 ■ *Web:* www.intrustbank.com	Wichita	KS	67202	316-383-1234	383-5805*
Investors Savings Bank 101 John F Kennedy Pkwy # 3 *TF:* 800-252-8119 ■ *Web:* www.isbnj.com	Short Hills	NJ	07078	973-376-5100	376-5357
Inwood National Bank 7621 Inwood Rd *Web:* www.inwoodbank.com	Dallas	TX	75209	214-358-5281	351-7381
Israel Discount Bank of New York (IDB Bank) 511 5th Ave *Web:* www.idbny.com	New York	NY	10017	212-551-8500	551-8511

Name / Address	City	State	Zip	Phone	Fax
James Polk Stone National Bank The PO Box 888 *Web:* www.portalesnb.com	Portales	NM	88130	575-356-6601	356-4788
Jeff Davis Bancshares Inc 507 N Main St PO Box 730 *Web:* www.jdbank.com/index.html	Jennings	LA	70546	337-824-3424	824-7283
Jefferson Federal Bank PO Box 1198 *Web:* www.jeffersonfederal.com	Morristown	TN	37814	423-586-8421	581-5134
Jersey Shore State Bank 300 Market St PO Box 967 *TF:* 888-412-5772 ■ *Web:* www.jssb.com	Williamsport	PA	17701	570-322-1111	398-2280
Johnson Bank 4001 N Main St *TF:* 800-236-8586 ■ *Web:* www.johnsonbank.com	Racine	WI	53402	262-639-6010	681-4627
JP Morgan Chase & Co 270 Pk Ave *Web:* www.jpmorganchase.com	New York	NY	10017	212-270-7325	648-5230
KBC Financial Products USA Inc 1177 Avenue of the Americas 7th Fl *Web:* www.kbcfp.com	New York	NY	10036	212-845-2000	845-2100
Kearny FSB 120 Passaic Ave **Fax Area Code:* 201 ■ *TF:* 800-273-3406 ■ *Web:* www.kearnyfederalsavings.com	Fairfield	NJ	07004	973-244-4500	991-6713*
Kennebec Savings Bank 150 State St PO Box 50 *TF:* 888-303-7788 ■ *Web:* www.kennebecsavings.com	Augusta	ME	04332	207-622-5801	626-2858
Kentucky Bank PO Box 157 *Web:* www.kybank.com	Paris	KY	40362	859-987-1795	987-5829
Key Bank 65 Dutch Hill Rd *TF Cust Svc:* 800-539-2968 ■ *Web:* www.key.com	Orangeburg	NY	10962	845-365-4816	365-5890
Key Bank USA NA 127 Public Sq *Web:* www.keybank.com	Cleveland	OH	44114	216-689-3000	
Kingston National Bank 2 N Main St PO Box 613 *TF:* 866-642-2191 ■ *Web:* www.kingstonnationalbank.com	Kingston	OH	45644	740-642-2191	642-2195
Kish Bancorp Inc 4255 E Main St PO Box 917 *PINK: KISB* ■ *Web:* www.kishbank.com	Belleville	PA	17004	717-935-2191	935-5511
Labette Bank 4th & Huston PO Box 497 *TF:* 800-711-5311 ■ *Web:* www.labettebank.com	Altamont	KS	67330	620-784-5311	784-5323
Lake Bank The 613 1st Ave *TF:* 888-852-4753 ■ *Web:* www.thelakebank.com	Two Harbors	MN	55616	218-834-2111	834-4373
Lakeside Bank 55 W Wacker Dr *TF:* 866-892-1572 ■ *Web:* www.lakesidebank.com	Chicago	IL	60601	312-435-5100	
LaPorte Savings BankThe 710 Indiana Ave *TF:* 866-362-7511 ■ *Web:* www.laportesavingsbank.com	LaPorte	IN	46350	219-362-7511	324-2269
Laurentian Bank of Canada 1981 McGill College Ave *TSE: LB* ■ *TF:* 800-252-1846 ■ *Web:* www.laurentianbank.ca	Montreal	QC	H3A3K3	514-284-4500	284-3988
Ledyard National Bank 320 Main St *Web:* www.ledyardbank.com	Norwich	VT	05055	802-649-2050	649-2060
Lehman Bros Bank FSB 1000 W St Suite 200 *TF:* 888-522-9295 ■ *Web:* www.aurorabankfsb.com	Wilmington	DE	19801	302-654-6179	428-3673
Liberty Bank 315 Main St *TF:* 800-622-6732 ■ *Web:* www.liberty-bank.com	Middletown	CT	06457	860-638-2922	
Liberty Bank & Trust Co PO Box 60131 *TF:* 800-883-3943 ■ *Web:* www.libertybank.net	New Orleans	LA	70160	504-240-5100	240-5153
Liberty Savings Bank FSB 2251 Rombach Ave *TF:* 800-627-7890 ■ *Web:* www.libertysavingsbank.com	Wilmington	OH	45177	937-382-6993	383-2208
Libertyville Bank & Trust Co 507 N Milwaukee Ave PO Box 7099 *Web:* www.libertyvillebank.com	Libertyville	IL	60048	847-367-6800	367-8444
Litchfield National Bank 316 N State St PO BOX 309	Litchfield	IL	62056	217-324-6161	324-3817
Little Bank Inc The 804 Carey Rd PO Box 279 *OTC: LTLB* ■ *Web:* www.thelittlebank.com	Kinston	NC	28501	252-939-9990	317-2837
Lloyds Bank Plc 1095 Avenue of the Americas # 35 *Web:* www.lloydstsb.com	New York	NY	10036	212-930-5000	930-5098
Lone Star National Bank Shares Neveda 100 W Ferguson St *Web:* www.lonestarnationalbank.com	Pharr	TX	78577	956-781-4321	
Lowell Five Cent Savings Bank The 1 Merrimack Plaza *Web:* www.lowellfive.com	Lowell	MA	01852	978-452-1300	441-6534
Lubbock National Bank 4811 50th St PO Box 6100 *Web:* www.lubbocknational.com	Lubbock	TX	79493	806-792-1000	792-0976
Luther Burbank Savings 804 4th St *Web:* www.lutherburbanksavings.com	Santa Rosa	CA	95404	707-578-9216	573-0316
M & I Bank 135 N Pennsylvania St First Indiana Plaza *Web:* www.mibank.com	Indianapolis	IN	46204	317-859-4838	269-1683
M & I Bank Northeast 310 W Walnut St *TF:* 888-464-5463 ■ *Web:* www.mibank.com	Green Bay	WI	54303	920-436-1800	436-1948
M & I Marshall & Ilsley Bank 770 N Water St *TF:* 800-342-2265 ■ *Web:* www.mibank.com	Milwaukee	WI	53202	414-765-7500	765-7436
M&T Bank 1 M & T Plaza 13th Fl *TF:* 800-724-2440 ■ *Web:* www.mtb.com	Buffalo	NY	14203	716-842-4470	842-5839
Machias Savings Bank 4 Ctr St PO Box 318 *TF:* 800-982-7179 ■ *Web:* www.machiassavings.com	Machias	ME	04654	207-255-3347	255-3170
Macquarie Infrastructure Co Inc 125 W 55th St *NYSE: MIC* ■ *Web:* www.macquarie.com	New York	NY	10019	212-231-1000	231-1010
Magyar Bancorp Inc 400 Somerset St *NASDAQ: MGYR* ■ *Web:* www.magbank.com/home/home	New Brunswick	NJ	08901	732-342-7600	342-7611
Magyar Bank 400 Somerset St *TF:* 800-472-3272 ■ *Web:* www.magbank.com	New Brunswick	NJ	08901	732-342-7600	
Main Source Bank 201 N Broadway PO Box 87 *Web:* www.mainsourcebank.com	Greensburg	IN	47240	812-663-4711	663-4904
Malvern FSB Inc 42 E Lancaster Ave *Web:* www.malvernfederal.com	Paoli	PA	19301	610-644-9400	644-1943
Marine Bank of Champaign-Urbana 2434 Village Green Pl *Web:* www.ibankmarine.com	Champaign	IL	61822	217-239-0100	
Marquette Savings Bank 920 Peach St *Web:* www.marquettesavings.com	Erie	PA	16501	814-455-4481	453-5345
Maspeth Federal Savings 56-18 69th St *TF:* 888-558-1300 ■ *Web:* www.maspethfederal.com	Maspeth	NY	11378	718-335-1300	335-4629
Mayflower Co-operative Bank 30 S Main St PO Box 311 *NASDAQ: MFLR* ■ *TF:* 800-552-4344 ■ *Web:* www.mayflowerbank.com	Middleboro	MA	02346	508-947-4343	923-0864
Mc Kenzie Banking Co (MBC) 676 N Main St *Web:* www.foundationbank.org	McKenzie	TN	38201	731-352-2262	352-7778
McHenry Savings Bank 353 Bank Dr *Web:* www.mchenrysavings.com	McHenry	IL	60050	815-385-3000	385-4433
Mcnb Bank & Trust Co PO Box 549 *TF:* 800-532-9553 ■ *Web:* www.mcnbbanks.com	Welch	WV	24801	304-436-4112	
Mechanics Bank 3170 Hilltop Mall Rd *TF:* 800-797-6324 ■ *Web:* www.mechanicsbank.com	Richmond	CA	94806	510-262-7980	262-7941
Mechanics Savings Bank 100 Minot Ave PO Box 400 *TF:* 877-886-1020 ■ *Web:* www.mechanicssavings.com/home/home	Auburn	ME	04210	207-786-5700	786-5709
Meramec Valley Bank 199 Clarkson Rd *Web:* www.meramecvalleybank.com	Ellisville	MO	63011	636-230-3500	230-3191
Mercantil Commercebank NA 220 Alhambra Cir *TF:* 888-629-0810 ■ *Web:* www.mercantilcb.com	Coral Gables	FL	33134	305-460-8701	460-4010
Merchants National Bank of Bangor Inc 25 Broadway PO Box 227 *Web:* www.merchantsbangor.com	Bangor	PA	18013	610-588-0981	588-6886
Meredith Village Savings Bank (MVSB) 24 State Rt 25 PO Box 177 *TF:* 800-922-6872 ■ *Web:* www.mvsb.com	Meredith	NH	03253	603-279-7986	279-5710
Meridian Bank NA PO Box 6630 *Web:* www.meridianbank.com	Peoria	AZ	85385	602-636-4939	274-7200
Metcalf Bank 609 N 291 Hwy *TF Cust Svc:* 888-860-7524 ■ *Web:* www.metcalfbank.com	Lee"s Summit	MO	64086	816-525-5300	
Midamerica National Bancshares 100 W Elm St *Web:* www.midnatbank.com	Canton	IL	61520	309-647-5000	647-8551
MidCarolina Financial Corp 3101 S Church St *OTC: MCFI* ■ *Web:* www.midcarolinabank.com	Burlington	NC	27215	336-538-1600	538-1603
Middlebury National Corp PO Box 189 *Web:* www.nationalbankmiddlebury.com	Middlebury	VT	05753	802-388-4982	
Middlesex Savings Bank 120 Flanders Rd *TF:* 877-463-6287 ■ *Web:* www.middlesexbank.com	Westborough	MA	01581	508-653-0300	389-9367
MidFirst Bank PO Box 76149 **Fax:* Cust Svc ■ *TF:* 888-643-3477 ■ *Web:* www.midfirst.com	Oklahoma City	OK	73147	405-943-8002	840-0862*
Midland National Bank 527 N Main *Web:* www.midlandnb.com	Newton	KS	67114	316-283-1700	283-3813
Midwest Bank 105 E Soo St PO Box 40 *TF:* 877-365-5155 ■ *Web:* www.midwestbank.net	Parkers Prairie	MN	56361	218-338-6054	338-5070
Mifflinburg Bank & Trust Co (MBTC) 250 E Chestnut St PO Box 186 *TF:* 888-966-3131 ■ *Web:* www.mbtc.com	Mifflinburg	PA	17844	570-966-1041	966-7432
Milford Bank 33 Broad St *TF:* 800-340-4862 ■ *Web:* www.milfordbank.com	Milford	CT	06460	203-783-5700	783-5755
Milford National Bank & Trust Co The 300 E Main St *Web:* www.milfordnational.com	Milford	MA	01757	508-634-4100	634-4107
Mitchell Bank 1039 W Mitchell St *Web:* www.mitchellbank.com	MILWAUKEE	WI	53204	414-645-0600	645-4020
Monarch Community Bancorp Inc 375 N Willowbrook Rd *NASDAQ: MCBF* ■ *TF:* 800-882-2911 ■ *Web:* www.monarchcb.com	Coldwater	MI	49036	517-278-4566	279-0221
Monarch Financial Holdings Inc 1435 Crossways Blvd Suite 301 *NASDAQ: MNRK* ■ *Web:* www.monarchbank.com	Chesapeake	VA	23320	757-389-5159	389-5100
Monroe Bank & Trust 102 E Front St **Fax:* Hum Res ■ *TF:* 800-321-0032 ■ *Web:* www.mbandt.com	Monroe	MI	48161	734-241-3431	242-3811*
Montecito Bank & Trust 1010 State St *Web:* www.montecito.com	Santa Barbara	CA	93101	805-963-7511	
Montgomery Bank 1 Montgomery Bank Plaza PO BOX 948 *Web:* www.montgomerybank.com	Sikeston	MO	63801	573-471-2275	472-5404
Mountain National Bancshares Inc 300 E Main St PO Box 6519 *OTC: MNBT* ■ *Web:* www.mountainnationalbank.com	Sevierville	TN	37862	865-428-7990	453-2588
Mountain Valley Bank 317 DAVIS Ave *Web:* www.mountainvalleybank.com	ELKINS	WV	26241	304-637-2265	637-2270
Mountain West Bank of Helena 1225 Cedar St PO Box 6013 *TF:* 800-775-1889 ■ *Web:* www.mtnwestbank.com	Helena	MT	59604	406-449-2265	449-0903
Mouvement des caisses Desjardins 100 des Commandeurs *TF:* 800-224-7737 ■ *Web:* www.desjardins.com	Levis	QC	G6V7N5	418-835-8444	833-4769
MSB Financial Corp 1902 Long Hill Rd *NASDAQ: MSBF* ■ *Web:* www.millingtonsbonline.com	Millington	NJ	07946	908-647-4000	647-6196
Mutual of Omaha Bank 9555 Hillwood Dr *TF:* 866-213-2112 ■ *Web:* www.mutualofomahabank.com	Las Vegas	NV	89134	702-880-3700	880-3600
N A Omnibank 4328 Old Spanish Trail *Web:* www.omnibank.com	Houston	TX	77021	713-747-9000	749-0664
National Australia Bank Americas 245 Pk Ave 28th Fl *TF:* 877-377-5480 ■ *Web:* www.national.com.au	New York	NY	10167	212-916-9631	697-8634
National Bank & Trust Co of Sycamore The 230 W State St *Web:* www.nabatco.com	Sycamore	IL	60178	815-895-2125	895-8961
National Bank & Trust Co The 48 N S St PO Box 711 *Web:* www.nbtdirect.com	Wilmington	OH	45177	937-382-1441	382-4385
National Bank of Arizona 335 N Wilmot Rd Suite 100 *TF:* 800-365-7455 ■ *Web:* www.nbarizona.com	Tucson	AZ	85711	520-571-1500	513-0134
National Bank of Blacksburg PO Box 90002 *TF:* 800-552-4123 ■ *Web:* www.nbbank.com	Blacksburg	VA	24062	540-552-2011	951-6337

Phone | Fax

National Bank of Canada
600 de La GauchetiFre W .... Montreal QC H3B4L2 514-394-5000 394-8258
TSE: NA ■ *TF:* 800-361-8688 ■ *Web:* www.nbc.ca
National Bank of Gatesville PO Box 779 .... Gatesville TX 76528 254-865-2211 865-8916
Web: www.natlbank.com
National Bank of Indianapolis Corp The
107 N Pennsylvania St Suite 100 .... Indianapolis IN 46204 317-261-9000 261-9696
TF: 877-233-9500 ■ *Web:* www.nbofi.com
National Bank of Kansas City (NBOFKC)
3510 W 95th St. .... Leawood KS 66206 913-341-1144 341-8989
TF: 888-431-0097 ■ *Web:* www.nbofkc.com
National Bank of South Carolina (NBSC)
1 Broad St PO Box 1798 .... Sumter SC 29151 800-708-5687
TF: 800-708-5687 ■ *Web:* www.nationalbanksc.com
National Bank The 852 Middle Rd .... Bettendorf IA 52722 563-344-3935 823-3350
Web: www.thenb.com
National Exchange Bank & Trust
130 S Main St PO Box 988 .... Fond Du Lac WI 54936 920-921-7700 923-7021
Web: www.nebat.com
National InterBank
45 N Pennsylvania St PO Box 1245 .... Indianapolis IN 46206 317-229-4011 435-8083*
**Fax Area Code:* 877 ■ *TF:* 877-468-7265 ■ *Web:* www.nationalinterbank.com
National Penn Bank PO Box 547 .... Boyertown PA 19512 610-367-6001 369-6501*
**Fax:* Mktg ■ *TF:* 800-822-3321 ■ *Web:* www.natpennbank.com
Naugatuck Valley Financial Corp
333 Church St .... Naugatuck CT 06770 203-720-5000 720-5016
NASDAQ: NVSL ■ *TF:* 800-251-2161 ■ *Web:* www.nvsl.com
NBT Bank NA 52 S Broad St PO Box 351 .... Norwich NY 13815 607-337-2265 336-8670
TF: 800-628-2265 ■ *Web:* www.nbtbank.com
NCAL Bancorp 12121 Wilshire Blvd. .... Brentwood CA 90025 310-882-4800 882-4890
OTC: NCAL ■ *Web:* www.nbcal.com
Neffs Bancorp Inc 5629 Rt 873 PO Box 10 .... Neffs PA 18065 610-767-3875 767-1890
PINK: NEFB ■ *Web:* www.neffsnatl.com
Nevada State Bank PO Box 990 .... Las Vegas NV 89125 702-383-0009
TF: 800-727-4743 ■ *Web:* www.nsbank.com
New Century Bank 700 W Cumberland St .... Dunn NC 28334 910-892-7080 892-9225
Web: www.newcenturybanknc.com
New Washington State Bank
402 E Main St PO Box 10 .... New Washington IN 47162 812-293-3321 293-3072
Web: www.newwashbank.com
New York Community Bank 615 Merrick Ave .... Westbury NY 11590 516-942-6000
Web: www.mynycb.com
NewBridge Bancorp
1501 Highwoods Blvd Suite 400 .... Greensboro NC 27410 336-369-0900 242-6201*
NASDAQ: NBBC ■ **Fax Area Code:* 910 ■ *Web:* www.newbridgebank.com
Newburyport Five Cents Savings Bank Inc The
63 State St PO Box 350 .... Newburyport MA 01950 978-462-3136 462-9672
Web: www.newburyportbank.com
Newfield National Bank 18 S W Blvd .... Newfield NJ 08344 856-692-3440 697-3114
Web: www.newfieldbank.com
Newtown Savings Bank Foundation Inc
39 Main St PO Box 497 .... Newtown CT 06470 203-426-2563 426-4510
TF: 800-461-0672 ■ *Web:* www.nsbonline.com
Nexity Bank 3680 Grandview Pkwy Suite 200 .... Birmingham AL 35243 205-298-6391 298-6395
TF: 877-738-6391 ■ *Web:* www.nexitybank.com
North American Savings Bank (NASB)
12520 S 71 Hwy. .... Grandview MO 64030 816-765-2200 316-4503*
**Fax:* Cust Svc ■ *TF:* 800-677-6272 ■ *Web:* www.nasb.com
North Community Bank 3639 N Broadway St .... Chicago IL 60613 773-244-7000 244-7016
Web: www.northcommunitybank.com
North Middlesex Savings Bank Inc
7 Main St PO Box 469 .... Ayer MA 01432 978-772-3306 772-9131
TF: 800-762-3306 ■ *Web:* www.nmsb.com
North Milwaukee State Bank (NMS)
5630 W Fond Du Lac Ave .... Milwaukee WI 53216 414-466-2344 466-6248
Web: www.nmsbank.com
North Shore Bank FSB 15700 W Bluemound Rd .... Brookfield WI 53005 262-785-1600 797-3850*
**Fax:* Cust Svc ■ *TF:* 800-236-4672 ■ *Web:* www.northshorebank.com
North Shore Trust & Savings
700 S Lewis Ave PO Box 980 .... Waukegan IL 60085 847-336-4430 336-4438
Web: www.northshoretrust.com
North Side Bank & Trust Co The
4125 Hamilton Ave PO Box 23128 .... Cincinnati OH 45223 513-542-7800 541-6941
Web: www.northsidebankandtrust.com
Northern Trust Bank of Florida NA
700 Brickell Ave .... Miami FL 33131 305-372-1000 789-1167*
**Fax:* Mktg ■ *TF:* 800-468-2352 ■ *Web:* www.ntrs.com
Northern Trust Co 50 S LaSalle St .... Chicago IL 60603 312-630-6000
TF: 888-289-6542 ■ *Web:* www.northerntrust.com
Northfield Savings Bank (NSB) PO Box 347 .... Northfield VT 05663 802-485-5871 485-7565
TF: 800-672-2274 ■ *Web:* www.nsbvt.com
Northrim BanCorp Inc 3111 C St. .... Anchorage AK 99503 907-562-0062 261-3594*
NASDAQ: NRIM ■ **Fax:* Mktg ■ *TF:* 800-478-3311 ■ *Web:* www.northrim.com
Northstar Bank of Texas 400 N Carroll Blvd .... Denton TX 76201 940-591-1200 384-1947
Web: www.nstarbank.com
Northwest Community Bank
86 Main St PO Box 1019 .... Winsted CT 06098 860-379-7561 379-9717
TF: 800-455-6668 ■ *Web:* www.nwcommunitybank.com
Northwest Georgia Bank
5063 Alabama Hwy PO Box 789 .... Ringgold GA 30736 706-965-3000
TF: 800-528-2273 ■ *Web:* www.northwestgabank.com
Northwest Savings Bank
100 Liberty St PO Box 128 .... Warren PA 16365 814-726-2140 728-7708*
**Fax:* Mktg ■ *TF:* 800-822-2009 ■ *Web:* www.northwestsavingsbank.com
Northwestern Bank
202 N Bridge St PO Box 49 .... Chippewa Falls WI 54729 715-723-4461 723-0586
Web: www.northwesternbank.com
NOVA Bank 1235 Westlakes Dr Suite 420 .... Berwyn PA 19312 610-993-4175
TF: 877-668-2226 ■ *Web:* www.novasavingsbank.com
OBA Financial Services Inc
20300 Seneca Meadows Pkwy .... Germantown MD 20876 301-916-6400
NASDAQ: OBAF ■ *Web:* www.obabank.com

Phone | Fax

Ocean Bank 780 NW 42nd Ave .... Miami FL 33126 305-442-2660 444-8153
TF: 877-688-2265 ■ *Web:* www.oceanbank.com
Ocean City Home Savings & Loan Inc
1001 Asbury Ave .... Ocean City NJ 08226 609-927-7722 399-3614
Web: www.ochome.com
OceanFirst Bank 975 Hooper Ave PO Box 2009 .... Toms River NJ 08753 732-240-4500 341-2579
TF: 888-623-2633 ■ *Web:* www.oceanfirstonline.com
Ocwen Federal Bank FSB
1661 Worthington Rd Suite 100 .... West Palm Beach FL 33409 561-682-8000 737-6211*
**Fax Area Code:* 407 ■ **Fax:* Hum Res ■ *TF:* 800-280-3863 ■ *Web:* www.ocwen.com
Old National Bank 1 Main St PO Box 718 .... Evansville IN 47708 812-464-1200 464-1551*
**Fax:* Cust Svc ■ *TF:* 800-677-1749 ■ *Web:* www.oldnational.com
OneUnited Bank 3683 Crenshaw Blvd. .... Los Angeles CA 90016 323-290-4848 389-0548
Web: www.oneunited.com
Orange County Trust Co PO Box 790 .... Middletown NY 10940 845-341-5000 341-3170
TF: 888-341-5100 ■ *Web:* www.orangecountytrust.com
Oritani Financial Corp
370 Pascack Rd PO Box 1329 .... Washington Township NJ 07676 201-664-5400 497-1223
NASDAQ: ORIT ■ *TF:* 888-674-8264 ■ *Web:* www.oritani.com
Oversea-Chinese Banking Corp Ltd
1700 Broadway 18th Fl. .... New York NY 10019 212-586-6222 586-0636
Web: www.ocbc.com
Oxford Bank PO Box 129 .... Addison IL 60101 630-629-5000 628-1575
TF: 800-236-2442 ■ *Web:* www.oxford-bank.com
Pacific City Financial Corp
3701 Wilshire Blvd Suite 402 .... Los Angeles CA 90010 213-210-2000 210-2032
OTC: PFCF ■ *Web:* www.paccitybank.com
Pacific Continental Corp
111 W 7th Ave PO Box 10727 .... Eugene OR 97440 541-686-8685 344-2807
NASDAQ: PCBK ■ *TF:* 877-231-2265 ■ *Web:* www.therightbank.com
Palmetto State Bank 601 First St W .... Hampton SC 29924 803-943-2671 943-5634
Web: www.palmettostatebank.com
Panhandle State Bank
414 Church St PO Box 967 .... Sandpoint ID 83864 208-263-0505 265-5295
Web: www.panhandlebank.com
Park National Bank 50 N 3rd St PO Box 3500 .... Newark OH 43058 740-349-8451 349-3931*
**Fax:* Cust Svc ■ *TF:* 888-545-4762 ■ *Web:* www.parknationalbank.com
Parkvale Savings Bank
4220 William Penn Hwy .... Monroeville PA 15146 412-373-7200 856-3943*
**Fax:* Hum Res ■ *Web:* www.parkvale.com
Parkway Bancorp Inc
4800 N Harlem Ave. .... Harwood Heights IL 60706 708-867-6600 867-1119
Web: www.parkwaybank.com
Penseco Financial Services Corp
150 N Washington Ave .... Scranton PA 18503 570-346-7741 969-2743
OTC: PFNS ■ *Web:* www.pennsecurity.com
Pentucket Bank 1 Merrimack St. .... Haverhill MA 01830 978-372-7731 372-4499
Web: www.pentucketbank.com
People Bank
201 N Bardstown Rd PO Box 95 .... Mount Washingt KY 40047 502-538-7301 538-6606
Web: www.peoplesbankmtw.com
People's United Bank
850 Main St Bridgeport Ctr. .... Bridgeport CT 06604 203-338-7171 338-2310
NASDAQ: PBCT ■ *TF:* 800-772-1090 ■ *Web:* www.peoples.com
Peoples Bank & Trust Co of Hazard PO Box 989 .... Hazard KY 41702 606-436-2161 439-9211
TF: 866-435-2161 ■ *Web:* www.peopleshazard.com
Peoples Bank Of Bullitt County
1612 Hwy 44 E .... Shepherdsville KY 40165 502-543-2226 543-3517
Web: www.pbofbc.com
Peoples Federal Bancshares Inc
435 Market St. .... Brighton MA 02135 617-254-0707
NASDAQ: PEOP ■ *Web:* www.pfsb.com
Peoples Financial Services Corp
82 Franklin Ave PO Box A .... Hallstead PA 18822 570-879-2175 879-4372
OTC: PFIS ■ *TF:* 888-868-3858 ■ *Web:* www.peoplesnatbank.com
Peoples Savings Bank (PSB)
414 N Adams PO Box 248 .... Wellsburg IA 50680 641-869-3721 869-3855
TF: 877-493-3799 ■ *Web:* www.bankpsb.com
Piedmont FSB (PFSB) 16 W 3rd St PO Box 215 .... Winston-Salem NC 27101 336-770-1000 770-1055
Web: www.piedmontfederal.com
Pine Country Bank 412 N Hwy 10 PO BOX 25 .... Royalton MN 56373 320-584-5522 584-8385
Web: www.pinecountrybank.com
Platte Valley Bank Of Missouri
2400 Prairie View Rd PO BOX 1250 .... Platte City MO 64079 816-858-5400 858-5300
Web: www.plattevalleybank.com
Plaza Bank 7460 W Irving Pk Rd .... Norridge866-957-7701 IL 60706 708-456-3440 583-3804
TF: 866-957-7701 ■ *Web:* www.plazabankillinois.com
Plums Bank 35 S Lindan Ave. .... Quincy CA 95971 530-283-7305 283-3557
NASDAQ: PLBC ■ *Web:* www.plumasbank.com
PNC Bank 110 Thomas Johnson Dr .... Frederick MD 21702 301-698-4606 695-3081*
**Fax:* Cust Svc ■ *TF:* 888-762-2265 ■ *Web:* www.pnc.com
PNC Bank 2 Hopkins Plaza .... Baltimore MD 21201 410-237-5505 237-5576
TF: 888-762-2265 ■ *Web:* www.pnc.com
PNC Bank 600 Grant St. .... Pittsburgh PA 15219 888-762-2265 835-5270*
NYSE: PNC ■ **Fax Area Code:* 202 ■ *TF:* 800-368-5800 ■ *Web:* www.pncbank.com
PNC Bank Delaware 300 Delaware Ave .... Wilmington DE 19899 302-429-1361 429-2872
TF: 888-762-2265 ■ *Web:* www.pnc.com
PNC Bank NA 249 5th Ave 1 PNC Plaza .... Pittsburgh PA 15222 412-762-2021 762-5798
TF: 888-762-2265 ■ *Web:* www.pnc.com
PNC Financial Services Group The
One PNC Plaza 249 Fifth Ave .... Pittsburgh PA 15222 412-762-7544
TF: 877-762-2000 ■ *Web:* www.pnc.com
Preferred Bank Los Angeles
601 S Figueroa St 29th Fl. .... Los Angeles CA 90017 213-891-1188 622-0369
NASDAQ: PFBC ■ *Web:* www.preferredbank.com
Premier Bank & Trust 2375 Benden Dr Suite C .... Wooster OH 44691 877-965-1113
TF: 877-965-1113 ■ *Web:* www.mypremierbankandtrust.com
Premier Commercial Bank NA
2400 E Katella Ave .... Anaheim CA 92806 714-978-2400 978-6100
Web: www.pcboc.com

	City	State	ZIP	Phone	Fax
Premier Valley Bank 255 E River Pk Cir Suite 180 *TF:* 877-438-2002 ■ *Web:* www.premiervalleybank.com	Fresno	CA	93720	559-438-2002	432-0572
PremierWest Bank 503 Airport Rd *NASDAQ: PRWT* ■ *Web:* www.premierwestbank.com	Medford	OR	97504	541-618-6003	618-6001
Presidential Online Bank 4520 East-West Hwy *TF:* 800-383-6266 ■ *Web:* www.presidential.com	Bethesda	MD	20814	301-652-0700	951-3582
Profile Bank 45 Wakefield St PO BOX 1808 *Web:* www.profilebank.com	Rochester	NH	03866	603-332-2610	332-2519
Progressive Bank NA 1090 E Bethlehem Blvd *TF:* 866-235-1923 ■ *Web:* www.progbank.com	Wheeling	WV	26003	304-238-0040	238-0045
Prosperity Bank 100 Suthpark Blvd *TF:* 800-347-9680 ■ *Web:* www.prosperitybank.com	Saint Augustine	FL	32086	904-824-9111	
Provident Bank 239 Washington St *NYSE: PFS* ■ *Web:* www.snl.com	Jersey City	NJ	07302	732-590-9200	
Provident Bank 38 New Main St *Web:* www.providentbanking.com	Haverstraw	NY	10927	845-942-3880	942-3885
Provident Savings Bank FSB 3756 Central Ave *TF:* 800-745-2217 ■ *Web:* www.myprovident.com	Riverside	CA	92506	951-686-6060	782-6157
Prudential Savings Bank 1834 W Oregon Ave *Web:* www.prudentialsavingsbank.com	Philadelphia	PA	19145	215-755-1500	336-7122
Pueblo Bank & Trust Co 301 W 5th St PO Box 639 *Web:* www.pbandt.com	Pueblo	CO	81002	719-545-1834	545-1844
Qnb Corp 15 N 3rd St PO Box 9005 *OTC: QNBC* ■ *TF:* 800-491-9070 ■ *Web:* www.qnb.com	Quakertown	PA	18951	215-538-5600	538-5765
Queens County Savings Bank 13665 Roosevelt Ave *Web:* www.mynycb.com	Flushing	NY	11354	718-460-4800	
Queenstown Bank of Maryland 7101 Main St PO BOX 120 *Web:* www.queenstown-bank.com	Queenstown	MD	21658	410-827-8881	827-8190
Rabo Bank 1026 Grand Ave *TF:* 800-473-7788 ■ *Web:* www.rabobankamerica.com	Arroyo Grande	CA	93420	800-942-6222	
Ramsey Financial Corp PO Box 160 *TF:* 800-726-0124 ■ *Web:* www.ramseybank.com	Devils Lake	ND	58301	701-662-4024	662-8900
Randall-Story State Bank 606 Broad St PO Box 278 *TF:* 800-535-2169 ■ *Web:* www.randallstory.com	Story City	IA	50248	515-733-4396	733-2068
Randolph Savings Bank 129 N Main St PO Box 354 *TF:* 877-963-2100 ■ *Web:* www.randolphsavings.com	Randolph	MA	02368	781-963-2100	961-7916
RBC Bank 301 Fayetteville St *Web:* www.rbcbankusa.com	Raleigh	NC	27601	919-839-4400	839-4806
RBC Royal Bank PO Box 6001 Suite A **Fax Area Code:* 514 ■ *TF:* 800-769-2599 ■ *Web:* www.rbcroyalbank.com	Montreal	QC	H3C3A9	800-769-2599	874-3055*
Regents Bank NA PO Box 9137 *TF:* 866-395-5800 ■ *Web:* www.regentsbank.com	La Jolla	CA	92038	858-729-7700	454-9052
Regions Bank 1900 5th Ave N *TF:* 800-284-4100 ■ *Web:* www.regions.com	Birmingham	AL	35203	205-326-5300	320-7185
Reliance Bancshares Inc 10401 Clayton Rd *OTC: RLBS* ■ *Web:* www.reliancebancshares.com	Frontenac	MO	63131	314-569-7200	
Renasant Bank 209 Troy St PO Box 709 *TF:* 800-680-1601 ■ *Web:* www.renasantbank.com	Tupelo	MS	38802	662-680-1001	680-1234
Republic Bank & Trust Co 601 W Market St *TF:* 888-584-3600 ■ *Web:* www.republicbank.com	Louisville	KY	40202	502-584-3600	584-3753
Republic Federal Bank 1001 Brickell Bay Dr *Web:* www.republicfederal.com	Miami	FL	33131	305-539-3400	539-3437
Ridgewood Savings Bank 71-02 Forest Ave *TF:* 800-250-4832 ■ *Web:* www.ridgewoodbank.com	Ridgewood	NY	11385	718-240-4800	240-4877
River City Bank PO Box 15247 *TF Cust Svc:* 800-564-7144 ■ *Web:* www.rcbank.com	Sacramento	CA	95851	916-567-2899	567-2784
Riverview Community Bank 900 Washington St Suite 100 PO Box 872290 *TF:* 800-822-2076 ■ *Web:* www.riverviewbank.com	Vancouver	WA	98687	360-693-6650	
Roselle Savings Bank Inc 235 Chestnut St PO Box 349 *Web:* www.rosellesavings.com	Roselle	NJ	07203	908-245-1885	245-2256
Royal Bank America 732 Montgomery Ave *Web:* www.royalbankamerica.com	Narberth	PA	19072	610-668-4700	668-1185
Royal Bank of Canada 200 Bay St 9th Fl S Tower *STE: RY* ■ *TF:* 800-769-2599 ■ *Web:* www.rbc.com	Toronto	ON	M5J2J5	416-955-7806	974-3535
S & T Bank 800 Philadelphia St PO Box 190 *TF Cust Svc:* 800-325-2265 ■ *Web:* www.stbank.com	Indiana	PA	15701	724-349-1800	465-6874
Safra National Bank of New York 545 5th Ave *Web:* www.safra.com	New York	NY	10017	212-704-5500	704-5527
Salem Five & Savings Bank 210 Essex St *TF:* 800-322-2265 ■ *Web:* www.salemfive.com	Salem	MA	01970	978-745-5555	498-0304
Sandhills Bank 300 King St E *Web:* www.sandhillsbank.com	Bethune	SC	29009	843-334-2265	334-6013
Sandy Spring National Bank of Maryland 17801 Georgia Ave *TF:* 800-399-5919 ■ *Web:* www.sandyspringbank.com	Olney	MD	20832	301-774-6400	483-6701
Santa Barbara Bank & Trust PO Box 60839 *TF Cust Svc:* 888-400-7228 ■ *Web:* www.sbbt.com	Santa Barbara	CA	93160	805-730-4968	564-6439
SCB Bancorp Inc 1501 E Eldorado St *TF:* 888-769-2265 ■ *Web:* www.soybank.com	Decatur	IL	62521	217-428-7781	
Scotiabank de Puerto Rico 273 Ponce de Leon Ave *TF:* 877-766-4999 ■ *Web:* www.scotiabankpr.com	Hato Rey	PR	00917	787-758-8989	766-7879
Sea Island Bank 2 E Main St PO Box 568 *Web:* www.seaislandbank.com	Statesboro	GA	30459	912-489-8661	
Seamen's Bank 221 Commercial St PO Box 659 *Web:* www.seamensbank.com	Provincetown	MA	02657	508-487-0035	487-8421
Seaway Bank & Trust Co 645 E 87th St *Web:* www.seawaybank.us	Chicago	IL	60619	773-487-4800	487-0452
Security Bank of Pulaski County 110 Lynn St PO Box S *Web:* www.sbpc.com	Waynesville	MO	65583	573-774-6417	774-6465
Security National Bank 40 S Limestone St *Web:* www.securitynationalbank.com	SPRINGFIELD	OH	45502	937-324-6800	324-6861
Security National Bank of Enid 201 W Maine Ave *Web:* www.snbenid.com	Enid	OK	73701	580-234-5151	249-9199
Security National Bank of Omaha (inc) 1120 S 101st St PO Box 31400 *Web:* www.snbconnect.com	Omaha	NE	68124	402-344-7300	334-6719
Security National Bank Of Sioux City Iowa PO Box 147 *Web:* www.snbonline.com	Sioux City	IA	51101	712-277-6666	
Security State Bank & Trust (inc) 201 W Main St PO Box 471 *Web:* www.ssbtexas.com	Fredericksburg	TX	78624	830-997-7575	997-7994
Severn Bancorp Inc 200 Westgate Cir Suite 200 *NASDAQ: SVBI* ■ *TF:* 800-752-5854 ■ *Web:* www.severnbank.com	Annapolis	MD	21401	410-260-2000	841-6296
Signature Bank 565 5th Ave 12th Fl *NASDAQ: SBNY* ■ *TF:* 866-744-5463 ■ *Web:* www.signatureny.com	New York	NY	10017	646-822-1500	822-1447
Silicon Valley Bank (SVB) 3003 Tasman Dr **Fax:* Mktg ■ *Web:* www.svb.com	Santa Clara	CA	95054	408-654-7400	654-6209*
Silvergate Bank 4275 Executive Sq Suite 800 *TF:* 800-595-5856 ■ *Web:* www.silvergatebank.com	La Jolla	CA	92037	858-362-6300	362-3300
Siuslaw Bank 777 Hwy 101 PO Box 280 *OTC: SFGP* ■ *Web:* www.clicksvb.com	Florence	OR	97439	541-997-3486	683-5663
Societe Generale USA 1221 Avenue of the Americas *TF:* 800-942-7575 ■ *Web:* www.sgcib.com	New York	NY	10020	212-278-7068	278-6789
Somerset Trust Co 151 W Main St PO Box 777 *TF:* 800-972-1651 ■ *Web:* www.somersettrust.com	Somerset	PA	15501	814-443-9200	
South Central Bank of Barren County Inc 208 S Broadway *TF:* 888-651-7466 ■ *Web:* www.southcentralbank.com	Glasgow	KY	42142	270-651-7466	651-6580
South Coastal Bank 279 Union St PO Box 533 *Web:* www.southcoastalbank.com	Rockland	MA	02370	781-878-6513	878-6635
South Louisiana Bank (SLB) 1362 W Tunnel Blvd PO BOX 1718 *Web:* www.ayeee.com	Houma	LA	70361	985-851-3434	879-3095
Southbridge Savings Bank Inc 253-257 Main St PO Box 370 *TF:* 800-939-9103 ■ *Web:* www.southbridgesavingsbank.com	Southbridge	MA	01550	508-765-9103	765-1187
Southern Michigan Bank & Trust 51 W Pearl St PO Box 309 *TF:* 800-379-7628 ■ *Web:* www.smb-t.com	Coldwater	MI	49036	517-279-5500	278-7358
Southwest Missouri Bank 2417 S Grand Ave *Web:* www.smbonline.com	CARTHAGE	MO	64836	417-358-1770	358-4081
Sovereign Bank FSB PO Box 12646 **Fax Area Code:* 888 ■ *TF Cust Svc:* 877-768-2265 ■ *Web:* www.sovereignbank.com	Reading	PA	19612	610-320-8400	433-8779*
Spencer Savings Bank PO Box 912 *TF:* 800-547-2885 ■ *Web:* www.spencersavingsbank.com	Spencer	MA	01562	508-885-5313	885-6505
Spencer Savings Bank SLA 611 River Dr *TF:* 800-363-8115 ■ *Web:* www.spencersavings.com	Elmwood Park	NJ	07407	973-772-6700	
St Martin Bank & Trust Co 301 S Main St *Web:* www.stmartinbank.com	Saint Martinville	LA	70582	337-394-7800	394-7831
Standard Bank & Trust Co 7800 W 95th St *TF:* 866-499-2265 ■ *Web:* www.standardbanks.com	Hickory Hills	IL	60457	708-598-7400	
Standard Bank PASB of Murrysville 4785 Old William Penn Hwy PO Box 114 *Web:* www.standardbankpa.com	Murrysville	PA	15668	724-327-0010	325-1967
Standard Chartered Bank 1 Madison Ave *TF:* 800-269-3101 ■ *Web:* www.standardchartered.com	New York	NY	10010	212-667-0700	667-0380
Star Bank 201 2nd Ave NW PO BOX 188 *Web:* www.starbank.net	Bertha	MN	56437	218-924-4055	924-2265
STAR Financial Group Inc PO Box 11409 *Web:* www.starfinancial.com	Fort Wayne	IN	46858	260-467-5507	
State Bank & Trust Co 1025 6th St PO Box 327 *Web:* www.banksbt.com	Nevada	IA	50201	515-382-2191	382-3826
State Bank Of Countryside Inc (SBC) 6734 Joliet Rd *Web:* www.statebankofcountryside.com/index.html	Countryside	IL	60525	708-485-3100	485-3106
State Bank of Cross Plains 1205 Main St PO Box 218 *Web:* www.crossplainsbank.com	Cross Plains	WI	53528	608-798-3961	298-3591
State Bank of Toledo 100 E High St PO Box 309 *Web:* www.banktoledo.com	Toledo	IA	52342	641-484-2980	484-2333
State Bank of Waterloo PO Box 148 *Web:* www.statebankofwaterloo.com	Waterloo	IL	62298	618-939-7194	939-4140
State Farm Financial Services FSB PO Box 2316 *TF:* 877-734-2265 ■ *Web:* www.statefarm.com/bank/bank.htm	Bloomington	IL	61702	877-734-2265	
State National Bank & Trust Co 122 Main St PO Box 130 *Web:* www.state-national-bank.com	Wayne	NE	68787	402-375-1130	375-1822
State Street Corp 1 Lincoln St **Fax:* Mktg ■ *Web:* www.statestreet.com	Boston	MA	02111	617-786-3000	664-6316*
Stephens Federal Bank 2859 Hwy 17 Alt PO BOX 40 *Web:* www.stephensfederalbank.com	Toccoa	GA	30577	706-886-2111	886-0107
Stephenson National Bank & Trust The 1820 Hall Ave PO Box 137 *Web:* www.snbt.com	Marinette	WI	54143	715-732-1732	732-1327
Sterling Bank 15000 NW Fwy *TF:* 888-777-8735 ■ *Web:* www.banksterling.com	Houston	TX	77040	713-507-7070	466-0765
Sterling Bank & Trust FSB 1 Town Sq 17th Fl *TF:* 866-619-2265 ■ *Web:* www.sterlingbank.com	Southfield	MI	48076	248-355-2400	355-3915
Sterling Savings Bank 111 N Wall St **Fax:* Hum Res ■ *TF:* 800-650-7141 ■ *Web:* www.sterlingsavingsbank.com	Spokane	WA	99201	509-624-4114	358-6118*
Stillman Banccorp NA PO Box 150 *Web:* www.stillmanbank.com	Stillman Valle	IL	61084	815-645-2000	645-2341

Phone | Fax

Stonebridge Bank
624 Willowbrook Ln Rt 202 West Chester PA 19382 800-807-1666 984-8225*
Fax Area Code: 888 ■ TF: 800-807-1666 ■ Web: www.stonebridgebank.com

Stoneham Savings Bank
359 Main St PO Box 80071 Stoneham MA 02180 781-438-9400 438-8596
Web: www.stonesav.com

Sturgis Bank & Trust Co
113-125 E Chicago Rd PO Box 600 Sturgis MI 49091 269-651-9345 651-5512*
*OTC: STBI ■ *Fax Area Code: 616 ■ Web: www.sturgisbank.com*

Sumitomo Mitsui Banking Corp (SMBC) 277 Pk Ave New York NY 10172 212-224-4000 593-9522
Web: www.smbcgroup.com

Sumitomo Trust & Banking Co (USA)
111 River St Hoboken NJ 07030 201-595-8969 983-3730*
**Fax Area Code: 718 ■ Web: www.sumitomotrustusa.com*

Summit Bank 2969 Broadway Oakland CA 94611 510-839-8800 839-8853
Web: www.summitbanking.com

Sun National Bank 226 Landis Ave Vineland NJ 08360 856-691-7700 786-9066
TF: 800-691-7701 ■ Web: www.sunnb.com

SunTrust Bank 25 Pk Pl NE Atlanta GA 30303 404-588-7610 575-2837
TF: 800-786-8787 ■ Web: www.suntrust.com

Suntrust Bank PO Box 4418 Atlanta GA 30302 800-786-8787 523-3310*
**Fax Area Code: 901 ■ TF: 800-786-8787 ■ Web: www.suntrust.com*

Susquehanna Bank
1570 Manheim Pike PO Box 3300 Lancaster PA 17604 717-735-8730
Web: www.susquehanna.net

Susquehanna Bank 26 N Cedar St PO Box 100 Lititz PA 17543 717-626-4721 626-4721
TF: 800-311-3182 ■ Web: www.susquehanna.net

Svenska Handelsbanken 875 3rd Ave 4th Fl New York NY 10022 212-326-5100 326-2705
Web: www.handelsbanken.se

Swedbank 1 Penn Plaza 15th Fl New York NY 10119 212-486-8400 486-3220
Web: www.swedbank.com

Swineford National Bank
1255 N Susquehanna Trial PO Box 241 Hummels Wharf PA 17831 570-743-7786 837-2671
TF: 866-762-1903 ■ Web: www.swineford.com

Tallahassee State Bank
2720 W Tennessee St Tallahassee FL 32304 850-576-1182 893-7192
Web: www.talstatebank.com

TCF National Bank 801 Marquette Ave Minneapolis MN 55402 612-661-6500 745-2773
TF: 800-533-1723 ■ Web: www.tcfbank.com

TD Bank NA 1701 Rt 70 E Cherry Hill NJ 08034 856-751-2739 751-0226
TF: 888-751-9000 ■ Web: www.tdbank.com

TD Banknorth Massachusetts 295 Pk Ave Worcester MA 01609 508-752-2584 751-8090
TF Cust Svc: 800-747-7000 ■ Web: www.tdbank.com

Tennessee Commerce Bank
381 Mallory Stn Rd Suite 207 Franklin TN 37067 615-599-2274 599-2275
TF: 877-684-2265 ■ Web: www.tncommercebank.com

Texas Bank & Trust Co
300 E Whaley PO Box 3188 Longview TX 75606 903-237-5500 237-1890
Web: www.texasbankandtrust.com

Texas Capital Bank 2000 McKinney Ave Suite 700 Dallas TX 75201 214-932-6600 932-6604
TF: 877-839-2737 ■ Web: www.texascapitalbank.com

Texas Star Bank
177 E Jefferson PO Box 608 Van Alstyne TX 75495 903-482-5234 482-5239
Web: www.texasstarbank.com

Third Federal Savings & Loan Assn of Cleveland
7007 Broadway Ave Cleveland OH 44105 216-429-5228 441-7030
TF: 888-844-7333 ■ Web: www.thirdfederal.com

Thomaston Savings Bank
203 Main St PO Box 907 Thomaston CT 06787 860-283-1874 283-6621
TF: 800-841-1267 ■ Web: www.thomastonsavingsbank.com

Tompkins Trust Co PO Box 460 Ithaca NY 14851 607-273-3210 277-6874
AMEX: TMP ■ TF: 888-273-3210 ■ Web: www.tompkinstrust.com

Toronto-Dominion Bank 55 King St W 10th Fl Toronto ON M5K1A2 416-982-8222 944-6931
TSE: TD ■ TF: 800-430-6095 ■ Web: www.td.com

Town Bank 850 W N Shore Dr Hartland WI 53029 262-367-1900
TF: 800-433-3076 ■ Web: www.townbank.us

Traditional Bank
49 W Main St PO Box 326 Mount Sterling KY 40353 859-498-0414 498-0643
TF: 800-498-0414 ■ Web: www.traditionalbank.com

Tri City Bankshares Corp 6400 S 27th St Oak Creek WI 53154 414-761-1610 761-2019
PINK: TRCY ■ Web: www.tcnb.com

Troy Bank & Trust Co 1000 Hwy 231 S PO Box 967 Troy AL 36081 334-566-4000 566-0578
TF: 888-258-8769 ■ Web: www.troybankandtrust.com

Trust Bank 600 E Main St PO Box 158 Olney IL 62450 618-395-4311 395-4312
TF: 800-766-3451 ■ Web: www.trustbank.net

Trustmark National Bank
248 E Capitol St PO Box 291 Jackson MS 39201 601-208-5111 208-6684*
**Fax: Hum Res ■ TF: 800-844-2000 ■ Web: www.trustmark.com*

Tulsa National Bancshares Inc PO Box 1051 Tulsa OK 74101 918-494-4884
Web: www.tulsanational.com

Twin River National Bank 1507 G St Lewiston ID 83501 208-746-4848 746-4949
Web: www.twinriverbank.com

UBS AG 1285 Avenue of the Americas New York NY 10019 212-713-2000
TF: 888-827-7275 ■ Web: www.ubs.com

Ulster Savings Bank
180 Schwenk Dr PO Box 3337 Kingston NY 12401 845-338-6322 339-9008
Web: www.ulstersavings.com/home/home

UMB Bank NA 1010 Grand Blvd Kansas City MO 64106 816-860-7000 860-7726
TF: 800-821-2171 ■ Web: www.umb.com

Umpqua Bank PO Box 1820 Roseburg OR 97470 503-727-4100 544-3750*
**Fax Area Code: 971 ■ TF: 866-486-7782 ■ Web: www.umpquabank.com*

Unibank For Savings 49 Church St Whitinsville MA 01588 508-234-8112 234-4648
TF: 800-578-4270 ■ Web: www.unibank.com

Unicredit Group 150 E 42nd St 29th Fl New York NY 10017 212-672-6000
TF: 800-493-2203

Union Bank & Trust Inc
312 Central Ave SE Minneapolis MN 55414 612-379-3222 379-8837
Web: www.ubtmn.com

Union Bank of California NA
400 California St 15th Fl San Francisco CA 94104 415-765-2000 765-3507
TF: 800-238-4486 ■ Web: www.unionbank.com

Union Savings Bank
223 W Stephenson St PO Box 540 Freeport IL 61032 815-235-0800 235-2017
Web: www.unionsavingsbank.com

Union State Bank
127 S Summit St PO Box 928 Arkansas City KS 67005 620-442-5200 442-8081
Web: www.myunionstate.com

United American Bank 101 S Ellsworth Ave San Mateo CA 94401 650-579-1500 579-1501
OTC: UABK ■ TF: 877-275-3342 ■ Web: www.unitedamericanbank.com

United Bank 11185 Fairfax Blvd Fairfax VA 22030 703-219-4850 352-8730
TF: 800-724-3259 ■ Web: www.unitedbank-dcmetro.com

United Bank of Philadelphia
30 S 15th St Suite 1200 Philadelphia PA 19102 215-351-4600
Web: www.ubphila.com

United Central Bank 4555 W Walnut St Garland TX 75042 972-487-1505 276-3972
TF: 800-585-3040 ■ Web: www.ucbtx.com

United Financial Bancorp Inc
95 Elm St PO Box 9020 West Springfield MA 01090 413-787-1700 737-7879
NASDAQ: UBNK ■ TF: 866-959-2265 ■ Web: www.bankatunited.com

United Overseas Bank Ltd (UOB)
592 5th Ave 10th Fl 48th St New York NY 10036 212-382-0088 382-1881
Web: www.uob.com.sg

United Security Bancshares
2126 Inyo St Dept 98 Fresno CA 93721 559-248-4943 320-1220
NASDAQ: UBFO ■ TF: 888-683-6030 ■ Web: www.unitedsecuritybank.com

United Western Bank 700 17th St Suite 100 Denver CO 80202 720-956-6500 956-6599
TF: 800-594-2079 ■ Web: www.uwbank.com

UPS Capital Business Credit
35 Glenlake Pkwy Ne Atlanta GA 30328 877-263-8772
TF: 877-263-8772 ■ Web: www.upscapital.com

US Bank NA 1900 N University Dr Fargo ND 58102 701-280-3547 280-3532
Web: www.usbank.com

US Bank NA 800 Nicollet Mall Minneapolis MN 55402 651-466-3000
TF: 800-872-2657 ■ Web: www.usbank.com

USAA FSB (USAAFSB) 10750 McDermott Fwy San Antonio TX 78288 800-531-8722 531-5717
TF: 800-531-8722 ■ Web: www.usaa.com

Valley Bank 2020 E Kimberly Rd Davenport IA 52807 563-441-6122 355-7020
TF: 866-462-5825 ■ Web: www.valleyb.com

Valley National Bank 615 Main Ave Passaic NJ 07055 973-777-6768 777-7963
TF: 800-522-4100 ■ Web: www.valleynationalbank.com

Vectra Bank Colorado NA
1650 S Colorado Blvd # 204 Denver CO 80222 720-947-7500 947-7760
TF: 888-648-7850 ■ Web: www.vectrabank.com

Viking Financial Services Corp
2237 NW 57th St PO Box 70546 Seattle WA 98107 206-784-2200 784-6650
Web: www.vikingbank.com

Village Bank & Trust 234 W NW Hwy Arlington Heights IL 60004 847-670-1000 670-7744
Web: www.bankatvillage.com

VirtualBank
3801 PGA Blvd Suite 700
PO Box 109638 Palm Beach Gardens FL 33410 561-514-4900 776-6378
TF: 877-998-2265 ■ Web: www.virtualbank.com

Wachovia Bank 11601 Wilshire Blvd Los Angeles CA 90025 310-477-8004 477-7324
TF: 800-922-4684 ■ Web: www.wachovia.com

Wachovia Bank NA
301 S College St Suite 4000 1 Wachovia Ctr Charlotte NC 28288 704-374-6161
TF: 800-922-4684 ■ Web: www.wachovia.com

Walpole Co-op Bank Inc 982 Main St PO Box 350 Walpole MA 02081 508-668-1080 660-2690
Web: www.walpolecoop.com

Washington Savings Bank FSB
4201 Mitchellville Rd Suite 200 Bowie MD 20716 301-352-3120 870-7891
AMEX: WSB ■ TF: 800-843-7250 ■ Web: www.twsb.com

Washington Trust Bank PO Box 2127 Spokane WA 99210 509-353-3875 353-3836
TF: 800-788-4578 ■ Web: www.watrust.com

Waterstone Bank 7500 W State St Wauwatosa WI 53213 414-258-5880
Web: www.wsbonline.com

Waukesha State Bank
151 E St Paul Ave PO Box 648 Waukesha WI 53187 262-549-8500 549-8593
Web: www.waukeshabank.com

Wcn Bancorp Inc 181 2nd St S Wisconsin Rapi WI 54494 715-423-7600 422-0300
Web: www.wcnbank.com

Weatherbank Inc 1015 Waterwood Pkwy Suite J Edmond OK 73034 405-359-0773 341-0115
TF: 800-687-3562 ■ Web: www.weatherbank.com

Webster Bank 145 Bank St Webster Plaza Waterbury CT 06702 203-578-2230 753-6511*
**Fax: Mktg ■ TF: 800-325-2424 ■ Web: www.websterbank.via.infonow.net*

Wells Fargo Bank 5622 3rd St Katy TX 77493 281-391-2101 391-1338
TF: 800-869-3557 ■ Web: www.wellsfargo.com

Wells Fargo Bank Indiana NA
111 E Wayne St Fort Wayne IN 46802 260-461-6401 461-6709
TF: 800-869-3557 ■ Web: www.wellsfargo.com

Wells Fargo Bank Iowa NA
666 Walnut St PO Box 837 Des Moines IA 50309 515-245-3304
Web: www.wellsfargo.com

Wells Fargo Bank Minnesota South NA
21 1st St SW Rochester MN 55902 507-285-2800
Web: www.wellsfargo.com

Wells Fargo Bank Montana NA 175 N 27th St Billings MT 59101 406-657-3503
Web: www.wellsfargo.com

Wells Fargo Bank NA 420 Montgomery St San Francisco CA 94104 415-396-3053 397-2987
TF: 800-869-3557 ■ Web: www.wellsfargo.com

Wells Fargo Bank Nebraska NA 1919 Douglas St Omaha NE 68102 402-536-2022
Web: www.wellsfargo.com

Wells Fargo Bank South Dakota NA
101 N Phillips Ave Sioux Falls SD 57104 605-575-6900
Web: www.wellsfargo.com

Wells Fargo Bank Texas NA
707 Castroville Rd San Antonio TX 78237 210-856-5000 856-5038
TF: 800-869-3557 ■ Web: www.wellsfargo.com

WesBanco Inc 1 Bank Plaza Wheeling WV 26003 304-234-9000 234-9298
TF: 800-328-3369 ■ Web: www.wesbanco.com

West Alabama Bank & Trust
509 1st Ave W PO Box 310 Reform AL 35481 205-375-6261 375-2289
Web: www.wabt.com

West Coast Bank 506 SW Coast Hwy Newport OR 97365 541-265-6666 265-8656
TF Cust Svc: 800-895-3345 ■ Web: www.wcb.com

				Phone	Fax
West Suburban Bank 711 Westmore Meyers Rd	Lombard	IL	60148	630-629-4200	629-0278
TF: 800-540-9257 ■ *Web:* www.westsuburbanbank.com					
Westamerica Bancorp 1108 Fifth Ave	San Rafael	CA	94901	415-257-8000	
TF: 800-848-1088 ■ *Web:* www.westamerica.com					
Western National Bank 508 W Wall Suite 1000	Midland	TX	79701	432-570-4181	
Web: www.wnbonline.com					
Western Security Bank 2812 1st Ave N	Billings	MT	59101	406-371-8200	371-8225
TF: 800-366-5120 ■ *Web:* www.westernsecuritybank.com					
Westpac Banking Corp Americas Div					
575 5th Ave 39th Fl	New York	NY	10017	212-551-1800	551-1999
TF: 800-937-8722 ■ *Web:* www.westpac.com.au					
WGNB Corp 201 Maple St	Carrollton	GA	30117	770-832-3557	214-7293
PINK: WGNB ■ *Web:* www.wgnb.com					
Whitney National Bank 228 St Charles Ave	New Orleans	LA	70130	504-586-7272	586-7383
TF: 800-347-7272 ■ *Web:* www.whitneybank.com					
Wilmington Trust Co 1100 N Market St	Wilmington	DE	19890	302-651-1000	651-8937*
**Fax:* Hum Res ■ *TF:* 800-441-7120 ■ *Web:* www.wilmingtontrust.com					
Wilshire State Bank					
3200 Wilshire Blvd Suite 1400	Los Angeles	CA	90010	213-368-7700	427-6562*
**Fax:* Cust Svc ■ *TF:* 866-886-2265 ■ *Web:* www.wilshirebank.com					
Wilson Bank Holding Co 623 W Main St	Lebanon	TN	37087	615-444-2265	443-7117
OTC: WBHC ■ *Web:* www.wilsonbank.com					
Winter Hill Bank 342 Broadway PO Box 9111	Somerville	MA	02145	617-666-8600	776-8197
TF: 800-444-4300 ■ *Web:* www.winterhillbank.com/Default.asp					
Woodforest Financial Group Inc					
PO Box 7889	The Woodlands	TX	77387	832-375-2000	375-3001
TF: 877-968-7962 ■ *Web:* www.woodforest.com					
Woodsville Guaranty Savings Bank					
10 Pleasant St PO Box 266	Woodsville	NH	03785	603-747-2735	747-3267
TF: 800-564-2735 ■ *Web:* www.theguarantybank.com					
Yadkin Valley Bank & Trust Co					
209 N Bridge St PO Box 888	Elkin	NC	28621	336-526-6312	526-5118
NASDAQ: YAVY ■ *TF:* 866-867-9979 ■ *Web:* www.yadkinvalleybank.com					
Yakima Federal Savings & Loan Assn					
118 E Yakima Ave	Yakima	WA	98901	509-248-2634	575-8405
TF: 800-331-3225 ■ *Web:* www.yakimafed.com					
York State Bank & Trust Co					
7th & Lincoln Ave PO Box 39	York	NE	68467	402-362-4411	362-4192
TF: 888-580-8002 ■ *Web:* www.yorkstatebank.com					
Zions First National Bank 1 S Main St	Salt Lake City	UT	84111	801-524-4711	524-4914
TF: 800-974-8800 ■ *Web:* www.zionsbank.com					

71 BANKS - FEDERAL RESERVE

				Phone	Fax
Federal Reserve System 20th & C St	Washington	DC	20551	202-452-3000	452-3819
Web: www.federalreserve.gov					
Bank of Sacramento 1750 Howe Ave Suite 100	Sacramento	CA	95825	916-648-2100	648-0548
Web: www.bankofsacramento.com					
Beacon Federal Bancorp Inc					
5000 Brittonfield Pkwy PO Box 186	East Syracuse	NY	13057	315-433-0111	
TF: 888-256-3800 ■ *Web:* www.beaconfederal.com					
Community FirstBank PO Box 22467	Charleston	SC	29413	843-723-7700	723-5446
Web: www.commfirstbank.com					
Eli Lilly Federal Credit Union					
225 S E St Suite 300	Indianapolis	IN	46202	317-276-2105	655-6171
TF: 800-621-2105 ■ *Web:* www.elfcu.org					
Federal Reserve Bank of Atlanta					
1000 Peachtree St NE	Atlanta	GA	30309	404-498-8353	
TF: 877-521-8500 ■ *Web:* www.frbatlanta.org					
Birmingham Branch 524 Liberty Pkwy	Birmingham	AL	35242	205-968-6700	968-6175
TF: 877-658-6700 ■ *Web:* www.frbatlanta.org					
Jacksonville Branch 800 Water St	Jacksonville	FL	32204	904-632-1000	
Miami Branch 9100 NW 36th St	Miami	FL	33178	305-591-2065	471-6240
Nashville Branch 301 Rosa L Parks	Nashville	TN	37203	615-251-7100	251-7189
New Orleans Branch 525 St Charles Ave	New Orleans	LA	70130	504-593-3200	593-3213
Web: www.frbatlanta.org					
Federal Reserve Bank of Boston					
600 Atlantic Ave	Boston	MA	02210	617-973-3000	973-3487
Web: www.bos.frb.org					
Federal Reserve Bank of Chicago					
230 S LaSalle St	Chicago	IL	60604	312-322-5322	322-5091
Web: www.chicagofed.org					
Detroit Branch 1600 E Warren Ave	Detroit	MI	48207	313-961-6880	
Federal Reserve Bank of Cleveland					
1455 E 6th St PO Box 6387	Cleveland	OH	44101	216-579-2000	579-3172
Web: www.clevelandfed.org					
Cincinnati Branch 150 E 4th St	Cincinnati	OH	45202	513-721-4787	455-4583
TF: 800-432-1343 ■ *Web:* www.clevelandfed.org					
Pittsburgh Branch 717 Grant St PO Box 867	Pittsburgh	PA	15219	412-261-7800	
Federal Reserve Bank of Dallas					
2200 N Pearl St PO Box 655906	Dallas	TX	75201	214-922-6000	922-5268
TF: 800-333-4460 ■ *Web:* www.dallasfed.org					
El Paso Branch 301 E Main St	El Paso	TX	79901	915-521-5200	521-8284
Web: www.dallasfed.org					
Houston Branch 1801 Allen Pkwy	Houston	TX	77019	713-483-3000	483-3638
TF: 800-392-4162 ■ *Web:* www.houstonfed.org					
San Antonio Branch 126 E Nueva St	San Antonio	TX	78204	210-978-1200	
TF: 800-333-4460 ■ *Web:* www.dallasfed.org					
Federal Reserve Bank of Kansas City					
1 Memorial Dr PO Box 1200	Kansas City	MO	64198	816-881-2000	881-2846
TF: 800-333-1010 ■ *Web:* www.kc.frb.org					
Denver Branch 1020 16th St	Denver	CO	80202	303-572-2300	572-2491
TF: 800-333-1020					
Oklahoma City Branch					
226 Dean A McGee Ave	Oklahoma City	OK	73102	405-270-8400	270-8676
TF: 800-333-1030 ■ *Web:* www.kc.frb.org					
Omaha Branch 2201 Farnam St	Omaha	NE	68102	402-221-5500	221-5715
TF: 800-333-1040 ■ *Web:* www.kansascityfed.org					
Federal Reserve Bank of Minneapolis					
90 Hennepin Ave	Minneapolis	MN	55401	612-204-5000	204-5339
TF: 800-553-9656 ■ *Web:* www.minneapolisfed.org					
Helena Branch 100 Neill Ave	Helena	MT	59601	406-447-3800	447-3808
Federal Reserve Bank of Philadelphia					
10 Independence Mall	Philadelphia	PA	19106	215-574-6000	
TF: 877-574-1776 ■ *Web:* www.phil.frb.org					
Federal Reserve Bank of Richmond					
701 E Byrd St	Richmond	VA	23219	804-697-8000	
Web: www.richmondfed.org					
Baltimore Branch 502 S Sharp St	Baltimore	MD	21201	410-576-3300	576-3353
Federal Reserve Bank of Saint Louis					
411 Locust St	Saint Louis	MO	63102	314-444-8444	444-8430
TF: 800-333-0810 ■ *Web:* www.stlouisfed.org					
Little Rock Branch					
111 Ctr St Suite 1000 Stephens Bldg	Little Rock	AR	72201	501-324-8300	324-8201
TF: 800-332-0813 ■ *Web:* www.stlouisfed.org					
Louisville Branch 101 S 5th St Suite 1920	Louisville	KY	40202	502-568-9200	568-9247
Web: www.stlouisfed.org					
Federal Reserve Bank of San Francisco					
101 Market St	San Francisco	CA	94105	415-974-2000	974-3340
TF: 800-227-4133 ■ *Web:* www.frbsf.org					
Los Angeles Branch 950 S Grand Ave	Los Angeles	CA	90015	213-683-2300	683-2488
Portland Branch 1500 SW 1st Ave Suite 100	Portland	OR	97201	503-276-3000	276-3002
TF: 800-227-4133 ■ *Web:* www.frbsf.org					
Salt Lake City Branch 120 S State St	Salt Lake City	UT	84111	801-322-7900	322-7845
TF: 800-523-3022					
First Federal of Northern Michigan					
100 S 2nd Ave	Alpena	MI	49707	989-356-9041	354-8671
NASDAQ: FFNM ■ *Web:* www.first-federal.com					
First FSB 633 La Salle St	Ottawa	IL	61350	815-434-3500	434-1775
TF: 800-443-8780 ■ *Web:* www.firstfedsavingsbank.com					
First Shore Federal					
108 S Division St PO Box 4248	Salisbury	MD	21803	410-546-1101	546-9590
TF: 800-634-6309 ■ *Web:* www.firstshorefederal.com					
Home Federal Bank					
221 S Locust St PO Box 1009	Grand Island	NE	68802	308-382-4000	382-9235
Web: www.homefedgi.com					
Hyde Park Savings Bank 1196 River St	Boston	MA	02136	617-361-6900	361-2662
TF: 800-361-6903 ■ *Web:* www.hydeparkbank.com					
Lake Shore Bancorp Inc 128 E 4th St	Dunkirk	NY	14048	716-366-4070	366-2965
NASDAQ: LSBK ■ *Web:* www.lakeshoresavings.com					
Lincoln FSB 1101 N St 68508 PO Box 80038	Lincoln	NE	68501	402-474-1400	474-1585
TF: 800-333-2158 ■ *Web:* www.lincolnfed.com					
Martha's Vineyard Savings Bank					
78 Main St PO Box 1069	Edgartown	MA	02539	508-627-4266	627-7588
Web: www.mvbank.com					
Milford Federal Savings & Loan Assn					
PO Box 210	Milford	MA	01757	508-634-2500	634-2500
TF: 800-478-6990 ■ *Web:* www.milfordfederal.com					
Naugatuck Savings Bank Foundation Inc					
251 Church St PO Box 370	Naugatuck	CT	06770	203-729-4442	
TF: 877-729-4442 ■ *Web:* www.naugatucksavingsbank.com					
Newport FSB 100 Bellevue Ave PO Box 210	Newport	RI	02840	401-847-5500	848-5910
TF: 888-660-6372 ■ *Web:* www.newportfederal.com					
OmniAmerican Bank					
1320 S University Dr Suite 110					
PO Box 150098	Fort Worth	TX	76107	817-367-4640	367-2786
NASDAQ: OABC ■ *TF:* 866-670-6664 ■ *Web:* www.omniamerican.com					
Passumpsic Savings Bank PO Box 38	Saint Johnsbur	VT	05819	802-748-3196	
TF: 800-581-1905 ■ *Web:* www.passumpsicbank.com					
Pioneer Savings Bank 21 2nd St PO Box 1048	Troy	NY	12181	518-274-4800	274-3560
Web: www.pioneersb.com/index.asp					
Ponce De Leon Fsb 2244 Westchester Ave	Bronx	NY	10462	718-931-9000	542-9733
Web: www.poncedeleonbank.com					
Putnam County Savings Bank (PCSB)					
2477 Rt 6 PO Box 417	Brewster	NY	10509	845-279-7101	279-9175
Web: www.pcsb.com					
Queen City FSB (QCFB)					
12th Ave S & Hwy 53 PO Box 1147	Virginia	MN	55792	218-741-2040	741-2042
Web: www.qcfb.com					
Roma Financial Corp 2300 Rt 33	Robbinsville	NJ	08691	800-223-8300	
NASDAQ: ROMA ■ *TF:* 888-440-7662 ■ *Web:* www.romabank.com					
SE Financial Corp 1901 E Passyunk Ave	Philadelphia	PA	19148	215-468-1700	462-7027
TF: 800-849-6599 ■ *Web:* www.stedmondsfsb.com					
Security Federal Bank (SFB) 238 Richland Ave W	Aiken	SC	29801	803-641-3000	502-2407
TF: 866-851-3000 ■ *Web:* www.securityfederalbank.com					
Sterling Federal Bank					
110 E 4th St PO Box 617	Sterling	IL	61081	815-626-0614	626-6921
Web: www.sterlingfederal.com					
Summit State Bank					
500 Bicentennial Way PO Box 6188	Santa Rosa	CA	95406	707-568-6000	568-7090
TF: 800-428-5008 ■ *Web:* www.summitstatebank.com					
Thomas County Federal Savings & Loan Assn Inc					
131 S Dawson St PO Box 1197	Thomasville	GA	31799	229-226-3221	226-3459
Web: www.tcfsl.com					
Webster First Federal Credit Union					
271 Greenwood St	Worcester	MA	01607	508-671-5140	
TF: 800-962-4452 ■ *Web:* www.websterfirst.com					

72 BAR ASSOCIATIONS - STATE

SEE ALSO Legal Professionals Associations p. 1458

				Phone	Fax
Alabama State Bar 415 Dexter Ave	Montgomery	AL	36104	334-269-1515	261-6310
Web: www.alabar.org					

				Phone	Fax
Alaska Bar Assn 550 W 7th Ave Suite 1900 PO Box 100279 *Web:* www.alaskabar.org	Anchorage	AK	99501	907-272-7469	272-2932
Arkansas Bar Assn 2224 Cottondale Ln *Web:* www.arkbar.com	Little Rock	AR	72202	501-375-4606	375-4901
Colorado Bar Assn 1900 Grant St Suite 900 *Web:* www.cobar.org	Denver	CO	80203	303-860-1115	894-0821
Connecticut Bar Assn 30 Bank St PO Box 350 *Web:* www.ctbar.org	New Britain	CT	06050	860-223-4400	223-4400
Delaware State Bar Assn 301 N Market St *Web:* www.dsba.org	Wilmington	DE	19801	302-658-5279	658-5212
District of Columbia Bar The 1101 K St NW Suite 200 *TF:* 877-333-2227 ■ *Web:* www.dcbar.org	Washington	DC	20005	202-737-4700	626-3453
Florida Bar 651 E Jefferson St *TF:* 800-342-8060 ■ *Web:* www.floridabar.org	Tallahassee	FL	32399	850-561-5600	561-1141
Hawaii State Bar Assn (HSBA) 1100 Alakea St Suite 1000 *Web:* www.hsba.org	Honolulu	HI	96813	808-537-1868	521-7936
Idaho State Bar 525 W Jefferson St *TF:* 800-221-3295 ■ *Web:* www.isb.idaho.gov	Boise	ID	83702	208-334-4500	334-4515
Illinois State Bar Assn 424 S 2nd St *TF:* 800-252-8908 ■ *Web:* www.isba.org	Springfield	IL	62701	217-525-1760	525-0712
Indiana State Bar Assn 1 Indiana Sq Suite 530 *Web:* www.inbar.org	Indianapolis	IN	46204	317-639-5465	266-2588
Iowa State Bar Assn 625 E Ct Ave *Web:* www.iowabar.org	Des Moines	IA	50309	515-243-3179	243-2511
Kansas Bar Assn 1200 SW Harrison St *Web:* www.ksbar.org	Topeka	KS	66612	785-234-5696	234-3813
Kentucky Bar Assn 514 W Main St *Web:* www.kybar.org	Frankfort	KY	40601	502-564-3795	564-3225
Louisiana State Bar Assn (LSBA) 601 St Charles Ave *TF:* 800-421-5722 ■ *Web:* www.lsba.org	New Orleans	LA	70130	504-566-1600	566-0930
Maine State Bar Assn 124 State St *TF:* 800-475-7523 ■ *Web:* www.mainebar.org	Augusta	ME	04330	207-622-7523	623-0083
Maryland State Bar Assn Inc 520 W Fayette St *TF:* 800-492-1964 ■ *Web:* www.msba.org	Baltimore	MD	21201	410-685-7878	685-1016
Massachusetts Bar Assn 20 W St *TF:* 866-627-7577 ■ *Web:* www.massbar.org	Boston	MA	02111	617-338-0500	338-0650
Minnesota State Bar Assn 600 Nicollet Mall Suite 380 *TF:* 800-882-6722 ■ *Web:* www.mnbar.org	Minneapolis	MN	55402	612-333-1183	333-4927
Mississippi Bar 643 N State St *Web:* www.msbar.org	Jackson	MS	39202	601-948-4471	355-8635
Missouri Bar The 326 Monroe St PO Box 119 *Web:* www.mobar.org	Jefferson City	MO	65102	573-635-4128	635-2811
Nebraska State Bar Assn 635 S 14th St Suite 200 *TF:* 800-927-0117 ■ *Web:* www.nebar.com	Lincoln	NE	68501	402-475-7091	475-7098
New Hampshire Bar Assn 2 Pillsbury St Suite 300 *Web:* www.nhbar.org	Concord	NH	03301	603-224-6942	224-2910
New Jersey State Bar Assn 1 Constitution Sq New Jersey Law Ctr *Web:* www.njsba.com	New Brunswick	NJ	08901	732-249-5000	249-2815
New York State Bar Assn 1 Elk St *TF:* 800-342-3661 ■ *Web:* www.nysba.org	Albany	NY	12207	518-463-3200	487-5517
North Carolina State Bar 208 Fayetteville St PO Box 25908 *TF:* 800-662-7407 ■ *Web:* www.ncbar.gov	Raleigh	NC	27601	919-828-4620	821-9168
Ohio State Bar Assn (OSBA) 1700 Lake Shore Dr *TF:* 800-282-6556 ■ *Web:* www.ohiobar.org	Columbus	OH	43204	614-487-2050	487-1008
Oklahoma Bar Assn 1901 N Lincoln Blvd PO Box 53036 *TF:* 800-522-8065 ■ *Web:* www.okbar.org	Oklahoma City	OK	73105	405-416-7000	416-7001
Oregon State Bar Assn 16037 SW Upper Boones Ferry Rd *Web:* www.osbar.org	Tigard	OR	97224	503-620-0222	684-1366
Pennsylvania Bar Assn 100 S St *TF:* 800-932-0311 ■ *Web:* www.pabar.org	Harrisburg	PA	17101	717-238-6715	238-1204
Rhode Island Bar Assn 115 Cedar St *Web:* www.ribar.com	Providence	RI	02903	401-421-5740	421-2703
South Carolina Bar 950 Taylor St *TF:* 877-797-2227 ■ *Web:* www.scbar.org	Columbia	SC	29201	803-799-6653	799-4118
State Bar Assn of North Dakota 504 N Washington St PO Box 2136 *TF:* 800-472-2685 ■ *Web:* www.sband.org	Bismarck	ND	58502	701-255-1404	224-1621
State Bar of Arizona 4201 N 24th St Suite 200 *TF:* 866-482-9227 ■ *Web:* www.azbar.org	Phoenix	AZ	85016	602-252-4804	271-4930
State Bar of California 180 Howard St *Web:* www.calbar.ca.gov	San Francisco	CA	94105	415-538-2000	538-2304
State Bar of Georgia 104 Marietta St NW Suite 100 *TF:* 800-334-6865 ■ *Web:* www.gabar.org	Atlanta	GA	30303	404-527-8700	527-8717
State Bar of Michigan 306 Townsend St *TF:* 800-968-1442 ■ *Web:* www.michbar.org	Lansing	MI	48933	517-346-6300	482-6248
State Bar of Montana PO Box 577 *Web:* www.montanabar.org	Helena	MT	59624	406-442-7660	442-7763
State Bar of Nevada 600 E Charleston Blvd *TF:* 800-254-2797 ■ *Web:* www.nvbar.org	Las Vegas	NV	89104	702-382-2200	385-2878
State Bar of New Mexico 5121 Masthead St NE PO Box 92860 *TF:* 800-876-6227 ■ *Web:* www.nmbar.org	Albuquerque	NM	87109	505-797-6000	828-3765
State Bar of South Dakota 222 E Capitol Ave Suite 3 *Web:* www.sdbar.org	Pierre	SD	57501	605-224-7554	224-0282
State Bar of Texas 1414 Colorado St *TF:* 800-204-2222 ■ *Web:* www.texasbar.com	Austin	TX	78701	512-427-1463	427-4100
State Bar of Wisconsin 5302 Eastpark Blvd *TF:* 800-728-7788 ■ *Web:* www.wisbar.org	Madison	WI	53718	608-257-3838	257-5502
Tennessee Bar Assn 221 4th Ave N Suite 400 *TF:* 800-899-6993 ■ *Web:* www.tba.org	Nashville	TN	37219	615-383-7421	297-8058
Utah State Bar 645 S 200 E *Web:* www.utahbar.org	Salt Lake City	UT	84111	801-531-9077	531-0660
Vermont Bar Assn (VBA) 35-37 Ct St PO Box 100 *Web:* www.vtbar.org	Montpelier	VT	05601	802-223-2020	223-1573
Virginia State Bar 707 E Main St Suite 1500 *Web:* www.vsb.org	Richmond	VA	23219	804-775-0500	775-0544
Washington State Bar Assn 1325 4th Ave Suite 600 *TF:* 800-945-9722 ■ *Web:* www.wsba.org	Seattle	WA	98101	206-727-8200	727-8320
West Virginia State Bar 2006 Kanawha Blvd E *TF:* 866-989-8227 ■ *Web:* www.wvbar.org	Charleston	WV	25311	304-558-2456	558-2467
Wyoming State Bar 4124 Laramie St *Web:* www.wyomingbar.org	Cheyenne	WY	82001	307-632-9061	632-3737

73 BASKETS, CAGES, RACKS, ETC - WIRE

SEE ALSO Pet Products p. 2411

				Phone	Fax
Adrian Fabricators Inc Cargotainer Div PO Box 518 *TF:* 800-221-3794	Adrian	MI	49221	517-266-5700	266-5751
Apco Products Inc PO Box 236 *Web:* www.apco-products.com	Essex	CT	06426	860-767-2108	767-7259
Archer Wire International Corp 7300 S Narragansett Ave *Web:* www.archerwire.com	Bedford Park	IL	60638	708-563-1700	563-1740
Bright Coop Inc 803 W Seale St *TF:* 800-562-0730 ■ *Web:* www.brightcoop.com	Nacogdoches	TX	75964	936-564-8378	564-3281
Equipment Fabricating Corp 729 45th Ave *Web:* www.equipmentfabricating.com	Oakland	CA	94601	510-261-0343	261-0715
Glamos Wire Products Co Inc 5561 N 152nd St *TF:* 800-428-6353 ■ *Web:* www.glamoswire.com	Hugo	MN	55038	651-429-5386	429-7733
InterMetro Industries Corp 651 N Washington St *Fax: Hum Res ■ *TF Cust Svc:* 800-992-1776 ■ *Web:* www.metro.com	Wilkes-Barre	PA	18705	570-825-2741	824-7520*
Kaspar Wire Works Inc PO Box 667 *TF:* 800-337-0610 ■ *Web:* www.kwire.com/wirewrk.htm	Shiner	TX	77984	361-594-3327	594-3311
Kewanna Metal Specialties Inc (KMS) 419 W Main St *Web:* www.kmswire.com	Kewanna	IN	46939	574-653-2554	653-2556
Lab Products Inc 742 Sussex Ave *TF:* 800-526-0469 ■ *Web:* www.labproductsinc.com	Seaford	DE	19973	302-628-4300	628-4309
Marlboro Wire 2403 N 24th St PO Box 5058 *Web:* www.marlborowire.com	Quincy	IL	62305	217-224-7989	224-7990
Midwest Wire Products Inc 800 Woodward Heights *TF:* 800-989-9881 ■ *Web:* www.midwestwire.com	Ferndale	MI	48220	248-399-5100	542-7104
Nashville Wire Products Mfg Co 199 Polk Ave *TF:* 888-743-2595 ■ *Web:* www.nashvillewire.com	Nashville	TN	37210	615-743-2500	242-4225
Nestaway Wire Fabricators 9501 Granger Rd *TF:* 888-587-9473 ■ *Web:* www.nestawaywire.com	Cleveland	OH	44125	216-587-1500	587-2774
Progress Wire Products Inc 3535 W 140th St *Web:* www.progresswire.com	Cleveland	OH	44111	216-251-2181	251-2699
Riverdale Mills Corp 130 Riverdale St PO Box 200 *TF:* 800-762-6374 ■ *Web:* www.riverdale.com	Northbridge	MA	01534	508-234-8715	234-9593
Stevens Wire Products Inc 351 NW 'F' St PO Box 1146 *Web:* www.stevenswire.com	Richmond	IN	47375	765-966-5534	962-3586
Technibilt Ltd 700 E P St PO Box 310 *Fax Area Code: 800 ■ *Web:* www.technibilt.com	Newton	NC	28658	828-464-7388	968-8934*
Tote Cart Co Inc 1802 Preston St *TF:* 800-435-5709 ■ *Web:* www.totecart.com	Rockford	IL	61102	815-963-3414	963-3892
Wirefab Inc 75 Blackstone River Rd *TF Sales:* 877-877-4445 ■ *Web:* www.wirefab.com	Worcester	MA	01607	508-754-5359	797-3620

74 BATTERIES

				Phone	Fax
A123 Systems Inc 200 W St *NASDAQ: AONE* ■ *Web:* www.a123systems.com	Waltham	MA	02451	617-778-5700	924-8910
Applied Energy Solutions LLC 1 Technology Pl *TF:* 800-836-2132 ■ *Web:* www.appliedenergysol.com	Caledonia	NY	14423	585-538-4421	538-6345
Atlantic Battery Co Inc 80 Elm St	Watertown	MA	02472	617-924-2868	924-5200
Bren-Tronics Inc 10 Brayton Ct *Web:* www.bren-tronics.com	Commack	NY	11725	631-499-5155	499-5504
C & D Technologies Inc 1400 Union Meeting Rd PO Box 3053 *NYSE: CHP* ■ *TF:* 800-543-8630 ■ *Web:* www.cdtechno.com	Blue Bell	PA	19422	215-619-2700	619-7899
Cell-con Inc 305 Commerce Dr Suite 300 *TF:* 800-771-7139 ■ *Web:* www.cell-con.com	Exton	PA	19341	610-280-7630	280-7685
Continental Battery Corp 4919 Woodall St *TF:* 800-442-0081 ■ *Web:* www.continentalbattery.com	Dallas	TX	75247	214-631-5701	634-7846
Crown Battery Mfg Co 1445 Majestic Dr *TF:* 800-487-2879 ■ *Web:* www.crownbattery.com	Fremont	OH	43420	419-334-7181	334-7416
Douglas Battery Mfg Co 500 Battery Dr *Fax: Hum Res ■ *TF:* 800-368-4527 ■ *Web:* www.douglasbattery.com	Winston-Salem	NC	27107	336-650-7000	650-7057*
Duracell 14 Research Dr Berkshire Corporate Pk *TF:* 800-243-9540 ■ *Web:* www.duracell.com	Bethel	CT	06801	203-796-4000	796-4483
Eagle-Picher Industries Inc 2424 John Daly Rd *Web:* www.epcorp.com	Inkster	MI	48141	313-278-5956	278-5982
Eagle-Picher Technologies LLC C & Porter St *Fax: Sales ■ *Web:* www.eaglepicher.com/EaglePicherInternet/Technologies	Joplin	MO	64801	417-623-8000	623-0850*
Ener1 Inc 500 W Cypress Creek Rd Suite 100 *Web:* www.ener1.com	Fort Lauderdale	FL	33309	954-556-4020	556-4031
Energizer Holdings Inc 533 Maryville University Dr *NYSE: ENR* ■ *TF:* 800-383-7323 ■ *Web:* www.energizerasiapacific.com	Saint Louis	MO	63141	314-985-2000	985-2200
EnerSys 2366 Bernville Rd *NYSE: ENS* ■ *TF:* 800-538-3627 ■ *Web:* www.enersysinc.com	Reading	PA	19605	610-208-1991	372-8457
EnerSys Inc 617 N Ridgeview Dr	Warrensburg	MO	64093	660-429-2165	429-2253

Phone | Fax

Web: www.enersysreservepower.com

Exide Technologies
13000 Deerfield Pkwy Bldg 200 .... Milton GA 30004 678-566-9000 566-9188
NASDAQ: XIDE ■ TF: 866-289-0645 ■ Web: www.exideworld.com

Hawker Powersource Inc
9404 Ooltewah Industrial Dr PO Box 808 .... Ooltewah TN 37363 423-238-5700 238-6060
TF: 800-238-8658 ■ Web: www.hawkerpowersource.com

Industrial Battery & Charger Inc
5831 Orr Rd PO Box 560978 .... Charlotte NC 28256 704-597-7330 597-0855
TF: 800-833-8412 ■ Web: www.ibciplusone.com

Johnson Controls Inc 5757 N Green Bay Ave .... Milwaukee WI 53209 414-524-1200 524-3232
NYSE: JCI ■ TF: 800-972-8040 ■ Web: www.johnsoncontrols.com

Keystone Battery Corp 35 Holton St .... Winchester MA 01890 781-729-8333 721-0127
Web: www.keystonebattery.com

MarathonNorco Aerospace Inc 8301 Imperial Dr .... Waco TX 76712 254-776-0650 776-6558
Web: www.mnaerospace.com

Mathews Assoc Inc 220 Power Ct .... Sanford FL 32771 407-323-3390 323-3115
Web: www.maifl.com

Medis Technologies Ltd (MTL)
805 3rd Ave 15th Fl .... New York NY 10022 212-935-8484 935-9216
NASDAQ: MDTL ■ Web: www.medistechnologies.com

Medtronic Energy & Component Ctr (MECC)
6700 Shingle Creek Pkwy .... Brooklyn Center MN 55430 763-514-1000 514-1170
TF: 800-328-2518

Micro Power Electronics Inc
13955 SW Millikan Way .... Beaverton OR 97005 503-693-7600 648-9625
TF: 800-576-6177 ■ Web: www.micro-power.com

Power Battery Co Inc 25 McLean Blvd .... Paterson NJ 07514 973-523-8630 523-3023*
*Fax: Sales ■ TF: 800-783-7697

R & D Batteries Inc
3300 Corporate Ctr Dr PO Box 5007 .... Burnsville MN 55306 952-890-0629 890-7912
TF: 800-950-1945 ■ Web: www.rdbatteries.net

Southwest Electronic Energy Corp PO Box 848 .... Stafford TX 77497 281-240-4000 240-5672
TF: 800-231-3612 ■ Web: www.swe.com

Spectrum Brands Inc
601 Rayovac Dr PO Box 44960 .... Madison WI 53711 608-275-3340 275-4577
NYSE: SPC ■ TF: 800-237-7000 ■ Web: www.spectrumbrands.com

Staab Battery Mfg Co 931 S 11th St .... Springfield IL 62703 217-528-0421

Web: www.staabbattery.com

Surefire LLC 18300 Mt Baldy Cir .... Fountain Valley CA 92708 714-545-9444 545-9537
TF: 800-828-8809 ■ Web: www.surefire.com

Tadiran Batteries
2001 Marcus Ave Suite 125E .... Lake Success NY 11042 516-621-4980 621-4517
TF: 800-537-1368 ■ Web: www.tadiranbat.com

TNR Technical Inc 301 Central Pk Dr .... Sanford FL 32771 407-321-3011 321-3208
TF: 800-346-0601 ■ Web: www.batterystore.com

Trojan Battery Co 12380 Clark St .... Santa Fe Springs CA 90670 562-236-3000 236-3282
TF Cust Svc: 800-423-6569 ■ Web: www.trojanbattery.com

Ultralife Batteries Inc 2000 Technology Pkwy .... Newark NY 14513 315-332-7100 331-7800
NASDAQ: ULBI ■ TF: 800-332-5000 ■ Web: www.ultralifecorporation.com

Valence Technology Inc
12303 Technology Blvd Suite 950 .... Austin TX 78727 512-527-2900 527-2910
TF: 888-825-3623 ■ Web: www.valence.com

Voltmaster Co Inc 2185 Hwy 2 PO Box 288 .... Corydon IA 50060 641-872-2044 872-2664

Yardney Technical Products Inc
82 Mechanic St .... Pawcatuck CT 06379 860-599-1100 599-3903
Web: www.yardney.com

75 BEARINGS - BALL & ROLLER

Phone | Fax

Accurate Bushing Co Inc 443 N Ave .... Garwood NJ 07027 908-789-1121 789-9429
TF Sales: 800-932-0076 ■ Web: www.smithbearing.com

Alinabal Inc 28 Woodmont Rd .... Milford CT 06460 203-877-3241 874-5063
TF: 800-254-6763 ■ Web: www.alinabal.com

AST Bearings 115 Main Rd .... Montville NJ 07045 973-335-2230 335-6987
TF: 800-526-1250 ■ Web: www.astbearings.com

Axsys Technologies Inc
175 Capital Blvd Suite 103 .... Rocky Hill CT 06067 860-257-0200 594-5750
Web: www.axsys.com

Barnes Engineering Co 2715 Delta Pl .... Colorado Springs CO 80910 719-390-6500 390-6700
TF: 800-995-6050

Bearing Inspection Inc 4422 Corporate Ctr Dr .... Los Alamitos CA 90720 714-484-2400 484-2428
TF Cust Svc: 800-416-8881 ■ Web: www.timken.com

Bearing Service Co of Pennsylvania
630 Alpha Dr CIDC Industrial Pk .... Pittsburgh PA 15238 412-963-7710 963-8005
TF: 800-783-2327 ■ Web: www.bearing-service.com

Berliss Bearing Co 644 Rt 10 .... Livingston NJ 07039 973-992-4242 992-6669
Web: www.berliss.com

C & S Engineering Corp 956 Old Colony Rd .... Meriden CT 06451 203-235-5727 237-7498

Carolina Forge PO Box 370 .... Wilson NC 27894 252-237-8181 237-2777
Web: www.carolinaforgeco.com

Emerson Power Transmission McGill Mfg Div
909 N Lafayette St .... Valparaiso IN 46383 219-465-2200 465-2290

Freeway Corp 9301 Allen Dr .... Cleveland OH 44125 216-524-9700 524-7396*
*Fax: Sales ■ Web: www.freewaycorp.com

General Bearing Corp 44 High St .... West Nyack NY 10994 845-358-6000 358-6277
TF Sales: 800-431-1766 ■ Web: www.generalbearing.com

Hartford Technologies 1022 Elm St .... Rocky Hill CT 06067 860-571-3601 571-3609
TF: 888-840-9565 ■ Web: www.hartfordtechnologies.com

Kaydon Corp 315 E Eisenhower Pkwy Suite 300 .... Ann Arbor MI 48108 734-747-7025 747-6565
NYSE: KDN ■ Web: www.kaydon.com

Koyo Corp of USA 29570 Clemens Rd .... Westlake OH 44145 440-835-1000 835-9347
TF Cust Svc: 800-248-5696 ■ Web: www.koyousa.com

Phone | Fax

LSB Industries Inc
16 S Pennsylvania Ave .... Oklahoma City OK 73107 405-235-4546 235-5067
AMEX: LXU ■ Web: www.lsb-okc.com

Lutco Bearings Inc 130 Higgins St .... Worcester MA 01606 508-853-2114 853-1105

Lutco Inc 677 Cambridge St .... Worcester MA 01610 508-756-6296 799-6848
TF: 888-588-0099 ■ Web: www.lutco.com

MRC Bearings Inc 402 Chandler St .... Jamestown NY 14701 716-661-2600 661-2740
TF Cust Svc: 800-672-7000

Nachi America Inc 715 Pushville Rd .... Greenwood IN 46143 317-530-1001
TF: 888-340-2747 ■ Web: www.nachi.com

National Bearing Co PO Box 4726 .... Lancaster PA 17604 717-569-0485 569-1605
Web: www.nationalbearings.com

New Hampshire Ball Bearings Inc
175 Jaffrey Rd .... Peterborough NH 03458 603-924-3311 924-4419*
*Fax: Cust Svc ■ Web: www.nhbb.com

Peer Bearing Co 2200 Norman Dr S .... Waukegan IL 60085 847-578-1000 578-1200*
*Fax: Orders ■ TF: 800-433-7337 ■ Web: www.peerbearing.com

Professional Instruments Co 7800 Powell Rd .... Hopkins MN 55343 952-933-1222 933-3315
Web: www.airbearings.com

RBC Bearings Inc 1 Tribology Ctr .... Oxford CT 06478 203-267-7001 267-5000
NASDAQ: ROLL ■ TF: 800-352-0079 ■ Web: www.rbcbearings.com

Roller Bearing Co of America
400 Sullivan Way .... West Trenton NJ 08628 609-882-5050 882-5533
Web: www.rbcbearings.com

Rotek Inc 1400 S Chillicothe Rd PO Box 312 .... Aurora OH 44202 330-562-4000 562-4620*
*Fax: Sales ■ TF: 800-221-8043 ■ Web: www.rotek-inc.com

S/n Precision Enterprises Inc 145 Jordan Rd .... Troy NY 12180 518-283-8002 283-8032
TF: 866-902-4998 ■ Web: www.pacamor.com

Schaeffler Group USA Inc
308 Springhill Farm Rd .... Fort Mill SC 29715 803-548-8500 548-8599
Web: www.ina.com/us

Schatz Bearing Corp 10 Fairview Ave .... Poughkeepsie NY 12601 845-452-6000 452-1660
TF: 800-554-1406

SKF USA Inc Roller Bearing Div
20 Industrial Dr .... Hanover PA 17331 717-637-8981 637-3395

Timken Co 1835 Dueber Ave SW .... Canton OH 44706 330-438-3000 458-6006
NYSE: TKR ■ TF: 800-223-1954 ■ Web: www.timken.com

Timken Rail Bearing Service
2122 Holston Bend Dr .... Mascot TN 37806 865-932-5800 932-5774
Web: www.timken.com

Universal Bearings Inc 431 N Birkey St .... Bremen IN 46506 574-546-2261 546-5085
Web: www.univbrg.com

Virginia Industries Inc 1022 Elm St .... Rocky Hill CT 06067 860-571-3600 571-3604

Wieland Metals Inc 567 Northgate Pkwy .... Wheeling IL 60090 847-537-3990 537-4085
Web: www.wielandus.com

Winsted Precision Ball Corp
159 Colebrook River Rd .... Winsted CT 06098 860-379-2788 379-9650
TF: 800-462-3075 ■ Web: www.winball.com

76 BEAUTY SALON EQUIPMENT & SUPPLIES

Phone | Fax

Beaute Craft Supply Co 600 W Maple Rd .... Troy MI 48084 248-362-0400 362-7996*
*Fax: Cust Svc ■ TF Cust Svc: 800-331-8277

Belvedere USA Corp 1 Belvedere Blvd .... Belvidere IL 61008 815-544-3131 544-6747
TF: 800-435-5491 ■ Web: www.belvedere.com

Betty Dain Creations Inc 3300 NW 110th St .... Miami FL 33167 305-769-3451 769-3451
TF: 800-327-5256 ■ Web: www.bettydain.com

Burmax Co 28 Barretts Ave .... Holtsville NY 11742 631-447-8700 289-7590
TF: 800-645-5118 ■ Web: www.burmax.com

Collins Mfg Co 2000 Bowser Rd .... Cookeville TN 38506 931-528-5151 528-5472
TF: 800-292-6450 ■ Web: www.collinsmfgco.com

Dr Kern USA Inc 221 S Franklin Rd .... Indianapolis IN 46219 317-472-0867 472-0873
TF: 800-908-9885 ■ Web: www.drkern.com

European Touch Ltd II 8301 W Parkland Ct .... Milwaukee WI 53223 414-357-7016 357-6360
TF: 800-626-6912 ■ Web: www.etspa.com

Kaemark Inc 1338 County Rd 208 .... Giddings TX 78942 979-542-3651 542-0039
Web: www.kaemark.com

Living Earth Crafts 3210 Executive Ridge Dr .... Vista CA 92081 760-597-2155 599-7374
TF: 800-358-8292 ■ Web: www.livingearthcrafts.com

Maly's of California Inc
28145 W Harrison Pkwy .... Valencia CA 91355 661-295-8317
TF: 800-446-2597 ■ Web: www.malys.com

National Salon Resources Inc
3109 Louisiana Ave N .... Minneapolis MN 55427 763-546-9500 546-5212
TF: 800-622-0003 ■ Web: www.nationalsalon.com

Pibbs Industries 133-15 32nd Ave .... Flushing NY 11354 718-445-8046 461-3910
TF: 800-551-5020 ■ Web: www.pibbs.com

Sally Beauty Co Inc 3001 Colorado Blvd .... Denton TX 76210 940-297-2000 297-2110
TF: 800-777-5706 ■ Web: www.sallybeauty.com

Takara Belmont USA Inc 101 Belmont Dr .... Somerset NJ 08873 732-469-5000 469-9430
Web: www.takara-belmont.com

TouchAmerica 437 Dimmocks Mill Rd .... Hillsborough NC 27278 919-732-6968 732-1173
TF: 800-678-6824 ■ Web: www.touchamerica.com

Valley Barber & Beauty Supply
413 W Harrison St .... Harlingen TX 78550 956-423-0727 423-0757
TF: 800-292-7548

William Marvy Co Inc 1540 St Clair Ave .... Saint Paul MN 55105 651-698-0726 698-4048
TF: 800-874-2651 ■ Web: www.wmmarvyco.com

77 BEAUTY SALONS

Phone | Fax

Beauty Brands Inc
4600 Madison St Suite 400 .... Kansas City MO 64112 816-531-2266
TF: 877-640-2248 ■ Web: www.beautybrands.com

	City	State	Zip	Phone	Fax
Beauty Management Inc					
270 Beavercreek Rd Suite 100	Oregon City	OR	97405	503-723-3200	723-3232
TF: 888-268-7577 ■ *Web:* www.perfectlooksalons.com					
Bumble & Bumble LLC 146 E 56th St	New York	NY	10022	212-521-6500	759-0867
TF: 800-728-6253 ■ *Web:* www.bumbleandbumble.com					
Charles Penzone Inc 1480 Manning Pkwy	Powell	OH	43065	614-985-0135	898-1194
Web: www.charlespenzone.com					
Elizabeth Arden Red Door Spas					
3822 E University Dr Suite 5	Phoenix	AZ	85034	602-864-8191	437-4220
TF: 800-592-7336 ■ *Web:* www.reddoorspas.com					
Fantastic Sams Inc 50 Dunham Rd 3rd Fl	Beverly	MA	01915	978-232-5600	232-5601
Web: www.fantasticsams.com					
First Choice Haircutters					
6465 Millcreek Dr Suite 210	Mississauga	ON	L5N5R6	905-821-8555	567-7000
TF: 800-361-2887 ■ *Web:* www.firstchoice.com					
Georgette Klinger Inc 501 Madison Ave	New York	NY	10022	212-838-3200	838-1181
TF: 800-554-6437					
Gino Morena Enterprises					
111 Starlite St	South San Francisco	CA	94080	650-871-0363	871-1379
Web: www.ginomorena.com					
Great Clips Inc					
7700 France Ave S Suite 425	Minneapolis	MN	55435	952-893-9088	844-3444
TF: 800-999-5959 ■ *Web:* www.greatclips.com					
Holiday Hair 7201 Metro Blvd	Minneapolis	MN	55439	952-947-7777	947-7301
Web: www.holidayhair.com					
Las Olas Beauty 1501 E Las Olas Blvd	Fort Lauderdale	FL	33301	954-779-2616	832-0165
Web: www.lasolasbeauty.com					
Lord's & Lady's Hair Salons					
1 Lord's & Lady's Way	West Roxbuy	MA	02132	617-323-4700	323-4059
TF: 877-323-4700 ■ *Web:* www.lordsandladys.com					
Mark Anthony Inc					
559 Jones Franklin Rd Suite 150	Raleigh	NC	27606	919-851-0962	851-2308
Web: www.mitchellshair.com					
Michael of the Carlyle					
750 Citadel Dr E Suite 1008	Colorado Springs	CO	80909	719-591-6188	
Web: www.regiscorp.com					
Premier Salons International					
8341 10th Ave N	Golden Valley	MN	55427	905-470-7850	470-8174
TF: 800-542-4247 ■ *Web:* www.premiersalons.com					
Premier Salons International					
3762 14th Ave Suite 200	Markham	ON	L3R0G7	800-749-0805	581-2108*
**Fax Area Code:* 866 ■ *TF:* 800-749-0805 ■ *Web:* www.halcyondayspa.com					
Ranter co 1577 Spring Hill Rd Suite 500	Vienna	VA	22182	703-269-5400	
TF: 800-874-6288 ■ *Web:* www.ratnerco.com					
Regis Corp 7201 Metro Blvd	Minneapolis	MN	55439	952-947-7777	
NYSE: RGS ■ *TF:* 888-888-7778 ■ *Web:* www.regiscorp.com					
Regis Corp MasterCuts Div					
7201 Metro Blvd	Minneapolis	MN	55439	952-947-7777	947-7801
TF: 888-888-7778 ■ *Web:* www.mastercuts.com					
Regis Corp Pro-Cuts Div 7201 Metro Blvd	Minneapolis	MN	55439	952-947-7777	
TF: 888-888-7778 ■ *Web:* www.procuts.com					
Regis Corp Regis Hairstylists Div					
7201 Metro Blvd	Minneapolis	MN	55439	952-947-7777	
TF: 888-888-7778 ■ *Web:* www.regissalons.com					
Regis Corp SmartStyle Div					
7201 Metro Blvd	Minneapolis	MN	55439	952-947-7777	
TF: 888-888-7778 ■ *Web:* www.smartstyle.com					
Regis Corp Supercuts Div 7201 Metro Blvd	Minneapolis	MN	55439	952-947-7777	947-7801
TF: 888-888-7778 ■ *Web:* www.supercuts.com					
Regis Corp Trade Secret Div					
7201 Metro Blvd	Minneapolis	MN	55439	952-947-7777	
TF: 888-888-7778 ■ *Web:* www.tradesecret.com					
Rios Golden Cut Inc 121 N Pk Blvd	San Antonio	TX	78204	210-227-4996	
Sport Clips Inc 110 Briarwood Dr	Georgetown	TX	78628	512-869-1201	869-0366
TF: 800-872-4247 ■ *Web:* www.sportclips.com					
Steiner Leisure Ltd					
770 S Dixie Hwy Suite 200	Coral Gables	FL	33146	305-358-9002	372-9310
NASDAQ: STNR ■ *Web:* www.steinerleisure.com					
Stewart School of Cosmetology					
604 N W Ave	Sioux Falls	SD	57104	605-336-2775	357-0288
TF: 800-537-2625 ■ *Web:* www.stewartschool.com					
Toni & Guy USA Inc 2311 Midway Rd	Carrollton	TX	75006	972-931-1567	248-0798
TF: 800-256-9391 ■ *Web:* www.toniguy.com					
Vidal Sassoon Salons 14 Newbury St	Boston	MA	02116	617-536-5496	536-6197
Visible Changes Inc 1303 Campbell Rd	Houston	TX	77055	713-984-8800	984-2632
Web: www.visiblechanges.com					

78 BETTER BUSINESS BUREAUS - CANADA

	City	Prov	Postal Code	Phone	Fax
Canadian Council of Better Business Bureaus					
2 St Clair Ave E	Toronto	ON	M4T2T5	416-644-4936	644-4945
Web: www.bbb.org					
Better Business Bureau of Eastern Ontario & the Outaouais Inc					
700 Industrial Ave Unit 505á	Ottawa	ON	K1G0Y9	613-237-4856	237-4878
Web: www.ottawa.bbb.org					
Better Business Bureau of Quebec					
1565 Boul de l'Avenir Suite 206	Laval	QC	H7S2N5	514-905-3893	663-6316*
**Fax Area Code:* 450 ■ *Web:* www.bbb-bec.com					
Better Business Bureau of Saskatchewan					
980 Albert St Suite 201	Regina	SK	S4R2P7	306-352-7601	565-6236
Web: www.sask.bbb.org					
Better Business Bureau of Southern Alberta					
7330 Fisher St SE Suite 350	Calgary	AB	T2H2H8	403-531-8784	640-2514
Web: calgary.bbb.org					
Better Business Bureau of the Maritime Provinces					
1888 Brunswick St Suite 805	Halifax	NS	B3J3J8	902-422-6581	429-6457
Web: maritimeprovinces.bbb.org					
Better Business Bureau of Vancouver Island					
1175 Cook St Suite 220	Victoria	BC	V8V4A1	250-386-6348	386-2367
TF: 877-826-4222 ■ *Web:* www.vi.bbb.org					
Better Business Bureau Serving Central & Northern Alberta					
9707 110th St Suite 888 Capital Pl	Edmonton	AB	T5K2L9	780-482-2341	482-1150
TF: 800-232-7298 ■ *Web:* edmonton.bbb.org					
Better Business Bureau Serving Mainland British Columbia					
788 Beatty St Suite 404	Vancouver	BC	V6B2M1	604-682-2711	681-1544
TF: 888-803-1222 ■ *Web:* mbc.bbb.org					
Better Business Bureau Serving Mid-Western & Central Ontario					
354 Charles St E	Kitchener	ON	N2G4L5	519-579-3080	570-0072
TF: 800-459-8875 ■ *Web:* www.bbbmwo.ca					
Better Business Bureau Serving South Central Ontario					
100 James St S	Hamilton	ON	L8P2Z2	905-526-1111	526-1225
Web: hamilton.bbb.org					
Better Business Bureau Serving Western Ontario					
200 Queens Ave Suite 308 PO Box 2153	London	ON	N6A4E3	519-673-3222	673-5966
TF: 877-283-9222 ■ *Web:* london.bbb.org					
Better Business Bureau Serving Windsor & Southwestern Ontario					
880 Ouellette Ave Suite 302	Windsor	ON	N9A1C7	519-258-7222	258-1198
Web: www.bbbwindsor.com					
Better Business Bureau Serving Winnipeg & Manitoba					
1030B Empress St	Winnipeg	MB	R3G3H4	204-989-9010	989-9016
TF: 800-385-3074 ■ *Web:* www.manitoba.bbb.org					

79 BETTER BUSINESS BUREAUS - US

SEE ALSO Consumer Interest Organizations p. 1421

	City	State	Zip	Phone	Fax
BBB OnLine					
The Council of Better Business Bureaus					
4200 Wilson Blvd Suite 800	Arlington	VA	22203	703-276-0100	525-8277
Web: www.bbb.org					
Better Business Bureau 50 W N St	Bethlehem	PA	18018	610-866-8780	868-8668
Web: dc-easternpa.bbb.org					
Better Business Bureau Heartland 11811 P St	Omaha	NE	68137	402-391-7612	391-7535
TF: 800-649-6814 ■ *Web:* www.nebraska.bbb.org					
Better Business Bureau In Alaska Oregon & Western Washington					
341 W Tudor Rd Suite 209	Anchorage	AK	99503	907-562-0704	644-5222
TF: 888-860-2221 ■ *Web:* alaskaoregonwesternwashington.bbb.org					
Better Business Bureau of Acadiana					
4007 W Congress St Suite B	Lafayette	LA	70506	337-981-3497	981-7559
Web: www.acadiana.bbb.org					
Better Business Bureau of Alaska Oregon & Western Washington					
1000 Stn Dr Suite 222	Dupont	WA	98327	206-431-2222	431-2200
Web: www.alaskaoregonwesternwashington.bbb.org					
Better Business Bureau of Ark-La-Tex					
401 Edwards St Suite 135	Shreveport	LA	71101	318-222-7575	222-7576
TF: 800-372-4222 ■ *Web:* www.shreveport.bbb.org					
Better Business Bureau of Arkansas					
12521 Kanis Rd	Little Rock	AR	72211	501-664-7274	664-0024
Web: www.arkansas.bbb.org					
Better Business Bureau of Asheville/Western North Carolina (BBB)					
112 Executive Pk	Asheville	NC	28801	828-253-2392	252-5039
Web: www.asheville.bbb.org					
Better Business Bureau of Brazos Valley & Deep East Texas					
418 Tarrow	College Station	TX	77840	979-260-2222	846-0276
Web: www.bryan.bbb.org					
Better Business Bureau of Canton Region/West Virginia					
1434 Cleveland Ave NW PO Box 8017	Canton	OH	44711	330-454-9401	456-8957
TF: 800-362-0494 ■ *Web:* www.canton.bbb.org					
Better Business Bureau of Central & Eastern Kentucky					
1460 Newtown Pike	Lexington	KY	40511	859-259-1008	259-1639
TF: 800-866-6668 ■ *Web:* www.bluegrass.bbb.org					
Better Business Bureau of Central & South Central Texas					
1005 La Posada Dr	Austin	TX	78752	512-445-2096	445-2096
Web: www.austin.bbb.org					
Better Business Bureau of Central Alabama & the Wiregrass Area					
4750 Woodmere Blvd Suite D	Montgomery	AL	36106	334-273-5530	273-5546
Web: www.birmingham-al.bbb.org					
Better Business Bureau of Central Alabama & the Wiregrass Area					
1971 S Brannon Stand Rd	Birmingham	AL	35205	205-558-2238	558-2239
Web: www.birmingham-al.bbb.org					
Better Business Bureau of Central Alabama & the Wiregrass Area Dothan Branch					
1971 S Brannon Stand Rd	Dothan	AL	36305	334-794-0492	794-0659
Web: www.birmingham-al.bbb.org					
Better Business Bureau of Central East Texas					
3600 Old Bullard Rd Bldg 1	Tyler	TX	75701	903-581-5704	534-8644
Web: www.tyler.bbb.org					
Better Business Bureau of Central East Texas Longview Branch					
2401 Judson Rd Suite 102	Longview	TX	75605	903-758-3222	758-3226
Web: www.longview.bbb.org					
Better Business Bureau of Central Florida					
1600 S Grant St	Longwood	FL	32750	407-621-3300	786-2625
Web: www.centralflorida.bbb.org					
Better Business Bureau of Central Georgia					
277 ML King Jr Blvd Suite 102	Macon	GA	31201	478-742-7999	742-8191
Web: www.centralgeorgia.bbb.org					
Better Business Bureau of Central Illinois					
112 Harrison St	Peoria	IL	61602	309-688-3741	681-7290
Web: www.heartofillinois.bbb.org					
Better Business Bureau of Central Indiana					
151 N Delaware St	Indianapolis	IN	46204	317-488-2222	488-2224
TF: 866-463-9222 ■ *Web:* www.indianapolis.bbb.org					
Better Business Bureau of Central Louisiana & Ark-La-Tex					
5220-C Rue Verdun	Alexandria	LA	71303	318-473-4494	473-8906
TF: 800-372-4222 ■ *Web:* www.alexandria-la.bbb.org					
Better Business Bureau of Central New England & Northeast Connecticut					
340 Main St Suite 802	Worcester	MA	01608	508-755-2548	754-4158
TF: 888-566-9222 ■ *Web:* www.central-westernma.bbb.org					

				Phone	Fax
Better Business Bureau of Central North Carolina					
3608 W Friendly Ave	Greensboro	NC	27410	336-852-4240	852-7540
Web: www.greensboro.bbb.org					
Better Business Bureau of Central Northeast Northwest & Southwest Arizona					
4428 N 12th St	Phoenix	AZ	85014	602-264-1721	263-0997
TF: 877-291-6222 ■ *Web:* www.central-northern-western-arizona.bbb.org					
Better Business Bureau of Central Ohio					
1169 Dublin Rd	Columbus	OH	43215	614-486-6336	486-6631
TF: 800-759-2400 ■ *Web:* www.columbus-oh.bbb.org					
Better Business Bureau of Central Oklahoma					
17 S Dewey Ave	Oklahoma City	OK	73102	405-239-6081	235-5891
Web: www.oklahomacity.bbb.org					
Better Business Bureau of Central South Carolina & the Charleston Area					
1515 Burnette Dr	Columbia	SC	29202	803-254-2525	779-3117
Web: www.columbia.bbb.org					
Better Business Bureau of Central Texas					
445 Central TX Expy Suite 1	Harker Heights	TX	76548	254-699-0694	699-0746
Web: www.centraltx.bbb.org					
Better Business Bureau of Central Virginia					
720 Moorefield Pk Dr Suite 300	Richmond	VA	23236	804-648-0016	320-0248
Web: www.richmond.bbb.org					
Better Business Bureau of Chicago & Northern Illinois					
330 N Wabash Ave Suite 2006	Chicago	IL	60611	312-832-0500	832-9985
Web: www.chicago.bbb.org					
Better Business Bureau of Cincinnati					
7 W 7th St Suite 1600	Cincinnati	OH	45202	513-421-3015	621-0907
Web: www.cincinnati.bbb.org					
Better Business Bureau of Coastal North & South Carolina					
314 Laurel St Suite 203	Conway	SC	29526	843-488-0238	488-0998
Web: myrtlebeach.bbb.org					
Better Business Bureau of Connecticut					
94 S Tpke Rd	Wallingford	CT	06492	203-269-2700	294-3694
Web: www.ct.bbb.org					
Better Business Bureau of Dayton/Miami Valley					
15 W 4th St Suite 300	Dayton	OH	45402	937-222-5825	222-3338
Web: www.dayton.bbb.org					
Better Business Bureau of Delaware					
60 Reads Way	New Castle	DE	19720	302-221-5255	221-5265
Web: www.delaware.bbb.org					
Better Business Bureau of Detroit & Eastern Michigan					
26777 Central Pk Blvd Suite 100	Southfield	MI	48076	248-223-9400	356-5135
Web: www.easternmichigan.bbb.org					
Better Business Bureau of Eastern Massachusetts Maine Rhode Island & Vermont					
290 Donald Lynch Blvd Suite 102	Marlborough	MA	01752	508-652-4800	652-4820
TF: 800-422-2811 ■ *Web:* boston.bbb.org					
Better Business Bureau of Eastern Missouri & Southern Illinois					
211 N Broadway #2060	Saint Louis	MO	63143	314-645-3300	645-2666
Web: www.stlouis.bbb.org					
Better Business Bureau of Eastern North Carolina					
5540 Munford Rd Suite 130	Raleigh	NC	27612	919-277-4222	277-4221
Web: www.easternnc.bbb.org					
Better Business Bureau of Eastern Oklahoma					
1722 S Carson Ave Suite 3200	Tulsa	OK	74119	918-492-1266	492-1276
Web: www.tulsa.bbb.org					
Better Business Bureau of Eastern Pennsylvania					
1880 JFK Blvd Suite 1330	Philadelphia	PA	19103	215-985-9313	563-4907
Web: www.mybbb.org					
Better Business Bureau of El Paso					
720 Arizona Ave	El Paso	TX	79902	915-577-0191	577-0209
Web: www.elpaso.bbb.org					
Better Business Bureau of Four Corners & Grand Junction Colorado					
308 N Locke Ave	Farmington	NM	87401	505-326-6501	327-7731
Web: www.newmexicoandsouthwestcolorado.bbb.org					
Better Business Bureau of Golden Gate					
1000 Broadway Suite 625	Oakland	CA	94607	510-844-2000	844-2100
TF: 866-411-2221 ■ *Web:* www.bbbgoldengate.org					
Better Business Bureau of Greater East Tennessee					
255 N Peters Rd Suite A PO Box 31377	Knoxville	TN	37923	865-692-1600	692-1590
Web: www.knoxville.bbb.org					
Better Business Bureau of Greater Iowa Quad Cities & Sioux Land Region					
505 5th Ave Suite 950	Des Moines	IA	50309	515-243-8137	243-2227
Web: www.iowa.bbb.org					
Better Business Bureau of Greater Kansas City					
8080 Ward Pkwy Suite 401	Kansas City	MO	64114	816-421-7800	472-5442
Web: www.kansascity.bbb.org					
Better Business Bureau of Greater Maryland					
502 S Sharp St Suite 1200	Baltimore	MD	21201	410-347-3990	347-3936
Web: www.greatermd.bbb.org					
Better Business Bureau of Greater New Orleans					
710 Baronne St Suite C	New Orleans	LA	70113	504-581-6222	524-9110
Web: www.neworleans.bbb.org					
Better Business Bureau of Hampton Roads					
586 Virginian Dr	Norfolk	VA	23505	757-531-1300	531-1388
Web: www.norfolk.bbb.org					
Better Business Bureau of Hawaii					
1132 Bishop St Suite 615	Honolulu	HI	96813	808-536-6956	628-3970
TF: 877-222-6551 ■ *Web:* www.hawaii.bbb.org					
Better Business Bureau of Kansas Inc					
345 N Riverview St Suite 720	Wichita	KS	67203	316-263-3146	263-3063
TF: 800-856-2417 ■ *Web:* www.wichita.bbb.org					
Better Business Bureau of Lancaster					
1337 N Front St	Harrisburg	PA	17102	717-364-3250	364-3251
Web: www.easternpa.bbb.org					
Better Business Bureau of Louisville Southern Indiana & Western Kentucky					
844 S 4th St	Louisville	KY	40203	502-583-6546	589-9940
Web: www.ky-in.bbb.org					
Better Business Bureau of Maine					
290 Donald Lynch Blvd Suite 102	Marlborough	MA	01752	508-652-4800	652-4820
TF: 800-422-2811 ■ *Web:* boston.bbb.org					
Better Business Bureau of Metro Washington DC & Eastern Pennsylvania					
1411 K St NW Suite 1000	Washington	DC	20005	202-393-8000	393-1198
Web: www.dc-easternpa.bbb.org					
Better Business Bureau of Metropolitan Atlanta					
503 Oak Pl Suite 590	Atlanta	GA	30349	404-766-0875	768-1085
Web: www.atlanta.bbb.org					
Better Business Bureau of Metropolitan Dallas & Northeast Texas					
1601 Elm St Suite 3838	Dallas	TX	75201	214-220-2000	740-0321
Web: www.dallas.bbb.org					
Better Business Bureau of Metropolitan Houston					
1333 W Loop S Suite 1200	Houston	TX	77027	713-868-9500	867-4947
Web: www.houston.bbb.org					
Better Business Bureau of Metropolitan New York					
257 Pk Ave S	New York	NY	10010	212-533-6200	477-4912
Web: www.newyork.bbb.org					
Better Business Bureau of Middle Tennessee Inc					
201 4th Ave N Suite 100 PO Box 198436	Nashville	TN	37219	615-242-4222	250-4245
Web: www.nashville.bbb.org					
Better Business Bureau of Minnesota & North Dakota					
2706 Gannon Rd	Saint Paul	MN	55116	651-699-1111	695-2488
Web: www.minnesota.bbb.org					
Better Business Bureau of Mississippi					
PO Box 3302	Ridgeland	MS	39158	601-707-0960	856-9331
Web: ms.bbb.org					
Better Business Bureau of New Hampshire					
25 Hall St Suite 102	Concord	NH	03301	603-228-3789	228-9035
Web: www.concord.bbb.org					
Better Business Bureau of New Jersey					
1700 Whitehorse-Hamilton Sq Rd Suite D-5	Trenton	NJ	08690	609-588-0808	588-0546
Web: www.trenton.bbb.org					
Better Business Bureau of North Central Texas					
4245 Kemp Blvd Suite 900	Wichita Falls	TX	76308	940-691-1172	691-1175
Web: www.wichitafalls.bbb.org					
Better Business Bureau of Northeast California					
3075 Beacon Blvd	West Sacramento	CA	95691	916-443-6843	443-0376
Web: www.necal.bbb.org					
Better Business Bureau of Northeast Florida & The Southeast Atlantic					
4417 Beach Blvd Suite 202	Jacksonville	FL	32207	904-721-2288	721-7373
TF: 800-713-6661 ■ *Web:* www.northeastflorida.bbb.org					
Better Business Bureau of Northeast Kansas					
501 SE Jefferson St Suite 24	Topeka	KS	66607	785-232-0454	232-9677
Web: www.kansasplains.bbb.org					
Better Business Bureau of Northeast Louisiana					
212 Walnut St Suite 210	Monroe	LA	71201	318-387-4600	361-0461
TF: 800-960-7756 ■ *Web:* www.bbbnela.org					
Better Business Bureau of Northeast Ohio					
3167 Westgate Mall Ave Plus Size Clothing Store	Cleveland	OH	44126	216-241-7678	861-6365
Web: www.cleveland.bbb.org					
Better Business Bureau of Northeastern & Central Pennsylvania					
4099 Birney Ave	Moosic	PA	18507	570-342-9129	342-1282
TF: 888-229-3222 ■ *Web:* www.nepa.bbb.org					
Better Business Bureau of Northern Alabama					
107 Lincoln St	Huntsville	AL	35804	256-533-1640	533-1177
Web: www.northalabama.bbb.org					
Better Business Bureau of Northern Colorado & East Central Wyoming					
8020 S County Rd 5 Suite 100	Fort Collins	CO	80528	970-484-1348	221-1239
TF: 800-564-0371 ■ *Web:* www.wynco.bbb.org					
Better Business Bureau of Northern Indiana					
4011 Parnell Ave	Fort Wayne	IN	46805	260-423-4433	423-3301
Web: www.michiana.bbb.org					
Better Business Bureau of Northern Nevada					
991 Bible Way	Reno	NV	89502	775-322-0657	322-8163
Web: www.reno.bbb.org					
Better Business Bureau of Northwest Florida					
912 E Gadsden St	Pensacola	FL	32501	850-429-0002	429-0006
Web: www.nwfl.bbb.org					
Better Business Bureau of Northwest Indiana					
7863 Broadway Suite 124	Merrillville	IN	46410	260-423-4433	884-2123*
**Fax Area Code:* 219 ■ *Web:* www.nwin.bbb.org					
Better Business Bureau of Northwest North Carolina					
500 W 5th St Suite 202	Winston-Salem	NC	27101	336-725-8348	777-3727
TF: 800-777-8348 ■ *Web:* www.nwnc.bbb.org					
Better Business Bureau of Northwest Ohio & Southeast Michigan					
7668 King's Pointe Rd	Toledo	OH	43617	419-531-3116	578-6001
TF: 800-743-4222 ■ *Web:* www.toledo.bbb.org					
Better Business Bureau of Rockford					
401 W State St	Rockford	IL	61101	815-963-2222	963-0329
Web: www.rockford.bbb.org					
Better Business Bureau of San Diego & Imperial Counties					
5050 Murphy Canyon Rd Suite 110	San Diego	CA	92123	858-637-6199	496-2141
Web: www.sandiego.bbb.org					
Better Business Bureau of South Alabama (BBB)					
960 S Schillinger Rd Suite I	Mobile	AL	36606	251-433-5494	438-3191
TF: 800-544-4714 ■ *Web:* www.mobile.bbb.org					
Better Business Bureau of South Central Louisiana					
748 Main St	Baton Rouge	LA	70802	225-346-5222	346-1029
Web: www.batonrouge.bbb.org					
Better Business Bureau of South Texas					
1333 W Loop S Suite 1200	Houston	TX	77027	713-868-9500	867-4947
Web: houston.bbb.org					
Better Business Bureau of Southeast Florida & the Caribbean					
4411 Beacon Cir Suite 4	West Palm Beach	FL	33407	561-842-1918	845-7234
TF: 800-834-6286 ■ *Web:* www.seflorida.bbb.org					
Better Business Bureau of Southeast Tennessee & Northwest Georgia					
1010 Market St Suite 200	Chattanooga	TN	37402	423-266-6144	267-1924
TF: 800-548-4456 ■ *Web:* www.chattanooga.bbb.org					
Better Business Bureau of Southeast Texas					
550 Fannin St Suite 100	Beaumont	TX	77701	409-835-5348	838-6858
Web: www.bbbsetexas.org					
Better Business Bureau of Southern Arizona					
434 S Williams Blvd Suite 102	Tucson	AZ	85711	520-888-5353	888-6262
Web: www.tucson.bbb.org					

Name / Address	City	State	Zip	Phone	Fax
Better Business Bureau of Southern Colorado 25 N Wahsatch Ave *Web:* www.southerncolorado.bbb.org	Colorado Springs	CO	80903	719-636-1155	636-5078
Better Business Bureau of Southern Nebraska 3633 'O' St Suite 1 *Web:* nebraska.bbb.org	Lincoln	NE	68510	402-436-2345	476-8221
Better Business Bureau of Southern Nevada 6040 S Jones Blvd *Web:* www.vegas.bbb.org	Las Vegas	NV	89118	702-320-4500	320-4560
Better Business Bureau of Southern Piedmont Carolinas 13860 Ballantyne Corporate Pl Suite 225 *Web:* www.charlotte.bbb.org	Charlotte	NC	28277	704-927-8611	927-8615
Better Business Bureau of Southwest Georgia PO Box 2587 *TF:* 800-768-4222 ■ *Web:* www.columbus-ga.bbb.org	Columbus	GA	31902	706-324-0712	324-2181
Better Business Bureau of Southwest Idaho & Eastern Oregon (BBB) 1200 N Curtis Rd PO Box 9817 *TF:* 800-218-1001 ■ *Web:* www.snake-river.bbb.org	Boise	ID	83706	208-342-4649	342-5116
Better Business Bureau of Southwest Louisiana Inc 2309 E Prien Lake Rd *TF:* 800-542-7085 ■ *Web:* www.lakecharles.bbb.org	Lake Charles	LA	70601	337-478-6253	474-8981
Better Business Bureau of Southwest Missouri 430 S Glenstone Ave *Web:* www.southwestmissouri.bbb.org	Springfield	MO	65802	417-862-4222	869-5544
Better Business Bureau of the Abilene Area 3300 S 14th St Suite 307 *Web:* www.abilene.bbb.org	Abilene	TX	79605	325-691-1533	691-0309
Better Business Bureau of the Akron Inc (BBB) 222 W Market St *TF:* 800-825-8887 ■ *Web:* www.akron.bbb.org	Akron	OH	44303	330-253-4590	253-6249
Better Business Bureau of the Bakersfield Area 1601 H St Suite 101 *TF:* 800-675-8118 ■ *Web:* www.bakersfield.bbb.org	Bakersfield	CA	93301	661-322-2074	322-8318
Better Business Bureau of the Denver-Boulder Metro Area 1020 Cherokee St *Web:* www.denver.bbb.org	Denver	CO	80204	303-758-2100	758-8321
Better Business Bureau of the Fort Worth Area 101 Summit Ave Suite 707 *Web:* www.fortworth.bbb.org	Fort Worth	TX	76102	817-332-7585	882-0566
Better Business Bureau of the Mid-Hudson 150 White Plains Rd Suite 107 *Web:* www.newyork.bbb.org	Tarrytown	NY	11735	914-333-0550	333-7519
Better Business Bureau of the Mid-South 3693 Tyndale Dr *TF:* 800-222-8754 ■ *Web:* www.midsouth.bbb.org	Memphis	TN	38125	901-759-1300	757-2997
Better Business Bureau of the Permian Basin Area of West Texas 10100 Liberator Ln *Web:* www.permianbasinbbb.org	Midland	TX	79706	432-563-1880	561-5506
Better Business Bureau of the San Angelo Area 3134 Executive Dr *Web:* www.sanangelo.bbb.org	San Angelo	TX	76904	325-949-2989	949-3514
Better Business Bureau of the Santa Clara Valley San Benito Santa Cruz & Monterey Inc 1112 S Bascom Ave *Web:* www.sanjose.bbb.org	San Jose	CA	95128	408-278-7400	278-7444
Better Business Bureau of the South Central Area 1800 NE Loop 410 Suite 400 *Web:* www.sanantonio.bbb.org	San Antonio	TX	78217	210-828-9441	828-3101
Better Business Bureau of the South Plains of Texas 3333 66th St *Web:* www.southplains.bbb.org	Lubbock	TX	79413	806-763-0459	744-9748
Better Business Bureau of the Southeast Atlantic 6606 Abercorn St Suite 108C *Web:* www.savannah.bbb.org	Savannah	GA	31405	912-354-7521	354-5068
Better Business Bureau of the Southland Inc 315 N La Cadena Dr *Web:* www.labbb.org	Colton	CA	92324	909-825-7280	825-6246
Better Business Bureau of the Southwest 2625 Pennsylvania St NE Suite 2050 *Web:* www.bbbsw.org	Albuquerque	NM	87110	505-346-0110	346-0696
Better Business Bureau of the Texas Panhandle 720 S Tyler St Suite B-112 *Web:* www.txpanhandle.bbb.org	Amarillo	TX	79101	806-379-6222	379-8206
Better Business Bureau of the Tri-Counties PO Box 129 *Web:* www.santabarbara.bbb.org	Santa Barbara	CA	93102	805-963-8657	962-8557
Better Business Bureau of the Tri-Parish Area 801 Barrow St Suite 400 *TF:* 866-695-4222 ■ *Web:* www.houma.bbb.org	Houma	LA	70360	985-868-3456	876-7664
Better Business Bureau of the Youngstown Area PO Box 1495 *Web:* www.youngstown.bbb.org	Youngstown	OH	44501	330-744-3111	744-7336
Better Business Bureau of Upstate New York 100 Bryant Woods S *Web:* www.upstateny.bbb.org	Amherst	NY	14228	716-881-5222	883-5349
Better Business Bureau of Utah 5673 S Redwood Rd Suite 22 *Web:* www.utah.bbb.org	Salt Lake City	UT	84123	801-892-6009	892-6002
Better Business Bureau of West Central Ohio 219 N McDonel St *Web:* www.wcohio.bbb.org	Lima	OH	45801	419-223-7010	229-2029
Better Business Bureau of West Florida 2655 McCormick Dr *TF:* 800-525-1447 ■ *Web:* www.westflorida.bbb.org	Clearwater	FL	33758	727-535-5522	539-6301
Better Business Bureau of West Georgia & East Alabama PO Box 2587 *TF:* 800-768-4222 ■ *Web:* www.columbus-ga.bbb.org	Columbus	GA	31902	706-324-0712	324-2181
Better Business Bureau of Western Massachusetts 35 Ctr St Suite 203 *TF:* 866-566-9222 ■ *Web:* www.central-westernma.bbb.org	Chicopee	MA	01013	413-594-2160	594-2167
Better Business Bureau of Western Michigan 40 Pearl St NW Suite 354 *Web:* www.grandrapids.bbb.org	Grand Rapids	MI	49503	616-774-8236	774-2014
Better Business Bureau of Western Pennsylvania 400 Holiday Dr Suite 220 *Web:* www.westernpennsylvania.bbb.org	Pittsburgh	PA	15220	412-456-2700	922-8656
Better Business Bureau of Western Virginia 31 W Campbell Ave Suite G *TF:* 800-533-5501 ■ *Web:* www.vawest.bbb.org	Roanoke	VA	24011	540-342-3455	345-2289
Better Business Bureau of Wisconsin 10101 W Greenfield Ave Suite 125 *Web:* www.wisconsin.bbb.org	Milwaukee	WI	53214	414-847-6000	302-0355
Better Business Bureau Serving Central California 4201 W Shaw Ave Suite 107 *TF:* 800-675-8118 ■ *Web:* www.cencal.bbb.org	Fresno	CA	93722	559-222-8111	228-6518
Better Business Bureau Serving Eastern Washington North Idaho & Montana Inc 152 S Jefferson St Suite 200 *Web:* www.bbb.org	Spokane	WA	99201	509-455-4200	838-1079
Better Business Bureau Upstate South Carolina 408 N Church St Suite C *Web:* www.greenville.bbb.org	Greenville	SC	29601	864-242-5052	271-9802
Council of Better Business Bureaus (CBBB) 4200 Wilson Blvd Suite 800 *Web:* www.bbb.org	Arlington	VA	22203	703-276-0100	525-8277
Tri-State Better Business Bureau 5401 Vogel Rd Suite 410 *Web:* www.evansville.bbb.org	Evansville	IN	47715	812-473-0202	473-3080

80 BEVERAGES - MFR

SSEE ALSO Breweries p. 1544; Water - Bottled p. 2772

80-1 Liquor - Mfr

Name / Address	City	State	Zip	Phone	Fax
A Bowman Smith Distillery Inc 1 Bowman Dr *Web:* www.asmithbowman.com	Fredericksburg	VA	22408	540-373-4555	371-2236
Anheuser-Busch Cos Inc 1 Busch Pl. *NYSE: BUD* ■ *TF:* 800-342-5283 ■ *Web:* www.anheuser-busch.com	Saint Louis	MO	63118	314-577-2000	577-2900
Bacardi Corp PO Box 363549 *Web:* www.bacardi.com	San Juan	PR	00936	787-788-1500	788-0340
Bacardi USA Inc 2100 Biscayne Blvd *TF:* 800-222-2734 ■ *Web:* www.bacardi.com	Miami	FL	33137	305-573-8511	573-7507
Black Prince Distillery Inc 691 Clifton Ave *Web:* www.blackprincedistillery.com	Clifton	NJ	07011	973-365-2050	365-0746
City Brewing Co LLC 925 S 3rd St *Web:* www.citybrewery.com	La Crosse	WI	54601	608-785-4200	785-4300
Diageo North America 801 Main Ave **Fax:* Hum Res ■ *TF:* 800-847-4109 ■ *Web:* www.diageo.com	Norwalk	CT	06851	203-229-2100	967-7682*
Dickel George A Co PO Box 490 *Web:* www.dickel.com	Tullahoma	TN	37388	931-857-3124	857-9313
Early Times Distillery Co PO Box 1105 *Web:* www.earlytimes.com	Louisville	KY	40201	502-774-2960	774-2103
Florida Distillers Co 530 Dakota Ave PO Box 1447 *Web:* www.ibrandsinc.com	Lake Alfred	FL	33850	863-956-1116	956-3979
Four Roses Distillery LLC 1224 Bonds Mill Rd *Web:* www.fourroses.us	Lawrenceburg	KY	40342	502-839-3436	839-8338
Gekkeikan Sake USA Inc 1136 Sibley St *Web:* www.gekkeikan-sake.com	Folsom	CA	95630	916-985-3111	985-2221
Heavenhill Distilleries Inc 1064 Loretto Rd *Web:* www.heaven-hill.com	Bardstown	KY	40004	502-348-3921	349-1512
Jack Daniel Distillery 280 Lynchburg Hwy *Web:* www.jackdaniels.com	Lynchburg	TN	37352	931-759-4221	759-6321
Jacquin Charles et Cie 2633 Trenton Ave *TF:* 800-523-3811	Philadelphia	PA	19125	215-425-9300	425-9438
Jim Beam Brands Worldwide Inc 510 Lake Cook Rd *Web:* www.jimbeam.com	Deerfield	IL	60015	847-948-8888	948-7883
Laird & Co 1 Laird Rd *TF:* 877-438-5247 ■ *Web:* www.lairdandcompany.com	Scobeyville	NJ	07724	732-542-0312	542-2244
Maker's Mark Distillery Inc 3350 Burke Spring Rd *Web:* www.makersmark.com	Loretto	KY	40037	270-865-2881	865-2196
McCormick Distilling Co Inc 1 McCormick Ln *Web:* www.mccormickdistilling.com	Weston	MO	64098	816-640-2276	640-3085
Montebello Brands Inc 1919 Willow Spring Rd	Baltimore	MD	21222	410-282-8800	282-8809
Paramount Distillers Inc 3116 Berea Rd *TF:* 800-821-2989 ■ *Web:* www.paramountdistillers.com	Cleveland	OH	44111	216-671-6300	671-2299
Pernod Ricard USA 100 Manhattanville Rd *TF:* 800-488-7539 ■ *Web:* www.pernod-ricard-usa.com	Purchase	NY	10577	914-848-4800	848-4777
Sazerac Co Inc 803 Jefferson Hwy PO BOX 52821 *Web:* www.sazerac.com	New Orleans	LA	70121	504-831-9450	831-2383
Skyy Spirits Inc 1 Beach St 3rd Fl *TF:* 800-367-7599 ■ *Web:* www.skyyspirits.com	San Francisco	CA	94133	415-315-8000	315-8001
Sunrich LLC 3824 SW 93rd St PO Box 128 *Web:* www.sunrich.com	Hope	MN	56046	507-451-4724	451-2910
Takara Sake USA Inc 708 Addison St *Web:* www.takarasake.com	Berkeley	CA	94710	510-540-8250	486-8758
Walker MS Inc 20 3rd Ave *TF:* 800-776-5808 ■ *Web:* www.mswalker.com	Somerville	MA	02143	617-776-6700	776-5808
White Rock Distilleries Inc 21 Saratoga St *TF:* 800-628-5441 ■ *Web:* www.whiterockdistilleries.com	Lewiston	ME	04240	207-783-1433	783-8409
Wild Turkey Distillery 1525 Tyrone Rd *Web:* www.wildturkeybourbon.com	Lawrenceburg	KY	40342	502-839-4544	839-3902

80-2 Soft Drinks - Mfr

Phone Fax

Adirondack Beverages Inc 701 Corporations Pk .... Scotia NY 12302 518-370-3621 370-3762
Web: www.adirondackbeverages.com

American Beverage Corp 1 Daily Way .... Verona PA 15147 412-828-9020 828-8876
Web: www.ambev.com

Beverage Corp International 3505 NW 107th St .... Miami FL 33167 305-714-7000 714-7134
TF: 800-226-5061 ■ *Web:* www.bcibeverages.com

Coca-Cola Co 1 Coca-Cola Plaza PO Box 1734 .... Atlanta GA 30313 404-676-2121 676-6792
NYSE: KO ■ *TF:* 800-438-2653 ■ *Web:* www.coca-cola.com

Cosco International Inc
1633 Sands Pl SE Cumberland Business Pk .... Marietta GA 30067 770-303-0797 303-0795
Web: www.coscous.com

Cott Corp 6525 Viscount Rd .... Mississauga ON L4V1H6 905-672-1900 203-8171*
NYSE: COT ■ **Fax Area Code:* 416 ■ *TF:* 800-994-2688 ■ *Web:* www.cott.com

Crystal Rock Holdings Inc
1050 Buckingham St .... Watertown CT 06795 860-945-0661 274-0397
AMEX: CRVP ■ *TF:* 800-525-0070 ■ *Web:* www.crystalrock.com

Davis Beverage Group 1530-A Bobali Dr .... Harrisburg PA 17104 717-914-1295 914-1296
TF: 800-360-7056

Double Cola Co USA
537 Market St Suite 100 .... Chattanooga TN 37402 423-267-5691 267-5691
TF: 877-325-2659

Dr Pepper/Seven-Up Inc 5301 Legacy Dr .... Plano TX 75024 972-673-7000 673-7000*
**Fax:* Hum Res ■ *TF:* 800-696-5891 ■ *Web:* www.drpeppersnapplegroup.com

Faygo Beverages Inc 3579 Gratiot Ave .... Detroit MI 48207 313-925-1600 571-7611
TF: 800-347-6591 ■ *Web:* www.faygo.com

Ferolito Vultaggio & Sons
5 Dakota Dr Suite 205 .... Lake Success NY 11024 516-812-0300 326-4988
TF: 800-832-3775

Fiji Water Co Llc
11444 W Olympic Blvd 2nd Fl .... Los Angeles CA 90064 310-312-2850 312-2828
TF: 888-426-3454 ■ *Web:* www.fijiwater.com

Global Beverage Co 130 Linden Oaks Dr .... Rochester NY 14625 585-381-3560 381-4025

Great Plains Coca-Cola Bottling Co Inc
600 N May Ave .... Oklahoma City OK 73107 405-280-2000 946-5739
TF: 800-753-2653 ■ *Web:* www.greatplainscocacola.com

Jones Soda Co 234 9th Ave N .... Seattle WA 98109 206-624-3357 624-6857
NASDAQ: JSDA ■ *TF:* 800-690-6903 ■ *Web:* www.jonessoda.com

Middlesboro Coca-Cola Bottling Works Inc
PO Box 1485 .... Middlesboro KY 40965 606-248-2660 248-1382
TF: 800-442-0102 ■ *Web:* www.mccbw.com

Monarch Beverage Co 1123 Zonolite Rd NE # 10 .... Atlanta GA 30306 404-262-4040 262-4001
TF: 800-241-3732

National Beverage Corp
8100 SW 10th St Suite 4000 .... Fort Lauderdale FL 33324 954-581-0922 473-4710
AMEX: FIZ ■ *TF:* 877-622-3499 ■ *Web:* www.nbcfiz.com

Oneta Co 1401 S Padre Island Dr .... Corpus Christi TX 78416 361-853-0123 853-5327
Web: www.onetacc.com

Polar Beverages Inc 1001 Southbridge St .... Worcester MA 01610 508-753-4300 793-0813
TF Cust Svc: 800-225-7410 ■ *Web:* www.polarbev.com

Procesadora Campo Fresco Inc PO Box 755 .... Santa Isabel PR 00757 787-845-4747 845-3490
Web: www.campofresco.com

Shasta Beverages Inc 26901 Industrial Blvd .... Hayward CA 94545 510-783-3200 785-3228*
**Fax:* Sales ■ *TF:* 800-326-8640 ■ *Web:* www.shastapop.com

Snapple Beverage Corp 900 King St .... Rye Brook NY 10573 800-964-7842 612-4100*
**Fax Area Code:* 914 ■ *TF:* 800-964-7842 ■ *Web:* www.snapple.com

South Beach Beverage Co 40 Richards Ave .... Norwalk CT 06854 203-899-7111 899-7177
TF Cust Svc: 800-588-0548 ■ *Web:* www.sobebev.com

Wallingford Coffee Mills Inc
11401 Rockfield Ct .... Cincinnati OH 45241 800-533-3690 771-3138*
**Fax Area Code:* 513 ■ *TF:* 800-533-3690 ■ *Web:* www.wallingfordcoffee.com

White Rock Products Corp
141-07 20th Ave Suite 403 .... Whitestone NY 11357 718-746-3400 767-0413
TF: 800-969-7625 ■ *Web:* www.whiterockbeverages.com

Yoo-Hoo Chocolate Beverage Corp
600 Commercial Ave .... Carlstadt NJ 07072 201-933-0070 933-5360
TF: 800-966-4669 ■ *Web:* www.drinkyoo-hoo.com

80-3 Wines - Mfr

Phone Fax

Banfi Vintners USA
1111 Cedar Swamp Rd .... Old Brookville NY 11545 516-626-9200 626-9218
TF: 800-645-6511 ■ *Web:* www.banfivintners.com

Beaulieu Vineyard 1960 St Helena Hwy .... Rutherford CA 94573 707-967-5200 963-5920
TF: 800-264-6918 ■ *Web:* www.bvwines.com

Benziger Family Winery
1883 London Ranch Rd .... Glen Ellen CA 95442 707-935-3000 935-3016
TF: 888-490-2739 ■ *Web:* www.benziger.com

Beringer Blass Wine Estates
610 Airpark Rd PO Box 4500 .... Napa CA 94558 707-259-4500 259-4542
Web: www.beringer.com

Bronco Wine Co 6342 Bystrum Rd .... Ceres CA 95307 209-538-3131 538-2178
TF: 800-692-5780

Brotherhood Winery
100 Brotherhood Plaza Dr PO Box 190 .... Washingtonville NY 10992 845-496-3662
Web: www.brotherhood-winery.com

Bully Hill Vineyards
8843 Greyton H Taylor Memorial Dr .... Hammondsport NY 14840 607-868-3610 868-3205
Web: www.bullyhill.com

Canandaigua Wine Co Inc 235 N Bloomfield Rd .... Naples NY 14424 585-396-7600 396-7831
TF: 888-659-7900 ■ *Web:* www.cwine.com

Chateau Montelena Winery 1429 Tubbs Ln .... Calistoga CA 94515 707-942-5106 942-4221
Web: www.montelena.com

Clos du Bois Wines
19410 Geyserville Ave PO Box 940 .... Geyserville CA 95441 707-857-1651 857-1667
TF Sales: 800-222-3189 ■ *Web:* www.closdubois.com

Columbia Crest Winery
Hwy 221 Columbia Crest Dr PO Box 231 .... Paterson WA 99345 509-875-4227 415-3657*
**Fax Area Code:* 425 ■ *TF:* 888-309-9463 ■ *Web:* www.columbiacrest.com

Delicato Vineyards 12001 S Hwy 99 .... Manteca CA 95336 209-824-3600 824-3400
TF: 888-599-4637 ■ *Web:* www.delicato.com

Diageo Chateau & Estate Wines Co
240 Gateway Rd W .... Napa CA 94558 707-299-2600 299-2600
Web: www.diageowines.com

Distillerie Stock USA Ltd
58-58 Laurel Hill Blvd .... Woodside NY 11377 718-651-9800 651-9800
TF: 800-323-1884

Dolce Winery Inc PO Box 327 .... Oakville CA 94562 707-944-8868 944-2312
Web: www.dolcewine.com

Domaine Chandon Inc 1 California Dr .... Yountville CA 94599 707-944-8844 944-1123
TF: 888-242-6366 ■ *Web:* www.chandon.com

E & J Gallo Winery 600 Yosemite Blvd .... Modesto CA 95354 209-341-3111 341-3307
TF: 800-322-2389 ■ *Web:* www.gallo.com

F Korbel & Bros Inc 13250 River Rd .... Guerneville CA 95446 707-824-7000 869-2981
TF: 800-656-7235 ■ *Web:* www.korbel.com

Franciscan Estates 1178 Galleron Rd .... Saint Helena CA 94574 707-963-7111 963-7867
TF: 800-529-9463 ■ *Web:* www.franciscan.com

Freixenet USA Inc 2355 Hwy 121 PO Box 1427 .... Sonoma CA 95476 707-996-7256 996-0720
Web: www.freixenetusa.com

Giumarra Vineyards Corp 11220 Edison Hwy .... Edison CA 93220 661-395-7000 366-7134

Hogue Cellars 2800 Lee Rd .... Prosser WA 99350 509-786-4557 786-4580
TF: 800-565-9779 ■ *Web:* www.hoguecellars.com

J Filippi Vintage Co
12467 Base Line Rd .... Rancho Cucamonga CA 91739 909-899-5755 899-9196
Web: www.josephfilippiwinery.com

Jefferson Vineyards LP
1353 Thmas Jefferson Pkwy .... Charlottesville VA 22902 434-977-3042
Web: www.jeffersonvineyards.com

Kendall-Jackson Wine Estates Ltd
425 Aviation Blvd .... Santa Rosa CA 95403 707-544-4000 569-0105
TF: 800-544-4413 ■ *Web:* www.kj.com

Laetitia Vineyards & Winery Inc
453 Laetitia Vineyard Dr .... Arroyo Grande CA 93420 805-481-1772 481-6920
TF: 800-809-8463 ■ *Web:* www.laetitiawine.com

Louis M Martini Winery
254 S St Helena Hwy PO Box 112 .... Saint Helena CA 94574 707-963-2736 963-8750
TF: 800-321-9463 ■ *Web:* www.louismartini.com

Malibu Hills Vineyards 29000 Newton Canyon Rd .... Malibu CA 90265 310-463-9532 916-1858*
**Fax Area Code:* 949 ■ *TF:* 800-814-0733 ■ *Web:* www.rosenthalestatewines.com

Meier's Wine Cellars Inc
6955 Plainfield Rd .... Cincinnati OH 45236 513-891-2900 891-6370
TF: 800-346-2941 ■ *Web:* www.meierswinecellars.com

Mendocino Wine Co 501 Parducci Rd .... Ukiah CA 95482 707-463-5350 462-7260
TF: 888-362-9463 ■ *Web:* www.mendocinowineco.com

Michel-schlumberger Partners LP
4155 Wine Creek Rd .... Healdsburg CA 95448 707-433-7427 433-0404
TF: 800-447-3060 ■ *Web:* www.michelschlumberger.com

Old Mill Winery 403 S Broadway .... Geneva OH 44041 800-227-6972 466-4417*
**Fax Area Code:* 440 ■ *TF:* 800-227-6972 ■ *Web:* www.ohiowines.org

Ozeki Sake (USA) Inc 249 Hillcrest Rd .... Hollister CA 95023 831-637-9217 637-0953
Web: www.ozekisake.com

Pine Ridge Winery LLC 5901 Silverado Trail .... Napa CA 94558 707-253-7500
TF: 800-575-9779 ■ *Web:* www.pineridgewinery.com

Ravenswood Winery Inc 18701 Gehricke Rd .... Sonoma CA 95476 707-938-1960
TF: 888-669-4679 ■ *Web:* www.ravenswoodwinery.com

Raymond Vineyard & Cellar Inc
849 Zinfandel Ln .... Saint Helena CA 94574 707-963-3141 525-5339*
**Fax Area Code:* 800 ■ *TF:* 800-525-2659 ■ *Web:* www.raymondwine.com

Renault Winery Resort
72 N Bremen Ave .... Egg Harbor City NJ 08215 609-965-2111 965-1847
Web: www.renaultwinery.com

Robert Mondavi Co Hwy 29 .... Oakville CA 94562 888-766-6328
TF: 888-766-6328 ■ *Web:* www.mondavi.com

Rodney Strong Vineyards
11455 Old Redwood Hwy .... Healdsburg CA 95448 707-433-6511 433-0939
TF: 800-678-4763 ■ *Web:* www.rodneystrong.com

Round Hill Vineyards & Cellars
1680 Silverado Trail .... Saint Helena CA 94574 707-968-3200 968-3239
Web: www.roundhillwines.com

Royal Wine Corp 63 Le Fante Ln .... Bayonne NJ 07002 718-384-2400 384-5329
TF: 800-382-8299 ■ *Web:* www.royalwines.com

Sebastiani Vineyards Inc 389 4th St E .... Sonoma CA 95476 707-938-5532 933-3370
TF: 800-888-5532 ■ *Web:* www.sebastiani.com

Simi Winery 16275 Healdsburg Ave .... Healdsburg CA 95448 707-433-6981 433-6253
TF: 800-746-4880 ■ *Web:* www.simiwinery.com

Ste Michelle Wine Estates
14111 NE 145th St .... Woodinville WA 98072 425-488-1133 415-3657
TF: 800-267-6793 ■ *Web:* www.ste-michelle.com

Trefethen Vineyards Winery Inc
1160 Oak Knoll Ave .... Napa CA 94558 707-255-7700 255-0793
TF: 800-556-4847 ■ *Web:* www.trefethen.com

Trinchero Family Estates
100 St Helena Hwy S PO Box 248 .... Saint Helena CA 94574 707-963-3104 963-2381*
**Fax:* Mktg ■ *Web:* www.tfewines.com

Vie-Del Co 11903 S Chestnut .... Fresno CA 93725 559-834-2525 834-1348

Vincor International Inc
441 Courtneypark Dr E .... Mississauga ON L5T2V3 905-564-6900 564-6909*
**Fax:* Sales ■ *TF:* 800-265-9463 ■ *Web:* www.vincorinternational.com

Warner Vineyards Inc 706 S Kalamazoo St .... Paw Paw MI 49079 269-657-3165 657-4154
TF: 800-756-5357

Weibel Vineyards 1 Winemaster Way .... Lodi CA 95240 209-365-9463 365-9469
TF: 800-932-9463 ■ *Web:* www.weibel.com

Willamette Valley Vineyards Inc
8800 Enchanted Way SE .... Turner OR 97392 503-588-9463 588-8894
NASDAQ: WVVI ■ *TF Sales:* 800-344-9463 ■ *Web:* www.wvv.com

Wine Group Inc
240 Stockton St Suite 800 .... San Francisco CA 94108 415-986-8700 986-4305

81 BEVERAGES - WHOL

81-1 Beer & Ale - Whol

Company / Address	City	State	Zip	Phone	Fax
All State Beverage Co 1580 Parallel St	Montgomery	AL	36104	334-265-0507	263-2367
TF: 800-489-1021					
Allentown Beverage Co Inc 1249 N Quebec St	Allentown	PA	18109	610-432-4581	821-8311
Arkansas Distributing Co LLC 800 E Barton Ave	West Memphis	AR	72301	870-735-3506	735-0052
TF: 877-735-3506					
Associated Distributors LLC 401 Woodlake Dr	Chesapeake	VA	23320	757-424-6300	424-4616
TF: 800-268-4200					
Atlas Distributing Corp 44 Southbridge St	Auburn	MA	01501	508-791-6221	791-0812
TF: 800-649-6221 ■ *Web:* www.atlasdistributing.com					
Banko Beverage Co 2124 Hanover Ave	Allentown	PA	18109	610-434-0147	434-2348
TF: 800-322-9295 ■ *Web:* www.bankobeverage.com					
Beauchamp Distributing Co 1911 S Santa Fe Ave	Compton	CA	90221	310-639-5320	537-8641
TF: 800-734-5102					
Bergseth Bros Co 501 23rd St N	Fargo	ND	58102	701-232-8818	232-8684
Big Sky Distributors Inc 14220 Wyandotte St	Kansas City	MO	64145	816-941-3300	897-3095*
**Fax Area Code:* 913 ■ *TF:* 800-926-4233 ■ *Web:* www.bigskydist.net					
Birmingham Beverage Co Inc PO Box 19457	Birmingham	AL	35219	205-942-9403	942-9411
Web: www.alabev.com					
Blach Distributing Co 131 W Main St	Elko	NV	89801	775-738-7111	738-6731
TF: 888-812-5224 ■ *Web:* www.abwholesaler.com					
Blue Ridge Beverage Co Inc 4446 Barley Dr PO Box 700	Salem	VA	24153	540-380-2000	380-2546
TF Cust Svc: 800-868-0354 ■ *Web:* www.blueridgebeverage.com					
Bob Hall LLC 5600 SE Crane Hwy	Upper Marlboro	MD	20772	301-627-1900	627-0613
TF: 800-451-6508					
Bonanza Beverage Co 6333 Ensworth St	Las Vegas	NV	89119	702-361-4166	361-6408
TF Cust Svc: 800-677-4166					
Buck Distributing Co Inc 15827 Commerce Ct	Upper Marlboro	MD	20774	301-952-0400	627-5380
TF Cust Svc: 800-750-2825 ■ *Web:* www.buckdistributing.com					
Burke Beverages Inc 4900 S Vernon	McCook	IL	60525	708-688-2000	688-2050
Calumet Breweries Inc 6535 Osborn Ave	Hammond	IN	46320	219-845-2242	845-2338
TF Cust Svc: 800-882-2739					
Capitol Distributors Inc PO Box 1148	Concord	NH	03302	603-223-2086	224-7832
Web: www.capitoldistributors.com					
Carenbauer Distributing Corp 1900 Jacob St	Wheeling	WV	26003	304-232-3000	232-3630
Web: www.abwholesaler.com					
Carter Distributing Co 1305 Broad St	Chattanooga	TN	37402	423-266-0056	265-1501
Central Distributors Inc 15 Foss Rd	Lewiston	ME	04240	207-784-4026	784-7869
TF Cust Svc: 800-427-5757 ■ *Web:* www.centraldistributors.com					
Central European Distribution Corp 2 Bala Plaza Suite 300	Bala Cynwyd	PA	19004	610-660-7817	667-3308
NASDAQ: CEDC ■ *Web:* www.ced-c.com					
Cherokee Distributing Co Inc 200 Miller Main Cir	Knoxville	TN	37919	865-588-7641	558-8941
TF: 800-362-9459					
Chicago Beverage Systems Inc 441 N Kilbourn Ave	Chicago	IL	60624	773-826-4100	826-8023
City Beverages of Orlando 10928 Florida Crown Dr	Orlando	FL	32824	407-851-7100	851-7100
TF: 800-717-7267 ■ *Web:* www.abwholesaler.com					
Clare Rose Inc 72 Clare Rose Blvd	Patchogue	NY	11772	631-475-1840	475-1840
TF: 800-427-2833 ■ *Web:* www.abwholesaler.com/Group03/clarerose/home					
Classic City Beverages LLC 530 Calhoun Dr	Athens	GA	30601	706-353-1650	353-1655
TF: 800-300-0218					
Coastal Beverage Co Inc 301 Harley Rd PO Box 10159	Wilmington	NC	28404	910-799-3011	392-3674
TF: 800-229-3884					
Columbia Distributing Co 6840 N Cutter Cir	Portland	OR	97217	503-289-9600	240-8666
TF: 800-275-4494 ■ *Web:* www.columbia-dist.com					
Commercial Distributing Co Inc 46 S Broad St	Westfield	MA	01085	413-562-9691	562-4618
TF Cust Svc: 800-332-8999 ■ *Web:* www.commercialdis.com					
Consolidated Beverages Inc 12 St Mark St	Auburn	MA	01501	508-832-5311	832-9831
TF: 800-922-8128					
Coors Distributing Co 5400 N Pecos St	Denver	CO	80221	303-433-6541	964-5577
TF: 800-642-6116 ■ *Web:* www.coors.com					
Couch Distributing Co Inc 104 Lee Rd	Watsonville	CA	95076	831-724-0649	724-4293
Web: www.couchdistributing.com					
Crescent Crown Distributing 5900 Almonaster Ave	New Orleans	LA	70136	504-240-5900	240-5500
Crest Beverage Co 8870 LIQUID Ct	San Diego	CA	92121	858-452-2300	
Web: www.crestbeverage.com					
D Canale Beverages Inc 45 Crump Blvd	Memphis	TN	38106	901-948-4543	948-6907
Web: www.abwholesaler.com/dcanalebeverages					
DET Distributing Co 301 Great Cir Rd	Nashville	TN	37228	615-244-4113	555-0122
Web: www.detdist.com					
Dutchess Beer Distributors Inc 5 Laurel St	Poughkeepsie	NY	12603	845-452-0940	452-0958
TF Cust Svc: 800-427-6308					
Eagle Distributing Co Inc 310 Radford Pl	Knoxville	TN	37917	865-637-3311	525-9530
TF: 800-467-3301					
Eagle Distributing Co Inc 1100 S Bud Blvd	Fremont	NE	68025	402-721-9723	721-0620
TF: 877-377-2283					
Eastown Distributors Co 14400 Oakland Ave	Highland Park	MI	48203	313-867-6900	867-6020
TF: 800-417-0080 ■ *Web:* www.eastown.com					
Fahr Beverage Inc PO Box 358	Waterloo	IA	50704	319-234-2605	234-5644
Web: www.fahrbeverage.com					
Five Star Distributing Inc 4055 E Parl 30 Dr	Columbia City	IN	46725	260-244-3775	
Web: www.fivestardistributing.net					
Fox Henry A Sales Co 4494 36th St SE	Kentwood	MI	49512	616-949-1210	949-7209
TF: 800-762-8730					
Frank B Fuhrer Wholesale Co 3100 E Carson St	Pittsburgh	PA	15203	412-488-8844	488-0195
TF: 800-837-2212 ■ *Web:* www.fuhrerwholesale.com					
Fred Nackard Wholesale Beverage Co 5660 E Pensdock Ave	Flagstaff	AZ	86004	928-526-2229	522-2171
TF: 800-622-5273					
Gambrinus Co The 14800 San Pedro Ave 3rd Fl	San Antonio	TX	78232	210-490-9128	490-9984
TF: 800-596-6486 ■ *Web:* www.gambrinusco.com					
General Distributing Co 5350 Amelia Earhart Dr	Salt Lake City	UT	84116	801-531-7895	363-4924
Georgia Crown Distributing Co 100 Georgia Crown Dr	McDonough	GA	30253	770-302-3000	305-9438
TF: 800-342-2350 ■ *Web:* www.georgiacrown.com					
Girardi Distributors LLC 5 Railroad Pl	Athol	MA	01331	978-249-3581	249-7894
TF: 800-322-1229					
Gold Coast Beverage Distributors Inc 3325 NW 70th Ave	Miami	FL	33122	305-591-9800	593-2392
Web: www.goldcoastbeverage.com					
Golden Brand Beverage Distributors 2225 Jerrold Ave	San Francisco	CA	94124	415-643-9900	643-9397
Web: www.goldenbrands.com					
Golden Eagle Distributors Inc 705 E Ajo Way	Tucson	AZ	85713	520-884-5999	884-1804
TF: 800-274-4283 ■ *Web:* www.gedaz.com					
Golden Eagle of Arkansas Inc 1900 E 15th St	Little Rock	AR	72202	501-372-2800	376-2404
Grantham Distributing Co Inc 2685 Hansrob Rd	Orlando	FL	32804	407-299-6446	295-7104
Great Bay Distributors Inc 2310 Starkey Rd	Largo	FL	33771	727-584-8626	585-9425
TF: 800-231-4283 ■ *Web:* www.greatbaybud.com					
Gretz Beer Co 710 E Main St	Norristown	PA	19401	610-275-0285	808-0075*
**Fax Area Code:* 866 ■ *TF:* 866-473-8926 ■ *Web:* www.abwholesaler.com/Group06/gretzbeer/home					
Grey Eagle Distributors Inc 2340 Millpark Dr	Maryland Heights	MO	63043	314-429-9100	429-9137
Web: www.greyeagle.com					
Guiffre Distributing Co 6839 Industrial Rd	Springfield	VA	22151	703-642-1700	642-2855
Gusto Brands Inc 707 Douglas St	LaGrange	GA	30240	706-882-2573	882-2412
TF: 800-241-3232					
H Dennert Distributing Corp 351 Wilmer Ave	Cincinnati	OH	45226	513-871-7272	871-7272
TF Cust Svc: 800-837-5659					
Halo Distributing Co 200 Lombrano St	San Antonio	TX	78207	210-735-1111	737-2139
Hartford Distributors Inc 131 Chapel Rd	Manchester	CT	06042	860-643-2337	646-3780
TF: 800-832-7211					
Hayes Beer Distributing Co 12160 S Central Ave	Alsip	IL	60803	708-389-8200	389-8287
Heineken USA 360 Hamilton Ave Suite 1103	White Plains	NY	10601	914-681-4100	681-1900
TF: 800-811-4951 ■ *Web:* www.heineken.com					
Hensley & Co 4201 N 45th Ave	Phoenix	AZ	85031	602-264-1635	247-7094*
**Fax Area Code:* 623 ■ *Web:* www.abwholesaler.com					
High Grade Beverage Inc 891 Georges Rd	Monmouth Junction	NJ	08852	732-821-7600	821-5953
TF: 800-221-1194 ■ *Web:* www.highgradebeverage.com					
Hill Distributing Co 2555 Harrison Rd	Columbus	OH	43204	614-276-6533	276-8888
Web: www.hilldistributing.com					
House of Schwan Inc 3636 Comotara St	Wichita	KS	67226	316-636-9100	636-6210
TF: 800-373-7773					
Hubert Distributors Inc 1200 Auburn Rd	Pontiac	MI	48342	248-858-2340	858-7777
Web: www.abwholesaler.com					
Iron City Distributing Co 2670 Commercial Ave	Mingo Junction	OH	43938	740-598-4171	598-4677
TF Cust Svc: 800-759-2671 ■ *Web:* www.ironcitydist.com					
JJ Taylor Cos Inc 655 N AIA	Jupiter	FL	33477	561-354-2900	354-2999
Web: www.jjtaylor.com					
JJ Taylor Distributing of Florida Inc 501 W 1st St	Tampa	FL	33619	813-247-4000	248-1231*
**Fax:* Mktg ■ *Web:* www.jjtaylor.com					
Koerner Distributors Inc 1305 W Wabash St PO Box 67	Effingham	IL	62401	217-347-7113	347-8736
TF: 800-475-5162 ■ *Web:* www.koernerdistributor.com					
Kramer Beverage Co Inc 161 S 2nd Rd	Hammonton	NJ	08037	609-704-7000	704-7100
TF Cust Svc: 800-321-4522 ■ *Web:* www.kramerbev.com					
Labatt Breweries of Canada 207 Queen's Quay W Suite 299	Toronto	ON	M5J1A7	416-361-5050	
TF Cust Svc: 800-268-2337 ■ *Web:* www.labatt.com					
Lake Beverage Corp 900 John St	West Henrietta	NY	14586	585-427-0090	427-0693
TF: 800-476-4049 ■ *Web:* www.abwholesaler.com/Group07/lakebeverage/home					
Leon Farmer & Co 100 Rail Ridge Rd PO Box 1352	Athens	GA	30603	706-353-1166	369-8922
TF: 800-282-7009 ■ *Web:* www.leonfarmer.com					
Lion Brewery Inc 700 N Pennsylvania Ave	Wilkes-Barre	PA	18705	570-823-8801	823-6686
TF: 800-233-8327 ■ *Web:* www.lionbrewery.com					
Louis Glunz Beer Inc 7100 N Capitol Dr	Lincolnwood	IL	60712	847-676-9500	675-5678
Web: www.glunzbeers.com					
Luce & Son Inc 2399 Valley Rd	Reno	NV	89512	775-785-7810	785-7834
TF: 888-296-7570					
Maple City Ice Co Inc 371 Cleveland Rd	Norwalk	OH	44857	419-668-2531	668-5291
TF Cust Svc: 800-736-6091					
Markstein Beverage Co 505 S Pacific St	San Marcos	CA	92079	760-744-9100	744-0082
Web: www.abwholesaler.com/markstein					
Mautino Distributing Co 500 N Richards St	Spring Valley	IL	61362	815-664-4311	664-2224
TF Cust Svc: 800-851-2756					
MBC United Wholesale 966 E I65 Service Rd N	Mobile	AL	36607	251-471-3486	479-5423
McLaughlin & Moran Inc 40 Slater Rd	Cranston	RI	02920	401-463-5454	463-3770
Merrimack Valley Distributing Co 50 Prince St	Danvers	MA	01923	978-777-2213	774-7487
TF: 800-698-0250					
Mesa Distributing Co Inc 8870 Liquid Ct	San Diego	CA	92121	858-452-2300	452-6242
Web: www.mesadistributing.com					

Company	City	State	Zip	Phone	Fax
Metz Beverage Co Inc 302 N Custer St *TF:* 800-821-4010	Sheridan	WY	82801	307-672-5848	672-6405
Mission Beverage Co 550 S Mission Rd	Los Angeles	CA	90033	323-266-6238	266-6559
Moon Distributors Inc 2800 Vance St	Little Rock	AR	72206	501-375-8291	375-7035
Muller Inc 2800 Grant Ave *TF:* 800-729-5483	Philadelphia	PA	19114	215-676-7575	698-0414
New Hampshire Distributors Inc 65 Regional Dr *TF:* 800-852-3781	Concord	NH	03301	603-224-9991	224-0415
NKS Distributors Inc 399 Churchmans Rd *TF:* 800-292-9509 ■ *Web:* www.abwholesaler.com	New Castle	DE	19720	302-322-1811	324-4024
Odom Corp 10500 NE 8th St Suite 2000 *TF:* 800-767-6366 ■ *Web:* www.odomcorp.com	Bellevue	WA	98004	425-456-3535	456-3536
Pacific Beverage Co 5305 Ekwill St *TF Cust Svc:* 800-325-2278	Santa Barbara	CA	93111	805-964-0611	683-4304
Paradise Beverages Inc 94-1450 Moaniani St **Fax:* Sales ■ *TF:* 800-252-3723	Waipahu	HI	96797	808-678-4000	677-8280*
Pepin Distributing Co 4121 N 50th St *Web:* www.pepindistributing.com	Tampa	FL	33610	813-626-6176	626-5800
Pike Distributors Inc 401 E John St PO Box 465	Newberry	MI	49868	906-293-8611	
Pine State Trading Co 8 Ellis Ave *TF:* 800-873-3825 ■ *Web:* www.pinestatetrading.com	Augusta	ME	04330	207-622-3741	626-0150
Powers Distributing Co Inc 3700 Giddings Rd *TF:* 800-498-4008 ■ *Web:* www.powers-dist.com	Orion	MI	48359	248-393-3700	393-1503
Premium Beverage Co Inc 928 N Railroad Ave	Opelika	AL	36801	334-745-4521	745-2179
Premium Distributors of Maryland LLC 530 Monocacy Blvd *TF:* 800-352-9165 ■ *Web:* www.reyesholdings.com	Frederick	MD	21701	301-662-0372	663-9488
Premium Distributors of Virginia 15001 Northridge Dr	Chantilly	VA	20151	703-227-1200	227-1202
Premium Distributors of Washington DC LLC 3500 Fort Lincoln Dr NE *TF:* 888-524-5483	Washington	DC	20018	202-526-3900	526-7417
Quality Beverage Inc 525 Miles Standish Blvd PO Box 671 *TF:* 800-525-8989	Taunton	MA	02780	508-822-6200	822-7051
Richland Beverage Assoc 2415 Midway Rd Suite 115 *TF:* 877-357-0248	Carrollton	TX	75006	214-357-0248	357-9581
Ritchie & Page Distributing Co Inc 292 3rd St *TF:* 800-257-9360	Trenton	NJ	08611	609-392-1146	392-8541
Saccani Distributing Co 2600 5th St PO Box 1764 *Web:* www.saccanidist.com	Sacramento	CA	95818	916-441-0213	441-0806
Sapporo USA Inc 11 E 44 St Suite 508 *Web:* www.sapporousa.com	New York	NY	10017	212-922-9165	922-9576
Saratoga Eagle Sales & Service Inc 319 Corinth Rd *TF:* 800-342-9565 ■ *Web:* www.abwholesaler.com	Glens Falls	NY	12804	518-792-3112	792-3247
Savannah Distributing Co Inc 5 Interchange Ct PO Box 1388 *TF:* 800-551-0777 ■ *Web:* www.gawine.com	Savannah	GA	31402	912-233-1167	233-1157
Seneca Beverage Corp 388 Upper Oakwood Ave *TF:* 800-724-0350	Elmira	NY	14903	607-734-6111	734-2415
Silver Eagle Distributors LP 7777 Washington Ave *Web:* www.wideworldofbud.com	Houston	TX	77007	713-869-4361	867-8112
Silver State Liquor & Wine Inc 100 Distribution Dr *TF:* 800-543-3867 ■ *Web:* www.renotahoedrinks.com	Sparks	NV	89441	775-331-3400	331-3474
Skokie Valley Beverage Co 199 Shepard Ave *Web:* www.svbco.com	Wheeling	IL	60090	847-541-1500	541-2059
Southern Wine & Spirits of Colorado 5270 Fox St PO Box 5603 *TF:* 800-332-9956 ■ *Web:* www.southernwine.com	Denver	CO	80217	303-292-1711	297-9967
Standard Beverage Corp 2416 E 37th St N *TF:* 800-999-7707 ■ *Web:* www.stdbev.com	Wichita	KS	67219	316-838-7707	838-1396
Standard Sales Co Inc 4800 E 42nd St Suite 400	Odessa	TX	79762	432-367-7662	367-9526
Star Distributors Inc 10 Eder Rd *TF:* 800-922-3501	West Haven	CT	06516	203-932-3636	932-5977
Stoudt Co 1618 Judson Rd PO Box 4147	Longview	TX	75606	903-753-7239	758-6479
Superior Distributing Co 22116 Washington Township Rd 218	Fostoria	OH	44830	419-435-1938	435-5231
Three Lakes Distributing Co 111 Overton St	Hot Springs	AR	71901	501-623-8201	624-4499
Town & Country Distributors Inc 1050 W Ardmore Ave	Itasca	IL	60143	630-250-0590	250-8946
Treu House of Munch Inc 8000 Arbor Dr *Web:* www.abwholesaler.com	Northwood	OH	43619	419-666-7770	666-5712
Tri-County Beverage Co 14301 Prospect Ave *Web:* www.tricountybeverage.com	Dearborn	MI	48126	313-584-7100	584-8364
United Distributors Inc 5500 United Dr *TF:* 800-282-7950	Smyrna	GA	30082	678-305-2000	305-2050
Virginia Distributing Co 2401 Patterson Ave SW	Roanoke	VA	24016	540-342-3105	345-1738
Watson Kunda & Sons Inc 349 S Henderson Rd *TF:* 800-262-2323 ■ *Web:* www.kundabev.com	King of Prussia	PA	19406	610-265-3113	265-3190
Western Beverages Inc 4545 E 51st Ave *TF:* 877-701-2337	Denver	CO	80216	303-388-5755	336-3336
Western Wyoming Beverages Inc 100 Reliance Rd *TF:* 800-551-8244	Rock Springs	WY	82901	307-362-6332	362-6335
Williams Distributing Corp 880 Burnett Rd *TF:* 800-332-9634	Chicopee	MA	01020	413-594-4900	594-4911
Wright Distributing Co Inc PO Box 460 *Web:* www.wrightdist.com	Bastrop	TX	78602	512-321-4411	321-4415
Wright Wisner Distributing Corp 3165 Brighton-Henrietta Town Line Rd	Rochester	NY	14623	585-427-2880	272-1216

81-2 Soft Drinks - Whol

Company	City	State	Zip	Phone	Fax
Admiral Beverage Corp PO Box 726 *Web:* www.admiralbeverage.com	Worland	WY	82401	307-347-4201	347-3571
All State Beverage Co 1580 Parallel St *TF:* 800-489-1021	Montgomery	AL	36104	334-265-0507	263-2367
Atlas Distributing Corp 44 Southbridge St *TF:* 800-649-6221 ■ *Web:* www.atlasdistributing.com	Auburn	MA	01501	508-791-6221	791-0812
Beverages Direct Inc 20 Danada Sq W *Web:* www.beveragesdirect.com	Wheaton	IL	60187	630-510-8925	
Buffalo Rock Co 111 Oxmoor Rd *TF:* 800-822-9799 ■ *Web:* www.buffalorock.com	Birmingham	AL	35209	205-942-3435	942-2601
Carolina Canners Inc PO Box 1628	Cheraw	SC	29520	843-537-5281	537-6743
Coca-Cola Bottling Co Consolidated 4100 Coca-Cola Plaza *NASDAQ: COKE* ■ *TF:* 800-777-2653 ■ *Web:* www.cokeconsolidated.com	Charlotte	NC	28211	704-551-4400	557-4646
Coca-Cola Bottling Co of New York 3 Skyline Dr	Hawthorne	NY	10532	914-345-3900	789-1814*
Coca-Cola Enterprises Inc 2500 Windy Ridge Pkwy *NYSE: CCE* ■ *Web:* www.cokecce.com	Atlanta	GA	30339	770-989-3000	989-3597
Flavia Beverage Systems 1301 Wilson Dr *TF:* 888-693-5284 ■ *Web:* www.us.myflavia.com	West Chester	PA	19380	610-430-2500	430-2652
Gusto Brands Inc 707 Douglas St *TF:* 800-241-3232	LaGrange	GA	30240	706-882-2573	882-2412
Honickman Affiliates 8275 Rt 130	Pennsauken	NJ	08110	856-665-6200	661-4560
Leading Brands Inc 1500 W Georgia St Suite 1800 *NASDAQ: LBIX* ■ *TF:* 866-685-5200 ■ *Web:* www.lbix.com	Vancouver	BC	V6G2Z6	604-685-5200	685-5249
Made-Rite Co PO Box 3283	Longview	TX	75606	903-753-8604	236-9743
Malolo Beverages & Supplies Ltd 120 Sand Island Access Rd	Honolulu	HI	96819	808-845-4830	845-4835
Markstein Beverage Co 505 S Pacific St *Web:* www.abwholesaler.com/markstein	San Marcos	CA	92079	760-744-9100	744-0082
Meadowbrook Distributing Corp 550 New Horizons Blvd	Amityville	NY	11701	631-226-9000	226-4233
Metz Beverage Co Inc 302 N Custer St *TF:* 800-821-4010	Sheridan	WY	82801	307-672-5848	672-6405
Noel Canning Corp 1011 N 3rd St	Yakima	WA	98901	509-248-4545	248-2843
Nor-Cal Beverage Co Inc 2286 Stone Blvd *Web:* www.ncbev.com	West Sacramento	CA	95691	916-372-0600	374-2602
PepsiCo International 700 Anderson Hill Rd	Purchase	NY	10577	914-253-2000	253-2070
Philadelphia Coca-Cola Bottling Co 725 E Erie Ave **Fax:* Hum Res ■ *TF Cust Svc:* 888-551-6800 ■ *Web:* www.phillycoke.com	Philadelphia	PA	19134	215-427-4500	427-4496*
Swire Coca-Cola USA 12634 S 265 W *TF:* 800-530-2653	Draper	UT	84020	801-816-5300	816-5423
Temple Bottling Co Ltd 3510 Pkwy Dr PO Box 308 *Web:* www.templebot.com	Temple	TX	76501	254-773-3376	778-5414
Vital Pharmaceuticals Inc 1600 N Pk Dr *TF:* 800-954-7904 ■ *Web:* www.vpxsports.com	Weston	FL	33326	954-641-0570	641-4960
Western Wyoming Beverages Inc 100 Reliance Rd *TF:* 800-551-8244	Rock Springs	WY	82901	307-362-6332	362-6335
Wis-Pak Inc 860 W St	Watertown	WI	53094	920-262-6300	262-9273

81-3 Wine & Liquor - Whol

Company	City	State	Zip	Phone	Fax
Alabama Crown Distributing 421 Industrial Ln *TF:* 800-548-1869	Birmingham	AL	35211	205-941-1155	942-3767
Bacardi Bottling Corp 12200 N Main St PO Box 26368	Jacksonville	FL	32226	904-757-1290	751-1397
Badger Liquor Co Inc 850 S Morris St *TF:* 800-242-9708 ■ *Web:* www.badgerliquor.com	Fond du Lac	WI	54936	920-922-0550	923-8169
Badger West Wine & Spirits LLC 5400 Old Town Hall Rd PO Box 869 *TF:* 800-472-6674 ■ *Web:* www.badgerwest.com	Eau Claire	WI	54701	715-836-8600	836-8609
Ben Arnold Beverage Co LP 101 Beverage Blvd **Fax:* Cust Svc ■ *TF Acctg:* 888-262-9787 ■ *Web:* www.benarnold-sunbelt.com	Ridgeway	SC	29130	803-337-3500	337-5310*
Beverage Distributors Co 14200 E Montcrieff Pl Suite D *TF:* 888-576-6464 ■ *Web:* www.charmer-sunbelt.com/beveragedistr/Pages/Welcome.aspx	Aurora	CO	80011	303-371-3421	373-5295
Blue Ridge Beverage Co Inc 4446 Barley Dr PO Box 700 *TF Cust Svc:* 800-868-0354 ■ *Web:* www.blueridgebeverage.com	Salem	VA	24153	540-380-2000	380-2546
Capitol-Husting Co Inc 12001 W Carmen Ave *TF:* 800-242-2231 ■ *Web:* www.capitol-husting.com	Milwaukee	WI	53225	414-353-1000	353-0768
Cardinal Distributing Co LLC 269 Jackrabbit Ln *Web:* www.cardinaldistributing.com	Bozeman	MT	59718	406-586-0241	587-1156
Castle Brands Inc 122 E 42nd St Suite 4700 *AMEX: ROX* ■ *TF:* 800-882-8140 ■ *Web:* www.castlebrandsinc.com	New York	NY	10168	646-356-0200	356-0222
Central Distributors Inc 15 Foss Rd *TF Cust Svc:* 800-427-5757 ■ *Web:* www.centraldistributors.com	Lewiston	ME	04240	207-784-4026	784-7869
Columbia Distributing Co 6840 N Cutter Cir *TF:* 800-275-4494 ■ *Web:* www.columbia-dist.com	Portland	OR	97217	503-289-9600	240-8666
Constellation Brands Inc 207 High Pt Dr Bldg 100 *NYSE: STZ* ■ *TF:* 888-724-2169 ■ *Web:* www.cbrands.com	Victor	NY	14564	585-678-7100	678-7103
Diageo Chateau & Estate Wines Co 240 Gateway Rd W *Web:* www.diageowines.com	Napa	CA	94558	707-299-2600	299-2600
Dichello Distributors Inc 55 Marsh Hill Rd PO Box 562 *Web:* www.dichello.com	Orange	CT	06477	203-891-2100	

	City	State	ZIP	Phone	Fax
Eber Bros Wine & Liquor Corp 155 Paragon Dr	Rochester	NY	14624	585-349-7700	349-7700
TF: 800-776-3237					
Edison Liquor Corp 21125 Enterprise Ave	Brookfield	WI	53045	262-821-0600	821-0363
Fedway Assoc Inc 56 Hackensack Ave	South Kearny	NJ	07032	973-624-6444	589-3556
TF: 800-433-3929 ■ *Web:* www.fedway.com					
Fox Henry A Sales Co 4494 36th St SE	Kentwood	MI	49512	616-949-1210	949-7209
TF: 800-762-8730					
Fred Nackard Wholesale Beverage Co 5660 E Pensdock Ave	Flagstaff	AZ	86004	928-526-2229	522-2171
TF: 800-622-5273					
Frederick Wildman & Sons Ltd 311 E 53rd St	New York	NY	10022	212-355-0700	355-4719
TF: 800-733-9463 ■ *Web:* www.frederickwildman.com					
General Beverage & Beer Sales Co 6169 McKee Rd PO Box 44326	Madison	WI	53744	608-271-1234	271-8625
TF: 800-362-3636					
General Wine & Liquor Co 373 Victor Ave	Highland Park	MI	48203	313-867-0521	867-4039
Web: www.gwlc.com					
Georgia Crown Distributing Co 100 Georgia Crown Dr	McDonough	GA	30253	770-302-3000	305-9438
TF: 800-342-2350 ■ *Web:* www.georgiacrown.com					
Glazer's Wholesale Drug Co Inc 14911 Quorum Dr Suite 400	Dallas	TX	75254	972-392-8200	702-8508
TF: 800-275-2854 ■ *Web:* www.glazers.com					
Goldring Gulf Distributing Co 675 S Pace Blvd	Pensacola	FL	32501	850-432-9883	432-5509
Web: www.goldringgulf.com					
Grantham Distributing Co Inc 2685 Hansrob Rd	Orlando	FL	32804	407-299-6446	295-7104
Hammer Co Inc 9450 Rosemont Dr	Streetsboro	OH	44241	330-422-9463	422-4727
TF: 800-258-9463					
Horizon Wine & Spirits Nashville 3851 Industrial Pkwy	Nashville	TN	37218	615-320-7292	321-4173
Web: www.hwas.com					
Horizon Wines Inc 13091 S Fwy	Houston	TX	77047	713-413-9463	
Web: www.horizonwinestx.com					
Johnson Bros Wholesale Liquor Co 1999 Shepard Rd	Saint Paul	MN	55116	651-649-5800	649-5894
TF: 800-723-2424 ■ *Web:* www.johnsonbrothers.com					
Kings Liquor Inc 2810 W Berry St	Fort Worth	TX	76109	817-923-3737	927-0021
Web: www.kingsliquor.com					
Luxco 5050 Kemper Ave	Saint Louis	MO	63139	314-772-2626	772-6021
Web: www.luxco.com					
Maisons Marques & Domaines USA Inc 383 4th St Suite 400	Oakland	CA	94607	510-286-2000	286-2010
Web: www.mmdusa.net					
Majestic Distilling Co Inc 2200 Monumental Rd	Baltimore	MD	21227	410-242-0200	247-7831
Web: www.majesticdistilling.com					
MBC United Wholesale 966 E I65 Service Rd N	Mobile	AL	36607	251-471-3486	479-5423
Mendez & Co PO Box 363348	San Juan	PR	00936	787-793-8888	783-9498
Merrimack Valley Distributing Co 50 Prince St	Danvers	MA	01923	978-777-2213	774-7487
TF: 800-698-0250					
Moet Hennessy USA 85 10th Ave	New York	NY	10011	212-251-8200	251-8388
Web: www.mhusa.com					
Moon Distributors Inc 2800 Vance St	Little Rock	AR	72206	501-375-8291	375-7035
National Wine & Spirits Inc PO Box 1602	Indianapolis	IN	46206	317-636-6092	685-8810
TF: 800-562-7359 ■ *Web:* www.nwscorp.com					
NKS Distributors Inc 399 Churchmans Rd	New Castle	DE	19720	302-322-1811	324-4024
TF: 800-292-9509 ■ *Web:* www.abwholesaler.com					
Odom Corp 10500 NE 8th St Suite 2000	Bellevue	WA	98004	425-456-3535	456-3536
TF: 800-767-6366 ■ *Web:* www.odomcorp.com					
Olinger Distributing Co 5337 W 78th St	Indianapolis	IN	46268	317-876-1188	876-3638
TF: 800-366-1090 ■ *Web:* www.olingerindiana.com					
Paradise Beverages Inc 94-1450 Moaniani St	Waipahu	HI	96797	808-678-4000	677-8280*
**Fax:* Sales ■ *TF:* 800-252-3723					
Paterno Wines International 900 Armour Dr	Lake Bluff	IL	60044	847-604-8900	604-5828
Web: www.terlatowines.com					
Pernod Ricard USA 100 Manhattanville Rd	Purchase	NY	10577	914-848-4800	848-4777
TF: 800-488-7539 ■ *Web:* www.pernod-ricard-usa.com					
Phillips Distributing Corp 3010 Nob Hill Rd	Madison	WI	53713	608-222-9177	222-0558
TF: 800-236-7269 ■ *Web:* www.phillipsdistributing.com					
Premier Beverage Co of Florida 9801 Premier Pkwy	Miramar	FL	33025	954-436-9200	436-9039
TF: 800-432-2002 ■ *Web:* www.charmer-sunbelt.com/premier/Pages/Welcome.aspx					
Premium Beverage Co Inc 928 N Railroad Ave	Opelika	AL	36801	334-745-4521	745-2179
Quality Beverage Inc 525 Miles Standish Blvd PO Box 671	Taunton	MA	02780	508-822-6200	822-7051
TF: 800-525-8989					
R & R Marketing LLC 10 Patton Dr	West Caldwell	NJ	07006	973-228-5100	403-8679
TF: 800-772-2096 ■ *Web:* www.rrmarketing.com					
Remy Cointreau USA Inc 1290 Avenue of the Americas	New York	NY	10104	212-399-4200	399-6909
TF: 800-858-9898 ■ *Web:* www.remycointreau.com					
Republic National Distributing Co (RNDC) 6511 Tri County Pkwy	Schertz	TX	78154	210-224-7531	227-7810
TF: 800-749-7532 ■ *Web:* www.rndc-usa.com					
Savannah Distributing Co Inc 5 Interchange Ct PO Box 1388	Savannah	GA	31402	912-233-1167	233-1157
TF: 800-551-0777 ■ *Web:* www.gawine.com					
Silver State Liquor & Wine Inc 100 Distribution Dr	Sparks	NV	89441	775-331-3400	331-3474
TF: 800-543-3867 ■ *Web:* www.renotahoedrinks.com					
Southern Wine & Spirits of America Inc 1600 NW 163rd St	Miami	FL	33169	305-625-4171	621-0388*
**Fax:* Cust Svc ■ *TF:* 800-432-6431 ■ *Web:* www.southernwine.com					
Southern Wine & Spirits of Colorado 5270 Fox St PO Box 5603	Denver	CO	80217	303-292-1711	297-9967
TF: 800-332-9956 ■ *Web:* www.southernwine.com					
Southern Wine & Spirits of Illinois 300 E Crossroads Pkwy Bolingbrook Corp Ctr	Bolingbrook	IL	60440	630-685-3000	685-3700
TF: 800-776-0180 ■ *Web:* www.southernwine.com					
Southern Wine & Spirits of New York 313 Underhill Blvd PO Box 9034	Syosset	NY	11791	516-921-9005	921-8526
Web: www.southernwine.com					
Southwest Services 4370 S Valley View Blvd	Las Vegas	NV	89103	702-367-7777	367-1143
Standard Beverage Corp 2416 E 37th St N	Wichita	KS	67219	316-838-7707	838-1396
TF: 800-999-7707 ■ *Web:* www.stdbev.com					
Ste. Michelle Wine Estates 14111 NE 145th St	Woodinville	WA	98072	425-488-1133	415-3657
Web: www.smwe.com					
Sterling Distributing Co 4433 S 96th St	Omaha	NE	68127	402-339-2300	339-3772
Sunbelt Beverage Corp 60 E 42nd St Suite 1915	New York	NY	10165	212-699-7000	699-7099
Web: www.charmer-sunbelt.com					
Terlato Wine Group 900 Armour Dr	Lake Bluff	IL	60044	847-604-8900	604-5829
TF: 800-950-7676 ■ *Web:* www.twg.com					
William Grant & Sons Inc 130 Fieldcrest Ave Raritan Ctr	Edison	NJ	08837	732-225-9000	225-0950
Web: www.grantusa.com					
Winebow Inc 75 Chestnut Ridge Rd	Montvale	NJ	07645	201-573-5500	
TF: 800-859-0689 ■ *Web:* www.winebow.com					
Wirtz Beverage Illinois (WBI) 1600 McConnor Pkwy 11th Fl	Schaumburg	IL	60193	847-228-9000	928-1985
TF: 800-548-8041 ■ *Web:* www.wirtzbeveragegroup.com					
Wisconsin Distributors Inc 900 Progress Way	Sun Prairie	WI	53590	608-834-2337	834-2300
TF: 800-373-2921 ■ *Web:* www.wisconsindistributors.com					
Young's Market Co LLC 500 S Central Ave	Los Angeles	CA	90013	213-612-1248	612-1238*
**Fax:* Hum Res ■ *TF:* 800-627-2777 ■ *Web:* www.youngsmarket.com					

82 BICYCLES & BICYCLE PARTS & ACCESSORIES

SEE ALSO Sporting Goods p. 2664; Toys, Games, Hobbies p. 2723

	City	State	ZIP	Phone	Fax
Burley Design Co-op Inc 4685 Cloudburst Way	Eugene	OR	97402	541-687-1644	687-0436
TF: 800-423-8445 ■ *Web:* www.burley.com					
Cane Creek Cycling Components 355 Cane Creek Rd	Fletcher	NC	28732	828-684-3551	684-1057
TF: 800-234-2725 ■ *Web:* www.canecreek.com					
Fuji Bikes 10940 Dutton Rd	Philadelphia	PA	19154	215-824-3854	824-1051
Web: www.fujibikes.com					
Giant Bicycle USA 3587 Old Conejo Rd	Newbury Park	CA	91320	805-267-4600	637-9704*
**Fax Area Code:* 800 ■ *TF:* 800-874-4268 ■ *Web:* www.giant-bicycles.com					
Haro Bicycles 1230 Avenida Chelsea	Vista	CA	92081	760-599-0544	599-1237
Web: www.harobikes.com					
Huffy Bicycle Co 225 Byers Rd	Springboro	OH	45342	800-872-2453	865-5470*
**Fax Area Code:* 937 ■ *TF:* 800-872-2453 ■ *Web:* www.huffybikes.com					
K2 Bike 1600 Calebs Path Ext Suite 203	Hauppauge	NY	11788	631-780-5360	780-5358
Web: www.eccyclesupply.com					
Pacific Cycle LLC 4902 Hammersley Rd	Madison	WI	53711	608-268-2468	
TF: 800-666-8813 ■ *Web:* www.pacific-cycle.com					
Raleigh America Inc Diamondback Div 6004 S 190th St Suite 101	Kent	WA	98032	800-222-5527	872-0257*
**Fax Area Code:* 253 ■ *TF:* 800-222-5527 ■ *Web:* www.diamondback.com					
Raleigh USA 6004 S 190th St Suite 101	Kent	WA	98032	253-395-1100	851-0807*
**Fax Area Code:* 800 ■ *TF:* 800-222-5527 ■ *Web:* www.raleighusa.com					
Serotta Competition Bicycles 41 Geyser Rd	Saratoga Springs	NY	12866	518-584-1221	584-8900
Web: www.serotta.com					
Shimano American Corp 1 Holland Dr	Irvine	CA	92618	949-951-5003	768-0920
Web: www.shimano.com					
Smith Mfg Co PO Box 3812	Jacksonville	FL	32206	904-354-3339	716-7598*
**Fax Area Code:* 888 ■ *TF:* 800-656-2376 ■ *Web:* www.aerofast.com					
Specialized Bicycle Components 15130 Concord Cir	Morgan Hill	CA	95037	408-779-6229	779-1631
TF: 877-808-8154 ■ *Web:* www.specialized.com					
SRAM Corp 1333 N Kingsbury St 4th Fl	Chicago	IL	60622	312-664-8800	664-8826
Web: www.sram.com					
Terry Precision Bicycles for Women Inc 1657 E Pk Dr	Macedon	NY	14502	315-986-2103	986-2104
TF Orders: 800-289-8379 ■ *Web:* www.terrybicycles.com					
Trek Bicycle Corp 801 W Madison St	Waterloo	WI	53594	920-478-2191	478-2774
Web: www.trekbikes.com					
Wald LLC 800 E 5th St	Maysville	KY	41056	606-564-4077	564-5248*
**Fax:* Sales ■ *Web:* www.waldllc.com					
Worksman Trading Corp 94-15 100th St	Ozone Park	NY	11416	718-322-2000	529-4803
Web: www.worksman.com					

83 BIO-RECOVERY SERVICES

Companies Listed Here Provide Services For Managing And Eliminating Biohazard Dangers That May Be Present After A Death Or Injury. These Services Include Cleaning, Disinfecting, And Deodorizing Biohazard Scenes Resulting From Accidents, Homicides, Suicides, Natural Deaths, And Similar Events.

	City	State	ZIP	Phone	Fax
AA Trauma Cleaning Service Inc 5500 NW 15th St M4	Margate	FL	33063	954-973-9502	973-8975
Web: www.aatraumacleaning.com					
Advanced Ozone Engineering Inc 6038 Oakwood Ave	Cincinnati	OH	45224	513-681-3871	681-3991
TF: 800-588-3871 ■ *Web:* www.advancedozone.com					
Allied Services PO Box 115	Thornton	IL	60476	708-339-6300	339-7551
TF: 877-570-1315 ■ *Web:* www.alliedcleaningservices.net					
Bio Pro LLC 955 W Sherri Dr	Gilbert	AZ	85233	602-234-6856	926-4985*
**Fax Area Code:* 480					

Phone Fax

Bio-Recovery Corp 51-49 47th St .... Woodside NY 11377 718-729-2600 472-1588
TF: 877-246-2532 ■ *Web:* www.biorecovery.com

Bio-Scene Recovery Inc
13191 Meadow St NE Suite A........................ Alliance OH 44601 330-823-5500 823-4405
TF: 877-380-5500 ■ *Web:* www.bioscene.com

Biocare Inc PO Box 817.............................. Easley SC 29641 864-855-3400 855-1185
TF: 800-875-9396

BioClean Inc PO Box 3062 .... Arlington WA 98223 360-435-8170 435-8180
TF: 888-412-6300 ■ *Web:* www.biocleanwa.com

Clean Scene Services LLC
9300 Louisiana 23 .... Belle Chasse LA 70037 504-433-5777

Commercial Detail Cleaning
11836 Judd Ct Suite 320 .... Dallas TX 75243 214-575-5060
Web: www.cdcllc.com

Crime & Death Scene Cleaning Inc (CADSC)
PO Box 828 .... Ipswich MA 01938 978-356-7007
TF: 877-366-8348 ■ *Web:* www.cadsc.com

Grangeville Environmental Services (GES)
GES Property Pros LLC 585 McAllister St.............Hanover PA 17331 717-637-6152 630-2713
TF: 866-437-5151 ■ *Web:* www.gespropertypros.com

JNL Cleaning & Restoration
4320 Chinchilla Ct .... Middleburg FL 32068 904-282-9617
Web: www.jnl.us

JP Maguire Assoc Inc 266 Brookside Rd............ Waterbury CT 06708 203-755-2297 573-8547
TF: 877-576-2484 ■ *Web:* www.fixmydamage.com

Loss Recovery Systems Inc 10 Dwight Pk Dr......... Syracuse NY 13209 315-451-9111 451-9222
TF: 800-724-3473 ■ *Web:* www.lrs911.com

Midwest Crisis Cleaning Inc 590 Meyerwood Rd .... Festus MO 63028 636-937-4862
TF: 877-937-4862 ■ *Web:* www.midwestcrisiscleaning.com

Peerless Cleaners Inc 1295 N 20th St .... Decatur IL 62521 217-423-7703
TF: 800-879-7056 ■ *Web:* www.peerlessrestoration.com

Red Alert Bio-Response Service Inc
PO Box 941629 ....Houston TX 77094 281-993-0016 232-2551
TF: 800-570-1833 ■ *Web:* www.wecleanall.com

Richey Restoration Inc 9574 Lebanon Rd.......... Mount Juliet TN 37122 615-758-8760 754-7160
Web: www.richeyrestoration.com

Rocky Mountain Remediation Contractors LLC
5870 S Walden Ct...............................Centennial CO 80015 303-667-0400 870-2696*
**Fax Area Code:* 720 ■ *Web:* www.rockymountainmold.com

Timbertown Cleaning & Restoration
106 Hoyt Ave ....Saginaw MI 48607 989-753-5139 754-0418
TF: 800-832-7060 ■ *Web:* www.timbertownservices.com

84 BIOMETRIC IDENTIFICATION EQUIPMENT & SOFTWARE

Phone Fax

AcSys Biometrics Corp
1100 Burloak Dr Suite 703........................Burlington ON L7L6B2 905-634-4111 634-1101
TF: 877-842-7687 ■ *Web:* www.acsysbiometrics.com

Aspect Business Solutions
7550 IH-10 W 14th Fl............................San Antonio TX 78229 210-298-5000 298-5001
TF: 800-609-8113

AuthenTec Inc 100 Rialto Pl # 100 ....Melbourne FL 32901 321-308-1300 308-1430
Web: www.authentec.com

Bio Medic Data Systems Inc 1 Silas Rd............... Seaford DE 19973 302-628-4100 628-4110
TF: 800-526-2637 ■ *Web:* www.bmds.com

BIO-key International Inc
300 Nickerson Rd................................Marlborough MA 01752 508-460-4000
Web: www.bio-key.com

Biometric Access Corp 2555 IH-35 Suite 200 ....Round Rock TX 78664 512-246-3760 246-3768
TF: 800-873-4133 ■ *Web:* www.biometricaccess.com

BNX Systems Corp 1953 Gallows Rd Suite 500 .... Vienna VA 22182 703-734-9200 734-6553
TF: 800-397-7561 ■ *Web:* www.bnx.com

Communication Intelligence Corp (CIC)
275 Shoreline Dr Suite 500 .... Redwood Shores CA 94065 650-802-7888 802-7777
OTC: CICI ■ *TF Sales:* 800-888-8242 ■ *Web:* www.cic.com

Count Me In LLC
601 W Golf Rd Suite 108 ....Mount Prospect IL 60056 847-981-8779 981-8878
TF: 800-958-8779 ■ *Web:* www.countmeinllc.com

Cross Match Technologies
3950 RCA Blvd Suite 5001................Palm Beach Gardens FL 33410 561-622-1650 622-9938
Web: www.crossmatch.com

Datastrip Inc 211 Welsh Pool Rd Suite 100 ....Exton PA 19341 610-594-6130 594-6065
TF: 800-548-2517 ■ *Web:* www.datastrip.com

Digital Persona Inc 720 Bay Rd Suite 100......... Redwood City CA 94063 650-474-4000 298-8313
TF: 877-378-2738 ■ *Web:* www.digitalpersona.com

Honeywell Aerospace 1944 E Sky Harbor Cir...........Phoenix AZ 85034 800-601-3099 365-3343*
**Fax Area Code:* 602 ■ *TF:* 800-601-3099 ■ *Web:* www.honeywell.com

International Biometric Group LLC
1 Battery Pk Plaza Suite 2901.......................New York NY 10004 212-809-9491 809-6197
TF: 888-424-8424 ■ *Web:* www.ibgweb.com

Lightning Powder Co Inc
13386 International Pkwy.........................Jacksonville FL 32218 904-741-5400 741-5403
Web: www.redwop.com

MorphoTrak Inc 113 S Columbus St 4th Fl............Alexandria VA 22314 703-797-2600 706-9549
TF: 800-601-6790 ■ *Web:* www.morphotrak.com

NEC Corp of America
10850 Gold Ctr Dr Suite 200 .... Rancho Cordova CA 95670 916-463-7000 636-5656
TF: 800-632-4636 ■ *Web:* www.necam.com

SecuGen Corp 2356 Walsh Ave..................... Santa Clara CA 95051 408-727-7787 727-7105
TF: 866-942-8800 ■ *Web:* www.secugen.com

Security First Corp
22362 Gilberto Suite 130 .... Rancho Santa Margarita CA 92688 949-858-7525 858-7092
Web: www.securityfirstcorp.com

Sensory Inc 1991 Russell Ave .... Santa Clara CA 95054 408-327-9000 727-4748
Web: www.sensoryinc.com

SIRCHIE Finger Print Laboratories Inc
100 Hunter Pl..................................... Youngsville NC 27596 919-554-2244 554-2266
TF: 800-356-7311 ■ *Web:* www.sirchie.com

Ultra-Scan Corp 4240 Ridge Lea Rd Suite 10............Amherst NY 14226 716-832-6269 832-2810
Web: www.ultra-scan.com

Phone Fax

Veridicom Inc 999 3rd Ave ....Seattle WA 98104 206-224-6206 224-6207
TF: 800-363-1418 ■ *Web:* www.veridicom.com

85 BIOTECHNOLOGY COMPANIES

SEE ALSO Diagnostic Products p. 1784; Medicinal Chemicals & Botanical Products p. 2231; Pharmaceutical Companies p. 2414; Pharmaceutical Companies - Generic Drugs p. 2416

Phone Fax

Aastrom Biosciences Inc
24 Frank Lloyd Wright Dr
Domino's Farms Lobby K.......................... Ann Arbor MI 48105 734-418-4400 665-0485
NASDAQ: ASTM ■ *Web:* www.aastrom.com

ACADIA Pharmaceuticals Inc
3911 Sorrento Valley Blvd .... San Diego CA 92121 858-558-2871 558-2872
NASDAQ: ACAD ■ *Web:* www.acadia-pharm.com

Access Pharmaceuticals Inc
2600 Stemmons Fwy Suite 176 .... Dallas TX 75207 214-905-5100 905-5101
Web: www.accesspharma.com

Acorda Therapeutics Inc 15 Skyline Dr ....Hawthorne NY 10532 914-347-4300 347-4560
NASDAQ: ACOR ■ *Web:* www.acorda.com

Acusphere Inc 99 Hayden Ave Suite 385 .... Lexington MA 02421 617-648-8800 863-9993*
PINK: ACUS ■ **Fax Area Code:* 978 ■ *TF:* 800-388-9429 ■ *Web:* www.acusphere.com

Adherex Technologies Inc
68 TW Alexander Dr
PO Box 13628 .... Research Triangle Park NC 27709 919-636-4530 890-0490
Web: www.adherex.com

Adolor Corp 700 Pennsylvania Dr ....Exton PA 19341 484-595-1500 595-1520
NASDAQ: ADLR ■ *TF:* 800-563-4450 ■ *Web:* www.adolor.com

ADVENTRX Pharmaceuticals Inc
6725 Mesa Ridge Rd Suite 100 .... San Diego CA 92121 858-552-0866 552-0876
AMEX: ANX ■ *Web:* www.adventrx.com

Aeolus Pharmaceuticals Inc
23811 Inverness Pl..........................Laguna Niguel CA 92677 949-481-9825 481-9829
TF: 888-290-0528 ■ *Web:* www.aeoluspharma.com

AEterna Zentaris Inc
1405 Parc Technologique Blvd....................... Quebec QC G1P4P5 418-652-8525 652-0881
NASDAQ: AEZS ■ *Web:* www.aezsinc.com/en/index.php

Affymax Inc 4001 Miranda Ave .... Palo Alto CA 94304 650-812-8700 424-0832
Web: www.affymax.com

Agenus Inc 3 Forbes Rd........................... Lexington MA 02421 781-674-4400 674-4200
NASDAQ: AGEN ■ *TF:* 800-962-2436 ■ *Web:* www.agenusbio.com

Alexion Pharmaceuticals Inc 352 Knotter Dr .... Cheshire CT 06410 203-272-2596 271-8198
NASDAQ: ALXN ■ *Web:* www.alxn.com

Alexza Pharmaceuticals Inc
2091 Stierlin Ct .... Mountain View CA 94043 650-944-7000 944-7999
NASDAQ: ALXA ■ *Web:* www.alexza.com

Alkermes Inc 852 WinteráSt .... Waltham MA 02451 781-609-6000 494-9263*
NASDAQ: ALKS ■ **Fax Area Code:* 617 ■ *TF:* 800-848-4876 ■ *Web:* www.alkermes.com

Allos Therapeutics Inc
11080 Cir Pt Rd Suite 200 .... Westminster CO 80020 303-426-6262 412-9160
NASDAQ: ALTH ■ *TF:* 888-255-6702 ■ *Web:* www.allos.com

Alnylam Pharmaceuticals Inc
300 3rd St 3rd Fl ....Cambridge MA 02142 617-551-8200 551-8101
NASDAQ: ALNY ■ *Web:* www.alnylam.com

Alseres Pharmaceuticals Inc 85 Main St .... Hopkinton MA 01748 508-497-2360 497-9964
Web: www.alseres.com

Amarillo Biosciences Inc
4134 Business Pk Dr ....Amarillo TX 79110 806-376-1741 376-9301
Web: www.amarbio.com

Ambrilia Biopharma Inc
1010 Sherbrooke St W Suite 1800 .... Montreal QC H3A2R7 514-751-2003 751-2502
TSX: AMB ■ *Web:* www.ambrilia.com

American Bio Medica Corp (ABMC) 122 Smith Rd... Kinderhook NY 12106 518-758-8158 758-8172
PINK: ABMC ■ *TF:* 800-227-1243 ■ *Web:* www.americanbiomedica.com

Amgen Canada Inc
6775 Financial Dr Suite 100..................... Mississauga ON L5N0A4 905-285-3000 285-3100
TF: 800-665-4273 ■ *Web:* www.amgen.ca

Amgen Inc 1 Amgen Ctr Dr..................... Thousand Oaks CA 91320 805-447-1000 447-1010
NASDAQ: AMGN ■ *TF:* 800-926-4369 ■ *Web:* www.amgen.com

AmpliPhi Biosciences Corp
601 Union St Suite 4200 ....Seattle WA 98101 206-623-7612 223-0288
PINK: APHB ■ *Web:* www.biocontrol-ltd.com

Antibodies Inc 25242 County Rd 95.....................Davis CA 95616 530-758-4400 758-6307
TF: 800-824-8540 ■ *Web:* www.antibodiesinc.com

Applera Corp 301 Merritt 7 ....Norwalk CT 06856 203-840-2000 841-2014
TF: 800-761-5381 ■ *Web:* www.applera.com

Applied Molecular Evolution Inc (AME)
10300 Campus Pt Dr # 200 .... San Diego CA 92121 858-597-4990 597-4950
Web: www.amevolution.com

Apricus Biosciences
6330 Nancy Ridge Dr Suite 103 .... San Diego CA 92121 858-222-8041 866-0482
NASDAQ: NEXM ■ *Web:* www.apricusbio.com

Arboretum The
1102 S Goodwin Ave Rm N-409
University of Illinois at Urbana-Champaign ....Urbana IL 61801 217-333-7579 244-3469
Web: www.arboretum.uiuc.edu

Ardea Biosciences Inc 4939 Directors Pl .... San Diego CA 92121 858-652-6500 625-0760
Web: www.ardeabiosciences.com

Arena Pharmaceuticals Inc
6166 Nancy Ridge Dr .... San Diego CA 92121 858-453-7200 453-7210
NASDAQ: ARNA ■ *Web:* www.arenapharm.com

ARIAD Pharmaceuticals Inc 26 Landsdowne St.......Cambridge MA 02139 617-494-0400 494-8144
NASDAQ: ARIA ■ *Web:* www.ariad.com

ArQule Inc 19 Presidential Way .... Woburn MA 01801 781-994-0300 376-6019
NASDAQ: ARQL ■ *TF:* 800-644-5000 ■ *Web:* www.arqule.com

Company	City	State	ZIP	Phone	Fax
Array BioPharma Inc 3200 Walnut St	Boulder	CO	80301	303-381-6600	449-5376
NASDAQ: ARRY ■ *TF:* 877-633-2436 ■ *Web:* www.arraybiopharma.com					
AtriCure Inc 6217 Centre Pk Dr	West Chester	OH	45069	513-755-4100	755-4567
NASDAQ: ATRC ■ *TF:* 888-347-6403 ■ *Web:* www.atricure.com					
Autoimmune Technologies LLC 1010 Common St Suite 1705	New Orleans	LA	70112	504-529-9944	529-8982
Web: www.autoimmune.com					
AVANIR Pharmaceuticals 101 Enterprise Suite 300	Aliso Viejo	CA	92656	949-389-6700	643-6800
NASDAQ: AVNR ■ *Web:* www.avanir.com					
AVAX Technologies Inc 2000 Hamilton St Suite 204	Philadelphia	PA	19130	215-241-9760	241-9684
Avecia Biotechnology Inc 125 Fortune Blvd	Milford	MA	01757	508-532-2500	532-2503
Web: www.avecia.com					
AVI BioPharma 3450 Monte Villa Pkwy	Bothell	WA	98021	425-354-5038	
NASDAQ: AVII ■ *Web:* www.avibio.com					
Bayer CropScience 2 T.W. Alexander Dr	Research Triangle Park	NC	27709	919-549-2000	
Web: www.bayercropscienceus.com					
BD Biosciences PharMingen 10975 Torreyana Rd	San Diego	CA	92121	858-812-8800	812-8888
TF: 800-848-6227 ■ *Web:* www.bdbiosciences.com					
Bellus Health Inc 275 Armand Frappier Blvd	Laval	QC	H7V4A7	450-680-4500	680-4501
NASDAQ: NRMX ■ *TF:* 877-680-4500 ■ *Web:* www.bellushealth.com					
BioCryst Pharmaceuticals Inc 2190 Pkwy Lake Dr	Birmingham	AL	35244	205-444-4600	444-4640
NASDAQ: BCRX ■ *Web:* www.biocryst.com					
BioDelivery Sciences International Inc (BDSI) 801 Corporate Ctr Dr Suite 210	Raleigh	NC	27607	919-582-9050	582-9051
NASDAQ: BDSI ■ *Web:* www.bdsi.com					
Biogen Idec Inc 133 Boston Post Rd	Weston	MA	02493	781-464-2000	679-2617*
NASDAQ: BIIB ■ **Fax Area Code:* 617 ■ *TF:* 877-750-8536 ■ *Web:* www.biogenidec.com					
BioMarin Pharmaceutical Inc 105 Digital Dr	Novato	CA	94949	415-884-6700	382-7889
NASDAQ: BMRN ■ *Web:* www.bmrn.com					
Bioniche Life Sciences Inc PO Box 1570	Belleville	ON	N8N5J2	613-966-8058	966-4177
TF: 800-265-5464 ■ *Web:* www.bioniche.com					
BioNumerik Pharmaceuticals Inc 8122 Datapoint Dr Suite 1250	San Antonio	TX	78229	210-614-1701	615-8030
Web: www.bionumerik.com					
Bioqual Corp 9600 Medical Ctr Dr Suite 200	Rockville	MD	20850	301-251-2801	251-1260
Web: www.bioqual.com					
BioReliance Corp 14920 Broschart Rd	Rockville	MD	20850	301-738-1000	610-2590
TF: 800-553-5372 ■ *Web:* www.bioreliance.com					
BioTime Inc 1301 Harbor Bay Pkwy	Alameda	CA	94502	510-521-3390	521-3389
Web: www.biotimeinc.com					
Callisto Pharmaceuticals Inc 420 Lexington Ave Suite 1609	New York	NY	10170	212-297-0010	297-0020
AMEX: KAL					
Cangene Corp 155 Innovation Dr	Winnipeg	MB	R3T5Y3	204-275-4200	269-7003
TSE: CNJ ■ *TF:* 800-768-2304 ■ *Web:* www.cangene.com					
Cardiome Pharma Corp 6190 Agronomy Rd 6th Fl	Vancouver	BC	V6T1Z3	604-677-6905	677-6915
NASDAQ: CRME ■ *TF:* 800-330-9928 ■ *Web:* www.cardiome.com					
CardioTech International Inc 229 Andover St	Wilmington	MA	01887	978-657-0075	657-0074
AMEX: CTE ■ *Web:* www.cardiotech-inc.com					
CEL-SCI Corp 8229 Boone Blvd Suite 802	Vienna	VA	22182	703-506-9460	506-9471
AMEX: CVM ■ *Web:* www.cel-sci.com					
Celera Genomics Group 1401 Harbor Bay Pkwy	Alameda	CA	94502	510-749-4200	
NYSE: CRA ■ *Web:* www.celera.com					
Celgene Corp 86 Morris Ave	Summit	NJ	07901	908-673-9000	673-9001
NASDAQ: CELG ■ *TF:* 800-742-3107 ■ *Web:* www.celgene.com					
Celgene Corp Signal Research Div 4550 Town Ctr Ct	San Diego	CA	92121	858-558-7500	552-8775
Web: www.signalpharm.com					
Cell Therapeutics Inc (CTI) 501 Elliott Ave W Suite 400	Seattle	WA	98119	206-282-7100	284-6206
NASDAQ: CTIC ■ *TF:* 800-215-2355 ■ *Web:* www.cticseattle.com					
Cephalon Inc 41 Moores Rd	Frazer	PA	19355	610-344-0200	344-0065
NASDAQ: CEPH ■ *TF:* 800-782-3656 ■ *Web:* www.cephalon.com					
Cerus Corp 2550 Stanwell Dr	Concord	CA	94520	925-288-6000	288-6001
NASDAQ: CERS ■ *TF:* 888-268-6115 ■ *Web:* www.cerus.com					
Cima Labs Inc 10000 Valley View Rd	Eden Prairie	MN	55344	952-947-8700	947-8770
Web: www.cimalabs.com					
CMC Biologics 22021 20th Ave SE	Bothell	WA	98021	425-485-1900	486-0300
Web: www.cmcbio.com					
CollaGenx Pharmaceuticals Inc 41 University Dr Suite 200	Newtown	PA	18940	215-579-7388	579-8577
NASDAQ: CGPI ■ *TF:* 800-613-7847					
Colorado Serum Co 4950 York St PO Box 16428	Denver	CO	80216	303-295-7527	295-1923
TF Orders: 800-525-2065 ■ *Web:* www.colorado-serum.com					
CombiMatrix Corp 300 Goddard Suite 100	Irvine	CA	92618	949-753-0624	753-1504
NASDAQ: CBMX ■ *TF:* 800-710-0624 ■ *Web:* www.combimatrix.com					
ConjuChem Inc 225 President Kennedy Ave Suite 3950	Montreal	QC	H2X3Y8	514-844-5558	844-1119
TSX: CJC					
Cook Biotech Inc 1425 Innovation Pl	West Lafayette	IN	47906	765-497-3355	497-2361
TF: 888-299-4224 ■ *Web:* www.cookbiotech.com					
Corcept Therapeutics Inc 149 Commonwealth Dr	Menlo Park	CA	94025	650-327-3270	327-3218
NASDAQ: CORT ■ *Web:* www.corcept.com					
Covance Inc 210 Carnegie Ctr	Princeton	NJ	08540	609-419-2240	
NYSE: CVD ■ *TF:* 888-268-2623 ■ *Web:* www.covance.com					
Cryolife Inc 1655 Roberts Blvd NW	Kennesaw	GA	30144	770-419-3355	426-0031
NYSE: CRY ■ *TF:* 800-438-8285 ■ *Web:* www.cryolife.com					
Cubist Pharmaceuticals Inc 65 Hayden Ave	Lexington	MA	02421	781-860-8660	861-0566
NASDAQ: CBST ■ *TF:* 877-528-2478 ■ *Web:* www.cubist.com					
Curacyte Inc 109 Connor Dr Bldg 1 Suite 2102	Chapel Hill	NC	27514	919-405-4002	405-4010
Web: www.curacyte.com					
Curis Inc 4 Maguire Rd	Lexington	MA	02421	617-503-6500	503-6501
NASDAQ: CRIS ■ *Web:* www.curis.com					
Cypress Bioscience Inc 4350 Executive Dr Suite 325	San Diego	CA	92121	858-452-2323	452-1222
NASDAQ: CYPB ■ *Web:* www.cypressbio.com					
Cytokinetics Inc 280 E Grand Ave	South San Francisco	CA	94080	650-624-3000	624-3010
NASDAQ: CYTK ■ *TF:* 877-394-2986 ■ *Web:* www.cytokinetics.com					
Cytomedix Inc 209 Perry Pkwy Suite 7	Rockville	MD	20877	240-499-2680	499-2690
OTC: CMXI ■ *TF:* 866-298-6633 ■ *Web:* www.cytomedix.com					
Cytori Therapeutics Inc 3020 Callan Rd	San Diego	CA	92121	858-458-0900	458-0994
NASDAQ: CYTX ■ *Web:* www.cytoritx.com					
CytRx Corp 11726 San Vicente Blvd Suite 650	Los Angeles	CA	90049	310-826-5648	826-6139
NASDAQ: CYTR ■ *TF:* 800-385-5790 ■ *Web:* www.cytrx.com					
Danisco US Inc Genencor Div 925 Page Mill Rd	Palo Alto	CA	94304	650-846-7500	845-6500
Web: www.genencor.com					
Dendreon Corp 3005 1st Ave	Seattle	WA	98121	206-256-4545	256-0571
NASDAQ: DNDN ■ *TF:* 877-256-4545 ■ *Web:* www.dendreon.com					
DepoMed Inc 1360 O'Brien Dr	Menlo Park	CA	94025	650-462-5900	462-9993
NASDAQ: DEPO ■ *Web:* www.depomedinc.com					
DexCom Inc 6340 Sequence Dr	San Diego	CA	92121	858-200-0200	200-0201
NASDAQ: DXCM ■ *TF:* 888-738-3646 ■ *Web:* www.dexcom.com					
diaDexus Inc 343 Oyster Pt Blvd	South San Francisco	CA	94080	650-246-6400	246-6499
Web: www.diadexus.com					
Discovery Laboratories Inc 2600 Kelly Rd Suite 100	Warrington	PA	18976	215-488-9300	488-9301
NASDAQ: DSCO ■ *TF:* 877-266-2411 ■ *Web:* www.discoverylabs.com					
Dow AgroSciences LLC 9330 Zionsville Rd	Indianapolis	IN	46268	317-337-3000	905-7326*
**Fax Area Code:* 800 ■ *TF:* 800-258-1470 ■ *Web:* www.dowagro.com					
DURECT Corp 2 Results Way	Cupertino	CA	95014	408-777-1417	777-3577
NASDAQ: DRRX ■ *Web:* www.durect.com					
DUSA Pharmaceuticals Inc 25 Upton Dr	Wilmington	MA	01887	978-657-7500	657-9193
NASDAQ: DUSA ■ *Web:* www.dusapharma.com					
Dyadic International Inc 140 Intracoastal Pointe Dr Suite 404	Jupiter	FL	33477	561-743-8333	743-8343
PINK: DYAI ■ *Web:* www.dyadic.com					
Dyax Corp 300 Technology Sq	Cambridge	MA	02139	617-225-2500	225-2501
NASDAQ: DYAX ■ *Web:* www.dyax.com					
Elan Corp PLC 1300 Gould Dr	Gainesville	GA	30504	770-534-8239	534-8247
NYSE: ELN ■ *TF:* 800-859-8586 ■ *Web:* www.elan.com					
Elite Pharmaceuticals Inc 165 Ludlow Ave	Northvale	NJ	07647	201-750-2646	750-2755
OTC: ELTP ■ *Web:* www.elitepharma.com					
EMD Serono Inc 1 Technology Pl	Rockland	MA	02370	781-982-9000	681-2914
TF: 800-283-8088 ■ *Web:* www.emdserono.com					
Emergent Biosolutions Inc 2273 Research Blvd Suite 400	Rockville	MD	20850	301-795-1800	795-1899
Web: www.emergentbiosolutions.com					
Emisphere Technologies Inc 240 Cedar Knolls Rd Suite 200	Cedar Knolls	NJ	07927	973-532-8000	532-8115
NASDAQ: EMIS ■ *Web:* www.emisphere.com					
Encore Medical Corp 9800 Metric Blvd	Austin	TX	78758	512-832-9500	834-6300
NASDAQ: ENMC ■ *TF:* 800-456-8696 ■ *Web:* www.djosurgical.com					
EntreMed Inc 9640 Medical Ctr Dr	Rockville	MD	20850	240-864-2600	864-2601
NASDAQ: ENMD ■ *TF:* 888-368-7363 ■ *Web:* www.entremed.com					
Enzo Biochem Inc 527 Madison Ave	New York	NY	10022	212-583-0100	583-0150
NYSE: ENZ ■ *TF:* 800-522-5052 ■ *Web:* www.enzo.com					
Enzon Pharmaceuticals Inc 20 Kingsbridge Rd	Piscataway	NJ	08854	732-980-4500	980-4585
NASDAQ: ENZN ■ *Web:* www.enzon.com					
Exelixis Inc 210 E Grand Ave PO Box 511	South San Francisco	CA	94080	650-837-7000	837-8300
NASDAQ: EXEL ■ *Web:* www.exelixis.com					
Galectin Therapeutics 7 Wells Ave Suite 34	Newton	MA	02459	617-559-0033	928-3450
TF: 800-488-6445 ■ *Web:* www.galectintherapeutics.com					
Generex Biotechnology Corp 33 Harbour Sq Suite 202	Toronto	ON	M5J2G2	416-364-2551	364-9363
OTC: GNBT ■ *TF:* 800-391-6755 ■ *Web:* www.generex.com					
Genitope Corp 6900 Dumbarton Cir	Fremont	CA	94555	510-284-3000	284-3100
PINK: GTOP ■ *TF:* 866-436-4867					
Genomic Health Inc 101 Galveston Dr	Redwood City	CA	94063	650-556-9300	556-1132
NASDAQ: GHDX ■ *TF:* 866-662-6897 ■ *Web:* www.genomichealth.com					
Genta Inc 200 Connell Dr	Berkeley Heights	NJ	07922	908-286-9800	464-1701
OTC: GNTA ■ *TF:* 888-322-2264 ■ *Web:* www.genta.com					
GenVec Inc 65 W Watkins Mill Rd	Gaithersburg	MD	20878	240-632-0740	632-0735
NASDAQ: GNVC ■ *TF:* 877-943-6832 ■ *Web:* www.genvec.com					
Genzyme Oncology 55 Cambridge Pkwy	Cambridge	MA	02142	617-252-7811	761-8783
Web: www.genzyme.com/molecularoncology.asp					
Geron Corp 230 Constitution Dr	Menlo Park	CA	94025	650-473-7700	473-7750
NASDAQ: GERN ■ *Web:* www.geron.com					
Gilead Sciences Inc 333 Lakeside Dr	Foster City	CA	94404	650-574-3000	578-9264
NASDAQ: GILD ■ *TF:* 800-445-3235 ■ *Web:* www.gilead.com					
Grifols USA Inc 5555 Valley Blvd	Los Angeles	CA	90032	323-225-2221	441-7968
TF: 800-421-0008 ■ *Web:* www.grifolsusa.com					
GTC Biotherapeutics Inc 175 Crossing Blvd	Framingham	MA	01702	508-620-9700	370-3797
Web: www.gtc-bio.com					
GTx Inc 175 Toyota Pl 7th Fl	Memphis	TN	38103	901-523-9700	644-8075
NASDAQ: GTXI ■ *Web:* www.gtxinc.com					
Harbor BioSciences Inc 9171 Towne Centre Dr Suite 180	San Diego	CA	92122	858-587-9333	558-6470
Web: www.harborbiosciences.com					
Heart Tronics Inc 4705 Laurel Canyon Blvd Suite 203	Studio City	CA	91607	818-432-4560	432-4567
Helix Biopharma Corp 305 Industrial Pkwy S Unit 3	Aurora	ON	L4G6X7	905-841-2300	841-2244
Web: www.helixbiopharma.com					
Hemispherx Biopharma Inc 1617 JFK Blvd 6th Fl	Philadelphia	PA	19103	215-988-0080	988-1739
AMEX: HEB ■ *Web:* www.hemispherx.net					
i3 Innovus 10 Cabot Rd Suite 304	Medford	MA	02155	781-338-9700	338-9522
TF: 866-322-0959 ■ *Web:* www.ingenix.com					
Idenix Pharmaceuticals Inc 60 Hampshire St	Cambridge	MA	02139	617-995-9800	995-9801
NASDAQ: IDIX ■ *TF:* 877-443-6491 ■ *Web:* www.idenix.com					
Idera Pharmaceuticals Inc 167 Sidney St	Cambridge	MA	02139	617-679-5500	679-5592
NASDAQ: IDRA ■ *Web:* www.iderapharma.com					

Company	City	State	ZIP	Phone	Fax
Illumina Inc 9885 Towne Centre Dr. NASDAQ: ILMN ■ TF: 800-809-4566 ■ Web: www.illumina.com	San Diego	CA	92121	858-202-4500	202-4545
ImClone Systems Inc 180 Varick St 6th Fl. *Fax Area Code: 212 ■ Web: www.imclone.com	New York	NY	10014	908-541-8000	645-2054*
ImmunoGen Inc 830 Winter St. NASDAQ: IMGN ■ Web: www.immunogen.com	Waltham	MA	02451	781-895-0600	895-0611
Immunomedics Inc 300 American Rd. NASDAQ: IMMU ■ TF: 800-327-7211 ■ Web: www.immunomedics.com	Morris Plains	NJ	07950	973-605-8200	605-8282
Incyte Corp Rt 141 & Henry Clay Rd Bldg E-336. NASDAQ: INCY ■ Web: www.incyte.com	Wilmington	DE	19880	302-498-6700	425-2750
Inhibitex Inc 9005 Westside Pkwy. NASDAQ: INHX ■ TF: 866-784-3510 ■ Web: www.inhibitex.com	Alpharetta	GA	30004	678-746-1100	746-1299
INSMED Inc 8720 Stony Pt Pkwy Suite 200. NASDAQ: INSM ■ Web: www.insmed.com	Richmond	VA	23235	804-565-3000	565-3500
Intarcia Therapeutics Inc 24650 Industrial Blvd. Web: www.intarcia.com	Hayward	CA	94545	510-782-7800	782-7801
Integra LifeSciences Holdings Corp 311 Enterprise Dr. NASDAQ: IART ■ TF: 800-654-2873 ■ Web: www.integra-ls.com	Plainsboro	NJ	08536	609-275-0500	799-3297
Irvine Scientific 2511 Daimler St. Web: www.irvinesci.com	Santa Ana	CA	92705	949-261-7800	261-6522
Isis Pharmaceuticals Inc 1896 Rutherford Rd. NASDAQ: ISIS ■ TF: 800-679-4747 ■ Web: www.isispharm.com	Carlsbad	CA	92008	760-931-9200	603-2700
ISTA Pharmaceuticals Inc 50 Technology Dr. NASDAQ: ISTA ■ TF: 866-264-8568 ■ Web: www.istavision.com	Irvine	CA	92618	949-788-6000	788-6010
Ivers-Lee Inc 31 Hansen Rd S. TF: 800-387-1188 ■ Web: ivers-lee.com	Brampton	ON	L6W3H7	905-451-5535	451-1255
Kosan Biosciences Inc 3832 Bay Ctr Pl. NASDAQ: KOSN ■ Web: www.kosan.com	Hayward	CA	94545	510-732-8400	732-8401
KV Pharmaceutical Co 2503 S Hanley Rd. Web: www.kvpharmaceutical.com	Saint Louis	MO	63144	314-645-6600	646-3751
La Jolla Pharmaceutical Co 4365 Executive Dr Suite 300. Web: www.ljpc.com	San Diego	CA	92121	858-452-6600	626-2851
Labopharm Inc 480 Armand Frappier Blvd. TF: 888-686-1017 ■ Web: www.labopharm.com	Laval	QC	H7V4B4	450-686-1017	686-9141
Leo Pharma Inc 123 Commerce Valley Dr E Suite 400. TF: 800-668-7234 ■ Web: www.leo-pharma.com	Thornhill	ON	L3T7W8	905-886-9822	886-6622
Lescarden Inc 420 Lexington Ave Suite 212. TF: 888-581-2076 ■ Web: www.lescarden.com	New York	NY	10170	212-687-1050	687-1051
Lexicon Pharmaceuticals Inc 8800 Technology Forest Pl. NASDAQ: LEXG ■ TF: 800-578-1972 ■ Web: www.lexicon-genetics.com	The Woodlands	TX	77381	281-863-3000	863-8088
LifeCore Biomedical LLC 3515 Lyman Blvd. TF Cust Svc: 800-752-2663 ■ Web: www.lifecore.com	Chaska	MN	55318	952-368-4300	368-3411
LiphaTech Inc 3600 W Elm St. *Fax Area Code: 414 ■ TF: 888-331-7900 ■ Web: www.liphatech.com	Milwaukee	WI	53209	888-331-7900	247-8166*
Lipid Sciences Inc 7068 Koll Ctr Pkwy Suite 401. NASDAQ: LIPD ■ TF: 866-254-7437 ■ Web: www.lipidsciences.com	Pleasanton	CA	94566	925-249-4000	249-4040
Lonza Biologics Inc 97 S St. Web: www.lonza.com	Hopkinton	MA	01748	508-497-0700	497-0777
Lorus Therapeutics Inc 2 Meridian Rd. Web: www.lorusthera.com	Toronto	ON	M9W4Z7	416-798-1200	798-2200
Lundbeck Canada Inc 1000 de la GauchetiFre W Suite 500. Web: www.lundbeck.com	Montreal	QC	H2Y1N9	514-844-8515	844-5495
MacroChem Corp 40 Washington St Suite 220. Web: www.macrochem.com	Wellesley Hills	MA	02481	781-489-7310	489-7311
MannKind Corp 28903 N Ave Paine. NASDAQ: MNKD ■ TF: 866-428-7348 ■ Web: www.mannkindcorp.com	Valencia	CA	91355	661-775-5300	775-2081
Martek Biosciences Corp 6480 Dobbin Rd. NASDAQ: MATK ■ Web: www.martek.com	Columbia	MD	21045	410-740-0081	740-2985
Maxygen Inc 301 Galveston Dr. NASDAQ: MAXY ■ TF: 888-629-9436 ■ Web: www.maxygen.com	Redwood City	CA	94063	650-298-5300	364-2715
Medicines Co 8 Sylvan Way. NASDAQ: MDCO ■ TF: 800-388-1183 ■ Web: www.themedicinescompany.com	Parsippany	NJ	07054	973-290-6000	656-9898
MediGene Inc 10660 Scripts Ranch Blvd Suite 200. TF: 888-586-1050 ■ Web: www.medigene.com	San Diego	CA	92131	858-586-2240	586-2241
MedImmune Inc 1 MedImmune Way. TF: 877-633-4411 ■ Web: www.medimmune.com	Gaithersburg	MD	20878	301-398-0000	
Mera Pharmaceuticals Inc 73-4460 Queen Kaahumanu Hwy Suite 110. TF: 800-480-6515 ■ Web: www.merapharma.com	Kailua-Kona	HI	96740	808-326-9301	326-9401
Microbix Biosystems Inc 115 Skyway Ave. TF: 800-794-6694 ■ Web: www.microbix.com	Toronto	ON	M9W4Z4	416-234-1624	234-1626
MicroIslet Inc 6370 Nancy Ridge Dr Suite 112. PINK: MIIS	San Diego	CA	92121	858-657-0287	657-0288
Micromet Inc 9201 Corporate Blvd Suite 400. NASDAQ: MITI ■ Web: www.micromet-inc.com	Rockville	MD	20850	240-752-1420	752-1425
Millennium Pharmaceuticals Inc 40 Lansdowne St. NASDAQ: MLNM ■ Web: www.millennium.com	Cambridge	MA	02139	617-577-1358	374-7788
Millipore Corp 290 Concord Rd. *Fax Area Code: 800 ■ TF: 800-645-5476 ■ Web: www.millipore.com	Billerica	MA	01821	781-533-6000	645-5439*
Momenta Pharmaceuticals Inc 675 W Kendall St. NASDAQ: MNTA ■ Web: www.momentapharma.com	Cambridge	MA	02142	617-491-9700	621-0431
Myriad Genetics Inc 320 Wakara Way. NASDAQ: MYGN ■ TF: 800-469-7423 ■ Web: www.myriad.com	Salt Lake City	UT	84108	801-584-3600	584-3640
N.E.T. Inc 5651 Palmer Way Suite C. TF: 800-888-4638 ■ Web: www.netmindbody.com	Carlsbad	CA	92010	760-929-5980	929-5981
Nabi Biopharmaceuticals 12276 Wilkins Ave. NASDAQ: NABI ■ TF: 800-685-5579 ■ Web: www.nabi.com	Rockville	MD	20852	301-770-3099	770-3097
Nektar Therapeutics 455 Mission Bay Blvd S. NASDAQ: NKTR ■ TF: 855-482-6587 ■ Web: www.nektar.com	San Francisco	CA	94158	415-482-5300	339-5300
Neurobiological Technologies Inc 2000 Powell St Suite 800. NASDAQ: NTII	Emeryville	CA	94608	510-595-6000	595-6006
Neurocrine Biosciences Inc 12790 El Camino Rl. NASDAQ: NBIX ■ Web: www.neurocrine.com	San Diego	CA	92130	858-617-7600	617-7601
Nordion Inc 447 March Rd. NYSE: NDZ ■ TF: 877-675-6777 ■ Web: www.mdsintl.com	Ottawa	ON	K2K1X8	613-592-2790	592-6937
Novartis Vaccines & Diagnostics 4560 Horton St. TF: 800-524-4766 ■ Web: www.novartis-vaccines.com	Emeryville	CA	94608	510-655-8730	655-9910
Novavax Inc 9920 Belward Campus Dr. NASDAQ: NVAX ■ TF: 888-669-9111 ■ Web: www.novavax.com	Rockville	MA	20850	240-268-2000	268-2100
NPS Pharmaceuticals Inc 550 Hills Dr 3rd Fl. NASDAQ: NPSP ■ Web: www.npsp.com	Bedminster	NJ	07921	908-450-5300	450-5351
Nucro-Technics 2000 Ellesmere Rd Unit 16. Web: www.nucro-technics.com	Scarborough	ON	M1H2W4	416-438-6727	438-3463
Nuvo Research Inc 7560 Airport Rd Suite 10. TSE: NRI ■ TF: 888-398-3463 ■ Web: www.nuvoresearch.com	Mississauga	ON	L4T4H4	905-673-6980	673-1842
Nycomed Canada Inc 435 N Service Rd W 1st Fl. TF: 888-367-3331 ■ Web: www.nycomed.ca	Oakville	ON	L6M4X8	905-469-9333	469-4883
Nymox Pharmaceutical Corp 9900 Cavendish Blvd. NASDAQ: NYMX ■ TF: 800-936-9669 ■ Web: www.nymox.com	Saint-Laurent	QC	H4M2V2	514-332-3222	332-2227
Oakwood Laboratories LLC 7670 1st Pl Suite A. TF: 888-625-9352 ■ Web: www.oakwoodlabs.com	Oakwood Village	OH	44146	440-359-0000	359-0001
Oncolytics Biotech Inc 1167 Kensington Crescent NW Suite 210. TSE: ONC ■ TF: 800-564-6253 ■ Web: www.oncolyticsbiotech.com	Calgary	AB	T2N1X7	403-670-7377	283-0858
Oncothyreon Inc 2601 Fourth Ave Suite 500. Web: www.oncothyreon.com	Seattle	WA	98121	206-801-2100	801-2101
Onyx Pharmaceuticals Inc 249 E Grand Av. NASDAQ: ONXX ■ TF: 877-669-9121 ■ Web: www.onyx-pharm.com	South San Francisco	CA	94080	650-266-0000	266-0100
OraPharma Inc 732 Louis Dr. TF: 866-273-7846 ■ Web: www.orapharma.com	Warminster	PA	18974	215-956-2200	443-9531
Organogenesis Inc 150 Dan Rd. Web: www.organogenesis.com	Canton	MA	02021	781-575-0775	575-0440
OSI Pharmaceuticals Inc 41 Pinelawn Rd. TF: 800-572-1932 ■ Web: www.osip.com	Melville	NY	11747	631-962-2000	752-3880
Osiris Therapeutics Inc 7015 Albert Einstein Dr. NASDAQ: OSIR ■ Web: www.osiristx.com	Columbia	MD	21046	443-545-1800	545-1701
Osteotech Inc 51 James Way. *Fax: Hum Res ■ TF: 800-469-4005 ■ Web: www.osteotech.com	Eatontown	NJ	07724	732-542-2800	542-9312*
OXiGENE Inc 701 Gateway Blvd Suite 210. NASDAQ: OXGN ■ Web: www.oxigene.com	South San Francisco	CA	94080	650-635-7000	635-7001
Oxis International Inc 468 N Camden Dr 2nd Fl. Web: www.oxis.com	Beverly Hills	CA	90210	310-860-5184	
Pacira Inc 10450 Science Ctr Dr. Web: www.pacira.com	San Diego	CA	92121	858-625-2424	625-2439
Palatin Technologies Inc 4-C Cedar Brook Dr. AMEX: PTN ■ Web: www.palatin.com	Cranbury	NJ	08512	609-495-2200	495-2201
Panacos Pharmaceuticals Inc 134 Coolidge Ave. NASDAQ: PANC ■ Web: www.panacos.com	Watertown	MA	02472	617-926-1551	923-2245
Paratek Pharmaceuticals Inc 75 Kneeland St. Web: www.paratekpharm.com	Boston	MA	02111	617-275-0040	275-0039
PDL BioPharma Inc 932 Southwood Blvd. NASDAQ: PDLI ■ Web: www.pdl.com	Incline Village	NV	89451	775-832-8500	832-8501
Peregrine Pharmaceuticals Inc 14272 Franklin Ave Suite 100. NASDAQ: PPHM ■ TF: 800-694-5334 ■ Web: www.peregrineinc.com	Tustin	CA	92780	714-508-6000	838-9433
Pharmachem Corp 719 Stefko Blvd. Web: www.pharmachemcorp.com	Bethlehem	PA	18018	610-867-4654	867-2971
Pharmacyclics Inc 995 E Arques Ave. NASDAQ: PCYC ■ TF: 800-458-0330 ■ Web: www.pharmacyclics.com	Sunnyvale	CA	94085	408-774-0330	774-0340
Poniard Pharmaceuticals Inc 750B Attery St Suite 330. NASDAQ: PARD ■ Web: www.poniard.com	South San Francisco	CA	94111	650-583-3774	583-3789
Pozen Inc 1414 Raleigh Rd Suite 400. NASDAQ: POZN ■ Web: www.pozen.com	Chapel Hill	NC	27517	919-913-1030	913-1039
PRA International 4130 Parklake Ave Suite 400. Web: www.prainternational.com	Raleigh	NC	27612	919-786-8200	786-8201
Pressure BioSciences Inc 14 Norfolk Ave. NASDAQ: PBIO ■ Web: www.pressurebiosciences.com	South Easton	MA	02375	508-230-1828	230-1829
Progenics Pharmaceuticals Inc 777 Old Saw Mill River Rd. NASDAQ: PGNX ■ Web: www.progenics.com	Tarrytown	NY	10591	914-789-2800	789-2817
Protein Polymer Technologies Inc 7660-H Fay Ave Suite 352. Web: www.ppti.com	La Jolla	CA	92037	858-558-6064	558-6477
Protein Sciences Corp 1000 Research Pkwy. TF: 800-488-7099 ■ Web: www.proteinsciences.com	Meriden	CT	06450	203-686-0800	686-0268
Proteome Systems Inc 6 Gill St. TF: 866-779-7836 ■ Web: www.proteomesystems.com	Woburn	MA	01801	781-932-9477	932-9294
pSivida Inc 400 Pleasant St. NASDAQ: PSDV ■ Web: www.psivida.com	Watertown	MA	02472	617-926-5000	926-5050
Psychemedics Corp 125 Nagog Pk Suite 200. AMEX: PMD ■ TF: 800-628-8073 ■ Web: www.psychemedics.com	Acton	MA	01720	978-206-8220	264-9236
QLT Inc 887 Great Northern Way Suite 101. TSE: QLT ■ TF: 800-663-5486 ■ Web: www.qltinc.com	Vancouver	BC	V5T4T5	604-707-7000	707-7001
Questcor Pharmaceuticals Inc 1300 N Kellogg Suite D. NASDAQ: QCOR ■ Web: www.questcor.com	Anaheim Hills	CA	92807	714-786-4200	789-4229

Company	City	State	Zip	Phone	Fax
Regeneron Pharmaceuticals Inc 777 Old Saw Mill River Rd *NASDAQ: REGN* ■ *TF:* 800-637-8322 ■ *Web:* www.regeneron.com	Tarrytown	NY	10591	914-347-7000	347-2847
Repligen Corp 41 Seyon St *NASDAQ: RGEN* ■ *TF Sales:* 800-622-2259 ■ *Web:* www.repligen.com	Waltham	MA	02453	781-250-0111	250-0115
Repros Therapeutics Inc 2408 Timberloch Pl Suite B-7 *NASDAQ: RPRX* ■ *Web:* www.reprosrx.com	The Woodlands	TX	77380	281-719-3400	719-3446
Research Triangle Park Laboratories 7201 Acc Blvd # 104 *Web:* www.rtp-labs.com	Raleigh	NC	27617	919-510-0228	510-0141
Revivicor Inc 1700 Kraft Dr Suite 2400 *Web:* www.revivicor.com	Blacksburg	VA	24060	540-961-5559	961-7958
Rigel Pharmaceuticals Inc 1180 Veterans Blvd. *NASDAQ: RIGL* ■ *Web:* www.rigel.com	South San Francisco	CA	94080	650-624-1100	624-1101
Roche Palo Alto LLC 3431 Hillview Ave.	Palo Alto	CA	94304	650-855-5050	855-5526
RTI Biologics Inc 11621 Research Cir *NASDAQ: RTIX* ■ *TF:* 877-343-6832 ■ *Web:* www.rtix.com	Alachua	FL	32615	386-418-8888	418-0342
SAFC 3050 Spruce St. *TF:* 800-244-1173 ■ *Web:* www.safcglobal.com	Saint Louis	MO	63103	314-534-4900	652-0000
Samaritan Pharmaceuticals Inc 101 Convention Ctr Dr Suite 310 *PINK: SPHC* ■ *Web:* www.samaritanpharma.com	Las Vegas	NV	89109	702-735-7001	737-7016
Sangamo BioSciences Inc 501 Canal Blvd Suite A100 *NASDAQ: SGMO* ■ *Web:* www.sangamo.com	Richmond	CA	94804	510-970-6000	236-8951
Sanofi Pasteur Inc Discovery Dr **Fax:* Hum Res ■ *TF Orders:* 800-822-2463 ■ *Web:* www.sanofipasteur.us	Swiftwater	PA	18370	570-839-7187	839-7187*
Sanofi-Aventis Canada 2150 St Elzear Blvd W *TF:* 800-363-6364 ■ *Web:* www.sanofi-aventis.ca	Laval	QC	H7L4A8	514-331-9220	334-8016
Santarus Inc 3721 Valley Centre Dr Suite 400 4th Fl. *NASDAQ: SNTS* ■ *TF Cust Svc:* 888-778-0887 ■ *Web:* www.santarus.com	San Diego	CA	92130	858-314-5700	314-5701
SCOLR Pharma Inc 19204 N Creek Pkwy Suite 100 *OTC: SCLR* ■ *Web:* www.scolr.com	Bothell	WA	98011	425-368-1050	368-1051
Seattle Genetics Inc 21823 30th Dr SE. *NASDAQ: SGEN* ■ *Web:* www.seagen.com	Bothell	WA	98021	425-527-4000	527-4001
Sequenom Inc 3595 John Hopkins Ct. *NASDAQ: SQNM* ■ *TF:* 877-443-6663 ■ *Web:* www.sequenom.com	San Diego	CA	92121	858-202-9000	202-9001
Sirna Therapeutics Inc 1700 Owens St 4th Fl *Web:* www.sirna.com	San Francisco	CA	94158	415-512-7200	512-7022
Soligenix Inc 29 Emmons Dr Suite C-10 *OTC: SNGX* ■ *Web:* www.dorbiopharma.com	Princeton	NJ	08540	609-538-8200	452-6467
Spectrum Pharmaceuticals Inc 11500 S Eastern Ave Suite 240 *NASDAQ: SPPI* ■ *Web:* www.spectrumpharm.com	Henderson	NV	89052	702-835-6300	260-7405
SuperGen Inc 4140 Dublin Blvd Suite 200 *NASDAQ: SUPG* ■ *TF:* 800-353-1075 ■ *Web:* www.supergen.com	Dublin	CA	94568	925-560-0100	560-0101
Supernus Pharmaceuticals Inc 1550 E Gude Dr	Rockville	MD	20850	301-838-2500	838-2501
Synthetech Inc 1290 Industrial Way *NASDAQ: NZYM* ■ *Web:* www.synthetech.com	Albany	OR	97322	541-967-6575	967-9424
Tamir Biotechnology Inc 11 Deer Pk Dr Suite 204 *NASDAQ: ACEL* ■ *Web:* www.alfacell.com	Monmouth Junction	NJ	08852	732-823-1003	652-4575
Tekmira Pharmaceuticals Corp 100 - 8900 Glenlyon Pkwy *Web:* www.tekmirapharm.com	Burnaby	BC	V5J5J8	604-419-3200	419-3201
Telik Inc 700 Hansen Way *NASDAQ: TELK* ■ *TF:* 800-254-2598 ■ *Web:* www.telik.com	Palo Alto	CA	94304	650-845-7700	845-7800
Thallion Pharmaceuticals Inc 7150 Alexander-Fleming *Web:* www.thallion.com	Montreal	QC	H4S2C8	514-940-3600	228-3622
Theratechnologies Inc 2310 Alfred Nobel Blvd. *Web:* www.theratech.com	Montreal	QC	H4S2B4	514-336-7800	336-7242
Theravance Inc 901 Gateway Blvd *NASDAQ: THRX* ■ *Web:* www.theravance.com	South San Francisco	CA	94080	650-808-6000	827-8690
Threshold Pharmaceuticals Inc 1300 Seaport Blvd Suite 500 *NASDAQ: THLD* ■ *Web:* www.thresholdpharm.com	Redwood City	CA	94063	650-474-8200	474-2529
Titan Pharmaceuticals Inc 400 Oyster Pt Blvd Suite 505 *OTC: TTNP* ■ *TF:* 800-860-2442 ■ *Web:* www.titanpharm.com	South San Francisco	CA	94080	650-244-4990	244-4956
TolerRx Inc 300 Technology Sq 3rd Fl *Web:* www.tolerrx.com	Cambridge	MA	02139	617-354-8100	354-8300
Trimeris Inc 3500 Paramount Pkwy *NASDAQ: TRMS* ■ *Web:* www.trimeris.com	Morrisville	NC	27560	919-419-6050	419-1816
Unigene Laboratories Inc 81 Fulton St. *Web:* www.unigene.com	Boonton	NJ	07005	973-265-1100	335-0972
United Biomedical Inc 25 Davids Dr *Web:* www.unitedbiomedical.com	Hauppauge	NY	11788	631-273-2828	273-1717
Urigen Pharmaceuticals Inc 1700 N Broadway Suite 330 *Web:* www.urigen.com	Walnut Creek	CA	94596	925-280-2861	280-2861
Vertex Pharmaceuticals Inc 130 Waverly St *NASDAQ: VRTX* ■ *TF:* 800-294-2465 ■ *Web:* www.vrtx.com	Cambridge	MA	02139	617-444-6100	444-6180
Vical Inc 10390 Pacific Ctr Ct *NASDAQ: VICL* ■ *Web:* www.vical.com	San Diego	CA	92121	858-646-1100	646-1150
Virexx Medical Corp 8223 Roper Rd NW. *Web:* www.virexx.com	Edmonton	AB	T6E6S4	780-433-4411	436-0068
ViroPharma Inc 730 Stockton Dr. *NASDAQ: VPHM* ■ *TF:* 888-651-0201 ■ *Web:* www.viropharma.com	Exton	PA	19341	610-458-7300	458-7380
Viventia Biotechnologies Inc 7895 Tranmere Dr Suite 204 *Web:* www.viventia.com	Mississauga	ON	L5S1V9	905-362-2973	362-2973
XenoPort Inc 3410 Central Expy *NASDAQ: XNPT* ■ *Web:* www.xenoport.com	Santa Clara	CA	95051	408-616-7200	616-7210
XOMA (US) LLC 2910 7th St. *NASDAQ: XOMA* ■ *TF:* 800-544-9662 ■ *Web:* www.xoma.com	Berkeley	CA	94710	510-204-7200	644-2011
YM Biosciences Inc 5045 Orbitor Dr Bldg 11 Suite 400 *AMEX: YMI* ■ *Web:* www.ymbiosciences.com	Mississauga	ON	L4W4Y4	905-629-9761	629-4959
ZymoGenetics Inc 1201 Eastlake Ave E *TF:* 800-775-6686 ■ *Web:* www.zymogenetics.com	Seattle	WA	98102	206-442-6600	442-6608

86 BLANKBOOKS & BINDERS

SEE ALSO Checks - Personal & Business p. 1598

Company	City	State	Zip	Phone	Fax
Abco Inc 1621 Wall St *TF:* 800-969-2226 ■ *Web:* www.abcoinc.com	Dallas	TX	75215	214-565-1191	428-8996
ACCO Canada Inc 5 Precido Ct *TF:* 800-268-3447 ■ *Web:* www.acco.ca	Brampton	ON	L6S6B7	905-595-3100	595-3130
Acme Sample Books Inc 2410 Schirra Pl *Web:* www.acmesample.com	High Point	NC	27263	336-883-4187	883-4565
AD Industries LLC PO Box 3316 *TF:* 800-233-4201 ■ *Web:* www.adind.com	Basalt	CA	81621	818-765-4200	765-4370
Advanced Looseleaf Technologies Inc 1424 Somerset Ave. *TF:* 800-339-6354 ■ *Web:* www.binder.com	Dighton	MA	02715	508-669-6354	669-6143
Allison Payment Systems LLC 2200 Production Dr *TF:* 800-755-2440 ■ *Web:* www.apsllc.com	Indianapolis	IN	46241	317-808-2400	808-2477
American Thermoplastic Co (ATC) 106 Gamma Dr *TF:* 800-245-6600 ■ *Web:* www.binders.com	Pittsburgh	PA	15238	412-967-0900	967-9990
Antioch Co PO Box 1839 *TF:* 800-328-2344 ■ *Web:* www.antiochcompany.com	Saint Cloud	MN	56301	320-251-3822	529-5863
Art Leather Mfg Co Inc 45-10 94th St. **Fax Area Code:* 800 ■ *TF:* 888-252-5286 ■ *Web:* www.artleather.com	Elmhurst	NY	11373	718-699-6300	882-5286*
Avery Dennison Corp 150 N Orange Grove Blvd *NYSE: AVY* ■ *TF Cust Svc:* 800-252-8379 ■ *Web:* www.averydennison.com	Pasadena	CA	91103	626-304-2000	304-2192
Blair Packaging Inc 116 E Missouri St *TF:* 800-624-3150 ■ *Web:* www.blairpkg.com	Scott City	MO	63780	573-264-2146	264-3730
Bobley Harmann Publishing Co 311 Crossways Pk Dr *TF Cust Svc:* 800-323-1692	Woodbury	NY	11797	516-364-1800	364-1899
Cardinal Brands Inc 643 Massachusetts St Suite 200 *TF:* 800-364-8713 ■ *Web:* www.cardinalbrands.com	Lawrence	KS	66044	785-344-1400	344-1200
Colad Group 801 Exchange St *TF:* 800-950-1755 ■ *Web:* www.colad.com	Buffalo	NY	14210	716-961-1776	961-1753
Columbia Loose Leaf Corp 50-02 5th St	Long Island City	NY	11101	718-937-8585	937-8585
Colwell Industries Inc 123 N 3rd St *Web:* www.colwellindustries.com	Minneapolis	MN	55401	612-340-0365	340-0231
Continental Binder & Specialty Corp 407 W Compton Blvd *TF:* 800-872-2897 ■ *Web:* www.continentalbinder.com	Gardena	CA	90248	310-324-8227	715-6740
Continental Loose Leaf Inc 1122 16th Ave *Web:* www.continentallooseleaf.com	Minneapolis	MN	55414	612-378-4800	378-7680
Custom Cover Service Inc 1600 W 92nd St *Web:* www.lithotechusa.com	Bloomington	MN	55431	952-884-5511	888-9014
D Davis Kenny Co Inc 4810 Greatland *Web:* www.topflightalbums.com	San Antonio	TX	78218	210-662-9882	662-9887
Daret Inc 33 Daret Dr	Ringwood	NJ	07456	973-962-6001	962-6091
Data Management Inc 537 New Britain Ave **Fax Area Code:* 800 ■ *TF Orders:* 800-243-1969 ■ *Web:* www.datamanage.com	Farmington	CT	06034	860-677-8586	428-1951*
Day Runner Inc 101 O'Neil Rd *TF:* 800-323-0500 ■ *Web:* www.dayrunner.com	Sydney	NY	13838	607-563-9411	563-8811
Day-Timers Inc 1 Willow Ln **Fax:* Hum Res ■ *TF:* 800-457-5702 ■ *Web:* www.daytimer.com	East Texas	PA	18046	610-398-1151	530-6500*
Dayton Legal Blank Inc 875 Congress Pk Dr *TF:* 800-262-8480 ■ *Web:* www.dlbinc.com	Dayton	OH	45459	937-435-4405	435-8352
Dilley Mfg Co 215 E 3rd St *TF:* 800-247-5087 ■ *Web:* www.dilleymfg.com	Des Moines	IA	50309	515-288-7289	288-4210
EBSCO Industries Inc Vulcan Information Packaging Div PO Box 29 *TF:* 800-633-4526 ■ *Web:* www.vulcan-online.com	Vincent	AL	35178	800-633-4526	344-8939
Eckhart & Co Inc 4011 W 54th St. *TF:* 800-443-3791 ■ *Web:* www.eckhartandco.com	Indianapolis	IN	46254	317-347-2665	347-2666
Eskco Inc 700 Liberty Ln *TF:* 800-783-7526 ■ *Web:* www.eskco.com	Dayton	OH	45449	937-865-0498	865-0070
Esselte Corp 225 Broadhollow Rd *TF:* 800-645-6051 ■ *Web:* www.esselte.com	Melville	NY	11747	631-675-5700	675-3456
Esselte Pendaflex Corp 1625 E Duane Blvd *TF:* 800-888-2115	Kankakee	IL	60901	815-933-3351	933-7922
Federal Business Products Inc 95 Main Ave. *TF:* 800-927-5123 ■ *Web:* www.feddirect.com	Clifton	NJ	07014	973-667-9800	667-7756
Fey Industries Blackbourn Media Packaging Div 200 4th Ave N. **Fax Area Code:* 507 ■ *TF:* 800-842-7550 ■ *Web:* www.blackbourn.com	Edgerton	MN	56128	800-842-7550	442-4313*
Fey Industries Inc 200 4th Ave N *TF:* 800-533-5340	Edgerton	MN	56128	507-442-4311	442-3686
Forbes Products Corp 45 High Tech Dr *TF:* 800-836-7237 ■ *Web:* www.forbesproducts.com	Rush	NY	14543	585-334-4800	334-6180
Formflex Inc PO Box 218 *TF:* 800-255-7659 ■ *Web:* www.formflexproducts.com	Bloomingdale	IN	47832	765-498-8900	498-5200
General Loose Leaf Bindery Co 3811 Hawthorn Ct. *TF:* 800-621-0493 ■ *Web:* www.looseleaf.com	Waukegan	IL	60087	847-244-9700	244-9741
General Products 4045 N Rockwell St *TF:* 800-888-1934 ■ *Web:* www.gpalbums.com	Chicago	IL	60618	773-463-2424	463-3028
HC Miller Co 3030 Lowell Dr *TF:* 800-829-6555 ■ *Web:* www.hcmiller.com	Green Bay	WI	54311	920-465-3030	465-3035
Holum & Sons Co Inc 740 Burr Oak Dr. *TF:* 800-447-4479 ■ *Web:* www.holumandsons.com	Westmont	IL	60559	630-654-8222	654-2929
Kurtz Bros Co Inc 400 Reed St PO Box 392 *TF:* 800-252-3811 ■ *Web:* www.kurtzbros.com	Clearfield	PA	16830	814-765-6561	765-8690
Leed Selling Tools Corp 9700 Hwy 57	Evansville	IN	47725	812-867-4340	867-4353

Company	City	State	ZIP	Phone	Fax
M & F Case International Inc 717 School St *TF Cust Svc:* 800-343-8820	Pawtucket	RI	02860	401-722-4830	724-5180
MeadWestvaco Consumer & Office Products 4751 Hempstead Stn Dr *TF:* 800-648-6323 ■ *Web:* www.meadwestvaco.com/cop.nsf	Kettering	OH	45429	937-495-6323	
Michael Lewis Simon Products Co Inc 201 Mittel Dr *TF:* 800-323-8808 ■ *Web:* www.mlco.com	Wood Dale	IL	60191	630-350-1060	350-1089
NAPCO Inc 120 Trojan Ave *TF:* 800-854-8621 ■ *Web:* www.napcousa.com	Sparta	NC	28675	336-372-5228	372-8602
Northeast Data Services 1316 College Ave *TF Cust Svc:* 800-845-3720 ■ *Web:* www.artisticlabels.com	Elmira	NY	14901	607-733-5541	735-4540
Pioneer Photo Albums Inc 9801 Deering Ave *TF:* 800-366-3686	Chatsworth	CA	91311	818-882-2161	882-6239
Roaring Spring Blank Book Co 740 Spang St PO Box 35 *TF Cust Svc:* 800-441-1653 ■ *Web:* www.rspaperproducts.com	Roaring Spring	PA	16673	814-224-5141	224-5429
Samsill Corp 5740 Hartman Rd *TF:* 800-255-1100 ■ *Web:* www.samsill.com	Fort Worth	TX	76119	817-536-1906	535-6900
Southwest Plastic Binding Co 109 Millwell Ct **Fax Area Code:* 800 ■ *TF:* 800-325-3628 ■ *Web:* www.swplastic.com	Maryland Heights	MO	63043	314-739-4400	942-2010*
Spiral Binding Co Inc 1 Maltese Dr **Fax:* Cust Svc ■ *TF:* 800-631-3572 ■ *Web:* www.spiralbinding.com	Totowa	NJ	07511	973-256-0666	256-5981*
Superior Press Inc 11930 Hamden Pl *TF Cust Svc:* 888-590-7998 ■ *Web:* www.superior-press.com	Santa Fe Springs	CA	90670	562-948-1866	948-4966
Trendex Inc 240 E Maryland Ave *TF:* 800-328-9200 ■ *Web:* www.trendex.com	Saint Paul	MN	55117	651-489-4655	489-4423
Unified Packaging Inc 500 E 76th Ave *Web:* www.unifiedpackaginginc.com	Denver	CO	80229	303-733-1000	733-6789
Union Group 649 Alden St *TF:* 800-289-3523 ■ *Web:* www.theuniongroup.com	Fall River	MA	02722	508-676-8580	677-0130
US Ring Binder 6800 Arsenal St *Web:* www.usring.com	Saint Louis	MO	63139	314-645-7880	645-7239
ViaTech Publishing Solutions 1440 5th Ave *TF:* 800-645-8558 ■ *Web:* www.viatechpub.com	Bay Shore	NY	11706	631-968-8500	968-8522
West Coast Samples Inc 14450 Central Ave *Web:* www.wcsample.com	Chino	CA	91710	909-464-1616	465-9982
Western Looseleaf 12160 Sherman Way *TF:* 800-233-4201	North Hollywood	CA	91605	818-765-4200	765-4370

87 BLINDS & SHADES

Company	City	State	ZIP	Phone	Fax
Aeroshade Inc 433 Oakland Ave *TF:* 800-331-7179 ■ *Web:* www.aeroshade.com	Waukesha	WI	53186	262-547-2101	547-0546
Beauti-Vue Products Inc 8555 194th Ave Bristol Industrial Pk **Fax Area Code:* 800 ■ *TF:* 800-558-9431 ■ *Web:* www.beautivue.com	Bristol	WI	53104	262-857-2306	329-9431*
Budget Blinds Inc 1927 N Glassell St *TF:* 800-800-9250 ■ *Web:* www.budgetblinds.com	Orange	CA	92865	714-637-2100	637-1400
C-Mor Co 7 Jewell St *TF:* 800-631-3830	Garfield	NJ	07026	973-478-3900	478-0249
Carnegie Fabrics Inc 110 N Centre Ave *Web:* www.carnegiefabrics.com	Rockville Centre	NY	11570	516-678-6770	678-6875
Comfortex Window Fashions Inc 21 Elm St **Fax Area Code:* 800 ■ *TF Cust Svc:* 800-843-4151 ■ *Web:* www.comfortex.com	Maplewood	NY	12189	518-273-3333	336-4580*
Delaine James Inc 10508C Boyer Blvd Suite 400 **Fax Area Code:* 800 ■ *TF Claims:* 800-999-5333 ■ *Web:* www.delainejames.com	Austin	TX	78758	512-835-5333	999-5555*
Dixon Blind & Awning Service 1800 Sunset Ave	Rocky Mount	NC	27804	252-442-2145	442-2146
Fashion Tech Inc 2010 SE 8th Ave *TF:* 800-444-8822 ■ *Web:* www.fashiontech.com	Portland	OR	97214	503-238-0666	231-6366
Hunter Douglas 2 Pkwy& Rt 17 S *TF:* 800-436-7366 ■ *Web:* www.hunterdouglas.com	Upper Saddle River	NJ	07458	201-327-8200	327-7938
Kenney Mfg Co 1000 Jefferson Blvd *TF Cust Svc:* 800-753-6639 ■ *Web:* www.kenney.com	Warwick	RI	02886	401-739-2200	821-4240
Lafayette Venetian Blind Inc 3000 N 300 W *TF:* 800-342-5523 ■ *Web:* www.lafvb.com	West Lafayette	IN	47906	765-464-2500	464-2680
Levolor Kirsch Window Fashions 4110 Premier Dr *TF:* 800-232-2028 ■ *Web:* www.levolor.com	High Point	NC	27265	336-812-8181	881-5991
Mill Supply Div 266 Morse St *TF:* 800-243-6648 ■ *Web:* www.millsupplydiv.com	Hamden	CT	06517	203-777-7668	777-4515
Nationwide Floorcover & Window Coverings 111 E Kilbourn Ave Suite 2400 *TF:* 800-366-8088 ■ *Web:* www.floorsandwindows.com	Milwaukee	WI	53202	414-765-9900	765-1300
Ralph Friedland & Bros Inc 17 Industrial Dr *TF:* 800-631-2162	Cliffwood Beach	NJ	07735	732-290-9800	290-2933
Southland Window Fashions 408 Arlington St **Fax Area Code:* 800 ■ *TF:* 800-299-9030 ■ *Web:* www.southlandwf.com	Houston	TX	77007	713-863-7761	299-7761*
Sun Control Products Inc 1908 2nd St SW *TF:* 800-533-0010	Rochester	MN	55902	507-282-2620	282-2377
Superior Shade & Blind Co Inc 1541 N Powerline Rd *TF:* 800-325-9018 ■ *Web:* www.superiorshade.com	Pompano Beach	FL	33069	954-975-8122	975-2938
Warm Co 5529 186th Pl SW *TF:* 800-234-9276 ■ *Web:* www.warmcompany.com	Lynnwood	WA	98037	425-248-2424	248-2422
Warren Steven Window Fashions 600 NE Hoover St *TF:* 800-937-0008 ■ *Web:* www.warrensteven.com	Minneapolis	MN	55413	612-331-5939	331-9116

88 BLISTER PACKAGING

Company	City	State	ZIP	Phone	Fax
Andex Industries Inc 1911 4th Ave N *TF:* 800-338-9882 ■ *Web:* www.andex.net	Escanaba	MI	49829	906-786-6070	786-3133
Card Pak Inc 29601 Solon Rd *TF:* 800-824-3342 ■ *Web:* www.cardpak.com	Solon	OH	44139	440-542-3100	542-3399
Display Pack 1340 Monroe Ave NW *Web:* www.displaypack.com	Grand Rapids	MI	49505	616-451-3061	451-8907
Jay Packaging Group (JPG) 100 Warwick Industrial Dr **Fax:* Cust Svc ■ *Web:* www.jaypack.com	Warwick	RI	02886	401-739-7200	738-5104*
Placon Corp 6096 McKee Rd *TF:* 800-541-1535 ■ *Web:* www.placon.com	Madison	WI	53719	608-271-5634	271-3162
Primary Packaging Inc 10810 Industrial Pkwy NW *TF:* 800-774-2247 ■ *Web:* www.primarypackaging.com	Bolivar	OH	44612	330-874-3131	874-3811
Sealed Air Corp 200 Riverfront Blvd *NYSE: SEE* ■ *Web:* www.sealedair.com	Elmwood Park	NJ	07407	201-791-7600	
Sharp Corp 23 Carland Rd *TF:* 800-892-6197 ■ *Web:* www.sharpcorporation.com	Conshohocken	PA	19428	610-279-3550	279-4712
Wynalda Packaging 8221 Graphic Dr NE PO Box 370 *TF:* 800-952-8668 ■ *Web:* www.wynalda.com	Belmont	MI	49306	616-866-1561	866-4316

89 BLOOD CENTERS

SEE ALSO Laboratories - Drug-Testing p. 2140; Laboratories - Genetic Testing p. 2140; Laboratories - Medical p. 2141

The Centers Listed Here Are Members Of America's Blood Centers (Abc), The National Network Of Non-Profit, Independent Community Blood Centers. Abc Members Are Licensed And Regulated By The Us Food & Drug Administration.

Company	City	State	ZIP	Phone	Fax
Belle Bonfils Memorial Blood Ctr 717 Yosemite St *TF:* 800-365-0006 ■ *Web:* www.bonfils.org	Denver	CO	80230	303-341-4000	340-2751
Blood & Tissue Center of Central Texas 4300 N Lamar Blvd *Web:* www.bloodandtissue.org	Austin	TX	78756	512-206-1266	458-3859
Blood Assurance Inc 705 E 4th St *TF:* 800-962-0628 ■ *Web:* www.bloodassurance.org	Chattanooga	TN	37403	423-756-0966	752-8460
Blood Bank of Alaska 4000 Laurel St *Web:* www.bloodbankofalaska.org	Anchorage	AK	99508	907-222-5600	563-1371
Blood Bank of Delmarva 100 Hygeia Dr *TF:* 888-825-6638 ■ *Web:* www.bloodbankofdelaware.org	Newark	DE	19713	302-737-8406	737-8233
Blood Bank of Hawaii 2043 Dillingham Blvd *TF:* 800-372-9966 ■ *Web:* www.bbh.org	Honolulu	HI	96819	808-845-9966	848-4737
Blood Bank of the Redwoods 2324 Bethards Dr *TF:* 800-425-6634 ■ *Web:* www.bbr.org	Santa Rosa	CA	95405	707-545-1222	575-8178
Blood Center of New Jersey 45 S Grove St *TF:* 800-652-5663 ■ *Web:* www.bloodnj.org	East Orange	NJ	07018	973-676-4700	676-4933
Blood Center of Northcentral Wisconsin 211 Forest St	Wausau	WI	54403	715-842-0761	845-6429
Blood Center The 2609 Canal St *TF:* 800-862-5663 ■ *Web:* www.thebloodcenter.org	New Orleans	LA	70112	504-524-1322	592-1580
Blood Centers of the Pacific 250 Bush St *TF:* 888-393-4483 ■ *Web:* www.bloodcenters.org	San Francisco	CA	94104	415-567-6400	749-6620
BloodCenter of Wisconsin 638 N 18th St *TF:* 800-257-3840 ■ *Web:* www.bcw.edu	Milwaukee	WI	53233	414-933-5000	937-6332
BloodSource 1625 Stockton Blvd **Fax Area Code:* 401 ■ *TF:* 800-995-4420 ■ *Web:* www.bloodsource.org	Sacramento	CA	95816	916-456-1500	739-8219*
Carter BloodCare 2205 Hwy 121 *TF:* 800-366-2834 ■ *Web:* www.carterbloodcare.org	Bedford	TX	76021	817-412-5000	412-5992
Cascade Regional Blood Services 220 S 'I' St *TF:* 877-242-5663 ■ *Web:* www.crbs.net	Tacoma	WA	98405	253-383-2553	572-6340
Central California Blood Ctr 4343 W Herndon Ave *Web:* www.cencalblood.org	Fresno	CA	93722	559-389-5433	225-1602
Central Illinois Community Blood Ctr 1134 S 7th St *TF:* 866-448-3256 ■ *Web:* www.cicbc.org	Springfield	IL	62703	217-753-1530	753-8116
Central Jersey Blood Ctr 494 Sycamore Ave *Web:* www.cjbc.org	Shrewsbury	NJ	07702	732-842-5750	842-1617
Central Kentucky Blood Ctr 3121 Beaumont Centre Cir *TF:* 800-775-2522 ■ *Web:* www.ckbc.org	Lexington	KY	40513	859-276-2534	233-4166
Central Pennsylvania Blood Bank 8167 Adams Dr *TF:* 800-771-0059 ■ *Web:* www.cpbb.org	Hummelstown	PA	17036	717-566-6161	566-7850
Coastal Bend Blood Ctr 209 N Padre Island Dr *TF:* 800-299-4943 ■ *Web:* www.coastalbendbloodcenter.org	Corpus Christi	TX	78406	361-855-4943	855-2641
Coffee Memorial Blood Ctr 7500 Wallace Dr *TF:* 800-658-6178 ■ *Web:* www.thegiftoflife.org	Amarillo	TX	79106	806-358-4563	358-2982
Community Blood Bank of Northwest Pennsylvania 2646 Peach St *Web:* www.fourhearts.org	Erie	PA	16508	814-456-4206	452-3966
Community Blood Center Inc 4406 W Spencer St *TF:* 800-280-4102 ■ *Web:* www.communityblood.org	Appleton	WI	54914	920-738-3131	738-3139
Community Blood Center of the Ozarks 220 W Plainview Rd *TF:* 800-280-5337 ■ *Web:* www.cbco.org	Springfield	MO	65810	417-227-5000	227-5400
Community Blood Ctr 349 S Main St *TF:* 800-388-4483 ■ *Web:* www.cbccts.org	Dayton	OH	45402	937-461-3450	461-9217
Community Blood Ctr 4040 Main St *TF:* 888-647-4040 ■ *Web:* www.savealifenow.org	Kansas City	MO	64111	816-753-4040	968-4047
Blue Springs Ctr 4040 Main St *Web:* www.savealifenow.org	Kansas City	MO	64111	816-753-4040	968-4047

Name / Address	City	State	ZIP	Phone	Fax
Gladstone Ctr 7265 N Oak Trafficway	Gladstone	MO	64118	816-468-9813	
Web: www.savealifenow.org					
Lawrence Ctr 1410 Kasold Rd	Lawrence	KS	66049	785-843-5383	
Web: www.savealifenow.org					
Olathe Ctr 1463 E 151st St	Olathe	KS	66061	913-829-3724	
Web: www.savealifenow.org					
Saint Joseph Ctr 3122 Frederick Ave	Saint Joseph	MO	64506	816-232-6791	232-3324
TF: 800-725-6791 ■ *Web:* www.savealifenow.org					
Community Blood Services					
970 Linwood Ave W PO Box 39	Paramus	NJ	07653	201-444-3900	670-6174
Web: www.communitybloodservices.org					
Community Blood Services of Illinois					
1408 W University Ave	Urbana	IL	61801	217-367-2202	367-6403
TF: 800-217-4483 ■ *Web:* www.bloodservices.org					
Delta Blood Bank 65 N Commerce St	Stockton	CA	95201	209-943-3831	462-0221
TF: 800-244-6794 ■ *Web:* www.deltabloodbank.org					
Florida Blood Services					
10100 Dr ML King Jr St N	Saint Petersburg	FL	33716	727-568-5433	568-1177
TF: 800-682-5663 ■ *Web:* www.fbsblood.org					
Florida Georgia Blood Alliance					
4500 San Pablo Rd S	Jacksonville	FL	32224	904-353-8263	355-6853
TF: 800-447-1479 ■ *Web:* www.fgba.org					
Florida's Blood Centers 8669 Commodity Cir	Orlando	FL	32819	407-248-5000	835-5505
TF Cust Svc: 888-936-6283 ■ *Web:* www.floridasbloodcenters.org					
Gulf Coast Regional Blood Ctr					
1400 La Concha Ln	Houston	TX	77054	713-790-1200	790-1007
TF: 888-482-5663 ■ *Web:* www.giveblood.org					
Heartland Blood Centers 1200 N Highland Ave	Aurora	IL	60506	630-892-7055	892-4590
TF: 800-786-4483 ■ *Web:* www.heartlandbc.org					
Hemacare Corp 15350 Sherman Way Suite 350	Van Nuys	CA	91406	818-226-1968	251-5300
TF: 888-481-1538 ■ *Web:* www.hemacare.com					
Houchin Blood Services 2600 G St	Bakersfield	CA	93301	661-327-8541	327-0509
Web: www.hcbb.com					
Hoxworth Blood Center University of Cincinnati Medical Ctr					
3130 Highland Ave ML0055	Cincinnati	OH	45267	513-558-1200	558-1300
TF: 800-265-1515 ■ *Web:* www.hoxworth.org					
Imperial Valley Blood Services					
1415 Ross Ave	El Centro	CA	92243	760-353-3554	339-7390
Inland Northwest Blood Ctr 210 W Cataldo Ave	Spokane	WA	99201	509-624-0151	232-4523
TF: 800-423-0151 ■ *Web:* www.inbc2.org					
Inland Northwest Blood Ctr					
1341 N Northwood Ctr Ct # B	Coeur d'Alene	ID	83814	208-667-5461	292-6103
TF: 800-423-0151 ■ *Web:* www.inbc2.org					
Institute for Transfusion Medicine					
5 PkwyCtr 875 Greentree Rd	Pittsburgh	PA	15220	412-209-7300	209-7330
TF: 800-431-0608 ■ *Web:* www.itxm.org					
Lane Memorial Blood Bank 2211 Willamette St	Eugene	OR	97405	541-484-9111	484-6976
Web: www.lanecountyblood.org					
Lifeblood Mid-South Regional Blood Ctr					
1040 Madison Ave	Memphis	TN	38104	901-522-8585	523-8671
TF: 888-543-3256 ■ *Web:* www.lifeblood.org					
Blytheville Ctr 320 N 6th St	Blytheville	AR	72315	870-763-8585	763-4117
Web: www.lifeblood.org					
DeSoto Ctr 577 Goodman Rd Suite 5	Southaven	MS	38671	901-271-1260	349-2427*
**Fax Area Code:* 662 ■ *Web:* www.lifeblood.org					
LifeServe Blood Ctr 431 E Locust St	Des Moines	IA	50309	515-288-0276	288-0833
TF: 800-287-4903 ■ *Web:* www.bloodonor.org					
LifeShare Blood Centers 8910 Linwood Ave	Shreveport	LA	71106	318-222-7770	222-8886
TF: 800-256-4483 ■ *Web:* www.lifeshare.org					
LifeShare Community Blood Services					
105 Cleveland St	Elyria	OH	44035	440-322-5700	322-6240
TF: 866-644-5433 ■ *Web:* www.lifeshare.cc					
LifeSource Blood Services					
1205 N Milwaukee Ave	Glenview	IL	60025	847-298-9660	298-4473
TF: 877-543-3768 ■ *Web:* www.lifesource.org					
LifeSouth Community Blood Centers					
1221 NW 13th St	Gainesville	FL	32601	352-334-1000	334-1066
Web: www.crbs.org					
LifeSouth Community Blood Centers Atlanta					
4891 Ashford Dunwoody Rd	Atlanta	GA	30338	404-329-1994	329-1707
TF: 888-795-2707 ■ *Web:* www.lifesouth.org					
Manatee Community Blood Ctr					
216 Manatee Ave E	Bradenton	FL	34208	941-746-7195	748-1711
Web: www.manateeblood.org					
Memorial Blood Centers (MBC) 737 Pelham Blvd	Saint Paul	MN	55114	651-332-7000	332-7001
TF Cust Svc: 888-448-3253 ■ *Web:* www.mbc.org					
Michigan Community Blood Centers					
1036 Fuller Ave NE	Grand Rapids	MI	49503	616-774-2300	233-8567
TF: 866-642-5663 ■ *Web:* www.miblood.org					
Michigan Community Blood Centers					
4005 Orchard Dr	Midland	MI	48670	989-839-3490	839-1315
TF: 866-642-5663 ■ *Web:* www.miblood.org					
Michigan Community Blood Centers Northwest					
2575 Aero Pk Dr	Traverse City	MI	49686	231-935-3030	935-1690
TF: 800-642-5663 ■ *Web:* www.miblood.org					
Miller-Keystone Blood Ctr					
1465 Valley Ctr Pkwy	Bethlehem	PA	18017	610-691-5850	691-5423
TF: 800-223-6667 ■ *Web:* www.hcsc.org					
Mississippi Blood Services 115 Tree St	Flowood	MS	39232	601-981-3232	
TF: 888-902-5663 ■ *Web:* www.msblood.com					
Mississippi Valley Regional Blood Ctr					
5500 Lakeview Pkwy	Davenport	IA	52807	563-359-5401	359-8603
TF: 800-747-5401 ■ *Web:* www.bloodcenter.org					
Nebraska Community Blood Bank 100 N 84th St	Lincoln	NE	68505	402-486-9400	486-9429
TF: 877-486-9414 ■ *Web:* www.ncbb.org					
New York Blood Ctr 310 E 67th St	New York	NY	10021	212-570-3000	570-3195
Web: www.nybloodcenter.org					
Northern California Community Blood Bank					
2524 Harrison Ave	Eureka	CA	95501	707-443-8004	443-8007
Web: www.nccbb.org					
Northwest Florida Blood Ctr 2209 N 9th Ave	Pensacola	FL	32503	850-434-2535	432-8941
Web: www.nfbcblood.org					
Oklahoma Blood Institute (OBI)					
1001 N Lincoln Blvd	Oklahoma City	OK	73104	405-297-5700	297-5513
TF: 800-827-5693 ■ *Web:* www.obi.org					
Puget Sound Blood Ctr 921 Terry Ave	Seattle	WA	98104	206-292-6500	292-8030
TF: 800-366-2831 ■ *Web:* www.psbc.org					
Rhode Island Blood Ctr 405 Promenade St	Providence	RI	02908	401-453-8360	453-8557
TF: 800-283-8385 ■ *Web:* www.ribc.org					
Rock River Valley Blood Ctr					
3065 N Perryville Rd # 105	Rockford	IL	61114	815-965-8751	965-8756
TF: 866-889-9073 ■ *Web:* www.rrvbc.org					
San Diego Blood Bank 440 Upas St	San Diego	CA	92103	619-296-6393	296-0126
TF: 800-479-3902 ■ *Web:* www.sandiegobloodbank.org					
SeraCare Life Sciences Inc 37 Birch St	Milford	MA	01757	508-244-6400	634-3394
NASDAQ: SRLS ■ *TF:* 800-676-1881 ■ *Web:* www.seracare.com					
Shepeard Community Blood Ctr					
1533 Wrightsboro Rd	Augusta	GA	30904	706-737-4551	733-5214
Web: www.shepeardblood.org					
Siouxland Community Blood Bank					
1019 Jones St	Sioux City	IA	51105	712-252-4208	252-1013
TF: 800-798-4208 ■ *Web:* www.siouxlandbloodbank.org					
South Texas Blood & Tissue Ctr					
6211 IH-10 W	San Antonio	TX	78201	210-731-5555	731-5501
TF: 800-292-5534 ■ *Web:* www.bloodntissue.org					
Southeast Iowa Blood Ctr					
1007 Pennsylvania Ave	Ottumwa	IA	52501	641-682-8149	682-9791
TF: 800-452-1097					
Southeastern Community Blood Ctr					
1731 Riggins Rd	Tallahassee	FL	32308	850-877-7181	877-7435
TF: 800-722-2218 ■ *Web:* www.scbcinfo.org					
Suncoast Communities Blood Bank					
1760 Mound St	Sarasota	FL	34236	941-954-1600	951-2629
Web: www.scbb.org					
Texoma Regional Blood Ctr 3911 N Texoma Pkwy	Sherman	TX	75090	903-893-4314	893-8628
United Blood Services					
6210 E Oak St PO Box 1867	Scottsdale	AZ	85257	480-946-4201	675-5767
TF: 800-288-2199 ■ *Web:* www.unitedbloodservices.org					
united blood services 4119 broad St	San luis obispo	CA	93401	831-751-1993	751-1985
Web: www.unitedbloodservices.org					
United Blood Services of Arizona					
Chandler 1989 W Elliot Rd Suite 33	Chandler	AZ	85224	480-732-9007	732-9009
Web: www.unitedbloodservices.org					
Glendale 18583 N 59th Ave Suite 113	Glendale	AZ	85308	602-843-1303	843-1476
Web: www.unitedbloodservices.org					
Mesa 1337 S Gilbert Rd Suite 101-103	Mesa	AZ	85204	480-892-6577	892-8343
TF: 800-288-2199 ■ *Web:* www.unitedbloodservices.org					
Phoenix 5757 N Black Canyon Hwy	Phoenix	AZ	85015	602-242-4697	242-7328
Web: www.unitedbloodservices.org					
San Luis Obispo					
4119 Broad St Suite 100	San Luis Obispo	CA	93401	805-543-4290	543-4926
Web: www.unitedbloodservices.org					
United Blood Services of Colorado					
146 Sawyer Dr	Durango	CO	81301	970-385-4601	385-4837
TF: 800-863-4524 ■ *Web:* www.unitedbloodservices.org					
United Blood Services of Louisiana					
Baton Rouge 8234 1 Calais Ave	Baton Rouge	LA	70806	225-769-7233	769-8633
Web: www.unitedbloodservices.org					
Lafayette 1503 Bertrand Dr	Lafayette	LA	70506	337-235-5433	232-5352
Web: www.unitedbloodservices.org					
Morgan City 1234 David Dr Suite 102	Morgan City	LA	70380	985-384-5671	384-5672
Web: www.unitedbloodservices.org					
United Blood Services of Mississippi					
Hattiesburg 805 S 28th Ave	Hattiesburg	MS	39402	601-264-0743	264-6717
Web: www.unitedbloodservices.org					
Meridian 1115 25th Ave	Meridian	MS	39301	601-482-2482	483-4204
TF: 877-582-2482 ■ *Web:* www.unitedbloodservices.org					
Tupelo 4326 S Eason Blvd	Tupelo	MS	38803	662-842-8870	680-9161
TF: 800-844-8870 ■ *Web:* www.unitedbloodservices.org					
United Blood Services of Montana					
Billings 1444 Grand Ave	Billings	MT	59102	406-248-9168	248-1025
TF: 800-365-4450 ■ *Web:* www.unitedbloodservices.org					
Butte 2201 Harrison Ave	Butte	MT	59701	406-723-3264	782-4475
Web: www.unitedbloodservices.org					
United Blood Services of Nevada					
Carson City 256 E Winnie Ln	Carson City	NV	89701	775-887-9111	887-9134
Web: www.unitedbloodservices.org					
Green Valley					
601 Whitney Ranch Dr Bldg D Suite 20	Henderson	NV	89014	702-434-1838	434-1007
Web: www.unitedbloodservices.org					
Las Vegas 6930 W Charleston Blvd	Las Vegas	NV	89117	702-228-4483	228-2374
Web: www.unitedbloodservices.org					
Las Vegas 4950 W Craig Rd Suite 1	Las Vegas	NV	89130	702-645-3600	645-3716
Web: www.unitedbloodservices.org					
Las Vegas 4950 W Craig Rd	Las Vegas	NV	89130	702-645-3600	
Web: www.unitedbloodservices.org/LV					
United Blood Services of New Mexico					
1515 University Blvd	Albe	NM	87102	505-843-6227	243-6820
TF: 800-333-8037 ■ *Web:* www.unitedbloodservices.org					
Albuquerque 1515 University Blvd NE	Albuquerque	NM	87102	505-843-6227	247-8835
TF: 800-333-8037 ■ *Web:* www.unitedbloodservices.org					
Farmington 475 E 20th St Suite A	Farmington	NM	87401	505-325-1505	327-1889
Web: www.unitedbloodservices.org					
Las Cruces 1200 Commerce Dr	Las Cruces	NM	88011	575-527-1322	527-5210
TF: 800-236-8053 ■ *Web:* www.unitedbloodservices.org					
Sante Fe 2801 Rodeo Rd Suite B-10	Santa Fe	NM	87505	505-438-0678	438-0783
Web: www.unitedbloodservices.org					

			Phone	Fax
United Blood Services of North Dakota				
Bismarck 517 S 7th St ... Bismarck	ND	58502	701-258-4512	223-0557
TF: 800-456-6159 ■ *Web:* www.unitedbloodservices.org				
Fargo 3231 11th St S ... Fargo	ND	58104	701-293-9453	293-9564
TF: 800-293-8203 ■ *Web:* www.unitedbloodservices.org				
Minot 1919 N Broadway ... Minot	ND	58703	701-852-2161	839-1503
Web: www.unitedbloodservices.org				
United Blood Services of South Dakota				
Rapid City 2209 W Omaha St ... Rapid City	SD	57702	605-342-8585	342-6662
Web: www.unitedbloodservices.org				
United Blood Services of Texas				
El Paso 424 S Mesa Hills ... El Paso	TX	79912	915-544-5422	544-5509
TF: 800-582-3146 ■ *Web:* www.unitedbloodservices.org				
Lubbock 2523 48th St ... Lubbock	TX	79413	806-797-6804	797-1824
Web: www.unitedbloodservices.org				
McAllen 1312 Pecan Blvd ... McAllen	TX	78501	956-682-1314	682-7578
TF: 888-827-4376 ■ *Web:* www.unitedbloodservices.org				
San Angelo 2020 W Beauregard St ... San Angelo	TX	76901	325-223-7500	223-7522
TF: 800-756-0024 ■ *Web:* www.unitedbloodservices.org				
United Blood Services of Wyoming				
Casper 167 S Conwell ... Casper	WY	82601	307-237-2328	237-1321
Web: www.unitedbloodservices.org				
Cheyenne 112 E 8th Ave ... Cheyenne	WY	82001	307-638-3326	635-6919
Web: www.unitedbloodservices.org				
Virginia Blood Services				
2401 Hydraulic Rd ... Charlottesville	VA	22903	434-977-8956	979-4860
TF: 800-989-4438 ■ *Web:* www.vablood.org				
Virginia Blood Services 2825 Emerywood Pkwy ... Richmond	VA	23294	804-359-5100	358-2786
Web: www.vablood.org				

90 BOATS - RECREATIONAL

			Phone	Fax
Action Craft Inc 2603 Andalusia Blvd ... Cape Coral	FL	33909	239-574-7008	574-1152
Web: www.actioncraft.com				
Advanced Outdoors Inc				
1250 NE 6th St PO Box 127 ... Hamlin	TX	79520	325-576-2144	576-2339
Albemarle Sportfishing Boats Inc				
140 Midway Dr ... Edenton	NC	27932	252-482-7600	482-8289
Web: www.albemarleboats.com				
Albin Marine Inc 143 River Rd PO Box 228 ... Cos Cob	CT	06807	203-661-4341	661-6040
Web: www.albinmarine.com				
Albury Bros Boats 1401 Broadway ... Riviera Beach	FL	33404	561-863-7006	863-7746
Web: www.alburybrothers.com				
Alpin Haus Ski Shop 4850 State Hwy 30 ... Amsterdam	NY	12010	518-843-4400	843-5159
Web: www.alpinhaus.com				
Aluma-Weld Inc 199 Extrusion Pl ... Hot Springs	AR	71901	501-262-5300	262-5053
Web: www.xpressboats.com				
Alumacraft Boat Co 315 St Julien St ... Saint Peter	MN	56082	507-931-1050	931-9056
Web: www.alumacraft.com				
Alumaweld Boats Inc 2000 Rouge River Dr ... Eagle Point	OR	97524	541-826-7171	826-6701
TF: 800-401-2628 ■ *Web:* www.alumaweldboats.com				
American Marine Sports LLC				
20150 Independence Blvd ... Groveland	FL	34736	352-429-8989	429-8388
Web: www.americanmarinesports.com				
Angler Boat Corp 7400 NW 37th Ave ... Miami	FL	33147	305-691-9975	691-9377
Web: www.anglerboats.com				
Aquasport Marine Corp 1651 Whitfield Ave ... Sarasota	FL	34243	941-751-7886	751-7851
TF: 800-755-1099				
Arima Marine International Inc 47 37th St NE ... Auburn	WA	98002	253-939-7980	939-1364
TF: 800-811-6440 ■ *Web:* www.arimaboats.com				
B & B Boats Inc 3568 Old Winter Garden Rd ... Orlando	FL	32805	407-299-2190	208-9800
Baha Cruiser Boats Inc				
668 N Fletcher Ave PO Box 1387 ... Mayo	FL	32066	386-294-2447	294-1311
Web: www.bahacruisers.com				
Baja Marine Corp				
1520 Isaac Beal Rd PO Box 151 ... Bucyrus	OH	44820	419-562-5377	562-0846
Web: www.bajamarine.com				
Bay Craft Inc 1785 Langley Ave ... DeLand	FL	32724	386-943-8877	943-8617
Web: www.baycraftinc.com				
Beneteau USA Inc 1313 Hwy 76 W ... Marion	SC	29541	843-629-5300	629-5309
Web: www.beneteauusa.com				
Bertram Yacht Inc 3663 NW 21st St ... Miami	FL	33142	305-633-8011	633-2868
Web: www.bertram.com				
Bluewater Inc 811 E Maple Ave ... Mora	MN	55051	320-679-3811	679-3820
TF: 800-733-7127 ■ *Web:* www.bluewater.ep2.channelbladelive.com				
Bone Boats 2901 N IH- 10 Service Rd E ... Metairie	LA	70002	504-828-5089	828-8986
Web: www.boneboats.com				
Boston Whaler Inc 100 Whaler Way ... Edgewater	FL	32141	877-294-5645	423-8589*
**Fax Area Code:* 386 ■ *TF:* 800-942-5379 ■ *Web:* www.whaler.com				
Briggs Boat Works Inc 370 Harbor Rd ... Wanchese	NC	27981	252-473-2393	473-2392
Web: www.briggsboatworks.com				
Brunswick Boat Group 800 S Gay St 17th Fl ... Knoxville	TN	37929	865-582-2200	582-2301
Web: www.brunswick.com/boats.html				
Brunswick Corp 1 N Field Ct ... Lake Forest	IL	60045	847-735-4700	735-4765
NYSE: BC ■ *Web:* www.brunswick.com				
Brunswick Corp Sea Ray Group				
2600 Sea Ray Blvd ... Knoxville	TN	37914	865-522-4181	971-6434
Web: www.searay.com				
C & C Mfg 6725 Bayline Dr ... Panama City	FL	32404	850-769-0311	769-0731
Web: www.cobiaboats.com				
Cabo Yachts Inc 110 N Glenburnie Rd ... New Bern	CA	28560	760-246-8917	634-4819*
**Fax Area Code:* 252 ■ **Fax:* Mktg ■ *Web:* www.caboyachts.com				
Cape Cod Shipbuilding Co 7 Narrows Rd ... Wareham	MA	02571	508-295-3550	295-3551
Web: www.capecodshipbuilding.com				
Caribiana Sea Skiffs 8920 County Rd 65 ... Foley	AL	36535	251-981-4442	981-3039
TF: 888-203-4883 ■ *Web:* www.caribiana.com				
Carolina Classic Boats Inc				
109 Anchors Way Dr PO Box 968 ... Edenton	NC	27932	252-482-3699	
Web: www.carolinaclassicboats.com				
Carolina Skiff Inc 3231 Fulford Rd ... Waycross	GA	31503	912-287-0547	287-0533
TF: 800-422-7282 ■ *Web:* www.carolinaskiff.com				
Carver Boat Corp LLC				
790 Markham Dr PO Box 1010 ... Pulaski	WI	54162	920-822-3214	
Web: www.carveryachts.com				
Catalina Yachts Inc				
21200 Victory Blvd ... Woodland Hills	CA	91367	818-884-7700	884-3810
Web: www.catalinayachts.com				
Catamarans New Zealand Ltd				
5021 Newport Ave ... San Diego	CA	92107	619-523-8891	223-9215
Cavileer Boatworks 2143 River Rd ... Lower Bank	NJ	08215	609-965-8650	965-7480
Web: www.cavileer.com				
Chaparral Boats Inc PO Box 928 ... Nashville	GA	31639	229-686-7481	686-3660
Web: www.chaparralboats.com				
Chris-Craft Boats 8161 15th St E ... Sarasota	FL	34243	941-351-4900	351-4900
Web: www.chriscraftboats.com				
Cigarette Racing Team LLC 4355 NW 128th St ... Opa Locka	FL	33054	305-931-4564	769-4355
TF: 800-347-4327 ■ *Web:* www.cigaretteracing.com				
Concept Boats Corp 2410 NW 147th St ... Opa Locka	FL	33054	305-635-8712	635-9543
TF: 888-635-8712 ■ *Web:* www.conceptboats.com				
Correct Craft Inc 14700 Aerospace Pkwy ... Orlando	FL	32809	407-855-4141	855-4141
TF: 800-346-2092 ■ *Web:* www.nautique.com				
Crestliner Inc 609 13th Ave NE ... Little Falls	MN	56345	320-632-6686	632-2127
Web: www.crestliner.com				
Crownline Boats Inc				
11884 Country Club Rd ... West Frankfort	IL	62896	618-937-6426	932-3426
Web: www.crownlineboats.com				
Defiant Marine 2234 Industrial Blvd ... Sarasota	FL	34234	941-351-8581	359-1516
Web: www.defiantmarine.com				
Donzi Marine PO Box 987 ... Tallevast	FL	34270	941-727-0622	758-5417
TF Cust Svc: 800-446-6725 ■ *Web:* www.donzimarine.com				
Ebbtide Corp 2545 Jones Creek Rd ... White Bluff	TN	37187	615-797-3193	797-4889
Web: www.ebbtideboats.com				
EdgeWater Power Boats 211 Dale St ... Edgewater	FL	32132	386-426-5457	427-9783
Web: www.edgewaterpowerboats.com				
Egg Harbor Yachts Inc				
801 Philadelphia Ave Po Box 702 ... Egg Harbor City	NJ	08215	609-965-2300	965-3517
Web: www.eggharboryachts.com				
Ercoa Industries Inc 40800 Hwy 65 NE ... Braham	MN	55006	320-396-3386	396-4107
Web: www.ercoa.com				
Everglades Boats 544 Air Pk Rd ... Edgewater	FL	32132	386-409-2202	409-7939
Web: www.evergladesboats.com				
Famous Craft Inc 7921 15th St E ... Sarasota	FL	34243	941-358-3121	351-5479
TF: 888-244-3244 ■ *Web:* www.famouscraft.com				
Fiberglass Engineering Inc 1715 N 8th St ... Neodesha	KS	66757	620-325-2653	325-2653
TF: 800-468-5764 ■ *Web:* www.cobaltboats.com				
Flats Cat Boats 1565 Patton Rd ... Rosenberg	TX	77471	281-342-3940	
Web: www.flatscat.com				
Fountain Powerboat Industries Inc				
1653 Whichards Beach Rd PO Box 457 ... Washington	NC	27889	252-975-2000	975-6793
TF: 800-438-2055 ■ *Web:* www.fountainpowerboats.com				
Four Winns Inc 925 Frisbie St ... Cadillac	MI	49601	231-775-1351	779-2348
Web: www.fourwinns.com				
Garlington Landeweer Marine Inc				
3370 SE Slater St ... Stuart	FL	34997	772-283-7124	220-1049
Web: www.garlingtonyachts.com				
Gibson Boats Inc 130 Davis St ... Portland	TN	37148	615-325-9320	325-9321
Web: www.gibsonboats.com				
Glacier Bay Catamarans 14298 169th Dr SE ... Monroe	WA	98272	360-794-0444	
Web: www.glacierbaycats.com				
Glastron Boats 925 Frisbie St ... Cadillac	MI	49601	231-779-2663	
TF: 855-272-2709 ■ *Web:* www.glastron.com				
Grady-White Boats Inc				
5121 Martin Luther King Jr Hwy ... Greenville	NC	27834	252-752-2111	752-4217
Web: www.gradywhite.com				
Grand Banks Yachts Ltd				
2288 W Commodore Way Suite 200 ... Seattle	WA	98199	206-352-0116	352-1711
Web: www.grandbanks.com				
Harris FloteBote 1 N Field Ct ... Lake Forest	IL	60045	847-735-4318	
Web: www.harrisflotebote.com				
Hatteras Yachts Inc 110 N Glenburnie Rd ... New Bern	NC	28560	252-633-3101	634-4813
Web: www.hatterasyachts.com				
Hinckley Co The 1 Little Harbor Landing ... Portsmouth	RI	02871	401-683-7005	
TF: 866-446-2553 ■ *Web:* www.hinckleyyachts.com				
Hobie Cat Co 4925 Oceanside Blvd ... Oceanside	CA	92056	760-758-9100	758-1841
TF: 800-462-4349 ■ *Web:* www.hobiecat.com				
Hunter Marine Corp 14700 NW US Hwy 441 ... Alachua	FL	32615	386-462-3077	462-4077
TF: 800-771-5556 ■ *Web:* www.huntermarine.com				
Intrepid Powerboats 11700 S Belcher Rd ... Largo	FL	33773	727-548-1260	544-1796
Web: www.intrepidboats.com				
Island Runner Boats				
1177 W Blue Heron Blvd PO Box 530098 ... Riviera Beach	FL	33404	561-863-9989	863-9987
Web: www.islandrunner.com				
Jefferson Yachts Inc				
700 E Market St PO Box 790 ... Jeffersonville	IN	47131	812-282-8111	288-7783
Web: www.jeffersonyachts.com				
Johnson Outdoors Inc 555 Main St ... Racine	WI	53403	262-631-6600	631-6601
NASDAQ: JOUT ■ *TF:* 800-299-2592 ■ *Web:* www.johnsonoutdoors.com				
Johnson Outdoors Watercraft Sport & Leisure Group				
5960 Tahoe Dr Suite 500 ... Grand Rapids	MI	49546	616-698-3000	698-2734
TF: 800-552-6287				
KCS International Inc Cruisers Div				
804 Pecor St ... Oconto	WI	54153	920-834-2211	834-2211*
**Fax:* Hum Res ■ *TF:* 800-743-3478				

Company	City	State	Zip	Phone	Fax
KenCraft Mfg Inc 4155 Dixie Inn Rd. *Web:* www.kencraftboats.com	Wilson	NC	27893	252-291-0271	291-0815
Key West Boats Inc 593 Ridgeville Rd PO Box 399 *Web:* www.keywestboatsinc.com	Ridgeville	SC	29472	843-873-0112	821-6334
Klamath Boat Co 5199 Fulton Dr Suite I *Web:* www.klamathboats.com	Fairfield	CA	94534	707-643-0447	643-0483
Knight & Carver Yachtcenter Inc 1313 Bay Marina Dr *Web:* www.knightandcarver.com	National City	CA	91950	619-336-4141	336-4050
L & H Boats Inc 3350 SE Slater St. *Web:* www.lhboats.com	Stuart	FL	34997	772-288-2291	288-9878
Larson Boats 700 Paul Larson Memorial Dr. *TF:* 800-255-3622 ■ *Web:* www.larsonboats.com	Little Falls	MN	56345	320-632-5481	632-1439
Lowe Boats 2900 Industrial Dr. *TF:* 800-641-4372 ■ *Web:* www.loweboats.com	Lebanon	MO	65536	417-532-9101	532-8991
Luhrs Corp 301 Riverside Dr. *TF:* 800-524-2804 ■ *Web:* www.luhrs.com	Millville	NJ	08332	856-825-4117	825-2064
Lund Boats 318 W Gilman St *Web:* www.lundboats.com	New York Mills	MN	56567	218-385-2235	385-2227
Magnum Marine Corp 2900 NE 188th St *Web:* www.magnummarine.com	Aventura	FL	33180	305-931-4292	931-0088
Mainship Corp 301 Riverside Dr **Fax Area Code:* 856 ■ *TF:* 800-524-2804 ■ *Web:* www.mainship.com	Millville	NJ	08332	800-524-2804	825-2064*
Marine Mfg Inc 1815 Peterson Ave. *Web:* www.capecraftfishingboats.com	Douglas	GA	31535	912-384-8943	384-8974
Marine Products Corp 2170 Piedmont Rd NE *NYSE: MPX* ■ *Web:* www.marineproductscorp.com	Atlanta	GA	30324	404-321-2140	321-5483
Marine Safety Corp PO Box 465	Farmingdale	NJ	07727	732-938-5661	938-4839
MarineMax Inc 18167 US 19 N Suite 300 *NYSE: HZO* ■ *Web:* www.marinemax.com	Clearwater	FL	33764	727-531-1700	531-0123
Maritime Skiff Inc PO Box 218	Duxbury	MA	02331	781-934-0010	934-0257
MasterCraft Boat Co 100 Cherokee Cove Dr *TF:* 800-443-8774 ■ *Web:* www.mastercraftboats.com	Vonore	TN	37885	423-884-2221	884-2295
Maurell Products Inc 2710 S M-52 PO Box 190 *Web:* www.crestpontoonboats.com	Owosso	MI	48867	989-725-5188	725-6849
Maverick Boat Co Inc 3207 Industrial 29th St *TF:* 888-742-5569 ■ *Web:* www.maverickboats.com	Fort Pierce	FL	34946	772-465-0631	489-2168
May-Craft Fiberglass Products Inc PO Box 450 *Web:* www.maycraftboats.com	Smithfield	NC	27577	919-934-3000	934-9014
Melges Boatworks Inc PO Box 1 *Web:* www.melges.com	Zenda	WI	53195	262-275-1110	275-8012
Merritt's Boat & Engine Works Inc 2931 NE 16th St *Web:* www.merrittboat.com	Pompano Beach	FL	33062	954-941-0118	942-1531
Monterey Boats 1579 SW 18th St. *Web:* www.montereyboats.com	Williston	FL	32696	352-528-2628	529-2628
Ocean Yachts Inc PO Box 312 *Web:* www.oceanyachtsinc.com	Egg Harbor City	NJ	08215	609-965-4616	965-4914
Pacific Seacraft PO Box 189 *Web:* www.pacificseacraft.com	Washington	NC	27889	252-948-1421	948-1422
Palmer Johnson Boats PO Box 109 *Web:* www.palmerjohnson.com	Sturgeon Bay	WI	54235	920-743-4412	
Palmer Marine of Washington Inc 5611 Imperial Way SW	Port Orchard	WA	98367	360-674-7090	674-7119
Parker Marine Enterprises Inc 2570 Nc Hwy 101 *Web:* www.parkerboats.net	Beaufort	NC	28516	252-728-5621	728-2770
Playbuoy Pontoon Mfg Inc 903 Michigan Ave PO Box 698 *TF:* 800-334-2913	Alma	MI	48801	989-463-2112	463-8226
Port Harbor Marine Inc 1 Spring Pt Dr PO Box 2350 *Web:* www.portharbormarine.com	South Portland	ME	04106	207-767-3254	767-5940
Porta-Bote International 1074 Independence Ave *TF:* 800-227-8882 ■ *Web:* www.porta-bote.com	Mountain View	CA	94043	650-961-5334	961-3800
Porter Inc 2200 W Monroe St *TF:* 800-736-7685 ■ *Web:* www.formulaboats.com	Decatur	IN	46733	260-724-9111	
PowerPlay Marine Inc 2740 NW 29th Terr	Fort Lauderdale	FL	33311	954-733-2500	733-2700
Pro-Line Boats Inc PO Box 1348 *TF:* 800-344-1281 ■ *Web:* www.prolineboats.com	Crystal River	FL	34423	352-795-4111	795-4374
Pursuit Boats 3901 St Lucie Blvd *TF:* 800-947-8778 ■ *Web:* www.pursuitboats.com	Fort Pierce	FL	34946	772-465-6006	465-6177
Regal Marine Industries Inc 2300 Jetport Dr. **Fax:* Sales ■ *TF:* 800-877-3425 ■ *Web:* www.regalboats.com	Orlando	FL	32809	407-851-4360	857-1256*
Rinalli Boats Ltd 1600 N King St *TF:* 866-746-2554 ■ *Web:* www.rinalliboats.com	Seguin	TX	78155	830-372-3300	
Riverside Marine Inc 11051 Pulaski Hwy *Web:* www.riversideboats.com	White Marsh	MD	21162	410-335-1500	344-1537
Rybovich Spencer Group 4200 N Flagler Dr *Web:* www.rybovich.com	West Palm Beach	FL	33407	561-844-1800	844-8393
Sabre Corp PO Box 134 *Web:* www.sabreyachts.com	South Casco	ME	04077	207-655-3831	655-5050
Scout Boats Inc 2531 US 78 *Web:* www.scoutboats.com	Summerville	SC	29483	843-821-0068	821-4786
Sea Cat Boats Inc 1005 Marina Rd. *Web:* www.seacatboats.com	Titusville	FL	32796	321-268-2628	269-8483
Sea Fox Boat Co Inc 2550 Hwy 52 *Web:* www.seafoxboats.com	Moncks Corner	SC	29461	843-761-6090	761-6139
Sea Sport Inc 4654 Guide Meridian PO Box 30678	Bellingham	WA	98228	360-733-3380	733-3653
SeaArk Boats 728 W Patton St *Web:* www.seaarkboats.com	Monticello	AR	71655	870-367-5317	460-3200
Seaswirl Boats PO Box 167 **Fax:* Cust Svc ■ *Web:* www.seaswirl.com	Culver	OR	97734	541-546-5011	546-7249*
Seminole Marine 2501 Milestone Industrial Pk *Web:* www.sailfishboats.com	Cairo	GA	39828	229-377-2125	377-1855
Silverton Marine Corp 301 Riverside Dr **Fax:* Mktg ■ *TF:* 800-524-2804 ■ *Web:* www.silverton.com	Millville	NJ	08332	856-825-4117	825-2064*
Skeeter Products Inc 2606 US Hwy 259 N *Web:* www.skeeterboats.com	Kilgore	TX	75662	903-984-0541	984-7856
Skier's Choice Inc 1717 Henry G Ln St *Web:* www.supraboats.com	Maryville	TN	37801	865-856-3035	
Smoker Craft Inc 68143 Clunette St *Web:* www.smokercraft.com	New Paris	IN	46553	574-831-2103	831-7003
Sonic USA 3600 N 29th Ave *Web:* www.sonicusaboats.com	Hollywood	FL	33020	954-922-5535	922-0578
Stamas Yacht Inc 300 Pampas Ave *TF Sales:* 800-782-6271 ■ *Web:* www.stamas.com	Tarpon Springs	FL	34689	727-937-4118	934-1339
Starcraft Marine LLC 201 Starcraft Dr PO Box 517 *TF:* 800-535-5722 ■ *Web:* www.starcraftmarine.com	Topeka	IN	46571	260-593-2500	593-2816
Stevens Marine Inc 9180 SW Burnham St *Web:* www.stevensmarine.com	Tigard	OR	97223	503-620-7023	684-8952
Stoltzfus RV's & Marine 1335 Wilmington Pike *Web:* www.stoltzfus-rec.com	West Chester	PA	19382	610-399-0628	399-1436
Sumerset Acquisition LLC 200 Sumerset Blvd *TF:* 888-786-3773 ■ *Web:* www.sumerset.com	Somerset	KY	42501	606-679-9393	678-0487
Sundance Boats Inc 6131 Sundance Rd *Web:* www.sundanceboats.com	Blackshear	GA	31516	912-449-0033	449-0038
Sylvan Marine Inc PO Box 65 **Fax Area Code:* 219 ■ *TF:* 866-766-9698 ■ *Web:* www.sylvanmarine.com	New Paris	IN	46553	574-831-2950	831-7012*
Tartan Yachts 1920 Fairport Nursery Rd *Web:* www.tartanyachts.com	Fairport Harbor	OH	44077	440-354-3111	354-6162
Tiara Yachts Inc 725 E 40th St *Web:* www.tiarayachts.com	Holland	MI	49423	616-392-7163	394-7466
Tracker Marine Group LLC 2500 E Kearney St **Fax:* Mktg ■ *Web:* www.trackermarine.com	Springfield	MO	65803	417-873-5900	873-5068*
Triumph Boats Marine 100 Golden Dr. *TF:* 800-564-4225 ■ *Web:* www.triumphboats.com	Durham	NC	27705	919-382-3149	382-0585
Valiant Yachts Inc 500 Harbour View Rd *Web:* www.valiantsailboats.com	Gordonville	TX	76245	903-523-4899	523-4077
Venture Marine Inc 1525 53rd St *TF:* 800-960-3434 ■ *Web:* www.venturemarine.com	West Palm Beach	FL	33407	561-845-8557	842-4239
Viking Yacht Co Inc 5738 US Hwy 9 *Web:* www.vikingyachts.com	New Gretna	NJ	08224	609-296-6000	296-3956
Weeres Industries Corp 1045 33rd St S *TF:* 800-397-6686 ■ *Web:* www.weeres.com	Saint Cloud	MN	56301	320-251-3551	654-9188
Wellcraft Marine Corp 1651 Whitfield Ave **Fax:* Sales ■ *TF:* 800-755-1099 ■ *Web:* www.wellcraft.com	Sarasota	FL	34243	941-753-7811	751-7808*
Willard Marine Inc 1250 N Grove St *Web:* www.willardmarine.com	Anaheim	CA	92806	714-666-2150	632-8136
Wood Mfg Co Inc PO Box 179 **Fax:* Hum Res ■ *Web:* www.rangerboats.com	Flippin	AR	72634	870-453-2222	704-2468*
Wooldridge Boats Inc 1303 S 96th St *Web:* www.wooldridgeboats.com	Seattle	WA	98108	206-722-8998	
World Cat 1090 W St James St. *TF:* 866-485-8899 ■ *Web:* www.worldcat.com	Tarboro	NC	27886	252-641-8000	641-9866
Yellowfin Yachts Inc 6611 19th St E *Web:* www.yellowfinyachts.com	Sarasota	FL	34243	941-753-7828	753-2540
Zodiac of North America Inc 540 Thompson Creek Rd *Web:* www.zodiacmilpro.com	Stevensville	MD	21666	410-643-4141	643-4491

91 BOILER SHOPS

Company	City	State	Zip	Phone	Fax
A & A Industries Inc 320 Jubilee Dr. *Web:* www.aandaindustries.com	Peabody	MA	01960	978-977-9660	977-3992
Ace Tank & Fueling Equipment 510 S Westgate Dr *TF:* 800-765-2080 ■ *Web:* www.acetank.com	Addison	IL	60101	847-364-1744	364-1744
Adamson Global Technology Corp 13101 N Eron Church Rd *TF:* 800-525-7703 ■ *Web:* www.adamsontank.com	Chester	VA	23836	804-748-6453	796-2037
Aerofin Corp 4621 Murray Pl PO Box 10819 **Fax:* Sales ■ *TF:* 800-237-6346 ■ *Web:* www.aerofin.com	Lynchburg	VA	24506	434-845-7081	528-6242*
Aesys Technologies LLC 693 N Hills Rd *Web:* www.aesystech.com	York	PA	17402	717-755-1081	755-0020
AlfaLaval Inc 5400 International Trade Dr *Web:* www.alfalaval.com	Richmond	VA	23231	804-222-5300	236-3276
American Welding & Tank Co 4718 Old Gettysburg Rd Suite 300 *TF:* 800-586-2657 ■ *Web:* www.awtank.com	Mechanicsburg	PA	17001	717-763-5080	763-5081
Amtrol Inc 1400 Division Rd *Web:* www.amtrol.com	West Warwick	RI	02893	401-884-6300	885-2567
API Heat Transfer Inc 2777 Walden Ave *TF:* 877-274-4328 ■ *Web:* www.apiheattransfer.com	Buffalo	NY	14225	716-684-6700	684-2129
Armstrong Engineering Assoc Inc 1101 W Strasburg Rd *Web:* www.rmarmstrong.com	West Chester	PA	19382	610-436-6080	436-0374
Arrow Tank & Engineering Co 650 N Emerson St. *TF:* 888-892-7769 ■ *Web:* www.arrowtank.com	Cambridge	MN	55008	763-689-3360	689-1263

Company	City	State	ZIP	Phone	Fax
AustinMohawk & Co Inc 2175 Beechgrove Pl.	Utica	NY	13501	315-793-3000	793-9370
TF: 800-765-3110 ■ *Web:* www.austinmohawk.com					
Babcock & Wilcox Co 20 S Van Buren Ave	Barberton	OH	44203	330-753-4511	860-1886
TF: 800-222-2625 ■ *Web:* www.babcock.com					
Babcock Power Inc 155 Ferncroft Rd Suite 210	Danvers	MA	01923	978-646-3300	646-3301
Web: www.babcockpower.com					
Baltimore Aircoil Co 7600 Dorsey Run Rd.	Baltimore	MD	20794	410-799-6200	799-6416
Web: www.baltaircoil.com					
Beaird Co Ltd 601 Benton Kelly St.	Shreveport	LA	71106	318-671-5400	671-5583
Web: www.beairdco.com					
Benicia Fabrication & Machine Inc					
101 E Ch Rd	Benicia	CA	94510	707-745-8111	745-8102
Web: www.beniciafab.com					
Bristol Metals LLC					
390 Bristol Metals Rd PO Box 1589	Bristol	TN	37620	423-989-4700	989-4790
Web: www.brismet.com					
Bryan Steam LLC 783 Chili Ave	Peru	IN	46970	765-473-6651	473-3074
Web: www.bryanboilers.com					
C Burgett & Assoc Inc					
104 Baker Ave PO Box 579	Scottsville	TX	75688	903-938-6638	938-6638
Caldwell Tanks Inc 4000 Tower Rd	Louisville	KY	40219	502-964-3361	966-8732
Web: www.caldwelltanks.com					
Chart Industries Inc					
1 Infinity Corporate Centre Dr					
Suite 300	Garfield Heights	OH	44125	440-753-1490	753-1491
Web: www.chart-ind.com					
Chicago Boiler Co 1300 Northwestern Ave	Gurnee	IL	60031	847-662-4000	662-4003
TF Cust Svc: 800-969-7343 ■ *Web:* www.cbmill.com					
Chicago Boiler Co CB Mills Div					
1300 Northwestern Ave	Gurnee	IL	60031	847-662-4000	662-4003
TF: 800-969-7343 ■ *Web:* www.cbmills.com					
Clawson Tank Co 4545 Clawson Tank Dr	Clarkston	MI	48346	248-625-8700	625-3066
TF: 800-325-8700 ■ *Web:* www.clawsontank.com					
Cleaver Brooks 11950 W Lake Pk Dr	Milwaukee	WI	53224	414-359-0600	577-3171
Cleaver Brooks Thomasville 221 Law St	Thomasville	GA	31792	229-226-3024	226-3027
Web: www.cleaver-brooks.com					
Coen Co Inc 1510 Tanforan Ave	Woodland	CA	95776	530-668-2100	668-2171
Web: www.coen.com					
Columbia Boiler Co					
390 Old Reading Pike PO Box 1070	Pottstown	PA	19464	610-323-2700	323-7292
Web: www.columbiaboiler.com					
Columbian Tectank 2101 S 21st St PO Box 996	Parsons	KS	67357	620-421-0200	421-9122
TF: 800-421-2788 ■ *Web:* www.tanks.com					
Connell LP 1 International Pl 31st Fl	Boston	MA	02110	617-737-2700	737-1617
TF: 800-276-4746 ■ *Web:* www.connell-lp.com					
CP Industries Inc (CPI) 2214 Walnut St.	McKeesport	PA	15132	412-664-6604	664-6653*
**Fax:* Sales ■ *Web:* www.cp-industries.com					
CP Industries Inc					
12767 Industrial Dr PO Box 690	Granger	IN	46530	574-273-3000	273-4000
Web: www.cpind.com					
DCI Inc 600 N 54th Ave	Saint Cloud	MN	56303	320-252-8200	252-0866
Web: www.dciinc.com					
Delta Industries 39 Bradley Pk Rd	East Granby	CT	06026	860-653-5041	653-5792
Web: www.delta-industries-ct.com					
Dynasteel Corp PO Box 27640	Memphis	TN	38167	901-358-6231	358-4401
Web: www.dynasteel.net					
Eaton Metal Products Co 4803 York St	Denver	CO	80216	303-296-4800	296-4800
TF: 800-208-2657 ■ *Web:* www.eatonsalesservice.com					
Ecodyne MRM 8203 Market St	Houston	TX	77029	713-675-3511	675-7922
Web: www.ecodynehx.com					
Enerfab Inc 4955 Spring Grove Ave.	Cincinnati	OH	45232	513-641-0500	641-1821
TF: 800-966-7323 ■ *Web:* www.enerfab.com					
Energy Exchanger Co 1844 N Garnett Rd.	Tulsa	OK	74116	918-437-3000	437-7144
Web: www.energyexchanger.com					
Engineered Storage Products Co					
345 Harvestore Dr.	DeKalb	IL	60115	815-756-1551	756-7821
Web: www.engstorage.com					
Erdle Perforating Co					
100 Pixley Industrial Pkwy	Rochester	NY	14624	585-247-4700	247-4716
TF: 800-627-4700 ■ *Web:* www.erdle.com					
Essick Air Products Inc 5800 Murray St.	Little Rock	AR	72209	501-562-1094	562-9485
TF: 800-643-8341 ■ *Web:* www.essickair.com					
Exothermics Inc 5040 Enterprise Blvd	Toledo	OH	43612	419-729-9726	729-9705
Web: www.exothermics.com					
Fabsco Shell & Tube LLC					
2410 Industrial Rd PO Box 988	Sapulpa	OK	74066	918-224-7550	224-3564
Fafco Inc 435 Otterson Dr	Chico	CA	95928	530-332-2100	332-2109
TF: 800-994-7652 ■ *Web:* www.fafco.com					
Fisher Tank Co 3131 W 4th St.	Chester	PA	19013	610-494-7200	485-0157
Web: www.fishertank.com					
GEA Rainey Corp 5202 W Ch Rd.	Catoosa	OK	74015	918-266-3060	266-2464
Web: www.gearainey.com					
Geiger & Peters Inc					
761 S Sherman Dr PO Box 33807	Indianapolis	IN	46203	317-359-9521	359-9525
Web: www.gpsteel.com					
General Welding Works Inc					
2060 N Loop W Suite 200 PO Box 925749	Houston	TX	77018	713-869-6401	869-5405
Web: www.generalwelding.com					
Goodhart Sons Inc 2515 Horseshoe Rd	Lancaster	PA	17605	717-656-2404	656-3301
Web: www.goodhartsons.com					
Hague International 6 Ivy Ct PO Box 449	Kennebunk	ME	04043	207-985-3540	985-9007
Web: www.hague.com					
Hammersmith Mfg & Sales Inc 401 Central Ave	Horton	KS	66439	785-486-2121	486-2454
TF: 800-375-8245 ■ *Web:* www.vailproducts.com					
Harsco Industrial Air-X-Changers					
5215 Arkansas Rd PO Box 1804	Catoosa	OK	74015	918-619-8000	384-5000
Web: www.harscoaxc.com					
HB Smith Co Inc					
47 Westfield Industrial Pk Rd	Westfield	MA	01085	413-568-3148	568-0525
Highland Tank & Mfg Co 1 Highland Rd	Stoystown	PA	15563	814-893-5701	893-6126
Web: www.highlandtank.com					
Holman Boiler Works Inc 1956 Singleton Blvd	Dallas	TX	75212	214-637-0020	637-2539
TF Sales: 800-331-1956 ■ *Web:* www.holmanboiler.com					
Hughes-Anderson Heat Exchangers Inc					
1001 N Fulton Ave	Tulsa	OK	74115	918-836-1681	836-5967
Web: www.hughesanderson.com					
Hurst Boiler & Welding Co Inc PO Box 530	Coolidge	GA	31738	229-346-3545	346-3074
TF: 877-994-8778 ■ *Web:* www.hurstboiler.com					
Indeck Energy Services Inc					
600 N Buffalo Grove Rd Suite 300	Buffalo Grove	IL	60089	847-520-3212	520-9883
Web: www.indeck-energy.com					
ITT Standard 175 Standard Pkwy.	Cheektowaga	NY	14227	716-897-2800	897-1777
TF: 800-447-7700 ■ *Web:* www.ittstandard.com					
Joseph Oat Corp 2500 S Broadway	Camden	NJ	08104	856-541-2900	541-0864
Web: www.josephoat.com					
Koch Heat Transfer Co LP 12602 FM 529	Houston	TX	77041	713-466-3535	466-3701
Web: www.kochheattransfer.com					
Krueger Engineering & Mfg Co					
12001 Hirsch Rd PO Box 11308	Houston	TX	77293	281-442-2537	442-6668
Web: www.kemco.net					
Loveless Mfg Co 1314 N Wheeling Ave	Tulsa	OK	74110	918-583-9129	583-6208
McAbee Construction Inc PO Box 1460	Tuscaloosa	AL	35403	205-349-2212	758-0762
Web: www.mcabeeconstruction.com					
Metalforms Mfg Inc PO Box 20118	Beaumont	TX	77720	409-842-1626	842-1503
Web: www.metalformsinc.com					
Mgs Inc 178 Muddy Creek Church Rd	Denver	PA	17517	717-336-7528	336-0514
TF: 800-952-4228 ■ *Web:* www.mgsincorporated.com					
Mississippi Tank & Mfg Co PO Box 1391	Hattiesburg	MS	39403	601-264-1800	264-0769
Web: www.mstank.com					
MiTek Industries Inc					
14515 N Outer 40 Rd Suite 300	Chesterfield	MO	63017	314-434-1200	434-9110
TF: 800-325-8075 ■ *Web:* www.mii.com/unitedstates					
Mitternight Boiler Works Inc					
5301 Hwy 43 N PO Box 489	Satsuma	AL	36572	251-675-2550	675-2671
Web: www.mitternight.com					
Modern Welding Co Inc 2880 New Hartford Rd.	Owensboro	KY	42303	270-685-4404	684-6972
TF: 800-922-1932 ■ *Web:* www.modweldco.com					
Nebraska Boiler Co Inc 6940 Cornhusker Hwy.	Lincoln	NE	68507	402-434-2000	434-2064
Ohmstede 895 N Main St	Beaumont	TX	77704	409-833-6375	839-4948
TF: 800-568-2328 ■ *Web:* www.ohmstede.com					
Ottenweller Co Inc					
3011 Congressional Pkwy	Fort Wayne	IN	46808	260-484-3166	484-9798
Web: www.ottenweller.com					
Pasadena Tank Corp 15915 Jacintoport Blvd	Houston	TX	77015	281-457-3996	
Web: www.ptctanks.com					
Pentair Water Treatment 200 Industrial Pkwy	Chardon	OH	44024	440-286-4116	942-7659*
**Fax Area Code:* 800 ■ *TF:* 800-922-8265 ■ *Web:* www.pentair.com/water.html					
Plant Maintenance Service Corp 3000 Fite Rd.	Memphis	TN	38127	901-353-9880	353-0882
TF: 800-459-9131 ■ *Web:* www.pmscmphs.com					
Precision Custom Components 500 Lincoln St.	York	PA	17404	717-848-1126	843-5733*
**Fax:* Mktg ■ *Web:* www.pcc-york.com					
Pressed Steel Tank Co Inc 1445 S 66th St.	West Allis	WI	53214	414-476-0500	476-7191
Web: www.pressedsteel.com					
PVI Industries LLC					
3209 Galvez Ave PO Box 7124	Fort Worth	TX	76111	817-335-9531	332-6742
TF: 800-784-8326 ■ *Web:* www.pvi.com					
Q3 JMC Inc 605 Miami St	Urbana	OH	43078	937-652-2181	653-8352
TF: 800-767-1422					
R. W. Fernstrum & Co					
1716 11th Ave PO Box 97	Menominee	MI	49858	906-863-5553	863-5634
Web: www.fernstrum.com					
Reco Constructors Inc 710 Hospital St	Richmond	VA	23219	804-644-2611	643-3561
Web: www.recoconstructors.com					
Redman Equipment & Mfg Co					
19800 Normandie Ave	Torrance	CA	90502	310-329-1134	324-5656
Web: www.redmaneq.com					
Rocky Mountain Fabrication Inc					
PO Box 16409	Salt Lake City	UT	84116	801-596-2400	322-2702
Web: www.rmf-slc.com					
Ross Technology Corp 104 N Maple Ave	Leola	PA	17540	717-656-2095	656-3281
TF: 800-345-8170 ■ *Web:* www.rosstechnology.com					
Roy E Hanson Jr Mfg					
1600 E Washington Blvd.	Los Angeles	CA	90021	213-747-7514	747-7724
TF: 800-421-9395 ■ *Web:* www.hansontank.com					
Sen-Dure Products Inc					
6785 NW 17th Ave	Fort Lauderdale	FL	33309	954-973-1260	968-7213
TF: 800-394-5112 ■ *Web:* www.sen-dure.com					
Silvan Industries Inc					
2121 Cleveland Ave PO Box 767	Marinette	WI	54143	715-735-9311	735-5488
TF: 800-247-8265 ■ *Web:* www.silvanind.com					
Sivalls Inc 2200 E 2nd St.	Odessa	TX	79761	432-337-3571	337-2624
Web: www.sivalls.com					
Smithco Engineering Inc 6312 S 39th W Ave	Tulsa	OK	74132	918-446-4406	445-2857
Web: www.smithco-eng.com					
Snap-Tite Autoclave Engineers Div					
8325 Hessinger Dr	Erie	PA	16509	814-838-5700	833-0145
TF: 800-458-0409 ■ *Web:* www.snap-tite.com/divisions/ae/index.html					

	City	State	Zip	Phone	Fax
SPX Cooling Technologies 7401 W 129th St *TF:* 800-462-7539 ■ *Web:* www.spxcooling.com	Overland Park	KS	66213	913-664-7400	664-7439
Super Steel Products Corp 7900 W Tower Ave *Web:* www.supersteel.com	Milwaukee	WI	53223	414-355-4800	355-0372
Superior Boiler Works Inc 3524 E 4th St PO Box 1527 *TF:* 800-444-6693 ■ *Web:* www.superiorboiler.com	Hutchinson	KS	67504	620-662-6693	662-7586
Superior Die Set Corp 900 W Drexel Ave **Fax Area Code:* 800 ■ *TF:* 800-558-6040 ■ *Web:* www.supdie.com	Oak Creek	WI	53154	414-764-4900	657-0855*
Superior Fabricators Inc 155 Gordy Ln PO Box 0539 *TF:* 800-960-7271 ■ *Web:* www.superiorfabricators.com	Baldwin	LA	70514	337-923-7271	923-7517
Sussman Automatic Corp 43-20 34th St *TF:* 800-727-8326 ■ *Web:* www.mrsteam.com	Long Island City	NY	11101	718-937-4500	786-4051
Tampa Tank Inc 2710 E 5th Ave *Web:* www.tampatank.com	Tampa	FL	33605	813-623-2675	622-7514
Taylor Forge Engineered Systems Inc 208 N Iron St *Web:* www.tfes.com	Paola	KS	66071	913-294-5331	294-5337
Taylor-Wharton 4718 Gettysburg Rd # 300 *Web:* www.taylorwharton.com	Mechanicsburg	PA	17055	717-763-5060	731-7988
Thermal Engineering International Inc 10375 Slusher Dr *Web:* www.babcockpower.com	Santa Fe Springs	CA	90670	323-726-0641	726-9592
Thermal Transfer Corp 50 N Linden St *Web:* www.hamon-thermaltransfer.com	Duquesne	PA	15110	412-460-4004	466-2899
ThermaSys Corp 2776 Gunter Pk Dr E Suite RS *Web:* www.thermasys.com	Montgomery	AL	36109	334-244-9240	244-9248
Thermodynetics Inc 651 Day Hill Rd *Web:* www.thermodynetics.com	Windsor	CT	06095	860-683-2005	285-0139
Titanium Fabrication Corp 110 Lehigh Dr *Web:* www.tifab.com	Fairfield	NJ	07004	973-227-5300	227-6541
Tranter Inc 1900 Old Burk Hwy *TF:* 800-414-6908 ■ *Web:* www.us.tranter.com	Wichita Falls	TX	76307	940-723-7125	723-5131
Trinity Industries Inc LPG Containers Div 2525 N Stemmons Fwy *TF:* 888-558-8265 ■ *Web:* www.trinitylpg.com	Dallas	TX	75207	214-589-8213	589-8303
Ultraflote Corp 8558 Katy Fwy Suite 100 *TF:* 877-461-2100 ■ *Web:* www.ultraflote.com	Houston	TX	77024	713-461-2100	461-2213
Weben-Jarco Inc 4007 Platinum Way *TF:* 800-527-6449 ■ *Web:* www.keldenequipment.com/Weben.aspx	Dallas	TX	75237	214-637-0530	330-6864
Weil-McLain Co 500 Blaine St *Web:* www.weil-mclain.com	Michigan City	IN	46360	219-879-6561	879-4025
Winbco Tank Co 1200 E Main St PO Box 618 *TF:* 800-822-1855 ■ *Web:* www.winbco.com	Ottumwa	IA	52501	641-683-1855	683-8265
Worthington Cylinder Corp 200 Old E Wilson Bridge Rd PO Box 391 *TF:* 866-928-2657 ■ *Web:* www.worthingtoncylinders.com	Columbus	OH	43085	614-438-3013	438-3083
Zak Inc 1 Tibbits Ave *Web:* www.zakinc.com	Green Island	NY	12183	518-273-3912	273-2744

92 BOOK BINDING & RELATED WORK

SEE ALSO Printing Companies - Book Printers p. 2451

	City	State	Zip	Phone	Fax
Area Trade Bindery Co 157 W Providencia Ave **Fax Area Code:* 313 ■ *TF:* 800-225-1343	Burbank	CA	91502	818-846-5581	849-3733*
Bindagraphics Inc 2701 Wilmarco Ave *TF:* 800-326-0300 ■ *Web:* www.bindagraphics.com	Baltimore	MD	21223	410-362-7200	362-7233
Bindtech Inc 1232 Antioch Pike *Web:* www.bindtechinc.com	Nashville	TN	37211	615-834-0404	
Bookbinders Co 2808 S Vail Ave	Los Angeles	CA	90040	323-838-8900	838-8905
Booklet Binding Inc 2200 W 16th St *Web:* www.bookletbinding.com	Broadview	IL	60155	708-345-0110	345-0289
Booksource Inc 1230 Macklind Ave **Fax Area Code:* 800 ■ *TF:* 800-444-0435 ■ *Web:* www.booksource.com	Saint Louis	MO	63110	314-647-0600	647-1923*
Bound to Stay Bound Books Inc (BTSB) 1880 W Morton Ave **Fax Area Code:* 800 ■ *TF:* 800-637-6586 ■ *Web:* www.btsb.com	Jacksonville	IL	62650	217-245-5191	747-2872*
Continental Bindery Corp 700 Fargo Ave	Elk Grove Village	IL	60007	847-439-6811	439-6847
Contract Converting LLC PO Box 247 **Fax Area Code:* 902 ■ *Web:* www.contractconverting.com	Greenville	WI	54942	920-757-4000	757-4004*
Dekker Bookbinding 2941 Clydon Ave SW *TF:* 800-299-2463 ■ *Web:* www.dekkerbook.com	Grand Rapids	MI	49519	616-538-5160	538-0720
Finishing Plus Inc 4546 W 47th St	Chicago	IL	60632	773-523-5510	523-9155
Form House Inc 7200 S Leamington Ave *Web:* www.theformhouse.com	Bedford Park	IL	60638	708-594-7300	594-7390
Fox Bindery Inc 2345 Milford Sq Pike *Web:* www.foxbind.com	Quakertown	PA	18951	215-538-5380	538-6109
HF Group The 8834 Mayfield Rd Suite A *TF:* 800-444-5117 ■ *Web:* www.boundtoplease.com	Chesterland	OH	44026	800-444-5117	
Kater-Crafts Bookbinders Inc 4860 Gregg Rd *Web:* www.katercrafts.com	Pico Rivera	CA	90660	562-692-0665	692-7920
Kolbus America Inc 812 Huron Rd E Suite 750	Cleveland	OH	44115	216-931-5100	931-5101
Lake Book Mfg Inc 2085 N Cornell Ave *Web:* www.lakebook.com	Melrose Park	IL	60160	708-345-7000	345-1544
Library Binding Service (LBS) 1801 Thompson Ave **Fax Area Code:* 800 ■ *TF:* 800-247-5323 ■ *Web:* www.lbsbind.com	Des Moines	IA	50316	515-262-3191	262-4091*
Macke Bros Inc 10355 Spartan Dr	Cincinnati	OH	45215	513-771-7500	771-3830
Marshall & Bruce Printing Co 689 Davidson St *Web:* www.marbruco.com	Nashville	TN	37213	615-256-3661	256-6803
McCain Bindery Systems Inc 3802 W 128th St *TF Cust Svc:* 800-225-9363 ■ *Web:* www.mccainbindery.com	Alsip	IL	60803	708-824-9600	824-0771
National Library Bindery Co 100 Hembree Pk Dr *TF:* 800-422-7908	Roswell	GA	30076	770-442-5490	442-0183
Parker Powis Inc 775 Heinz Ave *TF:* 800-321-2463 ■ *Web:* www.powis.com	Berkeley	CA	94710	510-848-2463	848-2462
Perma-Bound 617 E Vandalia Rd **Fax Area Code:* 800 ■ *TF:* 800-637-6581 ■ *Web:* www.perma-bound.com	Jacksonville	IL	62650	217-243-5451	551-1169*
Precision Technology Inc 39 Sheep Davis Rd *TF:* 800-362-7717	Pembroke	NH	03275	603-224-9989	
Reindl Bindery Co Inc W194 N11381 McCormick Dr *TF:* 800-878-1121 ■ *Web:* www.reindlbindery.com	Germantown	WI	53022	262-293-1444	293-1445
Rickard Circular Folding Co 325 N Ashland Ave *Web:* www.rickardbindery.com	Chicago	IL	60607	312-243-6300	243-6323
Riverside Group 655 Driving Pk Ave *TF:* 800-777-2463 ■ *Web:* www.riversidegroup.com	Rochester	NY	14613	585-458-2090	458-2123
Roswell Bookbinding Co 2614 N 29th Ave *TF:* 888-803-8883 ■ *Web:* www.roswellbookbinding.com	Phoenix	AZ	85009	602-272-9338	272-9786
Rotherwood Corp 301 Carlson Pkwy Suite 103	Minnetonka	MN	55305	952-835-2115	893-9036
Talas Inc 20 W 20th St 5th Fl *Web:* www.talas-nyc.com	New York	NY	10011	212-219-0770	219-0735
United Bindery Service Inc 1845 W Carroll Ave	Chicago	IL	60612	312-243-0240	243-3080
Wert Bookbinding Inc 9975 Allentown Blvd *TF Cust Svc:* 800-344-9378 ■ *Web:* www.wertbookbinding.com	Grantville	PA	17028	717-469-0626	469-0629

93 BOOK, MUSIC, VIDEO CLUBS

	City	State	Zip	Phone	Fax
African American Literature Book Club (AALBC) 55 W 116th St Suite 195 *TF:* 866-603-8394 ■ *Web:* www.aalbc.com	Harlem	NY	10026	866-603-8394	
Behavioral Science Book Service 1225 S Market St	Mechanicsburg	PA	17055	717-697-0311	
Black Expressions PO Box 916400 *Web:* www.blackexpressions.com	Rantoul	IL	61866	717-918-2665	
BMG Music Service PO Box 1958	Indianapolis	IN	46291	317-692-9200	542-6090
Booksfree.com 8453 Tyco Rd # P *Web:* www.booksfree.com	Vienna	VA	22182	703-748-2390	748-2394
BOOKSPAN 1225 S Market St *Web:* www.bookspan.com	Mechanicsburg	PA	17055	717-697-1948	
Children's Book-of-the-Month Club PO Box 916400 *Web:* www.cbomc.com	Rantoul	IL	61866	717-918-2665	
Columbia House Co 1400 N Fruitridge Ave **Fax:* Hum Res ■ *Web:* www.columbiahouse.com	Terre Haute	IN	47811	812-466-8111	466-6409*
Conservative Book Club (CBC) PO Box 97197 *TF:* 877-222-1964 ■ *Web:* www.conservativebookclub.com	Washington	DC	20090	202-216-0600	216-0615
Crossings Book Club PO Box 916400 *Web:* www.crossings.com	Rantoul	IL	61866	717-918-2665	
Disney Movie Club PO Box 738 *TF:* 800-382-4527 ■ *Web:* www.disney.videos.go.com	Neenah	WI	54957	920-521-4015	521-4020
Doubleday Book Club Doubleday Direct Inc 1225 S Market St *TF:* 800-688-4442 ■ *Web:* www.doubledaybookclub.com	Mechanicsburg	PA	17055	800-688-4442	
Doubleday Direct Inc 1225 S Market St	Mechanicsburg	PA	17055	717-697-0311	
Doubleday Large Print Home Library PO Box 916400 *Web:* www.doubledaylargeprint.com	Rantoul	IL	61866	717-918-2665	
Early Childhood Teachers' Club 1225 S Market St	Mechanicsburg	PA	17055	717-918-4120	
eMusic.com Inc 244 5th Ave # 2070 *Web:* www.emusic.com	New York	NY	10001	212-201-9240	201-9204
GameFly Inc PO Box 60018 **Fax Area Code:* 310 ■ *TF:* 888-986-6400 ■ *Web:* www.gamefly.com	City of Industry	CA	91716	888-986-6400	664-6788*
Gameznflix Inc 1535 Blackjack Rd **Fax Area Code:* 270 ■ *TF:* 888-542-6817 ■ *Web:* www.gameznflix.com	Franklin	KY	42134	888-542-6817	778-0025*
Good Cook The PO Box 916400 *TF:* 800-233-1066 ■ *Web:* www.thegoodcook.com	Rantoul	IL	61866	717-918-2665	
History Book Club PO Box 916400 *Web:* www.historybookclub.com	Rantoul	IL	61866	717-918-2665	
HomeStyle Books PO Box 916400 *Web:* www.homestylebooks.com	Rantoul	IL	61866	717-918-2665	
Intelliflix Inc 1401 Forum Way Suite 503 *Web:* www.intelliflix.com	West Palm Beach	FL	33401	561-697-8325	697-8320
Library of Speech-Language Pathology 1225 S Market St	Mechanicsburg	PA	17055	717-918-4120	
Literary Guild PO Box 916400 *Web:* www.literaryguild.com	Rantoul	IL	61866	717-918-2665	
Military Book Club PO Box 916400 *Web:* www.militarybookclub.com	Rantoul	IL	61866	717-918-2665	
Musical Heritage Society 1710 Hwy 35 *TF Cust Svc:* 800-558-9513 ■ *Web:* www.classicalstore.com	Oakhurst	NJ	07755	732-531-7000	517-0438
Mystery Guild PO Box 916400 *Web:* www.mysteryguild.com	Rantoul	IL	61866	717-918-2665	

	City	State	ZIP	Phone	Fax
NetFlix Inc 100 Winchester Cir	Los Gatos	CA	95032	408-540-3700	540-3737
NASDAQ: NFLX ■ *TF:* 888-638-3549 ■ *Web:* www.netflix.com					
One Spirit Book Club PO Box 916400	Rantoul	IL	61866	717-918-2665	
Web: www.onespirit.com					
Primary Teachers' Book Club 1225 S Market St	Mechanicsburg	PA	17055	717-918-4120	
Quality Paperback Book Club (QPBC) PO Box 916400	Rantoul	IL	61866	717-918-2665	
Web: www.qpb.com					
Reader's Subscription The 1225 S Market St	Mechanicsburg	PA	17055	717-918-4120	
Rhapsody Book Club Bookspan 1225 S Market St	Mechanicsburg	PA	17055	717-918-2665	
Web: www.rhapsodybookclub.com					
Scholastic Arrow Book Club 555 Broadway	New York	NY	10012	212-343-6100	223-4011*
**Fax Area Code:* 800 ■ *TF Orders:* 800-724-6527 ■ *Web:* www.teacher.scholastic.com/clubs					
Scholastic Seesaw Book Club 555 Broadway	New York	NY	10012	212-343-6458	
TF: 800-724-6527 ■ *Web:* www.teacher.scholastic.com					
Science Fiction Book Club PO Box 916400	Rantoul	IL	61866	717-918-2665	
Web: www.sfbc.com					
Writer's Digest Book Club 4700 E Galbraith Rd	Cincinnati	OH	45236	513-531-2690	531-4082
TF Cust Svc: 800-888-6880 ■ *Web:* www.writersdigest.com/wdbc					

94 BOOK PRODUCERS

Book Producers, Or Book Packagers, Work With Authors, Editors, Printers, Publishers, And Others To Provide All Publication Services Except Sales And Order Fulfillment. These Publication Services Include Editing Of Manuscripts, Formatting Of Computer Disks, Producing Books As A Finished Product, And Helping The Book Publisher To Develop Marketing Plans. Book Producers Listed Here Are Members Of The American Book Producers Association.

	City	State	ZIP	Phone	Fax
Agincourt Press 25 Main St	Chatham	NY	12037	518-392-2898	
AGS BookWorks PO Box 460313	San Francisco	CA	94146	415-285-8799	285-8790
Web: www.agsbookworks.com					
Ardent Media Inc 522 E 82nd St	New York	NY	10028	212-861-1501	861-0998
Becker & Mayer! Ltd 11120 NE 33rd Pl # 101	Bellevue	WA	98004	425-827-7120	828-9659
Web: www.beckermayer.com					
Charles Davey Design LLC 2 Deertrack Ln	Irvington	NY	10533	914-231-5120	
CMD Publishing 1250 Broadway 36th Fl	New York	NY	10001	212-771-7300	849-1180
Web: www.cmdny.com					
Dimensional Illustrators Inc 362 2nd St Pike Suite 112	SouthHampton	PA	18966	215-953-1415	953-1697
DreamBooks PO Box 10626	Burbank	CA	91510	818-841-9291	841-9691
Emprise Publishing Inc 1104 Murrayhill Rd	Vestal	NY	13850	607-772-0559	
Evanston Publishing Inc 4824 Brownsboro Ctr	Louisville	KY	40207	502-899-1919	896-0246
TF: 800-594-5190 ■ *Web:* www.evanstonpublishing.com					
Focus Strategic Communications Inc 535 Tipperton Crescent	Oakville	ON	L6L5E1	905-825-8757	825-5724
TF: 866-263-6287 ■ *Web:* www.focussc.com					
Garden Bench Books 109 Bell St	Seattle	WA	98121	206-443-8856	443-8862
GGP Publishing Inc 138 Chatsworth Ave Suite 3-5	Larchmont	NY	10538	914-834-8896	834-7566
Gonzalez Defino 7 E 14th St Suite 20-S	New York	NY	10003	212-414-1058	414-0876
Web: www.gonzalezdefino.com					
Grace Assoc 945 4th Ave Suite 200A	Huntington	WV	25701	304-697-3236	697-3399
Innovative USA Inc 18 Ann St	Norwalk	CT	06854	203-838-6400	855-5582
Web: www.innovativekids.com					
Learning Source Ltd 644 10th St	Brooklyn	NY	11215	718-768-0231	369-3467
Web: www.learningsourceltd.com					
Mountain Lion Inc 94 Voorhees Ct PO Box 799	Pennington	NJ	08534	609-730-1665	730-1286
Web: www.mtlioninc.com					
MTM Publishing Inc 121 W 27th St Suite 802	New York	NY	10016	212-645-2900	684-2526
Web: www.mtmpublishing.com					
Palace Press International Packaging 17 Paul Dr	San Rafael	CA	94903	415-526-1370	526-1394
Web: www.palacepress.com					
Philip Lief Group Inc 371 Sayre Dr	Princeton	NJ	08540	609-430-1000	430-0300
Web: www.philipliefgroup.com					
Rosa + Wesley Inc 400 S Knoll St Suite B	Wheaton	IL	60187	630-588-9801	588-9804
Web: www.rosawesley.com					
Roundtable Press Inc 20 E 9th St	New York	NY	10003	212-691-0500	691-1298
Web: www.roundtablepressinc.com					
Schlager Group Inc 1640 W Oakland Pk Blvd Suite 401	Oakland Park	FL	33311	954-730-8214	730-8212
Web: www.schlagergroup.com					
Shoreline Publishing Group 125 Santa Rosa Pl	Santa Barbara	CA	93109	805-564-1004	564-1156
Web: www.shorelinepublishing.com					
Sideshow Media 611 Broadway Suite 611	New York	NY	10012	212-674-5335	674-6116
Web: www.sideshowbooks.com					
Smallwood & Stewart Inc 5 E 20th St	New York	NY	10003	212-505-3268	505-3624
Web: www.smallwoodandstewart.com					
Spooky Cheetah Press 33 Glendale Dr	Stamford	CT	06906	203-357-1160	357-8096
Web: www.spookycheetah.com					
Stonesong Press LLC 27 W 24th St Suite 510	New York	NY	10010	212-929-4600	486-9123
Web: www.stonesong.com					
Victory Productions Inc 55 Linden St	Worcester	MA	01609	508-755-0051	755-0025
Web: www.victoryprd.com					
Welcome Enterprises Inc 6 W 18th St 3rd Fl	New York	NY	10011	212-989-3200	989-3205
Web: www.welcomebooks.com					

95 BOOK STORES

	City	State	ZIP	Phone	Fax
Alibris Inc 1250 45th St Suite 100	Emeryville	CA	94608	510-594-4500	652-2403
Web: www.alibris.com					
Amazon.com Inc 1200 12th Ave S Suite 1200	Seattle	WA	98144	206-266-1000	266-7601*
NASDAQ: AMZN ■ **Fax:* Hum Res ■ *TF Cust Svc:* 800-201-7575 ■ *Web:* www.amazon.com					
Antigone Books 411 N 4th Ave	Tucson	AZ	85705	520-792-3715	882-8802
Web: www.antigonebooks.com					
Archambault Group Inc 500 Rue Sainte-Catherine E	Montreal	QC	H2L2C6	514-849-6206	849-0764
TF: 877-849-8589 ■ *Web:* www.archambault.ca					
Atlantic Book Warehouse 979 Bethlehem Pike	Montgomeryville	PA	18936	215-661-0450	661-0472
TF: 800-237-7323 ■ *Web:* www.atlanticbooks.us					
Barbour Publishing Inc PO Box 719	Uhrichsville	OH	44683	740-922-6045	
Web: www.barbourbooks.com					
Barnes & Noble College Bookstores Inc 120 Mountain View Blvd	Basking Ridge	NJ	07920	908-991-2665	
Web: www.bkstore.com					
Barnes & Noble Inc 122 5th Ave	New York	NY	10011	212-633-3300	807-6105*
NYSE: BKS ■ **Fax:* Cust Svc ■ *Web:* www.barnesandnoble.com					
barnesandnoble.com Inc 76 9th Ave Fl 9	New York	NY	10011	212-414-6000	
TF: 800-843-2665 ■ *Web:* www.barnesandnoble.com					
Bear Pond Books 77 Main St	Montpelier	VT	05602	802-229-0774	229-1069
Web: www.bearpondbooks.com					
Becks Bookstores Inc 4520 N Broadway St 22	Chicago	IL	60640	773-784-7963	784-0066
Web: www.becksbooks.com					
Berean Christian Stores 9415 Meridiqan Way	West Chester	OH	45069	513-729-1500	728-6975
TF Cust Svc: 877-405-7194 ■ *Web:* www.berean.com					
Book Loft 631 S 3rd St	Columbus	OH	43206	614-464-1774	464-3443
Web: www.bookloft.com					
Book Passage 51 Tamal Vista Blvd	Corte Madera	CA	94925	415-927-0960	927-3069
TF: 800-999-7909 ■ *Web:* www.bookpassage.com					
Book Revue 313 New York Ave	Huntington	NY	11743	631-271-1442	271-5890
Web: www.bookrevue.com					
Book Soup 8818 Sunset Blvd	West Hollywood	CA	90069	310-659-3110	659-3410
TF: 800-764-2665 ■ *Web:* www.booksoup.com					
BookBuyers 317 Castro St	Mountain View	CA	94041	650-968-7323	
Web: www.bookbuyers.com					
BookCloseouts Inc 340 Welland Ave	Saint Catharines	ON	L2R7L9	905-680-7230	680-7218
TF: 888-402-7323 ■ *Web:* www.bookcloseouts.com					
BookPeople 603 N Lamar	Austin	TX	78703	512-472-5050	482-8495
TF: 800-853-9757 ■ *Web:* www.bookpeople.com					
Books & Books 265 Aragon Ave	Coral Gables	FL	33134	305-442-4408	444-9751
TF: 888-626-6576 ■ *Web:* www.booksandbooks.com					
Books on the Square 471 Angell St	Providence	RI	02906	401-331-9097	331-2845
TF: 888-669-9660 ■ *Web:* www.booksq.com					
Books-A-Million Inc 402 Industrial Ln	Birmingham	AL	35211	205-942-3737	945-1772
NASDAQ: BAMM ■ *TF:* 800-201-3550 ■ *Web:* www.booksamillion.com					
BookSense.com 200 White Plains Rd	Tarrytown	NY	10591	914-591-2665	591-2720
TF: 800-637-0037 ■ *Web:* www.indiebound.org					
Borders Group Inc 100 Phoenix Dr	Ann Arbor	MI	48108	734-477-1100	477-4545
NYSE: BGP ■ *TF:* 800-566-6616 ■ *Web:* www.borders.com					
Borders Properties Inc 100 Phoenix Dr	Ann Arbor	MI	48108	734-477-1100	477-4545
TF Cust Svc: 800-566-6616 ■ *Web:* www.borders.com					
Boulder Book Store 1107 Pearl St	Boulder	CO	80302	303-447-2074	447-3946
TF: 800-244-4651 ■ *Web:* www.boulderbookstore.com					
Brazos Bookstore 2421 Bissonnet	Houston	TX	77005	713-523-0701	523-1829
Web: www.brazosbookstore.com					
Brookline Booksmith 279 Harvard St	Brookline	MA	02446	617-566-6660	734-9125
Web: www.brooklinebooksmith.com					
Changing Hands Bookstore 6428 S McClintock Dr	Tempe	AZ	85283	480-730-0205	730-1196
Web: www.changinghands.com					
Chaucer's Books 3321 State St	Santa Barbara	CA	93105	805-682-6787	682-1129
Web: www.chaucersbooks.com					
City Lights Booksellers 261 Columbus Ave	San Francisco	CA	94133	415-362-8193	362-4921
Web: www.citylights.com					
Cody's Books Inc 1730 4th St	Berkeley	CA	94710	510-559-9500	
TF: 800-995-1180 ■ *Web:* www.codysbooks.com					
Curious George Goes to WordsWorth 1 John F Kennedy St	Cambridge	MA	02138	617-498-0062	498-0061
TF: 800-899-2202 ■ *Web:* www.curiousg.com					
Deseret Book Co 45 W S Temple	Salt Lake City	UT	84144	801-534-1515	453-3876*
**Fax Area Code:* 800 ■ *TF:* 800-453-4532 ■ *Web:* www.deseretbook.com					
Dickens Books Ltd 219 N Milwaukee St 3rd Fl	Milwaukee	WI	53202	414-270-3434	274-8690
TF: 800-236-7323 ■ *Web:* 800ceoread.com					
EBSCO Book Services PO Box 1943	Birmingham	AL	35201	205-991-6600	991-1479
TF Cust Svc: 800-815-9627 ■ *Web:* www.ebsco.com/home/about/ebs.asp					
eFollett.com 1818 Swift Dr	Oak Brook	IL	60522	800-381-5151	279-2569*
**Fax Area Code:* 630 ■ *TF:* 800-381-5151 ■ *Web:* www.efollett.com					
Elliott Bay Book Co 101 S Main St	Seattle	WA	98104	206-624-6600	903-1601
TF: 800-962-5311 ■ *Web:* www.elliottbaybook.com					
Family Christian Stores Inc 5300 Patterson Ave	Grand Rapids	MI	49530	616-554-8700	554-8608
Web: www.familychristian.com					
Follett Corp 2233 W St	River Grove	IL	60171	708-583-2000	452-0169
TF: 800-621-4345 ■ *Web:* www.follett.com					
Follett Higher Education Group 1818 Swift Dr	Oak Brook	IL	60523	630-279-2330	279-2569
TF: 800-323-4506 ■ *Web:* www.fheg.follett.com					

Name / Address	City	State	ZIP	Phone	Fax
Full Circle Bookstore 1900 NW Expy	Oklahoma City	OK	73118	405-842-2900	842-2894
TF: 800-683-7323 ■ *Web:* www.fullcirclebooks.com					
Grason PO Box 669007	Charlotte	NC	28254	800-487-0433	401-3031*
**Fax Area Code:* 704 ■ *TF:* 800-487-0433 ■ *Web:* www.billygrahambookstore.org					
Half Price Books Records & Magazines Inc 5803E NW Hwy	Dallas	TX	75231	214-360-0833	379-8010
Web: www.hpb.com					
Half.com Inc PO Box 1469	Draper	UT	84020	800-545-9857	349-5782*
**Fax Area Code:* 877 ■ *TF:* 800-545-9857 ■ *Web:* www.half.ebay.com					
Harvard Square Co-op Society 1400 Massachusetts Ave	Cambridge	MA	02238	617-499-2000	547-2768
TF: 800-368-1882 ■ *Web:* www.thecoop.com					
Hastings Entertainment Inc 3601 Plains Blvd	Amarillo	TX	79102	806-351-2300	351-2211
NASDAQ: HAST ■ *TF Cust Svc:* 877-427-8464 ■ *Web:* www.gohastings.com					
Indigo Books & Music Inc 468 King St W Suite 500	Toronto	ON	M5V1L8	416-364-4499	364-0355
TF: 800-974-7381 ■ *Web:* www.chapters.indigo.ca					
Kinokuniya Bookstores 1073 Avenue of the Americas	New York	NY	10018	212-869-1700	869-1703
Web: www.bookweb.kinokuniya.co.jp					
Lee Booksellers 1265 S Cotner Blvd #25 Piedmont Shops	Lincoln	NE	68510	402-488-4416	489-2770
TF: 888-665-0999					
Left Bank Books 399 N Euclid Ave	Saint Louis	MO	63108	314-367-6731	367-3256
Web: www.left-bank.com					
LibertyTree 100 Swan Way	Oakland	CA	94621	510-568-6047	568-6040
TF: 800-927-8733 ■ *Web:* www.liberty-tree.org					
Matthews Book Co 11559 Rock Island Ct	Maryland Heights	MO	63043	314-432-1400	432-7044
TF: 800-633-2665 ■ *Web:* www.matthewsbooks.com					
Micawber Books 110-114 Nassau St	Princeton	NJ	08542	609-577-0319	
Web: www.micawber.com					
Moe's Books 2476 Telegraph Ave	Berkeley	CA	94704	510-849-2087	849-9938
Web: www.moesbooks.com					
Newbury Comics Inc 5 Guest St	Brighton	MA	02135	617-254-1666	254-2540
Web: www.newbury.com					
Northshire Information Inc 4869 Main St	Manchester Center	VT	05255	802-362-2200	362-1233
TF: 800-437-3700 ■ *Web:* www.northshire.com					
Page One Bookstore 11018 Montgomery Blvd NE	Albuquerque	NM	87111	505-294-2026	323-9849
TF: 800-521-4122 ■ *Web:* www.page1book.com					
Parable Christian Stores 3563 Empleo St	San Luis Obispo	CA	93401	805-543-2644	543-2136
TF: 888-644-0500 ■ *Web:* www.parable.com					
Poisoned Pen Bookstore 4014 N Goldwater Blvd	Scottsdale	AZ	85251	480-947-2974	945-1023
TF: 888-560-9919 ■ *Web:* www.poisonedpen.com					
Politics & Prose Bookstore 5015 Connecticut Ave NW	Washington	DC	20008	202-364-1919	966-7532
TF: 800-722-0790 ■ *Web:* www.politics-prose.com					
Powell's Books Inc 7 NW 9th Ave	Portland	OR	97209	503-228-0540	228-1142
TF: 800-878-7323 ■ *Web:* www.powells.com					
Powell's City of Books 40 NW 10th Ave	Portland	OR	97209	503-228-4651	228-4631
TF: 800-878-7323 ■ *Web:* www.powells.com					
Prairie Lights Bookstore 15 S Dubuque St	Iowa City	IA	52240	319-337-2681	887-3084
TF: 800-295-2665 ■ *Web:* www.prairielights.com					
Regulator Bookshop 720 9th St	Durham	NC	27705	919-286-2700	286-6063
Web: www.regbook.com					
Seminary Co-op Bookstore 5757 S University Ave	Chicago	IL	60637	773-752-4381	752-8507
Web: www.semcoop.com					
Shaman Drum Bookshop 311-315 S State St	Ann Arbor	MI	48104	734-662-7407	662-0017
TF: 800-490-7023					
Skylight Books 1818 N Vermont Ave	Los Angeles	CA	90027	323-660-1175	660-0232
Web: www.skylightbooks.com					
Social Studies School Service 10200 Jefferson Blvd PO Box 802	Culver City	CA	90232	310-839-2436	944-5432*
**Fax Area Code:* 800 ■ *TF:* 800-421-4246 ■ *Web:* www.socialstudies.com					
Square Books 160 Courthouse Sq	Oxford	MS	38655	662-236-2262	234-9630
TF: 800-648-4001 ■ *Web:* www.squarebooks.com					
Steve's Books & Magazines 2612 S Harvard	Tulsa	OK	74114	918-743-3544	743-5912
TF: 888-743-0989 ■ *Web:* www.stevesbooksmags.com					
Tatnuck Bookseller 18 Lyman St	Westborough	MA	01581	508-366-4959	366-7929
Web: www.tatnuck.com					
Tattered Cover Book Store Inc 1628 16th St	Denver	CO	80202	303-436-1070	629-1704
TF: 800-833-9327 ■ *Web:* www.tatteredcover.com					
That Bookstore in Blytheville 316 W Main St	Blytheville	AR	72315	870-763-3333	763-1125
Web: www.tbib.com					
University of Oregon Bookstore Inc PO Box 3176	Eugene	OR	97403	541-346-4331	346-3645
Web: www.uoduckstore.com					
University Press Books (UPB) 2430 Bancroft Way	Berkeley	CA	94704	510-548-0585	849-9214
TF: 800-676-8722 ■ *Web:* www.universitypressbooks.com					
Valley Books 220 N Pleasant St	Amherst	MA	01002	413-256-1508	
Web: www.valleybooks.com					
Viewpoint Books 548 Washington St	Columbus	IN	47201	812-376-0778	376-1089
Web: www.viewpointbooks.com					
Walden Book Co Inc 100 Phoenix Dr	Ann Arbor	MI	48108	734-477-1100	973-4541*
**Fax:* Hum Res ■ *TF:* 800-566-6616					

96 BOOKS, PERIODICALS, NEWSPAPERS - WHOL

Name / Address	City	State	ZIP	Phone	Fax
21st Century Christian Inc PO Box 40526	Nashville	TN	37204	615-383-3842	
TF: 800-251-2477 ■ *Web:* www.21stcc.com					
Advanced Marketing Services Inc 5880 Oberlin Dr Suite 400	San Diego	CA	92121	858-457-2500	452-2167
NYSE: MKT ■ *TF:* 800-695-3580 ■ *Web:* www.csn.advmkt.com					
American Book Co 11130 Kingston Pike Suite 1	Knoxville	TN	37934	865-966-7454	675-0557
Web: www.americanbookco.com					
Anderson News Co 6016 Brookvale Ln Suite 151	Knoxville	TN	37919	865-584-9765	450-3159
Web: www.andersonnews.com					
Baker & Taylor Inc 2550 W Tyvola Rd Suite 300	Charlotte	NC	28217	704-998-3100	998-3316
TF: 800-775-1800 ■ *Web:* www.btol.com					
BMI Educational Services PO Box 800	Dayton	NJ	08810	732-329-6991	986-9393*
**Fax Area Code:* 800 ■ *TF:* 800-222-8100 ■ *Web:* www.bmiedserv.com					
Book Wholesalers Inc 1847 Mercer Rd Suite D	Lexington	KY	40511	859-231-9789	888-6319*
**Fax Area Code:* 800 ■ *TF:* 800-888-4478 ■ *Web:* www.bwibooks.com					
Bookazine Co Inc 75 Hook Rd	Bayonne	NJ	07002	201-339-7777	339-7778
TF: 800-221-8112 ■ *Web:* www.bookazine.com					
Booksource Inc 1230 Macklind Ave	Saint Louis	MO	63110	314-647-0600	647-1923*
**Fax Area Code:* 800 ■ *TF:* 800-444-0435 ■ *Web:* www.booksource.com					
Brodart Co Book Services Div 500 Arch St	Williamsport	PA	17701	570-326-2461	326-6769
TF: 800-233-8467 ■ *Web:* www.books.brodart.com					
Capitol Fiber Inc 6610 Electronics Dr	Springfield	VA	22151	703-658-0200	658-0212
Choice Books LLC 2387 Grace Chapel Rd	Harrisonburg	VA	22801	540-434-1827	434-9894
TF: 800-224-5006 ■ *Web:* www.choicebooks.org					
Comag Marketing Group LLC 155 Village Blvd 3rd Fl	Princeton	NJ	08540	609-524-1800	524-1629
TF: 800-397-9130 ■ *Web:* www.i-cmg.com					
Directory Distributing Assoc (DDA) 160 Corporate Woods Ct	Bridgeton	MO	63044	314-592-8600	592-8790
TF: 800-325-1964 ■ *Web:* www.ddai.com					
EBSCO Magazine Express 2517 State Hwy 35 Bldg C Suite 201	Belmar	NJ	07719	732-223-7177	223-7178
Web: www.magazineexpress.com					
EBSCO Reception Room Subscription Services PO Box 830460	Birmingham	AL	35283	800-527-5901	995-1621*
**Fax Area Code:* 205 ■ *TF:* 800-527-5901 ■ *Web:* www.ebsco.com					
EBSCO Subscription Services PO Box 1943	Birmingham	AL	35201	205-991-1220	995-1518
Web: www.ebsco.com/home/about/ess.asp					
Educational Development Corp 10302 E 55th Pl	Tulsa	OK	74146	918-622-4522	665-7919
NASDAQ: EDUC ■ *TF:* 800-611-1655 ■ *Web:* www.edcpub.com					
Fall River News Co 25 Westwood Ave	New London	CT	06320	860-442-4394	439-0773
Follett Corp 2233 W St	River Grove	IL	60171	708-583-2000	452-0169
TF: 800-621-4345 ■ *Web:* www.follett.com					
Follett Educational Services 1433 International Pkwy	Woodridge	IL	60517	630-972-5600	638-4424*
**Fax Area Code:* 800 ■ *TF:* 800-621-4272 ■ *Web:* www.fes.follett.com					
Follett Library Resources 1340 Ridgeview Dr	McHenry	IL	60050	815-759-1700	759-9831
TF: 888-511-5114 ■ *Web:* www.flr.follett.com					
Harlequin Enterprises Ltd Distribution Ctr 3010 Walden Ave	Depew	NY	14043	716-684-1800	684-5066
TF: 800-873-8635 ■ *Web:* www.eharlequin.com					
Independent Publishers Group 814 N Franklin St	Chicago	IL	60610	312-337-0747	337-5985
TF Orders: 800-888-4741 ■ *Web:* www.ipgbook.com					
Ingram Book Group 1 Ingram Blvd	La Vergne	TN	37086	615-793-5000	213-7140
TF: 800-937-8000 ■ *Web:* www.ingrambookgroup.com					
JA Majors Co 1401 Lakeway Dr	Lewisville	TX	75057	972-353-1100	353-1300
TF: 800-633-1851 ■ *Web:* www.majors.com					
Jim Pattison News Group 3320 S Service Rd 2nd Fl	Burlington	ON	L7N3M6	905-681-1113	323-2420*
**Fax Area Code:* 888					
Kable News Co Inc 14 Wall St # 4C	New York	NY	10005	212-705-4600	705-4666
Web: www.kable.com					
Levy Home Entertainment LLC 4201 Raymond Dr	Hillside	IL	60162	708-547-4400	547-4503
Web: www.levybooks.com					
MBS Textbook Exchange Inc 2711 W Ash St	Columbia	MO	65203	573-445-2243	446-5256
TF Cust Svc: 800-325-0530 ■ *Web:* www.mbsbooks.com					
Midwest Library Service Inc 11443 St Charles Rock Rd	Bridgeton	MO	63044	314-739-3100	739-1326
TF: 800-325-8833 ■ *Web:* www.midwestls.com					
Milligan News Co Inc 150 N Autumn St	San Jose	CA	95110	408-298-3322	293-5669
TF: 800-873-2387 ■ *Web:* www.milligannews.com					
MindBranch Inc 131 Ashland St Suite 200	North Adams	MA	01247	413-662-3700	664-9791
TF: 800-774-4410 ■ *Web:* www.mindbranch.com					
Nebraska Book Co 4700 S 19th St	Lincoln	NE	68512	402-421-7300	869-0399*
**Fax Area Code:* 800 ■ *TF:* 800-869-0366 ■ *Web:* www.nebook.com					
Product Development Corp 20 Ragsdale Dr Suite 100	Monterey	CA	93940	831-333-1100	333-1122
Publishers Group West 1400 65th St Suite 250	Emeryville	CA	94608	510-595-3664	595-4228
TF: 800-788-3123 ■ *Web:* www.pgw.com					
Publishers' Warehouse PO Box 101927	Irondale	AL	35210	205-956-2078	956-7265
TF: 800-956-2078					

Phone | Fax

Quality Books Inc 1003 W Pines Rd ... Oregon IL 61061 815-732-4450 732-4499
TF Cust Svc: 800-323-4241 ■ *Web:* www.quality-books.com

Rittenhouse Book Distributors Inc
511 Feheley Dr ... King of Prussia PA 19406 610-277-1414 223-7488*
**Fax Area Code:* 800 ■ **Fax:* Orders ■ *TF Cust Svc:* 800-345-6425 ■ *Web:* www.rittenhouse.com

Scholastic Book Fairs Inc
1080 Greenwood Blvd ... Lake Mary FL 32746 407-829-7300 829-7898*
**Fax:* Mktg ■ *TF:* 800-874-4809 ■ *Web:* www.scholastic.com/bookfairs

Source Interlink Cos Inc
27500 Riverview Ctr Blvd ... Bonita Springs FL 34134 239-949-4450 949-7689
TF: 866-276-5584 ■ *Web:* www.sourceinterlink.com

Southwestern/Great American
2451 Atrium Way ... Nashville TN 37214 615-391-2500 391-2503*
**Fax:* Cust Svc ■ *TF Cust Svc:* 800-251-1542 ■ *Web:* www.southwestern.com

Spring Arbor Distributors 1 Ingram Blvd ... La Vergne TN 37086 800-395-4340 213-7140*
**Fax Area Code:* 615 ■ **Fax:* Sales ■ *TF:* 800-395-4340 ■ *Web:* www.springarbor.com

Swets Information Services
904 Black Horse Pike ... Runnemede NJ 08078 856-312-2690 312-2000
TF: 800-645-6595 ■ *Web:* www.swets.com

Turtleback Books 5701 Manufacturers Dr ... Madison WI 53704 800-448-8939 828-0401*
**Fax:* Orders ■ *TF:* 800-448-8939 ■ *Web:* www.turtlebackbooks.com

Verizon Publishing 621 Mid-Atlantic Pkwy ... Martinsburg WV 25401 304-267-1100 267-1104

Vulcan Service PO Box 522 ... Birmingham AL 35201 205-991-1374 980-3891
TF: 800-841-9600 ■ *Web:* www.vulcanservice.com

YBP Library Services 999 Maple St ... Contoocook NH 03229 603-746-3102 746-5628
TF: 800-258-3774 ■ *Web:* www.ybp.com

97 BOTANICAL GARDENS & ARBORETA

SEE ALSO Zoos & Wildlife Parks p. 2780

Phone | Fax

Adkins Arboretum 12610 Eveland Rd PO Box 100 ... Ridgely MD 21660 410-634-2847 634-2878
Web: www.adkinsarboretum.org

Afton Villa Gardens 9247 N Hwy 61 ... Saint Francisville LA 70775 225-635-6773

Airlie Gardens 300 Airlie Rd ... Wilmington NC 28401 910-798-7700 256-5083
Web: www.airliegardens.org

Alaska Botanical Garden
4601 Campbell Airstrip Rd ... Anchorage AK 99520 907-770-3692 770-0555
Web: www.alaskabg.org

Aldridge Botanical Gardens 3530 Lorna Rd ... Hoover AL 35216 205-682-8019 682-8085
Web: www.aldridgegardens.com

Alexandra Botanic Gardens
Wellesley College 106 Central St ... Wellesley MA 02481 781-283-3094 283-3642
Web: www.wellesley.edu/FOH/greenhouse.html

Alfred B Maclay State Gardens
3540 Thomasville Rd ... Tallahassee FL 32309 850-487-4556 487-8808
Web: www.floridastateparks.org/maclaygardens

Allan Gardens Conservatory
19 Horticultural Ave ... Toronto ON M5A2P2 416-392-7288 392-0318
Web: www.torontobotanicalgarden.ca/tours/allangardens.htm

Alta Vista Gardens 200 Civic Ctr Dr PO Box 1988 ... Vista CA 92084 760-945-3954
Web: www.altavistagardens.org

Amarillo Botanical Gardens 1400 Streit Dr ... Amarillo TX 79106 806-352-6513 352-6227
Web: www.amarillobotanicalgardens.org

Amy BH Greenwell Ethnobotanical Garden
82-6188 Mamalahoa Hwy PO Box 1053 ... Captain Cook HI 96704 808-323-3318 323-2394
Web: www.bishopmuseum.org/greenwell

Anderson Japanese Gardens
318 Spring Creek Rd ... Rockford IL 61107 815-229-9390 229-9391
Web: www.andersongardens.org

Anna Scripps Whitcomb Conservatory
876 Picnic Way ... Detroit MI 48207 313-852-4064 852-4074
Web: www.bibsociety.org

Annmarie Garden 13480 Dowell Rd PO Box 99 ... Dowell MD 20629 410-326-4640 326-4887
Web: www.annmariegarden.org

Arboretum at Arizona State University
826 E Apache Blvd PO Box 87 ... Tempe AZ 85287 480-965-2682 965-9470
Web: www.cfo.asu.edu/fdm-arboretum

Arboretum at California State University Fresno
2351 E Barstow Ave ... Fresno CA 93740 559-278-6930 278-7698
Web: www.csufresno.edu

Arboretum at Flagstaff
4001 S Woody Mountain Rd ... Flagstaff AZ 86001 928-774-1442 774-1441
Web: www.thearb.org

Arboretum at Penn State
336 Forest Resources Bldg ... University Park PA 16802 814-865-9118 865-3725
Web: www.arboretum.psu.edu

Arboretum at Penn State Behrend
4701 College Dr Glenhill Farmhouse ... Erie PA 16563 814-898-6160 898-6461
Web: www.psbehrend.psu.edu

Arboretum at the University of California Santa Cruz
1156 High St ... Santa Cruz CA 95064 831-427-2998 427-1524
Web: www2.ucsc.edu/arboretum

Arboretum of the Barnes Foundation
300 N Latch's Ln ... Merion PA 19066 610-667-0290 664-4026
Web: www.barnesfoundation.org

Arboretum The
Arboretum Rd University of Guelph ... Guelph ON N1G2W1 519-824-4120 763-9598
Web: www.uoguelph.ca/arboretum

Arnold Arboretum of Harvard University
125 Arborway ... Jamaica Plain MA 02130 617-524-1718 524-1418
Web: www.arboretum.harvard.edu

Phone | Fax

Atlanta Botanical Garden
1345 Piedmont Ave NE ... Atlanta GA 30309 404-876-5859 876-7472
Web: www.atlantabotanicalgarden.org

Awbury Arboretum & Historic Estate
1 Awbury Rd Francis Cope House ... Philadelphia PA 19138 215-849-2855 849-0213
Web: www.awbury.org

Bartlett Arboretum & Gardens
151 Brookdale Rd ... Stamford CT 06903 203-322-6971 595-9168
Web: www.bartlettarboretum.org

Bartram's Garden
54th St & Lindbergh Blvd ... Philadelphia PA 19143 215-729-5281 729-1047
Web: www.bartramsgarden.org

Beardsley Zoo 1875 Noble Ave ... Bridgeport CT 06610 203-394-6565 394-6566
Web: www.beardsleyzoo.org

Bellagio Conservatory & Botanical Gardens
3600 S Las Vegas Blvd ... Las Vegas NV 89109 702-693-7111 693-8508
TF: 888-987-6667 ■
Web: www.bellagiolasvegas.com/amenities/botanical-garden.aspx

Bellevue Botanical Garden 12001 Main St ... Bellevue WA 98005 425-452-2750 452-2748
Web: www.bellevuebotanical.org

Bellingrath Gardens & Home
12401 Bellingrath Garden Rd ... Theodore AL 36582 251-973-2217 973-0540
TF: 800-247-8420 ■ *Web:* www.bellingrath.org

Belmont - The Gari Melchers Estate & Memorial Gallery
224 Washington St ... Fredericksburg VA 22405 540-654-1015 654-1785
Web: www.umw.edu/belm

Berkshire Botanical Garden
Rt 102 & 183 PO Box 826 ... Stockbridge MA 01262 413-298-3926 298-4897
Web: www.berkshirebotanical.org

Bernheim Arboretum & Research Forest
State Hwy 245 PO Box 130 ... Clermont KY 40110 502-955-8512 955-4039
Web: www.bernheim.org

Berry Botanic Garden The
11505 SW Summerville Ave ... Portland OR 97219 503-636-4112 636-7496
Web: www.berrybot.org

Better Homes & Gardens Test Garden
15th St & Grand Ave ... Des Moines IA 50309 515-284-3994

Betty Ford Alpine Gardens 183 Gore Creek Dr ... Vail CO 81657 970-476-0103 476-1685
Web: www.bettyfordalpinegardens.org

Bicentennial Gardens 1105 Hobbs Rd ... Greensboro NC 27410 336-297-4162 373-7941

Bickelhaupt Arboretum 340 S 14th St ... Clinton IA 52732 563-242-4771
Web: www.bickarb.org

Birmingham Botanical Gardens
2612 Ln Pk Rd ... Birmingham AL 35223 205-414-3900 414-3906
Web: www.bbgardens.org

Blithewold Mansion Gardens & Arboretum
101 Ferry Rd Rt 114 ... Bristol RI 02809 401-253-2707 253-0412
Web: www.blithewold.org

Bloedel Floral Conservatory
33rd Ave & Cambie St Queen Elizabeth Pk ... Vancouver BC V5X1C5 604-257-8584 257-2412
Web: www.vancouver.ca/parks/parks/bloedel/index.htm

Bloedel Reserve The
7571 NE Dolphin Dr ... Bainbridge Island WA 98110 206-842-7631 842-3295
Web: www.bloedelreserve.org

Boerner Botanical Gardens
9400 Boerner Dr ... Hales Corners WI 53130 414-525-5601 525-5610
Web: www.boernerbotanicalgardens.org

Botanic Garden of Smith College
Smith College ... NorthHampton MA 01063 413-585-2740 585-2744
Web: www.smith.edu/garden

Botanica the Wichita Gardens
701 N Amidon Ave ... Wichita KS 67203 316-264-0448 264-0587
Web: www.botanica.org

Botanical Garden of the Ozarks
4703 N Crossover Rd PO Box 10407 ... Fayetteville AR 72764 479-750-2620 756-1920
Web: www.bgozarks.org

Botanical Gardens at Asheville
151 WT Weaver Blvd ... Asheville NC 28804 828-252-5190 252-1211
Web: www.ashevillebotanicalgardens.org

Botanical Research Institute of Texas
500 E 4th St ... Fort Worth TX 76102 817-332-4441 332-4112
Web: www.brit.org

Bowman's Hill Wildflower Preserve
1635 River Rd PO Box 685 ... New Hope PA 18938 215-862-2924 862-1846
Web: www.bhwp.org

Boxerwood Nature Center & Woodland Garden
963 Ross Rd ... Lexington VA 24450 540-463-2697 463-1953
Web: www.boxerwood.org

Boyce Thompson Arboretum 37615 US Hwy 60 ... Superior AZ 85273 520-689-2723 689-5858
Web: www.ag.arizona.edu/bta

Brenton Arboretum 25141 260th St ... Dallas Center IA 50063 515-992-4211 992-3303
Web: www.thebrentonarboretum.org

Brookgreen Gardens 1931 Brookgreen Dr ... Murrells Inlet SC 29576 843-235-6000 235-6039
TF: 800-849-1931 ■ *Web:* www.brookgreen.org

Brooklyn Botanic Garden 1000 Washington Ave ... Brooklyn NY 11225 718-623-7200 857-2430
Web: www.bbg.org

	City	State	ZIP	Phone	Fax
Brookside Gardens 1800 Glenallan Ave *Web:* www.montgomeryparks.org	Wheaton	MD	20902	301-962-1400	962-7878
Buffalo & Erie County Botanical Gardens 2655 S Pk Ave *Web:* www.buffalogardens.com	Buffalo	NY	14218	716-827-1584	828-0091
Butchart Gardens The 800 Benvenuto Ave *TF:* 866-652-4422 ■ *Web:* www.butchartgardens.com	Brentwood Bay	BC	V8M1J8	250-652-4422	652-7751
Cabrillo College Environmental Horticultural Center & Botanic Gardens 6500 Soquel Dr www.cabrillo.edu/academics/horticulture/hortcenterhome.html	Aptos	CA	95003	831-479-6100	
Calgary Zoo Botanical Garden & Prehistoric Park 1300 Zoo Rd NE *TF:* 800-588-9993 ■ *Web:* www.calgaryzoo.ab.ca	Calgary	AB	T2M4R8	403-232-9300	237-7582
Camden Children's Garden 3 Riverside Dr *Web:* www.camdenchildrensgarden.org	Camden	NJ	08103	856-365-8733	365-8733
Cape Fear Botanical Garden 536 N Eastern Blvd PO Box 53485 *Web:* www.capefearbg.org	Fayetteville	NC	28301	910-486-0221	486-4209
Carleen Bright Arboretum 9001 Bosque Blvd *Web:* www.woodway-texas.com	Woodway	TX	76712	254-399-9204	399-9216
Cave Hill Cemetery & Arboretum 701 Baxter Ave *Web:* www.cavehillcemetery.com	Louisville	KY	40204	502-451-5630	451-5655
Cedar Valley Arboretum & Botanic Gardens 3336 Kimball Ave *Web:* www.cedarvalleyarboretum.org	Waterloo	IA	50702	319-226-4966	226-4966
Centennial Conservatory 1601 Dease St	Thunder Bay	ON	P7E6S4	807-622-7036	622-7602
Chanticleer Garden 786 Church Rd *Web:* www.chanticleergarden.org	Wayne	PA	19087	610-687-4163	293-0149
Charlotte Botanical Gardens & Sculpture Garden Biology Dept University of N Carolina Charlotte 9201 University City Blvd *Web:* gardens.uncc.edu	Charlotte	NC	28223	704-687-2364	687-3128
Cheekwood Museum of Art & Botanical Garden 1200 Forrest Pk Dr *TF:* 877-356-8150 ■ *Web:* www.cheekwood.org	Nashville	TN	37205	615-356-8000	353-0919
Chesapeake Arboretum 624 Oak Grove Rd *Web:* www.chesapeakearboretum.com	Chesapeake	VA	23328	757-382-7060	
Cheyenne Botanic Gardens 710 S Lions Pk Dr *Web:* www.botanic.org	Cheyenne	WY	82001	307-637-6458	637-6453
Chicago Botanic Garden 1000 Lake Cook Rd *Web:* www.chicagobotanic.org	Glencoe	IL	60022	847-835-5440	835-4484
Chihuahuan Desert Research Institute (CDRI) 43869 State Hwy 118 PO Box 905 *Web:* www.cdri.org	Fort Davis	TX	79734	432-364-2499	364-2686
Chimney Rock Park 431 Main St *TF:* 800-277-9611 ■ *Web:* www.chimneyrockpark.com	Chimney Rock	NC	28720	828-625-9611	625-9610
Cincinnati Zoo & Botanical Garden 3400 Vine St *TF:* 800-944-4776 ■ *Web:* www.cincinnatizoo.org	Cincinnati	OH	45220	513-281-4700	559-7790
Cleveland Botanical Garden 11030 E Blvd *TF:* 888-853-7091 ■ *Web:* www.cbgarden.org	Cleveland	OH	44106	216-721-1600	721-2056
Cleveland Metroparks Zoo 3900 Wildlife Way *Web:* www.clemetzoo.com	Cleveland	OH	44109	216-661-6500	
Clovis Botanical Garden 945 N Clovis Ave *Web:* www.clovisbotanicalgarden.org	Clovis	CA	93611	559-298-0391	
Coastal Maine Botanical Gardens PO Box 234 *Web:* www.mainegardens.org	Boothbay	ME	04537	207-633-4333	633-2366
Colasanti's Tropical Gardens 1550 Rd 3 E *Web:* www.colasanti.com	Kingsville	ON	N0P2G0	519-326-3287	322-2302
Como Zoo & Conservatory 1225 Estabrook Dr *Web:* www.ci.stpaul.mn.us/depts/parks/comopark	Saint Paul	MN	55103	651-487-8200	487-8254
Connecticut College Arboretum 270 Mohegan Ave PO Box 5201 *Web:* arboretum.conncoll.edu	New London	CT	06320	860-439-5020	439-5482
Conservatory Garden 14 E 60th St Central Pk *Web:* www.centralparknyc.org	New York	NY	10022	212-310-6600	860-1388
Conservatory of Flowers San Francisco Recreation & Pk Dept 100 John F Kennedy Dr *Web:* www.conservatoryofflowers.org	San Francisco	CA	94118	415-846-0538	666-7257
Cooley Gardens 225 W Main St *Web:* www.cooleygardens.org	Lansing	MI	48933	517-483-4277	483-6062
Cornell Plantations 1 Plantations Rd *Web:* www.plantations.cornell.edu	Ithaca	NY	14850	607-255-2400	255-2404
Cox Arboretum MetroPark 6733 Springboro Pike *Web:* www.metroparks.org/Parks/CoxArboretum	Dayton	OH	45449	937-434-9005	438-1221
Crosby Arboretum 370 Ridge Rd *Web:* www.msstate.edu	Picayune	MS	39466	601-799-2311	799-2372
CW Post Community Arboretum Long Island University 720 Northern Blvd *Web:* www.liu.edu	Brookville	NY	11548	516-299-2340	299-3223
Cylburn Arboretum 4915 Greenspring Ave *Web:* www.cylburnassociation.org	Baltimore	MD	21209	410-396-0180	367-8039
Dallas Arboretum & Botanical Garden 8525 Garland Rd *Web:* www.dallasarboretum.org	Dallas	TX	75218	214-515-6500	515-6522
Daniel Stowe Botanical Garden 6500 S New Hope Rd *Web:* www.dsbg.org	Belmont	NC	28012	704-825-4490	829-1240
Dawes Arboretum 7770 Jacksontown Rd SE *TF:* 800-443-2937 ■ *Web:* www.dawesarb.org	Newark	OH	43056	740-323-2355	323-4058
Delaware Center for Horticulture 1810 N DuPont St *Web:* www.thedch.org	Wilmington	DE	19806	302-658-6262	658-6267
Denver Botanic Gardens 1005 York St *Web:* www.botanicgardens.org	Denver	CO	80206	720-865-3500	865-3731
Des Moines Botanical Ctr 909 Robert D Ray Dr *Web:* www.botanicalcenter.com	Des Moines	IA	50316	515-323-6291	309-2484
Descanso Gardens 1418 Descanso Dr *Web:* www.descansogardens.org	La Canada	CA	91011	818-949-4200	790-3291
Desert Botanical Garden 1201 N Galvin Pkwy *Web:* www.dbg.org	Phoenix	AZ	85008	480-941-1225	481-8124
Devonian Botanic Garden University of Alberta *Web:* www.ales.ualberta.ca	Edmonton	AB	T6G2M7	780-987-3054	987-4141
Donald M Kendall Sculpture Gardens at PepsiCo Headquarters 700 Anderson Hill Rd	Purchase	NY	10577	914-253-2082	
Dothan Area Botanical Gardens 5130 Headland Ave *Web:* www.dabg.com	Dothan	AL	36303	334-793-3224	793-5275
Dow Gardens 1018 W Main St *TF:* 800-362-4874 ■ *Web:* www.dowgardens.org	Midland	MI	48640	989-631-2677	631-0675
Dr Sun Yat-Sen Classical Chinese Garden 578 Carrall St *Web:* www.vancouverchinesegarden.com	Vancouver	BC	V6B5K2	604-662-3207	682-4008
Dubuque Arboretum & Botanical Gardens 3800 Arboretum Dr *Web:* www.dubuquearboretum.com	Dubuque	IA	52001	563-556-2100	556-2443
Duke Farms 80 Rt 206 S *Web:* www.dukefarms.org	Hillsborough	NJ	08844	908-722-3700	
Dyck Arboretum of the Plains 177 W Hickory St *Web:* www.dyckarboretum.org	Hesston	KS	67062	620-327-8127	327-3151
Earl Burns Miller Japanese Garden 1250 Bellflower Blvd *Web:* www.csulb.edu/~jgarden	Long Beach	CA	90840	562-985-8885	985-5362
East Tennessee State University Arboretum Dept of Biological Studies PO Box 70703 *Web:* www.etsu.edu	Johnson City	TN	37614	423-439-8635	
East Texas Arboretum 1601 Legendary Ln *Web:* www.eastexasarboretum.org	Athens	TX	75751	903-675-5630	675-1618
Edith J Carrier Arboretum & Botanical Gardens at James Madison University 780 University Blvd MSC 3705 *Web:* www.jmu.edu	Harrisonburg	VA	22807	540-568-3194	568-5115
Elizabeth Gamble Garden 1431 Waverley St *Web:* www.gamblegarden.org	Palo Alto	CA	94301	650-329-1356	329-1688
Elizabeth Park Rose Gardens 150 Walbridge St *Web:* www.elizabethpark.org/rose_garden.htm	West Hartford	CT	06102	860-231-9443	
Elizabethan Gardens 1411 National Pk Dr *Web:* www.elizabethangardens.org	Manteo	NC	27954	252-473-3234	473-3244
Enid A Haupt Glass Garden 400 E 34th St NYU Medical Ctr Rusk Inst of Rehabilitative Medicine *Web:* www.med.nyu.edu	New York	NY	10016	212-263-6058	263-2091
Erie Zoo 423 W 38th St *Web:* www.eriezoo.org	Erie	PA	16508	814-864-4091	864-1140
Fairchild Tropical Botanic Garden 10901 Old Cutler Rd *Web:* www.fairchildgarden.org	Coral Gables	FL	33156	305-667-1651	661-8953
Fell Arboretum at Illnois State University PO Box 9000 *Web:* www.arboretum.illinoisstate.edu	Normal	IL	61790	309-438-2801	438-2089
Fellows Riverside Gardens 123 McKinley Ave	Youngstown	OH	44509	330-740-7116	740-7128
Fernwood Botanical Gardens & Nature Preserve 13988 Range Line Rd *Web:* www.fernwoodbotanical.org	Niles	MI	49120	269-695-6491	695-6688
Filoli 86 Canada Rd *Web:* www.filoli.org	Woodside	CA	94062	650-364-8300	366-7836
Flamingo Gardens 3750 S Flamingo Rd *Web:* www.flamingogardens.org	Davie	FL	33330	954-473-2955	473-1738
Florida Botanical Gardens 12520 Ulmerton Rd *Web:* www.flbg.org	Largo	FL	33774	727-582-2100	582-2149
Foellinger-Freimann Botanical Conservatory 1100 S Calhoun St *Web:* www.botanicalconservatory.org	Fort Wayne	IN	46802	260-427-6440	427-6450
For-Mar Nature Preserve & Arboretum 2142 N Genesee Rd *Web:* www.geneseecountyparks.org	Burton	MI	48509	810-789-8567	743-0541
Forestiere Underground Gardens 5021 W Shaw Ave *Web:* www.undergroundgardens.com	Fresno	CA	93722	559-271-0734	
Fort Worth Botanic Garden 3220 Botanic Garden Blvd *Web:* www.fwbg.org	Fort Worth	TX	76107	817-871-7686	871-7638
Foster Botanical Garden 50 N Vineyard Blvd *Web:* www.honolulu.gov/parks/hbg/fbg.htm	Honolulu	HI	96817	808-522-7066	522-7050
Founders Memorial Garden University of Georgia School of Environmental Design 609 Caldwell Hall *Web:* www.uga.edu/gardenclub/Founder.html	Athens	GA	30602	706-542-8972	542-4236
Franklin Park Conservatory & Chihuly Collection 1777 E Broad St *TF:* 800-241-7275 ■ *Web:* www.fpconservatory.org	Columbus	OH	43203	614-645-8733	645-5921
Frederik Meijer Gardens & Sculpture Park 1000 E Beltline Ave NE *Web:* www.meijergardens.org	Grand Rapids	MI	49525	616-957-1580	957-5792
Friends of the Topiary Park 480 E Town St *Web:* www.topiarygarden.org	Columbus	OH	43215	614-645-0197	645-0172
Fruit & Spice Park 24801 SW 187th Ave *Web:* www.floridaplants.com/fruit&spice	Homestead	FL	33031	305-247-5727	245-3369
Fullerton Arboretum 1900 Associated Rd *Web:* www.fullertonarboretum.org	Fullerton	CA	92831	657-278-3407	278-7066
Ganna Walska Lotusland 695 Ashley Rd *Web:* www.lotusland.org	Santa Barbara	CA	93108	805-969-3767	969-4423
Gardens of the American Rose Ctr 8877 Jefferson-Paige Rd *TF:* 800-637-6534 ■ *Web:* www.ars.org/ARC/gardens.htm	Shreveport	LA	71119	318-938-5402	938-5402
Gardens of the Fox Cities 1313 E Witzke Blvd *Web:* www.gardensfoxcities.org	Appleton	WI	54911	920-993-1900	993-9492

Name / Address	City	State	ZIP	Phone	Fax
Gardens on Spring Creek 2145 Centre Ave	Fort Collins	CO	80526	970-416-2486	416-2280
Web: www.fcgov.com					
Garfield Park Conservatory					
300 N Central Pk Ave	Chicago	IL	60624	312-746-5100	638-1777*
**Fax Area Code: 773* ■ *Web:* www.garfield-conservatory.org					
Garvan Woodland Gardens					
550 Arkridge Rd PO Box 22240	Hot Springs	AR	71903	501-262-9300	262-9301
TF: 800-366-4664 ■ *Web:* www.garvangardens.org					
George L Luthy Memorial Botanical Gardens					
2218 N Prospect Rd	Peoria	IL	61603	309-686-3362	685-6240
Web: www.peoriapark.org					
Georgeson Botanical Garden					
University of Alaska Fairbanks Campus					
117 W Tanana Dr PO Box 757200	Fairbanks	AK	99775	907-474-7222	474-1841
Web: www.georgesonbg.org					
Georgia Southern Botanical Garden					
1505 Bland Ave PO Box 8039	Statesboro	GA	30460	912-871-1149	871-1777
Web: www.ceps.georgiasouthern.edu					
Gifford Arboretum					
1301 Memorial Dr Rm 190					
University of Miami	Coral Gables	FL	33124	305-284-5364	284-3039
Web: www.bio.miami.edu/arboretum					
Gilroy Gardens Family Theme Park					
3050 Hecker Pass Hwy	Gilroy	CA	95020	408-840-7100	
Web: www.gilroygardens.org					
Glacier Gardens Rainforest Adventure					
7600 Old Glacier Hwy	Juneau	AK	99801	907-790-3377	790-3907
Web: www.glaciergardens.com					
Goodstay Gardens					
2600 Pennsylvania Ave					
University of Delaware Goodstay Ctr	Wilmington	DE	19806	302-573-4450	652-0116
Greater Philadelphia Gardens					
100 E Northwestern Ave					
c/o Morris Arboretum	Philadelphia	PA	19118	215-247-5777	247-7862
Web: www.greaterphiladelphiagardens.org					
Green Bay Botanical Garden 2600 Larsen Rd	Green Bay	WI	54303	920-490-9457	490-9461
TF: 877-355-4224 ■ *Web:* www.gbbg.org					
Green Spring Gardens Park					
4603 Green Spring Rd	Alexandria	VA	22312	703-642-5173	642-8095
Web: www.fairfaxcounty.gov/parks/gsgp					
Grotto The 8840 NE Skidmore St	Portland	OR	97220	503-254-7371	254-7948
Web: www.thegrotto.org					
Guadalupe River Park & Gardens					
438 Coleman Ave	San Jose	CA	95110	408-298-7657	288-9048
Web: www.grpg.org					
Halifax Public Gardens 5711 Sackville	Halifax	NS	B3H2C9	902-490-6509	435-8327
Web: www.halifaxpublicgardens.ca					
Harry P Leu Gardens 1920 N Forest Ave	Orlando	FL	32803	407-246-2620	246-2849
Web: www.leugardens.org					
Haverford College Arboretum					
370 Lancaster Ave	Haverford	PA	19041	610-896-1101	896-1095
Web: www.haverford.edu/Arboretum/home.htm					
Hawaii Tropical Botanical Garden					
27-717 Old Mamalahoa Hwy PO Box 80	Papaikou	HI	96781	808-964-5233	964-1338
Web: www.hawaiigarden.com					
Heathcote Botanical Gardens					
210 Savannah Rd	Fort Pierce	FL	34982	772-464-4672	489-2748
Web: www.heathcotebotanicalgardens.org					
Helen Avalynne Tawes Garden 580 Taylor Ave	Annapolis	MD	21401	410-260-8189	260-8191
TF: 800-830-3974 ■					
Web: www.dnr.state.md.us/publiclands/tawesgarden.html					
Hendricks Park & Gardens 1800 Skyline Blvd	Eugene	OR	97403	541-682-4812	
Web: www.eugene-or.gov					
Henry Schmieder Arboretum					
Delaware Valley College 700 E Butler Ave	Doylestown	PA	18901	215-489-2283	489-2404
Web: www.delval.edu					
Hershey Gardens 170 Hotel Rd	Hershey	PA	17033	717-534-3492	533-5095
Web: www.hersheygardens.org					
Hidden Lake Gardens 6214 Monroe Rd	Tipton	MI	49287	517-431-2060	431-9148
Web: www.hiddenlakegardens.msu.edu					
Highline SeaTac Botanical Gardens					
13735 24th Ave S PO Box 69384	SeaTac	WA	98168	206-391-4003	
Web: www.highlinegarden.org					
Highstead Arboretum					
127 Lonetown Rd PO Box 1097	Redding	CT	06875	203-938-8809	938-0343
Web: www.pages.prodigy.net/highsteadarboretum					
Hilltop Arboretum 11855 Highland Rd	Baton Rouge	LA	70810	225-767-6916	768-7740
Web: www.hilltop.lsu.edu/hilltop/hilltop.nsf/index					
Hilltop Garden & Nature Ctr					
Indiana University Campus 2367 E 10th St	Bloomington	IN	47408	812-855-2799	
Historic Bok Sanctuary 1151 Tower Blvd	Lake Wales	FL	33853	863-676-1408	676-6770
Web: www.boktower.org					
Hofstra University Arboretum					
129 Hofstra University	Hempstead	NY	11549	516-463-5924	463-5302
TF: 800-463-7872 ■ *Web:* www.hofstra.edu/COM/Arbor					
Holden Arboretum 9500 Sperry Rd	Kirtland	OH	44094	440-946-4400	602-3857
Web: www.holdenarb.org					
Honolulu Botanical Gardens					
50 N Vineyard Blvd	Honolulu	HI	96817	808-522-7060	522-7050
Web: www.honolulu.gov/parks/hbg					
Hoyt Arboretum 4000 SW Fairview Blvd	Portland	OR	97221	503-865-8733	823-5213
Web: www.hoytarboretum.org					
Hudson Gardens & Event Ctr					
6115 S Santa Fe Dr	Littleton	CO	80120	303-797-8565	797-8647
Web: www.hudsongardens.org					
Humber Arboretum 205 Humber College Blvd	Toronto	ON	M9W5L7	416-675-6622	675-2755
Web: www.humberarboretum.on.ca					
Humboldt Botanical Gardens 350 E St # 206	Eureka	CA	95501	707-442-5139	442-6634
Web: www.hbgf.org					
Huntington Library Art Collections & Botanical Gardens The					
1151 Oxford Rd	San Marino	CA	91108	626-405-2100	405-0225
Web: www.huntington.org					
Huntsville Botanical Garden					
4747 Bob Wallace Ave	Huntsville	AL	35805	256-830-4447	830-5314
TF: 877-930-4447 ■ *Web:* www.hsvbg.org					
Idaho Botanical Garden 2355 N Penitentiary Rd	Boise	ID	83712	208-343-8649	343-3601
TF: 877-527-8233 ■ *Web:* www.idahobotanicalgarden.org					
Inniswood Metro Gardens					
940 S Hempstead Rd	Westerville	OH	43081	614-895-6216	895-6352
Web: www.inniswood.org					
International Peace Garden					
Hwy 10 S PO Box 419	Boissevain	MB	R0K0E0	204-534-2510	263-3169*
**Fax Area Code: 701* ■ *TF:* 888-432-6733 ■ *Web:* www.peacegarden.com					
International Peace Garden Rt 1 PO Box 116	Dunseith	ND	58329	701-263-4390	263-3169
TF: 888-432-6733 ■ *Web:* www.peacegarden.com					
Iowa Arboretum 1875 Peach Ave	Madrid	IA	50156	515-795-3216	795-2619
Web: www.iowaarboretum.org					
Japanese Garden 611 SW Kingston Ave	Portland	OR	97205	503-223-4070	223-8303
Web: www.japanesegarden.com					
JC Raulston Arboretum					
North Carolina State University PO Box 7522	Raleigh	NC	27695	919-513-7457	515-5361
Web: www.ncsu.edu/jcraulstonarboretum					
Jenkins Arboretum (JA) 631 Berwyn Baptist Rd	Devon	PA	19333	610-647-8870	647-6664
Web: www.jenkinsarboretum.org					
JJ Neilson Arboretum					
Ridgetown College					
University of Guelph 120 Main St E	Ridgetown	ON	N0P2C0	519-674-1500	674-1515
Web: www.ridgetownc.on.ca/jjneilson					
Jungle Gardens Hwy 329	Avery Island	LA	70513	337-369-6243	369-6254
Jungle Island 1111 Parrot Jungle Trail	Miami	FL	33132	305-400-7000	400-7290
Web: www.jungleisland.com					
Kalmia Gardens of Coker College					
1624 W Carolina Ave	Hartsville	SC	29550	843-383-8145	383-8149
Web: www.coker.edu					
KC Irving Environmental Science Centre & Harriet Irving Botanical Gardens					
Acadia University					
32 University Ave PO Box 48	Wolfville	NS	B4P2R6	902-585-2665	585-1034
Web: www.acadiau.ca					
Kenilworth Aquatic Gardens					
1550 Anacostia Ave NE	Washington	DC	20019	202-426-6905	426-5991
Web: www.nps.gov/nace/keaq					
Key West Botanical Garden 5210 College Rd	Key West	FL	33040	305-296-1504	296-2242
Web: www.keywestbotanicalgarden.org					
Kingwood Ctr 900 Pk Ave	Mansfield	OH	44906	419-522-0211	
Web: www.kingwoodcenter.org					
Klehm Arboretum & Botanical Garden					
2701 S Main St	Rockford	IL	61102	815-965-8146	965-5914
TF: 888-419-0782 ■ *Web:* www.klehm.org					
Kruckeberg Botanic Garden					
20312 15th Ave NW	Shoreline	WA	98177	206-542-4777	
Web: www.kruckeberg.org					
Ladew Topiary Gardens 3535 Jarettsville Pike	Monkton	MD	21111	410-557-9466	557-7763
Web: www.ladewgardens.com					
Lady Bird Johnson Wildflower Ctr					
4801 LaCrosse Ave	Austin	TX	78739	512-292-4200	232-0156
TF: 877-945-3357 ■ *Web:* www.wildflower.org					
Lake Erie Arboretum at Frontier Park					
1650 Norcross Rd	Erie	PA	16510	814-825-1700	825-0775
Web: www.leaferie.org					
Lake Wilderness Arboretum					
22520 SE 248th St PO Box 72	Maple Valley	WA	98038	425-413-2572	
Web: www.lakewildernessarboretum.org					
Lakewold Gardens 12317 Gravelly Lake Dr SW	Lakewood	WA	98499	253-584-4106	584-3021
TF: 888-858-4106 ■ *Web:* www.lakewold.org					
Landis Arboretum 174 Lape Rd PO Box 186	Esperance	NY	12066	518-875-6935	875-6394
Web: www.landisarboretum.org					
Lauritzen Gardens Omaha's Botanical Ctr					
100 Bancroft St	Omaha	NE	68108	402-346-4002	346-8948
Web: www.omahabotanicalgardens.org					
Leach Botanical Garden					
6704 SE 122 Ave PO Box 90667	Portland	OR	97236	503-823-9503	823-9504
Web: www.leachgarden.org					
Leila Arboretum Society					
928 W Michigan Ave	Battle Creek	MI	49037	269-969-0270	969-0616
Web: www.leilaarboretumsociety.org					
Lewis Ginter Botanical Garden					
1800 Lakeside Ave	Richmond	VA	23228	804-262-9887	262-6329
Web: www.lewisginter.org					
Lincoln Botanical Garden & Arboretum (BGA)					
University of Nebraska 1309 N 17th St	Lincoln	NE	68588	402-472-2679	472-9615
Web: www.unl.edu/bga					
Living Desert Zoo & Gardens					
47900 Portola Ave	Palm Desert	CA	92260	760-346-5694	568-9685
Web: www.livingdesert.org					
Lockerly Arboretum 1534 Irwinton Rd	Milledgeville	GA	31061	478-452-2112	452-1020
Web: www.lockerly.org					
Locust Grove - Samuel Morse Historic Site					
2683 S Rd	Poughkeepsie	NY	12601	845-454-4500	485-7122
Web: www.lgny.org					
Long House Reserve 133 Hands Creek Rd	East Hampton	NY	11937	631-329-3568	329-4299
Web: www.longhouse.org					
Longwood Gardens PO Box 501	Kennett Square	PA	19348	610-388-1000	388-2079
TF: 800-737-5500 ■ *Web:* www.longwoodgardens.com					
Los Angeles County Arboretum & Botanic Garden					
301 N Baldwin Ave	Arcadia	CA	91007	626-821-3222	445-1217
Web: www.arboretum.org					
Los Angeles Zoo & Botanical Gardens					
5333 Zoo Dr	Los Angeles	CA	90027	323-644-4200	662-9786
Web: www.lazoo.org					
Lubbock Memorial Arboretum					
4111 University Ave	Lubbock	TX	79413	806-797-4520	
Web: www.lubbockarboretum.org					

Name / Address	City	State	Zip	Phone	Fax
Luther Burbank Home & Gardens 204 Santa Rosa Ave *Web:* www.lburbank.users.sonic.net	Santa Rosa	CA	95404	707-524-5445	524-5827
Mabery Gelvin Botanical Gardens 506 N Lombard St PO Box 1040 *Web:* www.ccfpd.org/Preserves/Attractions/BotanicalGarden.html	Mahomet	IL	61853	217-586-4630	586-6852
Magnolia Plantation & Gardens 3550 Ashley River Rd *TF:* 800-367-3517 ■ *Web:* www.magnoliaplantation.com	Charleston	SC	29414	843-571-1266	571-5346
Marie Selby Botanical Gardens 811 S Palm Ave *Web:* www.selby.org	Sarasota	FL	34236	941-366-5731	366-9807
Marjorie McNeely Conservatory at Como Park 1225 Estabrook Dr *Web:* www.comozooconservatory.org	Saint Paul	MN	55103	651-487-8201	487-8203
Markham Regional Arboretum 1202 La Vista Ave *Web:* www.markhamarboretum.org	Concord	CA	94521	925-681-2968	
Marywood University Arboretum 2300 Adams Ave *Web:* www.marywood.edu	Scranton	PA	18509	570-348-6218	
Matthaei Botanical Gardens 1800 N Dixboro Rd *Web:* www.lsa.umich.edu/mbg	Ann Arbor	MI	48105	734-647-7600	998-6205
McKee Botanical Garden 350 US 1 *Web:* www.mckeegarden.org	Vero Beach	FL	32962	772-794-0601	794-0602
Meadowlark Botanical Gardens 9750 Meadowlark Gardens Ct *Web:* www.nvrpa.org/park/meadowlark_botanical_gardens	Vienna	VA	22182	703-255-3631	255-2392
Memorial University of Newfoundland Botanical Garden Memorial University 306 Mt Scio Rd *Web:* www.mun.ca/botgarden	Saint John's	NL	A1C5S7	709-737-8590	737-8596
Memphis Botanic Garden 750 Cherry Rd *Web:* www.memphisbotanicgarden.com	Memphis	TN	38117	901-576-4100	682-1561
Mendocino Coast Botanical Gardens 18220 N Hwy 1 *Web:* www.gardenbythesea.org	Fort Bragg	CA	95437	707-964-4352	964-3114
Mepkin Abbey Botanical Garden 1098 Mepkin Abbey Rd *Web:* www.mepkinabbey.org	Moncks Corner	SC	29461	843-761-8509	761-6719
Mercer Arboretum & Botanic Gardens 22306 Aldine Westfield Rd *Web:* www.hcp4.net/mercer	Humble	TX	77338	281-443-8731	209-9767
Miami Beach Botanical Garden 2000 Convention Ctr Dr *Web:* www.mbgarden.org	Miami Beach	FL	33139	305-673-7256	
Minnesota Landscape Arboretum 3675 Arboretum Dr *Web:* www.arboretum.umn.edu	Chaska	MN	55318	952-443-1400	443-2521
Missouri Botanical Garden 4344 Shaw Blvd *TF:* 800-642-8842 ■ *Web:* www.mobot.org	Saint Louis	MO	63110	314-577-5100	577-9595
Missouri State Arboretum NW Missouri State University 800 University Dr *Web:* www.nwmissouri.edu/arboretum	Maryville	MO	64468	660-562-1329	562-1937
Mobile Botanical Gardens 5151 Museum Dr *Web:* www.mobilebotanicalgardens.org	Mobile	AL	36608	251-342-0555	342-3149
Montgomery Botanical Ctr 11901 Old Cutler Rd *Web:* www.montgomerybotanical.org	Miami	FL	33156	305-667-3800	661-5984
Montreal Botanical Garden 4101 Sherbrooke St E *Web:* www2.ville.montreal.qc.ca	Montreal	QC	H1X2B2	514-872-1400	872-1455
Morris Arboretum of the University of Pennsylvania 100 E Northwestern Ave *Web:* www.business-services.upenn.edu/arboretum	Philadelphia	PA	19118	215-247-5777	247-7862
Morton Arboretum 4100 Illinois Rt 53 *Web:* www.mortonarb.org	Lisle	IL	60532	630-968-0074	719-2433
Morven Museum & Gardens 55 Stockton St *Web:* www.historicmorven.org	Princeton	NJ	08540	609-924-8144	924-8331
Mount Holyoke College Botanic Garden 50 College St *Web:* www.mtholyoke.edu/offices/botan	South Hadley	MA	01075	413-538-2116	538-3243
Mount Pisgah Arboretum 34901 Frank Parrish Rd *Web:* mountpisgaharboretum.org	Eugene	OR	97405	541-747-1504	741-4904
Mountain Top Arboretum PO Box 379 *Web:* www.mtarbor.org	Tannersville	NY	12485	518-589-3903	589-3903
Mounts Botanical Garden 531 N Military Trail *Web:* www.mounts.org	West Palm Beach	FL	33415	561-233-1749	233-1782
Muttart Conservatory 9626 96A St *Web:* www.edmonton.ca	Edmonton	AB	T6C4L8	780-496-8755	496-8747
Mynelle Gardens 4736 Clinton Blvd *Web:* www.jacksonms.gov/visitors/mynellgardens	Jackson	MS	39209	601-960-1894	922-5759
Myriad Botanical Gardens/Crystal Bridge Tropical Conservatory 301 W Reno Ave *Web:* www.myriadgardens.com	Oklahoma City	OK	73102	405-297-3995	297-3620
Naples Botanical Garden 4820 Bayshore Dr *Web:* www.naplesgarden.org	Naples	FL	34112	239-643-7275	649-7306
National Garden 100 Maryland Ave *Web:* www.usbg.gov	Washington	DC	20001	202-225-8333	225-7910
National Tropical Botanical Garden 3530 Papalina Rd *Web:* www.ntbg.org	Kalaheo	HI	96741	808-332-7324	332-9765
Native Plant Center at Westchester Community College 75 Grasslands Rd *Web:* www.nativeplantcenter.org	Valhalla	NY	10595	914-606-7870	606-6143
Nebraska Statewide Arboretum University of Nebraska 206 Biochemistry Hall *Web:* www.arboretum.unl.edu	Lincoln	NE	68583	402-472-2971	472-8095
New Brunswick Botanical Gardens 15 Main St *Web:* www.jardinnbgarden.com	Saint-Jacques	NB	E7B1A3	506-737-4444	737-5389
New England Tropical Conservatory (NETC) 413 S St PO Box 4715 *Web:* www.netrop.org	Bennington	VT	05201	802-447-7419	681-4371
New England Wild Flower Society 180 Hemenway Rd *Web:* www.newfs.org	Framingham	MA	01701	508-877-7630	877-3658
Niagara Parks Botanical Gardens 2565 Niagara Pkwy N PO Box 150 *TF:* 877-642-7275 ■ *Web:* www.niagaraparks.com/garden/botanical.php	Niagara Falls	ON	L2E6T2	905-356-8554	356-5488
Nichols Arboretum *University of Michigan* 1600 Washington Heights *Web:* www.lsa.umich.edu	Ann Arbor	MI	48104	734-647-7600	
Nikka Yuko Japanese Garden PO Box 751 *Web:* www.nikkayuko.com	Lethbridge	AB	T1J3Z6	403-328-3511	328-0511
Norfolk Botanical Garden 6700 Azalea Garden Rd *Web:* www.norfolkbotanicalgarden.org/home	Norfolk	VA	23518	757-441-5830	441-5837
Normandale Community College Japanese Garden 9700 France Ave S *Web:* www.normandale.mnscu.edu/japanesegarden	Bloomington	MN	55431	952-487-8106	487-7066
North Carolina Arboretum 100 Frederick Law Olmsted Way *Web:* www.ncarboretum.org	Asheville	NC	28806	828-665-2492	665-2371
North Carolina Botanical Garden *The University of North Carolina* CB 3375 Totten Ctr *Web:* www.ncbg.unc.edu	Chapel Hill	NC	27599	919-962-0522	962-3531
Oklahoma Botanical Garden & Arboretum Oklahoma State University Dept of Horticulture 358 Ag Hall *Web:* www.osubotanicalgarden.okstate.edu	Stillwater	OK	74078	405-744-5415	744-9709
Olbrich Botanical Gardens 3330 Atwood Ave *Web:* www.olbrich.org	Madison	WI	53704	608-246-4551	246-4719
Oldfields - Lilly House & Gardens 4000 Michigan Rd *Web:* www.imamuseum.org	Indianapolis	IN	46208	317-923-1331	931-1978
Oregon Garden The 879 W Main St PO Box 155 *TF:* 877-674-2733 ■ *Web:* www.oregongarden.org	Silverton	OR	97381	503-874-8100	339-2996
Overfelt Gardens 2145 McKee Rd *Web:* www.sjparks.org	San Jose	CA	95116	408-251-3323	251-2865
Phipps Conservatory & Botanical Gardens 1 Schenley Pk *Web:* www.phipps.conservatory.org	Pittsburgh	PA	15213	412-622-6914	622-7363
Pine Tree State Arboretum 153 Hospital St	Augusta	ME	04330	207-621-0031	621-8245
Pinecrest Gardens 11000 Red Rd *Web:* www.pinecrest-fl.gov/gardens.htm	Pinecrest	FL	33156	305-669-6942	284-0911
Polly Hill Arboretum 809 State Rd PO Box 561 *Web:* www.pollyhillarboretum.org	West Tisbury	MA	02575	508-693-9426	693-5772
Powell Gardens 1609 NW US Hwy 50 *Web:* www.powellgardens.org	Kingsville	MO	64061	816-697-2600	697-2619
Quad City Botanical Ctr 2525 4th Ave *Web:* www.qcgardens.com	Rock Island	IL	61201	309-794-0991	794-1572
Quarryhill Botanical Garden 12841 Sonoma Hwy PO Box 232 *Web:* www.quarryhillbg.org	Glen Ellen	CA	95442	707-996-3166	996-3198
Queen Elizabeth II Sunken Gardens 2450 McDougall Rd	Windsor	ON	N8X3N6	519-253-2300	255-7990
Queens Botanical Garden 43-50 Main St *Web:* www.queensbotanical.org	Flushing	NY	11355	718-886-3800	463-0263
Rancho Santa Ana Botanic Garden 1500 N College Ave *Web:* www.rsabg.org	Claremont	CA	91711	909-625-8767	626-7670
Red Butte Garden & Arboretum 300 Wakara Way University of Utah *Web:* www.redbuttegarden.org	Salt Lake City	UT	84108	801-581-4747	585-6491
Reeves-Reed Arboretum 165 Hobart Ave *Web:* www.reeves-reedarboretum.org	Summit	NJ	07901	908-273-8787	273-6869
Reflection Riding Arboretum & Botanical Garden 400 Garden Rd *Web:* www.reflectionriding.org	Chattanooga	TN	37419	423-821-9582	
Reiman Gardens *Iowa State University* 1407 University Blvd *Web:* www.reimangardens.iastate.edu	Ames	IA	50011	515-294-2710	294-4817
Reynolda Gardens of Wake Forest University 100 Reynolda Village *Web:* www.reynoldagardens.org	Winston-Salem	NC	27106	336-758-5593	758-4132
Rhododendron Species Botanical Garden 2525 S 336th St PO Box 3798 *Web:* www.rhodygarden.org	Federal Way	WA	98063	253-838-4646	838-4686
Rio Grande Botanic Garden 2601 Central Ave NW *Web:* www.cabq.gov/biopark/garden	Albuquerque	NM	87104	505-764-6200	848-7192
Riverbanks Zoo & Botanical Garden 500 Wildlife Pkwy *Web:* www.riverbanks.org	Columbia	SC	29210	803-779-8717	253-6381
Robert Allerton Park & Conference Ctr 515 Old Timber Rd *Web:* www.allerton.uiuc.edu	Monticello	IL	61856	217-762-2721	762-3742
Rodef Shalom Biblical Botanical Garden 4905 5th Ave	Pittsburgh	PA	15213	412-621-6566	687-1977
Rotary Botanical Gardens 1455 Palmer Dr *Web:* www.rotarygardens.org	Janesville	WI	53545	608-752-3885	752-3853
Royal Botanical Gardens (RBG) 680 Plains Rd W *TF:* 800-694-4769 ■ *Web:* www.rbg.ca	Burlington	ON	L7T4H4	905-527-1158	577-0375
Royal Roads University Botanical Garden 2005 Sooke Rd *TF:* 866-391-2620	Victoria	BC	V9B5Y2	250-391-2511	391-2620
Rutgers Gardens 112 Ryders Ln Cook College/Rutgers University *Web:* www.rutgersgardens.rutgers.edu	New Brunswick	NJ	08901	732-932-8453	932-7060

Name / Address	City	State	Zip	Phone	Fax
Ruth Bancroft Garden 1552 Bancroft Rd *Web:* www.ruthbancroftgarden.org	Walnut Creek	CA	94598	925-210-9663	256-1889
San Antonio Botanical Garden & Lucile Halsell Conservatory 555 Funston Pl *Web:* www.sabot.org	San Antonio	TX	78209	210-207-3250	207-3274
San Diego Botanic Garden 230 Quail Gardens Dr *Web:* www.qbgardens.com	Encinitas	CA	92024	760-436-3036	632-0917
San Francisco Botanical Garden 9th Ave & Lincoln Way *Web:* www.sfbotanicalgarden.org	San Francisco	CA	94122	415-661-1316	661-3539
San Jose Heritage Rose Garden Taylor & Spring Sts. *Web:* www.grpg.org	San Jose	CA	95110	408-298-7657	288-9048
San Luis Obispo Botanical Garden 3450 Dairy Creek Rd. *Web:* www.slobg.org	San Luis Obispo	CA	93405	805-541-1400	541-1466
Sandhills Horticultural Gardens 3395 Airport Rd *Web:* www.sandhills.edu/lsg/hort.html	Pinehurst	NC	28374	910-695-3883	695-3894
Santa Barbara Botanic Garden 1212 Mission Canyon Rd *Web:* www.sbbg.org	Santa Barbara	CA	93105	805-682-4726	563-0352
Sarah P Duke Gardens 426 Anderson St PO Box 90341 *Web:* www.hr.duke.edu/dukegardens	Durham	NC	27708	919-684-3698	668-3610
Sawtooth Botanical Garden (SBG) 11 Gimlet Rd PO Box 928 *Web:* www.sbgarden.org	Ketchum	ID	83340	208-726-9358	726-5435
Schedel Arboretum & Gardens 19255 W Portage River S Rd *Web:* www.schedel-gardens.org	Elmore	OH	43416	419-862-3182	
Schoepfle Garden 12882 Diagonal Rd *TF:* 800-526-7275 ■ *Web:* www.metroparks.cc/reservation-schoepfle-garden.php	La Grange	OH	44050	440-458-5121	458-8924
Schreiner's Iris Gardens 3625 Quinaby Rd NE *TF:* 800-525-2367 ■ *Web:* www.schreinersgardens.com	Salem	OR	97303	503-393-3232	393-5590
Scott Arboretum of Swarthmore College 500 College Ave *Web:* www.scottarboretum.org	Swarthmore	PA	19081	610-328-8025	
Secrest Arboretum 1680 Madison Ave. *Web:* secrest.osu.edu	Wooster	OH	44691	330-263-3761	263-3886
Shambhala Mountain Ctr 4921 County Rd 68C *TF:* 888-788-7221 ■ *Web:* www.shambhalamountain.org	Red Feather Lakes	CO	80545	970-881-2184	881-2909
Shangri La Botanical Gardens & Nature Ctr 2111 W Pk Ave *Web:* www.shangrilagardens.org	Orange	TX	77630	409-670-9113	670-9341
Sherman Library & Gardens 2647 E Coast Hwy *Web:* www.slgardens.org	Corona del Mar	CA	92625	949-673-2261	675-5458
Sherwood Fox Arboretum *University of Western Ontario* 110 Staging Bldg *Web:* www.uwo.ca/biology/arboretum	London	ON	N6A5B7	519-850-2542	661-3935
Shinzen Japanese Friendship Gardens 7775 N Friant Rd *Web:* www.shinzenjapanesegarden.org	Fresno	CA	93755	559-621-2900	498-1588
Sister Mary Grace Burns Arboretum 900 Lakewood Ave *TF:* 800-458-8422 ■ *Web:* www.georgian.edu/arboretum/index.html	Lakewood	NJ	08701	732-987-2373	987-2010
Skylands PO Box 302 *Web:* www.njbg.org	Ringwood	NJ	07456	973-962-7527	962-1553
Slayton Arboretum of Hilsdale College 33 E College St *Web:* www.hillsdale.edu/arboretum	Hillsdale	MI	49242	517-607-2241	
Sonnenberg Gardens 151 Charlotte St *Web:* www.sonnenberg.org	Canandaigua	NY	14424	585-394-4922	394-2192
South Carolina Botanical Garden 150 Discovery Ln Clemson University *Web:* www.clemson.edu/public/scbg	Clemson	SC	29634	864-656-3405	656-6230
South Coast Botanic Garden 26300 Crenshaw Blvd. *Web:* www.palosverdes.com/botanicgardens	Palos Verdes Peninsula	CA	90274	310-544-6815	544-6820
South Texas Botanical Gardens & Nature Ctr 8545 S Staples St *Web:* www.stxbot.org	Corpus Christi	TX	78413	361-852-2100	852-7875
State Arboretum of Virginia 400 Blandy Farm Ln *Web:* www.virginia.edu	Boyce	VA	22620	540-837-1758	837-1523
State Botanical Garden of Georgia 2450 S Milledge Ave. *Web:* www.uga.edu/botgarden	Athens	GA	30605	706-542-1244	542-3091
Staten Island Botanical Garden 1000 Richmond Terr *Web:* www.sibg.org	Staten Island	NY	10301	718-273-8200	442-3645
Stonecrop Gardens 81 Stonecrop Ln *Web:* www.stonecrop.org	Cold Spring	NY	10516	845-265-2000	265-2405
Stranahan Arboretum 4131 Tantara Dr *Web:* www.utoledo.edu	Toledo	OH	43623	419-841-1007	530-4421
Sunken Gardens 1825 4th St N *Web:* www.stpete.org/sunken	Saint Petersburg	FL	33701	727-551-3102	551-3104
Texas Discovery Gardens 3601 Martin Luther King Junior Blvd *Web:* www.texasdiscoverygardens.org	Dallas	TX	75210	214-428-7476	428-5338
Tofino Botanical Gardens Foundation 1084 Pacific Rim Hwy PO Box 886 *Web:* www.tbgf.org	Tofino	BC	V0R2Z0	250-725-1220	725-2435
Tohono Chul Park 7366 N Paseo del Norte *Web:* www.tohonochulpark.org	Tucson	AZ	85704	520-742-6455	797-1213
Toledo Botanical Garden 5403 Elmer Dr *Web:* www.toledogarden.org	Toledo	OH	43615	419-936-2986	536-5574

Name / Address	City	State	Zip	Phone	Fax
Tower Hill Botanic Garden 11 French Dr PO Box 598 *Web:* www.towerhillbg.org	Boylston	MA	01505	508-869-6111	869-0314
Tryon Palace Historic Sites & Gardens 610 Pollock St *TF:* 800-767-1560 ■ *Web:* www.tryonpalace.org	New Bern	NC	28562	252-514-4900	514-4876
Tucson Botanical Gardens 2150 N Alvernon Way *Web:* www.tucsonbotanical.org	Tucson	AZ	85712	520-326-9255	324-0166
Tulsa Garden Ctr 2435 S Peoria Ave *Web:* www.tulsagardencenter.com	Tulsa	OK	74114	918-746-5125	746-5128
Tyler Arboretum 515 Painter Rd *Web:* www.tylerarboretum.org	Media	PA	19063	610-566-5431	891-1490
UC Davis Arboretum University of California La Ru Rd *Web:* arboretum.ucdavis.edu	Davis	CA	95616	530-752-4880	752-5796
University of Alabama Arboretum PO Box 870344 *Web:* www.arboretum.ua.edu	Tuscaloosa	AL	35487	205-553-3278	553-3728
University of Arizona Campus Arboretum PO Box 210036 *Web:* arboretum.arizona.edu/index.html	Tucson	AZ	85721	520-621-7074	621-7186
University of British Columbia Botanical Garden & Centre for Plant Research 6804 SW Marine Dr *Web:* www.botanicalgarden.ubc.ca	Vancouver	BC	V6T1Z4	604-822-4208	822-2016
University of California Botanical Garden at Berkeley 200 Centennial Dr. *Web:* www.botanicalgarden.berkeley.edu	Berkeley	CA	94720	510-643-2755	642-5045
University of California Riverside Botanic Gardens 900 University Ave *Web:* gardens.ucr.edu	Riverside	CA	92521	951-784-6962	784-6962
University of Chicago Botanic Garden 5555 S Ellis Ave *Web:* www.uchicago.edu	Chicago	IL	60637	773-702-1700	702-5814
University of Delaware Botanic Garden University of Delaware Plant & Soil Science Dept 152 Townsend Hall *Web:* www.ag.udel.edu/udbg	Newark	DE	19716	302-831-2531	831-0605
University of Idaho Arboretum & Botanical Garden 875 Perimeter Dr PO Box 442281 *Web:* www.uidaho.edu/arboretum	Moscow	ID	83844	208-885-6633	885-5748
University of Kentucky Lexington-Fayette Urban County Government Arboretum 500 Alumni Dr *Web:* www.ca.uky.edu/arboretum	Lexington	KY	40503	859-257-6955	
University of Missouri Botanic Garden 181 General Services Bldg *Web:* www.gardens.missouri.edu/faq/index.php	Columbia	MO	65211	573-882-4240	884-3032
University of Rochester Arboretum 612 Wilson Blvd. *Web:* www.facilities.rochester.edu/arboretum	Rochester	NY	14627	585-273-5627	461-3055
University of South Florida Botanical Gardens 4202 E Fowler Ave *Web:* www.cas.usf.edu/garden	Tampa	FL	33620	813-974-2329	974-4808
University of Southern Maine Arboretum 37 College Ave *TF:* 800-780-5520 ■ *Web:* www.usm.maine.edu/arboretum	Gorham	ME	04038	207-780-5443	780-5520
University of Tennessee Arboretum 901 S Illinois Ave *Web:* forestry.tennessee.edu/arboretum	Oak Ridge	TN	37830	865-483-3571	483-3572
University of Tennessee Gardens 2431 Joe Johnson Dr *Web:* utgardens.tennessee.edu	Knoxville	TN	37996	865-974-7324	974-1947
University of Wisconsin Arboretum 1207 Seminole Hwy *Web:* www.uwarboretum.org	Madison	WI	53711	608-263-7888	262-5209
US Botanic Garden 100 Maryland Ave *Web:* www.aoc.gov	Washington	DC	20001	202-225-8333	225-1561
US National Arboretum 3501 New York Ave NE *Web:* www.usna.usda.gov	Washington	DC	20002	202-245-2726	245-4575
Utah Botanical Ctr 725 S Sego Lily Dr PO Box 265 *Web:* www.utahbotanicalcenter.org	Kaysville	UT	84037	801-593-8969	593-5330
Van Vleck House & Gardens 21 Van Vleck St. *Web:* www.vanvleck.org	Montclair	NJ	07042	973-744-4752	746-1082
Vander Veer Botanical Park 215 W Central Pk Ave *Web:* www.cityofdavenportiowa.com	Davenport	IA	52803	563-326-7818	326-7955
Vermont Garden Park 1100 Dorset St *TF:* 800-538-7476 ■ *Web:* www.garden.org	South Burlington	VT	05403	802-864-5206	864-6889
Virginia Tech Horticulture Garden (VTHG) Virginia Tech 301 Saunders Hall *Web:* www.hort.vt.edu/VTHG	Blacksburg	VA	24061	540-231-5451	
Waddell Barnes Botanical Gardens 100 College Stn Dr Macon State College *Web:* www.maconstate.edu	Macon	GA	31206	478-471-2780	
Washington Park Arboretum 2300 Arboretum Dr E *Web:* www.depts.washington.edu	Seattle	WA	98112	206-543-8800	616-2871
Washington Park Botanical Garden 1740 W Fayette Ave *Web:* www.springfieldparks.org	Springfield	IL	62704	217-753-6228	546-0257
Wave Hill W 249th St & Independence Ave *Web:* www.wavehill.org	Bronx	NY	10471	718-549-3200	884-8952
Wegerzyn Gardens MetroPark 1301 E Siebenthaler Ave *Web:* www.metroparks.org	Dayton	OH	45414	937-275-7275	277-6546
Welkinweir 1328 Prizer Rd *Web:* www.welkinweir.org	Pottstown	PA	19465	610-469-7543	469-2218
West Virginia Botanic Garden 714 Venture Dr *Web:* www.wvbg.org	Morgantown	WV	26508	304-376-2717	

	City	State	ZIP	Phone	Fax
White River Gardens 1200 W Washington St PO Box 22309 *Web:* www.indianapoliszoo.com	Indianapolis	IN	46222	317-630-2001	630-5153
Wing Haven Gardens & Bird Sanctuary 248 Ridgewood Ave *Web:* www.winghavengardens.com	Charlotte	NC	28209	704-331-0664	331-9368
WJ Beal Botanical Garden Michigan State University 412 Olds Hall *Web:* www.cpp.msu.edu/beal/directions/direct_frames.htm	East Lansing	MI	48824	517-355-9582	432-1090
Woodland Cemetery & Arboretum Foundation 118 Woodland Ave *Web:* www.woodlandcemetery.org	Dayton	OH	45409	937-228-3221	222-7259
Wrigley Memorial & Botanical Garden 125 Claressa Ave *Web:* www.catalina.com/memorial.html	Avalon	CA	90704	310-510-2595	510-2325
WW Seymour Botanical Conservatory 316 S 'G' St	Tacoma	WA	98405	253-591-5330	627-2192
Yale University Marsh Botanical Gardens Yale University Corner of Prospect & Hillside St *Web:* www.yale.edu/marshgardens	New Haven	CT	06511	203-432-6320	
Yew Dell Gardens 6220 Old LaGrange Rd PO Box 1334 *Web:* www.yewdellgardens.org	Crestwood	KY	40014	502-241-4788	241-8338
Zilker Botanical Garden 2220 Barton Springs Rd *Web:* www.zilkergarden.org	Austin	TX	78746	512-477-8672	481-8254
ZooMontana & Botanical Gardens 2100 S Shiloh Rd *Web:* www.zoomontana.org	Billings	MT	59106	406-652-8100	652-9281

BOTTLES - GLASS

SEE Glass Jars & Bottles p. 1906

	City	State	ZIP	Phone	Fax
Wynton M Blount Cultural Park 6055 Vaughn Rd *Web:* www.blountculturalpark.org	Montgomery	AL	36116	334-244-5700	273-9666
Casa del Herrero 1387 E Valley Rd *Web:* www.casadelherrero.com	Santa Barbara	CA	93108	805-565-5653	969-2371
J Paul Getty Museum 1200 Getty Ctr Dr **Fax:* Hum Res ■ *Web:* www.getty.edu	Los Angeles	CA	90049	310-440-7300	440-7720*
Preservation Delaware Inc 1405 Greenhill Ave *Web:* www.preservationde.org	Wilmington	DE	19806	302-651-9617	651-9603
Winterthur Museum & Country Estate 5105 Kennett Pike *TF:* 800-448-3883 ■ *Web:* www.winterthur.org	Winterthur	DE	19735	302-888-4600	888-4880
Cathedral Church of Saint Peter & Saint Paul 3101 Wisconsin Ave NW *TF:* 800-622-6304 ■ *Web:* www.cathedral.org/cathedral	Washington	DC	20016	202-537-6200	364-6600
Hillwood Estate Museum & Gardens 4155 Linnean Ave NW *TF:* 877-445-5966 ■ *Web:* www.hillwoodmuseum.org	Washington	DC	20008	202-686-8500	966-7846
Goodwood Museum & Gardens 1600 Miccosukee Rd *Web:* www.goodwoodmuseum.org	Tallahassee	FL	32308	850-877-4202	877-3090
Callaway Gardens 17800 Hwy 27 *TF:* 800-225-5292 ■ *Web:* www.callawaygardens.com	Pine Mountain	GA	31822	706-663-2281	663-6812
Polynesian Cultural Ctr 55-370 Kamehameha Hwy *TF:* 800-367-7060 ■ *Web:* www.polynesia.com	Laie	HI	96762	808-293-3000	293-3027
Longue Vue House & Gardens 7 Bamboo Rd *Web:* www.longuevue.com	New Orleans	LA	70124	504-488-5488	486-7015
Applewood - the CS Mott Estate 1400 E Kearsley St	Flint	MI	48503	810-233-3031	232-6937
Clark County Museum 1830 S Boulder Hwy	Henderson	NV	89002	702-455-7955	455-7948
George Eastman House & Gardens 900 E Ave *Web:* www.eastmanhouse.org	Rochester	NY	14607	585-271-3361	271-3970
Stan Hywet Hall & Gardens 714 N Portage Path *TF:* 888-836-5533 ■ *Web:* www.stanhywet.org	Akron	OH	44403	330-836-5533	836-2680
Philbrook Museum of Art & Gardens 2727 S Rockford Rd *TF:* 800-324-7941 ■ *Web:* www.philbrook.org	Tulsa	OK	74114	918-749-7941	743-4230
Cedar Crest College 100 College Dr **Fax:* Admissions ■ *TF Admissions:* 800-360-1222 ■ *Web:* www.cedarcrest.edu	Allentown	PA	18104	610-437-4471	606-4647*
Journey Museum 222 New York St *Web:* www.journeymuseum.org	Rapid City	SD	57701	605-394-6923	394-6940
Dixon Gallery & Gardens 4339 Pk Ave *Web:* www.dixon.org	Memphis	TN	38117	901-761-5250	682-0943
Vanderbilt University 2201 W End Ave *TF:* 800-288-0432 ■ *Web:* www.vanderbilt.edu	Nashville	TN	37240	615-322-7311	343-7765
James Madison's Montpelier 11407 Constitution Hwy *Web:* www.montpelier.org	Montpelier Station	VA	22957	540-672-2728	672-0411
Monticello 931 Thomas Jefferson Pkwy PO Box 316 *Web:* www.monticello.org	Charlottesville	VA	22902	434-984-9822	977-7757
Old City Cemetery Museums & Arboretum 401 Taylor St *Web:* www.gravegarden.org	Lynchburg	VA	24501	434-847-1465	856-2004
Huntington Museum of Art Inc 2033 McCoy Rd *Web:* www.hmoa.org	Huntington	WV	25701	304-529-2701	529-7447

98 BOTTLES - PLASTICS

	City	State	ZIP	Phone	Fax
Abbott Industries Inc 1-11 Morris St	Paterson	NJ	07501	973-345-1116	345-9154
Alpha Packaging 1555 Page Industrial Blvd *TF:* 800-421-4772 ■ *Web:* www.alphap.com	Saint Louis	MO	63132	314-427-4300	427-5445
Amcor Packaging 6600 Valley View St *Web:* www.amcor.com/petpackaging	Buena Park	CA	90620	714-562-6000	562-6059
Ball Plastic Container Corp 9300 W 108th Cir *Web:* www.ball.com	Westminster	CO	80021	303-469-5511	
Colt's Plastics Co 969 N Main St PO Box 429 *TF:* 800-222-2658 ■ *Web:* www.coltsplastics.com	Dayville	CT	06241	860-774-2301	774-2301
Constar International Inc 1 Crown Way *Web:* www.constar.net	Philadelphia	PA	19154	215-552-3700	552-3715
Contour Packaging Corp 637 W Rockland St	Philadelphia	PA	19120	215-457-1600	457-1600
Custom Bottle Inc 10 Great Hill Rd *TF:* 800-537-6449 ■ *Web:* www.custombottle.com	Naugatuck	CT	06770	203-723-6681	723-6687
Drug Plastics & Glass Co Inc 1 Bottle Dr *Web:* www.drugplastics.com	Boyertown	PA	19512	610-367-5000	367-9800
Graham Packaging Co Inc 2401 Pleasant Valley Rd *Web:* www.grahampackaging.com	York	PA	17402	717-849-8500	854-4269
In Zone Brands Inc 2251 Corporate Plaza Pky Suite 220 *Web:* www.tummytickler.com	Smyrna	GA	30080	678-718-2000	718-2031
Midland Mfg Co Inc 101 E County Line Rd PO Box 899 *Web:* www.midlandmfgco.com	Monroe	IA	50170	641-259-2625	259-3216
NEW Plastics Corp 112 4th St *TF:* 800-666-5207 ■ *Web:* www.newplasticscorp.com	Luxemburg	WI	54217	920-845-2326	845-2439
Novapak Corp 370 Stevers Crossing Rd *TF:* 800-672-7721 ■ *Web:* www.novapakcorp.com	Philmont	NY	12565	518-672-7721	672-7728
Nutrifaster Inc 209 S Bennett St *TF:* 800-800-2641 ■ *Web:* www.nutrifaster.com	Seattle	WA	98108	206-767-5054	762-2209
Ozarks Coca-Cola Dr Pepper Bottling Co 1777 N Packer Rd *Web:* www.cocacolaozarks.com	Springfield	MO	65803	417-865-9900	865-7967
Paradigm Packaging 141 N 5th St *Web:* www.paradigmpackaging.com	Saddle Brook	NJ	07664	201-909-3400	291-3855
Penn Bottle & Supply Co 710 E 3rd St *TF:* 888-277-7366 ■ *Web:* www.pennbottle.com	Essington	PA	19029	610-521-6000	521-7200
Plastic Industries Inc 12400 Industry St	Garden Grove	CA	92841	714-897-2111	894-0124
Plastipak Packaging Inc 41605 Ann Arbor Rd PO Box 2500C *Web:* www.plastipak.com	Plymouth	MI	48170	734-455-3600	354-7391
Pluto Corp 8647 W State Rd 56 *Web:* www.plutocorp.com	French Lick	IN	47432	812-936-9988	936-2828
Poly-Tainer Inc 450 W Los Angeles Ave *Web:* www.polytainer.com	Simi Valley	CA	93065	805-526-3424	526-3430
Progressive Plastics Inc 14801 Emery Ave *TF:* 800-252-0053 ■ *Web:* www.progressive-plastics.com	Cleveland	OH	44135	216-252-5595	252-6327
Quality Containers of New England 247 Portland St Suite 300 *TF:* 800-639-1550 ■ *Web:* www.qualitycontainersne.com	Yarmouth	ME	04096	207-846-5420	846-3755
RN Fink Mfg Co Inc 1530 Noble Rd PO Box 245 *Web:* www.rnfink.com	Williamston	MI	48895	517-655-4351	655-5119
Silgan Plastics Corp 14515 N Outer Forty Suite 210 *TF:* 800-274-5426 ■ *Web:* www.silganplastics.com	Chesterfield	MO	63017	314-542-9223	523-4363
Weber International Packing Co LLC 318 Cornelia St *Web:* www.weberintl.com	Plattsburgh	NY	12901	518-561-8282	561-4509
Western Container Corp 1600 1st Ave	Big Spring	TX	79720	432-263-8361	263-8075

99 BOWLING CENTERS

	City	State	ZIP	Phone	Fax
AMF Bowling Worldwide Inc 8100 AMF Dr *TF:* 800-342-5263 ■ *Web:* www.amf.com	Mechanicsville	VA	23111	804-730-4000	730-0923
Bowl America Inc 6446 Edsall Rd *AMEX:* BWLa ■ *Web:* www.bowl-america.com	Alexandria	VA	22312	703-941-6300	256-2430
Brunswick Bowling & Billiards 1 N Field Ct *Web:* www.brunswick.com	Lake Forest	IL	60045	847-735-4700	735-4501
Don Carter Premier Bowling Centers 1389 NW 136 Ave	Sunrise	FL	33323	954-846-8400	846-8400
Mardi-Bob Management Inc PO Box 69	Poughkeepsie	NY	12602	845-471-2920	471-7202

100 BOXES - CORRUGATED & SOLID FIBER

	City	State	ZIP	Phone	Fax
Action Box Co Inc 6207 N Houston Rosslyn Rd *Web:* www.actionboxinc.com	Houston	TX	77091	713-869-7701	869-0103
Advance Packaging Corp 4459 40th St SE PO Box 888311 *Web:* www.advancepkg.com	Grand Rapids	MI	49588	616-949-6610	954-7373
Advanced Design & Packaging Inc 5090 McDougall Dr SW *TF:* 800-331-7835	Atlanta	GA	30336	404-699-1952	699-1825
Age Industries Ltd 3601 County Rd 316c *Web:* www.ageindustries.com	Cleburne	TX	76031	817-641-8178	641-2509
Akers Packaging Service Inc 2820 Lefferson Rd *Web:* www.akers-pkg.com	Middletown	OH	45044	513-422-6312	422-2829
Aldelano Packaging Corp 2010 S Lynx Ave *TF:* 800-972-2599 ■ *Web:* www.aldelano.com	Ontario	CA	91761	909-861-3970	861-6039
Amcor Sunclipse 6600 Valley View St	Buena Park	CA	90620	714-562-6000	562-6059
Anchor Bay Packaging Corp 30905 23 Mile Rd *Web:* www.anchorbaypackaging.com	New Baltimore	MI	48047	586-949-4040	949-9998
Artistic Carton Co 1975 Big Timber Rd *TF:* 877-784-7842 ■ *Web:* www.artisticcarton.com	Elgin	IL	60123	847-741-0247	741-8529
Arvco Container Corp 845 Gibson St *TF:* 800-968-9128 ■ *Web:* www.arvco.com	Kalamazoo	MI	49001	269-381-0900	381-2919

				Phone	Fax
Atlas Container Corp 8140 Telegraph Rd.	Severn	MD	21144	410-551-6300	551-2703
TF: 800-394-4894 ■ *Web:* www.atlascontainer.com					
Bates Container 6433 Davis Blvd.	North Richland Hills	TX	76180	817-498-3200	581-8802
TF: 800-792-8736 ■ *Web:* www.batescontainer.com					
Bay Cities Container Corp 8315 Hanan Way	Pico Rivera	CA	90660	562-948-3751	948-1503
Beacon Container Corp 700 W 1st St	Birdsboro	PA	19508	610-582-2222	582-3992
TF: 800-422-8383 ■ *Web:* www.beaconcontainer.com					
Bell Container Corp 615 Ferry St.	Newark	NJ	07105	973-344-4400	344-0817
Web: www.bellcontainer.com					
Buckeye Container Inc 3350 Long Rd	Wooster	OH	44691	330-264-6336	264-0127
TF: 800-686-8692 ■ *Web:* www.buckeyecontainer.com					
Buckeye Corrugated Inc 275 Springside Dr	Akron	OH	44333	330-576-0590	576-0600
Web: www.buckeyecorrugated.com					
Bulk-pack Inc 1025 N 9th St	Monroe	LA	71201	318-387-3260	387-6362
TF: 800-498-4215 ■ *Web:* www.bulk-pack.com					
Carolina Container Co 909 Prospect St.	High Point	NC	27260	336-883-7146	883-7576
TF: 800-627-0825 ■ *Web:* www.carolinacontainer.com					
Colorado Container Corp 4221 Monaco St.	Denver	CO	80216	303-331-0400	331-9455
Web: www.coloradocontainer.com					
Commander Packaging Corp 25777 Cleveland Ave.	Monee	IL	60449	708-367-4000	367-4010
Cornell Paper & Box Co 162 Van Dyke St	Brooklyn	NY	11231	718-875-3202	875-3281
Corrugated Supplies Corp (CSC) 5043 W 67th St.	Bedford Park	IL	60638	708-458-5525	458-0013
TF: 888-826-2738 ■ *Web:* www.csclive.com					
Cumberland Container Corp PO Box 250	Monterey	TN	38574	931-839-2227	839-3971
Web: www.cumberlandcontainer.com					
Delta Corrugated Paper Products Corp W Ruby Ave	Palisades Park	NJ	07650	201-941-1910	941-9399
TF: 800-932-6937 ■ *Web:* www.deltacorrugated.com					
Elgin Corrugated Box Co Inc 824 Raymond St.	Elgin	IL	60120	847-741-2200	741-3052
Ferguson Supply & Box Mfg Co 10820 Quality Dr	Charlotte	NC	28278	704-597-0310	597-5623
TF: 800-821-1023 ■ *Web:* www.fergusonbox.com					
Great Lakes Packaging Corp W 190 N 11393 Carnegie Dr.	Germantown	WI	53022	262-255-2100	255-7290
TF: 800-261-4572 ■ *Web:* www.glpc.com					
Great Northern Corp 395 Stroebe Rd	Appleton	WI	54914	920-739-3671	739-7096
TF: 800-236-3671 ■ *Web:* www.greatnortherncorp.com					
Green Bay Packaging Inc 1700 Webster Ct	Green Bay	WI	54302	920-433-5111	
TF: 800-558-4008 ■ *Web:* www.gbp.com					
High Country Container Inc 3700 Lima St	Denver	CO	80239	303-373-1430	373-2325
Web: www.delinebox.com					
Integrated Packaging Corp 122 Quentin Ave	New Brunswick	NJ	08901	732-247-5200	247-9559
Web: www.ipcboxes.com					
Key Container Corp 21 Campbell St.	Pawtucket	RI	02861	401-723-2000	725-5980
TF: 800-343-8811 ■ *Web:* www.keycontainercorp.com					
Lawrence Paper Co 2801 Lakeview Rd	Lawrence	KS	66049	785-843-8111	749-3904
TF: 800-535-4553 ■ *Web:* www.lpco.net					
Liberty Carton Co 870 Louisiana Ave S	Minneapolis	MN	55426	763-540-9600	540-9628
TF: 800-328-1784 ■ *Web:* www.libertycarton.com					
Lone Star Container 700 N Wildwood Dr.	Irving	TX	75061	972-579-1551	554-6081
TF: 800-552-6937 ■ *Web:* www.lonestarcontainer.com					
Longview Fibre Paper & Packaging Inc 300 Fibre Way PO Box 639	Longview	WA	98632	360-425-1550	230-5135
Web: www.longviewfibre.com					
Massillon Container Co 49 Ohio St.	Navarre	OH	44662	330-879-5653	879-2772
Web: www.vailpkg.com					
Menasha Corp 1645 Bergstrom Rd	Neenah	WI	54956	920-751-1000	751-1236
TF: 800-558-5073 ■ *Web:* www.menasha.com					
Menasha Packaging Co 1645 Bergstrom Rd.	Neenah	WI	54956	920-751-1000	751-2349
TF: 800-558-5073 ■ *Web:* www.menashapackaging.com					
Mystic Ltd 301 SW 27th St	Renton	WA	98057	425-251-5959	251-9378
TF: 800-423-0557 ■ *Web:* www.mysticsheets.com					
National Packaging Cos Display Group 105 Ave L	Newark	NJ	07105	973-589-2155	589-2414
TF: 800-589-5808					
New England Wooden Ware Corp 205 School St Suite 201	Gardner	MA	01440	978-632-3600	630-1513
Web: www.newoodenware.com					
North American Container Corp 1811 W Oak Pkwy Suite D	Marietta	GA	30062	770-431-4858	431-6957
TF: 800-929-3468 ■ *Web:* www.nacontainer.com					
Packaging Corp of America 1900 W Field Ct	Lake Forest	IL	60045	847-482-2000	615-6379
NYSE: PKG ■ *TF:* 888-828-2850 ■ *Web:* www.packagingcorp.com					
Pactiv Corp 1900 W Field Ct	Lake Forest	IL	60045	847-482-2000	482-4738
NYSE: PTV ■ *TF:* 888-828-2850 ■ *Web:* www.pactiv.com					
Progress Container Corp 635 Patrick Mill Rd SW	Winder	GA	30680	678-425-2000	
Web: www.progresscontainer.com					
Rand-Whitney Container Corp 1 Agrand St.	Worcester	MA	01607	508-791-2301	792-1578
TF: 800-370-9111 ■ *Web:* www.randwhitney.com					
Real Reel Corp Multi-Wall Corp Div 50 Taylor Dr	East Providence	RI	02916	401-434-1070	438-5203
TF Cust Svc: 800-992-4166 ■ *Web:* www.multiwall.com					
Rock TENN 1415 W 44th St	Chicago	IL	60609	773-254-1030	254-9092
TF: 800-621-1030					
Rock-Tenn Co 504 Thrasher St	Norcross	GA	30071	770-448-2193	
TF: 877-772-2999 ■ *Web:* www.rocktenn.com					
Royal Group 1301 S 47th Ave	Cicero	IL	60804	708-656-2020	656-2108
Web: www.royalbox.com					
Schiffenhaus Packaging Corp 2013 McCarter Hwy.	Newark	NJ	07104	973-484-5000	481-3630
Web: www.schifpack.com					
Southern Container Corp 115 Engineers Rd	Hauppauge	NY	11788	631-231-0400	231-0174
Web: www.southern-container.com					
Southern Container Ltd 10410 Papalote St Suite 130	Houston	TX	77041	713-466-5661	466-4223
Web: www.southerncontainer.com					
Stephen Gould Corp 35 S Jefferson Rd	Whippany	NJ	07981	973-428-1500	428-5274
TF: 800-253-1961 ■ *Web:* www.stephengould.com					
Stronghaven Inc 5090 McDougall Dr SW	Atlanta	GA	30336	404-699-9680	699-1825
TF: 800-233-2487 ■ *Web:* www.stronghaven.com					
Tecumseh Packaging Solutions Inc 1100 S St Frnacis	Tecumseh	MI	49286	517-423-2126	423-7240
TF: 800-866-8660					
Temple-Inland Inc 1300 S Mopac Expy	Austin	TX	78746	512-434-5800	434-8723
NYSE: TIN ■ *TF:* 800-826-8807 ■ *Web:* www.temple-inland.com					
Tharco Inc 2222 Grant Ave.	San Lorenzo	CA	94580	510-276-8600	322-4862*
**Fax Area Code: 800* ■ *TF:* 800-772-2332 ■ *Web:* www.tharco.com					
TimBar Packaging & Display 148 N Penn St PO Box 449	Hanover	PA	17331	717-632-4727	632-1243
TF: 800-572-6061 ■ *Web:* www.timbar.com					
Welch Packaging Group 1020 Herman St.	Elkhart	IN	46516	574-295-2460	295-1527
TF: 800-246-2475 ■ *Web:* www.welchpkg.com					
York Container Co 138 Mt Scion Rd PO Box 3008	York	PA	17402	717-757-7611	755-8090
TF: 800-772-9675 ■ *Web:* www.yorkcontainer.com					

101 BOXES - PAPERBOARD

Products Made By These Companies Include Setup, Folding, And Nonfolding Boxes.

				Phone	Fax
Advance Paper Box Co 6100 S Gramercy Pl	Los Angeles	CA	90047	323-750-2550	752-8133
Web: www.advancepaperbox.com					
AGI Inc 1950 N Ruby St.	Melrose Park	IL	60160	708-344-9103	344-9113
TF: 800-677-9110					
Aldelano Packaging Corp 2010 S Lynx Ave	Ontario	CA	91761	909-861-3970	861-6039
TF: 800-972-2599 ■ *Web:* www.aldelano.com					
Ample Industries Inc 4000 Commerce Ctr Dr	Franklin	OH	45005	937-746-9700	
TF: 888-818-9700 ■ *Web:* www.ampleindustries.com					
Apex Paper Box Co 5601 Walworth Ave	Cleveland	OH	44102	216-631-4000	416-2140*
**Fax: Sales* ■ *TF Cust Svc:* 800-438-2269					
Arkay Packaging Corp 22 Arkay Dr.	Hauppauge	NY	11788	631-273-2000	273-2478
TF: 888-327-5296 ■ *Web:* www.arkay.com					
Astronics Corp 130 Commerce Way	East Aurora	NY	14052	716-805-1599	655-0309
NASDAQ: ATRO ■ *Web:* www.astronics.com					
Boelter Industries Inc 202 Galewski Dr Airport Industrial Pk.	Winona	MN	55987	507-452-2315	452-2649
Web: www.boelterindustries.com					
Boutwell Owens & Co Inc 251 Authority Dr	Fitchburg	MA	01420	978-343-3067	343-9132
Web: www.boutwellowens.com					
Burd & Fletcher Co Inc 3000 W Geospace Dr	Independence	MO	64056	816-257-0291	257-9928
TF: 800-821-2776 ■ *Web:* www.burdfletcher.com					
Cadmus Communications Corp Whitehall Group Div 2750 Whitehall Pk Dr	Charlotte	NC	28273	704-583-6600	583-6781*
**Fax: Sales* ■ *TF:* 800-733-4318 ■ *Web:* www.cadmuswhitehall.com					
Calpine Containers Inc 9499 N Ford Wahington Rd Suite 103	Fresno	CA	93730	559-519-7199	279-1272*
**Fax Area Code: 925*					
Caraustar Industries Inc 5000 Austell-Powder Sprngs Rd Suite 300.	Austell	GA	30106	770-948-3100	
TF: 800-223-1373 ■ *Web:* www.caraustar.com					
Carton Service Inc First Quality Dr PO Box 702	Shelby	OH	44875	419-342-5010	342-4804
TF: 800-533-7744 ■ *Web:* www.cartonservice.com					
Colbert Packaging Corp 28355 N Bradley Rd	Lake Forest	IL	60045	847-367-5990	367-4403
Web: www.colbertpkg.com					
Complemar Partners 500 Lee Rd Suite 200	Rochester	NY	14606	585-647-5800	647-5800
TF: 866-742-5274 ■ *Web:* www.complemar.com					
Cornell Paper & Box Co 162 Van Dyke St	Brooklyn	NY	11231	718-875-3202	875-3281
Cortegra 6 Commerce Rd	Fairfield	NJ	07004	973-808-8000	808-8010
Web: www.cortegra.com					
Curtis Packaging Corp 44 Berkshire Rd	Sandy Hook	CT	06482	203-426-5861	426-2684
Web: www.curtispackaging.com					
Dee Paper Co Inc 100 Broomall St	Chester	PA	19013	610-876-9285	876-7040
TF: 800-359-0041 ■ *Web:* www.deepaper.com					
Diamond Packaging Co Inc 111 Commerce Dr PO Box 23620	Rochester	NY	14692	585-334-8030	334-9141
TF: 800-333-4079 ■ *Web:* www.diamondpkg.com					
Economy Folding Box Corp 2601 S La Salle St.	Chicago	IL	60616	312-225-2000	225-3082
Web: www.economyfoldingboxcorp.com					
F & S Carton Co 5265 Kellogg Woods Dr SE	Grand Rapids	MI	49548	616-538-9400	538-2650
Web: www.fscarton.com					
Fuller Box Co 150 Chestnut St.	North Attleboro	MA	02760	508-695-2525	695-2187
Web: www.fullerbox.com					
Gift Box Corp of America 7 W 34th St	New York	NY	10001	212-684-5113	684-5117
TF: 800-443-8269 ■ *Web:* www.800giftbox.com					
Graphic Packaging International 814 Livingston Ct	Marietta	GA	30067	770-644-3000	215-0766*
NYSE: GPK ■ **Fax Area Code: 303* ■ *TF:* 800-677-2886 ■ *Web:* www.graphicpkg.com					
House of Packaging Inc 13170 Temple Ave	City of Industry	CA	91746	626-369-3371	333-6115
Web: www.hopbox.com					
Hub Folding Box Co Inc 774 Norfolk St.	Mansfield	MA	02048	508-339-0005	339-0102
TF: 800-334-1113					
Knight Paper Box Co Inc 4651 W 72nd St	Chicago	IL	60629	773-585-2035	585-3824
Kramer Carton Co Inc 1800 61st St.	Sacramento	CA	95817	916-452-5363	451-3561
Web: www.kramercarton.com					
Mafcote Industries Inc 108 Main St.	Norwalk	CT	06851	203-847-8500	849-9177
TF Cust Svc: 800-221-3056 ■ *Web:* www.mafcote.com					
Malnove Inc 13434 F St.	Omaha	NE	68137	402-330-1100	330-2941
TF: 800-228-9877 ■ *Web:* www.malnove.com					
Massillon Container Co 49 Ohio St.	Navarre	OH	44662	330-879-5653	879-2772
Web: www.vailpkg.com					
MeadWestvaco Corp 501 S 5th St.	Richmond	VA	23219	804-444-1000	
Web: www.meadwestvaco.com					
Menasha Corp 1645 Bergstrom Rd	Neenah	WI	54956	920-751-1000	751-1236
TF: 800-558-5073 ■ *Web:* www.menasha.com					
MOD-PAC Corp 1801 Elmwood Ave.	Buffalo	NY	14207	716-873-0640	873-6008
NASDAQ: MPAC ■ *TF Cust Svc:* 800-666-3722 ■ *Web:* www.modpac.com					

Company	City	State	Zip	Phone	Fax
Pactiv Corp 1900 W Field Ct *NYSE: PTV* ■ *TF:* 888-828-2850 ■ *Web:* www.pactiv.com	Lake Forest	IL	60045	847-482-2000	482-4738
Panoramic Inc 1500 N Parker Dr *TF:* 800-333-1394 ■ *Web:* www.panoramicinc.com	Janesville	WI	53545	608-754-8850	754-5703
Paragon Packaging Inc 49-B Sherwood Terr *TF:* 888-615-0065 ■ *Web:* www.paragonpackaging.com	Lake Bluff	IL	60044	847-615-0065	615-0099
Rex Packaging 136 Eastport Rd *TF:* 800-821-0798 ■ *Web:* www.rexcorp.com	Jacksonville	FL	32218	904-757-5210	757-5353
Rice Packaging Inc 356 Somers Rd **Fax:* Sales ■ *TF:* 800-367-6725 ■ *Web:* www.ricepackaging.com	Ellington	CT	06029	860-872-8341	871-6834*
Rose City Printing & Packaging Inc 3100 NW Industrial St *TF:* 800-704-8693 ■ *Web:* www.rcpp.com	Portland	OR	97210	503-241-6486	241-3604
Royal Paper Box Co of California Inc PO Box 458 *Web:* www.royalpaperbox.com	Montebello	CA	90640	323-728-7041	722-2646
RTS Packaging LLC 504 Thrasher St *TF:* 800-558-6984 ■ *Web:* www.rtspackaging.com	Norcross	GA	30071	770-448-2244	449-0261
Rusken Packaging Inc PO Box 2100 *TF:* 800-232-8108 ■ *Web:* www.rusken.com	Cullman	AL	35056	256-734-0092	734-3008
Saint Joseph Packaging Inc 4515 Easton Rd *TF:* 800-383-3000	Saint Joseph	MO	64503	816-891-3486	233-2475
Seaboard Folding Box Corp 35 Daniels St *TF:* 800-225-6313	Fitchburg	MA	01420	978-342-8921	342-1105
Sheboygan Paper Box Co 716 Clara Ave PO Box 326 *TF:* 800-458-8373 ■ *Web:* www.spbox.com	Sheboygan	WI	53082	920-458-8373	458-2901
Sonoco 1 N 2nd St *NYSE: SON* ■ **Fax:* PR ■ *TF:* 800-377-2692 ■ *Web:* www.sonoco.com	Hartsville	SC	29550	843-383-7000	383-7008*
Southern Standard Cartons Inc 2415 Plantside Dr *Web:* www.sthestandardgroup.com	Louisville	KY	40299	502-491-2760	491-2767
Stephen Gould Corp 35 S Jefferson Rd *TF:* 800-253-1961 ■ *Web:* www.stephengould.com	Whippany	NJ	07981	973-428-1500	428-5274
Sterling Paper Co 2155 E Castor Ave *TF:* 800-745-5350	Philadelphia	PA	19134	215-744-5350	533-9577
Tetra Pak Inc 101 Corporate Woods Pkwy *TF:* 800-358-3872 ■ *Web:* www.tetrapak.com	Vernon Hills	IL	60061	847-955-6000	955-6500
Thoro-Packaging Inc 1467 Davril Cir *Web:* www.thoropkg.com	Corona	CA	92880	951-278-2100	
Triumph Packaging Group 515 W Crossroads Pkwy *Web:* www.triumphpackaging.com	Bolingbrook	IL	60440	630-771-0900	771-0522
Tropical Paper Box Co 7000 NW 25th St	Miami	FL	33122	305-592-5520	599-8966
Utah Paper Box Co Inc 340 W 200 S *Web:* www.upbslc.com	Salt Lake City	UT	84101	801-363-0093	363-9212
Winchester Carton Corp PO Box 597 *TF:* 800-633-5967 ■ *Web:* www.winchestercarton.com	Eutaw	AL	35462	205-372-3337	372-9226

102 BREWERIES

SEE ALSO Malting Products p. 2215

Company	City	State	Zip	Phone	Fax
Abita Brewing Co 21084 Hwy 36 *TF:* 800-737-2311 ■ *Web:* www.abita.com	Covington	LA	70433	985-893-3143	898-3546
Alaskan Brewing Co 5429 Shaune Dr *Web:* www.alaskanbeer.com	Juneau	AK	99801	907-780-5866	780-4514
Anchor Brewing Co 1705 Mariposa St *Web:* www.anchorbrewing.com	San Francisco	CA	94107	415-863-8350	552-7094
Anheuser-Busch InBev 250 Pk Ave *Web:* www.ab-inbev.com	New York	NY	10177	212-573-8800	
Asahi Beer USA Inc 20000 Mariner Ave Suite 300 *Web:* www.asahibeerusa.com	Torrance	CA	90503	310-921-4000	921-4001
Boston Beer Co 1 Design Ctr Pl Suite 850 *NYSE: SAM* ■ *TF:* 800-372-1131 ■ *Web:* www.bostonbeer.com	Boston	MA	02210	617-368-5000	368-5500
Boulder Beer Co 2880 Wilderness Pl *Web:* www.boulderbeer.com	Boulder	CO	80301	303-444-8448	444-4796
Boulevard Brewing Co 2501 SW Blvd *Web:* www.boulevard.com	Kansas City	MO	64108	816-474-7095	474-1722
Breckinridge Brewery Denver 2220 Blake St *Web:* www.breckbrew.com	Denver	CO	80205	303-297-3644	297-2341
BridgePort Brewing Co 1318 NW Northrup St *TF:* 888-834-7546 ■ *Web:* www.bridgeportbrew.com	Portland	OR	97209	503-241-7179	241-0625
Brooklyn Brewery The 79 N 11th St *Web:* www.brooklynbrewery.com	Brooklyn	NY	11211	718-486-7422	486-7440
Capital Brewery 7734 Terr Ave *Web:* www.capital-brewery.com	Middleton	WI	53562	608-836-7100	831-9155
Cold Spring Brewing Co 219 Red River Ave N PO Box 476 *Web:* www.coldspringbrewery.com	Cold Spring	MN	56320	320-685-8686	685-8318
Coors Brewing Co PO Box 4030 *TF:* 800-642-6116 ■ *Web:* www.coors.com	Golden	CO	80401	303-279-6565	277-6246
DG Yuengling & Son Inc 5th & Mahantongo St *Web:* www.yuengling.com	Pottsville	PA	17901	570-622-4141	622-4011
DL Geary Brewing Co Inc 38 Evergreen Dr *Web:* www.gearybrewing.com	Portland	ME	04103	207-878-2337	878-2388
Flying Dog Brewery LLC 2401 Blake St *Web:* www.flyingdogales.com	Denver	CO	80205	303-292-5027	296-0164
Great Lakes Brewing Co 2516 Market Ave *Web:* www.greatlakesbrewing.com	Cleveland	OH	44113	216-771-4404	771-2799
Harpoon Brewery 306 Northern Ave *TF:* 888-427-7666 ■ *Web:* www.harpoonbrewery.com	Boston	MA	02210	617-574-9551	482-9361
Heineken USA 360 Hamilton Ave Suite 1103 *TF:* 800-811-4951 ■ *Web:* www.heineken.com	White Plains	NY	10601	914-681-4100	681-1900
Humboldt Brews 856 10th St *Web:* www.humbrews.com	Arcata	CA	95521	707-826-2739	826-2045
Jacob Leinenkugel Brewing Co Hwy 124 N PO Box 368 *TF:* 888-534-6437 ■ *Web:* www.leinie.com	Chippewa Falls	WI	54729	715-723-5557	
John I Haas Inc 31 N 1st Ave *Web:* www.johnihaas.com	Yakima	WA	98902	509-469-4000	469-4089
Jones Brewing Co 260 2nd St *Web:* www.stoneysbeer.com	Smithton	PA	15479	724-872-6626	872-6538
Keurig Inc 55 Walkers Brook Dr *Web:* www.keurig.com	Reading	MA	01867	866-901-2739	
Kirin Brewery of America LLC 21241 S Western Ave Suite 110 *Web:* www.kirin.com	Torrance	CA	90501	310-354-3040	354-5955
Labatt Breweries of Canada 207 Queen's Quay W Suite 299 *TF Cust Svc:* 800-268-2337 ■ *Web:* www.labatt.com	Toronto	ON	M5J1A7	416-361-5050	
Latrobe Brewing Co 119 Jefferson St *Web:* www.rollingrock.com	Latrobe	PA	15650	724-537-5545	537-4035
Lion Brewery Inc 700 N Pennsylvania Ave *TF:* 800-233-8327 ■ *Web:* www.lionbrewery.com	Wilkes-Barre	PA	18705	570-823-8801	823-6686
Long Trail Brewing Co 5520 US Rt 4 *Web:* www.longtrail.com	Bridgewater Corners	VT	05035	802-672-5011	672-5012
Malt Products Corp 88 Market St *TF:* 800-526-0180 ■ *Web:* www.maltproducts.com	Saddle Brook	NJ	07663	201-845-4420	845-0028
Matt Brewing Co 811 Edward St *Web:* www.saranac.com	Utica	NY	13502	315-624-2400	624-2401
McMenamins 430 N Killingsworth *Web:* www.mcmenamins.com	Portland	OR	97217	503-223-0109	294-0837
Mendocino Brewing Co 455 Kunzler Ranch Rd *Web:* www.mendobrew.com	Ukiah	CA	95482	707-462-1697	462-1699
Minhas Craft Brewery 1208 14th Ave *Web:* www.minhasbrewery.com	Monroe	WI	53566	608-325-3191	325-3198
Molson Coors Brewing Co 1225 17th St Suite 3200 *NYSE: TAP* ■ *TF:* 800-642-6116 ■ *Web:* www.molsoncoors.com	Denver	CO	80202	303-927-2337	277-6246
New Belgium Brewing Co 500 Linden St *TF:* 888-622-4044 ■ *Web:* www.newbelgium.com	Fort Collins	CO	80524	970-221-0524	221-0535
North Coast Brewing Co Inc 455 N Main St *TF:* 866-955-4190 ■ *Web:* www.northcoastbrewing.com	Fort Bragg	CA	95437	707-964-2739	964-8768
Odell Brewing Co 800 E Lincoln Ave *TF:* 888-887-2797 ■ *Web:* www.odells.com	Fort Collins	CO	80524	970-498-9070	498-0706
Pabst Brewing Co PO Box 792627 *TF:* 800-935-2337 ■ *Web:* www.pabstbrewingco.com	San Antonio	TX	78279	210-226-0231	226-0231
Pittsburgh Brewing Co 3340 Liberty Ave	Pittsburgh	PA	15201	412-682-7400	692-1189
Prairie Malt Ltd (PML) PO Box 1150 *Web:* www.prairiemaltltd.com	Biggar	SK	S0K0M0	306-948-3500	948-3969
Pyramid Brewing Co 91 S Royal Brougham Way *Web:* www.pyramidbrew.com	Seattle	WA	98134	206-682-8322	682-8420
Redhook Ale Brewery Inc 929 N Russell St *NASDAQ: HOOK* ■ *Web:* www.craftbrewers.com	Portland	OR	97227	503-331-7270	331-7264
Rogue Ales Co 2320 OSU Dr *TF:* 800-850-1115 ■ *Web:* www.rogue.com	Newport	OR	97365	541-867-3660	867-3260
Saint Stan's Brewery 821 L St *Web:* www.ststans.com	Modesto	CA	95354	209-527-7826	524-4827
Sierra Nevada Brewing Co 1075 E 20th St *Web:* www.sierranevada.com	Chico	CA	95928	530-893-3520	893-1275
Summit Brewing Co 910 Montreal Cir *Web:* www.summitbrewing.com	Saint Paul	MN	55102	651-265-7800	265-7801
Widmer Bros Brewing Co 929 N Russell St *TF:* 800-943-6371 ■ *Web:* www.widmerbrothers.com	Portland	OR	97227	503-281-2437	281-1496

BROKERS

SEE Commodity Contracts Brokers & Dealers p. 1668; Electronic Communications Networks (ECNs) p. 1811; Freight Forwarders p. 1888; Insurance Agents, Brokers, Services p. 2111; Mortgage Lenders & Loan Brokers p. 2254; Real Estate Agents & Brokers p. 2518; Securities Brokers & Dealers p. 2646; Ticket Brokers p. 2714

103 BRUSHES & BROOMS

SEE ALSO Art Materials & Supplies - Mfr p. 1402

Company	City	State	Zip	Phone	Fax
A & B Brush Mfg Corp 1150 Three Ranch Rd	Duarte	CA	91010	626-303-8856	303-1207
Abco Cleaning Products 6800 NW 36th Ave *TF:* 888-694-2226 ■ *Web:* www.abcoproducts.com	Miami	FL	33147	305-694-2226	694-0451
Advanced Products Co 1015 Spring Garden St	Philadelphia	PA	19123	215-232-5926	232-3019
AJ Siris Corp Inc 59 Lewis St *TF:* 800-526-5300 ■ *Web:* www.ajsiris.com	Paterson	NJ	07501	973-684-7700	684-3251
American Brush Co Inc 300 Industrial Blvd *TF:* 800-225-0392	Claremont	NH	03743	603-542-9951	542-2086
Brush Research Mfg Co Inc 4642 Floral Dr *Web:* www.brushresearch.com	Los Angeles	CA	90022	323-261-2193	268-6587
Brushes Corp 5400 Smith Rd *TF Cust Svc:* 800-967-9697 ■ *Web:* www.brushescorp.com	Brook Park	OH	44142	216-267-8084	267-9077
Brushtech Inc 4 Matt Ave *TF:* 800-346-0818	Plattsburgh	NY	12901	518-563-8420	563-0581
Carlisle Sanitary Maintenance Products 402 S Black River St *TF:* 800-356-8366 ■ *Web:* www.carlislesmp.com	Sparta	WI	54656	608-269-2151	269-3293
Corona Brushes Inc 5065 Savarese Cir *TF:* 800-458-3483 ■ *Web:* www.coronabrushes.com	Tampa	FL	33634	813-885-2525	882-9810
Cosgrove Enterprises 16000 NW 49th Ave *TF Cust Svc:* 800-888-3396	Miami	FL	33014	305-623-6700	623-6935
Crystal Lake Mfg Inc 2225 Hwy 14 W PO Box 159 *TF:* 800-633-8720 ■ *Web:* www.crystallakemfg.com	Autaugaville	AL	36003	334-365-3342	365-3332
Danline Inc 1 Silver Ct *TF:* 800-552-7874 ■ *Web:* www.danlinebrushes.com	Springfield	NJ	07081	973-376-1000	376-9888
Detroit Quality Brush Mfg 32165 Schoolcraft Rd *TF:* 800-722-3037	Livonia	MI	48150	734-525-5660	525-0437

				Phone	Fax
Felton Brush Inc 7 Burton Dr	Londonderry	NH	03053	603-425-0200	425-0200
TF: 800-258-9702 ■ *Web:* www.feltoninc.com					
Fuller Brush Co The 1 Fuller Way	Great Bend	KS	67530	620-792-1711	792-1906
TF Cust Svc: 800-438-5537 ■ *Web:* www.fuller.com					
Gordon Brush Mfg Co Inc 6247 Randolph St	Commerce	CA	90040	323-724-7777	724-1111
TF: 800-950-7950 ■ *Web:* www.gordonbrush.com					
Greenwood Mop & Broom Inc 312 Palmer St PO Drawer 1426	Greenwood	SC	29648	864-227-8411	227-3200
TF: 800-635-6849 ■ *Web:* www.greenwoodmopandbroom.com					
Hamburg Industries Inc 218 Pine St	Hamburg	PA	19526	610-562-3031	562-0209
Web: www.hamburgindustries.com					
Harper Brush Works Inc 400 N 2nd St	Fairfield	IA	52556	641-472-5186	472-3187
TF: 800-223-7894 ■ *Web:* www.harperbrush.com					
Industrial Brush Co Inc 105 Clinton Rd	Fairfield	NJ	07004	973-575-0455	575-6169
TF: 800-241-9860 ■ *Web:* www.indbrush.com					
Industrial Brush Corp 1250 Philadelphia St	Pomona	CA	91766	909-591-9341	627-8916
TF: 800-228-6146 ■ *Web:* www.industrialbrush.com					
Industries for the Blind 3220 W Vliet St	Milwaukee	WI	53208	414-933-4319	933-4316
TF: 800-642-8778 ■ *Web:* www.ibmilw.com					
Industries of the Blind Inc 914 W Lee St # 920	Greensboro	NC	27403	336-274-1591	274-9207
Web: www.industriesoftheblind.com					
Keystone Plastics Inc 3451 County Rd 663	South Plainfield	NJ	07080	908-561-1300	561-3404
TF: 800-635-5238 ■ *Web:* www.keystonesweeperbrushes.com					
Laitner Brush Co 1561 Laitner Dr	Traverse City	MI	49686	231-929-3300	929-7219
TF Cust Svc: 800-423-6805 ■ *Web:* www.laitner.com					
Libman Co 220 N Sheldon St	Arcola	IL	61910	800-646-6262	268-4168*
**Fax Area Code:* 217 ■ *TF:* 800-646-6262 ■ *Web:* www.libman.com					
Linzer Products Corp 248 Wyandanch Ave	Wyandanch	NY	11798	631-253-3333	253-9750
TF: 800-221-0787 ■ *Web:* www.linzerproducts.com					
Magnolia Brush Mfg Inc 1000 N Cedar	Clarksville	TX	75426	903-427-2261	427-5230
TF: 800-248-2261 ■ *Web:* www.magnoliabrush.com					
Mill-Rose Co 7995 Tyler Blvd	Mentor	OH	44060	440-255-9171	255-5039
TF: 800-321-3533 ■ *Web:* www.millrose.com					
Newell Rubbermaid Inc Shur-Line Div 4051 S Iowa Ave	Saint Francis	WI	53235	414-481-4500	481-7642
TF: 800-558-3958 ■ *Web:* www.shurline.com					
O-Cedar/Vileda Inc 505 N Railroad Ave	North Lake	IL	60164	708-452-4100	452-9967
TF: 800-543-8105 ■ *Web:* www.ocedar.com					
Ohio Brush Co 2680 Lisbon Rd	Cleveland	OH	44104	216-791-3265	791-6615
TF: 888-411-3265 ■ *Web:* www.ohiobrush.com					
Osborn International 5401 Hamilton Ave	Cleveland	OH	44114	216-361-1900	361-1913
TF Cust Svc: 800-720-3358 ■ *Web:* www.osborn.com					
Padco Inc 2220 Elm St SE	Minneapolis	MN	55414	612-378-7270	378-9388
TF: 800-328-5513 ■ *Web:* www.padco.com					
PFERD Milwaukee Brush Co Inc 30 Jytek Dr	Leominster	MA	01453	978-840-6420	840-6421
TF: 800-342-9015 ■ *Web:* www.pferdusa.com					
Prager Brush Co Inc 730 Echo St NW	Atlanta	GA	30318	404-875-9292	872-1161
TF: 800-241-5696					
Rubberset Co 26466 Silver Ln	Crisfield	MD	21817	410-968-1050	968-0861
Web: www.rubberset.com					
Rutland Products 86 Ctr St PO Box 340	Rutland	VT	05702	802-775-5519	775-5262
TF: 800-544-1307 ■ *Web:* www.rutland.com					
Sanderson-MacLeod Inc 1199 S Main St PO Box 50	Palmer	MA	01069	413-283-3481	289-1919
TF: 866-522-3481 ■ *Web:* www.sandersonmacleod.com					
SM Arnold Inc 7901 Michigan Ave	Saint Louis	MO	63111	314-544-4103	544-3159
TF Cust Svc: 800-325-7865 ■ *Web:* www.smarnold.com					
Super Brush Co 800 Worcester St	Springfield	MA	01151	413-543-1442	543-1523
Web: www.superbrush.com					
Sweepster Inc 2800 N Zeeb Rd	Dexter	MI	48130	734-996-9116	996-9014
TF: 800-456-7100 ■ *Web:* www.paladinlightconstructiongroup.com					
Universal Brush Mfg Co 16200 Dixie Hwy	Markham	IL	60428	708-331-1700	331-4923
TF: 800-323-3474 ■ *Web:* www.universalbrush.com					
Weiler Corp 1 Wildwood Dr	Cresco	PA	18326	570-595-7495	595-2002
TF Cust Svc: 800-835-9999 ■ *Web:* www.weilercorp.com					
Wilen Products Inc 3760 S Side Industrial Pkwy	Atlanta	GA	30354	404-366-2111	361-8832
Web: www.wilen.com					
Wooster Brush Co 604 Madison Ave	Wooster	OH	44691	330-264-4440	263-0495
TF: 800-392-7246 ■ *Web:* www.woosterbrush.com					
Zephyr Mfg Co Inc 200 Mitchell Rd	Sedalia	MO	65301	660-827-0352	827-0713
TF: 800-821-7197 ■ *Web:* www.zephyrmfg.com					

104 BUILDING MAINTENANCE SERVICES

SEE ALSO Cleaning Services p. 1606

				Phone	Fax
Aid Maintenance Co 300 Roosevelt Ave PO Box 476	Pawtucket	RI	02860	401-722-6627	723-6860
Web: www.aidmaintenance.com					
American Bldg Maintenance Co 160 Pacific Ave Suite 222	San Francisco	CA	94111	415-733-4000	733-7333
TF: 888-225-2260					
Broadway Services Inc 3709 E Monument St	Baltimore	MD	21205	410-563-6900	563-6960
Web: www.broadwayservices.com					
Denali Ventures Inc 5613 DTC Pkwy Suite 200	Greenwood Village	CO	80111	303-716-5000	716-5145
TF: 877-290-5590 ■ *Web:* www.denaliventures.com					
FBG Service Corp 407 S 27th Ave	Omaha	NE	68131	402-346-4422	595-5044
TF: 800-777-8326 ■ *Web:* www.fbgservices.com					
Harvard Maintenance Co 570 7th Ave	New York	NY	10018	212-730-0001	398-6599
Web: www.harvardmaint.com					
Janitronics Bldg Services 29 Sawyer Rd	Waltham	MA	02453	781-647-5570	893-5878
Web: www.janitronics.com					
Powerplant Maintenance Specialists Inc (PMSI) 2900 Bristol St Suite H202	Costa Mesa	CA	92626	714-427-6900	427-6905
Web: www.pmsipower.com					
Style Crest Inc 2450 Enterprise St	Fremont	OH	43420	419-332-7369	332-8763
TF: 800-925-4440 ■ *Web:* www.stylecrestproducts.com					
Temco Service Industries Inc 1 Pk Ave	New York	NY	10016	212-889-6353	213-9854
Varsity Contractors Inc 315 S 5th Ave PO Box 1692	Pocatello	ID	83201	208-232-8598	232-6068
Web: www.varsitycontractors.com					

105 BUILDINGS - PREFABRICATED - METAL

				Phone	Fax
Aci Bldg Systems Inc PO Box 1316	Batesville	MS	38606	662-563-4574	563-1142
Web: www.acibuildingsystems.com					
American Buildings Co 1150 State Docks Rd	Eufaula	AL	36027	334-687-2032	688-2261
TF: 877-859-4313 ■ *Web:* www.americanbuildings.com					
American Modular Technologies 6306 Old 421 Rd	Liberty	NC	27298	336-622-6200	622-6473
Web: www.americanmodular.org					
American Steel Bldg Co Inc 12218 Robin Blvd	Houston	TX	77045	713-433-5661	433-0847
TF: 800-877-8335					
Behlen Mfg Co 4025 E 23rd St	Columbus	NE	68601	402-564-3111	563-7405
TF: 800-553-5520 ■ *Web:* www.behlenmfg.com					
Butler Mfg Co 1540 Genessee St	Kansas City	MO	64102	816-968-3000	968-6506*
**Fax:* Hum Res ■ *Web:* www.butlermfg.com					
California Expanded Metal Products Co (Inc) 263 N Covina Ln	City of Industry	CA	91746	626-369-3564	330-7598
TF: 800-775-2362 ■ *Web:* www.cemcosteel.com					
Ceco Bldg Systems 2400 Hwy 45 N	Columbus	MS	39705	662-328-6722	243-2781
Web: www.cecobuildings.com					
Clearspan Components Inc 6110 Old Hwy 80 W	Meridian	MS	39307	601-483-3941	483-3941
Conley's Mfg & Sales Inc 4344 Mission Blvd	Montclair	CA	91763	909-627-0981	628-3774
TF: 800-377-8441 ■ *Web:* www.conleys.com					
Dean Steel Buildings Inc 2929 Industrial Ave	Fort Myers	FL	33901	239-334-1051	334-0932
Web: www.deanintl.com					
DeRaffele Mfg Co Inc 2525 Palmer Ave	New Rochelle	NY	10801	914-636-6850	636-6596
Dura-Bilt Products Inc PO Box 188	Wellsburg	NY	14894	570-596-2000	596-3296
TF: 800-233-4251 ■ *Web:* www.durabilt.com					
Erect-A-Tube Inc 701 W Pk St PO Box 100	Harvard	IL	60033	815-943-4091	943-4095
TF: 800-624-9219 ■ *Web:* www.erect-a-tube.com					
Four Seasons Solar Products LLC 5005 Veterans Memorial Hwy	Holbrook	NY	11741	631-563-4000	563-4010
TF: 800-368-7732 ■ *Web:* www.fourseasonssunrooms.com					
Garco Bldg Systems 2714 S Garfield Rd	Airway Heights	WA	99001	509-244-5611	244-2850
TF: 800-941-2291 ■ *Web:* www.garcobuildings.com					
Gichner Systems Group Inc 490 E Locust St	Dallastown	PA	17313	717-244-7611	246-5475
Web: www.gichner.us					
Gulf States Manufacturers 101 Airport Rd PO Box 1128	Starkville	MS	39760	662-323-8021	324-2984
TF: 800-844-4853 ■ *Web:* www.gulfstatesmanufacturers.com					
Imperial Industries Inc 505 Industrial Pk Ave	Rothschild	WI	54474	715-359-0200	355-5349
TF: 800-558-2945 ■ *Web:* www.imperialind.com					
International Bldg Systems Inc 7150 Almeda Genoa Rd	Houston	TX	77075	713-991-7900	991-3939
Jewell Bldg Systems Inc 1932 Jordache Ct	Dallas	NC	28052	704-869-6169	
Kirby Bldg Systems Inc 124 Kirby Dr	Portland	TN	37148	615-325-4165	325-4700
TF: 800-348-7799 ■ *Web:* www.kirbybuildingsystems.com					
Lark Builders Inc 409 Dixon St	Vidalia	GA	30474	912-538-1888	538-0057
TF: 800-841-7844 ■ *Web:* www.larkbuilders.com					
Ludwig Buildings Inc 521 Timesaver Ave	Harahan	LA	70123	504-733-6260	733-7458
Madison Industries Inc of Georgia 1035 Iris Dr	Conyers	GA	30094	770-483-4401	785-6622
Web: www.madisonind.com					
Mesco Bldg Solutions 5244 Bear Creek Ct	Irving	TX	75061	214-687-9999	687-9736
TF: 800-556-3726 ■ *Web:* www.mescobldg.com					
Metal Bldg Components Inc 10943 Sam Houston Pkwy W	Houston	TX	77064	281-897-7788	477-9672
TF: 877-713-6224 ■ *Web:* www.mbci.com					
Metecno-ASI 725 Summerhill Dr	DeLand	FL	32724	386-626-6789	734-3289
TF: 888-882-5862 ■ *Web:* www.alumashield.com					
Metl-Span LLC 1720 Lakepointe Dr Suite 101	Lewisville	TX	75057	972-221-6656	420-9382
TF: 877-585-9969 ■ *Web:* www.metlspan.com					
Mid-West Steel Bldg Co 7301 Fairview St	Houston	TX	77041	713-466-7788	466-3194
TF: 800-777-9378 ■ *Web:* www.mid-weststeel.com					
Miracle Steel Corp 600 Oakwood Rd PO Box 1266	Watertown	SD	57201	605-886-7885	886-3036
TF: 888-508-4545 ■ *Web:* www.miracletruss.com					
Mobile Mini Inc 7420 S Kyrene Rd Suite 101	Tempe	AZ	85283	480-894-6311	894-1505
NASDAQ: MINI ■ *TF:* 800-288-5669 ■ *Web:* www.mobilemini.com					
Morton Buildings Inc 252 W Adams St PO Box 399	Morton	IL	61550	309-263-7474	266-5123
TF: 800-447-7436 ■ *Web:* www.mortonbuildings.com					
Mueller Inc 1913 Hutchins Ave	Ballinger	TX	76821	325-365-3555	365-8181
TF: 877-268-3553 ■ *Web:* www.muellerinc.com					
National Greenhouse Co 6 Industrial Dr	Pana	IL	62557	217-562-9333	562-2841
TF: 800-826-9314					
NCI Bldg Systems Inc 10943 N Sam Houston PkwyWest	Houston	TX	77064	281-897-7788	477-9674
NYSE: NCS ■ *TF:* 800-777-9378 ■ *Web:* www.ncilp.com					
Nucor Bldg Systems 305 Industrial Pkwy	Waterloo	IN	46793	260-837-7891	837-7384
Web: www.nucorbuildingsystems.com					
Package Industries Inc 15 Harback Rd	Sutton	MA	01590	508-865-5871	865-9130
TF: 800-225-7242 ■ *Web:* www.packagesteel.com					
Parkline Inc PO Box 65	Winfield	WV	25213	304-586-2113	586-3842
TF: 800-786-4855 ■ *Web:* www.parkline.com					
Porta-Fab Corp 18080 Chesterfield Airport Rd	Chesterfield	MO	63005	636-537-5555	537-2955
TF: 800-325-3781 ■ *Web:* www.portafab.com					
PorterCorp 4240 136th Ave	Holland	MI	49424	616-399-1963	399-9123
TF: 800-354-7721 ■ *Web:* www.portercorp.com					
Protect Controls Inc (PCI) 303 Little York Rd	Houston	TX	77076	713-691-5183	691-0159
Web: www.protectcontrols.com					
Red Dot Corp 1209 W Corsicana St	Athens	TX	75751	903-675-9181	675-9180
TF Cust Svc: 800-657-2234 ■ *Web:* www.reddotbuildings.com					

	City	State	ZIP	Phone	Fax
Rigid Bldg Systems Ltd					
18933 Aldine Westfield Rd	Houston	TX	77073	281-443-9065	443-9064
TF: 888-467-4443 ■ *Web:* www.rigidbuilding.com					
Ruffin Bldg Systems Inc 6914 Louisiana 2	Oak Grove	LA	71263	318-428-2305	428-2231
TF: 800-421-4232 ■ *Web:* www.ruffinbuildingsystems.com					
Safety Storage Inc 855 N 5th St	Charleston	IL	61920	831-637-5955	637-7405
TF: 800-344-6539 ■ *Web:* www.safetystorage.com					
Star Bldg Systems 8600 S I-35	Oklahoma City	OK	73149	405-636-2010	636-2419
TF: 800-879-7827 ■ *Web:* www.starbuildings.com					
Stuppy Greenhouse Mfg Inc 120 E 12th Ave	Kansas City	MO	64116	816-842-3071	423-1512
Tampa Tank Inc 2710 E 5th Ave	Tampa	FL	33605	813-623-2675	622-7514
Web: www.tampatank.com					
Temo Sunrooms Inc 20400 Hall Rd	Clinton Township	MI	48038	586-286-0410	286-5409
TF: 800-344-8366 ■ *Web:* www.temosunrooms.com					
Tj Truss Corp 2801 Industrial Ave 2	Fort Pierce	FL	34946	772-466-3388	466-9329
Web: www.tjtruss.com					
Trachte Bldg Systems Inc 314 Wilburn Rd	Sun Prairie	WI	53590	800-356-5824	981-9014
TF: 800-356-5824 ■ *Web:* www.trachte.com					
Truss-T Structures Inc 2100 N Pacific Hwy	Woodburn	OR	97071	503-981-9581	981-9584
TF: 800-727-7844 ■ *Web:* www.pbsbuildings.com					
Tyler Bldg Systems LP					
3535 Shiloh Rd PO Box 130819	Tyler	TX	75707	903-561-3000	561-7686
TF: 800-442-8979 ■ *Web:* www.tylerbuilding.com					
United Structures of America Inc					
1912 Buschong	Houston	TX	77039	281-442-8247	442-2125
Web: www.usabldg.com					
VP Buildings Inc 3200 Players Club Cir	Memphis	TN	38125	901-748-8000	748-9323
Web: www.vp.com					
WedgCor Bldg Systems Inc 6800 E Hampden Ave	Denver	CO	80224	303-759-3200	759-3025
TF: 800-964-8335 ■ *Web:* www.wedgcor.com					
Whirlwind Steel 8234 Hansen Rd	Houston	TX	77075	713-946-7140	553-4992*
**Fax Area Code:* 832 ■ *TF:* 800-324-9992 ■ *Web:* www.whirlwindsteel.com					
Winandy Greenhouse Co 2211 Peacock Rd	Richmond	IN	47374	765-935-2111	935-2110
XS Smith Inc PO Box X	Red Bank	NJ	07701	732-222-4600	222-7288
TF: 800-631-2226 ■ *Web:* www.xssmith.com					

106 BUILDINGS - PREFABRICATED - WOOD

	City	State	ZIP	Phone	Fax
Acorn Deck House Co 852 Main St	Acton	MA	01720	978-263-6800	263-4159
TF: 800-727-3325 ■ *Web:* www.deckhouse.com					
All American Homes LLC 309 S 13th St	Decatur	IN	46733	260-724-8044	724-8987
Web: www.allamericanhomes.com					
Barden & Robeson Corp 103 Kelly Ave	Middleport	NY	14105	716-735-3732	735-3752
TF: 800-724-0141 ■ *Web:* www.bardenhomes.com					
Blazer Industries Inc PO Box 489	Aumsville	OR	97325	503-749-1900	749-3969
TF: 877-211-3437 ■ *Web:* www.blazerind.com					
Cardinal Homes Inc					
525 Barnesville Hwy PO Box 10	Wylliesburg	VA	23976	434-735-8111	735-8824
Web: www.cardinalhomes.com					
Deluxe Bldg Systems Inc 499 W 3rd St	Berwick	PA	18603	570-752-5914	752-1525
TF: 800-843-7372 ■ *Web:* www.deluxehomes.com					
Design Homes Inc 600 N Marquette Rd	Prairie du Chien	WI	53821	608-326-6041	326-4233
TF: 800-627-9443 ■ *Web:* www.designhomes.com					
Dickinson Homes Inc					
404 S Stephenson Ave Hwy US-2	Iron Mountain	MI	49801	906-774-2186	774-2186
TF: 800-343-8179 ■ *Web:* www.dickinsonhomes.com					
Dynamic Homes LLC 525 Roosevelt Ave	Detroit Lakes	MN	56501	218-847-2611	847-2617*
**Fax:* Orders ■ *TF:* 800-492-4833 ■ *Web:* www.dynamichomes.com					
Farwest Homes 887 NW State Ave PO Box 480	Chehalis	WA	98532	360-748-3351	748-6443
TF: 800-752-0500 ■ *Web:* www.farwesthomes.com					
Fleetwood Homes of California Inc					
7007 Jurupa Ave	Riverside	CA	92504	951-688-5353	351-0378
TF: 800-999-9265 ■ *Web:* www.fleetwoodhomes.com					
Foremost Industries Inc					
2375 Buchanan Trail W	Greencastle	PA	17225	717-597-7166	597-5579
TF: 877-284-5334 ■ *Web:* www.foremosthomes.com					
Gary Doupnik Mfg Inc 3237 Rippey Rd PO Box 527	Loomis	CA	95650	916-652-9291	652-9021
Web: www.gdmfg.com					
Haven Homes Inc					
554 Eagle Valley Rd PO Box 178	Beech Creek	PA	16822	570-962-2111	962-3181
TF: 800-424-2836 ■ *Web:* www.havenhomes.com					
Heckaman Homes Inc 6 E	Nappanee	IN	46550	574-773-4167	773-2546
Web: www.heckamanhomes.com					
Heritage Log Homes Inc 1 Heritage Pl	Kodak	TN	37764	865-453-0140	429-4434
TF: 800-456-4663 ■ *Web:* www.heritagelog.com					
Homes by Keystone Inc					
13338 Midvale Rd PO Box 69	Waynesboro	PA	17268	717-762-1104	762-1106
TF: 800-890-7926 ■ *Web:* www.homesbykeystone.com					
International Homes of Cedar Inc					
8330 Maltby Rd # B	Woodinville	WA	98072	360-668-8511	668-5562
TF: 800-767-7674 ■ *Web:* www.ihoc.com					
KanBuild Inc 6317 Raytown Rd	Raytown	KS	64133	816-737-1900	528-4795*
**Fax Area Code:* 785 ■ *TF:* 866-963-8367 ■ *Web:* www.kanbuild.com					
Keiser Industries LLC					
56 Mechanic Falls Rd PO Box 9000	Oxford	ME	04270	888-333-1748	539-0944*
**Fax Area Code:* 207 ■ *TF:* 888-333-1748 ■ *Web:* www.keiserme.com					
KIT HomeBuilders West LLC 1124 Garber St	Caldwell	ID	83605	208-454-5000	455-2995
TF: 800-859-0347 ■ *Web:* www.kitwest.com					
Lester Bldg Systems LLC					
1111 2nd Ave S	Lester Prairie	MN	55354	320-395-2531	395-5393
TF: 800-826-4439 ■ *Web:* www.lesterbuildings.com					
Lindal Cedar Homes Inc 4300 S 104th Pl	Seattle	WA	98178	206-725-0900	725-1615
TF Prod Info: 800-426-0536 ■ *Web:* www.lindal.com					
Manufactured Structures Corp (MSC)					
3089 E Fort Wayne Rd PO Box 350	Rochester	IN	46975	574-223-4794	223-9051
TF: 800-662-5344 ■ *Web:* www.mscoffice.com					
Mod-U-Kraf Homes LLC					
260 Weaver St PO Box 573	Rocky Mount	VA	24151	540-483-0291	483-2228
TF: 888-663-5723 ■ *Web:* www.mod-u-kraf.com					
Morgan Bldg Systems Inc 2800 McCree Rd	Garland	TX	75041	972-864-7300	864-7307
TF: 800-935-0321 ■ *Web:* www.morganusa.com					
Muncy Homes Inc 1567 Rt 442	Muncy	PA	17756	570-546-2261	546-5903
TF: 800-788-1555 ■ *Web:* www.muncyhomesinc.com					
Nassal Co The 415 W Kaley St	Orlando	FL	32806	407-648-0400	648-0841
Web: www.nassal.com					
Nationwide Custom Homes 1100 Rives Rd	Martinsville	VA	24115	276-632-7101	632-1181
TF: 800-216-7001 ■ *Web:* www.nationwide-homes.com					
New England Homes 270 Ocean Rd	Greenland	NH	03840	603-436-8830	431-8540
TF: 800-800-8831 ■ *Web:* www.newenglandhomes.net					
Northeastern Log Homes Inc 10 Ames Rd	Kenduskeag	ME	04450	207-884-7000	884-3000
TF: 800-624-2797 ■ *Web:* www.northeasternlog.com					
Original Lincoln Logs Ltd					
5 Riverside Dr PO Box 135	Chestertown	NY	12817	518-494-5500	494-3008
TF: 800-833-2461 ■ *Web:* www.lincolnlogs.com					
Pacific Modern Homes Inc (PMHI)					
9723 Railroad St	Elk Grove	CA	95624	916-685-9514	685-1306
TF: 800-395-1011 ■ *Web:* www.pmhi.com					
Pan Abode Cedar Homes Inc 1100 Maple Ave SW	Renton	WA	98057	425-255-8260	255-8630
TF: 800-782-2633 ■ *Web:* www.panabodehomes.com					
Pittsville Homes Inc 5094 2nd Ave PO Box C	Pittsville	WI	54466	715-884-2511	884-2136
TF: 877-248-8371 ■ *Web:* www.pittsvillehomes.com					
Porta-Kamp 555 Gelhorn Dr	Houston	TX	77029	713-674-3163	674-4844
Web: www.portakamp.com					
Rocky Mountain Log Homes 1883 Hwy 93 S	Hamilton	MT	59840	406-363-5680	363-2109
Web: www.rmlh.com					
S & G Mfg Group LLC 4830 NW Pkwy	Hilliard	OH	43026	614-334-3600	334-3631
TF: 888-529-1992 ■ *Web:* www.sgmgroup.com					
Simplex Industries Inc 1 Simplex Dr	Scranton	PA	18504	570-346-5113	346-3731
TF: 800-233-4233 ■ *Web:* www.simplexind.com					
Sterling Bldg Systems PO Box 1967	Wausau	WI	54402	715-359-7108	359-2867
Stratford Homes LP 402 S Weber Ave	Stratford	WI	54484	715-687-3133	687-3453
TF: 800-448-1524 ■ *Web:* www.stratfordhomes.com					
Timberland Homes Inc 1201 37th St NW	Auburn	WA	98001	253-735-3435	939-8803
TF: 800-488-5036 ■ *Web:* www.timberland-homes.com					
Town & Country Cedar Homes					
4772 US Hwy 131 S	Petoskey	MI	49770	231-347-4360	347-7255
TF: 800-968-3178 ■ *Web:* www.cedarhomes.com					
Trading Post Homes 8103 Dixie Hwy	Louisville	KY	40258	502-937-1515	271-3010
Web: www.tradingposthomes.com					
Unibilt Industries Inc					
8005 Johnson Stn Rd PO Box 373	Vandalia	OH	45377	937-890-7570	890-8303
TF: 800-777-9942 ■ *Web:* www.unibiltcustomhomes.com					
Ward Cedar Log Homes 39 Bangor St PO Box 72	Houlton	ME	04730	207-532-6531	532-7806
TF Cust Svc: 800-341-1566 ■ *Web:* www.wardcedarloghomes.com					
Wausau Homes Inc PO Box 8005	Wausau	WI	54402	715-359-7272	359-2867
Web: www.wausauhomes.com					
Whitley Mfg Inc 201 W 1st St PO Box 496	South Whitley	IN	46787	260-723-5131	723-6949
Web: www.whitleyman.com					
Wisconsin Homes Inc 425 W McMillan St	Marshfield	WI	54449	715-384-2161	387-3627
Web: www.wisconsinhomesinc.com					

107 BUS SERVICES - CHARTER

	City	State	ZIP	Phone	Fax
A Yankee Line 370 W First St	Boston	MA	02127	617-268-8890	268-6960
TF: 800-942-8890 ■ *Web:* www.yankeeline.us					
Action Transit Enterprises Inc					
330 Poplar St	Pittsburgh	PA	15223	412-781-7906	781-8230
Agape Tours Inc 1210 US Hwy 281	Wichita Falls	TX	76310	940-767-4935	692-8477*
**Fax:* Sales ■ *TF:* 800-460-2641 ■ *Web:* www.agapetoursinc.com					
All West Coachlines Inc 7701 Wilbur Way	Sacramento	CA	95828	916-423-4000	689-5926
TF: 800-843-2121					
American Coach Lines Inc					
2328 10th Ave N Suite 501	Lake Worth	FL	33460	561-721-1170	721-2390
Web: www.americancoachlines.com					
Anderson Coach & Travel 1 Anderson Plaza	Greenville	PA	16125	724-588-8310	588-0257
TF: 800-345-3435 ■ *Web:* www.goanderson.com					
Arrow Line Inc 19 George St	East Hartford	CT	06108	860-289-1531	289-1535
TF: 800-243-9560 ■ *Web:* www.arrowline.com					
Arrow Stage Lines 720 E Norfolk Ave	Norfolk	NE	68701	402-371-3850	371-3267
TF: 800-672-8302 ■ *Web:* www.arrowstagelines.com					
Atlantic Express Transportation Group Inc					
7 N St	Staten Island	NY	10302	718-442-7000	442-7672
TF: 800-336-3886 ■ *Web:* www.atlanticexpress.com					
Audubon Trails Coach Lines Inc					
1807 Moll Ln	Evansville	IN	47725	812-867-2098	867-2833
TF: 800-255-5234 ■ *Web:* www.audubontrailscoachlines.com					
B & C Bus Lines 427 Continental Dr	Maryville	TN	37804	865-983-4653	983-5354
TF: 877-812-2287					
Badger Bus 5501 Femrite Dr	Madison	WI	53718	608-255-1511	258-3484
TF: 800-442-8259 ■ *Web:* www.badgerbus.com					
Blue Lakes Charters & Tours 12154 N Saginaw Rd	Clio	MI	48420	810-686-4287	686-9772
TF: 800-282-4287 ■ *Web:* www.bluelakes.com					
Boise-Winnemucca Stage Lines Inc					
1105 S La Pointe St	Boise	ID	83706	208-336-3300	336-3303
TF: 800-448-5692					
Brown Coach Inc 50 Venner Rd	Amsterdam	NY	12010	518-843-4700	843-3600
Web: www.browntours.com					
Butler Motor Transit Co Inc					
210 S Monroe St PO Box 1602	Butler	PA	16003	724-282-1000	282-3080
Web: www.coachusa.com/butler					
C & H Bus Lines Inc 448 Pine St	Macon	GA	31201	478-746-6441	743-5597
Carl R Bieber Tourways Inc					
320 Fair St PO Box 180	Kutztown	PA	19530	610-683-7333	683-5384
TF: 800-243-2374 ■ *Web:* www.biebertourways.com					
Central West of Texas Inc					
3426 Gilbert Rd	Grand Prairie	TX	75050	972-399-1059	986-7262
TF: 800-533-1939 ■ *Web:* www.bus-charter.com					

	City	State	Zip	Phone	Fax
Chenango Valley Bus Lines Inc 105 Chenango St	Binghamton	NY	13901	607-723-9408	723-8883
TF: 800-647-6471					
Chippewa Trails 510 E S Ave	Chippewa Falls	WI	54729	715-726-2440	726-2455
TF: 800-657-4469 ■ *Web:* www.chippewatrailstours.com					
Citizen Auto Stage Co 67 E Baffert Dr	Nogales	AZ	85621	520-281-0400	281-4818
Coach Tours Ltd 475 Federal Rd	Brookfield	CT	06804	203-740-1118	775-6851
TF: 800-822-6224 ■ *Web:* www.coachtour.com					
Colorado Charter Lines 4960 Locust St	Commerce City	CO	80022	303-287-0239	287-2819
TF: 800-821-7491 ■ *Web:* www.bus-charter.com/coloradocharter.htm					
Croswell Bus Lines Inc 975 W Main St	Williamsburg	OH	45176	513-724-2206	724-3261
TF: 800-782-8747 ■ *Web:* www.gocroswell.com					
Cyr Bus Lines 153 Gilman Falls Ave	Old Town	ME	04468	207-827-2335	827-6763
TF: 800-244-2335 ■ *Web:* www.cyrbustours.com					
DATTCO Inc 583 S St	New Britain	CT	06051	860-229-4878	826-1115
TF: 800-229-4879 ■ *Web:* www.dattco.com					
Delta Bus Lines Inc 3107 Hwy 82E	Greenville	MS	38701	662-335-2633	335-2634
Elite Coach 1685 W Main St	Ephrata	PA	17522	717-733-7710	733-7133
TF: 800-722-6206 ■ *Web:* www.elitecoach.com					
Eyre Bus Service Inc 13600 Triadelphia Rd PO Box 239	Glenelg	MD	21737	410-442-1330	442-0010
TF: 800-321-3973 ■ *Web:* www.eyre.com					
Free Enterprise System Inc 1254 S W St	Indianapolis	IN	46225	317-634-7433	632-6557
TF: 800-255-1337 ■ *Web:* www.freeenterprisesystem.com					
Good Time Tours 455 Corday St	Pensacola	FL	32503	850-476-0046	476-7637
TF: 800-446-0886 ■ *Web:* www.goodtimetours.com					
Gray Line Worldwide 1835 Gaylord St	Denver	CO	80206	303-394-6920	394-6950
Web: www.grayline.com					
Great American Coach Co 4220 Howard Ave	New Orleans	LA	70125	504-212-5925	212-5920
TF: 866-596-2698					
Great Southern Coaches Inc 900 Burke Ave	Jonesboro	AR	72401	870-935-5569	935-5572
TF: 800-251-5569					
Greyhound Canada Transportation Corp 180 Dundas St W Suite 300	Toronto	ON	M5G1Z8	416-594-0343	594-0345
Web: www.greyhound.ca					
Hampton Jitney Inc (HJ) 395 County Rd 39A Suite 6	SouthHampton	NY	11968	631-283-4600	287-4759
Web: www.hamptonjitney.com					
Harran Transportation Co Inc 30 Mahan St	West Babylon	NY	11704	631-491-9100	491-9057
TF: 800-666-4287 ■ *Web:* www.harran.com					
Hawkeye Stages Inc 703 Dudley St	Decorah	IA	52101	563-382-3639	382-3945
TF: 800-323-3368 ■ *Web:* www.hawkeyestages.com					
Hertz Northern Bus 333-A 105th St E	Saskatoon	SK	S7N1Z4	306-374-5161	374-2442
Indian Trails Inc 109 E Comstock St	Owosso	MI	48867	989-725-5105	725-9584
TF: 800-292-3831 ■ *Web:* www.indiantrails.com					
Industrial Bus Lines 230 S Country Club Dr	Mesa	AZ	85210	480-962-6202	962-5727
TF: 800-848-4728 ■ *Web:* www.allaboardamerica.com					
Jack Rabbit Lines Inc 301 N Dakota Ave	Sioux Falls	SD	57104	605-336-3339	336-1444
TF: 800-678-6543 ■ *Web:* www.jackrabbitlines.com					
Kerrville Bus Co 1 S Main St	Del Rio	TX	78840	830-775-7515	
TF: 800-474-3352 ■ *Web:* www.iridekbc.com					
Krapf Bus Cos 495 Thomas Jones Way Suite 300	Exton	PA	19341	610-594-2664	594-5011
Web: www.krapfbus.com					
Lamers Bus Lines Inc 2407 S Pt Rd	Green Bay	WI	54313	920-496-3600	496-3611
TF: 800-236-1240 ■ *Web:* www.golamers.com					
Leprechaun Cos Inc The 100 Leprechaun Ln	New Windsor	NY	12553	845-565-7900	
Magic Bus Co 520 Lakeshore Blvd E	Toronto	ON	M5A1C3	416-516-7827	516-6774
TF: 877-371-8747 ■ *Web:* www.magicbuscompany.com					
Marin Charter & Tours 8 Lovell Ave	San Rafael	CA	94901	415-256-8830	256-8839
Web: www.marinairporter.com					
Martz First Class Coach Co Inc 4783 37th St N	Saint Petersburg	FL	33714	727-526-9086	522-5548
TF: 800-282-8020 ■ *Web:* www.martzfirstclass.com					
Martz Group 239 Old River Rd	Wilkes-Barre	PA	18702	570-821-3838	821-3835
TF: 800-334-9608 ■ *Web:* www.martzgroup.com					
Mid-America Charter Lines 2513 E Higgins Rd	Elk Grove Village	IL	60007	847-437-3779	437-4978
TF: 800-323-0312 ■ *Web:* www.bus-charter.com/midamerica.html					
MV Transportation Inc 4620 W America Dr	Fairfield	CA	94534	707-863-8980	863-8944
Web: www.mvtransit.com					
New World Tours Inc 7920 Gainsford Ct	Bristow	VA	20136	703-392-8687	643-9527
TF: 800-322-7733 ■ *Web:* www.newworldtours.com					
Northern Tours 2740 Bauer St	Eau Claire	WI	54701	715-834-1463	834-8222
TF: 800-735-8687					
Northfield Lines Inc 32611 Northfield Blvd	Northfield	MN	55057	507-645-5267	645-5635
TF: 888-670-8068 ■ *Web:* www.northfieldlines.com					
Northwest Iowa Transportation Inc 2755 200th St PO Box 911	Fort Dodge	IA	50501	515-576-6494	955-1983
TF: 877-776-1700 ■ *Web:* www.nwitour.com					
Onondaga Coach Corp PO Box 277	Auburn	NY	13021	315-255-2216	255-0925
TF: 800-451-1570 ■ *Web:* www.onondagacoach.com					
Pacific Western Transportation Ltd 6999 Ordan Dr	Mississauga	ON	L5T1K6	905-564-3232	564-5959
TF: 800-387-6787 ■ *Web:* www.pacificwesterntoronto.com					
Peter Pan Bus Lines Inc 1776 Main St	Springfield	MA	01103	413-781-2900	731-9721
TF: 800-237-8747 ■ *Web:* www.peterpanbus.com					
Premier Coach Co Inc 67 Champlain Dr	Colchester	VT	05446	802-655-4456	655-4213
TF: 800-532-1811 ■ *Web:* www.premiercoach.net					
Raz Transportation 11655 SW Pacific Hwy	Portland	OR	97223	503-684-3322	968-3223
TF: 888-684-3322 ■ *Web:* www.portland.coachamerica.com					
Red Carpet Charters PO Box 94626	Oklahoma City	OK	73143	405-672-5100	672-9613
TF: 888-878-5100 ■ *Web:* www.redcarpetcharters.com					
Rimrock Stages Inc PO Box 988	Billings	MT	59103	406-245-5392	245-7696
TF: 800-255-7655 ■ *Web:* www.rimrocktrailways.com					
Riteway Bus Service Inc Motorcoach Div W201 N13900 Fond du Lac Ave	Richfield	WI	53076	414-677-3282	677-3121*
**Fax Area Code:* 262 ■ *TF:* 800-776-7026 ■ *Web:* www.ritewaybus.com					
Rockland Coaches Inc 180 Old Hook Rd	Westwood	NJ	07675	201-263-1254	664-8036
Web: www.coachusa.com/rockland					

	City	State	Zip	Phone	Fax
Rolling V Transportation Services 5008 Main St	South Fallsburg	NY	12779	845-434-0511	434-0259
Web: www.rollingv.com					
Salter Bus Lines Inc 212 Hudson Ave	Jonesboro	LA	71251	318-259-2522	259-2522
TF: 800-223-8056 ■ *Web:* www.salter.us					
SBS Transit Inc 3747 Colorado Ave	Sheffield Village	OH	44054	440-949-8121	949-2979
TF: 800-548-5304					
Silver Fox Tours & Motorcoaches 3 Silver Fox Dr	Millbury	MA	01527	508-865-6000	865-4660
TF: 800-342-5998 ■ *Web:* www.silverfoxcoach.com					
Southeastern Stages Inc 260 University Ave SW	Atlanta	GA	30315	404-874-2741	591-2745
Web: www.southeasternstages.com					
Southern Bus Stages Inc Shafer's Bus Lines Div 750 Harry L Dr	Johnson City	NY	13790	607-797-2006	797-1183
TF: 800-287-8986 ■ *Web:* www.shaferbus.com					
Star of America 8111 N SR 37	Bloomington	IN	47404	812-876-7851	876-9397
TF: 800-933-0097 ■ *Web:* www.charterstaramerica.com					
Starr Bus Charter & Tours 2531 E State St	Trenton	NJ	08619	609-587-0626	587-3052
TF: 800-782-7703 ■ *Web:* www.starrtours.com					
Storer Coachways 3519 McDonald Ave	Modesto	CA	95358	209-521-8250	578-4888
TF: 800-621-3383 ■ *Web:* www.storercoachways.com					
Sun Valley Stages Inc 119 S Pk Ave W PO Box 936	Twin Falls	ID	83301	208-733-3921	733-3993
TF: 800-574-8661					
Swarthout Coaches Inc 115 Graham Rd	Ithaca	NY	14850	607-257-2277	257-0218
TF: 800-772-7267 ■ *Web:* www.goswarthout.com					
Texas New Mexico & Oklahoma Coaches Inc PO Box 1800	Lubbock	TX	79408	806-763-5389	687-4535
Web: www.tnmo.com					
Trailways Transportation System Inc 3554 Chain Bridge Rd Suite 301	Fairfax	VA	22030	703-691-3052	691-9047
TF: 877-467-3346 ■ *Web:* www.trailways.com					
Triple J Tours Inc 4455 S Cameron St	Las Vegas	NV	89103	702-261-0131	736-5103
Web: www.lasvegasbus.com					
Van Galder Bus Co 715 S Pearl St	Janesville	WI	53548	608-752-5407	752-7120
TF: 800-747-0994 ■ *Web:* www.coachusa.com					
VIP Tour & Charter Bus Co 129-137 Fox St	Portland	ME	04101	207-772-4457	772-7020
TF: 800-337-4457 ■ *Web:* www.vipchartercoaches.com					
Wilson Bus Lines Inc 203 Patriots Rd PO Box 415	East Templeton	MA	01438	978-632-3894	632-9005
TF: 800-253-5235 ■ *Web:* www.wilsonbus.com					
Winn Transportation 1831 Westwood Ave	Richmond	VA	23227	804-358-9466	353-2606
TF: 800-296-9466 ■ *Web:* www.winnbus.com					
Wisconsin Coach Lines Inc 1520 Arcadian Ave	Waukesha	WI	53186	262-542-8861	542-2036
TF: 877-324-7767 ■ *Web:* www.coachusa.com					
Young Transportation & Tours 843 Riverside Dr	Asheville	NC	28804	828-258-0084	252-3342
TF: 800-622-5444 ■ *Web:* www.youngtransportation.com					

108 BUS SERVICES - INTERCITY & RURAL

SEE ALSO Bus Services - School p. 1548; Mass Transportation (Local & Suburban) p. 2220

	City	State	Zip	Phone	Fax
Adirondack Trailways 499 Hurley Ave	Hurley	NY	12443	845-339-4230	225-6815
TF: 800-858-8555 ■ *Web:* www.trailwaysny.com					
Carolina Coach Trailways Inc 1201 S Blount St	Raleigh	NC	27601	919-833-3601	833-0627
Web: www.trailways.com/member-company.asp?cid=25					
Colorado Valley Transit Inc 108 Cardinal Ln PO Box 940	Columbus	TX	78934	979-732-6281	732-6283
TF: 800-548-1068 ■ *Web:* www.gotransit.org					
Community & Rural Transportation Inc (CART) 850 Denver St	Idaho Falls	ID	83402	208-522-2278	529-5918
FirstGroup America 600 Vine St Suite 1400	Cincinnati	OH	45202	513-241-2200	381-0149
Web: www.firstgroup.com					
Geauga County Transit 12555 Merritt Rd	Chardon	OH	44024	440-279-2150	285-9476
TF Cust Svc: 888-287-7190 ■ *Web:* www.geaugatransit.org					
Greyhound Canada Transportation Corp 180 Dundas St W Suite 300	Toronto	ON	M5G1Z8	416-594-0343	594-0345
Web: www.greyhound.ca					
Jefferson Lines 2100 E 26th St	Minneapolis	MN	55404	612-359-3400	359-3437
TF Cust Svc: 800-767-5333 ■ *Web:* www.jeffersonlines.com					
Jefferson Partners LP 2100 E 26th St	Minneapolis	MN	55404	612-359-3400	359-3437
TF Cust Svc: 800-767-5333 ■ *Web:* www.jeffersonlines.com					
Martha's Vineyard Regional Transit Authority 11 A St MV Business Pk RR 1 PO Box 10	Edgartown	MA	02539	508-693-9440	693-9953
Web: www.vineyardtransit.com					
Martz Group 239 Old River Rd	Wilkes-Barre	PA	18702	570-821-3838	821-3835
TF: 800-334-9608 ■ *Web:* www.martzgroup.com					
Martz Trailways 239 Old River Rd	Wilkes-Barre	PA	18702	570-821-3838	821-3835
Web: www.martztrailways.com					
Merced Transportation Co 300 Grogan Ave	Merced	CA	95340	209-384-2575	384-3805
Moffit Bros LLC 918 Lostline Rd PO Box 156	Lostine	OR	97857	541-569-2284	569-2476
Ozark Regional Transit 2423 E Robinson Ave PO Box 785	Springdale	AR	72765	479-756-5901	756-2901
TF: 800-865-5901 ■ *Web:* www.ozark.org					
Pacific Transit System 216 N 2nd St	Raymond	WA	98577	360-875-9418	942-3193
Web: www.pacifictransit.org					
Pelivan Transit 333 S Oak St PO Drawer B	Big Cabin	OK	74332	918-783-5793	783-5786
TF: 800-482-4594					
Peter Pan Bus Lines Inc 1776 Main St	Springfield	MA	01103	413-781-2900	731-9721
TF: 800-237-8747 ■ *Web:* www.peterpanbus.com					
Pima County Dept of Transportation Transportation Systems Div 201 N Stone Ave 5th Fl	Tucson	AZ	85701	520-740-6403	740-6341
Web: www.dot.co.pima.az.us					
Powder River Transportation 1700 E Hwy 14-16 PO Box 218	Gillette	WY	82717	307-682-0960	682-4422
TF: 800-442-3682 ■ *Web:* www.coachusa.com					
Red Ball Stage Line Inc PO Box 1799	Klamath Falls	OR	97601	541-884-6460	884-6460

Company	City	State	Zip	Phone	Fax
Rides Mass Transit District (RMTD) PO Box 190 *TF*: 877-667-6122 ■ *Web*: www.ridesmtd.com	Rosiclare	IL	62982	618-285-3342	285-3340
Rimrock Stages Inc PO Box 988 *TF*: 800-255-7655 ■ *Web*: www.rimrocktrailways.com	Billings	MT	59103	406-245-5392	245-7696
Rural Community Transportation Inc 1161 Portland St *Web*: www.riderct.org	Saint Johnsbury	VT	05819	802-748-8170	748-5275
Rural Transit Enterprises Coordinated Inc (RTEC) 100 E Main St *TF*: 800-321-7832 ■ *Web*: www.4rtec.com	Mount Vernon	KY	40456	606-256-9835	256-2181
Southeastern Stages Inc 260 University Ave SW *Web*: www.southeasternstages.com	Atlanta	GA	30315	404-874-2741	591-2745
Suburban Transit Corp 750 Somerset St *TF*: 800-222-0492 ■ *Web*: www.coachusa.com	New Brunswick	NJ	08901	732-249-1100	545-7015
Thunderbird Rural Public Transportation System 5002 Knickerbocker St PO Box 60050 *TF*: 877-947-8286 ■ *Web*: www.cvcog.org/transportation.htm	San Angelo	TX	76906	325-944-9666	947-8286
Trans-Bridge Lines Inc 2012 Industrial Dr *TF*: 800-962-9135 ■ *Web*: www.transbridgelines.com	Bethlehem	PA	18017	610-868-6001	868-9057
Triboro Coach Corp 85-01 24th Ave *Web*: www.triborocoach.com	Jackson Heights	NY	11369	718-335-1000	397-1995
Valley Transit Co Inc 219 N 'A' St *TF*: 800-580-4710 ■ *Web*: www.valleytransitcompany.com	Harlingen	TX	78550	956-423-4710	423-4888
Viking Trailways 201 Glendale Rd *TF*: 800-400-2779 ■ *Web*: www.trailways.com/member-company.asp?cid=68	Joplin	MO	64804	417-781-2779	781-2778
White Mountain Passenger Lines Inc 1041 E Hall St PO Box 460 *TF*: 866-255-4819 ■ *Web*: www.wmlines.com	Show Low	AZ	85902	928-537-4539	532-6683

109 BUS SERVICES - SCHOOL

Company	City	State	Zip	Phone	Fax
A & E Transport Services Inc 101 W Utica St Suite 2 *TF*: 800-724-0614	Oswego	NY	13126	315-343-2804	343-0067
Action Transit Enterprises Inc 330 Poplar St	Pittsburgh	PA	15223	412-781-7906	781-8230
Atlantic Express Transportation Group Inc 7 N St *TF*: 800-336-3886 ■ *Web*: www.atlanticexpress.com	Staten Island	NY	10302	718-442-7000	442-7672
Beck Bus Transportation Corp 2201 Brownsville Rd PO Box 768 *Web*: www.beckbus.com	Mount Vernon	IL	62864	618-242-5685	242-4523
Birnie Bus Service Inc 248 Otis St *TF*: 800-734-3950 ■ *Web*: www.birniebus.tripod.com	Rome	NY	13441	315-336-3950	339-5957
Brown Bus Co 2111 E Sherman Ave *Web*: www.brownbuscompany.com	Nampa	ID	83686	208-466-4181	466-2861
Cook-Illinois Corp 4845 167th St Suite 300	Oak Forest	IL	60452	708-560-9840	560-0661
DATTCO Inc School Bus Div 583 S St *TF*: 800-229-4879 ■ *Web*: www.dattco.com	New Britain	CT	06051	860-229-4878	826-1115
Davidsmeyer Bus Service Inc 2513 E Higgins Rd *TF*: 800-323-0312 ■ *Web*: www.bus-charter.com/aboutus-dsm.htm	Elk Grove Village	IL	60007	847-437-3767	437-4978
Dean Transportation Inc 4812 Aurelius Rd *TF*: 800-282-3326	Lansing	MI	48910	517-319-8300	319-8385
First Student Inc 600 Vine St *Web*: www.firststudentinc.com	Cincinnati	OH	45202	513-241-2200	381-0149
George M Carroll Inc 7 SR 17K	Newburgh	NY	12550	845-565-8300	565-3196
Hastings Bus Co 425 31st St E *TF*: 888-290-2429 ■ *Web*: www.minnesotacoaches.com	Hastings	MN	55033	651-437-1888	438-3319
Hertz Northern Bus 333-A 105th St E	Saskatoon	SK	S7N1Z4	306-374-5161	374-2442
Independent Coach Corp 25 Wanser Ave	Inwood	NY	11096	516-239-1100	239-8641
John T Cyr & Sons Inc 153 Gilman Falls Ave *TF*: 800-244-2335 ■ *Web*: www.cyrbustours.com	Old Town	ME	04468	207-827-2335	827-6763
Johnson School Bus Services Inc 2151 W Washington St PO Box 285 *Web*: www.johnsonschoolbus.com	West Bend	WI	53095	262-334-3146	334-8019
Kobussen Buses Ltd W914 County Rd CE *TF*: 800-447-0116 ■ *Web*: www.kobussen.com	Kaukauna	WI	54130	920-766-0606	766-0797
Krapf Bus Cos School Bus Div 120 Springton Rd *Web*: www.krapfbus.com	Glenmoore	PA	19343	610-269-3897	942-2545
Krise Bus Service Inc 119 Bus Ln *Web*: www.krisebus.com	Punxsutawney	PA	15767	814-938-5250	938-5323
Laidlaw International Inc School Bus Div 3221 N Service Rd *TF*: 800-563-6072 ■ *Web*: www.laidlawschoolbus.com	Burlington	ON	L7R3Y8	905-336-1800	336-3976
Michael's Transportation Service Inc 140 Yolano Dr *TF Cust Svc*: 800-295-2448 ■ *Web*: www.bustransportation.com	Vallejo	CA	94589	707-643-2099	643-1906
Mid-Columbia Bus Co 73458 Bus Barn Ln *TF*: 888-291-7513 ■ *Web*: www.midcobus.com	Pendleton	OR	97801	541-276-5621	276-5205
Monroe School Transportation 970 Emerson St	Rochester	NY	14606	585-458-3230	458-9159
Palmer Bus Service Inc 521 County Rd 15 E	Saint Clair	MN	56080	507-386-0210	386-0211
Pioneer Transportation Corp 2890 Arthur Kill Rd	Staten Island	NY	10309	718-984-8077	984-6588
Riteway Bus Service Inc Motorcoach Div W201 N13900 Fond du Lac Ave **Fax Area Code*: 262 ■ *TF*: 800-776-7026 ■ *Web*: www.ritewaybus.com	Richfield	WI	53076	414-677-3282	677-3121*
Rocky Mountain Transportation Inc 1410 E Edgewood Dr *Web*: www.rockymountaintrans.com	Whitefish	MT	59937	406-863-1200	863-1213
Rolling V Transportation Services 5008 Main St *Web*: www.rollingv.com	South Fallsburg	NY	12779	845-434-0511	434-0259
Royal Coach Lines Inc 924 Broadway PO Box 191	Thornwood	NY	10594	914-747-9494	747-9497
Safe-Way Bus Co 6030 Carmen Ave	Inver Grove Heights	MN	55076	651-451-1375	451-3525
Safety Bus Service 7200 Pk Ave *Web*: www.safetytours.com	Pennsauken	NJ	08109	856-665-2662	665-0658
Sheppard Bus Service 35 Rockville Rd	Bridgeton	NJ	08302	856-451-4004	453-1620
Stock Transportation Ltd 25 Millard Ave W *Web*: www.stock-transport.com	Newmarket	ON	L3Y7R6	905-952-0878	952-0892
Student Transportation of America Inc (STA) 3349 Hwy 138 Bldg B Suite D *TF*: 888-942-2250 ■ *Web*: www.sta-ips.com/build/index.php	Wall	NJ	07719	732-280-4200	280-4214
Suffolk Transportation Service Inc 10 Moffitt Blvd *Web*: www.suffolkbus.com	Bay Shore	NY	11706	631-665-3245	665-3186
WE Transport Inc 75 Commercial St *Web*: www.wetransport.com	Plainview	NY	11803	516-349-8200	349-8275
Williams Bus Lines Inc PO Box 1272 *Web*: www.williamsbus.com	Springfield	VA	22151	703-560-5355	560-7851
WT Holmes Transportation Co 22 Myrtle St	Norfolk	MA	02056	508-528-4550	528-4728

110 BUSINESS FORMS

SEE ALSO Printing Companies - Commercial Printers p. 2451

Company	City	State	Zip	Phone	Fax
Ace Forms of Kansas Inc 2900 N Rotary Terr *TF*: 800-223-9287 ■ *Web*: www.aceforms.com	Pittsburg	KS	66762	620-232-9290	232-1111
Allison Payment Systems LLC 2200 Production Dr *TF*: 800-755-2440 ■ *Web*: www.apsllc.com	Indianapolis	IN	46241	317-808-2400	808-2477
Amsterdam Printing & Litho Corp 166 County Hwy 15 *TF*: 800-833-6231 ■ *Web*: www.amsterdamprinting.com	Amsterdam	NY	12010	518-842-6000	843-5204
Apex Color 200 N Lee St *TF*: 800-367-6790 ■ *Web*: www.apexcolor.net	Jacksonville	FL	32204	904-358-2928	358-8811
B & D Litho Inc 3820 N 38th Ave *TF Cust Svc*: 800-735-0375 ■ *Web*: www.bndlitho.com	Phoenix	AZ	85019	602-269-2526	269-2520
BBF Printing Solutions 10950 Belcher Rd S *Web*: www.bbfprinting.com	Largo	FL	33777	727-541-4641	541-1780
Bernadette Business Forms Inc 8950 Pershall Rd **Fax*: Mktg ■ *TF*: 800-862-7288 ■ *Web*: www.bbf.com	Saint Louis	MO	63042	314-522-1700	524-6161*
Bestforms Inc 1135 Avenida Acaso *TF*: 800-350-0618 ■ *Web*: www.bestforms.com	Camarillo	CA	93012	805-383-6993	987-5280
Business Forms Inc 3498 Grand Ave *TF*: 800-451-8086	Pittsburgh	PA	15225	412-331-3300	331-5566
Calibrated Forms Co Inc 537 N E Ave PO Box Drawer 191 *TF*: 800-237-7576 ■ *Web*: www.calforms.com	Columbus	KS	66725	800-237-7576	752-4396
CCH Insurance Services 130 Turner St Bldg 3 4th Fl **Fax Area Code*: 260 ■ *TF*: 800-481-1522 ■ *Web*: www.insurance.cch.com	Waltham	MA	02453	781-907-6677	925-6159*
Central States Business Forms Inc 2500 Industrial Pkwy *TF*: 800-331-0920 ■ *Web*: www.centralstates.net	Dewey	OK	74029	918-534-1280	534-3470
Champion Industries Inc 2450-90 First Ave PO Box 2968 *NASDAQ*: CHMP ■ *TF*: 800-624-3431 ■ *Web*: www.champion-industries.com	Huntington	WV	25728	304-528-2700	528-2765
Computer Stock Forms Inc 835 S High St *TF*: 800-543-5565 ■ *Web*: www.computerstockformsinc.com	Hillsboro	OH	45133	937-981-7751	981-2159
Curtis 1000 Inc 1725 Breckinridge Pkwy Suite 500 **Fax Area Code*: 800 ■ **Fax*: Mktg ■ *TF*: 800-683-8162 ■ *Web*: www.curtis1000.com	Duluth	GA	30096	678-380-9095	594-0518*
Custom Business Forms Inc 210 Edge Pl *TF*: 800-234-1221 ■ *Web*: www.cbfnet.com	Minneapolis	MN	55418	612-789-0002	789-6321
Data Business Forms Ltd (DBF) 9195 Torbram Rd *TF*: 800-268-0128 ■ *Web*: www.dbf.com	Brampton	ON	L6S6H2	905-791-3151	791-3277
Data Papers Inc 468 Industrial Pk Rd **Fax Area Code*: 888 ■ *TF*: 800-233-3032 ■ *Web*: www.datapapers.com	Muncy	PA	17756	570-546-2201	546-2366*
Data Source Inc 1400 Universal Ave *TF*: 800-829-3369 ■ *Web*: www.data-source.com	Kansas City	MO	64120	816-483-3282	483-3284
Datatel Resources Corp 1729 Pennsylvania Ave *TF*: 800-245-2688 ■ *Web*: www.datatelcorp.com	Monaca	PA	15061	724-775-5300	775-5300
DFS Group 12 S St *TF*: 800-225-9528 ■ *Web*: www.dfsbusiness.com	Townsend	MA	01469	800-225-9528	876-6337
Dupli-Systems Inc 8260 Dow Cir *TF*: 800-321-1610 ■ *Web*: www.dupli-systems.com	Strongsville	OH	44136	440-234-9415	234-2350
Eagle Graphics Inc 150 N Moyer St *Web*: www.eaglegraphic.com	Annville	PA	17003	717-867-5576	867-5579
Eastern Business Forms Inc 530 Old Sulphur Springs Rd	Greenville	SC	29607	864-288-2451	297-6492
Ennis Inc 2441 Presidential Pkwy *NYSE*: EBF ■ *Web*: www.ennis.com	Midlothian	TX	76065	972-775-9801	775-9820
Falcon Business Forms Inc PO Box 326 *TF*: 800-442-6262	Corsicana	TX	75151	903-874-6583	872-7960
Federal Business Products Inc 95 Main Ave *TF*: 800-927-5123 ■ *Web*: www.feddirect.com	Clifton	NJ	07014	973-667-9800	667-7756
Flesh Co 2118 59th St **Fax*: Sales ■ *TF*: 800-869-3330 ■ *Web*: www.fleshco.com	Saint Louis	MO	63110	314-781-4400	781-5546*
Forms Manufacturers Inc 312 E Forest Ave *TF*: 800-835-0614	Girard	KS	66743	620-724-8225	724-8188
Freedom Graphic Services Inc (FGS) 1101 S Janesville St *TF*: 800-334-3540 ■ *Web*: www.fgs.com	Milton	WI	53563	608-868-7007	868-7006
General Credit Forms Inc (GCF) 3595 Rider Trail S *TF*: 888-423-6397 ■ *Web*: www.gcfinc.com	Earth City	MO	63045	314-216-8600	216-8570
Genoa Business Forms Inc 445 Pk Ave *TF*: 800-383-2801 ■ *Web*: www.genoabusforms.com	Sycamore	IL	60178	815-895-2800	895-8206
Gulf Business Forms Inc 2460 S IH-35 PO Box 1073 *TF*: 800-433-4853 ■ *Web*: www.gulfforms.com	San Marcos	TX	78667	512-353-8313	353-8866

	City	State	Zip	Phone	Fax
Harland Clarke Holdings Corp 2939 Miller Rd. *TF:* 800-723-3690 ■ *Web:* www.harland.net	Decatur	GA	30035	770-981-9460	593-5347
Highland Computer Forms Inc 1025 W Main St. **Fax Area Code:* 800 ■ **Fax:* Sales ■ *TF:* 800-669-5213 ■ *Web:* www.hcf.com	Hillsboro	OH	45133	937-393-4215	842-6485*
Hospital Forms & Systems Corp 8900 Ambassador Row *TF:* 800-527-5081 ■ *Web:* www.hforms.com	Dallas	TX	75247	214-634-8900	905-3819
Howard Press Inc 450 W 1st Ave *Web:* www.howardpress.com	Roselle	NJ	07203	908-245-4400	245-1139
Hygrade Business Group Inc (HBG) 232 Entin Rd *TF:* 800-836-7714 ■ *Web:* www.hygradebusiness.com	Clifton	NJ	07014	973-249-6700	249-6109
Imperial Graphics Inc 3100 Walkent Dr NW *TF:* 800-777-2591 ■ *Web:* www.impgraphics.com	Grand Rapids	MI	49544	616-784-0100	784-8256
Integrated Print & Graphics 645 Stevenson Rd. *Web:* www.ipandginc.com	South Elgin	IL	60177	847-695-6777	741-4090
Interform Solutions 1901 Mayview Rd. **Fax:* Mktg ■ *TF:* 800-945-7746 ■ *Web:* www.interformsolutions.com	Bridgeville	PA	15017	412-221-3300	221-6585*
International Business Systems Inc (IBS) 431 Yerkes Rd. *TF:* 800-220-1255 ■ *Web:* www.ibsdm.com	King of Prussia	PA	19406	610-265-8210	265-7997
Kaye-Smith 4101 Oakesdale Ave SW *TF:* 800-822-9987 ■ *Web:* www.kayesmith.com	Renton	WA	98057	425-228-8600	271-0203
NCP Solutions 5200 E Lake Blvd *Web:* www.ncpsolutions.com	Birmingham	AL	35217	205-849-5200	849-2907
New England Business Service Inc (NEBS) 500 Main St **Fax Area Code:* 800 ■ **Fax:* Cust Svc ■ *TF Sales:* 800-225-6380 ■ *Web:* www.nebs.com	Groton	MA	01471	978-448-6111	333-4376*
New Jersey Business Forms Mfg Co 55 W Sheffield Ave *TF:* 800-466-6523 ■ *Web:* www.njbf.com	Englewood	NJ	07631	201-569-4500	569-1137
Paris Business Products 800 Highland Dr *TF Cust Svc:* 800-523-6454 ■ *Web:* www.pariscorp.com	Mount Holly	NJ	08060	609-265-9200	261-4853
Patterson Office Supplies 3310 N Duncan Rd PO Box 9009 **Fax Area Code:* 800 ■ *TF Cust Svc:* 800-637-1140 ■ *Web:* www.pattersonofficesupplies.com	Champaign	IL	60826	217-351-5400	843-3676*
Peachtree Business Products LLC PO Box 13290 *TF:* 800-241-4623 ■ *Web:* www.pbp1.com	Atlanta	GA	30324	770-420-1978	
Performance Office Papers 21673 Cedar Ave **Fax Area Code:* 800 ■ *TF:* 800-458-7189 ■ *Web:* www.perfpapers.com	Lakeville	MN	55044	952-469-1400	488-5058*
PrintEdd Products of North America 2641 N Forum Dr *TF:* 800-367-6728 ■ *Web:* www.printedd.com	Grand Prairie	TX	75052	972-988-3133	641-2564
Quality Forms 4317 W US Rt 36 **Fax Area Code:* 888 ■ *Web:* www.qualforms.com	Piqua	OH	45356	937-773-4595	550-3937*
Rapidforms Inc 301 Grove Rd. **Fax Area Code:* 800 ■ *TF Cust Svc:* 800-257-8354 ■ *Web:* www.rapidforms.com	Thorofare	NJ	08086	856-384-1144	348-8113*
Rotary Forms Press Inc 835 S High St *TF:* 800-654-2876 ■ *Web:* www.rotaryformspress.com	Hillsboro	OH	45133	937-393-3426	393-8473
Royal Business Forms Inc 3301 Ave E E. *TF:* 800-255-9303	Arlington	TX	76011	817-640-5248	633-2164
RR Donnelley & Sons Co 111 S Wacker Dr *NYSE: RRD* ■ **Fax:* Mail Rm ■ *Web:* www.rrdonnelley.com	Chicago	IL	60601	312-326-8000	326-8543*
Socrates Media LLC 111 S Wacker Dr. *TF:* 877-860-4649 ■ *Web:* www.socrates.com	Chicago	IL	60606	877-860-4649	
Source4 3944 S Morgan. *Web:* www.source4.com	Chicago	IL	60609	773-247-4141	247-1313
Specialized Printed Forms Inc 352 Ctr St. *TF:* 800-688-2381 ■ *Web:* www.spforms.com	Caledonia	NY	14423	585-538-2381	538-4922
Standard Register Co PO Box 1167. *NYSE: SR* ■ **Fax:* Sales ■ *TF:* 800-755-6405 ■ *Web:* www.stdreg.com	Dayton	OH	45401	937-221-1504	221-1205*
Sterling Business Forms PO Box 2486. *TF Cust Svc:* 800-759-3676 ■ *Web:* www.sbfnet.com	White City	OR	97503	800-759-3676	234-2409
Stry-Lenkoff Co Inc 1100 W Broadway St *TF:* 800-626-8247 ■ *Web:* www.strylenkoff.com	Louisville	KY	40232	502-587-6804	587-6822
United Business Forms Inc 8482 W Allens Bridge Rd *TF:* 800-547-5351	Greeneville	TN	37743	423-639-5551	639-7217
Unz & Co 201 Cir Dr N Suite 104 *TF:* 800-631-3098 ■ *Web:* www.unzco.com	Piscataway	NJ	08854	732-868-0706	868-0607
Victor Printing Inc 1 Victor Way *TF:* 800-443-2845 ■ *Web:* www.victorptg.com	Sharon	PA	16146	724-342-2106	342-6147
Ward-Kraft Inc 2401 Cooper St. *TF:* 800-821-4021 ■ *Web:* www.wardkraft.com	Fort Scott	KS	66701	620-223-5500	223-6953
Web Graphics PO Box 308 *TF:* 800-833-8863 ■ *Web:* www.printatweb.com	Glens Falls	NY	12801	518-792-6501	792-9353
Wilmer Service Line 515 W Sycamore St. **Fax Area Code:* 800 ■ *TF:* 800-494-5637 ■ *Web:* www.4wilmer.com	Coldwater	OH	45828	888-494-5637	553-4849*
Wise Business Forms Inc 555 McFarland 400 Dr *TF:* 888-815-9473 ■ *Web:* www.wbf.com	Alpharetta	GA	30004	770-442-1060	442-9849
Witt Printing Co Inc 301 Oak St. *TF:* 800-641-4342 ■ *Web:* www.wittprinting.com	El Dorado Springs	MO	64744	417-876-4721	876-4794
WorkflowOne 220 E Monument Ave. *TF:* 866-789-8999 ■ *Web:* www.workflowone.com	Dayton	OH	45402	877-735-4966	
Wright Business Forms Inc 2525 Braga Dr. *TF:* 800-487-2204	Broadview	IL	60155	708-865-7600	865-7626
Wright Business Graphics (WBG) 18440 NE San Rafael St PO Box 20489 *TF:* 800-547-8397 ■ *Web:* www.wrightbg.com	Portland	OR	97230	503-661-2525	661-0515

111 BUSINESS MACHINES - MFR

SEE ALSO Business Machines - Whol p. 1549; Calculators - Electronic p. 1552; Computer Equipment p. 1670; Photocopying Equipment & Supplies p. 2419

	City	State	Zip	Phone	Fax
Agissar Corp 526 Benton St. *TF:* 800-627-8256 ■ *Web:* www.agissar.com	Stratford	CT	06615	203-375-8662	375-5345
Amano Cincinnati Inc 140 Harrison Ave *TF:* 800-526-2559 ■ *Web:* www.amano.com	Roseland	NJ	07068	973-403-1900	364-1086
Atlantic Zeiser Inc 15 Patton Dr. *Web:* www.atlanticzeiser.com	West Caldwell	NJ	07006	973-228-0800	228-9064
Better Packages Inc 255 Canal St PO Box 711. *TF:* 800-237-9151 ■ *Web:* www.betterpackages.com	Shelton	CT	06484	203-926-3722	926-3706
Bidwell Industrial Group Inc 2055 S Main St. *TF:* 800-235-0999 ■ *Web:* www.bidwellinc.com	Middletown	CT	06457	860-346-9283	347-8775
BOWE Bell + Howell 3791 S Alston Ave *TF:* 800-220-3030 ■ *Web:* www.bowebellhowell.com	Durham	NC	27713	919-767-4401	
Brother International Corp 100 Somerset Corporate Blvd. *TF Cust Svc:* 800-276-7746 ■ *Web:* www.brother-usa.com	Bridgewater	NJ	08807	908-704-1700	704-8235
Canon USA Inc 1 Canon Plaza **Fax:* Hum Res ■ *TF:* 800-828-4040 ■ *Web:* www.usa.canon.com	Lake Success	NY	11042	516-328-5000	328-5069*
CP Bourg Inc 50 Samuel Barnet Blvd. *Web:* www.cpbourg.com	New Bedford	MA	02745	508-998-2171	998-2391
Cummins-Allison Corp 852 Feehanville Dr *TF:* 800-786-5528 ■ *Web:* www.cumminsallison.com	Mount Prospect	IL	60056	847-299-9550	299-9550
Diagraph Corp 1 Missouri Research Pk Dr **Fax Area Code:* 636 ■ *TF:* 800-526-2531 ■ *Web:* www.diagraph.com	Saint Charles	MO	63304	800-526-2531	300-2005*
Dynetics Engineering Corp 515 Bond St *TF:* 800-888-8110 ■ *Web:* www.dyneticsengineering.com	Lincolnshire	IL	60069	847-541-7300	541-7488
Ecco Business Systems Inc 60 W 38th St 4th Fl. *TF:* 800-682-3226 ■ *Web:* www.eccobusiness.com	New York	NY	10018	212-921-4545	921-2198
ECRM Inc 554 Clark Rd *Web:* www.ecrm.com	Tewksbury	MA	01876	978-851-0207	851-7016
Fellowes Inc 1789 Norwood Ave. **Fax:* Cust Svc ■ *TF:* 800-945-4545 ■ *Web:* www.fellowes.com	Itasca	IL	60143	630-893-1600	893-1600*
Global Payment Technologies Inc 170 Wilbur Pl *NASDAQ: GPTX* ■ *TF:* 800-472-2506 ■ *Web:* www.gptworld.com	Bohemia	NY	11716	631-563-2500	563-2630
Gradco USA Inc 871 Coronado Ctr Dr Suite 200 *Web:* www.gradco.com	Henderson	NV	89052	949-595-4374	595-4367
Imaging Business Machines LLC 2750 Crestwood Blvd *Web:* www.ibml.com	Birmingham	AL	35210	205-956-4071	956-5309
Industrial Paper Shredders Inc 707 S Ellsworth Ave PO Box 180 *TF:* 888-637-4733 ■ *Web:* www.industrialshredders.com	Salem	OH	44460	330-332-0024	332-4535
International Business Machines Corp (IBM) 1 New Orchard Rd. *NYSE: IBM* ■ *TF:* 800-426-4968 ■ *Web:* www.ibm.com	Armonk	NY	10504	914-766-1900	
Lathem Time Corp 200 Selig Dr SW. **Fax Area Code:* 800 ■ *TF:* 800-241-4990 ■ *Web:* www.lathem.com	Atlanta	GA	30336	404-691-0400	252-2208*
Lynde-Ordway Co Inc 3308 W Warner Ave. *TF:* 800-762-7057 ■ *Web:* www.lynde-ordway.com	Santa Ana	CA	92704	714-957-1311	433-2166
Martin Yale Industries Inc 251 Wedcor Ave. *TF:* 800-225-5644 ■ *Web:* www.martinyale.com	Wabash	IN	46992	260-563-0641	563-4575
Michael Business Machines Corp (MBM) 3134 Industry Dr. *TF Cust Svc:* 800-223-2508 ■ *Web:* www.mbmcorp.com	North Charleston	SC	29418	843-552-2700	552-2974
Neopost Inc 30955 Huntwood Ave. *TF Cust Svc:* 800-827-4543 ■ *Web:* www.neopost.com	Hayward	CA	94544	510-489-6800	475-5701
Neopost Inc Canada 150 Steelcase Rd W *TF:* 800-636-7678 ■ *Web:* www.neopost.ca	Markham	ON	L3R3J9	905-475-3722	475-7699
Newbold Corp 450 Weaver St *TF:* 800-552-3282 ■ *Web:* www.addressograph.com	Rocky Mount	VA	24151	540-489-4400	489-4393
Paymaster Technologies Inc 61 Garlisch Dr *TF:* 800-462-4477 ■ *Web:* www.paymastertech.com	Elk Grove Village	IL	60007	847-758-1234	758-0123
Pitney Bowes Inc 1 Elmcroft Rd. *NYSE: PBI* ■ *TF:* 800-672-6937 ■ *Web:* www.pb.com	Stamford	CT	06926	203-356-5000	460-3851
Pubco Corp 3830 Kelley Ave *TF:* 800-837-4323	Cleveland	OH	44114	216-881-5300	881-8380
Red Streak Corp 1627 Main St Suite 901. *Web:* www.redstreakcorp.com	Kansas City	MO	64108	816-471-6979	471-1143
Royal Consumer Information Products Inc 379 Campus Dr 2nd Fl. **Fax Area Code:* 800 ■ *TF Sales:* 888-261-4555 ■ *Web:* www.royal.com	Somerset	NJ	08873	732-627-9977	232-9769*
Security Check LLC 2612 Jackson Ave W PO Box 1211. *TF:* 800-634-4484	Oxford	MS	38655	662-234-0440	281-8400
Security Engineered Machinery Co Inc 5 Walkup Dr PO Box 1045 *TF Sales:* 800-225-9293 ■ *Web:* www.semshred.com	Westborough	MA	01581	508-366-1488	836-4154
Sharp Electronics Corp 1 Sharp Plaza. *TF:* 800-237-4277 ■ *Web:* www.sharpusa.com	Mahwah	NJ	07430	201-529-8200	529-8413
Staplex Co 777 5th Ave *TF Cust Svc:* 800-221-0822 ■ *Web:* www.staplex.com	Brooklyn	NY	11232	718-768-3333	965-0750
Swintec Corp 320 W Commercial Ave. *TF:* 800-225-0867 ■ *Web:* www.swintec.com	Moonachie	NJ	07074	201-935-0115	933-9745
Toshiba TEC America Retail Information Systems Inc 4401-A Bankers Cir *Web:* www.toshibatecusa.com	Atlanta	GA	30360	770-449-3040	449-1152

112 BUSINESS MACHINES - WHOL

SEE ALSO Business Machines - Mfr p. 1549; Computer Equipment & Software - Whol p. 1674; Photocopying Equipment & Supplies p. 2419

	City	State	Zip	Phone	Fax
Adams Remco Inc PO Box 3968. *Web:* www.adamsremco.com	South Bend	IN	46619	574-288-2113	288-1105

Phone | Fax

Blue Technologies 5885 Grant Ave Cleveland OH 44105 216-271-4800 271-0084
Web: www.bluetechnologiesinc.com

Canon Business Solutions-Central
425 N Martingale Rd Suite 1400. . . . . Schaumburg IL 60173 847-706-3400 706-3419*
**Fax:* Hum Res ■ *TF:* 800-706-3303 ■ *Web:* www.solutions.canon.com

Canon Business Solutions-Northeast Inc
125 Pk Ave 9th Fl . . . . New York NY 10017 212-850-1000 661-2779*
**Fax:* Mktg ■ *TF:* 800-627-2679 ■ *Web:* www.solutions.canon.com

Canon Business Solutions-Southeast Inc
300 Commerce Sq Blvd . . . . Burlington NJ 08016 609-387-8700 239-6489*
**Fax:* Mktg ■ *TF:* 800-220-4000 ■ *Web:* www.solutions.canon.com

Canon Business Solutions-West
110 W Walnut St. . . . . Gardena CA 90248 310-217-3000 715-7050
Web: www.solutions.canon.com

Carr Business Systems Inc 130 Spagnoli Rd . . . . Melville NY 11747 631-249-9880 249-0740
TF: 800-244-1880 ■ *Web:* www.carr-global.com

Copiers Northwest Inc 601 Dexter Ave N . . . . Seattle WA 98109 206-282-1200 282-2010
TF: 866-692-0700 ■ *Web:* www.copiersnw.com

Copytronics Inc 2461 Rolac Rd. . . . . Jacksonville FL 32207 904-731-5100 448-5897
Web: www.copytronics.com

CRS Inc 4851 White Bear Pkwy. Saint Paul MN 55110 651-294-2700 294-2900
TF: 800-333-4949 ■ *Web:* www.crs-usa.com

Daisy IT Supplies Sales & Service
8575 Red Oak Ave. . . . . Rancho Cucamonga CA 91730 909-989-5585 989-5585
TF: 800-266-5585 ■ *Web:* www.macs.itsdaisy.com

Datamax Office Systems Inc
6717 Waldemar Ave . . . . Saint Louis MO 63139 314-647-2500 647-2500
TF: 800-325-9299 ■ *Web:* www.datamaxstl.com

Dieterich-Post Co 616 Monterey Pass Rd . . . . Monterey Park CA 91754 626-289-5021 688-3729*
**Fax Area Code:* 800 ■ *TF:* 800-955-3729 ■ *Web:* www.dieterich-post.com

El Dorado Trading Group Inc
760 San Antonio Rd . . . . Palo Alto CA 94303 650-494-6600 494-1995
TF: 800-227-8292 ■ *Web:* www.edtg.com

FP Mailing Solutions 140 N Mitchell Ct . . . . Addison IL 60101 630-827-5500 241-9091
TF: 800-341-6052 ■ *Web:* www.fpusa.com

Global Imaging Systems Inc
3820 Northdale Blvd Suite 200A. . . . . Tampa FL 33624 813-960-5508 264-7877
TF: 888-628-7834 ■ *Web:* www.global-imaging.com

Gs Precision Inc
101 John Seitz Dr 1 Industrial Pk . . . . Brattleboro VT 05301 802-257-5200 257-7937
Web: www.gsprecision.com

Hughes-calihan Corp PO Box 10322 . . . . Phoenix AZ 85064 602-264-9631 234-2406
Web: www.hughes-calihan.com

IKON Office Solutions Inc
70 Valley Stream Pkwy . . . . Malvern PA 19355 610-296-8600 408-7026
NYSE: IKN ■ *TF:* 800-983-2898 ■ *Web:* www.ikon.com

Illinois Wholesale Cash Register Inc
2790 Pinnacle Dr . . . . Elgin IL 60124 847-310-4200 310-8490
TF: 800-544-5493 ■ *Web:* www.illinoiswholesale.com

Konica Minolta Business Solutions USA Inc
101 Williams Dr . . . . Ramsey NJ 07446 201-825-4000
Web: www.kmbs.konicaminolta.us

Merchants Solutions Co 4422 Roosevelt Rd. . . . . Hillside IL 60162 708-449-6650 449-1432
TF: 800-486-3214 ■ *Web:* www.merchants-solutions.com

Metro - Sales Inc 1640 E 78th St . . . . Minneapolis MN 55423 612-861-4000 866-8069
TF: 800-862-7414 ■ *Web:* www.metrosales.com

New Age Electronics Inc 21950 Arnold Ctr Rd. . . . . Carson CA 90810 310-549-0000 549-5722
TF: 800-234-0300 ■ *Web:* www.newageinc.com

Numeridex Inc 632 S Wheeling Rd . . . . Wheeling IL 60090 847-541-8840 541-8392
TF: 800-323-7737 ■ *Web:* www.numeridex.com

Pitney Bowes Inc 1 Elmcroft Rd . . . . Stamford CT 06926 203-356-5000 460-3851
NYSE: PBI ■ *TF:* 800-672-6937 ■ *Web:* www.pb.com

Ricoh Americas Corp 2300 Parklake Dr NE . . . . Atlanta GA 30345 770-496-9500 495-4199
TF: 800-727-1885 ■ *Web:* www.ricoh-usa.com

Secap USA Inc 10 Clipper Rd . . . . Conshohocken PA 19428 610-825-6205 825-6205
TF: 800-523-0320 ■ *Web:* www.secap.com

Seminole Office Products 762 Big Tree Dr. . . . . Longwood FL 32750 407-830-7950 830-1399
TF: 800-433-7950 ■ *Web:* www.sopfl.com

Standard Duplicating Machines Corp
10 Connector Rd. . . . . Andover MA 01810 978-470-1920 475-1900
TF: 800-526-4774 ■ *Web:* www.sdmc.com

Stewart Engineering Supply Inc
3221 E Pioneer Pkwy . . . . Arlington TX 76010 817-640-1767 633-7231
TF: 800-533-1265 ■ *Web:* www.sesisupply.com

Systel Business Equipment Co Inc
PO Box 35910 . . . . Fayetteville NC 28303 910-321-7700 483-2846
TF: 800-849-4600 ■ *Web:* www.systeloa.com

Transco Business Technologies (TBT)
34 Leighton Rd . . . . Augusta ME 04330 207-622-6251 621-8620
TF: 800-322-0003 ■ *Web:* www.transcobusiness.com

BUSINESS ORGANIZATIONS

SEE Management & Business Professional Associations p. 1460; Chambers of Commerce - Canadian p. 1562; Chambers of Commerce - International p. 1564; Chambers of Commerce - US - Local p. 1566; Chambers of Commerce - US - State p. 1597

113 BUSINESS SERVICE CENTERS

Phone | Fax

Advance Presort Service Inc 4258 N Knox Ave. . . . . Chicago IL 60641 773-736-8333 736-0691
Web: www.advancepresort.com

AIM Mail Centers 15550-D Rockfield Blvd. . . . . Irvine CA 92618 949-837-4151 837-4537
TF: 800-669-4246 ■ *Web:* www.aimmailcenters.com

Allegra Network LLC 21680 Haggerty Rd. . . . . Northville MI 48167 248-596-8600 596-8601
TF: 800-726-9050 ■ *Web:* www2.allegranetwork.com

Aloha Petroleum Ltd
1132 Bishop St Suite 1700. . . . . Honolulu HI 96813 808-522-9700 522-9707
Web: www.alohagas.com

Alphanumeric Systems Inc 3801 Wake Forest Rd . . . . Raleigh NC 27609 919-781-7575 872-1440
TF: 800-638-6556 ■ *Web:* www.alphanumeric.com

Annex Brands Inc
7580 Metropolitan Dr Suite 200 . . . . San Diego CA 92108 619-563-4800 563-9850
TF: 800-456-1525 ■ *Web:* www.gopackagingstore.com

Ares Corp 1440 Chapin Ave Suite 390 . . . . Burlingame CA 94010 650-401-7100 401-7101
Web: www.arescorporation.com

Asi System Integration Inc 48 W 37th St . . . . New York NY 10018 866-308-3920 629-3944*
**Fax Area Code:* 212 ■ *TF:* 866-308-3920 ■ *Web:* www.asisystem.com

B2B Workforce Inc 200 N Pt Ctr E Suite 150 . . . . Alpharetta GA 30022 770-667-7200 667-7201
Web: www.b2bworkforce.com

Belmark Inc 600 Heritage Rd PO Box 5310. . . . . De Pere WI 54115 920-336-2848 336-4577
Web: www.belmark.com

Brigade Corp 16 Brooke Ln Suite 220 . . . . South Barrington IL 60010 847-783-0400 483-0404
Web: www.brigade.com

Bright Trading LLC 4850 Harrison Dr . . . . Las Vegas NV 89121 702-739-1393 739-1398
Web: www.stocktrading.com

Color Reflections 3773 Richmond Ave. . . . . Houston TX 77046 713-626-4045 623-6810
Web: www.colorreflections.com

Composites Horizons Inc
1471 W Industrial Pk St . . . . Covina CA 91722 626-331-0861 339-3220
Web: www.chi-covina.com

Concentrix Corp 3750 Monroe Ave. . . . . Pittsford NY 14534 585-218-5300 218-5301
TF: 800-466-5500 ■ *Web:* www.concentrix.com

Core Bts Inc 3001 W Beltline Hwy . . . . Madison WI 53713 608-661-7700
TF: 866-661-7787 ■ *Web:* www.corebts.com

Corporation Service Co
2711 Centerville Rd Suite 400 . . . . Wilmington DE 19808 302-636-5400 636-5454
TF: 866-403-5272 ■ *Web:* www.cscglobal.com

Craters & Freighters 331 Corporate Cir Suite J. . . . . Golden CO 80401 800-736-3335 399-9964*
**Fax Area Code:* 303 ■ *TF:* 800-736-3335 ■ *Web:* www.cratersandfreighters.com

Dragonfly Technologies 48 Wall St Suite 1100. . . . . New York NY 10005 212-713-5250 202-4625
Web: www.dragonflytech.com

Duncan-Parnell Inc 900 S McDowell St. . . . . Charlotte NC 28204 704-372-7766 333-3845
TF: 800-849-7708 ■ *Web:* www.duncan-parnell.com

E4e Inc 10720 Gilroy Rd. . . . . Hunt Valley MD 21031 410-568-3076 527-1155
Web: www.e4e.com

Executive Service Corps of Southern California
520 S Lafayette Pk Pl Suite 210 . . . . Los Angeles CA 90057 213-381-2891 381-2893
TF: 800-466-4114 ■ *Web:* www.escsc.org

FedEx Kinko's Office & Print Services Inc
13155 Noel Rd Suite 1600 . . . . Dallas TX 75240 214-550-7000 550-7001

Group O Inc 4905 77th Ave . . . . Milan IL 61264 309-736-8300 736-8301
TF Cust Svc: 800-752-0730 ■ *Web:* www.groupo.com

Juran Institute Inc
555 Heritage Rd Suite 100 . . . . Southbury CT 06488 203-267-3445 267-3446
Web: www.juran.com

Mail Boxes Etc 6060 Cornerstone Ct W . . . . San Diego CA 92121 858-455-8800 546-7493
TF: 800-789-4623 ■ *Web:* www.mbe.com

Mid-West Fabricating Co 313 N Johns St . . . . Amanda OH 43102 740-969-4411 969-4433
Web: www.midwestfab.com

Miller Systems Inc 205 Portland St 2nd Fl. . . . . Boston MA 02114 617-266-4200 266-4449
Web: www.millersystems.com

Navis Logistics Network
5675 DTC Blvd Suite 280. . . . . Greenwood Village CO 80111 303-741-6626 741-6653
TF: 800-525-6309 ■ *Web:* www.gonavis.com

Navis Pack & Ship Centers
5675 DTC Blvd Suite 280. . . . . Greenwood Village CO 80111 303-741-6626 741-6653
TF: 800-525-6309 ■ *Web:* www.gonavis.com

Objectwin Technology Inc
14800 St Mary's Ln Suite 100. . . . . Houston TX 77079 713-782-8200 782-8283
Web: www.objectwin.com

Office Depot Inc 2200 Old Germantown Rd . . . . Delray Beach FL 33445 561-438-4800 438-4406*
NYSE: ODP ■ **Fax:* Hum Res ■ *TF:* 800-937-3600 ■ *Web:* www.officedepot.com

Pacific Event Productions Inc
6989 Corte Santa Fe. . . . . San Diego CA 92121 858-458-9908 458-1173
Web: www.pacificevents.com

Pak Mail Centers of America Inc
7173 S Havana St Suite 600. . . . . Englewood CO 80112 303-957-1000 790-9445
TF Cust Svc: 800-778-6665 ■ *Web:* www.pakmail.com

Parcel Plus Inc 12715 Telge Rd . . . . Cypress TX 77429 281-256-4100 256-4178
TF: 888-280-2053 ■ *Web:* www.parcelplus.com

Peachtree Planning Corp 5040 Roswell Rd NE . . . . Atlanta GA 30342 404-260-1600 260-1700
TF: 800-366-0839 ■ *Web:* www.peachtreeplanning.com

Postal Connections of America
1081 Camino del Rio S Suite 109. . . . . San Diego CA 92108 619-294-7550 294-4550
TF: 800-767-8257 ■ *Web:* www.postalconnections.com

PostalAnnex+ Inc
7580 Metropolitan Dr Suite 200 . . . . San Diego CA 92108 619-563-4800 563-9850
TF: 800-456-1525 ■ *Web:* www.postalannex.com

PostNet International Franchise Corp
1819 Wazee St . . . . Denver CO 80202 303-771-7100 771-7133
TF: 800-841-7171 ■ *Web:* www.postnet.com

Product Line Inc 5000 Lima St. . . . . Denver CO 80239 720-374-3800 374-3720
TF: 888-714-3700

Progressive Software Computing Inc (PSCI)
3505 Silverside Rd Plaza Center
Suite 201-B . . . . Wilmington DE 19810 302-479-9700 479-7573
Web: www.psci.com

Property One Inc
4141 Veterans Memorial Blvd Suite 300. . . . . Metairie LA 70002 504-681-3400 681-3438
Web: www.property-one.com

Quinstreet Inc 950 Tower Ln 6th Fl . . . . Foster City CA 94404 650-578-7700 578-7604
NASDAQ: QNST ■ *Web:* www.quinstreet.com

Reg.Net 9625 W 76th St. . . . . Eden Prairie MN 55344 952-646-5288 623-0399*
**Fax Area Code:* 719 ■ *TF:* 800-999-2734 ■ *Web:* www.reg.net

Schoeneckers Inc 7630 Bush Lake Rd. . . . . Minneapolis MN 55439 952-835-4800 831-7962
Web: www.biworldwide.com

Sharp Decisions Inc 1040 Avenue of the A . . . . New York NY 10018 212-481-5533 481-8751
Web: www.sharpdecisions.com

Shee Atika Inc 315 Lincoln St Suite 300. . . . . Sitka AK 99835 907-747-3534 747-5727
TF: 800-478-3534 ■ *Web:* www.sheeatika.com

Sir Speedy Inc 26722 Plaza Dr . . . . Mission Viejo CA 92691 949-348-5000 348-5010
TF: 800-854-8297 ■ *Web:* www.sirspeedy.com

Company	City	State	Zip	Phone	Fax
Stone Rudolph & Henry Plc					
124 Ctr Pointe Dr	Clarksville	TN	37040	931-648-4786	647-5445
Web: www.srhcpas.com					
Systems America Inc					
1901 S Bascom Ave Suite 850	Campbell	CA	95008	408-879-5400	281-3736
Web: www.systemsamerica.com					
Team National Inc 8210 W State Rd 84	Davie	FL	33324	954-584-2151	584-2747
Web: www.bign.com					
Technical Training Inc (TTI)					
2750 Product Dr	Rochester Hills	MI	48309	248-853-5550	853-2411
TF: 800-837-5222 ■ *Web:* www.ttinao.com					
Techno-sciences Inc					
11750 Bltsvlle Dr 3rd fl	Beltsville	MD	20705	301-577-6000	790-0605*
**Fax Area Code:* 240 ■ *Web:* www.technosci.com					
Total Energy Solutions LLC (TES)					
100 International Dr Suite 260	Portsmouth	NH	03801	603-436-9812	436-9837
Web: www.totalenergyllc.com					
TRM Corp 5208 NE 122nd Ave	Portland	OR	97230	503-257-8766	998-3712*
NASDAQ: TRMM ■ **Fax Area Code:* 800 ■ *TF:* 800-877-8762					
Ubics Inc 333 Technology Dr Suite 210	Canonsburg	PA	15317	724-746-6001	746-9597
PINK: UBIX ■ *Web:* www.ubics.com					
UPS Store The 6060 Cornerstone Ct W	San Diego	CA	92121	858-455-8800	546-7492
TF: 800-789-4623 ■ *Web:* www.theupsstore.com					
Zeller Corp 1000 University Ave Suite 800	Rochester	NY	14607	585-254-8840	254-0982
Web: www.zellercorp.com					
Zoom Information Inc 307 Waverley Oaks Rd	Waltham	MA	02452	781-693-7500	693-7510
Web: www.zoominfo.com					

114 BUYER'S GUIDES - ONLINE

SEE ALSO Investment Guides - Online p. 2133

Company	City	State	Zip	Phone	Fax
Ace Mart - San Antonio 1220 S St Mary's	San Antonio	TX	78210	210-224-0082	224-1629
Web: www.acemart.com					
CardWeb.com Inc 99 Vanderbilt Beach Rd Fl 2	Naples	FL	34108	239-325-5300	236-1607
TF: 800-260-7448 ■ *Web:* www.cardweb.com					
ConsumerREVIEW Inc					
100 Marine Pkwy Suite 550	Redwood Shores	CA	94065	650-264-4800	264-4841
Web: www.consumerreview.com					
Epinions Inc 8000 Marina Blvd 5th Fl	Brisbane	CA	94005	650-616-6500	
Web: www.epinions.com					
ePublicEye.com 1010 N Central Ave	Glendale	CA	91202	818-547-0222	
Web: www.epubliceye.com					
InsWeb Inc 11290 Pyrites Way Suite 200	Gold River	CA	95670	916-853-3300	853-3325
NASDAQ: INSW ■ *TF:* 888-446-7932 ■ *Web:* www.insweb.com					
LowerMyBills Inc					
4859 W Slauson Ave Suite 405	Los Angeles	CA	90056	310-348-6800	998-6999
Web: www.lowermybills.com					
Market America Inc 1302 Pleasant Ridge Rd	Greensboro	NC	27409	336-605-0040	605-0041
TF: 866-420-1709 ■ *Web:* www.marketamerica.com					
Parke-Bell Ltd. Inc 709 W 12th St	Huntingburg	IN	47542	812-683-3707	683-5921
TF: 800-457-7456 ■ *Web:* www.touchofclass.com					
PriceSCAN.com Inc 564 Nutt Rd Suite 103	Phoenixville	PA	19460	610-651-0760	
Web: www.pricescan.com					
Shopping.com Inc 8000 Marina Blvd 5th Fl	Brisbane	CA	94005	650-616-6500	616-6510
Web: www.shopping.com					

115 CABINETS - WOOD

SEE ALSO Carpentry & Flooring Contractors p. 1719; Household Furniture p. 1896

Company	City	State	Zip	Phone	Fax
American Woodmark Corp 3102 Shawnee Dr	Winchester	VA	22601	540-665-9100	665-9176
NASDAQ: AMWD ■ *TF:* 800-388-2483 ■ *Web:* www.americanwoodmark.com					
Ampco Products Inc 11400 NW 36th Ave	Miami	FL	33167	305-821-5700	557-0764
Web: www.ampco.com					
Bertch Cabinet Mfg Inc 4747 Crestwood Dr	Waterloo	IA	50702	319-296-2987	296-2315
Web: www.bertch.com					
Bloch Industries 140 Commerce Dr	Rochester	NY	14623	585-334-9600	521-9505*
**Fax Area Code:* 800 ■ *TF:* 800-992-5624 ■ *Web:* www.blochindustries.com					
Brandom Cabinets Co 404 Hawkins St	Hillsboro	TX	76645	254-580-1200	959-2801*
**Fax Area Code:* 800 ■ *TF Cust Svc:* 800-366-8001 ■ *Web:* www.brandom.com					
Cabinetry By Karman Inc					
6000 Stratler St	Salt Lake City	UT	84107	801-268-3581	261-0875
TF: 800-255-3581 ■ *Web:* www.cabinetrybykarman.com					
Cabinets 2000 Inc 11100 Firestone Blvd	Norwalk	CA	90650	562-868-0909	868-4131
Web: www.cabinets2000.com					
California Kitchen Cabinet Door Corp					
400 Cochrane Cir	Morgan Hill	CA	95037	408-782-5700	782-9000
TF: 888-225-3667 ■ *Web:* www.caldoor.com					
Cana Inc 29194 Phillips St	Elkhart	IN	46514	574-262-4664	262-0945
Candlelight Cabinetry Inc 24 Michigan St	Lockport	NY	14094	716-434-6543	434-6748
Web: www.candlelightcab.com					
Canyon Creek Cabinet Co 16726 Tye St SE	Monroe	WA	98272	360-348-4973	348-4810
TF: 800-228-1830 ■ *Web:* www.canyoncreek.com					
Capital Cabinet Corp 3645 Losee Rd	North Las Vegas	NV	89030	702-649-8733	649-6512
Web: www.capitalcabinet.com					
Cardell Cabinetry 3215 N Panam Expy	San Antonio	TX	78219	210-225-0290	212-5823
Web: www.cardellcabinetry.com					
Chandlers Plywood Products Inc					
3716 Waverly Rd	Huntington	WV	25704	304-429-1311	429-5886
TF: 800-624-3502 ■ *Web:* www.chandlerkitchens.com					
Commercial Wood Products Co 10019 Yucca Rd	Adelanto	CA	92301	760-246-4530	246-8226
Web: www.commercialwood.com					
Conestoga Wood Specialties Inc					
245 Reading Rd	East Earl	PA	17519	717-445-6701	638-7198*
**Fax Area Code:* 800 ■ *Web:* www.conestogawood.com					
Continental Cabinet Inc 2841 Pierce St	Dallas	TX	75233	214-467-4444	467-1132
TF: 800-786-6421 ■ *Web:* www.ccabinc.com					
Crystal Cabinet Works Inc 1100 Crystal Dr	Princeton	MN	55371	763-389-4187	389-5846
TF: 800-347-5045 ■ *Web:* www.ccworks.com					
Dalia Kitchen Design Inc					
1 Design Ctr Pl Suite 643	Boston	MA	02210	617-482-2566	482-2744
Web: www.alno.com					
Decore-ative Specialties Inc 2772 S Peck Rd	Monrovia	CA	91016	626-254-9191	254-1515
TF: 800-729-7277 ■ *Web:* www.decore.com					
Dewils Industries Inc 6307 NE 127th Ave	Vancouver	WA	98682	360-892-0300	253-2096
Web: www.dewils.com					
Dura Supreme Inc 300 Dura Dr	Howard Lake	MN	55349	320-543-3872	543-3310
Web: www.durasupreme.com					
Dutch Made Custom Cabinetry 10415 Roth Rd	Grabill	IN	46741	260-657-3311	657-5778
Web: www.dutchmade.com					
Evans Cabinet Corp 1321 N Franklin St	Dublin	GA	31021	478-272-2530	272-2731
Web: www.evanscabinet.com					
Fashion Cabinet Mfg Inc 5440 Axel Pk Rd	West Jordan	UT	84081	801-280-0646	280-8934
Web: www.fashioncabinet.com					
Fixture Exchange Corp 3000 W Pafford St	Fort Worth	TX	76110	817-429-2496	927-8451
Forest Wellborn Products Inc					
2212 Airport Blvd	Alexander City	AL	35010	256-234-7900	234-2750
TF: 800-846-2562 ■ *Web:* www.wellbornforest.com					
Fortune Brands Home & Hardware Inc					
520 Lake Cook Rd	Deerfield	IL	60015	847-484-4400	
Web: www.fortunebrands.com					
Grabill Cabinet Co Inc 13844 Sawmill Dr	Grabill	IN	46741	260-627-2131	627-3539
Web: www.grabillcabinets.com					
Grandview Products Co 1601 Superior Dr	Parsons	KS	67357	620-421-6950	421-4211
TF: 800-247-9105 ■ *Web:* www.grandviewcabinets.com					
Haas Cabinet Co Inc 625 W Utica St	Sellersburg	IN	47172	812-246-4431	246-5420
TF: 800-457-6458 ■ *Web:* www.haascabinet.com					
HomeCrest Cabinetry 1002 Eisenhower Dr N	Goshen	IN	46526	574-535-9300	533-3667
TF: 800-960-3660 ■ *Web:* www.homecrestcab.com					
Huntwood Industries 23800 E Apple Way	Liberty Lake	WA	99019	509-924-5858	928-6647
TF: 800-873-7350 ■ *Web:* www.huntwood.com					
Jim Bishop Cabinets Inc PO Box 11424	Montgomery	AL	36111	334-288-1381	386-2771
Web: www.jimbishopcabinets.com					
Kabinart Corp 3650 Trousdale Dr	Nashville	TN	37204	615-833-1961	834-8268
Kent Moore Cabinets Ltd 1460 Fountain Ave	Bryan	TX	77801	979-775-2906	775-0519
TF: 800-366-9233 ■ *Web:* www.kentmoorecabinets.com					
Kitchen Craft Cabinetry 1180 Springfield Rd	Winnipeg	MB	R2C2Z2	204-224-3211	665-3495*
**Fax Area Code:* 800 ■ *Web:* www.kitchencraft.com					
Kitchen Kompact Inc 911 E 11th St	Jeffersonville	IN	47130	812-282-6681	282-7880
Web: www.kitchenkompact.com					
Kountry Kraft Kitchens Inc PO Box 570	Newmanstown	PA	17073	610-589-4575	589-4986
TF: 877-677-9833 ■ *Web:* www.kountrykraft.com					
Kraftmaid Cabinetry Inc					
15535 S State Ave PO Box 1055	Middlefield	OH	44062	440-632-5333	632-5648
TF: 888-562-7744 ■ *Web:* www.kraftmaid.com					
Leedo Mfg Co Inc PO Box 520	East Bernard	TX	77435	979-335-4885	335-4109
TF: 866-995-3336 ■ *Web:* www.leedo.com					
Legacy Cabinets LLC 100 Legacy Blvd	Eastaboga	AL	36260	256-831-4888	831-4896
TF: 800-813-1112					
Legere Group Ltd PO Box 1527	Avon	CT	06001	860-674-0392	674-0469
Web: www.legeregroup.com					
Marsh Furniture Co PO Box 870	High Point	NC	27261	336-884-7363	884-3553
TF: 800-756-2774 ■ *Web:* www.marshfurniture.com					
Martin Cabinet Inc 336 S Washington St	Plainville	CT	06062	860-747-5769	747-9595
Masco Cabinetry LLC 5353 W US 223 PO Box 1946	Adrian	MI	49221	517-263-0771	265-3325
TF: 866-850-8557 ■ *Web:* www.merillat.com					
Masco Corp 21001 Van Born Rd	Taylor	MI	48180	313-274-7400	792-6135
NYSE: MAS ■ *Web:* www.masco.com					
MasterBrand Cabinets Inc					
1 MasterBrand Cabinets Dr PO Box 420	Jasper	IN	47547	812-482-2527	
Web: www.masterbrand.com					
Mastercraft Industries Inc 777 S St	Newburgh	NY	12550	845-565-8850	565-9392
TF: 800-835-7812 ■ *Web:* www.mastercraftusa.com					
McConnell Cabinets Inc					
13110 Louden Ln	City of Industry	CA	91746	626-937-2200	937-2207
TF: 800-794-7895					
Medallion Cabinetry 1 Medallion Way	Waconia	MN	55387	952-442-5171	442-4998
TF: 800-543-4074 ■ *Web:* www.medallioncabinetry.com					
Mid-America Cabinet Inc 20980 Marion Lee Rd	Gentry	AR	72734	479-736-2671	736-8086
Web: www.midamericacabinets.com					
Millbrook Millwork Inc 3565 Rt 20	Nassau	NY	12123	518-766-3033	766-3919
Mouser Custom Cabinetry					
2112 N Hwy 31 W	Elizabethtown	KY	42701	270-737-7477	737-7446
TF: 800-345-7537 ■ *Web:* www.mousercc.com					
Norcraft Cos 3020 Denmark Ave Suite 100	Eagan	MN	55121	651-234-3300	
TF: 866-802-7892 ■ *Web:* www.norcraftcompanies.com					
Northern Contours Inc					
1355 Mendota Heights Rd Suite 100	Mendota Heights	MN	55120	651-695-1698	695-1714
TF: 866-344-8132 ■ *Web:* www.northerncontours.com					
Omega Cabinetry Ltd 1205 Peters Dr	Waterloo	IA	50703	319-235-5700	235-5853*
**Fax:* Cust Svc ■ *Web:* www.omegacab.com					
Patella Industries Inc 161 Stirling Ave	LaSalle	QC	H8R3P3	514-364-1964	364-1270
TF: 800-265-1964					
Patrick Industries Inc					
107 W Franklin St PO Box 638	Elkhart	IN	46515	574-294-7511	522-5213
NASDAQ: PATK ■ *TF:* 800-331-2151 ■ *Web:* www.patrickind.com					
Plain & Fancy Custom Cabinetry Inc					
PO Box 519	Schaefferstown	PA	17088	717-949-6571	949-2114
TF: 800-447-9006 ■ *Web:* www.plainfancycabinetry.com					
Plato Woodwork Inc 200 Third St S W	Plato	MN	55370	320-238-2193	238-2131
TF: 800-328-5924 ■ *Web:* www.platowoodwork.com					
Prestige Inc 101 S 8th St	Neodesha	KS	66757	620-325-8500	325-8500
TF: 800-328-4006					
Quality Custom Cabinetry Inc					
125 Peters Rd	New Holland	PA	17557	717-656-2721	661-6901
TF: 800-909-6006 ■ *Web:* www.qcc.com					
Quality Wood Products Inc 7400 E 12th St	Kansas City	MO	64126	816-231-4601	231-4858
TF: 800-806-8531 ■ *Web:* www.qwpi.com					

	City	State	Zip	Phone	Fax
Regal Kitchens Inc 8600 NW S River Dr	Miami	FL	33166	305-885-0111	885-7419
TF: 800-432-0731 ■ *Web:* www.regalkitchensinc.com					
Republic Industries Inc 1400 Warren Dr.	Marshall	TX	75672	903-935-3680	935-3697
Web: www.republicind.com					
Rich Maid Kabinetry LLC 633 W Lincoln Ave	Myerstown	PA	17067	717-866-2112	866-5962
TF: 800-295-2912 ■ *Web:* www.richmaidkabinetry.com					
Rosebud Mfg Co Inc 111 W Ctr St	Madison	SD	57042	605-256-4561	256-3842
TF: 800-256-4561 ■ *Web:* www.rosebudmfg.com					
Royal Cabinets 1260 E Grand Ave.	Pomona	CA	91766	909-629-8565	629-7762
Web: www.royalcabinets.com					
RSI Home Products Inc 400 E Orangethorpe Ave.	Anaheim	CA	92801	714-449-2200	449-2222*
**Fax:* Cust Svc ■ *TF:* 888-774-8062 ■ *Web:* www.rsiholdingcorp.com					
Rutt HandCrafted Cabinetry					
215 Diller Ave.	New Holland	PA	17557	717-351-1700	351-1714
Web: www.rutt1.com					
Rynone Mfg Corp PO Box 128	Sayre	PA	18840	570-888-5272	888-1175
Web: www.rynone.com					
Shamrock Cabinet & Fixture Corp					
10201 E 65th St	Raytown	MO	64133	816-737-2300	356-7835
Web: www.shamrockcabinet.com					
Showplace Wood Products Inc					
1 Enterprise St	Harrisburg	SD	57032	605-743-2200	
Web: www.showplacewood.com					
Starmark Cabinetry 600 E 48th St N	Sioux Falls	SD	57104	605-335-8600	336-5574
Web: www.starmarkcabinetry.com					
Thomasville Furniture Industries Inc					
401 E Main St PO Box 339	Thomasville	NC	27361	336-472-4000	472-4085
Web: www.thomasville.com					
Tri-Star Cabinet & Top Co Inc 1000 S Cedar	New Lenox	IL	60451	815-485-2564	485-5747
Web: www.tristarcabinets.com					
Ultracraft Co 6163 Old 421 Rd	Liberty	NC	27298	336-622-4281	622-3474
TF: 800-262-4046 ■ *Web:* www.ultracraft.com					
US Home Systems Inc					
405 State Hwy 121 Bypass Bldg A Suite 250	Louisville	TX	75067	214-488-6300	
NASDAQ: USHS ■ *Web:* www.ushomesystems.com					
Valley Cabinet Inc 845 Prosper Rd	De Pere	WI	54115	920-336-3174	336-5956
TF: 800-236-8981 ■ *Web:* www.valleycabinetinc.com					
Wellborn Cabinet Inc 38669 Alabama 77	Ashland	AL	36251	256-354-7151	354-7022
TF: 800-762-4475 ■ *Web:* www.wellborn.com					
Wood-Mode Inc 1 2nd St	Kreamer	PA	17833	570-374-2711	374-2700
Web: www.wood-mode.com					
Woodcase Fine Cabinetry Inc 3255 W Osborn Rd.	Phoenix	AZ	85017	602-269-9731	269-1242
Web: www.woodcaseinc.net					
Woodcraft Industries Inc					
525 Lincoln Ave SE.	Saint Cloud	MN	56304	320-252-1503	656-2199
Web: www.woodcraftind.com					
WW Wood Products Inc 10182 Old Hwy 60	Dudley	MO	63936	573-624-7090	624-8576
Yorktowne Inc 100 Redco Ave.	Red Lion	PA	17356	717-244-4011	
TF: 800-777-0065 ■ *Web:* www.yorktownecabinetry.com					

116 CABLE & OTHER PAY TELEVISION SERVICES

	City	State	Zip	Phone	Fax
Advance/Newhouse Communications PO Box 4739	Syracuse	NY	13221	315-463-7675	463-4127
Armstrong Cable Services 660 S Benbrook Rd	Butler	PA	16001	724-482-4480	482-4884
Web: www.armstrongonewire.com					
Armstrong Group of Cos 1 Armstrong Pl.	Butler	PA	16001	724-283-0925	283-9655
Web: www.armstrongonewire.com					
Astral Media Inc					
1800 McGill CollegeáAve Suite 2700	Montreal	QC	H3H2T3	514-939-5000	939-1515
TSE: ACM.A ■ *Web:* www.astral.com					
Bresnan Communications 1 Manhattanville Rd	Purchase	NY	10577	914-641-3300	641-3301
TF: 888-909-4357 ■ *Web:* www.bresnan.com					
Buckeye CableSystem 5566 Southwick Blvd.	Toledo	OH	43614	419-724-9802	724-7074
Web: www.buckeyecablesystem.com					
Buford Media Group 6125 Paluxy Dr.	Tyler	TX	75703	903-561-4411	561-4031
Web: www.alliancecable.net					
Cable Line Inc 311 N 7th St PO Box 95.	Perkasie	PA	18944	215-258-1380	258-1388
Web: www.cable-line.com					
Cable One Inc 1314 N 3rd St 3rd Fl.	Phoenix	AZ	85004	602-364-6000	364-6010
Web: www.cableone.net					
CableAmerica Corp 4120 E Valley Auto Dr.	Mesa	AZ	85206	480-558-7260	892-7775
TF: 800-327-4375 ■ *Web:* www.cableamerica.com					
Cablevision Systems Corp 1111 Stewart Ave	Bethpage	NY	11714	516-803-2300	803-3134*
NYSE: CVC ■ **Fax:* Hum Res ■ *Web:* www.cablevision.com					
Capitol Connection					
George Mason University Television 4400 University Dr					
MS 1D2	Fairfax	VA	22030	703-993-3100	273-2417
Web: www.capitolconnection.gmu.edu					
Charter Communications Inc					
12405 Powerscourt Dr Suite 100	St. Louis	MO	63131	314-965-0555	965-9745
NASDAQ: CHTR ■ *TF:* 888-438-2427 ■ *Web:* www.charter.com					
Cogeco Cable Inc 5 Pl Ville-Marie Suite 915	Montreal	QC	H3B2G2	514-874-2600	874-2625
TF: 866-874-2600 ■ *Web:* www.cogeco.ca					
Comcast Cable Communications LLC					
1701 John F Kennedy Blvd	Oaks	PA	19103	215-665-1700	981-7790
Web: www.comcast.com					
Comcast Corp Cable Div 1500 Market St	Philadelphia	PA	19102	215-665-1700	981-7790
Web: www.comcast.com					
Cox Communications Inc 1400 Lake Hearn Dr	Atlanta	GA	30319	404-843-5000	843-5000
Web: www.ww2.cox.com					
DIRECTV Inc 2230 E Imperial Hwy	El Segundo	CA	90245	310-535-5000	535-5315*
**Fax:* Hum Res ■ *TF Cust Svc:* 800-531-5000 ■ *Web:* www.directv.com					
DISH Network LLC 9601 S Meridian Blvd	Englewood	CO	80112	303-723-1000	723-2727*
NASDAQ: DISH ■ **Fax:* Cust Svc ■ *TF:* 800-333-3474 ■ *Web:* www.dishnetwork.com					
EchoStar Communications Corp					
9601 S Meridian Blvd.	Englewood	CO	80112	303-723-1000	723-1399*
NASDAQ: DISH ■ **Fax:* Hum Res ■ *TF:* 800-333-3474 ■ *Web:* www.dishnetwork.com					
High Power Technical Services Inc (HPTS)					
2230 Ampere Dr	Louisville	KY	40299	502-254-0768	271-2483
TF: 866-398-3474 ■ *Web:* www.hpts.tv					
Insight Communications Co Inc 810 7th Ave	New York	NY	10019	917-286-2300	286-2301
Web: www.myinsight.com					
Insight Interactive LLC					
5601 N MacArthur Blvd Suite 201	Irving	TX	75038	469-524-0116	
TF: 877-494-6077					
Knology Inc 1241 OG Skinner Dr.	West Point	GA	31833	706-645-8553	645-1446
NASDAQ: KNOL ■ *TF:* 877-566-5649 ■ *Web:* www.knology.com					
LodgeNet Entertainment Corp					
3900 W Innovation St.	Sioux Falls	SD	57107	605-988-1330	988-1532
NASDAQ: LNET ■ *TF:* 888-563-4363 ■ *Web:* www.lodgenet.com					
Mediacom Communications Corp					
100 Crystal Run Rd.	Middletown	NY	10941	845-695-2600	695-2669
NASDAQ: MCCC ■ *TF:* 888-692-9090 ■ *Web:* www.mediacomcc.com					
Midcontinent Communications PO Box 5010.	Sioux Falls	SD	57117	605-229-1775	330-4089*
**Fax:* Cust Svc ■ *TF:* 800-888-1300 ■ *Web:* www.midcocomm.com					
National Cable Television Co-op Inc (NCTC)					
11200 Corporate Ave	Lenexa	KS	66219	913-599-5900	599-5903
TF: 800-888-6282 ■ *Web:* www.ncta.com					
Oceanic Time Warner Cable 200 Akamainui St	Mililani	HI	96789	808-625-2100	625-5888
Web: www.oceanic.com					
Omega Communications Inc					
41 E Washington Suite 110	Indianapolis	IN	46204	317-264-4010	264-4020
TF: 800-622-6728 ■ *Web:* www.omegac.com					
Paragould Light & Water Commission (PLWC)					
1901 Jones Rd PO Box 9	Paragould	AR	72451	870-239-7700	239-7798
Web: www.clwc.com					
Persona Inc 17 Duffy Pl	Saint John's	NL	A1B4L1	709-754-3775	754-3883
TF: 866-737-7662 ■ *Web:* www.personainc.ca					
Phoenix Cable Inc					
17 S Franklin Tpke Suite 100B	Ramsey	NJ	07446	201-825-9090	825-8794
Quebecor Media Inc 612 Rue St Jacques	Montreal	QC	H3C4M8	514-597-2231	594-8844
Web: www.quebecor.com					
Resort Television Cable Co Inc					
115 E Capitol Ave	Little Rock	AR	72201	501-378-3529	376-8594
Rifkin & Assoc Inc 360 S Monroe St Suite 600	Denver	CO	80209	303-333-1215	322-3553
Web: www.rifkinco.com					
Selectronics Corp PO Box 9.	Waitsfield	VT	05673	802-496-3391	496-8342
TF: 800-496-3391 ■ *Web:* www.wcvt.com					
Service Electric Cable TV & Communications					
2260 Ave A.	Bethlehem	PA	18017	610-865-9100	865-7888
TF: 800-232-9100 ■ *Web:* www.sectv.com					
Shaw Communications Inc 630 3rd Ave SW	Calgary	AB	T2P4L4	403-750-4500	750-4501*
NYSE: SJR ■ **Fax:* Mktg ■ *TF:* 888-472-2222 ■ *Web:* www.shaw.ca					
Suddenlink PO Box 139400.	Tyler	TX	75713	800-999-8876	561-5485*
**Fax Area Code:* 903 ■ *TF:* 877-423-2743 ■ *Web:* www.suddenlink.com					
Tele-Media Corp PO Box 39	Bellefonte	PA	16823	814-355-4729	353-2072
Web: www.tele-media.com					
Time Warner Cable of New York City					
120 E 23rd St	New York	NY	10010	212-598-7200	
TiVo Inc 2160 Gold St.	Alviso	CA	95002	408-519-9100	519-5330
NASDAQ: TIVO ■ *TF:* 877-367-8486 ■ *Web:* www.tivo.com					
US Cable Corp 28 W Grand Ave.	Montvale	NJ	07645	201-930-9000	930-9232
Web: www.uscablegroup.com					
Videotron Ltee 405 Ogilvy Ave	Montreal	QC	H2X3W4	514-281-1232	773-1877*
**Fax Area Code:* 800 ■ **Fax:* Cust Svc ■ *Web:* www.videotron.com					
Wavevision 10300 Wstffice Dr Suite 200	Houston	TX	77042	832-495-4109	
Web: www.wavevision.com					
Wireless Cable International Inc					
5 Mountain Blvd Suite 6	Warren	NJ	07059	908-769-1731	769-4078

117 CABLE REELS

	City	State	Zip	Phone	Fax
American Reeling Devices Inc					
15 Airpark Vista Blvd	Dayton	NV	89403	775-246-1000	246-1002
TF Sales: 800-354-7335 ■ *Web:* www.americanreeling.com					
Conductix 10102 F St.	Omaha	NE	68127	402-339-9300	339-9627
TF: 800-521-4888 ■ *Web:* www.conductix.us					
Coxreels 6720 S Clementine Ct	Tempe	AZ	85283	480-820-6396	820-5132
TF Cust Svc: 800-269-7335 ■ *Web:* www.coxreels.com					
Gleason Reel Corp 600 S Clark St	Mayville	WI	53050	920-387-4120	387-4189
TF: 800-571-0166 ■ *Web:* www.hubbell-gleason.com					
Hannay Reels Inc 553 SR 143	Westerlo	NY	12193	518-797-3791	797-3259
TF: 877-467-3357 ■ *Web:* www.hannay.com					
Tayloreel Corp PO Box 476.	Oakwood	GA	30566	770-503-1612	503-9614
Web: www.tayloreel.com					

118 CALCULATORS - ELECTRONIC

	City	State	Zip	Phone	Fax
Calculated Industries Inc 4840 Hytech Dr	Carson City	NV	89706	775-885-4900	885-4949
TF: 800-854-8075 ■ *Web:* www.calculated.com					
Sharp Electronics Corp 1 Sharp Plaza	Mahwah	NJ	07430	201-529-8200	529-8413
TF: 800-237-4277 ■ *Web:* www.sharpusa.com					
Sweda Co LLC 17411 Valley Blvd	City of Industry	CA	91744	626-357-9999	357-6080
Web: www.swedausa.com					
Texas Instruments Inc 12500 TI Blvd	Dallas	TX	75243	972-995-3773	927-6377
NYSE: TXN ■ *TF Cust Svc:* 800-336-5236 ■ *Web:* www.ti.com					
Victor Technology Inc 780 W Belden Ave	Addison	IL	60101	630-268-8400	268-8450
TF: 800-628-2420 ■ *Web:* www.victortech.com					

119 CAMERAS & RELATED SUPPLIES - RETAIL

	City	State	Zip	Phone	Fax
Abe's of Maine Cameras & Electronics					
1957 Coney Island Ave.	Brooklyn	NY	11223	718-645-0900	998-5216
TF: 800-992-2237 ■ *Web:* www.abesofmaine.com					

Company	City	State	Zip	Phone	Fax
Adorama Camera Inc 42 W 18th St *TF:* 800-223-2500 ■ *Web:* www.adorama.com	New York	NY	10011	212-741-0052	463-7223
B & H Photo-Video-Pro Audio Corp 420 9th Ave. *TF:* 800-947-9954 ■ *Web:* www.bhphotovideo.com	New York	NY	10001	212-444-6600	239-7770
Beach Camera 203 Rt 22 E *Web:* www.beachcamera.com	Green Brook	NJ	08812	732-968-6400	968-7709
Black Photo Corp 371 Gough Rd *TF:* 800-668-3826 ■ *Web:* www.blackphoto.com	Markham	ON	L3R4B6	905-475-2777	475-8814
Calumet Photographic Inc 890 Supreme Dr. *TF Cust Svc:* 800-453-2550 ■ *Web:* www.calumetphoto.com	Bensenville	IL	60106	630-860-7447	860-7481
Camasco Group 550-B Guy St. *TF:* 877-361-4472 ■ *Web:* www.cameraexpert.com	Granby	QC	J2G7J8	800-361-4472	
Cambridge Camera 34 Franklin Ave *TF:* 800-221-2253 ■ *Web:* www.cambridgeworld.com	Brooklyn	NY	11205	718-858-5002	858-5437
Camera Corner Inc PO Box 1899 *TF:* 800-868-2462 ■ *Web:* www.camcor.com	Burlington	NC	27216	336-228-0251	222-8011
CameraWorld.com 2010 Main St Suite 400 **Fax Area Code:* 877 ■ **Fax:* Orders ■ *TF:* 800-226-3721 ■ *Web:* www.cameraworld.com	Irvine	CA	92614	800-226-3721	333-9957*
Canoga Camera Corp 22065 Sherman Way *TF:* 800-201-4201 ■ *Web:* www.canogacamera.com	Canoga Park	CA	91303	818-346-5506	346-9376
Cress Photo PO Box 4262 *Web:* www.flashbulbs.com	Wayne	NJ	07474	973-694-1280	694-6965
Dodd Co 2077 E 30th St *TF:* 800-507-1676 ■ *Web:* www.doddcamera.com	Cleveland	OH	44115	216-361-6800	361-6819
Dury's 701 Ewing Ave *TF:* 800-824-2379 ■ *Web:* www.durys.com	Nashville	TN	37203	615-255-3456	255-3506
F-11 Photographic Supplies 16 E Main St. *TF Sales:* 888-548-0203 ■ *Web:* www.f11photo.com	Bozeman	MT	59715	406-586-3281	587-3277
Focus Camera Inc 905 McDonald Ave *TF:* 800-221-0828 ■ *Web:* www.focuscamera.com	Brooklyn	NY	11219	718-431-7900	437-8895
Foto Source Canada Inc 1075 Meyerside Dr Unit 10. *Web:* www.fotosource.com	Mississauga	ON	L5T1M3	905-795-1771	795-0433
Get Smart Products PO Box 0018 **Fax Area Code:* 866 ■ *TF:* 800-827-0673 ■ *Web:* www.pfile.com	Maryknoll	NY	10545	914-762-3500	827-0673*
Helix Ltd 310 S Racine Ave. *TF:* 800-334-3549 ■ *Web:* www.helixphoto.com	Chicago	IL	60607	312-421-6000	421-1586
Island Camera & Gift Shop Inc 670 Queen St	Honolulu	HI	96813	808-592-4800	592-4858
Kenmore Camera Inc 18031 67th Ave NE PO Box 82467 *TF:* 888-485-7447 ■ *Web:* www.kenmorecamera.com	Kenmore	WA	98028	425-485-7447	489-2843
Lawrence Photo & Video Inc 2550 S Campbell St *Web:* www.lawrencephotovideo.com	Springfield	MO	65807	417-883-8300	883-8305
Porter's Camera Store PO Box 628 *TF:* 800-553-2001 ■ *Web:* www.porterscamerastore.com	Cedar Falls	IA	50613	319-268-0104	277-5254
Ritz Camera & Image 6711 Ritz Way *TF Cust Svc:* 877-999-7489 ■ *Web:* www.ritzcamera.com	Beltsville	MD	20705	301-419-0000	419-2995
Samy's Camera Inc 431 S Fairfax Ave *TF:* 800-321-4726 ■ *Web:* www.samys.com	Los Angeles	CA	90036	323-938-2420	692-0750

120 CAMPERS, TRAVEL TRAILERS, MOTOR HOMES

Company	City	State	Zip	Phone	Fax
Airstream Inc 419 W Pike St *Web:* www.airstream-rv.com	Jackson Center	OH	45334	937-596-6111	596-7939
Alaskan Campers Inc 420 NE Alaskan Way *Web:* www.alaskancamper.net	Chehalis	WA	98532	360-748-6494	748-1475
Alfa Leisure Inc 13501 5th St *TF:* 800-373-3372	Chino	CA	91710	909-628-5574	591-7902
Coach House Inc 3480 Technology Dr *TF:* 800-235-0984 ■ *Web:* www.coachhouserv.com	Nokomis	FL	34275	941-485-0984	488-4095
Coachmen Industries Inc 2831 Dexter Dr PO Box 3300 *NYSE:* COA ■ *Web:* www.allamericangroupinc.com	Elkhart	IN	46515	574-266-2500	266-2559
Cool Amphibious Manufacturers International LLC 31 Hawkes Rd *TF:* 888-926-6553 ■ *Web:* www.camillc.com	Bluffton	SC	29910	843-757-4133	757-6774
Cruise America 11 W Hampton Ave *TF:* 800-671-8042 ■ *Web:* www.cruiseamerica.com	Mesa	AZ	85210	480-464-7300	464-7321
Custom Fiberglass Mfg Corp *Snugtop* 1711 Harbor Ave PO Box 121 *TF:* 800-768-4867 ■ *Web:* www.snugtop.com	Long Beach	CA	90813	562-432-5454	435-2992
Dexter Chassis Group 501 Miller Dr *TF:* 800-669-7681 ■ *Web:* www.dexterchassisgroup.com	White Pigeon	MI	49099	269-483-7681	483-9089
Dutchmen Mfg Inc 2164 Caragana Court PO Box 2164 *Web:* www.dutchmen-rv.com	Goshen	IN	46527	574-537-0600	533-3807
Fleetwood RV 3125 Myers St *NYSE:* FLE ■ *TF:* 877-887-2921 ■ *Web:* www.fleetwood.com	Riverside	CA	92503	877-887-2921	
Forest River Inc 58277 SR 19 S *Web:* www.forestriverinc.com	Elkhart	IN	46517	574-296-7700	295-8749
Foretravel Motorcoach Inc 1221 NW Stallings Dr *TF:* 800-955-6226 ■ *Web:* www.foretravel.com	Nacogdoches	TX	75964	936-564-8367	564-0391
Four Wheel Campers 1460 Churchill Downs Ave *TF:* 800-242-1442 ■ *Web:* www.fourwheelcampers.com	Woodland	CA	95776	530-666-1442	666-1486
Gulf Stream Coach Inc 503 S Oakland Ave PO Box 1005 *TF:* 800-289-8787 ■ *Web:* www.gulfstreamcoach.com	Nappanee	IN	46550	574-773-7761	773-5761
Jayco Inc 903 S Main St *TF Cust Svc:* 800-283-8267 ■ *Web:* www.jayco.com	Middlebury	IN	46540	574-825-5861	825-7354
Keystone RV Co 2642 Hackberry Dr PO Box 2000 *TF:* 866-425-4369 ■ *Web:* www.keystonerv.com	Goshen	IN	46527	574-535-2100	535-2199
Lance Camper Mfg Corp 43120 Venture St. *TF:* 800-423-7996 ■ *Web:* www.lancecampers.com	Lancaster	CA	93535	661-949-3322	949-1262
Monaco Coach Corp 91320 Coburg Industrial Way **Fax:* Hum Res ■ *TF:* 800-634-0855 ■ *Web:* www.monaco-online.com	Coburg	OR	97408	541-686-8011	681-8037*
New Horizons RV Corp 2401 Lacy Dr. *TF:* 800-235-3140 ■ *Web:* www.horizonsrv.com	Junction City	KS	66441	785-238-7575	238-4992
Newell Coach Corp 6411 S Hwy 69 PO Box 511 *TF:* 888-363-9355 ■ *Web:* www.newellcoach.com	Miami	OK	74354	918-542-3344	542-2028
Newmar Corp 355 Delaware St. *TF:* 800-731-8300 ■ *Web:* www.newmarcorp.com	Nappanee	IN	46550	574-773-7791	773-2007
Nu-Wa Industries Inc 3701 Johnson Rd *TF:* 800-835-0676 ■ *Web:* www.nuwa.com	Chanute	KS	66720	620-431-2088	431-2513
Palomino RV 1047 E M86 *Web:* www.palominorv.com	Colon	MI	49040	269-432-3271	432-2516
Peterson Industries Inc 616 E Hwy 36 *TF:* 800-368-3759 ■ *Web:* www.petersonind.com	Smith Center	KS	66967	785-282-6825	282-3810
Renegade/Kibbi LLC 52216 State Rd 15 **Fax:* Sales ■ *TF:* 888-522-1126 ■ *Web:* www.renegaderv.com	Bristol	IN	46507	574-848-1126	848-1127*
Rexhall Industries Inc 46147 7th St W **Fax:* Sales ■ *TF:* 800-444-9720 ■ *Web:* www.rexhall.com	Lancaster	CA	93534	661-726-0565	726-5811*
Skyline Corp 2520 By-Pass Rd *NYSE:* SKY ■ *TF:* 800-348-7469 ■ *Web:* www.skylinecorp.com	Elkhart	IN	46514	574-294-6521	295-8601
Starcraft RV Inc 536 Michigan St PO Box 458 *TF:* 800-945-4787 ■ *Web:* www.starcraftrv.com	Topeka	IN	46571	260-593-2550	593-2876
Teton Homes 3283 N 9 Mile Rd **Fax Area Code:* 800 ■ *Web:* www.tetonhomes.com	Casper	WY	82604	307-235-1525	733-3792*
Thor Industries Inc 419 W Pike St *NYSE:* THO ■ *Web:* www.thorindustries.com	Jackson Center	OH	45334	937-596-6849	596-7929
Tiffin Motor Homes Inc (TMH) 105 2nd St NW *Web:* www.tiffinmotorhomes.com	Red Bay	AL	35882	256-356-8661	356-8219
Truck Accessories Group Inc 2400 Commercial Rd *TF:* 888-231-2686 ■ *Web:* www.pace-edwards.com	Centralia	WA	98531	360-736-9991	736-9992
Viking Recreational Vehicles LLC 580 W Burr Oak St PO Box 549	Centreville	MI	49032	269-467-6321	467-6021
Winnebago Industries Inc 605 W Crystal Lake Rd PO Box 152 *NYSE:* WGO ■ *TF:* 800-643-4892 ■ *Web:* www.winnebagoind.com	Forest City	IA	50436	641-585-3535	585-6966

121 CAMPGROUND OPERATORS

Company	City	State	Zip	Phone	Fax
Kampgrounds of America Inc (KOA) PO Box 30558 **Fax Area Code:* 406 ■ *TF:* 888-562-0000 ■ *Web:* www.koa.com	Billings	MT	59114	888-562-0000	255-7402*
Leisure Systems Inc 50 W Techne Ctr Dr Suite G *TF:* 866-928-9644 ■ *Web:* www.leisuresystemsinc.com	Milford	OH	45150	513-831-2100	576-8670
Thousand Trails Inc 3801 Parkwood Blvd Suite 100. *TF:* 888-509-6791 ■ *Web:* www.thousandtrails.com	Frisco	TX	75034	214-618-7200	618-7324
Western Horizon Resorts (WHR) 103 W Tomichi Ave Suite 201A. *TF:* 800-378-3709 ■ *Web:* www.westernhorizonresorts.com	Gunnison	CO	81230	970-641-5387	642-4591
Holiday Trails Resorts(Western) Inc 53730 Bridal Falls Rd *TF:* 800-663-2265 ■ *Web:* www.holidaytrailsresorts.com	Rosedale	BC	V0X1X0	604-794-7876	794-3756

122 CANDLES

SEE ALSO Gift Shops p. 1905

Company	City	State	Zip	Phone	Fax
Blyth Inc 1 E Weaver St *NYSE:* BTH ■ *Web:* www.blyth.com	Greenwich	CT	06831	203-661-1926	661-1969
Dadant & Sons Inc 51 S 2nd St *TF:* 800-922-1293 ■ *Web:* www.dadant.com	Hamilton	IL	62341	217-847-3324	847-3660
General Wax & Candle Co 6858 Beck Ave PO Box 9398 *TF:* 800-543-0642 ■ *Web:* www.generalwax.com	North Hollywood	CA	91609	818-765-5800	764-3878
Knorr Beeswax Products Inc 1965 Kellogg Ave. *TF:* 800-807-2337 ■ *Web:* www.knorrbeeswax.com	Carlsbad	CA	92008	760-431-2007	431-8977
Lumi-Lite Candle Co Inc 102 Sundale Rd PO Box 97 *TF:* 800-288-2340	Norwich	OH	43767	740-872-3248	872-3312
Mason Candlelight Co 8729 Aviation Blvd **Fax Area Code:* 310 ■ *TF:* 800-556-2766 ■ *Web:* www.masoncandle.com	Inglewood	CA	90301	800-556-2766	348-0135*
Reed Candle Co 1531 W Poplar St PO Box 7261	San Antonio	TX	78207	210-734-4243	734-2342
Root Candles Co 623 W Liberty St *TF:* 800-289-7668 ■ *Web:* www.rootcandles.com	Medina	OH	44256	330-725-6677	725-5624
Swans Candles 8933 Gravelly Lake Dr SW *TF:* 888-848-7926 ■ *Web:* www.swanscandles.com	Lakewood	WA	98499	253-584-4666	584-2874
White Barn Candle Co 7 Limited Pkwy E *TF Cust Svc:* 800-395-1001 ■ *Web:* www.limitedbrands.com	Reynoldsburg	OH	43068	614-856-6000	856-6313
Will & Baumer Inc 100 Buckley St *TF:* 800-733-7337 ■ *Web:* www.willbaumer.com	Liverpool	NY	13288	315-451-1000	451-0120

123 CANDY STORES

Company	City	State	Zip	Phone	Fax
Candy Bouquet International Inc 510 Mclean St *TF:* 877-226-3901 ■ *Web:* www.candybouquet.com	Little Rock	AR	72202	501-375-9990	375-9998
Candy Express 3320 Greencastle Rd	Burtonsville	MD	20866	301-384-5889	384-1788
Gardners Candies Inc 2600 Adams Ave PO Box E *TF:* 800-242-2639 ■ *Web:* www.gardnerscandies.com	Tyrone	PA	16686	814-684-3925	684-3928
Gertrude Hawk Chocolates Inc 9 Keystone Pk *TF:* 800-822-2032 ■ *Web:* www.gertrudehawkchocolates.com	Dunmore	PA	18512	570-342-7556	342-0261
Gorant Candies Inc 8301 Market St *TF:* 800-572-4139	Youngstown	OH	44512	330-726-8821	726-0325
Hebert Candy Mansion 575 Hartford Tpke. *TF:* 866-432-3781 ■ *Web:* www.hebertcandies.com	Shrewsbury	MA	01545	508-845-8051	842-3065

Phone | Fax

JaCiva's Chocolate 4733 SE Hawthorne Ave .... Portland OR 97215 503-234-8115 234-6076
Web: www.jacivas.com

Karmelkorn Shoppes Inc 7505 Metro Blvd .... Minneapolis MN 55439 952-830-0200 830-0270
Web: www.karmelkorn.com

Kilwin's Quality Confections
355 N Division Rd .... Petoskey MI 49770 231-347-3800 347-6951
TF: 800-454-5946 ■ *Web:* www.kilwins.com

Lammes Candies Since 1885 Inc
200 B Parker Dr Suite 500 .... Austin TX 78728 512-310-1885 310-2280
TF Cust Svc: 800-252-1885 ■ *Web:* www.lammes.com

Nirvana Chocolates 66 Central St Suite 7 .... Wellesley MA 02482 781-283-5787 237-1787
TF: 877-463-8543 ■ *Web:* www.nirvanachocolates.com

Provide Commerce Inc 4840 Eastgate mall .... San Diego CA 92121 858-638-4900 909-4201
TF Cust Svc: 800-776-3569 ■ *Web:* www.prvd.com

Rocky Mountain Chocolate Factory Inc (RMCF)
265 Turner Dr .... Durango CO 81303 970-259-0554 259-5895
NASDAQ: RMCF ■ *TF Cust Svc:* 888-525-2462 ■ *Web:* www.rockymountainchocolatefactory.com

See's Candies Inc
210 El Camino Real .... South San Francisco CA 94080 650-761-2490 875-6825
TF Cust Svc: 800-951-7337 ■ *Web:* www.sees.com

Sweets From Heaven USA LP
PO Box 882829 .... Steamboat Springs CO 80486 970-870-2770 870-8618
TF: 877-247-2770 ■ *Web:* www.sweetsfromheaven.com

Van Duyn Chocolate Inc PO Box 10384 .... Portland OR 97296 503-227-1927 227-1510
Web: www.vanduyns.com

124 CANS - METAL

SEE ALSO Containers - Metal (Barrels, Drums, Kegs) p. 1743

Phone | Fax

Allstate Can Corp 1 Wood Hollow Rd .... Parsippany NJ 07054 973-560-9030 560-9217
Web: www.allstatecan.com

Ball Metal Beverage Container Corp
9300 W 108th Cir .... Westminster CO 80021 303-469-5511 460-5256
Web: www.ball.com

Ball Metal Food Container Corp
1200 S Crutcher St .... Springdale AR 72764 479-751-4666 872-4800
Web: www.ball.com

Bertels Can Co 485 Stewart Rd .... Wilkes-Barre PA 18706 570-829-0524 829-6544*
**Fax Area Code:* 800 ■ *TF Cust Svc:* 800-829-0578 ■ *Web:* www.bertelscan.com

BWAY Corp 8607 Roberts Dr Suite 250 .... Atlanta GA 30350 770-645-4800 645-4810
TF: 800-527-2267 ■ *Web:* www.bwaycorp.com

Can Corp of America Inc
326 june Ave PO Box 170 .... Blandon PA 19510 610-926-3044 926-5041
TF: 800-441-0876

Ccl Container Corp 1 Llodio Dr .... Hermitage PA 16148 724-981-4420
Web: www.cclcontainer.com

Central Can Co 3200 S Kilbourn Ave .... Chicago IL 60623 773-254-8700 254-9127

Champion Container Corp
180 Essex Ave PO Box 90 .... Avenel NJ 07001 732-636-6700 855-8663
Web: www.championcontainer.com

Container Supply Co Inc
12571 Western Ave .... Garden Grove CA 92841 714-892-8321 892-3824

Crown Holdings Inc 1 Crown Way .... Philadelphia PA 19154 215-698-5100 698-5201
NYSE: CCK ■ *TF:* 800-523-3644 ■ *Web:* www.crowncork.com

Eagle Mfg Co Inc 2400 Charles St .... Wellsburg WV 26070 304-737-3171 737-3171
Web: www.eagle-mfg.com

Independent Can Co 1300 Brass Mill Rd .... Belcamp MD 21017 410-272-0090 273-7500
Web: www.independentcan.com

JL Clark Mfg Co 923 23rd Ave .... Rockford IL 61104 815-962-8861 962-6356
TF: 877-878-1940 ■ *Web:* www.jlclark.com

JL Clark Mfg Co Lancaster Div
303 N Plum St .... Lancaster PA 17602 717-392-4125 392-5587
Web: www.jlclark.com

Protectoseal Co 225 W Foster Ave .... Bensenville IL 60106 630-595-0800 595-8059
TF: 800-323-2268 ■ *Web:* www.protectoseal.com

Rexam Beverage Can Americas
8770 W Bryn Mawr Ave .... Chicago IL 60631 773-399-3000

Rexam Inc 4201 Congress St Suite 340 .... Charlotte NC 28209 704-551-1500 551-1571
TF: 800-289-2800 ■ *Web:* www.rexam.com

Ring Container Technology 1 Industrial Pk Dr .... Oakland TN 38060 901-465-3607 465-1179*
**Fax:* Hum Res ■ *TF:* 800-280-6333

Silgan Containers Corp
21800 Oxnard St Suite 600 .... Woodland Hills CA 91367 818-348-3700 593-2255
Web: www.silgancontainers.com

Silgan Holdings Inc 4 Landmark Sq Suite 400 .... Stamford CT 06901 203-975-7110 975-7902
NASDAQ: SLGN ■ *Web:* www.silganholdings.com

Simmons Metal Container 103 E Benge Rd .... Fort Gibson OK 74434 918-478-2117 478-4526

125 CANS, TUBES, DRUMS - PAPER (FIBER)

Phone | Fax

Acme Spirally Wound Paper Products Inc
4810 W 139th St PO Box 35320 .... Cleveland OH 44135 216-267-2950 267-0239
TF: 800-274-2797 ■ *Web:* www.acmespiral.com

American Paper Products Co Inc
2113 E Rush St .... Philadelphia PA 19134 215-739-5718 739-3019
Web: www.americanpaperproducts.com

American Tube & Paper Co Inc PO Box 68 .... Totowa NJ 07511 973-256-3600 785-3341

Armbrust Paper Tubes Inc 6255 S Harlem Ave .... Chicago IL 60638 773-586-3232 586-8997
Web: www.tubesrus.com

Callenor Co Inc
N 60 W 15725 Kohler Ln .... Menomonee Falls WI 53051 262-252-3343 252-3873
Web: www.callenor.com

Caraustar Industries Inc
5000 Austell-Powder Sprngs Rd Suite 300 .... Austell GA 30106 770-948-3100
TF: 800-223-1373 ■ *Web:* www.caraustar.com

Phone | Fax

Chicago Mailing Tube Co 400 N Leavitt St .... Chicago IL 60612 312-243-6050 243-6545
Web: www.mailing-tube.com

Custom Paper Tubes Inc
15900 Industrial Pkwy .... Cleveland OH 44135 216-362-2964 362-2980
TF: 800-766-2527 ■ *Web:* www.custompapertubes.com

FiberCorp Inc 670 17th St NW .... Massillon OH 44647 330-837-5151 837-9109

Greif Inc 425 Winter Rd .... Delaware OH 43015 740-549-6000 549-6100
NYSE: GEF ■ *TF:* 800-354-7343 ■ *Web:* www.greif.com

Industrial Paper Tube Inc 1335 E Bay Ave .... Bronx NY 10474 718-893-5000 378-0055
TF: 800-345-0960 ■ *Web:* www.mailingtubes-ipt.com

LCH Paper Tube & Core Co
11930 Larc Industrial Blvd .... Burnsville MN 55337 952-358-3587 224-0087
TF: 800-472-3477 ■ *Web:* www.lchpackaging.com

Marshall Paper Tube Co PO Box 304 .... Randolph MA 02368 781-963-5555 961-7291

Master Package Corp 200 Madson St .... Owen WI 54460 715-229-2156 229-2689
Web: www.masterpackage.com

Michael's Cooperage Co Inc 363 W Pershing Rd .... Chicago IL 60609 773-268-6281 268-8088
TF: 800-262-6281

Midwest Paper Tube & Can Corp
PO Box 510006 .... New Berlin WI 53151 262-782-7300 782-7330
TF Cust Svc: 800-577-1400

New England Paper Tube Co Inc PO Box 186 .... Pawtucket RI 02862 401-725-2610 726-4920

NYSCO Products Inc 2350 Lafayette Ave .... Bronx NY 10473 718-792-9000 792-7732
TF: 800-227-8685 ■ *Web:* www.nysco.com

Ohio Paper Tube Co 3424 Navarre Rd SW .... Canton OH 44706 330-478-5171 478-9511
Web: www.ohiopapertube.com

Ox Paper Tube & Core Inc 331 Maple Ave .... Hanover PA 17331 717-630-0230 630-0820
TF: 800-414-2476 ■ *Web:* www.mailingtube.com

Pacific Paper Tube Inc 1025 98th Ave .... Oakland CA 94603 510-562-8823 562-9002
TF: 888-377-8823 ■ *Web:* www.pacificpapertube.com

Precision Paper Tube Co Inc 1033 S Noel Ave .... Wheeling IL 60090 847-537-4250 537-5777
Web: www.pptube.com

Precision Paper Tube Co Resinite Corp Div
1033 S Noel Ave .... Wheeling IL 60090 847-537-4250 537-5777
Web: www.pptube.com

Real Reel Corp Multi-Wall Corp Div
50 Taylor Dr .... East Providence RI 02916 401-434-1070 438-5203
TF Cust Svc: 800-992-4166 ■ *Web:* www.multiwall.com

Self-Seal Container Corp 401 E 4th St .... Bridgeport PA 19405 610-275-2300 275-4430
TF: 800-334-1428 ■ *Web:* www.selfsealtubes.com

Sonoco 1 N 2nd St .... Hartsville SC 29550 843-383-7000 383-7008*
NYSE: SON ■ **Fax:* PR ■ *TF:* 800-377-2692 ■ *Web:* www.sonoco.com

TEKPAK Inc 1410 Washington St .... Marion AL 36756 334-683-6121 683-9920
TF: 800-876-8841 ■ *Web:* www.tekpakinc.com

Trend-Pak of Canada 71 Railside Rd .... Toronto ON M3A1B2 416-510-3129 510-8371
Web: www.trendpak.com

Yankee Containers 110 Republic Dr .... North Haven CT 06473 203-288-3851 288-9936
Web: www.yankeecontainers.com

Yazoo Mills Inc PO Box 369 .... New Oxford PA 17350 717-624-8993 624-4420
TF Cust Svc: 800-242-5216 ■ *Web:* www.yazoomills.com

Yorktowne Paperboard Corp 1001 Loucksmill Rd .... York PA 17402 717-843-8061 843-3426

126 CAR RENTAL AGENCIES

SEE ALSO Fleet Leasing & Management p. 1849; Truck Rental & Leasing p. 2734

Phone | Fax

A Betterway Rent-a-car Inc
1110 Northchase Pkwy SE .... Marietta GA 30067 770-984-8228 240-3340
TF: 800-527-0700 ■ *Web:* www.budgetatl.com

Ace Rent-A-Car 5806 W Washington St .... Indianapolis IN 46241 317-243-6336 248-5691
TF: 800-242-7368 ■ *Web:* www.acerentacar.com

Advantage Rent-A-Car
6660 1st Pk Ten Blvd Suite 116 .... San Antonio TX 78216 210-344-4712 679-2589
TF Cust Svc: 800-777-5500 ■ *Web:* www.advantage.com

Affordable Car Rental LC 105 Hwy 36 .... Eatontown NJ 07724 732-380-0888 380-0404
TF: 800-367-5159 ■ *Web:* www.sensiblecarrental.com

Alamo Rent A Car Inc
6929 N Lakewood Ave Suite 100 .... Tulsa OK 74117 918-401-6000
TF: 800-327-9633 ■ *Web:* www.alamo.com

Auto Europe 39 Commercial St .... Portland ME 04101 207-842-2000 842-2222
TF: 800-223-5555 ■ *Web:* www.autoeurope.com

Avis Budget Group Inc 6 Sylvan Way .... Parsippany NJ 07054 973-496-4700 413-1924*
NYSE: CAR ■ **Fax Area Code:* 212 ■ *Web:* www.avisbudgetgroup.com

Avis Rent A Car System Inc 6 Sylvan Way .... Parsippany NJ 07054 973-496-3500 496-3785*
**Fax:* Sales ■ *TF:* 800-331-1212 ■ *Web:* www.avis.com

Budget Rent A Car System Inc 6 Sylvan Way .... Parsippany NJ 07054 973-496-3500 496-3895
TF: 800-527-0700 ■ *Web:* www.budget.com

Car Rental Express 2817 138th St .... Surrey BC V4P1T6 604-714-5911 731-5772
TF: 888-557-8188 ■ *Web:* www.carrentalexpress.com

Car Rentals Inc 1570 S Washington Ave .... Piscataway NJ 08854 732-752-6800 981-1953
Web: www.avisnj.com

Dewey Ford Inc 3055 SE Delaware Ave .... Ankeny IA 50021 515-289-4949 289-4956
TF: 888-378-8516 ■ *Web:* www.deweyford.com

Discount Car & Truck Rentals Ltd
720 Arrow Rd .... North York ON M9M2M1 866-742-5968 744-8340*
**Fax Area Code:* 416 ■ *TF:* 866-742-5968 ■ *Web:* www.discountcar.com

Dollar Rent A Car Inc 5330 E 31st St .... Tulsa OK 74135 918-669-3000 669-3007*
**Fax:* Sales ■ *TF:* 800-800-4000 ■ *Web:* www.dollarcar.com

Dollar Thrifty Automotive Group Inc
5330 E 31st St PO Box 35985 .... Tulsa OK 74135 918-669-2119
NYSE: DTG ■ *TF:* 800-800-4000 ■ *Web:* www.dtag.com

Enterprise Rent-A-Car
600 Corporate Pk Dr .... Saint Louis MO 63105 314-512-5000 512-5940
TF: 800-325-8007 ■ *Web:* www.enterprise.com

Europe by Car Inc 62 William St 7th Fl .... New York NY 10005 212-581-3040 581-3040
TF: 800-223-1516 ■ *Web:* www.europebycarblog.com

Hertz Global Holdings Inc 225 Brae Blvd .... Park Ridge NJ 07656 201-307-2000 307-2644
NYSE: HTZ ■ *TF:* 800-654-3131 ■ *Web:* www.hertz.com

			Phone	Fax
Kemwel Inc 39 Commercial St. . . . . Portland	ME	04112	207-842-2285	842-2147
TF: 800-678-0678 ■ Web: www.kemwel.com				
National Car Rental 6929 N Lakewood Ave Suite 100 . . . . Tulsa	OK	74117	918-401-6000	
TF: 800-227-7368 ■ Web: www.nationalcar.com				
Payless Car Rental System Inc 2350-N 34th St N . . . . Saint Petersburg	FL	33713	727-321-6352	323-3529
TF: 800-729-5377 ■ Web: www.paylesscar.com				
Rent-A-Wreck of America LLC 105 Main St. . . . . . . Laurel	MD	20707	240-581-1350	
TF: 800-944-7501 ■ Web: www.rentawreck.com				
Sensible Car Rental 105 Hwy 36 . . . . Eatontown	NJ	07724	800-367-5159	380-0404*
*Fax Area Code: 732 ■ TF: 800-631-2290 ■ Web: www.affiliatedcarrental.com				
Sutton Leasing Inc 3555 14 Mile Rd . . . . Sterling Heights	MI	48310	586-759-5777	759-5781
Web: www.suttonleasing.com				
Thrifty Car Rental 5330 E 31st St. . . . . . . Tulsa	OK	74135	918-665-3930	669-2228
TF: 800-367-2277 ■ Web: www.thrifty.com				
U-Save Auto Rental of America Inc 4780 I-55 N Suite 300 . . . . Jackson	MS	39211	601-713-4333	713-4317
TF: 800-438-2300 ■ Web: www.usave.com				
Vanguard Car Rental USA 6929 N Lakewood Ave Suite 100 . . . . Tulsa	OK	74117	918-401-6000	
TF: 800-837-0032 ■ Web: www.vanguardcar.com				
Yellow Checker Cab Co Inc 1880 S 7th St . . . . San Jose	CA	95112	408-286-3400	293-0301
Web: www.yellowcheckercab.com				

127 CARBON & GRAPHITE PRODUCTS

			Phone	Fax
Advance Carbon Products Inc 2036 National Ave. . . . . Hayward	CA	94545	510-293-5930	293-5939
TF: 800-283-1249 ■ Web: www.advancecarbon.com				
Carbone of America Graphite Materials Div 215 Stackpole St. . . . . Saint Marys	PA	15857	814-781-1234	781-8570
Energy Conversion Systems 1 Morganite Dr . . . . Dunn	NC	28334	910-892-8081	892-9600
Fiber Materials Inc 5 Morin St . . . . Biddeford	ME	04005	207-282-5911	282-7529
Web: www.fibermaterialsinc.com				
GrafTech International Holdings Inc 12900 Snow Rd . . . . Parma	OH	44130	216-676-2000	676-2600
NYSE: GTI ■ Web: www.graftech.com				
Graphite Machining Inc 240 N Main St . . . . Topton	PA	19562	610-682-0080	
Web: www.graphitemachininginc.com				
Graphite Systems Inc 1613 Danciger Dr . . . . Fort Worth	TX	76112	817-457-1851	457-2664
Helwig Carbon Products Inc 8900 W Tower Ave . . . . Milwaukee	WI	53224	414-354-2411	354-2421
TF: 800-365-3113 ■ Web: www.helwigcarbon.com				
Mersen USA BN Corp 400 Myrtle Ave. . . . . Boonton	NJ	07005	973-541-4720	334-6394
TF Cust Svc: 800-526-0877 ■ Web: www.carbonebrush.com				
Micro Mech Inc 33 Tpke Rd . . . . Ipswich	MA	01938	978-356-2966	356-4019
Web: www.micro-mech.com				
National Electrical Carbon Products Inc 251 Forrester Dr . . . . Greenville	SC	29607	800-999-6322	281-0180*
*Fax Area Code: 864 ■ TF: 800-999-6322 ■ Web: www.morganamt.com/nl/Products-and-Materials/Koolborstels.htm				
Oxbow Carbon & Minerals Inc 1601 Forum Pl Suite 1400 . . . . West Palm Beach	FL	33401	561-697-4300	640-8727
Web: www.oxbow.com				
Process Engineering Corp PO Box 279 . . . . Crystal Lake	IL	60039	815-459-1734	459-3676
Web: www.pecfrictionfighters.com				
Pyrotek Inc 9503 E Montgomery Ave. . . . . Spokane	WA	99503	509-926-6212	927-2408
Web: www.pyrotek-inc.com				
Saint Marys Carbon Co 259 Eberl St. . . . . Saint Marys	PA	15857	814-781-7333	834-9201
Web: www.stmaryscarbon.com				
Saturn Industries Inc 157 Union Tpke. . . . . Hudson	NY	12534	518-828-9956	828-9868
TF: 800-775-1651 ■ Web: www.saturnedm.com				
SGL Carbon Corp 307 Jamestown Rd . . . . Morganton	NC	28655	828-437-3221	432-5885*
*Fax: Sales ■ TF: 800-828-6601 ■ Web: www.sglgroup.com				
Superior Graphite Co 10 S Riverside Plaza Suite 1470. . . . . Chicago	IL	60606	312-559-2999	559-9064
TF Orders: 800-325-0337 ■ Web: www.graphitesgc.com				
US Graphite Inc 1620 E Holland Ave. . . . . Saginaw	MI	48601	989-755-0441	755-0445
Web: www.usgraphite.net				
Zoltek Cos Inc 3101 McKelvey Rd. . . . . St. Louis	MO	63044	314-291-5110	291-8536
NASDAQ: ZOLT ■ TF: 800-325-4409 ■ Web: www.zoltek.com				

128 CARBURETORS, PISTONS, PISTON RINGS, VALVES

SEE ALSO Aircraft Engines & Engine Parts p. 1387; Automotive Parts & Supplies - Mfr p. 1497

			Phone	Fax
C Lee Cook Co 916 S 8th St. . . . . Louisville	KY	40203	502-587-6783	515-6992
TF: 877-266-5226 ■ Web: www.cleecook.com				
Compressor Products International 4410 Greenbriar Dr. . . . . Stafford	TX	77477	281-207-4600	207-4611
TF: 800-675-6646 ■ Web: www.c-p-i.com				
Dexter Automatic Products Co 2500 Bishop Cir E . . . . Dexter	MI	48130	734-426-8900	426-2622
Web: www.dapcoind.com				
Grant Piston Rings 1360 Jefferson St. . . . . Anaheim	CA	92807	714-996-0050	524-6607
TF: 800-854-3540 ■ Web: www.grantpistonrings.com				
Grover Corp 2759 S 28th St . . . . Milwaukee	WI	53234	414-384-9472	384-0201
TF: 800-776-3602 ■ Web: www.grovercorp.com				
Hastings Mfg Co 325 N Hanover St . . . . Hastings	MI	49058	269-945-2491	945-4667
TF: 800-776-1088 ■ Web: www.hastingsmfg.com				
Helio Precision Products Inc 601 N Skokie Hwy . . . . Lake Bluff	IL	60044	847-473-1300	473-1306
Web: www.helioprecision.com				
Holley Performance Products Inc 1801 Russellville Rd. . . . . Bowling Green	KY	42101	270-782-2900	781-9940*
*Fax: Cust Svc ■ TF Sales: 800-638-0032 ■ Web: www.holley.com				
Hydreco 1500 County Naple Blvd . . . . Charlotte	NC	28273	704-295-7575	295-7574
Web: www.hydreco.com				
IMPCO Technologies Inc 3030 S Susan St . . . . Santa Ana	CA	92704	714-656-1200	656-1400*
NASDAQ: IMCO ■ *Fax: Sales ■ Web: www.impcotechnologies.com				
LE Jones Co 1200 34th Ave . . . . Menominee	MI	49858	906-863-4411	863-4867
TF: 800-535-6637 ■ Web: www.lejones.com				
MAHLE Engine Components USA Inc 2020 Sanford St . . . . Muskegon	MI	49444	231-722-1300	724-1940
TF: 800-717-5398 ■ Web: www.us.mahle.com				
MAHLE Industries Inc 1 Mahle Dr PO Box 748 . . . . Morristown	TN	37814	423-581-6603	587-5170
Web: www.us.mahle.com				
Martin Wells Industries PO Box 01406 . . . . Los Angeles	CA	90001	323-581-6266	589-2334
TF: 800-421-6000				
Pacific Piston Ring Co Inc 3620 Eastham Dr . . . . Culver City	CA	90232	310-836-3322	836-3327
Safety Seal Piston Ring Co 4000 Airport Rd . . . . Marshall	TX	75672	903-938-9241	938-9317*
*Fax: Sales ■ TF Sales: 800-962-3631 ■ Web: www.sswesco.com				
Total Seal Inc 22642 N 15th Ave. . . . . Phoenix	AZ	85027	623-587-7400	587-7600
TF: 800-874-2753 ■ Web: www.totalseal.com				
United Engine & Machine Co Inc 1040 Corbett St . . . . Carson City	NV	89706	775-882-7790	882-7773
TF: 800-648-7970 ■ Web: www.kb-silvolite.com				
Wiseco Piston Inc 7201 Industrial Pk Blvd . . . . Mentor	OH	44060	440-951-6600	951-6606
TF: 800-321-1364 ■ Web: www.wiseco.com				
Zenith Fuel Systems Inc 14570 Industrial Pk Rd. . . . . Bristol	VA	24202	276-669-5555	645-8696
Web: www.zenithfuelsystems.com				

129 CARD SHOPS

SEE ALSO Gift Shops p. 1905

			Phone	Fax
American Greetings Corp Carlton Cards Div 1 American Rd . . . . Cleveland	OH	44144	216-252-7300	252-6778
TF: 800-321-3040 ■ Web: www.corporate.americangreetings.com				
Elm Tree Cards & Gifts Inc 4300 Prince William Pkwy . . . . Woodbridge	VA	22192	703-680-2548	730-2439
Evenson Card Shops Inc 2440 Pershing Rd Suite 200 PO Box 419218. . . . . Kansas City	MO	64108	816-274-5111	274-4800
Hallmark Cards Inc 2501 McGee St. . . . . Kansas City	MO	64108	816-274-5111	545-2305*
*Fax: Mail Rm ■ TF: 800-425-5627 ■ Web: www.hallmark.com				
Papyrus Franchise Corp 500 Chadbourne Rd. . . . . Fairfield	CA	94533	707-428-8006	428-0641
TF: 800-333-6724 ■ Web: www.papyrusonline.com				
Recycled Paper Greetings Inc 111 N Canal St # 700 . . . . Chicago	IL	60606	773-348-6410	929-7123
TF: 800-777-9494 ■ Web: www.recycledpapergreetings.com				

130 CARDS - GREETING - MFR

			Phone	Fax
Alfred Mainzer Inc 35-27 35th St. . . . . Long Island City	NY	11106	718-392-4200	392-2681
TF: 800-222-2737 ■ Web: www.alfredmainzer.com				
Alice Briggs Illustration 11 Possum Hollow Ln . . . . Natick	MA	01760	508-651-1607	647-0090
Web: www.alicebriggs-illustration.com				
Allen & John Inc 2505 N Shirk Rd . . . . Visalia	CA	93278	800-803-7527	421-5291
TF: 800-803-7527				
Amber Lotus Publishing PO Box 11329 . . . . Portland	OR	97211	503-284-6400	284-6417
TF: 800-326-2375 ■ Web: www.amberlotus.com				
American Artists Group Inc 178 Dearing St. . . . . Athens	GA	30605	706-227-0708	
Web: www.americanartistsgroup.com				
American Greetings Corp 1 American Rd . . . . Cleveland	OH	44144	216-252-7300	252-6778
NYSE: AM ■ TF Sales: 800-321-3040 ■ Web: www.corporate.americangreetings.com				
Ancient Images Greeting Cards 44 N 100 W. . . . . Moab	UT	84532	435-259-4087	259-6635
TF: 800-891-6635 ■ Web: www.ancientimagescards.com				
Anne Taintor Inc PO Box 9 . . . . Youngsville	NM	87064	505-638-5919	
AtticSalt Greetings Inc 1548 Erie St . . . . North Kansas City	MO	64116	816-587-1600	587-1121
Web: www.atticsaltgreetings.com				
Avanti Press Inc 155 W Congress St Suite 200 . . . . Detroit	MI	48226	313-961-0022	875-9690*
*Fax Area Code: 800 ■ TF: 800-228-2684 ■ Web: www.avantipress.com				
B Designs Letterpress 23 Noel St Suite 2 . . . . Amesbury	MA	01913	978-388-1052	388-3759
TF: 800-978-3575 ■ Web: www.bdesignsletterpress.com				
Bayview Press 30 Knox St PO Box 153. . . . . Thomaston	ME	04861	207-354-9919	354-9919
TF: 800-903-2346 ■ Web: www.bayviewpress.com				
Birchcraft Studios Inc 10 Railroad St . . . . Abington	MA	02351	781-878-5152	678-5151*
*Fax Area Code: 800 ■ TF: 800-333-0405 ■ Web: www.birchcraft.com				
Bizou PhotoGreetings 29311 Castle Hill Dr. . . . . Agoura Hills	CA	91301	818-640-7575	889-5881
Blue Mountain Arts Inc PO Box 4549. . . . . Boulder	CO	80306	303-449-0536	417-6496*
*Fax: Cust Svc ■ TF Sales: 800-545-8573 ■ Web: www.bluemountain.com				
Blue Turtle Studio 4884 Broiles Rd . . . . Christiana	TN	37037	615-896-9830	890-0191
Web: www.blueturtlestudio.com				
Bonair Daydreams PO Box 3741 . . . . Farmington	NM	87499	910-617-3887	326-1683*
*Fax Area Code: 505 ■ TF: 888-226-6247 ■ Web: www.bonairdaydreams.com				
Candy Care Inc 774 White Plains Rd. . . . . Edgemont	NY	10019	212-421-1234	421-1191
TF: 888-423-8823				
Carole Joy Creations Inc 1087 Federal Rd Unit 8. . . . . Brookfield	CT	06804	203-740-4490	740-4495
TF Sales: 800-223-6945 ■ Web: www.carolejoy.com				
Charnette Messe Embracing Life 100 Phoenix Dr . . . . Groton	CT	06340	860-449-0798	
Web: www.charnettemesse.com				
Checkerboard Ltd 216 W Boylston St. . . . . West Boylston	MA	01583	508-835-2475	835-4843
Claudiam Publications Inc PO Box 925. . . . . Huntington	NY	11743	631-424-7074	424-4614
Web: www.claudiampublications.com				
Cockeyed Creations 1442-A Walnut St Suite 412. . . . . Berkeley	CA	94709	510-559-1897	525-9509
Web: www.cockeyedcreations.com				

Company	City	State	Zip	Phone	Fax
Colors By Design 7723 Densmore Ave *TF:* 800-832-8436 ■ *Web:* www.cbdcards.com	Van Nuys	CA	91406	800-832-8436	824-2530
Cow Pie Greeting Cards PO Box 655	Springville	UT	84663	801-491-4300	226-6214
Creative Contrasts 303 W Lancaster Ave PMB #316 *Web:* www.creativecontrasts.com	Wayne	PA	19087	610-220-0081	975-0864
Curiosities Greeting Cards 21 Ashwood Ct *TF:* 877-424-4401 ■ *Web:* www.curiosities.com	Lancaster	NY	14086	716-681-2801	685-2141
DaySpring Cards Inc 21154 Hwy 16 E *TF:* 800-944-8000 ■ *Web:* www.dayspring.com	Siloam Springs	AR	72761	479-524-9301	524-8813
Design Design Inc 19 La Grave SE *TF:* 800-334-3348 ■ *Web:* www.designdesign.us	Grand Rapids	MI	49503	616-774-2448	774-4020
Different Drumbeats 400 Murrasy Hollow Rd *Web:* www.differentdrumbeats.com	Shushan	NY	12873	518-854-7446	
Eclectik 1332 W Lake St *Web:* www.eclectik.com	Chicago	IL	60607	773-480-0911	751-2075
Egreetings Network Inc 1 American Rd *TF:* 800-321-3040 ■ *Web:* www.egreetings.com	Cleveland	OH	44144	216-252-7300	252-6778
Eunco 168 Mason Way Suite B-3	Industry	CA	91746	626-435-0177	435-0178
Executive Greetings Inc 120 Greenwoods Industrial Pk *TF Cust Svc:* 800-562-5468 ■ *Web:* www.executive-greetings.com	New Hartford	CT	06057	860-379-9911	379-7124
Fantus Paper Products 5730 N Tripp Ave *TF Sales:* 800-621-8823 ■ *Web:* www.psg-fpp.com	Chicago	IL	60646	773-267-6069	267-6055
Fat Pat Productions LLC 4313 Columbine Dr *TF:* 800-856-0234 ■ *Web:* www.fatpatcards.com	Austin	TX	78727	800-856-0234	
Fotofolio Inc 561 Broadway *TF Sales:* 800-955-3686 ■ *Web:* www.fotofolio.com	New York	NY	10012	212-226-0923	226-0072
Freedom Greeting Card Co Inc 774 American Dr *TF Sales:* 800-359-3301 ■ *Web:* www.freedomgreetings.com	Bensalem	PA	19020	215-604-0300	604-0436
FSG Crest LLC 354 W Armory Dr *TF:* 877-747-1225 ■ *Web:* www.fsgcrest.com	South Holland	IL	60473	708-210-0800	210-0808
Gallant Greetings Corp 4300 United Pkwy *TF:* 800-621-4279 ■ *Web:* www.gallantgreetings.com	Schiller Park	IL	60176	847-671-6500	671-5900
Gina B Designs Inc 12700 Industrial Pk Blvd Suite 40 *TF:* 800-228-4856 ■ *Web:* www.ginabdesigns.com	Plymouth	MN	55441	763-559-7595	559-3899
Goodge Street Press PO Box 9172 *Web:* www.goodge.com	Peoria	IL	61612	309-674-5477	674-1799
Graphique De France 9 State St *TF Sales:* 800-444-1464 ■ *Web:* www.graphiquedefrance.com	Woburn	MA	01801	781-935-3405	935-5145
Great Arrow Graphics 2495 Main St Suite 457 *TF:* 800-835-0490 ■ *Web:* www.greatarrow.com	Buffalo	NY	14214	716-836-0408	836-0702
Hallmark Cards Inc 2501 McGee St **Fax:* Mail Rm ■ *TF:* 800-425-5627 ■ *Web:* www.hallmark.com	Kansas City	MO	64108	816-274-5111	545-2305*
Hallmark International PO Box 419034 *TF:* 800-425-5627 ■ *Web:* www.hallmark.com	Kansas City	MO	64141	816-274-5111	545-2305
Hazy Jean Inc 41 Crewe Ave *TF:* 866-270-5798 ■ *Web:* www.hazyjean.com	Toronto	ON	M4C2J2	416-425-4299	429-5882
Head Cards 1 Morton Sq *Web:* www.headcards.com	Bronx	NY	10014	917-952-3491	
Heart-Felt Greetings II Inc 1367 Fairview Blvd PO Box 1025 *TF:* 800-818-9099 ■ *Web:* www.heartfeltgreetings.com	Fairview	TN	37062	615-799-8562	799-7945
Highland Creations Inc PO Box 3512 *Web:* www.highlandcreations.com	Westport	MA	02790	508-636-4598	636-2414
Hunkydory Paper Products PO Box 90081 **Fax Area Code:* 866 ■ *TF:* 866-617-1259 ■ *Web:* www.hunkydorycards.com	San Antonio	TX	78209	201-731-6646	617-8424*
InterArt Distribution 1145 Sunrise Greetings Ct *TF Sales:* 800-457-4045 ■ *Web:* www.interartdistribution.com	Bloomington	IN	47404	812-336-9900	336-8712
JewishCard 304 Darwin St *Web:* www.jewishcard.com	Santa Cruz	CA	95062	831-469-8883	469-8803
Karen & Co Greeting Cards Inc PO Box 972 *Web:* www.sistathingcards.com	East Stroudsburg	PA	18301	570-424-8528	424-8529
KDi Studios LLC 206 New Rd	Avon	CT	06001	860-913-4123	693-1952
Kenzig Kards Inc 2300 Julia Goldbach Ave	Ronkonkoma	NY	11779	631-737-1584	
Kisses to You Greetings 300 DeWittshire Rd S	DeWitt	NY	13214	315-446-2505	256-9210
Laughing Elephant 3645 Interlake Ave N *TF:* 800-354-0400 ■ *Web:* www.laughingelephant.com	Seattle	WA	98103	206-447-9229	447-9189
Laura & Co Inc PO Box 1238 *TF:* 866-439-1715 ■ *Web:* www.lauraandcompany.com	Yelm	WA	98597	360-894-1418	894-1419
Laurel Ink 911 N 145th St *TF Cust Svc:* 800-850-0081 ■ *Web:* www.laurelink.com	Seattle	WA	98133	206-767-4000	
Leanin' Tree Inc 6055 Longbow Dr *TF:* 800-777-8716 ■ *Web:* www.leanintree.com	Boulder	CO	80301	303-530-1442	530-7283
Legacy Greetings LLC 2030 Byberry Rd *TF:* 866-438-5342 ■ *Web:* www.legacygreetings.com	Philadelphia	PA	19116	215-677-7111	677-7119
Marian Heath Greeting Cards Inc 9 Kendrick Rd *TF Sales:* 800-338-3740 ■ *Web:* www.marianheath.com	Wareham	MA	02571	508-291-0766	291-2976
Masterpiece Studios 2080 Lookout Dr *TF:* 800-447-0219 ■ *Web:* www.masterpiecestudios.com	North Mankato	MN	56003	507-388-8788	344-4601
Max & Lucy 116 W Mcdowell Rd # 100 *TF:* 877-975-5050 ■ *Web:* www.maxandlucy.com	Phoenix	AZ	85003	602-275-5050	275-5700
Meri Meri 525 Harbor Blvd *TF:* 800-733-4770 ■ *Web:* www.merimeri.com	Belmont	CA	94002	650-508-2300	508-2301
Miya & Me 29 Floribel Ave	San Anselmo	CA	94960	415-460-1658	
Morning Center Cards 37 Stratford Dr	Brick	NJ	08724	732-295-3923	295-3922
Museum Facsimiles 117 4th St *TF:* 800-499-0020 ■ *Web:* www.museumfacsimiles.com	Pittsfield	MA	01201	413-499-0020	442-3011
Naos Graphics Inc 103 Edgevale Rd *Web:* www.naosgraphics.com	Baltimore	MD	21210	410-435-0031	435-1849
NCPL Inc 5035 Timberlea Blvd Unit 9 *TF:* 877-627-7444 ■ *Web:* www.northerncards.com	Mississauga	ON	L4W2K9	905-625-4944	625-5995
New England Art Publisher Inc PO Box 328 **Fax Area Code:* 800 ■ *TF:* 800-333-0405 ■ *Web:* www.birchcraft.com	Rockland	MA	02370	781-878-5151	678-5151*
No Name Girl 691 Bridgeway *Web:* www.nonamegirl.com	Sausalito	CA	94965	415-332-7633	332-1263
NobleWorks Inc 500 Paterson Plank Rd *TF:* 800-346-6253 ■ *Web:* www.nobleworkscards.com	Union City	NJ	07087	201-420-0095	420-0679
Northern Cards 5035 Timberlea Blvd Suite 9 *TF:* 877-627-7444 ■ *Web:* www.northerncards.com	Mississauga	ON	L4W2W9	905-625-4944	625-5995
Northern Exposure Greeting Cards 2301 Circadian Way Suite 300 *TF:* 800-237-3524 ■ *Web:* www.northernexposurecards.com	Santa Rosa	CA	95407	707-546-2153	546-0875
Nouvelles Images Inc 22 Eagle Rd *TF:* 800-345-1383 ■ *Web:* www.nouvellesimage.com	Danbury	CT	06810	203-730-1004	730-0516
NRN Designs 5142 Argosy Ave *TF:* 800-421-6958	Huntington Beach	CA	92649	714-898-6363	898-0015
Oatmeal Studios Inc 440 State Garage Rd PO box 138 *TF Cust Svc:* 800-628-6325 ■ *Web:* www.oatmealstudios.com	Rochester	VT	05767	802-767-3171	767-9890
Palm Press Inc 1442A Walnut St PMB 120 *TF:* 800-322-7256 ■ *Web:* www.palmpressinc.com	Berkeley	CA	94709	510-486-0502	486-1158
Paper Magic Group Inc 401 Adams Ave Suite 501 **Fax:* Cust Svc ■ *TF Cust Svc:* 800-258-1044 ■ *Web:* www.papermagic.com	Scranton	PA	18510	570-961-3863	961-2628*
Paper Prince 2001 Kennedy St NE *TF:* 800-717-1574	Minneapolis	MN	55413	612-378-4691	617-4155
Paperdoll Co 4944 Encino Ave *TF:* 866-223-1145	Encino	CA	91316	818-906-8411	907-0225
Paradachs Pictures Inc 17 W 64th St Suite 9C **Fax Area Code:* 845 ■ *TF:* 877-896-7877	New York	NY	10023	877-896-7877	657-2808*
Paramount Cards Inc 400 Pine St **Fax:* Hum Res ■ *TF:* 800-554-5017 ■ *Web:* www.paramountcards.com	Pawtucket	RI	02860	401-726-0800	727-0370*
Patriot Greetings LLC 13736 Santa Rosa Ct *Web:* www.patriotgreetings.com	Manassas	VA	20112	703-725-6642	852-7229
Peaceable Kingdom Press 950 Gilman St Suite 200 *TF:* 877-444-5195 ■ *Web:* www.peaceablekingdom.com	Berkeley	CA	94710	510-558-2051	558-2052
Penny Laine Papers 2211 Century Ctr Blvd Suite 110 *TF:* 800-456-6484	Irving	TX	75062	972-812-3000	812-3004
Perma-Greetings Inc 2470 Schuetz Rd	Maryland Heights	MO	63043	314-567-4606	567-0674
Persimmon Press PO Box 297 *TF:* 800-910-5080 ■ *Web:* www.persimmoncards.com	Belmont	CA	94002	800-910-5080	910-5095
Pixel Ditties LLC 3980 S Bellaire St	Cherry Hills Village	CO	80110	303-757-8097	759-3895
Portal Publications Ltd 201 Alameda Del Prado *TF:* 800-227-1720 ■ *Web:* www.portalpub.com	Novato	CA	94949	415-884-6200	382-3377
PostMark Press Inc 16 Spruce St *TF:* 888-924-3520 ■ *Web:* www.postmarkpress.com	Watertown	MA	02472	617-924-3520	924-1371
Posty Cards 1600 Olive St **Fax Area Code:* 888 ■ *TF:* 800-821-7968 ■ *Web:* www.postycards.com	Kansas City	MO	64127	816-231-2323	577-3800*
Potluck Press 1229 21st Ave E *TF:* 877-818-5500 ■ *Web:* www.potluckpress.com	Seattle	WA	98112	206-323-8310	328-4633
Princeton Mint Inc PO Drawer M *Web:* www.princetonmint.com	Jackson	NJ	08527	732-928-2777	928-2660
Recycled Paper Greetings Inc 111 N Canal St # 700 *TF:* 800-777-9494 ■ *Web:* www.recycledpapergreetings.com	Chicago	IL	60606	773-348-6410	929-7123
Scarlet's Feathers PO Box 638 *Web:* www.zazzle.com/scarletsfeathers	Montclair	NJ	07042	973-509-9427	
Schurman Fine Papers 500 Chadbourne Rd PO Box 6030 *TF Sales:* 800-333-6724 ■ *Web:* www.papyrusonline.com	Fairfield	CA	94533	707-428-0200	428-0641
Sillies Greeting Card Co 14762 Oak Run Ln *TF:* 800-355-9148	Burnsville	MN	55306	952-892-5666	435-8036
Smorganbord Ltd/Pumps Greetings 165 N Canal Suite 519 *Web:* www.pumpsgreetings.com	Chicago	IL	60606	312-382-1557	382-1614
Sole Source Inc 1 Idea Way *TF:* 800-285-1657 ■ *Web:* www.sole-source.com	Caldwell	ID	83605	800-285-1657	455-0642
Spirit Inspired PO Box 7904 *TF:* 877-474-8460 ■ *Web:* www.spiritinspired.com	Atlanta	GA	30357	404-792-3664	792-8168
StellArt 2012 Waltzer Rd *TF:* 866-621-1987 ■ *Web:* www.stellart.com	Santa Rosa	CA	95403	707-569-1378	569-1379
Studio 1970 Inc 1813 Clarence St Suite 8	Dallas	TX	75215	214-207-3465	565-1766
Sunshine Business Class 150 Kingswood Rd PO Box 8465 *TF:* 800-873-7681 ■ *Web:* www.sunshinebusinessclass.com	Mankato	MN	56002	800-873-7681	232-6366
Sunshine Girl Creations Inc 11111 Excelsior Blvd *TF:* 866-899-3632 ■ *Web:* www.sunshinegirlcreations.com	Hopkins	MN	55343	952-931-2464	931-2575
Tagline Greetings 1100 Irvine Blvd Suite 123	Tustin	CA	92780	323-857-5337	857-5338
Touchstone Designs 111 Providence St	Mendon	MA	01756	508-243-3824	473-6489
Up With Paper 6049 Hi-Tek Ct **Fax Area Code:* 800 ■ *TF:* 800-852-7677 ■ *Web:* www.upwithpaper.com	Mason	OH	45040	513-759-7473	293-8471*
US Allegiance Inc 63075 NE 18th St *TF:* 800-327-1402 ■ *Web:* www.ipledge.com	Bend	OR	97701	541-330-6282	330-6268
USA Greetings Inc 268 Bush St Suite 3438 *Web:* www.usagreetings.com	San Francisco	CA	94104	415-269-6931	707-2103
Victorian Trading Co 15600 W 99th St **Fax Area Code:* 800 ■ *TF Cust Svc:* 800-700-2035 ■ *Web:* www.victoriantradingco.com	Lenexa	KS	66219	913-438-3995	724-7697*
Viktorina Cards 89 Stonehurst Ave Suite 311 *Web:* www.amazzzingcards.com	Ottawa	ON	K1Y4R6	613-627-4149	
Vivyland 350 Detroit St Suite 206 *TF:* 888-621-5266 ■ *Web:* www.vivyland.com	Denver	CO	80206	303-893-8038	329-0877
William Arthur Inc 7 Alewive Pk Rd *TF:* 800-985-6581 ■ *Web:* www.williamarthur.com	West Kennebunk	ME	04094	207-985-6581	985-0407
Willow Creek Press Inc 9931 Hwy 70 W PO Box 147 *TF Cust Svc:* 800-850-9453 ■ *Web:* www.willowcreekpress.com	Minocqua	WI	54548	715-358-7010	358-2807
World Paper Inc 76 Ethel Ave *TF:* 800-385-5911	Hawthorne	NJ	07506	973-238-1750	238-1740
Yahoo! Greetings 701 1st Ave *Web:* www.yahoo.americangreetings.com	Sunnyvale	CA	94089	408-349-3300	349-3301
Your True Greetings 2215 Farmersville Rd *TF:* 800-241-2704	Bethlehem	PA	18020	610-694-8028	694-8708

	City	State	Zip	Phone	Fax
ZPR International Inc 24000 Mercantile Rd Unit 8	Beachwood	OH	44122	216-464-2667	464-2668

131 CARPETS & RUGS

SEE ALSO Flooring - Resilient p. 1849; Tile - Ceramic (Wall & Floor) p. 2714

The Companies Listed Here Include Carpet Finishers And Makers Of Mats And Padding.

	City	State	Zip	Phone	Fax
Apache Mills Inc 18 Passaic Ave Unit 1 — *TF:* 800-456-7791	Fairfield	NJ	07004	973-227-9080	808-8330
Artisans Inc 716 River St — *TF:* 800-311-8756 ■ *Web:* www.artisanscarpet.com	Calhoun	GA	30701	706-629-9265	629-4247
Atlas Carpet Mills Inc 2200 Saybrook Ave — *TF:* 800-272-8527 ■ *Web:* www.atlascarpetmills.com	City of Commerce	CA	90040	323-724-9000	724-4526
Bacova Guild Ltd 1000 Commerce Ctr Dr — *Web:* www.bacova.com	Covington	VA	24457	540-863-2600	863-2645
Barrett Carpet Mills Inc 2216 Abutment Rd — *TF:* 800-241-4064 ■ *Web:* www.barrettcarpet.com	Dalton	GA	30720	706-277-2114	277-3250
Beaulieu of America Inc 1502 Coronet Dr PO Box 1248 — *TF:* 800-227-7211 ■ *Web:* www.blissflooring.com	Dalton	GA	30722	800-227-7211	
Bentley Prince Street 14641 E Don Julian Rd — **Fax Area Code:* 800 ■ *TF:* 800-423-4709 ■ *Web:* www.bentleyprincestreet.com	City of Industry	CA	91746	626-333-4585	741-7420*
Blue Ridge Carpet Mills 1546 Progress Rd — *TF:* 800-241-5945 ■ *Web:* www.blueridgecarpet.com	Ellijay	GA	30540	706-276-2001	276-2005
Camelot Carpet Mills Inc 17111 Red Hill Ave — *TF:* 800-854-3258 ■ *Web:* www.camelotcarpetmills.com	Irvine	CA	92614	949-477-2299	553-8238
Capel Inc 831 N Main St — *TF:* 800-334-3711 ■ *Web:* www.capelrugs.com	Troy	NC	27371	910-572-7000	572-7040
Carousel Carpet Mills Inc 1 Carousel Ln — *TF:* 866-227-6873	Ukiah	CA	95482	707-485-0333	485-5911
Carpet Cushions & Supplies Inc 1520 Pratt Blvd — *TF:* 800-626-5572 ■ *Web:* www.carpetcushions.com	Elk Grove Village	IL	60007	847-364-6760	364-6785
Collins & Aikman Corp Floorcoverings Div 311 Smith Industrial Blvd PO Box 1447 — **Fax:* Mktg ■ *TF:* 800-248-2878 ■ *Web:* www.tandus.com	Dalton	GA	30722	706-259-9711	259-9711*
Couristan Inc 2 Executive Dr — *TF:* 800-223-6186 ■ *Web:* www.couristan.com	Fort Lee	NJ	07024	201-585-8500	585-8552
Delaware Valley Corp 500 Broadway — *Web:* www.dvc500.com	Lawrence	MA	01842	978-688-6995	688-5825
Dixie Group Inc 104 Nowlin Ln Suite 101 PO Box 25107 — *NASDAQ: DXYN* ■ *TF:* 866-606-7475 ■ *Web:* www.thedixiegroup.com	Chattanooga	TN	37422	423-510-7000	510-7015
Dorsett Industries Inc 1304 May St PO Box 805 — *TF:* 800-241-4035 ■ *Web:* www.dorsettind.com	Dalton	GA	30721	706-278-1961	217-1775
Durkan Patterned Carpet Inc 405 Virgil Dr — *TF:* 800-241-4580 ■ *Web:* www.durkan.com	Dalton	GA	30721	706-278-7037	428-8270
F Schumacher & Co 79 Madison Ave — *TF:* 800-523-1200 ■ *Web:* www.fschumacher.com	New York	NY	10016	212-213-7900	213-7848
Garland Sales Inc PO Box 1870 — *TF:* 800-524-0361 ■ *Web:* www.garlandrug.com	Dalton	GA	30722	706-278-7880	275-0284
Gulistan Carpet Inc 3140 NC Hwy 5 — *TF:* 800-869-2727 ■ *Web:* www.gulistan.com	Aberdeen	NC	28315	910-944-2371	944-6359
Interface Inc 2859 Paces Ferry Rd Suite 2000 — *NASDAQ: IFSIA* ■ *Web:* www.interfaceglobal.com	Atlanta	GA	30339	770-437-6800	803-6950
J & J Industries Inc 818 J & J Dr PO Box 1287 — *TF:* 800-241-4585 ■ *Web:* www.jjindustries.com	Dalton	GA	30722	706-278-4454	275-4433
Langhorne Carpet Co 201 W Lincoln Hwy PO Box 7175 — *Web:* www.langhornecarpets.com	Penndel	PA	19047	215-757-5155	757-2212
Lexmark Carpet Mills Inc 543 Callahan Rd SE — *TF:* 800-871-3211 ■ *Web:* www.lexmarkcarpet.com	Dalton	GA	30721	706-277-3000	277-6236
Maples Industries Inc 2210 Moody Ridge Rd — *TF Hum Res:* 800-537-3304	Scottsboro	AL	35768	256-259-1327	259-2072
Marglen Industries Inc 1748 Ward Mountain Rd NE	Rome	GA	30161	706-295-5621	295-0706
Masland Carpets Inc 716 Bill Myles Dr — *TF:* 800-633-0468 ■ *Web:* www.maslandcarpets.com	Saraland	AL	36571	251-675-9080	675-5808
Milliken & Co 920 Milliken Rd — **Fax:* Hum Res ■ *Web:* www.milliken.com	Spartanburg	SC	29303	864-503-2020	503-2100*
Milliken & Co KEX Div 201 Lukken Industrial Dr W MS 801 — **Fax Area Code:* 706 ■ **Fax:* Cust Svc ■ *TF:* 800-342-5539 ■ *Web:* www.milliken.dk/Americas/Pages/NewHome.aspx	LaGrange	GA	30240	800-342-5539	880-5358*
Mohawk Carpet Corp 160 S Industrial Blvd — *TF:* 800-241-4494 ■ *Web:* www.mohawkcarpet.com	Calhoun	GA	30701	706-629-7721	
Mohawk Commercial Business 443 Nathaniel Dr — **Fax:* Cust Svc ■ *TF:* 800-554-6637 ■ *Web:* www.bigelowcommercial.com	East Dublin	GA	31027	478-272-7711	275-9539*
Mohawk Home 3032 Sugar Valley Rd NW — *TF:* 800-843-4473 ■ *Web:* www.mohawkhome.com	Sugar Valley	GA	30746	706-629-7916	625-3544
Mohawk Industries Inc 160 S Industrial Blvd — *NYSE: MHK* ■ **Fax:* Hum Res ■ *TF:* 800-241-4494 ■ *Web:* www.mohawkind.com	Calhoun	GA	30703	706-629-7721	625-4576*
Mohawk Industries Inc Bigelow Commercial Div 160 S Industrial Blvd PO Box 12069 — *TF Cust Svc:* 800-241-4494 ■ *Web:* www.bigelowcommercial.com	Calhoun	GA	30701	706-629-7721	
Mohawk Industries Inc Karastan Div 335 Summit Rd — **Fax Area Code:* 800 ■ **Fax:* Cust Svc ■ *TF Cust Svc:* 800-845-8877 ■ *Web:* www.karastan.com	Eden	NC	27288	336-627-7200	533-3263*
Mohawk Industries Inc Lees Carpets Div 706 Green Valley Rd Suite 300 — **Fax Area Code:* 866 ■ *TF:* 800-523-5647 ■ *Web:* www.leescarpets.com	Greensboro	NC	27408	336-378-9162	250-3590*
Natco Products Corp 155 Brookside Ave	West Warwick	RI	02893	401-828-0300	823-7670
Netchannel Inc 8310 Rio Grande Blvd NW — *TF:* 888-843-8282 ■ *Web:* www.netchannel.com	Albuquerque	NM	87106	505-843-8282	890-6012
Oriental Weavers Group Sphinx Div 3252 Lower Dug Gap Rd SW — *TF:* 800-832-8020 ■ *Web:* www.owsphinx.com	Dalton	GA	30720	706-277-9666	277-9665
Rieter Automotive North America - Carpet 480 W 5th St	Bloomsburg	PA	17815	570-784-4100	784-4106
Royalty Carpet Mills Inc 17111 Red Hill Ave — *TF:* 800-854-8331 ■ *Web:* www.royaltycarpetmills.com	Irvine	CA	92614	949-474-4000	553-8238
RW Beattie Carpet Industries Inc 333 S Dixie Hwy Suite 41 PO Box 4 — *Web:* www.beattiecarpet.com	Dalton	GA	30720	706-694-8416	694-8416
S & S Mills Inc 3007 Parquet Dr PO Box 1568 — *TF:* 800-392-6890 ■ *Web:* www.ssmills.com	Dalton	GA	30722	706-277-3677	277-3922
Scottdel Inc 400 Church St — *Web:* www.scottdel.com	Swanton	OH	43558	419-825-2341	825-1523
Shaw Industries Inc 616 E Walnut Ave — **Fax:* Mail Rm ■ *TF:* 800-720-7429 ■ *Web:* www.shawfloors.com	Dalton	GA	30721	706-278-3812	275-3040*
Stainmaster 175 Town Pk Dr — **Fax Area Code:* 770 ■ *TF:* 800-438-7668 ■ *Web:* www.stainmaster.com	Kennesaw	GA	30144	877-446-8478	792-4215*
Subaru of Indiana Automotive Inc 5500 State Rd 38 E — *Web:* www.subaru-sia.com	Lafayette	IN	47905	765-449-1111	449-6952
Syntec Industries LLC 438 Lavender Dr PO Box 1653 — *Web:* www.syntecind.com	Rome	GA	30162	706-235-1158	235-1768
Unique Carpets Ltd 7360 Jurupa Ave — *TF:* 800-547-8266 ■ *Web:* www.uniquecarpetsltd.com	Riverside	CA	92504	951-352-8125	352-8140
World Carpets Inc 160 S Industrial Blvd — *TF:* 800-241-4494	Calhoun	GA	30701	706-278-8000	

132 CASINO COMPANIES

SEE ALSO Games & Gaming p. 1901

	City	State	Zip	Phone	Fax
Ameristar Casinos Inc 3773 Howard Hughes Pkwy Suite 490-S — *NASDAQ: ASCA* ■ *TF:* 866-921-9229 ■ *Web:* www.ameristar.com	Las Vegas	NV	89169	702-567-7000	369-8860
Archon Corp 4336 Losee Rd Suite 5	North Las Vegas	NV	89030	702-732-9120	732-9465
Barden Cos Inc 163 Madison Ave Suite 2000	Detroit	MI	48226	313-496-2900	496-8400
Boomtown Inc PO Box 399 — **Fax:* Hum Res ■ *TF:* 877-526-6686 ■ *Web:* www.boomtownreno.com	Verdi	NV	89439	775-345-6000	345-8695*
Boyd Gaming Corp 3883 Howard Hughes Pkwy 9th Fl — *NYSE: BYD* ■ *TF:* 800-695-2455 ■ *Web:* www.boydgaming.com	Las Vegas	NV	89109	702-792-7200	792-7354
Century Casinos Inc 2860 S Cir Dr Suite 350 — *NASDAQ: CNTY* ■ *TF:* 888-966-2257 ■ *Web:* www.cnty.com	Colorado Springs	CO	80906	719-527-8300	527-8301
Coast Casinos Inc 4500 W Tropicana Ave — *TF:* 888-365-7111 ■ *Web:* www.coastcasinos.com	Las Vegas	NV	89103	702-365-7111	365-7102
Delaware North Cos Gaming & Entertainment 40 Fountain Plaza — *TF:* 800-828-7240 ■ *Web:* www.delawarenorth.com	Buffalo	NY	14202	716-858-5000	858-5926
Empire Resorts Inc 204 Rt 17B — *NASDAQ: NYNY* ■ *Web:* www.empireresorts.com	Monticello	NY	12701	845-794-4100	791-1402
Fond du Lac Band of Lake Superior Chippewa 1720 Big Lake Rd — *TF:* 800-365-1613	Cloquet	MN	55720	218-879-4593	879-4146
Full House Resorts Inc 4670 S Fort Apache Rd Suite 190 — *AMEX: FLL* ■ *Web:* www.fullhouseresorts.com	Las Vegas	NV	89147	702-221-7800	221-8101
Granite Gaming Group 115 N 1st St	Las Vegas	NV	89101	702-385-4250	385-4935
Great Canadian Gaming Corp 13775 Commerce Pkwy Suite 350 — *TSE: GC* ■ *Web:* www.greatcanadiancasinos.com	Richmond	BC	V6V2V4	604-303-1000	279-8605
Harrah's Entertainment Inc 1 Harrah's Ct — *TF:* 800-442-6443 ■ *Web:* www.totalrewards.com/brands/harrahs/hotel-casinos/harrahs-brand.shtml	Las Vegas	NV	89119	702-407-6000	407-6022
HTMI GAMING CORP 71 S Wacker Dr — *Web:* www.htmigaming.com	Chicago	IL	60606	312-750-1234	780-6223
Kerzner International Ltd 1000 S Pine Island Rd Suite 800 — *TF:* 800-321-3000 ■ *Web:* www.kerzner.com	Plantation	FL	10019	954-809-2000	809-2337
Lakes Entertainment Inc 130 Cheshire Ln Suite 101 — *TF:* 800-946-9464 ■ *Web:* www.lakesentertainment.com	Minnetonka	MN	55305	952-449-9092	449-9353
Majestic Investor Holdings LLC 1 Buffington Harbor Dr — *TF:* 888-225-8259 ■ *Web:* www.majesticstar.com	Gary	IN	46406	219-977-7777	977-7811
Mille Lacs Band of Ojibwe 43408 Oodena Dr — *TF:* 800-709-6445 ■ *Web:* www.millelacsband.com	Onamia	MN	56359	320-532-4181	532-7505
Nevada Gold 50 Briar Hollow Ln W Suite 500 — *AMEX: UWN* ■ *Web:* www.nevadagold.com	Houston	TX	77027	713-621-2245	621-6919
Palace Casino 158 Howard Ave — **Fax:* Mktg ■ *TF:* 800-725-2239 ■ *Web:* www.palacecasinoresort.com	Biloxi	MS	39530	228-432-8888	386-2314*
Pinnacle Entertainment Inc 8918 Spanish Ridge Ave — *NYSE: PNK* ■ *TF:* 877-764-8750 ■ *Web:* www.pnkinc.com	Las Vegas	NV	89169	702-784-7777	784-7778
Primm Valley Resorts 31900 S Las Vegas Blvd — *TF:* 800-386-7867 ■ *Web:* www.primmvalleyresorts.com	Primm	NV	89019	702-386-7867	679-5633
Red Lake Gaming Enterprises Inc PO Box 543 — *TF:* 800-568-6649 ■ *Web:* www.sevenclanscasino.com	Red Lake	MN	56671	218-679-2111	679-2191
Station Casinos Inc 1505 S Pavilion Ctr Dr — *TF Resv:* 800-634-3101 ■ *Web:* www.stationcasinos.com	Las Vegas	NV	89135	702-495-3000	
Trump Hotels & Casino Resorts Inc 1000 Boardwalk — *Web:* www.trump.com	Atlantic City	NJ	08401	609-449-6515	449-6586

133 CASINOS

SEE ALSO Games & Gaming p. 1901

Listings For Casinos Are Alphabetized By States.

	City	State	Zip	Phone	Fax
Baccarat Casino 10128 104th Ave *TF:* 877-616-5695 ■ *Web:* www.gatewaycasinos.com	Edmonton	AB	T5J4Y8	780-413-3178	413-3177
Deerfoot Inn & Casino 1000 11500 35th St SE *TF:* 877-236-5225 ■ *Web:* www.deerfootinn.com	Calgary	AB	T2Z3W4	403-236-7529	252-4767
Palace Casino 2710 8882-170th St W Edmonton Mall *Web:* www.palacecasino.com	Edmonton	AB	T5T4J2	780-444-2112	444-1155
Stampede Casino 421 - 12 Ave SE *TF:* 888-610-8946 ■ *Web:* www.stampedecasino.com	Calgary	AB	T2G1A5	403-514-0900	532-8171
Casino Arizona at Salt River 524 N 92nd St *TF:* 877-724-4687 ■ *Web:* www.casinoaz.com	Scottsdale	AZ	85256	480-850-7777	850-7741
Fort McDowell Casino 10424 N Fort McDowell Rd **Fax:* Mktg ■ *TF:* 800-843-3678 ■ *Web:* www.fortmcdowellcasino.com	Scottsdale	AZ	85264	480-837-1424	837-4756*
River Rock Casino Resort 8811 River Rd *TF:* 866-748-3718 ■ *Web:* www.riverrock.com	Richmond	BC	V6X3P8	604-247-8900	247-2641
Agua Caliente Casino Resort Spa 32-250 Bob Hope Dr *TF:* 888-999-1995 ■ *Web:* www.hotwatercasino.com	Rancho Mirage	CA	92270	760-321-2000	
Augustine Casino 84-001 Ave 54 *TF:* 888-752-9294 ■ *Web:* www.augustinecasino.com	Coachella	CA	92236	760-391-9500	398-4447
Barona Resort & Casino 1932 Wildcat Canyon Rd *TF:* 888-722-7662 ■ *Web:* www.barona.com	Lakeside	CA	92040	619-443-2300	443-1794
Bicycle Casino The 7301 Eastern Ave *TF:* 800-292-0015 ■ *Web:* www.thebike.com	Bell Gardens	CA	90201	562-806-4646	806-3576
Chumash Casino 3400 E Hwy 246 *TF:* 800-728-9997 ■ *Web:* www.chumashcasino.com	Santa Ynez	CA	93460	805-686-0855	
Commerce Casino 6131 Telegraph Rd **Fax:* Cust Svc ■ *Web:* www.commercecasino.com	Commerce	CA	90040	323-721-2100	838-3472*
Eagle Mountain Casino 681 S Tule Reservation Rd *TF:* 800-903-3353 ■ *Web:* www.eaglemtncasino.com	Porterville	CA	93257	559-788-6220	788-6223
Fantasy Springs Resort Casino 84-245 Indio Springs Pkwy *TF Cust Svc:* 800-827-2946 ■ *Web:* www.fantasyspringsresort.com	Indio	CA	92203	760-342-5000	
Hawaiian Gardens Casino 11871 Carson St *Web:* www.thegardenscasino.com	Hawaiian Gardens	CA	90716	562-860-5887	860-6762
Pala Casino Resort & Spa 35008 Pala-Temecula Rd *TF:* 877-946-7252 ■ *Web:* www.palacasino.com	Pala	CA	92059	760-510-5100	510-5191
Pechanga Resort & Casino 45000 Pechanga Pkwy *TF:* 877-711-2946 ■ *Web:* www.pechanga.com	Temecula	CA	92592	951-693-1819	695-7410
San Manuel Indian Bingo & Casino 777 San Manuel Blvd *TF:* 800-359-2464 ■ *Web:* www.sanmanuel.com	Highland	CA	92346	909-864-5050	864-3557
Spa Resort Casino 401 E Amado Rd *TF:* 888-999-1995 ■ *Web:* www.sparesortcasino.com	Palm Springs	CA	92262	888-999-1995	
Spotlight 29 Casino 46-200 Harrison Pl *TF:* 866-377-6829 ■ *Web:* www.spotlight29.com	Coachella	CA	92236	760-775-5566	775-7677
Sycuan Casino & Resort 5469 Casino Way *TF:* 800-279-2826 ■ *Web:* www.sycuancasino.com	El Cajon	CA	92019	619-445-6002	445-1961
Sycuan Resort & Casino 3007 Dehesa Rd *TF:* 800-457-5568 ■ *Web:* www.sycuan.com/sycuan_resort	El Cajon	CA	92019	619-442-3425	442-9574
Viejas Casino 5000 Willows Rd *TF:* 800-847-6537 ■ *Web:* www.viejas.com	Alpine	CA	91901	619-445-5400	659-1954
Black Hawk Station Casino 141 Gregory St PO Box 477 *Web:* www.wildcargcasino.com	Black Hawk	CO	80422	303-582-5582	582-5590
Bronco Billy's Casino 233 E Bennett Ave PO Box 590 *TF:* 877-989-2142 ■ *Web:* www.broncobillyscasino.com	Cripple Creek	CO	80813	719-689-2142	689-2869
Bullwhackers Casino 101 Gregory St *TF:* 800-426-2855 ■ *Web:* www.bullwhackers.com	Black Hawk	CO	80422	303-271-2506	271-2501
Canyon Casino 131 Main St PO Box 30 *Web:* www.canyoncasino.com	Black Hawk	CO	80422	303-777-1111	582-0311
Doc Holliday Casino 131 Main St PO Box 639	Central City	CO	80427	303-582-1400	582-3800
Dostal Alley Casino 1 Dostal Alley *Web:* www.centralcitycolorado.com	Central City	CO	80427	303-582-1610	582-0143
Double Eagle Hotel & Casino 442 E Bennett Ave *TF:* 800-711-7234 ■ *Web:* www.doubleeaglehotelandcasino.com	Cripple Creek	CO	80813	719-689-5000	689-5096
Famous Bonanza Casino 107 Main St *Web:* www.famousbonanza.com	Central City	CO	80427	303-582-5914	582-0447
Fitzgeralds Casino 101 Main St *TF:* 800-538-5825 ■ *Web:* www.fitzgeraldsbh.com	Black Hawk	CO	80422	303-582-6100	582-6170
Fortune Valley Hotel & Casino 321 Gregory St *TF Resv:* 800-924-6646 ■ *Web:* www.fortunevalleycasino.com	Central City	CO	80427	303-582-0800	327-2224
Gilpin Hotel Casino 111 Main St PO Box 554	Black Hawk	CO	80422	303-582-1133	582-1154
Golden Gates Casino 300 Main St *Web:* thegoldengatescasino.com	Black Hawk	CO	80422	303-582-5600	582-5700
Golden Mardi Gras 300 Main St *Web:* goldenmardigras.com	Black Hawk	CO	80422	303-582-5600	582-5700
Grande Plateau Casino 131 Main St *Web:* www.blackhawkcolorado.com	Black Hawk	CO	80422	303-777-1111	582-0311
Isle of Capri Casino 401 Main St *TF resv:* 800-843-4753 ■ *Web:* www.isleofcapricasinos.com	Black Hawk	CO	80422	303-998-7777	582-9601
Lodge Casino 240 Main St PO Box 50 *Web:* www.thelodgecasino.com	Black Hawk	CO	80422	303-582-1771	582-6464
Midnight Rose Hotel & Casino 256 E Bennett Ave *TF:* 800-635-5825	Cripple Creek	CO	80813	719-689-2446	689-3413
Red Dolly Casino 530 Gregory St PO Box 28	Black Hawk	CO	80422	303-582-1100	582-1435
Riviera Casino 444 Main St PO Box 9 **Fax Area Code:* 720 ■ *Web:* www.rivierablackhawk.com	Black Hawk	CO	80422	303-582-1000	406-3812*
Sky Ute Casino 14826 Hwy 172 N *TF:* 888-842-4180 ■ *Web:* www.skyutecasino.com	Ignacio	CO	81131	970-563-3000	563-9546
Ute Mountain Casino 3 Weeminuche Dr *TF:* 800-258-8007 ■ *Web:* www.utemountaincasino.com	Towaoc	CO	81334	970-565-8800	565-6553
Wild Card Saloon & Casino 120 Main St *Web:* www.thewildcardsaloon.com	Black Hawk	CO	80422	303-582-3412	582-3508
Wild Horse Casino 353 Myers Ave	Cripple Creek	CO	80813	719-687-7777	689-0305
Foxwoods Resort Casino 39 Norwich Westerly Rd *TF:* 800-752-9244 ■ *Web:* www.foxwoods.com	Ledyard	CT	06339	860-312-3000	396-3639
Mohegan Sun Resort & Casino 1 Mohegan Sun Blvd *TF:* 888-226-7711 ■ *Web:* www.mohegansun.com	Uncasville	CT	06382	860-862-8000	862-7824
Palm Beach Casino Line 1 E 11th St Suite 500 *TF:* 800-841-7447	Riviera Beach	FL	33404	561-845-7447	845-2188
Seminole Casino Hollywood 4150 N State Rd 7 *TF:* 866-222-7466 ■ *Web:* www.seminolehollywoodcasino.com	Hollywood	FL	33021	954-961-3220	961-3401
Seminole Casino Immokalee 506 S 1st St **Fax Area Code:* 239 ■ *TF:* 800-218-0007 ■ *Web:* www.seminoleimmokaleecasino.com	Immokalee	FL	34142	800-218-0007	658-1515*
Seminole Hard Rock Hotel & Casino Tampa (SHRH & C) 5223 N Orient Rd *TF:* 800-282-7016 ■ *Web:* www.seminolehardrocktampa.com	Tampa	FL	33610	813-627-7625	627-7655
Argosy's Alton Belle Casino 1 Piasa St *TF:* 800-711-4263 ■ *Web:* www.argosyalton.com	Alton	IL	62002	800-711-4263	
Casino Queen 200 S Front St *TF:* 800-777-0777 ■ *Web:* www.casinoqueen.com	East Saint Louis	IL	62201	618-874-5000	874-5008
Grand Victoria Casino Elgin 250 S Grove Ave *TF:* 888-508-1900 ■ *Web:* www.grandvictoria-elgin.com	Elgin	IL	60120	847-468-7000	468-7251
Harrah's Joliet 151 N Joliet St *TF:* 800-427-7247 ■ *Web:* www.harrahsjoliet.com	Joliet	IL	60432	815-740-7800	740-2223
Hollywood Casino Joliet 777 Hollywood Blvd *TF:* 888-436-7737 ■ *Web:* www.hollywoodcasinojoliet.com	Joliet	IL	60436	815-744-9400	744-9455
Argosy Casino Cincinnati 777 Argosy Pkwy *TF Resv:* 888-274-6797	Lawrenceburg	IN	47025	812-539-8000	539-8441
Belterra Casino Resort 777 Belterra Dr *TF:* 888-235-8377 ■ *Web:* www.belterracasino.com	Florence	IN	47020	812-427-7777	427-7812
Blue Chip Casino Inc 777 Blue Chip Dr *TF:* 888-879-7711 ■ *Web:* www.bluechipcasino.com	Michigan City	IN	46360	219-879-7711	877-2112
Casino Aztar 421 NW Riverside Dr *TF:* 800-342-5386 ■ *Web:* www.casinoaztar.com	Evansville	IN	47708	812-433-4000	433-4384
Grand Victoria Casino & Resort by Hyatt 600 Grand Victoria Dr **Fax Area Code:* 812 ■ *TF:* 800-472-6311 ■ *Web:* www.grandvictoria.com	Rising Sun	IN	47040	800-472-6311	438-5151*
Horseshoe Casino 777 Casino Ctr Dr *TF:* 866-711-7463 ■ *Web:* www.totalrewards.com	Hammond	IN	46320	219-473-7000	473-6115
Majestic Star Casino & Hotel 1 Buffington Harbor Dr *TF:* 888-218-7867 ■ *Web:* www.majesticstar.com	Gary	IN	46406	219-977-7777	977-7211
Ameristar Casino Hotel Council Bluffs 2200 River Rd **Fax:* Mktg ■ *TF:* 866-667-3386 ■ *Web:* www.ameristarcasinos.com	Council Bluffs	IA	51501	712-328-8888	329-6984*
Harrah's Council Bluffs 2701 23rd Ave *TF:* 888-598-8451 ■ *Web:* www.harrahscouncilbluffs.com	Council Bluffs	IA	51501	712-329-6000	329-6491
Horseshoe Council Bluffs 2701 23rd Ave *Web:* www.totalrewards.com	Council Bluffs	IA	51501	712-323-2500	
Meskwaki Bingo Hotel Casino 1504 305th St *TF:* 800-728-4263 ■ *Web:* www.meskwaki.com	Tama	IA	52339	641-484-2108	484-1618
Rhythm City Casino 101 W River Dr *TF:* 800-724-5825 ■ *Web:* www.davenport.isleofcapricasinos.com	Davenport	IA	52801	563-322-2628	322-2583
Prairie Band Casino & Resort 12305 150th Rd *TF:* 888-727-4946 ■ *Web:* www.pbpgaming.com	Mayetta	KS	66509	785-966-7777	966-7799
Belle of Baton Rouge Casino 103 France St *TF:* 800-676-4847 ■ *Web:* www.belleofbatonrouge.com	Baton Rouge	LA	70802	225-378-6000	344-8056
Boomtown Casino New Orleans 4132 Peters Rd *TF:* 800-366-7711 ■ *Web:* www.boomtownneworleans.com	Harvey	LA	70058	504-366-7711	364-8796
Boomtown Hotel Casino 300 Riverside Dr *TF:* 877-862-4428 ■ *Web:* www.boomtownbossier.com	Bossier City	LA	71111	318-746-0711	226-9434
Coushatta Casino Resort 777 Coushatta Dr PO Box 1510 *TF:* 800-584-7263 ■ *Web:* www.gccoushatta.com	Kinder	LA	70648	337-738-7300	738-7386
DiamondJacks Casino Resort 711 Diamond Jacks Blvd *TF:* 866-552-9629 ■ *Web:* www.diamondjacks.com/bossiercity.aspx	Bossier City	LA	71111	318-678-7777	424-1470
Eldorado Resort Casino Shreveport 451 Clyde Fant Pkwy *TF:* 877-602-0711 ■ *Web:* www.eldoradoshreveport.com	Shreveport	LA	71101	318-220-0711	220-0160
Hollywood Casino Baton Rouge 1717 River Rd N *TF:* 800-447-6843 ■ *Web:* www.hollywoodbr.com	Baton Rouge	LA	70802	225-709-7777	709-7770
Horseshoe Casino & Hotel 711 Horseshoe Blvd **Fax:* Mktg ■ *TF:* 800-895-0711 ■ *Web:* www.horseshoebossiercity.com/casinos/horseshoe-bossier-city/hotel-casino	Bossier City	LA	71111	318-742-0711	741-7728*
Isle of Capri Lake Charles 100 W Lake Ave *TF:* 800-843-4753 ■ *Web:* www.lake-charles.isleofcapricasinos.com	West Lake	LA	70669	337-430-0711	430-0083
Paragon Casino Resort 711 Paragon Pl *TF:* 800-946-1946 ■ *Web:* www.paragoncasinoresort.com	Marksville	LA	71351	318-253-1946	253-2028
Sam's Town Hotel & Casino Shreveport 315 Clyde Fant Pkwy *TF:* 877-429-0711 ■ *Web:* www.samstownshreveport.com	Shreveport	LA	71101	318-424-7777	424-5658
Treasure Chest Casino 5050 Williams Blvd *TF:* 800-298-0711 ■ *Web:* www.treasurechest.com	Kenner	LA	70065	504-443-8000	469-4115
Kewadin Casinos 3015 Mackinac Tr *TF:* 800-539-2346 ■ *Web:* www.kewadin.com	Saint Ignace	MI	49781	906-643-7071	643-8472
Leelanau Sands Casino 2521 NW Bay Shore Dr *TF:* 800-922-2946 ■ *Web:* www.casino2win.com	Peshawbestown	MI	49682	251-534-8100	

Name / Address	City	State	Zip	Phone	Fax
MGM Grand Detroit 1777 3rd St *TF:* 877-888-2121 ■ *Web:* www.mgmgranddetroit.com	Detroit	MI	48226	313-465-1777	
MotorCity Casino Hotel 2901 Grand River Ave *TF:* 866-752-9622 ■ *Web:* www.motorcitycasino.com	Detroit	MI	48201	313-237-7711	961-3312
Soaring Eagle Casino & Resort 6800 E Soaring Eagle Blvd **Fax Area Code:* 989 ■ *TF:* 877-232-4532 ■ *Web:* www.soaringeaglecasino.com	Mount Pleasant	MI	48858	888-732-4537	775-5383*
Black Bear Casino Resort 1785 Hwy 210 PO Box 777 *TF:* 888-771-0777 ■ *Web:* www.blackbearcasinohotel.com	Carlton	MN	55718	218-878-2327	878-2414
Grand Casino Hinckley 777 Lady Luck Dr *TF:* 800-472-6321 ■ *Web:* www.grandcasinomn.com	Hinckley	MN	55037	320-384-7777	384-4775
Grand Casino Mille Lacs 777 Grand Ave PO Box 343 *TF:* 800-626-5825 ■ *Web:* www.grandcasinomn.com	Onamia	MN	56359	320-532-7777	532-8103
Jackpot Junction Casino Hotel 39375 County Hwy 24 PO Box 420 *TF:* 800-946-2274 ■ *Web:* www.jackpotjunction.com	Morton	MN	56270	507-697-8000	644-2529
Mystic Lake Casino Hotel 2400 Mystic Lake Blvd *TF:* 800-262-7799 ■ *Web:* www.mysticlake.com	Prior Lake	MN	55372	952-445-9000	403-5210
Treasure Island Resort & Casino 5734 Sturgeon Lake Rd *TF:* 800-222-7077 ■ *Web:* www.treasureislandcasino.com	Welch	MN	55089	651-388-6300	385-2906
Ameristar Casino Hotel Vicksburg 4116 Washington St **Fax:* Mktg ■ *TF:* 866-667-3386 ■ *Web:* www.ameristarcasinos.com	Vicksburg	MS	39180	601-638-1000	630-3742*
Bally's Casino Tunica 1450 Bally's Blvd Casino Ctr *TF:* 800-382-2559 ■ *Web:* www.ballystunica.com	Robinsonville	MS	38664	662-357-1500	357-1756
Bayou Caddy's Jubilee Casino 199 N Lakefront Rd *Web:* www.ayoucaddyjublee.com	Greenville	MS	38701	662-335-1111	335-2700
Boomtown Casino Biloxi 676 Bayview Ave *TF:* 800-627-0777 ■ *Web:* www.boomtownbiloxi.com	Biloxi	MS	39530	228-435-7000	435-7964
Fitzgeralds Casino & Hotel Tunica 711 Lucky Ln *TF:* 888-766-5825 ■ *Web:* www.fitzgeraldstunica.com	Robinsonville	MS	38664	662-363-5825	363-3579
Gold Strike Casino Resort 1010 Casino Ctr Dr *TF Resv:* 888-245-7829 ■ *Web:* www.goldstrikemississippi.com	Tunica Resorts	MS	38664	662-357-1111	357-1306
Grand Biloxi Casino Hotel & Spa 280 Beach Blvd *TF:* 800-946-2946 ■ *Web:* www.totalrewards.com	Biloxi	MS	39530	228-436-2946	
Hard Rock Hotel & Casino Biloxi 777 Beach Blvd *TF:* 877-877-6256 ■ *Web:* www.hardrockbiloxi.com	Biloxi	MS	39530	228-374-7625	276-7655
Harrah's Tunica 13615 Old Hwy 61 N *TF:* 800-946-4946 ■ *Web:* www.harrahstunica.com	Robinsonville	MS	38664	800-946-4946	
Hollywood Casino Bay Saint Louis 711 Hollywood Blvd **Fax:* Hum Res ■ *TF:* 866-758-2591 ■ *Web:* www.hollywoodbsl.com	Bay Saint Louis	MS	39520	228-467-9257	467-3080*
Hollywood Casino Tunica 1150 Casino Strip Blvd PO Box 218 *TF:* 800-871-0711 ■ *Web:* www.hollywoodcasinotunica.com	Robinsonville	MS	38664	662-357-7700	357-7800
Horseshoe Tunica Casino & Hotel 1021 Casino Ctr Dr **Fax Area Code:* 662 ■ *TF:* 800-303-7463 ■ *Web:* www.horseshoetunica.com	Robinsonville	MS	38664	800-303-7463	357-5561*
IP Casino Resort & Spa 850 Bayview Ave *TF:* 800-436-3000 ■ *Web:* www.ipbiloxi.com	Biloxi	MS	39530	228-436-3000	432-3260
Island View Casino Resort 3300 W Beach Blvd PO Box 1600 *TF:* 877-774-8439 ■ *Web:* www.islandviewcasino.com	Gulfport	MS	39502	228-314-2100	314-2221
Isle of Capri Casino 777 Isle of Capri Pkwy *TF:* 800-789-5825 ■ *Web:* www.lula.isleofcapricasinos.com	Lula	MS	38644	662-363-4600	337-2738
Isle of Capri Casino Resort 151 Beach Blvd *TF:* 800-843-4753 ■ *Web:* www.biloxi.isleofcapricasinos.com	Biloxi	MS	39530	228-436-4753	436-7834
Lighthouse Point Casino 199 N Lakefront Rd *TF:* 800-878-1777 ■ *Web:* www.lighthouse-casino.com	Greenville	MS	38701	662-334-7711	378-2024
Pearl River Resort 13541 Hwy 16 W **Fax:* Mktg ■ *TF:* 800-557-0711 ■ *Web:* www.pearlriverresort.com	Philadelphia	MS	39350	601-650-1234	650-1351*
Resorts Tunica 1100 Casino Strip Blvd PO Box 750 *TF Resv:* 866-797-7111 ■ *Web:* www.resortstunica.com	Robinsonville	MS	38664	662-363-7777	357-2300
Sam's Town Hotel & Gambling Hall 1477 Casino Strip Blvd **Fax:* Hum Res ■ *TF:* 800-456-0711 ■ *Web:* www.samstowntunica.com	Robinsonville	MS	38664	662-363-0711	363-0895*
Silver Slipper Casino 5000 S Beach Blvd *TF:* 866-775-4773 ■ *Web:* www.silverslipper-ms.com	Lakeshore	MS	39558	228-469-2777	469-2805
Ameristar Casino Saint Charles 1260 S Main St PO Box 720 *TF:* 800-325-7777 ■ *Web:* www.ameristarcasinos.com	Saint Charles	MO	63301	636-940-4300	940-4391
Argosy Casino Kansas City 777 NW Argosy Pkwy *TF Resv:* 800-270-7711 ■ *Web:* www.stayargosy.com	Riverside	MO	64150	816-746-3100	741-5423
Harrah's Saint Louis Casino & Hotel 777 Casino Ctr Dr *TF:* 800-427-7247 ■ *Web:* www.harrahsstlouis.com	Maryland Heights	MO	63043	314-770-8100	770-8399
Isle of Capri Casino 1800 E Front St *TF:* 800-843-4753 ■ *Web:* www.kansas-city.isleofcapricasinos.com	Kansas City	MO	64120	816-855-7777	855-4247
President Casino on the Admiral 802 N First St *TF:* 800-772-3647	Saint Louis	MO	63102	314-622-3000	622-3049
Aquarius Casino Resort 1900 S Casino Dr *TF:* 888-662-5825 ■ *Web:* www.aquariuscasinoresort.com	Laughlin	NV	89029	702-298-5111	
Arizona Charlie's Boulder Casino & Hotel 4575 Boulder Hwy *TF:* 800-362-4040 ■ *Web:* www.arizonacharliesboulder.com	Las Vegas	NV	89121	702-951-9000	951-1046
Arizona Charlie's Decatur Casino & Hotel 740 S Decatur Blvd *TF:* 888-236-8645 ■ *Web:* www.arizonacharliesdecatur.com	Las Vegas	NV	89107	702-258-5111	258-5192
Atlantis Casino Resort 3800 S Virginia St *TF:* 800-723-6500 ■ *Web:* www.atlantiscasino.com	Reno	NV	89502	775-825-4700	332-2211
Bally's Las Vegas 3645 Las Vegas Blvd S *TF Resv:* 800-338-2127 ■ *Web:* www.ballyslasvegas.com	Las Vegas	NV	89109	702-967-4111	866-1700
Binion's Horseshoe Hotel & Casino 128 Fremont St *TF:* 800-237-6537 ■ *Web:* www.binions.com	Las Vegas	NV	89101	702-382-1600	384-1574
Boomtown Casino & Hotel Reno 2100 Garson Rd *NYSE: PNK* ■ *TF:* 800-648-3790 ■ *Web:* www.boomtownreno.com	Verdi	NV	89439	775-345-6000	345-8696
Boulder Station Hotel & Casino 4111 Boulder Hwy *TF:* 800-683-7777 ■ *Web:* www.boulderstation.com	Las Vegas	NV	89121	702-432-7777	432-7744
Buffalo Bill's Resort & Casino 31900 Las Vegas Blvd S *TF:* 888-386-7867 ■ *Web:* www.primmvalleyresorts.com/hotel_buffalobill.php	Primm	NV	89019	702-386-7867	679-7766
Cactus Jack's Casino 420 N Carson St	Carson City	NV	89702	775-882-8770	882-9147
California Hotel & Casino 12 E Ogden Ave *TF:* 800-634-6505 ■ *Web:* www.thecal.com	Las Vegas	NV	89101	702-385-1222	388-2660
Carson Horseshoe Club Casino 402 N Carson St	Carson City	NV	89702	775-883-2211	883-2262
Carson Nugget Casino 507 N Carson St *TF:* 800-426-5239 ■ *Web:* www.ccnugget.com	Carson City	NV	89703	775-882-1626	883-1106
Casino Fandango 3800 S Carson St *Web:* www.casinofandango.com	Carson City	NV	89701	775-885-7000	885-7008
Casino Royale Hotel 3411 Las Vegas Blvd S *TF:* 800-854-7666 ■ *Web:* www.casinoroyalehotel.com	Las Vegas	NV	89109	702-737-3500	650-4743
Circus Circus Hotel & Casino Reno 500 N Sierra St *TF:* 800-648-5010 ■ *Web:* www.circusreno.com	Reno	NV	89503	775-329-0711	328-9652
Circus Circus Hotel Casino & Theme Park Las Vegas 2880 Las Vegas Blvd S *TF Resv:* 800-634-3450 ■ *Web:* www.circuscircus.com	Las Vegas	NV	89109	702-734-0410	794-3816
Colorado Belle Hotel & Casino 2100 S Casino Dr **Fax:* Hum Res ■ *TF Resv:* 877-460-0777 ■ *Web:* www.coloradobelle.com	Laughlin	NV	89029	702-298-4000	298-3697*
Don Laughlin's Riverside Resort & Casino 1650 Casino Dr *TF:* 800-227-3849 ■ *Web:* www.riversideresort.com	Laughlin	NV	89029	702-298-2535	298-2695
Edgewater Hotel & Casino 2020 S Casino Dr **Fax:* Mktg ■ *TF Resv:* 800-677-4837 ■ *Web:* www.edgewater-casino.com	Laughlin	NV	89029	702-298-2453	298-5606*
El Cortez Hotel & Casino 600 E Fremont St *TF:* 800-634-6703 ■ *Web:* www.elcortezhotelcasino.com	Las Vegas	NV	89101	702-385-5200	474-3633
Eldorado Hotel Casino 345 N Virginia St *TF Resv:* 800-879-8879 ■ *Web:* www.eldoradoreno.com	Reno	NV	89501	775-786-5700	322-7124
Excalibur Hotel & Casino 3850 Las Vegas Blvd S PO Box 96776 *TF:* 877-750-5464 ■ *Web:* www.excalibur.com	Las Vegas	NV	89109	702-597-7777	597-7009
Fiesta Rancho Casino Hotel 2400 N Rancho Dr *TF Resv:* 888-899-7700 ■ *Web:* www.fiestarancholasvegas.com	Las Vegas	NV	89130	702-631-7000	638-3645
Fitzgeralds Casino & Hotel Reno 255 N Virginia St PO Box 40130 *TF:* 800-535-5825	Reno	NV	89504	775-785-3300	785-3318
Flamingo Las Vegas 3555 Las Vegas Blvd S *TF:* 800-902-9929 ■ *Web:* www.totalrewards.com	Las Vegas	NV	89109	702-697-2711	733-3528
Fremont Hotel & Casino 200 Fremont St *TF:* 800-634-6460 ■ *Web:* www.fremontcasino.com	Las Vegas	NV	89101	702-385-3232	385-6270
Gold Coast Hotel & Casino 4000 W Flamingo Rd *TF:* 800-331-5334 ■ *Web:* www.goldcoastcasino.com	Las Vegas	NV	89103	702-367-7111	367-8575
Gold Ranch Casino & RV Resort Hwy 80 W Exit 2 PO Box 160 *TF:* 877-927-6789 ■ *Web:* www.goldranchrvcasino.com	Verdi	NV	89439	775-345-6789	345-2356
Gold Spike Hotel & Casino 217 Las Vegas Blvd N *TF:* 866-600-8600 ■ *Web:* www.goldspike.com	Las Vegas	NV	89101	702-384-8444	382-6428
Gold Strike Hotel & Gambling Hall 1 Main St PO Box 19278 *TF:* 800-634-1359 ■ *Web:* www.goldstrike-jean.com	Jean	NV	89019	702-477-5000	671-1665
Golden Nugget Laughlin 2300 S Casino Dr *TF:* 800-950-7700 ■ *Web:* www.goldennugget.com	Laughlin	NV	89029	702-298-7111	298-7122
Grand Sierra Resort & Casino 2500 E 2nd St *TF:* 800-501-2651 ■ *Web:* www.grandsierraresort.com	Reno	NV	89595	775-789-2000	789-1678
Green Valley Ranch Resort Casino & Spa 2300 Paseo Verde Pkwy *TF:* 866-617-0777 ■ *Web:* www.greenvalleyranchresort.com	Henderson	NV	89052	702-617-7777	617-7778
Harrah's Lake Tahoe PO Box 8 *TF:* 800-427-7247 ■ *Web:* www.harrahs.com/our_casinos/tah	Stateline	NV	89449	775-588-6611	586-6607
Harrah's Laughlin 2900 S Casino Dr *TF:* 800-427-7247 ■ *Web:* www.totalrewards.com	Laughlin	NV	89029	702-298-4600	298-6802
Harveys Lake Tahoe 18 Hwy 50 PO Box 128 *TF:* 800-427-8397 ■ *Web:* www.harveystahoe.com	Lake Tahoe	NV	89449	775-588-2411	588-6643
Hyatt Regency Lake Tahoe Resort & Casino 111 Country Club Dr *TF:* 800-233-1234 ■ *Web:* www.laketahoe.hyatt.com	Incline Village	NV	89451	775-832-1234	831-2171
Imperial Palace Hotel & Casino 3535 Las Vegas Blvd S *TF:* 800-634-6441 ■ *Web:* www.imperialpalace.com	Las Vegas	NV	89109	702-731-3311	735-8328
John Ascuaga's Nugget Hotel Casino 1100 Nugget Ave **Fax:* Resv ■ *TF:* 800-648-1177 ■ *Web:* www.janugget.com	Sparks	NV	89431	775-356-3300	356-3434*
Lake Tahoe Horizon Casino 50 Hwy 50 *TF:* 800-648-3322 ■ *Web:* www.horizoncasino.com	Stateline	NV	89449	775-588-6211	586-4048
Las Vegas Club Hotel & Casino (LVC) 18 E Fremont St *TF:* 800-634-6532 ■ *Web:* www.vegasclubcasino.net	Las Vegas	NV	89101	702-385-1664	380-5793
Las Vegas Hilton 3000 Paradise Rd *TF:* 888-732-5111 ■ *Web:* www.lvhilton.com	Las Vegas	NV	89109	702-732-5111	732-5778
Luxor Hotel & Casino 3900 Las Vegas Blvd S *TF Resv:* 800-288-1000 ■ *Web:* www.luxor.com	Las Vegas	NV	89119	702-262-4000	262-4404

				Phone	Fax
Mandalay Bay Resort & Casino 3950 Las Vegas Blvd S *TF*: 877-632-7800 ■ *Web*: www.mandalaybay.com	Las Vegas	NV	89119	702-632-7777	632-7234
MGM Grand Hotel & Casino 3799 Las Vegas Blvd S *TF*: 877-880-0880 ■ *Web*: www.mgmgrand.com	Las Vegas	NV	89109	702-891-1111	891-3036
Monte Carlo Resort & Casino 3770 Las Vegas Blvd S *TF*: 800-311-8999 ■ *Web*: www.montecarlo.com	Las Vegas	NV	89109	702-730-7777	730-7200
New York New York Hotel & Casino 3790 Las Vegas Blvd S *TF*: 800-689-1797 ■ *Web*: www.newyorknewyork.com	Las Vegas	NV	89109	702-740-6969	740-6700
Orleans Las Vegas Hotel & Casino 4500 W Tropicana Ave *TF*: 800-675-3267 ■ *Web*: www.orleanscasino.com	Las Vegas	NV	89103	702-365-7111	365-7500
Palace Station Hotel & Casino 2411 W Sahara Ave *TF*: 800-634-3101 ■ *Web*: www.palacestation.com	Las Vegas	NV	89102	702-367-2411	367-2478
Palms Casino Resort 4321 W Flamingo Rd *TF*: 866-942-7777 ■ *Web*: www.palms.com	Las Vegas	NV	89103	702-942-7777	942-7001
Peppermill Hotel & Casino 2707 S Virginia St *TF*: 800-648-6992 ■ *Web*: www.peppermillreno.com	Reno	NV	89502	775-826-2121	826-7041
Railroad Pass Hotel & Casino 2800 S Boulder Hwy *TF*: 800-654-0877 ■ *Web*: www.railroadpass.com	Henderson	NV	89002	702-294-5000	294-0092
Red Rock Resort Spa & Casino 11011 W Charleston Blvd *TF*: 866-767-7773 ■ *Web*: www.redrocklasvegas.com	Las Vegas	NV	89135	702-797-7777	797-7890
River Palms Resort & Casino 2700 S Casino Dr *TF*: 800-835-7904 ■ *Web*: www.river-palms.com	Laughlin	NV	89029	702-298-2242	298-2117
Riviera Hotel & Casino 2901 Las Vegas Blvd S *TF Resv*: 800-634-6753 ■ *Web*: www.rivierahotel.com	Las Vegas	NV	89109	702-734-5110	794-9663
Sahara Hotel & Casino 2535 Las Vegas Blvd S *TF*: 888-696-2121 ■ *Web*: www.saharavegas.com	Las Vegas	NV	89109	702-737-2111	791-2027
Sam's Town Hotel & Gambling Hall 5111 Boulder Hwy *TF*: 800-897-8696 ■ *Web*: www.samstownlv.com	Las Vegas	NV	89122	702-456-7777	454-8107
Santa Fe Station 4949 N Rancho Dr *TF*: 800-634-3101 ■ *Web*: www.santafestationlasvegas.com	Las Vegas	NV	89130	702-658-4900	658-4919
Silver Legacy Resort & Casino 407 N Virginia St *TF*: 800-687-8733 ■ *Web*: www.silverlegacyreno.com	Reno	NV	89501	775-325-7401	325-7474
Silverton Hotel & Casino 3333 Blue Diamond Rd *TF*: 866-722-4608 ■ *Web*: www.silvertoncasino.com	Las Vegas	NV	89139	702-263-7777	263-7002
Slots-A-Fun Casino 2890 Las Vegas Blvd S	Las Vegas	NV	89109	702-734-0410	794-3816
South Point Hotel & Casino 9777 Las Vegas Blvd S *TF*: 866-796-7111 ■ *Web*: www.southpointcasino.com	Las Vegas	NV	89183	702-796-7111	797-8041
Stratosphere Tower Hotel & Casino 2000 S Las Vegas Blvd *Fax: Sales ■ *TF*: 800-998-6937 ■ *Web*: www.stratospherehotel.com	Las Vegas	NV	89104	702-380-7777	383-4755*
Suncoast Hotel & Casino 9090 Alta Dr *TF*: 877-677-7111 ■ *Web*: www.suncoastcasino.com	Las Vegas	NV	89145	702-636-7111	636-7288
Sunset Station Hotel & Casino 1301 W Sunset Rd *TF*: 888-786-7389 ■ *Web*: www.sunsetstation.com	Henderson	NV	89014	702-547-7777	547-7744
Texas Station Gambling Hall & Hotel 2101 Texas Star Ln *TF Resv*: 800-654-8888 ■ *Web*: www.texasstation.com	North Las Vegas	NV	89032	702-631-1000	631-8120
Treasure Island Hotel & Casino 3300 Las Vegas Blvd S *TF*: 800-288-7206 ■ *Web*: www.treasureisland.com	Las Vegas	NV	89109	702-894-7111	894-7414
Tropicana Express 2121 S Casino Dr *TF*: 800-243-6846 ■ *Web*: www.tropicanax.com	Laughlin	NV	89029	702-298-4200	298-6403
Tuscany Suites & Casino 255 E Flamingo Rd *TF Resv*: 877-887-2261 ■ *Web*: www.tuscanylv.com	Las Vegas	NV	89109	702-893-8933	947-5994
Western Village Inn & Casino 815 Nichols Blvd *Fax: PR ■ *TF*: 800-648-1170 ■ *Web*: www.westernvillagesparks.com	Sparks	NV	89434	775-331-1069	331-4834*
Westin Casuarina Las Vegas Hotel Casino & Spa 160 E Flamingo Rd *Web*: www.starwoodhotels.com	Las Vegas	NV	89109	702-836-5900	836-9776
Whiskey Pete's Hotel & Casino 100 W Primm Blvd *TF*: 800-386-7867 ■ *Web*: www.primmvalleyresorts.com	Primm	NV	89019	702-386-7867	679-5195
Wynn Las Vegas 3131 Las Vegas Blvd S *TF*: 877-321-9966 ■ *Web*: www.wynnlasvegas.com	Las Vegas	NV	89109	702-770-7000	770-1571
Atlantic City Hilton Casino Resort Boston Ave & The Boardwalk *TF*: 800-257-7075 ■ *Web*: www.hiltonac.com	Atlantic City	NJ	08401	609-347-7111	340-7128
Harrah's Resort Atlantic City 777 Harrah's Blvd *TF*: 800-645-6774 ■ *Web*: www.harrahsresort.com/casinos/harrahs-atlantic-city	Atlantic City	NJ	08401	609-441-5000	340-8621
Resorts Casino Hotel 1133 Boardwalk *TF*: 800-334-6378 ■ *Web*: www.resortsac.com	Atlantic City	NJ	08401	800-334-6378	
Showboat Atlantic City 801 Boardwalk *TF*: 800-427-7247 ■ *Web*: www.harrahs.com/our_casinos/sac	Atlantic City	NJ	08401	609-343-4000	343-4057
Tropicana Entertainment 2831 Boardwalk *TF*: 800-843-8767 ■ *Web*: www.tropicana.net	Atlantic City	NJ	08401	609-340-4000	340-4457
Trump Taj Mahal Casino Resort 1000 Boardwalk & Virginia Ave *TF*: 800-825-8786 ■ *Web*: www.trumptaj.com	Atlantic City	NJ	08401	609-449-1000	449-6818
Camel Rock Casino 17486A Hwy 84/285 *TF*: 800-462-2635 ■ *Web*: www.camelrockcasino.com	Santa Fe	NM	87506	505-984-8414	989-9234
Cities of Gold Casino 10-B Cities of Gold Rd *TF*: 800-455-3313 ■ *Web*: www.citiesofgold.com	Santa Fe	NM	87506	505-455-3313	455-7188
Route 66 Casino Hotel 14500 Central Ave *TF*: 866-352-7866 ■ *Web*: www.rt66casino.com	Albuquerque	NM	87121	505-352-7866	352-7880
Sandia Resort & Casino 30 Rainbow Rd NE *TF*: 800-526-9366 ■ *Web*: www.sandiacasino.com	Albuquerque	NM	87113	505-796-7500	796-7605
Seneca Niagara Casino 310 4th St *TF*: 877-873-6322 ■ *Web*: www.senecaniagaracasino.com	Niagara Falls	NY	14303	716-299-1100	299-1099
Turning Stone Casino Resort 5218 Patrick Rd *TF*: 800-771-7711 ■ *Web*: www.turning-stone.com	Verona	NY	13478	315-361-7711	361-7901
Harrah's Cherokee Casino & Hotel 777 Casino Dr *TF*: 800-427-7247 ■ *Web*: www.harrahscherokee.com/casinos/harrahs-cherokee/hotel-casino	Cherokee	NC	28719	828-497-7777	497-5076
Prairie Knights Casino & Resort 7932 Hwy 24 *TF*: 800-425-8277 ■ *Web*: www.prairieknights.com	Fort Yates	ND	58538	701-854-7777	854-7786
Casino Nova Scotia 1983 Upper Water St *TF*: 888-642-6376 ■ *Web*: www.casinonovascotia.com	Halifax	NS	B3J3Y5	902-425-7777	428-7846
Osage Nation Million Dollar Elm Casino 301 Blackjack Dr *TF*: 877-246-8777 ■ *Web*: www.milliondollarelm.com	Sand Springs	OK	74063	918-699-7777	699-7700
Caesars Windsor 377 Riverside Dr E *TF*: 800-991-7777 ■ *Web*: www.caesarswindsor.com	Windsor	ON	N9A7H7	519-258-7878	258-0434
Casino Niagara 5705 Falls Ave *TF*: 888-325-5788 ■ *Web*: www.casinoniagara.com	Niagara Falls	ON	L2E6T3	905-374-3598	353-6727
Fallsview Casino Resort 6380 Fallsview Blvd *TF*: 888-325-5788 ■ *Web*: www.fallsviewcasinoresort.com	Niagara Falls	ON	L2G7X5	905-358-3255	371-7952
Presque Isle Downs Casino & Racetrack 8199 Perry Hwy *TF*: 866-374-3386 ■ *Web*: www.presqueisledowns.com	Erie	PA	16509	814-860-8999	
Speaking Rock Entertainment Centre 122 S Old Pueblo Rd *Web*: www.speakingrock.com	El Paso	TX	79907	915-860-7777	860-7745
Emerald Queen Casino (EQC) 2024 E 29th St *TF*: 888-831-7655 ■ *Web*: www.emeraldqueen.com	Tacoma	WA	98404	253-594-7777	272-6725
Great American Casino 10117 S Tacoma Way *Web*: www.greatamericancasino.com	Lakewood	WA	98499	253-396-0500	882-1001
Lucky Eagle Casino 12888 188th Ave SW *TF*: 800-720-1788 ■ *Web*: www.luckyeagle.com	Rochester	WA	98579	360-273-2000	273-2366
Muckleshoot Indian Casino 2402 Auburn Way S *TF*: 800-804-4944 ■ *Web*: www.muckleshootcasino.com	Auburn	WA	98002	253-939-7484	939-7702
Northern Quest Casino 100 N Hayford Rd *TF*: 888-603-7051 ■ *Web*: www.northernquest.com	Airway Heights	WA	99001	509-242-7000	343-2163
Red Wind Casino 12819 Yelm Hwy *TF*: 866-946-2444 ■ *Web*: www.redwindcasino.com	Olympia	WA	98513	360-412-5000	455-0364
Skagit Valley Casino Resort 5984 N Darrk Ln *TF*: 877-275-2448 ■ *Web*: www.theskagit.com	Bow	WA	98232	360-724-7777	724-0222
Tulalip Casino 10200 Quil Ceda Blvd *TF*: 888-272-1111 ■ *Web*: www.tulalipcasino.com	Tulalip	WA	98271	360-651-1111	651-3119
Ho-Chunk Casino S 3214 Hwy 12 *TF*: 800-746-2486 ■ *Web*: www.ho-chunk.com	Baraboo	WI	53913	608-356-6210	355-1500
Lake of the Torches Resort Casino 510 Old Abe Rd *TF*: 800-258-6724 ■ *Web*: www.lakeofthetorches.com	Lac du Flambeau	WI	54538	715-588-7070	588-9508
Oneida Bingo & Casino 2020 Airport Dr *TF*: 800-238-4263 ■ *Web*: www.oneidabingoandcasino.net	Green Bay	WI	54313	920-497-8118	496-3745
Saint Croix Casino & Hotel 777 US Hwys 8 & 63 *TF*: 800-846-8946 ■ *Web*: www.stcroixcasino.com	Turtle Lake	WI	54889	715-986-4777	986-2877

134 CASKETS & VAULTS

SEE ALSO Mortuary, Crematory, Cemetery Products & Services p. 2255

				Phone	Fax
American Wilbert Vault Corp 1015 Troost Ave	Forest Park	IL	60130	708-366-3210	366-3281
Batesville Casket Co 1 Batesville Blvd *TF Cust Svc*: 800-622-8373 ■ *Web*: www.batesville.com	Batesville	IN	47006	812-934-7500	934-8300
Brown-Wilbert Inc 2280 Hamline Ave N *Web*: www.wilbert.net	Saint Paul	MN	55113	651-631-1234	631-1428
Casket Shells Inc 432 1st St PO Box 172 *Web*: www.casketshellsinc.com	Eynon	PA	18403	570-876-2642	876-5613
Clark Grave Vault Co 375 E 5th Ave *TF*: 800-848-3570 ■ *Web*: www.clarkvault.com	Columbus	OH	43201	614-294-3761	299-2324
DeltAurora LLC 10944 Marsh Rd PO Box 29 *Fax: Cust Svc ■ *TF Cust Svc*: 800-457-5111 ■ *Web*: www.auroracasket.com	Aurora	IN	47001	812-926-1111	926-1148*
JM Hutton & Co Inc 1501 S 8th St *Web*: www.jmhutton.com	Richmond	IN	47374	765-962-3591	966-0149
Matthews International Corp 2 Northshore Ctr Suite 200 *NASDAQ: MATW* ■ *TF*: 800-223-4964	Pittsburgh	PA	15212	412-442-8200	442-8291
Norwalk-Wilbert Vault Co 136 James St *TF*: 800-826-9406 ■ *Web*: www.norwalkwilbert.com	Bridgeport	CT	06604	203-366-5678	337-5433
Paul Casket Co 505 S Green St *TF*: 800-521-8202	Cambridge City	IN	47327	765-478-3991	962-0911
Pettigrew & Sons Casket Co 6151 Power Inn Rd *Web*: www.pettigrewcaskets.com	Sacramento	CA	95824	916-383-0777	383-2445
Providence Casket Co 1 Industrial Cir *TF*: 800-848-2999	Lincoln	RI	02865	401-726-1700	726-1702
Sound Casket Inc 20350 71st Ave NE Suite F *TF*: 800-735-7274 ■ *Web*: www.soundcasket.com	Arlington	WA	98223	360-403-7939	403-7939
Wilbert Inc PO Box 147 *TF*: 800-323-7188	Forest Park	IL	60130	708-865-1600	865-1646
York Group Inc 2 Northshore Ctr Suite 100 *Fax Area Code: 800 ■ *TF*: 800-223-4964 ■ *Web*: www.yorkgrp.com	Pittsburgh	PA	15212	412-995-1600	201-4338*
Zane Casket Co 1201 Hall Ave	Zanesville	OH	43702	740-452-4680	452-8993

135 CEMENT

				Phone	Fax
Alamo Cement Co PO Box 34807	San Antonio	TX	78265	210-208-1880	208-1881

Name / Address	City	State	ZIP	Phone	Fax
Alamo Concrete Products Ltd PO Box 34210	San Antonio	TX	78265	210-208-1880	208-1501
Ash Grove Cement Co 8900 Indian Creek Pkwy *TF:* 800-545-1886 ■ *Web:* www.ashgrove.com	Overland Park	KS	66210	913-451-8900	451-8324
Ash Grove Texas LP PO Box 520 **Fax Area Code:* 972 ■ *TF Cust Svc:* 800-545-1882 ■ *Web:* www.ashgrove.com	Midlothian	TX	76065	913-451-8900	534-1231*
Buzzi Unicem USA Inc 100 Brodhead Rd Suite 230 *Web:* www.buzziunicem.com	Bethlehem	PA	18017	610-866-4400	866-9430
California Portland Cement Co 2025 E Financial Way Suite 200 *TF Cust Svc:* 800-272-1891 ■ *Web:* www.calportland.com	Glendora	CA	91741	626-852-6200	691-2269
Cemex Puerto Rico Inc RT 165 KM 2.7 Industrial Amelia Pk *Web:* www.cemex.com	Bucahna Guaynabo	PR	00968	787-783-3000	781-8850
Cemex USA 840 Gessner Suite 1400 *NYSE:* CX ■ *TF:* 800-999-8529 ■ *Web:* www.cemex.com	Houston	TX	77024	713-650-6200	722-5105
CGM Inc 1445 Ford Rd *TF:* 800-523-6570 ■ *Web:* www.cgmbuildingproducts.com	Bensalem	PA	19020	215-638-4400	638-7949
Coastal Cement Corp 36 Drydock Ave *TF:* 800-828-8352	Boston	MA	02210	617-350-0183	350-0186
Continental Cement Co LLC 14755 N Outer 40 Suite 514 *TF:* 800-625-1144 ■ *Web:* www.continentalcement.com	Chesterfield	MO	63017	636-532-7440	532-7445
Dragon Products Co 960 Ocean Ave *TF:* 800-828-8352 ■ *Web:* www.dragonproducts.com	Portland	ME	04103	207-774-6355	761-5694
Eagle Materials Inc 3811 Turtle Creek Blvd Suite 1100 *NYSE:* EXP ■ *TF:* 800-759-7625 ■ *Web:* www.eaglematerials.com	Dallas	TX	75219	214-432-2000	432-2100
Eastern Cement Corp 13250 Eastern Ave *TF:* 800-282-7798	Palmetto	FL	34221	941-729-7311	729-8124
ESSROC Materials Inc 3251 Bath Pike *TF:* 800-523-9238 ■ *Web:* www.essroc.com	Nazareth	PA	18064	610-837-6725	837-9614
Federal White Cement Ltd PO Box 1609 *TF Sales:* 800-265-1806 ■ *Web:* www.federalwhitecement.com	Woodstock	ON	N4S0A8	519-485-5410	485-5892
Giant Cement Holding Inc 320-D Midland Pkwy *TF:* 800-845-1174	Summerville	SC	29485	843-851-9898	851-9881
Hawaiian Cement 99-1300 Halawa Valley St *Web:* www.hawaiiancement.com	Aiea	HI	96701	808-532-3400	532-3499
Holcim (US) Inc 6211 Ann Arbor Rd **Fax Area Code:* 734 ■ *TF:* 800-831-9507 ■ *Web:* www2.holcim.com/USA	Dundee	MI	48131	800-831-9507	821-7057*
Illinois Cement Co PO Box 442	La Salle	IL	61301	815-224-2112	224-4358
Keystone Cement Co PO Box A *TF:* 800-523-5442	Bath	PA	18014	610-837-1881	837-2267
Knife River Corp 1150 W Century Ave *TF:* 800-982-5339 ■ *Web:* www.kniferiver.com	Bismarck	ND	58503	701-530-1400	530-1451
Lafarge North America Inc 12950 Worldgate Dr Suite 600 *Web:* www.lafargenorthamerica.com	Herndon	VA	20170	703-480-3600	480-3899
Lehigh Inland Cement Ltd 12640 Inland Way *TF:* 800-252-9304 ■ *Web:* www.lehighinland.com	Edmonton	AB	T5V1K2	780-420-2500	420-2550
Lehigh Northwest Cement Ltd 3600 Lysander Ln Suite 320 *Web:* www.lehighnw.com	Richmond	BC	V7B1C3	604-279-6600	261-7241
Monarch Cement Co 449 1200 St PO Box 1000 *TF:* 800-362-0570 ■ *Web:* www.monarchcement.com	Humboldt	KS	66748	620-473-2222	473-2447
Mountain Cement Co 5 Sand Creek Rd *Web:* www.mountaincement.com	Laramie	WY	82070	307-745-4879	742-4534
National Cement Co Inc PO Box 530010	Birmingham	AL	35253	205-423-2600	870-5777
Phoenix Cement Co 8800 E Chaparral Rd Suite 155 *Web:* www.srmaterials.com	Scottsdale	AZ	85250	480-850-5757	850-5758
Prairie Group Inc 7601 W 79th St *TF Sales:* 800-649-3690 ■ *Web:* www.prairiegroup.com	Bridgeview	IL	60455	708-458-0400	458-6007
Texas Industries Inc 1341 W Mockingbird Ln Suite 700W *NYSE:* TXI ■ *Web:* www.txi.com	Dallas	TX	75247	972-647-6700	647-3878
Titan America Inc 1151 Azalea Garden Rd *TF:* 800-468-7622 ■ *Web:* www.titanamerica.com	Norfolk	VA	23502	757-858-6500	855-7707

136 CEMETERIES - NATIONAL

SEE ALSO Historic Homes & Buildings p. 1477; Parks - National - US p. 2340

Name / Address	City	State	ZIP	Phone	Fax
Alexandria National Cemetery 209 E Shamrock St *Web:* www.cem.va.gov	Pineville	LA	71360	318-449-1793	449-9327
Alton National Cemetery 600 Pearl St *TF:* 800-535-1117 ■ *Web:* www.cem.va.gov	Alton	IL	62003	314-845-8320	260-8723
Annapolis National Cemetery 800 W St *Web:* www.cem.va.gov	Annapolis	MD	21401	410-644-9696	644-1563
Balls Bluff National Cemetery Rt 7 *Web:* www.cem.va.gov	Leesburg	VA	22075	540-825-0027	825-6684
Baltimore National Cemetery 5501 Frederick Ave *Web:* www.cem.va.gov/nchp/baltimore.htm	Baltimore	MD	21228	410-644-9696	644-1563
Barrancas National Cemetery Naval Air Stn 80 Hovey Rd *Web:* www.cem.va.gov	Pensacola	FL	32508	850-453-4108	453-4635
Bath National Cemetery VA Medical Ctr *Web:* www.cem.va.gov	Bath	NY	14810	607-664-4853	664-4761
Battleground National Cemetery 6625 Georgia Ave NW *Web:* www.nps.gov	Washington	DC	20240	202-895-6070	
Bay Pines National Cemetery 10000 Bay Pines Blvd *Web:* www.cem.va.gov	Saint Petersburg	FL	33708	727-398-9426	398-9520
Beaufort National Cemetery 1601 Boundary St *Web:* www.cem.va.gov	Beaufort	SC	29902	843-524-3925	524-8538
Beverly National Cemetery 916 Bridgeboro Rd **Fax Area Code:* 609 ■ *Web:* www.cem.va.gov/cems/nchp/beverly.asp	Beverly	NJ	08010	215-504-5610	871-4691*
Biloxi National Cemetery 400 Veterans Ave *Web:* www.cem.va.gov	Biloxi	MS	39531	228-388-6668	523-5784
Black Hills National Cemetery 20901 Pleasant Valley Dr *Web:* www.cem.va.gov	Sturgis	SD	57785	605-347-3830	720-7298
Calverton National Cemetery 210 Princeton Blvd *Web:* www.cem.va.gov	Calverton	NY	11933	631-727-5410	727-5815
Camp Butler National Cemetery 5063 Camp Butler Rd *Web:* www.cem.va.gov/cems/nchp/campbutler.asp	Springfield	IL	62707	217-492-4070	492-4072
Camp Nelson National Cemetery 6980 Danville Rd *Web:* www.cem.va.gov	Nicholasville	KY	40356	859-885-5727	887-4860
Cave Hill National Cemetery 701 Baxter Ave *Web:* www.cem.va.gov/nchp/cavehill.htm	Louisville	KY	40204	502-893-3852	893-6612
Chattanooga National Cemetery 1200 Bailey Ave *Web:* www.cem.va.gov	Chattanooga	TN	37404	423-855-6590	855-6597
City Point National Cemetery 10th Ave & Davis St *Web:* www.cem.va.gov/cems/nchp/citypoint.asp	Hopewell	VA	23860	804-795-2031	795-1064
Cold Harbor National Cemetery 6038 Cold Harbor Rd *Web:* www.cem.va.gov/nchp/coldharbor.htm	Mechanicsville	VA	23111	804-795-2031	795-1064
Corinth National Cemetery 1551 Horton St *Web:* www.cem.va.gov	Corinth	MS	38834	901-386-8311	382-0750
Crown Hill National Cemetery 700 W 38th St *Web:* www.cem.va.gov	Indianapolis	IN	46208	317-920-2633	
Culpeper National Cemetery 305 US Ave *Web:* www.cem.va.gov/cems/nchp/culpeper.asp	Culpeper	VA	22701	540-825-0027	825-6684
Cypress Hills National Cemetery 625 Jamaica Ave *Web:* www.cem.va.gov/cems/nchp/cypresshills.asp	Brooklyn	NY	11208	631-454-4949	694-5422
Danville National Cemetery 721 Lee St *Web:* www.cem.va.gov/cems/nchp/danvilleva.asp	Danville	VA	24541	704-636-2661	636-1115
Danville National Cemetery 1900 E Main St *Web:* www.cem.va.gov	Danville	IL	61832	217-554-4550	554-4803
Dayton National Cemetery 4100 W 3rd St *Web:* www.cem.va.gov	Dayton	OH	45428	937-262-2115	262-2187
Eagle Point National Cemetery 2763 Riley Rd *Web:* www.cem.va.gov	Eagle Point	OR	97524	541-826-2511	826-2888
Fayetteville National Cemetery 700 S Government Ave *Web:* www.cem.va.gov	Fayetteville	AR	72701	479-444-5051	444-5094
Finn's Point National Cemetery Fort Mott Rd RD 3 PO Box 542 *Web:* www.cem.va.gov/cems/nchp/finnspoint.asp	Salem	NJ	08079	215-504-5610	504-5611
Florence National Cemetery 803 E National Cemetery Rd *Web:* www.cem.va.gov	Florence	SC	29506	843-669-8783	662-8318
Florida National Cemetery 6502 SW 102nd Ave *Web:* www.cem.va.gov	Bushnell	FL	33513	352-793-7740	793-9560
Fort Bayard National Cemetery 200 Camino De Paz PO Box 189 *Web:* www.cem.va.gov/cems/nchp/ftbayard.asp	Fort Bayard	NM	88036	915-564-0201	564-3746
Fort Bliss National Cemetery PO Box 6342 *Web:* www.cem.va.gov	El Paso	TX	79906	915-564-0201	564-3746
Fort Custer National Cemetery 15501 Dickman Rd *Web:* www.cem.va.gov	Augusta	MI	49012	269-731-4164	731-2428
Fort Gibson National Cemetery 1423 Cemetery Rd *Web:* www.cem.va.gov	Fort Gibson	OK	74434	918-478-2334	478-2661
Fort Harrison National Cemetery 8620 Varina Rd *Web:* www.cem.va.gov/nchp/ftharrision.htm	Richmond	VA	23231	804-795-2031	795-1064
Fort Leavenworth National Cemetery 395 Biddle Blvd *Web:* www.cem.va.gov	Fort Leavenworth	KS	66027	913-758-4105	758-4136
Fort Logan National Cemetery 4400 W Kenyon Ave *Web:* www.cem.va.gov	Denver	CO	80235	303-761-0117	781-9378
Fort Lyon National Cemetery 15700 County Rd HH *Web:* www.cem.va.gov	Las Animas	CO	81054	303-761-0117	781-9378
Fort Mitchell National Cemetery 553 Hwy 165 *Web:* www.cem.va.gov	Fort Mitchell	AL	36856	334-855-4731	855-4740
Fort Richardson National Cemetery Bldg 58-512, Davis Hwy PO Box 5-498 *Web:* www.cem.va.gov/cems/nchp/ftrichardson.asp	Fort Richardson	AK	99505	907-384-7075	384-7111
Fort Rosecrans National Cemetery PO Box 6237 *Web:* www.cem.va.gov/cems/nchp/ftrosecrans.asp	San Diego	CA	92166	619-553-2084	553-6593
Fort Sam Houston National Cemetery 1520 Harry Wurzbach Rd *Web:* www.cem.va.gov/nchp/ftsamhouston.htm	San Antonio	TX	78209	210-820-3891	820-3445
Fort Scott National Cemetery 900 E National Ave *Web:* www.cem.va.gov/cems	Fort Scott	KS	66701	620-223-2840	223-2505
Fort Smith National Cemetery 522 Garland Ave *Web:* www.cem.va.gov	Fort Smith	AR	72901	479-783-5345	785-4189

Name / Address	City	State	Zip	Phone	Fax
Fort Snelling National Cemetery 7601 34th Ave. *Web:* www.cem.va.gov	Minneapolis	MN	55450	612-726-1127	726-9119
Glendale National Cemetery 8301 Willis Church Rd *Web:* www.cem.va.gov/nchp/glendale.htm	Richmond	VA	23231	804-795-2031	795-1064
Golden Gate National Cemetery 1300 Sneath Ln *Web:* www.cem.va.gov/nchp/goldengate.htm	San Bruno	CA	94066	650-589-7737	873-6578
Grafton National Cemetery 431 Walnut St. *Web:* www.cem.va.gov	Grafton	WV	26354	304-265-2044	265-4336
Hampton National Cemetery Cemetery Rd at Marshall Ave *Web:* www.cem.va.gov	Hampton	VA	23669	757-723-7104	728-3144
Houston National Cemetery 10410 Veterans Memorial Dr *Web:* www.cem.va.gov	Houston	TX	77038	281-447-8686	447-0580
Indiantown Gap National Cemetery RR 2 PO Box 484 *Web:* www.cem.va.gov/cems/nchp/indiantowngap.asp	Annville	PA	17003	717-865-5254	865-5256
Jefferson Barracks National Cemetery 2900 Sheridan Rd *Web:* www.cem.va.gov/nchp/jeffersonbarracks.htm	Saint Louis	MO	63125	314-845-8320	845-8355
Jefferson City National Cemetery 1024 E McCarty St *Web:* www.cem.va.gov/cems/nchp/jeffersoncity.asp	Jefferson City	MO	65101	314-845-8320	845-8355
Keokuk National Cemetery 1701 J St **Fax Area Code: 319* ■ *Web:* www.cem.va.gov/cems/nchp/keokuk.asp	Keokuk	IA	52632	309-782-2094	524-8118*
Kerrville National Cemetery 3600 Memorial Blvd *Web:* www.cem.va.gov	Kerrville	TX	78028	210-820-3891	820-3445
Knoxville National Cemetery 939 Tyson St NW *Web:* www.cem.va.gov/cems/nchp/knoxville.asp	Knoxville	TN	37917	423-855-6590	855-6597
Leavenworth National Cemetery 150 Muncie Rd *Web:* www.cem.va.gov/cems	Leavenworth	KS	66048	913-758-4105	758-4136
Lebanon National Cemetery 20 Hwy 208 *Web:* www.cem.va.gov	Lebanon	KY	40033	270-692-3390	692-0018
Little Rock National Cemetery 2523 Confederate Blvd *Web:* www.cem.va.gov	Little Rock	AR	72206	501-324-6401	324-7182
Long Island National Cemetery 2040 Wellwood Ave *Web:* www.cem.va.gov/cems/nchp/longisland.asp	Farmingdale	NY	11735	631-454-4949	694-5422
Los Angeles National Cemetery 950 S Sepulveda Blvd. *Web:* www.cem.va.gov	Los Angeles	CA	90049	310-268-4494	268-3257
Loudon Park National Cemetery 3445 Frederick Rd *Web:* www.cem.va.gov/cems/nchp/loudonpark.asp	Baltimore	MD	21228	410-644-9696	644-1563
Marietta National Cemetery 500 Washington Ave. *TF:* 866-236-8159 ■ *Web:* www.cem.va.gov	Marietta	GA	30060	770-428-5631	479-9311
Marion National Cemetery 1700 E 38th St. *Web:* www.cem.va.gov	Marion	IN	46953	765-674-0284	674-4521
Massachusetts National Cemetery Conery Rd *Web:* www.cem.va.gov	Bourne	MA	02532	508-563-7113	564-9946
Memphis National Cemetery 3568 Townes Ave. *Web:* www.cem.va.gov	Memphis	TN	38122	901-386-8311	382-0750
Mill Springs National Cemetery 9044 W Hwy 80 *Web:* www.cem.va.gov/cems/nchp/millsprings.asp	Nancy	KY	42544	859-885-5727	887-4860
Mobile National Cemetery 1202 Virginia St. *Web:* www.cem.va.gov	Mobile	AL	36604	850-453-4108	453-4635
Mound City National Cemetery Hwy 37 & 51 PO Box 128 *Web:* www.cem.va.gov/cems/nchp/moundcity.asp	Mound City	IL	62963	314-845-8320	845-8355
Mountain Home National Cemetery PO Box 8 *Web:* www.cem.va.gov/cems/nchp/mountainhome.asp	Mountain Home	TN	37684	423-979-3535	979-3521
Nashville National Cemetery 1420 Gallatin Rd S *Web:* www.cem.va.gov	Madison	TN	37115	615-860-0086	860-8691
Natchez National Cemetery 41 Cemetery Rd *Web:* www.cem.va.gov	Natchez	MS	39120	601-445-4981	445-8815
National Memorial Cemetery of Arizona 23029 N Cave Creek Rd *Web:* www.cem.va.gov	Phoenix	AZ	85024	480-513-3600	513-1412
New Albany National Cemetery 1943 Ekin Ave. *Web:* www.cem.va.gov/cems/nchp/newalbany.asp	New Albany	IN	47150	502-893-3852	893-6612
New Bern National Cemetery 1711 National Ave. *Web:* www.cem.va.gov	New Bern	NC	28560	252-637-2912	637-7145
Philadelphia National Cemetery Haines St & Limekiln Pike *Web:* www.cem.va.gov/cems/nchp/philadelphia.asp	Philadelphia	PA	19138	215-504-5610	504-5611
Poplar Grove National Cemetery 8005 Vaughan Rd *Web:* www.nps.gov/pogr/index.htm	Petersburg	VA	23805	804-732-3531	732-3615
Port Hudson National Cemetery 20978 Port Hickey Rd. *Web:* www.cem.va.gov	Zachary	LA	70791	225-654-3767	654-3728
Prescott National Cemetery 500 Hwy 89 N. *Web:* www.cem.va.gov/nchp/prescott.htm	Prescott	AZ	86313	480-513-3600	513-1412
Quantico National Cemetery 18424 Joplin Rd. *Web:* www.cem.va.gov	Triangle	VA	22172	703-221-2183	221-2185
Quincy National Cemetery 36th & Main Sts. *Web:* www.cem.va.gov/cems/nchp/quincy.asp	Quincy	IL	62301	309-782-2094	782-2097
Raleigh National Cemetery 501 Rock Quarry Rd *Web:* www.cem.va.gov/cems/nchp/raleigh.asp	Raleigh	NC	27610	252-637-2912	637-7145
Richmond National Cemetery 1701 Williamsburg Rd *Web:* www.cem.va.gov/nchp/richmond.htm	Richmond	VA	23231	804-795-2031	795-1064
Riverside National Cemetery 22495 Van Buren Blvd *Web:* www.cem.va.gov	Riverside	CA	92518	951-653-8417	653-5233
Rock Island National Cemetery Bldg 118 *Web:* www.cem.va.gov/cems/nchp/rockisland.asp	Rock Island	IL	61299	309-782-2094	782-2097
Roseburg National Cemetery 1770 Harvard Blvd *Web:* www.cem.va.gov/cems/nchp/roseburg.asp	Roseburg	OR	97470	541-826-2511	826-2111
Saint Augustine National Cemetery 104 Marine St. *Web:* www.cem.va.gov/cems/nchp/staugustine.asp	Saint Augustine	FL	32084	352-793-7740	793-9560
Salisbury National Cemetery 501 Statesville Blvd *Web:* www.cem.va.gov/cems/nchp/salisbury.asp	Salisbury	NC	28144	704-636-2661	636-1115
San Antonio National Cemetery c/o Port San Houston National Cemetery 1520 Harry Wurzback Rd *Web:* www.cem.va.gov	San Antonio	TX	78209	210-820-3891	820-3445
San Francisco National Cemetery Presidio of San Francisco 1 Lincoln Blvd *Web:* www.cem.va.gov/cems/nchp/sanfrancisco.asp	San Francisco	CA	94129	650-589-7737	873-6578
San Joaquin Valley National Cemetery 32053 W McCabe Rd *Web:* www.cem.va.gov/cems/nchp/sanjoaquinvalley.asp	Santa Nella	CA	95322	209-854-1040	854-3944
Santa Fe National Cemetery 501 N Guadalupe St *Web:* www.cem.va.gov	Santa Fe	NM	87501	505-988-6400	988-6497
Seven Pines National Cemetery 400 E Williamsburg Rd *Web:* www.cem.va.gov/cems/nchp/sevenpines.asp	Sandston	VA	23150	804-795-2031	795-1064
Sitka National Cemetery 803 Sawmill Creek Rd. *Web:* www.cem.va.gov	Sitka	AK	99835	907-384-7075	384-7111
Springfield National Cemetery 1702 E Seminole St *Web:* www.cem.va.gov	Springfield	MO	65804	417-881-9499	881-7862
Staunton National Cemetery 901 Richmond Ave. *Web:* www.cem.va.gov/cems/nchp/staunton.asp	Staunton	VA	24401	540-825-0027	825-6684
Tahoma National Cemetery 18600 SE 240th St *Web:* www.cem.va.gov	Kent	WA	98042	425-413-9614	413-9618
Togus National Cemetery VA Regional Office Center *Web:* www.cem.va.gov/cems/nchp/togus.asp	Togus	ME	04330	508-563-7113	564-9946
West Virginia National Cemetery Rt 2 PO Box 127 *Web:* www.cem.va.gov/cems/nchp/westvirginia.asp	Grafton	WV	26354	304-265-2044	265-4336
Willamette National Cemetery 11800 SE Mt Scott Blvd *Web:* www.cem.va.gov	Portland	OR	97266	503-273-5250	273-5330
Wilmington National Cemetery 2011 Market St **Fax Area Code: 252* ■ *Web:* www.cem.va.gov	Wilmington	NC	28403	910-815-4877	637-7145*
Winchester National Cemetery 401 National Ave. *Web:* www.cem.va.gov/cems/nchp/winchester.asp	Winchester	VA	22601	540-825-0027	825-6684
Wood National Cemetery 5000 W National Ave Bldg 1301 *Web:* www.cem.va.gov	Milwaukee	WI	53295	414-382-5300	382-5321
Woodlawn National Cemetery 1825 Davis St *Web:* www.cem.va.gov	Elmira	NY	14901	607-732-5411	732-1769
Yorktown National Cemetery PO Box 210 *Web:* www.nps.gov/york/index.htm	Yorktown	VA	23690	757-898-2410	898-6346
Zachary Taylor National Cemetery 4701 Brownsboro Rd *Web:* www.cem.va.gov	Louisville	KY	40207	502-893-3852	893-6612

137 CHAMBERS OF COMMERCE - CANADIAN

Listings Are Organized By Provinces And Then Are Alphabetized Within Each Province Grouping According To The Name Of The City In Which Each Chamber Is Located.

Name / Address	City	Province	Postal Code	Phone	Fax
Brooks & District Chamber of Commerce 2 Ave W Suite 6 PO Box 400 *Web:* www.brookschamber.ab.ca	Brooks	AB	T1R1B4	403-362-7641	362-6893
Calgary Chamber of Commerce 100 6th Ave SW *Web:* www.calgarychamber.com	Calgary	AB	T2P0P5	403-750-0400	266-3413
Alberta Chambers of Commerce 10025 - 102A Ave Suite 1808 Edmonton Ctr *TF:* 800-272-8854 ■ *Web:* www.abchamber.ca	Edmonton	AB	T5J2Z2	780-425-4180	429-1061
Edmonton Chamber of Commerce 9990 Jasper Ave Suite 700 *Web:* www.edmontonchamber.com	Edmonton	AB	T5J1P7	780-426-4620	424-7946
Fort McMurray Chamber of Commerce 9612 Franklin Ave Suite 304 *Web:* www.fortmcmurraychamber.ca	Fort McMurray	AB	T9H2J9	780-743-3100	790-9757
Grande Prairie & District Chamber of Commerce 11330 106th St Suite 217 *Web:* www.grandeprairiechamber.com	Grande Prairie	AB	T8V7X9	780-532-5340	532-2926
Lethbridge Chamber of Commerce 529 6th St S Suite 200 *Web:* lethbridgechamber.com	Lethbridge	AB	T1J2E1	403-327-1586	327-1001
Medicine Hat & District Chamber of Commerce 413 6th Ave SE *Web:* www.medicinehatchamber.com	Medicine Hat	AB	T1A2S7	403-527-5214	527-5182
Peace River Chamber of Commerce PO Box 6599 *Web:* www.peaceriverchamber.com	Peace River	AB	T8S1S4	780-624-4166	624-4663
Red Deer Chamber of Commerce 3017 Gaetz Ave. *Web:* www.reddeerchamber.com	Red Deer	AB	T4N5Y6	403-347-4491	343-6188

Organization	City	Prov	Postal Code	Phone	Fax
Saint Albert Chamber of Commerce 71 St Albert Rd *Web:* www.stalbertchamber.com	Saint Albert	AB	T8N6L5	780-458-2833	458-6515
Abbotsford Chamber of Commerce 32900 S Fraser Way Unit 207 *Web:* www.abbotsfordchamber.com	Abbotsford	BC	V2S5A1	604-859-9651	850-6880
Burnaby Board of Trade 4555 Kings Way Suite 201 *Web:* www.bbot.ca	Burnaby	BC	V5H4T8	604-412-0100	412-0102
Campbell River & District Chamber of Commerce 900 Alder St PO Box 400 *Web:* www.campbellriverchamber.ca	Campbell River	BC	V9W2P6	250-287-4636	286-6490
Chilliwack Chamber of Commerce 46093 Yale Rd Suite 201 *Web:* www.chilliwackchamber.com	Chilliwack	BC	V2P2L8	604-793-4323	793-4303
Tri-Cities Chamber of Commerce 1209 Pinetree Way *Web:* www.tricitieschamber.com	Coquitlam	BC	V3B7Y3	604-464-2716	464-6796
Comox Valley Chamber of Commerce 2040 Cliffe Ave *TF:* 888-357-4471 ■ *Web:* www.comoxvalleychamber.com	Courtenay	BC	V9N2L3	250-334-3234	334-4908
Delta Chamber of Commerce 6201 60th Ave *Web:* www.deltachamber.ca	Delta	BC	V4K4E2	604-946-4232	946-5285
Duncan Cowichan Chamber of Commerce 381 Trans Canada Hwy *Web:* duncancc.bc.ca	Duncan	BC	V9L3R5	250-748-1111	746-8222
Fort Saint John & District Chamber of Commerce 9325 100th St Suite 202 *Web:* www.fsjchamber.com	Fort Saint John	BC	V1J4N4	250-785-6037	785-6050
Kamloops Chamber of Commerce 1290 W Trans-Canada Hwy *Web:* www.kamloopschamber.bc.ca	Kamloops	BC	V2C6R3	250-372-7722	828-9500
Kelowna Chamber of Commerce 544 Harvey Ave *Web:* www.kelownachamber.org	Kelowna	BC	V1Y6C9	250-861-3627	861-3624
Langley Chamber of Commerce 5761 Glover Rd Unit 1 *Web:* www.langleychamber.com	Langley	BC	V3A8M8	604-530-6656	530-7066
Maple Ridge Chamber of Commerce 22238 Lougheed Hwy *Web:* www.ridgemeadowschamber.com	Maple Ridge	BC	V2X2T2	604-463-3366	463-3201
Mission Regional Chamber of Commerce 34033 Lougheed Hwy *Web:* www.missionchamber.bc.ca	Mission	BC	V2V5X8	604-826-6914	826-5916
Greater Nanaimo Chamber of Commerce 2133 Bowen Rd *Web:* www.nanaimochamber.bc.ca	Nanaimo	BC	V9S1H8	250-756-1191	756-1584
New Westminster Chamber of Commerce 601 Queens Ave *Web:* www.newwestchamber.com	New Westminster	BC	V3M1L1	604-521-7781	521-0057
North Vancouver Chamber of Commerce 124 W 1st St Suite 102 *TF:* 877-880-4699 ■ *Web:* www.nvchamber.bc.ca	North Vancouver	BC	V7M3N3	604-987-4488	987-8272
Parksville Chamber of Commerce (PDCC) PO Box 99 *Web:* www.parksvillechamber.com	Parksville	BC	V9P2G3	250-248-3613	248-5210
Penticton & Wine Country Chamber of Commerce 553 Railway St *TF:* 800-663-5052 ■ *Web:* www.penticton.org	Penticton	BC	V2A8S3	250-492-4103	492-6119
Alberni Valley Chamber of Commerce 2533 Port Alberni Hwy *Web:* www.avcoc.com	Port Alberni	BC	V9Y8P2	250-724-6535	724-6560
Prince George Chamber of Commerce 890 Vancouver St *Web:* www.pgchamber.bc.ca	Prince George	BC	V2L2P5	250-562-2454	562-6510
Richmond Chamber of Commerce 5811 Cooney Rd Suite 101 *Web:* www.richmondchamber.ca	Richmond	BC	V6X3M1	604-278-2822	278-2972
Saanich Peninsula Chamber of Commerce 209-2453 Beacon Ave *Web:* www.spcoc.org	Sidney	BC	V8L1X7	250-656-3616	656-7111
Surrey Board of Trade 14439 104th Ave Suite 101 *Web:* www.businessinsurrey.com	Surrey	BC	V3R1M1	604-581-7130	588-7549
British Columbia Chamber of Commerce 750 W Pender St Suite 1201 *Web:* www.bcchamber.org	Vancouver	BC	V6C2T8	604-683-0700	683-0416
Vancouver Board of Trade 999 Canada Pl Suite 400 *Web:* www.boardoftrade.com	Vancouver	BC	V6C3E1	604-681-2111	681-0437
Greater Vernon Chamber of Commerce 701 Hwy 97 S *Web:* www.vernonchamber.ca	Vernon	BC	V1B3W4	250-545-0771	545-3114
Greater Victoria Chamber of Commerce 852 Fort St Suite 100 *Web:* www.victoriachamber.ca	Victoria	BC	V8W1H8	250-383-7191	385-3552
West Shore Chamber of Commerce 2830 Aldwynd Rd *TF:* 877-912-1780 ■ *Web:* www.westshore.bc.ca	Victoria	BC	V9B3S7	250-478-1130	478-1584
West Vancouver Chamber of Commerce 1846 Marine Dr *TF:* 888-471-9996 ■ *Web:* www.westvanchamber.com	West Vancouver	BC	V7V1J6	604-926-6614	925-7220
Westbank & District Chamber of Commerce 2372 Dobbin Rd *TF:* 866-768-3378 ■ *Web:* www.westbankchamber.com	Westbank	BC	V4T2H9	250-768-3378	768-3465
Brandon Chamber of Commerce 1043 Rosser Ave *Web:* www.brandonchamber.ca	Brandon	MB	R7A0L5	204-571-5340	571-5347
Portage & District Chamber of Commerce 11 2nd St NE *Web:* www.portagechamber.com	Portage la Prairie	MB	R1N1R8	204-857-7778	857-4095
Saint-Boniface Chamber of Commerce 383 boul Provencher PO Box 204 *Web:* www.ccfsb.mb.ca	Saint-Boniface	MB	R2H3B4	204-235-1406	233-1017
Selkirk & District Chamber of Commerce (SDCC) 200 Eaton Ave *Web:* www.selkirkanddistrictchamber.ca	Selkirk	MB	R1A0W6	204-482-7176	482-5448
Manitoba Chambers of Commerce 227 Portage Ave *Web:* www.mbchamber.mb.ca	Winnipeg	MB	R3B2A6	204-948-0100	948-0110
Winnipeg Chamber of Commerce The 259 Portage Ave Suite 100 *Web:* www.winnipeg-chamber.com	Winnipeg	MB	R3B2A9	204-944-8484	944-8492
Enterprise Fredericton 570 Queen St Suite 102 *TF:* 800-200-1180 ■ *Web:* www.gfedc.nb.ca	Fredericton	NB	E3B6Z6	506-444-4686	444-4649
Fredericton Chamber of Commerce 270 Rookwood Rd PO Box 275 *Web:* www.frederictonchamber.ca	Fredericton	NB	E3B4Y9	506-458-8006	451-1119
Miramichi Chamber of Commerce PO Box 342 *Web:* www.greatermiramichi.com	Miramichi	NB	E1N3A7	506-622-5522	622-5959
Atlantic Provinces Chamber of Commerce 236 St George St Suite 21 *Web:* www.apcc.ca	Moncton	NB	E1C1W1	506-857-3980	859-6131
Greater Moncton Chamber of Commerce 910 Main St Suite 100 *Web:* www.gmcc.nb.ca	Moncton	NB	E1C1G6	506-857-2883	857-9209
Saint John Board of Trade (SJBT) 40 King St PO Box 6037 *Web:* www.sjboardoftrade.com	Saint John	NB	E2L4R5	506-634-8111	632-2008
Greater Corner Brook Board of Trade 11 Confederation Dr PO Box 475 *Web:* www.gcbbt.com	Corner Brook	NL	A2H6E6	709-634-5831	639-9710
Gander & Area Chamber of Commerce 109 Trans Canada Hwy *Web:* www.ganderchamber.nf.ca	Gander	NL	A1V1P6	709-256-7110	256-4080
Saint John's Board of Trade 34 Harvey Rd PO Box 5127 *Web:* www.bot.nf.ca	Saint John's	NL	A1C5V5	709-726-2961	726-2003
Northwest Territories Chamber of Commerce 4910 50th Ave YK Ctr PO Box 13 *Web:* www.nwtchamber.com	Yellowknife	NT	X1A3S5	867-920-9505	873-4174
Bridgewater & Area Chamber of Commerce 220 N St *Web:* www.bridgewaterchamber.com	Bridgewater	NS	B4V2V6	902-543-4263	543-1156
Metropolitan Halifax Chamber of Commerce 656 Windmill Rd Suite 200 *Web:* www.halifaxchamber.com	Dartmouth	NS	B3B1B8	902-468-7111	468-7333
Pictou County Chamber of Commerce 980 E River Rd *Web:* www.pictouchamber.com	New Glasgow	NS	B2H3S8	902-755-3463	755-2848
Sydney & Area Chamber of Commerce PO Box 131 *Web:* www.sydneyareachamber.ca	Sydney	NS	B1P6G9	902-564-6453	539-7487
Truro & District Chamber of Commerce 605 Prince St PO Box 54 *Web:* www.trurochamber.com	Truro	NS	B2N1G2	902-895-6328	897-6641
Yarmouth Chamber of Commerce 342 Main St Suite 1 PO Box 532 *Web:* www.yarmouthchamberofcommerce.com	Yarmouth	NS	B5A4B4	902-742-3074	749-1383
Aurora Chamber of Commerce 6-14845 Yonge St Suite 321 *Web:* www.aurorachamber.on.ca	Aurora	ON	L4G6H8	905-727-7262	841-6217
Greater Barrie Chamber of Commerce 97 Toronto St *Web:* www.barriechamber.com	Barrie	ON	L4N1V1	705-721-5000	726-0973
Belleville & District Chamber of Commerce 5 Moira St E *TF:* 888-852-9992 ■ *Web:* www.bellevillechamber.ca	Belleville	ON	K8N5B3	613-962-4597	962-3911
Caledon Chamber of Commerce PO Box 626 *Web:* www.caledonchamber.com	Bolton	ON	L7E5T5	905-857-7393	857-7405
Brampton Board of Trade 33 Queen St W 2nd Fl *Web:* www.bramptonbot.com	Brampton	ON	L6Y1L9	905-451-1122	450-0295
Brantford Brant Chamber of Commerce (BBCC) 77 Charlotte St *Web:* www.brantfordbrantchamber.com	Brantford	ON	N3T2W8	519-753-2617	753-0921
Burlington Chamber of Commerce 414 Locust St Suite 201 *Web:* www.burlingtonchamber.com	Burlington	ON	L7S1T7	905-639-0174	333-3956
Cambridge Chamber of Commerce 750 Hespeler Rd *TF:* 800-749-7560 ■ *Web:* www.cambridgechamber.com	Cambridge	ON	N3H5L8	519-622-2221	622-0662
Chatham-Kent Chamber of Commerce 54 4th St *Web:* www.chatham-kentchamber.ca	Chatham	ON	N7M2G2	519-352-7540	352-8741
Vaughan Chamber of Commerce 160 Applewood Crescent Unit 32 *TF:* 888-828-4426 ■ *Web:* www.vaughanchamber.ca	Concord	ON	L4K4H2	905-761-1366	761-1918
Cornwall & Area Chamber of Commerce 113 2nd St E *Web:* www.chamber.cornwall.on.ca	Cornwall	ON	K6J1Y5	613-933-4004	933-8466
Dryden District Chamber of Commerce 284 Government St *Web:* www.cityofdryden.on.ca	Dryden	ON	P8N2P3	807-223-2622	223-2626
Halton Hills Chamber of Commerce 328 Guelph St *Web:* www.haltonhillschamber.on.ca	Georgetown	ON	L7G4B5	905-877-5116	877-5117
Guelph Chamber of Commerce 485 Silver Creek Pkwy N Unit 15 *Web:* www.guelphchamber.com	Guelph	ON	N1H7K5	519-822-8081	822-8451
Hamilton Chamber of Commerce 555 Bay St N *Web:* www.hamiltonchamber.on.ca	Hamilton	ON	L8L1H1	905-522-1151	522-1154
Greater Kingston Chamber of Commerce 67 Brock St *Web:* www.kingstonchamber.on.ca	Kingston	ON	K7L1R8	613-548-4453	548-4743
Chamber of Commerce of Kitchener & Waterloo 80 Queen St N PO Box 2367 *TF:* 888-672-4282 ■ *Web:* www.greaterkwchamber.com	Kitchener	ON	N2H6L4	519-576-5000	742-4760

				Phone	Fax
Leamington District Chamber of Commerce PO Box 321	Leamington	ON	N8H3W3	519-326-2721	326-3204
TF: 800-250-3336 ■ *Web:* www.leamingtonchamber.com					
London Chamber of Commerce 244 Pall Mall St Suite 101	London	ON	N6A5P6	519-432-7551	432-8063
Web: www.londonchamber.com					
Markham Board of Trade 80 F Centurian Dr Suite 206	Markham	ON	L3R8C1	905-474-0730	474-0685
Web: www.markhamboard.com					
Southern Georgia Bay Chamber of Commerce 208 King St.	Midland	ON	L4R3L9	705-526-7884	526-1744
Web: www.southerngeorgianbay.on.ca					
Milton Chamber of Commerce 251 Main St E Suite 104	Milton	ON	L9T1P1	905-878-0581	878-4972
Web: www.miltonchamber.ca					
Mississauga Board of Trade 77 City Centre Dr Suite 701	Mississauga	ON	L5B1M5	905-273-6151	273-4937
Web: www.mbot.com					
Newmarket Chamber of Commerce 470 Davis Dr	Newmarket	ON	L3Y2P3	905-898-5900	853-7271
Web: www.newmarketchamber.com					
Niagara Falls Canada Chamber of Commerce 4056 Dorchester Rd	Niagara Falls	ON	L2E6M9	905-374-3666	374-2972
Web: www.niagarafallschamber.com					
North Bay & District Chamber of Commerce 1375 Seymour St PO Box 747	North Bay	ON	P1B8J8	705-472-8480	472-8027
TF: 888-249-8998 ■ *Web:* www.northbaychamber.com					
Oakville Chamber of Commerce 2521 Wyecroft Rd	Oakville	ON	L6L6P8	905-845-6613	845-6475
Web: www.oakvillechamber.com					
Greater Dufferin Area Chamber of Commerce PO Box 101	Orangeville	ON	L9W2Z5	519-941-0490	941-0492
Web: www.gdacc.ca					
Greater Oshawa Chamber of Commerce 44 Richmond St W Suite 100	Oshawa	ON	L1G1C7	905-728-1683	432-1259
Web: www.oshawachamber.com					
Canadian Chamber of Commerce 350 Albert St Suite 420	Ottawa	ON	K1R7X7	613-238-4000	238-7643
Web: www.chamber.ca					
Ottawa Chamber of Commerce 328 Somerset St W	Ottawa	ON	K2P0J9	613-236-3631	236-7498
Web: www.ottawachamber.ca					
Upper Ottawa Valley Chamber of Commerce 2 International Dr	Pembroke	ON	K8A6W5	613-732-1492	732-5793
Web: www.upperottawavalleychamber.com					
Perth & District Chamber of Commerce 34 Herriott St	Perth	ON	K7H1T2	613-267-3200	267-6797
Web: www.perthchamber.com					
Greater Peterborough Chamber of Commerce 175 George St N	Peterborough	ON	K9J3G6	705-748-9771	743-2331
TF: 877-640-4037 ■ *Web:* www.peterboroughchamber.ca					
Port Colborne-Wainfleet Chamber of Commerce 76 Main St W	Port Colborne	ON	L3K3V2	905-834-9765	834-1542
Web: www.pcwchamber.com					
Richmond Hill Chamber of Commerce (RHCOC) 376 Church St S	Richmond Hill	ON	L4C9V8	905-884-1961	884-1962
Web: www.rhcoc.com					
Saint Catharines Chamber of Commerce 1 St Paul St Ste103 PO Box 940	Saint Catharines	ON	L2R6Z4	905-684-2361	684-2100
Web: www.sctchamber.com					
Saint Thomas & District Chamber of Commerce 555 Talbot St.	Saint Thomas	ON	N5P1C5	519-631-1981	631-0466
Web: www.stthomaschamber.on.ca					
Sault Sainte Marie Chamber of Commerce 334 Bay St	Sault Sainte Marie	ON	P6A1X1	705-949-7152	759-8166
Web: www.ssmcoc.com					
Scarborough Chamber of Commerce 940 Progress Ave	Scarborough	ON	M1G3T5	416-439-4140	439-4147
Web: www.scarboroughchamber.com					
Timmins Chamber of Commerce PO Box 985	Schumacher	ON	P4N7H6	705-360-1900	360-1193
Web: www.timminschamber.on.ca					
Simcoe & District Chamber of Commerce 95 Queensway W	Simcoe	ON	N3Y2M8	519-426-5867	428-7718
Web: www.simcoechamber.on.ca					
Stratford & District Chamber of Commerce 55 Lorne Ave E	Stratford	ON	N5A6S4	519-273-5250	273-2229
Web: www.stratfordchamber.com					
Greater Sudbury Chamber of Commerce 40 Elm St Suite 1	Sudbury	ON	P3C1S8	705-673-7133	673-2944
Web: www.sudburychamber.ca					
Thunder Bay Chamber of Commerce 200 Syndicated Ave S Suite 102	Thunder Bay	ON	P7E1C9	807-624-2626	622-7752
Web: www.tb-chamber.on.ca					
Canadian Chamber of Commerce Toronto Office 55 University Ave Suite 901	Toronto	ON	M5J2H7	416-868-6415	868-0189
Web: www.chamber.ca					
Ontario Chamber of Commerce 180 Dundas St W Suite 505	Toronto	ON	M5G1Z8	416-482-5222	482-5879
Web: www.occ.on.ca					
Flamborough Chamber of Commerce PO Box 1030	Waterdown	ON	L0R2H0	905-689-7650	689-1313
Web: www.flamboroughchamber.ca					
Welland/Pelham Chamber of Commerce 32 E Main St.	Welland	ON	L3B3W3	905-732-7515	732-7175
Web: www.chamber.iaw.com					
Whitby Chamber of Commerce 128 Brock St S	Whitby	ON	L1N4J8	905-668-4506	668-1894
Web: www.whitbychamber.org					
Windsor & District Chamber of Commerce 2575 Ouellette Pl	Windsor	ON	N8X1L9	519-966-3696	966-0603
Web: www.windsorchamber.org					
Woodstock District Chamber of Commerce 425 Dundas St Suite 3	Woodstock	ON	N4S1B8	519-539-9411	456-1611
Web: www.woodstockchamber.on.ca					
Greater Charlottetown Area Chamber of Commerce PO Box 67	Charlottetown	PE	C1A7K2	902-628-2000	368-3570
Web: www.charlottetownchamber.com					
La Chambre de Commerce de Drummond 234 Rue St Marcel CP 188	Drummondville	QC	J2B6V7	819-477-7822	477-2823
Web: www.ccid.qc.ca					
Chambre de Commerce Haute-Yamaska Region (CDCHY) 650 Rue Principale	Granby	QC	J2G8L4	450-372-6100	372-3161
Web: www.chambredecommerce.org					
Laval Chamber of Commerce 1555 boul Chomedey Suite 200	Laval	QC	H7V3Z1	450-682-5255	682-5735
Web: www.ccilaval.qc.ca					
Mont-Laurier Chamber of Commerce 445 Rue Du Pont	Mont-Laurier	QC	J9L2R8	819-623-3642	623-5220
Web: www.ccmont-laurier.com					
Board of Trade of Metropolitan Montreal 380 St Antoine St W Suite 6000	Montreal	QC	H2Y3X7	514-871-4000	871-1255
Web: www.btmm.qc.ca/en					
Canadian Chamber of Commerce Montreal Office 1155 University St Suite 709	Montreal	QC	H3B3A7	514-866-4334	866-7296
Web: www.chamber.ca					
Chambre de Commerce du Quebec 249 Rue St Jacques Bureau 302	Montreal	QC	H2Y1M6	514-522-1885	522-9468
TF: 888-595-8110 ■ *Web:* www.ccquebec.ca					
Chambre de Commerce et d'Industrie du Quebec Metropolitain 17 St Louis St	Quebec	QC	G1R3Y8	418-692-3853	694-2286
Web: www.ccquebec.ca					
Haut-Richelieu Chamber of Commerce 315 Rue MacDonald Bureau 232	Saint-Jean-sur-Richelieu	QC	J3B8J3	450-346-2544	346-3812
Web: www.cchautrichelieu.qc.ca					
Sept-Iles Chamber of Commerce 700 boul Laure Bureau 237	Sept-Iles	QC	G4R1Y1	418-968-3488	968-3432
Web: www.ccseptiles.com					
Chambre de Commerce de la Region Sherbrookoise 75 Rue Welligton N Suite 402	Sherbrooke	QC	J1H5A9	819-822-6151	822-6156
Web: www.ccsherbrooke.ca					
Trois-Rivieres & District Chamber of Commerce 168 Rue Bonaventure CP 1045	Trois-Rivieres	QC	G9A5K4	819-375-9628	375-9083
Web: www.ccdtr.com					
Moose Jaw & District Chamber of Commerce 88 Saskatchewan St E	Moose Jaw	SK	S6H0V4	306-692-6414	694-6463
Web: www.mjchamber.com					
Battlefords Chamber of Commerce PO Box 1000	North Battleford	SK	S9A3E6	306-445-6226	445-6633
Web: www.battlefordschamber.com					
Prince Albert & District Chamber of Commerce 1084 Central Ave Suite 347	Prince Albert	SK	S6V7P3	306-764-6222	922-4727
Web: www.thechamberofcom.com					
Regina Chamber of Commerce 2145 Albert St	Regina	SK	S4P2V1	306-757-4658	757-4668
Web: www.reginachamber.com					
Greater Saskatoon Chamber of Commerce 345 3rd Ave S	Saskatoon	SK	S7K1M6	306-244-2151	244-8366
Web: www.eboardoftrade.com					
Whitehorse Chamber of Commerce 302 Steele St Suite 101	Whitehorse	YT	Y1A2C5	867-667-7545	667-4507
Web: www.whitehorsechamber.com					
Yukon Chamber of Commerce 307 Jarvis St Suite 101	Whitehorse	YT	Y1A2H3	867-667-2000	667-2001
Web: www.yukonchamber.com					

138 CHAMBERS OF COMMERCE - INTERNATIONAL

SEE ALSO Chambers of Commerce - Canadian p. 1562

Included Here Are Organizations That Work To Promote Business And Trade Relationships Between The United States And Other Countries.

				Phone	Fax
African Chamber of Commerce Dallas/Fort Worth 1402 Coringh St Suite 249	Dallas	TX	75215	214-421-6155	421-6158
Web: www.africanchamberdfw.org					
America-Israel Chamber of Commerce & Industry (AICCI) 70 W 36 St Suite 700	New York	NY	10018	646-467-8037	365-3366
Web: www.aicci.net					
America-Israel Chamber of Commerce - Chicago 247 S State St 15th Fl.	Chicago	IL	60604	312-235-0586	641-0724
Web: www.americaisrael.org					
American Egyptian Cooperation Foundation 28 E Jackson Blvd Suite 809	Chicago	IL	60604	312-427-9368	
Web: www.americanegyptiancoop.org					
American Egyptian Cooperation Foundation 1535 W Loop S Suite 200	Houston	TX	77027	713-624-7113	
Web: www.americanegyptiancoop.org					
American Egyptian Cooperation Foundation 235 E 40th St # 22A	New York	NY	10016	212-867-2323	697-0465
Web: www.americanegyptiancoop.org					
American Egyptian Cooperation Foundation 870 Market St Suite 855	San Francisco	CA	94102	347-470-4622	
Web: www.americanegyptiancoop.org					
American-Indonesian Chamber of Commerce 317 Madison Ave Suite 1619	New York	NY	10017	212-687-4505	687-5844
Web: www.aiccusa.org					
American-Israel Chamber of Commerce & Industry of Minnesota 13100 Wayzata Blvd Suite 130	Minnetonka	MN	55305	952-593-8666	593-8668
Web: www.aiccmn.org/index.html					
American-Israel Chamber of Commerce Southeast Region 1150 Lake Hearn Dr Suite 650	Atlanta	GA	30342	404-843-9426	843-1416
Web: www.aiccse.org					
American-Russian Chamber of Commerce & Industry 1101 Pennsylvania Ave NW 6th Fl	Washington	DC	20004	202-756-4943	362-4634
Web: www.arcci.org					

Organization / Address	City	State	ZIP	Phone	Fax
Argentine-American Chamber of Commerce Inc 630 5th Ave 25th Fl *Web:* www.argentinechamber.org	New York	NY	10111	212-698-2238	698-2239
Assn of American Chambers of Commerce in Latin America 1615 H St NW 3rd Fl *Web:* www.aaccla.org	Washington	DC	20062	202-463-5485	463-3126
Australian American Chamber of Commerce of Houston 2400 Augusta Suite 426 *Fax Area Code: 832 ■ *Web:* www.aacc-houston.org	Houston	TX	77057	713-527-9688	415-0545*
Australian New Zealand American Chambers of Commerce 28150 N Alma School Pkwy Suite 103-250 *Web:* www.usa.embassy.gov.au/whwh/AACCinUS.html	Scottsdale	AZ	85262	480-784-7377	
Australian-American Chamber of Commerce - San Francisco PO Box 210508 *Web:* www.sfaussies.com	San Francisco	CA	94121	415-485-6718	345-1766
Australian-American Chamber of Commerce of Hawaii 1000 Bishop St *Web:* aacchawaii.org	Honolulu	HI	96813	808-526-2242	534-0475
Belgian-American Chamber of Commerce in the US (BACC) 101 Hudson St 21st Fl *Web:* www.belcham.org	Jersey City	NJ	07302	201-631-8065	631-8067
Brazilian-American Chamber of Commerce Inc 509 Madison Ave Suite 304 *Web:* www.brazilcham.com	New York	NY	10022	212-751-4691	751-7692
Brazilian-American Chamber of Commerce of Florida PO Box 310038 *Web:* www.brazilchamber.org	Miami	FL	33231	305-579-9030	579-9756
Brazilian-American Chamber of Commerce of Southeast Inc PO Box 93411 *Web:* www.bacc-ga.com	Atlanta	GA	30377	404-880-1551	880-1555
British-American Business Council (BABC) 52 Vanderbilt Ave 20th Fl *Web:* www.babc.org	New York	NY	10017	212-661-4060	661-4074
British-American Business Council of Los Angeles 11766 Wilshire Blvd Suite 1230 *Web:* www.babcla.org	Los Angeles	CA	90025	310-312-1962	312-1914
British-American Chamber of Commerce Great Lakes Region 1120 Chester Ave Suite 470 *Web:* www.baccgl.org	Cleveland	OH	44114	216-621-0222	696-2582
British-American Chamber of Commerce of Miami 200 S Biscayne Blvd Suite 4143	Miami	FL	33131	305-377-0992	448-7605
British-American Chamber of Commerce of San Francisco 703 Market St # 1314 *Web:* www.baccsf.org	San Francisco	CA	94103	415-296-8645	296-9649
Central American Chamber of Commerce 1395 Brickell Ave 13th Fl	Miami	FL	33131	305-569-9113	735-2445
Chile-US Chamber of Commerce 800 Brickell Ave Suite 900 *Fax Area Code: 305 ■ *Web:* www.chileus.org	Miami	FL	33131	786-419-2092	374-4270*
Chinese Chamber of Commerce of Hawaii 8 S King St *Web:* www.chinesechamber.com	Honolulu	HI	96817	808-533-3181	533-6967
Chinese Chamber of Commerce of Los Angeles 977 N Broadway Ground Fl Suite E *Web:* www.lachinesechamber.org	Los Angeles	CA	90012	213-617-0396	617-2128
Chinese Chamber of Commerce of San Francisco 730 Sacramento St	San Francisco	CA	94108	415-982-3000	982-4720
Colombian American Chamber of Commerce 250 Catalonia Ave Suite 407 *Web:* www.colombiachamber.com	Coral Gables	FL	33134	305-446-2542	446-2038
Danish-American Chamber of Commerce 885 2nd Ave 18th Fl *Web:* www.daccny.com	New York	NY	10017	212-705-4945	754-1904
Ecuadorian-American Chamber of Commerce of Greater Miami 1390 Brickell Ave Suite 220 *Web:* www.ecuachamber.com	Miami	FL	33131	305-539-0010	539-8001
European-American Business Council 919 18th St NW Suite 220 *Web:* www.eabc.org	Washington	DC	20006	202-828-9104	828-9106
Finnish American Chamber of Commerce Inc 866 United Nations Plaza Suite 250 *Web:* www.facc-ny.com	New York	NY	10017	212-821-0225	750-4418
Finnish-American Chamber of Commerce on the Pacific Coast PO Box 3058 *Web:* www.faccpacific.com	Tustin	CA	92781	714-573-0604	242-9153
French American Chamber of Commerce - Louisiana Chapter PO Box 57255 *Web:* www.facc-la.com	New Orleans	LA	70157	504-458-3528	865-0323
French-American Chamber of Commerce of Atlanta 3399 Peachtree Rd NE Suite 500 *Web:* www.facc-atlanta.com	Atlanta	GA	30326	404-997-6800	997-6810
French-American Chamber of Commerce of Chicago (FACC) 35 E Wacker Dr Suite 670 *Web:* www.facc-chicago.com	Chicago	IL	60601	312-578-0444	578-0445
French-American Chamber of Commerce of Dallas 2665 Villa Creek Dr Suite 214 *Web:* www.faccdallas.com	Dallas	TX	75234	972-241-0111	241-0901
French-American Chamber of Commerce of Florida 168 SE First St Suite 1102 *Web:* www.faccmiami.com	Miami	FL	33131	305-374-5000	358-8203
French-American Chamber of Commerce of Houston 5373 W Alabama St Suite 209 *Web:* www.facchouston.com	Houston	TX	77056	713-960-0575	960-0495
French-American Chamber of Commerce of Los Angeles 8222 Melrose Ave Suite 203 *Web:* www.frenchchamberla.org	Los Angeles	CA	90046	323-651-4741	651-2547
French-American Chamber of Commerce of New York 122 E 42nd St Suite 2015 *Web:* www.ccife.org	New York	NY	10168	212-867-0123	867-9050
French-American Chamber of Commerce of Philadelphia (FACC) 1528 Walnut St Suite 2020 *Web:* www.faccphila.org	Philadelphia	PA	19102	215-545-0123	545-0144
French-American Chamber of Commerce of San Francisco 26 O'Farrell St Suite 500 *Web:* www.faccsf.com	San Francisco	CA	94108	415-442-4717	442-4621
French-American Chamber of Commerce of the Pacific Northwest 2200 Alaskan Way Suite 490 *Web:* www.ccife.org	Seattle	WA	98121	206-443-4703	448-4218
German-American Chamber of Commerce Inc 75 Broad St 21st Fl *Web:* www.gaccny.com	New York	NY	10004	212-974-8830	974-8867
German-American Chamber of Commerce Inc - Philadelphia 1617 John F Kennedy Blvd Suite 340 1 Penn Ctr *Web:* www.gaccphiladelphia.com	Philadelphia	PA	19103	215-665-1585	665-0375
German-American Chamber of Commerce of the Midwest Inc 321 N Clark St Suite 1425 *Web:* www.gaccom.org	Chicago	IL	60654	312-644-2662	644-0738
German-American Chamber of Commerce of the Southern US Inc 1170 Howell Mill Rd #300 *Web:* www.gaccsouth.com	Atlanta	GA	30318	404-586-6800	586-6820
Hellenic-American Chamber of Commerce 780 3rd Ave 16th Fl *Web:* www.hellenicamerican.cc	New York	NY	10017	212-629-6380	564-9281
Honolulu-Japanese Chamber of Commerce 2454 S Beretania St Suite 201 *Web:* www.honolulujapanesechamber.org	Honolulu	HI	96826	808-949-5531	949-3020
Icelandic-American Chamber of Commerce 800 3rd Ave 36th Fl *Web:* www.iceland.org/us/nyc/consulate-general/chamber-of-commerce	New York	NY	10022	212-593-2700	593-6269
Ireland Chamber of Commerce in the US 556 Central Ave *Web:* www.iccusa.org	New Providence	NJ	07974	908-286-1300	286-1200
Italian American Chamber of Commerce of Chicago 30 S Michigan Ave Suite 504 *Web:* www.italianchamber.us	Chicago	IL	60603	312-553-9137	553-9142
Italy-America Chamber of Commerce Inc 730 5th Ave Suite 600 *Web:* www.italchamber.org	New York	NY	10019	212-459-0044	459-0090
Italy-America Chamber of Commerce of Texas Inc 1800 W Loop S Suite 1120 *Web:* www.iacctexas.com	Houston	TX	77027	713-626-9303	626-9309
Italy-America Chamber of Commerce Southeast Inc 2 S Biscayne Blvd # 1880 *Web:* www.iacc-miami.com	Miami	FL	33131	305-577-9868	577-3956
Italy-America Chamber of Commerce West Inc 10537 Santa Monica Blvd # 210 *Web:* www.italchambers.net	Los Angeles	CA	90025	310-557-3017	557-1217
Japanese Chamber of Commerce & Industry of Chicago 541 N Fairbanks Ct Suite 2050 *Web:* www.jccc-chi.org/en	Chicago	IL	60611	312-245-8344	245-8355
Japanese Chamber of Commerce & Industry of Hawaii 400 Hualani St Suite 20B	Hilo	HI	96720	808-934-0177	934-0178
Japanese Chamber of Commerce & Industry of New York Inc 145 W 57th St 6th Fl *Web:* www.jcciny.org	New York	NY	10019	212-246-8001	246-8002
Japanese Chamber of Commerce of Northern California 1875 S Grant St Suite 760 *Web:* www.jccnc.org	San Mateo	CA	94402	650-522-8500	522-8300
Korean Chamber of Commerce 3435 Wilshire Blvd # 2450	Los Angeles	CA	90010	213-480-1115	480-7521
Korean Chamber of Commerce & Industry in the USA Inc 460 Park Ave Suite 410 *Web:* www.kocham.org	New York	NY	10022	212-644-0140	644-9106
Latin Chamber of Commerce of the US (CAMACOL) 1417 W Flagler St *Web:* www.camacol.org	Miami	FL	33135	305-642-3870	642-0653
Luxembourg-American Chamber of Commerce 17 Beekman Pl *Web:* www.luxembourgbusiness.org	New York	NY	10022	212-888-6701	935-5896
National US-Arab Chamber of Commerce 8921 S Sepulveda Blvd Suite 206 *Web:* www.nusacc.org	Los Angeles	CA	90045	310-646-1499	646-2462
National US-Arab Chamber of Commerce 1023 15th St NW Suite 400 *Web:* www.nusacc.org	Washington	DC	20005	202-289-5920	289-5938
National US-Arab Chamber of Commerce 420 Lexington Ave Suite 2034 *Web:* www.nusacc.org	New York	NY	10170	212-986-8024	986-0216
National US-Arab Chamber of Commerce 1330 Post Oak Blvd Suite 1600 *Web:* www.nusacc.org	Houston	TX	77056	713-963-4620	963-4609
Netherlands Chamber of Commerce in the US Inc 267 5th Ave Suite 301 *Web:* www.netherlands.org	New York	NY	10016	212-265-6460	265-6402
Nicaraguan-American Chamber of Commerce PO Box 310835 *Web:* www.naccflorida.com	Miami	FL	33231	305-776-3206	
Norwegian-American Chamber of Commerce Inc 835 3rd Ave 38th Fl *Web:* www.nacc.no	New York	NY	10022	212-421-1655	838-0374
Norwegian-American Chamber of Commerce Inc The PO Box 583782 *Fax Area Code: 212 ■ *Web:* www.naccminneapolis.org	Minneapolis	MN	55458	612-859-8927	681-3900*
Norwegian-American Chamber of Commerce Inc The 655 Third Ave Suite 1810 *Web:* www.naccusa.org	New York	NY	10017	212-885-9737	885-9710
Norwegian-American Chamber of Commerce Southern California Chapter PO Box 3251 *Web:* www.naccla.org	Thousand Oaks	CA	91359	818-735-0019	735-0032
Norwegian-American Chamber of Commerce Southwest Chapter (NACC) 5219 Pine Arbor Dr *Web:* www.nacchouston.org	Houston	TX	77066	281-537-6879	587-9284

Organization / Address	City	State	Zip	Phone	Fax
Peruvian American Chamber of Commerce 7600 S Red Rd Suite 304 *Web:* www.peruvianchamber.org	South Miami	FL	33143	305-661-8288	
Philippine American Chamber of Commerce Inc The 317 Madison Ave Suite 520 *Web:* www.philamchamber.org	New York	NY	10017	212-972-9326	687-5844
Portugal-US Chamber of Commerce 590 5th Ave 4th Fl *Web:* www.portugal-us.com	New York	NY	10036	212-354-4627	575-4737
Puerto Rican Chamber of Commerce of South Florida 3550 Biscayne Blvd Suite 306 *Web:* www.puertoricanchamber.com	Miami	FL	33137	305-571-8007	571-8007
Representative of German Industry & Trade 1776 I St NW # 1000 *Web:* www.rgit-usa.com	Washington	DC	20006	202-659-4777	659-4779
Russian Americans Chamber of Commerce 28 E County Line Rd *Web:* www.rachamber.com	Feasterville	PA	19053	215-396-9001	396-8388
Spain-US Chamber of Commerce 350 5th Ave Suite 2600 *Web:* www.spainuscc.org	New York	NY	10118	212-967-2170	564-1415
Swedish-American Chamber of Commerce Atlanta Inc 4775 Peachtree Industrial Blvd Bldg 300 Suite 300 *Web:* www.sacc-atlanta.org	Norcross	GA	30092	770-670-2480	670-2500
Swedish-American Chamber of Commerce Chicago Inc 150 N Michigan Ave Suite 2800 *Web:* www.sacc-usa.org/chicago	Chicago	IL	60601	312-863-8592	624-7701
Swedish-American Chamber of Commerce Inc Minnesota Chapter American Swedish Institute 2600 Park Ave *Web:* www.sacc-minnesota.org	Minneapolis	MN	55407	612-991-3001	
Swedish-American Chamber of Commerce Inc New York Chapter 570 Lexington Ave 20th Fl *Web:* www.saccny.org	New York	NY	10022	212-838-5530	755-7953
Swedish-American Chamber of Commerce New England 253 Summer St Suite 203 *Web:* www.sacc-ne.org	Boston	MA	02210	617-395-8534	
Swedish-American Chamber of Commerce of Colorado Inc 1720 S Bellaire St Suite 310 *Web:* sacc-usa.org	Denver	CO	80222	720-515-9421	889-2606
Swedish-American Chamber of Commerce San Diego 9710 Scranton Rd Suite 160 *Web:* www.sacc-sandiego.org	San Diego	CA	92121	858-729-8819	598-4809
Swedish-American Chamber of Commerce San Francisco/Silicon Valley 452 Tehama St *Web:* www.sacc-sf.org	San Francisco	CA	94104	415-781-4188	781-4189
Swedish-American Chamber of Commerce Washington DC INC 2900 K St NW *Web:* sacc-usa.org	Washington	DC	20007	202-536-1570	
Swedish-American Chambers of Commerce of the Utah Inc 200 S Peyton St Second Fl *Web:* www.sacc-usa.org	Alexandria	VA	22314	703-836-6560	836-6561
Swiss-American Chamber of Commerce *New York Chapter* 500 5th Ave Rm 1800 *Web:* www.amcham.ch	New York	NY	10110	212-246-7789	246-1366
US Federation of Philippine American Chambers of Commerce 2887 College Ave Suite 1 PO Box 106 *Web:* www.fpacc.com	Berkeley	CA	94705	510-548-7952	
US-Angola Chamber of Commerce 1100 17th St NW Suite 1000 *Web:* www.us-angola.org	Washington	DC	20036	202-857-0789	223-0551
US-Austrian Chamber of Commerce 165 W 46th St *Web:* www.usatchamber.com	New York	NY	10036	212-819-0117	819-0345
US-Mexico Chamber of Commerce 1300 Pennsylvania Ave NW Suite 0003 *Web:* www.usmcoc.org	Washington	DC	20004	202-312-1520	312-1530
US-Mexico Chamber of Commerce California Pacific Chapter 2450 Colorado Ave Suite 400E *Web:* www.usmcocca.org	Santa Monica	CA	90404	310-586-7901	586-7800
US-Mexico Chamber of Commerce Inter-American Chapter 1441 Brickell Ave Suite 1400 *Web:* www.usmcoc.org	Miami	FL	33131	305-374-7401	374-7405
USA-China Chamber of Commerce 55 W Monroe St Suite 630 *Web:* www.usccc.org	Chicago	IL	60603	312-368-9911	368-9922
Venezuelan-American Chamber of Commerce of the US 1600 Ponce de Leon Suite 1004 *Web:* venezuelanchamber.org	Coral Gables	FL	33134	786-350-1190	350-1191
Vietnamese-American Chamber of Commerce of Hawaii PO Box 2011 *Web:* www.vacch.org	Honolulu	HI	96805	808-545-1889	734-2315

139 CHAMBERS OF COMMERCE - US - LOCAL

SEE ALSO Civic & Political Organizations p. 1417

Chambers Listed Here Represent Areas With A Population Of 25,000 Or More. Listings Are Organized By States And Then Are Alphabetized Within Each State Grouping According To The Name Of The City In Which Each Chamber Is Located.

ALABAMA

Organization / Address	City	State	Zip	Phone	Fax
Alexander City Chamber of Commerce 120 Tallapoosa St *Web:* www.alexandercity.org	Alexander City	AL	35010	256-234-3461	234-0094
Calhoun County Chamber of Commerce 1330 Quintard Ave *TF:* 800-489-1087 ■ *Web:* www.calhounchamber.com	Anniston	AL	36201	256-237-3536	237-0126
Greater Limestone County Chamber of Commerce 101 S Beaty St *TF:* 866-953-6565 ■ *Web:* www.tourathens.com	Athens	AL	35611	256-232-2600	232-2609
Auburn Chamber of Commerce 714 E Glenn Ave PO Box 1370 *Web:* www.auburnchamber.com	Auburn	AL	36831	334-887-7011	821-5500
North Baldwin Chamber of Commerce 301 McMeans Ave *Web:* www.northbaldwinchamber.com	Bay Minette	AL	36507	251-937-5665	937-5670
Bessemer Area Chamber of Commerce 321 N 18th St *TF:* 888-423-7736 ■ *Web:* www.bessemerchamber.com	Bessemer	AL	35020	205-425-3253	425-4979
Birmingham Business Alliance 505 N 20th St Suite 200 *Web:* www.birminghamchamber.com	Birmingham	AL	35203	205-241-8100	324-2560
Chilton County Chamber of Commerce 500 5th Ave N *TF:* 800-553-0493 ■ *Web:* www.chiltoncountychamber.com	Clanton	AL	35045	205-755-2400	755-8444
Cullman Area Chamber of Commerce 301 2nd Ave SW *TF:* 800-313-5114 ■ *Web:* www.cullmanchamber.org	Cullman	AL	35055	256-734-0454	737-7443
Eastern Shore Chamber of Commerce 29750 Larry Dee Cawyer Dr PO Box 310 *Web:* www.eschamber.com	Daphne	AL	36526	251-621-8222	621-8001
Decatur-Morgan County Chamber of Commerce 515 6th Ave NE *TF:* 800-353-0005 ■ *Web:* www.dcc.org	Decatur	AL	35601	256-353-5312	353-2384
Dothan Area Chamber of Commerce 102 Jamestown Blvd *TF:* 800-221-1027 ■ *Web:* www.dothan.com	Dothan	AL	36301	334-792-5138	794-4796
Eufaula/Barbour County Chamber of Commerce 333 E Broad St *TF:* 800-524-7529 ■ *Web:* www.eufaula-barbourchamber.com	Eufaula	AL	36027	334-687-6664	687-5240
Shoals Chamber of Commerce 20 Hightower Pl *TF:* 877-764-4661 ■ *Web:* www.shoalschamber.com	Florence	AL	35630	256-764-4661	766-9017
South Baldwin Chamber of Commerce 104 N McKenzie St *Web:* www.southbaldwinchamber.com	Foley	AL	36535	251-943-3291	943-6810
Gadsden & Etowah County Chamber 1 Commerce Sq *TF:* 800-238-6924 ■ *Web:* www.gadsdenchamber.com	Gadsden	AL	35901	256-543-3472	543-9887
Greenville Area Chamber of Commerce 1 Depot Sq *TF:* 800-959-0717	Greenville	AL	36037	334-382-3251	382-3181
Hoover Chamber of Commerce PO Box 36005 *Web:* www.hooverchamber.org	Hoover	AL	35236	205-988-5672	988-8383
Chamber of Commerce of Huntsville/Madison County 225 Church St *Web:* www.huntsvillealabamausa.com	Huntsville	AL	35801	256-535-2000	535-2015
Walker County Chamber of Commerce 204 19th St E Suite 101 *TF:* 888-384-4571 ■ *Web:* www.walkerchamber.us	Jasper	AL	35501	205-384-4571	384-4901
Greater Valley Area Chamber of Commerce 2102 S Broad Ave PO Box 205 *Web:* www.greatervalleyarea.com	Lanett	AL	36863	334-642-1411	642-1410
Mobile Area Chamber of Commerce 451 Government St *TF:* 800-422-6951 ■ *Web:* www.mobilechamber.com	Mobile	AL	36602	251-433-6951	432-1143
Monroeville Area Chamber of Commerce 63 N Mt Pleasant Ave *Web:* www.monroecountyal.com	Monroeville	AL	36460	251-743-2879	743-2189
Montgomery Area Chamber of Commerce 41 Commerce St PO Box 79 *Web:* www.montgomerychamber.com	Montgomery	AL	36104	334-834-5200	265-4745
Lawrence County Chamber of Commerce 12001 Alabama 157 *Web:* www.lawrencealabama.com	Moulton	AL	35650	256-974-1658	974-2400
Blount County-Oneonta Chamber of Commerce 225 2nd Ave E *Web:* www.blountoneontachamber.org	Oneonta	AL	35121	205-274-2153	274-2099
Ozark Area Chamber of Commerce 294 Painter Ave *TF:* 800-582-8497 ■ *Web:* www.ozarkalchamber.com	Ozark	AL	36360	334-774-9321	774-8736
Greater Shelby County Chamber of Commerce 1301 County Services Dr *Web:* www.shelbychamber.org	Pelham	AL	35124	205-663-4542	663-4524
Phenix City-Russell County Chamber of Commerce 1107 Broad St *TF:* 800-892-2248 ■ *Web:* www.pc-rcchamber.com	Phenix City	AL	36867	334-298-3639	298-3846
Franklin County Chamber of Commerce 103 N Jackson Ave *Web:* www.franklincountychamber.org	Russellville	AL	35653	256-332-1760	332-1740
Greater Jackson County Chamber of Commerce PO Box 973 *TF:* 800-259-5508 ■ *Web:* www.jacksoncountychamber.com	Scottsboro	AL	35768	256-259-5500	259-4447
Selma-Dallas County Chamber of Commerce 912 Selma Ave *TF:* 800-457-3562 ■ *Web:* www.selmaalabama.com	Selma	AL	36701	334-875-7241	875-7142
Greater Talladega Area Chamber of Commerce 210 East St S PO Box A *Web:* www.talladegachamber.com	Talladega	AL	35160	256-362-9075	362-9093
Pike County Chamber of Commerce 246 US Highway 231 N	Troy	AL	36081	334-566-2294	566-2298
Chamber of Commerce of West Alabama 2200 University Blvd *Web:* www.tuscaloosachamber.com	Tuscaloosa	AL	35401	205-758-7588	391-0565

ALASKA

Organization / Address	City	State	Zip	Phone	Fax
Anchorage Chamber of Commerce 1016 W 6th Ave Suite 303 *Web:* www.anchoragechamber.org	Anchorage	AK	99501	907-272-2401	272-4117
Chugiak-Eagle River Chamber of Commerce 11401 Old Glenn Hwy Suite 105 *Web:* www.cer.org	Eagle River	AK	99577	907-694-4702	694-1205

	City	State	ZIP	Phone	Fax
Fairbanks Chamber of Commerce 100 Cushman St Suite 102 *Web:* www.fairbankschamber.org	Fairbanks	AK	99701	907-452-1105	456-6968
Juneau Chamber of Commerce 3100 Ch Dr Suite 300 *Web:* www.juneauchamber.com	Juneau	AK	99801	907-463-3488	463-3489

ARIZONA

	City	State	ZIP	Phone	Fax
Apache Junction Chamber of Commerce 567 W Apache Trail *TF:* 800-252-3141 ■ *Web:* www.apachejunctioncoc.com	Apache Junction	AZ	85220	480-982-3141	982-3234
Bullhead Area Chamber of Commerce 1251 Hwy 95 *TF:* 800-987-7457 ■ *Web:* www.bullheadchamber.com	Bullhead City	AZ	86429	928-754-4121	754-5514
Chandler Chamber of Commerce 25 S Arizona Pl Suite 201 *TF:* 800-963-4571 ■ *Web:* www.chandlerchamber.com	Chandler	AZ	85225	480-963-4571	963-0188
Cottonwood Chamber of Commerce 1010 S Main St *Web:* www.cottonwoodchamberaz.org	Cottonwood	AZ	86326	928-634-7593	634-7594
Flagstaff Chamber of Commerce 101 W Rt 66 *Web:* www.flagstaffchamber.com	Flagstaff	AZ	86001	928-774-4505	779-1209
Gilbert Chamber of Commerce 119 N Gilbert Rd Suite 101 PO Box 527 **Fax Area Code:* 602 ■ *Web:* www.gilbertaz.com	Gilbert	AZ	85299	480-892-0056	892-1980*
Glendale Chamber of Commerce 7105 N 59th Ave *TF:* 800-437-8669 ■ *Web:* www.glendaleazchamber.org	Glendale	AZ	85301	623-937-4754	937-3333
Southwest Valley Chamber of Commerce 289 N Litchfield Rd *Web:* www.southwestvalleychamber.org	Goodyear	AZ	85338	623-932-2260	932-9057
Kingman Area Chamber of Commerce 120 W Andy Devine Ave *Web:* www.kingmanchamber.org	Kingman	AZ	86401	928-753-6253	753-1049
Lake Havasu Area Chamber of Commerce 314 London Bridge Rd *Web:* www.havasuchamber.com	Lake Havasu City	AZ	86403	928-855-4115	680-0010
Mesa Chamber of Commerce 120 N Ctr St *Web:* www.mesachamber.org	Mesa	AZ	85201	480-969-1307	827-0727
Nogales Chamber of Commerce 123 W Kino Pk *Web:* www.thenogaleschamber.com	Nogales	AZ	85621	520-287-3685	287-3687
Rim Country Regional Chamber of Commerce 100 W Main St *TF:* 800-672-9766 ■ *Web:* www.rimcountrychamber.com	Payson	AZ	85547	928-474-4515	474-8812
Peoria Chamber of Commerce 8631 W Union Hill Dr Bldg 203 *TF:* 800-580-2645 ■ *Web:* www.peoriachamber.com	Peoria	AZ	85382	623-979-3601	486-4729
Greater Phoenix Chamber of Commerce 201 N Central Ave Suite 2700 *Web:* www.phoenixchamber.com	Phoenix	AZ	85004	602-495-2195	495-8913
North Phoenix Chamber of Commerce 12601 N Cave Creek Rd Suite 104 *Web:* www.northphoenixchamber.com	Phoenix	AZ	85022	602-482-3344	482-3344
Prescott Chamber of Commerce 117 W Goodwin St *TF:* 800-266-7534 ■ *Web:* www.prescott.org	Prescott	AZ	86303	928-445-2000	445-0068
Prescott Valley Chamber of Commerce 3001 N Main St Suite 2A *Web:* www.pvchamber.org	Prescott Valley	AZ	86314	928-772-8857	772-4267
Graham County Chamber of Commerce 1111 Thatcher Blvd *TF:* 888-837-1841 ■ *Web:* www.graham-chamber.com	Safford	AZ	85546	928-428-2511	428-0744
Scottsdale Area Chamber of Commerce 4725 N Scottsdale Rd Suite 210 *Web:* www.scottsdalechamber.com	Scottsdale	AZ	85251	480-355-2700	355-2710
Greater Sierra Vista Area Chamber of Commerce 21 E Wilcox Dr *Web:* www.sierravistachamber.org	Sierra Vista	AZ	85635	520-458-6940	452-0878
Northwest Valley Chamber of Commerce 12801 W Bell Rd Suite 14 *Web:* www.northwestvalley.com	Surprise	AZ	85374	623-583-0692	583-0694
Tempe Chamber of Commerce 909 E Apache Blvd *Web:* www.tempechamber.org	Tempe	AZ	85281	480-967-7891	966-5365
Tucson Metropolitan Chamber of Commerce 465 W St Mary's Rd PO Box 991 *Web:* www.tucsonchamber.org	Tucson	AZ	85702	520-792-2250	882-5704
Yuma County Chamber of Commerce 180 W 1st St Suite A *Web:* www.yumachamber.org	Yuma	AZ	85364	928-782-2567	343-0038

ARKANSAS

	City	State	ZIP	Phone	Fax
Bentonville/Bella Vista Chamber of Commerce (BBVCC) 200 E Central St PO Box 330 *Web:* www.bbvchamber.com	Bentonville	AR	72712	479-273-2841	273-2180
Berryville Chamber of Commerce 506 S Main PO Box 402 *Web:* www.berryvillear.com	Berryville	AR	72616	870-423-3704	
Conway Area Chamber of Commerce 900 Oak St *Web:* www.conwayarkcc.org	Conway	AR	72032	501-327-7788	327-7790
El Dorado Chamber of Commerce 542 Main St *Web:* www.eldoradocounty.org	El Dorado	AR	95667	530-621-5885	642-1624
Fayetteville Chamber of Commerce 123 W Mountain St *Web:* www.fayettevillear.com	Fayetteville	AR	72702	479-521-1710	521-1791
Fort Smith Regional Chamber of Commerce 612 Garrison Ave *Web:* www.fortsmithchamber.com	Fort Smith	AR	72901	479-783-3111	783-6110
Phillips County Chamber of Commerce 111 Hickory Hill Dr PO Box 447 *Web:* www.phillipscountychamber.org	Helena	AR	72342	870-338-8327	338-8882
Greater Hot Springs Chamber of Commerce 659 Ouachita Ave *TF:* 800-467-4636 ■ *Web:* www.hotspringschamber.com	Hot Springs	AR	71901	501-321-1700	321-3551
Jacksonville Chamber of Commerce 200 Dupree Dr *Web:* www.jacksonville-arkansas.com	Jacksonville	AR	72076	501-982-1511	982-1464
Jonesboro Regional Chamber of Commerce 1709 E Nettleton St *Web:* www.jonesborochamber.org	Jonesboro	AR	72401	870-932-6691	933-5758
Little Rock Regional Chamber of Commerce 1 Chamber Plaza *Web:* www.littlerockchamber.com	Little Rock	AR	72201	501-374-2001	374-6018
Magnolia-Columbia County Chamber of Commerce 529 E Main St *Web:* www.magnoliachamber.com	Magnolia	AR	71753	870-234-4352	234-7937
Mountain Home Area Chamber of Commerce 1023 Hwy 62 *TF:* 800-822-3536 ■ *Web:* www.enjoymountainhome.com	Mountain Home	AR	72653	870-425-5111	425-4446
North Little Rock Chamber of Commerce 100 Main St *Web:* www.nlrchamber.org	North Little Rock	AR	72114	501-372-5959	372-5955
Paragould Regional Chamber of Commerce 300 W Ct St *Web:* www.paragould.org	Paragould	AR	72450	870-236-7684	236-7142
Greater Pine Bluff Chamber of Commerce 510 S Main St *Web:* www.pinebluffchamber.com	Pine Bluff	AR	71601	870-535-0110	535-1643
Rogers-Lowell Area Chamber of Commerce 317 W Walnut St *TF:* 800-364-1240 ■ *Web:* www.rogerslowell.com	Rogers	AR	72756	479-636-1240	636-5485
Russellville Area Chamber of Commerce 708 W Main St *Web:* www.russellvillechamber.org	Russellville	AR	72801	479-968-2530	968-5894
Springdale Chamber of Commerce 202 W Emma *TF:* 800-972-7261 ■ *Web:* www.springdale.com	Springdale	AR	72765	479-872-2222	751-4699
West Memphis Chamber of Commerce 108 W Broadway *Web:* www.wmcoc.com	West Memphis	AR	72301	870-735-1134	735-6283

CALIFORNIA

	City	State	ZIP	Phone	Fax
Alameda Chamber of Commerce 2210D S Shore Ctr *Web:* www.alamedachamber.com	Alameda	CA	94501	510-522-0414	522-7677
Alhambra Chamber of Commerce 104 S 1st St *Web:* www.alhambrachamber.org	Alhambra	CA	91801	626-282-8481	282-5596
Altadena Chamber of Commerce 730 E Altadena Dr *Web:* www.abacus-es.com	Altadena	CA	91001	626-794-3988	794-6015
Anaheim Chamber of Commerce 201 E Ctr St *Web:* www.anaheimchamber.org	Anaheim	CA	92805	714-758-0222	758-0468
Antioch Chamber of Commerce 101 H St #4 *Web:* www.antiochchamber.com	Antioch	CA	94509	925-757-1800	757-5286
Apple Valley Chamber of Commerce 16010 Apple Valley Rd *Web:* www.avchamber.org	Apple Valley	CA	92307	760-242-2753	242-0303
Aptos Chamber of Commerce 7605-A Old Dominion Ct *Web:* www.aptoschamber.com	Aptos	CA	95003	831-688-1467	688-6961
Arcadia Chamber of Commerce 388 W Huntington Dr *Web:* www.arcadiachamber.com	Arcadia	CA	91007	626-447-2159	445-0273
Atascadero Chamber of Commerce 6904 El Camino Real *TF:* 800-756-5592 ■ *Web:* www.atascaderochamber.org	Atascadero	CA	93422	805-466-2044	466-9218
Atwater Chamber of Commerce 1181 3rd St *Web:* www.atwaterchamber.com	Atwater	CA	95301	209-358-4251	358-0934
Auburn Area Chamber of Commerce 601 Lincoln Way *Web:* www.auburnchamber.net	Auburn	CA	95603	530-885-5616	885-5854
Azusa Chamber of Commerce 240 W Foothill Blvd *Web:* www.azusachamber.org	Azusa	CA	91702	626-334-1507	334-5217
Greater Bakersfield Chamber of Commerce 1725 Eye St *Web:* www.bakersfieldchamber.org	Bakersfield	CA	93301	661-327-4421	327-8751
Kern County Board of Trade 2101 Oak St *TF:* 800-500-5376 ■ *Web:* www.visitkern.com	Bakersfield	CA	93301	661-868-5376	868-5376
Baldwin Park Chamber of Commerce 3942 Maine Ave *Web:* www.bpchamber.com	Baldwin Park	CA	91706	626-960-4848	960-2990
Beaumont Chamber of Commerce 726 Beaumont Ave *Web:* www.beaumontcachamber.com	Beaumont	CA	92223	951-845-9541	769-9080
Bell Chamber of Commerce 4401 Gage Ave	Bell	CA	90201	323-560-8755	560-2060
Bell Gardens Chamber 7535 Perry Rd *Web:* www.bellgardenschamber.org	Bell Gardens	CA	90201	562-806-2355	806-1585
Bellflower Chamber of Commerce 16730 Bellflower Blvd	Bellflower	CA	90706	562-867-1744	866-7545
Belmont Chamber of Commerce 1059 Alameda De Las Pulgas *Web:* www.belmontchamber.org	Belmont	CA	94002	650-595-8696	595-8731
Benicia Chamber of Commerce 601 1st St Suite 100 *Web:* www.beniciachamber.com	Benicia	CA	94510	707-745-2120	745-2275
Berkeley Chamber of Commerce 1834 University Ave *Web:* www.berkeleychamber.com	Berkeley	CA	94703	510-549-7000	549-1789

	City	State	Zip	Phone	Fax
Beverly Hills Chamber of Commerce 239 S Beverly Dr. *TF:* 800-345-2210 ■ *Web:* www.beverlyhillschamber.com	Beverly Hills	CA	90212	310-248-1000	248-1020
Blythe Area Chamber of Commerce 201 S Broadway *Web:* www.blytheareachamberofcommerce.com	Blythe	CA	92225	760-922-8166	922-4010
Brea Chamber of Commerce 1 Civic Ctr Cir *Web:* www.breachamber.com	Brea	CA	92821	714-529-4938	529-6103
Buena Park Chamber of Commerce 6601 Beach Blvd. *Web:* www.buenaparkchamber.org	Buena Park	CA	90621	714-521-0261	521-1851
Burbank Chamber of Commerce 200 W Magnolia Blvd *Web:* www.burbankchamber.org	Burbank	CA	91502	818-846-3111	846-0109
Burlingame Chamber of Commerce 290 California Dr *Web:* www.burlingamechamber.org	Burlingame	CA	94010	650-344-1735	344-1763
Camarillo Chamber of Commerce 2400 Ventura Blvd *Web:* www.camarillochamber.org	Camarillo	CA	93010	805-484-4383	484-1395
Campbell Chamber of Commerce 1628 W Campbell Ave *Web:* www.campbellchamber.com	Campbell	CA	95008	408-378-6252	378-0192
Canoga Park/West Hills Chamber of Commerce 7248 Owensmouth Ave. *Web:* www.cpwhchamber.com	Canoga Park	CA	91303	818-884-4222	884-4604
Carlsbad Chamber of Commerce 5934 Priestly Dr *Web:* www.carlsbad.org	Carlsbad	CA	92008	760-931-8400	931-9153
Carmichael Chamber of Commerce 6825 Fair Oaks Blvd Suite 100 *Web:* www.carmichaelchamber.com	Carmichael	CA	95608	916-481-1002	481-1003
Carson Chamber of Commerce 530 E Del Amo Blvd *Web:* www.carsonchamber.com	Carson	CA	90746	310-217-4590	217-4591
Castro Valley Chamber of Commerce 3467 Castro Valley Blvd *Web:* www.edenareachamber.com	Castro Valley	CA	94546	510-537-5300	537-5335
Cathedral City Chamber of Commerce 68950 E Palm Canyon Dr *Web:* www.cathedralcitycc.com	Cathedral City	CA	92234	760-328-1213	321-0659
Ceres Chamber of Commerce 2503 Lawrence St. *Web:* www.cereschamber.org	Ceres	CA	95307	209-537-2601	537-2699
Cerritos Chamber of Commerce 13259 S St. *Web:* www.cerritos.org	Cerritos	CA	90703	562-467-0800	467-0840
Chatsworth Chamber of Commerce 10038 Old Depot Plaza Rd *Web:* www.chatsworthchamber.com	Chatsworth	CA	91311	818-341-2428	341-4930
Chico Chamber of Commerce 300 Salem St *TF:* 800-852-8570 ■ *Web:* www.chicochamber.com	Chico	CA	95928	530-891-5556	891-3613
Chino Valley Chamber of Commerce 13150 7th St *Web:* www.chinovalleychamber.com	Chino	CA	91710	909-627-6177	627-4180
Chula Vista Chamber of Commerce 233 4th Ave. *Web:* www.chulavistachamber.org	Chula Vista	CA	91910	619-420-6602	420-1269
Citrus Heights Chamber of Commerce 7115 Greenback Ln # A *Web:* www.chchamber.com	Citrus Heights	CA	95611	916-722-4545	722-4543
Claremont Chamber of Commerce 205 Yale Ave *Web:* www.claremontchamber.org	Claremont	CA	91711	909-624-1681	624-6629
Clovis Chamber of Commerce 325 Pollasky Ave *Web:* www.clovischamber.com	Clovis	CA	93612	559-299-7363	299-2969
Colton Chamber of Commerce 655 N La Cadena Dr	Colton	CA	92324	909-825-2222	824-1650
Compton Chamber of Commerce 700 N Bullis Rd Suite 6A *Web:* www.comptonchamberofcommerce.com	Compton	CA	90221	310-631-8611	631-2066
Greater Concord Chamber of Commerce 2280 Diamond Blvd Suite 200 *Web:* www.concordchamber.com	Concord	CA	94520	925-685-1181	685-5623
Corona Chamber of Commerce 904 E 6th St. *Web:* www.coronachamber.org	Corona	CA	92879	951-737-3350	737-3531
Coronado Chamber of Commerce 875 Orange Ave Suite 102 *Web:* www.coronadochamber.com	Coronado	CA	92118	619-435-9260	522-6577
Costa Mesa Chamber of Commerce 1700 Adams Ave Suite 101 *Web:* www.costamesachamber.com	Costa Mesa	CA	92626	714-885-9092	885-9094
Covina Chamber of Commerce 935 W Badillo St Suite 100 *Web:* www.covina.org	Covina	CA	91722	626-967-4191	966-9660
Culver City Chamber of Commerce 4249 Overland Ave *Web:* www.culvercitychamber.com	Culver City	CA	90230	310-287-3850	287-1350
Cupertino Chamber of Commerce 20455 Silverado Ave. *Web:* www.cupertino-chamber.org	Cupertino	CA	95014	408-252-7054	252-0638
Cypress Chamber of Commerce 5550 Cerritos Ave Suite D *Web:* www.cypresschamber.org	Cypress	CA	90630	714-827-2430	827-1229
Daly City-Colma Chamber of Commerce 355 Gellert Blvd Suite 138 *Web:* www.dalycity-colmachamber.org	Daly City	CA	94015	650-755-3900	755-5160
Dana Point Chamber of Commerce 24681 La Plaza Suite 115 *Web:* www.danapoint-chamber.com	Dana Point	CA	92629	949-496-1555	496-5321
Davis Chamber of Commerce 604 3 St *Web:* www.davischamber.com	Davis	CA	95616	530-756-5160	756-5190
San Diego Coastal Chamber of Commerce 1104 Camino Del Mar Suite 1 *Web:* www.delmarchamber.org	Del Mar	CA	92014	858-755-4844	793-5293
Regional Chamber of Commerce San Gabriel Valley 21845 Copley Dr # 1170 *Web:* www.regionalchambersgv.com	Diamond Bar	CA	91765	909-860-1904	860-6064
Downey Chamber of Commerce 11131 Brookshire Ave. *Web:* www.downeychamber.com	Downey	CA	90241	562-923-2191	869-0461
Dublin Chamber of Commerce 7080 Donlon Way Suite 110 *Web:* www.dublinchamberofcommerce.org	Dublin	CA	94568	925-828-6200	828-4247
San Diego East County Chamber of Commerce 201 S Magnolia Ave *Web:* www.eastcountychamber.org	El Cajon	CA	92020	619-440-6161	440-6164
El Centro Chamber of Commerce & Visitors Bureau 1095 S 4th St *Web:* www.elcentrochamber.org	El Centro	CA	92243	760-352-3681	352-3246
El Monte/South El Monte Chamber of Commerce 10505 Valley Blvd Suite 312 *Web:* www.emsem.com	El Monte	CA	91731	626-443-0180	443-0463
Elk Grove Chamber of Commerce 9370 Studio Ct Suite 110 *Web:* www.elkgroveca.com	Elk Grove	CA	95758	916-691-3760	691-3810
Encinitas Chamber of Commerce 527 Encinitas Blvd *TF:* 800-953-6041 ■ *Web:* www.encinitaschamber.com	Encinitas	CA	92024	760-753-6041	753-6270
Encino Chamber of Commerce 4933 Balboa Blvd *Web:* www.encinochamber.org	Encino	CA	91316	818-789-4711	789-2485
Escondido Chamber of Commerce 720 N Broadway *Web:* www.escondidochamber.org	Escondido	CA	92025	760-745-2125	745-1183
Greater Eureka Chamber of Commerce 2112 Broadway *TF:* 800-356-6381 ■ *Web:* www.eurekachamber.com	Eureka	CA	95501	707-442-3738	442-0079
Fair Oaks Chamber of Commerce 10224 Fair Oaks Blvd PO Box 352 *Web:* www.fairoakschamber.com	Fair Oaks	CA	95628	916-967-2903	967-8536
Fairfield-Suisun Chamber of Commerce 1111 Webster St *Web:* www.ffsc-chamber.com	Fairfield	CA	94533	707-425-4625	425-0826
Fallbrook Chamber of Commerce 233 E Mission Rd *Web:* www.fallbrookchamberofcommerce.org	Fallbrook	CA	92028	760-728-5845	728-4031
Folsom Chamber of Commerce 200 Wool St. *Web:* www.folsomchamber.com	Folsom	CA	95630	916-985-2698	985-4117
Fontana Chamber of Commerce 8491 Sierra Ave *Web:* www.fontanachamber.com	Fontana	CA	92335	909-822-4433	822-6238
Mendocino Coast Chamber of Commerce 217 S Main St PO Box 1141 *TF:* 800-726-2780 ■ *Web:* www.mendocinocoast.com	Fort Bragg	CA	95437	707-961-6300	964-2056
Foster City Chamber of Commerce 1031 E Hillsdale Blvd Suite F *Web:* www.fostercitychamber.com	Foster City	CA	94404	650-573-7600	573-5201
Fountain Valley Chamber of Commerce 8840 Warner Ave Suite 207 *Web:* www.fvchamber.com	Fountain Valley	CA	92708	714-841-3822	841-3877
Fremont Chamber of Commerce 39488 Stevenson Pl Suite 100 *Web:* www.fremontbusiness.com	Fremont	CA	94539	510-795-2244	795-2240
Fresno Chamber of Commerce 2331 Fresno St. *Web:* www.fresnochamber.com	Fresno	CA	93721	559-495-4800	495-4811
Fullerton Chamber of Commerce 444 N Harbor Blvd Suite 200 *Web:* www.fullertonchamber.com	Fullerton	CA	92832	714-871-3100	871-2871
Garden Grove Chamber of Commerce 12866 Main St Suite 102 *TF:* 800-959-5560 ■ *Web:* www.gardengrovechamber.org	Garden Grove	CA	92840	714-638-7950	636-6672
Gardena Valley Chamber of Commerce 1204 W Gardena Blvd Suite E *Web:* www.gardenachamber.com	Gardena	CA	90247	310-532-9905	329-7307
Gilroy Chamber of Commerce 7471 Monterey St. *Web:* www.gilroy.org	Gilroy	CA	95020	408-842-6437	842-6010
Glendale Chamber of Commerce 200 S Louise St *Web:* www.glendalechamber.com	Glendale	CA	91205	818-240-7870	240-2872
Glendora Chamber of Commerce 131 E Foothill Blvd *Web:* www.glendora-chamber.org	Glendora	CA	91741	626-963-4128	914-4822
Goleta Valley Chamber of Commerce 271 N Fairview Ave Suite 104 *TF:* 800-646-5382 ■ *Web:* www.goletavalley.com	Goleta	CA	93117	805-967-2500	967-4615
Granada Hills Chamber of Commerce 17723 Chatsworth St *Web:* www.granadachamber.com	Granada Hills	CA	91344	818-368-3235	366-7425
Hanford Chamber of Commerce 109 W 7th St. *Web:* www.hanfordchamber.com	Hanford	CA	93230	559-582-0483	582-0960
Hawthorne Chamber of Commerce 12629 Crenshaw Blvd. *Web:* www.hawthorne-chamber.com	Hawthorne	CA	90250	310-676-1163	676-7661
Hayward Chamber of Commerce 22561 Main St. *Web:* www.hayward.org	Hayward	CA	94541	510-537-2424	537-2730
Hemet Jacinto Valley Chamber of Commerce 615 N San Jacinto St *TF:* 800-334-9344 ■ *Web:* www.hemetsanjacintochamber.com	Hemet	CA	92543	951-658-3211	766-5013
Hesperia Chamber of Commerce 16816 Main St Suite D *Web:* www.hesperiachamber.org	Hesperia	CA	92345	760-244-2135	244-1333
Highland Area Chamber of Commerce 27255 Messina St. *Web:* www.highlandchamber.org	Highland	CA	92346	909-864-4073	864-4583
San Benito County Chamber of Commerce 650 San Benito St Suite 130 *Web:* www.sanbenitocountychamber.com	Hollister	CA	95023	831-637-5315	637-1008
Hollywood Chamber of Commerce 7018 Hollywood Blvd *Web:* www.hollywoodchamber.net	Hollywood	CA	90028	323-469-8311	469-2805

	City	State	ZIP	Phone	Fax
Huntington Beach Chamber of Commerce 19891 Beach Blvd Suite 140 *Web:* www.hbchamber.org	Huntington Beach	CA	92648	714-536-8888	960-7654
Greater Huntington Park Area Chamber of Commerce 6330 Pacific Blvd Suite 208 *Web:* www.hpchamber1.com	Huntington Park	CA	90255	323-585-1155	585-2176
Imperial Beach Chamber of Commerce & Visitors Bureau 702 Seacoast Dr *Web:* www.ib-chamber.com	Imperial Beach	CA	91932	619-424-3151	424-3008
Indio Chamber of Commerce 82921 Indio Blvd *TF:* 800-775-8440 ■ *Web:* www.indiochamber.org	Indio	CA	92201	760-347-0676	347-6069
Inglewood Chamber of Commerce 330 E Queen St *Web:* www.inglewoodchamber.com	Inglewood	CA	90301	310-677-1121	677-1001
Irvine Chamber of Commerce 2485 McCabe Way Suite 150 *TF:* 800-558-4262 ■ *Web:* www.irvinechamber.com	Irvine	CA	92614	949-660-9112	660-0829
Orange County Business Council 2 Pk Plaza Suite 100 *Web:* www.ocbc.org	Irvine	CA	92614	949-476-2242	476-9240
Amador County Chamber of Commerce 571 S Hwy 49 PO Box 596 *TF:* 800-649-4988 ■ *Web:* www.amadorcountychamber.com	Jackson	CA	95642	209-223-0350	223-4425
Crescenta Valley Chamber of Commerce 3131 Foothill Blvd Suite D *Web:* www.lacrescenta.org	La Crescenta	CA	91214	818-248-4957	248-9625
La Habra Area Chamber of Commerce 321 E La Habra Blvd *Web:* www.lahabrachamber.com	La Habra	CA	90631	562-697-1704	697-8359
La Jolla Town Council PO Box 1101	La Jolla	CA	92038	858-454-1444	454-1848
La Mirada Chamber of Commerce 11900 La Mirada Blvd *Web:* www.lmchamber.org	La Mirada	CA	90638	562-902-1970	902-1218
La Verne Chamber of Commerce 2078 Bonita Ave *Web:* www.lavernechamber.org	La Verne	CA	91750	909-593-5265	596-0579
Laguna Beach Chamber of Commerce 357 Glenneyre St *Web:* www.lagunabeachchamber.org	Laguna Beach	CA	92651	949-494-1018	376-8916
Laguna Niguel Chamber of Commerce 28062 Forbes Rd Suite C *Web:* www.lagunaniguelchamber.net	Laguna Niguel	CA	92677	949-363-0136	363-9026
Lake Elsinore Valley Chamber of Commerce 132 W Graham Ave *Web:* www.lakeelsinorechamber.com	Lake Elsinore	CA	92530	951-245-8848	245-9127
Lakeport Regional Chamber of Commerce 875 Lakeport Blvd PO Box 295 *TF:* 866-525-3767 ■ *Web:* www.lakeportchamber.com	Lakeport	CA	95453	707-263-5092	263-5104
Lakeside Chamber of Commerce 9924 Vine St *Web:* www.lakesideca.com	Lakeside	CA	92040	619-561-1031	561-7951
Lakewood Chamber of Commerce 24 Lakewood Ctr Mall *Web:* www.lakewoodchamber.com	Lakewood	CA	90712	562-531-9733	
Antelope Valley Board of Trade 548 W Lancaster Blvd Suite 103 *Web:* www.avbot.org	Lancaster	CA	93534	661-942-9581	723-9279
Antelope Valley Chambers of Commerce 554 W Lancaster Blvd *Web:* www.avchambers.com	Lancaster	CA	93534	661-948-4518	949-1212
South Orange County Regional Chambers of Commerce 26111 Antonio Pkwy Suite 400 *Web:* www.socchambers.com	Las Flores	CA	92688	949-635-5800	635-1635
Livermore Chamber of Commerce 2157 1st St *Web:* www.livermorechamber.org	Livermore	CA	94550	925-447-1606	447-1641
Lodi District Chamber of Commerce 35 S School St *Web:* www.lodichamber.com	Lodi	CA	95240	209-367-7840	369-9344
Lompoc Valley Chamber of Commerce & Visitors Bureau PO Box 626 *TF:* 800-240-0999 ■ *Web:* www.lompoc.com	Lompoc	CA	93438	805-736-4567	737-0453
Long Beach Area Chamber of Commerce 1 World Trade Ctr Suite 206 *Web:* www.lbchamber.com	Long Beach	CA	90831	562-436-1251	436-7099
Los Altos Chamber of Commerce 321 University Ave *Web:* www.losaltoschamber.org	Los Altos	CA	94022	650-948-1455	948-6238
Century City Chamber of Commerce 2029 Century Pk E Concourse Level *Web:* www.centurycitycc.com	Los Angeles	CA	90067	310-553-2222	553-4623
Eagle Rock Chamber of Commerce PO Box 41354 *Web:* www.eaglerockchamberofcommerce.com	Los Angeles	CA	90041	323-257-2197	257-4245
East Los Angeles Chamber of Commerce PO Box 63220	Los Angeles	CA	90063	323-263-2005	722-2405
Lincoln Heights Chamber of Commerce 2716 N Broadway Suite 210	Los Angeles	CA	90031	323-221-6571	221-1513
Los Angeles Area Chamber of Commerce 350 S Bixel St *Web:* www.lachamber.com	Los Angeles	CA	90017	213-580-7500	580-7511
Westchester/LAX- Coastal Chamber Of Commerce 9100 S Sepulveda Blvd Suite 210	Los Angeles	CA	90045	310-645-5151	645-0130
Los Gatos Chamber of Commerce 349 N Santa Cruz Ave *Web:* www.losgatoschamber.com	Los Gatos	CA	95030	408-354-9300	399-1594
Lynwood Chamber of Commerce 3651 E Imperial Hwy	Lynwood	CA	90262	310-527-1431	537-8143
Madera District Chamber of Commerce 120 N E St **Fax:* Acctg ■ *Web:* www.maderachamber.com	Madera	CA	93638	559-673-3563	673-5009*
Malibu Chamber of Commerce 23805 Stuart Ranch Rd Suite 210 *Web:* www.malibu.org	Malibu	CA	90265	310-456-9025	456-0195
Manhattan Beach Chamber of Commerce 425 15th St *Web:* www.manhattanbeachchamber.net	Manhattan Beach	CA	90266	310-545-5313	545-7203
Manteca Chamber of Commerce 107 N Lincoln Ave *Web:* www.manteca.org	Manteca	CA	95336	209-823-6121	239-6131
Marina Chamber of Commerce PO Box 425 *Web:* www.marinachamber.com	Marina	CA	93933	831-384-0155	
Martinez Area Chamber of Commerce 603 Marina Vista *Web:* www.martinezchamber.com	Martinez	CA	94553	925-228-2345	228-2356
Yuba-Sutter Chamber of Commerce 429 10th St *Web:* www.yubasutterchamber.com	Marysville	CA	95901	530-743-6501	741-8645
Menlo Park Chamber of Commerce 1100 Merrill St *Web:* www.menloparkchamber.com	Menlo Park	CA	94025	650-325-2818	325-0920
Greater Merced Chamber of Commerce 1640 N St # 120 *Web:* www.merced-chamber.com	Merced	CA	95340	209-384-7092	384-8472
Merced County Chamber of Commerce 860 W 18th St *Web:* www.mercedcountychamber.com	Merced	CA	95341	209-722-3864	722-2406
Modesto Chamber of Commerce 1114 J St PO Box 844 *Web:* www.modchamber.org	Modesto	CA	95353	209-577-5757	577-2673
Monrovia Chamber of Commerce 620 S Myrtle Ave *Web:* www.monroviacc.com	Monrovia	CA	91016	626-358-1159	357-6036
Montclair Chamber of Commerce 5220 Benito St *Web:* www.montclairchamber.com	Montclair	CA	91763	909-624-4569	625-2009
Montebello Chamber of Commerce 109 N 19th St *Web:* www.montebellochamber.org	Montebello	CA	90640	323-721-1153	721-7946
Monterey Peninsula Chamber of Commerce 30 Ragsdale Dr #200 *Web:* www.mpcc.com	Monterey	CA	93940	831-648-5360	649-3502
Monterey Park Chamber of Commerce 700 El Mercado Ave	Monterey Park	CA	91754	626-570-9429	570-9491
Moorpark Chamber of Commerce 18 E High St *Web:* www.moorparkchamber.com	Moorpark	CA	93021	805-529-0322	529-5304
Moreno Valley Chamber of Commerce 12625 Frederick St *Web:* www.movalchamber.org	Moreno Valley	CA	92553	951-697-4404	697-0995
Morgan Hill Chamber of Commerce 17485 Monterey St # 105 *Web:* www.morganhill.org	Morgan Hill	CA	95037	408-779-9444	779-5405
Chamber of Commerce Mountain View 580 Castro St *Web:* www.chambermv.org	Mountain View	CA	94041	650-968-8378	968-5668
Murrieta Chamber of Commerce 24801 Monroe Ave *Web:* www.murrietachamber.org	Murrieta	CA	92562	951-677-7916	677-9976
Napa Chamber of Commerce 1556 1st St *Web:* www.napachamber.org	Napa	CA	94559	707-226-7455	226-1171
National City Chamber of Commerce 901 National City Blvd *TF:* 800-292-4624 ■ *Web:* www.nationalcitychamber.org	National City	CA	91950	619-477-9339	477-5018
Newark Chamber of Commerce 6066 Civic Terr Ave Suite 8 *Web:* www.newark-chamber.com	Newark	CA	94560	510-744-1000	744-1003
Newport Beach Chamber of Commerce 1470 Jamboree Rd *Web:* www.newportbeach.com	Newport Beach	CA	92660	949-729-4400	729-4417
Universal City-North Hollywood Chamber of Commerce 6369 Bellingham Ave *Web:* www.noho.org	North Hollywood	CA	91606	818-508-5155	508-5156
North Valley Regional Chamber of Commerce 9401 Reseda Blvd Suite 100 *Web:* www.nvrcc.com	Northridge	CA	91324	818-349-5676	349-4343
Norwalk Chamber of Commerce 12040 Foster Rd *Web:* www.norwalkchamber.com	Norwalk	CA	90650	562-864-7785	864-8539
Novato Chamber of Commerce 807 DeLong Ave *TF:* 800-897-1164 ■ *Web:* www.novatochamber.com	Novato	CA	94945	415-897-1164	898-9097
Oakhurst Area Chamber of Commerce 49074 Civic Cir *Web:* www.oakhurstchamber.com	Oakhurst	CA	93644	559-683-7766	658-2942
Oakland Metropolitan Chamber of Commerce 475 14th St Suite 100 *Web:* www.oaklandchamber.com	Oakland	CA	94612	510-874-4800	839-8817
Oceanside Chamber of Commerce 928 N Coast Hwy *Web:* www.oceansidechamber.com	Oceanside	CA	92054	760-722-1534	722-8336
Ojai Valley Chamber of Commerce 201 S Signal St *Web:* www.ojaichamber.org	Ojai	CA	93023	805-646-8126	646-9762
Ontario Chamber of Commerce 500 E E St Suite 200 *Web:* www.ontario.org	Ontario	CA	91764	909-984-2458	984-6439
Orange Chamber of Commerce 439 E Chapman Ave *TF:* 800-938-0073 ■ *Web:* www.orangechamber.com	Orange	CA	92866	714-538-3581	532-1675
Orangevale Chamber of Commerce 9267 Greenback Ln Suite B-91 *Web:* www.orangevalechamber.com	Orangevale	CA	95662	916-988-0175	988-1049
Oroville Area Chamber of Commerce 1789 Montgomery St *TF:* 800-655-4653 ■ *Web:* www.orovillechamber.net	Oroville	CA	95965	530-538-2542	538-2546
Oxnard Chamber of Commerce 400 E Esplanade Dr Suite 302 *Web:* www.oxnardchamber.org	Oxnard	CA	93036	805-983-6118	604-7331
Pacifica Chamber of Commerce 225 Rockaway Beach Ave Suite 1 *Web:* www.pacificachamber.com	Pacifica	CA	94044	650-355-4122	355-6949
Palm Desert Chamber of Commerce (PDCC) 72559 Hwy 111 *Web:* www.pdcc.org	Palm Desert	CA	92260	760-346-6111	346-3263

Name / Address	City	State	ZIP	Phone	Fax
Palm Springs Chamber of Commerce 190 W Amado Rd *Web:* www.pschamber.org	Palm Springs	CA	92262	760-325-1577	325-8549
Palmdale Chamber of Commerce 817 E Ave Q-9 *Web:* www.palmdalechamber.org	Palmdale	CA	93550	661-273-3232	273-8508
Palo Alto Chamber of Commerce 400 Mitchell Ln *Web:* www.paloaltochamber.com	Palo Alto	CA	94301	650-324-3121	324-1215
Paradise Chamber of Commerce 5550 Sky Way Suite 1 *TF:* 888-845-2769 ■ *Web:* www.paradisechamber.com	Paradise	CA	95969	530-877-9356	877-1865
Paramount Chamber of Commerce 15357 Paramount Blvd *Web:* www.paramountchamber.org	Paramount	CA	90723	562-634-3980	634-0891
Pasadena Chamber of Commerce & Civic Assn 844 E Green St # 208 *Web:* www.pasadena-chamber.org	Pasadena	CA	91101	626-795-3355	795-5603
Petaluma Area Chamber of Commerce 6 Petaluma Blvd N Suite A-2 *Web:* www.petalumachamber.com	Petaluma	CA	94952	707-762-2785	762-4721
Pico Rivera Chamber of Commerce 5016 Passons Blvd *Web:* www.picoriverachamber.org	Pico Rivera	CA	90660	562-949-2473	949-8320
Pittsburg Chamber of Commerce 985 Railroad Ave *Web:* pittsburgchamber.org	Pittsburg	CA	94565	925-432-7301	427-5555
Placentia Chamber of Commerce 201 E Yorba Linda Blvd Suite C *Web:* www.placentiachamber.com	Placentia	CA	92870	714-528-1873	528-1879
El Dorado County Chamber of Commerce 542 Main St *TF:* 800-457-6279 ■ *Web:* www.eldoradocounty.org	Placerville	CA	95667	530-621-5885	642-1624
Pleasant Hill Chamber of Commerce 91 Gregory Ln Suite 11 *Web:* www.pleasanthillchamber.com	Pleasant Hill	CA	94523	925-687-0700	676-7422
Pleasanton Chamber of Commerce 777 Peters Ave *Web:* www.pleasanton.org	Pleasanton	CA	94566	925-846-5858	846-9697
Pomona Chamber of Commerce 101 W Mission Blvd Suite 223 *Web:* www.pomonachamberofcommerce.homestead.com	Pomona	CA	91766	909-622-1256	620-5986
Porterville Chamber of Commerce 93 N Main St Suite A *Web:* www.portervillechamber.org	Porterville	CA	93257	559-784-7502	784-0770
Poway Chamber of Commerce 13381 County Hwy S4 *Web:* www.poway.com	Poway	CA	92064	858-748-0016	748-1710
Ramona Chamber of Commerce 960 Main St *Web:* www.ramonachamber.com	Ramona	CA	92065	760-789-1311	789-1317
Rancho Cordova Chamber of Commerce 2729 Prospect Pk Dr Suite 117 *Web:* www.ranchocordova.org	Rancho Cordova	CA	95670	916-273-5688	273-5727
Rancho Cucamonga Chamber of Commerce 7945 Vineyard Ave Suite D5 *Web:* www.ranchochamber.org	Rancho Cucamonga	CA	91730	909-987-1012	987-5917
Greater Redding Chamber of Commerce 747 Auditorium Dr *Web:* www.reddingchamber.com	Redding	CA	96001	530-225-4433	225-4398
Redlands Chamber of Commerce 1 E Redlands Blvd *Web:* www.redlandschamber.org	Redlands	CA	92373	909-793-2546	335-6388
Redondo Beach Chamber of Commerce & Visitors Bureau 200 N Pacific Coast Hwy *Web:* www.redondochamber.org	Redondo Beach	CA	90277	310-376-6911	374-7373
Redwood City-San Mateo County Chamber of Commerce 1450 Veterans Blvd Suite 125 *Web:* www.redwoodcitychamber.com	Redwood City	CA	94063	650-364-1722	364-1729
Rialto Chamber of Commerce 120 N Riverside Ave *Web:* www.rialtochamber.org	Rialto	CA	92376	909-875-5364	875-6790
Richmond Chamber of Commerce 3925 Macdonald Ave *Web:* www.rcoc.com	Richmond	CA	94805	510-234-3512	234-3540
Ridgecrest Chamber of Commerce 128-B E California Ave Suite B *Web:* www.ridgecrestchamber.com	Ridgecrest	CA	93555	760-375-8331	375-0365
Greater Riverside Chambers of Commerce 3985 University Ave *Web:* www.riverside-chamber.com	Riverside	CA	92501	951-683-7100	683-2670
Jurupa Chamber of Commerce 8175 Limonite Ave # A1	Riverside	CA	92509	951-681-9242	681-2720
Rocklin Area Chamber of Commerce 3700 Rocklin Rd *Web:* www.rocklinchamber.com	Rocklin	CA	95677	916-624-2548	624-5743
Rohnert Park Chamber of Commerce 101 Golf Course Dr Suite C-7 *Web:* www.rohnertparkchamber.org	Rohnert Park	CA	94928	707-584-1415	584-2945
Palos Verdes Peninsula Chamber of Commerce 707 Silver Spur Rd Suite 100 *Web:* www.palosverdeschamber.com	Rolling Hills Estates	CA	90274	310-377-8111	377-0614
Rosemead Chamber of Commerce 3953 Muscatel Ave	Rosemead	CA	91770	626-288-0811	288-2514
Roseville Chamber of Commerce 650 Douglas Blvd *Web:* www.rosevillechamber.com	Roseville	CA	95678	916-783-8136	783-5261
Sacramento Metro Chamber of Commerce 1 Capital Mall Suite 300 *Web:* www.metrochamber.org	Sacramento	CA	95814	916-552-6800	443-2672
Salinas Valley Chamber of Commerce 119 E Alisal St *Web:* www.salinaschamber.com	Salinas	CA	93901	831-751-7725	424-8639
San Bernardino Area Chamber of Commerce PO Box 658 *Web:* www.sbachamber.org	San Bernardino	CA	92402	909-885-7515	384-9979
San Bruno Chamber of Commerce 618 San Mateo Ave *Web:* www.sanbrunochamber.com	San Bruno	CA	94066	650-588-0180	588-6473
San Carlos Chamber of Commerce 1500 Laurel St Suite B *Web:* www.sancarloschamber.org	San Carlos	CA	94070	650-593-1068	593-9108
San Clemente Chamber of Commerce 1100 N El Camino Real *Web:* www.scchamber.com	San Clemente	CA	92672	949-492-1131	492-3764
Peninsula Chamber of Commerce PO Box 6015 *Web:* www.peninsulachamber.com	San Diego	CA	92166	619-223-9767	225-1294
San Diego North Chamber of Commerce 11650 Iberia Pl Suite 220 *Web:* www.sdncc.com	San Diego	CA	92128	858-487-1767	487-8051
San Diego Regional Chamber of Commerce 402 W Broadway Suite 1000 *Web:* www.sdchamber.org	San Diego	CA	92101	619-544-1300	
San Dimas Chamber of Commerce 246 E Bonita Ave *Web:* www.sandimaschamber.com	San Dimas	CA	91773	909-592-3818	592-8178
San Francisco Chamber of Commerce 235 Montgomery St 12th Fl *Web:* www.sfchamber.com	San Francisco	CA	94104	415-392-4520	392-0485
San Francisco Hispanic Chamber of Commerce 703 Market St Suite 611 *Web:* www.sfhcc.com	San Francisco	CA	94103	415-278-9611	
San Gabriel Chamber of Commerce 620 W Santa Anita St *Web:* www.sangabrielchamber.com	San Gabriel	CA	91776	626-576-2525	289-2901
San Jose Silicon Valley Chamber of Commerce (SJSVCC) 101 W Santa Clara St *Web:* www.sjchamber.com	San Jose	CA	95113	408-291-5250	286-5019
San Juan Capistrano Chamber of Commerce 31421 La Matanza St *Web:* www.sanjuanchamber.com	San Juan Capistrano	CA	92675	949-493-4700	489-2695
San Leandro Chamber of Commerce 15555 E 14th St Suite 100 *Web:* www.sanleandrochamber.com	San Leandro	CA	94578	510-317-1400	317-1404
San Luis Obispo Chamber of Commerce 1039 Chorro St *Web:* www.slochamber.org	San Luis Obispo	CA	93401	805-781-2777	543-1255
San Marcos Chamber of Commerce 939 Grand Ave *Web:* www.sanmarcoschamber.com	San Marcos	CA	92078	760-744-1270	744-5230
San Mateo Area Chamber of Commerce 385 1st Ave *Web:* www.sanmateoca.org	San Mateo	CA	94401	650-401-2440	401-2446
San Pablo Chamber of Commerce 13925 San Pablo Ave	San Pablo	CA	94806	510-234-2067	234-0604
San Pedro Peninsula Chamber of Commerce 390 W 7th St *TF:* 888-447-3376 ■ *Web:* www.sanpedrochamber.com	San Pedro	CA	90731	310-832-7272	832-0685
San Rafael Chamber of Commerce 817 Mission Ave *TF:* 800-454-4163 ■ *Web:* www.sanrafaelchamber.com	San Rafael	CA	94901	415-454-4163	454-7039
San Ramon Chamber of Commerce 2410 Camino Ramon #125 *Web:* www.sanramon.org	San Ramon	CA	94583	925-242-0600	242-0603
San Ysidro Chamber of Commerce 663 E San Ysidro Blvd *Web:* www.sanysidrochamber.org	San Ysidro	CA	92173	619-428-1281	428-1294
Santa Ana Chamber of Commerce 2020 N Broadway 2nd Fl *Web:* www.santaanachamber.com	Santa Ana	CA	92706	714-541-5353	541-2238
Santa Barbara Region Chamber of Commerce 924 Anacapa St Suite 1 *Web:* www.sbchamber.org	Santa Barbara	CA	93101	805-965-3023	966-5954
Santa Clara Chamber of Commerce 1850 Warburton Ave *TF:* 800-272-6822 ■ *Web:* www.santaclarachamber.org	Santa Clara	CA	95050	408-244-8244	244-7830
Santa Clarita Valley Chamber of Commerce 27451 Tourney Rd Suite 160 *Web:* www.scvchamber.com	Santa Clarita	CA	91355	661-702-6977	702-6980
Santa Cruz Chamber of Commerce 611 Ocean St Suite 1 *Web:* www.santacruzchamber.org	Santa Cruz	CA	95060	831-457-3713	423-1847
Santa Maria Valley Chamber of Commerce 614 S Broadway *TF:* 800-331-3779 ■ *Web:* www.santamaria.com	Santa Maria	CA	93454	805-925-2403	928-7559
Santa Monica Chamber of Commerce 1234 6th St Suite 100 *Web:* www.smchamber.com	Santa Monica	CA	90401	310-393-9825	394-1868
Santa Paula Chamber of Commerce 200 N 10th St *Web:* www.santapaulachamber.com	Santa Paula	CA	93060	805-525-5561	525-8950
Santa Rosa Chamber of Commerce 637 1st St *Web:* www.santarosachamber.com	Santa Rosa	CA	95404	707-545-1414	545-6914
Santee Chamber of Commerce 10315 Mission Gorge Rd *Web:* www.santee-chamber.org	Santee	CA	92071	619-449-6572	562-7906
Saratoga Chamber of Commerce 14485 Big Basin Way *Web:* www.saratogachamber.org	Saratoga	CA	95070	408-867-0753	867-5213
Seal Beach Chamber & Business Assn 201 8th St Suite 120 *Web:* www.sealbeachchamber.org	Seal Beach	CA	90740	562-799-0179	795-5637
Sebastopol Area Chamber of Commerce 265 S Main St *TF:* 877-828-4748 ■ *Web:* www.sebastopol.org	Sebastopol	CA	95472	707-823-3032	823-8439
Greater Sherman Oaks Chamber of Commerce 14827 Ventura Blvd Suite 207 *Web:* www.shermanoakschamber.org	Sherman Oaks	CA	91403	818-906-1951	783-3100

			Phone	Fax
Simi Valley Chamber of Commerce 40 W Cochran St Suite 100 . . . Simi Valley *Web:* www.simivalleychamber.org	CA	93065	805-526-3900	526-6234
Sonoma Valley Chamber of Commerce 651A Broadway . . . Sonoma *Web:* www.sonomachamber.org	CA	95476	707-996-1033	996-9402
Tuolumne County Chamber of Commerce 222 S Shepherd St . . . Sonora *TF:* 877-532-4212 ■ *Web:* www.tcchamber.com	CA	95370	209-532-4212	532-8068
South Gate Chamber of Commerce 3350 Tweedy Blvd . . . South Gate	CA	90280	323-567-1203	567-1204
South Tahoe Chamber of Commerce 2572 Lake Tahoe Blvd Suite 3 . . . South Lake Tahoe *Web:* www.tahoechamber.org	CA	96150	530-542-5060	
South San Francisco Chamber of Commerce 213 Linden Ave . . . South San Francisco *Web:* www.ssfchamber.com	CA	94080	650-588-1911	588-2534
Spring Valley Chamber of Commerce 3322 Sweetwater Springs Blvd Suite 202 . . . Spring Valley *Web:* www.springvalleychamber.org	CA	91977	619-670-9902	670-9924
Stanton Chamber of Commerce 8381 Katella Ave Suite H . . . Stanton *Web:* www.stantonchamber.org	CA	90680	714-995-1485	995-1184
Greater Stockton Chamber of Commerce 445 W Weber Ave Suite 220 . . . Stockton *Web:* www.stocktonchamber.org	CA	95203	209-547-2770	466-5271
Studio City Chamber of Commerce 4024 Radford Ave Edit 2 Suite F . . . Studio City *Web:* www.studiocitychamber.com	CA	91604	818-769-3213	655-8392
Greater Menifee Valley Chamber of Commerce 29683 New Hub Dr # C . . . Sun City *Web:* www.menifeevalleychamber.com	CA	92586	951-672-1991	672-4022
Sun Valley Area Chamber of Commerce 11501 Strathern St Po Box 308 . . . Sun Valley *Web:* www.svacc.com	CA	91352	818-768-2014	767-1947
Sunland-Tujunga Chamber of Commerce 8250 Foothill Blvd Suite A . . . Sunland *Web:* www.stchamber.com	CA	91040	818-352-4433	353-7551
Sunnyvale Chamber of Commerce 260 S Sunnyvale Ave Suite 4 . . . Sunnyvale *Web:* www.svcoc.org	CA	94086	408-736-4971	736-1919
Lassen County Chamber of Commerce 75 N Weatherlow St . . . Susanville *Web:* www.lassencountychamber.org	CA	96130	530-257-4323	251-2561
Greater Tehachapi Chamber of Commerce 209 E Tehachapi Blvd PO Box 401 . . . Tehachapi *TF:* 866-822-4180 ■ *Web:* www.tehachapi.com	CA	93581	661-822-4180	822-9036
Temecula Valley Chamber of Commerce (TVCC) 26790 Ynez Ct Suite A . . . Temecula *TF:* 866-676-5090 ■ *Web:* www.temecula.org	CA	92591	951-676-5090	694-0201
Temple City Chamber of Commerce 9050 Las Tunas Dr . . . Temple City *Web:* www.templecitychamber.org	CA	91780	626-286-3101	286-2590
Harbor City-Harbor Gateway Chamber of Commerce 19401 S Vermont Ave Suite G104 . . . Torrance *Web:* www.hchgchamber.com	CA	90502	310-516-7933	516-7734
Torrance Area Chamber of Commerce 3400 Torrance Blvd Suite 100 . . . Torrance *Web:* www.torrancechamber.com	CA	90503	310-540-5858	540-7662
Tracy Chamber of Commerce 223 E 10th St . . . Tracy *Web:* www.tracychamber.org	CA	95376	209-835-2131	833-9526
Greater Tulare Chamber of Commerce 220 E Tulare Ave . . . Tulare *Web:* www.tularechamber.org	CA	93274	559-686-1547	686-4915
Turlock Chamber of Commerce 115 S Golden State Blvd . . . Turlock	CA	95380	209-632-2221	632-5289
Tustin Chamber of Commerce 700 W 1st St # 5 . . . Tustin *Web:* www.tustinchamber.org	CA	92780	714-544-5341	544-2083
Twentynine Palms Chamber of Commerce 73660 Civic Ctr Dr Suite D . . . Twentynine Palms *Web:* www.29chamber.com	CA	92277	760-367-3445	367-3366
Ukiah Chamber of Commerce 200 S School St . . . Ukiah *Web:* www.ukiahchamber.com	CA	95482	707-462-4705	462-2088
Union City Chamber of Commerce 3939 Smith St . . . Union City *Web:* www.unioncitychamber.com	CA	94587	510-952-9637	952-9647
Upland Chamber of Commerce 215 N 2nd Ave Suite D . . . Upland *Web:* www.uplandchamber.org	CA	91786	909-204-4465	204-4464
Vacaville Chamber of Commerce 300 Main St . . . Vacaville *Web:* www.vacavillechamber.com	CA	95688	707-448-6424	448-0424
Vallejo Chamber of Commerce 427 York St . . . Vallejo *Web:* www.vallejochamber.com	CA	94590	707-644-5551	644-5590
Mid Valley Chamber of Commerce 7120 Hayvenhurst Ave Suite 114 . . . Van Nuys *Web:* www.midvalleychamber.com	CA	91406	818-989-0300	989-3836
Venice Chamber of Commerce 327 Washington Blvd PO Box 202 . . . Venice *Web:* www.venicechamber.net	CA	90294	310-822-5425	664-7938
Ventura Chamber of Commerce 505 Poli St 2nf Fl . . . Ventura *Web:* www.venturachamber.org	CA	93003	805-643-7222	650-1414
Victorville Chamber of Commerce 14174 Green Tree Blvd . . . Victorville *Web:* www.vvchamber.com	CA	92395	760-245-6506	245-6505
Visalia Chamber of Commerce 220 N Santa Fe St . . . Visalia *TF:* 877-847-2542 ■ *Web:* www.visaliachamber.org	CA	93292	559-734-5876	734-7479
Vista Chamber of Commerce 201 Washington St . . . Vista *Web:* www.vistachamber.org	CA	92084	760-726-1122	726-8654
Walnut Creek Chamber of Commerce 1777 Botelho Dr Suite 103 . . . Walnut Creek *Web:* www.walnut-creek.com	CA	94596	925-934-2007	934-2404
Pajaro Valley Chamber of Commerce 449 Union St . . . Watsonville *Web:* www.pajarovalleychamber.com	CA	95076	831-724-3900	728-5300
West Covina Chamber of Commerce 811 S Sunset Ave . . . West Covina *Web:* www.westcovinachamber.com	CA	91790	626-338-8496	960-0511
West Hollywood Chamber of Commerce 8272 Santa Monica Blvd . . . West Hollywood *Web:* www.wehochamber.com	CA	90046	323-650-2688	650-2689
West Sacramento Chamber of Commerce 1414 Merkley Ave Suite 1 . . . West Sacramento *Web:* www.westsacramentochamber.com	CA	95691	916-371-7042	371-7007
Greater Conejo Valley Chamber of Commerce 600 Hampshire Rd Suite 200 . . . Westlake Village *Web:* www.towlvchamber.org	CA	91361	805-370-0035	370-1083
Westminster Chamber of Commerce 1025 Westminster Mall . . . Westminster *Web:* www.westminsterchamber.org	CA	92683	714-898-9648	373-1499
Whittier Area Chamber of Commerce 8158 Painter Ave . . . Whittier *Web:* www.whittierchamber.com	CA	90602	562-698-9554	693-2700
Willows Chamber of Commerce 118 W Sycamore . . . Willows *TF:* 888-799-4254	CA	95988	530-934-8150	934-8710
Wilmington Chamber of Commerce 544 N Avalon Blvd Suite 104 . . . Wilmington *Web:* www.wilmington-chamber.com	CA	90744	310-834-8586	834-8887
Woodland Chamber of Commerce 307 1st St . . . Woodland *TF:* 888-843-2636 ■ *Web:* www.woodlandchamber.org	CA	95695	530-662-7327	662-4086
Woodland Hills Chamber of Commerce 20121 Ventura Blvd Suite 309 . . . Woodland Hills *Web:* www.woodlandhillscc.net	CA	91364	818-347-4737	347-3321
Yorba Linda Chamber of Commerce 17670 Yorba Linda Blvd . . . Yorba Linda *Web:* www.yorbalindachamber.org	CA	92886	714-993-9537	993-7764
Yucaipa Valley Chamber of Commerce 35139 Yucaipa Blvd . . . Yucaipa *Web:* www.yucaipachamber.com	CA	92399	909-790-1841	363-7373
Yucca Valley Chamber of Commerce 56711 29 Palms Hwy . . . Yucca Valley *Web:* www.yuccavalley.org	CA	92284	760-365-6323	365-0763

COLORADO

			Phone	Fax
Arvada Chamber of Commerce 7305 Grandview Ave . . . Arvada *Web:* www.arvadachamber.org	CO	80002	303-424-0313	424-5370
Aspen Chamber Resort Assn 425 Rio Grande Pl . . . Aspen *TF:* 800-670-0792 ■ *Web:* www.aspenchamber.org	CO	81611	970-925-1940	920-1173
Aurora Chamber of Commerce 14305 E Alameda Ave Suite 300 . . . Aurora *Web:* www.aurorachamber.org	CO	80012	303-344-1500	344-1564
Vail Valley Chamber of Commerce 191 Fawcett Rd Suite 240 . . . Avon *TF:* 800-525-3875 ■ *Web:* www.visitvailvalley.com	CO	81620	970-476-1000	476-6008
Boulder Chamber of Commerce 2440 Pearl St . . . Boulder *Web:* www.boulderchamber.com	CO	80302	303-442-1044	938-8837
Broomfield Chamber of Commerce 350 Interlocken Blvd Suite 250 . . . Broomfield *Web:* www.broomfieldchamber.com	CO	80021	303-466-1775	466-4481
Canon City Chamber of Commerce 403 Royal Gorge Blvd . . . Canon City *TF:* 800-876-7922 ■ *Web:* www.canoncity.com	CO	81212	719-275-2331	275-2332
South Metro Denver Chamber of Commerce 6840 S University Blvd . . . Centennial *Web:* www.bestchamber.com	CO	80122	303-795-0142	795-7520
Colorado Springs Chamber of Commerce 6 S Tejon St Suite 700 . . . Colorado Springs *Web:* www.coloradospringschamber.org	CO	80903	719-635-1551	635-1571
Delta Area Chamber of Commerce 301 Main St . . . Delta *Web:* www.deltacolorado.org	CO	81416	970-874-8616	874-8618
Denver Metro Chamber of Commerce 1445 Market St . . . Denver *Web:* www.denverchamber.org	CO	80202	303-534-8500	534-3200
MetroNorth Chamber of Commerce 2921 W 120th Ave Suite 210 . . . Denver *Web:* www.metronorthchamber.com	CO	80234	303-288-1000	227-1050
Durango Area Chamber of Commerce 111 S Camino del Rio . . . Durango *TF:* 888-414-0835 ■ *Web:* www.durangobusiness.org	CO	81303	970-247-0312	385-7884
Fort Collins Area Chamber of Commerce 225 S Meldrum St . . . Fort Collins *Web:* www.fcchamber.org	CO	80521	970-482-3746	482-3774
Fort Morgan Area Chamber of Commerce 300 Main St . . . Fort Morgan *TF:* 800-354-8660 ■ *Web:* www.fortmorganchamber.org	CO	80701	970-867-6702	867-6121
Greater Golden Chamber of Commerce 1010 Washington Ave . . . Golden *Web:* www.goldencochamber.org	CO	80401	303-279-3113	279-0332
West Chamber of Commerce 1667 Cole Blvd Bldg 19 Suite 400 . . . Golden *Web:* www.westchamber.org	CO	80401	303-233-5555	237-7633
Grand Junction Area Chamber of Commerce 360 Grand Ave . . . Grand Junction *TF:* 800-352-5286 ■ *Web:* www.gjchamber.org	CO	81501	970-242-3214	242-3694
Greeley-Weld Chamber of Commerce 902 7th Ave . . . Greeley *TF:* 800-449-3866 ■ *Web:* www.greeleychamber.com	CO	80631	970-352-3566	352-3572
La Veta/Cuchara Chamber of Commerce 132 W Ryus Ave . . . La Veta *TF:* 866-615-3676 ■ *Web:* www.lavetacucharachamber.com	CO	81055	719-742-3676	
Longmont Area Chamber of Commerce 528 Main St . . . Longmont *Web:* www.longmontchamber.org	CO	80501	303-776-5295	776-5657

	City	State	ZIP	Phone	Fax
Loveland Chamber of Commerce 5400 Stone Creek Cir Suite 200 *Web:* www.loveland.org	Loveland	CO	80538	970-667-6311	667-5211
Montrose Chamber of Commerce 1519 E Main St *TF:* 800-923-5515 ■ *Web:* www.montroseact.com	Montrose	CO	81401	970-249-5000	249-2907
Parker Chamber of Commerce 19751 E Main St Unit R-12 *Web:* www.parkerchamber.com	Parker	CO	80134	303-841-4268	841-8061
Greater Pueblo Chamber of Commerce 302 N Santa Fe Ave. *TF:* 800-233-3446 ■ *Web:* www.pueblochamber.org	Pueblo	CO	81003	719-542-1704	542-1624

CONNECTICUT

	City	State	ZIP	Phone	Fax
Branford Chamber of Commerce 239 N Main St PO Box 375 *Web:* www.branfordct.com	Branford	CT	06405	203-488-5500	488-5046
Bridgeport Regional Business Council 10 Middle St 14th Fl *Web:* www.brbc.org	Bridgeport	CT	06604	203-335-3800	366-0105
Greater Bristol Chamber of Commerce 200 Main St *Web:* www.bristol-chamber.org	Bristol	CT	06010	860-584-4718	584-4722
Cheshire Chamber of Commerce 195 S Main St *Web:* www.cheshirechamber.com	Cheshire	CT	06410	203-272-2345	271-3044
Greater Danbury Chamber of Commerce 39 W St *Web:* www.danburychamber.com	Danbury	CT	06810	203-743-5565	794-1439
Northeastern Connecticut Chamber of Commerce 3 Central St *Web:* www.newenglanditgroup.com/nectcc	Danielson	CT	06239	860-774-8001	774-4299
East Hartford Chamber of Commerce 1137 Main St *Web:* www.ehcoc.com	East Hartford	CT	06108	860-289-0239	289-0230
East Haven Chamber of Commerce 157 Main St *Web:* www.easthavenchamber.com	East Haven	CT	06512	203-467-4305	469-2299
Fairfield Chamber of Commerce 1597 Post Rd *Web:* www.fairfieldctchamber.com	Fairfield	CT	06824	203-255-1011	256-9990
Chamber of Commerce of Eastern Connecticut Inc 39 Kings Hwy PO Box 726 *Web:* www.chamberect.com	Gales Ferry	CT	06335	860-464-7373	464-7374
Glastonbury Chamber of Commerce 2400 Main St *Web:* www.glastonburychamber.org	Glastonbury	CT	06033	860-659-3587	659-0102
Greenwich Chamber of Commerce 45 E Putnam Ave Suite 121 *Web:* www.greenwichchamber.com	Greenwich	CT	06830	203-869-3500	869-3502
Hamden Chamber of Commerce 2969 Whitney Ave *Web:* www.hamdenchamber.com	Hamden	CT	06518	203-288-6431	288-4499
MetroHartford Alliance 31 Pratt St Suite 5 *Web:* www.metrohartford.com	Hartford	CT	06103	860-525-4451	293-2592
Greater Manchester Chamber of Commerce 20 Hartford Rd *Web:* www.manchesterchamber.com	Manchester	CT	06040	860-646-2223	646-5871
Greater Meriden Chamber of Commerce 3 Colony St Suite 301 *Web:* www.meridenchamber.com	Meriden	CT	06451	203-235-7901	686-0172
Middlesex County Chamber of Commerce 393 Main St *Web:* www.middlesexchamber.com	Middletown	CT	06457	860-347-6924	346-1043
Milford Chamber of Commerce 5 Broad St *Web:* www.milfordct.com	Milford	CT	06460	203-878-0681	876-8517
Mystic Chamber of Commerce 14 Holmes St PO Box 143 *TF:* 866-572-9578 ■ *Web:* www.mysticchamber.org	Mystic	CT	06355	860-572-9578	572-9273
Waterbury/Naugatuck Chamber of Commerce 195 Water St	Naugatuck	CT	06770	203-729-4511	729-4512
New Britain Chamber of Commerce 1 Ct St 4th Fl *Web:* www.newbritainchamber.com	New Britain	CT	06051	860-229-1665	223-8341
Greater New Haven Chamber of Commerce 900 Chapel St 10th Fl *Web:* www.gnhcc.com	New Haven	CT	06510	203-787-6735	782-4329
Greater New Milford Chamber of Commerce 11 Railroad St *Web:* www.newmilford-chamber.com	New Milford	CT	06776	860-354-6080	354-8526
Greater Norwalk Chamber of Commerce 101 E Ave *Web:* www.norwalkchamberofcommerce.com	Norwalk	CT	06851	203-866-2521	852-0583
Old Saybrook Chamber of Commerce 1 Main St *Web:* www.oldsaybrookchamber.com	Old Saybrook	CT	06475	860-388-3266	388-9433
Greater Valley Chamber of Commerce 900 Bridgeport Ave 2nd Fl *Web:* www.greatervalleychamber.com	Shelton	CT	06484	203-925-4981	925-4984
Greater Southington Chamber of Commerce 1 Factory Sq Suite 201 *Web:* www.southingtoncoc.com	Southington	CT	06489	860-628-8036	276-9696
Business Council of Fairfield County (SACIA) 1 Landmark Sq Suite 300 *Web:* www.sacia.org	Stamford	CT	06901	203-359-3220	967-8294
Stamford Chamber of Commerce 733 Summer St Suite 104 *Web:* www.stamfordchamber.com	Stamford	CT	06901	203-359-4761	363-5069
Chamber of Commerce of Northwest Connecticut 333 Kennedy Dr Suite R 101 *Web:* www.northwestchamber.org	Torrington	CT	06790	860-482-6586	489-8851
Tolland County Chamber of Commerce 30 Lafayette Sq *Web:* www.tollandcountychamber.org	Vernon	CT	06066	860-872-0587	872-0588
Quinnipiac Chamber of Commerce 100 S Turnpike Rd *Web:* www.quinncham.com	Wallingford	CT	06492	203-269-9891	269-1358
Greater Waterbury Chamber of Commerce 83 Bank St PO Box 1469 *Web:* www.waterburychamber.org	Waterbury	CT	06721	203-757-0701	756-3507
West Hartford Chamber of Commerce 948 Farmington Ave *Web:* www.whchamber.com	West Hartford	CT	06107	860-521-2300	521-1996
West Haven Chamber of Commerce 334 Main St *Web:* www.westhavenchamber.com	West Haven	CT	06516	203-933-1500	931-1940
Windham Region Chamber of Commerce 1010 Main St *Web:* www.windhamchamber.com	Willimantic	CT	06226	860-423-6389	423-8235
Windsor Chamber of Commerce 261 Broad St *Web:* www.windsorcc.org	Windsor	CT	06095	860-688-5165	688-0809

DELAWARE

	City	State	ZIP	Phone	Fax
Rehoboth Beach-Dewey Beach Chamber of Commerce 501 Rehoboth Ave. *TF:* 800-441-1329 ■ *Web:* www.beach-fun.com	Rehoboth Beach	DE	19971	302-227-2233	227-8351

FLORIDA

	City	State	ZIP	Phone	Fax
Amelia Island-Fernandina Beach-Yulee Chamber of Commerce 961687 Gateway Blvd Suite 101-G *Web:* www.islandchamber.com	Amelia Island	FL	32034	904-261-3248	261-6997
Apalachicola Bay Chamber of Commerce 122 Commerce St *Web:* www.apalachicolabay.org	Apalachicola	FL	32320	850-653-9419	653-8219
DeSoto County Chamber of Commerce 16 S Volusia Ave *Web:* www.desotochamber.net	Arcadia	FL	34266	863-494-4033	494-3312
Florida Gold Coast Chamber of Commerce 1100 Kane Concourse Suite 210	Bay Harbor Islands	FL	33154	305-866-6020	866-0635
Belleview-South Marion Chamber of Commerce 5301 SE Abshier Blvd	Belleview	FL	34420	352-245-2178	245-7673
Lower Keys Chamber of Commerce 31020 Overseas Hwy *TF:* 800-872-3722 ■ *Web:* www.lowerkeyschamber.com	Big Pine Key	FL	33043	305-872-2411	872-0752
Greater Boca Raton Chamber of Commerce 1800 N Dixie Hwy *Web:* www.bocaratonchamber.com	Boca Raton	FL	33432	561-395-4433	392-3780
Bonita Springs Area Chamber of Commerce 25071 Chamber of Commerce Dr *TF:* 800-226-2943 ■ *Web:* www.bonitaspringschamber.com	Bonita Springs	FL	34135	239-992-2943	992-5011
Greater Boynton Beach Chamber of Commerce 1880 N Congress Ave Suite 106 *Web:* www.boyntonbeach.org	Boynton Beach	FL	33426	561-732-9501	734-4304
Manatee Chamber of Commerce 222 10th St W *Web:* www.manateechamber.com	Bradenton	FL	34205	941-748-3411	745-1877
Greater Brandon Chamber of Commerce 330 Pauls Dr Suite 100 *Web:* www.brandonchamber.com	Brandon	FL	33511	813-689-1221	689-9440
Greater Hernando County Chamber of Commerce 15588 Aviation Loop Dr *Web:* www.hernandochamber.com	Brooksville	FL	34604	352-796-0697	796-3704
Cape Coral Chamber of Commerce 2051 Cape Coral Pkwy E *TF:* 800-226-9609 ■ *Web:* www.capecoralchamber.com	Cape Coral	FL	33904	239-549-6900	549-9609
Clearwater Regional Chamber of Commerce 401 Cleveland St *TF:* 888-425-3279 ■ *Web:* www.clearwaterflorida.org	Clearwater	FL	33755	727-461-0011	449-2889
Coral Gables Chamber of Commerce 224 Catalonia *Web:* www.cg.wliinc2.com	Coral Gables	FL	33134	305-446-1657	446-9900
Coral Springs Chamber of Commerce 11805 Heron Bay Blvd *Web:* www.cschamber.com	Coral Springs	FL	33076	954-752-4242	827-0543
Crestview Area Chamber of Commerce 1447 Commerce Dr *Web:* www.crestviewchamber.com	Crestview	FL	32539	850-682-3212	682-7413
Citrus County Chamber of Commerce 28 NW Us Hwy 19 *Web:* www.citruscountychamber.com	Crystal River	FL	34428	352-795-3149	795-4260
Davie-Cooper City Chamber of Commerce 4185 Davie Rd *Web:* www.davie-coopercity.org	Davie	FL	33314	954-581-0790	581-9684
Daytona Beach-Halifax Area Chamber of Commerce 126 E Orange Ave *Web:* www.daytonachamber.com	Daytona Beach	FL	32114	386-255-0981	258-5104
Greater Deerfield Beach Chamber of Commerce 1601 E Hillsboro Blvd *Web:* www.deerfieldchamber.com	Deerfield Beach	FL	33441	954-427-1050	427-1056
DeLand Area Chamber of Commerce 336 N Woodland Blvd *Web:* www.delandchamber.org	DeLand	FL	32720	386-734-4331	734-4333
Greater Delray Beach Chamber of Commerce 64-A SE 5th Ave *Web:* www.delraybeach.com	Delray Beach	FL	33483	561-278-0424	278-0555
Destin Area Chamber of Commerce 4484 Legendary Dr Suite A *Web:* www.destinchamber.com	Destin	FL	32541	850-837-6241	654-5612
Dunedin Chamber of Commerce 301 Main St *Web:* www.dunedin-fl.com	Dunedin	FL	34698	727-733-3197	734-8942
Dunnellon Area Chamber of Commerce 20500 E Pennsylvania Ave *TF:* 800-830-2087 ■ *Web:* www.dunnellonchamber.org	Dunnellon	FL	34432	352-489-2320	489-6846

Chamber / Address	City	State	ZIP	Phone	Fax
Englewood-Cape Haze Area Chamber of Commerce 601 S Indiana Ave TF: 800-603-7198 ■ Web: www.englewoodchamber.com	Englewood	FL	34223	941-474-5511	475-9257
Broward County Chamber of Commerce 2425 E Commercial Blvd #103 Web: www.browardbiz.com	Fort Lauderdale	FL	33308	954-565-5750	566-3398
Greater Fort Lauderdale Chamber of Commerce 512 NE 3rd Ave Web: www.ftlchamber.com	Fort Lauderdale	FL	33301	954-462-6000	527-8766
Chamber of Southwest Florida 5237 Summerlin Commons Blvd Suite 114 Web: www.chamber-swflorida.com	Fort Myers	FL	33907	239-278-4001	275-2103
Greater Fort Myers Chamber of Commerce 2310 Edwards Dr TF: 800-366-3622 ■ Web: www.fortmyers.org	Fort Myers	FL	33901	239-332-3624	332-7276
Fort Myers Beach Chamber of Commerce 17200 San Carlos Blvd TF: 800-782-9283 ■ Web: www.fmbchamber.com	Fort Myers Beach	FL	33931	239-454-7500	454-7910
Greater Fort Walton Beach Chamber of Commerce 34 Miracle Strip PkwySE Web: www.fwbchamber.org	Fort Walton Beach	FL	32548	850-244-8191	244-1935
Gainesville Area Chamber of Commerce 300 E University Ave Suite 100 Web: www.gainesvillechamber.com	Gainesville	FL	32601	352-334-7100	334-7141
Hallandale Beach Chamber of Commerce 400 S Federal Hwy Suite 192 Web: www.hallandalebeachchamber.com	Hallandale Beach	FL	33009	954-454-0541	454-0930
Seminole County Regional Chamber of Commerce 1055 Triple A Dr Suite 153 Web: www.seminolebusiness.org	Heathrow	FL	32746	407-333-4748	708-4615
Camara de Comercio Hispana de Hialeah 4696 E 10 Ct	Hialeah	FL	33013	305-557-5060	
Hialeah Chamber of Commerce & Industries 240 E 1st Ave Suite 217 Web: www.hialeahchamber.org	Hialeah	FL	33010	305-888-7780	888-7804
Greater Hollywood Chamber of Commerce 330 N Federal Hwy TF: 800-231-5562 ■ Web: www.hollywoodchamber.org	Hollywood	FL	33020	954-923-4000	923-8737
Greater Homestead/Florida City Chamber of Commerce 212 NW 1st Ave TF: 888-352-4891 ■ Web: www.chamberinaction.com	Homestead	FL	33030	305-247-2332	224-9101
Citrus County Chamber of Commerce 401 Tompkins St Web: www.citruscountychamber.com	Inverness	FL	34450	352-726-2801	637-1921
Islamorada Chamber of Commerce PO Box 915 TF: 800-322-5397 ■ Web: www.islamoradachamber.com	Islamorada	FL	33036	305-664-4503	664-4289
Jacksonville Chamber of Commerce 3 Independent Dr Web: www.myjaxchamber.com	Jacksonville	FL	32202	904-366-6600	632-0617
Jacksonville Chamber of Commerce Beaches Div 3 Independent Dr Web: www.myjaxchamber.com	Jacksonville	FL	32202	904-366-6600	632-0617
North Palm Beach County Chamber of Commerce 800 N US Hwy 1 Web: www.npbchamber.com	Jupiter	FL	33477	561-694-2300	745-7519
Northern Palm Beach County Chamber of Commerce 800 N US Hwy 1 TF: 800-616-7402 ■ Web: www.npbchamber.com	Jupiter	FL	33477	561-746-7111	746-7715
Key Largo Chamber of Commerce 106000 Overseas Hwy Web: www.keylargo.org	Key Largo	FL	33037	305-451-1414	451-4726
Key West Chamber of Commerce 402 Wall St TF: 800-527-8539 ■ Web: www.keywestchamber.org	Key West	FL	33040	305-294-2587	294-7806
Kissimmee/Osceola County Chamber of Commerce 1425 E Vine St Web: www.kissimmeechamber.com	Kissimmee	FL	34744	407-847-3174	870-8607
Lake City/Columbia County Chamber of Commerce 162 S Marion Ave Web: www.lakecitychamber.com	Lake City	FL	32025	386-752-3690	755-7744
Sumter County Chamber of Commerce 102 N County Rd 470 Web: www.gosumter.com	Lake Panasoffkee	FL	33538	352-793-3099	793-2120
Greater Lake Placid Chamber of Commerce 18 N Oak Ave Web: www.lpfla.com	Lake Placid	FL	33852	863-465-4331	465-2588
Lake Wales Area Chamber of Commerce 340 W Central Ave Web: www.lakewaleschamber.com	Lake Wales	FL	33859	863-676-3445	676-3446
Greater Lake Worth Chamber of Commerce 501 Lake Ave Web: www.lwchamber.com	Lake Worth	FL	33460	561-582-4401	547-8300
Lakeland Area Chamber of Commerce 35 Lake Morton Dr Web: www.lakelandchamber.com	Lakeland	FL	33801	863-688-8551	683-7454
Central Pasco Chamber of Commerce 2810 Land O' Lakes Blvd Web: www.centralpascochamber.com	Land O' Lakes	FL	34639	813-909-2722	909-0827
Greater Largo Chamber of Commerce 151 3rd St NW Web: www.largochamber.com	Largo	FL	33770	727-584-2321	586-3112
Lehigh Acres Chamber of Commerce 25 Homestead Rd N Web: www.lehighacreschamber.org	Lehigh Acres	FL	33971	239-369-3322	368-0500
Suwannee County Chamber of Commerce 816 Ohio Ave S Web: www.suwanneechamber.com	Live Oak	FL	32064	386-362-3071	362-4758
Palms West Chamber of Commerce 13901 Southern Blvd TF: 800-790-2364 ■ Web: www.palmswest.com	Loxahatchee	FL	33470	561-790-6200	791-2069
Maitland Area Chamber of Commerce 110 N Maitland Ave Web: www.maitlandchamber.com	Maitland	FL	32751	407-644-0741	539-2529
Greater Marathon Chamber of Commerce 12222 Overseas Hwy TF: 800-262-7284 ■ Web: www.floridakeysmarathon.com	Marathon	FL	33050	305-743-5417	289-0183
Marco Island Chamber of Commerce 1102 N Collier Blvd TF: 800-788-6272 ■ Web: www.marcoislandchamber.org	Marco Island	FL	34145	239-394-7549	394-3061
Jackson County Chamber of Commerce PO Box 130 Web: www.jacksoncounty.com	Marianna	FL	32447	850-482-8061	482-8002
Melbourne-Palm Bay Area Chamber of Commerce 1005 E Strawbridge Ave TF: 800-771-9922 ■ Web: www.melpb-chamber.org	Melbourne	FL	32901	321-724-5400	725-2093
Cocoa Beach Area Chamber of Commerce 400 Fortenberry Rd TF: 877-321-8474 ■ Web: www.cocoabeachchamber.com	Merritt Island	FL	32952	321-459-2200	459-2232
Greater Miami Chamber of Commerce 1601 Biscayne Blvd TF: 888-660-5955 ■ Web: www.greatermiami.com	Miami	FL	33132	305-350-7700	374-6902
Miami-Dade Chamber of Commerce 11380 NW 27th Ave Suite 1328 Web: www.m-dcc.org	Miami	FL	33167	305-751-8648	758-3839
North Dade Regional Chamber of Commerce 1300 NW 167th St Suite 2 Web: www.thechamber.cc	Miami	FL	33169	305-690-9123	690-9124
Miami Beach Chamber of Commerce 1920 Meridian Ave 3rd Fl Web: www.miamibeachchamber.com	Miami Beach	FL	33139	305-672-1270	538-4336
Santa Rosa County Chamber of Commerce 5247 Stewart St Web: www.srcchamber.com	Milton	FL	32570	850-623-2339	623-4413
Greater Naples Chamber of Commerce The 2390 Tamiami Trail N Suite 210 Web: www.napleschamber.org	Naples	FL	34103	239-262-6376	262-8374
West Pasco Chamber of Commerce 5443 Main St Web: www.westpasco.com	New Port Richey	FL	34652	727-842-7651	848-0202
Southeast Volusia Chamber of Commerce 115 Canal St TF: 877-460-8410 ■ Web: www.sevchamber.com	New Smyrna Beach	FL	32168	386-428-2449	423-3512
Niceville-Valparaiso Chamber of Commerce 1055 E John Sims Pkwy Web: www.nicevillechamber.com	Niceville	FL	32578	850-678-2323	678-2602
North Fort Myers Chamber of Commerce 2787 N Tamiami Trail Unit 10 Web: www.nfmchamber.com	North Fort Myers	FL	33903	239-997-9111	997-4026
Greater North Miami Chamber of Commerce 13100 W Dixie Hwy Web: www.northmiamichamber.com	North Miami	FL	33161	305-891-7811	893-8522
North Miami Beach Chamber of Commerce 1870 NE 171st St Web: www.nmbchamber.com	North Miami Beach	FL	33162	305-944-8500	944-8191
Ocala-Marion County Chamber of Commerce 310 SE 3rd St Web: www.ocalacc.com	Ocala	FL	34471	352-629-8051	629-7651
Okeechobee Chamber of Commerce 55 S Parrott Ave Web: www.okeechobeechamberofcommerce.com	Okeechobee	FL	34972	863-763-6464	763-3467
Upper Tampa Bay Regional Chamber of Commerce 163 SR 580 W Web: www.utbchamber.com	Oldsmar	FL	34677	813-855-4233	854-1237
Clay County Chamber of Commerce 1734 Kingsley Ave Web: www.claychamber.org	Orange Park	FL	32073	904-264-2651	264-0070
East Orlando Chamber of Commerce 10111 E Colonial Dr Web: www.eocc.org	Orlando	FL	32817	407-277-5951	381-1720
Orlando Regional Chamber of Commerce 75 S Ivanhoe Blvd Web: www.orlando.org	Orlando	FL	32804	407-425-1234	835-2500
Ormond Beach Chamber of Commerce 165 W Granada Blvd Web: www.ormondchamber.com	Ormond Beach	FL	32174	386-677-3454	677-4363
Putnam County Chamber of Commerce 1100 Reid St Web: www.putnamcountychamber.org	Palatka	FL	32177	386-328-1503	328-7076
Flagler County Chamber of Commerce 20 Airport Rd Suite C TF: 800-881-1022 ■ Web: www.flaglerpcchamber.org	Palm Coast	FL	32164	386-437-0106	437-5700
Greater Palm Harbor Area Chamber of Commerce 1151 Nebraska Ave Web: www.palmharborcc.org	Palm Harbor	FL	34683	727-784-4287	786-2336
Bay County Chamber of Commerce 235 W 5th St Web: www.panamacity.org	Panama City	FL	32401	850-785-5206	763-6229
Panama City Beaches Chamber of Commerce 309 Richard Jackson Blvd Web: www.pcbeach.org	Panama City Beach	FL	32407	850-234-3193	235-2301
Miramar-Pembroke Pines Regional Chamber of Commerce 10100 Pines Blvd 4th Fl Web: www.miramarpembrokepines.org	Pembroke Pines	FL	33026	954-432-9808	432-9193
Pensacola Area Chamber of Commerce 117 W Garden St Web: www.pensacolachamber.com	Pensacola	FL	32502	850-438-4081	438-6369
Pinellas Park Mid-County Chamber of Commerce 5851 Pk Blvd Web: www.pinellasparkchamber.com	Pinellas Park	FL	33781	727-544-4777	209-0837
Greater Plant City Chamber of Commerce 106 N Evers St TF: 800-760-2315 ■ Web: www.plantcity.org	Plant City	FL	33563	813-754-3707	752-8793
Greater Plantation Chamber of Commerce 7401 NW 4th St Web: www.plantationchamber.org	Plantation	FL	33317	954-587-1410	587-1886

	City	State	Zip	Phone	Fax
Greater Pompano Beach Chamber of Commerce 2200 E Atlantic Blvd *Web:* www.pompanobeachchamber.com	Pompano Beach	FL	33062	954-941-2940	785-8358
Charlotte County Chamber of Commerce 2702 Tamiami Trail *Web:* www.charlottecountychamber.org	Port Charlotte	FL	33952	941-627-2222	627-9730
Port Orange-South Daytona Chamber of Commerce 3431 S Ridgewood Ave *Web:* www.pschamber.com	Port Orange	FL	32129	386-761-1601	788-9165
Charlotte County Chamber of Commerce 311 W Retta Esplanade *Web:* www.charlottecountychamber.org	Punta Gorda	FL	33950	941-639-2222	639-6330
Gadsden County Chamber of Commerce 208 N Adams St *TF:* 800-627-9231 ■ *Web:* www.gadsdencc.com	Quincy	FL	32351	850-627-9231	875-3299
Greater Riverview Chamber of Commerce 10011 Water Works Ln *Web:* www.riverviewchamber.com	Riverview	FL	33578	813-234-5944	234-5945
Ruskin Chamber of Commerce 315 S US Hwy 41 *Web:* www.ruskinchamber.org	Ruskin	FL	33570	813-645-3808	645-2099
Saint Johns County Chamber of Commerce 1 Riberia St *Web:* www.stjohnscountychamber.com	Saint Augustine	FL	32084	904-829-5681	829-6477
Saint Cloud/Greater Osceola Chamber of Commerce 1200 New York Ave *Web:* www.stcloudflchamber.com	Saint Cloud	FL	34769	407-892-3671	892-5289
Tampa Bay Beaches Chamber of Commerce 6990 Gulf Blvd *TF:* 800-944-1847 ■ *Web:* www.tampabaybeaches.com	Saint Pete Beach	FL	33706	727-360-6957	360-2233
Saint Petersburg Area Chamber of Commerce 100 2nd Ave N Suite 150 *Web:* www.stpete.com	Saint Petersburg	FL	33701	727-821-4069	895-6326
Sanford Chamber of Commerce 400 E 1st St *Web:* www.sanfordchamber.com	Sanford	FL	32771	407-322-2212	322-8160
Sanibel & Captiva Islands Chamber of Commerce 1159 Cswy Rd *Web:* www.sanibel-captiva.org	Sanibel	FL	33957	239-472-1080	472-1070
Walton Area Chamber of Commerce 63 S Centry Trail *Web:* www.waltoncountychamber.com	Santa Rosa Beach	FL	32459	850-267-0683	267-0603
Greater Sarasota Chamber of Commerce 1945 Fruitville Rd *Web:* www.sarasotachamber.com	Sarasota	FL	34236	941-955-8187	366-5621
Sebastian River Area Chamber of Commerce 700 Main St *TF:* 888-881-7568 ■ *Web:* www.sebastianchamber.com	Sebastian	FL	32958	772-589-5969	589-5993
Greater Sebring Chamber of Commerce 227 US 27 N *Web:* www.sebringflchamber.com	Sebring	FL	33870	863-385-8448	385-8810
Greater Seffner Area Chamber of Commerce 11816 US Hwy 92 E PO Box 1920 *Web:* www.seffnerchamber.com	Seffner	FL	33583	813-627-8686	627-8699
Greater Seminole Area Chamber of Commerce 8400 113th St *Web:* www.seminolechamber.net	Seminole	FL	33772	727-392-3245	397-7753
Chamber South 6410 SW 80th St *Web:* www.chambersouth.com	South Miami	FL	33143	305-661-1621	666-0508
Stuart-Martin County Chamber of Commerce 1650 S Kanner Hwy *Web:* www.goodnature.org	Stuart	FL	34994	772-287-1088	220-3437
Sunny Isles Beach Tourism & Marketing Council 18070 Collins Ave *Web:* www.sunnyislesbeachmiami.com	Sunny Isles Beach	FL	33160	305-792-1952	792-1672
Sunrise Chamber of Commerce 12717 W Sunrise Blvd Suite 318 *Web:* www.sunrisechamber.org	Sunrise	FL	33323	954-835-2428	523-0607
Greater Tallahassee Chamber of Commerce 115 N Calhoun St *Web:* www.talchamber.com	Tallahassee	FL	32301	850-224-8116	561-3860
Tamarac Chamber of Commerce 7525 NW 88th Ave # 103 *Web:* www.tamaracchamber.org	Tamarac	FL	33321	954-722-1520	721-2725
Greater Tampa Chamber of Commerce 201 N Franklin St Suite 201 *TF:* 800-298-2672 ■ *Web:* www.tampachamber.com	Tampa	FL	33602	813-228-7777	223-7899
North Tampa Chamber of Commerce PO Box 82043 *Web:* www.northtampachamber.com	Tampa	FL	33682	813-961-2420	961-2903
Ybor City Chamber of Commerce 1800 E 9th Ave *Web:* www.ybor.org	Tampa	FL	33605	813-248-3712	247-1764
Tarpon Springs Chamber of Commerce 11 E Orange St *Web:* tarponspringschamber.com	Tarpon Springs	FL	34689	727-937-6109	937-2879
Titusville Area Chamber of Commerce 2000 S Washington Ave *Web:* www.titusville.org	Titusville	FL	32780	321-267-3036	264-0127
Venice Area Chamber of Commerce 597 Tamiami Trail S *Web:* www.venicechamber.com	Venice	FL	34285	941-488-2236	484-5903
Indian River County Chamber of Commerce 1216 21st St *Web:* www.indianriverchamber.com	Vero Beach	FL	32960	772-567-3491	778-3181
Chamber of Commerce of the Palm Beaches 401 N Flagler Dr *Web:* www.palmbeaches.org	West Palm Beach	FL	33401	561-833-3711	833-5582
Weston Area Chamber of Commerce 1290 Weston Rd Suite 312 *Web:* www.westonchamber.com	Weston	FL	33326	954-389-0600	384-6133
West Orange Chamber of Commerce 12184 W Colonial Dr *Web:* www.wochamber.com	Winter Garden	FL	34787	407-656-1304	656-0221
Greater Winter Haven Area Chamber of Commerce 401 Ave 'B' NW *Web:* winterhavenchamber.com	Winter Haven	FL	33881	863-293-2138	297-5818
Goldenrod Area Chamber of Commerce 4960 N Oak Ave *Web:* www.goldenrodchamber.com	Winter Park	FL	32792	407-677-5980	677-4928
Winter Park Chamber of Commerce 150 N New York Ave *TF:* 877-972-4262 ■ *Web:* www.winterpark.org	Winter Park	FL	32789	407-644-8281	644-7826
Zephyrhills Chamber of Commerce 38550 5th Ave *Web:* www.lschamber.com	Zephyrhills	FL	33542	813-782-1913	783-6060

GEORGIA

	City	State	Zip	Phone	Fax
Albany Area Chamber of Commerce 225 W Broad Ave *TF:* 800-475-8700 ■ *Web:* www.albanyga.com	Albany	GA	31701	229-434-8700	434-8716
Greater North Fulton Chamber of Commerce (GNFCC) 11605 Haynes Bridge Rd Suite 100 *TF:* 866-840-5770 ■ *Web:* www.gnfcc.com	Alpharetta	GA	30009	770-993-8806	594-1059
Americus-Sumter County Chamber of Commerce 409 Elm Ave Suite A *Web:* www.americus-sumterchamber.com	Americus	GA	31709	229-924-2646	924-8784
Athens Area Chamber of Commerce 246 W Hancock Ave *Web:* www.athenschamber.net	Athens	GA	30601	706-549-6800	549-5636
Cobb Chamber of Commerce 240 IH- N Pkwy *Web:* www.cobbchamber.org	Atlanta	GA	30339	770-980-2000	980-9510
Metro Atlanta Chamber of Commerce 235 International Blvd NW *Web:* www.metroatlantachamber.com	Atlanta	GA	30303	404-880-9000	586-8426
Augusta Metro Chamber of Commerce 701 Greene St PO Box 1837 *TF:* 888-639-8188 ■ *Web:* www.augustachamber.net	Augusta	GA	30901	706-821-1300	821-1330
Bainbridge-Decatur County Chamber of Commerce 100 Earl May Boat Basin Cir *TF:* 800-246-4774 ■ *Web:* www.bainbridgega.com	Bainbridge	GA	39819	229-246-4774	243-7633
Brunswick-Golden Isles Chamber of Commerce 4 Glynn Ave *Web:* brunswick-georgia.com/chamber	Brunswick	GA	31520	912-265-0620	265-0629
Gordon County Chamber of Commerce 300 S Wall St *TF:* 800-887-3811 ■ *Web:* www.gordonchamber.org	Calhoun	GA	30701	706-625-3200	625-5062
Cherokee County Chamber of Commerce 3605 Marietta Hwy *Web:* www.cherokee-chamber.com	Canton	GA	30114	770-345-0400	345-0030
Carroll County Chamber of Commerce 200 Northside Dr *Web:* www.carroll-ga.org	Carrollton	GA	30117	770-832-2446	832-1300
Cartersville-Bartow County Chamber of Commerce 122 W Main St PO Box 307 *Web:* www.cartersvillechamber.com	Cartersville	GA	30120	770-382-1466	382-2704
Chatsworth-Murray County Chamber of Commerce 126 N 3rd Ave *TF:* 800-969-9490 ■ *Web:* www.murraycountychamber.com	Chatsworth	GA	30705	706-695-6060	517-0198
White County Chamber of Commerce 122 N Main St *TF:* 800-392-8279 ■ *Web:* www.whitecountychamber.org	Cleveland	GA	30528	706-865-5356	865-0758
Greater Columbus Chamber of Commerce 1200 6th Ave PO Box 1200 *TF:* 800-360-8552 ■ *Web:* www.columbusgachamber.com	Columbus	GA	31902	706-327-1566	327-7512
Conyers-Rockdale Chamber of Commerce 1186 Scott St *Web:* www.conyers-rockdale.com	Conyers	GA	30012	770-483-7049	922-8415
Habersham County Chamber of Commerce 668 Clarkesville St *TF:* 800-835-2559 ■ *Web:* www.habershamchamber.com	Cornelia	GA	30531	706-778-4654	776-1416
Newton County Chamber of Commerce 2100 Washington St *Web:* www.newtonchamber.com	Covington	GA	30014	770-786-7510	786-1294
Cumming-Forsyth County Chamber of Commerce 212 Kelly Mill Rd *Web:* www.cummingforsythchamber.org	Cumming	GA	30040	770-887-6461	781-8800
Paulding County Chamber of Commerce 455 Jimmy Campbell Pkwy *Web:* www.pauldingchamber.org	Dallas	GA	30132	770-445-6016	445-3050
Dalton-Whitfield Chamber of Commerce 890 College Dr *Web:* www.daltonchamber.org	Dalton	GA	30720	706-278-7373	226-8739
Douglas-Coffee County Chamber of Commerce 211 S Gaskin Ave *TF:* 888-426-3334 ■ *Web:* www.douglasga.org	Douglas	GA	31533	912-384-1873	383-6304
Douglas County Chamber of Commerce 6658 Church St *Web:* www.douglascountygeorgia.com	Douglasville	GA	30134	770-942-5022	942-5876
Dublin-Laurens County Chamber of Commerce 1200 Bellvue *Web:* www.dublin-georgia.com	Dublin	GA	31021	478-272-5546	275-0811
Gwinnett Chamber of Commerce 6500 Sugarloaf Pkwy *Web:* www.gwinnettchamber.org	Duluth	GA	30097	770-232-3000	232-8807
Columbia County Chamber of Commerce 4424 Evans to Locks Rd *Web:* www.columbiacountychamber.com	Evans	GA	30809	706-651-0018	651-0023
Fayette County Chamber of Commerce 200 Courthouse Sq *Web:* www.fayettechamber.org	Fayetteville	GA	30214	770-461-9983	461-9622
Greater Hall Chamber of Commerce 230 EE Butler Pkwy *Web:* www.ghcc.com	Gainesville	GA	30501	770-532-6206	535-8419
Griffin-Spalding Chamber of Commerce 143 N Hill St *Web:* www.griffinchamber.com	Griffin	GA	30223	770-228-8200	228-8031

				Phone	Fax
Liberty County Chamber of Commerce 425 W Oglethorpe Hwy *Web:* www.libertycounty.org	Hinesville	GA	31313	912-368-4445	368-4677
Jackson County Area Chamber of Commerce 270 Athens St PO Box 629 *Web:* www.jacksoncountyga.com	Jefferson	GA	30549	706-387-0300	387-0304
Clayton County Chamber of Commerce 2270 Mt Zion Rd. *Web:* www.claytonchamber.org	Jonesboro	GA	30236	678-610-4021	610-4025
LaGrange-Troup County Chamber of Commerce 111 Bull St *Web:* www.lagrangechamber.com	LaGrange	GA	30240	706-884-8671	882-8012
Greater Macon Chamber of Commerce 305 Coliseum Dr *Web:* www.maconchamber.com	Macon	GA	31217	478-621-2000	621-2021
Henry County Chamber of Commerce 1709 Hwy 20 W W Ridge Business Ctr. *TF:* 800-436-7926 ■ *Web:* www.henrycounty.com	McDonough	GA	30253	770-957-5786	957-8030
Milledgeville-Baldwin County Chamber of Commerce 130 S Jefferson St *Web:* www.milledgevillega.com	Milledgeville	GA	31061	478-453-9311	453-0051
Walton County Chamber of Commerce 132 E Spring St *Web:* www.waltonchamber.org	Monroe	GA	30655	770-267-6594	267-0961
Moultrie-Colquitt County Chamber of Commerce 116 1st Ave SE *TF:* 888-408-4748 ■ *Web:* www.moultriechamber.com	Moultrie	GA	31768	229-985-2131	890-2638
Newnan-Coweta Chamber of Commerce 23 Bullsboro Dr *Web:* www.newnancowetachamber.org	Newnan	GA	30263	770-253-2270	253-2271
Catoosa County Area Chamber of Commerce 264 Catoosa Cir *TF:* 877-965-5201 ■ *Web:* www.catoosachamberofcommerce.com	Ringgold	GA	30736	706-965-5201	965-8224
Walker County Chamber of Commerce 10052 N Hwy 27 *Web:* www.walkercochamber.com	Rock Spring	GA	30739	706-375-7702	375-7797
Polk County Chamber of Commerce/Development Authority 604 Goodyear St. *TF:* 800-226-2517 ■ *Web:* www.polk.ofgeorgia.org	Rockmart	GA	30153	770-684-8760	684-9155
Greater Rome Chamber of Commerce 1 Riverside Pkwy *TF:* 800-234-3154 ■ *Web:* www.romega.com	Rome	GA	30161	706-291-7663	232-5755
Camden County Chamber of Commerce 2603 Osborne Rd Suite R *Web:* www.camdenchamber.com	Saint Marys	GA	31558	912-729-5840	576-7924
Savannah Area Chamber of Commerce 101 E Bay St. *TF:* 877-728-2662 ■ *Web:* www.savannahchamber.com	Savannah	GA	31401	912-644-6400	644-6499
Effingham County Chamber of Commerce 520 W 3rd St PO Box 1078. *TF:* 866-754-3301 ■ *Web:* www.effinghamcounty.com	Springfield	GA	31329	912-754-3301	754-1236
Statesboro-Bulloch Chamber of Commerce 102 S Main St. *Web:* www.statesboro-chamber.org	Statesboro	GA	30458	912-764-6111	489-3108
Thomaston-Upson Chamber of Commerce 110 W Main St *Web:* www.thomastonchamber.com	Thomaston	GA	30286	706-647-9686	647-1703
Thomasville-Thomas County Chamber of Commerce 401 S Broad St *Web:* www.thomasvillechamber.com	Thomasville	GA	31792	229-226-9600	226-9603
Tifton-Tift County Chamber of Commerce 100 Central Ave *TF:* 800-550-8438 ■ *Web:* www.tiftonchamber.org	Tifton	GA	31794	229-382-6200	386-2232
Toccoa-Stephens County Chamber of Commerce 160 N Alexander St. *Web:* www.toccoagachamber.com	Toccoa	GA	30577	706-886-2132	886-2133
DeKalb Chamber of Commerce 100 Crescent Centre Pkwy Suite 680 *Web:* www.dekalbchamber.org	Tucker	GA	30084	404-378-8000	378-3397
Valdosta-Lowndes County Chamber of Commerce 416 N Ashley St *Web:* www.valdostachamber.com	Valdosta	GA	31601	229-247-8100	245-0071
Warner Robins Area Chamber of Commerce 1228 Watson Blvd. *Web:* www.warner-robins.com	Warner Robins	GA	31093	478-922-8585	328-7745
Waycross-Ware County Chamber of Commerce 315 Plant Ave Suite B *Web:* www.waycrosschamber.org	Waycross	GA	31501	912-283-3742	283-0121
Barrow County Chamber of Commerce PO Box 456 *Web:* www.barrowchamber.com	Winder	GA	30680	770-867-9444	867-6366

HAWAII

				Phone	Fax
Hawaii Island Chamber of Commerce 117 Keawe St *Web:* www.hicc.bic	Hilo	HI	96720	808-935-7178	961-4435
Maui Chamber of Commerce 313 Ano St. *Web:* www.mauichamber.com	Kahului	HI	96732	808-871-7711	871-0706
Kailua Chamber of Commerce 600 Kailua Rd Suite 107 *TF:* 888-261-7997 ■ *Web:* www.kailuachamber.com	Kailua	HI	96734	808-261-2727	
Kona-Kohala Chamber of Commerce 75-5737 Kuakini Hwy Suite 208 *Web:* www.kona-kohala.com	Kailua-Kona	HI	96740	808-329-1758	329-8564
Kaua'i Chamber of Commerce 2970 Kele St # 112 *Web:* www.kauaichamber.org	Lihue	HI	96766	808-245-7363	245-8815

IDAHO

				Phone	Fax
Boise Metro Chamber of Commerce PO Box 2368 *Web:* www.boisechamber.org	Boise	ID	83701	208-472-5205	472-5201
Caldwell Chamber of Commerce 704 Blaine St *Web:* www.chamber.cityofcaldwell.com	Caldwell	ID	83605	208-459-7493	454-1284
Coeur d'Alene Area Chamber of Commerce 105 N 1st St Suite 100 *TF:* 877-782-9232 ■ *Web:* www.cdachamber.com	Coeur d'Alene	ID	83814	208-664-3194	667-9338
Mini-Cassia Chamber of Commerce (MCC) 1177 7th St. *Web:* www.minicassiachamber.com	Heyburn	ID	83336	208-679-4793	679-4794
Greater Idaho Falls Chamber of Commerce 630 W Broadway. *TF:* 866-365-6943 ■ *Web:* www.idahofallschamber.com	Idaho Falls	ID	83402	208-523-1010	523-2255
Lewiston Chamber of Commerce 111 Main St Suite 120 *TF:* 800-473-3543 ■ *Web:* www.lcvalleychamber.org	Lewiston	ID	83501	208-743-3531	743-2176
Meridian Chamber of Commerce 215 E Franklin Rd. *Web:* www.meridianchamber.org	Meridian	ID	83642	208-888-2817	888-2682
Moscow Chamber of Commerce 411 S Main St *TF:* 800-380-1801 ■ *Web:* www.moscowchamber.com	Moscow	ID	83843	208-882-1800	882-6186
Nampa Chamber of Commerce 315 11th Ave S *Web:* www.nampa.com	Nampa	ID	83651	208-466-4641	466-4677
Greater Pocatello Chamber of Commerce 324 S Main St. *Web:* www.pocatelloidaho.com	Pocatello	ID	83204	208-233-1525	233-1527
Sun Valley/Ketchum Chamber & Visitors Bureau PO Box 2420 *TF:* 800-634-3347 ■ *Web:* www.visitsunvalley.com	Sun Valley	ID	83353	208-726-3423	726-4533
Twin Falls Area Chamber of Commerce 858 Blue Lakes Blvd N *TF:* 866-894-6325 ■ *Web:* www.twinfallschamber.com	Twin Falls	ID	83301	208-733-3974	733-9216

ILLINOIS

				Phone	Fax
Addison Chamber of Commerce & Industry 777 W Army Trail Blvd # D *Web:* www.addisonchamber.org	Addison	IL	60101	630-543-4300	543-4355
Arlington Heights Chamber of Commerce 311 S Arlington Heights Rd Suite 20 *Web:* www.arlingtonhtschamber.com	Arlington Heights	IL	60005	847-253-1703	253-9133
Aurora Chamber of Commerce 43 W Galena Blvd *Web:* www.aurorachamber.com	Aurora	IL	60506	630-256-3180	256-3189
Barrington Area Chamber of Commerce 325 N Hough St *Web:* www.barringtonchamber.com	Barrington	IL	60010	847-381-2525	381-2540
Bartlett Chamber of Commerce 138 S Oak Ave *Web:* www.bartlettchamber.com	Bartlett	IL	60103	630-830-0324	830-9724
Belvidere Area Chamber of Commerce 130 S State St Suite 300. *Web:* www.belviderechamber.com	Belvidere	IL	61008	815-544-4357	547-7654
Berwyn Development Corp 3322 S Oak Pk Ave 2nd Fl *Web:* www.berwyn.net	Berwyn	IL	60402	708-788-8100	788-0966
McLean County Chamber of Commerce 210 S E St. *Web:* www.mcleancochamber.org	Bloomington	IL	61701	309-829-6344	827-3940
Bolingbrook Area Chamber of Commerce & Industry 201 Canterbury Ln Unit B. *Web:* www.bolingbrookchamber.org	Bolingbrook	IL	60440	630-226-8420	226-8426
Bradley-Bourbonnais Chamber of Commerce 1690 Newtown Dr. *Web:* www.bbchamber.com	Bourbonnais	IL	60914	815-932-2222	932-3294
Kankakee Regional Chamber of Commerce 1137 E 5000 N Rd *Web:* www.kankakee.org	Bourbonnais	IL	60914	815-933-7721	933-7675
Buffalo Grove Area Chamber of Commerce 50 1/2 Raupp Blvd PO Box 7124 *Web:* www.bgacc.org	Buffalo Grove	IL	60089	847-541-7799	541-7819
Calumet City Chamber of Commerce 80 River Oaks Ctr Westwood Bldg ARC 6 *Web:* www.calumetcitychamber.com	Calumet City	IL	60409	708-891-5888	891-8877
Carbondale Chamber of Commerce 131 S Illinois Ave *Web:* www.carbondalechamber.com	Carbondale	IL	62901	618-549-2146	529-5063
Northern Kane County Chamber of Commerce 2429 Randall Rd Suite B. *Web:* www.nkcchamber.com	Carpentersville	IL	60110	847-426-8565	426-1098
Champaign County Chamber of Commerce 1817 S Neil St Suite 201 *Web:* www.ccchamber.org	Champaign	IL	61820	217-359-1791	359-1809
Charleston Area Chamber of Commerce 501 Jackson Ave. *Web:* www.charlestonchamber.com	Charleston	IL	61920	217-345-7041	345-7042
Albany Park Chamber of Commerce 3403 W Lauren Ave Suite 201 *Web:* www.albanyparkchamber.org	Chicago	IL	60625	773-478-0202	478-0282
Business Partners the Chamber for Uptown 4753 N Broadway St Suite 822 *Web:* www.uptownbusinesspartners.com	Chicago	IL	60640	773-878-1184	878-3678
Chicagoland Chamber of Commerce 200 E Randolph St Suite 2200 *Web:* www.chicagolandchamber.org	Chicago	IL	60601	312-494-6700	861-0660
Cosmopolitan Chamber of Commerce 203 N Wabash Ave Suite 518 *Web:* www.cosmococ.org	Chicago	IL	60601	312-499-0611	701-0095
East Side Chamber of Commerce 3501 E 106th St Suite 200 *Web:* www.eastsidechamber.com	Chicago	IL	60617	773-721-7948	721-7446
Hyde Park Chamber of Commerce 5211 S Harper Ave # D *Web:* www.hydeparkchamberchicago.org	Chicago	IL	60615	773-288-0124	288-0464

Phone | Fax

Jefferson Park Chamber of Commerce
4849 N Milwaukee Ave Suite 305 .... Chicago IL 60630 773-736-6697 685-3316
Web: www.jeffersonpark.net

Lincoln Park Chamber of Commerce
1925 N Clybourn Ave Suite 301 .... Chicago IL 60614 773-880-5200 880-0266
Web: www.lincolnparkchamber.com

Portage Park Chamber of Commerce
5758 W Irving Pk Rd. .... Chicago IL 60634 773-777-2020 777-0202
Web: www.portageparkchamber.org

Cicero Chamber of Commerce & Industry
5801 W Cermak Rd. .... Cicero IL 60804 708-863-6000 863-8981
Web: www.cicerochamber.org

Collinsville Chamber of Commerce
221 W Main St .... Collinsville IL 62234 618-344-2884 344-7499
Web: www.discovercollinsville.com

Crete Area Chamber of Commerce
1182 Main St PO Box 263 .... Crete IL 60417 708-672-9216 672-7640
Web: www.cretechamber.com

Crystal Lake Chamber of Commerce
427 W Virginia St .... Crystal Lake IL 60014 815-459-1300 459-0243
Web: www.clchamber.com

Vermillion Advantage 28 W N St. .... Danville IL 61832 217-442-1887 442-6228
TF: 800-373-6201 ■ *Web:* www.vermillionadvantage.com

Greater Decatur Chamber of Commerce
132 S Water St #103 .... Decatur IL 62523 217-422-2200 422-4576
Web: www.decaturchamber.com

Deerfield Bannockburn & Riverwoods Chamber of Commerce
601 Deerfield Rd Suite 200 .... Deerfield IL 60015 847-945-4660 940-0381
Web: www.dbrchamber.com

DeKalb Chamber of Commerce 164 E Lincoln Hwy .... DeKalb IL 60115 815-756-6306 756-5164
Web: www.dekalb.org

Des Plaines Chamber of Commerce & Industry
1401 E Oakton St .... Des Plaines IL 60018 847-824-4200 824-7932
Web: www.dpchamber.com

Downers Grove Area Chamber of Commerce & Industry
2001 Butterfield Rd Suite 105 .... Downers Grove IL 60515 630-968-4050 968-8368
Web: www.downersgrove.org

Elgin Area Chamber of Commerce 31 S Grove Ave .... Elgin IL 60120 847-741-5660 741-5677
Web: www.elginchamber.com

Greater O'Hare Assn of Industry & Commerce
PO Box 1516 .... Elk Grove Village IL 60009 630-773-2944 350-2979
TF: 877-355-4768 ■ *Web:* www.greater-ohare.com

Elmhurst Chamber of Commerce & Industry
242 N York St .... Elmhurst IL 60126 630-834-6060 834-6002
Web: www.elmhurstchamber.org

Mont Clare-Elmwood Park Chamber of Commerce
11 W Conti Pkwy .... Elmwood Park IL 60707 708-456-8000 456-8680
Web: www.mcepchamber.org

Evanston Chamber of Commerce 1840 Oak Ave .... Evanston IL 60201 847-328-1500 328-1510
Web: www.evchamber.com

Evergreen Park Chamber of Commerce
3960 W 95 St 3rd Fl .... Evergreen Park IL 60805 708-423-1118 423-1859
Web: www.evergreenparkchamber.org

Freeport Area Chamber of Commerce
27 W Stephenson St .... Freeport IL 61032 815-233-1350 235-4038
Web: www.freeportilchamber.com

Galesburg Area Chamber of Commerce
185 S Kellogg St .... Galesburg IL 61401 309-343-1194 343-1195
Web: www.galesburg.org

Glen Ellyn Chamber of Commerce
800 Roosevelt Rd Bldg D Suite 108 .... Glen Ellyn IL 60137 630-469-0907 469-0426
Web: www.glenellynchamber.com

Glenview Chamber of Commerce
2320 Glenview Rd. .... Glenview IL 60025 847-724-0900 724-0202
Web: www.glenviewchamber.com

Growth Assn of Southwestern Illinois
5800 Godfrey Rd Alden Hall .... Godfrey IL 62035 618-467-2280 466-8289
Web: www.growthassociation.com

Chamber of Commerce of Southwestern Madison County
3600 Nameoki Rd Suite 202 .... Granite City IL 62040 618-876-6400 876-6448
Web: www.chamberswmadisoncounty.com

Lake County Chamber of Commerce
5221 Grand Ave .... Gurnee IL 60031 847-249-3800 249-3892
Web: www.lakecountychamber.com

Highland Park Chamber of Commerce
508 Central Ave Suite 206 .... Highland Park IL 60035 847-432-0284 432-2802
Web: www.chamberhp.com

West Suburban Chamber of Commerce
9440 Joliet Rd Suite B .... Hodgkins IL 60525 708-387-7550 387-7556
Web: www.westsuburbanchamber.org

Hoffman Estates Chamber of Commerce
2200 W Higgins Rd Suite 201 .... Hoffman Estates IL 60169 847-781-9100 781-9172
Web: www.hechamber.com

Chicago Southland Chamber of Commerce
920 W 175th St. .... Homewood IL 60430 708-957-6950 957-6968
Web: www.chicagosouthland.com

Jacksonville Area Chamber of Commerce
155 W Morton Ave .... Jacksonville IL 62650 217-245-2174 245-0661
Web: www.jacksonvilleil.org

Joliet Region Chamber of Commerce & Industry
63 N Chicago St .... Joliet IL 60432 815-727-5371 727-5374
Web: www.jolietchamber.com

Joliet/Will County Center for Economic Development
116 N Chicago St Suite 101 .... Joliet IL 60432 815-723-1800 723-6972
Web: www.willcountyced.com

Illinois Valley Area Chamber of Commerce & Economic Development
300 Bucklin St .... La Salle IL 61301 815-223-0227 223-4827
Web: www.ivaced.org

Algonquin/Lake in the Hills Chamber of Commerce
2114 W Algonquin Rd .... Lake In the Hills IL 60156 847-658-5300 658-6546
Web: www.alchamber.com

Lake Zurich Area Chamber of Commerce
1st Bank Plaza Suite 308 .... Lake Zurich IL 60047 847-438-5572 438-5574
Web: www.lzacc.com

Lansing Chamber of Commerce 3404 Lake St. .... Lansing IL 60438 708-474-4170 474-7393

GLMV Chamber of Commerce
1123 S Milwaukee Ave .... Libertyville IL 60048 847-680-0750 680-0760
Web: www.glmvchamber.org

Lincoln/Logan County Chamber of Commerce
1555 5th St. .... Lincoln IL 62656 217-735-2385 735-9205
Web: www.lincolnillinois.com

Lombard Area Chamber of Commerce 10 Lilac Ln. .... Lombard IL 60148 630-627-5040 627-5519
Web: www.lombardchamber.com

Parks Chamber of Commerce 100 Heart Blvd .... Loves Park IL 61111 815-633-3999 633-4057
Web: www.parkschamber.com

Macomb Area Chamber of Commerce & Downtown Development Corp
214 N Lafayette St. .... Macomb IL 61455 309-837-4855 837-4857
Web: www.macombareachamber.com

Greater Marion Area Chamber of Commerce
2305 W Main St .... Marion IL 62959 618-997-6311 997-4665
TF: 800-699-1760 ■ *Web:* www.marionillinois.com

McHenry Area Chamber of Commerce
1257 N Green St .... McHenry IL 60050 815-385-4300 385-9142
Web: www.mchenrychamber.com

Illinois Quad City Chamber of Commerce
622 19th St. .... Moline IL 61265 309-757-5416 757-5435
Web: www.quadcitychamber.com

Grundy County Chamber of Commerce & Industry
909 Liberty St .... Morris IL 60450 815-942-0113 942-0117
Web: www.grundychamber.com

Mount Prospect Chamber of Commerce
107 S Main St. .... Mount Prospect IL 60056 847-398-6616 398-6780
Web: www.mountprospectchamber.org

Jefferson County Chamber of Commerce
200 Potomac Blvd .... Mount Vernon IL 62864 618-242-5725 242-5130
Web: www.southernillinois.com

Naperville Area Chamber of Commerce
55 S Main St Suite 351 .... Naperville IL 60540 630-355-4141 355-8335
Web: www.naperville.net

Niles Chamber of Commerce
8060 W Oakton St Suite 101 .... Niles IL 60714 847-268-8180 268-8186
Web: www.nileschamber.org

Northbrook Chamber of Commerce & Industry
2002 Walters Ave .... Northbrook IL 60062 847-498-5555 498-5510
Web: www.northbrookchamber.org

Oak Forest Chamber of Commerce
15440 S Central Ave. .... Oak Forest IL 60452 708-687-4600 687-7878
Web: www.oakforestchamber.org

Oak Lawn Chamber of Commerce 5314 W 95th St ..... Oak Lawn IL 60453 708-424-8300 229-2236
Web: www.oaklawnchamber.com

Orland Park Area Chamber of Commerce
8799 W 151 St .... Orland Park IL 60462 708-349-2972 349-7454
Web: www.orlandparkchamber.org

Palatine Area Chamber of Commerce
579 First Bank Dr #205 .... Palatine IL 60067 847-359-7200 359-7246
Web: www.palatinechamber.com

Paris Area Chamber of Commerce & Tourism
105 N Central Ave. .... Paris IL 61944 217-465-4179 465-4170
Web: www.parisilchamber.com

Matteson Area Chamber of Commerce
298 Main St .... Park Forest IL 60466 708-747-6000 747-6054

Park Ridge Chamber of Commerce
32 Main St Suite C .... Park Ridge IL 60068 847-825-3121 825-3122
Web: www.secure.parkridgechamber.org

Pekin Area Chamber of Commerce 402 Ct St. .... Pekin IL 61554 309-346-2106 346-2104
Web: www.pekin.net

Peoria Area Chamber of Commerce
100 SW Water St. .... Peoria IL 61602 309-676-0755 676-7534
Web: www.peoriachamber.org

Quincy Area Chamber of Commerce
300 Civic Ctr Plaza Suite 245 .... Quincy IL 62301 217-222-7980 222-3033
Web: www.quincychamber.org

Oak Park-River Forest Chamber of Commerce
7727 Lake St. .... River Forest IL 60305 708-771-5760 848-8182
Web: www.oprfchamber.org

Rockford Chamber of Commerce
308 W State St Suite 190 .... Rockford IL 61101 815-987-8100 987-8122
Web: www.rockfordchamber.com

Rolling Meadows Chamber of Commerce
2775 Algonquin Rd Suite 310 .... Rolling Meadows IL 60008 847-398-3730 398-3745
Web: www.rmchamber.com

Round Lake Area Chamber of Commerce & Industry
2007 Civic Center Way .... Round Lake Beach IL 60073 847-546-2002 546-2254
Web: www.rlchamber.org

Skokie Chamber of Commerce
5002 Oakton St PO Box 106 .... Skokie IL 60077 847-673-0240 673-0249
Web: www.skokiechamber.org

Greater Springfield Chamber of Commerce The
1011 S 2nd St. .... Springfield IL 62701 217-525-1173 525-8768
Web: www.gscc.org

Illinois Assn of Chamber of Commerce Executives
215 E Adams St .... Springfield IL 62701 217-522-5512 522-5518
Web: www.iacce.org

Streamwood Chamber of Commerce
22 W Streamwood Blvd PO Box 545. .... Streamwood IL 60107 630-837-5200 837-5251
Web: www.streamwoodchamber.com

Streator Area Chamber of Commerce & Industry
320 E Main St PO Box 360 .... Streator IL 61364 815-672-2921 672-1768
Web: www.streatorchamber.com

Tinley Park Chamber of Commerce
17316 Oak Pk Ave. .... Tinley Park IL 60477 708-532-5700 532-1475
Web: www.tinleychamber.org

Wheaton Chamber of Commerce 108 E Wesley St ..... Wheaton IL 60187 630-668-6464 668-2744
Web: www.wheatonchamber.com

Organization / Address	City	State	Zip	Phone	Fax
Wheeling/Prospect Heights Area Chamber of Commerce & Industry 395 E Dundee Rd Suite 300 *Web:* www.wphchamber.com	Wheeling	IL	60090	847-541-0170	541-0296
Wilmette Chamber of Commerce (WCC) 1150 Wilmette Ave Suite A *Web:* www.wilmettechamber.org	Wilmette	IL	60091	847-251-3800	251-6321
Woodridge Area Chamber of Commerce 6440 Main St Suite 330 *Web:* www.woodridgechamber.org	Woodridge	IL	60517	630-960-7080	852-2316
Woodstock Chamber of Commerce & Industry 136 Cass St *Web:* www.woodstockilchamber.com	Woodstock	IL	60098	815-338-2436	338-2927
Chicago Ridge-Worth Chamber of Commerce PO Box 356 *Web:* www.crwchamber.com	Worth	IL	60482	708-923-2050	930-0090

INDIANA

Organization / Address	City	State	Zip	Phone	Fax
Madison County Chamber of Commerce The 2701 Enterprise Dr Suite 109 *Web:* www.getlinkedmadison.com	Anderson	IN	46013	765-642-0264	642-0266
Angola Area Chamber of Commerce 211 E Maumee St Suite B *Web:* www.angolachamber.org	Angola	IN	46703	260-665-3512	665-7418
Auburn Chamber of Commerce 208 S Jackson St *Web:* www.chamberinauburn.com	Auburn	IN	46706	260-925-2100	925-2199
Greater Bloomington Chamber of Commerce 400 W 7th St Suite 102 *Web:* www.chamberbloomington.org	Bloomington	IN	47404	812-336-6381	336-0651
Warrick County Chamber of Commerce 224 W Main St *Web:* www.warrickcounty.us	Boonville	IN	47601	812-897-2340	897-2360
Carmel-Clay Chamber of Commerce 37 E Main St Suite 300 *Web:* www.carmelchamber.com	Carmel	IN	46032	317-846-1049	844-6843
Columbia City Area Chamber of Commerce 201 N Line St *Web:* www.whitleychamber.com	Columbia City	IN	46725	260-248-8131	248-8162
Columbus Area Chamber of Commerce 500 Franklin St *Web:* www.columbusareachamber.com	Columbus	IN	47201	812-379-4457	378-7308
Connersville/Fayette County Chamber of Commerce 504 N Central Ave	Connersville	IN	47331	765-825-2561	825-4613
Chamber of Commerce of Harrison County 119 E Beaver St *Web:* www.harrisonchamber.org	Corydon	IN	47112	812-738-2137	738-6438
Crawfordsville-Montgomery County Chamber of Commerce 309 N Green St *Web:* www.crawfordsvillechamber.com	Crawfordsville	IN	47933	765-362-6800	362-6900
Greater Elkhart Chamber of Commerce 418 S Main St *Web:* www.elkhart.org	Elkhart	IN	46516	574-293-1531	294-1859
Chamber of Commerce of Southwest Indiana 100 NW 2nd St Suite 100 *Web:* www.evansvillechamber.com	Evansville	IN	47708	812-425-8147	421-5883
Greater Fort Wayne Chamber of Commerce 826 Ewing St *Web:* www.fwchamber.org	Fort Wayne	IN	46802	260-424-1435	426-7232
Clinton County Chamber of Commerce 259 E Walnut St *Web:* www.ccinchamber.org	Frankfort	IN	46041	765-654-5507	654-9592
Gary Chamber of Commerce 839 Broadway Suite S-103 *Web:* www.garychamber.com	Gary	IN	46402	219-885-7407	885-7408
Goshen Chamber of Commerce 232 S Main St *TF:* 800-307-4204 ■ *Web:* www.goshen.org	Goshen	IN	46526	574-533-2102	533-2103
Greencastle Chamber of Commerce 16 S Jackson St *Web:* www.gogreencastle.com	Greencastle	IN	46135	765-653-4517	653-6385
Greater Greenwood Chamber of Commerce 65 Airport Pkwy *Web:* www.greenwood-chamber.com	Greenwood	IN	46143	317-888-4856	865-2609
Lakeshore Chamber of Commerce 5246 Hohman Ave Suite 100 *Web:* www.lakeshorechamber.com	Hammond	IN	46320	219-931-1000	937-8778
Greater Indianapolis Chamber of Commerce 111 Monument Cir Suite 1950 *Web:* www.indychamber.com	Indianapolis	IN	46204	317-464-2200	464-2217
Greater Lawrence Township Chamber of Commerce 9120 Otis Ave Suite 100 *Web:* www.lawrencechamberofcommerce.org	Indianapolis	IN	46216	317-541-9876	541-9875
Kokomo/Howard County Chamber of Commerce 325 N Main St *Web:* www.kokomochamber.com	Kokomo	IN	46901	765-457-5301	452-4564
Lafayette-West Lafayette Chamber of Commerce 337 Columbia St *Web:* www.lafayettechamber.com	Lafayette	IN	47901	765-742-4041	742-6276
LaGrange County Chamber of Commerce 901 S Detroit St Suite A *Web:* www.lagrangechamber.org	LaGrange	IN	46761	260-463-2443	463-2683
Dearborn County Chamber of Commerce 320 Walnut St *TF:* 800-322-8198 ■ *Web:* www.dearborncountychamber.org	Lawrenceburg	IN	47025	812-537-0814	537-0845
Boone County Chamber of Commerce 221 N Lebanon St *Web:* www.boonechamber.org	Lebanon	IN	46052	765-482-1320	482-3114
Logansport/Cass County Chamber of Commerce 300 E Broadway Suite 103 *TF:* 800-425-2071 ■ *Web:* www.logan-casschamber.com	Logansport	IN	46947	574-753-6388	735-0909
Madison Area Chamber of Commerce 301 E Main St *Web:* www.madisonchamber.org	Madison	IN	47250	812-265-3135	265-9784
Marion-Grant County Chamber of Commerce 215 S Adams St *Web:* www.marionchamber.org	Marion	IN	46952	765-664-5107	668-5443
Michigan City Area Chamber of Commerce 200 E Michigan Blvd *Web:* www.michigancitychamber.com	Michigan City	IN	46360	219-874-6221	873-1204
Greater Monticello Chamber of Commerce 116 N Main St *Web:* www.monticelloin.com	Monticello	IN	47960	574-583-7220	583-3399
Muncie-Delaware County Chamber of Commerce 401 S High St *TF:* 800-336-1373 ■ *Web:* www.muncie.com	Muncie	IN	47305	765-288-6681	751-9151
One Southern Indiana 4100 Charlestown Rd *Web:* www.1si.org	New Albany	IN	47150	812-945-0266	948-4664
Noblesville Chamber of Commerce 601 Conner St *Web:* www.noblesvillechamber.com	Noblesville	IN	46060	317-773-0086	773-1966
Jennings County Chamber of Commerce 524 N State St PO Box 340 *Web:* www.jenningscountychamber.org	North Vernon	IN	47265	812-346-2339	346-2065
Miami County Chamber of Commerce 13 E Main St *Web:* www.miamicochamber.com	Peru	IN	46970	765-472-1923	472-7099
Greater Portage Chamber of Commerce 2642 Eleanor St *Web:* www.portageinchamber.com	Portage	IN	46368	219-762-3300	763-2450
Wayne County Area Chamber of Commerce 33 S 7th St Suite 2 *Web:* www.rwchamber.org	Richmond	IN	47374	765-962-1511	966-0882
Schererville Chamber of Commerce 13 W Joliet St *Web:* www.scherervillechamber.com	Schererville	IN	46375	219-322-5412	322-0598
Shelby County Chamber of Commerce 501 N Harrison St *TF:* 800-318-4083 ■ *Web:* www.shelbychamber.net	Shelbyville	IN	46176	317-398-6647	392-3901
Chamber of Commerce of Saint Joseph County 401 E Colfax Ave Suite 310 *Web:* www.sjchamber.org	South Bend	IN	46617	574-234-0051	289-0358
Winchester Area Chamber of Commerce 112 W Washington St *Web:* www.winchesterchamber.org	Winchester	IN	47394	765-584-3731	584-5544

IOWA

Organization / Address	City	State	Zip	Phone	Fax
Ames Chamber of Commerce 1601 Golden Aspen Dr Suite 110 *Web:* www.ameschamber.com	Ames	IA	50010	515-232-2310	232-6716
Burlington/West Burlington Area Chamber of Commerce 610 N 4th St Suite 200 *TF:* 800-827-4837 ■ *Web:* www.growburlington.com	Burlington	IA	52601	319-752-6365	752-6454
Greater Cedar Falls Chamber of Commerce 10 Main St *Web:* www.cedarfalls.org	Cedar Falls	IA	50613	319-266-3593	277-4325
Cedar Rapids Area Chamber of Commerce 424 1st Ave NE *Web:* www.cedarrapids.org	Cedar Rapids	IA	52401	319-398-5317	398-5228
Clinton Area Chamber of Commerce 721 S 2nd St *TF:* 800-828-5702 ■ *Web:* www.clintonia.com	Clinton	IA	52732	563-242-5702	242-5803
Council Bluffs Area Chamber of Commerce 7 N 6th St *TF:* 800-228-6878 ■ *Web:* www.councilbluffsiowa.com	Council Bluffs	IA	51503	712-325-1000	322-5698
DavenportOne 130 W 2nd St *Web:* www.davenportone.com	Davenport	IA	52801	563-322-1706	322-7804
Greater Des Moines Partnership 700 Locust St Suite 100 *TF:* 800-376-9059 ■ *Web:* www.desmoinesmetro.com	Des Moines	IA	50309	515-286-4950	286-4974
Dubuque Area Chamber of Commerce 300 Main St Suite 200 *TF:* 800-798-4748 ■ *Web:* www.dubuquechamber.com	Dubuque	IA	52001	563-557-9200	557-1591
Fort Dodge Chamber of Commerce 1406 Central Ave *Web:* www.fortdodgechamber.com	Fort Dodge	IA	50501	515-955-5500	955-3245
Iowa City Area Chamber of Commerce 325 E Washington St Suite 100 *Web:* www.iowacityarea.com	Iowa City	IA	52240	319-337-9637	338-9958
Keokuk Area Chamber of Commerce 329 Main St *Web:* www.keokukchamber.com	Keokuk	IA	52632	319-524-5055	524-5016
Marion Chamber of Commerce 1225 6th Ave Suite 100 *Web:* www.cedarrapids.org	Marion	IA	52302	319-377-6316	377-1576
Marshalltown Area Chamber of Commerce 709 S Ctr St PO Box 1000 *Web:* www.marshalltown.org	Marshalltown	IA	50158	641-753-6645	752-8373
Mason City Area Chamber of Commerce 25 W State St *Web:* www.masoncityia.com	Mason City	IA	50401	641-423-5724	423-5725
Ottumwa Area Chamber of Commerce 217 E Main St *TF:* 800-564-5274 ■ *Web:* www.ottumwaiowa.com	Ottumwa	IA	52501	641-682-3465	682-3466
Siouxland Chamber of Commerce 101 Pierce St *Web:* www.siouxlandchamber.com	Sioux City	IA	51101	712-255-7903	258-7578
Urbandale Chamber of Commerce 3600 NW 86th St *Web:* www.urbandalechamber.com	Urbandale	IA	50322	515-331-6855	331-2987
Greater Cedar Valley Chamber of Commerce 315 E 5th St *Web:* www.waterloochamber.org	Waterloo	IA	50703	319-233-8431	233-4580

	City	State	Zip	Phone	Fax
West Des Moines Chamber of Commerce 4200 Mills Civic Pkwy Suite E-200 *Web:* www.wdmchamber.org	West Des Moines	IA	50265	515-225-6009	225-7129

KANSAS

	City	State	Zip	Phone	Fax
Arkansas City Area Chamber of Commerce PO Box 795 *Web:* www.arkcity.org	Arkansas City	KS	67005	620-442-0230	441-0048
Dodge City Area Chamber of Commerce 311 W Spruce St *Web:* www.dodgechamber.com	Dodge City	KS	67801	620-227-3119	227-2957
Emporia Area Chamber of Commerce 719 Commercial St *Web:* www.emporia.com	Emporia	KS	66801	620-342-1600	342-3223
Garden City Area Chamber of Commerce 1511 E Fulton Terr *Web:* www.gardencity.net	Garden City	KS	67846	620-276-3264	276-3290
Hutchinson/Reno County Chamber of Commerce 117 N Walnut St *TF:* 800-691-4262 ■ *Web:* www.hutchchamber.com	Hutchinson	KS	67501	620-662-3391	662-2168
Junction City Area Chamber of Commerce 701 N Jefferson *Web:* www.junctioncitychamber.org	Junction City	KS	66441	785-762-2632	762-3353
Kansas City Kansas Area Chamber of Commerce 727 Minnesota Ave *Web:* www.kckchamber.com	Kansas City	KS	66117	913-371-3070	371-3732
Women's Chamber of Commerce PO Box 171337 *Web:* www.womenschamberkck.org	Kansas City	KS	66117	913-371-3165	
Leavenworth-Lansing Area Chamber of Commerce 518 Shawnee St *TF:* 800-844-4114 ■ *Web:* www.leavenworth-lansingareachamberofcommerce.com	Leavenworth	KS	66048	913-682-4112	682-8170
Lenexa Chamber of Commerce 11180 Lackman Rd *TF:* 800-950-7867 ■ *Web:* www.lenexa.org	Lenexa	KS	66219	913-888-1414	888-3770
Liberal Area Chamber of Commerce PO Box 676 *Web:* www.liberalkschamber.com	Liberal	KS	67905	620-624-3855	624-8851
Manhattan Area Chamber of Commerce 501 Poyntz Ave *TF:* 800-759-0134 ■ *Web:* www.manhattan.org	Manhattan	KS	66502	785-776-8829	776-0679
Olathe Chamber of Commerce 18001 W 106th St Suite 160 *TF:* 800-921-5678 ■ *Web:* www.olathe.com	Olathe	KS	66061	913-764-1050	782-4636
Overland Park Chamber of Commerce 9001 W 110th St Suite 150 *Web:* www.opks.org	Overland Park	KS	66210	913-491-3600	491-0393
Pittsburg Area Chamber of Commerce 117 W 4th St *TF:* 800-879-1112 ■ *Web:* www.pittsburgareachamber.com	Pittsburg	KS	66762	620-231-1000	231-3178
Salina Area Chamber of Commerce 120 W Ash St *Web:* www.salinakansas.org	Salina	KS	67401	785-827-9301	827-9758
Shawnee Chamber of Commerce 15100 W 67th St Suite 202 *TF:* 888-550-7282 ■ *Web:* www.shawneekschamber.com	Shawnee	KS	66217	913-631-6545	631-9628
Greater Topeka Chamber of Commerce 120 SE 6th St Suite 110 *Web:* www.topekachamber.org	Topeka	KS	66603	785-234-2644	234-8656
Wichita Area Chamber of Commerce 350 W Douglas Ave *Web:* www.wichitachamber.org	Wichita	KS	67202	316-265-7771	265-7502

KENTUCKY

	City	State	Zip	Phone	Fax
Ashland Alliance Chamber of Commerce 1733 Winchester Ave *TF:* 888-524-6860 ■ *Web:* www.ashlandalliance.com	Ashland	KY	41101	606-324-5111	325-4607
Knox County Chamber of Commerce 196 Daniel Boone Dr Suite 205 *Web:* www.knoxcochamber.com	Barbourville	KY	40906	606-546-4300	
Bardstown-Nelson County Chamber of Commerce 1 Ct Sq *TF:* 866-894-9545 ■ *Web:* www.bardstownchamber.com	Bardstown	KY	40004	502-348-9545	348-6478
Marshall County Chamber of Commerce 17 US Hwy 68 W *Web:* www.marshallcounty.net	Benton	KY	42025	270-527-7665	527-9193
Bowling Green Area Chamber of Commerce 710 College St *Web:* www.bgchamber.com	Bowling Green	KY	42101	270-781-3200	843-0458
Danville-Boyle County Chamber of Commerce 304 S 4th St Suite 201 *Web:* www.betterindanville.com	Danville	KY	40422	859-236-2805	236-3197
Elizabethtown-Hardin County Chamber of Commerce 111 W Dixie Ave *Web:* www.elizabethtownchamber.org	Elizabethtown	KY	42701	270-765-4334	737-0690
Northern Kentucky Chamber of Commerce 300 Buttermilk Pike Suite 330 *Web:* www.nkychamber.com	Fort Mitchell	KY	41017	859-578-8800	578-8802
Frankfort Area Chamber of Commerce 100 Capitol Ave *Web:* www.frankfortky.info	Frankfort	KY	40601	502-223-8261	223-5942
Georgetown-Scott County Chamber of Commerce 160 E Main St *Web:* www.gtown.org	Georgetown	KY	40324	502-863-5424	863-5756
Glasgow-Barren County Chamber of Commerce 118 E Public Sq *TF:* 800-264-3161 ■ *Web:* www.glasgowbarrenchamber.com	Glasgow	KY	42141	270-651-3161	651-3122
Greenville-Muhlenberg County Chamber of Commerce PO Box 313	Greenville	KY	42345	270-338-5422	338-5440
Harlan County Chamber of Commerce 115 N Cumberland Ave *Web:* www.harlancountychamber.com	Harlan	KY	40831	606-573-4717	573-4717
Henderson-Henderson County Chamber of Commerce 230 2nd St # 320 *Web:* www.hendersonky.com	Henderson	KY	42420	270-826-9531	827-4461
Hopkinsville-Christian County Chamber of Commerce 2800 Port Campbell Blvd *TF:* 800-842-9959 ■ *Web:* www.commercecenter.org	Hopkinsville	KY	42240	270-885-9096	886-2059
Jeffersontown Chamber of Commerce 10434 Watterson Tr *Web:* www.jtownchamber.com	Jeffersontown	KY	40299	502-267-1674	267-6874
Oldham County Chamber of Commerce 412 E Main St *TF:* 800-813-9953 ■ *Web:* www.oldhamcountychamber.com	LaGrange	KY	40031	502-222-1635	222-3159
Greater Lexington Chamber of Commerce Inc 330 E Main St Suite 100 *Web:* www.commercelexington.com	Lexington	KY	40507	859-254-4447	233-3304
Greater Louisville Inc 614 W Main St *TF:* 800-500-1066 ■ *Web:* www.greaterlouisville.com	Louisville	KY	40202	502-625-0000	625-0010
Madisonville-Hopkins County Chamber of Commerce 15 E Ctr St *Web:* www.madisonville-hopkinschamber.com	Madisonville	KY	42431	270-821-3435	821-9190
Mayfield-Graves County Chamber of Commerce 201 E College St *Web:* www.mayfieldchamber.com	Mayfield	KY	42066	270-247-6101	247-6110
Bell County Chamber of Commerce PO Box 788 *Web:* www.bellcountychamber.com	Middlesboro	KY	40965	606-248-1075	248-8851
Murray-Calloway County Chamber of Commerce 805 N 12th St *TF:* 800-900-5171 ■ *Web:* www.murraylink.com	Murray	KY	42071	270-753-5171	753-0948
Jessamine County Chamber of Commerce 508 N Main St Suite A *Web:* www.jessaminechamber.com	Nicholasville	KY	40356	859-887-4351	887-1211
Greater Owensboro Chamber of Commerce 200 E 3rd St PO Box 825 *Web:* www.owensboro.com	Owensboro	KY	42302	270-926-1860	926-3364
Paducah Area Chamber of Commerce 401 Kentucky Ave *Web:* www.paducahchamber.org	Paducah	KY	42003	270-443-1746	442-9152
Pike County Chamber of Commerce 787 Hambley Blvd *Web:* www.pikecountychamber.org	Pikeville	KY	41501	606-432-5504	432-7295
Radcliff Hardin County Chamber of Commerce 306 N Wilson Rd *Web:* www.hardinchamber.com	Radcliff	KY	40160	270-351-4450	352-4449
Logan County Chamber of Commerce 116 S Main St *Web:* www.loganchamber.com	Russellville	KY	42276	270-726-2206	726-2237
Shelby County Chamber of Commerce 316 Main St *Web:* www.shelbycountykychamber.com	Shelbyville	KY	40065	502-633-1636	633-7501
Bullitt County Chamber of Commerce 505 Buffalo Run Rd # 101 *Web:* www.bullittcounty.org	Shepherdsville	KY	40165	502-543-6727	543-1765
Somerset-Pulaski County Chamber of Commerce 445 S Hwy 27 Suite 101 *Web:* www.spcchamber.com	Somerset	KY	42501	606-679-7323	679-1744
Winchester-Clark County Chamber of Commerce 2 S Maple St *Web:* www.winchesterkychamber.com	Winchester	KY	40391	859-744-6420	744-9229

LOUISIANA

	City	State	Zip	Phone	Fax
Central Louisiana Chamber of Commerce 1118 3rd St PO Box 992 *Web:* www.cenlachamber.org	Alexandria	LA	71309	318-442-6671	442-6734
Bastrop-Morehouse Parish Chamber of Commerce 110 N Franklin St *Web:* www.bastrop-morehouse.com	Bastrop	LA	71220	318-281-3794	281-3781
Greater Baton Rouge Chamber of Commerce 564 Laurel St *Web:* www.brac.org	Baton Rouge	LA	70801	225-381-7125	336-4306
Bossier Chamber of Commerce 710 Benton Rd *Web:* www.bossierchamber.com	Bossier City	LA	71111	318-746-0252	746-0357
Saint Tammany West Chamber of Commerce 610 Hollycrest Blvd *Web:* www.sttammanychamber.org	Covington	LA	70433	985-892-3216	893-4244
Livingston Parish Chamber of Commerce PO Box 591	Denham Springs	LA	70726	225-665-8155	665-2411
Greater Beauregard Chamber of Commerce 111 N Washington St PO Box 309	DeRidder	LA	70634	337-463-5533	463-2244
Ascension Chamber of Commerce 1006 W Hwy 30 *Web:* www.ascensionchamber.com	Gonzales	LA	70737	225-647-7487	647-5124
Houma-Terrebonne Chamber of Commerce 6133 Louisiana 311 *Web:* www.houmachamber.com	Houma	LA	70360	985-876-5600	876-5611
Greater Jennings Chamber of Commerce 246 N Main St *Web:* www.jenningschamber.com	Jennings	LA	70546	337-824-0933	824-0934
Greater Lafayette Chamber of Commerce 804 E St Mary Blvd *Web:* www.lafchamber.org	Lafayette	LA	70503	337-233-2705	234-8671
Chamber/Southwest Louisiana 120 W Pujo St *Web:* www.chamberswla.org	Lake Charles	LA	70601	337-433-3632	436-3727
Chamber of Lafourche & the Bayou Region 107 W 26th St *Web:* www.lafourchechamber.com	Larose	LA	70373	985-693-6700	693-6702

Chamber	City	State	ZIP	Phone	Fax
Greater Vernon Chamber of Commerce PO Box 1228 *Web:* www.chambervernonparish.com	Leesville	LA	71496	337-238-0349	238-0340
DeSoto Parish Chamber of Commerce 115 N Washington Ave *Web:* www.desotoparishchamber.net	Mansfield	LA	71052	318-872-1310	871-1875
Jefferson Chamber of Commerce 3421 N Cswy Blvd Suite 203 *Web:* www.jeffersonchamber.org	Metairie	LA	70002	504-835-3880	835-3828
Monroe Chamber of Commerce 212 Walnut St Suite 100 *TF:* 888-531-9535 ■ *Web:* www.monroe.org	Monroe	LA	71201	318-323-3461	322-7594
Saint Mary Parish Chamber of Commerce 7332 Hwy 182 *Web:* www.stmarychamberofcommerce.com	Morgan City	LA	70380	985-384-3830	384-0771
Natchitoches Area Chamber of Commerce 560 2nd St *Web:* www.natchitocheschamber.com	Natchitoches	LA	71457	318-352-6894	352-5385
Greater Iberia Chamber of Commerce 111 W Main St	New Iberia	LA	70560	337-364-1836	367-7405
New Orleans Chamber of Commerce 1515 Poydras St Suite 1010 *Web:* www.neworleanschamber.org	New Orleans	LA	70112	504-522-7226	799-4259
Iberville Parish Chamber of Commerce 23675 Church St *Web:* www.ibervillechamber.com	Plaquemine	LA	70764	225-687-3560	687-3575
Ruston/Lincoln Chamber of Commerce 211 N Trenton *TF:* 800-392-9032 ■ *Web:* www.rustonlincoln.org	Ruston	LA	71270	318-255-2031	255-3481
Greater Shreveport Chamber of Commerce 400 Edwards St *TF:* 800-448-5432 ■ *Web:* www.shreveportchamber.org	Shreveport	LA	71101	318-677-2500	677-2541
Greater Slidell Area Chamber of Commerce 118 W Hall Ave *TF:* 800-471-3758 ■ *Web:* www.slidellchamber.com	Slidell	LA	70460	985-643-5678	649-2460
Thibodaux Chamber of Commerce 318 E Bayou Rd PO Box 467 *Web:* www.thibodauxchamber.com	Thibodaux	LA	70302	985-446-1187	446-1191

MAINE

Chamber	City	State	ZIP	Phone	Fax
Kennebec Valley Chamber of Commerce 21 University Dr *Web:* www.augustamaine.com	Augusta	ME	04330	207-623-4559	626-9342
Bangor Region Chamber of Commerce 519 Main St *Web:* www.bangorregion.com	Bangor	ME	04401	207-947-0307	990-1427
Bar Harbor Chamber of Commerce 2 Cottage St *TF:* 888-540-9990 ■ *Web:* www.barharborinfo.com	Bar Harbor	ME	04609	207-288-5103	667-9080
Belfast Area Chamber of Commerce 14 Main St *Web:* www.belfastmaine.org	Belfast	ME	04915	207-338-5900	338-3808
Saint Croix Valley Chamber of Commerce 39 Union St *TF:* 888-422-3112 ■ *Web:* www.visitcalais.com	Calais	ME	04619	207-454-2308	454-2308
Ellsworth Area Chamber of Commerce 163 High St *Web:* www.ellsworthchamber.org	Ellsworth	ME	04605	207-667-5584	667-2617
Androscoggin County Chamber of Commerce PO Box 59 *Web:* www.androscoggincounty.com	Lewiston	ME	04243	207-783-2249	783-4481
Greater Lincoln Lakes Region Chamber of Commerce 256 W Broadway *Web:* www.lincolnmechamber.org	Lincoln	ME	04457	207-794-8065	
Portland Regional Chamber 60 Pearl St *Web:* www.portlandregion.com	Portland	ME	04101	207-772-2811	772-1179
Biddeford-Saco Chamber of Commerce & Industry 138 Main St Suite 101 *Web:* www.biddefordsacochamber.org	Saco	ME	04072	207-282-1567	282-3149
Sanford-Springvale Chamber of Commerce & Economic Development 917 Main St Suite B *Web:* www.sanfordchamber.org	Sanford	ME	04073	207-324-4280	324-8290
Oxford Hills Chamber of Commerce 4 Western Ave *Web:* www.oxfordhillsmaine.com	South Paris	ME	04281	207-743-2281	743-0687
Southern Midcoast Maine Chamber 2 Main St Border Trust Business Ctr *TF:* 877-725-8797 ■ *Web:* www.midcoastmaine.com	Topsham	ME	04086	207-725-8797	725-9787
Mid-Maine Chamber of Commerce 50 Elm St *Web:* www.midmainechamber.com	Waterville	ME	04901	207-873-3315	877-0087

MARYLAND

Chamber	City	State	ZIP	Phone	Fax
Annapolis & Anne Arundel County Chamber of Commerce 49 Old Solomons Island Rd Suite 204 *Web:* www.annapolischamber.com	Annapolis	MD	21401	410-266-3960	266-8270
Harford County Chamber of Commerce 108 S Bond St *TF:* 800-682-8536 ■ *Web:* www.harfordchamber.org	Bel Air	MD	21014	410-838-2020	893-4715
Greater Bethesda-Chevy Chase Chamber of Commerce 7910 Woodmont Ave Suite 1204 *Web:* www.bccchamber.org	Bethesda	MD	20814	301-652-4900	657-1973
Greater Bowie Chamber of Commerce 1525 Pointer Ridge Pl Suite 302 *Web:* www.bowiechamber.org	Bowie	MD	20715	301-262-0920	262-0921
Saint Mary's County Chamber of Commerce 44200 Airport Rd Suite B *Web:* www.smcchamber.com	California	MD	20619	301-737-3001	737-0089
Dorchester Chamber of Commerce 528 Poplar St *Web:* www.dorchesterchamber.org	Cambridge	MD	21613	410-228-3575	228-6848
Queen Anne's County Chamber of Commerce 1561 Postal Rd *Web:* www.qacchamber.com	Chester	MD	21619	410-643-8530	643-8477
Howard County Chamber of Commerce 5560 Sterrett Pl Suite 105 *Web:* www.howardchamber.com	Columbia	MD	21044	410-730-4111	730-4584
Greater Crofton Chamber of Commerce 1561 Eton Way *Web:* www.croftonchamber.com	Crofton	MD	21114	410-721-9131	721-0785
Allegany County Chamber of Commerce 24 Frederick St *Web:* www.alleganycountychamber.com	Cumberland	MD	21502	301-722-2820	722-5995
Caroline County Chamber of Commerce 24820 Meeting House Rd Suite 113 *Web:* www.carolinechamber.org	Denton	MD	21629	410-479-4638	479-4862
Talbot County Chamber of Commerce 101 Marlboro Ave Suite 53 *Web:* www.talbotchamber.org	Easton	MD	21601	410-822-4606	822-7922
Cecil County Chamber of Commerce 106 E Main St #101a *Web:* www.cecilchamber.com	Elkton	MD	21921	410-392-3833	392-6225
Frederick County Chamber of Commerce 8420 Gas House Pike # B *TF:* 800-999-3613 ■ *Web:* www.frederickchamber.org	Frederick	MD	21701	301-662-4164	846-4427
Gaithersburg-Germantown Chamber of Commerce 4 Professional Dr Suite 132 *Web:* www.ggchamber.org	Gaithersburg	MD	20879	301-840-1400	963-3918
Northern Anne Arundel County Chamber of Commerce 7477 Baltimore-Annapolis Blvd Suite 204 *Web:* www.naaccc.com	Glen Burnie	MD	21061	410-766-8282	766-5722
Hagerstown-Washington County Chamber of Commerce 28 W Washington St *Web:* www.hagerstown.org	Hagerstown	MD	21740	301-739-2015	739-1278
Charles County Chamber of Commerce 101 Centennial St Suite A *Web:* www.charlescountychamber.org	La Plata	MD	20646	301-932-6500	932-3945
Prince George's Chamber of Commerce 4640 Forbes Blvd Suite 130 *Web:* www.pgcoc.org	Lanham	MD	20706	301-731-5000	731-5013
Baltimore/Washington Corridor Chamber of Commerce 312 Marshall Ave Suite 104 *Web:* www.baltwashchamber.org	Laurel	MD	20707	301-725-4000	725-0776
Garrett County Chamber of Commerce 15 Visitors Ctr Dr *TF:* 800-387-5237 ■ *Web:* www.visitdeepcreek.com	McHenry	MD	21541	301-387-4386	387-2080
Essex-Middle River-White Marsh Chamber of Commerce 405 Williams Ct Suite 108 *Web:* www.emrchamber.org	Middle River	MD	21220	443-317-8763	317-8772
Greater Ocean City Chamber of Commerce 12320 Ocean Gateway *TF:* 888-626-3386 ■ *Web:* www.oceancity.org	Ocean City	MD	21842	410-213-0144	213-7521
West Anne Arundel County Chamber of Commerce 8385 Piney Orchard Pkwy *Web:* www.waaccc.org	Odenton	MD	21113	410-672-3422	672-3475
Olney Chamber of Commerce 3460 Olney-Laytonsville Rd Suite 211 *Web:* www.olneymd.org	Olney	MD	20832	301-774-7117	774-4944
Pikesville Chamber of Commerce 7 Church Ln Suite 14 *Web:* www.pikesvillechamber.org	Pikesville	MD	21208	410-484-2337	484-4151
Calvert County Chamber of Commerce PO Box 9 **Fax Area Code:* 443 ■ *Web:* www.calvertchamber.org	Prince Frederick	MD	20678	410-535-2577	295-7213*
Reisterstown-Owings Mills-Glyndon Chamber of Commerce 100 Owings Ct Suite 9	Reistertown	MD	21136	410-702-7074	702-7075
Montgomery County Chamber of Commerce 51 Monroe St Suite 1800 *Web:* www.montgomerycountychamber.com	Rockville	MD	20850	301-738-0015	738-8792
Rockville Chamber of Commerce 1 Research Ct # 450 *Web:* www.rockvillechamber.org	Rockville	MD	20850	301-424-9300	762-7599
Salisbury Area Chamber of Commerce 144 E Main St *Web:* www.salisburyarea.com	Salisbury	MD	21801	410-749-0144	860-9925
Greater Severna Park Chamber of Commerce 1 Holly Ave *Web:* www.severnaparkchamber.com	Severna Park	MD	21146	410-647-3900	647-3999
Greater Silver Spring Chamber of Commerce 8601 Georgia Ave Suite 203 *Web:* www.silverspringchamber.com	Silver Spring	MD	20910	301-565-3777	565-3377
Snow Hill Chamber of Commerce 100 Pearl St *Web:* www.snowhillmd.com	Snow Hill	MD	21863	410-632-0809	632-3158
Baltimore County Chamber of Commerce 102 W Pennsylvania Ave Suite 101 *Web:* www.baltcountycc.com	Towson	MD	21204	410-825-6200	821-9901
Eastern Baltimore Area Chamber of Commerce 102 W Pennsylvania Ave Suite 101 *Web:* www.baltcountycc.com	Towson	MD	21204	410-825-6200	821-9901
Carroll County Chamber of Commerce 700 Corporate Ctr Ct # L *Web:* www.carrollcountychamber.org	Westminster	MD	21157	410-876-7212	876-1023
Wheaton-Kensington Chamber of Commerce 2401 Blueridge Ave Suite 101 *Web:* www.wkchamber.org	Wheaton	MD	20902	301-949-0080	949-0081

MASSACHUSETTS

Chamber	City	State	ZIP	Phone	Fax
Middlesex West Chamber of Commerce 77 Great Rd Suite 214 *Web:* www.mwcoc.com	Acton	MA	01720	978-263-0010	264-0303
Amherst Area Chamber of Commerce 28 Amity St *Web:* www.amherstarea.com	Amherst	MA	01002	413-253-0700	256-0771

Name / Address	City	State	ZIP	Phone	Fax
Arlington Chamber of Commerce 1 Whittemore Pk *Web:* www.arlcc.org	Arlington	MA	02474	781-643-4600	646-5581
North Quabbin Chamber of Commerce 427 Main St *Web:* www.northquabbinchamber.com	Athol	MA	01331	978-249-3849	249-7151
Beverly Chamber of Commerce 28 Cabot St *Web:* www.beverlychamber.com	Beverly	MA	01915	978-232-9559	232-9372
Greater Boston Chamber of Commerce 265 Franklin St 12th Fl *Web:* www.bostonchamber.com	Boston	MA	02110	617-227-4500	227-7505
Metro South Chamber of Commerce 60 School St *Web:* www.metrosouthchamber.com	Brockton	MA	02301	508-586-0500	587-1340
Brookline Chamber of Commerce 251 Harvard St Suite 1 *Web:* www.brooklinechamber.com	Brookline	MA	02446	617-739-1330	739-1200
Cape Cod Canal Regional Chamber of Commerce 70 Main St *Web:* www.capecodcanalchamber.org	Buzzards Bay	MA	02532	508-759-6000	759-6965
Cambridge Chamber of Commerce 859 Massachusetts Ave *Web:* www.cambridgechamber.org	Cambridge	MA	02139	617-876-4100	354-9874
Cape Cod Chamber of Commerce 5 Shoot Flying Hill Rd *TF:* 888-332-2732 ■ *Web:* www.capecodchamber.org	Centerville	MA	02632	508-362-3225	362-3698
Chicopee Chamber of Commerce 264 Exchange St *Web:* www.chicopeechamber.org	Chicopee	MA	01013	413-594-2101	594-2103
Wachusett Chamber of Commerce 167 Church St PO Box 703 *Web:* www.wachusettchamber.com	Clinton	MA	01510	978-368-7687	368-7689
North Shore Chamber of Commerce 5 Cherry Hill Dr Suite 100 *Web:* www.northshorechamber.org	Danvers	MA	01923	978-774-8565	774-3418
Nashoba Valley Chamber of Commerce 100 Sherman Ave *Web:* www.nvcoc.com	Devens	MA	01434	978-772-6976	772-3503
East Boston Chamber of Commerce 296 Bennington St 2nd Fl *Web:* www.eastbostonchamber.com	East Boston	MA	02128	617-569-5000	569-1945
Everett Chamber of Commerce 467 Broadway *Web:* www.everettmachamber.com	Everett	MA	02149	617-387-9100	389-6655
Fall River Area Chamber of Commerce & Industry 200 Pocasset St *Web:* www.fallriverchamber.com	Fall River	MA	02721	508-676-8226	675-5932
Falmouth Chamber of Commerce 20 Academy Ln *TF:* 800-526-8532 ■ *Web:* www.falmouthchamber.com	Falmouth	MA	02540	508-548-8500	548-8521
North Central Massachusetts Chamber of Commerce 860 S St *Web:* www.northcentralmass.com	Fitchburg	MA	01420	978-353-7600	353-4896
Metro West Chamber of Commerce 1671 Worcester Rd Suite 201 *Web:* www.metrowest.org	Framingham	MA	01701	508-879-5600	875-9325
United Regional Chamber of Commerce 4 W St *Web:* www.unitedchamber.org	Franklin	MA	02038	508-528-2800	520-7864
Greater Gardner Chamber of Commerce 210 Main St *Web:* www.gardnerma.com	Gardner	MA	01440	978-632-1780	630-1767
Cape Ann Chamber of Commerce 33 Commercial St *Web:* www.capeannchamber.com	Gloucester	MA	01930	978-283-1601	283-4740
Franklin County Chamber of Commerce 395 Main St *Web:* www.co.franklin.ma.us	Greenfield	MA	01301	413-773-5463	773-7008
Greater Haverhill Chamber of Commerce 87 Winter St *Web:* www.haverhillchamber.com	Haverhill	MA	01830	978-373-5663	373-8060
Greater Holyoke Chamber of Commerce 177 High St *Web:* www.holycham.com	Holyoke	MA	01040	413-534-3376	534-3385
Assabet Valley Chamber of Commerce 18 Church St PO Box 578 *Web:* www.assabetvalleychamber.org	Hudson	MA	01749	978-568-0360	562-4118
Hyannis Area Chamber of Commerce 397 Main St *TF:* 800-492-6647 ■ *Web:* www.hyannis.com	Hyannis	MA	02601	508-775-2201	362-9499
Merrimack Valley Chamber of Commerce 264 Essex St *Web:* www.merrimackvalleychamber.com	Lawrence	MA	01840	978-686-0900	794-9953
Lexington Chamber of Commerce 1875 Massachusetts Ave *Web:* www.lexingtonchamber.org	Lexington	MA	02420	781-862-2480	862-5995
Greater Lowell Chamber of Commerce 131 Merrimack St *Web:* www.glcc.biz	Lowell	MA	01852	978-459-8154	452-4145
Lynn Area Chamber of Commerce 583 Chestnut St Unit 38	Lynn	MA	01901	781-592-2900	592-2903
Malden Chamber of Commerce 200 Pleasant St Suite 416 *Web:* www.maldenchamber.org	Malden	MA	02148	781-322-4500	322-4866
Marlborough Regional Chamber of Commerce 11 Florence St *Web:* www.marlboroughchamber.org	Marlborough	MA	01752	508-485-7746	481-1819
Medford Chamber of Commerce 1 Shipyard Way Suite 308 *Web:* www.medfordchamberma.com	Medford	MA	02155	781-396-1277	396-1278
Melrose Chamber of Commerce 1 W Foster St *Web:* www.melrosechamber.org	Melrose	MA	02176	781-665-3033	665-5595
Cranberry Country Chamber of Commerce 40 N Main St *Web:* www.cranberrycountry.org	Middleboro	MA	02346	508-947-1499	947-1446
Milford Area Chamber of Commerce 258 Main St PO Box 621 *Web:* www.milfordchamber.org	Milford	MA	01757	508-473-6700	473-8467
New Bedford Area Chamber of Commerce 794 Purchase St *Web:* www.newbedfordchamber.com	New Bedford	MA	02740	508-999-5231	999-5237
Newton-Needham Chamber of Commerce 281 Needham St *Web:* www.nnchamber.com	Newton	MA	02464	617-244-5300	244-5302
United Regional Chamber of Commerce 31 N Washington St Suite 5 *Web:* www.unitedregionalchamber.com	North Attleboro	MA	02761	508-695-6011	695-6096
Greater Northampton Chamber of Commerce 99 Pleasant St *Web:* www.explorenorthampton.com	NorthHampton	MA	01060	413-584-1900	584-1934
Neposet Valley Chamber of Commerce 190 Vanderbilt Ave *Web:* www.nvcc.com	Norwood	MA	02062	781-769-1126	769-0808
Quaboag Valley Chamber of Commerce 3 Converse St Suite 103 *Web:* www.quaboagvalley.org	Palmer	MA	01069	413-283-2418	289-1355
Peabody Chamber of Commerce 24 Main St Suite 28 *Web:* www.peabody-chamber.com	Peabody	MA	01960	978-531-0384	532-7227
Berkshire Chamber of Commerce 75 N St Suite 360 *Web:* www.berkshirechamber.com	Pittsfield	MA	01201	413-499-4000	447-9641
Plymouth Area Chamber of Commerce 10 Cordage Pk Cir Suite 231 *Web:* www.plymouthchamber.com	Plymouth	MA	02360	508-830-1620	830-1621
South Shore Chamber of Commerce PO Box 690625 *Web:* www.southshorechamber.org	Quincy	MA	02269	617-479-1111	479-9274
Reading-North Reading Chamber of Commerce PO Box 771 *Web:* www.readingnreadingchamber.org	Reading	MA	01867	781-944-8824	944-6125
Revere Chamber of Commerce 270 Broadway Suite 10 *Web:* www.reverechamber.org	Revere	MA	02151	781-289-8009	289-2166
Salem Chamber of Commerce 265 Essex St *Web:* www.salem-chamber.org	Salem	MA	01970	978-744-0004	745-3855
Saugus Chamber of Commerce 394 Lincoln Ave *Web:* www.sauguschamber.org	Saugus	MA	01906	781-233-8407	231-1145
Somerville Chamber of Commerce 2 Alpine St PO Box 44034 *Web:* www.somervillechamber.org	Somerville	MA	02144	617-776-4100	
Affiliated Chamber of Commerce of Greater Springfield 1441 Main St *Web:* www.myonlinechamber.com	Springfield	MA	01003	413-787-1555	731-8530
West Springfield Chamber of Commerce 1441 Main St *Web:* www.myonlinechamber.com	Springfield	MA	01103	413-787-1555	731-8530
Taunton Area Chamber of Commerce 12 Taunton Green Suite 201 *Web:* www.tauntonareachamber.org	Taunton	MA	02780	508-824-4068	884-8222
Wakefield Chamber of Commerce 467 Main St PO Box 585 *Web:* www.wakefieldma.org	Wakefield	MA	01880	781-245-0741	245-0755
Waltham/West Suburban Chamber of Commerce 84 S St *Web:* www.walthamchamber.com	Waltham	MA	02453	781-894-4700	894-1708
Watertown-Belmont Chamber of Commerce 440 Arsenal St *Web:* www.wbcc.org	Watertown	MA	02472	617-926-1017	926-2322
Wellesley Chamber of Commerce 1 Hollis St Suite 232 *Web:* www.wellesleychamber.org	Wellesley	MA	02482	781-235-2446	235-7326
Greater Westfield Chamber of Commerce 53 Ct St *Web:* www.westfieldbiz.org	Westfield	MA	01085	413-568-1618	572-1453
Blackstone Valley Chamber of Commerce 110 Church St *TF:* 800-841-0919 ■ *Web:* www.blackstonevalley.org	Whitinsville	MA	01588	508-234-9090	234-5152
North Suburban Chamber of Commerce 76-R Winn St Suite 3D *Web:* www.northsuburbanchamber.com	Woburn	MA	01801	781-933-3499	933-1071
Worcester Regional Chamber of Commerce 446 Main St Suite 200 *Web:* www.worcesterchamber.org	Worcester	MA	01608	508-753-2924	754-8560

MICHIGAN

Name / Address	City	State	ZIP	Phone	Fax
Lenawee Economic Development Corp 5285 W US Hwy 223 Suite A *Web:* www.lenaweeeconomicdevelopment.org	Adrian	MI	49221	517-265-5141	263-6065
Allen Park Chamber of Commerce 6543 Allen Rd *Web:* www.allenparkchamber.org	Allen Park	MI	48101	313-382-7303	382-4409
Gratiot Area Chamber of Commerce 110 W Superior St PO Box 516 *Web:* www.gratiot.org	Alma	MI	48801	989-463-5525	463-6588
Alpena Area Chamber of Commerce 235 W Chisholm St *TF:* 800-425-7362 ■ *Web:* www.alpenachamber.com	Alpena	MI	49707	989-354-4181	356-3999
Ann Arbor Area Chamber of Commerce 115 W Heron 3rd Fl *Web:* www.annarborchamber.org	Ann Arbor	MI	48104	734-665-4433	665-4191
Battle Creek Area Chamber of Commerce 77 E Michigan Ave Suite 80 *Web:* www.battlecreek.org/chamber	Battle Creek	MI	49017	269-962-4076	962-6309
Bay Area Chamber of Commerce 901 Saginaw St *Web:* www.baycityarea.com	Bay City	MI	48708	989-893-4567	895-5594

				Phone	Fax
Belleville Area Chamber of Commerce 248 Main St . . . Belleville *Web:* www.bellevillech.org		MI	48111	734-697-7151	697-1415
Cornerstone Alliance Chamber Services 38 W Wall St. . . . Benton Harbor *Web:* www.cstonealliance.org		MI	49022	269-925-6100	925-4471
Mecosta County Area Chamber of Commerce 246 N State St. . . . Big Rapids *Web:* www.mecostacounty.com		MI	49307	231-796-7649	796-1625
Birmingham-Bloomfield Chamber of Commerce 725 S Adams Rd #130 . . . Birmingham *Web:* www.bbcc.com		MI	48009	248-644-1700	644-0286
Greater Brighton Area Chamber of Commerce 131 Hyne St . . . Brighton *Web:* www.brightoncoc.org		MI	48116	810-227-5086	227-5940
Brooklyn-Irish Hills Chamber of Commerce 131 N Main St PO Box 805. . . . Brooklyn *Web:* www.brooklynmi.com		MI	49230	517-592-8907	
Cadillac Area Chamber of Commerce 222 N Lake St. . . . Cadillac *Web:* www.cadillac.org		MI	49601	231-775-9776	775-1440
Canton Chamber of Commerce 45525 Hanford Rd . . . Canton *Web:* www.cantonchamber.com		MI	48187	734-453-4040	453-4503
Clarkston Area Chamber of Commerce 5856 S Main St. . . . Clarkston *Web:* www.clarkston.org		MI	48346	248-625-8055	625-8041
Branch County Area Chamber of Commerce 20 Division St. . . . Coldwater *Web:* www.branch-county.com		MI	49036	517-278-5985	278-8369
Davison Area Chamber of Commerce 709 S State Rd # A . . . Davison *Web:* www.davisonchamberofcommerce.com		MI	48423	810-653-6266	653-0669
Dearborn Chamber of Commerce 22100 Michigan Ave. . . . Dearborn *Web:* www.dearbornchamber.org		MI	48124	313-584-6100	584-9818
Dearborn Heights Chamber of Commerce 24951 W Warren St # 2. . . . Dearborn Heights *Web:* www.dearbornheightschamber.com		MI	48127	313-274-7480	724-0757
Detroit Regional Chamber 1 Woodward Ave Suite 1900 . . . Detroit *Web:* www.detroitchamber.com		MI	48226	313-964-4000	964-0183
Eastpointe-Roseville Chamber of Commerce 24840 Gratiot Ave Suite B. . . . Eastpointe *Web:* www.epchamber.com		MI	48021	586-776-5520	776-7808
Delta County Area Chamber of Commerce 230 Ludington St . . . Escanaba *TF:* 888-335-8264 ■ *Web:* www.deltami.org		MI	49829	906-786-2192	786-8830
Farmington/Farmington Hills Chamber of Commerce 27555 Executive Dr Suite 145. . . . Farmington Hills *Web:* www.ffhchamber.com		MI	48331	248-474-3440	474-9235
Ferndale Chamber of Commerce 407 E 9-Mile Rd . . . Ferndale *Web:* www.ferndalechamber.com		MI	48220	248-542-2160	542-8979
Genesee Regional Chamber of Commerce 519 S Saginaw St Suite 200 . . . Flint *Web:* www.thegrcc.org		MI	48502	810-600-1404	600-1461
Garden City Chamber of Commerce 30120 Ford Rd Suite D. . . . Garden City *Web:* www.gardencity.org		MI	48135	734-422-4448	422-1601
Grand Blanc Chamber of Commerce 512 E Grand Blanc Rd. . . . Grand Blanc *Web:* www.grandblancchamber.org		MI	48439	810-695-4222	695-0053
Chamber of Commerce - Grand Haven-Spring Lake-Ferrysburg 1 S Harbor Dr . . . Grand Haven *Web:* www.grandhavenchamber.org		MI	49417	616-842-4910	842-0379
Grand Rapids Area Chamber of Commerce 111 Pearl St NW. . . . Grand Rapids *Web:* www.grandrapids.org		MI	49503	616-771-0300	771-0318
Hillsdale County Chamber of Commerce 22 N Manning St . . . Hillsdale *Web:* www.hillsdalecountychamber.com		MI	49242	517-437-6401	437-6408
Holland Area Chamber of Commerce 272 E 8th St . . . Holland *Web:* www.hollandchamber.org		MI	49423	616-392-2389	392-7379
Keweenaw Peninsula Chamber of Commerce 902 College Ave PO Box 336 . . . Houghton *TF:* 866-304-5722 ■ *Web:* www.keweenaw.org		MI	49931	906-482-5240	482-5241
Howell Area Chamber of Commerce (HACC) 123 E Washington St . . . Howell *Web:* www.howell.org		MI	48843	517-546-3920	546-4115
Dickinson Area Partnership 600 S Stephenson Ave . . . Iron Mountain *TF:* 800-236-2447 ■ *Web:* www.dickinsonchamber.com		MI	49801	906-774-2002	774-2004
Greater Jackson Chamber of Commerce 141 S Jackson St . . . Jackson *Web:* www.gjcc.org		MI	49201	517-782-8221	780-3688
Kalamazoo Regional Chamber of Commerce 346 W Michigan Ave. . . . Kalamazoo *Web:* www.kazoochamber.com		MI	49007	269-381-4000	343-0430
Orion Area Chamber of Commerce 1520 S Lapeer Rd # 112. . . . Lake Orion *Web:* www.orion.lib.mi.us		MI	48360	248-693-6300	693-9227
Lansing Regional Chamber of Commerce 500 E Michigan Ave Suite 200 . . . Lansing *Web:* www.lansingchamber.org		MI	48912	517-487-6340	484-6910
Lapeer Area Chamber of Commerce 108 W Pk St . . . Lapeer *Web:* www.lapeerareachamber.org		MI	48446	810-664-6641	664-4349
Lincoln Park Chamber of Commerce 1335 Southfield Rd PO Box 382. . . . Lincoln Park		MI	48146	313-386-0140	386-0140
Livonia Chamber of Commerce 33233 5 Mile Rd . . . Livonia *Web:* www.livonia.org		MI	48154	734-427-2122	427-6055
Madison Heights-Hazel Park Chamber of Commerce 724 W 11 Mile Rd. . . . Madison Heights *Web:* www.madisonheightschamber.org		MI	48071	248-542-5010	542-6821

				Phone	Fax
Midland Area Chamber of Commerce 300 Rodd St Suite 101 . . . Midland *Web:* www.macc.org		MI	48640	989-839-9901	835-3701
Huron Valley Chamber of Commerce 317 Union St . . . Milford *Web:* www.huronvcc.com		MI	48381	248-685-7129	685-9047
Monroe County Chamber of Commerce 1645 N Dixie Hwy Suite 20. . . . Monroe *Web:* www.monroemi.usachamber.com		MI	48162	734-384-3366	384-3367
Macomb County Chamber 28 1st St Suite B. . . . Mount Clemens *Web:* www.macombchamber.com		MI	48043	586-268-6430	268-6397
Macomb County Chamber of Commerce 28 1st St. . . . Mount Clemens *Web:* www.central-macomb.com		MI	48043	586-493-7600	493-7602
Mount Pleasant Area Chamber of Commerce 114 E Broadway . . . Mount Pleasant *Web:* www.mt-pleasant.net		MI	48858	989-772-2396	773-2656
Muskegon Area Chamber of Commerce 380 W Western Suite 202. . . . Muskegon *Web:* www.muskegon.org		MI	49440	231-722-3751	728-7251
Anchor Bay Chamber of Commerce (ABCC) 36341 Front St Suite 2 . . . New Baltimore *Web:* www.suscc.com		MI	48047	586-725-5148	725-5369
Four Flags Area Chamber of Commerce 321 E Main St. . . . Niles *TF:* 888-683-8361 ■ *Web:* www.nilesmi.com		MI	49120	269-683-3720	683-3722
Novi Chamber of Commerce 41875 W 11 Mile Rd Suite 201. . . . Novi *Web:* www.novichamber.com		MI	48375	248-349-3743	349-9719
Petoskey Regional Chamber of Commerce 401 E Mitchell St . . . Petoskey *Web:* www.petoskey.com		MI	49770	231-347-4150	348-1810
Plymouth Community Chamber of Commerce 850 W Ann Arbor Trail . . . Plymouth *Web:* www.plymouthchamber.org		MI	48170	734-453-1540	453-1724
Pontiac Regional Chamber of Commerce 402 N Telegraph Rd . . . Pontiac *Web:* www.pontiacchamber.com		MI	48341	248-335-9600	335-9601
Blue Water Area Chamber of Commerce 512 McMorran Blvd . . . Port Huron *TF:* 800-361-0526 ■ *Web:* www.bluewaterchamber.com		MI	48060	810-985-7101	985-7311
Redford Township Chamber of Commerce 26050 5-Mile Rd . . . Redford *Web:* www.redfordchamber.org		MI	48239	313-535-0960	535-6356
Greater Rochester Chamber of Commerce 71 Walnut Blvd Suite 110. . . . Rochester *Web:* www.rochesterregionalchamber.com		MI	48307	248-651-6700	651-5270
Rockford Area Chamber of Commerce 598 Byrne Industrial Dr. . . . Rockford *Web:* www.rockfordmichamber.com		MI	49341	616-866-2000	866-2141
Romeo-Washington Chamber of Commerce 228 N Main St PO Box 175. . . . Romeo *Web:* www.rwchamber.com		MI	48065	586-752-4436	752-2835
Greater Royal Oak Chamber of Commerce 200 S Washington Ave . . . Royal Oak *Web:* www.virtualroyaloak.com		MI	48067	248-547-4000	547-0504
Saginaw County Chamber of Commerce 515 N Washington Ave 2nd Fl . . . Saginaw *Web:* www.saginawchamber.org		MI	48607	989-752-7161	752-9055
Metro East Chamber of Commerce 27601 Jefferson Ave. . . . Saint Clair Shores *Web:* www.metroeastchamber.com		MI	48081	586-777-2741	777-4811
Sault Area Chamber of Commerce 2581 I-75 Business Spur . . . Sault Sainte Marie *Web:* www.saultstemarie.org		MI	49783	906-632-3301	632-2331
South Lyon Area Chamber of Commerce 125 N Lafayette St. . . . South Lyon *Web:* www.southlyonchamber.com		MI	48178	248-437-3257	437-4116
Southfield Chamber of Commerce 17515 W 9-Mile Rd Suite 190 . . . Southfield *Web:* www.southfieldchamber.com		MI	48075	248-557-6661	557-3931
Sterling Heights Area Chamber of Commerce 12900 Hall Rd Suite 190. . . . Sterling Heights *Web:* www.suscc.com		MI	48313	586-731-5400	731-3521
Southern Wayne County Regional Chamber 20600 Eureka Rd Suite 315 . . . Taylor *Web:* www.swccc.org		MI	48180	734-284-6000	284-0198
Traverse City Area Chamber of Commerce 202 E Grandview Pkwy . . . Traverse City *Web:* www.tcchamber.org		MI	49684	231-947-5075	946-2565
Troy Chamber of Commerce 4555 Investment Dr Suite 300 . . . Troy *Web:* www.troychamber.com		MI	48098	248-641-8151	641-0545
Lakes Area Chamber of Commerce 305 N Pontiac Trail Suite B. . . . Walled Lake *Web:* www.lakesareachamber.com		MI	48390	248-624-2826	624-2892
West Bloomfield Chamber of Commerce 6668 Orchard Lake Rd Suite 207 . . . West Bloomfield *Web:* www.westbloomfieldchamber.com		MI	48322	248-626-3636	626-4218
Westland Chamber of Commerce 36900 Ford Rd. . . . Westland *Web:* www.westlandchamber.com		MI	48185	734-326-7222	326-6040
Wyoming-Kentwood Area Chamber of Commerce 590 32nd St SE. . . . Wyoming *Web:* www.southkent.org		MI	49548	616-531-5990	531-0252
Ypsilanti Area Chamber of Commerce 301 W Michigan Ave Suite 101 . . . Ypsilanti *Web:* www.ypsichamber.org		MI	48197	734-482-4920	482-2021

MINNESOTA

Organization	City	State	ZIP	Phone	Fax
Albert Lea-Freeborn County Chamber of Commerce 701 Marshall St *Web:* www.albertlea.org	Albert Lea	MN	56007	507-373-3938	373-0344
Alexandria Lakes Area Chamber of Commerce 206 Broadway *TF:* 800-235-9441 ■ *Web:* www.alexandriamn.org	Alexandria	MN	56308	320-763-3161	763-6857
Anoka Area Chamber of Commerce 12 Bridge Sq *Web:* www.anokaareachamber.com	Anoka	MN	55303	763-421-7130	421-0577
Apple Valley Chamber of Commerce 14800 Galaxie Ave # 101 *TF:* 800-301-9435 ■ *Web:* www.applevalleychamber.com	Apple Valley	MN	55124	952-432-8422	432-7964
Bemidji Area Chamber of Commerce 300 Bemidji Ave *TF:* 800-458-2223 ■ *Web:* www.bemidji.org	Bemidji	MN	56601	218-444-3541	444-4276
Brainerd Lakes Area Chamber of Commerce 124 N 6th St PO Box 356 *TF:* 800-450-2838 ■ *Web:* www.explorebrainerdlakes.com	Brainerd	MN	56401	218-829-2838	829-8199
Burnsville Chamber of Commerce 101 W Burnsville Pkwy Suite 150 *Web:* www.burnsvillechamber.com	Burnsville	MN	55337	952-435-6000	435-6972
Cloquet Area Chamber of Commerce 225 Sunnyside Dr *TF:* 800-554-4350 ■ *Web:* www.cloquet.com	Cloquet	MN	55720	218-879-1551	878-0223
Detroit Lakes Regional Chamber of Commerce 700 Summit Ave *TF:* 800-542-3992 ■ *Web:* www.visitdetroitlakes.com	Detroit Lakes	MN	56501	218-847-9202	847-9082
Duluth Area Chamber of Commerce 5 W 1st St Suite 101 *Web:* www.duluthchamber.com	Duluth	MN	55802	218-722-5501	722-3223
Dakota County Regional Chamber of Commerce 1121 Town Ctr Dr Suite 102 *Web:* www.ndcchambers.com	Eagan	MN	55123	651-452-9872	452-8978
Eden Prairie Chamber of Commerce 11455 Viking Dr Suite 270 *Web:* www.epchamber.org	Eden Prairie	MN	55344	952-944-2830	944-0229
Forest Lake Area Chamber of Commerce 56 E Broadway Ave *Web:* www.flacc.org	Forest Lake	MN	55025	651-464-3200	464-3201
Grand Rapids Area Chamber of Commerce 1 NW 3rd St *TF:* 800-472-6366 ■ *Web:* www.grandmn.com	Grand Rapids	MN	55744	218-326-6619	326-4825
Hastings Area Chamber of Commerce & Tourism Bureau 111 E 3rd St *TF:* 888-612-6122 ■ *Web:* www.hastingsmn.org	Hastings	MN	55033	651-437-6775	437-2697
River Heights Chamber of Commerce 5782 Blackshire Path *Web:* www.riverheights.com	Inver Grove Heights	MN	55076	651-451-2266	451-0846
Lakeville Area Chamber of Commerce & Convention & Visitors Bureau 19950 Dodd Blvd Suite 101 *TF:* 888-525-3845 ■ *Web:* www.lakevillechamber.org	Lakeville	MN	55044	952-469-2020	469-2028
Minneapolis Regional Chamber of Commerce 81 S 9th St Suite 200 *Web:* www.minneapolischamber.org	Minneapolis	MN	55402	612-370-9100	370-9195
Chamber of Commerce of Fargo Moorhead 202 1st Ave N *Web:* www.fmchamber.com	Moorhead	MN	56560	218-233-1100	233-1200
Twin Cities North Chamber of Commerce 5394 Edgewood Dr Suite 100 *Web:* www.twincitiesnorth.org	Mounds View	MN	55112	763-571-9781	572-7950
North Hennepin Chamber of Commerce 229 1st Ave NE *Web:* www.nhachamber.com	Osseo	MN	55369	763-424-6744	424-6927
Owatonna Area Chamber of Commerce & Tourism 320 Hoffman Dr *TF:* 800-423-6466 ■ *Web:* www.owatonna.org	Owatonna	MN	55060	507-451-7970	451-7972
TwinWest Chamber of Commerce 10700 Old County Rd 15 *Web:* www.twinwest.com	Plymouth	MN	55441	763-450-2220	450-2221
Richfield Chamber of Commerce 6601 Lyndale Ave S Suite 106 *Web:* www.richfieldchambercvb.org	Richfield	MN	55423	612-866-5100	861-8302
Rochester Area Chamber of Commerce 220 S Broadway Suite 100 *Web:* www.rochestermnchamber.com	Rochester	MN	55904	507-288-1122	282-8960
Saint Cloud Area Chamber of Commerce 110 6th Ave S *TF:* 800-264-2040 ■ *Web:* www.stc.stcloudareachamber.com	Saint Cloud	MN	56301	320-251-2940	251-0081
Saint Paul Area Chamber of Commerce 401 N Robert St Suite 150 *Web:* www.saintpaulchamber.com	Saint Paul	MN	55101	651-223-5000	223-5119
Lake Minnetonka Chamber of Commerce 4165 Shoreline Dr Suite 130 *Web:* www.lakeminnetonkachamber.com	Spring Park	MN	55384	952-471-5492	471-5449
Greater Stillwater Chamber of Commerce 1950 Northwestern Ave S #101 *Web:* www.ilovestillwater.com	Stillwater	MN	55082	651-439-4001	439-4035
Leech Lake Area Chamber of Commerce 205 Minnesota Ave E *TF:* 800-833-1118 ■ *Web:* www.leech-lake.com	Walker	MN	56484	218-547-1313	547-1338
White Bear Lake Area Chamber of Commerce 4801 Hwy 61 Suite 305 *Web:* www.whitebearchamber.com	White Bear Lake	MN	55110	651-429-8593	429-8592
Willmar Lakes Area Chamber of Commerce 2104 Hwy 12 E *Web:* www.willmarareachamber.com	Willmar	MN	56201	320-235-0300	231-1948
Winona Area Chamber of Commerce 67 Main St PO Box 870 *Web:* www.winonachamber.com	Winona	MN	55987	507-452-2272	454-8814

MISSISSIPPI

Organization	City	State	ZIP	Phone	Fax
Monroe County Chamber of Commerce 124 W Commerce St *Web:* www.gomonroe.org	Aberdeen	MS	39730	662-369-6488	369-6489
Panola Partnership Inc 150-A Public Sq *TF:* 888-872-6652 ■ *Web:* www.panolacounty.com	Batesville	MS	38606	662-563-3126	563-0704
Hancock County Chamber of Commerce 412 Hwy 90 Suite 6 *Web:* www.hancockchamber.org	Bay Saint Louis	MS	39520	228-467-9048	467-6033
Rankin County Chamber of Commerce 101 Service Dr *Web:* www.rankinchamber.com	Brandon	MS	39043	601-825-2268	825-1977
Brookhaven-Lincoln County Chamber of Commerce 230 S Whitworth Ave *TF:* 800-613-4667 ■ *Web:* www.brookhavenchamber.com	Brookhaven	MS	39601	601-833-1411	833-1412
Clarksdale-Coahoma County Chamber of Commerce & Industrial Foundation 1540 DeSoto Ave *TF:* 800-626-3764 ■ *Web:* www.clarksdale.com	Clarksdale	MS	38614	662-627-7337	627-1313
Cleveland-Bolivar County Chamber of Commerce 600 3rd St *TF:* 800-295-7473 ■ *Web:* www.clevelandmschamber.com	Cleveland	MS	38732	662-843-2712	843-2718
Marion County Development Partnership (MCDP) 412 Courthouse Sq PO Box 272 *Web:* www.mcdp.info	Columbia	MS	39429	601-736-6385	736-6392
Alliance The 810 Tate St *TF:* 877-347-0545 ■ *Web:* www.corinth.ms	Corinth	MS	38834	662-287-5269	287-5260
Delta Economic Development Ctr 342 Washington Ave Suite 201 PO box 933 *Web:* www.greenvilleareachamber.com	Greenville	MS	38702	662-378-3141	378-3143
Greenwood-Leflore County Chamber of Commerce 402 Hwy 82 *Web:* www.greenwoodms.com	Greenwood	MS	38930	662-453-4152	453-8003
Gulfport Chamber of Commerce 11975-E Seaway Rd *Web:* www.mscoastchamber.com	Gulfport	MS	39503	228-604-0014	604-0105
Mississippi Gulf Coast Chamber of Commerce 11975-E Seaway Rd *Web:* www.mscoastchamber.com	Gulfport	MS	39503	228-604-0014	604-0105
Area Development Partnership 1 Convention Ctr Plaza *TF:* 800-238-4288 ■ *Web:* www.theadp.com	Hattiesburg	MS	39401	601-296-7500	296-7505
Horn Lake Chamber of Commerce 3010 Goodman Rd W Suite B *Web:* www.hornlakechamber.com	Horn Lake	MS	38637	662-393-9897	393-2942
Greater Jackson Chamber Partnership PO Box 22548 *Web:* www.greaterjacksonpartnership.com	Jackson	MS	39225	601-948-7575	352-5539
Jones County Chamber of Commerce PO Box 527 *TF General:* 800-392-9629	Laurel	MS	39441	601-428-0574	428-2047
Pike County Chamber of Commerce & Economic Development District 112 N Railroad Blvd *TF:* 800-399-4404 ■ *Web:* www.pikeinfo.com	McComb	MS	39648	601-684-2291	684-4899
East Mississippi Business Development Corp 1901 Front St Union Stn Suite A *Web:* www.embdc.org	Meridian	MS	39302	601-693-1306	693-5638
Natchez-Adams County Chamber of Commerce 108 S Commerce St *Web:* www.natchezchamber.com	Natchez	MS	39120	601-445-4611	445-9361
Olive Branch Chamber of Commerce 9123 Pigeon Roost PO Box 608 *Web:* www.olivebranchms.com	Olive Branch	MS	38654	662-895-2600	895-2625
Oxford-Lafayette County Chamber of Commerce 299 W Jackson Ave *TF:* 800-880-6967 ■ *Web:* www.oxfordms.com	Oxford	MS	38655	662-234-4651	234-4655
Jackson County Chamber of Commerce 720 Krebs Ave *Web:* www.jcchamber.com	Pascagoula	MS	39567	228-762-3391	769-1726
Community Development Partnership 410 Poplar Ave 256 W Beacon *TF:* 877-752-2643 ■ *Web:* www.neshoba.org	Philadelphia	MS	39350	601-656-1000	656-1066
Madison County Chamber of Commerce 618 Crescent Blvd Suite 101 *Web:* www.madisoncountychamber.com	Ridgeland	MS	39157	601-605-2554	605-2260
Southaven Chamber of Commerce 8700 NW Dr Suite 100 *TF:* 800-272-6551 ■ *Web:* www.southavenchamber.com	Southaven	MS	38671	662-342-6114	342-6365
Greater Starkville Development Partnership 200 E Main St *TF:* 800-649-8687 ■ *Web:* www.starkville.org	Starkville	MS	39759	662-323-3322	323-5815
Vicksburg-Warren County Chamber of Commerce 2020 Mission 66 *TF:* 888-842-5728 ■ *Web:* www.vicksburgchamber.org	Vicksburg	MS	39180	601-636-1012	636-4422
Yazoo County Chamber of Commerce 212 E Broadway PO Box 172 *TF:* 800-748-8875 ■ *Web:* www.yazoochamber.org	Yazoo City	MS	39194	662-746-1273	746-7238

MISSOURI

Organization	City	State	ZIP	Phone	Fax
Affton Chamber of Commerce 10203 Gravois Rd *Web:* www.afftonchamber.com	Affton	MO	63123	314-849-6499	849-6399
Blue Springs Chamber of Commerce 1000 W Main St *Web:* www.bluespringschamber.com	Blue Springs	MO	64015	816-229-8558	229-1244
Branson/Lakes Area Chamber of Commerce PO Box 1897 *TF:* 800-214-3661 ■ *Web:* www.bransonchamber.com	Branson	MO	65615	417-334-4084	334-4139
Northwest Chamber of Commerce 11965 St Charles Rock Rd Suite 203 *Web:* www.northwestchamber.com	Bridgeton	MO	63044	314-291-2131	291-2153
Cape Girardeau Area Chamber of Commerce 1267 N Mt Auburn Rd *Web:* www.capechamber.com	Cape Girardeau	MO	63701	573-335-3312	335-4686
Cassville Area Chamber of Commerce 504 Main St *Web:* www.cassville.com	Cassville	MO	65625	417-847-2814	847-0804

Chamber	Address	City	State	ZIP	Phone	Fax	TF / Web
Chesterfield Chamber of Commerce	101 Chesterfield Business Pkwy	Chesterfield	MO	63005	636-532-3399	532-7446	TF: 888-242-4262 ■ Web: www.chesterfieldmochamber.com
Columbia Chamber of Commerce	300 S Providence Rd	Columbia	MO	65203	573-874-1132	443-3986	Web: www.columbiamochamber.com
Twin City Area Chamber of Commerce	114 Main St	Festus	MO	63028	636-931-7697	937-0925	Web: www.twincity.org
Greater North County Chamber of Commerce	420 W Washington St	Florissant	MO	63031	314-831-3500	831-9682	Web: www.greaternorthcountychamber.com
Kingdom of Callaway Chamber of Commerce	409 Ct St	Fulton	MO	65251	573-642-3055	642-5182	TF: 800-257-3554 ■ Web: www.callawaychamber.com
Gladstone Area Chamber of Commerce	6913 N Cherry	Gladstone	MO	64118	816-436-4523	436-4352	Web: www.gladstonechamber.com
Grandview Area Chamber of Commerce	12500 S US Hwy 71	Grandview	MO	64030	816-761-6505	763-8460	Web: www.grandview.org
Independence Chamber of Commerce	210 W Truman Rd	Independence	MO	64050	816-252-4745	252-4917	Web: www.independencechamber.com
Jefferson City Area Chamber of Commerce	213 Adams St	Jefferson City	MO	65101	573-634-3616	634-3805	Web: www.jcchamber.org
Joplin Area Chamber of Commerce	320 E 4th St	Joplin	MO	64801	417-624-4150	624-4303	Web: www.joplincc.com
Greater Kansas City Chamber of Commerce	911 Main St Suite 2600	Kansas City	MO	64105	816-221-2424	221-7440	Web: www.kcchamber.com
Northland Regional Chamber of Commerce	634 NW Englewood Rd	Kansas City	MO	64118	816-455-9911	455-9933	Web: www.northlandchamber.com
South Kansas City Chamber of Commerce	406 E Bannister Rd # F	Kansas City	MO	64131	816-761-7660	761-7340	Web: www.southkcchamber.com
Kirkwood-Des Peres Area Chamber of Commerce	108 W Adams Ave	Kirkwood	MO	63122	314-821-4161	821-5229	Web: www.kirkwoodarea.com
Lebanon Area Chamber of Commerce	186 N Adams St	Lebanon	MO	65536	417-588-3256	588-3251	TF: 888-588-5710 ■ Web: www.lebanonmissouri.com
Lee's Summit Chamber of Commerce	220 SE Main St	Lee's Summit	MO	64063	816-524-2424	524-5246	TF: 888-816-5757 ■ Web: www.lschamber.com
West Saint Louis County Chamber of Commerce	134 Enchanted Pkwy Suite 204	Manchester	MO	63021	636-230-9900	230-9912	Web: www.westcountychamber.com
Neosho Area Chamber of Commerce	216 W Spring St	Neosho	MO	64850	417-451-1925	451-8097	Web: www.neoshocc.com
O'Fallon Chamber of Commerce	1299 Bryan Rd	O'Fallon	MO	63366	636-240-1818		Web: www.ofallonchamber.org
Park Hills Leadington Chamber of Commerce (PHLCOC)	5 Municipal Dr	Park Hills	MO	63601	573-431-1051	431-2327	Web: www.phlcoc.net
Raytown Area Chamber of Commerce	5909 Raytown Trafficway	Raytown	MO	64133	816-353-8500	353-8525	Web: www.raytownchamber.com
Rolla Area Chamber of Commerce	1311 Kingshighway	Rolla	MO	65401	573-364-3577	364-5222	TF: 888-809-3817 ■ Web: www.rollachamber.org
Saint Charles Chamber of Commerce	2201 First Capitol Dr	Saint Charles	MO	63301	636-946-0633	946-0301	Web: www.stcharleschamber.org
Saint Joseph Area Chamber of Commerce	3003 Frederick Ave	Saint Joseph	MO	64506	816-232-4461	364-4873	TF: 800-748-7856 ■ Web: www.saintjoseph.com
Maryland Heights Chamber of Commerce	547 W Port Plaza	Saint Louis	MO	63146	314-576-6603	576-6855	Web: www.mhcc.com
North County Chamber of Commerce	119 Church St Suite 135	Saint Louis	MO	63135	314-521-6000	521-2897	
Saint Louis Regional Commerce & Growth Assn	1 Metropolitan Sq Suite 1300	Saint Louis	MO	63102	314-231-5555	444-1122	TF: 877-785-7242 ■ Web: www.stlrcga.org
South County Chamber of Commerce	6921 S Lindburg Blvd	Saint Louis	MO	63125	314-894-6800	894-6888	Web: www.scountychamber.org
Saint Peters Chamber of Commerce	1236 Jungermann Rd Suite C	Saint Peters	MO	63376	636-447-3336	447-3337	Web: www.stpeterschamber.com
Waynesville-Saint Robert Area Chamber of Commerce	137 St Robert Blvd Suite B	Saint Robert	MO	65584	573-336-5121	336-5472	Web: www.waynesville-strobertchamber.com
Sedalia Area Chamber of Commerce	600 E 3rd St	Sedalia	MO	65301	660-826-2222	826-2223	TF: 800-827-5295 ■ Web: www.sedaliachamber.com
Springfield Area Chamber of Commerce	202 S John Q Hammons Pkwy	Springfield	MO	65806	417-862-5567	862-1611	TF: 800-879-7504 ■ Web: www.springfieldchamber.com
Washington Area Chamber of Commerce	323 W Main St	Washington	MO	63090	636-239-2715	239-1381	TF: 888-792-7466 ■ Web: www.washmo.org

MONTANA

Chamber	Address	City	State	ZIP	Phone	Fax	TF / Web
Billings Area Chamber of Commerce	815 S 27th St	Billings	MT	59101	406-245-4111	245-7333	TF: 800-735-2635 ■ Web: www.billingschamber.com
Bozeman Area Chamber of Commerce	2000 Commerce Way	Bozeman	MT	59715	406-586-5421	586-8286	Web: www.bozemanchamber.com
Butte-Silver Bow Chamber of Commerce	1000 George St	Butte	MT	59701	406-723-3177	723-1215	TF: 800-735-6814 ■ Web: www.butteinfo.org
Great Falls Area Chamber of Commerce	100 1st Ave N	Great Falls	MT	59401	406-761-4434	761-6129	TF: 800-735-8535 ■ Web: www.greatfallschamber.org
Bitterroot Valley Chamber of Commerce	105 E Main St	Hamilton	MT	59840	406-363-2400	363-2402	Web: www.bvchamber.com
Helena Area Chamber of Commerce	225 Cruse Ave	Helena	MT	59601	406-442-4120	447-1532	TF: 800-743-5362 ■ Web: www.helenachamber.com
Kalispell Area Chamber of Commerce	15 Depot Pk	Kalispell	MT	59901	406-758-2800	758-2805	Web: www.kalispellchamber.com
Missoula Area Chamber of Commerce	825 E Front St	Missoula	MT	59802	406-543-6623	543-6625	Web: www.missoulachamber.com

NEBRASKA

Chamber	Address	City	State	ZIP	Phone	Fax	TF / Web
Bellevue Chamber of Commerce	1102 Galvin Rd S	Bellevue	NE	68005	402-898-3000	291-8729	Web: www.bellevuenebraska.com
Grand Island Area Chamber of Commerce	309 W 2nd St	Grand Island	NE	68802	308-382-9210	382-1154	Web: www.gichamber.com
Kearney Area Chamber of Commerce	1007 2nd Ave PO Box 607	Kearney	NE	68848	308-237-3101	237-3103	TF: 800-227-8340 ■ Web: www.kearneycoc.org
Lincoln Chamber of Commerce	1135 M St PO Box 83006	Lincoln	NE	68508	402-436-2350	436-2360	Web: www.lcoc.com
North Platte Area Chamber & Development	502 S Dewey St	North Platte	NE	69101	308-532-4966	532-4827	Web: www.nparea.com
Greater Omaha Chamber of Commerce	13206 Grover St	Omaha	NE	68144	402-346-5000	346-7050	Web: www.omahachamber.org
Sarpy County Chamber of Commerce	7775 Olson Dr Suite 207	Papillion	NE	68046	402-339-3050	339-9968	Web: www.sarpychamber.org

NEVADA

Chamber	Address	City	State	ZIP	Phone	Fax	TF / Web
Carson City Area Chamber of Commerce	1900 S Carson St Suite 200	Carson City	NV	89701	775-882-1565	882-4179	Web: www.carsoncitychamber.com
Elko Area Chamber of Commerce	1405 Idaho St	Elko	NV	89801	775-738-7135	738-7136	TF: 800-428-7143 ■ Web: www.elkonevada.com
Fallon Chamber of Commerce	85 N Taylor St	Fallon	NV	89406	775-423-2544	423-0540	Web: www.fallonchamber.com
Carson Valley Chamber of Commerce & Visitors Authority	1477 Hwy 395 N Suite A	Gardnerville	NV	89410	775-782-8144	782-1025	TF: 800-727-7677 ■ Web: www.carsonvalleynv.org
Henderson Chamber of Commerce	590 S Boulder Hwy	Henderson	NV	89015	702-565-8951	565-3115	Web: www.hendersonchamber.com
Las Vegas Chamber of Commerce	6671 Las Vegas Blvd S Suite 300	Las Vegas	NV	89119	702-735-1616	735-0406	Web: www.lvchamber.com
Latin Chamber of Commerce	300 N 13th St	Las Vegas	NV	89101	702-385-7367	385-2614	Web: www.lvlcc.com
North Las Vegas Chamber of Commerce	3365 W Craig Rd Suite 25	North Las Vegas	NV	89032	702-642-9595	642-0439	Web: www.nlvchamber.org
Reno-Sparks Chamber of Commerce	1 E 1st St 16th Fl	Reno	NV	89501	775-337-3030	337-3038	Web: www.reno-sparkschamber.org
Northern Nevada Chamber of Commerce	1420 Scheels Dr Suite E-108	Sparks	NV	89434	775-358-1976	358-1992	Web: www.sparkschamber.org
Lake Tahoe Chamber of Commerce	169 Hwy 50	Stateline	NV	89449	775-588-1728	588-1941	Web: www.tahoechamber.org
Tonopah Chamber of Commerce	301 Brougher Ave	Tonopah	NV	89049	775-482-3859		Web: www.tonopahnevada.com

NEW HAMPSHIRE

Chamber	Address	City	State	ZIP	Phone	Fax	TF / Web
Souhegan Valley Chamber of Commerce	69 New Hampshire 101A	Amherst	NH	03033	603-673-4360	673-5018	Web: www.souhegan.net
Greater Concord Chamber of Commerce	40 Commercial St	Concord	NH	03301	603-224-2508	224-8128	Web: www.concordnhchamber.com
Greater Derry Chamber of Commerce	29 W Broadway	Derry	NH	03038	603-432-8205	432-7938	Web: www.derry-chamber.org
Greater Dover Chamber of Commerce	550 Central Ave	Dover	NH	03820	603-742-2218	749-6317	Web: www.dovernh.org

Name / Address	City	State	ZIP	Phone	Fax
Exeter Area Chamber of Commerce 120 Water St *Web:* www.exeterarea.org	Exeter	NH	03833	603-772-2411	772-9965
Hampton Area Chamber of Commerce 1 Layfayette Rd *Web:* www.hamptonchamber.com	Hampton	NH	03842	603-926-8718	926-9977
Hanover Area Chamber of Commerce 47 S Main St *Web:* www.hanoverchamber.org	Hanover	NH	03755	603-643-3115	643-5606
Greater Keene Chamber of Commerce 48 Central Sq *Web:* www.keenechamber.com	Keene	NH	03431	603-352-1303	358-5341
Greater Laconia-Weirs Beach Chamber of Commerce 11 Veterans Sq *Web:* www.laconia-weirs.org	Laconia	NH	03246	603-524-5531	524-5534
Greater Manchester Chamber of Commerce 889 Elm St 3rd Fl *Web:* www.manchester-chamber.org	Manchester	NH	03101	603-666-6600	626-0910
Greater Nashua Chamber of Commerce 151 Main St *Web:* www.nashuachamber.com	Nashua	NH	03060	603-881-8333	881-7323
Greater Portsmouth Chamber of Commerce 500 Market St PO Box 239 *Web:* www.portsmouthchamber.org	Portsmouth	NH	03802	603-610-5510	436-5118
Greater Rochester Chamber of Commerce 18 S Main St *Web:* www.rochesternh.org	Rochester	NH	03867	603-332-5080	332-5216
Greater Salem Chamber of Commerce 224 N Broadway *Web:* www.salemnhchamber.org	Salem	NH	03079	603-893-3177	894-5158

NEW JERSEY

Name / Address	City	State	ZIP	Phone	Fax
Asbury Park Chamber of Commerce 308 Main St *Web:* www.asburyparkchamber.com	Asbury Park	NJ	07712	732-775-7676	775-7675
Greater Atlantic City Chamber 9 Gordon's Alley *Web:* www.atlanticcitychamber.com	Atlantic City	NJ	08401	609-345-4524	345-1666
Bayonne Chamber of Commerce 621 Ave C *Web:* www.bayonnenj.org	Bayonne	NJ	07002	201-436-4333	436-8546
Brick Township Chamber of Commerce 270 Chambers Bridge Rd *Web:* www.brickchamber.org	Brick	NJ	08723	732-477-4949	477-5788
Bridgeton Area Chamber of Commerce 76 Magnolia Ave PO Box 1063 *Web:* www.baccnj.com	Bridgeton	NJ	08302	856-455-1312	453-9795
Somerset County Business Partnership 360 Grove St *Web:* www.somersetbusinesspartnership.com	Bridgewater	NJ	08807	908-218-4300	722-7823
Mount Olive Area Chamber of Commerce PO Box 192 *Web:* www.mtolivechambernj.com	Budd Lake	NJ	07828	973-691-0109	691-0110
Cape May County Chamber of Commerce 13 Crest Haven Rd PO Box 74 *Web:* www.capemaycountychamber.com	Cape May Court House	NJ	08210	609-465-7181	465-5017
Salem County Chamber of Commerce 91 S Virginia Ave # A *Web:* www.salemnjchamber.homestead.com	Carneys Point	NJ	08069	856-299-6699	299-0299
Cherry Hill Regional Chamber of Commerce 1060 Kings Hwy N Suite 200 *Web:* www.cherryhillregional.com	Cherry Hill	NJ	08034	856-667-1600	667-1464
North Jersey Regional Chamber of Commerce 1033 US Hwy 46 # A103 *Web:* www.njrcc.org	Clifton	NJ	07013	973-470-9300	470-9245
Edison Chamber of Commerce 336 Raritan Ctr Pkwy *Web:* www.edisonchamber.com	Edison	NJ	08837	732-738-9482	738-9485
Gateway Regional Chamber of Commerce 135 Jefferson Ave PO Box 300 *Web:* www.gatewaychamber.com	Elizabeth	NJ	07207	908-352-0900	352-0865
Englewood Chamber of Commerce 2-10 N Van Brunt St *Web:* www.englewood-chamber.com	Englewood	NJ	07631	201-567-2381	871-4549
Fair Lawn Chamber of Commerce 12-45 River Rd *Web:* www.fairlawnchamber.org	Fair Lawn	NJ	07410	201-796-7050	475-0619
Hunterdon County Chamber of Commerce 14 Mine St *Web:* www.hunterdon-chamber.org	Flemington	NJ	08822	908-782-7115	782-7283
Greater Fort Lee Chamber of Commerce (GFLCOC) 210 Whiteman St *Web:* www.fortleechamber.com	Fort Lee	NJ	07024	201-944-7575	944-5168
Greater Monmouth Chamber of Commerce 17 Broad St *Web:* www.greatermonmouthchamber.com	Freehold	NJ	07728	732-462-3030	462-2123
Greater Hackensack Chamber of Commerce 5 University Plaza Dr *Web:* www.hackensackchamber.org	Hackensack	NJ	07601	201-489-3700	489-1741
Greater Hammonton Chamber of Commerce 790 E Commerce St PO Box 554 *Web:* www.hammontonnj.us	Hammonton	NJ	08037	609-561-9080	561-9411
Northern Monmouth Chamber of Commerce 1340 State Hwy 36 Suite 22 PO Box 5007 *Web:* www.northernmonmouthchamber.com	Hazlet	NJ	07730	732-203-0340	203-0341
Howell Chamber of Commerce 103 W 2nd St # 2 *Web:* www.howellchamber.com	Howell	NJ	07731	732-363-4114	363-8747
Irvington Chamber of Commerce PO Box 323 *Web:* www.irvington-nj.com	Irvington	NJ	07111	973-372-4100	673-5828
Hudson County Chamber of Commerce 857 Bergen Ave 3rd Fl *Web:* www.hudsonchamber.org	Jersey City	NJ	07306	201-386-0699	386-8480
Parsippany Area Chamber of Commerce 12-14 N Beverwyck Rd *Web:* www.parsippanychamber.org	Lake Hiawatha	NJ	07034	973-402-6400	206-5856
Lakewood Chamber of Commerce 395 New Jersey 70 *Web:* www.mylakewoodchamber.com	Lakewood	NJ	08701	732-363-0012	367-4453
Greater Long Branch Chamber of Commerce 228 Broadway PO Box 628 *Web:* www.longbranchchamber.org	Long Branch	NJ	07740	732-222-0400	571-3385
Matawan-Aberdeen Chamber of Commerce 201 Broad St PO Box 522	Matawan	NJ	07747	732-290-1125	290-1125
Mercer Regional Chamber of Commerce 1A Quakerbridge Plaza Dr Suite 2 *Web:* www.mercerchamber.org	Mercerville	NJ	08619	609-689-9960	586-9989
Millville Chamber of Commerce 4 City Pk Dr *Web:* www.millville-nj.com	Millville	NJ	08332	856-825-2600	825-5333
Morris County Chamber of Commerce 25 Lindsley Dr Suite 105 *Web:* www.morrischamber.org	Morristown	NJ	07960	973-539-3882	539-3960
Randolph Area Chamber of Commerce PO Box 391 *Web:* www.randolphchamber.org	Mount Freedom	NJ	07970	973-361-3462	895-3297
Burlington County Chamber of Commerce 100 Technology Way Suite 110 *Web:* www.bccoc.com	Mount Laurel	NJ	08054	856-439-2520	439-2523
Middlesex County Regional Chamber of Commerce 109 Church St *Web:* www.mcrcc.org	New Brunswick	NJ	08901	732-745-8090	745-8098
Newark Regional Business Partnership 744 Broad St 26th Fl *Web:* www.newarkrbp.org	Newark	NJ	07102	973-522-0099	824-6587
Sussex County Chamber of Commerce 120 Hampton House Rd *Web:* www.sussexcountychamber.org	Newton	NJ	07860	973-579-1811	579-3031
Nutley Chamber of Commerce 172 Chestnut St *Web:* www.nutleychamber.com	Nutley	NJ	07110	973-667-5300	
Orange Chamber of Commerce PO Box 1178 *Web:* www.orangechamber.biz	Orange	NJ	07050	973-676-8725	673-5828
Commerce & Industry Assn of New Jersey 61 S Paramus Rd # 2 *Web:* www.new.cianj.org	Paramus	NJ	07652	201-368-2100	368-3438
Greater Paramus Chamber of Commerce 58 E Midland Ave *Web:* www.paramuschamber.com	Paramus	NJ	07652	201-261-3344	261-3346
Greater Paterson Chamber of Commerce 100 Hamilton Plaza Suite 1201 *Web:* www.greaterpatersoncc.org	Paterson	NJ	07505	973-881-7300	881-8233
Perth Amboy Chamber of Commerce 69 Smith St # A *Web:* www.perthamboychamber.com	Perth Amboy	NJ	08861	732-442-7400	442-7450
Piscataway/Middlesex/South Plainfield Chamber of Commerce 2 Lakeview Ave Suite 303	Piscataway	NJ	08854	732-394-0220	394-0223
Point Pleasant Beach Chamber of Commerce 517-A Arnold Ave *Web:* www.pointchamber.com	Point Pleasant Beach	NJ	08742	732-899-2424	899-0103
Princeton Regional Chamber of Commerce 9 Vandeventer Ave *Web:* www.princetonchamber.org	Princeton	NJ	08542	609-924-1776	924-5776
Eastern Monmouth Area Chamber of Commerce 47 Reckless Pl Suite A *Web:* www.emacc.org	Red Bank	NJ	07701	732-741-0055	741-6778
Ridgewood Chamber of Commerce 27 Chestnut St *Web:* www.webridgewood.com	Ridgewood	NJ	07450	201-445-2600	251-1958
Meadowlands Regional Chamber of Commerce 201 Rt 17 *Web:* www.meadowlands.org	Rutherford	NJ	07070	201-939-0707	939-0522
Southern Ocean County Chamber of Commerce 265 W 9th St *TF:* 800-292-6372 ■ *Web:* www.visitlbiregion.com	Ship Bottom	NJ	08008	609-494-7211	494-5807
Franklin Township Chamber of Commerce 675 Franklin Blvd *Web:* www.franklinchamber.com	Somerset	NJ	08873	732-545-7044	545-7043
Suburban Chambers of Commerce 71 Summit Ave *Web:* www.suburbanchambers.org	Summit	NJ	07901	908-522-1700	522-9252
Toms River-Ocean County Chamber of Commerce 1200 Hooper Ave *Web:* www.oc-chamber.com	Toms River	NJ	08753	732-349-0220	349-1252
Union Township Chamber of Commerce 355 Chestnut St 2nd Fl *Web:* www.unionchamber.com	Union	NJ	07083	908-688-2777	688-0338
Greater Vineland Chamber of Commerce 2115 S Delsea Dr *TF:* 800-309-0019 ■ *Web:* www.vinelandchamber.org	Vineland	NJ	08360	856-691-7400	691-2113
Chamber of Commerce of Southern New Jersey 6014 Main St *Web:* www.chambersnj.com	Voorhees	NJ	08043	856-424-7776	424-8180
Southern Monmouth Chamber of Commerce 2510 Belmar Blvd Suite I-20 *Web:* www.southernmonmouthchamber.com	Wall	NJ	07719	732-280-8800	280-8505
Warren County Regional Chamber of Commerce 10 Brasscastle Rd *Web:* www.warrencountychamber.org	Washington	NJ	07882	908-835-9200	835-9296
Tri-County Chamber of Commerce 2055 Hamburg Tpke *Web:* www.tricounty.org	Wayne	NJ	07470	973-831-7788	831-9112
North Essex Chamber of Commerce 3 Fairfield Ave *Web:* www.northessexchamber.com	West Caldwell	NJ	07006	973-226-5500	403-9335
West Milford Chamber of Commerce PO Box 192 *Web:* www.westmilford.com	West Milford	NJ	07480	973-728-3150	697-5177

	City	State	ZIP	Phone	Fax
Westfield Area Chamber of Commerce (WACC) 173 Elm St 3rd Fl *Web:* www.westfieldareachamber.com	Westfield	NJ	07090	908-233-3021	654-8183
Woodbridge Metro Chamber of Commerce 52 Main St *Web:* www.woodbridgechamber.com	Woodbridge	NJ	07095	732-636-4040	636-3492

NEW MEXICO

	City	State	ZIP	Phone	Fax
Alamogordo Chamber of Commerce 1301 N White Sands Blvd *TF:* 800-826-0294 ■ *Web:* www.alamogordo.com	Alamogordo	NM	88310	575-437-6120	437-6334
Greater Albuquerque Chamber of Commerce 115 Gold Ave SW # 201 *Web:* www.abqchamber.com	Albuquerque	NM	87102	505-764-3700	764-3714
Carlsbad Chamber of Commerce 302 S Canal St PO Box 910 *TF:* 866-822-9226 ■ *Web:* www.carlsbadchamber.com	Carlsbad	NM	88220	575-887-6516	885-1455
Clovis/Curry County Chamber of Commerce 105 E 3rd St *TF:* 800-261-7656 ■ *Web:* www.clovisnm.org	Clovis	NM	88101	575-763-3435	763-7266
Espanola Valley Chamber of Commerce 710 N Paseo De Onate *Web:* www.espanolanmchamber.com	Espanola	NM	87532	505-753-2831	753-1252
Farmington Chamber of Commerce 100 W Broadway *TF:* 888-325-0279 ■ *Web:* www.gofarmington.com	Farmington	NM	87401	505-325-0279	327-7556
Grants/Cibola County Chamber of Commerce 100 N Iron Ave *TF:* 800-748-2142 ■ *Web:* www.grants.org	Grants	NM	87020	505-287-4802	287-8224
Hobbs Chamber of Commerce 400 N Marland Blvd *TF:* 800-658-6291 ■ *Web:* www.hobbschamber.org	Hobbs	NM	88240	575-397-3202	397-1689
Greater Las Cruces Chamber of Commerce 760 W Picacho Ave *Web:* www.lascruces.org	Las Cruces	NM	88005	575-524-1968	527-5546
Las Vegas-San Miguel Chamber of Commerce 503 6th St PO Box 128 *TF:* 800-832-5947 ■ *Web:* www.lasvegasnm.org	Las Vegas	NM	87701	505-425-8631	425-3057
Rio Rancho Chamber of Commerce 4001 Southern Blvd SE *Web:* www.rrchamber.org	Rio Rancho	NM	87124	505-892-1533	892-6157
Roswell Chamber of Commerce 131 W 2nd St *TF:* 877-849-7679 ■ *Web:* www.roswellnm.org	Roswell	NM	88202	575-623-5695	624-6870
Santa Fe Chamber of Commerce 8380 Cerrillos Rd Suite 302 *Web:* www.santafechamber.com	Santa Fe	NM	87507	505-988-3279	984-2205
Silver City-Grant County Chamber of Commerce 201 N Hudson St *TF:* 800-548-9378 ■ *Web:* www.silvercity.org	Silver City	NM	88061	575-538-3785	538-3786

NEW YORK

	City	State	ZIP	Phone	Fax
Albany-Colonie Regional Chamber of Commerce 1 Computer Dr S *Web:* www.acchamber.org	Albany	NY	12205	518-434-1214	431-1402
Orleans County Chamber of Commerce 102 N Main St Suite 1 *Web:* www.orleanschamber.com	Albion	NY	14411	585-589-7727	589-7326
Cayuga County Chamber of Commerce 2 State St *Web:* www.cayugacountychamber.com	Auburn	NY	13021	315-252-7291	255-3077
Greater Baldwinsville Chamber of Commerce 3 Marble St *Web:* www.b-ville.com	Baldwinsville	NY	13027	315-638-0550	
Genesee County Chamber of Commerce 210 E Main St *TF:* 800-622-2686 ■ *Web:* www.geneseeny.com	Batavia	NY	14020	585-343-7440	343-7487
Greater Bath Area Chamber of Commerce 10 Pulteney Sq W	Bath	NY	14810	607-776-7122	776-7122
Bay Shore Chamber of Commerce 77 E Main St PO Box 5110 *Web:* www.bayshorecommerce.com	Bay Shore	NY	11706	631-665-7003	665-5204
Chamber of Commerce of the Bellmores 1514 Bellmore Ave *Web:* www.bellmorechamber.com	Bellmore	NY	11710	516-679-1875	409-0544
Greater Binghamton Chamber of Commerce 49 Ct St *TF:* 800-836-6740 ■ *Web:* www.greaterbinghamtonchamber.com	Binghamton	NY	13901	607-772-8860	722-4513
Bronx Chamber of Commerce 1200 Waters Pl Suite 305 *Web:* www.bronxmall.com	Bronx	NY	10461	718-828-3900	409-3748
Brooklyn Chamber of Commerce 25 Elm Pl Suite 200 *Web:* www.ibrooklyn.com	Brooklyn	NY	11201	718-875-1000	237-4274
Buffalo Niagara Partnership 665 Main St Suite 200 *TF:* 800-241-0474 ■ *Web:* www.thepartnership.org	Buffalo	NY	14203	716-852-7100	852-2761
Saint Lawrence County Chamber of Commerce 101 Main St *TF:* 877-228-7810 ■ *Web:* www.northcountryguide.com	Canton	NY	13617	315-386-4000	379-0134
Greene County Chamber of Commerce 1 Bridge St 2nd Fl *Web:* www.greenecounty-chamber.com	Catskill	NY	12414	518-943-4222	943-1700
Cheektowaga Chamber of Commerce 2875 Union Rd Suite 50 *Web:* www.cheektowaga.org	Cheektowaga	NY	14227	716-684-5838	684-5571
Chamber of Southern Saratoga County 15 Pk Ave Suite 7-B *Web:* www.southernsaratoga.org	Clifton Park	NY	12065	518-371-7748	371-5025
Corning Area Chamber of Commerce 1 W Market St Suite 302 *TF:* 866-463-6264 ■ *Web:* www.corningny.com	Corning	NY	14830	607-936-4686	936-4685
Cortland County Chamber of Commerce 37 Church St *Web:* www.cortlandchamber.com	Cortland	NY	13045	607-756-2814	756-4698
Delaware County Chamber of Commerce 5 1/2 Main St *TF:* 866-775-4425 ■ *Web:* www.delawarecounty.org	Delhi	NY	13753	607-746-2281	746-3571
Bethlehem Chamber of Commerce 318 Delaware Ave Suite 11 *Web:* www.bethlehemchamber.com	Delmar	NY	12054	518-439-0512	475-0910
Chautauqua County Chamber of Commerce 10785 Bennett Rd *Web:* www.chautauquachamber.org	Dunkirk	NY	14048	716-366-6200	366-4276
Greater East Aurora Chamber of Commerce 652 Main St *Web:* www.eanycc.com	East Aurora	NY	14052	716-652-8444	652-8384
Chemung County Chamber of Commerce 400 E Church St *TF:* 800-627-5892 ■ *Web:* www.chemungchamber.org	Elmira	NY	14901	607-734-5137	734-4490
Montgomery County Chamber of Commerce 12 S Bridge St PO Box 836 *TF:* 800-743-7337 ■ *Web:* www.montgomerycountyny.com	Fonda	NY	12068	518-853-1800	853-1813
Livingston County Chamber of Commerce 4635 Millennium Dr *TF:* 800-538-7365 ■ *Web:* www.fingerlakeswest.com	Geneseo	NY	14454	585-243-2222	243-4824
Adirondack Regional Chambers of Commerce 136 Glen St # 3 *TF:* 888-516-7247 ■ *Web:* www.adirondackchamber.org	Glens Falls	NY	12801	518-798-1761	792-4147
Fulton County Regional Chamber of Commerce 2 N Main St *TF:* 800-676-3858 ■ *Web:* www.fultoncountyny.org	Gloversville	NY	12078	518-725-0641	725-0643
Guilderland Chamber of Commerce 2050 Western Ave Suite 109 *Web:* www.guilderlandchamber.com	Guilderland	NY	12084	518-456-6611	456-6690
Hamburg Chamber of Commerce 8 S Buffalo St *TF:* 877-322-6890 ■ *Web:* www.hamburg-chamber.org	Hamburg	NY	14075	716-649-7917	649-6362
Hempstead Village Chamber of Commerce 1776 Nichols Ct *Web:* www.hempsteadchamber.org	Hempstead	NY	11550	516-483-2000	483-2000
Hicksville Chamber of Commerce 10 W Marie St *Web:* www.hicksvillechamber.com	Hicksville	NY	11801	516-931-7170	931-8546
Southern Ulster County Chamber of Commerce 33 Main St *Web:* www.southernulsterchamber.org	Highland	NY	12528	845-691-6070	691-9194
Columbia County Chamber of Commerce 507 Warren St *Web:* www.columbiachamber-ny.com	Hudson	NY	12534	518-828-4417	822-9539
Huntington Township Chamber of Commerce 164 Main St *TF:* 888-361-5710 ■ *Web:* www.huntingtonchamber.com	Huntington	NY	11743	631-423-6100	351-8276
Hyde Park Chamber of Commerce PO Box 17 *Web:* www.hydeparkchamber.org	Hyde Park	NY	12538	845-229-8612	229-8638
Tompkins County Chamber of Commerce 904 E Shore Dr *Web:* www.tompkinschamber.org	Ithaca	NY	14850	607-273-7080	272-7617
Queens Chamber of Commerce 75-20 Astoria Blvd Suite 140 *Web:* www.queenschamber.org	Jackson Heights	NY	11370	718-898-8500	898-8599
Jamaica Chamber of Commerce 90-25 161st St Suite 505	Jamaica	NY	11432	718-657-4800	658-4642
Chautauqua County Chamber of Commerce 512 Falconer St *Web:* www.chautauquachamber.org	Jamestown	NY	14701	716-484-1101	487-0785
Kenmore-Town of Tonawanda Chamber of Commerce 3411 Delaware Ave *TF:* 888-281-1680 ■ *Web:* www.ken-ton.org	Kenmore	NY	14217	716-874-1202	874-3151
Chamber of Commerce of Ulster County 55 Albany Ave *Web:* www.ulsterchamber.org	Kingston	NY	12401	845-338-5100	338-0968
Lake Placid/Essex County Visitors Bureau 49 Parkside Dr *TF:* 800-447-5224 ■ *Web:* www.lakeplacid.com	Lake Placid	NY	12946	518-523-2445	523-2605
Greater Liverpool Chamber of Commerce 314 2nd St *Web:* www.liverpoolchamber.com	Liverpool	NY	13088	315-457-3895	234-3226
Long Beach Chamber of Commerce 350 National Blvd *Web:* www.thelongbeachchamber.com	Long Beach	NY	11561	516-432-6000	432-0273
Lewis County Chamber of Commerce 7576 S State St *TF:* 800-724-0242 ■ *Web:* www.lewiscountychamber.org	Lowville	NY	13367	315-376-2213	376-0326
Greater Mahopacs-Carmel Chamber of Commerce 953 S Lake Blvd PO Box 160 *Web:* www.mahopaccarmelonline.com	Mahopac	NY	10541	845-628-5553	628-5962
Chamber of Commerce of the Massapequas Inc 674 Broadway *Web:* www.massapequachamber.com	Massapequa	NY	11758	516-541-1443	541-8625
Long Island Assn 300 Broadhollow Rd Suite 110-W *Web:* www.longislandassociation.org	Melville	NY	11747	631-499-4400	499-2194
Herkimer County Chamber of Commerce 28 W Main St *TF:* 877-984-4636 ■ *Web:* www.herkimercountychamber.com	Mohawk	NY	13407	315-866-7820	866-7833
Orange County Chamber of Commerce 30 Scott's Corners Dr *Web:* www.orangeny.com	Montgomery	NY	12549	845-457-9700	457-8799
Sullivan County Chamber of Commerce 457 W Broadway Suite 1 *Web:* www.catskills.com	Monticello	NY	12701	845-791-4200	791-4220
Mount Vernon Chamber of Commerce 65 Haven Ave *Web:* www.mtvernonchamber.org	Mount Vernon	NY	10553	914-667-7500	699-0139

Name / Address	City	State	ZIP	Phone	Fax
Chamber of Commerce of New Rochelle 459 Main St *Web:* www.newrochellechamber.org	New Rochelle	NY	10801	914-632-5700	632-0708
Greater New York Chamber of Commerce 20 W 44th St 4th Fl *Web:* www.ny-chamber.com	New York	NY	10036	212-686-7220	686-7232
Manhattan Chamber of Commerce 1375 Broadway 3rd F *Web:* www.manhattancc.org	New York	NY	10018	212-479-7772	473-8074
New York City Partnership & Chamber of Commerce Inc 1 Battery Pk Plaza 5th Fl *Web:* www.pfnyc.org	New York	NY	10004	212-493-7400	344-3344
Chamber of Commerce of the Tonawandas 15 Webster St *Web:* www.the-tonawandas.com	North Tonawanda	NY	14120	716-692-5120	692-1867
Commerce Chenango 19 Eaton Ave *Web:* www.chenangony.org	Norwich	NY	13815	607-334-1400	336-6963
Oceanside Chamber of Commerce 2721 Harrison Ave	Oceanside	NY	11572	516-763-9177	
Greater Olean Area Chamber of Commerce 120 N Union St *Web:* www.oleanny.com	Olean	NY	14760	716-372-4433	372-7912
Otsego County Chamber 189 Main St Suite 201 *TF:* 877-568-7346 ■ *Web:* www.otsegocountychamber.com	Oneonta	NY	13820	607-432-4500	432-4506
Orchard Park Chamber of Commerce 4211 N Buffalo St Suite 14 *Web:* www.orchardparkchamber.com	Orchard Park	NY	14127	716-662-3366	662-5946
Greater Oswego-Fulton Chamber of Commerce (GOFCC) 44 E Bridge St *Web:* www.oswegofultonchamber.com	Oswego	NY	13126	315-343-7681	342-0831
Tioga County Chamber of Commerce 80 N Ave *Web:* www.tiogachamber.com	Owego	NY	13827	607-687-2020	687-9028
Hudson Valley Gateway Chamber of Commerce 1 S Division St *Web:* www.hvgatewaychamber.com	Peekskill	NY	10566	914-737-3600	737-0541
Plattsburgh North Country Chamber of Commerce 7061 Rt 9 *Web:* www.northcountrychamber.com	Plattsburgh	NY	12901	518-563-1000	563-1028
Tri-State Chamber of Commerce 5 S Broome St	Port Jervis	NY	12771	845-856-6694	856-6695
Port Washington Chamber of Commerce 329 Main St *Web:* www.pwguide.com	Port Washington	NY	11050	516-883-6566	883-6591
Dutchess County Regional Chamber of Commerce 1 Civic Ctr Plaza Suite 400 *Web:* www.dutchesscountyregionalchamber.org	Poughkeepsie	NY	12601	845-454-1700	454-1702
Rochester Business Alliance 150 State St *Web:* www.rochesterbusinessalliance.com	Rochester	NY	14614	585-454-2220	263-3679
Rome Area Chamber of Commerce 139 W Dominick St *Web:* www.romechamber.com	Rome	NY	13440	315-337-1700	337-1715
Niagara USA Chamber of Commerce 6311 Inducon Corporate Dr Suite 2 *Web:* www.niagarachamber.org	Sanborn	NY	14132	716-285-9141	285-0941
Saratoga County Chamber of Commerce 28 Clinton St *TF:* 800-526-8970 ■ *Web:* www.saratoga.org	Saratoga Springs	NY	12866	518-584-3255	587-0318
Chamber of Schenectady County 306 State St *TF:* 800-962-8007 ■ *Web:* www.schenectadychamber.net	Schenectady	NY	12305	518-372-5656	370-3217
Schoharie County Chamber of Commerce 113 Pk Pl Suite 2 *TF:* 800-418-4748 ■ *Web:* www.schohariechamber.com	Schoharie	NY	12157	518-295-6550	295-7453
Seneca County Chamber of Commerce 2020 Rt 5 & 20 W *Web:* www.senecachamber.org	Seneca Falls	NY	13148	315-568-2906	568-1730
Smithtown Chamber of Commerce 79 E Main St Suite E *Web:* www.smithtownchamber.org	Smithtown	NY	11787	631-979-8069	979-2206
Southampton Chamber of Commerce 76 Main St *Web:* www.southamptonchamber.com	SouthHampton	NY	11968	631-283-0402	283-8707
Staten Island Chamber of Commerce 130 Bay St *Web:* www.sichamber.com	Staten Island	NY	10301	718-727-1900	727-2295
Greater Syracuse Chamber of Commerce 572 S Salina St *Web:* www.syracusechamber.com	Syracuse	NY	13202	315-470-1800	471-8545
Rensselaer County Regional Chamber of Commerce 255 River St *Web:* www.renscochamber.com	Troy	NY	12180	518-274-7020	272-7729
Mohawk Valley Chamber of Commerce 200 Genesee St *Web:* www.mvchamber.org	Utica	NY	13502	315-724-3151	724-3177
Greater Southern Dutchess Chamber of Commerce 2582 S Ave *Web:* www.gsdcc.org	Wappingers Falls	NY	12590	845-296-0001	296-0006
Warwick Valley Chamber of Commerce (WVCC) PO Box 202 *Web:* www2.warwickcc.org	Warwick	NY	10990	845-986-2720	986-6982
Greater Watertown-North Country Chamber of Commerce 1241 Coffeen St *Web:* www.watertownny.com	Watertown	NY	13601	315-788-4400	788-3369
Webster Chamber of Commerce 1110 Crosspointe Ln Suite C *Web:* www.websterchamber.com	Webster	NY	14580	585-265-3960	265-3702
Business Council of Westchester 108 Corporate Pk Dr Suite 101 *Web:* www.westchesterny.org	White Plains	NY	10604	914-948-2110	948-0122
Amherst Chamber of Commerce 350 Essjay Rd Suite 200 *Web:* www.amherst.org	Williamsville	NY	14221	716-632-6905	632-0548
Yonkers Chamber of Commerce 55 Main St 2nd Fl *Web:* www.yonkerschamber.com	Yonkers	NY	10701	914-963-0332	963-0455

NORTH CAROLINA

Name / Address	City	State	ZIP	Phone	Fax
Ahoskie Chamber of Commerce PO Box 7 *Web:* www.ashokiechamber.com	Ahoskie	NC	27910	252-332-2042	332-8617
Stanly County Chamber of Commerce 116 E N St *Web:* www.stanlychamber.org	Albemarle	NC	28001	704-982-8116	983-5000
Archdale-Trinity Chamber of Commerce 213 Balfour Dr *Web:* www.archdaletrinitychamber.com	Archdale	NC	27263	336-434-2073	431-5845
Asheboro/Randolph Chamber of Commerce 317 E Dixie Dr *Web:* www.chamber.asheboro.com	Asheboro	NC	27203	336-626-2626	626-7077
Asheville Area Chamber of Commerce 36 Montford Ave *TF:* 800-257-1300 ■ *Web:* www.ashevillechamber.org	Asheville	NC	28802	828-258-6101	251-0926
Black Mountain-Swannanoa Chamber of Commerce 201 E State St *TF:* 800-669-2301 ■ *Web:* www.blackmountain.org	Black Mountain	NC	28711	828-669-2300	669-1407
Blowing Rock Chamber of Commerce 7738 Valley Blvd *TF:* 800-295-7851 ■ *Web:* www.blowingrock.com	Blowing Rock	NC	28605	828-295-7851	295-4643
Brevard-Transylvania Chamber of Commerce 175 E Main St *TF:* 800-648-4523 ■ *Web:* www.brevardncchamber.org	Brevard	NC	28712	828-883-3700	883-8550
Alamance County Area Chamber of Commerce 610 S Lexington Ave *Web:* www.alamancechamber.com	Burlington	NC	27215	336-228-1338	228-1330
Cary Chamber of Commerce 307 N Academy St *TF:* 800-919-2279 ■ *Web:* www.carychamber.com	Cary	NC	27513	919-467-1016	469-2375
Chapel Hill-Carrboro Chamber of Commerce 104 S Estes Dr *Web:* www.carolinachamber.org	Chapel Hill	NC	27515	919-967-7075	968-6874
Charlotte Chamber of Commerce PO Box 32785 *Web:* www.charlottechamber.com	Charlotte	NC	28232	704-378-1300	374-1903
Lake Norman Chamber of Commerce 19900 W Catawba Ave *TF:* 800-305-2508 ■ *Web:* www.lakenormanchamber.org	Cornelius	NC	28031	704-987-3300	892-5313
Greater Durham Chamber of Commerce 300 W Morgan St Suite 1400 PO Box 3829 *Web:* www.durhamchamber.org	Durham	NC	27702	919-328-8700	688-8351
Elizabeth City Area Chamber of Commerce 502 E Ehringhaus St *TF:* 888-258-4832 ■ *Web:* www.elizcity.com	Elizabeth City	NC	27909	252-335-4365	335-5732
Yadkin Valley Chamber of Commerce 116 E Market St PO Box 496 *Web:* www.yadkinvalley.org	Elkin	NC	28621	336-526-1111	526-1879
Cumberland County Business Council 201 Hay St 4th Fl *Web:* www.ccbusinesscouncil.org	Fayetteville	NC	28301	910-483-8133	483-0263
Fuquay-Varina Area Chamber of Commerce 121 N Main St *Web:* www.fuquay-varina.com	Fuquay-Varina	NC	27526	919-552-4947	552-1029
Gaston Chamber of Commerce 601 W Franklin Blvd *TF:* 800-348-8461 ■ *Web:* www.gastonchamber.com	Gastonia	NC	28052	704-864-2621	854-8723
Wayne County Chamber of Commerce 308 N Williams St *Web:* www.waynecountychamber.com	Goldsboro	NC	27530	919-734-2241	734-2247
Greensboro Area Chamber of Commerce 342 N Elm St *Web:* www.greensborochamber.com	Greensboro	NC	27401	336-387-8300	275-9299
Greenville-Pitt County Chamber of Commerce 302 S Greene St *Web:* www.greenvillenc.org	Greenville	NC	27834	252-752-4101	752-5934
Henderson-Vance County Chamber of Commerce 414 S Garnett St *Web:* www.hendersonvance.org	Henderson	NC	27536	252-438-8414	492-8989
Hendersonville County Chamber of Commerce 204 Kanuga Rd *Web:* www.hendersonvillechamber.org	Hendersonville	NC	28739	828-692-1413	693-8802
Catawba County Chamber of Commerce 1055 Southgate Corporate Pk SW PO Box 1828 *Web:* www.catawbachamber.org	Hickory	NC	28603	828-328-6111	328-1175
High Point Chamber of Commerce 1634 N Main St *Web:* www.highpointchamber.org	High Point	NC	27262	336-882-5000	889-9499
Jacksonville/Onslow Chamber of Commerce 1099 Gum Branch Rd *Web:* www.jacksonvilleonline.org	Jacksonville	NC	28541	910-347-3141	347-4705
Cabarrus Regional Chamber of Commerce 3003 Dale Earnhardt Blvd *Web:* www.cabarruschamber.org	Kannapolis	NC	28083	704-782-4000	782-4050
Outer Banks Chamber of Commerce 101 Town Hall Dr PO Box 1757 *Web:* www.outerbankschamber.com	Kill Devil Hills	NC	27948	252-441-8144	441-0339
Kinston-Lenoir County Chamber of Commerce 301 N Queen St *Web:* www.kinstonchamber.com	Kinston	NC	28501	252-527-1131	527-1914
Laurinburg/Scotland County Area Chamber of Commerce 606 Atkinson St *Web:* www.laurinburgchamber.org	Laurinburg	NC	28353	910-276-7420	277-8785
Caldwell County Chamber of Commerce 1909 Hickory Blvd SE *Web:* www.caldwellcochamber.org	Lenoir	NC	28645	828-726-0616	726-0385
Lincolnton-Lincoln County Chamber of Commerce 101 E Main St *Web:* www.lincolnchambernc.org	Lincolnton	NC	28092	704-735-3096	735-5449

Chamber / Address	City	State	ZIP	Phone	Fax
Greater Franklin County Chamber of Commerce 112 E Nash St PO Box 62 *Web:* www.franklin-chamber.org	Louisburg	NC	27549	919-496-3056	496-0422
Lumberton Area Chamber of Commerce 800 N Chestnut St *Web:* www.lumbertonchamber.com	Lumberton	NC	28358	910-739-4750	671-9722
Western Rockingham Chamber of Commerce 112 W Murphy St *Web:* www.westernrockinghamchamber.com	Madison	NC	27025	336-548-6248	548-4466
McDowell County Chamber of Commerce 1170 W Tate St *Web:* www.mcdowellchamber.com	Marion	NC	28752	828-652-4240	659-9620
Davie County Chamber of Commerce 135 S Salisbury St *Web:* www.daviecounty.com	Mocksville	NC	27028	336-751-3304	751-5697
Union County Chamber of Commerce 903 Skyway Dr Po Box 1789 *Web:* www.unioncountycoc.com	Monroe	NC	28110	704-289-4567	282-0122
Mooresville-South Iredell Chamber of Commerce 149 E Iredell Ave. *Web:* www.mooresvillenc.org	Mooresville	NC	28115	704-664-3898	664-2549
Carteret County Chamber of Commerce 801 Arendell St Suite 1 *TF:* 800-622-6278 ■ *Web:* www.nccoastchamber.com	Morehead City	NC	28557	252-726-6350	726-3505
Burke County Chamber of Commerce 110 E Meeting St *Web:* www.burkecounty.org	Morganton	NC	28655	828-437-3021	437-1613
Greater Mount Airy Chamber of Commerce 200 N Main St *TF:* 800-948-0949 ■ *Web:* www.mtairyncchamber.org	Mount Airy	NC	27030	336-786-6116	786-1488
Mount Olive Area Chamber of Commerce 123 N Ctr St *Web:* www.moachamber.com	Mount Olive	NC	28365	919-658-3113	658-3125
Cherokee County Chamber of Commerce (CCCC) 805 W US 64 Hwy *Web:* www.cherokeecountychamber.com	Murphy	NC	28906	828-837-2242	837-6012
New Bern Area Chamber of Commerce 316 S Front St *Web:* www.newbernchamber.com	New Bern	NC	28560	252-637-3111	637-7541
Wilkes Chamber of Commerce 717 Main St *Web:* www.wilkesnc.org	North Wilkesboro	NC	28659	336-838-8662	838-3728
Granville County Chamber of Commerce 124 Hillsboro St *Web:* www.granville-chamber.com	Oxford	NC	27565	919-693-6125	693-6126
Raeford-Hoke Chamber of Commerce 101 N Main St *Web:* www.raefordhokechamber.com	Raeford	NC	28376	910-875-5929	875-1010
Greater Raleigh Chamber of Commerce PO Box 2978 *Web:* www.raleighchamber.org	Raleigh	NC	27602	919-664-7000	664-7097
Roanoke Valley Chamber of Commerce 1640 Julian R Allsbrook Hwy *Web:* www.rvchamber.com	Roanoke Rapids	NC	27870	252-537-3513	535-5767
Richmond County Chamber of Commerce 505 Rockingham Rd *TF:* 800-858-1688 ■ *Web:* www.richmondcountychamber.com	Rockingham	NC	28379	910-895-9058	895-9056
Rocky Mount Area Chamber of Commerce 100 Coastline St # 200 *Web:* www.rockymountchamber.org	Rocky Mount	NC	27804	252-446-0323	446-5103
Roxboro Area Chamber of Commerce 211 N Main St *Web:* www.roxboronc.com	Roxboro	NC	27573	336-599-8333	599-8335
Rutherford County Chamber of Commerce 162 N Main St *Web:* www.rutherfordcoc.org	Rutherfordton	NC	28139	828-287-3090	287-0799
Rowan County Chamber of Commerce 204 E Innes St Suite 110 *Web:* www.rowanchamber.com	Salisbury	NC	28144	704-633-4221	639-1200
Sanford Area Chamber of Commerce 143 Charlotte Ave Suite 101 *Web:* www.sanford-nc.com	Sanford	NC	27330	919-775-7341	776-6244
Brunswick County Chamber of Commerce 4948 Main St *TF:* 800-426-6644 ■ *Web:* www.brunswickcountychamber.org	Shallotte	NC	28459	910-754-6644	754-6539
Cleveland County Chamber of Commerce 200 S Lafayette St *Web:* www.clevelandchamber.org	Shelby	NC	28150	704-487-8521	487-7458
Chatham Chamber of Commerce 1609 E 11th St *Web:* www.ccucc.net	Siler City	NC	27344	919-742-3333	742-1333
Greater Smithfield-Selma Area Chamber of Commerce 1115 Industrial Pk Dr *Web:* www.smithfieldselma.com	Smithfield	NC	27577	919-934-9166	934-1337
Moore County Chamber of Commerce 10677 Hwy 15-501 *Web:* www.moorecountychamber.com	Southern Pines	NC	28387	910-692-3926	692-0619
Jackson County Chamber of Commerce 773 W Main St *TF:* 800-962-1911 ■ *Web:* www.mountainlovers.com	Sylva	NC	28779	828-586-2155	586-4887
Tarboro Edgecombe Chamber of Commerce 509 Trade St *Web:* www.tarborochamber.com	Tarboro	NC	27886	252-823-7241	823-1499
Alexander County Chamber of Commerce 16 W Main Ave *Web:* www.alexandercountychamber.com	Taylorsville	NC	28681	828-632-8141	632-1096
Thomasville Area Chamber of Commerce 6 W Main St *Web:* www.thomasvillechamber.net	Thomasville	NC	27360	336-475-6134	475-4802
Carolina Foothills Chamber of Commerce 2753 Lynn Rd Suite A *Web:* www.polkchamber.org	Tryon	NC	28782	828-859-6236	859-2301
Washington-Beaufort County Chamber of Commerce 102 Stewart Pkwy PO Box 665 *Web:* www.wbcchamber.com	Washington	NC	27889	252-946-9168	946-9169
Haywood County Chamber of Commerce 591 N Main St *TF:* 877-456-3073 ■ *Web:* www.haywood-nc.com	Waynesville	NC	28786	828-456-3021	452-7265
Martin County Chamber of Commerce 413 E Blvd *Web:* www.martincountync.com	Williamston	NC	27892	252-792-4131	792-1013
Greater Wilmington Chamber of Commerce 1 Estell Lee Pl *Web:* www.wilmingtonchamber.org	Wilmington	NC	28401	910-762-2611	762-9765
Wilson Chamber of Commerce 200 Nash St NE *Web:* www.wilsonncchamber.com	Wilson	NC	27893	252-237-0165	243-7931
Windsor-Bertie Area Chamber of Commerce 102 N York St *Web:* www.albemarle-nc.com	Windsor	NC	27983	252-794-4277	794-5070
Greater Winston-Salem Chamber of Commerce PO Box 1408 *Web:* www.winstonsalem.com	Winston-Salem	NC	27102	336-725-2361	721-2209
Yadkin County Chamber of Commerce 205 S Jackson St PO Box 1840 *Web:* www.yadkinchamber.org	Yadkinville	NC	27055	336-679-2200	679-3034

NORTH DAKOTA

Chamber / Address	City	State	ZIP	Phone	Fax
Bismarck Mandan Chamber of Commerce 1640 Burnt Boat Dr *Web:* www.bismarckmandan.com	Bismarck	ND	58502	701-223-5660	255-6125
Grand Forks Chamber of Commerce 202 N 3rd St *Web:* www.gochamber.org	Grand Forks	ND	58203	701-772-7271	772-9238
Jamestown Area Chamber of Commerce 120 2nd St SE PO Box 1530 *Web:* www.jamestownchamber.com	Jamestown	ND	58401	701-252-4830	952-4837
Minot Area Chamber of Commerce 1020 20th Ave SW *Web:* www.minotchamber.org	Minot	ND	58701	701-852-6000	838-2488

OHIO

Chamber / Address	City	State	ZIP	Phone	Fax
Greater Akron Chamber 1 Cascade Plaza 17th Fl *TF:* 800-621-8001 ■ *Web:* www.greaterakronchamber.org	Akron	OH	44308	330-376-5550	379-3164
Alliance Area Chamber of Commerce 210 E Main St *Web:* www.allianceohiochamber.org	Alliance	OH	44601	330-823-6260	823-4434
Ashtabula Area Chamber of Commerce 4536 Main Ave *Web:* www.ashtabulachamber.net	Ashtabula	OH	44004	440-998-6998	992-8216
Athens Area Chamber of Commerce 449 E State St Suite 1 *Web:* www.athenschamber.com	Athens	OH	45701	740-594-2251	594-2252
Barberton South Summitt Chamber of Commerce 503 W Pk Ave *Web:* www.southsummitchamber.org	Barberton	OH	44203	330-745-3141	777-0597
Beavercreek Chamber of Commerce 3299 Kemp Rd *Web:* www.beavercreekchamber.org	Beavercreek	OH	45431	937-426-2202	426-2204
Logan County Chamber of Commerce 100 S Main St *Web:* www.logancountyohio.com	Bellefontaine	OH	43311	937-599-5121	599-2411
Muskingum Valley Area Chamber of Commerce 531 5th St *Web:* www.mvacc.com	Beverly	OH	45715	740-984-8259	
Bowling Green Chamber of Commerce (BGCC) 163 N Main St PO Box 31 *Web:* www.bgchamber.net	Bowling Green	OH	43402	419-353-7945	353-3693
Brunswick Area Chamber of Commerce 3511 Center Rd Suite A-B *Web:* www.brunswickareachamber.org	Brunswick	OH	44212	330-225-8411	273-8172
Cambridge Area Chamber of Commerce 918 Wheeling Ave *Web:* www.cambridgeohiochamber.com	Cambridge	OH	43725	740-439-6688	439-6689
Canton Regional Chamber of Commerce 222 Market Ave N *TF:* 800-533-4302 ■ *Web:* www.cantonchamber.org	Canton	OH	44702	330-456-7253	452-7786
Carroll County Chamber of Commerce & Economic Development 61 N Lisbon St *TF:* 800-956-4684 ■ *Web:* www.carrollohchamber.com	Carrollton	OH	44615	330-627-4811	627-3647
Celina-Mercer County Chamber of Commerce 226 N Main St *Web:* www.celinamercer.com	Celina	OH	45822	419-586-2219	586-8645
Chagrin Valley Chamber of Commerce 79 N Main St *Web:* www.cvcc.org	Chagrin Falls	OH	44022	440-247-6607	
Chillicothe-Ross Chamber of Commerce 45 E Main St *Web:* www.chillicotheohio.com	Chillicothe	OH	45601	740-702-2722	702-2727
Anderson Area Chamber of Commerce 7850 Five Mile Rd *Web:* www.andersonareachamber.com	Cincinnati	OH	45230	513-474-4802	474-4857
Cincinnati USA Regional Chamber 441 Vine St Suite 300 *Web:* www.cincinnatichamber.com	Cincinnati	OH	45202	513-579-3100	579-3102
Clermont Chamber of Commerce 4355 Ferguson Dr Suite 150 *Web:* www.clermontchamber.com	Cincinnati	OH	45145	513-576-5000	576-5001
Pickaway County Chamber of Commerce 325 W Main St *Web:* www.pickaway.com	Circleville	OH	43113	740-474-4923	477-6800

Name / Address	City	State	ZIP	Phone	Fax
Greater Cleveland Partnership 100 Public Sq Suite 210 *TF:* 800-562-7121 ■ *Web:* www.gcpartnership.com	Cleveland	OH	44113	216-621-3300	621-6013
Columbus Chamber of Commerce 150 S Front St # 200 *TF:* 800-950-1321 ■ *Web:* www.columbus.org	Columbus	OH	43215	614-221-1321	221-9360
Coshocton County Chamber of Commerce 401 Main St *Web:* www.coshoctoncounty.net	Coshocton	OH	43812	740-622-5411	622-9902
Cuyahoga Falls Chamber of Commerce (CFCC) 151 Portage Trail Suite 1 *Web:* www.cfchamber.com	Cuyahoga Falls	OH	44221	330-929-6756	929-4278
Dayton Area Chamber of Commerce 1 Chamber Plaza Suite 200 *Web:* www.daytonchamber.org	Dayton	OH	45402	937-226-1444	226-8254
South Metro Regional Chamber of Commerce 7887 Washington Village Dr Suite 265 *Web:* www.smrcoc.org	Dayton	OH	45459	937-433-2032	433-6881
Defiance Area Chamber of Commerce 615 W 3rd St *Web:* www.defiancechamber.com	Defiance	OH	43512	419-782-7946	782-0111
East Liverpool Area Chamber of Commerce 529 Market St PO Box 94 *Web:* www.elchamber.com	East Liverpool	OH	43920	330-385-0845	385-0581
Eaton-Preble County Chamber of Commerce 122 W Decatur St PO Box 303 *Web:* www.preblecountyohio.com	Eaton	OH	45320	937-456-4949	456-4949
Lorain County Chamber of Commerce 226 Middle Ave *Web:* www.loraincountychamber.com	Elyria	OH	44035	440-328-2550	328-2557
Englewood-Northmont Chamber of Commerce PO Box 62 *Web:* www.northmont-area-coc.org	Englewood	OH	45322	937-836-2550	836-2485
Euclid Chamber of Commerce 21935 Lake Shore Blvd *Web:* www.euclidchamberofcommerce.com	Euclid	OH	44123	216-731-9322	731-8354
Fairborn Area Chamber of Commerce 12 N Central Ave *Web:* www.fairborn.com	Fairborn	OH	45324	937-878-3191	878-3197
Fairfield Chamber of Commerce 670 Wessel Dr *Web:* www.fairfieldchamber.com	Fairfield	OH	45014	513-881-5500	881-5503
Findlay-Hancock County Chamber of Commerce 123 E Main Cross St *Web:* www.greaterfindlayinc.com	Findlay	OH	45840	419-422-3313	422-9508
Fostoria Area Chamber of Commerce (FACC) 121 N Main St *Web:* www.fostoriaohio.org	Fostoria	OH	44830	419-435-7789	435-0936
Chamber of Commerce of Sandusky County 101 S Front St *Web:* www.scchamber.org	Fremont	OH	43420	419-332-1591	332-8666
Gahanna Area Chamber of Commerce 181 Granville St Suite 200 *Web:* www.gahannaareachamber.com	Gahanna	OH	43230	614-471-0451	471-5122
Gallia County Chamber of Commerce 16 State St PO Box 465 *Web:* www.galliacounty.org	Gallipolis	OH	45631	740-446-0596	446-7031
Garfield Heights Chamber of Commerce 5284 Transportation Blvd *Web:* www.garfieldchamber.com	Garfield Heights	OH	44125	216-475-7775	475-2237
Geneva Area Chamber of Commerce 866 E Main St *Web:* www.genevachamber.org	Geneva	OH	44041	440-466-8694	466-0823
Brown County Chamber of Commerce 110 E State St PO Box 21606 *TF:* 888-276-9664 ■ *Web:* www.browncountyohiochamber.com	Georgetown	OH	45121	937-378-4784	378-1634
Darke County Chamber of Commerce 622 S Broadway *Web:* www.darkecountyohio.com	Greenville	OH	45331	937-548-2102	548-5608
Greater Hamilton Chamber of Commerce 201 Dayton St *Web:* www.hamilton-ohio.com	Hamilton	OH	45011	513-844-1500	844-1999
Highland County Chamber of Commerce 1575 N High St Suite 400 *Web:* www.highlandcountychamber.com	Hillsboro	OH	45133	937-393-1111	393-9604
Huber Heights Chamber of Commerce 4756 Fishburg Rd *Web:* www.huberheightschamber.com	Huber Heights	OH	45424	937-233-5700	233-5769
Jackson Area Chamber of Commerce 234 Broadway St *Web:* www.jacksonohio.org	Jackson	OH	45640	740-286-2722	286-8443
Jackson-Beldon Chamber of Commerce 5735 Wales Ave NW *Web:* www.jbcc.org	Jackson Township	OH	44646	330-833-4400	833-4456
Kent Area Chamber of Commerce 138 E Main St Suite 102 *Web:* www.kentbiz.com	Kent	OH	44240	330-673-9855	673-9860
Hardin County Chamber of Commerce (HCCBA) 225 S Detroit St *TF:* 888-642-7346 ■ *Web:* www.hardinohio.org	Kenton	OH	43326	419-673-4131	674-4876
Kettering-Moraine-Oakwood Area Chamber of Commerce 2977 Far Hills Ave *Web:* www.kmo-coc.org	Kettering	OH	45419	937-299-3852	299-3851
Lakewood Chamber of Commerce 16017 Detroit Ave *Web:* www.lakewoodchamber.org	Lakewood	OH	44107	216-226-2900	226-1340
Lancaster-Fairfield County Chamber of Commerce 109 N Broad St # 100 *Web:* www.lancoc.org	Lancaster	OH	43130	740-653-8251	653-7074
Lima/Allen County Chamber of Commerce 147 S Main St *Web:* www.limachamber.com	Lima	OH	45801	419-222-6045	229-0266
Logan-Hocking Chamber of Commerce 4 E Hunter St *TF:* 800-414-6731 ■ *Web:* www.logan-hockingchamber.com	Logan	OH	43138	740-385-6836	385-7259
Madison-Perry Area Chamber of Commerce 5965 N Ridge Rd *Web:* www.mpacc.org	Madison	OH	44057	440-428-3760	428-6668
Mansfield-Richland Area Chamber of Commerce 55 N Mulberry St *Web:* www.mrachamber.com	Mansfield	OH	44902	419-522-3211	526-6853
Marietta Area Chamber of Commerce 100 Front St Suite 200 *Web:* www.mariettachamber.com	Marietta	OH	45750	740-373-5176	373-7808
Marion Area Chamber of Commerce 205 W Ctr St Suite 100 *Web:* www.marionareachamber.org	Marion	OH	43302	740-382-2181	387-7722
Union County Chamber of Commerce 227 E 5th St *TF:* 800-642-0087 ■ *Web:* www.unioncounty.org	Marysville	OH	43040	937-642-6279	644-0422
Massillon Area Chamber of Commerce 137 Lincoln Way E *Web:* www.massillonohchamber.com	Massillon	OH	44646	330-833-3146	833-8944
Mentor Chamber of Commerce 6972 Spinach Dr *Web:* www.mentorchamber.org	Mentor	OH	44060	440-255-1616	255-1717
Chamber of Commerce serving Middletown Monroe & Trenton 1500 Central Ave *Web:* www.mmvchamber.org	Middletown	OH	45044	513-422-4551	422-6831
Milford-Miami Township Chamber of Commerce 983 Lila Ave *Web:* www.milfordmiamitownship.com	Milford	OH	45150	513-831-2411	831-3547
Holmes County Chamber of Commerce 35 N Monroe St *Web:* www.holmescountychamber.com	Millersburg	OH	44654	330-674-3975	674-3976
Morrow County Chamber of Commerce 17 1/2 W High St PO Box 174 *Web:* www.morrowchamber.org	Mount Gilead	OH	43338	419-946-2821	946-3861
Mount Vernon-Knox County Chamber of Commerce 400 S Gay St *Web:* www.knoxchamber.com	Mount Vernon	OH	43050	740-393-1111	393-1590
Napoleon/Henry County Chamber of Commerce 611 N Perry St *Web:* www.ohiohenrycounty.com	Napoleon	OH	43545	419-592-1786	592-4945
Perry County Chamber of Commerce (PCCC) 121 S Main St *Web:* www.perrycountyohiochamber.com	New Lexington	OH	43764	740-342-3547	342-9124
Tuscarawas County Chamber of Commerce 1323 4th St NW *Web:* www.tuschamber.com	New Philadelphia	OH	44663	330-343-4474	343-6526
Licking County Chamber of Commerce 50 W Locust St *Web:* www.lickingcountychamber.com	Newark	OH	43055	740-345-9757	345-5141
North Canton Area Chamber of Commerce 121 S Main St *Web:* www.northcantonchamber.org	North Canton	OH	44720	330-499-5100	499-7181
North Olmsted Chamber of Commerce 28938 Lorain Rd Suite 204 *Web:* www.nolmstedchamber.org	North Olmsted	OH	44070	440-777-3368	777-9361
North Royalton Chamber of Commerce 13737 State Rd *Web:* www.nroyaltonchamber.com	North Royalton	OH	44133	440-237-6180	237-6181
Eastern Maumee Bay Chamber of Commerce 2460 Navaree Ave *Web:* www.embchamber.org	Oregon	OH	43616	419-693-5580	693-9990
Painesville Area Chamber of Commerce 1 Victoria Pl Suite 265-A *Web:* www.painesvilleohchamber.org	Painesville	OH	44077	440-357-7572	357-8752
Parma Area Chamber of Commerce 7908 Day Dr *Web:* www.parmaareachamber.org	Parma	OH	44129	440-886-1700	886-1770
Perrysburg Area Chamber of Commerce 105 W Indiana Ave *Web:* www.perrysburgchamber.com	Perrysburg	OH	43551	419-874-9147	872-9347
Portsmouth Area Chamber of Commerce 342 2nd St PO Box 509 *TF:* 800-648-2574 ■ *Web:* www.portsmouth.org	Portsmouth	OH	45662	740-353-7647	353-5824
Reynoldsburg Area Chamber of Commerce 1580 Brice Rd *Web:* www.reynoldsburgchamber.com	Reynoldsburg	OH	43068	614-866-4753	866-7313
Salem Area Chamber of Commerce 713 E State St *Web:* www.salemohiochamber.com	Salem	OH	44460	330-337-3473	337-3474
Erie County Chamber of Commerce 225 W Washington Row *Web:* www.eriecountyohiocofc.com	Sandusky	OH	44870	419-625-6421	625-7914
Shelby Chamber of Commerce 142 N Gamble St Suite A *TF:* 888-245-2426 ■ *Web:* www.shelbyoh.com	Shelby	OH	44875	419-342-2426	342-2189
Sidney-Shelby County Chamber of Commerce 101 S Ohio Ave 2nd Fl *Web:* www.sidneyshelbychamber.com	Sidney	OH	45365	937-492-9122	498-2472
Greater Lawrence County Area Chamber of Commerce 216 Collins Ave *TF:* 800-408-1334 ■ *Web:* www.lawrencecountyohio.org	South Point	OH	45680	740-377-4550	377-2091
Jefferson County Chamber of Commerce 630 Market St *Web:* www.jeffersoncountychamber.com	Steubenville	OH	43952	740-282-6226	282-6285
Stow-Munroe Falls Chamber of Commerce 4381 Hudson Dr Suite K2 *Web:* www.smfcc.com	Stow	OH	44224	330-688-1579	688-6234
Strongsville Chamber of Commerce 18829 Royalton Rd *Web:* www.strongsvillechamber.com	Strongsville	OH	44136	440-238-3366	238-7010
Sylvania Area Chamber of Commerce 5632 Main St *Web:* www.sylvaniachamber.org	Sylvania	OH	43560	419-882-2135	885-7740
Tiffin Area Chamber of Commerce 62 S Washington St *TF:* 800-253-3314 ■ *Web:* www.tiffinchamber.com	Tiffin	OH	44883	419-447-4141	447-5141

				Phone	Fax
Toledo Regional Chamber of Commerce 300 Madison Ave Suite 200 *Web:* www.toledochamber.com	Toledo	OH	43604	419-243-8191	241-8302
Trotwood Chamber of Commerce 5790 Denlinger Rd *Web:* www.trotwoodchamber.org	Trotwood	OH	45426	937-837-1484	837-1508
Upper Arlington Area Chamber of Commerce 2152 Tremont Ctr *Web:* www.uachamber.org	Upper Arlington	OH	43221	614-481-5710	481-5711
Champaign County Chamber of Commerce 113 Miami St *TF:* 877-873-5764 ■ *Web:* www.ccchamber.org	Urbana	OH	43078	937-653-5764	652-1599
Van Wert Area Chamber of Commerce 1199 Professional Dr *Web:* www.vanwertchamber.com	Van Wert	OH	45891	419-238-4390	238-4589
Vandalia-Butler Chamber of Commerce 544 W National Rd *Web:* www.vandaliabutlerchamber.org	Vandalia	OH	45377	937-898-5351	898-5491
Fayette County Chamber of Commerce 101 E E St *Web:* www.fayettecountyohio.com	Washington Court House	OH	43160	740-335-0761	335-0762
West Chester Chamber Alliance 7617 Voice of America Centre Dr *TF:* 877-924-3783 ■ *Web:* www.westchesterchamberalliance.com	West Chester	OH	45069	513-777-3600	777-0188
Adams County Chamber of Commerce 509 E Main St *TF:* 877-232-6764 ■ *Web:* www.adamscountyohchamber.org	West Union	OH	45693	937-544-5454	544-6957
Westerville Area Chamber of Commerce 99 Commerce Pk Dr # A *Web:* www.westervillechamber.com	Westerville	OH	43082	614-882-8917	882-2085
West Shore Chamber of Commerce 1100 Crocker Rd Westlake Holiday Inn *Web:* www.westshorechamber.org	Westlake	OH	44145	440-835-8787	835-8798
Willougby Area Chamber of Commerce 28 Public Sq *Web:* www.willoughbyareachamber.com	Willoughby	OH	44094	440-942-1632	942-0586
Wilmington Clinton County Chamber of Commerce 40 N S St *Web:* www.wccchamber.com	Wilmington	OH	45177	937-382-2737	383-2316
Wooster Area Chamber of Commerce 377 W Liberty St *Web:* www.woosterchamber.com	Wooster	OH	44691	330-262-5735	262-5745
Worthington Area Chamber of Commerce 25 W New England Ave Suite 100 *Web:* www.worthingtonchamber.org	Worthington	OH	43085	614-888-3040	841-4842
Xenia Area Chamber of Commerce 334 W Market St *Web:* www.xacc.com	Xenia	OH	45385	937-372-3591	372-2192
Youngstown Warren Regional Chamber 11 Central Sq Suite 1600 *Web:* www.regionalchamber.com	Youngstown	OH	44503	330-744-2131	746-0330
Zanesville-Muskingum County Chamber of Commerce 205 N 5th St *TF:* 800-743-2303 ■ *Web:* www.zmchamber.com	Zanesville	OH	43701	740-455-8282	454-2963

OKLAHOMA

				Phone	Fax
Ada Area Chamber of Commerce 209 W Main St *Web:* www.adachamber.com	Ada	OK	74820	580-332-2506	332-3265
Ardmore Chamber of Commerce 410 W Main St *Web:* www.ardmore.org	Ardmore	OK	73401	580-223-7765	223-7825
Bartlesville Area Chamber of Commerce 201 S Keeler Ave *TF:* 800-364-8708 ■ *Web:* www.bartlesville.com	Bartlesville	OK	74003	918-336-8708	337-0216
Broken Arrow Chamber of Commerce 123 N Main St *Web:* www.brokenarrow.org	Broken Arrow	OK	74012	918-251-1518	251-1777
Del City Chamber of Commerce PO Box 15643 *Web:* www.Delcitychamber.com	Del City	OK	73155	405-677-1910	
Durant Area Chamber of Commerce 215 N 4th St *Web:* www.durantchamber.org	Durant	OK	74701	580-924-0848	924-0348
Edmond Area Chamber of Commerce 825 E 2nd St *Web:* www.edmondchamber.com	Edmond	OK	73034	405-341-2808	340-5512
Greater Enid Chamber of Commerce PO Box 907 *TF:* 888-229-2443 ■ *Web:* www.enidchamber.com	Enid	OK	73702	580-237-2494	237-2497
Lawton Chamber of Commerce & Industry 629 SW 'C' Ave Suite A *TF:* 800-872-4540 ■ *Web:* www.lawtonfortsillchamber.com	Lawton	OK	73501	580-355-3541	357-3642
Midwest City Chamber of Commerce PO Box 10980 *Web:* www.midwestcityok.com/chamber.html	Midwest City	OK	73140	405-733-3801	733-5633
Moore Chamber of Commerce 305 W Main St *Web:* www.moorechamber.com	Moore	OK	73160	405-794-3400	794-8555
Greater Muskogee Area Chamber of Commerce PO Box 797 *Web:* www.muskogeechamber.org	Muskogee	OK	74402	918-682-2401	682-2403
Norman Chamber of Commerce 115 E Gray St *Web:* www.normanok.org	Norman	OK	73069	405-321-7260	360-4679
Greater Oklahoma City Chamber of Commerce 123 Pk Ave *TF:* 800-616-1114 ■ *Web:* www.okcchamber.com	Oklahoma City	OK	73102	405-297-8900	297-8916
South Oklahoma City Chamber of Commerce 701 W I 240 Service Rd *Web:* www.southokc.com	Oklahoma City	OK	73139	405-634-1436	634-1462
Owasso Chamber of Commerce 315 S Cedar St *Web:* www.owassochamber.com	Owasso	OK	74055	918-272-2141	272-8564
Ponca City Area Chamber of Commerce 420 E Grand Ave *Web:* www.poncacitychamber.com	Ponca City	OK	74601	580-765-4400	765-2798
Poteau Chamber of Commerce 201 S Broadway *Web:* poteauchamber.com	Poteau	OK	74953	918-647-9178	647-4099
Sallisaw Chamber of Commerce 301 E Cherokee Ave *Web:* www.sallisawchamber.com	Sallisaw	OK	74955	918-775-2558	775-4021
Greater Shawnee Area Chamber of Commerce 131 N Bell Ave *Web:* www.shawneechamber.com	Shawnee	OK	74801	405-273-6092	275-9851
Stillwater Chamber of Commerce 409 S Main St *TF:* 800-593-5573 ■ *Web:* www.stillwaterchamber.org	Stillwater	OK	74075	405-372-5573	372-4316
Tulsa Metro Chamber 2 W 2nd St Suite 105 Williams Ctr Tower II **Fax:* Hum Res ■ *TF:* 800-558-3311 ■ *Web:* www.tulsachamber.com	Tulsa	OK	74103	918-585-1201	585-8016*
Yukon Chamber of Commerce 510 Elm St *Web:* www.yukoncc.com	Yukon	OK	73099	405-354-3567	350-0724

OREGON

				Phone	Fax
Albany Area Chamber of Commerce 435 W 1st Ave W *Web:* www.albanychamber.com	Albany	OR	97321	541-926-1517	926-7064
Beaverton Area Chamber of Commerce 12655 SW Ctr St Suite 140 *Web:* www.beaverton.org	Beaverton	OR	97005	503-644-0123	526-0349
Bend Chamber of Commerce 777 NW Wall St Suite 200 *TF:* 800-905-2363 ■ *Web:* www.bendchamber.org	Bend	OR	97701	541-382-3221	385-9929
Bay Area Chamber of Commerce 145 Central Ave *Web:* www.oregonsbayarea.org	Coos Bay	OR	97420	541-266-0868	267-6704
Corvallis Area Chamber of Commerce 420 NW 2nd St *Web:* www.corvallischamber.com	Corvallis	OR	97330	541-757-1505	766-2996
Cottage Grove Area Chamber of Commerce 700 E Gibbs Ave Suite C *Web:* www.cgchamber.com	Cottage Grove	OR	97424	541-942-2411	767-0783
Eugene Chamber of Commerce 1401 Willamette St *Web:* www.eugenechamber.com	Eugene	OR	97401	541-484-1314	484-4942
Florence Area Chamber of Commerce 290 Hwy 101 *TF:* 800-524-4864 ■ *Web:* www.florencechamber.com	Florence	OR	97439	541-997-3128	997-4101
Grants Pass Chamber of Commerce 1995 NW Vine St PO Box 970 *TF:* 800-547-5927 ■ *Web:* www.grantspasschamber.org	Grants Pass	OR	97528	541-476-7717	476-9574
Gresham Area Chamber of Commerce 701 NE Hood Ave *Web:* www.greshamchamber.org	Gresham	OR	97030	503-665-1131	666-1041
Hermiston Chamber of Commerce 415 S Hwy 395 PO Box 185 *Web:* www.hermistonchamber.com	Hermiston	OR	97838	541-567-6151	564-9109
Hillsboro Chamber of Commerce 5193 NE Elam Young Pkwy Suite A *Web:* www.hillchamber.org	Hillsboro	OR	97124	503-648-1102	681-0535
Keizer Chamber of Commerce 980 Chemawa Rd NE *Web:* www.keizerchamber.com	Keizer	OR	97303	503-393-9111	393-1003
Klamath County Chamber of Commerce 205 Riverside Dr *TF:* 877-552-6284 ■ *Web:* www.klamath.org	Klamath Falls	OR	97601	541-884-5193	884-5195
La Grande-Union County Chamber of Commerce 102 Elm St *Web:* www.unioncountychamber.org	La Grande	OR	97850	541-963-8588	963-3936
Lake Oswego Chamber of Commerce 242 B Ave *Web:* www.lake-oswego.com	Lake Oswego	OR	97034	503-636-3634	636-7427
Chamber of Medford/Jackson County 101 E 8th St *Web:* www.medfordchamber.com	Medford	OR	97501	541-779-4847	776-4808
North Clackamas County Chamber of Commerce 7740 SE Harmony Rd *Web:* www.yourchamber.com	Milwaukie	OR	97222	503-654-7777	653-9515
Greater Newport Chamber of Commerce 555 SW Coast Hwy *TF:* 800-262-7844 ■ *Web:* www.newportchamber.org	Newport	OR	97365	541-265-8801	265-5589
Oregon City Chamber of Commerce 1201 Washington St *Web:* www.oregoncity.org	Oregon City	OR	97045	503-656-1619	656-2274
Portland Business Alliance 200 SW Market St Suite 150 *Web:* www.portlandalliance.com	Portland	OR	97201	503-224-8684	323-9186
Salem Area Chamber of Commerce 1110 Commercial St NE *Web:* www.salemchamber.org	Salem	OR	97301	503-581-1466	581-0972
Springfield Chamber of Commerce 101 S 'A' St PO Box 155 *TF:* 866-346-1651 ■ *Web:* www.springfield-chamber.org	Springfield	OR	97477	541-746-1651	726-4727
Tigard Area Chamber of Commerce (TACC) 12345 SW Main St *Web:* www.tigardareachamber.org	Tigard	OR	97223	503-639-1656	639-6302

PENNSYLVANIA

				Phone	Fax
Greater Lehigh Valley Chamber of Commerce 840 Hamilton St Suite 205 *Web:* www.lehighvalleychamber.org	Allentown	PA	18101	610-841-5800	437-4907
Two Rivers Area Chamber of Commerce 840 Hamilton St Suite 205 *Web:* www.lehighvalleychamber.org	Allentown	PA	18101	610-841-5800	437-4907
Altoona-Blair County Chamber of Commerce 3900 Industrial Pk Dr Suite 12 *Web:* www.blairchamber.com	Altoona	PA	16602	814-943-8151	943-5239

Organization / Address	City	State	ZIP	Phone	Fax
Beaver County Chamber of Commerce 300 S Walnut Ln Suite 202 *Web:* www.bcchamber.com	Beaver	PA	15009	724-775-3944	728-9737
Bedford County Chamber of Commerce 137 E Pitt St *Web:* www.bedfordcountychamber.org	Bedford	PA	15522	814-623-2233	623-6089
Bellefonte Intervalley Chamber of Commerce 320 W High St *Web:* www.bellefonte.com	Bellefonte	PA	16823	814-355-2917	355-2761
Lehigh Valley Chamber of Commerce 561 Main St Suite 200 *Web:* www.lehighvalleychamber.org	Bethlehem	PA	18018	610-841-5862	758-9533
Bloomsburg Area Chamber of Commerce 238 Market St *Web:* www.bloomsburg.org	Bloomsburg	PA	17815	570-784-2522	784-2661
Columbia Montour chamber of Commerce The 238 Market St *Web:* www.columbiamontourchamber.com	Bloomsburg	PA	17815	570-784-2522	784-2661
Butler County Chamber of Commerce 101 E Diamond St # 116 *Web:* www.butlercountychamber.com	Butler	PA	16001	724-283-2222	283-0224
West Shore Chamber of Commerce 4211 E Trindle Rd *Web:* www.wschamber.org	Camp Hill	PA	17011	717-761-0702	761-4315
Greater Chambersburg Chamber of Commerce 100 Lincoln Way E Suite A *Web:* www.chambersburg.org	Chambersburg	PA	17201	717-264-7101	267-0399
Clarion Area Chamber of Business & Industry 21 N 6th Ave *Web:* www.clarionpa.com	Clarion	PA	16214	814-226-9161	226-4903
Perkiomen Valley Chamber of Commerce 351 E Main St *Web:* www.pvchamber.net	Collegeville	PA	19426	610-489-6660	454-1270
Greater Connellsville Chamber of Commerce 923 W Crawford Ave *Web:* www.greaterconnellsville.org	Connellsville	PA	15425	724-628-5500	628-5676
Central Bucks Chamber of Commerce 252 W Swamp Rd Suite 23 *Web:* www.centralbuckschamber.com	Doylestown	PA	18901	215-348-3913	348-7154
Montgomery County Chamber of Commerce PO Box 200 *Web:* www.montgomerycountychamber.org	Eagleville	PA	19408	610-265-1776	265-0473
Erie Regional Chamber & Growth Partnership 208 E Bayfront Pkwy *TF:* 800-524-3743 ■ *Web:* www.eriepa.com	Erie	PA	16507	814-454-7191	459-0241
Exton Region Chamber of Commerce 967 E Swedesford Rd Suite 409 *Web:* www.ercc.net	Exton	PA	19341	610-644-4985	644-2370
Lower Bucks County Chamber of Commerce 409 Hood Blvd *Web:* www.lbccc.org	Fairless Hills	PA	19030	215-943-7400	943-7404
Franklin Area Chamber of Commerce (FACC) 1259 Liberty St *TF:* 888-547-2377 ■ *Web:* www.franklinareachamber.org	Franklin	PA	16323	814-432-5823	437-2453
Gettysburg-Adams County Area Chamber of Commerce 18 Carlisle St Suite 203 *Web:* www.gettysburg-chamber.org	Gettysburg	PA	17325	717-334-8151	334-3368
Westmoreland Chamber of Commerce 241 Tollgate Hill Rd *Web:* www.westmorelandchamber.com	Greensburg	PA	15601	724-834-2900	837-7635
Hanover Area Chamber of Commerce 146 Carlisle St *Web:* www.hanoverchamber.com	Hanover	PA	17331	717-637-6130	637-9127
Harrisburg Regional Chamber 3211 N Front St Suite 201 *TF:* 877-883-8339 ■ *Web:* www.harrisburgregionalchamber.org	Harrisburg	PA	17110	717-232-4099	232-5184
Wayne County Chamber of Commerce 32 Commercial St *TF:* 800-433-9008 ■ *Web:* www.waynecountycc.com	Honesdale	PA	18431	570-253-1960	253-1517
Huntingdon County Business & Industry 419 14th St *Web:* www.hcbi.com	Huntingdon	PA	16652	814-641-6697	506-1282
Indiana County Chamber of Commerce 1019 Philadelphia St *Web:* www.indianapa.com	Indiana	PA	15701	724-465-2511	465-3706
Norwin Chamber of Commerce 321 Main St *Web:* www.norwinchamber.com	Irwin	PA	15642	724-863-0888	863-5133
Greater Johnstown/Cambria County Chamber of Commerce 245 Market St Suite 100 *TF:* 800-790-4522 ■ *Web:* www.johnstownchamber.com	Johnstown	PA	15901	814-536-5107	539-5800
Southern Chester County Chamber of Commerce 217 W State St *Web:* www.scccc.com	Kennett Square	PA	19348	610-444-0774	444-5105
King of Prussia Chamber of Commerce 101 Bill Smith Blvd *Web:* www.gvfcc.com	King of Prussia	PA	19406	610-265-1776	265-0473
Armstrong County Chamber of Commerce 124 Market St *Web:* www.armstrongchamber.org	Kittanning	PA	16201	724-543-1305	548-2951
Lancaster Chamber of Commerce & Industry PO Box 1558 *Web:* www.lcci.com	Lancaster	PA	17608	717-397-3531	293-3159
North Penn Chamber of Commerce 229 S Broad St *Web:* www.northpenn.org	Lansdale	PA	19446	215-362-9200	362-0393
Latrobe Area Chamber of Commerce 326 McKinley Ave Suite 102 *Web:* www.latrobearea.com	Latrobe	PA	15650	724-537-2671	537-2690
Lebanon Valley Chamber of Commerce 604 Cumberland St *Web:* www.lvchamber.org	Lebanon	PA	17042	717-273-3727	273-7940
Juniata Valley Area Chamber of Commerce 1 W Market St Suite 119 *TF:* 877-568-9739 ■ *Web:* www.juniatavalleychamber.org	Lewistown	PA	17044	717-248-6713	248-6714
Clinton County Economic Partnership 212 N Jay St *TF:* 888-388-6991 ■ *Web:* www.clintoncountyinfo.com	Lock Haven	PA	17745	570-748-5782	893-0433
Meadville-Western Crawford County Chamber of Commerce 908 Diamond Pk *Web:* www.meadvillechamber.com	Meadville	PA	16335	814-337-8030	337-8022
Delaware County Chamber of Commerce 602 E Baltimore Pike *Web:* www.delcochamber.org	Media	PA	19063	610-565-3677	565-1606
Pike County Chamber of Commerce 209 E Hartford St *Web:* www.pikechamber.com	Milford	PA	18337	570-296-8700	296-3921
Monroeville Area Chamber of Commerce 4268 Northern Pike *TF:* 888-753-5522 ■ *Web:* www.monroevillechamber.com	Monroeville	PA	15146	412-856-0622	856-1030
Pittsburgh Airport Area Chamber of Commerce 850 Beaver Grade Rd *Web:* www.paacc.com	Moon Township	PA	15108	412-264-6270	264-1575
Laurel Highlands Chamber of Commerce 537 W Main St *Web:* www.laurelhighlandschamber.com	Mount Pleasant	PA	15666	724-547-7521	547-5530
Allegheny Valley Chamber of Commerce 1 Acee Dr Suite 2 *Web:* www.alleghenyvalleychamber.com	Natrona Heights	PA	15065	724-224-3400	224-3442
Nazareth Area Chamber of Commerce 201 N Main St PO Box 173 *Web:* www.nazarethchamber.com	Nazareth	PA	18064	610-759-9188	759-5262
Lawrence County Chamber of Commerce 138 W Washington St *Web:* www.lawrencecountychamber.com	New Castle	PA	16101	724-654-5593	654-3330
Pennridge Chamber of Commerce 538 W Market St *Web:* www.pennridge.com	Perkasie	PA	18944	215-257-5390	257-6840
Greater Northeast Philadelphia Chamber of Commerce 8601 E Roosevelt Blvd *Web:* www.gnpcc.org	Philadelphia	PA	19152	215-332-3400	332-6050
Greater Philadelphia Chamber of Commerce 200 S Broad St Suite 700 *Web:* www.greaterphilachamber.com	Philadelphia	PA	19102	215-545-1234	790-3600
Moshannon Valley Economic Development Partnership 200 Shady Ln *Web:* www.mvedp.org	Philipsburg	PA	16866	814-342-2260	342-2878
Phoenixville Regional Chamber of Commerce 171 Bridge St *Web:* www.phoenixvillechamber.org	Phoenixville	PA	19460	610-933-3070	917-0503
East Liberty Quarter Chamber of Commerce 5907 Penn Ave Suite 305 *Web:* www.eastlibertychamber.org	Pittsburgh	PA	15206	412-661-9660	661-9661
Greater Pittsburgh Chamber of Commerce 425 6th Ave Suite 1100 *TF:* 800-843-8772 ■ *Web:* www.alleghenyconference.org	Pittsburgh	PA	15219	412-392-4500	392-1040
North Side Chamber of Commerce 809 Middle St *Web:* www.northsidechamberofcommerce.com	Pittsburgh	PA	15212	412-231-6500	321-6760
Penn Hills Chamber of Commerce 12013 Frankstown Rd *Web:* www.pennhillschamber.org	Pittsburgh	PA	15235	412-795-8741	795-7993
South Hills Chamber of Commerce 1910 Cochran Rd Suite 140 *Web:* www.shchamber.org	Pittsburgh	PA	15220	412-306-8090	306-8093
South Side Chamber of Commerce 1910 E Carson St # 2	Pittsburgh	PA	15203	412-431-3360	
Greater Pittston Chamber of Commerce 104 Kennedy Blvd PO Box 704 *Web:* www.pittstonchamber.org	Pittston	PA	18640	570-655-1424	655-0336
Tri County Area Chamber of Commerce 152 E High St # 360 *Web:* www.tricountyareachamber.com	Pottstown	PA	19464	610-326-2900	970-9705
Schuylkill Chamber of Commerce 91 S Progress Ave *TF:* 800-755-1942 ■ *Web:* www.schuylkillchamber.com	Pottsville	PA	17901	570-622-1942	622-1638
Upper Bucks Chamber of Commerce 2170 Portzer Rd *Web:* www.ubcc.org	Quakertown	PA	18951	215-536-3211	536-7767
Greater Reading Chamber of Commerce & Industry 201 Penn St *Web:* www.greaterreadingchamber.org	Reading	PA	19601	610-376-6766	376-4135
Greater Scranton Chamber of Commerce 222 Mulberry St *Web:* www.scrantonchamber.com	Scranton	PA	18503	570-342-7711	347-6262
Greater Susquehanna Valley Chamber of Commerce 2859 N Susquehanna Trail PO Box 10 *TF:* 800-410-2880 ■ *Web:* www.gsvcc.org	Shamokin Dam	PA	17876	570-743-4100	743-1221
Shenango Valley Chamber of Commerce 41 Chestnut St *Web:* www.svchamber.com	Sharon	PA	16146	724-981-5880	981-5480
Shippensburg Area Chamber of Commerce 53 W King St *Web:* www.shippensburg.org	Shippensburg	PA	17257	717-532-5509	532-7501
Somerset County Chamber of Commerce 601 N Ctr Ave *Web:* www.somersetcntypachamber.org	Somerset	PA	15501	814-445-6431	443-4313
Chamber of Business & Industry of Centre County 200 Innovation Blvd Suite 150 *Web:* www.cbicc.org	State College	PA	16803	814-234-1829	234-5869
Pocono Mountains Chamber of Commerce 556 Main St	Stroudsburg	PA	18360	570-421-4433	424-7281
Indian Valley Chamber of Commerce 100 Penn Ave *Web:* www.indianvalleychamber.com	Telford	PA	18969	215-723-9472	723-2490
Fayette Chamber of Commerce 65 W Main St *TF:* 800-916-9365 ■ *Web:* www.fayettechamber.com	Uniontown	PA	15401	724-437-4571	438-3304

Chamber	City	State	Zip	Phone	Fax
StrongLand Chamber of Commerce 1129 Industrial Pk Rd Suite 108 PO Box 10 *Web:* www.strongland.org	Vandergrift	PA	15690	724-845-5426	845-5428
Warren County Chamber of Commerce (WCCBI) 308 Market St *Web:* www.wccbi.org	Warren	PA	16365	814-723-3050	723-6024
Washington County Chamber of Commerce 20 E Beau St *Web:* www.washcochamber.com	Washington	PA	15301	724-225-3010	228-7337
Main Line Chamber of Commerce 175 Strafford Ave Suite 130 *Web:* www.mlcc.org	Wayne	PA	19087	610-687-6232	687-8085
Greater Waynesboro Chamber of Commerce 5 Roadside Ave *Web:* www.waynesboro.org	Waynesboro	PA	17268	717-762-7123	762-7124
Greater West Chester Chamber of Commerce 119 N High St *Web:* www.greaterwestchester.com	West Chester	PA	19380	610-696-4046	696-9110
Greater Wilkes-Barre Chamber of Business & Industry 2 Public Sq PO Box 5340 *Web:* www.wilkes-barre.org	Wilkes-Barre	PA	18710	570-823-2101	822-5951
Williamsport/Lycoming Chamber of Commerce 100 W 3rd St *Web:* www.williamsport.org	Williamsport	PA	17701	570-326-1971	321-1208
York County Chamber of Commerce 96 S George St Suite 300 *Web:* www.yorkchamber.com	York	PA	17401	717-848-4000	843-6737

RHODE ISLAND

Chamber	City	State	Zip	Phone	Fax
Greater Cranston Chamber of Commerce 875 Oaklawn Ave Suite 1 *Web:* www.cranstonchamber.com	Cranston	RI	02910	401-785-3780	785-3782
East Providence Chamber of Commerce 1011 Waterman Ave *Web:* www.eastprovchamber.com	East Providence	RI	02914	401-438-1212	435-4581
North Central Chamber of Commerce 255 Greenville Ave *Web:* www.ncrichamber.com	Johnston	RI	02919	401-349-4674	349-4676
Northern Rhode Island Chamber of Commerce 6 Blackstone Valley Pl Suite 301 *Web:* www.nrichamber.com	Lincoln	RI	02865	401-334-1000	334-1009
Newport County Chamber of Commerce 35 Valley Rd *Web:* www.newportchamber.com	Middletown	RI	02842	401-847-1600	849-5848
North Kingstown Chamber of Commerce 8045 Post Rd *Web:* www.northkingstown.com	North Kingstown	RI	02852	401-295-5566	295-5582
Greater Providence Chamber of Commerce 30 Exchange Terr *Web:* www.providencechamber.com	Providence	RI	02903	401-521-5000	621-6109
South Kingstown Chamber of Commerce 230 Old Tower Hill Rd *Web:* www.skchamber.com	Wakefield	RI	02879	401-783-2801	789-3120
East Bay Chamber of Commerce 16 Cutler St Suite 102 *TF:* 888-278-9948 ■ *Web:* www.eastbaychamberri.org	Warren	RI	02885	401-245-0750	245-0110
Central Rhode Island Chamber of Commerce 3288 Post Rd *Web:* www.centralrichamber.com	Warwick	RI	02886	401-732-1100	732-1107
Pawtuxet Valley Chamber of Commerce 1192 Main St *Web:* www.pvccommerce.org	West Warwick	RI	02893	401-823-3349	823-8162

SOUTH CAROLINA

Chamber	City	State	Zip	Phone	Fax
Greater Abbeville Chamber of Commerce 107 Ct Sq *Web:* www.visitabbevillesc.com	Abbeville	SC	29620	864-366-4600	366-4068
Greater Aiken Chamber of Commerce 121 Richland Ave E PO Box 892 *TF:* 800-542-4536 ■ *Web:* www.aikenchamber.net	Aiken	SC	29802	803-641-1111	641-4174
Anderson Area Chamber of Commerce 907 N Main St Suite 200 *Web:* www.andersonscchamber.com	Anderson	SC	29621	864-226-3454	226-3300
Kershaw County Chamber of Commerce 607 S Broad St *TF:* 800-968-4037 ■ *Web:* www.kershawcountychamber.org	Camden	SC	29020	803-432-2525	432-4181
West Metro Chamber of Commerce 1006 12th St *TF:* 866-720-5400 ■ *Web:* www.visitwestmetro.com	Cayce	SC	29033	803-794-6504	794-6505
Chester County Chamber of Commerce 109 Gadsden St *Web:* www.chesterchamber.com	Chester	SC	29706	803-581-4142	581-2431
Laurens County Chamber of Commerce 291 Professional Pk Rd *Web:* www.laurenscounty.org	Clinton	SC	29325	864-833-2716	833-6935
Greater Columbia Chamber of Commerce 930 Richland St *Web:* www.columbiachamber.com	Columbia	SC	29201	803-733-1110	733-1149
Conway Area Chamber of Commerce 203 Main St *Web:* www.conwayscchamber.com	Conway	SC	29526	843-248-2273	248-0003
Greater Darlington Chamber of Commerce 38 Public Sq *Web:* www.darlingtonchamber.com	Darlington	SC	29532	843-393-2641	393-8059
Dillon County Chamber of Commerce 100 N MacArthur Ave *TF:* 800-444-6838 ■ *Web:* www.dilloncitysc.com	Dillon	SC	29536	843-774-8551	774-0114
Greater Easley Chamber of Commerce 2001 E Main St PO Box 241 *Web:* www.easleychamber.org	Easley	SC	29641	864-859-2693	859-1941
Greater Florence Chamber of Commerce 610 W Palmetto St *Web:* www.florencescchamber.com	Florence	SC	29501	843-665-0515	662-2010
Cherokee County Chamber of Commerce 225 S Limestone St *Web:* www.cherokeechamber.org	Gaffney	SC	29340	864-489-5721	487-3399
Georgetown County Chamber of Commerce 531 Front St *TF:* 800-777-7705 ■ *Web:* www.visitgeorge.com	Georgetown	SC	29440	843-546-8436	520-4876
Greater Greenville Chamber of Commerce 24 Cleveland St **Fax:* PR ■ *Web:* www.greenvillechamber.org	Greenville	SC	29601	864-242-1050	282-8509*
Greenwood Chamber of Commerce 110 Phoenix St *Web:* www.greenwoodscchamber.org	Greenwood	SC	29646	864-223-8431	229-9785
Greater Hartsville Chamber of Commerce 214 N 5th St *Web:* www.hartsvillechamber.org	Hartsville	SC	29550	843-332-6401	332-8017
Hilton Head Island-Bluffton Chamber of Commerce 1 Chamber Dr *TF:* 800-523-3373 ■ *Web:* www.hiltonheadisland.org	Hilton Head Island	SC	29928	843-785-3673	785-7110
Williamsburg Hometown Chamber of Commerce 130 E Main St *Web:* www.williamsburgsc.org	Kingstree	SC	29556	843-355-6431	355-3343
Lancaster County Chamber of Commerce PO Box 430 *Web:* www.lancasterchambersc.org	Lancaster	SC	29721	803-283-4105	286-4360
Lexington Chamber of Commerce 321 S Lake Dr *Web:* www.lexingtonsc.org	Lexington	SC	29072	803-359-6113	359-0634
Clarendon County Chamber of Commerce 19 N Brooks St *TF:* 800-731-5253 ■ *Web:* www.clarendoncounty.com	Manning	SC	29102	803-435-4405	435-4406
Berkeley County Chamber of Commerce PO Box 968 *TF:* 800-882-0337 ■ *Web:* www.berkeleysc.org	Moncks Corner	SC	29461	843-761-8238	899-6491
Myrtle Beach Area Chamber of Commerce 1200 N Oak St *TF:* 800-356-3016 ■ *Web:* www.myrtlebeachinfo.com	Myrtle Beach	SC	29577	843-626-7444	626-0009
Newberry County Chamber of Commerce 1109 Main St PO Box 396 *Web:* www.newberrycounty.org	Newberry	SC	29108	803-276-4274	276-4373
North Augusta Chamber of Commerce 406 W Ave *Web:* www.northaugustachamber.org	North Augusta	SC	29841	803-279-2323	279-0003
Charleston Metro Chamber of Commerce 4500 Leeds Ave Suite 100 *Web:* www.charlestonchamber.net	North Charleston	SC	29405	843-577-2510	723-4853
Orangeburg County Chamber of Commerce 1570 John C Calhoun Dr SW *TF:* 800-545-6153 ■ *Web:* www.orangeburgchamber.com	Orangeburg	SC	29118	803-534-6821	531-9435
York County Regional Chamber of Commerce 116 E Main St *Web:* www.yorkcountychamber.com	Rock Hill	SC	29731	803-324-7500	324-1889
Spartanburg Area Chamber of Commerce 105 N Pine St *Web:* www.spartanburgchamber.com	Spartanburg	SC	29302	864-594-5000	594-5055
Greater Summerville-Dorchester County Chamber of Commerce 402 N Main St *Web:* www.gsdcchamber.org	Summerville	SC	29483	843-873-2931	875-4464
Greater Sumter Chamber of Commerce 32 E Calhoun St *Web:* www.sumterchamber.com	Sumter	SC	29150	803-775-1231	775-0915
Union County Chamber of Commerce 135 W Main St *TF:* 877-202-8755 ■ *Web:* www.unionsc.com	Union	SC	29379	864-427-9039	427-9030
Walterboro-Colleton Chamber of Commerce 109 Benson St *Web:* www.walterboro.org	Walterboro	SC	29488	843-549-9595	549-5775

SOUTH DAKOTA

Chamber	City	State	Zip	Phone	Fax
Aberdeen Area Chamber of Commerce 516 S Main St *TF:* 800-874-9038 ■ *Web:* www.aberdeen-chamber.com	Aberdeen	SD	57401	605-225-2860	225-2437
Pierre Area Chamber of Commerce 800 W Dakota Ave *TF:* 800-962-2034 ■ *Web:* www.pierre.org	Pierre	SD	57501	605-224-7361	224-6485
Rapid City Area Chamber of Commerce 444 Mt Rushmore Rd N *Web:* www.rapidcitychamber.com	Rapid City	SD	57701	605-343-1744	343-6550
Sioux Falls Area Chamber of Commerce 200 N Phillips Ave Suite 102 *Web:* www.siouxfalls.com	Sioux Falls	SD	57104	605-336-1620	336-6499

TENNESSEE

Chamber	City	State	Zip	Phone	Fax
Cheatham County Chamber of Commerce 575 S Main St Suite 101 *Web:* www.cheathamchamber.org	Ashland City	TN	37015	615-792-6722	792-5001
Bartlett Area Chamber of Commerce 2969 Elmore Pk Rd *Web:* www.bartlettchamber.org	Bartlett	TN	38134	901-372-9457	372-9488
Bristol Chamber of Commerce 20 Volunteer Pkwy *Web:* www.bristolchamber.org	Bristol	TN	37620	423-989-4850	989-4867
Chattanooga Area Chamber of Commerce 811 Broad St *Web:* www.chattanoogachamber.com	Chattanooga	TN	37402	423-756-2121	267-7242

				Phone	Fax
Clarksville Area Chamber of Commerce 25 Jefferson St Suite 300 *TF:* 800-530-2487 ■ *Web:* www.clarksvillechamber.com	Clarksville	TN	37040	931-647-2331	645-1574
Cleveland/Bradley Chamber of Commerce 225 Keith St *TF:* 800-472-6588 ■ *Web:* www.clevelandchamber.com	Cleveland	TN	37311	423-472-6587	472-2019
Anderson County Chamber of Commerce 245 N Main St Suite 200 *Web:* www.andersoncountychamber.org	Clinton	TN	37716	865-457-2559	463-7480
Collierville Chamber of Commerce 485 Halle Pk Dr *TF:* 888-853-1949 ■ *Web:* www.colliervillechamber.com	Collierville	TN	38017	901-853-1949	853-2399
Maury Alliance 106 W 6th St *Web:* www.mauryalliance.com	Columbia	TN	38401	931-388-2155	380-0335
Cookeville Area-Putnam County Chamber of Commerce 1 W 1st St *TF:* 800-264-5541 ■ *Web:* www.cookevillechamber.com	Cookeville	TN	38501	931-526-2211	526-4023
Covington-Tipton County Chamber of Commerce 106 W Liberty St *Web:* www.covington-tiptoncochamber.com	Covington	TN	38019	901-476-9727	476-0056
Crossville Cumberland County Chamber of Commerce 34 S Main St *TF:* 877-465-3861 ■ *Web:* www.crossville-chamber.com	Crossville	TN	38555	931-484-8444	484-7511
Jefferson County Chamber of Commerce 532 Patriot Dr *TF:* 877-237-3847 ■ *Web:* www.jefferson-tn-chamber.org	Dandridge	TN	37725	865-397-9642	397-0164
Dickson County Chamber of Commerce 119 Hwy 70 E *TF:* 877-718-4967 ■ *Web:* www.dicksoncountychamber.com	Dickson	TN	37055	615-446-2349	441-3112
Weakley County Chamber of Commerce 114 W Maple St PO Box 67 *Web:* www.weakleycountychamber.com	Dresden	TN	38225	731-364-3787	364-2099
Dyersburg/Dyer County Chamber of Commerce 2000 Commerce Ave. *Web:* www.dyerchamber.com	Dyersburg	TN	38024	731-285-3433	286-4926
Elizabethton/Carter County Chamber of Commerce Hwy 19 E *Web:* www.elizabethtonchamber.com	Elizabethton	TN	37644	423-547-3850	547-3854
Fayetteville-Lincoln County Chamber of Commerce 208 S Elk Ave *TF:* 888-433-1238 ■ *Web:* www.fayettevillelincolncountychamber.com	Fayetteville	TN	37334	931-433-1234	433-9087
Williamson County-Franklin Chamber of Commerce 134 2nd Ave N *TF:* 800-356-3445 ■ *Web:* www.williamson-franklinchamber.com	Franklin	TN	37065	615-794-1225	790-5337
Germantown Area Chamber of Commerce 2195 S Germantown Rd *Web:* www.germantownchamber.com	Germantown	TN	38138	901-755-1200	755-9168
Greene County Partnership & Chamber of Commerce 115 Academy St *Web:* www.greenecountypartnership.com	Greeneville	TN	37743	423-638-4111	638-5345
Hendersonville Area Chamber of Commerce 100 Country Dr Suite 104 *Web:* www.hendersonvillechamber.com	Hendersonville	TN	37075	615-824-2818	250-3637
Carroll County Chamber of Commerce 20740 Main St E *Web:* www.carrollcounty-tn-chamber.com	Huntingdon	TN	38344	731-986-4664	986-2029
Jackson Area Chamber of Commerce 197 Auditorium St *TF:* 800-858-5596 ■ *Web:* www.jacksontn.com	Jackson	TN	38301	731-423-2200	424-4860
Johnson City/Jonesborough/Washington County Chamber of Commerce 603 E Market St *TF:* 800-852-3392 ■ *Web:* www.johnsoncitytnchamber.com	Johnson City	TN	37601	423-461-8000	461-8047
Kingsport Area Chamber of Commerce 151 E Main St *Web:* www.kingsportchamber.org	Kingsport	TN	37660	423-392-8800	246-7234
Roane County Chamber of Commerce 1209 N Kentucky St *Web:* www.roanealliance.org	Kingston	TN	37763	865-376-5572	376-4978
Knoxville Area Chamber Partnership 17 Market Sq Suite 201 *Web:* www.knoxvillechamber.com	Knoxville	TN	37902	865-637-4550	523-2071
Lawrence County Chamber of Commerce 1609 N Locust Ave PO Box 86 *TF:* 877-388-4911 ■ *Web:* www.selectlawrence.com	Lawrenceburg	TN	38464	931-762-4911	762-3153
Lebanon-Wilson County Chamber of Commerce 149 Public Sq *Web:* www.lebanonwilsontnchamber.org	Lebanon	TN	37087	615-444-5503	443-0596
Loudon County Chamber of Commerce (LCCC) 318 Angel Row *Web:* www.loudoncountychamberofcommerce.com	Loudon	TN	37774	865-458-2067	458-1206
Madison Rivergate Area Chamber of Commerce 301 Madison St *Web:* www.madisonrivergatechamber.com	Madison	TN	37115	615-865-5400	865-0448
Monroe County Chamber of Commerce 520 Cook St Suite A *Web:* www.monroecountychamber.org	Madisonville	TN	37354	423-442-4588	442-9016
Blount County Chamber of Commerce 201 S Washington St *Web:* www.blountchamber.com	Maryville	TN	37804	865-983-2241	984-1386
McMinnville-Warren County Chamber of Commerce 110 S Ct Sq *Web:* www.warrentn.com	McMinnville	TN	37110	931-473-6611	473-4741
Memphis Regional Chamber of Commerce 22 N Front St Suite 200 *Web:* www.memphischamber.com	Memphis	TN	38103	901-543-3500	543-3510
Morristown Area Chamber of Commerce 825 W 1st N St *Web:* www.morristownchamber.com	Morristown	TN	37814	423-586-6382	586-6576
Mount Juliet/West Wilson County Chamber of Commerce 46 W Caldwell St *Web:* www.mtjulietchamber.com	Mount Juliet	TN	37122	615-758-3478	754-8595
Rutherford County Chamber of Commerce 501 Memorial Blvd *TF:* 800-716-7560 ■ *Web:* www.rutherfordchamber.org	Murfreesboro	TN	37129	615-893-6565	890-7600
Donelson-Hermitage Chamber of Commerce PO Box 140200 *Web:* www.d-hchamber.com	Nashville	TN	37214	615-883-7896	391-4880
Nashville Chamber of Commerce 211 Commerce St Suite 100 *Web:* www.nashvillechamber.com	Nashville	TN	37201	615-743-3000	743-3004
Newport/Cocke County Chamber of Commerce 433 Prospect Ave # B *Web:* www.cockecounty.org	Newport	TN	37821	423-623-7201	623-7216
Oak Ridge Chamber of Commerce 1400 Oak Ridge Tpke *Web:* www.orcc.org	Oak Ridge	TN	37830	865-483-1321	483-1678
Paris-Henry County Chamber of Commerce 2508 Eastwood St *TF:* 800-345-1103 ■ *Web:* www.paristnchamber.com	Paris	TN	38242	731-642-3431	642-3454
Giles County Chamber of Commerce 110 N 2nd St *Web:* www.gilescountychamber.com	Pulaski	TN	38478	931-363-3789	363-7279
Rogersville/Hawkins County Chamber of Commerce 107 E Main St Suite 100 *Web:* www.rogersvillechamber.us	Rogersville	TN	37857	423-272-2186	272-2186
Shelbyville-Bedford County Chamber of Commerce 100 N Cannon Blvd *TF:* 888-662-2525 ■ *Web:* www.shelbyvilletn.com	Shelbyville	TN	37160	931-684-3482	684-3483
Fayette County Chamber of Commerce 13145 N Main St PO Box 411 *Web:* www.fayettecountychamber.com	Somerville	TN	38068	901-465-8690	465-6497
Springfield-Robertson County Chamber of Commerce 503 W Ct Sq	Springfield	TN	37172	615-384-3800	384-1260
Claiborne County Chamber of Commerce 1732 Main St PO Box 649 *TF:* 800-332-8164 ■ *Web:* www.claibornecounty.com	Tazewell	TN	37879	423-626-4149	626-1611
Greater Gibson County Area Chamber of Commerce 200 E Eaton St *Web:* www.gibsoncountytn.com	Trenton	TN	38382	731-855-0973	855-0979
Obion County Chamber of Commerce 214 E Church St *TF:* 877-885-0211 ■ *Web:* www.obioncounty.org	Union City	TN	38261	731-885-0211	885-7155
Franklin County Chamber of Commerce 44 Chamber Way PO Box 280 *Web:* www.franklincountychamber.com	Winchester	TN	37398	931-967-6788	967-9418

TEXAS

				Phone	Fax
Abilene Chamber of Commerce 174 Cypress St Suite 200 *Web:* www.abilenechamber.com	Abilene	TX	79601	325-677-7241	677-0622
Alice Chamber of Commerce (ACC) 612 E Main St PO Box 1609 *TF:* 877-992-5423 ■ *Web:* www.alicetxchamber.org	Alice	TX	78333	361-664-3454	664-2291
Allen Chamber of Commerce 210 W McDermott Dr *Web:* www.allenchamber.com	Allen	TX	75013	972-727-5585	727-9000
Alvin-Manvel Area Chamber of Commerce 105 W Willis St *TF:* 800-331-4063 ■ *Web:* www.alvinmanvelchamber.org	Alvin	TX	77511	281-331-3944	585-8662
Amarillo Chamber of Commerce 1000 S Polk St *Web:* www.amarillo-chamber.org	Amarillo	TX	79101	806-373-7800	373-3909
Arlington Chamber of Commerce 505 E Border St *Web:* www.arlingtontx.com	Arlington	TX	76010	817-275-2613	701-0893
Atlanta Area Chamber of Commerce 101 N E St *Web:* www.atlantatexas.org	Atlanta	TX	75551	903-796-3296	796-5711
Greater Austin Chamber of Commerce 210 Barton Springs Rd Suite 400 *TF:* 800-856-5602 ■ *Web:* www.austinchamber.org	Austin	TX	78704	512-478-9383	478-6389
Bastrop Chamber of Commerce 927 Main St *Web:* www.bastropchamber.com	Bastrop	TX	78602	512-321-2419	303-0305
Baytown Chamber of Commerce 1300 Rolling Brook Suite 400 *Web:* www.baytownchamber.com	Baytown	TX	77521	281-422-8359	428-1758
Beaumont Chamber of Commerce 1110 Pk St *Web:* www.bmtcoc.org	Beaumont	TX	77701	409-838-6581	833-6718
Hurst-Euless-Bedford Chamber of Commerce 2109 Martin Dr *Web:* www.heb.org	Bedford	TX	76021	817-283-1521	267-5111
Bee County Chamber of Commerce 1705 N St Mary's St *Web:* www.beecountychamber.org	Beeville	TX	78102	361-358-3267	358-3966
Greater Southwest Houston Chamber of Commerce 6900 S Rice Ave *TF:* 866-517-8114 ■ *Web:* www.gswhcc.org	Bellaire	TX	77401	713-666-1521	666-1523
Bonham Area Chamber of Commerce 110 E 1st St *Web:* www.bonhamchamber.com	Bonham	TX	75418	903-583-4811	583-7972
Washington County Chamber of Commerce 314 S Austin St *TF:* 888-273-6426 ■ *Web:* www.brenhamtexas.com	Brenham	TX	77833	979-836-3695	836-2540
Brownsville Chamber of Commerce 1600 University Blvd *Web:* www.brownsvillechamber.com	Brownsville	TX	78520	956-542-4341	504-3348
Brownwood Area Chamber of Commerce 600 E Depot St *Web:* www.brownwoodchamber.org	Brownwood	TX	76801	325-646-9535	643-6686
Bryan-College Station Chamber of Commerce 4001 E 29th St Suite 175 *TF:* 800-777-8292 ■ *Web:* www.bcschamber.org	Bryan	TX	77802	979-260-5200	260-5208
Burleson Area Chamber of Commerce 1044 SW Wilshire Blvd *Web:* www.burlesonareachamber.com	Burleson	TX	76028	817-295-6121	295-6192
Canyon Chamber of Commerce 1518 5th Ave *TF:* 800-999-9481 ■ *Web:* www.canyonchamber.org	Canyon	TX	79015	806-655-7815	655-4608

	City	State	ZIP	Phone	Fax
Panola County Chamber of Commerce 300 W Panola St *Web:* www.carthagetexas.com	Carthage	TX	75633	903-693-6634	693-8578
Cleburne Chamber of Commerce PO Box 701 *Web:* www.cleburnechamber.com	Cleburne	TX	76033	817-645-2455	641-3069
Greater Conroe-Lake Conroe Area Chamber of Commerce 505 W Davis St *TF:* 800-283-6645 ■ *Web:* www.conroe.org	Conroe	TX	77301	936-756-6644	756-6462
Greater Conroe/Lake Conroe Area Chamber of Commerce PO Box 2347 *TF:* 800-283-6645 ■ *Web:* www.conroe.org	Conroe	TX	77305	936-756-6644	756-6462
Coppell Chamber of Commerce 509 W Bethel Rd Suite 200 *Web:* www.coppellchamber.org	Coppell	TX	75019	972-393-2829	393-0659
Copperas Cove Chamber of Commerce 204 E Robertson Ave *Web:* www.copperascove.com	Copperas Cove	TX	76522	254-547-7571	547-5015
Corpus Christi Chamber of Commerce 1201 N Shoreline Blvd *Web:* www.corpuschristichamber.org	Corpus Christi	TX	78401	361-881-1800	882-4256
Corsicana Area Chamber of Commerce 120 N 12th St *TF:* 877-376-7477 ■ *Web:* www.corsicana.org	Corsicana	TX	75110	903-874-4731	874-4187
Cy-Fair Houston Chamber of Commerce 11734 Barker Cypress Suite 105 *Web:* www.cyfairchamber.com	Cypress	TX	77433	281-373-1390	373-1394
Greater Dallas Chamber of Commerce 700 N Pearl St Suite 1200 *Web:* www.dallaschamber.org	Dallas	TX	75201	214-746-6600	746-6799
Greater East Dallas Chamber of Commerce 9543 Losa Dr Suite 118 *Web:* www.dallasnortheastchamber.net	Dallas	TX	75214	214-328-4100	328-4124
Metrocrest Chamber of Commerce 5100 Belt Line Rd Suite 430 *Web:* www.metrocrestchamber.com	Dallas	TX	75254	469-587-0420	587-0428
North Dallas Chamber of Commerce 10707 Preston Rd *Web:* www.ndcc.org	Dallas	TX	75230	214-368-6485	691-5584
Oak Cliff Chamber of Commerce 400 S Zang Blvd Suite 110 *Web:* www.oakcliffchamber.org	Dallas	TX	75208	214-943-4567	943-4582
Southeast Dallas Chamber of Commerce 802 S Buckner Blvd *Web:* www.sedcc.org	Dallas	TX	75217	214-398-9590	398-9591
Deer Park Chamber of Commerce 110 Ctr St *Web:* www.deerpark.org	Deer Park	TX	77536	281-479-1559	476-4041
Del Rio Chamber of Commerce (DRCoC) 1915 Veterans Blvd *TF:* 800-889-8149 ■ *Web:* www.drchamber.com	Del Rio	TX	78840	830-775-3551	774-1813
Denton Chamber of Commerce 414 W Pkwy St *TF:* 888-381-1818 ■ *Web:* www.denton-chamber.org	Denton	TX	76201	940-382-9693	382-0040
DeSoto Chamber of Commerce 2010 N Hampton Rd Suite 200 *Web:* www.desotochamber.org	DeSoto	TX	75115	972-224-3565	354-1022
North Galveston County Chamber of Commerce 218 FM 517 W *Web:* www.northgalvestoncountychamber.com	Dickinson	TX	77539	281-534-4380	534-4389
Duncanville Chamber of Commerce 300 E Wheatland Rd *Web:* www.duncanvillechamber.org	Duncanville	TX	75116	972-780-4990	298-9370
Eagle Pass Chamber of Commerce 400 E Garrison St *TF:* 888-355-3224 ■ *Web:* www.eaglepasstexas.com	Eagle Pass	TX	78852	830-773-3224	773-8844
Edinburg Chamber of Commerce 602 W University Dr *TF:* 800-800-7214 ■ *Web:* www.edinburg.com	Edinburg	TX	78540	956-383-4974	383-6942
Greater El Paso Chamber of Commerce 10 Civic Ctr Plaza *TF:* 800-651-8065 ■ *Web:* www.elpaso.org	El Paso	TX	79901	915-534-0500	534-0510
Farmers Branch Chamber of Commerce 12875 Josey Ln Suite 150 *Web:* www.fbchamber.com	Farmers Branch	TX	75234	972-243-8966	243-8968
Flower Mound Chamber of Commerce 700 Parker Sq Suite 100 *Web:* www.flowermoundchamber.com	Flower Mound	TX	75028	972-539-0500	539-4307
Fort Worth Chamber of Commerce 777 Taylor St Suite 900 *Web:* www.fortworthcoc.org	Fort Worth	TX	76102	817-336-2491	877-4034
Friendswood Chamber of Commerce 1100 S Friendswood Dr *Web:* www.friendswood-chamber.com	Friendswood	TX	77546	281-482-3329	482-3911
Gainesville Area Chamber of Commerce 311 S Weaver St *TF:* 888-585-4468 ■ *Web:* www.gogainesville.net	Gainesville	TX	76240	940-665-2831	665-2833
Galveston Chamber of Commerce 519 25th St *Web:* www.galvestonchamber.com	Galveston	TX	77550	409-763-5326	763-8271
Garland Chamber of Commerce 914 S Garland Ave *Web:* www.garlandchamber.com	Garland	TX	75040	972-272-7551	276-9261
Georgetown Chamber of Commerce 100 Stadium Dr *Web:* www.georgetownchamber.org	Georgetown	TX	78626	512-930-3535	930-3587
Gilmer Area Chamber of Commerce 106 Buffalo St *Web:* www.gilmerareachamber.com	Gilmer	TX	75644	903-843-2413	843-3759
Lake Granbury Area Chamber of Commerce 3408 E Hwy 377 *Web:* www.granburychamber.com	Granbury	TX	76049	817-573-1622	573-0805
Grapevine Chamber of Commerce 200 Vine St *Web:* www.grapevinechamber.org	Grapevine	TX	76051	817-481-1522	424-5208
Northeast Tarrant Chamber of Commerce 5001 Denton Hwy *Web:* www.netarrant.org	Haltom City	TX	76117	817-281-9376	281-9379
Harlingen Area Chamber of Commerce 311 E Tyler St *TF:* 800-531-7346 ■ *Web:* www.harlingen.com	Harlingen	TX	78550	956-423-5440	425-3870
Henderson Area Chamber of Commerce 201 N Main St *Web:* www.hendersontx.com	Henderson	TX	75652	903-657-5528	657-9454
Clear Lake Area Chamber of Commerce 1201 NASA Pkwy *Web:* www.clearlakearea.com	Houston	TX	77058	281-488-7676	488-8981
Galleria Area Chamber of Commerce 5005 Woodway Suite 215 *Web:* www.galleriachamber.com	Houston	TX	77056	713-629-5555	629-6403
Greater Heights Area Chamber of Commerce 545 W 19th St 2nd Fl *Web:* www.heightschamber.com	Houston	TX	77008	713-861-6735	861-9310
Greater Houston Partnership 1200 Smith St Suite 700 *Web:* www.houston.org	Houston	TX	77002	713-844-3600	844-0200
Houston Northwest Chamber of Commerce 3920 FM 1960 Rd W # 120 *Web:* www.hnwcc.com	Houston	TX	77068	281-440-4160	440-5302
Houston West Chamber of Commerce 10370 Richmond Ave Suite 125 *Web:* www.hwcoc.org	Houston	TX	77042	713-785-4922	785-4944
North Ch Area Chamber of Commerce 13301 E Fwy # 100 *Web:* www.northchannelarea.com	Houston	TX	77015	713-450-3600	450-0700
North Houston-Greenspoint Chamber of Commerce 250 N Sam Houston Pkwy E Suite 200 *Web:* www.nhgcc.org	Houston	TX	77060	281-260-3163	260-3161
South Belt-Ellington Chamber of Commerce 10500 Scarsdale Blvd *Web:* www.southbeltchamber.com	Houston	TX	77089	281-481-5516	922-7045
Humble Area Chamber of Commerce 110 W Main St *Web:* www.humbleareachamber.org	Humble	TX	77338	281-446-2128	446-7483
Huntsville-Walker County Chamber of Commerce 1327 11th St *TF:* 800-289-0389 ■ *Web:* www.chamber.huntsville.tx.us	Huntsville	TX	77340	936-295-8113	295-0571
Greater Irving & Las Colinas Chamber of Commerce 5201 N O'Connor Blvd Suite 100 *Web:* www.irvingchamber.com	Irving	TX	75039	214-217-8484	389-2513
Kerrville Area Chamber of Commerce 1700 Sidney Baker St Suite 100 *Web:* www.kerrvilletx.com	Kerrville	TX	78028	830-896-1155	896-1175
Greater Killeen Chamber of Commerce 1 Santa Fe Plaza *TF:* 866-790-4769 ■ *Web:* www.killeenchamber.com	Killeen	TX	76540	254-526-9551	526-6090
Kingsville Chamber of Commerce 635 E King Ave # 124 *Web:* www.kingsville.org	Kingsville	TX	78363	361-592-6438	592-0866
La Porte-Bayshore Chamber of Commerce 712 W Fairmont Pkwy *Web:* www.laportechamber.org	La Porte	TX	77571	281-471-1123	471-1710
Brazosport Area Chamber of Commerce 300 Abner Jackson Pkwy *TF:* 888-477-2505 ■ *Web:* www.brazosport.org	Lake Jackson	TX	77566	979-285-2501	285-2505
Laredo-Webb County Chamber of Commerce 2310 San Bernardo Ave *TF:* 800-292-2122 ■ *Web:* www.laredochamber.com	Laredo	TX	78042	956-722-9895	791-4503
Lewisville Chamber of Commerce 551 N Valley Pkwy *Web:* www.lewisvillechamber.org	Lewisville	TX	75067	972-436-9571	436-5949
Liberty-Dayton Area Chamber of Commerce 1801 Trinity St *Web:* www.libertydaytonchamber.com	Liberty	TX	77575	936-336-5736	336-1159
Livingston-Polk County Chamber of Commerce (LPCC) 1001 US Hwy 59 Loop N PO Box 600 *TF:* 800-918-1305 ■ *Web:* www.lpcchamber.com	Livingston	TX	77351	936-327-4929	327-2660
Longview Partnership 410 N Ctr St *Web:* www.longviewchamber.com	Longview	TX	75601	903-237-4000	237-4049
Lubbock Chamber of Commerce 1500 Broadway Suite 101 *Web:* www.lubbockchamber.com	Lubbock	TX	79401	806-761-7000	761-7013
Lufkin/Angelina County Chamber of Commerce 1615 S Chestnut St *TF:* 800-409-5659 ■ *Web:* www.lufkintexas.org	Lufkin	TX	75901	936-634-6644	634-8726
Greater Cedar Creek Lake Area Chamber of Commerce 604 S 3rd St Suite E *TF:* 877-222-5253 ■ *Web:* www.cclake.net	Mabank	TX	75147	903-887-3152	887-3695
Greater Marshall Chamber of Commerce 213 W Austin St *TF:* 800-953-7868 ■ *Web:* www.marshall-chamber.com	Marshall	TX	75670	903-935-7868	935-9982
McAllen Chamber of Commerce 1200 Ash Ave *TF:* 877-622-5536 ■ *Web:* www.mcallenchamber.com	McAllen	TX	78501	956-682-2871	687-2917
McKinney Chamber of Commerce 2150 S Central Expy # 150 *Web:* www.mckinneytx.org	McKinney	TX	75070	972-542-0163	548-0876
Mesquite Chamber of Commerce 617 N Ebrite St *TF:* 800-541-2355 ■ *Web:* www.mesquitechamber.com	Mesquite	TX	75149	972-285-0211	285-3535
Midland Chamber of Commerce 109 N Main St *TF:* 800-624-6435 ■ *Web:* www.midlandtxchamber.com	Midland	TX	79701	432-683-3381	686-3556
Mineral Wells Area Chamber of Commerce 511 E Hubbard St *TF:* 800-252-6989 ■ *Web:* www.mineralwellstx.com	Mineral Wells	TX	76067	940-325-2557	328-0850
Mission Chamber of Commerce 202 W Tom Landry St *TF:* 800-580-2700 ■ *Web:* www.missionchamber.com	Mission	TX	78572	956-585-2727	585-3044
Mount Pleasant-Titus County Chamber of Commerce 1604 N Jefferson Ave *Web:* www.mtpleasanttx.com	Mount Pleasant	TX	75455	903-572-8567	572-0613

Name / Address	City	State	ZIP	Phone	Fax
Nacogdoches County Chamber of Commerce 2516 N St; *Web:* www.nacogdoches.org	Nacogdoches	TX	75965	936-560-5533	560-3920
New Braunfels Chamber of Commerce 390 S Seguin St; *TF:* 800-572-2626 ■ *Web:* www.nbcham.org	New Braunfels	TX	78130	830-625-2385	625-7918
Odessa Chamber of Commerce 700 N Grant St Suite 200; *TF:* 800-780-4678 ■ *Web:* www.odessachamber.com	Odessa	TX	79761	432-332-9111	333-7858
Greater Orange Area Chamber of Commerce 1012 Green Ave; *Web:* www.goacc.org	Orange	TX	77630	409-883-3536	886-3247
Lamar County Chamber of Commerce 1125 Bonham St; *TF:* 800-727-4789 ■ *Web:* www.paristexas.com	Paris	TX	75460	903-784-2501	784-2503
Pasadena Chamber of Commerce 4334 Fairmont Pkwy; *Web:* www.pasadenachamber.org	Pasadena	TX	77504	281-487-7871	487-5530
Pearland Area Chamber of Commerce 6117 Broadway St; *Web:* www.pearlandchamber.com	Pearland	TX	77581	281-485-3634	485-2420
Greater Pflugerville Chamber of Commerce 101 S 3rd St PO Box 483; *Web:* www.pfchamber.com	Pflugerville	TX	78691	512-251-7799	251-7802
Pharr Chamber of Commerce 308 W Pk St; *Web:* www.pharrchamber.com	Pharr	TX	78577	956-787-1481	787-7972
Plainview Chamber of Commerce 1906 W 5th St; *TF:* 800-658-2685 ■ *Web:* www.plainviewtexaschamber.com	Plainview	TX	79072	806-296-7431	296-0819
Plano Chamber of Commerce 1200 E 15th St; *Web:* www.planochamber.org	Plano	TX	75074	972-424-7547	422-5182
Greater Port Arthur Chamber of Commerce 4749 Twin City Hwy Suite 300; *Web:* www.portarthurtexas.com	Port Arthur	TX	77642	409-963-1107	962-1997
Richardson Chamber of Commerce 411 Belle Grove Dr; *Web:* www.richardsonchamber.com	Richardson	TX	75080	972-792-2800	792-2825
Rockwall County Chamber of Commerce 697 E IH- 30; *Web:* www.rockwallchamber.org	Rockwall	TX	75087	972-771-5733	772-3642
Rosenberg-Richmond Area Chamber of Commerce 4120 Ave H; *Web:* www.roserichchamber.org	Rosenberg	TX	77471	281-342-5464	342-2990
Round Rock Chamber of Commerce 212 E Main St; *TF:* 800-747-3479 ■ *Web:* www.roundrockchamber.org	Round Rock	TX	78664	512-255-5805	255-3345
Rowlett Chamber of Commerce 3910 Main St; *TF:* 800-796-8644 ■ *Web:* www.rowlettchamber.com	Rowlett	TX	75088	972-475-3200	463-1699
Greater San Antonio Chamber of Commerce 602 E Commerce St; *Web:* www.sachamber.org	San Antonio	TX	78205	210-229-2100	229-1600
North San Antonio Chamber of Commerce 12930 Country Pkwy; *Web:* www.northsachamber.com	San Antonio	TX	78216	210-344-4848	525-8207
South San Antonio Chamber of Commerce 7902 Challenger Dr; *Web:* www.southsachamber.org	San Antonio	TX	78235	210-533-1600	533-1611
San Marcos Area Chamber of Commerce 202 N CM Allen Pkwy; *TF:* 888-200-5620 ■ *Web:* www.sanmarcostexas.com	San Marcos	TX	78666	512-393-5900	393-5912
Seguin Area Chamber of Commerce 116 N Camp St; *TF:* 800-580-7322 ■ *Web:* www.seguinchamber.com	Seguin	TX	78155	830-379-6382	379-6971
Springtown Chamber of Commerce 112 S Main St; *Web:* www.springtowntexas.com	Springtown	TX	76082	817-220-7828	523-3268
Fort Bend Chamber of Commerce 445 Commerce Green Blvd; *Web:* www.visitfortbend.com	Sugar Land	TX	77478	281-491-0800	491-0112
Hopkins County Chamber of Commerce 300 Connally St; *Web:* www.sulphursprings-tx.com	Sulphur Springs	TX	75482	903-885-6515	885-6516
Temple Chamber of Commerce 2 N 5th St; *Web:* www.templetx.org	Temple	TX	76501	254-773-2105	773-0661
Texarkana Chamber of Commerce 819 N State Line Ave; *TF:* 877-275-5289 ■ *Web:* www.texarkanachamber.com	Texarkana	TX	75501	903-792-7191	793-4304
Texas City-La Marque Chamber of Commerce 9702 Emmett F Lowry Expy; *TF:* 877-986-8791 ■ *Web:* www.texascitychamber.com	Texas City	TX	77591	409-935-1408	316-0901
Colony Chamber of Commerce The 6900 Main St PO Box 560006; *Web:* www.thecolonychamber.com	The Colony	TX	75056	972-625-8027	625-8027
South Montgomery County Woodlands Chamber of Commerce 1400 Woodloch Forest Dr Suite 300; *Web:* www.woodlandschamber.org	The Woodlands	TX	77380	281-367-5777	292-1655
Tyler Area Chamber of Commerce 315 N Broadway Ave; *TF:* 800-235-5712 ■ *Web:* www.tylertexas.com	Tyler	TX	75702	903-592-1661	593-2746
Randolph Metrocom Chamber of Commerce 1001 Pat Booker Rd Suite 206; *Web:* www.randolphmetrocomchamber.org	Universal City	TX	78148	210-658-8322	658-1817
Victoria Chamber of Commerce 3404 N Ben Wilson St; *Web:* www.victoriachamber.org	Victoria	TX	77901	361-573-5277	573-5911
Greater Waco Chamber of Commerce 101 S 3rd St; *Web:* www.wacochamber.com	Waco	TX	76701	254-752-6551	752-6618
Weatherford Chamber of Commerce 401 Fort Worth St; *TF:* 888-594-3801 ■ *Web:* www.weatherford-chamber.com	Weatherford	TX	76086	817-596-3801	613-9216
Rio Grande Valley Chamber of Commerce 322 S Missouri St; *Web:* www.valleychamber.com	Weslaco	TX	78596	956-968-3141	968-0210
Weslaco Area Chamber of Commerce 301 W Railroad; *TF:* 888-968-2102 ■ *Web:* www.weslaco.com	Weslaco	TX	78596	956-968-2102	968-6451
Lake Tawakoni Regional Chamber of Commerce 100 Hwy 276 W PO Box 1149; *Web:* www.laketawakonichamber.org	West Tawakoni	TX	75474	903-447-3020	447-3820
Wichita Falls Board of Commerce & Industry 900 8th St Suite 218; *Web:* www.wichitafallscommerce.com	Wichita Falls	TX	76301	940-723-2741	723-8773

UTAH

Name / Address	City	State	ZIP	Phone	Fax
Davis Chamber of Commerce 450 Simmons Way # 220; *Web:* www.davischamberofcommerce.com	Kaysville	UT	84037	801-593-2200	593-2212
Cache Chamber of Commerce 160 N Main St; *Web:* www.cachechamber.com	Logan	UT	84321	435-752-2161	753-5825
Murray Area Chamber of Commerce (MACC) 5250 S Commerce Dr Suite 180; *Web:* www.murraychamber.org	Murray	UT	84107	801-263-2632	263-8262
Ogden/Weber Chamber of Commerce 2484 Washington Blvd Suite 400; *TF:* 866-990-1299 ■ *Web:* www.echamber.cc	Ogden	UT	84401	801-621-8300	392-7609
Commission for Economic Development in Orem 777 S State St; *Web:* www.cedo.org	Orem	UT	84058	801-226-1538	226-2678
Provo/Orem Chamber of Commerce 51 S University Ave Suite 215; *Web:* thechamber.org	Provo	UT	84601	801-379-2555	851-2557
Saint George Area Chamber of Commerce 97 E St George Blvd; *Web:* www.stgeorgechamber.com	Saint George	UT	84770	435-628-1658	673-1587
Salt Lake City Chamber of Commerce 175 E University Blvd 400 S Suite 600; *Web:* www.slchamber.com	Salt Lake City	UT	84111	801-364-3631	328-5098
Sandy Area Chamber of Commerce 8807 S 700 E; *Web:* www.sandychamber.com	Sandy	UT	84070	801-566-0344	566-0346
South Salt Lake Chamber of Commerce 220 E Morris Ave Suite 150; *Web:* www.sslchamber.com	South Salt Lake	UT	84115	801-466-3377	467-3322
Tooele County Chamber of Commerce 86 S Main PO Box 460; *TF:* 800-378-0690 ■ *Web:* www.tooelechamber.com	Tooele	UT	84074	435-882-0690	833-0946
West Jordan Chamber of Commerce 8000 Redwood Rd; *Web:* www.westjordanchamber.com	West Jordan	UT	84088	801-569-5151	569-5153
ChamberWest 1241 W Village Main Dr Suite B; *Web:* www.chamberwest.org	West Valley City	UT	84119	801-977-8755	977-8329

VERMONT

Name / Address	City	State	ZIP	Phone	Fax
Great Falls Region Chamber of Commerce 17 Depot St; *Web:* www.gfrcc.org	Bellows Falls	VT	05101	802-463-4280	
Bennington Area Chamber of Commerce 100 Veterans Memorial Dr; *TF:* 800-229-0252 ■ *Web:* www.bennington.com	Bennington	VT	05201	802-447-3311	447-1163
Central Vermont Chamber of Commerce 33 Stewart Rd; *TF:* 877-887-3678 ■ *Web:* www.central-vt.com	Berlin	VT	05602	802-229-5711	229-5713
Brattleboro Area Chamber of Commerce 180 Main St; *TF:* 877-254-4565 ■ *Web:* www.brattleborochamber.org	Brattleboro	VT	05301	802-254-4565	254-5675
Lake Champlain Regional Chamber of Commerce 60 Main St Suite 100; *TF:* 877-686-5253 ■ *Web:* www.vermont.org	Burlington	VT	05401	802-863-3489	863-1538
Addison County Chamber of Commerce 93 Ct St; *TF:* 800-733-8376 ■ *Web:* www.addisoncounty.com	Middlebury	VT	05753	802-388-7951	388-8066
Vermont's North Country Chamber of Commerce 246 Cswy St; *TF:* 800-635-4643 ■ *Web:* www.vtnorthcountry.org	Newport	VT	05855	802-334-7782	334-7238
Franklin County Regional Chamber of Commerce 2 N Main St Suite 101; *Web:* www.stalbanschamber.com	Saint Albans	VT	05478	802-524-2444	527-2256
Northeast Kingdom Chamber of Commerce 51 Depot Sq Suite 3; *TF:* 800-639-6379 ■ *Web:* www.nekchamber.com	Saint Johnsbury	VT	05819	802-748-3678	748-0731

VIRGINIA

Name / Address	City	State	ZIP	Phone	Fax
Washington County Chamber of Commerce 179 E Main St; *Web:* www.washingtonvachamber.org	Abingdon	VA	24210	276-628-8141	628-3984
Alexandria Chamber of Commerce 801 N Fairfax St Suite 402; *Web:* www.alexchamber.com	Alexandria	VA	22314	703-549-1000	739-3805
Mount Vernon-Lee Chamber of Commerce 6911 Richmond Hwy #320; *Web:* www.mtvernon-leechamber.org	Alexandria	VA	22306	703-360-6925	360-6928
Amherst County Chamber of Commerce 154 S Main St; *Web:* www.amherstvachamber.com	Amherst	VA	24521	434-946-0990	946-0879
Annandale Chamber of Commerce 7263 Maple Pl Suite 207; *Web:* www.annandalechamber.com	Annandale	VA	22003	703-256-7232	256-7233

			Phone	Fax
Arlington Chamber of Commerce 2009 14th St N Suite 111 . . . Arlington *Web:* www.arlingtonchamber.org	VA	22201	703-525-2400	
Bedford Area Chamber of Commerce 305 E Main St . . . Bedford *TF:* 800-933-9535 ■ *Web:* www.bedfordareachamber.com	VA	24523	540-586-9401	587-6650
Montgomery County Chamber of Commerce 103 Professional Pk Dr . . . Blacksburg *Web:* www.montgomerycc.org	VA	24060	540-552-2636	552-2639
Danville Pittsylvania County Chamber of Commerce 8653 US Hwy 29 PO Box 99 . . . Blairs *Web:* www.dpchamber.org	VA	24527	434-836-6990	836-6955
Charlottesville Regional Chamber of Commerce 209 5th St NE . . . Charlottesville *Web:* www.cvillechamber.com	VA	22902	434-295-3141	295-3144
Culpeper County Chamber of Commerce & Visitors Ctr 109 S Commerce St . . . Culpeper *TF:* 888-285-7373 ■ *Web:* www.culpepervachamber.com	VA	22701	540-825-8628	825-1449
Pulaski County Chamber of Commerce 4440 Cleburne Blvd Suite B . . . Dublin *Web:* www.pulaskichamber.info	VA	24084	540-674-1991	674-4163
Central Fairfax Chamber of Commerce 11166 Fairfax Blvd Suite 407 . . . Fairfax *Web:* www.cfcc.org	VA	22030	703-591-2450	591-2820
Botetourt County Chamber of Commerce 13 W Main St . . . Fincastle *Web:* www.bot-co-chamber.com	VA	24090	540-473-8280	473-8365
Greater Augusta Regional Chamber of Commerce 30 Ladd Rd PO Box 1107 . . . Fishersville *Web:* www.augustachamber.org	VA	22939	540-949-8203	949-7740
Franklin-Southampton Area Chamber of Commerce 108 W 3rd Ave PO Box 531 . . . Franklin *Web:* www.fsachamber.com	VA	23851	757-562-4900	562-6138
Fredericksburg Regional Chamber of Commerce 2300 Fall Hill Ave Suite 240 . . . Fredericksburg *Web:* www.fredericksburgchamber.org	VA	22401	540-373-9400	373-9570
Front Royal-Warren County Chamber of Commerce 104 E Main St . . . Front Royal *Web:* www.frontroyalchamber.com	VA	22630	540-635-3185	635-9758
Galax-Carroll-Grayson Chamber of Commerce 405 N Main St . . . Galax *Web:* www.gcgchamber.com	VA	24333	276-236-2184	236-1338
Gloucester County Chamber of Commerce 6688 Main St . . . Gloucester	VA	23061	804-693-2425	693-7193
Virginia Peninsula Chamber of Commerce 21 Enterprise Pkwy Suite 100 . . . Hampton *TF:* 800-556-1822 ■ *Web:* www.vpcc.org	VA	23666	757-262-2000	262-2009
Harrisonburg-Rockingham Chamber of Commerce 800 Country Club Rd . . . Harrisonburg *Web:* www.hrchamber.org	VA	22802	540-434-3862	434-4508
Carroll County Chamber of Commerce 515 N Main St PO Box 1184 . . . Hillsville *Web:* www.carrollvachamber.com	VA	24343	276-728-5397	728-7825
Hopewell-Prince George Chamber of Commerce 210 N 2nd Ave . . . Hopewell *Web:* www.hpgchamber.org	VA	23860	804-458-5536	458-0041
Loudoun County Chamber of Commerce 19301 Winmeade Dr Suite 210 . . . Lansdowne *Web:* www.loudounchamber.org	VA	20176	703-777-2176	777-1392
Russell County Chamber of Commerce 133 Highland Dr . . . Lebanon *Web:* www.russellcountyva.org	VA	24266	276-889-8041	889-8002
Lexington-Rockbridge County Chamber of Commerce 100 E Washington St . . . Lexington *Web:* www.lexrockchamber.com	VA	24450	540-463-5375	463-3567
Lynchburg Regional Chamber of Commerce 2015 Memorial Ave . . . Lynchburg *Web:* www.lynchburgchamber.org	VA	24501	434-845-5966	522-9592
Prince William County-Greater Manassas Chamber of Commerce 9720 Capital Ct #203 . . . Manassas *Web:* www.pwcgmcc.org	VA	20110	703-368-6600	368-4733
Chamber of Commerce of Smyth County 214 W Main St . . . Marion *Web:* www.smythchamber.org	VA	24354	276-783-3161	783-8003
Martinsville-Henry County Chamber of Commerce 115 Broad St . . . Martinsville *Web:* www.martinsville.com	VA	24112	276-632-6401	632-5059
Hanover Assn of Businesses & Chamber of Commerce 9097 Atlee Stn Rd Suite 117 . . . Mechanicsville *Web:* www.habcc.com	VA	23116	804-798-8130	798-0014
Eastern Shore of Virginia Chamber of Commerce 19056 Pkwy Rd . . . Melfa *Web:* www.esvachamber.org	VA	23410	757-787-2460	787-8687
Hampton Roads Chamber of Commerce 500 E Main St Suite 700 . . . Norfolk *Web:* www.hamptonroadschamber.com	VA	23510	757-622-2312	622-5563
Wise County Chamber of Commerce 765 Park Ave PO Box 226 . . . Norton *Web:* www.wisecountychamber.org	VA	24273	276-679-0961	679-2655
Petersburg Chamber of Commerce 325 E Washington St PO Box 928 . . . Petersburg *Web:* www.petersburgvachamber.com	VA	23804	804-733-8131	733-9891
Prince William Regional Chamber of Commerce 4320 Ridgewood Ctr Dr . . . Prince William *Web:* www.regionalchamber.org	VA	22192	703-590-5000	590-9815
Greater Reston Chamber of Commerce 1763 Fountain Dr . . . Reston *Web:* www.restonchamber.org	VA	20190	703-707-9045	707-9049
Greater Richmond Chamber of Commerce 600 E Main St 7th Fl . . . Richmond *Web:* www.grcc.com	VA	23219	804-648-1234	783-9366
Roanoke Regional Chamber of Commerce 210 S Jefferson St . . . Roanoke *Web:* www.roanokechamber.org	VA	24011	540-983-0700	983-0723
Franklin County Chamber of Commerce 52 Franklin St PO Box 158 . . . Rocky Mount *Web:* www.franklincountyva.gov	VA	24151	540-483-9542	483-0653
Salem/Roanoke County Chamber of Commerce 611 E Main St . . . Salem *Web:* www.s-rcchamber.org	VA	24153	540-387-0267	387-4110
Halifax County Chamber of Commerce 515 Broad St . . . South Boston *Web:* www.halifaxchamber.net	VA	24592	434-572-3085	572-1733
Greater Springfield Chamber of Commerce 6434 Brandon Ave Suite 3A . . . Springfield *Web:* www.springfieldchamber.org	VA	22150	703-866-3500	866-3501
Hampton Roads Chamber of Commerce-Suffolk 127 E Washington St Suite 100 . . . Suffolk *Web:* www.hamptonroadschamber.com	VA	23434	757-622-2312	622-5563
Tazewell Area Chamber of Commerce 185 Tazewell Mall Cir . . . Tazewell *Web:* www.tazewellchamber.org	VA	24651	276-988-5091	988-5093
Fairfax County Chamber of Commerce (FCCC) 8230 Old Courthouse Rd Suite 350 . . . Vienna *Web:* www.fairfaxchamber.org	VA	22182	703-749-0400	749-9075
Vienna-Tysons Regional Chamber of Commerce 513 Maple Ave W 2nd Fl . . . Vienna *Web:* www.vtrcc.org	VA	22180	703-281-1333	242-1482
Fauquier County Chamber of Commerce 205-1 Keith St . . . Warrenton *Web:* www.fauquierchamber.org	VA	20186	540-347-4414	347-7510
Williamsburg Area Chamber of Commerce 421 N Boundary St PO Box 3495 . . . Williamsburg *TF:* 800-368-6511 ■ *Web:* www.williamsburgcc.com	VA	23187	757-229-6511	253-1397
Top of Virginia Regional Chamber 407 S Loudoun St . . . Winchester *Web:* www.regionalchamber.biz	VA	22601	540-662-4118	722-6365
Wytheville-Wythe-Bland Chamber of Commerce Inc 150 E Monroe St PO Box 563 . . . Wytheville *Web:* www.wwbchamber.com	VA	24382	276-223-3365	223-3412

WASHINGTON

			Phone	Fax
Grays Harbor Chamber of Commerce 506 Duffy St . . . Aberdeen *TF:* 800-321-1924 ■ *Web:* www.graysharbor.org	WA	98520	360-532-1924	533-7945
Auburn Area Chamber of Commerce 108 S Division St Suite B . . . Auburn *Web:* www.auburnareawa.org	WA	98001	253-833-0700	735-4091
Bellevue Chamber of Commerce 302 Bellevue Sq 3rd Fl . . . Bellevue *Web:* www.bellevuechamber.org	WA	98004	425-454-2464	462-4660
Bellingham/Whatcom Chamber of Commerce & Industry 119 N Commercial St Suite 110 . . . Bellingham *Web:* www.bellingham.com	WA	98225	360-734-1330	734-1332
Bremerton Area Chamber of Commerce 286 Fourth St . . . Bremerton *Web:* www.bremertonchamber.org	WA	98337	360-479-3579	479-1033
Camas-Washougal Chamber of Commerce 422 NE 4th Ave . . . Camas *Web:* www.cwchamber.com	WA	98607	360-834-2472	834-9171
Centralia-Chehalis Chamber of Commerce 500 NW Chamber of Commerce Way . . . Chehalis *Web:* www.chamberway.com	WA	98532	360-748-8885	748-8763
Greater Edmonds Chamber of Commerce 121 5th Ave N . . . Edmonds *Web:* www.edmondswa.com	WA	98020	425-670-1496	712-1808
Enumclaw Area Chamber of Commerce 1421 Cole St . . . Enumclaw *Web:* www.enumclawchamber.com	WA	98022	360-825-7666	825-8369
Everett Area Chamber of Commerce 2000 Hewitt Ave Suite 205 . . . Everett *Web:* www.everettchamber.com	WA	98201	425-257-3222	257-2074
Greater Federal Way Chamber of Commerce 31919 1st Ave S Suite 202 . . . Federal Way *Web:* www.federalwaychamber.com	WA	98003	253-838-2605	661-9050
Gig Harbor/Peninsula Area Chamber of Commerce 3311 Harborview Dr Suite 101 . . . Gig Harbor *Web:* www.gigharborchamber.com	WA	98332	253-851-6865	851-6881
Greater Issaquah Chamber of Commerce 155 NW Gilman Blvd . . . Issaquah *Web:* www.issaquahchamber.com	WA	98027	425-392-7024	392-8101
Tri-City Area Chamber of Commerce 7130 W Grandridge Blvd . . . Kennewick *Web:* www.tcrchamber.com	WA	99336	509-736-0510	783-1733
Kent Chamber of Commerce 524 W Meeker St Suite 1 . . . Kent *Web:* www.kentchamber.com	WA	98032	253-854-1770	854-8567
Greater Kirkland Chamber of Commerce 401 Pk Pl Suite 102 . . . Kirkland *Web:* www.kirklandchamber.org	WA	98033	425-822-7066	827-4878
Lacey-Thurston County Chamber of Commerce 8300 Quinault Dr NE # A . . . Lacey *Web:* www.laceychamber.com	WA	98516	360-491-4141	491-9403
Lakewood Chamber of Commerce 4650 Steilacoom Blvd SW Bldg 19 Suite 109 . . . Lakewood *Web:* www.lakewood-wa.com	WA	98499	253-582-9400	581-5241
Kelso Longview Chamber of Commerce 1563 Olympia Way . . . Longview *Web:* www.kelsolongviewchamber.org	WA	98632	360-423-8400	423-0432
South Snohomish County Chamber of Commerce 3815 196th St SW Suite 136 . . . Lynnwood *Web:* www.sscchamber.org	WA	98036	425-774-0507	774-4636
Greater Maple Valley-Black Diamond Chamber of Commerce 23745 225th Way SE Suite 205 . . . Maple Valley *Web:* www.maplevalley.com	WA	98038	425-432-0222	413-8017

Name / Address	City	State	Zip	Phone	Fax
Moses Lake Area Chamber of Commerce 324 S Pioneer Way *TF:* 800-992-6234 ■ *Web:* www.moseslake.com	Moses Lake	WA	98837	509-765-7888	765-7891
Greater Oak Harbor Chamber of Commerce 32630 SR 20 PO Box 883 *Web:* www.oakharborchamber.com	Oak Harbor	WA	98277	360-675-3755	679-1624
Olympia/Thurston County Chamber of Commerce 809 Legion Way *Web:* www.thurstonchamber.com	Olympia	WA	98501	360-357-3362	357-3376
Greater Pasco Area Chamber of Commerce 1925 N 20th Ave *Web:* www.pascochamber.org	Pasco	WA	99301	509-547-9755	547-9756
Port Orchard Chamber of Commerce 1014 Bay St Suite 8 *Web:* www.portorchard.com	Port Orchard	WA	98366	360-876-3505	895-1920
Pullman Chamber of Commerce 415 N Grand Ave *TF:* 800-365-6948 ■ *Web:* www.pullmanchamber.com	Pullman	WA	99163	509-334-3565	332-3232
Eastern Pierce County Chamber of Commerce 323 N Meridian Suite A-1 *Web:* www.puyallupchamber.com	Puyallup	WA	98371	253-845-6755	848-6164
Redmond Chamber of Commerce 16210 NE 80th St *Web:* www.redmondchamber.org	Redmond	WA	98052	425-885-4014	882-0996
Greater Renton Chamber of Commerce 300 Rainier Ave N *Web:* www.gorenton.com	Renton	WA	98057	425-226-4560	226-4287
Ballard Chamber of Commerce 2208 NW Market St Suite 100 *Web:* www.ballardchamber.com	Seattle	WA	98107	206-784-9705	783-8154
Greater Seattle Chamber of Commerce 1301 5th Ave Suite 2500 *Web:* www.seattlechamber.com	Seattle	WA	98101	206-389-7200	389-7288
Greater University Chamber of Commerce 4710 University Way NE Suite 114 *Web:* www.udistrictchamber.org	Seattle	WA	98105	206-547-4417	547-5266
Lake City Chamber of Commerce 12345 30th Ave NE Suite FG *Web:* www.lakecitychamber.org	Seattle	WA	98125	206-363-3287	363-6456
White Center Chamber of Commerce 1327 SW 102nd St	Seattle	WA	98146	206-763-4196	763-1042
Shelton-Mason County Chamber of Commerce 215 W Railroad Ave PO Box 2389 *TF:* 800-576-2021 ■ *Web:* www.sheltonchamber.org	Shelton	WA	98584	360-426-2021	426-8678
Shoreline Chamber of Commerce 18560 1st Ave NE *Web:* www.shorelinechamber.com	Shoreline	WA	98155	206-361-2260	361-2268
Greater Spokane Inc 801 W Riverside Ave Suite 100 *TF:* 800-776-5263 ■ *Web:* www.greaterspokane.org	Spokane	WA	99201	509-321-3601	747-0077
Spokane Valley Chamber of Commerce 9507 E Sprague Ave *Web:* www.spokanevalleychamber.org	Spokane Valley	WA	99206	509-924-4994	924-4992
Tacoma-Pierce County Chamber of Commerce 950 Pacific Ave Suite 300 *Web:* www.tacomachamber.org	Tacoma	WA	98402	253-627-2175	597-7305
Southwest King County Chamber of Commerce 14220 Interurban Ave S Suite 134 *TF:* 800-638-8613 ■ *Web:* www.swkcc.org	Tukwila	WA	98168	206-575-1633	575-2007
Greater Vancouver Chamber of Commerce 1101 Broadway Suite 100 *Web:* www.vancouverusa.com	Vancouver	WA	98660	360-694-2588	693-8279
Walla Walla Valley Chamber of Commerce 29 E Sumach St *TF:* 877-998-4748 ■ *Web:* www.wwvchamber.com	Walla Walla	WA	99362	509-525-0850	522-2038
Wenatchee Valley Chamber of Commerce 2 S Mission St *Web:* www.wenatchee.org	Wenatchee	WA	98801	509-662-2116	663-2022
Greater Yakima Chamber of Commerce 10 N 9th St *Web:* www.yakima.org	Yakima	WA	98901	509-248-2021	248-0601

WEST VIRGINIA

Name / Address	City	State	Zip	Phone	Fax
Beckley-Raleigh County Chamber of Commerce 245 N Kanawha St *TF:* 877-987-3847 ■ *Web:* www.brccc.com	Beckley	WV	25801	304-252-7328	252-7373
Buckhannon-Upshur Chamber of Commerce 16 S Kanawha St PO Box 442 *Web:* www.buchamber.com	Buckhannon	WV	26201	304-472-1722	472-4938
Jefferson County Chamber of Commerce 29 Keyes Ferry Rd Suite 200 PO Box 426 *TF:* 800-624-0577 ■ *Web:* www.jeffersoncountywvchamber.org	Charles Town	WV	25414	304-725-2055	728-8307
Charleston Regional Chamber of Commerce 1116 Smith St *TF:* 800-792-4326 ■ *Web:* www.charlestonareaalliance.org	Charleston	WV	25301	304-340-4253	340-4275
Harrison County Chamber of Commerce 520 W Main St *Web:* www.harrisoncountychamber.com	Clarksburg	WV	26301	304-624-6331	624-5190
Elkins-Randolph County Chamber of Commerce (ERCCC) 200 Executive Plaza *Web:* www.erccc.com	Elkins	WV	26241	304-636-2717	636-8046
Marion County Chamber of Commerce 110 Adams St *TF:* 800-296-3379 ■ *Web:* www.marionchamber.com	Fairmont	WV	26554	304-363-0442	363-0480
Huntington Regional Chamber of Commerce 720 4th Ave *Web:* www.huntingtonchamber.org	Huntington	WV	25701	304-525-5131	525-5158
Mineral County Chamber of Commerce 1 Grand Central Pk # 2011 *Web:* www.mineralcounty.info	Keyser	WV	26726	304-788-2513	788-3887
Preston County Chamber of Commerce 200 W Main St # A *Web:* www.prestonchamber.com	Kingwood	WV	26537	304-329-0576	329-1407
Greater Greenbrier Chamber of Commerce 540 N Jefferson St Suite N PO Box 17 *TF:* 800-833-2068 ■ *Web:* www.jeffersoncountywvchamber.org	Lewisburg	WV	24901	304-645-2818	647-3001
Logan County Chamber of Commerce 214 Stratton St *Web:* www.logancountychamberofcommerce.com	Logan	WV	25601	304-752-1324	752-5988
Martinsburg-Berkeley County Chamber of Commerce 198 Viking Way *TF:* 800-332-9007 ■ *Web:* www.berkeleycounty.org	Martinsburg	WV	25401	304-267-4841	263-4695
Morgantown Area Chamber of Commerce 1029 University Ave Suite 101 *TF:* 800-618-2525 ■ *Web:* www.morgantownchamber.com	Morgantown	WV	26505	304-292-3311	296-6619
Marshall County Chamber of Commerce 609 Jefferson Ave *Web:* www.marshallcountychamber.com	Moundsville	WV	26041	304-845-2773	845-2773
Wetzel County Chamber of Commerce 201 Main St PO Box 271 *Web:* www.wetzelcountychamber.com	New Martinsville	WV	26155	304-455-3825	455-3637
Fayette County Chamber of Commerce 310 Oyler Ave *TF:* 800-927-0263 ■ *Web:* www.fayettecounty.com	Oak Hill	WV	25901	304-465-5617	465-5618
Chamber of Commerce of Mid-Ohio Valley 214 8th St	Parkersburg	WV	26101	304-422-3588	422-3580
Mason County Area Chamber of Commerce 305 Main St *Web:* www.masoncountychamber.org	Point Pleasant	WV	25550	304-675-1050	675-1601
Princeton-Mercer County Chamber of Commerce 1522 N Walker St *Web:* www.pmccc.com	Princeton	WV	24740	304-487-1502	425-0227
Wheeling Area Chamber of Commerce 1310 Market St *Web:* www.wheelingchamber.com	Wheeling	WV	26003	304-233-2575	233-1320
Tug Valley Chamber of Commerce PO Box 376 *Web:* www.tugvalleychamber.com	Williamson	WV	25661	304-235-5240	235-4509
Putnam County Chamber of Commerce 5664 SR 34 N *Web:* www.putnamchamber.org	Winfield	WV	25213	304-757-6510	757-6562

WISCONSIN

Name / Address	City	State	Zip	Phone	Fax
Fox Cities Chamber of Commerce & Industry 125 N Superior St *TF:* 800-999-3224 ■ *Web:* www.foxcitieschamber.com	Appleton	WI	54911	920-734-7101	734-7161
Greater Beloit Chamber of Commerce 500 Public Ave *TF:* 800-683-2774 ■ *Web:* www.greaterbeloitchamber.com	Beloit	WI	53511	608-365-8835	365-6850
Greater Brookfield Chamber of Commerce 1305 N Barker Rd Suite 5 *Web:* www.brookfieldchamber.com	Brookfield	WI	53045	262-786-1886	786-1959
Chippewa Falls Area Chamber of Commerce 10 S Bridge St *TF:* 888-723-0024 ■ *Web:* www.chippewachamber.org	Chippewa Falls	WI	54729	715-723-0331	723-0332
Eau Claire Area Chamber of Commerce 101 N Farwell St Suite 101 *Web:* www.eauclairechamber.org	Eau Claire	WI	54703	715-834-1204	834-1956
Fond du Lac Area Assn of Commerce 207 N Main St *Web:* www.fdlac.com	Fond du Lac	WI	54935	920-921-9500	921-9559
Green Bay Area Chamber of Commerce PO Box 1660 *Web:* www.titletown.org	Green Bay	WI	54305	920-437-8704	437-1024
Greenfield Chamber of Commerce 4818 S 76th St Suite 129 *Web:* www.greenfieldchamber.org	Greenfield	WI	53220	414-327-8500	421-6797
Heart of the Valley Chamber of Commerce 101 E Wisconsin Ave *Web:* www.heartofthevalleychamber.com	Kaukauna	WI	54130	920-766-1616	766-5504
Kenosha Area Chamber of Commerce 600 52nd St Suite 130 *Web:* www.kenoshaareachamber.com	Kenosha	WI	53140	262-654-1234	654-4655
Greater La Crosse Area Chamber of Commerce 712 Main St *TF:* 800-889-0539 ■ *Web:* www.lacrossechamber.com	La Crosse	WI	54601	608-784-4880	784-4919
Greater Madison Chamber of Commerce PO Box 71 *Web:* www.greatermadisonchamber.com	Madison	WI	53701	608-256-8348	256-0333
Manitowoc-Two Rivers Area Chamber of Commerce 1515 Memorial Dr *TF:* 866-727-5575 ■ *Web:* www.manitowocchamber.com	Manitowoc	WI	54220	920-684-5575	684-1915
Menomonee Falls Chamber of Commerce N 88 W 16621 Appleton Ave *Web:* www.menomoneefallschamber.com	Menomonee Falls	WI	53052	262-251-2430	251-0969
Greater Menomonie Area Chamber of Commerce 342 E Main St *TF:* 800-283-1862 ■ *Web:* www.menomoniechamber.org	Menomonie	WI	54751	715-235-9087	235-2824
Merrill Area Chamber of Commerce 705 N Ctr Ave *TF:* 877-907-2757 ■ *Web:* www.merrillchamber.com	Merrill	WI	54452	715-536-9474	539-2043
Metropolitan Milwaukee Assn of Commerce 756 N Milwaukee St *Web:* www.mmac.org	Milwaukee	WI	53202	414-287-4100	271-7753
Monroe Chamber of Commerce & Industry 1505 9th St *Web:* www.monroechamber.org	Monroe	WI	53566	608-325-7648	328-2241
New Berlin Chamber of Commerce 13825 W National Ave *Web:* www.nb-chamber.org	New Berlin	WI	53151	262-786-5280	786-9165
SECUB-Southeastern Chamber United in Business 8580 S Howell Ave *Web:* www.secub.net	Oak Creek	WI	53154	414-768-5845	768-5848

Organization / Address	City	State	Zip	Phone	Fax
Oconomowoc Area Chamber of Commerce 175 E Wisconsin Ave *Web:* www.oconomowoc.org	Oconomowoc	WI	53066	262-567-2666	567-3477
Oshkosh Chamber of Commerce 120 Jackson St *Web:* www.oshkoshchamber.com	Oshkosh	WI	54901	920-303-2266	303-2263
Racine Area Mfg & Commerce 300 5th St. *Web:* www.racinechamber.com	Racine	WI	53403	262-634-1931	634-7422
Ripon Area Chamber of Commerce 127 Jefferson St *Web:* www.ripon-wi.com	Ripon	WI	54971	920-748-6764	748-6784
Shawano Country Chamber of Commerce 1263 S Main St. *TF:* 800-235-8528 ■ *Web:* www.shawanocountry.com	Shawano	WI	54166	715-524-2139	524-3127
Sheboygan County Chamber of Commerce 621 S 8th St *TF:* 800-457-9497 ■ *Web:* www.sheboygan.org	Sheboygan	WI	53081	920-457-9491	457-6269
Portage County Business Council 5501 Vern Holmes Dr *Web:* www.portagecountybiz.com	Stevens Point	WI	54481	715-344-1940	344-4473
Superior-Douglas County Chamber of Commerce 205 Belknap St *TF:* 800-942-5313 ■ *Web:* www.superiorchamber.org	Superior	WI	54880	715-394-7716	394-3810
Waukesha County Chamber of Commerce 2717 N Grandview Blvd Suite 204 *Web:* www.waukesha.org	Waukesha	WI	53188	262-542-4249	542-8068
Wausau Area Chamber of Commerce 200 Washington St Suite 120 *Web:* www.wausauchamber.com	Wausau	WI	54403	715-845-6231	845-6235
West Suburban Chamber of Commerce 2300 N Mayfair Rd Suite 380 *Web:* www.westsuburbanchamber.com	Wauwatosa	WI	53226	414-453-2330	453-2336
West Allis-West Milwaukee Chamber of Commerce 7447 W Greenfield Ave *Web:* www.wawmchamber.com	West Allis	WI	53214	414-302-9901	302-9918
West Bend Area Chamber of Commerce 304 S Main St. *TF:* 888-338-8666 ■ *Web:* www.wbachamber.org	West Bend	WI	53095	262-338-2666	338-1771
Heart of Wisconsin Business & Economic Alliance 1120 Lincoln St *Web:* www.heartofwi.com	Wisconsin Rapids	WI	54494	715-423-1830	423-1865

WYOMING

Organization / Address	City	State	Zip	Phone	Fax
Casper Area Chamber of Commerce 500 N Ctr St *TF:* 866-234-5311 ■ *Web:* www.casperwyoming.org	Casper	WY	82601	307-234-5311	265-2643
Greater Cheyenne Chamber of Commerce 121 W 15th St Suite 204 *Web:* www.cheyennechamber.org	Cheyenne	WY	82001	307-638-3388	778-1407
Campbell County Chamber of Commerce 314 S Gillette Ave *Web:* www.gillettechamber.com	Gillette	WY	82716	307-682-3673	682-0538
Jackson Hole Chamber of Commerce 112 Ctr St. *Web:* www.jacksonholechamber.com	Jackson	WY	83001	307-733-3316	733-5585
Laramie Area Chamber of Commerce 800 S 3rd St *TF:* 866-876-1012 ■ *Web:* www.laramie.org	Laramie	WY	82070	307-745-7339	745-4624
Rock Springs Chamber of Commerce 1897 Dewar Dr *TF:* 800-463-8637 ■ *Web:* www.rockspringswyoming.net	Rock Springs	WY	82901	307-362-3771	362-3838
Sheridan County Chamber of Commerce 1517 E 5th St *TF:* 800-453-3650 ■ *Web:* www.sheridanwyomingchamber.org	Sheridan	WY	82801	307-672-2485	672-7321

140 CHAMBERS OF COMMERCE - US - STATE

Organization / Address	City	State	Zip	Phone	Fax
US Chamber of Commerce 1615 H St NW *TF:* 800-638-6582 ■ *Web:* www.uschamber.com	Washington	DC	20062	202-659-6000	463-5836
Alaska State Chamber of Commerce 217 2nd St Suite 201 *Web:* www.alaskachamber.com	Juneau	AK	99801	907-586-2323	463-5515
Arizona Chamber of Commerce & Industry 1221 E Osborn Rd # 100 *TF:* 800-498-6973 ■ *Web:* www.azchamber.com	Phoenix	AZ	85014	602-248-9172	265-1262
Arkansas State Chamber of Commerce 1200 W Capitol Ave PO Box 3645 *Web:* www.arkansasstatechamber.com	Little Rock	AR	72203	501-372-2222	372-2722
Assn of Washington Business PO Box 658 *TF:* 800-521-9325 ■ *Web:* www.awb.org	Olympia	WA	98507	360-943-1600	943-5811
Business Council of Alabama 2 N Jackson St PO Box 76 *TF:* 800-665-9647 ■ *Web:* www.bcatoday.org	Montgomery	AL	36101	334-834-6000	262-7371
Business Council of New York State Inc 152 Washington Ave. *TF:* 800-358-1202 ■ *Web:* www.bcnys.org	Albany	NY	12210	518-465-7511	465-4389
California Chamber of Commerce 1215 K St Suite 1400 PO Box 1736 *Web:* www.calchamber.com	Sacramento	CA	95812	916-444-6670	325-1272
Colorado Assn of Commerce & Industry 1600 Broadway Suite 1000 *Web:* www.cochamber.com	Denver	CO	80202	303-831-7411	860-1439
Connecticut Business & Industry Assn 350 Church St *Web:* www.cbia.com	Hartford	CT	06103	860-244-1900	278-8562
Delaware State Chamber of Commerce 1201 N Orange St Suite 200 PO Box 671 *TF:* 800-292-9507 ■ *Web:* www.dscc.com	Wilmington	DE	19899	302-655-7221	654-0691
District of Columbia Chamber of Commerce 506 9th St NW *Web:* www.dcchamber.org	Washington	DC	20004	202-347-7201	638-6762
Florida Chamber of Commerce 136 S Bronough St PO Box 11309 *TF:* 877-521-1200 ■ *Web:* www.flchamber.com	Tallahassee	FL	32302	850-521-1200	521-1219
Georgia Chamber of Commerce 233 Peachtree St NE Suite 2000 *TF:* 800-241-2286 ■ *Web:* www.gachamber.com	Atlanta	GA	30303	404-223-2264	223-2290
Hawaii Chamber of Commerce 1132 Bishop St Suite 402 *TF:* 800-464-2924 ■ *Web:* www.cochawaii.com	Honolulu	HI	96813	808-545-4300	545-4369
Idaho Assn of Commerce & Industry 816 W Bannock St *Web:* www.iaci.org	Boise	ID	83701	208-343-1849	338-5623
Illinois State Chamber of Commerce 300 S Wacker Dr Suite 1600 *Web:* www.ilchamber.org	Chicago	IL	60606	312-983-7100	983-7101
Indiana State Chamber of Commerce 115 W Washington St Suite 850-S *Web:* www.indianachamber.com	Indianapolis	IN	46204	317-264-3110	264-6855
Iowa Assn of Business & Industry 400 E Ct Ave # 100 *TF:* 800-383-4224 ■ *Web:* www.iowaabi.org	Des Moines	IA	50309	515-280-8000	244-8907
Kansas Chamber of Commerce & Industry 835 SW Topeka Blvd. *Web:* www.kansaschamber.org	Topeka	KS	66612	785-357-6321	357-4732
Kentucky Chamber of Commerce 464 Chenault Rd *Web:* www.kychamber.com	Frankfort	KY	40601	502-695-4700	695-6824
Louisiana Assn of Business & Industry 3113 Valley Creek Dr PO Box 80258 *TF:* 888-816-5224 ■ *Web:* www.labi.org	Baton Rouge	LA	70898	225-928-5388	929-6054
Maine State Chamber of Commerce 125 Community Dr Suite 101 *Web:* www.mainechamber.org	Augusta	ME	04330	207-623-4568	622-7723
Maryland Chamber of Commerce 60 W St Suite 100 *Web:* www.mdchamber.org	Annapolis	MD	21401	410-269-0642	269-5247
Michigan Chamber of Commerce 600 S Walnut St. *TF:* 800-748-0266 ■ *Web:* www.michamber.com	Lansing	MI	48933	517-371-2100	371-7224
Minnesota Chamber of Commerce 400 Robert St N Suite 1500 *TF:* 800-821-2230 ■ *Web:* www.mnchamber.com	Saint Paul	MN	55101	651-292-4650	292-4656
Mississippi Economic Council PO Box 23276 *TF:* 800-748-7626 ■ *Web:* www.msmec.com	Jackson	MS	39225	601-969-0022	353-0247
Missouri Chamber of Commerce 428 E Capitol Ave PO Box 149 *Web:* www.mochamber.org	Jefferson City	MO	65102	573-634-3511	634-8855
Montana Chamber of Commerce 2030 11th Ave. *Web:* www.montanachamber.com	Helena	MT	59601	406-442-2405	442-2409
Nebraska Chamber of Commerce & Industry 1320 Lincoln Mall # 201A *Web:* www.nechamber.com	Lincoln	NE	68508	402-474-4422	474-5681
New England Council Inc 98 N Washington St Suite 201 *Web:* www.newenglandcouncil.com	Boston	MA	02114	617-723-4009	723-3943
New Hampshire Business & Industry Assn 122 N Main St 3rd Fl *Web:* www.nhbia.org	Concord	NH	03301	603-224-5388	224-2872
New Jersey State Chamber of Commerce 216 W State St *Web:* www.njchamber.com	Trenton	NJ	08608	609-989-7888	989-9696
New Mexico Assn of Commerce & Industry (ACI) 2201 Buena Vista Dr SE Suite 410 PO Box 9706 *Web:* www.aci.nm.org	Albuquerque	NM	87106	505-842-0644	842-0734
North Carolina Chamber 701 Corporate Ctr Dr Suite 400 *Web:* www.ncchamber.net/mx/hm.asp?id=home	Raleigh	NC	27607	919-836-1400	836-1425
North Dakota Chamber of Commerce PO Box 2639 *TF:* 800-382-1405 ■ *Web:* www.gnda.com	Bismarck	ND	58502	701-222-0929	222-1611
Ohio Chamber of Commerce 230 E Town St PO Box 15159 *TF:* 800-622-1893 ■ *Web:* www.ohiochamber.com	Columbus	OH	43215	614-228-4201	228-6403
Oklahoma State Chamber 330 NE 10th St *TF:* 800-364-6465 ■ *Web:* www.okstatechamber.com	Oklahoma City	OK	73104	405-235-3669	235-3670
Pennsylvania Chamber of Business & Industry 417 Walnut St. *TF:* 800-225-7224 ■ *Web:* www.pachamber.org	Harrisburg	PA	17101	717-255-3252	255-3298
Puerto Rico Chamber of Commerce PO Box 9024033 *Web:* www.camarapr.org	San Juan	PR	00902	787-721-6060	723-1891
Rhode Island Economic Development Corp 315 Iron Horse Way Suite 101 *Web:* www.riedc.com	Providence	RI	02908	401-278-9100	273-8270
South Carolina Chamber of Commerce 1201 Main St Suite 1700 *TF:* 800-799-4601 ■ *Web:* www.scchamber.net	Columbia	SC	29201	803-799-4601	779-6043
South Dakota Chamber of Commerce & Industry 108 N Euclid Ave *Web:* www.sdchamber.biz	Pierre	SD	57501	605-224-6161	224-7198
Tennessee Chamber of Commerce & Industry 611 Commerce St Suite 3030 *Web:* www.tnchamber.org	Nashville	TN	37203	615-256-5141	256-6726
Texas Assn of Business 1209 Nueces St. *Web:* www.txbiz.org	Austin	TX	78701	512-477-6721	477-0836
Vermont Chamber of Commerce PO Box 37 *Web:* www.vtchamber.com	Montpelier	VT	05601	802-223-3443	223-4257
Virginia Chamber of Commerce 9 S 5th St *TF:* 800-477-7682 ■ *Web:* www.vachamber.com	Richmond	VA	23219	804-644-1607	783-6112

	City	State	ZIP	Phone	Fax
West Virginia Chamber of Commerce 1624 Kanawha Blvd E *Web:* www.wvchamber.com	Charleston	WV	25311	304-342-1115	342-1130
Wisconsin Manufacturers & Commerce PO Box 352 *Web:* www.wmc.org	Madison	WI	53701	608-258-3400	258-3413

141 CHECK CASHING SERVICES

	City	State	ZIP	Phone	Fax
ACE Cash Express Inc 1231 Greenway Dr Suite 600 *TF Sales:* 800-713-3338 ■ *Web:* www.acecashexpress.com	Irving	TX	75038	972-550-5000	550-5150
Advance America Cash Advance Centers Inc 135 N Church St *NYSE: AEA* ■ *TF:* 866-640-4227 ■ *Web:* www.advanceamerica.net	Spartanburg	SC	29306	864-342-5600	342-5612
Cash Plus Inc 3002 Dow Ave Suite 120 *TF:* 888-707-2274 ■ *Web:* www.cashplusinc.com	Tustin	CA	92780	714-731-2274	731-2099
CashZone Check Cashing Service 365 7th Ave *Web:* www.cashzoneusa.com	New York	NY	10001	212-564-4705	268-7312
Check Cashing Store (CCS) 6340 NW 5th Way *Web:* www.ccsfinancial.com	Fort Lauderdale	FL	33309	954-938-3550	938-3565
Dollar Financial Corp 1436 Lancaster Ave Suite 300 *NASDAQ: DLLR* ■ *Web:* www.dfg.com	Berwyn	PA	19312	610-296-3400	296-7844
First Cash Financial Services Inc 690 E Lamar Blvd Suite 400 *NASDAQ: FCFS* ■ *Web:* www.firstcash.com	Arlington	TX	76011	817-460-3947	461-7019
Mister Money Investment 2057 Vermont Dr *TF:* 800-827-7296 ■ *Web:* www.mistermoney.com	Fort Collins	CO	80525	970-493-0574	490-2099
Nix Check Cashing 17019 Kingsview Ave *Web:* www.nixcheckcashing.com	Carson	CA	90746	310-538-2242	538-0131
Pay-O-Matic Corp 160 Oak Dr *TF:* 888-729-3773 ■ *Web:* www.payomatic.com	Syosset	NY	11791	516-496-4900	496-2282
QC Holdings Inc 9401 Indian Creek Pkwy Suite 1500 *NASDAQ: QCCO* ■ *Web:* www.qcholdings.com	Overland Park	KS	66210	866-660-2243	
TeleCheck International Inc 5251 Westheimer Rd *TF:* 800-835-3243 ■ *Web:* www.telecheck.com	Houston	TX	77056	713-331-7600	331-7740
United Financial Services Group 325 Chestnut St # 3000 *TF:* 800-826-0787 ■ *Web:* www.unitedfsg.com	Philadelphia	PA	19106	215-238-0300	238-9056

142 CHECKS - PERSONAL & BUSINESS

	City	State	ZIP	Phone	Fax
Artistic Checks Inc 11501 Otter Creek Rd S PO Box 1000 **Fax Area Code: 866* ■ *TF:* 800-243-2577 ■ *Web:* www.artisticchecks.com	Mabelvale	AR	72103	410-679-3300	567-5560*
Check Printers Inc 1530 Antioch Pike *TF:* 800-766-1217 ■ *Web:* www.check-printers.com	Antioch	TN	37013	615-277-7100	831-0153
CheckCrafters Inc PO Box 100 *TF:* 888-404-5245 ■ *Web:* www.checkcrafters.com	Edgewood	MD	21040	410-679-3300	679-4658
Checks In The Mail Inc 2435 Goodwin Ln **Fax Area Code: 877* ■ *TF:* 888-325-3614 ■ *Web:* www.secure.checksinthemail.com	New Braunfels	TX	78135	830-609-5500	397-1541*
Checks Unlimited 8245 N Union Blvd PO Box 35630 **Fax Area Code: 866* ■ *TF:* 800-565-8332 ■ *Web:* www.checksunlimited.com	Colorado Springs	CO	80935	800-565-8332	231-7024*
Clarke American Checks Inc 10931 Laureate Dr *TF:* 800-382-0818 ■ *Web:* www.clarkeamerican.com	San Antonio	TX	78249	210-697-8888	696-1676
Classic Checks Inc PO Box 2 *TF:* 800-354-3588 ■ *Web:* www.classicchecks.com	Edgewood	MD	21040	410-679-3300	676-1510
Custom Direct LLC 1802 Fashion Ct *TF:* 800-354-3540 ■ *Web:* www.cdi-us.com	Joppa	MD	21085	410-679-3300	676-0950
Deluxe Business Forms 3680 Victoria St N **Fax Area Code: 800* ■ **Fax: Sales* ■ *TF Cust Svc:* 800-328-7205 ■ *Web:* www.deluxe.com	Shoreview	MN	55126	651-483-7111	447-1407*
Deluxe Paper Payment Systems LLC 3660 Victoria St N	Saint Paul	MN	55126	651-490-8000	490-8569
Harland Clarke Holdings Corp 2939 Miller Rd *TF:* 800-723-3690 ■ *Web:* www.harland.net	Decatur	GA	30035	770-981-9460	593-5347
Image Checks Inc PO Box 548 *TF:* 800-562-8768 ■ *Web:* www.imagechecks.com	Little Rock	AR	72203	501-455-1600	455-4299
Safeguard Business Systems Inc 8585 N Stemmons Fwy Suite 600 N *TF:* 800-523-2422 ■ *Web:* www.gosafeguard.com	Dallas	TX	75247	800-523-2422	439-3423

CHEMICALS - AGRICULTURAL

SEE Fertilizers & Pesticides p. 1843

143 CHEMICALS - INDUSTRIAL (INORGANIC)

	City	State	ZIP	Phone	Fax
Advance Research Chemicals Inc 1110 Keystone Ave *Web:* www.fluoridearc.com	Catoosa	OK	74015	918-266-6789	266-6796
Air Liquide America LP 2700 Post Oak Blvd Suite 1800 **Fax: Mktg* ■ *TF:* 877-855-9533 ■ *Web:* www.airliquide.com	Houston	TX	77056	713-624-8000	624-8793*
Air Products & Chemicals Inc 7201 Hamilton Blvd *NYSE: APD* ■ **Fax: Sales* ■ *TF Prod Info:* 800-345-3148 ■ *Web:* www.airproducts.com	Allentown	PA	18195	610-481-4911	481-3855*
AkzoNobel Surface Chemistry LLC 525 W Van Buren St *TF Cust Svc:* 877-565-8432 ■ *Web:* www.akzonobel.com	Chicago	IL	60607	312-544-7006	544-7410
Almatis Inc 501 W Pk Rd *TF:* 800-643-8771 ■ *Web:* www.almatis.com	Leetsdale	PA	15056	412-630-2800	630-2900
American Chemet Corp 740 Waukegan Rd *Web:* www.chemet.com	Deerfield	IL	60015	847-948-0800	948-0811
Americhem Inc 2000 Americhem Way *TF:* 800-228-3476 ■ *Web:* www.americhem.com	Cuyahoga Falls	OH	44221	330-929-4213	929-4144
Ampacet Corp 660 White Plains Rd *TF Cust Svc:* 800-888-4267 ■ *Web:* www.ampacet.com	Tarrytown	NY	10591	914-631-6600	631-7197
Ashta Chemicals Inc 3509 Middle Rd *TF Cust Svc:* 800-492-5082 ■ *Web:* www.ashtachemicals.com	Ashtabula	OH	44004	440-997-5221	992-0151
Baerlocherßproduction USABllc 5890 Highland Ridge Dr *Web:* www.baerlocher.com	Cincinnati	OH	45232	513-482-6300	242-9213
BASF Canada 100 Milverton Dr 5th Fl *TF Cust Svc:* 866-485-2273 ■ *Web:* www2.basf.us/basf-canada	Mississauga	ON	L5R4H1	289-360-1300	360-6000
BASF Corp 100 Campus Dr *NYSE: BF* ■ *TF:* 800-526-1072 ■ *Web:* www.basf.com	Florham Park	NJ	07932	973-245-6000	895-8002
Bio-Lab Inc 1735 N Brown Rd *TF:* 800-859-7946	Lawrenceville	GA	30043	678-502-4000	502-4702
BWX Technologies Inc 1570 Mt Athos Rd *Web:* www.babcock.com	Lynchburg	VA	24504	434-522-6000	522-5922
Cabot Corp 2 Seaport Ln Suite 1300 *NYSE: CBT* ■ *TF:* 800-853-5407 ■ *Web:* www.cabot-corp.com	Boston	MA	02210	617-345-0100	342-6103
Calgon Carbon Corp 500 Calgon Carbon Dr *NYSE: CCC* ■ *TF Cust Svc:* 800-422-7266 ■ *Web:* www.calgoncarbon.com	Pittsburgh	PA	15205	412-787-6700	787-6676
Carus Corp 315 5th St *TF:* 800-435-6856 ■ *Web:* www.caruschem.com	Peru	IL	61354	815-223-1500	224-6697
Chemical Products Corp 102 Old Mill Rd *Web:* www.chemicalproductscorp.com	Cartersville	GA	30120	770-382-2144	386-6053
Circle-Prosco Inc 401 N Gates Dr *Web:* www.circleprosco.com	Bloomington	IN	47404	812-339-3653	331-2566
Cormetech Inc 5000 International Dr *Web:* www.cormetech.com	Durham	NC	27712	919-620-3000	620-3001
Criterion Catalysts & Technologies 16825 Northchase Dr Suite 1000 *TF:* 800-777-2650 ■ *Web:* www.criterioncatalysts.com	Houston	TX	77060	281-874-2600	874-2641
Dow Chemical Co 2030 Dow Ctr *NYSE: DOW* ■ *TF Cust Svc:* 800-422-8193 ■ *Web:* www.dow.com	Midland	MI	48674	989-636-1463	636-1830
DuPont Titanium Technologies 1007 Market St *TF:* 800-441-7515 ■ *Web:* www2.dupont.com	Wilmington	DE	19898	302-774-1000	999-5166
Elementis Chromium 3800 Buddy Lawrence Dr *TF Cust Svc:* 800-531-3188 ■ *Web:* www.elementis.com	Corpus Christi	TX	78407	361-883-6421	883-5145
Energy Research & Generation Inc 900 Stanford Ave *Web:* www.ergaerospace.com	Oakland	CA	94608	510-658-9785	658-7428
Enersul LP 7210 Blackfood Terr SE *Web:* www.enersul.com	Calgary	AB	T2H1M5	403-253-5969	259-2771
Erachem Comilog Inc 610 Pittman Rd *TF:* 800-789-2686 ■ *Web:* www.erachem-comilog.com	Baltimore	MD	21226	410-789-8800	636-7134
ExxonMobil Chemical Co 13501 Katy Fwy *Web:* www.exxonmobilchemical.com	Houston	TX	77079	281-870-6000	870-6661
Ferro Corp Color Div 251 W Wylie Ave PO Box 519	Washington	PA	15301	724-223-5900	223-5901
Ferro Corp Electronic Materials Div 4150 E 56th St	Cleveland	OH	44105	216-641-8580	750-7339
FMC Corp 1735 Market St *NYSE: FMC* ■ *Web:* www.fmc.com	Philadelphia	PA	19103	215-299-6000	299-5998
FMC Corp Industrial Chemicals Group 1735 Market St *TF:* 800-323-7107 ■ *Web:* www.fmcchemicals.com	Philadelphia	PA	19103	215-299-6000	299-6728
General Chemical Group Inc 90 E Halsey Rd *TF Cust Svc:* 800-631-8050 ■ *Web:* www.genchem.com	Parsippany	NJ	07054	973-515-0900	515-3232
Georgia Gulf Corp 115 Perimeter Ctr Pl Suite 460 *NYSE: GGC* ■ *Web:* www.ggc.com	Atlanta	GA	30346	770-395-4500	395-4529
Giles Chemical Corp 102 Commerce St *Web:* www.gileschemical.com	Waynesville	NC	28786	828-452-4784	452-4786
Green Plains Renewable Energy Inc 9420 Underwood Ave Suite 100 *NASDAQ: GPRE* ■ *Web:* www.gpreinc.com	Omaha	NE	68114	402-884-8700	884-8776
Hammond Lead Products Inc 2308 165th St *Web:* www.hammondleadproducts.com	Hammond	IN	46320	219-931-9360	931-2140
Hawkins Inc 3100 E Hennepin Ave *NASDAQ: HWKN* ■ *TF:* 800-328-5460 ■ *Web:* www.hawkinschemical.com	Minneapolis	MN	55413	612-331-6910	331-5304
Henkel Corp 2200 Renaissance Blvd Suite 200 *TF:* 800-521-5317 ■ *Web:* www.henkel.com	Gulph Mills	PA	19406	610-270-8100	270-8102
Heucotech Ltd 99 Newbold Rd *TF:* 800-438-2224	Fairless Hills	PA	19030	215-736-0712	736-2249
Horsehead Corp 4955 Steubenville Pike Suite 405 *TF Cust Svc:* 800-648-8897 ■ *Web:* www.horsehead.net	Pittsburgh	PA	15205	724-774-1020	773-2299
INEOS Silicas Americas 111 Ingalls Ave *TF:* 800-775-3651 ■ *Web:* www.ineossilicas.com	Joliet	IL	60435	815-727-3651	727-5312
Interstate Chemical Co Inc 2797 Freedland Rd *TF:* 800-422-2436 ■ *Web:* www.interstatechemical.com	Hermitage	PA	16148	724-981-3771	981-8383
Johnson Matthey Inc Catalysts & Chemicals Div 2001 Nolte Dr *TF:* 800-444-1411 ■ *Web:* www.chemicals.matthey.com	West Deptford	NJ	08066	856-853-8000	384-7282
Jones Hamilton Co 30354 Tracy Rd *TF:* 877-797-5426 ■ *Web:* www.jones-hamilton.com	Walbridge	OH	43465	419-666-9838	662-5049
Kanto Corp 13424 N Woodrush Way *TF:* 866-609-5571 ■ *Web:* www.kantocorp.com	Portland	OR	97203	503-283-0405	240-0409
Keystone Aniline Corp 2501 W Fulton St *TF:* 800-522-4393 ■ *Web:* www.dyes.com	Chicago	IL	60612	312-666-2015	666-8530
LSB Industries Inc 16 S Pennsylvania Ave *AMEX: LXU* ■ *Web:* www.lsb-okc.com	Oklahoma City	OK	73107	405-235-4546	235-5067
Martin Marietta Magnesia Specialties Inc 8140 Corporate Dr Suite 220 *TF:* 800-648-7400 ■ *Web:* www.magspecialties.com	Baltimore	MD	21236	410-780-5500	780-5777

	City	State	Zip	Phone	Fax
Matheson Tri-Gas Inc 959 Rt 46 E	Parsippany	NJ	07054	973-257-1100	257-9393
Web: www.mathesongas.com					
Minerals Technologies Inc					
622 3rd Ave 38th Fl	New York	NY	10017	212-878-1831	878-1801
NYSE: MTX ■ *Web:* www.mineralstech.com					
Moravek Biochemicals Inc 577 Mercury Ln	Brea	CA	92821	714-990-2018	990-1824
Web: www.moravek.com					
National Welders Supply Co Inc					
810 Gesco St	Charlotte	NC	28208	704-333-5475	342-0260
TF: 800-866-4422 ■ *Web:* www.nwsco.com					
NL Industries Inc					
16825 Northchase Dr Suite 1200	Houston	TX	77060	281-423-3300	423-3258
NYSE: NL ■ *TF:* 800-866-5600 ■ *Web:* www.nl-ind.com					
Noah Technologies Corp of Texas					
1 Noah Pk	San Antonio	TX	78249	210-691-2000	691-2600
Web: www.noahtech.com					
Norit Americas Inc					
3200 W University Ave PO Box 790	Marshall	TX	75671	903-923-1000	938-9701
TF: 800-641-9245 ■ *Web:* www.norit-americas.com					
Nuclear Fuel Services Inc 1205 Banner Hill Rd	Erwin	TN	37650	423-743-9141	743-9025
Web: www.nuclearfuelservices.com					
Occidental Chemical Corp 5005 LBJ Fwy	Dallas	TX	75244	972-404-3300	404-3669
TF: 800-752-5151 ■ *Web:* www.oxychem.com					
Occidental Petroleum Corp					
10889 Wilshire Blvd	Los Angeles	CA	90024	310-208-8800	443-6690
NYSE: OXY ■ *TF:* 800-752-5151 ■ *Web:* www.oxy.com					
Old Bridge Chemicals Inc PO Box 175	Old Bridge	NJ	08857	732-727-2225	727-2653
TF: 800-275-3924 ■ *Web:* www.oldbridgechem.com					
Olin Corp Olin Chlor Alkali Products Div					
490 Stuart Rd NE	Cleveland	TN	37312	423-336-4850	336-4830
Web: www.chloralkali.com					
OMYA Inc 61 Main St	Proctor	VT	05765	802-459-3311	459-6327
TF: 800-451-4468 ■ *Web:* www.omya-na.com					
Phibro Animal Health Corp					
65 Challenger Rd 3rd Fl	Ridgefield Park	NJ	07660	201-329-7300	329-7399
TF: 800-223-0434 ■ *Web:* www.phibrochem.com					
Plasticolors Inc					
2600 Michigan Ave PO Box 816	Ashtabula	OH	44005	440-997-5137	992-3613
TF: 888-997-5137 ■ *Web:* www.plasticolors.com					
Potash Corp 1101 Skokie Blvd	Northbrook	IL	60062	847-849-4200	849-4695
TF: 800-645-2183 ■ *Web:* www.potashcorp.com					
Praxair Inc 39 Old Ridgebury Rd	Danbury	CT	06810	203-837-2000	837-2731
NYSE: PX ■ *TF:* 800-772-9247 ■ *Web:* www.praxair.com					
Rutgers Organics Corp 201 Struble Rd	State College	PA	16801	814-238-2424	238-1567
TF: 800-458-3434 ■ *Web:* www.ruetgers-organics-corp.com					
Shepherd Chemical Co 4900 Beech St	Cincinnati	OH	45212	513-731-1110	731-1532
Web: www.shepchem.com					
Silberline Mfg Co Inc 130 Lincoln Dr PO Box B	Tamaqua	PA	18252	570-668-6050	668-0197
TF: 800-348-4824 ■ *Web:* www.silberline.com					
Solutia Inc 575 Maryville Centre Dr	Saint Louis	MO	63141	314-674-1000	674-1585*
**Fax:* Hum Res ■ *TF:* 800-325-4330 ■ *Web:* www.solutia.com					
Solvay America Inc 3333 Richmond Ave	Houston	TX	77098	713-525-6000	525-7887
TF: 800-231-6313 ■ *Web:* www.solvay.com					
Southern Ionics Inc 201 Commerce St	West Point	MS	39773	662-494-3055	495-2590
TF: 800-953-3585 ■ *Web:* www.southernionics.com					
Sud-Chemie Inc PO Box 32370	Louisville	KY	40232	502-634-7200	637-3732
Web: www.sud-chemie.com					
Synalloy Corp					
2155 W Croft Cir PO Box 5627	Spartanburg	SC	29304	864-585-3605	596-1501
NASDAQ: SYNL ■ *TF Orders:* 800-763-1001 ■ *Web:* www.synalloy.com					
Tanner Systems Inc 625 19th Ave NE	Saint Joseph	MN	56374	320-363-1800	362-1812
TF: 800-461-6454 ■ *Web:* www.tannersystems.com					
TETRA Technologies Inc 25025 I-45 N	The Woodlands	TX	77380	281-367-1983	364-4306
NYSE: TTI ■ *TF:* 800-327-7817 ■ *Web:* www.tetratec.com					
Texas United Corp 4800 San Felipe St	Houston	TX	77056	713-877-1793	877-2664
TF: 800-554-8658					
TOR Minerals International Inc					
722 Burleson St	Corpus Christi	TX	78302	361-882-5175	883-7619
NASDAQ: TORM ■ *TF:* 888-464-0147 ■ *Web:* www.torminerals.com					
Tronox Inc 3301 NW 150th St	Oklahoma City	OK	73134	405-775-5000	775-5155
PINK: TRXAQ ■ *TF:* 866-775-5009 ■ *Web:* www.tronox.com					
UOP LLC 25 E Algonquin Rd	Des Plaines	IL	60017	847-391-2000	391-2253
TF: 800-877-6184 ■ *Web:* www.uop.com					
USEC Inc 6903 Rockledge Dr 4th Fl	Bethesda	MD	20817	301-564-3200	564-3201
NYSE: USU ■ *TF:* 800-273-7754 ■ *Web:* www.usec.com					
Vulcan Materials Co					
1200 Urban Ctr Dr PO Box 385014	Birmingham	AL	35238	205-298-3000	298-2942
NYSE: VMC ■ *TF:* 800-615-4331 ■ *Web:* www.vulcanmaterials.com					
Westlake Chemical Corp					
2801 Post Oak Blvd Suite 600	Houston	TX	77056	713-960-9111	963-1562
NYSE: WLK ■ *TF:* 888-953-3623 ■ *Web:* www.westlakechemical.com					

144 CHEMICALS - INDUSTRIAL (ORGANIC)

	City	State	Zip	Phone	Fax
Abengoa Bioenergy Corp					
16150 Main Cir Dr Suite 300	Chesterfield	MO	63017	636-728-0508	728-1148
Web: www.abengoabioenergy.com					
Advanced Chemtech Inc 5609 Fern Vly Rd	Louisville	KY	40228	502-969-0000	968-1000
Web: www.advancedchemtech.com					
Ag Rx Inc 751 S Rose Ave	Oxnard	CA	93030	805-487-0696	483-6146
Web: www.agrx.com					
Altair Nanotechnologies Inc 204 Edison Way	Reno	NV	89502	775-856-2500	856-1619
NASDAQ: ALTI ■ *Web:* www.altairnano.com					
American Natural Soda Ash Corp					
15 Riverside Ave	Westport	CT	06880	203-226-9056	227-1484
Web: www.ansac.com					
Ampacet Corp 660 White Plains Rd	Tarrytown	NY	10591	914-631-6600	631-7197
TF Cust Svc: 800-888-4267 ■ *Web:* www.ampacet.com					
Arizona Chemical Co Inc					
4600 Touchton Rd E # 1500	Jacksonville	FL	32246	904-928-8700	928-8778
Web: www.arizonachemical.com					
Badger State Ethanol LLC					
820 W 17th St PO Box 317	Monroe	WI	53566	608-329-3900	329-3866
Web: www.badgerstateethanol.com					
Bayer Corp 100 Bayer Rd	Pittsburgh	PA	15205	412-777-2000	778-4430
TF: 800-422-9374 ■ *Web:* www.bayerus.com					
Bayer Corp Chemicals Div 100 Bayer Rd	Pittsburgh	PA	15205	412-777-2000	777-7626
TF: 800-662-2927 ■ *Web:* www.bayerus.com					
Bayer Inc 77 Belfield Rd	Toronto	ON	M9W1G6	416-248-0771	248-1297*
**Fax:* Hum Res ■ *TF:* 800-622-2937 ■ *Web:* www.bayer.ca					
BP Plc 28100 Torch Pkwy	Warrenville	IL	60555	630-420-5111	298-0738*
NYSE: BP ■ **Fax Area Code:* 281 ■ *TF:* 866-427-6947 ■ *Web:* www.bp.com					
Cambrex Corp					
1 Meadowlands Plaza 15th Fl	East Rutherford	NJ	07073	201-804-3000	804-9852
NYSE: CBM ■ *TF:* 800-638-8174 ■ *Web:* www.cambrex.com					
Cardolite Corp 500 Doremus Ave	Newark	NJ	07105	973-344-5015	344-1197
Web: www.cardolite.com					
Celanese Corp 1601 W LBJ Fwy	Dallas	TX	75234	972-443-4000	443-8557
NYSE: CE ■ *Web:* www.celanese.com					
Chemical Exchange Industries Inc					
900 Clinton Dr PO Box 67	Galena Park	TX	77547	713-526-8291	455-8959
Web: www.cxi.com					
Chemstar Products Co 3915 Hiawatha Ave	Minneapolis	MN	55406	612-722-0079	722-2473
TF: 800-328-5037 ■ *Web:* www.chemstar.com					
Chevron Phillips Chemical Co LP					
10001 Six Pines Dr	The Woodlands	TX	77380	832-813-4100	
TF: 800-231-1212 ■ *Web:* www.cpchem.com					
Cognis Corp 5051 Estecreek Dr	Cincinnati	OH	45232	513-482-3000	482-5503
TF Cust Svc: 800-254-1029 ■ *Web:* www.na.cognis.com					
Colgate-Palmolive Co Institutional Products Div					
191 E Hanover Ave	Morristown	NJ	07962	973-630-1500	292-6172*
**Fax:* Hum Res ■ *TF:* 888-276-0783					
Colorcon Inc 415 Moyer Blvd	West Point	PA	19486	215-699-7733	661-2605
Web: www.colorcon.com					
Corsicana Technologies Inc 2733 E Hwy 31	Corsicana	TX	75110	903-874-9500	874-9595
TF: 800-477-5353 ■ *Web:* www.corsicanatech.com					
Dodge Chemical Co Inc The					
165 Cambridgepark Dr	Cambridge	MA	02140	617-661-0500	661-1428
TF: 800-443-6343 ■ *Web:* www.dodgeco.com					
Dow Chemical Canada Inc (DCCI)					
450 1st St SW Suite 2100	Calgary	AB	T2P5H1	403-267-3500	267-3597
TF: 800-447-4369 ■ *Web:* www.dow.com					
Dow Chemical Co 2030 Dow Ctr	Midland	MI	48674	989-636-1463	636-1830
NYSE: DOW ■ *TF Cust Svc:* 800-422-8193 ■ *Web:* www.dow.com					
Dow Corning Corp PO Box 994	Midland	MI	48686	989-496-4000	496-1886*
**Fax:* Hum Res ■ *TF Cust Svc:* 800-248-2481 ■ *Web:* www.dowcorning.com					
DSM Chemicals North America Inc					
1 Columbia Nitrogen Rd	Augusta	GA	30901	706-849-6600	849-6760*
**Fax:* Cust Svc ■ *TF:* 800-825-4376 ■ *Web:* www.dsm.com					
Eastman Chemical Co 200 S Wilcox Dr	Kingsport	TN	37660	423-229-2000	229-1194*
NYSE: EMN ■ **Fax:* Mktg ■ *TF Cust Svc:* 800-327-8626 ■ *Web:* www.eastman.com					
Elan Chemical Co 268 Doremus Ave	Newark	NJ	07105	973-344-8014	344-8014
Web: www.elan-chemical.com					
Ferro Corp Grant Chemical Div 111 W Irene Rd	Zachary	LA	70791	225-654-6801	654-3268
TF: 800-325-3578 ■ *Web:* www.ferro.com					
Ferro Corp Polymer Additives Div					
7050 Krick Rd	Walton Hills	OH	44146	216-641-8580	439-7686*
**Fax Area Code:* 440 ■ *TF:* 800-321-9946					
First Chemical Corp 1001 Industrial Rd	Pascagoula	MS	39581	228-762-0870	769-5355
TF: 877-243-6178 ■ *Web:* www.firstchem.com					
GE Petrochemicals Inc SR 892	Washington	WV	26181	304-863-7778	863-7791
TF: 800-643-4346 ■ *Web:* www.ge.com					
Heucotech Ltd 99 Newbold Rd	Fairless Hills	PA	19030	215-736-0712	736-2249
TF: 800-438-2224					
Huntsman Corp 500 Huntsman Way	Salt Lake City	UT	84108	801-584-5700	584-5781
NYSE: HUN ■ *TF:* 800-421-2411 ■ *Web:* www.huntsman.com					
ICC Industries Inc 460 Pk Ave	New York	NY	10022	212-521-1700	521-1794
TF: 800-422-1720 ■ *Web:* www.iccchem.com					
Innospec Inc 8375 S Willow St	Littleton	CO	80124	303-792-5554	451-1380*
NYSE: IOP ■ **Fax Area Code:* 302 ■ *Web:* www.innospecinc.com					
Inolex Chemical Co 2101 S Swanson St	Philadelphia	PA	19148	215-271-0800	271-6282*
**Fax:* Cust Svc ■ *TF Cust Svc:* 800-521-9891 ■ *Web:* www.inolex.com					
International Flavors & Fragrances Inc (IFF)					
521 W 57th St	New York	NY	10019	212-765-5500	708-7132
NYSE: IFF ■ *Web:* www.iff.com					
International Specialty Products Inc (ISP)					
1361 Alps Rd	Wayne	NJ	07470	973-628-4000	628-3311
TF: 800-622-4423 ■ *Web:* www.online1.ispcorp.com					
Kingsford Products Co Inc 1221 Broadway	Oakland	CA	94612	510-271-7000	832-1463
Web: www.kingsford.com					
Lifeline Foods LLC 2811 S 11th St Rd	Saint Joseph	MO	64503	816-279-1651	232-6926
Web: www.lifeline-foods.com					
Light Fabrications Inc 40 Hytec Cir	Rochester	NY	14606	585-426-5330	426-5239
TF: 800-836-6920 ■ *Web:* www.lightfab.com					
Methanex Corp					
1800 Waterfront Centre 200 Burrard St	Vancouver	BC	V6C3M1	604-661-2600	661-2676
NASDAQ: MEOH ■ *TF:* 800-661-8851 ■ *Web:* www.methanex.com					
Millennium Chemicals Inc					
20 Wight Ave Suite 100	Hunt Valley	MD	21030	410-229-4400	229-5003
TF: 866-225-5642 ■ *Web:* www.millenniumchem.com					
Mitsubishi Chemical Holdings America					
1 N Lexington Ave	White Plains	NY	10601	914-286-3600	286-3677
Web: www.mitsubishichemical.com					
Mitsui Chemicals America Inc					
800 Westchester Ave	Rye Brook	NY	10573	914-253-0777	253-0790*
**Fax:* PR ■ *TF:* 800-682-2377 ■ *Web:* www.mitsuichemicals.com					
National Enzyme Co Inc 15366 US Hwy 160	Forsyth	MO	65653	417-546-4796	546-2329
TF: 800-825-8545 ■ *Web:* www.nationalenzyme.com					
Niacet Corp 400 47th St	Niagara Falls	NY	14304	716-285-1474	285-1497
TF: 800-828-1207 ■ *Web:* www.niacet.com					

	City	State	ZIP	Phone	Fax
Norquay Technology Inc 800 W Front St PO Box 468	Chester	PA	19013	610-874-4330	874-3575
Web: www.norquaytech.com					
Oakwood Products Inc 1741 Old Dunbar Rd	West Columbia	SC	29172	803-739-8800	739-6957
TF: 800-467-3386 ■ *Web:* www.oakwoodchemical.com					
Pacer Fuels Retail Inc 1950 Royal Indus Blvd	Austell	GA	30106	678-217-7100	217-7103
Web: www.pacerfuels.com					
Pencco Inc 831 Bartlett Rd PO Box 600	San Felipe	TX	77473	979-885-0005	885-3208
TF: 800-864-1742 ■ *Web:* www.pencco.com					
Perstorp Polyols Inc 600 Matzinger Rd	Toledo	OH	43612	419-729-5448	729-3291
TF Cust Svc: 800-537-0280 ■ *Web:* www.perstorppolyols.com					
PMC Specialties Group Inc 501 Murray Rd	Cincinnati	OH	45217	513-242-3300	482-7315
TF: 800-543-2466 ■ *Web:* www.pmcsg.com					
PPG Industries Inc 1 PPG Pl	Pittsburgh	PA	15272	412-434-3131	434-2011*
NYSE: PPG ■ **Fax:* Hum Res ■ *Web:* www.ppg.com					
RT Vanderbilt Co Inc 30 Winfield St	Norwalk	CT	06855	203-853-1400	853-1452
TF Cust Svc: 800-243-6064 ■ *Web:* www.rtvanderbilt.com					
Sachem Inc 821 Woodward St	Austin	TX	78704	512-444-3626	440-7324
Web: www.sacheminc.com					
Sasol North America Inc 900 Threadneedle St Suite 100	Houston	TX	77079	281-588-3000	588-3144
Web: www.sasolnorthamerica.com					
Selee Corp 700 Shepherd St	Hendersonville	NC	28792	828-606-2532	693-1868
Web: www.selee.com					
Shell Chemical Co 910 Louisiana St	Houston	TX	77002	713-241-6161	241-4044
Web: www.shellchemicals.com					
Shin-Etsu Silicones of America 1150 Damar Dr	Akron	OH	44305	330-630-9860	630-9855
TF: 800-544-1745 ■ *Web:* www.shinetsusilicones.com					
Solutia Inc 575 Maryville Centre Dr	Saint Louis	MO	63141	314-674-1000	674-1585*
**Fax:* Hum Res ■ *TF:* 800-325-4330 ■ *Web:* www.solutia.com					
Struktol Co Of America Inc PO Box 1649	Stow	OH	44224	330-928-5188	928-8726
TF: 800-327-8649 ■ *Web:* www.struktol.com					
Sun Chemical Corp 35 Waterview Blvd	Parsippany	NJ	07054	973-404-6000	404-6001
Web: www.sunchemical.com					
Sunoco Chemicals 1735 Market St Suite LL	Philadelphia	PA	19103	215-977-3000	977-3470
TF: 800-786-6261 ■ *Web:* www.sunocochem.com					
Sunoco Inc 1735 Market St Suite LL	Philadelphia	PA	19103	215-977-3000	977-3409
NYSE: SUN ■ *TF:* 800-786-6261 ■ *Web:* www.sunocoinc.com					
Synalloy Corp 2155 W Croft Cir PO Box 5627	Spartanburg	SC	29304	864-585-3605	596-1501
NASDAQ: SYNL ■ *TF Orders:* 800-763-1001 ■ *Web:* www.synalloy.com					
Tedia Co Inc 1000 Tedia Way	Fairfield	OH	45014	513-874-5340	874-5346
TF: 800-787-4891 ■ *Web:* www.tedia.com					
Texas Petrochemicals LP (TPC group) 5151 San Felipe Suite 800	Houston	TX	77056	713-627-7474	626-3650
TF: 877-584-3256 ■ *Web:* www.tpcgrp.com					
Velsicol Chemical Corp 10400 W Higgins Rd Suite 600	Rosemont	IL	60018	847-298-9000	298-9018
TF Cust Svc: 800-843-7759 ■ *Web:* www.velsicol.com					
Vulcan Materials Co 1200 Urban Ctr Dr PO Box 385014	Birmingham	AL	35238	205-298-3000	298-2942
NYSE: VMC ■ *TF:* 800-615-4331 ■ *Web:* www.vulcanmaterials.com					
Wacker Chemical Corp 3301 Sutton Rd	Adrian	MI	49221	517-264-8500	264-8246
TF: 888-922-5374 ■ *Web:* www.wacker.com					
Waterworks America Inc 5005 Rockside Rd Crown Centre 6th Fl	Cleveland	OH	44131	440-237-0909	
Web: www.1water.com					
Wausau Chemical Corp 2001 N River Dr	Wausau	WI	54403	715-842-2285	842-9059
TF: 800-950-6656 ■ *Web:* www.wausauchemical.com					
Western Polymer Corp 32 Rd 'R' SE	Moses Lake	WA	98837	509-765-1803	765-0327
Web: www.westernpolymer.com					
Wyoming Ethanol LLC PO Box 178	Torrington	WY	82240	307-532-2449	532-8964
Web: www.ethanol.org					

CHEMICALS - MEDICINAL

SEE Medicinal Chemicals & Botanical Products p. 2231

145 CHEMICALS - SPECIALTY

	City	State	ZIP	Phone	Fax
ADA-ES Inc 8100 Southpark Way Suite B	Littleton	CO	80120	303-734-1727	734-0330
NASDAQ: ADES ■ *TF:* 888-822-8617 ■ *Web:* www.adaes.com					
Afton Chemical Corp 500 Spring St	Richmond	VA	23219	804-788-5800	788-5184
Web: www.aftonchemical.com					
Airosol Co Inc 1206 Illinois St	Neodesha	KS	66757	620-325-2666	325-2602
TF: 800-633-9576 ■ *Web:* www.airosol.com					
Akzo Nobel Chemicals Inc 10 Finderne Ave	Bridgewater	NJ	08807	888-331-6212	707-3664*
**Fax Area Code:* 908 ■ *TF:* 888-331-6212 ■ *Web:* www.akzonobel.com					
Alex C Fergusson Inc 5000 Letterkenny Rd Suite 220	Chambersburg	PA	17201	717-264-9147	264-9147
TF: 800-345-1329 ■ *Web:* www.afcocare.us					
Alfa Aesar Co 26 Parkridge Rd 2nd Fl	Ward Hill	MA	01835	978-521-6300	322-4757*
**Fax Area Code:* 800 ■ *TF:* 800-343-0660 ■ *Web:* www.alfa.com					
Allied Diagnostic Imaging Resources Inc 5440 Oakbrook Pkwy	Norcross	GA	30093	770-448-0250	995-2443*
**Fax Area Code:* 201 ■ *TF:* 800-262-9333 ■ *Web:* www.alliedautex.com					
Altana Inc *nycomed Inc* 60 Baylis Rd	Melville	NY	11747	631-454-7677	756-7017
Web: www.altana.com					
AM Todd Co 1717 Douglas Ave	Kalamazoo	MI	49007	269-343-2603	343-3399
TF: 800-968-2603 ■ *Web:* www.amtodd.com					
American Pacific Corp (AMPAC) 3883 Howard Hughes Pkwy Suite 700	Las Vegas	NV	89169	702-735-2200	735-4876
NASDAQ: APFC ■ *Web:* www.american-pacific-corp.com					
American Polywater Corp 11222 60th St N	Stillwater	MN	55082	651-430-2270	430-3634
TF: 800-328-9384 ■ *Web:* www.polywater.com					
American Radiolabeled Chemicals Inc (ARC) 101 ARC Dr	Saint Louis	MO	63146	314-991-4545	991-4692
TF: 800-331-6661 ■ *Web:* www.arc-inc.com					
American Vanguard Corp 4695 MacArthur Ct	Newport Beach	CA	92660	949-260-1200	260-1201
AMEX: AVD ■ *Web:* www.american-vanguard.com					
Ameron International Corp 245 S Los Robles Ave	Pasadena	CA	91101	626-683-4000	683-4060
NYSE: AMN ■ *Web:* www.ameron.com					
AMJAY Chemicals PO Box 218786	Houston	TX	77218	281-492-2000	
AMPAC Fine Chemicals (AFC) Hwy 50 & Hazel Ave PO Box 1718 MS 1007	Rancho Cordova	CA	95741	916-357-6880	353-3523
TF: 800-311-9668 ■ *Web:* www.ampacfinechemicals.com					
AMREP Inc 990 Industrial Pk Dr	Marietta	GA	30062	770-422-2071	422-1737
TF Cust Svc: 800-241-7766 ■ *Web:* www.amrep.com					
Anderson Chemical Co 325 S Davis Ave PO Box 1041	Litchfield	MN	55355	320-693-2477	693-8238
TF: 800-366-2477 ■ *Web:* www.andersonchemco.com					
Anderson Development Co 1415 E Michigan St	Adrian	MI	49221	517-263-2121	263-1000
Web: www.andersondevelopment.com					
Angstrom Technologies Inc 7880 Foundation Dr	Florence	KY	41042	859-282-0020	282-8577
TF Cust Svc: 800-543-7358 ■ *Web:* www.angstromtechnologies.com					
Apollo Chemical Co LLC 1105 Southerland St	Graham	NC	27253	336-226-1161	226-7494
TF: 800-374-3827 ■ *Web:* www.apollochemical.com					
Arch Chemicals Inc 501 Merritt Seven PO Box 5204	Norwalk	CT	06856	203-229-2900	229-2880
NYSE: ARJ ■ *TF:* 800-636-3786 ■ *Web:* www.archchemicals.com					
Ashland Specialty Chemical Co 1745 Cottage St	Ashland	OH	44805	419-289-9588	
Web: www.ashland.com					
Athea Laboratories Inc 6161 N 64th St	Milwaukee	WI	53218	414-354-6417	354-9219
TF: 800-743-6417 ■ *Web:* www.athea.com					
Atlas Refinery Inc 142 Lockwood St	Newark	NJ	07105	973-589-2002	589-7377
Web: www.atlasrefinery.com					
Baker Hughes Inc Baker Petrolite Div 12645 W Airport Blvd	Sugar Land	TX	77478	281-276-5400	275-7392*
**Fax:* Hum Res ■ *TF:* 800-231-3606 ■ *Web:* www.bakerhughes.com					
Barclay Water Management Inc 150 Coolidge Ave	Watertown	MA	02472	617-926-3400	924-5467
Web: www.barclaywm.com					
Baroid Drilling Fluids 3000 N Sam Houston Pkwy E Bldg J	Houston	TX	77032	281-871-5900	871-5565*
**Fax:* Hum Res ■ *Web:* www.baroid.com					
BASF Admixture Systems 23700 Chagrin Blvd	Beachwood	OH	44122	216-839-7500	839-8821
TF: 800-628-9990 ■ *Web:* www.basf-admixtures.com					
BASF Wall Systems 3550 St Johns Bluff Rd S	Jacksonville	FL	32224	904-996-6000	996-6300
TF: 800-221-9255 ■ *Web:* www.wallsystems.basf.com					
Bedoukian Research Inc 21 Finance Dr	Danbury	CT	06810	203-830-4000	830-4010
Web: www.bedoukian.com					
Berje Inc 5 Lawrence St	Bloomfield	NJ	07003	973-748-8980	680-9618
Web: www.berjeinc.com					
Birchwood Laboratories Inc 7900 Fuller Rd	Eden Prairie	MN	55344	952-937-7900	937-7979
TF: 800-328-6156 ■ *Web:* www.birchwoodcasey.com					
Blue Grass Chemical Specialties LP 895 Industrial Blvd	New Albany	IN	47150	812-948-1115	948-1561
TF: 800-638-7197					
Brewster Foods Inc 7121 Candy Ave PO Box 306	Reseda	CA	91335	818-881-4268	881-6370
Web: www.testlabinc.com					
Brulin & Co Inc 2920 Dr AJ Brown Ave	Indianapolis	IN	46205	317-923-3211	925-4596
TF: 800-776-7149 ■ *Web:* www.brulin.com					
Buckman Laboratories Inc 1256 N McLean Blvd	Memphis	TN	38108	901-278-0330	
TF: 800-282-5626 ■ *Web:* www.buckman.com					
Bullen Midwest 900 E 103rd St	Chicago	IL	60628	773-785-2300	785-9969
TF: 800-621-8553 ■ *Web:* www.nuancesol.com					
Cabot Corp 2 Seaport Ln Suite 1300	Boston	MA	02210	617-345-0100	342-6103
NYSE: CBT ■ *TF:* 800-853-5407 ■ *Web:* www.cabot-corp.com					
Cabot Microelectronics Corp 870 N Commons Dr	Aurora	IL	60504	630-375-6631	375-5539
NASDAQ: CCMP ■ *TF:* 800-811-2756 ■ *Web:* www.cabotcmp.com					
Cabot Specialty Fluids Inc Waterway Plaza Two 10001 Woodlock Forest Dr Suite 275	The Woodlands	TX	77380	281-298-9955	298-6190
TF: 888-273-7455 ■ *Web:* www.formatebrines.com					
Cal-Pac Chemical Co Inc 6231 Maywood Ave	Huntington Park	CA	90255	323-585-2178	585-3087
Cambridge Isotope Laboratories Inc 50 Frontage Rd	Andover	MA	01810	978-749-8000	749-2768
Web: www.isotope.com					
Champion Technologies Inc 3200 SW Fwy Suite 2700	Houston	TX	77027	713-627-3303	627-7603
Web: www.champ-tech.com					
Chem Lab Products Inc 5180 E Airport Dr	Ontario	CA	91761	909-390-9912	390-9911
TF: 800-745-4536 ■ *Web:* www.kem-tek.com					
Chemtool Inc 8200 Ridgefield Rd	Crystal Lake	IL	60039	815-459-1250	459-1955
Web: www.chemtool.com					
Chippewa Valley Ethanol Co LLC 270 20th St NW	Benson	MN	56215	320-843-4813	843-4800
Web: www.cvec.com					
CHT R Beitlich Corp 5046 Old Pineville Rd	Charlotte	NC	28217	704-529-1274	522-8142
TF: 800-277-4941 ■ *Web:* www.cht-group.com					
Citrus & Allied Essences Ltd 3000 Marcus Ave Suite 3E11	Lake Success	NY	11042	516-354-1200	354-1262
Web: www.citrusandallied.com					
Claire Mfg Co 1005 S Westgate Ave	Addison	IL	60101	630-543-7600	543-4310
TF Sales: 800-252-4731 ■ *Web:* www.clairemfg.com					
Cognis Corp 5051 Estecreek Dr	Cincinnati	OH	45232	513-482-3000	482-5503
TF Cust Svc: 800-254-1029 ■ *Web:* www.na.cognis.com					
Columbian Chemicals Co 1800 W Oak Commons Ct	Marietta	GA	30062	770-792-9400	792-9623
TF: 800-235-4003 ■ *Web:* www.columbianchemicals.com					
Coral Chemical Co 1915 Industrial Blvd	Zion	IL	60099	847-246-6666	246-6667
TF: 800-228-4646 ■ *Web:* www.coral.com					

Company	City	State	ZIP	Phone	Fax
Cortec Corp 4119 White Bear Pkwy *TF:* 800-426-7832 ■ *Web:* www.cortecvci.com	Saint Paul	MN	55110	651-429-1100	429-1122
CPC Aeroscience Inc 2700 SW 14th St *TF Cust Svc:* 800-327-1835 ■ *Web:* www.terandstore.com	Pompano Beach	FL	33069	954-974-5440	977-7513
CRC Industries Inc 885 Louis Dr *TF Cust Svc:* 800-556-5074 ■ *Web:* www.crcindustries.com	Warminster	PA	18974	215-674-4300	674-2196
Croda Inc 300 Columbus Cir # A *TF:* 888-252-7632 ■ *Web:* www.croda.com	Edison	NJ	08837	732-417-0800	417-0804
Cytec Industries Inc 5 Garret Mountain Plaza *NYSE: CYT* ■ *TF:* 800-652-6013 ■ *Web:* www.cytec.com	West Paterson	NJ	07424	973-357-3100	357-3060
Delta Chemical Corp 2601 Cannery Ave *TF:* 800-282-5322 ■ *Web:* www.deltachemical.com	Baltimore	MD	21226	410-354-0100	354-1021
Detrex Corp 24901 Northwestern Hwy Suite 410 *Web:* www.detrex.com	Southfield	MI	48075	248-358-5800	799-7192
Dexter Chemical LLC 845 Edgewater Rd *TF:* 800-339-9111	Bronx	NY	10474	718-542-7700	542-7700
Diversified Chemical Technologies Inc (DCT) 15477 Woodrow Wilson St *TF:* 800-243-1424 ■ *Web:* www.diversifiedchemicalinc.com	Detroit	MI	48238	313-867-5444	867-3831
Dober Chemical Group 11230 Katherine Crossing *TF:* 800-323-4983 ■ *Web:* www.dobergroup.com	Woodridge	IL	60517	630-410-7300	410-7444
Dover Chemical Corp 3000 Sheffield Ave *TF:* 800-426-3042 ■ *Web:* www.doverchem.com	Hammond	IN	46327	219-931-2630	853-9703
DSM Desotech Inc 1122 St Charles St **Fax:* Sales ■ *TF:* 800-222-7189 ■ *Web:* www.dsm.com	Elgin	IL	60120	847-697-0400	468-7785*
DuPont Chemical Solutions 1007 Market St *TF:* 800-441-7515 ■ *Web:* www.dupont.com	Wilmington	DE	19898	302-774-1000	355-4013
Dynaloy LLC 6445 Olivia Ln *TF:* 800-669-5709 ■ *Web:* www.dynaloy.com	Indianapolis	IN	46226	317-788-5694	788-5690
Eastman Gelatine Corp 227 Washington St *Web:* www.eastmangelatine.com	Peabody	MA	01960	978-573-3700	573-3880
ELANTAS PDG INC 5200 N 2nd St *TF:* 800-325-7492 ■ *Web:* www.elantas.com	Saint Louis	MO	63147	314-621-5700	436-1030
Elementis Specialities Inc 329 Wyckoffs Mill Rd PO Box 700 *TF Cust Svc:* 800-418-5196 ■ *Web:* www.elementisspecialities.com	Hightstown	NJ	08520	609-443-2500	443-2422
Eltech Systems Corp 100 7th Ave Suite 300 *TF:* 800-795-6832 ■ *Web:* www.denora.com	Chardon	OH	44024	440-285-0300	285-0300
Enthone Inc 350 Frontage Rd *TF:* 800-496-8326 ■ *Web:* www.enthone.com	West Haven	CT	06516	203-934-8611	932-5061
Excelda Mfg Co 12785 Emerson Dr *TF:* 800-550-4062 ■ *Web:* www.excelda.com	Brighton	MI	48116	248-486-3800	486-3810
Fabric Chemical Corp 61 Cornelison Ave	Jersey City	NJ	07304	201-432-0440	432-7997
FMC Corp Specialty Chemicals Group 1735 Market St *Web:* www.fmc.com	Philadelphia	PA	19103	215-299-6000	299-5998
Foseco Metallurgical Inc 20200 Sheldon Rd *TF:* 800-321-3132 ■ *Web:* www.fosecomet.com	Cleveland	OH	44142	440-826-4548	826-3434
Frac Tech Services LLC 16858 IH- 20 *TF:* 866-877-1008 ■ *Web:* www.fractech.net	Cisco	TX	76437	817-850-1008	850-1026
Freezetone Products Inc 7986 NW 14th St *Web:* www.freezetone-usa.com	Doral	FL	33126	305-640-0414	640-0454
Fremont Industries Inc 4400 Valley Industrial Blvd N PO Box 67 *TF:* 800-436-1238 ■ *Web:* www.fremontind.com	Shakopee	MN	55379	952-445-4121	496-3027
GE Betz 4636 Somerton Rd **Fax Area Code:* 888 ■ *TF Cust Svc:* 866-439-8372	Trevose	PA	19053	866-755-5936	422-5878*
Genieco Inc 200 N Laflin St *TF:* 800-223-8217 ■ *Web:* www.gonesh.net	Chicago	IL	60607	312-421-2383	421-3042
GEO Specialty Chemicals Inc 401 S Earl Suite 3-A *Web:* www.geosc.com	Lafayette	IN	47904	765-448-9412	448-6728
Gold Eagle Co 4400 S Kildare Ave **Fax Area Code:* 773 ■ *TF:* 800-367-3245 ■ *Web:* www.goldeagle.com	Chicago	IL	60632	800-367-3245	376-5749*
Goulston Technologies Inc 700 N Johnson St *Web:* www.goulston.com	Monroe	NC	28110	704-289-6464	296-6400
Grace Construction Products 62 Whittemore Ave *Web:* www.na.graceconstruction.com	Cambridge	MA	02140	617-876-1400	498-4311
Grace Davison 7500 Grace Dr *TF:* 800-638-6014 ■ *Web:* www.grace.com	Columbia	MD	21044	410-531-4197	531-4197
H Krevit & Co Inc 73 Welton St *Web:* www.hkrevit.com	New Haven	CT	06511	203-772-3350	776-0730
Hanson-Loran Chemical Co 6700 Caballero Blvd *Web:* www.hansonloran.com	Buena Park	CA	90620	714-522-5700	522-5834
Harcros Chemicals Inc 5200 Speaker Rd *TF:* 800-765-4748 ■ *Web:* www.harcroschem.com	Kansas City	KS	66106	913-321-3131	621-7718
Hercules Inc Pulp & Paper Div 1313 N Market St *NYSE: ASH* ■ *TF:* 800-274-5263 ■ *Web:* www.ashland.com	Wilmington	DE	19894	302-594-5000	594-5400
Hexion Specialty Chemicals Inc 180 E Broad St *Web:* www.hexionchem.com	Columbus	OH	43215	614-225-4000	
Hitachi Chemical Co America Ltd 10080 N Wolfe Rd Suite SW3-200 *Web:* www.hitachi-chemical.com	Cupertino	CA	95014	408-873-2200	873-2284
Honeywell Fluorine Products 101 Columbia Rd *TF:* 800-951-1527 ■ *Web:* www51.honeywell.com/sm/genetron	Morristown	NJ	07962	973-455-2000	455-6394
Honeywell Specialty Chemical Solutions 101 Columbia Rd *TF:* 800-222-0094 ■ *Web:* www.hpsweb.honeywell.com	Morristown	NJ	07962	973-455-2145	455-6154
Houghton Chemical Corp 52 Cambridge St *TF:* 800-777-2466 ■ *Web:* www.houghton.com	Boston	MA	02134	617-254-1010	254-2713
Hybrid Plastics 55 WL Runnels Industrial Dr *Web:* www.hybridplastics.com	Hattiesburg	MS	92708	601-544-3466	545-3103
I-K-I Mfg Co Inc 116 Swift St *Web:* www.ikimfg.com	Edgerton	WI	53534	608-884-3411	884-4712
Intercontinental Chemical Corp 4660 Spring Grove Ave *TF:* 800-543-2075 ■ *Web:* www.icc-chemicals.com	Cincinnati	OH	45232	513-541-7100	541-6880
International Chemical Co 2628 N Mascher St *TF:* 800-541-2504 ■ *Web:* www.e-icc.com	Philadelphia	PA	19133	215-739-2313	423-7171
ITW Chemtronics Inc 8125 Cobb Centre Dr *TF:* 800-645-5244 ■ *Web:* www.chemtronics.com	Kennesaw	GA	30152	770-424-4888	423-0748
JM Huber Corp 499 Thornall St 8th Fl **Fax:* Hum Res ■ *Web:* www.huber.com	Edison	NJ	08837	732-549-8600	549-2239*
Kao Specialties Americas LLC 243 Woodline St PO Box 2316 *TF:* 800-727-2214 ■ *Web:* www.ksallc.com	High Point	NC	27261	336-884-2214	884-8786
Kester Inc 800 W Thorndale Ave *TF:* 800-253-7837 ■ *Web:* www.kester.com	Itasca	IL	60143	630-616-4000	616-4044
Kik Custom Products 2825 Middlebury St *Web:* www.kikcorp.com	Elkhart	IN	46516	574-295-0000	296-1711
King Industries Inc 1 Science Rd *TF:* 800-431-7900 ■ *Web:* www.kingindustries.com	Norwalk	CT	06852	203-866-5551	866-1268
Kmco LP 16503 Ramsey Rd *Web:* www.kmcoinc.com	Crosby	TX	77532	281-272-4100	328-9528
Kolene Corp 12890 Westwood Ave *TF:* 800-521-4182 ■ *Web:* www.kolene.com	Detroit	MI	48223	313-273-9220	273-5207
Koppers Inc 436 7th Ave *NYSE: KOP* ■ *TF:* 800-321-9876 ■ *Web:* www.koppers.com	Pittsburgh	PA	15219	412-227-2001	227-2333
Kronos Worldwide Inc 5430 LBJ Pkwy Suite 1700 *NYSE: KRO* ■ *Web:* www.kronostio2.com	Dallas	TX	75240	972-233-1700	448-1445
Leadership Performance Sustainability Laboratories 4647 Hugh Howell Rd *TF:* 800-241-8334 ■ *Web:* www.lpslabs.com	Tucker	GA	30084	770-934-7800	243-8899
Lloyd Laboratories Inc 24 Fitch Ct PO Box 256	Wakefield	MA	01880	781-224-0083	245-1557
Lubrizol Corp 29400 Lakeland Blvd *NYSE: LZ* ■ *TF:* 800-522-4125 ■ *Web:* www.lubrizol.com	Wickliffe	OH	44092	440-943-4200	347-3583
MacDermid Inc 1401 Blake St *TF:* 800-325-4158 ■ *Web:* www.macdermid.com	Denver	CO	80202	720-479-3060	
McGean-Rohco Inc 2910 Harvard Ave *TF Orders:* 800-932-7006 ■ *Web:* www.mcgean.com	Cleveland	OH	44105	216-441-4900	441-1377
MeadWestvaco Chemical Div PO Box 118005 *Web:* www.meadwestvaco.com/chemicals.nsf	Charleston	SC	29423	843-745-3000	740-2147
Micro Powders Inc 580 White Plains Rd *Web:* www.micropowders.com	Tarrytown	NY	10591	914-793-4058	472-7098
Microchem Corp 90 Oak St *Web:* www.microchem.com	Newton	MA	02464	617-965-5511	965-5818
Milacron Inc 3010 Disney St *NYSE: MZ* ■ *Web:* www.milacron.com	Cincinnati	OH	45209	513-487-5000	487-5086
Millennium Specialty Chemicals 601 Crestwood St *TF:* 800-231-6728	Jacksonville	FL	32208	904-768-5800	768-2200
Miller-Stephenson Chemical Co 55 Backus Ave *TF Tech Supp:* 800-992-2424 ■ *Web:* www.miller-stephenson.com	Danbury	CT	06810	203-743-4447	791-8702
Momar Inc 1830 Ellsworth Industrial Dr **Fax Area Code:* 800 ■ *TF:* 800-556-3967 ■ *Web:* www.momar.com	Atlanta	GA	30318	404-355-4580	849-5684*
Monroe Fluid Technology Inc 36 Draffin Rd PO Box 810 *TF:* 800-828-6351 ■ *Web:* www.monroefluid.com	Hilton	NY	14468	585-392-3434	392-2691
Montana Sulphur & Chemical Co PO Box 31118 *Web:* www.montanasulphur.com	Billings	MT	59107	406-252-9324	252-8250
Montello Inc 6106 E 32nd Pl Suite 100 *TF:* 800-331-4628 ■ *Web:* www.montelloinc.com	Tulsa	OK	74135	918-665-1170	665-1480
Moses Lake Industries Inc 8248 Randolph Rd Ne *Web:* www.mlindustries.com	Moses Lake	WA	98837	509-762-5336	762-5981
Mount Pulaski Products Inc 908 N Vine St *TF:* 800-577-2627 ■ *Web:* www.mtpulaski.com	Mount Pulaski	IL	62548	217-792-3211	792-5040
Multisorb Technologies Inc 325 Harlem Rd *TF Cust Svc:* 800-445-9890 ■ *Web:* www.multisorb.com	West Seneca	NY	14224	716-824-8900	824-4128
Nalco Co 1601 W Diehl Rd *NYSE: NLC* ■ *TF:* 800-288-0879 ■ *Web:* www.nalco.com	Naperville	IL	60563	630-305-1000	305-2900
Nanophase Technologies Corp 1319 Marquette Dr *NASDAQ: NANX* ■ *Web:* www.nanophase.com	Romeoville	IL	60446	630-771-6700	771-0825
Nanostellar Inc 3696 Haven Ave Suite B *Web:* www.nanostellar.com	Redwood City	CA	94063	650-368-1010	368-1101
National Starch & Chemical Co 10 Finderne Ave *TF:* 866-961-6285 ■ *Web:* www.nationalstarch.com	Bridgewater	NJ	08807	908-685-5000	685-5005
Northern Technologies International Corp (NTIC) 4201 Woodland Rd *NASDAQ: NTIC* ■ *TF:* 800-328-2433	Circle Pines	MN	55014	763-225-6600	225-6645
Nox-Crete Inc 1444 S 20th St *TF:* 800-369-9800 ■ *Web:* www.nox-crete.com	Omaha	NE	68108	402-341-2080	341-9752
Octagon Process Inc 450 Raritan Ctr Pkwy Suite F *Web:* www.octagonprocess.com	Edison	NJ	08837	732-346-8000	346-8010
OM Group Inc 811 Sharon Dr *NYSE: OMG* ■ *TF:* 800-321-9696 ■ *Web:* www.omgi.com	Westlake	OH	44145	440-899-2950	808-7114
OMNOVA Solutions Inc 175 Ghent Rd *NYSE: OMN* ■ *Web:* www.omnova.com	Fairlawn	OH	44333	330-869-4200	869-4288
OMNOVA Solutions Inc Performance Chemicals Div 165 S Cleveland Ave **Fax:* Cust Svc ■ *TF Cust Svc:* 888-353-4173 ■ *Web:* www.omnova.com/pc.htm	Mogadore	OH	44260	330-628-9925	628-6500*
Ortec Inc 505 Gentry Memorial Hwy PO Box 1469 *Web:* www.ortecinc.com	Easley	SC	29641	864-859-1471	859-8580
Pacific Ethanol Corp 400 Capitol Mall Suite 2060 *NASDAQ: PEIX* ■ *TF:* 866-508-4969 ■ *Web:* www.pacificethanol.net	Sacramento	CA	95814	916-403-2123	446-3937
Pavco Inc 1935 John Crosland Jr Dr *TF Orders:* 800-321-7735 ■ *Web:* www.pavco.com	Charlotte	NC	28208	704-496-6800	496-6810

Company	City	State	Zip	Phone	Fax
Peach State Labs Inc (PSL) 180 Burlington Rd PO Box 1087 — TF: 800-634-1653 ■ Web: www.peachstatelabs.com	Rome	GA	30162	706-291-8743	291-4888
Penford Corp 7094 S Revere Pkwy — NASDAQ: PENX ■ TF: 800-204-7369 ■ Web: www.penx.com	Centennial	CO	80112	303-649-1900	649-1700
Peninsula Copper Industries Inc 52430 Duncan Ave — Web: www.pencopper.com	Hubbell	MI	49934	906-296-9918	296-0033
Penray Cos Inc 440 Denniston Ct — TF: 800-373-6729 ■ Web: www.penray.com	Wheeling	IL	60090	847-459-5000	459-5043
PMC Global Inc 12243 Branford St — TF: 800-423-5632 ■ Web: www.pmcglobalinc.com	Sun Valley	CA	91352	818-896-1101	686-2531
Polarome International Inc 200 Theodore Conrad Dr — Web: www.polarome.com	Jersey City	NJ	07305	201-309-4500	433-0638
Precision Laboratories Inc 1429 S Shields Dr — TF: 800-323-6280 ■ Web: www.precisionlab.com	Waukegan	IL	60085	847-596-3001	596-3017
Premier Colors Inc 100 Industrial Dr — TF: 800-245-6944 ■ Web: www.premiercolorsinc.com	Union	SC	29379	864-427-0338	427-5824
Prime Leather Finishes Co Inc 205 S 2nd St — TF: 800-558-7285 ■ Web: www.primeleatherfinishes.com	Milwaukee	WI	53204	414-276-1668	276-9462
PVS Chemicals Inc 10900 Harper Ave — TF: 800-787-6659 ■ Web: www.pvschemicals.com	Detroit	MI	48213	313-921-1200	921-1378
Quaker Chemical Corp 901 Hector St — NYSE: KWR ■ TF: 800-523-7010 ■ Web: www.quakerchem.com	Conshohocken	PA	19428	610-832-4000	832-8682
Qualitek International Inc 315 Fairbank St — Web: www.qualitek.com	Addison	IL	60101	630-628-8083	628-6543
Radiator Specialty Co 1900 Wilkinson Blvd — TF: 877-464-4865 ■ Web: www.gunk.com	Charlotte	NC	28208	704-377-6555	688-2383
Rentech Inc 10877 Wilshire Blvd Suite 710 — AMEX: RTK ■ Web: www.rentechinc.com	Los Angeles	CA	90024	310-571-9800	571-9799
Rochester Midland Corp 333 Hollenbeck St — TF: 800-836-1627 ■ Web: www.rochestermidland.com	Rochester	NY	14621	585-336-2200	467-4406
Rockwood Specialties Group Inc 100 Overlook Ctr — Web: www.rockwoodspecialties.com	Princeton	NJ	08540	609-514-0300	514-8722
Roebic Laboratories Inc 25 Connair Rd PO Box 927 — Web: www.roebic.com	Orange	CT	06477	203-795-1283	795-5227
Rohm & Haas Co 100 Independence Mall W — *Fax: Hum Res ■ Web: www.rohmhaas.com	Philadelphia	PA	19106	215-592-3000	592-3377*
Royal Chemical Co 1755 Entp Pkwy Suite 100 — Web: www.royalchemical.com	Twinsburg	OH	44087	330-467-1300	405-0975
SA Day Mfg Co Inc 1489 Niagara St — Web: www.saday.com	Buffalo	NY	14213	716-881-3030	881-4353
Scholler Inc 95 James Way Suite 100 — TF: 800-220-1504	SouthHampton	PA	18966	215-942-0200	942-0255
Senomyx Inc 4767 Nexus Centre Dr — NASDAQ: SNMX ■ Web: www.senomyx.com	San Diego	CA	92121	858-646-8300	404-0752
Sid Richardson Carbon & Energy Cos 201 Main St — Web: www.sidrich.com	Fort Worth	TX	76102	817-390-8600	
Sigma-Aldrich Corp 3050 Spruce St — NASDAQ: SIAL ■ *Fax Area Code: 800 ■ TF: 800-325-3010 ■ Web: www.sigmaaldrich.com	Saint Louis	MO	63103	314-771-5765	325-5052*
Sika Corp 201 Polito Ave — TF: 800-933-7452 ■ Web: www.usa.sika.com	Lyndhurst	NJ	07071	201-933-8800	
Solutek Corp 94 Shirley St — TF: 800-403-0770 ■ Web: www.solutekcorporation.com	Boston	MA	02119	617-445-5335	445-9623
Spartan Chemical Co Inc 1110 Spartan Dr — TF: 800-537-8990 ■ Web: www.spartanchemical.com	Maumee	OH	43537	419-531-5551	536-8423
Specco Industries Inc 13087 Main St — TF: 800-441-6646 ■ Web: www.specco.com	Lemont	IL	60439	630-257-5060	257-9006
Spectra Gases Inc 1 Greenwich St — Web: www.spectragases.com	Somerville	NJ	08886	908-329-9700	329-9740
Sprayway Inc 500 S Vista Ave — TF: 800-332-9000 ■ Web: www.spraywayinc.com	Addison	IL	60101	630-628-3000	543-7797
Stapleton Technologies Inc 1350 W 12th St — TF: 800-266-0541 ■ Web: www.stapletontech.com	Long Beach	CA	90813	562-437-0541	437-8632
Stepan Co 22 W Frontage Rd — TF Cust Svc: 800-745-7837 ■ Web: www.stepan.com	Northfield	IL	60093	847-446-7500	501-2100
SulphCo Inc 4333 W.Sam Houston Pkwy N. Suite 190 — AMEX: SUF ■ Web: www.sulphco.com	Houston	TX	77043	713-896-9100	896-8803
Sunland Chemical & Research Corp 5447 San Fernando Rd W — Web: www.sunlandchemical.com	Los Angeles	CA	90039	818-244-9600	246-0478
Sweetwater Technologies PO Box 1473 — TF: 888-711-7575 ■ Web: www.sweetwatertech.com	Temecula	CA	92593	951-303-0999	344-8388
Sybron Chemicals Inc 200 Birmingham Rd PO Box 66 — *Fax Area Code: 412 ■ TF: 800-678-0020 ■ Web: www.sybronchemicals.com	Birmingham	NJ	08011	609-845-1500	809-1124*
Symrise Inc 300 N St — TF: 800-422-1559 ■ Web: www.symrise.com	Teterboro	NJ	07608	201-288-3200	288-0843
Technic Inc 47 Molter St — Web: www.technic.com	Cranston	RI	02910	401-781-6100	781-2890
Technical Chemical Co 3327 Pipeline Rd — TF: 800-527-0885 ■ Web: www.technicalchemical.com	Cleburne	TX	76033	817-645-6088	556-0694
Thatcher Co 1905 Fortune Rd — TF: 800-348-0034 ■ Web: www.thatchercompany.com	Salt Lake City	UT	84127	801-972-4587	972-4606
United Color Mfg Inc (UCM) PO Box 480 — TF: 800-852-5942 ■ Web: www.unitedcolor.com	Newtown	PA	18940	215-860-2165	860-8560
United Laboratories Inc 320 37th Ave — *Fax: Sales ■ TF: 800-323-2594 ■ Web: www.beearthsmart.com	Saint Charles	IL	60174	630-377-0900	443-2087*
United Salt Corp 4800 San Felipe St — TF: 800-554-8658 ■ Web: www.unitedsalt.com	Houston	TX	77056	713-877-2600	877-2604
Univertical Corp 203 Weatherhead St — Web: www.univertical.com	Angola	IN	46703	260-665-1500	665-1400
Vertellus Specialties Inc 300 N Meridian St Suite 1500 — Web: www.vertellus.com	Indianapolis	IN	46204	317-247-8141	248-6472
Watcon Inc 2215 S Main St — TF: 800-492-8266 ■ Web: www.watcon-inc.com	South Bend	IN	46613	574-287-3397	287-2427
WR Grace & Co 7500 Grace Dr — NYSE: GRA ■ TF: 888-398-4646 ■ Web: www.grace.com	Columbia	MD	21044	410-531-4000	531-4367
Wynn's Oil Co 1050 W 5th St — TF: 800-989-8363 ■ Web: www.wynnsusa.com	Azusa	CA	91702	626-334-0231	
XL Brands 4284 S Dixie Hwy — TF: 800-367-4583 ■ Web: www.xlbrands.com	Resaca	GA	30735	706-625-0025	226-9210
Zinkan Enterprises Inc 1919 Case Pkwy N — *Fax Area Code: 330 ■ Web: www.zinkan.com	Twinsburg	OH	44087	800-229-6801	425-8202*

146 CHEMICALS & RELATED PRODUCTS - WHOL

Company	City	State	Zip	Phone	Fax
Airgas Inc 259 N Radnor-Chester Rd Suite 100 — NYSE: ARG ■ TF: 800-255-2165 ■ Web: www.airgas.com	Radnor	PA	19087	610-687-5253	687-1052
Amfine Chemical Corp 10 Montnview Rd Suite 215N — Web: www.amfine.com	Upper Saddle River	NJ	07458	201-818-0159	818-0259
Ashland Distribution Co 5200 Blazer Pkwy PO Box 2219 — Web: www.ashland.com	Columbus	OH	43216	614-790-3333	790-4119
Astro Chemicals Inc 126 Memorial Dr — TF: 800-223-0776 ■ Web: www.astrochemicals.com	Springfield	MA	01104	413-781-7240	781-7246
Austin Chemical Co Inc 1565 Barclay Blvd — Web: www.austinchemical.com	Buffalo Grove	IL	60089	847-520-9600	520-9160
Barton Solvents Inc 1920 NE Broadway Ave — TF: 800-383-6488 ■ Web: www.barsol.com	Des Moines	IA	50313	515-265-7998	265-0259
Basic Chemical Solutions (BCS) 525 Seaport Blvd — TF: 888-810-4787 ■ Web: www.basicchem.com	Redwood City	CA	94063	650-363-1661	363-0713
Berryman Products Inc 3800 E Randol Mill Rd — TF: 800-433-1704 ■ Web: www.berrymanproducts.com	Arlington	TX	76011	817-640-2376	640-4850
Brandt Technologies Inc 231 W Grand Ave — Web: www.brandttech.com	Bensenville	IL	60106	630-787-1800	787-1801
Brenntag Canada Inc 35 Vulcan St — TF: 866-516-9707 ■ Web: www.brenntag.ca/en	Rexdale	ON	M9W1L3	416-243-9615	243-9731
Brenntag Great Lakes LLC PO Box 444 — *Fax: Sales ■ TF: 800-558-8501 ■ Web: www.brenntaggreatlakes.com	Butler	WI	53007	262-252-3550	252-5250*
Brenntag Mid-South Inc 1405 Hwy 136 W — *Fax: Hum Res ■ TF: 800-950-1727 ■ Web: www.brenntagmid-south.com	Henderson	KY	42419	270-830-1200	827-3990*
Brenntag North America Inc 5083 Pottsville Pike PO Box 13786 — Web: www.brenntag.com	Reading	PA	19605	610-926-6100	926-0411
Brenntag Northeast Inc 81 W Huller Ln PO Box 13788 — Web: www.brenntagnortheast.com	Reading	PA	19605	610-926-4151	926-4160
Brenntag Pacific 4545 Ardine St	South Gate	CA	90280	323-832-5000	773-0909
Brenntag Southeast Inc 2000 E Pedigree St — TF: 800-849-7000 ■ Web: www.brenntagsoutheast.com	Durham	NC	27703	919-596-0681	598-0681
Brenntag Southwest Inc 610 Fisher Rd — TF: 800-945-1858 ■ Web: www.brenntagsouthwest.com	Longview	TX	75604	903-759-7151	759-3145
Budenheim USA Inc 2219 Westbrooke Dr — Web: www.budenheim.com	Columbus	OH	43228	614-345-2400	
Cal-chlor Corp 627 Jefferson St — TF: 800-245-6743 ■ Web: www.cal-chlor.com	Lafayette	LA	70501	337-264-1449	264-9359
Callahan Chemical Co 200 Industrial Ave — TF: 800-526-7000 ■ Web: www.calchem.com	Richfield Park	NJ	07660	201-440-9000	440-5441
Canada Colors & Chemicals Ltd 175 Bloor St E Suite 1300 N Tower — Web: www.canadacolors.com	Toronto	ON	M4W3R8	416-443-5500	449-9039
Canpotex Ltd 111 2nd Ave S Suite 400 PO Box 1600 — Web: www.canpotex.com	Saskatoon	SK	S7K3R7	306-931-2200	653-5505
Cardinal Color Inc 50-56 1st Ave — Web: www.cardinalcolor.com	Paterson	NJ	07524	973-684-1919	684-0865
Charkit Chemical Corp 32 Haviland St Unit 1 — Web: www.charkit.com	Norwalk	CT	06854	203-299-3230	299-1355
Chembridge Corp 16981 Via Tazon Suite G — TF: 800-964-6143 ■ Web: www.chembridge.com	San Diego	CA	92127	858-451-7400	451-7401
Chemetall Foote Corp 348 Holiday Inn Dr — TF: 800-523-7116 ■ Web: www.chemetalllithium.com	Kings Mountain	NC	28086	704-739-2501	734-2718
Chemicals Inc 270 Osborne Dr — Web: www.chemgroup.com	Fairfield	OH	37686	513-682-2000	682-2008
Chemroy Canada Inc 106 Summerlea Rd — TF: 888-243-6769 ■ Web: www.chemroy.ca	Brampton	ON	L6T4X3	905-789-0701	789-7170
Chemsolv Inc 1140 Industry Ave SE — TF: 800-523-3099 ■ Web: www.chemsolv.com	Roanoke	VA	24103	540-427-4000	427-3207
Coastal Chemical Co Inc 3520 Veterans Memorial — TF Cust Svc: 800-535-3862 ■ Web: www.coastalchem.com	Abbeville	LA	70510	337-893-3862	892-1185
Cole Chemical & Distributing Inc 1500 S Dairy Ashford St # 450 — Web: www.colechem.com	Houston	TX	77077	713-465-2653	461-3462
Connell Bros Co Ltd 345 California St 27th Fl — Web: www.connellbrothers.com	San Francisco	CA	94104	415-772-4000	772-4100
Dar-tech Inc 16485 Rockside Rd — TF: 800-228-7347 ■ Web: www.dar-tech.com	Cleveland	OH	44137	216-663-7600	663-8007
DB Becker Co Inc 46 Leigh St — TF: 800-394-3991 ■ Web: www.dbbecker.com	Clinton	NJ	08809	908-730-6010	730-9118
DH Litter Co Inc 565 Taxter Rd Suite 610 — TF: 800-551-1039 ■ Web: www.dhlitter.com	Elmsford	NY	10523	914-592-1077	592-1499
Dm Figley Co Inc 10 Kelly Ct — TF: 800-292-9919 ■ Web: www.dmfigley.com	Menlo Park	CA	94025	650-329-8700	329-0601
Dorsett & Jackson Inc 3800 Noakes St — Web: www.dorsettandjackson.com	Los Angeles	CA	90023	323-268-1815	268-9082
Durr Marketing Assoc Inc PO Box 17600 — TF: 800-937-3877 ■ Web: www.durrmarketing.com	Pittsburgh	PA	15235	412-829-2300	829-7680

	City	State	ZIP	Phone	Fax
Eliokem LLC 1452 E Archwood Ave 240	Akron	OH	44306	330-734-1100	734-1101
TF: 866-354-6536 ■ *Web:* www.eliokem.com					
Ellsworth Corp PO Box 1002	Germantown	WI	53022	262-253-8600	253-8619
TF: 877-454-9224 ■ *Web:* www.ellsworth.com					
EMCO Chemical Distributors Inc					
2100 Commonwealth Ave	North Chicago	IL	60064	847-689-2200	689-8470
Web: www.emcochem.com					
ET Horn Co 16141 Heron Ave	La Mirada	CA	90638	714-523-8050	670-6851
TF: 800-442-4676 ■ *Web:* www.ethorn.com					
EW Kaufmann Co 1320 Industrial Hwy	SouthHampton	PA	18966	215-364-0240	364-4397
TF: 800-635-5358 ■ *Web:* www.ewkaufmann.com					
Fitz Chem Corp 450 E Devon Ave Suite 175	Itasca	IL	60143	630-467-8383	467-1183
Web: www.fitzchem.com					
FutureFuel Corp 8235 Forsyth Blvd 4th Fl	Clayton	MO	63105	805-565-9800	565-0800
NYSE: FF ■ *Web:* www.futurefuelcorporation.com					
Gallade Chemical Inc 1230 E St Gertrude Pl	Santa Ana	CA	92707	714-546-9901	546-2501
TF: 800-325-8431 ■ *Web:* www.galladechem.com					
General Air Service & Supply Co Inc					
1105 Zuni St	Denver	CO	80204	303-892-7003	595-9036
TF: 877-782-8434 ■ *Web:* www.generalair.com					
George S Coyne Chemical Co 3015 State Rd	Croydon	PA	19021	215-785-3000	785-1585
TF: 800-523-1230 ■ *Web:* www.coynechemical.com					
GJ Chemical Co 370 Adams St	Newark	NJ	07105	973-589-1450	589-5786
Web: www.gjchemical.com					
GS Robins & Co 126 Chouteau Ave	Saint Louis	MO	63102	314-621-5165	621-1216
TF: 800-777-5155 ■ *Web:* www.gsrobins.com					
Hand Industries/Dirilyte Line 315 S Hand Ave	Warsaw	IN	46580	574-267-3525	267-7349
Web: www.dirilyte.com					
Harcros Chemicals Inc 5200 Speaker Rd	Kansas City	KS	66106	913-321-3131	621-7718
TF: 800-765-4748 ■ *Web:* www.harcroschem.com					
Haviland Enterprises Inc 421 Ann St NW	Grand Rapids	MI	49504	616-361-6691	361-9772
TF: 800-456-1134 ■ *Web:* www.havilandusa.com					
Helm US Chemical Corp 1110 Centennial Ave	Piscataway	NJ	08854	732-981-1116	981-0528
Web: www.helmusa.com					
Hill Bros Chemical Co 1675 N Main St	Orange	CA	92867	714-998-8800	998-6310
TF: 800-994-8801 ■ *Web:* www.hillbrothers.com					
HM Royal Inc 689 Pennington Ave	Trenton	NJ	08618	609-396-9176	396-3185
TF: 800-257-9452 ■ *Web:* www.hmroyal.com					
Hubbard-Hall Inc 563 S Leonard St	Waterbury	CT	06708	203-756-5521	756-9017
TF: 800-331-6871 ■ *Web:* www.hubbardhall.com					
Hydrite Chemical Co 300 N Patrick Blvd	Brookfield	WI	53045	262-792-1450	792-8721
TF: 800-543-4560 ■ *Web:* www.hydrite.com					
ICC Chemical Corp 460 Pk Ave	New York	NY	10022	212-521-1700	521-1794
TF: 800-422-1720 ■ *Web:* www.iccchem.com					
Ideal Chemical & Supply Co 4025 Air Pk St	Memphis	TN	38118	901-363-7720	366-0864
TF: 800-232-6776 ■ *Web:* www.idealchemical.com					
Independent Chemical Corp 7951 Cooper Ave	Glendale	NY	11385	718-894-0700	894-9224
TF: 800-892-2578 ■ *Web:* www.independentchemical.com					
Industrial Chemicals Inc 2042 Montreat Dr	Birmingham	AL	35216	205-823-7330	978-0485
TF Cust Svc: 800-476-2042					
Innophos Holdings Inc					
259 Prospect Plains Rd	Cranbury	NJ	08512	609-495-2495	560-0138
NASDAQ: IPHS ■ *Web:* www.innophos.com					
Island Import & Export Co 7570 Hwy 65 NE	Fridley	MN	55432	763-783-7338	783-1106
Web: www.i-i-e.com					
JLM Marketing Inc 8675 Hidden River Pkwy	Tampa	FL	33637	813-632-3300	632-3301
TF: 800-457-3743					
John R Hess & Co Inc 400 Stn St PO Box 3615	Cranston	RI	02910	401-785-9300	785-2510
TF: 800-828-4377 ■ *Web:* www.jrhess.com					
John R White Co Inc PO Box 10043	Birmingham	AL	35202	205-595-8381	595-8386
TF: 800-245-1183 ■ *Web:* www.johnrwhite.com					
KA Steel Chemicals Inc					
15185 Main St PO Box 729	Lemont	IL	60439	630-257-3900	257-3922
TF: 800-677-8335 ■ *Web:* www.kasteelchemicals.com					
Kraft Chemical Co 1975 N Hawthorne Ave	Melrose Park	IL	60160	708-345-5200	345-4005
TF: 800-345-5200 ■ *Web:* www.kraftchemical.com					
LidoChem Inc 20 Village Ct	Hazlet	NJ	07730	732-888-8000	264-2751
Web: www.lidochem.com					
Lipo Chemicals Inc 207 19th Ave	Paterson	NJ	07504	973-345-8600	345-8365
Web: www.lipochemicals.com					
LV Lomas Ltd 99 Summerlea Rd	Brampton	ON	L6T4V2	905-458-1555	458-0722
TF: 800-575-3382 ■ *Web:* www.lvlomas.com					
Maroon Inc 1390 Jaycox Rd	Avon	OH	44011	440-937-1000	937-1001
TF: 877-627-6661 ■ *Web:* www.marooninc.com					
Mays Chemical Co 5611 E 71st St	Indianapolis	IN	46220	317-842-8722	576-9630
TF: 800-525-4803 ■ *Web:* www.mayschem.com					
McCullough & Assoc 1746 NE Expy PO Box 29803	Atlanta	GA	30329	404-325-1606	329-0208
TF: 800-969-1606 ■ *Web:* www.mccanda.com					
MF Cachat Co 14600 Detroit Ave Suite 600	Lakewood	OH	44107	216-228-8900	228-9916
TF: 800-729-8900 ■ *Web:* www.mfcachat.com					
Milport Enterprises Inc 2829 S 5th Ct	Milwaukee	WI	53207	414-769-7350	769-0167
Web: www.milport.com					
Mitsubishi International Corp 655 3rd Ave	New York	NY	10017	212-605-2000	
Web: www.micusa.com					
Mitsui & Co (Canada) Ltd					
20 Adelaide St E Suite 1400	Toronto	ON	M5C1T6	416-365-3800	865-1486
Web: www.mitsui.ca					
Mozel 1900 W Gate Dr	Columbia	IL	62236	618-281-3040	281-9176
TF: 800-260-5348 ■ *Web:* www.mozel.com					
Nagase America Corp 546 5th Ave 16th Fl	New York	NY	10036	212-703-1340	398-0687
Web: www.nagase.com					
NuCo2 Inc 2800 SE Marketplace	Stuart	FL	34997	772-221-1754	781-3500
TF: 800-472-2855 ■ *Web:* www.nuco2.com					
Pain Enterprises Inc 101 Daniels Way	Bloomington	IN	47404	812-330-1400	330-1544
Web: www.painenterprises.com					
Palmer Holland Inc					
24950 Country Club Blvd Suite 400	North Olmsted	OH	44070	440-686-2300	686-2180
TF: 800-635-4822 ■ *Web:* www.palmerholland.com					
Pidilite USA Inc 401 Maplewood Dr Suite 18	Jupiter	FL	33458	561-775-9600	622-1055
Web: www.cyclo.com					
Plaza Group Inc 10375 Richmond Ave Suite 1620	Houston	TX	77042	713-266-0707	266-8660
TF: 800-876-3738 ■ *Web:* www.theplazagrp.com					
Pride Solvents & Chemical Co of New York Inc					
6 Long Island Ave	Holtsville	NY	11742	631-758-0200	758-0290
TF: 800-645-5255 ■ *Web:* www.pridesol.com					
Purity Cylinder Gases Inc PO Box 9390	Grand Rapids	MI	49509	616-532-2375	532-5626
Web: www.puritygas.com					
Quadra Chemicals Ltd					
3901 Fixtessier	Vaudreuil-Dorion	QC	J7V5V5	450-424-0161	424-9458*
**Fax:* Hum Res ■ *TF:* 800-665-6553 ■ *Web:* www.quadra.ca					
Ribelin Sales Inc 3857 Miller Pk Dr	Garland	TX	75042	972-272-1594	474-2354*
**Fax Area Code:* 877 ■ *TF:* 800-374-1594 ■ *Web:* www.ribelin.com					
Rockwood Specialties Group Inc					
100 Overlook Ctr	Princeton	NJ	08540	609-514-0300	514-8722
Web: www.rockwoodspecialties.com					
Rowell Chemical Corp					
15 Salt Creek Ln Suite 205	Hinsdale	IL	60521	630-920-8833	920-8994
Web: www.rowellchemical.com					
SARCOM Inc AEP Colloids Div 6299 Rt 9N	Hadley	NY	12835	518-696-9900	696-9997
TF: 800-848-0658 ■ *Web:* www.aepcolloids.com					
Sasol Wax North America Corp					
21325-B Cabot Blvd	Hayward	CA	94545	510-783-9295	670-8659
Web: www.sasolwax.com					
Sessions Specialty Co					
5090 Styers Ferry Rd	Lewisville	NC	27023	336-766-2880	723-0055*
**Fax Area Code:* 800 ■ *Web:* www.sessionsusa.com					
Solvents & Chemicals Inc					
4704 Shank Rd PO Box 490	Pearland	TX	77581	281-485-5377	485-6129
TF: 800-622-3990 ■ *Web:* www.solvchem.com					
Specified Technologies Inc					
200 Evans Way Suite 2	Somerville	NJ	08876	908-526-8000	526-9623
TF: 800-992-1180 ■ *Web:* www.stifirestop.com					
Spectra Colors Corp 25 Rizzolo Rd	Kearny	NJ	07032	201-997-0606	997-0504
TF: 800-527-8588 ■ *Web:* www.spectracolors.com					
Sumitomo Chemical America Inc					
335 Madison Ave Suite 830	New York	NY	10017	212-572-8200	572-8234
Web: www.sumitomo-chem.co.jp					
Sunbelt Chemicals Corp 71 Hargrove Grade	Palm Coast	FL	32137	386-446-4595	446-4627
Web: www.sunbeltchemicals.com					
Superior Solvents & Chemicals					
1402 N Capitol Ave Suite 100	Indianapolis	IN	46204	317-781-4400	781-4401
TF: 800-553-5480 ■ *Web:* www.superioroil.com/solv					
Sweetlake Chemical Ltd 446 Heights Blvd	Houston	TX	77007	713-827-8707	
TF: 888-752-1998 ■ *Web:* www.sweetlakechem.com					
Tanner Industries Inc					
735 Davisville Rd 3rd Fl	SouthHampton	PA	18966	215-322-1238	322-7791*
**Fax:* Sales ■ *TF:* 800-643-6226 ■ *Web:* www.tannerind.com					
Tarr LLC 2429 N Borthwick St	Portland	OR	97227	503-288-5294	288-0421
TF: 800-422-5069 ■ *Web:* www.tarr-inc.com					
TCR Industries 26 Centerpointe Dr Suite 120	La Palma	CA	90623	714-521-5222	521-1636
Web: www.tcrindustries.com					
Tilley Chemical Co Inc					
501 Chesapeake Pk Plaza	Baltimore	MD	21220	410-574-4500	391-6665
TF: 800-638-6968 ■ *Web:* www.tilleychem.com					
Tm Deer Park Services LP					
2525 Battleground Rd PO Box 1914	Deer Park	TX	77536	281-930-2525	930-2535
Web: www.texasmolecular.com					
TR International Trading Co Inc					
1218 3rd Ave Suite 2100	Seattle	WA	98101	206-505-3500	505-3501
Web: www.tritrading.com					
TransChemical Inc 419 E DeSoto Ave	Saint Louis	MO	63147	314-231-6905	231-5851
TF: 888-873-6481 ■ *Web:* www.transchemical.com					
Tulstar Products Inc 5510 S Lewis Ave	Tulsa	OK	74105	918-749-9060	747-1444
TF: 800-988-5782 ■ *Web:* www.tulstar.com					
Union Carbide Corp 1254 Enclave Pkwy	Houston	TX	77077	281-966-2016	966-2394
Web: www.unioncarbide.com					
United Mineral & Chemical Corp					
1100 Valley Brook Ave	Lyndhurst	NJ	07071	201-507-3300	507-1506
TF: 800-777-0505 ■ *Web:* www.umccorp.com					
Univar Canada Ltd PO Box 2009	Richmond	BC	V6B3R2	604-273-1441	273-2046
Web: www.univarcanada.com					
Univar USA Inc 17425 NE Union Hill Rd	Redmond	WA	98052	425-889-3400	889-4100
TF: 800-234-4588 ■ *Web:* www.univar.com					
Van Horn Metz & Co 201 E Elm St	Conshohocken	PA	19428	610-828-4500	828-0936
TF: 800-523-0424 ■ *Web:* www.vanhornmetz.com					
Walsh & Assoc Inc 1400 Macklind Ave	Saint Louis	MO	63110	314-781-2520	781-9424
TF: 800-949-2574 ■ *Web:* www.walsh-assoc.com					
Webb Chemical Service Corp 2708 Jarman St	Muskegon	MI	49444	231-733-2181	739-5454
Web: www.webbchemical.com					
Wego Chemical & Mineral Corp					
239 Great Neck Rd	Great Neck	NY	11021	516-487-3510	487-3794
TF: 877-489-6645 ■ *Web:* www.wegochem.com					
Whitaker Oil Co 1557 Marietta Rd NW	Atlanta	GA	30318	404-355-8220	355-8217
TF: 800-221-0521 ■ *Web:* www.whitakeroil.com					
Wilson Industrial Sales Co Inc					
201 S Wilson St PO Box 425	Brook	IN	47922	219-275-7333	275-9622
TF: 800-633-5427 ■ *Web:* www.wilsonindustrial.com					

147 CHILD CARE MONITORING SYSTEMS - INTERNET

	City	State	ZIP	Phone	Fax
Jewish Child Care Assn of New York					
120 Wall St FL 12	New York	NY	10005	212-425-3333	425-9397
Web: www.jccany.org					
Mississippi Action For Progress Inc (MAP)					
1751 Morson Rd	Jackson	MS	39209	601-923-4100	923-4114
TF: 800-924-4615 ■ *Web:* www.mapheadstart.org					
ParentWatch Inc 45 Kensico Dr	Mount Kisco	NY	10549	914-919-1700	919-0495
TF: 800-696-2664 ■ *Web:* www.parentwatch.com					

148 CHILDREN'S LEARNING CENTERS

Company	City	State	Zip	Phone	Fax
Abrakadoodle Inc 1800 Robert Fulton Dr Web: www.abrakadoodle.com	Reston	VA	22191	703-860-6570	860-6574
Bright Horizons Family Solutions LLC 200 Talcott Ave S TF: 800-324-4386 ■ Web: www.brighthorizons.com	Watertown	MA	02472	617-673-8000	673-8001
Child Care Links 1020 Serpentine Ln TF: 888-886-9660 ■ Web: www.childcarelinks.org	Pleasanton	CA	94566	925-417-8733	417-8740
Child Care of Southwest Florida Inc 4315 Metro Pkwy Suite 400 TF: 800-435-7352 ■ Web: www.ccswfl.org	Fort Myers	FL	33916	239-278-1002	
Child Development Assoc Inc 678 3rd Ave Suite 201 TF: 888-755-2445 ■ Web: www.cdasandiego.com	Chula Vista	CA	91910	619-427-4411	205-6294
Childcare Network Inc 1501-D 13th St TF Cust Svc: 877-424-4530 ■ Web: www.childcarenetwork.net	Columbus	GA	31901	706-562-8600	562-0600
Children S Friend Inc PO Box 8989 TF: 866-713-0455 ■ Web: www.childrensfriend.com	Warner Robins	GA	31095	478-923-0961	328-8989
Children's Home + Aid 125 S Wacker Dr Fl 14 Web: www.childrenshomeandaid.org	Chicago	IL	60606	312-424-0200	
Colonial Intermediate Unit 20 6 Danforth Rd Web: www.ciu20.org	Easton	PA	18045	610-252-5550	252-5740
Computer Explorers 12715 Telge Rd TF: 800-531-5053 ■ Web: www.computerexplorers.com	Cypress	TX	77429	281-256-4100	373-4450
DePelchin Children's Ctr 4950 Memorial Dr Web: www.depelchin.org	Houston	TX	77007	713-730-2335	802-3801
FasTracKids International Ltd 6900 E Belleview Ave Suite 100 TF: 888-576-6888 ■ Web: www.fastrackids.com	Greenwood Village	CO	80111	303-224-0200	224-0222
Goddard Systems Inc 1016 W Ninth Ave TF: 800-463-3273 ■ Web: www.goddardschool.com	King of Prussia	PA	19406	610-265-8510	265-8867
Gymboree Corp Play & Music Program 500 Howard St TF: 800-520-7529 ■ Web: www.gymboree.com	San Francisco	CA	94105	415-278-7000	278-7100
Head Start of Greater Dallas Inc 3954 Gannon Ln Web: www.hsgd.org	Dallas	TX	75237	972-283-6400	
Honors Learning Ctr 5959 Shallowford Rd Suite 515 Web: www.honorslearningcenter.com	Chattanooga	TN	37421	423-892-1800	892-1800
Huntington Learning Centers Inc 23 Jefferson Ave TF: 800-226-5327 ■ Web: www.westwood.huntingtonlearning.com	Westwood	NJ	07675	201-261-8600	
KinderCare Learning Centers Inc 650 NE Holladay St Suite 1400 PO Box 6760 TF: 888-525-2780 ■ Web: www.kindercare.com	Portland	OR	97228	503-872-1300	872-1349
Knowledge Learning Corp 650 NE Holladay St Suite 1400 TF: 888-525-2780 ■ Web: www.kueducation.com	Portland	OR	97225	503-872-1300	872-1349
Knowledge Universe 650 NE Holladay St Suite 1400 *Fax: Cust Svc ■ TF: 800-633-1488 ■ Web: www.knowledgeuniverse.com	Portland	OR	97232	503-872-1300	872-1345*
Kumon North America Inc 300 Frank W Burr Blvd Glenpointe Ctr E Suite 6 TF: 877-586-6673 ■ Web: www.kumon.com	Teaneck	NJ	07666	201-928-0444	928-0044
Learning Care Group Inc 21333 Haggerty Rd Suite 300 TF: 866-244-5384 ■ Web: learningcaregroup.com	Novi	MI	48375	248-697-9000	697-9002
Miami Valley Child Development Centers 215 Horace St Web: www.mvcdc.org	Dayton	OH	45402	937-226-5664	
New Horizon Kids Quest Inc 16355 36th Ave N Suite 700 TF Cust Svc: 800-941-1007 ■ Web: www.kidsquest.com	Plymouth	MN	55446	763-557-1111	383-6101
Oxford Learning Centers Inc 97B S Livingston Ave TF: 888-559-2212 ■ Web: www.oxfordlearning.com	Livingston	NJ	07039	973-597-4300	
Primrose School Franchising Co 3660 Cedarcrest Rd TF: 800-745-0677 ■ Web: www.primroseschools.com	Acworth	GA	30101	770-529-4100	529-1551
Rural Resources Community Action 956 S Main St Suite A TF: 800-678-3346 ■ Web: www.ruralresources.org	Colville	WA	99114	509-684-8421	684-4740
Talladega Clay Randolph Child Care Corp 925 N St E Web: www.tcrchildcarecorporation.org	Talladega	AL	35160	256-362-3852	
Yeled V'yalda Early Childhood Center Inc 1312 38th St Web: www.yeled.org	Brooklyn	NY	11218	718-686-3700	

149 CIRCUS, CARNIVAL, FESTIVAL OPERATORS

Company	City	State	Zip	Phone	Fax
Big Apple Circus 505 8th Ave 19th Fl TF: 800-899-2775 ■ Web: www.bigapplecircus.org	New York	NY	10018	212-268-2500	268-3163
Carson & Barnes Circus PO Box J Web: www.carsonbarnescircus.com	Hugo	OK	74743	580-326-3173	326-7466
Cirque du Soleil Inc 8400 2nd Ave TF: 800-678-2119 ■ Web: www.cirquedusoleil.com	Montreal	QC	H1Z4M6	514-722-2324	722-3692
Culpepper & Merriweather Circus PO Box 813 TF: 866-244-8676 ■ Web: www.cmcircus.com	Hugo	OK	74743	580-326-8833	326-8866
Feld Entertainment Inc 8607 Westwood Ctr Dr TF: 800-298-3858 ■ Web: www.feldentertainment.com	Vienna	VA	22182	703-448-4000	448-4100
International Renaissance Festivals Ltd PO Box 315 TF: 800-296-7304 ■ Web: www.rennfest.com	Crownsville	MD	21032	410-266-7304	573-1508
Ringling Bros & Barnum & Bailey Circus 8607 Westwood Ctr Dr Web: www.ringling.com	Vienna	VA	22182	703-448-4000	448-4100

150 CLAY PRODUCTS - STRUCTURAL

SEE ALSO Brick, Stone, Related Materials p. 1732

Company	City	State	Zip	Phone	Fax
Acme Brick Co 3024 Acme Brick Plaza TF: 800-433-5650 ■ Web: www.acmebrick.com	Fort Worth	TX	76109	817-332-4101	390-2404
Belden Brick Co Inc 700 Tuscarawas St W Web: www.beldenbrick.com	Canton	OH	44702	330-456-0031	456-2694
Boral Bricks Inc 1630 Arthern Rd TF: 800-580-3842 ■ Web: www.boralbricks.com	Augusta	GA	30903	706-823-8802	724-0302
Bowerston Shale Co 515 Main St PO Box 199 Web: www.bowerstonshale.com	Bowerston	OH	44695	740-269-2921	269-5456
Brampton Brick Ltd 225 Wanless Dr Web: www.bramptonbrick.com	Brampton	ON	L7A1E9	905-840-1011	840-1535
Brick & Tile Corp of Lawrenceville 16024 Governor Harrison Pkwy PO Box 45 TF: 877-274-2582 ■ Web: www.lawrencevillebrick.co	Lawrenceville	VA	23868	434-848-3151	848-4000
Cherokee Brick & Tile Co Inc 3250 Waterville Rd TF: 800-277-2745 ■ Web: www.cherokeebrick.com	Macon	GA	31206	478-781-6800	781-8964
Colloid Environmental Technologies Co (CETCO) 1500 W Shure Dr TF: 800-527-9948 ■ Web: www.cetco.com	Arlington Heights	IL	60004	847-392-5800	577-6150
Cunningham Brick Co Inc 701 N Main St TF: 800-672-6181 ■ Web: www.cunninghambrick.com	Lexington	NC	27292	336-248-8541	224-0002
Elgin-Butler Brick Co 1007 E 40th St Web: www.elginbutler.com	Austin	TX	78751	512-453-7366	281-3003
Endicott Clay Products Co 57120 707 Rd TF: 800-927-9179 ■ Web: www.endicott.com	Endicott	NE	68350	402-729-3315	729-5804
Endicott Tile LLC 57120 707 Rd TF: 800-927-9179 ■ Web: www.endicott.com	Endicott	NE	68350	402-729-3315	729-5804
General Shale Products LLC 3015 Bristol Hwy TF: 800-414-4661 ■ Web: www.generalshale.com	Johnson City	TN	37601	423-282-4661	952-4104
Glen-Gery Corp 1166 Spring St PO Box 7001 Web: www.glengerybrick.com	Wyomissing	PA	19610	610-374-4011	374-1622
Henry Brick Co Inc 3409 Water Ave TF: 800-548-7576 ■ Web: www.henrybrick.com	Selma	AL	36703	334-875-2600	875-7842
I-XL Industries Ltd 612 Porcelain Ave SE Web: www.ixlbrick.com	Medicine Hat	AB	T1A8S4	403-526-5901	526-7680
International Chimney Corp 55 S Long St TF: 800-828-1446 ■ Web: www.internationalchimney.com	Williamsville	NY	14221	716-634-3967	634-3983
Jenkins Brick Co Inc 201 N 6th St PO Box 91 Web: www.jenkinsbrick.com	Montgomery	AL	36104	334-834-2210	262-6817
Kansas Brick & Tile Inc PO Box 450 TF Cust Svc: 800-999-0480 ■ Web: www.kansasbrick.com	Hoisington	KS	67544	620-653-2157	653-7609
Kinney Brick Co 100 Prosperity Rd PO Box 1804 TF: 800-464-4605 ■ Web: www.kinneybrick.com	Albuquerque	NM	87103	505-877-4550	877-4557
Lee Brick & Tile Co 3704 Hawkins Ave PO Box 1027 TF: 800-672-7559 ■ Web: www.leebrickonline.com	Sanford	NC	27330	919-774-4800	774-7557
Logan Clay Products Co 201 S Walnut St TF: 800-848-2141 ■ Web: www.loganclaypipe.com	Logan	OH	43138	740-385-2184	385-9336
Ludowici Roof Tile Inc 4757 Tile Plant Rd PO Box 69 TF Cust Svc: 800-945-8453 ■ Web: www.ludowici.com	New Lexington	OH	43764	740-342-1995	342-0025
Marion Ceramics Inc PO Box 1134 TF: 800-845-4010 ■ Web: www.marionceramics.com	Marion	SC	29571	843-423-1311	423-1515
McNear Brick & Block 1 McNear Brickyard Rd PO Box 151380 TF: 888-442-6811 ■ Web: www.mcnear.com	San Rafael	CA	94901	415-453-7702	453-3141
MCP Industries Inc Mission Clay Products Div 708 S Temescal St Suite 101 TF: 800-795-6067 ■ Web: www.mcpind.com	Corona	CA	92879	951-736-1881	549-8280
Morin Brick Co 130 Morin Brick Rd PO Box 1510 Web: www.morinbrick.com	Auburn	ME	04210	207-784-9375	784-2013
Mutual Materials Co 605 119th Ave NE TF: 800-477-3008 ■ Web: www.mutualmaterials.com	Bellevue	WA	98005	425-452-2300	454-7732
Old Virginia Brick Co 2500 W Main St TF: 800-879-8227 ■ Web: www.oldvirginiabrick.com	Salem	VA	24153	540-389-2357	389-4716
Pacific Clay Products Inc 14741 Lake St Web: www.pacificclay.com	Lake Elsinore	CA	92530	951-674-2131	674-4909
Palmetto Brick Co 3501 Brickyard Rd TF: 800-922-4423 ■ Web: www.palmettobrick.com	Wallace	SC	29596	843-537-7861	537-4802
Phoenix Brick Yard Corp 1814 S 7th Ave Web: www.phxbrickyard.com	Phoenix	AZ	85007	602-258-7158	258-1751
Pine Hall Brick Co 2701 Shorefair Dr TF: 800-952-7425 ■ Web: www.pinehallbrick.com	Winston-Salem	NC	27116	336-721-7536	725-3940
Potomac Valley Brick & Supply Co 15810 Indianola Dr Suite 100 Web: www.pvbrick.com	Rockville	MD	20855	301-309-9600	309-0929
Redland Brick Inc 15718 Clear Spring Rd TF: 800-366-2742 ■ Web: www.redlandbrick.com	Williamsport	MD	21795	301-223-7700	223-6675
Richards Brick Co 234 Springer Ave Web: www.richardsbrick.com	Edwardsville	IL	62025	618-656-0230	656-0944
Sioux City Brick & Tile Co 310 S Floyd Blvd Web: www.siouxcitybrick.com	Sioux City	IA	51101	712-258-6571	252-3215
Statesville Brick Co 391 Brickyard Rd TF: 800-522-4716 ■ Web: www.statesvillebrick.com	Statesville	NC	28677	704-872-4123	872-4125
Summitville Tiles Inc SR-644 Web: www.summitville.com	Summitville	OH	43962	330-223-1511	223-1414

	City	State	Zip	Phone	Fax
Superior Clay Corp 6566 Superior Rd SE *TF:* 800-848-6166 ■ *Web:* www.superiorclay.com	Uhrichsville	OH	44683	740-922-4122	922-6626
Taylor Clay Products Co 185 Peeler Rd PO Box 2128 *Web:* www.taylorclay.com	Salisbury	NC	28145	704-636-2411	636-2413
Tri-State Brick & Tile Co Inc 2050 Forest Ave *TF:* 800-962-2101 ■ *Web:* www.tsbrick.com	Jackson	MS	39286	601-981-1410	366-2205
Triangle Brick Co 6523 Hwy 55 *TF:* 800-672-8547 ■ *Web:* www.trianglebrick.com	Durham	NC	27713	919-544-1796	544-3904
US Tile Co Inc 909 Railroad St *TF:* 800-252-9548 ■ *Web:* www.ustile.com	Corona	CA	92882	951-737-0200	734-9591
Whitacre Greer Fireproofing Inc 1400 S Mahoning Ave *TF Cust Svc:* 800-947-2837 ■ *Web:* www.wgpaver.com	Alliance	OH	44601	330-823-1610	823-5502
Yankee Hill Brick & Tile 3705 S Coddington Ave *Web:* www.yankeehillbrick.com	Lincoln	NE	68522	402-477-6663	477-2832

151 CLEANING PRODUCTS

SEE ALSO Brushes & Brooms p. 1544; Mops, Sponges, Wiping Cloths p. 2254

	City	State	Zip	Phone	Fax
3M Automotive Aftermarket Div 3M Ctr Bldg 0223-06-N-01 *TF:* 800-364-3577 ■ *Web:* www.3m.com/product/business-units/automotive-aftermarket.html	Saint Paul	MN	55144	651-733-5547	737-2653
3M Commercial Care Div 3M Ctr Bldg 0223-04-N-14 *TF:* 800-852-9722 ■ *Web:* www.3m.com/product/business-units/commercial-care.html	Saint Paul	MN	55144	651-737-6501	733-5261
ABC Compounding Co Inc & Acme Wholesale 6970 Jonesboro Rd *TF:* 800-795-9222 ■ *Web:* www.abccompounding.com	Morrow	GA	30260	770-968-9222	968-7281
Abso-Clean Industries Inc 199 Wales Ave *TF:* 800-837-5000	Tonawanda	NY	14150	716-693-2111	693-2155
Adco Inc 900 W Main St *TF:* 800-821-7556 ■ *Web:* www.adco-inc.com	Sedalia	MO	65301	660-826-3300	826-1361
AJ Funk & Co 1471 Timber Dr *TF:* 877-225-3865 ■ *Web:* www.glasscleaner.com	Elgin	IL	60123	847-741-6760	741-6767
American Cleaning Solutions 39-30 Review Ave *TF:* 888-929-7587 ■ *Web:* www.cleaning-solutions.com	Long Island City	NY	11101	718-392-8080	482-9366
Angelus Shoe Polish Co 13500 Excelsior Dr *TF:* 800-722-4848 ■ *Web:* www.angelusshoepolish.com	Santa Fe Springs	CA	90670	562-229-0521	229-0702
Armor All 1221 Broadway PO Box 24305 *TF:* 800-222-7784 ■ *Web:* www.armorall.com	Oakland	CA	94623	510-271-7000	832-1463
Arrow-Magnolia International 2646 Rodney Ln *TF:* 800-527-2101 ■ *Web:* www.arrowmagnolia.com	Dallas	TX	75229	972-247-7111	484-2896
Aztec International Inc 5225 Middlebrook Pike *TF:* 800-369-5357 ■ *Web:* www.candlemaking.com/cms/Contact+Us/30.html	Knoxville	TN	37921	865-588-5357	558-6214
BAF Industries Inc 1910 S Yale St *TF:* 800-437-9893 ■ *Web:* www.prowax.com	Santa Ana	CA	92704	714-540-3850	545-2367
Blue Cross Laboratories Inc 20950 Ctr Pointe Pkwy *Web:* www.bc-labs.com	Santa Clarita	CA	91350	661-255-0955	255-3628
Buckeye International Inc 2700 Wagner Pl *TF:* 800-321-2583 ■ *Web:* www.buckeyeinternational.com	Maryland Heights	MO	63043	314-291-1900	298-2850
Bullen Cos 1640 Delmar Dr PO Box 37 *TF:* 800-444-8900 ■ *Web:* www.bullenairx.com	Folcroft	PA	19032	610-534-8900	534-8912
Butcher Co 8310 16th St *TF:* 800-795-9550	Austin	WI	53177	800-795-9550	786-7337
C & H Chemical Inc 222 Starkey St *TF:* 800-966-2909 ■ *Web:* www.chchemical.com	Saint Paul	MN	55107	651-227-4343	227-2485
Camco Chemical Co 8150 Holton Dr *TF Cust Svc:* 800-354-1001 ■ *Web:* www.camco-chem.com	Florence	KY	41042	859-727-3200	727-1508
Canberra Corp 3610 Holland Sylvania Rd *Web:* www.canberracorp.com	Toledo	OH	43615	419-841-6616	841-7597
Car-Freshner Corp 21205 Little Tree Dr PO Box 719 *TF:* 800-545-5454 ■ *Web:* www.little-trees.com	Watertown	NY	13601	315-788-6250	788-7467
Carroll Co 2900 W Kingsley Rd *TF:* 800-527-5722 ■ *Web:* www.carrollco.com	Garland	TX	75041	972-278-1304	840-0678
Cello Professional Products 1354 Old Post Rd *TF:* 800-638-4850 ■ *Web:* www.cello-online.com	Havre de Grace	MD	21078	410-939-1234	939-3028
Champion Chemical Co 8319 S Greenleaf Ave **Fax Area Code:* 800 ■ *TF:* 800-621-7868 ■ *Web:* www.championchemical.com	Whittier	CA	90602	562-945-1456	898-8064*
Chemical Specialties Mfg Corp 901 N Newkirk St *TF Sales:* 800-638-7370 ■ *Web:* www.chemspecworld.com	Baltimore	MD	21205	410-675-4800	675-0038
Chemstar 3670 Scarlet Oak Blvd *TF:* 800-325-3312 ■ *Web:* www.navybrand.com	Saint Louis	MO	63122	636-861-5500	861-5509
Church & Dwight Co Inc 469 N Harrison St *NYSE: CHD* ■ *Web:* www.churchdwight.com	Princeton	NJ	08543	609-683-5900	
Clorox Co 1221 Broadway *NYSE: CLX* ■ *TF Cust Svc:* 800-292-2808 ■ *Web:* www.thecloroxcompany.com	Oakland	CA	94612	510-271-7000	832-1463
Clorox Co The 1221 Broadway PO Box 24305 *Web:* www.thecloroxcompany.com	Oakland	CA	94612	510-271-7000	832-1463
Colgate-Palmolive Co 300 Pk Ave *NYSE: CL* ■ *Web:* www.colgate.com	New York	NY	10022	212-310-2000	310-2595
Concord Chemical Co 1700 Federal St *TF:* 800-282-2436	Camden	NJ	08105	856-966-1526	966-1526
Continental Commercial Products 305 Rock Industrial Pk **Fax Area Code:* 800 ■ *TF:* 800-325-1051 ■ *Web:* www.continentalcommercialproducts.com	Bridgeton	MO	63044	314-739-8585	327-5492*
Copper Brite Inc 1482 E Valley Rd Suite 29 PO Box 50610 *Web:* www.copperbrite.com	Santa Barbara	CA	93108	805-565-1566	565-1394
Correlated Products Inc 5616 Progress Rd *TF:* 800-428-3266 ■ *Web:* www.cpicorrelated.com	Indianapolis	IN	46242	317-243-3248	244-8461
Crain Chemical Co 2624 Andjon Dr	Dallas	TX	75220	214-358-3301	358-3304
Damon Industries Inc 12435 Rockhill Ave NE PO Box 2120 *TF:* 800-362-9850 ■ *Web:* www.damonq.com	Alliance	OH	44601	330-821-5310	821-6355
Delta Carbona LP 376 Hollywood Ave Suite 208 *TF:* 888-746-5599 ■ *Web:* www.carbona.com	Fairfield	NJ	07004	973-808-6260	808-5661
DeSoto LLC 900 Washington St PO Box 609	Joliet	IL	60433	815-727-4931	727-4333
Diamond Chemical Co Inc Union Ave & Dubois St *TF:* 800-654-7627 ■ *Web:* www.diamondchem.com	East Rutherford	NJ	07073	201-935-4300	935-6997
Dubois Chemicals Inc 200 Crowne Pt Pl **Fax Area Code:* 800 ■ *TF:* 800-543-4906 ■ *Web:* www.duboischemicals.com	Sharonville	OH	45241	513-326-8800	543-1720*
Dura Wax Co 4101 W Albany St *TF:* 800-435-5705 ■ *Web:* www.janitorialsuppliesandequipment.com	McHenry	IL	60050	815-385-5000	344-8056
Ecolab Inc 370 N Wabasha St *NYSE: ECL* ■ *TF:* 800-352-5326 ■ *Web:* www.ecolab.com	Saint Paul	MN	55102	651-293-2233	293-2069
Elco Laboratories Inc 2545 Palmer Ave *Web:* www.elcolabs.com	University Park	IL	60466	708-534-3000	534-0445
Empire Cleaning Supply 12821 S Figueroa St *TF:* 888-868-7336 ■ *Web:* www.empirecleaningsupply.com	Los Angeles	CA	90061	310-715-6500	715-1166
Emulso Corp 2750 Kenmore Ave *TF:* 800-724-7667 ■ *Web:* www.emulso.com	Tonawanda	NY	14150	716-854-2889	854-2809
Falcon Safety Products Inc 25 Chubb Way *TF:* 800-332-5266 ■ *Web:* www.falconsafety.com	Branchburg	NJ	08876	908-707-4900	707-8855
Faultless Starch/Bon Ami Co The 1025 W 8th St *TF Cust Svc:* 800-821-5565 ■ *Web:* www.bonami.com	Kansas City	MO	64101	816-842-1230	842-3417
Fine Organics Corp 420 Kuller Rd PO Box 2277 **Fax:* Sales ■ *TF:* 800-526-7480 ■ *Web:* www.fineorganicscorp.com	Clifton	NJ	07015	973-478-1000	478-6120*
Frank B Ross Co 970-H New Brunswick Ave *Web:* www.frankbross.com	Rahway	NJ	07065	732-669-0810	669-0814
Frank Miller & Sons Inc 13831 S Emerald Ave *TF:* 800-423-6358	Riverdale	IL	60827	708-201-7200	841-8073
Gent-l-kleen Products Inc 3445 Board Rd *TF:* 800-233-9382 ■ *Web:* www.gentlkleen.com	York	PA	17406	717-767-6881	767-6888
Glissen Chemical Co Inc 1321 58th St *TF:* 800-356-9922	Brooklyn	NY	11219	718-436-4200	
Goodwin Co 12102 Industry St *Web:* www.goodwininc.com	Garden Grove	CA	92841	714-894-0531	897-7673
Granitize Products Inc 11022 Vulcan St *TF:* 800-553-6866 ■ *Web:* www.granitize.com	South Gate	CA	90280	562-923-5438	861-3475
Heritage-Crystal Clean Inc 2175 Pt Blvd Suite 375 *TF:* 877-938-7948 ■ *Web:* www.crystal-clean.com	Elgin	IL	60123	847-836-5670	836-5677
Hill Mfg Co Inc 1500 Jonesboro Rd SE **Fax Area Code:* 800 ■ *TF:* 800-445-5123 ■ *Web:* www.soap.com	Atlanta	GA	30315	404-522-8364	789-1754*
Hillyard Chemical Co Inc 302 N 4th St **Fax Area Code:* 800 ■ *TF:* 800-365-1555 ■ *Web:* www.hillyard.com	Saint Joseph	MO	64501	816-233-1321	861-0256*
Impact Products LLC 2840 Centennial Rd *TF Cust Svc:* 800-333-1541 ■ *Web:* www.impact-products.com	Toledo	OH	43617	419-841-2891	841-7861
Implus Footcare LLC 9221 Globe Ctr Dr *TF:* 800-446-7587 ■ *Web:* www.implus.com	Morrisville	NC	27560	919-544-7900	
ITW Dymon 805 E Old 56 Hwy *TF:* 800-443-9536 ■ *Web:* www.dymon.com	Olathe	KS	66061	913-829-6296	397-8707
James Austin Co 115 Downieville Rd PO Box 827 *TF:* 800-245-1942 ■ *Web:* www.jamesaustin.com	Mars	PA	16046	724-625-1535	625-3288
JohnsonDiversey Inc 8310 16th St PO Box 902 *Web:* www.diversey.com	Sturtevant	WI	53177	262-631-4001	631-4282
Kay Chemical Co 8300 Capital Dr *TF:* 800-333-4300 ■ *Web:* www.ecolab.com	Greensboro	NC	27409	336-668-7290	668-9763
Kitter Corp 100 S Cleveland St *TF:* 800-299-5488 ■ *Web:* www.kitter.com	Amarillo	TX	79105	806-376-1448	555-0199
Koger/Air Corp PO Box 2098 *TF:* 800-368-2096 ■ *Web:* www.kogerair.com	Martinsville	VA	24113	276-638-8821	638-4305
KozaK Auto DryWash Inc 6 Lyon St *TF:* 800-237-9927 ■ *Web:* www.kozak.com	Batavia	NY	14020	585-343-8111	343-3732
Leadership Performance Sustainability Laboratories 4647 Hugh Howell Rd *TF:* 800-241-8334 ■ *Web:* www.lpslabs.com	Tucker	GA	30084	770-934-7800	243-8899
Lincoln Shoe Polish Co 172 Commercial St *Web:* www.lincolnshoepolish.com	Sunnyvale	CA	94086	408-732-5120	732-0659
Lonn Mfg Co Inc 5450 W 84th St *Web:* www.lonn.net	Indianapolis	IN	46228	317-897-1440	898-4561
Luseaux Laboratories Inc 16816 S Gramercy Pl	Gardena	CA	90247	310-324-1555	
M-Chem Technologies Inc 1607 Derwent Way **Fax Area Code:* 604 ■ *TF:* 800-663-9925 ■ *Web:* www.mchem.com	Delta	BC	V3M6K8	800-663-9925	526-1618*
Madison Chemical Co Inc 3141 Clifty Dr *TF:* 800-345-1915 ■ *Web:* www.madchem.com	Madison	IN	47250	812-273-6000	273-6002
Magic American Corp 26901 Cannon Rd Suite 190 *TF Cust Svc:* 800-321-6330 ■ *Web:* www.magicamerican.com	Bedford Heights	OH	44146	440-786-3100	786-3101
Malco Products Inc 361 Fairview Ave PO Box 892 *TF:* 800-253-2526 ■ *Web:* www.malcopro.com	Barberton	OH	44203	330-753-0361	753-2025
Matchless Metal Polish Co 840 W 49th Pl *Web:* www.matchlessmetal.com	Chicago	IL	60609	773-924-1515	924-5513
Meguiar's Inc 17991 Mitchell S *TF Cust Svc:* 800-347-5700 ■ *Web:* www.meguiars.com	Irvine	CA	92614	949-752-8000	752-5784
Micro Care Corp 595 John Downey Dr *TF:* 800-638-0125 ■ *Web:* www.microcare.com	New Britain	CT	06051	860-827-0626	827-8105

				Phone	Fax
Mission Laboratories 2433 Birkdale St. *TF:* 888-201-8866 ■ *Web:* www.missionlabs.net	Los Angeles	CA	90031	323-223-1405	223-9968
Morgan Gallacher Inc 8707 Millergrove Dr. *TF:* 877-344-2346 ■ *Web:* www.customchem.com	Santa Fe Springs	CA	90670	562-695-1232	
Mother's Polishes Waxes & Cleaners 5456 Industrial Dr. *TF:* 800-221-8257 ■ *Web:* www.mothers.com	Huntington Beach	CA	92649	714-891-3364	893-1827
National Chemical Laboratories Inc 401 N 10th St. *TF:* 800-628-2436 ■ *Web:* www.nclonline.com	Philadelphia	PA	19123	215-922-1200	922-5517
National Chemicals Inc 105 Liberty St PO box 32. **Fax Area Code:* 877 ■ *TF Cust Svc:* 800-533-0027 ■ *Web:* www.nationalchemicals.com	Winona	MN	55987	507-454-5640	858-4141*
NCH Corp 2727 Chemsearch Blvd. *TF:* 800-527-9919 ■ *Web:* www.nch.com	Irving	TX	75062	972-438-0211	438-0707
New Pig Corp 1 Pork Ave. **Fax Area Code:* 800 ■ *TF:* 800-468-4647 ■ *Web:* www.newpig.com	Tipton	PA	16684	814-684-0101	621-7447*
Nord-Viscount Corp PO Box 300166. **Fax Area Code:* 866 ■ *TF:* 866-278-7674	Brooklyn	NY	11230	718-854-5586	660-7000*
Northern Labs Inc 5800 W Dr PO Box 850. *TF:* 800-558-7621 ■ *Web:* www.northernlabs.com	Manitowoc	WI	54221	920-684-7137	684-6573
Nuvite Chemical Compounds Corp 213 Freeman St. *TF:* 800-394-8351 ■ *Web:* www.nuvitechemical.com	Brooklyn	NY	11222	718-383-8351	383-0008
Ocean Bio-Chem Inc (OBCI) 4041 SW 47th Ave. *NASDAQ:* OBCI ■ *TF:* 800-327-8583 ■ *Web:* www.oceanbiochem.com	Fort Lauderdale	FL	33314	954-587-6280	587-2813
Paramount Chemical Specialties Inc PO Box 124. *TF:* 877-846-7826 ■ *Web:* www.kidsnpetsbrand.com	Redmond	WA	98073	425-882-2673	881-1486
Prestige Brands International Inc 90 N Broadway. *NYSE:* PBH ■ *Web:* www.prestigebrandsinc.com	Irvington	NY	10533	914-524-6810	524-6815
Prosoco Inc 3741 Greenway Cir. **Fax Area Code:* 785 ■ *Web:* www.prosoco.com	Lawrence	KS	66046	800-255-4255	830-9797*
Reckitt Benckiser Inc 399 Interpace Pkwy PO Box 225. *TF Cust Svc:* 800-333-3899 ■ *Web:* www.rb.com	Parsippany	NJ	07054	973-404-2600	404-5700
Safeguard Chemical Corp 411 Wales Ave. *TF:* 800-536-3170 ■ *Web:* www.safeguardchemical.com	Bronx	NY	10454	718-585-3170	585-3657
Safetec Of America Inc 887 Kensington Ave. *TF:* 800-456-7077 ■ *Web:* www.safetec.com	Buffalo	NY	14215	716-895-1822	895-2969
SC Johnson & Son Inc 1525 Howe St. *TF:* 800-494-4855 ■ *Web:* www.scjohnson.com	Racine	WI	53403	262-260-2154	260-2632
Scott Fetzer Co Scot Laboratories Div 16841 Pk Cir Dr. *TF:* 800-486-7268 ■ *Web:* www.scotlabs.com	Chagrin Falls	OH	44023	440-543-3033	543-1825
Scott's Liquid Gold Inc 4880 Havana St. *TF:* 800-447-1919 ■ *Web:* www.scottsliquidgold.com	Denver	CO	80239	303-373-4860	
Selig Chemical Industries Inc 115 Kendall Pk Ln. *TF:* 800-447-3544 ■ *Web:* www.seligind.com	Atlanta	GA	30336	800-447-3544	999-3566
Seventh Generation Inc 60 Lake St. *TF:* 800-456-1191 ■ *Web:* www.seventhgeneration.com	Burlington	VT	05401	802-658-3773	658-1771
Share Corp 7821 N Faulkner Rd. *TF:* 800-776-7192 ■ *Web:* www.sharecorp.com	Milwaukee	WI	53224	414-355-4000	355-0516
Simoniz USA 201 Boston Tpke. *TF:* 800-227-5536 ■ *Web:* www.simonizusa.com	Bolton	CT	06043	860-646-0172	645-6070
Snyder Mfg Corp 1541 W Cowles St. *Web:* www.snydermanufacturing.com	Long Beach	CA	90813	562-432-2038	432-1603
State Industrial Products 3100 Hamilton Ave. **Fax Area Code:* 888 ■ *TF:* 800-782-2436 ■ *Web:* www.stateindustrial.com	Cleveland	OH	44114	216-861-7114	771-9670*
Stearns Packaging Corp 4200 Sycamore Ave. *TF:* 800-655-5008 ■ *Web:* www.stearnspkg.com	Madison	WI	53714	608-246-5150	246-5149
Summit Industries Inc 839 Pickens Industrial Dr. *TF:* 800-241-6996 ■ *Web:* www.summitinds.com	Marietta	GA	30062	770-590-0600	590-0714
Sun Products Corp The 60 Danbury Rd. *TF:* 800-298-2408 ■ *Web:* www.sunproductscorp.com	Wilton	CT	06897	203-254-6700	256-0585
Sunshine Makers Inc 15922 Pacific Coast Hwy. *TF:* 800-228-0709 ■ *Web:* www.simplegreen.com	Huntington Harbour	CA	92649	562-795-6000	592-3034
Turtle Wax Inc PO Box 247. *TF:* 800-887-8539 ■ *Web:* www.turtlewax.com	Westmont	IL	60559	800-887-8539	
Unit Chemical Corp 7360 Commercial Way. *TF:* 800-879-8648 ■ *Web:* www.unitchemical.com	Henderson	NV	89015	702-564-6454	564-6629
UNX Inc 707 E Arlington Blvd PO Box 7206. *Web:* www.unxinc.com	Greenville	NC	27835	252-756-8616	756-2764
Venus Laboratories Inc 855 Lively Blvd. *TF:* 800-592-1900 ■ *Web:* www.venuslabs.com	Wood Dale	IL	60191	630-595-1900	595-3252
Warsaw Chemical Co Inc 390 Argonne Rd. *TF:* 800-548-3396 ■ *Web:* www.warsaw-chem.com	Warsaw	IN	46580	574-267-3251	267-3884
WD-40 Co 1061 Cudahy Pl. *NASDAQ:* WDFC ■ *TF:* 800-448-9340 ■ *Web:* www.wd40company.com	San Diego	CA	92110	619-275-1400	275-5823
Webco Chemical Corp 420 W Main St. *Web:* www.webcochemical.com	Dudley	MA	01571	508-943-2337	987-0366
West Penetone Corp 700 Gotham Pkwy. *TF:* 800-631-1652 ■ *Web:* www.west-penetone.com	Carlstadt	NJ	07072	201-567-3000	510-3973
Willert Home Products Inc 4044 Pk Ave. *TF:* 800-325-9680 ■ *Web:* www.willert.com	Saint Louis	MO	63110	314-772-2822	772-3506
ZEP Inc 1310 Seaboard Industrial Blvd NW. *NYSE:* ZEP ■ *TF:* 877-428-9937 ■ *Web:* www.zepinc.com	Atlanta	GA	30318	404-352-1680	603-7958
Zep Mfg Co 1310 Seaboard Industrial Blvd NW. *TF:* 877-428-9937 ■ *Web:* www.zepmfg.com	Atlanta	GA	30318	404-352-1680	

152 CLEANING SERVICES

SEE ALSO Bio-Recovery Services p. 1524; Building Maintenance Services p. 1545

				Phone	Fax
1-800-Water Damage 1167 Mercer St. *TF:* 800-940-9745 ■ *Web:* www.1800waterdamage.com	Seattle	WA	98109	206-381-3041	381-3052
ABM Janitorial Services 420 Taylor St 2nd Fl.	San Francisco	CA	94102	415-351-4450	351-4581
BearCom Bldg Services 7022 S 400 W. *TF:* 888-569-9533 ■ *Web:* www.bearcomservices.com	Midvale	UT	84047	801-569-9500	569-8400
Bonus Bldg Care Inc 14331 Proton Rd. *TF:* 800-931-1102 ■ *Web:* www.bonusbuildingcare.com	Dallas	TX	75244	972-789-9400	789-9399
Bonus of America Inc Rt 2 PO Box 132-C. *TF:* 800-931-1102 ■ *Web:* www.bonusbuildingcare.com	McAlester	OK	74501	918-823-4990	823-4994
Boston's Best Chimney Sweep 76 Bacon St. *TF Cust Svc:* 800-660-6708 ■ *Web:* www.bestchimney.com	Waltham	MA	02451	781-893-6611	893-1132
Braco Window Cleaning Service Inc 1 Braco International Blvd. *TF Cust Svc:* 877-878-7091 ■ *Web:* www.bracowindowcleaning.com	Wilder	KY	41076	859-442-6000	442-6001
Chem-Dry 1530 N 1000 W. *TF:* 800-243-6379 ■ *Web:* www.chemdry.com	Logan	UT	84321	435-755-0099	755-0021
Clean Power LLC 124 N 121st St. *TF:* 888-566-1717 ■ *Web:* www.cleanpower1.com	Milwaukee	WI	53226	414-302-3000	302-3015
Clean-Tech Co 211 S Jefferson Ave. **Fax Area Code:* 800 ■ *TF:* 800-852-2388	Saint Louis	MO	63103	314-652-2388	762-7910*
Cleaning Authority 6994 Columbia Gateway Dr Suite 100. **Fax Area Code:* 866 ■ *TF:* 800-783-6243 ■ *Web:* www.thecleaningauthority.com	Columbia	MD	21046	410-740-1900	685-6243*
CleanNet USA 9861 Brokenland Pkwy Suite 208. *TF:* 800-735-8838 ■ *Web:* www.cleannetusa.com	Columbia	MD	21046	410-720-6444	720-5307
Cleanol Services Inc 40 adesso Dr concord. *TF:* 800-263-9430 ■ *Web:* www.cleanol.com	North York	ON	I4K3C6	416-745-5221	745-5209
Coverall Cleaning Concepts 5201 Congress Ave Suite 275. *TF:* 800-537-3371 ■ *Web:* www.coverall.com	Boca Raton	FL	33487	561-922-2500	922-2423
Deluxe Carpet Cleaning Co Inc 5907 High Grove Rd.	Grandview	MO	64030	816-763-3331	763-3331
Diversified Maintenance Systems Inc 5110 Eisenhower Blvd Suite 150. *TF:* 800-351-1557 ■ *Web:* www.diveinc.com	Tampa	FL	33634	813-383-0238	
Duraclean International Inc 220 W Campus Dr # A. *TF:* 800-251-7070 ■ *Web:* www.duraclean.com	Arlington Heights	IL	60004	847-704-7100	704-7101
Federal Bldg Services Inc 1641 Barclay Blvd. *TF:* 800-982-9234 ■ *Web:* www.federalbuildingservice.com	Buffalo Grove	IL	60089	847-279-7360	215-7600
Fish Window Cleaning Services Inc 200 Enchanted Pkwy. *TF:* 877-707-3474 ■ *Web:* www.fishwindowcleaning.com	Saint Louis	MO	63021	636-530-7334	530-7856
GCA Services Group 1350 Euclid Ave Suite 1500. *TF:* 800-422-8760 ■ *Web:* www.gcaservices.com	Cleveland	OH	44115	216-535-4900	583-0481
GCI Services 2324 Ridgepoint Dr Suite A. *TF:* 800-833-2923 ■ *Web:* www.gciservices.com	Austin	TX	78754	512-615-3400	615-3509
Healthcare Services Group Inc (HCSG) 3220 Tillman Dr Suite 300. *NASDAQ:* HCSG ■ *TF:* 800-363-4274 ■ *Web:* www.hcsgcorp.com	Bensalem	PA	19020	215-639-4274	639-2152
Heaven's Best Carpet & Upholstery Cleaning PO Box 607. *TF:* 800-359-2095 ■ *Web:* www.heavensbest.com	Rexburg	ID	83440	208-359-1106	359-1236
Hospital Housekeeping Systems 322 Congress Ave 2nd Fl. *TF:* 800-229-2028 ■ *Web:* www.hhs1.com	Austin	TX	78701	512-478-1888	478-1971
Ih Services Inc PO Box 5033. *TF:* 800-868-3777 ■ *Web:* www.ihservices.com	Greenville	SC	29606	864-297-3748	297-9219
Jan-Pro International Inc (JPI) 2520 Northwinds Pkwy Suite 375. *TF:* 866-355-1064 ■ *Web:* www.jan-pro.com	Alpharetta	GA	30009	678-336-1780	336-1781
Jani-King International Inc 16885 Dallas Pkwy. **Fax Area Code:* 800 ■ *TF:* 800-552-5264 ■ *Web:* www.janiking.com	Addison	TX	75001	972-991-0900	526-4546*
Linc Services Mid-Atlantic LLC 3701 Saunders Ave. *TF:* 800-238-5462 ■ *Web:* www.lincservice.com	Richmond	VA	23227	804-254-5790	
Maid Brigade USA/Minimaid Canada 4 Concourse Pkwy Suite 200. *TF:* 800-722-6243 ■ *Web:* www.maidbrigade.com	Atlanta	GA	30328	770-551-9630	391-9092
MaidPro Corp 180 Canal St. *TF:* 888-624-3776 ■ *Web:* www.maidpro.com	Boston	MA	02114	617-742-8787	720-0700
Maids International 9394 W Dodge Rd Suite 1400. *TF:* 800-843-6243 ■ *Web:* www.maids.com	Omaha	NE	68114	402-558-5555	558-4112
Merry Maids 3839 Forrest Hill-Irene Rd. *TF:* 800-798-8000 ■ *Web:* www.merrymaids.com	Memphis	TN	38125	901-597-8100	597-8140
Molly Maid Inc 3948 Ranchero Dr. *TF:* 800-665-5962 ■ *Web:* www.mollymaid.com	Ann Arbor	MI	48108	734-822-6800	822-6888
MPW Industrial Services Group Inc 9711 Lancaster Rd SE PO Box 10. *TF:* 800-827-8790 ■ *Web:* www.mpwgroup.com	Hebron	OH	43025	740-927-8790	928-8140
Neighbors Stores Inc 1314 Old Hwy 601 S PO Box 48. *Web:* www.neighborsstores.com	Mount Airy	NC	27030	336-789-5561	789-7067
OctoClean Franchising Systems 3357 Chicago Ave. *Web:* www.octoclean.com	Riverside	CA	92507	951-683-5859	779-0270
Platinum Maintenance Services Corp 120 Broadway FL 36. *TF:* 888-535-7528 ■ *Web:* www.platinummaintenance.com	New York	NY	10271	212-535-9700	480-2699
Professional Carpet Systems Inc (PCS) 4211 Atlantic Ave. *TF:* 800-925-5055 ■ *Web:* www.professionalcarpetsystems.com	Raleigh	NC	27604	919-875-8871	875-9855

	City	State	ZIP	Phone	Fax
Professional Contract Services Inc 718 W FM 1626 *Web:* www.pcsiinc.com	Austin	TX	78748	512-358-8887	358-8890
Professional Janitorial Service Of Houston Inc 2303 Nance St *Web:* www.pjs.com	Houston	TX	77020	713-850-0287	963-9420
Pyramid Bldg Maintenance Corp 2175 Martin Ave *TF:* 800-605-8263 ■ *Web:* www.pmc-ibm.com	Santa Clara	CA	95050	408-727-9393	727-9344
Rainbow International 1010 N University Pk Dr *TF:* 800-583-9100 ■ *Web:* www.rainbowintl.com	Waco	TX	76707	254-745-2444	745-2592
Serv-U-Clean 207 Edgeley Blvd Unit 5 **Fax Area Code:* 905 ■ *Web:* www.serv-u-clean.com	Concord	ON	L4K4B5	416-667-0696	660-0550*
Service Management Systems 7135 Charlotte Pike Suite 100 *Web:* www.smsclean.com	Nashville	TN	37209	615-399-1839	399-1438
ServiceMaster Clean 3839 Forrest Hill Irene Rd *TF:* 800-633-5703 ■ *Web:* www.servicemaster.com	Memphis	TN	38125	901-597-7500	597-7600
Servpro Industries Inc 801 Industrial Blvd *TF:* 800-826-9586 ■ *Web:* www.servpro.com	Gallatin	TN	37066	615-451-0600	451-4861
Sharian Inc 368 W Ponce de Leon Ave	Decatur	GA	30030	404-373-2274	370-1812
Sparkle International Inc 26851 Richmond Rd *TF:* 800-321-0770 ■ *Web:* www.sparklewash.com	Cleveland	OH	44146	216-464-4212	464-8869
Spencer Bldg Maintenance Inc 1336 Dixieanne Ave *Web:* www.spencerservices.com	Sacramento	CA	95815	916-922-1900	641-8250
St Moritz Bldg Services Inc 4616 Clairton Blvd *Web:* www.bsinc.com	Pittsburgh	PA	15236	412-885-2100	885-3953
Steam Bros Inc 2400 Vermont Ave *TF:* 800-767-5064 ■ *Web:* www.steambrothers.com	Bismarck	ND	58502	701-222-1263	222-1372
Steamatic Inc 33 quorum Dr *TF:* 800-544-1303 ■ *Web:* www.steamatic.com	Fort Worth	TX	76137	817-332-1575	332-5349
Support Services of America Inc 12440 Firestone Blvd Suite 312 *TF:* 888-564-0005 ■ *Web:* www.supportservicesamerica.com	Norwalk	CA	90650	562-868-3550	868-7811
Swisher Hygiene Co 4725 Piedmont Row Dr **Fax Area Code:* 800 ■ *TF:* 800-444-4138 ■ *Web:* www.swisherhygiene.com	Charlotte	NC	28210	704-364-7707	444-4565*
T.u.c.s. Cleaning Service Inc 166 Central Ave *TF:* 800-992-5998 ■ *Web:* www.tucscleaning.com	Orange	NJ	07050	973-673-0700	
Vanguard Cleaning Systems Inc 655 Mariners Island Blvd Suite 303 *TF:* 800-564-6422 ■ *Web:* www.vanguardcleaning.com	San Mateo	CA	94404	650-594-1500	591-1545
Venoco Inc 370 17th St Suite 3900 *NYSE: VQ* ■ *Web:* www.venocoinc.com	Denver	CO	80202	303-626-8300	626-8315
Window Gang 405 Arendell St *TF:* 877-946-4264 ■ *Web:* www.windowgang.com	Morehead City	NC	28557	252-726-1463	726-2837

153 CLOCKS, WATCHES, RELATED DEVICES, PARTS

	City	State	ZIP	Phone	Fax
Baume & Mercier Inc 645 5th Ave *TF:* 800-683-2286 ■ *Web:* www.baume-et-mercier.com	New York	NY	10022	212-593-0444	755-3138
Borg Indak Inc 701 Enterprise Dr *Web:* www.borgindak.com	Delavan	WI	53115	262-728-5531	728-3788
Bulova Corp 1 Bulova Ave *TF:* 800-228-5682 ■ *Web:* www.bulova.com	Woodside	NY	11377	718-204-3300	204-3546
Canterbury International 5632 W Washington Blvd *TF:* 800-935-7111 ■ *Web:* www.canterburyintl.com	Los Angeles	CA	90016	323-936-7111	936-7115
Citizen Watch Co of America Inc 1200 Wall St W *TF:* 800-321-1023 ■ *Web:* www.citizenwatch.com	Lyndhurst	NJ	07071	201-438-8150	438-4161
Colibri/Park Lane Assoc Inc Linden Div 100 Niantic Ave *TF Sales:* 800-556-7354	Providence	RI	02907	401-943-2100	943-4230
E Gluck Corp 29-10 Thompson Ave *TF:* 800-937-0051 ■ *Web:* www.armitron.com	Long Island City	NY	11101	718-784-0700	482-2702
Emperor Clock LLC 340 Industrial Pk Dr **Fax Area Code:* 434 ■ *TF:* 800-642-0011 ■ *Web:* www.emperorclock.com	Amherst	VA	24521	800-642-0011	946-7747*
Fossil Inc 2280 N Greenville Ave *NASDAQ: FOSL* ■ *TF:* 800-969-0900 ■ *Web:* www.fossil.com	Richardson	TX	75082	972-234-2525	699-2169
Hamilton Watch Co Inc 1200 Harbor Blvd *TF Cust Svc:* 800-456-5354 ■ *Web:* www.hamiltonwatch.com	Weehawken	NJ	07086	201-271-4680	271-4633
Howard Miller Clock Co 860 E Main Ave *Web:* www.howardmiller.com	Zeeland	MI	49464	616-772-7277	772-1670
Invicta Watch Co of America Inc 1 Invicta WY 3069 Taft St *TF:* 800-327-7682 ■ *Web:* www.invictawatch.com	Hollywood	FL	33021	954-921-2444	921-4222
Marcel Watch Corp 200 Meadowland Pkwy **Fax:* Cust Svc ■ *TF:* 800-422-6053 ■ *Web:* www.marcelwatch.com	Secaucus	NJ	07094	201-330-5600	330-0218*
Movado Group Inc 650 From Rd Suite 375 *NYSE: MOV* ■ *TF:* 800-810-2311 ■ *Web:* www.movadogroupinc.com	Paramus	NJ	07652	201-267-8000	267-8070
MZ Berger & Co Inc 29-76 Northern Blvd 4th Fl *TF:* 800-221-0131 ■ *Web:* www.mzberger.com	Long Island City	NY	11101	718-472-7500	472-7691
Pyramid Technologies Inc 45 Gracey Ave *TF:* 888-479-7264 ■ *Web:* www.pyramidtechnologies.com	Meriden	CT	06451	203-238-0550	237-9497
RADO USA 1200 Harbor Blvd *TF:* 877-839-5223 ■ *Web:* www.rado.ch	Weehawken	NJ	07086	201-271-1400	271-4633
Seiko Corp of America 1111 MacArthur Blvd **Fax:* Cust Svc ■ *TF Cust Svc:* 800-782-2510 ■ *Web:* www.seikousa.com	Mahwah	NJ	07430	201-529-5730	529-5985*
Seiko Instruments USA Inc 1309 Rutherford Ln *TF:* 800-358-0880 ■ *Web:* www.seikoinstruments.com	Austin	TX	78753	512-349-3800	349-3000
Skagen Designs Inc 640 Maestro Dr Suite 100 *TF:* 800-791-6784 ■ *Web:* www.skagen.com	Reno	NV	89511	775-850-5500	850-5530
Sligh Furniture Co 217 E 24th St Suite 102 *TF:* 866-277-0258 ■ *Web:* www.sligh.com	Holland	MI	49423	616-392-7101	392-9495
Swatch Group 1200 Harbor Blvd 7th Fl *TF:* 800-456-5354 ■ *Web:* www.swatchgroup.com	Weehawken	NJ	07087	201-271-1400	271-4633
Telechron Inc 2025 Trade St	Leland	NC	28451	910-371-1132	371-1133
Timex Group USA Inc 555 Christian Rd PO Box 310 *TF:* 800-367-8463 ■ *Web:* www.timex.com	Middlebury	CT	06762	203-346-5000	346-5139
Verdin Co The 444 Reading Rd *TF:* 800-543-0488 ■ *Web:* www.verdin.com	Cincinnati	OH	45202	513-241-4010	241-1855
Vulcan Inc 410 E Berry Ave *TF:* 800-633-6845 ■ *Web:* www.vulcaninc.com	Foley	AL	36535	251-943-1541	943-9270
World of Watches 14051 NW 14th St Bay 6 *TF:* 800-222-0077 ■ *Web:* www.worldofwatches.com	Sunrise	FL	33323	954-453-2821	453-2950

154 CLOSURES - METAL OR PLASTICS

	City	State	ZIP	Phone	Fax
Alcoa Closure Systems International Inc 6625 Network Way Suite 200 *Web:* www.alcoa.com/csi	Indianapolis	IN	46278	317-390-5000	390-5137
Alliance Plastics Inc 3123 Stn Rd *TF:* 877-728-9227 ■ *Web:* www.allianceplastics.com	Erie	PA	16510	814-899-7671	898-1638
AptarGroup Inc 475 W Terra Cotta Ave Suite E *NYSE: ATR* ■ *Web:* www.aptar.com	Crystal Lake	IL	60014	815-477-0424	477-0481
Caplugs LLC 2150 Elmwood Ave *TF cust svc:* 888-227-5847 ■ *Web:* www.caplugs.com	Buffalo	NY	14207	716-876-9855	874-1680
Carpin Mfg Inc 411 Austin Rd *TF:* 800-227-7461 ■ *Web:* www.carpin.com	Waterbury	CT	06705	203-574-2556	753-8771
Champion Container Corp 180 Essex Ave PO Box 90 *Web:* www.championcontainer.com	Avenel	NJ	07001	732-636-6700	855-8663
Magenta Corp 3800 N Milwaukee Ave *TF:* 800-387-4378 ■ *Web:* www.magentacorp.com	Chicago	IL	60641	773-777-5050	777-4055
Penn-Wheeling Metal Closure & Caps 1701 Wheeling Ave *TF:* 800-999-2567	Glen Dale	WV	26038	304-845-3402	843-5475
Phoenix Closures Inc 1899 High Grove Ln *Web:* www.phoenixclosures.com	Naperville	IL	60540	630-420-4750	420-4774
Polytop Corp 110 Graham Dr *Web:* www.polytop.com	Slatersville	RI	02876	401-767-2400	765-2694
Portola Tech International Inc 85 Fairmount St *TF:* 800-556-7630 ■ *Web:* www.portolatech.com	Woonsocket	RI	02895	401-765-0600	766-8324
Rexam Closures & Containers 3245 Kansas Rd *Web:* www.rexamclosures.com	Evansville	IN	47725	812-867-6671	867-6861
Silgan Holdings Inc 4 Landmark Sq Suite 400 *NASDAQ: SLGN* ■ *Web:* www.silganholdings.com	Stamford	CT	06901	203-975-7110	975-7902
StockCap 123 Manufacturers Dr *TF:* 800-827-2277 ■ *Web:* www.stockcap.com	Arnold	MO	63010	636-282-6800	282-6888
Stull Technologies Inc 17 Veronica Ave *Web:* www.stulltech.com	Somerset	NJ	08873	732-873-5000	873-1295
Tipper Tie Inc 2000 Lufkin Rd *TF:* 800-331-2905 ■ *Web:* www.tippertie.com	Apex	NC	27502	919-362-8811	362-7058
Van Blarcom Closures Inc 156 Sandford St *Web:* www.vbcpkg.com	Brooklyn	NY	11205	718-855-3810	935-9855
Weatherchem Corp 2222 Highland Rd *Web:* www.weatherchem.com	Twinsburg	OH	44087	330-425-4206	425-1385
West Penn Plastic Inc 4117 Pulaski Rd *Web:* www.westpennplastic.com	New Castle	PA	16101	724-654-2081	654-5126

155 CLOTHING & ACCESSORIES - MFR

SEE ALSO Baby Products p. 1504; Clothing & Accessories - Whol p. 1613; Fashion Design Houses p. 1842; Footwear p. 1876; Leather Goods - Personal p. 2149; Personal Protective Equipment & Clothing p. 2409

155-1 Athletic Apparel

	City	State	ZIP	Phone	Fax
Bogner of America Inc 172 Bogner Dr *TF:* 800-415-4477 ■ *Web:* www.bogner.com	Newport	VT	05855	802-334-6507	334-6870
Bristol Products Corp 700 Shelby St *TF Orders:* 800-336-8775 ■ *Web:* www.bristolproducts.com	Bristol	TN	37620	423-968-4140	968-2084
Champion Athletic Wear 1000 E Hanes Mill Rd *TF:* 800-999-2249 ■ *Web:* www.championforwomen.com	Winston-Salem	NC	27105	336-519-4400	519-6501
Choi Bros Inc 3401 W Division St *TF:* 800-524-2464 ■ *Web:* www.choibrothers.com	Chicago	IL	60651	773-489-2800	489-3030
Columbia Sportswear Co 14375 NW Science Pk Dr *NASDAQ: COLM* ■ *TF:* 800-547-8066 ■ *Web:* www.columbia.com	Portland	OR	97229	503-985-4000	985-5800
Cutter & Buck Inc 701 N 34th St Suite 400 *TF:* 800-929-9299 ■ *Web:* www.cutterbuck.com	Seattle	WA	98103	206-622-4191	448-0589
Dodger Industries 1702 21st St *TF:* 800-247-7879 ■ *Web:* www.dodgerindustries.com	Eldora	IA	50627	641-939-5464	939-5185
Elite Sportswear LP 2136 N 13th St *TF Cust Svc:* 800-345-4087 ■ *Web:* www.gk-elitesportswear.com	Reading	PA	19604	610-921-1469	921-0208
Gear for Sports Inc 9700 Commerce Pkwy *TF:* 800-423-5044 ■ *Web:* www.gearforsports.com	Lenexa	KS	66219	913-693-3200	693-3908
Hilton Apparel Group 510 Maryville University Dr Suite 110 *TF:* 800-323-5590 ■ *Web:* www.hiltoncc.com	Saint Louis	MO	63141	314-819-2800	819-2988

Company	City	State	Zip	Phone	Fax
Jantzen Inc 424 NE 18th Ave *TF:* 800-626-0215 ■ *Web:* www.jantzen.com	Portland	OR	97232	503-238-5000	238-5930
King Louie International Inc 13500 15th St. *TF:* 800-521-5212 ■ *Web:* www.kinglouie.com	Grandview	MO	64030	816-765-5212	765-3228
Marika Group Inc 8960 Carroll Way *TF:* 800-666-2927 ■ *Web:* www.marika.com	San Diego	CA	92121	858-537-5300	537-5400
MJ Soffe Co 1 Soffe Dr *TF:* 800-723-4223 ■ *Web:* www.mjsoffe.com	Fayetteville	NC	28312	910-483-2500	486-9030
Moving Comfort Inc 4500 Southgate Pl Suite 800 *TF:* 800-763-6000 ■ *Web:* www.movingcomfort.com	Chantilly	VA	20151	703-631-1000	631-1001
No Fear 1812 Aston Ave *TF:* 800-266-3327 ■ *Web:* www.nofear.com	Carlsbad	CA	92008	760-931-9550	931-9741
Onfield Apparel Group LLC 8677 LogoAthletic Ct *TF:* 800-955-6467	Indianapolis	IN	46219	317-895-7000	895-7250
Powers Mfg Co 1340 Sycamore St PO Box 2157 *Web:* www.powersathletic.com	Waterloo	IA	50704	319-233-6118	234-8048
Race Face Components Inc 100 Braid St Unit 100 *TF:* 800-527-9244 ■ *Web:* www.raceface.com	New Westminster	BC	V3L3P4	604-527-9996	527-9959
Royal Textile Mills Inc 929 Firetower Rd. *TF:* 800-334-9361 ■ *Web:* www.dukeathletic.com	Yanceyville	NC	27379	336-694-4121	694-9084
Russell Corp 755 Lee St. *NYSE: RML* ■ *TF:* 800-729-2905	Alexander City	AL	35010	256-500-4000	500-5045
Russell Corp Russell Athletic Div Fruit of the Loom Dr PO Box 90015 *Web:* www.russellathletic.com	Bowling Green	KY	42102	270-781-6400	438-1372
Scotty's Fashions Inc 636 Pen Argyl St. *Web:* www.scottysfashions.com	Pen Argyl	PA	18072	610-863-6454	863-6490
Shaffer Sportswear Mfg Inc 224 N Washington St *TF Orders:* 800-643-3300	Neosho	MO	64850	417-451-9444	451-6451
Southland Athletic Mfg Co PO Box 280 *TF:* 800-527-7637 ■ *Web:* www.southland-athletic.com	Terrell	TX	75160	972-563-3321	563-0943
Speedline Athletic Wear 1804 N Habana Ave. *Web:* www.speedlineathletic.com	Tampa	FL	33607	813-876-1375	873-8714
Sports Belle Inc 6723 Pleasant Ridge Rd *TF Sales:* 800-888-2063 ■ *Web:* www.sportsbelle.com	Knoxville	TN	37921	865-938-2063	947-4466
Stone International LLC 317 Neely Ferry Rd. *TF Cust Svc:* 800-762-2637 ■ *Web:* www.stonellc.com	Mauldin	SC	29662	864-288-4822	288-1478
Tighe Industries Inc 333 E 7th Ave *TF:* 800-839-1039 ■ *Web:* www.tighe.com	York	PA	17404	717-252-1578	852-6982
Under Armour Inc 1020 Hull St 3rd Fl *NYSE: UA* ■ *TF:* 888-427-6687 ■ *Web:* www.underarmour.com	Baltimore	MD	21230	410-454-6428	454-6535
Volcom Inc 1740 Monrovia Ave *NASDAQ: VLCM* ■ *Web:* www.volcom.com	Costa Mesa	CA	92627	949-646-2175	646-5247

155-2 Belts (Leather, Plastics, Fabric)

Company	City	State	Zip	Phone	Fax
Chambers Belt Co Inc 3230 E Broadway Rd Suite A-200 *TF:* 800-528-1388 ■ *Web:* www.chambersbelt.com	Phoenix	AZ	85040	602-276-0016	276-0210
Circa Corp 1330 Fitzgerald Ave *Web:* www.circacorp.com	San Francisco	CA	94124	415-822-1600	822-1700
French Craft Leather Goods Co Inc 234 W 24th St. *TF:* 800-541-0088	Los Angeles	CA	90007	213-746-6771	746-4610
Gem Dandy Inc 200 W Academy St *TF:* 800-334-5101 ■ *Web:* www.gem-dandy.com	Madison	NC	27025	336-548-9624	427-7105
Leegin Creative Leather Co 14022 Nelson Ave. *TF:* 800-235-8748 ■ *Web:* www.brighton.com	City of Industry	CA	91746	626-961-9381	369-1771
Max Leather Group Inc 14-15 Redfern Ave	Far Rockaway	NY	11691	718-471-3300	471-3707
Swank Inc 90 Pk Ave 13th Fl *Web:* www.swankinc.com	New York	NY	10016	212-867-2600	370-1039
Tandy Brands Accessories Inc 690 E Lamar Blvd Suite 200 *NASDAQ: TBAC* ■ *TF:* 800-570-7443 ■ *Web:* www.tandybrands.com	Arlington	TX	76011	817-548-0090	548-1144

155-3 Casual Wear (Men's & Women's)

Company	City	State	Zip	Phone	Fax
Alps Sportswear Mfg Co 15 Union St *TF:* 800-262-7010 ■ *Web:* www.alps-sportswear.com	Lawrence	MA	01840	978-683-2438	686-8051
Attraction Inc 672 Rue du Parc *TF:* 800-567-6095 ■ *Web:* www.attraction.com	Lac-Drolet	QC	G0Y1C0	819-549-2477	549-2734
Badger Sportswear Inc 111 Badger Ln *TF:* 888-871-0990 ■ *Web:* www.badgersportswear.com	Statesville	NC	28677	704-871-0990	
Bobby Jones Retail Corp 1155 N Clinton Ave. **Fax Area Code:* 800 ■ **Fax:* Sales ■ *TF Cust Svc:* 888-603-8968 ■ *Web:* www.bobbyjonesshop.com	Rochester	NY	14621	585-467-7021	987-8953*
California Mfg Co 2270 Weldon Pkwy *TF:* 888-567-7004 ■ *Web:* www.cmcbrands.com	Saint Louis	MO	63146	314-567-4404	567-5062
Champion Products Inc 1000 E Hanes Mill Rd. **Fax:* Hum Res ■ *TF:* 800-999-2249 ■ *Web:* www.saralee.com	Winston-Salem	NC	27105	336-519-6500	519-6501*
Cherokee Inc 6835 Valjean Ave. *NASDAQ: CHKE* ■ *Web:* www.thecherokeegroup.com	Van Nuys	CA	91406	818-908-9868	908-9191
Columbia Sportswear Co 14375 NW Science Pk Dr *NASDAQ: COLM* ■ *TF:* 800-547-8066 ■ *Web:* www.columbia.com	Portland	OR	97229	503-985-4000	985-5800
Crazy Shirts Inc 99-969 Iwaena St *TF:* 800-771-2720 ■ *Web:* www.crazyshirts.com	Aiea	HI	96701	808-487-9919	486-1276
Deckers Outdoor Corp 495-A S Fairview Ave *NASDAQ: DECK* ■ *TF:* 800-858-5342 ■ *Web:* www.deckers.com	Goleta	CA	93117	805-967-7611	967-9722
Delta Apparel Inc 2750 Premier Pkwy Suite 100 *AMEX: DLA* ■ *TF:* 800-285-4456 ■ *Web:* www.deltaapparel.com	Duluth	GA	30097	678-775-6900	775-6992
Fortune Dogs Inc 121 Gray Ave **Fax:* Hum Res ■ *TF Orders:* 800-642-3647 ■ *Web:* www.bigdogs.com	Santa Barbara	CA	93101	805-963-8727	899-2917*
Fruit of the Loom Inc 1 Fruit of the Loom Dr PO Box 90015 *TF:* 888-378-4829 ■ *Web:* www.fruitactivewear.com	Bowling Green	KY	90015	270-781-6400	781-1754
Fun-Tees Inc 209 S Chestnut St *Web:* www.funtees.com	Lumberton	NC	28358	910-738-6231	739-1753
Gildan 600 Maisonneuve W 3rd Fl *TSE: GIL* ■ *TF:* 866-755-2023 ■ *Web:* www.gildan.com	Montreal	QC	H3A3J2	514-735-2023	735-6810
Hamrick Inc 742 Peachoid Rd *TF:* 800-487-5411 ■ *Web:* www.hamricks.com	Gaffney	SC	29341	864-489-6095	489-9514
Harper Industries Inc 52 Virginia St	Lucedale	MS	39452	601-947-2746	947-4739
IC Isaacs & Co Inc 3840 Bank St *TF:* 800-537-5995 ■ *Web:* www.icisaacs.com	Baltimore	MD	21224	410-342-8200	276-4087
L & L Mfg Co 815 N Nash St	El Segundo	CA	90245	310-615-0000	615-4549
Ms. Bubbles Inc 2731 S Alameda St. **Fax Area Code:* 213 ■ *Web:* www.msbubbles.com	Los Angeles	CA	90058	323-544-0300	239-9709*
Nemanco Inc 1028 Hopewell Rd	Philadelphia	MS	39350	601-656-7361	656-7645
Ocean Pacific Apparel Corp 3 Studebaker *TF:* 800-562-3269 ■ *Web:* www.op.com	Irvine	CA	92618	949-580-1888	580-1870
Peruvian Connection Ltd Inc PO Box 990 *Web:* www.peruvianconnection.com	Tonganoxie	KS	66086	913-845-2450	573-7378
Phat Fashions LLC 512 Fashion Ave # 4300 *Web:* www.phatfarm.com	New York	NY	10018	212-391-9443	391-9448
Quiksilver Inc 15202 Graham St *NYSE: ZQK* ■ *TF:* 800-576-4004 ■ *Web:* www.quiksilver.com	Huntington Beach	CA	92649	714-889-2200	889-3700
Rothschild & Co Inc 500 7th Ave.	New York	NY	10018	212-354-8550	382-1187
Russell Corp Jerzees Div 1 Fruit of the Loom Dr PO Box 90015. *TF:* 888-378-4829 ■ *Web:* www.jerzees.com	Bowling Green	KY	42102	270-781-6400	781-1754
Sherry Mfg Co Inc 3287 NW 65th St *TF:* 800-741-4750 ■ *Web:* www.sherrymanufacturing.com	Miami	FL	33147	305-693-7000	691-6132
Sport-Haley Inc 4600 E 48th Ave *NASDAQ: SPOR* ■ *TF:* 800-627-9211 ■ *Web:* www.sporthaley.com	Denver	CO	80216	303-320-8800	320-8822
Stussy Inc 17426 Daimler St *Web:* www.stussy.com	Irvine	CA	92614	949-474-9255	474-8229
Surf Line Hawaii Ltd 1451 Kalani St. *Web:* www.jamsworld.com	Honolulu	HI	96817	808-847-5985	841-5254
Tonix Corp 40910 Encyclopedia Cir *Web:* www.tonixteams.com	Fremont	CA	94538	510-651-8050	651-8052
Val D'Or Inc 475 Pk Ave S 9th Fl **Fax Area Code:* 212	New York	NY	10016	631-784-7810	564-0043*
VF Corp 105 Corporate Ctr Blvd *NYSE: VFC* ■ *Web:* www.vfc.com	Greensboro	NC	27408	336-424-6000	424-7634
Walking Co Holdings Inc The 121 Gray Ave *PINK: WALK* ■ *TF Sales:* 800-244-3647 ■ *Web:* www.bigdogs.com	Santa Barbara	CA	93101	805-963-8727	962-9460
Whisper Knits Inc 175 E New Hampshire *Web:* www.whisperknits.com	Southern Pines	NC	28387	910-246-0450	246-0550
Wolf Mfg Co 1801 W Waco Dr PO Box 3100 **Fax Area Code:* 257 ■ *TF:* 800-437-0940 ■ *Web:* www.wolfmfg.com	Waco	TX	76707	254-753-7301	753-8919*

155-4 Children's & Infants' Clothing

Company	City	State	Zip	Phone	Fax
Baby Togs Inc 100 W 33rd St # 1100 *Web:* www.babytogs.com	New York	NY	10001	212-868-2100	947-2039
Byer California 66 Potrero Ave *TF:* 800-998-2937 ■ *Web:* www.byer.com	San Francisco	CA	94103	415-626-7844	626-7865
Candlesticks Inc 112 W 34th St Suite 901	New York	NY	10120	212-947-8900	643-9653
Carter's Inc 1170 Peachtree St NE Suite 900 *NYSE: CRI* ■ *TF:* 888-782-9548 ■ *Web:* www.carters.com	Atlanta	GA	30309	404-745-2700	892-0968
Devil Dog Mfg Co Inc 400 E Gannon Ave	Zebulon	NC	27597	919-269-7485	269-5962
Donegal Industries Inc 860 Anderson Ferry Rd	Mount Joy	PA	17552	717-653-1486	653-6658
Eiseman Co LLC 342 N Water St *Web:* www.florenceeiseman.com	Milwaukee	WI	53202	414-272-3222	272-4274
Gerber Childrenswear Inc 7005 Pelham Rd Suite D *TF:* 800-642-4452 ■ *Web:* www.gerberchildrenswear.com	Greenville	SC	29602	864-987-5200	987-5264
Gerson & Gerson Inc 112 W 34th St 17th Fl *Web:* bonniejean.com	New York	NY	10120	212-244-6775	244-6794
Good Lad Apparel 431 E Tioga St *Web:* www.goodlad.com	Philadelphia	PA	19134	215-739-0200	739-5150
Happy Kids Inc 100 W 33rd St Suite 1100	New York	NY	10001	212-695-1151	736-0397
IFG Corp 100 W 33rd St *TF:* 800-873-5511	New York	NY	10001	212-629-9600	629-6699
Irwin Mfg Corp 398 Fitzgerald Hwy	Ocilla	GA	31774	229-468-9481	468-9484
Isfel Co Inc 900 Hart St *TF:* 800-927-8760	Rahway	NJ	07065	732-382-3100	388-0587
Kahn Lucas Lancaster Inc 112 W 34th St # 600 *Web:* www.kahnlucas.com	New York	NY	10120	212-244-4500	643-1345
LT Apparel Group 100 W 33rd St Suite 1012 *TF:* 800-262-5437 ■ *Web:* www.lollytogs.com	New York	NY	10001	212-502-6000	268-5160
Mayfair Co Absorba Div 100 W 33rd St Suite 813	New York	NY	10001	212-279-3211	714-0401
Mayfair Infant Wear Co 100 Wesley White Rd	Carteret	NJ	07008	732-382-4055	381-4020
Mini Togs Inc 3030 Aurora Ave *TF:* 800-588-6227	Monroe	LA	71211	318-388-4916	323-1899
New ICM LP 112 W 34th St Suite 1108 *TF:* 800-978-9008 ■ *Web:* www.newicm.com	New York	NY	10020	212-695-8554	268-0422
OshKosh B'Gosh Inc 112 Otter Ave. *TF:* 800-282-4674 ■ *Web:* www.oshkoshbgosh.com	Oshkosh	WI	54901	920-231-8800	231-8621
Royal Park Uniforms Co 14139 Hwy 86 S *Web:* www.royal-park.com	Prospect Hill	NC	27314	336-562-3345	562-3832
S Schwab Co Inc 12101 Upper Potomac Industrial Pk St *TF:* 800-533-5437	Cumberland	MD	21502	301-729-4488	729-4057
Samara Bros Inc 112 W 34th St Suite 1101	New York	NY	10120	212-695-0210	695-0267
Star Children's Dress Co Inc 100 W 33rd St Suite 1005 *Web:* www.rareedicions.com	New York	NY	10001	212-279-1524	967-4915

155-5 Coats (Overcoats, Jackets, Raincoats, etc)

Company	City	State	Zip	Phone	Fax
Alpha Industries Inc 14200 Pk Meadow Dr #110s *Web:* www.alphaindustries.com	Chantilly	VA	20151	703-378-1420	378-4910
Essex Mfg Inc 350 5th Ave Suite 501 *TF:* 800-648-6010 ■ *Web:* www.baum-essex.com	New York	NY	10118	212-239-0080	714-2958
G-III Apparel Group Ltd 512 7th Ave 35th Fl *NASDAQ: GIII* ■ *Web:* www.g-iii.com	New York	NY	10018	212-403-0600	403-0551
Helly Hansen US Inc 3326 160th Ave *TF:* 800-435-5901 ■ *Web:* www.hellyhansen.com	Bellevue	WA	98008	425-378-8700	649-3740
High Sierra Sport Co 880 Corporate Woods Pkwy *TF:* 800-323-9590 ■ *Web:* www.hssc.com	Vernon Hills	IL	60061	847-913-1100	913-1145
Holloway Sportswear Inc 2633 Campbell Rd **Fax:* Cust Svc ■ *TF:* 800-331-5156 ■ *Web:* www.hollowayusa.com	Sidney	OH	45365	937-596-7575	497-1555*
Item House Inc 2920 S Steele St *TF All:* 800-426-8990	Tacoma	WA	98409	253-627-7168	627-1070
London Fog Industries 1700 Westlake Ave N Suite 200 *TF:* 800-877-8878 ■ *Web:* www.londonfog.com	Seattle	WA	98109	206-270-5300	270-5301
MECA Sportswear Inc 3499 Lexington Ave N Suite 205 *TF:* 800-729-6322 ■ *Web:* www.mecasportswear.com	Arden Hills	MN	55126	651-638-3800	
Pendleton Woolen Mills Inc 220 NW Broadway *TF:* 800-760-4844 ■ *Web:* www.pendleton-usa.com	Portland	OR	97209	503-226-4801	535-5502
RefrigiWear Inc 54 Breakstone Dr *TF Cust Svc:* 800-645-3744 ■ *Web:* www.refrigiwear.com	Dahlonega	GA	30533	706-864-5757	864-5898
Rennoc Corp 3501 SE Blvd *TF Cust Svc:* 800-252-2538 ■ *Web:* www.rennoc.com	Vineland	NJ	08360	856-327-5400	327-0197
Sport Obermeyer Ltd USA Inc 115 AABC *TF:* 800-525-4203 ■ *Web:* www.obermeyer.com	Aspen	CO	81611	970-925-5060	925-9203
Sport-Haley Inc 4600 E 48th Ave *NASDAQ: SPOR* ■ *TF:* 800-627-9211 ■ *Web:* www.sporthaley.com	Denver	CO	80216	303-320-8800	320-8822
Standard Mfg Co Inc 750 2nd Ave *TF Cust Svc:* 800-227-1056 ■ *Web:* www.sportsmaster.com	Troy	NY	12182	518-235-2200	235-2668
Whaling Mfg Co 451 Quarry St *TF:* 800-225-8554 ■ *Web:* www.newportharboronline.com	Fall River	MA	02723	508-678-9061	678-9726
Woolrich Inc 2 Mill St *TF:* 800-995-1299 ■ *Web:* www.woolrich.com	Woolrich	PA	17779	570-769-6464	769-6470

155-6 Costumes

Company	City	State	Zip	Phone	Fax
Art Stone Enterprises 1795 Express Dr N PO Box 2505 *TF:* 800-522-8897 ■ *Web:* www.artstonecostumes.com	Smithtown	NY	11787	631-582-9500	582-9541
Bevan Mfg Co 4451 Rt 130 *TF:* 800-222-8125 ■ *Web:* www.costumegallery.net	Burlington	NJ	08016	609-386-6501	386-0677
Cleveland Costume & Display 18489 Pearl Rd	Strongsville	OH	44136	440-846-9292	846-9294
Costume Specialists Inc 211 N 5th St *TF:* 800-596-9357 ■ *Web:* www.costumespecialists.com	Columbus	OH	43215	614-464-2115	464-2114
Curtain Call Costumes 333 E 7th Ave **Fax Area Code:* 800 ■ *TF:* 888-808-0801 ■ *Web:* www.curtaincallcostumes.com	York	PA	17404	717-852-6910	839-1039*
Disguise 12120 Kear Pl *TF:* 800-786-4864 ■ *Web:* www.disguise.com	Poway	CA	92064	858-391-3600	391-3601
Morris Costumes Inc 4300 Monroe Rd	Charlotte	NC	28205	704-333-4653	348-3032
Rubie's Costume Co Inc 120-08 Jamaica Ave *Web:* www.rubies.com	Richmond Hill	NY	11418	718-846-1008	846-6174
Sew Biz Industries 174 Cross St	Central Falls	RI	02863	401-724-8410	726-9845
Stagecraft Costuming Inc 3950 Spring Grove Ave *Web:* www.stagecraftinc.com	Cincinnati	OH	45223	513-541-7150	541-7159

155-7 Fur Goods

Company	City	State	Zip	Phone	Fax
American Legend Co-op PO Box 58308 *Web:* www.americanlegend.com	Seattle	WA	98138	425-251-3200	251-3222
Blum & Fink Inc 158 W 29th St 12th Fl	New York	NY	10001	212-695-2606	967-8123
Corn Furs Inc 337 7th Ave **Fax Area Code:* 646	New York	NY	10001	212-695-3914	473-1380*
Corniche Furs Inc 345 7th Ave 20th Fl *Web:* www.cornichefurs.com	New York	NY	10001	212-239-8655	239-1811
Goodman Couture 224 W 30 St Suite 902	New York	NY	10001	212-244-7422	594-0657
Jerry Sorbara Furs Inc 12 W 32nd St 11th Fl	New York	NY	10001	212-594-3897	643-9098
Kaitery Furs Ltd 25-29 49th St	Long Island City	NY	11103	718-204-1396	204-0721
LA Rockler Fur Co 16 N 4th St	Minneapolis	MN	55401	612-332-8643	332-2926
Michaels Furs 2270 W Washington Blvd *Web:* michaelsfurs.com	Los Angeles	CA	90018	310-273-5262	273-7270
Mohl Fur Co Inc 345 7th Ave 3rd Fl	New York	NY	10001	212-736-7676	629-4832
Sekas International Ltd 345 7th Ave 4th Fl *Web:* sekasinternational.com/default.aspx	New York	NY	10001	212-629-6095	629-6097
Steve's Original Furs Inc 150 W 30th St 8th Fl *Web:* www.stevesoriginalfurs.com	New York	NY	10001	212-967-8007	967-3871

155-8 Gloves & Mittens

Company	City	State	Zip	Phone	Fax
Berlin Glove Co Inc 150 W Franklin St *TF:* 800-236-3367 ■ *Web:* www.berlingloveco.com	Berlin	WI	54923	920-361-5050	361-5055
Boss Mfg Co 1221 Page St *TF:* 800-447-4581 ■ *Web:* www.bossgloves.com	Kewanee	IL	61443	309-852-2131	852-0848
Brookville Glove Mfg Co Inc 5 Western Ave # 15 *TF:* 800-322-7324 ■ *Web:* www.brookvilleglove.com	Brookville	PA	15825	814-849-7324	849-6874
Carolina Glove Co Inc PO Drawer 820 *TF:* 800-438-6888 ■ *Web:* www.carolinaglove.com	Newton	NC	28658	828-464-1132	464-1710
Fownes Bros & Co Inc 16 E 34th St *TF All:* 800-345-6837	New York	NY	10016	212-683-0150	683-2832
Gloves Inc 50 Suffolk Rd *TF:* 800-225-6076	Mansfield	MA	02048	508-339-2590	339-3181
Grandoe Corp 74 Bleecker St *TF:* 800-472-6363 ■ *Web:* www.grandoe.com	Gloversville	NY	12078	518-725-8641	725-9088
Guard-Line Inc 215 S Louise St PO Box 1030 **Fax:* Orders ■ *TF:* 800-527-8822 ■ *Web:* www.guardline.com	Atlanta	TX	75551	903-796-4111	796-7262*
Illinois Glove Co 3701 Commercial Ave *TF:* 800-342-5458 ■ *Web:* www.illinoisglove.com	Northbrook	IL	60062	847-291-1700	291-7722
Kinco International 4286 NE 185th Ave *TF:* 800-547-8410 ■ *Web:* www.kinco.com	Portland	OR	97230	503-674-9002	674-3513
Magid Glove & Safety Mfg Co 2060 N Kolmar Ave *TF:* 800-444-8010 ■ *Web:* www.magidglove.com	Chicago	IL	60639	773-384-2070	384-6677
Manzella Productions 80 Sonwil Dr *TF:* 800-645-6837 ■ *Web:* www.manzella.com	Buffalo	NY	14225	716-681-8880	681-6888
MCR Safety 5321 E Shelby Dr **Fax Area Code:* 800 ■ **Fax:* Sales ■ *TF:* 800-955-6887 ■ *Web:* www.mcrsafety.com	Memphis	TN	38118	901-795-5810	999-3908*
Midwest Quality Gloves Inc 835 Industrial Rd *TF:* 800-821-3028 ■ *Web:* www.midwestglove.com	Chillicothe	MO	64601	660-646-2165	646-6933
Montpelier Glove & Safety Co Inc 129 N Main St PO Box 7 *TF:* 800-645-3931 ■ *Web:* www.montpeliergsp.com	Montpelier	IN	47359	765-728-2481	728-5239
Nationwide Glove Co 924 Bauman Ln PO Box K	Harrisburg	IL	62946	618-252-6303	252-4497
North Star Glove Co 2916 S Steele St *TF:* 800-423-1616 ■ *Web:* www.northstarglove.com	Tacoma	WA	98409	253-627-7107	627-0597
Perfect Fit Glove Co Inc 85 Innsbruck Dr *TF:* 800-245-6837 ■ *Web:* www.perfectfitglove.com	Buffalo	NY	14227	716-668-2000	668-3224
Saranac Glove Co 999 LOmbardi Ave *TF:* 800-727-2622 ■ *Web:* www.saranacglove.com	Green Bay	WI	54304	920-435-3737	435-7618
Seal Glove Mfg Inc 525 N St *TF:* 800-992-5444 ■ *Web:* www.sealglove.com	Millersburg	PA	17061	717-692-4747	692-5442
Slate Springs Glove Co 148 Vance St	Calhoun City	MS	38916	662-637-2222	637-2515
Southern Glove Mfg Co Inc 749 AC Little Dr *TF Cust Svc:* 800-222-1113 ■ *Web:* www.southernglove.com	Newton	NC	28658	828-464-4884	464-7968
Swany America Corp 115 Corp Dr *TF:* 800-237-9269 ■ *Web:* www.swanyamerica.com	Johnstown	NY	12095	518-725-3333	725-2026
Totes Isotoner Corp 9655 International Blvd *TF:* 800-762-8712 ■ *Web:* www.totes-isotoner.com	Cincinnati	OH	45246	513-682-8200	682-8600
Wells Lamont Corp 6640 W Touhy Ave *TF:* 800-323-2830 ■ *Web:* www.wellslamont.com	Niles	IL	60714	847-647-8200	647-6943
Wells Lamont Industry Group 6640 W Touhy Ave **Fax Area Code:* 847 ■ *TF:* 800-247-3295 ■ *Web:* www.wellslamontindustry.com	Niles	IL	60714	800-247-3295	647-6943*

155-9 Hats & Caps

Company	City	State	Zip	Phone	Fax
180s Inc 700 S Caroline St *TF:* 877-725-4386 ■ *Web:* www.180s.com	Baltimore	MD	21231	410-534-6320	534-6321
Ahead 270 Samuel Barnet Blvd **Fax:* Cust Svc ■ *TF:* 800-282-2246 ■ *Web:* www.aheadweb.com	New Bedford	MA	02745	508-999-4466	985-3091*
American Needle Inc 1275 Bush Pkwy *TF:* 800-356-7589 ■ *Web:* www.americanneedle.com	Buffalo Grove	IL	60089	847-215-0011	215-0013
Arlington Hat Co Inc 4725 34th St	Long Island City	NY	11101	718-361-3000	361-8713
Bancroft Cap Co Inc 1122 S 2nd St *TF:* 800-345-8784 ■ *Web:* www.bancroftcaps.com	Cabot	AR	72023	501-843-6561	843-8996
Bollman Hat Co 110 E Main St PO Box 517 *TF:* 800-451-4287 ■ *Web:* www.bollmanhats.com	Adamstown	PA	19501	717-484-4361	484-2139
F & M Hat Co Inc 103 Walnut St PO Box 40 *TF:* 800-953-4287 ■ *Web:* www.fmhat.com	Denver	PA	17517	717-336-5505	336-0501
Greg Norman Collection 134 W 37th St # 4	New York	NY	10018	646-840-5200	
Julie Hat Co Inc 5948 Industrial Blvd PO Box 518 *TF:* 800-841-2592 ■ *Web:* www.juliehat.com	Patterson	GA	31557	912-647-2031	647-2605
Korber Hats Inc 394 Kilburn St *TF Cust Svc:* 800-428-9911	Fall River	MA	02724	508-672-7033	673-0762
Kraft Hat Mfg Inc 725 Whittier St *Web:* www.krafthat.com	Bronx	NY	10474	718-620-6100	620-0127
M & B Headwear Co Inc 2323 E Main St PO Box 8180	Richmond	VA	23223	804-648-1603	648-1613
MPC Promotions Inc 2026 Shepherdsville Rd *TF:* 800-331-0989 ■ *Web:* www.mpcpromotions.com	Louisville	KY	40218	502-451-4900	451-5075
New Era Cap Co Inc 8061 Erie Rd *TF:* 800-989-0445 ■ *Web:* www.neweracap.com	Derby	NY	14047	716-549-0445	549-5424
Onfield Apparel Group LLC 8677 LogoAthletic Ct *TF:* 800-955-6467	Indianapolis	IN	46219	317-895-7000	895-7250
Paramount Apparel International Inc 1 Paramount Dr PO Box 98 *TF:* 800-255-4287	Bourbon	MO	65441	573-732-4411	732-5211
Pro-Line Cap Co 1332 N Main St *TF:* 800-227-2456 ■ *Web:* www.prolinecap.com	Fort Worth	TX	76106	817-246-1978	367-1585
Stetson Hat Co 4500 Stetson Trail	Saint Joseph	MO	64503	816-233-8031	233-8032
Stratton Hats Inc 3200 Randolph St *Web:* www.strattonhats.com	Bellwood	IL	60104	708-544-5220	544-5243
Texace Corp 5405 Vandera Rd Suite 121 *TF:* 800-835-8973 ■ *Web:* www.texace.com	San Antonio	TX	78238	210-227-7551	227-4237
Town Talk Inc 6310 Cane Run Rd PO Box 58157 *TF:* 800-626-2220 ■ *Web:* www.ttcaps.com	Louisville	KY	40268	502-933-7575	933-7599

155-10 Hosiery & Socks

	City	State	Zip	Phone	Fax
Acme-McCrary Corp 159 N St *Web:* www.acme-mccrary.com	Asheboro	NC	27203	336-625-2161	629-2263
Americal Corp 389 Americal Rd PO Box 1419 *TF:* 800-633-9707	Henderson	NC	27536	252-762-2000	762-0439
Auburn Hosiery Mills Inc 113 E Main St PO Box 95	Auburn	KY	42206	270-542-4175	542-7120
Bossong Hosiery Mills Inc 840 W Salisbury St *TF:* 800-833-8895	Asheboro	NC	27203	336-625-2175	626-6607
Carolina Hosiery Mills Inc 710 Plantation Dr PO Box 850	Burlington	NC	27216	336-226-5581	226-9721
Clayson Knitting Co 734 S Main St PO Box 39	Star	NC	27356	910-428-2171	428-1133
Commonwealth Hosiery Mills Inc 4964 Island Ford Rd *Web:* www.commonwealth-hosiery.com	Randleman	NC	27317	336-498-2621	498-5560
Cooper Hosiery Mills Inc 4005 Gault Ave N PO Box 680909	Fort Payne	AL	35968	256-845-1491	845-3554
Crescent Inc 527 E Willson St *TF:* 877-807-7625 ■ *Web:* www.crescenthosiery.com	Niota	TN	37826	423-568-2101	568-2104
DeSoto Mills Inc 3850 Sand Valley Rd PO Box 680228 *TF:* 800-551-7625	Fort Payne	AL	35968	256-845-6700	845-9658
Emby Hosiery Corp 3905 2nd Ave *TF:* 800-287-6916 ■ *Web:* www.embyhosiery.com	Brooklyn	NY	11232	718-499-6300	499-7156
Fox River Mills Inc 227 Poplar Stq PO Box 298 *TF:* 800-247-1815 ■ *Web:* www.foxsox.com	Osage	IA	50461	641-732-3798	732-3375
Harriss & Covington Hosiery Mills Inc 1250 Hickory Chapel Rd	High Point	NC	27260	336-882-6811	889-2412
HCI Direct Inc 3050 Tillman Dr *TF:* 800-989-3695 ■ *Web:* www.silkies.com	Bensalem	PA	19020	215-244-9600	244-0328
Highland Mills Inc 340 E 16th St *Web:* www.highlandmills.com	Charlotte	NC	28206	704-375-3333	342-0391
Holt Hosiery Mills Inc 733 Koury Dr PO Box 1757	Burlington	NC	27216	336-227-1431	227-8614
Hosiery Mills Industry Inc 140 58th St Suite 8 E PO Box 172 *Web:* www.hosierymills.net	Brooklyn	NY	11220	718-567-9290	567-9291
Jefferies Socks LLC 1176 N Church St *TF Cust Svc:* 800-334-6831 ■ *Web:* www.jefferiessocks.com	Burlington	NC	27217	336-226-7315	226-8217
Jockey International Inc 2300 60th St PO Box 1417 *TF:* 800-562-5391 ■ *Web:* www.jockey.com	Kenosha	WI	53140	262-658-8111	658-1942
Johnson Hosiery Mills Inc 2808 Main Ave NW *TF:* 800-438-1511 ■ *Web:* www.johnsonhosiery.com	Hickory	NC	28601	828-322-6185	322-6539
Kayser-Roth Corp 102 Corporate Ctr Blvd **Fax:* Acctg ■ *Web:* www.kayser-roth.com	Greensboro	NC	27408	336-852-2030	632-1921*
Keepers International Inc 20720 Marilla St *TF:* 800-797-6257 ■ *Web:* www.keepers.com	Chatsworth	CA	91311	818-882-5000	700-1152
Lea-wayne Knitting Mills Inc 5937 Commerce Blvd *Web:* www.lea-wayne.com	Morristown	TN	37814	423-586-7513	586-6437
Lemco Mills Inc 766 Koury Dr PO Box 2098	Burlington	NC	27216	336-226-5548	226-6356
Mauney Hosiery Mills Inc PO Box 1279	Kings Mountain	NC	28086	704-739-3621	734-0608
Mayer Berkshire Corp 25 Edison Dr *TF:* 800-245-6789 ■ *Web:* www.berkshirestore.com	Wayne	NJ	07470	973-696-6200	696-6203
Mayo Knitting Mills Inc 2204 Austin St PO Box 160	Tarboro	NC	27886	252-823-3101	823-0368
Menzies Southern Hosiery Mills Inc 953 Central Ave SE	Hickory	NC	28601	828-328-5201	328-2896
Moretz Inc 514 W 21st St *TF:* 800-438-9127 ■ *Web:* www.moretzsports.com	Newton	NC	28658	828-464-0751	465-4203
Mountain High Hosiery Ltd 675 Gateway Ctr Dr *TF:* 800-528-5355 ■ *Web:* www.mtnhighinc.com	San Diego	CA	92102	619-262-9202	262-9682
Neuville Industries Inc 9451 Neuville Ave PO Box 286 *TF:* 800-334-2587	Hildebran	NC	28637	828-397-5566	397-2377
Parker Hosiery Co Inc 78 Catawba Ave	Old Fort	NC	28762	828-668-7628	668-2081
Paul Lavitt Mills Inc 1517 'F' Ave SE *TF:* 800-825-7285 ■ *Web:* www.paullavittmills.com	Hickory	NC	28602	828-328-2463	328-5908
Premiere Direct/Legwear Express 227 Avery Ave *TF Orders:* 800-280-1222	Morganton	NC	28655	828-439-8724	439-8571
Renfro Corp 661 Linville Rd *TF:* 800-334-9091 ■ *Web:* www.renfro.com	Mount Airy	NC	27030	336-719-8000	719-8215
Slane Hosiery Mills Inc 313 S Centennial St *Web:* www.slanehosiery.com	High Point	NC	27261	336-883-4138	886-4543
Tefron USA Inc 720 W Main St *TF:* 800-554-5541 ■ *Web:* www.tefron.com	Valdese	NC	28690	828-879-6500	879-6579
Thor-Lo Inc 2210 Newton Dr *TF:* 888-846-7567 ■ *Web:* www.thorlo.com	Statesville	NC	28677	704-872-6522	838-7010
Trimfit Inc 1900 Frost Rd Suite 111 *TF:* 800-347-7697 ■ *Web:* www.trimfit.com	Bristol	PA	19007	215-781-0600	781-1803
Twin City Knitting Co Inc 104 Rock Barn Rd NE PO Box 1179 **Fax Area Code:* 800 ■ *TF Cust Svc:* 800-438-6884 ■ *Web:* www.twincityknitting.com	Conover	NC	28613	828-464-4830	497-6257*
Wigwam Mills Inc 3402 Crocker Ave *TF:* 800-558-7760 ■ *Web:* www.wigwam.com	Sheboygan	WI	53082	920-457-5551	457-0311
WY Shugart & Sons Inc 405 Beeson Gap Rd NE *Web:* www.wyshugart.com	Fort Payne	AL	35968	256-845-1251	845-4502

155-11 Jeans

	City	State	Zip	Phone	Fax
Aalfs Mfg Co 1005 4th St *TF:* 888-412-2537	Sioux City	IA	51101	712-252-1877	252-5205
Ditto Apparel of California Inc Hwy 8 E PO Box 226	Colfax	LA	71417	318-627-3264	627-3446
Elk Brand Mfg Co 1601 County Hospital Rd *Web:* www.elkbrand.com	Nashville	TN	37218	615-254-4300	242-3137
Flynn Enterprises Inc 2203 Walnut St PO Box 1047	Hopkinsville	KY	42241	270-886-0223	886-0573
Guess Inc 1444 S Alameda St *NYSE: GES* ■ *TF:* 800-224-8377 ■ *Web:* www.guess.com	Los Angeles	CA	90021	213-765-3100	765-3226
Jordache Enterprises 1400 Broadway 15th Fl *TF:* 888-295-3267 ■ *Web:* www.jordache.com	New York	NY	10018	212-643-8400	629-9223
Kayo of California Inc 161 W 39th St *TF:* 800-233-6140	Los Angeles	CA	90037	323-233-6107	231-4828
Lee Jeans 9001 W 67th St *TF Cust Svc:* 800-453-3348 ■ *Web:* www.lee.com	Merriam	KS	66202	913-384-4000	384-0190
Levi Strauss & Co 1155 Battery St *TF:* 800-872-5384 ■ *Web:* www.levistrauss.com	San Francisco	CA	94111	415-501-6000	501-7112
Miller International Inc Rocky Mountain Clothing Co Div 8500 Zuni St *TF:* 800-688-4449 ■ *Web:* www.rockymountainclothing.com	Denver	CO	80260	303-428-5696	430-1130
Reed Mfg Co Inc 1321 S Veterans Blvd *TF:* 800-647-1280 ■ *Web:* www.reedmanufacturing.com	Tupelo	MS	38801	662-842-4472	680-9644
VF Jeanswear LP 335 Church Ct PO Box 21488 **Fax Area Code:* 800 ■ *TF Orders:* 800-888-8010 ■ *Web:* www.vfc.com	Greensboro	NC	27420	336-332-3400	283-3113*
Vintage Blue 13087 E Temple Ave	City of Industry	CA	91746	626-934-4144	934-4145

155-12 Men's Clothing

	City	State	Zip	Phone	Fax
After Six Inc 240 Collins Industrial Dr *TF Cust Svc:* 800-554-8212 ■ *Web:* www.aftersix.com	Athens	GA	30601	706-543-5286	549-5430
American Apparel LLC 747 Warehouse St *Web:* www.americanapparel.net	Los Angeles	CA	90021	213-488-0226	488-0334
American Trouser Inc 605 17th St S	Columbus	MS	39701	662-328-1556	329-8115
Anniston Sportswear Corp 919 W 9th St	Anniston	AL	36201	256-237-9411	237-7569
Antigua Sportswear Inc 16651 N 84 Ave *TF:* 800-528-3133 ■ *Web:* www.antigua.com	Peoria	AZ	85382	623-523-6000	523-6001
Barry Better Menswear 309 McLaws Cir Suite D *Web:* www.bettermenswear.com	Williamsburg	VA	23185	757-345-0971	345-6224
Calvin Klein Inc 205 W 39th St 3rd Fl *TF Cust Svc:* 800-388-9122 ■ *Web:* www.pvh.com	New York	NY	10018	212-719-2600	730-4818
Capital Mercury Apparel 1359 Broadway 19th Fl	New York	NY	10018	212-704-4800	704-4996
Charles Navasky & Co Inc 124 Walton St	Philipsburg	PA	16866	814-342-1160	342-1920
Cluett American Group 48 W 38th St 8th Fl	New York	NY	10018	212-984-8900	984-8925
Crown Clothing Corp 340 Vanderbilt Ave *TF:* 800-225-8950 ■ *Web:* www.crownclothingcorp.com	Norwood	MA	02062	781-769-0001	769-7337
David Peyser Sportswear Inc 8890 Spence St *TF:* 800-367-7900	Bay Shore	NY	11706	631-231-7788	435-8018
Ely & Walker Co 208 Hartmann Dr	Lebanon	TN	37087	615-443-1878	443-2214
English American Tailoring Co 411 N Cranberry Rd *Web:* www.englishamericanco.com	Westminster	MD	21157	410-857-5774	386-0417
Fishman & Tobin Inc 625 Ridge Pike Bldg E Suite 320 *TF:* 800-367-2772	Conshohocken	PA	19428	610-828-8400	828-4426
Franklin Clothing Co Inc 208 Lurgan Ave	Shippensburg	PA	17257	717-532-4146	532-6836
Gitman & Co 2309 Chestnut St *TF:* 800-526-3929	Ashland	PA	17921	570-875-3100	875-2841
Gitman Bros Shirt Co Inc 641 Lexington Ave 19th Fl *TF Cust Svc:* 800-526-3929 ■ *Web:* www.gitmanco.com	New York	NY	10019	212-581-6968	581-6960
Granite Knitwear Inc 805 S Salberry Ave Hwy 52S *TF Cust Svc:* 800-476-9944 ■ *Web:* www.calcru.com	Granite Quarry	NC	28072	704-279-5526	279-8205
Greg Norman Collection 134 W 37th St # 4	New York	NY	10018	646-840-5200	
H Freeman & Son Inc 411 N Cranberry Rd *TF:* 800-468-0689 ■ *Web:* www.hfreemanco.com	Westminster	MD	21157	410-857-5774	857-1560
Haggar Clothing Co 11511 Luna Rd Two Colinas Crossing *TF:* 800-942-4427 ■ *Web:* www.haggar.com	Dallas	TX	75234	214-352-8481	
Hardwick Clothes Inc 3800 Old Tasso Rd NE **Fax Area Code:* 800 ■ *TF:* 800-251-6392	Cleveland	TN	37312	423-476-6534	442-7394*
Hartmarx Inc 101 N Wacker Dr *TF:* 800-327-4466 ■ *Web:* www.hartschaffnermarx.com	Chicago	IL	60606	312-372-6300	444-2710
Hartz & Co 1341 Hughes Ford Rd *TF:* 800-638-8170	Frederick	MD	21701	301-662-7500	662-0800
Hickey-Freeman Co Inc 1155 N Clinton Ave *TF Cust Svc:* 800-295-2000 ■ *Web:* www.hickeyfreeman.com	Rochester	NY	14621	585-467-7240	467-1236
Hugo Boss Fashions Inc 601 W 26th St Suite 845 *TF Cust Svc:* 800-484-6207 ■ *Web:* www.hugo.com	New York	NY	10001	212-940-0600	940-0616
Indiana Knitwear Corp 230 E Osage St	Greenfield	IN	46140	317-462-4413	462-0994
Individualized Shirts Co 581 Cortland St *TF:* 888-474-4787	Perth Amboy	NJ	08861	732-826-8400	826-6382
John H Daniel Co Inc 120 W Jackson Ave *Web:* www.johnhdaniel.com	Knoxville	TN	37902	865-637-6441	523-6435
Jos A Bank Clothiers 500 Hanover Pike *NASDAQ: JOSB* ■ *TF Cust Svc:* 800-999-7472 ■ *Web:* www.josbank.com	Hampstead	MD	21074	410-239-2700	239-5700
Kenneth Gordon IAG Inc 1209 Distributors Row *TF Cust Svc:* 800-234-1433	New Orleans	LA	70123	504-734-1433	733-1625
Merrill-Sharpe Ltd 250 Clearbrook Rd *TF:* 800-832-0159 ■ *Web:* www.merrillsharpe.com	Elmsford	NY	10523	914-347-8686	347-8861
Nautica Enterprises Inc 40 W 57th St 3rd Fl **Fax:* Cust Svc ■ *Web:* www.nautica.com	New York	NY	10019	212-541-5990	245-4724*

Company	City	State	Zip	Phone	Fax
Nitches Inc 10280 Camino Santa Fe *NASDAQ: NICH*	San Diego	CA	92121	858-625-2633	625-0746
Nu-Look Fashions Inc 5080 Sinclair Rd Suite 200 *TF:* 800-800-4500	Columbus	OH	43229	614-885-4936	885-4193
Oxford Industries Inc 222 Piedmont Ave NE *NYSE: OXM* ■ *Web:* www.oxfordinc.com	Atlanta	GA	30308	404-659-2424	525-3650
Oxxford Clothes Inc 1220 W Van Buren St *TF:* 888-469-9367 ■ *Web:* www.oxxfordclothes.com	Chicago	IL	60607	312-829-3600	829-6075
Perry Ellis International Inc 3000 NW 107th Ave *NASDAQ: PERY* ■ *TF:* 800-327-7587 ■ *Web:* www.perryelliscorporate.com	Miami	FL	33172	305-592-2830	594-2307
Phillips-Van Heusen Corp 200 Madison Ave *NYSE: PVH* ■ *TF:* 800-777-1726 ■ *Web:* www.pvh.com	New York	NY	10016	212-381-3500	381-3950
PremiumWear Inc 5500 Feltl Rd *TF Cust Svc:* 800-347-6098 ■ *Web:* www.premiumwear.com	Minnetonka	MN	55343	952-979-1700	979-1717
R Siskind & Co Inc 1385 Broadway 24th Fl	New York	NY	10018	212-840-0880	840-0969
Savane International Div 4902 W Waters Ave *TF:* 800-327-2464 ■ *Web:* www.savane.com	Tampa	FL	33634	813-249-4900	
Scotty's Fashions Inc 636 Pen Argyl St *Web:* www.scottysfashions.com	Pen Argyl	PA	18072	610-863-6454	863-6490
Seitchik Industries Inc 920 E Lycoming St *TF:* 800-523-0814	Philadelphia	PA	19124	215-743-0400	743-5914
Smart Apparel US Inc 1400 Broadway 10th Fl	New York	NY	10018	212-329-3400	329-3486
Southwick Clothing LLC 50 Island St *Web:* www.southwickclothing.com	Lawrence	MA	01840	978-686-3833	738-0802
Thorngate Ltd 1507 Independence St *Web:* www.thorngate.com	Cape Girardeau	MO	63703	573-334-7723	
Tom James Co 424 S Lynn Riggs Blvd *TF:* 800-237-2140 ■ *Web:* www.tomjamesco.com	Claremore	OK	74017	918-341-3773	343-1711
Warren Sewell Clothing Co 126 Hamilton Ave *TF:* 800-876-9722 ■ *Web:* www.warrensewell.com	Bremen	GA	30110	770-537-2391	537-6898
Weatherproof Garment Co 1071 Avenue of the Americas 12th Fl *TF:* 800-645-7788	New York	NY	10018	212-695-7716	239-9786

155-13 Neckwear

Company	City	State	Zip	Phone	Fax
Bost Neckwear Co Inc 503 Industrial Pk PO Box 1065 *TF:* 800-334-8441	Asheboro	NC	27204	336-625-6650	626-7667
Burma Bibas Inc 597 5th Ave 10th Fl *TF:* 800-362-0037	New York	NY	10017	212-750-2500	750-2834
Carter & Holmes 3750 N Lake Shore Dr # 4C *TF:* 800-621-4646 ■ *Web:* www.carterholmes.com	Chicago	IL	60613	773-588-2626	588-3092
Echo Design Group 10 E 40th St 16th Fl *TF:* 800-331-3246 ■ *Web:* www.echodesign.com	New York	NY	10016	212-686-8771	686-5017
Fendrich Industries Inc 7025 Augusta Rd *TF:* 800-845-2744	Greenville	SC	29605	864-299-0600	299-0603
Handcraft Mfg Corp 10 E 34th St 2nd Fl	New York	NY	10016	212-251-0022	251-0076
Mallory & Church LLC 676 S Industrial Way *TF:* 800-255-8437 ■ *Web:* www.malloryandchurch.com	Seattle	WA	98108	206-587-2100	587-2971
MMG Corp 1717 Olive St *TF:* 800-264-8437	Saint Louis	MO	63103	314-421-2182	421-4912
Paris Accessories Inc 350 5th Ave 70th Fl *TF:* 800-223-7557	New York	NY	10118	212-868-0500	967-4936
Ralph Marlin & Co 1701 Pearl St Suite 4 *TF:* 800-922-8437 ■ *Web:* www.ralphmarlin.com	Waukesha	WI	53186	262-549-5100	549-5122
Robert Talbott Inc 2901 Salinas Hwy *Web:* www.roberttalbott.com	Monterey	CA	93940	831-649-6000	
Superba Inc 1735 S Santa Fe Ave *Web:* www.superbainc.com	Los Angeles	CA	90021	213-688-7970	623-3226
White Mountain Traders 100 Factory St *TF:* 800-648-6505 ■ *Web:* www.whitemountaintraders.com	Nashua	NH	03060	603-889-5115	889-3126
Wolfmark 1026 W Van Buren St *TF Cust Svc:* 800-621-3435 ■ *Web:* www.wolfmarkties.com	Chicago	IL	60607	312-563-5510	563-0280
Zanzara International Ltd 1160 S Rogers Cir Suite 1	Boca Raton	FL	33487	561-998-8898	998-9711

155-14 Robes (Ceremonial)

Company	City	State	Zip	Phone	Fax
Academic Apparel 20644 Superior St *TF:* 800-626-5000 ■ *Web:* www.academicapparel.com	Chatsworth	CA	91311	818-886-8697	886-8743
CM Almy Inc 1 Ruth Rd *TF:* 800-225-2569 ■ *Web:* www.almy.com	Pittsfield	ME	04967	207-487-3232	487-3240
Jostens Inc 3601 Minnesota Ave Suite 400 **Fax:* Hum Res ■ *TF:* 800-235-4774 ■ *Web:* www.jostens.com	Minneapolis	MN	55435	952-830-3300	830-3309*
Oak Hall Industries 840 Union St *TF:* 800-456-7623 ■ *Web:* www.oakhalli.com	Salem	VA	24153	540-387-0000	387-2034
Robert Gaspard Co Inc 200 N Janacek Rd *TF:* 800-784-6868 ■ *Web:* www.robertgaspardco.com	Brookfield	WI	53045	262-784-6800	784-7567
Thomas Creative Apparel Inc 1 Harmony Pl *TF:* 800-537-2575 ■ *Web:* www.thomasrobes.com	New London	OH	44851	419-929-1506	929-0122
Willsie Cap & Gown Co 1220 S 13th St *TF:* 800-234-4696 ■ *Web:* www.willsieco.com	Omaha	NE	68108	402-341-6536	341-6551

155-15 Sleepwear

Company	City	State	Zip	Phone	Fax
Isaco International Corp 5980 Miami Lakes Dr *Web:* www.isaco.com	Miami	FL	33014	305-594-4455	594-4496
LSC LLC 525 Brannan St Suite 410 *TF:* 800-421-0731 ■ *Web:* www.eileenwest.com	San Francisco	CA	94107	415-957-9378	495-8628
Magnolia Garment Corp 101 Ostrover Dr	Tower Town	MS	39667	601-876-6524	876-6069
Milco Industries Inc 550 E 5th St *TF:* 800-867-0288	Bloomsburg	PA	17815	570-784-0400	387-8433
Miss Elaine Inc 8430 Valcour Ave *TF:* 800-458-1422 ■ *Web:* www.misselaine.com	Saint Louis	MO	63123	314-631-1900	631-7577
Movie Star Inc 1303 E Algonquin Rd *AMEX: MSI* ■ *Web:* www.motorolasolutions.com	Schaumburg	IL	60196	847-576-5000	576-5372
O'Bryan Bros Inc 4220 W Belmont Ave *TF:* 800-627-9262	Chicago	IL	60641	773-283-3000	283-2470
Roytex Inc 16 E 34th St 17th Fl *Web:* www.roytex.com	New York	NY	10016	212-686-3500	686-4336
Russell-Newman Ltd 600 N Loop 288	Denton	TX	76209	940-898-8888	382-6453
VF Intimates 3025 Windward Plaza Suite 600 *TF:* 800-366-8339 ■ *Web:* www.vanityfairlingerie.com	Alpharetta	GA	30005	770-753-0900	753-5050
Wormser Co 820 W Jackson Blvd Suite 400 *Web:* www.wormser.com	Chicago	IL	60607	312-525-2670	525-0108

155-16 Sweaters (Knit)

Company	City	State	Zip	Phone	Fax
AM Knitwear Corp 681 Grand Blvd	Deer Park	NY	11729	631-586-3200	586-3657
Binghamton Knitting Co Inc 11 Alice St PO Box 1646 *Web:* www.brimwick.com	Binghamton	NY	13902	607-722-6941	722-4621
Mamiye Bros Inc Group 112 W 34th St Suite 1000 *Web:* www.mamiye.com	New York	NY	10120	212-279-4150	279-4115

155-17 Swimwear

Company	City	State	Zip	Phone	Fax
A & H Sportswear Co Inc 500 Williams St	Pen Argyl	PA	18072	610-863-4176	863-7838
AH Schreiber Co 460 W 34th St 10th Fl *TF:* 800-724-1612	New York	NY	10001	212-564-2700	594-7234
Apparel Ventures Inc 13809 S Figueroa St *TF:* 800-289-7946	Los Angeles	CA	90061	310-538-4980	538-0515
Blue Sky Swimwear 729 E International Speedway Blvd *TF Orders:* 800-799-6445 ■ *Web:* www.blueskyswimwear.com	Daytona Beach	FL	32118	386-255-9009	253-5938
Christina America Inc *Trimera group* 5555 Cypihot St *TF Cust Svc:* 800-463-7946 ■ *Web:* www.trimeragroup.com	Ville Saint-Laurent	QC	H3L2R3	514-381-2365	381-8202
Jantzen Inc 424 NE 18th Ave *TF:* 800-626-0215 ■ *Web:* www.jantzen.com	Portland	OR	97232	503-238-5000	238-5930
Manhattan Beachwear Inc 6600 Katella Ave *TF:* 800-279-2987 ■ *Web:* www.manhattanbeachwear.com	Cypress	CA	90630	714-892-7354	799-5381
Quiksilver Inc 15202 Graham St *NYSE: ZQK* ■ *TF:* 800-576-4004 ■ *Web:* www.quiksilver.com	Huntington Beach	CA	92649	714-889-2200	889-3700
TYR Sport 15391 Springdale St *TF:* 800-252-7878 ■ *Web:* www.tyr.com	Huntington Beach	CA	92649	714-897-0799	897-6420
Venus Swimwear 11711 Marco Beach Dr 1 Venus Plaza **Fax Area Code:* 800 ■ *TF:* 800-366-7946 ■ *Web:* www.venus.com	Jacksonville	FL	32224	904-645-6000	648-0411*

155-18 Undergarments

Company	City	State	Zip	Phone	Fax
Alpha Mills Corp 122 Margaretta St	Schuylkill Haven	PA	17972	570-385-0511	385-0467
Biflex Intimates Group 180 Madison Ave 6th Fl *Web:* www.biflex.com	New York	NY	10016	212-532-8340	696-3485
Carter's Inc 1170 Peachtree St NE Suite 900 *NYSE: CRI* ■ *TF:* 888-782-9548 ■ *Web:* www.carters.com	Atlanta	GA	30309	404-745-2700	892-0968
Champion Athletic Wear 1000 E Hanes Mill Rd *TF:* 800-999-2249 ■ *Web:* www.championforwomen.com	Winston-Salem	NC	27105	336-519-4400	519-6501
Cupid Foundations Inc 475 Pk Ave S 17th Fl	New York	NY	10016	212-686-6224	481-9357
Delta Galil USA 150 Meadowland Pkwy *TF:* 800-645-4461 ■ *Web:* www.deltagalil.com	Secaucus	NJ	07094	201-902-0055	902-0070
Eveden Ltd 65 Sprague St *TF:* 800-733-8964 ■ *Web:* www.eveden.com	Hyde Park	MA	02136	617-361-7559	361-7527
Gelmart Industries Inc 136 Madison Ave 4th Fl *TF:* 800-746-0014 ■ *Web:* www.gelmart.com	New York	NY	10016	212-743-6900	725-7248
Glamorise Foundations Inc 135 Madison Ave	New York	NY	10016	212-684-5025	689-7793
Hanesbrands Inc 1000 E Hanes Mill Rd *NYSE: HBI* ■ *Web:* www.hanesbrands.com	Winston-Salem	NC	27105	336-519-4400	519-8746
Indera Mills Co 350 W Maple St PO Box 309 *TF:* 800-334-8605 ■ *Web:* www.inderamills.com	Yadkinville	NC	27055	336-679-4440	679-4475
JE Morgan Knitting Mills Inc 143 Mahanoy Ave PO Box 390 *TF:* 800-448-8240	Tamaqua	PA	18252	570-668-3330	668-9016
Jockey International Inc 2300 60th St PO Box 1417 *TF:* 800-562-5391 ■ *Web:* www.jockey.com	Kenosha	WI	53140	262-658-8111	658-1942
Leading Lady Cos 24050 Commerce Pk *TF Cust Svc:* 800-321-4804 ■ *Web:* www.leadinglady.com	Beachwood	OH	44122	216-464-5490	464-9365
Movie Star Inc 1303 E Algonquin Rd *AMEX: MSI* ■ *Web:* www.motorolasolutions.com	Schaumburg	IL	60196	847-576-5000	576-5372
Reliable of Milwaukee Inc 1126 S 70th St # 112 *TF:* 800-336-6876 ■ *Web:* www.reliableofmilwaukee.com	Milwaukee	WI	53214	414-272-5084	272-6443
Robinson Mfg Co Inc 798 Market St PO Box 338 *TF:* 800-251-7286 ■ *Web:* www.robinsonmfg.com	Dayton	TN	37321	423-775-2212	775-0489
Spencers Inc 238 Willow St *TF:* 800-633-9111	Mount Airy	NC	27030	336-789-9111	789-6824
Spirite Industries Inc 150 S Dean St *TF:* 800-272-6897 ■ *Web:* www.spirite.com	Englewood	NJ	07631	201-871-4910	871-9790

	City	State	ZIP	Phone	Fax
Under Armour Performance Apparel 1020 Hull St	Baltimore	MD	21230	410-468-2512	927-6687*
*Fax Area Code: 866 ■ TF: 888-427-6687 ■ Web: www.underarmour.com					
VF Corp 105 Corporate Ctr Blvd	Greensboro	NC	27408	336-424-6000	424-7634
NYSE: VFC ■ Web: www.vfc.com					
VF Intimates 3025 Windward Plaza Suite 600	Alpharetta	GA	30005	770-753-0900	753-5050
TF: 800-366-8339 ■ Web: www.vanityfairlingerie.com					
Wacoal America 50 Polito Ave	Lyndhurst	NJ	07071	201-933-8400	635-0208
TF: 800-526-6286 ■ Web: www.wacoal-america.com					
Warnaco Inc 501 7th Ave	New York	NY	10018	212-287-8000	
Web: www.warnaco.com					
Windsong Allegiance Group LLC 1599 Post Rd E	Westport	CT	06880	203-319-3600	319-3610

155-19 Uniforms & Work Clothes

	City	State	ZIP	Phone	Fax
Action Sports Systems Inc 617 Carbon City Rd	Morganton	NC	28655	828-584-8000	584-8440
TF: 800-631-1091					
Algy Costume & Uniform Co 440 NE 1st Ave	Hallandale	FL	33009	954-457-8100	928-2282*
*Fax Area Code: 888 ■ TF: 800-458-2549 ■ Web: www.algyteam.com					
All-Bilt Uniform Fashion 4545 Malsbary Rd	Cincinnati	OH	45242	866-638-5390	793-2725*
*Fax Area Code: 513 ■ TF: 800-221-2980					
American Apparel Inc 107 Selma Bypass PO Box 1310	Selma	AL	36702	334-872-6337	872-2449
American Uniform Co 4363 Ocoee St N # 3	Cleveland	TN	37312	423-476-6561	559-3855
Web: www.amuniform.com					
Anson Shirt Co 620 Anson Shirt Apparel Rd PO Box 311	Wadesboro	NC	28170	704-694-5148	694-6679
Barco Uniforms Inc 350 W Rosecrans Ave	Gardena	CA	90248	310-323-7315	324-5274*
*Fax: Cust Svc ■ TF: 800-421-1874 ■ Web: www.barcouniforms.com					
Berne Apparel Co 2210 Summit St	New Haven	IN	46774	260-469-3136	469-8193
TF: 800-843-7657 ■ Web: www.berneapparel.com					
Blauer Mfg Co Inc 20 Aberdeen St	Boston	MA	02215	617-536-6606	536-6948
TF: 800-225-6715 ■ Web: www.blauer.com					
Blue Generation Div of M Rubin & Sons Inc 34-01 38th Ave	Long Island City	NY	11101	718-361-2800	361-2680
TF: 888-336-4687 ■ Web: www.bluegeneration.com					
Carhartt Inc 5750 Mercury Dr	Dearborn	MI	48126	313-271-8460	271-3455
TF: 800-358-3825 ■ Web: www.carhartt.com					
Choi Bros Inc 3401 W Division St	Chicago	IL	60651	773-489-2800	489-3030
TF: 800-524-2464 ■ Web: www.choibrothers.com					
City Shirt Co Inc 242 Frackville Industrial Pk Rd	Frackville	PA	17931	570-874-4251	874-0593
DeMoulin Bros & Co Inc 1025 S 4th St	Greenville	IL	62246	618-664-2000	664-1712
TF: 800-228-8134 ■ Web: www.demoulin.com					
Dennis Uniform Mfg Co Inc 135 SE Hawthorne Blvd	Portland	OR	97214	503-238-7123	238-2529
TF: 800-544-7123 ■ Web: www.dennisuniform.com					
Dickson Industries Inc 2425 Dean Ave	Des Moines	IA	50317	515-262-8061	262-1844
Web: www.dicksonindustries.com					
Earl's Apparel Inc 908 S 4th St PO Box 939	Crockett	TX	75835	936-544-5521	544-7973
TF: 800-527-3148 ■ Web: www.stanray.us					
Elbeco Inc 4418 Pottsville Pike	Reading	PA	19605	610-921-0651	921-8651
TF: 800-468-4654 ■ Web: www.elbeco.com					
Elder Mfg Co Inc 999 Executive Pkwy Suite 300	Saint Louis	MO	63141	314-469-1120	
TF: 800-829-8880 ■ Web: www.elderwearwecare.com					
Encompass Group LLC 615 Macon Rd	McDonough	GA	30253	770-957-3981	957-8728
TF: 800-284-4540 ■ Web: www.encompassgroup.net					
Euclid Garment Mfg Co 333 Martinel Dr PO Box 550	Kent	OH	44240	330-673-7413	673-0228
Web: www.euclidgarment.com					
Fechheimer Bros Co Inc 4545 Malsbary Rd	Cincinnati	OH	45242	513-793-5400	793-7819
TF: 800-543-1939 ■ Web: www.fechheimer.com					
Fechheimer Martin Plant Co 1445 Main St	Martin	TN	38237	731-587-3861	587-9292
Web: www.fechheimer.com					
French Toast 3003 Scarlett St Suite 25	Brunswick	CA	31520	800-378-6248	
TF: 800-378-6248 ■ Web: www.frenchtoast.com					
Gibson & Barnes 1675 Pioneer Way	El Cajon	CA	92020	619-440-6976	748-6694*
*Fax Area Code: 800 ■ TF: 800-748-6693 ■ Web: www.gibson-barnes.com					
Globe Corp 490 E McMillan St	Cincinnati	OH	45206	513-961-0200	961-0101
Golden Mfg Co Inc 125 Hwy 366 PO Box 390	Golden	MS	38847	662-454-3428	454-9240
Web: www.goldenmfg.com					
Howard Uniform Co 1915 Annapolis Rd	Baltimore	MD	21230	410-727-3086	727-3142
TF: 800-628-8299 ■ Web: www.howarduniform.com					
I Spiewak & Sons Inc 469 7th Ave 10th Fl	New York	NY	10018	212-695-1620	629-4803
TF Cust Svc: 800-223-6850 ■ Web: www.spiewak.com					
Integrated Textile Solutions Inc 865 Cleveland Ave	Salem	VA	24153	540-389-8113	387-5855
Web: www.intextile.com					
Key Industries Inc 400 Marble Rd	Fort Scott	KS	66701	620-223-2000	223-5822
TF: 800-835-0365 ■ Web: www.keyindustriesinc.com					
Landau Uniforms Inc 8410 W Sandidge Rd	Olive Branch	MS	38654	662-895-7200	895-5099
TF: 800-238-7513 ■ Web: www.landau.com					
LC King Mfg Co Inc 24 7th St PO Box 367	Bristol	TN	37620	423-764-5188	764-6809
TF: 800-826-2510 ■ Web: www.pointerbrand.com					
Leventhal Ltd 1295 Northern Blvd	Manhasset	NY	11030	516-365-9540	365-9547
TF: 800-847-4095 ■ Web: www.leventhalltd.com					
Lion Apparel Inc 7200 Poe Ave Suite 400	Dayton	OH	45414	937-898-1949	898-2848*
*Fax: Hum Res ■ TF: 800-548-6614 ■ Web: www.lionprotects.com					
National Spirit Group Ltd 2010 Merritt Dr	Garland	TX	75041	972-840-1233	840-4077
TF: 800-527-4366 ■ Web: www.nationalspirit.com					
Nationwide Uniform Corp 235 Shepherdsville Rd	Hodgenville	KY	42748	270-358-4173	358-8255
OshKosh B'Gosh Inc 112 Otter Ave	Oshkosh	WI	54901	920-231-8800	231-8621
TF: 800-282-4674 ■ Web: www.oshkoshbgosh.com					
Polkton Mfg Co Inc 6713 E Marshville Blvd PO Box 220	Marshville	NC	28103	704-624-3200	624-6128
TF: 800-445-0044 ■ Web: www.seafarer.com					
Riverside Mfg Co 301 Riverside Dr	Moultrie	GA	31768	229-985-5210	890-2932
TF: 800-841-8677 ■ Web: www.riversideuniforms.com					
Royal Park Uniforms Co 14139 Hwy 86 S	Prospect Hill	NC	27314	336-562-3345	562-3832
Web: www.royal-park.com					
Rubin Bros Inc 2241 S Halsted St	Chicago	IL	60608	312-942-1111	942-1871
TF: 800-632-2308					
School Apparel Inc 1099 Sneath Ln	San Bruno	CA	94066	650-827-7400	277-2272*
*Fax Area Code: 800 ■ TF: 888-628-9020 ■ Web: www.schoolapparel.com					
SCORE American Soccer Co Inc 726 E Anaheim St	Wilmington	CA	90744	310-830-6161	426-1222*
*Fax Area Code: 800 ■ TF: 800-626-7774 ■ Web: www.scoresports.com					
Scotty's Fashions Inc 636 Pen Argyl St	Pen Argyl	PA	18072	610-863-6454	863-6490
Web: www.scottysfashions.com					
Stanbury Uniforms Inc 108 Stanbury Industrial Dr PO Box 100	Brookfield	MO	64628	660-258-2246	258-5781
TF: 800-826-2246 ■ Web: www.stanbury.com					
Standard Textile Co Inc 1 Knollcrest Dr	Cincinnati	OH	45237	513-761-9255	761-0467
TF: 800-888-5000 ■ Web: www.standardtextile.com					
Superior Uniform Group Inc 10055Seminole Blvd	Seminole	FL	33772	727-397-9611	391-5401
AMEX: SGC ■ TF Cust Svc: 800-727-8643 ■ Web: www.superiorsurgicalmfg.com					
Tennessee Apparel Corp 401 N Atlantic St	Tullahoma	TN	37388	931-455-3468	455-1209
Topps Safety Apparel Inc 2516 E State Rd 14	Rochester	IN	46975	574-223-4311	223-8622
TF: 800-348-2990 ■ Web: www.toppssafetyapparel.com					
Universal Overall Co 1060 W Van Buren St	Chicago	IL	60607	312-226-3336	226-1986
TF Cust Svc: 800-621-3344 ■ Web: www.universaloverall.com					
Varsity Spirit Div Varsity Brands Inc 6745 Lenox Ctr Ct Suite 300	Memphis	TN	38115	901-387-4370	387-4357
Web: www.varsity.com					
Walls Industries Inc 1905 N Main St	Cleburne	TX	76033	817-645-4366	645-4366
TF: 800-433-1765					
Wenaas AGS Inc 202 E Larkspur St	Victoria	TX	77904	361-576-2668	576-2674
TF: 888-576-2668 ■ Web: www.wenaasusa.com					
Williamson-Dickie Mfg Co 509 W Vickery Blvd	Fort Worth	TX	76104	817-336-7201	336-8643*
*Fax Area Code: 800 ■ TF: 800-336-7201 ■ Web: www.dickies.com					

155-20 Western Wear (Except Hats & Boots)

	City	State	ZIP	Phone	Fax
Darwood Mfg Co 620 W Railroad St S PO Box 625	Pelham	GA	31779	229-294-4932	294-9323
Web: www.darwoodmfg.com					
Karman Inc 14707 E 2nd Ave 3rd Fl	Aurora	CO	80011	303-893-2320	571-2248
TF: 800-825-6555 ■ Web: www.roperusa.com					
Miller International Inc Rocky Mountain Clothing Co Div 8500 Zuni St	Denver	CO	80260	303-428-5696	430-1130
TF: 800-688-4449 ■ Web: www.rockymountainclothing.com					
Niver Western Wear Inc PO Box 10122	Fort Worth	TX	76185	817-924-4299	924-4296
TF Orders: 800-433-5752					
Rockmount Ranch Wear Mfg Co 1626 Wazee St	Denver	CO	80202	303-629-7777	629-5836
TF: 800-776-2566 ■ Web: www.rockmount.com					
Sidran Inc 14280 Gillis Rd	Farmers Branch	TX	75244	214-352-7979	352-0439
TF Cust Svc: 800-969-5015 ■ Web: www.sidraninc.com					

155-21 Women's Clothing

	City	State	ZIP	Phone	Fax
Adrianna Papell Ltd 512 7th Ave 8th Fl	New York	NY	10018	212-695-5244	714-1871
Web: www.adriannapapell.com					
Alfred Angelo Inc 1301 Virginia Dr Suite 110	Fort Washington	PA	19034	215-659-5300	659-1532
TF: 800-504-7263 ■ Web: www.alfredangelo.com					
Anne Klein & Co 1129 Westchester Ave	White Plains	NY	10604	888-841-2229	
Web: www.anneklein.com					
Bari-Jay Fashions Inc 225 W 37th St 7th Fl	New York	NY	10018	212-921-1551	391-0165
Web: www.barijay.com					
Basham Industries Hwy 56 & Industrial Dr	Coalmont	TN	37313	931-692-3218	692-3481
bebe stores Inc 400 Valley Dr	Brisbane	CA	94005	415-715-3900	715-3939
NASDAQ: BEBE ■ TF: 877-232-3777 ■ Web: www.bebe.com					
Bernard Chaus Inc 530 7th Ave 18th Fl	New York	NY	10018	212-354-1280	768-2954
Web: www.bernardchaus.com					
Bill Blass Ltd 236 5th Ave 2nd Fl	New York	NY	10001	212-689-8957	213-5485
Web: www.billblass.com					
Bleyle Inc 67 Liberty Church Rd	Carrollton	GA	30116	678-853-0023	853-0029
TF Cust Svc: 800-241-3437 ■ Web: www.bleyle.com					
Byer California 66 Potrero Ave	San Francisco	CA	94103	415-626-7844	626-7865
TF: 800-998-2937 ■ Web: www.byer.com					
Calvin Klein Inc 205 W 39th St 3rd Fl	New York	NY	10018	212-719-2600	730-4818
TF Cust Svc: 800-388-9122 ■ Web: www.pvh.com					
Carole Wren Inc 30-00 47th Ave 5th Fl	Long Island City	NY	11101	718-552-3800	937-5812
Web: www.carolewren.com					
Christine Alexander Inc 34210 9th Ave S Suite 101 PO Box 24960	Federal Way	WA	98093	253-874-5570	927-4516
Web: www.christinealexander.com					
Crown Clothing Corp 340 Vanderbilt Ave	Norwood	MA	02062	781-769-0001	769-7337
TF: 800-225-8950 ■ Web: www.crownclothingcorp.com					
Darue of California Inc 14102 S Broadway	Los Angeles	CA	90061	310-323-1350	323-8133
TF: 800-733-3375 ■ Web: www.darue.com					
Depeche Mode Inc 520 8th Ave 11th Fl	New York	NY	10018	212-643-6633	643-1184
Web: www.depecheco.com					
Donna Karan International Inc 550 7th Ave 15th Fl	New York	NY	10018	212-789-1500	789-1821
TF: 800-231-0884 ■ Web: www.donnakaran.com					
ENC 13071 E Temple Ave	City of Industry	CA	91746	626-934-4111	
Gator of Florida Inc 5002 N Howard Ave	Tampa	FL	33603	813-877-8267	876-3372
Graff Californiawear 1515 E 15th St	Los Angeles	CA	90021	213-749-0171	746-5754
TF: 800-421-8692 ■ Web: www.graffwear.com					
Halmode Apparel Inc 1400 Broadway 11th Fl	New York	NY	10018	212-564-7800	398-6462
TF: 800-388-0938					

	City	State	Zip	Phone	Fax
Hartstrings Inc 270 E Conestoga Rd	Wayne	PA	19087	610-687-6900	
TF: 866-346-4242 ■ *Web:* www.hartstrings.com					
Jessica McClintock Inc 1400 16th St	San Francisco	CA	94103	415-553-8200	553-8329
TF: 800-333-5301 ■ *Web:* www.jessicamcclintock.com					
JLM Couture Inc 525 Seventh Ave Suite 1703	New York	NY	10018	212-221-8203	921-7608
TF: 800-924-6475 ■ *Web:* www.jlmcouture.com					
Jones Apparel Group Inc Evan-Picone Dress Div 498 7th Ave 10th Fl	New York	NY	10018	215-785-4000	785-1795
TF: 800-848-8668 ■ *Web:* www.jonesgroupinc.com/index.php?option=com_content&view=article&id=38&Itemid=45					
Jones Apparel Group Inc Jones New York Collection Div 1411 Broadway	New York	NY	10018	215-642-3860	
TF: 800-848-8668 ■ *Web:* www.jonesgroupinc.com/index.php?option=com_content&view=article&id=8&Itemid=13					
Jones Apparel Group Inc Jones New York Dress Div 1411 Broadway	New York	NY	10018	215-642-3860	
TF: 800-848-8668 ■ *Web:* www.jonesgroupinc.com/index.php?option=com_content&view=article&id=9&Itemid=14					
Kellwood Co 600 Kellwood Pkwy	Chesterfield	MO	63017	314-576-3100	576-3460
Web: www.kellwood.com					
Koret Co 505 14th St	Oakland	CA	94612	510-622-7000	622-7294
TF: 800-468-6006 ■ *Web:* www.koretcompany.com					
Leon Levin Inc 250 W 39th St 5th Fl	New York	NY	10018	212-575-1900	944-1482
TF: 800-822-3363 ■ *Web:* www.leonlevin.com					
Leon Max Inc 3100 New York Dr	Pasadena	CA	91107	626-797-6886	797-8555
TF: 800-345-3813 ■ *Web:* www.maxstudio.com					
Liz Claiborne Inc 1441 Broadway 22nd Fl	New York	NY	10018	212-354-4900	354-4900
NYSE: LIZ ■ *Web:* www.lizclaiborneinc.com					
Maggy London International Ltd 530 7th Ave 16th Fl	New York	NY	10018	212-944-7199	840-2483
Marisa Christina Inc 8101 Tonnelle Ave	North Bergen	NJ	07047	201-758-9800	861-9767
Web: www.marisachristina.com					
Nitches Inc 10280 Camino Santa Fe	San Diego	CA	92121	858-625-2633	625-0746
NASDAQ: NICH					
Paquette Alfred Inc 1201 Rio Vista Ave	Los Angeles	CA	90023	323-266-4561	267-1086
TF: 800-585-2937					
Robespierre Inc 225 W 35th St	New York	NY	10001	212-764-8810	764-8796
TF: 877-537-6734 ■ *Web:* www.nanettelepore.com					
S & S Mfg Co 175 Old Airport Rd	Roebuck	SC	29376	864-574-5807	574-3694
Sag Harbor 1407 Broadway	New York	NY	10018	212-391-8666	730-2040
Web: www.sag-harbor.com					
Saint John Knits Inc 17622 Armstrong Ave	Irvine	CA	92614	949-863-1171	261-9585
Web: www.sjk.com					
Sally Lou Fashions Corp 1400 Broadway 6th Fl	New York	NY	10018	212-354-9670	819-0166
TF: 800-258-1540					
Scotty's Fashions Inc 636 Pen Argyl St	Pen Argyl	PA	18072	610-863-6454	863-6490
Web: www.scottysfashions.com					
Tahari Ltd Inc 11 W 42nd St	New York	NY	10036	212-763-2000	763-2299
Web: www.elietahari.com					
Tama Mfg Co Inc 100 Cascade Dr	Allentown	PA	18109	610-231-3100	231-3180
Web: www.tamamfg.com					
Tanner Cos LLC 581Rock Rd	Rutherfordton	NC	28139	828-287-4205	286-2072
TF: 800-669-3662					
Tarrant Apparel Group 801 S Figueroa St	Los Angeles	CA	90017	323-780-8250	780-0751
Web: www.tags.com					
Taylor Togs Inc 621 Micaville Loop PO Box 180	Micaville	NC	28755	828-675-4153	675-9602
TF: 800-872-4290 ■ *Web:* www.taylortogs.com					
Ursula of Switzerland Inc 31 Mohawk Ave	Waterford	NY	12188	518-237-2580	237-3038
TF: 800-826-4041 ■ *Web:* www.ursula.com					
Young Stuff Apparel Group Inc 1372 broad way 6th Fl 36th st	New York	NY	10018	646-839-7000	846-7001

156 CLOTHING & ACCESSORIES - WHOL

	City	State	Zip	Phone	Fax
Alternative Apparel Inc 1650 Indian Brook Way	Norcross	GA	30093	678-380-1890	380-1894
TF: 888-481-4287 ■ *Web:* www.iceboxonline.com					
Bounty Trading Corp 1370 Broadway 14th Fl	New York	NY	10018	212-279-5900	564-5950
TF: 800-526-8689 ■ *Web:* www.bountytrading.com					
Broder Bros Co 45555 Port St	Plymouth	MI	48170	734-454-4800	454-8971
TF: 800-521-0850 ■ *Web:* www.broderbros.com					
Crew Outfitters 579 W High St	Aurora	MO	65605	888-567-2739	678-6277*
**Fax Area Code: 417* ■ *TF:* 888-567-2739 ■ *Web:* www.crewoutfitters.com					
Foria International Inc 18689 Arenth Ave	City of Industry	CA	91748	626-912-6100	964-9933
Web: www.foria.com					
Herman's Inc 2820 Blackhawk Rd	Rock Island	IL	61201	309-788-9568	786-8296
TF Cust Svc: 800-447-1295 ■ *Web:* www.hermansinc.com					
Jacob Ash Co Inc 301 Munson Ave	McKees Rocks	PA	15136	412-331-6660	331-6347
TF: 800-245-6111 ■ *Web:* www.jacobash.com					
Marmaxx Group 770 Cochituate Rd	Framingham	MA	01701	508-390-1000	390-3132
Mast Industries Inc 3425 Morse Crossing	Columbus	OH	43219	614-337-5600	337-5080
Web: www.mast.com					
Mid-Continent Imports Inc 12920 Metcalf Ave Suite 170	Overland Park	KS	66213	913-681-0090	681-0091
Nike Team Sports 15550 SW Milikan Way	Beaverton	OR	97006	503-532-6874	532-6704
Web: www.niketeam.com					
Noamex Inc 625 Wortman Ave	Brooklyn	NY	11208	718-342-2278	342-2258
Web: www.noamex.com					
Poushak Inc 11800 W Olympic Blvd	Los Angeles	CA	90064	310-478-8660	478-6935
Web: www.zanetti.com					
Romerovski Corp 450 W Westfield Ave	Roselle Park	NJ	07204	908-241-3000	241-6662
TF: 800-852-9944 ■ *Web:* www.romerovski.com					
Scope Imports Inc 8020 Blankenship Dr	Houston	TX	77055	713-688-0077	688-8768
Smokin Joes Cigars LLC 2293 Saunders Settlement Rd	Sanborn	NY	14132	716-215-2000	754-4184
Web: www.smokinjoes.com					
Soex West USA LLC 3294 E 26th St	Los Angeles	CA	90058	323-264-8300	227-6845
Web: www.soexgroup.com					
Sussex Co Inc PO Box 749	Milford	DE	19963	302-422-8037	422-8244
TF: 800-537-5995					
Topwin Corp 3415 Kashiwa St	Torrance	CA	90505	310-325-2255	325-1877
Web: www.topwin.co.jp					
TSC Apparel LLC 12080 Mosteller Rd	Cincinnati	OH	45241	513-771-1138	248-1069*
**Fax Area Code: 800* ■ *TF:* 800-543-7230 ■ *Web:* www.tscapparel.com					
Tucker Rocky Distributing Inc 4900 Alliance Gateway Fwy	Fort Worth	TX	76177	817-258-9000	258-9095*
**Fax: Cust Svc* ■ *TF:* 800-283-8787 ■ *Web:* www.tuckerrocky.com					
William B Coleman Co Inc 4001 Earhart Blvd	New Orleans	LA	70125	504-822-1000	822-3152
World Wide Dreams LLC 350 5th Ave Suite 2101	New York	NY	10118	212-273-9200	273-9599
TF: 800-221-8828					
WS Emerson Co Inc 15 Acme Rd	Brewer	ME	04412	207-989-3410	989-8540
TF: 800-789-6120 ■ *Web:* www.wsemerson.com					

157 CLOTHING STORES

SEE ALSO Department Stores p. 1783

157-1 Children's Clothing Stores

	City	State	Zip	Phone	Fax
Babies 'R' Us 545 Rt 17 S	Paramus	NJ	07652	201-251-3191	251-2469
Web: www.babiesrus.com					
Children's Place Retail Stores Inc 500 Plaza Dr	Secaucus	NJ	07094	201-558-2400	558-2819*
NASDAQ: PLCE ■ **Fax: Cust Svc* ■ *TF:* 877-752-2387 ■ *Web:* www.childrensplace.com					
Gymboree Corp 500 Howard St	San Francisco	CA	94105	415-278-7000	278-7100
NASDAQ: GYMB ■ *TF:* 877-449-6932 ■ *Web:* www.gymboree.com					
Kid to Kid 170 S 1000E	Salt Lake City	UT	84102	801-359-0071	359-3207
TF: 888-543-2543 ■ *Web:* www.kidtokid.com					
Strasburg Children 9810 Industrial Blvd	Lenexa	KS	66215	913-888-1115	495-9413
Web: www.strasburgchildren.com					
Tween Brands Inc 8323 Walton Pkwy	New Albany	OH	43054	614-775-3500	775-3938
TF: 800-934-4496 ■ *Web:* www.tooinc.com					
Valor Brands LLC 3159 Royal Dr Suite 360	Alpharetta	GA	30022	770-346-9250	
TF: 866-949-9098 ■ *Web:* www.valorbrands.com					
Winmark Corp 605ßHwy 169 N Suite 400	Minneapolis	MN	55421	763-520-8500	520-8410
NASDAQ: WINA ■ *TF:* 800-433-2540 ■ *Web:* www.winmarkcorporation.com					

157-2 Family Clothing Stores

	City	State	Zip	Phone	Fax
Benetton USA Corp 601 5th Ave	New York	NY	10017	212-593-0290	371-1438
Bob's Stores Inc 160 Corporate Ct	Meriden	CT	06450	203-235-5775	634-1185
TF: 866-333-2627 ■ *Web:* www.bobstores.com					
Citi Trends Inc 104 Coleman Blvd	Savannah	GA	31408	912-443-3650	443-3085
NASDAQ: CTRN ■ *TF:* 800-605-8174 ■ *Web:* www.cititrends.com					
Daffy's Inc 1 Secaucus Area	Secaucus	NJ	07094	201-902-0800	902-9016
Web: www.daffys.com					
Dawahares Inc 1845 Alexandria Dr	Lexington	KY	40504	859-278-0422	514-3298
TF: 800-677-9108 ■ *Web:* www.dawahares.com					
De Byles Inc PO Box 128	Rhinelander	WI	54501	715-362-4406	362-1772
Eblens Casual Clothing 299 Industrial Ln	Torrington	CT	06790	860-489-3073	496-7446
TF: 800-464-2898 ■ *Web:* www.eblens.com					
Foursome Inc 3570 Vicksveurg Ln N Suite 100	Plymouth	MN	55447	952-473-4667	504-5555*
**Fax Area Code: 763* ■ *TF:* 888-368-7766 ■ *Web:* www.thefoursome.com					
Goody's Family Clothing Inc PO Box 22000	Knoxville	TN	37933	865-966-2000	777-4220*
**Fax: Hum Res* ■ *TF:* 800-224-3114 ■ *Web:* www.goodysonline.com					
Hammer's 102 1st Ave SE	Winchester	TN	37398	931-967-3787	962-0717
Kittery Trading Post 301 US 1	Kittery	ME	03904	207-439-2700	439-8001
TF: 888-587-6246 ■ *Web:* www.kitterytradingpost.com					
Marshalls Inc 770 Cochituate Rd	Framingham	MA	01701	508-390-1000	390-3147*
**Fax: Hum Res* ■ *Web:* www.marshallsonline.com					
Name Brands Inc 7215 S Memorial Dr	Tulsa	OK	74133	918-307-0284	307-0294
Web: www.halfofhalf.com					
National Stores Inc 15001 S Figueroa St	Gardena	CA	90248	310-324-9962	324-0696
Web: www.factory2-u.com					
Palais Royal 10201 S Main St	Houston	TX	77025	713-667-5601	669-2709
TF: 800-324-3244 ■ *Web:* www.palaisroyal.com					
Peter Harris Clothes 952 Troy-Schenectady Rd	Latham	NY	12110	518-785-1650	785-0100
TF: 800-444-1650 ■ *Web:* www.peterharrisclothes.com					
Puritan of Cape Cod 408 Main St	Hyannis	MA	02601	508-775-2400	771-3277
TF: 800-924-0606 ■ *Web:* www.puritancapecod.com					
Rogers Dept Store Inc 1001 28th St SW	Grand Rapids	MI	49509	616-538-6000	538-0613
TF: 800-727-7643					
Ross Stores Inc 4440 Rosewood Dr	Pleasanton	CA	94588	925-965-4400	965-4388
NASDAQ: ROST ■ *TF:* 800-289-7677 ■ *Web:* www.rossstores.com					
Sealfons Inc 410 Springfield Ave	Summit	NJ	07901	908-277-1777	277-3054
Sharpe Dry Goods Co Inc 200 N Broadway St	Checotah	OK	74426	918-473-2233	473-2755
TF: 800-238-6491 ■ *Web:* www.sharpeclothing.com					
Syms Corp 1 Syms Way	Secaucus	NJ	07094	201-902-9600	902-9874
NASDAQ: SYM ■ *TF:* 800-322-7967 ■ *Web:* www.syms.com					
TJ Maxx 770 Cochituate Rd	Framingham	MA	01701	508-390-1000	
TF Cust Svc: 800-926-6299 ■ *Web:* www.tjmaxx.com					
Wakefield's Inc 1212 Quintard Ave	Anniston	AL	36201	256-237-9521	236-9253
TF: 800-333-1552 ■ *Web:* www.wakefields.com					
Zumiez Inc 6300 Merrill Creek Pkwy Suite B	Everett	WA	98203	425-551-1500	551-1555
NASDAQ: ZUMZ ■ *TF:* 877-828-6929 ■ *Web:* www.zumiez.com					

157-3 Men's Clothing Stores

				Phone	Fax
Brooks Bros Inc 346 Madison Ave TF: 800-444-1613 ■ Web: www.brooksbrothers.com	New York	NY	10017	212-682-8800	309-7273
C & R Clothiers Inc 5803 Glenmont Dr *Fax: Hum Res ■ TF: 800-447-8487	Houston	TX	77081	713-295-7200	592-7008*
Caplan's Mens Shops Inc 916 3rd St	Alexandria	LA	71301	318-487-4231	443-8816
Carroll & Co 425 N Canon Dr TF: 800-238-9400 ■ Web: www.carrollandco.com	Beverly Hills	CA	90210	310-273-9060	273-7974
Casual Male Inc 555 Tpke St *Fax: Hum Res ■ TF: 800-767-0319 ■ Web: www.casualmale.com	Canton	MA	02021	781-828-9300	828-5059*
Casual Male Retail Group Inc 555 Tpke St NASDAQ: CMRG ■ Web: www.casualmale.com	Canton	MA	02021	781-828-9300	821-1366
Culwell & Son Inc 6319 Hillcrest Ave Web: www.culwell.com	Dallas	TX	75205	214-522-7000	521-7329
Dahle Management Corp 4065 S Commerce Dr Suite 300-W Web: www.dahles-bigandtall.com	Murray	UT	84107	801-892-2555	892-2556
Dr. Denim Inc 1136 Market St TF: 888-761-6520 ■ Web: www.drdenim.com	Philadelphia	PA	19107	215-564-5152	564-2984
Gushner Bros Inc 1818 Chestnut St Web: www.boydsphila.com	Philadelphia	PA	19103	215-564-9000	564-2876
H & M Hennes & Mauritz Corp 1328 Broadway 3rd Fl Web: www.hm.com	New York	NY	10001	646-473-1165	473-1165
Harold's Men's Wear 350 W 19th St	Houston	TX	77008	713-864-2647	864-9830
Hugestore.com 427 S Illinois St TF: 800-259-7283 ■ Web: www.hugestore.com	Indianapolis	IN	46225	317-321-9999	321-9988
International Male 741 F St TF: 800-293-9333 ■ Web: www.internationalmale.com	San Diego	CA	92101	619-544-9900	881-3940
Ja Apparel Corp 650 5th Ave FL 20 Web: www.josephabboud.com	New York	NY	10019	212-586-9140	397-9360
Jos A Bank Clothiers 500 Hanover Pike NASDAQ: JOSB ■ TF Cust Svc: 800-999-7472 ■ Web: www.josbank.com	Hampstead	MD	21074	410-239-2700	239-5700
Joseph Davidson Inc 412 S Jefferson St	Roanoke	VA	24011	540-343-2441	345-6021
K & G Men's Center Inc 1225 Chattahoochee Ave NW TF: 800-351-7987 ■ Web: www.kgmens.com	Atlanta	GA	30318	404-351-7987	351-8038
Kizan International Inc 100 W Hill Dr Web: www.louisraphael.com	Brisbane	CA	94005	415-468-7360	468-0444
Louis Boston 234 Berkeley St TF: 800-225-5135 ■ Web: www.louisboston.com	Boston	MA	02116	617-262-6100	266-4586
Lourie's Inc 1601 Main St Web: www.louries.com	Columbia	SC	29201	803-765-9200	256-1906
Marsh's Men's Shop 270 Main St	Huntington	NY	11743	631-423-1660	423-1670
Men's Wearhouse Inc 6380 Rogerdale Rd NYSE: MW ■ TF: 800-777-8580 ■ Web: www.menswearhouse.com	Houston	TX	77072	281-776-7000	776-7038
Miltons Inc 250 Granite St TF: 800-645-8667 ■ Web: www.miltons.com	Braintree	MA	02184	781-848-1880	848-1090
Norton Ditto Co Inc 2425 W Alabama St Web: www.nortonditto.com	Houston	TX	77098	713-688-9800	621-3875
Patrick James Inc 3457 W Shaw Ave TF: 888-427-6003 ■ Web: www.patrickjames.com	Fresno	CA	93711	559-275-4300	275-0137
Paul Fredrick Menstyle 223 W Poplar St TF: 800-247-1417 ■ Web: www.paulfredrick.com	Fleetwood	PA	19522	610-944-0909	944-6452
Rochester Big & Tall 700 Mission St TF: 800-282-8200 ■ Web: www.rochesterclothing.com	San Francisco	CA	94103	415-982-6455	227-0727
Rubenstein Bros Inc 102 St Charles Ave TF: 800-725-7823	New Orleans	LA	70130	504-581-6666	582-6982

157-4 Men's & Women's Clothing Stores

				Phone	Fax
Abercrombie & Fitch Co 6301 Fitch Pass NYSE: ANF ■ TF: 800-666-2595 ■ Web: www.abercrombie.com	New Albany	OH	43054	614-283-6500	283-6565
American Eagle Outfitters Inc 77 Hot Metal St NYSE: AEO ■ *Fax Area Code: 724 ■ TF Cust Svc: 888-232-4535 ■ Web: www.ae.com	Pittsburgh	PA	15203	412-432-3300	776-6160*
Barneys New York Inc 575 5th Ave *Fax: Hum Res ■ Web: www.barneys.com	New York	NY	10017	212-450-8700	450-8489*
Bergdorf Goodman Inc 754 5th Ave TF Cust Svc: 800-558-1855 ■ Web: www.bergdorfgoodman.com	New York	NY	10019	212-753-7300	872-8886
Buckle Inc 2407 W 24th St NYSE: BKE ■ TF: 800-626-1255 ■ Web: www.buckle.com	Kearney	NE	68845	308-236-4461	236-4493
Burberry Ltd (New York) 9 E 57th St Web: www.burberry.com	New York	NY	10022	212-407-7100	355-9870
Cohoes Fashions Inc 43 Mohawk St TF: 800-736-8765 ■ Web: www.cohoesfashions.com	Cohoes	NY	12047	518-237-0524	237-0234
Cygne Designs Inc 11 W 42nd St	New York	NY	10036	212-997-7767	245-7761
Eddie Bauer Inc 15010 NE 36th St *Fax Area Code: 800 ■ TF Orders: 800-426-8020 ■ Web: www.eddiebauer.com	Redmond	WA	98052	425-755-6100	414-6110*
Gap Inc 2 Folsom St NYSE: GPS ■ TF: 800-333-7899 ■ Web: www.gapinc.com	San Francisco	CA	94105	650-952-4400	874-7803
Guntersville Outlet Inc 701 Railroad Ave TF: 888-713-3984 ■ Web: www.factory-connection.com	Albertville	AL	35951	256-878-2866	878-0629
J Crew Group Inc 770 Broadway TF: 800-932-0043 ■ Web: www.jcrew.com	New York	NY	10003	212-209-2500	209-2666
J Hirshleifer & Son Inc 2080 Northern Blvd TF: 800-401-9313 ■ Web: www.hirshleifers.com	Manhasset	NY	11030	516-627-3566	627-3579
J McLaughlin 1008 Lexington Ave	New York	NY	10021	212-879-9565	879-0066
Jack Henry Clothing Co Inc 612 W 47th St	Kansas City	MO	64112	816-753-3800	753-0284
James Davis 400 S Grove Pk Rd	Memphis	TN	38117	901-767-4640	682-3338
Joe's Jeans Inc 2340 S Eastern Ave NASDAQ: JOEZ ■ TF: 877-413-7467 ■ Web: www.joesjeans.com	Commerce	CA	90040	323-837-3700	837-3790
John B Malouf Inc 8201 Quaker Ave Suite 106 Web: www.maloufs.com	Lubbock	TX	79424	806-794-9500	798-3428
Jones & Mitchell Sportswear Inc 11880 College Blvd Suite 400 TF: 800-345-7973 ■ Web: www.jonesmitchell.com	Overland Park	KS	66210	913-324-2700	324-2799
Limited Brands Inc 3 Limited Pkwy NYSE: LTD ■ *Fax: Mail Rm ■ TF: 800-945-9000 ■ Web: www.limitedbrands.com	Columbus	OH	43230	614-415-7000	415-2491*
Mark Fore & Strike Inc 6500 Pk of Commerce Blvd TF Orders: 800-327-3627 ■ Web: www.markforeandstrike.com	Boca Raton	FL	33487	561-241-1700	241-1055
Mark Shale 10441 Beaudin Blvd Suite 100 TF: 800-488-2686 ■ Web: www.markshale.com	Woodridge	IL	60517	630-427-1100	427-1200
Maurices Inc 105 W Superior St TF: 866-977-1542 ■ Web: www.maurices.com	Duluth	MN	55802	218-727-8431	720-2102
Oak Hall Inc 6150 Poplar Ave Suite 146 Web: www.oakhall.com	Memphis	TN	38119	901-761-3580	761-5731
Pacific Sunwear of California Inc 3450 E Miraloma Ave NASDAQ: PSUN ■ TF: 800-444-6770	Anaheim	CA	92806	714-414-4000	414-4251
Patagonia Inc 259 W Santa Clara St PO Box 150 TF Cust Svc: 800-638-6464 ■ Web: www.patagonia.com	Ventura	CA	93001	805-643-8616	653-6355
Paul Stuart Inc Madison Ave & 45th St TF Orders: 800-678-8278 ■ Web: www.paulstuart.com	New York	NY	10017	212-682-0320	983-2742
Plato's Closet 4200 Dahlberg Dr Suite 100 Web: www.platoscloset.com	Minneapolis	MN	55422	763-520-8500	520-8410
Specialty Retailers Inc 10201 S Main St TF: 800-579-2302 ■ Web: www.stagestoresinc.com	Houston	TX	77025	800-579-2302	
Stanley Korshak 500 Crescent Ct Suite 100 TF: 800-972-5959 ■ Web: www.stanleykorshak.com	Dallas	TX	75201	214-871-3600	871-3617
TJX Cos Inc 770 Cochituate Rd NYSE: TJX ■ TF: 800-926-6299 ■ Web: www.tjx.com	Framingham	MA	01701	508-390-1000	390-2091
Town & County Inc 2660 S Glenstone Ave	Springfield	MO	65804	417-883-6131	883-7271
Urban Outfitters Inc 30 Industrial Park Blvd NASDAQ: URBN ■ Web: www.urbanoutfitters.com	Trenton	SC	29847	800-282-2200	959-8795
Watch LA 1138 Wall St Web: www.watchla.com	Los Angeles	CA	90015	213-747-1838	747-2888
Wicked Fashions Inc 222 Bridge Plaza S Web: www.wickedfashionsinc.com	Fort Lee	NJ	07024	201-242-5900	242-8466

157-5 Specialty Clothing Stores

Specialty Clothing Stores Are Those Which Sell A Specific Type Of Clothing, Such As Western Wear, Uniforms, Etc.

				Phone	Fax
5.11 Inc 4300 Spyres Way TF: 866-451-1726 ■ Web: www.511tactical.com	Modesto	CA	95356	209-527-4511	527-1511
Aeropostale Inc 112 W 34th St 22nd Fl NYSE: ARO ■ Web: www.aeropostale.com	New York	NY	10120	646-485-5410	485-5440
Alvin's Stores Inc 14520 Front Beach Rd Web: www.alvinsisland.com	Panama City	FL	32413	850-234-8897	235-2250
Brigade Quartermasters Ltd 1025 Cobb Intl Dr NW Suite 100 Web: www.brigadeqm.com	Kennesaw	GA	30156	770-428-1248	426-7726
Carlen Enterprises Inc 1760 Apollo Ct Web: www.carlen.com	Seal Beach	CA	90740	562-296-1055	296-1052
Cavender's 2025 SW Loop 323 Web: www.cavenders.com	Tyler	TX	75701	903-561-4992	561-4849
Country Curtains PO Box 955 Web: www.countrycurtains.com	Stockbridge	MA	01262	413-243-1474	243-1067
Dunham's Sports 5000 Dixie Hwy Web: www.dunhamssports.com	Waterford	MI	48329	248-674-4991	674-1407
Flynn & Ohara Of Virginia Inc 10905 Dutton Rd TF: 800-441-4122 ■ Web: www.flynnohara.com	Philadelphia	PA	19154	215-637-4600	637-6392
Hat World Corp 8142 Woodland Dr Web: www.lids.com	Indianapolis	IN	46278	317-334-9428	337-1428
Hilo Hattie 700 N Nimitz Hwy TF: 800-233-8912 ■ Web: www.hilohattie.com	Honolulu	HI	96817	808-524-3966	533-6809
Hot Topic Inc 18305 E San Jose Ave NASDAQ: HOTT ■ Web: www.hottopic.com	City of Industry	CA	91748	626-839-4681	839-4686
Libertyville Saddle Shop Inc 306 Peterson Rd Hwy 137 TF: 800-872-3353 ■ Web: www.saddleshop.com	Libertyville	IL	60048	847-362-0570	680-2491
Life Uniform Co 2132 Kratky Rd *Fax Area Code: 800 ■ TF: 800-325-8033 ■ Web: www.lifeuniform.com	Saint Louis	MO	63114	314-824-2900	327-8070*
Mark's Work Warehouse 30-1035 64th Ave SE TF: 800-663-6275 ■ Web: www2.marks.com	Calgary	AB	T2H2J7	403-255-9220	255-6005
Modell's Sporting Goods 498 7th Ave 20th Fl TF: 800-250-7405 ■ Web: www.modells.com	New York	NY	10018	212-822-1000	822-1090
Niver Western Wear Inc PO Box 10122 TF Orders: 800-433-5752	Fort Worth	TX	76185	817-924-4299	924-4296
Northwest Designs Ink Inc 1 Lake Bellevue Dr Suite 205 *Fax Area Code: 877 ■ TF: 800-925-9327 ■ Web: www.northwestdesigns.com	Bellevue	WA	98005	800-925-9327	925-9327*
Overland Sheepskin Co Inc 2096 Nutmeg Ave TF: 800-683-7526 ■ Web: www.overland.com	Fairfield	IA	52556	641-472-8484	472-8474
Post & Nickel 144 N 14th St Web: www.postandnickel.com	Lincoln	NE	68508	402-476-3432	476-3454
Pro Image Franchise LC 233 N 1250 W Suite 200 TF: 888-477-6326 ■ Web: www.proimage.net	Centerville	UT	84014	801-296-9999	296-1319
Sheplers Inc 6501 W Kellogg Dr Web: www.sheplers.com	Wichita	KS	67209	316-946-3838	946-3778
Smartphone Experts Inc 3151 E Thomas St TF: 888-599-8998 ■ Web: www.smartphoneexperts.com	Inverness	FL	34453	352-400-4400	
U S Cavalry Inc 2855 Centennial Ave TF: 800-777-7172 ■ Web: www.uscav.com	Radcliff	KY	40160	270-351-1164	352-0266
Watumull Bros Ltd 307 Lewers St Suite 600	Honolulu	HI	96815	808-971-8800	971-8824
Wilsons Leather Inc 7401 Boone Ave N TF: 800-967-6270 ■ Web: www.wilsonsleather.com	Brooklyn Park	MN	55428	763-391-4000	391-4535
Work 'n Gear Stores 2300 crown colony Dr Suite 300 *Fax Area Code: 781 ■ TF: 800-659-9675 ■ Web: www.workngear.com	quincy	MA	02169	800-987-0218	746-0180*

157-6 Women's Clothing Stores

				Phone	Fax
5-7-9 Shops 1000 Pennsylvania Ave	Brooklyn	NY	11207	718-485-3000	485-3807
TF: 877-695-9858 ■ Web: www.579.com					
A & E Stores Inc 1000 Huyler St	Teterboro	NJ	07608	201-393-0600	393-0233
Web: www.aestores.com					
A Nose For Clothes 14271 SW 120th St Suite 102	Miami	FL	33186	305-253-8631	235-4370
TF: 877-870-6673 ■ Web: www.anoseforclothes.com					
ABS by Allan Schwartz					
1231 Long Beach Ave	Los Angeles	CA	90021	213-895-4400	891-2812*
*Fax: Hum Res ■ TF: 800-499-5534 ■ Web: www.absstyle.com					
Ann Inc 7 Times Sq	New York	NY	10036	212-541-3300	541-3299
NYSE: ANN ■ TF: 800-677-6788 ■ Web: www.anninc.com					
AnnTaylor Inc 7 Times Sq	New York	NY	10036	212-541-3300	541-3379
TF: 800-677-6788 ■ Web: www.anntaylor.com					
Avenue Stores Inc 365 W Passaic St	Rochelle Park	NJ	07662	201-845-0880	909-2216*
*Fax: Mktg ■ TF: 877-708-8740 ■ Web: www.avenue.com					
B Moss Clothing Co Ltd 550 Meadowland Pkwy	Secaucus	NJ	07094	201-866-6677	866-0387
TF: 800-524-0639					
Balliet's Inc 1900 NW Expy	Oklahoma City	OK	73118	405-848-7811	848-9632
TF: 877-841-8078 ■ Web: www.balliets.com					
Ben Thylan Furs Corp 345 7th Ave 5th Fl	New York	NY	10001	212-753-7700	643-2082
Big M Inc 12 Vreeland Ave	Totowa	NJ	07512	973-890-0021	890-1923
Bluefly Inc 42 W 39th St 9th Fl	New York	NY	10018	212-944-8000	354-3400
NASDAQ: BFLY ■ TF Cust Svc: 877-258-3359 ■ Web: www.bluefly.com					
Body Shops of America Inc					
6225 Powers Ave	Jacksonville	FL	32217	904-737-0811	737-6509
Web: www.bodyc.com					
Cache Inc 1440 Broadway 5th Fl	New York	NY	10018	212-575-3200	575-3225
NASDAQ: CACH ■ TF: 800-788-2224 ■ Web: www.cache.com					
Cato Corp The 8100 Denmark Rd	Charlotte	NC	28273	704-554-8510	
TF: 800-488-0619 ■ Web: www.catofashions.com					
Cgs Industries Inc 3409 Queens Blvd	Long Island City	NY	11101	718-482-0700	482-1385
Web: www.rigolletto.com					
Charlotte Russe Holding Inc					
4645 Morena Blvd	San Diego	CA	92117	858-587-1500	587-0902
TF: 877-266-9327 ■ Web: www.corp.charlotterusse.com					
Charming Shoppes Inc 450 Winks Ln	Bensalem	PA	19020	215-245-9100	633-4748
NASDAQ: CHRS ■ Web: www.charmingshoppes.com					
Chico's FAS Inc 11215 Metro Pkwy	Fort Myers	FL	33966	239-277-6200	277-5237
NYSE: CHS ■ TF: 888-855-4986 ■ Web: www.chicosfas.com					
Christopher & Banks Corp 2400 Xenium Ln N	Plymouth	MN	55441	763-551-5000	551-5198
NYSE: CBK ■ Web: www.christopherandbanks.com					
Claire's Accessories					
2400 W Central Rd	Hoffman Estates	IL	60192	847-765-1100	765-4676
TF: 800-252-4737 ■ Web: www.claires.com					
Country Casuals 311 E Mitchell St	Petoskey	MI	49770	231-347-6501	
Daffodil 163 Pearl St	Essex Junction	VT	05452	802-879-0212	872-3221
TF: 800-795-1305					
Danice Stores Inc 482 Fulton St	Brooklyn	NY	11201	718-875-0664	797-1895
Web: www.danicestores.com					
David's Bridal Inc 1001 Washington St	Conshohocken	PA	19428	610-943-5000	943-5020*
*Fax: Cust Svc ■ TF: 800-823-2403 ■ Web: www.davidsbridal.com					
Deb Shops Inc 9401 Blue Grass Rd	Philadelphia	PA	19114	215-676-6000	698-7151
TF: 866-803-4803 ■ Web: www.debshops.com					
Destination Maternity Corp 456 N 5th St	Philadelphia	PA	19123	215-873-2200	625-3843*
NASDAQ: DEST ■ *Fax: Cust Svc ■ TF: 800-291-7800 ■ Web: www.motherswork.com					
Drapers & Damons 9 Pasteur Suite 200	Irvine	CA	92618	949-784-3000	784-3300
TF: 800-843-1174 ■ Web: www.drapers.com					
Dress Barn Inc 30 Dunnigan Dr	Suffern	NY	10901	845-369-4500	
TF Cust Svc: 800-373-7722 ■ Web: www.dressbarn.com					
EC Dittrich & Co 7373 3rd Ave	Detroit	MI	48202	313-873-8300	873-8300
Web: www.dittrichfurs.com					
EM Scarbrough & Sons Inc					
4001 N Lamar Blvd Bldg 400	Austin	TX	78756	512-452-4220	452-6608
Embry's & Co 3363 Tates Creek Rd Suite 212	Lexington	KY	40502	859-266-9785	266-9785
TF: 800-236-2797					
Express 1 Limited Pkwy	Columbus	OH	43230	614-415-4000	415-4340
TF: 888-397-1980 ■ Web: www.express.com					
Fashion Bug 450 Winks Ln	Bensalem	PA	19020	215-245-9100	633-4640*
NASDAQ: CHRS ■ *Fax: Hum Res ■ TF: 888-693-8683 ■ Web: www.charmingshoppes.com					
Fendi NA Inc 720 5th Ave 5th Fl	New York	NY	10019	212-920-8100	767-0545
TF: 800-336-3469 ■ Web: www.fendi.com					
Flemington Fur Co 8 Spring St	Flemington	NJ	08822	908-782-2212	782-2773
Web: www.flemingtonfurs.com					
Forever 21 Inc 2001 S Alameda St	Los Angeles	CA	90058	213-741-5100	741-5161
TF Cust Svc: 800-966-1355 ■ Web: www.forever21.com					
Fox's 79 MN St	Mineola	NY	11501	516-294-8321	294-2682
Web: www.foxs.com					
Frederick's of Hollywood Inc					
6255 Sunset Blvd Suite 600	Hollywood	CA	90028	323-466-5151	962-9935
TF: 800-323-9525 ■ Web: www.fredericks.com					
Gartenhaus Furs 6950 Wisconsin Ave	Chevy Chase	MD	20815	301-656-2800	656-2819
Girlshop Inc 154 W 14th St 9th Fl	New York	NY	10011	212-645-6240	645-5554
TF: 888-450-7467 ■ Web: www.net-a-porter.com					
Gucci Group Inc 50 Hartz Way	Secaucus	NJ	07094	201-867-8800	617-2398*
*Fax: Hum Res ■ Web: www.guccigroup.com					
GWK Enterprises 120 S State St	Geneseo	IL	61254	309-944-6516	944-8262
H & M Hennes & Mauritz Corp					
1328 Broadway 3rd Fl	New York	NY	10001	646-473-1165	473-1165
Web: www.hm.com					
Henig Inc 4135 Carmichael Rd	Montgomery	AL	36106	334-277-7610	272-3562
TF: 800-521-2037 ■ Web: www.henigfurs.com					
Henri Bendel Inc 712 5th Ave	New York	NY	10019	212-247-1100	
TF: 800-423-6335 ■ Web: www.limitedbrands.com					
Hyman Family LP 620 S Wanamaker Ave	Ontario	CA	91761	909-510-4800	510-4801
Web: www.susiesdeals.com					
Irresistibles 7 Hawkes St	Marblehead	MA	01945	781-631-1248	631-8965
TF: 800-555-9865 ■ Web: www.irresistibles.com					
Joyce Leslie Inc 135 W Commercial Ave	Moonachie	NJ	07074	201-804-7800	804-8841
TF: 800-526-6216 ■ Web: www.joyceleslie.com					
L & L Wings Inc 666 Broadway 2nd Fl	New York	NY	10012	212-481-8299	481-8218
Web: www.wingsbeachwear.com					
Lady Grace Stores Inc					
5 Commonwealth Ave Suite 1	Woburn	MA	01801	781-569-0727	437-9123*
*Fax Area Code: 800 ■ TF: 800-922-0504 ■ Web: www.ladygrace.com					
Lane Bryant Inc 3344 Morse Crossing	Columbus	OH	43219	614-463-5200	463-5240*
*Fax: Mktg ■ TF: 800-876-8728 ■ Web: www.lanebryant.com					
Limited Brands Inc 3 Limited Pkwy	Columbus	OH	43230	614-415-7000	415-2491*
NYSE: LTD ■ *Fax: Mail Rm ■ TF: 800-945-9000 ■ Web: www.limitedbrands.com					
Loehmann's Holdings Inc 2500 Halsey St	Bronx	NY	10461	718-409-2000	518-2766
Web: www.loehmanns.com					
Louis Vuitton NA Inc 19 E 57th St	New York	NY	10022	212-931-2000	931-2097*
*Fax: Mktg ■ TF Cust Svc: 866-884-8866					
Ltd The 3 Limited Pkwy	Columbus	OH	43230	614-415-7000	
Web: www.limitedbrands.com					
Lucy Activewear Inc					
222 SW Columbia St Suite 300	Portland	OR	97201	503-228-2142	228-2144
Web: www.lucy.com					
Maison Weiss 4500 I-55 at Highland Village	Jackson	MS	39211	601-981-4621	981-4671
Mandee Shop 80 Enterprise Ave S	Secaucus	NJ	07094	201-601-4284	617-8666
TF: 866-601-7321 ■ Web: www.mandee.com					
Marshall Retail Group LLC					
2330 Industrial Rd	Las Vegas	NV	89102	702-385-5233	385-2842
Web: www.marshallretailgroup.com					
Miken Sales Inc 539 S Mission Rd	Los Angeles	CA	90033	323-266-2560	266-2580
Motherhood Maternity 456 N 5th St	Philadelphia	PA	19123	215-873-2200	625-3843*
*Fax: Cust Svc ■ TF: 800-291-7800 ■ Web: www.motherhood.com					
New York & Co 450 W 33rd St 5th Fl	New York	NY	10001	800-324-1952	
TF: 800-678-4906 ■ Web: www.nyandcompany.com					
Orva Stores Inc 155 E 86th St	New York	NY	10028	212-369-3448	722-6904
Rainbow Apparel Cos 1000 Pennsylvania Ave	Brooklyn	NY	11207	718-485-3000	
TF: 877-695-9858 ■ Web: www.rainbowshops.com					
Right On Casuals 2496 Central Ave	Yonkers	NY	10710	914-337-7300	337-5266
rue21 Inc 800 Commonwealth Dr Suite 100	Warrendale	PA	15086	724-776-9780	776-4111
TF: 888-871-2744 ■ Web: www.rue21.com					
Saks Jandel 5510 Wisconsin Ave	Chevy Chase	MD	20815	301-652-2250	652-2044
Schweser's Stores Inc 630 N Pk Ave	Fremont	NE	68025	402-721-1700	727-4925
Silver Fox Inc 1207 3rd St S Suite 7	Naples	FL	34102	239-262-7598	262-5382
Star Of India Fashions Inc 1038 W Southern Ave	Tempe	AZ	85282	480-968-6195	966-4452
Web: www.soifashions.net					
Styles for Less 12728 Shoemaker Ave	Santa Fe Springs	CA	90670	562-229-3400	229-3401
TF: 800-929-3466 ■ Web: www.stylesforless.com					
Swim 'n Sport Retail Inc 2396 NW 96th Ave	Miami	FL	33172	305-593-5071	593-2669
TF: 800-497-2111 ■ Web: www.swimnsport.com					
Talbots Inc 1 Talbots Dr	Hingham	MA	02043	781-749-7600	741-4369
NYSE: TLB ■ TF: 800-225-8200 ■ Web: www.talbotsinc.com					
Twigland Fashions Ltd					
12460 Network Blvd Suite 106	San Antonio	TX	78249	210-377-3393	377-1546
TF: 866-362-4224					
Vanity Shop of Grand Forks Inc					
2410 Great Northern Dr	Fargo	ND	58102	701-237-3330	237-4692
TF: 866-247-7920 ■ Web: www.evanity.com					
Victoria's Secret Stores 4 Limited Pkwy	Reynoldsburg	OH	43068	614-577-7000	577-7047
TF: 800-411-5116 ■ Web: www.victoriassecret.com					
Wet Seal Inc 26972 Burbank Ave	Foothill Ranch	CA	92610	949-699-3900	699-4722
NASDAQ: WTSLA ■ TF: 866-746-7938 ■ Web: www.wetseal.com					
White House/Black Market (WHBM)					
11215 Metro Pkwy	Fort Meyers	FL	33966	239-277-6200	277-0259
TF: 877-948-2525 ■ Web: www.whitehouseblackmarket.com					
Willow Tree 2944 Biddle Ave	Wyandotte	MI	48192	734-285-7020	285-0895
Web: www.willowtreefashions.com					
Windsor Inc 4533 Pacific Blvd	Vernon	CA	90058	323-282-9000	973-4224
TF: 888-494-6376 ■ Web: www.windsorstore.com					
Wrapper & Just For Wraps Inc					
5815 Smithway St	Commerce	CA	90040	213-239-0503	239-0515
Web: www.wrapper.com					

158 COAST GUARD INSTALLATIONS

				Phone	Fax
Astoria Coast Guard Air Station					
2185 SE 12th Pl	Warrenton	OR	97146	503-861-6220	861-6358
Web: www.uscg.mil/d13/sectcolrvr/default.asp					
Atlantic City Coast Guard Air Station					
Atlantic City International Airport					
Bldg 350	Atlantic City	NJ	08505	609-677-2222	677-2228
Barbers Point Coast Guard Air Station					
1 Coral Sea Rd	Kapolei	HI	96707	808-682-2771	
Web: www.uscg.mil					
Borinquen Coast Guard Air Station					
260 Guard Rd	Aguadilla	PR	00603	787-890-8400	890-8407
Web: www.uscg.mil/d7/airstaborinquen					
Cape Cod Coast Guard Air Station					
2300 Wilson Blvd Suite 500	Arlington	VA	20598	202-372-4620	
TF: 877-669-8724 ■ Web: www.uscg.mil/d1/units/ascapecod					
Charleston Coast Guard Base 196 Tradd St	Charleston	SC	29401	843-724-7600	724-7633
Web: www.uscg.mil					
Clearwater Coast Guard Air Station					
15100 Rescue Way	Clearwater	FL	33762	727-535-1437	
Web: www.uscg.mil/d7/units/as-clearwater					
Coast Guard Group/Air Station Humboldt Bay					
1001 Lyconing Ave	McKinleyville	CA	95519	707-839-6121	839-6129
Web: www.uscg.mil/d11/grphumboldtbay					
Coast Guard Sector Detroit					
110 Mt Elliott Ave	Detroit	MI	48207	313-568-9525	568-9469
Web: www.uscg.mil					
Coast Guard Sector Sault Sainte Marie					
337 Water St	Sault Sainte Marie	MI	49783	906-635-3217	
Web: www.uscg.mil/d9/sectSaultSteMarie					
Corpus Christi Coast Guard Air Station					
8930 Ocean Dr	Corpus Christi	TX	78419	361-939-6200	939-6377
Web: www.uscg.mil/history/stations/airsta_corpuschristi.asp					

	City	State	Zip	Phone	Fax
Elizabeth City Coast Guard Air Station					
1664 Weeksville Rd Bldg 35	Elizabeth City	NC	27909	252-335-6000	335-6185
TF: 800-338-6215 ■ *Web:* www.uscg.mil/d5/airstation/ecity					
Galveston Coast Guard Base PO Box 1943	Galveston	TX	77553	409-766-5620	766-4702
Houston Coast Guard Air Station					
1178 Ellington Field	Houston	TX	77034	713-578-3000	
Web: www.uscg.mil/d8/airstahouston					
Integrated Support Command Miami Beach					
100 MacArthur Cswy	Miami Beach	FL	33139	305-535-4300	535-4491
Web: www.uscg.mil/d7/sectmiami					
Ketchikan Integrated Support Command					
1300 Stedman St	Ketchikan	AK	99901	907-228-0340	228-0342
Web: www.uscg.mil					
Los Angeles Coast Guard Air Station					
7159 World Way W	Los Angeles	CA	90045	310-215-2112	215-1348
Web: www.uscg.mil/d11/airstationla					
Mayport Coast Guard Base					
4200 Ocean St	Atlantic Beach	FL	32233	904-564-7521	564-7533
Web: www.uscg.mil					
Miami Coast Guard Air Station					
Opa Locka Airport 14750 NW 44th Ct	Opa Locka	FL	33054	305-953-2130	
Web: www.uscg.mil					
Milwaukee Coast Guard Base					
2420 S Lincoln Memorial Dr	Milwaukee	WI	53207	414-747-7100	747-7108
Web: www.uscg.mil					
Mobile Coast Guard Base S Broad St	Mobile	AL	36615	251-441-6217	
New Orleans Coast Guard Air Station					
400 Russell Ave	New Orleans	LA	70143	504-393-6005	393-6016
North Bend Coast Guard Air Station					
2000 Connecticut Ave	North Bend	OR	97459	541-756-9210	756-9203
Web: www.uscg.mil/d13/units/grunbend					
Port Angeles Coast Guard Air Station					
Ediz Hook Rd	Port Angeles	WA	98362	360-417-5840	457-5849
Web: www.uscg.mil					
Sacramento Coast Guard Air Station					
6037 Price Ave	McClellan	CA	95652	916-643-7659	643-7700
Web: www.uscg.mil					
San Diego Coast Guard Air Station					
2710 N Harbor Dr PO Box 45A	San Diego	CA	92101	619-278-7670	683-6474
Web: www.uscg.mil/d11/stasandiego					
San Francisco Coast Guard Air Station					
SFO International Airport Bldg 1020	San Francisco	CA	94128	650-808-2900	808-2916
Web: www.uscg.mil/d11/airstasanfrancisco					
San Juan Coast Guard Base					
5 La Puntilla Final	San Juan	PR	00901	787-729-6800	729-1017
Traverse City Coast Guard Air Station					
1175 Airport Access Rd	Traverse City	MI	49686	231-922-8210	922-8213
Web: www.uscg.mil/d9/astc/astc.htm					
United States Coast Guard/Personnel Services & Support Unit					
400 Sand Island Pkwy	Honolulu	HI	96816	808-842-2062	842-2026
Web: www.uscg.mil					
US Coast Guard Air Station Detroit					
1461 N Perimeter Rd Selfridge ANGB	Selfridge	MI	48045	586-307-6700	307-6705
Web: www.uscg.mil/d9/airstaDetroit					
US Coast Guard Air Station Savannah					
1297 N Lightning Rd Hunter AAF	Savannah	GA	31409	912-652-4646	
Web: www.uscg.mil/d7/airstasavannah					

159 COFFEE & TEA STORES

	City	State	Zip	Phone	Fax
Ahh-Some Gourmet Coffee Inc 900 Elm St	Manchester	NH	03101	603-665-9487	669-7040
Bad Ass Coffee Co of Hawaii Inc					
155 W Malvern Ave	Salt Lake City	UT	84115	801-463-1966	463-2606
TF: 888-422-3277 ■ *Web:* www.badasscoffee.com					
Barnie's Coffee & Tea Co Inc					
2126 Landstreet Rd Suite 300	Orlando	FL	32809	407-854-6600	854-6601
TF: 800-854-1416 ■ *Web:* www.barniescoffee.com					
Brewster's Coffee Co Inc					
500 Lake Cook Rd Suite 475	Deerfield	IL	60015	847-948-7520	405-8140
TF: 800-251-6101 ■ *Web:* www.babcorp.com					
Bucks County Coffee Co 2250 W Cabot Blvd	Langhorne	PA	19047	215-741-1855	741-1799
TF Sales: 800-844-8790 ■ *Web:* www.buckscountycoffee.com					
Caribou Coffee Co Inc					
3900 Lakebreeze Ave N	Brooklyn Center	MN	55429	763-592-2200	592-2300
NASDAQ: CBOU ■ *TF Cust Svc:* 888-227-4268 ■ *Web:* www.cariboucoffee.com					
Coffee Bean & Tea Leaf The					
1945 S La Cienega Blvd	Los Angeles	CA	90034	310-237-2326	
TF: 800-832-5323 ■ *Web:* coffeebean.com					
Coffee Beanery LTD The 3429 Pierson Pl	Flushing	MI	48433	810-733-1020	733-1536
TF: 800-728-2326 ■ *Web:* www.coffeebeanery.com					
Coffee People Inc 28 Executive Pk Suite 200	Irvine	CA	92614	949-260-1600	260-1610
TF: 800-354-5282 ■ *Web:* www.greenmountaincoffee.com					
Dunkin' Donuts 130 Royall St	Canton	MA	02021	781-737-3000	737-4000
TF Cust Svc: 800-859-5339 ■ *Web:* www.dunkindonuts.com					
Hawaii Coffee Co Inc 1555 Kalani St	Honolulu	HI	96817	808-847-3600	972-0777*
**Fax Area Code:* 800 ■ *TF:* 800-338-8353 ■ *Web:* www.hicoffeeco.com					
International Coffee & Tea Inc					
1945 S La Cienega Blvd	Los Angeles	CA	90034	310-237-2326	815-2520
TF: 800-854-6252 ■ *Web:* www.coffeebean.com					
It's A Grind Inc					
6272 E Pacific Coast Hwy Suite E	Long Beach	CA	90803	562-594-5600	594-4100
TF: 866-424-5282 ■ *Web:* www.itsagrind.com					
McNulty's Tea & Coffee Co Inc					
109 Christopher St	New York	NY	10014	212-242-5351	
TF: 800-356-5200 ■ *Web:* www.mcnultys.com					
Montana Coffee Traders Inc 5810 Hwy 93 S	Whitefish	MT	59937	406-862-7633	862-7680
TF: 800-345-5282 ■ *Web:* www.coffeetraders.com					
Moxie Java International LLC					
4990 W Chinden Blvd	Boise	ID	83714	208-322-7773	321-0279
TF: 800-659-6963 ■ *Web:* www.moxiejava.com					
New World Coffee 100 Horizon Ctr Blvd	Hamilton	NJ	08691	609-631-7000	631-7068
TF: 800-308-2457					
Peet's Coffee & Tea Inc 1400 Pk Ave	Emeryville	CA	94608	510-594-2100	594-2180*
NASDAQ: PEET ■ **Fax:* Orders ■ *TF Orders:* 800-999-2132 ■ *Web:* www.peets.com					
PJS's Coffee					
109 New Camellia Blvd Suite 201	Covington	LA	70433	985-792-5899	792-1201
Web: www.pjscoffee.com					
Seattle's Best Coffee Co 2401 Utah Ave S	Seattle	WA	98134	800-611-7793	318-0772*
**Fax Area Code:* 206 ■ *TF:* 800-611-7793 ■ *Web:* www.seattlesbest.com					
Second Cup Ltd 6303 Airport Rd	Mississauga	ON	L4V1R8	877-212-1818	
TF: 877-212-1818 ■ *Web:* www.secondcup.com					
Shefield Group 2265 W Railway St	Abbotsford	BC	V2S2E3	604-859-1014	859-1711
Web: www.shefield.com					
Starbucks Coffee Co 2401 Utah Ave S	Seattle	WA	98134	206-447-1575	318-3432
NASDAQ: SBUX ■ *TF:* 800-782-7282 ■ *Web:* www.starbucks.com					
Tully's Coffee Corp 3100 Airport Way	Seattle	WA	98134	206-233-2070	233-2077
TF: 800-968-8559 ■ *Web:* www.tullys.com					

160 COLLECTION AGENCIES

	City	State	Zip	Phone	Fax
ABC-Amega Inc 1100 Main St	Buffalo	NY	14209	716-885-4444	878-2872
Web: www.abc-amega.com					
Alden Curtis & Michaels Ltd					
1170 Broadway Suite 316	New York	NY	10001	212-532-7996	213-6731
TF: 800-569-3877 ■ *Web:* www.aldencurtis.com					
Alexander & Hamilton Inc 2618 Edenborn Ave	Metairie	LA	70002	504-887-9153	887-8620
TF: 800-627-2539					
Alliance One Inc 4797 Ruffner St	San Diego	CA	92111	858-560-6000	560-0250
TF: 866-855-0727 ■ *Web:* www.allianceoneinc.com					
Allied International Credit Corp					
16635 Young St Unit 26	Newmarket	ON	L3X1V6	905-470-8181	470-8155
TF: 888-478-8181 ■ *Web:* www.aiccorp.com					
American Accounts & Advisors Inc					
3904 Cedarvale Dr	Eagan	MN	55122	651-405-9760	405-9846
TF: 800-732-9115					
American Agencies Co Inc					
21 E Ogden Ave Suite 201	Westmont	IL	60559	630-493-1776	493-1781
Asset Acceptance Capital Corp (AACC)					
28405 Van Dyke Ave PO Box 2036	Warren	MI	48090	586-939-9600	446-7837
NASDAQ: AACC ■ *TF:* 800-545-9931 ■ *Web:* www.assetacceptance.com					
Associated Creditors Exchange Inc (ACE)					
3443 N Central Ave Suite 1100	Phoenix	AZ	85012	602-954-6554	650-5949
TF: 800-280-3800 ■ *Web:* www.ace-collects.com					
Atlantic Credit & Finance Inc					
3353 Orange Ave	Roanoke	VA	24012	540-772-7800	
TF: 800-888-9419 ■ *Web:* www.atlanticcreditfinance.com					
Bonneville Billing & Collection Inc					
1186 E 4600 S Suite 100	Ogden	UT	84403	801-621-7880	393-5808
TF: 800-660-6138 ■ *Web:* www.bonncoll.com					
Capital Asset Research Corp Ltd					
3980 RCA Blvd Suite 8012	Palm Beach Gardens	FL	33410	561-776-5000	776-5030*
**Fax:* Cust Svc ■ *TF:* 800-888-8293					
Cardon Health Care Network Inc					
4185 Technology Forest Blvd Suite 200					
PO Box 4950	The Woodlands	TX	77381	281-296-1771	
TF: 800-417-4845 ■ *Web:* www.cardonhealthcare.com					
Collectcorp Corp 415 Yonge St Suite 700	Toronto	ON	M5B2E7	416-961-9622	432-2923*
**Fax Area Code:* 888 ■ *TF:* 800-900-4238					
Collecto Inc 700 Longwater Dr 2nd Fl	Norwell	MA	02061	781-681-4300	681-4340
TF: 800-886-9177					
Communications Credit & Recovery Corp (CCR)					
100 Garden City Plaza Suite 222	Garden City	NY	11530	516-294-6800	294-5682
TF: 800-327-3618 ■ *Web:* www.ccrcollect.com					
Computer Credit Inc 640 W 4th St	Winston-Salem	NC	27101	336-761-1524	761-8852
TF: 800-942-2995					
Credit Collections Inc					
2915 N Classen Blvd Suite 100	Oklahoma City	OK	73106	405-290-2000	290-2043
TF: 866-723-2455 ■ *Web:* www.cciokc.com					
Credit Control Services Inc (CCS)					
2 Wells Ave Suite 1	Newton	MA	02459	617-965-2000	
TF: 800-998-5000					
Credit Management LP					
4200 International Pkwy	Carrollton	TX	75007	972-862-4200	862-4355
TF: 800-377-7723 ■ *Web:* www.thecmigroup.com					
Diversified Adjustment Service Inc					
600 Coon Rapids Blvd	Coon Rapids	MN	55433	800-348-2274	780-9338*
**Fax Area Code:* 763 ■ *TF:* 800-279-3733 ■ *Web:* www.diversifiedadjustment.com					
Diversified Collection Services Inc					
333 N Canyons Pkwy Suite 100	Livermore	CA	94551	925-960-4800	960-4880
TF: 800-327-9467					
Dun & Bradstreet Receivable Management Services					
899 Eaton Ave	Bethlehem	PA	18025	610-882-7000	882-6005
TF: 800-999-3867 ■ *Web:* www.dnbcollections.com					
Dynamic Recovery Services Inc					
4101 McEwen Rd Suite 150	Farmers Branch	TX	75244	972-241-5611	241-9552
TF: 800-886-8088 ■ *Web:* www.dynamicrecoveryservices.com					
Encore Capital Group Inc					
8875 Aero Dr Suite 200	San Diego	CA	92123	858-560-2600	306-4443*
NASDAQ: ECPG ■ **Fax Area Code:* 800 ■ *TF:* 877-445-4581 ■ *Web:* www.encorecapital.com					
Enhanced Recovery Corp 8014 Bayberry Rd	Jacksonville	FL	32256	904-645-0049	
TF: 800-617-0049 ■ *Web:* www.erccollections.com					
Focus Receivables Management LLC					
1130 Northchase Pkwy Suite 150	Marietta	GA	30067	678-228-0000	228-0019
TF: 877-362-8766 ■ *Web:* www.focusrm.com					
GC Services LP 6330 Gulfton St	Houston	TX	77081	713-777-4441	776-6558
TF: 800-756-6524 ■ *Web:* www.gcserv.com					
General Revenue Corp 11501 Northlake Dr	Cincinnati	OH	45249	513-469-1472	469-7428
TF: 800-234-1472 ■ *Web:* www.generalrevenue.com					

	City	State	Zip	Phone	Fax
Gulf Coast Collection Bureau Inc 5630 Marquesas Cir *TF:* 888-839-6999 ■ *Web:* www.gulfcoastcollection.com	Sarasota	FL	34233	941-927-6999	684-4023
Hill Top Collections Inc 38 W 32nd St Suite 1510 *TF:* 800-564-2322	New York	NY	10001	212-564-2322	564-4322
Hospital Billing & Collection Service Ltd 118 Lukens Dr *TF:* 877-254-9580 ■ *Web:* www.hbcs.org	New Castle	DE	19720	302-552-8000	254-3750
LC Financial Inc 66111 Valjean Ave Suite 109 *TF:* 800-800-4523 ■ *Web:* www.lcf.net	Van Nuys	CA	91406	818-780-9300	780-3112
LTD Financial Services LP 7322 SW Fwy Suite 1600 *TF Cust Svc:* 800-414-2101	Houston	TX	77074	713-414-2100	414-2120
Nationwide Credit Inc (NCI) 2002 Summit Blvd Suite 600 *TF:* 800-456-4729 ■ *Web:* www.ncirm.com	Atlanta	GA	30319	770-644-7400	612-7340
Nationwide Recovery Systems Inc 3000 Kellway Dr *TF:* 800-458-6357 ■ *Web:* www.nationwide-recovery.com	Carrollton	TX	75006	972-798-1000	798-1020
NCO Financial Systems Inc 507 Prudential Rd *TF:* 800-220-2274 ■ *Web:* www.ncogroup.com	Horsham	PA	19044	215-441-3000	442-8470
NCO Group Inc 507 Prudential Rd *TF:* 800-220-2274 ■ *Web:* www.ncogroup.com	Horsham	PA	19044	215-441-3000	441-3929
Pentagroup Financial LLC 5959 Corp Dr Suite 1400 *TF:* 800-385-9060 ■ *Web:* www.pentagroup.us	Houston	TX	77036	832-615-2100	
Portfolio Recovery Assoc LLC 120 Corporate Blvd Suite 100, Reverside Commerce Ctr *NASDAQ: PRAA* ■ **Fax Area Code:* 757 ■ *TF:* 888-772-7326 ■ *Web:* www.portfoliorecovery.com	Norfolk	VA	23502	888-772-7326	518-0901*
Preferred Collection Management Services Inc 1 Davis Blvd Suite 703 *Web:* www.preferredcms.com	Tampa	FL	33606	813-251-0802	254-7026
Recovery's Unlimited Inc 225 Broadhollow Rd Suite 405-E *TF:* 800-356-7402 ■ *Web:* www.ruicreditservices.com	Melville	NY	11747	516-222-1200	222-1144
Richmond North Assoc Inc 4232 Ridge Lea Rd Suite 12 *TF:* 888-228-9112 ■ *Web:* www.rnacollects.com	Amherst	NY	14226	716-832-5668	832-4236
Sterling Phillips & Assoc Inc 4739 Utica St Suite 212 *TF:* 800-375-5773 ■ *Web:* www.s-p-a.com	Metairie	LA	70006	504-887-0202	887-0701
Transworld Systems Inc 2235 Mercury Way Suite 275 *TF:* 888-446-4733 ■ *Web:* www.transworldsystems.com	Santa Rosa	CA	95407	707-236-3800	
Twenty-First Century Assoc 266 Summit Ave *Web:* www.tfc-associates.com	Hackensack	NJ	07601	201-678-1144	678-9088
United Recovery Systems LP 5800 N Course Dr *TF:* 800-568-0399 ■ *Web:* www.unitedrecoverysystems.com	Houston	TX	77072	713-977-1234	977-0119
United Resource Systems Inc 10075 W Colfax Ave *TF:* 800-441-7364 ■ *Web:* www.urs-inc.com	Lakewood	CO	80215	303-205-0152	205-0153
Van Ru Credit Corp 1350 E Touhy Ave Suite 300E *TF:* 800-337-8331 ■ *Web:* www.vanru.com	Des Plaines	IL	60018	847-824-2414	824-0769
Vengroff Williams & Assoc Inc 7441 Lincoln Way *TF:* 888-374-2600 ■ *Web:* www.vwainc.com	Garden Grove	CA	92841	714-889-6200	889-6300

161 COLLEGES - BIBLE

SEE ALSO Colleges & Universities - Christian p. 1636

	City	State	Zip	Phone	Fax
Alaska Bible College 200 College Rd *TF:* 800-478-7884 ■ *Web:* www.akbible.edu	Glennallen	AK	99588	907-822-3201	822-5027
Allegheny Wesleyan College 2161 Woodsdale Rd *TF:* 800-292-3153 ■ *Web:* www.awc.edu	Salem	OH	44460	330-337-6403	337-6255
American Baptist College 1800 Baptist World Ctr Dr *Web:* www.abcnash.edu	Nashville	TN	37207	615-256-1463	226-7855
Baptist Bible College 538 Venard Rd *TF:* 800-451-8668 ■ *Web:* www.bbc.edu	Clarks Summit	PA	18411	570-586-2400	585-9400
Baptist Bible College 628 E Kearney St **Fax:* Admissions ■ *TF:* 800-228-5754 ■ *Web:* www.baptist.edu	Springfield	MO	65803	417-268-6060	268-6694*
Baptist University of the Americas 8019 S Pan Am Expy *TF:* 800-721-1396 ■ *Web:* www.bua.edu	San Antonio	TX	78224	210-924-4338	924-2701
Barclay College 607 N Kingman St *TF:* 800-862-0226 ■ *Web:* www.barclaycollege.edu	Haviland	KS	67059	620-862-5252	862-5403
Bethesda Christian University 730 N Euclid *Web:* www.bcu.edu	Anaheim	CA	92801	714-517-1945	563-0623
Beulah Heights Bible College 892 Berne St SE PO Box 18145 **Fax:* Admissions ■ *TF:* 888-777-2422 ■ *Web:* www.beulah.org	Atlanta	GA	30316	404-627-2681	627-0702*
Boise Bible College 8695 W Marigold St *TF:* 800-893-7755 ■ *Web:* www.boisebible.edu	Boise	ID	83714	208-376-7731	376-7743
Calvary Bible College & Theological Seminary 15800 Calvary Rd **Fax:* Admissions ■ *TF:* 800-326-3960 ■ *Web:* www.calvary.edu	Kansas City	MO	64147	816-322-3960	331-4474*
Central Bible College 3000 N Grant Ave *TF:* 800-831-4222 ■ *Web:* www.cbcag.edu	Springfield	MO	65803	417-833-2551	833-5478
Central Christian College of the Bible 911 E Urbandale Dr *TF:* 888-263-3900 ■ *Web:* www.cccb.edu	Moberly	MO	65270	660-263-3900	263-3936
Cincinnati Christian University 2700 Glenway Ave *TF:* 800-949-4228 ■ *Web:* www.ccuniversity.edu	Cincinnati	OH	45204	513-244-8100	244-8140
Circleville Bible College PO Box 458 *TF:* 800-701-0222 ■ *Web:* www.hocking.edu	Circleville	OH	43113	740-474-8896	477-7755
Clear Creek Baptist Bible College 300 Clear Creek Rd *Web:* www.ccbbc.edu	Pineville	KY	40977	606-337-3196	337-2372
College of Biblical Studies-Houston 7000 Regency Sq Blvd Suite 110 *Web:* www.cbshouston.edu	Houston	TX	77036	713-785-5995	532-8150
Columbia International University 7435 Monticello Rd *TF:* 800-777-2227 ■ *Web:* www.ciu.edu	Columbia	SC	29203	803-754-4100	786-4209
Crossroads Bible College 601 N Shortridge Rd *TF:* 800-822-3119 ■ *Web:* www.crossroads.edu	Indianapolis	IN	46219	317-352-8736	352-9145
Crossroads College 920 Mayowood Rd SW *TF:* 800-456-7651 ■ *Web:* www.crossroadscollege.edu	Rochester	MN	55902	507-288-4563	288-9046
Crown College 8700 College View Dr *TF:* 800-682-7696 ■ *Web:* www.crown.edu	Saint Bonifacius	MN	55375	952-446-4100	446-4149
Dallas Christian College 2700 Christian Pkwy *TF:* 800-688-1029 ■ *Web:* www.dallas.edu	Dallas	TX	75234	972-241-3371	241-8021
Davis College 400 Riverside Dr *TF:* 800-331-4137 ■ *Web:* www.davisny.edu	Johnson City	NY	13790	607-729-1581	729-2962
Ecclesia College 9653 Nations Dr *TF:* 800-735-9926 ■ *Web:* www.ecclesiacollege.org	Springdale	AR	72762	479-248-7236	248-1455
Emmaus Bible College 2570 Asbury Rd *TF:* 800-397-2425 ■ *Web:* www.emmaus.edu	Dubuque	IA	52001	563-588-8000	588-1216
Eugene Bible College 2155 Bailey Hill Rd **Fax:* Admissions ■ *TF:* 800-322-2638 ■ *Web:* www.ebc.edu	Eugene	OR	97405	541-485-1780	343-5801*
Faith Baptist Bible College 1900 NW 4th St *TF:* 888-324-8448 ■ *Web:* www.faith.edu	Ankeny	IA	50023	515-964-0601	964-1638
Florida Christian College 1011 Bill Beck Blvd **Fax Area Code:* 321 ■ *TF:* 888-468-6322 ■ *Web:* www.fcc.edu	Kissimmee	FL	34744	407-847-8966	206-2007*
Free Will Baptist Bible College 3606 W End Ave *TF:* 800-763-9222 ■ *Web:* www.fwbbc.edu	Nashville	TN	37205	615-383-1340	269-6028
God's Bible School & College 1810 Young St *TF:* 800-486-4637 ■ *Web:* www.gbs.edu	Cincinnati	OH	45202	513-721-7944	721-1357
Grace Bible College 1011 Aldon St SW PO Box 910 *TF:* 800-968-1887 ■ *Web:* www.gbcol.edu	Wyoming	MI	49509	616-538-2330	538-0599
Grace University 1311 S 9th St *TF:* 800-383-1422 ■ *Web:* www.graceuniversity.edu	Omaha	NE	68108	402-449-2800	341-9587
Great Lakes Christian College 6211 W Willow Hwy *TF Admissions:* 800-937-4522 ■ *Web:* www.glcc.edu	Lansing	MI	48917	517-321-0242	321-5902
Heritage Christian University 3625 Helton Dr PO Box HCU *TF:* 800-367-3565 ■ *Web:* www.hcu.edu	Florence	AL	35630	256-766-6610	760-0981
Hobe Sound Bible College PO Box 1065 *TF:* 800-881-5534 ■ *Web:* www.hsbc.edu	Hobe Sound	FL	33475	772-546-5534	545-1422
John Wesley College 2314 N Centennial St *Web:* www.johnwesley.edu	High Point	NC	27265	336-889-2262	889-2261
Johnson Bible College 7900 Johnson Dr *TF:* 800-827-2122 ■ *Web:* www.jbc.edu	Knoxville	TN	37998	865-251-2309	251-2336
Kentucky Mountain Bible College 855 Hwy 541 PO Box 10 *TF:* 800-879-5622 ■ *Web:* www.kmbc.edu	Vancleve	KY	41385	606-693-5000	693-4884
King's College & Seminary 14800 Sherman Way *Web:* www.kingscollege.edu	Los Angeles	CA	91405	818-779-8040	779-8429
Kuyper College 3333 E Beltline Ave NE *TF:* 800-511-3749 ■ *Web:* www.kuyper.edu	Grand Rapids	MI	49525	616-222-3000	222-3045
Lancaster Bible College 901 Eden Rd PO Box 83403 *TF:* 800-544-7335 ■ *Web:* www.lbc.edu	Lancaster	PA	17608	717-569-7071	560-8213
Life Pacific College 1100 W Covina Blvd *TF:* 877-886-5433 ■ *Web:* www.lifepacific.edu	San Dimas	CA	91773	909-599-5433	599-6690
Lincoln Christian College Seminary 100 Campus View Dr *TF:* 888-522-5228 ■ *Web:* www.lccs.edu	Lincoln	IL	62656	217-732-3168	732-4078
Manhattan Christian College 1415 Anderson Ave *Web:* www.mccks.edu	Manhattan	KS	66502	785-539-3571	776-9251
Moody Bible Institute 820 N La Salle St **Fax:* Admissions ■ *TF:* 800-967-4624 ■ *Web:* www.moody.edu	Chicago	IL	60610	312-329-4400	329-8955*
Multnomah Bible College & Biblical Seminary 8435 NE Glisan St *TF:* 800-275-4672 ■ *Web:* www.multnomah.edu	Portland	OR	97220	503-255-0332	254-1268
Nazarene Bible College 1111 Academy Pk Loop *TF:* 800-873-3873 ■ *Web:* www.nbc.edu	Colorado Springs	CO	80910	719-884-5000	884-5199
Oak Hills Christian College 1600 Oak Hills Rd SW *TF:* 888-751-8670 ■ *Web:* www.oakhills.edu	Bemidji	MN	56601	218-751-8670	751-8825
Ozark Christian College 1111 N Main St *TF:* 800-299-4622 ■ *Web:* www.occ.edu	Joplin	MO	64801	417-624-2518	624-0090
Philadelphia Biblical University 200 Manor Ave **Fax:* Admissions ■ *TF:* 800-366-0049 ■ *Web:* www.pbu.edu	Langhorne	PA	19047	215-752-5800	702-4248*
Pillsbury Baptist Bible College 315 S Grove Ave *TF:* 800-747-4557 ■ *Web:* www.pillsbury.edu	Owatonna	MN	55060	507-451-2710	451-0156
Puget Sound Christian College 2610 Wetmore Ave *TF:* 888-775-8699 ■ *Web:* www.pscc.edu	Everett	WA	98201	425-257-3090	258-1488
Rio Grande Bible Institute 4300 S Business Hwy 281 *Web:* www.nbc.edu	Edinburg	TX	78539	956-380-8100	380-8101
Roanoke Bible College 715 N Poindexter St *TF:* 800-722-8980 ■ *Web:* www.roanokebible.edu	Elizabeth City	NC	27909	252-334-2070	334-2071
Rosedale Bible College 2270 Rosedale Rd **Fax Area Code:* 877 ■ *Web:* www.rosedale.edu	Irwin	OH	43029	740-857-1311	857-1312*

	City	State	Zip	Phone	Fax
Saint Louis Christian College					
1360 Grandview Dr	Florissant	MO	63033	314-837-6777	837-8291
TF Admissions: 800-887-7522 ■ *Web:* www.slcconline.edu					
Somerset Christian College 10 College Way	Zarephath	NJ	08890	732-356-1595	356-4846
TF: 800-234-9305 ■ *Web:* www.somerset.edu					
Southeastern Baptist College 4229 Hwy 15 N	Laurel	MS	39440	601-426-6346	426-6347
Web: www.southeasternbaptist.edu					
Southwestern College 2625 E Cactus Rd	Phoenix	AZ	85032	602-489-5300	404-2159
TF: 800-247-2697 ■ *Web:* www.swcaz.edu					
Toccoa Falls College 328 Chappel Dr	Toccoa Falls	GA	30598	706-886-6831	282-6012
TF: 800-868-3257 ■ *Web:* www.tfc.edu					
Tri-State Bible College 506 Margaret St	South Point	OH	45680	740-377-2520	377-0001
TF: 800-261-2947 ■ *Web:* www.tsbc.edu					
Trinity Bible College 50 6th Ave N	Ellendale	ND	58436	701-349-3621	349-5786
TF: 800-523-1603 ■ *Web:* www.trinitybiblecollege.edu					
Trinity College of Florida 2430 Welbilt Blvd	Trinity	FL	34655	727-376-6911	569-1410
TF: 800-388-0869 ■ *Web:* www.trinitycollege.edu					
Vennard College					
2300 8th Ave E PO Box 29	University Park	IA	52595	641-673-8391	673-8365
TF: 800-686-8391					
Washington Bible College/Capital Bible Seminary					
6511 Princess Garden Pkwy	Lanham	MD	20706	301-552-1400	552-2775
TF: 877-793-7227 ■ *Web:* www.bible.edu					
Zion Bible College 27 Middle Hwy	Barrington	RI	02806	401-246-0900	246-0906
TF: 800-356-4014 ■ *Web:* www.zbc.edu					

162 COLLEGES - COMMUNITY & JUNIOR

SEE ALSO Colleges - Fine Arts p. 1634; Colleges - Tribal p. 1635; Colleges & Universities - Four-Year p. 1638; Vocational & Technical Schools p. 2763

Institutions That Offer Academic Degrees That Can Be Transferred To A Four-Year College Or University.

ALABAMA

	City	State	Zip	Phone	Fax
Central Alabama Community College					
1675 Cherokee Rd	Alexander City	AL	35010	256-215-4255	234-0384*
**Fax:* Admissions ■ *TF:* 800-643-2657 ■ *Web:* www.cacc.cc.al.us					
Atmore 6574 Hwy 21 N	Atmore	AL	36502	251-368-8118	368-8211
Web: www.jeffdavis.cc.al.us					
Faulkner State Community College					
Bay Minette 1900 S US Hwy 31	Bay Minette	AL	36507	251-580-2100	580-2285
TF: 800-231-3752 ■ *Web:* www.faulkner.cc.al.us					
Jefferson State Community College					
2601 Carson Rd	Birmingham	AL	35215	205-853-1200	856-6070*
**Fax:* Admissions ■ *TF:* 800-239-5900 ■ *Web:* www.jeffstateonline.com					
Snead State Community College					
220 N Walnut St PO Box 734	Boaz	AL	35957	256-593-5120	593-7180*
**Fax:* Admissions ■ *Web:* www.snead.edu					
Jefferson Davis Community College					
Brewton 220 Alco Dr	Brewton	AL	36426	251-867-4832	809-1596
Web: www.jdcc.edu					
Childersburg 34091 US Hwy 280	Childersburg	AL	35044	256-378-5576	378-5281
Web: www.cacc.edu					
Calhoun Community College PO Box 2216	Decatur	AL	35609	256-306-2500	306-2941
TF: 800-626-3628 ■ *Web:* www.calhoun.cc.al.us					
Wallace Community College 1141 Wallace Dr	Dothan	AL	36303	334-983-3521	983-6066*
**Fax:* Admissions ■ *TF:* 800-543-2426 ■ *Web:* www.wallace.edu					
Enterprise-Ozark Community College					
600 Plaza Dr PO Box 1300	Enterprise	AL	36331	334-393-3752	393-6223
Web: www.eocc.edu					
Fairhope 440 Fairhope Ave	Fairhope	AL	36532	251-990-0420	580-2285*
**Fax:* Admissions ■ *TF:* 800-231-3752 ■ *Web:* www.faulkner.cc.al.us					
Bevill State Community College					
2631 Temple Ave N	Fayette	AL	35555	205-932-3221	932-3294*
**Fax:* Admissions ■ *Web:* www.bscc.edu					
Gadsden State Community College					
1001 George Wallace Dr PO Box 227	Gadsden	AL	35902	256-549-8200	549-8205*
**Fax:* Admissions ■ *TF:* 800-226-5563 ■ *Web:* www.gadsdenst.cc.al.us					
Gulf Shores 3301 Gulf Shores Pkwy	Gulf Shores	AL	36542	251-968-3101	968-3120
TF: 800-231-3752 ■ *Web:* www.faulkner.cc.al.us					
Wallace State Community College					
801 Main St	Hanceville	AL	35077	256-352-8000	352-8129
Web: www.wallacestate.edu					
Huntsville 102B Wynn Dr	Huntsville	AL	35805	256-890-4701	890-4775*
**Fax:* Admissions ■ *Web:* www.calhoun.edu					
Jasper 1411 Indiana Ave	Jasper	AL	35501	205-387-0511	387-5191*
**Fax:* Admissions ■ *Web:* www.bscc.edu					
Marion Military Institute 1101 Washington St	Marion	AL	36756	334-683-2306	683-2383
TF: 800-664-1842 ■ *Web:* www.marionmilitary.edu					
Community College of the Air Force					
CCAF/RRA 130 W Maxwell Blvd	Maxwell AFB	AL	36112	334-953-8409	953-3621
Web: www.au.af.mil					
Bishop State Community College 351 N Broad St	Mobile	AL	36603	251-690-6412	438-5403*
**Fax:* Admissions ■ *Web:* www.bishop.edu					
Baker-Gaines Central 1365 Dr ML King Jr Ave	Mobile	AL	36603	251-662-5400	405-4427
Web: www.bscc.cc.al.us					
Carver 414 Stanton St	Mobile	AL	36617	251-473-8692	473-7915*
**Fax:* Admissions ■ *Web:* www.bishop.edu/carvercp.htm					
Southwest 925 Dauphin Island Pkwy	Mobile	AL	36605	251-665-4100	478-5170*
**Fax:* Admissions ■ *Web:* www.bishop.edu/sw_camp.htm					
Alabama Southern Community College					
2800 Alabama Ave	Monroeville	AL	36460	251-575-3156	575-5356
Web: www.ascc.edu					
Muscle Shoals 800 George Wallace Blvd	Muscle Shoals	AL	35661	256-331-5200	331-5366*
**Fax:* Admissions ■ *Web:* www.nwscc.edu					
Opelika 1701 Lafayette Pkwy	Opelika	AL	36801	334-745-6437	742-9418*
**Fax:* Admissions ■ *Web:* www.suscc.edu					
Chattahoochee Valley Community College					
2602 College Dr	Phenix City	AL	36869	334-291-4900	291-4994*
**Fax:* Admissions ■ *Web:* www.cv.edu					
Northwest-Shoals Community College					
Phil Campbell 2080 College Rd	Phil Campbell	AL	35581	256-331-6200	331-6272*
**Fax:* Admissions ■ *Web:* www.nwscc.edu					
Northeast Alabama Community College					
PO Box 159	Rainsville	AL	35986	256-228-6001	228-6861
Web: www.nacc.edu					
Redstone Arsenal 6250 Hwy 31 N	Tanner	AL	35671	256-306-2500	306-2941
TF: 800-626-3628 ■ *Web:* www.calhoun.edu					
Alabama Southern Community College					
30755 Hwy 43	Thomasville	AL	36784	334-636-9642	636-1380
Web: www.ascc.edu					
Shelton State Community College					
9500 Old Greensboro Rd	Tuscaloosa	AL	35405	205-759-1541	391-3910*
**Fax:* Admissions ■ *Web:* www.sheltonstate.edu					
Valley 321 Fob James Dr	Valley	AL	36854	334-756-4151	756-5183*
**Fax:* Admissions ■ *Web:* www.suscc.edu					
Southern Union State Community College					
Wadley 750 Roberts St PO Box 1000	Wadley	AL	36276	256-395-2211	745-6368*
**Fax Area Code:* 334 ■ **Fax:* Admissions ■ *Web:* www.suscc.edu					

ALASKA

	City	State	Zip	Phone	Fax
University of Alaska Southeast Ketchikan					
2600 7th Ave	Ketchikan	AK	99901	907-225-6177	225-3624
Web: www.ketch.alaska.edu					
University of Alaska Anchorage Kodiak College					
117 Benny Benson Dr	Kodiak	AK	99615	907-486-4161	486-1264
TF: 800-486-7660 ■ *Web:* www.koc.alaska.edu					
Northwest 400 E Front St PO Box 400	Nome	AK	99762	907-443-2201	443-5602
TF: 800-478-2202 ■ *Web:* www.nwc.uaf.edu					
University of Alaska Anchorage Matanuska-Susitna College					
PO Box 2889	Palmer	AK	99645	907-745-9774	745-9747
Web: www.matsu.alaska.edu					
University of Alaska Southeast Sitka					
1332 Seward Ave	Sitka	AK	99835	907-747-6653	747-7768
TF: 800-478-6653 ■ *Web:* www.uas.alaska.edu					
University of Alaska Anchorage Kenai Peninsula College					
34820 College Dr	Soldotna	AK	99669	907-262-5801	262-0322
Web: www.kpc.alaska.edu					
University of Alaska					
Prince William Sound Community College					
PO Box 97	Valdez	AK	99686	907-834-1600	834-1691
Web: www.pwscc.edu					

ARIZONA

	City	State	Zip	Phone	Fax
Estrella Mountain Community College					
3000 N Dysart Rd	Avondale	AZ	85323	623-935-8000	935-8870*
**Fax:* Admissions ■ *Web:* www.emc.maricopa.edu					
Bullhead City 3400 Hwy 95	Bullhead City	AZ	86442	928-758-3926	704-9460
TF: 866-664-2832 ■ *Web:* www.mohave.edu					
Chandler-Gilbert Community College					
Pecos 2626 E Pecos Rd	Chandler	AZ	85225	480-732-7000	732-7099*
**Fax:* Admissions ■ *Web:* www.cgc.maricopa.edu					
Verde Valley 601 Black Hills Dr	Clarkdale	AZ	86324	928-634-7501	634-6549*
**Fax:* Admissions ■ *TF:* 800-922-6787 ■ *Web:* www.yc.edu					
North Mohave PO Box 980	Colorado City	AZ	86021	928-875-2799	875-2831*
**Fax:* Admissions ■ *TF:* 800-678-3992 ■ *Web:* www.mohave.edu					
Central Arizona College 8470 N Overfield Rd	Coolidge	AZ	85228	520-494-5444	494-5083*
**Fax:* Admissions ■ *TF:* 800-237-9814 ■ *Web:* www.centralaz.edu					
Cochise College 4190 W Hwy 80	Douglas	AZ	85607	520-364-7943	417-4006*
**Fax:* Admissions ■ *TF:* 800-966-7943 ■ *Web:* www.cochise.edu					
Coconino Community College					
Lonetree 2800 S Lone Tree Rd	Flagstaff	AZ	86001	928-527-1222	226-4110*
**Fax:* Admissions ■ *TF:* 800-350-7122 ■ *Web:* www.coconino.edu					
Glendale Community College 6000 W Olive Ave	Glendale	AZ	85302	623-845-3000	845-3303*
**Fax:* Admissions ■ *Web:* www.gc.maricopa.edu					
North 5727 W Happy Valley Rd	Glendale	AZ	85310	623-845-4000	845-4010
Web: www.gc.maricopa.edu/gccnorth					
Northland Pioneer College PO Box 610	Holbrook	AZ	86025	928-532-6111	536-3382*
**Fax:* Admissions ■ *TF:* 800-266-7845 ■ *Web:* www.npc.edu					
Mohave Community College					
Kingman 1971 Jagerson Ave	Kingman	AZ	86409	928-757-0879	757-0808*
**Fax:* Admissions ■ *TF:* 866-664-2832 ■ *Web:* www.mohave.edu					
Lake Havasu 1977 W Acoma Blvd	Lake Havasu City	AZ	86403	928-855-7812	680-5955*
**Fax:* Admissions ■ *TF:* 866-664-2832 ■ *Web:* www.mohave.edu					
Williams 7360 E Tahoe Ave	Mesa	AZ	85212	480-988-8000	988-8993
Web: www.cgc.maricopa.edu					
Mesa Community College 1833 W Southern Ave	Mesa	AZ	85202	480-461-7000	461-7321*
**Fax:* Admissions ■ *TF:* 866-532-4983 ■ *Web:* www.mc.maricopa.edu					
Red Mountain 7110 E McKellips Rd	Mesa	AZ	85207	480-654-7200	654-7379
Web: www.mc.maricopa.edu					
GateWay Community College 108 N 40th St	Phoenix	AZ	85034	602-392-5000	286-8072*
**Fax:* Admissions ■ *Web:* www.gatewaycc.edu					

	City	State	ZIP	Phone	Fax
Paradise Valley Community College					
18401 N 32nd St	Phoenix	AZ	85032	602-787-6500	787-7025*
*Fax: Admissions ■ Web: www.pvc.maricopa.edu					
Phoenix College 1202 W Thomas Rd	Phoenix	AZ	85013	602-285-7800	285-7700
Web: www.pc.maricopa.edu					
South Mountain Community College					
7050 S 24th St	Phoenix	AZ	85042	602-243-8000	243-8199*
*Fax: Admissions ■ Web: www.southmountaincc.edu					
Yavapai College 1100 E Sheldon St	Prescott	AZ	86301	928-445-7300	776-2151*
*Fax: Admissions ■ TF: 800-922-6787 ■ Web: www.yc.edu					
Scottsdale Community College					
9000 E Chaparral Rd	Scottsdale	AZ	85256	480-423-6000	423-6200*
*Fax: Admissions ■ Web: www.scottsdalecc.edu					
Tohono O'odham Community College PO Box 3129	Sells	AZ	85634	520-383-8401	383-8403
Web: www.tocc.cc.az.us					
Sierra Vista 901 N Colombo Ave	Sierra Vista	AZ	85635	520-515-0500	515-5452*
*Fax: Admissions ■ TF: 800-966-7943 ■ Web: www.cochise.edu					
Rio Salado College 2323 W 14th St	Tempe	AZ	85281	480-517-8540	517-8199
TF: 800-729-1197 ■ Web: www.riosalado.edu					
Eastern Arizona College 615 N Stadium Ave	Thatcher	AZ	85552	928-428-8472	428-2578
TF: 800-678-3808 ■ Web: www.eac.edu					
Dine College PO Box 67	Tsaile	AZ	86556	928-724-6600	724-3327*
*Fax: Admissions ■ TF: 877-988-3463 ■ Web: www.dinecollege.edu					
Pima Community College					
401 N Bonita Ave Suite B-220	Tucson	AZ	85709	520-206-2733	206-4790*
*Fax: Admissions ■ TF: 800-860-7462 ■ Web: www.pima.edu					
Desert Vista 5901 S Calle Santa Cruz	Tucson	AZ	85709	520-206-5000	206-5050*
*Fax: Admissions ■ Web: www.dv.pima.edu					
East 8181 E Irvington Rd	Tucson	AZ	85709	520-206-7000	206-7875*
*Fax: Admissions ■ Web: www.ecc.pima.edu					
West 2202 W Anklam Rd	Tucson	AZ	85709	520-206-6600	206-6728*
*Fax: Admissions ■ TF: 800-860-7462 ■ Web: www.wc.pima.edu					
Arizona Western College 2020 S Ave 8 E	Yuma	AZ	85366	928-317-6000	344-7543
TF: 888-293-0392 ■ Web: www.azwestern.edu					

ARKANSAS

	City	State	ZIP	Phone	Fax
NorthWest Arkansas Community College					
1 College Dr	Bentonville	AR	72712	479-636-9222	619-2229*
*Fax: Admissions ■ TF: 800-995-6922 ■ Web: www.nwacc.edu					
Arkansas Northeastern College					
2501 S Division St PO Box 1109	Blytheville	AR	72316	870-762-1020	763-1654*
*Fax: Admissions ■ Web: www.anc.edu					
South Arkansas Community College					
PO Box 7010	El Dorado	AR	71731	870-862-8131	864-7134*
*Fax: Admissions ■ TF: 800-955-2289 ■ Web: www.southark.edu					
East Arkansas Community College					
1700 Newcastle Rd	Forrest City	AR	72335	870-633-4480	633-3840*
*Fax: Admissions ■ TF: 877-797-3222 ■ Web: www.eacc.edu					
Fort Smith PO Box 3649	Fort Smith	AR	72913	479-788-7000	788-7016
TF: 888-512-5466 ■ Web: www.uafortsmith.edu					
North Arkansas College 1515 Pioneer Dr	Harrison	AR	72601	870-743-3000	391-3339
TF: 800-679-6622 ■ Web: www.northark.edu					
Phillips Community College PO Box 785	Helena	AR	72342	870-338-6474	338-7542
Web: www.pccua.edu					
National Park Community College					
101 College Dr	Hot Springs	AR	71913	501-760-4222	760-4236*
*Fax: Admissions ■ TF: 800-760-1825 ■ Web: www.npcc.edu					
Ouachita Technical College 1 College Cir	Malvern	AR	72104	501-337-5000	337-9382
Web: www.otcweb.edu					
Ozarka College 218 College Dr	Melbourne	AR	72556	870-368-7371	368-2091
TF: 800-821-4335 ■ Web: www.ozarka.edu					
Rich Mountain Community College 1100 College Dr	Mena	AR	71953	479-394-7622	394-2760*
*Fax: Admissions ■ Web: www.rmcc.edu					
Arkansas State University Mountain Home					
1600 S College St	Mountain Home	AR	72653	870-508-6100	508-6287
Web: www.asumh.edu					
Arkansas State University Newport					
7648 Victory Blvd	Newport	AR	72112	870-512-7800	512-7825*
*Fax: Admissions ■ TF: 800-976-1676 ■ Web: www.asun.edu					
Pulaski Technical College					
3000 W Scenic Dr	North Little Rock	AR	72118	501-812-2200	771-2844
Web: www.pulaskitech.edu					
Shorter College 604 N Locust St	North Little Rock	AR	72114	501-374-6305	374-9333*
*Fax: Admissions ■ Web: www.shortercollege.4t.com					
Crowley's Ridge College 100 College Dr	Paragould	AR	72450	870-236-6901	236-7748*
*Fax: Admissions ■ TF: 800-264-1096 ■ Web: www.crc.edu					
Southeast Arkansas College 1900 Hazel St	Pine Bluff	AR	71603	870-543-5900	543-5956
Web: www.seark.org					
Black River Technical College					
1410 Hwy 304 E	Pocahontas	AR	72455	870-248-4000	248-4100
Web: www.blackrivertech.org					
Mid-South Community College					
2000 W Broadway	West Memphis	AR	72301	870-733-6722	733-6719*
*Fax: Admissions ■ Web: www.midsouthcc.edu					

CALIFORNIA

	City	State	ZIP	Phone	Fax
College of Alameda					
555 Ralph Appezzato Meml Pkwy	Alameda	CA	94501	510-522-7221	769-6019
Web: www.alameda.peralta.edu					
Cabrillo College 6500 Soquel Dr	Aptos	CA	95003	831-479-6100	479-5782*
*Fax: Admitting ■ Web: www.cabrillo.edu					
Bakersfield College 1801 Panorama Dr	Bakersfield	CA	93305	661-395-4011	395-4500*
*Fax: Admissions ■ Web: www.bakersfieldcollege.edu					
Barstow College 2700 Barstow Rd	Barstow	CA	92311	760-252-2411	252-6754
TF: 877-336-6868 ■ Web: www.barstow.cc.ca.us					
Berkeley City College 2050 Center St	Berkeley	CA	94704	510-981-2800	841-7333
Web: berkeley.peralta.edu					
Bishop 4090 W Line St	Bishop	CA	93514	760-872-1565	872-5319*
*Fax: Admissions ■ TF: 888-537-6932 ■ Web: www.cerrocoso.edu					
Palo Verde College 1 College Dr	Blythe	CA	92225	760-921-5500	921-3608*
*Fax: Admissions ■ Web: www.paloverde.edu					
San Elijo 3333 Manchester Ave	Cardiff	CA	92007	760-944-4449	634-7875
TF: 888-201-8480 ■ Web: www.miracosta.cc.ca.us					
Southwestern College 900 Otay Lakes Rd	Chula Vista	CA	91910	619-421-6700	482-6489*
*Fax: Admissions ■ Web: www.swc.cc.ca.us					
West Hills College					
Coalinga 300 Cherry Ln	Coalinga	CA	93210	559-934-2000	935-3788*
*Fax: Admissions ■ TF: 800-266-1114 ■ Web: www.westhillscollege.com					
Compton Ctr 1111 E Artesia Blvd	Compton	CA	90221	310-637-2660	900-1662*
*Fax: Admissions ■ Web: www.compton.cc.ca.us					
Orange Coast College					
2701 Fairview Rd PO Box 5005	Costa Mesa	CA	92628	714-432-5735	432-5957*
*Fax: Admissions ■ Web: www.orangecoastcollege.com					
Del Norte 883 W Washington Blvd	Crescent City	CA	95531	707-465-2300	464-6867*
*Fax: Admissions ■ TF: 800-641-0400 ■ Web: www.redwoods.edu					
West Los Angeles College					
9000 Overland Ave	Culver City	CA	90230	310-287-4200	287-4327*
*Fax: Admissions ■ Web: www.wlac.edu					
DeAnza College 21250 Stevens Creek Blvd	Cupertino	CA	95014	408-864-5678	864-8329*
*Fax: Admissions ■ Web: www.deanza.edu					
Cypress College 9200 Valley View St	Cypress	CA	90630	714-484-7000	484-7446*
*Fax: Admissions ■ Web: www.cypresscollege.edu					
South Kern 140 Methusa Ave	Edwards AFB	CA	93524	661-258-8644	258-0651*
*Fax: Admissions ■ Web: www.cerrocoso.edu/sk					
Cuyamaca College 900 Rancho San Diego Pkwy	El Cajon	CA	92019	619-660-4000	660-4575*
*Fax: Admissions ■ Web: www.cuyamaca.net					
Grossmont College 8800 Grossmont College Dr	El Cajon	CA	92020	619-644-7000	644-7933*
*Fax: Admissions ■ TF: 866-476-7766 ■ Web: www.grossmont.edu					
College of the Redwoods 7351 Tompkins Hill Rd	Eureka	CA	95501	707-476-4100	476-4406*
*Fax: Admissions ■ TF: 800-641-0400 ■ Web: www.redwoods.edu					
Solano Community College					
4000 Suisun Valley Rd	Fairfield	CA	94534	707-864-7171	864-7175*
*Fax: Admissions ■ Web: www.solano.edu					
Mendocino Coast 440 Alger St	Fort Bragg	CA	95437	707-962-2600	961-0943
TF: 800-641-0400 ■ Web: www.redwoods.edu					
Coastline Community College					
11460 Warner Ave	Fountain Valley	CA	92708	714-546-7600	241-6288*
*Fax: Admissions ■ Web: www.coastline.edu					
Ohlone College 43600 Mission Blvd	Fremont	CA	94539	510-659-6000	659-7321*
*Fax: Admissions ■ Web: www.ohlone.edu					
Queen of the Holy Rosary College					
43326 Mission Blvd	Fremont	CA	94539	510-657-2468	657-1734*
*Fax: Admissions ■ Web: www.msjdominicans.org					
Fresno City College 1101 E University Ave	Fresno	CA	93741	559-442-4600	237-4232*
*Fax: Admissions ■ TF: 866-245-3276 ■ Web: www.fresnocitycollege.edu					
Fullerton College 321 E Chapman Ave	Fullerton	CA	92832	714-992-7000	870-7751*
*Fax: Admissions ■ Web: www.fullcoll.edu					
Gavilan College 5055 Santa Teresa Blvd	Gilroy	CA	95020	408-847-1400	846-4940*
*Fax: Admissions ■ Web: www.gavilan.edu					
Glendale Community College					
1500 N Verdugo Rd	Glendale	CA	91208	818-240-1000	551-5255*
*Fax: Admissions ■ Web: www.glendale.edu					
Citrus College 1000 W Foothill Blvd	Glendora	CA	91741	626-963-0323	914-8613*
*Fax: Admissions ■ Web: www.citruscollege.edu					
Sierra College					
Nevada County 250 Sierra College Dr	Grass Valley	CA	95945	530-274-5300	274-5324*
*Fax: Admissions ■ TF: 800-242-4004 ■ Web: www.sierracollege.edu					
Golden West College					
15744 Golden W St PO Box 2748	Huntington Beach	CA	92647	714-892-7711	895-8960*
*Fax: Admissions ■ Web: www.gwc.info					
Imperial Valley College					
380 E Aten Rd PO Box 158	Imperial	CA	92251	760-352-8320	355-2663*
*Fax: Admissions ■ Web: www.imperial.cc.ca.us					
Irvine Valley College 5500 Irvine Ctr Dr	Irvine	CA	92618	949-451-5100	451-5443*
*Fax: Admissions ■ Web: www.ivc.edu					
Copper Mountain College					
6162 Rotary Way PO Box 1398	Joshua Tree	CA	92252	760-366-3791	366-5257*
*Fax: Admissions ■ TF: 866-366-3791 ■ Web: www.cmccd.cc.ca.us					
College of Marin 835 College Ave	Kentfield	CA	94904	415-457-8811	460-0773*
*Fax: Admissions ■ Web: www.marin.cc.ca.us					
Kern River Valley					
5520 Lake Isabella Blvd	Lake Isabella	CA	93240	760-379-5501	379-5547*
*Fax: Admissions ■ TF: 888-537-6932 ■ Web: www.cerrocoso.edu					
Antelope Valley College 3041 W Ave K	Lancaster	CA	93536	661-722-6300	722-6531*
*Fax: Admissions ■ Web: www.avc.edu					
Lemoore 555 College Ave	Lemoore	CA	93245	559-925-3000	924-1539
Web: www.westhillscollege.com					
Las Positas College 3033 Collier Canyon Rd	Livermore	CA	94551	925-424-1000	443-0742
Web: www.laspositascollege.edu					
Lompoc Valley 1 Hancock Dr	Lompoc	CA	93436	805-735-3366	736-9368
Web: www.hancock.cc.ca.us					
Long Beach City College 4901 E Carson St	Long Beach	CA	90808	562-938-4111	938-4858*
*Fax: Admissions ■ Web: www.lbcc.edu					
Foothill College 12345 El Monte Rd	Los Altos Hills	CA	94022	650-949-7777	949-7048*
*Fax: Admissions ■ Web: www.foothill.edu					
Los Angeles City College					
855 N Vermont Ave	Los Angeles	CA	90029	323-953-4000	953-4013*
*Fax: Admissions ■ Web: www.lacitycollege.edu					
Los Angeles Southwest College					
1600 W Imperial Hwy	Los Angeles	CA	90047	323-241-5225	
Web: www.lasc.edu					
Los Angeles Trade Technical College					
400 W Washington Blvd	Los Angeles	CA	90015	213-763-7000	763-5386*
*Fax: Admissions ■ Web: www.lattc.edu					

	City	State	Zip	Phone	Fax
Mount Saint Mary's College Doheny 10 Chester Pl	Los Angeles	CA	90007	213-477-2561	477-2569*
**Fax:* Admissions ■ *TF Admissions:* 800-999-9893 ■ *Web:* www.msmc.la.edu					
Mammoth 101 College Pkwy PO Box 1865	Mammoth Lakes	CA	93546	760-934-2875	924-1613*
**Fax:* Admissions ■ *TF:* 888-537-6932 ■ *Web:* www.cerrocoso.edu					
Menifee Valley 28237 La Piedra Rd	Menifee	CA	92584	951-672-6752	
Web: www.msjc.edu					
Merced College 3600 M St	Merced	CA	95348	209-384-6000	384-6339*
**Fax:* Admissions ■ *Web:* www.merced.cc.ca.us					
Saddleback College 28000 Marguerite Pkwy	Mission Viejo	CA	92692	949-582-4500	347-8315*
**Fax:* Admissions ■ *Web:* www.saddleback.edu					
Modesto Junior College 435 College Ave	Modesto	CA	95350	209-575-6550	575-6859*
**Fax:* Admissions ■ *Web:* www.mjc.edu					
Monterey Peninsula College 980 Fremont St	Monterey	CA	93940	831-646-4000	646-4015*
**Fax:* Admissions ■ *Web:* www.mpc.edu					
East Los Angeles College 1301 Avenida Cesar Chavez	Monterey Park	CA	91754	323-265-8650	265-8688*
**Fax:* Admissions ■ *Web:* www.elac.edu					
Moorpark College 7075 Campus Rd	Moorpark	CA	93021	805-378-1400	378-1583*
**Fax:* Admissions ■ *Web:* www.moorpark.cc.ca.us					
Moreno Valley 16130 Lasselle St	Moreno Valley	CA	92551	951-571-6100	571-6188*
**Fax:* Admissions ■ *Web:* www.rcc.edu					
Napa Valley College 2277 Napa-Vallejo Hwy	Napa	CA	94558	707-253-3005	253-3064
TF: 800-826-1077 ■ *Web:* www.napavalley.edu					
Norco 2001 3rd St	Norco	CA	92860	951-372-7000	372-7054*
**Fax:* Admissions ■ *Web:* www.rcc.edu					
Cerritos College 11110 Alondra Blvd	Norwalk	CA	90650	562-860-2451	467-5068*
**Fax:* Admitting ■ *Web:* www.cerritos.edu					
Indian Valley 1800 Ignacio Blvd	Novato	CA	94949	415-883-2211	884-0429*
**Fax:* Admissions ■ *Web:* www.marin.cc.ca.us					
Laney College 900 Fallon St	Oakland	CA	94607	510-834-5740	466-7394*
**Fax:* Admissions ■ *Web:* www.peralta.cc.ca.us					
Merritt College 12500 Campus Dr	Oakland	CA	94619	510-531-4911	436-2405*
**Fax:* Admissions ■ *Web:* www.merritt.edu					
MiraCosta College *Oceanside* 1 Barnard Dr Suite 7	Oceanside	CA	92056	760-757-2121	795-6626*
**Fax:* Admissions ■ *TF:* 888-201-8480 ■ *Web:* www.miracosta.edu					
Santiago Canyon College 8045 E Chapman Ave	Orange	CA	92869	714-628-4900	628-4723*
**Fax:* Admissions ■ *Web:* www.sccollege.edu					
Butte College 3536 Butte Campus Dr	Oroville	CA	95965	530-895-2511	879-4313*
**Fax:* Admissions ■ *TF Hum Res:* 800-933-8322 ■ *Web:* www.butte.edu					
Oxnard College 4000 S Rose Ave	Oxnard	CA	93033	805-986-5800	986-5943*
**Fax:* Admissions ■ *Web:* www.oxnardcollege.edu					
College of the Desert 43-500 Monterey Ave	Palm Desert	CA	92260	760-346-8041	862-1379*
**Fax:* Admissions ■ *Web:* www.collegeofthedesert.edu					
Pasadena City College 1570 E Colorado Blvd	Pasadena	CA	91106	626-585-7123	585-7915*
**Fax:* Admissions ■ *Web:* www.pasadena.edu					
North County 2800 Buena Vista Dr	Paso Robles	CA	93446	805-591-6200	591-6370
Web: www.academic.cuesta.edu					
Los Medanos College 2700 E Leland Rd	Pittsburg	CA	94565	925-439-2181	427-1599
Web: www.losmedanos.edu					
Diablo Valley College 312 Golf Club Rd	Pleasant Hill	CA	94523	925-685-1230	609-8085
Web: www.dvc.edu					
Porterville College 100 E College Ave	Porterville	CA	93257	559-791-2200	791-2349*
**Fax:* Admissions ■ *Web:* www.pc.cc.ca.us					
Feather River College 570 Golden Eagle Ave	Quincy	CA	95971	530-283-0202	283-9961*
**Fax:* Admissions ■ *TF:* 800-442-9799 ■ *Web:* www.frc.edu					
Chaffey College 5885 Haven Ave	Rancho Cucamonga	CA	91737	909-987-1737	466-2875*
**Fax:* Admissions ■ *Web:* www.chaffey.edu					
Canada College 4200 Farm Hill Blvd	Redwood City	CA	94061	650-306-3100	306-3113*
**Fax:* Admissions ■ *Web:* www.canadacollege.edu					
Reedley College 995 N Reed Ave	Reedley	CA	93654	559-638-3641	638-5040
Web: www.reedleycollege.edu					
Cerro Coso Community College *Indian Wells Valley* 3000 College Heights Blvd	Ridgecrest	CA	93555	760-384-6100	384-6377*
**Fax:* Admissions ■ *TF:* 888-537-6932 ■ *Web:* www.cerrocoso.edu					
Riverside Community College *Riverside* 4800 Magnolia Ave	Riverside	CA	92506	951-222-8000	328-3503*
**Fax:* Admissions ■ *Web:* www.rcc.edu					
Sierra Community College 5000 Rocklin Rd	Rocklin	CA	95677	916-624-3333	781-0403*
**Fax:* Admissions ■ *Web:* www.sierra.cc.ca.us					
American River College 4700 College Oak Dr	Sacramento	CA	95841	916-484-8011	484-8864*
**Fax:* Admissions ■ *Web:* www.arc.losrios.edu					
Cosumnes River College 8401 Ctr Pkwy	Sacramento	CA	95823	916-691-7410	691-7467*
**Fax:* Admissions ■ *Web:* www.crc.losrios.edu					
Sacramento City College 3835 Freeport Blvd	Sacramento	CA	95822	916-558-2351	558-2190*
**Fax:* Admissions ■ *Web:* www.scc.losrios.edu					
Hartnell College 156 Homestead Ave	Salinas	CA	93901	831-755-6700	759-6014*
**Fax:* Admissions ■ *Web:* www.hartnell.edu					
San Bernardino Valley College 701 S Mt Vernon Ave	San Bernardino	CA	92410	909-888-6511	889-4988
Web: www.valleycollege.edu					
Skyline College 3300 College Dr	San Bruno	CA	94066	650-738-4100	738-4222*
**Fax:* Admissions ■ *Web:* www.skylinecollege.edu					
San Diego City College 1313 Pk Blvd	San Diego	CA	92101	619-230-2400	388-3505*
**Fax:* Admissions ■ *Web:* www.sdcity.edu					
San Diego Mesa College 7250 Mesa College Dr	San Diego	CA	92111	619-388-2600	388-2960
Web: www.sandiegomesacollege.net					
San Diego Miramar College 10440 Black Mountain Rd	San Diego	CA	92126	619-388-7844	388-7915*
**Fax:* Admissions ■ *Web:* www.miramarcollege.net					
City College of San Francisco 50 Phelan Ave	San Francisco	CA	94112	415-239-3000	239-3936*
**Fax:* Admissions ■ *Web:* www.ccsf.edu					
Mount San Jacinto College 1499 N State St	San Jacinto	CA	92583	951-487-6752	654-6738*
**Fax:* Admissions ■ *TF:* 800-624-5561 ■ *Web:* www.msjc.edu					
Evergreen Valley College 3095 Yerba Buena Rd	San Jose	CA	95135	408-274-7900	223-9351*
**Fax:* Admissions ■ *Web:* www.evc.edu					
San Jose City College 2100 Moorpark Ave	San Jose	CA	95128	408-298-2181	298-1935*
**Fax:* Admissions ■ *Web:* www.sjcc.edu					
Cuesta College PO Box 8106	San Luis Obispo	CA	93403	805-546-3100	546-3975*
**Fax:* Admissions ■ *Web:* www.cuesta.edu					
Palomar College 1140 W Mission Rd	San Marcos	CA	92069	760-744-1150	744-8123*
**Fax:* Admissions ■ *Web:* www.palomar.edu					
College of San Mateo 1700 W Hillsdale Blvd	San Mateo	CA	94402	650-574-6161	574-6506*
**Fax:* Admissions ■ *Web:* www.collegeofsanmateo.edu					
Contra Costa College 2600 Mission Bell	San Pablo	CA	94806	510-235-7800	412-0769
Web: www.contracosta.cc.ca.us					
Santa Ana College 1530 W 17th St	Santa Ana	CA	92706	714-564-6000	564-6455*
**Fax:* Admissions ■ *Web:* www.sac.edu					
Santa Barbara City College 721 Cliff Dr	Santa Barbara	CA	93109	805-965-0581	963-7222*
**Fax:* Admissions ■ *Web:* www.sbcc.edu					
Mission College 3000 Mission College Blvd	Santa Clara	CA	95054	408-988-2200	980-8980*
**Fax:* Admissions ■ *Web:* www.missioncollege.org					
College of the Canyons 26455 Rockwell Canyon Rd	Santa Clarita	CA	91355	661-259-7800	362-5566*
**Fax:* Admissions ■ *Web:* www.canyons.edu					
Allan Hancock College 800 S College Dr	Santa Maria	CA	93454	805-922-6966	922-3477*
**Fax:* Admissions ■ *Web:* www.hancockcollege.edu					
Santa Monica College 1900 Pico Blvd	Santa Monica	CA	90405	310-434-4000	434-3645*
**Fax:* Admissions ■ *Web:* www.smc.edu					
Santa Rosa Junior College 1501 Mendocino Ave	Santa Rosa	CA	95401	707-527-4011	527-4798
TF: 800-564-7752 ■ *Web:* www.santarosa.edu					
West Valley College 14000 Fruitvale Ave	Saratoga	CA	95070	408-867-2200	867-5033*
**Fax:* Admissions ■ *Web:* www.westvalley.edu					
Columbia College 11600 Columbia College Dr	Sonora	CA	95370	209-588-5100	588-5104
Web: www.columbia.yosemite.cc.ca.us					
Lake Tahoe Community College 1 College Dr	South Lake Tahoe	CA	96150	530-541-4660	542-1781*
**Fax:* Admissions ■ *Web:* www.ltcc.edu					
San Joaquin Delta College 5151 Pacific Ave	Stockton	CA	95207	209-954-5151	954-5769*
**Fax:* Admissions ■ *Web:* www.deltacollege.edu					
Lassen Community College 478-200 Hwy 139 PO Box 3000	Susanville	CA	96130	530-257-6181	251-8802*
**Fax:* Admissions ■ *TF:* 800-461-9389 ■ *Web:* www.lassen.cc.ca.us					
Los Angeles Mission College 13356 Eldridge Ave	Sylmar	CA	91342	818-364-7600	364-7806*
**Fax:* Admissions ■ *Web:* www.lamission.edu					
Taft College 29 Emmons Pk Dr	Taft	CA	93268	661-763-7700	763-7758*
**Fax:* Admissions ■ *TF:* 800-379-6784 ■ *Web:* www.taftcollege.edu					
El Camino College 16007 Crenshaw Blvd	Torrance	CA	90506	310-532-3670	660-3818
Web: www.elcamino.edu					
Mendocino College 1000 Hensley Creek Rd	Ukiah	CA	95482	707-468-3000	468-3430*
**Fax:* Admissions ■ *Web:* www.mendocino.edu					
Los Angeles Valley College 5800 Fulton Ave	Valley Glen	CA	91401	818-947-2600	947-2501*
**Fax:* Admissions ■ *Web:* www.lavc.cc.ca.us					
Ventura College 4667 Telegraph Rd	Ventura	CA	93003	805-654-6400	654-6357*
**Fax:* Admissions ■ *Web:* www.venturacollege.edu					
Victor Valley Community College 18422 Bear Valley Rd	Victorville	CA	92392	760-245-4271	245-9745
Web: www.vvc.edu					
College of the Sequoias 915 S Mooney Blvd	Visalia	CA	93277	559-730-3700	737-4820*
**Fax:* Admissions ■ *Web:* www.cos.edu					
Mount San Antonio College 1100 N Grand Ave	Walnut	CA	91789	909-594-5611	468-4068*
**Fax:* Admissions ■ *Web:* www.mtsac.edu					
College of the Siskiyous 800 College Ave	Weed	CA	96094	530-938-4461	938-5367*
**Fax:* Admissions ■ *TF:* 888-397-4339 ■ *Web:* www.siskiyous.edu					
Rio Hondo College 3600 Workman Mill Rd	Whittier	CA	90601	562-692-0921	699-7386
Web: www.riohondo.edu					
Los Angeles Harbor College 1111 Figueroa Pl	Wilmington	CA	90744	310-233-4000	233-4223
Web: www.lahc.cc.ca.us					
Pierce College 6201 Winnetka Ave	Woodland Hills	CA	91371	818-719-6401	710-9844
Web: www.piercecollege.edu					
Crafton Hills College 11711 Sand Canyon Rd	Yucaipa	CA	92399	909-794-2161	389-9141*
**Fax:* Admissions ■ *Web:* www.craftonhills.edu					

COLORADO

	City	State	Zip	Phone	Fax
Aspen 0255 Sage Way	Aspen	CO	81611	970-925-7740	925-6045
Web: www.coloradomtn.edu					
Community College of Aurora 16000 E Centretech Pkwy	Aurora	CO	80011	303-360-4700	361-7432*
**Fax:* Admissions ■ *Web:* www.ccaurora.edu					
Pikes Peak Community College *Centennial* 5675 S Academy Blvd	Colorado Springs	CO	80906	719-576-7711	540-7092*
**Fax:* Claims ■ *TF:* 800-456-6847 ■ *Web:* www.ppcc.edu					
Downtown Studio 100 W Pikes Peak Ave	Colorado Springs	CO	80903	719-502-2000	527-6010
TF: 800-456-6847 ■ *Web:* www.ppcc.edu					
Rampart Range 11195 Hwy 83	Colorado Springs	CO	80921	719-502-2000	538-5144
TF: 800-456-6847 ■ *Web:* www.ppcc.edu					
Craig 50 College Dr	Craig	CO	81625	970-824-7071	824-1134*
**Fax:* Admissions ■ *TF:* 800-562-1105 ■ *Web:* www.cncc.edu					
Community College of Denver 1111 E Colfax Ave	Denver	CO	80218	303-556-2600	556-2431
Web: www.ccd.edu					

				Phone	Fax
Larimer 4616 S Shields St	Fort Collins	CO	80526	970-226-2500	204-8484
TF: 800-289-3722 ■ *Web:* www.frontrange.edu					
Fort Lupton 260 County Rd 29 1/2	Fort Lupton	CO	80621	303-857-4022	352-5443*
**Fax Area Code:* 970 ■ *Web:* www.aims.edu					
Morgan Community College 920 Barlow Rd	Fort Morgan	CO	80701	970-542-3100	867-6608
TF: 800-622-0216 ■ *Web:* www.morgancc.edu					
Colorado Mountain College					
Roaring Fork-Spring Valley					
3000 County Rd 114	Glenwood Springs	CO	81601	970-945-7481	928-9668
TF: 800-621-8559 ■ *Web:* www.coloradomtn.edu					
Aims Community College 5401 W 20th St	Greeley	CO	80634	970-330-8008	506-6958*
**Fax:* Admissions ■ *TF:* 800-301-5388 ■ *Web:* www.aims.edu					
Otero Junior College 1802 Colorado Ave	La Junta	CO	81050	719-384-6831	384-6933*
**Fax:* Admissions ■ *Web:* www.ojc.edu					
Red Rocks Community College 13300 W 6th Ave	Lakewood	CO	80228	303-914-6600	914-6666
Web: www.rrcc.edu					
Lamar Community College 2401 S Main St	Lamar	CO	81052	719-336-2248	336-2400*
**Fax:* Admissions ■ *TF:* 800-968-6920 ■ *Web:* www.lcc.cccoes.edu					
Timberline 901 US Hwy 24	Leadville	CO	80461	719-486-2015	486-3212
Web: www.coloradomtn.edu					
Arapahoe Community College					
5900 S Santa Fe Dr	Littleton	CO	80160	303-794-1550	797-5970*
**Fax:* Admissions ■ *Web:* www.arapahoe.edu					
Boulder County 2190 Miller Dr	Longmont	CO	80501	303-678-3722	678-3699*
**Fax:* Admissions ■ *Web:* www.frontrange.edu					
Pueblo Community College 900 W Orman Ave	Pueblo	CO	81004	719-549-3200	543-7566*
**Fax:* Admissions ■ *TF:* 888-642-6017 ■ *Web:* www.pueblocc.edu					
Colorado Northwestern Community College					
500 Kennedy Dr	Rangely	CO	81648	970-675-2261	675-3343*
**Fax:* Admissions ■ *TF:* 800-562-1105 ■ *Web:* www.cncc.edu					
Alpine 1330 Bob Adams Dr	Steamboat Springs	CO	80487	970-870-4444	870-4535*
**Fax:* Admissions ■ *TF:* 800-621-8559 ■ *Web:* www.coloradomtn.edu					
Northeastern Junior College 100 College Ave	Sterling	CO	80751	970-521-6600	522-4664
TF: 800-626-4637 ■ *Web:* www.njc.edu					
Trinidad State Junior College					
600 Prospect St	Trinidad	CO	81082	719-846-5011	846-5620*
**Fax:* Admissions ■ *TF:* 800-621-8752 ■ *Web:* www.trinidadstate.edu					
Front Range Community College (FRCC)					
Westminster 3645 W 112th Ave	Westminster	CO	80031	303-404-5000	466-1623*
**Fax:* Admissions ■ *Web:* www.frontrange.edu					

CONNECTICUT

				Phone	Fax
Housatonic Community College					
900 Lafayette Blvd	Bridgeport	CT	06604	203-332-5000	332-5123*
**Fax:* Admissions ■ *Web:* www.hctc.commnet.edu					
Quinebaug Valley Community College					
742 Upper Maple St	Danielson	CT	06239	860-774-1130	779-2998*
**Fax:* Admissions ■ *Web:* www.qvctc.commnet.edu					
Asnuntuck Community College 170 Elm St	Enfield	CT	06082	860-253-3000	253-3014*
**Fax:* Admissions ■ *TF:* 800-501-3967 ■ *Web:* www.acc.commnet.edu					
Tunxis Community College					
271 Scott Swamp Rd	Farmington	CT	06032	860-677-7701	676-8906
Web: www.tunxis.commnet.edu					
Avery Point 1084 Shennecossett Rd	Groton	CT	06340	860-405-9019	405-9018
Web: www.averypoint.uconn.edu					
Capital Community College 950 Main St	Hartford	CT	06103	860-906-5000	906-5129
TF: 800-894-6126 ■ *Web:* www.ccc.commnet.edu					
Manchester Community College PO Box 1046	Manchester	CT	06045	860-646-4900	512-3221*
**Fax:* Admissions ■ *Web:* www.mcc.commnet.edu					
Middlesex Community College					
100 Training Hill Rd	Middletown	CT	06457	860-343-5800	344-7488*
**Fax:* Admissions ■ *Web:* www.mxctc.commnet.edu					
Gateway Community College 60 Sargent Dr	New Haven	CT	06510	203-285-2000	285-2260*
**Fax:* Admissions ■ *Web:* www.gwcc.commnet.edu					
Norwalk Community College 188 Richards Ave	Norwalk	CT	06854	203-857-7060	857-3335*
**Fax:* Admissions ■ *Web:* www.ncc.commnet.edu					
Three Rivers Community College Mohegan					
7 Mahan Dr	Norwich	CT	06360	860-885-2300	885-1684*
**Fax:* Admissions ■ *Web:* www.trcc.commnet.edu					
Three Rivers Community College Thames Valley					
7 Mahan Dr	Norwich	CT	06360	860-886-0177	892-5753*
**Fax:* Admissions ■ *Web:* www.trcc.commnet.edu					
Torrington 855 University Dr	Torrington	CT	06790	860-626-6800	626-6847
Web: www.torrington.uconn.edu					
Naugatuck Valley Community College					
750 Chase Pkwy	Waterbury	CT	06708	203-575-8078	596-8766*
**Fax:* Admissions ■ *Web:* www.nvcc.commnet.edu					
Waterbury 99 E Main St	Waterbury	CT	06702	203-236-9800	236-9805
Web: www.waterbury.uconn.edu					
Greater Hartford 85 Lawler Rd	West Hartford	CT	06117	860-570-9214	570-9210
Web: www.hartford.uconn.edu					
Northwestern Connecticut Community College					
Park Pl E	Winsted	CT	06098	860-738-6300	738-6437*
**Fax:* Admissions ■ *Web:* www.nwctc.commnet.edu					

FLORIDA

				Phone	Fax
South Florida Community College					
600 W College Dr	Avon Park	FL	33825	863-453-6661	453-2365*
**Fax:* Admissions ■ *Web:* www.southflorida.edu					
Belle Glade 1977 College Dr	Belle Glade	FL	33430	561-993-1121	993-1129*
**Fax:* Admissions ■ *Web:* www.pbcc.edu					
Boca Raton 3000 St Lucie Ave	Boca Raton	FL	33431	561-862-4340	862-4350
Web: www.pbcc.edu					
Manatee Community College 5840 26th St W	Bradenton	FL	34207	941-752-5000	727-6380
Web: www.mccfl.edu					
North 11415 Ponce de Leon Blvd	Brooksville	FL	34601	352-796-6726	797-5133
TF: 877-879-7422 ■ *Web:* www.pacc.edu					
Levy County 114 Rodgers Blvd	Chiefland	FL	32626	352-493-9533	493-9994
Web: www.cf.edu					
Saint Petersburg College					
Clearwater 2465 Drew St	Clearwater	FL	33765	727-791-2473	791-2423
Web: www.spcollege.edu/clw					
South Lake 1250 N Hancock Rd	Clermont	FL	34711	352-243-5722	243-0117
Web: www.lscc.edu					
Brevard Community College					
Cocoa 1519 Clearlake Rd	Cocoa	FL	32922	321-632-1111	433-7357*
**Fax:* Admissions ■ *TF:* 888-747-2802 ■ *Web:* www.brevard.cc.fl.us					
Broward Community College					
North 1000 Coconut Creek Blvd	Coconut Creek	FL	33066	954-201-2240	201-2242*
**Fax:* Admissions ■ *Web:* www.broward.edu					
East 36727 Blanton Rd	Dade City	FL	33523	352-567-6701	518-1225
Web: www.pasco-hernandocc.com					
Central 3501 SW Davie Rd	Davie	FL	33314	954-201-6500	201-6954
Web: www.broward.edu					
Daytona Beach Community College					
1200 W International Speedway Blvd	Daytona Beach	FL	32114	386-506-3222	
Web: www.dbcc.edu					
Downtown Ctr 111 E Las Olas Blvd	Fort Lauderdale	FL	33301	954-201-7350	201-7466*
**Fax:* Admissions ■ *Web:* www.broward.edu					
Edison College					
Lee County 8099 College Pkwy SW	Fort Myers	FL	33919	239-489-9054	489-9372*
**Fax:* Admissions ■ *TF:* 800-749-2322 ■ *Web:* www.edison.edu/lee					
Indian River Community College					
3209 Virginia Ave	Fort Pierce	FL	34981	772-462-4700	462-4699*
**Fax:* Admissions ■ *TF:* 866-866-4722 ■ *Web:* www.ircc.edu					
Florida National College 4425 W 20th Ave	Hialeah	FL	33012	305-821-3333	362-0595*
**Fax:* Acctg ■ *Web:* www.florida-national.edu					
North-Hialeah Ctr 1780 W 49th St	Hialeah	FL	33012	305-237-8700	237-8771*
**Fax:* Admissions ■ *Web:* www.mdc.edu					
Homestead 500 College Terr Rm A230	Homestead	FL	33030	305-237-5555	237-5019*
**Fax:* Admissions ■ *Web:* www.mdc.edu/homestead					
Florida Community College at Jacksonville					
Downtown 101 State St W	Jacksonville	FL	32202	904-633-8100	633-8400
TF: 877-633-5950 ■ *Web:* www.fccj.org					
Kent 3939 Roosevelt Blvd	Jacksonville	FL	32205	904-381-3400	381-3771*
**Fax:* Admissions ■ *Web:* www.fccj.org					
North 4501 Capper Rd	Jacksonville	FL	32218	904-766-6500	713-6002
Web: www.fccj.org					
South 11901 Beach Blvd	Jacksonville	FL	32246	904-646-2111	646-2124*
**Fax:* Admissions ■ *Web:* www.fccj.org					
Florida Keys Community College					
5901 College Rd	Key West	FL	33040	305-296-9081	292-5155*
**Fax:* Admissions ■ *Web:* www.fkcc.edu					
Osceola 1800 Denn John Ln PO Box 3028	Kissimmee	FL	32802	407-299-5000	
Web: www.valenciacc.edu/osceola					
Lake City Community College					
149 SE College Pl	Lake City	FL	32025	386-752-1822	754-4581*
**Fax:* Admissions ■ *Web:* www.lakecitycc.edu					
Palm Beach Community College					
Lake Worth 4200 Congress Ave	Lake Worth	FL	33461	561-868-3350	868-3584*
**Fax:* Admissions ■ *TF:* 866-576-7222 ■ *Web:* www.pbcc.edu					
Citrus County 3800 S Lecanto Hwy	Lecanto	FL	34461	352-746-6721	249-1218
Web: www.cf.edu					
Lake-Sumter Community College					
9501 US Hwy 441	Leesburg	FL	34788	352-787-3747	365-3553*
**Fax:* Admissions ■ *Web:* www.lscc.edu					
North Florida Community College					
321 NW Turner Davis Dr	Madison	FL	32340	850-973-2288	973-1696
Web: www.nfcc.edu					
Melbourne 3865 N Wickham Rd	Melbourne	FL	32935	321-632-1111	433-5770*
**Fax:* Admissions ■ *TF:* 888-747-2802 ■ *Web:* www.brevardcc.edu					
Miami Dade College					
Kendall 11011 SW 104th St	Miami	FL	33176	305-237-2000	237-2964*
**Fax:* Admissions ■ *Web:* www.mdc.edu/kendall					
Medical Ctr 950 NW 20th St	Miami	FL	33127	305-237-4100	237-4339
Web: www.mdc.edu/medical					
North 11380 NW 27th Ave	Miami	FL	33167	305-237-1000	237-8070*
**Fax:* Admissions ■ *Web:* www.mdc.edu/north					
Wolfson 300 NE 2nd Ave	Miami	FL	33132	305-237-3000	237-3669*
**Fax:* Admissions ■ *Web:* www.mdc.edu/wolfson					
Collier County 7007 Lely Cultural Pkwy	Naples	FL	34113	239-732-3701	732-3761*
**Fax:* Admissions ■ *TF:* 800-749-2322 ■ *Web:* www.edison.edu					
Pasco-Hernando Community College					
10230 Ridge Rd	New Port Richey	FL	34654	727-847-2727	816-3389*
**Fax:* Admissions ■ *TF:* 877-879-7422 ■ *Web:* www.phcc.edu					
Okaloosa-Walton Community College					
100 College Blvd	Niceville	FL	32578	850-678-5111	729-5273
Web: www.owcc.cc.fl.us					
Central Florida Community College					
Ocala 3001 SW College Rd	Ocala	FL	34474	352-237-2111	291-4450
Web: www.gocfcc.com					
Orange Park 283 College Dr	Orange Park	FL	32065	904-276-6800	276-6888*
**Fax:* Admissions ■ *Web:* www.sjrcc.edu					
Valencia Community College PO Box 3028	Orlando	FL	32802	407-299-5000	582-1450
Web: www.valenciacc.edu					
East 701 N Econlockhatchee Trail	Orlando	FL	32825	407-299-5000	582-2621
Web: www.valenciacc.edu/east					
Oviedo 2505 Lockwood Blvd	Oviedo	FL	32765	407-971-5000	971-5012
Web: www.scc-fl.edu					

				Phone	Fax
Saint Johns River Community College					
5001 Saint Johns Ave	Palatka	FL	32177	386-312-4200	312-4048*
*Fax: Admissions ■ TF: 888-757-2293 ■ Web: www.sjrcc.edu/palcamp.html					
Palm Bay 250 Community College Pkwy	Palm Bay	FL	32909	321-632-1111	433-5325*
*Fax: Admissions ■ TF: 888-747-2802 ■ Web: www.brevardcc.edu					
Palm Beach Gardens 3160 PGA Blvd	Palm Beach Gardens	FL	33410	561-207-5300	207-5315
TF: 866-576-7222 ■ Web: www.pbcc.edu					
Gulf Coast Community College					
5230 W Hwy 98	Panama City	FL	32401	850-769-1551	913-3308*
*Fax: Admissions ■ TF: 800-311-3685 ■ Web: www.gc.cc.fl.us					
Pines 16957 Sheridan St	Pembroke Pines	FL	33331	954-201-3601	201-3614
Web: www.broward.edu/locations/pines					
South 7200 Hollywood/Pines Blvd	Pembroke Pines	FL	33024	954-201-8835	201-8060*
*Fax: Admissions ■ Web: www.broward.edu					
Pensacola Junior College 1000 College Blvd	Pensacola	FL	32504	850-484-1000	484-1829*
*Fax: Admissions ■ TF: 888-897-3605 ■ Web: www.pjc.edu					
Warrington 5555 W Hwy 98	Pensacola	FL	32507	850-484-2200	484-2375
Web: www.pjc.edu					
Plant City 1206 N Pk Rd	Plant City	FL	33566	813-757-2102	757-2187
Web: www.hccfl.edu					
Charlotte 26300 Airport Rd	Punta Gorda	FL	33950	941-637-5629	637-3538*
*Fax: Admissions ■ TF: 800-749-2322 ■ Web: www.edison.edu					
Saint Augustine 2990 College Dr	Saint Augustine	FL	32084	904-808-7400	808-7420*
*Fax: Admissions ■ Web: www.sjrcc.edu					
Gibbs PO Box 13489	Saint Petersburg	FL	33733	727-341-4772	341-4792
Web: www.spcollege.edu					
Seminole Community College 100 Weldon Blvd	Sanford	FL	32773	407-328-4722	328-2395*
*Fax: Admissions ■ Web: www.scc-fl.edu					
Seminole 9200 113th St N	Seminole	FL	33772	727-394-6134	394-6132
Web: www.spcollege.edu/se/campus					
Sumter 1405 CR 526A	Sumterville	FL	33585	352-568-0001	568-7515
Web: www.lscc.edu					
Tallahassee Community College					
444 Appleyard Dr	Tallahassee	FL	32304	850-201-6200	201-8474*
*Fax: Admissions ■ Web: www.tcc.fl.edu					
Hillsborough Community College					
Brandon 10414 E Columbus Dr	Tampa	FL	33619	813-253-7801	
Web: www.hccfl.edu/campus/br					
Dale Mabry 4001 Tampa Bay Blvd	Tampa	FL	33614	813-253-7000	253-7400*
*Fax: Admissions ■ Web: www.hccfl.edu					
Ybor City 2112 N 15th St	Tampa	FL	33675	813-253-7602	
Web: www.hccfl.edu/campus/yb					
Titusville 1311 N US 1	Titusville	FL	32796	321-632-1111	433-5115*
*Fax: Admissions ■ TF: 888-747-2802 ■ Web: www.brevardcc.edu					
South 8000 S Tamiami Trail	Venice	FL	34293	941-408-1300	727-6380*
*Fax: Admissions ■ Web: www.mccfl.edu					
Polk Community College 999 Ave H NE	Winter Haven	FL	33881	863-297-1000	297-1060*
*Fax: Admissions ■ Web: www.polk.edu					
Lakeland 999 Ave H NE	Winter Haven	FL	33881	863-297-1000	297-1023
Web: www.polk.edu					

GEORGIA

				Phone	Fax
Darton College 2400 Gillionville Rd	Albany	GA	31707	229-430-6742	317-6607*
*Fax: Admissions ■ TF: 866-775-1214 ■ Web: www.darton.edu					
Atlanta Metropolitan College					
1630 Metropolitan Pkwy SW	Atlanta	GA	30310	404-756-4000	756-4407*
*Fax: Admissions ■ Web: www.atlm.edu					
Gordon College 419 College Dr	Barnesville	GA	30204	770-358-5000	358-5080*
*Fax: Admissions ■ Web: www.gdn.edu					
Coastal Georgia Community College					
3700 Altama Ave	Brunswick	GA	31520	912-264-7235	262-3072*
*Fax: Admissions ■ TF: 800-675-7235 ■ Web: www.cgcc.edu					
Cartersville 5441 Hwy 20 NE	Cartersville	GA	30121	678-872-8000	872-8013
Web: www.highlands.edu					
Clarkston 555 N Indian Creek Dr	Clarkston	GA	30021	678-891-3200	
Web: www.gpc.edu					
Middle Georgia College 1100 2nd St SE	Cochran	GA	31014	478-934-6221	934-3403*
*Fax: Admissions ■ Web: www.mgc.edu					
Andrew College 501 College St	Cuthbert	GA	39840	229-732-2171	732-2176
TF: 800-664-9250 ■ Web: www.andrewcollege.edu					
Georgia Perimeter College					
Decatur 3251 Panthersville Rd	Decatur	GA	30034	678-891-2300	
Web: www.gpc.edu					
Dunwoody 2101 Womack Rd	Dunwoody	GA	30338	770-274-5000	551-3148
Web: www.gpc.edu					
Gainesville State College					
3820 Mundy Mill Rd PO Box 1358	Gainesville	GA	30566	770-718-3639	718-3751*
*Fax: Admissions ■ Web: www.gsc.edu					
Georgia Military College					
201 E Green St	Milledgeville	GA	31061	478-445-2700	445-6520*
*Fax: Admissions ■ TF: 800-342-0413 ■ Web: www.gmc.cc.ga.us					
Emory University Oxford College					
100 Hamill St PO Box 1418	Oxford	GA	30054	770-784-8328	784-8359
TF: 800-723-8328 ■ Web: www.emory.edu					
Georgia Highlands College					
Floyd 3175 Cedartown Hwy	Rome	GA	30161	706-802-5000	295-6341
TF: 800-332-2406 ■ Web: www.highlands.edu					
East Georgia College 131 College Cir	Swainsboro	GA	30401	478-289-2000	289-2140*
*Fax: Admissions ■ Web: www.ega.edu					
Abraham Baldwin Agricultural College					
2802 Moore Hwy ABAC 3	Tifton	GA	31793	229-386-3236	391-5002*
*Fax: Admissions ■ TF: 800-733-3653 ■ Web: www.abac.edu					
Waycross College 2001 S Georgia Pkwy	Waycross	GA	31503	912-285-6130	285-6158*
*Fax: Admissions ■ Web: www.waycross.edu					
Young Harris College PO Box 116	Young Harris	GA	30582	706-379-3111	379-3108*
*Fax: Admissions ■ TF: 800-241-3754 ■ Web: www.yhc.edu					

HAWAII

				Phone	Fax
Hawaii Community College 200 W Kawili St	Hilo	HI	96720	808-974-7662	974-7692*
*Fax: Admissions ■ Web: www.hawcc.hawaii.edu					
University of Hawaii					
Honolulu Community College					
874 Dillingham Blvd	Honolulu	HI	96817	808-845-9129	847-9829*
*Fax: Admissions ■ Web: www.honolulu.hawaii.edu					
Kapiolani Community College					
4303 Diamond Head Rd	Honolulu	HI	96816	808-734-9000	734-9896
Web: www.kcc.hawaii.edu					
Maui Community College 310 W Kaahumanu Ave	Kahului	HI	96732	808-984-3267	242-9618*
*Fax: Admissions ■ TF: 800-479-6692 ■ Web: www.maui.hawaii.edu					
Windward Community College					
45-720 Keaahala Rd	Kaneohe	HI	96744	808-235-7400	235-9148*
*Fax: Admissions ■ Web: www.wcc.hawaii.edu					
Kauai Community College 3-1901 Kaumualii Hwy	Lihue	HI	96766	808-245-8311	245-8220
Web: www.kauai.hawaii.edu					
Leeward Community College 96-045 Ala Ike	Pearl City	HI	96782	808-455-0011	454-8804*
*Fax: Admissions ■ Web: www.lcc.hawaii.edu					
Leeward Community College					
96-045 Ala Ike St	Pearl City	HI	96782	808-455-0001	454-8804*
*Fax: Admissions ■ Web: www.lcc.hawaii.edu					

IDAHO

				Phone	Fax
North Idaho College 1000 W Garden Ave	Coeur d'Alene	ID	83814	208-769-3300	769-3399*
*Fax: Library ■ TF: 877-404-4536 ■ Web: www.nic.edu					
College of Southern Idaho PO Box 1238	Twin Falls	ID	83303	208-733-9554	736-3014*
*Fax: Admissions ■ Web: www.csi.edu					

ILLINOIS

				Phone	Fax
Southwestern Illinois College					
2500 Carlyle Ave	Belleville	IL	62221	618-235-2700	222-9768*
*Fax: Admissions ■ TF: 800-222-5131 ■ Web: www.southwestern.cc.il.us					
Spoon River College 23235 N County 22	Canton	IL	61520	309-647-4645	649-6393*
*Fax: Admissions ■ TF: 800-334-7337 ■ Web: www.spoonrivercollege.net					
John A Logan College					
700 Logan College Rd	Carterville	IL	62918	618-985-3741	985-4433*
*Fax: Admissions ■ Web: www.jal.cc.il.us					
Parkland College 2400 W Bradley Ave	Champaign	IL	61821	217-351-2200	353-2640*
*Fax: Admissions ■ Web: www.parkland.edu					
Harold Washington College 30 E Lake St	Chicago	IL	60601	312-553-6000	553-3075*
*Fax: Admissions ■ Web: hwashington.ccc.edu					
Harry S Truman College 1145 W Wilson Ave	Chicago	IL	60640	773-878-1700	907-4464*
*Fax: Admissions ■ Web: www.trumancollege.cc					
Kennedy-King College 6301 S Halsted St	Chicago	IL	60621	773-602-5000	602-5247*
*Fax: Admissions ■ Web: www.kennedyking.ccc.edu					
Malcolm X College 1900 W Van Buren St	Chicago	IL	60612	312-850-7000	850-7092
Web: www.malcolmx.ccc.edu					
Olive-Harvey College 10001 S Woodlawn Ave	Chicago	IL	60628	773-291-6100	291-6185*
*Fax: Admissions ■ Web: www.oliveharvey.ccc.edu					
Richard J Daley College 7500 S Pulaski Rd	Chicago	IL	60652	773-838-7500	838-7605*
*Fax: Admissions ■ Web: www.daley.ccc.edu					
Saint Augustine College 1345 W Argyle St	Chicago	IL	60640	773-878-8756	878-0937*
*Fax: Admissions ■ Web: www.staugustine.edu					
Wilbur Wright College					
4300 N Narragansett Ave	Chicago	IL	60634	773-777-7900	481-8185
Web: www.wright.ccc.edu					
Prairie State College					
202 S Halsted St	Chicago Heights	IL	60411	708-709-3500	709-3951*
*Fax: Admissions ■ Web: www.prairiestate.edu					
Morton College 3801 S Central Ave	Cicero	IL	60804	708-656-8000	656-9592*
*Fax: Admitting ■ Web: www.morton.edu					
McHenry County College 8900 US Hwy 14	Crystal Lake	IL	60012	815-455-3700	455-3766
Web: www.mchenry.edu					
Danville Area Community College					
2000 E Main St	Danville	IL	61832	217-443-3222	443-8560*
*Fax: Hum Res ■ TF: 888-455-3222 ■ Web: www.dacc.cc.il.us					
Richland Community College 1 College Pk	Decatur	IL	62521	217-875-7200	875-6965*
*Fax: Hum Res ■ Web: www.richland.edu					
Oakton Community College 1600 E Golf Rd	Des Plaines	IL	60016	847-635-1600	635-1890*
*Fax: Admissions ■ Web: www.oakton.edu					
Sauk Valley Community College					
173 Illinois Rt 2	Dixon	IL	61021	815-288-5511	288-3190*
*Fax: Admissions ■ Web: www.svcc.cc.il.us					
Illinois Central College 1 College Dr	East Peoria	IL	61635	309-694-5011	694-8461*
*Fax: Admissions ■ Web: www.icc.edu					
Elgin Community College 1700 Spartan Dr	Elgin	IL	60123	847-697-1000	608-5458*
*Fax: Admissions ■ Web: www.elgin.edu					
Fountain Square 51 S Spring St	Elgin	IL	60120	847-214-6900	608-5458*
*Fax: Admissions ■ Web: www.elgin.edu					
Frontier Community College 2 Frontier Dr	Fairfield	IL	62837	618-842-3711	842-3412*
*Fax: Admissions ■ TF: 877-464-3687 ■ Web: www.iecc.cc.il.us					
Highland Community College					
2998 W Pearl City Rd	Freeport	IL	61032	815-235-6121	235-6130*
*Fax: Admissions ■ Web: www.highland.cc.il.us					
Carl Sandburg College					
2400 Tom L Wilson Blvd	Galesburg	IL	61401	309-344-2518	344-3291
TF: 877-236-1862 ■ Web: www.sandburg.edu					
College of DuPage 425 Fawell Blvd	Glen Ellyn	IL	60137	630-858-2800	790-2686*
*Fax: Admissions ■ Web: www.cod.edu					

	City	State	Zip	Phone	Fax
Lewis & Clark Community College					
5800 Godfrey Rd	Godfrey	IL	62035	618-466-3411	468-2310*
*Fax: Admissions ■ Web: www.lc.edu					
Granite City 4950 Maryville Rd	Granite City	IL	62040	618-931-0600	931-1598
Web: www.southwestern.cc.il.us					
College of Lake County					
Grayslake 19351 W Washington St	Grayslake	IL	60030	847-223-6601	543-3061*
*Fax: Admissions ■ Web: www.clcillinois.edu					
Southeastern Illinois College					
3575 College Rd	Harrisburg	IL	62946	618-252-6376	252-3062*
*Fax: Admissions ■ TF: 866-338-2742 ■ Web: www.sic.edu					
Rend Lake College 468 N Ken Gray Pkwy	Ina	IL	62846	618-437-5321	437-5677*
*Fax: Admitting ■ TF: 800-369-5321 ■ Web: www.rlc.cc.il.us					
Joliet Junior College 1215 Houbolt Rd	Joliet	IL	60431	815-729-9020	280-2493*
*Fax: Admissions ■ TF: 800-636-9886 ■ Web: www.jjc.edu					
Kankakee Community College 100 College Dr	Kankakee	IL	60901	815-933-0345	802-8101*
*Fax: Admissions ■ Web: www.kcc.edu					
Black Hawk College					
East 1501 State Hwy 78	Kewanee	IL	61443	309-852-5671	856-6005*
*Fax: Admissions ■ TF: 800-233-5671 ■ Web: www.bhc.edu					
Lincoln College 300 Keokuk St	Lincoln	IL	62656	217-732-3155	732-8859
TF: 800-569-0556 ■ Web: www.lincolncollege.edu					
Kishwaukee College 21193 Malta Rd	Malta	IL	60150	815-825-2086	825-2306
Web: www.kishwaukeecollege.edu					
Lake Land College 5001 Lake Land Blvd	Mattoon	IL	61938	217-234-5253	234-5390*
*Fax: Admissions ■ Web: www.lakeland.cc.il.us					
Quad Cities 6600 34th Ave	Moline	IL	61265	309-796-5000	796-5209*
*Fax: Admissions ■ TF: 800-334-1311 ■ Web: www.bhc.edu					
Wabash Valley College 2200 College Dr	Mount Carmel	IL	62863	618-262-8641	262-8641*
*Fax: Admissions ■ TF: 866-982-4322 ■ Web: www.iecc.cc.il.us					
Heartland Community College 1500 W Raab Rd	Normal	IL	61761	309-268-8000	268-7992
Web: www.hcc.cc.il.us					
Illinois Valley Community College					
815 N Orlando Smith Ave	Oglesby	IL	61348	815-224-2720	224-3033*
*Fax: Admissions ■ Web: www.ivcc.edu					
Olney Central College 305 N W St	Olney	IL	62450	618-395-4351	395-1261*
*Fax: Admissions ■ TF: 866-622-4322 ■ Web: www.iecc.cc.il.us					
Harper College 1200 W Algonquin Rd	Palatine	IL	60067	847-925-6000	925-6044*
*Fax: Admissions ■ Web: www.harpercollege.edu					
Moraine Valley Community College					
9000 W College Pkwy	Palos Hills	IL	60465	708-974-4300	974-0974
Web: www.morainevalley.edu					
Pittsfield 1308 W Washington St	Pittsfield	IL	62363	217-285-5319	641-4192
Web: www.jwcc.edu					
John Wood Community College 1301 S 48th St	Quincy	IL	62305	217-224-6500	641-4192*
*Fax: Admissions ■ Web: www.jwcc.edu					
Red Bud 500 W S 4th St	Red Bud	IL	62278	618-282-6682	282-6568
Web: www.southwestern.cc.il.us					
Triton College 2000 N 5th Ave	River Grove	IL	60171	708-456-0300	583-3147*
*Fax: Admissions ■ TF: 800-942-7404 ■ Web: www.triton.edu					
Lincoln Trail College 11220 State Hwy 1	Robinson	IL	62454	618-544-8657	544-4705*
*Fax: Admissions ■ TF: 866-582-4322 ■ Web: www.iecc.cc.il.us					
Rock Valley College 3301 N Mulford Rd	Rockford	IL	61114	815-921-7821	921-4269*
*Fax: Admissions ■ TF: 800-973-7821 ■ Web: www.rockvalleycollege.edu					
North 1125 135th St	Romeoville	IL	60446	815-886-3000	886-4331
TF: 800-636-9886 ■ Web: www.jjc.edu					
Skokie Campus 7701 N Lincoln Ave	Skokie	IL	60077	847-635-1600	635-1497
Web: www.oakton.edu					
South Suburban College					
15800 S State St	South Holland	IL	60473	708-596-2000	225-5806*
*Fax: Admissions ■ Web: www.southsuburbancollege.edu					
Lincoln Land Community College					
5250 Shepherd Rd PO Box 19256	Springfield	IL	62794	217-786-2200	786-2468
TF: 800-727-4161 ■ Web: www.llcc.edu					
Springfield College in Illinois - Benedictine University					
1500 N 5th St	Springfield	IL	62702	217-525-1420	525-1497
TF: 800-635-7289 ■ Web: www.sci.edu					
Waubonsee Community College					
Rt 47 At Waubonsee Dr	Sugar Grove	IL	60554	630-466-7900	466-4964*
*Fax: Admissions ■ Web: www.waubonsee.edu					
Shawnee Community College					
8364 Shawnee College Rd	Ullin	IL	62992	618-634-3200	634-3300*
*Fax: Admitting ■ Web: www.shawneecc.edu					
Lakeshore 33 N Genessee St	Waukegan	IL	60085	847-623-8686	543-2170*
*Fax: Admissions ■ Web: www.clcillinois.edu					

INDIANA

	City	State	Zip	Phone	Fax
Jasper 850 College Ave	Jasper	IN	47546	812-482-3030	481-5960*
*Fax: Admissions ■ TF: 800-809-8852 ■ Web: www.vujc.vinu.edu					
Vincennes University 1002 N 1st St	Vincennes	IN	47591	812-888-4313	888-5707*
*Fax: Admissions ■ TF: 800-742-9198 ■ Web: www.vinu.edu					

IOWA

	City	State	Zip	Phone	Fax
Des Moines Area Community College					
Ankeny 2006 S Ankeny Blvd	Ankeny	IA	50021	515-964-6200	964-6391*
*Fax: Admissions ■ TF: 800-362-2127 ■ Web: www.dmacc.edu					
Scott Community College 500 Belmont Rd	Bettendorf	IA	52722	563-441-4001	441-4131*
*Fax: Admissions ■ TF: 888-336-3907 ■ Web: www.eicc.edu					
Boone 1125 Hancock Dr	Boone	IA	50036	515-432-7203	433-5033*
*Fax: Admissions ■ TF: 800-362-2127 ■ Web: www.dmacc.edu					
Northeast Iowa Community College					
Calmar 1625 Hwy 150 S PO Box 400	Calmar	IA	52132	563-562-3263	562-4369*
*Fax: Admissions ■ TF: 800-728-2256 ■ Web: www.nicc.edu					
Carroll 906 N Grant Rd	Carroll	IA	51401	712-792-1755	792-6358
TF: 800-622-3334 ■ Web: www.dmacc.edu					
Kirkwood Community College					
6301 Kirkwood Blvd SW	Cedar Rapids	IA	52404	319-398-5411	398-1244*
*Fax: Admissions ■ TF: 800-332-2055 ■ Web: www.kirkwood.edu					
Iowa Western Community College					
Clarinda 923 E Washington St	Clarinda	IA	51632	712-542-5117	542-4608*
*Fax: Admissions ■ TF: 800-521-2073 ■ Web: www.iwcc.cc.ia.us					
Clinton Community College 1000 Lincoln Blvd	Clinton	IA	52732	563-244-7001	244-7107*
*Fax: Library ■ Web: www.eicc.edu					
Southwestern Community College					
1501 W Townline St	Creston	IA	50801	641-782-7081	782-3312*
*Fax: Admissions ■ TF: 800-247-4023 ■ Web: www.swcciowa.edu					
Urban/Des Moines 1100 7th St	Des Moines	IA	50314	515-244-4226	248-7253
TF: 800-622-3334 ■ Web: www.dmacc.edu					
Iowa Lakes Community College					
300 S 18th St	Estherville	IA	51334	712-362-2604	362-8363*
*Fax: Admissions ■ TF: 800-242-5106 ■ Web: www.iowalakes.edu					
Iowa Central Community College 330 Ave M	Fort Dodge	IA	50501	515-576-7201	576-7724*
*Fax: Admissions ■ TF: 800-362-2793 ■ Web: www.iccc.cc.ia.us					
Ellsworth Community College					
1100 College Ave	Iowa Falls	IA	50126	641-648-4611	648-3128*
*Fax: Admissions ■ TF: 800-322-9235 ■ Web: www.iavalley.cc.ia.us					
Southeastern Community College South					
335 Messenger Rd	Keokuk	IA	52632	319-524-3221	524-8621*
*Fax: Admissions ■ Web: www.secc.cc.ia.edu					
Marshalltown Community College					
3700 S Ctr St	Marshalltown	IA	50158	641-752-7106	752-8149
TF: 866-622-4748 ■ Web: www.iavalley.cc.ia.us					
North Iowa Area Community College					
500 College Dr	Mason City	IA	50401	641-423-1264	422-4385*
*Fax: Admissions ■ TF: 888-466-4222 ■ Web: www.niacc.cc.ia.us					
Muscatine Community College					
152 Colorado St	Muscatine	IA	52761	563-288-6001	288-6104*
*Fax: Admissions ■ TF: 888-336-3907 ■ Web: www.eicc.edu					
Indian Hills Community College					
525 Grandview Ave	Ottumwa	IA	52501	641-683-5111	683-5741
TF: 800-726-2585 ■ Web: www.ihcc.cc.ia.us					
Peosta 10250 Sundown Rd	Peosta	IA	52068	563-556-5110	557-0347*
*Fax: Admissions ■ TF: 800-728-7367 ■ Web: www.nicc.edu					
Northwest Iowa Community College 603 W Pk St	Sheldon	IA	51201	712-324-5061	324-4136
TF: 800-352-4907 ■ Web: www.nwicc.edu					
Hawkeye Community College 1501 E Orange Rd	Waterloo	IA	50704	319-296-2320	296-2874*
*Fax: Admissions ■ TF: 800-670-4769 ■ Web: www.hawkeye.cc.ia.us					
Southeastern Community College North					
1500 W Agency Rd	West Burlington	IA	52655	319-752-2731	758-6725*
*Fax: Admissions ■ Web: www.secc.cc.ia.us					

KANSAS

	City	State	Zip	Phone	Fax
Cowley County Community College & Area Vocational-Technical School					
PO Box 1147	Arkansas City	KS	67005	620-442-0430	441-5350
TF: 800-593-2222 ■ Web: www.cowley.edu					
Neosho County Community College					
800 W 14th St	Chanute	KS	66720	620-431-2820	431-6056*
*Fax: Admissions ■ Web: www.neosho.edu					
Coffeyville Community College					
400 W 11th St	Coffeyville	KS	67337	620-251-7700	252-7010*
*Fax: Admissions ■ TF: 800-782-4732 ■ Web: www.coffeyville.edu					
Colby Community College 1255 S Range Ave	Colby	KS	67701	785-462-3984	460-4691*
*Fax: Admissions ■ TF: 888-634-9350 ■ Web: www.colbycc.edu					
Cloud County Community College					
2221 Campus Dr	Concordia	KS	66901	785-243-1435	243-1040*
*Fax: Admissions ■ TF: 800-729-5101 ■ Web: www.cloud.edu					
Dodge City Community College					
2501 N 14th Ave	Dodge City	KS	67801	620-225-1321	227-9277*
*Fax: Admissions ■ TF: 800-367-3222 ■ Web: www.dc3.edu					
Butler Community College					
901 S Haverhill Rd	El Dorado	KS	67042	316-321-2222	322-3316*
*Fax: Admissions ■ Web: www.butlercc.edu					
Fort Scott Community College					
2108 S Horton St	Fort Scott	KS	66701	620-223-2700	223-6530*
*Fax: Admissions ■ TF: 800-874-3722 ■ Web: www.fortscott.edu					
Garden City Community College					
801 N Campus Dr	Garden City	KS	67846	620-276-7611	276-9573
TF: 800-658-1696 ■ Web: www.gcccks.edu					
Barton County Community College					
245 NE 30th Rd	Great Bend	KS	67530	620-792-2701	786-1160*
*Fax: Admissions ■ TF: 800-722-6842 ■ Web: www.bartonccc.edu					
Hesston College 325 S College Dr PO Box 3000	Hesston	KS	67062	620-327-4221	327-8300
TF: 800-995-2757 ■ Web: www.hesston.edu					
Highland Community College 606 W Main St	Highland	KS	66035	785-442-6000	442-6106*
*Fax: Admissions ■ Web: www.highlandcc.edu					
Hutchinson Community College & Area Vocational School					
1300 N Plum St	Hutchinson	KS	67501	620-665-3500	728-8199*
*Fax: Admissions ■ TF: 800-289-3501 ■ Web: www.hutchcc.edu					
Independence Community College					
1057 W College Ave PO Box 708	Independence	KS	67301	620-331-4100	331-0946*
*Fax: Admissions ■ TF: 800-842-6063 ■ Web: www.indy.cc.ks.us					
Allen County Community College					
1801 N Cottonwood St	Iola	KS	66749	620-365-5116	365-7406*
*Fax: Admissions ■ Web: www.allencc.edu					
Donnelly College 608 N 18th St	Kansas City	KS	66102	913-621-6070	621-8734*
*Fax: Admissions ■ Web: www.donnelly.edu					
Kansas City Kansas Community College					
7250 State Ave	Kansas City	KS	66112	913-334-1100	288-7648*
*Fax: Admissions ■ Web: www.kckcc.edu					
Seward County Community College					
1801 N Campus Ave PO Box 1137	Liberal	KS	67905	620-624-1951	629-2725
TF: 800-373-9951 ■ Web: www.sccc.edu					

Phone Fax

Ottawa 226 S Beech St. Ottawa KS 66067 785-242-2067 242-2068*
*Fax: Admissions ■ Web: www.neosho.edu
Johnson County Community College
12345 College Blvd Overland Park KS 66210 913-469-8500 469-2524*
*Fax: Admissions ■ TF: 866-896-5893 ■ Web: www.jccc.net
Labette Community College 200 S 14th St Parsons KS 67357 620-421-6700 421-0180*
*Fax: Admissions ■ TF: 888-522-3883 ■ Web: www.labette.cc.ks.us
Pratt Community College 348 NE SR-61 Pratt KS 67124 620-672-5641 672-5288*
*Fax: Admissions ■ Web: www.prattcc.edu

KENTUCKY

Phone Fax

Ashland Community & Technical College
1400 College Dr Ashland KY 41101 606-329-2999 326-2192*
*Fax: Admissions ■ TF: 800-928-4256 ■ Web: www.ashland.kctcs.edu
Southeast Kentucky Community & Technical College
Cumberland 700 College Rd Cumberland KY 40823 606-589-2145 589-3175*
*Fax: Admissions ■ TF: 888-274-7322 ■ Web: www.secc.kctcs.edu
Elizabethtown Community & Technical College
600 Cs-1124-30 Elizabethtown KY 42701 270-769-2371 769-0736
TF: 877-246-2322 ■ Web: www.elizabethtown.kctcs.edu
Hazard Community & Technical College
1 Community College Dr Hazard KY 41701 606-436-5721 439-2988
TF: 800-246-7521 ■ Web: www.hazcc.kctcs.edu
Hazard Campus 101 Vo Tech Dr Hazard KY 41701 606-435-6101 487-8417
TF: 800-246-7521 ■ Web: www.hazcc.kctcs.edu
Henderson Community College
2660 S Green St Henderson KY 42420 270-827-1867 831-9612*
*Fax: Admissions ■ Web: www.hencc.kctcs.net
Hopkinsville Community College 720 N Dr. Hopkinsville KY 42240 270-886-3921 886-0237*
*Fax: Admissions ■ Web: www.hopcc.kctcs.net
Lees Campus 601 Jefferson Ave Jackson KY 41339 606-666-7521
TF: 800-246-7521 ■ Web: www.hazard.kctcs.edu
Bluegrass Community & Technical College
Cooper Campus 470 Cooper Dr Lexington KY 40506 859-246-6200 246-4666
TF: 866-774-4872 ■ Web: www.bluegrass.kctcs.edu
Jefferson Community & Technical College
109 E Broadway Louisville KY 40202 502-584-0181 213-2540*
*Fax: Admissions ■ Web: www.jefferson.kctcs.edu
Madisonville Community College
2000 College Dr Madisonville KY 42431 270-821-2250 824-1864*
*Fax: Admissions ■ TF: 866-227-4812 ■ Web: www.madisonville.kctcs.edu
Maysville Community & Technical College
1755 US 68 Maysville KY 41056 606-759-7141 759-5818
Web: www.maysville.kctcs.edu
Middlesboro 1300 Chichester Ave. Middlesboro KY 40965 606-242-2145 248-3233
TF: 888-274-7322 ■ Web: www.secc.kctcs.edu
West Kentucky Community & Technical College
4810 Alben Barkley Dr PO Box 7380 Paducah KY 42001 270-554-9200 554-6203*
*Fax: Admissions ■ Web: www.westkentucky.kctcs.edu
Mayo 513 3rd St Paintsville KY 41240 606-789-5321 789-9753
Web: www.kctcs.net
Big Sandy Community & Technical College
1 Bert T Combs Dr Prestonsburg KY 41653 606-886-3863 886-6943*
*Fax: Admissions ■ TF: 888-641-4132 ■ Web: www.bigsandy.kctcs.edu
Saint Catharine College
2735 Bardstown Rd Saint Catharine KY 40061 859-336-5082 336-5031*
*Fax: Admissions ■ Web: www.sccky.edu
Somerset Community College
808 Monticello St. Somerset KY 42501 606-679-8501 676-9065
TF: 877-629-9722 ■ Web: www.somerset.kctcs.edu
Whitesburg 2 Long Ave. Whitesburg KY 41858 606-633-0279 589-3377
TF: 888-274-7322 ■ Web: www.secc.kctcs.edu

LOUISIANA

Phone Fax

Baton Rouge Community College
5310 Florida Blvd. Baton Rouge LA 70806 225-216-8000 216-8010*
*Fax: Admissions ■ TF: 800-601-4558 ■ Web: www.brcc.cc.la.us
Bossier Parish Community College
6220 E Texas St Bossier City LA 71111 318-678-6000 678-6390
Web: www.bpcc.edu
Elaine P Nunez Community College
3710 Paris Rd. Chalmette LA 70043 504-278-7497 278-7480
TF: 866-825-1954 ■ Web: www.nunez.edu
Eunice PO Box 1129 Eunice LA 70535 337-457-7311 550-1306*
*Fax: Admissions ■ Web: www.lsue.edu
Louisiana Delta Community College
1201 Bayou Dr Monroe LA 71203 318-342-3700 342-3747
TF: 866-500-5322 ■ Web: www.ladelta.cc.la.us
Southern University
Shreveport 3050 ML King Jr Dr. Shreveport LA 71107 318-674-3300 674-3344*
*Fax: Admissions ■ TF: 800-458-1472 ■ Web: www.susla.edu

MAINE

Phone Fax

Washington County Community College
1 College Dr Calais ME 04619 207-454-1000 454-1092
Web: www.wccc.me.edu
Kennebec Valley Community College
92 Western Ave. Fairfield ME 04937 207-453-5000 453-5010
TF: 800-528-5882 ■ Web: www.kvcc.me.edu
York County Community College 112 College Dr Wells ME 04090 207-646-9282 641-0837
TF: 800-580-3820 ■ Web: www.yccc.edu

MARYLAND

Phone Fax

Baltimore City Community College
2901 Liberty Heights Ave Baltimore MD 21215 410-462-8000 462-8345*
*Fax: Admissions ■ TF: 888-203-1261 ■ Web: www.bccc.edu
Dundalk 7200 Sollers Pt Rd. Baltimore MD 21222 410-282-6700 285-9903
Web: www.ccbcmd.edu
Essex 7201 Rossville Blvd. Baltimore MD 21237 410-682-6000 686-9503*
*Fax: Admissions ■ TF: 800-832-0262 ■ Web: www.ccbcmd.edu
Harford Community College 401 Thomas Run Rd Bel Air MD 21015 410-879-8920 836-4169*
*Fax: Admissions ■ Web: www.harford.edu
Community College of Baltimore County
Catonsville 800 S Rolling Rd. Catonsville MD 21228 410-455-6050 719-6546*
*Fax: Admissions ■ Web: www.ccbcmd.edu
Howard Community College
10901 Little Patuxent Pkwy. Columbia MD 21044 410-772-4800 772-4589*
*Fax: Admissions ■ TF: 800-234-9981 ■ Web: www.howardcc.edu
Allegany College of Maryland
12401 Willowbrook Rd SE Cumberland MD 21502 301-784-5000 784-5027*
*Fax: Admissions ■ Web: www.allegany.edu
Frederick Community College
7932 Opossumtown Pike Frederick MD 21702 301-846-2400 846-2498
Web: www.frederick.edu
Hagerstown Community College
11400 Robinwood Dr Hagerstown MD 21742 301-790-2800 791-9165*
*Fax: Admissions ■ Web: www.hagerstowncc.edu
Hunt Valley 11101 McCormick Rd. Hunt Valley MD 21031 410-771-6835 527-0993
Web: www.ccbcmd.edu
La Plata 8730 Mitchell Rd PO Box 910 La Plata MD 20646 301-934-2251 870-3008
Web: www.csmd.edu
Prince George's Community College 301 Largo Rd Largo MD 20774 301-336-6000 322-0119*
*Fax: Admissions ■ Web: www.pgcc.edu
College of Southern Maryland
Leonardtown 22950 Hollywood Rd Leonardtown MD 20650 240-725-5300 725-5400*
*Fax: Admissions ■ TF: 800-933-9177 ■ Web: www.csmd.edu
Garrett College 687 Mosser Rd McHenry MD 21541 301-387-3000 387-3038*
*Fax: Admissions ■ Web: www.garrettcollege.edu
Cecil Community College 1 Seahawk Dr. North East MD 21901 410-287-6060 287-1001*
*Fax: Admissions ■ Web: www.cecilcc.edu
Owings Mills 110 Painters Mill Rd Owings Mills MD 21117 410-363-4111 363-6575
Web: www.ccbcmd.edu
Prince Frederick
115 J W Williams Rd Prince Frederick MD 20678 443-550-6000 550-6100
TF: 800-933-9177 ■ Web: www.csmd.edu
Montgomery College Rockville
51 Mannakee St Rockville MD 20850 301-279-5000 279-5037*
*Fax: Admissions ■ Web: www.montgomerycollege.edu/rvhome
Wor-Wic Community College 32000 Campus Dr Salisbury MD 21804 410-334-2800 334-2954*
*Fax: Admissions ■ Web: www.worwic.edu
Carroll Community College
1601 Washington Rd Westminster MD 21157 410-386-8000 386-8431*
*Fax: Admissions ■ Web: www.carrollcc.edu
Chesapeake College PO Box 8 Wye Mills MD 21679 410-758-1537 827-5878*
*Fax: Admissions ■ Web: www.chesapeake.edu

MASSACHUSETTS

Phone Fax

Attleboro 11 Field St Attleboro MA 02703 508-226-2484 222-7638
TF: 888-710-8999 ■ Web: www.srvweb.bristol.mass.edu
Middlesex Community College 590 Springs Rd Bedford MA 01730 781-275-8910 280-3603
Web: www.middlesex.mass.edu
Bunker Hill Community College
Charlestown 250 New Rutherford Ave Boston MA 02129 617-228-2000 228-2082*
*Fax: Admissions ■ Web: www.bhcc.mass.edu
Fisher College 118 Beacon St. Boston MA 02116 617-236-8800 236-5473*
*Fax: Admissions ■ TF: 800-446-1226 ■ Web: www.fisher.edu
Massasoit Community College
1 Massasoit Blvd Brockton MA 02302 508-588-9100 427-1255*
*Fax: Admissions ■ Web: www.massasoit.mass.edu
Chelsea 175 Hawthorne St Bellingham Sq Chelsea MA 02150 617-228-2101 228-2106
Web: www.bhcc.mass.edu
North Shore Community College 1 Ferncroft Rd Danvers MA 01923 978-762-4000 762-4015*
*Fax: Admissions ■ Web: www.northshore.edu
Bristol Community College 777 Elsbree St. Fall River MA 02720 508-678-2811 730-3255*
*Fax: Admissions ■ Web: www.bristol.mass.edu
Framingham 19 Flagg Dr. Framingham MA 01702 508-270-4000 872-4067
Web: www.massbay.edu
Dean College 99 Main St. Franklin MA 02038 508-541-1508 541-8726*
*Fax: Admissions ■ TF: 877-879-3326 ■ Web: www.dean.edu
Mount Wachusett Community College
444 Green St. Gardner MA 01440 978-632-6600 630-9554*
*Fax: Admissions ■ Web: www.mwcc.mass.edu
Greenfield Community College 1 College Dr. Greenfield MA 01301 413-775-1837 775-1838*
*Fax: Admissions ■ Web: www.gcc.mass.edu
Northern Essex Community College
100 Elliott St. Haverhill MA 01830 978-556-3000 556-3729*
*Fax: Admissions ■ Web: www.necc.mass.edu
Holyoke Community College 303 Homestead Ave Holyoke MA 01040 413-538-7000 552-2192*
*Fax: Admissions ■ Web: www.hcc.edu
New Bedford 188 Union St New Bedford MA 02740 508-984-8226 730-3264
Web: www.srvweb.bristol.mass.edu
Berkshire Community College 1350 W St Pittsfield MA 01201 413-499-4660 447-7840
Web: www.berkshirecc.edu
Plymouth 36 Cordage Pk Cir Plymouth MA 02360 508-747-0400 747-8168
Web: www.quincycollege.edu
Quincy College 150 Newport Ave Ext # 1 Quincy MA 02171 617-984-1600 984-1794
TF: 800-698-1700 ■ Web: www.quincycollege.edu

	City	State	ZIP	Phone	Fax
Roxbury Community College					
1234 Columbus Ave	Roxbury Crossing	MA	02120	617-541-5310	427-5316*
**Fax:* Admitting ■ *Web:* www.rcc.mass.edu					
Springfield Technical Community College					
1 Armory Sq PO Box 900	Springfield	MA	01102	413-781-7822	746-0344*
**Fax:* Admissions ■ *Web:* www.stcc.edu					
Marian Court College 35 Littles Pt Rd	Swampscott	MA	01907	781-595-6768	595-3560*
**Fax:* Admissions ■ *TF:* 800-418-9868 ■ *Web:* www.mariancourt.edu					
Massachusetts Bay Community College					
Wellesley Hills 50 Oakland St	Wellesley Hills	MA	02481	781-239-3000	239-1047
Web: www.massbay.edu					
Cape Cod Community College					
2240 Iyanough Rd	West Barnstable	MA	02668	508-362-2131	375-4089*
**Fax:* Admissions ■ *TF:* 877-846-3672 ■ *Web:* www.capecod.edu					
Quinsigamond Community College					
670 W Boylston St	Worcester	MA	01606	508-853-2300	854-4357*
**Fax:* Admissions ■ *Web:* www.qcc.edu					

MICHIGAN

	City	State	ZIP	Phone	Fax
Alpena Community College 666 Johnson St	Alpena	MI	49707	989-356-9021	358-7561
TF: 888-468-6222 ■ *Web:* www.alpena.cc.mi.us					
Washtenaw Community College					
4800 E Huron River Dr PO Box 1610	Ann Arbor	MI	48106	734-973-3300	677-5408*
**Fax:* Admissions ■ *Web:* www.wccnet.edu					
Auburn Hills 2900 Featherstone Rd	Auburn Hills	MI	48326	248-232-4100	
Web: www.oaklandcc.edu					
Keweenaw Bay Ojibwa Community College					
111 Beartown Rd	Baraga	MI	49908	906-353-4600	353-8107
Web: www.kbocc.org					
Kellogg Community College 450 N Ave	Battle Creek	MI	49017	269-965-3931	966-4089*
**Fax:* Admissions ■ *Web:* www.kellogg.cc.mi.us					
Western 9555 Haggerty Rd	Belleville	MI	48111	734-699-7008	699-7152
Web: www.wcccd.edu					
Lake Michigan College					
2755 E Napier Ave	Benton Harbor	MI	49022	269-927-3571	927-6875*
**Fax:* Admissions ■ *Web:* www.lakemichigancollege.edu					
Oakland Community College					
2480 Opdyke Rd	Bloomfield Hills	MI	48304	248-341-2000	341-2199
Web: www.oaklandcc.edu					
Southfield 2480 Opdyke Rd	Bloomfield Hills	MI	48304	248-341-2000	233-2828*
**Fax:* Library ■ *Web:* www.oaklandcc.edu					
Bay Mills Community College					
12214 W Lakeshore Dr	Brimley	MI	49715	906-248-3354	248-3351
TF: 800-844-2622 ■ *Web:* www.bmcc.edu					
Glen Oaks Community College					
62249 Shimmel Rd	Centreville	MI	49032	269-467-9945	467-9068*
**Fax:* Admissions ■ *TF:* 888-994-7818 ■ *Web:* www.glenoaks.edu					
Macomb Community College					
Center 44575 Garfield Rd	Clinton Township	MI	48038	586-286-2000	286-4787*
**Fax:* Admissions ■ *TF:* 866-622-6624 ■ *Web:* www.macomb.edu					
Henry Ford Community College					
5101 Evergreen Rd	Dearborn	MI	48128	313-845-9600	845-9891*
**Fax:* Admissions ■ *TF:* 800-585-4322 ■ *Web:* www.hfcc.edu					
Downtown 1001 W Fort St	Detroit	MI	48226	313-496-2758	961-9648
Web: www.wcccd.edu					
Eastern 5901 Conner	Detroit	MI	48213	313-922-3311	922-1104
Web: www.wcccd.edu					
Northwest 8200 W Outer Dr	Detroit	MI	48219	313-943-4000	943-4025
Web: www.wcccd.edu					
Southwestern Michigan College					
58900 Cherry Grove Rd	Dowagiac	MI	49047	269-782-1000	782-1331*
**Fax:* Admissions ■ *TF:* 800-456-8675 ■ *Web:* www.smc.cc.mi.us					
Bay de Noc Community College					
2001 N Lincoln Rd	Escanaba	MI	49829	906-786-5802	786-8515*
**Fax:* Admissions ■ *TF:* 800-221-2001 ■ *Web:* www.baydenoc.cc.mi.us					
Orchard Ridge 27055 Orchard Lake Rd	Farmington Hills	MI	48334	248-522-3400	522-3530*
**Fax:* Library ■ *Web:* www.oaklandcc.edu					
Charles Stewart Mott Community College					
1401 E Ct St	Flint	MI	48503	810-762-0200	762-5611
Web: www.mcc.edu					
Grand Rapids Community College					
143 Bostwick Ave NE	Grand Rapids	MI	49503	616-234-4000	234-4107*
**Fax:* Admissions ■ *Web:* www.grcc.edu					
Mid Michigan Community College					
1375 S Clare Ave	Harrison	MI	48625	989-386-6622	386-6613*
**Fax:* Admissions ■ *Web:* www.midmich.cc.mi.us					
Hillsdale 3120 W Carleton Rd PO Box 712	Hillsdale	MI	49242	517-437-3343	437-0232
Web: www.jccmi.edu					
West 1401 S Carpenter Ave	Iron Mountain	MI	49801	906-774-8547	774-1910
Web: www.baydenoc.cc.mi.us					
Gogebic Community College E 4946 Jackson Rd	Ironwood	MI	49938	906-932-4231	932-0868*
**Fax:* Admissions ■ *TF:* 800-682-5910 ■ *Web:* www.gogebic.cc.mi.us					
Jackson Community College 2111 Emmons Rd	Jackson	MI	49201	517-787-0800	796-8631*
**Fax:* Admissions ■ *TF:* 888-522-7344 ■ *Web:* www.jccmi.edu					
Kalamazoo Valley Community College					
Arcadia Commons 202 N Rose St	Kalamazoo	MI	49003	269-373-7800	373-7892
Web: www.puma.kvcc.edu					
Texas Township 6767 W 'O' Ave	Kalamazoo	MI	49003	269-488-4400	488-4161*
**Fax:* Admissions ■ *Web:* www.kvcc.edu					
Lansing Community College					
419 N Washington Sq	Lansing	MI	48933	517-483-1957	483-9668
TF: 800-644-4522 ■ *Web:* www.lansing.cc.mi.us					
Schoolcraft College 18600 Haggerty Rd	Livonia	MI	48152	734-462-4400	462-4553*
**Fax:* Admissions ■ *Web:* www.schoolcraft.edu					
Monroe County Community College					
1555 S Raisinville Rd	Monroe	MI	48161	734-242-7300	242-9711*
**Fax:* Admissions ■ *TF:* 877-937-6222 ■ *Web:* www.monroeccc.edu					
Mount Pleasant 5805 E Pickard Ave	Mount Pleasant	MI	48858	989-773-6622	772-2386
Web: www.midmich.cc.mi.us					
Saginaw Chippewa Tribal College					
2274 Enterprise Dr	Mount Pleasant	MI	48858	989-775-4123	775-4528
Web: www.sagchip.org					
Muskegon Community College					
221 S Quarterline Rd	Muskegon	MI	49442	231-773-9131	777-0255*
**Fax:* Admissions ■ *TF:* 866-711-4622 ■ *Web:* www.muskegon.cc.mi.us					
Bertrand Crossing 1905 Foundation Dr	Niles	MI	49120	269-695-1391	695-2999
TF: 800-252-1562 ■ *Web:* www.lakemichigancollege.edu					
Niles Area 2229 US 12 E	Niles	MI	49120	269-687-1600	684-2281
TF: 800-456-8675 ■ *Web:* www.smc.cc.mi.us					
North Central Michigan College					
1515 Howard St	Petoskey	MI	49770	231-348-6605	348-6672*
**Fax:* Admissions ■ *TF:* 888-298-6605 ■ *Web:* www.ncmich.edu					
Saint Clair County Community College					
323 Erie St PO Box 5015	Port Huron	MI	48061	810-984-3881	989-5541
Web: www.sc4.edu					
Kirtland Community College					
10775 N St Helen Rd	Roscommon	MI	48653	989-275-5121	275-6789
Web: www.kirtland.edu					
Royal Oak 739 S Washington Ave	Royal Oak	MI	48067	248-246-2400	246-2520*
**Fax:* Library ■ *Web:* www.oaklandcc.edu					
West Shore Community College PO Box 277	Scottville	MI	49454	231-845-6211	845-3944*
**Fax:* Admissions ■ *TF:* 800-848-9722 ■ *Web:* www.westshore.edu					
Montcalm Community College 2800 College Dr	Sidney	MI	48885	989-328-2111	328-2950*
**Fax:* Admissions ■ *Web:* www.montcalm.edu					
South Haven 125 Veterans Blvd	South Haven	MI	49090	269-639-8442	637-7515
TF: 800-252-1562 ■ *Web:* www.lakemichigancollege.edu					
Wayne County Community College					
Downriver 21000 Northline Rd	Taylor	MI	48180	734-946-3500	374-0240
Web: www.wcccd.edu					
Northwestern Michigan College					
1701 E Front St	Traverse City	MI	49686	231-995-1000	995-1339*
**Fax:* Admissions ■ *TF:* 800-748-0566 ■ *Web:* www.nmc.edu					
Delta College 1961 Delta Rd	University Center	MI	48710	989-686-9000	667-2202*
**Fax:* Admissions ■ *Web:* www.delta.edu					
South 14500 E 12-Mile Rd	Warren	MI	48088	586-445-7000	445-7140*
**Fax:* Admissions ■ *TF:* 866-622-6624 ■ *Web:* www.macomb.edu					
Highland Lakes 7350 Cooley Lake Rd	Waterford	MI	48327	248-942-3100	942-3113
Web: www.oaklandcc.edu					

MINNESOTA

	City	State	ZIP	Phone	Fax
Riverland Community College 1900 8th Ave NW	Austin	MN	55912	507-433-0600	433-0515
TF: 800-247-5039 ■ *Web:* www.riverland.edu					
Normandale Community College					
9700 France Ave S	Bloomington	MN	55431	952-487-8200	487-8230*
**Fax:* Admissions ■ *TF:* 866-880-8740 ■ *Web:* www.normandale.edu					
Central Lakes College					
Brainerd 501 W College Dr	Brainerd	MN	56401	218-855-8199	855-8057*
**Fax:* Admissions ■ *TF:* 800-933-0346 ■ *Web:* www.clcmn.edu					
North Hennepin Community College					
7411 85th Ave N	Brooklyn Park	MN	55445	763-424-0702	424-0929*
**Fax:* Admissions ■ *TF:* 800-818-0395 ■ *Web:* www.nhcc.edu					
Cambridge 300 Polk St S	Cambridge	MN	55008	763-689-7000	433-1841*
**Fax:* Admissions ■ *Web:* www.anokaramsey.edu					
Leech Lake Tribal College					
6945 Little Wolf Rd NW	Cass Lake	MN	56633	218-335-4200	335-4209
TF: 800-627-3529 ■ *Web:* www.lltc.org					
Fond du Lac Tribal & Community College					
2101 14th St	Cloquet	MN	55720	218-879-0800	879-0814
TF: 800-657-3712 ■ *Web:* www.fdltcc.edu					
Anoka-Ramsey Community College					
11200 Mississippi Blvd NW	Coon Rapids	MN	55433	763-433-1100	433-1521
Web: www.anokaramsey.edu					
Detroit Lakes 900 Hwy 34E	Detroit Lakes	MN	56501	218-846-3700	846-3794
TF: 800-492-4836 ■ *Web:* www.minnesota.edu					
Lake Superior College 2101 Trinity Rd	Duluth	MN	55811	218-733-7600	733-5945*
**Fax:* Admissions ■ *TF:* 800-432-2884 ■ *Web:* www.lsc.cc.mn.us					
East Grand Forks					
2022 Central Ave NE	East Grand Forks	MN	56721	218-773-3441	793-2842
TF: 800-451-3441 ■ *Web:* www.northlandcollege.edu					
Vermilion Community College 1900 E Camp St	Ely	MN	55731	218-365-7200	365-7218
TF: 800-657-3608 ■ *Web:* www.vcc.edu					
Mesabi Range Community & Technical College					
1100 Industrial Pk Dr PO Box 648	Eveleth	MN	55734	218-741-3095	744-7466
TF: 800-657-3860 ■ *Web:* www.mr.mnscu.edu					
South Central College					
Faribault 1225 3rd St	Faribault	MN	55021	507-332-5800	332-5888
TF: 800-422-0391 ■ *Web:* www.southcentral.edu					
Minnesota State Community & Technical College					
Fergus Falls 1414 College Way	Fergus Falls	MN	56537	218-736-1500	736-1510*
**Fax:* Admissions ■ *TF:* 877-450-3322 ■ *Web:* www.minnesota.edu					
Itasca Community College					
1851 E Us Hwy 169	Grand Rapids	MN	55744	218-327-4460	327-4350
TF: 800-996-6422 ■ *Web:* www.itascacc.edu					
Hibbing Community College 1515 E 25th St	Hibbing	MN	55746	218-262-6700	262-6717*
**Fax:* Admissions ■ *TF:* 800-224-4422 ■ *Web:* www.hcc.mnscu.edu					
Rainy River Community College					
1501 Hwy 71	International Falls	MN	56649	218-285-7722	285-2239*
**Fax:* Admissions ■ *TF:* 800-456-3996 ■ *Web:* www.rrcc.mnscu.edu					
Inver Hills Community College					
2500 80th St E	Inver Grove Heights	MN	55076	651-450-8500	450-8677*
**Fax:* Admissions ■ *Web:* www.inverhills.edu					

	City	State	Zip	Phone	Fax
White Earth Tribal & Community College					
124 S 1st St	Mahnomen	MN	56557	218-935-0417	936-5736
Web: www.wetcc.org					
Minneapolis Community & Technical College					
1501 Hennepin Ave.	Minneapolis	MN	55403	612-659-6200	659-6210*
**Fax:* Admissions ■ *TF:* 800-247-0911 ■ *Web:* www.minneapolis.edu					
Moorhead 1900 28th Ave S	Moorhead	MN	56560	218-299-6500	299-6584*
**Fax:* Admissions ■ *TF:* 800-426-5603 ■ *Web:* www.minnesota.edu					
Mankato 1920 Lee Blvd	North Mankato	MN	56003	507-389-7200	388-9951
TF: 800-722-9359 ■ *Web:* www.southcentral.edu					
Rochester Community & Technical College					
851 30th Ave SE	Rochester	MN	55904	507-285-7210	280-3529*
**Fax:* Admissions ■ *TF:* 800-247-1296 ■ *Web:* www.rctc.edu					
Staples 1830 Airport Rd	Staples	MN	56479	218-894-5100	894-5185
TF: 800-247-6836 ■ *Web:* www.clcmn.edu					
Northland Community & Technical College					
1101 US Hwy 1 E	Thief River Falls	MN	56701	218-681-0701	681-0774*
**Fax:* Admissions ■ *TF:* 800-959-6282 ■ *Web:* www.northlandcollege.edu					
Century College 3300 Century Ave N	White Bear Lake	MN	55110	651-779-3200	773-1796*
**Fax:* Admissions ■ *TF:* 800-228-1978 ■ *Web:* www.century.cc.mn.us					
Minnesota West Community & Technical College					
1450 Collegeway	Worthington	MN	56187	507-372-3400	372-5803*
**Fax:* Admissions ■ *TF:* 800-657-3966 ■ *Web:* www.mnwest.edu					

MISSISSIPPI

	City	State	Zip	Phone	Fax
Northeast Mississippi Community College					
101 Cunningham Blvd	Booneville	MS	38829	662-728-7751	720-7405*
**Fax:* Admissions ■ *TF:* 800-555-2154 ■ *Web:* www.nemcc.edu					
East Central Community College PO Box 129	Decatur	MS	39327	601-635-2126	635-4060*
**Fax:* Admissions ■ *TF:* 877-462-3222 ■ *Web:* www.eccc.cc.ms.us					
Jones County Junior College 900 S Ct St	Ellisville	MS	39437	601-477-4000	477-4258*
**Fax:* Admissions ■ *Web:* www.jcjc.cc.ms.us					
Itawamba Community College					
Fulton 602 W Hill St	Fulton	MS	38843	662-862-8000	862-8234*
**Fax:* Admissions ■ *Web:* www.iccms.edu					
Jackson County 2300 Hwy 90	Gautier	MS	39553	228-497-9602	497-7873
TF: 866-735-1122 ■ *Web:* www.mgccc.edu					
Holmes Community College 232 Hill St	Goodman	MS	39079	662-472-2312	472-9152
TF: 800-465-6374 ■ *Web:* www.holmescc.edu					
Jefferson Davis 2226 Switzer Rd	Gulfport	MS	39507	228-896-3355	896-2520*
**Fax:* Admissions ■ *TF:* 866-735-1122 ■ *Web:* www.mgccc.edu					
Meridian Community College 910 Hwy 19 N	Meridian	MS	39307	601-483-8241	484-8838*
**Fax:* Admissions ■ *TF:* 800-622-8431 ■ *Web:* www.mcc.cc.ms.us					
Mississippi Delta Community College					
PO Box 668	Moorhead	MS	38761	662-246-6322	246-6288
Web: www.msdelta.edu					
Natchez 11 Co-Lin Cir	Natchez	MS	39120	601-442-9111	446-1225*
**Fax:* Admissions ■ *Web:* www.colin.edu					
Rankin 3805 Hwy 80 E	Pearl	MS	39208	601-932-5237	936-1833*
**Fax:* Admissions ■ *Web:* www.hindscc.edu					
Mississippi Gulf Coast Community College					
51 Main St PO Box 548	Perkinston	MS	39573	601-928-5211	928-6345*
**Fax:* Admitting ■ *TF:* 866-735-1122 ■ *Web:* www.mgccc.edu					
Pearl River Community College					
101 Hwy 11 N	Poplarville	MS	39470	601-403-1000	403-1339*
**Fax:* Admissions ■ *Web:* www.prcc.edu					
Hinds Community College					
501 E Main St PO Box 1100	Raymond	MS	39154	601-857-5261	857-3539*
**Fax:* Admissions ■ *TF:* 800-446-3722 ■ *Web:* www.hindscc.edu					
East Mississippi Community College					
1512 Kemper St PO Box 158	Scooba	MS	39358	662-476-8442	476-5038*
**Fax:* Admissions ■ *Web:* www.emcc.cc.ms.us					
Northwest Mississippi Community College					
4975 Hwy 51 N	Senatobia	MS	38668	662-562-3200	562-3221
Web: www.northwestms.edu					
Southwest Mississippi Community College					
1156 College Dr	Summit	MS	39666	601-276-2000	276-3888
Web: www.smcc.edu					
Tupelo 2176 S Eason Blvd	Tupelo	MS	38804	662-620-5000	620-5315*
**Fax:* Admissions ■ *Web:* www.iccms.edu					
Utica Hwy 18 W	Utica	MS	39175	601-354-2327	885-6026*
**Fax:* Admissions ■ *TF:* 800-446-3722 ■ *Web:* www.hindscc.edu					
Copiah-Lincoln Community College					
1001 Copiah-Lincoln Ln	Wesson	MS	39191	601-643-5101	643-8225*
**Fax:* Admissions ■ *Web:* www.colin.edu					

MISSOURI

	City	State	Zip	Phone	Fax
Watley Ctr 504 E 13th St	Cassville	MO	65625	417-847-1706	847-1367
Web: www.crowder.edu					
Jefferson College 1000 Viking Dr	Hillsboro	MO	63050	636-789-3951	789-5103*
**Fax:* Admissions ■ *Web:* www.jeffco.edu					
Metropolitan Community College Blue River					
20301 E 78 Hwy	Independence	MO	64057	816-220-6500	220-6577*
**Fax:* Admissions ■ *Web:* www.mcckc.edu					
Maple Woods Community College					
2601 NE Barry Rd	Kansas City	MO	64156	816-437-3000	437-3351*
**Fax:* Admissions ■ *Web:* www.mcckc.edu					
Metropolitan Community College Penn Valley					
3201 SW Trafficway	Kansas City	MO	64111	816-759-4000	759-4161
Web: www.mcckc.edu					
Meramec 11333 Big Bend Blvd	Kirkwood	MO	63122	314-984-7500	984-7051*
**Fax:* Admissions ■ *Web:* www.stlcc.edu					
Metropolitan Community College Longview					
500 SW Longview Rd	Lee's Summit	MO	64081	816-672-2000	672-2378*
**Fax:* Admissions ■ *Web:* www.mcckc.edu					
Moberly Area Community College					
101 College Ave	Moberly	MO	65270	660-263-4110	263-2406
TF: 800-622-2070 ■ *Web:* www.macc.edu					
Crowder College 601 Laclede Ave	Neosho	MO	64850	417-451-3223	455-5731*
**Fax:* Admissions ■ *TF:* 866-238-7788 ■ *Web:* www.crowder.edu					
Cottey College 1000 W Austin Blvd	Nevada	MO	64772	417-667-8181	667-8103*
**Fax:* Admissions ■ *TF:* 888-526-8839 ■ *Web:* www.cottey.edu					
Mineral Area College					
5270 Frat River Rd PO Box 1000	Park Hills	MO	63601	573-431-4593	518-2166*
**Fax:* Admissions ■ *Web:* www.mineralarea.edu					
Three Rivers Community College					
2080 Three Rivers Blvd	Poplar Bluff	MO	63901	573-840-9600	840-9058*
**Fax:* Admissions ■ *TF:* 877-879-8722 ■ *Web:* www.trcc.edu					
Saint Louis Community College (STLCC)					
300 S Broadway	Saint Louis	MO	63102	314-539-5000	539-5170*
**Fax:* Admissions ■ *Web:* www.stlcc.edu					
Florissant Valley 3400 Pershall Rd	Saint Louis	MO	63135	314-595-4200	595-2224*
**Fax:* Admissions ■ *Web:* www.stlcc.edu/fv					
Forest Park 5600 Oakland Ave	Saint Louis	MO	63110	314-644-9100	644-9375*
**Fax:* Admissions ■ *Web:* www.stlcc.edu/fp					
Saint Charles Community College					
4601 Mid Rivers Mall Dr	Saint Peters	MO	63376	636-922-8000	922-8236
Web: www.stchas.edu					
State Fair Community College 3201 W 16th St	Sedalia	MO	65301	660-530-5800	596-7472*
**Fax:* Admissions ■ *Web:* www.sfcc.cc.mo.us					
Ozarks Technical Community College					
1001 E Chestnut Expy	Springfield	MO	65802	417-447-7500	447-6906*
**Fax:* Admissions ■ *Web:* www.otc.edu					
North Central Missouri College 1301 Main St	Trenton	MO	64683	660-359-3948	359-2211*
**Fax:* Admissions ■ *TF:* 800-880-6180 ■ *Web:* www.ncmc.cc.mo.us					
East Central College 1964 Prairie Dell Rd	Union	MO	63084	636-583-5193	583-1897*
**Fax:* Admissions ■ *Web:* www.eastcentral.edu					

MONTANA

	City	State	Zip	Phone	Fax
Blackfeet Community College PO Box 819	Browning	MT	59417	406-338-5421	338-3272*
**Fax:* Admissions ■ *TF:* 800-549-7457 ■ *Web:* www.bfcc.org					
Dawson Community College PO Box 421	Glendive	MT	59330	406-377-3396	377-8132*
**Fax:* Admissions ■ *TF:* 800-821-8320 ■ *Web:* www.dawson.edu					
Flathead Valley Community College					
777 Grandview Dr	Kalispell	MT	59901	406-756-3822	756-3815
TF: 800-313-3822 ■ *Web:* www.fvcc.edu					
Chief Dull Knife College PO Box 98	Lame Deer	MT	59043	406-477-6215	477-6219
Web: www.cdkc.edu					
Libby 225 Commerce Way	Libby	MT	59923	406-293-2721	293-5112*
**Fax:* Admissions ■ *Web:* www.fvcc.edu					
Miles Community College 2715 Dickinson St	Miles City	MT	59301	406-874-6100	874-6283*
**Fax:* Admissions ■ *TF:* 800-541-9281 ■ *Web:* www.milescc.edu					
Salish Kootenai College PO Box 70	Pablo	MT	59855	406-275-4800	275-4801*
**Fax:* Admissions ■ *TF:* 877-752-6553 ■ *Web:* www.skc.edu					
Fort Peck Community College PO Box 398	Poplar	MT	59255	406-768-6300	768-6301
Web: www.fpcc.edu					

NEBRASKA

	City	State	Zip	Phone	Fax
Beatrice 4771 W Scott Rd	Beatrice	NE	68310	402-228-3468	228-2218*
**Fax:* Admissions ■ *TF:* 800-233-5027 ■ *Web:* www.southeast.edu					
Columbus 4500 63rd St PO Box 1027	Columbus	NE	68602	402-564-7132	562-1201*
**Fax:* Admissions ■ *Web:* www.cccneb.edu					
Elkhorn Valley 829 N 204th	Elkhorn	NE	68022	402-289-1200	
Web: www.mccneb.edu					
Grand Island 3134 W Hwy 34 PO Box 4903	Grand Island	NE	68802	308-398-4222	398-7399*
**Fax:* Admissions ■ *Web:* www.cccneb.edu					
Central Community College					
Hastings 550 Technical Blvd	Hastings	NE	68901	402-463-9811	461-2454
Web: www.cccneb.edu					
Southeast Community College					
Lincoln 8800 'O' St	Lincoln	NE	68520	402-471-3333	437-2404*
**Fax:* Admissions ■ *TF:* 800-642-4075 ■ *Web:* www.southeast.edu					
Nebraska Indian Community College PO Box 428	Macy	NE	68039	402-837-5078	837-4183*
**Fax:* Admissions ■ *Web:* www.thenicc.edu					
McCook Community College 1205 E 3rd St	McCook	NE	69001	308-345-8100	345-8180*
**Fax:* Admissions ■ *TF:* 800-658-4348 ■ *Web:* www.mpcc.edu					
Northeast Community College					
801 E Benjamin Ave PO Box 469	Norfolk	NE	68702	402-371-2020	844-7396*
**Fax:* Admissions ■ *Web:* www.northeastcollege.com					
North Platte Community College					
North 1101 Halligan Dr	North Platte	NE	69101	308-535-3601	534-5767*
**Fax:* Admissions ■ *TF:* 800-658-4308 ■ *Web:* www.mpcc.edu					
South 601 W State Farm Rd	North Platte	NE	69101	308-535-3700	535-3794
TF: 800-658-4308 ■ *Web:* www.mpcc.edu					
Metropolitan Community College PO Box 3777	Omaha	NE	68103	402-457-2400	457-2788*
**Fax:* Admissions ■ *TF:* 800-228-9553 ■ *Web:* www.mccneb.edu					
Western Nebraska Community College					
1601 E 27th St	Scottsbluff	NE	69361	308-635-3606	635-6732
TF: 800-348-4435 ■ *Web:* www.wncc.net					
Little Priest Tribal College PO Box 270	Winnebago	NE	68071	402-878-2380	878-2355
Web: www.lptc.bia.edu					

NEVADA

	City	State	Zip	Phone	Fax
Fallon 160 Campus Way	Fallon	NV	89406	775-423-7565	423-8029
Web: www.wncc.edu					

	City	State	ZIP	Phone	Fax
Henderson 700 College Dr	Henderson	NV	89002	702-651-3000	651-3509*
*Fax: Admissions ■ Web: www.ccsn.nevada.edu					
West Charleston 6375 W Charleston Blvd	Las Vegas	NV	89146	702-651-5610	651-7495*
*Fax: Admissions ■ Web: www.ccsn.nevada.edu					
Western Nevada Community College					
Douglas 1680 Bently Pkwy S	Minden	NV	89423	775-782-2413	782-2415
Web: www.wnc.edu					
Community College of Southern Nevada					
Cheyenne 3200 E Cheyenne Ave	North Las Vegas	NV	89030	702-651-4000	651-4811*
*Fax: Admissions ■ TF: 800-492-5728 ■ Web: www.ccsn.nevada.edu					
Truckee Meadows Community College					
7000 Dandini Blvd Red Mountain Bldg Rm 319	Reno	NV	89512	775-673-7000	673-7028*
*Fax: Admissions ■ Web: www.tmcc.edu					

NEW HAMPSHIRE

	City	State	ZIP	Phone	Fax
White Mountains Community College (WMCC)					
2020 Riverside Dr	Berlin	NH	03570	603-752-1113	752-6335
TF: 800-445-4525 ■ Web: www.wmcc.edu					
Community College System of New Hampshire (CCSNH)					
26 College Dr	Concord	NH	03301	603-271-2722	271-2725
Web: www.ccsnh.edu					
NHTI Concord's Community College					
31 College Dr	Concord	NH	03301	603-271-6484	271-7139
TF: 800-247-0179 ■ Web: www.nhti.edu					
Lakes Region Community College (LRCC)					
379 Belmont Rd	Laconia	NH	03246	603-524-3207	524-8084
TF: 800-357-2992 ■ Web: www.lrcc.edu					
Manchester Community College					
1066 Front St	Manchester	NH	03102	603-206-8000	668-5354
TF: 800-924-3445 ■ Web: www.manchestercommunitycollege.edu					
New Hampshire Community Technical College					
Nashua 505 Amherst St	Nashua	NH	03063	603-882-6923	882-8690
TF: 800-247-3420					
Stratham 277 Portsmouth Ave	Stratham	NH	03885	603-772-1194	772-1198*
*Fax: Admissions ■ Web: ms.nhctc.edu					

NEW JERSEY

	City	State	ZIP	Phone	Fax
Camden County College 200 College Dr	Blackwood	NJ	08012	856-227-7200	374-4917
TF: 888-228-2466 ■ Web: www.camdencc.edu					
Camden City 200 N Broadway # 1	Camden	NJ	08102	856-338-1817	968-1399
Web: www.camdencc.edu					
Salem Community College					
460 Hollywood Ave	Carneys Point	NJ	08069	856-299-2100	351-2763*
*Fax: Admissions ■ Web: www.salemcc.edu					
Union County College 1033 Springfield Ave	Cranford	NJ	07016	908-709-7000	709-7125*
*Fax: Admissions ■ Web: www.ucc.edu					
Middlesex County College					
2600 Woodbridge Ave PO Box 3050	Edison	NJ	08818	732-548-6000	906-7728*
*Fax: Admissions ■ Web: www.middlesex.cc.nj.us					
Hudson County Community College					
162 Sip Ave	Jersey City	NJ	07306	201-714-7200	714-2136*
*Fax: Admissions ■ Web: www.hccc.edu					
Brookdale Community College					
765 Newman Springs Rd	Lincroft	NJ	07738	732-842-1900	224-2271*
*Fax: Admissions ■ Web: www.brookdalecc.edu					
Assumption College for Sisters					
350 Bernardsville Rd	Mendham	NJ	07945	973-543-6528	543-1738
Web: www.acs350.org					
Essex County College 303 University Ave	Newark	NJ	07102	973-877-3000	877-3446*
*Fax: Admissions ■ Web: www.essex.edu					
Sussex County Community College					
1 College Hill Rd	Newton	NJ	07860	973-300-2100	579-5226*
*Fax: Admissions ■ Web: www.sussex.edu					
Bergen Community College 400 Paramus Rd	Paramus	NJ	07652	201-447-7200	670-7973*
*Fax: Admissions ■ Web: www.bergen.edu					
Passaic County Community College					
1 College Blvd	Paterson	NJ	07505	973-684-6800	684-6778*
*Fax: Admissions ■ Web: www.pccc.cc.nj.us					
Burlington County College					
601 Pemberton Browns Mills Rd	Pemberton	NJ	08068	609-894-9311	726-0401*
*Fax: Admissions ■ Web: www.bcc.edu					
County College of Morris 214 Ctr Grove Rd	Randolph	NJ	07869	973-328-5000	328-5199*
*Fax: Admissions ■ TF: 888-226-8001 ■ Web: www.ccm.edu					
Gloucester County College 1400 Tanyard Rd	Sewell	NJ	08080	856-468-5000	468-8498*
*Fax: Admissions ■ Web: www.gccnj.edu					
Raritan Valley Community College					
PO Box 3300	Somerville	NJ	08876	908-526-1200	704-3442*
*Fax: Admissions ■ Web: www.raritanval.edu					
Ocean County College PO Box 2001	Toms River	NJ	08754	732-255-0400	255-0444
Web: www.ocean.edu					
Mercer County Community College PO Box B	Trenton	NJ	08690	609-586-4800	586-6944
TF: 800-392-6222 ■ Web: www.mccc.edu					
Kerney Ctr N Broad & Academy St	Trenton	NJ	08608	609-586-4800	570-3106
TF: 800-392-6222 ■ Web: www.mccc.edu					
Cumberland County College 3322 College Dr	Vineland	NJ	08360	856-691-8600	691-6157*
*Fax: Admissions ■ Web: www.cccnj.net					
Warren County Community College					
475 Rt 57 W	Washington	NJ	07882	908-835-9222	689-5824*
*Fax: Admissions ■ Web: www.warren.edu					
West Essex 730 Bloomfield Ave	West Caldwell	NJ	07006	973-877-3175	
Web: www.essex.edu					
West Windsor 1200 Old Trenton Rd	West Windsor	NJ	08550	609-586-4800	570-3861*
*Fax: Admissions ■ TF: 800-392-6222 ■ Web: www.mccc.edu					

NEW MEXICO

	City	State	ZIP	Phone	Fax
Alamogordo 2400 N Scenic Dr	Alamogordo	NM	88310	575-439-3600	439-3760
Web: www.nmsua.edu					
New Mexico State University					
Carlsbad 1500 University Dr	Carlsbad	NM	88220	505-234-9200	885-4951*
*Fax: Admissions ■ TF: 888-888-2199 ■ Web: artemis.nmsu.edu					
Clovis Community College (CCC) 417 Schepps Blvd	Clovis	NM	88101	575-769-2811	769-4190*
*Fax: Admissions ■ TF: 800-769-1409 ■ Web: www.clovis.edu					
Northern New Mexico College					
921 Paseo de Onate	Espanola	NM	87532	505-747-2100	747-5449
Web: www.nnmc.edu					
San Juan College 4601 College Blvd	Farmington	NM	87402	505-326-3311	566-3500*
*Fax: Admissions ■ Web: www.sanjuancollege.edu					
Grants 1500 3rd St	Grants	NM	87020	505-287-7981	287-2329*
*Fax: Admissions ■ Web: www.grants.nmsu.edu					
New Mexico Junior College 1 Thunderbird Cir	Hobbs	NM	88240	505-392-4510	392-0322
TF: 800-657-6260 ■ Web: www.nmjc.edu					
Dona Ana Branch Community College (DACC)					
2800 N Sonoma Ranch Blvd PO Box 30001	Las Cruces	NM	88011	575-528-7000	528-7300*
*Fax: Admissions ■ TF: 800-903-7503 ■ Web: dabcc.nmsu.edu					
Luna Community College 366 Luna Dr	Las Vegas	NM	87701	505-454-2500	454-2519
TF: 800-588-7232 ■ Web: www.luna.cc.nm.us					
Valencia 280 La Entrada	Los Lunas	NM	87031	505-925-8580	925-8563*
*Fax: Admissions ■ TF: 800-225-5866 ■ Web: www.unm.edu					
Eastern New Mexico University Roswell					
52 University Blvd PO Box 6000	Roswell	NM	88202	505-624-7000	624-7144*
*Fax: Admissions ■ TF: 800-243-6687 ■ Web: www.roswell.enmu.edu					
New Mexico Military Institute (NMMI)					
101 W College Blvd	Roswell	NM	88201	505-624-8478	624-8058*
*Fax: Admissions ■ TF Admitting: 800-421-5376 ■ Web: www.nmmi.edu					
Santa Fe Community College					
6401 Richards Ave	Santa Fe	NM	87508	505-428-1000	395-4118*
*Fax Area Code: 352 ■ *Fax: Admissions ■ Web: www.sfcc.edu					
Mesalands Community College 911 S 10th St	Tucumcari	NM	88401	505-461-4413	461-1901
Web: www.mesalands.edu					

NEW YORK

	City	State	ZIP	Phone	Fax
Maria College 700 New Scotland Ave	Albany	NY	12208	518-438-1368	453-1366
Web: www.mariacollege.edu					
College of Technology at Alfred					
10 Upper College Dr	Alfred	NY	14802	607-587-4215	587-4299*
*Fax: Admissions ■ TF: 800-425-3733 ■ Web: www.alfredstate.edu					
Cayuga Community College 197 Franklin St	Auburn	NY	13021	315-255-1743	255-2117
Web: www.cayuga-cc.edu					
Genesee Community College 1 College Rd	Batavia	NY	14020	585-343-0068	345-6810
Web: www.genesee.edu					
Queensborough Community College					
222-05 56th Ave	Bayside	NY	11364	718-631-6262	281-5189*
*Fax: Admissions ■ Web: www.qcc.cuny.edu					
Broome Community College 901 Front St	Binghamton	NY	13905	607-778-5000	778-5442*
*Fax: Admissions ■ TF: 800-836-0689 ■ Web: www.sunybroome.edu					
Suffolk County Community College					
Grant 1001 Crooked Hill Rd	Brentwood	NY	11717	631-851-6700	851-6819*
*Fax: Admissions ■ Web: www.sunysuffolk.edu					
Bronx Community College 2155 University Ave	Bronx	NY	10453	718-289-5100	289-6003*
*Fax: Admissions ■ Web: www.bcc.cuny.edu					
Hostos Community College 500 Grand Concourse	Bronx	NY	10451	718-518-4444	518-4256*
*Fax: Admissions ■ Web: www.hostos.cuny.edu					
Kingsborough Community College					
2001 Oriental Blvd	Brooklyn	NY	11235	718-368-5000	368-5356*
*Fax: Admissions ■ Web: www.kbcc.cuny.edu					
Erie Community College 121 Ellicott St	Buffalo	NY	14203	716-842-2770	851-1129
TF: 800-836-0981 ■ Web: www.ecc.edu					
Trocaire College 360 Choate Ave	Buffalo	NY	14220	716-826-1200	828-6107*
*Fax: Admissions ■ Web: www.trocaire.edu					
Villa Maria College 240 Pine Ridge Rd	Buffalo	NY	14225	716-896-0700	896-0705
Web: www.villa.edu					
Finger Lakes Community College					
4340 Lakeshore Dr	Canandaigua	NY	14424	585-394-3500	394-5005
Web: www.fingerlakes.edu					
Canton 34 Cornell Dr	Canton	NY	13617	315-386-7011	386-7929
TF: 800-388-7123 ■ Web: www.canton.edu					
Corning Community College 1 Academic Dr	Corning	NY	14830	607-962-9011	962-9582*
*Fax: Admissions ■ Web: www.corning-cc.edu					
Delhi 2 Main St	Delhi	NY	13753	607-746-4000	746-4104
TF: 800-963-3544 ■ Web: www.delhi.edu					
Tompkins Cortland Community College 170 N St	Dryden	NY	13053	607-844-8211	844-6541*
*Fax: Admissions ■ TF: 888-567-8211 ■ Web: www.tc3.edu					
Nassau Community College 1 Education Dr	Garden City	NY	11530	516-572-7500	572-9743
Web: www.ncc.edu					
Herkimer County Community College					
100 Reservoir Rd	Herkimer	NY	13350	315-866-0300	866-0062*
*Fax: Admissions ■ Web: www.herkimer.edu					
Columbia-Greene Community College 4400 Rt 23	Hudson	NY	12534	518-828-4181	828-8543
Web: www.sunycgcc.edu					
Jamestown Community College					
525 Faulkner St	Jamestown	NY	14702	716-665-5220	338-1466
TF: 800-388-8557 ■ Web: www.sunyjcc.edu					
Fulton-Montgomery Community College					
2805 New York 67	Johnstown	NY	12095	518-762-4651	762-4334
Web: www.fmcc.suny.edu					
Sullivan County Community College					
112 College Rd	Loch Sheldrake	NY	12759	845-434-5750	434-0923*
*Fax: Admissions ■ Web: www.sullivan.suny.edu					

				Phone	Fax
LaGuardia Community College					
31-10 Thomson Ave	Long Island City	NY	11101	718-482-5000	609-2033*
*Fax: Admissions ■ Web: www.lagcc.cuny.edu					
Orange County Community College 115 S St	Middletown	NY	10940	845-344-6222	342-8662
Web: www.sunyorange.edu					
Bank Street College Library 610 W 112th St	New York	NY	10025	212-875-4595	875-4594
Web: www.bankstreet.edu					
Borough of Manhattan Community College					
199 Chambers St Rm S-300	New York	NY	10007	212-220-1265	220-2366
TF: 877-669-2622 ■ Web: www.bmcc.cuny.edu					
Cattaraugus County 260 N Union St PO Box 5901	Olean	NY	14760	716-376-7500	376-7020*
*Fax: Admissions ■ TF: 800-388-9776 ■ Web: www.sunyjcc.edu					
South 4041 Southwestern Blvd	Orchard Park	NY	14127	716-851-1003	851-1687*
*Fax: Admissions ■ TF: 800-836-0983 ■ Web: www.ecc.edu					
Clinton Community College					
136 Clinton Pt Dr	Plattsburgh	NY	12901	518-562-4200	562-4158
TF: 800-552-1160 ■ Web: clintoncc.suny.edu					
Dutchess Community College					
53 Pendell Rd	Poughkeepsie	NY	12601	845-431-8010	431-8605
TF: 800-763-3933 ■ Web: www.sunydutchess.edu					
Adirondack Community College 640 Bay Rd	Queensbury	NY	12804	518-743-2200	745-1433
Web: www.sunyacc.edu					
Eastern 121 Speonk-Riverhead Rd	Riverhead	NY	11901	631-548-2500	548-2504*
*Fax: Admissions ■ Web: www.sunysuffolk.edu					
Monroe Community College					
1000 E Henrietta Rd	Rochester	NY	14623	585-292-2000	292-3860
Web: www.monroecc.edu					
Niagara County Community College					
3111 Saunders Settlement Rd	Sanborn	NY	14132	716-614-6222	614-6820*
*Fax: Admissions ■ Web: www.niagaracc.suny.edu					
North Country Community College					
23 Santanoni Ave	Saranac Lake	NY	12983	518-891-2915	891-2915
TF: 888-879-6222 ■ Web: www.nccc.edu					
Schenectady County Community College					
78 Washington Ave	Schenectady	NY	12305	518-381-1200	381-1477
Web: www.sunysccc.edu					
Ammerman 533 College Rd	Selden	NY	11784	631-451-4110	451-4094
Web: www.sunysuffolk.edu					
Ulster County Community College					
Cottekill Rd	Stone Ridge	NY	12484	845-687-5000	687-5090
TF: 800-724-0833 ■ Web: www.sunyulster.edu					
Rockland Community College 145 College Rd	Suffern	NY	10901	845-574-4000	574-4433
TF: 800-722-7666 ■ Web: www.sunyrockland.edu					
Onondaga Community College 4941 Onondaga Rd	Syracuse	NY	13215	315-498-2622	498-2107
Web: www.sunyocc.edu					
Hudson Valley Community College					
80 Vandenburgh Ave	Troy	NY	12180	518-629-4822	629-4576*
*Fax: Admissions ■ TF: 877-325-4822 ■ Web: www.hvcc.edu					
Mohawk Valley Community College					
1101 Sherman Dr	Utica	NY	13501	315-792-5400	792-5527
Web: www.mvcc.edu					
Westchester Community College					
75 Grasslands Rd	Valhalla	NY	10595	914-606-6600	785-6540*
*Fax: Admissions ■ Web: www.sunywcc.edu					
Jefferson Community College					
1220 Coffeen St	Watertown	NY	13601	315-786-2200	786-2459
TF: 888-435-6522 ■ Web: www.sunyjefferson.edu					
North 6205 Main St	Williamsville	NY	14221	716-634-0800	851-1429
Web: www.ecc.edu					

NORTH CAROLINA

				Phone	Fax
Roanoke-Chowan Community College					
109 Community College Rd	Ahoskie	NC	27910	252-862-1200	862-1355*
*Fax: Admissions ■ Web: www.roanoke.cc.nc.us					
Randolph Community College					
629 Industrial Pk Ave PO Box 1009	Asheboro	NC	27204	336-633-0200	629-4695*
*Fax: Admissions ■ Web: www.randolph.cc.nc.us					
Asheville-Buncombe Technical Community College					
340 Victoria Rd	Asheville	NC	28801	828-254-1921	251-6718*
*Fax: Admissions ■ Web: www.abtech.edu					
Watauga 294 Community College Dr PO Box 3318	Boone	NC	28607	828-297-3811	297-4174
Web: www.caldwell.cc.nc.us					
Transylvania 45 Oak Pk Dr	Brevard	NC	28712	828-883-2520	884-5725
Web: www.blueridge.edu					
Central Piedmont Community College					
1201 Elizabeth Ave	Charlotte	NC	28204	704-330-2722	330-6136*
*Fax: Admissions ■ Web: www.cpcc.edu					
Cato 8120 Grier Rd PO Box 35009	Charlotte	NC	28235	704-330-4801	330-4884*
*Fax: Admissions ■ Web: www.cpcc.edu					
Harper 315 W Hebron St	Charlotte	NC	28273	704-330-4400	330-4444
Web: www.cpcc.edu					
Sampson Community College PO Box 318	Clinton	NC	28329	910-592-8081	592-8048*
*Fax: Admissions ■ Web: www.sampson.cc.nc.us					
Haywood Community College 185 Freedlander Dr	Clyde	NC	28721	828-627-2821	627-4513*
*Fax: Admissions ■ Web: www.haywood.edu					
South 1531 Trinity Church Rd	Concord	NC	28027	704-788-3197	788-2168*
*Fax: Admissions ■ Web: www.rowancabarrus.edu					
South PO Box 39	Creedmoor	NC	27522	919-528-4737	528-1201*
*Fax: Admissions ■ Web: www.vgcc.edu					
Gaston College 201 Hwy 321-S	Dallas	NC	28034	704-922-6200	922-2344*
*Fax: Admissions ■ Web: www.gaston.cc.nc.us					
Surry Community College 630 S Main St	Dobson	NC	27017	336-386-8121	386-3690*
*Fax: Admissions ■ Web: www.surry.cc.nc.us					
Bladen Community College PO Box 266	Dublin	NC	28332	910-879-5556	879-5513
Web: www.bladencc.edu					
Durham Technical Community College					
1637 E Lawson St	Durham	NC	27703	919-686-3300	686-3669*
*Fax: Admissions ■ Web: www.durhamtech.edu					
College of the Albemarle PO Box 2327	Elizabeth City	NC	27906	252-335-0821	335-2011*
*Fax: Admissions ■ Web: www.albemarle.edu					
Fayetteville Technical Community College					
2201 Hull Rd	Fayetteville	NC	28303	910-678-8400	678-8407
Web: www.faytechcc.edu					
Blue Ridge Community College					
180 W Campus Dr	Flat Rock	NC	28731	828-694-1700	694-1690
Web: www.blueridge.edu					
Wayne Community College					
3000 Wayne Memorial Dr PO Box 8002	Goldsboro	NC	27533	919-735-5151	736-9425*
*Fax: Admissions ■ TF: 866-414-5064 ■ Web: www.waynecc.edu					
Alamance Community College PO Box 8000	Graham	NC	27253	336-578-2002	578-3964*
*Fax: Acctg ■ Web: www.alamance.cc.nc.us					
Pamlico Community College PO Box 185	Grantsboro	NC	28529	252-249-1851	249-2377*
*Fax: Library ■ Web: www.pamlico.cc.nc.us					
Richmond Community College PO Box 1189	Hamlet	NC	28345	910-582-7000	582-7102*
*Fax: Admissions ■ Web: www.richmondcc.edu					
Vance-Granville Community College					
200 Community College Rd	Henderson	NC	27537	252-492-2061	430-0460
Web: www.vgcc.edu					
Catawba Valley Community College					
2550 US Hwy 70 SE	Hickory	NC	28602	828-327-7000	327-7276
Web: www.cvcc.edu					
Caldwell Community College & Technical Institute					
2855 Hickory Blvd	Hudson	NC	28638	828-726-2200	726-2216*
*Fax: Admissions ■ Web: www.caldwell.cc.nc.us					
North 11930 Verhoeff Dr	Huntersville	NC	28078	704-330-4100	330-4113*
*Fax: Admissions ■ Web: www.cpcc.edu/campuses/north					
Coastal Carolina Community College					
444 Western Blvd	Jacksonville	NC	28546	910-455-1221	455-7027*
*Fax: Admissions ■ Web: www.coastal.cc.nc.us					
Guilford Technical Community College					
601 Highpoint Rd PO Box 309	Jamestown	NC	27282	336-334-4822	819-2022*
*Fax: Admissions ■ Web: www.gtcc.edu					
James Sprunt Community College					
133 James Sprunt Dr	Kenansville	NC	28349	910-296-2400	296-1636*
*Fax: Admissions ■ Web: www.sprunt.com					
Lenoir Community College PO Box 188	Kinston	NC	28502	252-527-6223	233-6879
TF: 800-848-5497 ■ Web: www.lenoir.cc.nc.us					
Davidson County Community College					
PO Box 1287	Lexington	NC	27293	336-249-8186	224-0240*
*Fax: Admissions ■ Web: www.davidson.cc.nc.us					
Louisburg College 501 N Main St	Louisburg	NC	27549	919-496-2521	496-1788*
*Fax: Admissions ■ TF: 800-775-0208 ■ Web: www.louisburg.edu					
Franklin 8100 Nc 56 Hwy	Louisburg	NC	27549	919-496-1567	496-6604
Web: www.vgcc.edu					
Robeson Community College PO Box 1420	Lumberton	NC	28359	910-272-3700	272-3328*
*Fax: Admissions ■ Web: www.robeson.cc.nc.us					
McDowell Technical Community College					
54 College Dr	Marion	NC	28752	828-652-6021	652-1014*
*Fax: Admissions ■ Web: www.mcdowelltech.cc.nc.us					
Madison 4646 US Hwy 25-70	Marshall	NC	28753	828-649-2947	281-9859
Web: www.abtech.edu					
Levine 2800 Campus Ridge Rd	Matthews	NC	28105	704-330-4200	330-4210
Web: www.cpcc.edu/it-old/campuses-locations/levine-campus					
Carteret Community College					
3505 Arendell St	Morehead City	NC	28557	252-222-6000	222-6265
Web: www.carteret.edu					
Western Piedmont Community College					
1001 Burkemont Ave	Morganton	NC	28655	828-438-6000	
Web: www.wpcc.edu					
Tri-County Community College 21 Campus Cir	Murphy	NC	28906	828-837-6810	837-3266
Web: www.tricountycc.edu					
Craven Community College 800 College Ct	New Bern	NC	28562	252-638-4131	638-4649*
*Fax: Admissions ■ Web: www.cravencc.edu					
Sandhills Community College					
3395 Airport Rd	Pinehurst	NC	28374	910-692-6185	695-3981*
*Fax: Admissions ■ TF: 800-338-3944 ■ Web: www.sandhills.edu					
South Piedmont Community College 680 Hwy 74	Polkton	NC	28135	704-272-7635	272-5303*
*Fax: Admissions ■ TF: 800-766-0319 ■ Web: www.spcc.edu					
Wake Technical Community College					
9101 Fayetteville Rd	Raleigh	NC	27603	919-662-3500	661-0117*
*Fax: Admissions ■ Web: www.waketech.edu					
Nash Community College PO Box 7488	Rocky Mount	NC	27804	252-443-4011	443-0828*
*Fax: Admissions ■ Web: www.nashcc.edu					
Piedmont Community College					
1715 College Dr PO Box 1197	Roxboro	NC	27573	336-599-1181	597-3817*
*Fax: Admissions ■ Web: www.piedmont.cc.nc.us					
Rowan-Cabarrus Community College					
North 1333 Jake Alexander Blvd PO Box 1595	Salisbury	NC	28145	704-637-0760	633-6804*
*Fax: Admissions ■ Web: www.rowancabarrus.edu					
Central Carolina Community College					
1105 Kelly Dr	Sanford	NC	27330	919-775-5401	718-7380*
*Fax: Admissions ■ Web: www.cccc.edu					
Cleveland Community College 137 S Post Rd	Shelby	NC	28152	704-484-4000	484-5305*
*Fax: Admissions ■ Web: www.cleveland.cc.nc.us					
Johnston Community College 245 College Rd	Smithfield	NC	27577	919-934-3051	989-7862*
*Fax: Admissions ■ Web: www.johnston.cc.nc.us					
Isothermal Community College					
806 ICC Loop Rd PO Box 804	Spindale	NC	28160	828-286-3636	286-8109*
*Fax: Admissions ■ Web: www.isothermal.edu					
Mayland Community College					
200 Mayland Dr PO Box 547	Spruce Pine	NC	28777	828-765-7351	765-0728*
*Fax: Admissions ■ TF: 800-462-9526 ■ Web: www.mayland.edu					
Mitchell Community College					
500 W Broad St	Statesville	NC	28677	704-878-3200	878-0872
Web: www.mitchellcc.edu					
Brunswick Community College PO Box 30	Supply	NC	28462	910-754-6900	754-9609*
*Fax: Admissions ■ TF: 800-754-1050 ■ Web: www.brunswick.cc.nc.us					
Southwestern Community College 447 College Dr	Sylva	NC	28779	828-586-4091	586-3129*
*Fax: Admissions ■ TF: 800-447-4091 ■ Web: www.southwest.cc.nc.us					

	City	State	Zip	Phone	Fax
Edgecombe Community College 2009 W Wilson St *Fax: Admissions ■ Web: www.edgecombe.cc.nc.us	Tarboro	NC	27886	252-823-5166	823-6817*
Montgomery Community College 1011 Page St TF: 800-839-6222 ■ Web: www.montgomery.cc.nc.us	Troy	NC	27371	910-576-6222	576-2176
Warren County PO Box 207 *Fax: Admissions ■ Web: www.vgcc.edu	Warrenton	NC	27536	252-257-1900	257-3612*
Beaufort County Community College 5337 Hwy 264 E *Fax: Admissions ■ Web: www.beaufort.cc.nc.us	Washington	NC	27889	252-946-6194	940-6393*
Halifax Community College 100 College Dr Web: www.halifaxcc.edu	Weldon	NC	27890	252-536-2551	536-4144
Rockingham Community College 215 Wrenn Memorial Rd Web: www.rockinghamcc.edu	Wentworth	NC	27375	336-342-4261	342-1809
Southeastern Community College PO Box 151 *Fax: Admissions ■ Web: www.sccnc.edu	Whiteville	NC	28472	910-642-7141	642-1267*
Wilkes Community College 1328 S Collegiate Dr PO Box 120 Web: www.wilkes.cc.nc.us	Wilkesboro	NC	28697	336-838-6100	838-6547
Martin Community College 1161 Kehukee Pk Rd Web: www.martin.cc.nc.us	Williamston	NC	27892	252-792-1521	792-0826
Cape Fear Community College 411 N Front St *Fax: Admissions ■ Web: www.cfcc.edu	Wilmington	NC	28401	910-362-7000	362-7080*
Wilson Technical Community College PO Box 4305 Web: www.wilsontech.cc.nc.us	Wilson	NC	27893	252-291-1195	246-1384
Pitt Community College 1986 Pitt Tech Rd *Fax: Admissions ■ Web: www.pitt.cc.nc.us	Winterville	NC	28590	252-321-4200	321-4209*
Caswell County 331 Piedmont Dr PO Box 1150 Web: www.piedmont.cc.nc.us	Yanceyville	NC	27379	336-694-5707	694-7086

NORTH DAKOTA

	City	State	Zip	Phone	Fax
Turtle Mountain Community College 10145 BIA Rd 7 Web: www.tm.edu	Belcourt	ND	58316	701-477-7862	477-7892
Bismarck State College 1500 Edwards Ave *Fax: Admissions ■ TF: 800-445-5073 ■ Web: www.bismarckstate.edu	Bismarck	ND	58501	701-224-5400	224-5643*
Minot State University Bottineau 105 Simrall Blvd *Fax: Admissions ■ TF: 800-542-6866 ■ Web: www.misu-b.nodak.edu	Bottineau	ND	58318	701-228-5451	228-5499*
Lake Region State College 1801 College Dr N *Fax: Admissions ■ TF: 800-443-1313 ■ Web: www.lrsc.nodak.edu	Devils Lake	ND	58301	701-662-1514	662-1581*
Cankdeska Cikana Community College 214 1st Ave PO Box 269 TF: 888-783-1463 ■ Web: www.littlehoop.cc	Fort Totten	ND	58335	701-766-4415	766-4077
Fort Berthold Community College PO Box 490 *Fax: Admissions ■ Web: www.fbcc.bia.edu	New Town	ND	58763	701-627-3665	627-3609*
North Dakota State College of Science 800 6th St N *Fax: Admissions ■ TF: 800-342-4325 ■ Web: www.ndscs.nodak.edu	Wahpeton	ND	58076	701-671-2401	671-2201*
Williston State College 1410 University Ave PO Box 1326 *Fax: Admissions ■ TF: 888-863-9455 ■ Web: www.wsc.nodak.edu	Williston	ND	58802	701-774-4200	774-4211*

OHIO

	City	State	Zip	Phone	Fax
Ashtabula 3300 Lake Rd W *Fax: Admissions ■ Web: www.ashtabula.kent.edu	Ashtabula	OH	44004	440-964-3322	964-4269*
University of Cincinnati Clermont College 4200 Clermont College Dr *Fax: Admissions ■ TF: 866-446-2822 ■ Web: www.clc.uc.edu	Batavia	OH	45103	513-732-5200	732-5303*
Geauga 14111 Claridon-Troy Rd *Fax: Admissions ■ Web: www.geauga.kent.edu	Burton	OH	44021	440-834-4187	834-8846*
Wright State University Lake 7600 Lake Campus Dr *Fax: Admissions ■ TF: 800-237-1477 ■ Web: www.wright.edu/lake	Celina	OH	45822	419-586-0300	586-0358*
Cincinnati State Technical & Community College 3520 Central Pkwy *Fax: Admissions ■ TF: 877-569-0115 ■ Web: www.cincinnatistate.edu	Cincinnati	OH	45223	513-569-1500	569-1562*
Raymond Walters College 9555 Plainfield Rd *Fax: Admissions ■ Web: www.rwc.uc.edu	Cincinnati	OH	45236	513-745-5600	745-5768*
Cuyahoga Community College *Metropolitan* 2900 Community College Ave *Fax: Admitting ■ TF: 800-954-8742 ■ Web: www.tri-c.edu	Cleveland	OH	44115	216-987-4200	696-2567*
Columbus State Community College 550 E Spring St *Fax: Admissions ■ TF: 800-621-6407 ■ Web: www.cscc.edu	Columbus	OH	43215	614-287-2400	287-6019*
Sinclair Community College 444 W 3rd St *Fax: Admissions ■ Web: www.sinclair.edu	Dayton	OH	45402	937-512-2500	512-2393*
Lorain County Community College 1005 N Abbe Rd TF: 800-995-5222 ■ Web: www.loraincc.edu	Elyria	OH	44035	440-365-5222	366-4167
Findlay 3200 Bright Rd TF: 800-346-3529 ■ Web: www.owens.edu	Findlay	OH	45840	419-429-3500	424-5194
Terra Community College 2830 Napoleon Rd TF: 800-334-3886 ■ Web: www.terra.edu	Fremont	OH	43420	419-334-8400	334-9035
Eastern 4250 Richmond Rd *Fax: Admissions ■ TF: 800-954-8742 ■ Web: www.tri-c.edu	Highland Hills	OH	44122	216-987-2024	987-2214*
Bowling Green State University Firelands 1 University Dr *Fax: Admissions ■ Web: www.firelands.bgsu.edu	Huron	OH	44839	419-433-5560	433-9696*
Kettering College of Medical Arts 3737 Southern Blvd *Fax: Admissions ■ TF: 800-433-5262 ■ Web: www.kcma.edu	Kettering	OH	45429	937-395-8601	395-8338*
Lakeland Community College 7700 Clocktower Dr *Fax: Admissions ■ TF: 800-589-8520 ■ Web: www.lakeland.cc.oh.us	Kirtland	OH	44094	440-525-7000	525-7651*
Washington State Community College 710 Colegate Dr Web: www.wscc.edu	Marietta	OH	45750	740-374-8716	376-0257
University of Akron Wayne College 1901 Smucker Rd TF: 800-221-8308 ■ Web: www.wayne.uakron.edu	Orrville	OH	44667	330-683-2010	684-8989
Western 11000 Pleasant Valley Rd *Fax: Admissions ■ TF: 800-954-8742 ■ Web: www.tri-c.edu	Parma	OH	44130	216-987-5000	987-5071*
Owens Community College *Toledo* 30335 Oregon Rd *Fax: Admissions ■ TF: 800-466-9367 ■ Web: www.owens.edu	Perrysburg	OH	43551	419-661-7000	661-7734*
Edison Community College 1973 Edison Dr TF: 800-922-3722 ■ Web: www.edisonohio.edu	Piqua	OH	45356	937-778-8600	778-1920
University of Rio Grande Rio Grande Community College 218 N College Ave *Fax: Admissions ■ TF: 800-282-7201 ■ Web: www.urgrgcc.edu	Rio Grande	OH	45674	740-245-5353	245-7260*
Chatfield College 20918 SR-251 *Fax: Admissions ■ Web: www.chatfield.edu	Saint Martin	OH	45118	513-875-3344	875-3912*
South 12681 US Rt 62 *Fax: Admissions ■ Web: www.sscc.edu	Sardinia	OH	45171	937-695-0307	695-8093*
Clark State Community College 300 S Fountain Ave Web: www.clarkstate.edu	Springfield	OH	45506	937-325-0691	328-6097
Southern State Community College *North* 1850 Davids Dr *Fax: Admissions ■ Web: www.sscc.edu	Wilmington	OH	45177	937-382-6645	383-1206*

OKLAHOMA

	City	State	Zip	Phone	Fax
Western Oklahoma State College 2801 N Main St Web: www.wosc.edu	Altus	OK	73521	580-477-2000	477-7723
Rogers State University Bartlesville 401 E Adams Rd *Fax: Admissions ■ TF: 800-256-7511 ■ Web: www.rsu.edu	Bartlesville	OK	74003	918-335-3500	338-8095*
Redlands Community College 1300 S Country Club Rd *Fax: Admissions ■ TF: 866-415-6367 ■ Web: www.redlandscc.edu	El Reno	OK	73036	405-262-2552	422-1200*
Comanche Nation College 1608 SW 9th St TF: 877-591-0203 ■ Web: www.cnc.cc.ok.us	Lawton	OK	73501	580-591-0203	353-7075
Northeastern Oklahoma A&M College 200 I St NE *Fax: Admissions ■ Web: www.neoam.edu	Miami	OK	74354	918-542-8441	540-6946*
Rose State College 6420 SE 15th St *Fax: Admissions ■ Web: www.rose.edu	Midwest City	OK	73110	405-733-7311	736-0309*
Oklahoma City Community College 7777 S May Ave *Fax: Admissions ■ Web: www.occc.edu	Oklahoma City	OK	73159	405-682-1611	682-7521*
Oklahoma City 900 N Portland Ave *Fax: Admissions ■ TF: 800-560-4099 ■ Web: www.osuokc.edu	Oklahoma City	OK	73107	405-947-4421	945-9120*
Carl Albert State College 1507 S McKenna St Web: www.carlalbert.edu	Poteau	OK	74953	918-647-1300	647-1306
Rogers State University Pryor 421 S Elliott St *Fax: Admissions ■ Web: www.rsu.edu	Pryor	OK	74361	918-825-6117	825-6135*
Southwestern Oklahoma State University Sayre 409 E Mississippi St *Fax: Admissions ■ Web: www.swosu.edu/sayre	Sayre	OK	73662	580-928-5533	928-1140*
Seminole State College 2701 Boren Blvd PO Box 351 *Fax: Admissions ■ Web: www.ssc.cc.ok.us	Seminole	OK	74818	405-382-9950	382-9524*
Murray State College 1 Murray Campus *Fax: Admissions ■ TF: 800-342-0698 ■ Web: www.mscok.edu	Tishomingo	OK	73460	580-371-2371	371-9844*
Northern Oklahoma College 1220 E Grand St PO Box 310 *Fax: Admissions ■ TF: 888-429-5715 ■ Web: www.north-ok.edu	Tonkawa	OK	74653	580-628-6200	628-6371*
Tulsa Community College *Metro* 909 S Boston Ave *Fax: Admissions ■ Web: www.tulsacc.edu	Tulsa	OK	74119	918-595-7000	595-7347*
Northeast 3727 E Apache St Web: www.tulsacc.edu	Tulsa	OK	74115	918-595-7000	595-7594
Southeast 10300 E 81st St Web: www.tulsacc.edu	Tulsa	OK	74133	918-595-7000	595-7748
West 7505 W 41st St Web: www.tulsacc.edu	Tulsa	OK	74107	918-595-7000	595-8130
Connors State College 1000 College Rd Web: www.connors.cc.ok.us	Warner	OK	74469	918-463-2931	463-6324
Eastern Oklahoma State College 1301 W Main St Web: www.eosc.edu	Wilburton	OK	74578	918-465-2361	465-4417

OREGON

	City	State	Zip	Phone	Fax
Linn-Benton Community College 6500 Pacific Blvd SW *Fax: Admissions ■ Web: www.linnbenton.edu	Albany	OR	97321	541-917-4999	917-4838*
Clatsop Community College 1653 Jerome Ave TF: 866-252-8767 ■ Web: www.clatsopcc.edu	Astoria	OR	97103	503-325-0910	325-5738
Central Oregon Community College 2600 NW College Way *Fax: Admissions ■ Web: www.cocc.edu	Bend	OR	97701	541-383-7700	383-7506*
Southwestern Oregon Community College 1988 Newmark Ave TF: 800-962-2838 ■ Web: www.socc.edu	Coos Bay	OR	97420	541-888-2525	888-1513

	City	State	Zip	Phone	Fax
Cottage Grove 1275 S River Rd PO Box 96	Cottage Grove	OR	97424	541-463-4202	942-5186
Web: www.lanecc.edu					
Lane Community College 4000 E 30th Ave	Eugene	OR	97405	541-463-3000	463-3995*
**Fax:* Admissions ■ *Web:* www.lanecc.edu					
Florence 3149 Oak St	Florence	OR	97439	541-997-8444	997-8448
Web: www.lanecc.edu					
Rogue Community College 3345 Redwood Hwy	Grants Pass	OR	97527	541-956-7500	471-3585*
**Fax:* Admissions ■ *TF:* 800-411-6508 ■ *Web:* www.roguecc.edu					
Mount Hood Community College					
26000 SE Stark St	Gresham	OR	97030	503-491-6422	491-7388*
**Fax:* Admissions ■ *Web:* www.mhcc.edu					
Klamath Community College					
7390 S 6th St	Klamath Falls	OR	97603	541-882-3521	885-7758
Web: www.kcc.cc.or.us					
Riverside 117 S Central	Medford	OR	97501	541-245-7500	245-7648
Web: www.roguecc.edu					
Treasure Valley Community College					
650 College Blvd	Ontario	OR	97914	541-881-8822	881-2721*
**Fax:* Admissions ■ *Web:* www.tvcc.cc.or.us					
Clackamas Community College					
19600 S Molalla Ave	Oregon City	OR	97045	503-657-8400	722-5864*
**Fax:* Admissions ■ *Web:* www.clackamas.edu					
Blue Mountain Community College					
2411 NW Carden Ave PO Box 100	Pendleton	OR	97801	541-276-1260	278-5871*
**Fax:* Admissions ■ *Web:* www.bluecc.edu					
Portland Community College					
Sylvania 12000 SW 49th Ave	Portland	OR	97219	503-244-6111	977-4740*
**Fax:* Admissions ■ *Web:* www.pcc.edu					
Umpqua Community College					
1140 Umpqva College Rd PO Box 967	Roseburg	OR	97470	541-440-4600	440-4612
Web: www.umpqua.edu					
Chemeketa Community College					
4000 Lancaster Dr NE PO Box 14007	Salem	OR	97309	503-399-5006	399-3918*
**Fax:* Admissions ■ *Web:* www.chemek.cc.or.us					
Tillamook Bay Community College					
4301 3rd St	Tillamook	OR	97141	503-842-8222	842-2214
TF: 888-306-8222 ■ *Web:* www.tbcc.cc.or.us					

PENNSYLVANIA

	City	State	Zip	Phone	Fax
Northampton Community College					
3835 Green Pond Rd	Bethlehem	PA	18020	610-861-5300	861-4560*
**Fax:* Admissions ■ *TF:* 877-543-0998 ■ *Web:* www.northampton.edu					
Montgomery County Community College					
Central 340 DeKalb Pike	Blue Bell	PA	19422	215-641-6300	619-7188*
**Fax:* Admitting ■ *Web:* www.mc3.edu					
Bristol 1280 New Rodgers Rd	Bristol	PA	19007	215-781-3939	781-3928
Web: www.bucks.edu					
Harcum College 750 Montgomery Ave	Bryn Mawr	PA	19010	610-525-4100	526-6147*
**Fax:* Admissions ■ *TF:* 800-345-2600 ■ *Web:* www.harcum.edu					
Butler County Community College					
107 College Dr	Butler	PA	16002	724-287-8711	285-6047
TF: 888-826-2829 ■ *Web:* www.bc3.edu					
Downingtown 100 Bond Dr	Downington	PA	19335	484-237-6200	237-6305
Web: www.dccc.edu/locations/about_dtown					
DuBois 1 College Pl	Du Bois	PA	15801	814-375-4700	375-4784*
**Fax:* Admissions ■ *TF:* 800-346-7627 ■ *Web:* www.ds.psu.edu					
Worthington Scranton 120 Ridge View Dr	Dunmore	PA	18512	570-963-2500	963-2524*
**Fax:* Admissions ■ *Web:* www.sn.psu.edu					
Pennsylvania Highlands Community College					
881 Hills Plaza Dr Suite 450	Ebensburg	PA	15931	814-262-6446	262-6420
Web: www.pennhighlands.edu					
Lehigh Valley 8380 Mohr Ln PO Box 549	Fogelsville	PA	18051	610-285-5000	285-5220*
**Fax:* Admissions ■ *Web:* www.lv.psu.edu					
Gettysburg 731 Old Harrisburg Rd	Gettysburg	PA	17325	717-337-3855	337-3015*
**Fax:* Admissions ■ *TF:* 800-222-4222 ■ *Web:* www.hacc.edu					
Harrisburg Area Community College					
1 HACC Dr	Harrisburg	PA	17110	717-780-2300	231-7674*
**Fax:* Admissions ■ *TF:* 800-222-4222 ■ *Web:* www.hacc.edu					
Hazleton 76 University Dr	Hazleton	PA	18202	570-450-3000	450-3182*
**Fax:* Admissions ■ *TF:* 800-279-8495 ■ *Web:* www.hn.psu.edu					
Manor College 700 Fox Chase Rd	Jenkintown	PA	19046	215-885-2360	576-6564*
**Fax:* Admissions ■ *Web:* www.manor.edu					
Lebanon 735 Cumberland St	Lebanon	PA	17042	717-270-4222	270-6385
TF: 800-222-4222 ■ *Web:* www.hacc.edu					
Wilkes-Barre Old Rt 115 PO Box PSU	Lehman	PA	18627	570-675-2171	675-9113*
**Fax:* Admissions ■ *Web:* www.wb.psu.edu					
McKeesport 4000 University Dr	McKeesport	PA	15132	412-675-9000	675-9056*
**Fax:* Admissions ■ *Web:* www.mk.psu.edu					
Delaware County Community College					
901 Media Line Rd	Media	PA	19063	610-359-5000	359-5343
TF: 800-543-0146 ■ *Web:* www.dccc.edu					
Community College of Beaver County					
1 Campus Dr	Monaca	PA	15061	724-775-8561	728-7599*
**Fax:* Admissions ■ *TF:* 800-335-0222 ■ *Web:* www.ccbc.edu					
Beaver 100 University Dr	Monaca	PA	15061	724-773-3500	773-3578*
**Fax:* Admissions ■ *TF:* 877-564-6778 ■ *Web:* www.br.psu.edu					
Boyce 595 Beatty Rd	Monroeville	PA	15146	724-325-6614	325-6859*
**Fax:* Admissions ■ *Web:* www.ccac.edu					
Mont Alto 1 Campus Dr	Mont Alto	PA	17237	717-749-6000	749-6132*
**Fax:* Admissions ■ *TF:* 800-392-6173 ■ *Web:* www.ma.psu.edu					
Luzerne County Community College					
1333 S Prospect St	Nanticoke	PA	18634	570-740-0200	740-0238*
**Fax:* Admissions ■ *TF:* 800-377-5222 ■ *Web:* www.luzerne.edu					
New Kensington 3550 7th St Rd Rt 780	New Kensington	PA	15068	724-334-6000	334-6111
Web: www.nk.psu.edu					
Bucks County Community College 275 Swamp Rd	Newtown	PA	18940	215-968-8000	968-8110*
**Fax:* Admissions ■ *Web:* www.bucks.edu					
Upper County 1 Hillendale Dr	Perkasie	PA	18944	215-258-7700	258-7749
Web: www.bucks.edu					
Community College of Philadelphia					
1700 Spring Garden St	Philadelphia	PA	19130	215-751-8000	751-8001*
**Fax:* Admissions ■ *Web:* www.ccp.edu					
Community College of Allegheny County					
Allegheny 808 Ridge Ave	Pittsburgh	PA	15212	412-237-2525	237-4581*
**Fax:* Admissions ■ *Web:* www.ccac.edu					
North 8701 Perry Hwy	Pittsburgh	PA	15237	412-366-7000	369-3635*
**Fax:* Admissions ■ *Web:* www.ccac.edu					
Pottstown 101 College Dr	Pottstown	PA	19464	610-718-1800	718-1999
Web: www.mc3.edu					
Berks PO Box 7009	Reading	PA	19610	610-396-6000	396-6077
Web: www.bk.psu.edu					
Reading Area Community College					
10 S 2nd St PO Box 1706	Reading	PA	19603	610-372-4721	607-6290*
**Fax:* Admissions ■ *TF:* 800-626-1665 ■ *Web:* www.racc.edu					
Lehigh Carbon Community College					
4525 Education Pk Dr	Schnecksville	PA	18078	610-799-2121	799-1527
TF: 800-414-3975 ■ *Web:* www.lccc.edu					
Schuylkill 200 University Dr	Schuylkill Haven	PA	17972	570-385-6000	385-6272*
**Fax:* Admissions ■ *Web:* www.sl.psu.edu					
Lackawanna College 501 Vine St	Scranton	PA	18509	570-961-7810	961-7843*
**Fax:* Admissions ■ *TF:* 877-346-3552 ■ *Web:* www.lackawanna.edu					
Shenango 147 Shenango Ave	Sharon	PA	16146	724-983-2803	983-2820*
**Fax:* Admissions ■ *Web:* www.shenango.psu.edu					
Southeast 2000 Elmwood Ave	Sharon Hill	PA	19079	610-957-5700	957-5787
Web: www.dccc.edu					
Morgan Ctr 234 High St	Tamaqua	PA	18252	570-668-6880	668-7296
TF: 888-414-3975 ■ *Web:* www.lccc.edu					
Monroe 3 Old Mill Rd PO Box 530	Tannersville	PA	18372	570-620-9221	620-9317
TF: 877-543-0998 ■ *Web:* www.northampton.edu					
Titusville 504 E Main St	Titusville	PA	16354	814-827-5668	827-4519*
**Fax:* Admissions ■ *TF:* 888-878-0462 ■ *Web:* www.upt.pitt.edu					
Fayette Rt 119 N PO Box 519	Uniontown	PA	15401	724-430-4100	430-4175*
**Fax:* Admissions ■ *TF:* 877-568-4130 ■ *Web:* www.fe.psu.edu					
Valley Forge Military Academy & College					
1001 Eagle Rd	Wayne	PA	19087	610-989-1300	688-1545*
**Fax:* Admissions ■ *TF:* 800-234-8362 ■ *Web:* www.vfmac.edu					
South 1750 Clairton Rd Rt 885	West Mifflin	PA	15122	412-469-1100	469-6291*
**Fax:* Admissions ■ *Web:* www.ccac.edu					
York 1031 Edgecomb Ave	York	PA	17403	717-771-4000	771-4005*
**Fax:* Admissions ■ *TF:* 800-778-6227 ■ *Web:* www.yk.psu.edu					
Westmoreland County Community College					
145 Pavilion Ln	Youngwood	PA	15697	724-925-4000	925-5802*
**Fax:* Admissions ■ *TF:* 800-262-2103 ■ *Web:* www.wccc-pa.edu					

QUEBEC

	City	State	Zip	Phone	Fax
College Merici 755 ch St-Louis	Quebec City	QC	G1S1C1	418-683-1591	685-8938
TF: 800-208-1463 ■ *Web:* www.college-merici.qc.ca					

RHODE ISLAND

	City	State	Zip	Phone	Fax
Community College of Rhode Island					
Flanagan 1762 Louisquisset Pike	Lincoln	RI	02865	401-333-7000	333-7122*
**Fax:* Admissions ■ *Web:* www.ccri.edu					
Liston 1 Hilton St	Providence	RI	02905	401-455-6000	455-6014
Web: www.ccri.edu					
Knight 400 E Ave	Warwick	RI	02886	401-825-1000	825-2394*
**Fax:* Admissions ■ *Web:* www.ccri.edu					

SOUTH CAROLINA

	City	State	Zip	Phone	Fax
Salkehatchie PO Box 617	Allendale	SC	29810	803-584-3446	584-5038
TF: 800-922-5500 ■ *Web:* www.uscsalkehatchie.sc.edu					
Northeastern Technical College 1201 E Blvd	Cheraw	SC	29520	843-921-6900	921-1476
Web: www.netc.edu					
Midlands Technical College PO Box 2408	Columbia	SC	29202	803-738-1400	790-7524*
**Fax:* Admissions ■ *TF:* 800-922-8038 ■ *Web:* www.midlandstech.edu					
Aiken Technical College					
2276 Jefferson Davis Pkwy PO Drawer 696	Graniteville	SC	29829	803-593-9231	593-6526*
**Fax:* Admissions ■ *Web:* www.atc.edu					
Greenville Technical College					
Barton 506 S Pleasantburg Dr	Greenville	SC	29606	864-250-8000	250-8534*
**Fax:* Admissions ■ *TF:* 800-723-0673 ■ *Web:* greenvilletech.com/barton					
Brashier PO Box 5616	Greenville	SC	29606	864-228-5000	228-5009
TF: 800-723-0673 ■ *Web:* www.greenvilletech.com					
Williamsburg Technical College					
601 MLK Jr Ave	Kingstree	SC	29556	843-355-4110	355-4289*
**Fax:* Admissions ■ *TF:* 800-768-2021 ■ *Web:* www.williamsburgtech.com					
Lancaster PO Box 889	Lancaster	SC	29721	803-313-7471	313-7106*
**Fax:* Admissions ■ *Web:* www.usclancaster.sc.edu					
Orangeburg-Calhoun Technical College					
3250 St Matthews Rd NE	Orangeburg	SC	29118	803-536-0311	535-1368*
**Fax:* Admissions ■ *Web:* www.octech.org					
Clinton Junior College 1029 Crawford Rd	Rock Hill	SC	29730	803-327-7402	327-3261*
**Fax:* Admissions ■ *Web:* www.clintonjuniorcollege.edu					
York Technical College 452 S Anderson Rd	Rock Hill	SC	29730	803-327-8000	327-8059
TF: 800-922-8324 ■ *Web:* www.yorktech.com					

Phone Fax

Spartanburg Methodist College
1000 Powell Mill Rd. . . . Spartanburg SC 29301 864-587-4000 587-4355*
*Fax: Admissions ■ Web: www.smcsc.edu
Greer 2522 Locust Hill Rd. . . . Taylors SC 29607 864-848-2000 848-2982*
*Fax: Admissions ■ TF: 800-723-0673 ■ Web: www.greenvilletech.com
North Greenville University
7801 N Tigerville Rd PO Box 1892. . . . Tigerville SC 29688 864-977-7000 977-7177*
*Fax: Admissions ■ TF: 800-468-6642 ■ Web: www.ngu.edu
Union 401 E Main St. . . . Union SC 29379 864-429-8728 427-3682
TF: 800-768-5566 ■ Web: www.uscunion.sc.edu

SOUTH DAKOTA

Phone Fax

Mitchell Technical Institute
821 N Capital St. . . . Mitchell SD 57301 605-995-3024 996-3299
TF: 800-952-0042 ■ Web: www.mitchelltech.com
Kilian Community College 300 E 6th St. . . . Sioux Falls SD 57103 605-221-3100 336-2606*
*Fax: Admissions ■ TF: 800-888-1147 ■ Web: www.kilian.edu
Sisseton Wahpeton College 12572 BIA Hwy 700. . . . Sisseton SD 57262 605-698-3966 742-0394
Web: www.swc.tc
Lake Area Technical Institute
230 11th St NE PO Box 730. . . . Watertown SD 57201 605-882-5284 882-6299
TF: 800-657-4344 ■ Web: www.lati.tec.sd.us

TENNESSEE

Phone Fax

Chattanooga State Technical Community College
4501 Amnicola Hwy. . . . Chattanooga TN 37406 423-697-4400 697-3115*
*Fax: Admissions ■ TF: 866-547-3733 ■ Web: www.chattanoogastate.edu
Cleveland State Community College
3535 Adkisson Dr. . . . Cleveland TN 37312 423-472-7141 478-6255
Web: www.clevelandstatecc.edu
Clifton 795 Main St. . . . Clifton TN 38425 931-676-6966 676-6941
Web: www.columbiastate.edu
Columbia State Community College
PO Box 1315 . . . . Columbia TN 38402 931-540-2722 540-2830*
*Fax: Admissions ■ Web: www.columbiastate.edu
Dyersburg State Community College
1510 Lake Rd. . . . Dyersburg TN 38024 731-286-3200 286-3325*
*Fax: Admissions ■ Web: www.dscc.edu
Volunteer State Community College
1480 Nashville Pike . . . . Gallatin TN 37066 615-452-8600 230-4875*
*Fax: Admissions ■ TF: 888-335-8722 ■ Web: www.volstate.edu
Roane State Community College 276 Patton Ln. . . . Harriman TN 37748 865-354-3000 882-4562*
*Fax: Admitting ■ TF: 800-343-9104 ■ Web: www.rscc.cc.tn.us
Jackson State Community College 2046 N Pkwy. . . . Jackson TN 38301 731-424-3520 425-9559*
*Fax: Admissions ■ Web: www.jscc.edu
Pellissippi State Technical Community College
10915 Hardin Valley Rd . . . . Knoxville TN 37933 865-694-6400 539-7217*
*Fax: Admissions ■ Web: www.pstcc.edu
Lexington-Henderson County 932 E Church St. . . . Lexington TN 38351 731-968-5722 968-1539
Web: www.jscc.edu
Motlow State Community College PO Box 8500 . . . . Lynchburg TN 37352 931-393-1500 393-1971*
*Fax: Admissions ■ TF: 800-654-4877 ■ Web: www.mscc.cc.tn.us
Hiwassee College
225 Hiwassee College Dr . . . . Madisonville TN 37354 423-442-2001 442-8521*
*Fax: Admissions ■ TF: 800-356-2187 ■ Web: www.hiwassee.edu
Southwest Tennessee Community College
PO Box 780 . . . . Memphis TN 38101 901-333-5000 333-4473
TF: 877-717-7822 ■ Web: www.southwest.tn.edu
Walters State Community College
500 S Davy Crockett Pkwy . . . . Morristown TN 37813 423-585-2600 585-6786*
*Fax: Admissions ■ TF: 800-225-4770 ■ Web: www.ws.edu

TEXAS

Phone Fax

Abilene 717 E Industrial Blvd. . . . Abilene TX 79602 325-794-4400 442-5100*
*Fax Area Code: 254 ■ Web: www.cisco.cc.tx.us
Abilene 650 E Hwy 80 . . . . Abilene TX 79601 325-672-7091 734-3658
Web: www.westtexas.tstc.edu
Amarillo College 2201 S Washington St. . . . Amarillo TX 79109 806-371-5000 371-5066
Web: www.actx.edu
Tarrant County College
Southeast 2100 SE Pkwy. . . . Arlington TX 76018 817-515-3100 515-3182*
*Fax: Admissions ■ Web: www.tccd.edu
Trinity Valley Community College
Athens 100 Cardinal Dr. . . . Athens TX 75751 903-675-6200 675-6209*
*Fax: Admissions ■ TF: 866-882-2937 ■ Web: www.tvcc.edu
Austin Community College
5930 Middle Fiskville Rd . . . . Austin TX 78752 512-223-7000 223-7665*
*Fax: Admissions ■ Web: www.austincc.edu
Eastview 3401 Webberville Rd. . . . Austin TX 78702 512-223-5100 223-5900*
*Fax: Admissions ■ Web: www.austincc.edu/evc
Northridge 11928 Stonehollow Dr. . . . Austin TX 78758 512-223-4000 223-4651*
*Fax: Admissions ■ Web: www.austincc.edu/nrg
Pinnacle 7748 Hwy 290 W. . . . Austin TX 78736 512-223-8001 223-8122
Web: www.austincc.edu/locations/pin.php
Rio Grande 1212 Rio Grande St. . . . Austin TX 78701 512-223-3000 223-3444*
*Fax: Admissions ■ Web: www.austincc.edu/rgc
Riverside 1020 Grove Blvd . . . . Austin TX 78741 512-223-6000 223-6767*
*Fax: Admissions ■ Web: www.austincc.edu/rvs
Lee College 200 Lee Dr . . . . Baytown TX 77520 281-427-5611 425-6831
Web: www.lee.edu

Phone Fax

Coastal Bend College
Beeville 3800 Charco Rd . . . . Beeville TX 78102 361-358-2838 354-2254*
*Fax: Admissions ■ TF: 866-722-2838 ■ Web: www.vct.coastalbend.edu
Howard College 1001 Birdwell Ln. . . . Big Spring TX 79720 432-264-5000 264-5082*
*Fax: Admissions ■ Web: www.howardcollege.edu
Southwest Collegiate Institute for the Deaf
3200 Ave C . . . . Big Spring TX 79720 432-264-3700 264-3707*
*Fax: Admissions ■ Web: www.howardcollege.edu
Frank Phillips College PO Box 5118. . . . Borger TX 79008 806-457-4200 273-7642*
*Fax: Admissions ■ TF: 800-687-2056 ■ Web: www.fpc.cc.tx.us
Bowie 810 S Mill St. . . . Bowie TX 76230 940-872-4002 872-3065
Web: www.nctc.edu
Blinn College 902 College Ave . . . . Brenham TX 77833 979-830-4000 830-4110*
*Fax: Admissions ■ Web: www.blinn.edu
Texas Southmost College 80 Fort Brown St . . . . Brownsville TX 78520 956-882-8200 882-8832
TF: 800-850-0160 ■ Web: www.utb.edu
Panola College 1109 W Panola St . . . . Carthage TX 75633 903-693-2000 693-2031*
*Fax: Admissions ■ Web: www.panola.edu
Cypress Creek 1555 County Rd 182 . . . . Cedar Park TX 78613 512-223-2000 223-2048
Web: www.austincc.edu
Cisco Junior College 101 College Heights . . . . Cisco TX 76437 254-442-2567 442-5100*
*Fax: Admissions ■ Web: www.cisco.cc.tx.us
Clarendon College
1122 College Dr PO Box 968 . . . . Clarendon TX 79226 806-874-3571 874-5080*
*Fax: Admissions ■ TF: 800-687-9737 ■ Web: www.clarendoncollege.edu
Montgomery College 3200 College Pk Dr. . . . Conroe TX 77384 936-273-7000 273-7234*
*Fax: Admissions ■ Web: www.montgomery-college.com
Del Mar College
East 101 Baldwin Blvd. . . . Corpus Christi TX 78404 361-698-1200 698-1595*
*Fax: Admissions ■ TF: 800-652-3357 ■ Web: www.delmar.edu
Navarro College 3200 W 7th Ave . . . . Corsicana TX 75110 903-874-6501 875-7353*
*Fax: Admissions ■ TF: 800-628-2776 ■ Web: www.navarrocollege.edu
El Centro College 801 Main St. . . . Dallas TX 75202 214-860-2037 860-2233*
*Fax: Admissions ■ Web: www.ecc.dcccd.edu
Mountain View College 4849 W Illinois Ave. . . . Dallas TX 75211 214-860-8600 860-8570*
*Fax: Admissions ■ Web: www.mvc.dcccd.edu
Richland College 12800 Abrams Rd. . . . Dallas TX 75243 972-238-6100 238-6346*
*Fax: Admissions ■ Web: www.rlc.dcccd.edu
Grayson County College 6101 Grayson Dr . . . . Denison TX 75020 903-465-6030 463-5284*
*Fax: Admissions ■ Web: www.grayson.edu
El Paso Community College
Mission Del Paso 10700 Gateway E . . . . El Paso TX 79927 915-831-7017
Web: www.epcc.edu
Northwest 6701 S Desert Blvd. . . . El Paso TX 79932 915-831-8803 831-8926
Web: www.epcc.edu
Rio Grande 100 W Rio Grande Ave . . . . El Paso TX 79902 915-831-4000 831-4409*
*Fax: Admissions ■ Web: www.epcc.edu
Transmountain 9570 Gateway Blvd N . . . . El Paso TX 79924 915-831-5030 831-5209*
*Fax: Admissions ■ Web: www.epcc.edu
Valle Verde 919 Hunter Dr. . . . El Paso TX 79915 915-831-2000 831-2161*
*Fax: Admissions ■ Web: www.epcc.edu
Brookhaven College
3939 Valley View Ln. . . . Farmers Branch TX 75244 972-860-4700 860-4886*
*Fax: Admitting ■ Web: www.brookhavencollege.edu
Northwest 4801 Marine Creek Pkwy . . . . Fort Worth TX 76179 817-515-7100 515-7732*
*Fax: Admissions ■ Web: www.tccd.edu
South 5301 Campus Dr. . . . Fort Worth TX 76119 817-515-4100 515-4110*
*Fax: Admissions ■ Web: www.tccd.edu
Preston Ridge 9700 Wade Blvd . . . . Frisco TX 75035 972-377-1790 377-1723*
*Fax: Admissions ■ Web: www.ccccd.edu
North Central Texas College
1525 W California St . . . . Gainesville TX 76240 940-668-7731 665-7075*
*Fax: Admissions ■ Web: www.nctc.edu
Galveston College 4015 Ave Q. . . . Galveston TX 77550 409-763-6551 944-1501*
*Fax: Admissions ■ Web: www.gc.edu
Harlingen 1902 N Loop 499 . . . . Harlingen TX 78550 956-364-4000 364-5117
TF: 800-852-8784 ■ Web: www.harlingen.tstc.edu
Hill College 112 Lamar Dr PO Box 619. . . . Hillsboro TX 76645 254-659-7500 582-7591*
*Fax: Admissions ■ Web: www.hillcollege.edu
Houston Community College
Central College 1300 Holman . . . . Houston TX 77004 713-718-6000 718-6112
Web: www.ccollege.hccs.edu
NortheastCollege 4638 Airline Dr . . . . Houston TX 77022 713-718-8100
Web: www.hccs.edu
North Harris College 2700 WW Thorne Rd . . . . Houston TX 77073 281-618-5400 618-7141*
*Fax: Admissions ■ Web: www.northharriscollege.com
North 5800 Uvalde Rd. . . . Houston TX 77049 281-458-4050 459-7688*
*Fax: Admissions ■ Web: www.sjcd.edu
South 13735 Beamer Rd . . . . Houston TX 77089 281-922-3431 922-3485
Web: www.sjcd.edu
Northeast 828 Harwood Rd . . . . Hurst TX 76054 817-515-8223 515-6988*
*Fax: Admissions ■ Web: www.tccd.edu/Campuses_and_Centers/Northeast_Campus.html
North Lake College 5001 N MacArthur Blvd . . . . Irving TX 75038 972-273-3000 273-3112*
*Fax: Admissions ■ Web: www.northlakecollege.edu
Jacksonville College
105 BJ Albritton Dr. . . . Jacksonville TX 75766 903-586-2518 586-0743*
*Fax: Admissions ■ TF: 800-256-8522 ■ Web: www.jacksonville-college.edu
Lon Morris College
800 College Ave Administrative Bldg . . . . Jacksonville TX 75766 903-589-4000 589-4006*
*Fax: Admissions ■ TF: 800-259-5753 ■ Web: www.lonmorris.edu
Kilgore College 1100 Broadway . . . . Kilgore TX 75662 903-984-8531 988-7531*
*Fax: Admissions ■ Web: www.kilgore.edu
Central Texas College
6200 W Central Texas Expy. . . . Killeen TX 76549 254-526-1696 526-1111*
*Fax: Admissions ■ TF: 800-792-3348 ■ Web: www.online.ctcd.edu
Kingwood College 20000 Kingwood Dr. . . . Kingwood TX 77339 281-312-1600 312-1477*
*Fax: Admissions ■ TF: 800-883-7939 ■ Web: www.kcweb.nhmccd.edu
Brazosport College 500 College Dr . . . . Lake Jackson TX 77566 979-230-3000 230-3443*
*Fax: Admissions ■ Web: www.brazosport.edu

	City	State	ZIP	Phone	Fax
Cedar Valley College 3030 N Dallas Ave	Lancaster	TX	75134	972-860-8200	860-8001*
*Fax: Admissions ■ *Web:* www.dcccd.edu					
Laredo Community College					
West End Washington St.	Laredo	TX	78040	956-722-0521	721-5493*
*Fax: Admissions ■ *Web:* www.laredo.cc.tx.us					
South Plains College 1401 S College Ave	Levelland	TX	79336	806-894-9611	897-3167*
*Fax: Admissions ■ *Web:* www.southplainscollege.edu					
Collin County Community College					
Central Park 2200 W University Dr	McKinney	TX	75070	972-548-6790	548-6702*
*Fax: Admissions ■ *Web:* www.cccd.edu					
Eastfield College 3737 Motley Dr.	Mesquite	TX	75150	972-860-7100	860-8306
Web: www.eastfieldcollege.com					
Midland College 3600 N Garfield St	Midland	TX	79705	432-685-4500	685-4623*
*Fax: Admissions ■ *Web:* www.midland.edu					
Northeast Texas Community College					
1735 Chapel Hill Rd	Mount Pleasant	TX	75455	903-572-1911	572-6712*
*Fax: Admissions ■ *TF:* 800-870-0142 ■ *Web:* www.ntcc.edu					
Odessa College 201 W University Blvd.	Odessa	TX	79764	432-335-6400	335-6824
Web: www.odessa.edu					
Lamar State College					
Orange 410 Front St	Orange	TX	77630	409-883-7750	882-3055*
*Fax: Admissions ■ *Web:* www.lsco.edu					
Palestine PO Box 2530	Palestine	TX	75802	903-729-0256	729-2325
Web: www.tvcc.edu					
Paris Junior College 2400 Clarksville St	Paris	TX	75460	903-785-7661	782-0427*
*Fax: Admissions ■ *TF:* 800-232-5804 ■ *Web:* www.parisjc.edu					
San Jacinto College					
Central 8060 Spencer Hwy	Pasadena	TX	77505	281-476-1501	478-2720
Web: www.sjcd.edu					
Spring Creek 2800 E Spring Creek Pkwy.	Plano	TX	75074	972-881-5790	881-5174*
*Fax: Admissions ■ *Web:* www.cccd.edu					
Port Arthur PO Box 310	Port Arthur	TX	77641	409-983-4921	984-6025*
*Fax: Admissions ■ *TF:* 800-477-5872 ■ *Web:* www.pa.lamar.edu					
Ranger College 1100 College Cir	Ranger	TX	76470	254-647-3234	647-3739*
*Fax: Admissions ■ *Web:* www.ranger.cc.tx.us					
Western Texas College 6200 College Ave.	Snyder	TX	79549	325-573-8511	573-9321*
*Fax: Admissions ■ *TF:* 888-468-6982 ■ *Web:* www.wtc.edu					
Southwest College 9910 Cash Rd	Stafford	TX	77477	713-718-7802	718-7793
Web: www.swc2.hccs.edu					
Sugar Land 550 Julie Rivers Dr.	Sugar Land	TX	77478	281-243-8410	243-8432*
*Fax: Admissions ■ *TF:* 800-561-9252 ■ *Web:* www.wcjc.edu					
Texas State Technical College					
Sweetwater 300 Homer K Taylor Dr	Sweetwater	TX	79556	325-235-7300	235-7443
Web: www.westtexas.tstc.edu					
Temple College 2600 S 1st St.	Temple	TX	76504	254-298-8300	298-8288*
*Fax: Admissions ■ *TF Admissions:* 800-460-4636 ■ *Web:* www.templejc.edu					
Terrell 1200 IH- 20	Terrell	TX	75160	972-563-9573	563-1667
Web: www.tvcc.edu					
Texarkana College 2500 N Robison Rd	Texarkana	TX	75599	903-838-4541	832-5030*
*Fax: Admissions ■ *Web:* www.texarkanacollege.edu					
College of the Mainland 1200 N Amburn Rd	Texas City	TX	77591	409-938-1211	938-1306
Web: www.com.edu					
Tomball College 30555 Tomball Pkwy	Tomball	TX	77375	281-351-3300	351-3384*
*Fax: Admissions ■ *Web:* www.tomballcollege.com					
Tyler Junior College PO Box 9020.	Tyler	TX	75711	903-510-2523	510-2161*
*Fax: Admissions ■ *TF:* 800-687-5680 ■ *Web:* www.tjc.edu					
Southwest Texas Junior College					
2401 Garner Field Rd	Uvalde	TX	78801	830-278-4401	591-7396*
*Fax: Admissions ■ *Web:* www.swtjc.net					
Vernon College 4400 College Dr.	Vernon	TX	76384	940-552-6291	553-1753
Web: www.vernoncollege.edu					
Victoria College 2200 E Red River St.	Victoria	TX	77901	361-573-3291	582-2525
Web: www.vc.cc.tx.us					
McLennan Community College 1400 College Dr.	Waco	TX	76708	254-299-8000	299-8694*
*Fax: Admissions ■ *Web:* www.mclennan.edu					
Waco 3801 Campus Dr	Waco	TX	76705	254-799-3611	867-3044
TF: 800-792-8784 ■ *Web:* www.waco.tstc.edu					
Weatherford College 225 College Pk Dr	Weatherford	TX	76086	817-594-5471	598-6205*
*Fax: Admissions ■ *TF:* 800-287-5471 ■ *Web:* www.wc.edu					
Wharton County Junior College 911 Boling Hwy	Wharton	TX	77488	979-532-4560	532-6494*
*Fax: Admissions ■ *TF:* 800-561-9252 ■ *Web:* www.wcjc.edu					

UTAH

	City	State	ZIP	Phone	Fax
San Juan 639 W 100 S	Blanding	UT	84511	435-678-2201	678-2220*
*Fax: Admissions ■ *TF:* 800-395-2969 ■ *Web:* sjc.ceu.edu					
Snow College 150 College Ave PO Box 1028	Ephraim	UT	84627	435-283-7000	283-7157*
*Fax: Admissions ■ *Web:* www.snow.edu					
Stevens Henager College 1890 S 1350 W	Ogden	UT	84401	801-394-7791	621-0853
TF: 800-622-2640 ■ *Web:* www.stevenshenager.edu					
Utah Valley State College 800 W University Pkwy.	Orem	UT	84058	801-863-8000	225-4677*
*Fax: Admissions ■ *Web:* www.uvsc.edu					
College of Eastern Utah 451 E 400 N	Price	UT	84501	435-637-2120	613-5814*
*Fax: Admissions ■ *TF:* 800-336-2381 ■ *Web:* www.ceu.edu					
Salt Lake Community College					
Redwood 4600 S Redwood Rd.	Salt Lake City	UT	84130	801-957-4111	957-4444
Web: www.slcc.edu					
South City 1575 S State St	Salt Lake City	UT	84115	801-957-3413	957-3150
Web: www.slcc.edu					

VERMONT

	City	State	ZIP	Phone	Fax
Bennington 324 Main St	Bennington	VT	05201	802-447-2361	447-3246*
*Fax: Admissions ■ *Web:* www.ccv.edu/locations/bennington					
Brattleboro 70 Landmark Hill Suite 101	Brattleboro	VT	05301	802-254-6370	257-2593
Web: www.ccv.edu/locations/brattleboro					
Burlington 119 Pearl St	Burlington	VT	05401	802-865-4422	865-3323*
*Fax: Admissions ■ *Web:* www.ccv.edu/burlington_college					
Middlebury 10 Merchants Row Suite 223	Middlebury	VT	05753	802-388-3032	388-4686*
*Fax: Admissions ■ *Web:* www.ccv.edu					
Montpelier 32 College St.	Montpelier	VT	05602	802-828-4060	828-2801*
*Fax: Admissions ■ *Web:* www.ccv.edu					
Morrisville 197 Harrell St Suite 2	Morrisville	VT	05661	802-888-4258	888-2554*
*Fax: Admissions ■ *Web:* www.ccv.edu					
Newport 100 Main St Suite 150.	Newport	VT	05855	802-334-3387	334-5373*
*Fax: Admissions ■ *Web:* www.ccv.edu/locations/newport					
Landmark College 1 River Road S PO Box 820	Putney	VT	05346	802-387-6718	387-6868*
*Fax: Admissions ■ *Web:* www.landmarkcollege.org					
Rutland 24 Evelyn St	Rutland	VT	05701	802-786-6996	786-4980*
*Fax: Admissions ■ *Web:* www.ccv.edu					
Saint Albans 142 S Main St Suite 2	Saint Albans	VT	05478	802-524-6541	524-5216*
*Fax: Admissions ■ *Web:* www.ccv.edu					
Saint Johnsbury 1197 Main St Suite 3	Saint Johnsbury	VT	05819	802-748-6673	748-5014*
*Fax: Admissions ■ *Web:* www.ccv.edu					
Springfield 307 S St	Springfield	VT	05156	802-885-8360	885-8373
Web: www.ccv.edu					
Community College of Vermont					
Waterbury 103 S Main St.	Waterbury	VT	05676	802-241-3535	241-3526*
*Fax: Admissions ■ *Web:* www.ccv.vsc.edu					
Upper Valley					
145 Billings Farm Rd	White River Junction	VT	05001	802-295-8822	295-8862*
*Fax: Admissions ■ *Web:* www.ccv.edu					

VIRGINIA

	City	State	ZIP	Phone	Fax
Virginia Highlands Community College					
100 VHCC Dr PO Box 828	Abingdon	VA	24212	276-739-2400	739-2590*
*Fax: Admissions ■ *Web:* www.vhcc.edu					
Southside Virginia Community College					
109 County Rd 378.	Alberta	VA	23821	434-949-1000	949-7863
TF: 888-220-7822 ■ *Web:* www.sv.vccs.edu					
Alexandria 3001 N Beauregard St	Alexandria	VA	22311	703-845-6200	845-6046*
*Fax: Admissions ■ *Web:* www.nvcc.edu					
Northern Virginia Community College					
Annandale 8333 Little River Tpke	Annandale	VA	22003	703-323-3000	323-3367*
*Fax: Admissions ■ *TF:* 877-408-2028 ■ *Web:* www.nvcc.edu/campuses-and-centers/annandale/index.html					
Mountain Empire Community College					
3441 Mountain Empire Rd	Big Stone Gap	VA	24219	276-523-2400	523-8297*
*Fax: Admissions ■ *Web:* www.me.cc.va.us					
Piedmont Virginia Community College					
501 College Dr	Charlottesville	VA	22902	434-977-3900	961-5425*
*Fax: Admissions ■ *Web:* www.pvcc.edu					
Chesapeake 1428 Cedar Rd.	Chesapeake	VA	23322	757-822-5100	822-5122
TF: 800-371-0898 ■ *Web:* www.tcc.edu					
John Tyler Community College					
13101 Jefferson Davis Hwy	Chester	VA	23831	804-796-4000	796-4362*
*Fax: Admissions ■ *Web:* www.jtcc.edu					
Dabney S Lancaster Community College					
1000 Dabney Dr PO Box 1000	Clifton Forge	VA	24422	540-863-2800	863-2915
Web: www.dl.vccs.edu					
Danville Community College 1008 S Main St	Danville	VA	24541	434-797-2222	797-8541*
*Fax: Admissions ■ *Web:* www.dcc.vccs.edu					
New River Community College					
5251 College PO Box 1127	Dublin	VA	24084	540-674-3600	674-3644*
*Fax: Admissions ■ *TF:* 866-462-6722 ■ *Web:* www.nr.edu					
Paul D Camp Community College					
100 N College Dr PO Box 737	Franklin	VA	23851	757-569-6700	569-6795*
*Fax: Admissions ■ *Web:* www.pdc.edu					
Fredericksburg					
10000 Germanna Point Dr	Fredericksburg	VA	22408	540-891-3000	710-2092*
*Fax: Admissions ■ *Web:* www.germanna.edu					
Rappahannock Community College					
Glenns 12745 College Dr	Glenns	VA	23149	804-758-6700	758-6830*
*Fax: Admissions ■ *TF:* 800-836-9381 ■ *Web:* www.rappahannock.edu					
Thomas Nelson Community College					
99 Thomas Nelson Dr	Hampton	VA	23666	757-825-2700	825-2763*
*Fax: Admissions ■ *Web:* www.tncc.vccs.edu					
Blue Ridge Community College Harrisonburg					
160 N Mason St	Harrisonburg	VA	22802	540-432-3690	
Web: www.brcc.edu					
Germanna Community College					
Locust Grove 2130 Germanna Hwy	Locust Grove	VA	22508	540-423-9030	727-3207
Web: www.germanna.edu					
Central Virginia Community College					
3506 Wards Rd.	Lynchburg	VA	24502	434-832-7600	832-7793*
*Fax: Admissions ■ *Web:* www.cv.cc.va.us					
Manassas 6901 Sudley Rd	Manassas	VA	20109	703-257-6600	257-6565*
*Fax: Admitting ■ *Web:* www.nvcc.edu					
Patrick Henry Community College					
645 Patriot Ave PO Box 5311	Martinsville	VA	24112	276-638-8777	656-0352*
*Fax: Admissions ■ *Web:* www.ph.vccs.edu					
Eastern Shore Community College					
29300 Lankford Hwy.	Melfa	VA	23410	757-787-5900	789-1737*
*Fax: Admissions ■ *Web:* www.es.vccs.edu					
Lord Fairfax Community College					
Middletown 173 Skirmisher Ln	Middletown	VA	22645	540-868-7000	868-7005*
*Fax: Admissions ■ *TF:* 800-906-5322 ■ *Web:* www.lfcc.edu					
Norfolk 315 Granby St.	Norfolk	VA	23510	757-822-1110	822-1154
TF: 800-371-0898 ■ *Web:* www.tcc.edu/welcome/locations/norfolk					

	City	State	ZIP	Phone	Fax
Richard Bland College 11301 Johnson Rd	Petersburg	VA	23805	804-862-6100	862-6490*
**Fax:* Admissions ■ *Web:* www.rbc.edu					
Tidewater Community College					
Portsmouth 7000 College Dr	Portsmouth	VA	23703	757-822-2124	822-2002*
**Fax:* Admissions ■ *TF:* 800-371-0898 ■ *Web:* www.tcc.edu					
Southwest Virginia Community College					
PO Box SWCC	Richlands	VA	24641	276-964-2555	964-7716*
**Fax:* Admissions ■ *TF:* 800-822-7822 ■ *Web:* www.sw.edu					
J Sargeant Reynolds Community College					
1701 E Parham Rd	Richmond	VA	23228	804-371-3000	371-3650*
**Fax:* Admissions ■ *Web:* www.reynolds.edu					
Downtown 700 E Jackson St	Richmond	VA	23219	804-523-5455	371-3650
Web: www.jsr.vccs.edu					
Virginia Western Community College					
3094 Colonial Ave PO Box 14007	Roanoke	VA	24038	540-857-8922	857-6102*
**Fax:* Admissions ■ *Web:* www.virginiawestern.edu					
Loudoun 1000 Harry Flood Byrd Hwy	Sterling	VA	20164	703-450-2500	450-2536
Web: www.nvcc.edu					
Hobbs Suffolk 271 Kenyon Rd	Suffolk	VA	23434	757-925-6300	925-6370*
**Fax:* Admissions ■ *Web:* www.pdc.edu/hobbs-suffolk-campus					
Virginia Beach 1700 College Crescent	Virginia Beach	VA	23453	757-822-7100	822-7350
TF: 800-371-0898 ■ *Web:* www.tcc.edu					
Fauquier 6480 College St	Warrenton	VA	20187	540-351-1505	351-1530*
**Fax:* Admissions ■ *Web:* www.lfcc.edu					
Warsaw 52 Campus Dr	Warsaw	VA	22572	804-333-6700	333-0106*
**Fax:* Admissions ■ *Web:* www.rcc.vccs.edu					
Blue Ridge Community College					
1 College Ln PO Box 80	Weyers Cave	VA	24486	540-234-9261	453-2437*
**Fax:* Admissions ■ *Web:* www.brcc.edu					
Woodbridge 15200 Neabsco Mills Rd	Woodbridge	VA	22191	703-323-3000	878-5692*
**Fax:* Admissions ■ *TF:* 877-408-2028 ■ *Web:* www.nvcc.edu					
Wytheville Community College					
1000 E Main St	Wytheville	VA	24382	276-223-4700	223-4860*
**Fax:* Admissions ■ *Web:* www.wcc.vccs.edu					

WASHINGTON

	City	State	ZIP	Phone	Fax
Grays Harbor College 1620 Edward P Smith Dr	Aberdeen	WA	98520	360-532-9020	538-4293*
**Fax:* Admissions ■ *Web:* www.ghc.ctc.edu					
Green River Community College					
12401 SE 320th St	Auburn	WA	98092	253-833-9111	288-3454*
**Fax:* Admissions ■ *Web:* www.greenriver.edu					
Bellevue Community College					
3000 Landerholm Cir SE	Bellevue	WA	98007	425-564-1000	564-4065*
**Fax:* Admissions ■ *Web:* www.bcc.ctc.edu					
Northwest Indian College 2522 Kwina Rd	Bellingham	WA	98226	360-676-2772	392-4333*
**Fax:* Admissions ■ *TF:* 866-676-2772 ■ *Web:* www.nwic.edu					
Whatcom Community College					
237 W Kellogg Rd	Bellingham	WA	98226	360-676-2170	676-2171
Web: www.whatcom.ctc.edu					
Olympic College 1600 Chester Ave	Bremerton	WA	98337	360-792-6050	475-7202*
**Fax:* Admissions ■ *TF:* 800-259-6718 ■ *Web:* www.olympic.edu					
Centralia College 600 W Locust St	Centralia	WA	98531	360-736-9391	330-7503*
**Fax:* Admissions ■ *Web:* www.centralia.edu					
Everett Community College 2000 Tower St	Everett	WA	98201	425-388-9100	388-9129*
**Fax:* Admissions ■ *Web:* www.everettcc.edu					
Grandview 500 W Main St	Grandview	WA	98930	509-882-7000	882-7012
Web: www.yvcc.edu					
Clover Park Technical College					
4500 Steilacoom Blvd SW	Lakewood	WA	98499	253-589-5800	589-5750
Web: www.cptc.edu					
Pierce College 9401 Farwest Dr SW	Lakewood	WA	98498	253-964-6500	964-6427*
**Fax:* Admissions ■ *Web:* www.pierce.ctc.edu					
Lower Columbia College					
1600 Maple St PO Box 3010	Longview	WA	98632	360-442-2301	442-2379*
**Fax:* Admissions ■ *Web:* www.lowercolumbia.edu					
Edmonds Community College 20000 68th Ave W	Lynnwood	WA	98036	425-640-1500	640-1159
Web: www.edcc.edu					
Big Bend Community College					
7662 Chanute St	Moses Lake	WA	98837	509-762-5351	762-6243*
**Fax:* Admissions ■ *Web:* www.bigbend.edu					
Skagit Valley College					
2405 E College Way	Mount Vernon	WA	98273	360-416-7600	416-7890*
**Fax:* Admissions ■ *TF:* 877-385-5360 ■ *Web:* www.skagit.edu					
Whidbey Island 1900 SE Pioneer Way	Oak Harbor	WA	98277	360-679-5330	679-5375*
**Fax:* Admissions ■ *Web:* www.skagit.edu					
South Puget Sound Community College					
2011 Mottman Rd SW	Olympia	WA	98512	360-754-7711	596-5709*
**Fax:* Admissions ■ *Web:* www.spscc.ctc.edu					
Omak 116 W Apple Ave PO Box 2058	Omak	WA	98841	509-422-7803	422-7801*
**Fax:* Admissions ■ *Web:* www.wvc.edu					
Columbia Basin College 2600 N 20th Ave	Pasco	WA	99301	509-547-0511	546-0401
Web: www.columbiabasin.edu					
Peninsula College 1502 E Lauridsen Blvd	Port Angeles	WA	98362	360-452-9277	417-6581*
**Fax:* Admissions ■ *Web:* www.pc.ctc.edu					
Puyallup 1601 39th Ave SE	Puyallup	WA	98374	253-840-8400	840-8449*
**Fax:* Admissions ■ *Web:* www.pierce.ctc.edu					
Renton Technical College 3000 NE 4th St	Renton	WA	98056	425-235-2352	235-7832
Web: www.rtc.edu					
North Seattle Community College					
9600 College Way N	Seattle	WA	98103	206-527-3600	527-3671
Web: www.northseattle.edu					
Seattle Central Community College					
1701 Broadway	Seattle	WA	98122	206-587-3800	587-6321*
**Fax:* Admissions ■ *Web:* www.seattlecentral.org					
South Seattle Community College					
6000 16th Ave SW	Seattle	WA	98106	206-764-5300	764-7947
Web: www.southseattle.edu					
Shelton 937 W Alpine Way	Shelton	WA	98584	360-427-2119	432-5412*
**Fax:* Admissions ■ *TF:* 800-259-6718 ■ *Web:* www.olympic.edu					
Shoreline Community College					
16101 Greenwood Ave N	Shoreline	WA	98133	206-546-4101	546-5835
Web: www.shoreline.edu					
Spokane Community College 1810 N Greene St	Spokane	WA	99217	509-533-7000	533-8181
TF: 800-248-5644 ■ *Web:* www.scc.spokane.edu					
Spokane Falls Community College					
3410 W Fort George Wright Dr	Spokane	WA	99224	509-533-3500	533-3237*
**Fax:* Admissions ■ *TF:* 888-509-7944 ■ *Web:* www.spokanefalls.edu					
Bates Technical College 1101 S Yakima Ave	Tacoma	WA	98405	253-680-7000	680-7001*
**Fax:* Admissions ■ *Web:* www.bates.ctc.edu					
Tacoma Community College 6501 S 19th St	Tacoma	WA	98466	253-566-5000	566-6011*
**Fax:* Admissions ■ *Web:* www.tacomacc.edu					
Clark College 1800 E McLoughlin Blvd	Vancouver	WA	98663	360-992-2000	992-2876*
**Fax:* Admissions ■ *Web:* www.clark.edu					
Walla Walla Community College					
500 Tausick Way	Walla Walla	WA	99362	509-522-2500	527-3661*
**Fax:* Admissions ■ *TF:* 877-992-9922 ■ *Web:* www.wwcc.edu					
Wenatchee Valley College 1300 5th St	Wenatchee	WA	98801	509-682-6800	682-6801*
**Fax:* Admissions ■ *TF:* 877-982-4968 ■ *Web:* www.wvc.edu					
Yakima Valley Community College					
1015 S 16th Ave	Yakima	WA	98902	509-574-4600	574-4649
Web: www.yvcc.edu					

WEST VIRGINIA

	City	State	ZIP	Phone	Fax
Potomac State College 101 Fort Ave	Keyser	WV	26726	304-788-6800	788-6939*
**Fax:* Admissions ■ *TF:* 800-262-7332 ■ *Web:* www.potomacstatecollege.edu					
Eastern West Virginia Community & Technical College					
316 Eastern Dr	Moorefield	WV	26836	304-434-8000	434-7000
TF: 877-982-2322 ■ *Web:* www.eastern.wvnet.edu					
Southern West Virginia Community & Technical College					
Logan 2900 Dempsey Branch Rd PO Box 2900	Mount Gay	WV	25637	304-792-7098	792-7028*
**Fax:* Admissions ■ *Web:* www.southernwv.edu					
West Virginia Northern Community College					
1704 Market St	Wheeling	WV	26003	304-233-5900	232-8187
Web: www.northern.wvnet.edu					

WISCONSIN

	City	State	ZIP	Phone	Fax
Baraboo/Sauk County 1006 Connie Rd	Baraboo	WI	53913	608-355-5200	356-0752*
**Fax:* Admissions ■ *Web:* www.baraboo.uwc.edu					
Fond du Lac 400 University Dr	Fond du Lac	WI	54935	920-929-3600	929-3626*
**Fax:* Admissions ■ *Web:* www.fdl.uwc.edu					
Lac Courte Oreilles Ojibwa Community College					
13466 W Trepania Rd	Hayward	WI	54843	715-634-4790	634-5049*
**Fax:* Admissions ■ *TF:* 888-526-6221 ■ *Web:* www.lco.edu					
Rock County 2909 Kellogg Ave	Janesville	WI	53546	608-758-6523	758-6579
Web: www.rock.uwc.edu					
College of Menominee Nation PO Box 1179	Keshena	WI	54135	715-799-5600	799-4392*
**Fax:* Admissions ■ *TF:* 800-567-2344 ■ *Web:* www.menominee.edu					
Manitowoc 705 Viebahn St	Manitowoc	WI	54220	920-683-4700	683-4776
Web: www.uwmanitowoc.uwc.edu					
Marinette 750 W Bay Shore St	Marinette	WI	54143	715-735-4300	735-4304*
**Fax:* Admissions ■ *Web:* www.marinette.uwc.edu					
Marshfield/Wood County 2000 W 5th St	Marshfield	WI	54449	715-389-6530	384-1718
Web: www.marshfield.uwc.edu					
Fox Valley 1478 Midway Rd	Menasha	WI	54952	920-832-2600	832-2674
Web: www.uwfox.uwc.edu					
Nicolet Area Technical College					
PO Box 518	Rhinelander	WI	54501	715-365-4410	365-4901*
**Fax:* Admissions ■ *TF:* 800-544-3039 ■ *Web:* www.nicolet.tec.wi.us					
University of Wisconsin					
Barron County 1800 College Dr	Rice Lake	WI	54868	715-234-8176	234-1975
Web: www.barron.uwc.edu					
Richland 1200 Hwy 14 W	Richland Center	WI	53581	608-647-6186	647-2275*
**Fax:* Admissions ■ *Web:* richland.uwc.edu					
Sheboygan 1 University Dr	Sheboygan	WI	53081	920-459-6600	459-6602*
**Fax:* Admissions ■ *Web:* sheboygan.uwc.edu					
Waukesha 1500 N University Dr	Waukesha	WI	53188	262-521-5200	521-5491*
**Fax:* Admissions ■ *Web:* waukesha.uwc.edu					
Marathon County 518 S 7th Ave	Wausau	WI	54401	715-261-6100	261-6331
TF: 888-367-8962 ■ *Web:* www.marathon.uwc.edu					
Washington County 400 S University Dr	West Bend	WI	53095	262-335-5200	335-5220
Web: washington.uwc.edu					

WYOMING

	City	State	ZIP	Phone	Fax
Casper College 125 College Dr	Casper	WY	82601	307-268-2110	268-2611*
**Fax:* Admissions ■ *TF:* 800-442-2963 ■ *Web:* www.caspercollege.edu					
Laramie County Community College					
1400 E College Dr	Cheyenne	WY	82007	307-778-5222	778-1350*
**Fax:* Admissions ■ *TF:* 800-522-2993 ■ *Web:* www.lccc.cc.wy.us					
Gillette 300 W Sinclair St	Gillette	WY	82718	307-686-0254	686-0339*
**Fax:* Admissions ■ *Web:* www.sheridan.edu					
Albany County 1125 Boulder Dr	Laramie	WY	82070	307-721-5138	772-4266
TF: 800-522-2993 ■ *Web:* www.lccc.wy.edu					
Northwest College 231 W 6th St	Powell	WY	82435	307-754-6000	754-6249*
**Fax:* Admissions ■ *TF:* 800-560-4692 ■ *Web:* www.northwestcollege.edu					
Central Wyoming College 2660 Peck Ave	Riverton	WY	82501	307-855-2000	855-2092
TF: 800-735-8418 ■ *Web:* www.cwc.edu					

Phone | Fax

Western Wyoming Community College
2500 College Dr .... Rock Springs WY 82901 307-382-1600 382-1636*
*Fax: Admissions ■ TF: 800-226-1181 ■ Web: www.wwcc.wy.edu

Sheridan College
3059 Coffeen Ave PO Box 1500 .... Sheridan WY 82801 307-674-6446 674-7205
TF: 800-913-9139 ■ Web: www.sheridan.edu

Eastern Wyoming College 3200 W 'C' St .... Torrington WY 82240 307-532-8200 532-8222*
*Fax: Admissions ■ TF: 800-658-3195 ■ Web: www.ewc.wy.edu

163 COLLEGES - CULINARY ARTS

Phone | Fax

Arizona Culinary Institute
10585 N 114th St Suite 401 .... Scottsdale AZ 85259 480-603-1066 603-1067
TF: 866-294-2433 ■ Web: www.azculinary.com

Baltimore International College
17 Commerce St .... Baltimore MD 21202 410-752-4710 752-3730*
*Fax: Admissions ■ TF: 800-624-9926 ■ Web: www.bic.edu

California Culinary Academy Inc
625 Polk St .... San Francisco CA 94102 415-771-3500 771-2194*
*Fax: Admissions ■ TF: 800-229-2433 ■ Web: www.baychef.com

Cambridge School of Culinary Arts
2020 Massachusetts Ave .... Cambridge MA 02140 617-354-2020 576-1963
Web: www.cambridgeculinary.com

Capital Culinary Institute of Keiser College
Melbourne 900 S Babcock St .... Melbourne FL 32901 321-255-2255 725-3766
Web: www.keisercollege.edu/culinary.html
Sarasota 6151 Lake Osprey Dr .... Sarasota FL 34240 941-907-3900 907-2016
TF: 866-534-7372 ■ Web: www.keisercollege.edu

Capital Culinary Institute of Keiser Institute
Tallahassee 1700 Halstead Blvd Bldg 4 .... Tallahassee FL 32309 850-906-9494 906-0069
TF: 877-243-3123 ■ Web: www.capitalculinaryinstitute.com

Cascade Culinary Institute 2600 NW College Way .... Bend OR 97701 541-383-7700
Web: www.culinary.cocc.edu

Center for Culinary Arts 106 Sebethe Dr .... Cromwell CT 06416 860-613-3350 613-3353
Web: www.centerforculinaryarts.com

Chef John Folse Culinary Institute
PO Box 2099 .... Thibodaux LA 70310 985-449-7100 449-7089
Web: www.nicholls.edu

Connecticut Culinary Institute
85 Sigourney St .... Hartford CT 06105 860-895-6100 895-6101
TF: 800-762-4337 ■ Web: www.ctculinary.edu
Suffield 1760 Mapleton Ave .... Suffield CT 06032 860-668-3500 668-3518
TF: 866-672-4337 ■ Web: www.ctculinary.com

Cook Street School of Fine Cooking
1937 Market St .... Denver CO 80202 303-308-9300 308-9400
Web: www.cookstreet.com

Cooking & Hospitality Institute of Chicago
361 W Chestnut St .... Chicago IL 60610 312-944-0882 944-8557
TF: 888-295-7222 ■ Web: www.chic.edu

Culinard-the Culinary Institute of Virginia College
65 Bagby Dr .... Birmingham AL 35209 205-802-1200 943-3940
TF: 877-812-8428 ■ Web: www.culinard.com

Culinary Academy of Long Island
125 Michael Dr .... Syosset NY 11791 516-364-4344 364-1894
Web: www.culinaryacademyli.com
Manhattan 154 W 14th St 11th Fl .... New York NY 10011 212-675-6655 463-9194
Web: www.culinaryacademyli.com

Culinary Institute Alain & Marie LeNotre
7070 Allensby .... Houston TX 77022 713-692-0077 692-7399
TF: 888-536-6873 ■ Web: www.lenotre-alain-marie.com

Culinary Institute of America
1946 Campus Dr .... Hyde Park NY 12538 845-452-9430 451-1068
TF Admissions: 800-285-4627 ■ Web: www.ciachef.edu

Culinary Institute of America at Greystone
2555 Main St .... Saint Helena CA 94574 707-967-2350
Web: www.ciachef.edu

Culinary Institute of Charleston
7000 Rivers Ave .... Charleston SC 29406 843-574-6111 820-5060
TF: 877-349-7184 ■ Web: www.tridenttech.edu

Florida Culinary Institute
2410 Metro Centre Blvd .... West Palm Beach FL 33407 561-688-2001 688-9882
TF: 800-262-9986 ■ Web: www.floridaculinary.com

French Culinary Institute 462 Broadway .... New York NY 10013 212-219-8890 431-3065*
*Fax: Admissions ■ TF: 888-324-2433 ■ Web: www.frenchculinary.com

Institute of Culinary Education
50 W 23rd St .... New York NY 10010 212-847-0700 847-0723
TF: 800-522-4610 ■ Web: www.iceculinary.com

JNA Institute of Culinary Arts
1212 S Broad St .... Philadelphia PA 19146 215-468-8800 468-8838
Web: www.culinaryarts.com

Kendall College 900 N N Branch St .... Chicago IL 60622 312-752-2000 752-2010*
*Fax: Admissions ■ TF: 866-667-3344 ■ Web: www.kendall.edu

Kitchen Academy 6370 W Sunset Blvd .... Los Angeles CA 90028 323-203-3967 460-4198
TF: 866-548-2223 ■ Web: www.kitchenacademy.com

L'Academie de Cuisine Inc
16006 Industrial Dr .... Gaithersburg MD 20877 301-670-8670 670-0450
TF: 800-664-2433 ■ Web: www.lacademie.com

L'Ecole de Cuisine 3050 Hempland Rd .... Lancaster PA 17601 717-295-1100 295-1135
TF: 866-984-2433 ■ Web: www.chefs.yti.edu

Le Cordon Bleu College of Culinary Arts
Atlanta 1927 Lakeside Pkwy .... Tucker GA 30084 770-938-4711 938-4571
TF: 866-315-2433 ■ Web: www.atlantaculinary.com
Las Vegas 1451 Ctr Crossing Rd .... Las Vegas NV 89144 702-365-7690 365-7911
Web: www.vegasculinary.com
Miami 3221 Enterprise Way .... Miramar FL 33025 954-628-4400 438-9519
TF: 866-762-2433 ■ Web: www.miamiculinary.com

Lincoln Tech Center for Culinary Arts
8 Progress Dr .... Shelton CT 06484 203-929-0592 929-0763
Web: www.centerforculinaryarts.com

Phone | Fax

Louisiana Culinary Institute
5837 Essen Ln .... Baton Rouge LA 70810 225-769-8820 769-8792*
*Fax: Admissions ■ TF: 877-769-8820 ■ Web: www.louisianaculinary.com

New England Culinary Institute
56 College St .... Montpelier VT 05602 802-223-6324 225-3280
TF: 877-223-6324 ■ Web: www.neci.edu

Oregon Coast Culinary Institute
1988 Newmark Ave .... Coos Bay OR 97420 541-888-2525 888-7247
TF: 877-895-2433 ■ Web: www.occi.net

Orlando Culinary Academy
8511 Commodity Cir Suite 100 .... Orlando FL 32819 407-888-4000 888-4019
TF: 800-622-2433 ■ Web: www.orlandoculinary.com

Pennsylvania Culinary Institute
717 Liberty Ave .... Pittsburgh PA 15222 412-566-2433 566-2434
TF: 800-432-2433 ■ Web: www.pci.edu

Restaurant School at Walnut Hill College
4207 Walnut St .... Philadelphia PA 19104 215-222-4200 222-2811*
*Fax: Admissions ■ Web: www.walnuthillcollege.com

Robert Morris University Institute of Culinary Arts
401 S State St .... Chicago IL 60605 312-935-4100 935-4182*
*Fax: Admissions ■ TF: 800-762-5960 ■ Web: www.robertmorris.edu/culinary
Dupage 905 Meridian Lake Dr .... Aurora IL 60504 800-762-5960 375-8020*
*Fax Area Code: 630 ■ TF: 800-762-5960 ■ Web: www.robertmorris.edu

San Diego Culinary Institute
8072 La Mesa Blvd .... La Mesa CA 91941 619-644-2100 644-2106
Web: www.sdci-inc.com

Sclafani's Cooking School Inc
107 Gennaro Pl .... Metairie LA 70001 504-833-7861 833-7872
TF: 800-583-1282 ■ Web: www.sclafanicookingschool.com

Scottsdale Culinary Institute
8100 E Camelback Rd Suite 1001 .... Scottsdale AZ 85251 480-990-3773 990-0351
TF: 800-848-2433 ■ Web: www.chefs.edu

Stratford University School of Culinary Arts
7777 Leesburg Pike .... Falls Church VA 22043 703-821-8570 734-5336
TF: 800-444-0804 ■ Web: www.stratford.edu/?page=home_culinary

Sullivan University National Center for Hospitality Studies
3101 Bardstown Rd .... Louisville KY 40205 502-456-6505 456-0040
TF: 800-844-1354 ■ Web: www.sullivan.edu/nchs

Tante Marie's Cooking School
271 Francisco St .... San Francisco CA 94133 415-788-6699 788-8924
Web: www.tantemarie.com

Texas Culinary Academy
11400 Burnet Rd Suite 2100 .... Austin TX 78758 512-837-2665 977-7753*
*Fax: Admissions ■ TF: 888-553-2433 ■ Web: www.tca.edu

164 COLLEGES - FINE ARTS

SEE ALSO Colleges & Universities - Four-Year p. 1638; Vocational & Technical Schools p. 2763

Phone | Fax

American Academy of Art
332 S Michigan Ave 3rd Fl .... Chicago IL 60604 312-461-0600 294-9570
TF: 888-461-0600 ■ Web: www.aaart.edu

American Academy of Dramatic Arts
120 Madison Ave .... New York NY 10016 212-686-9244 545-7934
TF: 800-463-8990 ■ Web: www.aada.org

Antonelli Institute 300 Montgomery Ave .... Erdenheim PA 19038 215-836-2222 836-2794
TF: 800-722-7871 ■ Web: www.antonelli.org

Art Academy of Cincinnati 1212 Jackson St .... Cincinnati OH 45202 513-562-6262 562-8778
TF: 800-323-5692 ■ Web: www.artacademy.edu

Art Ctr College of Design 1700 Lida St .... Pasadena CA 91103 626-396-2200 795-0578
Web: www.artcenter.edu

Art Institute of Atlanta
6600 Peachtree Dunwoody Rd NE
100 Embassy Row .... Atlanta GA 30328 770-394-8300 394-0008
TF: 800-275-4242 ■ Web: www.artinstitutes.edu

Art Institute of Boston at Lesley
700 Beacon St Suite 202 .... Boston MA 02215 617-585-6600 585-6721
TF: 800-773-0494 ■ Web: web.lesley.edu/aib

Art Institute of California
Inland Empire 630 E Brier Dr .... San Bernardino CA 92408 909-915-2100
TF: 800-353-0812 ■ Web: www.artinstitutes.edu
Los Angeles 2900 31st St .... Santa Monica CA 90405 310-752-4700 752-4708
TF: 888-646-4610 ■ Web: www.artinstitutes.edu
Orange County 3601 W Sunflower Ave .... Santa Ana CA 92704 714-830-0200 556-1923
TF: 888-549-3055 ■ Web: www.artinstitutes.edu
San Diego 7650 Mission Valley Rd .... San Diego CA 92108 858-598-1200 291-3206*
*Fax Area Code: 619 ■ TF: 800-591-2422 ■ Web: www.artinstitutes.edu
San Francisco 1170 Market St .... San Francisco CA 94102 415-865-0198 863-6344
TF: 888-493-3261 ■ Web: www.artinstitutes.edu

Art Institute of Charlotte
2110 Water Ridge Pkwy 3 LakePointe Plaza .... Charlotte NC 28217 704-357-8020 357-1133
TF: 800-872-4417 ■ Web: www.artinstitutes.edu

Art Institute of Colorado 1200 Lincoln St .... Denver CO 80203 303-837-0825 860-8520
TF: 800-275-2420 ■ Web: www.artinstitutes.edu

Art Institute of Dallas 8080 Pk Ln Suite 100 .... Dallas TX 75231 214-692-8080 750-9460
TF: 800-275-4243 ■ Web: www.artinstitutes.edu

Art Institute of Fort Lauderdale
1799 SE 17th St .... Fort Lauderdale FL 33316 954-463-3000 728-8637
TF: 800-275-7603 ■ Web: www.artinstitutes.edu

Art Institute of Houston 1900 Yorktown St .... Houston TX 77056 713-623-2040 966-2700
TF: 800-275-4244 ■ Web: www.artinstitutes.edu

Art Institute of Indianapolis
3500 Depauw Blvd .... Indianapolis IN 46268 317-613-4800 613-4808
TF: 866-441-9031 ■ Web: www.artinstitutes.edu

Art Institute of Las Vegas
2350 Corporate Cir .... Henderson NV 89074 702-369-9944 992-8458
TF: 800-833-2678 ■ Web: www.artinstitutes.edu

				Phone	Fax
Art Institute of New York City					
75 Varisk St 16th Fl	New York	NY	10013	212-226-5500	625-6065
Web: www.artinstitutes.edu					
Art Institute of Ohio					
Cincinnati					
8845 Covernor's Hill Dr Suite 100	Cincinnati	OH	45249	513-833-2400	833-2411
TF: 866-613-5184 ■ *Web:* www.artinstitutes.edu					
Art Institute of Philadelphia					
1622 Chestnut St	Philadelphia	PA	19103	215-567-7080	405-6398
TF: 800-275-2474 ■ *Web:* www.artinstitutes.edu					
Art Institute of Phoenix 2233 W Dunlap Ave	Phoenix	AZ	85021	602-678-4300	331-5301
TF: 800-474-2479 ■ *Web:* www.artinstitutes.edu					
Art Institute of Pittsburgh					
420 Blvd of the Allies	Pittsburgh	PA	15219	412-263-6600	263-6667
TF: 800-275-2470 ■ *Web:* www.artinstitutes.edu					
Art Institute of Portland 1122 NW Davis St	Portland	OR	97209	503-228-6528	227-1945*
**Fax:* Admissions ■ *TF:* 888-228-6528 ■ *Web:* www.artinstitutes.edu					
Art Institute of Seattle 2323 Elliott Ave	Seattle	WA	98121	206-448-0900	448-2501
TF: 800-275-2471 ■ *Web:* www.artinstitutes.edu					
Art Institute of Tampa					
4401 N Himes Ave Suite 150	Tampa	FL	33614	813-873-2112	873-2171
TF: 866-703-3277 ■ *Web:* www.artinstitutes.edu					
Art Institute of Washington					
1820 N Fort Myer Dr	Arlington	VA	22209	703-358-9550	358-9759
TF: 877-303-3771 ■ *Web:* www.artinstitutes.edu/arlington					
Art Institutes International Minnesota					
15 S 9th St	Minneapolis	MN	55402	612-332-3361	332-3934
TF: 800-777-3643 ■ *Web:* www.artinstitutes.edu					
Bradley Academy for the Visual Arts					
1409 Williams Rd	York	PA	17402	717-755-2300	840-1951
TF: 800-864-7725 ■ *Web:* www.artinstitutes.edu					
Brooks College 4825 E Pacific Coast Hwy	Long Beach	CA	90804	562-498-2441	597-2661
TF: 800-421-3775 ■ *Web:* www.brookscollege.edu					
California College of the Arts					
Oakland 5212 Broadway	Oakland	CA	94618	510-594-3600	594-3601
TF: 800-447-1278 ■ *Web:* www.cca.edu					
San Francisco 1111 8th St	San Francisco	CA	94107	415-703-9500	703-9539
TF: 800-447-1278 ■ *Web:* www.cca.edu					
California Design College					
3440 Wilshire Blvd 10th Fl	Los Angeles	CA	90010	213-251-3636	385-3545
TF: 877-468-6232 ■ *Web:* www.artinstitutes.edu					
California Institute of the Arts					
24700 McBean Pkwy	Valencia	CA	91355	661-255-1050	253-7710
TF: 800-545-2787 ■ *Web:* www.calarts.edu					
Cleveland Institute of Art 11141 E Blvd	Cleveland	OH	44106	216-421-7400	754-3634
TF: 800-754-3355 ■ *Web:* www.cia.edu					
College for Creative Studies 201 E Kirby St	Detroit	MI	48202	313-664-7425	872-2739
TF: 800-952-2787 ■ *Web:* www.collageforcreativestudies.edu					
Columbus College of Art & Design					
60 Cleveland Ave	Columbus	OH	43215	614-224-9101	222-4040
Web: www.ccad.edu					
Corcoran College of Art & Design					
500 17th St NW	Washington	DC	20006	202-639-1800	639-1802
TF: 888-267-2672 ■ *Web:* www.corcoran.edu					
Cornish College of the Arts 710 E Roy St	Seattle	WA	98121	206-323-1400	720-1011
TF: 800-726-2787 ■ *Web:* www.cornish.edu					
Fashion Institute of Design & Merchandising					
Los Angeles 919 S Grand Ave	Los Angeles	CA	90015	213-624-1200	624-4777
TF Admissions: 800-624-1200 ■ *Web:* www.fidm.com					
Orange County 17590 Gillette Ave	Irvine	CA	92614	949-851-6200	851-6808
TF: 888-974-3436 ■ *Web:* www.fidm.com					
San Diego 350 Tenth Ave	San Diego	CA	92101	619-235-2049	232-4322
TF: 800-243-3436 ■ *Web:* www.fidm.com					
San Francisco 55 Stockton St	San Francisco	CA	94108	415-675-5200	296-7299
TF: 800-422-3436 ■ *Web:* www.fidm.com					
Fashion Institute of Technology					
227 W 27th St	New York	NY	10001	212-217-7650	217-7481
TF: 800-999-9923 ■ *Web:* www.fitnyc.edu					
Florida School of the Arts 5001 St Johns Ave	Palatka	FL	32177	386-312-4300	312-4306
Web: floarts.org					
Hussian School of Art					
111 S Independence Mall E	Philadelphia	PA	19106	215-574-9600	864-9115
Web: www.hussianart.edu					
Illinois Institute of Art					
Chicago 350 N Orleans St Suite 136-L	Chicago	IL	60654	312-280-3500	280-8562
TF: 800-351-3450 ■ *Web:* www.ilia.aii.edu					
Schaumburg 1000 N Plaza Dr	Schaumburg	IL	60173	847-619-3450	619-3064
TF: 800-314-3450 ■ *Web:* www.artinstitutes.edu					
Institute of American Indian Arts					
83 Avan Nu Po Rd	Santa Fe	NM	87508	505-424-2300	424-4500
TF Admissions: 800-804-6422 ■ *Web:* www.iaiancad.org					
International Academy of Design & Technology					
Chicago 1 N State St Suite 500	Chicago	IL	60602	312-980-9200	541-3929
TF: 888-318-6111 ■ *Web:* www.iadtchicago.com					
Las Vegas 2495 Village View Dr	Henderson	NV	89074	702-990-0150	990-0161
TF: 866-400-4238 ■ *Web:* www.iadtvegas.com					
Tampa 5104 Eisenhower Blvd	Tampa	FL	33634	813-881-0007	881-0008
TF: 800-222-3369 ■ *Web:* www.academy.edu					
Kansas City Art Institute					
4415 Warwick Blvd	Kansas City	MO	64111	816-474-5224	802-3309
TF: 800-522-5224 ■ *Web:* www.kcai.edu					
Maine College of Art 97 Spring St	Portland	ME	04101	207-775-3052	772-5069
TF: 800-639-4808 ■ *Web:* www.meca.edu					
Maryland Institute College of Art					
1300 W Mt Royal Ave	Baltimore	MD	21217	410-669-9200	225-2337
Web: www.mica.edu					
Memphis College of Art 1930 Poplar Ave	Memphis	TN	38104	901-272-5100	272-5158
TF: 800-727-1088 ■ *Web:* www.mca.edu					
Miami International University of Art & Design					
1501 Biscayne Blvd	Miami	FL	33132	305-428-5700	374-5933
TF: 800-225-9023 ■ *Web:* www.artinstitutes.edu/miami					
Minneapolis College of Art & Design					
2501 Stevens Ave	Minneapolis	MN	55404	612-874-3760	874-3701
TF: 800-874-6223 ■ *Web:* www.mcad.edu					
Montclair Kimberley Academy The					
201 Valley Rd	Montclair	NJ	07042	973-746-9800	783-5777
Web: www.montclairkimberley.org					
Moore College of Art & Design					
1940 Race St	Philadelphia	PA	19103	215-965-4014	568-3547
TF: 800-523-2025 ■ *Web:* www.moore.edu					
New England Institute of Art					
10 Brookline Pl W	Brookline	MA	02245	617-739-1700	582-4500
TF: 800-903-4425 ■ *Web:* www.artinstitutes.edu					
North Carolina School of the Arts					
1533 S Main St	Winston-Salem	NC	27127	336-770-3399	770-3370
Web: www.ncarts.edu					
Otis College of Art & Design					
9045 Lincoln Blvd	Los Angeles	CA	90045	310-665-6820	665-6821
TF: 800-527-6847 ■ *Web:* www.otis.edu					
Pennsylvania Academy of the Fine Arts					
School of Fine Arts 118 N Broad St	Philadelphia	PA	19102	215-972-7600	569-0153
Web: www.pafa.org					
Pennsylvania College of Art & Design					
204 N Prince St PO Box 59	Lancaster	PA	17608	717-396-7833	396-1339
Web: www.pcad.edu					
Rhode Island School of Design					
2 College St	Providence	RI	02903	401-454-6100	454-6309
TF: 800-364-7473 ■ *Web:* www.risd.edu					
Ringling College of Art & Design					
2700 N Tamiami Trail	Sarasota	FL	34234	941-351-5100	359-7517
TF: 800-255-7695 ■ *Web:* www.ringling.edu					
San Francisco Art Institute					
800 Chestnut St	San Francisco	CA	94133	415-771-7020	749-1951
TF: 800-345-7324 ■ *Web:* www.sfai.edu					
Savannah College of Art & Design					
342 Bull St PO Box 2072	Savannah	GA	31402	912-525-5100	525-5983
TF: 800-869-7223 ■ *Web:* www.scad.edu					
Atlanta 1600 Peachtree St PO Box 77300	Atlanta	GA	30357	404-253-2700	253-3466
TF: 877-722-3285 ■ *Web:* www.scad.edu					
School of Visual Arts 209 E 23rd St	New York	NY	10010	212-592-2000	592-2116
TF: 800-436-4204 ■ *Web:* www.schoolofvisualarts.edu					
University of the Arts 320 S Broad St	Philadelphia	PA	19102	215-717-6049	717-6000
TF: 800-616-2787 ■ *Web:* www.uarts.edu					
Virginia Marti College of Art & Design					
11724 Detroit Ave	Lakewood	OH	44107	216-221-8584	221-2311
TF: 800-473-4350 ■ *Web:* www.virginiamarticollege.com					
Watkins College of Art & Design					
2298 Rose Parks Blvd	Nashville	TN	37228	615-383-4848	383-4849
TF: 866-877-6395 ■ *Web:* www.watkins.edu					
New Hampshire Institute of Art					
148 Concord St	Manchester	NH	03104	603-623-0313	647-0658
TF: 866-241-4918 ■ *Web:* www.nhia.edu					

165 COLLEGES - TRIBAL

SEE ALSO Colleges - Community & Junior p. 1618

Tribal Colleges Generally Serve Geographically Isolated American Indian Populations That Have No Other Means Of Accessing Education Beyond The High School Level. They Are Unique Institutions That Combine Personal Attention With Cultural Relevance.

				Phone	Fax
Fort Belknap College PO Box 159	Harlem	MT	59526	406-353-2607	353-2898*
**Fax:* Admissions ■ *Web:* www.fbcc.edu					
Institute of American Indian Arts					
83 Avan Nu Po Rd	Santa Fe	NM	87508	505-424-2300	424-4500
TF Admissions: 800-804-6422 ■ *Web:* www.iaiancad.org					
Little Big Horn College					
1 Forestry Ln PO Box 370	Crow Agency	MT	59022	406-638-3104	638-3169
Web: www.lbhc.edu					
Sinte Gleska University					
101 Antelope Lake Cir Dr PO Box 105	Mission	SD	57555	605-856-8100	856-4194
Web: www.sintegleska.edu					
Sitting Bull College 9299 Hwy 24	Fort Yates	ND	58538	701-854-8000	854-3403*
**Fax:* Admissions ■ *Web:* www.sittingbull.edu					
Stone Child College					
8294 Upper Box Elder Rd	Box Elder	MT	59521	406-395-4875	395-4836*
**Fax:* Admissions ■ *Web:* www.stonechild.edu					
Wind River Tribal College PO Box 8300	Ethete	WY	82520	307-335-8243	335-8148
TF: 866-701-8385 ■ *Web:* www.wrtribalcollege.com					
Tohono O'odham Community College PO Box 3129	Sells	AZ	85634	520-383-8401	383-8403
Web: www.tocc.cc.az.us					
Dine College PO Box 67	Tsaile	AZ	86556	928-724-6600	724-3327*
**Fax:* Admissions ■ *TF:* 877-988-3463 ■ *Web:* www.dinecollege.edu					
Haskell Indian Nations University					
155 Indian Ave PO Box 5031	Lawrence	KS	66046	785-749-8454	749-8429*
**Fax:* Admissions ■ *Web:* www.haskell.edu					
Keweenaw Bay Ojibwa Community College					
111 Beartown Rd	Baraga	MI	49908	906-353-4600	353-8107
Web: www.kbocc.org					
Bay Mills Community College					
12214 W Lakeshore Dr	Brimley	MI	49715	906-248-3354	248-3351
TF: 800-844-2622 ■ *Web:* www.bmcc.edu					
Saginaw Chippewa Tribal College					
2274 Enterprise Dr	Mount Pleasant	MI	48858	989-775-4123	775-4528
Web: www.sagchip.org					
Leech Lake Tribal College					
6945 Little Wolf Rd NW	Cass Lake	MN	56633	218-335-4200	335-4209
TF: 800-627-3529 ■ *Web:* www.lltc.org					

Phone Fax

Fond du Lac Tribal & Community College
2101 14th St. .... Cloquet MN 55720 218-879-0800 879-0814
TF: 800-657-3712 ■ Web: www.fdltcc.edu

White Earth Tribal & Community College
124 S 1st St .... Mahnomen MN 56557 218-935-0417 936-5736
Web: www.wetcc.org

Blackfeet Community College PO Box 819. .... Browning MT 59417 406-338-5421 338-3272*
*Fax: Admissions ■ TF: 800-549-7457 ■ Web: www.bfcc.org

Chief Dull Knife College PO Box 98 .... Lame Deer MT 59043 406-477-6215 477-6219
Web: www.cdkc.edu

Salish Kootenai College PO Box 70 .... Pablo MT 59855 406-275-4800 275-4801*
*Fax: Admissions ■ TF: 877-752-6553 ■ Web: www.skc.edu

Fort Peck Community College PO Box 398 .... Poplar MT 59255 406-768-6300 768-6301
Web: www.fpcc.edu

Nebraska Indian Community College PO Box 428. .... Macy NE 68039 402-837-5078 837-4183*
*Fax: Admissions ■ Web: www.thenicc.edu

Little Priest Tribal College PO Box 270. .... Winnebago NE 68071 402-878-2380 878-2355
Web: www.lptc.bia.edu

Navajo Technical College PO Box 849. .... Crownpoint NM 87313 505-786-4100 786-5644
Web: www.navajotech.edu

Southwestern Indian Polytechnic Institute
9169 Coors Blvd NW PO Box 10146 .... Albuquerque NM 87120 505-346-2306 346-2311
TF: 800-586-7474 ■ Web: www.sipi.edu

United Tribes Technical College
3315 University Dr .... Bismarck ND 58504 701-255-3285 530-0640
Web: www.uttc.edu

Turtle Mountain Community College
10145 BIA Rd 7 .... Belcourt ND 58316 701-477-7862 477-7892
Web: www.tm.edu

Cankdeska Cikana Community College
214 1st Ave PO Box 269. .... Fort Totten ND 58335 701-766-4415 766-4077
TF: 888-783-1463 ■ Web: www.littlehoop.cc

Fort Berthold Community College PO Box 490 ...... New Town ND 58763 701-627-3665 627-3609*
*Fax: Admissions ■ Web: www.fbcc.bia.edu

Comanche Nation College 1608 SW 9th St .... Lawton OK 73501 580-591-0203 353-7075
TF: 877-591-0203 ■ Web: www.cnc.cc.ok.us

Oglala Lakota College PO Box 629. .... Martin SD 57551 605-685-6407 685-6887
Web: www.olc.edu

Sisseton Wahpeton College 12572 BIA Hwy 700. ...... Sisseton SD 57262 605-698-3966 742-0394
Web: www.swc.tc

Northwest Indian College 2522 Kwina Rd .... Bellingham WA 98226 360-676-2772 392-4333*
*Fax: Admissions ■ TF: 866-676-2772 ■ Web: www.nwic.edu

Lac Courte Oreilles Ojibwa Community College
13466 W Trepania Rd .... Hayward WI 54843 715-634-4790 634-5049*
*Fax: Admissions ■ TF: 888-526-6221 ■ Web: www.lco.edu

College of Menominee Nation PO Box 1179. .... Keshena WI 54135 715-799-5600 799-4392*
*Fax: Admissions ■ TF: 800-567-2344 ■ Web: www.menominee.edu

166 COLLEGES - WOMEN'S (FOUR-YEAR)

Phone Fax

Moore College of Art & Design
1940 Race St .... Philadelphia PA 19103 215-965-4014 568-3547
TF: 800-523-2025 ■ Web: www.moore.edu

Judson College 302 Bibb St .... Marion AL 36756 334-683-5110 683-5282*
*Fax: Admissions ■ TF Admissions: 800-447-9472 ■ Web: www.judson.edu

Mills College 5000 MacArthur Blvd. .... Oakland CA 94613 510-430-2135 430-3298*
*Fax: Admissions ■ TF Admissions: 800-876-4557 ■ Web: www.mills.edu

Mount Saint Mary's College
12001 Chalon Rd .... Los Angeles CA 90049 310-954-4250 954-4259*
*Fax: Admissions ■ TF Admissions: 800-999-9893 ■ Web: www.msmc.la.edu

Scripps College 1030 Columbia Ave. .... Claremont CA 91711 909-621-8149 607-7508*
*Fax: Admissions ■ TF: 800-770-1333 ■ Web: www.scrippscol.edu

Women's College of the University of Denver
1901 E Asbury Ave .... Denver CO 80208 303-871-6848 871-6897
Web: www.womenscollege.du.edu

Saint Joseph College 1678 Asylum Ave .... West Hartford CT 06117 860-232-4571 231-5744*
*Fax: Admissions ■ TF Admissions: 866-442-8753 ■ Web: www.sjc.edu

Trinity University 125 Michigan Ave NE. .... Washington DC 20017 202-884-9000 884-9403*
*Fax: Admissions ■ TF Admissions: 800-492-6882 ■ Web: www.trinitydc.edu

Agnes Scott College 141 E College Ave .... Decatur GA 30030 404-471-6000 471-6414*
*Fax: Admissions ■ TF: 800-868-8602 ■ Web: www.agnesscott.edu

Brenau University 500 Washington St .... Gainesville GA 30501 770-534-6299 538-4701*
*Fax: Admissions ■ TF: 800-252-5119 ■ Web: www.brenau.edu

Spelman College 350 Spelman Ln SW .... Atlanta GA 30314 404-681-3643 270-5201*
*Fax: Admissions ■ TF Admissions: 800-982-2411 ■ Web: www.spelman.edu

Wesleyan College 4760 Forsyth Rd .... Macon GA 31210 478-477-1110 757-4030*
*Fax: Admissions ■ TF: 800-447-6610 ■ Web: www.wesleyancollege.edu

Saint Mary's College Le Mans Hall Rm 122 .... Notre Dame IN 46556 574-284-4587 284-4841*
*Fax: Admissions ■ TF Admissions: 800-551-7621 ■ Web: www.saintmarys.edu

Saint Mary-of-the-Woods College
3301 St Mary Rd. .... Saint Mary-of-the-Woods IN 47876 812-535-5106 535-5010*
*Fax: Admissions ■ TF: 800-926-7692 ■ Web: www.smwc.edu

Midway College 512 E Stephens St .... Midway KY 40347 859-846-5346 846-5787*
*Fax: Admissions ■ TF: 800-755-0031 ■ Web: www.midway.edu

Newcomb College Institute for Women
43 Newcomb Pl .... New Orleans LA 70118 504-865-5422 862-8589
TF: 888-862-8589 ■ Web: www.newcomb.tulane.edu

College of Notre Dame of Maryland
4701 N Charles St .... Baltimore MD 21210 410-435-0100 532-6287*
*Fax: Admissions ■ TF Admissions: 800-435-0300 ■ Web: www.ndm.edu

Bay Path College 588 Longmeadow St. .... Longmeadow MA 01106 413-567-0621 565-1105
TF: 800-782-7284 ■ Web: www.baypath.edu

Mount Holyoke College 50 College St .... South Hadley MA 01075 413-538-2000 538-2409
Web: www.mtholyoke.edu

Pine Manor College 400 Heath St .... Chestnut Hill MA 02467 617-731-7104 731-7102
TF: 800-762-1357 ■ Web: www.pmc.edu

Regis College 235 Wellesley St. .... Weston MA 02493 781-768-7000 768-7071
TF: 866-438-7344 ■ Web: www.regiscollege.edu

Simmons College 300 The Fenway .... Boston MA 02115 617-521-2000 521-3190*
*Fax: Admissions ■ TF: 800-345-8468 ■ Web: www.simmons.edu

Smith College 7 College Ln. .... NorthHampton MA 01063 413-584-2700 585-2527
TF: 800-383-3232 ■ Web: www.smith.edu

Wellesley College 106 Central St. .... Wellesley MA 02481 781-283-1000 283-3678*
*Fax: Admissions ■ Web: www.wellesley.edu

College of Saint Benedict
37 S College Ave .... Saint Joseph MN 56374 320-363-5011 363-3206*
*Fax: Admissions ■ TF: 800-249-9840 ■ Web: www.csbsju.edu

College of Saint Catherine
2004 Randolph Ave. .... Saint Paul MN 55105 651-690-6000 690-6024*
*Fax: Admissions ■ TF: 800-945-4599 ■ Web: www.stkate.edu
Minneapolis 601 25th Ave S .... Minneapolis MN 55454 651-690-7700 690-7849*
*Fax: Admissions ■ TF: 800-945-4599 ■ Web: www.stkate.edu

Blue Mountain College PO Box 160 .... Blue Mountain MS 38610 662-685-4161 685-4776*
*Fax: Admissions ■ TF: 800-235-0136 ■ Web: www.bmc.edu

Stephens College 1200 E Broadway PO Box 2121 .... Columbia MO 65215 573-876-7207 876-7237*
*Fax: Admissions ■ TF Admissions: 800-876-7207 ■ Web: www.stephens.edu

College of Saint Mary 7000 Mercy Rd .... Omaha NE 68106 402-399-2400 399-2412*
*Fax: Admissions ■ TF: 800-926-5534 ■ Web: www.csm.edu

College of Saint Elizabeth 2 Convent Rd .... Morristown NJ 07960 973-290-4700 290-4710*
*Fax: Admissions ■ TF Admissions: 800-210-7900 ■ Web: www.cse.edu

Georgian Court University 900 Lakewood Ave .... Lakewood NJ 08701 732-987-2760 987-2000*
*Fax: Admissions ■ TF: 800-458-8422 ■ Web: www.georgian.edu

Barnard College Columbia University
3009 Broadway .... New York NY 10027 212-854-2014 854-6220*
*Fax: Admissions ■ Web: www.barnard.edu

College of New Rochelle 29 Castle Pl .... New Rochelle NY 10805 914-654-5452 654-5464
TF: 800-933-5923 ■ Web: www.cnr.edu
Westchester 400 Westchester Ave .... West Harrison NY 10604 914-332-8295 332-7442
TF: 800-724-4312 ■ Web: www.fordham.edu

Russell Sage College 45 Ferry St .... Troy NY 12180 518-244-2217 244-6880*
*Fax: Admissions ■ TF Admissions: 888-837-9724 ■ Web: www.sage.edu

Bennett College 900 E Washington St .... Greensboro NC 27401 336-370-8624 517-2166*
*Fax: Admissions ■ TF Admissions: 800-413-5323 ■ Web: www.bennett.edu

Meredith College 3800 Hillsborough St. .... Raleigh NC 27607 919-760-8581 760-2348*
*Fax: Admissions ■ TF: 800-637-3348 ■ Web: www.meredith.edu

Peace College 15 E Peace St .... Raleigh NC 27604 919-508-2000 508-2326*
*Fax: Admissions ■ TF: 800-732-2347 ■ Web: www.peace.edu

Salem College 601 S Church St .... Winston-Salem NC 27101 336-721-2600 917-5572*
*Fax: Admissions ■ TF Admissions: 800-327-2536 ■ Web: www.salem.edu

Ursuline College 2550 Lander Rd. .... Pepper Pike OH 44124 440-449-4200 684-6138*
*Fax: Admissions ■ TF: 888-877-8546 ■ Web: www.ursuline.edu

Bryn Mawr College 101 N Merion Ave. .... Bryn Mawr PA 19010 610-526-5000 526-7471*
*Fax: Admissions ■ TF Admissions: 800-262-1885 ■ Web: www.brynmawr.edu

Carlow University 3333 5th Ave .... Pittsburgh PA 15213 412-578-6000 578-6689
TF: 800-333-2275 ■ Web: www.carlow.edu

Cedar Crest College 100 College Dr .... Allentown PA 18104 610-437-4471 606-4647*
*Fax: Admissions ■ TF Admissions: 800-360-1222 ■ Web: www.cedarcrest.edu

Chatham University 5700 W Woodland Rd .... Pittsburgh PA 15232 412-365-1100 365-1609
TF: 800-837-1290 ■ Web: www.chatham.edu

Rosemont College 1400 Montgomery Ave. .... Rosemont PA 19010 610-527-0200 520-4399*
*Fax: Admissions ■ TF Admissions: 800-331-0708 ■ Web: www.rosemont.edu

Wilson College 1015 Philadelphia Ave .... Chambersburg PA 17201 717-264-4141 264-1578*
*Fax: Admissions ■ TF Admissions: 800-421-8402 ■ Web: www.wilson.edu

Columbia College 1301 Columbia College Dr .... Columbia SC 29203 803-786-3012 786-3674
TF: 800-277-1301 ■ Web: www.columbiacollegesc.edu

Converse College 580 E Main St .... Spartanburg SC 29302 864-596-9000 596-9225*
*Fax: Admissions ■ TF Admissions: 800-766-1125 ■ Web: www.converse.edu

Texas Woman's University
304 Administration Dr PO Box 425589. .... Denton TX 76204 940-898-3188 898-3081*
*Fax: Admissions ■ TF: 866-809-6130 ■ Web: www.twu.edu

Hollins University 7916 Williamson Rd .... Roanoke VA 24020 540-362-6401 362-6218*
*Fax: Admissions ■ TF Admissions: 800-456-9595 ■ Web: www.hollins.edu

Mary Baldwin College 318 Prospect St. .... Staunton VA 24401 540-887-7019 887-7292*
*Fax: Admissions ■ TF Admissions: 800-468-2262 ■ Web: www.mbc.edu

Randolph College 2500 Rivermont Ave .... Lynchburg VA 24503 434-947-8000 947-8996*
*Fax: Admissions ■ TF Admissions: 800-745-7692 ■ Web: www.randolphcollege.edu

Sweet Briar College 134 Chappel Rd. .... Sweet Briar VA 24595 434-381-6100 381-6152*
*Fax: Admissions ■ TF Admissions: 800-381-6142 ■ Web: www.sbc.edu

Alverno College PO Box 343922. .... Milwaukee WI 53234 414-382-6100 382-6055
TF: 800-933-3401 ■ Web: www.alverno.edu

Mount Mary College
2900 N Menomonee River Pkwy. .... Milwaukee WI 53222 414-256-1219 256-0180*
*Fax: Admissions ■ TF Admissions: 800-321-6265 ■ Web: www.mtmary.edu

167 COLLEGES & UNIVERSITIES - CHRISTIAN

SEE ALSO Colleges - Bible p. 1617; Colleges & Universities - Jesuit p. 1668

The Institutions Listed Here Are Members Of The Council For Christian Colleges & Universities (Cccu). Although Many Other Colleges And Universities Describe Themselves As "Religiously Affiliated," Members Of Cccu Are Intentionally Christ-Centered. Among The Criteria For Membership In Cccu, Schools Must Have Curricular And Extra-Curricular Programs That Reflect The Integration Of Scholarship, Biblical Faith, And Service.

Phone Fax

Crown College 8700 College View Dr .... Saint Bonifacius MN 55375 952-446-4100 446-4149
TF: 800-682-7696 ■ Web: www.crown.edu

King's University College 9125 50th St .... Edmonton AB T6B2H3 780-465-3500 465-3534
TF: 800-661-8582 ■ Web: www.kingsu.ab.ca

Redeemer University College 777 Garner Rd E. .... Ancaster ON L9K1J4 905-648-2131 648-2134
TF: 877-779-0913 ■ Web: www.redeemer.on.ca

Trinity Western University 7600 Glover Rd .... Langley BC V2Y1Y1 604-888-7511 513-2064*
*Fax: Admissions ■ TF: 888-468-6898 ■ Web: www.twu.ca

Judson College 302 Bibb St .... Marion AL 36756 334-683-5110 683-5282*
*Fax: Admissions ■ TF Admissions: 800-447-9472 ■ Web: www.judson.edu

Institution	City	State	ZIP	Phone	Fax
John Brown University 2000 W University St	Siloam Springs	AR	72761	479-524-3131	524-4196*
*Fax: Admissions ■ TF Admissions: 877-528-4636 ■ Web: www.jbu.edu					
Williams Baptist College 60 W Fulbright St	Walnut Ridge	AR	72476	870-886-6741	886-3924*
*Fax: Admissions ■ TF: 800-722-4434 ■ Web: www.wbcoll.edu					
Azusa Pacific University 901 E Alosta Ave PO Box 7000	Azusa	CA	91702	626-969-3434	812-3096
TF: 800-825-5278 ■ Web: www.apu.edu					
Biola University 13800 Biola Ave	La Mirada	CA	90639	562-903-6000	903-4709*
*Fax: Admissions ■ TF Admissions: 800-652-4652 ■ Web: www.biola.edu					
California Baptist University 8432 Magnolia Ave	Riverside	CA	92504	951-689-5771	343-4525*
*Fax: Admissions ■ TF: 877-228-8866 ■ Web: www.calbaptist.edu					
Fresno Pacific University 1717 S Chestnut Ave PO Box 2005	Fresno	CA	93702	559-453-2039	453-7151*
*Fax: Admissions ■ TF: 800-660-6089 ■ Web: www.fresno.edu					
Hope International University 2500 E Nutwood Ave	Fullerton	CA	92831	714-879-3901	526-0231*
*Fax: Admissions ■ TF: 866-722-4673 ■ Web: www.hiu.edu					
Master's College 21726 Placerita Canyon Rd	Santa Clarita	CA	91321	661-259-3540	288-1037*
*Fax: Admissions ■ TF: 800-568-6248 ■ Web: www.masters.edu					
Point Loma Nazarene University 3900 Lomaland Dr	San Diego	CA	92106	619-849-2200	849-2601*
*Fax: Admissions ■ TF Admissions: 800-733-7770 ■ Web: www.pointloma.edu					
Simpson University 2211 College View Dr	Redding	CA	96003	530-226-4606	226-4861*
*Fax: Admissions ■ TF: 888-974-6776 ■ Web: www.simpsonu.edu					
Vanguard University of Southern California 55 Fair Dr	Costa Mesa	CA	92626	714-556-3610	966-5471*
*Fax: Admissions ■ TF Admissions: 800-722-6279 ■ Web: www.vanguard.edu					
Westmont College 955 La Paz Rd	Santa Barbara	CA	93108	805-565-6000	565-6234*
*Fax: Admissions ■ TF Admissions: 800-777-9011 ■ Web: www.westmont.edu					
Colorado Christian University 8787 W Alameda Ave	Lakewood	CO	80226	303-963-3200	963-3201
TF: 800-443-2484 ■ Web: www.ccu.edu					
Palm Beach Atlantic University PO Box 24708	West Palm Beach	FL	33416	561-803-2000	803-2115*
*Fax: Admissions ■ TF: 888-468-6722 ■ Web: www.pba.edu					
Southeastern University 1000 Longfellow Blvd	Lakeland	FL	33801	863-667-5000	667-5200*
*Fax: Admissions ■ TF Admissions: 800-500-8760 ■ Web: www.seuniversity.edu					
Warner Southern College 13895 Hwy 27	Lake Wales	FL	33859	863-638-1426	638-7290*
*Fax: Admissions ■ TF: 800-949-7248 ■ Web: www.warner.edu					
Covenant College 14049 Scenic Hwy	Lookout Mountain	GA	30750	706-820-1560	419-1044*
*Fax: Admissions ■ TF: 888-451-2683 ■ Web: www.covenant.edu					
Northwest Nazarene University 623 Holly St	Nampa	ID	83686	208-467-8000	467-8645*
*Fax: Admissions ■ TF Admissions: 877-668-4968 ■ Web: www.nnu.edu					
Greenville College 315 E College Ave	Greenville	IL	62246	618-664-7100	664-9841*
*Fax: Admissions ■ TF: 800-345-4440 ■ Web: www.greenville.edu					
Judson University 1151 N State St	Elgin	IL	60123	847-628-2500	628-2526*
*Fax: Admissions ■ TF Admissions: 800-879-5376 ■ Web: www.judsonu.edu					
North Park University 3225 W Foster Ave	Chicago	IL	60625	773-244-5500	244-4953
TF: 800-888-6728 ■ Web: www.northpark.edu					
Olivet Nazarene University 1 University Ave	Bourbonnais	IL	60914	815-939-5011	935-4998*
*Fax: Admissions ■ TF: 800-648-1463 ■ Web: www.olivet.edu					
Trinity Christian College 6601 W College Dr	Palos Heights	IL	60463	866-874-6463	239-4826*
*Fax Area Code: 708 ■ TF: 800-748-0085 ■ Web: www.trnty.edu					
Trinity International University 2065 Half Day Rd	Deerfield	IL	60015	847-317-7000	317-8097
TF: 800-822-3225 ■ Web: www.tiu.edu					
Wheaton College 501 College Ave	Wheaton	IL	60187	630-752-5000	752-5285
TF: 800-222-2419 ■ Web: www.wheaton.edu					
Anderson University 1100 E 5th St	Anderson	IN	46012	765-649-9071	641-4091*
*Fax: Admissions ■ TF Admissions: 800-428-6414 ■ Web: www.anderson.edu					
Bethel College 1001 W McKinley Ave	Mishawaka	IN	46545	574-257-3339	257-3335*
*Fax: Admissions ■ TF Admissions: 800-422-4101 ■ Web: www.bethelcollege.edu					
Goshen College 1700 S Main St	Goshen	IN	46526	574-535-7000	535-7609*
*Fax: Admissions ■ TF: 800-348-7422 ■ Web: www.goshen.edu					
Grace College 200 Seminary Dr	Winona Lake	IN	46590	574-372-5100	372-5120*
*Fax: Admissions ■ TF: 800-544-7223 ■ Web: www.grace.edu					
Huntington University 2303 College Ave	Huntington	IN	46750	260-356-6000	358-3699*
*Fax: Admissions ■ TF Admissions: 800-642-6493 ■ Web: www.huntington.edu					
Indiana Wesleyan University 4201 S Washington St	Marion	IN	46953	765-677-2138	677-2333*
*Fax: Admissions ■ TF: 800-332-6901 ■ Web: www.indwes.edu					
Taylor University 236 W Reade Ave	Upland	IN	46989	765-998-2751	998-4925*
*Fax: Admissions ■ TF: 800-882-3456 ■ Web: www.taylor.edu					
Dordt College 498 4th Ave NE	Sioux Center	IA	51250	712-722-6080	722-1198
TF: 800-343-6738 ■ Web: www.dordt.edu					
Northwestern College 101 7th St SW	Orange City	IA	51041	712-707-7000	707-7164*
*Fax: Admissions ■ TF: 800-747-4757 ■ Web: www.nwciowa.edu					
MidAmerica Nazarene University 2030 E College Way	Olathe	KS	66062	913-782-3750	791-3481*
*Fax: Admissions ■ TF: 800-800-8887 ■ Web: www.mnu.edu					
Sterling College 125 W Cooper	Sterling	KS	67579	620-278-2173	278-4418
TF: 800-346-1017 ■ Web: www.sterling.edu					
Tabor College 400 S Jefferson St	Hillsboro	KS	67063	620-947-3121	947-6276*
*Fax: Admissions ■ TF Admissions: 800-822-6799 ■ Web: www.tabor.edu					
Asbury College 1 Macklem Dr	Wilmore	KY	40390	859-858-3511	858-3921*
*Fax: Admissions ■ TF Admissions: 800-888-1818 ■ Web: www.asbury.edu					
Campbellsville University 1 University Dr	Campbellsville	KY	42718	270-789-5000	789-5071*
*Fax: Admissions ■ TF Admissions: 800-264-6014 ■ Web: www.campbellsville.edu					
Kentucky Christian University 100 Academic Pkwy	Grayson	KY	41143	606-474-3000	474-3155*
*Fax: Admissions ■ TF Admissions: 800-522-3181 ■ Web: www.kcu.edu					
Louisiana College 1140 College Dr	Pineville	LA	71359	318-487-7011	487-7550*
*Fax: Admissions ■ TF: 800-487-1906 ■ Web: www.lacollege.edu					
Eastern Nazarene College 23 E Elm Ave	Quincy	MA	02170	617-745-3000	745-3929
TF: 800-883-6288 ■ Web: www.enc.edu					
Gordon College 255 Grapevine Rd	Wenham	MA	01984	978-927-2300	867-4682*
*Fax: Admissions ■ TF: 800-343-1379 ■ Web: www.gordon.edu					
Calvin College 3201 Burton St SE	Grand Rapids	MI	49546	616-526-6000	526-6777*
*Fax: Admissions ■ TF: 800-688-0122 ■ Web: www.calvin.edu					
Cornerstone University 1001 E Beltline Ave NE	Grand Rapids	MI	49525	616-222-1426	222-1418*
*Fax: Admissions ■ TF Admissions: 800-787-9778 ■ Web: www.cornerstone.edu					
Spring Arbor University 106 E Main St	Spring Arbor	MI	49283	517-750-1200	750-6620*
*Fax: Admissions ■ TF Admissions: 800-968-0011 ■ Web: www.spring.arbor.edu					
Belhaven College 1500 Peachtree St PO Box 153	Jackson	MS	39202	601-968-5940	968-8946*
*Fax: Admissions ■ TF: 800-960-5940 ■ Web: www.belhaven.edu					
Mississippi College 200 S Capitol St PO Box 4026	Clinton	MS	39058	601-925-3000	925-3950*
*Fax: Admissions ■ TF: 800-738-1236 ■ Web: www.mc.edu					
College of the Ozarks 1 Industrial Dr PO Box 17	Point Lookout	MO	65726	417-334-6411	335-2618*
*Fax: Admissions ■ TF Admissions: 800-222-0525 ■ Web: www.cofo.edu					
Evangel University 1111 N Glenstone Ave	Springfield	MO	65802	417-865-2815	865-9599
TF: 800-382-6435 ■ Web: www.evangel.edu					
Missouri Baptist University 1 College Pk Dr	Saint Louis	MO	63141	314-434-1115	434-7596
TF: 877-434-1115 ■ Web: www.mobap.edu					
Southwest Baptist University 1600 University Ave	Bolivar	MO	65613	417-326-5281	328-1808*
*Fax: Admissions ■ TF: 800-526-5859 ■ Web: www.sbuniv.edu					
Houghton College 1 Willard Ave PO Box 128	Houghton	NY	14744	585-567-9200	567-9522*
*Fax: Admissions ■ TF: 800-777-2556 ■ Web: www.houghton.edu					
Nyack College 1 S Blvd	Nyack	NY	10960	845-358-1710	358-3047*
*Fax: Admissions ■ TF Admissions: 800-336-9225 ■ Web: www.nyackcollege.edu					
Roberts Wesleyan College 2301 Westside Dr	Rochester	NY	14624	585-594-6000	594-6371*
*Fax: Admissions ■ TF Admissions: 800-777-4792 ■ Web: www.roberts.edu					
Montreat College 310 Gaither Cir PO Box 1267	Montreat	NC	28757	828-669-8011	669-0120
TF: 800-622-6968 ■ Web: www.montreat.edu					
Bluffton University 1 University Dr	Bluffton	OH	45817	419-358-3000	358-3081*
*Fax: Admissions ■ TF: 800-488-3257 ■ Web: www.bluffton.edu					
Cedarville University 251 N Main St	Cedarville	OH	45314	937-766-7700	766-7575*
*Fax: Admissions ■ TF: 800-233-2784 ■ Web: www.cedarville.edu					
Malone College 515 25th St NW	Canton	OH	44709	330-471-8100	471-8149*
*Fax: Admissions ■ TF: 800-521-1146 ■ Web: www.malone.edu					
Mount Vernon Nazarene University 800 Martinsburg Rd	Mount Vernon	OH	43050	740-392-6868	
TF Admissions: 866-782-2435 ■ Web: www.mvnu.edu					
Oklahoma Baptist University 500 W University St	Shawnee	OK	74804	405-275-2850	878-2068*
*Fax: Admissions ■ TF: 800-654-3285 ■ Web: www.okbu.edu					
Oklahoma Christian University PO Box 11000	Oklahoma City	OK	73136	405-425-5000	425-5069*
*Fax: Admissions ■ TF: 800-877-5010 ■ Web: www.oc.edu					
Oklahoma Wesleyan University 2201 Silver Lake Rd	Bartlesville	OK	74006	918-333-6200	335-6229*
*Fax: Admissions ■ TF: 800-468-6292 ■ Web: www.okwu.edu					
Oral Roberts University 7777 S Lewis Ave	Tulsa	OK	74171	918-495-6161	495-6222*
*Fax: Admissions ■ TF: 800-678-8876 ■ Web: www.oru.edu					
Southern Nazarene University 6729 NW 39th Expy	Bethany	OK	73008	405-789-6400	491-6320*
*Fax: Admissions ■ TF: 800-648-9899 ■ Web: www.snu.edu					
Corban College 5000 Deer Pk Dr SE	Salem	OR	97317	503-581-8600	585-4316
TF: 800-845-3005 ■ Web: www.corban.edu					
George Fox University 414 N Meridian St	Newberg	OR	97132	503-538-8383	554-3110*
*Fax: Admissions ■ TF: 800-765-4369 ■ Web: www.georgefox.edu					
Northwest Christian College 828 E 11th Ave	Eugene	OR	97401	541-684-7201	684-7317*
*Fax: Admissions ■ TF: 877-463-6622 ■ Web: www.nwcc.edu					
Warner Pacific College 2219 SE 68th Ave	Portland	OR	97215	503-517-1020	517-1352
TF: 800-804-1510 ■ Web: www.warnerpacific.edu					
Eastern University 1300 Eagle Rd	Saint Davids	PA	19087	610-341-5800	341-1723*
*Fax: Admissions ■ TF Admissions: 800-452-0996 ■ Web: www.eastern.edu					
Geneva College 3200 College Ave	Beaver Falls	PA	15010	724-847-6500	847-6776*
*Fax: Admissions ■ TF: 800-847-8255 ■ Web: www.geneva.edu					
Messiah College PO Box 3005	Grantham	PA	17027	717-691-6000	796-5374*
*Fax: Admissions ■ TF: 800-233-4220 ■ Web: www.messiah.edu					
Waynesburg College 51 W College St	Waynesburg	PA	15370	724-627-8191	627-8124*
*Fax: Admissions ■ TF Admissions: 800-225-7393 ■ Web: www.waynesburg.edu					
Erskine College PO Box 176	Due West	SC	29639	864-379-2131	379-3048*
*Fax: Admissions ■ TF Admissions: 800-241-8721 ■ Web: www.erskine.edu					
Southern Wesleyan University 907 Wesleyan Dr	Central	SC	29630	864-644-5000	644-5972*
*Fax: Admissions ■ TF: 800-282-8798 ■ Web: www.swu.edu					
North Greenville University 7801 N Tigerville Rd PO Box 1892	Tigerville	SC	29688	864-977-7000	977-7177*
*Fax: Admissions ■ TF: 800-468-6642 ■ Web: www.ngu.edu					
University of Sioux Falls 1101 W 22nd St	Sioux Falls	SD	57105	605-331-6600	331-6615
TF: 800-888-1047 ■ Web: www.thecoo.edu					
Bryan College 721 Bryan Dr PO Box 7000	Dayton	TN	37321	423-775-2041	775-7199
TF: 800-277-9522 ■ Web: www.bryan.edu					
Carson-Newman College 1646 Russell Ave	Jefferson City	TN	37760	865-475-9061	471-3502*
*Fax: Admissions ■ TF: 800-678-9061 ■ Web: www.cn.edu					
Crichton College 255 N Highland Ave	Memphis	TN	38111	901-320-9797	320-9791*
*Fax: Admissions ■ TF: 800-960-9777 ■ Web: www.crichton.edu					
King College 1350 King College Rd	Bristol	TN	37620	423-652-4861	968-4456
TF Admissions: 800-362-0014 ■ Web: www.king.edu					
Lee University 1120 N Ocoee St	Cleveland	TN	37311	423-614-8000	614-8533*
*Fax: Admissions ■ TF: 800-533-9930 ■ Web: www.leeuniversity.edu					
Lipscomb University 3901 Granny White Pike	Nashville	TN	37204	615-966-1000	966-1804*
*Fax: Admissions ■ TF: 800-333-4358 ■ Web: www.lipscomb.edu					
Milligan College PO Box 500	Milligan College	TN	37682	423-461-8730	461-8982*
*Fax: Admissions ■ TF: 800-262-8337 ■ Web: www.milligan.edu					
Trevecca Nazarene University 333 Murfreesboro Rd	Nashville	TN	37210	615-248-1200	248-7406*
*Fax: Admissions ■ TF: 888-210-4868 ■ Web: www.trevecca.edu					
Union University 1050 Union University Dr	Jackson	TN	38305	731-661-5210	661-5589*
*Fax: Admissions ■ TF: 800-338-6466 ■ Web: www.uu.edu					

	Phone	Fax
Dallas Baptist University 3000 Mountain Creek Pkwy ... Dallas TX 75211	214-333-7100	333-5447*
**Fax:* Admissions ■ *TF:* 800-460-1328 ■ *Web:* www.dbu.edu		
East Texas Baptist University 1209 N Grove St ... Marshall TX 75670	903-935-7963	923-2001*
**Fax:* Admissions ■ *TF:* 800-804-3828 ■ *Web:* www.etbu.edu		
Hardin-Simmons University 2200 Hickory St ... Abilene TX 79698	325-670-1206	671-2115*
**Fax:* Admissions ■ *TF:* 877-464-7889 ■ *Web:* www.hsutx.edu		
Houston Baptist University 7502 Fondren Rd ... Houston TX 77074	281-649-3000	649-3217*
**Fax:* Admissions ■ *TF Admissions:* 800-969-3210 ■ *Web:* www.hbu.edu		
Howard Payne University 1000 Fisk Ave ... Brownwood TX 76801	325-646-2502	649-8901*
**Fax:* Admissions ■ *TF:* 800-950-8465 ■ *Web:* www.hputx.edu		
LeTourneau University 2100 S Mobberly Ave ... Longview TX 75602	903-753-0231	233-4301*
**Fax:* Admissions ■ *TF:* 800-759-8811 ■ *Web:* www.letu.edu		
Wayland Baptist University 1900 W 7th St ... Plainview TX 79072	806-291-1000	291-1973*
**Fax:* Admissions ■ *TF:* 800-588-1928 ■ *Web:* www.wbu.edu		
Eastern Mennonite University 1200 Pk Rd ... Harrisonburg VA 22802	540-432-4118	432-4444*
**Fax:* Admissions ■ *TF Admissions:* 800-368-2665 ■ *Web:* www.emu.edu		
Northwest University 5520 108th Ave NE ... Kirkland WA 98033	425-822-8266	889-5224*
**Fax:* Admissions ■ *TF Admissions:* 800-669-3781 ■ *Web:* www.northwestu.edu		
Seattle Pacific University 3307 3rd Ave W ... Seattle WA 98119	206-281-2000	281-2544*
**Fax:* Admissions ■ *TF:* 800-366-3344 ■ *Web:* www.spu.edu		
Whitworth College 300 W Hawthorne Rd ... Spokane WA 99251	509-777-3212	777-3758*
**Fax:* Admissions ■ *TF Admissions:* 800-533-4668 ■ *Web:* www.whitworth.edu		

168 COLLEGES & UNIVERSITIES - FOUR-YEAR

SEE ALSO Colleges - Community & Junior p. 1618; Colleges - Fine Arts p. 1634; Colleges - Women's (Four-Year) p. 1636; Colleges & Universities - Christian p. 1636; Colleges & Universities - Graduate & Professional Schools p. 1659; Colleges & Universities - Historically Black p. 1666; Colleges & Universities - Jesuit p. 1668; Military Service Academies p. 2248; Universities - Canadian p. 2746; Vocational & Technical Schools p. 2763

ALABAMA

	Phone	Fax
Alabama Agricultural & Mechanical University 4900 Meridian St PO Box 1087 ... Huntsville AL 35810	256-372-5783	372-5906
TF: 800-553-0816 ■ *Web:* www.aamu.edu		
Alabama State University 915 S Jackson St ... Montgomery AL 36104	334-229-4100	229-4984*
**Fax:* Admissions ■ *TF Admissions:* 800-253-5037 ■ *Web:* www.alasu.edu		
Amridge University 1200 Taylor Rd ... Montgomery AL 36117	334-387-3877	387-3878
TF: 888-790-8080 ■ *Web:* www.amridgeuniversity.edu		
Auburn University 202 Mary Martin Hall ... Auburn University AL 36849	334-844-6425	844-6436*
**Fax:* Admissions ■ *TF Admissions:* 800-282-8769 ■ *Web:* www.auburn.edu		
Montgomery 7440 E Dr ... Montgomery AL 36117	334-244-3000	244-3795
TF: 800-227-2649 ■ *Web:* www.aum.edu		
Birmingham-Southern College 900 Arkadelphia Rd ... Birmingham AL 35254	205-226-4600	226-3074*
**Fax:* Admissions ■ *TF:* 800-523-5793 ■ *Web:* www.bsc.edu		
Concordia College Selma 1804 Green St ... Selma AL 36703	334-874-5700	874-5755
Web: www.concordiaselma.edu		
Faulkner University 5345 Atlanta Hwy ... Montgomery AL 36109	334-272-5820	260-6137*
**Fax:* Admissions ■ *TF:* 800-879-9816 ■ *Web:* www.faulkner.edu		
Huntingdon College 1500 E Fairview Ave ... Montgomery AL 36106	334-833-4497	833-4497*
**Fax:* Admissions ■ *TF Admissions:* 800-763-0313 ■ *Web:* www.huntingdon.edu		
Jacksonville State University 700 Pelham Rd N ... Jacksonville AL 36265	256-782-5781	782-5953*
**Fax:* Admissions ■ *TF:* 800-231-5291 ■ *Web:* www.jsu.edu		
Judson College 302 Bibb St ... Marion AL 36756	334-683-5110	683-5282*
**Fax:* Admissions ■ *TF Admissions:* 800-447-9472 ■ *Web:* www.judson.edu		
Miles College 5500 Myron Massey Blvd ... Fairfield AL 35064	205-929-1000	929-1627*
**Fax:* Admissions ■ *TF Admissions:* 800-445-0708 ■ *Web:* www.miles.edu		
Oakwood College 7000 Adventist Blvd ... Huntsville AL 35896	256-726-7356	726-7154*
**Fax:* Admissions ■ *TF:* 800-824-5312 ■ *Web:* www.oakwood.edu		
Samford University 800 Lakeshore Dr ... Birmingham AL 35229	205-726-3673	726-2171*
**Fax:* Admissions ■ *TF Admissions:* 800-888-7218 ■ *Web:* www.samford.edu		
Selma University 1501 Lapsley St ... Selma AL 36701	334-872-2533	872-7746
South University *Montgomery* 5355 Vaughn Rd ... Montgomery AL 36116	334-395-8800	395-8859*
**Fax:* Admissions ■ *TF:* 866-629-2962 ■ *Web:* www.southuniversity.edu		
Spring Hill College 4000 Dauphin St ... Mobile AL 36608	251-380-4000	460-2186*
**Fax:* Admissions ■ *TF Admissions:* 800-742-6704 ■ *Web:* www.shc.edu		
Stillman College 3601 Stillman Blvd ... Tuscaloosa AL 35401	205-349-4240	366-8941
TF: 800-841-5722 ■ *Web:* www.stillman.edu		
Talladega College 627 W Battle St ... Talladega AL 35160	256-362-0206	362-0274*
**Fax:* Admissions ■ *TF:* 866-540-3956 ■ *Web:* www.talladega.edu		
Troy University 600 University Ave ... Troy AL 36082	334-670-3100	670-3733*
**Fax:* Admissions ■ *TF:* 800-551-9716 ■ *Web:* www.troy.edu		
Dothan PO Box 8368 ... Dothan AL 36304	334-983-6556	556-1040*
**Fax:* Admissions ■ *TF:* 866-291-0317 ■ *Web:* www.dothan.troy.edu		
Montgomery 231 Montgomery St PO Box 4419 ... Montgomery AL 36103	334-834-1400	241-5448*
**Fax:* Admissions ■ *TF:* 800-414-5756 ■ *Web:* montgomery.troy.edu		
Phenix City 1 University Pl ... Phenix City AL 36869	334-297-1007	448-5229*
**Fax:* Admissions ■ *Web:* www.phenix.troy.edu		
Tuskegee University 102 Old Admissions Blvd ... Tuskegee AL 36088	334-727-8011	727-5750*
**Fax:* Admissions ■ *TF Admissions:* 800-622-6531 ■ *Web:* www.tuskegee.edu		
University of Alabama PO Box 870132 ... Tuscaloosa AL 35487	205-348-6010	348-9046*
**Fax:* Admissions ■ *TF Admissions:* 800-933-2262 ■ *Web:* www.ua.edu		
Birmingham 1530 3rd Ave S HUC260 ... Birmingham AL 35294	205-934-8221	975-7114*
**Fax:* Admissions ■ *TF:* 800-421-8743 ■ *Web:* www.uab.edu		
Huntsville 301 Sparkman Dr ... Huntsville AL 35899	256-824-2733	824-7780*
**Fax:* Admissions ■ *TF:* 800-824-2255 ■ *Web:* www.uah.edu		
University of Mobile 5735 College Pkwy ... Mobile AL 36613	251-675-5990	442-2498*
**Fax:* Admissions ■ *TF:* 800-946-7267 ■ *Web:* www.umobile.edu		
University of Montevallo Stn 6030 ... Montevallo AL 35115	205-665-6030	665-6032*
**Fax:* Admissions ■ *TF Admissions:* 800-292-4349 ■ *Web:* www.montevallo.edu		
University of North Alabama 1 Harrison Plaza ... Florence AL 35632	256-765-4100	765-4960*
**Fax:* Admissions ■ *TF:* 800-825-5862 ■ *Web:* www.una.edu		
University of South Alabama 2500 Meisler Hall ... Mobile AL 36688	251-460-6141	460-7876
TF: 800-872-5247 ■ *Web:* www.usouthal.edu		
University of West Alabama Stn 4 UWA ... Livingston AL 35470	205-652-3400	652-3522*
**Fax:* Admissions ■ *TF Admissions:* 800-621-8044 ■ *Web:* www.uwa.edu		

ALASKA

	Phone	Fax
Alaska Pacific University 4101 University Dr ... Anchorage AK 99508	907-564-8248	567-8317*
**Fax:* Admissions ■ *TF:* 800-252-7528 ■ *Web:* www.alaskapacific.edu		
Sheldon Jackson College 801 Lincoln St ... Sitka AK 99835	907-747-5221	747-6366*
**Fax:* Admissions ■ *TF Admissions:* 800-478-4556 ■ *Web:* www.sj-alaska.edu		
University of Alaska Anchorage 3211 Providence Dr ... Anchorage AK 99508	907-786-1800	786-4888*
**Fax:* Admissions ■ *Web:* www.uaa.alaska.edu		
University of Alaska Fairbanks PO Box 757480 ... Fairbanks AK 99775	907-474-7500	474-5379*
**Fax:* Admissions ■ *TF:* 800-478-1823 ■ *Web:* www.uaf.edu		
Bristol Bay 527 Seward St PO Box 1070 ... Dillingham AK 99576	907-842-5109	842-5692*
**Fax:* Admissions ■ *TF:* 800-478-5109 ■ *Web:* www.uaf.edu		
Kuskokwim PO Box 368 ... Bethel AK 99559	907-543-4500	543-4551
Web: www.kuskokwim.bethel.alaska.edu		
University of Alaska Southeast 11120 Glacier Hwy ... Juneau AK 99801	907-796-6000	796-6365
TF: 877-465-4827 ■ *Web:* www.jun.alaska.edu		
Wayland Baptist University Anchorage 7801 E 32 Ave ... Anchorage AK 99504	907-333-2277	337-8122
Web: www.wbu.edu		

ARIZONA

	Phone	Fax
American Indian College of the Assemblies of God 10020 N 15th Ave ... Phoenix AZ 85021	602-944-3335	943-8299
TF: 800-933-3828 ■ *Web:* www.aicag.edu		
Arizona State University 1151 S Forest Ave PO Box 870312 ... Tempe AZ 85281	480-965-9011	727-6453
Web: www.asu.edu		
East 7001 E Williams Field Rd ... Mesa AZ 85212	480-727-3278	965-3610
Web: www.poly.asu.edu		
West PO Box 37100 ... Phoenix AZ 85069	602-543-5500	543-8312*
**Fax:* Admissions ■ *Web:* www.west.asu.edu		
Embry-Riddle Aeronautical University Prescott 3700 Willow Creek Rd ... Prescott AZ 86301	928-777-3728	777-6606*
**Fax:* Admissions ■ *TF:* 800-888-3728 ■ *Web:* www.erau.edu		
Grand Canyon University 3300 W Camelback Rd ... Phoenix AZ 85017	602-639-7500	639-7835*
**Fax:* Library ■ *TF:* 800-800-9776 ■ *Web:* www.gcu.edu		
Indian Bible College 2918 N Aris Ave ... Flagstaff AZ 86004	928-774-3890	774-2655
Web: www.indianbible.org		
International Baptist College 2150 E Southern Ave ... Tempe AZ 85282	480-838-7070	505-3299
TF: 800-422-4858 ■ *Web:* www.tricityministries.org		
Northern Arizona University PO Box 4084 ... Flagstaff AZ 86011	928-523-5511	523-6023*
**Fax:* Admissions ■ *TF Admissions:* 888-628-2968 ■ *Web:* www.nau.edu		
Ottawa University Phoenix 10020 N 25th Ave ... Phoenix AZ 85021	602-371-1188	371-0035
TF: 800-235-9586 ■ *Web:* www.ottawa.edu		
Prescott College 220 Grove Ave ... Prescott AZ 86301	928-778-2090	776-5242*
**Fax:* Admissions ■ *TF:* 877-350-2100 ■ *Web:* www.prescott.edu		
University of Arizona 1401 E University Blvd ... Tucson AZ 85721	520-621-2211	621-9799*
**Fax:* Admissions ■ *Web:* www.arizona.edu		
University of Phoenix 4605 E Elwood St ... Phoenix AZ 85040	480-966-7400	
TF: 800-366-9699 ■ *Web:* www.phoenix.edu		
Western International University 9215 N Black Canyon Hwy ... Phoenix AZ 85021	602-943-2311	371-8637
TF: 866-948-4636 ■ *Web:* www.wintu.edu		

ARKANSAS

	Phone	Fax
Arkansas State University PO Box 1630 ... State University AR 72467	870-972-3024	972-3406
TF: 800-382-3030 ■ *Web:* www.astate.edu		
Harding University 900 E Ctr Ave ... Searcy AR 72149	501-279-4000	279-4129
TF: 800-477-4407 ■ *Web:* www.harding.edu		
Henderson State University 1100 Henderson St ... Arkadelphia AR 71999	870-230-5000	230-5066*
**Fax:* Admissions ■ *TF:* 800-228-7333 ■ *Web:* www.hsu.edu		
Hendrix College 1600 Washington Ave ... Conway AR 72032	501-329-6811	450-3843*
**Fax:* Admissions ■ *TF:* 800-277-9017 ■ *Web:* www.hendrix.edu		
John Brown University 2000 W University St ... Siloam Springs AR 72761	479-524-3131	524-4196*
**Fax:* Admissions ■ *TF Admissions:* 877-528-4636 ■ *Web:* www.jbu.edu		
Ouachita Baptist University 410 Ouachita St ... Arkadelphia AR 71998	870-245-5000	245-5500*
**Fax:* Admissions ■ *TF Admissions:* 800-342-5628 ■ *Web:* www.obu.edu		
Philander Smith College 900 Daisy Bates Dr ... Little Rock AR 72202	501-370-5221	370-5225*
**Fax:* Admissions ■ *TF:* 800-446-6772 ■ *Web:* www.philander.edu		

				Phone	Fax
Southern Arkansas University					
100 E University St	Magnolia	AR	71753	870-235-4000	235-5005*
**Fax:* Admissions ■ *TF:* 800-332-7286 ■ *Web:* www.saumag.edu					
University of Arkansas					
232 Silas Hunt Hall	Fayetteville	AR	72701	479-575-5346	575-7515*
**Fax:* Admissions ■ *TF Admissions:* 800-377-8632 ■ *Web:* www.uark.edu					
Little Rock 2801 S University Ave	Little Rock	AR	72204	501-569-3000	569-8956
Web: www.ualr.edu					
Monticello PO Box 3600	Monticello	AR	71656	870-460-1026	460-1926*
**Fax:* Admissions ■ *TF:* 800-844-1826 ■ *Web:* www.uamont.edu					
Pine Bluff 1200 N University Dr	Pine Bluff	AR	71601	870-575-8000	575-4608*
**Fax:* Admissions ■ *TF Admissions:* 800-264-6585 ■ *Web:* www.uapb.edu					
University of Central Arkansas					
201 Donaghey Ave	Conway	AR	72035	501-450-5000	450-5228*
**Fax:* Admissions ■ *TF Admissions:* 800-243-8245 ■ *Web:* www.uca.edu					
University of the Ozarks					
415 N College Ave	Clarksville	AR	72830	479-979-1227	979-1417*
**Fax:* Admissions ■ *TF Admissions:* 800-264-8636 ■ *Web:* www.ozarks.edu					
Williams Baptist College					
60 W Fulbright St	Walnut Ridge	AR	72476	870-886-6741	886-3924*
**Fax:* Admissions ■ *TF:* 800-722-4434 ■ *Web:* www.wbcoll.edu					

CALIFORNIA

				Phone	Fax
Academy of Art University					
79 New Montgomery St	San Francisco	CA	94105	415-274-2200	618-6287
TF: 800-544-2787 ■ *Web:* www.academyart.edu					
Alliant International University					
10455 Pomerado Rd	San Diego	CA	92131	858-635-4772	635-4739*
**Fax:* Admissions ■ *TF:* 866-825-5426 ■ *Web:* www.alliant.edu					
American InterContinental University Los Angeles					
12655 W Jefferson Blvd	Los Angeles	CA	90066	310-302-2000	302-2001*
**Fax:* Admissions ■ *TF:* 888-594-9888 ■ *Web:* www.la.aiuniv.edu					
Azusa Pacific University					
901 E Alosta Ave PO Box 7000	Azusa	CA	91702	626-969-3434	812-3096
TF: 800-825-5278 ■ *Web:* www.apu.edu					
Bethany University of the Assemblies of God					
800 Bethany Dr	Scotts Valley	CA	95066	831-438-3800	438-6104*
**Fax:* Admissions ■ *TF Admissions:* 800-843-9410 ■ *Web:* www.bethany.edu					
Biola University 13800 Biola Ave	La Mirada	CA	90639	562-903-6000	903-4709*
**Fax:* Admissions ■ *TF Admissions:* 800-652-4652 ■ *Web:* www.biola.edu					
Brooks Institute					
1321 Alameda Padre Serra	Santa Barbara	CA	93103	805-966-3888	564-1475
TF: 888-276-4999 ■ *Web:* www.brooks.edu					
California Baptist University					
8432 Magnolia Ave	Riverside	CA	92504	951-689-5771	343-4525*
**Fax:* Admissions ■ *TF:* 877-228-8866 ■ *Web:* www.calbaptist.edu					
California Christian College					
4881 E University Ave	Fresno	CA	93703	559-251-4215	251-4231*
**Fax:* Admissions ■ *Web:* www.calchristiancollege.org					
California Institute of Technology					
1200 E California Blvd	Pasadena	CA	91125	626-395-6811	683-3026*
**Fax:* Admissions ■ *TF:* 800-568-8324 ■ *Web:* www.caltech.edu					
California International University					
3130 Wilshire Blvd	Los Angeles	CA	90010	213-381-3719	381-6990*
**Fax:* Admissions ■ *Web:* www.ciula.edu					
California Lutheran University					
60 W Olsen Rd	Thousand Oaks	CA	91360	805-493-3135	493-3114
TF: 877-258-3678 ■ *Web:* www.callutheran.edu					
California Maritime Academy					
200 Maritime Academy Dr	Vallejo	CA	94590	707-654-1330	654-1336*
**Fax:* Admissions ■ *TF:* 800-561-1945 ■ *Web:* www.csum.edu					
California Pacific University					
1017 E Grand Ave	Escondido	CA	92025	760-739-7730	
TF: 800-458-9667 ■ *Web:* www.cpu.edu					
California Polytechnic State University					
1 Grand Ave	San Luis Obispo	CA	93407	805-756-1111	756-5400
Web: www.calpoly.edu					
California State Polytechnic University Pomona					
3801 W Temple Ave	Pomona	CA	91768	909-869-7659	869-4555*
**Fax:* Admissions ■ *Web:* www.csupomona.edu					
California State University					
Bakersfield 9001 Stockdale Hwy	Bakersfield	CA	93311	661-654-2011	654-3389*
**Fax:* Admissions ■ *Web:* www.csubak.edu					
Ch Islands 1 University Dr	Camarillo	CA	93012	805-437-8400	437-8509*
**Fax:* Admissions ■ *Web:* www.csuci.edu					
Chico CSU Chico	Chico	CA	95929	530-898-6321	898-6456*
**Fax:* Admissions ■ *TF Admissions:* 800-542-4426 ■ *Web:* www.csuchico.edu					
Dominguez Hills 1000 E Victoria St	Carson	CA	90747	310-243-3300	516-4573*
**Fax:* Admissions ■ *TF:* 888-278-3448 ■ *Web:* www.csudh.edu					
East Bay 25800 Carlos Bee Blvd	Hayward	CA	94542	510-885-3000	885-4059
Web: www.csueastbay.edu					
Fresno 5241 N Maple Ave	Fresno	CA	93740	559-278-4240	278-4812*
**Fax:* Admissions ■ *Web:* www.csufresno.edu					
Fullerton 800 N State College Blvd	Fullerton	CA	92834	714-278-2011	278-2300
Web: www.fullerton.edu					
Long Beach 1250 Bellflower Blvd	Long Beach	CA	90840	562-985-4111	985-4973*
**Fax:* Admissions ■ *Web:* www.csulb.edu					
Los Angeles 5151 State University Dr	Los Angeles	CA	90032	323-343-3000	343-6306*
**Fax:* Admissions ■ *Web:* www.calstatela.edu					
Monterey Bay 100 Campus Ctr	Seaside	CA	93955	831-582-3518	582-3738*
**Fax:* Admissions ■ *Web:* www.csumb.edu					
Northridge 18111 Nordhoff St	Northridge	CA	91330	818-677-1200	677-3766
Web: www.csun.edu					
Sacramento 6000 J St	Sacramento	CA	95819	916-278-3901	278-7473
Web: www.csus.edu					
San Bernardino 5500 University Pkwy	San Bernardino	CA	92407	909-537-5188	537-7034
Web: www.csusb.edu					
San Marcos 333 S Twin Oaks Valley Rd	San Marcos	CA	92096	760-750-4000	750-3248*
**Fax:* Admissions ■ *Web:* www.csusm.edu					
Stanislaus 1 University Cir	Turlock	CA	95382	209-667-3152	667-3788
Web: www.csustan.edu					
Chapman University 1 University Dr	Orange	CA	92866	714-997-6815	997-6713*
**Fax:* Admissions ■ *TF:* 888-282-7759 ■ *Web:* www.chapman.edu					
University College Irvine					
7545 Irvine Ctr Dr Suite 150	Irvine	CA	92618	949-753-4774	753-7875
Web: www.chapman.edu					
Charles R Drew University of Medicine & Science					
1731 E 120th St	Los Angeles	CA	90059	323-563-4800	563-4957*
**Fax:* Admissions ■ *Web:* www.cdrewu.edu					
City University Los Angeles PO Box 45227	Los Angeles	CA	90045	310-671-0783	293-1691*
**Fax Area Code:* 323 ■ **Fax:* Admissions ■ *Web:* www.cula.edu					
Claremont McKenna College 500 E 9th St	Claremont	CA	91711	909-621-8088	621-8516
Web: www.claremontmckenna.edu					
Cogswell Polytechnical College					
1175 Bordeaux Dr	Sunnyvale	CA	94089	408-541-0100	747-0764*
**Fax:* Admissions ■ *TF:* 800-264-7955 ■ *Web:* www.cogswell.edu					
Coleman College 8888 Balboa Ave	San Diego	CA	92123	858-499-0202	499-0233
Web: www.coleman.edu					
Columbia College Hollywood 18618 Oxnard St	Tarzana	CA	91356	818-345-8414	345-9053
TF: 800-785-0585 ■ *Web:* www.columbiacollege.edu					
Concordia University Irvine 1530 Concordia W	Irvine	CA	92612	949-854-8002	854-6894
TF: 800-229-1200 ■ *Web:* www.cui.edu					
Design Institute of San Diego					
8555 Commerce Ave	San Diego	CA	92121	858-566-1200	566-2711
Web: www.disd.edu					
Dominican University of California					
50 Acacia Ave	San Rafael	CA	94901	415-457-4440	485-3214*
**Fax:* Admissions ■ *TF Admissions:* 888-323-6763 ■ *Web:* www.dominican.edu					
Escondido Bible College 927 Idaho Ave	Escondido	CA	92025	760-745-9826	
Web: www.cotvbiblecollege.edu					
Fresno Pacific University					
1717 S Chestnut Ave PO Box 2005	Fresno	CA	93702	559-453-2039	453-7151*
**Fax:* Admissions ■ *TF:* 800-660-6089 ■ *Web:* www.fresno.edu					
Harvey Mudd College					
301 Platt Blvd Kingston Hall	Claremont	CA	91711	909-621-8011	607-7046*
**Fax:* Admissions ■ *Web:* www.hmc.edu					
Hebrew Union College Los Angeles					
3077 University Ave	Los Angeles	CA	90007	213-749-3424	747-6128*
**Fax:* Admissions ■ *TF:* 800-899-0925 ■ *Web:* www.huc.edu					
Holy Names University 3500 Mountain Blvd	Oakland	CA	94619	510-436-1000	436-1325*
**Fax:* Admissions ■ *TF:* 800-430-1321 ■ *Web:* www.hnu.edu					
Hope International University					
2500 E Nutwood Ave	Fullerton	CA	92831	714-879-3901	526-0231*
**Fax:* Admissions ■ *TF:* 866-722-4673 ■ *Web:* www.hiu.edu					
Humboldt State University 1 Harpst St	Arcata	CA	95521	707-826-3011	826-6190*
**Fax:* Admissions ■ *TF:* 866-850-9556 ■ *Web:* www.humboldt.edu					
Humphreys College 6650 Inglewood Ave	Stockton	CA	95207	209-478-0800	478-8721
Web: www.humphreys.edu					
John F Kennedy University					
100 Ellinwood Way	Pleasant Hill	CA	94523	925-969-3300	969-3101*
**Fax:* Admissions ■ *TF:* 800-696-5358 ■ *Web:* www.jfku.edu					
La Sierra University 4500 Riverwalk Pkwy	Riverside	CA	92515	951-785-2000	785-2901
TF: 800-874-5587 ■ *Web:* www.lasierra.edu					
Laguna College of Art & Design					
2222 Laguna Canyon Rd	Laguna Beach	CA	92651	949-376-6000	376-6009*
**Fax:* Admissions ■ *TF:* 800-255-0762 ■ *Web:* www.lagunacollege.edu					
Lincoln University 401 15th St	Oakland	CA	94612	510-628-8010	628-8012*
**Fax:* Admissions ■ *TF:* 888-810-9998 ■ *Web:* www.lincolnuca.edu					
Loma Linda University 11234 Anderson St	Loma Linda	CA	92354	909-558-1000	
Web: www.llu.edu					
Loyola Marymount University 1 LMU Dr	Los Angeles	CA	90045	310-338-2700	338-2797
TF: 800-568-4636 ■ *Web:* www.lmu.edu					
Master's College					
21726 Placerita Canyon Rd	Santa Clarita	CA	91321	661-259-3540	288-1037*
**Fax:* Admissions ■ *TF:* 800-568-6248 ■ *Web:* www.masters.edu					
Menlo College 1000 El Camino Real	Atherton	CA	94027	650-543-3753	543-4496
TF: 800-556-3656 ■ *Web:* www.menlo.edu					
Mills College 5000 MacArthur Blvd	Oakland	CA	94613	510-430-2135	430-3298*
**Fax:* Admissions ■ *TF Admissions:* 800-876-4557 ■ *Web:* www.mills.edu					
Mount Saint Mary's College					
12001 Chalon Rd	Los Angeles	CA	90049	310-954-4250	954-4259*
**Fax:* Admissions ■ *TF Admissions:* 800-999-9893 ■ *Web:* www.msmc.la.edu					
National Hispanic University 14271 Story Rd	San Jose	CA	95127	408-254-6900	254-1369*
**Fax:* Admissions ■ *Web:* www.nhu.edu					
National University 11255 N Torrey Pines Rd	La Jolla	CA	92037	858-642-8000	642-8709
TF: 800-628-8648 ■ *Web:* www.nu.edu					
New College of California					
777 Valencia St	San Francisco	CA	94110	415-437-3400	437-3470*
**Fax:* Admissions ■ *TF:* 888-437-3460 ■ *Web:* www.newcollege.edu					
Northwestern Polytechnic University					
47671 Westinghouse Dr	Fremont	CA	94539	510-657-5913	657-8975
Web: www.npu.edu					
Notre Dame de Namur University					
1500 Ralston Ave	Belmont	CA	94002	650-508-3600	508-3426*
**Fax:* Admissions ■ *TF:* 800-263-0545 ■ *Web:* www.ndnu.edu					
Occidental College 1600 Campus Rd	Los Angeles	CA	90041	323-259-2700	341-4875*
**Fax:* Admissions ■ *TF Admissions:* 800-825-5262 ■ *Web:* www.oxy.edu					
Pacific Union College 1 Angwin Ave	Angwin	CA	94508	707-965-6336	965-6432*
**Fax:* Admissions ■ *TF:* 800-862-7080 ■ *Web:* www.puc.edu					
Patten University 2433 Coolidge Ave	Oakland	CA	94601	510-261-8500	534-4344*
**Fax:* Admissions ■ *TF:* 877-472-8836 ■ *Web:* www.patten.edu					
Pepperdine University 24255 Pacific Coast Hwy	Malibu	CA	90263	310-506-4000	506-4861*
**Fax:* Admissions ■ *Web:* www.pepperdine.edu					
Pitzer College 1050 N Mills Ave	Claremont	CA	91711	909-621-8129	621-8770*
**Fax:* Admissions ■ *TF:* 800-748-9371 ■ *Web:* www.pitzer.edu					
Point Loma Nazarene University					
3900 Lomaland Dr	San Diego	CA	92106	619-849-2200	849-2601*
**Fax:* Admissions ■ *TF Admissions:* 800-733-7770 ■ *Web:* www.pointloma.edu					
Pomona College 333 N College Way	Claremont	CA	91711	909-621-8134	621-8952*
**Fax:* Admissions ■ *Web:* www.pomona.edu					
Ryokan College					
11965 Venice Blvd Suite 304	Los Angeles	CA	90066	310-390-7560	391-9756*
**Fax:* Admissions ■ *TF:* 866-796-5261 ■ *Web:* www.ryokan.edu					
Saint Mary's College of California					
1928 St Mary's Rd	Moraga	CA	94556	925-631-4000	376-7193*
**Fax:* Admissions ■ *TF Admissions:* 800-800-4762 ■ *Web:* www.stmarys-ca.edu					
Samuel Merritt College 370 Hawthorne Ave	Oakland	CA	94609	510-869-6576	869-6525*

				Phone	Fax
**Fax:* Admissions ■ *TF Admissions:* 800-607-6377 ■ *Web:* www.samuelmerritt.edu					
San Diego Christian College					
2100 Greenfield Dr	El Cajon	CA	92019	619-441-2200	590-1739*
**Fax:* Admissions ■ *TF:* 800-676-2242 ■ *Web:* www.sdcc.edu					
San Diego State University					
5500 Campanile Dr	San Diego	CA	92182	619-594-5200	594-1250*
**Fax:* Admissions ■ *Web:* www.sdsu.edu					
Imperial Valley 720 Heber Ave	Calexico	CA	92231	760-768-5520	768-5589*
**Fax:* Admissions ■ *Web:* www.ivcampus.sdsu.edu					
San Francisco Conservatory of Music					
50 Oak St	San Francisco	CA	94102	415-864-7326	503-6299
Web: www.sfcm.edu					
San Francisco State University					
1600 Holloway Ave	San Francisco	CA	94132	415-338-1111	338-7196*
**Fax:* Admissions ■ *Web:* www.sfsu.edu					
San Jose State University 1 Washington Sq	San Jose	CA	95192	408-924-1000	924-2050
Web: www.sjsu.edu					
Santa Clara University					
500 El Camino Real	Santa Clara	CA	95053	408-554-4000	554-5255
Web: www.scu.edu					
Scripps College 1030 Columbia Ave	Claremont	CA	91711	909-621-8149	607-7508*
**Fax:* Admissions ■ *TF:* 800-770-1333 ■ *Web:* www.scrippscol.edu					
Simpson University 2211 College View Dr	Redding	CA	96003	530-226-4606	226-4861*
**Fax:* Admissions ■ *TF:* 888-974-6776 ■ *Web:* www.simpsonu.edu					
Sonoma State University					
1801 E Cotati Ave	Rohnert Park	CA	94928	707-664-2880	664-2060*
**Fax:* Admissions ■ *Web:* www.sonoma.edu					
South Baylo University 1126 N Brookhurst St	Anaheim	CA	92801	714-533-1495	533-6040
TF: 888-642-2956 ■ *Web:* www.southbaylo.edu					
Southern California Institute of Architecture					
960 E 3rd St	Los Angeles	CA	90013	213-613-2200	613-2260*
**Fax:* Admissions ■ *Web:* www.sciarc.edu					
Southern California Seminary					
2075 E Madison Ave	El Cajon	CA	92019	619-442-9841	442-4510
Web: www.socalsem.edu					
Stanford University 450 Serra Mall	Stanford	CA	94305	650-723-2091	725-2846
Web: www.stanford.edu					
Thomas Aquinas College 10000 N Ojai Rd	Santa Paula	CA	93060	805-525-4417	525-9342
TF: 800-634-9797 ■ *Web:* www.thomasaquinas.edu					
Trinity Life Bible College					
5225 Hillsdale Blvd	Sacramento	CA	95842	916-348-4689	334-2315*
**Fax:* Admissions ■ *Web:* www.tlbc.edu					
University of California					
Berkeley 110 Sproul Hall MC	Berkeley	CA	94720	510-642-6000	643-7333
Web: berkeley.edu					
Davis 1 Shields Ave	Davis	CA	95616	530-752-2971	752-1280
Web: www.ucdavis.edu					
Irvine 204 Administration Bldg	Irvine	CA	92697	949-824-5011	824-2711
Web: www.uci.edu					
Los Angeles 405 Hilgard Ave	Los Angeles	CA	90095	310-825-4321	206-1206*
**Fax:* Admissions ■ *Web:* www.ucla.edu					
Merced PO Box 2039	Merced	CA	95344	209-724-4400	724-4244*
**Fax:* Admissions ■ *TF:* 866-270-7301 ■ *Web:* www.ucmerced.edu					
Riverside					
900 University Ave 1120 Hinderaker Hall	Riverside	CA	92521	951-827-3411	827-6344
Web: www.ucr.edu					
San Diego 9500 Gilman Dr	La Jolla	CA	92093	858-534-2230	534-4831*
**Fax:* Admissions ■ *Web:* www.ucsd.edu					
San Francisco 505 Parnassus Ave	San Francisco	CA	94122	415-353-1553	353-3925
Web: www.ucsf.edu					
Santa Barbara 1210 Cheadle Hall	Santa Barbara	CA	93106	805-893-8000	893-2676
Web: www.ucsb.edu					
Santa Cruz 1156 High St Hahn Bldg Rm 150	Santa Cruz	CA	95064	831-459-2131	459-4163
Web: www.ucsc.edu					
University of California Irvine College of Health Sciences					
101 Theory Suite 200	Irvine	CA	92697	949-824-9267	824-2118
Web: www.cohs.uci.edu					
University of Judaism 15600 Mulholland Dr	Bel Air	CA	90077	310-476-9777	471-3657*
**Fax:* Admissions ■ *TF:* 877-862-5852 ■ *Web:* www.ajula.edu					
University of La Verne 1950 3rd St	La Verne	CA	91750	909-593-3511	392-2714*
**Fax:* Admissions ■ *TF Admissions:* 800-876-4858 ■ *Web:* www.ulv.edu					
University of Redlands					
1200 E Colton Ave PO Box 3080	Redlands	CA	92373	909-793-2121	335-4089*
**Fax:* Admissions ■ *TF:* 800-455-5064 ■ *Web:* www.redlands.edu					
University of San Diego 5998 Alcala Pk	San Diego	CA	92110	619-260-4506	260-6836
TF: 800-248-4873 ■ *Web:* www.sandiego.edu					
University of San Francisco					
2130 Fulton St	San Francisco	CA	94117	415-422-5555	422-2217*
**Fax:* Admissions ■ *TF Admissions:* 800-225-5873 ■ *Web:* www.usfca.edu					
University of Southern California					
University Park Campus	Los Angeles	CA	90089	213-740-2311	821-3716*
**Fax:* Admissions ■ *Web:* www.usc.edu					
University of the Pacific 3601 Pacific Ave	Stockton	CA	95211	209-946-2211	946-2413
TF: 800-959-2867 ■ *Web:* www.web.pacific.edu					
Vanguard University of Southern California					
55 Fair Dr	Costa Mesa	CA	92626	714-556-3610	966-5471*
**Fax:* Admissions ■ *TF Admissions:* 800-722-6279 ■ *Web:* www.vanguard.edu					
Weimar College 20601 W Paoli Ln PO Box 486	Weimar	CA	95736	530-637-4111	422-7949
TF: 800-525-9192 ■ *Web:* www.weimarcollege.com					
Westmont College 955 La Paz Rd	Santa Barbara	CA	93108	805-565-6000	565-6234*
**Fax:* Admissions ■ *TF Admissions:* 800-777-9011 ■ *Web:* www.westmont.edu					
Whittier College 13406 E Philadelphia St	Whittier	CA	90608	562-907-4200	907-4870*
**Fax:* Admissions ■ *Web:* www.whittier.edu					
William Jessup University 333 Sunset Blvd	Rocklin	CA	95765	916-577-2200	577-2220*
**Fax:* Admissions ■ *TF:* 800-355-7522 ■ *Web:* www.jessup.edu					
Woodbury University 7500 Glenoaks Blvd	Burbank	CA	91510	818-767-0888	767-7520
TF: 800-784-9663 ■ *Web:* www.woodbury.edu					
World University 107 N Ventura St PO Box 1567	Ojai	CA	93024	805-646-1444	646-1217
Web: www.worldu.edu					

COLORADO

				Phone	Fax
Adams State College 208 Edgemont Blvd	Alamosa	CO	81102	719-587-7712	587-7522
TF: 800-824-6494 ■ *Web:* www.adams.edu					
Auraria Higher Education Ctr 1201 5th St	Denver	CO	80204	303-556-3291	
Web: www.ahec.edu					
Beth-El College of Nursing & Health Sciences					
3955 Craigwood Dr	Colorado Springs	CO	80918	719-262-4422	262-4416
Web: www.web.uccs.edu					
Colorado Baptist College					
3615 Vickers Dr	Colorado Springs	CO	80918	719-593-7887	593-1798
Colorado Christian University					
8787 W Alameda Ave	Lakewood	CO	80226	303-963-3200	963-3201
TF: 800-443-2484 ■ *Web:* www.ccu.edu					
Loveland 1750 Foxtail Dr Suite 100	Loveland	CO	80538	970-669-8700	669-8701*
**Fax:* Admissions ■ *TF:* 800-443-2484 ■ *Web:* www.ccu.edu					
Colorado College					
14 E Cache La Poudre St	Colorado Springs	CO	80903	719-389-6344	389-6816*
**Fax:* Admissions ■ *TF:* 800-542-7214 ■ *Web:* www.coloradocollege.edu					
Colorado School of Mines 1600 Maple St	Golden	CO	80401	303-273-3000	273-3509
TF: 800-446-9488 ■ *Web:* www.mines.edu					
Colorado State University 200 W Lake St	Fort Collins	CO	80523	970-491-1101	491-7799*
**Fax:* Admissions ■ *Web:* www.colostate.edu					
Pueblo 2200 Bonforte Blvd	Pueblo	CO	81001	719-549-2100	549-2419
Web: www.colostate-pueblo.edu					
Colorado Technical University					
4435 N Chestnut St	Colorado Springs	CO	80907	719-598-0200	590-6825*
**Fax:* Admissions ■ *TF:* 800-559-9287 ■ *Web:* www.ctucoloradosprings.com					
Fort Lewis College 1000 Rim Dr	Durango	CO	81301	970-247-7010	247-7179*
**Fax:* Admissions ■ *Web:* www.fortlewis.edu					
Johnson & Wales University Denver					
7150 E Montview Blvd	Denver	CO	80220	303-256-9300	256-9333
TF: 877-598-3368 ■ *Web:* www.jwu.edu					
Mesa State College 1100 N Ave	Grand Junction	CO	81501	970-248-1020	248-1973*
**Fax:* Admissions ■ *TF:* 800-982-6372 ■ *Web:* www.mesastate.edu					
Metropolitan State College of Denver					
CB 44 PO Box 173362	Denver	CO	80217	303-556-3058	556-6345*
**Fax:* Admissions ■ *Web:* www.mscd.edu					
Naropa University 2130 Arapahoe Ave	Boulder	CO	80302	303-444-0202	546-3536
TF: 800-772-6951 ■ *Web:* www.naropa.edu					
National American University Colorado Springs					
5125 N Academy Blvd	Colorado Springs	CO	80918	719-277-0588	590-8305
Web: www.national.edu					
National American University Denver					
1325 S Colorado Blvd Bldg B Suite 100	Denver	CO	80222	303-758-6700	876-7105*
**Fax:* Admissions ■ *Web:* www.national.edu					
Regis University 3333 Regis Blvd	Denver	CO	80221	303-458-4100	964-5534
TF Admissions: 800-568-8932 ■ *Web:* www.regis.edu					
Colorado Springs					
7450 Campus Dr Suite 100	Colorado Springs	CO	80920	800-568-8932	264-7095*
Fax Area Code: 719 ■ **Fax:* Admissions ■ *TF:* 800-568-8932 ■ *Web:* www.regis.edu					
Fort Collins 1501 Academy Ct	Fort Collins	CO	80524	970-472-2208	472-2201*
**Fax:* Admissions ■ *TF:* 800-390-0891 ■ *Web:* www.regis.edu					
University of Colorado					
Boulder CB 552	Boulder	CO	80309	303-492-1411	492-7115*
**Fax:* Admissions ■ *Web:* www.colorado.edu					
Colorado Springs PO Box 7150	Colorado Springs	CO	80933	719-262-3000	262-3116*
**Fax:* Admissions ■ *TF:* 800-990-8227 ■ *Web:* www.uccs.edu					
University of Colorado at Denver					
1250 14th St PO Box 173364	Denver	CO	80217	303-556-2704	556-4838*
**Fax:* Admissions ■ *Web:* www.ucdenver.edu/Pages/UCDWelcomePage.aspx					
University of Denver 2199 S University Blvd	Denver	CO	80210	303-871-2036	871-3301
TF: 800-525-9495 ■ *Web:* www.du.edu					
University of Northern Colorado					
501 20th St CB 10	Greeley	CO	80639	970-351-2881	351-2984*
**Fax:* Admissions ■ *TF Admissions:* 888-700-4862 ■ *Web:* www.unco.edu					
US Air Force Academy (USAFA)					
2304 Cadet Dr Suite 2300	Usaf Academy	CO	80840	719-333-1110	333-3012
TF: 800-443-9266 ■ *Web:* www.usafa.af.mil					
Western State College of Colorado					
600 N Adams St	Gunnison	CO	81231	970-943-2119	943-2363*
**Fax:* Admissions ■ *TF Admissions:* 800-876-5309 ■ *Web:* www.western.edu					
Women's College of the University of Denver					
1901 E Asbury Ave	Denver	CO	80208	303-871-6848	871-6897
Web: www.womenscollege.du.edu					
Yeshiva Toras Chaim Talmudical Seminary					
1555 Stuart St PO Box 40067	Denver	CO	80204	303-629-8200	623-5949

CONNECTICUT

				Phone	Fax
Albertus Magnus College 700 Prospect St	New Haven	CT	06511	203-773-8550	773-5248*
**Fax:* Admissions ■ *TF Admissions:* 800-578-9160 ■ *Web:* www.albertus.edu					
Briarwood College 2279 Mt Vernon Rd	Southington	CT	06489	860-628-4751	628-6444*
**Fax:* Admissions ■ *TF:* 800-952-2444 ■ *Web:* www.briarwood.edu					

	City	State	ZIP	Phone	Fax
Central Connecticut State University 1615 Stanley St	New Britain	CT	06050	860-832-3200	832-2295
Web: www.ccsu.edu					
Connecticut College 270 Mohegan Ave	New London	CT	06320	860-439-2000	439-4301*
**Fax:* Admissions ■ *TF:* 888-553-8760 ■ *Web:* www.connecticutcollege.edu					
Eastern Connecticut State University 83 Windham St	Willimantic	CT	06226	860-465-5000	465-5544*
**Fax:* Admissions ■ *TF Admissions:* 877-353-3278 ■ *Web:* www.easternct.edu					
Fairfield University 1073 N Benson Rd	Fairfield	CT	06824	203-254-4000	254-4199*
**Fax:* Admissions ■ *Web:* www.fairfield.edu					
Hartford Seminary 77 Sherman St	Hartford	CT	06105	860-509-9500	509-9509*
**Fax:* Admissions ■ *Web:* www.hartsem.edu					
Mitchell College 437 Pequot Ave	New London	CT	06320	860-701-5000	444-1209*
**Fax:* Admissions ■ *TF Admitting:* 800-443-2811 ■ *Web:* www.mitchell.edu					
Paier College of Art Inc 20 Gorham Ave	Hamden	CT	06514	203-287-3031	287-3021
Web: www.paiercollegeofart.edu					
Post University 800 Country Club Rd	Waterbury	CT	06723	203-596-4500	756-5810*
**Fax:* Admissions ■ *TF:* 800-345-2562 ■ *Web:* www.post.edu					
Quinnipiac University 275 Mt Carmel Ave	Hamden	CT	06518	203-582-8600	582-8906*
**Fax:* Admissions ■ *TF Admissions:* 800-462-1944 ■ *Web:* www.quinnipiac.edu					
Sacred Heart University 5151 Pk Ave	Fairfield	CT	06825	203-371-7999	365-7609
Web: www.sacredheart.edu					
Saint Joseph College 1678 Asylum Ave	West Hartford	CT	06117	860-232-4571	231-5744*
**Fax:* Admissions ■ *TF Admissions:* 866-442-8753 ■ *Web:* www.sjc.edu					
Southern Connecticut State University 501 Crescent St	New Haven	CT	06515	203-392-5200	392-5727
TF: 888-500-7278 ■ *Web:* www.southernct.edu					
Trinity College 300 Summit St	Hartford	CT	06106	860-297-2180	297-2287*
**Fax:* Admissions ■ *Web:* www.trincoll.edu					
University of Bridgeport 126 Pk Ave	Bridgeport	CT	06604	203-576-4000	576-4941*
**Fax:* Admissions ■ *TF:* 800-392-3582 ■ *Web:* www.bridgeport.edu					
University of Connecticut 2131 Hillside Rd Unit 3088	Storrs	CT	06269	860-486-2000	486-1476*
**Fax:* Admissions ■ *Web:* www.uconn.edu					
Stamford 1 University Pl	Stamford	CT	06901	203-251-8400	251-8556
Web: www.stamford.uconn.edu					
University of Hartford 200 Bloomfield Ave	West Hartford	CT	06117	860-768-4296	768-4961
TF: 800-947-4303 ■ *Web:* www.hartford.edu					
University of New Haven 300 Boston Post Rd	West Haven	CT	06516	203-932-7319	931-6093*
**Fax:* Admissions ■ *TF:* 800-342-5864 ■ *Web:* www.newhaven.edu					
US Coast Guard Academy 15 Mohegan Ave	New London	CT	06320	860-444-8500	701-6700
TF: 800-883-8724 ■ *Web:* www.cga.edu					
Wesleyan University 70 Wyllys Ave	Middletown	CT	06459	860-685-3000	685-3001*
**Fax:* Admissions ■ *Web:* www.wesleyan.edu					
Western Connecticut State University 181 White St	Danbury	CT	06810	203-837-8200	837-8338
TF: 877-837-9278 ■ *Web:* www.wcsu.ctstateu.edu					
Yale University 3800 Hill House Ave PO Box 208234 Yale Stn	New Haven	CT	06520	203-432-4771	432-9392*
**Fax:* Admissions ■ *Web:* www.yale.edu					

DELAWARE

	City	State	ZIP	Phone	Fax
Delaware State University 1200 N DuPont Hwy	Dover	DE	19901	302-857-6351	857-6352*
**Fax:* Admissions ■ *TF Admissions:* 800-845-2544 ■ *Web:* www.desu.edu					
Goldey Beacom College 4701 Limestone Rd	Wilmington	DE	19808	302-998-8814	996-5408*
**Fax:* Admissions ■ *TF:* 800-833-4877 ■ *Web:* www.goldey.gbc.edu					
University of Delaware Hullihen Hall Rm 209	Newark	DE	19716	302-831-2792	831-6905*
**Fax:* Admissions ■ *Web:* www.udel.edu					
Wesley College 120 N State St	Dover	DE	19901	302-736-2300	736-2382
TF: 800-937-5398 ■ *Web:* www.wesley.edu					
Wilmington University 320 N DuPont Hwy	New Castle	DE	19720	302-356-6739	328-5902*
**Fax:* Admissions ■ *TF Admissions:* 877-967-5464 ■ *Web:* www.wilmu.edu					

DISTRICT OF COLUMBIA

	City	State	ZIP	Phone	Fax
American University 4400 Massachusetts Ave NW	Washington	DC	20016	202-885-1000	885-2558
Web: www.american.edu					
Catholic University of America 620 Michigan Ave NE	Washington	DC	20064	202-319-5000	319-6533
Web: www.cua.edu					
Gallaudet University 800 Florida Ave NE	Washington	DC	20002	202-651-5000	651-5744
Web: www.gallaudet.edu					
George Washington University 2121 'I' St NW	Washington	DC	20052	202-994-1000	994-9619
Web: www.gwu.edu					
Mount Vernon College 2100 Foxhall Rd NW	Washington	DC	20007	202-242-6672	994-0325*
**Fax:* Admissions ■ *TF:* 800-447-3765 ■ *Web:* www.gwu.edu					
Georgetown University 37th & 'O' Sts NW	Washington	DC	20057	202-687-3600	687-5084
Web: www.georgetown.edu					
Howard University 2400 6th St NW	Washington	DC	20059	202-806-6100	806-4465*
**Fax:* Admissions ■ *TF:* 800-822-6363 ■ *Web:* www.howard.edu					
Strayer University 1133 15th St NW	Washington	DC	20005	202-408-2400	419-1425*
**Fax:* Admissions ■ *TF:* 888-360-1588 ■ *Web:* www.strayer.edu					
Takoma Park 6830 Laurel St NW	Washington	DC	20012	202-722-8100	722-8108*
**Fax:* Admissions ■ *TF:* 888-360-1588 ■ *Web:* www.strayer.edu					
Trinity University 125 Michigan Ave NE	Washington	DC	20017	202-884-9000	884-9403*
**Fax:* Admissions ■ *TF Admissions:* 800-492-6882 ■ *Web:* www.trinitydc.edu					
University of the District of Columbia 4200 Connecticut Ave NW	Washington	DC	20008	202-274-5000	274-5552
Web: www.udc.edu					

FLORIDA

	City	State	ZIP	Phone	Fax
American Intercontinental University South Florida 2250 N Commerce Pkwy	Weston	FL	33326	954-446-6100	
TF: 866-248-4723 ■ *Web:* www.aiufl.edu					
Ave Maria University 5050 Ave Maria Blvd	Naples	FL	34119	239-280-2500	280-2556*
**Fax:* Admissions ■ *TF:* 877-283-8648 ■ *Web:* www.naples.avemaria.edu					
Baptist College of Florida 5400 College Dr	Graceville	FL	32440	850-263-3261	263-7506*
**Fax:* Admissions ■ *TF:* 800-328-2660 ■ *Web:* www.baptistcollege.edu					
Barry University 11300 NE 2nd Ave	Miami Shores	FL	33161	305-899-3000	899-2971*
**Fax:* Admissions ■ *TF:* 800-756-6000 ■ *Web:* www.barry.edu					
Boynton Beach 1501 Corporate Dr Suite 230	Boynton Beach	FL	33426	561-364-8220	364-8113
Orlando 1650 Sandlake Rd Suite 390	Orlando	FL	32809	407-438-4150	438-9774*
Tallahassee 325 John Knox Rd Bldg A	Tallahassee	FL	32303	850-385-2279	385-7576*
Bethune-Cookman College 640 Dr Mary McLeod Bethune Blvd	Daytona Beach	FL	32114	386-255-1401	481-2601*
**Fax:* Admissions ■ *TF Admissions:* 800-448-0228 ■ *Web:* www.cookman.edu					
Chipola College 3094 Indian Cir	Marianna	FL	32446	850-526-2761	718-2287*
**Fax:* Admissions ■ *Web:* www.chipola.edu					
Clearwater Christian College 3400 Gulf to Bay Blvd	Clearwater	FL	33759	727-726-1153	726-8597*
**Fax:* Admissions ■ *TF Admissions:* 800-348-4463 ■ *Web:* www.clearwater.edu					
Columbia College Orlando 2600 Technology Dr Suite 100	Orlando	FL	32804	407-293-9911	293-8530*
**Fax:* Admissions ■ *Web:* www.ccis.edu					
Eckerd College 4200 54th Ave S	Saint Petersburg	FL	33711	727-867-1166	866-2304*
**Fax:* Admissions ■ *TF Admissions:* 800-456-9009 ■ *Web:* www.eckerd.edu					
Edward Waters College 1658 Kings Rd	Jacksonville	FL	32209	904-470-8200	470-8048*
**Fax:* Admissions ■ *TF Admissions:* 888-898-3191 ■ *Web:* www.ewc.edu					
Embry-Riddle Aeronautical University *Daytona Beach* 600 S Clyde Morris Blvd	Daytona Beach	FL	32114	386-226-6000	226-7070*
**Fax:* Admissions ■ *TF:* 800-862-2416 ■ *Web:* www.erau.edu					
Flagler College 74 King St	Saint Augustine	FL	32084	904-829-6481	819-6466*
**Fax:* Admissions ■ *TF Admissions:* 800-304-4208 ■ *Web:* www.flagler.edu					
Florida A & M University 1700 Lee Hall Dr Rm G-7 Foote-Hilyer Administration Ctr	Tallahassee	FL	32307	850-599-3000	599-3069
Web: www.famu.edu					
Florida Atlantic University 777 Glades Rd	Boca Raton	FL	33431	561-297-3000	297-2758*
**Fax:* Admissions ■ *TF Admissions:* 800-299-4328 ■ *Web:* www.fau.edu					
Davie 2912 College Ave	Davie	FL	33314	954-236-1012	236-1184*
**Fax:* Admissions ■ *TF:* 800-764-2222 ■ *Web:* www.broward.fau.edu					
Fort Lauderdale 111 E Las Olas Blvd	Fort Lauderdale	FL	33301	954-762-5200	236-1184*
**Fax:* Admissions ■ *TF:* 800-764-2222 ■ *Web:* www.broward.fau.edu					
MacArthur 5353 Parkside Dr	Jupiter	FL	33458	561-799-8500	799-8721*
**Fax:* Admissions ■ *Web:* www.fau.edu/jupiter					
Treasure Coast 500 NW California Blvd	Port Saint Lucie	FL	34986	772-873-3300	873-3304*
**Fax:* Admissions ■ *Web:* www.fau.edu					
Florida College 119 N Glen Arven Ave	Temple Terrace	FL	33617	813-988-5131	899-6772*
**Fax:* Admissions ■ *TF:* 800-326-7655 ■ *Web:* www.floridacollege.edu					
Florida Gulf Coast University 10501 FGCU Blvd S	Fort Myers	FL	33965	239-590-1000	590-7894*
**Fax:* Admissions ■ *TF:* 800-590-3428 ■ *Web:* www.fgcu.edu					
Florida Institute of Technology 150 W University Blvd	Melbourne	FL	32901	321-674-8000	674-8004*
**Fax:* Admissions ■ *TF:* 800-888-4348 ■ *Web:* www.fit.edu					
Florida International University 11200 SW 8th St	Miami	FL	33199	305-348-2000	348-3648
Web: www.fiu.edu					
Florida Memorial University 15800 NW 42nd Ave	Miami	FL	33054	305-626-3600	623-1462*
**Fax:* Admissions ■ *TF:* 800-822-1362 ■ *Web:* www.fmuniv.edu					
Florida Southern College 111 Lake Hollingsworth Dr	Lakeland	FL	33801	863-680-4131	680-4120*
**Fax:* Admissions ■ *TF Admissions:* 800-274-4131 ■ *Web:* www.flsouthern.edu					
Florida State University 296 Champions Way ; Rm 6100C UCC	Tallahassee	FL	32306	850-644-2525	645-4670
Web: www.fsu.edu					
Hodges University 2655 Northbrooke Dr	Naples	FL	34119	239-513-1122	598-6254*
**Fax:* Admissions ■ *TF:* 800-466-8017 ■ *Web:* www.hodges.edu					
Fort Myers 4501 Colonial Blvd	Fort Myers	FL	33966	239-482-0019	938-7891*
**Fax:* Admissions ■ *TF:* 800-466-0019 ■ *Web:* www.internationalcollege.edu					
Jacksonville University 2800 University Blvd N	Jacksonville	FL	32211	904-256-8000	256-7012*
**Fax:* Admissions ■ *TF:* 800-225-2027 ■ *Web:* www.ju.edu					
Johnson & Wales University North Miami 1701 NE 127th St	North Miami	FL	33181	305-892-7551	892-7020
TF: 866-598-3567 ■ *Web:* www.jwu.edu					
Jones College 5353 Arlington Expy	Jacksonville	FL	32211	904-743-1122	371-1182*
**Fax:* Admissions ■ *TF:* 800-331-0176 ■ *Web:* www.jones.edu					
Logos Christian College 9000 Regency Sq Blvd	Jacksonville	FL	32211	904-745-3311	743-8866*
**Fax:* Admissions ■ *TF:* 800-252-4253 ■ *Web:* www.logos.edu					
Lynn University 3601 N Military Trail	Boca Raton	FL	33431	561-237-7900	237-7100*
**Fax:* Admissions ■ *TF Admissions:* 800-544-8035 ■ *Web:* www.lynn.edu					
New College of Florida 5800 Bay Shore Rd	Sarasota	FL	34243	941-487-5000	487-5010*
**Fax:* Admissions ■ *Web:* www.ncf.edu					
Northwood University Florida 2600 N Military Trail	West Palm Beach	FL	33409	561-478-5500	681-7901*
**Fax:* Admissions ■ *TF Admissions:* 800-458-8325 ■ *Web:* www.northwood.edu					
Nova Southeastern University 3301 College Ave	Davie	FL	33314	954-262-8000	262-3811*
**Fax:* Admissions ■ *TF:* 800-541-6682 ■ *Web:* www.nova.edu					
Palm Beach Atlantic University PO Box 24708	West Palm Beach	FL	33416	561-803-2000	803-2115*
**Fax:* Admissions ■ *TF:* 888-468-6722 ■ *Web:* www.pba.edu					
Pensacola Christian College 250 Brent Ln	Pensacola	FL	32503	850-478-8496	722-3355*
**Fax Area Code:* 800 ■ *TF:* 800-722-4636 ■ *Web:* www.pcci.edu					
Rollins College 1000 Holt Ave	Winter Park	FL	32789	407-646-2000	646-1502*
**Fax:* Admissions ■ *Web:* www.rollins.edu					
Saint Leo University 33701 State Rd 52	Saint Leo	FL	33574	352-588-8200	588-8257*
**Fax:* Admissions ■ *TF:* 800-334-5532 ■ *Web:* www.saintleo.edu					

				Phone	Fax
Key West Ctr 718 Essex Ct Bldg A	Key West	FL	33040	305-293-2847	296-7296*
Palatka Ctr 33701 State Rd 52 PO Box 6665	Saint Leo	FL	33574	352-588-8200	
TF: 800-334-5532 ■ *Web:* www.saintleo.edu					
Saint Thomas University 16401 NW 37th Ave	Miami Gardens	FL	33054	305-628-6546	628-6591
TF: 800-367-9010 ■ *Web:* www.stu.edu					
South University West Palm Beach 1760 N Congress Ave	West Palm Beach	FL	33409	561-697-9200	697-9944*
**Fax:* Admissions ■ *TF:* 866-629-2902 ■ *Web:* www.southuniversity.edu					
Southeastern University 1000 Longfellow Blvd	Lakeland	FL	33801	863-667-5000	667-5200*
**Fax:* Admissions ■ *TF Admissions:* 800-500-8760 ■ *Web:* www.seuniversity.edu					
Stetson University 421 N Woodland Blvd Unit 8378	DeLand	FL	32723	386-822-7100	822-7112*
**Fax:* Admissions ■ *TF Admissions:* 800-688-0101 ■ *Web:* www.stetson.edu					
Trinity International University South Florida 8190 W SR 84	Davie	FL	33324	954-382-6400	382-6420
TF: 877-392-3586 ■ *Web:* www.tiu.edu					
University of Central Florida 4000 Central Florida Blvd PO Box 160000	Orlando	FL	32816	407-823-2000	823-5625*
**Fax:* Admissions ■ *Web:* www.ucf.edu					
University of Florida 201 Criser Hall PO Box 114000	Gainesville	FL	32611	352-392-1365	392-2115*
**Fax:* Admissions ■ *TF:* 866-876-4472 ■ *Web:* www.ufl.edu					
University of Miami 1252 Memorial Dr	Coral Gables	FL	33146	305-284-4323	284-2507
Web: www.miami.edu					
University of North Florida 4567 St Johns Bluff Rd S	Jacksonville	FL	32224	904-620-1000	620-2414
Web: www.unf.edu					
University of South Florida					
Lakeland 3433 Winter Lake Rd	Lakeland	FL	33803	863-667-7000	667-7096*
**Fax:* Admissions ■ *TF:* 800-873-5636 ■ *Web:* www.lklnd.usf.edu					
Saint Petersburg 140 7th Ave S	Saint Petersburg	FL	33701	727-553-1142	873-4525
Web: www.stpt.usf.edu					
Sarasota-Manatee 8350 N Tamiami Trail	Sarasota	FL	34243	941-359-4200	359-4236*
**Fax:* Admissions ■ *TF:* 877-873-2855 ■ *Web:* www.sarasota.usf.edu					
Tampa 4202 E Fowler Ave	Tampa	FL	33620	813-974-2011	974-4346
TF: 877-873-2855 ■ *Web:* www.usf.edu					
University of Tampa 401 W Kennedy Blvd	Tampa	FL	33606	813-253-6228	258-7398
TF: 800-733-4773 ■ *Web:* www.ut.edu					
University of West Florida 11000 University Pkwy	Pensacola	FL	32514	850-474-2230	474-3360*
**Fax:* Admissions ■ *TF:* 800-263-1074 ■ *Web:* www.uwf.edu					
Warner Southern College 13895 Hwy 27	Lake Wales	FL	33859	863-638-1426	638-7290*
**Fax:* Admissions ■ *TF:* 800-949-7248 ■ *Web:* www.warner.edu					
Webber International University 1201 N Scenic Hwy	Babson Park	FL	33827	863-638-2910	638-1591*
**Fax:* Admissions ■ *TF:* 800-741-1844 ■ *Web:* www.webber.edu					

GEORGIA

				Phone	Fax
Agnes Scott College 141 E College Ave	Decatur	GA	30030	404-471-6000	471-6414*
**Fax:* Admissions ■ *TF:* 800-868-8602 ■ *Web:* www.agnesscott.edu					
Albany State University 504 College Dr Rd	Albany	GA	31705	229-430-4646	430-4105*
**Fax:* Admissions ■ *Web:* asuweb.asurams.edu/asu					
American InterContinental University					
Atlanta 6600 Peachtree Dunwoody Rd 500 Embassy Row NE	Atlanta	GA	30328	404-965-5700	965-5858
TF: 877-252-5221 ■ *Web:* www.aiuniv.edu					
Dunwoody 6600 Peachtree-Dunwoody Rd 500 Embassy Row	Atlanta	GA	30328	404-965-6500	604-9650*
**Fax Area Code:* 770 ■ **Fax:* Admissions ■ *TF:* 800-353-1744 ■ *Web:* www.aiudunwoody.com					
Armstrong Atlantic State University 11935 Abercorn St	Savannah	GA	31419	912-344-2675	344-3470
TF: 800-633-2349 ■ *Web:* www.armstrong.edu					
Atlanta Christian College 2605 Ben Hill Rd	East Point	GA	30344	404-761-8861	460-2451*
**Fax:* Admissions ■ *TF:* 800-776-1222 ■ *Web:* www.acc.edu					
Augusta State University 2500 Walton Way	Augusta	GA	30904	706-737-1632	667-4355
TF: 800-341-4373 ■ *Web:* www.aug.edu					
Berry College 2277 Martha Berry Hwy PO Box 490159	Mount Berry	GA	30149	706-232-5374	290-2178*
**Fax:* Admissions ■ *TF:* 800-237-7942 ■ *Web:* www.berry.edu					
Brenau University 500 Washington St	Gainesville	GA	30501	770-534-6299	538-4701*
**Fax:* Admissions ■ *TF:* 800-252-5119 ■ *Web:* www.brenau.edu					
Brewton-Parker College 201 David-Eliza Fountain Cir Hwy 280 PO Box 197	Mount Vernon	GA	30445	912-583-2241	583-3598*
**Fax:* Admissions ■ *TF:* 800-342-1087 ■ *Web:* www.bpc.edu					
Carver Bible College 3870 Cascade Rd	Atlanta	GA	30331	404-527-4520	527-4524
Web: www.carver.edu					
Clark Atlanta University 223 James P Brawley Dr SW	Atlanta	GA	30314	404-880-8000	880-6174*
**Fax:* Admissions ■ *TF Admissions:* 800-688-3228 ■ *Web:* www.cau.edu					
Clayton State University 2000 Clayton State Blvd	Morrow	GA	30260	678-466-4000	466-4149*
**Fax:* Admissions ■ *Web:* www.clayton.edu					
Columbus State University 4225 University Ave	Columbus	GA	31907	706-507-8800	568-5091
TF: 866-264-2035 ■ *Web:* www.colstate.edu					
Covenant College 14049 Scenic Hwy	Lookout Mountain	GA	30750	706-820-1560	419-1044*
**Fax:* Admissions ■ *TF:* 888-451-2683 ■ *Web:* www.covenant.edu					
Dalton State College 650 N College Dr	Dalton	GA	30720	706-272-4436	272-2530*
**Fax:* Admissions ■ *TF:* 800-829-4436 ■ *Web:* www.daltonstate.edu					
Emmanuel College PO Box 129	Franklin Springs	GA	30639	706-245-7226	245-2876*
**Fax:* Admissions ■ *TF:* 800-860-8800 ■ *Web:* www.emmanuelcollege.edu					
Emory University 200 B Jones Ctr	Atlanta	GA	30322	404-727-6036	727-4303
TF Admissions: 800-727-6036 ■ *Web:* www.emory.edu					
Fort Valley State University 1005 State University Dr	Fort Valley	GA	31030	478-825-6211	825-6169*
**Fax:* Admissions ■ *TF:* 877-462-3878 ■ *Web:* www.fvsu.edu					
Georgia College & State University 231 W Hancock St CB 23	Milledgeville	GA	31061	478-445-5004	445-3653*
**Fax:* Admissions ■ *TF:* 800-342-0471 ■ *Web:* www.gcsu.edu					
Macon 433 Cherry St	Macon	GA	31206	478-752-4278	752-1064
TF: 800-342-0471 ■ *Web:* www.gcsu.edu/macon					
Georgia Institute of Technology 225 N Ave NW	Atlanta	GA	30332	404-894-2000	894-9511*
**Fax:* Admissions ■ *Web:* www.gatech.edu					
Georgia Southern University PO Box 8024	Statesboro	GA	30460	912-478-5391	478-7240
Web: www.georgiasouthern.edu					
Georgia Southwestern State University 800 Gsw State University Dr	Americus	GA	31709	229-928-1273	931-2983
TF Admissions: 800-338-0082 ■ *Web:* www.gsw.edu					
Georgia State University 33 Gilmer St SE # 200	Atlanta	GA	30303	404-413-2000	413-2002
Web: www.gsu.edu					
Kennesaw State University 1000 Chastain Rd	Kennesaw	GA	30144	770-423-6000	420-4435*
**Fax:* Admissions ■ *Web:* www.kennesaw.edu					
LaGrange College 601 Broad St	LaGrange	GA	30240	706-880-8005	880-8010*
**Fax:* Admissions ■ *TF Admissions:* 800-593-2885 ■ *Web:* www.lagrange.edu					
Macon State College 100 College Stn Dr	Macon	GA	31206	478-471-2700	471-5343*
**Fax:* Admissions ■ *TF:* 800-272-7619 ■ *Web:* www.maconstate.edu					
Warner Robins 100 University Blvd	Warner Robins	GA	31093	478-929-6700	929-6726
Web: www.maconstate.edu/wrc					
Medical College of Georgia 1120 15th St	Augusta	GA	30912	706-721-0211	721-7028
TF: 800-736-2273 ■ *Web:* www.mcg.edu					
Mercer University 1400 Coleman Ave	Macon	GA	31207	478-301-2650	301-2828*
**Fax:* Admissions ■ *TF:* 800-637-2378 ■ *Web:* www.mercer.edu					
Cecil B Day 3001 Mercer University Dr	Atlanta	GA	30341	678-547-6089	547-6367
TF: 800-840-8577 ■ *Web:* www.mercer.edu					
Morehouse College 830 Westview Dr SW	Atlanta	GA	30314	404-681-2800	572-3668*
**Fax:* Admissions ■ *Web:* www.morehouse.edu					
North Georgia College & State University 82 College Cir	Dahlonega	GA	30597	706-864-1800	864-1478*
**Fax:* Admissions ■ *TF:* 800-498-9581 ■ *Web:* www.ngcsu.edu					
Oglethorpe University 3000 Woodrow Way NE	Atlanta	GA	30319	404-364-8307	364-8491
TF: 800-428-4484 ■ *Web:* www.oglethorpe.edu					
Paine College 1235 15th St	Augusta	GA	30901	706-821-8200	821-8293*
**Fax:* Admissions ■ *TF:* 800-476-7703 ■ *Web:* www.paine.edu					
Piedmont College 165 Central Ave	Demorest	GA	30535	706-776-0103	776-6635*
**Fax:* Admissions ■ *TF:* 800-277-7020 ■ *Web:* www.piedmont.edu					
Reinhardt College 7300 Reinhardt College Cir	Waleska	GA	30183	770-720-5526	720-5899*
**Fax:* Admissions ■ *TF:* 877-346-4273 ■ *Web:* www.reinhardt.edu					
Savannah State University 3219 College St	Savannah	GA	31404	912-356-2186	356-2256*
**Fax:* Admissions ■ *TF Admissions:* 800-788-0478 ■ *Web:* www.savstate.edu					
Shorter College 315 Shorter Ave	Rome	GA	30165	706-233-7319	233-7224*
**Fax:* Admissions ■ *TF:* 800-868-6980 ■ *Web:* www.shorter.edu					
South University Savannah 709 Mall Blvd	Savannah	GA	31406	912-691-6000	201-8117*
**Fax:* Admissions ■ *TF:* 866-629-2901 ■ *Web:* www.southuniversity.edu					
Southern Polytechnic State University 1100 S Marietta Pkwy	Marietta	GA	30060	678-915-4188	915-7292*
**Fax:* Admissions ■ *TF Admissions:* 800-635-3204 ■ *Web:* www.spsu.edu					
Spelman College 350 Spelman Ln SW	Atlanta	GA	30314	404-681-3643	270-5201*
**Fax:* Admissions ■ *TF Admissions:* 800-982-2411 ■ *Web:* www.spelman.edu					
Thomas University 1501 Millpond Rd	Thomasville	GA	31792	229-226-1621	226-1653*
**Fax:* Admissions ■ *TF:* 800-538-9784 ■ *Web:* www.thomasu.edu					
Truett-McConnell College 100 Alumni Dr	Cleveland	GA	30528	706-865-2134	865-7615*
**Fax:* Admissions ■ *TF:* 800-226-8621 ■ *Web:* www.truett.edu					
University of Georgia 212 Terrell Hall	Athens	GA	30602	706-542-3000	542-1466
TF: 866-423-2947 ■ *Web:* www.uga.edu					
University of West Georgia 1600 Maple St	Carrollton	GA	30117	678-839-5000	839-4747
Web: www.westga.edu					
Valdosta State University 1500 N Patterson St	Valdosta	GA	31698	229-333-5800	333-5482*
**Fax:* Admissions ■ *TF:* 800-618-1878 ■ *Web:* www.valdosta.edu					
Wesleyan College 4760 Forsyth Rd	Macon	GA	31210	478-477-1110	757-4030*
**Fax:* Admissions ■ *TF:* 800-447-6610 ■ *Web:* www.wesleyancollege.edu					

HAWAII

				Phone	Fax
Brigham Young University Hawaii 55-220 Kulanui St	Laie	HI	96762	808-293-3211	293-3741*
**Fax:* Admissions ■ *Web:* www.byuh.edu					
Chaminade University 3140 Waialae Ave	Honolulu	HI	96816	808-735-4711	735-4735*
**Fax:* Admissions ■ *TF:* 800-735-3733 ■ *Web:* www.chaminade.edu					
Hawaii Pacific University 1164 Bishop St Suite 200	Honolulu	HI	96813	808-544-0200	544-1136*
**Fax:* Admissions ■ *TF:* 866-225-5478 ■ *Web:* www.hpu.edu					
Windward Hawaii Loa 45-045 Kamehameha Hwy	Kaneohe	HI	96744	808-236-3500	544-1136
TF Admissions: 866-225-5478					

IDAHO

				Phone	Fax
Boise State University 1910 University Dr	Boise	ID	83725	208-426-1156	426-3765
TF: 800-824-7017 ■ *Web:* www.idbsu.edu					
Brigham Young University Idaho 525 S Ctr	Rexburg	ID	83460	208-496-2011	496-1220*
**Fax:* Admissions ■ *Web:* www.byui.edu					
College of Idaho 2112 Cleveland Blvd	Caldwell	ID	83605	208-459-5011	459-5757*
**Fax:* Admissions ■ *TF Admissions:* 800-224-3246 ■ *Web:* www.collegeofidaho.edu					
Idaho State University 921 S 8th Ave	Pocatello	ID	83209	208-236-0211	282-4511*
**Fax:* Admissions ■ *Web:* www.isu.edu					
Lewis-Clark State College 500 8th Ave	Lewiston	ID	83501	208-792-5272	792-2210*
**Fax:* Admissions ■ *TF:* 800-933-5272 ■ *Web:* www.lcsc.edu					
Northwest Nazarene University 623 Holly St	Nampa	ID	83686	208-467-8000	467-8645*
**Fax:* Admissions ■ *TF Admissions:* 877-668-4968 ■ *Web:* www.nnu.edu					

Phone Fax

University of Idaho
709 Deakin Ave PO Box 444264 ... Moscow ID 83844 208-885-6111 885-9119*
*Fax: Admissions ■ TF: 888-884-3246 ■ Web: www.uihome.uidaho.edu
Boise 322 E Front St Suite 190 ... Boise ID 83702 208-334-2999 364-4035
TF: 866-264-7384 ■ Web: www.boise.uidaho.edu

ILLINOIS

Phone Fax

American Islamic College 640 W Irving Pk Rd ... Chicago IL 60613 773-281-4700 281-8552*
*Fax: Admissions ■ Web: www.aicusa.edu
Augustana College 639 38th St ... Rock Island IL 61201 309-794-7000 794-7174*
*Fax: Admissions ■ TF: 800-798-8100 ■ Web: www.augustana.edu
Aurora University 347 S Gladstone Ave ... Aurora IL 60506 630-844-5533 844-5535
TF: 800-742-5281 ■ Web: www.aurora.edu
Benedictine University 5700 College Rd ... Lisle IL 60532 630-829-6300 829-6301
TF: 888-829-6363 ■ Web: www.ben.edu
Blackburn College 700 College Ave ... Carlinville IL 62626 217-854-3231 854-3713*
*Fax: Admissions ■ TF: 800-233-3550 ■ Web: www.blackburn.edu
Bradley University 1501 W Bradley Ave ... Peoria IL 61625 309-676-7611 677-2797
TF Admissions: 800-447-6460 ■ Web: www.bradley.edu
Chicago State University 9501 S King Dr ... Chicago IL 60628 773-995-2513 995-3820*
*Fax: Admissions ■ Web: www.csu.edu
Christian Life College
404 E Gregory St ... Mount Prospect IL 60056 847-259-1840 259-3888
Web: www.christianlifecollege.edu
Columbia College 600 S Michigan Ave 3rd Fl ... Chicago IL 60605 312-663-1600 344-8024*
*Fax: Admissions ■ Web: www.colum.edu
Concordia University Chicago
7400 Augusta St ... River Forest IL 60305 708-771-8300 209-3347
TF: 800-285-2668 ■ Web: www.cuchicago.edu
DePaul University 1 E Jackson Blvd Suite 9100 ... Chicago IL 60614 312-362-8300 362-5749
TF: 800-433-7285 ■ Web: www.depaul.edu
Dominican University 7900 W Division St ... River Forest IL 60305 708-366-2490 524-6864*
*Fax: Admissions ■ TF: 800-828-8475 ■ Web: www.dom.edu
East-West University 819 S Wabash Ave # 800 ... Chicago IL 60605 312-939-0111 939-0083
TF: 877-398-9376 ■ Web: www.eastwest.edu
Eastern Illinois University
600 Lincoln Ave ... Charleston IL 61920 217-581-2223 581-7060*
*Fax: Admissions ■ TF Admissions: 800-252-5711 ■ Web: www.eiu.edu
Elmhurst College 190 Prospect Ave ... Elmhurst IL 60126 630-617-3400 617-5501
TF: 800-697-1871 ■ Web: www.elmhurst.edu
Eureka College 300 E College Ave ... Eureka IL 61530 309-467-6350 467-6576*
*Fax: Admissions ■ TF Admissions: 888-438-7352 ■ Web: www.eureka.edu
Governors State University
1 University Pkwy ... University Park IL 60466 708-534-5000 534-1640*
*Fax: Admissions ■ TF: 800-478-8478 ■ Web: www.govst.edu
Greenville College 315 E College Ave ... Greenville IL 62246 618-664-7100 664-9841*
*Fax: Admissions ■ TF: 800-345-4440 ■ Web: www.greenville.edu
Harrington College of Design
410 S Michigan Ave ... Chicago IL 60605 312-939-4975 697-8032
TF: 877-939-4975 ■ Web: www.interiordesign.edu
Illinois College 1101 W College Ave ... Jacksonville IL 62650 217-245-3030 245-3034*
*Fax: Admissions ■ TF Admissions: 866-464-5265 ■ Web: www.ic.edu
Illinois Institute of Technology
10 W 33rd St ... Chicago IL 60616 312-567-3025 567-6939*
*Fax: Admissions ■ TF: 800-448-2329 ■ Web: www.iit.edu
Rice 201 E Loop Rd ... Wheaton IL 60189 630-682-6000 682-6010*
*Fax: Admissions ■ Web: www.iit.edu/rice
Illinois State University
CB 2200 Hovey Hall 201 ... Normal IL 61790 309-438-2181 438-3932*
*Fax: Admissions ■ TF Admissions: 800-366-2478 ■ Web: www.ilstu.edu
Illinois Wesleyan University 1312 Pk St ... Bloomington IL 61701 309-556-3031 556-3820*
*Fax: Admissions ■ TF Admissions: 800-332-2498 ■ Web: www.iwu.edu
Judson University 1151 N State St ... Elgin IL 60123 847-628-2500 628-2526*
*Fax: Admissions ■ TF Admissions: 800-879-5376 ■ Web: www.judsonu.edu
Knox College 2 E S St ... Galesburg IL 61401 309-341-7100 341-7070*
*Fax: Admissions ■ TF Admissions: 800-678-5669 ■ Web: www.knox.edu
Lake Forest College 555 N Sheridan Rd ... Lake Forest IL 60045 847-234-3100 735-6271
TF: 800-828-4751 ■ Web: www.lakeforest.edu
Lewis University
1 University Pkwy Unit 297 ... Romeoville IL 60446 815-836-5250 836-5002
TF: 800-897-9000 ■ Web: www.lewisu.edu
Loyola University Chicago
Lake Shore 6525 N Sheridan Rd ... Chicago IL 60626 773-508-3075 508-8926
Web: www.luc.edu
Water Tower 820 N Michigan Ave ... Chicago IL 60611 312-915-6500 915-7216*
*Fax: Admissions ■ TF Admissions: 800-262-2373 ■ Web: www.luc.edu
MacMurray College 447 E College Ave ... Jacksonville IL 62650 217-479-7056 291-0702*
*Fax: Admissions ■ TF: 800-252-7485 ■ Web: www.mac.edu
McKendree College 701 College Rd ... Lebanon IL 62254 618-537-4481 537-6496*
*Fax: Admissions ■ TF: 800-232-7228 ■ Web: www.mckendree.edu
Millikin University 1184 W Main St ... Decatur IL 62522 217-424-6211 425-4669*
*Fax: Admissions ■ TF: 800-373-7733 ■ Web: www.millikin.edu
Monmouth College 700 E Broadway Ave ... Monmouth IL 61462 309-457-2311 457-2310
TF: 888-827-8268 ■ Web: www.monm.edu
National University of Health Sciences
200 E Roosevelt Rd ... Lombard IL 60148 630-629-2000 889-6554
TF: 800-826-6285 ■ Web: www.nuhs.edu
National-Louis University 1000 Capitol Dr ... Wheeling IL 60090 847-947-5718 465-5730*
*Fax: Admissions ■ TF: 800-443-5522 ■ Web: www.nl.edu
Chicago 122 S Michigan Ave ... Chicago IL 60603 312-261-3096 465-5730*
*Fax Area Code: 847 ■ *Fax: Admissions ■ TF: 800-443-5522 ■ Web: www.nl.edu
North Central College 30 N Brainard St ... Naperville IL 60540 630-637-5800 637-5819*
*Fax: Admissions ■ TF: 800-411-1861 ■ Web: www.noctrl.edu
North Park University 3225 W Foster Ave ... Chicago IL 60625 773-244-5500 244-4953
TF: 800-888-6728 ■ Web: www.northpark.edu
Northeastern Illinois University
5500 N St Louis Ave ... Chicago IL 60625 773-442-4050 442-4020*
*Fax: Admissions ■ Web: www.neiu.edu
Northern Illinois University PO Box 3001 ... DeKalb IL 60115 815-753-1000 753-8312*
*Fax: Admissions ■ TF: 800-892-3050 ■ Web: www.niu.edu
Northwestern University 1801 Hinman Ave ... Evanston IL 60208 847-491-7271 467-2331*
*Fax: Admissions ■ Web: www.northwestern.edu
Olivet Nazarene University
1 University Ave ... Bourbonnais IL 60914 815-939-5011 935-4998*
*Fax: Admissions ■ TF: 800-648-1463 ■ Web: www.olivet.edu
Principia College 1 Maybeck Pl ... Elsah IL 62028 618-374-2131 374-4000*
*Fax: Admissions ■ TF: 800-277-4648 ■ Web: www.prin.edu
Quincy University 1800 College Ave ... Quincy IL 62301 217-228-5210 228-5479*
*Fax: Admissions ■ TF: 800-688-4295 ■ Web: www.quincy.edu
Robert Morris College
Chicago 401 S State St ... Chicago IL 60605 312-935-6800 935-4182
TF: 800-762-5960 ■ Web: www.robertmorris.edu
DuPage 905 Meridian Lake Dr ... Aurora IL 60504 630-375-8100 375-8020*
*Fax: Admissions ■ TF Admissions: 800-762-5960 ■ Web: www.robertmorris.edu
Orland Park 43 Orland Sq Dr ... Orland Park IL 60462 708-226-3800 226-5350
TF: 800-225-1520 ■ Web: www.robertmorris.edu
Springfield 3101 Montvale Dr ... Springfield IL 62704 217-793-2500 793-4210*
*Fax: Admitting ■ TF: 800-762-5960 ■ Web: www.robertmorris.edu
Rockford College 5050 E State St ... Rockford IL 61108 815-226-4000 226-2822*
*Fax: Admissions ■ TF: 800-892-2984 ■ Web: www.rockford.edu
Roosevelt University 430 S Michigan Ave ... Chicago IL 60605 312-341-3500 341-3523*
*Fax: Admissions ■ TF Admissions: 877-277-5978 ■ Web: www.roosevelt.edu
Albert A Robin 1400 N Roosevelt Blvd ... Schaumburg IL 60173 847-619-8600 619-8636*
*Fax: Admissions ■ TF Admissions: 877-277-5978 ■ Web: www.roosevelt.edu
Rush University 600 S Paulina St Rm 440 ... Chicago IL 60612 312-942-7100 942-2219*
*Fax: Admissions ■ Web: www.rushu.rush.edu
Saint Xavier University 3700 W 103rd St ... Chicago IL 60655 773-298-3000 298-3076*
*Fax: Admissions ■ TF: 800-462-9288 ■ Web: www.sxu.edu
School of the Art Institute of Chicago
36 S Wabash Ave ... Chicago IL 60603 312-629-6100 629-6101*
*Fax: Admissions ■ TF Admissions: 800-232-7242 ■ Web: www.artic.edu
Shimer College 3424 S State St ... Chicago IL 60616 312-235-3506 235-3501*
*Fax: Admissions ■ TF: 800-215-7173 ■ Web: www.shimer.edu
Southern Illinois University
Edwardsville SR 157 ... Edwardsville IL 62026 618-650-2000 650-5013*
*Fax: Admissions ■ TF: 888-328-5168 ■ Web: www.siue.edu
Southern Illinois University Carbondale
900 S Normal Ave Woody Hall MC 4716 ... Carbondale IL 62901 618-453-2121 453-3250*
*Fax: Admissions ■ Web: www.gradschool.siuc.edu
Trinity Christian College
6601 W College Dr ... Palos Heights IL 60463 866-874-6463 239-4826*
*Fax Area Code: 708 ■ TF: 800-748-0085 ■ Web: www.trnty.edu
Trinity International University
2065 Half Day Rd ... Deerfield IL 60015 847-317-7000 317-8097
TF: 800-822-3225 ■ Web: www.tiu.edu
University of Chicago 5801 S Ellis Ave ... Chicago IL 60637 773-702-1234 702-4199*
*Fax: Admissions ■ Web: www.uchicago.edu
University of Illinois
Chicago 601 S Morgan ... Chicago IL 60607 312-996-7000 413-7628
Web: www.uic.edu
Springfield
1 University Plaza MS UHB 1080 ... Springfield IL 62703 217-206-4847 206-6620*
*Fax: Admissions ■ TF: 888-977-4847 ■ Web: www.uis.edu
Urbana-Champaign 901 W Illinois St ... Urbana IL 61801 217-333-0302 244-4614*
*Fax: Admissions ■ TF Admissions: 800-252-1352 ■ Web: www.uiuc.edu
VanderCook College of Music
3140 S Federal St ... Chicago IL 60616 312-225-6288 225-5211*
*Fax: Admissions ■ Web: www.vandercook.edu
West Suburban College of Nursing 3 Erie Ct ... Oak Park IL 60302 708-763-6530 763-1531*
*Fax: Admissions ■ Web: www.wscn.edu
Western Illinois University 1 University Cir ... Macomb IL 61455 309-298-1414 298-3111*
*Fax: Admissions ■ TF Admissions: 877-742-5948 ■ Web: www.wiu.edu
Quad Cities 3561 60th St ... Moline IL 61265 309-762-9481 764-7172*
*Fax: Admissions ■ Web: www.wiu.edu
Wheaton College 501 College Ave ... Wheaton IL 60187 630-752-5000 752-5285
TF: 800-222-2419 ■ Web: www.wheaton.edu

INDIANA

Phone Fax

American Conservatory of Music
252 Wildwood Rd ... Hammond IN 46324 219-931-6000 931-6089*
*Fax: Admissions ■ Web: www.americanconservatory.edu
Anderson University 1100 E 5th St ... Anderson IN 46012 765-649-9071 641-4091*
*Fax: Admissions ■ TF Admissions: 800-428-6414 ■ Web: www.anderson.edu
Ball State University 2000 W University Ave ... Muncie IN 47306 765-289-1241 285-1632*
*Fax: Admissions ■ TF: 800-382-8540 ■ Web: cms.bsu.edu
Bethel College 1001 W McKinley Ave ... Mishawaka IN 46545 574-257-3339 257-3335*
*Fax: Admissions ■ TF Admissions: 800-422-4101 ■ Web: www.bethelcollege.edu
Butler University 4600 Sunset Ave ... Indianapolis IN 46208 317-940-8100 940-8150*
*Fax: Admissions ■ TF: 800-368-6852 ■ Web: www.butler.edu
Calumet College of Saint Joseph
2400 New York Ave ... Whiting IN 46394 219-473-4215 473-4336*
*Fax: Admissions ■ TF: 877-700-9100 ■ Web: www.ccsj.edu
DePauw University 101 E Seminary St ... Greencastle IN 46135 765-658-4006 658-4007*
*Fax: Admissions ■ TF: 800-447-2495 ■ Web: www.depauw.edu
Earlham College 801 National Rd W ... Richmond IN 47374 765-983-1600 983-1560*
*Fax: Admissions ■ TF: 800-327-5426 ■ Web: www.earlham.edu
Franklin College 101 Branigin Blvd ... Franklin IN 46131 317-738-8000 738-8274*
*Fax: Admissions ■ TF: 800-852-0232 ■ Web: www.franklincollege.edu
Goshen College 1700 S Main St ... Goshen IN 46526 574-535-7000 535-7609*
*Fax: Admissions ■ TF: 800-348-7422 ■ Web: www.goshen.edu
Grace College 200 Seminary Dr ... Winona Lake IN 46590 574-372-5100 372-5120*
*Fax: Admissions ■ TF: 800-544-7223 ■ Web: www.grace.edu
Hanover College 484 Ball Dr ... Hanover IN 47243 812-866-7000 866-7098
TF: 800-213-2178 ■ Web: www.hanover.edu

	City	State	ZIP	Phone	Fax
Holy Cross College 54515 SR 933 N	Notre Dame	IN	46556	574-239-8400	239-8323*
*Fax: Admissions ■ Web: www.hcc-nd.edu					
Huntington University 2303 College Ave.	Huntington	IN	46750	260-356-6000	358-3699*
*Fax: Admissions ■ TF Admissions: 800-642-6493 ■ Web: www.huntington.edu					
Indiana Institute of Technology					
1600 E Washington Blvd.	Fort Wayne	IN	46803	260-422-5561	422-7696*
*Fax: Admissions ■ TF: 800-937-2448 ■ Web: www.indianatech.edu					
Indiana State University 218 N 6th St	Terre Haute	IN	47809	812-237-2121	237-8023
TF: 800-468-6478 ■ Web: www.indstate.edu					
Indiana University 300 N Jordan Ave.	Bloomington	IN	47405	812-855-0661	855-5102
Web: www.indiana.edu					
East 2325 Chester Blvd	Richmond	IN	47374	765-973-8208	973-8288*
*Fax: Admissions ■ TF: 800-959-3278 ■ Web: www.iue.edu					
Kokomo 2300 S Washington St PO Box 9003	Kokomo	IN	46904	765-455-9217	455-9537*
*Fax: Admissions ■ TF: 888-875-4485 ■ Web: www.iuk.edu					
Northwest 3400 Broadway	Gary	IN	46408	219-980-6500	981-4219*
*Fax: Admissions ■ TF: 888-968-7486 ■ Web: www.iun.edu					
South Bend 1700 Mishawaka Ave PO Box 7111	South Bend	IN	46634	574-520-4870	523-4834*
*Fax: Admissions ■ TF: 877-462-4872 ■ Web: www.iusb.edu					
Southeast 4201 Grant Line Rd	New Albany	IN	47150	812-941-2212	941-2595
Web: www.ius.edu					
Indiana University-Purdue University					
Columbus 4601 Central Ave	Columbus	IN	47203	812-348-7311	348-7257
Web: www.columbus.iupui.edu					
Fort Wayne 2101 E Coliseum Blvd	Fort Wayne	IN	46805	260-481-6100	481-6880*
*Fax: Hum Res ■ TF: 800-324-4739 ■ Web: www.ipfw.edu					
Indianapolis 425 University Blvd.	Indianapolis	IN	46202	317-274-5555	278-1862
Web: www.iupui.edu					
Indiana Wesleyan University					
4201 S Washington St	Marion	IN	46953	765-677-2138	677-2333*
*Fax: Admissions ■ TF: 800-332-6901 ■ Web: www.indwes.edu					
Manchester College					
604 E College Ave.	North Manchester	IN	46962	260-982-5000	982-5239*
*Fax: Admissions ■ TF Admissions: 800-852-3648 ■ Web: www.manchester.edu					
Marian College 3200 Cold Spring Rd.	Indianapolis	IN	46222	317-955-6000	955-6401*
*Fax: Admissions ■ TF Admissions: 800-772-7264 ■ Web: www.marian.edu					
Martin University 2171 Avondale Pl.	Indianapolis	IN	46218	317-543-3235	543-4790
TF: 866-344-3114 ■ Web: www.martin.edu					
Oakland City University					
138 N Lucretia St	Oakland City	IN	47660	812-749-4781	749-1433
TF: 800-737-5125 ■ Web: www.oak.edu					
Purdue University					
Schleman Hall 475 Stadium Mall Dr.	West Lafayette	IN	47907	765-494-1776	494-0544*
*Fax: Admissions ■ Web: www.purdue.edu					
Calumet 2200 169th St	Hammond	IN	46323	219-989-2400	989-2775*
*Fax: Admissions ■ TF: 800-447-8738 ■ Web: www.calumet.purdue.edu					
North Central 1401 S US Hwy 421	Westville	IN	46391	219-785-5200	785-5538*
*Fax: Admissions ■ Web: www.pnc.edu					
Rose-Hulman Institute of Technology					
5500 Wabash Ave.	Terre Haute	IN	47803	812-877-1511	877-8941
TF Admissions: 800-248-7448 ■ Web: www.rose-hulman.edu					
Saint Mary's College Le Mans Hall Rm 122	Notre Dame	IN	46556	574-284-4587	284-4841*
*Fax: Admissions ■ TF Admissions: 800-551-7621 ■ Web: www.saintmarys.edu					
Saint Mary-of-the-Woods College					
3301 St Mary Rd.	Saint Mary-of-the-Woods	IN	47876	812-535-5106	535-5010*
*Fax: Admissions ■ TF: 800-926-7692 ■ Web: www.smwc.edu					
Taylor University 236 W Reade Ave	Upland	IN	46989	765-998-2751	998-4925*
*Fax: Admissions ■ TF: 800-882-3456 ■ Web: www.taylor.edu					
Fort Wayne 915 W Rudisill Blvd	Fort Wayne	IN	46807	260-744-8790	745-4974
TF: 800-233-3922 ■ Web: www.fw.taylor.edu					
Tri-State University 1 University Blvd	Angola	IN	46703	260-665-4100	665-4578*
*Fax: Admissions ■ TF: 800-347-4878 ■ Web: www.tristate.edu					
University of Evansville 1800 Lincoln Ave	Evansville	IN	47722	812-488-2000	488-4076*
*Fax: Admissions ■ TF: 800-423-8633 ■ Web: www.evansville.edu					
University of Indianapolis					
1400 E Hanna Ave.	Indianapolis	IN	46227	317-788-3368	788-3300*
*Fax: Admissions ■ TF: 800-232-8634 ■ Web: www.uindy.edu					
University of Notre Dame 220 Main Bldg.	Notre Dame	IN	46556	574-631-7505	631-8665*
*Fax: Admissions ■ Web: www.nd.edu					
University of Saint Francis					
2701 Spring St	Fort Wayne	IN	46808	260-434-3100	434-7526*
*Fax: Admissions ■ TF: 800-729-4732 ■ Web: www.sfc.edu					
University of Southern Indiana					
8600 University Blvd	Evansville	IN	47712	812-464-1765	465-7154
TF: 800-467-1965 ■ Web: www.usi.edu					
Valparaiso University 1700 Chapel Dr	Valparaiso	IN	46383	219-464-5011	464-6898*
*Fax: Admissions ■ TF: 888-468-2576 ■ Web: www.valpo.edu					
Wabash College					
410 W Wabash Ave PO Box 352	Crawfordsville	IN	47933	765-361-6225	361-6437*
*Fax: Admissions ■ TF: 800-345-5385 ■ Web: www.wabash.edu					

IOWA

	City	State	ZIP	Phone	Fax
Ashford University 400 N Bluff Blvd.	Clinton	IA	52732	563-242-4023	243-6102*
*Fax: Admissions ■ TF: 800-242-4153 ■ Web: www.ashford.edu					
Briar Cliff University 3303 Rebecca St	Sioux City	IA	51104	712-279-5321	279-1632*
*Fax: Admissions ■ TF: 800-662-3303 ■ Web: www.briarcliff.edu					
Buena Vista University 610 W 4th St	Storm Lake	IA	50588	712-749-2235	749-2035
TF: 800-383-9600 ■ Web: www.bvu.edu					
Central College 812 University St CB 5100	Pella	IA	50219	641-628-5285	628-5983
TF: 877-462-3687 ■ Web: www.central.edu					
Clarke College 1550 Clarke Dr	Dubuque	IA	52001	563-588-6316	588-6789*
*Fax: Admissions ■ TF: 888-825-2753 ■ Web: www.clarke.edu					
Coe College 1220 1st Ave NE	Cedar Rapids	IA	52402	319-399-8500	399-8816
TF: 877-225-5263 ■ Web: www.coe.edu					
Cornell College 600 1st St SW	Mount Vernon	IA	52314	319-895-4215	895-4451*
*Fax: Admissions ■ TF Admissions: 800-747-1112 ■ Web: www.cornellcollege.edu					
Divine Word College 102 Jacoby Dr SW	Epworth	IA	52045	563-876-3353	876-3407*
*Fax: Admissions ■ Web: www.dwci.edu					
Dordt College 498 4th Ave NE	Sioux Center	IA	51250	712-722-6080	722-1198
TF: 800-343-6738 ■ Web: www.dordt.edu					
Drake University 2507 University Ave.	Des Moines	IA	50311	515-271-3181	271-2831
TF: 800-443-7253 ■ Web: www.drake.edu					
Graceland University 1 University Pl.	Lamoni	IA	50140	641-784-5000	784-5480*
*Fax: Admissions ■ Web: www.graceland.edu					
Grand View College 1200 Grandview Ave	Des Moines	IA	50316	515-263-2800	263-2974*
*Fax: Admissions ■ TF: 800-444-6083 ■ Web: www.gvc.edu					
Grinnell College 1103 Pk St	Grinnell	IA	50112	641-269-3600	269-4800
TF: 800-247-0113 ■ Web: www.grinnell.edu					
Iowa State University 100 Alumni Hall	Ames	IA	50011	515-294-4111	294-2592*
*Fax: Admissions ■ TF Admissions: 800-262-3810 ■ Web: www.iastate.edu					
Iowa Wesleyan College 601 N Main St.	Mount Pleasant	IA	52641	319-385-8021	385-6240*
*Fax: Admissions ■ TF: 800-582-2383 ■ Web: www.iwc.edu					
Loras College 1450 Alta Vista St	Dubuque	IA	52001	563-588-7100	588-7119*
*Fax: Admissions ■ TF: 800-245-6727 ■ Web: www.loras.edu					
Luther College 700 College Dr	Decorah	IA	52101	563-387-2000	387-2159*
*Fax: Admissions ■ TF: 800-458-8437 ■ Web: www.luther.edu					
Maharishi University of Management					
1000 N 4th St	Fairfield	IA	52557	641-472-1110	472-1179
TF: 800-369-6480 ■ Web: www.mum.edu					
Morningside College 1501 Morningside Ave.	Sioux City	IA	51106	712-274-5000	274-5101*
*Fax: Admissions ■ TF: 800-831-0806 ■ Web: www.morningside.edu					
Mount Mercy College 1330 Elmhurst Dr NE	Cedar Rapids	IA	52402	319-368-6460	861-2390
TF: 800-248-4504 ■ Web: www.mtmercy.edu					
Northwestern College 101 7th St SW	Orange City	IA	51041	712-707-7000	707-7164*
*Fax: Admissions ■ TF: 800-747-4757 ■ Web: www.nwciowa.edu					
Saint Ambrose University 518 W Locust St	Davenport	IA	52803	563-333-6000	333-6243*
*Fax: Admissions ■ TF Admissions: 800-383-2627 ■ Web: www.sau.edu					
Simpson College 701 N 'C' St.	Indianola	IA	50125	515-961-6251	961-1870*
*Fax: Admissions ■ TF: 800-362-2454 ■ Web: www.simpson.edu					
University of Dubuque 2000 University Ave	Dubuque	IA	52001	563-589-3000	589-3690*
*Fax: Admissions ■ TF: 800-722-5583 ■ Web: www.dbq.edu					
University of Iowa 107 Calvin Hall	Iowa City	IA	52242	319-335-3847	335-1535
TF: 800-553-4692 ■ Web: www.uiowa.edu					
University of Northern Iowa					
1222 W 27th St.	Cedar Falls	IA	50614	319-273-2281	273-2885*
*Fax: Admissions ■ TF Admissions: 800-772-2037 ■ Web: www.uni.edu					
Upper Iowa University					
605 Washington St PO Box 1857	Fayette	IA	52142	563-425-5200	425-5323*
*Fax: Admissions ■ TF Admissions: 800-553-4150 ■ Web: www.uiu.edu					
Waldorf College 106 S 6th St	Forest City	IA	50436	641-585-2450	585-8184*
*Fax: Admissions ■ TF: 800-292-1903 ■ Web: www.waldorf.edu					
Wartburg College 100 Wartburg Blvd.	Waverly	IA	50677	319-352-8264	352-8579*
*Fax: Admissions ■ TF: 800-772-2085 ■ Web: www.wartburg.edu					
William Penn University 201 Trueblood Ave.	Oskaloosa	IA	52577	641-673-1001	673-2113*
*Fax: Admissions ■ TF: 800-779-7366 ■ Web: www.wmpenn.edu					

KANSAS

	City	State	ZIP	Phone	Fax
Benedictine College 1020 N 2nd St	Atchison	KS	66002	913-367-5340	367-5462*
*Fax: Admissions ■ TF: 800-467-5340 ■ Web: www.benedictine.edu					
Bethany College 421 N 1st St.	Lindsborg	KS	67456	785-227-3311	227-8993*
*Fax: Admissions ■ TF Admissions: 800-826-2281 ■ Web: www.bethanylb.edu					
Bethel College 300 E 27th St	North Newton	KS	67117	316-283-2500	284-5286*
*Fax: Admissions ■ TF: 800-522-1887 ■ Web: www.bethelks.edu					
Central Christian College PO Box 1403	McPherson	KS	67460	620-241-0723	241-6032*
*Fax: Admissions ■ TF: 800-835-0078 ■ Web: www.centralchristian.edu					
Emporia State University					
1200 Commercial St CB 4034	Emporia	KS	66801	620-341-1200	341-5599
TF: 877-468-6378 ■ Web: www.emporia.edu					
Fort Hays State University 600 Pk St	Hays	KS	67601	785-628-4000	628-4187*
*Fax: Admissions ■ TF Admissions: 800-628-3478 ■ Web: www.fhsu.edu					
Friends University 2100 University St	Wichita	KS	67213	316-295-5000	295-5701*
*Fax: Admissions ■ TF: 800-794-6945 ■ Web: www.friends.edu					
Haskell Indian Nations University					
155 Indian Ave PO Box 5031	Lawrence	KS	66046	785-749-8454	749-8429*
*Fax: Admissions ■ Web: www.haskell.edu					
Kansas State University 119 Anderson Hall	Manhattan	KS	66506	785-532-6250	532-6393*
*Fax: Admissions ■ TF Admissions: 800-432-8270 ■ Web: www.k-state.edu					
Kansas State University-Salina					
College of Technology & Aviation					
2310 Centennial Rd	Salina	KS	67401	785-826-2640	826-2938*
*Fax: Admissions ■ Web: www.sal.ksu.edu					
Kansas University					
Edwards 12600 Quivira Rd	Overland Park	KS	66213	913-897-8400	897-8490*
*Fax: Admissions ■ Web: www.edwardscampus.ku.edu					
Kansas Wesleyan University 100 E Claflin Ave	Salina	KS	67401	785-827-5541	827-0927*
*Fax: Admissions ■ TF: 800-874-1154 ■ Web: www.kwu.edu					
McPherson College PO Box 1402	McPherson	KS	67460	620-241-0731	241-8443*
*Fax: Admissions ■ TF: 800-365-7402 ■ Web: www.mcpherson.edu					
MidAmerica Nazarene University					
2030 E College Way	Olathe	KS	66062	913-782-3750	791-3481*
*Fax: Admissions ■ TF: 800-800-8887 ■ Web: www.mnu.edu					
Newman University 3100 McCormick Ave	Wichita	KS	67213	316-942-4291	942-4483*
*Fax: Admissions ■ TF: 877-639-6268 ■ Web: www.newmanu.edu					
Ottawa University 1001 S Cedar St	Ottawa	KS	66067	785-242-5200	229-1008*
*Fax: Admissions ■ TF Admissions: 800-755-5200 ■ Web: www.ottawa.edu					
Pittsburg State University					
1701 S Broadway St	Pittsburg	KS	66762	620-235-4251	235-6003*
*Fax: Admissions ■ TF: 800-854-7488 ■ Web: www.pittstate.edu					
Southwestern College 100 College St.	Winfield	KS	67156	620-229-6236	229-6344*
*Fax: Admissions ■ TF: 800-846-1543 ■ Web: www.sckans.edu					
Sterling College 125 W Cooper	Sterling	KS	67579	620-278-2173	278-4418
TF: 800-346-1017 ■ Web: www.sterling.edu					
Tabor College 400 S Jefferson St	Hillsboro	KS	67063	620-947-3121	947-6276*
*Fax: Admissions ■ TF Admissions: 800-822-6799 ■ Web: www.tabor.edu					
University of Kansas 1502 Iowa St	Lawrence	KS	66045	785-864-2700	864-5017
Web: www.ku.edu					

	City	State	ZIP	Phone	Fax
University of Saint Mary 4100 S 4th St *Fax: Admissions ■ TF: 800-752-7043 ■ Web: www.stmary.edu	Leavenworth	KS	66048	913-682-5151	758-6140*
Washburn University 1700 SW College Ave TF: 800-332-0291 ■ Web: www.washburn.edu	Topeka	KS	66621	785-670-1010	670-1113
Wichita State University 1845 Fairmount St *Fax: Admissions ■ TF Admissions: 800-362-2594 ■ Web: www.wichita.edu	Wichita	KS	67260	316-978-3456	978-3174*

KENTUCKY

	City	State	ZIP	Phone	Fax
Alice Lloyd College 100 Purpose Rd *Fax: Admissions ■ TF Admissions: 888-280-4252 ■ Web: www.alc.edu	Pippa Passes	KY	41844	606-368-2101	368-6215*
Asbury College 1 Macklem Dr *Fax: Admissions ■ TF Admissions: 800-888-1818 ■ Web: www.asbury.edu	Wilmore	KY	40390	859-858-3511	858-3921*
Bellarmine University 2001 Newburg Rd TF: 800-274-4723 ■ Web: www.bellarmine.edu	Louisville	KY	40205	502-452-8000	452-8002
Berea College 101 Chestnut St *Fax: Admissions ■ TF: 800-326-5948 ■ Web: www.berea.edu	Berea	KY	40403	859-985-3500	985-3512*
Brescia University 717 Frederica St *Fax: Admissions ■ TF Admissions: 877-273-7242 ■ Web: www.brescia.edu	Owensboro	KY	42301	270-685-3131	686-4314*
Campbellsville University 1 University Dr *Fax: Admissions ■ TF Admissions: 800-264-6014 ■ Web: www.campbellsville.edu	Campbellsville	KY	42718	270-789-5000	789-5071*
Centre College 600 W Walnut St TF: 800-423-6236 ■ Web: www.centre.edu	Danville	KY	40422	859-238-5350	238-5373
Eastern Kentucky University 521 Lancaster Ave TF: 800-465-9191 ■ Web: www.eku.edu	Richmond	KY	40475	859-622-2106	622-8024
Georgetown College 400 E College St *Fax: Admissions ■ TF Admissions: 800-788-9985 ■ Web: www.georgetowncollege.edu	Georgetown	KY	40324	502-863-8000	868-7733*
Kentucky Christian University 100 Academic Pkwy *Fax: Admissions ■ TF Admissions: 800-522-3181 ■ Web: www.kcu.edu	Grayson	KY	41143	606-474-3000	474-3155*
Kentucky State University 400 E Main St *Fax: Admissions ■ TF Admissions: 800-325-1716 ■ Web: www.kysu.edu	Frankfort	KY	40601	502-597-6000	597-5814*
Kentucky Wesleyan College 3000 Frederica St *Fax: Admissions ■ TF Admissions: 800-999-0592 ■ Web: www.kwc.edu	Owensboro	KY	42301	270-852-3120	852-3133*
Lindsey Wilson College 210 Lindsey Wilson St *Fax: Admissions ■ TF: 800-264-0138 ■ Web: www.lindsey.edu	Columbia	KY	42728	270-384-2126	384-8591*
Louisville Bible College PO Box 91046 TF: 888-676-7458 ■ Web: www.louisvillebiblecollege.org	Louisville	KY	40291	502-231-5221	231-5222
Mid-Continent University 99 Powell Rd E *Fax: Admissions ■ Web: www.midcontinent.edu	Mayfield	KY	42066	270-247-8521	247-3115*
Midway College 512 E Stephens St *Fax: Admissions ■ TF: 800-755-0031 ■ Web: www.midway.edu	Midway	KY	40347	859-846-5346	846-5787*
Morehead State University 100 Admissions Ctr *Fax: Admissions ■ TF: 800-585-6781 ■ Web: www.morehead-st.edu	Morehead	KY	40351	606-783-2000	783-5038*
Murray State University 100 Sparks Hall *Fax: Admissions ■ TF: 800-272-4678 ■ Web: www.murraystate.edu	Murray	KY	42071	270-809-3741	809-3780*
Hopkinsville 5305 Fort Campbell Blvd	Hopkinsville	KY	42240	270-707-1525	707-1535*
Northern Kentucky University Nunn Dr *Fax: Admissions ■ TF Admissions: 800-637-9948 ■ Web: www.nku.edu	Highland Heights	KY	41099	859-572-5220	572-6665*
Pikeville College 147 Sycamore St *Fax: Admissions ■ TF: 866-232-7700 ■ Web: www.pc.edu	Pikeville	KY	41501	606-218-5250	218-5255*
Spalding University 851 S 4th St TF: 800-896-8941 ■ Web: www.spalding.edu	Louisville	KY	40203	502-585-9911	585-7158
Sullivan University 3101 Bardstown Rd TF: 800-844-1354 ■ Web: www.sullivan.edu	Louisville	KY	40205	502-456-6505	456-0040
Thomas More College 333 Thomas More Pkwy TF: 800-825-4557 ■ Web: www.thomasmore.edu	Crestview Hills	KY	41017	859-344-3332	344-3444
Transylvania University 300 N Broadway TF: 800-872-6798 ■ Web: www.transy.edu	Lexington	KY	40508	859-233-8242	233-8797
Union College 310 College St *Fax: Admissions ■ TF: 800-489-8646 ■ Web: www.unionky.edu	Barbourville	KY	40906	606-546-4151	546-1667*
University of Kentucky 800 Rose St TF: 866-900-4685 ■ Web: www.uky.edu	Lexington	KY	40536	859-257-9000	257-3823
University of Louisville 2301 S 3rd St TF: 800-334-8635 ■ Web: louisville.edu	Louisville	KY	40292	502-852-5555	852-6526
University of the Cumberlands 816 Walnut St *Fax: Admissions ■ TF: 800-343-1609 ■ Web: www.cumberlandcollege.edu	Williamsburg	KY	40769	606-549-2200	539-4303*
Western Kentucky University 1906 College Heights Blvd *Fax: Admissions ■ TF Admissions: 800-495-8463 ■ Web: www.wku.edu	Bowling Green	KY	42101	270-745-0111	745-6133*

LOUISIANA

	City	State	ZIP	Phone	Fax
Centenary College of Louisiana 2911 Centenary Blvd *Fax: Admissions ■ TF Admissions: 800-234-4448 ■ Web: www.centenary.edu	Shreveport	LA	71104	318-869-5131	869-5005*
Grambling State University 403 Main St TF: 800-569-4714 ■ Web: www.gram.edu	Grambling	LA	71245	318-247-3811	
Louisiana College 1140 College Dr *Fax: Admissions ■ TF: 800-487-1906 ■ Web: www.lacollege.edu	Pineville	LA	71359	318-487-7011	487-7550*
Louisiana State University *Alexandria* 8100 US Hwy 71 S *Fax: Admissions ■ TF Admissions: 888-473-6417 ■ Web: www.lsua.edu	Alexandria	LA	71302	318-445-3672	473-6418*
Baton Rouge 110 Thomas Boyd Hall *Fax: Admissions ■ Web: www.lsu.edu	Baton Rouge	LA	70803	225-578-3202	578-4433*
Shreveport 1 University Pl *Fax: Admissions ■ Web: www.lsus.edu	Shreveport	LA	71115	318-797-5000	797-5286*
Louisiana Tech University 305 Wisteria St *Fax: Admissions ■ TF Admissions: 800-528-3241 ■ Web: www.latech.edu	Ruston	LA	71272	318-257-0211	257-2499*
Loyola University *New Orleans* 6363 St Charles Ave CB 18 *Fax: Admissions ■ TF Admissions: 800-456-9652 ■ Web: www.loyno.edu	New Orleans	LA	70118	504-865-3240	865-3383*
McNeese State University 4205 Ryan St *Fax: Admissions ■ TF: 800-622-3352 ■ Web: www.mcneese.edu	Lake Charles	LA	70609	337-475-5000	475-5151*
Newcomb College Institute for Women 43 Newcomb Pl TF: 888-862-8589 ■ Web: www.newcomb.tulane.edu	New Orleans	LA	70118	504-865-5422	862-8589
Nicholls State University 906 E 1st St *Fax: Admissions ■ TF Admissions: 877-642-4655 ■ Web: www.nicholls.edu	Thibodaux	LA	70301	985-448-4507	448-4929*
Northwestern State University 200 Central Ave TF: 800-767-8115 ■ Web: www.nsula.edu	Natchitoches	LA	71497	318-357-6361	357-4660
Our Lady of Holy Cross College 4123 Woodland Dr TF: 800-259-7744 ■ Web: www.olhcc.edu	New Orleans	LA	70131	504-394-7744	394-1182
Our Lady of the Lake College 7434 Perkins Rd *Fax: Admissions ■ TF Admissions: 877-242-3509 ■ Web: www.ololcollege.edu	Baton Rouge	LA	70808	225-768-1700	768-1726*
Southeastern Louisiana University 752 University Stn *Fax: Admissions ■ TF: 800-222-7358 ■ Web: www.selu.edu	Hammond	LA	70402	985-549-2062	549-5632*
Southern University & A & M College Branch Post Office *Fax: Admissions ■ TF Admissions: 800-256-1531 ■ Web: www.subr.edu	Baton Rouge	LA	70813	225-771-4500	771-2500*
Tulane University 6823 St Charles Ave *Fax: Admissions ■ TF Admissions: 800-873-9283 ■ Web: www.tulane.edu	New Orleans	LA	70118	504-865-5000	862-8715*
University of Louisiana *Lafayette* 611 McKinley St TF: 800-752-6553 ■ Web: www.louisiana.edu	Lafayette	LA	70504	337-482-1000	482-1317
Monroe 700 University Ave *Fax: Admissions ■ TF Admissions: 800-372-5127 ■ Web: www.ulm.edu	Monroe	LA	71209	318-342-5430	342-1953*
University of New Orleans Administrative Bldg Rm 103 Lakefront TF Admissions: 800-256-5866 ■ Web: www.uno.edu	New Orleans	LA	70148	504-280-6000	280-5522
Xavier University of Louisiana 3437 Audubon Ct TF: 877-928-4378 ■ Web: www.xula.edu	New Orleans	LA	70125	504-486-7411	485-7941

MAINE

	City	State	ZIP	Phone	Fax
Bates College 2 Andrews Rd Ln Hall *Fax: Admissions ■ Web: www.bates.edu	Lewiston	ME	04240	207-786-6255	786-6025*
Bowdoin College 5000 College Stn *Fax: Admissions ■ Web: www.bowdoin.edu	Brunswick	ME	04011	207-725-3000	725-3101*
Colby College 4800 Mayflower Hill *Fax: Admissions ■ TF Admissions: 800-723-3032 ■ Web: www.colby.edu	Waterville	ME	04901	207-859-4800	859-4828*
College of the Atlantic 105 Eden St *Fax: Admissions ■ TF Admissions: 800-528-0025 ■ Web: www.coa.edu	Bar Harbor	ME	04609	207-288-5015	288-4126*
Husson College 1 College Cir *Fax: Admissions ■ TF: 800-448-7766 ■ Web: www.husson.edu	Bangor	ME	04401	207-941-7000	941-7935*
Maine Maritime Academy 66 Pleasant St *Fax: Admissions ■ TF Admissions: 800-227-8465 ■ Web: www.mainemaritime.edu	Castine	ME	04420	207-326-4311	326-2515*
New England Bible College 879 Sawyer St PO Box 2886 *Fax: Admissions ■ TF: 800-286-1859 ■ Web: www.nebc.edu	South Portland	ME	04116	207-799-5979	799-6586*
Saint Joseph's College of Maine 278 Whites Bridge Rd *Fax: Admissions ■ TF Admissions: 800-338-7057 ■ Web: www.sjcme.edu	Standish	ME	04084	207-893-7746	893-7862*
Thomas College 180 W River Rd *Fax: Admissions ■ TF Admissions: 800-339-7001 ■ Web: www.thomas.edu	Waterville	ME	04901	207-859-1111	859-1114*
Unity College 90 Quaker Hill Rd *Fax: Admissions ■ TF: 800-624-1024 ■ Web: www.unity.edu	Unity	ME	04988	207-948-3131	948-2928*
University of Maine 5713 Chadbourne Hall *Fax: Admissions ■ TF Admissions: 877-486-2364 ■ Web: www.umaine.edu	Orono	ME	04469	207-581-1110	581-1213*
Augusta 46 University Dr *Fax: Admissions ■ Web: www.uma.edu	Augusta	ME	04330	207-621-3000	621-3333*
Farmington 111 S St *Fax: Admissions ■ Web: www.umf.maine.edu	Farmington	ME	04938	207-778-7000	778-8182*
Fort Kent 23 University Dr *Fax: Admissions ■ TF Admissions: 888-879-8635 ■ Web: www.umfk.maine.edu	Fort Kent	ME	04743	207-834-7500	834-7609*
Machias 9 O'Brien Ave *Fax: Admissions ■ TF Admissions: 888-468-6866 ■ Web: www.umm.maine.edu	Machias	ME	04654	207-255-1200	255-1363*
Presque Isle 181 Main St *Fax: Admissions ■ Web: www.umpi.maine.edu	Presque Isle	ME	04769	207-768-9400	768-9777*
University of New England 11 Hills Beach Rd *Fax: Admissions ■ TF Admissions: 800-477-4863 ■ Web: www.une.edu	Biddeford	ME	04005	207-283-0171	602-5900*
Westbrook College 716 Stevens Ave *Fax: Admissions ■ TF Admissions: 800-477-4863 ■ Web: www.une.edu	Portland	ME	04103	207-797-7261	878-4889*
University of Southern Maine 96 Falmouth St TF: 800-800-4876 ■ Web: www.usm.maine.edu	Portland	ME	04103	207-780-4141	780-5640
Gorham 37 College Ave *Fax: Admissions ■ TF: 800-800-4876 ■ Web: www.usm.maine.edu	Gorham	ME	04038	207-780-5670	780-5640*
Lewiston-Auburn College 51 Westminster St *Fax: Admissions ■ TF: 800-800-4876 ■ Web: www.usm.maine.edu	Lewiston	ME	04240	207-753-6500	753-6555*

MARYLAND

	City	State	ZIP	Phone	Fax
Bowie State University 14000 Jericho Pk Rd TF: 877-772-6943 ■ Web: www.bowiestate.edu	Bowie	MD	20715	301-860-4000	860-3518
Capitol College 11301 Springfield Rd *Fax: Admissions ■ TF: 800-950-1992 ■ Web: www.capitol-college.edu	Laurel	MD	20708	301-369-2800	953-1442*
College of Notre Dame of Maryland 4701 N Charles St *Fax: Admissions ■ TF Admissions: 800-435-0300 ■ Web: www.ndm.edu	Baltimore	MD	21210	410-435-0100	532-6287*

	City	State	ZIP	Phone	Fax
Columbia Union College 7600 Flower Ave *TF:* 800-835-4212 ■ *Web:* www.cuc.edu	Takoma Park	MD	20912	301-891-4000	891-4167
Coppin State University 2500 W N Ave **Fax:* Admissions ■ *TF Admissions:* 800-635-3674 ■ *Web:* www.coppin.edu	Baltimore	MD	21216	410-951-3600	523-7351*
Frostburg State University 101 Braddock Rd **Fax:* Admissions ■ *Web:* www.frostburg.edu	Frostburg	MD	21532	301-687-4000	687-7074*
Goucher College 1021 Dulaney Valley Rd **Fax:* Admissions ■ *TF:* 800-468-2437 ■ *Web:* www.goucher.edu	Baltimore	MD	21204	410-337-6000	337-6354*
Hood College 401 Rosemont Ave **Fax:* Admissions ■ *TF:* 800-922-1599 ■ *Web:* www.hood.edu	Frederick	MD	21701	301-696-3400	696-3819*
Johns Hopkins University 3400 N Charles St *Web:* www.jhu.edu	Baltimore	MD	21218	410-516-8000	516-6025
Loyola College 4501 N Charles St **Fax:* Admissions ■ *TF:* 800-221-9107 ■ *Web:* www.loyola.edu	Baltimore	MD	21210	410-617-5012	617-2176*
McDaniel College 2 College Hill **Fax:* Admissions ■ *TF Admissions:* 800-638-5005 ■ *Web:* www.mcdaniel.edu	Westminster	MD	21157	410-857-2230	857-2757*
Morgan State University 1700 E Cold Spring Ln **Fax:* Admissions ■ *TF:* 800-319-4678 ■ *Web:* www.morgan.edu	Baltimore	MD	21251	443-885-3333	885-8260*
Mount Saint Mary's University 16300 Old Emmitsburg Rd **Fax:* Admissions ■ *TF Admissions:* 800-448-4347 ■ *Web:* www.msmary.edu	Emmitsburg	MD	21727	301-447-5214	447-5860*
Peabody Institute of the Johns Hopkins University *Peabody Conservatory of Music* 1 E Mt Vernon Pl *TF:* 800-368-2521 ■ *Web:* www.peabody.jhu.edu	Baltimore	MD	21202	410-659-8110	659-8102
Saint John's College 60 College Ave **Fax:* Admissions ■ *TF Admissions:* 800-727-9238 ■ *Web:* www.sjca.edu	Annapolis	MD	21401	410-263-2371	269-7916*
Saint Mary's College of Maryland 18952 E Fisher Rd **Fax:* Admissions ■ *TF Admissions:* 800-492-7181 ■ *Web:* www.smcm.edu	Saint Mary's City	MD	20686	240-895-2000	895-5001*
Salisbury University 1200 Camden Ave **Fax:* Admissions ■ *TF:* 888-543-0148 ■ *Web:* www.salisbury.edu	Salisbury	MD	21801	410-543-6000	546-6016*
Sojourner-Douglass College 200 N Central Ave *TF:* 800-732-2630 ■ *Web:* www.sdc.edu	Baltimore	MD	21202	410-276-0306	675-1810
Strayer University Prince George's 4710 Auth Pl Suite 100 **Fax:* Admissions ■ *TF:* 866-344-3297 ■ *Web:* www.strayer.edu	Suitland	MD	20746	301-423-3600	423-3999*
Towson University 8000 York Rd *TF:* 888-486-9766 ■ *Web:* www.towson.edu	Towson	MD	21252	410-704-2113	704-3030
University of Baltimore 1420 N Charles St *TF Admitting:* 888-661-5622 ■ *Web:* www.ubalt.edu	Baltimore	MD	21201	410-837-4200	837-4793
University of Maryland 7050 Baltimore Ave **Fax:* Admissions ■ *TF Admissions:* 800-422-5867 ■ *Web:* www.umd.edu	College Park	MD	20742	301-405-1000	314-9693*
Baltimore County 1000 Hilltop Cir *TF:* 800-862-2482 ■ *Web:* www.umbc.edu	Baltimore	MD	21250	410-455-1000	455-1094
Eastern Shore 30665 Student Services Ctr Ln *Web:* www.umes.edu	Princess Anne	MD	21853	410-651-2200	651-7922
University of Maryland University College 3501 University Blvd E **Fax:* Admissions ■ *TF:* 800-888-8682 ■ *Web:* www.umuc.edu	Adelphi	MD	20783	301-985-7000	985-7978*
US Naval Academy 121 Blake Rd **Fax:* Admissions ■ *TF Admissions:* 888-249-7707 ■ *Web:* www.usna.edu	Annapolis	MD	21402	410-293-1000	293-4348*
Villa Julie College 1525 Green Spring Valley Rd **Fax Area Code:* 443 ■ *TF:* 877-468-6852 ■ *Web:* www.vjc.edu	Stevenson	MD	21153	410-486-7001	352-4440*
Washington College 300 Washington Ave *TF:* 800-422-1782 ■ *Web:* www.washcoll.edu	Chestertown	MD	21620	410-778-2800	778-7287

MASSACHUSETTS

	City	State	ZIP	Phone	Fax
American International College 1000 State St **Fax:* Admissions ■ *TF Admissions:* 800-242-3142 ■ *Web:* www.aic.edu	Springfield	MA	01109	413-205-3201	205-3051*
Amherst College 220 S Pleasant St **Fax:* Admissions ■ *Web:* www.amherst.edu	Amherst	MA	01002	413-542-2000	542-2040*
Assumption College 500 Salisbury St *TF:* 888-882-7786 ■ *Web:* www.assumption.edu	Worcester	MA	01609	508-767-7000	799-4412
Atlantic Union College 338 Main St *TF:* 800-282-2030 ■ *Web:* www.auc.edu	South Lancaster	MA	01561	978-368-2000	368-2517
Babson College 231 Forest St **Fax:* Admissions ■ *TF Admissions:* 800-488-3696 ■ *Web:* www.babson.edu	Babson Park	MA	02457	781-235-1200	239-4006*
Bay Path College 588 Longmeadow St *TF:* 800-782-7284 ■ *Web:* www.baypath.edu	Longmeadow	MA	01106	413-567-0621	565-1105
Becker College 61 Sever St **Fax:* Admissions ■ *TF:* 877-523-2537 ■ *Web:* www.becker.edu	Worcester	MA	01609	508-791-9241	890-1500*
Bentley College 175 Forest St **Fax:* Admissions ■ *TF Admissions:* 800-523-2354 ■ *Web:* www.bentley.edu	Waltham	MA	02452	781-891-2244	891-3414*
Berklee College of Music 1140 Boylston St **Fax:* Admissions ■ *TF:* 800-421-0084 ■ *Web:* www.berklee.edu	Boston	MA	02215	617-747-2221	747-2047*
Boston College 140 Commonwealth Ave *TF:* 800-360-2522 ■ *Web:* www.bc.edu	Chestnut Hill	MA	02467	617-552-3100	552-0798
Boston Conservatory of Music Dance & Theater 8 Fenway **Fax:* Admissions ■ *Web:* www.bostonconservatory.edu	Boston	MA	02215	617-536-6340	247-3159*
Boston University 1 Sherborn St **Fax:* Admissions ■ *Web:* www.web.bu.edu	Boston	MA	02215	617-353-2000	353-9695*
Brandeis University 415 S St *TF:* 800-622-0622 ■ *Web:* www.brandeis.edu	Waltham	MA	02454	781-736-3500	736-3536
Bridgewater State College 131 Summer St **Fax:* Admissions ■ *Web:* www.bridgew.edu	Bridgewater	MA	02325	508-531-1000	531-1746*
Clark University 950 Main St *TF:* 800-462-5275 ■ *Web:* www.clarku.edu	Worcester	MA	01610	508-793-7711	793-8821
College of the Holy Cross 1 College St *TF:* 800-442-2421 ■ *Web:* www.holycross.edu	Worcester	MA	01610	508-793-2011	793-3888
Curry College 1071 Blue Hill Ave *TF:* 800-669-0686 ■ *Web:* www.curry.edu	Milton	MA	02186	617-333-2210	333-2114
Eastern Nazarene College 23 E Elm Ave *TF:* 800-883-6288 ■ *Web:* www.enc.edu	Quincy	MA	02170	617-745-3000	745-3929
Elms College 291 Springfield St **Fax:* Admissions ■ *TF Admissions:* 800-255-3567 ■ *Web:* www.elms.edu	Chicopee	MA	01013	413-592-3189	594-2781*
Emerson College 10 Boylston Pl *Web:* www.emerson.edu	Boston	MA	02116	617-824-8500	824-8609
Emmanuel College 400 Fenway *Web:* www.emmanuel.edu	Boston	MA	02115	617-277-9340	735-9801
Endicott College 376 Hale St **Fax:* Admissions ■ *TF Admissions:* 800-325-1114 ■ *Web:* www.endicott.edu	Beverly	MA	01915	978-232-2021	232-2520*
Fitchburg State College 160 Pearl St **Fax:* Admissions ■ *Web:* www.fsc.edu	Fitchburg	MA	01420	978-345-2151	665-4540*
Framingham State College 100 State St PO Box 9101 **Fax:* Admissions ■ *Web:* www.framingham.edu	Framingham	MA	01701	508-620-1220	626-4017*
Franklin W Olin College of Engineering 1000 Olin Way **Fax:* Admissions ■ *Web:* www.olin.edu	Needham	MA	02492	781-292-2300	292-2210*
Gordon College 255 Grapevine Rd **Fax:* Admissions ■ *TF:* 800-343-1379 ■ *Web:* www.gordon.edu	Wenham	MA	01984	978-927-2300	867-4682*
Hampshire College 893 W St **Fax:* Admissions ■ *TF Admissions:* 877-937-4267 ■ *Web:* www.hampshire.edu	Amherst	MA	01002	413-549-4600	559-5631*
Harvard University 12 Holyoke St *Web:* www.harvard.edu	Cambridge	MA	02138	617-495-1000	495-8821
Hebrew College 160 Herrick Rd *TF:* 800-866-4814 ■ *Web:* www.hebrewcollege.edu	Newton Center	MA	02459	617-559-8610	559-8601
Hellenic College-Holy Cross School of Theology 50 Goddard Ave **Fax:* Admissions ■ *Web:* www.hchc.edu	Brookline	MA	02445	617-731-3500	850-1460*
Lasell College 1844 Commonwealth Ave **Fax:* Admissions ■ *TF Admissions:* 888-527-3554 ■ *Web:* www.lasell.edu	Newton	MA	02466	617-243-2225	243-2380*
Lesley University 29 Everett St *TF:* 800-999-1959 ■ *Web:* www.lesley.edu	Cambridge	MA	02138	617-868-9600	349-8313
Massachusetts College of Art 621 Huntington Ave *Web:* www.massart.edu	Boston	MA	02115	617-879-7222	879-7250
Massachusetts College of Liberal Arts 375 Church St *Web:* www.mcla.edu	North Adams	MA	01247	413-662-5000	662-5179
Massachusetts College of Pharmacy & Health Sciences 179 Longwood Ave *TF:* 800-225-5506 ■ *Web:* www.mcphs.edu	Boston	MA	02115	617-732-2850	732-2118
Massachusetts Institute of Technology 77 Massachusetts Ave Bldg 3 Rm 108 *Web:* www.web.mit.edu	Cambridge	MA	02139	617-253-1000	258-8304
Massachusetts Maritime Academy 101 Academy Dr **Fax:* Admissions ■ *TF Admissions:* 800-544-3411 ■ *Web:* www.maritime.edu	Buzzards Bay	MA	02532	508-830-5000	830-5077*
Merrimack College 315 Tpke St **Fax:* Admissions ■ *Web:* www.merrimack.edu	North Andover	MA	01845	978-837-5000	837-5133*
Montserrat College of Art 23 Essex St PO Box 26 **Fax:* Admissions ■ *TF:* 800-836-0487 ■ *Web:* www.montserrat.edu	Beverly	MA	01915	978-921-4242	921-4241*
Mount Holyoke College 50 College St *Web:* www.mtholyoke.edu	South Hadley	MA	01075	413-538-2000	538-2409
Mount Ida College 777 Dedham St **Fax:* Admissions ■ *Web:* www.mountida.edu	Newton Center	MA	02459	617-928-4500	928-4507*
New England Conservatory 290 Huntington Ave **Fax:* Admissions ■ *Web:* www.newenglandconservatory.edu	Boston	MA	02115	617-585-1100	585-1115*
Newbury College 129 Fisher Ave **Fax:* Admitting ■ *TF:* 800-639-2879 ■ *Web:* www.newbury.edu	Brookline	MA	02445	617-730-7000	731-9618*
Nichols College 124 Ctr Rd *TF:* 800-470-3379 ■ *Web:* www.nichols.edu	Dudley	MA	01571	508-218-1560	943-9885
Northeastern University 360 Huntington Ave **Fax:* Admissions ■ *Web:* www.northeastern.edu	Boston	MA	02115	617-373-2000	373-8780*
Pine Manor College 400 Heath St *TF:* 800-762-1357 ■ *Web:* www.pmc.edu	Chestnut Hill	MA	02467	617-731-7104	731-7102
Regis College 235 Wellesley St *TF:* 866-438-7344 ■ *Web:* www.regiscollege.edu	Weston	MA	02493	781-768-7000	768-7071
Salem State College 352 Lafayette St *Web:* www.salemstate.edu	Salem	MA	01970	978-542-6000	542-6893
School of the Museum of Fine Arts 230 The Fenway **Fax:* Admissions ■ *TF Admissions:* 800-643-6078 ■ *Web:* www.smfa.edu	Boston	MA	02115	617-369-3626	369-4264*
Simmons College 300 The Fenway **Fax:* Admissions ■ *TF:* 800-345-8468 ■ *Web:* www.simmons.edu	Boston	MA	02115	617-521-2000	521-3190*
Simon's Rock College of Bard 84 Alford Rd **Fax:* Admissions ■ *Web:* www.simons-rock.edu	Great Barrington	MA	01230	413-528-0771	528-7380*
Smith College 7 College Ln *TF:* 800-383-3232 ■ *Web:* www.smith.edu	NorthHampton	MA	01063	413-584-2700	585-2527
Springfield College 263 Alden St **Fax:* Admissions ■ *TF Admissions:* 800-343-1257 ■ *Web:* www.spfldcol.edu	Springfield	MA	01109	413-748-3136	748-3694*
Stonehill College 320 Washington St **Fax:* Admissions ■ *Web:* www.stonehill.edu	Easton	MA	02357	508-565-1000	565-1545*
Suffolk University 8 Ashburton Pl *TF:* 800-678-3365 ■ *Web:* www.suffolk.edu	Boston	MA	02108	617-573-8460	557-1574
Tufts University 4 Colby St *Web:* www.tufts.edu	Medford	MA	02155	617-628-5000	627-4079
University of Massachusetts *Amherst* 181 Presidents Dr **Fax:* Admissions ■ *Web:* www.umass.edu	Amherst	MA	01003	413-545-0111	545-4312*
Boston 100 Morrissey Blvd Campus Ctr **Fax:* Admitting ■ *Web:* www.umb.edu	Boston	MA	02125	617-287-6100	287-5999*
Dartmouth 285 Old Westport Rd **Fax:* Admissions ■ *Web:* www.umassd.edu	North Dartmouth	MA	02747	508-999-8000	999-8755*
Lowell 1 University Ave **Fax:* Admissions ■ *Web:* www.uml.edu	Lowell	MA	01854	978-934-4000	934-3086*
Wellesley College 106 Central St **Fax:* Admissions ■ *Web:* www.wellesley.edu	Wellesley	MA	02481	781-283-1000	283-3678*

	City	State	Zip	Phone	Fax
Wentworth Institute of Technology 550 Huntington Ave	Boston	MA	02115	617-989-4590	989-4010*
*Fax: Admissions ■ *TF:* 800-556-0610 ■ *Web:* www.wit.edu					
Western New England College 1215 Wilbraham Rd	Springfield	MA	01119	413-782-3111	782-1777*
*Fax: Admissions ■ *TF:* 800-325-1122 ■ *Web:* www.wnec.edu					
Westfield State University 577 Western Ave	Westfield	MA	01086	413-572-5300	572-0520*
*Fax: Admissions ■ *Web:* www.westfield.ma.edu					
Wheaton College 26 Main St	Norton	MA	02766	508-286-8200	286-8271
TF Admissions: 800-394-6003 ■ *Web:* www.wheatonma.edu					
Wheelock College 200 The Riverway	Boston	MA	02215	617-879-2206	879-2449
TF: 800-734-5212 ■ *Web:* www.wheelock.edu					
Williams College 33 Stetson Ct	Williamstown	MA	01267	413-597-3131	597-4052*
*Fax: Admissions ■ *Web:* www.williams.edu					
Worcester Polytechnic Institute 100 Institute Rd	Worcester	MA	01609	508-831-5000	831-5875*
*Fax: Admissions ■ *Web:* www.wpi.edu					
Worcester State College 486 Chandler St	Worcester	MA	01602	508-793-8000	929-8193
TF: 866-972-2255 ■ *Web:* www.worcester.edu					

MICHIGAN

	City	State	Zip	Phone	Fax
Adrian College 110 S Madison St	Adrian	MI	49221	517-265-5161	264-3331*
*Fax: Admissions ■ *TF Admissions:* 800-877-2246 ■ *Web:* www.adrian.edu					
Albion College 611 E Porter St	Albion	MI	49224	517-629-1000	629-0569
TF: 800-858-6770 ■ *Web:* www.albion.edu					
Alma College 614 W Superior St	Alma	MI	48801	989-463-7139	463-7057
TF: 800-321-2562 ■ *Web:* www.alma.edu					
Andrews University 3976 Rose Dr	Berrien Springs	MI	49103	269-471-7771	471-2670
TF: 800-253-2874 ■ *Web:* www.andrews.edu					
Baker College					
Auburn Hills 1500 University Dr	Auburn Hills	MI	48326	248-340-0600	340-0608*
*Fax: Admissions ■ *TF:* 888-429-0410 ■ *Web:* www.baker.edu					
Cadillac 9600 E 13th St	Cadillac	MI	49601	231-876-3100	876-3440
TF: 888-313-3463 ■ *Web:* www.baker.edu					
Clinton Township 34950 Little Mack Ave	Clinton Township	MI	48035	586-791-6610	791-5790*
*Fax: Admissions ■ *TF:* 888-272-2842 ■ *Web:* www.baker.edu					
Flint 1050 W Bristol Rd	Flint	MI	48507	810-767-7600	766-4255*
*Fax: Admissions ■ *TF:* 800-964-4299 ■ *Web:* www.baker.edu					
Jackson 2800 Springport Rd	Jackson	MI	49202	517-788-7800	788-6187
TF: 888-343-3683 ■ *Web:* www.baker.edu					
Owosso 1020 S Washington St	Owosso	MI	48867	989-729-3300	729-3359*
*Fax: Admissions ■ *TF:* 800-879-3797 ■ *Web:* www.baker.edu					
Port Huron 3403 Lapeer Rd	Port Huron	MI	48060	810-985-7000	985-7066
TF: 888-262-2442 ■ *Web:* www.baker.edu					
Calvin College 3201 Burton St SE	Grand Rapids	MI	49546	616-526-6000	526-6777*
*Fax: Admissions ■ *TF:* 800-688-0122 ■ *Web:* www.calvin.edu					
Central Michigan University 102 Warriner Hall	Mount Pleasant	MI	48859	989-774-4000	774-7267*
*Fax: Admissions ■ *TF Admissions:* 888-292-5366 ■ *Web:* www.cmich.edu					
Concordia University Ann Arbor 4090 Geddes Rd	Ann Arbor	MI	48105	734-995-7322	995-4610
TF: 800-253-0680 ■ *Web:* www.cuaa.edu					
Cornerstone University 1001 E Beltline Ave NE	Grand Rapids	MI	49525	616-222-1426	222-1418*
*Fax: Admissions ■ *TF Admissions:* 800-787-9778 ■ *Web:* www.cornerstone.edu					
Davenport University					
Dearborn 4801 Oakman Blvd	Dearborn	MI	48126	313-581-4400	581-4480
TF: 800-585-1479 ■ *Web:* www.davenport.edu					
Flint 4318 Miller Rd Suite A	Flint	MI	48507	810-732-9977	732-9128*
*Fax: Admissions ■ *TF:* 800-727-1443 ■ *Web:* www.davenport.edu					
Lansing 220 E Kalamazoo St	Lansing	MI	48933	517-484-2600	484-1132*
*Fax: Admissions ■ *TF:* 800-686-1600 ■ *Web:* www.davenport.edu					
Lettinga Campus 6191 Kraft Ave SE	Grand Rapids	MI	49512	616-698-7111	554-5214
TF: 866-925-3884 ■ *Web:* www.davenport.edu					
Saginaw 5300 Bay Rd	Saginaw	MI	48604	989-799-7800	799-9696*
*Fax: Admissions ■ *TF:* 800-968-8133 ■ *Web:* www.davenport.edu					
Warren 27650 Dequindre Rd	Warren	MI	48092	586-558-8700	558-7868*
*Fax: Admissions ■ *TF:* 800-724-7708 ■ *Web:* www.davenport.edu					
Eastern Michigan University 1000 College Pl	Ypsilanti	MI	48197	734-487-1849	487-6559*
*Fax: Admissions ■ *TF:* 800-468-6368 ■ *Web:* www.emich.edu					
Ferris State University 1201 S State St	Big Rapids	MI	49307	231-591-2000	591-3944*
*Fax: Admissions ■ *TF:* 800-433-7747 ■ *Web:* www.ferris.edu					
Traverse City 2200 Dendrinos Dr Suite 200H	Traverse City	MI	49684	231-995-1734	995-1736*
*Fax: Admissions ■ *TF:* 866-857-1954 ■ *Web:* www.ferris.edu					
Finlandia University 601 Quincy St	Hancock	MI	49930	906-482-5300	487-7383*
*Fax: Admissions ■ *TF:* 800-682-7604 ■ *Web:* www.finlandia.edu					
Grand Valley State University 1 N Campus Dr	Allendale	MI	49401	616-331-5000	331-2000
TF: 800-748-0246 ■ *Web:* www.gvsu.edu					
Hillsdale College 33 E College St	Hillsdale	MI	49242	517-437-7341	437-3923*
*Fax: Admissions ■ *Web:* www.hillsdale.edu					
Hope College 69 E 10th St PO Box 9000	Holland	MI	49422	616-395-7850	395-7130*
*Fax: Admissions ■ *TF Admissions:* 800-968-7850 ■ *Web:* www.hope.edu					
Kalamazoo College 1200 Academy St	Kalamazoo	MI	49006	269-337-7166	337-7390*
*Fax: Admissions ■ *TF Admissions:* 800-253-3602 ■ *Web:* www.kzoo.edu					
Kendall College of Art & Design of Ferris State University 17 Fountain St NW	Grand Rapids	MI	49503	616-451-2787	831-9689
TF: 800-676-2787 ■ *Web:* www.kcad.edu					
Kettering University 1700 University Ave	Flint	MI	48504	810-762-9500	762-9837
TF: 800-955-4464 ■ *Web:* www.kettering.edu					
Lake Superior State University 650 W Easterday Ave	Sault Sainte Marie	MI	49783	906-632-6841	635-6696*
*Fax: Admissions ■ *TF Admissions:* 888-800-5778 ■ *Web:* www.lssu.edu					
Lawrence Technological University 21000 W 10-Mile Rd	Southfield	MI	48075	248-204-3160	204-3188*
*Fax: Admissions ■ *TF:* 800-225-5588 ■ *Web:* www.ltu.edu					
Madonna University 36600 Schoolcraft Rd	Livonia	MI	48150	734-432-5339	432-5424
TF: 800-852-4951 ■ *Web:* www.madonna.edu					
Marygrove College 8425 W McNichols Rd	Detroit	MI	48221	313-927-1200	927-1399*
*Fax: Admissions ■ *TF Admissions:* 866-313-1927 ■ *Web:* www.marygrove.edu					
Michigan State University 250 Hannah Administration Bldg	East Lansing	MI	48824	517-355-1855	353-1647
Web: www.msu.edu					
Michigan Technological University 1400 Townsend Dr	Houghton	MI	49931	906-487-2335	487-2125*
*Fax: Admissions ■ *TF:* 888-688-1885 ■ *Web:* www.mtu.edu					
Northern Michigan University 1401 Presque Isle Ave	Marquette	MI	49855	906-227-2650	227-1747*
*Fax: Admissions ■ *TF:* 800-682-9797 ■ *Web:* www.nmu.edu					
Northwood University Michigan 4000 Whiting Dr	Midland	MI	48640	989-837-4200	837-4490*
*Fax: Admissions ■ *TF:* 800-457-7878 ■ *Web:* www.northwood.edu					
Oakland University 2200 Squirrel Rd	Rochester	MI	48309	248-370-2100	370-4462*
*Fax: Admissions ■ *TF Admissions:* 800-625-8648 ■ *Web:* www.oakland.edu					
Olivet College 320 S Main St	Olivet	MI	49076	269-749-7000	749-6617*
*Fax: Admissions ■ *TF:* 800-456-7189 ■ *Web:* www.olivetcollege.edu					
Rochester College 800 W Avon Rd	Rochester Hills	MI	48307	248-218-2011	218-2025*
*Fax: Admissions ■ *TF:* 800-521-6010 ■ *Web:* www.rc.edu					
Saginaw Valley State University 7400 Bay Rd	University Center	MI	48710	989-964-4200	790-0180
TF: 800-968-9500 ■ *Web:* www.svsu.edu					
Siena Heights University 1247 E Siena Heights Dr	Adrian	MI	49221	517-263-0731	264-7745*
*Fax: Admissions ■ *TF:* 800-521-0009 ■ *Web:* www.sienahts.edu					
Spring Arbor University 106 E Main St	Spring Arbor	MI	49283	517-750-1200	750-6620*
*Fax: Admissions ■ *TF Admissions:* 800-968-0011 ■ *Web:* www.spring.arbor.edu					
University of Detroit Mercy 4001 W McNichols Rd	Detroit	MI	48221	313-993-1000	993-3326*
*Fax: Admissions ■ *TF Admissions:* 800-635-5020 ■ *Web:* www.udmercy.edu					
University of Detroit Mercy School of Dentistry *Corktown Campus* 2700 MLK Dr	Detroit	MI	48219	313-494-6611	
Web: www.udmercy.edu					
University of Michigan 515 E Jefferson St	Ann Arbor	MI	48109	734-764-1817	
Web: www.umich.edu					
Dearborn 4901 Evergreen Rd	Dearborn	MI	48128	313-593-5100	436-9167*
*Fax: Admissions ■ *Web:* www.umd.umich.edu					
Flint 303 E Kearsley St	Flint	MI	48502	810-762-3000	762-3272
TF: 800-942-5636 ■ *Web:* www.flint.umich.edu					
Wayne State University 42 W Warren	Detroit	MI	48202	313-577-3577	577-7536*
*Fax: Admissions ■ *TF:* 877-978-4636 ■ *Web:* www.wayne.edu					
Western Michigan University 1903 W Michigan Ave	Kalamazoo	MI	49008	269-387-1000	387-2096*
*Fax: Admissions ■ *Web:* www.wmich.edu					

MINNESOTA

	City	State	Zip	Phone	Fax
Apostolic Bible Institute Inc 6944 Hudson Blvd N	Saint Paul	MN	55128	651-739-7686	730-8669*
*Fax: Admissions ■ *Web:* www.apostolic.org					
Argosy University 1515 Central Pkwy	Eagan	MN	55121	651-846-2882	994-7956*
*Fax: Admissions ■ *TF:* 888-844-2004 ■ *Web:* www.argosyu.edu					
Augsburg College 2211 Riverside Ave	Minneapolis	MN	55454	612-330-1000	330-1590
TF: 800-788-5678 ■ *Web:* www.augsburg.edu					
Bemidji State University 1500 Birchmont Dr NE	Bemidji	MN	56601	218-755-2001	755-4048
TF Admissions: 800-475-2001 ■ *Web:* www.bemidjistate.edu					
Bethany Lutheran College 700 Luther Dr	Mankato	MN	56001	507-344-7000	344-7376*
*Fax: Admissions ■ *TF:* 800-944-3066 ■ *Web:* www.blc.edu					
Bethel University 3900 Bethel Dr	Saint Paul	MN	55112	651-638-6400	635-1490*
*Fax: Admissions ■ *TF:* 800-255-8706 ■ *Web:* www.bethel.edu					
Carleton College 100 S College St	Northfield	MN	55057	507-646-4000	646-4526*
*Fax: Admissions ■ *TF Admissions:* 800-995-2275 ■ *Web:* www.carleton.edu					
College of Saint Benedict 37 S College Ave	Saint Joseph	MN	56374	320-363-5011	363-3206*
*Fax: Admissions ■ *TF:* 800-249-9840 ■ *Web:* www.csbsju.edu					
College of Saint Catherine 2004 Randolph Ave	Saint Paul	MN	55105	651-690-6000	690-6024*
*Fax: Admissions ■ *TF:* 800-945-4599 ■ *Web:* www.stkate.edu					
Minneapolis 601 25th Ave S	Minneapolis	MN	55454	651-690-7700	690-7849*
*Fax: Admissions ■ *TF:* 800-945-4599 ■ *Web:* www.stkate.edu					
College of Saint Scholastica 1200 Kenwood Ave	Duluth	MN	55811	218-723-6046	723-5991*
*Fax: Admissions ■ *TF:* 800-447-5444 ■ *Web:* www.css.edu					
Concordia College 901 8th St S	Moorhead	MN	56562	218-299-4000	299-4720
TF: 800-699-9897 ■ *Web:* www.cord.edu					
Concordia University Saint Paul 275 Syndicate St N	Saint Paul	MN	55104	651-641-8278	603-6320*
*Fax: Admissions ■ *TF:* 800-333-4705 ■ *Web:* www.csp.edu					
Gustavus Adolphus College 800 Gustavus Adolphus College	Saint Peter	MN	56082	507-933-8000	933-7474
TF: 800-487-8288 ■ *Web:* www.gustavus.edu					
Hamline University 1536 Hewitt Ave	Saint Paul	MN	55104	651-523-2207	523-2458
TF: 800-753-9753 ■ *Web:* www.hamline.edu					
Macalester College 1600 Grand Ave	Saint Paul	MN	55105	651-696-6357	696-6724*
*Fax: Admissions ■ *TF Admissions:* 800-231-7974 ■ *Web:* www.macalester.edu					
Martin Luther College 1995 Luther Ct	New Ulm	MN	56073	507-354-8221	354-8225*
*Fax: Admissions ■ *TF:* 877-652-1995 ■ *Web:* www.mlc-wels.edu					
Metropolitan State University 700 E 7th St	Saint Paul	MN	55106	651-793-1200	793-1310*
*Fax: Admissions ■ *Web:* www.metrostate.edu					
Minnesota State University *Mankato* 122 Taylor Ctr	Mankato	MN	56001	507-389-1822	389-1511
TF Admissions: 800-722-0544 ■ *Web:* www.mnsu.edu					

Phone | Fax

Moorhead 1104 7th Ave S .... Moorhead MN 56563 218-477-2161 477-4374*
*Fax: Admissions ■ TF: 800-593-7246 ■ Web: www.mnstate.edu

National American University Roseville
1550 W Hwy 36 .... Roseville MN 55113 651-644-1265 855-6305*
*Fax: Admissions ■ TF: 800-843-8892 ■ Web: www.national.edu

North Central University
910 Elliot Ave S .... Minneapolis MN 55404 612-343-4460 343-4146*
*Fax: Admissions ■ TF Admissions: 800-289-6222 ■ Web: www.northcentral.edu

Northwestern College
3003 Snelling Ave N PO Box 130517 .... Saint Paul MN 55113 651-631-5100 631-5680
TF: 800-692-4020 ■ Web: www.nwc.edu/web/guest

Saint Cloud State University
720 4th Ave S .... Saint Cloud MN 56301 320-308-2244 308-2243*
*Fax: Admissions ■ TF: 877-654-7278 ■ Web: www.stcloudstate.edu

Saint John's University PO Box 2000 .... Collegeville MN 56321 320-363-2196 363-3206*
*Fax: Admissions ■ TF Admissions: 800-544-1489 ■ Web: www.csbsju.edu

Saint Mary's University of Minnesota
700 Terr Heights .... Winona MN 55987 507-452-4430 457-1722*
*Fax: Admissions ■ TF: 800-635-5987 ■ Web: www.smumn.edu

Saint Olaf College 1520 St Olaf Ave .... Northfield MN 55057 507-646-3025 646-3832*
*Fax: Admissions ■ TF Admissions: 800-800-3025 ■ Web: www.stolaf.edu

Southwest Minnesota State University
1501 State St .... Marshall MN 56258 507-537-6286 537-7145*
*Fax: Admissions ■ TF: 800-642-0684 ■ Web: www.southwest.msus.edu

University of Minnesota
Crookston 2900 University Ave 170 Owen Hall .... Crookston MN 56716 218-281-8569 281-8575*
*Fax: Admissions ■ TF: 800-862-6466 ■ Web: www.crk.umn.edu
Duluth 1049 University Dr .... Duluth MN 55812 218-726-8000 726-6394*
*Fax: Admissions ■ TF: 800-232-1339 ■ Web: www.d.umn.edu
Morris 600 E 4th St .... Morris MN 56267 320-589-6035 589-1673*
*Fax: Admissions ■ TF: 800-992-8863 ■ Web: www.morris.umn.edu
Rochester 111 S Broadway .... Rochester MN 55904 507-280-2838 280-2820
TF: 800-947-0117 ■ Web: www.r.umn.edu
Twin Cities 3 Morrill Hall .... Minneapolis MN 55455 612-625-5000 626-1693
TF: 800-752-1000 ■ Web: www.umn.edu

University of Saint Thomas
2115 Summit Ave .... Saint Paul MN 55105 651-962-5000 962-6160*
*Fax: Admissions ■ TF: 800-328-6819 ■ Web: www.stthomas.edu

Winona State University 175 W Mark St .... Winona MN 55987 507-457-5000 457-5620*
*Fax: Admissions ■ TF: 800-342-5978 ■ Web: www.winona.edu

MISSISSIPPI

Phone | Fax

Belhaven College 1500 Peachtree St PO Box 153 .... Jackson MS 39202 601-968-5940 968-8946*
*Fax: Admissions ■ TF: 800-960-5940 ■ Web: www.belhaven.edu

Blue Mountain College PO Box 160 .... Blue Mountain MS 38610 662-685-4161 685-4776*
*Fax: Admissions ■ TF: 800-235-0136 ■ Web: www.bmc.edu

Delta State University 1003 W Sunflower Rd .... Cleveland MS 38733 662-846-4020 846-4684*
*Fax: Admissions ■ TF: 800-468-6378 ■ Web: www.deltastate.edu

Jackson State University
1400 John R Lynch St .... Jackson MS 39217 601-979-2121 979-3445*
*Fax: Admissions ■ TF: 800-848-6817 ■ Web: www.jsums.edu

Magnolia Bible College 822 S Huntington St .... Kosciusko MS 39090 662-289-2896 289-1850*
*Fax: Admissions ■ TF: 800-748-8655 ■ Web: www.magnolia.edu

Millsaps College 1701 N State St .... Jackson MS 39210 601-974-1000 974-1335*
*Fax: Admissions ■ TF Admissions: 800-352-1050 ■ Web: www.millsaps.edu

Mississippi College
200 S Capitol St PO Box 4026 .... Clinton MS 39058 601-925-3000 925-3950*
*Fax: Admissions ■ TF: 800-738-1236 ■ Web: www.mc.edu

Mississippi State University
PO Box 6305 .... Mississippi State MS 39762 662-325-2224 325-7360*
*Fax: Admissions ■ Web: www.msstate.edu

Mississippi University for Women
1100 College St MUW-1613 .... Columbus MS 39701 662-329-4750 241-7481*
*Fax: Admissions ■ TF: 877-462-8439 ■ Web: www.muw.edu

Mississippi Valley State University
14000 Hwy 82 .... Itta Bena MS 38941 662-254-9041 254-3759
TF: 800-844-6885 ■ Web: www.mvsu.edu

Rust College 150 Rust Ave .... Holly Springs MS 38635 662-252-8000 252-2258*
*Fax: Admissions ■ TF: 888-806-8492 ■ Web: www.rustcollege.edu

Tougaloo College 500 W County Line Rd .... Tougaloo MS 39174 601-977-7700 977-4501*
*Fax: Admissions ■ TF Admissions: 888-424-2566 ■ Web: www.tougaloo.edu

University of Mississippi PO Box 1848 .... University MS 38677 662-915-7211 915-5869*
*Fax: Admissions ■ Web: www.olemiss.edu
Tupelo 1918 Briar Ridge Rd .... Tupelo MS 38804 662-844-5622 844-5625*
*Fax: Admissions ■ Web: www.outreach.olemiss.edu

University of Southern Mississippi
118 College Dr .... Hattiesburg MS 39406 601-266-1000 266-5148*
*Fax: Admissions ■ Web: www.usm.edu
Gulf Park 730 E Beach Blvd .... Long Beach MS 39560 228-865-4500 865-4587*
*Fax: Admissions ■ Web: www.usm.edu

Wesley College PO Box 1070 .... Florence MS 39073 601-845-5746 845-2266*
*Fax: Admissions ■ TF: 800-748-9972 ■ Web: www.wesleycollege.edu

William Carey University 498 Tuscan Ave .... Hattiesburg MS 39401 601-318-6051 318-6454*
*Fax: Admissions ■ TF: 800-962-5991 ■ Web: www.wmcarey.edu

MISSOURI

Phone | Fax

Avila University 11901 Wornall Rd .... Kansas City MO 64145 816-501-2400 501-2453
TF: 800-462-8452 ■ Web: www.avila.edu

Central Methodist University
411 Central Methodist Sq .... Fayette MO 65248 660-248-3391 248-1872*
*Fax: Admissions ■ TF: 877-268-1854 ■ Web: www.centralmethodist.edu

Chamberlain College of Nursing
11830 Westline Industrial # 106 .... Saint Louis MO 63146 314-768-7501 768-5673
TF: 800-942-4310 ■ Web: www.chamberlain.edu

College of the Ozarks
1 Industrial Dr PO Box 17 .... Point Lookout MO 65726 417-334-6411 335-2618*
*Fax: Admissions ■ TF Admissions: 800-222-0525 ■ Web: www.cofo.edu

Columbia College 1001 Rogers St .... Columbia MO 65216 573-875-8700 875-7506*
*Fax: Admissions ■ TF: 800-231-2391 ■ Web: www.ccis.edu

Columbia College Jefferson City
3314 Emerald Ln .... Jefferson City MO 65109 573-634-3250 634-8507*
*Fax: Admissions ■ Web: ccis.edu/jeffcity

Columbia College Lake of the Ozarks
900 College Blvd .... Osage Beach MO 65065 573-348-6463 348-1791
Web: www.ccis.edu

Culver-Stockton College 1 College Hill .... Canton MO 63435 573-288-6000 288-6618*
*Fax: Admissions ■ TF Admissions: 800-537-1883 ■ Web: www.culver.edu

Drury University 900 N Benton Ave .... Springfield MO 65802 417-873-7879 866-3873
TF: 800-922-2274 ■ Web: www.drury.edu

Evangel University 1111 N Glenstone Ave .... Springfield MO 65802 417-865-2815 865-9599
TF: 800-382-6435 ■ Web: www.evangel.edu

Fontbonne University 6800 Wydown Blvd .... Saint Louis MO 63105 314-862-3456 889-1451*
*Fax: Admissions ■ TF: 800-205-5862 ■ Web: www.fontbonne.edu

Graceland University Independence
1401 W Truman Rd .... Independence MO 64050 816-833-0524 833-2990*
*Fax: Admissions ■ TF: 800-833-0524 ■ Web: www.graceland.edu

Hannibal-LaGrange College 2800 Palmyra Rd .... Hannibal MO 63401 573-221-3675 221-6594
TF Admissions: 800-454-1119 ■ Web: www.hlg.edu

Harris-Stowe State University
3026 Laclede Ave .... Saint Louis MO 63103 314-340-3366 340-3555
Web: www.hssu.edu

Lincoln University
820 Chestnut St B-7 Young Hall .... Jefferson City MO 65102 573-681-5599 681-5889*
*Fax: Admissions ■ TF Admissions: 800-521-5052 ■ Web: www.lincolnu.edu

Lindenwood University
209 S Kingshighway .... Saint Charles MO 63301 636-949-2000 949-4989*
*Fax: Admissions ■ Web: www.lindenwood.edu

Maryville University
650 Maryville University Dr .... Saint Louis MO 63141 314-529-9300 529-9927*
*Fax: Admissions ■ TF: 800-627-9855 ■ Web: www.maryville.edu

Missouri Baptist University
1 College Pk Dr .... Saint Louis MO 63141 314-434-1115 434-7596
TF: 877-434-1115 ■ Web: www.mobap.edu
Troy/Wentzville Extension
75 College Campus Dr .... Moscow Mills MO 63362 636-366-4363 356-4119*
*Fax: Admissions ■ Web: www.mobap.edu

Missouri Southern State University
3950 Newman Rd .... Joplin MO 64801 417-625-9300 659-4429
TF: 866-818-6778 ■ Web: www.mssu.edu

Missouri State University (MSU)
901 S National Ave .... Springfield MO 65897 417-836-5000 836-6334
TF: 800-492-7900 ■ Web: www.missouristate.edu

Missouri University of Science & Technology
Rolla 1870 Miner Cir G2 Parker Hall .... Rolla MO 65409 573-341-4111 341-4082*
*Fax: Admissions ■ TF: 800-522-0938 ■ Web: www.mst.edu

Missouri Valley College 500 E College St .... Marshall MO 65340 660-831-4000 831-4233*
*Fax: Admissions ■ Web: www.moval.edu

Missouri Western State University
4525 Downs Dr .... Saint Joseph MO 64507 816-271-4266 271-5833
TF: 800-662-7041 ■ Web: www.missouriwestern.edu

National American University Independence
3620 Arrowhead Ave .... Independence MO 64057 816-412-7700 412-7705
TF: 866-628-1288 ■ Web: www.national.edu

Northwest Missouri State University
800 University Dr .... Maryville MO 64468 660-562-1148 562-1821*
*Fax: Admissions ■ TF: 800-633-1175 ■ Web: www.nwmissouri.edu

Ozark Bible Institute & College
906 Summit St PO Box 398 .... Neosho MO 64850 417-451-2057 451-2059*
*Fax: Admissions ■ Web: www.obiweb.org

Park University 8700 NW River Pk Dr .... Parkville MO 64152 816-741-2000 741-9668
TF: 800-745-7275 ■ Web: www.park.edu

Rockhurst University 1100 Rockhurst Rd .... Kansas City MO 64110 816-501-4000 501-4241*
*Fax: Admissions ■ TF: 800-842-6776 ■ Web: www.rockhurst.edu

Saint Louis College of Pharmacy
4588 Parkview Pl .... Saint Louis MO 63110 314-367-8700 446-8304*
*Fax: Admissions ■ TF: 800-278-5267 ■ Web: www.stlcop.edu

Saint Louis University 221 N Grand Blvd .... Saint Louis MO 63103 314-977-2100 977-7136*
*Fax: Admissions ■ TF: 800-758-3678 ■ Web: www.slu.edu
Parks College of Engineering Aviation & Technology
3450 Lindell Blvd .... Saint Louis MO 63103 314-977-8203 977-8403
Web: parks.slu.edu

Southeast Missouri State University
1 University Plaza .... Cape Girardeau MO 63701 573-651-2000 651-5936*
*Fax: Admissions ■ Web: www.semo.edu

Southwest Baptist University
1600 University Ave .... Bolivar MO 65613 417-326-5281 328-1808*
*Fax: Admissions ■ TF: 800-526-5859 ■ Web: www.sbuniv.edu

Stephens College 1200 E Broadway PO Box 2121 .... Columbia MO 65215 573-876-7207 876-7237*
*Fax: Admissions ■ TF Admissions: 800-876-7207 ■ Web: www.stephens.edu

Truman State University 100 E Normal St .... Kirksville MO 63501 660-785-4000 785-7456*
*Fax: Admissions ■ TF: 800-892-7792 ■ Web: www.truman.edu

University of Central Missouri
PO Box 800 .... Warrensburg MO 64093 660-543-4111 543-8517*
*Fax: Admissions ■ TF: 877-729-8266 ■ Web: www.ucmo.edu

University of Missouri
Columbia 104 Jesse Hall .... Columbia MO 65211 573-882-6333 882-7887*
*Fax: Admissions ■ TF: 800-856-2181 ■ Web: www.missouri.edu
Kansas City 5100 Rockhill Rd .... Kansas City MO 64110 816-235-1000 235-5544
TF: 800-775-8652 ■ Web: www.umkc.edu
Saint Louis 1 University Blvd .... Saint Louis MO 63121 314-516-5000 516-5310*
*Fax: Admissions ■ TF Admissions: 888-462-8675 ■ Web: www.umsl.edu

Washington University in Saint Louis
1 Brookings Dr .... Saint Louis MO 63130 314-935-5000 935-4290
TF: 800-638-0700 ■ Web: www.wustl.edu

Webster University 470 E Lockwood Ave .... Saint Louis MO 63119 314-968-6900 968-7115*
*Fax: Admissions ■ TF Admissions: 800-753-6765 ■ Web: www.webster.edu

	City	State	ZIP	Phone	Fax
Westminster College 501 Westminster Ave *TF Admissions:* 800-475-3361 ■ *Web:* www.wcmo.edu	Fulton	MO	65251	573-592-5251	592-5255
William Jewell College					
500 College Hill WJC PO Box 1002 *TF:* 888-253-9355 ■ *Web:* www.jewell.edu	Liberty	MO	64068	816-781-7700	415-5040
William Woods University 1 University Ave *Fax: Admissions ■ *TF Admissions:* 800-995-3159 ■ *Web:* www.williamwoods.edu	Fulton	MO	65251	573-592-4221	592-1146*

MONTANA

	City	State	ZIP	Phone	Fax
Carroll College 1601 N Benton Ave *TF:* 800-992-3648 ■ *Web:* www.carroll.edu	Helena	MT	59625	406-447-4300	447-4533
Montana State University					
Billings 1500 University Dr *Fax: Admissions ■ *Web:* www.msubillings.edu	Billings	MT	59101	406-657-2011	657-2302*
Bozeman PO Box 172190 *Fax: Admissions ■ *TF Admissions:* 888-678-2287 ■ *Web:* www.montana.edu	Bozeman	MT	59717	406-994-2452	994-7360*
Northern PO Box 7751 *Fax: Admissions ■ *TF:* 800-662-6132 ■ *Web:* www.montana.edu	Havre	MT	59501	406-265-3700	265-3792*
Montana Tech of the University of Montana					
1300 W Pk St *Fax: Admissions ■ *TF Admissions:* 800-445-8324 ■ *Web:* www.mtech.edu	Butte	MT	59701	406-496-4718	496-4710*
Rocky Mountain College 1511 Poly Dr *Fax: Admissions ■ *TF:* 800-877-6259 ■ *Web:* www.rocky.edu	Billings	MT	59102	406-657-1000	657-1189*
University of Great Falls 1301 20th St S *Fax: Admissions ■ *TF Admissions:* 800-856-9544 ■ *Web:* www.ugf.edu	Great Falls	MT	59405	406-761-8210	791-5209*
University of Montana 32 Campus Dr *Fax: Admissions ■ *TF Admissions:* 800-462-8636 ■ *Web:* www.umt.edu	Missoula	MT	59812	406-243-6266	243-5711*
Western 710 S Atlantic St *Fax: Admissions ■ *TF Admissions:* 877-683-7331 ■ *Web:* www.umwestern.edu	Dillon	MT	59725	406-683-7011	683-7493*
Yellowstone Baptist College					
1515 S Shiloh Rd *Fax: Admissions ■ *TF:* 800-487-9950 ■ *Web:* www.yellowstonebaptist.edu	Billings	MT	59106	406-656-9950	656-3737*

NEBRASKA

	City	State	ZIP	Phone	Fax
Bellevue University 1000 Galvin Rd S *Fax: Admissions ■ *TF:* 800-756-7920 ■ *Web:* www.bellevue.edu	Bellevue	NE	68005	402-291-8100	293-2020*
Chadron State College 1000 Main St *TF:* 800-242-3766 ■ *Web:* www.csc.edu	Chadron	NE	69337	308-432-6263	432-6229
Clarkson College 101 S 42nd St *Fax: Admissions ■ *TF:* 800-647-5500 ■ *Web:* www.clarksoncollege.edu	Omaha	NE	68131	402-552-3100	552-6057*
College of Saint Mary 7000 Mercy Rd *Fax: Admissions ■ *TF:* 800-926-5534 ■ *Web:* www.csm.edu	Omaha	NE	68106	402-399-2400	399-2412*
Lincoln 4600 Valley Rd Suite 403 *Fax: Admissions ■ *TF:* 800-727-6546 ■ *Web:* www.csm.edu	Lincoln	NE	68510	402-489-2900	489-4306*
Concordia University Nebraska					
800 N Columbia Ave *Fax: Admissions ■ *TF:* 800-535-5494 ■ *Web:* www.cune.edu	Seward	NE	68434	402-643-3651	643-4073*
Creighton University 2500 California Plaza *Fax: Admissions ■ *TF:* 800-282-5835 ■ *Web:* www.creighton.edu	Omaha	NE	68178	402-280-2700	280-2685*
Dana College 2848 College Dr *Fax: Admissions ■ *TF Admissions:* 800-444-3262 ■ *Web:* www.dana.edu	Blair	NE	68008	402-426-9000	426-7225*
Doane College 1014 Boswell Ave *TF:* 800-333-6263 ■ *Web:* www.doane.edu	Crete	NE	68333	402-826-2161	826-8600
Grand Island 3180 W US Hwy 34 *Web:* www.doane.edu	Grand Island	NE	68801	308-398-0800	398-7279
Lincoln 303 N 52nd St *TF:* 888-803-6263 ■ *Web:* www.doane.edu	Lincoln	NE	68504	402-466-4774	466-4228
Hastings College 710 N Turner Ave *Fax: Admissions ■ *TF:* 800-532-7642 ■ *Web:* www.hastings.edu	Hastings	NE	68901	402-463-2402	461-7490*
Midland Lutheran College 900 N Clarkson St *Fax: Admissions ■ *TF:* 800-642-8382 ■ *Web:* www.mlc.edu	Fremont	NE	68025	402-721-5480	941-6513*
Nebraska Wesleyan University					
5000 St Paul Ave *Fax: Admissions ■ *TF:* 800-541-3818 ■ *Web:* www.nebrwesleyan.edu	Lincoln	NE	68504	402-466-2371	465-2177*
Peru State College 600 Hoyt St PO Box 10 *Fax: Admissions ■ *TF:* 800-742-4412 ■ *Web:* www.peru.edu	Peru	NE	68421	402-872-3815	872-2296*
Summit Christian College 2025 21st St *TF:* 888-305-8083 ■ *Web:* www.summitcc.net	Gering	NE	69341	308-632-6933	632-8599
Union College 3800 S 48th St *Fax: Admissions ■ *TF Admissions:* 800-228-4600 ■ *Web:* www.ucollege.edu	Lincoln	NE	68506	402-486-2504	486-2566*
University of Nebraska					
Kearney 905 W 25th St *Fax: Admissions ■ *TF:* 800-532-7639 ■ *Web:* www.unk.edu	Kearney	NE	68849	308-865-8441	865-8987*
Lincoln 1410 Q St *Fax: Admissions ■ *TF:* 800-742-8800 ■ *Web:* www.unl.edu	Lincoln	NE	68588	402-472-2023	472-0607*
Omaha 6001 Dodge St *Fax: Admissions ■ *TF:* 800-858-8648 ■ *Web:* www.unomaha.edu	Omaha	NE	68182	402-554-2200	554-3472*
Wayne State College 1111 Main St *Fax: Admissions ■ *TF:* 800-228-9972 ■ *Web:* www.wsc.edu	Wayne	NE	68787	402-375-7000	375-7180*
York College 1125 E 8th St *Fax: Admissions ■ *TF:* 800-950-9675 ■ *Web:* www.york.edu	York	NE	68467	402-362-4441	363-5623*

NEVADA

	City	State	ZIP	Phone	Fax
Great Basin College 1500 College Pkwy *Fax: Admissions ■ *Web:* www.gbcnv.edu	Elko	NV	89801	775-738-8493	753-2311*
Morrison University					
10315 Professional Cir Suite 201 *Web:* www.morrison.neumont.edu	Reno	NV	89521	775-850-0700	850-0711
Sierra Nevada College 999 Tahoe Blvd *Fax: Admissions ■ *TF:* 866-412-4636 ■ *Web:* www.sierranevada.edu	Incline Village	NV	89451	775-831-1314	831-1347*
University of Nevada					
Las Vegas 4505 S Maryland Pkwy *Fax: Admissions ■ *Web:* www.unlv.edu	Las Vegas	NV	89154	702-895-3011	895-1118*
Reno 1664 N Virginia St *Fax: Admissions ■ *TF:* 866-263-8232 ■ *Web:* www.unr.edu	Reno	NV	89557	775-784-1110	784-4283*

NEW HAMPSHIRE

	City	State	ZIP	Phone	Fax
Chester College of New England 40 Chester St *Fax: Admissions ■ *TF:* 800-974-6372 ■ *Web:* www.chestercollege.edu	Chester	NH	03036	603-887-4401	887-1777*
Colby-Sawyer College 541 Main St *Fax: Admissions ■ *TF Admissions:* 800-272-1015 ■ *Web:* www.colby-sawyer.edu	New London	NH	03257	603-526-3700	526-3452*
Daniel Webster College 20 University Dr *TF:* 800-325-6876 ■ *Web:* www.dwc.edu	Nashua	NH	03063	603-577-6000	577-6001
Dartmouth College 6016 McNutt Hall *Web:* www.dartmouth.edu	Hanover	NH	03755	603-646-1110	646-1216
Franklin Pierce University					
Concord 5 Chenell Dr *Fax: Admissions ■ *TF:* 800-437-0048 ■ *Web:* www.franklinpierce.edu	Concord	NH	03301	603-228-1155	229-4590*
Keene 17 Bradco St *Fax: Admissions ■ *TF:* 800-325-1090 ■ *Web:* www.franklinpierce.edu	Keene	NH	03431	603-357-0079	899-1062*
Lebanon 24 Airport Rd Suite 19 *Fax: Admissions ■ *TF:* 800-325-1090 ■ *Web:* www.franklinpierce.edu	West Lebanon	NH	03784	603-298-5549	899-1065*
Manchester 670 N Commercial St *TF Admissions:* 800-437-0048 ■ *Web:* www.franklinpierce.edu	Manchester	NH	03101	603-626-4972	626-4815
Portsmouth 73 Corporate Dr *Fax: Admissions ■ *TF:* 800-325-1090 ■ *Web:* www.franklinpierce.edu	Portsmouth	NH	03801	603-433-2000	899-1067*
Rindge 40 University Dr *Fax: Admissions ■ *TF Admissions:* 800-437-0048 ■ *Web:* www.franklinpierce.edu	Rindge	NH	03461	603-899-4000	899-4394*
Granite State College 8 Old Suncook Rd *TF:* 888-228-3000 ■ *Web:* www.granite.edu	Concord	NH	03301	603-228-3000	513-1389
Berlin 2020 Riverside Dr Rm 144 *Web:* www.granite.edu	Berlin	NH	03570	603-752-2479	752-6335
Portsmouth 51 International Dr *Web:* www.granite.edu	Portsmouth	NH	03801	603-334-6060	334-6313
Hesser College 3 Sundial Ave *Fax: Admissions ■ *TF:* 800-526-9231 ■ *Web:* www.hesser.edu	Manchester	NH	03103	603-668-6660	621-8994*
Keene State College 229 Main St *Fax: Admissions ■ *TF:* 800-572-1909 ■ *Web:* www.keene.edu	Keene	NH	03435	603-352-1909	358-2767*
Magdalen College 511 Kearsarge Mountain Rd *TF:* 877-498-1723 ■ *Web:* www.magdalen.edu	Warner	NH	03278	603-456-2656	456-2660
New England College 102 Bridge St *Fax: Admissions ■ *TF Admissions:* 800-521-7642 ■ *Web:* www.nec.edu	Henniker	NH	03242	603-428-2223	428-3155*
Plymouth State University 17 High St *Fax: Admissions ■ *TF:* 800-842-6900 ■ *Web:* www.plymouth.edu	Plymouth	NH	03264	603-535-2237	535-2714*
Rivier College 420 S Main St *Fax: Admissions ■ *TF:* 800-447-4843 ■ *Web:* www.rivier.edu	Nashua	NH	03060	603-888-1311	891-1799*
Saint Anselm College 100 St Anselm Dr *TF:* 888-426-7356 ■ *Web:* www.anselm.edu	Manchester	NH	03102	603-641-7500	641-7550
Southern New Hampshire University					
2500 N River Rd *TF:* 800-642-4968 ■ *Web:* www.snhu.edu	Manchester	NH	03106	603-668-2211	645-9693
University of New Hampshire					
3 Garrison Ave Grant House *Fax: Admissions ■ *Web:* www.unh.edu	Durham	NH	03824	603-862-1234	862-0077*
Manchester 400 Commercial St *Web:* www.unhm.unh.edu	Manchester	NH	03101	603-641-4321	641-4305

NEW JERSEY

	City	State	ZIP	Phone	Fax
Beth Medrash Govoha 601 Private Way	Lakewood	NJ	08701	732-367-1060	367-7487
Bloomfield College 467 Franklin St *TF:* 800-848-4555 ■ *Web:* www.bloomfield.edu	Bloomfield	NJ	07003	973-748-9000	748-0916
Caldwell College 9 Ryerson Ave *Fax: Admissions ■ *TF Admissions:* 888-864-9516 ■ *Web:* www.caldwell.edu	Caldwell	NJ	07006	973-618-3500	618-3600*
Centenary College 400 Jefferson St *Fax: Admissions ■ *TF Admissions:* 800-236-8679 ■ *Web:* www.centenarycollege.edu	Hackettstown	NJ	07840	908-852-1400	852-3454*
College of New Jersey					
2000 Pennington Rd PO Box 7718 *Fax: Admissions ■ *Web:* www.tcnj.edu	Ewing	NJ	08628	609-771-1855	637-5174*
College of Saint Elizabeth 2 Convent Rd *Fax: Admissions ■ *TF Admissions:* 800-210-7900 ■ *Web:* www.cse.edu	Morristown	NJ	07960	973-290-4700	290-4710*
Douglass College 100 George St *Web:* www.douglass.rutgers.edu	New Brunswick	NJ	08901	732-932-9500	932-8877
Drew University 36 Madison Ave *Fax: Admissions ■ *Web:* www.drew.edu	Madison	NJ	07940	973-408-3000	408-3068*
Fairleigh Dickinson University					
285 Madison Ave *Fax: Admissions ■ *TF:* 800-338-8803 ■ *Web:* www.fdu.edu	Madison	NJ	07940	973-593-8500	443-8088*
Metropolitan 1000 River Rd *TF:* 800-338-8803 ■ *Web:* www.fdu.edu	Teaneck	NJ	07666	201-692-2000	692-2560
Felician College 262 S Main St *Fax: Admissions ■ *Web:* www.felician.edu	Lodi	NJ	07644	201-559-6000	559-6138*
Rutherford 223 Montross Ave *Web:* www.felician.edu	Rutherford	NJ	07070	201-559-6000	559-3578
Georgian Court University 900 Lakewood Ave *Fax: Admissions ■ *TF:* 800-458-8422 ■ *Web:* www.georgian.edu	Lakewood	NJ	08701	732-987-2760	987-2000*
Kean University 1000 Morris Ave Kean Hall *Fax: Admissions ■ *Web:* www.kean.edu	Union	NJ	07083	908-737-7100	737-7105*
Monmouth University 400 Cedar Ave *Fax: Admissions ■ *TF:* 800-543-9671 ■ *Web:* www.monmouth.edu	West Long Branch	NJ	07764	732-571-3456	263-5166*
Montclair State University 1 Normal Ave *Fax: Admissions ■ *TF Admissions:* 800-331-9205 ■ *Web:* www.montclair.edu	Montclair	NJ	07043	973-655-4000	655-7700*
New Jersey City University 2039 JFK Blvd *TF:* 888-441-6528 ■ *Web:* www.njcu.edu	Jersey City	NJ	07305	201-200-2000	200-2044
New Jersey Institute of Technology					
University Heights *TF:* 800-926-6548 ■ *Web:* www.njit.edu	Newark	NJ	07102	973-596-3000	596-3461

				Phone	Fax
Princeton University 33 Washington Rd	Princeton	NJ	08544	609-258-3000	258-6743*
*Fax: Admissions ■ *Web:* www.princeton.edu					
Rabbinical College of America 226 Sussex Ave PO Box 1996	Morristown	NJ	07962	973-267-9404	267-5208
Web: www.rca.edu					
Ramapo College of New Jersey 505 Ramapo Valley Rd	Mahwah	NJ	07430	201-684-7500	684-7964*
*Fax: Admissions ■ *Web:* www.ramapo.edu					
Richard Stockton College of New Jersey PO Box 195	Pomona	NJ	08240	609-652-1776	748-5541*
*Fax: Admissions ■ *Web:* www.stockton.edu					
Rider University 2083 Lawrenceville Rd	Lawrenceville	NJ	08648	609-896-5000	895-6645*
*Fax: Admissions ■ *TF:* 800-257-9026 ■ *Web:* www.rider.edu					
Westminster Choir College 101 Walnut Ln	Princeton	NJ	08540	609-921-7100	921-2538*
*Fax: Admissions ■ *TF:* 800-962-4647 ■ *Web:* westminster.rider.edu					
Rowan University 201 Mullica Hill Rd	Glassboro	NJ	08028	856-256-4200	256-4430*
*Fax: Admissions ■ *TF Admissions:* 877-787-6926 ■ *Web:* www.rowan.edu					
Rutgers the State University of New Jersey					
Camden 406 Penn St	Camden	NJ	08102	856-225-6104	225-6498*
*Fax: Admissions ■ *Web:* www.camden.rutgers.edu					
New Brunswick/Piscataway 57 US Hwy 1	New Brunswick	NJ	08854	732-932-1766	445-0237
Web: nbp.rutgers.edu					
Newark 249 University Ave Rm 100	Newark	NJ	07102	973-353-5205	353-1440*
*Fax: Admissions ■ *Web:* www.newark.rutgers.edu					
Saint Peter's College 2641 JFK Blvd	Jersey City	NJ	07306	201-915-9000	761-7105*
*Fax: Admissions ■ *TF:* 888-772-9933 ■ *Web:* www.spc.edu					
Seton Hall University 400 S Orange Ave	South Orange	NJ	07079	973-761-9332	275-2321*
*Fax: Admissions ■ *TF:* 800-738-6648 ■ *Web:* www.shu.edu					
Stevens Institute of Technology Castle Pt on the Hudson	Hoboken	NJ	07030	201-216-5194	216-8348*
*Fax: Admissions ■ *TF:* 800-458-5323 ■ *Web:* www.stevens.edu					
Thomas Edison State College 101 W State St	Trenton	NJ	08608	609-984-1102	984-8447*
*Fax: Admissions ■ *TF:* 888-442-8372 ■ *Web:* www.tesc.edu					
William Paterson University 300 Pompton Rd	Wayne	NJ	07470	973-720-2000	720-2910*
*Fax: Admissions ■ *TF:* 877-978-3923 ■ *Web:* www.ww2.wpunj.edu					

NEW MEXICO

				Phone	Fax
College of Santa Fe 1600 St Michaels Dr	Santa Fe	NM	87505	505-473-6011	473-6129*
*Fax: Admissions ■ *TF:* 800-456-2673 ■ *Web:* www.csf.edu					
College of the Southwest 6610 N Lovington Hwy	Hobbs	NM	88240	575-392-6561	392-6006*
Fax Area Code: 505 ■ *Fax: Admissions ■ *TF:* 800-530-4400 ■ *Web:* www.usw.edu					
Eastern New Mexico University 1500 S Ave K Stn 7	Portales	NM	88130	575-562-1011	562-2118*
Fax Area Code: 505 ■ *Fax: Admissions ■ *TF:* 800-367-3668 ■ *Web:* www.enmu.edu					
National American University Albuquerque 4775 Indian School Rd NE Suite 200	Albuquerque	NM	87110	505-265-7517	348-3705
Web: www.national.edu					
New Mexico Highlands University 901 University Ave	Las Vegas	NM	87701	505-425-7511	454-3552
TF: 877-850-9064 ■ *Web:* www.nmhu.edu					
New Mexico Institute of Mining & Technology (NMT) 801 Leroy Pl	Socorro	NM	87801	505-835-5434	835-5989*
*Fax: Admissions ■ *TF Admissions:* 800-428-8324 ■ *Web:* www.nmt.edu					
New Mexico State University PO Box 30001 MSC-3A	Las Cruces	NM	88003	575-646-3121	646-6330*
*Fax: Admissions ■ *TF Admissions:* 800-662-6678 ■ *Web:* www.nmsu.edu					
Saint John's College Santa Fe 1160 Camino Cruz Blanca	Santa Fe	NM	87505	505-984-6060	984-6162*
*Fax: Admissions ■ *TF Admissions:* 800-331-5232 ■ *Web:* www.sjcsf.edu					
Santa Fe University of Art & Design 1600 St Michaels Dr	Santa Fe	NM	87505	800-456-2673	473-6011*
Fax Area Code: 505 ■ *Fax: Admissions ■ *TF:* 800-456-2673 ■ *Web:* www.santafeuniversity.edu					
University of New Mexico (UNM) 1 University of New Mexico	Albuquerque	NM	87131	505-277-0111	277-6686
TF: 800-225-5866 ■ *Web:* www.unm.edu					
Gallup 200 College Rd	Gallup	NM	87301	505-863-7500	863-7610
TF: 800-225-5866 ■ *Web:* www.gallup.unm.edu					
Western New Mexico University 1000 W College St PO Box 680	Silver City	NM	88061	505-538-6011	538-6278*
Fax Area Code: 575 ■ *TF Admissions:* 800-872-9668 ■ *Web:* www.wnmu.edu					

NEW YORK

				Phone	Fax
Adelphi University PO Box 701	Garden City	NY	11530	516-877-3050	877-3039*
*Fax: Admissions ■ *TF:* 800-233-5744 ■ *Web:* www.adelphi.edu					
Manhattan Ctr 75 Varick St 2nd Fl	New York	NY	10013	212-965-8340	431-5161
TF: 800-233-5744 ■ *Web:* www.adelphi.edu					
Albany College of Pharmacy 106 New Scotland Ave	Albany	NY	12208	518-694-7221	694-7322*
*Fax: Admissions ■ *TF:* 888-203-8010 ■ *Web:* www.acp.edu					
Albert A List College of Jewish Studies 3080 Broadway	New York	NY	10027	212-678-8832	280-6022*
*Fax: Admissions ■ *Web:* www.jtsa.edu/x670.xml					
Bard College PO Box 5000	Annandale-on-Hudson	NY	12504	845-758-7472	758-5208
Web: www.bard.edu					
Barnard College Columbia University 3009 Broadway	New York	NY	10027	212-854-2014	854-6220*
*Fax: Admissions ■ *Web:* www.barnard.edu					
Baruch College 55 Lexington Ave at 24th St	New York	NY	10010	646-312-1000	312-1362
Web: www.baruch.cuny.edu					
Binghamton University PO Box 6000	Binghamton	NY	13902	607-777-2000	777-4445*
*Fax: Admissions ■ *Web:* www.binghamton.edu					
Boricua College 3755 Broadway	New York	NY	10032	212-694-1000	694-1015*
*Fax: Admissions ■ *Web:* www.boricuacollege.edu					
Brooklyn College 2900 Bedford Ave	Brooklyn	NY	11210	718-951-5000	951-4506*
*Fax: Admissions ■ *Web:* www.brooklyn.cuny.edu					
Buffalo State College 1300 Elmwood Ave	Buffalo	NY	14222	716-878-4000	878-6100*
*Fax: Admissions ■ *Web:* www.buffalostate.edu					
Canisius College 2001 Main St	Buffalo	NY	14208	716-888-2200	888-3230*
*Fax: Admissions ■ *TF:* 800-843-1517 ■ *Web:* www.canisius.edu					
Cazenovia College 8 Sullivan St	Cazenovia	NY	13035	315-655-7208	655-4860
TF: 800-654-3210 ■ *Web:* www.cazenovia.edu					
City College of New York 138th St & Convent Ave	New York	NY	10031	212-650-6448	650-6417*
*Fax: Admissions ■ *TF Admissions:* 800-286-9937 ■ *Web:* www.ccny.cuny.edu					
Clarkson University 10 Clarkson Ave	Potsdam	NY	13699	315-268-6480	268-7647*
*Fax: Admissions ■ *TF Admissions:* 800-527-6577 ■ *Web:* www.clarkson.edu					
Colgate University 13 Oak Dr	Hamilton	NY	13346	315-228-1000	228-7544*
*Fax: Admissions ■ *Web:* www.colgate.edu					
College of Mount Saint Vincent 6301 Riverdale Ave	Riverdale	NY	10471	718-405-3304	549-7945*
*Fax: Admissions ■ *TF:* 800-665-2678 ■ *Web:* www.mountsaintvincent.edu					
College of New Rochelle 29 Castle Pl	New Rochelle	NY	10805	914-654-5452	654-5464
TF: 800-933-5923 ■ *Web:* www.cnr.edu					
College of Saint Rose 432 Western Ave	Albany	NY	12203	518-454-5150	454-2013*
*Fax: Admissions ■ *TF:* 800-637-8556 ■ *Web:* www.strose.edu					
College of Staten Island 2800 Victory Blvd	Staten Island	NY	10314	718-982-2000	982-2500
Web: www.csi.cuny.edu					
Columbia University 2960 Broadway	New York	NY	10027	212-854-1754	
Web: www.columbia.edu					
Concordia College New York 171 White Plains Rd	Bronxville	NY	10708	914-337-9300	395-4636*
*Fax: Admissions ■ *TF Admissions:* 800-937-2655 ■ *Web:* www.concordia-ny.edu					
Cooper Union for the Advancement of Science & Art 30 Cooper Sq	New York	NY	10003	212-353-4120	353-4342*
*Fax: Admissions ■ *Web:* www.cooper.edu					
Cornell University 410 Thurston Ave	Ithaca	NY	14850	607-255-5241	254-5175*
*Fax: Admissions ■ *Web:* www.cornell.edu					
D'Youville College 320 Porter Ave	Buffalo	NY	14201	716-829-7600	829-7900*
*Fax: Admissions ■ *TF:* 800-777-3921 ■ *Web:* www.dyc.edu					
Daemen College 4380 Main St	Amherst	NY	14226	716-839-8225	839-8229*
*Fax: Admissions ■ *TF:* 800-462-7652 ■ *Web:* www.daemen.edu					
Dominican College 470 Western Hwy	Orangeburg	NY	10962	845-359-7800	365-3150*
*Fax: Admissions ■ *TF:* 866-432-4636 ■ *Web:* www.dc.edu					
Dowling College 150 Idle Hour Blvd	Oakdale	NY	11769	631-244-3000	244-1059*
*Fax: Admissions ■ *TF:* 800-369-5464 ■ *Web:* www.dowling.edu					
Elmira College 1 Pk Pl	Elmira	NY	14901	607-735-1724	735-1718*
*Fax: Admissions ■ *TF Admissions:* 800-935-6472 ■ *Web:* www.elmira.edu					
Eugene Lang College 65 W 11th St	New York	NY	10011	212-229-5665	229-5355*
*Fax: Admissions ■ *Web:* www.newschool.edu/lang					
Excelsior College 7 Columbia Cir	Albany	NY	12203	518-464-8500	464-8833*
*Fax: Admissions ■ *TF:* 888-647-2388 ■ *Web:* www.excelsior.edu					
Farmingdale State University of New York 2350 Broadhollow Rd	Farmingdale	NY	11735	631-420-2000	420-2633
TF: 877-432-7646 ■ *Web:* www.farmingdale.edu					
Fordham University 441 E Fordham Rd	Bronx	NY	10458	718-817-5067	367-9404*
*Fax: Admissions ■ *TF:* 800-367-3426 ■ *Web:* www.fordham.edu					
College at Lincoln Ctr 113 W 60th St	New York	NY	10023	212-636-6710	636-7002
TF: 800-367-3426 ■ *Web:* www.fordham.edu					
Westchester 400 Westchester Ave	West Harrison	NY	10604	914-332-8295	332-7442
TF: 800-724-4312 ■ *Web:* www.fordham.edu					
Hamilton College 198 College Hill Rd	Clinton	NY	13323	315-859-4421	859-4457*
*Fax: Admissions ■ *TF Admissions:* 800-843-2655 ■ *Web:* www.hamilton.edu					
Hartwick College 1 Hartwick Dr	Oneonta	NY	13820	607-431-4150	431-4154*
*Fax: Admissions ■ *TF:* 888-427-8942 ■ *Web:* www.hartwick.edu					
Hebrew Union College					
Jewish Institute of Religion 1 W 4th St	New York	NY	10012	212-824-2207	388-1720*
*Fax: Admissions ■ *TF:* 800-424-1336 ■ *Web:* www.huc.edu					
Hilbert College 5200 S Pk Ave	Hamburg	NY	14075	716-649-7900	649-1152
TF: 800-649-8003 ■ *Web:* www.hilbert.edu					
Hobart & William Smith Colleges 300 Pulteney St	Geneva	NY	14456	315-781-3000	781-3914*
*Fax: Admissions ■ *TF Admissions:* 800-852-2256 ■ *Web:* www.hws.edu					
Hofstra University 100 Hofstra University	Hempstead	NY	11549	516-463-6700	463-5100*
*Fax: Admissions ■ *TF:* 800-463-7872 ■ *Web:* www.hofstra.edu/home/index.html					
Houghton College 1 Willard Ave PO Box 128	Houghton	NY	14744	585-567-9200	567-9522*
*Fax: Admissions ■ *TF:* 800-777-2556 ■ *Web:* www.houghton.edu					
West Seneca 810 Union Rd	West Seneca	NY	14224	716-674-6363	674-0250
TF: 800-247-6448					
Hunter College 695 Pk Ave N Bldg Rm 203	New York	NY	10065	212-772-4490	650-3472
Web: www.hunter.cuny.edu					
Iona College 715 N Ave	New Rochelle	NY	10801	914-633-2502	633-2642
TF: 800-231-4662 ■ *Web:* www.iona.edu					
Ithaca College 953 Danby Rd	Ithaca	NY	14850	607-274-3124	274-1900*
*Fax: Admissions ■ *TF Admissions:* 800-429-4274 ■ *Web:* www.ithaca.edu					
Jewish Theological Seminary 3080 Broadway	New York	NY	10027	212-678-8832	678-6022
Web: www.jtsa.edu					
John Jay College of Criminal Justice 445 W 59th St	New York	NY	10019	212-237-8000	237-8777
Web: www.jjay.cuny.edu					
Juilliard School 144 W 66th St	New York	NY	10023	212-799-5000	769-6420
Web: www.juilliard.edu					
Keuka College 141 Central Ave	Keuka Park	NY	14478	315-279-5254	536-5386*
*Fax: Admissions ■ *TF Admissions:* 800-335-3852 ■ *Web:* www.keuka.edu					
Laboratory Institute of Merchandising 12 E 53rd St	New York	NY	10022	212-752-1530	832-6708*
*Fax: Admissions ■ *TF:* 800-677-1323 ■ *Web:* www.limcollege.edu					
Le Moyne College 1419 Salt Springs Rd	Syracuse	NY	13214	315-445-4100	445-4711*
*Fax: Admissions ■ *TF Admissions:* 800-333-4733 ■ *Web:* www.lemoyne.edu					
Lehman College 250 Bedford Pk Blvd W	Bronx	NY	10468	718-960-8000	960-8712*
*Fax: Admissions ■ *Web:* www.lehman.cuny.edu					
Long Island University					
Brentwood 100 2nd Ave	Brentwood	NY	11717	631-273-5112	273-3155
Web: www.liunet.edu					

Phone Fax

Brooklyn 1 University Plaza........................ Brooklyn NY 11201 718-488-1011 797-2399*
*Fax: Admissions ■ TF: 800-548-7526 ■ Web: www.brooklyn.liu.edu
CW Post 720 Northern Blvd...................... Greenvale NY 11548 516-299-2000 299-2137*
*Fax: Admissions ■ TF: 800-548-7526 ■ Web: www.cwpost.liu.edu
Manhattan College 4513 Manhattan College Pkwy........Bronx NY 10471 718-862-8000 862-8019*
*Fax: Admissions ■ TF: 800-622-9235 ■ Web: www.manhattan.edu
Manhattan School of Music 120 Claremont Ave.......New York NY 10027 212-749-2802 749-3025*
*Fax: Admissions ■ Web: www.msmnyc.edu
Manhattanville College 2900 Purchase St............Purchase NY 10577 914-323-5464 694-1732
TF: 800-328-4553 ■ Web: www.mville.edu
Mannes College of Music 150 W 85th St............New York NY 10024 212-580-0210 580-1738*
*Fax: Admissions ■ Web: www.mannes.edu
Marist College 3399 N Rd..................... Poughkeepsie NY 12601 845-575-3000 575-3215
TF: 800-436-5483 ■ Web: www.marist.edu
Marymount Manhattan College 221 E 71st St........New York NY 10021 212-517-0400 517-0448
TF: 800-627-9668 ■ Web: www.marymount.mmm.edu
Medaille College 18 Agassiz Cir.......................Buffalo NY 14214 716-880-2200 880-2007*
*Fax: Admissions ■ TF: 800-292-1582 ■ Web: www.medaille.edu
Medgar Evers College 1650 Bedford Ave............. Brooklyn NY 11225 718-270-4900 270-6411*
*Fax: Admissions ■ Web: www.mec.cuny.edu
Mercy College 555 Broadway.....................Dobbs Ferry NY 10522 914-693-4500 674-7382*
*Fax: Admissions ■ TF: 800-637-2969 ■ Web: www.mercy.edu
Manhattan 66 W 35th St..........................New York NY 10001 212-615-3313 967-2993
TF: 800-637-2969 ■ Web: www.mercy.edu
White Plains 277 Martine Ave.................. White Plains NY 10601 914-948-3666 948-6732
TF: 800-637-2969 ■ Web: www.mercy.edu
Yorktown Heights 2651 Strang Blvd.......... Yorktown Heights NY 10598 914-245-6100 962-0931*
*Fax: Admissions ■ TF: 800-637-2969 ■ Web: www.mercy.edu
Metropolitan College of New York
431 Canal St...................................New York NY 10013 212-343-1234 343-7399*
*Fax: Admissions ■ TF: 800-338-4465 ■ Web: www.metropolitan.edu
Molloy College
1000 Hempstead Ave PO Box 5002............ Rockville Centre NY 11571 516-678-5000 256-2247*
*Fax: Admissions ■ TF Admissions: 888-466-5569 ■ Web: www.molloy.edu
Morrisville State College
80 Eaton St PO Box 901.........................Morrisville NY 13408 315-684-6000 684-6427*
*Fax: Admissions ■ TF Admissions: 800-258-0111 ■ Web: www.morrisville.edu
Mount Saint Mary College 330 Powell Ave.......... Newburgh NY 12550 845-569-3248 562-6762
TF: 888-937-6762 ■ Web: www.msmc.edu
Nazareth College of Rochester 4245 E Ave.......... Rochester NY 14618 585-389-2860 389-2826
TF: 800-462-3944 ■ Web: www.naz.edu
New School 66 W 12th St..........................New York NY 10011 212-229-5600 989-3887*
*Fax: Admissions ■ Web: www.newschool.edu
New York City College of Technology
300 Jay St.................................... Brooklyn NY 11201 718-260-5000 260-5504*
*Fax: Admissions ■ Web: www.citytech.cuny.edu
New York Institute of Technology
New York Institute of Technology Northern Blvd
PO Box 8000...............................Old Westbury NY 11568 516-686-1000 686-7613*
*Fax: Admissions ■ TF: 800-345-6948 ■ Web: www.nyit.edu
Islip PO Box 9029........................Central Islip NY 11722 631-348-3200 348-0912*
*Fax: Admissions ■ TF: 800-345-6948 ■ Web: www.nyit.edu
Manhattan 1855 Broadway........................New York NY 10023 212-261-1500 261-1505*
*Fax: Admissions ■ TF: 800-345-6948 ■ Web: www.nyit.edu
New York School of Interior Design
170 E 70th St.................................New York NY 10021 212-472-1500 472-1867*
*Fax: Admissions ■ TF: 800-336-9743 ■ Web: www.nysid.edu
New York University 22 Washington Sq N............New York NY 10011 212-998-4500 995-4902*
*Fax: Admissions ■ Web: www.nyu.edu
Niagara University
5795 Lewiston Rd PO Box 2011.............Niagara University NY 14109 716-286-8700 286-8710*
*Fax: Admissions ■ TF: 800-462-2111 ■ Web: www.niagara.edu
Nyack College 1 S Blvd............................. Nyack NY 10960 845-358-1710 358-3047*
*Fax: Admissions ■ TF Admissions: 800-336-9225 ■ Web: www.nyackcollege.edu
Pace University 1 Pace Plaza......................New York NY 10038 212-346-1200 346-1040*
*Fax: Admissions ■ TF: 866-874-7223 ■ Web: www.pace.edu
Pleasantville/Briarcliff
861 Bedford Rd........................... Pleasantville NY 10570 914-773-3200 773-3851*
*Fax: Admissions ■ TF: 866-722-3338 ■ Web: www.pace.edu
Parsons New School for Design
65 5th Ave Rm 103..............................New York NY 10003 212-229-8989 229-8975*
*Fax: Admissions ■ TF Admissions: 800-252-0852 ■ Web: www.parsons.edu
Paul Smith's College
Rt 30 & 86 PO Box 265.........................Paul Smiths NY 12970 518-327-6227 327-6016*
*Fax: Admissions ■ TF Admissions: 800-421-2605 ■ Web: www.paulsmiths.edu
Polytechnic University
Long Island 105 Maxess Rd.......................Melville NY 11747 631-755-4300 755-4404*
*Fax: Admissions ■ TF Admissions: 800-765-9832 ■ Web: www.poly.edu
Pratt Institute 200 Willoughby Ave................... Brooklyn NY 11205 718-636-3669 636-3670
TF: 800-331-0834 ■ Web: www.pratt.edu
Purchase College 735 Anderson Hill Rd............. Purchase NY 10577 914-251-6000 251-6314*
*Fax: Admissions ■ Web: www.purchase.edu
Queens College 65-30 Kissena Blvd................. Flushing NY 11367 718-997-5000 997-5617
Web: www.qc.cuny.edu
Rensselaer Polytechnic Institute 110 8th St.............Troy NY 12180 518-276-6216 276-4072*
*Fax: Admissions ■ TF: 800-448-6562 ■ Web: www.rpi.edu
Roberts Wesleyan College 2301 Westside Dr........ Rochester NY 14624 585-594-6000 594-6371*
*Fax: Admissions ■ TF Admissions: 800-777-4792 ■ Web: www.roberts.edu
Rochester Institute of Technology
1 Lomb Memorial Dr........................... Rochester NY 14623 585-475-2411 475-7424*
*Fax: Admissions ■ Web: www.rit.edu
Russell Sage College 45 Ferry St......................Troy NY 12180 518-244-2217 244-6880*
*Fax: Admissions ■ TF Admissions: 888-837-9724 ■ Web: www.sage.edu
Sage College of Albany 140 New Scotland Ave..........Albany NY 12208 518-292-1730 292-1912*
*Fax: Admissions ■ TF Admissions: 888-837-9724 ■ Web: www.sage.edu
Saint Bonaventure University
PO Box D..............................Saint Bonaventure NY 14778 716-375-2400 375-4005*
*Fax: Admissions ■ TF: 800-462-5050 ■ Web: www.sbu.edu
Saint Francis College
180 Remsen St 3rd Fl......................Brooklyn Heights NY 11201 718-522-2300 802-0453*
*Fax: Admissions ■ Web: www.stfranciscollege.edu

Saint John Fisher College 3690 E Ave.............. Rochester NY 14618 585-385-8064 385-8386*
*Fax: Admissions ■ TF Admissions: 800-444-4640 ■ Web: www.sjfc.edu
Saint John's University 8000 Utopia Pkwy...............Jamaica NY 11439 718-990-2000 990-2096*
*Fax: Admissions ■ TF: 888-978-5646 ■ Web: www.stjohns.edu
Staten Island 300 Howard Ave.................. Staten Island NY 10301 718-447-4343 390-4298*
*Fax: Admissions ■ Web: www.stjohns.edu
Saint Joseph's College
Brooklyn 245 Clinton Ave......................... Brooklyn NY 11205 718-636-6800 636-8303*
*Fax: Admissions ■ Web: www.sjcny.edu
Suffolk 155 W Roe Blvd.......................... Patchogue NY 11772 631-447-3200 447-1731*
*Fax: Admissions ■ Web: www.sjcny.edu
Saint Lawrence University 23 Romoda Dr..............Canton NY 13617 315-229-5261 229-5818*
*Fax: Admissions ■ TF Admissions: 800-285-1856 ■ Web: www.stlawu.edu
Saint Thomas Aquinas College 125 Rt 340........... Sparkill NY 10976 845-398-4000 398-4114
TF: 800-999-7822 ■ Web: www.stac.edu
Sarah Lawrence College 1 Meadway............... Bronxville NY 10708 800-888-2858 395-2515*
*Fax Area Code: 914 ■ *Fax: Admissions ■ TF: 800-888-2858 ■ Web: www.slc.edu
Siena College 515 Loudon Rd......................Loudonville NY 12211 518-783-2200 783-2436*
*Fax: Admissions ■ TF Admissions: 888-287-4362 ■ Web: www.siena.edu
Skidmore College 815 N Broadway............Saratoga Springs NY 12866 518-580-5000 580-5584*
*Fax: Admissions ■ TF: 800-867-6007 ■ Web: www.skidmore.edu
State University of New York
Brockport 350 New Campus Dr.....................Brockport NY 14420 585-395-2751 395-5452
Web: www.brockport.edu
College at Oneonta Ravine Pkwy....................Oneonta NY 13820 607-436-3500 436-3074*
*Fax: Admissions ■ TF: 800-786-9123 ■ Web: www.oneonta.edu
College of Agriculture & Technology at Cobleskill
Rt 7...................................... Cobleskill NY 12043 518-255-5525 255-6769*
*Fax: Admissions ■ TF: 800-295-8988 ■ Web: www.cobleskill.edu
College of Environmental Science & Forestry
1 Forestry Dr.................................Syracuse NY 13210 315-470-6500 470-6933*
*Fax: Admissions ■ TF Admissions: 800-777-7373 ■ Web: www.esf.edu
Cortland PO Box 2000........................... Cortland NY 13045 607-753-2011 753-5998*
*Fax: Admissions ■ Web: www.cortland.edu
Empire State College 1 Union Ave............Saratoga Springs NY 12866 518-587-2100 587-9759*
*Fax: Admissions ■ TF: 800-847-3000 ■ Web: www.esc.edu
Fredonia 178 Central Ave......................... Fredonia NY 14063 716-673-3251 673-3249*
*Fax: Admissions ■ TF: 800-252-1212 ■ Web: www.fredonia.edu
Geneseo 1 College Cir............................ Geneseo NY 14454 585-245-5571 245-5550*
*Fax: Admitting ■ TF Admitting: 866-245-5211 ■ Web: www.geneseo.edu
Institute of Technology PO Box 3050.................. Utica NY 13504 315-792-7500 792-7837*
*Fax: Admissions ■ TF: 800-786-9832 ■ Web: www.sunyit.edu
Maritime College 6 Pennyfield Ave Fort Schuyler..........Bronx NY 10465 718-409-7200 409-7465
Web: www.sunymaritime.edu
New Paltz 1 Hawk Dr............................New Paltz NY 12561 845-257-3212 257-3209*
*Fax: Admissions ■ TF: 877-696-7411 ■ Web: www.newpaltz.edu
Oswego 7060 SR 104............................ Oswego NY 13126 315-312-2500 312-3260*
*Fax: Admissions ■ Web: www.oswego.edu
Plattsburgh 101 Broad St....................... Plattsburgh NY 12901 518-564-2040 564-2045*
*Fax: Admissions ■ TF Admissions: 888-673-0012 ■ Web: www.plattsburgh.edu
Potsdam 44 Pierrpont Ave......................... Potsdam NY 13676 315-267-2180 267-2163*
*Fax: Admissions ■ TF Admissions: 877-768-7326 ■ Web: www.potsdam.edu
The College at Old Westbury
223 Store Hill Rd PO Box 307................Old Westbury NY 11568 516-876-3073 876-3307*
*Fax: Admissions ■ Web: www.oldwestbury.edu
University at Buffalo 12 Capen Hall....................Buffalo NY 14260 716-645-2450 645-6411*
*Fax: Admissions ■ TF: 888-822-3648 ■ Web: www.buffalo.edu
Stern College for Women of Yeshiva University
245 Lexington Ave..............................New York NY 10016 212-340-7701 340-7788*
*Fax: Admissions ■ Web: www.yu.edu/stern
Stony Brook University 100 Nicolls Rd............Stony Brook NY 11794 631-689-6000 632-9898
Web: www.sunysb.edu
Syracuse University 900 S Crouse Ave............... Syracuse NY 13244 315-443-3611 443-4226*
*Fax: Admissions ■ Web: www.syr.edu
Touro College 27-33 W 23rd St......................New York NY 10010 212-463-0400 627-9144
Web: www.touro.edu
Lander College for Men
75-31 150th St.........................Kew Gardens Hills NY 11367 718-820-4884 820-4838
Web: www.touro.edu
Union College 807 Union St.................... Schenectady NY 12308 518-388-6112 388-6986*
*Fax: Admissions ■ TF Admissions: 888-843-6688 ■ Web: www.union.edu
University at Albany 1400 Washington Ave.............Albany NY 12222 518-442-3300 442-5383*
*Fax: Admissions ■ TF: 800-293-7869 ■ Web: www.albany.edu
University of Rochester
Wallace Hall PO Box 270251...................... Rochester NY 14627 585-275-2121 461-4595*
*Fax: Admissions ■ TF Admissions: 888-822-2256 ■ Web: www.rochester.edu
US Merchant Marine Academy
300 Steamboat Rd............................Kings Point NY 11024 516-773-5000 773-5390*
*Fax: Admissions ■ TF: 866-546-4778 ■ Web: www.usmma.edu
US Military Academy
Admissions Bldg 606 3rd Fl.......................West Point NY 10996 845-938-5746 938-8121
TF: 800-822-8762 ■ Web: www.usma.edu
Utica College 1600 Burrstone Rd...................... Utica NY 13502 315-792-3111 792-3003*
*Fax: Admissions ■ TF Admissions: 800-782-8884 ■ Web: www.utica.edu
Vassar College 124 Raymond Ave............... Poughkeepsie NY 12604 845-437-7000 437-7063
TF: 800-827-7270 ■ Web: www.vassar.edu
Vaughn College of Aeronautics & Technology
86-01 23rd Ave............................ East Elmhurst NY 11369 718-429-6600 779-2231*
*Fax: Admissions ■ TF: 800-776-2376 ■ Web: www.vaughn.edu
Wagner College 1 Campus Rd................... Staten Island NY 10301 718-390-3411 390-3105
TF Admissions: 800-221-1010 ■ Web: www.wagner.edu
Webb Institute 298 Crescent Beach Rd............... Glen Cove NY 11542 516-671-2213 674-9838*
*Fax: Admissions ■ TF: 866-708-9322 ■ Web: www.webb-institute.edu
Wells College 170 Main St PO Box 500................ Aurora NY 13026 315-364-3370 364-3227*
*Fax: Admissions ■ TF Admissions: 800-952-9355 ■ Web: www.wells.edu

Institution	City	State	Zip	Phone	Fax
Yeshiva University 500 W 185th St *Fax: Admissions ■ *Web:* www.yu.edu	New York	NY	10033	212-960-5400	960-0086*
York College 94-20 Guy R Brewer Blvd *Fax: Admissions ■ *Web:* www.york.cuny.edu	Jamaica	NY	11451	718-262-2000	262-2601*

NORTH CAROLINA

Institution	City	State	Zip	Phone	Fax
Barton College PO Box 5000 *TF:* 800-345-4973 ■ *Web:* www.barton.edu	Wilson	NC	27893	252-399-6300	399-6572
Belmont Abbey College 100 Belmont-Mt Holly Rd *Fax: Admissions ■ *TF:* 888-222-0110 ■ *Web:* www.belmontabbeycollege.edu	Belmont	NC	28012	704-825-6700	825-6220*
Bennett College 900 E Washington St *Fax: Admissions ■ *TF Admissions:* 800-413-5323 ■ *Web:* www.bennett.edu	Greensboro	NC	27401	336-370-8624	517-2166*
Brevard College 1 Brevard College Dr *Fax: Admissions ■ *TF Admissions:* 800-527-9090 ■ *Web:* www.brevard.edu	Brevard	NC	28712	828-883-8292	884-3790*
Campbell University 450 Leslie Campbell Ave PO Box 546 *Fax: Admissions ■ *TF:* 800-334-4111 ■ *Web:* www.campbell.edu	Buies Creek	NC	27506	910-893-1290	893-1288*
Catawba College 2300 W Innes St *Fax: Admissions ■ *TF:* 800-228-2922 ■ *Web:* www.catawba.edu	Salisbury	NC	28144	704-637-4111	637-4222*
Chowan University 1 University Pl *Fax: Admissions ■ *TF Admissions:* 800-488-4101 ■ *Web:* www.chowan.edu	Murfreesboro	NC	27855	252-398-6500	398-1190*
Davidson College PO Box 7156 *Fax: Admissions ■ *TF:* 800-768-0380 ■ *Web:* www.davidson.edu	Davidson	NC	28035	704-894-2000	894-2016*
Duke University 2138 Campus Dr PO Box 90586 *Fax: Admissions ■ *Web:* www.duke.edu	Durham	NC	27708	919-684-3214	681-8941*
East Carolina University E 5th St *Web:* www.ecu.edu	Greenville	NC	27858	252-328-6131	328-6640
Elizabeth City State University 1704 Weeksville Rd CB 901 *Fax: Admissions ■ *TF Admissions:* 800-347-3278 ■ *Web:* www.ecsu.edu	Elizabeth City	NC	27909	252-335-3305	335-3537*
Elon University 314 E Haggard Ave *TF:* 800-334-8448 ■ *Web:* www.elon.edu	Elon	NC	27244	336-278-2000	278-7699
Fayetteville State University 1200 Murchison Rd *Fax: Admissions ■ *TF Admissions:* 800-222-2594 ■ *Web:* www.uncfsu.edu	Fayetteville	NC	28301	910-672-1371	672-1414*
Gardner-Webb University PO Box 817 *Fax: Admissions ■ *TF:* 800-253-6472 ■ *Web:* www.gardner-webb.edu	Boiling Springs	NC	28017	704-406-4498	406-4488*
Greensboro College 815 W Market St *Fax: Admissions ■ *TF:* 800-346-8226 ■ *Web:* www.gborocollege.edu	Greensboro	NC	27401	336-272-7102	378-0154*
Guilford College 5800 W Friendly Ave *Fax: Admissions ■ *TF Admissions:* 800-992-7759 ■ *Web:* www.guilford.edu	Greensboro	NC	27410	336-316-2000	316-2954*
Heritage Bible College PO Box 1628 *Fax: Admissions ■ *TF:* 800-297-6351 ■ *Web:* www.heritagebiblecollege.org	Dunn	NC	28335	910-892-4268	891-1660*
High Point University 833 Montlieu Ave *Fax: Admissions ■ *TF:* 800-345-6993 ■ *Web:* www.highpoint.edu	High Point	NC	27262	336-841-9216	888-6382*
Johnson & Wales University Charlotte 801 W Trade St *Fax: Admissions ■ *TF:* 866-598-2427 ■ *Web:* www.jwu.edu	Charlotte	NC	28202	980-598-1100	598-1111*
Johnson C Smith University 100 Beatties Ford Rd *Fax: Admissions ■ *TF Admissions:* 800-782-7303 ■ *Web:* www.jcsu.edu	Charlotte	NC	28216	704-378-1000	378-1242*
Lees-McRae College 191 Main St W *TF:* 800-280-4562 ■ *Web:* www.lmc.edu	Banner Elk	NC	28604	828-898-5241	898-8707
Lenoir-Rhyne College 510 7th Ave NE PO Box 7227 *TF:* 800-277-5721 ■ *Web:* www.lrc.edu	Hickory	NC	28603	828-328-7300	328-7378
Livingstone College 701 W Monroe St *TF:* 800-835-3435 ■ *Web:* www.livingstone.edu	Salisbury	NC	28144	704-216-6000	216-6215
Mars Hill College 100 Athletics St *Fax: Admissions ■ *TF:* 866-642-4968 ■ *Web:* www.mhc.edu	Mars Hill	NC	28754	828-689-1201	689-1473*
Meredith College 3800 Hillsborough St *Fax: Admissions ■ *TF:* 800-637-3348 ■ *Web:* www.meredith.edu	Raleigh	NC	27607	919-760-8581	760-2348*
Methodist University 5400 Ramsey St *Fax: Admissions ■ *TF:* 800-488-7110 ■ *Web:* www.methodist.edu	Fayetteville	NC	28311	910-630-7000	630-7285*
Montreat College 310 Gaither Cir PO Box 1267 *TF:* 800-622-6968 ■ *Web:* www.montreat.edu	Montreat	NC	28757	828-669-8011	669-0120
Mount Olive College 634 Henderson St *Fax: Admissions ■ *TF:* 800-653-0854 ■ *Web:* www.moc.edu	Mount Olive	NC	28365	919-658-2502	658-9816*
North Carolina A & T State University 1601 E Market St *Fax: Admissions ■ *TF Admissions:* 800-443-8964 ■ *Web:* www.ncat.edu	Greensboro	NC	27411	336-334-7946	334-7478*
North Carolina Central University 1801 Fayetteville St *Fax: Admissions ■ *TF Admissions:* 877-667-7533 ■ *Web:* www.nccu.edu	Durham	NC	27707	919-530-6100	530-7625*
North Carolina State University 2200 Hillsborough St *Fax: Admissions ■ *TF:* 800-662-7301 ■ *Web:* www.ncsu.edu	Raleigh	NC	27695	919-515-2011	515-5039*
North Carolina Wesleyan College 3400 N Wesleyan Blvd *Fax: Admissions ■ *TF Admissions:* 800-488-6292 ■ *Web:* www.ncwc.edu	Rocky Mount	NC	27804	252-985-5100	985-5295*
Peace College 15 E Peace St *Fax: Admissions ■ *TF:* 800-732-2347 ■ *Web:* www.peace.edu	Raleigh	NC	27604	919-508-2000	508-2326*
Pfeiffer University 48380 Hwy 52 N *Fax: Admissions ■ *TF:* 800-338-2060 ■ *Web:* www.pfeiffer.edu	Misenheimer	NC	28109	704-463-1360	463-1363*
Piedmont Baptist College 420 S Broad St *Fax: Admissions ■ *TF Admissions:* 800-937-5097 ■ *Web:* www.pbc.edu	Winston-Salem	NC	27101	336-725-8344	725-5522*
Queens University of Charlotte 1900 Selwyn Ave *Fax: Admissions ■ *TF:* 800-849-0202 ■ *Web:* www.queens.edu	Charlotte	NC	28274	704-337-2212	337-2403*
Saint Andrews Presbyterian College 1700 Dogwood Mile *Fax: Admissions ■ *TF:* 800-763-0198 ■ *Web:* www.sapc.edu	Laurinburg	NC	28352	910-277-5000	277-5087*
Saint Augustine's College 1315 Oakwood Ave *Fax: Admissions ■ *TF Admissions:* 800-948-1126 ■ *Web:* www.st-aug.edu	Raleigh	NC	27610	919-516-4016	516-5805*
Salem College 601 S Church St *Fax: Admissions ■ *TF Admissions:* 800-327-2536 ■ *Web:* www.salem.edu	Winston-Salem	NC	27101	336-721-2600	917-5572*
Shaw University 118 E S St *Fax: Admissions ■ *TF Admissions:* 800-214-6683 ■ *Web:* www.shawu.edu	Raleigh	NC	27601	919-546-8275	546-8271*
University of North Carolina					
Asheville 1 University Heights CPO 1320 *Fax: Admissions ■ *TF:* 800-531-9842 ■ *Web:* www.unca.edu	Asheville	NC	28804	828-251-6481	251-6482*
Chapel Hill Jackson Hall CB 2200 *Fax: Admissions ■ *Web:* www.unc.edu	Chapel Hill	NC	27599	919-966-3621	962-3045*
Charlotte 9201 University City Blvd *Web:* www.uncc.edu	Charlotte	NC	28223	704-687-2000	687-6483
Greensboro 1400 Spring Garden St *TF:* 800-346-8226 ■ *Web:* www.uncg.edu	Greensboro	NC	27412	336-334-5000	334-4180
Pembroke PO Box 1510 *Fax: Admissions ■ *TF:* 800-949-8627 ■ *Web:* www.uncp.edu	Pembroke	NC	28372	910-521-6000	521-6497*
Wilmington 601 S College Rd *Fax: Admissions ■ *TF:* 800-228-5571 ■ *Web:* www.uncwil.edu	Wilmington	NC	28403	910-962-3000	962-3038*
Wake Forest University 1834 Wake Forest Rd *Fax: Admissions ■ *Web:* www.wfu.edu	Winston-Salem	NC	27106	336-758-5255	758-4324*
Warren Wilson College 701 Warren Wilson Rd *Fax: Admissions ■ *TF Admissions:* 800-934-3536 ■ *Web:* www.warren-wilson.edu	Swannanoa	NC	28778	828-298-3325	298-1440*
Western Carolina University (WCU) 1 University Dr *TF:* 877-928-4968 ■ *Web:* www.wcu.edu	Cullowhee	NC	28723	828-227-7211	227-7319
Wingate University 315 E Wilson St *TF:* 800-755-5550 ■ *Web:* www.wingate.edu	Wingate	NC	28174	704-233-8000	233-8110
Winston-Salem State University 601 S ML King Jr Dr 206 Thompson Ctr *Fax: Admissions ■ *TF Admissions:* 800-257-4052 ■ *Web:* www.wssu.edu	Winston-Salem	NC	27110	336-750-2000	750-2079*

NORTH DAKOTA

Institution	City	State	Zip	Phone	Fax
Dickinson State University 291 Campus Dr *Fax: Admissions ■ *TF:* 800-279-4295 ■ *Web:* www.dickinsonstate.com	Dickinson	ND	58601	701-483-2331	483-9959*
Jamestown College 6000 College Ln *TF:* 800-336-2554 ■ *Web:* www.jc.edu	Jamestown	ND	58405	701-252-3467	253-4318
Mayville State University 330 3rd St NE *Fax: Admissions ■ *TF:* 800-437-4104 ■ *Web:* www.masu.nodak.edu	Mayville	ND	58257	701-788-2301	788-4748*
Minot State University 500 University Ave W *TF:* 800-777-0750 ■ *Web:* www.minotstateu.edu	Minot	ND	58707	701-858-3000	858-3888
North Dakota State University 1301 12th Ave N *Fax: Admissions ■ *TF:* 800-488-6378 ■ *Web:* www.ndsu.edu	Fargo	ND	58105	701-231-8643	231-8802*
University of Mary 7500 University Dr *Fax: Admissions ■ *TF Admissions:* 800-288-6279 ■ *Web:* www.umary.edu	Bismarck	ND	58504	701-255-7500	255-7687*
University of North Dakota PO Box 8357 *Fax: Admissions ■ *TF:* 800-225-5863 ■ *Web:* www.und.nodak.edu	Grand Forks	ND	58202	701-777-2011	777-2721*
Valley City State University 101 College St SW *TF:* 800-532-8641 ■ *Web:* www.vcsu.edu	Valley City	ND	58072	701-845-7990	845-7299

OHIO

Institution	City	State	Zip	Phone	Fax
Ashland University 401 College Ave *TF:* 800-882-1548 ■ *Web:* www.ashland.edu	Ashland	OH	44805	419-289-4142	289-5999
Baldwin-Wallace College 275 Eastland Rd *Fax: Admissions ■ *TF:* 877-292-7759 ■ *Web:* www.bw.edu	Berea	OH	44017	440-826-2222	826-3830*
Bluffton University 1 University Dr *Fax: Admissions ■ *TF:* 800-488-3257 ■ *Web:* www.bluffton.edu	Bluffton	OH	45817	419-358-3000	358-3081*
Bowling Green State University 1001 E Wooster St *TF:* 866-246-6732 ■ *Web:* www.bgsu.edu	Bowling Green	OH	43403	419-372-2531	372-6955
Capital University College & Main St *Fax: Admissions ■ *TF:* 866-544-6175 ■ *Web:* www.capital.edu	Columbus	OH	43209	614-236-6101	236-6926*
Case Western Reserve University 2061 Cornell Rd *TF:* 800-967-8898 ■ *Web:* www.case.edu	Cleveland	OH	44106	216-368-2000	368-5111
Cedarville University 251 N Main St *Fax: Admissions ■ *TF:* 800-233-2784 ■ *Web:* www.cedarville.edu	Cedarville	OH	45314	937-766-7700	766-7575*
Central State University 1400 Brush Row Rd PO Box 1004 *Fax: Admissions ■ *TF:* 800-388-2781 ■ *Web:* www.centralstate.edu	Wilberforce	OH	45384	937-376-6011	376-6648*
Cleveland Institute of Music 11021 E Blvd *Web:* www.cim.edu	Cleveland	OH	44106	216-791-5000	791-3063
Cleveland State University 2121 Euclid Ave *Fax: Admissions ■ *TF:* 888-278-6446 ■ *Web:* www.csuohio.edu	Cleveland	OH	44115	216-687-2000	687-9210*
College of Mount Saint Joseph 5701 Delhi Rd *TF:* 800-654-9314 ■ *Web:* www.msj.edu	Cincinnati	OH	45233	513-244-4200	244-4601
College of Wooster 1189 Beall Ave *TF:* 800-877-9905 ■ *Web:* www.wooster.edu	Wooster	OH	44691	330-263-2000	263-2621
Defiance College 701 N Clinton St *Fax: Admissions ■ *TF:* 800-520-4632 ■ *Web:* www.defiance.edu	Defiance	OH	43512	419-784-4010	783-2468*
Denison University 100 Chapel St *Fax: Admissions ■ *TF:* 800-336-4766 ■ *Web:* www.denison.edu	Granville	OH	43023	740-587-0810	587-6306*
Franklin University 201 S Grant Ave *TF:* 877-341-6300 ■ *Web:* www.franklin.edu	Columbus	OH	43215	614-797-4700	947-6729
Hebrew Union College Cincinnati 3101 Clifton Ave *Fax: Admissions ■ *Web:* www.huc.edu	Cincinnati	OH	45220	513-221-1875	221-0321*
Heidelberg College 310 E Market St *Fax: Admissions ■ *TF Admissions:* 800-434-3352 ■ *Web:* www.heidelberg.edu	Tiffin	OH	44883	419-448-2000	448-2334*
Hiram College PO Box 67 *Fax: Admissions ■ *TF Admissions:* 800-362-5280 ■ *Web:* www.hiram.edu	Hiram	OH	44234	330-569-5169	569-5944*
John Carroll University 20700 N Pk Blvd *Fax: Admissions ■ *TF:* 888-335-6800 ■ *Web:* www.jcu.edu	University Heights	OH	44118	216-397-1886	397-4981*
Kent State University 1500 Summit St PO Box 5190 *Fax: Admissions ■ *TF:* 800-988-5368 ■ *Web:* www.kent.edu	Kent	OH	44242	330-672-2121	672-2499*
East Liverpool 400 E 4th St *Fax: Admissions ■ *Web:* www.kenteliv.kent.edu	East Liverpool	OH	43920	330-385-3805	382-7566*

	City	State	Zip	Phone	Fax
Salem 2491 SR-45 S	Salem	OH	44460	330-332-0361	337-4122*
*Fax: Admissions ■ *Web:* www.salem.kent.edu					
Stark 6000 Frank Ave NW	North Canton	OH	44720	330-499-9600	499-0301*
*Fax: Admissions ■ *Web:* www.stark.kent.edu					
Trumbull Campus 4314 Mahoning Ave NW	Warren	OH	44483	330-847-0571	675-8888*
*Fax: Admissions ■ *Web:* www.trumbull.kent.edu					
Tuscarawas 330 University Dr NE	New Philadelphia	OH	44663	330-339-3391	339-3321*
*Fax: Admissions ■ *Web:* www.tusc.kent.edu					
Kenyon College 103 College Dr	Gambier	OH	43022	740-427-5000	427-5770
TF: 800-848-2468 ■ *Web:* www.kenyon.edu					
Lake Erie College 391 W Washington St	Painesville	OH	44077	440-375-7050	375-7005*
*Fax: Admissions ■ *TF:* 800-533-4996 ■ *Web:* www.lec.edu					
Lourdes College 6832 Convent Blvd	Sylvania	OH	43560	419-885-5291	882-3987*
*Fax: Admissions ■ *TF:* 800-878-3210 ■ *Web:* www.lourdes.edu					
Malone College 515 25th St NW	Canton	OH	44709	330-471-8100	471-8149*
*Fax: Admissions ■ *TF:* 800-521-1146 ■ *Web:* www.malone.edu					
Marietta College 215 5th St	Marietta	OH	45750	740-376-4000	376-8888*
*Fax: Admissions ■ *TF Admissions:* 800-331-7896 ■ *Web:* www.marietta.edu					
Miami University 501 E High St	Oxford	OH	45056	513-529-1809	529-1550*
*Fax: Admissions ■ *Web:* www.miami.muohio.edu					
Middletown 4200 E University Blvd	Middletown	OH	45042	513-727-3200	727-3223
TF: 866-426-4643 ■ *Web:* www.mid.muohio.edu					
Mount Union College 1972 Clark Ave	Alliance	OH	44601	330-823-2590	823-5097*
*Fax: Admissions ■ *TF Admissions:* 800-334-6682 ■ *Web:* www.muc.edu					
Mount Vernon Nazarene University					
800 Martinsburg Rd	Mount Vernon	OH	43050	740-392-6868	
TF Admissions: 866-782-2435 ■ *Web:* www.mvnu.edu					
Muskingum College 163 Stormont St	New Concord	OH	43762	740-826-8211	826-8100*
*Fax: Admissions ■ *TF Admissions:* 800-752-6082 ■ *Web:* www.muskingum.edu					
Myers University 3921 Chester Ave	Cleveland	OH	44114	216-391-6937	361-9274*
*Fax: Admissions ■ *TF:* 877-366-9377 ■ *Web:* www.myers.edu					
Notre Dame College of Ohio					
4545 College Rd	South Euclid	OH	44121	216-381-1680	373-5278*
*Fax: Admissions ■ *TF:* 877-632-6446 ■ *Web:* www.ndc.edu					
Oberlin College 101 N Professor St	Oberlin	OH	44074	440-775-8121	775-6905
Web: www.oberlin.edu					
Ohio Dominican University 1216 Sunbury Rd	Columbus	OH	43219	614-251-4500	251-0156*
*Fax: Admissions ■ *TF:* 800-955-6446 ■ *Web:* www.ohiodominican.edu					
Ohio Northern University 525 S Main St	Ada	OH	45810	419-772-2000	772-2313*
*Fax: Admissions ■ *TF Admissions:* 888-408-4668 ■ *Web:* www.onu.edu					
Ohio State University 154 W 12th Ave	Columbus	OH	43210	614-292-3980	292-4818*
*Fax: Admissions ■ *Web:* www.osu.edu					
Lima 4240 Campus Dr	Lima	OH	45804	419-995-8600	995-8483
Web: www.lima.osu.edu					
Mansfield 1760 University Dr	Mansfield	OH	44906	419-755-4011	755-3091*
*Fax: Admissions ■ *Web:* mansfield.osu.edu					
Marion 1465 Mt Vernon Ave	Marion	OH	43302	614-292-9133	292-5817*
*Fax: Admissions ■ *Web:* www.marion.ohio-state.edu					
Newark 1179 University Dr	Newark	OH	43055	740-366-9333	364-9645*
*Fax: Admissions ■ *TF:* 800-963-9275 ■ *Web:* newark.osu.edu					
Ohio University 120 Chubb Hall	Athens	OH	45710	740-593-1000	593-0560*
*Fax: Admissions ■ *Web:* www.ohio.edu					
Chillicothe 101 University Dr	Chillicothe	OH	45601	740-774-7200	774-7214*
*Fax: Admissions ■ *TF:* 877-462-6824 ■ *Web:* www.oucweb.chillicothe.ohiou.edu					
Eastern 45425 National Rd	Saint Clairsville	OH	43950	740-695-1720	695-7079*
*Fax: Admissions ■ *TF:* 800-648-3331 ■ *Web:* www.eastern.ohiou.edu					
Lancaster 1570 Granville Pike	Lancaster	OH	43130	740-654-6711	687-9497*
*Fax: Admissions ■ *Web:* www.lancaster.ohiou.edu					
Southern 1804 Liberty Ave	Ironton	OH	45638	740-533-4600	533-4632*
*Fax: Admissions ■ *TF:* 800-626-0513 ■ *Web:* www.southern.ohiou.edu					
Zanesville 1425 Newark Rd	Zanesville	OH	43701	740-453-0762	453-6161
Web: www.zanesville.ohiou.edu					
Ohio Wesleyan University					
61 S Sandusky St Slocum Hall	Delaware	OH	43015	740-368-3020	368-3314*
*Fax: Admissions ■ *Web:* web.owu.edu					
Otterbein College 1 Otterbein College	Westerville	OH	43081	614-823-1500	823-1200*
*Fax: Admissions ■ *TF Admissions:* 800-488-8144 ■ *Web:* www.otterbein.edu					
Shawnee State University 940 2nd St	Portsmouth	OH	45662	740-351-3221	351-3111
TF: 800-959-2778 ■ *Web:* www.shawnee.edu					
Tiffin University 155 Miami St	Tiffin	OH	44883	419-447-6442	443-5006
TF: 800-968-6446 ■ *Web:* www.tiffin.edu					
Union Institute & University					
440 E McMillan St	Cincinnati	OH	45206	513-861-6400	861-0779*
*Fax: Admissions ■ *TF:* 800-486-3116 ■ *Web:* www.tui.edu					
University of Akron 277 E Buchtel Ave	Akron	OH	44325	330-972-7100	972-7022
TF Admissions: 800-655-4884 ■ *Web:* www.uakron.edu					
University of Cincinnati					
2600 Clifton Ave PO Box 210091	Cincinnati	OH	45221	513-556-1100	556-1105*
*Fax: Admissions ■ *Web:* www.uc.edu					
University of Dayton 300 College Pk	Dayton	OH	45469	937-229-4411	229-4729*
*Fax: Admissions ■ *TF:* 800-837-7433 ■ *Web:* www.udayton.edu					
University of Findlay 1000 N Main St	Findlay	OH	45840	419-422-8313	434-4822
TF: 800-472-9502 ■ *Web:* www.findlay.edu					
University of Rio Grande					
218 N College Ave	Rio Grande	OH	45674	740-245-5353	245-7260*
*Fax: Admissions ■ *TF:* 800-282-7201 ■ *Web:* www.rio.edu					
University of Toledo 2801 W Bancroft St	Toledo	OH	43606	419-530-4636	530-5745*
*Fax: Admissions ■ *TF:* 800-586-5336 ■ *Web:* www.utoledo.edu					
Urbana University 579 College Way	Urbana	OH	43078	937-484-1400	652-6871*
*Fax: Admissions ■ *TF:* 800-787-2262 ■ *Web:* www.urbana.edu					
Ursuline College 2550 Lander Rd	Pepper Pike	OH	44124	440-449-4200	684-6138*
*Fax: Admissions ■ *TF:* 888-877-8546 ■ *Web:* www.ursuline.edu					
Walsh University 2020 E Maple St	North Canton	OH	44720	330-499-7090	490-7165*
*Fax: Admissions ■ *TF Admissions:* 800-362-9846 ■ *Web:* www.walsh.edu					
Wilberforce University					
1055 N Bickett Rd PO Box 1001	Wilberforce	OH	45384	937-376-2911	376-4751*
*Fax: Admissions ■ *TF Admissions:* 800-367-8568 ■ *Web:* www.wilberforce.edu					
Wilmington College of Ohio					
1870 Quaker Way	Wilmington	OH	45177	937-382-6661	383-8542*
*Fax: Admissions ■ *TF:* 800-341-9318 ■ *Web:* www.wilmington.edu					
Wittenberg University					
200 W Ward St PO Box 720	Springfield	OH	45501	937-327-6314	327-6379*
*Fax: Admissions ■ *TF:* 800-677-7558 ■ *Web:* www.wittenberg.edu					
Wright State University					
3640 Colonel Glenn Hwy	Dayton	OH	45435	937-775-5740	775-5795*
*Fax: Admissions ■ *TF Admissions:* 800-247-1770 ■ *Web:* www.wright.edu					
Xavier University 3800 Victory Pkwy	Cincinnati	OH	45207	513-745-3000	745-4319*
*Fax: Admissions ■ *TF:* 800-344-4698 ■ *Web:* www.xavier.edu					
Youngstown State University					
1 University Plaza	Youngstown	OH	44555	330-941-3000	941-3694*
*Fax: Admissions ■ *TF Admissions:* 877-468-6978 ■ *Web:* www.ysu.edu					
Ashtabula 3300 Lake Rd W	Ashtabula	OH	44004	440-964-3322	964-4269*
*Fax: Admissions ■ *Web:* www.ashtabula.kent.edu					

OKLAHOMA

	City	State	Zip	Phone	Fax
Bacone College 2299 Old Bacone Rd	Muskogee	OK	74403	918-683-4581	781-7416*
*Fax: Admissions ■ *TF Admissions:* 888-682-5514 ■ *Web:* www.bacone.edu					
Cameron University 2800 W Gore Blvd	Lawton	OK	73505	580-581-2289	581-5514*
*Fax: Admissions ■ *TF Admissions:* 888-454-7600 ■ *Web:* www.cameron.edu					
East Central University 1100 E 14th St	Ada	OK	74820	580-332-8000	310-5432*
*Fax: Admissions ■ *Web:* www.ecok.edu					
Hillsdale Free Will Baptist College					
PO Box 7208	Moore	OK	73153	405-912-9000	912-9050*
*Fax: Admissions ■ *Web:* www.hc.edu					
Langston University Hwy 33 PO Box 1500	Langston	OK	73050	405-466-3428	466-3391
TF: 877-466-2231 ■ *Web:* www.lunet.edu					
Mid-America Christian University					
3500 SW 119th St	Oklahoma City	OK	73170	405-691-3800	692-3165*
*Fax: Admissions ■ *Web:* www.macu.edu					
Broken Arrow 3100 E New Orleans	Broken Arrow	OK	74014	918-449-6000	449-6190*
*Fax: Admissions ■ *TF:* 800-772-9614 ■ *Web:* www.nsuba.edu					
Muskogee 2400 W Shawnee	Muskogee	OK	74401	918-683-0040	458-2106
TF: 800-722-9614 ■ *Web:* www.nsuok.edu					
Tahlequah 600 N Grand Ave	Tahlequah	OK	74464	918-456-5511	458-2342
TF: 800-722-9614 ■ *Web:* www.nsuok.edu					
Northwestern Oklahoma State University					
709 Oklahoma Blvd	Alva	OK	73717	580-327-1700	327-8699
Web: www.nwalva.edu					
Oklahoma Baptist University					
500 W University St	Shawnee	OK	74804	405-275-2850	878-2068*
*Fax: Admissions ■ *TF:* 800-654-3285 ■ *Web:* www.okbu.edu					
Oklahoma Christian University					
PO Box 11000	Oklahoma City	OK	73136	405-425-5000	425-5069*
*Fax: Admissions ■ *TF:* 800-877-5010 ■ *Web:* www.oc.edu					
Oklahoma City University					
2501 N Blackwelder Ave	Oklahoma City	OK	73106	405-208-5050	208-5916*
*Fax: Admissions ■ *TF Admissions:* 800-633-7242 ■ *Web:* www.okcu.edu					
Oklahoma Panhandle State University					
323 Eagle Blvd	Goodwell	OK	73939	580-349-2611	349-2302*
*Fax: Admitting ■ *TF:* 800-664-6778 ■ *Web:* www.opsu.edu					
Oklahoma State University					
219 Student Union Bldg	Stillwater	OK	74078	405-744-5000	744-7092
TF: 800-852-1255 ■ *Web:* www.okstate.edu					
Tulsa 700 N Greenwood Ave	Tulsa	OK	74106	918-594-8000	594-8202
TF: 800-364-0710 ■ *Web:* www.osu-tulsa.okstate.edu					
Oklahoma Wesleyan University					
2201 Silver Lake Rd	Bartlesville	OK	74006	918-333-6200	335-6229*
*Fax: Admissions ■ *TF:* 800-468-6292 ■ *Web:* www.okwu.edu					
Oral Roberts University 7777 S Lewis Ave	Tulsa	OK	74171	918-495-6161	495-6222*
*Fax: Admissions ■ *TF:* 800-678-8876 ■ *Web:* www.oru.edu					
Rogers State University					
1701 W Will Rogers Blvd	Claremore	OK	74017	918-343-7546	343-7595*
*Fax: Admissions ■ *TF:* 800-256-7511 ■ *Web:* www.rsu.edu					
Saint Gregory's University					
1900 W MacArthur St	Shawnee	OK	74804	405-878-5100	878-5198
TF Admissions: 888-784-7347 ■ *Web:* www.stgregorys.edu					
Southeastern Oklahoma State University					
1405 N 4th St	Durant	OK	74701	580-745-2000	745-7502*
*Fax: Admissions ■ *TF:* 800-435-1327 ■ *Web:* www.se.edu					
Southern Nazarene University					
6729 NW 39th Expy	Bethany	OK	73008	405-789-6400	491-6320*
*Fax: Admissions ■ *TF:* 800-648-9899 ■ *Web:* www.snu.edu					
Southwestern Christian University					
7210 NW 39th Expy PO Box 340	Bethany	OK	73008	405-789-7661	495-0078*
*Fax: Admissions ■ *TF:* 888-418-9272 ■ *Web:* www.swcu.edu					
Southwestern College 100 Campus Dr	Weatherford	OK	73096	580-772-6611	774-3795
Web: www.swosu.edu					
University of Central Oklahoma					
100 N University Dr	Edmond	OK	73034	405-974-2000	974-3841*
*Fax: Admissions ■ *Web:* www.ucok.edu					
University of Oklahoma 1000 Asp Ave	Norman	OK	73019	405-325-0311	325-7124
TF: 877-522-0772 ■ *Web:* www.ou.edu					
University of Sciences & Arts of Oklahoma					
1727 W Alabama Ave	Chickasha	OK	73018	405-224-3140	574-1220*
*Fax: Admissions ■ *TF:* 800-933-8726 ■ *Web:* www.usao.edu					
University of Tulsa 800 S Tucker Rd	Tulsa	OK	74104	918-631-2307	631-5003*
*Fax: Admissions ■ *TF:* 800-331-3050 ■ *Web:* www.utulsa.edu					

OREGON

	City	State	Zip	Phone	Fax
Concordia University Portland					
2811 NE Holman St	Portland	OR	97211	503-288-9371	280-8531*
*Fax: Admissions ■ *TF:* 800-321-9371 ■ *Web:* www.cu-portland.edu					
Corban College 5000 Deer Pk Dr SE	Salem	OR	97317	503-581-8600	585-4316
TF: 800-845-3005 ■ *Web:* www.corban.edu					

				Phone	Fax
Eastern Oregon University 1 University Blvd	La Grande	OR	97850	541-962-3393	962-3418*
*Fax: Admissions ■ TF: 800-452-8639 ■ Web: www.eou.edu					
George Fox University 414 N Meridian St	Newberg	OR	97132	503-538-8383	554-3110*
*Fax: Admissions ■ TF: 800-765-4369 ■ Web: www.georgefox.edu					
Gutenberg College 1883 University St	Eugene	OR	97403	541-683-5141	683-6997
Web: www.gutenberg.edu					
Lewis & Clark College 0615 SW Palatine Hill Rd	Portland	OR	97219	503-768-7040	768-7055*
*Fax: Admissions ■ TF Admissions: 800-444-4111 ■ Web: www.lclark.edu					
Linfield College 900 SE Baker St	McMinnville	OR	97128	503-883-2213	883-2472*
*Fax: Admissions ■ TF Admissions: 800-640-2287 ■ Web: www.linfield.edu					
Marylhurst University 17600 Pacific Hwy 43 PO Box 261	Marylhurst	OR	97036	503-636-8141	635-6585*
*Fax: Admissions ■ TF: 800-634-9982 ■ Web: www.marylhurst.edu					
Northwest Christian College 828 E 11th Ave	Eugene	OR	97401	541-684-7201	684-7317*
*Fax: Admissions ■ TF: 877-463-6622 ■ Web: www.nwcc.edu					
Oregon Health & Science University Hospital 3181 SW Sam Jackson Pk Rd	Portland	OR	97239	503-494-8311	494-3400
Web: www.ohsu.edu					
Oregon Institute of Technology 3201 Campus Dr	Klamath Falls	OR	97601	541-885-1150	885-1024*
*Fax: Admissions ■ TF: 800-422-2017 ■ Web: www.oit.edu					
Oregon State University 104 Kerr Administration Bldg	Corvallis	OR	97331	541-737-4411	737-2482
TF: 800-291-4192 ■ Web: www.oregonstate.edu					
Pacific Northwest College of Art 1241 NW Johnson St	Portland	OR	97209	503-226-4391	821-8978
TF: 888-390-7499 ■ Web: www.pnca.edu					
Pacific University 2043 College Way	Forest Grove	OR	97116	503-352-2794	352-2975*
*Fax: Admissions ■ TF Admissions: 800-677-6712 ■ Web: www.pacificu.edu					
Portland State University 1825 SW Broadway	Portland	OR	97201	503-725-3000	725-5525
TF: 800-547-8887 ■ Web: www.pdx.edu					
Reed College 3203 SE Woodstock Blvd	Portland	OR	97202	503-777-7511	777-7553
TF Admissions: 800-547-4750 ■ Web: www.reed.edu					
Southern Oregon University 1250 Siskiyou Blvd Britt Hall	Ashland	OR	97520	541-552-6411	552-8403*
*Fax: Admissions ■ TF: 800-482-7672 ■ Web: www.sou.edu					
University of Oregon 1585 E 13th Ave	Eugene	OR	97403	541-346-1000	346-5815*
*Fax: Admissions ■ TF Admissions: 800-232-3825 ■ Web: www.uoregon.edu					
University of Portland 5000 N Willamette Blvd	Portland	OR	97203	503-943-7147	943-7315*
*Fax: Admissions ■ TF: 888-627-5601 ■ Web: www.up.edu					
Warner Pacific College 2219 SE 68th Ave	Portland	OR	97215	503-517-1020	517-1352
TF: 800-804-1510 ■ Web: www.warnerpacific.edu					
Western Oregon University 345 Monmouth Ave N	Monmouth	OR	97361	503-838-8000	838-8067
TF Admissions: 877-877-1593 ■ Web: www.wou.edu					
Willamette University 900 State St	Salem	OR	97301	503-370-6303	375-5363*
*Fax: Admissions ■ TF: 877-542-2787 ■ Web: www.willamette.edu					

PENNSYLVANIA

				Phone	Fax
Albright College 1621 N 13th St	Reading	PA	19604	610-921-2381	921-7294
TF: 800-252-1856 ■ Web: www.albright.edu					
Allegheny College 520 N Main St	Meadville	PA	16335	814-332-4351	337-0431
TF: 800-521-5293 ■ Web: www.allegheny.edu					
Alvernia College 540 Upland Ave	Reading	PA	19611	610-796-8200	790-2873
TF: 888-258-3764 ■ Web: www.alvernia.edu					
Arcadia University 450 S Easton Rd	Glenside	PA	19038	215-572-2900	881-8767*
*Fax: Admissions ■ TF: 888-232-8373 ■ Web: www.arcadia.edu					
Bloomsburg University 400 E 2nd St	Bloomsburg	PA	17815	570-389-3900	389-4741*
*Fax: Admissions ■ TF: 800-745-7320 ■ Web: www.bloomu.edu					
Bryn Mawr College 101 N Merion Ave	Bryn Mawr	PA	19010	610-526-5000	526-7471*
*Fax: Admissions ■ TF Admissions: 800-262-1885 ■ Web: www.brynmawr.edu					
Bucknell University 701 Moore Ave	Lewisburg	PA	17837	570-577-2000	577-1345*
*Fax: Admissions ■ Web: www.bucknell.edu					
Cabrini College 610 King of Prussia Rd	Radnor	PA	19087	610-902-8552	902-8508*
*Fax: Acctg ■ TF: 800-848-1003 ■ Web: www.cabrini.edu					
California University of Pennsylvania 250 University Ave	California	PA	15419	724-938-4000	938-4564
Web: www.cup.edu					
Carlow University 3333 5th Ave	Pittsburgh	PA	15213	412-578-6000	578-6689
TF: 800-333-2275 ■ Web: www.carlow.edu					
Carnegie Mellon University 5000 Forbes Ave	Pittsburgh	PA	15213	412-268-2000	268-7838*
*Fax: Admissions ■ Web: www.cmu.edu					
Cedar Crest College 100 College Dr	Allentown	PA	18104	610-437-4471	606-4647*
*Fax: Admissions ■ TF Admissions: 800-360-1222 ■ Web: www.cedarcrest.edu					
Chatham University 5700 W Woodland Rd	Pittsburgh	PA	15232	412-365-1100	365-1609
TF: 800-837-1290 ■ Web: www.chatham.edu					
Chestnut Hill College 9601 Germantown Ave	Philadelphia	PA	19118	215-248-7001	248-7082*
*Fax: Admissions ■ TF: 800-248-0052 ■ Web: www.chc.edu					
Cheyney University of Pennsylvania 1837 University Cir PO Box 200	Cheyney	PA	19319	610-399-2275	399-2099*
*Fax: Admissions ■ TF: 800-243-9639 ■ Web: www.cheyney.edu					
Clarion University of Pennsylvania 840 Wood St	Clarion	PA	16214	814-393-2306	393-2030*
*Fax: Admissions ■ TF: 800-672-7171 ■ Web: www.clarion.edu					
Venango 1801 W 1st St	Oil City	PA	16301	814-676-6591	676-1348
TF: 800-672-7171 ■ Web: www.clarion.edu					
Curtis Institute of Music 1726 Locust St	Philadelphia	PA	19103	215-893-5252	893-9065
Web: www.curtis.edu					
Delaware Valley College 700 E Butler Ave	Doylestown	PA	18901	215-489-2211	230-2968
TF Admissions: 800-233-5825 ■ Web: www.devalcol.edu					
DeSales University 2755 Stn Ave	Center Valley	PA	18034	610-282-1100	282-0131
TF: 877-433-7253 ■ Web: www.desales.edu					
Dickinson College PO Box 1773	Carlisle	PA	17013	717-243-5121	245-1442*
*Fax: Admissions ■ TF: 800-644-1773 ■ Web: www.dickinson.edu					
Drexel University 3141 Chestnut St	Philadelphia	PA	19104	215-895-2000	895-5939*
*Fax: Admissions ■ TF Admissions: 800-237-3935 ■ Web: www.drexel.edu					
Duquesne University 600 Forbes Ave	Pittsburgh	PA	15282	412-396-6000	396-6223*
*Fax: Admissions ■ TF: 800-456-0590 ■ Web: www.duq.edu					
East Stroudsburg University 200 Prospect St	East Stroudsburg	PA	18301	570-422-3542	422-3933*
*Fax: Admissions ■ TF Admissions: 877-230-5547 ■ Web: www.esu.edu					
Eastern University 1300 Eagle Rd	Saint Davids	PA	19087	610-341-5800	341-1723*
*Fax: Admissions ■ TF Admissions: 800-452-0996 ■ Web: www.eastern.edu					
Edinboro University of Pennsylvania 200 E Normal St	Edinboro	PA	16444	814-732-2761	732-2420*
*Fax: Admissions ■ TF: 888-846-2676 ■ Web: www.edinboro.edu					
Elizabethtown College 1 Alpha Dr	Elizabethtown	PA	17022	717-361-1000	361-1365*
*Fax: Admissions ■ Web: www.etown.edu					
Franklin & Marshall College PO Box 3003	Lancaster	PA	17604	717-291-3951	291-4389*
*Fax: Admissions ■ TF: 877-678-9111 ■ Web: www.fandm.edu					
Gannon University 109 University Sq	Erie	PA	16541	814-871-7000	871-5803
TF Admissions: 800-426-6668 ■ Web: www.gannon.edu					
Geneva College 3200 College Ave	Beaver Falls	PA	15010	724-847-6500	847-6776*
*Fax: Admissions ■ TF: 800-847-8255 ■ Web: www.geneva.edu					
Gettysburg College 300 N Washington St	Gettysburg	PA	17325	717-337-6000	337-6145*
*Fax: Admissions ■ TF: 800-431-0803 ■ Web: www.gettysburg.edu					
Gratz College 7605 Old York Rd	Melrose Park	PA	19027	215-635-7300	635-7320*
*Fax: Admissions ■ TF: 800-475-4635 ■ Web: www.gratz.edu					
Grove City College 100 Campus Dr	Grove City	PA	16127	724-458-2000	458-3395*
*Fax: Admissions ■ Web: www.gcc.edu					
Gwynedd-Mercy College 1325 Sunneytown Pike PO Box 901	Gwynedd Valley	PA	19437	215-646-7300	641-5556*
*Fax: Admissions ■ TF Admissions: 800-342-5462 ■ Web: www.gmc.edu					
Haverford College 370 Lancaster Ave	Haverford	PA	19041	610-896-1000	896-1338
Web: www.haverford.edu					
Holy Family University 9801 Frankford Ave	Philadelphia	PA	19114	215-637-7700	281-1022*
*Fax: Admissions ■ TF: 877-438-4643 ■ Web: www.hfc.edu					
Immaculata University 1145 King Rd	Immaculata	PA	19345	610-647-4400	640-0836*
*Fax: Admissions ■ TF: 877-428-6329 ■ Web: www.immaculata.edu					
Indiana University of Pennsylvania Sutton Hall 1011 S Dr Suite 117	Indiana	PA	15705	724-357-2230	357-6281*
*Fax: Admissions ■ TF: 800-442-6830 ■ Web: www.iup.edu					
Juniata College 1700 Moore St	Huntingdon	PA	16652	814-641-3000	641-3100*
*Fax: Admissions ■ TF: 877-586-4282 ■ Web: www.juniata.edu					
Keystone College 1 College Green	La Plume	PA	18440	570-945-8000	945-7916*
*Fax: Admissions ■ TF: 800-824-2764					
King's College 133 N River St	Wilkes-Barre	PA	18711	570-208-5858	208-5971*
*Fax: Admissions ■ TF: 800-955-5777 ■ Web: www.kings.edu					
Kutztown University 15200 Kutztown Rd	Kutztown	PA	19530	610-683-4000	683-1375
TF: 877-628-1915 ■ Web: www.kutztown.edu					
La Roche College 9000 Babcock Blvd	Pittsburgh	PA	15237	412-367-9300	536-1048*
*Fax: Admissions ■ TF Admissions: 800-838-4572 ■ Web: www.laroche.edu					
La Salle University 1900 W Olney Ave	Philadelphia	PA	19141	215-951-1500	951-1656*
*Fax: Admissions ■ TF: 800-328-1910 ■ Web: www.lasalle.edu					
Lafayette College 730 High St	Easton	PA	18042	610-330-5000	330-5355*
*Fax: Admissions ■ Web: www.lafayette.edu					
Lebanon Valley College 101 N College Ave	Annville	PA	17003	717-867-6181	867-6026*
*Fax: Admissions ■ TF: 866-582-4236 ■ Web: www.lvc.edu					
Lehigh University 27 Memorial Dr W	Bethlehem	PA	18015	610-758-3000	758-4361*
*Fax: Admissions ■ Web: www.lehigh.edu					
Lincoln University 1570 Old Baltimore Pike PO Box 179	Lincoln University	PA	19352	484-365-8000	365-8109*
*Fax: Admissions ■ TF Admissions: 800-790-0191 ■ Web: www.lincoln.edu					
Lock Haven University 401 N Fairview St	Lock Haven	PA	17745	570-484-2011	484-2201*
*Fax: Admissions ■ TF: 800-233-8978 ■ Web: www.lhup.edu					
Lycoming College 700 College Pl	Williamsport	PA	17701	570-321-4000	321-4317*
*Fax: Admissions ■ TF: 800-345-3920 ■ Web: www.lycoming.edu					
Mansfield University Alumni Hall	Mansfield	PA	16933	570-662-4000	662-4121
TF Admissions: 800-577-6826 ■ Web: www.mansfield.edu					
Marywood University 2300 Adams Ave	Scranton	PA	18509	570-348-6234	961-4763*
*Fax: Admissions ■ TF: 866-279-9663 ■ Web: www.marywood.edu					
Mercyhurst College 501 E 38th St	Erie	PA	16546	814-824-2202	824-3634*
*Fax: Admissions ■ TF: 800-825-1926 ■ Web: www.mercyhurst.edu					
Messiah College PO Box 3005	Grantham	PA	17027	717-691-6000	796-5374*
*Fax: Admissions ■ TF: 800-233-4220 ■ Web: www.messiah.edu					
Millersville University of Pennsylvania PO Box 1002	Millersville	PA	17551	717-872-3011	871-2147*
*Fax: Admissions ■ TF: 800-682-3648 ■ Web: www.muweb.millersville.edu					
Misericordia University 301 Lake St	Dallas	PA	18612	570-674-6400	675-2441*
*Fax: Admissions ■ TF: 866-262-6363 ■ Web: www.misericordia.edu					
Moravian College 1200 Main St	Bethlehem	PA	18018	610-861-1300	625-7930*
*Fax: Admissions ■ Web: www.moravian.edu					
Mount Aloysius College 7373 Admiral Perry Hwy	Cresson	PA	16630	814-886-6383	886-6441
TF: 888-823-2220 ■ Web: www.mtaloy.edu					
Muhlenberg College 2400 Chew St	Allentown	PA	18104	484-664-3100	664-3234
Web: www.muhlberg.edu					
Neumann College 1 Neumann Dr	Aston	PA	19014	610-459-0905	459-1370*
*Fax: Admissions ■ TF: 800-963-8626 ■ Web: www.neumann.edu					
Peirce College 1420 Pine St	Philadelphia	PA	19102	215-545-6400	670-9366*
*Fax: Admissions ■ TF: 888-467-3472 ■ Web: www.peirce.edu					
Pennsylvania State University 201 Shields Bldg Office of Admissions	University Park	PA	16802	814-865-4700	863-7590
Web: www.psu.edu					
Abington College 1600 Woodland Rd	Abington	PA	19001	215-881-7300	881-7412*
*Fax: Admissions ■ Web: www.abington.psu.edu					
Altoona 3000 Ivyside Pk	Altoona	PA	16601	814-949-5466	949-5564*
*Fax: Admissions ■ TF: 800-848-9843 ■ Web: www.aa.psu.edu					
Brandywine 25 Yearsley Mill Rd	Media	PA	19063	610-892-1200	892-1357*
*Fax: Admissions ■ Web: www.brandywine.psu.edu					
Harrisburg 777 W Harrisburg Pike	Middletown	PA	17057	717-948-6250	948-6325*
*Fax: Admissions ■ TF: 800-222-2056 ■ Web: www.hbg.psu.edu					

	City	State	Zip	Phone	Fax
Pennsylvania State University at Erie *Behrend College* 4701 College Dr *Fax: Admissions ■ TF: 866-374-3378 ■ Web: www.pserie.psu.edu	Erie	PA	16563	814-898-6000	898-6044*
Philadelphia University 4201 Henry Ave. *Fax: Admissions ■ TF Admissions: 800-951-7287 ■ Web: www.philau.edu	Philadelphia	PA	19144	215-951-2800	951-2907*
Point Park University 201 Wood St. *Fax: Admissions ■ TF Admissions: 800-321-0129 ■ Web: www.pointpark.edu	Pittsburgh	PA	15222	412-391-4100	392-3902*
Robert Morris University 6001 University Blvd TF: 800-762-0097 ■ Web: www.rmu.edu	Moon Township	PA	15108	412-262-8200	397-2425
Rosemont College 1400 Montgomery Ave *Fax: Admissions ■ TF Admissions: 800-331-0708 ■ Web: www.rosemont.edu	Rosemont	PA	19010	610-527-0200	520-4399*
Saint Francis University 167 Lakeview Dr *Fax: Admissions ■ TF: 866-342-5738 ■ Web: www.saintfrancisuniversity.edu	Loretto	PA	15940	814-472-3000	472-3335*
Saint Joseph's University 5600 City Ave *Fax: Admissions ■ TF: 888-232-4295 ■ Web: www.sju.edu	Philadelphia	PA	19131	610-660-1000	660-1314*
Saint Vincent College 300 Fraser Purchase Rd. *Fax: Admissions ■ TF: 800-782-5549 ■ Web: www.stvincent.edu	Latrobe	PA	15650	724-532-6600	805-2953*
Seton Hill University 1 Seton Hill Dr *Fax: Admissions ■ TF: 800-826-6234 ■ Web: www.setonhill.edu	Greensburg	PA	15601	724-838-4255	830-1294*
Shippensburg University 1871 Old Main Dr *Fax: Admissions ■ TF: 800-822-8028 ■ Web: www.ship.edu	Shippensburg	PA	17257	717-477-1231	477-4016*
Slippery Rock University 1 Morrow Way *Fax: Admissions ■ TF: 800-929-4778 ■ Web: www.sru.edu	Slippery Rock	PA	16057	724-738-9000	738-2913*
Susquehanna University 514 University Ave TF: 800-326-9672 ■ Web: www.susqu.edu	Selinsgrove	PA	17870	570-374-0101	372-2722
Swarthmore College 500 College Ave *Fax: Admissions ■ TF Admissions: 800-667-3110 ■ Web: www.swarthmore.edu	Swarthmore	PA	19081	610-328-8300	328-8580*
Temple University 1801 N Broad St Web: www.temple.edu	Philadelphia	PA	19122	215-204-7000	204-5694
Thiel College 75 College Ave *Fax: Admissions ■ TF: 800-248-4435 ■ Web: www.thiel.edu	Greenville	PA	16125	724-589-2000	589-2013*
Thomas Jefferson University 1020 Walnut St. Web: www.jefferson.edu	Philadelphia	PA	19107	215-955-6000	955-5151
University of Pennsylvania 3451 Walnut St. *Fax: Admissions ■ Web: www.upenn.edu	Philadelphia	PA	19104	215-898-5000	898-9670*
University of Pittsburgh 4227 5th Ave *Fax: Admissions ■ Web: www.pitt.edu	Pittsburgh	PA	15260	412-624-4141	648-8815*
Bradford 300 Campus Dr. TF: 800-872-1787 ■ Web: www.upb.pitt.edu	Bradford	PA	16701	814-362-7555	362-5150
Greensburg 150 Finoli Dr *Fax: Admissions ■ Web: www.upg.pitt.edu	Greensburg	PA	15601	724-837-7040	836-7160*
Johnstown 157 Blackington Hall TF: 800-765-4875 ■ Web: www.upj.pitt.edu	Johnstown	PA	15904	814-269-7050	269-7044
University of Scranton 800 Linden St St Thomas Hall *Fax: Admissions ■ TF: 888-727-2686 ■ Web: www.matrix.scranton.edu	Scranton	PA	18510	570-941-7400	941-5928*
University of the Sciences in Philadelphia 600 S 43rd St *Fax: Admissions ■ TF: 866-304-8747 ■ Web: www.usip.edu	Philadelphia	PA	19104	215-596-8800	596-8821*
Ursinus College 601 E Main St PO Box 1000 *Fax: Admissions ■ Web: www.ursinus.edu	Collegeville	PA	19426	610-409-3200	409-3662*
Valley Forge Christian College 1401 Charlestown Rd *Fax: Admissions ■ TF: 800-432-8322 ■ Web: www.vfcc.edu	Phoenixville	PA	19460	610-935-0450	917-2069*
Villanova University 800 Lancaster Ave. TF: 800-634-8773 ■ Web: www.villanova.edu	Villanova	PA	19085	610-519-4500	519-6450
Washington & Jefferson College 60 S Lincoln St. *Fax: Admissions ■ TF: 888-926-3529 ■ Web: www.washjeff.edu	Washington	PA	15301	724-222-4400	223-6534*
Waynesburg College 51 W College St. *Fax: Admissions ■ TF Admissions: 800-225-7393 ■ Web: www.waynesburg.edu	Waynesburg	PA	15370	724-627-8191	627-8124*
West Chester University 700 S High St TF: 877-315-2165 ■ Web: www.wcupa.edu	West Chester	PA	19383	610-436-1000	436-2907
Westminster College 319 S Market St. *Fax: Admissions ■ TF: 800-942-8033 ■ Web: www.westminster.edu	New Wilmington	PA	16172	724-946-8761	946-6171*
Widener University 1 University Pl. *Fax: Admissions ■ TF Admissions: 888-943-3637 ■ Web: www.widener.edu	Chester	PA	19013	610-499-4000	499-4676*
Wilkes University 84 W S St. *Fax: Admissions ■ TF: 800-945-5378 ■ Web: www.wilkes.edu	Wilkes-Barre	PA	18766	570-824-4651	408-4904*
Wilson College 1015 Philadelphia Ave *Fax: Admissions ■ TF Admissions: 800-421-8402 ■ Web: www.wilson.edu	Chambersburg	PA	17201	717-264-4141	264-1578*
York College of Pennsylvania 441 Country Club Rd *Fax: Hum Res ■ Web: www.ycp.edu	York	PA	17403	717-846-7788	815-6862*

RHODE ISLAND

	City	State	Zip	Phone	Fax
Brown University 45 Prospect St *Fax: Admissions ■ Web: www.brown.edu	Providence	RI	02912	401-863-2378	863-9300*
Bryant University 1150 Douglas Pike *Fax: Admissions ■ TF Admissions: 800-622-7001 ■ Web: www.bryant.edu	Smithfield	RI	02917	401-232-6000	232-6741*
Johnson & Wales University *Providence* 8 Abbott Pk Pl TF: 800-342-5598 ■ Web: www.jwu.edu	Providence	RI	02903	401-598-1000	598-4641
Providence College 549 River Ave. *Fax: Admissions ■ TF Admissions: 800-721-6444 ■ Web: www.providence.edu	Providence	RI	02918	401-865-1000	865-2826*
Rhode Island College 600 Mt Pleasant Ave TF: 800-669-5760 ■ Web: www.ric.edu	Providence	RI	02908	401-456-8000	456-8817
Roger Williams University 1 Old Ferry Rd *Fax: Admissions ■ TF: 800-458-7144 ■ Web: www.rwu.edu	Bristol	RI	02809	401-254-3500	254-3557*
Salve Regina University 100 Ochre Pt Ave *Fax: Admissions ■ TF: 888-467-2583 ■ Web: www.salve.edu	Newport	RI	02840	401-847-6650	848-2823*
University of Rhode Island 14 Upper College Rd *Fax: Admissions ■ Web: www.uri.edu	Kingston	RI	02881	401-874-7100	874-5523*
Feinstein Providence 80 Washington St Web: www.uri.edu	Providence	RI	02903	401-277-5000	277-5168

SOUTH CAROLINA

	City	State	Zip	Phone	Fax
Allen University 1530 Harden St. *Fax: Mail Rm ■ TF: 877-625-5368 ■ Web: www.allenuniversity.edu	Columbia	SC	29204	803-376-5700	376-5733*
Anderson University 316 Blvd TF: 800-542-3594 ■ Web: www.ac.edu	Anderson	SC	29621	864-231-2030	231-2033
Benedict College 1600 Harden St TF: 800-868-6598 ■ Web: www.benedict.edu	Columbia	SC	29204	803-256-5000	
Bob Jones University 1700 Wade Hampton Blvd *Fax Area Code: 800 ■ *Fax: Admissions ■ TF Admissions: 800-252-6363 ■ Web: www.bju.edu	Greenville	SC	29614	864-242-5100	232-9258*
Cathedral Bible College 803 Howard Pkwy	Myrtle Beach	SC	29577	843-477-1503	477-1627
Charleston Southern University 9200 University Blvd TF: 800-947-7474 ■ Web: www.csuniv.edu	Charleston	SC	29423	843-863-7050	863-7070
Citadel The 171 Moultrie St. TF: 800-868-1842 ■ Web: www.citadel.edu	Charleston	SC	29409	843-953-5230	953-7036
Claflin University 400 Magnolia St. TF: 800-922-1276 ■ Web: www.claflin.edu	Orangeburg	SC	29115	803-535-5000	535-5385
Clemson University 105 Sikes Hall *Fax: Admissions ■ Web: www.clemson.edu	Clemson	SC	29634	864-656-3311	656-2464*
Coastal Carolina University PO Box 261954 TF: 800-277-7000 ■ Web: www.coastal.edu	Conway	SC	29528	843-349-2170	349-2127
Coker College 300 E College Ave *Fax: Admissions ■ TF: 800-950-1908 ■ Web: www.coker.edu	Hartsville	SC	29550	843-383-8000	383-8056*
College of Charleston 66 George St Web: www.cofc.edu	Charleston	SC	29424	843-805-5507	953-6322
Columbia College 1301 Columbia College Dr TF: 800-277-1301 ■ Web: www.columbiacollegesc.edu	Columbia	SC	29203	803-786-3012	786-3674
Converse College 580 E Main St *Fax: Admissions ■ TF Admissions: 800-766-1125 ■ Web: www.converse.edu	Spartanburg	SC	29302	864-596-9000	596-9225*
Erskine College PO Box 176 *Fax: Admissions ■ TF Admissions: 800-241-8721 ■ Web: www.erskine.edu	Due West	SC	29639	864-379-2131	379-3048*
Francis Marion University PO Box 100547 *Fax: Admissions ■ TF: 800-368-7551 ■ Web: www.fmarion.edu	Florence	SC	29501	843-661-1231	661-4635*
Furman University 3300 Poinsett Hwy *Fax: Admissions ■ Web: www.furman.edu	Greenville	SC	29613	864-294-2000	294-2018*
Lander University 320 Stanley Ave. *Fax: Admissions ■ TF Admissions: 888-452-6337 ■ Web: www.lander.edu	Greenwood	SC	29649	864-388-8307	388-8125*
Limestone College 1115 College Dr. *Fax: Admissions ■ TF: 800-795-7151 ■ Web: www.limestone.edu	Gaffney	SC	29340	864-489-7151	488-8206*
Medical University of South Carolina 41 Bee St MSC 203 *Fax: Admissions ■ TF: 800-424-6872 ■ Web: www.musc.edu	Charleston	SC	29425	843-792-3281	792-3764*
Morris College 100 W College St *Fax: Admissions ■ TF Admissions: 866-853-1345 ■ Web: www.morris.edu	Sumter	SC	29150	803-934-3200	773-8241*
Newberry College 2100 College St. *Fax: Admissions ■ TF: 800-845-4955 ■ Web: www.newberry.edu	Newberry	SC	29108	803-276-5010	321-5138*
Presbyterian College 503 S Broad St *Fax: Admissions ■ TF: 800-476-7272 ■ Web: www.presby.edu	Clinton	SC	29325	864-833-2820	833-8481*
South Carolina State University 300 College St NE PO Box 7127 TF Admissions: 800-260-5956 ■ Web: www.scsu.edu	Orangeburg	SC	29117	803-536-7000	536-8990
South University Columbia 9 Science Ct *Fax: Admissions ■ TF: 866-629-3031 ■ Web: www.southuniversity.edu	Columbia	SC	29203	803-799-9082	935-4382*
Southern Wesleyan University 907 Wesleyan Dr. *Fax: Admissions ■ TF: 800-282-8798 ■ Web: www.swu.edu	Central	SC	29630	864-644-5000	644-5972*
University of South Carolina 1600 Hampton St *Fax: Admissions ■ TF: 800-868-5872 ■ Web: www.sc.edu	Columbia	SC	29208	803-777-7000	777-0101*
Aiken 471 University Pkwy *Fax: Admissions ■ TF: 888-969-8722 ■ Web: www.usca.edu	Aiken	SC	29801	803-648-6851	641-3727*
Beaufort 801 Carteret St. *Fax: Admissions ■ Web: www.sc.edu	Beaufort	SC	29902	843-521-4100	521-4198*
Sumter 200 Miller Rd *Fax: Admissions ■ TF: 888-872-7868 ■ Web: www.uscsumter.edu	Sumter	SC	29150	803-775-8727	938-3901*
Upstate 800 University Way *Fax: Admissions ■ TF: 800-277-8727 ■ Web: www.uscupstate.edu	Spartanburg	SC	29303	864-503-5246	503-5727*
Voorhees College 213 Wiggins Dr PO Box 678 TF Admissions: 800-446-6250 ■ Web: www.voorhees.edu	Denmark	SC	29042	803-793-3351	753-9077
Winthrop University 701 Oakland Ave *Fax: Admissions ■ Web: www.winthrop.edu	Rock Hill	SC	29733	803-323-2211	323-2137*
Wofford College 429 N Church St *Fax: Admissions ■ Web: www.wofford.edu	Spartanburg	SC	29303	864-597-4000	597-4149*

SOUTH DAKOTA

	City	State	Zip	Phone	Fax
Augustana College 2001 S Summit Ave. *Fax: Admissions ■ TF: 800-727-2844 ■ Web: www.augie.edu	Sioux Falls	SD	57197	605-274-0770	274-5518*
Black Hills State University 1200 University St Unit 9502 TF: 800-255-2478 ■ Web: www.bhsu.edu	Spearfish	SD	57799	605-642-6011	642-6254
Dakota State University 820 N Washington Ave. TF: 888-378-9988 ■ Web: www.dsu.edu	Madison	SD	57042	605-256-5139	256-5020
Dakota Wesleyan University 1200 W University Ave TF: 800-333-8506 ■ Web: www.dwu.edu	Mitchell	SD	57301	605-995-2600	995-2699
Mount Marty College 1105 W 8th St. *Fax: Admissions ■ TF Admissions: 800-658-4552 ■ Web: www.mtmc.edu	Yankton	SD	57078	605-668-1545	668-1508*
National American University 321 Kansas City St *Fax: Admissions ■ TF: 800-843-8892 ■ Web: www.national.edu	Rapid City	SD	57701	605-394-4800	394-4871*

	City	State	Zip	Phone	Fax
Sioux Falls 2801 S Kiwanis Ave Suite 100	Sioux Falls	SD	57105	605-336-4600	336-4605*
**Fax:* Admissions ■ *TF:* 800-388-5430 ■ *Web:* www.national.edu					
Northern State University 1200 S Jay St	Aberdeen	SD	57401	605-626-3011	626-2587*
**Fax:* Admissions ■ *TF:* 800-678-5330 ■ *Web:* www.northern.edu					
Oglala Lakota College PO Box 629	Martin	SD	57551	605-685-6407	685-6887
Web: www.olc.edu					
Presentation College 1500 N Main St	Aberdeen	SD	57401	605-225-1634	229-8425
TF: 800-437-6060 ■ *Web:* www.presentation.edu					
South Dakota School of Mines & Technology					
501 E St Joseph St	Rapid City	SD	57701	605-394-2414	394-1268
TF: 800-544-8162 ■ *Web:* www.hpcnet.org					
South Dakota State University PO Box 2201	Brookings	SD	57007	605-688-4121	688-6891
TF: 800-952-3541 ■ *Web:* www.sdstate.edu					
University of Sioux Falls 1101 W 22nd St	Sioux Falls	SD	57105	605-331-6600	331-6615
TF: 800-888-1047 ■ *Web:* www.thecoo.edu					
University of South Dakota 414 E Clark St	Vermillion	SD	57069	605-677-5341	677-6323*
**Fax:* Admissions ■ *TF:* 877-269-6837 ■ *Web:* www.usd.edu					

TENNESSEE

	City	State	Zip	Phone	Fax
Aquinas College 4210 Harding Rd	Nashville	TN	37205	615-297-7545	297-7970*
**Fax:* Admissions ■ *TF Admissions:* 800-649-9956 ■ *Web:* www.aquinas-tn.edu					
Austin Peay State University					
601 College St	Clarksville	TN	37044	931-221-7661	221-6168*
**Fax:* Admissions ■ *TF Admissions:* 800-844-2778 ■ *Web:* www.apsu.edu					
Belmont University 1900 Belmont Blvd	Nashville	TN	37212	615-460-6000	460-5434*
**Fax:* Admissions ■ *TF:* 800-563-6765 ■ *Web:* www.belmont.edu					
Bethel College 325 Cherry Ave	McKenzie	TN	38201	731-352-4000	352-4241*
**Fax:* Admissions ■ *Web:* www.bethel-college.edu					
Bryan College 721 Bryan Dr PO Box 7000	Dayton	TN	37321	423-775-2041	775-7199
TF: 800-277-9522 ■ *Web:* www.bryan.edu					
Carson-Newman College					
1646 Russell Ave	Jefferson City	TN	37760	865-475-9061	471-3502*
**Fax:* Admissions ■ *TF:* 800-678-9061 ■ *Web:* www.cn.edu					
Christian Bros University 650 E Pkwy S	Memphis	TN	38104	901-321-3000	321-3494*
**Fax:* Admissions ■ *TF Admissions:* 800-288-7576 ■ *Web:* www.cbu.edu					
Crichton College 255 N Highland Ave	Memphis	TN	38111	901-320-9797	320-9791*
**Fax:* Admissions ■ *TF:* 800-960-9777 ■ *Web:* www.crichton.edu					
Cumberland University 1 Cumberland Sq	Lebanon	TN	37087	615-444-2562	444-2569
TF: 800-467-0562 ■ *Web:* www.cumberland.edu					
East Tennessee State University					
PO Box 70731	Johnson City	TN	37614	423-439-4213	439-4630
TF: 800-462-3878 ■ *Web:* www.etsu.edu					
Fisk University 1000 17th Ave N	Nashville	TN	37208	615-329-8500	329-8774
TF: 800-443-3475 ■ *Web:* www.fisk.edu					
Freed-Hardeman University 158 E Main St	Henderson	TN	38340	731-989-6651	989-6047
TF: 800-630-3480 ■ *Web:* www.fhu.edu					
King College 1350 King College Rd	Bristol	TN	37620	423-652-4861	968-4456
TF Admissions: 800-362-0014 ■ *Web:* www.king.edu					
Lambuth University 705 Lambuth Blvd	Jackson	TN	38301	731-425-2500	425-3496*
**Fax:* Admissions ■ *TF:* 800-526-2884 ■ *Web:* www.lambuth.edu					
Lane College 545 Ln Ave	Jackson	TN	38301	731-426-7500	426-7559*
**Fax:* Admissions ■ *TF Admissions:* 800-960-7532 ■ *Web:* www.lanecollege.edu					
Lee University 1120 N Ocoee St	Cleveland	TN	37311	423-614-8000	614-8533*
**Fax:* Admissions ■ *TF:* 800-533-9930 ■ *Web:* www.leeuniversity.edu					
LeMoyne-Owen College 807 Walker Ave	Memphis	TN	38126	901-435-1000	435-1524*
**Fax:* Admissions ■ *TF Admissions:* 800-737-7778 ■ *Web:* www.loc.edu					
Lincoln Memorial University					
6965 Cumberland Gap Pkwy	Harrogate	TN	37752	423-869-3611	869-6444
TF: 800-325-0900 ■ *Web:* www.lmunet.edu					
Lipscomb University 3901 Granny White Pike	Nashville	TN	37204	615-966-1000	966-1804*
**Fax:* Admissions ■ *TF:* 800-333-4358 ■ *Web:* www.lipscomb.edu					
Martin Methodist College 433 W Madison St	Pulaski	TN	38478	931-363-9804	363-9803*
**Fax:* Admissions ■ *TF:* 800-467-1273 ■ *Web:* www.martinmethodist.edu					
Maryville College					
502 E Lamar Alexander Pkwy	Maryville	TN	37804	865-981-8000	981-8005*
**Fax:* Admissions ■ *TF:* 800-597-2687 ■ *Web:* www.maryvillecollege.edu					
Middle Tennessee State University					
1301 E Main St	Murfreesboro	TN	37132	615-898-2111	898-5478*
**Fax:* Admissions ■ *TF Admissions:* 800-433-6878 ■ *Web:* www.mtsu.edu					
Milligan College PO Box 500	Milligan College	TN	37682	423-461-8730	461-8982*
**Fax:* Admissions ■ *TF:* 800-262-8337 ■ *Web:* www.milligan.edu					
O'More College of Design 423 S Margin St	Franklin	TN	37064	615-794-4254	790-1662
TF: 888-662-1970 ■ *Web:* www.omorecollege.edu					
Rhodes College 2000 N Pkwy	Memphis	TN	38112	901-843-3700	843-3631*
**Fax:* Admissions ■ *TF:* 800-844-5969 ■ *Web:* www.rhodes.edu					
Southern Adventist University					
4881 Taylor Cir	Collegedale	TN	37315	423-236-2000	236-1000
TF: 800-768-8437 ■ *Web:* www.southern.edu					
Tennessee State University					
3500 John A Merritt Blvd PO Box 9609	Nashville	TN	37209	615-963-5000	963-5108
TF Admissions: 888-463-6878 ■ *Web:* www.tnstate.edu					
Tennessee Technological University					
1 William L Jones Dr	Cookeville	TN	38505	931-372-3888	372-6250
TF: 800-255-8881 ■ *Web:* www.tntech.edu					
Tennessee Temple University					
1815 Union Ave	Chattanooga	TN	37404	423-493-4100	493-4497*
**Fax:* Admissions ■ *TF:* 800-553-4050 ■ *Web:* www.tntemple.edu					
Tennessee Wesleyan College					
204 E College St PO Box 40	Athens	TN	37371	423-745-7504	744-9968
TF: 800-742-5892 ■ *Web:* www.twcnet.edu					
Trevecca Nazarene University					
333 Murfreesboro Rd	Nashville	TN	37210	615-248-1200	248-7406*
**Fax:* Admissions ■ *TF:* 888-210-4868 ■ *Web:* www.trevecca.edu					
Tusculum College 60 Shiloh Rd Hwy 107	Greeneville	TN	37743	423-636-7300	798-1622*
**Fax:* Admissions ■ *TF:* 800-729-0256 ■ *Web:* www.tusculum.edu					
Union University 1050 Union University Dr	Jackson	TN	38305	731-661-5210	661-5589*
**Fax:* Admissions ■ *TF:* 800-338-6466 ■ *Web:* www.uu.edu					
University of Memphis Wilder Tower Rm 101	Memphis	TN	38152	901-678-2101	678-3053*
**Fax:* Admissions ■ *TF:* 800-669-2678 ■ *Web:* www.memphis.edu					
University of Tennessee					
1331 Cir Park Dr 320 Student Services Bldg	Knoxville	TN	37996	865-974-1000	974-3851*
**Fax:* Admissions ■ *Web:* www.utk.edu					
Chattanooga 615 McCallie Ave	Chattanooga	TN	37403	423-425-4111	425-4157*
**Fax:* Admissions ■ *TF:* 800-882-6627 ■ *Web:* www.utc.edu					
Health Science Ctr 800 Madison Ave	Memphis	TN	38163	901-448-5000	448-7772
Web: www.utmem.edu					
Martin 544 University St	Martin	TN	38238	731-881-7020	881-7029
TF: 800-829-8861 ■ *Web:* www.utm.edu					
University of the South 735 University Ave	Sewanee	TN	37383	931-598-1238	598-3248*
**Fax:* Admissions ■ *TF:* 800-522-2234 ■ *Web:* www.sewanee.edu					
Vanderbilt University 2201 W End Ave	Nashville	TN	37240	615-322-7311	343-7765
TF: 800-288-0432 ■ *Web:* www.vanderbilt.edu					

TEXAS

	City	State	Zip	Phone	Fax
Abilene Christian University 1705 Campus Ct	Abilene	TX	79601	325-674-2000	674-2130
TF: 800-460-6228 ■ *Web:* www.acu.edu					
Angelo State University					
2601 W Ave N ASU Stn 11014	San Angelo	TX	76909	325-942-2041	942-2078*
**Fax:* Admissions ■ *TF:* 800-946-8627 ■ *Web:* www.angelo.edu					
Arlington Baptist College					
3001 W Division St	Arlington	TX	76012	817-461-8741	274-1138*
**Fax:* Admissions ■ *Web:* www.abconline.edu					
Austin College 900 N Grand Ave	Sherman	TX	75090	903-813-3000	813-3198*
**Fax:* Admissions ■ *TF:* 800-526-4276 ■ *Web:* www.austincollege.edu					
Austin Graduate School of Theology					
7640 Guadalupe St	Austin	TX	78752	512-476-2772	476-3919
TF: 866-287-4723 ■ *Web:* www.austingrad.edu					
Baylor University 1311 S 5th St 1 Bear Pl 98013	Waco	TX	76798	254-710-3718	710-1066
TF: 800-229-5678 ■ *Web:* www.baylor.edu					
Concordia University Austin 3400 IH-35 N	Austin	TX	78705	512-486-2000	486-1350
TF: 800-865-4282 ■ *Web:* www.concordia.edu					
Criswell College 4010 Gaston Ave	Dallas	TX	75246	214-821-5433	818-1310*
**Fax:* Admissions ■ *TF:* 800-899-0012 ■ *Web:* www.criswell.edu					
Dallas Baptist University					
3000 Mountain Creek Pkwy	Dallas	TX	75211	214-333-7100	333-5447*
**Fax:* Admissions ■ *TF:* 800-460-1328 ■ *Web:* www.dbu.edu					
East Texas Baptist University					
1209 N Grove St	Marshall	TX	75670	903-935-7963	923-2001*
**Fax:* Admissions ■ *TF:* 800-804-3828 ■ *Web:* www.etbu.edu					
Hardin-Simmons University 2200 Hickory St	Abilene	TX	79698	325-670-1206	671-2115*
**Fax:* Admissions ■ *TF:* 877-464-7889 ■ *Web:* www.hsutx.edu					
Houston Baptist University 7502 Fondren Rd	Houston	TX	77074	281-649-3000	649-3217*
**Fax:* Admissions ■ *TF Admissions:* 800-969-3210 ■ *Web:* www.hbu.edu					
Howard Payne University 1000 Fisk Ave	Brownwood	TX	76801	325-646-2502	649-8901*
**Fax:* Admissions ■ *TF:* 800-950-8465 ■ *Web:* www.hputx.edu					
Huston-Tillotson University 900 Chicon St	Austin	TX	78702	512-505-3000	505-3192*
**Fax:* Admissions ■ *TF:* 877-505-3028 ■ *Web:* www.htu.edu					
Jarvis Christian College PO Box 1470	Hawkins	TX	75765	903-769-5700	769-1282*
**Fax:* Admissions ■ *Web:* www.jarvis.edu					
Lamar University 4400 ML King Jr Pkwy	Beaumont	TX	77710	409-880-7011	880-8463
Web: www.lamar.edu					
LeTourneau University 2100 S Mobberly Ave	Longview	TX	75602	903-753-0231	233-4301*
**Fax:* Admissions ■ *TF:* 800-759-8811 ■ *Web:* www.letu.edu					
Lubbock Christian University 5601 19th St	Lubbock	TX	79407	806-720-7151	720-7162*
**Fax:* Admissions ■ *TF:* 800-933-7601 ■ *Web:* www.lcu.edu					
McMurry University S 14 St & Sayles Blvd	Abilene	TX	79697	325-793-4700	793-4701
TF: 800-460-2395 ■ *Web:* www.mcm.edu					
Midwestern State University					
3410 Taft Blvd	Wichita Falls	TX	76308	940-397-4000	397-4672*
**Fax:* Admissions ■ *TF Admissions:* 800-842-1922 ■ *Web:* www.mwsu.edu					
Northwood University					
Texas 1114 W FM 1382	Cedar Hill	TX	75104	972-291-1541	291-3824
TF: 800-927-9663 ■ *Web:* www.northwood.edu					
Our Lady of the Lake University					
411 SW 24th St	San Antonio	TX	78207	210-434-6711	431-4036*
**Fax:* Admissions ■ *TF:* 800-436-6558 ■ *Web:* www.ollusa.edu					
Paul Quinn College 3837 Simpson Stuart Rd	Dallas	TX	75241	214-376-1000	302-3648*
**Fax:* Admissions ■ *TF:* 800-237-2648 ■ *Web:* www.pqc.edu					
Prairie View A & M University					
PO Box 519	Prairie View	TX	77446	936-857-2626	261-1079*
**Fax:* Admissions ■ *TF:* 800-787-7826 ■ *Web:* www.pvamu.edu					
Rice University 6100 Main St	Houston	TX	77005	713-348-0000	348-5323*
**Fax:* Admissions ■ *TF:* 800-527-6957 ■ *Web:* www.rice.edu					
Saint Edward's University 3001 S Congress Ave	Austin	TX	78704	512-448-8500	464-8877
TF: 800-555-0164 ■ *Web:* www.stedwards.edu					
Saint Mary's University					
1 Camino Santa Maria	San Antonio	TX	78228	210-436-3126	431-6742*
**Fax:* Admissions ■ *TF Admissions:* 800-367-7868 ■ *Web:* www.stmarytx.edu					
Sam Houston State University					
1903 University Ave	Huntsville	TX	77340	936-294-1111	294-3758*
**Fax:* Admissions ■ *TF:* 866-232-7528 ■ *Web:* www.shsu.edu					
Schreiner University 2100 Memorial Blvd	Kerrville	TX	78028	830-792-7217	792-7226*
**Fax:* Admissions ■ *TF:* 800-343-4919 ■ *Web:* www.schreiner.edu					
Southern Methodist University 6425 Boaz Ln	Dallas	TX	75205	214-768-2000	768-0202*
**Fax:* Admissions ■ *TF:* 800-323-0672 ■ *Web:* www.smu.edu					
Southwestern Adventist University					
100 W Hillcrest Dr PO Box 567	Keene	TX	76059	817-645-3921	556-4753
TF Admissions: 888-732-7928 ■ *Web:* www.swau.edu					
Southwestern Assemblies of God University					
1200 Sycamore St	Waxahachie	TX	75165	972-937-4010	923-0006*
**Fax:* Admissions ■ *TF:* 888-937-7248 ■ *Web:* www.sagu.edu					
Southwestern Christian College PO Box 10	Terrell	TX	75160	972-524-3341	563-7133
TF: 800-925-9357 ■ *Web:* www.swcc.edu					
Southwestern University PO Box 770	Georgetown	TX	78627	512-863-1200	863-9601*
**Fax:* Admissions ■ *TF:* 800-252-3166 ■ *Web:* www.southwestern.edu					

	City	State	ZIP	Phone	Fax
Stephen F Austin State University					
1936 N St PO Box 13051	Nacogdoches	TX	75962	936-468-2504	468-3149*
*Fax: Admissions ■ *Web:* www.sfasu.edu					
Sul Ross State University E Hwy 90	Alpine	TX	79832	432-837-8011	837-8431*
*Fax: Admissions ■ *TF:* 888-722-7778 ■ *Web:* www.sulross.edu					
Tarleton State University PO Box T-0030	Stephenville	TX	76402	254-968-9125	968-9951*
*Fax: Admissions ■ *TF:* 800-687-8236 ■ *Web:* www.tarleton.edu					
Texas A & M International University					
5201 University Blvd	Laredo	TX	78041	956-326-2001	326-2199
Web: www.tamiu.edu					
Texas A & M University PO Box 30018	College Station	TX	77842	979-845-3211	458-0434*
*Fax: Admissions ■ *Web:* www.tamu.edu					
Commerce PO Box 3011	Commerce	TX	75429	903-886-5081	468-8685
TF: 888-868-2682 ■ *Web:* www.tamu-commerce.edu					
Corpus Christi 6300 Ocean Dr.	Corpus Christi	TX	78412	361-825-7024	825-5887*
*Fax: Admissions ■ *Web:* www.tamucc.edu					
Galveston 200 Seawolf Pkwy Bldg 3026	Galveston	TX	77553	409-740-4428	740-4731
TF: 877-322-4443 ■ *Web:* www.tamug.edu					
Kingsville 700 University Blvd CB 128	Kingsville	TX	78363	361-593-2111	593-2195*
*Fax: Admissions ■ *Web:* www.tamuk.edu					
Texarkana 7101 University Ave	Texarkana	TX	75503	903-223-3000	223-3140
Web: www.tamut.edu					
Texas Christian University					
TCU PO Box 297013	Fort Worth	TX	76129	817-257-7490	257-7268
TF: 800-828-3764 ■ *Web:* www.tcu.edu					
Texas College 2404 N Grand Ave	Tyler	TX	75702	903-593-8311	536-0001*
*Fax: Admissions ■ *TF:* 800-306-6299 ■ *Web:* www.texascollege.edu					
Texas Lutheran University 1000 W Ct St	Seguin	TX	78155	830-372-8000	372-8096
TF: 800-771-8521 ■ *Web:* www.tlu.edu					
Texas Southern University 3100 Cleburne St	Houston	TX	77004	713-313-7011	313-1859
Web: www.tsu.edu					
Texas State University					
San Marcos 601 University Dr.	San Marcos	TX	78666	512-245-2340	245-8044*
*Fax: Admissions ■ *TF Admissions:* 866-798-2287 ■ *Web:* www.txstate.edu					
Texas Tech University PO Box 45005	Lubbock	TX	79409	806-742-1480	742-0062*
*Fax: Admissions ■ *TF:* 888-270-3369 ■ *Web:* www.ttu.edu					
Texas Wesleyan University					
1201 Wesleyan St	Fort Worth	TX	76105	817-531-4422	531-7515*
*Fax: Admissions ■ *TF:* 800-580-8980 ■ *Web:* www.txwesleyan.edu					
Texas Woman's University					
304 Administration Dr PO Box 425589	Denton	TX	76204	940-898-3188	898-3081*
*Fax: Admissions ■ *TF:* 866-809-6130 ■ *Web:* www.twu.edu					
Trinity University 1 Trinity Pl	San Antonio	TX	78212	210-999-7011	999-8164*
*Fax: Admissions ■ *TF:* 800-874-6489 ■ *Web:* www.trinity.edu					
University of Dallas 1845 E Northgate Dr	Irving	TX	75062	972-721-5266	721-5017*
*Fax: Admissions ■ *TF Admissions:* 800-628-6999 ■ *Web:* www.udallas.edu					
University of Houston 4800 Calhoun Rd	Houston	TX	77004	713-743-1000	743-9665
Web: www.uh.edu					
Clear Lake 2700 Bay Area Blvd	Houston	TX	77058	281-283-7600	283-2522*
*Fax: Admissions ■ *Web:* www.cl.uh.edu					
Downtown 1 Main St	Houston	TX	77002	713-221-8000	221-8157*
*Fax: Admissions ■ *Web:* www.dt.uh.edu					
Victoria 3007 N Ben Wilson St	Victoria	TX	77901	361-570-4848	570-4114*
*Fax: Admissions ■ *TF:* 877-970-4848 ■ *Web:* www.uhv.edu					
University of Mary Hardin-Baylor					
900 College St PO Box 8004	Belton	TX	76513	254-295-8642	295-5049*
*Fax: Admissions ■ *TF:* 800-727-8642 ■ *Web:* www.umhb.edu					
University of North Texas PO Box 311277	Denton	TX	76203	940-565-2681	565-2408*
*Fax: Admissions ■ *TF:* 800-868-8211 ■ *Web:* www.unt.edu					
University of Saint Thomas					
3800 Montrose Blvd	Houston	TX	77006	713-522-7911	525-3558*
*Fax: Admissions ■ *TF:* 800-856-8565 ■ *Web:* www.stthom.edu					
University of Texas					
Allied Health Sciences School					
5323 Harry Hines Blvd.	Dallas	TX	75390	214-648-3111	648-3289
Web: www3.utsouthwestern.edu					
Arlington 701 S Nedderman Dr PO Box 19111	Arlington	TX	76019	817-272-6287	272-3435*
*Fax: Admissions ■ *Web:* www.uta.edu					
Austin 2400 Inner Campus Dr Mail Bldg Rm 7	Austin	TX	78712	512-475-7399	475-7399*
*Fax: Admissions ■ *Web:* www.utexas.edu					
Brownsville 80 Fort Brown St	Brownsville	TX	78520	956-882-8200	882-7810*
*Fax: Admissions ■ *TF:* 800-892-3348 ■ *Web:* www.utb.edu					
Dallas 800 W Campbell Rd # Be3.204	Richardson	TX	75080	972-883-2111	883-2599
TF: 800-889-2443 ■ *Web:* www.utdallas.edu					
El Paso 500 W University Ave	El Paso	TX	79968	915-747-5000	747-8893*
*Fax: Admissions ■ *TF Admissions:* 877-746-4637 ■ *Web:* www.utep.edu					
Pan American 1201 W University Dr	Edinburg	TX	78539	956-381-8872	381-2212
TF: 866-441-8872 ■ *Web:* www.utpa.edu					
Permian Basin 4901 E University Blvd.	Odessa	TX	79762	432-552-2000	552-3605*
*Fax: Admissions ■ *TF Admissions:* 866-552-8872 ■ *Web:* www.utpb.edu					
San Antonio 6900 N Loop 1604 W	San Antonio	TX	78249	210-458-4011	458-7716*
*Fax: Admissions ■ *TF:* 800-669-0919 ■ *Web:* www.utsa.edu					
Tyler 3900 University Blvd.	Tyler	TX	75799	903-566-7000	566-7068*
*Fax: Admissions ■ *TF:* 800-888-9537 ■ *Web:* www.uttyler.edu					
University of the Incarnate Word					
4301 Broadway St	San Antonio	TX	78209	210-829-6000	829-3921*
*Fax: Admissions ■ *TF Admissions:* 800-749-9673 ■ *Web:* www.uiw.edu					
Wayland Baptist University 1900 W 7th St	Plainview	TX	79072	806-291-1000	291-1973*
*Fax: Admissions ■ *TF:* 800-588-1928 ■ *Web:* www.wbu.edu					
West Texas A & M University 2501 4th Ave	Canyon	TX	79016	806-651-2020	651-5285*
*Fax: Admissions ■ *TF:* 800-999-8268 ■ *Web:* www.wtamu.edu					
Wiley College 711 Wiley Ave.	Marshall	TX	75670	903-927-3311	927-3366*
*Fax: Admissions ■ *TF Admissions:* 800-658-6889 ■ *Web:* www.wileyc.edu					

UTAH

	City	State	ZIP	Phone	Fax
Brigham Young University 770 E University Pkwy	Provo	UT	84604	801-422-4636	422-0005
Web: www.home.byu.edu					
Dixie State College of Utah 225 S 700 E	Saint George	UT	84770	435-652-7500	656-4005*
*Fax: Admissions ■ *TF:* 888-324-2998 ■ *Web:* www.new.dixie.edu					
Southern Utah University 351 W Ctr St	Cedar City	UT	84720	435-586-7700	865-8223*
*Fax: Admissions ■ *Web:* www.suu.edu					
University of Utah					
201 S Campus Dr Rm 270	Salt Lake City	UT	84112	801-581-3612	581-7880*
*Fax: Admissions ■ *Web:* www.utah.edu					
Utah State University 1600 Old Main Hill	Logan	UT	84322	435-797-1116	797-1110
Web: www.usu.edu					
Weber State University 3848 Harrison Blvd	Ogden	UT	84408	801-626-6000	626-6747
TF: 800-848-7770 ■ *Web:* www.weber.edu					
Davis 2750 N University Pk Blvd	Layton	UT	84041	801-395-3473	395-3538*
*Fax: Admissions ■ *TF:* 800-848-7770 ■ *Web:* www.weber.edu					
Westminster College 1840 S 1300 E	Salt Lake City	UT	84105	801-832-2200	832-3101*
*Fax: Admissions ■ *TF:* 800-748-4753 ■ *Web:* www.westminstercollege.edu					

VERMONT

	City	State	ZIP	Phone	Fax
Bennington College 1 College Dr.	Bennington	VT	05201	802-442-5401	447-4269
TF: 800-833-6845 ■ *Web:* www.bennington.edu					
Burlington College 95 N Ave	Burlington	VT	05401	802-862-9616	660-4331
TF: 800-862-9616 ■ *Web:* www.burlingtoncollege.edu					
Castleton State College 86 Seminary St	Castleton	VT	05735	802-468-5611	468-1476*
*Fax: Admissions ■ *TF:* 800-639-8521 ■ *Web:* www.csc.vsc.edu					
Champlain College 163 S Willard St	Burlington	VT	05401	802-860-2700	860-2767
TF: 800-570-5858 ■ *Web:* www.champlain.edu					
College of Saint Joseph in Vermont					
71 Clement Rd	Rutland	VT	05701	802-773-5900	776-5258*
*Fax: Admissions ■ *TF Admissions:* 877-270-9998 ■ *Web:* www.csj.edu					
Goddard College 123 Pitkin Rd	Plainfield	VT	05667	802-454-8311	454-1029*
*Fax: Admissions ■ *TF:* 800-468-4888 ■ *Web:* www.goddard.edu					
Green Mountain College 1 Brennan Cir	Poultney	VT	05764	802-287-8000	287-8099
TF Admissions: 800-776-6675 ■ *Web:* www.greenmtn.edu					
Johnson State College 337 College Hill	Johnson	VT	05656	802-635-2356	635-1230*
*Fax: Admissions ■ *TF:* 800-635-2356 ■ *Web:* www.jsc.vsc.edu					
Lyndon State College					
1001 College Rd PO Box 919	Lyndonville	VT	05851	802-626-6413	626-6335
TF: 800-225-1998 ■ *Web:* www.lyndonstate.edu					
Marlboro College 2582 S Rd PO Box A	Marlboro	VT	05344	802-257-4333	451-7555
TF: 800-343-0049 ■ *Web:* www.marlboro.edu					
Middlebury College 131 S Main St	Middlebury	VT	05753	802-443-3000	443-2056*
*Fax: Admissions ■ *Web:* www.middlebury.edu					
Norwich University 158 Harmon Dr	Northfield	VT	05663	802-485-2001	485-2032
TF: 800-468-6679 ■ *Web:* www.norwich.edu					
Saint Michael's College 1 Winooski Pk	Colchester	VT	05439	802-654-2000	654-2906
TF: 800-762-8000 ■ *Web:* www.smcvt.edu					
Southern Vermont College 982 Manison Dr.	Bennington	VT	05201	802-442-5427	447-4695*
*Fax: Admissions ■ *TF:* 800-378-2782 ■ *Web:* www.svc.edu					
Union Institute & University Vermont College					
36 College St	Montpelier	VT	05602	802-828-8500	828-8855*
*Fax: Admissions ■ *TF:* 800-336-6794 ■ *Web:* www.tui.edu					
University of Vermont 85 S Prospect St	Burlington	VT	05405	802-656-3131	656-8611
Web: www.uvm.edu					

VIRGINIA

	City	State	ZIP	Phone	Fax
Bluefield College 3000 College Dr	Bluefield	VA	24605	276-326-3682	326-4395*
*Fax: Admissions ■ *TF:* 800-872-0175 ■ *Web:* www.bluefield.edu					
Bridgewater College 402 E College St	Bridgewater	VA	22812	540-828-5375	828-5481
TF: 800-759-8328 ■ *Web:* www.bridgewater.edu					
Christendom College 134 Christendom Dr	Front Royal	VA	22630	540-636-2900	636-1655*
*Fax: Admissions ■ *TF:* 800-877-5456 ■ *Web:* www.christendom.edu					
Christopher Newport University					
1 University Pl	Newport News	VA	23606	757-594-7015	594-7333*
*Fax: Admissions ■ *TF Admissions:* 800-333-4268 ■ *Web:* www.cnu.edu					
College of William & Mary PO Box 8795	Williamsburg	VA	23187	757-221-4000	221-1242*
*Fax: Admissions ■ *Web:* www.wm.edu					
Eastern Mennonite University 1200 Pk Rd	Harrisonburg	VA	22802	540-432-4118	432-4444*
*Fax: Admissions ■ *TF Admissions:* 800-368-2665 ■ *Web:* www.emu.edu					
Emory & Henry College PO Box 10	Emory	VA	24327	276-944-4121	944-6935*
*Fax: Admissions ■ *TF Admissions:* 800-848-5493 ■ *Web:* www.ehc.edu					
Ferrum College 215 Ferrum Mountain Rd	Ferrum	VA	24088	540-365-2121	365-4266
TF: 800-868-9797 ■ *Web:* www.ferrum.edu					
George Mason University					
4400 University Dr MS N3A4	Fairfax	VA	22030	703-993-1000	993-2392
TF: 888-627-6612 ■ *Web:* www.gmu.edu					
Prince William 10900 University Blvd	Manassas	VA	20110	703-993-8350	993-8378
Web: www.princewilliam.gmu.edu					
Hampden-Sydney College PO Box 667	Hampden-Sydney	VA	23943	434-223-6120	223-6120*
*Fax: Admissions ■ *TF Admissions:* 800-755-0733 ■ *Web:* www.hsc.edu					
Hampton University 11 Frissell Ave	Hampton	VA	23669	757-727-5000	727-5095
TF: 800-624-3328 ■ *Web:* www.hamptonu.edu					
Hollins University 7916 Williamson Rd	Roanoke	VA	24020	540-362-6401	362-6218*
*Fax: Admissions ■ *TF Admissions:* 800-456-9595 ■ *Web:* www.hollins.edu					
James Madison University 800 S Main St	Harrisonburg	VA	22807	540-568-6211	568-3332*
*Fax: Admissions ■ *Web:* www.jmu.edu					
Liberty University 1971 University Blvd	Lynchburg	VA	24502	434-582-2000	542-2311*
Fax Area Code: 800 ■ *Fax: Admissions ■ *TF:* 800-543-5317 ■ *Web:* www.liberty.edu					
Longwood University 201 High St	Farmville	VA	23909	434-395-2060	395-2332*
*Fax: Admissions ■ *TF:* 800-281-4677 ■ *Web:* www.longwood.edu					
Lynchburg College 1501 Lakeside Dr	Lynchburg	VA	24501	434-544-8100	544-8653*
*Fax: Admissions ■ *TF:* 800-426-8101 ■ *Web:* www.lynchburg.edu					
Mary Baldwin College 318 Prospect St	Staunton	VA	24401	540-887-7019	887-7292*
*Fax: Admissions ■ *TF Admissions:* 800-468-2262 ■ *Web:* www.mbc.edu					
Marymount University 2807 N Glebe Rd	Arlington	VA	22207	703-522-5600	522-0349
TF: 800-548-7638 ■ *Web:* www.marymount.edu					

Phone | Fax

Norfolk State University 700 Pk Ave. . . . . Norfolk VA 23504 757-823-8600 823-2078*
*Fax: Admissions ■ TF: 800-274-1821 ■ Web: www.nsu.edu

Old Dominion University Rollins Hall . . . . Norfolk VA 23529 757-683-3685 683-3255*
*Fax: Admissions ■ TF: 800-348-7926 ■ Web: www.odu.edu

Radford University 801 E Main St . . . . Radford VA 24142 540-831-5371 831-5038*
*Fax: Admissions ■ TF Admissions: 800-890-4265 ■ Web: www.radford.edu

Randolph College 2500 Rivermont Ave . . . . Lynchburg VA 24503 434-947-8000 947-8996*
*Fax: Admissions ■ TF Admissions: 800-745-7692 ■ Web: www.randolphcollege.edu

Randolph-Macon College PO Box 5005. . . . . Ashland VA 23005 804-752-7200 752-4707*
*Fax: Admissions ■ TF: 800-888-1762 ■ Web: www.rmc.edu

Roanoke College 221 College Ln. . . . . Salem VA 24153 540-375-2270 375-2267*
*Fax: Admissions ■ TF Admissions: 800-388-2276 ■ Web: www.roanoke.edu

Saint Paul's College 115 College Dr . . . . Lawrenceville VA 23868 434-848-3111 848-1846*
*Fax: Admissions ■ TF: 800-678-7071 ■ Web: www.saintpauls.edu

Shenandoah University 1460 University Dr. . . . . Winchester VA 22601 540-665-4581 665-4627*
*Fax: Admissions ■ TF: 800-432-2266 ■ Web: www.su.edu

Southern Virginia University
1 University Hill Dr. . . . . Buena Vista VA 24416 540-261-8400 261-8559*
*Fax: Admissions ■ TF: 800-229-8420 ■ Web: www.southernvirginia.edu

Strayer University Alexandria
2730 Eisenhower Ave . . . . Alexandria VA 22314 703-329-9100 329-9602*
*Fax: Admissions ■ TF: 888-478-7293 ■ Web: www.strayer.edu

Strayer University Arlington
2121 15th St N . . . . Arlington VA 22201 703-892-5100 769-2677*
*Fax: Admissions ■ TF: 888-478-7293 ■ Web: www.strayer.edu

Strayer University Fredericksburg
150 Riverside Pkwy Jefferson Bldg. . . . . Fredericksburg VA 22406 540-374-4300 374-4330*
*Fax: Admissions ■ TF: 800-765-8680 ■ Web: www.strayer.edu

Strayer University Loudoun
45150 Russell Branch Pkwy Suite 200 . . . . Ashburn VA 20147 703-729-8800 729-8820
Web: www.strayer.edu

Strayer University Manassas
9990 Battleview Pkwy. . . . . Manassas VA 20109 703-330-8400 330-8135*
*Fax: Admissions ■ Web: www.strayer.edu

Strayer University Woodbridge
13385 Minnieville Rd . . . . Woodbridge VA 22192 703-878-2800 878-2993
Web: www.strayer.edu

Sweet Briar College 134 Chappel Rd. . . . . Sweet Briar VA 24595 434-381-6100 381-6152*
*Fax: Admissions ■ TF Admissions: 800-381-6142 ■ Web: www.sbc.edu

Tabernacle Baptist Bible College & Theological Seminary
717 N Whitehurst Landing Rd. . . . . Virginia Beach VA 23464 757-424-4673 424-3014*
*Fax: Admissions ■ Web: www.tbbcts.org

University of Mary Washington
1301 College Ave . . . . Fredericksburg VA 22401 540-654-2000 654-1857*
*Fax: Admissions ■ TF Admissions: 800-468-5614 ■ Web: www.umw.edu

University of Richmond 28 Westhampton Way . . . . Richmond VA 23173 804-289-8000 287-6003
TF: 800-700-1662 ■ Web: www.richmond.edu
Westhampton College
The Deanery
28 Westhampton Way . . . . University of Richmond VA 23173 804-289-8640 287-6003
TF: 800-700-1662 ■ Web: www.oncampus.richmond.edu

University of Virginia
Peabody Hall PO Box 400160. . . . . Charlottesville VA 22903 434-982-3200 924-3587*
*Fax: Admissions ■ Web: www.virginia.edu

University of Virginia's College at Wise
1 College Ave . . . . Wise VA 24293 276-328-0102 328-0251*
*Fax: Admissions ■ TF Admissions: 888-282-9324 ■ Web: www.uvawise.edu

Virginia Commonwealth University
910 W Franklin St. . . . . Richmond VA 23284 804-828-0100 828-1899
TF: 800-841-3638 ■ Web: www.vcu.edu

Virginia Intermont College 1013 Moore St . . . . Bristol VA 24201 276-669-6101 466-7855*
*Fax: Admissions ■ TF: 800-451-1842 ■ Web: www.vic.edu

Virginia Military Institute
319 Letcher Ave . . . . Lexington VA 24450 540-464-7211 464-7746*
*Fax: Admissions ■ TF: 800-767-4207 ■ Web: www.vmi.edu

Virginia Polytechnic Institute & State University
112 Burruss Hall. . . . . Blacksburg VA 24061 540-231-6000 231-3242*
*Fax: Admissions ■ Web: www.vt.edu

Virginia State University 1 Hayden Dr . . . . Petersburg VA 23806 804-524-5000 524-5055
TF Admissions: 800-871-7611 ■ Web: www.vsu.edu

Virginia Union University
1500 N Lombardy St. . . . . Richmond VA 23220 804-342-3570 342-3511*
*Fax: Admissions ■ TF: 800-368-3227 ■ Web: www.vuu.edu

Virginia Wesleyan College 1584 Wesleyan Dr. . . . . Norfolk VA 23502 757-455-3208 461-5238*
*Fax: Admissions ■ TF: 800-737-8684 ■ Web: www.vwc.edu

Washington & Lee University
204 W Washington St. . . . . Lexington VA 24450 540-458-8710 458-8062*
*Fax: Admissions ■ Web: www.wlu.edu

WASHINGTON

Phone | Fax

Antioch University 2326 6th Ave . . . . Seattle WA 98121 206-441-5352 268-4242
TF: 888-268-4477 ■ Web: www.antiochsea.edu

Central Washington University
400 E University Way . . . . Ellensburg WA 98926 509-963-1111 963-3022*
*Fax: Admissions ■ TF Admissions: 866-298-4968 ■ Web: www.cwu.edu

City University 11900 NE 1st St . . . . Bellevue WA 98005 425-637-1010 709-5361
TF Admissions: 800-426-5596 ■ Web: www.cityu.edu

Eastern Washington University 526 5th St . . . . Cheney WA 99004 509-359-6200 359-6692*
*Fax: Admissions ■ Web: www.ewu.edu

Evergreen State College 2700 Evergreen Pkwy . . . . Olympia WA 98505 360-867-6000 867-5114
Web: www.evergreen.edu

Gonzaga University 502 E Boone Ave. . . . . Spokane WA 99258 509-323-6572 323-5780*
*Fax: Admissions ■ TF: 800-986-9585 ■ Web: www.gonzaga.edu

Heritage University 3240 Fort Rd. . . . . Toppenish WA 98948 509-865-8500 865-8659*
*Fax: Admissions ■ TF: 888-272-6190 ■ Web: www.heritage.edu

Northwest University 5520 108th Ave NE . . . . Kirkland WA 98033 425-822-8266 889-5224*
*Fax: Admissions ■ TF Admissions: 800-669-3781 ■ Web: www.northwestu.edu

Pacific Lutheran University 1010 122nd St S . . . . Tacoma WA 98444 253-531-6900 536-5136*
*Fax: Admissions ■ TF: 800-274-6758 ■ Web: www.plu.edu

Saint Martin's University 5300 Pacific Ave SE . . . . Lacey WA 98503 360-438-4311 412-6189*
*Fax: Admissions ■ TF Admissions: 800-368-8803 ■ Web: www.stmartin.edu

Phone | Fax

Seattle Bible College
11625 Airport Rd Suite B . . . . Everett WA 98204 425-212-3530 212-3532*
*Fax: Admissions ■ TF: 877-722-9673 ■ Web: www.seattlebiblecollege.edu

Seattle Pacific University 3307 3rd Ave W . . . . Seattle WA 98119 206-281-2000 281-2544*
*Fax: Admissions ■ TF: 800-366-3344 ■ Web: www.spu.edu

Seattle University 901 12th Ave. . . . . Seattle WA 98122 206-296-6000 296-5656*
*Fax: Admissions ■ TF: 800-426-7123 ■ Web: www.seattleu.edu

University of Puget Sound 1500 N Warner St. . . . . Tacoma WA 98416 253-879-3611 879-3993*
*Fax: Admissions ■ TF: 800-396-7191 ■ Web: www.ups.edu

University of Washington PO Box 355852. . . . . Seattle WA 98195 206-543-2100 685-3655*
*Fax: Admissions ■ Web: www.washington.edu

Walla Walla University
204 S College Ave . . . . College Place WA 99324 509-527-2327 527-2397
TF: 800-541-8900 ■ Web: www.wallawalla.edu

Washington State University PO Box 641040 . . . . Pullman WA 99164 509-335-3564 335-4902
TF: 888-468-6978 ■ Web: www.wsu.edu
Spokane 310 N Riverpoint Blvd PO Box 1495. . . . . Spokane WA 99210 509-358-7978 358-7538
Web: spokane.wsu.edu
Vancouver 14204 NE Salmon Creek Ave. . . . . Vancouver WA 98686 360-546-9788 546-9030*
*Fax: Admissions ■ Web: www.vancouver.wsu.edu

Western Washington University 516 High St . . . . Bellingham WA 98225 360-650-3000 650-7369
Web: www.wwu.edu

Whitman College 345 Boyer Ave . . . . Walla Walla WA 99362 509-527-5111 527-4967*
*Fax: Admissions ■ TF Admissions: 877-462-9448 ■ Web: www.whitman.edu

Whitworth College 300 W Hawthorne Rd. . . . . Spokane WA 99251 509-777-3212 777-3758*
*Fax: Admissions ■ TF Admissions: 800-533-4668 ■ Web: www.whitworth.edu

WEST VIRGINIA

Phone | Fax

Alderson-Broaddus College
101 College Hill Rd CB 2003 . . . . Philippi WV 26416 304-457-1700 457-6239*
*Fax: Admissions ■ TF Admissions: 800-263-1549 ■ Web: www.ab.edu

Bethany College 1 Main St. . . . . Bethany WV 26032 304-829-7000 829-7142*
*Fax: Admissions ■ TF: 800-922-7611 ■ Web: www.bethanywv.edu

Bluefield State College 219 Rock St. . . . . Bluefield WV 24701 304-327-4000 325-7747*
*Fax: Admissions ■ TF: 800-654-7798 ■ Web: www.bluefield.wvnet.edu

Concord University PO Box 1000. . . . . Athens WV 24712 304-384-3115 384-3218*
*Fax: Admissions ■ TF: 800-344-6679 ■ Web: www.concord.edu

Davis & Elkins College 100 Campus Dr . . . . Elkins WV 26241 304-637-1900 637-1800*
*Fax: Admissions ■ TF: 800-624-3157 ■ Web: www.davisandelkins.edu

Fairmont State University 1201 Locust Ave. . . . . Fairmont WV 26554 304-367-4892 367-4789*
*Fax: Admissions ■ TF Admissions: 800-641-5678 ■ Web: www.fairmontstate.edu

Glenville State College 200 High St . . . . Glenville WV 26351 304-462-7361 462-8619*
*Fax: Admissions ■ TF Admissions: 800-924-2010 ■ Web: www.glenville.edu

Marshall University 1 John Marshall Dr . . . . Huntington WV 25755 304-696-3170 696-3135*
*Fax: Admissions ■ TF: 877-642-3463 ■ Web: www.marshall.edu

Mountain State University 609 S Kanawha St . . . . Beckley WV 25801 304-253-7351 253-5072*
*Fax: Admissions ■ TF: 800-766-6067 ■ Web: www.mountainstate.edu
Martinsburg 214 Viking Way. . . . . Martinsburg WV 25401 304-263-4381 263-4674*
*Fax: Admissions ■ TF: 888-612-7800 ■ Web: www.martinsburg.mountainstate.edu

Ohio Valley University 1 Campus View Dr. . . . . Vienna WV 26105 304-865-6000 865-6175*
*Fax: Admissions ■ TF Admissions: 877-446-8668 ■ Web: www.ovu.edu

Salem International University 223 W Main St. . . . . Salem WV 26426 304-326-1109 326-1592*
*Fax: Admissions ■ TF: 800-283-4562 ■ Web: www.salemiu.edu

Shepherd University 301 N King St . . . . Shepherdstown WV 25443 304-876-5000 876-5165*
*Fax: Admissions ■ TF: 800-344-5231 ■ Web: www.shepherd.edu

University of Charleston
2300 MacCorkle Ave SE. . . . . Charleston WV 25304 304-357-4800 357-4715*
*Fax: Admissions ■ TF Admissions: 800-995-4682 ■ Web: www.ucwv.edu

West Liberty State College PO Box 295. . . . . West Liberty WV 26074 304-336-5000 336-8403*
*Fax: Admissions ■ TF: 866-937-8542 ■ Web: www.westliberty.edu

West Virginia State University
Barron Dr Rt 25 E PO Box 1000 . . . . Institute WV 25112 304-766-3000 766-5182*
*Fax: Admissions ■ TF: 800-987-2112 ■ Web: www.wvstateu.edu

West Virginia University PO Box 6009. . . . . Morgantown WV 26506 304-293-2121 293-3080
TF: 800-344-9881 ■ Web: www.wvu.edu
Institute of Technology 405 Fayette Pike . . . . Montgomery WV 25136 304-442-3032 442-3737*
*Fax: Admissions ■ TF: 888-554-8324 ■ Web: www.wvutech.edu

West Virginia Wesleyan College
59 College Ave. . . . . Buckhannon WV 26201 304-473-8000 473-8108*
*Fax: Admissions ■ TF Admitting: 800-722-9933 ■ Web: www.wvwc.edu

Wheeling Jesuit University
316 Washington Ave. . . . . Wheeling WV 26003 304-243-2000 243-2397*
*Fax: Admissions ■ TF: 800-624-6992 ■ Web: www.wju.edu

WISCONSIN

Phone | Fax

Alverno College PO Box 343922. . . . . Milwaukee WI 53234 414-382-6100 382-6055
TF: 800-933-3401 ■ Web: www.alverno.edu

Bellin College of Nursing PO Box 23400 . . . . Green Bay WI 54305 920-433-3560 433-7416
TF: 800-236-8707 ■ Web: www.bcon.edu

Beloit College 700 College St. . . . . Beloit WI 53511 608-363-2500 363-2075*
*Fax: Admissions ■ TF Admissions: 800-356-0751 ■ Web: www.beloit.edu

Cardinal Stritch University
6801 N Yates Rd . . . . Milwaukee WI 53217 414-410-4000 410-4058*
*Fax: Admissions ■ TF: 800-347-8822 ■ Web: www.stritch.edu

Carroll College 100 N E Ave . . . . Waukesha WI 53186 262-547-1211 951-3037*
*Fax: Admissions ■ TF: 800-227-7655 ■ Web: www.cc.edu

Carthage College 2001 Alford Pk Dr . . . . Kenosha WI 53140 262-551-8500 551-5762*
*Fax: Admissions ■ TF Admissions: 800-351-4058 ■ Web: www.carthage.edu

Columbia College of Nursing
2121 E Newport Ave . . . . Milwaukee WI 53211 414-961-3530 961-4205
Web: www.ccon.edu

Concordia University Wisconsin
12800 N Lake Shore Dr . . . . Mequon WI 53097 262-243-5700 243-4545*
*Fax: Admissions ■ TF Admissions: 888-628-9472 ■ Web: www.cuw.edu

Edgewood College 1000 Edgewood College Dr . . . . Madison WI 53711 608-663-2294 663-2214
TF: 800-444-4861 ■ Web: www.edgewood.edu

	City	State	Zip	Phone	Fax
Lakeland College PO Box 359	Sheboygan	WI	53082	920-565-2111	565-1215*
*Fax: Admissions ■ *TF:* 800-569-2166 ■ *Web:* www.lakeland.edu					
Lawrence University 115 S Drew St	Appleton	WI	54911	920-832-7000	832-6782
TF: 888-201-6017 ■ *Web:* www.lawrence.edu					
Maranatha Baptist Bible College 745 W Main St	Watertown	WI	53094	920-261-2327	261-9109*
*Fax: Admissions ■ *TF:* 800-622-2947 ■ *Web:* www.mbbc.edu					
Marian College of Fond du Lac 45 S National Ave	Fond du Lac	WI	54935	920-923-7650	923-8755*
*Fax: Admissions ■ *TF:* 800-262-7426 ■ *Web:* www.mariancollege.edu					
Marquette University 1217 W Wisconsin Ave	Milwaukee	WI	53233	414-288-7302	288-3764*
*Fax: Admissions ■ *TF Admissions:* 800-222-6544 ■ *Web:* www.marquette.edu					
Milwaukee Institute of Art & Design 273 E Erie St	Milwaukee	WI	53202	414-276-7889	291-8077*
*Fax: Admissions ■ *TF:* 888-749-6423 ■ *Web:* www.miad.edu					
Milwaukee School of Engineering 1025 N Broadway St	Milwaukee	WI	53202	414-277-6763	277-7475*
*Fax: Admissions ■ *TF:* 800-332-6763 ■ *Web:* www.msoe.edu					
Mount Mary College 2900 N Menomonee River Pkwy	Milwaukee	WI	53222	414-256-1219	256-0180*
*Fax: Admissions ■ *TF Admissions:* 800-321-6265 ■ *Web:* www.mtmary.edu					
Northland Baptist Bible College W10085 Pike Plains Rd	Dunbar	WI	54119	715-324-6900	324-6133*
*Fax: Admissions ■ *TF Admissions:* 888-466-7845 ■ *Web:* www.nbbc.edu					
Northland College 1411 Ellis Ave	Ashland	WI	54806	715-682-1224	682-1258*
*Fax: Admissions ■ *TF:* 800-753-1840 ■ *Web:* www.northland.edu					
Ripon College 300 Seward St	Ripon	WI	54971	920-748-8337	748-8335*
*Fax: Admissions ■ *TF Admissions:* 800-947-4766 ■ *Web:* www.ripon.edu					
Saint Norbert College 100 Grant St	De Pere	WI	54115	920-403-3005	403-4072*
*Fax: Admissions ■ *TF Admissions:* 800-236-4878 ■ *Web:* www.snc.edu					
Silver Lake College 2406 S Alverno Rd	Manitowoc	WI	54220	920-686-6175	684-7082*
*Fax: Admissions ■ *TF:* 800-236-4752 ■ *Web:* www.sl.edu					
Eau Claire 105 Garfield Ave PO Box 4004	Eau Claire	WI	54701	715-836-2637	836-2409*
*Fax: Admissions ■ *Web:* www.uwec.edu					
Green Bay 2420 Nicolet Dr	Green Bay	WI	54311	920-465-2000	465-5754*
*Fax: Admissions ■ *Web:* www.uwgb.edu					
La Crosse 1725 State St 115 Graff Main Hall	La Crosse	WI	54601	608-785-8000	785-6695
Web: www.uwlax.edu					
Madison 702 W Johnson St Suite 1101	Madison	WI	53715	608-262-3961	262-7706*
*Fax: Admissions ■ *Web:* www.wisc.edu					
Milwaukee PO Box 413	Milwaukee	WI	53201	414-229-1122	229-6940*
*Fax: Admissions ■ *Web:* www.uwm.edu					
Oshkosh 800 Algoma Blvd PO Box 2423	Oshkosh	WI	54903	920-424-0202	424-1207*
*Fax: Admissions ■ *Web:* www.uwosh.edu					
Parkside 900 Wood Rd	Kenosha	WI	53141	262-595-2345	595-2008*
*Fax: Admissions ■ *Web:* www.uwp.edu					
Platteville 1 University Plaza	Platteville	WI	53818	608-342-1125	342-1122*
*Fax: Admissions ■ *TF:* 800-362-5515 ■ *Web:* www.uwplatt.edu					
River Falls 410 S 3rd St B3 E Hathorn Hall	River Falls	WI	54022	715-425-3911	425-0698
Web: www.uwrf.edu					
Stevens Point 2100 Main St	Stevens Point	WI	54481	715-346-0123	346-3296*
*Fax: Admissions ■ *Web:* www.uwsp.edu					
Stout 802 S Broadway	Menomonie	WI	54751	715-232-1232	232-1667*
*Fax: Admissions ■ *TF Admissions:* 800-447-8688 ■ *Web:* www.uwstout.edu					
Superior Belknap St & Caitlin Ave PO Box 2000	Superior	WI	54880	715-394-8101	394-8407
TF: 800-442-6459 ■ *Web:* www.uwsuper.edu					
Whitewater 800 W Main St	Whitewater	WI	53190	262-472-1440	472-1515*
*Fax: Admissions ■ *Web:* www.uww.edu					
Viterbo University 900 Viterbo Dr	La Crosse	WI	54601	608-796-3000	796-3020*
*Fax: Admissions ■ *TF:* 800-848-3726 ■ *Web:* www.viterbo.edu					
Wisconsin Lutheran College 8800 W Bluemound Rd	Milwaukee	WI	53226	414-443-8800	443-8514*
*Fax: Admissions ■ *TF:* 888-947-5884 ■ *Web:* www.wlc.edu					

WYOMING

	City	State	Zip	Phone	Fax
University of Wyoming 1000 E University Ave Dept 3435	Laramie	WY	82071	307-766-5160	766-4042*
*Fax: Admissions ■ *TF Admissions:* 800-342-5996 ■ *Web:* www.uwyo.edu					

169 COLLEGES & UNIVERSITIES - GRADUATE & PROFESSIONAL SCHOOLS

	City	State	Zip	Phone	Fax
American Public University System (AMU) 111 W Congress St	Charles Town	WV	25414	304-724-3700	
TF: 877-777-9081 ■ *Web:* www.amu.apus.edu					
Kern Community College District 2100 Chester Ave	Bakersfield	CA	93301	661-336-5100	
Web: www.kccd.edu					

169-1 Law Schools

Law Schools Listed Here Are Approved By The American Bar Association.

	City	State	Zip	Phone	Fax
Albany Law School of Union University 80 New Scotland Ave	Albany	NY	12208	518-445-2326	445-2369
Web: www.als.edu					
American University Washington College of Law 4801 Massachusetts Ave NW	Washington	DC	20016	202-274-4101	274-4107
Web: www.wcl.american.edu					
Appalachian School of Law 1169 Edgewater Dr	Grundy	VA	24614	276-935-4349	935-8261
TF: 800-895-7411 ■ *Web:* www.asl.edu					
Ave Maria University School of Law 3475 Plymouth Rd	Ann Arbor	MI	48105	734-827-8040	622-0123
Web: www.avemarialaw.edu					
Barry University Dwayne O Andreas School of Law 6441 E Colonial Dr	Orlando	FL	32807	321-206-5600	206-5662
Web: www.barry.edu					
Baylor University School of Law 1114 S University Parks Dr 1 Bear Pl 97288	Waco	TX	76798	254-710-1911	710-2316
Web: www.law.baylor.edu					
Benjamin N Cardozo School of Law Yeshiva University 55 5th Ave Brookdale Ctr	New York	NY	10003	212-790-0200	790-0256
Web: www.cardozo.yu.edu					
Boston College Law School 885 Centre St	Newton	MA	02459	617-552-8550	552-2615
Web: www.bc.edu					
Boston University School of Law 765 Commonwealth Ave	Boston	MA	02215	617-353-3100	353-0578
Web: www.bu.edu/law					
Brigham Young University J Reuben Clark Law School JRCB Bldg PO Box 28000	Provo	UT	84602	801-422-2414	422-0389*
*Fax: Admissions ■ *Web:* www.law.byu.edu					
Brooklyn Law School 250 Joralemon St	Brooklyn	NY	11201	718-780-7906	780-0395*
*Fax: Admissions ■ *Web:* www.brooklaw.edu					
California Western School of Law 225 Cedar St	San Diego	CA	92101	619-525-1401	615-1401
TF: 800-255-4252 ■ *Web:* www.cwsl.edu					
Campbell University Norman Adrian Wiggins School of Law 113 Main St	Buies Creek	NC	27506	910-893-1750	893-1780
TF: 800-334-4111 ■ *Web:* www.law.campbell.edu					
Capital University Law School 303 E Broad St	Columbus	OH	43215	614-236-6500	236-6972
Web: www.law.capital.edu					
Case Western Reserve University School of Law 11075 E Blvd	Cleveland	OH	44106	216-368-3600	368-1042*
*Fax: Admissions ■ *TF:* 800-756-0036 ■ *Web:* www.lawcwru.edu					
Catholic University of America Columbus School of Law 3600 John McCormack Rd NE	Washington	DC	20064	202-319-5140	319-4459
Web: www.law.edu					
Chapman University School of Law 1 University Dr Kennedy Hall	Orange	CA	92866	714-628-2500	628-2501*
*Fax: Admissions ■ *TF:* 888-242-1913 ■ *Web:* www.chapman.edu					
Chicago-Kent College of Law Illinois Institute of Technology 565 W Adams St	Chicago	IL	60661	312-906-5000	906-5280
Web: www.kentlaw.edu					
City University of New York School of Law 65-21 Main St	Flushing	NY	11367	718-340-4200	340-4435*
*Fax: Admissions ■ *Web:* www.law.cuny.edu					
Cleveland State University Cleveland-Marshall College of Law 1801 Euclid Ave LB 138	Cleveland	OH	44115	216-687-2344	687-6881
Web: www.law.csuohio.edu					
Columbia University School of Law 435 W 116th St	New York	NY	10027	212-854-2640	854-1109
Web: www.law.columbia.edu					
Cornell Law School 226 Myron Taylor Hall	Ithaca	NY	14853	607-255-5141	255-7193
Web: www.lawschool.cornell.edu					
Creighton University School of Law 2133 California St	Omaha	NE	68178	402-280-2872	280-3161*
*Fax: Admissions ■ *Web:* www.culaw2.creighton.edu					
DePaul University College of Law 25 E Jackson Blvd	Chicago	IL	60604	312-362-8701	362-5280*
*Fax: Admissions ■ *Web:* www.law.depaul.edu					
Drake University School of Law 2507 University Ave	Des Moines	IA	50311	515-271-2824	271-1958
TF: 800-443-7253 ■ *Web:* www.law.drake.edu					
Duke University School of Law Science Dr & Towerview Rd PO Box 90393	Durham	NC	27708	919-613-7001	613-7231
TF: 888-529-2586 ■ *Web:* www.law.duke.edu					
Duquesne University School of Law 600 Forbes Ave	Pittsburgh	PA	15282	412-396-6300	396-1073
Web: www.law.duq.edu/law					
Emory University School of Law 1301 Clifton Rd	Atlanta	GA	30322	404-727-6816	727-6802*
*Fax: Admissions ■ *Web:* www.law.emory.edu					
Florida Coastal School of Law 8787 Bay Pine Rd	Jacksonville	FL	32256	904-680-7700	680-7692*
*Fax: Admissions ■ *TF:* 877-210-2591 ■ *Web:* www.fcsl.edu					
Florida State University College of Law 425 W Jefferson St	Tallahassee	FL	32306	850-644-3400	644-5487
Web: www.law.fsu.edu					
Fordham University School of Law 140 W 62nd St	New York	NY	10023	212-636-6810	636-7984*
*Fax: Admissions ■ *Web:* www.law.fordham.edu					
Franklin Pierce Law Ctr 2 White St	Concord	NH	03301	603-228-1541	228-1074*
*Fax: Admissions ■ *Web:* www.law.una.edu					
George Mason University School of Law 3301 N Fairfax Dr New Bldg A01	Arlington	VA	22201	703-993-8000	993-8088
Web: www.gmu.edu/departments/law					
George Washington University Law School 2000 H St NW	Washington	DC	20052	202-994-6261	994-7230*
*Fax: Admissions ■ *Web:* www.law.gwu.edu					
Georgetown University Law Ctr 600 New Jersey Ave NW	Washington	DC	20001	202-662-9000	662-9439*
*Fax: Admissions ■ *Web:* www.law.georgetown.edu					
Georgia State University College of Law 140 Decatur St	Atlanta	GA	30303	404-651-2048	651-1244*
*Fax: Admissions ■ *Web:* www.law.gsu.edu					
Golden Gate University School of Law 536 Mission St	San Francisco	CA	94105	415-442-6600	442-6609
TF: 800-448-4968 ■ *Web:* www.ggu.edu/school_of_law					
Gonzaga University School of Law 721 N Cincinnati St	Spokane	WA	99258	509-328-4220	323-5532*
*Fax: Admissions ■ *TF Admissions:* 800-986-9585 ■ *Web:* www.law.gonzaga.edu					

Phone | Fax

Hamline University School of Law
1536 Hewitt Ave . . . . Saint Paul MN 55104 651-523-2461 523-3064*
*Fax: Admissions ■ TF: 800-388-3688 ■ Web: www.hamline.edu/law
Harvard Law School 1515 Massachusetts Ave. . . . . Cambridge MA 02138 617-495-3109
Web: www.law.harvard.edu
Hofstra University School of Law
121 Hofstra University . . . . Hempstead NY 11549 516-463-5916 463-5100*
*Fax: Admissions ■ TF: 800-463-7872 ■ Web: www.hofstra.edu/Academics/Law
Howard University School of Law
2900 Van Ness St NW. . . . . Washington DC 20008 202-806-8000 806-8162*
*Fax: Admissions ■ Web: www.law.howard.edu
Indiana University School of Law Bloomington
211 S Indiana Ave. . . . . Bloomington IN 47405 812-855-7995 855-0555
Web: www.law.indiana.edu
Indiana University School of Law Indianapolis
Lawrence W Inlow Hall 530 W New York St . . . . Indianapolis IN 46202 317-274-8523 274-3955
Web: www.indylaw.indiana.edu
Inter American University School of Law
PO Box 70351 . . . . San Juan PR 00936 787-751-1912
Web: www.derecho.inter.edu
John Marshall Law School 315 S Plymouth Ct. . . . . Chicago IL 60604 312-427-2737 427-5136*
*Fax: Admissions ■ Web: www.jmls.edu
Lewis & Clark Law School
10015 SW Terwilliger Blvd . . . . Portland OR 97219 503-768-6600 768-6793*
*Fax: Admissions ■ Web: www.lclark.edu
Louis D Brandeis School of Law at the Univeristy of Louisville
2301 S 3rd St . . . . Louisville KY 40208 502-852-6358 852-0862
Web: www.law.louisville.edu
Louisiana State University Paul M Hebert Law Ctr
Paul M Hebert Law Ctr . . . . Baton Rouge LA 70803 225-578-8646 578-8647
Web: www.law.lsu.edu
Loyola Marymount Law School
919 Albany St . . . . Los Angeles CA 90015 213-736-1000 736-6523
Web: www.lls.edu
Loyola University New Orleans College of Law
7214 St Charles Ave PO Box 901 . . . . New Orleans LA 70118 504-861-5550
Web: www.law.loyno.edu
Marquette University Law School
1215 W Michigan St. . . . . Milwaukee WI 53233 414-288-7090 288-6403
Web: www.law.marquette.edu
Mercer University Walter F George School of Law
1021 Georgia Ave. . . . . Macon GA 31207 478-301-2605 301-2989*
*Fax: Admissions ■ TF: 800-637-2378 ■ Web: www.law.mercer.edu
Michigan State University College of Law
368 Law College Bldg. . . . . East Lansing MI 48824 517-432-6810 432-0098*
*Fax: Admissions ■ TF: 800-844-9352 ■ Web: www.law.msu.edu
Mississippi College School of Law
151 E Griffith St . . . . Jackson MS 39201 601-925-7100 925-7166*
*Fax: Admissions ■ Web: www.law.mc.edu
New England School of Law 154 Stuart St. . . . . Boston MA 02116 617-451-0010 457-3033*
*Fax: Admissions ■ Web: www.nesl.edu
New York Law School 185 W Broadway. . . . . New York NY 10013 212-431-2100 966-1522
TF: 877-937-6957 ■ Web: www.nyls.edu
New York University School of Law
110 W 3rd St . . . . New York NY 10012 212-998-6100 995-4527*
*Fax: Admissions ■ Web: www.law.nyu.edu
North Carolina Central University School of Law
1512 S Alston Ave . . . . Durham NC 27707 919-530-6333 530-6339
Web: www.nccu.edu
Northeastern University School of Law
400 Huntington Ave . . . . Boston MA 02115 617-373-2395 373-8865
Web: www.northeastern.edu/law
Northern Illinois University College of Law
1425 W Lincoln Hwy . . . . DeKalb IL 60115 815-753-8559 753-4501
TF: 800-892-3050 ■ Web: www.law.niu.edu
Northern Kentucky University Salmon P Chase College of Law
1 Nunn Dr. . . . . Highland Heights KY 41099 859-572-5340 572-5342*
*Fax: Admissions ■ Web: www.chaselaw.nku.edu
Northwestern University School of Law
357 E Chicago Ave . . . . Chicago IL 60611 312-503-3100 503-0178*
*Fax: Admissions ■ Web: www.law.northwestern.edu
Notre Dame Law School
University of Notre Dame 103 Law School . . . . Notre Dame IN 46556 574-631-6627 631-4197
Web: www.law.nd.edu
Nova Southeastern University Shepard Broad Law Ctr
3305 College Ave . . . . Fort Lauderdale FL 33314 954-262-6100 262-3844*
*Fax: Admissions ■ TF: 800-986-6529 ■ Web: www.nsulaw.nova.edu
Ohio Northern University Claude W Pettit College of Law
525 S Main St. . . . . Ada OH 45810 419-772-2211 772-3042
TF: 888-452-9668 ■ Web: www.law.onu.edu
Ohio State University Moritz College of Law
55 W 12th Ave . . . . Columbus OH 43210 614-292-2631 292-1492
Web: www.moritzlaw.osu.edu
Oklahoma City University School of Law
2501 N Blackwelder Ave . . . . Oklahoma City OK 73106 405-208-5000 521-5802
TF: 800-230-3012 ■ Web: www.okcu.edu
Pace University School of Law
78 N Broadway . . . . White Plains NY 10603 914-422-4210 989-8714*
*Fax: Admissions ■ Web: www.law.pace.edu
Pennsylvania State University Dickinson School of Law
150 S College St. . . . . Carlisle PA 17013 717-240-5000 241-3503*
*Fax: Admissions ■ TF: 800-840-1122 ■ Web: www.dsl.psu.edu
Pepperdine University School of Law
24255 Pacific Coast Hwy . . . . Malibu CA 90263 310-506-4631 506-7668*
*Fax: Admissions ■ Web: www.law.pepperdine.edu
Pontifical Catholic University of Puerto Rico School of Law
2250 Ave Las Americas. . . . . Ponce PR 00717 787-651-2000
Web: www.pucpr.edu
Quinnipiac University School of Law
275 Mt Carmel Ave. . . . . Hamden CT 06518 203-582-3400 582-3339
TF: 800-462-1944 ■ Web: law.quinnipiac.edu

Regent University School of Law
1000 Regent University Dr
Regent Hall 239 . . . . Virginia Beach VA 23464 757-226-4584 226-4139*
*Fax: Admissions ■ TF: 877-267-5072 ■ Web: www.regent.edu/acad/schlaw
Roger Williams University Ralph R Papitto School of Law
10 Metacom Ave. . . . . Bristol RI 02809 401-254-4500 254-4516*
*Fax: Admissions ■ TF: 800-633-2727 ■ Web: www.law.rwu.edu
Rutgers University School of Law Newark
123 Washington St Center for Law & Justice . . . . Newark NJ 07102 973-353-5557 353-3459*
*Fax: Admissions ■ Web: www.law.newark.rutgers.edu
Saint John's University School of Law
8000 Utopia Pkwy. . . . . Jamaica NY 11439 718-990-6611 990-2526
TF: 888-978-5646 ■ Web: www.new.stjohns.edu
Saint Louis University School of Law
3700 Lindell Blvd . . . . Saint Louis MO 63108 314-977-2766 977-3333
Web: www.law.slu.edu
Saint Mary's University School of Law
1 Camino Santa Maria . . . . San Antonio TX 78228 210-436-3523 431-4202*
*Fax: Admissions ■ TF: 866-639-5831 ■ Web: www.stmarytx.edu/law
Saint Thomas University School of Law
16401 NW 37th Ave . . . . Miami Gardens FL 33054 305-623-2310 623-2357*
*Fax: Admissions ■ TF: 800-245-4569 ■ Web: www.stu.edu/lawschool
Samford University Cumberland School of Law
800 Lakeshore Dr . . . . Birmingham AL 35229 205-726-2400 726-2057
Web: cumberland.samford.edu/cumberland1.asp?ID=2
Santa Clara University School of Law
500 El Camino Real . . . . Santa Clara CA 95053 408-554-4361 554-5095*
*Fax: Admissions ■ Web: www.scu.edu
Seattle University School of Law
901 12th Ave Sullivan Hall . . . . Seattle WA 98122 206-398-4000 398-4058*
*Fax: Admissions ■ Web: www.law.seattleu.edu
Seton Hall University School of Law
1 Newark Ctr. . . . . Newark NJ 07102 973-642-8747 642-8876*
*Fax: Admissions ■ TF: 888-415-7271 ■ Web: www.law.shu.edu
South Texas College of Law
1303 San Jacinto St . . . . Houston TX 77002 713-659-8040 646-2906*
*Fax: Admissions ■ Web: www.stcl.edu
Southern Illinois University School of Law
1209 W Chautauqua Rd . . . . Carbondale IL 62901 618-453-8858 453-8921*
*Fax: Admissions ■ TF: 800-739-9187 ■ Web: www.law.siu.edu
Southern Methodist University Dedman School of Law
3300 University Blvd . . . . Dallas TX 75205 214-768-2550 768-2549*
*Fax: Admissions ■ TF: 888-768-5291 ■ Web: www.law.smu.edu
Southern University Law Ctr
2 Roosevelt Steptoe Dr PO Box 9294 . . . . Baton Rouge LA 70813 225-771-6297 771-2121
TF: 800-537-1135 ■ Web: www.sulc.edu
Southwestern University School of Law
3050 Wilshire Blvd. . . . . Los Angeles CA 90010 213-738-6700 738-6899
Web: www.swlaw.edu
Stanford University Law School
559 Nathan Abbott Way Crown Quadrangle . . . . Stanford CA 94305 650-723-2465 723-0838*
*Fax: Admissions ■ Web: www.law.stanford.edu
Stetson University College of Law
1401 61st St S . . . . Gulfport FL 33707 727-562-7800 343-0136*
*Fax: Admissions ■ Web: www.law.stetson.edu
Suffolk University Law School 120 Tremont St . . . . Boston MA 02108 617-573-8144 523-1367*
*Fax: Admissions ■ Web: www.law.suffolk.edu
Syracuse University College of Law
300 White St. . . . . Syracuse NY 13244 315-443-1962 443-9568
Web: www.law.syr.edu
Temple University James E Beasley School of Law
1719 N Broad St . . . . Philadelphia PA 19122 215-204-7861 204-1185
Web: www.law.temple.edu
Texas Southern University Thurgood Marshall School of Law
3100 Cleburne St . . . . Houston TX 77004 713-313-4455 313-1049*
*Fax: Admissions ■ Web: www.tsu.edu/academics/law
Texas Tech University School of Law
1802 Hartford Ave. . . . . Lubbock TX 79409 806-742-3990 742-1629
Web: www.law.ttu.edu
Texas Wesleyan University School of Law
1515 Commerce St. . . . . Fort Worth TX 76102 817-212-4000 212-4141*
*Fax: Admissions ■ TF: 800-733-9529 ■ Web: www.law.txwes.edu
Thomas Jefferson School of Law
1155 Island Ave . . . . San Diego CA 92101 619-297-9700 294-4713
TF: 800-956-5070 ■ Web: www.tjsl.edu
Thomas M Cooley Law School 300 S Capitol Ave . . . . Lansing MI 48933 517-371-5140 334-5752
Web: www.cooley.edu
Touro College Jacob D Fuchsberg Law Ctr
225 Eastview Dr . . . . Central Islip NY 11722 631-421-2244 421-2675
Web: www.tourolaw.edu
Tulane University Law School
6329 Freret St Weinmann Hall . . . . New Orleans LA 70118 504-865-5939 865-6710*
*Fax: Admissions ■ TF: 800-734-6031 ■ Web: www.law.tulane.edu
University at Buffalo Law School
John Lord O'Brian Hall . . . . Buffalo NY 14260 716-645-2052 645-2064
Web: www.law.buffalo.edu
University of Akron School of Law
150 University Ave . . . . Akron OH 44325 330-972-7331 258-2343
Web: www.uakron.edu
University of Arizona James E Rogers College of Law
1201 E Speedway Blvd PO Box 210176 . . . . Tucson AZ 85721 520-621-1373 626-1839
Web: www.law.arizona.edu
University of Arkansas at Little Rock William H Bowen School of Law
1201 McMath Ave. . . . . Little Rock AR 72202 501-324-9903 324-9909
Web: www.law.ualr.edu
University of Arkansas School of Law
1045 W Maple St . . . . Fayetteville AR 72701 479-575-5601 575-3937*
*Fax: Admissions ■ Web: www.law.uark.edu
University of Baltimore School of Law
1415 Maryland Ave. . . . . Baltimore MD 21201 410-837-4468 837-4450
TF: 877-277-5982 ■ Web: www.law.ubalt.edu
University of California Berkeley School of Law
2600 Bancroft Way 5 Boalt Hall . . . . Berkeley CA 94720 510-642-2274 643-6222*
*Fax: Admissions ■ Web: www.law.berkeley.edu

				Phone	Fax
University of California Davis School of Law 400 Mrak Hall Dr *TF:* 866-752-6622 ■ *Web:* www.law.ucdavis.edu	Davis	CA	95616	530-752-0243	754-8371
University of California Hastings College of the Law 200 McAllister St **Fax:* Admissions ■ *Web:* www.uchastings.edu	San Francisco	CA	94102	415-565-4600	581-8946*
University of California Los Angeles School of Law 71 Dodd Hall PO Box 951445 *Web:* www.law.ucla.edu	Los Angeles	CA	90095	310-825-4841	
University of Chicago Law School 1111 E 60th St *Web:* www.law.uchicago.edu	Chicago	IL	60637	773-702-9494	834-0942
University of Cincinnati College of Law 2540 Clifton Ave *Web:* www.law.uc.edu	Cincinnati	OH	45221	513-556-6805	556-2391
University of Colorado School of Law 4050 Kittredge Loop Dr *Web:* www.colorado.edu/law	Boulder	CO	80309	303-492-7203	492-1757
University of Connecticut School of Law 45 Elizabeth St **Fax:* Admissions ■ *Web:* www.law.uconn.edu	Hartford	CT	06105	860-570-5100	570-5153*
University of Dayton School of Law 300 College Pk **Fax:* Admissions ■ *Web:* www.law.udayton.edu	Dayton	OH	45469	937-229-3211	229-4194*
University of Denver College of Law 2255 E Evans Ave *Web:* www.law.du.edu	Denver	CO	80208	303-871-6000	871-6378
University of Detroit Mercy School of Law 651 E Jefferson Ave **Fax:* Admissions ■ *TF:* 866-428-1610 ■ *Web:* www.law.udmercy.edu	Detroit	MI	48226	313-596-0264	596-0280*
University of Florida Fredric G Levin College of Law 2500 SW 2nd Ave **Fax:* Admissions ■ *TF:* 877-429-1297 ■ *Web:* www.law.ufl.edu	Gainesville	FL	32611	352-273-0890	392-4087*
University of Georgia School of Law 120 Herty Dr *Web:* www.lawsch.uga.edu	Athens	GA	30602	706-542-5191	542-5556
University of Houston Law Ctr 100 Law Ctr **Fax:* Admissions ■ *Web:* www.law.uh.edu	Houston	TX	77204	713-743-2100	743-2194*
University of Idaho College of Law 6th & Rayburn St PO Box 442321 *TF:* 888-884-3246 ■ *Web:* www.law.uidaho.edu	Moscow	ID	83844	208-885-4977	885-5709
University of Illinois College of Law 504 E Pennsylvania Ave *Web:* www.law.uiuc.edu	Champaign	IL	61820	217-333-0930	244-1478
University of Iowa College of Law 130 Byington Rd *TF:* 800-553-4692 ■ *Web:* www.law.uiowa.edu	Iowa City	IA	52242	319-335-9034	335-9019
University of Kansas School of Law 1535 W 15th St *Web:* www.law.ku.edu	Lawrence	KS	66045	785-864-4550	864-5054
University of Kentucky College of Law 620 S Limestone St *Web:* www.uky.edu/Law	Lexington	KY	40506	859-257-1678	323-1061
University of Maine School of Law 246 Deering Ave *Web:* www.mainelaw.maine.edu	Portland	ME	04102	207-780-4355	780-4239
University of Maryland School of Law 500 W Baltimore St **Fax:* Admissions ■ *Web:* www.law.umaryland.edu	Baltimore	MD	21201	410-706-3492	706-1793*
University of Memphis Cecil C Humphreys School of Law 3715 Central Ave *Web:* www.law.memphis.edu	Memphis	TN	38152	901-678-2421	678-5210
University of Miami School of Law 1311 Miller Dr **Fax:* Admissions ■ *Web:* www.law.miami.edu	Coral Gables	FL	33146	305-284-2339	284-3084*
University of Michigan Law School 625 S State St **Fax:* Admissions ■ *Web:* www.law.umich.edu	Ann Arbor	MI	48109	734-764-1358	647-3218*
University of Minnesota Law School 229 19th Ave S Walter F Mondale Hall **Fax:* Admissions ■ *Web:* www.law.umn.edu	Minneapolis	MN	55455	612-625-1000	626-1874*
University of Mississippi School of Law 301 Grove Loop PO Box 1848 **Fax:* Admissions ■ *Web:* www.law.olemiss.edu	University	MS	38677	662-915-7361	915-1289*
University of Missouri Columbia School of Law 203 Hulston Hall *Web:* www.law.missouri.edu	Columbia	MO	65211	573-882-6487	882-4984
University of Missouri Kansas City School of Law 500 E 52nd St **Fax:* Admissions ■ *Web:* www.law.umkc.edu	Kansas City	MO	64110	816-235-1644	235-5276*
University of Montana School of Law 32 Campus Dr **Fax:* Admissions ■ *Web:* www.umt.edu/law	Missoula	MT	59812	406-243-4311	243-2576*
University of Nebraska College of Law 1875 N 42nd St *Web:* www.unl.edu	Lincoln	NE	68583	402-472-2161	472-5185
University of Nevada Las Vegas William S Boyd School of Law 4505 Maryland Pkwy *Web:* www.law.unlv.edu	Las Vegas	NV	89154	702-895-3671	895-1095
University of New Mexico School of Law 1117 Stanford Dr NE *Web:* www.lawschool.unm.edu	Albuquerque	NM	87106	505-277-2146	277-0068
University of North Carolina School of Law 160 Ridge Rd *Web:* www.law.unc.edu	Chapel Hill	NC	27599	919-962-5106	843-7939
University of North Dakota School of Law 2901 University Ave **Fax:* Admissions ■ *TF:* 800-225-5863 ■ *Web:* www.law.und.nodak.edu	Grand Forks	ND	58202	701-777-2104	777-2721*
University of Oklahoma College of Law 300 Timberdell Rd Andrew M Coats Hall *Web:* www.law.ou.edu	Norman	OK	73019	405-325-4699	325-7474
University of Oregon School of Law 1515 Agate St *Web:* www.law.uoregon.edu	Eugene	OR	97403	541-346-3852	346-1564
University of Pennsylvania Law School 3400 Chestnut St *Web:* www.law.upenn.edu	Philadelphia	PA	19104	215-898-7483	573-2025
University of Pittsburgh School of Law 3900 Forbes Ave *Web:* www.law.pitt.edu	Pittsburgh	PA	15260	412-648-1400	648-2647
University of Richmond School of Law 28 W Hampton Way *Web:* www.law.richmond.edu	University of Richmond	VA	23173	804-289-8740	289-8992
University of Saint Thomas School of Law 1000 LaSalle Ave **Fax:* Admissions ■ *TF:* 800-328-6819 ■ *Web:* www.stthomas.edu	Minneapolis	MN	55403	651-962-4892	962-4876*
University of San Diego School of Law 5998 Alcala Pk **Fax:* Admissions ■ *TF:* 800-248-4873 ■ *Web:* www.sandiego.edu/usdlaw	San Diego	CA	92110	619-260-4528	260-2218*
University of San Francisco School of Law 2130 Fulton St **Fax:* Admissions ■ *Web:* www.usfca.edu/law	San Francisco	CA	94117	415-422-6586	422-5442*
University of South Carolina School of Law 701 S Main St **Fax:* Admissions ■ *Web:* www.law.sc.edu	Columbia	SC	29208	803-777-6605	777-7751*
University of South Dakota School of Law 414 E Clark St *TF:* 877-269-6837 ■ *Web:* www.usd.edu/law	Vermillion	SD	57069	605-677-5443	677-5417
University of Southern California Law School 699 Exposition Blvd **Fax:* Admissions ■ *Web:* www.lawweb.usc.edu	Los Angeles	CA	90089	213-740-2523	740-4570*
University of Tennessee College of Law 1505 Cumberland Ave *Web:* www.law.utk.edu	Knoxville	TN	37916	865-974-2521	974-6595
University of Texas School of Law 727 E Dean Keeton St *Web:* www.utexas.edu/law	Austin	TX	78705	512-471-5151	471-6988
University of the District of Columbia David A Clarke School of Law 4200 Connecticut Ave NW *Web:* www.law.udc.edu	Washington	DC	20008	202-274-7341	274-5583
University of the Pacific McGeorge School of Law 3200 5th Ave **Fax:* Admissions ■ *Web:* www.mcgeorge.edu	Sacramento	CA	95817	916-739-7105	739-7134*
University of Toledo College of Law 2801 W Bancroft St **Fax:* Admissions ■ *Web:* www.utlaw.edu	Toledo	OH	43606	419-530-4131	530-4345*
University of Tulsa College of Law 3120 E 4th Pl *Web:* www.law.utulsa.edu	Tulsa	OK	74104	918-631-2401	631-3630
University of Utah SJ Quinney College of Law 332 S 1400 E Rm 101 *Web:* www.law.utah.edu	Salt Lake City	UT	84112	801-581-6833	581-6897
University of Virginia School of Law 580 Massie Rd *Web:* www.law.virginia.edu	Charlottesville	VA	22903	434-924-7354	924-7536
University of Washington School of Law William H Gates Hall PO Box 353020 *Web:* www.law.washington.edu	Seattle	WA	98195	206-543-4078	543-5671
University of Wisconsin Law School 975 Bascom Mall *Web:* www.law.wisc.edu	Madison	WI	53706	608-262-2240	262-5485
University of Wyoming College of Law 1000 E University Ave Dept 3035 *Web:* www.uwadmnweb.uwyo.edu	Laramie	WY	82071	307-766-6416	766-6417
Valparaiso University School of Law 651 College Ave *TF:* 888-825-7652 ■ *Web:* www.valpo.edu	Valparaiso	IN	46383	219-465-7829	465-7808
Vanderbilt University Law School 131 21st Ave S *Web:* www.law.vanderbilt.edu	Nashville	TN	37203	615-322-2615	322-6631
Vermont Law School 168 Chelsea St PO Box 96 *TF:* 800-227-1395 ■ *Web:* www.vermontlaw.edu	South Royalton	VT	05068	802-831-1001	763-7071
Villanova University School of Law 299 N Spring Mill Rd **Fax:* Admissions ■ *Web:* www.law.villanova.edu	Villanova	PA	19085	610-519-7000	519-6291*
Wake Forest University School of Law Worrell Professional Ctr Wake Forest Rd **Fax:* Admissions ■ *Web:* www.law.wfu.edu	Winston-Salem	NC	27109	336-758-5435	758-3930*
Washburn University School of Law 1700 SW College Ave *Web:* www.washburnlaw.edu	Topeka	KS	66621	785-231-1060	670-1024
Washington & Lee University School of Law Sydney Lewis Hall 4th Fl **Fax:* Admissions ■ *Web:* www.law.wlu.edu	Lexington	VA	24450	540-458-8502	458-8586*
Washington University School of Law 1 Brookings Dr Anheuser-Busch Hall **Fax:* Admissions ■ *Web:* www.wulaw.wustl.edu	Saint Louis	MO	63130	314-935-6400	935-8778*
Wayne State University Law School 471 W Palmer St **Fax:* Admissions ■ *Web:* www.law.wayne.edu	Detroit	MI	48202	313-577-3937	993-8129*
West Virginia University College of Law PO Box 6130 *Web:* law.wvu.edu	Morgantown	WV	26506	304-293-5301	
Western New England College School of Law 1215 Wilbraham Rd **Fax:* Admissions ■ *Web:* www.law.wnec.edu	Springfield	MA	01119	413-782-1412	796-2067*
Western State University College of Law 1111 N State College Blvd **Fax:* Admissions ■ *TF:* 800-978-4529 ■ *Web:* www.wsulaw.edu	Fullerton	CA	92831	714-738-1000	441-1748*
Whittier Law School 3333 Harbor Blvd **Fax:* Admissions ■ *TF:* 800-808-8188 ■ *Web:* www.law.whittier.edu	Costa Mesa	CA	92626	714-444-4141	444-0250*

				Phone	Fax
Widener University School of Law Harrisburg 3800 Vartan Way	Harrisburg	PA	17110	717-541-3900	541-3999
TF: 888-943-3637 ■ *Web:* www.law.widener.edu					
Widener University School of Law Wilmington 4601 Concord Pike	Wilmington	DE	19803	302-477-2100	477-2224*
**Fax:* Admissions ■ *TF:* 888-943-3637 ■ *Web:* www.law.widener.edu					
Willamette University College of Law 245 Winter St SE	Salem	OR	97301	503-370-6282	370-6087*
**Fax:* Admissions ■ *Web:* www.willamette.edu/wucl					
William & Mary Law School 613 S Henry St	Williamsburg	VA	23185	757-221-3800	221-3261*
**Fax:* Admissions ■ *Web:* www.wm.edu					
William Mitchell College of Law 875 Summit Ave	Saint Paul	MN	55105	651-227-9171	290-6414
TF: 888-962-5529 ■ *Web:* www.wmitchell.edu					
Yale Law School 127 Wall St	New Haven	CT	06511	203-432-4992	432-2112
Web: www.law.yale.edu					

169-2 Medical Schools

Medical Schools Listed Here Are Accredited, Md-Grantingmembers Of The Association Of American Medical Colleges. Accredited Canadian Schools That Do Not Offer Classes In English Are Not Included Among These Listings.

				Phone	Fax
Albany Medical College 47 New Scotland Ave MC 3	Albany	NY	12208	518-262-5521	262-5887
Web: www.amc.edu					
Albert Einstein College of Medicine of Yeshiva University 1300 Morris Pk Ave	Bronx	NY	10461	718-430-2000	430-4098
Web: www.aecom.yu.edu					
Baylor College of Medicine 1 Baylor Plaza MS BCM365	Houston	TX	77030	713-798-7766	798-1518
Web: www.bcm.edu					
Boston University School of Medicine 715 Albany St	Boston	MA	02118	617-638-8000	638-5258*
**Fax:* Admissions ■ *Web:* www.bumc.bu.edu					
Brody School of Medicine at East Carolina University 600 Moye Blvd	Greenville	NC	27834	252-744-1020	744-1926*
**Fax:* Admissions ■ *TF:* 800-722-3281 ■ *Web:* www.ecu.edu/med					
Brown Medical School 97 Waterman St	Providence	RI	02912	401-863-2149	863-2660*
**Fax:* Admissions ■ *Web:* www.bms.brown.edu					
Case Western Reserve University School of Medicine 10900 Euclid Ave	Cleveland	OH	44106	216-368-3450	368-6011*
**Fax:* Admissions ■ *Web:* www.medismeds.cwru.edu					
Cincinnati Children's Hospital Medical Ctr 3333 Burnet Ave	Cincinnati	OH	45229	513-636-4200	636-3733*
**Fax:* Admitting ■ *TF:* 800-344-2462 ■ *Web:* www.cincinnatichildrens.org					
Columbia University College of Physicians & Surgeons 630 W 168th St	New York	NY	10032	212-305-3806	305-3601*
**Fax:* Admissions ■ *Web:* www.cpmcnet.columbia.edu					
Creighton University School of Medicine 2500 California Plaza	Omaha	NE	68178	402-280-2799	280-1241*
**Fax:* Admissions ■ *TF:* 800-325-4405 ■ *Web:* www.medicine.creighton.edu					
Dalhousie University Faculty of Medicine CRC Bldg Rm C-132	Halifax	NS	B3H4H7	902-494-1874	494-6369*
**Fax:* Admissions ■ *Web:* www.medicine.dal.ca					
Dartmouth Medical School 1 Rope Ferry Rd	Dartmouth	NH	03755	603-650-1200	650-1202
TF: 877-367-1797 ■ *Web:* www.dms.dartmouth.edu					
David Geffen School of Medicine at UCLA Center for Health Sciences 10833 Leconte Ave	Los Angeles	CA	90095	310-825-6081	
Web: www.dgsom.healthsciences.ucla.edu					
Drexel University College of Medicine 2900 Queen Ln	Philadelphia	PA	19129	215-991-8202	843-1766
Web: www.drexelmed.edu					
Duke University School of Medicine Office of Medical School Admissions DUMC 3710 Duke University Medical Ctr	Durham	NC	27710	919-684-2985	668-3714*
**Fax:* Admissions ■ *TF:* 877-684-2985 ■ *Web:* www.medschool.duke.edu					
East Tennessee State University James H Quillen College of Medicine PO Box 70580	Johnson City	TN	37614	423-439-2033	439-2110
Web: com.etsu.edu					
Eastern Virginia Medical School 700 W Olney Rd PO Box 1980	Norfolk	VA	23501	757-446-5812	446-5896*
**Fax:* Admissions ■ *Web:* www.evms.edu					
Emory University School of Medicine 1440 Clifton Rd NE Rm 115	Atlanta	GA	30322	404-727-5660	727-5456*
**Fax:* Admissions ■ *Web:* www.med.emory.edu					
Florida State University College of Medicine 1115 W Call St	Tallahassee	FL	32306	850-644-1855	645-2846*
**Fax:* Admissions ■ *Web:* www.med.fsu.edu					
George Washington University School of Medicine & Health Sciences 2300 'I' St NW Ross Hall 716	Washington	DC	20037	202-994-3506	994-1753
Web: www.gwumc.edu					
Georgetown University School of Medicine 13900 Reservoir Rd NW	Washington	DC	20007	202-687-1154	687-3079*
**Fax:* Admissions ■ *Web:* www.som.georgetown.edu					
Harvard Medical School 25 Shattuck St	Boston	MA	02115	617-432-1550	432-3307*
**Fax:* Admissions ■ *Web:* www.hms.harvard.edu					
Howard University College of Medicine 520 W St NW	Washington	DC	20059	202-806-6270	806-7934
Web: www.med.howard.edu					
Indiana University School of Medicine 545 Barnhill Dr # Eh435	Indianapolis	IN	46202	317-274-3772	278-0211
Web: www.medicine.iu.edu					
Jefferson Medical College of Thomas Jefferson University 1015 Walnut St	Philadelphia	PA	19107	215-955-6983	955-5151
Web: www.jefferson.edu/JMC					
Joan & Sanford Weill Medical College of Cornell University 445 E 69th St	New York	NY	10021	212-746-5454	746-8052*
**Fax:* Admissions ■ *Web:* www.med.cornell.edu					
Joan C Edwards School of Medicine at Marshall University 1600 Medical Ctr Dr	Huntington	WV	25701	304-691-1700	691-1726
TF: 877-691-1600 ■ *Web:* www.musom.marshall.edu					
Johns Hopkins University School of Medicine 601 N Caroline St	Baltimore	MD	21205	410-955-3080	955-0826
Web: www.hopkinsmedicine.org					
Keck School of Medicine of the University of Southern California 1975 Zonal Ave KAM 100	Los Angeles	CA	90089	323-442-1100	442-2433*
**Fax:* Admissions ■ *Web:* www.usc.edu					
Loma Linda University School of Medicine 11175 Campus St	Loma Linda	CA	92350	909-558-4467	558-0359
TF: 800-422-4558 ■ *Web:* www.llu.edu/llu/medicine					
Louisiana State University School of Medicine in New Orleans 433 Bolivar St	New Orleans	LA	70112	504-568-6262	568-7701
Web: www.medschool.lsuhsc.edu					
Louisiana State University School of Medicine in Shreveport 1501 Kings Hwy PO Box 33932	Shreveport	LA	71130	318-675-5069	675-5000
Web: www.sh.lsuhsc.edu					
Loyola University Chicago Stritch School of Medicine 2160 S 1st Ave Bldg 120 Rm 200	Maywood	IL	60153	708-216-3229	216-9160*
**Fax:* Admissions ■ *Web:* www.meddean.luc.edu					
Mayo Medical School 200 1st St SW	Rochester	MN	55905	507-284-3671	284-2634
Web: www.mayo.edu/mms					
McGill University Faculty of Medicine 3655 Promenade Sir-William-Osler 6th Fl	Montreal	QC	H3G1Y6	514-398-3517	398-4631*
**Fax:* Admissions ■ *Web:* www.med.mcgill.ca					
McMaster University School of Medicine 1200 Main St W Health Sciences Ctr Rm 1B7	Hamilton	ON	L8N3Z5	905-525-9140	546-0349
Web: www.fhs.mcmaster.ca					
Medical College of Georgia School of Medicine 1120 15th St	Augusta	GA	30912	706-721-0211	721-7279*
**Fax:* Admissions ■ *TF:* 800-736-2273 ■ *Web:* www.georgiahealth.edu					
Medical College of Wisconsin 8701 Watertown Plank Rd	Milwaukee	WI	53226	414-456-8296	456-6506
Web: www.mcw.edu					
Medical University of South Carolina College of Medicine 96 Jonathan Lucas St	Charleston	SC	29425	843-792-2300	792-3126*
**Fax:* Admissions ■ *Web:* find.musc.edu					
Meharry Medical College School of Medicine 1005 Doctor D B Todd Junior Blvd	Nashville	TN	37203	615-327-6111	327-6228
Web: www.mmc.edu					
Memorial University of Newfoundland Faculty of Medicine 300 Prince Phillip Dr Rm 1751 Health Sciences Ctr	Saint John's	NL	A1B3V6	709-777-6615	777-8422
Web: www.med.mun.ca					
Mercer University School of Medicine 1550 College St	Macon	GA	31207	478-301-2542	301-2547
TF: 800-342-0841 ■ *Web:* www.medicine.mercer.edu					
Michigan State University College of Human Medicine A-239 Life Sciences Bldg	East Lansing	MI	48824	517-353-9620	432-0021
Web: www.humanmedicine.msu.edu					
Morehouse School of Medicine 720 Westview Dr SW	Atlanta	GA	30310	404-752-1500	752-1512*
**Fax:* Admissions ■ *Web:* www.msm.edu					
Mount Sinai School of Medicine 1 Gustave L Levy Pl	New York	NY	10029	212-241-6696	828-4135*
**Fax:* Admissions ■ *Web:* www.mssm.edu					
New Jersey Medical School 185 S Orange Ave Rm C-653 PO Box 1709	Newark	NJ	07101	973-972-4631	972-7986
Web: www.njms.umdnj.edu					
New York Medical College Administration Bldg	Valhalla	NY	10595	914-594-4507	594-4976*
**Fax:* Admissions ■ *Web:* www.nymc.edu					
New York University School of Medicine 560 1st Ave	New York	NY	10016	212-263-7300	263-0720
Web: www.med.nyu.edu					
Northeastern Ohio Universities College of Medicine 4209 State Rt 44 PO Box 95	Rootstown	OH	44272	330-325-2511	325-8372*
**Fax:* Admissions ■ *TF:* 800-686-2511 ■ *Web:* www.neoucom.edu					
Northwestern University Feinberg School of Medicine 303 E Chicago Ave	Chicago	IL	60611	312-503-8649	503-6978
Web: www.medschool.northwestern.edu					
Ohio State University College of Medicine & Public Health 370 W 9th Ave 155 Meiling Hall	Columbus	OH	43210	614-292-2220	247-7959*
**Fax:* Admitting ■ *Web:* www.medicine.osu.edu					
School of Medicine 3181 SW Sam Jackson Pk Rd L-109	Portland	OR	97239	503-494-7800	494-4629
TF: 800-775-5460 ■ *Web:* www.ohsu.edu					
Pennsylvania State University College of Medicine 500 University Dr Rm C1805 PO Box 850	Hershey	PA	17033	717-531-8755	531-6225*
**Fax:* Admissions ■ *Web:* www.hmc.psu.edu					
Queen's University Faculty of Health Sciences School of Medicine 68 Barrie St	Kingston	ON	K7L3N6	613-533-2542	533-3190
Web: www.meds.queensu.ca					
Robert Wood Johnson Medical School 675 Hoes Ln	Piscataway	NJ	08854	732-235-4576	235-5078
Web: www.rwjms.umdnj.edu					
Rosalind Franklin University of Medicine & Science 3333 Green Bay Rd	North Chicago	IL	60064	847-578-3205	578-3284
Web: www.rosalindfranklin.edu					
Rush Medical College of Rush University 600 S Paulina St	Chicago	IL	60612	312-942-6913	942-2333*
**Fax:* Admissions ■ *Web:* www.rushu.rush.edu					
Saint Louis University School of Medicine 1402 S Grand Blvd Rm 226	Saint Louis	MO	63104	314-977-9870	977-9825
Web: www.slu.edu/colleges/med					
Schulich School of Medicine & Dentistry Health Sciences Addition Rm HSA 110	London	ON	N6A5C1	519-661-3459	661-3797*
**Fax:* Admissions ■ *Web:* www.med.uwo.ca					
Southern Illinois University School of Medicine 520 N 4th St # 202	Springfield	IL	62702	217-545-8000	
TF: 800-342-5748 ■ *Web:* www.siumed.edu					

Phone | Fax

Stanford University School of Medicine
291 Campus Dr Rm LK3C02 . . . . Stanford CA 94305 650-725-3900 725-7368
Web: med.stanford.edu

State University of New York Downstate Medical Ctr
450 Clarkson Ave PO Box 60M . . . . Brooklyn NY 11203 718-270-1000 270-7592
Web: www.downstate.edu

State University of New York Upstate Medical University
766 Irving Ave . . . . Syracuse NY 13210 315-464-4570 464-8867
TF: 800-736-2171 ■ *Web:* www.upstate.edu

Stony Brook University Health Sciences Center School of Medicine
Nichols Rd
Health Sciences Ctr Level 4 Rm 158. . . . . Stony Brook NY 11794 631-444-2113 444-6032*
**Fax:* Admissions ■ *Web:* www.hsc.stonybrook.edu/som

Temple University School of Medicine
3340 N Broad St SFC Suite 305 . . . . Philadelphia PA 19140 215-707-3656 707-6932
Web: www.temple.edu/medicine

Texas A & M University System Health Science Ctr
301 Tarrow St 7th Fl . . . . College Station TX 77840 979-458-7200 458-7202
Web: www.tamhsc.edu
College of Medicine
159 Joe H Reynolds Medical Bldg . . . . College Station TX 77843 979-845-7743 845-5533
Web: www.medicine.tamu.edu

Tufts University School of Medicine
136 Harrison Ave . . . . Boston MA 02111 617-636-7000 636-3805
Web: www.tufts.edu

Tulane University School of Medicine
1555 Poydras St Suite 1000. . . . . New Orleans LA 70118 504-988-5462 988-2945
Web: www.som.tulane.edu

University at Buffalo School of Medicine & Biomedical Sciences
131 Biomedical Education Bldg . . . . Buffalo NY 14214 716-829-3466 829-3849*
**Fax:* Admissions ■ *Web:* www.wings.buffalo.edu

University of Alabama at Birmingham School of Medicine
1670 University Blvd Volker Hall . . . . Birmingham AL 35294 205-934-2330 934-8724
Web: www.uab.edu/uasom

University of Alberta Faculty of Medicine & Dentistry
2-45 Medical Sciences Bldg. . . . . Edmonton AB T6G2H7 780-492-6350 492-9531
Web: www.med.ualberta.ca

University of Arizona College of Medicine
1501 N Campbell Ave. . . . . Tucson AZ 85724 520-626-4555 626-6252
Web: www.medicine.arizona.edu

University of British Columbia Faculty of Medicine
317-2194 Health Sciences Mall . . . . Vancouver BC V6T1Z3 604-822-2421 822-6061
Web: www.med.ubc.ca

University of Calgary Faculty of Medicine
3330 Hospital Dr NW
Health Sciences Ctr Rm G331. . . . . Calgary AB T2N4N1 403-220-7448 270-0178
Web: www.faculty.med.ucalgary.ca

University of California Davis School of Medicine
4610 X St Suite 1202 . . . . Sacramento CA 95817 916-734-4800 734-4050*
**Fax:* Admissions ■ *Web:* www.som.ucdavis.edu

University of California Irvine School of Medicine
Medical Education Bldg 802. . . . . Irvine CA 92697 949-824-5388 824-2485
TF: 800-824-5388 ■ *Web:* www.ucihs.uci.edu

University of California San Diego School of Medicine
9500 Gilman Dr
Rm 180 Medical Teaching Facility . . . . La Jolla CA 92093 858-534-0830 534-6573
Web: medicine.ucsd.edu

University of California San Francisco School of Medicine
521 Parnassus Ave. . . . . San Francisco CA 94143 415-476-4044
Web: medschool.ucsf.edu

University of Chicago Pritzker School of Medicine
924 E 57th St . . . . Chicago IL 60637 773-702-1939 702-2598
Web: www.pritzker.uchicago.edu

University of Cincinnati College of Medicine
231 Albert Sabin Way PO Box 670552 . . . . Cincinnati OH 45267 513-558-5575 558-1100
Web: www.med.uc.edu

University of Connecticut School of Medicine
263 Farmington Ave Rm AG036 MC 3906 . . . . Farmington CT 06030 860-679-4306 679-1899*
**Fax:* Admissions ■ *Web:* www.medicine.uchc.edu

University of Florida College of Medicine
1600 SW Archer Rd Rm M-108 . . . . Gainesville FL 32610 352-392-4569 392-1307
Web: www.med.ufl.edu

University of Illinois College of Medicine
808 S Wood St Rm 165 . . . . Chicago IL 60612 312-996-5635 996-6693*
**Fax:* Admissions ■ *Web:* www.uic.edu/depts/mcam

University of Iowa Roy J & Lucille A Carver College of Medicine
200 CMAB . . . . Iowa City IA 52242 319-335-6707 335-8318
Web: www.medicine.uiowa.edu

University of Kansas School of Medicine
3901 Rainbow Blvd 3030 Murphy MS1049 . . . . Kansas City KS 66160 913-588-5200 588-5259
Web: www.kumc.edu/som

University of Kentucky College of Medicine
Office of Medical Education MN 104 UKMC. . . . . Lexington KY 40536 859-323-6161 323-2076
Web: www.mc.uky.edu

University of Louisville School of Medicine
323 E Chestnut St Abell Bldg Rm 413 . . . . Louisville KY 40202 502-852-5193 852-0302
TF: 800-334-8635 ■ *Web:* www.louisville.edu/medschool

University of Manitoba Faculty of Medicine
727 McDermot Ave Rm 260 . . . . Winnipeg MB R3E3P5 204-789-3557 789-3928
Web: www.umanitoba.ca

University of Maryland School of Medicine
685 W Baltimore St
1-005 Bressler Research Bldg . . . . Baltimore MD 21201 410-706-7478 706-0467*
**Fax:* Admissions ■ *Web:* www.medschool.umaryland.edu
Graduate School of Biomedical Sciences
30 Bergen St ADMC 110 . . . . Newark NJ 07107 973-972-4511 972-7148
Web: www.gsbs.umdnj.edu

University of Minnesota Medical School Twin Cities
420 Delaware St SE Mayo MC 293. . . . . Minneapolis MN 55455 612-624-1188 626-4911
Web: www.ahc.umn.edu

University of Mississippi School of Medicine
2500 N State St. . . . . Jackson MS 39216 601-984-1080 984-1079
Web: som.umc.edu

University of Missouri-Columbia School of Medicine
1 Hospital Dr Rm MA 215. . . . . Columbia MO 65212 573-882-2923 884-2988
Web: www.muhealth.org/%7Emedicine

University of Missouri-Kansas City School of Medicine
2411 Holmes St . . . . Kansas City MO 64108 816-235-1111 235-5277
TF: 800-735-2466 ■ *Web:* www.research.med.umkc.edu

University of Nebraska School of Medicine
986585 Nebraska Medical Ctr . . . . Omaha NE 68198 402-559-2259 559-6840*
**Fax:* Admissions ■ *TF:* 800-626-8431 ■ *Web:* www.unmc.edu/UNCOM

University of Nevada School of Medicine
1664 N Virginia St
Pennington Medical Education Bldg 357 . . . . Reno NV 89557 775-784-6063 784-6194
Web: www.unr.edu

University of New Mexico School of Medicine
1 University of New Mexico
BMB Rm 177 MSC08-4720. . . . . Albuquerque NM 87131 505-272-2321 272-6581
Web: www.hsc.unm.edu

University of North Dakota School of Medicine & Health Sciences
501 N Columbia Rd . . . . Grand Forks ND 58203 701-777-5046 777-4942*
**Fax:* Admissions ■ *Web:* www.med.und.nodak.edu

University of Oklahoma College of Medicine
PO Box 26901 . . . . Oklahoma City OK 73190 405-271-2265 271-3032
Web: www.medicine.ouhsc.edu

University of Ottawa Faculty of Medicine
451 Smyth Rd. . . . . Ottawa ON K1H8M5 613-562-5700 562-5323
TF: 877-868-8292 ■ *Web:* www.uottawa.ca

University of Pennsylvania School of Medicine
3450 Hamilton Walk
Stemmler Hall Suite 100. . . . . Philadelphia PA 19104 215-898-8004 573-6645*
**Fax:* Admissions ■ *Web:* www.med.upenn.edu

University of Pittsburgh School of Medicine
3550 Terrace St 518 Scaife Hall . . . . Pittsburgh PA 15261 412-648-9891 648-8768*
**Fax:* Admissions ■ *Web:* www.medschool.pitt.edu

University of Rochester School of Medicine & Dentistry
601 Elmwood Ave. . . . . Rochester NY 14642 585-275-0017 756-5479*
**Fax:* Admissions ■ *Web:* www.urmc.rochester.edu/SMD

University of Saskatchewan College of Medicine
107 Wiggins Rd B103 Health Sciences Bldg . . . . Saskatoon SK S7N5E5 306-966-6135 966-6164
Web: www.usask.ca

University of South Alabama College of Medicine
307 N University Blvd. . . . . Mobile AL 36688 251-460-6101 460-6278
Web: www.southalabama.edu

University of South Carolina School of Medicine
6439 Garners Ferry Rd . . . . Columbia SC 29209 803-733-3210 733-3335
Web: www.med.sc.edu

University of South Dakota School of Medicine
414 E Clark St S Dakota Union Bldg 17 . . . . Vermillion SD 57069 605-677-5233 677-5109
Web: www.usd.edu/med

University of South Florida College of Medicine
12901 Bruce B Downs Blvd MDC PO Box 3. . . . . Tampa FL 33612 813-974-2229 974-4990*
**Fax:* Admissions ■ *Web:* www.med.usf.edu

University of Tennessee Health Science Center College of Medicine
800 Medicine Ave. . . . . Memphis TN 38163 901-448-5529 448-1430*
**Fax:* Admissions ■ *Web:* www.utmem.edu

University of Texas Medical Branch
301 University Blvd . . . . Galveston TX 77555 409-772-2618 747-2909*
**Fax:* Admissions ■ *TF:* 800-228-1841 ■ *Web:* www.utmb.edu

University of Texas Medical School at Houston
6431 Fannin St. . . . . Houston TX 77030 713-500-3333 500-3356
Web: www.med.uth.tmc.edu

University of Texas Medical School at San Antonio
7703 Floyd Curl Dr. . . . . San Antonio TX 78229 210-567-4420 567-6962*
**Fax:* Admissions ■ *Web:* www.som.uthscsa.edu

University of Toledo College of Medicine
3045 Arlington Ave Mulford Library Bldg. . . . . Toledo OH 43614 419-383-4229 383-4229
Web: www.hsc.utoledo.edu

University of Toronto Faculty of Medicine
500 University Ave 2nd Fl. . . . . Toronto ON M5G1V7 416-978-6976 978-7144
Web: www.facmed.utoronto.ca

University of Utah School of Medicine
30 N 1900 E . . . . Salt Lake City UT 84132 801-581-7201 585-3300
Web: uuhsc.utah.edu/som

University of Vermont College of Medicine
89 Beaumont Ave E-126 Given Bldg. . . . . Burlington VT 05405 802-656-2156 656-8577
Web: www.med.uvm.edu

University of Virginia School of Medicine
1300 Jefferson Pk Ave PO Box 800725 . . . . Charlottesville VA 22908 434-924-5571 982-2586
Web: www.medicine.virginia.edu

University of Washington School of Medicine
A-300 Health Sciences Bldg PO Box 356340. . . . . Seattle WA 98195 206-543-5560 616-3341
Web: www.uwmedicine.org

University of Wisconsin Medical School
750 Highland Ave Rm 2130 . . . . Madison WI 53705 608-263-4925 262-4226*
**Fax:* Admissions ■ *Web:* www.med.wisc.edu

Vanderbilt University School of Medicine
215 Light Hall. . . . . Nashville TN 37232 615-322-2145 343-8397
Web: www.mc.vanderbilt.edu/medschool

Virginia Commonwealth University School of Medicine
1101 E Marshall St PO Box 980565 . . . . Richmond VA 23298 804-828-9629 828-1246*
**Fax:* Admissions ■ *Web:* www.medschool.vcu.edu

Wake Forest University School of Medicine
Medical Ctr Blvd. . . . . Winston-Salem NC 27157 336-716-4264 716-9593
Web: www.wakehealth.edu

Washington University in Saint Louis School of Medicine
660 Euclid Ave CB 8107. . . . . Saint Louis MO 63110 314-362-6858 362-4658*
**Fax:* Admissions ■ *Web:* www.medinfo.wustl.edu

Wayne State University School of Medicine
540 E Canfield St 1310 Scott Hall. . . . . Detroit MI 48201 313-577-1466 577-9420*
**Fax:* Admitting ■ *Web:* www.med.wayne.edu

Phone Fax

West Virginia University School of Medicine
Medical Ctr Dr
Health Sciences Ctr N Rm 1146 . . . Morgantown WV 26506 304-293-2408 293-7814
TF: 800-543-5650 ■ *Web:* www.hsc.wvu.edu/som

Wright State University Boonshoft School of Medicine
3640 Col Glenn Hwy PO Box 1751 . . . Dayton OH 45401 937-775-2934 775-3322*
**Fax:* Admissions ■ *Web:* www.med.wright.edu

Yale University School of Medicine
367 Cedar St . . . New Haven CT 06510 203-785-2643 785-3234
Web: www.info.med.yale.edu

169-3 Theological Schools

Theological Schools Listed Here Are Members Of The Association Of Theological Schools (Ats), An Organization Of Graduate Schools In The U.S. And Canada That Conduct Post-Baccalaureate Professional And Academic Degree Programs To Educate Persons For The Practice Of Ministry And For Teaching And Research In The Theological Disciplines. Listings Include Ats Accredited Member Schools, Candidates For Accredited Membership, And Associate Member Schools.

Phone Fax

Acadia Divinity College 31 Horton Ave . . . Wolfville NS B4P2R6 902-585-2210 585-2233
TF: 866-875-8975 ■ *Web:* www.adc.acadiau.ca

Alliance Theological Seminary
350 N Highland Ave . . . Nyack NY 10960 845-353-2020 358-2651
TF: 800-541-6891 ■ *Web:* www.alliance.edu

American Baptist Seminary of the West
2606 Dwight Way . . . Berkeley CA 94704 510-841-1905 841-2446
Web: www.absw.edu

Andover Newton Theological School
210 Herrick Rd . . . Newton Centre MA 02459 617-964-1100 965-9756
TF: 800-964-2687 ■ *Web:* www.ants.edu

Andrews University Seventh-day Adventist Theological Seminary
4145 E Campus Cir Dr
Andrews University . . . Berrien Springs MI 49104 269-471-3537 471-6202
TF: 800-253-2874 ■ *Web:* www.andrews.edu/SEM

Aquinas Institute of Theology
23 S Spring Ave . . . Saint Louis MO 63108 314-256-8800 256-8888
TF: 800-977-3869 ■ *Web:* www.ai.edu

Asbury Theological Seminary
204 N Lexington Ave . . . Wilmore KY 40390 859-858-3581 858-2173
TF: 800-227-2879 ■ *Web:* www.asburyseminary.edu

Ashland Theological Seminary 910 Ctr St . . . Ashland OH 44805 419-289-5161 289-5969
Web: www.ashland.edu

Assemblies of God Theological Seminary
1435 N Glenstone Ave . . . Springfield MO 65802 417-268-1000 268-1001
TF: 800-467-2487 ■ *Web:* www.agts.edu

Associated Mennonite Biblical Seminary
3003 Benham Ave . . . Elkhart IN 46517 574-295-3726 295-0092
TF: 800-964-2627 ■ *Web:* www.ambs.edu

Athenaeum of Ohio 6616 Beechmont Ave . . . Cincinnati OH 45230 513-231-2223 231-3254
Web: www.mtsm.org

Atlantic School of Theology 660 Francklyn St . . . Halifax NS B3H3B5 902-423-6939 492-4048
Web: www.astheology.ns.ca

Austin Presbyterian Theological Seminary
100 E 27th St . . . Austin TX 78705 512-472-6736 479-0738
Web: www.austinseminary.edu

Bangor Theological Seminary 300 Union St . . . Bangor ME 04401 207-942-6781 990-1267
TF: 800-287-6781 ■ *Web:* www.bts.edu

Baptist Missionary Assn Theological Seminary
1530 E Pine St . . . Jacksonville TX 75766 903-586-2501 586-0378
TF: 800-259-5673 ■ *Web:* www.bmats.edu

Baptist Theological Seminary at Richmond
3400 Brook Rd . . . Richmond VA 23227 804-355-8135 355-8182
TF: 888-345-2877 ■ *Web:* www.btsr.edu

Berkeley Divinity School 409 Prospect St . . . New Haven CT 06511 203-432-9285 432-9353
Web: www.research.yale.edu

Bethany Theological Seminary
615 National Rd W . . . Richmond IN 47374 765-983-1800 983-1840
TF: 800-287-8822 ■ *Web:* www.bethanyseminary.edu

Bethel Seminary 3949 Bethel Dr . . . Saint Paul MN 55112 651-638-6288 638-6002
TF: 800-255-8706 ■ *Web:* seminary.bethel.edu

Bexley Hall Seminary 26 Broadway St . . . Rochester NY 14607 585-546-2160 546-1969
Web: www.bexley.edu

Biblical Theological Seminary 200 N Main St . . . Hatfield PA 19440 215-368-5000 368-2301
TF: 800-235-4021 ■ *Web:* www.biblical.edu

Blessed John XXIII National Seminary
558 S Ave . . . Weston MA 02493 781-899-5500 899-5500
Web: www.blessedjohnxxiii.edu

Briercrest College & Seminary
510 College Dr . . . Caronport SK S0H0S0 306-756-3200 756-5500
TF: 888-232-0531 ■ *Web:* www.briercrest.ca

Byzantine Catholic Seminary of SS Cyril & Methodius
3605 Perrysville Ave . . . Pittsburgh PA 15214 412-321-8383 321-9936
Web: www.byzcathsem.org

Calvin Theological Seminary
3233 Burton St SE . . . Grand Rapids MI 49546 616-957-6036 957-8621
TF: 800-388-6034 ■ *Web:* www.calvinseminary.edu

Canadian Southern Baptist Seminary
200 Seminary View . . . Cochrane AB T4C2G1 403-932-6622 932-7049
TF: 877-922-2727 ■ *Web:* www.csbs.ca

Canadian Theological Seminary
630-833 4th Ave SW . . . Calgary AB T2P3T5 403-410-2000 571-2556
TF: 800-461-1222 ■ *Web:* www.auc-nuc.ca

Carey Theological College 5920 Iona Dr . . . Vancouver BC V6T1J6 604-224-4308 224-5014
Web: www.careytheologicalcollege.ca

Carolina Evangelical Divinity School
1208 Eastchester Dr Suite 101 . . . High Point NC 27265 336-882-3370 882-3370

Catholic Theological Union
5416 S Cornell Ave . . . Chicago IL 60615 773-324-8000 324-4360
Web: www.ctu.edu

Central Baptist Theological Seminary
6601 Monticello Rd . . . Shawnee KS 66226 913-667-5700 371-5110
TF: 800-677-2287 ■ *Web:* www.cbts.edu

Phone Fax

Chicago Theological Seminary
5757 S University Ave . . . Chicago IL 60637 773-752-5757 752-0905
Web: www.chgosem.edu

Christ The King Seminary 711 Knox Rd . . . East Aurora NY 14052 716-652-8900 652-8903
Web: www.cks.edu

Christian Theological Seminary
1000 W 42nd St . . . Indianapolis IN 46208 317-924-1331 923-1961
TF: 800-585-0108 ■ *Web:* www.cts.edu

Christian Witness Theological Seminary
1040 Oak Grove Rd . . . Concord CA 94518 925-676-5002 676-5220
Web: www.cwts.edu

Church Divinity School of the Pacific
2451 Ridge Rd . . . Berkeley CA 94709 510-204-0700 644-0712
TF: 800-353-2377 ■ *Web:* www.cdsp.edu

Church of God Theological Seminary
900 Walker St NE . . . Cleveland TN 37311 423-478-1131 478-7711
TF: 800-228-9126 ■ *Web:* www.cogts.edu

Cincinnati Christian University
2700 Glenway Ave . . . Cincinnati OH 45204 513-244-8100 244-8140
TF: 800-949-4228 ■ *Web:* www.ccuniversity.edu

Claremont School of Theology
1325 N College Ave . . . Claremont CA 91711 909-626-3521 447-6290*
**Fax:* Admissions ■ *TF:* 866-274-6500 ■ *Web:* www.cst.edu

Colgate Rochester Crozer Divinity School
1100 S Goodman St . . . Rochester NY 14620 585-271-1320 271-8013
TF: 888-937-3732 ■ *Web:* www.crcds.edu

Columbia International University
7435 Monticello Rd . . . Columbia SC 29203 803-754-4100 786-4209
TF: 800-777-2227 ■ *Web:* www.ciu.edu

Columbia Theological Seminary
701 S Columbia Dr . . . Decatur GA 30030 404-378-8821 377-9696
Web: www.ctsnet.edu

Concordia Lutheran Seminary 7040 Ada Blvd . . . Edmonton AB T5B4E3 780-474-1468 479-3067
Web: www.concordiasem.ab.ca

Concordia Lutheran Theological Seminary
470 Glenridge Ave . . . Saint Catharines ON L2T4C3 905-688-2362 688-9744
Web: www.concordia-seminary.ca

Concordia Seminary 801 Seminary Pl . . . Saint Louis MO 63105 314-505-7000 505-7001
TF: 800-822-9545 ■ *Web:* www.csl.edu

Concordia Theological Seminary
6600 N Clinton St . . . Fort Wayne IN 46825 260-452-2100 452-2121
TF: 800-481-2155 ■ *Web:* www.ctsfw.edu

Covenant Theological Seminary
12330 Conway Rd . . . Saint Louis MO 63141 314-434-4044 434-4819
TF: 800-264-8064 ■ *Web:* www.covenantseminary.edu

Dallas Theological Seminary 3909 Swiss Ave . . . Dallas TX 75204 214-824-3094 841-3664
TF: 800-992-0998 ■ *Web:* www.dts.edu

Denver Seminary 6399 S Santa Fe Dr . . . Littleton CO 80120 303-761-2482 761-8060
TF: 800-922-3040 ■ *Web:* www.denverseminary.edu

Dominican House of Studies
487 Michigan Ave NE . . . Washington DC 20017 202-529-5300 636-1700
Web: www.dhs.edu

Dominican School of Philosophy & Theology
2301 Vine St . . . Berkeley CA 94708 510-849-2030 849-1372
TF: 888-450-3778 ■ *Web:* www.dspt.edu

Drew University Theological School
36 Madison Ave . . . Madison NJ 07940 973-408-3258 408-3068
Web: www.drew.edu

Duke University Divinity School
2 Chapel Dr PO Box 90968 . . . Durham NC 27708 919-660-3400 660-3535
TF: 888-246-3853 ■ *Web:* www.divinity.duke.edu

Earlham School of Religion 228 College Ave . . . Richmond IN 47374 765-983-1423 983-1688
TF: 800-432-1377 ■ *Web:* www.esr.earlham.edu

Ecumenical Theological Seminary (ETS)
2930 Woodward Ave . . . Detroit MI 48201 313-831-5200 831-1353
Web: www.etseminary.org

Eden Theological Seminary
475 E Lockwood Ave . . . Saint Louis MO 63119 314-961-3627 918-2626
TF: 800-969-3627 ■ *Web:* www.eden.edu

Emmanuel School of Religion 1 Walker Dr . . . Johnson City TN 37601 423-926-1186 926-6198
Web: www.esr.edu

Episcopal Divinity School 99 Brattle St . . . Cambridge MA 02138 617-868-3450 864-5385
TF: 800-433-7669 ■ *Web:* www.eds.edu

Episcopal Theological Seminary of the Southwest
606 Rathervue Pl . . . Austin TX 78705 512-472-4133 472-3098
Web: www.etss.edu

Erskine Theological Seminary 210 S Main St . . . Due West SC 29639 864-379-8885 379-2171
TF: 877-811-8117 ■ *Web:* www.erskine.edu

Evangelical School of Theology
121 S College St . . . Myerstown PA 17067 717-866-5775 866-4667
TF: 800-532-5775 ■ *Web:* www.evangelical.edu

Franciscan School of Theology
1712 Euclid Ave . . . Berkeley CA 94709 510-848-5232 549-9466
TF: 800-793-1378 ■ *Web:* www.fst.edu

Fuller Theological Seminary
135 N Oakland Ave . . . Pasadena CA 91182 626-584-5200 795-8767
TF: 800-235-2222 ■ *Web:* www.fuller.edu

Gardner-Webb University M Christopher White School of Divinity
110 S Main St Noel Hall . . . Boiling Springs NC 28017 704-406-4400 406-4734
TF: 800-619-3761 ■ *Web:* www.divinity.gardner-webb.edu

Garrett-Evangelical Theological Seminary
2121 Sheridan Rd . . . Evanston IL 60201 847-866-3900 866-3957
TF: 800-736-4627 ■ *Web:* www.garrett.northwestern.edu

General Theological Seminary 440 W 21st St . . . New York NY 10011 212-243-5150 727-3907
TF: 888-487-5649 ■ *Web:* www.gts.edu

George Fox Evangelical Seminary
12753 SW 68th Ave . . . Portland OR 97223 503-554-6150 554-6111
TF: 800-493-4937 ■ *Web:* www.georgefox.edu

Golden Gate Baptist Theological Seminary
201 Seminary Dr . . . Mill Valley CA 94941 415-380-1300 380-1302
TF: 888-444-8701 ■ *Web:* www.ggbts.edu

Name / Address	City	State	ZIP	Phone	Fax
Gordon-Conwell Theological Seminary 130 Essex St *TF:* 800-428-7329 ■ *Web:* www.gordonconwell.edu	South Hamilton	MA	01982	978-468-7111	468-6691
Grace Theological Seminary 200 Seminary Dr *TF:* 800-544-7223 ■ *Web:* gts.grace.edu	Winona Lake	IN	46590	574-372-5100	372-5113
Graduate Theological Union 2400 Ridge Rd *TF:* 800-826-4488 ■ *Web:* www.gtu.edu	Berkeley	CA	94709	510-649-2400	649-1730
Harding University Graduate School of Religion 1000 Cherry Rd *TF:* 800-680-0809 ■ *Web:* www.hugsr.edu	Memphis	TN	38117	901-761-1352	761-1358
Hood Theological Seminary 1810 Days Inn Dr *Web:* www.hoodseminary.edu	Salisbury	NC	28144	704-636-7611	636-7699
Houston Graduate School of Theology 2501 Central Pkwy *Web:* www.hgst.edu	Houston	TX	77092	713-942-9505	942-9506
Howard University School of Divinity 1400 Shepherd St NE *Web:* www.howard.edu	Washington	DC	20017	202-806-0500	806-0711
Iliff School of Theology 2201 S University Blvd *TF:* 800-678-3360 ■ *Web:* www.iliff.edu	Denver	CO	80210	303-744-1287	777-0164
Interdenominational Theological Ctr 700 Martin Luther King Jr Dr *Web:* www.itc.edu	Atlanta	GA	30314	404-527-7700	527-0901
Jesuit School of Theology at Berkeley 1735 LeRoy Ave *TF:* 800-824-0122 ■ *Web:* www.jstb.edu	Berkeley	CA	94709	510-549-5000	841-8536
Kenrick-Glennon Seminary 5200 Glennon Dr *Web:* www.kenrick.edu	Saint Louis	MO	63119	314-792-6100	792-6500
Knox College 59 St George St *Web:* www.utoronto.ca	Toronto	ON	M5S2E6	416-978-4500	971-2133
Lancaster Theological Seminary 555 W James St *TF:* 800-393-0654 ■ *Web:* www.lancasterseminary.edu	Lancaster	PA	17603	717-393-0654	393-4254
Lexington Theological Seminary 631 S Limestone St *TF:* 866-296-6087 ■ *Web:* www.lextheo.edu	Lexington	KY	40508	859-252-0361	281-6042
Lincoln Christian College Seminary 100 Campus View Dr *TF:* 888-522-5228 ■ *Web:* www.lccs.edu	Lincoln	IL	62656	217-732-3168	732-4078
Logos Evangelical Seminary 9358 Telstar Ave *Web:* www.logos-seminary.edu	El Monte	CA	91731	626-571-5110	571-5119
Louisville Presbyterian Theological Seminary 1044 Alta Vista Rd *TF:* 800-264-1839 ■ *Web:* www.lpts.edu	Louisville	KY	40205	502-895-3411	895-1096
Luther Seminary 2481 Como Ave *Web:* www.luthersem.edu	Saint Paul	MN	55108	651-641-3456	641-3425
Lutheran School of Theology at Chicago 1100 E 55th St *TF:* 800-635-1116 ■ *Web:* www.lstc.edu	Chicago	IL	60615	773-256-0700	256-0782
Lutheran Theological Seminary 114 Seminary Crescent *Web:* www.usask.ca	Saskatoon	SK	S7N0X3	306-966-7850	966-7852
Lutheran Theological Seminary at Gettysburg 61 Seminary Ridge *TF:* 800-658-8437 ■ *Web:* www.ltsg.edu	Gettysburg	PA	17325	717-334-6286	334-3469
Lutheran Theological Seminary at Philadelphia 7301 Germantown Ave *TF:* 800-286-4616 ■ *Web:* www.ltsp.edu	Philadelphia	PA	19119	215-248-4616	248-4577
Lutheran Theological Southern Seminary 4201 N Main St *TF:* 800-804-5233 ■ *Web:* www.ltss.edu	Columbia	SC	29203	803-786-5150	786-6499
McCormick Theological Seminary 5460 S University Ave *TF:* 800-228-4687 ■ *Web:* www.mccormick.edu	Chicago	IL	60615	773-947-6300	288-2612
Meadville Lombard Theological School 5701 S Woodlawn Ave *Web:* www.meadville.edu	Chicago	IL	60637	773-256-3000	256-3007
Memphis Theological Seminary 168 E Pkwy S *TF:* 800-822-0687 ■ *Web:* www.memphisseminary.edu	Memphis	TN	38104	901-458-8232	452-4051
Mennonite Brethren Biblical Seminary 4824 E Butler Ave *TF:* 800-251-6227 ■ *Web:* www.mbseminary.com	Fresno	CA	93727	559-251-8628	251-7212
Methodist Theological School in Ohio 3081 Columbus Pike *TF:* 800-333-6876 ■ *Web:* www.mtso.edu	Delaware	OH	43015	740-363-1146	362-3135
Michigan Theological Seminary 41550 E Ann Arbor Trail *TF:* 888-687-2737 ■ *Web:* www.mts.edu	Plymouth	MI	48170	734-207-9581	207-9582
Mid-America Reformed Seminary 229 Seminary Dr *TF:* 888-440-6277 ■ *Web:* www.midamerica.edu	Dyer	IN	46311	219-864-2400	864-2410
Midwestern Baptist Theological Seminary 5001 N Oak Trafficway *TF:* 877-414-3720 ■ *Web:* www.mbts.edu	Kansas City	MO	64118	816-414-3700	414-3799
Moravian Theological Seminary 1200 Main St *Web:* www.moravianseminary.edu	Bethlehem	PA	18018	610-861-1516	861-1569
Mount Angel Seminary 1 Abbey Dr *Web:* www.mtangel.edu	Saint Benedict	OR	97373	503-845-3951	845-3126
Multnomah Bible College & Biblical Seminary 8435 NE Glisan St *TF:* 800-275-4672 ■ *Web:* www.multnomah.edu	Portland	OR	97220	503-255-0332	254-1268
Nashotah House 2777 Mission Rd *TF:* 800-627-4682 ■ *Web:* www.nashotah.edu	Nashotah	WI	53058	262-646-6500	646-6504
Nazarene Theological Seminary 1700 E Meyer Blvd *TF:* 800-831-3011 ■ *Web:* www.nts.edu	Kansas City	MO	64131	816-333-6254	333-6271
New Brunswick Theological Seminary 17 Seminary Pl *TF:* 800-445-6287 ■ *Web:* www.nbts.edu	New Brunswick	NJ	08901	732-247-5241	249-5412
New Orleans Baptist Theological Seminary 3939 Gentilly Blvd *TF:* 800-662-8701 ■ *Web:* www.nobts.edu	New Orleans	LA	70126	504-282-4455	816-8023
New York Theological Seminary 475 Riverside Dr Suite 500 *Web:* www.nyts.edu	New York	NY	10115	212-870-1211	870-1236
Newman Theological College 15611 St Albert Trail *Web:* www.newman.edu	Edmonton	AB	T6V1H3	780-447-2993	447-2685
North American Baptist Seminary 1525 S Grange Ave *TF:* 800-440-6227 ■ *Web:* www.nabs.edu	Sioux Falls	SD	57105	605-336-6588	335-9090
North Park Theological Seminary 3225 W Foster Ave *TF:* 800-964-0101 ■ *Web:* www.northpark.edu	Chicago	IL	60625	773-244-6210	244-6244
Northern Seminary 660 E Butterfield Rd *TF:* 800-937-6287 ■ *Web:* www.seminary.edu	Lombard	IL	60148	630-620-2100	620-2190
Notre Dame Seminary 2901 S Carrollton Ave *Web:* www.nds.edu	New Orleans	LA	70118	504-866-7426	866-3119
Oblate School of Theology 285 Oblate Dr *Web:* www.ost.edu	San Antonio	TX	78216	210-341-1366	341-4519
Pacific Lutheran Theological Seminary 2770 Marin Ave *TF:* 800-235-7587 ■ *Web:* www.plts.edu	Berkeley	CA	94708	510-524-5264	524-2408
Pacific School of Religion 1798 Scenic Ave *TF:* 800-999-0528 ■ *Web:* www.psr.edu	Berkeley	CA	94709	510-848-0528	845-8948
Palmer Theological Seminary 6 Lancaster Ave *TF:* 800-220-3287 ■ *Web:* www.palmerseminary.edu	Wynnewood	PA	19096	610-896-5000	649-3834
Payne Theological Seminary 1230 Wilberforce Clifton Rd *TF:* 888-816-8933 ■ *Web:* www.payne.edu	Wilberforce	OH	45384	937-376-2946	376-3330
Phillips Theological Seminary 901 N Mingo Rd *TF:* 800-843-4675 ■ *Web:* www.ptstulsa.edu	Tulsa	OK	74116	918-610-8303	610-8404
Phoenix Seminary 4222 E Thomas Rd Suite 400 *TF:* 888-443-1020 ■ *Web:* www.phoenixseminary.edu	Phoenix	AZ	85018	602-850-8000	850-8080
Pittsburgh Theological Seminary 616 N Highland Ave *TF:* 800-451-4194 ■ *Web:* www.pts.edu	Pittsburgh	PA	15206	412-362-5610	363-3260
Pontifical College Josephinum 7625 N High St *TF:* 888-252-5812 ■ *Web:* www.pcj.edu	Columbus	OH	43235	614-885-5585	885-2307
Princeton Theological Seminary 64 Mercer St *TF:* 800-622-6767 ■ *Web:* www.ptsem.edu	Princeton	NJ	08540	609-921-8300	924-2973
Protestant Episcopal Theological Seminary in Virginia 3737 Seminary Rd *TF:* 800-941-0083 ■ *Web:* www.vts.edu	Alexandria	VA	22304	703-370-6600	370-6234
Providence College & Seminary 10 College Crescent *TF:* 800-668-7768 ■ *Web:* www.prov.ca	Otterburne	MB	R0A1G0	204-433-7488	433-3046
Queen's College Faculty of Theology 210 Prince Philip Dr Suite 3000 *TF:* 877-753-0116 ■ *Web:* www.mun.ca/queens	Saint John's	NL	A1B3R6	709-753-0116	753-1214
Queen's Theological College Theological Hall 99 University Ave Rm 212 *Web:* www.queensu.ca	Kingston	ON	K7L3N6	613-533-2110	533-6879
Reformed Episcopal Seminary 826 2nd Ave *Web:* www.reseminary.edu	Blue Bell	PA	19422	610-292-9852	292-9853
Reformed Presbyterian Theological Seminary 7418 Penn Ave *TF:* 866-778-7338 ■ *Web:* www.rpts.edu	Pittsburgh	PA	15208	412-731-8690	731-4834
Reformed Theological Seminary 5422 Clinton Blvd *TF:* 800-543-2703 ■ *Web:* www.rts.edu	Jackson	MS	39209	601-923-1600	923-1654
Regent College 5800 University Blvd *TF:* 800-663-8664 ■ *Web:* www.regent-college.edu	Vancouver	BC	V6T2E4	604-224-3245	224-3097
Regent University School of Divinity 1000 Regent University Dr Robertson Hall 303 *TF:* 800-723-6162 ■ *Web:* www.regent.edu/acad/schdiv	Virginia Beach	VA	23464	757-226-4537	226-4597
Regis College 15 St Mary St *Web:* www.regiscollege.ca	Toronto	ON	M4Y2R5	416-922-5474	922-2898
Sacred Heart Major Seminary 2701 Chicago Blvd *Web:* www.aodonline.org	Detroit	MI	48206	313-883-8501	868-6440
Sacred Heart School of Theology 7335 S Hwy 100 *Web:* www.shst.edu	Franklin	WI	53132	414-425-8300	529-6999
Saint Andrew's College 1121 College Dr *TF:* 877-664-8970 ■ *Web:* www.usask.ca	Saskatoon	SK	S7N0W3	306-966-8970	644-8981
Saint Augustine's Seminary of Toronto 2661 Kingston Rd *Web:* www.staugustines.on.ca	Toronto	ON	M1M1M3	416-261-7207	261-2529
Saint Bernard's School of Theology & Ministry 120 French Rd *Web:* www.stbernards.edu	Rochester	NY	14618	585-271-3657	271-2045
Saint Charles Borromeo Seminary 100 E Wynnewood Rd *Web:* www.scs.edu	Wynnewood	PA	19096	610-667-3394	
Saint Francis Seminary 3257 S Lake Dr *Web:* www.sfs.edu	Saint Francis	WI	53235	414-747-6400	747-6442
Saint John Vianney Theological Seminary 1300 S Steele St *Web:* www.sjvdenver.org	Denver	CO	80210	303-282-3427	282-3453
Saint John's Seminary 127 Lake St *Web:* www.sjs.edu	Brighton	MA	02135	617-254-2610	787-2336
Saint John's Seminary 5012 Seminary Rd *Web:* www.stjohnsem.edu	Camarillo	CA	93012	805-482-2755	484-4074
Saint Joseph's Seminary 201 Seminary Ave *Web:* www.archny.org	Yonkers	NY	10704	914-968-6200	376-2019
Saint Mary Seminary & Graduate School of Theology 28700 Euclid Ave *Web:* www.stmarysem.edu	Wickliffe	OH	44092	440-943-7600	943-7577

Name / Address	City	State	Zip	Phone	Fax
Saint Mary's Seminary & University 5400 Roland Ave. *Web:* www.stmarys.edu	Baltimore	MD	21210	410-864-4000	864-4278
Saint Meinrad School of Theology 200 Hill Dr *Web:* www.saintmeinrad.edu	Saint Meinrad	IN	47577	812-357-6611	357-6964
Saint Patrick's Seminary & University 320 Middlefield Rd *Web:* www.stpatricksseminary.org	Menlo Park	CA	94025	650-325-5621	323-5447
Saint Paul School of Theology 5123 Truman Rd *TF:* 800-825-0378 ■ *Web:* www.spst.edu	Kansas City	MO	64127	816-483-9600	483-9605
Saint Peter's Seminary 1040 Waterloo St N *Web:* www.stpetersseminary.ca	London	ON	N6A3Y1	519-432-1824	432-0964
Saint Tikhon's Orthodox Theological Seminary St Tikhon's Rd PO Box 130 *Web:* www.stots.edu	South Canaan	PA	18459	570-561-1818	937-3100
Saint Vincent de Paul Regional Seminary 10701 S Military Trail *Web:* www.svdp.edu	Boynton Beach	FL	33436	561-732-4424	737-2205
Saint Vincent Seminary 300 Fraser Purchase Rd *Web:* www.benedictine.stvincent.edu	Latrobe	PA	15650	724-537-4592	532-5052
Saint Vladimir's Orthodox Theological Seminary 575 Scarsdale Rd *Web:* www.svots.edu	Crestwood	NY	10707	914-961-8313	961-4507
San Francisco Theological Seminary 105 Seminary Rd *TF:* 800-447-8820 ■ *Web:* www.sfts.edu	San Anselmo	CA	94960	415-451-2800	451-2851
Seabury-Western Theological Seminary 2122 Sheridan Rd *TF:* 800-275-8235 ■ *Web:* www.seabury.edu	Evanston	IL	60201	847-328-9300	328-9624
Seminary of the Immaculate Conception 440 W Neck Rd *Web:* www.icseminary.edu	Huntington	NY	11743	631-423-0483	423-2346
Seton Hall University Immaculate Conception Seminary 400 S Orange Ave *Web:* www.theology.shu.edu	South Orange	NJ	07079	973-761-9575	761-9577
Southeastern Baptist Theological Seminary 120 S Wingate St *TF:* 800-284-6317 ■ *Web:* www.sebts.edu	Wake Forest	NC	27587	919-556-3101	556-0998
Southern Baptist Theological Seminary 2825 Lexington Rd **Fax:* Admitting ■ *TF:* 800-626-5525 ■ *Web:* www.sbts.edu	Louisville	KY	40280	502-897-4011	897-4723*
Southwestern Baptist Theological Seminary PO Box 22740 *Web:* www.swbts.edu	Fort Worth	TX	76122	817-923-1921	921-8758
SS Cyril & Methodius Seminary 3535 Indian Trail *Web:* www.orchardlakeseminary.org	Orchard Lake	MI	48324	248-683-0310	738-6735
Starr King School for the Ministry 2441 LeConte Ave *Web:* www.sksm.edu	Berkeley	CA	94709	510-845-6232	845-6273
Taylor University College & Seminary 11525 23rd Ave *TF:* 800-567-4988 ■ *Web:* www.taylor-edu.ca	Edmonton	AB	T6J4T3	780-431-5200	436-9416
Toronto School of Theology 47 Queen's Pk Crescent E *Web:* www.tst.edu	Toronto	ON	M5S2C3	416-978-4039	978-7821
Trinity Episcopal School for Ministry 311 11th St *TF:* 800-874-8754 ■ *Web:* www.tesm.edu	Ambridge	PA	15003	724-266-3838	266-4617
Trinity Lutheran Seminary 2199 E Main St *TF:* 866-610-8571 ■ *Web:* www.trinitylutheranseminary.edu	Columbus	OH	43209	614-235-4136	238-0263
Trinity Western University 7600 Glover Rd **Fax:* Admissions ■ *TF:* 888-468-6898 ■ *Web:* www.twu.ca	Langley	BC	V2Y1Y1	604-888-7511	513-2064*
Tyndale University College & Seminary 25 Ballyconnor Ct *TF:* 877-896-3253 ■ *Web:* www.tyndale.ca	Toronto	ON	M2M4B3	416-226-6380	226-6746
Union Theological Seminary 3041 Broadway *Web:* www.uts.columbia.edu	New York	NY	10027	212-662-7100	280-1416
Union Theological Seminary & Presbyterian School of Christian Education 3401 Brook Rd *TF:* 800-229-2990 ■ *Web:* www.union-psce.edu	Richmond	VA	23227	804-355-0671	355-3919
United Theological Seminary 4501 Denlinger Rd **Fax:* Admissions ■ *Web:* www.united.edu	Trotwood	OH	45426	937-529-2201	529-2292*
United Theological Seminary of the Twin Cities 3000 5th St NW *TF:* 800-937-1316 ■ *Web:* www.unitedseminary-mn.org	New Brighton	MN	55112	651-633-4311	633-4315
University of Dubuque Theological Seminary 2000 University Ave *TF:* 800-369-8387 ■ *Web:* www.udts.dbq.edu	Dubuque	IA	52001	563-589-3122	589-3110
University of Saint Mary of the Lake Mundelein Seminary 1000 E Maple Ave *Web:* www.usml.edu	Mundelein	IL	60060	847-566-6401	566-7330
University of Saint Michael's College Faculty of Theology 81 St Mary St *Web:* www.utoronto.ca	Toronto	ON	M5S1J4	416-926-1300	926-7276
University of Saint Thomas School of Theology 9845 Memorial Dr *Web:* www.stthom.edu	Houston	TX	77024	713-686-4345	683-8673
Urshan Graduate School of Theology 704 Howder Shell Rd *Web:* www.ugst.org	Florissant	MO	63031	314-921-9290	921-9203
Vancouver School of Theology 6000 Iona Dr *TF:* 866-822-9031 ■ *Web:* www.vst.edu	Vancouver	BC	V6T1L4	604-822-9031	822-9212
Wartburg Theological Seminary 333 Wartburg Pl *TF:* 800-225-5987 ■ *Web:* www.wartburgseminary.edu	Dubuque	IA	52003	563-589-0200	589-0333
Washington Baptist University 4302 Evergreen Ln *Web:* www.wbcs.edu	Annandale	VA	22003	703-333-5904	333-5906
Washington Bible College/Capital Bible Seminary 6511 Princess Garden Pkwy *TF:* 877-793-7227 ■ *Web:* www.bible.edu	Lanham	MD	20706	301-552-1400	552-2775
Washington Theological Union 6896 Laurel St NW *TF:* 800-334-9922 ■ *Web:* www.wtu.edu	Washington	DC	20012	202-726-8800	726-1716
Waterloo Lutheran Seminary 75 University Ave W **Fax:* Admissions ■ *Web:* www.info.wlu.ca	Waterloo	ON	N2L3C5	519-884-1970	884-8826*
Wesley Biblical Seminary 787 E Northside Dr *TF:* 800-788-9571 ■ *Web:* www.wbs.edu	Jackson	MS	39206	601-366-8880	366-8832
Wesley Theological Seminary 4500 Massachusetts Ave NW *TF:* 800-882-4987 ■ *Web:* www.wesleysem.edu	Washington	DC	20016	202-885-8600	885-8605
Western Seminary 5511 SE Hawthorne Blvd *TF:* 877-517-1800 ■ *Web:* www.westernseminary.edu	Portland	OR	97215	503-517-1800	517-1801
Western Theological Seminary 101 E 13th St *TF:* 800-392-8554 ■ *Web:* www.westernsem.edu	Holland	MI	49423	616-392-8555	392-7717
Westminster Theological Seminary 2960 Church Rd *TF:* 800-373-0119 ■ *Web:* www.wts.edu	Glenside	PA	19038	215-887-5511	887-5404
Westminster Theological Seminary in California 1725 Bear Valley Pkwy *Web:* www.wscal.edu	Escondido	CA	92027	760-480-8474	480-0252
Weston Jesuit School of Theology 3 Phillips Pl *Web:* www.wjst.edu	Cambridge	MA	02138	617-492-1960	492-5833
Winebrenner Theological Seminary 950 N Main St *TF:* 800-992-4987 ■ *Web:* www.winebrenner.edu	Findlay	OH	45840	419-434-4200	434-4267
Samford University 800 Lakeshore Dr **Fax:* Admissions ■ *TF Admissions:* 800-888-7218 ■ *Web:* www.samford.edu	Birmingham	AL	35229	205-726-3673	726-2171*
Azusa Pacific University 901 E Alosta Ave PO Box 7000 *TF:* 800-825-5278 ■ *Web:* www.apu.edu	Azusa	CA	91702	626-969-3434	812-3096
Biola University 13800 Biola Ave **Fax:* Admissions ■ *TF Admissions:* 800-652-4652 ■ *Web:* www.biola.edu	La Mirada	CA	90639	562-903-6000	903-4709*
La Sierra University 4500 Riverwalk Pkwy *TF:* 800-874-5587 ■ *Web:* www.lasierra.edu	Riverside	CA	92515	951-785-2000	785-2901
Hartford Seminary 77 Sherman St **Fax:* Admissions ■ *Web:* www.hartsem.edu	Hartford	CT	06105	860-509-9500	509-9509*
Catholic University of America 620 Michigan Ave NE *Web:* www.cua.edu	Washington	DC	20064	202-319-5000	319-6533
Barry University 11300 NE 2nd Ave **Fax:* Admissions ■ *TF:* 800-756-6000 ■ *Web:* www.barry.edu	Miami Shores	FL	33161	305-899-3000	899-2971*
Trinity International University 2065 Half Day Rd *TF:* 800-822-3225 ■ *Web:* www.tiu.edu	Deerfield	IL	60015	847-317-7000	317-8097
Anderson University 1100 E 5th St **Fax:* Admissions ■ *TF Admissions:* 800-428-6414 ■ *Web:* www.anderson.edu	Anderson	IN	46012	765-649-9071	641-4091*
Oakland City University 138 N Lucretia St *TF:* 800-737-5125 ■ *Web:* www.oak.edu	Oakland City	IN	47660	812-749-4781	749-1433
Mount Saint Mary's University 16300 Old Emmitsburg Rd **Fax:* Admissions ■ *TF Admissions:* 800-448-4347 ■ *Web:* www.msmary.edu	Emmitsburg	MD	21727	301-447-5214	447-5860*
Hellenic College-Holy Cross School of Theology 50 Goddard Ave **Fax:* Admissions ■ *Web:* www.hchc.edu	Brookline	MA	02445	617-731-3500	850-1460*
Cornerstone University 1001 E Beltline Ave NE **Fax:* Admissions ■ *TF Admissions:* 800-787-9778 ■ *Web:* www.cornerstone.edu	Grand Rapids	MI	49525	616-222-1426	222-1418*
University of Saint Thomas 2115 Summit Ave **Fax:* Admissions ■ *TF:* 800-328-6819 ■ *Web:* www.stthomas.edu	Saint Paul	MN	55105	651-962-5000	962-6160*
Roberts Wesleyan College 2301 Westside Dr **Fax:* Admissions ■ *TF Admissions:* 800-777-4792 ■ *Web:* www.roberts.edu	Rochester	NY	14624	585-594-6000	594-6371*
Campbell University 450 Leslie Campbell Ave PO Box 546 **Fax:* Admissions ■ *TF:* 800-334-4111 ■ *Web:* www.campbell.edu	Buies Creek	NC	27506	910-893-1290	893-1288*
Shaw University 118 E S St **Fax:* Admissions ■ *TF Admissions:* 800-214-6683 ■ *Web:* www.shawu.edu	Raleigh	NC	27601	919-546-8275	546-8271*
Oral Roberts University 7777 S Lewis Ave **Fax:* Admissions ■ *TF:* 800-678-8876 ■ *Web:* www.oru.edu	Tulsa	OK	74171	918-495-6161	495-6222*
Lipscomb University 3901 Granny White Pike **Fax:* Admissions ■ *TF:* 800-333-4358 ■ *Web:* www.lipscomb.edu	Nashville	TN	37204	615-966-1000	966-1804*
University of the South 735 University Ave **Fax:* Admissions ■ *TF:* 800-522-2234 ■ *Web:* www.sewanee.edu	Sewanee	TN	37383	931-598-1238	598-3248*
Eastern Mennonite University 1200 Pk Rd **Fax:* Admissions ■ *TF Admissions:* 800-368-2665 ■ *Web:* www.emu.edu	Harrisonburg	VA	22802	540-432-4118	432-4444*
Virginia Union University 1500 N Lombardy St **Fax:* Admissions ■ *TF:* 800-368-3227 ■ *Web:* www.vuu.edu	Richmond	VA	23220	804-342-3570	342-3511*

170 COLLEGES & UNIVERSITIES - HISTORICALLY BLACK

Historically Black Colleges & Universities (Hbcus) Are Colleges Or Universities That Were Established Before 1964 With The Intention Of Serving The African-American Community. (Prior To 1964, African-Americans Were Almost Always Excluded From Higher Education Opportunities At The Predominantly White Colleges And Universities.)

Name / Address	City	State	Zip	Phone	Fax
Interdenominational Theological Ctr 700 Martin Luther King Jr Dr *Web:* www.itc.edu	Atlanta	GA	30314	404-527-7700	527-0901
Meharry Medical College School of Medicine 1005 Doctor D B Todd Junior Blvd *Web:* www.mmc.edu	Nashville	TN	37203	615-327-6111	327-6228

	City	State	ZIP	Phone	Fax
Morehouse School of Medicine 720 Westview Dr SW	Atlanta	GA	30310	404-752-1500	752-1512*
*Fax: Admissions ■ Web: www.msm.edu					
H Councill Trenholm State Technical College 1225 Air Base Blvd	Montgomery	AL	36108	334-832-9000	420-4206
Web: www.trenholmtech.cc.al.us					
Miles College 5500 Myron Massey Blvd	Fairfield	AL	35064	205-929-1000	929-1627*
*Fax: Admissions ■ TF Admissions: 800-445-0708 ■ Web: www.miles.edu					
Oakwood College 7000 Adventist Blvd	Huntsville	AL	35896	256-726-7356	726-7154*
*Fax: Admissions ■ TF: 800-824-5312 ■ Web: www.oakwood.edu					
Selma University 1501 Lapsley St	Selma	AL	36701	334-872-2533	872-7746
Stillman College 3601 Stillman Blvd	Tuscaloosa	AL	35401	205-349-4240	366-8941
TF: 800-841-5722 ■ Web: www.stillman.edu					
Tuskegee University 102 Old Admissions Blvd	Tuskegee	AL	36088	334-727-8011	727-5750*
*Fax: Admissions ■ TF Admissions: 800-622-6531 ■ Web: www.tuskegee.edu					
Bishop State Community College 351 N Broad St	Mobile	AL	36603	251-690-6412	438-5403*
*Fax: Admissions ■ Web: www.bishop.edu					
Shelton State Community College 9500 Old Greensboro Rd	Tuscaloosa	AL	35405	205-759-1541	391-3910*
*Fax: Admissions ■ Web: www.sheltonstate.edu					
Shorter College 604 N Locust St	North Little Rock	AR	72114	501-374-6305	374-9333*
*Fax: Admissions ■ Web: www.shortercollege.4t.com					
Charles R Drew University of Medicine & Science 1731 E 120th St	Los Angeles	CA	90059	323-563-4800	563-4957*
*Fax: Admissions ■ Web: www.cdrewu.edu					
Delaware State University 1200 N DuPont Hwy	Dover	DE	19901	302-857-6351	857-6352*
*Fax: Admissions ■ TF Admissions: 800-845-2544 ■ Web: www.desu.edu					
Howard University 2400 6th St NW	Washington	DC	20059	202-806-6100	806-4465*
*Fax: Admissions ■ TF: 800-822-6363 ■ Web: www.howard.edu					
University of the District of Columbia 4200 Connecticut Ave NW	Washington	DC	20008	202-274-5000	274-5552
Web: www.udc.edu					
Bethune-Cookman College 640 Dr Mary McLeod Bethune Blvd	Daytona Beach	FL	32114	386-255-1401	481-2601*
*Fax: Admissions ■ TF Admissions: 800-448-0228 ■ Web: www.cookman.edu					
Edward Waters College 1658 Kings Rd	Jacksonville	FL	32209	904-470-8200	470-8048*
*Fax: Admissions ■ TF Admissions: 888-898-3191 ■ Web: www.ewc.edu					
Florida A & M University 1700 Lee Hall Dr Rm G-7 Foote-Hilyer Administration Ctr	Tallahassee	FL	32307	850-599-3000	599-3069
Web: www.famu.edu					
Florida Memorial University 15800 NW 42nd Ave	Miami	FL	33054	305-626-3600	623-1462*
*Fax: Admissions ■ TF: 800-822-1362 ■ Web: www.fmuniv.edu					
Albany State University 504 College Dr Rd	Albany	GA	31705	229-430-4646	430-4105*
*Fax: Admissions ■ Web: asuweb.asurams.edu/asu					
Clark Atlanta University 223 James P Brawley Dr SW	Atlanta	GA	30314	404-880-8000	880-6174*
*Fax: Admissions ■ TF Admissions: 800-688-3228 ■ Web: www.cau.edu					
Fort Valley State University 1005 State University Dr	Fort Valley	GA	31030	478-825-6211	825-6169*
*Fax: Admissions ■ TF: 877-462-3878 ■ Web: www.fvsu.edu					
Morehouse College 830 Westview Dr SW	Atlanta	GA	30314	404-681-2800	572-3668*
*Fax: Admissions ■ Web: www.morehouse.edu					
Paine College 1235 15th St	Augusta	GA	30901	706-821-8200	821-8293*
*Fax: Admissions ■ TF: 800-476-7703 ■ Web: www.paine.edu					
Savannah State University 3219 College St	Savannah	GA	31404	912-356-2186	356-2256*
*Fax: Admissions ■ TF Admissions: 800-788-0478 ■ Web: www.savstate.edu					
Spelman College 350 Spelman Ln SW	Atlanta	GA	30314	404-681-3643	270-5201*
*Fax: Admissions ■ TF Admissions: 800-982-2411 ■ Web: www.spelman.edu					
Kentucky State University 400 E Main St	Frankfort	KY	40601	502-597-6000	597-5814*
*Fax: Admissions ■ TF Admissions: 800-325-1716 ■ Web: www.kysu.edu					
Grambling State University 403 Main St	Grambling	LA	71245	318-247-3811	
TF: 800-569-4714 ■ Web: www.gram.edu					
Southern University & A & M College Branch Post Office	Baton Rouge	LA	70813	225-771-4500	771-2500*
*Fax: Admissions ■ TF Admissions: 800-256-1531 ■ Web: www.subr.edu					
Xavier University of Louisiana 3437 Audubon Ct	New Orleans	LA	70125	504-486-7411	485-7941
TF: 877-928-4378 ■ Web: www.xula.edu					
Southern University *Shreveport* 3050 ML King Jr Dr	Shreveport	LA	71107	318-674-3300	674-3344*
*Fax: Admissions ■ TF: 800-458-1472 ■ Web: www.susla.edu					
Bowie State University 14000 Jericho Pk Rd	Bowie	MD	20715	301-860-4000	860-3518
TF: 877-772-6943 ■ Web: www.bowiestate.edu					
Coppin State University 2500 W N Ave	Baltimore	MD	21216	410-951-3600	523-7351*
*Fax: Admissions ■ TF Admissions: 800-635-3674 ■ Web: www.coppin.edu					
Morgan State University 1700 E Cold Spring Ln	Baltimore	MD	21251	443-885-3333	885-8260*
*Fax: Admissions ■ TF: 800-319-4678 ■ Web: www.morgan.edu					
Lewis College of Business 17370 Meyers Rd	Detroit	MI	48235	313-862-6300	862-1027*
*Fax: Admissions ■ Web: www.lewiscollege.edu					
Jackson State University 1400 John R Lynch St	Jackson	MS	39217	601-979-2121	979-3445*
*Fax: Admissions ■ TF: 800-848-6817 ■ Web: www.jsums.edu					
Mississippi Valley State University 14000 Hwy 82	Itta Bena	MS	38941	662-254-9041	254-3759
TF: 800-844-6885 ■ Web: www.mvsu.edu					
Rust College 150 Rust Ave	Holly Springs	MS	38635	662-252-8000	252-2258*
*Fax: Admissions ■ TF: 888-806-8492 ■ Web: www.rustcollege.edu					
Tougaloo College 500 W County Line Rd	Tougaloo	MS	39174	601-977-7700	977-4501*
*Fax: Admissions ■ TF Admissions: 888-424-2566 ■ Web: www.tougaloo.edu					
Hinds Community College 501 E Main St PO Box 1100	Raymond	MS	39154	601-857-5261	857-3539*
*Fax: Admissions ■ TF: 800-446-3722 ■ Web: www.hindscc.edu					
Harris-Stowe State University 3026 Laclede Ave	Saint Louis	MO	63103	314-340-3366	340-3555
Web: www.hssu.edu					
Lincoln University 820 Chestnut St B-7 Young Hall	Jefferson City	MO	65102	573-681-5599	681-5889*
*Fax: Admissions ■ TF Admissions: 800-521-5052 ■ Web: www.lincolnu.edu					
Bennett College 900 E Washington St	Greensboro	NC	27401	336-370-8624	517-2166*
*Fax: Admissions ■ TF Admissions: 800-413-5323 ■ Web: www.bennett.edu					
Elizabeth City State University 1704 Weeksville Rd CB 901	Elizabeth City	NC	27909	252-335-3305	335-3537*
*Fax: Admissions ■ TF Admissions: 800-347-3278 ■ Web: www.ecsu.edu					
Fayetteville State University 1200 Murchison Rd	Fayetteville	NC	28301	910-672-1371	672-1414*
*Fax: Admissions ■ TF Admissions: 800-222-2594 ■ Web: www.uncfsu.edu					
Johnson C Smith University 100 Beatties Ford Rd	Charlotte	NC	28216	704-378-1000	378-1242*
*Fax: Admissions ■ TF Admissions: 800-782-7303 ■ Web: www.jcsu.edu					
Livingstone College 701 W Monroe St	Salisbury	NC	28144	704-216-6000	216-6215
TF: 800-835-3435 ■ Web: www.livingstone.edu					
North Carolina A & T State University 1601 E Market St	Greensboro	NC	27411	336-334-7946	334-7478*
*Fax: Admissions ■ TF Admissions: 800-443-8964 ■ Web: www.ncat.edu					
North Carolina Central University 1801 Fayetteville St	Durham	NC	27707	919-530-6100	530-7625*
*Fax: Admissions ■ TF Admissions: 877-667-7533 ■ Web: www.nccu.edu					
Saint Augustine's College 1315 Oakwood Ave	Raleigh	NC	27610	919-516-4016	516-5805*
*Fax: Admissions ■ TF Admissions: 800-948-1126 ■ Web: www.st-aug.edu					
Shaw University 118 E S St	Raleigh	NC	27601	919-546-8275	546-8271*
*Fax: Admissions ■ TF Admissions: 800-214-6683 ■ Web: www.shawu.edu					
Winston-Salem State University 601 S ML King Jr Dr 206 Thompson Ctr	Winston-Salem	NC	27110	336-750-2000	750-2079*
*Fax: Admissions ■ TF Admissions: 800-257-4052 ■ Web: www.wssu.edu					
Central State University 1400 Brush Row Rd PO Box 1004	Wilberforce	OH	45384	937-376-6011	376-6648*
*Fax: Admissions ■ TF: 800-388-2781 ■ Web: www.centralstate.edu					
Wilberforce University 1055 N Bickett Rd PO Box 1001	Wilberforce	OH	45384	937-376-2911	376-4751*
*Fax: Admissions ■ TF Admissions: 800-367-8568 ■ Web: www.wilberforce.edu					
Langston University Hwy 33 PO Box 1500	Langston	OK	73050	405-466-3428	466-3391
TF: 877-466-2231 ■ Web: www.lunet.edu					
Cheyney University of Pennsylvania 1837 University Cir PO Box 200	Cheyney	PA	19319	610-399-2275	399-2099*
*Fax: Admissions ■ TF: 800-243-9639 ■ Web: www.cheyney.edu					
Lincoln University 1570 Old Baltimore Pike PO Box 179	Lincoln University	PA	19352	484-365-8000	365-8109*
*Fax: Admissions ■ TF Admissions: 800-790-0191 ■ Web: www.lincoln.edu					
Allen University 1530 Harden St	Columbia	SC	29204	803-376-5700	376-5733*
*Fax: Mail Rm ■ TF: 877-625-5368 ■ Web: www.allenuniversity.edu					
Benedict College 1600 Harden St	Columbia	SC	29204	803-256-5000	
TF: 800-868-6598 ■ Web: www.benedict.edu					
Claflin University 400 Magnolia St	Orangeburg	SC	29115	803-535-5000	535-5385
TF: 800-922-1276 ■ Web: www.claflin.edu					
Morris College 100 W College St	Sumter	SC	29150	803-934-3200	773-8241*
*Fax: Admissions ■ TF Admissions: 866-853-1345 ■ Web: www.morris.edu					
South Carolina State University 300 College St NE PO Box 7127	Orangeburg	SC	29117	803-536-7000	536-8990
TF Admissions: 800-260-5956 ■ Web: www.scsu.edu					
Voorhees College 213 Wiggins Dr PO Box 678	Denmark	SC	29042	803-793-3351	753-9077
TF Admissions: 800-446-6250 ■ Web: www.voorhees.edu					
Clinton Junior College 1029 Crawford Rd	Rock Hill	SC	29730	803-327-7402	327-3261*
*Fax: Admissions ■ Web: www.clintonjuniorcollege.edu					
Fisk University 1000 17th Ave N	Nashville	TN	37208	615-329-8500	329-8774
TF: 800-443-3475 ■ Web: www.fisk.edu					
Lane College 545 Ln Ave	Jackson	TN	38301	731-426-7500	426-7559*
*Fax: Admissions ■ TF Admissions: 800-960-7532 ■ Web: www.lanecollege.edu					
LeMoyne-Owen College 807 Walker Ave	Memphis	TN	38126	901-435-1000	435-1524*
*Fax: Admissions ■ TF Admissions: 800-737-7778 ■ Web: www.loc.edu					
Tennessee State University 3500 John A Merritt Blvd PO Box 9609	Nashville	TN	37209	615-963-5000	963-5108
TF Admissions: 888-463-6878 ■ Web: www.tnstate.edu					
Huston-Tillotson University 900 Chicon St	Austin	TX	78702	512-505-3000	505-3192*
*Fax: Admissions ■ TF: 877-505-3028 ■ Web: www.htu.edu					
Jarvis Christian College PO Box 1470	Hawkins	TX	75765	903-769-5700	769-1282*
*Fax: Admissions ■ Web: www.jarvis.edu					
Paul Quinn College 3837 Simpson Stuart Rd	Dallas	TX	75241	214-376-1000	302-3648*
*Fax: Admissions ■ TF: 800-237-2648 ■ Web: www.pqc.edu					
Prairie View A & M University PO Box 519	Prairie View	TX	77446	936-857-2626	261-1079*
*Fax: Admissions ■ TF: 800-787-7826 ■ Web: www.pvamu.edu					
Southwestern Christian College PO Box 10	Terrell	TX	75160	972-524-3341	563-7133
TF: 800-925-9357 ■ Web: www.swcc.edu					
Texas College 2404 N Grand Ave	Tyler	TX	75702	903-593-8311	536-0001*
*Fax: Admissions ■ TF: 800-306-6299 ■ Web: www.texascollege.edu					
Texas Southern University 3100 Cleburne St	Houston	TX	77004	713-313-7011	313-1859
Web: www.tsu.edu					
Wiley College 711 Wiley Ave	Marshall	TX	75670	903-927-3311	927-3366*
*Fax: Admissions ■ TF Admissions: 800-658-6889 ■ Web: www.wileyc.edu					
Hampton University 11 Frissell Ave	Hampton	VA	23669	757-727-5000	727-5095
TF: 800-624-3328 ■ Web: www.hamptonu.edu					
Norfolk State University 700 Pk Ave	Norfolk	VA	23504	757-823-8600	823-2078*
*Fax: Admissions ■ TF: 800-274-1821 ■ Web: www.nsu.edu					
Saint Paul's College 115 College Dr	Lawrenceville	VA	23868	434-848-3111	848-1846*
*Fax: Admissions ■ TF: 800-678-7071 ■ Web: www.saintpauls.edu					
Virginia State University 1 Hayden Dr	Petersburg	VA	23806	804-524-5000	524-5055
TF Admissions: 800-871-7611 ■ Web: www.vsu.edu					
Virginia Union University 1500 N Lombardy St	Richmond	VA	23220	804-342-3570	342-3511*
*Fax: Admissions ■ TF: 800-368-3227 ■ Web: www.vuu.edu					
Bluefield State College 219 Rock St	Bluefield	WV	24701	304-327-4000	325-7747*
*Fax: Admissions ■ TF: 800-654-7798 ■ Web: www.bluefield.wvnet.edu					
West Virginia State University Barron Dr Rt 25 E PO Box 1000	Institute	WV	25112	304-766-3000	766-5182*
*Fax: Admissions ■ TF: 800-987-2112 ■ Web: www.wvstateu.edu					

171 COLLEGES & UNIVERSITIES - JESUIT

The Institutions Listed Here Are Members Of The Association Of Jesuit Colleges & Universities.

	City	State	Zip	Phone	Fax
Spring Hill College 4000 Dauphin St	Mobile	AL	36608	251-380-4000	460-2186*
*Fax: Admissions ■ TF Admissions: 800-742-6704 ■ Web: www.shc.edu					
Loyola Marymount University 1 LMU Dr	Los Angeles	CA	90045	310-338-2700	338-2797
TF: 800-568-4636 ■ Web: www.lmu.edu					
Santa Clara University					
500 El Camino Real	Santa Clara	CA	95053	408-554-4000	554-5255
Web: www.scu.edu					
University of San Francisco					
2130 Fulton St	San Francisco	CA	94117	415-422-5555	422-2217*
*Fax: Admissions ■ TF Admissions: 800-225-5873 ■ Web: www.usfca.edu					
Regis University 3333 Regis Blvd.	Denver	CO	80221	303-458-4100	964-5534
TF Admissions: 800-568-8932 ■ Web: www.regis.edu					
Fairfield University 1073 N Benson Rd	Fairfield	CT	06824	203-254-4000	254-4199*
*Fax: Admissions ■ Web: www.fairfield.edu					
Georgetown University 37th & 'O' Sts NW	Washington	DC	20057	202-687-3600	687-5084
Web: www.georgetown.edu					
Loyola University Chicago					
Lake Shore 6525 N Sheridan Rd	Chicago	IL	60626	773-508-3075	508-8926
Web: www.luc.edu					
Water Tower 820 N Michigan Ave	Chicago	IL	60611	312-915-6500	915-7216*
*Fax: Admissions ■ TF Admissions: 800-262-2373 ■ Web: www.luc.edu					
Loyola University					
New Orleans 6363 St Charles Ave CB 18	New Orleans	LA	70118	504-865-3240	865-3383*
*Fax: Admissions ■ TF Admissions: 800-456-9652 ■ Web: www.loyno.edu					
Loyola College 4501 N Charles St.	Baltimore	MD	21210	410-617-5012	617-2176*
*Fax: Admissions ■ TF: 800-221-9107 ■ Web: www.loyola.edu					
Boston College 140 Commonwealth Ave	Chestnut Hill	MA	02467	617-552-3100	552-0798
TF: 800-360-2522 ■ Web: www.bc.edu					
College of the Holy Cross 1 College St.	Worcester	MA	01610	508-793-2011	793-3888
TF: 800-442-2421 ■ Web: www.holycross.edu					
University of Detroit Mercy					
4001 W McNichols Rd	Detroit	MI	48221	313-993-1000	993-3326*
*Fax: Admissions ■ TF Admissions: 800-635-5020 ■ Web: www.udmercy.edu					
University of Detroit Mercy School of Dentistry					
Corktown Campus 2700 MLK Dr.	Detroit	MI	48219	313-494-6611	
Web: www.udmercy.edu					
Rockhurst University 1100 Rockhurst Rd	Kansas City	MO	64110	816-501-4000	501-4241*
*Fax: Admissions ■ TF: 800-842-6776 ■ Web: www.rockhurst.edu					
Saint Louis University 221 N Grand Blvd	Saint Louis	MO	63103	314-977-2100	977-7136*
*Fax: Admissions ■ TF: 800-758-3678 ■ Web: www.slu.edu					
Creighton University 2500 California Plaza	Omaha	NE	68178	402-280-2700	280-2685*
*Fax: Admissions ■ TF: 800-282-5835 ■ Web: www.creighton.edu					
Saint Peter's College 2641 JFK Blvd.	Jersey City	NJ	07306	201-915-9000	761-7105*
*Fax: Admissions ■ TF: 888-772-9933 ■ Web: www.spc.edu					
Canisius College 2001 Main St	Buffalo	NY	14208	716-888-2200	888-3230*
*Fax: Admissions ■ TF: 800-843-1517 ■ Web: www.canisius.edu					
Fordham University 441 E Fordham Rd	Bronx	NY	10458	718-817-5067	367-9404*
*Fax: Admissions ■ TF: 800-367-3426 ■ Web: www.fordham.edu					
College at Lincoln Ctr 113 W 60th St	New York	NY	10023	212-636-6710	636-7002
TF: 800-367-3426 ■ Web: www.fordham.edu					
Le Moyne College 1419 Salt Springs Rd	Syracuse	NY	13214	315-445-4100	445-4711*
*Fax: Admissions ■ TF Admissions: 800-333-4733 ■ Web: www.lemoyne.edu					
John Carroll University					
20700 N Pk Blvd.	University Heights	OH	44118	216-397-1886	397-4981*
*Fax: Admissions ■ TF: 888-335-6800 ■ Web: www.jcu.edu					
Xavier University 3800 Victory Pkwy	Cincinnati	OH	45207	513-745-3000	745-4319*
*Fax: Admissions ■ TF: 800-344-4698 ■ Web: www.xavier.edu					
Saint Joseph's University 5600 City Ave	Philadelphia	PA	19131	610-660-1000	660-1314*
*Fax: Admissions ■ TF: 888-232-4295 ■ Web: www.sju.edu					
University of Scranton					
800 Linden St St Thomas Hall	Scranton	PA	18510	570-941-7400	941-5928*
*Fax: Admissions ■ TF: 888-727-2686 ■ Web: www.matrix.scranton.edu					
Gonzaga University 502 E Boone Ave.	Spokane	WA	99258	509-323-6572	323-5780*
*Fax: Admissions ■ TF: 800-986-9585 ■ Web: www.gonzaga.edu					
Seattle University 901 12th Ave.	Seattle	WA	98122	206-296-6000	296-5656*
*Fax: Admissions ■ TF: 800-426-7123 ■ Web: www.seattleu.edu					
Wheeling Jesuit University					
316 Washington Ave.	Wheeling	WV	26003	304-243-2000	243-2397*
*Fax: Admissions ■ TF: 800-624-6992 ■ Web: www.wju.edu					
Marquette University 1217 W Wisconsin Ave.	Milwaukee	WI	53233	414-288-7302	288-3764*
*Fax: Admissions ■ TF Admissions: 800-222-6544 ■ Web: www.marquette.edu					

172 COMMODITY CONTRACTS BROKERS & DEALERS

SEE ALSO Investment Advice & Management p. 2129; Securities Brokers & Dealers p. 2646

	City	State	Zip	Phone	Fax
ADM Investor Services Inc					
141 W Jackson Blvd 1600A Board of Trade Bldg	Chicago	IL	60604	312-435-7000	435-7045
Web: www.admis.com					
Barclays Capital Futures					
200 Cedar Knolls Rd.	Whippany	NJ	07981	973-576-3000	
Web: www.barcap.com/futures					
Basic Commodities Inc 863 S Orlando Ave.	Winter Park	FL	32789	407-629-2000	740-0200
TF: 800-338-7006					
Cargill Investor Services Inc					
233 S Wacker Dr Suite 2300	Chicago	IL	60606	312-460-4000	460-4015
Commerzbank Capital Markets Corp					
2 World Financial Ctr 31st Fl	New York	NY	10281	212-703-4000	266-7235
Web: www.commerzbank.com					
Country Hedging Inc PO Box 64089	Saint Paul	MN	55164	651-355-5151	355-3723
TF: 800-328-6530 ■ Web: www.countryhedging.com					
GFI Group Inc 55 Water St	New York	NY	10041	212-968-4100	968-2386
NYSE: GFIG ■ Web: www.gfigroup.com					
Imperial Commodities Corp					
17 Battery Pl Suite 636	New York	NY	10004	212-837-9400	269-9878
Keeley Investment Corp					
401 S La Salle St Suite 1201	Chicago	IL	60605	312-786-5000	786-5002
TF: 800-533-5344 ■ Web: www.keeleyfunds.com					
Koch Mineral Services LLC 4111 E 37th St N	Wichita	KS	67220	316-828-5500	
Web: www.kochind.com					
Koch Supply & Trading LP 4111 E 37th St N	Wichita	KS	67220	316-828-5500	828-5752
TF: 800-245-2243 ■ Web: www.kochoil.com					
Lind-Waldock 141 W Jackson Blvd # 1400A	Chicago	IL	60604	312-788-2800	788-2815
TF: 800-327-3562 ■ Web: www.lind-waldock.com					
Marubeni America Corp 375 Lexington Ave	New York	NY	10017	212-450-0100	450-0700
Web: www.marubeni-usa.com					
Marubeni Canada Ltd					
40 University Ave Suite 600	Toronto	ON	M5J1T1	416-368-1171	947-9004
OptionsXpress Inc 311 W Monroe Suite 1000	Chicago	IL	60606	312-630-3300	629-5256
NASDAQ: OXPS ■ TF: 888-280-8020 ■ Web: www.optionsxpress.com					
Orion Futures 1905 W Busch Blvd.	Tampa	FL	33612	813-876-9662	876-5530
TF: 888-769-9399 ■ Web: www.orionfutures.com					
Paragon Investments Inc					
9941 NW Hwy 24 Suite 3	Silver Lake	KS	66539	758-582-9527	582-0121*
*Fax Area Code: 785 ■ TF: 888-452-8751 ■ Web: www.paragoninvestments.com					
PS International Ltd					
1414 Raleigh Rd Suite 205	Chapel Hill	NC	27517	919-933-7400	933-7441
Web: www.psinternational.net					
Rand Financial Services Inc					
141 W Jackson Blvd Suite 1950	Chicago	IL	60604	312-559-8800	559-8801
TF: 800-842-7263 ■ Web: www.rand-usa.com					
RJ O'Brien & Assoc					
222 S Riverside Plaza Suite 900	Chicago	IL	60606	312-373-5000	373-5238
TF: 866-438-7564 ■ Web: www.rjobrien.com					
Rosenthal Collins Group LLC (RCG)					
216 W Jackson Blvd Suite 400	Chicago	IL	60606	312-460-9200	795-7887*
*Fax: Hum Res ■ Web: www.rcgdirect.com					
Zaner Group LLC 150 S Wacker Dr Suite 2350	Chicago	IL	60606	312-277-0050	277-0150
TF: 800-621-1414 ■ Web: www.zaner.com					

173 COMMUNICATIONS TOWER OPERATORS

SEE ALSO Communications Lines & Towers Construction p. 1713

Listed Here Are Companies That Own, Operate, Lease, Maintain, And/Or Manage Towers Used By Telecommunications Services And Radio Broadcast Companies, Including Free-Standing Towers As Well As Antenna Systems Mounted On Monopoles Or Rooftops. Many Of These Companies Also Build Their Communications Towers, But Companies That Only Do The Building Are Classified As Heavy Construction Contractors.

	City	State	Zip	Phone	Fax
American Tower Corp 116 Huntington Ave 11th Fl	Boston	MA	02116	617-375-7500	375-7575
NYSE: AMT ■ TF: 877-282-7483 ■ Web: www.americantower.com					
Atlantic Tower Corp 10197 Maple Leaf Ct	Ashland	VA	23005	804-550-7490	550-7493
TF: 800-826-8616 ■ Web: www.atlantic-tower.com					
Centerpointe Communications					
2106 W Pioneer Pkwy Suite 131	Arlington	TX	76013	817-277-6811	277-6768
TF: 877-277-6811 ■ Web: www.cencom.com					
CLS Group 609 S Kelly Ave Suite D	Edmond	OK	73003	405-348-5460	341-6334
TF: 800-580-5460 ■ Web: www.clsgroup.com					
Crown Castle International Corp					
1220 Augusta Dr Suite 500	Houston	TX	77057	713-570-3000	570-3100
NYSE: CCI ■ TF: 877-486-9377 ■ Web: www.crowncastle.com					
Crown Communication Inc 2000 Corporate Dr.	Canonsburg	PA	15317	724-416-2000	416-2200
DukeNet Communications Inc 400 S Tryon St.	Charlotte	NC	28285	704-382-7111	
TF: 800-873-3853 ■ Web: www.dc.duke-energy.com					
LTS Wireless Inc 311 S LHS Dr	Lumberton	TX	77657	409-755-4038	755-7409
TF: 800-255-5471 ■ Web: www.ltswireless.com					
Millennium Telecom LLC 320 60th St NW	Sauk Rapids	MN	56379	320-654-6249	
SBA Communications Corp					
5900 Broken Sound Pkwy NW	Boca Raton	FL	33487	561-995-7670	995-7626
NASDAQ: SBAC ■ TF: 800-487-7483 ■ Web: www.sbasite.com					
SCANA Communications Inc 1426 Main St MC 107	Columbia	SC	29201	803-217-7383	217-9721
TF Cust Svc: 800-679-5463 ■ Web: www.scana.com/SCANA+Communications					
Shaffer Communications Group Inc					
8584 Katy Fwy Suite 300	Houston	TX	77024	713-463-0022	647-0045
TF: 800-243-7525 ■ Web: www.shafcomm.com					
Tower Innovations 2855 Hwy 261	Newburgh	IN	47630	812-853-0595	853-6652
TF: 800-664-8222 ■ Web: www.centraltower.com					
US RealTel Inc 15 Piedmont Ctr NE Suite 100	Atlanta	GA	30305	404-442-0126	869-2525
Web: www.usrealtel.com					

174 COMMUNITIES - ONLINE

SEE ALSO Internet Service Providers (ISPs) p. 2128

	City	State	Zip	Phone	Fax
Allnurses.com Inc 8930 177th St W.	Lakeville	MN	55044	612-816-8773	
Web: allnurses.com					
Alloy Inc 151 W 26th St 11th Fl	New York	NY	10001	212-244-4307	244-4311
TF Cust Svc: 888-452-5569 ■ Web: www.alloy.com					
America Online Inc (AOL) 22000 AOL Way	Dulles	VA	20166	703-265-1000	265-5769
TF Orders: 888-265-8002 ■ Web: www.aol.com					
AOL Black Voices 435 N Michigan Ave Suite L2	Chicago	IL	60611	312-222-4326	222-4502
TF: 877-765-1350 ■ Web: www.blackvoices.aol.com					
AsianAvenue.com 205 Hudson St 6th Fl	New York	NY	10013	212-431-4477	505-3478
Web: www.asianavenue.com					
AudienceScience Inc					
1110 112th Ave NE Suite 300	Bellevue	WA	98004	425-216-1700	216-1777
Web: www.audiencescience.com					
Beliefnet Inc 115 E 23rd St Suite 400	New York	NY	10010	212-533-1400	
Web: www.beliefnet.com					
BET Interactive LLC 1235 W St NE	Washington	DC	20018	202-608-2000	533-1999
Web: www1.bet.com					

	City	State	Zip	Phone	Fax
BlackPlanet.com 205 Hudson St 6th Fl	New York	NY	10013	212-431-4477	505-3478
Web: www.blackplanet.com					
Children with Diabetes 5689 Chancery Pl	Hamilton	OH	45011	513-755-0186	755-9963
Web: www.childrenwithdiabetes.com					
China Crescent Enterprises Inc 14860 Montfort Dr Suite 210	Dallas	TX	75254	214-722-3040	777-3094*
PINK: CCTR ■ **Fax Area Code:* 303 ■ *Web:* www.chinacrescent.com					
Christianity.com Inc 1423 Powhatan St Suite 1 2nd Fl	Alexandria	VA	22314	703-548-8900	548-8940
Web: www.christianity.com					
Internet Broadcasting Systems Inc 355 Randolph Ave	Saint Paul	MN	55102	651-365-4000	365-4430
Web: www.ibsys.com					
Internet World 18 S Main St	Norwalk	CT	06854	203-945-2070	945-2078
Internet.com 950 Tower Ln Fl 6	Foster City	CA	94404	650-578-7700	350-1423
Web: www.internet.com					
iVillage 500 7th Ave 14th Fl	New York	NY	10018	212-664-4444	600-6100
TF: 800-977-1436 ■ *Web:* www.ivillage.com					
Knot Inc The 462 Broadway 6th Fl	New York	NY	10013	212-219-8555	219-1929
NASDAQ: KNOT ■ *Web:* www.theknotinc.com					
lawyers.com Martindale-Hubbell 121 Chanlon Rd	New Providence	NJ	07974	908-464-6800	464-3553
TF: 800-526-4902 ■ *Web:* www.lawyers.com					
Logical Information Machines Inc 22 W Washington St	Chicago	IL	60602	312-244-7170	244-7185
TF: 800-546-9646 ■ *Web:* www.lim.com					
MaMaMedia Inc 110 Greene St Suite 708	New York	NY	10012	212-334-3277	249-5599*
**Fax Area Code:* 404 ■ *Web:* www.mamamedia.com					
Merit Network Inc 1000 Oakbrook Dr Suite 200	Ann Arbor	MI	48104	734-764-9430	527-5790
Web: www.merit.edu					
MiGente.com 205 Hudson St 6th Fl	New York	NY	10013	212-431-4477	
Web: www.migente.com					
Military Advantage Inc 799 Market St 7th Fl	San Francisco	CA	94103	415-820-3434	820-0552
Web: www.military.com					
Nominum Inc 2000 Seaport Blvd Suite 400	Redwood City	CA	94063	650-381-6000	381-6055
TF: 877-249-1559 ■ *Web:* www.nominum.com					
One Call Concepts Inc 7223 Pkwy Dr Suite 210	Hanover	MD	21076	410-712-0082	712-0838
Web: www.occinc.com					
OnePlace LLC 9401 Courthouse Rd Suite 300	Chesterfield	VA	23832	804-768-9404	768-9359
Web: www.oneplace.com					
Salon.com 101 Spear St Suite 203	San Francisco	CA	94105	415-645-9200	645-9204
Web: www.salon.com					
Schlesinger Assoc New York Inc 10 Parsonage Rd Suite 400	Edison	NJ	08837	732-906-1122	906-8792
TF: 800-672-7676 ■ *Web:* www.schlesingerassociates.com					
SeniorNet 900 Lafayette St Suite 604	Santa Clara	CA	95050	408-615-0699	615-0928
TF: 800-747-6848 ■ *Web:* www.seniornet.org					
Sensitech Inc 800 Cummings Ctr Suite 258x	Beverly	MA	01915	978-927-7033	921-2112
TF: 800-999-7926 ■ *Web:* www.sensitech.com					
SHRM Global Forum 1800 Duke St	Alexandria	VA	22314	703-548-3440	535-6490
TF: 800-283-7476 ■ *Web:* www.shrm.org/global					
Spark Networks PLC 8383 Wilshire Blvd Suite 800	Beverly Hills	CA	90211	323-836-3000	836-3333
AMEX: LOV ■ *Web:* www.spark.net					
ThirdAge LLC 2618 San Miguel Suite 175	Newport Beach	CA	92660	415-267-4400	330-6601*
**Fax Area Code:* 949 ■ *Web:* www.thirdage.com					
Video Monitoring Services Of America LP 1500 Broadway	New York	NY	10036	212-736-2010	329-5292
TF: 800-867-2002 ■ *Web:* www.vmsinfo.com					
WELL The c/o Salon.com 101 Spear St Suite 203	San Francisco	CA	94105	415-645-9300	645-9309
Web: www.well.com					

COMPRESSORS - AIR CONDITIONING & REFRIGERATION

SEE Air Conditioning & Heating Equipment - Commercial/Industrial p. 1382

175 COMPRESSORS - AIR & GAS

	City	State	Zip	Phone	Fax
Airtek Inc PO Box 466	Irwin	PA	15642	724-863-1350	864-7853
TF: 800-424-7835 ■ *Web:* www.airtek-inc.com					
American Air Compressor Services 185 Lackawanna Ave	West Paterson	NJ	07424	201-865-4848	890-5991*
**Fax Area Code:* 973					
Atlas Copco Compressors LLC 94 N Elm St 4th Fl	Westfield	MA	01085	413-536-0600	536-0091
Web: www.atlascopco.com					
Bauer Compressors Inc 1328 Azalea Garden Rd	Norfolk	VA	23502	757-855-6006	855-6224
Web: www.bauercomp.com					
Cameron Compression Systems 16250 Port NW Dr	Houston	TX	77041	713-354-1900	354-1923
TF: 888-423-7463 ■ *Web:* www.c-a-m.com					
Cameron Turbocompressor 3101 Broadway	Buffalo	NY	14225	716-896-6600	896-1233
TF: 877-805-7911 ■ *Web:* www.c-a-m.com					
Champion A Gardner Denver Co 1301 N Euclid Ave	Princeton	IL	61356	815-875-3321	872-0421
Web: www.gardnerdenver.com					
Chapin International Inc 700 Ellicott St	Batavia	NY	14021	585-343-3140	344-1775
Web: www.chapinmfg.com					
Compressed Air Systems Inc 9303 Stannum St	Tampa	FL	33619	813-626-8177	628-0187
TF: 800-626-8177 ■ *Web:* www.compressedairsystems.com					
Compressor Engineering Corp (CECO) 5440 Alder Dr	Houston	TX	77081	713-664-7333	664-6444
TF: 800-879-2326 ■ *Web:* www.compressor-engineering.com					
Corken Inc 3805 NW 36th St	Oklahoma City	OK	73112	405-946-5576	948-6664
TF: 800-631-4929 ■ *Web:* www.corken.com					
CSI Compressor Systems Inc 3809 S FM 1788 PO Box 60760	Midland	TX	79711	432-563-1170	563-0820
TF: 800-365-1170 ■ *Web:* www.compressor-systems.com					
Curtis Dyna-Fog Ltd 17335 US Hwy 31 N	Westfield	IN	46074	317-896-2561	896-3788
TF: 800-544-8990 ■ *Web:* www.dynafog.com					
Curtis-Toledo Inc 1905 Kienlen Ave	Saint Louis	MO	63133	314-383-1300	383-1300
TF: 800-925-5431 ■ *Web:* www.us.fscurtis.com					
Devilbiss Air Power Co PO Box 2468	Jackson	TN	38302	800-888-2468	888-9036
TF: 800-888-2468 ■ *Web:* www.devap.com					
Dresser-Rand Co Paul Clark Dr PO Box 560	Olean	NY	14760	716-375-3000	375-3178
Web: www.dresser-rand.com					
Dresser-Rand Co Reciprocating Products Div 100 Chemung St	Painted Post	NY	14870	800-345-4302	937-2100*
**Fax Area Code:* 607 ■ *TF:* 800-345-4302 ■ *Web:* www.dresser-rand.com					
Elliott Group 901 N 4th St	Jeannette	PA	15644	724-527-2811	600-8442
TF: 800-635-2208 ■ *Web:* www.elliott-turbo.com					
Federal Equipment Co 928 Low Ave	Waukegan	IL	60085	847-775-1300	775-1310
Web: www.speedysprayer.com					
Fountainhead Group Inc 23 Garden St	New York Mills	NY	13417	315-736-0037	768-4220
TF: 800-311-9903 ■ *Web:* www.thefountainheadgroup.com					
Gardner Denver Compressor Div 1800 Gardner Expwy	Quincy	IL	62301	217-222-5400	223-5897
TF: 800-682-9868 ■ *Web:* www.gardnerdenver.com					
Gardner Denver Inc 1800 Gardner Expy	Quincy	IL	62305	217-222-5400	223-5897
NYSE: GDI ■ *TF:* 800-682-9868 ■ *Web:* www.gardnerdenver.com					
Gardner Denver Nash 1800 Gardner Expy	Quincy	IL	62301	217-222-5400	223-5897
TF: 800-682-9868 ■ *Web:* www.gardnerdenver.com					
Gardner Denver Water Jetting Systems Inc 12300 N Houston Rosslyn Rd	Houston	TX	77086	281-448-5800	448-7500*
**Fax:* Sales ■ *TF:* 800-231-3628 ■ *Web:* www.gardnerdenver.com					
Gast Mfg Inc 2300 M-139 Hwy PO Box 97	Benton Harbor	MI	49023	269-926-6171	925-8288
TF: 800-952-4278 ■ *Web:* www.gastmfg.com					
Goodrich Corp Delavan Spray Technologies Div 4334 Main Hwy PO Box 969	Bamberg	SC	29003	803-245-4347	245-4146
TF: 800-621-9357 ■ *Web:* www.delavan.com					
Guardair Corp 54 2nd Ave	Chicopee	MA	01020	413-594-4400	594-4884
TF: 800-482-7324 ■ *Web:* www.guardaircorp.com					
Ingersoll Rand Air Solutions Group 800-D Beaty St	Davidson	NC	28036	704-896-4000	896-4459
Web: www.company.ingersollrand.com					
ITW Industrial Finishing 195 International Blvd	Glendale Heights	IL	60139	630-237-5000	246-5012*
**Fax Area Code:* 888 ■ **Fax:* Sales ■ *TF:* 800-992-4657					
ITW Ransburg 320 Phillips Ave	Toledo	OH	43612	419-470-2000	470-2270
TF Cust Svc: 800-726-8097 ■ *Web:* www.itwransburg.com					
Kaeser Compressors Inc PO Box 946	Fredericksburg	VA	22404	540-898-5500	898-5520
Web: www.kaeser.com					
Magnum Venus Plastech 5148 113th Ave N	Clearwater	FL	33760	727-573-2955	571-3636
Web: www.mvpind.com					
Manchester Tank 1000 Corp Centre Dr Suite 300	Franklin	TN	37067	615-370-6300	370-6150
Web: www.mantank.com					
Master Mfg Co 747 N Yale Ave	Villa Park	IL	60181	630-833-7060	833-7094
Mattson Spray Equipment 230 W Coleman St	Rice Lake	WI	54868	715-234-1617	236-7032
TF: 800-877-4857					
Michigan Automotive Compressor Inc (MACI) 2400 N Dearing Rd	Parma	MI	49269	517-622-7000	
Web: www.michauto.com					
Norwalk Compressor Co 1650 Stratford Ave	Stratford	CT	06615	203-386-1234	386-1300
TF: 800-556-5001 ■ *Web:* www.norwalkcompressor.com					
Quincy Compressor 3501 Wismann Ln	Quincy	IL	62305	217-222-7700	222-5109
Web: www.quincycompressor.com					
Riley Industrial Services Inc 2615 San Juan Blvd PO Box 2014	Farmington	NM	87401	505-327-4947	326-0305
Web: www.rileyindustrial.com					
Saylor Beall Mfg Co Inc 400 N Kibbee St	Saint Johns	MI	48879	989-224-2371	224-8788
TF: 800-248-9001 ■ *Web:* www.saylor-beall.com					
Scales Air Compressor Corp 110 Voice Rd	Carle Place	NY	11514	516-248-9096	248-9639
TF: 800-777-9096 ■ *Web:* www.scalesair.com					
SIHI Pumps Inc 303 Industrial Blvd	Grand Island	NY	14072	716-773-6450	773-2330
Web: www.sihi-pumps.com					
Spencer Turbine Co 600 Day Hill Rd	Windsor	CT	06095	860-688-8361	688-0098
TF: 800-232-4321 ■ *Web:* www.spencerturbine.com					
Sullair Corp 3700 E Michigan Blvd	Michigan City	IN	46360	219-879-5451	874-1273*
**Fax:* Mktg ■ *TF:* 800-785-5247 ■ *Web:* www.sullair.com					
Sullivan-Palatek Inc 386 River Rd	Claremont	NH	03743	603-543-3131	543-0014
TF: 800-334-5022 ■ *Web:* www.sullivanind.com					
Sulzer Metco US Inc 1101 Prospect Ave	Westbury	NY	11590	516-334-1300	338-2414*
**Fax:* Sales ■ *TF:* 800-638-2699 ■ *Web:* www.sulzermetco.com					
Tafa Inc 146 Pembroke Rd	Concord	NH	03301	603-224-9585	225-4342
Web: www.praxair.com					
Tecumseh Products Co 1136 Oak Valley Dr	Ann Arbor	MI	48108	734-585-9500	352-3700
Web: www.tecumseh.com					
Thermionics Laboratory Inc PO Box 3711	Hayward	CA	94540	510-538-3304	538-2889
Web: www.thermionics.com					
Tuthill Vacuum Systems 4840 W Kearney St	Springfield	MO	65803	417-865-8715	865-2950
TF: 800-225-3810 ■ *Web:* www.tuthill.com					
Varian Vacuum Technologies 121 Hartwell Ave	Lexington	MA	02421	781-861-7200	860-5437
TF Cust Svc: 800-882-7426 ■ *Web:* www.varianinc.com					
Wagner Spray Tech Corp 1770 Fernbrook Ln	Plymouth	MN	55447	763-553-0759	553-7288
TF: 800-328-8251 ■ *Web:* www.wagnerspraytech.com					
Wittemann Co LLC The 1 Industry Dr	Palm Coast	FL	32137	386-445-4200	445-7042
Web: www.pureco2nfidence.com					
Zeks Compressed Air Solutions 1302 Goshen Pkwy	West Chester	PA	19380	610-692-9100	692-9192
TF: 800-888-2323 ■ *Web:* www.zeks.com					

176 COMPUTER EQUIPMENT

SEE ALSO Automatic Teller Machines (ATMs) p. 1489; Business Machines - Mfr p. 1549; Calculators - Electronic p. 1552; Modems p. 1671; Computer Networking Products & Systems p. 1676; Flash Memory Devices p. 1848; Point-of-Sale (POS) & Point-of-Information (POI) Systems p. 2436

176-1 Computer Input Devices

Company	City	State	ZIP	Phone	Fax
3M Touch Systems 501 Griffin Brook Dr *TF:* 866-407-6666 ■ *Web:* www.3m.com	Methuen	MA	01844	978-659-9000	659-9103
Aten Technology Inc 23 Hubble *Web:* www.aten-usa.com	Irvine	CA	92618	949-428-1111	428-1100
CH Products 970 Pk Ctr Dr *Web:* www.chproducts.com	Vista	CA	92081	760-598-2518	598-2524
Chicony America Inc 53 Parker *Web:* www.chicony.com.tw	Irvine	CA	92618	949-380-0928	380-8201
Cirque Corp 2463 S 3850 W Suite A *TF:* 800-454-3375 ■ *Web:* www.cirque.com	Salt Lake City	UT	84120	801-467-1100	467-0208
Cortron Inc 1 Aegean Dr *Web:* www.cortroninc.com	Methuen	MA	01844	978-975-5445	975-0357
Digit Professional Inc 3926 Varsity Dr *TF:* 877-767-8862 ■ *Web:* www.digitprofessional.com	Ann Arbor	MI	48108	734-677-0840	677-3027
Elo TouchSystems Inc 301 Constitution Dr *TF:* 800-557-1458 ■ *Web:* www.elotouch.com	Menlo Park	CA	94025	650-361-4700	361-4747
Esterline -Advanced Input Devices Inc 600 W Wilbur Ave *TF:* 800-444-5923 ■ *Web:* www.advanced-input.com	Coeur D'Alene	ID	83815	208-765-8000	292-2275
Fujitsu Components America Inc 250 E Caribbean Dr *Web:* www.fujitsu.com	Sunnyvale	CA	94089	408-745-4900	745-4970
GTCO CalComp Inc 7125 Riverwood Dr *TF:* 800-344-4723 ■ *Web:* www.gtco.com	Columbia	MD	21046	410-381-6688	290-9065
Guillemot North America 5800 Rue St Denis Suite 1001 *Web:* www.us.guillemot.com	Montreal	QC	H2S3L5	514-279-9960	279-4954
Gyration Inc 12930 Saratoga Ave *TF:* 888-340-0033 ■ *Web:* www.gyration.com	Saratoga	CA	95070	408-973-7070	255-9075
Immersion Corp 801 Fox Ln *NASDAQ: IMMR* ■ *TF:* 888-467-1900 ■ *Web:* www.immersion.com	San Jose	CA	95131	408-467-1900	467-1901
Innovative Global Solutions Co LLC 511 5th St Unit F *Web:* www.igsco.net	San Fernando	CA	91340	818-837-9495	837-9526
Interlink Electronics Inc 546 Flynn Rd *PINK: LINK* ■ *Web:* www.interlinkelec.com	Camarillo	CA	93012	805-484-8855	484-8989
Kensington Computer Products Group 333 Twin Dolphin Dr 6th Fl *TF:* 800-535-4242 ■ *Web:* www.kensington.com	Redwood Shores	CA	94065	650-572-2700	267-2800
Kinesis Corp 22121 17th Ave SE Suite 112 *TF:* 800-454-6374 ■ *Web:* www.kinesis.com	Bothell	WA	98021	425-402-8100	402-8181
KYE Systems Corp 1301 NW 84th Ave Suite 127 *Web:* www.geniusnet.com	Doral	FL	33126	305-468-9250	468-9251
Lite-On Trading USA Inc 720 S Hillview Dr *Web:* www.us.liteon.com	Milpitas	CA	95035	408-946-4873	941-4597
Logitech Inc 6505 Kaiser Dr *TF Sales:* 800-231-7717 ■ *Web:* www.logitech.com	Fremont	CA	94555	510-795-8500	792-8901
Macally USA Mace Group Inc 4601 E Airport Dr *TF:* 800-644-1132 ■ *Web:* www.macally.com	Ontario	CA	91761	909-230-6888	230-6889
Mad Catz Interactive Inc 7480 Mission Valley Rd Suite 101 *AMEX: MCZ* ■ *TF:* 800-659-2287 ■ *Web:* www.madcatz.com	San Diego	CA	92108	619-683-9830	683-9839
NaturalPoint Inc 33872 SE Eastgate Cir *Web:* www.naturalpoint.com	Corvallis	OR	97333	541-753-6645	753-6689
NMB Technologies Corp 9730 Independence Ave *Web:* www.nmbtech.com	Chatsworth	CA	91311	818-341-3355	341-8207
Numonics Corp 101 Commerce Dr PO Box 1005 *TF:* 800-523-6716 ■ *Web:* www.numonics.com	Montgomeryville	PA	18936	215-362-2766	361-0167
PolyVision Corp 3970 Johns Creek Ct Suite 325 *TF:* 800-620-7659 ■ *Web:* www.polyvision.com	Suwanee	GA	30024	678-542-3100	542-3200
SMART Modular Technologies Inc 39870 Eureka Dr *NASDAQ: SMOD* ■ *TF:* 800-956-7627 ■ *Web:* www.smartm.com	Newark	CA	94560	510-623-1231	623-1434
SMART Technologies Inc 1207 11th Ave SW Suite 300 *TF:* 888-427-6278 ■ *Web:* www.smarttech.com	Calgary	AB	T3C0M5	403-245-0333	245-0366
Synaptics Inc 3120 Scott Blvd Suite 130 *NASDAQ: SYNA* ■ *Web:* www.synaptics.com	Santa Clara	CA	95054	408-454-5100	454-5200
TouchSystems Corp 220 Tradesmen Dr *TF:* 800-320-5944 ■ *Web:* www.touchsystems.com	Hutto	TX	78634	512-846-2424	846-2425
Ultra Electronics Measurement Systems Inc 50 Barnes Pk N Suite 102 *Web:* www.ultra-msi.com	Wallingford	CT	06492	203-949-3500	949-3598
Virtual Ink Corp 150 CambridgePark Dr *TF:* 877-696-4646 ■ *Web:* www.mimio.com	Cambridge	MA	02140	617-902-2040	902-2041
Wacom Technology Corp 1311 SE Cardinal Ct *TF:* 800-922-9348 ■ *Web:* www.wacom.com	Vancouver	WA	98683	360-896-9833	896-9724

176-2 Computers

Company	City	State	ZIP	Phone	Fax
Aberdeen LLC 9130 Norwalk Blvd **Fax:* Sales ■ *Web:* www.aberdeeninc.com	Santa Fe Springs	CA	90670	562-699-6998	695-5570*
Acer America Corp 333 W San Carlos St Suite 1500 **Fax:* Sales ■ *TF:* 800-571-2237 ■ *Web:* www.acer.com	San Jose	CA	95110	408-533-7700	533-4574*
ACMA Computers Inc 1565 Reliance Way *TF Sales:* 800-786-6888 ■ *Web:* www.acma.com	Fremont	CA	94539	510-623-1212	651-0629
ACME Portable Machines Inc 1330 Mountain View Cir *Web:* www.acmeportable.com	Azusa	CA	91702	626-610-1888	610-1881
Amax Engineering Corp 1565 Reliance Way *TF Cust Svc:* 800-889-2629 ■ *Web:* www.amax.com	Fremont	CA	94539	510-651-8886	651-0629
Apple Inc 1 Infinite Loop *NASDAQ: AAPL* ■ **Fax:* Mail Rm ■ *TF Cust Svc:* 800-275-2273 ■ *Web:* www.apple.com	Cupertino	CA	95014	408-996-1010	996-0275*
Aries Research Inc 46750 Fremont Blvd Suite 107 *TF:* 800-282-7437 ■ *Web:* www.ari.com	Fremont	CA	94538	510-413-0288	226-0781
Au Optronics Corp 9720 Cypresswood Dr Suite 241	Houston	TX	77070	832-678-3610	678-3630
Azul Systems Inc 1600 Plymouth St *TF:* 800-258-4199 ■ *Web:* www.azulsystems.com	Mountain View	CA	94043	650-230-6500	230-6600
Bytespeed LLC 3131 24th Ave S *TF:* 877-553-0777 ■ *Web:* www.bytespeed.com	Moorhead	MN	56560	218-227-0445	
Chem USA Corp 38507 Cherry St *TF:* 800-866-2436 ■ *Web:* www.chemusa.com	Newark	CA	94560	510-608-8818	608-8828
Cognex Corp 1 Vision Dr *NASDAQ: CGNX* ■ *TF:* 877-926-4639 ■ *Web:* www.cognex.com	Natick	MA	01760	508-650-4141	650-3333
Comark Corp 93 W St *TF:* 800-280-8522 ■ *Web:* www.comarkcorp.com	Medfield	MA	02052	508-359-8161	359-2267
Computer Management Corp 260 Lackland Dr *Web:* www.cmcusa.com	Middlesex	NJ	08846	732-356-3500	356-3501
Corvallis Microtechnology Inc 413 SW Jefferson Ave *Web:* www.cmtinc.com	Corvallis	OR	97333	541-752-5456	752-4117
Cray Inc 901 Fifth Ave Suite 1000 *NASDAQ: CRAY* ■ *Web:* www.cray.com	Seattle	WA	98164	206-701-2000	701-2500
CSP Inc 43 Manning Rd *TF:* 800-325-3110 ■ *Web:* www.cspi.com	Billerica	MA	01821	978-663-7598	663-0150
CSS Laboratories Inc 1641 McGaw Ave *TF:* 800-852-2680 ■ *Web:* www.csslabs.com	Irvine	CA	92614	949-852-8161	852-0410
Csts Inc 735 Challenger St *Web:* www.csts.com	Brea	CA	92821	714-990-2787	482-9090
Cyberchron Corp 2700 Rt 9 PO Box 160 *Web:* www.cyberchron.com	Cold Spring	NY	10516	845-265-3700	265-4154
Cytec Corp 1017 William D Tate Ave Suite 107 *TF:* 888-349-8881 ■ *Web:* www.cytecsys.com	Grapevine	TX	76051	214-349-8881	
Daisy Data Displays Inc 2850 Lewisberry Rd *Web:* www.d3inc.net	York Haven	PA	17370	717-932-9999	932-8000
Datalux Corp 155 Aviation Dr *TF:* 800-328-2589 ■ *Web:* www.datalux.com	Winchester	VA	22602	540-662-1500	662-1682
Dedicated Computing N26 W23880 Commerce Cir *TF:* 877-523-3301 ■ *Web:* www.dedicatedcomputing.com	Waukesha	WI	53188	262-951-7200	523-2222
Dell Inc 1 Dell Way *NASDAQ: DELL* ■ *TF:* 800-854-6214 ■ *Web:* www.dell.com	Round Rock	TX	78682	512-338-4400	283-6161
Diamond Flower Electric Instrument Co USA Inc (DFI) 732-C Striker Ave *TF:* 800-909-4334	Sacramento	CA	95834	916-568-1234	568-1234
Diversified Technology Inc 476 Highland Colony Pkwy *TF:* 800-443-2667 ■ *Web:* www.dtims.com	Ridgeland	MS	39157	601-856-4121	856-2888
Drive Thru Technology Inc 1755 N Main St *TF:* 800-933-8388 ■ *Web:* www.dttusa.com	Los Angeles	CA	90031	323-576-1400	576-1470
DRS Tactical Systems Inc 1110 W Hibiscus Blvd *Web:* www.drs-ts.com	Melbourne	FL	32901	321-727-3672	725-0496
Ectaco Inc 31-21 31st St *TF:* 800-710-7920 ■ *Web:* www.ectaco.com	Long Island City	NY	11106	718-728-6110	728-4023
Electrovaya Inc 2645 Royal Windsor Dr *TSE: EFL* ■ *TF:* 800-388-2865 ■ *Web:* www.electrovaya.com	Mississauga	ON	L5J1K9	905-855-4610	822-7953
EliteGroup Computer Systems Inc (ECS) 44259 Nobel Dr *TF:* 800-829-8890 ■ *Web:* www.ecsusa.com	Fremont	CA	94538	510-226-7333	771-0250
eMachines Inc 14350 Myford Rd Bldg 100 *TF:* 877-566-3463 ■ *Web:* www.e4me.com	Irvine	CA	92606	714-481-2828	368-9896
Encore Real Time Computing Inc 105 E Dr *TF Cust Svc:* 800-936-2673 ■ *Web:* www.encore.com	Melbourne	FL	32904	321-727-2211	727-7009
ENGlobal Corp 654 N Sam Houston Pkwy E Suite 400 *AMEX: ENG* ■ *TF:* 800-411-6040 ■ *Web:* www.englobal.com	Houston	TX	77060	281-878-1000	878-1010
Equus Computer Systems Inc 5801 Clearwater Dr *TF:* 866-378-8727 ■ *Web:* www.equuscs.com	Minnetonka	MN	55343	612-617-6200	617-6298
Franklin Electronic Publishers Inc 1 Franklin Plaza 8 Terri Ln *TF:* 800-266-5626 ■ *Web:* www.franklin.com	Burlington	NJ	08016	609-386-2500	239-5948
Fujitsu America Inc 1250 E Arques Ave *TF:* 800-538-8460 ■ *Web:* www.fujitsu.com	Sunnyvale	CA	95085	408-746-6200	746-6260
Gateway Inc 7565 Irvine Ctr Dr *NYSE: GTW* ■ *TF:* 800-846-2000 ■ *Web:* www.gateway.com	Irvine	CA	92618	949-471-7000	471-7001
Granite Microsystems Inc 10202 N Enterprise Dr *Web:* www.granitemicrosystems.com	Mequon	WI	53092	262-242-8800	242-8825
Hewlett-Packard (Canada) Ltd (HP) 5150 Spectrum Way *TF:* 888-447-4636 ■ *Web:* www.hp.com/country/ca/eng/welcome.html	Mississauga	ON	L4W5G1	905-206-4725	206-4739
Hewlett-Packard Co 3000 Hanover St *NYSE: HPQ* ■ *TF Sales:* 800-752-0900 ■ *Web:* www.hp.com	Palo Alto	CA	94304	650-857-1501	857-5518
IBM Canada Ltd 3600 Steeles Ave E *Web:* www.ibm.com/ca/en	Markham	ON	L3R9Z7	905-316-5000	
Immecor Corp 2351 Circadian Way *Web:* www.immecor.com	Santa Rosa	CA	95407	707-636-2550	636-2565
International Business Machines Corp (IBM) 1 New Orchard Rd *NYSE: IBM* ■ *TF:* 800-426-4968 ■ *Web:* www.ibm.com	Armonk	NY	10504	914-766-1900	
Keydata International Inc 201 Cir Dr N *TF:* 800-486-4800 ■ *Web:* www.keydata-pc.com	Piscataway	NJ	08854	732-868-0588	868-6536
Kontron Mobile Computing Inc 7631 Anagram Dr *TF:* 888-343-5396 ■ *Web:* www.kontronmobile.com	Eden Prairie	MN	55344	952-974-7000	974-0859

Company	City	State	Zip	Phone	Fax
LXE Inc 125 Technology Pkwy. *TF:* 800-664-4593 ■ *Web:* www.lxe.com	Norcross	GA	30092	770-447-4224	447-4405
MaxVision Corp 495 Production Ave. *TF:* 800-533-5805 ■ *Web:* www.maxvision.com	Madison	AL	35758	256-772-3058	772-3078
Mercury Computer Systems Inc 201 Riverneck Rd *NASDAQ: MRCY* ■ *TF:* 866-627-6951 ■ *Web:* www.mc.com	Chelmsford	MA	01824	978-967-1401	
Micro Center Online 2701 Charter St Suite A *TF:* 800-468-1633 ■ *Web:* www.microcenter.com	Columbus	OH	43228	614-334-1496	
Micro Electronics Inc 4119 Leap Rd. *TF:* 800-634-3478 ■ *Web:* www.microelectronics.com	Hilliard	OH	43026	614-850-3000	850-3001
Micro Express Inc 8 Hammond Dr Suite 105 *TF:* 800-989-9900 ■ *Web:* www.microexpress.net	Irvine	CA	92618	949-460-9911	269-3070
Micro/Sys Inc 3730 Pk Pl *Web:* www.embeddedsys.com	Montrose	CA	91020	818-244-4600	244-4246
Microtech Computers Inc 4921 Legends Dr. *TF Tech Supp:* 800-828-9533 ■ *Web:* www.microtechcomp.com	Lawrence	KS	66049	785-841-9513	841-1809
Microway Inc 12 Richards Rd *Web:* www.microway.com	Plymouth	MA	02360	508-746-7341	746-4678
Miltope Corp 500 Richardson Rd S *TF Cust Svc:* 800-645-8673 ■ *Web:* www.miltope.com	Hope Hull	AL	36043	334-284-8665	613-6302
Myricom Inc 325 N Santa Anita Ave. *Web:* www.myri.com	Arcadia	CA	91006	626-821-5555	821-5316
Oqo Inc 583 Shotwell St *Web:* www.oqo.com	San Francisco	CA	94110	415-430-6200	430-6201
Panasonic Solutions Co 1 Panasonic Way *TF:* 888-223-1012 ■ *Web:* www.panasonic.com/business/toughbook/contact-toughbook.asp	Secaucus	NJ	07094	888-223-1012	
Pinnacle Data Systems Inc 6600 Port Rd Suite 100 *AMEX: PNS* ■ *TF:* 800-882-8282 ■ *Web:* www.pinnacle.com	Groveport	OH	43125	614-748-1150	748-1209
QEI Inc 60 Fadem Rd. *Web:* www.qeiinc.com	Springfield	NJ	07081	973-379-7400	379-2138
Quantum3D Inc 6330 San Ignacio Ave *TF:* 888-747-1020 ■ *Web:* www.quantum3d.com	San Jose	CA	95119	408-361-9999	361-9980
Recortec Inc 1620 Berryessa Rd Suite A. *TF:* 888-732-6783 ■ *Web:* www.recortec.com	San Jose	CA	95133	408-928-1480	729-3661
Research In Motion Ltd 295 Phillip St *NASDAQ: RIMM* ■ *Web:* www.rim.net	Waterloo	ON	N2L3W8	519-888-7465	888-7884
Roper Mobile Technology 875 Charest Blvd W Suite 200 *TF:* 800-363-1993 ■ *Web:* www.daptech.com	Quebec City	QC	G1N2C9	418-681-9394	681-7734
Roper Mobile Technology 7450 S Priest Dr *Web:* www.ropermobile.com	Tempe	AZ	85283	480-705-4200	705-4216
Sharp Electronics Corp 1 Sharp Plaza. *TF:* 800-237-4277 ■ *Web:* www.sharpusa.com	Mahwah	NJ	07430	201-529-8200	529-8413
Socket Mobile Inc 39700 Eureka Dr. *NASDAQ: SCKT* ■ *Web:* www.socketmobile.com	Newark	CA	94560	510-933-3000	933-3030
Sony Electronics Inc 1 Sony Dr. **Fax:* Hum Res ■ *TF Cust Svc:* 800-222-7669 ■ *Web:* www.sony.com	Park Ridge	NJ	07656	201-930-1000	358-4058*
SRC Computers LLC 4240 N Nevada Ave *Web:* www.srccomp.com	Colorado Springs	CO	80907	719-262-0213	262-0223
Stealth Computer Corp 530 Rowntree Dairy Rd Bldg 4 *TF:* 888-783-2584 ■ *Web:* www.stealth.ca	Woodbridge	ON	L4L8H2	905-264-9000	264-7440
Superchips Inc 1790 E Airport Blvd *TF:* 888-227-2447 ■ *Web:* www.superchips.com	Sanford	FL	32773	407-585-7000	585-1900
Sys Technology Inc 17358 Railroad St. *TF:* 888-797-7248 ■ *Web:* www.sys.com	City of Industry	CA	91748	714-952-8767	
Systemax Inc 11 Harbor Pk Dr. *NYSE: SYX* ■ **Fax:* Sales ■ *TF:* 800-845-6225 ■ *Web:* www.systemaxpc.com	Port Washington	NY	11050	516-625-3663	608-7744*
Tangent Computer Inc 197 Airport Blvd *TF Sales:* 800-342-9388 ■ *Web:* www.tangent.com	Burlingame	CA	94010	650-342-9388	342-0615
Technology Advancement Group Inc 22355 Tag Way *TF:* 800-824-7693 ■ *Web:* www.tag.com	Dulles	VA	20166	703-406-3000	948-9720
TeleVideo Inc 2345 Harris Way *Web:* www.televideo.com	San Jose	CA	95131	408-954-8333	954-0622
Toshiba America Inc 1251 Avenue of the Americas Suite 4100 *TF:* 800-457-7777 ■ *Web:* www.toshiba.com	New York	NY	10020	212-596-0600	593-3875
Toshiba America Information Systems Inc 9740 Irvine Blvd *TF Cust Svc:* 800-457-7777 ■ *Web:* www.us.toshiba.com	Irvine	CA	92618	949-583-3000	
TouchStar Solutions LLC *Touchstar Group* 5147 S Garnett Rd Suite D *Web:* www.touchstargroup.com	Tulsa	OK	74146	918-307-7100	307-7190
Transource Computers Corp 2405 W Utopia Rd. *TF:* 800-486-3715 ■ *Web:* www.transource.com	Phoenix	AZ	85027	623-879-8882	879-8887
Twinhead Corp 48303 Fremont Blvd **Fax Area Code:* 510 ■ *TF Sales:* 800-995-8946 ■ *Web:* www.twinhead.com.tw	Fremont	CA	94538	800-995-8946	492-0820*
Versalogic Corp 4211 W 11th Ave *TF:* 800-824-3163 ■ *Web:* www.versalogic.com	Eugene	OR	97402	541-485-8575	485-5712
Win Enterprises Inc 300 Willow St S *Web:* www.win-ent.com	North Andover	MA	01845	978-688-2000	
Wyse Technology Inc 3471 N 1st St *TF:* 800-800-9973 ■ *Web:* www.wyse.com	San Jose	CA	95134	408-473-1200	473-2080
Xybernaut Corp 12701 Fair Lakes Cir Suite 550 *TF:* 888-992-3777 ■ *Web:* www.xybernaut.com	Fairfax	VA	22033	703-631-6925	631-6734

176-3 Modems

Company	City	State	Zip	Phone	Fax
ActionTec Electronics Inc 760 N Mary Ave *TF:* 800-752-7820 ■ *Web:* www.actiontec.com	Sunnyvale	CA	94085	408-752-7700	541-9003
Avocent Corp 4991 Corporate Dr. *TF:* 866-286-2368 ■ *Web:* www.avocent.com	Huntsville	AL	35805	256-430-4000	430-4030
Aztech Labs Inc 4005 Clipper Ct *Web:* www.aztech.com	Fremont	CA	94538	510-683-9800	683-9803
Best Data Products Inc 20740 Plummer St. *Web:* www.bestdata.com	Chatsworth	CA	91311	818-773-9600	717-3101
Biscom Inc 321 Billerica Rd *TF:* 800-477-2472 ■ *Web:* www.biscom.com	Chelmsford	MA	01824	978-250-1800	250-4449
Canoga Perkins Corp 20600 Prairie St *TF Tech Supp:* 800-360-6642 ■ *Web:* www.canoga.com	Chatsworth	CA	91311	818-718-6300	718-6312
Cermetek Microelectronics Inc 374 Turquoise St. *Web:* www.cermetek.com	Milpitas	CA	95035	408-752-5000	942-1346
Circuit Research Corp 5 Northern Blvd Suite 12	Amherst	NH	03031	603-880-4000	880-8297
Comspec Digital Products Inc PO Box 178. *TF:* 800-490-6893 ■ *Web:* www.comspecdpi.com	Jacksonville	TX	75766	832-443-4487	443-4487
Comtech EF Data Corp 2114 W 7th St. *Web:* www.comtechefdata.com	Tempe	AZ	85281	480-333-2200	333-2540
Copia International Ltd 1220 Iroquois Dr Suite 180 **Fax:* Sales ■ *TF Sales:* 800-689-8898 ■ *Web:* www.copia.com	Naperville	IL	60563	630-778-8898	778-8848*
CXR Larus Corp 894 Faulstich Ct *TF:* 800-999-9946 ■ *Web:* www.cxrlarus.com	San Jose	CA	95112	408-573-2700	573-2708
Data-Linc Group 3535 Factoria Blvd SE Suite 100 *Web:* www.data-linc.com	Bellevue	WA	98006	425-882-2206	867-0865
Dataforth Corp 3331 E Hemisphere Loop *TF:* 800-444-7644 ■ *Web:* www.dataforth.com	Tucson	AZ	85706	520-741-1404	741-0762
Eiger Technology Inc 144 Front St W Suite 700 *TSX: AXA* ■ *Web:* www.eigertechnology.com	Toronto	ON	ONTM5J	416-216-8659	216-1164
Electronic Systems Technology Inc 415 N Quay St Bldg B-1 *Web:* www.esteem.com	Kennewick	WA	99336	509-735-9092	783-5475
Encore Networks Inc 45472 Holiday Dr Suite 3. *Web:* www.encorenetworks.com	Dulles	VA	20166	703-318-7750	787-4625
Engage Communications Inc 9565 Soquel Dr. *Web:* www.engagecom.com	Aptos	CA	95003	831-688-1021	688-1421
FreeWave Technologies Inc 1880 S Flatiron Ct Suite F *TF Cust Svc:* 800-548-5616 ■ *Web:* www.freewave.com	Boulder	CO	80301	303-444-3862	786-8393
GRE America Inc 425 Harbor Blvd *TF:* 800-233-5973 ■ *Web:* www.greamerica.com	Belmont	CA	94002	650-591-1400	591-2001
Motorola Canada Ltd 8133 Warden Ave *TF:* 800-268-3395 ■ *Web:* www.motorola.ca	Markham	ON	L6G1B3	905-948-5200	948-5250
Multi-Tech Systems 2205 Woodale Dr. *TF Cust Svc:* 800-328-9717 ■ *Web:* www.multitech.com	Mounds View	MN	55112	763-785-3500	785-9874
Nayna Networks Inc 4699 Old Ironsides Dr Suite 420 *Web:* www.nayna.com	Santa Clara	CA	95054	408-956-8000	956-8730
Novatel Wireless Inc 9645 Scranton Rd Suite 205. *NASDAQ: NVTL* ■ *TF:* 888-888-9231 ■ *Web:* www.novatelwireless.com	San Diego	CA	92121	858-320-8400	812-3402
Phoebe Micro Inc 47606 Kato Rd. *Web:* www.phoebemicro.com	Fremont	CA	94538	510-360-0800	360-0818
Sierra Wireless Inc 13811 Wireless Way *NASDAQ: SWIR* ■ *Web:* www.sierrawireless.com	Richmond	BC	V6V3A4	604-231-1100	231-1109
Teldat Corp 1001 Brickell Bay Dr Suite 2810. *Web:* www.teldat.com	Miami	FL	33131	305-372-3480	372-8759
Telenetics Corp 39 Parker.	Irvine	CA	92618	949-455-4000	455-4010
Teletronics International Inc 2 Choke Cherry Rd *Web:* www.teletronics.com	Rockville	MD	20850	301-309-8500	309-8851
Unlimited Systems Corp Inc 5550 Oberlin Dr. *TF:* 800-275-6354 ■ *Web:* www.konexx.com	San Diego	CA	92121	858-537-5010	550-7330
US Robotics Corp 1300 E Woodfield Dr # 506. *TF:* 877-710-0884 ■ *Web:* www.usr.com	Schaumburg	IL	60173	847-874-2000	874-2001
Western Datacom Co Inc 959 Bassett Rd Unit B. *TF Cust Svc:* 800-262-3311 ■ *Web:* www.western-data.com	Westlake	OH	44145	440-835-1510	835-9146
Western Telematic Inc 5 Sterling *TF:* 800-854-7226 ■ *Web:* www.wti.com	Irvine	CA	92618	949-586-9950	583-9514
Wi-LAN Inc 11 Holland Ave Suite 608 *Web:* www.wi-lan.com	Ottawa	ON	K1Y4S1	613-688-4900	688-4894
Works Computing Inc 1801 American Blvd E Suite 12 *TF:* 866-222-4077 ■ *Web:* www.workscomputing.com	Bloomington	MN	55425	952-746-1580	746-1585
Zoom Technologies Inc 207 S St. *NASDAQ: ZOOM* ■ *TF:* 800-666-6191 ■ *Web:* www.zoomtel.com	Boston	MA	02111	617-423-1072	423-5536
ZyXEL Communications Inc 1130 N Miller St. *TF:* 800-255-4101 ■ *Web:* www.zyxel.com	Anaheim	CA	92806	714-632-0882	632-0858

176-4 Monitors & Displays

Company	City	State	Zip	Phone	Fax
Aydin Displays Inc 1 Riga Ln *TF:* 866-367-2934 ■ *Web:* www.aydindisplays.com	Birdsboro	PA	19508	610-404-7400	404-8190
Barco Folsom LLC 11101 Trade Ctr Dr *TF:* 888-414-7226	Rancho Cordova	CA	95670	916-859-2500	859-2515
BarcoView LLC 3059 Premiere Pkwy. **Fax:* Hum Res ■ *Web:* www.barco.com	Duluth	GA	30097	678-475-8000	475-8160*
Computron Display Systems Inc 1697 W Imperial Ct.	Mount Prospect	IL	60056	847-952-8800	952-0832
Conrac Inc 5124 Commerce Dr *Web:* www.conrac.com	Baldwin Park	CA	91706	626-480-0095	480-0077
CopyTele Inc 900 Walt Whitman Rd. *Web:* www.copytele.com	Melville	NY	11747	631-549-5900	549-5974
CTX Technology Corp 16728 E Gale Ave **Fax:* Cust Svc ■ *TF Cust Svc:* 877-688-3288 ■ *Web:* www.ctxintl.com	City of Industry	CA	91745	626-363-9328	363-9390*
Daisy Data Displays Inc 2850 Lewisberry Rd *Web:* www.d3inc.net	York Haven	PA	17370	717-932-9999	932-8000
Daktronics Inc 201 Daktronics Dr. *NASDAQ: DAKT* ■ *TF:* 800-843-9878 ■ *Web:* www.daktronics.com	Brookings	SD	57006	605-692-0200	697-4700

Company	City	State	ZIP	Phone	Fax
Dotronix Inc 160 1st St SE *TF:* 800-720-7218 ■ *Web:* www.dotronix.com	New Brighton	MN	55112	651-633-1742	633-7025
Eizo Nanao Technologies Inc 5710 Warland Dr *TF:* 800-800-5202 ■ *Web:* www.eizo.com	Cypress	CA	90630	562-431-5011	431-4811
eMagin Corp 3006 Northup Way Suite 103 *AMEX: EMA* ■ *Web:* www.emagin.com	Bellevue	WA	98004	425-284-5200	284-5201
Envision Peripherals Inc (EPI) 47490 Seabridge Dr *TF Tech Supp:* 888-838-6388 ■ *Web:* www.aocdisplay.com	Fremont	CA	94538	510-770-9988	770-1088
Futaba Corp of America 1605 E Penny Ln *Web:* www.futaba.com	Schaumburg	IL	60173	847-884-1444	884-1635
General Digital Corp 8 Nutmeg Rd S *TF:* 800-952-2535 ■ *Web:* www.generaldigital.com	South Windsor	CT	06074	860-282-2900	282-2244
Gunze USA 2113 Wells Branch Pkwy Suite 5400 *Web:* www.gunzeusa.com	Austin	TX	78728	512-990-3400	252-1181
Hantronix Inc 10080 Bubb Rd *Web:* www.hantronix.com	Cupertino	CA	95014	408-252-1100	252-1123
Iiyama North America Inc 65 W St Rd Suite 101-B *TF:* 800-394-4335 ■ *Web:* www.iiyama.com	Warminster	PA	18974	215-682-9050	682-9066
La Cie Ltd 22985 NW Evergreen Pkwy **Fax:* Mktg ■ *Web:* www.lacie.com	Hillsboro	OR	97124	503-844-4500	844-4508*
LG Electronics USA Inc 1000 Sylvan Ave *TF Tech Supp:* 800-243-0000 ■ *Web:* www.us.lge.com	Englewood Cliffs	NJ	07632	201-816-2000	816-0636
Lite-On Trading USA Inc 720 S Hillview Dr *Web:* www.us.liteon.com	Milpitas	CA	95035	408-946-4873	941-4597
NEC Corp of America 10850 Gold Ctr Dr Suite 200 *TF:* 800-632-4636 ■ *Web:* www.necam.com	Rancho Cordova	CA	95670	916-463-7000	636-5656
NEC Display Solutions of America Inc 500 Pk Blvd Suite 1100 **Fax:* Sales ■ *TF Cust Svc:* 800-632-4662 ■ *Web:* www.necdisplay.com	Itasca	IL	60143	630-467-3000	467-3050*
OSRAM Sylvania Inc 100 Endicott St *Web:* www.sylvania.com	Danvers	MA	01923	978-777-1900	750-2152
Pioneer Electronics (USA) Inc 1925 E Dominguez St *TF:* 800-421-1404 ■ *Web:* www.pioneerelectronics.com	Long Beach	CA	90810	310-952-2000	952-2402
Planar Systems Inc 1195 NW Compton Dr *NASDAQ: PLNR* ■ *TF:* 866-475-2627 ■ *Web:* www.planar.com	Beaverton	OR	97006	503-748-1100	748-1244
Proview Technology 7373 Hunt Ave *TF:* 800-776-8439 ■ *Web:* www.proview.net	Garden Grove	CA	92841	714-799-3899	891-3751
Sampo Technology 5550 Peachtree Industrial Blvd Suite 100	Norcross	GA	30071	770-449-6220	447-1109
Sharp Electronics Corp 1 Sharp Plaza *TF:* 800-237-4277 ■ *Web:* www.sharpusa.com	Mahwah	NJ	07430	201-529-8200	529-8413
Sharp Microelectronics of the Americas 5700 NW Pacific Rim Blvd *Web:* www.sharpsma.com	Camas	WA	98607	360-834-2500	834-8903
Sony Electronics Inc 1 Sony Dr **Fax:* Hum Res ■ *TF Cust Svc:* 800-222-7669 ■ *Web:* www.sony.com	Park Ridge	NJ	07656	201-930-1000	358-4058*
Tatung Co of America Inc 2850 El Presidio St *TF:* 800-827-2850 ■ *Web:* www.tatungusa.com	Long Beach	CA	90810	310-637-2105	
Trans-Lux Corp 26 Pearl St *AMEX: TLX* ■ **Fax:* Sales ■ *TF:* 800-243-5544 ■ *Web:* www.trans-lux.com	Norwalk	CT	06850	203-853-4321	854-6891*
Trans-Lux Fair-Play Inc 1700 Delaware Ave *TF:* 800-247-0265 ■ *Web:* www.fair-play.com	Des Moines	IA	50317	515-265-5305	265-3364
Video Display Corp 1868 Tucker Industrial Rd *NASDAQ: VIDE* ■ *TF Cust Svc:* 800-241-5005 ■ *Web:* www.videodisplay.com	Tucker	GA	30084	770-938-2080	493-3903
ViewSonic Corp 381 Brea Canyon Rd *TF:* 800-888-8583 ■ *Web:* www.viewsonic.com	Walnut	CA	91789	909-444-8888	468-1240
Wells-Gardner Electronics Corp 9500 W 55th St Suite A *AMEX: WGA* ■ *TF:* 800-336-6630 ■ *Web:* www.wellsgardner.com	McCook	IL	60525	708-290-2100	290-2200

176-5 Multimedia Equipment & Supplies

Company	City	State	ZIP	Phone	Fax
Boston Acoustics Inc 300 Jubilee Dr *TF:* 800-288-6148 ■ *Web:* www.bostonacoustics.com	Peabody	MA	01960	978-538-5000	538-5199
Corsair Memory Inc 46221 Landing Pkwy *TF:* 888-222-4346 ■ *Web:* www.corsair.com	Fremont	CA	94538	510-657-8747	657-8748
Creative Labs Inc 1901 McCarthy Blvd *TF Cust Svc:* 800-998-1000 ■ *Web:* www.us.creative.com	Milpitas	CA	95035	408-428-6600	428-6611
Cyber Acoustics LLC 3109 NE 109th Ave *Web:* www.cyberacoustics.com	Vancouver	WA	98682	360-883-0333	883-4888
Faroudja Laboratories 180 Baytech Dr Suite 100 *Web:* www.faroudja.com/internet/faroudja/content/home.jsp	San Jose	CA	95134	408-735-1492	735-8571
Focus - A VITEC Co 1370 Dell Ave *NASDAQ: FCSE* ■ *TF:* 800-338-3348 ■ *Web:* www.focusinfo.com	Campbell	CA	95008	408-866-8300	866-4859
Kinyo Co Inc 14235 Lomitas Ave *TF:* 800-735-4696 ■ *Web:* www.kinyo.com	La Puente	CA	91746	626-333-3711	961-9114
Matrox Electronic Systems Ltd 1055 St Regis Blvd *Web:* www.matrox.com	Dorval	QC	H9P2T4	514-822-6000	822-6363
Pinnacle Systems Inc 280 Bernardo Ave *TF:* 800-522-8783 ■ *Web:* www.pinnaclesys.com	Mountain View	CA	94043	650-526-1600	526-1601
SpeakerCraft Inc 940 Columbia Ave *TF:* 800-448-0976 ■ *Web:* www.speakercraft.com	Riverside	CA	92507	951-787-0543	787-8747
Vocollect Inc 703 Rodi Rd *Web:* www.vocollect.com	Pittsburgh	PA	15235	412-829-8145	829-0972

176-6 Printers

Company	City	State	ZIP	Phone	Fax
Addmaster Corp 225 Huntington Dr *Web:* www.addmaster.com	Monrovia	CA	91016	626-358-2395	358-2784
AMT Datasouth Corp 803 Camarillo Springs Rd # D *TF:* 800-216-9192 ■ *Web:* www.amtdatasouth.com	Camarillo	CA	93012	805-388-5799	484-5282
Astro-Med Inc 600 E Greenwich Ave *NASDAQ: ALOT* ■ *TF:* 877-757-7978 ■ *Web:* www.astro-medinc.com	West Warwick	RI	02893	401-828-4000	822-2430
Avery Dennison Printer Systems Div 7722 Dungan Rd *TF:* 800-395-2282 ■ *Web:* www.machines.averydennison.com	Philadelphia	PA	19111	215-725-4700	725-6850
Canon USA Inc 1 Canon Plaza **Fax:* Hum Res ■ *TF:* 800-828-4040 ■ *Web:* www.usa.canon.com	Lake Success	NY	11042	516-328-5000	328-5069*
Citizen Systems America Corp 363 Van Ness Way Suite 404 *TF:* 800-421-6516 ■ *Web:* www.citizen-systems.com	Torrance	CA	90501	310-781-1460	781-9152
Craden Peripherals Corp 7860 Airport Hwy *Web:* www.craden.com	Pennsauken	NJ	08109	856-488-0700	488-0925
Datamax Corp 4501 Pkwy Commerce Blvd *TF:* 800-321-2233 ■ *Web:* www.datamaxcorp.com	Orlando	FL	32808	407-578-8007	578-8377
Digital Design Inc 67 Sand Pk Rd *TF:* 800-967-7746 ■ *Web:* www.genesisinkjet.com/ddiworldwide	Cedar Grove	NJ	07009	973-857-0900	857-9375
Eastman Kodak Co 343 State St *NYSE: EK* ■ *Web:* www.kodak.com	Rochester	NY	14650	585-724-4000	724-0663
Encad Inc A Kodak Co 6059 Cornerstone Ct W *TF Sales:* 800-453-6223 ■ *Web:* www.encad.com	San Diego	CA	92121	858-452-0882	452-0891
Epson America Inc 3840 Kilroy Airport Way *TF:* 800-463-7766 ■ *Web:* www.epson.com	Long Beach	CA	90806	562-981-3840	290-5220
Fujitsu Components America Inc 250 E Caribbean Dr *Web:* www.fujitsu.com	Sunnyvale	CA	94089	408-745-4900	745-4970
GCC Printers USA 209 Burlington Rd *TF Sales:* 800-422-7777 ■ *Web:* www.gccprinters.com	Bedford	MA	01730	781-275-5800	275-1115
Hewlett-Packard (Canada) Ltd (HP) 5150 Spectrum Way *TF:* 888-447-4636 ■ *Web:* www.hp.com/country/ca/eng/welcome.html	Mississauga	ON	L4W5G1	905-206-4725	206-4739
Hewlett-Packard Co 3000 Hanover St *NYSE: HPQ* ■ *TF Sales:* 800-752-0900 ■ *Web:* www.hp.com	Palo Alto	CA	94304	650-857-1501	857-5518
Imaging Technologies Corp (ITEC) 9449 Balboa Ave Suite 211	San Diego	CA	92123	858-277-5300	277-3448
International Business Machines Corp (IBM) 1 New Orchard Rd *NYSE: IBM* ■ *TF:* 800-426-4968 ■ *Web:* www.ibm.com	Armonk	NY	10504	914-766-1900	
Konica Minolta Business Solutions USA Inc 101 Williams Dr *Web:* www.kmbs.konicaminolta.us	Ramsey	NJ	07446	201-825-4000	
Kroy LLC 3830 Kelley Ave *TF Cust Svc:* 888-888-5769 ■ *Web:* www.kroy.com	Cleveland	OH	44114	216-426-5600	426-5601
Lexmark International Inc 740 W New Cir Rd *NYSE: LXK* ■ *TF Cust Svc:* 800-539-6275 ■ *Web:* www.lexmark.com	Lexington	KY	40550	859-232-2000	
Mutoh America Inc 2602 S 47th St Suite 102 *TF:* 800-999-0097 ■ *Web:* www.mutoh.com	Phoenix	AZ	85034	480-968-7772	968-7990
NEC Corp of America 10850 Gold Ctr Dr Suite 200 *TF:* 800-632-4636 ■ *Web:* www.necam.com	Rancho Cordova	CA	95670	916-463-7000	636-5656
Oce-USA Inc 5450 N Cumberland Ave 6th Fl *TF:* 800-877-6232 ■ *Web:* www.oceusa.com	Chicago	IL	60656	773-714-8500	693-7634
Oki America Inc 785 N Mary Ave *TF:* 800-654-3282 ■ *Web:* www.oki.com	Sunnyvale	CA	94085	408-720-1900	720-1918
Oki Data Americas Inc 2000 Bishops Gate Blvd *TF Cust Svc:* 800-654-3282 ■ *Web:* www.okidata.com	Mount Laurel	NJ	08054	856-235-2600	222-5320
Paxar Corp 105 Corporate Pk Dr *TF:* 888-447-2927 ■ *Web:* www.paxar.com	White Plains	NY	10604	914-697-6800	697-6894
Pentax Imaging Co 600 12th St Suite 300 *TF:* 800-877-0155 ■ *Web:* www.pentaximaging.com	Golden	CO	80401	303-799-8000	728-0122
Plastic Card Systems Inc 31 Pierce St PO Box 1070 *TF:* 800-742-2273 ■ *Web:* www.plasticard-systems.com	Northborough	MA	01532	508-351-6210	351-6211
Practical Automation Inc 45 Woodmont Rd *Web:* www.practicalautomation.com	Milford	CT	06460	203-882-5640	882-5648
Primera Technology Inc 2 Carlson Pkwy N Suite 375 *TF:* 800-797-2772 ■ *Web:* www.primera.com	Plymouth	MN	55447	763-475-6676	475-6677
Printek Inc 1517 Townline Rd *TF:* 800-368-4636 ■ *Web:* www.printek.com	Benton Harbor	MI	49022	269-925-3200	925-8539
Printronix Inc 14600 Myford Rd *TF:* 800-665-6210 ■ *Web:* www.printronix.com	Irvine	CA	92606	714-368-2300	368-2600
Ricoh Corp 5 Dedrick Pl **Fax:* Mail Rm ■ *TF:* 800-637-4264 ■ *Web:* www.ricoh-usa.com	West Caldwell	NJ	07006	973-882-2000	244-2605*
Ricoh Printing Systems America Inc 2390 Ward Ave # A *TF:* 800-887-8848 ■ *Web:* www.rpsa.ricoh.com	Simi Valley	CA	93065	805-578-4000	578-4001
RISO Inc 300 Rosewood Dr Suite 210 *TF:* 800-876-7476 ■ *Web:* www.riso.com	Danvers	MA	01923	978-777-7377	777-2517
Roland DGA Corp 15363 Barranca Pkwy *TF:* 800-542-2307 ■ *Web:* www.rolanddga.com	Irvine	CA	92618	949-727-2100	727-2112
Sato America Inc 10350A Nations Ford Rd *TF:* 888-871-8741 ■ *Web:* www.satoamerica.com	Charlotte	NC	28273	704-644-1650	644-1662
Seiko Instruments USA Inc 1309 Rutherford Ln *TF:* 800-358-0880 ■ *Web:* www.seikoinstruments.com	Austin	TX	78753	512-349-3800	349-3000
Seiko Instruments USA Inc Business & Home Office Products Div 2990 Lomita Blvd *Web:* www.siibusinessproducts.com/corp/index.html	Torrance	CA	90505	310-517-7700	517-7051
Seiko Instruments USA Inc Micro Printer Div 2990 Lomita Blvd *TF:* 800-553-6570 ■ *Web:* www.siibusinessproducts.com	Torrance	CA	90505	310-517-7778	517-8154
Sharp Electronics Corp 1 Sharp Plaza *TF:* 800-237-4277 ■ *Web:* www.sharpusa.com	Mahwah	NJ	07430	201-529-8200	529-8413
SiPix Imaging Inc 47485 Seabridge Dr *Web:* www.sipix.com	Fremont	CA	94538	510-743-2849	
Star Micronics America Inc 1150 King George's Post Rd **Fax:* Sales ■ *TF:* 800-782-7636 ■ *Web:* www.starmicronics.com	Edison	NJ	08837	732-623-5500	623-5590*

	City	State	Zip	Phone	Fax
Stratix 4920 Avalon Ridge Pkwy	Norcross	GA	30071	770-326-7580	326-7593
TF: 800-883-8300 ■ *Web:* www.stratixcorp.com					
TallyGenicom 4500 Daly Dr Suite 100	Chantilly	VA	20151	703-633-8700	222-7629
TF: 800-436-4266 ■ *Web:* www.tallygenicom.com					
Telpar Inc 19111 N Dallas Pakwy Suite 100	Lewisville	TX	75287	972-532-2513	407-7391
TF: 800-872-4886 ■ *Web:* www.telpar.com					
Toshiba America Inc					
1251 Avenue of the Americas Suite 4100	New York	NY	10020	212-596-0600	593-3875
TF: 800-457-7777 ■ *Web:* www.toshiba.com					
Toshiba TEC America Retail Information Systems Inc					
4401-A Bankers Cir	Atlanta	GA	30360	770-449-3040	449-1152
Web: www.toshibatecusa.com					
TransAct Technologies Inc					
One Hamden Ctr, 2319 Whitney Ave Suite 3B	Hamden	CT	06518	203-859-6800	949-9048
NASDAQ: TACT ■ *TF:* 800-243-8941 ■ *Web:* www.transact-tech.com					
Unimark Products 9818 Pflumm Rd	Lenexa	KS	66215	913-649-2424	649-5795
TF Cust Svc: 800-255-6356 ■ *Web:* www.unimark.com					
Xante Corp 2800 Dauphin St Suite 100	Mobile	AL	36606	251-473-6502	473-6503
TF: 800-926-8839 ■ *Web:* www.store.xante.com					
Xerox Corp 45 Glover Ave PO Box 4505	Norwalk	CT	06856	203-968-3000	968-3218
NYSE: XRX ■ *TF:* 800-842-0024 ■ *Web:* www.xerox.com					
Zebra Technologies Corp					
475 Half Day Rd Suite 500	Lincolnshire	IL	60069	847-634-6700	913-8766
NASDAQ: ZBRA ■ *TF:* 800-423-0422 ■ *Web:* www.zebra.com					

176-7 Scanning Equipment

	City	State	Zip	Phone	Fax
Accu-Sort Systems Inc 511 School House Rd	Telford	PA	18969	215-723-0981	721-5551
TF: 800-227-2633 ■ *Web:* www.accusort.com					
AirClic Inc 411 S State St 3rd Fl	Newtown	PA	18940	215-504-0560	504-0565
Web: www.airclic.com					
BenQ America Corp 15375 Barranca Suite A205	Irvine	CA	92618	949-255-9500	255-9600
TF: 866-600-2367 ■ *Web:* www.benq.us					
BOWE Bell + Howell 760 S Wolf Rd	Wheeling	IL	60090	847-675-7600	423-7503
TF: 800-327-4608 ■ *Web:* www.bowebellhowell.com					
Canon USA Inc 1 Canon Plaza	Lake Success	NY	11042	516-328-5000	328-5069*
**Fax:* Hum Res ■ *TF:* 800-828-4040 ■ *Web:* www.usa.canon.com					
CardScan Inc 25 First St Suite 107	Cambridge	MA	02141	617-492-4200	492-6659
TF: 800-942-6739 ■ *Web:* www.cardscan.com					
Computerwise Inc 302 N Winchester Ln	Olathe	KS	66062	913-829-0600	829-0810
TF: 800-255-3739 ■ *Web:* www.computerwise.com					
Datalogic Scanning 959 Terry St	Eugene	OR	97402	541-683-5700	345-7140
TF: 800-695-5700 ■ *Web:* www.datalogic.com					
Eastman Kodak Co 343 State St	Rochester	NY	14650	585-724-4000	724-0663
NYSE: EK ■ *Web:* www.kodak.com					
GTCO CalComp Inc 7125 Riverwood Dr	Columbia	MD	21046	410-381-6688	290-9065
TF: 800-344-4723 ■ *Web:* www.gtco.com					
Hewlett-Packard Co 3000 Hanover St	Palo Alto	CA	94304	650-857-1501	857-5518
NYSE: HPQ ■ *TF Sales:* 800-752-0900 ■ *Web:* www.hp.com					
Hitachi Canada Ltd					
5750 Explore Dr Suit 301	Mississauga	ON	L4W0A9	905-821-4545	290-0141
TF: 800-906-4482 ■ *Web:* www.hitachi.ca					
iCAD Inc 4 Townsend W Suite 17	Nashua	NH	03063	603-882-5200	880-3843
NASDAQ: ICAD ■ *TF:* 866-280-2239 ■ *Web:* www.icadmed.com					
InPath Devices 3610 Dodge St Suite 200	Omaha	NE	68131	402-345-9200	526-5920*
**Fax Area Code:* 888 ■ *TF:* 800-988-1914 ■ *Web:* www.inpath.com					
Microtek Lab Inc					
9960 Bell Ranch Dr Unit #103	Santa Fe Springs	CA	90670	310-687-5800	687-5950
Web: www.store2.microtek.com/shop/index.php?osCsid=q2edtovid0g77i4ldqd3bd5tm1					
Mustek Inc 15271 Barranca Pkwy	Irvine	CA	92618	949-790-3800	788-3670
TF: 800-308-7226 ■ *Web:* www.mustek.com					
Oce-USA Inc 5450 N Cumberland Ave 6th Fl	Chicago	IL	60656	773-714-8500	693-7634
TF: 800-877-6232 ■ *Web:* www.oceusa.com					
Order-Matic Corp					
320 S Bryant Pl PO Box 25463	Oklahoma City	OK	73115	405-672-1487	672-5349
TF: 800-767-6733 ■ *Web:* www.ordermatic.com					
Peripheral Dynamics Inc					
5150 Campus Dr					
Whitemarsh Industrial Pk	Plymouth Meeting	PA	19462	610-825-7090	834-7708
TF: 800-523-0253 ■ *Web:* www.pdiscan.com					
Ricoh Corp 5 Dedrick Pl	West Caldwell	NJ	07006	973-882-2000	244-2605*
**Fax:* Mail Rm ■ *TF:* 800-637-4264 ■ *Web:* www.ricoh-usa.com					
Ricoh Electronics Inc 1100 Valencia Ave	Tustin	CA	92780	714-566-2500	
Web: www.rei.ricoh.com					
Roland DGA Corp 15363 Barranca Pkwy	Irvine	CA	92618	949-727-2100	727-2112
TF: 800-542-2307 ■ *Web:* www.rolanddga.com					
Scan-Optics Inc 169 Progress Dr	Manchester	CT	06043	860-645-7878	645-7995
TF: 800-543-8681 ■ *Web:* www.scanoptics.com					
Scantron Corp 34 Parker	Irvine	CA	92618	949-639-7500	639-7710
TF: 800-722-6876 ■ *Web:* www.scantron.com					
Scion Corp 82 Wormans Mill Ct Suite H	Frederick	MD	21701	301-695-7870	695-0035
SPYRUS Inc 2355 Oakland Rd Suite 1	San Jose	CA	95131	408-953-0700	953-9835
TF: 800-277-9787 ■ *Web:* www.spyrus.com					
Stratix 4920 Avalon Ridge Pkwy	Norcross	GA	30071	770-326-7580	326-7593
TF: 800-883-8300 ■ *Web:* www.stratixcorp.com					
Techville Inc 11343 N Central Expwy	Dallas	TX	75238	214-739-7033	739-7042
Web: www.umax.com					
Videx Inc 1105 NE Cir Blvd	Corvallis	OR	97330	541-738-5500	738-5501
Web: www.videx.com					
Visioneer Inc 5673 Gibraltar Dr Suite 150	Pleasanton	CA	94588	925-251-6300	416-8600
TF Cust Svc: 888-229-4172 ■ *Web:* www.visioneer.com					
Wizcom Technologies Inc					
Boston Post Rd W 33 Suite 320	Marlborough	MA	01752	508-251-5388	251-5394
TF: 888-777-0552 ■ *Web:* www.wizcomtech.com					
ZBA Inc 94 Old Camplain Rd	Hillsborough	NJ	08844	908-359-2070	595-0909
TF: 866-468-6912 ■ *Web:* www.zbaus.com					

176-8 Storage Devices

	City	State	Zip	Phone	Fax
Ampex Data Systems Corp 500 Broadway	Redwood City	CA	94063	650-367-2011	367-3536
Web: www.ampexdata.com					
Appro International Inc 446 S Abbott Ave	Milpitas	CA	95035	408-941-8100	941-8111
TF: 800-927-5464 ■ *Web:* www.appro.com					
Apricorn Inc 12191 Kirkham Rd	Poway	CA	92064	858-513-2000	513-2020
TF: 800-458-5448 ■ *Web:* www.apricorn.com					
Atp Electronics Inc 750 N Mary Ave	Sunnyvale	CA	94085	408-732-5000	732-5055
Web: www.atpinc.com					
BlueArc Corp 50 Rio Robles Dr	San Jose	CA	95134	408-576-6600	576-6601
Web: www.bluearc.com					
Cirrascale Corp 12140 Community Rd	Poway	CA	92064	858-874-3800	874-3838
TF: 888-942-3800 ■ *Web:* www.cirrascale.com					
CMS Peripherals Inc 3095 Redhill Ave	Costa Mesa	CA	92626	714-424-5520	435-9504
TF Sales: 800-327-5773 ■ *Web:* www.cmsproducts.com					
Creative Labs Inc 1901 McCarthy Blvd	Milpitas	CA	95035	408-428-6600	428-6611
TF Cust Svc: 800-998-1000 ■ *Web:* www.us.creative.com					
CRU Acquisitions Group LLC					
1000 SE Tech Ctr Dr Suite 160	Vancouver	WA	98683	360-816-1800	816-1831
TF: 800-260-9800 ■ *Web:* www.cru-dataport.com					
Cybernetics Inc 111 Cybernetics Way	Yorktown	VA	23693	757-833-9100	833-9300
Web: www.cybernetics.com					
DataDirect Networks 9320 Lurline Ave	Chatsworth	CA	91311	818-700-7600	700-7601
TF: 800-837-2298 ■ *Web:* www.datadirectnet.com					
Datalink Corp 8170 Upland Cir	Chanhassen	MN	55317	952-944-3462	944-7869
NASDAQ: DTLK ■ *TF:* 800-448-6314 ■ *Web:* www.datalink.com					
Digital Peripheral Solutions Inc					
8015 E Crystal Dr	Anaheim	CA	92807	877-998-3440	692-5516*
**Fax Area Code:* 714 ■ *TF:* 800-559-4777 ■ *Web:* www.qps-inc.com					
Disc Makers 7905 N Rt 130	Pennsauken	NJ	08110	856-663-9030	661-3458
TF: 800-468-9353 ■ *Web:* www.discmakers.com					
Donlin Teleproduction Engineering Ltd					
14 Marion Ave	Norwood	MA	02062	781-688-3102	688-3104
TF: 800-485-7137 ■ *Web:* raq4.buydonlin.com					
Dynamic Network Factory Inc 21353 Cabot Blvd	Hayward	CA	94545	510-265-1122	265-1565
Web: www.dnfstorage.com					
Edge Electronics Inc 75 Orville Dr	Bohemia	NY	11716	631-471-3343	471-3405
TF: 800-647-3343 ■ *Web:* www.edgeelectronics.com					
Exabyte Corp 2108 55th St	Boulder	CO	80301	303-442-4333	442-4333*
**Fax:* Mktg ■ *TF Cust Svc:* 800-445-7736					
Fujitsu Computer Products of America Inc					
1255 E Arques Ave	Sunnyvale	CA	94085	408-746-7000	746-6910
TF: 800-626-4686 ■ *Web:* www.fcpa.com					
Fusion-io Inc					
2855 E Cottonwood Pkwy Suite 100	Salt Lake City	UT	84121	801-424-5500	
Web: www.fusionio.com					
Genica Corp 1890 Ord Way	Oceanside	CA	92056	760-639-4500	639-4599
Web: www.genica.com					
Hewlett-Packard (Canada) Ltd (HP)					
5150 Spectrum Way	Mississauga	ON	L4W5G1	905-206-4725	206-4739
TF: 888-447-4636 ■ *Web:* www.hp.com/country/ca/eng/welcome.html					
Hewlett-Packard Co 3000 Hanover St	Palo Alto	CA	94304	650-857-1501	857-5518
NYSE: HPQ ■ *TF Sales:* 800-752-0900 ■ *Web:* www.hp.com					
Hitachi America Ltd Computer Div					
2000 Sierra Pt Pkwy	Brisbane	CA	94005	650-244-7929	244-7776
TF: 800-225-1741 ■ *Web:* www.hitachi-america.us					
Hitachi Data Systems Corp					
750 Central Expy	Santa Clara	CA	95050	408-970-1000	727-8036
TF: 800-227-1930 ■ *Web:* www.hds.com					
I/O Magic Corp 4 Marconi	Irvine	CA	92618	949-707-4800	855-3550
Web: www.iomagic.com					
Imation Corp 1 Imation Pl	Oakdale	MN	55128	651-704-4000	704-7100
NYSE: IMN ■ *TF:* 888-466-3456 ■ *Web:* www.imation.com					
Interactive Media Corp 1360 Main St	Millis	MA	02054	508-376-4245	376-4462
TF Sales: 888-526-4878 ■ *Web:* www.kanguru.com					
International Business Machines Corp (IBM)					
1 New Orchard Rd	Armonk	NY	10504	914-766-1900	
NYSE: IBM ■ *TF:* 800-426-4968 ■ *Web:* www.ibm.com					
ITCN Inc 591 Congress Pk Dr	Dayton	OH	45459	937-439-9223	439-9173
Web: www.itcninc.com					
La Cie Ltd 22985 NW Evergreen Pkwy	Hillsboro	OR	97124	503-844-4500	844-4508*
**Fax:* Mktg ■ *Web:* www.lacie.com					
LG Electronics USA Inc					
1000 Sylvan Ave	Englewood Cliffs	NJ	07632	201-816-2000	816-0636
TF Tech Supp: 800-243-0000 ■ *Web:* www.us.lge.com					
Luminex Software Inc 871 Marlborough Ave	Riverside	CA	92507	951-781-4100	781-4105
TF Sales: 888-586-4639 ■ *Web:* www.luminex.com					
Microboards Technology LLC					
8150 Mallory Ct PO Box 846	Chanhassen	MN	55317	952-556-1600	556-1620
TF: 800-646-8881 ■ *Web:* www.microboards.com					
Mitsumi Electronics Corp 5808 W Campus Cir Dr	Irving	TX	75063	972-550-7300	550-7424
TF Tech Supp: 800-648-7864 ■ *Web:* www.mitsumi.com					
NEC Corp of America					
10850 Gold Ctr Dr Suite 200	Rancho Cordova	CA	95670	916-463-7000	636-5656
TF: 800-632-4636 ■ *Web:* www.necam.com					
Nexsan Corp 555 St Charles Dr Suite 202	Thousand Oaks	CA	91360	805-418-2700	418-2799
TF: 866-263-9726 ■ *Web:* www.nexsan.com					
Perifitech of Ohio Inc 23108 Felch St	Cleveland	OH	44128	216-332-0655	332-0656
Web: www.perifitech.com					
Phoenix International 812 W Southern Ave	Orange	CA	92865	714-283-4800	283-1169
Web: www.phenxint.com					
Pillar Data Systems 2840 Junction Ave	San Jose	CA	95134	408-503-4000	503-4050
TF: 877-252-3706 ■ *Web:* www.pillardata.com					
Pioneer Electronics (USA) Inc					
1925 E Dominguez St	Long Beach	CA	90810	310-952-2000	952-2402
TF: 800-421-1404 ■ *Web:* www.pioneerelectronics.com					
Qualstar Corp 3990-B Heritage Oak Ct	Simi Valley	CA	93063	805-583-7744	583-7749
NASDAQ: QBAK ■ *TF:* 800-468-0680 ■ *Web:* www.qualstar.com					
Quantum Corp 1650 Technology Dr Suite 700	San Jose	CA	95110	408-944-4000	944-4040
NYSE: QTM ■ *TF Tech Supp:* 800-826-8022 ■ *Web:* www.quantum.com					
Quantum/ATL PO Box 57100	Irvine	CA	92619	949-856-7800	856-7799
TF: 800-677-6268 ■ *Web:* www.quantum.com					

	City	State	Zip	Phone	Fax
Rimage Corp 7725 Washington Ave S *NASDAQ: RIMG* ■ *TF:* 800-445-8288 ■ *Web:* www.rimage.com	Minneapolis	MN	55439	952-944-8144	944-7808
Seagate Technology LLC 10200 S De Anza Blvd *NYSE: STX* ■ *Web:* www.seagate.com	Cupertino	CA	95014	831-438-6550	
Shaffstall Corp 8531 Bash St *TF:* 800-923-8439 ■ *Web:* www.shaffstall.com	Indianapolis	IN	46250	317-842-2077	915-9045
Sony Electronics Inc 1 Sony Dr **Fax:* Hum Res ■ *TF Cust Svc:* 800-222-7669 ■ *Web:* www.sony.com	Park Ridge	NJ	07656	201-930-1000	358-4058*
Storage Computer Corp 11 Riverside St	Nashua	NH	03062	603-880-3005	889-7232
TDK USA Corp 901 Franklin Ave PO Box 9302 **Fax:* Sales ■ *TF:* 800-835-8273 ■ *Web:* www.tdk.com	Garden City	NY	11530	516-535-2600	294-7751*
TEAC America Inc 7733 Telegraph Rd *Web:* www.teac.com	Montebello	CA	90640	323-726-0303	727-7656
Themis Computer 47200 Bayside Pkwy *Web:* www.themis.com	Fremont	CA	94538	510-252-0870	490-5529
Toshiba America Inc 1251 Avenue of the Americas Suite 4100 *TF:* 800-457-7777 ■ *Web:* www.toshiba.com	New York	NY	10020	212-596-0600	593-3875
VeriStor Systems Inc 3308 Peachtree Industrial Blvd *TF:* 866-956-2948 ■ *Web:* www.veristor.com	Duluth	GA	30096	678-990-1593	990-1597
Voltaire Ltd 6 Fortune Dr *TF:* 800-865-8247 ■ *Web:* www.voltaire.com	Billerica	MA	01821	978-439-5400	439-5401
Western Digital Corp 3355 Michelson Dr Suite 100 *NYSE: WDC* ■ *TF:* 800-832-4778 ■ *Web:* www.westerndigital.com	Irvine	CA	92612	949-672-7000	672-5498

177 COMPUTER EQUIPMENT & SOFTWARE - WHOL

SEE ALSO Business Machines - Whol p. 1549; Electrical & Electronic Equipment & Parts - Whol p. 1804

	City	State	Zip	Phone	Fax
Agilysys Inc 28925 Fountain Pkwy *NASDAQ: AGYS* ■ *TF:* 800-362-9127 ■ *Web:* www.agilysys.com	Solon	OH	44139	440-519-8700	720-8501
Ahearn & Soper Inc 100 Woodbine Downs Blvd *TF:* 800-263-4258 ■ *Web:* www.ahearn.com	Rexdale	ON	M9W5S6	416-675-3999	675-6589
Alexander Open Systems Inc 12851 Foster St *TF:* 800-473-1110 ■ *Web:* www.aos5.com	Overland Park	KS	66213	913-307-2300	307-2380
American Business Network Inc 2544 S 156th Cir *TF:* 800-338-1531 ■ *Web:* www.theupgradeplace.com	Omaha	NE	68130	402-691-8248	691-8548
American Portwell Technology Inc 44200 Christy St *TF:* 877-278-8899 ■ *Web:* www.portwell.com	Fremont	CA	94538	510-403-3399	403-3184
Amex Inc 2724 Summer St NE *Web:* www.amexinc.com	Minneapolis	MN	55413	612-331-3063	331-3180
Arrow Electronics Corp 7459 S Lima St *NASDAQ: ARW* ■ *Web:* www.arrow.com	Englewood	CO	80112	303-824-4000	
Arrow Electronics Inc 50 Marcus Dr *NYSE: ARW* ■ *TF Sales:* 800-777-2776 ■ *Web:* www.arrow.com	Melville	NY	11747	631-847-2000	847-2222
Arrow Enterprise Computing Solutions 7459 S Lima St Bldg 2 *Web:* www.arrowecs.com	Englewood	CO	80112	303-824-7650	
Arrow Enterprise Storage Solutions 7629 Anagram Dr *TF:* 800-229-3475	Eden Prairie	MN	55344	952-949-0053	949-0453
Asa Tire Systems Inc 651 S Stratford Dr *TF:* 800-241-8472 ■ *Web:* www.asatire.com	Meridian	ID	83642	208-855-0781	
ASI Corp 48289 Fremont Blvd **Fax:* Sales ■ *TF:* 800-210-0274 ■ *Web:* www.asipartner.com	Fremont	CA	94538	510-226-8000	226-8858*
Atlantix Global Systems 1 Sun Ct *TF:* 888-786-2727 ■ *Web:* www.atlantixglobal.com	Norcross	GA	30092	770-248-7700	448-7726
Avnet Inc 2211 S 47th St *NYSE: AVT* ■ *TF:* 888-822-8638 ■ *Web:* www.avnet.com	Phoenix	AZ	85034	480-643-2000	
Avnet Technology Solutions 8700 S Price Rd *TF:* 800-409-1483 ■ *Web:* www.ats.avnet.com	Tempe	AZ	85284	480-794-6900	
Axiom Memory Solutions LLC 19651 Descartes *TF:* 888-658-3326 ■ *Web:* www.axiommemory.com	Foothill Ranch	CA	92610	949-581-1450	
Axxion Group Corp 1855 Northwestern Dr *TF:* 800-828-6475 ■ *Web:* www.axxion.com	El Paso	TX	79912	915-225-8888	225-8800
Azerty Inc 13 Centre Dr *TF:* 800-888-8080 ■ *Web:* www.azerty.com	Orchard Park	NY	14127	716-662-0200	662-7616
Best Computer Supplies 895 E Patriot Blvd Suite 110 *TF:* 800-544-3472 ■ *Web:* www.theschoolsupplier.com	Reno	NV	89511	775-850-2600	850-2610
CAD/CAM Consulting Services Inc (CCCS) 996 Lawrence Dr Suite 101 *TF:* 888-375-7676 ■ *Web:* www.cad-cam.com	Newbury Park	CA	91320	805-375-7676	375-7678
Cadec Corp 645 Harvey Rd *TF:* 888-287-9400 ■ *Web:* www.cadec.com	Manchester	NH	03103	603-668-1010	623-0604
Champion Solutions Group 791 Pk of Commerce Blvd Suite 200 *TF:* 800-771-7000 ■ *Web:* www.championsg.com	Boca Raton	FL	33487	561-997-2900	997-4043
Columbia Ultimate Business Systems Inc 4400 NE 77th Ave Suite 100 *TF:* 800-488-4420 ■ *Web:* www.columbiaultimate.com	Vancouver	WA	98662	360-256-7358	256-1614
Column Technologies Inc 1400 Opus Pl Suite 110 *Web:* www.columnit.com	Downers Grove	IL	60515	630-515-6660	271-1508
Comprehensive Traffic Systems Inc 4860 Robb St Suite 205 *TF:* 888-396-1328 ■ *Web:* www.cts-worldwide.com	Wheat Ridge	CO	80033	303-940-3890	432-2605
Computer Connection of Central New York Inc 11206 Cosby Manor Rd *TF:* 800-566-4786 ■ *Web:* www.ccny.com	Utica	NY	13502	315-724-2209	
Computer Dynamics Inc 7640 Pelham Rd *Web:* www.cdynamics.com	Greenville	SC	29615	864-627-8800	675-0106
Comstor Inc 14850 Conference Ctr Dr Suite 200 **Fax:* Sales ■ *TF:* 800-955-9590 ■ *Web:* www.comstor.com	Chantilly	VA	20151	703-345-5100	345-5572*
Cranel Inc 8999 Gemini Pkwy *TF:* 800-288-3475 ■ *Web:* www.cranel.com	Columbus	OH	43240	614-431-8000	431-8388
Crown Micro 48363 Fremont Blvd *Web:* www.crownmicro.com	Fremont	CA	94538	510-490-8187	490-8068
D & H Distributing Co Inc 2525 N 7th St *TF:* 800-340-1001 ■ *Web:* www.dandh.com	Harrisburg	PA	17110	800-340-1001	340-1001
Data Impressions 17418 Studebaker Rd *TF:* 800-777-6488 ■ *Web:* www.ecom.dataimpressions.com	Cerritos	CA	90703	562-207-9050	207-9053
Data Sales Co Inc 3450 W Burnsville Pkwy *TF:* 800-328-2730 ■ *Web:* www.datasales.com	Burnsville	MN	55337	952-890-8838	895-3369
Digital Storage Inc 7611 Green Meadows Dr **Fax Area Code:* 800 ■ *TF:* 800-232-3475 ■ *Web:* www.digitalstorage.com	Lewis Center	OH	43035	740-548-7179	803-8030*
Dlt Solutions 13861 Sunrise Valley Dr Suite 400 *TF:* 800-262-4358 ■ *Web:* www.dlt.com	Herndon	VA	20170	703-709-7172	709-8450
Dynamic Computer Corp 23400 Industrial Pk Ct *TF:* 866-257-2111 ■ *Web:* www.dcc-online.com	Farmington Hills	MI	48335	248-848-1183	473-2201
E-max Group Inc 12070 Miramar Pkwy *TF:* 888-335-3282 ■ *Web:* www.databazaar.com	Miramar	FL	33025	954-843-0483	843-0429
Electrograph Systems Inc 50 Marcus Blvd *TF:* 800-632-9877	Hauppauge	NY	11788	631-436-5050	435-2113
Electronic Environments Corp 410 Forest St *TF:* 800-342-5332 ■ *Web:* www.eecnet.com	Marlborough	MA	01752	508-229-1400	303-0579
En Pointe Technologies Inc 100 N Sepulveda Blvd 19th Fl *TF:* 800-800-4214 ■ *Web:* www.enpointe.com	El Segundo	CA	90245	310-725-5200	725-1141
Enigma Inc 200 Wheeler Rd *TF:* 888-364-4624 ■ *Web:* www.enigma.com	Burlington	MA	01803	781-273-3600	273-4400
Expresspoint Technology Services Inc 1109 Zane Ave N *TF:* 866-473-7247 ■ *Web:* www.expresspoint.com	Golden Valley	MN	55422	763-543-6000	543-5900
Gar Enterprises 418 E Live Oak Ave *Web:* www.kgselectronics.com	Arcadia	CA	91006	626-574-1175	574-0553
General Data Co Inc 4354 Ferguson Dr **Fax:* Sales ■ *TF:* 800-733-5252 ■ *Web:* www.general-data.com	Cincinnati	OH	45245	513-752-7978	752-6947*
Global Computer Supplies Inc 11 Harbor Pk Dr *TF:* 800-446-9662 ■ *Web:* www.globalcomputer.com	Port Washington	NY	11050	516-625-6200	
Graphic Products Inc PO Box 4030 *TF:* 888-326-9244 ■ *Web:* www.graphicproducts.com	Beaverton	OR	97076	503-644-5572	646-0183
GST/E-Systems 13043 166th St *TF Cust Svc:* 877-778-8930 ■ *Web:* www.gstes.com	Cerritos	CA	90703	562-345-8700	345-8701
GTSI Corp 2553 Dulles View Dr Suite 100 *NASDAQ: GTSI* ■ *TF:* 800-999-4874 ■ *Web:* www.gtsi.com	Herndon	VA	20171	703-502-2000	463-5101
Helmel Engineering Products Inc 6520 Lockport Rd *TF:* 800-237-8266 ■ *Web:* www.helmel.com	Niagara Falls	NY	14305	716-297-8644	297-9405
Iceptstechnology Group Inc 1301 Fulling Mill Rd *Web:* www.icepts.com	Middletown	PA	17057	717-704-1000	704-1010
Infotel Distributors 6990 SR 36 **Fax Area Code:* 800 ■ **Fax:* Cust Svc ■ *TF:* 800-682-0422 ■ *Web:* www.infoteldistributors.com	Fletcher	OH	45326	937-368-2650	262-6622*
Ingram Micro Inc 1600 E St Andrew Pl *NYSE: IM* ■ **Fax Area Code:* 716 ■ **Fax:* Cust Svc ■ *TF Sales:* 800-456-8000 ■ *Web:* www.ingrammicro.com	Santa Ana	CA	92705	714-566-1000	565-8899*
INTCOMEX Holdings LLC 9835 NW 14th St *Web:* www.intcomex.com	Miami	FL	33172	305-477-6230	477-5694
Itochu Technology Inc 3945 Freedom Cir Suite 350 *Web:* www.itochu.net	Santa Clara	CA	95054	408-727-8810	727-4619
Journey Education Marketing Inc 13755 Hutton Dr Suite 500 *TF:* 800-874-9001 ■ *Web:* www.journeyed.com	Dallas	TX	75234	972-481-2000	245-3585
LA Computer Ctr 463 N Oak St *TF:* 800-689-3933 ■ *Web:* www.lacc.com	Inglewood	CA	90302	310-671-4444	671-9565
Lake Cos Inc The 2980 Walker Dr *Web:* www.lakeco.com	Green Bay	WI	54311	920-406-3030	406-3040
Laser Pros International 1 International Ln *TF:* 888-558-5277 ■ *Web:* www.laserpros.com	Rhinelander	WI	54501	715-369-5995	369-5910
Leadman Electronic USA Inc 2995 Gordon Ave *TF:* 877-532-3626 ■ *Web:* www.leadman.com	Santa Clara	CA	95051	408-738-1751	738-2620
Lyme Computer Systems Inc PO Box 290 *TF:* 800-370-1095 ■ *Web:* www.lyme.com	Lyme	NH	03768	603-795-4000	795-4800
M & A Technology Inc 2045 Chenault Dr *TF:* 800-225-1452 ■ *Web:* www.macomp.com	Carrollton	TX	75006	972-490-5803	490-0616
MA Laboratories Inc 2075 N Capitol Ave *Web:* www.malabs.com	San Jose	CA	95132	408-941-0808	941-0909
Max Group Corp 17011 Green Dr *TF:* 800-256-9040 ■ *Web:* www.maxgroup.com	City of Industry	CA	91745	626-935-0050	935-0056
Media Sciences International Inc 8 Allerman Rd *PINK: MSII* ■ *TF:* 888-376-8348 ■ *Web:* www.mediasciences.com	Oakland	NJ	07436	201-677-9311	677-1440
Merisel Inc 127 W 30th St 5th Fl *Web:* www.merisel.com	New York	NY	10001	212-594-4800	
Micro Technology Concepts Inc (MTC) 17837 Rowland St *Web:* www.mtcdirect.com	City of Industry	CA	91748	626-839-6800	839-6899
Microland Electronics Corp 1883 Ringwood Ave *Web:* www.microlandusa.com	San Jose	CA	95131	408-441-1688	441-1766
MontaVista Software Inc 2929 Patrick Henry Dr *TF:* 888-624-4846 ■ *Web:* www.mvista.com	Santa Clara	CA	95054	408-572-8000	572-8005

Company	City	State	Zip	Phone	Fax
Navarre Corp 7400 49th Ave N *NASDAQ:* NAVR ■ *TF:* 800-728-4000 ■ *Web:* www.navarre.com	New Hope	MN	55428	763-535-8333	533-2156
Netstar-1 Inc 9713 Key W Ave Suite 400 **Fax Area Code:* 310 ■ *Web:* www.netstar-1.com	Rockville	MD	20850	240-425-4200	309-0338*
Network Hardware Resale LLC 26 Castilian Dr Suite A *TF:* 800-451-3407 ■ *Web:* www.networkhardware.com	Santa Barbara	CA	93117	805-964-9975	964-9405
Open Systems of Cleveland Inc 22999 Forbes Rd Suite A *TF:* 888-881-6660 ■ *Web:* www.osinc.com	Cleveland	OH	44146	440-439-2332	439-3794
PCNet Inc 100 Technology Dr *Web:* www.pcnet-inc.com	Trumbull	CT	06611	203-452-8500	452-8644
Peak Technologies Inc 10330 Old Columbia Rd *TF:* 800-950-6372 ■ *Web:* www.peaktech.com	Columbia	MD	21046	410-312-6000	312-7381
Phoenix Computer Assoc Inc 10 Sasco Hill Rd *TF:* 800-432-1815	Fairfield	CT	06824	203-319-3060	319-3069
Programmer's Paradise Inc 1157 Shrewsbury Ave Suite C *NASDAQ:* PROG ■ *TF:* 800-441-1511 ■ *Web:* www.pparadise.com	Shrewsbury	NJ	07702	732-389-8950	389-0010
Promark Technology Inc 10900 Pump House Rd Suite B **Fax Area Code:* 301 ■ *TF:* 800-634-0255 ■ *Web:* www.promarktech.com	Annapolis Junction	MD	20701	240-280-8030	725-7869*
Prostar Computer Inc 837 Lawson St *TF:* 888-576-4742 ■ *Web:* www.pro-star.com	City of Industry	CA	91748	626-839-6472	854-3438
Provantage Corp 7249 Whipple Ave NW *TF:* 800-336-1166 ■ *Web:* www.provantage.com	North Canton	OH	44720	330-494-3781	494-5260
Rave Computer Assn Inc 7171 Sterling Ponds Ct *TF:* 800-966-7283 ■ *Web:* www.rave.net	Sterling Heights	MI	48312	586-939-8230	939-7431
Rippey Corp 5000 Hillsdale Cir *Web:* www.rippey.com	El Dorado Hills	CA	95762	916-939-4332	939-4338
Rorke Data Inc 7626 Golden Triangle Dr *TF:* 800-328-8147 ■ *Web:* www.rorke.com	Eden Prairie	MN	55344	952-829-0300	829-0988
Rpl Supplies Inc 141 Lanza Ave Bldg 3A *TF:* 800-524-0914 ■ *Web:* www.rplsupplies.com	Garfield	NJ	07026	973-767-0880	772-6601
Sanyo Denki America Inc 468 Amapola Ave *Web:* www.sanyo-denki.com	Torrance	CA	90501	310-783-5400	212-6545
ScanSource Inc 6 Logue Ct *NASDAQ:* SCSC ■ *TF:* 800-944-2432 ■ *Web:* www.scansourceinc.com	Greenville	SC	29615	864-288-2432	288-1165
Scivantage Inc 10 Exchange Pl Unit 13 *TF:* 866-724-8268 ■ *Web:* www.scivantage.com	Jersey City	NJ	07302	646-452-0050	452-0049
SED International Inc 4916 N Royal Atlanta Dr *TF Sales:* 800-444-8962 ■ *Web:* www.sedonline.com	Tucker	GA	30084	770-491-8962	938-2814
Softmart Inc 450 Acorn Ln *TF Cust Svc:* 800-328-1319 ■ *Web:* www.softmart.com	Downingtown	PA	19335	610-518-4000	518-3014
Software House International (SHI) 2 Riverview Dr NULL *TF:* 888-764-8888 ■ *Web:* www.shi.com	Somerset	NJ	08873	732-764-8888	764-8889
Solution Systems Inc 3201 Tollview Dr *TF:* 888-477-7989 ■ *Web:* www.solsyst.com	Rolling Meadows	IL	60008	847-590-3000	590-0912
Stardock Systems Inc 15090 N Beck Rd Suite 300 *TF:* 888-782-7362 ■ *Web:* www.stardock.com	Plymouth	MI	48170	734-927-0677	927-0678
Static Control Components Inc 3010 Lee Ave PO Box 152 *TF:* 800-488-2426 ■ *Web:* www.scc-inc.com	Sanford	NC	27331	919-774-3808	774-1287
SYNNEX Canada 200 Ronson Dr **Fax:* Hum Res ■ *Web:* www.synnex.ca	Etobicoke	ON	M9W5Z9	416-240-7012	240-2622*
Synnex Corp 44201 Nobel Dr *NYSE:* SNX ■ *TF Cust Svc:* 800-756-1888 ■ *Web:* www.synnex.com	Fremont	CA	94538	510-656-3333	668-3777
Tech Data Corp 5350 Tech Data Dr *NASDAQ:* TECD ■ **Fax:* Hum Res ■ *TF:* 800-237-8931 ■ *Web:* www.techdata.com	Clearwater	FL	33760	727-539-7429	538-7054*
TigerDirect Inc 7795 W Flagler St Suite 35 *TF:* 800-800-8300 ■ *Web:* www.tigerdirect.com	Miami	FL	33144	305-415-2200	415-2177
Topdek Inc 2926 NW 72nd Ave **Fax Area Code:* 786 ■ *Web:* www.topdek.com	Miami	FL	33122	305-599-0006	845-8668*
Transcend Information Inc 1645 N Brian St *Web:* www.transcendusa.com	Orange	CA	92867	714-921-2000	921-2111
Ubmatrix Inc 803 Kirkland Ave Suite 200 *Web:* www.ubmatrix.com	Kirkland	WA	98033	425-285-0299	285-0299
Us Micro Corp 7000 Highlnds Pkwy SE *TF:* 888-876-4276 ■ *Web:* www.usmicrocorp.com	Smyrna	GA	30082	770-437-0706	437-0855
Vistamax Inc 6723 Mowry Ave *TF:* 866-758-4782 ■ *Web:* www.vistamaxinc.com	Newark	CA	94560	510-578-0001	791-1378
Voda One Corp *Westcon Convergence* 1010 S 120th St Suite 100 *TF:* 877-642-7750 ■ *Web:* www.us.convergencepoint.westcon.com	Omaha	NE	68154	402-334-4537	334-4537
VSS LLC 303 Brame Rd *Web:* www.vss-inc.com	Ridgeland	MS	39157	601-853-8550	853-8560
WDL Systems 220 Chatham Business Dr *TF Sales:* 800-548-2319 ■ *Web:* www.wdlsystems.com	Pittsboro	NC	27312	919-545-2500	545-2559
Westcon Group Inc 520 White Plains Rd 2nd Fl *TF:* 800-527-9516 ■ *Web:* www.westcongroup.com	Tarrytown	NY	10591	914-829-7000	829-7089
Westham Trade Co Ltd 3620 NW 114th Ave *Web:* www.wtrade.com	Doral	FL	33178	305-717-5400	593-0316
Wintec Industries Inc 4280 Technology Dr **Fax:* Tech Supp ■ *Web:* www.wintecindustries.com	Fremont	CA	94538	510-360-6300	770-9338*
Woodard Technology & Investments LLC 4937 S 78th E Ave *TF:* 800-400-8999 ■ *Web:* www.sagenet.com	Tulsa	OK	74145	918-270-7000	270-7195
Woot Inc 4121 International Pkwy *Web:* www.synmicro.com	Carrollton	TX	75007	972-417-3959	418-9245
Zones Inc 1102 15th St SW *TF:* 800-258-2088 ■ *Web:* www.zones.com	Auburn	WA	98001	253-205-3000	205-3500

COMPUTER & INTERNET TRAINING PROGRAMS

SEE Training & Certification Programs - Computer & Internet p. 2724

178 COMPUTER MAINTENANCE & REPAIR

Company	City	State	Zip	Phone	Fax
Accram Inc 2901 W Clarendon Ave *TF:* 800-786-0288 ■ *Web:* www.accram.com	Phoenix	AZ	85017	602-264-0288	264-1440
Advanced Microelectronics Inc 6001 E Old Hwy 50 *TF:* 800-264-8851 ■ *Web:* www.advancedmicro.com	Vincennes	IN	47591	812-726-4500	726-4551
ATCI Consultants 11720 Chairman Dr Suite 108 *Web:* www.atcicomputer.com	Dallas	TX	75243	214-343-0600	343-0716
Cera Services 10960 E Crystal Falls Pkwy Suite 300 *TF:* 800-966-3070	Leander	TX	78641	512-259-5151	
Computer Repair & Sales 2930 W Main St *Web:* www.computerrepair.org	Rapid City	SD	57702	605-399-0278	342-6141
Computer Specialists Inc 904 Wind River Ln Suite 100 *TF:* 800-505-4365 ■ *Web:* www.csi-csi.com	Gaithersburg	MD	20878	301-921-8860	921-4679
Computer Troubleshooters USA 755 Commerce Dr Suite 412 **Fax Area Code:* 770 ■ *TF:* 877-704-1702 ■ *Web:* www.comptroub.com	Decatur	GA	30030	404-477-1300	234-6162*
Computing Concepts Inc 185 E Union Ave *Web:* www.computingconceptsinc.com	East Rutherford	NJ	07073	201-935-4100	935-3150
Comtek Computer Systems 2751 Mercantile Dr Suite 100 *TF:* 800-823-4450 ■ *Web:* www.comtekcomsys.com	Rancho Cordova	CA	95742	916-859-7000	859-7012
CPT of South Florida Inc 2699 Stirling Rd Suite A 101 *Web:* www.cpt-florida.com	Fort Lauderdale	FL	33312	954-963-2775	963-5781
CRV Inc 1111 Navarro St *Web:* www.crvinc.com	San Antonio	TX	78205	210-828-8552	828-5042
Data Exchange Corp 3600 Via Pescador *TF:* 800-237-7911 ■ *Web:* www.dex.com	Camarillo	CA	93012	805-388-1711	389-1726
Data Service Ctr 324 Remington St *Web:* www.dataservicecenter.com	Fort Collins	CO	80524	970-282-7000	484-0693
Datatech Depot 11390 Knott St *TF:* 800-888-8181 ■ *Web:* www.dtdi.com	Garden Grove	CA	92841	714-908-5370	908-5380
DBK Concepts Inc 12905 SW 129 Ave *TF:* 800-725-7226 ■ *Web:* www.dbk.com	Miami	FL	33186	305-596-7226	596-7222
DecisionOne Corp 426 W Lancaster Ave *TF:* 800-767-2876 ■ *Web:* www.decisiononecorporate.com	Devon	PA	19355	610-296-6000	296-6045
Essential Technologies Inc 805 Virginia Dr *Web:* www.acsisupport.com	Orlando	FL	32803	407-896-8155	897-6603
Everprint International Inc 18021 Cortney Ct *TF:* 800-984-5777 ■ *Web:* www.everprint.com	City of Industry	CA	91748	626-913-2888	913-5702
Ex-Cel Solutions Inc 14618 Grover St **Fax:* Cust Svc ■ *Web:* www.excels.com	Omaha	NE	68144	402-333-6541	333-3124*
Friendly Computers 3440 W Cheyenne Suite 100 *TF:* 800-656-3115 ■ *Web:* www.friendlycomputers.com	North Las Vegas	NV	89032	702-458-2780	869-2780
Genesis Computer Repair & Sales 121 F Grafton Stn Ln *Web:* buygenesiscomputers.com/repair.html	Yorktown	VA	23692	757-833-6262	833-8757
ICM Corp 4025 Steve Reynolds Blvd Suite 120 *TF Cust Svc:* 800-654-8013 ■ *Web:* www.icmcorp.com	Norcross	GA	30093	770-381-2947	279-6036
Integration Technologies Group Inc 2745 Hartland Rd Suite 200 *TF:* 800-835-7823 ■ *Web:* www.itgonline.com	Falls Church	VA	22043	703-698-8282	698-0305
Interactive Services Group Inc 600 Delran Pkwy Suite C **Fax Area Code:* 856 ■ *TF:* 800-566-3310 ■ *Web:* www.isg-service.com	Delran	NJ	08075	800-566-3310	824-9415*
Jaguar Computer Systems Inc 4135 Indus Way *Web:* www.jaguar.net	Riverside	CA	92503	951-273-7950	734-5615
Just Service Inc 2940 N Clark St *Web:* www.justservice.com	Chicago	IL	60657	773-871-7171	
Matthijssen Inc 14 Rt 10 *TF:* 800-845-2200 ■ *Web:* www.mattnj.com	East Hanover	NJ	07936	973-887-1100	887-2453
MCPconnect 21555 Drake Rd *TF:* 800-486-0060 ■ *Web:* www.mcpc.com	Strongsville	OH	44149	440-238-0102	238-4546
Midwest Computer Support 3315 N Centennial Rd *Web:* www.callmcs.com	Sylvania	OH	43560	419-843-9410	843-9411
Nations First Office Repair 1555 E Flamingo Rd Suite 202 *Web:* www.laptoprepairs.com	Las Vegas	NV	89119	702-699-5657	699-5468
NCE Computer Group 1973 Friendship Dr Suite B *TF Cust Svc:* 800-767-2587 ■ *Web:* www.ncegroup.com	El Cajon	CA	92020	619-212-3000	212-3036
Nexicore 3949 Heritage Oak Ct *TF:* 800-644-4494 ■ *Web:* www.nexicore.com	Simi Valley	CA	93063	805-306-2500	306-2599
Ockers Co 1340 Belmont St *Web:* www.ockers.com	Brockton	MA	02301	508-586-4642	584-9180
PCHero Digital Imaging 2055 Jeff Davis Hwy *Web:* www.pchero.biz	Stafford	VA	22554	540-657-9555	659-6291
Precision Computer Services Inc (PCS) 175 Constitution Blvd S *Web:* www.precisiongroup.com	Shelton	CT	06484	203-929-0000	929-8800
Rescuecom Corp 2560 Burnet Ave **Fax Area Code:* 315 ■ *TF:* 800-737-2837 ■ *Web:* www.rescuecom.com	Syracuse	NY	13206	800-737-2837	433-5228*
Scantron Service Group 2020 S 156th Cir *TF:* 800-228-3628 ■ *Web:* www.scantronservicegroup.com	Omaha	NE	68130	402-697-3000	697-3350
Systems Maintenance Services Inc (SMS) 9013 Perimeter Woods Dr Suite E *Web:* www.sysmaint.com	Charlotte	NC	28216	980-939-7008	
Technology Innovations Inc 555 E Easy St *TF Cust Svc:* 800-286-0651 ■ *Web:* www.tsli.com	Simi Valley	CA	93065	805-426-1000	579-9588

179 COMPUTER NETWORKING PRODUCTS & SYSTEMS

SEE ALSO Modems p. 1671; Systems & Utilities Software p. 1691; Telecommunications Equipment & Systems p. 2682

Company	City	State	ZIP	Phone	Fax
Accton Technology Corp 1362 Borregas Ave *Web:* www.accton.com	Sunnyvale	CA	94089	408-747-0994	747-0982
Alcatel-Lucent 600 Mountain Ave *Web:* www.alcatel-lucent.com	Murray Hill	NJ	07974	908-508-8080	508-2576
Allied Telesyn International Corp 19800 N Creek Pkwy Suite 100 **Fax:* Sales ■ *TF:* 800-424-4284 ■ *Web:* www.alliedtelesis.com	Bothell	WA	98011	425-481-3895	481-3899*
Alvarion Ltd 2495 Leghorn St *NASDAQ: ALVR* ■ *Web:* www.alvarion.com	Mountain View	CA	94043	650-314-2500	967-3966
Am Networks Inc 1900 AM Dr *TF:* 800-248-9004 ■ *Web:* www.amcomm.com	Quakertown	PA	18951	215-538-8700	538-8779
American Megatrends Inc (AMI) 5555 Oakbrook Pkwy Bldg 200 *TF:* 800-828-9264 ■ *Web:* www.ami.com	Norcross	GA	30093	770-246-8600	246-8790
American Research Corp 602 Monterey Pass Rd *TF:* 888-462-3899 ■ *Web:* www.800findarc.com	Monterey Park	CA	91754	626-284-1904	281-0767
ASA Computers Inc 645 National Ave *TF:* 800-732-5727 ■ *Web:* www.asacomputers.com	Mountain View	CA	94043	650-230-8000	230-8090
Asante Technologies Inc 673 S Milpitas Blvd Suite 100 *TF:* 800-303-9121 ■ *Web:* www.asante.com	Milpitas	CA	95035	408-435-8388	719-8594
Avaya Inc 211 Mt Airy Rd *TF:* 800-462-8292 ■ *Web:* www.avaya.com	Basking Ridge	NJ	07920	908-953-6000	953-7609
Axis Communications Inc (ACI) 100 Apollo Dr *TF:* 800-444-2947 ■ *Web:* www.axis.com	Chelmsford	MA	01824	978-614-2000	614-2100
Belobox Networks Inc 18 Technology Dr Suite 103 *TF:* 800-235-6269 ■ *Web:* www.belobox.com	Irvine	CA	92618	949-727-4115	727-2149
Black Box Corp 1000 Pk Dr *NASDAQ: BBOX* ■ **Fax Area Code:* 800 ■ *TF:* 877-877-2269 ■ *Web:* www.blackbox.com	Lawrence	PA	15055	724-746-5500	321-0746*
Blue Coat Systems Inc 420 N Mary Ave *NASDAQ: BCSI* ■ *TF:* 888-462-3569 ■ *Web:* www.bluecoat.com	Sunnyvale	CA	94085	408-220-2200	220-2250
Brocade Communications Systems Inc 130 Holger Way *NASDAQ: BRCD* ■ *Web:* www.brocade.com	San Jose	CA	95134	408-333-8000	333-8101
Bytex Corp 113 Cedar St 495 Commerce Pk Suite S6 *TF:* 800-227-1145	Milford	MA	01757	508-422-9422	422-9410
Cambex Corp 337 Tpke Rd *TF:* 800-325-5565 ■ *Web:* www.cambex.com	Westborough	MA	01772	508-281-0209	281-0214
Chatsworth Products Inc 31425 Agoura Rd *TF:* 800-834-4969 ■ *Web:* www.chatsworth.com	Westlake Village	CA	91361	818-735-6100	735-6199
CIENA Corp Metro Transport Div 1185 Sanctuary Pkwy	Alpharetta	GA	30004	678-867-5100	867-5101
Cisco Systems Inc 170 W Tasman Dr *NASDAQ: CSCO* ■ *TF:* 800-553-6387 ■ *Web:* www.cisco.com	San Jose	CA	95134	408-526-4000	526-4100
CNet Technology Inc 1455 McCandless Dr *TF:* 800-486-2638 ■ *Web:* www.cnet.com.tw	Milpitas	CA	95035	408-934-0800	934-0900
Communication Devices Inc 1 Forstmann Ct *TF:* 800-359-8561 ■ *Web:* www.commdevices.com	Clifton	NJ	07011	973-772-6997	772-0747
Compex Inc 840 Columbia St Suite B **Fax:* Sales ■ *TF:* 800-279-8891 ■ *Web:* www.compex.com.sg	Brea	CA	92821	714-482-0333	482-0332*
CompuCom Systems Inc 7171 Forest Ln *TF Cust Svc:* 800-597-0555 ■ *Web:* www.compucom.com	Dallas	TX	75230	972-856-3600	
Comtrol Corp 6655 Wedgewood Rd Suite 120 *TF:* 800-926-6876 ■ *Web:* www.comtrol.com	Maple Grove	MN	55311	763-494-4100	494-4199
Comverse Technology Inc 100 Quannapowitt Pkwy *NASDAQ: CMVT* ■ *Web:* www.cmvt.com	Wakefield	MA	01880	781-246-9000	224-8135
Contemporary Control Systems Inc 2431 Curtiss St *Web:* www.ccontrols.com	Downers Grove	IL	60515	630-963-7070	963-0109
Continental Resources Inc 175 Middlesex Tpke *TF:* 800-937-4688 ■ *Web:* www.conres.com	Bedford	MA	01730	781-275-0850	275-6563
Crossroads Systems Inc 8300 N MoPac Expy *TF:* 800-643-7148 ■ *Web:* www.crossroads.com	Austin	TX	78759	512-349-0300	795-8309
Crystal Group Inc 850 Kacena Rd *TF:* 877-279-7863 ■ *Web:* www.crystalrugged.com	Hiawatha	IA	52233	319-378-1636	393-2338
Cubix Corp 2800 Lockheed Way *TF Sales:* 800-829-0554 ■ *Web:* www.cubix.com	Carson City	NV	89706	775-883-7611	888-1002
Cyberdata Corp 3 Justin Ct *TF:* 800-292-3738 ■ *Web:* www.cyberdata.net	Monterey	CA	93940	831-373-2601	373-4193
D-Link Systems Inc 17595 Mt Herrmann St **Fax Area Code:* 866 ■ *TF:* 800-326-1688 ■ *Web:* www.dlink.com	Fountain Valley	CA	92708	714-885-6000	743-4905*
Daly Computers Inc 22521 Gateway Ctr Dr *TF:* 800-955-3259 ■ *Web:* www.daly.com	Clarksburg	MD	20871	301-670-0381	963-1516
Datacomm Management Sciences Inc 25 Van Zant St	East Norwalk	CT	06855	203-838-7183	838-1751
Dell Inc 1 Dell Way *NASDAQ: DELL* ■ *TF:* 800-854-6214 ■ *Web:* www.dell.com	Round Rock	TX	78682	512-338-4400	283-6161
Digi International Inc 11001 Bren Rd E *NASDAQ: DGII* ■ *TF:* 877-912-3444 ■ *Web:* www.digi.com	Minnetonka	MN	55343	952-912-3444	912-4991
Digilog Inc 2360 Maryland Rd *TF Cust Svc:* 800-344-4564 ■ *Web:* www.digilog.com	Willow Grove	PA	19090	215-830-9400	830-9444
Dot Hill Systems Corp 1351 S Sunset St *NASDAQ: HILL* ■ *TF:* 800-872-2783 ■ *Web:* www.dothill.com	Longmont	CO	80501	303-845-3200	845-3655
Echelon Corp 550 Meridian Ave *NASDAQ: ELON* ■ *TF:* 800-324-3566 ■ *Web:* www.echelon.com	San Jose	CA	95126	408-938-5200	790-3800
Egenera Inc 80 Central St *TF:* 800-316-3976 ■ *Web:* www.egenera.com	Boxborough	MA	01719	978-206-6300	206-6436
Electronics for Imaging Inc 303 Velocity Way *NASDAQ: EFII* ■ *TF:* 800-568-1917 ■ *Web:* www.efi.com	Foster City	CA	94404	650-357-3500	357-3500
EMC Corp 176 S St *NYSE: EMC* ■ *TF:* 877-362-6973 ■ *Web:* www.emc.com	Hopkinton	MA	01748	508-435-1000	497-6912
Emulex Corp 3333 Susan St *NYSE: ELX* ■ *TF:* 800-854-7112 ■ *Web:* www.emulex.com	Costa Mesa	CA	92626	714-662-5600	241-0792
Enterasys Networks Inc 50 Minuteman Rd *Web:* www.enterasys.com	Andover	MA	01810	978-684-1000	684-1658
eSoft Inc 295 Interlocken Blvd Suite 500 *TF:* 888-903-7638 ■ *Web:* www.esoft.com	Broomfield	CO	80021	303-444-1600	444-1640
Extreme Networks Inc 3585 Monroe St *NASDAQ: EXTR* ■ *TF:* 888-257-3000 ■ *Web:* www.extremenetworks.com	Santa Clara	CA	95051	408-579-2800	579-3000
Ezenia! Inc 14 Celina Ave Unit 17 **Fax Area Code:* 603 ■ *TF:* 800-966-2301 ■ *Web:* www.ezenia.com	Nashua	NH	03063	781-505-2100	880-4978*
F5 Networks Inc 401 Elliott Ave W *NASDAQ: FFIV* ■ *TF:* 888-882-4447 ■ *Web:* www.f5.com	Seattle	WA	98119	206-272-5555	272-5556
Finisar Corp 1389 Moffett Pk Dr *NASDAQ: FNSR* ■ *Web:* www.finisar.com	Sunnyvale	CA	94089	408-548-1000	541-6129
Forsythe Technology Inc 7770 Frontage Rd *TF:* 800-843-4488 ■ *Web:* www.forsythe.com	Skokie	IL	60077	847-675-8000	213-7770
Fujitsu Computer Systems Corp 1250 E Arques Ave *TF:* 800-538-8460 ■ *Web:* www.computers.us.fujitsu.com	Sunnyvale	CA	94085	408-746-6000	
FusionWare Corp 5605 NE Elam Young Pkwy *TF:* 866-266-2326	Hillsboro	OR	97124	604-633-9891	633-9892
Futurex Inc 864 Old Boerne Rd *TF:* 800-251-5112 ■ *Web:* www.futurex.com	Bulverde	TX	78163	830-980-9782	438-8782
General DataComm Inc 6 Rubber Ave *Web:* www.gdc.com	Naugatuck	CT	06770	203-729-0271	729-2883
GlassHouse Technologies Inc 200 Crossing Blvd *Web:* www.glasshouse.com	Framingham	MA	01702	508-879-5729	879-7319
High Point Solutions Inc 5 Gail Ct *Web:* www.highpt.com	Sparta	NJ	07871	973-940-0040	940-0041
iGo Inc 17800 N Perimeter Dr Suite 200 *NASDAQ: MOBE* ■ *Web:* corporate.igo.com	Scottsdale	AZ	85255	480-596-0061	596-0349
iLinc Communications Inc 2999 N 44th St Suite 650 *TF:* 877-736-8347 ■ *Web:* www.ilinc.com	Phoenix	AZ	85018	602-952-1200	952-0544
IMC Networks Corp 19772 Pauling *TF:* 800-624-1070 ■ *Web:* www.imcnetworks.com	Foothill Ranch	CA	92610	949-465-3000	465-3020
Informer Computer Systems Inc 12833 Monarch St *TF:* 800-650-4636 ■ *Web:* www.informer911.com	Garden Grove	CA	92841	714-891-1112	898-2624
Interphase Corp 2901 N Dallas Pkwy Suite 200 *NASDAQ: INPH* ■ *TF:* 800-327-8638 ■ *Web:* www.interphase.com	Plano	TX	75093	214-654-5000	654-5500
ISDN*Tek 3000 Hwy 84 PO Box 3000 *Web:* www.isdntek.com	San Gregorio	CA	94074	650-712-3000	712-3003
Juniper Networks Inc 1194 N Mathilda Ave *NASDAQ: JNPR* ■ *TF:* 888-586-4737 ■ *Web:* www.juniper.net	Sunnyvale	CA	94089	408-745-2000	745-2100
LightSand Communications Inc 101 E Park Blvd Suite 600 *Web:* www.lightsand.com	Plano	TX	75074	972-516-3740	516-3741
Link Computer Corp Inc PO Box 250 *Web:* www.linkcorp.com	Bellwood	PA	16617	814-742-7700	742-7900
MAPSYS Inc 920 Michigan Ave *Web:* www.mapsysinc.com	Columbus	OH	43215	614-224-5193	224-6048
Marathon Technologies Corp 295 Foster St *TF:* 800-884-6425 ■ *Web:* www.marathontechnologies.com	Littleton	MA	01460	978-489-1100	489-1101
Marvell Semiconductor Inc 5488 Marvell Ln *TF Cust Svc:* 800-752-3334 ■ *Web:* www.marvell.com	Santa Clara	CA	95054	408-222-2500	
Medical Knowledge Systems Inc 440 Burroughs Suite 130 *Web:* www.mksi.com	Detroit	MI	48202	313-483-0955	731-0591
Micro Design International Inc (MDI) 45 Skyline Dr Suite 1017 *TF:* 800-228-0891 ■ *Web:* www.mdi.com	Lake Mary	FL	32746	407-472-6000	472-6100
MTM Technologies Inc 1200 High Ridge Rd *NASDAQ: MTMC* ■ *Web:* www.mtm.com	Stamford	CT	06905	203-975-3700	975-3701
NEC Corp of America 10850 Gold Ctr Dr Suite 200 *TF:* 800-632-4636 ■ *Web:* www.necam.com	Rancho Cordova	CA	95670	916-463-7000	636-5656
Netopia Inc 6001 Shellmound St 4th Fl *Web:* www.netopia.com	Emeryville	CA	94608	510-420-7400	420-7601
Netplanner Systems Inc 3100 Northwoods Pl Suite B *TF:* 800-795-1975 ■ *Web:* www.netplanner.com	Norcross	GA	30071	770-662-5482	441-3773
Network Appliance Inc 495 E Java Dr *NASDAQ: NTAP* ■ *TF Sales:* 800-443-4537 ■ *Web:* www.netapp.com	Sunnyvale	CA	94089	408-822-6000	822-4422
Network Dynamics Inc 640 Brooker Creek Blvd Suite 410 *TF:* 877-818-8597 ■ *Web:* www.ndiwebsite.com	Oldsmar	FL	34677	813-818-8597	818-9659
Network Engines Inc (NEI) 25 Dan Rd *NASDAQ: NENG* ■ *TF:* 800-977-4002 ■ *Web:* www.networkengines.com	Canton	MA	02021	781-332-1000	770-2000
Network Equipment Technologies Inc 6900 Paseo Padre Pkwy *NYSE: NWK* ■ *TF:* 888-828-8080 ■ *Web:* www.net.com	Fremont	CA	94555	510-713-7300	574-4000
Network Management Corp (NMC) 111 Derek Pl *TF:* 888-455-4662 ■ *Web:* www.netmgmt.com	Roseville	CA	95678	916-772-2020	772-2323
Newman Group 7400 Newman Blvd *Web:* www.newman.com	Dexter	MI	48130	734-426-3200	426-0777
Overland Storage Inc 4820 Overland Ave *NASDAQ: OVRL* ■ *TF:* 800-729-8725 ■ *Web:* www.overlandstorage.com	San Diego	CA	92123	858-571-5555	571-0982
OvisLink Technologies Corp 20266 Paseo Robles *Web:* www.ovislink.com	Walnut	CA	91789	909-869-8666	869-8585
Patton Electronics Co 7622 Rickenbacker Dr *Web:* www.patton.com	Gaithersburg	MD	20879	301-975-1000	869-9293
Peak 10 733 Barret Ave *TF:* 866-732-5836 ■ *Web:* www.peak10.com	Louisville	KY	40204	502-315-6000	315-6035
Performance Technologies Inc 205 Indigo Creek Dr *NASDAQ: PTIX* ■ *Web:* www.pt.com	Rochester	NY	14626	585-256-0200	256-0791
Plaintree Systems Inc 90 Decosta Pl Suite 100 *TF:* 800-461-0062 ■ *Web:* www.plaintree.com	Arnprior	ON	K7S0B5	613-623-3434	623-4647

Company / Address	City	State	ZIP	Phone	Fax
Polycom Inc 4750 Willow Rd	Pleasanton	CA	94588	925-924-6000	924-6101*
NASDAQ: PLCM ■ **Fax:* Hum Res ■ *TF:* 866-476-5926 ■ *Web:* www.polycom.com					
PrimeArray Systems Inc 127 Riverneck Rd	Chelmsford	MA	01824	978-654-6250	654-6249
TF: 800-433-5133 ■ *Web:* www.primearray.com					
Quantum Corp 11431 Willows Rd NE	Redmond	WA	98052	425-881-8004	881-2296
TF: 800-336-1233 ■ *Web:* www.quantum.com					
Quick Eagle Networks Inc 830 Maude Ave	Mountain View	CA	94043	650-962-8282	962-7950
Racore Technology Corp 4125 S 6000 W	West Valley City	UT	84128	801-973-9779	973-2005
TF: 877-252-9779 ■ *Web:* www.racore.com					
RADVISION Inc 17-17 State Hwy 208 Suite 300	Fair Lawn	NJ	07410	201-689-6300	689-6301
NASDAQ: RVSN ■ *Web:* www.radvision.com					
Raytheon Computer Products 1001 Boston Post Rd	Marlborough	MA	01752	508-490-1000	490-2675
Web: www.raytheon.com					
Ringdale Inc 101 Halmar Cove	Georgetown	TX	78628	512-288-9080	288-7210
TF: 888-288-9080 ■ *Web:* www.ringdale.com					
Safari Circuits Inc 411 Washington St	Otsego	MI	49078	269-694-9471	692-2651
TF: 888-694-7230 ■ *Web:* www.safaricircuits.com					
SafeNet Inc 4690 Millennium Dr	Belcamp	MD	21017	410-931-7500	931-7524
TF Sales: 800-533-3958 ■ *Web:* www.safenet-inc.com					
SARCOM Inc 8337 Green Meadows Dr N Suite A	Lewis Center	OH	43035	614-854-1300	854-1800*
**Fax:* Sales ■ *TF:* 800-326-3962 ■ *Web:* www.sarcom.com					
segNET Technologies Inc 325 Mt Support Rd PO Box 610	Lebanon	NH	03766	603-643-5883	643-9854
TF: 800-763-5556 ■ *Web:* www.segnet.com					
Server Technology Inc 1040 Sandhill Dr	Reno	NV	89521	775-284-2000	284-2065
TF: 800-835-1515 ■ *Web:* www.servertech.com					
Siemens Subscriber Networks LLC 4849 Alpha Rd	Dallas	TX	75244	972-852-1000	852-1001
SIGCOM 4230 Beechwood Dr	Greensboro	NC	27410	336-547-9700	547-1449
TF: 877-474-4266 ■ *Web:* www.sigcom.net/employment.htm					
Silicon Graphics Inc (SGI) 1140 E Argues Ave	Sunnyvale	CA	94085	650-960-1980	933-0908
Web: www.sgi.com					
Skyline Network Engineering LLC 6200 Georgetwn Blvd Suite C	Eldersburg	MD	21784	410-795-2700	
Web: www.skylinenet.net					
Soapstone Networks Inc 101 Billerica Ave	North Billerica	MA	01862	978-964-2000	964-2100
PINK: SOAP ■ *TF:* 877-292-8424					
SOHOware Inc 1250 Oakmead Pkwy Suite 210	Sunnyvale	CA	95085	408-565-9888	565-9889
TF: 800-632-1118 ■ *Web:* www.sohoware.com					
Solectek Corp 6370 Nancy Ridge Dr Suite 109	San Diego	CA	92121	858-450-1220	457-2681
TF: 800-437-1518 ■ *Web:* www.solectek.com					
SonicWALL Inc 2001 Logic Dr	San Jose	CA	95124	408-745-9600	745-9300
NASDAQ: SNWL ■ *TF:* 888-557-6642 ■ *Web:* www.sonicwall.com					
Spectrum Communications Cabling Services Inc 226 N Lincoln Ave	Corona	CA	92882	951-371-0549	270-3833
TF: 800-319-8711 ■ *Web:* www.spectrumccsi.com					
SteelCloud Inc 20110 Ashbrook Pl Suite 270	Ashburn	VA	20147	703-674-5500	674-5506
PINK: SCLD ■ *TF:* 800-296-3866 ■ *Web:* www.steelcloud.com					
StoneFly Inc 21353 Cabot Blvd	Hayward	CA	94545	510-265-1616	265-1565
Web: www.stonefly.com					
Storage Engine Inc 1 Sheila Dr Bldg 6A	Tinton Falls	NJ	07724	732-747-6995	747-6542
TF: 866-734-8899 ■ *Web:* www.storageengine.com					
Strictly Business Computer Systems Inc 848 4th Ave Suite 200	Huntington	WV	25701	888-529-0401	781-2590*
**Fax Area Code:* 304 ■ *Web:* www.sbcs.com					
Sycamore Networks Inc 220 Mill Rd	Chelmsford	MA	01824	978-250-2900	256-3434
NASDAQ: SCMR ■ *TF:* 877-792-2667 ■ *Web:* www.sycamorenet.com					
Symon Communications Inc 500 N Central Expy Suite 175	Plano	TX	75074	972-578-8484	422-1680
TF: 800-827-9666 ■ *Web:* www.symon.com					
Systech Corp 16510 Via Esprillo	San Diego	CA	92127	858-674-6500	613-2400
TF: 800-800-8970 ■ *Web:* www.systech.com					
Systemax Inc 11 Harbor Pk Dr	Port Washington	NY	11050	516-625-3663	608-7744*
NYSE: SYX ■ **Fax:* Sales ■ *TF:* 800-845-6225 ■ *Web:* www.systemaxpc.com					
TalkPoint Communications Inc 100 William St 9th Fl	New York	NY	10038	212-909-2900	909-2901
TF: 866-323-8660 ■ *Web:* www.talkpointcommunications.com					
Technology Integration Group (TIG) 7810 Trade St	San Diego	CA	92121	858-566-1900	566-8794
TF: 800-858-0549 ■ *Web:* www.tig.com					
Tekworks Inc 13000 Gregg St Suite B	Poway	CA	92064	877-835-9675	
Web: www.tekworks.com					
Telebyte Inc 355 Marcus Blvd	Hauppauge	NY	11788	631-423-3232	385-8184
TF: 800-835-3298 ■ *Web:* www.telebyteusa.com					
TeleSoft International Inc 11502 Saddle Mountain Trail	Austin	TX	78739	512-373-4224	373-4181
Web: www.telesoft-intl.com					
Telkonet Inc 10200 W Innovation Dr Suite 300	Milwaukee	WI	53226	414-223-0473	258-8307
PINK: TKOI ■ *TF Sales:* 888-703-9398 ■ *Web:* www.telkonet.com					
Transition Networks Inc 6103 City W Pkwy	Eden Prairie	MN	55344	952-941-7600	941-2322
TF: 800-526-9267 ■ *Web:* www.transition.com					
TransNet Corp 45 Columbia Rd	Somerville	NJ	08876	908-253-0500	253-0600
TF: 800-526-4965 ■ *Web:* www.transnet.com					
Transource Computers Corp 2405 W Utopia Rd	Phoenix	AZ	85027	623-879-8882	879-8887
TF: 800-486-3715 ■ *Web:* www.transource.com					
Trendware International Inc 20675 Manhattan Pl	Torrance	CA	90501	310-961-5500	961-5511
TF: 888-326-6061 ■ *Web:* www.trendnet.com					
Ultera Systems Inc 26081 Merit Cir # 123	Laguna Hills	CA	92653	949-367-8800	367-0758
Web: www.ultera.com					
UNICOM 565 Brea Canyon Rd Suite A	Walnut	CA	91789	626-964-7873	964-7880*
**Fax:* Mktg ■ *TF:* 800-346-6668 ■ *Web:* www.unicomlink.com					
Unimark Products 9818 Pflumm Rd	Lenexa	KS	66215	913-649-2424	649-5795
TF Cust Svc: 800-255-6356 ■ *Web:* www.unimark.com					
US Robotics Corp 1300 E Woodfield Dr # 506	Schaumburg	IL	60173	847-874-2000	874-2001
TF: 877-710-0884 ■ *Web:* www.usr.com					
ViewCast Corp 3701 W Plano Pkwy Suite 300	Plano	TX	75075	972-488-7200	488-7299
TF: 800-540-4119 ■ *Web:* www.viewcast.com					
Virtela Technology Services Inc 5680 Greenwood Plaza Blvd Suite 200	Greenwood Village	CO	80111	720-475-4000	475-4001
TF: 877-803-9629 ■ *Web:* www.virtela.net					
Visara International Inc 2700 Gateway Centre Blvd Suite 600	Morrisville	NC	27560	919-882-0200	882-0163
TF: 888-334-4380 ■ *Web:* www.visara.com					
WatchGuard Technologies Inc 505 5th Ave S Suite 500	Seattle	WA	98104	206-613-6600	521-8342
NASDAQ: WGRD ■ *TF Sales:* 800-734-9905 ■ *Web:* www.watchguard.com					
WAV Inc 2380 Prospect Dr	Aurora	IL	60504	630-818-1000	818-4450
TF: 800-678-2419 ■ *Web:* www.wavonline.com					
WideBand Corp 401 W Grand St	Gallatin	MO	64640	660-663-3000	663-3736
TF: 888-663-3050 ■ *Web:* www.wband.com					
Winchester Systems Inc 101 Billerica Ave Bldg 5	Burlington	MA	01862	781-265-0200	265-0201
TF Cust Svc: 800-325-3700 ■ *Web:* www.winsys.com					
Works Computing Inc 1801 American Blvd E Suite 12	Bloomington	MN	55425	952-746-1580	746-1585
TF: 866-222-4077 ■ *Web:* www.workscomputing.com					
World Data Products Inc 121 Cheshire Ln	Minnetonka	MN	55305	952-476-9000	476-1903
TF: 888-210-7636 ■ *Web:* www.wdpi.com					
Xyratex International 2031 Concourse Dr	San Jose	CA	95131	408-894-0800	894-0880
Web: www.xyratex.com					
ZT Group International Inc 350 Meadowlands Pkwy	Secaucus	NJ	07094	201-559-1000	559-1004
TF: 888-984-8899 ■ *Web:* www.ztsystems.com					

180 COMPUTER PROGRAMMING SERVICES - CUSTOM

SEE ALSO Computer Software p. 1679; Computer Systems Design Services p. 1694

Company / Address	City	State	ZIP	Phone	Fax
Abaris Inc PO Box 1210	Lake Forest	CA	92609	949-333-3500	597-1120
Web: www.abaris-inc.com					
Access Innovations Inc 4725 Indian School Rd NE # 100	Albuquerque	NM	87110	505-265-3591	256-1080
TF: 800-926-8328 ■ *Web:* www.accessinn.com					
AccuCode Inc 6886 S Yosemite St Suite 100	Centennial	CO	80112	303-639-6111	639-6178
TF: 866-705-9879 ■ *Web:* www.accucode.com					
ACS International Resources Inc 1290 Baltimore Pike 2nd Fl, Unit 118	Chadds Ford	PA	19317	610-387-6005	387-6018
Web: www.acs-intl.com					
Actsoft Inc 8910 N Dale Mabry Hwy	Tampa	FL	33614	813-936-2331	936-7541
TF: 888-732-6638 ■ *Web:* www.actsoft.com					
Advanced Digital Data Inc 6 Laurel Dr	Flanders	NJ	07836	973-584-4026	584-3205
TF: 800-922-0972 ■ *Web:* www.addsys.com					
Advanced Health Media LLC 420 Mountain Ave	Murray Hill	NJ	07974	908-393-8700	393-8701
Web: www.ahmdirect.com					
Advanced Solutions International Inc 901 N Pitt St Suite 200	Alexandria	VA	22314	703-739-3100	739-3218
Web: www.advsol.com					
Alliance Consulting 2001 Market St 8th Fl	Philadelphia	PA	19103	215-569-8722	500-0808*
**Fax Area Code:* 800 ■ *TF:* 800-706-3339 ■ *Web:* www.alliance-consulting.com					
Alphanumerica Inc 8000 Marina Blvd Suite 600	Brisbane	CA	94005	650-228-2500	228-2501
TF: 888-532-6823 ■ *Web:* www.collab.net					
Analytical Graphics Inc 220 Valley Creek Blvd	Exton	PA	19341	610-981-8000	981-8001
TF: 800-220-4785 ■ *Web:* www.agi.com					
Archibus Inc 18 Tremont St	Boston	MA	02108	617-227-2508	227-2509
Web: www.archibus.com					
Argo Data Resource Corp 1500 N Greenville Ave	Richardson	TX	75081	972-866-3300	866-3301
Web: www.argodata.com					
Aricent Inc 1 Tower Ctr Blvd 18th Fl	East Brunswick	NJ	08816	732-837-1200	837-1190
Web: www.aricent.com					
Arsin Corp 4800 Great America Pkwy	Santa Clara	CA	95054	408-653-2020	653-2030
Web: www.arsin.com					
Aruba Networks Inc 1344 Crossman Ave	Sunnyvale	CA	94089	408-227-4500	752-0626
NASDAQ: ARUN ■ *Web:* www.arubanetworks.com					
Atlantic Internet Technologies Inc 628 Shrewsbury Ave	Red Bank	NJ	07701	732-758-0505	758-0869
Avineon Inc 4825 Mark Ctr Dr Suite 700	Alexandria	VA	22311	703-671-1900	671-1901
Web: www.avineon.com					
Big Creek Software LLC 201 N 3rd St Suite E	Polk City	IA	50226	515-984-6243	
Web: www.bigcreek.com					
Boingo Wireless Inc 10960 Wilshire Blvd Suite 800	Los Angeles	CA	90024	310-586-5180	586-4060
TF: 800-880-4117 ■ *Web:* www.boingo.com					
C-Sharp Technologies Inc 5837 Karric Sq Dr Suite 340	Dublin	OH	43016	614-529-2393	
Web: www.c-sharp.com					
CareerCast Inc 5963 La Pl Ct Suite 100	Carlsbad	CA	92008	760-602-9502	602-9260
Web: www.careercast.com					
Carnegie Learning Inc 437 Grant St	Pittsburgh	PA	15219	412-690-6284	690-2444
TF: 888-851-7094 ■ *Web:* www.carnegielearning.com					
Channelnet 3 Harbor Dr Suite 206	Sausalito	CA	94965	800-667-6858	332-1635*
**Fax Area Code:* 415 ■ *TF:* 800-667-6858 ■ *Web:* www.channelnet.com					
Charles River Analytics Inc 625 Mt Auburn St Suite 3	Cambridge	MA	02138	617-491-3474	868-0780
Web: www.cra.com					
Cherryroad Technologies Inc 301 Gibraltar Dr Suite 2C	Morris Plains	NJ	07950	973-402-7802	402-7808
TF: 877-402-7804 ■ *Web:* www.cherryroad.com					
Cimarron Software Services Inc 1115 Gemini	Houston	TX	77058	281-226-5100	226-5190
Web: www.cimarroninc.com					

Company	City	State	ZIP	Phone	Fax
CMA Consulting Services Inc 700 Troy Schenectady Rd *TF:* 800-276-6101 ■ *Web:* www.cma.com	Latham	NY	12110	518-783-9003	783-5093
Commercial Programming Systems Inc 4400 Coldwater Canyon Ave. **Fax Area Code:* 888 ■ *TF:* 888-277-4562 ■ *Web:* www.cpsinc.com	Studio City	CA	91604	323-851-2681	812-5966*
Comnet International Co 1 Trans Am Plaza Dr Suite 520 *Web:* www.comneti.com	Oakbrook Terrace	IL	60181	630-615-2000	678-2919
Companion Professional Services LLC 1800 St Julian Pl Suite 100 *TF:* 800-780-1170 ■ *Web:* www.tmfloyd.com	Columbia	SC	29204	803-765-1310	765-1431
Compusearch Software Systems Inc 21251 Ridgetop Cir *Web:* www.compusearch.com	Dulles	VA	20166	703-481-3699	481-3442
Computer Aid Inc (CAI) 1390 Ridgeview Dr. *Web:* www.compaid.com	Allentown	PA	18104	610-530-5000	530-5298
Computer Guidance Corp 15035 N 75th St. *TF:* 888-361-4551 ■ *Web:* www.computer-guidance.com	Scottsdale	AZ	85260	480-444-7000	444-7001
Computer Software Innovations Inc (CSI) 900 E Main St Suite T. *OTC:* CSWI ■ *TF:* 800-953-6847 ■ *Web:* www.csioutfitters.com	Easley	SC	29640	864-855-3900	855-1429
Computrition Inc 19808 Nordhoff Pl. *TF:* 800-222-4488 ■ *Web:* www.computrition.com	Chatsworth	CA	91311	818-701-5544	701-1702
Construx Software 11820 Northup Way Suite E-200 *TF:* 866-296-6300 ■ *Web:* www.construx.com	Bellevue	WA	98005	425-636-0100	636-0159
Control Systems International Inc 8040 Nieman Rd. *Web:* www.csiks.com	Lenexa	KS	66214	913-599-5010	599-5013
Corptax LLC 1751 Lake Cook Rd Suite 200 *Web:* www.corptax.com	Deerfield	IL	60015	847-236-8213	236-8011
Credant Technologies Inc 15303 Dallas Pkwy Suite 1420. *TF:* 800-929-8331 ■ *Web:* www.credant.com	Addison	TX	75001	972-458-5400	458-5454
Cyber-Ark Software Inc 57 Wells Ave Suite 20A *TF:* 888-808-9005 ■ *Web:* www.cyber-ark.com	Newton	MA	02459	617-965-1544	965-1644
CyberThink Inc 1125 US Hwy 22 Suite 1 *Web:* www.cyberthink.com	Bridgewater	NJ	08807	908-429-8008	429-8004
Dataflux Corp 940 NW Cary Pkwy Suite 201 *TF:* 877-846-3589 ■ *Web:* www.dataflux.com	Cary	NC	27513	919-447-3000	447-3100
DecisionPoint Systems Inc 19655 Descartes. *TF:* 800-336-3670 ■ *Web:* www.decisionpt.com	Foothill Ranch	CA	92610	949-465-0065	215-9642
Dekker Ltd 3633 Inland Empire Blvd *TF:* 800-433-5537 ■ *Web:* www.dekkerltd.com	Ontario	CA	91764	909-912-1500	889-9163
Digital ChoreoGraphics PO Box 8268. *Web:* www.dcgfx.com	Newport Beach	CA	92658	949-548-1969	
Digital Intelligence Systems Corp 4151 Lafayette Ctr Dr *TF:* 877-503-4797 ■ *Web:* www.disys.com	Chantilly	VA	20151	703-802-0500	
Dime Soft Business Solutions Inc 20710 Havenhurst Dr PO Box 1089 *Web:* www.dimesoftinc.com	Nuevo	CA	92567	951-928-1990	928-1171
Distribution Services Of America (DSA) 208 N St *Web:* www.dsa-inc.com	Foxboro	MA	02035	508-543-9700	543-7408
Divx Inc 4780 Eastgate Mall *Web:* www.divx.com	San Diego	CA	92121	858-882-0600	882-0601
Documation Inc PO Box 5265. **Fax Area Code:* 845 ■ *Web:* www.documationinc.com	Coeur d'Alene	ID	83814	208-665-1410	350-8198*
eCybersuite 9330 Eton Ave *Web:* www.ecybersuite.com	Chatsworth	CA	91311	818-676-0790	610-0509
Edge Systems LLC 3S721 W Ave Suite 200 *TF Tech Supp:* 800-352-3343 ■ *Web:* www.edge.com	Warrenville	IL	60555	630-810-9669	810-9228
Edgenet Inc 3445 Peachtree Rd Ne *TF:* 866-865-6602 ■ *Web:* www.edgenet.com	Atlanta	GA	30326	615-371-3848	371-3023
Einstruction Corp 308 N Carroll Blvd. *TF:* 888-707-6819 ■ *Web:* www.einstruction.com	Denton	TX	76201	940-565-0004	565-0959
Everest Consulting Group Inc 3840 Pk Ave Suite 203 *Web:* www.everestconsulting.net	Edison	NJ	08820	732-548-2700	548-9181
Experts Inc The 2400 E Commercial Blvd Suite 614 *TF:* 800-336-8359 ■ *Web:* www.expertsit.com	Fort Lauderdale	FL	33308	954-493-8040	493-8844
Extensis 1800 SW 1st Ave Suite 500 *TF:* 800-796-9798 ■ *Web:* www.extensis.com	Portland	OR	97201	503-274-2020	274-0530
Fgm Inc 12021 Sunset Hills Rd Suite 400 *Web:* www.fgm.com	Reston	VA	20190	703-885-1000	885-0130
Full Spectrum Software 225 Tpke Rd Suite 504 *Web:* www.fullspectrumsoftware.com	Southborough	MA	01772	508-620-6400	
FusionStorm 2 Bryant St Suite 150 *TF:* 800-228-8324 ■ *Web:* www.fusionstorm.com	San Francisco	CA	94105	415-623-2626	623-2630
Future Tech Enterprise Inc 101-8 Colin Dr *Web:* www.ftei.com	Holbrook	NY	11741	631-472-5500	472-6599
GDI Infotech Inc 3775 Varsity Dr *TF:* 800-608-7682 ■ *Web:* www.gdii.com	Ann Arbor	MI	48108	734-477-6900	477-7100
Genesisfour Corp PO Box 773 *TF:* 800-937-4364 ■ *Web:* www.service2k.com	Andrews	SC	29510	978-443-4440	856-2209
Global Solutions Network Inc 121 Congressional Ln Suite 302 **Fax Area Code:* 703 ■ *Web:* www.gsnhome.com	Rockville	MD	20852	301-881-7012	881-7014*
Gnuco LLC 20 N Wacker Dr Suite 1870 *TF:* 800-441-0566 ■ *Web:* www.emergenow.com	Chicago	IL	60606	312-669-9600	
Gst Information Technology Solutions 13043 166th St. *TF:* 800-833-0128 ■ *Web:* www.gstes.com	Cerritos	CA	90703	562-345-8700	345-8701
H & W Computer Systems Inc PO Box 46019 *TF:* 800-338-6692 ■ *Web:* www.hwcs.com	Boise	ID	83711	208-377-0336	377-0069
Health Care Software Inc PO Box 2430 *TF:* 800-524-1038 ■ *Web:* www.hcsinteractant.com	Farmingdale	NJ	07727	732-938-5600	938-5380
Healthcare Automation Inc 41 Sharpe Dr *TF:* 800-738-8850 ■ *Web:* www.healthcare-automation.com	Cranston	RI	02920	401-572-3040	572-3350
Hubspan Inc 505 5th Ave S Suite 350 *Web:* www.hubspan.com	Seattle	WA	98104	206-838-5400	838-5449
Human Factors International Inc 410 W Lowe Ave *TF:* 800-242-4480 ■ *Web:* www.humanfactors.com	Fairfield	IA	52556	641-472-4480	472-5412
Inbit Inc PO Box 391674 *Web:* www.inbit.com	Mountain View	CA	94039	408-730-9819	730-1756
Information Systems of Florida Inc (ISF) 9550 Regency Sq Blvd Suite 1000 *Web:* www.isf.com	Jacksonville	FL	32225	904-724-2277	723-3561
Inforonics LLC 25 Porter Rd *Web:* www.inforonics.com	Littleton	MA	01460	978-698-7300	698-7500
Infosource Inc 1300 City View Ctr *TF:* 800-393-4636 ■ *Web:* www.infosourcelearning.com	Oviedo	FL	32765	407-677-0300	796-5190
Inmedius Inc 4900 Perry Hwy Suite 200 **Fax Area Code:* 412 ■ *TF:* 800-697-7110 ■ *Web:* www.inmedius.com	Pittsburgh	PA	15229	800-697-7110	459-0311*
Innovasystems International LLC 2385 Northside Dr Suite 300 *Web:* www.innovasi.com	San Diego	CA	92108	619-955-5800	955-5801
Innovative Systems Group Inc 799 Roosevelt Rd *TF:* 800-739-2400 ■ *Web:* www.innovativesys.com	Glen Ellyn	IL	60137	630-858-8500	858-8532
Insurance Technology Consultants Inc 681 S Parker St Suite 260. *Web:* www.itc-systems.com	Orange	CA	92868	714-836-0671	836-0737
Integrated Data Services Inc 700 Veterans Hwy Suite 35. *Web:* www.idserve.com	Hauppauge	NY	11788	631-265-7162	366-4317
Intelligent Software Solutions Inc 5450 Tech Ctr Dr. *Web:* www.issinc.com	Colorado Springs	CO	80919	719-457-0690	457-0693
International Technology Solutions Inc 100 Plainfield Ave Suite 5. *Web:* www.itcsolutions.com	Edison	NJ	08817	732-985-5900	985-4955
Isis Papyrus America Inc 301 Bank St *Web:* www.isis-papyrus.com	Southlake	TX	76092	817-416-2345	
J&b Software Inc 510 Township Line Rd *Web:* www.tmsimage.com	Blue Bell	PA	19422	215-641-1500	641-1181
JBoss Inc 3340 Peachtree Rd Suite 1200 *Web:* www.jboss.com	Atlanta	GA	30326	404-467-8555	948-1496
Justice Systems Inc 4600 McLeod NE *Web:* www.justicesystems.com	Albuquerque	NM	87109	505-883-3987	883-2845
K-micro Inc 2050 S Westgate Ave *Web:* www.corpinfo.com	Los Angeles	CA	90025	310-442-3200	442-3201
Lake Superior Software Inc 6423 City W Pkwy *Web:* www.lssdata.com	Eden Prairie	MN	55344	952-941-1000	829-4309
Learnframe Inc 12637 S 265 W # 300 *TF:* 800-738-9800 ■ *Web:* www.learnframe.com	Draper	UT	84020	801-523-8000	523-8012
Logikos Inc 2914 Independence Dr *Web:* www.logikos.com	Fort Wayne	IN	46808	260-483-3638	484-5268
Lynx Medical Systems Inc 15325 SE 30th Pl Suite 200 *TF:* 800-767-5969 ■ *Web:* www.lynxmed.com	Bellevue	WA	98007	425-641-4451	
M2S Inc 12 Commerce Ave. *Web:* www.m2s.com	West Lebanon	NH	03784	603-298-5509	298-5055
ManTech International Corp 678 Third Ave Suite 305 *Web:* www.mtcsc.com	Chula Vista	CA	91910	619-585-2100	585-2101
Melillo Consulting Inc 285 Davidson Ave Suite 202. *Web:* www.mjm.com	Somerset	NJ	08873	732-563-8400	563-8450
Merge CAD Inc 11040 Main St Suite 100 *Web:* www.merge.com	Bellevue	WA	98004	425-691-1400	691-1599
Meridian Technology Group Inc 12909 SW 68th Pkwy Suite 340 *TF:* 800-755-1038 ■ *Web:* www.meridiangroup.com	Portland	OR	97223	503-697-1600	697-8600
Midwave Corp 10050 Crosstown Cir Suite 500 *Web:* www.midwave.com	Eden Prairie	MN	55344	952-279-5900	279-5601
Mil Corp 4000 Mitchellville Rd *Web:* www.milcorp.com	Bowie	MD	20716	301-805-8500	805-8505
Mission Critical Technologies Inc 2041 Rosecrans Ave *Web:* www.mctinc.net	El Segundo	CA	90245	310-246-4455	246-9540
Misys International Banking Systems Inc 45 Broadway 2ne Fl *Web:* www.misys.com	New York	NY	10006	212-898-9500	898-9510
Money Tree Software Ltd 1600 SW Western Blvd. *TF:* 877-421-9815 ■ *Web:* www.moneytree.com	Corvallis	OR	97333	541-754-3701	738-6522
Mortgageflex Systems Inc 10151 Deerwood Pk Blvd *TF:* 800-326-3539 ■ *Web:* www.mortgageflex.com	Jacksonville	FL	32256	904-356-2490	356-1099
Mysql Inc 20400 Stevens Creek Blvd *TF:* 866-221-0634 ■ *Web:* www.mysql.com	Cupertino	CA	95014	408-213-6600	213-2807
nCircle Network Security Inc 101 2nd St Suite 400 *TF:* 888-464-2900 ■ *Web:* www.ncircle.com	San Francisco	CA	94105	415-625-5900	625-5982
Neon Enterprise Software 14100 SW Fwy Suite 400. *TF:* 888-338-6366 ■ *Web:* www.neonesoft.com	Sugar Land	TX	77478	281-491-6366	207-4973
Ness Technologies Inc 300 Frank W Burr Blvd 7th Fl *TF:* 866-637-7380 ■ *Web:* www.ness.com	Teaneck	NJ	07666	201-488-7222	488-5040
Network Dynamics Inc 640 Brooker Creek Blvd Suite 410 *TF:* 877-818-8597 ■ *Web:* www.ndiwebsite.com	Oldsmar	FL	34677	813-818-8597	818-9659
Neudesic LLC 8105 Irvine Ctr Dr *TF:* 800-805-1805 ■ *Web:* www.neudesic.com	Irvine	CA	92618	949-754-4500	754-6800

	City	State	Zip	Phone	Fax
New World Systems Corp 888 W Big Beavr Rd TF: 800-333-9673 ■ Web: www.newworldsystems.com	Troy	MI	48084	248-269-1000	269-1020
Noetix Corp 5010 148th Ave NE Suite 100 *Fax Area Code: 866 ■ TF: 866-466-3849 ■ Web: www.noetix.com	Redmond	WA	98052	425-372-2699	436-0406*
Nomadix Inc 30851 Agoura Rd Suite 102 Web: www.nomadix.com	Agoura Hills	CA	91301	818-597-1500	597-1502
Objectwin Technology Inc 14800 St Mary's Ln Suite 100 Web: www.objectwin.com	Houston	TX	77079	713-782-8200	782-8283
Oeconnection LLC 4205 Highlander Pkwy TF: 888-776-5792 ■ Web: www.oeconnection.com	Richfield	OH	44286	330-523-1830	523-1700
Ontario Systems Corp 1150 W Kilgore Ave Web: www.ontariosystems.com	Muncie	IN	47305	765-751-7000	751-7099
Orchard Software Corp 701 Congressional Blvd Suite 360 TF: 800-856-1948 ■ Web: www.orchardsoft.com	Carmel	IN	46032	317-573-6663	573-2633
Paladin Data Systems Corp 19362 Powder Hill Pl NE TF: 800-532-8448 ■ Web: www.paladindata.com	Poulsbo	WA	98370	360-779-2400	779-2600
Panasas Inc 969 W Maude Ave TF: 800-726-2727 ■ Web: www.panasas.com	Sunnyvale	CA	94085	408-215-6800	215-6801
Patel Consultants Corp 1525 Morris Ave Web: www.patelcorp.com	Union	NJ	07083	908-964-7575	964-3176
Patni Americas Inc 1 Broadway FL 15 TF: 877-209-0463 ■ Web: www.patni.com	Cambridge	MA	02142	617-914-8000	914-8200
Patriot Technologies Inc 5108 Pegasus Ct Suite F TF: 888-417-9899 ■ Web: www.patriot-tech.com	Frederick	MD	21704	301-695-7500	695-4711
Performance Software 2095 W Pinnacle Peak Rd Suite 120 *Fax Area Code: 602 ■ *Fax: Sales ■ Web: www.psware.com	Phoenix	AZ	85027	623-337-8003	308-8688*
Prenia Corp 16625 Redmond Way Suite M-418 Web: www.prenia.com	Redmond	WA	98052	425-898-8300	898-8301
Prime Controls LP 815 Office Pk Cir Web: www.prime-controls.com	Lewisville	TX	75057	972-221-4849	420-4842
Process Control Technology Inc 4335 Piedras Dr W Suite 175 Web: www.gopct.com	San Antonio	TX	78228	210-735-9141	735-9775
Progeny Linux Systems Inc 8335 Allison Pointe Trail Suite 160 Web: www.progeny.com	Indianapolis	IN	46250	317-578-8882	578-8920
Programming Concepts Inc 640 Johnson Ave Suite 5 Web: www.programmingconcepts.com	Bohemia	NY	11716	631-563-3800	563-3898
Quantum Compliance Systems Inc 2111 Golfside Rd Web: www.qcs-facts.com	Ypsilanti	MI	48197	734-572-1000	572-8815
Quorum Business Solutions Inc 3010 Briarpark Dr Suite 450 Web: www.qbsol.com	Houston	TX	77042	713-430-8601	430-8697
RDA Corp 303 International Cir Suite 340 Web: www.rdacorp.com	Hunt Valley	MD	21030	410-308-9300	308-9600
Rediker Software Inc 2 Wilbraham Rd TF: 800-213-9860 ■ Web: www.rediker.com	Hampden	MA	01036	413-566-3463	455-2274
Rei Systems Inc 200 Fairbrook Dr Suite 104 Web: www.reisys.com	Herndon	VA	20170	703-480-9100	689-4680
Research Design Resources Inc (RDR) 5900 Fort Dr Suite 300 Web: www.rdr.com	Centreville	VA	20121	703-263-0347	961-1637
Rose International 16401 Swingley Ridge Rd SUIte 300 Web: www.roseint.com	Chesterfield	MO	63017	636-812-4000	812-0076
S & K Technologies Inc 63066 Old Hwy 93 PO Box 339 TF: 866-758-2677 ■ Web: www.sktcorp.com	Saint Ignatius	MT	59865	406-745-7500	745-7506
Satmetrix Systems Inc 1100 Pk Pl TF: 866-697-2103 ■ Web: www.satmetrix.com	San Mateo	CA	94403	650-227-8300	227-8301
School-Link Technologies Inc PO Box 2410 TF: 800-423-2113 ■ Web: www.sl-tech.net	Santa Monica	CA	90407	310-656-6840	656-6845
Shaw Systems Assoc Inc 6200 Savoy Dr Suite 600 TF: 800-731-3612 ■ Web: www.shawsystems.com	Houston	TX	77036	713-782-7730	782-4158
SingleTap Inc PO Box 178586 *Fax Area Code: 858 ■ TF: 800-536-1256 ■ Web: www.singletap.com	San Diego	CA	92117	800-536-1256	794-8213*
Smartronix Inc 44150 Smartronix Way TF: 866-442-7767 ■ Web: www.smartronix.com	Hollywood	MD	20636	301-373-6000	373-7171
Softerware Inc 132 Welsh Rd Suite 140 TF: 800-220-8111 ■ Web: www.softerware.com	Horsham	PA	19044	215-628-0400	628-0585
Solers Inc 950 N Glebe Rd Suite 1100 Web: www.solers.com	Arlington	VA	22203	703-526-0001	908-9353
Sparta Systems Inc Holmdel Corporate Plaza, 2137 Hwy 35 TF: 888-261-5948 ■ Web: www.spartasystems.com	Holmdel	NJ	07733	732-203-0400	203-0375
Stenograph LLC 1500 Bishop Ct TF: 800-323-4247 ■ Web: www.stenograph.com	Mount Prospect	IL	60056	847-803-1400	803-1089
Surgical Information Systems LLC 11605 Haynes Bridge Rd TF: 800-930-0895 ■ Web: www.sisfirst.com	Alpharetta	GA	30009	678-507-1610	507-1616
Susquehanna Technologies 600 Pegasus Ct Suite 100 TF: 888-603-0304 ■ Web: www.susqtech.com	Winchester	VA	22602	540-723-8700	722-9547
Sycamore.us Inc 241 E 4th St Suite 105 Web: www.sycamore.us	Frederick	MD	21701	301-668-4681	
Syclo LLC 1721 Moon Lake Blvd Suite 300 TF: 800-567-9256 ■ Web: www.syclo.com	Hoffman Estates	IL	60169	847-230-3800	230-3801
Synecticsworld Inc 20 University Rd Web: www.synecticsworld.com	Cambridge	MA	02138	617-868-6530	354-2923
Systalex Corp 1901 RES Blvd Suite 240 Web: www.systalex.com	Rockville	MD	20850	301-251-8889	251-8505
Systems Integration & Management Inc 2611 Jefferson Davis Hwy Web: www.simincsd.com	Arlington	VA	22202	703-412-5068	412-5069
Systems Products & Solutions Inc 4950 Corp Dr NW Suite 115 Web: www.services-sps.com	Huntsville	AL	35805	256-319-2135	
Systems Technology Group Inc 3155 W Big Beaver Rd Web: www.stgit.com	Troy	MI	48084	248-643-9010	643-9250
Tallan Inc 628 Hebron Ave Bldg 2 Suite 502 TF: 800-677-3693 ■ Web: www.tallan.com	Glastonbury	CT	06033	860-633-3693	633-5361
Tangoe Inc 35 Executive Blvd TF: 877-571-4737 ■ Web: www.tangoe.com	Orange	CT	06477	203-859-9300	859-9427
Tapestry Solutions Inc 5643 Copley Dr Web: www.tapestrysolutions.com	San Diego	CA	92111	858-503-1990	
Technosoft Corp 28411 Northwestern Hwy Suite 640 Web: www.technosoftcorp.com	Southfield	MI	48034	248-603-2600	603-2599
TopCoder Inc 95 Glastonbury Blvd TF: 866-867-2633 ■ Web: www.topcoder.com	Glastonbury	CT	06033	860-633-5540	657-4276
Triple Point Technology Inc 301 Riverside Ave Web: www.tpt.com	Westport	CT	06880	203-291-7979	291-7977
Tririga Inc 6720 Via Austi Pkwy Suite 500 TF: 888-874-7442 ■ Web: www.tririga.com	Las Vegas	NV	89119	702-932-4444	932-4445
Ultra Electronics Advanced Tactical Systems Inc 4101 Smith School Rd Web: www.ultra-ats.com	Austin	TX	78744	512-327-6795	327-8043
United Systems & Software Inc PO Box 958444 TF: 800-522-8774 ■ Web: www.ussincorp.com	Lake Mary	FL	32795	407-875-2120	
Visibility Corp 200 Minuteman Rd Web: www.visibility.com	Andover	MA	01887	978-269-6500	269-6501
Vision Systems Group Inc 101 Durham Ave Suite 300 Web: www.vsginc.com	South Plainfield	NJ	07080	732-537-9000	537-9990
Vision Technologies Inc 530 McCormick Dr Suite G Web: www.visiontechnologiesinc.net	Glen Burnie	MD	21061	410-424-2183	424-2208
Vpisystems Corp 943 Holmdel Rd Web: www.vpisystems.com	Holmdel	NJ	07733	732-332-0233	
Vtls Inc 1701 Kraft Dr Web: www.vtls.com	Blacksburg	VA	24060	540-557-1200	557-1210
Weidenhammer Systems Corp 935 Berkshire Blvd Web: www.hammer.net	Reading	PA	19610	610-378-1149	378-9409
Winware Inc 1955 W Oak Cir TF: 888-419-1399 ■ Web: www.cribmaster.com	Marietta	GA	30062	770-419-1399	281-8501
Wolfram Research Inc 100 Trade Ctr Dr TF: 800-965-3726 ■ Web: www.wolfram.com	Champaign	IL	61820	217-398-0700	398-0747
Youngsoft Inc 49197 Wixom Tech Dr Suite B TF: 888-470-4553 ■ Web: www.youngsoft.com	Wixom	MI	48393	248-675-1200	675-1201
Z-Law Software Inc PO Box 40602 TF: 800-526-5588 ■ Web: www.z-law.com	Providence	RI	02940	401-273-5588	421-5334

COMPUTER RESELLERS

SEE Computer Equipment & Software - Whol p. 1674

181 COMPUTER SOFTWARE

SEE ALSO Application Service Providers (ASPs) p. 1398; Computer Equipment & Software - Whol p. 1674; Computer Networking Products & Systems p. 1676; Computer Programming Services - Custom p. 1677; Computer Stores p. 1694; Computer Systems Design Services p. 1694; Educational Materials & Supplies p. 1791

	City	State	Zip	Phone	Fax
Calypso Technology Inc 595 Market St Suite 1800 Web: www.calypso.com	San Francisco	CA	94105	415-817-2400	284-1222
Williamson Law Book Co 790 Canning Pkwy TF: 800-733-9522 ■ Web: www.wlbonline.com	Victor	NY	14564	585-924-3400	924-4153

181-1 Business Software (General)

Companies Listed Here Make General-Purpose Software Products That Are Designed For Use By All Types Of Businesses, Professionals, And, To Some Extent, Personal Users.

	City	State	Zip	Phone	Fax
1MAGE Software Inc 384 Inverness Pkwy Suite 206 TF: 800-844-1468 ■ Web: www.1mage.com	Englewood	CO	80112	303-773-1424	796-0587
4D Inc 3031 Tisch Way Suite 900 TF: 800-785-3303 ■ Web: www.4d.com	San Jose	CA	95128	408-557-4600	261-9879
ACI Worldwide 4965 Preston Pk Blvd Suite 100 TF: 800-527-4131 ■ Web: www.aciworldwide.com	Plano	TX	75093	972-599-5600	599-5610
ACOM Solutions Inc 2850 E 29th St TF: 800-347-3638 ■ Web: www.acom.com	Long Beach	CA	90806	562-424-7899	424-8662
Action Technologies Inc 10970 International Blvd 2nd Fl TF: 800-967-5356 ■ Web: www.actiontech.com	Oakland	CA	94603	510-638-8300	638-8115
Actuate Corp 2207 Bridgepointe Pkwy Suite 500 NASDAQ: BIRT ■ TF Sales: 800-914-2259 ■ Web: www.actuate.com	San Mateo	CA	94404	650-645-3000	

Company	City	State	Zip	Phone	Fax
Aderant North America 3525 Piedmont Rd Bldg 6 Suite 620 *TF:* 877-608-4369 ■ *Web:* www.aderant.com	Atlanta	GA	30305	404-720-3600	720-3601
Adexa Inc 5933 W Century Blvd 12th Fl *TF:* 888-300-7692 ■ *Web:* www.adexa.com	Los Angeles	CA	90045	310-642-2100	338-9878
Adobe Systems Inc 345 Pk Ave *NASDAQ: ADBE* ■ *TF:* 800-833-6687 ■ *Web:* www.adobe.com	San Jose	CA	95110	408-536-6000	537-6000
AdStar Inc 4553 Glencoe Ave Suite 300 *NASDAQ: ADST* ■ *TF:* 800-752-5187	Marina del Rey	CA	90292	310-577-8255	577-8266
Advent Software Inc 600 Townsend St Suite 500 PO Box 20 *NASDAQ: ADVS* ■ *TF:* 800-727-0605 ■ *Web:* www.advent.com	San Francisco	CA	94103	415-543-7696	556-0607
AgilQuest Corp 9407 Hull St Rd *TF:* 888-745-7455 ■ *Web:* www.agilquest.com	Richmond	VA	23236	804-745-0467	745-6243
Alpha Software Inc 70 Blanchard Rd Suite 206 *Web:* www.alphasoftware.com	Burlington	MA	01803	781-229-4500	272-4876
Alterian Inc 35 E Wacker Dr Suite 200 *Web:* www.alterian.com	Chicago	IL	60601	312-704-1700	704-1701
American Business Systems Inc 315 Littleton Rd *TF:* 800-356-4034 ■ *Web:* www.abs-software.com	Chelmsford	MA	01824	978-250-9600	250-8027
American Software Inc 470 E Paces Ferry Rd *NASDAQ: AMSWA* ■ *TF:* 800-726-2946 ■ *Web:* www.amsoftware.com	Atlanta	GA	30305	404-264-5296	264-5206
Amethyst 478 Arlington *Web:* www.ameth.com	Elmhurst	IL	60126	630-530-4997	530-0940
An chorPad Security Inc 5576 Corporate Ave *TF:* 800-626-2467 ■ *Web:* www.anchorpad.com	Cypress	CA	90630	714-827-8888	827-5576
Appian Corp 1875 Explorer St 4th Fl *Web:* www.appian.com	Reston	VA	20190	703-442-8844	442-8919
APPX Software Inc 11363 San Jose Blvd Suite 301 *TF:* 800-879-2779 ■ *Web:* www.appx.com	Jacksonville	FL	32223	904-880-5560	880-6635
AquiTec International 547 W Jackson Blvd 9th Fl	Chicago	IL	60661	312-264-1900	264-1991
Architecture Technology Corp 9977 Valley View Rd Suite 300 *Web:* www.atcorp.com	Eden Prairie	MN	55344	952-829-5864	829-5868
Artemis International Solutions Corp 6011 W Courtyard Dr *TF:* 800-477-8900 ■ *Web:* www.aisc.com	Austin	TX	78730	512-874-3030	874-8900
AskSam Systems Inc 121 S Jefferson St *TF:* 800-800-1997 ■ *Web:* www.asksam.com	Perry	FL	32347	850-584-6590	584-7481
Astaro Corp 260A Fordham Rd *TF:* 877-927-8276 ■ *Web:* www.astaro.com	Wilmington	MA	01887	978-974-2600	974-2626
Astea International Inc 240 Gibraltar Rd Suite 300 *NASDAQ: ATEA* ■ *TF:* 800-878-4657 ■ *Web:* www.astea.com	Horsham	PA	19044	215-682-2500	682-2515
athenahealth Inc 311 Arsenal St *NASDAQ: ATHN* ■ *TF:* 800-981-5084 ■ *Web:* www.athenahealth.com	Watertown	MA	02472	617-402-1000	402-1099
Atos Origin 5599 San Felipe St Suite 300 *TF:* 866-875-8902 ■ *Web:* www.na.atosorigin.com	Houston	TX	77056	713-513-3000	403-7204
AttachmateWRQ 1500 Dexter Ave N *TF Sales:* 800-872-2829 ■ *Web:* www.attachmate.com	Seattle	WA	98109	206-217-7500	217-7515
Attunity Inc 70 Blanchard Rd **Fax Area Code:* 877 ■ *TF:* 866-288-8648 ■ *Web:* www.attunity.com	Burlington	MA	01803	781-730-4070	896-2760*
Avue Technologies Corp 1145 Broadway Plaza Suite 800 *Web:* www.avuetech.com	Tacoma	WA	98402	253-573-1877	573-1876
Baudville Inc 5380 52nd St SE *TF Orders:* 800-728-0888 ■ *Web:* www.baudville.com	Grand Rapids	MI	49512	616-698-0889	698-0554
Blackbaud Inc 2000 Daniel Island Dr *NASDAQ: BLKB* ■ *TF:* 800-468-8996 ■ *Web:* www.blackbaud.com	Charleston	SC	29492	843-216-6200	216-6100
BMC Software Inc 2101 City W Blvd *NYSE: BMC* ■ *TF:* 800-841-2031 ■ *Web:* www.bmc.com	Houston	TX	77042	713-918-8800	918-8000
Borland Software Corp 20450 Stevens Creek Blvd Suite 500 *TF:* 800-287-1329 ■ *Web:* www.borland.com	Cupertino	CA	95014	408-863-2800	
Bottomline Technologies 325 Corporate Dr *NASDAQ: EPAY* ■ *TF:* 800-243-2528 ■ *Web:* www.bottomline.com	Portsmouth	NH	03801	603-436-0700	436-0300
Bradmark Technologies Inc 4265 San Felipe St Suite 700 *TF:* 800-621-2808 ■ *Web:* www.bradmark.com	Houston	TX	77027	713-621-2808	621-1639
Brady Identification Solutions 6555 W Good Hope Rd **Fax Area Code:* 800 ■ **Fax:* Cust Svc ■ *TF Cust Svc:* 800-537-8791 ■ *Web:* www.bradyid.com	Milwaukee	WI	53223	414-358-6600	292-2289*
Brainworks Software Inc 100 S Main St *TF:* 800-755-1111 ■ *Web:* www.brainworks.com	Sayville	NY	11782	631-563-5000	563-6320
BroadSoft Inc 9737 Washingtonian Blvd Suite 350 *NASDAQ: BSFT* ■ *Web:* www.broadsoft.com	Gaithersburg	MD	20877	301-977-9440	977-8846
Business Computer Design International Inc 950 N York Rd # 206 *Web:* www.bcdsoftware.com	Hinsdale	IL	60521	630-986-0800	986-0926
CA Inc 1 CA Plaza *NYSE: CA* ■ *TF:* 800-225-5224 ■ *Web:* www.ca.com	Islandia	NY	11749	631-342-6000	342-6800
Champs Software Inc 1255 N Vantage Pt Dr *TF:* 800-322-6647 ■ *Web:* www.champsinc.com	Crystal River	FL	34429	352-795-2362	795-9100
Cicero Inc 8000 Regency Pkwy Suite 542 *OTC: CICN* ■ *TF:* 866-538-3588 ■ *Web:* www.ciceroinc.com	Cary	NC	27511	919-380-5000	380-5121
Cincom Systems Inc 55 Merchant St *TF:* 800-888-0115 ■ *Web:* www.cincom.com	Cincinnati	OH	45246	513-612-2300	612-2000
Clarity Systems Ltd 2 Sheppard Ave E Suite 800 *TF:* 877-410-5070 ■ *Web:* www.claritysystems.com	Toronto	ON	M2N5Y7	416-250-5500	250-5533
ClearStory Systems Inc 1 Research Dr Suite 200-B *TF:* 800-298-9795 ■ *Web:* www.clearstorysystems.com	Westborough	MA	01581	508-870-4000	870-5585
Commence Corp 200 Tornillo Way Suite 200 *TF:* 800-933-9069 ■ *Web:* www.commence.com	Tinton Falls	NJ	07712	732-380-9100	380-9170
Commercial Data Systems Inc 50 S Beretania St Suite C-208B **Fax Area Code:* 808 ■ *TF:* 800-527-2970 ■ *Web:* www.cdsinc.com	Honolulu	HI	96813	800-527-2970	527-2030*
Computershare Plans Software 2 Enterprise Dr *TF:* 888-340-4267 ■ *Web:* www.transcentive.com	Shelton	CT	06484	203-944-7300	944-7325
Computing Technologies Inc 3028 Javier Rd Suite 400 *Web:* www.cots.com	Fairfax	VA	22031	703-280-8800	280-8804
Compuware Corp 1 Campus Martius St *NASDAQ: CPWR* ■ *TF:* 800-292-7432 ■ *Web:* www.compuware.com	Detroit	MI	48226	313-227-7300	
Comsquared Systems Inc 5125 Peachtree Industrial Blvd *TF:* 800-592-3766 ■ *Web:* www.comsquared.com	Norcross	GA	30092	770-734-5300	734-5379
Concur Technologies Inc 18400 NE Union Hill Rd *NASDAQ: CNQR* ■ *TF:* 800-358-0610 ■ *Web:* www.concur.com	Redmond	WA	98052	425-702-8808	702-8828
Current Analysis Inc 21335 Signal Hill Plaza Suite 200 *TF:* 877-787-8947 ■ *Web:* www.currentanalysis.com	Sterling	VA	20164	703-404-9200	404-9300
Cyma Systems Inc 2330 W University Dr Suite 4 *TF:* 800-292-2962 ■ *Web:* www.cyma.com	Tempe	AZ	85281	480-303-2962	303-2969
D&B Sales & Marketing Solutions 460 Totten Pond Rd *TF:* 800-590-0065 ■ *Web:* www2.zapdata.com	Waltham	MA	02451	781-672-9200	672-9290
Data Direct Technologies 14100 SW Fwy Suite 500 *TF:* 800-505-6366 ■ *Web:* www.datadirect.com	Sugar Land	TX	77478	281-491-4200	242-3880
Data Pro Accounting Software Inc 111 2nd Ave NE Suite 1200 *TF:* 800-237-6377 ■ *Web:* www.dpro.com	Saint Petersburg	FL	33701	727-803-1500	803-1535
Datalogics Inc 101 N Wacker Dr Suite 1800 *Web:* www.datalogics.com	Chicago	IL	60606	312-853-8200	853-8282
Datamatics Management Services Inc 330 New Brunswick Ave *TF:* 800-673-0366 ■ *Web:* www.datamaticsinc.com	Fords	NJ	08863	732-738-9600	738-9603
Deltek Inc 13880 Dulles Corner Ln *TF:* 800-456-2009 ■ *Web:* www.deltek.com	Herndon	VA	20171	703-734-8606	734-0346
DeskNet Inc 10 Exchange Pl 20th Fl *Web:* www.desknetinc.com	Jersey City	NJ	07302	201-946-7080	946-7081
DLGL Ltd 850 Michele-Bohec Blvd *Web:* www.dlgl.com	Blainville	QC	J7C5E2	450-979-4646	979-4650
Drake Software 235 E Palmer St **Fax Area Code:* 828 ■ *TF:* 800-890-9500 ■ *Web:* www.drakesoftware.com	Franklin	NC	28734	800-890-9500	369-9928*
DST Systems Inc 333 W 11th St *NYSE: DST* ■ *Web:* www.dstsystems.com	Kansas City	MO	64105	816-435-1000	435-8630
Dynalogic Inc 1110 N 175th St Suite 216 *TF:* 800-735-0433 ■ *Web:* www.dynalogicinc.com	Shoreline	WA	98133	206-533-1050	542-1326
E*Trade Financial Corp Corporate Services 4500 Bohannon Dr *TF:* 800-786-2575 ■ *Web:* www.us.etrade.com/e/t/corporateservices	Menlo Park	CA	94025	650-331-6000	331-6801
Echo Group The PO Box 2150 *TF:* 800-635-8209 ■ *Web:* www.echoman.com	Conway	NH	03818	603-447-8600	447-8680
eCredit.com Inc 20 CareMatrix Dr *TF:* 800-276-2321 ■ *Web:* www.ecredit.com	Dedham	MA	02026	781-752-1200	752-1400
Edge Technologies Inc 3702 Pender Dr Suite 420 *TF:* 888-771-3343 ■ *Web:* www.edge-technologies.com	Fairfax	VA	22030	703-691-7900	691-4020
Elcom International Inc 10 Oceana Way *TF:* 800-713-3993 ■ *Web:* www.elcominternational.com	Norwood	MA	02062	781-501-4000	501-4070
EMC Corp Documentum Div 6801 Koll Ctr Pkwy *Web:* www.emc.com	Pleasanton	CA	94566	925-600-6800	600-6850
EMC Document Sciences Corp 5958 Priestly Dr *TF:* 877-372-8500 ■ *Web:* www.docscience.com	Carlsbad	CA	92008	760-602-1400	602-1450
Emerging Technology Solutions Inc 145 Sandy Hollow Trail Suite 100 PO Box 1024 *Web:* www.etsgroup.com	Franktown	CO	80116	303-688-1987	484-5080
Empagio Inc 225 E Robinson St Suite 240 *Web:* www.empagio.com	Orlando	FL	32801	407-488-1500	488-1505
Emptoris Inc 200 Wheeler Rd *Web:* www.emptoris.com	Burlington	MA	01803	781-993-9212	993-9213
EntComm Inc 879 W 190th St 12th Fl *Web:* www.entcomm.com	Gardena	CA	90248	310-436-3800	436-3700
Entrade Inc 500 Central Ave	Northfield	IL	60093	847-441-6650	441-6959
ePartners Inc 6565 N MacArthur Blvd Suite 950 *TF:* 888-883-9797 ■ *Web:* www.epartnersolutions.com	Irving	TX	75039	469-587-5660	587-5661
Epicor Software Corp 18200 Von Karman Dr Suite 1000 *TF:* 800-999-1809 ■ *Web:* www.epicor.com	Irvine	CA	92612	949-585-4000	585-4091
Epsilon Inc 4301 Regent Blvd *TF:* 800-309-0505 ■ *Web:* www.epsilon.com	Irving	TX	75063	972-582-9600	582-9700
Equitrac Corp 1000 S Pine Island Rd Suite 900 *Web:* www.equitrac.com	Plantation	FL	33324	954-888-7800	475-7295
Escalate Inc 5505 Morehouse Dr Suite 300 **Fax Area Code:* 858 ■ *TF Sales:* 888-777-6811 ■ *Web:* www.escalate.com	San Diego	CA	92121	800-854-2263	457-2145*
Escalate Retail 1615 S Congress Ave Suite 200 *Web:* www.escalateretail.com	Delray Beach	FL	33445	561-265-2700	454-4800
eSignal 3955 Salt Way *TF:* 800-367-4670 ■ *Web:* www.esignal.com	Hayward	CA	94545	510-266-6000	266-6100
Essex Corp 1235 Evans Rd *TF:* 800-289-2923	Melbourne	FL	32904	321-837-7000	837-7000
eTEK International Inc 5445 DTC Pkwy PH-4 **Fax Area Code:* 866 ■ *TF:* 800-888-6894	Greenwood Village	CO	80111	303-488-3499	743-5254*
ETS Inc 1115 E Brigadoon Ct *TF:* 800-387-7003 ■ *Web:* www.protext.com	Salt Lake City	UT	84117	801-265-2497	
Evolutionary Technologies International Inc 6011 W Courtyard Dr # 300 *TF:* 800-856-8800 ■ *Web:* www.eti.com	Austin	TX	78730	512-383-3000	383-3300
FatWire Corp 330 Old Country Rd Suite 207 *TF:* 800-801-8504 ■ *Web:* www.fatwire.com	Mineola	NY	11501	516-328-9473	739-5069

Company	City	State	ZIP	Phone	Fax
Fidessa Corp 17 State St 42nd Fl *Web:* www.royalblue.com	New York	NY	10004	212-269-9000	943-0353
FileMaker Inc 5201 Patrick Henry Dr **Fax:* Cust Svc ■ *TF Cust Svc:* 800-325-2747 ■ *Web:* www.filemaker.com	Santa Clara	CA	95054	408-987-7000	987-3932*
Fischer International Systems Corp 5801 Pelican Bay Blvd # 300 *TF:* 800-776-7258 ■ *Web:* www.fisc.com	Naples	FL	34108	239-643-1500	643-3772
FlexiInternational Software Inc 2 Enterprise Dr *TF:* 800-353-9492 ■ *Web:* www.flexi.com	Shelton	CT	06484	203-925-3040	925-3044
Formscan Inc 517 E Lancaster Ave Suite 101 **Fax Area Code:* 610	Downingtown	PA	19355	484-696-4200	269-5247*
FrontRange Solutions USA Inc 5675 Gibraltar Dr *TF:* 800-776-7889 ■ *Web:* www.frontrange.com	Pleasanton	CA	94588	925-398-1800	
Gemmar Systems International Inc 11450 Cote de Liesse *Web:* www.gsi.ca	Dorval	QC	H9P1A9	514-631-3336	631-7722
Gemstone Systems Inc 1260 NW Waterhouse Ave Suite 200 *Web:* www.gemstone.com	Beaverton	OR	97006	503-533-3000	629-8556
Genesys Software Systems Inc 5 Branch St **Fax Area Code:* 801 ■ *Web:* www.genesys-soft.com	Methuen	MA	01844	978-685-5400	761-2015*
Global Shop Solutions Inc 975 Evergreen Cir *TF Sales:* 800-364-5958 ■ *Web:* www.globalshopsolutions.com	The Woodlands	TX	77380	281-681-1959	681-2663
Global Software Inc 3201 Beechleaf Ct # 170 *TF:* 800-326-3444 ■ *Web:* www.glbsoft.com	Raleigh	NC	27604	919-872-7800	876-8205
Glovia International Inc 1940 E Mariposa Ave Suite 200 *TF:* 888-245-6842 ■ *Web:* www.glovia.com	El Segundo	CA	90245	310-563-7000	563-7300
Goodwin Systems Inc 1403 Princeton Ave *TF:* 800-203-1358	Silverton	OR	97381	503-873-8695	
Grandite Inc 1220 Lebourgneuf Blvd Suite 120 *TF:* 800-361-0528 ■ *Web:* www.grandite.com	Quebec	QC	G2K2G4	418-622-4892	622-7001
GSE Systems Inc 1332 Londontown Blvd Suite 200 *AMEX:* GVP ■ *TF Cust Svc:* 800-638-7912 ■ *Web:* www.gses.com	Sykesville	MD	21784	410-970-7800	970-7997
Gt Nexus Inc 300 Lakeside Dr Suite 400 *Web:* www.gtnexus.com	Oakland	CA	94612	510-808-2222	808-2220
Halogen Software 495 March Rd Suite 500 *TF:* 866-566-7778 ■ *Web:* www.halogensoftware.com	Kanata	ON	K2K3G1	613-270-1011	270-8311
HarrisData 13555 Bishops Ct Suite 300 *TF:* 800-225-0585 ■ *Web:* www.harrisdata.com	Brookfield	WI	53005	262-784-9099	784-5994
HighJump Software 6455 City W Pkwy *TF:* 800-328-3271 ■ *Web:* www.highjump.com	Eden Prairie	MN	55344	952-947-4088	947-0440
HK Systems Inc 2855 S James Dr *TF:* 800-424-7365 ■ *Web:* www.hksystems.com	New Berlin	WI	53151	262-860-7000	860-7014
I-many Inc 1735 Market St 37th Fl *NASDAQ:* IMNY ■ *TF:* 877-774-2451 ■ *Web:* www.imany.com	Philadelphia	PA	19103	215-344-1900	344-1919
IBM WebSphere Information Integration 50 Washington St *Web:* www.ibm.ascential.com	Westborough	MA	01581	508-366-3888	366-3669
iCIMS Inc 1301 Hwy 36 Bldg 1 Suite 102 *TF:* 800-889-4422 ■ *Web:* www.icims.com	Hazlet	NJ	07730	732-847-1941	876-0422
Iconixx Software 100 Congress Ave Suite 2000 **Fax Area Code:* 512 ■ *TF:* 877-426-6499 ■ *Web:* www.iconixxsoftware.com	Austin	TX	78701	877-426-6499	651-3111*
iEmployee 699 Fall River Ave *TF:* 800-884-6504 ■ *Web:* www.iemployee.com	Seekonk	MA	02771	508-336-4441	336-5894
IFS North America Inc 5451 E Williams Blvd # 181 *TF:* 800-807-7610 ■ *Web:* www.ifsworld.com	Tucson	AZ	85711	520-512-2000	512-2001
Image Process Design 36800 Woodward Ave Suite 300 *TF:* 888-842-0455 ■ *Web:* www.ipdsolution.com	Bloomfield Hills	MI	48304	248-723-9733	203-2566
Info Directions Inc 833 Phillips Rd *TF:* 888-924-4110 ■ *Web:* www.infodirections.com	Victor	NY	14564	585-924-4110	924-1821
Infoglide Software 6500 River Pl Blvd Bldg 2 *TF:* 800-338-2441 ■ *Web:* www.infoglide.com	Austin	TX	78730	512-532-3500	532-3505
Informatica Corp 100 Cardinal Way *NASDAQ:* INFA ■ *TF:* 800-653-3871 ■ *Web:* www.informatica.com	Redwood City	CA	94063	650-385-5000	385-5500
Information & Computing Services Inc 1650 Prudential Dr Suite 300 *Web:* www.icsfl.com	Jacksonville	FL	32207	904-399-8500	398-7855
Infospectrum 5412 Clareton Cr Suite 260 *Web:* www.info-spectrum.com	Agoura Hills	CA	91301	818-874-9226	874-9227
Infosys Technologies Ltd 1 Spectrum Pointe Suite 350 *Web:* www.infosys.com	Lake Forest	CA	92630	949-206-8400	206-8499
InfoVista Corp 12950 Worldgate Dr Suite 250 *Web:* www.infovista.com	Herndon	VA	20170	703-435-2435	435-5122
Innovative Systems Inc 790 Holiday Dr Bldg 11 *TF:* 800-622-6390 ■ *Web:* www.innovativesystems.com	Pittsburgh	PA	15220	412-937-9300	937-9309
Inova Solutions Inc 110 Avon St *TF:* 866-686-8774 ■ *Web:* www.inovasolutions.com	Charlottesville	VA	22902	434-817-8000	817-8002
Inspiration Software Inc 7412 SW Beaverton-Hillsdale Hwy Suite 300 *TF:* 800-877-4292 ■ *Web:* www.inspiration.com	Beaverton	OR	97005	503-297-3004	297-4676
Integrated Business Systems & Services Inc 1601 Shop Rd Suite E *Web:* www.ibss.net	Columbia	SC	29201	803-736-5595	736-5639
Integrated Decisions & Systems Inc 8500 Normandale Lake Blvd Suite 1200 *Web:* www.ideas.com	Minneapolis	MN	55437	952-698-4200	698-4299
Intellicorp Inc 2900 Lakeside Dr Suite 221 *Web:* www.intellicorp.com	Santa Clara	CA	95054	408-454-3500	454-3529
International Business Machines Corp (IBM) 1 New Orchard Rd *NYSE:* IBM ■ *TF:* 800-426-4968 ■ *Web:* www.ibm.com	Armonk	NY	10504	914-766-1900	
InterraTech Corp 11 Federal St *TF:* 888-589-4889 ■ *Web:* www.interratech.com	Camden	NJ	08103	856-854-5100	854-5102
InterSystems Corp 1 Memorial Dr *Web:* www.intersys.com	Cambridge	MA	02142	617-621-0600	494-1631
Intuitive Research & Technology Corp 5030 Bradford Dr NW # 205 *Web:* www.irtc-hq.com	Huntsville	AL	35805	256-922-9300	922-1122
Invensys Operations Management 33 Commercial St *TF:* 866-746-6477 ■ *Web:* www.invensys.com	Foxboro	MA	02035	508-543-8750	
ISG Novasoft 7901 Stoneridge Dr Suite 499 *Web:* www.isgn.com	Pleasanton	CA	94588	925-847-9090	847-0800
ITT Visual Information Solutions 4990 Pearl E Cir *Web:* www.ittvis.com	Boulder	CO	80301	303-786-9900	786-9909
K-Systems Inc 2104 Aspen Dr *TF:* 800-221-0204 ■ *Web:* www.ksystemsinc.com	Mechanicsburg	PA	17055	717-795-7711	795-7715
Kalido 1 Wall St # 3 *Web:* www.kalido.com	Burlington	MA	01803	781-202-3200	202-3299
Lawson Software 380 St Peter St *Web:* www.lawson.com	Saint Paul	MN	60173	651-767-6154	767-5645
Lawson Software Americas Inc 380 St Peter St *NASDAQ:* LWSN ■ *TF:* 800-477-1357 ■ *Web:* www.lawson.com	Saint Paul	MN	55102	651-767-7000	767-7141
Levi Ray & Shoup Inc 2401 W Monroe St *Web:* www.lrs.com	Springfield	IL	62704	217-793-3800	787-3286
Logility Inc 470 E Paces Ferry Rd *TF:* 800-762-5207 ■ *Web:* www.logility.com	Atlanta	GA	30305	404-261-9777	264-5206
Longview Solutions 100 Matsonford Rd Suite 230 **Fax Area Code:* 484 ■ *TF:* 888-456-6484 ■ *Web:* www.longview.com	Radnor	PA	19087	610-977-0995	367-1153*
M2 Technology Inc 21702 Hardy Oak Suite 100 *TF:* 800-267-1760 ■ *Web:* www.m2ti.com	San Antonio	TX	78258	210-566-3773	566-3993
M86 Security Inc 8845 Irvine Ctr Dr *Web:* www.m86security.com	Irvine	CA	92618	949-932-1000	932-1086
Malvern Systems Inc 81 Lancaster Ave Suite 219 *TF:* 800-296-9642 ■ *Web:* www.malvernsys.com	Malvern	PA	19355	610-296-9642	889-2254
Maverick Technologies 265 Admiral Trost Rd PO Box 470 *TF:* 888-917-9109 ■ *Web:* www.mavtechglobal.com	Columbia	IL	62236	618-281-9100	281-9191
Mayflowers Software 30 Great Rd *Web:* www.maysoft.com	Acton	MA	01720	978-371-3900	371-1696
Mediagrif Interactive Technologies Inc 1111 St-Charles St W E Tower Suite 255 *TSE:* MDF ■ *TF:* 877-677-9088 ■ *Web:* www.mediagrif.com	Longueuil	QC	J4K5G4	450-449-0102	449-8725
Mediaplex Inc 177 Steuart St 6th Fl *TF:* 866-417-1271 ■ *Web:* www.mediaplex.com	San Francisco	CA	94105	415-808-1900	348-0374
Meridian Systems 1720 Prairie City Rd Suite 120 *TF:* 800-850-2660 ■ *Web:* www.meridiansystems.com	Folsom	CA	95630	916-294-2000	294-2001
Meridium Inc 207 Bullitt Ave SE *Web:* www.meridium.com	Roanoke	VA	24013	540-344-9205	345-7083
Metastorm Inc 500 E Pratt St Suite 1250 *TF:* 877-321-6382 ■ *Web:* www.metastorm.com	Baltimore	MD	21202	443-874-1300	874-1336
MicroBiz Corp 17075 Newhope St Suite A *TF:* 800-385-0072 ■ *Web:* www.microbiz.com	Fountain Valley	CA	92708	201-785-1311	785-1568
Microlink Enterprise Inc 20955 Pathfinder Rd Suite 100 *TF:* 800-829-3688 ■ *Web:* www.microlinkenterprise.com	Diamond Bar	CA	91745	562-205-1888	205-1886
Microsoft Corp 1 Microsoft Way *NASDAQ:* MSFT ■ *Web:* www.microsoft.com	Redmond	WA	98052	425-882-8080	936-7329
Microsoft Great Plains Business Solutions 3900 Great Plains Dr S *TF:* 888-477-7877	Fargo	ND	58104	701-281-6500	
Microsystems 3025 highland Pkwy Suite 450 *Web:* www.microsystems.com	Lombard	IL	60515	630-598-1100	598-9520
Motive Inc 12515 Research Blvd Bldg 5 *Web:* www.motive.com	Austin	TX	78759	512-339-8335	339-9040
Multi-Ad Inc 1720 W Detweiller Dr *TF:* 800-348-6485 ■ *Web:* www.multi-ad.com	Peoria	IL	61615	309-692-1530	692-6566
MYOB US Inc 300 Roundhill Dr *TF Cust Svc:* 800-322-6962 ■ *Web:* www.myob.com	Rockaway	NJ	07866	973-586-2200	586-2229
Nakoma Group 16735 Von Karman Ave Suite 225 *TF:* 877-891-2811 ■ *Web:* www.nakomagroup.com	Irvine	CA	92606	949-222-0244	222-0144
Netec International Inc PO Box 180549 *Web:* www.netec2000.com	Dallas	TX	75218	214-343-9744	343-9009
NetMotion Wireless Inc 701 N 34th St Suite 250 *TF:* 877-818-7626 ■ *Web:* www.netmotionwireless.com	Seattle	WA	98103	206-691-5500	691-5501
New Century Education Corp 220 Old New Brnswk Rd *TF:* 800-833-6232 ■ *Web:* www.ncecorp.com	Piscataway	NJ	08854	732-981-0820	981-0552
NewlineNoosh Inc 625 Ellis St Suite 300 *TF:* 888-286-6674 ■ *Web:* www.newlinenoosh.com	Mountain View	CA	94043	650-637-6000	965-1377
Newport Wave Inc 15 McLean *TF:* 800-999-2611 ■ *Web:* www.newportwave.com	Irvine	CA	92620	949-651-1099	786-0167
North Atlantic Publishing Systems Inc 182 Woodridge Rd *Web:* www.napsys.com	Concord	MA	01742	978-371-8989	371-8989
Novell Inc 1800 S Novell Pl **Fax:* Sales ■ *TF:* 800-529-3400 ■ *Web:* www.novell.com	Provo	UT	84606	801-861-4272	373-6798*
Object/FX Corp 1200 Washington Ave S Suite 340 *TF:* 866-900-2002 ■ *Web:* www.objectfx.com	Minneapolis	MN	55415	612-312-2002	312-2555
Objectivity Inc 640 W California Ave Suite 210 *TF:* 800-767-6259 ■ *Web:* www.objectivity.com	Sunnyvale	CA	94086	408-992-7100	992-7171
OMD Corp 3705 Missouri Blvd *TF:* 866-440-8664 ■ *Web:* www.omdcorp.com	Jefferson City	MO	65109	573-893-8930	893-3487

Company / Address	City	State	ZIP	Phone	Fax
Open Link Financial Inc 1502 RXR Plaza 15th Fl W Tower *Web:* www.olf.com	Uniondale	NY	11556	516-227-6600	227-1799
Open Systems Inc 4301 Dean Lakes Blvd *TF Sales:* 800-328-2276 ■ *Web:* www.osas.com	Shakopee	MN	55379	952-496-2465	403-5870
OpenLink Software Inc 10 Burlington Mall Rd Suite 265 *TF:* 800-495-6322 ■ *Web:* www.openlinksw.com	Burlington	MA	01803	781-273-0900	229-8030
Oracle Corp 500 Oracle Pkwy *NASDAQ: ORCL* ■ *TF Sales:* 800-392-2999 ■ *Web:* www.oracle.com	Redwood Shores	CA	94065	650-506-7000	506-7200
Oracle Information Rights Management 500 Oracle Pkwy *Web:* www.oracle.com	Redwood Shores	CA	94065	650-506-0024	
Oracle USA 500 Oracle Pkwy *TF:* 800-392-2999 ■ *Web:* www.oracle.com	Redwood Shores	CA	94065	800-392-2999	
Palisade Corp 798 Cascadilla St *TF:* 800-432-7475 ■ *Web:* www.palisade.com	Ithaca	NY	14850	607-277-8000	277-8001
Paperclip Software Inc 1 University Plaza **Fax:* Hum Res ■ *TF:* 800-929-3503 ■ *Web:* www.paperclip.com	Hackensack	NJ	07601	201-525-1221	525-1511*
Passport Corp 85 Chestnut Ridge Rd *TF:* 800-926-6736 ■ *Web:* www.passportcorp.com	Montvale	NJ	07645	201-573-0038	573-0082
Payformance Corp 7751 Belfort Pkwy Suite 200 *TF:* 800-733-0908 ■ *Web:* www.payformance.com	Jacksonville	FL	32256	904-997-6777	997-6955
PDI 3407 S 31st St PO Box 5550 *Web:* www.profdata.com	Lubbock	TX	79408	254-771-7100	771-7117
Pegasystems Inc 101 Main St *NASDAQ: PEGA* ■ *Web:* www.pega.com	Cambridge	MA	02142	617-374-9600	374-9620
Pentagon 2000 Software Inc 15 W 34th St 5th Fl *TF:* 800-643-1806 ■ *Web:* www.pentagon2000.com	New York	NY	10001	212-629-7521	629-7513
Percussion Software Inc 600 Unicorn Pk Dr *TF:* 800-283-0800 ■ *Web:* www.percussion.com	Woburn	MA	01801	781-438-9900	438-9955
Performance Solutions Technology LLC 1198 Pacific Coast Hwy Suite D515 **Fax Area Code:* 800 ■ *Web:* www.managepro.com	Seal Beach	CA	90740	562-430-7096	645-6618*
Personnel Data Systems Inc (PDS) 470 Norritown Rd Suite 202 *TF:* 800-243-8737 ■ *Web:* www.pdssoftware.com	Blue Bell	PA	19422	610-238-4600	238-4550
Pilgrim Software 2807 W Busch Blvd Suite 200 *Web:* www.pilgrimsoftware.com	Tampa	FL	33618	813-915-1663	915-1948
Pitney Bowes Group 1 Software 4200 Parliament Pl Suite 600 *TF:* 800-368-5806 ■ *Web:* www.g1.com	Lanham	MD	20706	301-731-2300	731-0360
Planview Inc 8300 N Mopac Suite 100 *TF:* 800-856-8600 ■ *Web:* www.planview.com	Austin	TX	78759	512-346-8600	346-9180
Platform Computing Inc 3760 14th Ave *TF:* 877-528-3676 ■ *Web:* www.platform.com	Markham	ON	L3R3T7	905-948-8448	948-9975
Polygon Industries Inc PO Box 24096 **Fax Area Code:* 708 ■ *TF:* 800-326-7083 ■ *Web:* www.polygonindustries.com	New Orleans	LA	70184	504-451-5721	575-4195*
Portrait Software Inc 125 Summer St 16th Fl *TF:* 800-821-8031 ■ *Web:* www.portraitsoftware.com	Boston	MA	02110	617-457-5200	457-5299
Print-O-Stat Inc 1011 W Market St PO Box 15046 *Web:* www.printostat.com	York	PA	17404	717-854-7821	846-4084
Process Control Technology Inc 4335 Piedras Dr W Suite 175 *Web:* www.gopct.com	San Antonio	TX	78228	210-735-9141	735-9775
Progress Software Corp 14 Oak Pk *NASDAQ: PRGS* ■ *TF:* 800-477-6473 ■ *Web:* www.web.progress.com/en/index.html	Bedford	MA	01730	781-280-4000	280-4095
Provue Development Corp 18685-A Main St PMB 356 *TF:* 800-966-7878 ■ *Web:* www.provue.com	Huntington Beach	CA	92648	714-841-7779	
QAD Inc 100 Innovation Pl *NASDAQ: QADB* ■ *TF:* 888-641-4141 ■ *Web:* www.qad.com	Santa Barbara	CA	93108	805-684-6614	565-4202
QNX Software Sytems 175 Terence Matthews Crescent *TF:* 800-676-0566 ■ *Web:* www.qnx.com	Ottawa	ON	K2M1W8	613-591-0931	591-3579
Quest Software Inc 5 Polairis Way *NASDAQ: QSFT* ■ *TF:* 800-306-9329 ■ *Web:* www.quest.com	Aliso Viejo	CA	92656	949-754-8000	754-8999
Quick Solutions Inc 440 Polaris Pkwy Suite 500 *Web:* www.quicksolutions.com	Westerville	OH	43082	614-825-8000	825-8006
Quorum Business Solutions Inc 3010 Briarpark Dr Suite 450 *Web:* www.qbsol.com	Houston	TX	77042	713-430-8601	430-8697
Realtime Software Corp 24 Deane Rd *TF:* 866-418-0590 ■ *Web:* www.realtimesw.com	Bernardston	MA	01337	847-803-1100	954-4764
Red Wing Software Inc 491 Hwy 19 *TF:* 800-732-9464 ■ *Web:* www.redwingsoftware.com	Red Wing	MN	55066	651-388-1106	388-7950
Redemtech Inc 4115 Leap Rd *TF:* 800-743-3499 ■ *Web:* www.redemtech.com	Columbus	OH	43026	614-850-3366	850-3354
RedPrairie Corp 20700 Swenson Dr Suite 400 *TF:* 800-990-9632 ■ *Web:* www.redprairie.com	Waukesha	WI	53186	262-317-2000	317-2001
Relavis Corp 40 Wall St 33rd Fl *Web:* www.relavis.com	New York	NY	10005	212-995-2900	995-2206
Rentrak Corp 7700 NE Ambassador Pl 3rd Fl *NASDAQ: RENT* ■ *TF:* 866-333-6210 ■ *Web:* www.rentrak.com	Portland	OR	97220	503-284-7581	
Rockwell Software Inc 2424 S 102nd St	West Allis	WI	53227	440-646-5800	646-5801
Sage Business Solutions 8800 N Gainey Ctr Dr Suite 200 *TF:* 800-643-6400 ■ *Web:* www.sagenorthamerica.com	Scottsdale	AZ	85258	480-383-5200	
Sage Fixed Assets 2325 Dulles Corner Blvd Suite 700 *TF:* 800-368-2405 ■ *Web:* www.sagefas.com	Herndon	VA	20171	703-793-2700	793-2770
Sage Software Inc Small Business Div 1715 N Brown Rd *TF Sales:* 800-285-0999 ■ *Web:* www.sagesoftware.com	Lawrenceville	GA	30043	770-724-4000	
Sand Technology Inc 215 Redfern St Suite 410 *TF:* 877-468-2538	Westmount	QC	H3Z3L5	514-939-3477	939-2042
SAP America Inc 3999 W Chester Pike *Web:* www.sap.com	Newtown Square	PA	19073	610-661-1000	
SAP Triversity 100 Consilium Pl *TF:* 888-287-4629 ■ *Web:* www.sap.com	Scarborough	ON	M1H3E3	416-791-7100	791-7101
Sapphire International 101 Merritt Blvd Suite 107 *Web:* www.dataease.com	Trumbull	CT	06611	203-375-8668	375-1965
SAS Institute Inc 100 SAS Campus Dr *TF:* 800-707-0025 ■ *Web:* www.sas.com	Cary	NC	27513	919-677-8000	677-4444
Satori Software Inc 1301 5th Ave Suite 2200 *TF:* 800-553-6477 ■ *Web:* www.satorisoftware.com	Seattle	WA	98101	206-357-2900	357-2901
SchoolDESX Technologies LLC 4150 S 100 E Ave Suite 1000 *TF:* 800-324-9393 ■ *Web:* www.schooldesx.com	Tulsa	OK	74146	918-664-8383	665-1999
Sciforma Corp 985 University Ave Suite 5 *TF Sales:* 800-533-9876 ■ *Web:* www.sciforma.com	Los Gatos	CA	95032	408-354-0144	354-0122
SCO Group Inc 355 S 520 W Suite 170 *PINK: SCOX* ■ *TF:* 888-553-3305 ■ *Web:* www.sco.com	Lindon	UT	84042	801-765-4999	765-1313
SDL International 1292 Hammerwood Ave *TF:* 888-487-2367 ■ *Web:* www.sdl.com	Sunnyvale	CA	94089	408-743-3500	743-3600
Selectica Inc 1740 Technology Dr Suite 450 *NASDAQ: SLTC* ■ *TF:* 877-712-9560 ■ *Web:* www.selectica.com	San Jose	CA	95110	408-570-9700	570-9705
SERENA Software Inc 1900 Seaport Blvd 2nd Fl *TF:* 800-457-3736 ■ *Web:* www.serena.com	Redwood City	CA	94063	650-481-3400	481-3700
Sierra Atlantic Inc 6522 Kaiser Dr *Web:* www.sierraatlantic.com	Fremont	CA	94555	510-742-4100	742-4101
Silvon Software Inc 900 Oakmont Ln Suite 400 *TF:* 800-874-5866 ■ *Web:* www.silvon.com	Westmont	IL	60559	630-655-3313	655-3377
Simul8 Corp 225 Franklin St 26th Fl **Fax Area Code:* 800 ■ *Web:* www.simul8.com	Boston	MA	02110	708-579-4073	547-6389*
Siwel Consulting Inc 71 W 23rd St Suite1907 *Web:* www.siwel.com	New York	NY	10010	212-691-9326	929-6815
Skybridge Global Inc 161 Vllage Pkwy NE Bldg 7 *Web:* www.skybridgeglobal.com	Marietta	GA	30067	770-373-2300	953-8360
Soffront Software Inc 45437 Warm Springs Blvd *TF:* 800-763-3766 ■ *Web:* www.soffront.com	Fremont	CA	94539	510-413-9000	413-9027
Software AG USA 11700 Plaza America Dr Suite 700 *TF:* 877-724-4965 ■ *Web:* www.softwareagusa.com	Reston	VA	20190	703-860-5050	391-6975
Source Technologies 2910 Whitehall Pk Dr *TF:* 800-922-8501 ■ *Web:* www.sourcetech.com	Charlotte	NC	28273	704-969-7500	969-7595
SourceForge Inc 46939 Bayside Pkwy *TF:* 877-825-4689 ■ *Web:* www.web.sourceforge.com	Fremont	CA	94538	510-687-7000	687-7155
SP Systems Inc 7500 Greenway Ctr Dr Suite 850 *Web:* www.sp-systems.com	Greenbelt	MD	20770	301-614-1322	614-1328
Speedware Corp 6380 Cote de Liesse Suite 110 *TF:* 800-361-6782 ■ *Web:* www.speedware.com	Saint-Laurent	QC	H4T1E3	514-747-7007	747-3380
Stamps.com Inc 12959 Coral Tree Pl *NASDAQ: STMP* ■ *TF:* 888-434-0055 ■ *Web:* www.stamps.com	Los Angeles	CA	90066	310-482-5800	450-3474
Sterling Commerce Inc 4600 Lakehurst Ct PO Box 8000 *TF:* 800-876-9772 ■ *Web:* www.sterlingcommerce.com	Dublin	OH	43016	614-793-7000	793-4040
StrataCare Inc 17838 Gillette Ave **Fax Area Code:* 949 ■ *TF:* 800-277-6512 ■ *Web:* www.stratacare.com	Irvine	CA	92614	800-277-6512	743-1299*
Superior Software Inc 16055 Ventura Blvd Suite 650 *TF:* 800-421-3264 ■ *Web:* www.superior-software.com	Encino	CA	91436	818-990-1135	783-5846
Sybase Inc 1 Sybase Dr *TF:* 800-792-2735 ■ *Web:* www.sybase.com	Dublin	CA	94568	925-236-5000	236-4321
SYSPRO 959 S Coast Dr Suite 100 *TF:* 800-369-8649 ■ *Web:* www.syspro.com	Costa Mesa	CA	92626	714-437-1000	437-1407
Systar Inc 8618 Westwood Ctr Dr Suite 240 *Web:* www.systar.com	Vienna	VA	22182	703-556-8400	556-8430
Taleo Corp 4140 Dublin Blvd Suite 400 *NASDAQ: TLEO* ■ *TF:* 888-836-3669 ■ *Web:* www.taleo.com	Dublin	CA	94568	925-452-3000	452-3001
TCG Software Services Inc 333 Thornall St 2nd Fl *Web:* www.tcgsoftwareinc.com	Edison	NJ	08837	732-632-3439	
TECSYS Inc 1 Pl Alexis Nihon Suite 800 *TF:* 800-922-8649 ■ *Web:* www.tecsys.com	Montreal	QC	H3C2M7	514-866-0001	866-1805
TenFold Corp 698 W 10000 S Suite 200 *TF:* 800-836-3653 ■ *Web:* www.tenfold.com	South Jordan	UT	84095	801-495-1010	495-0353
Tenrox 3452 E Foothill Blvd Suite 720 *Web:* www.tenrox.com	Pasadena	CA	91107	626-796-6640	796-6662
Thomson Tax & Accounting 7322 Newman Blvd *TF Cust Svc:* 800-968-0600 ■ *Web:* www.cs.thomson.com	Dexter	MI	48130	734-426-5860	426-3750
TIBCO Software Inc 3303 Hillview Ave *NASDAQ: TIBX* ■ *Web:* www.tibco.com	Palo Alto	CA	94304	650-846-5000	846-1005
Tomax Corp 224 S 200 W *TF:* 800-255-8120 ■ *Web:* www.tomax.com	Salt Lake City	UT	84101	801-990-0909	924-3400
TradeBeam Inc 2 Waters Pk Dr Suite 200 *TF:* 888-311-1415 ■ *Web:* www.tradebeam.com	San Mateo	CA	94403	650-653-4800	653-4801
TreeAge Software Inc 1075 Main St *TF:* 800-254-1911 ■ *Web:* www.treeage.com	Williamstown	MA	01267	413-458-0104	458-0105
TREEV LLCMetavante Image Solutions 13454 Sunrise Valley Dr Suite 400 *TF:* 800-254-0994 ■ *Web:* www.metavanteimage.com	Herndon	VA	20171	703-478-2260	481-6920
Trilogy Enterprises Inc 6011 W Courtyard Dr Suite 300 *Web:* www.trilogy.com	Austin	TX	78730	512-874-3100	874-8900
Trintech Inc 15851 Dallas Pkwy Suite 900 *NASDAQ: TTPA* ■ *TF:* 800-416-0075 ■ *Web:* www.trintech.com	Addison	TX	75001	972-701-9802	701-9337
Tritek Solutions Inc 7617 Little River Tpke Suite 800 *Web:* www.triteksol.com	Annandale	VA	22003	703-333-3060	333-3071
Ultimate Software Group Inc 2000 Ultimate Way *NASDAQ: ULTI* ■ *TF:* 800-432-1729 ■ *Web:* www.ultimatesoftware.com	Weston	FL	33326	954-331-7000	331-7306
Unica Corp 170 Tracer Ln *Web:* www.unicacorp.com	Waltham	MA	02451	781-839-8000	890-0012
Unz & Co 201 Cir Dr N Suite 104 *TF:* 800-631-3098 ■ *Web:* www.unzco.com	Piscataway	NJ	08854	732-868-0706	868-0607

Company	City	State	Zip	Phone	Fax
Valiant Solutions Inc 110 Crossways Pk Dr *TF:* 800-699-8869 ■ *Web:* www.valiant.com	Woodbury	NY	11797	516-390-1100	390-1111
Validar 801 1st Ave S Suite 200 *TF:* 888-784-8455 ■ *Web:* www.validar.com	Seattle	WA	98134	206-855-8494	223-8455
Ventyx 3301 Windy Ridge Pkwy Suite 200 *TF:* 800-554-6387 ■ *Web:* www.ventyx.com	Atlanta	GA	30339	770-952-8444	989-4231
Versant Corp 255 Shoreline Dr Suite 450 *NASDAQ: VSNT* ■ *TF:* 800-837-7268 ■ *Web:* www.versant.com	Redwood City	CA	94065	650-232-2400	232-2401
Versata Inc 6011 W Courtyard Dr *TF:* 800-984-7638 ■ *Web:* www.versata.com	Austin	TX	87830	512-874-3000	874-8900
Vertex Inc 1041 Old Cassatt Rd *TF:* 800-355-3500 ■ *Web:* www.vertexinc.com	Berwyn	PA	19312	610-640-4200	640-5892
Vertro Inc 143 Varick St *NASDAQ: VTRO* ■ *Web:* www.vertro.com	New York	NY	10013	212-231-2000	809-0926
VFA Inc 226 Summer St # 2 *TF:* 800-693-3132 ■ *Web:* www.vfa.com	Boston	MA	02210	617-451-5100	350-7087
Viador Inc 4677 Old Ironsides Dr Suite 300 *Web:* www.viador.com	Santa Clara	CA	95054	408-567-6030	567-6001
Vignette Corp 1301 S Mopac Expy Suite 100 *TF:* 888-608-9900 ■ *Web:* www.vignette.com	Austin	TX	78746	512-741-4300	741-1537
ViryaNet Inc 2 Willow St *NASDAQ: VRYA* ■ *TF:* 800-661-7096 ■ *Web:* www.viryanet.com	Southborough	MA	01745	508-490-5900	490-8666
Visible Systems Corp 201 Spring St *TF Sales:* 800-684-7425 ■ *Web:* www.visible.com	Lexington	MA	02421	781-778-0200	778-0208
Vitria Technology Inc 945 Stewart Dr *STO: VITR* ■ *TF:* 877-365-5935 ■ *Web:* www.vitria.com	Sunnyvale	CA	94085	408-212-2700	212-2720
Volunteer Software 628 S 2nd St **Fax Area Code:* 303 ■ *TF:* 800-391-9446 ■ *Web:* www.volsoft.com	Missoula	MT	59801	406-721-0113	265-9288*
Wave Systems Corp 480 Pleasant St *NASDAQ: WAVX* ■ *TF:* 888-669-9283 ■ *Web:* www.wavesys.com	Lee	MA	01238	413-243-1600	243-0045
Waypoint Global LLC 6910 N Shadeland Ave *TF:* 800-964-9004 ■ *Web:* www.powerwayinc.com	Indianapolis	IN	46220	317-624-4000	624-4040
Wizdom Systems Inc 1300 Iroquois Ave *Web:* www.wizdom.com	Naperville	IL	60563	630-357-3000	357-3059
Worden Bros Inc 4905 Pine Cone Dr *TF:* 800-776-4940 ■ *Web:* www.worden.com	Durham	NC	27707	919-408-0542	408-0545
Xaware Inc 3300 Irvine Ave Suite 261 *Web:* www.xaware.com	Newport Beach	CA	92660	719-884-5410	325-8943
ZyLAB North America LLC 1577 Spring Hill Rd Suite 420 *Web:* www.zylab.com	Vienna	VA	22182	703-448-1420	991-2508

181-2 Computer Languages & Development Tools

Company	City	State	Zip	Phone	Fax
Amzi! inc 1 Galax Ave *Web:* www.amzi.com	Asheville	NC	28806	828-350-0350	
Applied Dynamics International Inc 3800 Stone School Rd *Web:* www.adi.com	Ann Arbor	MI	48108	734-973-1300	668-0012
BSQUARE Corp 110 110th Ave NE Suite 200 *NASDAQ: BSQR* ■ *TF:* 888-820-4500 ■ *Web:* www.bsquare.com	Bellevue	WA	98004	425-519-5900	519-5999
BulletProof Corp 2400 E Las Olas Blvd Suite 332 **Fax Area Code:* 954 ■ *TF:* 800-505-0105 ■ *Web:* www.bulletproof.com	Fort Lauderdale	FL	33301	800-505-0105	337-0768*
Calypso Technology Inc 595 Market St Suite 1800 *Web:* www.calypso.com	San Francisco	CA	94105	415-817-2400	284-1222
Data Access Corp 14000 SW 119th Ave *TF:* 800-451-3539 ■ *Web:* www.daccess.com	Miami	FL	33186	305-238-0012	238-0012
DDC-I Inc 4600 E Shea Blvd Suite #102 *TF:* 800-221-8643 ■ *Web:* www.ddci.com	Phoenix	AZ	85028	602-275-7172	252-6054
Diamond Edge Inc 184 S 300 W *Web:* www.diamondedge.com	Lindon	UT	84042	801-785-8473	
Embarcadero Technologies Inc 100 California St 12th Fl *Web:* www.embarcadero.com	San Francisco	CA	94111	415-834-3131	434-1721
Empress Software Inc 11785 Beltsville Dr *TF:* 866-626-8888 ■ *Web:* www.empress.com	Beltsville	MD	20705	301-220-1919	220-1997
Fgm Inc 12021 Sunset Hills Rd Suite 400 *Web:* www.fgm.com	Reston	VA	20190	703-885-1000	885-0130
FMS Inc 8150 Leesburg Pike Suite 600 *TF:* 866-367-7801 ■ *Web:* www.fmsinc.com	Vienna	VA	22182	703-356-4700	448-3861
Forth Inc 5959 W Century Blvd Suite 700 *TF:* 800-553-6784 ■ *Web:* www.forth.com	Los Angeles	CA	90045	310-999-6784	943-3806
Green Hills Software Inc 30 W Sola St *TF:* 800-765-4733 ■ *Web:* www.ghs.com	Santa Barbara	CA	93101	805-965-6044	965-6343
Gt Nexus Inc 300 Lakeside Dr Suite 400 *Web:* www.gtnexus.com	Oakland	CA	94612	510-808-2222	808-2220
Infinite Software 28202 Cabot Rd *TF:* 800-474-4047 ■ *Web:* www.infinitesoftware.com	Laguna Niguel	CA	92677	949-498-9300	498-9201
Instantiations Inc 4412 SE 185th Ct Suite 1325B *TF:* 855-476-2558 ■ *Web:* www.instantiations.com	Vancouver	WA	98661	503-649-3836	684-8355
Integrated Computer Solutions Inc (ICS) 54 Middlesex Tpke Suite B *TF:* 800-800-4271 ■ *Web:* www.ics.com	Bedford	MA	01730	617-621-0060	621-9555
LANSA Inc 3010 Highland Pkwy Suite 275 *Web:* www.lansa.com	Downers Grove	IL	60515	630-874-7000	874-7001
Lattice Inc 1751 S Naperville Rd Suite 100 *TF Sales:* 800-444-4309 ■ *Web:* www.lattice.com	Wheaton	IL	60187	630-949-3250	949-3299
Mix Software Inc 1203 Berkeley Dr *TF:* 800-333-0330 ■ *Web:* www.mixsoftware.com	Richardson	TX	75081	972-231-0949	
MKS Inc 410 Albert St *TF Sales:* 800-265-2797 ■ *Web:* www.mks.com	Waterloo	ON	N2L3V3	519-884-2251	884-8861
NIS Inc 12995 Thomas Creek Rd *Web:* www.nis.com	Reno	NV	89511	775-852-0640	852-0640
Numara Software Inc 2202 NW Shore Blvd Suite 650 *TF Sales:* 800-557-3031 ■ *Web:* www.numarasoftware.com	Tampa	FL	33607	813-227-4500	227-4501
Object/FX Corp 1200 Washington Ave S Suite 340 *TF:* 866-900-2002 ■ *Web:* www.objectfx.com	Minneapolis	MN	55415	612-312-2002	312-2555
Primus Software Corp 3061 Peachtree Industrial Blvd Suite 110 *Web:* www.primussoft.com	Duluth	GA	30097	770-300-0004	300-0005
Prolifics 22 Cortlandt St # 18 *TF:* 800-458-3313 ■ *Web:* www.prolifics.com	New York	NY	10007	212-267-7722	608-6753
Recital Corp 100 Cummings Ctr Suite 318J *TF:* 800-873-7443 ■ *Web:* www.recital.com	Beverly	MA	01915	978-921-5594	921-4005
Revelation Software 99 Kinderkamack Rd *TF:* 800-262-4747 ■ *Web:* www.revelation.com	Westwood	NJ	07675	201-594-1422	722-9815
Rogue Wave Software Inc 5500 Flatiron Pkwy *TF:* 800-487-3217 ■ *Web:* www.roguewave.com	Boulder	CO	80301	303-473-9118	473-9137
Savitar Corp 3000 Kent Ave	West Lafayette	IN	47906	765-742-5400	742-5432
SemWare Corp 730 Elk Cove Ct *Web:* www.semware.com	Kennesaw	GA	30152	678-355-9810	355-9812
Shaw Systems Assoc Inc 6200 Savoy Dr Suite 600 *TF:* 800-731-3612 ■ *Web:* www.shawsystems.com	Houston	TX	77036	713-782-7730	782-4158
SlickEdit Inc 3000 Aerial Ctr Pkwy Suite 120 *TF:* 800-934-3348 ■ *Web:* www.slickedit.com	Morrisville	NC	27560	919-473-0070	473-0080
Sunbelt Computer Systems Inc 13090 Swan Lake Rd CR 468 *TF Sales:* 800-359-5907 ■ *Web:* www.sunbelt-plb.com	Tyler	TX	75704	903-881-0400	
Synactive Inc 950 Tower Ln Suite 750 *Web:* www.synactive.net	Foster City	CA	94404	650-341-3310	341-3610
Thoroughbred Software International Inc 285 Davidson Ave Suite 302 *TF:* 800-524-0430 ■ *Web:* www.thoroughbredsoftware.com	Somerset	NJ	08873	732-560-1377	560-1594
Zortec International 25 Century Blvd Suite 103 *TF:* 800-361-7005 ■ *Web:* www.zortec.com	Nashville	TN	37214	615-361-7000	361-3800

181-3 Educational & Reference Software

Company	City	State	Zip	Phone	Fax
Allen Communication Learning Services 175 W 200 S Suite 100 *TF:* 866-310-7800 ■ *Web:* www.allencomm.com	Salt Lake City	UT	84101	801-537-7800	537-7805
American Education Corp 7506 Broadway Ext *TF:* 800-222-2811 ■ *Web:* www.amered.com	Oklahoma City	OK	73116	405-840-6031	848-3960
Atari Inc 417 5th Ave 8th Fl *TF:* 800-898-1438 ■ *Web:* www.atari.com	New York	NY	10016	212-726-6500	252-8603
Automated Training Systems Corp 4545 E Industrial St Suite 5B *TF:* 800-426-8737 ■ *Web:* www.ibmuser.com	Simi Valley	CA	93063	805-520-1509	520-1067
Blackboard Inc 1899 L St NW 5th Fl *NASDAQ: BBBB* ■ *TF:* 800-424-9299 ■ *Web:* www.blackboard.com	Washington	DC	20036	202-463-4860	463-4863
CBT Direct LLC 25400 US Hwy 19N Suite 285 *TF:* 877-872-4646 ■ *Web:* www.cbtdirect.com	Clearwater	FL	33763	727-724-8994	726-6922
CompassLearning Inc 203 Colorado St *TF:* 800-232-9556 ■ *Web:* www.compasslearning.com	Austin	TX	78701	512-478-9600	492-6193
Cosmi Corp 1351 Charles Willard St *Web:* www.cosmi.com	Carson	CA	90746	310-603-5800	886-3500
Deep River Interactive 7 Custom House St 2nd Fl	Portland	ME	04101	207-775-6405	775-5668
Electronic Courseware Systems Inc 1713 S State St *TF Orders:* 800-832-4965	Champaign	IL	61820	217-359-7099	359-7099
Gamco Industries Inc 325 N Kirkwood Rd Suite 200 *TF:* 888-726-8100 ■ *Web:* www.gamco.com	Saint Louis	MO	63122	314-909-1670	984-8063
Individual Software Inc 4255 Hopyard Rd Suite 2 *TF:* 800-822-3522 ■ *Web:* www.individualsoftware.com	Pleasanton	CA	94588	925-734-6767	734-8337
Inscape Publishing Inc 6465 Wayzata Blvd Suite 800 *TF:* 800-395-0957 ■ *Web:* www.inscapepublishing.com	Minneapolis	MN	55426	763-765-2222	765-2277
Insightful Corp 1700 Westlake Ave N Suite 500 *NASDAQ: IFUL* ■ *TF:* 800-569-0123 ■ *Web:* www.insightful.com	Seattle	WA	98109	206-283-8802	283-8691
Inspiration Software Inc 7412 SW Beaverton-Hillsdale Hwy Suite 300 *TF:* 800-877-4292 ■ *Web:* www.inspiration.com	Beaverton	OR	97005	503-297-3004	297-4676
Language Engineering Co 135 Beaver St Suite 204 *Web:* www.lec.com	Waltham	MA	02452	781-642-8900	642-8904
Ldp Inc 75 Kiwanis Blvd PO Box O *Web:* www.leaderservices.com	West Hazleton	PA	18201	800-522-8413	
MedTech USA PO Box 351150 **Fax Area Code:* 310 ■ *TF:* 800-640-8000 ■ *Web:* www.medtech.com	Los Angeles	CA	90048	323-964-1000	280-0411*
Milliken Publishing Co Inc 3190 Rider Trail S *TF:* 800-325-4136 ■ *Web:* www.millikenpub.com	Earth City	MO	63045	314-991-4220	991-4807
MindPlay Educational Software 440 S Williams Blvd Suite 206 *TF:* 800-221-7911 ■ *Web:* www.mindplay.com	Tucson	AZ	85711	520-888-1800	888-7904
NCS Pearson Inc 5601 Green Valley Dr Suite 220 *TF:* 800-431-1421 ■ *Web:* www.ncspearson.com	Bloomington	MN	55437	952-681-3000	681-3580
Nordic Software Inc 917 Carlos Dr PO Box 5403 *TF:* 800-306-6502 ■ *Web:* www.nordicsoftware.com	Lincoln	NE	68505	402-489-1557	489-1560
Optimum Resource Inc 18 Hunter Rd *TF:* 888-784-2592 ■ *Web:* www.stickybear.com	Hilton Head Island	SC	29926	843-689-8000	689-8008
PLATO Learning Inc 5600 W 83rd St Suite 300 *TF:* 800-869-2000 ■ *Web:* www.plato.com	Bloomington	MN	55437	952-832-1000	832-1200

				Phone	Fax
Queue Inc 1 Controls Dr. *Fax Area Code: 800 ■ *TF:* 800-232-2224 ■ *Web:* www.queueinc.com	Shelton	CT	06484	203-446-8100	775-2729*
Quicksilver Software Inc 18261 McDermott *Web:* www.quicksilver.com	Irvine	CA	92614	949-474-2150	
Renaissance Learning Inc 2911 Peach St *NASDAQ: RLRN* ■ *TF:* 800-338-4204 ■ *Web:* www.renlearn.com	Wisconsin Rapids	WI	54494	715-424-3636	424-4242
Saba Software Inc 2400 Bridge Pkwy *NASDAQ: SABA* ■ *TF:* 877-803-1900 ■ *Web:* www.saba.com	Redwood Shores	CA	94065	650-696-3840	696-1773
Scientific Learning Corp 300 Frank H Ogawa Plaza Suite 600 *NASDAQ: SCIL* ■ *TF:* 888-665-9707 ■ *Web:* www.scilearn.com	Oakland	CA	94612	510-444-3500	444-3580
Siboney Corp 325 N Kirkwood Rd Suite 300 PO Box 221029 *TF:* 888-726-8100 ■ *Web:* www.siboney.com	Saint Louis	MO	63122	314-822-3163	822-3197
Sunburst Technology 1550 Executive Dr *TF:* 800-321-7511 ■ *Web:* www.commerce.sunburst.com	Elgin	IL	60123	888-492-8817	800-3028
Tom Snyder Productions Inc 100 Talcott Ave *TF:* 800-342-0236 ■ *Web:* www.tomsnyder.com	Watertown	MA	02472	617-926-6000	926-6222
Transparent Language Inc 12 Murphy Dr. *Fax Area Code: 603 ■ *TF:* 800-538-8867 ■ *Web:* www.transparent.com	Nashua	NH	03062	800-538-8867	262-6476*
True BASIC Inc 245 Main St PO Box 500 *TF:* 800-436-2111 ■ *Web:* www.truebasic.com	Bethel	VT	05032	802-705-1403	234-6378
VCampus Corp 1850 Centennial Pk Dr Suite 200 *NASDAQ: VCMP* ■ *TF:* 800-915-9298	Reston	VA	20191	703-893-7800	893-1905
Ventura Educational Systems 2780 Sevada Ln *Fax Area Code: 800 ■ *TF:* 800-336-1022 ■ *Web:* www.venturaes.com	Arroyo Grande	CA	93420	805-473-7387	493-7380*
Wordsmart Corp 10025 Mesa Rim Rd. *Web:* www.wordsmart.com	San Diego	CA	92121	858-565-8068	565-8413
Wright Group/McGraw-Hill 130 E Randolph St Suite 400 *TF:* 800-648-2970 ■ *Web:* www.wrightgroup.com	Chicago	IL	60601	312-233-6500	233-6511

181-4 Electronic Purchasing & Procurement Software

				Phone	Fax
Apptis Inc 4800 Westfields Blvd. *TF:* 800-277-8478 ■ *Web:* www.apptis.com	Chantilly	VA	20151	703-745-6016	691-4911
Ariba Inc 807 11th Ave *NASDAQ: ARBA* ■ *TF:* 888-237-3131 ■ *Web:* www.ariba.com	Sunnyvale	CA	94089	650-390-1000	390-1100
CA Inc 1 CA Plaza *NYSE: CA* ■ *TF:* 800-225-5224 ■ *Web:* www.ca.com	Islandia	NY	11749	631-342-6000	342-6800
Covisint 1 Campus Martius *TF:* 888-222-1700 ■ *Web:* www.covisint.com	Detroit	MI	48226	313-227-7300	227-6410
Elavon 1 Concourse Pkwy Suite 300 *Fax Area Code: 865 ■ *TF:* 800-725-1243 ■ *Web:* www.elavon.com	Atlanta	GA	30328	678-731-5000	577-0661*
Epylon Corp 3675 Mt Diablo Blvd Suite 110 *TF:* 888-211-7438 ■ *Web:* www.epylon.com	Lafayette	CA	94549	925-407-1020	407-1021
Fiserv Lending Solutions 455 S Gulph Rd Suite 125 *Web:* www.fiservlemans.com	King of Prussia	PA	19406	610-337-8686	337-7206
GXS Inc 9711 Washingtonian Blvd *TF:* 800-560-4347 ■ *Web:* www.gxs.com	Gaithersburg	MD	20878	301-340-4000	340-5840
International Business Machines Corp (IBM) 1 New Orchard Rd. *NYSE: IBM* ■ *TF:* 800-426-4968 ■ *Web:* www.ibm.com	Armonk	NY	10504	914-766-1900	
MarketAxess Holdings Inc 299 Pk Ave 10th Fl. *NASDAQ: MKTX* ■ *Web:* www.marketaxess.com	New York	NY	10171	212-813-6000	813-6390
SciQuest Inc 6501 Weston Pkwy Suite 200 *TF:* 888-638-7322 ■ *Web:* www.sciquest.com	Cary	NC	27513	919-659-2100	659-2199
Verian Technologies Inc 1245 Rosemont Dr. *TF:* 800-672-8776 ■ *Web:* www.procureit.com	Indian Land	SC	29707	800-672-8776	

181-5 Engineering Software

				Phone	Fax
Accelrys Inc 10188 Telesis Ct Suite 100 *NASDAQ: ACCL* ■ *TF:* 888-249-2284 ■ *Web:* www.accelrys.com	San Diego	CA	92121	858-799-5000	799-5100
Advanced Visual Systems Inc (AVS) 300 5th Ave *TF Sales:* 800-728-1600 ■ *Web:* www.avs.com	Waltham	MA	02451	781-890-4300	890-8287
Altium Inc 3207 Grey Hawk Ct Suite 100 *TF Sales:* 800-544-4186 ■ *Web:* www.altium.com	Carlsbad	CA	92010	760-231-0760	231-0761
ANSYS Inc 275 Technology Dr *NASDAQ: ANSS* ■ *TF:* 800-937-3321 ■ *Web:* www.ansys.com	Canonsburg	PA	15317	724-746-3304	514-9494
Ashlar Inc 12710 Research Blvd Suite 308 *TF:* 800-877-2745 ■ *Web:* www.ashlar.com	Austin	TX	78759	512-250-2186	250-5811*
Aspen Technology Inc 200 Wheeler Rd *NASDAQ: AZPN* ■ *Web:* www.aspentech.com	Burlington	MA	02141	781-221-6400	221-6410
Autodesk Inc 111 McInnis Pkwy *NASDAQ: ADSK* ■ *TF Tech Supp:* 800-964-6432 ■ *Web:* www.autodesk.com	San Rafael	CA	94903	415-507-5000	507-5100
Bentley Systems Inc 685 Stockton Dr *TF:* 800-236-8539 ■ *Web:* www.bentley.com	Exton	PA	19341	610-458-5000	458-1060
Bohannan Huston Inc 7500 Jefferson St NE Courtyard 1 *TF:* 800-877-5332 ■ *Web:* www.bhinc.com	Albuquerque	NM	87109	505-823-1000	798-7988
CACI MTL Systems Inc 3481 Dayton-Xenia Rd *Web:* www.caci.com	Dayton	OH	45432	937-426-3111	426-8301
Cadalog Inc 1448 King St *Web:* www.cadalog-inc.com	Bellingham	WA	98229	360-647-2426	647-2890
Cadence Design Systems Inc 2655 Seely Ave *NASDAQ: CDNS* ■ *TF Cust Svc:* 800-746-6223 ■ *Web:* www.cadence.com	San Jose	CA	95134	408-943-1234	428-5001
CambridgeSoft Corp 100 CambridgePark Dr *TF:* 800-315-7300 ■ *Web:* www.cambridgesoft.com	Cambridge	MA	02140	617-588-9100	588-9190
Comarco Inc 25541 Commerce Ctr Dr. *NASDAQ: CMRO* ■ *TF:* 800-792-0250 ■ *Web:* www.comarco.com	Lake Forest	CA	92630	949-599-7400	599-1415
CSA Inc 280 IH- N Cir SE Suite 250 *Web:* www.csaatl.com	Atlanta	GA	30339	770-955-3518	956-8748
Data Description Inc 840 Hanshaw Rd 2nd Fl. *Fax:* Sales ■ *TF:* 800-573-5121 ■ *Web:* www.datadesk.com	Ithaca	NY	14850	607-257-1000	257-4146*
Direct Source Inc 8176 Mallory Ct *TF:* 800-934-8055 ■ *Web:* www.directsource.com	Chanhassen	MN	55317	952-934-8000	934-8030
Disk Software Inc 205 Ridgestone Dr. *TF:* 800-635-7760 ■ *Web:* www.disksoft.com	Murphy	TX	75094	972-423-7288	633-0718
Dp Technology Corp 1150 Avenida Acaso *TF:* 800-627-8479 ■ *Web:* www.dptechnology.com	Camarillo	CA	93012	805-388-6000	388-3085
Engineered Software Inc 615 Guilford Jamestown Rd *Web:* www.engsw.com	Greensboro	NC	27409	336-299-4843	852-2067
Evolution Computing 7000 N 16th St Suite 120 #514 *TF:* 800-874-4028 ■ *Web:* www.fastcad.com	Phoenix	AZ	85020	480-659-5658	
Geocomp Corp 1145 Massachusetts Ave. *TF Cust Svc:* 800-822-2669 ■ *Web:* www.geocomp.com	Boxborough	MA	01719	978-635-0012	635-0266
Gibbs & Assoc 323 Science Dr *TF Cust Svc:* 800-654-9399 ■ *Web:* www.gibbsnc.com	Moorpark	CA	93021	805-523-0004	523-0006
IDC Digital Solutions 111 E 1st St *Web:* www.geneseo.com	Geneseo	IL	61254	309-944-4115	944-9475
Infinite Graphics Inc 4611 E Lake St *TF:* 800-679-0676 ■ *Web:* www.igi.com	Minneapolis	MN	55406	612-721-6283	721-3802
Intergraph Corp 19 Interpro Rd *TF:* 800-345-4856 ■ *Web:* www.intergraph.com	Madison	AL	35758	256-730-2000	730-2048
Kubotek USA 2 Mt Royal Ave # 500 *TF:* 800-372-3872 ■ *Web:* www.kubotekusa.com	Marlborough	MA	01752	508-229-2020	229-2121
LINDO Systems Inc 1415 N Dayton St *TF Sales:* 800-441-2378 ■ *Web:* www.lindo.com	Chicago	IL	60622	312-988-7422	988-9065
Magma Design Automation Inc 1650 Technology Dr *NASDAQ: LAVA* ■ *Web:* www.magma-da.com	San Jose	CA	95110	408-565-7500	565-7501
Manufacturing & Consulting Services Inc 401-B W Main St *TF:* 800-932-9329 ■ *Web:* www.mcsaz.com	Payson	AZ	85541	480-991-8700	991-8732
Mathworks Inc 3 Apple Hill Dr *Web:* www.mathworks.com	Natick	MA	01760	508-647-7000	647-7001
Mentor Graphics Corp 8005 SW Boeckman Rd *NASDAQ: MENT* ■ *TF:* 800-592-2210 ■ *Web:* www.mentor.com	Wilsonville	OR	97070	503-685-7000	685-1204
MSC.Software Corp 2 MacArthur Pl. *TF:* 800-345-2078 ■ *Web:* www.mscsoftware.com	Santa Ana	CA	92707	714-540-8900	784-4056
National Instruments Corp 11500 N Mopac Expy *NASDAQ: NATI* ■ *TF Cust Svc:* 800-433-3488 ■ *Web:* www.ni.com	Austin	TX	78759	512-794-0100	683-8411
Numerical Control Computer Sciences 4685 MacArthur Ct Suite 200 *Web:* www.nccs.com	Newport Beach	CA	92660	949-553-1077	553-1911
Parametric Technology Corp (PTC) 140 Kendrick St *Web:* www.ptc.com	Needham	MA	02494	781-370-5000	370-6000
Planit Solutions Inc 3800 Palisades Dr *TF:* 800-280-6932 ■ *Web:* www.planit.com	Tuscaloosa	AL	35405	205-556-9199	556-9210
PMS Systems Corp 2800 28th St Suite 109 *TF:* 800-755-3968 ■ *Web:* www.assetsmart.com	Santa Monica	CA	90405	310-450-2566	450-1311
Science Application International Corp (SAIC) 4600 Powder Mill Rd Suite 400 *Web:* www.saic.com	Beltsville	MD	20705	301-931-2900	931-3797
Tripos Inc 1699 S Hanley Rd *TF:* 800-323-2960 ■ *Web:* www.tripos.com	Saint Louis	MO	63144	314-647-1099	647-9241
Triton Services Inc 2014 Industrial Dr *Web:* www.tritonsvc.com	Annapolis	MD	21401	443-716-0600	716-0601
Zuken USA 238 Littleton Rd Suite 100 *TF:* 800-447-7332 ■ *Web:* www.zuken.com	Westford	MA	01886	978-692-4900	692-4725

181-6 Games & Entertainment Software

				Phone	Fax
Abacus Software Inc 5130 Patterson St SE *TF Sales:* 800-451-4319 ■ *Web:* www.abacuspub.com	Grand Rapids	MI	49512	616-698-0330	698-0325
Activision Inc 3100 Ocean Pk Blvd *NASDAQ: ATVI* ■ *Web:* www.activision.com	Santa Monica	CA	90405	310-255-2000	479-4005
Alienware Corp 14591 SW 120th St *Fax Area Code: 786 ■ *TF:* 866-287-6727 ■ *Web:* www.alienware.com	Miami	FL	33186	305-251-9797	388-5719*
Apogee Software Inc 1999 S Bascom Ave Suite 325 *TF:* 800-854-6705 ■ *Web:* www.apogee1.com	Campbell	CA	95008	408-369-9001	369-9018
Bethesda Softworks LLC 1370 Piccard Dr Suite 120 *Web:* www.bethsoft.com	Rockville	MD	20850	301-926-8300	926-8010
Buena Vista Game Entertainment Studio *Disney Interactive Studios* 500 S Bunavista St *TF:* 800-228-0988 ■ *Web:* www.disney.com	Bubank	CA	91521	818-553-5000	567-0284
Buena Vista Games 500 S Buena Vista St *Fax Area Code: 818 ■ *TF:* 800-228-0988 ■ *Web:* www.disney.go.com/DisneyInteractive	Burbank	CA	91521	800-228-0988	567-0284*
Capcom USA Inc 800 Concar Dr Suite 300 *Web:* www.capcom.com	San Mateo	CA	94406	650-350-6500	350-6655
Cyan Worlds Inc 14617 N Newport Hwy *Web:* www.cyan.com	Mead	WA	99021	509-468-0807	467-2209
Disney Consumer Products 500 S Buena Vista St *Fax:* Cust Svc ■ *TF PR:* 800-723-4763	Burbank	CA	91521	818-560-1000	560-1930*
Eidos Inc 1300 Seaport Blvde *Web:* www.eidos.com	Redwood City	CA	94063	650-421-7600	421-6701
Electronic Arts Inc (EA) 209 Redwood Shores Pkwy *NASDAQ: ERTS* ■ *TF Sales:* 877-324-2637 ■ *Web:* www.ea.com	Redwood City	CA	94065	650-628-1500	628-1414
Her Interactive Inc 1150 114th Ave SE Suite 200 *TF Orders:* 800-461-8787 ■ *Web:* www.herinteractive.com	Bellevue	WA	98004	425-460-8787	460-8788
iEntertainment Network Inc 124 Quade Dr *TF:* 800-438-4263 ■ *Web:* www.ient.com	Cary	NC	27513	919-678-8301	678-8302

Company	City	State	ZIP	Phone	Fax
Jim Henson Co 1416 N La Brea Ave *Web:* www.henson.com	Hollywood	CA	90028	323-802-1500	802-1825
Learningware Inc 700 Raymond Ave *TF:* 800-457-5661 ■ *Web:* www.learningware.com	Saint paul	MN	55114	612-904-6878	904-1781
Lucasfilm Ltd LucasArts Entertainment Div 1110 Gorgas St *Web:* www.lucasarts.com	San Francisco	CA	94129	415-746-8000	746-8923
Macrovision 2830 de la Cruz Blvd *NASDAQ: ROVI* ■ *Web:* www.rovicorp.com	Santa Clara	CA	95050	408-562-8400	567-1800
MakeMusic! Inc 7615 Golden Triangle Dr Suite M *NASDAQ: MMUS* ■ *TF:* 800-843-2066 ■ *Web:* www.makemusic.com	Eden Prairie	MN	55344	952-937-9611	937-9760
Mythic Entertainment Inc 4035 Ridge Top Rd 8th Fl *Web:* www.mythicentertainment.com	Fairfax	VA	22030	703-934-0169	934-0447
Nintendo of America Inc 4820 150th Ave NE *TF Cust Svc:* 800-255-3700 ■ *Web:* www.nintendo.com	Redmond	WA	98052	425-882-2040	882-3585
NovaLogic Inc 27489 Agoura Rd *Web:* www.novalogic.com	Agoura Hills	CA	91301	818-880-1997	865-6405
Quicksilver Software Inc 18261 McDermott *Web:* www.quicksilver.com	Irvine	CA	92614	949-474-2150	
SEGA of America Inc 650 Townsend St Suite 650 *Web:* www.sega.com	San Francisco	CA	94103	415-701-6000	701-6018
Southpeak Interactive LLC 2900 Polo Pkwy *OTC: SOPYW* ■ *Web:* www.southpeakgames.com	Midlothian	VA	23113	804-378-5100	
Take-Two Interactive Software Inc 622 Broadway *NASDAQ: TTWO* ■ *Web:* www.take2games.com	New York	NY	10012	646-536-2842	536-2926
Take-Two Licensing Inc 8550 Balboa Blvd *Web:* www.tdk-mediactive.com	Northridge	CA	91325	818-707-7063	672-8040
THQ Inc 29903 Agoura Rd *NASDAQ: THQI*	Agoura Hills	CA	91301	818-871-5000	871-7400
TreyArch 3420 Ocean Pk Blvd Suite 1000 *Web:* www.treyarch.com	Santa Monica	CA	90405	310-581-4700	581-4702
Walt Disney Interactive 601 Cir 7 Dr *TF:* 800-228-0988 ■ *Web:* www.disney.go.com	Glendale	CA	91201	818-553-5000	547-9035
WildTangent Inc 18578 NE 67th Ct Redmond E Office Complex Bldg 5 *Web:* www.wildtangent.com	Redmond	WA	98052	425-497-4500	497-4501
ZeniMax Media Inc 1370 Piccard Dr Suite 120 *TF:* 800-677-0700 ■ *Web:* www.zenimax.com	Rockville	MD	20850	301-948-2200	926-8010
Zoo Entertainment Inc 3805 Edwards Rd Suite 400 *NASDAQ: ZOOG* ■ *TF:* 866-663-2510 ■ *Web:* www.zoogamesinc.com	Cincinnati	OH	45209	513-824-8297	351-0464
@Comm Corp 150 Dow St *TF:* 800-641-5400 ■ *Web:* www.atcomm.com	Manchester	NH	03101	650-375-8188	342-1139

181-7 Internet & Communications Software

Company	City	State	ZIP	Phone	Fax
Activeworlds Inc 95 Parker St *Web:* www.activeworlds.com	Newburyport	MA	01950	978-499-0222	499-0221
Adaptive Micro Systems Inc 7840 N 86th St *TF:* 800-558-4187 ■ *Web:* www.ams-i.com	Milwaukee	WI	53224	414-357-2020	357-2029
Akamai Technologies Inc 8 Cambridge Ctr *NASDAQ: AKAM* ■ *TF:* 877-425-2624 ■ *Web:* www.akamai.com	Cambridge	MA	02142	617-444-3000	444-3001
Alexa Internet PO Box 29141 *Web:* www.alexa.com	San Francisco	CA	94129	415-561-6900	561-6795
Amcom Software Inc 10400 Yellow Cir Dr *TF:* 800-852-8935 ■ *Web:* www.amcomsoft.com	Eden Prairie	MN	55343	952-230-5200	230-5510
Anonymizer Inc 6755 Mira Mesa Blvd *TF:* 888-270-0141 ■ *Web:* www.anonymizer.com	San Diego	CA	92121	858-866-1300	866-0164
Answers Corp 237 W 35th St Suite 1101 *Web:* www.answers.com	New York	NY	10001	646-502-4778	502-4778
AnyDoc Software Inc 1 Tampa City Ctr Suite 800 *TF:* 800-775-3222 ■ *Web:* www.anydocsoftware.com	Tampa	FL	33602	813-222-0414	222-0018
Apex Voice Communications Inc 21031 Ventura Blvd 2nd Fl *TF:* 800-727-3970 ■ *Web:* www.apexvoice.com	Woodland Hills	CA	91364	818-379-8400	379-8410
Ariba Inc 807 11th Ave *NASDAQ: ARBA* ■ *TF:* 888-237-3131 ■ *Web:* www.ariba.com	Sunnyvale	CA	94089	650-390-1000	390-1100
Asure Softwar 110 Wild Basin Rd *NASDAQ: ASUR* ■ *TF:* 888-323-8835 ■ *Web:* www.asuresoftware.com	Austin	TX	78746	512-437-2700	437-2365
AttachmateWRQ 1500 Dexter Ave N *TF Sales:* 800-872-2829 ■ *Web:* www.attachmate.com	Seattle	WA	98109	206-217-7500	217-7515
Authorize.Net Corp PO Box 8999 *TF:* 877-447-3938 ■ *Web:* www.authorize.net	San Francisco	UT	94128	801-492-6450	492-6489
Automation Technology Inc 2001 Gateway Pl Suite 100 *Web:* www.atinet.com	San Jose	CA	95110	408-350-7020	350-7021
Autonomy Inc One Market Plaza Spear Tower Suite 19 *Web:* www.autonomy.com	San Francisco	CA	94105	415-243-9955	243-9984
Avanquest Software USA 1333 W 120th Ave Suite 314 **Fax Area Code:* 303 ■ *Web:* www.avanquest.com	Denver	CO	80234	720-330-1345	450-1154*
Avistar Communications Corp 1875 S Grant St 10th Fl *NASDAQ: AVSR* ■ *TF:* 800-803-0153 ■ *Web:* www.avistar.com	San Mateo	CA	94402	650-525-3300	525-1360
Axeda Systems Inc 25 Forbes Blvd *TF:* 800-700-0362 ■ *Web:* www.axeda.com	Mansville	MA	02035	508-337-9200	337-9201
BackWeb Technologies Inc 2077 Gateway Pl Suite 500 *PINK: BWEB* ■ *TF:* 800-863-0100 ■ *Web:* www.backweb.com	San Jose	CA	95110	408-933-1747	933-1800
Big Sky Technologies 9325 Sky Pk Ct Suite 120 *TF:* 800-736-2751 ■ *Web:* www.bigskytech.com	San Diego	CA	92123	858-715-5000	715-5010
Blast Inc 220 Chatham Business Dr *TF:* 800-242-5278 ■ *Web:* www.blast.com	Pittsboro	NC	27312	919-533-0143	542-5955
Callware Technologies Inc 2755 E Cottonwood Pkwy 4th Fl *TF:* 800-888-4226 ■ *Web:* www.callware.com	Salt Lake City	UT	84121	801-937-6800	937-6820
Century Software 6465 S 3000 E Suite 104 *TF:* 800-877-3088 ■ *Web:* www.censoft.com	Salt Lake City	UT	84121	801-268-3088	268-2772
Certeon Inc 4 Van de Graaff Dr *TF:* 877-221-6688 ■ *Web:* www.certeon.com	Burlington	MA	01803	781-425-5200	425-5210
CertifiedMail.com Inc 35 Airport Rd Suite 120 *TF:* 800-672-7233 ■ *Web:* www.certifiedmail.com	Morristown	NJ	07960	973-455-1245	455-0750
ClickSoftware Inc 35 Corporate Dr Suite 400 *NASDAQ: CKSW* ■ *TF:* 800-438-3308 ■ *Web:* www.clicksoftware.com	Burlington	MA	01803	781-272-5903	272-6409
CommTouch Software Ltd 292 Gibraltar Dr Suite 107 *NASDAQ: CTCH* ■ *TF:* 800-638-6824 ■ *Web:* www.commtouch.com	Sunnyvale	CA	94089	650-864-2000	864-2002
Conquest Systems Inc 7617 Arlington Rd **Fax Area Code:* 301 ■ *TF:* 800-719-8817 ■ *Web:* www.conquestsystems.com	Bethesda	MD	20814	800-719-8817	556-2454*
Continuous Computing Corp 9450 Carroll Pk Dr *Web:* www.ccpu.com	San Diego	CA	92121	858-882-8800	777-3388
Cothern Computer Systems Inc 1640 Lelia Dr Suite 200 *TF:* 800-844-1155 ■ *Web:* www.ccslink.com	Jackson	MS	39216	601-969-1155	969-1184
CyberSource Corp 1295 Charleston Rd PO Box 8999 *TF:* 800-709-7779 ■ *Web:* www.cybersource.com	San Francisco	CA	94128	650-965-6000	625-9145
Cykic Software Inc PO Box 3098 *Web:* www.cykic.com	San Diego	CA	92163	619-459-8799	
DealerTrack Holdings Inc 1111 Marcus Ave Suite M04 *NASDAQ: TRAK* ■ *TF:* 877-357-8725 ■ *Web:* www.dealertrack.com	Lake Success	NY	11042	516-734-3600	
Deerfield.com 4241 Old US 27 S PO Box 851 *TF:* 800-599-8856 ■ *Web:* www.deerfield.com	Gaylord	MI	49735	989-732-8856	731-9299
Digisoft 9 E 40th St *Web:* www.digisoft.com	New York	NY	10016	212-687-1810	687-1781
Digital Insight Corp 26025 Mureau Rd *NASDAQ: DGIN* ■ *TF:* 888-344-4674 ■ *Web:* www.ifs.intuit.com	Calabasas	CA	91302	818-871-0000	878-7555
Dynamic Instruments Inc 3860 Calle Fortunada *TF:* 800-793-3358 ■ *Web:* www.dynamicinst.com	San Diego	CA	92123	858-278-4900	278-6700
eAcceleration Corp 1050 NE Hostmark St Suite 100-B *TF:* 800-811-1485 ■ *Web:* www.eacceleration.com	Poulsbo	WA	98370	360-779-6301	598-2450
Elance Inc 441 Logue Ave Suite 150 *TF:* 877-435-2623 ■ *Web:* www.elance.com	Mountain View	CA	94043	650-316-7500	316-7501
Enterprise Messaging Services 10 Mystic Ln **Fax Area Code:* 484 ■ *TF:* 877-367-5050 ■ *Web:* www.emessages.com	Malvern	PA	19355	610-701-7002	653-1070*
EXTOL International Inc 529 Terry Reiley Way *TF:* 888-334-3986 ■ *Web:* www.extol.com	Pottsville	PA	17901	570-628-5500	628-6983
FutureSoft Inc 1417 Upland Dr *TF:* 800-989-8908 ■ *Web:* www.futuresoft.com	Houston	TX	77043	281-496-9400	496-1090
GeoTrust Inc 350 Ellis St Bldg J *TF:* 866-511-4141 ■ *Web:* www.geotrust.com	Mountain View	CA	94043	650-426-5010	237-8871
Grassroots Enterprise Inc 120 Montgomery St Suite 1970 *Web:* www.grassroots.com	San Francisco	CA	94104	415-633-1100	633-1101
Hilgraeve Inc 115 E Elm Ave *TF Sales:* 800-826-2760 ■ *Web:* www.hilgraeve.com	Monroe	MI	48162	734-243-0576	243-0645
HtmlGear.com 100 5th Ave **Fax:* Hum Res ■ *Web:* www.htmlgear.lycos.com	Waltham	MA	02451	781-370-2700	370-3415*
Hyland Software Inc 28500 Clemens Rd *Web:* www.hyland.com	Westlake	OH	44145	440-788-5000	788-5100
ICQ Inc 22000 AOL Way *TF:* 800-827-6364 ■ *Web:* www.icq.com	Dulles	VA	20166	703-265-1000	
Ikanos Communications 47669 Fremont Blvd *NASDAQ: IKAN* ■ *Web:* www.ikanos.com	Fremont	CA	94538	510-979-0400	979-0500
Imecom Group 8 Governor Wentworth Hwy *TF:* 800-329-9099 ■ *Web:* www.imecominc.com	Wolfeboro	NH	03894	603-569-0600	569-0609
InfoNow Corp 1875 Lawrence St Suite 1100 *Web:* www.infonow.com	Denver	CO	80202	303-293-0212	293-0213
Information Builders Inc 2 Penn Plaza *TF:* 800-969-4636 ■ *Web:* www.informationbuilders.com	New York	NY	10121	212-736-4433	967-6406
IntelliNet Technologies Inc 1990 W New Haven Ave Suite 303 *TF:* 888-726-0686 ■ *Web:* www.intellinet-tech.com	Melbourne	FL	32904	321-726-0686	726-0683
Interact Inc 1225 L St Suite 600 *TF:* 800-242-8649 ■ *Web:* www.iivip.com	Lincoln	NE	68508	402-476-8786	476-7473
Interactive Intelligence Inc 7601 Interactive Way *NASDAQ: ININ* ■ *TF:* 800-267-1364 ■ *Web:* www.inin.com	Indianapolis	IN	46278	317-872-3000	872-3000
InternetSafety.com Inc 3979 S Main St Suite 230 *TF:* 877-944-8080 ■ *Web:* www.internetsafety.com	Acworth	GA	30101	877-944-8080	
Intrinsyc Software International Inc 700 W Pender St 10th Fl *TF:* 800-474-7644 ■ *Web:* www.intrinsyc.com	Vancouver	BC	V6C1G8	604-801-6461	801-6417
Ion Networks Inc 120 Corporate Blvd Suite A *TF:* 800-722-8986 ■ *Web:* www.ion-networks.com	South Plainfield	NJ	07080	908-546-3900	546-3901
Jones Cyber Solutions Ltd 9697 E Mineral Ave *Web:* www.jonescyber.com	Centennial	CO	80112	303-784-3600	784-3797
KANA Software Inc 181 Constitution Dr *Web:* www.kana.com	Menlo Park	CA	94025	650-614-8300	614-8301
Keynote Systems Inc 777 Mariners Island Blvd *NASDAQ: KEYN* ■ *TF:* 888-539-7978 ■ *Web:* www.keynote.com	San Mateo	CA	94404	650-403-2400	403-5500

	City	State	Zip	Phone	Fax
Knexa 1600-409 Granville St *Web:* www.knexa.com	Vancouver	BC	V6C1T2	604-682-2421	682-7576
Language Automation Inc 1670 S Amphlett Blvd Suite 214 *Web:* www.lai.com	San Mateo	CA	94402	650-571-7877	378-8542
LassoSoft LLC PO Box 33 *TF:* 888-286-7753 ■ *Web:* www.lassosoft.com	Manchester	WA	98353	954-302-3526	302-3526
LOGIKA Corp 3717 N Ravenswood Ave Suite 244 *Web:* www.logika.net	Chicago	IL	60613	773-529-3482	529-3483
Mark/Space Softworks 200 S Santa Cruz Ave *TF:* 800-799-1718 ■ *Web:* www.markspace.com	Los Gatos	CA	95030	408-293-7299	293-7298
Metric Stream Inc 2600 E Bayshore Rd *Web:* www.metricstream.com	Palo Alto	CA	94303	650-620-2900	632-1953
Mirror Image Internet Inc 2 Highwood Dr *TF:* 800-353-2923 ■ *Web:* www.mirror-image.com	Tewksbury	MA	01876	781-376-1100	376-1110
Mize Houser & Co 534 S Kansas Ave Suite 700 *Web:* www.mizehouser.com	Topeka	KS	66603	785-233-0536	233-1078
Moai Technologies Inc 100 1st Ave Suite 900 *Web:* www.moai.com	Pittsburgh	PA	15222	412-454-5550	454-5555
MODCOMP Inc 1500 S Powerline Rd *TF:* 800-940-1111 ■ *Web:* www.modcomp.com	Deerfield Beach	FL	33442	954-571-4600	571-4700
Momentum Systems Ltd 41 Twosome Dr Suite 9 *TF:* 800-279-1384 ■ *Web:* www.momsys.com	Moorestown	NJ	08057	856-727-0777	273-3765
NetDIVE Inc 41 Sutter St Suite 1142 **Fax Area Code:* 843 ■ *Web:* www.netdive.com	San Francisco	CA	94104	415-378-8200	216-6843*
Netrics Inc 707 State Rd Suite 212 *Web:* www.netrics.com	Princeton	NJ	08540	609-683-4002	651-4809
NetScout Systems Inc 310 Littleton Rd *NASDAQ: NTCT* ■ *TF:* 800-999-5946 ■ *Web:* www.netscout.com	Westford	MA	01886	978-614-4000	614-4004
NetVillage.com LLC 342 Main St PO Box 1241 *Web:* www.netvillage.com	Laurel	MD	20707	301-498-7797	498-8110
NICE Systems Inc 301 Rt 17 N 10th Fl *TF:* 888-577-6423 ■ *Web:* www.nice.com	Rutherford	NJ	07070	201-964-2600	964-2610
Northcore Technologies Inc 302 E Mall Suite 300 *TF:* 888-287-7467 ■ *Web:* www.northcore.com	Etobicoke	ON	M9B6C7	416-640-0400	640-0412
Norton-Lambert Corp PO Box 4085 *Web:* www.norton-lambert.com	Santa Barbara	CA	93140	805-964-6767	683-5679
Nuance Communications Inc 1 Wayside Rd *NASDAQ: NUAN* ■ *TF:* 800-654-1187 ■ *Web:* www.nuance.com	Burlington	MA	01803	781-565-5000	565-5012
ObjectVideo Inc 11600 Sunrise Valley Dr Suite 290 *Web:* www.objectvideo.com	Reston	VA	20191	703-654-9300	654-9399
OmTool Ltd 6 Riverside Dr *NASDAQ: OMTL* ■ *TF:* 800-886-7845 ■ *Web:* www.omtool.com	Andover	MA	01810	978-327-5700	659-1323
One Touch Systems Inc 2346 Bering Dr *TF:* 800-721-8682 ■ *Web:* www.onetouchsys.com	San Jose	CA	95131	408-436-4600	436-4699
Open Text Corp 275 Frank Tompa Dr *NASDAQ: OTEX* ■ *TF Sales:* 888-450-2547 ■ *Web:* www.opentext.com	Waterloo	ON	N2L0A1	519-888-7111	888-0677
Open Text Corp (USA) 100 Tri-State International Pkwy 3rd Fl *TF Sales:* 800-507-5777 ■ *Web:* www.opentext.com	Lincolnshire	IL	60069	847-267-9330	267-9332
OpenCon Systems Inc 377 Hoes Ln *Web:* www.opencon.com	Piscataway	NJ	08854	732-463-3131	463-3557
OpenConnect Systems Inc 2711 LBJ Fwy Suite 700 *TF:* 800-551-5881 ■ *Web:* www.oc.com	Dallas	TX	75234	972-484-5200	484-6100
OpenTV Corp 275 Sacramento St *TF:* 800-962-5000 ■ *Web:* www.opentv.com	San Francisco	CA	94111	415-962-5000	962-5300
Openwave Systems Inc 2100 Seaport Blvd *NASDAQ: OPWV* ■ *Web:* www.openwave.com	Redwood City	CA	94063	650-480-8000	480-8100
Paloma Systems Inc 11250 Waples Mill Rd *Web:* www.palomasys.com	Fairfax	VA	22030	703-563-2060	591-0985
PCTEL Inc 471 Brighton Dr *NASDAQ: PCTI* ■ *Web:* www.pctel.com	Bloomingdale	IL	60108	630-372-6800	372-8077
Planetweb Inc 300 Twin Dolphin Dr Suite 600 *Web:* www.planetweb.com	Redwood Shores	CA	94065	650-632-4356	632-4328
Powersteering Software Inc 25 First St *TF:* 866-390-9088 ■ *Web:* www.powersteeringsoftware.com	Cambridge	MA	02141	617-492-0707	492-9444
Propel Software Corp 1010 Rincon Cir *Web:* www.propel.com	San Jose	CA	95131	408-571-6300	577-1070
QSA ToolWorks LLC 64 W 48th St Suite 905 **Fax Area Code:* 570 ■ *TF:* 800-784-7018 ■ *Web:* www.qsatoolworks.com	New York	NY	10036	516-935-9151	662-2636*
Quadbase Systems Inc 275 Saratoga Ave Suite 203 *Web:* www.quadbase.com	Santa Clara	CA	95050	408-982-0835	982-0838
Qualcomm Inc 5775 Morehouse Dr *NASDAQ: QCOM* ■ *Web:* www.qualcomm.com	San Diego	CA	92121	858-587-1121	658-2100
Resonate Inc 2883 Junction Ave *TF:* 877-737-6628 ■ *Web:* www.resonate.com	San Jose	CA	95134	408-545-5500	545-5516
RuleSpace LLC 1925 NW AmberGlen Pkwy Suite 210 *TF:* 800-387-8373 ■ *Web:* www.rulespace.com	Beaverton	OR	97006	503-290-5100	290-5200
S4F Inc PO Box 150 *TF:* 888-390-2224 ■ *Web:* centipedenetworks.com	Owasso	OK	74055	918-524-1010	524-1011
Saqqara Systems Inc 3155 Kearney St Suite 220 *Web:* www.saqqara.com	Fremont	CA	94538	510-360-5361	413-0079
Selectica Inc 1740 Technology Dr Suite 450 *NASDAQ: SLTC* ■ *TF:* 877-712-9560 ■ *Web:* www.selectica.com	San Jose	CA	95110	408-570-9700	570-9705
Sendmail Inc 6475 Christie Ave Suite 350 *TF:* 888-594-3150 ■ *Web:* www.sendmail.com	Emeryville	CA	94608	510-594-5400	594-5429
Smith Micro Software Inc 51 Columbia St Suite 200 *NASDAQ: SMSI* ■ *TF:* 800-964-7674 ■ *Web:* www.smithmicro.com	Aliso Viejo	CA	92656	949-362-5800	362-2300
Software 602 Inc 500 Oceola Ave *TF:* 888-468-6602 ■ *Web:* www.software602.com	Jacksonville Beach	FL	32250	904-642-5400	565-6024
Soliton Inc 44 Victoria St Suite 820 *TF:* 888-327-9457 ■ *Web:* www.soliton.com	Toronto	ON	M5C1Y2	416-364-9355	364-6159
Sterling Commerce 900 Chelmsford St *TF:* 888-292-6872 ■ *Web:* www.sterlingcommerce.com	Lowell	MA	01851	978-513-6000	513-6006
SupportSoft Inc 1900 Seaport Blvd 3rd Fl *NASDAQ: SPRT* ■ *TF:* 877-493-2778 ■ *Web:* www.support.com	Redwood City	CA	94063	650-556-9440	556-1195
Surety LLC 12020 Sunrise Valley Dr Suite 250 *TF:* 800-298-3115 ■ *Web:* www.surety.com	Reston	VA	20191	571-748-5800	748-5810
Sybase Inc 1 Sybase Dr *TF:* 800-792-2735 ■ *Web:* www.sybase.com	Dublin	CA	94568	925-236-5000	236-4321
Symantec Corp 350 Ellis St *NASDAQ: SYMC* ■ *TF:* 800-441-7234 ■ *Web:* www.symantec.com	Mountain View	CA	94043	650-527-8000	527-8050
Symphony SMS 14881 Quorum Dr Suite 800 *Web:* www.symphonysms.com	Dallas	TX	75254	972-581-7300	581-7301
SyVox 1850 I-30 *TF Cust Svc:* 866-436-3782 ■ *Web:* www.genesta.com	Rockwall	TX	75087	972-771-1653	722-1179
Teknowledge Corp 1800 Embarcadero Rd *TF:* 800-285-0500	Palo Alto	CA	94303	650-424-0500	493-2645
Telenity Inc 755 Main St Suite 7 *Web:* www.telenity.com	Monroe	CT	06468	203-445-2000	268-1860
Tenebril Inc 959 Concord St *TF:* 800-722-7770 ■ *Web:* www.tenebril.com	Framingham	MA	01701	508-879-6994	879-0042
Timecruiser Computing Corp 9 Law Dr 2rd Fl *TF:* 877-450-9482 ■ *Web:* www.campuscruiser.com	Fairfield	NJ	07004	973-244-7856	244-7859
Transend Corp 225 Emerson St *Web:* www.transend.com	Palo Alto	CA	94301	650-324-5370	324-5377
UmeVoice Inc 20C Pimentel Ct Suite 1 *TF:* 888-230-3300 ■ *Web:* www.umevoice.com	Novato	CA	94949	415-883-1500	883-1711
UNET 80 E 11th St *Web:* www.unet.net	New York	NY	10003	212-777-5463	777-5534
Unify Corp 1420 Rocky Ridge Dr Suite 380 *TF:* 800-248-6439 ■ *Web:* www.unify.com	Roseville	CA	95661	916-218-4700	218-4378
Vendio Services Inc 2800 Campus Dr Suite 150 *Web:* www.vendio.com	San Mateo	CA	94403	650-293-3500	
Verint Systems Inc 9 Polito Ave 9th Fl *TF:* 888-637-2661 ■ *Web:* www.verint.com	Lyndhurst	NJ	07071	201-507-8800	507-5554
Vertical Communications Inc 3940 Freedom Cr 10th Fl *PINK: VRCC* ■ *TF Sales:* 800-914-9985 ■ *Web:* www.vertical.com	Santa Clara	CA	95054	408-404-1600	969-9601
VillageEDOCS Inc 1401 N Tustin Ave Suite 230 *TF:* 800-866-0883 ■ *Web:* www.villageedocs.com	Santa Ana	CA	92705	714-734-1030	734-1040
Visto Corp 101 Redwood Shores Pkwy Suite 400 *Web:* www.visto.com	Redwood Shores	CA	94065	650-486-6000	622-9590
VMware Inc 3401 Hillview Ave *NYSE: VMW* ■ *TF:* 877-486-9273 ■ *Web:* www.vmware.com	Palo Alto	CA	94304	650-427-5000	427-5001
Voice Information Systems Inc 2118 Wilshire Blvd *TF:* 800-234-3948 ■ *Web:* www.voiceinfo.com	Santa Monica	CA	90403	310-392-8780	392-5511
Vovici Corp 45365 Vintage Pk Plaza Suite 250 **Fax Area Code:* 703 ■ *TF:* 800-787-8755 ■ *Web:* www.vovici.com	Dulles	VA	20166	571-521-0592	783-0069*
Voxware Inc 300 American Metro Blvd Suite 155 *Web:* www.voxware.com	hamilton	NJ	08619	609-514-4100	514-4101
Wave Three Software Inc 1770 N Research Pkwy Suite 140 *TF:* 888-408-8422	Logan	UT	84341	435-787-0555	787-0516
WaveLink Corp 1011 Western Ave Suite 601 *TF Tech Supp:* 888-699-9283 ■ *Web:* www.wavelink.com	Seattle	WA	98104	206-274-4280	652-2329
WebBalanced Technologies LLC 6206 Discount Dr *TF:* 866-331-3465	Fort Wayne	IN	46818	866-331-3465	
Websense Inc 10240 Sorrento Valley Rd *NASDAQ: WBSN* ■ *TF:* 800-723-1166 ■ *Web:* www.websense.com	San Diego	CA	92121	858-320-8000	458-2950
Wexcel Inc 222 S Riverside Plaza	Chicago	IL	60606	312-347-0955	347-0908
WildBlue Communications Inc 349 Inverness Dr S *Web:* www.wildblue.com	Englewood	CO	80112	720-554-7400	554-7500
WorldFlash Software Inc 3853 Marcasel Ave *Web:* www.worldflash.com	Los Angeles	CA	90066	310-775-3633	
XAP Corp 3534 Hayden Ave *Web:* www.xap.com	Culver City	CA	90232	310-842-9800	842-9898
YellowBrix Inc 500 Montgomery St # 700 *TF:* 888-325-9366 ■ *Web:* www.yellowbrix.com	Alexandria	VA	22314	703-548-3300	548-9151
Yodlee Inc 3600 Bridge Pkwy Suite 200 *Web:* www.corporate.yodlee.com	Redwood City	CA	94065	650-980-3600	980-3602
Zone Alarm 800 Bridge Pkwy *TF:* 877-966-5221 ■ *Web:* www.zonealarm.com	Redwood City	CA	94065	415-633-4500	633-4501

181-8 Multimedia & Design Software

	City	State	Zip	Phone	Fax
3D Systems Inc 333 Three D Systems Cir *NASDAQ: TDSC* ■ *TF:* 800-653-1993 ■ *Web:* www.3dsystems.com	Rock Hill	SC	29730	803-326-3900	324-4311
ACD Systems International Inc 200-1312 Blanshard St *TSX: ASA* ■ *TF:* 800-579-5309 ■ *Web:* www.acdsee.com	Victoria	BC	V8W2J1	250-419-6700	419-6745
Adobe Systems Inc 345 Pk Ave *NASDAQ: ADBE* ■ *TF:* 800-833-6687 ■ *Web:* www.adobe.com	San Jose	CA	95110	408-536-6000	537-6000
Apple Inc 1 Infinite Loop *NASDAQ: AAPL* ■ **Fax:* Mail Rm ■ *TF Cust Svc:* 800-275-2273 ■ *Web:* www.apple.com	Cupertino	CA	95014	408-996-1010	996-0275*
Arts & Letters Corp 2201 Midway Rd Suite 106 *TF:* 888-853-9292 ■ *Web:* www.arts-letters.com	Carolton	TX	75006	972-661-8960	934-2333
Auto FX Software 141 Village St Suite 2 *TF:* 800-839-2008 ■ *Web:* www.autofx.com	Birmingham	AL	35242	205-980-0056	980-1121
Autodesk 210 King St E *Web:* usa.autodesk.com	Toronto	ON	M5A1J7	416-362-9181	369-6140
Autodessys Inc 2011 Riverside Dr *Web:* www.formz.com	Columbus	OH	43221	614-488-8838	488-0848
Autonomy Virage 1 Market St Spear Tower **Fax Area Code:* 650 ■ *Web:* www.virage.com	San Francisco	CA	94105	415-243-9955	243-9984*

Company / Address	City	State	ZIP	Phone	Fax
Avid Technology Inc 1 Pk W Metropolitan Technology Pk *NASDAQ: AVID* ■ *TF:* 800-949-2843 ■ *Web:* www.avid.com	Tewksbury	MA	01876	978-640-6789	640-3366
Bitstream Inc 500 Nickerson Rd *NASDAQ: BITS* ■ *TF:* 800-522-3668 ■ *Web:* www.bitstream.com	Marlborough	MA	01752	617-497-6222	868-0784
Blue Zone Inc 329 Railway St 4th Fl	Vancouver	BC	V6A1A4	604-685-4310	685-4391
Brilliant Digital Entertainment Inc 14011 Ventura Blvd Suite 501 *Web:* www.brilliantdigital.com	Sherman Oaks	CA	91423	818-386-2180	615-0995
Caligari Corp 1959 Landings Dr *TF:* 800-351-7620 ■ *Web:* www.caligari.com	Mountain View	CA	94043	650-390-9600	390-9755
Chyron Corp 5 Hub Dr **Fax:* Sales ■ *Web:* www.chyron.com	Melville	NY	11747	631-845-2000	845-3895*
Concurrent 4375 River Green Pkwy Suite 100 *NASDAQ: CCUR* ■ *TF:* 877-978-7363 ■ *Web:* www.ccur.com	Duluth	GA	30096	678-258-4000	258-4300
Corel Corp 1600 Carling Ave *TF Orders:* 800-772-6735 ■ *Web:* www.corel.ca	Ottawa	ON	K1Z8R7	613-728-8200	761-9176
Dassault Systèmes 166 Valley St *Web:* www.simulia.com	Providence	RI	02909	401-276-4400	276-4408
DeLorme 2 DeLorme Dr PO Box 298 **Fax Area Code:* 800 ■ *TF Sales:* 800-452-5931 ■ *Web:* www.delorme.com	Yarmouth	ME	04096	207-846-7000	561-5105*
EI Technology Group LLC 10860 Gulfdale *Web:* www.eitechnologygroup.com	San Antonio	TX	78216	210-377-2525	579-6668
Enliven Marketing Technologies Corp 498 7th Ave Suite 1810 *TF:* 866-843-9764 ■ *Web:* www.viewpoint.com	New York	NY	10018	212-201-0800	201-0801
Equilibrium Inc 3 Harbor Dr *Web:* www.equilibrium.com	Sausalito	CA	94965	415-332-4343	331-8374
eWorkplace Solutions Inc 24461 Ridge Rt Dr Suite 210 *TF:* 866-235-3492 ■ *Web:* www.eworkplace.com	Laguna Hills	CA	92653	949-583-1646	271-4620
Fonthead Design Inc 3210 Lansdowne Dr **Fax Area Code:* 866 ■ *Web:* www.fonthead.com	Wilmington	DE	19810	302-479-7922	806-1006*
Global 360 5400 LBJ Fwy #300 *Web:* www.global360.com	Dallas	TX	75219	214-520-1660	219-0476
HydroCAD Software Solutions LLC 216 Chocorua Mountain Hwy *TF:* 800-927-7246 ■ *Web:* www.hydrocad.net	Chocorua	NH	03817	603-323-8666	323-7467
Image Labs International PO Box 1545 *TF:* 800-785-5995 ■ *Web:* www.imagelabs.com	Belgrade	MT	59714	406-585-7225	388-0998
Innovatv 12730 High Bluff Dr Suite 120	San Diego	CA	92130	858-259-4120	259-4104
International Microcomputer Software Inc 25 Leveroni Ct *TF:* 800-833-8082 ■ *Web:* www.imsidesign.com	Novato	CA	94949	415-483-8000	884-9023
Kofax PLC 15211 Laguna Canyon Rd *Web:* www.kofax.com	Irvine	CA	92618	949-783-1000	727-3144
La Cie Ltd 22985 NW Evergreen Pkwy **Fax:* Mktg ■ *Web:* www.lacie.com	Hillsboro	OR	97124	503-844-4500	844-4508*
Liquid Digital Media Inc 999 Main St *TF:* 800-222-8132 ■ *Web:* www.liquiddigitalmedia.com	Redwood City	CA	94063	650-549-2000	549-2001
Media 100 Inc 260 Cedar Hill St **Fax Area Code:* 508 ■ *TF:* 800-922-3220 ■ *Web:* www.media100.com	Marlborough	MA	01752	703-462-1640	481-8627*
MicroVision Development Inc 5541 Fermi Ct Suite 120 *TF:* 800-998-4555 ■ *Web:* www.mvd.com	Carlsbad	CA	92008	760-438-7781	438-7406
Minds-Eye-View Inc 103 Remsen St Suite 201 *NASDAQ: IPIX* ■ *Web:* www.ipix.com	Cohoes	NY	12047	518-237-1975	
Mitek Systems Inc 8911 Balboa Ave Suite B *Web:* www.miteksys.com	San Diego	CA	92123	858-503-7810	503-7820
Monotype Imaging Inc 500 Unicorn Pk Dr *Web:* www.monotypeimaging.com	Woburn	MA	01801	781-970-6000	970-6001
Nemetschek North America 7150 Riverwood Dr *TF:* 888-646-4223 ■ *Web:* www.nemetschek.net	Columbia	MD	21046	410-290-5114	290-8050
NewTek Inc 5131 Beckwith Blvd *TF Cust Svc:* 800-862-7837 ■ *Web:* www.newtek.com	San Antonio	TX	78249	210-370-8000	370-8001
Octopus Media LLC 412 8th Ave *Web:* www.hypercd.com	New York	NY	10001	212-967-5191	967-5199
Onyx Computing 10 Avon St *Web:* www.onyxtree.com	Cambridge	MA	02138	617-876-3876	868-8033
Overwatch Geospatial Operations 21660 Ridgetop Cir Suite 110 *Web:* www.overwatch.com	Sterling	VA	20166	703-437-7651	437-0039
PaceWorks Inc 16780 Lark Ave *Web:* www.paceworks.com	Los Gatos	CA	95032	408-354-5711	884-2281
Patton & Patton Software Corp 1796 W Wimbledon Way *TF:* 800-525-0082 ■ *Web:* www.patton-patton.com	Tucson	AZ	85737	520-638-8738	888-2937
PC/Nametag 124 Horizon Dr PO Box 8604 **Fax Area Code:* 800 ■ *TF:* 800-369-8622 ■ *Web:* www.pcnametag.com	Verona	WI	53593	877-626-3824	233-9787*
Peerless Systems Corp 300 Atlantic St Suite 301 *NASDAQ: PRLS* ■ *Web:* www.peerless.com	Stamford	CT	06901	203-350-0040	
Prediction Systems Inc 309 Morris Ave Suite G *Web:* www.predictsys.com	Spring Lake	NJ	07762	732-449-6800	449-0897
Presagis 1301 W George Bush Fwy Suite 120 **Fax Area Code:* 469 ■ *TF:* 800-361-6424 ■ *Web:* www.presagis.com	Richardson	TX	75080	972-943-2400	467-4564*
Quark Inc 1800 Grant St *TF Cust Svc:* 800-676-4575 ■ *Web:* www.quark.com	Denver	CO	80203	303-894-8888	894-3399
RealNetworks Inc 2601 Elliott Ave Suite 1000 *NASDAQ: RNWK* ■ *TF Cust Svc:* 888-768-3248 ■ *Web:* www.realnetworks.com	Seattle	WA	98121	206-674-2700	674-2699
Scan-Optics Inc 169 Progress Dr *TF:* 800-543-8681 ■ *Web:* www.scanoptics.com	Manchester	CT	06043	860-645-7878	645-7995
Sigma Design 5521 Jackson St *TF Sales:* 888-990-0900 ■ *Web:* www.arriscad.com	Alexandria	LA	71303	318-449-9900	449-9901
Silicon Graphics Inc (SGI) 1140 E Argues Ave *Web:* www.sgi.com	Sunnyvale	CA	94085	650-960-1980	933-0908
SoftPress Systems Inc 3020 Bridgeway Suite 408 *TF:* 800-853-6454 ■ *Web:* www.softpress.com	Sausalito	CA	94965	415-331-4820	331-4824
Spatial Corp 310 Interlocken Pkwy Suite 200 *Web:* www.spatial.com	Broomfield	CO	80021	303-544-2900	544-3000
TechSmith Corp 2405 Woodlake Dr *TF:* 800-517-3001 ■ *Web:* www.techsmith.com	Okemos	MI	48864	517-381-2300	381-2336
Telestream Inc 848 Gold Flat Rd Suite 1 *Web:* www.telestream.net	Nevada City	CA	95959	530-470-1300	470-1301
think3 Inc 7723 Tylers Pl Blvd Suite 106 **Fax Area Code:* 513 ■ *TF:* 800-323-6770 ■ *Web:* www.think3.com	West Chester	OH	45069	800-323-6770	263-6777*
Three D Graphics Inc 11340 W Olympic Blvd Suite 352 *TF:* 800-913-0008 ■ *Web:* www.threedgraphics.com	Los Angeles	CA	90064	310-231-3330	231-3303
Videotex Systems Inc 10255 Miller Rd *TF:* 800-888-4336 ■ *Web:* www.videotexsystems.com	Dallas	TX	75238	972-231-9200	231-2420
Worlds.com Inc 11 Royal Rd *Web:* www.worlds.com	Brookline	MA	02445	617-725-8900	975-3888
Xaos Tools Inc 582 San Luis Rd	Berkeley	CA	94707	510-525-5465	

181-9 Personal Software

Company / Address	City	State	ZIP	Phone	Fax
Actioneer Inc 56 John F Kennedy St 3rd Fl *Web:* www.actioneer.com	Cambridge	MA	02138	617-864-1400	864-1401
APEX Analytix Inc 1501 Highwoods Blvd Suite 200-A **Fax:* Hum Res ■ *TF:* 866-577-8183 ■ *Web:* www.apexanalytix.com	Greensboro	NC	27410	336-422-7371	387-1775*
Approva Corp 13454 Sunrise Valley Dr Suite 500 *Web:* www.approva.net	Herndon	VA	20171	703-956-8300	956-8350
Avery Dennison Corp 150 N Orange Grove Blvd *NYSE: AVY* ■ *TF Cust Svc:* 800-252-8379 ■ *Web:* www.averydennison.com	Pasadena	CA	91103	626-304-2000	304-2192
Block Financial Corp 10 Fawcett St 1st Fl *Web:* www.blocksoft.com	Cambridge	MA	02138	617-491-1800	491-9981
Corel Corp 1600 Carling Ave *TF Orders:* 800-772-6735 ■ *Web:* www.corel.ca	Ottawa	ON	K1Z8R7	613-728-8200	761-9176
Equis International 90 S 400 W Suite 620 *TF Sales:* 800-882-3040 ■ *Web:* www.equis.com	Salt Lake City	UT	84101	801-265-9996	265-3999
HowardSoft 7852 Ivanhoe Ave **Fax Area Code:* 800 ■ *Web:* www.howardsoft.com	La Jolla	CA	92037	858-454-0121	248-2937*
Intuit Inc 2632 Marine Way *NASDAQ: INTU* ■ **Fax:* Hum Res ■ *TF Cust Svc:* 800-446-8848 ■ *Web:* www.intuit.com	Mountain View	CA	94043	650-944-6000	944-2788*
Logos Bible Software 1313 Commercial St *Web:* www.logos.com	Bellingham	WA	98225	360-527-1700	527-1701
Micro Logic Corp 666 Godwin Ave *Web:* www.miclog.com	Midland Park	NJ	07432	201-447-6991	447-6921
Microsoft Corp 1 Microsoft Way *NASDAQ: MSFT* ■ *Web:* www.microsoft.com	Redmond	WA	98052	425-882-8080	936-7329
MOTU Inc 1280 Massachusetts Ave *Web:* www.motu.com	Cambridge	MA	02138	617-576-2760	576-3609
Musicam USA 670 N Beers St Bldg 4 *Web:* www.musicamusa.com	Holmdel	NJ	07733	732-739-5600	739-1818
Nolo.com 950 Parker St *TF:* 800-728-3555 ■ *Web:* www.nolo.com	Berkeley	CA	94710	800-728-3555	645-0895
Radialpoint 2050 Bleury St Suite 300 *TF:* 866-286-2636 ■ *Web:* www.radialpoint.com	Montreal	QC	H3A2J5	514-286-2636	286-0558
Smyth Systems Inc 101 Greenwood Ave **Fax Area Code:* 215 ■ *TF:* 800-767-6984 ■ *Web:* www.smythsystems.com	Jenkintown	PA	19046	800-767-6984	887-9871*
Sony Creative Software 1617 Sherman Ave *TF:* 800-577-6642 ■ *Web:* www.sonycreativesoftware.com	Madison	WI	53704	608-256-3133	250-1745
Stevens Creek Software PO Box 2126 *TF:* 800-823-4279 ■ *Web:* www.stevenscreek.com	Cupertino	CA	95015	408-725-0424	366-1954
Symantec Corp 350 Ellis St *NASDAQ: SYMC* ■ *TF:* 800-441-7234 ■ *Web:* www.symantec.com	Mountain View	CA	94043	650-527-8000	527-8050

181-10 Professional Software (Industry-Specific)

Companies Listed Here Manufacture Software Designed For Specific Professions Or Business Sectors (I.E., Architecture, Banking, Investment, Physical Sciences, Real Estate, Etc.).

Company / Address	City	State	ZIP	Phone	Fax
a4 Health Systems 5501 Dillard Dr	Cary	NC	27511	919-851-6177	851-5991
Access International Group Inc 248 Columbia Tpk *Web:* www.accessig.com	Florham Park	NJ	07932	973-360-0750	360-0710
ACI Worldwide Inc 6060 Coventry Dr *NASDAQ: ACIW* ■ *Web:* www.tsainc.com	Elkhorn	NE	68022	402-390-7600	
Adacel Technologies Ltd 5945 Hazeltine National Dr *Web:* www.adacelinc.com	Orlando	FL	32822	407-581-1560	581-1581
AGRIS Corp 1600 N Lorraine St *TF:* 800-795-7995 ■ *Web:* www.agris.com	Hutchinson	KS	67501	620-669-9811	694-4450
Algorithmics Inc 185 Spadina Ave *Web:* www.algorithmics.com	Toronto	ON	M5T2C6	416-217-1500	971-6100
Allot Communications 300 Tradecenter Suite 4680 *TF:* 877-255-6826 ■ *Web:* www.allot.com	Woburn	MA	01801	781-939-9300	939-9393
Allscripts Healthcare Solutions 222 Merchandise Mart Plaza Suite 2024 *NASDAQ: MDRX* ■ *TF:* 800-654-0889 ■ *Web:* www.allscripts.com	Chicago	IL	60654	800-654-0889	
Alogent Corp 4005 Windward Plaza 2nd Fl *TF:* 888-333-6030 ■ *Web:* www.alogent.com	Alpharetta	GA	30005	770-752-6400	752-6500
Alternative System Concepts Inc 22 Haverhill Rd PO Box 128 *Web:* www.ascinc.com	Windham	NH	03087	603-437-2234	437-2722
Amdocs Ltd 1390 Timberlake Manor Pkwy *NYSE: DOX* ■ *TF:* 866-426-8003 ■ *Web:* www.amdocs.com	Chesterfield	MO	63017	314-212-7000	212-7500
AMS Services Inc 3 Waterside Crossing **Fax:* PR ■ *TF Sales:* 800-444-4813 ■ *Web:* www.vertafore.com	Windsor	CT	06095	860-602-6000	602-6006*
Anchor Computer Inc 1900 New Hwy *TF:* 800-728-6262 ■ *Web:* www.anchorcomputer.com	Farmingdale	NY	11735	631-293-6100	293-0891

Phone | Fax

Applied Information Management Sciences Inc
235 Desiard . . . Monroe LA 71201 318-323-2467 322-3472
TF: 800-729-2467 ■ *Web:* www.aims1.com

ARI Network Services Inc
10850 W Pk Pl Suite 1200 . . . Milwaukee WI 53224 414-973-4300 283-4357
TF: 800-233-6997 ■ *Web:* www.arinet.com

ASI DataMyte Inc 2800 Campus Dr Suite 60 . . . Plymouth MN 55441 763-553-1040 553-1041
TF: 800-207-5631 ■ *Web:* www.asidatamyte.com

Aspyra Inc 4360 Pk Terr Dr Suite 100 . . . Westlake Village CA 91361 818-880-6700 880-4398
PINK: APY ■ *TF:* 800-437-9000 ■ *Web:* www.aspyra.com

Avantus 15 W Strong St Suite 20A . . . Pensacola FL 32501 850-470-9336 600-2508*
**Fax Area Code:* 800 ■ *TF:* 800-600-2510 ■ *Web:* www.advantagecredit.com

Avaya Government Solutions Inc
12730 Fair Lakes Cir . . . Fairfax VA 22033 703-653-8000 653-8001
TF: 800-492-6769 ■ *Web:* www.avayagov.com

BatchMaster Software Inc
24461 Ridge Rt Dr Suite 210 . . . Laguna Hills CA 92653 949-583-1646 271-4620
TF: 866-235-3492 ■ *Web:* www.batchmaster.com

Baxter Planning Systems Inc
7801 N Capital of Texas Hwy Suite 250 . . . Austin TX 78731 512-323-5959 323-5354
Web: www.bybaxter.com

Bbn Technologies 10 Moulton St . . . Cambridge MA 02138 617-873-8000 873-4463
Web: www.bbn.com

BenefitMall Inc 4851 LBJ Fwy Suite 1100 . . . Dallas TX 75244 469-791-3300 791-3313
TF: 888-338-6293 ■ *Web:* www.benefitmall.com

Brodart Co 500 Arch St . . . Williamsport PA 17701 570-326-2461 326-6769
TF: 800-233-8467 ■ *Web:* www.brodart.com

C & S Marketing
10360 Old Placerville Rd Suite 100 . . . Sacramento CA 95827 916-438-3160 455-3851
TF: 888-288-2009

C-Solutions Inc 1900 Folsom St Suite 205 . . . Boulder CO 80302 303-786-9461 786-9469
Web: www.gmsworks.com

CACI MTL Systems Inc 3481 Dayton-Xenia Rd . . . Dayton OH 45432 937-426-3111 426-8301
Web: www.caci.com

CAM Commerce Solutions Inc
17075 Newhope St Suite A . . . Fountain Valley CA 92708 714-241-9241 241-9893
TF: 800-726-3282 ■ *Web:* www.camcommerce.com

Capital Management Sciences
2901 28th St Suite 300 . . . Santa Monica CA 90405 310-479-9715 479-6333
Web: www.interactivedata.com

Capital Technology Information Services Inc
1 Research Ct Suite 200 . . . Rockville MD 20850 301-948-3033 948-2242
Web: www.ctisinc.com

CareCentric Inc 2839 Paces Ferry Rd SE # 900 . . . Atlanta GA 30339 678-264-4400 384-1650*
**Fax Area Code:* 770 ■ *TF:* 800-254-9872 ■ *Web:* www.carecentric.com

Carousel Industries of North America Inc
659 S County Trail . . . Exeter RI 02822 401-284-1925 284-1984
TF: 800-401-0760 ■ *Web:* www.carouselindustries.com

Cash Technologies Inc 1434 W 11th St . . . Los Angeles CA 90015 213-745-2000 745-2005
AMEX: TQ ■ *Web:* www.cashtechnologies.com

Catalyst International Inc
8989 N Deerwood Dr . . . Milwaukee WI 53223 414-362-6800 377-6263*
**Fax Area Code:* 262 ■ *TF:* 800-236-4600 ■ *Web:* www.catalystwms.com

Cedara Software Corp
6509 Airport Rd Suite 500 . . . Mississauga ON L4V1R8 905-364-8000 364-8100
TF: 800-724-5970 ■ *Web:* www.merge.com

Cerner DHT Inc 2800 Rockcreek Pkwy . . . Kansas City MO 64117 816-221-1024 474-1742
Web: www.cerner.com

Charles River Development Inc
7 New England Executive Pk . . . Burlington MA 01803 781-238-0099 238-0088
Web: www.crd.com

Circa Information Technologies Inc
12001 Woodruff Ave Suite H . . . Downey CA 90241 562-803-1594 803-5898
TF: 877-992-4722 ■ *Web:* www.circausa.com

CliniComp International 9655 Towne Ctr Dr . . . San Diego CA 92121 858-546-8202 546-1801
TF: 800-350-8202 ■ *Web:* www.clinicomp.com

Cobalt Group Inc 2200 1st Ave S Suite 400 . . . Seattle WA 98134 206-269-6363 269-6350
TF: 800-909-8244 ■ *Web:* www.cobaltgroup.com

CodeCorrect Inc 1200 Chesterly Dr Suite 260 . . . Yakima WA 98902 509-453-0400
TF: 877-937-3600 ■ *Web:* www.codecorrect.com

Command Alkon Inc
1800 International Pk Dr Suite 400 . . . Birmingham AL 35243 205-879-3282 870-1405
TF: 800-624-1872 ■ *Web:* www.commandalkon.com

Commerx Corp 555 11th Ave SW Suite 200 . . . Calgary AB T2R1P6 403-301-3883 294-1664
TF: 877-301-3883 ■ *Web:* www.commerx.com

Community Computer Service Inc PO Box 980 . . . Auburn NY 13021 315-255-1751 255-3539
Web: www.medent.com

Compumedics USA Ltd 7850 Paseo del Norte . . . El Paso TX 79912 915-845-5600 845-2965
TF: 877-717-3975 ■ *Web:* www.compumedics.com

Computac Inc 162 N Main St . . . West Lebanon NH 03784 603-298-5721 298-6189
Web: www.computac.com

Computers Unlimited 2407 Montana Ave . . . Billings MT 59101 406-255-9500 255-9595
Web: www.cu.net

Construction Software Technologies Inc
4430 Carver Woods Dr . . . Cincinnati OH 45242 513-645-8004 645-8005
Web: www.isqft.com

Construction Systems Software Inc
494 Covered Bridge . . . Schertz TX 78154 210-979-6494 979-0007
TF: 800-979-6494

Continental Computer Corp
2200 E Matthews Ave . . . Jonesboro AR 72401 870-932-0081 931-1273
TF: 800-874-1413 ■ *Web:* www.continentalcomputers.com

CoStar Group Inc
2 Bethesda Metro Ctr 10th Fl . . . Bethesda MD 20814 301-215-8300 218-2444
NASDAQ: CSGP ■ *TF:* 800-613-1303 ■ *Web:* www.costar.com

CryptoLogic Inc 55 St Claire Ave W 3rd Fl . . . Toronto ON M4V2Y7 416-545-1455 545-1454
NASDAQ: CRYP ■ *Web:* www.cryptologic.com

CSG Systems International Inc
9555 Maroon Cir . . . Englewood CO 80112 303-200-2000 804-4088
NASDAQ: CSGS ■ *TF:* 800-366-2744 ■ *Web:* www.csgsystems.com

CSSC Inc 130 Campus Dr . . . Edison NJ 08837 732-225-5555 417-0482
Web: www.csscinc.com

DataCert Inc 3040 Post Oak Blvd # 1900 . . . Houston TX 77056 713-572-3282 572-3286
TF: 800-770-5121 ■ *Web:* www.datacert.com

Phone | Fax

Datatel Inc 4375 Fair Lakes Ct . . . Fairfax VA 22033 703-968-9000 968-4625
TF: 800-328-2835 ■ *Web:* www.datatel.com

DataTRAK International Inc
6150 Parkland Blvd Suite 100 . . . Mayfield Heights OH 44124 440-443-0082 442-3482
NASDAQ: DATA ■ *TF Sales:* 888-677-3282 ■ *Web:* www.datatrak.net

DealerTrack Holdings Inc
1111 Marcus Ave Suite M04 . . . Lake Success NY 11042 516-734-3600
NASDAQ: TRAK ■ *TF:* 877-357-8725 ■ *Web:* www.dealertrack.com

Deltagen Inc 1900 S Norfolk St Suite 105 . . . San Mateo CA 94403 650-345-7602
Web: www.deltagen.com

Demand Management Inc
165 N Meramec Ave Suite 300 . . . Saint Louis MO 63105 314-727-4448 727-4782

Digineer 600 S Hwy 169 Suite 1640 . . . Saint Louis Park MN 55426 763-544-3400 544-3402
Web: www.digineer.com

Digital Harbor Inc 1851 A Bell Dr Suite 200 . . . Reston VA 20191 703-476-7339
Web: www.digitalharbor.com

Digital Technology International
1180 Mountain Springs Pkwy S . . . Springville UT 84663 801-853-5000 853-5001
Web: www.dtint.com

DIS Corp 1315 Cornwall Ave . . . Bellingham WA 98225 360-733-7610 647-6921
TF Cust Svc: 800-426-8870 ■ *Web:* www.dis-corp.com

Document Security Systems Inc
28 E Main St Suite 1525 . . . Rochester NY 14614 585-325-3610 325-2977
AMEX: DMC ■ *TF:* 877-276-0293 ■ *Web:* www.documentsecurity.com

DynTek Inc 4440 Von Karman Suite 200 . . . Newport Beach CA 92660 949-271-6700 271-0801
Web: www.dyntek.com

Eagle Point Software Corp 4131 Westmark Dr . . . Dubuque IA 52002 563-556-8392 556-5321
TF: 800-678-6565 ■ *Web:* www.eaglepoint.com

Emerging Information Systems Inc (EISI)
330 St Mary Ave Suite 500 . . . Winnipeg MB R3C3Z5 204-943-3474 942-5100
TF: 888-692-3474 ■ *Web:* www.naviplan.com

Emptoris Rivermine Inc
3975 Fair Ridge Dr Suite 350 S . . . Fairfax VA 22033 703-995-6000 995-6060
Web: www.rivermine.com

Enghouse Systems Ltd 80 Tiverton Ct Suite 800 . . . Markham ON L3R0G4 905-946-3200 946-3201
TF: 866-772-8425 ■ *Web:* www.enghouse.com

Environmental Systems Research Institute Inc
380 New York St . . . Redlands CA 92373 909-793-2853 793-5953
TF Sales: 800-447-9778 ■ *Web:* www.esri.com

Envision Telephony Inc 520 Pike St Suite 1600 . . . Seattle WA 98101 206-225-0800 225-0801
Web: www.envisioninc.com

EPIQ Systems Inc 501 Kansas Ave . . . Kansas City KS 66105 913-621-9500 321-1243
NASDAQ: EPIQ ■ *Web:* www.epiqsystems.com

Equis International
90 S 400 W Suite 620 . . . Salt Lake City UT 84101 801-265-9996 265-3999
TF Sales: 800-882-3040 ■ *Web:* www.equis.com

eResearch Technology Inc 30 S 17th St . . . Philadelphia PA 19103 215-972-0420 972-0414
NASDAQ: ERES ■ *TF:* 800-704-9698 ■ *Web:* www.ert.com

Experior Corp 5710 Coventry Ln . . . Fort Wayne IN 46804 260-432-2020 432-4753
Web: www.experior.com

Final Draft Inc 26707 W Agoura Rd Suite 205 . . . Calabasas CA 91302 818-995-8995 995-4422
TF: 800-231-4055 ■ *Web:* www.finaldraft.com

Financial Engines Inc 1804 Embarcadero Rd . . . Palo Alto CA 94303 650-565-4900 565-4905
TF: 888-443-8577 ■ *Web:* www.corp.financialengines.com

First DataBank Inc
1111 Bayhill Dr Suite 350 . . . San Bruno CA 94066 650-588-5454 588-4003
TF: 800-633-3453 ■ *Web:* www.firstdatabank.com

Follett Software Co 1391 Corporate Dr . . . McHenry IL 60050 815-344-8700 344-8774
TF: 800-323-3397 ■ *Web:* www.follettsoftware.com

Fxcm Inc 32 Old Slip . . . New York NY 10005 212-897-7660 229-0004*
NYSE: FXCM ■ **Fax Area Code:* 877 ■ *TF:* 888-503-6739 ■ *Web:* www.fxcm.com

Gene Logic Inc 50 W Watkins Mill Rd . . . Gaithersburg MD 20878 301-987-1700 987-1701
TF: 800-436-3564 ■ *Web:* www.genelogic.com

General Dynamics C4 Systems
400 John Quincy Adams Rd Bldg 80 . . . Taunton MA 02780 508-880-4000 880-4800
TF: 888-483-2472 ■ *Web:* www.gdc4s.com

Geofields Inc 1180 W Peachtree St Suite 1250 . . . Atlanta GA 30309 404-253-1000 875-2442
Web: www.geofields.com

GeoFocus Inc 3651 FAU Blvd Suite 215 . . . Boca Raton FL 33431 561-955-1480 955-1481
Web: www.geofocus.com

Geokinetics Inc 1500 CityWest Blvd Suite 800 . . . Houston TX 77042 713-850-7600 850-7330
AMEX: GOK ■ *Web:* www.geokinetics.com

Ghg Corp 960 Clear Lake City Blvd . . . Webster TX 77598 281-488-8806 488-1838
TF: 866-380-4146 ■ *Web:* www.ghg.com

Glimmerglass Networks Inc
26142 Eden Landing Rd . . . Hayward CA 94545 510-723-1900 780-9851
TF: 877-723-1900 ■ *Web:* www.glimmerglass.com

Global Turnkey Systems Inc
2001 US Hwy 46 # 203 . . . Parsippany NJ 07054 973-331-1010 331-0042
TF: 800-221-1746 ■ *Web:* www.gtsystems.com

GoldenSource Corp 22 Cortlandt St 22nd Fl . . . New York NY 10007 212-798-7100 798-7275
Web: www.ftintl.com

gomembers Inc
11720 Sunrise Valley Dr Suite 300 . . . Reston VA 20191 703-620-9600 620-4858
TF: 888-288-4634 ■ *Web:* www.gomembers.com

Guidance Software Inc
215 N Marengo Ave 2nd Fl . . . Pasadena CA 91101 626-229-9191 229-9199
Web: www.guidancesoftware.com

Heartlab Inc 1 Crosswind Rd . . . Westerly RI 02891 401-596-0592 596-8562
TF: 800-959-3205 ■ *Web:* www.heartlab.com

HRsmart 2929 N Central Expwy Suite 110 . . . Richardson TX 75080 972-783-3000 853-5319*
**Fax Area Code:* 214 ■ *Web:* www.hrsmart.com

Hyphen Solutions Inc
5055 Keller Springs Rd Suite 200 . . . Addison TX 75001 972-728-8100 386-0992
TF: 877-508-2547

iHealth Technologies
6666 Powers Ferry Rd Suite 200 . . . Atlanta GA 30339 770-379-2800 379-2803*
**Fax:* Hum Res ■ *Web:* www.ihealthtechnologies.com

IHS Energy Group 15 Inverness Way E . . . Englewood CO 80112 303-736-3000 397-2923*
**Fax:* Hum Res ■ *TF:* 800-645-3282 ■ *Web:* www.ihs.com

Phone | Fax

ImageWare Systems Inc
10815 Rancho Bernardo Rd Suite 310 San Diego CA 92127 858-673-8600 673-1770
AMEX: IW ■ *TF:* 800-842-4199 ■ *Web:* www.iwsinc.com
Incyte Corp
Rt 141 & Henry Clay Rd Bldg E-336 Wilmington DE 19880 302-498-6700 425-2750
NASDAQ: INCY ■ *Web:* www.incyte.com
Info Tech Inc 5700 SW 34th St Suite 1235 Gainesville FL 32608 352-381-4400 381-4444
Web: www.infotechfl.com
Infor Global Solutions
13560 Morris Rd Suite 4100 Alpharetta GA 30004 678-319-8000 319-8682
TF: 866-244-5479 ■ *Web:* www.infor.com
Inmagic Inc 200 Unicorn Pk Dr Woburn MA 01801 781-938-4444 938-4446
TF: 800-229-8398 ■ *Web:* www.inmagic.com
Innovative Technologies Corp (ITC)
1020 Woodman Dr Suite 100 Dayton OH 45432 937-252-2145 254-6853
TF: 800-745-8050 ■ *Web:* www.itc-1.com
Input 1 LLC
21820 Burbank Blvd Suite 300 Woodland Hills CA 91367 818-676-2133 340-1261
TF: 888-882-2554 ■ *Web:* www.input1.com
Insurance Information Technologies Inc (INSTEC)
1811 Centre Pt Cir Suite 115 Naperville IL 60563 630-955-9200 955-9240
Web: www.instec-corp.com
Interactive Technology Solutions LLC
8757 Georgia Ave Suite 500 Silver Spring MD 20910 301-495-5545 495-7750
Web: www.itsolutions-llc.com
Intercim LLC 1915 Plaza Dr Eagan MN 55122 651-289-5700 289-3420
TF: 800-343-3734 ■ *Web:* www.intercim.com
IPC Systems Inc 1500 Plaza 10 15th Fl Jersey City NJ 07311 201-253-2000 253-2361
Web: www.ipc.com
Isg Technology Inc 127 N 7th St Salina KS 67401 785-823-1555 827-3310
Web: www.isgdirect.com
Island Pacific Inc
19800 MacArthur Blvd Suite 1200 Irvine CA 92612 949-476-2212 476-0199
TF: 800-944-3847 ■ *Web:* www.islandpacific.com
Ita Software Inc 141 Portland St Cambridge MA 02139 617-714-2100 621-3913
Web: www.itasoftware.com
iWay Software 2 Penn Plaza New York NY 10121 212-736-4433 967-6406
TF: 800-736-6130 ■ *Web:* www.iwaysoftware.com
JDA Software Group Inc 14400 N 87th St Scottsdale AZ 85260 480-308-3000 308-3001
NASDAQ: JDAS ■ *Web:* www.jda.com
Jenzabar Inc 5 Cambridge Ctr 11th Fl Cambridge MA 02142 617-492-9099 492-9081
TF: 877-536-0222 ■ *Web:* www.jenzabar.net
JPMorgan Chase Vastera
45025 Aviation Dr Suite 200 Dulles VA 20166 703-661-9006 742-4580
TF: 800-275-1374
Kaba Benzing America 5753 Miami Lakes Dr Miami Lakes FL 33014 305-819-4000 819-4001
Web: www.kaba-benzing-usa.com
Kewill Systems PLC 100 Nickerson Rd Marlborough MA 01752 508-229-4400 229-4404
TF: 877-872-2379 ■ *Web:* www.kewill.com
Kinaxis 700 Silver Seven Rd Ottawa ON K2V1C3 613-592-5780 592-0584
TF: 877-546-2947 ■ *Web:* www.kinaxis.com
Knorr Assoc Inc 10 Pk Pl PO Box 400 Butler NJ 07405 973-492-8500 492-0453
Web: www.knorrassociates.com
Knovalent Inc 3135 S State St Suite 300 Ann Arbor MI 48108 734-996-8300 996-2754
Web: www.knovalent.com
Knowlagent 3157 Royal Dr Alpharetta GA 30022 678-356-3500
Web: www.knowlagent.com
Koyosha Graphics of America Inc (KGA)
465 California St Suite 610 San Francisco CA 94104 415-283-1800 283-1801
Web: www.koyoshausa.com
Labware Inc 3 Mill Rd Suite 102 Wilmington DE 19806 302-658-8444 658-7894
Web: www.labware.com
Land & Legal Solutions Inc
300 S Hamilton Ave Greensburg PA 15601 724-853-8992 853-3221
TF: 800-245-7900 ■ *Web:* www.landlegal.com
Landacorp Inc 2080 E 20th St # 170 Chico CA 95928 530-891-0853 891-8428
Web: www.landacorp.com
Learnsomething Inc 2457 Care Dr Tallahassee FL 32308 877-399-4925 385-7964*
**Fax Area Code: 850* ■ *Web:* www.learnsomething.com
Library Corp The 3801 E Florida Ave Suite 300 Denver CO 80210 303-758-3030 758-0606
TF: 888-439-2275 ■ *Web:* www.tlcdelivers.com
Loan Protector Insurance Services
6001 Cochran Rd Solon OH 44139 800-545-6580 498-9370*
**Fax Area Code: 440* ■ *Web:* www.loanprotector.com
Logic Trends Inc 1040 Crown Pointe Pkwy Atlanta GA 30338 770-551-5050 551-5055
Web: www.logictrends.com
Logiplex Corp 4855 N Lagoon Portland OR 97217 503-978-6726 240-7410
Lumedx Corp 555 12th St Suite 2060 Oakland CA 94607 510-419-1000 419-3699
TF: 800-966-0699 ■ *Web:* www.lumedx.com
Lumigent Technologies Inc 289 Great Rd Acton MA 01720 978-206-3700 206-3699
TF: 866-586-4436 ■ *Web:* www.lumigent.com
Luminex Molecular Diagnostics
439 University Ave Suite 900 Toronto ON M5G1Y8 416-593-4323 593-1066
Web: www.luminexcorp.com
LynuxWorks Inc 855 Embedded Way San Jose CA 95138 408-979-3900 979-3920
TF: 800-255-5969 ■ *Web:* www.lynuxworks.com
Management Information Control Systems Inc (MICS)
2025 9th St Los Osos CA 93402 805-543-7000 543-0373
TF: 800-838-6427 ■ *Web:* www.bissoftware.com
Managing Editor Inc 610 York Rd # 250 Jenkintown PA 19046 215-886-5662 886-5681
Web: www.maned.com
Manhattan Assoc Inc
2300 Windy Ridge Pkwy 7th Fl Atlanta GA 30339 770-955-7070 955-0302
NASDAQ: MANH ■ *TF:* 877-414-7999 ■ *Web:* www.manh.com
Market Scan Information Systems Inc
811 Camarillo Springs Suite B Camarillo CA 93012 818-575-2000 631-6275*
**Fax Area Code: 866* ■ *TF:* 800-658-7226 ■ *Web:* www.marketscan.com
MarketTools Inc 150 Spear St San Francisco CA 94105 415-957-2200 957-2180
TF: 866-396-6014 ■ *Web:* www.markettools.com
Marshall & Swift
911 Wilshire Blvd Suite 1600 Los Angeles CA 90017 213-683-9000 683-9010
TF: 800-544-2678 ■ *Web:* www.marshallswift.com
MAXxess Systems Inc 1040 N Tustin Ave Anaheim CA 92802 714-772-1000 399-9358
TF: 800-842-0221 ■ *Web:* www.maxxess-systems.com

Phone | Fax

McDonald Bradley Inc
2250 Corporate Pk Dr Suite 500 Herndon VA 20171 703-326-1000 326-1004
Web: www.mcdonaldbradley.com
McKesson Information Solutions
5995 Windward Pkwy Alpharetta GA 30005 404-338-6000 338-5116*
**Fax: Sales* ■ *TF:* 800-981-8601 ■ *Web:* www.customerportal.mckesson.com
Mdi Achieve 7690 Golden Triangle Dr Eden Prairie MN 55344 952-995-9800 995-9735
TF: 800-869-1322 ■ *Web:* www.mdiachieve.com
MEDecision Inc 601 Lee Rd Chesterbrook Corp Ctr Wayne PA 19087 610-540-0202 540-0270
Web: www.medecision.com
Media Cybernetics Inc 4340 E W Hwy Suite 400 Bethesda MD 20814 301-495-3305 495-5964
TF Sales: 800-263-2088 ■ *Web:* www.mediacy.com
Medical Information Technology Inc
1 Meditech Cir Westwood MA 02090 781-821-3000 821-2199
Web: www.meditech.com
MedPlus Inc 4690 Pkwy Dr Mason OH 45040 513-229-5500 229-5505
TF: 800-444-6235 ■ *Web:* www.medplus.com
Megaputer Intelligence Inc
120 W 7th St Suite 314 Bloomington IN 47404 812-330-0110 330-0150
Web: www.megaputer.com
Merrick Systems Inc 4801 Woodway Suite 100E Houston TX 77056 713-355-6800 355-7202
TF: 800-842-8389 ■ *Web:* www.merricksystems.com
MicroBilt Corp 1640 Airport Rd Suite 115 Kennesaw GA 30144 800-884-4747 218-4997*
**Fax Area Code: 770* ■ *TF:* 800-884-2733 ■ *Web:* www.microbilt.com
Midrange Software Inc 12716 Riverside Dr Studio City CA 91607 818-762-8539 762-6256
TF: 800-737-6766 ■ *Web:* www.midrangesoftware.com
Minitab Inc
Quality Plaza 1829 Pine Hall Rd State College PA 16801 814-238-3280 238-1702
Web: www.minitab.com
Moody's Analytics Inc
7 World Trade Ctr 250 Greenwich St New York NY 94597 212-553-1653
Web: www.moodys.com
Mortgage Builders Software
24370 Northwestern Hwy Suite 200 Southfield MI 48075 800-850-8060 208-6142*
**Fax Area Code: 248* ■ *TF:* 800-850-8060 ■ *Web:* www.mortgagebuilder.com
MSGI Security Solutions Inc
575 Madison Ave 10th Fl New York NY 10022 212-605-0245 605-0222
NASDAQ: MSGI ■ *Web:* www.msgisecurity.com
Mzinga Inc 230 3rd Ave Waltham MA 02451 781-930-5430 930-5430
TF: 888-694-6428 ■ *Web:* www.mzinga.com
Navtech Inc 295 Hagey Blvd Suite 200 Waterloo ON N2L6R5 519-747-1170 747-1003
Web: www.navtechinc.com
Nestor Inc
400 Massasoit Ave Suite 200 East Providence RI 02914 401-434-5522 434-5809
NASDAQ: NEST
netGuru Inc 1240 N Van Buren St Suite 104 Anaheim CA 92807 714-638-4878 414-0200
Web: www.netguru.com
Netsol Technologies Inc
23901 Calabasas Rd Suite 2072 Calabasas CA 91302 818-222-9195 222-9197
NASDAQ: NTWK ■ *Web:* www.netsoltech.com
New England Computer Services Inc
168 Boston Post Rd Suites 6 & 7 Madison CT 06443 203-245-3999 245-4513
TF Sales: 800-766-6327 ■ *Web:* www.necs.com
NIC Inc 25501 W Valley Pkwy Suite 300 Olathe KS 66061 913-498-3468 498-3472
NASDAQ: EGOV ■ *TF:* 877-234-3468 ■ *Web:* www.egov.com
Nissho Electronics USA Corp
3945 Freedom Cir Suite 240 Santa Clara CA 95054 408-969-9700 969-0155
Web: www.nelco.com
OATSystems Inc 309 Waverley Oaks Rd Suite 306 Waltham MA 02452 781-907-6100 907-6098
Web: www.oatsystems.com
Olson Research Assoc Inc
10290 Old Columbia Rd Columbia MD 21046 410-290-6999 290-6726
TF: 888-657-6680 ■ *Web:* www.olsonresearch.com
OpenTable Inc 799 Market St 4th Fl San Francisco CA 94103 415-344-4200 267-0944
TF: 800-673-6822 ■ *Web:* www.opentable.com
Opex Corp 305 Commerce Dr Moorestown NJ 08057 856-727-1100 727-1955
Web: www.opex.com
OSI Software Inc 777 Davis St Suite 250 San Leandro CA 94577 510-297-5800 357-8136
Web: www.osisoft.com
OverDrive Inc 8555 Sweet Valley Dr Unit C Cleveland OH 44125 216-573-6886 573-6888
Web: www.overdrive.com
Packet Design Inc 2455 Augustine Dr Santa Clara CA 95054 408-490-1000 562-0080
Web: www.packetdesign.com
Pason Systems Inc 6130 3rd St SE Calgary AB T2H1K4 403-301-3400 301-3499
TSE: PSI ■ *TF:* 877-255-3158 ■ *Web:* www.pason.com
Passport Health Communications Inc
720 Cool Springs Blvd Suite 200 Franklin TN 37067 615-661-5657 376-3552
TF: 888-661-5657 ■ *Web:* www.passporthealth.com
Pavilion Technologies
9500 Arboretum Blvd Suite 400 Austin TX 78759 512-438-1400 438-1401
TF: 800-880-5432 ■ *Web:* www.pavtech.com
PCi Services Inc 30 Winter St 12th Fl Boston MA 02108 617-535-3000 535-3155
TF: 800-261-3111 ■ *Web:* www.pciwiz.com
PDF Solutions Inc
333 W San Carlos St Suite 700 San Jose CA 95110 408-280-7900 280-7915
NASDAQ: PDFS ■ *Web:* www.pdf.com
Peopleware Inc 110 110th Ave NE Suite 590 Bellevue WA 98004 425-454-6444 454-7634
TF: 800-869-7166 ■ *Web:* www.peopleware.com
Phase Forward Inc 77 Fourth Ave Waltham MA 02451 781-890-7878 890-4848
TF: 888-703-1122 ■ *Web:* www.phaseforward.com
Picis Inc 100 Quannapowitt Pkwy Suite 405 Wakefield MA 01880 781-557-3000 557-3140
PKC Corp 1 Mill St C13 Suite 355 Burlington VT 05401 802-658-5351 658-3078
TF: 800-752-5351 ■ *Web:* www.pkc.com
Planet Payment Inc 670 Long Beach Blvd Long Beach NY 11561 516-670-3200 670-3520
Web: www.planetpayment.com
Poinserve Inc 110 Wild Basin Rd Suite 300 Austin TX 78746 512-617-5300 617-0466
TF: 877-943-9433 ■ *Web:* www.pointserve.com
Pragmatics Inc 1761 Business Ctr Dr Reston VA 20190 703-761-4033 438-1779
Web: www.pragmatics.com
ProCard Inc 1819 Denver W Dr Bldg 26 Suite 265 Golden CO 80401 303-279-2255 279-1044
TF: 800-469-6578 ■ *Web:* www.procard.com

Company	City	State	Zip	Phone	Fax
Promodel Corp 3400 Bath Pike Suite 200 *TF:* 888-900-3090 ■ *Web:* www.promodel.com	Bethlehem	PA	18017	610-867-1553	867-8240
Pros Holdings Inc 3100 Main St Suite 900 *NYSE: PRO* ■ *Web:* www.prospricing.com	Houston	TX	77002	713-335-5151	335-8144
PSI International Inc 4000 Legato Rd Suite 850 *Web:* www.psiint.com	Fairfax	VA	22033	703-621-5825	352-8236
QlikTech International AB 150 N Radnor Chester Rd Suite E220 *NASDAQ: QLIK* ■ **Fax Area Code:* 610 ■ *TF:* 888-828-9768 ■ *Web:* www.qlikview.com	Radnor	PA	19087	888-828-9768	975-5987*
QS/1 Data Systems PO Box 6052 *TF:* 800-845-7558 ■ *Web:* www.qs1.com	Spartanburg	SC	29304	864-253-8600	253-8690
Quality Systems Inc (QSI) 18111 Von Karman Ave Suite 600 *NASDAQ: QSII* ■ *TF Cust Svc:* 800-888-7955 ■ *Web:* www.qsii.com	Irvine	CA	92612	949-255-2600	255-2605
QUMAS 66 York St *TF Sales:* 800-577-1545 ■ *Web:* www.qumas.com	Jersey City	NJ	07302	973-805-8600	377-8687
Qvidian Corp 175 Cabot St Suite 210 **Fax Area Code:* 978 ■ *TF:* 800-272-0047 ■ *Web:* www.qvidian.com	Lowell	MA	01854	513-631-1155	703-7631*
RainMaker Software Inc 475 Sentry Pkwy E Suite 4000 *TF Cust Svc:* 800-341-4012 ■ *Web:* www.rainmakerlegal.com	Blue Bell	PA	19422	610-567-3400	567-3449
Ramesys Hospitality Inc 1 Cragwood Rd Suite 202 *TF:* 800-888-8819	South Plainfield	NJ	07080	908-941-1300	941-1312
Raytheon Solipsys 8170 Maple Lawn Blvd Suite 300 *TF:* 888-837-1210 ■ *Web:* www.solipsys.com	Fulton	MD	20759	240-554-8100	554-8101
RealLegal 221 Main St Suite 1250 **Fax Area Code:* 415 ■ *TF:* 800-290-9378 ■ *Web:* www.reallegal.com	San Francisco	CA	94105	888-584-9988	321-2301*
Red Wing Software Inc 491 Hwy 19 *TF:* 800-732-9464 ■ *Web:* www.redwingsoftware.com	Red Wing	MN	55066	651-388-1106	388-7950
RESUMate Inc 135 E Bennett St Suite 5 *TF Cust Svc:* 800-530-9310 ■ *Web:* www.resumate.com	Saline	MI	48176	734-429-8510	429-4228
Retail Pro International LLC 400 Plaza Dr Suite 200 *PINK: RTPRQ* ■ **Fax Area Code:* 949 ■ *TF:* 800-738-2457 ■ *Web:* www.retailpro.com	Folsom	CA	95630	916-605-7200	476-0177*
Reynolds & Reynolds Co 1 Reynolds Way *TF:* 800-756-5310 ■ *Web:* www.reyrey.com	Kettering	OH	45430	800-756-5310	
Risk Management Solutions Inc 7575 Gateway Blvd *Web:* www.rms.com	Newark	CA	94560	510-505-2500	505-2501
RiskWatch Inc 2568A Riva Rd Suite 300 *TF:* 800-448-4666 ■ *Web:* www.riskwatch.com	Annapolis	MD	21401	410-224-4773	224-4995
S1 Corp 3500 Lenox Rd Suite 200 *NASDAQ: SONE* ■ *TF:* 888-457-2237 ■ *Web:* www.s1.com	Atlanta	GA	30326	404-923-3500	923-6727
Sapiens International Corp 4000 CentreGreen Way Suite 150 *NASDAQ: SPNS* ■ *Web:* www.sapiens.com	Cary	NC	27513	919-405-1500	405-1700
Satori Group Inc 555 N Ln Suite 6100 *Web:* www.satorigroupinc.com	Conshohocken	PA	19428	610-862-6300	862-6350
Savi Technology Inc 3601 Eisenhower Ave Suite 280 *Web:* www.savi.com	Mountain View	CA	94041	571-227-7950	227-7960
Scantron Corp 34 Parker *TF:* 800-722-6876 ■ *Web:* www.scantron.com	Irvine	CA	92618	949-639-7500	639-7710
Schlumberger Information Solutions (SIS) 5599 San Felipe St Suite 100 *Web:* www.slb.com	Houston	TX	77056	713-513-2000	513-2006
Serendipity Systems Inc PO Box 10477 *Web:* www.serendipsys.com	Sedona	AZ	86339	928-282-6831	282-4383
Siemens Product Lifecycle Management Software Inc 5800 Granite Pkwy Suite 600 *TF:* 800-498-5351 ■ *Web:* www.plm.automation.siemens.com	Plano	TX	75024	972-987-3000	987-3399
Simulation Systems Technologies Inc 520 Fellowship Rd Unit A-110 *Web:* www.s-s-t-i.com	Mount Laurel	NJ	08054	856-231-7711	231-4663
Simulations Plus Inc 42505 10th St W *AMEX: SLP* ■ *TF:* 888-266-9294 ■ *Web:* www.simulations-plus.com	Lancaster	CA	93534	661-723-7723	723-5524
Simunet Corp PO Box 7289 **Fax Area Code:* 808 ■ *TF:* 800-326-5155 ■ *Web:* www.adaptive-research.com	Alhambra	CA	91802	626-688-4565	356-0128*
SM & A 4695 MacArthur Ct 8th Fl *Web:* www.smawins.com	Newport Beach	CA	92660	949-975-1550	975-1624
SmartLabs Inc 16542 Millikan Ave *TF:* 800-762-7846 ■ *Web:* www.smartlabsinc.com	Irvine	CA	92606	949-477-5505	221-9240
Snap-on Diagnostics 420 Barclay Blvd *TF:* 800-424-7226 ■ *Web:* www1.snapon.com	Lincolnshire	IL	60069	847-478-0700	478-7311
Snowbound Software 309 Waverley Oaks Rd Suite 401 *Web:* www.snowbound.com	Waltham	MA	02542	617-607-2000	607-2002
Software Consulting Services LLC 630 Selvaggio Dr Suite 420 *Web:* www.newspapersystems.com	Nazareth	PA	18064	610-746-7700	746-7900
Solid Oak Software Inc PO Box 6826 *Web:* www.solidoak.com	Santa Barbara	CA	93160	805-967-9853	967-1614
SolidWorks Corp 300 Baker Ave *TF:* 800-693-9000 ■ *Web:* www.solidworks.com	Concord	MA	01742	978-371-5011	371-7303
Solucient 1007 Church St Suite 700 *TF:* 800-366-7526 ■ *Web:* www.solucient.com	Evanston	IL	60201	847-424-4400	332-1768
Spillman Technologies Inc 4625 Lake Pk Blvd *TF:* 800-860-8026 ■ *Web:* www.spillman.com	Salt Lake City	UT	84120	801-902-1200	902-1210
SQN Signature Systems 65 Indel Ave 2nd Fl *TF:* 888-744-7226 ■ *Web:* www.sqnsigs.com	Rancocas	NJ	08073	609-261-5500	265-9517
StatSoft Inc 2300 E 14th St *Web:* www.statsoft.com	Tulsa	OK	74104	918-749-1119	749-2217
Stok Software Inc 373 Nesconset Hwy Suite 287 *TF:* 888-448-8668 ■ *Web:* www.stok.com	Hauppauge	NY	11788	631-232-2228	
Sungard Business Systems LLC 1660 Prudential Dr PO Box 47470 *TF:* 800-326-7235 ■ *Web:* www.relius.net	Jacksonville	FL	32207	904-399-5888	399-5551
SunGard Collegis Inc 2300 Maitland Ctr Pkwy Suite 340 *TF:* 800-800-1874 ■ *Web:* www.sungardcollegis.com	Maitland	FL	32751	407-660-1199	660-8008
SunGard HTE Inc 1000 Business Ctr Dr **Fax:* Mktg ■ *TF:* 800-727-8088 ■ *Web:* www.sungard.com	Lake Mary	FL	32746	407-304-3235	304-1005*
SunGard Trust Systems Inc 5510 77 Ctr Dr *Web:* www.sungardtrust.com	Charlotte	NC	28217	704-527-6300	527-9617
SXC Health Solutions Corp 555 Industrial Dr *Web:* www.sxc.com	Milton	ON	L9T5E1	905-876-4741	878-8869
Synergex International Corp 2330 Gold Meadow Way *TF:* 800-366-3472 ■ *Web:* www.synergex.com	Rancho Cordova	CA	95670	916-635-7300	635-6549
Synopsys Inc 700 E Middlefield Rd *NASDAQ: SNPS* ■ *TF:* 800-541-7737 ■ *Web:* www.synopsys.com	Mountain View	CA	94043	650-584-5000	965-8637
System Automation 7110 Samuel Morse Dr 1st Fl *TF:* 800-839-4729 ■ *Web:* www.systemautomation.com	Columbia	MD	21046	301-837-8000	837-8001
System Innovators Inc 10550 Deerwood Pk Blvd Suite 700 *TF:* 800-963-5000	Jacksonville	FL	32256	904-281-9090	281-0075
T2 Systems Inc 7835 Woodland Dr Suite 250 *TF:* 800-434-1502 ■ *Web:* www.t2systems.com	Indianapolis	IN	46278	317-524-5500	524-5501
Tableau Software Inc 837 N 34th St Suite 400 *Web:* www.tableausoftware.com	Seattle	WA	98103	206-633-3400	633-3004
Tax Management Inc BNA Software Div 1250 23rd St NW *TF:* 800-424-2938 ■ *Web:* www.bnasoftware.com	Washington	DC	20037	202-728-7962	728-7964
Telcordia Technologies Inc 1 Telcordia Dr *TF:* 800-521-2673 ■ *Web:* www.telcordia.com	Piscataway	NJ	08854	732-699-2000	
Telos OK 111 SW 'C' Ave	Lawton	OK	73501	580-355-9280	355-9381
Thomson Elite 5100 W Goldleaf Cir Suite 100 *TF Cust Svc:* 800-274-9287 ■ *Web:* www.elite.com	Los Angeles	CA	90056	323-642-5200	642-5400
TMA Resources Inc 1919 Gallows Rd 4th Fl *Web:* www.tmaresources.com	Vienna	VA	22182	703-564-5200	564-5201
Tmw Systems Inc 21111 Chagrin Blvd *TF:* 800-401-6682 ■ *Web:* www.tmwsystems.com	Beachwood	OH	44122	216-831-6606	831-3606
Track Data Corp 95 Rockwell Pl *NASDAQ: TRAC* ■ *TF:* 800-223-0113 ■ *Web:* www.trackdata.com	Brooklyn	NY	11217	212-943-4555	612-2014
TradeStation Group Inc 8050 SW 10th St Suite 2000 *NASDAQ: TRAD* ■ *TF:* 800-871-3577 ■ *Web:* www.tradestation.com	Plantation	FL	33324	954-652-7000	652-7899
Transentric 1400 Douglas St Suite 0840 *Web:* www.transentric.com	Omaha	NE	68179	402-544-2984	501-2984
TransWorks 9910 Dupont Cir Dr E Suite 200 *TF:* 800-435-4691 ■ *Web:* www.trnswrks.com	Fort Wayne	IN	46825	260-487-4400	
TRX Inc 2970 Clairmont Rd Suite 300 *PINK: TRXI* ■ **Fax:* Hum Res ■ *Web:* www.trx.com	Atlanta	GA	30329	404-929-6100	929-5270*
Tyler Technologies Inc 5949 Sherry Ln Suite 1400 *NYSE: TYL* ■ *Web:* www.tylertech.com	Dallas	TX	75225	972-713-3700	713-3741
Universal Tax Systems 6 Mathis Dr *TF Sales:* 800-755-9473 ■ *Web:* www.taxwise.com	Rome	GA	30165	706-232-7757	236-9168
Urchin Software Corp 2165 India St *TF Sales:* 888-887-2446 ■ *Web:* www.urchin.com	San Diego	CA	92101	619-233-1400	374-2478
US Dataworks Inc One Sugar Creek Ctr Blvd Fifth Fl *AMEX: UDW* ■ *TF:* 866-337-5477 ■ *Web:* www.usdataworks.com	Sugar Land	TX	77478	281-504-8000	
US Digital Corp 1400 NE 136th Ave *TF:* 800-736-0194 ■ *Web:* www.usdigital.com	Vancouver	WA	98684	360-260-2468	260-2469
VantageMed Corp 3017 Kilgore Rd Suite 180 *TF:* 877-879-8633 ■ *Web:* www.vantagemed.net	Rancho Cordova	CA	95670	916-638-4744	638-0504
Verdasys Inc 404 Wyman St Suite 320 *TF:* 800-886-5369 ■ *Web:* www.verdasys.com	Waltham	MA	02451	781-788-8180	788-8188
Vermont Systems Inc 12 Market Pl *TF:* 877-883-8757 ■ *Web:* www.vermontsystems.com	Essex Junction	VT	05452	802-879-6993	879-5368
VersaForm Systems Corp 591 W Hamilton Ave Suite 201 *TF Sales:* 800-678-1111 ■ *Web:* www.versaform.com	Campbell	CA	95008	408-370-2662	370-3393
Viewlocity Inc 3475 Piedmont Rd Suite 1700 *TF:* 877-512-8900 ■ *Web:* www.viewlocity.com	Atlanta	GA	30305	404-267-6400	267-6500
ViPS Inc 1 W Pennsylvania Ave Suite 700 *TF:* 888-289-8477 ■ *Web:* www.vips.com	Baltimore	MD	21204	410-832-8300	832-8315
Vital Images Inc 5850 Opus Pkwy Suite 300 *NASDAQ: VTAL* ■ *TF:* 800-208-3005 ■ *Web:* www.vitalimages.com	Minnetonka	MN	55343	952-487-9500	487-9510
VoltDelta Resources Inc 560 Lexington Ave 14th Fl *Web:* www.voltdelta.com	New York	NY	10022	212-827-2600	827-2650
Votenet Solutions Inc 1420 K St *Web:* www.votenet.com	Washington	DC	20005	202-737-2277	737-2283
VT M-K 68 Moulton St *Web:* www.mak.com	Cambridge	MA	02138	617-876-8085	876-9208
Wausau Financial Systems Inc 875 Indianhead Dr PO Box 37 *Web:* www.wausaufs.com	Mosinee	WI	54455	715-359-0427	241-2288
Weather Services International 400 Minuteman Rd *Web:* www.wsi.com	Andover	MA	01810	978-983-6300	983-6400
Wizsoft Inc 6800 Jericho Tpke Suite 120W *Web:* www.wizsoft.com	Syosset	NY	11791	516-393-5841	393-5842
Wonderware Corp 26561 Rancho Pkwy S *Web:* www.global.wonderware.com	Lake Forest	CA	92630	949-727-3200	727-3270
Worksoft Inc 15851 Dallas Pkwy Suite 855 **Fax Area Code:* 972 ■ *TF:* 866-836-1773 ■ *Web:* www.worksoft.com	Addison	TX	75240	214-239-0400	250-9900*
X-Rite Inc 3100 44th St SW *NASDAQ: XRIT* ■ *TF:* 800-248-9748 ■ *Web:* www.xrite.com	Grandville	MI	49418	616-534-7664	534-0723
Xybernet Inc 10640 Scripps Ranch Blvd *TF Cust Svc:* 800-228-9026 ■ *Web:* www.xyber.net	San Diego	CA	92131	858-530-1900	530-1419

181-11 Service Software

	City	State	Zip	Phone	Fax
Alorica Inc 14726 Ramona Ave 3rd Fl *Web:* www.alorica.com	Chino	CA	91710	909-606-3600	606-7708
Applied Systems Inc 200 Applied Pkwy **Fax:* Hum Res ■ *TF Sales:* 800-999-5368 ■ *Web:* www.appliedsystems.com	University Park	IL	60466	708-534-5575	534-8016*
Aprimo Inc 900 E 96th St Suite 400 *Web:* www.aprimo.com	Indianapolis	IN	46240	317-814-6465	844-2256
Aptech Computer Systems Inc 135 Delta Dr *TF:* 800-245-0720 ■ *Web:* www.aptech-inc.com	Pittsburgh	PA	15238	412-963-7440	963-9799
ARINC Inc 2551 Riva Rd *TF:* 800-492-2182 ■ *Web:* www.arinc.com	Annapolis	MD	21401	410-266-4000	266-4040
Aristotle Inc 205 Pennsylvania Ave SE **Fax:* Sales ■ *TF Sales:* 800-296-2747 ■ *Web:* www.aristotle.com	Washington	DC	20003	202-543-8345	543-6407*
ASA International Ltd 10 Speen St *Web:* www.asaint.com	Framingham	MA	01701	508-626-2727	626-0645
Automated Financial Systems Inc 123 Summit Dr *Web:* www.afsvision.com	Exton	PA	19341	610-524-0400	524-7977
Bankers Systems Inc 6815 Saukview Dr *TF:* 800-397-2341 ■ *Web:* www.bankerssystems.com	Saint Cloud	MN	56303	320-251-3060	251-8110
Camstar Systems Inc 13024 Ballantyne Corporate Pl Suite 300 *TF:* 800-237-2841 ■ *Web:* www.camstar.com	Charlotte	NC	28277	704-227-6600	227-6783
Capital Growth Systems Inc 180 N LaSalle St Suite 2430 *PINK: CGSYQ* ■ *Web:* www.globalcapacity.com	Chicago	IL	60601	312-673-2400	673-2422
CaseSoft Div 5000 Sawgrass Village Cir Suite 21 *Web:* www.casesoft.com	Ponte Vedra Beach	FL	32082	904-273-5000	273-5001
Cerner Corp 2800 Rockcreek Pkwy *NASDAQ: CERN* ■ *TF:* 800-255-1024 ■ *Web:* www.cerner.com	North Kansas City	MO	64117	816-221-1024	274-1742
Computer Technology Corp 4900 College Blvd	Overland Park	KS	66211	913-677-0095	677-0185
Datamann Inc 1994 Hartford Ave *TF:* 800-451-4263 ■ *Web:* www.datamann.com	Wilder	VT	05088	802-295-6600	296-3623
Dhi Computing Service Inc 1525 W 820 N PO Box 51427 *TF:* 800-992-1344 ■ *Web:* www.dhiprovo.com	Provo	UT	84601	801-373-8518	374-5316
Digital Solutions Inc 4200 Industrial Pk Dr *TF Cust Svc:* 888-222-3081 ■ *Web:* www.dsicdi.com	Altoona	PA	16602	814-944-0405	949-3307
DPSI Inc 1801 Stanley Rd # 301 *TF:* 800-897-7233 ■ *Web:* www.dpsi.com	Greensboro	NC	27407	336-854-7700	854-7715
Dr Schueler's Health Informatics Inc 703 Rockledge Dr *Web:* www.dshisystems.com	Rockledge	FL	32955	321-637-0321	637-0021
Ebix Inc 5 Concourse Pkwy Suite 3200 *NASDAQ: EBIX* ■ *Web:* www.ebix.com	Atlanta	GA	30328	678-281-2020	281-2019
EOS International 2292 Faraday Ave *TF:* 888-728-8746 ■ *Web:* www.eosintl.com	Carlsbad	CA	92008	760-431-8400	431-8448
Firstwave Technologies Inc 7000 Central Pkwy Suite 330 *NASDAQ: FSTW* ■ *TF:* 800-289-6070 ■ *Web:* www.firstwave.com	Atlanta	GA	30328	678-672-3100	672-3130
Fiserv Mortgage Products 3575 Moreau Ct Suite 2 *Web:* www.fiserve.com	South Bend	IN	46628	574-282-3300	282-3366
Galaxy Hotel Systems LLC 15621 Red Hill Ave Suite 100 *Web:* www.galaxyhotelsystems.com	Tustin	CA	92780	714-258-5800	258-5880
Gallagher Financial Systems 7301 SW 57th Ct Suite 570 *TF:* 800-989-9998 ■ *Web:* www.gogallagher.com	South Miami	FL	33143	305-665-5099	665-0547
Goldleaf Financial Solutions Inc PO Box 1603 *NASDAQ: PBIZ* ■ **Fax Area Code:* 615 ■ *TF:* 800-235-5584 ■ *Web:* www.privatebusiness.com	Brentwood	TN	37024	800-235-5584	565-7425*
H & M Systems Software Inc 600 E Crescent Ave Suite 203 *TF Cust Svc:* 800-367-3366 ■ *Web:* www.hm-software.com	Upper Saddle River	NJ	07458	201-934-3414	934-9206
IHS Inc 321 Inverness Dr S *NYSE: IHS* ■ *TF:* 800-525-7052 ■ *Web:* www.ihs.com	Englewood	CO	80112	303-790-0600	397-2599
Incontact Inc 7730 S Union Pk Ave Suite 500 *NASDAQ: SAAS* ■ *TF:* 800-363-6177 ■ *Web:* www.incontact.com	Salt Lake City	UT	84047	801-320-3200	320-3330
Inmass/MRP PO Box 41000 *Web:* www.inmass.com	Tucson	AZ	85717	520-795-6800	323-2505
Insurance Data Processing Inc (IDP) 8101 Washington Ln PO Box 137 *TF:* 800-523-6745 ■ *Web:* www.idpnet.com	Wyncote	PA	19095	215-885-2150	887-4621
Intelligent Health Systems (HIS) 2251 San Diego Ave Suite A-141 *TF:* 800-487-5772 ■ *Web:* www.ihshealthcare.com	San Diego	CA	92110	619-243-8300	241-7724
Jack Henry & Assoc Inc 663 W Hwy 60 PO Box 807 *NASDAQ: JKHY* ■ *TF:* 800-299-4222 ■ *Web:* www.jackhenry.com	Monett	MO	65708	417-235-6652	235-8406
Jobscope Corp 355 Woodruff Rd # 211 *TF:* 800-443-5794 ■ *Web:* www.jobscope.com	Greenville	SC	29607	864-458-3100	234-4852
Keane Care Inc 8383 158th Ave NE Suite 100 **Fax Area Code:* 425 ■ *TF:* 800-426-2675 ■ *Web:* www.keanecare.com	Redmond	WA	98052	800-426-2675	307-2220*
Key Information Systems Inc 21700 Oxnard St Suite 250 *TF:* 877-442-3249 ■ *Web:* www.keyisit.com	Woodland Hills	CA	91367	818-992-8950	992-8970
Kronos Inc 297 Billerica Rd *NASDAQ: KRON* ■ *TF:* 800-432-2351 ■ *Web:* www.kronos.com	Chelmsford	MA	01824	978-250-9800	367-5900
LegalEdge Software 175 Stratford Ave Suite 1 *Web:* www.legaledge.com	Wayne	PA	19087	610-975-5888	975-5884
Liquent Inc 101 Gibraltar Rd Suite 200 *TF:* 800-515-3777 ■ *Web:* www.liquent.com	Horsham	PA	19044	215-328-4444	328-4445
M86 Security Inc 8845 Irvine Ctr Dr *Web:* www.m86security.com	Irvine	CA	92618	949-932-1000	932-1086
Management Technology America Ltd 4742 N 24th St Suite 410 *TF:* 800-366-6633 ■ *Web:* www.mtanet.com	Phoenix	AZ	85016	602-381-5100	251-0903
Manatron Inc 510 E Milham Ave *NASDAQ: MANA* ■ *TF Cust Svc:* 866-471-2900 ■ *Web:* www.manatron.com	Portage	MI	49002	269-567-2900	567-2930
McCallie Assoc Inc 3906 Raynor Pkwy Suite 200 *Web:* www.mccallie.com	Bellevue	NE	68123	402-291-2203	291-8221
Medical Manager MacHealth 210 Gateway Mall Suite 102 *TF:* 800-888-4344	Lincoln	NE	68505	402-466-8100	466-9044
Mediware Information Systems Inc 11711 W 79th St *NASDAQ: MEDW* ■ *TF:* 800-255-0026 ■ *Web:* www.mediware.com	Lenexa	KS	66214	913-307-1000	307-1111
Meta Health Technology Inc 330 7th Ave 14th Fl *TF:* 800-334-6840 ■ *Web:* www.metahealth.com	New York	NY	10001	212-695-5870	643-2913
Metafile Information Systems Inc 2900 43rd St NW *TF Sales:* 800-638-2445 ■ *Web:* www.metaviewer.com	Rochester	MN	55901	507-286-9232	286-9065
MicroMass Communications Inc 11000 Regency Pkwy Suite 300 *Web:* www.micromass.com	Cary	NC	27511	919-851-3182	851-3188
MicroStrategy Inc 1861 International Dr *NASDAQ: MSTR* ■ *TF:* 866-966-6787	McLean	VA	22102	703-848-8600	848-8610
Mincron Software Systems 333 N Sam Houston Pkwy E Suite 1100 *Web:* www.mincron.com	Houston	TX	77060	281-999-7010	999-6329
Mortgage Computer Applications Inc 2650 Washington Blvd Suite 203 *TF Cust Svc:* 800-421-3277 ■ *Web:* www.mcoffice.com	Ogden	UT	84401	801-621-3900	627-2537
MPSI Systems Inc 4343 S 118th E Ave *TF Cust Svc:* 800-727-6774 ■ *Web:* www.mpsisys.com	Tulsa	OK	74146	918-877-6774	877-6960
Narus Inc 570 Maude Ct *TF:* 877-310-6700 ■ *Web:* www.narus.com	Sunnyvale	CA	94085	408-215-4300	215-4301
Netsmart Technologies Inc 3500 Sunrise Hwy Suite D-122 *TF:* 800-421-7503 ■ *Web:* www.ntst.com	Great River	NY	11739	631-968-2000	968-2123
Newmarket International Inc 135 Commerce Way *Web:* www.newmarketinc.com	Portsmouth	NH	03801	603-436-7500	436-1826
Online Resources Corp 4795 Meadow Wood Ln Suite 300 *NASDAQ: ORCC* ■ *TF:* 866-606-3000 ■ *Web:* www.orcc.com	Chantilly	VA	20151	703-653-3100	653-3105
Pactolus Communications Software Corp 200 Nickerson Rd *Web:* www.pactolus.com	Marlborough	MA	01752	508-616-0900	616-0901
Parallels Holding 500 SW 39th St Suite 200 *Web:* www.parallels.com	Renton	WA	37763	425-282-6400	282-6444
Proscape Technologies Inc 1155 Business Ctr Dr Suite 180 *TF:* 800-459-9300 ■ *Web:* www.proscape.com	Horsham	PA	19044	215-441-0300	441-0600
Radware Inc 575 Corporate Dr Lbby 2 *TF:* 888-234-5763 ■ *Web:* www.radware.com	Mahwah	NJ	07430	201-512-9771	512-9774
Real Soft Inc 2540 Rt 130 N Suite 118 *Web:* www.realsoftinc.com	Cranbury	NJ	08512	609-409-3636	409-3637
Retalix Ltd USA 6100 Tennyson Pkwy Suite 150 *TF:* 866-893-7722 ■ *Web:* www.retalix.com	Plano	TX	75024	469-241-8400	241-0771
Right On Computer Software 27 Bowdon Rd - Suite B *Web:* www.rightonlibrarysoftware.com	Greenlawn	NY	11740	631-424-7777	424-7207
Sandata Technologies Inc 26 Harbor Pk Dr *TF Sales:* 800-544-7263 ■ *Web:* www.sandata.com	Port Washington	NY	11050	516-484-4400	484-6084
Settlement Services Corp 1004 W Taft Ave *TF Sales:* 800-767-7832	Orange	CA	92865	714-998-1111	998-4866
SS & C Technologies Inc 80 Lamberton Rd *Web:* www.ssctech.com	Windsor	CT	06095	860-298-4500	298-4900
Strictly Business Computer Systems Inc 848 4th Ave Suite 200 **Fax Area Code:* 304 ■ *Web:* www.sbcs.com	Huntington	WV	25701	888-529-0401	781-2590*
Successfactors Inc 1500 Fashion Island Blvd Suite 300 *NYSE: SFSF* ■ *TF:* 800-809-9920 ■ *Web:* www.successfactors.com	San Mateo	CA	94404	650-645-2000	645-2099
SunGard Pentamation Inc 3 W Broad St Suite 1 *TF Cust Svc:* 800-333-3619 ■ *Web:* www.sungardps.com	Bethlehem	PA	18018	610-691-3616	691-1031
Symphony Technology Group LLC (STG) 2475 Hanover St *Web:* www.symphonytg.com	Palo Alto	CA	94304	650-935-9500	935-9501
Synergistics Inc 15 Tech Cir *TF:* 800-433-7616 ■ *Web:* www.synergisticsinc.com	Natick	MA	01760	508-655-1340	651-2902
Technalysis Inc 7172 Waldemar Dr *Web:* www.technalysis.com	Indianapolis	IN	46268	317-291-1985	291-7281
Technical Services Assoc Inc (TSA) 2 Kacey Ct *TF:* 800-388-1415 ■ *Web:* www.pox.com	Mechanicsburg	PA	17055	717-691-5691	691-5690
Thermeon Corp 12241 Newport Ave Suite 111 *Web:* www.thermeon.com	Santa Ana	CA	92705	714-731-9191	731-5938
TimeValue Software 22 Nauchoi *TF Sales:* 800-426-4741 ■ *Web:* www.timevalue.com	Irvine	CA	92618	949-727-1800	727-3268
TMA Systems LLC 5100 E Skelly Dr Suite 900 *TF:* 800-862-1130 ■ *Web:* www.tmasystems.com	Tulsa	OK	74135	918-858-6600	858-6655
Velos Inc 2201 Walnut Ave Suite 208 *Web:* www.velos.com	Fremont	CA	94538	510-739-4010	739-4018
Xactware Solutions Inc 1 Xactware Plaza *TF:* 800-758-9228 ■ *Web:* www.xactware.com	Orem	UT	84097	801-764-5900	932-8013
Xora Inc 1890 N Shoreline Blvd *TF:* 877-477-9672 ■ *Web:* www.xora.com	Mountain View	CA	94043	650-314-6460	938-8401

181-12 Systems & Utilities Software

	City	State	Zip	Phone	Fax
Accelr8 Technology Corp 7000 Broadway Bldg 3-307 *AMEX: AXK* ■ *TF:* 800-582-8898 ■ *Web:* www.accelr8.com	Denver	CO	80221	303-863-8088	863-1218

Company / Address	City	State	Zip	Phone	Fax
ACCESS Systems Americas Inc					
1188 E Arques Ave	Sunnyvale	CA	94085	408-400-3000	400-1500
Web: www.access-company.com					
ActivCard Inc 6623 Dumbarton Cir	Fremont	CA	94555	510-574-0100	574-0101
NASDAQ: ACTI ■ *TF:* 800-529-9499 ■ *Web:* www.actividentity.com					
activePDF Inc					
27405 Puerta Real Suite 100	Mission Viejo	CA	92691	949-582-9002	582-9004
TF: 866-468-6733 ■ *Web:* www.activepdf.com					
Adaptive Solutions Inc					
1301 Azalea Rd Suite 101	Mobile	AL	36619	251-666-3045	660-1788
TF: 800-299-3045 ■ *Web:* www.talksight.com					
Advantage IQ Inc 1313 N Atlantic St 5th Fl	Spokane	WA	99201	509-329-7600	
TF: 877-828-8208 ■ *Web:* www.advantageiq.com					
AEP Networks Inc 347 Elizabeth Ave Suite 100	Somerset	NJ	08873	732-652-5200	764-8862
TF: 877-638-4552 ■ *Web:* www.aepnetworks.com					
Allen Systems Group Inc (ASG) 1333 3rd Ave S	Naples	FL	34102	239-435-2200	325-2555*
**Fax Area Code:* 800 ■ *TF:* 800-932-5536 ■ *Web:* www.asg.com					
Aonix North America Inc					
5040 Shoreham Pl Suite 100	San Diego	CA	92122	858-457-2700	824-0212
TF: 800-972-6649 ■ *Web:* www.aonix.com					
Apex CoVantage LLC					
198 Van Buren St 200 Presidents Plaza	Herndon	VA	20170	703-709-3000	709-0333
TF: 800-628-2739 ■ *Web:* www.apexcovantage.com					
AREVA T & D					
1 International Plaza Suite 300	Philadelphia	PA	19113	484-766-8100	766-8150
Web: www.areva-td.com					
Aspect Business Solutions					
7550 IH-10 W 14th Fl	San Antonio	TX	78229	210-298-5000	298-5001
TF: 800-609-8113					
Authentium Inc					
7121 Fairway Dr Suite 102	Palm Beach Gardens	FL	33418	561-575-3200	575-3026
TF: 800-423-9147 ■ *Web:* www.authentium.com					
Auto-trol Technology Corp					
12500 N Washington St	Denver	CO	80241	303-452-4919	252-2249
TF: 800-233-2882 ■ *Web:* www.auto-trol.com					
Avatier Corp 111 Deerwood Rd	San Ramon	CA	94583	925-217-5170	275-0853
TF: 800-609-8610 ■ *Web:* www.avatier.com					
BakBone Software Inc					
9540 Town Centre Dr Suite 100	San Diego	CA	92121	858-450-9009	450-9929
TF: 877-939-2663 ■ *Web:* www.bakbone.com					
Basis International Ltd					
5901 Jefferson St NE	Albuquerque	NM	87109	505-345-5232	345-5082
TF Orders: 800-423-1394 ■ *Web:* www.basis.com					
BenchmarkQA Inc					
3800 American Blvd W Suite 1580	Minneapolis	MN	55431	952-392-2381	392-2382
TF: 877-425-2581 ■ *Web:* www.benchmarkqa.com					
Beta Systems Software of North America Inc					
8300 Greensboro Dr Suite 1150	McLean	VA	22102	703-889-1240	889-1241
TF: 800-475-1168 ■ *Web:* www.betasystems.com					
Blue Lance Inc 1401 McKinney St Suite 950	Houston	TX	77010	713-255-4800	590-0040
TF: 800-856-2583 ■ *Web:* www.bluelance.com					
bNimble Technologies					
45987 Paseo Padre Pkwy Suite 7	Fremont	CA	94539	510-870-2312	445-0625
Web: www.bnimbletech.com					
CA Inc 1 CA Plaza	Islandia	NY	11749	631-342-6000	342-6800
NYSE: CA ■ *TF:* 800-225-5224 ■ *Web:* www.ca.com					
CardLogix 16 Hughes Suite 100	Irvine	CA	92618	949-380-1312	380-1428
Web: www.cardlogix.com					
Certicom Corp 4701 Tahoe Blvd Bldg A	Mississauga	ON	L4W0B5	905-507-4220	507-4230
TF: 800-561-6100 ■ *Web:* www.certicom.com					
Check Point Software Technologies Ltd					
800 Bridge Pkwy	Redwood City	CA	94065	650-628-2000	654-4233
NASDAQ: CHKP ■ *TF:* 800-429-4391 ■ *Web:* www.checkpoint.com					
Cincom Systems Inc 55 Merchant St	Cincinnati	OH	45246	513-612-2300	612-2000
TF: 800-888-0115 ■ *Web:* www.cincom.com					
Citrix Systems Inc					
851 W Cypress Creek Rd	Fort Lauderdale	FL	33309	954-267-3000	267-9319
NASDAQ: CTXS ■ *TF:* 800-393-1888 ■ *Web:* www.citrix.com					
Cognetics Corp PO Box 386	Princeton Junction	NJ	08550	609-799-5005	
Web: www.cognetics.com					
Columbia Data Products Inc					
925 Sunshine Ln Suite 1080	Altamonte Springs	FL	32714	407-869-6700	862-4725
TF Sales: 800-613-6288 ■ *Web:* www.cdpi.com					
Communication Intelligence Corp (CIC)					
275 Shoreline Dr Suite 500	Redwood Shores	CA	94065	650-802-7888	802-7777
OTC: CICI ■ *TF Sales:* 800-888-8242 ■ *Web:* www.cic.com					
CommuniGate Systems Inc					
655 Redwood Hwy Suite 275	Mill Valley	CA	94941	415-383-7164	383-7461
TF: 800-262-4722 ■ *Web:* www.stalker.com					
ComponentOne LLC					
201 S Highland Ave, 3rd Fl Suite 500	Pittsburgh	PA	15206	412-681-4343	681-4384
TF: 800-858-2739 ■ *Web:* www.componentone.com					
Configuresoft Inc					
4390 Arrowswest Dr	Colorado Springs	CO	80907	719-447-4600	447-4601
Web: www.configuresoft.com					
CSI International Inc 8120 State Rt 138	Williamsport	OH	43164	740-420-5400	333-7335
TF: 800-795-4914 ■ *Web:* www.csi-international.com					
CSP Inc 43 Manning Rd	Billerica	MA	01821	978-663-7598	663-0150
TF: 800-325-3110 ■ *Web:* www.cspi.com					
CYA Technologies Inc 4 Research Dr	Shelton	CT	06484	203-513-3111	513-3139
Web: www.cya.com					
CyberTeams Inc 205 Broadway St	Frederick	MD	21701	301-473-7778	473-9751
TF: 888-449-5575 ■ *Web:* www.cyberteams.com					
DataDirect Technologies					
3202 Tower Oaks Blvd	Rockville	MD	20852	301-468-8501	
TF: 800-876-3101 ■ *Web:* www.datadirect.com					
DataPath Inc					
3095 Satellite Blvd Bldg 800 Suite 600	Duluth	GA	30096	678-597-0300	252-4101
TF: 866-855-3800 ■ *Web:* www.datapath.com					
DataViz Inc 612 Wheelers Farms Rd	Milford	CT	06460	203-874-0085	874-4345
TF: 800-733-0030 ■ *Web:* www.dataviz.com					
Datawatch Corp 271 Mill Rd	Chelmsford	MA	01824	978-441-2200	441-1114
NASDAQ: DWCH ■ *TF:* 800-445-3311 ■ *Web:* www.datawatch.com					
Descartes Systems Group Inc 120 Randall Dr	Waterloo	ON	N2V1C6	519-746-8110	747-0082
NASDAQ: DSGX ■ *TF:* 800-419-8495 ■ *Web:* www.descartes.com					
Digicomp Research Corp 930 Danby Rd	Ithaca	NY	14850	607-273-5900	273-8779
TF Cust Svc: 800-457-6000 ■ *Web:* www.digicomp.com					
Digimarc Corp 9405 SW Gemini Dr	Beaverton	OR	97008	503-469-4800	469-4780
NASDAQ: DMRC ■ *TF:* 800-344-4627 ■ *Web:* www.digimarc.com					
Digital Persona Inc 720 Bay Rd Suite 100	Redwood City	CA	94063	650-474-4000	298-8313
TF: 877-378-2738 ■ *Web:* www.digitalpersona.com					
Diskeeper Corp 7590 N Glenoaks Blvd	Burbank	CA	91504	818-771-1600	252-5514
TF Sales: 800-829-6468 ■ *Web:* www.diskeeper.com					
Distinct Corp 3315 Almaden Expy Suite 10	San Jose	CA	95118	408-445-3270	445-3274
Web: www.distinct.com					
Diversified International Sciences Corp					
4550 Forbes Blvd Suite 300	Lanham	MD	20706	301-731-9070	731-9070
Diversinet Corp					
2225 Sheppard Ave E Suite 1700	Toronto	ON	M2J5B5	416-756-2324	756-7346
Web: www.diversinet.com					
E-Net Corp 300 Valley St Suite 204	Sausalito	CA	94965	415-332-6200	339-9592
Web: www.enet.com					
EasyLink Services Corp					
6025 The Corners Pwy Suite 100	Norcross	GA	30092	678-823-4600	
NASDAQ: ESIC ■ *TF:* 800-209-6245 ■ *Web:* www.easylink.com					
Electronic Scriptorium Ltd					
26 Fairfax St SE Suite K	Leesburg	VA	20175	703-779-0376	779-0378
Web: www.electronicscriptorium.com					
eMag Solutions LLC					
3495 Piedmont Rd 11 Piedmont Ctr Suite 500	Atlanta	GA	30305	404-995-6060	872-8247
TF: 800-364-9838 ■ *Web:* www.emaglink.com					
EMC Corp 176 S St	Hopkinton	MA	01748	508-435-1000	497-6912
NYSE: EMC ■ *TF:* 877-362-6973 ■ *Web:* www.emc.com					
EMC Legato 2831 Mission College Blvd	Santa Clara	CA	95054	408-566-2000	566-2701
TF Tech Supp: 877-534-2867 ■ *Web:* www.emc.com					
Empirix Inc 20 Crosby Dr	Bedford	MA	01730	781-266-3200	266-3201
Web: www.empirix.com					
Entegrity Solutions Corp 410 Amherst St	Nashua	NH	03063	603-882-1306	882-6092
TF: 800-525-4343					
Entrust Inc 5400 LBJ Fwy Suite 1340	Dallas	TX	75240	972-728-0447	728-0440
TF Sales: 888-690-2424 ■ *Web:* www.entrust.com					
Esker Inc 1212 Deming Way Suite 350	Madison	WI	53717	608-828-6000	828-6001
TF: 800-368-5283 ■ *Web:* www.esker.com					
Expert Choice Inc 1501 Lee Hwy Suite 302	Arlington	VA	22209	703-243-5595	243-5587
TF: 888-259-6400 ■ *Web:* www.expertchoice.com					
F-Secure Inc 100 Century Ctr Ct Suite 700	San Jose	CA	95112	408-938-6700	938-6701
Web: www.f-secure.com					
FalconStor Software Inc					
2 Huntington Quad Suite 2S01	Melville	NY	11747	631-777-5188	501-7633
NASDAQ: FALC ■ *Web:* www.falconstor.com					
FileStream Inc 333 Glen Head Rd	Glen Head	NY	11545	516-759-4100	759-3011
Web: www.filestream.com					
Forvus Research Inc 742-200 McKnight Dr	Knightdale	NC	27545	919-954-0063	954-9254
TF: 888-323-4887 ■ *Web:* www.forvus.com					
GroupSystems 228 Pk Ave S Suite 49066	New York	NY	10003	800-368-6338	468-8681*
**Fax Area Code:* 303 ■ *TF:* 800-368-6338 ■ *Web:* www3.groupsystems.com					
harmon.ie 698 Tasman Dr	Milpitas	CA	95035	408-907-1339	351-4984
TF: 800-624-6946 ■ *Web:* harmon.ie					
Heroix Corp 57 Wells Ave	Newton	MA	02459	617-527-1550	527-6132
TF: 800-229-6500 ■ *Web:* www.heroix.com					
Hitachi Data Systems Corp					
750 Central Expy	Santa Clara	CA	95050	408-970-1000	727-8036
TF: 800-227-1930 ■ *Web:* www.hds.com					
Infosystems Technology Inc					
7700 Leesburg Pike Suite 402	Falls Church	VA	22043	703-448-0002	448-9898
Web: www.rubix.com					
Innodata-Isogen Inc 3 University Plaza Dr	Hackensack	NJ	07601	201-371-8000	
NASDAQ: INOD ■ *TF:* 877-454-8400 ■ *Web:* www.innodata-isogen.com					
Innovative Security Systems Inc					
1809 Woodfield Dr	Savoy	IL	61874	217-355-6308	355-1433
Web: www.argus-systems.com					
Integralis US					
111 Founders Plaza 13th Fl	East Hartford	CT	06108	860-291-0851	291-0847
TF: 877-557-1475 ■ *Web:* www.us.integralis.com					
International Business Machines Corp (IBM)					
1 New Orchard Rd	Armonk	NY	10504	914-766-1900	
NYSE: IBM ■ *TF:* 800-426-4968 ■ *Web:* www.ibm.com					
InterTrust Technologies Corp					
955 Stewart Dr	Sunnyvale	CA	94085	408-616-1600	616-1626
Web: www.intertrust.com					
Intrusion Inc 1101 E Arapaho Rd	Richardson	TX	75081	972-234-6400	234-1467
TF: 800-862-6637 ■ *Web:* www.intrusion.com					
Ipswitch Inc 83 Hartwell Ave	Lexington	MA	02421	781-676-5700	676-5710
TF: 800-793-4825 ■ *Web:* www.ipswitch.com					
Kroll Ontrack Inc 9023 Columbine Rd	Eden Prairie	MN	55347	952-937-5161	937-5750
TF: 800-872-2599 ■ *Web:* www.krollontrack.com					
LapLink Software Inc					
14335 NE 24th St Suite 201	Bellevue	WA	98007	425-952-6000	952-6002
TF: 800-343-8080 ■ *Web:* www.laplink.com					
Lattice Inc 1751 S Naperville Rd Suite 100	Wheaton	IL	60187	630-949-3250	949-3299
TF Sales: 800-444-4309 ■ *Web:* www.lattice.com					
Lenel System International Inc					
1212 Pittsford-Victor Rd	Pittsford	NY	14534	585-248-9720	248-9185
Web: www.lenel.com					
Linspire Inc					
5960 Cornerstone Ct W Suite 200	San Diego	CA	92121	858-587-6700	587-8095
Web: www.linspire.com					
Luminex Software Inc 871 Marlborough Ave	Riverside	CA	92507	951-781-4100	781-4105
TF Sales: 888-586-4639 ■ *Web:* www.luminex.com					
Magic Software Enterprises Inc					
23046 Avenida de la Carlotta Suite 300	Laguna Hills	CA	92653	949-250-1718	250-7404
NASDAQ: MGIC ■ *TF:* 800-345-6244 ■ *Web:* www.magic-sw.com					

				Phone	Fax
Mainstay 1320 Flynn Rd Suite 401	Camarillo	CA	93012	805-484-9400	484-9428
TF Orders: 800-362-2605 ■ *Web:* www.mstay.com					
Management Science Assoc Inc					
6565 Penn Ave	Pittsburgh	PA	15206	412-362-2000	363-8878
TF: 800-672-4636 ■ *Web:* www.msa.com					
Mandarin Library Automation Inc					
1100 Holland Dr	Boca Raton	FL	33487	561-995-4010	995-4065
TF: 800-426-7477 ■ *Web:* www.mlasolutions.com					
Mangosoft Inc 108 Village Sq Suite 315	Somers	NY	10589	914-669-5333	277-3385*
**Fax Area Code:* 866 ■ *TF:* 888-886-2646 ■ *Web:* www.mangosoft.com					
MARX Software Security Inc					
2900 Chamblee-Tucker Rd Bldg 9 Suite 100	Atlanta	GA	30341	770-986-8887	986-8891
TF: 800-627-9468 ■ *Web:* www.cryptotech.com					
Maxum Development Corp PO Box 315	Crystal Lake	IL	60039	815-444-0100	444-0301*
**Fax:* Sales ■ *TF:* 800-813-3410 ■ *Web:* www.maxum.com					
McAfee Inc 2821 Mission College Blvd	Santa Clara	CA	95054	408-988-3832	970-9727
NYSE: MFE ■ *TF Cust Svc:* 888-847-8766 ■ *Web:* www.mcafee.com					
McCabe & Assoc Inc					
9730 Patuxent Dr Suite 400	Columbia	MD	21045	410-381-3710	381-7912
TF: 800-638-6316 ■ *Web:* www.mccabe.com					
Mediafour Corp 1101 5th St	West Des Moines	IA	50266	515-225-7409	225-6370
Web: www.mediafour.com					
Micro 2000 Inc 700 N Central Ave Suite 6	Glendale	CA	91203	818-547-0125	543-7092
TF: 800-864-8008 ■ *Web:* www.micro2000pcdiagnostics.com					
Micro Logic Corp 666 Godwin Ave	Midland Park	NJ	07432	201-447-6991	447-6921
Web: www.miclog.com					
Microsoft Corp 1 Microsoft Way	Redmond	WA	98052	425-882-8080	936-7329
NASDAQ: MSFT ■ *Web:* www.microsoft.com					
Mindjet Corp 1160 Battery St E 4th Fl	San Francisco	CA	94111	415-229-4200	229-4201
Web: www.mindjet.com					
Mitem Corp 640 Menlo Ave	Menlo Park	CA	94025	650-323-1500	323-1511
TF Sales: 800-826-4836 ■ *Web:* www.mitem.com					
MTI Systems Inc I-59 Dr	WEST SPRINGFIELD	MA	00108	413-733-1972	739-9250
TF: 800-644-4318 ■ *Web:* www.mtisystems.com					
NetIQ Corp 1233 W Loop S	Houston	TX	77027	713-548-1700	548-1771
TF Sales: 888-323-6768 ■ *Web:* www.netiq.com					
Network Appliance Inc 495 E Java Dr	Sunnyvale	CA	94089	408-822-6000	822-4422
NASDAQ: NTAP ■ *TF Sales:* 800-443-4537 ■ *Web:* www.netapp.com					
New Year Tech Inc 12330 Pinecrest Rd Suite 100	Reston	VA	20191	703-564-0290	564-0296
Web: www.nyt1.net					
Norman Data Defense Systems Inc					
9302 Lee Hwy Suite 950A	Fairfax	VA	22031	703-267-6109	934-6368
TF: 888-466-6762 ■ *Web:* www.norman.com					
NovaStor Corp 80-B W Cochran St	Simi Valley	CA	93065	805-579-6700	579-6710*
**Fax:* Sales ■ *TF:* 800-668-2786 ■ *Web:* www.novastor.com					
NTP Software 20A NW Blvd Suite 136	Nashua	NH	03063	603-622-4400	263-2375
TF: 800-226-2755 ■ *Web:* www.ntpsoftware.com					
Numara Software Inc					
2202 NW Shore Blvd Suite 650	Tampa	FL	33607	813-227-4500	227-4501
TF Sales: 800-557-3031 ■ *Web:* www.numarasoftware.com					
Open Door Networks Inc 110 S Laurel St	Ashland	OR	97520	541-488-4127	
Web: www.opendoor.com					
Open Systems Management Inc					
1511 3rd Ave Suite 905	Seattle	WA	98101	206-583-8373	583-8374
TF: 866-601-8011 ■ *Web:* www.osmcorp.com					
OPNET Technologies Inc 7255 Woodmont Ave	Bethesda	MD	20814	240-497-3000	497-3001
NASDAQ: OPNT ■ *Web:* www.opnet.com					
Optical Research Assoc 3280 E Foothill Blvd	Pasadena	CA	91107	626-795-9101	795-9102
Web: www.opticalres.com					
Oracle Corp 500 Oracle Pkwy	Redwood Shores	CA	94065	650-506-7000	506-7200
NASDAQ: ORCL ■ *TF Sales:* 800-392-2999 ■ *Web:* www.oracle.com					
Panda Software					
230 N Maryland Ave Suite 303 PO Box 10578	Glendale	CA	91209	818-553-0599	543-6910
Web: www.pandasecurity.com					
Peoplesmith Software Inc					
50 Cole Pkwy Suite 34	Scituate	MA	02066	781-545-7300	545-7717
TF Sales: 800-777-2460 ■ *Web:* www.peoplesmith.com					
Perceptics Corp 9737 Cogdill Rd Suite 200	Knoxville	TN	37932	865-966-9200	966-9330
TF: 800-448-8544 ■ *Web:* www.perceptics.com					
Pervasive Software Inc					
12365 Riata Trace Pkwy Bldg B	Austin	TX	78727	512-231-6000	231-6010
NASDAQ: PVSW ■ *TF:* 800-287-4383 ■ *Web:* www.pervasive.com					
Phoenix Technologies Ltd					
915 Murphy Ranch Rd	Milpitas	CA	95035	408-570-1000	570-1001
TF: 800-677-7305 ■ *Web:* www.phoenix.com					
PKWare Inc 648 N Plankinton Ave Suite 220	Milwaukee	WI	53203	414-354-8699	289-9789
Web: www.pkware.com/company					
Plex Systems Inc 1731 Harmon Rd	Auburn Hills	MI	48326	248-391-8001	393-1799
Web: www.plex.com					
Pragma Systems Inc					
13708 Research Blvd Suite 675	Austin	TX	78750	512-219-7270	219-7110
TF Sales: 800-224-1675 ■ *Web:* www.pragmasys.com					
Process Software Corp 959 Concord St	Framingham	MA	01701	508-879-6994	879-0042
TF: 800-722-7770 ■ *Web:* www.process.com					
RadView Software Inc					
111 Deerwood Rd Suite 200	San Ramon	CA	94583	925-831-4808	831-4807
TF: 888-723-8439 ■ *Web:* www.radview.com					
Raxco Software Inc					
6 Montgomery Village Ave Suite 500	Gaithersburg	MD	20879	301-527-0803	519-7711
TF Tech Supp: 800-546-9728 ■ *Web:* www.raxco.com					
RDKS Inc 17861 Cartwright Rd	Irvine	CA	92614	949-851-1085	851-8588*
**Fax:* Sales ■ *Web:* www.litronic.com					
Red Hat Inc 1801 Varsity Dr	Raleigh	NC	27606	919-754-3700	754-3701
NYSE: RHAT ■ *TF:* 888-733-4281 ■ *Web:* www.redhat.com					
Relais International					
1690 Woodward Dr Suite 215	Ottawa	ON	K2C3R8	613-226-5571	226-0998
TF: 888-294-5244 ■ *Web:* www.relais-intl.com					
Rhintek Inc 8835 Columbia 100 Pkwy Suite C	Columbia	MD	21045	410-730-2575	730-5960
Web: www.rhintek.com					
RSA Security Inc 174 Middlesex Tpke	Bedford	MA	01730	781-515-5000	515-5010
NASDAQ: RSAS ■ *TF:* 877-772-4900 ■ *Web:* www.rsa.com					

				Phone	Fax
ScriptLogic Corp					
6000 Broken Sound Pkwy NW	Boca Raton	FL	33487	561-886-2400	886-2499
Web: www.scriptlogic.com					
Sensory Inc 1991 Russell Ave	Santa Clara	CA	95054	408-327-9000	727-4748
Web: www.sensoryinc.com					
Serengeti Systems Inc 812 W 11th St 3rd Fl	Austin	TX	78701	512-345-2211	480-8729
TF: 800-634-3122 ■ *Web:* www.serengeti.com					
Silicon Graphics Inc (SGI) 1140 E Argues Ave	Sunnyvale	CA	94085	650-960-1980	933-0908
Web: www.sgi.com					
Simtrol Inc 2200 Norcross Pkwy Suite 255	Norcross	GA	30071	770-242-7566	441-1823
TF: 800-423-0769 ■ *Web:* www.simtrol.com					
Skyward Inc 5233 Coye Dr	Stevens Point	WI	54481	715-341-9406	341-1370
TF: 800-236-0001 ■ *Web:* www.skyward.com					
Smart Card Integrators Inc (SCI)					
2424 N Ontario St	Burbank	CA	91504	818-847-1022	847-1454
Web: www.sci-s.com					
Smart Card Solutions LLC 229 E Capitol Dr	Hartland	WI	53029	262-369-3400	369-3401
TF: 888-225-6442 ■ *Web:* www.sc-solutions.com					
Smart Dynamics LLC					
3601 Wilson Blvd Suite 500	Arlington	VA	22201	703-312-7383	812-5190
Web: www.smartdynamics.com					
SNMP Research International Inc					
3001 Kimberlin Heights Rd	Knoxville	TN	37920	865-579-3311	579-6565
Web: www.snmp.com					
Software Engineering of America Inc (SEA)					
1230 Hempstead Tpke	Franklin Square	NY	11010	516-328-7000	354-4015
TF: 800-272-7322 ■ *Web:* www.seasoft.com					
Software Pursuits Inc 1900 S Norfolk St	San Mateo	CA	94403	650-372-0900	372-2912
TF: 800-367-4823 ■ *Web:* www.softwarepursuits.com					
Soliton Inc 44 Victoria St Suite 820	Toronto	ON	M5C1Y2	416-364-9355	364-6159
TF: 888-327-9457 ■ *Web:* www.soliton.com					
SPSS Inc ShowCase Div 233 S Wacker Dr 11th Fl	Chicago	IL	60606	312-651-3000	
TF: 800-259-1028 ■ *Web:* www.spss.com					
SPYRUS Inc 2355 Oakland Rd Suite 1	San Jose	CA	95131	408-953-0700	953-9835
TF: 800-277-9787 ■ *Web:* www.spyrus.com					
Stirling Networks Inc 2751 Currier Ave	Simi Valley	CA	93065	805-579-8998	579-8190
Web: www.businessbasic.com					
Stratus Technologies 111 Powdermill Rd	Maynard	MA	01754	978-461-7000	461-5210
TF: 800-787-2887 ■ *Web:* www.stratus.com					
Symantec Corp 350 Ellis St	Mountain View	CA	94043	650-527-8000	527-8050
NASDAQ: SYMC ■ *TF:* 800-441-7234 ■ *Web:* www.symantec.com					
Syncsort Inc 50 Tice Blvd	Woodcliff Lake	NJ	07677	201-930-9700	930-8290
Web: www.syncsort.com					
TeamQuest Corp 1 TeamQuest Way	Clear Lake	IA	50428	641-357-2700	357-2778
TF: 800-551-8326 ■ *Web:* www.teamquest.com					
TechSmith Corp 2405 Woodlake Dr	Okemos	MI	48864	517-381-2300	381-2336
TF: 800-517-3001 ■ *Web:* www.techsmith.com					
Tecsec Inc 1953 Gallows Rd Suite 220	Vienna	VA	22182	703-506-9069	506-1484
Web: www.tecsec.com					
Telesensory Inc 38083 Cherry St	Newark	CA	94560	510-793-3075	793-2017
Web: www.telesensory.com					
Tenebril Inc 959 Concord St	Framingham	MA	01701	508-879-6994	879-0042
TF: 800-722-7770 ■ *Web:* www.tenebril.com					
Thales e-Security Inc					
2200 N Commerce Pkwy Suite 200	Weston	FL	33326	954-888-6200	888-6211
TF: 888-744-4976 ■ *Web:* www.thales-esecurity.com					
TigerLogic Corp 25-A Technology Dr	Irvine	CA	92618	949-442-4400	250-8187
NASDAQ: RDTA ■ *TF:* 800-367-7425 ■ *Web:* www.rainingdata.com					
TouchStone Software Corp 1538 Tpke St	North Andover	MA	01845	978-686-6468	683-1630
TF: 800-800-2467					
TrendMicro Inc					
10101 N De Anza Blvd Suite 200	Cupertino	CA	95014	408-257-1500	257-2003
TF: 800-228-5651 ■ *Web:* www.us.trendmicro.com					
Tripwire Inc 101 SW Main St # 1500	Portland	OR	97204	503-276-7500	223-0182
TF: 800-874-7947 ■ *Web:* www.tripwire.com					
TurboLinux Inc					
600 Townsend St Suite 120E	San Francisco	CA	94103	415-503-4330	437-2892
Web: www.turbolinux.com					
UltraBac Software 15015 Main St Suite 200	Bellevue	WA	98007	425-644-6000	644-8222
Web: www.ultrabac.com					
UniSoft Corp 10 Rollins Rd Suite 118	Millbrae	CA	94030	650-259-1290	259-1299
Web: www.unisoft.com					
US Design Corp 9075 Guilford Rd	Columbia	MD	21046	410-381-3000	381-3235
VanDyke Software Inc					
4848 Tramway Ridge Dr NE Suite 101	Albuquerque	NM	87111	505-332-5700	332-5701
Web: www.vandyke.com					
Vcg LLC 1805 Old Alabama Rd	Roswell	GA	30076	770-246-2300	449-3638
TF: 800-318-4983 ■ *Web:* www.vcgsoftware.com					
Vendant Inc 26 Parker St	Newburyport	MA	01950	978-462-0737	462-4755
TF: 800-714-4900 ■ *Web:* www.vedanthealth.com					
Vision Solutions Inc 15300 Barranca Pkwy	Irvine	CA	92618	949-253-6500	253-6501
TF: 800-683-4667 ■ *Web:* www.visionsolutions.com					
VisionAIR Inc 5601 Barbados Blvd	Castle Hayne	NC	28429	910-675-9117	602-6190
TF: 800-882-2108 ■ *Web:* www.visionair.com					
Visual Automation Inc					
403 S Clinton St Suite 4	Grand Ledge	MI	48837	517-622-1850	622-1761
Web: www.visualautomation.com					
Webroot Software Inc 2560 55th St	Boulder	CO	80301	303-442-3813	442-3846
TF: 800-772-9383 ■ *Web:* www.webroot.com					
WildPackets Inc					
1340 Treat Blvd Suite 500	Walnut Creek	CA	94597	925-937-3200	937-3211*
**Fax:* Sales ■ *TF:* 800-466-2447 ■ *Web:* www.wildpackets.com					
Wilson WindowWare Inc 5421 California Ave SW	Seattle	WA	98136	206-938-1740	935-7129
TF: 800-762-8383 ■ *Web:* www.windowware.com					
Wind River Systems Inc 500 Wind River Way	Alameda	CA	94501	510-748-4100	749-2010
TF: 800-545-9463 ■ *Web:* www.windriver.com					
WinZip Computing Inc PO Box 540	Mansfield	CT	06268	860-429-3539	429-3542
Web: www.winzip.com					
Xinet Inc 2560 9th St Suite 312	Berkeley	CA	94710	510-845-0555	644-2680
Web: www.xinet.com					
XIOtech Corp					
9950 Federal Dr Suite 100	Colorado Springs	CO	80921	719-388-5500	
TF: 866-472-6764 ■ *Web:* www.xiotech.com					

				Phone	Fax
Yrrid Software Inc 507 Monroe St *TF:* 800-443-0065 ■ *Web:* www.yrrid.com	Chapel Hill	NC	27516	919-968-7858	968-7856
Zix Corp 2711 N Haskell Ave Suite 2300-LB *NASDAQ: ZIXI* ■ *TF:* 888-771-4049 ■ *Web:* www.zixcorp.com	Dallas	TX	75204	214-370-2000	370-2070
Zone Alarm 800 Bridge Pkwy *TF:* 877-966-5221 ■ *Web:* www.zonealarm.com	Redwood City	CA	94065	415-633-4500	633-4501

182 COMPUTER STORES

SEE ALSO Appliance & Home Electronics Stores p. 1396

				Phone	Fax
A Matter of Fax 105 Harrison Ave *TF:* 800-433-3329 ■ *Web:* www.amatteroffax.com	Harrison	NJ	07029	973-482-3700	482-0715
Aaron Industries Inc 28966 Hwy 76 E *TF:* 800-525-2558 ■ *Web:* www.aaronindustriesinc.com	Clinton	SC	29325	864-833-0178	833-5493
Aberdeen LLC 9130 Norwalk Blvd **Fax:* Sales ■ *Web:* www.aberdeeninc.com	Santa Fe Springs	CA	90670	562-699-6998	695-5570*
Adtech Solutions LLC 1880 McFarland Pkwy **Fax Area Code:* 678 ■ *Web:* www.adtechglobal.com	Alpharetta	GA	30005	770-205-2346	679-2333*
Aspyr Media Inc 1221 S MoPac Expwy Suite 50 *Web:* www.aspyr.com	Austin	TX	78746	512-708-8100	708-9595
Barcoding Inc 2220 Boston St *TF:* 888-412-7226 ■ *Web:* www.barcoding.com	Baltimore	MD	21231	410-385-8532	385-8559
CDW Corp 200 N Milwaukee Ave *TF:* 800-828-4239 ■ *Web:* www.cdw.com	Vernon Hills	IL	60061	847-465-6000	465-6800
Computer Renaissance 500 S Florida Ave Suite 400 **Fax Area Code:* 800 ■ *Web:* www.compren.com	Lakeland	FL	33801	863-669-1155	665-6324*
ConnectWise Inc 2803 W Busch Blvd Suite 204 *TF:* 866-476-8781 ■ *Web:* www.connectwise.com	Tampa	FL	33618	813-463-4700	
Datel Systems Inc 5636 Ruffin Rd *Web:* www.datelsys.com	San Diego	CA	92123	858-571-3100	571-0452
GameStop Corp 625 Westport Pkwy *NYSE: GME* ■ *TF:* 800-883-8895 ■ *Web:* www.gamestop.com	Grapevine	TX	76051	817-424-2000	424-2002
Gateway Inc 7565 Irvine Ctr Dr *NYSE: GTW* ■ *TF:* 800-846-2000 ■ *Web:* www.gateway.com	Irvine	CA	92618	949-471-7000	471-7001
Geeks.com 1890 Ord Way *Web:* www.geeks.com	Oceanside	CA	92056	760-726-7700	726-7723
Govconnection Inc 7503 Standish Pl **Fax Area Code:* 603 ■ *TF:* 888-213-0607 ■ *Web:* www.govconnection.com	Rockville	MD	20855	800-998-0009	423-6192*
Hartco LP 9393 Boul Louis H Lafontaine *Web:* www.hartco.com	Ville d'Anjou	QC	H1J1Y8	514-354-3810	354-1998
Innovative Information Solutions Inc 61 I- Ln *TF:* 800-343-8121 ■ *Web:* www.innovativeis.com	Waterbury	CT	06705	203-756-4243	756-4244
Insight Enterprises Inc 6820 S Harl Ave *NASDAQ: NSIT* ■ *TF:* 800-467-4448 ■ *Web:* www.insight.com	Tempe	AZ	85283	480-333-3000	760-3330
Intalio Inc 644 Emerson St Suite 200 *Web:* www.intalio.com	Palo Alto	CA	94301	650-596-1800	249-0439
Knowledge Information Solutions Inc 2877 Guardian Ln Suite 201 *Web:* www.kisinc.net	Virginia Beach	VA	23452	757-463-0033	463-3971
Mda Mindbox Inc 350 S Grand Ave 34th Fl **Fax Area Code:* 415 ■ *TF:* 877-650-6463 ■ *Web:* www.mindbox.com	Los Angeles	CA	90071	877-650-6463	785-3055*
Mphasis Corp 460 Pk Ave S Rm 1101 *Web:* www.mphasis.com	New York	NY	10016	212-686-6655	
Newegg Inc 16839 E Gale Ave *TF:* 800-390-1119 ■ *Web:* www.newegg.com	City of Industry	CA	91745	626-271-9700	271-9403
PC Connection Inc 730 Milford Rd Rt 101A *NASDAQ: PCCC* ■ *TF:* 800-800-1111 ■ *Web:* www.pcconnection.com	Merrimack	NH	03054	603-683-2000	683-5766
PC Connection Inc MacConnection Div 730 Milford Rd Rt 101A *TF:* 800-800-0014 ■ *Web:* www.macconnection.com	Merrimack	NH	03054	603-683-2000	683-5766
PC Mall Inc 2555 W 190th St *NASDAQ: MALL* ■ **Fax:* Mktg ■ *TF:* 800-413-3833 ■ *Web:* www.pcmall.com	Torrance	CA	90504	310-354-5600	353-7475*
Physmark Inc 13140 Coit Rd Suite 410 *Web:* www.physmark.com	Dallas	TX	75240	972-231-8000	231-1410
Recursion Software Inc 2591 Dallas Pkwy Suite 200 *TF:* 800-727-8674 ■ *Web:* www.recursionsw.com	Frisco	TX	75034	972-731-8800	731-8881
Tech Depot 6 Cambridge Dr **Fax:* Cust Svc ■ *TF Cust Svc:* 800-585-4080 ■ *Web:* www.4sure.com	Trumbull	CT	06611	203-615-7000	615-7005*
Topics Entertainment Inc 3401 Lind Ave SW *Web:* www.topics-ent.com	Renton	WA	98057	425-656-3621	656-8013
Translations.com Inc 3 Pk Ave 40th Fl *TF:* 800-688-7205 ■ *Web:* www.translations.com	New York	NY	10016	212-689-1616	685-9797
Tritech Software Systems 9860 Mesa Rim Rd *Web:* www.tritech.com	San Diego	CA	92121	858-799-7000	799-7010
Tukatech Inc 5527 E Slauson Ave *Web:* www.tukatech.com	Los Angeles	CA	90040	323-726-3836	726-3866

183 COMPUTER SYSTEMS DESIGN SERVICES

SEE ALSO Web Site Design Services p. 2774

Companies That Plan And Design Computer Systems That Integrate Hardware, Software, And Communication Technologies.

				Phone	Fax
3t Systems Inc 999 18th St Suite 2100 *TF:* 800-485-1180 ■ *Web:* www.3tsystems.com	Denver	CO	80202	303-858-8800	790-9784
Abacus Technology Corp 5454 Wisconsin Ave Suite 1100 *TF:* 800-225-2135 ■ *Web:* www.abacustech.com	Chevy Chase	MD	20815	301-907-8500	907-8508
Acumen Solutions Inc 8614 Westwood Ctr Dr Suite 700 *Web:* www.acumensolutions.com	Vienna	VA	22182	703-600-4000	600-4001
Advanced Information Systems Group Inc 11315 Corporate Blvd Suite 210 *Web:* www.aisg.com	Orlando	FL	32817	407-581-2929	581-2935
Advanced Resource Technologies Inc 1555 King St Suite 400 *TF:* 800-796-9936 ■ *Web:* www.team-arti.com	Alexandria	VA	22314	703-682-4740	682-4820
Advent Global Solutions Inc 12777 Jones Rd Suite 445 *TF:* 877-727-2247 ■ *Web:* www.adventglobal.com	Houston	TX	77070	832-678-3889	
AETEA Information Technology Inc 1445 Research Blvd Suite 300 *TF:* 888-772-3832 ■ *Web:* www.aetea.com	Rockville	MD	20850	301-721-4200	721-1730
AGSI 3390 Peachtree Rd NE Suite 350 *TF:* 800-768-2474 ■ *Web:* www.agsi.com	Atlanta	GA	30326	404-816-7577	816-7578
All Native Systems LLC 1 Mission Dr PO Box 458 *Web:* www.allnativesystems.com	Winnebago	NE	68071	402-878-2700	878-2560
Allied Technology Inc 1803 Research Blvd Suite 601 *Web:* www.alliedtech.com	Rockville	MD	20850	301-309-1234	309-0978
Allin Corp 381 Mansfield Ave Suite 400 *Web:* www.allin.com	Pittsburgh	PA	15220	412-928-8800	928-0887
AlphaSoft Services Corp 2121 N California Blvd Suite 345 *Web:* www.alphasoftservices.com	Walnut Creek	CA	94596	925-952-6300	932-3743
AmberWave Inc 13 Garabedian Dr *Web:* www.amberwave.com	Salem	NH	03079	603-870-8700	870-8607
American Systems Corp 14151 Pk Meadow Dr # 500 *TF:* 800-733-2721 ■ *Web:* www.2asc.com	Chantilly	VA	20151	703-968-6300	968-5151
Amtex Systems Inc 50 Broad St Suite 801 *Web:* www.amtexsystems.com	New York	NY	10004	212-269-6448	269-6458
Analysts International Corp 3601 W 76th St *NASDAQ: ANLY* ■ *TF:* 800-800-5044 ■ *Web:* www.analysts.com	Minneapolis	MN	55435	952-835-5900	897-4555
Arlington Computer Products Inc 851 Commerce Ct *TF Orders:* 800-548-5105 ■ *Web:* www.arlingtoncp.com	Buffalo Grove	IL	60089	847-541-6333	541-6881
Arrow Strategies LLC 30300 Telegraph Rd Suite 117 *Web:* www.arrowstrategies.com	Bingham Farms	MI	48025	248-502-2500	502-2525
Automation Image Inc 2650 Valley View Ln Suite 100 *Web:* www.ccentrix.com	Dallas	TX	75234	972-247-8816	243-2814
Automation Technologies Inc 8219 Leesburg Pike *Web:* www.ati4it.com	Vienna	VA	22182	703-883-1410	883-1435
Bay State Computers Inc 4201 Northview Dr Suite 408 *TF:* 800-266-3783 ■ *Web:* www.bayst.com	Bowie	MD	20716	301-352-7878	352-6925
Bell Industries Inc Tech.logix Group 5777 Decatur Blvd *TF:* 800-722-1599 ■ *Web:* www.belltechlogix.com	Indianapolis	IN	46241	317-227-6700	704-0064
Berbee Information Networks Corp 5520 Research Pk Dr *TF:* 888-888-8835 ■ *Web:* www.berbee.com	Madison	WI	53711	608-288-3000	288-3007
Blytheco LLC 23161 Mill Creek Dr *TF:* 800-425-9843 ■ *Web:* www.blytheco.com	Laguna Hills	CA	92653	949-583-9500	583-0649
Bull HN Information Systems Inc 285 Billerica Rd *Web:* www.bull.com	Billerica	MA	01821	978-294-6000	294-7999
CACI International Inc 1100 N Glebe Rd *NYSE: CACI* ■ *TF:* 888-868-1908 ■ *Web:* www.caci.com	Arlington	VA	22201	703-841-7800	841-7882
Cadre Computer Resources Co 255 E 5th St Suite 1200 *TF:* 888-862-2373 ■ *Web:* www.ccr.com	Cincinnati	OH	45202	513-762-7350	762-6502
Calence Inc 1560 W Fountainhead Pkwy # 2 *TF:* 877-225-3623 ■ *Web:* www.calence.com	Tempe	AZ	85282	480-889-9500	889-9599
Calibre Systems Inc 6354 Walker Ln Suite 300, Metro Pk *TF:* 888-225-4273 ■ *Web:* www.calibresys.com	Alexandria	VA	22310	703-797-8500	797-8501
Camber Corp 635 Discovery Dr NW *TF:* 800-998-7988 ■ *Web:* www.camber.com	Huntsville	AL	35806	256-922-0200	922-3599
Capgemini US LLC 623 5th Ave # 33 *Web:* www.us.capgemini.com	New York	NY	10022	917-934-8000	934-8001
Carreker Corp 4055 Valley View Ln Suite 1000 *TF:* 800-486-1981 ■ *Web:* www.carreker.fiserv.com	Dallas	TX	75244	972-458-1981	701-0758
Catapult Systems Inc 1221 S MoPac Expwy Suite 350 *Web:* www.catapultsystems.com	Austin	TX	78746	512-328-8181	328-0584
CD Group Inc 5550 Triangle Pkwy *Web:* www.cdgroup.com	Norcross	GA	30092	678-268-2000	268-2001
Cdo Technologies Inc 5200 Sprngfeld St Suite 320 *TF:* 866-307-6616 ■ *Web:* www.cdotech.com	Dayton	OH	45431	937-258-0022	258-1614
Cexec Inc 11440 Commerce Pk Dr Suite 600 *Web:* www.cexec.com	Reston	VA	20191	703-435-0099	766-8539
CGI Group Inc 1130 Sherbrooke St W 7th Fl *NYSE: GIB* ■ *TF:* 800-828-8377 ■ *Web:* www.cgi.ca	Montreal	QC	H3A2M8	514-841-3200	841-3299
Cherokee Information Services Inc 1225 S Clark St Suite 1300 *Web:* www.cherokee-inc.com	Arlington	VA	22202	703-416-0720	416-1045
CIBER Inc 6363 S Fiddler's Green Cir Suite 1400 *NYSE: CBR* ■ *TF:* 800-242-3799 ■ *Web:* www.ciber.com	Greenwood Village	CO	80111	303-220-0100	220-7100
Clarkston Consulting 1007 Slater Rd Suite 400 *TF:* 800-652-4274 ■ *Web:* www.clarkstonconsulting.com	Durham	NC	27703	919-484-4400	484-4450
Clever Devices Ltd 137 Commercial St *TF:* 800-872-6129 ■ *Web:* www.cleverdevices.com	Plainview	NY	11803	516-433-6100	433-5088
CodeSoft International Inc 6470 E Johns Crossing Suite 450 *Web:* www.codesoft.net	Duluth	GA	30097	770-913-0101	913-0611

Company / Address	City	State	ZIP	Phone	Fax
Cognizant Technology Solutions Corp 500 Frank W Burr Blvd	Teaneck	NJ	07666	201-801-0233	801-0243*
NASDAQ: CTSH ■ *Fax: Mktg ■ TF: 888-937-3277 ■ Web: www.cognizant.com					
COLSA Corp 6728 Odyssey Dr	Huntsville	AL	35806	256-964-5555	964-5418
Web: www.colsa.com					
Compri Consulting Inc 2601 Blake St # 110	Denver	CO	80205	303-860-1533	860-1557
Web: www.compri.com					
CompuCom Systems Inc Excell Data Div 1756 114th Ave SE Suite 220	Bellevue	WA	98004	425-974-2000	974-2001
TF: 800-539-2355 ■ Web: www.excell.com					
Computech Inc 7735 Old Georgetown Rd	Bethesda	MD	20814	301-656-4030	656-7060
Web: www.computechinc.com					
Computer Analytical Systems Inc (CASI) 1418 S 3rd St	Louisville	KY	40208	502-635-2019	636-9157
TF: 800-977-3475 ■ Web: www.c-a-s-i.com					
Computer Horizons Corp 49 Old Bloomfield Ave	Mountain Lakes	NJ	07046	973-299-4000	299-4000
NASDAQ: CHRZ ■ TF: 800-321-2421					
Computer Methods Corp 525 Rt 73 S Suite 300	Marlton	NJ	08053	856-596-4360	596-4362
TF: 800-969-4360 ■ Web: www.computermethods.com					
Computer Sciences Corp 2100 E Grand Ave	El Segundo	CA	90245	310-615-0311	640-2648
NYSE: CSC ■ TF: 800-342-5272 ■ Web: www.csc.com					
Computer Task Group Inc (CTG) 800 Delaware Ave	Buffalo	NY	14209	716-882-8000	887-7464
NASDAQ: CTGX ■ TF: 800-992-5350 ■ Web: www.ctg.com					
Computer Technology Assoc (CTA) 12530 Parklawn Dr Suite 470	Rockville	MD	20852	301-581-3200	581-3201
TF: 800-753-9201 ■ Web: www.cta.com					
Covansys Corp 32605 W 12 Mile Rd Suite 250	Farmington Hills	MI	48334	248-488-2088	488-2088
NASDAQ: CVNS					
Custom Computer Specialists Inc (CCS) 70 Suffolk Ct	Hauppauge	NY	11788	631-864-6699	543-2512
TF: 800-598-8989 ■ Web: www.customonline.com					
Cybertech Systems & Software Inc 1250 E Diehl Rd Suite 403	Naperville	IL	60563	630-472-3200	472-3299
TF: 800-874-1985 ■ Web: www.cybertech.com					
Data Systems Analysts Inc (DSA) 8 Neshaminy Interplex Suite 209	Trevose	PA	19053	215-245-4800	245-4375
Web: www.dsainc.com					
Delta CompuTec Inc 900 Huyler St	Teterboro	NJ	07608	201-440-8585	440-3985
TF: 800-477-8586 ■ Web: www.dcis.com					
Delta Corporate Services Inc 129 Littleton Rd	Parsippany	NJ	07054	973-334-6260	331-0144
TF: 800-335-8220 ■ Web: www.deltacorp.com					
Denali Advance Integration (DAI) 17735 NE 65th St Suite 130	Redmond	WA	98052	425-885-4000	467-1127
TF: 877-467-8008 ■ Web: www.denaliai.com					
Design Strategy Corp 600 3rd Ave 25th Fl	New York	NY	10016	212-370-0000	949-3648
TF: 800-331-8726 ■ Web: www.designstrategy.com					
DPE Systems Inc 425 Pontius Ave N Suite 430	Seattle	WA	98109	206-223-3737	223-0859
TF: 800-541-6566 ■ Web: www.dpes.com					
DRS Technical Services Inc 4041 Powder Mill Rd Suite 700	Calverton	MD	20705	301-595-0710	937-5236
TF: 800-282-6727 ■ Web: www.drs.com					
Dynamics Research Corp (DRC) Two Tech Dr	Andover	MA	01810	978-289-1500	289-1887
NASDAQ: DRCO ■ TF: 800-522-4321 ■ Web: www.drc.com					
Dyonyx LP 1235 N Loop W	Houston	TX	77008	713-485-7000	
TF: 855-749-6758 ■ Web: www.dyonyx.com					
E.magination Network Llc 1030 Hull St Suite 300	Baltimore	MD	21230	410-234-1500	234-1485
Web: www.emagination.com					
EA Consulting Inc 1130 Iron Pt Rd Suite 288	Folsom	CA	95630	916-357-6588	200-0368
TF: 800-399-2828 ■ Web: www.ea-inc.com					
Echota Technologies Corp 3286 Northpark Blvd Suite A	Alcoa	TN	37701	865-273-1270	273-1277
Web: www.echotatech.com					
Edgewater Technology Inc 20 Harvard Mill Sq	Wakefield	MA	01880	781-246-3343	246-5903
NASDAQ: EDGW ■ TF: 800-233-7924 ■ Web: www.edgewater.com					
Electronic Consulting Services Inc 2750 Prosperity Ave Suite 510	Fairfax	VA	22031	703-270-1540	270-1541
Web: www.ecs-federal.com					
Electronic Warfare Assoc Inc (EWA Inc) 13873 Pk Ctr Rd Suite 500	Herndon	VA	20171	703-904-5700	904-5779
TF: 888-392-0002 ■ Web: www.ewa.com					
EMC Microsoft Practice 98 Inverness Dr E Suite 150	Englewood	CO	80112	303-542-7100	790-0908
Web: www.emc.com/mspractice					
ePartners Inc 6565 N MacArthur Blvd Suite 950	Irving	TX	75039	469-587-5660	587-5661
TF: 888-883-9797 ■ Web: www.epartnersolutions.com					
eVerge Group Inc 4965 Preston Pk Blvd Suite 700	Plano	TX	75093	972-608-1803	608-1893
TF: 888-548-1973 ■ Web: www.evergegroup.com					
Facilite Informatique Canada Inc 1010 Sherbrooke St W Office 2510	Montreal	QC	H3A2R7	514-284-5636	284-9529
Web: www.facilite.com					
Force 3 Inc 2151 Priest Bridge Dr Suite 7	Crofton	MD	21114	301-261-0204	721-5624*
*Fax Area Code: 410 ■ TF: 800-391-0204 ■ Web: www.force3.com					
Frontier Computer Corp 1275 Business Pk Dr	Traverse City	MI	49686	231-929-1386	
TF: 866-226-6344 ■ Web: www.frontiercomputercorp.com					
Fujitsu Consulting 1450 American Ln # 1700	Schaumburg	IL	60173	847-706-4000	706-4020
TF: 800-453-0347 ■ Web: www.fujitsu.com					
Fyi Systems Inc 3799 US Hwy 46	Parsippany	NJ	07054	973-331-9050	331-9055
Web: www.fyisolutions.com					
G&b Solutions Inc 1861 Wiehle Ave Suite 200	Reston	VA	20190	703-883-1140	883-1143
Web: www.gbsolutionsinc.com					
General Dynamics Information Technology 3211 Jermantown Rd	Fairfax	VA	22030	703-246-0200	246-0351
TF: 800-242-0230 ■ Web: www.gdit.com					
Genesis Corp 950 3rd Ave FL 26	New York	NY	10022	212-688-5522	421-6292
TF: 800-261-1776 ■ Web: www.genesis10.com					
GeoLogics Corp 5285 Shawnee Rd Suite 300	Alexandria	VA	22312	703-750-4000	750-4010
TF: 800-684-3455 ■ Web: www.corporateweb.geologics.com					
Getronics 290 Concord Rd	Billerica	MA	01821	978-625-5000	
TF: 800-225-0654 ■ Web: www.getronics.com					
Global Consultants Inc 25 Airport Rd	Morristown	NJ	07960	973-889-5200	292-1643
TF: 877-264-6424 ■ Web: www.collabera.com					
Global Management Systems Inc (GMSI) 2201 Wisconsin Ave NW Suite 300	Washington	DC	20007	202-471-4674	625-9016
Web: www.gmsi.com					
Global Technology Resources Inc 990 S Broadway Suite 400	Denver	CO	80209	303-455-8800	803-6520*
*Fax Area Code: 888 ■ TF: 877-603-1984 ■ Web: www.gtri.com					
Globalspec Inc 350 Jordan Rd	Troy	NY	12180	518-880-0200	880-0250
TF: 800-261-2052 ■ Web: www.globalspec.com					
GramTel USA 211 W Washington St # 2	South Bend	IN	46601	574-472-4726	472-0904
TF: 866-481-7622 ■ Web: www.gramtel.com					
Greenpages Inc 33 Badgers Island W	Kittery	ME	03904	207-439-7310	439-7334
TF: 888-687-4876 ■ Web: www.greenpages.com					
Harris Information Technology Services 13665 Dulles Technology Dr Suite 250	Herndon	VA	20171	703-480-2607	480-2610
TF: 800-339-8828 ■ Web: www.maxnet.harris.com					
Hartford Computer Group Inc 3949 Heritage Oak Ct	Simi Valley	CA	93063	805-306-2500	836-3600*
*Fax Area Code: 224 ■ TF: 800-680-4424 ■ Web: www.hcgi.com					
Helios & Matheson North America Inc 200 Pk Ave S Suite 901	New York	NY	10003	732-499-8229	979-2517*
*Fax Area Code: 212 ■ Web: www.tact.com					
Hexaware Technologies Inc 1095 Cranbury Rd	Jamesburg	NJ	08831	609-409-6950	409-6910
Web: www.hexaware.com					
Howard Systems International 290 Harbor Dr 1st Fl	Stamford	CT	06902	203-324-4600	324-7722*
*Fax: Hum Res ■ TF: 800-326-4860 ■ Web: www.howardsystems.com					
Ibaset 27442 Portola Pkwy	Foothill Ranch	CA	92610	949-598-5200	598-2600
TF: 877-422-7381 ■ Web: www.ibaset.com					
Iconixx Software 100 Congress Ave Suite 2000	Austin	TX	78701	877-426-6499	651-3111*
*Fax Area Code: 512 ■ TF: 877-426-6499 ■ Web: www.iconixxsoftware.com					
Ikon Office Solutions Inc 5100 W Lemon St Suite 250	Tampa	FL	33609	813-261-2000	261-2500
Web: www.ikon.com					
iMakeNews Inc 200 Fifth Ave	Waltham	MA	02451	781-890-4700	890-4701
TF: 866-964-6397 ■ Web: www.imninc.com					
Indotronix International Corp (IIC) 331 Main St	Poughkeepsie	NY	12601	845-473-1137	473-1197
TF: 800-800-8442 ■ Web: www.iic.com					
Infinite Technology Group Inc 28c W Jefryn Blvd	Deer Park	NY	11729	631-392-0962	392-0965
Web: www.itgl.net					
Infinity Software Development Inc 1901 Commonwealth Ln	Tallahassee	FL	32303	850-383-1011	383-1015
Web: www.infinity-software.com					
Information Analysis Inc 11240 Waples Mill Rd Suite 400	Fairfax	VA	22030	703-383-3000	293-7979
TF: 800-829-7614 ■ Web: www.infoa.com					
Information Systems & Networks Corp (ISN) 10411 Motor City Dr 7th Fl	Bethesda	MD	20817	301-469-0400	469-0767
Web: www.isncorp.com					
Innovative Logistics Techniques Inc 8300 Greensboro Dr # 225	McLean	VA	22102	703-506-1555	506-4559
TF: 800-466-6564 ■ Web: www.innolog.com					
Insite One Inc 135 N Plains Indus Rd	Wallingford	CT	06492	203-265-6111	265-1144
TF: 800-441-0091 ■ Web: www.insiteone.com					
Integrated Systems Analysts Inc 2001 N Beauregard St Suite 600	Alexandria	VA	22311	703-824-0700	379-6321
TF: 800-929-3436 ■ Web: www.isa.com					
Integro Inc 7670 S Chester St Suite 180	Englewood	CO	80112	303-575-9300	575-9633
TF: 888-575-9300 ■ Web: www.integro.com					
Intelligent Decisions Inc 21445 Beaumeade Cir	Ashburn	VA	20147	703-554-1600	
TF: 800-929-8331 ■ Web: www.intelligent.net					
Intelliswift Software Inc 39120 Argonaut Way	Fremont	CA	94538	510-490-9240	
Web: www.intelliswift.com					
Interactive Business Systems Inc 2625 Butterfield Rd	Oak Brook	IL	60523	630-571-9100	571-2490
TF: 800-555-5427 ■ Web: www.ibs.com					
Intermedia Group Inc 5 Hanover Sq 15th Fl	New York	NY	10004	212-248-0100	248-0600
Web: www.intermediagroup.com					
Inventa Technologies Inc 2040 Briggs Rd # B	Mount Laurel	NJ	08054	856-914-5200	608-7970
Web: www.inventa.com					
Iris Software Inc 200 Metroplex Dr Suite 300	Edison	NJ	08817	732-393-0034	393-0035
Web: www.irissoftinc.com					
Jacer Corp 10340 Democracy Ln	Fairfax	VA	22030	703-352-1964	352-5057
TF: 866-522-3726 ■ Web: www.jacer.com					
James River Technical Inc 4439 Cox Rd	Glen Allen	VA	23060	804-935-0150	935-0165
Web: www.jrti.com					
Jyacc Inc 114 W 47th St Fl 20	New York	NY	10036	800-458-3313	608-6753*
*Fax Area Code: 212 ■ TF: 800-458-3313 ■ Web: www.jyacc.com					
Karta Technologies Inc 5555 NW Pkwy	San Antonio	TX	78249	210-582-3000	582-3002
Web: www.karta.com					
Keane Inc 100 City Sq	Boston	MA	02129	877-885-3263	241-9507*
*Fax Area Code: 617 ■ TF: 877-885-3263 ■ Web: www.keane.com					
Kemtah Group Inc 6565 Americas Pkwy NE	Albuquerque	NM	87110	505-346-4900	
TF: 877-753-6824 ■ Web: www.kemtah.com					
KForce Government Soultions 2750 Prosperity Ave Suite 300	Fairfax	VA	22031	703-245-7350	245-7560
TF: 800-200-7465 ■ Web: www.kforcegov.com					
L-3 Communications Government Services Inc 3750 Centerview Dr	Chantilly	VA	20151	703-708-1400	708-5700
Web: www.l-3gsi.com					
Lighthouse Computer Services Inc 6 Blackstone Valley Pl Suite 205	Lincoln	RI	02865	401-334-0799	334-0719
TF: 888-542-8030 ■ Web: www.lighthousecs.com					
Logikal Solutions 3915 N 1800e Rd	Herscher	IL	60941	815-949-1593	949-1012
Web: www.logikalsolutions.com					

Company / Address	City	State	ZIP	Phone	Fax
Logistics Management Resources Inc 4300 Crossings Blvd *Web:* www.lmr-inc.com	Prince George	VA	23875	804-541-6193	541-2559
Lucrum Inc 7755 Montgomery Rd *TF:* 888-272-5797 ■ *Web:* www.lucruminc.com	Cincinnati	OH	45236	513-241-5949	241-6731
Maden Technologies 2110 Washington Blvd Suite 200 *TF:* 888-769-9333 ■ *Web:* www.madentech.com	Arlington	VA	22204	703-769-4440	769-4424
Mainline Information Systems Inc 1700 Summit Lake Dr *TF:* 800-811-4429 ■ *Web:* www.mainline.com	Tallahassee	FL	32317	850-219-5000	219-5050
Managed Business Solutions 12325 Oracle Blvd Suite 200 *Web:* www.thinkmbs.com	Colorado Springs	CO	80921	719-314-3400	314-3499
MANDEX Inc 12500 Fair Lakes Cir Suite 125 *TF:* 888-662-6339 ■ *Web:* www.mandex.com	Fairfax	VA	22033	703-227-0900	227-0910
ManTech International Corp 12015 Lee Jackson Hwy *NASDAQ: MANT* ■ *Web:* www.mantech.com	Fairfax	VA	22033	703-218-6000	218-6005
Maryville Technologies 540 Maryville Ctr Suite 300 *Web:* www.maryville.com	Saint Louis	MO	63141	636-519-4100	519-4141
Mercom Inc 235 Commerce Dr Unit 303 *TF:* 877-223-8330 ■ *Web:* www.mercomcorp.com	Pawleys Island	SC	29585	843-979-9957	979-9956
Meridian Group 9 PkwyN Suite 500 *TF:* 800-811-2674 ■ *Web:* www.onlinemeridian.com	Deerfield	IL	60015	847-940-1200	964-2662
Metters Industries Inc 8200 Greensboro Dr Suite 500 *TF:* 800-638-8377 ■ *Web:* www.metters.com	McLean	VA	22102	703-821-3300	821-3996
NCI Inc 11730 Plaza America Dr Suite 700 *NASDAQ: NCIT* ■ *Web:* www.nciinc.com	Reston	VA	20190	703-707-6900	707-6901
NCI Information Systems Inc 11730 Plaza America Dr Suite 700 *TF:* 888-409-5457 ■ *Web:* www.nciinc.com	Reston	VA	20190	703-707-6900	707-6901
New Technologies Inc 133386 International Pkwy *TF:* 800-773-8294 ■ *Web:* www.forensics-intl.com	Jacksonville	FL	32218	800-773-8294	588-0399
NewAgeSys Inc 231 Clarksville Rd Suite 200 *TF:* 888-863-9243 ■ *Web:* www.newagesys.com	Princeton Junction	NJ	08550	609-919-9800	919-9830
NuWare Technology Corp Inc 120 Wood Ave S Suite 404 *Web:* www.nuware.com	Iselin	NJ	08830	732-494-0550	494-4586
Odyssey Systems Consulting Group Ltd 201 Edgewater Dr Suite 270 *Web:* www.odysseyconsult.com	Wakefield	MA	01880	781-245-0111	245-5858
Omicron Consulting LLC PO Box 1047 *Web:* www.omicron.com	Bryn Mawr	PA	19010	610-822-3100	822-3200
Omni Resources Inc 155 S Executive Dr *Web:* www.omniresources.com	Brookfield	WI	53005	262-797-0600	797-8866
Open Systems Solutions Inc 2325 Maryland Rd Suite 100 *TF:* 866-483-9827 ■ *Web:* www.ossi.net	Willow Grove	PA	19090	215-659-4440	659-4550
Openpages Inc 201 Jones Rd *Web:* www.openpages.com	Waltham	MA	02451	781-647-3800	647-4300
PacificNet Inc 655 N Central Ave 17th Fl **Fax Area Code:* 646 ■ *TF:* 888-250-6478	Glendale	CA	91203	888-250-6478	349-1096*
Paradigm Solutions 9715 Key W Ave 3rd Fl *Web:* www.paradigmsolutions.com	Rockville	MD	20850	301-468-1200	468-1201
Paragon Computer Professionals Inc 11 Commerce Dr 3rd Fl *TF:* 800-462-5582	Cranford	NJ	07016	908-276-9260	709-8071
Perot Systems Corp 12320 Racetrack Rd *TF:* 800-872-2992 ■ *Web:* www.perotsystems.com	Tampa	FL	33626	813-891-6084	891-6138
Planned Systems International Inc 10632 Little Patuxent Pkwy *Web:* www.plan-sys.com	Columbia	MD	21044	410-964-8000	964-8001
Pointe Technology Group Inc 7272 Pk Cir Dr Suite 200 *TF:* 800-730-6171 ■ *Web:* www.pointetech.com	Hanover	MD	21076	410-712-9425	712-9435
Pomeroy IT Solutions Inc 1020 Petersburg Rd *NASDAQ: PMRY* ■ *TF:* 800-846-8727 ■ *Web:* www.pomeroy.com	Hebron	KY	41048	859-586-0600	586-4414
Preferred Systems Solutions Inc 1945 Old Gallows Rd Suite 450 *Web:* www.pssfed.com	Vienna	VA	22182	703-663-2777	663-2780
Presidio Networked Solutions Inc 7601 Ora Glen Dr Suite 100 *TF:* 800-452-6926 ■ *Web:* www.presidio.com	Greenbelt	MD	20770	301-313-2000	313-2400
Professional Software Engineering Inc 780 Lynnhaven Pkwy Suite 350 *TF:* 800-951-5161 ■ *Web:* www.prosoft-eng.com	Virginia Beach	VA	23452	757-431-2400	463-1071
RCG Information Technology Inc 379 Thornall St 14th Fl *TF:* 800-333-7816 ■ *Web:* www.rcgit.com	Edison	NJ	08837	732-744-3500	744-3501
Remtech Services Inc (RSI) 804 Middle Ground Blvd Suite A *Web:* www.remtech.com	Newport News	VA	23606	757-873-8733	873-8403
Resource One Computer Systems Inc 1159 Dublin Rd *Web:* www.rocs.com	Columbus	OH	43215	614-485-4800	485-4848
RiverPoint Group LLC 2200 E Devon Ave Unit 385 *TF:* 800-297-5601 ■ *Web:* www.riverpoint.com	Des Plains	IL	60018	847-233-9600	233-9602
Rolta Tusc Inc 377 E Butterfield Rd Suite 100 *TF:* 800-755-8872 ■ *Web:* www.tusc.com	Lombard	IL	60148	630-960-2909	960-2938
RWD Technologies 5521 Research Pk Dr *TF:* 877-952-8301 ■ *Web:* www.rwd.com	Baltimore	MD	21228	410-869-1000	869-3002
Salira Optical Netwk Systems Inc 3920 Freedom Cir Suite 101 *Web:* www.salira.com	Santa Clara	CA	95054	408-845-5200	845-5205
San Vision Technology Inc 50 Broadway *Web:* www.svtinc.com	New York	NY	10004	212-571-6904	571-3588
Sayers Group LLC 1150 Feehanville Dr *TF:* 800-323-5357 ■ *Web:* www.sayers.com	Mount Prospect	IL	60056	847-391-4040	294-0750
Scc Soft Computer Inc 5400 Tech Data Dr *TF:* 800-763-8352 ■ *Web:* www.softcomputer.com	Clearwater	FL	33760	727-789-0100	789-0124
SecureInfo Corp 211 N Loop 1604 E Suite 200 *TF:* 888-677-9351 ■ *Web:* www.secureinfo.com	San Antonio	TX	78232	210-403-5600	403-5702
Servigistics Sns Inc 2300 Windy Ridge Pkwy 450 N Tower *Web:* www.servigistics.com	Atlanta	GA	30339	770-565-2340	565-8767
Siemens IT Solutions & Services Inc 101 Merritt 7 *TF:* 888-368-1112 ■ *Web:* www.it-solutions.siemens.com	Norwalk	CT	06851	203-642-2300	642-2399
SMS Data Products Group Inc 1501 Farm Credit Dr Suite 2000 *TF:* 800-331-1767 ■ *Web:* www.sms.com	McLean	VA	22102	703-709-9898	356-4831
Social & Scientific Systems Inc 8757 Georgia Ave 12th Fl *Web:* www.s-3.com	Silver Spring	MD	20910	301-628-3000	628-3001
Software Information Systems Inc 455 Pk Pl Suite 301 *Web:* www.thinksis.com	Lexington	KY	40511	859-977-4747	977-4750
Software Technology Group 555 S 300 E *TF:* 888-595-1001 ■ *Web:* www.swtg.com	Salt Lake City	UT	84111	801-595-1000	595-1080
Solutions Consulting LLC 370 Southpointe Blvd 4th Fl	Canonsburg	PA	15317	724-514-5000	514-5050
Southeastern Computer Consultants Inc 5166 Potomac Dr Suite 400 *Web:* www.teamscci.com	King George	VA	22485	301-695-5311	695-6101
Spo America Inc 650 Worcester Rd Suite 102 *Web:* www.spo-us.com	Framingham	MA	01702	508-875-9900	875-5177
SRA International Inc 4300 Fair Lakes Ct *NYSE: SRX* ■ *Web:* www.sra.com	Fairfax	VA	22033	703-803-1500	803-1509
Starpoint Solutions 22 Cortlandt St # 14 *Web:* www.starpoint.com	New York	NY	10007	212-962-1550	967-7175
Stefanini TechTeam Inc 27335 W Eleven-Mile Rd *TF:* 800-522-4451 ■ *Web:* www.techteam.com	Southfield	MI	48034	248-357-2866	357-2570
Stg International Inc 4900 Seminary Rd Suite 1100 *Web:* www.stginternational.com	Alexandria	VA	22311	703-578-6030	578-4474
Strategic Technologies Inc 301 Gregson Dr *Web:* www.stratech.com	Cary	NC	27511	919-379-8000	379-8100
Sumaria Systems Inc 99 Rosewood Dr *Web:* www.sumariasystems.com	Danvers	MA	01923	978-739-4200	739-4850
Sun Technologies Inc 2400 Pleasant Hill Rd *Web:* www.suntechnologies.com	Duluth	GA	30096	770-418-0630	
Svam International Inc 233 E Shore Rd Suite 201 *TF:* 800-903-6716 ■ *Web:* www.svam.com	Great Neck	NY	11023	516-466-6655	466-8260
Sykes Enterprises Inc 400 N Ashley Dr Suite 2800 *NASDAQ: SYKE* ■ *TF:* 800-867-9537 ■ *Web:* www.sykes.com	Tampa	FL	33602	813-274-1000	273-0148
Syntel Inc 525 E Big Beaver Rd Suite 300 *NASDAQ: SYNT* ■ *Web:* www.syntelinc.com	Troy	MI	48083	248-619-2800	619-2888
Sysorex Federal Inc 13921 Pk Ctr Rd Suite 2204 *Web:* www.sysorex.com	Herndon	VA	20171	703-356-2900	734-4825
System Development Integration Inc (SDI) 33 W Monroe St Suite 400 *Web:* www.sdienterprises.com	Chicago	IL	60603	312-580-7500	580-7600
TASC Inc 4805 Stonecroft Blvd *Web:* www.tasc.com	Chantilly	VA	20151	703-633-8300	449-3400
Technica Corp 45245 Business Ct Suite 300 *Web:* www.technicacorp.com	Dulles	VA	20166	703-662-2000	662-2001
Technology Infrastructure Solutions Inc (TIS) 621 NW 53rd St Suite 395 *TF:* 800-667-6506 ■ *Web:* www.deploytis.com	Boca Raton	FL	33487	561-994-3077	994-3018
Technology Solutions Co (TSC) 55 E Monroe St Suite 2600 *NASDAQ: TSCC* ■ *TF:* 800-819-2250 ■ *Web:* www.techsol.com	Chicago	IL	60603	312-228-4500	228-4501
Telesciences Inc 2000 Midlantic Dr Suite 410	Mount Laurel	NJ	08054	856-866-1000	866-0185
Telos Corp 19886 Ashburn Rd *PINK: TLSRP* ■ *TF:* 800-444-9268 ■ *Web:* www.telos.com	Ashburn	VA	20147	703-724-3800	724-3868
Thaumaturgix Inc 19 W 44th St Suite 810 *Web:* www.tgix.com	New York	NY	10036	212-918-5000	918-5001
ThruPoint Inc 1040 Avenue of the Americas 19th Fl *Web:* www.thrupoint.net	New York	NY	10018	646-562-6000	562-6100
Tier Technologies Inc 11130 Sunrise Valley Dr Suite 300 *NASDAQ: TIER* ■ *Web:* www.tier.com	Reston	VA	20191	571-382-1000	382-1002
TRI-COR Industries Inc 4403 Forbes Blvd Suite 205 *Web:* www.tricorind.com	Lanham	MD	20706	301-731-6140	306-6740
Universal Software Corp 20 Industrial Pk Dr *Web:* www.universal-sw.com	Nashua	NH	03062	603-689-2600	598-0739
US-Analytics Solutions Group LLC 600 E Las Colinas Blvd Suite 2222 *TF:* 877-828-8727 ■ *Web:* www.us-analytics.com	Irving	TX	75039	214-630-0081	630-0082
Valuemomentum Inc 3001 Hadley Rd Suite 8 *Web:* www.valuemomentum.com	South Plainfield	NJ	07080	908-755-0050	755-0393
Ventera Corp 8444 Westpark Dr Suite 800 *TF:* 877-836-8372 ■ *Web:* www.ventera.com	McLean	VA	22102	703-760-4600	760-9494
Visionary Integration Professionals Inc 80 Iron Pt Cir Suite 100 *TF:* 800-434-2673 ■ *Web:* www.vipconsulting.com	Folsom	CA	95630	916-985-9625	985-9632
Vistronix Inc 1851 Alexander Bell Dr Suite 350 *TF:* 800-483-2434 ■ *Web:* www.vistronix.com	Reston	VA	20191	703-734-2270	483-2500

				Phone	Fax
Volt Information Sciences Inc Maintech Div 39 Paterson Ave	Wallington	NJ	07057	973-330-3200	330-3187*
Fax: Sales ■ *TF:* 800-426-8324 ■ *Web:* www.maintech.com					
Washington Consulting Group Inc 4915 Auburn Ave Suite 301	Bethesda	MD	20814	301-656-2330	656-1996
Web: www.washcg.com					
WidePoint Corp 18W100 22nd St # 124	Oakbrook Terrace	IL	60181	630-629-0003	629-7559
Web: www.widepoint.com					
Wisdom Infotech Ltd 18650 W Corp Dr Suite 120	Brookfield	WI	53045	262-792-0200	792-0202
Web: www.wisdominfotech.com					
Wolcott Systems Group LLC 3700 Embassy Pkwy Suite 430	Fairlawn	OH	44333	330-666-5900	666-5600
Web: www.wolcottgroup.com					
Xoriant Corp 1248 Reamwood Ave	Sunnyvale	CA	94089	408-743-4400	743-4490
Web: www.xoriant.com					
Xtria 2435 N Central Expy Suite 700	Richardson	TX	75080	972-301-4000	699-4025
TF: 866-769-2987 ■ *Web:* www.xtria.com					
ZyQuest Inc 1385 W Main Ave	De Pere	WI	54115	920-499-0533	490-3218
TF: 800-992-0533 ■ *Web:* www.zyquest.com					

184 CONCERT, SPORTS, OTHER LIVE EVENT PRODUCERS & PROMOTERS

				Phone	Fax
AMS Entertainment 226 E Cannon Perdido Suite H	Santa Barbara	CA	93101	805-899-4000	899-4184
TF: 800-267-3548 ■ *Web:* www.amsentertainment.com					
Capital Sports & Entertainment (CSE) 300 W 6th St Suite 2150	Austin	TX	78701	512-370-1919	470-1920
Web: www.planetcse.com					
Cinnabar California Inc 4571 Electronics Pl	Los Angeles	CA	90039	818-842-8190	842-0563
Web: www.cinnabar.com					
Contemporary Productions LLC 190 Carondelet Plaza Suite 1111	Saint Louis	MO	63105	314-721-9090	721-9091
Web: www.contemporaryproductions.com					
Don King Productions Inc 501 Fairway Dr	Deerfield Beach	FL	33441	954-418-5800	418-0166
Web: www.donking.com					
Executive Visions Inc 7000 Miller Ct E	Norcross	GA	30071	770-416-6100	416-6300
Web: www.executivevisions.com					
Gilmore Entertainment Group 8901-A Business 17 N PO Box 7576	Myrtle Beach	SC	29572	843-449-4444	913-1441
TF: 800-843-6779 ■ *Web:* www.cgp.net					
Harlem Globetrotters International Inc 400 E Van Buren St Suite 300	Phoenix	AZ	85004	602-258-0000	258-5925
TF: 800-641-4667 ■ *Web:* www.harlemglobetrotters.com					
House of Blues Entertainment Inc 7060 Hollywood Blvd # 1100	Hollywood	CA	90028	323-769-4600	769-4792
TF: 800-843-2583 ■ *Web:* www.houseofblues.com					
IMG Inc 1360 E 9th St IMG Ctr Suite 100	Cleveland	OH	44114	216-522-1200	522-1145
Web: www.imgworld.com					
JAM Productions Ltd 207 W Goethe St	Chicago	IL	60610	312-266-6262	266-9568
Web: www.jamusa.com					
Live Nation Inc 9348 Civic Ctr Dr	Beverly Hills	CA	90210	310-867-7000	867-7001
NYSE: LYV ■ *Web:* www.livenation.com					
Miss Universe LP 1370 Avenue of the Americas 16th Fl	New York	NY	10019	212-373-4999	315-5378
Web: www.missuniverse.com					
Nocturne Productions 3000 Harvestore Dr	DeKalb	IL	60115	815-756-9600	756-9377
Web: www.nocturneproductions.com					
On Stage Entertainment Inc 4625 W Nevso Dr	Las Vegas	NV	89103	702-253-1333	253-1122
Radio City Entertainment LLC 1260 6th Ave	New York	NY	10020	212-485-7200	472-0603*
Fax: PR ■ *Web:* www.radiocity.com					
Shubert Organization Inc 234 W 44th St	New York	NY	10036	212-944-3700	944-3841
Speedway Motorsports Inc 5555 Concord Pkwy	Concord	NC	28027	704-455-3239	455-2168
NYSE: TRK ■ *TF:* 800-455-7267 ■ *Web:* www.speedwaymotorsports.com					
Top Rank Inc 3980 Howard Hughes Pkwy Suite 580	Las Vegas	NV	89109	702-732-2717	733-8232
Web: www.toprank.com					
Walt Disney Theatrical Productions 500 S Buena Vista St	Burbank	CA	91521	818-553-5342	
Web: www.disney.go.com/disneytheatrical					
Willy Bietak Productions Inc 1404 3rd St Promenade Suite 200	Santa Monica	CA	90401	310-576-2400	576-2405
Web: www.iceshows.com					
World Wrestling Entertainment Inc 1241 E Main St	Stamford	CT	06902	203-352-8600	359-5151
NYSE: WWE ■ *TF:* 866-993-7467 ■ *Web:* www.wwe.com					

185 CONCRETE - READY-MIXED

				Phone	Fax
A Teichert & Son Inc 3500 American River Dr	Sacramento	CA	95864	916-484-3011	484-6506
Web: www.teichert.com					
AJ Walker Construction Co 421 S 21st St	Mattoon	IL	61938	217-235-5647	235-5939
Alamo Concrete 2301 Industrial Crossway PO Box 531808	Harlingen	TX	78550	956-423-6380	425-3336
Anderson Concrete Corp 400 Frank Rd	Columbus	OH	43207	614-443-0123	443-4001
Web: www.andersonconcrete.com					
Antioch Bldg Materials Co PO Box 870	Antioch	CA	94509	925-432-0171	432-9441
AVR Inc 14698 Galaxy Ave	Apple Valley	MN	55124	952-432-7132	432-7530
Web: www.avrconcrete.com					
Axim Italcementi Group 8282 Middlebranch Rd PO Box 234	Middlebranch	OH	44652	330-966-0444	499-9275
TF: 800-899-8795 ■ *Web:* www.aximconcrete.com					
Baccala Concrete Corp 100 Armento St	Johnston	RI	02919	401-231-8300	232-3965
TF: 866-705-2382 ■ *Web:* www.baccalaconcrete.com					
BARD Materials 2021 325th Ave PO Box 246	Dyersville	IA	52040	563-875-7145	875-7860
Big Horn Redi-Mix Inc 600 Industrial Pk PO Box 672	Greybull	WY	82426	307-765-4610	765-4462
Bode Concrete 385 Mendell St	San Francisco	CA	94124	415-920-7100	920-7106
Web: www.bodegravel.com					
Bonded Concrete Inc 303 Rt 155	Watervliet	NY	12189	518-273-5800	273-0848
TF: 800-252-8589 ■ *Web:* www.bondedconcrete.com					
Bornhoft Concrete Products Inc 150 County Rd 8	Tyler	MN	56178	507-247-5575	247-5576
TF: 800-257-5576 ■ *Web:* www.bornhoftconcrete.com					
Boston Sand & Gravel Co Inc 100 N Washington St PO Box 9187	Boston	MA	02114	617-227-9000	523-7947
TF: 800-624-2724 ■ *Web:* www.bostonsand.com					
Builders Redi-Mix Inc 1384 Lake Lansing Rd	Lansing	MI	48912	517-372-9765	372-0222
Web: www.buildersredimix.com					
Building Products Corp 950 Freeburg Ave	Belleville	IL	62220	618-233-4427	233-2031
TF: 800-233-1996 ■ *Web:* www.buildingproductscorp.com					
Cadman Inc 7554 185th Ave NE Suite 100 PO Box 97038	Redmond	WA	98052	425-868-1234	961-7390
TF: 888-322-6847 ■ *Web:* www.cadman.com					
CalPortland Co 5975 E Marginal Way S PO Box 1730	Seattle	WA	98134	206-764-3000	764-3012
TF: 800-750-0123 ■ *Web:* www.calportland.com					
Campbell Concrete & Materials LP 9500 Harwin Dr	Houston	TX	77036	713-783-4761	783-4761
Cemex Puerto Rico Inc RT 165 KM 2.7 Industrial Amelia Pk	Bucahna Guaynabo	PR	00968	787-783-3000	781-8850
Web: www.cemex.com					
Cemex USA 840 Gessner Suite 1400	Houston	TX	77024	713-650-6200	722-5105
NYSE: CX ■ *TF:* 800-999-8529 ■ *Web:* www.cemex.com					
Cemstone Products Co 2025 Centre Pointe Blvd Suite 300	Mendota Heights	MN	55120	651-688-9292	688-0124
TF: 800-236-7866 ■ *Web:* www.cemstone.com					
Centex Materials Inc 3019 Alvin Devane Blvd Suite 100	Austin	TX	78741	512-460-3003	444-9809
Central Builders Supply Co Inc 125 Bridge Ave PO Box 152	Sunbury	PA	17801	570-286-6461	286-5108
TF: 800-326-9361					
Central Concrete Supermix Inc 4300 SW 74th Ave	Miami	FL	33155	305-262-3250	267-0698
Web: www.supermix.com					
Central Concrete Supply Co Inc 755 Stockton Ave	San Jose	CA	95126	408-293-6272	294-3162
TF: 866-404-1000 ■ *Web:* www.centralconcrete.com					
Century Ready-Mix Corp 3250 Armand St PO Box 4420	Monroe	LA	71211	318-322-4444	322-7299
TF: 800-732-3969					
Champion Inc 180 Traders Mine Rd PO Box 490	Iron Mountain	MI	49801	906-779-2300	779-2326
TF: 800-962-5615 ■ *Web:* www.championinc.com					
Chandler Concrete Co Inc 1006 S Church St PO Box 131	Burlington	NC	27216	336-226-1181	226-2969
TF: 800-237-1259 ■ *Web:* www.chandlerconcrete.com					
CJ Horner Co Inc 105 W Grand Ave	Hot Springs	AR	71901	501-321-9600	321-9623
Clayton Cos The PO Box 3015	Lakewood	NJ	08701	732-905-3154	751-7623
TF: 800-905-3154 ■ *Web:* www.claytonco.com					
Conco Cos 510 N Sherman Pkwy	Springfield	MO	65802	417-862-9336	862-9336
Web: www.concocompanies.com					
Concrete Materials Corp 106 Industry Rd	Richmond	KY	40475	859-623-4238	623-4255
TF: 877-623-4238 ■ *Web:* www.concretematerialscompany.com					
Concrete Nor'West Inc 663 Pease Rd	Burlington	WA	98233	360-757-3121	757-3816
Concrete Supply Co 3823 Raleigh St	Charlotte	NC	28206	704-372-2930	334-8650
Web: www.concretesupplyco.com					
Cornejo & Sons Inc 2060 E Tulsa	Wichita	KS	67216	316-522-5100	522-8187
Web: www.cornejocorp.com					
Cumberland Concrete Corp Narrows Pk Rt 40 PO Box 3369	LaVale	MD	21504	301-724-2000	724-6416
Delta Concrete Products Co Inc 425 Florida Blvd PO Box 1589	Denham Springs	LA	70727	225-665-6103	665-6103
Devine Bros Inc 38 Commerce St	Norwalk	CT	06850	203-866-4421	857-4609
Web: www.devinebioheat.com					
Dolese Bros Co 20 NW 13th St	Oklahoma City	OK	73103	405-235-2311	297-8329
TF: 800-375-2311					
Dragon Products Co 960 Ocean Ave	Portland	ME	04103	207-774-6355	761-5694
TF: 800-828-8352 ■ *Web:* www.dragonproducts.com					
DuBrook Inc 40 Hoover Ave PO Box 388	Du Bois	PA	15801	814-371-3113	371-3113
TF: 866-950-3111 ■ *Web:* www.dubrook.com					
Dunham Price Inc 210 Mike Hooks Rd PO Box 760	Westlake	LA	70669	337-433-3900	433-8895
Web: www.dunhamprice.com					
DW Dickey & Son Inc 7896 Dickey Dr PO Box 189	Lisbon	OH	44432	330-424-1441	424-1441
Web: www.dwdickey.com/dwdickey					
Eagle Materials Inc 3811 Turtle Creek Blvd Suite 1100	Dallas	TX	75219	214-432-2000	432-2100
NYSE: EXP ■ *TF:* 800-759-7625 ■ *Web:* www.eaglematerials.com					
Eastern Concrete Materials Inc 475 Market St	Elmwood Park	NJ	07407	201-797-7979	791-9631*
Fax: Sales ■ *TF:* 800-822-7242 ■ *Web:* www.us-concrete.com					
Eastern Industries Inc 4401 Camp Meeting Rd Suite 200	Center Valley	PA	18034	610-866-0932	867-1886
Web: www.eastern-ind.com					
Elkins Builders Supply Co 5 11th St	Elkins	WV	26241	304-636-2640	636-8078
Web: www.wvbuilders.com					
Ernst Enterprises Inc 3361 Successful Way	Dayton	OH	45414	937-233-5555	233-9203
TF: 800-353-1555 ■ *Web:* ernstconcrete.com					
Federal Materials Concrete 2425 Wayne Sullivan Dr	Paducah	KY	42003	270-442-5496	443-6484
Web: www.fmc1.com					
Flemington Block & Supply Co 207 Everitts Rd PO Box 2050	Flemington	NJ	08822	908-782-8545	782-2378
Foley Products Co 5526 Schatulga Rd PO Box 7877	Columbus	GA	31908	706-563-7882	563-1869
TF: 800-762-6773 ■ *Web:* www.theconcretecompany.com					
Fulton Concrete Co Inc PO Box 534	Alpharetta	GA	30009	770-475-0044	664-9573
TF: 800-615-4331 ■ *Web:* www.fultonconcrete.com					

				Phone	Fax
Gallup Sand & Gravel Co 601 Round House Rd *TF:* 800-257-3818 ■ *Web:* www.gallupsand-gravel.com	Gallup	NM	87301	505-863-3818	863-4720
Garrott Bros Continous Mix Inc PO Box 419 *Web:* www.garrottbros.com	Gallatin	TN	37066	615-452-2385	452-8952
Geiger Ready Mix Co Inc PO Box 50 *Web:* www.geigerreadymix.com	Leavenworth	KS	66048	913-772-4010	772-8661
Geneva Rock Products Inc 730 N 1500 *TF:* 800-464-2003 ■ *Web:* www.genevarock.com	Orem	UT	84057	801-765-7800	765-7830
Hanson Structural Precast Pacific Inc 13131 Los Angeles St *Web:* www.hansonstructural.com	Irwindale	CA	91706	626-962-8751	962-8752
Hardaway Concrete Co Inc 2001 Taylor St PO Box 4128	Columbia	SC	29240	803-254-4350	343-2408
Hawaiian Cement 99-1300 Halawa Valley St *Web:* www.hawaiiancement.com	Aiea	HI	96701	808-532-3400	532-3499
Hempt Bros Inc 205 Creek Rd	Camp Hill	PA	17011	717-737-3411	761-5019
Hilltop Basic Resources Inc 1 W 4th St Suite 1100 *Web:* www.hilltopbasicresources.com	Cincinnati	OH	45202	513-651-5000	684-8222
Hunterdon Concrete Inc 207 Everett Rd PO Box 2050	Flemington	NJ	08822	908-782-3619	782-2378
Irving Materials Inc (IMI) 8032 N SR-9 *Web:* www.irvmat.com	Greenfield	IN	46140	317-326-7799	326-7727
Irving Ready-Mix Inc 13415 Coldwater Rd *TF:* 888-637-3101	Fort Wayne	IN	46845	260-637-3101	637-3104
Jackson Ready Mix Concrete Inc 100 W Woodrow Wilson Dr	Jackson	MS	39213	601-354-3801	292-3924
Janesville Sand & Lycon Co 1110 Harding St *TF:* 800-955-7702 ■ *Web:* www.jsandg.com	Janesville	WI	53547	608-754-7701	754-8555
Joe Brown Co Inc 20 3rd St NE PO Box 1669 *TF:* 800-444-4293	Ardmore	OK	73402	580-223-4555	223-2546
Jones & Sons Inc PO Box 2357 *Web:* www.jonesandsons.com	Washington	IN	47501	812-254-4731	254-3293
King's Material Inc 650 12th Ave SW PO Box 368 *TF:* 800-332-5298 ■ *Web:* www.kingsmaterial.com	Cedar Rapids	IA	52406	319-363-0233	366-0249
Kirkpatrick Concrete Co 2000-A Southbridge Pkwy Suite 610 *TF:* 800-489-0205	Birmingham	AL	35209	205-423-2630	423-2626
Kloepfer Concrete & Paving Co 505 E Ellis PO Box 875 *Web:* www.kloepfer.com	Paul	ID	83347	208-438-4525	438-5030
Knife River Corp 1150 W Century Ave *TF:* 800-982-5339 ■ *Web:* www.kniferiver.com	Bismarck	ND	58503	701-530-1400	530-1451
Krehling Industries Inc 1399 Hagy Way *Web:* www.krehlingcountertops.com	Harrisburg	PA	17110	717-232-7936	236-8810
Kuert Concrete Inc 3402 Lincoln Way W *TF:* 866-465-8378 ■ *Web:* www.kuert.com	South Bend	IN	46628	574-232-9911	232-9977
Kuhlman Corp 1845 Indian Woods Cir *TF:* 800-669-3309 ■ *Web:* www.kuhlman-corp.com	Maumee	OH	43537	419-897-6000	897-6061
L Suzio Concrete Co Inc 975 Westfield Rd *TF:* 888-789-4626 ■ *Web:* www.suzioyorkhill.com	Meriden	CT	06450	203-237-8421	238-9177
Lafarge North America Inc 12950 Worldgate Dr Suite 600 *Web:* www.lafargenorthamerica.com	Herndon	VA	20170	703-480-3600	480-3899
Loveland Ready Mix Concrete Inc 644 N County Rd 19 E	Loveland	CO	80539	970-667-1108	667-0092
LTM Inc PO Box 1145	Medford	OR	97501	541-770-2960	664-4567
Lycon Inc 110 Harding St PO Box 427 *TF:* 800-955-8758 ■ *Web:* www.lyconinc.com	Janesville	WI	53547	608-754-7701	754-8555
Manitou Construction Co Inc 1260 Jefferson Rd	Rochester	NY	14623	585-424-6410	424-1846
Mid-Continent Concrete Co 431 W 23rd St *Fax: Sales ■ *TF:* 800-771-7334 ■ *Web:* www.midcoconcrete.com	Tulsa	OK	74107	918-582-8111	560-4601*
MMC Materials Inc 1052 Highland Colony Pkwy Suite 201 *Web:* www.mmcmaterials.com	Ridgeland	MS	39157	601-898-4000	898-4030
Moraine Materials Co Inc 1400 Commerce Ctr Dr *TF:* 888-667-2463 ■ *Web:* www.mormat.com	Franklin	OH	45005	937-743-0650	743-0651
National Cement Co of California Inc 15821 Ventura Blvd Suite 475 *Web:* www.vicat.com	Encino	CA	91436	818-728-5200	788-0615
New Holland Concrete 828 E Earl Rd PO Box 218 *Fax Area Code: 888 ■ *TF:* 800-543-3860 ■ *Web:* www.newhollandconcrete.com	New Holland	PA	17557	800-543-3860	428-7538*
Pacific Concrete Industries 4170 Holz Rd PO Box J	Bellingham	WA	98227	360-734-0910	354-5677
Paramount Ready Mix Concrete Inc 13949 E Stage Rd PO Box 2823 *TF:* 888-404-4125	Santa Fe Springs	CA	90670	562-404-4125	802-3792
Pennsy Supply Inc 1001 Paxton St *Web:* www.pennsysupply.com	Harrisburg	PA	17104	717-233-4511	238-7312
Pine Bluff Sand & Gravel Inc 1501 Heart Wood	white hall	AR	71602	870-534-7120	534-2980
Prairie Group Inc 7601 W 79th St *TF Sales:* 800-649-3690 ■ *Web:* www.prairiegroup.com	Bridgeview	IL	60455	708-458-0400	458-6007
Prestige Concrete Products 8529 S Pk Cr Suite 320 *Web:* www.prestige-gunite.com	Orlando	FL	32819	407-802-3540	226-0359
Ready Mix Concrete Co 3610 Bush St PO Box 27326 *TF:* 800-849-0668 ■ *Web:* www.rmcc.info	Raleigh	NC	27611	919-790-1520	981-7475
Ready Mixed Concrete Co 4315 Cuming St	Omaha	NE	68131	402-556-3600	556-5171
RiverStone Group Inc 1701 5th Ave *TF:* 800-906-2489 ■ *Web:* www.riverstonegrp.com	Moline	IL	61265	309-757-8250	757-8257
RMX Holdings Inc 4602 E Thomas Rd *Web:* www.readymixinc.com	Phoenix	AZ	85018	602-249-5814	
Robar Enterprises Inc 17671 Bear Valley Rd *Web:* www.robarenterprises.com	Hesperia	CA	92345	760-244-5456	948-3251
Rockville Fuel & Feed Co Inc 14901 S Lawn Ln PO Box 1707	Rockville	MD	20849	301-762-3988	309-3894
S & G Concrete Co 2110 Philadelphia Rd	Edgewood	MD	21040	410-679-0500	679-3293
Sequatchie Concrete Service Inc 406 Cedar Ave *TF:* 800-824-0824 ■ *Web:* www.seqconcrete.com	South Pittsburg	TN	37380	423-837-7913	837-7479
Shamrock Materials Inc 548 DuBois St *TF:* 800-779-5777 ■ *Web:* www.shamrockmat.com	San Rafael	CA	94901	415-455-1576	453-6429
Shelby Materials Inc 157 E 150 N *TF:* 800-548-9516 ■ *Web:* www.shelbymaterials.com	Shelbyville	IN	46176	317-398-4485	398-2727
Silvi Concrete Products Inc 355 Newbold Rd *TF:* 800-367-2667 ■ *Web:* www.silvi.com	Fairless Hills	PA	19030	215-295-0777	295-0630
Smith Ready Mix Inc 251 W Lincolnway *TF:* 888-632-5656 ■ *Web:* www.smithreadymix.com	Valparaiso	IN	46383	219-462-3191	465-4025
Speedway Redi Mix Inc 1201 N Taylor Rd *TF:* 800-227-5649 ■ *Web:* www.speedwayredimix.com	Garrett	IN	46783	260-357-6885	357-0238
Starvaggi Industries Inc 401 Pennsylvania Ave *Web:* www.starvaggi.com	Weirton	WV	26062	304-748-1400	797-5208
Stocker Concrete Co 7574 US Rt 36 PO Box 176 *Web:* www.stockerconcrete.com	Gnadenhutten	OH	44629	740-254-4626	254-9108
Superior Ready Mix Concrete LP 1508 Mission Rd *Web:* www.superiorrm.com	Escondido	CA	92029	760-745-0556	740-9557
Texas Industries Inc 1341 W Mockingbird Ln Suite 700W *NYSE: TXI* ■ *Web:* www.txi.com	Dallas	TX	75247	972-647-6700	647-3878
Thomas Bennett & Hunter Inc 70 John St *Web:* www.tbhconcrete.com	Westminster	MD	21157	410-848-9030	876-0733
Thomas Concrete Inc 2500 Cumberland Pkwy Suite 200 *Web:* www.thomasconcrete.com	Atlanta	GA	30339	770-431-3300	431-3308
Tilcon Connecticut Inc PO Box 1357 *Web:* www.tilconct.com	New Britain	CT	06050	860-224-6005	225-1865
Titan America Inc 1151 Azalea Garden Rd *TF:* 800-468-7622 ■ *Web:* www.titanamerica.com	Norfolk	VA	23502	757-858-6500	855-7707
Transit Mix Concrete & Materials Co 505 Orleans St *TF:* 800-835-4933 ■ *Web:* www.transitmixconcrete.com	Beaumont	TX	77726	409-835-4933	981-1364
Union Sand & Supply Corp 1037 Banks St PO Box 1457	Painesville	OH	44077	440-354-4347	354-0847
United Cos of Mesa County Inc 2273 River Rd	Grand Junction	CO	81505	970-243-4900	243-5945
United Materials LLC 561 Pavement Rd *Web:* www.umconcrete.com	Lancaster	NY	14086	716-683-1432	683-0270
US Concrete Inc 2925 Briarpark Dr Suite 1050 *NASDAQ: USCR* ■ *Web:* www.us-concrete.com	Houston	TX	77042	713-499-6200	499-6201
Van Der Vaart Inc 1436 S 15th St	Sheboygan	WI	53081	920-459-2400	459-2410
Westroc Inc 670 W 220 S *Web:* www.westrocinc.com	Pleasant Grove	UT	84062	801-785-5600	785-7408
WG Block Co 1414 Mississippi Blvd PO Box 280 *TF:* 800-397-1651 ■ *Web:* www.wgblock.com	Bettendorf	IA	52722	563-823-2080	823-2071
Willcan Inc PO Box 1357 *Web:* www.basicreadymix.com	Calhoun	GA	30703	706-629-2256	625-0587

186 CONCRETE PRODUCTS - MFR

				Phone	Fax
A Duchini Inc 2550 McKinley Ave *TF:* 800-937-7317 ■ *Web:* www.duchini.com	Erie	PA	16514	814-456-7027	454-0737
Abresist Corp PO Box 38 *TF:* 800-348-0717 ■ *Web:* www.abresist.com	Urbana	IN	46990	260-774-3327	774-3882
AC Miller Concrete Products Inc 312 E Bridge St PO Box 199 *TF:* 800-229-2922 ■ *Web:* www.acmiller.com	Spring City	PA	19475	610-948-4600	948-9750
Accord Industries 4001 Forsyth Rd *TF:* 800-866-5699 ■ *Web:* www.accordindustries.com	Winter Park	FL	32792	407-671-5200	679-2297
Adams Products Co 5701 McCrimmon Pkwy PO Box 189 *TF:* 800-672-3131 ■ *Web:* www.adamsproducts.com	Morrisville	NC	27560	919-467-2218	469-0509
American Concrete Pipe Co Inc 2448 Century Rd PO Box 10508 *Web:* www.spancrete.com	Green Bay	WI	54307	920-494-0274	494-7901
Ameron International Corp 245 S Los Robles Ave *NYSE: AMN* ■ *Web:* www.ameron.com	Pasadena	CA	91101	626-683-4000	683-4060
Ameron International Water Transmission Group 10681 Foothill Blvd Suite 450 *Web:* www.ameronpipe.com	Rancho Cucamonga	CA	91730	909-944-4100	944-4112
Angelus Block Co Inc 11374 Tuxford St *Web:* www.angelusblock.com	Sun Valley	CA	91352	818-767-8576	768-3124
Arkansas Precast Corp 2601 Cory Dr PO Box 425 *Web:* www.arkansasprecast.com	Jacksonville	AR	72078	501-982-1547	982-4001
Atlantic Concrete Products Inc 8900 Old Rt 13 *Web:* www.atlanticconcrete.com	Tullytown	PA	19007	215-945-5600	946-3102
Basalite Concrete Products LLC 605 Industrial Way *TF:* 800-776-6690 ■ *Web:* www.basalite.paccoast.com	Dixon	CA	95620	707-678-1901	678-6268
Bayshore Concrete Products Corp 1134 Bayshore Rd PO Box 230 *Web:* www.usa.skanska.com	Cape Charles	VA	23310	757-331-2300	331-2501
Beavertown Block Co Inc 3612 Paxtonville Rd PO Box 337 *TF Cust Svc:* 800-597-2565 ■ *Web:* www.beavertownblock.com	Middleburg	PA	17842	570-837-1744	837-1591
Bend Industries Inc 2200 S Main St *TF:* 800-686-2363 ■ *Web:* www.bendindustries.com	West Bend	WI	53095	262-338-5700	306-8257

Company	City	State	ZIP	Phone	Fax
Best Block Co PO Box 13707	Milwaukee	WI	53213	262-781-7200	781-7253
TF: 800-782-7708 ■ Web: www.bestblock.com					
Binkley & Ober Inc 2742 Lancaster Rd PO Box 7	East Petersburg	PA	17545	717-560-6730	569-5066
TF: 800-860-8716 ■ Web: www.binkleyandober.com					
Blakeslee Construction 200 N Branford Rd	Branford	CT	06405	203-488-2500	488-4538
TF: 800-922-6203					
Blakeslee Prestress Inc Rt 139 McDermott Rd PO Box 510	Branford	CT	06405	203-481-5306	481-3562
Web: www.blakesleeprestress.com					
Block USA 327 Fiberglass Rd	Jackson	TN	38301	731-421-4624	421-4625
TF: 888-942-5625 ■ Web: www.specblockusa.com					
Blocklite Corp 1201 Golden State Blvd PO Noc 540	Selma	CA	93662	559-896-0753	896-9652
Web: www.blocklite.com					
BNZ Materials Inc 6901 S Pierce St Suite 260	Littleton	CO	80128	303-978-1199	978-0308
TF: 800-999-0890 ■ Web: www.bnzmaterials.com					
Bomat Ltd 91-400 Komohana St	Kapolei	HI	96707	808-673-2000	673-2025
TF: 877-726-6333 ■ Web: www.bondedmaterials.com					
Bonsal American Inc 8201 Arrowridge Blvd PO Box 241148	Charlotte	NC	28224	704-525-1621	529-5261
TF: 800-738-1621 ■ Web: www.bonsalamerican.com/html/contact.html					
Buehner Block Co 2800 S W Temple	Salt Lake City	UT	84115	801-467-5456	467-0866
TF: 800-999-2565 ■ Web: www.buehnerblock.com					
Burtco Inc Rt 123 PO Box 40	Westminster Station	VT	05159	802-722-3358	722-9088
TF: 800-451-4401					
Cary Concrete Products Inc 211 Dean St Suite 1D	Woodstock	IL	60098	815-338-2301	337-5801
Web: www.caryconcrete.com					
Cement Industries Inc 2782 Ford St	Fort Myers	FL	33916	239-332-1440	332-0370
TF: 800-332-1440 ■ Web: www.cementindustries.com					
Cement Products & Supply Co Inc 516 W Main St	Lakeland	FL	33815	863-686-5141	683-2034
Century Group Inc The 1106 W Napoleon St PO Box 228	Sulphur	LA	70664	337-527-5266	527-8028
TF: 800-527-5232 ■ Web: www.centurygrp.com					
Chaney Enterprises 12480 Mattawoman Dr PO Box 548	Waldorf	MD	20604	301-932-5000	843-9123*
*Fax: Sales ■ TF: 888-244-0411 ■ Web: www.chaney-ent.com					
Cinder & Concrete Block Corp 10111 Beaver Dam Rd PO Box 9	Cockeysville	MD	21030	410-666-2350	666-8781
Clayton Block Co 515 Lakewood New Egypt Rd	Lakewood	NJ	08701	732-751-7600	751-7618
TF Orders: 800-662-3044 ■ Web: www.claytonco.com					
Clayton Cos The PO Box 3015	Lakewood	NJ	08701	732-905-3154	751-7623
TF: 800-905-3154 ■ Web: www.claytonco.com					
Con Forms 777 Maritime Dr	Port Washington	WI	53074	262-284-7800	284-7878
TF: 800-223-3676 ■ Web: www.conforms.com					
Conart Inc PO Box 335	Cobb	GA	31735	229-853-5000	853-5010
Web: www.conartinc.com					
Concrete Technology Corp 1123 Port of Tacoma Rd PO Box 2259	Tacoma	WA	98401	253-383-3545	572-9386
Web: www.concretetech.com					
Concrete Tie Corp 130 E Oris St	Compton	CA	90222	310-886-1000	638-8363
Web: www.concretetie.net					
Construction Products Inc 1631 Ashport Rd	Jackson	TN	38305	731-668-7305	668-1361
TF: 800-238-8226 ■ Web: www.cpi-tn.com					
Cook Concrete Products Inc 5461 Eastside Rd	Redding	CA	96001	530-243-2562	243-6881
Web: www.cookconcreteproducts.com					
Coreslab International 332 Jones Rd Unit 8	Stoney Creek	ON	L8E5N2	905-643-0220	643-0233
Web: www.coreslab.com					
Coreslab Structures Inc 150 W Placentia Ave	Perris	CA	92571	951-943-9119	943-7571
Web: www.coreslab.com					
Cranesville Block Co Inc 774 State Hwy 5 S PO Box 430	Amsterdam	NY	12010	518-887-5560	887-2560
Web: www.cranesville.com					
Creative Stone Mfg Inc 11191 Calabash Ave	Fontana	CA	92337	909-357-8295	357-7362
TF: 800-847-8663 ■ Web: www.coronado.com					
Cretex Cos Inc 311 Lowell Ave	Elk River	MN	55330	763-441-2121	441-3585
Web: www.cretexinc.com					
Crom Corp 250 SW 36th Terr	Gainesville	FL	32607	352-372-3436	372-6209
TF: 800-289-2766 ■ Web: www.cromgnv.com					
Cumberland Concrete Corp Narrows Pk Rt 40 PO Box 3369	LaVale	MD	21504	301-724-2000	724-6416
Dolese Bros Co 20 NW 13th St	Oklahoma City	OK	73103	405-235-2311	297-8329
TF: 800-375-2311					
Dura-Stress Inc 11325 County Rd 44	Leesburg	FL	34788	352-787-1422	787-0080
TF: 800-342-9239 ■ Web: www.durastress.com					
Dutchland Inc PO Box 549	Gap	PA	17527	717-442-8282	442-9330
Web: www.dutchlandinc.com					
DYK Inc 351 Cypress Ln	El Cajon	CA	92020	619-440-8181	440-8653
TF: 800-227-8181 ■ Web: www.dyk.com					
E Dillon & Co 2522 Swords Creek Rd PO Box 160	Swords Creek	VA	24649	276-873-6816	873-4208
TF: 800-234-8970 ■ Web: www.edillon.com					
Echo Rock Ventures 13620 Lincoln Way Suite 380	Auburn	CA	95603	530-823-9600	823-9650
Egyptian Concrete Co 749 W Commercial St PO Box 488	Salem	IL	62881	618-548-1190	548-1190
Elk River Concrete Products Co 6550 Wedgwood Rd PO Box 1660	Maple Grove	MN	55311	763-545-7473	545-7473
TF: 800-557-7473 ■ Web: www.ercp.com					
EP Henry Corp 201 Pk Ave	Woodbury	NJ	08096	856-845-6200	845-0023
TF: 800-444-3679 ■ Web: www.ephenry.com					
Ernest Maier Inc 4700 Annapolis Rd	Bladensburg	MD	20710	301-927-8300	779-8924
TF: 888-927-8303 ■ Web: www.emcoblock.com					
Fabcon Inc 6111 Hwy 13 W	Savage	MN	55378	952-890-4444	890-6657
TF: 800-727-4444 ■ Web: www.fabcon-usa.com					
Featherlite Bldg Products Corp 508 McNeil St	Round Rock	TX	78681	512-255-2573	255-2572
Web: www.featherlitetexas.com					
Federal Block Corp 247 Walsh Ave	New Windsor	NY	12553	845-561-4108	561-5344
TF: 800-724-1999 ■ Web: www.montfortgroup.com					
Fendt Builders Supply Inc 22005 Gill Rd	Farmington Hills	MI	48335	248-474-3211	474-8110
TF: 888-706-9974 ■ Web: www.fendtbuilderssupply.com					
Finfrock Industries Inc PO Box 607754	Orlando	FL	32860	407-293-4000	
Web: www.finfrockindustries.com					
Fizzano Bros Concrete Products Inc 1776 Chester Pike	Crum Lynne	PA	19022	610-833-1100	833-5347
Web: www.fizzano.com					
Flexicore of Texas PO Box 450049	Houston	TX	77245	281-437-5700	437-8913
TF: 888-359-4267 ■ Web: www.flexicoreoftexas.com					
Florence Concrete Products Inc PO Box 5506	Florence	SC	29502	843-662-2549	667-0729
Web: www.florenceconcreteproducts.com					
Fritz Industries Inc PO Box 170040	Dallas	TX	75217	972-285-5471	270-0179
TF: 800-955-1323 ■ Web: www.fritztile.com					
Frontier Precast LLC 2633 Waterford Rd	Marietta	OH	45750	740-373-3211	373-5678
TF: 800-633-9969					
General Shale Products LLC 3015 Bristol Hwy	Johnson City	TN	37601	423-282-4661	952-4104
TF: 800-414-4661 ■ Web: www.generalshale.com					
Glen-Gery Corp 1166 Spring St PO Box 7001	Wyomissing	PA	19610	610-374-4011	374-1622
Web: www.glengerybrick.com					
Goria Enterprises 108 Buchanan Church Rd PO Box 14489	Greensboro	NC	27415	336-375-5821	375-8259
TF: 800-828-5879					
Grand Blanc Cement Products 10709 Ctr Rd	Grand Blanc	MI	48439	810-694-7500	694-2995
TF: 800-875-7500 ■ Web: www.grandblanccement.com					
Gulf Coast Pre-stress Inc PO Box 825	Pass Christian	MS	39571	228-452-9486	452-9495
Web: www.gcprestress.com					
Hancock Concrete Products Inc 17 Atlantic Ave	Hancock	MN	56244	320-392-5207	392-5155
TF: 800-992-8982 ■ Web: www.hancockconcrete.com					
Hanson Bldg Products North America 3500 Maple Ave	Dallas	TX	75219	214-525-5500	525-5563
TF: 800-527-2362 ■ Web: www.heidelbergcement.com					
Hanson Pipe & Products PO Box 368	Green Cove Springs	FL	32043	904-284-3213	284-9865
TF: 800-432-0030					
Hartford Concrete Products Inc 1400 N Walbash Ave PO Box 660	Hartford City	IN	47348	765-348-3506	348-3121
TF: 800-428-8110 ■ Web: www.oldcastleprecast.com/Plants/hartford					
Hastings Pavement Co LLC 200 Henry St	Lindenhurst	NY	11757	631-669-0600	669-8052
Web: www.hastingsarchitectural.com					
High Concrete Structures Inc 125 Denver Rd	Denver	PA	17517	717-336-9300	336-9301*
*Fax: Sales ■ TF: 800-773-2278 ■ Web: www.highconcrete.com					
High Industries Inc 1853 William Penn Way	Lancaster	PA	17601	717-293-4444	293-4416
Web: www.high.net					
Hunterdon Concrete Inc 207 Everett Rd PO Box 2050	Flemington	NJ	08822	908-782-3619	782-2378
Illinois Concrete Co Inc 702 N Edwin St	Champaign	IL	61821	217-352-4181	352-9601
Web: www.illinois-concrete.com					
Iowa Prestressed Concrete Inc 601 SW 9th St Suite B	Des Moines	IA	50309	515-243-5118	243-5502
TF: 800-826-0464					
Isabel Bloom LLC 736 Federal St Suite 2100	Davenport	IA	52803	563-333-2040	333-2044
TF: 800-273-5436 ■ Web: www.ibloom.com					
Jensen Precast 625 Bergin Way	Sparks	NV	89431	775-359-6200	359-1038
TF: 800-648-1134 ■ Web: www.jensenprecast.com					
JW Peters Inc 500 W Market St	Burlington	WI	53105	262-763-2401	763-2401
TF: 800-877-9040					
K & S Contractors Supply Co Inc 1971 Gunnville Rd	Lancaster	NY	14086	716-759-6911	759-2129
Kerr Concrete Pipe Co Inc 1920 12th St PO Box 312	Hammonton	NJ	08037	609-561-3400	
Kieft Bros Inc 837 S Riverside Dr	Elmhurst	IL	60126	630-832-8090	834-5765
Web: www.kieftbros.com					
King's Material Inc 650 12th Ave SW PO Box 368	Cedar Rapids	IA	52406	319-363-0233	366-0249
TF: 800-332-5298 ■ Web: www.kingsmaterial.com					
Kistner Concrete Products Inc 8713 Read Rd	East Pembroke	NY	14056	585-762-8216	762-8315
TF: 800-809-2801 ■ Web: www.kistner.com					
L M Scofield Co 6533 Bandini Blvd	Los Angeles	CA	90040	323-720-8810	722-7826
TF: 800-800-9900 ■ Web: www.scofield.com					
Lafarge North America Inc 12950 Worldgate Dr Suite 600	Herndon	VA	20170	703-480-3600	480-3899
Web: www.lafargenorthamerica.com					
Lakelands Concrete Products Inc 7520 E Main St	Lima	NY	14485	585-624-1990	624-2102
Web: www.lakelandsconcrete.com					
Landis Block Co 711 N County Line Rd PO Box 64418	Souderton	PA	18964	215-723-5506	723-5500
Web: www.landisbc.com					
Lombard Co 4245 W 123rd St	Alsip	IL	60803	708-389-1060	389-7120
Martin Fireproofing Corp 2200 Military Rd	Tonawanda	NY	14150	716-692-3680	693-3402
TF: 800-766-3969 ■ Web: www.martinfireproofing.com					
Mathis-Akins Concrete Block Co Inc PO Box 45	Macon	GA	31202	478-746-5154	746-3030
TF: 888-469-0680 ■ Web: www.mathisakins.com					
Metro Supply Co 4950 White Lake Rd	Clarkston	MI	48346	248-625-8080	625-7820
Web: www.premark.com					
Metromont Corp PO Box 2486	Greenville	SC	29602	864-295-0295	295-0295
TF: 888-295-0383 ■ Web: www.metromont.com					
Metromont Materials Corp 475 Simuel Rd	Spartanburg	SC	29303	864-585-4241	582-8435*
*Fax: Sales ■ TF: 888-826-2662					
Midwest Tile & Concrete Products Inc 4309 Webster Rd	Woodburn	IN	46797	260-749-5173	493-2477
TF: 800-359-4701 ■ Web: www.midwesttile.net					
MMC Materials Inc 1052 Highland Colony Pkwy Suite 201	Ridgeland	MS	39157	601-898-4000	898-4030
Web: www.mmcmaterials.com					
Modern Inc/Environmental & Wastewater 210 Durham Rd	Ottsville	PA	18942	610-847-5112	847-2468
Web: www.modcon.com					
Molin Concrete Products Co 415 Lilac St	Lino Lakes	MN	55014	651-786-7722	786-0229
TF: 800-336-6546 ■ Web: www.molin.com					

Company	City	State	ZIP	Phone	Fax
MonierLifetile Inc					
7575 Irvine Ctr Dr Suite 100	Irvine	CA	92618	949-756-1605	756-2401
TF: 800-224-2024 ■ *Web:* www.monierlifetile.com					
Montfort Bros Inc 44 Elm St	Fishkill	NY	12524	845-896-6225	896-0021
TF: 800-724-1777 ■ *Web:* www.montfortgroup.com					
Montfort Group The 44 Elm St	Fishkill	NY	12524	845-896-6225	896-0021
TF: 800-724-1777 ■ *Web:* www.montfortgroup.com					
Mutual Materials Co 605 119th Ave NE	Bellevue	WA	98005	425-452-2300	454-7732
TF: 800-477-3008 ■ *Web:* www.mutualmaterials.com					
National Concrete Products Co 939 S Mill St	Plymouth	MI	48170	734-453-8448	453-1890
NC Products Corp 920 Withers Rd PO Box 27077	Raleigh	NC	27611	919-772-6301	772-1209
TF: 800-662-1983					
New Holland Concrete					
828 E Earl Rd PO Box 218	New Holland	PA	17557	800-543-3860	428-7538*
**Fax Area Code:* 888 ■ *TF:* 800-543-3860 ■ *Web:* www.newhollandconcrete.com					
New Milford Block & Supply					
574 Danbury Rd	New Milford	CT	06776	860-355-1101	355-3772
Web: www.montfortgroup.com					
Nitterhouse Concrete Products Inc					
2655 Molly Pitcher Hwy	Chambersburg	PA	17202	717-264-6154	267-4518
Web: www.nitterhouse.com					
Oldcastle Inc 375 N Ridge Rd Suite 350	Atlanta	GA	30350	770-804-3363	804-3369
TF: 800-899-8455 ■ *Web:* www.oldcastle.com					
Olson Precast Co (OPC) 2750 Marion Dr	Las Vegas	NV	89115	702-643-4371	643-4510
TF: 800-876-8374 ■ *Web:* www.olsonprecastcompany.com					
Orco Block Co Inc 11100 Beach Blvd	Stanton	CA	90680	714-527-2239	889-1280
TF: 800-473-6726 ■ *Web:* www.orco.com					
Pavestone Plus Inc RR 2 1081 Rife Rd	Cambridge	ON	N1R5S3	519-740-6000	740-2543
TF: 800-265-6496 ■ *Web:* www.pavestoneplus.com					
Pontchartrain Materials Corp					
3819 France Rd	New Orleans	LA	70126	504-949-7571	944-3338
TF: 800-255-9848					
Pre-Cast Specialties Inc					
1380 NE 48th St	Pompano Beach	FL	33064	954-781-4040	781-3539
TF: 800-749-4041 ■ *Web:* www.precastspecialties.com					
Preload Inc 60 Commerce Dr	Hauppauge	NY	11788	631-231-8100	231-8881
Web: www.preload.com					
Premarc Corp 7505 E M 71	Durand	MI	48429	989-288-2661	288-6366
TF: 800-968-2662 ■ *Web:* www.premarc.com					
Prestress Engineering Corp 2220 Rt 176	Prairie Grove	IL	60014	815-459-4545	459-6855
Web: www.pre-stress.com					
Prestress Services Inc 7855 NW Winchester Rd	Decatur	IN	46733	260-724-7117	724-3349
Web: www.prestressservices.com					
QUIKRETE Cos 3490 Piedmont Rd Suite 1300	Atlanta	GA	30305	404-634-9100	842-1424
TF: 800-282-5828 ■ *Web:* www.quikrete.com					
Rancho Bldg Materials Co 4701 Wible Rd	Bakersfield	CA	93313	661-831-0831	831-0244
RCP Block & Brick Inc 8240 Broadway	Lemon Grove	CA	91945	619-460-7250	460-3926
TF: 800-732-7425 ■ *Web:* www.rcpblock.com					
Reading Precast Inc 5494 Pottsville Pike	Leesport	PA	19533	610-926-5000	926-0894
TF: 800-724-4881 ■ *Web:* www.readingprecast.com					
Reading Rock Inc 4600 Devitt Dr	Cincinnati	OH	45246	513-874-2345	874-2520
TF: 800-482-6466 ■ *Web:* www.readingrock.com					
RI Lampus Co 816 RI Lampus Ave PO Box 167	Springdale	PA	15144	412-362-3800	274-2181*
**Fax Area Code:* 724 ■ *TF:* 800-872-7310 ■ *Web:* www.lampus.com					
Rinker Materials Corp Concrete Pipe Div					
8311 W Carder Ct	Littleton	CO	80125	303-791-1600	791-1710
TF: 800-285-2902 ■ *Web:* www.rinkermaterials.com					
Rockwood Retaining Walls Inc 7200 Hwy 63 N	Rochester	MN	55906	507-288-8850	288-3810
TF: 800-535-2375 ■ *Web:* www.rockwoodwalls.com					
Royal Concrete Pipe Inc PO Box 430	Stacy	MN	55079	651-462-2130	462-6990
TF: 800-817-3240 ■ *Web:* www.royalenterprises.net					
Schuster's Bldg Products Inc					
901 E Troy Ave	Indianapolis	IN	46203	317-787-3201	788-5906
TF: 800-424-0190 ■ *Web:* www.schusters.com					
Sequatchie Concrete Service Inc					
406 Cedar Ave	South Pittsburg	TN	37380	423-837-7913	837-7479
TF: 800-824-0824 ■ *Web:* www.seqconcrete.com					
Sherman International Corp					
1400 Urban Ctr Dr Suite 200	Birmingham	AL	35242	205-970-7500	970-7555
TF: 800-277-6920 ■ *Web:* www.shermaninternational.com					
Smith-Midland Corp 5119 Catlett Rd PO Box 300	Midland	VA	22728	540-439-3266	439-1232
Web: www.smithmidland.com					
Spancrete Industries Inc					
N 16 W 23415 Stone Ridge Dr PO Box 828	Waukesha	WI	53187	414-290-9000	290-9125
Web: www.spancrete.com					
Speed Fab-Crete Corp International					
PO Box 15580	Fort Worth	TX	76119	817-478-1137	561-2544
TF: 800-758-1137 ■ *Web:* www.speedfab-crete.com					
ST Griswold & Co Inc					
193 Industrial Ave PO Box 849	Williston	VT	05495	802-658-0201	658-6869
TF: 800-339-4565 ■ *Web:* www.stgriswold.com					
Stanley Hardware 480 Myrtle St	New Britain	CT	06053	860-225-5111	529-4254*
**Fax Area Code:* 877 ■ **Fax:* Cust Svc ■ *TF Cust Svc:* 800-337-4393 ■ *Web:* www.stanleyhardware.com					
Stoneway Concrete Co 9125 10th Ave S	Seattle	WA	98108	206-762-9125	763-4178
Superlite Block Co Inc 4150 W Turney Ave	Phoenix	AZ	85019	602-269-3561	352-3813
TF: 800-366-7877 ■ *Web:* www.superliteblock.com					
Terre Hill Silo Co Inc PO Box 10	Terre Hill	PA	17581	717-445-3100	445-3109
TF: 800-242-1509 ■ *Web:* www.terrehill.com					
Texas Concrete Co 4702 N Vine St	Victoria	TX	77904	361-573-9145	578-5859
TF: 800-242-3511					
Tindall Corp					
3076 N Blackstock Rd PO Box 1778	Spartanburg	SC	29301	864-576-3230	587-8828
TF: 800-849-4521 ■ *Web:* www.tindallcorp.com					
Trenwyth Industries Inc					
1 Connely Rd PO Box 438	Emigsville	PA	17318	717-767-6868	767-4023
TF Cust Svc: 800-233-1924 ■ *Web:* www.trenwyth.com					
TXI Operations LP PO Box 5396	Bossier City	LA	71171	318-742-3111	742-4047
TF: 800-894-5422					
Unistress Corp 550 Cheshire Rd PO Box 1145	Pittsfield	MA	01202	413-499-1441	499-9930
TF: 800-927-9468 ■ *Web:* www.unistresscorp.com					
United Precast Inc PO Box 991	Mount Vernon	OH	43050	740-393-1121	392-9708
TF: 800-366-8740 ■ *Web:* www.unitedprecast.net					
Universal Concrete Products Corp					
400 Old Reading Pike Suite 100	Stowe	PA	19464	610-323-0700	323-4046
Web: www.universalconcrete.com					
Valley Blox Inc 210 Stone Spring Rd	Harrisonburg	VA	22801	540-434-6725	434-6514*
**Fax:* Acctg ■ *TF:* 800-648-6725					
Walters & Wolf Precast 41777 Boyce Rd	Fremont	CA	94538	510-226-9800	226-0360
Web: www.waltersandwolf.com					
Wausau Tile Inc PO Box 1520	Wausau	WI	54402	715-359-3121	355-4627
TF: 800-388-8728 ■ *Web:* www.wausautile.com					
Wieser Concrete Products Inc					
W3716 US Hwy 10	Maiden Rock	WI	54750	715-647-2311	647-5181
TF: 800-325-8456 ■ *Web:* www.wieserconcrete.com					
Wilbert Inc PO Box 147	Forest Park	IL	60130	708-865-1600	865-1646
TF: 800-323-7188					
Wingra Stone Co 2975 Kapec Rd PO Box 44284	Madison	WI	53744	608-271-5555	271-3142
TF: 800-249-6908 ■ *Web:* www.wingrastone.com					
Wyoming Concrete Products Co					
725 Bryan Stock Trail	Casper	WY	82609	307-265-3100	265-0013
York Bldg Products Co 950 Smile Way	York	PA	17404	717-848-2831	854-9156
TF: 800-673-2408 ■ *Web:* www.yorkbuilding.com					

187 CONFERENCE & EVENTS COORDINATORS

Company	City	State	ZIP	Phone	Fax
Accent on Cincinnati 915 W 8th St	Cincinnati	OH	45203	513-721-8687	721-1542
Web: www.accentcinti.com					
Accenting Chicago Events & Tours Inc					
333 N Michigan Ave Suite 425	Chicago	IL	60601	312-819-5363	819-5366
Web: www.accentingchicago.com					
Action Motivation					
465 Forbes Blvd	South San Francisco	CA	94080	650-416-2400	416-2499
Web: www.amotive.com					
Ambassadors International Inc					
1071 Camelback St	Newport Beach	CA	92660	949-759-5900	759-5909
NASDAQ: AMIE ■ *TF:* 800-325-7103 ■ *Web:* www.ambassadors.com					
ASD 6255 Sunset Blvd 19th Fl	Los Angeles	CA	90028	323-817-2200	481-1900*
**Fax Area Code:* 310 ■ *TF:* 800-421-4511 ■ *Web:* www.asdonline.com					
At Your Service of the Low Country Inc					
355 E Broad St	Savannah	GA	31401	912-232-6866	234-8437
TF: 800-868-6867 ■ *Web:* www.savannah.com					
Bixel & Co 8721 Sunset Blvd Suite 101	Los Angeles	CA	90069	310-854-3828	854-0115
Web: www.bixelco.com					
Briggs Inc 1501 Broadway Suite 406	New York	NY	10036	212-354-9440	382-1560
Web: www.briggsnyc.com					
Cappa & Graham Inc					
401 Terry A Francois Blvd Suite 200	San Francisco	CA	94158	415-512-6967	512-6982
Web: www.cappa-graham.com					
Casey & Hayes Exhibits Inc Brede Exposition Services Div					
100 Industrial Pk Rd	Hingham	MA	02043	781-741-5900	741-5902
TF: 800-835-3976 ■ *Web:* www.brede.com					
Celebrity International Entertainment Inc					
1800 Century Pk E Suite 600	Los Angeles	CA	90067	323-848-2300	848-2303*
**Fax Area Code:* 310 ■ *Web:* www.celebintl.com					
Centennial Conferences					
901 Front St Suite 130	Louisville	CO	80027	303-499-2299	499-2599
Web: www.centennialconferences.com					
COMCOR Event & Meeting Production					
1040 Bayview Dr # 407	Fort Lauderdale	FL	33304	954-491-3233	491-6466
Web: www.comcorevents.com					
Complete Conference					
1540 River Pk Dr Suite 111	Sacramento	CA	95815	916-583-8560	922-7379
Web: www.completeconference.com					
Conference & Logistics Consultants Inc					
31 Old Solomans Island Rd	Annapolis	MD	21401	410-571-0590	571-0592
Web: www.gomeeting.com					
Conference & Travel 5701 Coventry Ln	Fort Wayne	IN	46804	260-434-6600	436-3177
TF: 800-346-9807 ■ *Web:* www.conftvl.com					
Conference Consultants 445 El Escarpado	Stanford	CA	94305	650-324-1653	326-7751
Conference Group Inc 1580 Fishinger Rd	Columbus	OH	43221	614-488-2030	488-5747
Conference Hotels Unlimited 51 Harborview Rd	Hull	MA	02045	781-925-4000	925-2474
Conference Management Assoc Inc					
45 Lyme Rd Suite 304	Hanover	NH	03755	603-643-2325	643-1444
Conference Management Services PO Box 2506	Monterey	CA	93942	831-622-7772	622-0711
TF: 800-882-1891 ■ *Web:* www.conferencemanagement.net					
Conference Solutions Inc					
2545 SW Spring Garden St Suite 150	Portland	OR	97219	503-244-4294	244-2401
Web: www.conferencesolutionsinc.com					
Convention Consultants Historic Savannah Foundation					
117 W Perry St	Savannah	GA	31401	912-234-4088	
TF: 800-627-5030 ■ *Web:* www.savtours.com					
Convention Planning Services Inc					
2453 Orlando Central Pkwy	Orlando	FL	32809	407-851-5122	851-5122
TF: 800-777-5333 ■ *Web:* www.cpsorlando.com					
Courtesy Assoc 2025 M St NW Suite 800	Washington	DC	20036	202-331-2000	331-0111
TF: 800-647-4689 ■ *Web:* www.courtesyassociates.com					
Creative Convention Services					
1300 6th Ave	Beaver Falls	PA	15010	724-843-7501	843-7501
TF: 800-365-8501					
Creative Impact Group Inc					
666 Dundee Rd # 902	Northbrook	IL	60062	847-945-7401	945-7405
TF: 800-445-2171 ■ *Web:* www.creativeimpactgroup.com					
Crescent City Consultants 3701 Canal St	New Orleans	LA	70119	504-561-1191	561-5894
TF: 800-899-1191 ■ *Web:* www.ccc-nola.com					
David Price & Assoc Inc 8410 SW 156 St	Palmetto Bay	FL	33157	305-259-7903	259-7416
Web: www.dprice.com					
Destination Marketing Assn International					
2025 M St NW Suite 500	Washington	DC	20036	202-296-7888	296-7889
Web: www.destinationmarketing.org					
Destination Resources					
5435 Balboa Blvd Suite 206	Encino	CA	91316	818-995-7915	990-6129
TF: 800-234-7027 ■ *Web:* www.destinationresources.com					

	City	State	ZIP	Phone	Fax
Destination Services of Colorado Inc 0020 Eagle Rd Bldg 1	Avon	CO	81620	970-476-6565	476-6565
TF: 800-372-7686					
Event Planning International Corp 10900 Granite St	Charlotte	NC	28273	980-233-3777	233-3800
TF: 800-940-2164 ■ *Web:* www.epicreg.com					
Executive Arrangements 2460 Fairmount Blvd Suite 205	Cleveland	OH	44106	216-231-9311	
Web: www.executivearrangements.com					
Experient Inc 2500 E Enterprise Pkwy	Twinsburg	OH	44087	330-425-8333	425-3299
Web: www.experient-inc.com					
Expo Group The 5931 W Campus Cir Dr	Irving	TX	75063	972-580-9000	738-0008
TF: 800-736-7775 ■ *Web:* www.theexpogroup.com					
Fox Premier Meetings & Incentives 2150 S Washburn St	Oshkosh	WI	54904	920-236-8030	236-8006
TF: 800-236-5095 ■ *Web:* www.gofoxpremier.com					
Freeman Cos 1600 Viceroy Suite 100	Dallas	TX	75235	214-445-1000	445-0200
Web: www.freemanco.com					
Gavel International Corp 300 Tri State International Suite 320	Lincolnshire	IL	60069	847-945-8150	945-6569
TF: 800-544-2835 ■ *Web:* www.gavelintl.com					
Gene Bayliss Productions 208 Goodhill Rd	Weston	CT	06883	203-227-7521	454-1032
GES Exposition Services 950 Grier Dr	Las Vegas	NV	89119	702-263-1500	263-1528
TF: 800-443-9767 ■ *Web:* www.ges.com					
Great Events & TEAMS Inc 2170 S Parker Rd Suite 290	Denver	CO	80231	303-394-2022	394-3450
Web: www.geteams.com					
GT Consultants Inc 3050 Eagle Watch Dr	Woodstock	GA	30189	770-591-1343	591-1559
TF: 800-659-0345 ■ *Web:* www.gtconsultantsinc.com					
Henry V Events 6360 ML King Blvd	Portland	OR	97211	503-232-6666	239-8556
TF: 877-463-3846 ■ *Web:* www.henryvevents.com					
Holiday Models Convention Services 3651 Lindell Rd Suite D140	Las Vegas	NV	89103	702-735-7353	796-5676
Web: www.holidaymodels.com					
Hughes Production 1625 Berger Ln PO Box 3556	Jackson	WY	83001	307-733-6505	733-0542
Web: www.hughesproduction.com					
IDG World Expo 3 Speen St Suite 320	Framingham	MA	01701	508-879-6700	620-6668
Web: www.idgworldexpo.com					
Incentive Travel & Meetings (ITM) 970 Clementstone Dr Suite 100	Atlanta	GA	30342	404-252-2728	252-8328
Web: www.usaitm.com					
Individualized Events Inc 34893 Staccato St	Palm Desert	CA	92211	760-200-8700	200-8770
Web: www.individualizedevents.com					
International Meeting Managers Inc 4550 Post Oak Pl Suite 342	Houston	TX	77027	713-965-0566	960-0488
TF: 800-423-7175 ■ *Web:* www.meetingmanagers.com					
International Meeting Planners Ltd (IMP) 4863 Hampshire Ct Suite 303	Naples	FL	34112	239-775-1467	775-1472
Web: www.internationalplanners.com					
International Trade Information Inc 6233 Randi Ave Suite 308	Woodland Hills	CA	91367	818-591-2255	591-2289
Web: www.internationaltradeinformation.com					
Key Event Group LLC The 3815 Hilldale Dr	Nashville	TN	37215	615-352-6900	385-4976
Web: www.nashvilledmc.com					
Kraus-Anderson Communications Group 523 S 8th St	Minneapolis	MN	55404	612-375-1080	342-2239
Web: www.kacommunications.com					
LMS Meetings & Incentives 300 Corporate Pointe Suite 310	Culver City	CA	90230	310-641-4222	641-5222
Lydon Co 143 St Clair Dr	Saint Simons Island	GA	31522	912-638-0901	638-2451
Management International Inc 1828 SE 1st Ave	Fort Lauderdale	FL	33316	954-763-8811	425-1995*
**Fax Area Code:* 800 ■ *Web:* www.currentreviews.com					
Maxcel Co 6600 LBJ Fwy Suite 109	Dallas	TX	75240	972-644-0880	680-2488
Web: www.maxcel.net					
McNabb Roick & Assoc Inc 414 E 52 St Suite 18	New York	NY	10022	212-944-7784	944-7786
Web: www.mcnabbroick.com					
Meeting & Event Design Inc 5010 Dodge St	Omaha	NE	68132	402-554-4422	554-4433
Meeting Connection Inc The 893 High St	Worthington	OH	43085	614-888-2568	888-1684
Web: www.the-meeting-connection.com					
Meeting Consultants Inc 1350 Ctr Dr Bldg 1350 Suite 100	Atlanta	GA	30338	770-399-3190	399-3170
Web: www.meetingconsultants.com					
Meeting Services Unlimited 135 S Mitthoeffer Rd	Indianapolis	IN	46229	317-841-7171	578-0621
Web: www.conventionmanagers.com					
Meetings & Incentives Group 21760 Stevens Creek Blvd	Cupertino	CA	95014	408-973-1915	973-9712
TF: 800-752-9202 ■ *Web:* www.migr.com					
Meetings & Media 4730 W 72nd St	Indianapolis	IN	46268	317-254-0316	872-1480
Moshman Assoc Inc 4340 E W Hwy S Tower Suite 1105	Bethesda	MD	20814	301-229-3000	654-6940
MP Assoc Inc 1721 Boxelder St Suite 107	Louisville	CO	80027	303-530-4562	530-4334
Web: www.mpassociates.com					
National Trade Productions Inc 313 S Patrick St	Alexandria	VA	22314	703-683-8500	836-4486
TF: 800-687-7469 ■ *Web:* www.ntpshow.com					
On the Scene 500 N Dearborn St Suite 550	Chicago	IL	60610	312-661-1440	661-1182
TF: 800-621-5327 ■ *Web:* www.onthescenechicago.com					
Pacific Agenda PO Box 10142	Portland	OR	97296	503-223-8633	
Pearson & Pipkin Inc 1101 Pennsylvania Ave SE Suite 201	Washington	DC	20003	202-547-7177	546-3091
Pearson Group Inc 904 Princess Anne St Suite 103	Fredericksburg	VA	22401	540-373-4493	373-8893
Presenting Baltimore 3501 Century Ave	Baltimore	MD	21227	410-539-1344	461-9994
Web: www.presentingbaltimore.com					
Prestige Accommodations International 1231 E Dyer Rd Suite 240	Santa Ana	CA	92705	714-957-9100	957-9112
TF: 800-321-6338 ■ *Web:* www.meetingplanners.com					

	City	State	ZIP	Phone	Fax
Productions USA 1960 N Lincoln Pk W Suite 1704	Chicago	IL	60614	773-296-6200	296-6333
Web: www.productionsusa.com					
Professional Meetings International Inc 130 Spruce St Penn's Landing Sq Suite 16B	Philadelphia	PA	19106	215-922-3222	922-5282
Web: www.pmimeetings.com					
Publicis Meetings USA 340 N Primrose Dr	Orlando	FL	32803	407-513-3700	513-3705
TF: 800-944-9797 ■ *Web:* www.publicismeetingsusa.com					
Resource Connection Inc 161 S Main St	Middleton	MA	01949	978-777-9333	777-3360
TF: 800-649-5228 ■ *Web:* www.resource-connection.com					
Robustelli Corporate Services 30 Spring St	Stamford	CT	06902	203-905-8100	905-8121
Web: www.rcsltd.com					
Rx Worldwide Meetings Inc 3060 Communications Pkwy Suite 200	Plano	TX	75093	214-291-2920	291-2930
TF: 800-562-1713 ■ *Web:* www.rx-worldwide.net					
Sand Assoc 3560 Green St	Harrisburg	PA	17110	717-238-5558	238-4626
Web: www.sandassociates.com					
Schneider Group 5400 Bosque Blvd Suite 680	Waco	TX	76710	254-776-3550	776-3767
TF: 800-375-7363 ■ *Web:* www.sgmeet.com					
Seattle Hospitality Group 1500 4th Ave Suite 200	Seattle	WA	98101	206-623-2090	623-2540
Web: www.seattlehospitality.com					
Secretariat 910 N Union St	Wilmington	DE	19805	302-654-4479	654-4117
Web: www.secevents.com					
Shepard Exposition Services 1531 Carroll Dr NW	Atlanta	GA	30318	404-720-8600	720-8750
Web: www.shepardes.com					
Showcase Assoc Inc 911 Cypress Ave	Elkins Park	PA	19027	215-884-6205	884-2306
Southwest Events Etc 3200 N Hayden Rd Suite 280	Scottsdale	AZ	85251	480-947-6800	947-6888
Star Meetings & Events 1025 Acuff Rd	Bloomington	IN	47404	812-331-8800	331-6669
TF: 866-546-1687 ■ *Web:* www.starmeetingsandevents.com					
TBA Global LLC 21700 Oxnard St Suite 1430	Woodland Hills	CA	91367	818-226-2800	226-2801
Web: www.tbaglobal.com					
Transeair Travel LLC 2813 McKinley Pl NW	Washington	DC	20015	202-362-6100	362-7411
Web: www.transeairtravel.com					
Travel Meetings & Leisure Services 1152 Brantley Estates Dr	Altamonte Springs	FL	32714	407-774-6474	
Travizon Meeting Management 10 State St 2nd Fl	Woburn	MA	01801	781-994-1200	343-6128
TF: 888-625-6338 ■ *Web:* www.meetingmakers.com					
Universal Odyssey Inc 1601 Dove St Suite 260	Newport Beach	CA	92660	949-263-1222	263-0983
Web: www.universalodyssey.com					
Vega Group 7220 Washington Ave	New Orleans	LA	70125	504-488-5222	488-5214
TF: 800-771-2979 ■ *Web:* www.vegagroup.com					
Weston & Assoc Inc 110 Thomas St	Winston-Salem	NC	27101	336-725-1147	725-0551
Web: www.westoninc.com					
Wings Unlimited Inc 397 Boston Post Rd Suite 104	Darien	CT	06820	203-656-9591	656-1141
Web: www.wingsunlimited.net					

188 CONGLOMERATES

SEE ALSO Holding Companies p. 2012

A Business Conglomerate Is Defined Here As A Corporation That Consists Of Many Business Units In Different Industries.

	City	State	ZIP	Phone	Fax
3M Co 3M Ctr	Saint Paul	MN	55144	651-733-1110	733-9973*
NYSE: MMM ■ **Fax:* Mail Rm ■ *TF:* 800-364-3577 ■ *Web:* www.3m.com					
Alberto-Culver Co 2525 Armitage Ave	Melrose Park	IL	60160	708-450-3000	450-3419*
NYSE: ACV ■ **Fax:* Hum Res ■ *TF:* 800-333-0005 ■ *Web:* www.alberto.com					
Alexander & Baldwin Inc 822 Bishop St	Honolulu	HI	96813	808-525-6611	525-6652
NASDAQ: ALEX ■ *Web:* www.alexanderbaldwin.com					
Alleghany Corp 7 Times Sq Tower	New York	NY	10036	212-752-1356	759-8149
NYSE: Y ■ *Web:* www.alleghany.com					
Alsco Inc 505 E S Temple	Salt Lake City	UT	84102	801-328-8831	363-5680
TF: 800-408-0208 ■ *Web:* www.alsco.com					
Alticor Inc 7575 Fulton St E	Ada	MI	49355	616-787-6000	787-4195*
**Fax:* Hum Res ■ *Web:* www.alticor.com					
Altria Group Inc 6601 W Broad St	Richmond	VA	23230	804-274-2200	484-8231
NYSE: MO ■ *Web:* www.altria.com					
AMERCO 1325 Airmotive Way Suite 100	Reno	NV	89502	775-688-6300	688-6338
NASDAQ: UHAL ■ *Web:* www.amerco.com					
Andersons Inc 480 W Dussel Dr	Maumee	OH	43537	419-893-5050	891-6393*
NASDAQ: ANDE ■ **Fax:* Hum Res ■ *TF:* 800-537-3370 ■ *Web:* www.andersonsinc.com					
APi Group Inc 1100 Old Hwy 8 NW	New Brighton	MN	55112	651-636-4320	636-0312
TF: 800-223-4922 ■ *Web:* www.apigroupinc.com					
ARAMARK Corp 1101 Market St Aramark Tower	Philadelphia	PA	19107	215-238-3000	238-3333
NYSE: RMK ■ *TF:* 800-999-8989 ■ *Web:* www.aramark.com					
Archer Daniels Midland Co (ADM) 4666 E Faries Pkwy	Decatur	IL	62526	217-424-5200	424-5580*
NYSE: ADM ■ **Fax:* PR ■ *TF:* 800-637-5824 ■ *Web:* www.admworld.com					
Ashland Inc 50 E River Ctr Blvd PO Box 391	Covington	KY	41012	859-815-3333	815-3559
NYSE: ASH ■ *TF:* 877-546-2782 ■ *Web:* www.ashland.com					
Ball Corp 10 Longs Peak Dr	Broomfield	CO	80021	303-469-3131	460-5256*
NYSE: BLL ■ **Fax:* Sales ■ *Web:* www.ball.com					
Berkshire Hathaway Inc 3555 Farnam St Suite 1440	Omaha	NE	68131	402-346-1400	346-3375
NYSE: BRKa ■ *Web:* www.berkshirehathaway.com					
Berwind Group 1500 Market St 3000 Centre Sq W	Philadelphia	PA	19102	215-563-2800	575-2314
Web: www.berwind.com					
BFC Financial Corp 2100 W Cypress Creek Raod	Fort Lauderdale	FL	33309	954-940-4900	940-5320
NASDAQ: BFCF ■ *Web:* www.bfcfinancial.com					
Brink's Co 1801 Bayberry Ct PO Box 18100	Richmond	VA	23226	804-289-9600	289-9770*
NYSE: BCO ■ **Fax:* Mail Rm ■ *TF:* 877-877-9119 ■ *Web:* www.brinkscompany.com					

Company / Address	City	State	Zip	Phone	Fax
Brown-Forman Corp 850 Dixie Hwy PO Box 1080 *NYSE: BF.B* ■ *TF:* 800-418-6423 ■ *Web:* www.brown-forman.com	Louisville	KY	40210	502-585-1100	774-6633
Canadian Tire Corp Ltd 2180 Yonge St PO Box 770 Stn K *TSX: CTR* ■ *TF:* 800-387-8803 ■ *Web:* www.corp.canadiantire.ca	Toronto	ON	M4P2V8	416-480-3000	544-7715
Carlson Cos Inc 701 Carlson Pkwy *Web:* www.carlson.com	Minnetonka	MN	55305	763-212-5000	
Ceridian Corp 3311 E Old Shakopee Rd *TF:* 800-767-4969 ■ *Web:* www.ceridian.com	Minneapolis	MN	55425	952-853-8100	
Chemed Corp 255 E 5th St Chemed Ctr Suite 2600 *NYSE: CHE* ■ *TF:* 800-224-3633 ■ *Web:* www.chemed.com	Cincinnati	OH	45202	513-762-6900	762-6919
Clear Ch Communications Inc 200 E Basse Rd *NYSE: CCU* ■ *TF:* 888-937-6131 ■ *Web:* www.clearchannel.com	San Antonio	TX	78209	210-822-2828	822-2299
Clorox Co 1221 Broadway *NYSE: CLX* ■ *TF Cust Svc:* 800-292-2808 ■ *Web:* www.thecloroxcompany.com	Oakland	CA	94612	510-271-7000	832-1463
Colgate-Palmolive Co 300 Pk Ave *NYSE: CL* ■ *Web:* www.colgate.com	New York	NY	10022	212-310-2000	310-2595
Connell Co 200 Connell Dr # 4th *TF:* 800-233-3240 ■ *Web:* www.connellco.com	Berkeley Heights	NJ	07922	908-673-3700	673-3800
Continental Grain Co 277 Pk Ave *Web:* www.contigroup.com	New York	NY	10172	212-207-5100	207-5181
Cook Group Inc PO Box 1608 *TF:* 800-457-4500 ■ *Web:* www.cookgroup.com	Bloomington	IN	47402	812-331-1025	331-8990
Cox Enterprises Inc 1400 Lake Hearn Dr **Fax:* PR ■ *Web:* www.coxenterprises.com	Atlanta	GA	30319	404-843-5000	843-5775*
CSX Corp 500 Water St 15th Fl *NYSE: CSX* ■ **Fax Area Code:* 804 ■ *Web:* www.csx.com	Jacksonville	FL	32202	904-359-3200	782-1409*
Deere & Co 1 John Deere Pl *NYSE: DE* ■ *Web:* www.deere.com	Moline	IL	61265	309-765-8000	765-4609
Delaware North Cos Inc 40 Fountain Plaza *TF:* 800-828-7240 ■ *Web:* www.delawarenorth.com	Buffalo	NY	14202	716-858-5000	858-5266
Deseret Management Corp 60 E S Temple St Suite 575 *Web:* www.deseretmanagement.com	Salt Lake City	UT	84111	801-538-0651	538-0655
Dover Corp 3005 Highland Pkwy Suite 200 *NYSE: DOV* ■ *Web:* www.dovercorporation.com	Downers Grove	IL	60515	630-541-1540	743-2671
Dyson-Kissner-Moran Corp (DKM) 565 5th Ave 4th Fl *Web:* www.dkmcorp.com	New York	NY	10017	212-661-4600	986-7169
EBSCO Industries Inc 5724 Hwy 280 *TF:* 800-527-5901 ■ *Web:* www.ebscoind.com	Birmingham	AL	35242	205-991-6600	995-1636
Empire Co Ltd 115 King St *TSX: EMP.a* ■ *Web:* www.empireco.ca	Stellarton	NS	B0K1S0	902-755-4440	755-6477
Ergon Inc 2829 Lakeland Dr **Fax:* Hum Res ■ *TF:* 800-824-2626 ■ *Web:* www.ergon.com	Jackson	MS	39232	601-933-3000	933-3373*
Federal Signal Corp 1415 W 22nd St Suite 1100 *NYSE: FSS* ■ *Web:* www.federalsignal.com	Oak Brook	IL	60523	630-954-2000	954-2030
FirstService Corp 1140 Bay St FirstService Bldg Suite 4000 *TSE: FSV* ■ *Web:* www.firstservice.com	Toronto	ON	M5S2B4	416-960-9500	960-5333
Fortune Brands Inc 520 Lake Cook Rd *NYSE: FO* ■ *TF:* 800-225-2719 ■ *Web:* www.fortunebrands.com	Deerfield	IL	60015	847-484-4400	478-0073
GenCorp Inc Hwy 50 & Aerojet Rd PO Box 537012 *NYSE: GY* ■ *Web:* www.GenCorp.com	Rancho Cordova	CA	95742	916-355-4000	355-2459
General Electric Co (GE) 3135 Easton Tpke *NYSE: GE* ■ *TF Cust Svc:* 800-626-2000 ■ *Web:* www.ge.com	Fairfield	CT	06828	203-373-2211	373-3131
Griffon Corp 100 Jericho Quadrangle Suite 224 *NYSE: GFF* ■ *Web:* www.griffoncorp.com	Jericho	NY	11753	516-938-5544	938-5644
H & R Block Inc 4400 Main St *NYSE: HRB* ■ *TF:* 800-829-7733 ■ *Web:* www.hrblock.com	Kansas City	MO	64111	816-753-6900	753-5346
Halliburton Co 1401 McKinney Ave *NYSE: HAL* ■ *Web:* www.halliburton.com	Houston	TX	77010	713-759-2600	759-2635
Hallwood Group Inc 3710 Rawlins St Suite 1500 *AMEX: HWG* ■ *TF:* 800-225-0135 ■ *Web:* www.hallwood.com	Dallas	TX	75219	214-528-5588	528-8855
Harsco Corp 350 Poplar church Rd *NYSE: HSC* ■ *Web:* www.harsco.com	Camp Hill	PA	17011	717-763-7064	763-6424
Hawaiian Electric Industries Inc 900 Richards St *NYSE: HE* ■ *Web:* www.hei.com	Honolulu	HI	96813	808-543-5662	543-7966
Hitachi America Ltd 50 Prospect Ave *TF:* 800-448-2244 ■ *Web:* www.hitachi.com	Tarrytown	NY	10591	914-332-5800	332-5555
HNI Corp 408 E 2nd St PO Box 1109 *NYSE: HNI* ■ *TF:* 800-336-8398 ■ *Web:* www.hnicorp.com	Muscatine	IA	52761	563-264-7400	272-7655
Holiday Cos 4567 American Blvd W *TF Cust Svc:* 800-745-7411 ■ *Web:* www.holidaystations.com	Bloomington	MN	55437	952-830-8700	832-8551
Honeywell International Inc 101 Columbia Rd *NYSE: HON* ■ *TF Cust Svc:* 800-707-4555 ■ *Web:* www.honeywell.com	Morristown	NJ	07962	973-455-2000	455-4807
HT Hackney Co 502 S Gay St *TF:* 800-406-1291 ■ *Web:* www.hthackney.com	Knoxville	TN	37902	865-546-1291	546-1501
IAC/InterActiveCorp 555 W 18th St *NASDAQ: IACI* ■ *Web:* www.iac.com	New York	NY	10011	212-314-7300	314-7309
Ilitch Holdings Inc 2211 Woodward Ave *TF:* 800-722-3727 ■ *Web:* www.ilitchholdings.com	Detroit	MI	48201	313-983-6000	983-6494
Intermec Inc 6001 36th Ave W *NYSE: IN* ■ *TF:* 800-755-5505 ■ *Web:* www.intermec.com	Everett	WA	98203	425-348-2600	267-2983
Jim Pattison Group 1067 W Cordova St Suite 1800 *Web:* www.jimpattison.com	Vancouver	BC	V6C1C7	604-688-6764	687-2601
Johnson & Johnson 1 Johnson & Johnson Plaza *NYSE: JNJ* ■ *TF:* 800-635-6789 ■ *Web:* www.jnj.com	New Brunswick	NJ	08933	732-524-0400	214-0332
Jordan Industries Inc (JII) 1751 Lake Cook Rd Suite 550	Deerfield	IL	60015	847-945-5591	945-5698
Kaman Corp PO Box 1 *NASDAQ: KAMN* ■ *Web:* www.kaman.com	Bloomfield	CT	06002	860-243-7100	
Kimball International Inc 1600 Royal St *NASDAQ: KBALB* ■ **Fax:* Hum Res ■ *TF:* 800-482-1616 ■ *Web:* www.kimball.com	Jasper	IN	47549	812-482-1600	482-8803*
Koch Enterprises Inc 14 S 11th Ave *Web:* www.kochenterprises.com	Evansville	IN	47744	812-465-9800	465-9613
Koch Industries Inc 4111 E 37th St N *Web:* www.kochind.com	Wichita	KS	67220	316-828-5500	828-5327
Kohler Co Inc 444 Highland Dr **Fax:* Mktg ■ *TF:* 800-456-4537 ■ *Web:* www.kohlerco.com	Kohler	WI	53044	920-457-4441	459-1796*
Kraus-Anderson Inc 525 S 8th St *Web:* www.krausanderson.com	Minneapolis	MN	55404	612-332-7281	332-8739
Lancaster Colony Corp 37 W Broad St Suite 500 *NASDAQ: LANC* ■ *Web:* www.lancastercolony.com	Columbus	OH	43215	614-224-7141	469-8219
Larry H Miller Group 9350 S 150 E Suite 1000 *Web:* www.lhm.com	Sandy	UT	84070	801-563-4100	563-4198
LDI Ltd 54 Monument Cir Suite 800 *Web:* www.ldiltd.com	Indianapolis	IN	46204	317-237-2251	237-2280
Leucadia National Corp 315 Pk Ave S 20th Fl *NYSE: LUK* ■ *Web:* www.leucadia.com	New York	NY	10010	212-460-1900	598-4869
LGL Group Inc The 2525 Shader Rd *AMEX: LGL* ■ *Web:* www.lglgroup.com	Orlando	FL	32804	407-298-2000	
Loews Corp 667 Madison Ave *NYSE: LTR* ■ **Fax:* Mktg ■ *TF:* 800-235-6397 ■ *Web:* www.loews.com	New York	NY	10021	212-521-2000	521-2379*
MacAndrews & Forbes Holdings Inc 35 E 62nd St *Web:* www.macandrewsandforbes.com	New York	NY	10065	212-572-8600	572-8400
Marmon Group LLC The 181 W Madison St 26th Fl *Web:* www.marmon.com	Chicago	IL	60602	312-372-9500	845-5305
Mars Inc 6885 Elm St *Web:* www.mars.com	McLean	VA	22101	703-821-4900	448-9678
MAXXAM Inc 1330 Post Oak Blvd Suite 2000 *AMEX: MXM* ■ **Fax:* Hum Res	Houston	TX	77056	713-975-7600	267-3701*
McRae Industries Inc PO Box 1239 *TF:* 800-768-5248 ■ *Web:* www.mcraeindustries.com	Mount Gilead	NC	27306	910-439-6147	439-4190
MDU Resources Group Inc 1200 W Century Ave PO Box 5650 *NYSE: MDU* ■ *TF:* 866-760-4852 ■ *Web:* www.mdu.com	Bismarck	ND	58506	701-530-1000	530-1698
Metromedia Co 810 7th Ave 29th Fl *TF:* 800-461-8368	New York	NY	10019	212-606-4400	397-3802
NACCO Industries Inc 5875 Landerbrook Dr Suite 300 *NYSE: NC* ■ *TF:* 800-531-3964 ■ *Web:* www.nacco.com	Cleveland	OH	44124	440-449-9600	
NESCO Inc 6140 Parkland Blvd	Mayfield Heights	OH	44124	440-461-6000	449-3111
Newell Rubbermaid Inc 3 Glenlake Pkwy *NYSE: NWL* ■ *TF:* 800-752-9677 ■ *Web:* www.newellrubbermaid.com	Atlanta	GA	30328	770-418-7000	677-8662
Nicor Inc PO Box 2020 *NYSE: GAS* ■ **Fax:* Hum Res ■ *Web:* www.nicor.com	Aurora	IL	60507	630-305-9500	983-9296*
Olin Corp 190 Carondelet Plaza Suite 1530 *NYSE: OLN* ■ *Web:* www.olin.com	Clayton	MO	63105	314-480-1400	862-7406
Onex Corp 161 Bay St PO Box 700 *Web:* www.onex.com	Toronto	ON	M5J2S1	416-362-7711	362-5765
Oxbow Corp 1601 Forum Pl Suite 1400 **Fax:* Hum Res ■ *Web:* www.oxbow.com	West Palm Beach	FL	33401	561-697-4300	640-8727*
PepsiCo Inc 700 Anderson Hill Rd *NYSE: PEP* ■ *TF PR:* 800-433-2652 ■ *Web:* www.pepsico.com	Purchase	NY	10577	914-253-2000	253-2070
Power Corp of Canada 751 Victoria Sq *TSX: POW* ■ *TF:* 800-890-7440 ■ *Web:* www.powercorporation.com	Montreal	QC	H2Y2K3	514-286-7400	286-7424
Procter & Gamble Co (PG) 1 Procter & Gamble Plaza *NYSE: PG* ■ *Web:* www.pg.com	Cincinnati	OH	45201	513-983-1100	
Raleigh Enterprises 100 Wilshire Blvd 8th Fl *TF:* 866-669-7685 ■ *Web:* www.raleighenterprises.com	Santa Monica	CA	90401	310-899-8900	899-8910
Raytheon Co 870 Winter St *NYSE: RTN* ■ *Web:* www.raytheon.com	Waltham	MA	02451	781-522-3000	522-3001
RB Pamplin Corp 805 SW Broadway Suite 2400 *Web:* www.pamplin.org	Portland	OR	97205	503-248-1133	248-1175
Renco Group 1 Rockefeller Plaza # 29 *Web:* www.rencogroup.net	New York	NY	10020	212-541-6000	541-6197
Roll International Corp 11444 W Olympic Blvd 10th Fl *Web:* www.roll.com	Los Angeles	CA	90064	310-966-5700	914-4747
Rowan Cos Inc 2800 Postoak Blvd Suite 5450 *NYSE: RDC* ■ *Web:* www.rowancompanies.com	Houston	TX	77056	713-621-7800	960-7560
Ruddick Corp 301 S Tryon St Suite 1800 *NYSE: RDK* ■ *Web:* www.ruddickcorp.com	Charlotte	NC	28202	704-372-5404	372-6409
Sammons Enterprises Inc 5949 Sherry Ln Suite 1900 *Web:* www.sammonsenterprises.com	Dallas	TX	75225	214-210-5000	210-5099
Seaboard Corp 9000 W 67th St *AMEX: SEB* ■ *TF:* 800-388-4647 ■ *Web:* www.seaboardcorp.com	Shawnee Mission	KS	66202	913-676-8800	676-8872
Sequa Corp 3000 Bayport Dr Suite 880 *Web:* www.sequa.com	Tampa	FL	33607	813-434-4522	
Siemens Corp 153 E 53rd St 56th Fl **Fax:* Mktg ■ *TF:* 800-743-6367 ■ *Web:* www.usa.siemens.com	New York	NY	10022	212-258-4000	258-4099*
Sotheby's Holdings Inc 1334 York Ave *NYSE: BID* ■ *Web:* www.sothebys.com	New York	NY	10021	212-606-7000	606-7107
SPX Corp 13515 Ballantyne Corporate Pl *NYSE: SPW* ■ *TF:* 800-446-2617 ■ *Web:* www.spx.com	Charlotte	NC	28277	704-752-4400	752-4505
Standex International Corp 11 Keewaydin Dr *NYSE: SXI* ■ *Web:* www.standex.com	Salem	NH	03079	603-893-9701	893-7324
Sten Corp 13828 Lincoln St NE *NASDAQ: STEN* ■ *TF:* 800-328-7958 ■ *Web:* www.stencorporation.com	Ham Lake	MN	55304	763-755-9516	755-9466
Tang Industries Inc 3773 Howard Hughes Pkwy Suite 350N	Las Vegas	NV	89109	702-734-3700	734-6766
TECO Energy Inc 702 N Franklin St *NYSE: TE*	Tampa	FL	33602	813-228-1111	228-1670
Teleflex Inc 155 S Limerick Rd *NYSE: TFX* ■ *TF:* 866-246-6990 ■ *Web:* www.teleflex.com	Limerick	PA	19468	610-948-5100	948-0811
Temple-Inland Inc 1300 S Mopac Expy *NYSE: TIN* ■ *TF:* 800-826-8807 ■ *Web:* www.temple-inland.com	Austin	TX	78746	512-434-5800	434-8723
Textron Inc 40 Westminster St *NYSE: TXT* ■ *Web:* www.textron.com	Providence	RI	02903	401-421-2800	421-2878

Phone Fax

Time Warner Inc 1 Time Warner Ctr .... New York NY 10019 212-484-8000
NYSE: *TWX* ■ *Web:* www.timewarner.com

Topa Equities Ltd
1800 Avenue of the Stars Suite 1400 .... Los Angeles CA 90067 310-203-9199 557-1837
Web: www.topa.com

Trinity Industries Inc 2525 Stemmons Fwy .... Dallas TX 75207 214-631-4420 589-8501
NYSE: *TRN* ■ *TF:* 800-631-4420 ■ *Web:* www.trin.net

United Services Automobile Assn (USAA)
10750 McDermott Fwy .... San Antonio TX 78288 800-531-8722 531-5717
TF: 800-531-8722 ■ *Web:* www.usaa.com

United Technologies Corp 1 Financial Plaza .... Hartford CT 06103 860-728-7000 728-7028*
NYSE: *UTX* ■ **Fax:* Hum Res ■ *Web:* www.utc.com

Universal Corp
1501 N Hamilton St PO Box 25099 .... Richmond VA 23260 804-359-9311 254-3582
NYSE: *UVV* ■ *Web:* www.universalcorp.com

Valhi Inc
5430 LBJ Fwy Suite 1700 3 Lincoln Ctr .... Dallas TX 75240 972-233-1700 448-1444*
NYSE: *VHI* ■ **Fax:* Acctg ■ *Web:* www.valhi.net

Viacom Inc 1515 Broadway 28th Fl .... New York NY 10036 212-258-6000 258-6100
NYSE: *VIA* ■ *Web:* www.viacom.com

Viad Corp 1850 N Central Ave Suite 800 .... Phoenix AZ 85004 602-207-4000 207-5455*
NYSE: *VVI* ■ **Fax:* Hum Res ■ *Web:* www.viad.com

Volt Information Sciences Inc
560 Lexington Ave .... New York NY 10022 212-704-2400 704-2417
Web: www.volt.com

Walt Disney Co 500 S Buena Vista St .... Burbank CA 91510 818-560-1000 553-7210*
NYSE: *DIS* ■ **Fax:* Mail Rm ■ *Web:* www.corporate.disney.go.com

Washington Post Co 1150 15th St NW .... Washington DC 20071 202-334-6000
NYSE: *WPO* ■ *TF:* 800-627-1150 ■ *Web:* www.washpostco.com

Watkins Associated Industries
1958 Monroe Dr NE .... Atlanta GA 30324 404-872-3841

Wesco Financial Corp
301 E Colorado Blvd Suite 300 .... Pasadena CA 91101 626-585-6700 449-1455
AMEX: *WSC* ■ *Web:* www.wescofinancial.com

Weyerhaeuser Co 33663 Weyerhaeuser Way S .... Federal Way WA 98003 253-924-2345 924-2685
NYSE: *WY* ■ *TF:* 800-525-5440 ■ *Web:* www.weyerhaeuser.com

Wirtz Corp 680 N Lake Shore Dr Suite 1900 .... Chicago IL 60611 312-943-7000 943-9017

189 CONSTRUCTION - BUILDING CONTRACTORS - NON-RESIDENTIAL

Phone Fax

A & E Construction Co 152 Garrett Rd .... Upper Darby PA 19082 610-449-3152 449-6325
Web: www.aeconstruction.com

A D Morgan Corp The 716 N Renellie Dr .... Tampa FL 33609 813-832-3033 831-9860
Web: www.admorgan.com

A J Martini Inc 5 Lowell Ave .... Winchester MA 01890 781-569-6900 838-6868
Web: www.ajmartini.com

Abrams Construction Inc
1945 The Exchange Suite 350 .... Atlanta GA 30339 770-952-3555 952-4010
TF: 800-935-9350 ■ *Web:* www.abrams-properties.com/construction

Absher Construction Co Inc 1001 Shaw Rd .... Puyallup WA 98372 253-845-9544 841-0925
Web: www.abshernw.com

Adolfson & Peterson Construction Inc
6701 W 23rd St .... Minneapolis MN 55426 952-544-1561 525-2333
Web: www.adolfsonpeterson.com

Advanced Industrial Services Inc
3250 Susquehanna Trial .... York PA 17406 717-764-9811 767-3606
TF: 800-544-5080 ■ *Web:* www.ais-york.com

Air Ride Transport
11911 Shady Meadow St Suite 127 .... Houston TX 77039 940-566-1962 382-9217

Ajax Bldg Corp 1080 Commerce Blvd .... Midway FL 32343 850-224-9571 224-2496
Web: www.ajaxbuilding.com

Alan Utz & Assoc Inc (AU& A) PO Box 131857 .... Tyler TX 75713 903-566-9797 566-9393
Web: www.auainc.com

Alberici Constructors 8800 Page Ave .... Saint Louis MO 63114 314-733-2000 733-2001
Web: www.alberici.com

Albert M Higley Co 2926 Chester Ave .... Cleveland OH 44114 216-861-2050 861-0038
Web: www.amhigley.com

Alcan Electrical & Engineering Inc
6670 Arctic Spur Rd .... Anchorage AK 99518 907-563-3787 562-6286
Web: www.alcanelectric.com

Alex E. Paris Contracting Co
1595 Smith Township State .... Atlasburg PA 15004 724-947-2235 947-3820
Web: www.alexparis.com

All Pool & Spa Inc 905 Kalanianaole Hwy .... Kailua HI 96734 808-261-8991 263-6158
Web: www.allpoolandspa.com

Alliance Construction Solutions LLC
2725 Rocky Mountain Ave Suite 100 .... Loveland CO 80538 970-663-9700 663-9750
Web: www.allianceconstruction.com

Allstate Construction Inc 5718 Tower Rd .... Tallahassee FL 32303 850-514-1004 514-1206
Web: www.allstateconstruction.com

Alpha Bldg Corp 24850 Blanco Rd Suite 200 .... San Antonio TX 78260 210-491-9925 491-9717
Web: www.alphabuilding.com

Alvin H Butz Inc 840 W Hamilton St # 600 .... Allentown PA 18101 610-395-6871 395-3363
Web: www.butz.com

AMEC Construction Management
1979 Lakeside Pkwy Suite 400 .... Tucker GA 30084 770-688-2500 688-2501
Web: www.amec.com

Andersen Construction Co Inc
6712 N Cutter Cir .... Portland OR 97217 503-283-6712 283-3607
Web: www.andersen-const.com

Ansco & Assoc LLC PO Box 18445 .... Greensboro GA 27419 336-852-3433 852-4027
Web: www.anscoinc.com

Armada Hoffler
222 Central Pk Ave Suite 2100 .... Virginia Beach VA 23462 757-366-4000 523-0782
Web: www.armadahoffler.com

Ashton Co Inc The
2727 S Country Club Rd PO Box 26927 .... Tucson AZ 85713 520-624-5500 791-9059
Web: www.ashtoncoinc.com

Asi Constructors Inc
1850 E Platteville Blvd .... Pueblo West CO 81007 719-647-2821 647-2890
Web: www.asiconstructors.com

Phone Fax

Atlas General Contractors LLC
8218 E 121st St S .... Bixby OK 74008 918-369-3910
TF: 800-480-5208 ■ *Web:* www.atlasgc.com

Austin Co 6095 Parkland Blvd .... Cleveland OH 44124 440-544-2600 544-2661
Web: www.theaustin.com

Austin Commercial Inc 3535 Travis Suite 300 .... Dallas TX 75204 214-443-5700 443-5791*
**Fax:* Acctg ■ *Web:* www.austin-ind.com

B&b Contractors & Developers Inc
2781 Salt Springs Rd .... Youngstown OH 44509 330-270-5020 270-5035
Web: www.bbcdonline.com

B. H. Craig Construction Co Inc 835 Wall St .... Florence AL 35630 256-766-3350 767-0367
Web: www.bhcraigconst.com

Baldwin & Shell Construction Co Inc
1000 W Capitol PO Box 1750 .... Little Rock AR 72203 501-374-8677 375-7649
Web: www.baldwinshell.com

Bank of the Orient 233 Sansome St .... San Francisco CA 94104 415-338-0843 398-0619
Web: www.bankorient.com/home

Barlovento LLC 431 Technology Dr .... Dothan AL 36303 334-983-9979 983-9983
TF: 877-498-6039 ■ *Web:* www.barlovento8a.com

Barnhill Contracting Co 2311 N Main St .... Tarboro NC 27886 252-823-1021 823-0137
Web: www.barnhillcontracting.com

Barr & Barr Inc 460 W 34th St 16th Fl .... New York NY 10001 212-563-2330 967-2297
Web: www.barrandbarr.com

Barrier Island Station Inc
1 Cypress Knee Trial .... Kitty Hawk NC 27949 252-261-4610 261-1425
Web: www.bistation.com

Barton Malow Enterprises Inc
26500 American Dr .... Southfield MI 48034 248-436-5000 436-5001
Web: www.bmco.com

Batson-Cook Co Inc 815 5th Ave .... West Point GA 31833 706-643-2500 643-2199
Web: www.batson-cook.com

Bay Electric Co Inc 627 36th St .... Newport News VA 23607 757-595-2300 595-6112
Web: www.bayelectricco.com

Baybutt Construction Corp PO Box 463 .... Keene NH 03431 603-352-6846 352-6633
Web: www.baybutt.com

Bayley Construction Co
8005 SE 28th St # 100 .... Mercer Island WA 98040 206-621-8884 343-7728
TF: 800-598-8884 ■ *Web:* www.bayley.net

BBL Construction Services Inc
302 Washington Ave Ext .... Albany NY 12203 518-452-8200 452-2897
Web: www.bblinc.com

BE & K Bldg Group
5605 Carnegie Blvd Suite 200 .... Charlotte NC 28209 704-551-2700 551-2799
Web: www.bekbuildinggroup.com

Beauchamp Construction Co
2100 Ponce De Leon Blvd Suite 825 .... Coral Gables FL 33134 305-445-0819 447-0941
Web: www.beauchampco.com

Beck Group The 1807 Ross Ave Suite 500 .... Dallas TX 75201 214-303-6200 303-6300
Web: www.beckgroup.com

Becker Bros Inc 401 Main St Suite 110 .... Peoria IL 61602 309-674-1200 674-5454

Belt Group The
11521 Milnor Ave PO Box 1210 .... Cumberland MD 21502 301-729-8900 729-0921
TF: 888-729-1616 ■ *Web:* www.thebeltgroup.com

Benning Construction Co Inc (BCC)
4695 S Atlanta Rd PO Box 724375 .... Atlanta GA 31139 404-792-1911 792-2337
Web: www.benningnet.com

Bergenfield Public School District
225 W Clinton Ave .... Bergenfield NJ 07621 201-385-8801
Web: www.bergenfield.org

Berry Contracting LP 1414 Valero Way .... Corpus Christi TX 78469 361-693-2100 693-2841
Web: www.bayltd.com

Berschauer Phillips Construction Co
2823 29th Ave SW .... Tumwater WA 98512 360-754-5788 943-5868
Web: www.bp-construction.com

Bertie County Schools 222 County Farm Rd .... Windsor NC 27983 252-794-3174 794-9727
Web: www.bertieschools.com

BL Harbert International Inc
PO Box 531390 .... Birmingham AL 35253 205-802-2800 802-2801
Web: www.bharbert.com

Blach Construction Co
469 El Cmino Real Suite 100 .... Santa Clara CA 95050 408-244-7100 244-2220
Web: www.blach.com

Blaine Construction Corp PO Box 10147 .... Knoxville TN 37939 865-693-8900 691-7606
TF: 800-424-0426 ■ *Web:* www.blaineconstruction.com

BlueScope Construction Inc
1540 Genessee St .... Kansas City MO 64102 816-245-6000 245-6099
Web: www.bucon.com

Bond Bros Inc 145 Spring St .... Everett MA 02149 617-387-3400 389-1412
Web: www.bondbrothers.com

Bonnette Page & Stone Corp 91 Bisson Ave .... Laconia NH 03246 603-524-3411 524-4641
Web: www.bpsnh.com

Bor-Son Construction Inc
2001 Killebrew Dr Suite 400 .... Bloomington MN 55425 952-854-8444 854-8910
Web: www.borson.com

Boran Craig Barber Engel Construction Co Inc
3606 Enterprise Ave .... Naples FL 34104 239-643-3343 643-4548
Web: www.bcbe.com

Bovis Lend Lease 200 Pk Ave 9th Fl .... New York NY 10166 212-592-6700 592-6988
Web: www.bovis.com

Bowen & Watson Inc PO Box 877 .... Toccoa GA 30577 706-886-3197 886-3010
Web: www.bowen-watson.com

Boyertown Area School District (BASD)
911 Montgomery Ave .... Boyertown PA 19512 610-367-6031 369-7620
Web: www.boyertownasd.org

Brackett Builders Inc 185 Marybill Dr S .... Troy OH 45373 937-339-7505
Web: www.brackettbuilders.com

Bradbury & Stamm Construction Co Inc
7110 2nd St NW .... Albuquerque NM 87107 505-765-1200 842-5419
Web: www.bradburystamm.com

Brae Burn Construction Co PO Box 742288 .... Houston TX 77274 713-777-0063 995-9649
Web: www.braeburnconstruction.com

Phone | Fax

Branagh Inc 750 Kevin Ct ... Oakland CA 94621 510-638-6455 562-8371
Web: www.branaghinc.com

Branch Group Inc PO Box 40004 ... Roanoke VA 24022 540-982-1678 982-4127
Web: www.branchgroup.com

Brannan Paving Coltd 111 Elk Dr PO Box 3403 ... Victoria TX 77903 361-573-3130 573-6211
TF: 800-626-7064 ■ *Web:* www.brannanpaving.com

Brasfield & Gorrie LLC 729 30th St S ... Birmingham AL 35233 205-328-4000 251-1304
TF: 800-239-8017 ■ *Web:* www.brasfieldgorrie.com

Breiholz Construction Co
202 Des Moines St ... Des Moines IA 50309 515-288-6077 288-6335
Web: www.breiholz.com

Brice Bldg Co Inc 201 Sunbelt Pkwy ... Birmingham AL 35211 205-930-9911 918-1850
Web: www.bricebuilding.com

Brookstone LP 3715 Dacoma St ... Houston TX 77092 713-683-8800 680-0088
Web: www.brookstone-tx.com

BSI Constructors Inc 6767 SW Ave ... Saint Louis MO 63143 314-781-7820 781-1354
TF: 800-769-8090 ■ *Web:* www.bsistl.com

BT Mancini Co Inc 876 S Milpitas Blvd ... Milpitas CA 95036 408-942-7900 945-1360
TF: 800-488-4286 ■ *Web:* www.btmancini.com

BT Mancini Co Inc Brookman Div
876 S Milpitas Blvd ... Milpitas CA 95035 408-942-7900 945-1360
TF: 800-488-4286 ■ *Web:* www.btmancini.com

Budreck Truck Lines Inc 8040 S Roberts Rd ... Bridgeview IL 60455 708-496-0522 496-0568
TF: 800-621-0013 ■ *Web:* www.budreck.com

Buford-Thompson Co
3005 Medlin Dr PO Box 150449 ... Arlington TX 76015 817-467-4981 467-5619
Web: www.buford-thompson.com

Bulley & Andrews LLC 1453 W 38th St ... Chicago IL 60609 773-235-2433 235-2471
Web: www.bulley.com

Buquet & LeBlanc Inc PO Box 549 ... Baton Rouge LA 70821 225-753-4150 751-1922
Web: www.buquet-leblanc.com

Butters Construction & Development Inc
6820 Lyons Technology Ctr Suite 100 ... Coconut Creek FL 33073 954-312-2415 570-8844
Web: www.butters.com

C Construction Co Inc PO Box 8270 ... Tyler TX 75711 903-597-1500 597-0567
Web: www.cconstruction.net

C Erickson & Sons Inc
2200 ARCH St Suite 200 ... Philadelphia PA 19103 215-568-3120 496-9460
Web: www.cerickson.com

C Overaa & Co Inc 200 Parr Blvd ... Richmond CA 94801 510-234-0926 237-2435
Web: www.overaa.com

C. Martin Co Inc 3395 W Cheyenne Ave ... North Las Vegas NV 89032 702-656-8080
Web: www.cmartin.com

C.a. Murren & Sons Co Inc
2275 Loganville Hwy ... Grayson GA 30017 770-682-2940 682-1802
Web: www.camurren.com

C.t. Wilson Construction Co PO Box 2011 ... Durham NC 27702 919-383-2535 382-0044
Web: www.ctwilson.com

Ca Lindman Inc 10401 Guilford Rd ... Jessup MD 20794 301-470-4700 470-4708
TF: 877-737-8675 ■ *Web:* www.calindman.com

Caddell Construction Co Inc
2700 Lagoon Pk Dr ... Montgomery AL 36109 334-272-7723 394-0189
Web: www.caddell.com

Camosy Construction Inc 43451 N US Hwy 41 ... Zion IL 60099 847-395-6800 395-6891
Web: www.camosy.com

Campbell/Manix Inc 21520 Bridge St ... Southfield MI 48033 248-354-5100 354-0058
Web: www.campbell-manix.com

Carbondale Elementary School District 95
925 S Giant City Rd ... Carbondale IL 62902 618-457-3591 457-2043
Web: www.ces95.org

Cardinal Construction Inc 800 Waterloo Bldg ... Waterloo IA 50704 319-232-5400 232-3149
Web: www.cardinalconst.com

Careage Inc PO Box 1969 ... Gig Harbor WA 98335 253-853-4457 853-5280
Web: www.careage.com

Carmel Contractors Inc 8030 England St ... Charlotte NC 28273 704-552-2338 552-0397
Web: www.carmelcontractors.com

Carroll County School District
605-9 Pine St ... Hillsville VA 24343 276-730-3200 728-3195
Web: www.ccpsd.k12.va.us

Cavico Corp
17011 Beach Blvd Suite 1230 ... Huntington Beach CA 92647 714-843-5456 843-5451
NASDAQ: CAVO ■ *Web:* www.cavicocorp.com

CD Moody Construction Co Inc 6017 Redan Rd ... Lithonia GA 30058 770-482-7778 482-7727
Web: www.cdmoodyconstruction.com

CD Smith Construction Inc
889 E Johnson St PO Box 1006 ... Fond du Lac WI 54936 920-924-2900 924-2910
Web: www.cd-smith.com

CDI Contractors LLC 3000 Cantrell Rd ... Little Rock AR 72202 501-666-4300 666-4741
Web: www.cdicon.com

Cedar Grove Composting Inc
7343 E Marginal Way S ... Seattle WA 98108 206-832-3000 832-3030
TF: 888-832-3008 ■ *Web:* www.cedar-grove.com

Centex Construction Co Inc
3100 McKinnon St 7th Fl ... Dallas TX 75201 214-468-4700 468-4505

Centex Construction Inc
2636 Elm Hill Pike Suite 120 ... Nashville TN 37214 615-889-4400 872-1107

Centex Rooney Construction Co Inc
7901 SW 6th Ct ... Plantation FL 33324 954-585-4000 585-4501

Century Concrete Inc
1364 Air Rail Ave ... Virginia Beach VA 23455 757-460-5366 460-3296
Web: www.centuryconcreteinc.com

CF Jordan Construction LLC 7700 CF Jordan Dr ... El Paso TX 79912 915-877-3333 877-3999
Web: www.cfjordan.com

CG Schmidt Inc 11777 W Lake Pk Dr ... Milwaukee WI 53224 414-577-1177 577-1155
TF: 800-248-1254 ■ *Web:* www.cgschmidt.com

Charles C Brandt Construction Co
1505 N Sherman Dr ... Indianapolis IN 46201 317-375-1111 375-4321
Web: www.ccbrandt.com

Charles N White Construction Co
600 Crescent Blvd # A ... Ridgeland MS 39157 601-898-5180 989-5190
Web: www.whiteconst.com

Charles Pankow Builders Ltd
3280 E Foothill Blvd Suite 100 ... Pasadena CA 91107 626-304-1190 696-1782
Web: www.pankow.com

Choate Construction Co
8200 Roberts Dr Suite 600 ... Atlanta GA 30350 678-892-1200 892-1202
Web: www.choateco.com

Christman Co Inc 208 N Capitol Ave ... Lansing MI 48933 517-482-1488 482-3520
Web: www.christmanco.com

Clancy & Theys Construction Co PO Box 27608 ... Raleigh NC 27611 919-834-3601 834-2439
Web: www.clancytheys.com

Clark Construction Group LLC
7500 Old Georgetown Rd ... Bethesda MD 20814 301-272-8100 272-8414
TF: 800-827-4422 ■ *Web:* www.clarkconstruction.com

Clark Transfer Inc 800A Paxton St ... Harrisburg PA 17104 717-238-6581 238-4865
TF: 800-488-7585 ■ *Web:* www.clarktransfer.com

Clarksdale Municipal School District
101 McGuire St PO Box 1088 ... Clarksdale MS 38614 662-627-8500 627-8542
Web: www.cmsd.k12.ms.us

Clayco Construction Co
2199 Innerbelt Business Ctr Dr ... Saint Louis MO 63114 314-429-5100 429-3137
TF: 888-429-3330 ■ *Web:* www.claycorp.com

Comanco 4301 Sterling Commerce Dr ... Plant City FL 33566 813-988-8829 988-8779
Web: www.comanco.net

Commercial Bldg Specialist 401 Derek Pl ... Roseville CA 95678 916-780-9680 780-9685

Commodore Builders 80 Bridge St ... Newton MA 02458 617-614-3500 965-8354
Web: www.commodorebuilders.com

Concord Cos Inc 4215 E McDowell Rd Suite 201 ... Mesa AZ 85215 480-962-8080 962-0707
Web: www.concordinc.com

Condon-Johnson & Assoc Inc PO Box 12368 ... Oakland CA 94604 510-636-2100 568-9316
Web: www.condonjohnson.com

Condotte America Inc 10790 NW 127th St ... Medley FL 33178 305-670-7585 670-7462
Web: www.condotteamerica.com

Congleton Hacker Co PO Box 22640 ... Lexington KY 40522 859-254-6481 253-0442
Web: www.congleton-hacker.com

Conlan Co The 1800 Pkwy Pl Suite 1010 ... Marietta GA 30067 770-423-8000 423-8010
Web: www.conlancompany.com

Corna/Kokosing Construction Co
6235 Westerville Rd ... Westerville OH 43081 614-901-8844 212-5599
Web: www.corna.com

Corporate Construction Ltd
7617 Mineral Pt Rd ... Madison WI 53717 608-827-6001 827-6066
Web: www.corporate-construction.com

CR Meyer & Sons Co 895 W 20th Ave ... Oshkosh WI 54902 920-235-3350 235-3419
Web: www.crmeyer.com

Creative Business Interiors Inc
11217 W Becher St ... Milwaukee WI 53227 414-545-8500 545-8588
Web: www.creativebusinessinteriors.com

Crossland Construction Co Inc PO Box 45 ... Columbus KS 66725 620-429-1414 429-1412
Web: www.crosslandconstruction.com

Culp Construction Co 2320 S Main St ... Salt Lake City UT 84115 801-486-2064 485-4755
Web: www.culpco.com

CW Driver General Contractors Inc
468 N Rosemead Blvd ... Pasadena CA 91107 626-351-8800 351-8880
Web: www.cwdriver.com

D & D Construction Services Of Orlando Inc
2707 Rew Cir ... Ocoee FL 34761 407-654-7545
Web: www.ddconstructionservices.com

D'annunzio & Sons Inc 136 Central Ave Suite 102 ... Clark NJ 07066 732-574-1300 574-1244
Web: www.dannunziocorp.com

D.s.simmons Inc
112 W Chestnut St PO Box 287 ... Goldsboro NC 27533 919-734-4700 736-3218
Web: www.dssimmons.com

Dallman Industrial Corp
201 N Illinois St Suite 156 ... Indianapolis IN 46204 317-613-1300 613-1313
Web: www.dallmancorp.com

Dalmac Construction
111 W Spring Valley Rd Suite 200 ... Richardson TX 75081 972-725-3400 725-3700
Web: www.dalmac.com

Danis Bldg Construction Co
3233 Newmark Dr ... Miamisburg OH 45342 937-228-1225 228-7443
Web: www.danisbuilding.com

Daryl Flood Inc 450 Airline Dr Suite 100 ... Coppell TX 75019 972-471-1496 745-9629
TF: 866-496-1020 ■ *Web:* www.darylflood.com

Davis & Assoc Inc 2852 N Webster Ave ... Indianapolis IN 46219 317-263-9947 238-9209
Web: www.davisassocindy.com

Daw Inc 12552 S 125 W ... Draper UT 84020 801-553-9111 553-2345
TF Sales: 800-748-4778 ■ *Web:* www.dawinc.com

Dawson Construction Inc PO Box 30920 ... Bellingham WA 98225 360-756-1000 756-1001
Web: www.dawson.com

DBT Holding Co 24 2nd Ave SE PO Box 3668 ... Moultrie GA 31768 866-616-6020
TF: 866-713-6498 ■ *Web:* www.darbybank.com

Dean Snyder Construction Co
913 N 14th St PO Box 181 ... Clear Lake IA 50428 641-357-2283 357-2232
Web: www.deansnyderconst.com

Deerfield Construction Co Inc
8960 Glendale Milford Rd ... Loveland OH 45140 513-984-4096 984-3035
Web: www.deerfieldconstruction.com

Deig Bros Lumber & Construction Inc
2804 A St ... Evansville IN 47712 812-423-4201 421-5058
Web: www.deigbros.com

Deltec Homes Inc 69 Bingham Rd ... Asheville NC 28806 828-253-0483 254-1880
TF: 800-642-2508 ■ *Web:* www.deltechomes.com

Demar Ltd 6200 Savoy Dr Suite 800 ... Houston TX 77036 713-963-0930 963-0941
Web: www.demar-ltd.com

DeMaria Bldg Co Inc 45500 Grand River Ave ... Novi MI 48374 248-348-8710 348-6251
Web: www.demariabldgco.com

Denver Commercial Builders Inc (DCB)
909 E 62nd Ave ... Denver CO 80216 303-287-5525 287-3697
Web: www.dcb1.com

Design Partnership The
1412 Van Ness Ave ... San Francisco CA 94109 415-777-3737 777-3476
Web: www.dpsf.com

Company / Address	City	State	ZIP	Phone	Fax
Design Transportation Services Inc PO Box 560686 *Fax Area Code: 817 ■ Web: www.designtransport.net	Dallas	TX	75356	214-688-6900	624-8931*
Designed Mobile Systems Industries PO Box 367 Web: www.dmsi-inc.com	Patterson	CA	95363	209-892-6298	892-5018
Devcon Construction Inc 690 Gibraltar Dr Web: www.devcon-const.com	Milpitas	CA	95035	408-942-8200	942-8200
DiCarlo Construction Co 33 E 2nd St Web: www.dicarlo.com	Kansas City	MO	64106	816-471-3300	471-3311
Dick Corp 1900 Rt 51 TF: 800-245-6577	Large	PA	15025	412-384-1000	384-1000
Dick Pacific Construction Co Ltd 707 Richards St Suite 400	Honolulu	HI	96813	808-533-5000	533-5320
Diffenbaugh Inc 6865 Airport Dr. TF: 800-394-5334 ■ Web: www.diffenbaugh.com	Riverside	CA	92504	951-351-6865	351-6880
Dimeo Construction Co 75 Chapman St Web: www.dimeo.com	Providence	RI	02905	401-781-9800	461-4580
DL Withers Construction LC 3220 E Harbour Dr. Web: www.dlwithers.com	Phoenix	AZ	85034	602-438-9500	438-9600
Don Chapin Co Inc The 560 Crazy Horse Canyon Rd. Web: www.donchapin.com	Salinas	CA	93907	831-449-4273	449-0700
Donohoe Cos Inc 2101 Wisconsin Ave NW. TF: 877-366-6463 ■ Web: www.donohoe.com	Washington	DC	20007	202-333-0880	342-3924
Doster Construction Co 2100 International Pk Dr. Web: www.dosterconstruction.com	Birmingham	AL	35243	205-956-5902	951-2612
DPR Construction Inc 1450 Veterans Blvd. Web: www.dpr.com	Redwood City	CA	94063	650-474-1450	474-1451
Duffield Assoc Inc 5400 Limestone Rd Web: www.duffnet.com	Wilmington	DE	19808	302-239-6634	239-8485
Dugan & Meyers 11110 Kenwood Rd Web: www.dugan-meyers.com	Cincinnati	OH	45242	513-891-4300	891-0704
Dunn Investment Co 3900 Airport Hwy	Birmingham	AL	35222	205-592-8908	595-4734
Dyad Constructors Inc 8505 Holt St TF: 877-223-4333 ■ Web: www.dyad-inc.com	Houston	TX	77054	713-799-9380	799-2021
E C Kenyon Construction Co Inc 10028 San Jose Blvd Web: www.eckenyon.com	Jacksonville	FL	32257	904-389-2353	389-2395
E Kent Halvorson Inc 9840 Willows Rd Ne Web: www.ekhi.com	Redmond	WA	98052	425-885-1983	861-8433
Ecological Restoration & Management Inc (ER&M) 9475 Deereco Rd Suite 406 Web: www.er-m.com	Timonium	MD	21093	410-337-4899	583-5678
Ed Taylor Construction South Inc 2713 N Falkenburg Rd Web: www.edtaylor.net	Tampa	FL	33619	813-623-3724	621-1439
EE Reed Construction Co 333 Commerce Green Blvd. Web: www.eereed.com	Sugar Land	TX	77478	281-933-4000	933-4852
Elder-Jones Inc 1120 E 80th St Suite 211. Web: www.elderjones.com	Minneapolis	MN	55420	952-854-2854	854-2703
Elite Retails Services Inc PO Box 618 Web: www.elite-construction.com	Lake Jackson	TX	77566	979-285-0712	285-0714
Ellis Stone Construction 3201 Stanley St PO Box 366. Web: www.ellisstone.com	Stevens Point	WI	54481	715-345-5000	345-5007
Ellis-Walker Builders Inc PO Box 41109 Web: www.elliswalkerbuilders.com	Fayetteville	NC	28309	910-485-8111	438-9122
EMJ Corp 2034 Hamilton Pl Blvd # 400 Web: www.emjcorp.com	Chattanooga	TN	37421	423-855-1550	855-6857
Energy Services of America Corp 100 Industrial Ln AMEX: ESA ■ Web: www.energyservicesofamerica.com	Huntington	WV	25702	304-399-6300	399-1096
Engel Holdings Inc 1311 First St TF: 866-950-9862 ■ Web: cabrillohoist.com	Coronado	CA	92118	310-834-3430	834-3439
Esa Construction Inc 3435 Girard Blvd Ne Suite A. Web: www.esaconstruction.com	Albuquerque	NM	87107	505-884-2171	
Eutaw Construction Co Inc 109 1/2 W Commerce St PO Box 36. Web: www.eutawconstruction.com	Aberdeen	MS	39730	662-369-8868	369-7770
Ewing Construction Co Inc PO Box 4235. Web: www.ewingcc.com	Corpus Christi	TX	78469	361-882-6525	882-8424
FA Wilhelm Construction Co Inc 3914 Prospect St Web: www.fawilhelm.com	Indianapolis	IN	46203	317-359-5411	359-8346
Facility Construction Services Inc 8200 Lovett Ave Web: www.fcsdallas.com	Dallas	TX	75227	214-381-0101	275-4744
Facility Group Inc 2233 Lake Pk Dr Suite 100 TF: 800-525-2463 ■ Web: www.facilitygroup.com	Smyrna	GA	30080	770-437-2700	437-7554
Fairfield Banchshares Inc 220 E Main St PO Box 429. Web: www.fairfieldnb.com	Fairfield	IL	62837	618-842-2107	842-5849
FaulknerUSA Inc 535 E 5th St. Web: www.faulknerusa.com	Austin	TX	78701	512-652-4000	652-4001
Fcl Builders Inc 1150 Spring Lake Dr. Web: www.fclbuilders.com	Itasca	IL	60143	630-773-0050	773-4030
Ferguson Construction Co 400 Canal St Web: www.ferguson-construction.com	Sidney	OH	45365	937-498-2381	498-1796
Findorff JH & Son Inc 300 S Bedford St Web: www.findorff.com	Madison	WI	53703	608-257-5321	257-5306
Fisher Development Inc 201 Spear St Suite 220. TF: 800-227-4392 ■ Web: www.fisherinc.com	San Francisco	CA	94105	415-228-3060	468-6241
Flintco Inc 1624 W 21st St TF: 800-947-2828 ■ Web: www.flintco.com	Tulsa	OK	74107	918-587-8451	582-7506
Flintco LLC 1624 W 21st St. TF: 800-947-2828 ■ Web: www.flintco.com	Tulsa	OK	74107	918-587-8451	582-7506
Fluor Constructors International Inc 352 Halton Rd Suite 200.	Greenville	CA	29607	864-234-7335	234-5476
Fluor Daniel Inc 3 Polaris Way Web: www.fluor.com	Aliso Viejo	CA	92698	949-349-2000	349-2585
Ford Development Corp 11148 Woodward Ln. Web: www.forddevelopment.com	Cincinnati	OH	45241	513-772-1521	772-1556
Fortney & Weygandt Inc 31269 Bradley Rd. Web: www.fortneyweygandt.com	North Olmsted	OH	44070	440-716-4000	716-4010
Foushee & Assoc Inc 3260 118th Ave SE Web: www.foushee.com	Bellevue	WA	98005	425-746-1000	746-3737
Francis Tuttle Technology Center School District 21 12777 N Rockwell Ave Web: www.francistuttle.com	Oklahoma City	OK	73142	405-717-7799	
Frederick Quinn Corp 103 S Church St. Web: www.fquinncorp.com	Addison	IL	60101	630-628-8500	628-8595
Fru-Con Construction LLC 4310 Prince William Pkwy Suite 200 Web: www.fru-con.com	Woodbridge	VA	22192	703-586-6100	586-6101
Furino & Son Inc 66 Columbia Rd Web: www.furinoandsons.com	Branchburg	NJ	08876	908-756-7736	756-3783
G & D Transportation Inc 50 Commerce Dr TF: 800-451-6680 ■ Web: www.gdintegrated.com	Morton	IL	61550	309-284-6700	266-1450
G. L. Wilson Bldg Co 190 Wilson Pk Rd. Web: www.glwilson.com	Statesville	NC	28625	704-872-2411	872-8281
Gaines Motor Lines Inc 2349 13th Ave SW PO Box 1549 TF: 800-438-7311 ■ Web: www.gainesml.com	Hickory	NC	28603	828-322-2000	324-7026
Gamma Construction Co PO Box 22047 Web: www.gammaconst.com	Houston	TX	77227	713-963-0086	963-0961
Garling Construction Inc 1120 11th St. Web: www.garlingconstruction.com	Belle Plaine	IA	52208	319-444-3409	444-2437
GE Johnson Construction Co 25 N Cascade Ave Suite 400. Web: www.gejohnson.com	Colorado Springs	CO	80903	719-473-5321	473-5324
Geis Cos The 10020 Aurora Hudson Rd. Web: www.geisco.net	Streetsboro	OH	44241	330-528-3500	528-0008
Geneva Construction Co (GCCO) 1350 Aurora Ave Web: www.genevaconstruction.net	Aurora	IL	60507	630-892-4357	892-7738
Gerace Construction Co Inc 4055 S Saginaw Rd. Web: www.geraceconstruction.com	Midland	MI	48640	989-496-2440	496-2465
Gerald H Phipps Inc 5995 Greenwood Florida Blvd Web: www.ghpd.com	Greenwood Village	CO	80111	303-571-5377	629-7467
Gerloff Co Inc 14955 Bulverde Rd. TF: 800-486-3621 ■ Web: www.gerloffinc.com	San Antonio	TX	78247	210-490-2777	494-0610
Geupel DeMars Hagerman Inc 7930 Castleway Dr Web: www.hagermangc.com/geupel_demars_manage.htm	Indianapolis	IN	46250	317-713-0632	713-0641
Gilbane Bldg Co Mid-Atlantic Regional Office 7901 Sandy Spring Rd Suite 500 TF: 800-445-2263 ■ Web: www.gilbaneco.com	Laurel	MD	20707	301-317-6100	317-6155
Gilbane Bldg Co New England Regional Office 7 Jackson Walkway. Web: www.gilbaneco.com	Providence	RI	02903	401-456-5800	456-5936
Gilbane Bldg Co Southwest Regional Office 1331 Lamar St Suite 1170 TF: 800-445-2263 ■ Web: www.gilbaneco.com	Houston	TX	77010	713-209-1873	651-0541
Giordano Construction Co Inc 1155 Main St. Web: www.giordano-construction.com	Branford	CT	06405	203-488-7264	481-5764
GLY Construction Inc 15 Lake Belview Dr Suite 200. Web: www.gly.com	Bellevue	WA	98004	425-451-8877	453-5680
Gomez Construction Co 7100 SW 44th St. Web: www.gomezconstruction.com	Miami	FL	33155	305-661-7660	661-0504
Grae-Con Construction Inc PO Box 1778. Web: www.graecon.com	Steubenville	OH	43952	740-282-6830	282-6849
Granger Construction Co 6267 Aurelius Rd Web: www.grangerconstruction.com	Lansing	MI	48911	517-393-1670	393-1382
Grant Parish School Board (GPSB) 512 Main St PO Box 208 Web: www.gpsb.org	Colfax	LA	71417	318-627-3274	627-5931
Gray Construction 10 Quality St. TF: 800-950-4729 ■ Web: www.gray.com	Lexington	KY	40507	859-281-5000	252-5300
Graycor Inc 1 Graycor Dr. Web: www.graycor.com	Homewood	IL	60430	708-206-0500	206-0505
Greenway Enterprises Inc PO Box 5553. Web: www.greenwayent.com	Helena	MT	59604	406-458-9411	458-6516
Grunley Construction Co Inc 15020 Shady Grove Rd Suite 500. Web: www.grunley.com	Rockville	MD	20850	240-399-2000	399-2001
Guntersville City Schools Board of Education 2208 Ringgold St Web: www.guntersvilleboe.com	Guntersville	AL	35987	256-582-3159	
Gurosky Myrick & Assoc 4 River Chase RdG TF: 888-860-2442 ■ Web: www.mgandassociates.com	Birmingham	AL	35244	205-313-3020	313-3049
Gutirrez Co The 1 Wall St Web: www.gutierrezco.com	Burlington	MA	01803	781-272-7000	272-3130
H & M Construction Co Inc 50 Security Dr. Web: www.hmcompany.com	Jackson	TN	38305	731-664-6300	664-1358
Hagerman Construction Corp PO Box 10690. Web: www.hagermancorp.com	Fort Wayne	IN	46853	260-424-1470	422-3129
Haley Construction Inc 900 Orange Ave Web: www.haleyconstruction.com	Daytona Beach	FL	32114	386-944-0470	944-0471
Hansen Co Inc The 5665 Greendale Rd Suite A Web: www.hansencompany.com	Johnston	IA	50131	515-270-1117	270-3829
Harbison-Mahony-Higgins Inc 15 Business Pkwy Suite 101. Web: www.hmh.com	Sacramento	CA	95828	916-383-4825	383-6014
Harbour Contractors Inc 23830 W Main St. Web: www.harbour-cm.com	Plainfield	IL	60544	815-254-5500	254-5505
Hardaway Group 615 Main St. Web: www.hardaway.net	Nashville	TN	37206	615-254-5461	254-4518

	City	State	ZIP	Phone	Fax
Hardin Construction Group Inc					
3301 Windy Ridge Pkwy#400	Atlanta	GA	30339	404-264-0404	264-3514
Web: www.hardinconstruction.com					
Hardy Bros Inc 6406 Siloam Rd	Siloam	NC	27047	336-374-5050	374-5045
TF: 800-525-5354 ■ *Web:* www.hardybros.com					
Harkins Builders Inc 2201 Warwick Way	Marriottsville	MD	21104	410-750-2600	480-4299
TF: 888-224-5697 ■ *Web:* www.harkinsbuilders.com					
Harman Construction Inc 1633 Rogers Rd	Fort Worth	TX	76107	817-336-5780	336-5797
Web: www.harmanandson.com					
Harrell Construction Group LLC PO Box 12850	Jackson	MS	39236	601-206-7600	206-7601
Web: www.harrellcontracting.com					
Haselden Construction Inc					
6950 S Potomac St Suite 100	Centennial	CO	80112	303-751-1478	751-1627
Web: www.haselden.com					
Haskell Co 111 Riverside Ave	Jacksonville	FL	32202	904-791-4500	791-4699
TF: 800-733-4275 ■ *Web:* www.thehaskellco.com					
Haskell Corp PO Box 917	Bellingham	WA	98227	360-734-1200	734-5538
Web: www.haskellcorp.com					
Hatcher Nolan Construction Services LLC					
PO Box 806	Tuttle	OK	73089	405-381-9478	381-9480
Web: www.hatcherconstructionservices.com					
Hathaway Dinwiddie Construction Co					
275 Battery St Suite 300	San Francisco	CA	94111	415-986-2718	956-5669
Web: www.hdcco.com					
Hawkins Construction Co 2516 Deer Pk Blvd	Omaha	NE	68105	402-342-1607	342-3221
Web: www.hawkins1.com					
HBE Corp 11330 Olive Blvd	Saint Louis	MO	63141	314-567-9000	567-1045
Web: www.hbecorp.com					
Heartland Bldg Co 119 William St	Middlesex	NJ	08846	732-302-9277	356-9286
Web: www.njheartland.com					
Hellas Construction Inc					
12710 RES Blvd Suite 240	Austin	TX	78759	512-250-2910	
Web: www.hellasconstruction.com					
Henderson Corp 575 State Hwy 28	Raritan	NJ	08869	908-685-1300	595-1131
Web: www.henco.com					
Henning Construction Co Inc PO Box 394	Johnston	IA	50131	515-253-0943	253-0942
Web: www.henningconstruction.com					
Hensel Phelps Construction Co					
420 6th Ave PO Box 0	Greeley	CO	80631	970-352-6565	352-9311
TF: 800-826-6309 ■ *Web:* www.henselphelps.com					
HG Reynolds Co Inc 113 Contract Dr PO Box 2728	Aiken	SC	29802	803-641-1401	641-1037
Web: www.hgreynolds.net					
Hilco Transport Inc 7700 Kenmont Rd	Greensboro	NC	27409	336-273-9441	273-9701
Web: www.hilcotransport.com					
Hitt Contracting Inc 2704 Dorr Ave	Fairfax	VA	22031	703-846-9000	846-9110
Web: www.hitt-gc.com					
HJ Russell & Co 504 Fair St SW	Atlanta	GA	30313	404-330-1000	330-0922
Web: www.hjrussell.com					
Hoar Construction Inc					
2 Metroplex Dr # 400	Birmingham	AL	35209	205-803-2121	423-2323
Web: www.hoarllc.com					
Hoffman Construction Corp					
805 SW Broadway Suite 2100	Portland	OR	97205	503-221-8811	221-8934
Web: www.hoffmancorp.com					
Hoffman Corp 805 SW Broadway Suite 2100	Portland	OR	97205	503-221-8811	221-8934
Web: www.hoffmancorp.com					
Holder Construction Co					
3333 Riverwood Pkwy Suite 400	Atlanta	GA	30339	770-988-3000	988-3265
Web: www.holderconstruction.com					
Holloman Corp					
333 N Sam Houston Pkwy E Suite 600	Houston	TX	77060	281-878-2600	272-1227
Web: www.hollomancorp.com					
Horst Group Inc					
320 Granite Run Dr PO Box 3330	Lancaster	PA	17604	717-581-9800	581-9816
Web: www.horstgroup.com					
Housley Communications Inc					
3550 S Bryant Blvd	San Angelo	TX	76903	325-944-9905	944-1781
TF: 800-880-9905 ■ *Web:* www.hc-inc.com					
HSU Development Co					
1335 Rockville Pike Suite 255	Rockville	MD	20852	301-881-3500	881-3505
Web: www.hsubuilders.com					
Hunt Construction Group					
2450 S Tibbs Ave	Indianapolis	IN	46241	317-227-7800	227-7810
TF: 800-223-6301 ■ *Web:* www.huntconstructiongroup.com					
Hunzinger Construction Co					
21100 Enterprise Ave	Brookfield	WI	53045	262-797-0797	797-0474
Web: www.hunzinger.com					
Ibc Southwest Inc 23027 N 15th Ln Suite A	Phoenix	AZ	85027	623-581-5300	581-0608
Web: www.ibcsouthwest.net					
Ideal Co Inc The PO Box 149	Clayton	OH	45315	937-836-8683	832-2133
Web: www.idealco.net					
Ideal Interiors Inc 575 8th Ave 12th Fl	New York	NY	10018	212-262-7005	262-7024
Web: www.ideal-interiors.com					
Industrial Contractors Inc (ICI)					
401 NW First St	Evansville	IN	47708	812-423-7832	464-7255
Web: www.industrialcontractors.com					
Industrial Resources Inc PO Box 2648	Fairmont	WV	26555	304-363-4100	367-9737
Web: www.indres.com					
Inman-emj Construction 88 Union Ave Suite 400	Memphis	TN	38103	901-682-4100	682-0755
Web: www.inmanconstruction.com					
Interface Construction Corp					
8401 Wabash Ave	Saint Louis	MO	63134	314-522-1011	522-1022
Web: www.interfaceconstruction.com					
Irmscher Inc 1030 Osage St	Fort Wayne	IN	46808	260-422-5572	424-1487
Web: www.irmscherinc.com					
Irwin Industries Inc 1580 W Carson St	Long Beach	CA	90810	310-233-3000	834-9402
Web: www.irwinind.com					
J Kokolakis Contracting Inc 1500 Ocean Ave	Bohemia	NY	11716	631-744-6147	744-6156
Web: www.jkokolakis.com					
J T Turner Construction Co Inc					
2250 E Victory Dr Suite 104	Savannah	GA	31414	912-356-5611	356-5615
Web: www.jttconst.com					
J.C.N. Construction Co Inc PO Box 1600	Manchester	NH	03105	603-624-7080	
Web: www.jcnconstruction.com					
J.R. Abbot Construction Inc 3408 1st Ave S	Seattle	WA	98134	206-467-8500	447-1885
Web: www.jrabbott.com					
JA Tiberti Construction Co					
1806 Industrial Rd	Las Vegas	NV	89102	702-248-4000	382-5361
Web: www.tiberti.com					
Jackson Local Schools District (JLSD)					
7602 Fulton Dr	Massillon	OH	44646	330-830-8000	830-8008
Web: jackson.stark.k12.oh.us					
Jacobsen Construction Co Inc					
3131 W 2210 S	Salt Lake City	UT	84119	801-973-0500	973-7496
Web: www.jacobsen-const.com					
James G Davis Construction Corp					
12530 Parklawn Dr Suite 100	Rockville	MD	20852	301-881-2990	468-3918
Web: www.davisconstruction.com					
Jaynes Corp 2906 Broadway NE	Albuquerque	NM	87107	505-345-8591	345-8598
TF: 800-432-5204 ■ *Web:* www.jaynescorp.com					
JE Dunn Construction Co 1001 Locust St	Kansas City	MO	64106	816-474-8600	391-2510
Web: www.jedunn.com					
Jeffrey M. Brown Assoc LLC					
2337 Philmont Ave	Huntingdon Valley	PA	19006	215-938-5000	938-5005
Web: www.jmbassociates.com					
JESCO Inc 2020 McCullough Blvd	Tupelo	MS	38801	662-842-3240	680-6123
John Deklewa & Sons Inc					
1273 Washington Pike	Bridgeville	PA	15017	412-257-9000	257-4486
Web: www.deklewa.com					
John E Jones Oil Co Inc					
1016 S Cedar PO Box 546	Stockton	KS	67669	785-425-6746	425-6323
TF: 800-323-9821 ■ *Web:* www.jonesoil.net					
John Gallin & Son Inc 102 Madison Ave 9th Fl	New York	NY	10016	212-252-8900	
Web: www.gallin.com					
John M Olson Corp					
26210 Harper Ave	Saint Clair Shores	MI	48081	586-771-9330	771-2440
John S Clark Co Inc 210 Airport Rd	Mount Airy	NC	27030	336-789-1000	789-7609
Web: www.jsclark.com					
Joseph A Natoli Construction Corp					
293 Changebridge Rd	Pine Brook	NJ	07058	973-575-1500	575-8216
Web: www.jnatoli.com					
Joseph Construction Co Inc PO Box 10563	Knoxville	TN	37939	865-584-3945	584-3120
Web: www.josephconst.com					
JP Jansen Co Inc 8355 W Bradley Rd	Milwaukee	WI	53223	414-357-8800	357-8830
K L House Construction Co Inc					
6409 Acoma Rd SE	ALBUQUERQUE	NM	87108	505-268-4361	268-9266
Web: www.klhouse.com					
Kane Is Able Inc PO Box 931	Scranton	PA	18517	570-344-9801	207-2244
TF: 888-356-5263 ■ *Web:* www.kaneisable.com					
Kapp Construction Co					
329 Mt Vernon Ave PO Box 629	Springfield	OH	45503	937-324-0134	324-3406
Web: www.kappconstruction.com					
Kcc Contractor Inc 2664 E Kearney St	Springfield	MO	65803	417-883-1204	887-7338
Web: www.killco.com					
Keating Bldg Corp 1600 Arch St Suite 300	Philadelphia	PA	19103	610-668-4100	668-4060
Web: www.keatingweb.com					
Kelsey Construction Inc 306 E Princeton St	Orlando	FL	32804	407-898-4101	898-0172
Web: www.kelseyconstruction.com					
Kenmore Construction Co Inc 700 Home Ave	Akron	OH	44310	330-762-9373	762-2135
Web: www.kenmorecompanies.com					
Kenny Construction Co					
2215 Sanders Rd Suite 400	Northbrook	IL	60062	847-541-8200	272-5421
Web: www.kennyconstruction.com					
Kickerillo Cos 1306 S Fry Rd	Katy	TX	77450	713-951-0666	492-2018*
**Fax Area Code: 281* ■ *Web:* www.kickerillo.com					
Kinsley Construction Inc 1110 E Princess St	York	PA	17403	717-741-3841	741-9054
TF: 800-546-7539 ■ *Web:* www.rkinsley.com					
Kirila Contractors Inc					
505 Bedford Rd PO Box 179	Brookfield	OH	44403	330-448-4055	454-4054
Web: www.kirila.com					
Kitchell Corp 1707 E Highland Ave Suite 100	Phoenix	AZ	85016	602-264-4411	631-6121*
**Fax: Hum Res* ■ *Web:* www.kitchell.com					
Kjellstrom & Lee Inc 1607 Ownby Ln	Richmond	VA	23220	804-288-0082	285-4288
Web: www.kjellstromandlee.com					
Knutson Construction Services Inc					
5500 Wayzata Blvd # 300	Minneapolis	MN	55416	763-546-1400	546-2226
Web: www.knutsonconstruction.com					
Koll Construction LP					
4343 Von Karman Ave Suite 150	Newport Beach	CA	92660	949-833-3030	250-4344
Web: www.koll.com					
Koll Development Co					
4343 Von Karman Ave	Newport Beach	CA	92660	949-833-3030	250-4344
Web: www.koll.com					
Korte Construction Co 12441 US Hwy 40	Highland	IL	62249	618-654-8611	654-4999
Web: www.korteco.com					
Korte Construction Co 5700 Oakland Ave	Saint Louis	MO	63110	314-231-3700	231-4682
Web: www.korteco.com					
KPRS Construction Services Inc 2850 Saturn St	Brea	CA	92821	714-672-0800	672-0871
Web: www.kprsinc.com					
Kraemer Bros Inc 925 Pk Ave	Plain	WI	53577	608-546-2411	546-2509
Web: www.kraemerbrothers.com					
Kraus-Anderson Construction Co					
525 S 8th St	Minneapolis	MN	55404	612-332-7281	332-8739
Web: www.kraus-anderson.com/construction/home.html					
L Kelley Construction Co					
2901 Falling Springs Rd	East Saint Louis	IL	62206	314-421-5933	421-2266
Web: www.lkeeley.com					
L L Pelling Co					
1425 W Penn St PO Box 230	North Liberty	IA	52317	319-626-4600	626-4605
Web: www.llpelling.com					
La Habra City School District (LHCSD)					
500 N Walnut St PO Box 307	La Habra	CA	90631	562-690-2305	
Web: www.lhcsd.k12.ca.us					
Lakeview Construction Inc					
10505 Corp Dr Suite 200	Pleasant Prairie	WI	53158	262-857-3336	857-3424
Web: www.lvconstruction.com					

Company	City	State	ZIP	Phone	Fax
Lampasas Isd 207 W 8th St *Web:* www.lampasas.k12.tx.us	Lampasas	TX	76550	512-556-6224	556-8711
Landau Bldg Co 9855 Rinaman Rd *Web:* www.landau-bldg.com	Wexford	PA	15090	724-935-8800	935-6510
Landis Construction LLC 241 Industrial Ave *Web:* www.landisllc.com	Jefferson	LA	70121	504-833-6070	833-6662
Latco Inc 2265 E Pridemore PO Box 9 *Web:* www.latcoinc.com	Lincoln	AR	72744	479-824-3282	824-3983
Lathrop Co 460 W Dussel Dr *Web:* www.turnerconstruction.com	Maumee	OH	43537	419-893-7000	893-1741
Law Co Inc The 345 Riverview St Suite 300 *Web:* www.law-co.com	Wichita	KS	67203	316-268-0200	268-0210
Lease Crutcher Lewis 107 Spring St *Web:* www.lewisbuilds.com	Seattle	WA	98104	206-622-0500	343-6541
Lee Lewis Construction Inc 7810 Orlando Ave *Web:* www.leelewis.com	Lubbock	TX	79423	806-797-8400	797-8492
Leonard Construction Co Inc PO Box 14547	Saint Louis	MO	63178	314-275-5814	275-5998
Leopardo Cos Inc 5200 Prairie Stone Pkwy *Web:* www.leopardo.com	Hoffman Estates	IL	60192	847-783-3000	783-3001
Letsos Co 8435 Westglen Dr PO Box 36927 *Web:* www.letsos.com	Houston	TX	77063	713-783-3200	972-7880
Lewis & Michael Inc 1827 Woodman Dr *TF:* 800-543-3524 ■ *Web:* www.atlasagent.com/atlaslm	Dayton	OH	45420	937-252-6683	258-7862
Lewis Contractors LLC 55 Gwynns Mill Ct *Web:* www.hhlewis.com	Owings Mills	MD	21117	410-356-4200	356-7732
LF Driscoll Co Inc 9 Presidential Blvd *Web:* www.lfdriscoll.com	Bala Cynwyd	PA	19004	610-668-0950	668-9425
Linbeck Construction Corp 3900 Essex Ln Suite 1200 PO Box 22500 *Fax: Mktg ■ *Web:* www.linbeck.com	Houston	TX	77027	713-621-2350	341-9436*
Lippert Bros Inc 2211 E I-44 Service Rd PO Box 17450 *Web:* www.lippertbros.com	Oklahoma City	OK	73136	405-478-3580	478-3301
Lloyd Bilyeu Construction Co Inc 11421 Blnknbker Access Dr *Web:* www.lloydbilyeu.com	Louisville	KY	40299	502-452-1151	454-0291
Loebl Schlossman & Hackl Inc 233 N Michigan Ave Suite 3000 *Web:* www.lshdesign.com	Chicago	IL	60601	312-565-1800	565-5912
Logan Trucking Inc 3224 Navarre Rd SW *Web:* www.logantrucking.com	Canton	OH	44706	330-478-1404	478-6706
Louis P Ciminelli Construction Corp 369 Franklin St *Web:* www.lpciminelli.com	Buffalo	NY	14202	716-855-1200	854-6655
Luckett & Farley Architects Engineers & Construction Managers Inc 737 S 3rd St *Web:* www.luckett-farley.com	Louisville	KY	40202	502-585-4181	587-0488
Lusardi Construction Co Inc 1570 Linda Vista Dr *Web:* www.lusardi.com	San Marcos	CA	92078	760-744-3133	744-9064
Lyda Builders Inc 12400 Hwy 281 N Suite 200 *TF:* 800-846-7026 ■ *Web:* www.lydabuilders.com	San Antonio	TX	78216	210-684-1770	684-1859
Lydig Construction Inc 11001 E Montgomery St *Web:* www.lydig.com	Spokane	WA	99206	509-534-0451	535-6622
M. M. Parrish Construction Co 3455 SW 42nd Ave *Web:* www.mmparrishconstruction.com	Gainesville	FL	32608	352-378-1571	377-0669
MA Angeliades Inc 5-44 47th Ave *Web:* www.ma-angeliades.com	Long Island City	NY	11101	718-786-5555	786-4700
MA Mortenson Co 700 Meadow Ln N *Web:* www.mortenson.com	Minneapolis	MN	55422	763-522-2100	287-5430
Magnum Construction Inc 6201 SW 70th St 2nd Fl *Web:* www.mcmcorp.com	Miami	FL	33143	305-541-0000	541-9771
Maloney & Bell General Contractors Inc 2620 Mercantile Dr *Web:* www.maloneyandbell.com	Rancho Cordova	CA	95742	916-635-7600	635-5829
Marco Enterprises Inc 3504 Watkins Ave *Web:* www.marcoenterprises.com	Landover	MD	20785	301-773-5656	773-0422
Market Contractors Ltd of Oregon 10250 NE Marx St *TF:* 800-793-1448 ■ *Web:* www.marketcontractors.com	Portland	OR	97220	503-255-0977	262-4280
Marlborough Public Schools (MPS) 17 Washington St *Web:* www.mps-edu.org	Marlborough	MA	01752	508-460-3509	
Martin Allgeier & Assoc Inc 7231 E 24th St *Web:* www.amce.com	Joplin	MO	64804	417-680-7200	680-7300
Martin-Harris Construction Co 3030 S Highland Dr *Web:* www.martinharris.com	Las Vegas	NV	89109	702-385-5257	474-8257
Mathiowetz Construction Co 30676 County Rd 24 *Web:* www.mathiowetzconst.com	Sleepy Eye	MN	56085	507-794-6953	794-3514
Matous Construction Ltd 8602 State Hwy 317 *Web:* www.matousconstruction.com	Belton	TX	76513	254-780-1400	780-2599
Matthews Construction Co Inc 210 1st Ave S *Web:* www.matthewsconstruction.com	Conover	NC	28613	828-464-7325	465-6747
Max J. Kuney Co 120 N Ralph Str PO Box 4008 *Web:* www.maxkuney.com	Spokane	WA	99220	509-535-0651	534-6828
MB Kahn Construction Co Inc Moore GE Div PO Box 1179 *Web:* www.mbkahn.com	Columbia	SC	29202	803-736-2950	699-6413
McBride Construction Resources Inc 224 Nickerson St *Web:* www.mcbrideconstruction.com	Seattle	WA	98109	206-283-7121	284-5670
McCarthy Bldg Cos Inc 1341 N Rock Hill Rd *Fax: Mktg ■ *Web:* www.mccarthy.com	Saint Louis	MO	63124	314-968-3300	968-4642*
Mcdr Inc 5100 Wheelis Dr Suite 200 *Web:* www.mcdr.com	Memphis	TN	38117	901-761-0911	761-1054
McGough Construction Co Inc 2737 Fairview Ave N *Web:* www.mcgough.com	Saint Paul	MN	55113	651-633-5050	633-5673
Mcgraw/Kokosing Inc 101 Clark Blvd *Web:* www.mcgrawkokosing.com	Middletown	OH	45044	513-422-4521	423-5384
Mehlville School District 3120 Lemay Ferry Rd *Web:* www.mehlvilleschooldistrict.com	Saint Louis	MO	63125	314-467-5000	467-5099
Merced Irrigation District PO Box 2288 *Web:* www.mercedid.org	Merced	CA	95344	209-722-5761	722-6421
Messer Construction Co 5158 Fishwick Dr *Web:* www.messer.com	Cincinnati	OH	45216	513-242-1541	242-6467
Meyer & Najem Inc 13099 Parkside Dr *Web:* www.meyer-najem.com	Fishers	IN	46038	317-577-0007	577-0286
MGM Mirage Design Group Inc 3260 Industrial Rd *TF:* 800-477-5110	Las Vegas	NV	89109	702-792-4600	792-4790
Mid Valley School District 52 Underwood Rd *Web:* www.mvsd.us	Throop	PA	18512	570-307-1150	307-1107
Midstate Construction Corp 1180 Holm Rd *Web:* www.midstateconstruction.com	Petaluma	CA	94954	707-762-3200	762-0700
Milcord Co 9801 Industrial Dr *TF:* 888-664-5673 ■ *Web:* www.milord.com	Bridgeview	IL	60455	708-598-7900	598-7991
Millie & Severson Inc 3601 Serpentine Dr *Web:* www.mandsinc.com	Los Alamitos	CA	90720	562-493-3611	598-6871
Mine & Mill Industrial Supply Co Inc 2500 S Combee Rd *Fax Area Code: 813 ■ *TF:* 800-282-8489 ■ *Web:* www.mineandmillindustrialsupplyco.com	Lakeland	FL	33801	863-665-5601	623-6999*
Miron Construction Co Inc 1471 McMahon Dr *Web:* www.mironconst.com	Neenah	WI	54956	920-969-7000	969-7393
Mlb Construction Services LLC 1 Stonebreak Rd *Web:* www.mlbind.com	Malta	NY	12020	518-289-1371	289-1652
Monarch Construction Co Inc PO Box 12249 *Web:* www.monarchconstruction.cc	Cincinnati	OH	45212	513-351-6900	351-0979
Montgomery Martin Contractors LLC 8245 Tournament Dr Suite 300 *Web:* www.montgomerymartin.com	Memphis	TN	38125	901-374-9400	374-9402
Moores Electrical & Mechanical PO Box 119 *Web:* www.mooreselectric.com	Altavista	VA	24517	434-369-4374	369-7402
Morganti Group Inc 100 Mill Plain Rd 4th Fl *Fax: Sales ■ *Web:* www.morganti.com	Danbury	CT	06811	203-743-2675	792-8066*
Morley Group 2901 28th St Suite 100 *Web:* www.morleybuilders.com	Santa Monica	CA	90405	310-399-1600	314-7347
Morris Group Inc The 3 Office Pk Cir Suite 302 *Web:* www.morrisgroupinc.net	Birmingham	AL	35223	205-871-3500	871-3963
Moseley Architects PC 3200 Norfolk St *Web:* www.moseleyarchitects.com	Richmond	VA	23230	804-794-7555	355-5690
Mosser Group Inc 122 S Wilson Ave *Web:* www.mossergrp.com	Fremont	OH	43420	419-334-3801	332-1534
Motor Service Inc 130 Byassee Dr *TF:* 800-966-5080 ■ *Web:* www.motorserviceinc.net	Hazelwood	MO	63042	314-731-4111	731-1213
Murnane Bldg Contractors Inc 99 Boynton Ave *Web:* www.murnanebuilding.com	Plattsburgh	NY	12901	518-561-4010	561-5926
Murphy & Sons Inc 9148 Corporate Dr PO Box 492 *Web:* www.murphyandsons.com	Southaven	MS	38671	662-393-3130	393-8111
Muse Concrete Contractors Inc 8599 Commercial Way *Web:* www.museconcrete.com	Redding	CA	96002	530-226-5151	226-5155
Muskegon Construction Co 111 W Western Ave PO Box 477 *Web:* www.muskegonconstruction.com	Muskegon	MI	49442	231-726-3177	728-3547
Nabholz Construction Corp PO Box 2090 *Web:* www.nabholz.com	Conway	AR	72033	501-327-7781	327-8231
Nastos Construction Inc 1421 Kenilworth Ave Ne *Web:* www.nastos.com	Washington	DC	20019	202-398-5500	398-5501
Neenan Co 2620 E Prospect Rd Suite 100 *Web:* www.neenan.com	Fort Collins	CO	80525	970-493-8747	493-5869
New Era Builders Inc 36445 Biltmore Pl Suite A *Web:* www.new-era-builders.com	Willoughby	OH	44094	440-942-4900	942-5800
New Philadelphia City School District (NPCS) 248 Front Ave SW *Web:* www.npschools.org	New Philadelphia	OH	44663	330-364-0600	364-9310
Nibbi Bros Inc 180 Hubbell St *Web:* www.nibbi.com	San Francisco	CA	94107	415-863-1820	863-7488
Nor-Son Inc 7900 Hastings Rd *TF:* 800-858-1722 ■ *Web:* www.nor-son.com	Baxter	MN	56425	218-828-1722	828-0487
Norfolk Dredging Co 110 CentervilleßTpke N *Web:* www.norfolkdredging.com	Chesapeake	VA	23320	757-547-9391	547-2833
Norsouth Corp The 329 Commercial Dr Suite 110 *Web:* www.norsouth.net	Savannah	GA	31406	912-354-6096	352-3451
North Salem Elementary School 140 Zion Hill Rd *Web:* www.sau57.org/northsalem/Pages/Home.aspx	Salem	NH	03079	603-893-7062	893-7062
Norwood Co 530 Brandywine Pkwy *Web:* www.norwdco.com	West Chester	PA	19380	610-431-3500	431-7197
O & G Industries Inc 112 Wall St *Web:* www.ogind.com	Torrington	CT	06790	860-489-9261	489-9261
O'Connor Constructors Inc 45 Industrial Dr	Canton	MA	02021	781-828-0271	828-8248
O'Harrow Construction Co 4575 Ann Arbor Rd *Web:* www.oharrow.net	Jackson	MI	49202	517-764-4770	764-5564
Oak Contracting 1000 Cromwell Bridge Rd *Web:* www.oakcontracting.com	Baltimore	MD	21286	410-828-1000	828-7488
Oakview Construction Inc 1981 G Ave *Web:* www.oakviewconst.com	Red Oak	IA	51566	712-623-4927	623-9402

	City	State	ZIP	Phone	Fax
Oceanside Unified School District (OUSD) 2111 Mission Ave. *Web:* www.oside.k12.ca.us	Oceanside	CA	92058	760-966-4000	439-6023
Odebrecht Construction Inc 201 Alhambra Cir Suite 1400 *Web:* www.odebrecht.com.br	Coral Gables	FL	33134	305-341-8800	569-1500
Oltmans Construction Co 10005 Mission Mill Rd PO Box 985 *Web:* www.oltmans.com	Whittier	CA	90608	562-948-4242	695-5299
Omega General Contractors Inc 1778 September Ave. *Web:* www.omegagc.com	Memphis	TN	38116	901-345-6600	
Oneonta City School District 189 Main St. *Web:* www.oneontacsd.org	Oneonta	NY	13820	607-433-8200	433-8290
Opus Group of Cos 10350 Bren Rd W *Web:* www.opus-group.com	Minnetonka	MN	55343	952-656-4444	656-4529
Opus South Corp 4200 W Cypress St Suite 444	Tampa	FL	33607	813-877-4444	877-1222
Orcutt/Winslow 3003 N Central Ave *Web:* www.owp.com	Phoenix	AZ	85012	602-257-1764	257-9029
Oregon Mainline Paving LLC PO Box 768 *Web:* www.oregonmainline.com	McMinnville	OR	97128	503-472-4155	472-0393
Osborne Construction Co Inc 10602 NE 38th Pl # 100 *TF:* 888-270-8221 ■ *Web:* www.osborne.cc	Kirkland	WA	98033	425-827-4221	828-4314
Oscar J Boldt Construction Co 2525 N Roemer Rd *Web:* www.theboldtcompany.com	Appleton	WI	54911	920-739-6321	739-4409
Owen-Ames-Kimball Co 300 Ionia Ave NW *Web:* www.owen-ames-kimball.com	Grand Rapids	MI	49503	616-456-1521	458-0770
Ozanne Construction Co Inc 1635 E 25th St *Web:* www.ozanne.com	Cleveland	OH	44114	216-696-2876	696-8613
P & C Construction Co 2133 NW York St *Web:* www.builtbypandc.com	Portland	OR	97210	503-665-0165	667-2565
P A Landers Inc 351 Winter St *TF:* 800-660-6404 ■ *Web:* www.palanders.com	Hanover	MA	02339	781-826-8818	829-8934
Pacific Construction Systems Inc 2275 116th Ave Ne Suite 100 *Web:* www.paconsys.com	Bellevue	WA	98004	425-455-3000	462-8268
Palace Construction Co Inc 7 S Galapago St. *Web:* www.palaceconst.com	Denver	CO	80223	303-777-7999	777-5256
Pangere Corp 4050 W 4th Ave. *Web:* www.pangere.com	Gary	IN	46406	219-949-1368	944-3028
Parent Co The PO Box 5036 *Web:* www.theparentco.com	Brentwood	TN	37024	615-221-7000	221-7013
Parkway Construction & Assoc LP 1000 Civic Cir *Web:* www.parkwayconstruction.com	Lewisville	TX	75067	972-221-1979	219-0061
PCL Construction Enterprises Inc 2000 S Colorado Blvd Tower 2 Suite 2-500 *Web:* www.pcl.com	Denver	CO	80222	303-365-6500	
PCL Construction Group Inc 5400 99th St *Web:* www.pcl.ca	Edmonton	AB	T6E3N7	780-435-9600	435-9654
PDC Facilities Inc 700 Walnut Ridge Dr. *TF:* 800-545-5998 ■ *Web:* www.pdcbiz.com	Hartland	WI	53029	262-367-7700	367-7744
Peacock Construction Inc PO Box 1818 *Web:* www.peacockconstruction.com	Lafayette	CA	94549	925-283-4550	283-0784
Pence Kelly Construction LLC 2747 Pence Loop SE *Web:* www.pencekelly.com	Salem	OR	97302	503-399-7223	585-7477
Penfield Fire Co Inc 1838 Penfield Rd. *Web:* www.penfieldfire.org	Penfield	NY	14526	585-586-2413	387-6610
Pepper Cos Inc 643 N Orleans St *Web:* www.pepperconstruction.com	Chicago	IL	60610	312-266-4703	266-2792
Perini Corp 73 Mt Wayte Ave PO Box 9160 *NYSE:* TPC ■ *Web:* www.tutorperini.com	Framingham	MA	01701	508-628-2000	628-2821
Peris Cos Inc 282 N Washington St. *Web:* www.peris.com	Falls Church	VA	22046	703-533-4700	533-4710
Perry Construction Group Inc 1440 W 21st St. *Web:* www.perryconst.com	Erie	PA	16502	814-459-8551	453-5653
Peter R Brown Construction Inc 13830 58th St N Suite 401 *Web:* www.peterbrownconst.com	Clearwater	FL	33760	727-535-6407	539-8485
Phipps Houses 902 Broadway FL 13 *Web:* www.phippsny.org	New York	NY	10010	212-243-9090	727-1639
Piedmont Construction Group LLC (PCG) 107 Gateway Dr Suite B *Web:* www.piedmontconstructiongroup.com	Macon	GA	31210	478-405-8907	405-8908
Pierson Co 1200 W Harris St *Web:* www.piersoncompany.com	Eureka	CA	95503	707-268-1800	268-1801
Pike Co 1 Cir St *Web:* www.pikeco.com	Rochester	NY	14607	585-271-5256	271-3101
Pinkard Construction Co 9195 W 6th Ave *Web:* www.pinkardcc.com	Lakewood	CO	80215	303-986-4555	985-5050
Pinkerton & Laws Inc 1165 N Chase Pkwy Suite 100	Marietta	GA	30067	770-956-9000	618-8688
Pioneer Construction Co Inc 550 Kirtland St SW *Web:* www.pioneerinc.com	Grand Rapids	MI	49507	616-247-6966	247-0186
Pioneer Contract Services Inc 8090 Kempwood Dr *Web:* www.pioneercontract.com	Houston	TX	77055	713-464-8200	464-7100
Pizzagalli Construction Co 50 Joy Dr *TF:* 800-760-7607 ■ *Web:* www.pizzagalli.com	South Burlington	VT	05403	802-658-4100	651-1360
PJ Dick Inc PO Box 98100	Pittsburgh	PA	15227	412-462-9300	462-8961
Plant Process Equipment Inc 280 Reynolds Ave. *Web:* www.plant-process.com	League City	TX	77573	281-332-2589	332-6280
Platt Construction Inc PO Box 320160 *Web:* www.plattcon.net	Franklin	WI	53132	414-761-3868	761-3591
PM Construction Co Inc PO Box 728 *Web:* www.pmconstruction.com	Saco	ME	04072	207-282-7697	283-4549
Pnb Holding Co 223 N Mill St PO Box 680	Pontiac	IL	61764	815-844-3171	842-2958
Polhemus Savery DaSilva Architects Builders 101 Depot Rd *Web:* www.psdab.com	Chatham	MA	02633	508-945-4500	945-9803
Port Jervis City School District PO Box 1104 *Web:* www.pjschools.org	Port Jervis	NY	12771	845-858-3100	856-1885
Power Construction Co LLC 2360 Palmer Dr *TF:* 800-307-4048 ■ *Web:* www.powerconstruction.net	Schaumburg	IL	60173	847-925-1300	925-1372
Powers & Sons Construction Co Inc 2636 W 15th Ave *Web:* www.powersandsons.com	Gary	IN	46404	219-949-3100	949-5906
Prime Contractors Inc 525 N Sam Houston Pkwy E *Web:* www.primecontractorsinc.com	Houston	TX	77060	281-999-0875	999-0885
Primus Builders Inc 8294 Hwy 92 Suite 210 *Web:* www.primusbuilders.com	Woodstock	GA	30189	770-928-7120	928-6548
Prince George County Public Schools 6410 Cts Dr PO Box 400 *Web:* www.pgs.k12.va.us	Prince George	VA	23875	804-733-2700	733-2737
Progressive Contracting Co Inc 10 N Ritters Ln *Web:* www.progressivecci.com	Owings Mills	MD	21117	410-356-9096	356-9098
Quadrants Inc 30475 Wixom Rd Suite 100 *Web:* www.quadrants.com	Wixom	MI	48393	248-960-3900	960-9867
Quandel Group Inc 3003 N Front St # 201 *Web:* www.quandel.com	Harrisburg	PA	17110	717-657-0909	652-6282
R E Purcell Construction Co 1550 Starkey Rd *Web:* www.repurcell.com	Largo	FL	33771	727-584-3329	587-6560
R W Mercer Co 2322 Brooklyn Rd PO Box 180 *Web:* www.rwmercer.com	Jackson	MI	49204	517-787-2960	787-8111
R Zoppo Corp 160 Old Maple St. *Web:* www.zoppo.com	Stoughton	MA	02072	781-344-8822	344-7382
Raco General Contractors 1401 Dalon Rd Ne *Web:* www.racogc.com	Atlanta	GA	30306	404-873-3567	876-1394
Rafn Co 1721 132nd Ave Ne *Web:* www.rafn.com	Bellevue	WA	98005	425-702-6600	
Ragnar Benson Construction LLC 250 S NW Hwy *Web:* www.ragnarbenson.com	Park Ridge	IL	60068	847-698-4900	692-9320
Ramtech Bldg Systems Inc 1400 Hwy 287 S *Web:* www.ramtechgroup.com	Mansfield	TX	76063	817-473-9376	
Rand Construction Co 1428 W 9th St *Web:* www.randsc.com	KANSAS CITY	MO	64101	816-421-4143	421-4144
Randolph & Son Builders Inc PO Box 410283 *Web:* www.randolphbuilders.com	Charlotte	NC	28241	704-588-7116	588-8280
RD Olson Construction 2955 Main St 3rd Fl *Web:* www.rdolson.com	Irvine	CA	92614	949-474-2001	474-1534
Renfrow Bros Inc 855 Gossett Rd PO Box 4786 *TF:* 888-522-5958 ■ *Web:* www.renfrowbros.com	Spartanburg	SC	29305	864-579-0558	579-1782
Reno Contracting Inc 1450 Frazee Rd Suite 100 *Web:* www.renocon.com	San Diego	CA	92108	619-220-0224	220-0029
Rentenbach Constructors Inc 2400 Sutherland Ave. *Web:* www.rentenbach.com	Knoxville	TN	37919	865-546-2440	546-3414
Retrotech Inc 610 Fishers Run *TF:* 866-915-2777 ■ *Web:* www.retrotech.com	Victor	NY	14564	585-924-6333	924-6334
Riddleberger Bros Inc (RBI) 6127 S Valley Pike *Web:* www.rbiva.com	Mount Crawford	VA	22841	540-434-1731	432-1691
Ringland-Johnson Construction PO Box 5165 *Web:* www.ringland.com	Rockford	IL	61125	815-332-8600	332-8411
River City Construction LLC 101 Hoffer Ln *Web:* www.rccllc.com	East Peoria	IL	61611	309-694-3120	435-2457
RM Shoemaker Co 100 Front St 13th Fl *Web:* www.shoemakerco.com	West Conshohocken	PA	19428	610-941-5500	941-5526
Robins & Morton Group 400 Shades Creek Pkwy Suite 200 *Web:* www.robinsmorton.com	Birmingham	AL	35209	205-870-1000	871-0906
Roche Constructors Inc 361 71st Ave. *Web:* www.rocheconstructors.com	Greeley	CO	80634	970-356-3611	356-3619
Rochon Corp 3650 Annapolis Ln N Suite 101 *Web:* www.rochoncorp.com	Minneapolis	MN	55447	763-559-9393	559-8101
Rockdale Pipeline Inc PO Box 1157 *Web:* www.rockdalepipeline.com	Conyers	GA	30012	770-922-4123	614-5723
Roebbelen Construction Inc 1241 Hawks Flight Ct *Web:* www.roebbelen.com	El Dorado Hills	CA	95762	916-939-4000	939-4028
Roel Construction Co Inc 3366 Kurtz St *TF:* 800-662-7635 ■ *Web:* www.roel.com	San Diego	CA	92110	619-297-4156	297-1522
Rogers-o'brien Construction USA 1901 Regal Row *Web:* www.rogers-obrien.com	Dallas	TX	75235	214-962-3000	962-3001
Rooney Holdings 5601 S 122nd E Ave *Web:* www.rooneyholdings.com	Tulsa	OK	74146	918-583-6900	592-4334
Roy Anderson Corp 11400 Reichold Rd *TF:* 800-688-4003 ■ *Web:* www.rac.com	Gulfport	MS	39503	228-896-4000	896-4086
Roy Kirby & Sons Inc 1421 Clarkview Rd Suite 130 *Web:* www.roykirby.com	Baltimore	MD	21209	410-583-0808	583-0799
RSH Architects 100 N Wren Dr Suite 2 *Web:* www.rsharc.com	Pittsburgh	PA	15243	412-429-1555	279-7285
Rudolph & Sletten Inc 1600 Seaport Blvd Suite 350 *Web:* www.rsconstruction.com	Redwood City	CA	94063	650-216-3600	599-9030
Rudolph/Libbe Inc 6494 Latcha Rd. *Web:* www.rlcos.com	Walbridge	OH	43465	419-241-5000	837-9373
Ruhlin Co Inc PO Box 190 *Web:* www.ruhlin.com	Sharon Center	OH	44274	330-239-2800	239-1828

Company / Address	City	State	ZIP	Phone	Fax
Ruscilli Construction Co Inc 2041 Arlingate Ln; *Web:* www.ruscilli.com	Columbus	OH	43228	614-876-9484	771-2634
Rushforth Construction Co Inc 6021 12th St E Suite 100; *Web:* www.rushforth.com	Tacoma	WA	98424	253-922-1884	922-2089
RW Allen LLC 1015 Broad St; *Web:* www.rwallen.com	Augusta	GA	30901	706-733-2800	733-3879
Rw Setterlin Bldg Co 560 Harmon Ave; *Web:* www.setterlin.com	Columbus	OH	43223	614-459-7077	459-0960
Ryan Cos US Inc 50 S 10th St Suite 300; *Web:* www.ryancompanies.com	Minneapolis	MN	55403	612-492-4000	492-3000
Rycon Construction Inc 2525 Liberty Ave; *Web:* www.ryconinc.com	Pittsburgh	PA	15222	412-392-2525	392-2526
S C & A Construction Inc PO Box 7202; *Web:* www.scaconstructs.com	Wilmington	DE	19803	302-478-6030	478-3775
S D Deacon Corp 17681 Mitchell N Suite 100; *Web:* www.deacon.com	Irvine	CA	92614	949-222-9060	222-0596
Safeway Transportation Co Inc 634 Hwy 190 W PO Box 147; *TF:* 800-555-1212	Port Allen	LA	70767	225-387-6623	387-6664
Sain Construction Co 713 Vincent St Po Box 1078; *Web:* www.sainconstruction.com	Manchester	TN	37355	931-728-7644	728-7944
Sambe Construction Co Inc 1650 Hylton Rd; *Web:* www.sambe.net	Pennsauken	NJ	08110	856-663-7751	663-5859
Samet Corp 309 Gallimore Dairy Rd Suite 102 PO Box 8050; *Web:* www.sametcorp.com	Greensboro	NC	27409	336-544-2600	544-2638
Satterfield & Pontikes Construction Inc 11000 Equity Dr Suite 100; *Web:* www.satpon.com	Houston	TX	77041	713-996-1300	996-1400
Saugus Union School The 24930 Ave Stanford; *Web:* www.saugususd.org	Santa Clarita	MA	01906	661-294-5300	
Saunders Construction Inc 6950 S Jordan Rd; *Web:* www.saundersci.com	Centennial	CO	80112	303-699-9000	680-7448
Saxon Group Inc The 790 Brogdon Rd PO Box 606; *Web:* www.thesaxongroupinc.com	Suwanee	GA	30024	770-271-2174	271-2176
Schimenti Construction Co 650 Danbury Rd; *Web:* www.schimenti.com	Ridgefield	CT	06877	914-244-9100	244-9103
SCR Construction Co Inc 5420 FM 2218 Rd; *Web:* www.scrconstruction.net	Richmond	TX	77469	281-344-0700	344-0099
SDB INC 810 W 1st St; *Web:* www.sdb.com	Tempe	AZ	85281	480-967-5810	967-5841
Seaboard Construction Group 1518 Hwy 138; *Web:* www.seaboardconstruction.com	Wall	NJ	07719	732-556-0080	556-0084
Sedalco Inc 2554 E Long Ave; *Web:* www.sedalco.com	Fort Worth	TX	76137	817-831-2245	831-2248
Sellen Construction Co Inc 227 Westlake Ave N; *Web:* www.sellen.com	Seattle	WA	98109	206-682-7770	623-5206
Septagon Industries 113 E 3rd St; *TF:* 800-733-5999 ■ *Web:* www.septagon.com	Sedalia	MO	65301	660-827-2115	826-8058
Service Products Buildings Inc 460 W Dussel Dr	Maumee	OH	43537	419-897-0708	897-0938
Servidyne Inc 1945 The Exchange Suite 325; *NASDAQ: SERV* ■ *TF:* 800-241-8996 ■ *Web:* www.servidyne.com	Atlanta	GA	30339	770-933-4200	953-9922
Shaw - Lundquist Assoc Inc 2757 W Service Rd; *Web:* www.shawlundquist.com	Saint Paul	MN	55121	651-454-0670	454-7982
Shaw Construction Co LLC 300 Kalamath St; *Web:* www.shawconstruction.net	Denver	CO	80223	303-825-4740	825-6403
Shawmut Design & Construction 560 Harrison Ave; *Web:* www.shawmut.com	Boston	MA	02118	617-622-7000	622-7001
Shiel Sexton Co Inc 902 N Capitol Ave; *Web:* www.shielsexton.com	Indianapolis	IN	46204	317-423-6000	423-6300
Shingobee Builders Inc PO Box 8; *Web:* www.shingobee.com	Loretto	MN	55357	763-479-1300	479-3267
Shioi Construction Inc 98-724 Kuaho Pl	Pearl City	HI	96782	808-487-2441	487-2445
Sigal Construction Corp 2231 Crystal Dr Suite 200; *Web:* www.sigal.com	Arlington	VA	22202	703-302-1500	302-1520
Sjostrom & Sons Inc PO Box 5766; *Web:* www.sjostromconstruction.com	Rockford	IL	61125	815-226-0330	226-8868
Skaf Construction Co 7205 Corporate Center Dr Suite 301; *Web:* www.bestinteriorco.com	Miami	FL	33126	305-640-3010	640-3011
Skanska USA Inc 16-16 Whitestone Expy; *Web:* www.skanska.com	Whitestone	NY	11357	718-767-2600	767-2663
Sletten Construction Co Inc 1000 25th St N; *Web:* www.slettencompanies.com	Great Falls	MT	59401	406-761-7920	761-0923
SM Wilson & Co PO Box 5210; *Web:* www.smwilson.com	Saint Louis	MO	63139	314-645-9595	645-1700
Small Mine Development LLC 967 E Parkcenter Blvd; *Web:* www.undergroundmining.com	Boise	ID	83706	208-338-8880	338-8881
Smoot Construction Co The 1907 Leonard Ave Suite 200; *Web:* www.smootconstruction.com	Columbus	OH	43219	614-253-9000	258-9998
Snyder Langston Inc 17962 Cowan St; *TF:* 800-899-4122 ■ *Web:* www.snyder-langston.com	Irvine	CA	92614	949-863-9200	863-1087
Solo Construction Corp 3855 Commerce Pkwy	Miramar	FL	33025	954-447-2800	447-6768
Soltek of San Diego 2424 Congress St Suite A; **Fax:* Mktg ■ *Web:* www.soltekpacific.com	San Diego	CA	92110	619-296-6247	296-0730*
Sordoni Construction Services Inc 45 Owen St; *Web:* www.sordoni.com	Forty Fort	PA	18704	570-287-3161	287-0298
South Brunswick Public Schools 231 Black Horse Ln PO Box 181; *Web:* www.sbschools.org	Monmouth Junct	NJ	08852	732-297-7800	
Southwestern Carriers Inc 1085 Jarvis Rd PO Box 79550	Saginaw	TX	76179	817-232-4220	232-0256
Speed Fab-Crete Corp International PO Box 15580; *TF:* 800-758-1137 ■ *Web:* www.speedfab-crete.com	Fort Worth	TX	76119	817-478-1137	561-2544
Stellar Group 2900 Hartley Rd; **Fax:* Sales ■ *TF:* 800-488-2900 ■ *Web:* www.tsgjax.com	Jacksonville	FL	32257	904-260-2900	268-4932*
Stenstrom Cos Ltd 2420 20th St PO Box 5866; *Web:* www.rstenstrom.com	Rockford	IL	61125	815-398-2420	398-0041
Sterling Construction Co Inc 20810 Fernbush Ln; *NASDAQ: STRL* ■ *Web:* www.sterlingconstructionco.com	Houston	TX	77073	281-821-9091	821-2995
Stevens Construction Corp PO Box 7726; *Web:* www.stevensconstruction.com	Madison	WI	53707	608-222-5100	222-5930
Stidham Trucking Inc PO Box 308; *Web:* www.stidhamtrucking.com	Yreka	CA	96097	530-842-4161	842-2047
Stiles Construction Co 300 SE 2nd St; *Web:* www.stiles.com/construction_about_us.htm	Fort Lauderdale	FL	33301	954-627-9300	627-9305
Story Construction Co 300 S Bell Ave PO Box 1668; *Web:* www.storycon.com	Ames	IA	50010	515-232-4358	232-0599
Streeter Assoc Inc 101 E Woodlawn Ave PO Box 118; *Web:* www.streeterassociates.com	Elmira	NY	14902	607-734-4151	732-2952
Structure Tone Inc 770 Broadway 9th Fl; *Web:* www.structuretone.com	New York	NY	10003	212-481-6100	685-9267
Suffolk Construction Co Inc 65 Allerton St; *Web:* www.suffolkconstruction.com	Boston	MA	02119	617-445-3500	541-2128
Summit Builders Construction Co 3333 E Camelback Rd Suite 122; *Web:* www.summitbuilders.com	Phoenix	AZ	85018	602-840-7700	955-5898
Sun Builders Co 5870 6 N Hwy Suite 206; *Web:* www.sunbuildersco.com	Houston	TX	77084	281-815-1020	815-1021
Sun Eagle Corp 461 N Dean Ave; *Web:* www.suneaglecorporation.com	Chandler	AZ	85226	480-961-0004	940-0160
Sundt Construction Inc 4101 E Irvington Rd; **Fax:* Mktg ■ *TF:* 800-467-5544 ■ *Web:* www.sundt.com	Tucson	AZ	85714	520-748-7555	750-6266*
Swinerton Builders 260 Townsend St; *Web:* www.swinerton.com	San Francisco	CA	94107	415-421-2980	984-1384
Swinerton Inc 260 Townsend St; **Fax:* Hum Res ■ *Web:* www.swinerton.com	San Francisco	CA	94107	415-421-2980	984-1306*
T&g Constructors Inc 8623 Commodity Cir; *Web:* www.t-and-g.com	Orlando	FL	32819	407-352-4443	352-0778
Taisei Construction Corp 6261 Katella Ave Suite 200; *Web:* www.taisei.com	Cypress	CA	90630	714-886-1530	886-1546
Talladega City Schools 501 S St E; *Web:* www.talladega.com	Talladega	AL	35160	256-315-5600	315-5606
Tarlton Corp 5500 W Pk Ave; *TF:* 888-827-5866 ■ *Web:* www.tarltoncorp.com	Saint Louis	MO	63110	314-633-3300	647-1940
Tbi Construction & Construction Management Inc 1960 the Alameda Suite 100; *Web:* www.tbionline.com	San Jose	CA	95126	408-246-3691	241-9983
Tci Architects/Engineers/Contractors Inc 1718 State Rd 16; *Web:* www.tciaec.com	La Crosse	WI	54601	608-781-5700	781-5705
TCS Communications LLC 2045 W Union Ave Bldg E; *Web:* www.tcscomm.com	Englewood	CO	80110	303-377-3800	377-8300
Tedco Construction Corp Tedco Pl; *Web:* www.tedco.com	Carnegie	PA	15106	412-276-8080	276-6804
Teng Inc 205 N Michigan Ave Suite 3600; *Web:* www.teng.com	Chicago	IL	60601	312-616-0000	616-6069
Tepsco 2909 Aaron St; *Web:* www.tepsco.com	Deer Park	TX	77536	281-604-0309	930-0788
Tesoro Corp 5250 Challedon Dr; *TF:* 800-645-2059 ■ *Web:* www.tetratechtesoro.com	Virginia Beach	VA	23462	757-518-8491	518-8589
Thomas & Marker Construction Co 2084 US 68 S PO Box 250; *Web:* www.thomasmarker.com	Bellefontaine	OH	43311	937-599-2160	599-6170
Thomas S Byrne Ltd 900 Summit Ave; *Web:* www.tsbyrne.com	Fort Worth	TX	76102	817-429-0452	877-5507
Thompson Thrift Construction Inc 901 Wabash Ave Suite 300; *Web:* www.thompsonthrift.com	Terre Haute	IN	47807	812-235-5959	235-8122
Titan Construction Organization Inc 11865 S Conley St; *Web:* www.titanbuilt.com	Olathe	KS	66061	913-782-6700	829-2785
Titan Global Technologies Ltd 5005 3rd Ave S	Seattle	WA	98134	206-832-8165	832-8161
TN Ward Co 129 Coulter Ave PO Box 191; *Web:* www.tnward.com	Ardmore	PA	19003	610-649-0400	649-1790
Tomlinson-Hawley-Patterson Inc 2225 Reservoir Ave; *Web:* www.thp-gc.com	Trumbull	CT	06611	203-372-3583	371-7549
Torcon Inc 328 Newman Springs Rd; *Web:* www.torcon.com	Red Bank	NJ	07701	732-704-9800	704-9810
Torti Gallas & Partners Inc 1300 Spring St Suite 400; *Web:* www.tortigallas.com	Silver Spring	MD	20910	301-588-4800	650-2255
Tredyffrin-Easttown School District (TESD) 940 W Valley Rd Suite 1700; *Web:* www.tesd.k12.pa.us	Wayne	PA	19087	610-240-1900	
Trehel Corp PO Box 1707; *TF:* 800-319-7006 ■ *Web:* www.trehel.com	Clemson	SC	29633	864-654-6582	654-7788
Tri-state Design Construction Inc 7401 Old York Rd; *Web:* www.tristatedesign.net	Elkins Park	PA	19027	215-782-8200	782-8282
Tribble & Stephens Construction Ltd 8588 Katy Fwy Suite 100; *Web:* www.tribblestephens.com	Houston	TX	77024	713-465-8550	973-7107

				Phone	Fax
Tristar Constructors Inc 531 Wasatch Rd Web: www.tristarconstructors.com	Evanston	WY	82930	307-789-4508	789-4516
Turelk Inc 3700 Santa Fe Ave PO Box 93101 Web: www.turelk.com	Long Beach	CA	90810	310-835-3736	835-5909
Turner Construction Co 375 Hudson St *Fax: Mktg ■ Web: www.turnerconstruction.com	New York	NY	10014	212-229-6000	229-6185*
Turner Universal 336 James Record Rd Web: www.turnerconstruction.com	Huntsville	AL	35824	256-461-0568	461-6737
Tutor-Saliba Corp 15901 Olden St Web: www.tutorsaliba.com	Sylmar	CA	91342	818-362-8391	367-5379
U S Group Inc 100 Executive Ctr Dr Suite 217 Web: www.usgroupinc.com	Columbia	SC	29210	803-798-1420	798-1450
Ukpeagvik Inupiat Corp 1250 Agvik St PO Box 890 Web: www.ukpik.com	Barrow	AK	99723	907-852-4460	852-4459
United Steel Structures Inc 14925 Memorial Dr Suite 250 Web: www.ussi.com	Houston	TX	77079	281-496-1300	496-1314
Universal Construction Co Inc 11200 W 79th St Web: www.universalconstruction.net	Lenexa	KS	66214	913-342-1150	342-1151
University Moving & Storage Co 23305 Commerce Dr TF: 800-448-6683 ■ Web: www.universitymoving.com	Farmington Hills	MI	48335	248-615-7000	615-8515
USM Inc 1880 Markley St TF: 800-355-4000 ■ Web: www.usmservices.com	Norristown	PA	19178	610-278-9000	275-8023
Uw Marx Inc 20 Gurley Ave Web: www.uwmarx.com	Troy	NY	12182	518-272-2541	272-1196
Valley Construction Co PO Box 2020 Web: www.valleyconstruction.com	Rock Island	IL	61204	309-787-0292	787-7048
Valley View Bldg Services Inc 106 W 2950 S Web: www.wecleanutah.com	Salt Lake City	UT	84115	801-576-0067	816-1599
Van Hoose Construction 101 NE 70th St Web: www.vhcon.com	Oklahoma City	OK	73105	405-848-0415	848-3911
Van-Pak Inc 255 Cadwell Dr TF: 800-628-8388 ■ Web: www.hirschbach.com/drive/vanpak.htm	Springfield	MA	01104	413-736-9168	731-9824
Vaughn Construction 10355 Westpark Dr Web: www.vaughnconstruction.com	Houston	TX	77042	713-243-8300	243-8350
Vinco Inc PO Box 907 Web: www.vinco-inc.com	Forest Lake	MN	55025	651-982-4642	
Virtexco Corp 977 Norfolk Sq TF: 800-766-1082 ■ Web: www.virtexco.com	Norfolk	VA	23502	757-466-1114	466-1115
Vratsinas Construction PO Box 2596 Web: www.vccconstruction.com	Little Rock	AR	72203	501-376-0017	376-4145
VRH Construction Corp 320 Grand Ave Web: www.vrhcorp.com	Englewood	NJ	07631	201-871-4422	871-6727
W. L. Butler Construction Inc 204 Franklin St Web: www.wlbutler.com	Redwood City	CA	94063	650-361-1270	361-8657
W. Rogers Co 649 Bizzell Dr Web: www.wrogers.com	Lexington	KY	40510	859-231-6290	233-2066
WA Klinger LLC 2015 E 7th St PO Box 8800 Web: www.waklinger.com	Sioux City	IA	51102	712-277-3901	277-5300
Wakefield Corp The PO Box 31198 TF: 866-691-1365 ■ Web: www.thewakefieldcorp.com	Knoxville	TN	37930	865-675-1550	675-1582
Walbridge Aldinger Co 777 Woodward Ave #300 Web: www.walbridge.com	Detroit	MI	48226	313-963-8000	963-8129
Wallick Construction Co Inc PO Box 1023 Web: www.wallickcos.com	Columbus	OH	43216	614-863-4640	863-1725
Walsh Construction Co 2905 SW 1st Ave Web: www.walshconstructionco.com	Portland	OR	97201	503-222-4375	274-7676
Walsh Group Inc 929 W Adams St TF: 800-759-2574 ■ Web: www.walshgroup.com	Chicago	IL	60607	312-563-5400	563-5466
Walton Construction Co 3252 Roanoke Rd Web: www.waltoncci.com	Kansas City	MO	64111	816-531-4396	753-6161
Walton County Board of Education 200 Double Springs Church Rd Web: www.walton.k12.ga.us	Monroe	GA	30656	770-266-4520	
Wanzek Construction Inc PO Box 2019 TF: 877-492-6935 ■ Web: www.wanzek.com	Fargo	ND	58107	701-282-6171	282-6166
Ware County Board of Education 1301 Bailey St PO Box 1789 Web: www.ware.k12.ga.us	Waycross	GA	31502	912-283-8656	283-8698
Warfel Construction Co 1110 Enterprise Rd Web: www.warfelconst.com	East Petersburg	PA	17520	717-299-4500	299-4628
Warren Paving Inc 562 Elks Lake Rd PO Box 572 Web: www.warrenpaving.com	Hattiesburg	MS	39403	601-544-7811	544-2005
Washington Local Schools 3505 W Lincolnshire Blvd Web: www.washloc.k12.oh.us	Toledo	OH	43606	419-473-8251	473-8247
Washtenaw County Road Commission 555 N Zeeb Rd Web: www.wcroads.org	Ann Arbor	MI	48103	734-761-1500	761-3239
Waterbury Public School District (WPSD) 236 Grand St Suite 1 Web: www.waterbury.k12.ct.us	Waterbury	CT	06702	203-574-8000	574-8010
WE O'Neil Construction Co Inc 2751 N Clybourn Ave Web: www.weoneil.com	Chicago	IL	60614	773-755-1611	327-4784
Weaver Cooke Construction LLC 8401 Key Blvd Web: www.weavercooke.com	Greensboro	NC	27409	336-378-7900	378-7901
Webcor Builders Inc 951 Mariners Island Blvd 7th Fl Web: www.webcor.com	San Mateo	CA	94404	650-349-2727	524-7399
Weber Group Inc 5233 Progress Way Web: www.webergroupinc.com	Sellersburg	IN	47172	812-246-2100	246-2109
Wehr Constructors Inc 2517 Plantside Dr Web: www.wehrconstructors.com	Louisville	KY	40299	502-491-9250	491-3540
Weis Builders Inc 2227 7th St NW Web: www.weisbuilders.com	Rochester	MN	55901	507-288-2041	288-7979
Weitz Co Inc 5901 Thornton Ave Web: www.weitz.com	Des Moines	IA	50321	515-698-4260	
Weitz/Cohen Construction Co 4725 S Monaco St Suite 100 Web: www.weitz.com	Denver	CO	80237	303-860-6600	860-6698
Welbro Bldg Corp 2301 Maitland Ctr Pkwy Suite 250 Web: www.welbro.com	Maitland	FL	32751	407-475-0800	475-0801
Wentz Group 555 Twin Dolphin Dr Suite 160 Web: www.wentzgroup.com	Redwood Shores	CA	94065	650-592-3950	593-5632
West Bay Builders Inc 250 Bel Marin Keys Blvd Web: www.westbaybuilders.com	Novato	CA	94949	415-456-8972	459-0665
West Construction Inc 318 S Dixie Hwy Suite 4-5 Web: www.westconstructioninc.net	Lake Worth	FL	33460	561-588-2027	582-9419
Western Summit Constructors Inc 5470 N Valley Hwy Web: www.westernsummit.com	Denver	CO	80216	303-298-9500	298-9501
WG Yates & Sons Construction Co Inc 1 Gulley Ave PO Box 456 Web: www.wgyates.com	Philadelphia	MS	39350	601-656-5411	656-8958
Whitaker Construction Co 44 S 1050 W Web: www.whitcon.com	Brigham City	UT	84302	435-723-2921	723-5808
Whiting-Turner Contracting Co 300 E Joppa Rd 8th Fl TF: 800-638-4279 ■ Web: www.whiting-turner.com	Baltimore	MD	21286	410-821-1100	337-5770
Whittenberg Construction Co PO Box 9429 Web: www.wccbuild.com	Louisville	KY	40209	502-361-8891	368-9192
Wild Bldg Contractors Inc 225 W 1st N St Suite 102 Web: www.wildbuilding.com	Morristown	TN	37814	423-581-5639	587-4037
William Blanchard Co 199 Mountain Ave	Springfield	NJ	07081	973-376-9100	376-9154
Williams Co of Orlando Inc 2301 Silver Star Rd Web: www.williamsco.com	Orlando	FL	32804	407-295-2530	297-0459
Williams Service Group Inc 2076 W Pk Pl *Fax: Acctg ■ TF: 800-892-0992	Stone Mountain	GA	30087	770-879-4000	469-0251*
Winter Construction Co 191 Peachtree St NE Web: www.wintercompanies.com	Atlanta	GA	30309	404-588-3300	223-1146
Winter Group of Cos 191 Peachtree St NE *Fax: Acctg ■ Web: www.wintercompanies.com	Atlanta	GA	30309	404-588-3300	223-1146*
Winter Park Construction Co 221 Cir Dr Web: www.wpc.com	Maitland	FL	32751	407-644-8923	645-1972
WM Brode Co 100 Elizabeth St PO Box 299 TF: 800-848-9217 ■ Web: www.wmbrode.com	Newcomerstown	OH	43832	740-498-5121	498-8553
WM Jordan Co Inc 11010 Jefferson Ave Web: www.wmjordan.com	Newport News	VA	23601	757-596-6341	596-7425
Wolverine Bldg Group Inc 4045 Barden SE Web: www.wolvgroup.com	Grand Rapids	MI	49512	616-949-3360	949-6211
Woodfield Inc 3161 Hwy 376 S TF: 800-501-6020 ■ Web: www.woodfieldinc.com	Camden	AR	71701	870-231-6020	231-6070
Worth Construction Co Inc 24 Taylor Ave Web: www.worthconstruction.com	Bethel	CT	06801	203-797-8788	791-2515
Wright Construction Corp 5811 Youngquist Rd Web: www.wrightconstructioncorp.com	Fort Myers	FL	33912	239-481-5000	481-2448
WS Bellows Construction Corp 1906 Afton St Web: www.wsbellows.com	Houston	TX	77055	713-680-2132	680-2614
Zachry Nuclear Inc 527 Logwood Ave Web: www.zhi.com	San Antonio	TX	78221	210-588-5000	475-8060
Zandri Construction Corp PO Box 140 Web: www.zandricc.com	Cohoes	NY	12047	518-237-1411	237-1485
Zeeland Public Schools (ZPS) 183 W Roosevelt Ave Web: www.zps.org	Zeeland	MI	49464	616-748-3000	748-3033

190 CONSTRUCTION - BUILDING CONTRACTORS - RESIDENTIAL

				Phone	Fax
Agbayani Construction Corp 88 Dixon Ct *Fax Area Code: 415 ■ Web: www.agbayani.com	Daly City	CA	94014	650-994-9380	665-9470*
Air Contact Transport Inc PO Box 570 Web: actovernight.com	Budd Lake	NJ	07828	973-691-7077	691-0127
Albert D Seeno Construction Co Inc 4021 Port Chicago Hwy Web: www.seenohomes.com	Concord	CA	94520	925-671-7711	689-7752
Alcan Electrical & Engineering Inc 6670 Arctic Spur Rd Web: www.alcanelectric.com	Anchorage	AK	99518	907-563-3787	562-6286
Alexander Co Inc The 145 E Badger Rd Suite 200 Web: www.alexandercompany.com	Madison	WI	53713	608-258-5580	258-5599
All American Group Inc 2831 Dexter Dr PO Box 3300 Web: www.allamericangroupinc.com	Elkhart	IN	46514	574-266-2500	266-2559
Alliance Construction Solutions LLC 2725 Rocky Mountain Ave Suite 100 Web: www.allianceconstruction.com	Loveland	CO	80538	970-663-9700	663-9750
Apartment House Builders Inc PO Box 959	North Little Rock	AR	72115	501-758-2842	758-1903
Arthur Rutenberg Homes Inc 13922 58th St N TF: 800-274-6637 ■ Web: www.arthurrutenberghomes.com	Clearwater	FL	33760	727-536-5900	538-9089
Ashton Woods Homes Inc 11375 W Sam Houston Pkwy S Suite 100 Web: www.ashtonwoods.com	Houston	TX	77031	281-561-7773	561-7774
Aui Contractors LLC 4775 N Fwy Web: www.auigc.com	Fort Worth	TX	76106	817-926-4377	926-4387

Company	City	State	Zip	Phone	Fax
Ball Homes LLC 3609 Walden Dr. *TF:* 888-268-1101 ■ *Web:* www.ballhomes.com	Lexington	KY	40517	859-268-1191	268-9093
Barbour & Short Inc PO Box 6509	Norman	OK	73070	405-321-0482	360-8950
Barlow Homes LLC 3473 Yorkshire Blvd. *Web:* www.barlowhomes.com	Lexington	KY	40509	859-277-1600	
Blandford Development Corp 3321 E Baseline Rd.	Gilbert	AZ	85234	480-892-4492	892-5106
Bob Schmitt Homes Inc 8501 Woodbridge Ct. *Web:* www.bobschmitthomes.com	North Ridgeville	OH	44039	440-327-9495	327-7540
Bozzuto Group 7850 Walker Dr Suite 400 *TF:* 800-718-0200 ■ *Web:* www.bozzuto.com	Greenbelt	MD	20770	301-220-0100	220-3738
Breeden Homes Inc 366 E 40th Ave *TF Sales:* 800-322-3198 ■ *Web:* www.breedenhomes.com	Eugene	OR	97405	541-686-9431	686-0918
Burnsteads The 11980 NE 24th St Suite 200 *Web:* www.burnstead.com	Bellevue	WA	98005	425-454-1900	454-4543
Bush Construction Corp 4029 Ironbound Rd Suite 200	Williamsburg	VA	23188	757-220-2874	229-2542
Calcon Constructors Inc 2270 W Bates Ave *Web:* www.calconci.com	Englewood	CO	80110	303-762-1554	762-1948
Capital Pacific Holdings Inc 4100 MacArthur Blvd Suite 150 *Web:* www.capitalpacifichomes.com/corp	Newport Beach	CA	92660	949-622-8400	622-8404
Century-Crowell Communities Inc 1535 S 'D' St Suite 200	San Bernardino	CA	92408	909-381-6007	381-2617
Churchill Development Corp 5 Choke Cherry Rd Suite 360 *Web:* www.churchillbuilders.com	Rockville	MD	20850	240-243-1000	
City Dash 949 Laidlaw Ave *Web:* www.citydash.com	Cincinnati	OH	45237	513-562-2000	482-7206
Clark-Pacific Corp 1980 S River Rd *Web:* www.clarkpacific.com	West Sacramento	CA	95691	916-371-0305	372-0323
Coastal Contractors Inc PO Box 759 *Web:* www.coastalcontractors.net	Beaufort	SC	29901	843-524-3191	524-8468
Colson & Colson Construction Co 2260 McGilchrist St S E *Web:* www.colson-colson.com	Salem	OR	97302	503-586-7401	370-4205
Construction Enterprises Inc (CEI) 325 Seaboard Ln Suite 170 *Web:* www.constructionenterprises.com	Franklin	TN	37067	615-332-8880	771-0818
Crossgates Inc 3555 Washington Rd *Web:* www.crossgatesinc.com	McMurray	PA	15317	724-941-9240	941-4339
Damuth Trane 1100 Cavalier Blvd *Web:* www.damuth.com	Chesapeake	VA	23323	757-558-0200	558-9715
Dick Pacific Construction Co Ltd 707 Richards St Suite 400	Honolulu	HI	96813	808-533-5000	533-5320
Dot-Line Transportation PO Box 8739 *TF:* 800-423-3780 ■ *Web:* www.dotline.net	Fountain Valley	CA	92728	323-780-9010	780-1552
DRC Group The 740 Museum Dr *TF:* 888-721-4473 ■ *Web:* www.drcusa.com	Mobile	AL	36608	251-343-3581	343-5554
Drees Co 211 Grandview Dr *TF:* 800-647-1711 ■ *Web:* www.dreeshomes.com	Fort Mitchell	KY	41017	859-578-4200	578-4200
Du Bois Area School District Inc 500 Liberty Blvd *Web:* www.dasd.k12.pa.us	Du Bois	PA	15801	814-371-2700	
Edward Rose & Sons 30057 Orchard Lake Rd PO Box 9070 *Web:* www.edwardrose.com	Farmington Hills	MI	48334	248-539-2130	539-2125
Eid-Co Buildings Inc 1701 32nd Ave S *Web:* www.eid-co.com	Fargo	ND	58103	701-237-0510	239-4702
Ellicott Development Co 295 Main St Rm 210 *Web:* www.ellicottdevelopment.com	Buffalo	NY	14203	716-854-0060	852-2829
Excel Homes Inc 10642 S Susquehanna Trail *TF Sales:* 800-521-8599 ■ *Web:* www.excelhomes.com	Liverpool	PA	17045	717-444-3395	444-7577
Eyde Construction Co PO Box 4218 *TF:* 800-442-3933 ■ *Web:* www.eyde.com	East Lansing	MI	48826	517-351-2480	351-3946
F D Rich Co 222 Summer St *Web:* www.fdrich.com	Stamford	CT	06901	203-359-2900	328-7980
Farmington School District R-7 1022 Suite Genevieve Ave. *Web:* www.farmington.k12.mo.us	Farmington	MO	63640	573-701-1300	701-1309
Faxongillis Homes Inc 825 Timber Creek Dr *Web:* www.faxongillis.com	Cordova	TN	38018	901-759-7000	756-4449
FH Martin Constructors 28740 Mound Rd *Web:* www.fhmartin.com	Warren	MI	48092	586-558-2100	558-2921
Fish Enterprises 905 S Fair Oaks Ave. *Web:* www.fishenterprises.com	Pasadena	CA	91105	626-773-8800	773-8820
Forbes Homes Inc PO Box 597 *Web:* www.forbeshomes.com	Getzville	NY	14068	716-688-5597	688-6674
Fox Ridge Homes Inc 93 Seaboard Ln Suite 201 *Web:* www.foxridgehomes.com	Brentwood	TN	37027	615-377-6840	377-6864
Franklin Development Co 21260 Gathering Oak Suite 101 *Web:* www.franklindevelopment.net	San Antonio	TX	78260	210-694-2223	
Fulton Homes Corp 9140 S Kyrene Rd Suite 202 *Web:* www.fultonhomes.com	Tempe	AZ	85284	480-753-6789	753-5554
Galaxy Builders Ltd 4729 College Pk *Web:* www.thegalaxycompanies.com	San Antonio	TX	78249	210-493-0550	493-1238
Gioffre Cos Inc 6262 Eiterman Rd *Web:* www.gioffreconstruction.com	Dublin	OH	43016	614-764-0032	764-1620
Glen Construction Co Inc 9055 Comprint Ct Suite 100	Gaithersburg	MD	20878	301-258-2700	417-6990
Godley Builders Inc 415 Minuet Ln Suite D	Charlotte	NC	28217	704-522-6146	525-4657
Green Valley Corp 777 N 1st St 5th Fl *Web:* www.barryswensonbuilder.com	San Jose	CA	95112	408-287-0246	998-1737
Grupe Co 3255 W March Ln Suite 400 *Web:* www.grupe.com	Stockton	CA	95219	209-473-6000	473-6001
Hardaway Group 615 Main St *Web:* www.hardaway.net	Nashville	TN	37206	615-254-5461	254-4518
Harkins Builders Inc 2201 Warwick Way *TF:* 888-224-5697 ■ *Web:* www.harkinsbuilders.com	Marriottsville	MD	21104	410-750-2600	480-4299

Company	City	State	Zip	Phone	Fax
Harper Corp General Contractors 35 W Ct St Suite 400 *Web:* www.harpercorp.com	Greenville	SC	29601	864-527-2500	527-2536
Hasbrouck Heights Board of Education 379 Blvd *Web:* www.hhschools.org	Hasbrouck Heights	NJ	07604	201-288-6150	
Hawaii Modular Space Inc 91-282 Kalaeloa Blvd *Web:* www.hawaiimodularspace.com	Kapolei	HI	96707	808-682-5559	682-5199
Haywood County School District 900 E Main St *Web:* www.haywoodnc.net	Brownsville	TN	38012	731-772-9613	772-3275
Henry Fischer Builder Inc 2670 Chancellor Dr Suite 300 *Web:* www.fischerhomes.com	Crestview Hills	KY	41017	859-341-4709	344-5900
Hernandez Cos Inc 3734 E Anne St *Web:* www.hernandezcompanies.com	Phoenix	AZ	85040	602-438-7825	438-6558
Hitt Contracting Inc 2704 Dorr Ave *Web:* www.hitt-gc.com	Fairfax	VA	22031	703-846-9000	846-9110
House Doctors 575 Chamber Dr *TF:* 800-319-3359 ■ *Web:* www.housedoctors.com	Milford	OH	45150	513-831-0100	831-6010
HRH Construction LLC 11 Martine Ave 10th Fl *Web:* www.hrhconstruction.com	White Plains	NY	10606	914-993-5500	993-5700
Integra Construction Inc (ICI) 210 I- N Pkwy SE Suite 150 *Web:* www.integraconstruction.com	Atlanta	GA	30339	770-953-1200	953-1122
JA Jones/Tompkins Builders 1110 Vermont Ave NW # 200 *Web:* www.tompkinsbuilders.com	Washington	DC	20005	202-789-0770	898-2531
James A Cummings Inc 3575 NW 53rd St *Web:* www.jamesacummings.com	Fort Lauderdale	FL	33309	954-733-4211	415-9055
JB Sandlin Cos 5137 Davis Blvd *TF:* 800-821-4663 ■ *Web:* www.sandlinhomes.com	Fort Worth	TX	76180	817-281-3509	656-0719
Jim Walter Homes Inc PO Box 31601 *TF:* 800-492-5837 ■ *Web:* www.jimwalterhomes.com	Tampa	FL	33631	813-871-4811	
John Cannon Homes Inc 6710 Professional Pkwy W *Web:* www.johncannonhomes.com	Sarasota	FL	34240	941-924-5935	924-4129
Jokake Construction Co 5013 E Washington St Suite 100 *Web:* www.jokake.com	Phoenix	AZ	85034	602-224-4500	667-5500
Jones Co 16640 Chesterfield Grove Rd Suite 200 *TF:* 866-675-6637 ■ *Web:* www.thejonesco.com	Chesterfield	MO	63005	636-537-7000	537-9952
Joseph J. Henderson & Son Inc 4288 Old Grand Ave PO Box 9 *Web:* www.jjhenderson.com	Gurnee	IL	60031	847-244-3222	244-9572
Kalian Cos 225 Hwy 35 Navesink N *Web:* www.kalian.com	Red Bank	NJ	07701	732-741-0054	741-3404
Keith Waters & Assoc Inc 6216 Baker Rd Suite 110 *Web:* www.keithwaters.com	Eden Prairie	MN	55346	952-974-0004	974-0005
Kickerillo Cos 1306 S Fry Rd **Fax Area Code:* 281 ■ *Web:* www.kickerillo.com	Katy	TX	77450	713-951-0666	492-2018*
Kopf Builders Inc 420 Avon Belden Rd *TF:* 800-242-8913 ■ *Web:* www.kopf.net	Avon Lake	OH	44012	440-933-6908	933-6956
Landstar Homes Inc 550 Biltmore Way Suite 1110 *Web:* www.landstarhomes.com	Coral Gables	FL	33134	305-461-2440	461-3190
Lane Co 303 Perimeter Ctr N Suite 201 *Web:* www.lanecompany.com	Atlanta	GA	30346	404-459-6100	
LAS Enterprises Inc 2413 L & A Rd *TF:* 800-264-1527 ■ *Web:* www.lasenterprises.com	Metairie	LA	70001	504-887-1515	832-0036
Lennar Corp 700 NW 107th Ave Suite 400 *NYSE: LEN* ■ *TF:* 800-741-4663 ■ *Web:* www.lennar.com	Miami	FL	33172	305-559-4000	226-4158
Lewis Builders Inc 54 Sawyer Ave *Web:* www.lewisbuilders.com	Atkinson	NH	03811	603-362-5333	362-4936
Lizardos Engineering Assoc Pc 200 Old Country Rd Suite 670 *Web:* www.leapc.com	Mineola	NY	11501	516-484-1020	484-0926
Lowder Construction Co Inc 5272 Hampstead High St # 200 *Web:* www.lowder-construction.com	Montgomery	AL	36116	334-270-6524	270-6540
Mayer Homes Inc 755 S New Ballas Rd Suite 210	Saint Louis	MO	63141	314-997-2300	997-3322
McBride & Son Inc 16091 Swingley Ridge Rd Suite 300 *Web:* www.mcbridehomes.com	Chesterfield	MO	63005	636-537-2000	537-2546
Mercy Housing Inc 1999 Broadway Suite 1000 *TF:* 866-338-0557 ■ *Web:* www.mercyhousing.org	Denver	CO	80202	303-830-3300	
Michaels Group LLC 10 Blacksmith Dr Suite 1 *Web:* www.michaelsgroup.com	Malta	NY	12020	518-899-6311	899-6260
Morgan Group Inc 5606 S Rice Ave *Web:* www.morgangroup.com	Houston	TX	77081	713-361-7200	361-7299
Morris General Bldg Co PO Box 3632	Chatsworth	CA	91313	818-341-5135	
Nordaas American Homes Co Inc 10091 State Hwy 22 *TF:* 800-658-7076 ■ *Web:* www.nordaashomes.com	Minnesota Lake	MN	56068	507-462-3331	462-3211
Norris School District 6940 Calloway Dr *Web:* www.norris.k12.ca.us	Bakersfield	CA	93312	661-387-7000	399-9750
NVR Inc 11700 Plaza America Dr Suite 500 *AMEX: NVR* ■ *Web:* www.nvrinc.com	Reston	VA	20190	703-956-4000	956-4750
O'Harrow Construction Co 4575 Ann Arbor Rd *Web:* www.oharrow.net	Jackson	MI	49202	517-764-4770	764-5564
OakHill Properties PO Box 2308 *Web:* www.oakhillproperties.com	Leesburg	VA	20141	540-751-9010	
Obayashi USA LLC 420 E 3rd St Suite 906 *Web:* www.ocac.com	Los Angeles	CA	90013	213-687-8700	687-3700
Ole South Properties Inc 201 E Main St Suite 300 *Web:* www.olesouth.com	Murfreesboro	TN	37130	615-896-0019	896-9380

	City	State	Zip	Phone	Fax
Olgoonik Development LLC					
3201 C St Suite 700	Anchorage	AK	99503	907-562-8728	562-8751
Web: www.olgoonik.com					
Olympus Homes Inc PO Box 2999	Westerville	OH	43086	614-436-4100	
Web: www.olympushomes.com					
Pardee Homes					
10880 Wilshire Blvd Suite 1900	Los Angeles	CA	90024	310-475-3525	446-1291
Web: www.pardeehomes.com					
Paul H Schwendener Inc 1000 Vandustrial Dr	Westmont	IL	60559	630-971-3303	971-0355
Perry Homes PO Box 34306	Houston	TX	77234	713-947-1750	
TF: 800-247-3779 ■ *Web:* www.perryhomes.com					
Prestige Builders Partners LLC					
14160 Palmetto Frontage Rd Suite 21	Miami Lakes	FL	33016	305-827-5665	827-6263
Prince Telecom Inc 34 Blevins Dr Suite 5	New Castle	DE	19720	302-324-1800	324-1850
Web: www.princetelecom.com					
Providence Homes Inc					
4901 Belfort Rd Suite 140	Jacksonville	FL	32256	904-262-9898	262-9861
TF: 866-836-0981 ■ *Web:* www.providencehomesinc.com					
Purcell Construction Co 1550 Starkey Rd	Largo	FL	33771	888-568-1555	587-6560*
**Fax Area Code:* 727 ■ *TF:* 888-568-1555					
Purcell Construction Inc 277 Dennis St	Humble	TX	77338	281-548-1000	548-2998
Web: www.purcellc.com					
Pyramid Construction Inc 275 N Franklin Tpke	Ramsey	NJ	07446	201-327-1919	327-0054
R L Turner Corp 1000 W Oak St	Zionsville	IN	46077	317-873-2712	873-1262
Web: www.rlturner.com					
Realen Homes LP 1040 Stoney Hill Rd Suite 100	Yardley	PA	19067	215-497-0600	497-9550*
**Fax:* Cust Svc ■ *TF:* 800-732-5368 ■ *Web:* www.realenhomes.com					
Regency Homes Inc 2840 University Dr	Coral Springs	FL	33065	954-755-1775	341-8873
Reimers & Jolivette Inc 2344 NW 24th Ave	Portland	OR	97210	503-228-7691	228-2721
Rio Verde Development Inc					
18934 Avenida Del Ray Suite V	Rio Verde	AZ	85263	480-471-1962	471-0107
TF: 800-233-7103 ■ *Web:* www.theverdes.com					
Robert W Gottfried Inc					
340 Royal Poinciana Way Suite 315	Palm Beach	FL	33480	561-655-7107	833-8889
Rockford Homes Inc					
999 Polaris Pkwy Suite 200	Columbus	OH	43240	614-785-0015	785-9181
Web: www.rockfordhomes.net					
Rohde Construction Co Inc 4087 Brockton Dr	Kentwood	MI	49512	616-698-0880	698-1850
Rs Mowery & Sons Inc					
1000 Bent Creek Blvd	Mechanicsburg	PA	17050	717-506-1000	506-1010
Web: www.rsmowery.com					
Russell Construction Co Inc 4600 E 53rd St	Davenport	IA	52807	563-459-4600	
Web: www.russellco.com					
Rust Constructors Inc					
2 Perimeter Pk South Suite 300 W	Birmingham	AL	35243	205-995-7171	995-3873
Web: www.rustconstructors.com					
Ryan Homes Corp					
11460 Cronridge Dr Suite 128	Owings Mills	MD	21117	410-654-5720	654-0069
Web: www.ryanhomes.com					
Schneider Homes Inc					
6510 Southcenter Blvd Suite 1	Tukwila	WA	98188	206-248-2471	242-4209
Web: www.schneiderhomes.com					
Schuck & Sons Construction Co Inc					
8205 N 67th Ave	Glendale	AZ	85302	623-931-3661	937-3435
Web: www.schuckaz.com					
Selmer Co The 2200 Woodale Ave PO Box 11415	Green Bay	WI	54307	920-434-0230	434-0454
TF: 800-473-5637 ■ *Web:* www.theselmerco.com					
Shaw Construction Co LLC 300 Kalamath St	Denver	CO	80223	303-825-4740	825-6403
Web: www.shawconstruction.net					
Shepherd Public School District PO Box 219	Shepherd	MI	48883	989-828-5520	
Web: www.shepherd.edzone.net					
Shreve Land Co Inc 666 Travis St Suite 100	Shreveport	LA	71101	318-226-0056	226-0064
TF: 800-259-0056 ■ *Web:* www.shreveland.com					
Shugart Enterprises LLC					
221 Jonestown Rd	Winston Salem	NC	27104	336-765-9661	765-1295
Web: www.shugartenterprises.com					
Silverton Construction Co LLC					
1080 River Oaks Dr Suite A 150	Flowood	MS	39232	601-420-2525	420-2524
Web: www.silvertonconstruction.com					
Simonini Builders Inc 1910 S Blvd Suite 200	Charlotte	NC	28203	704-358-9940	358-9978
Web: www.simonini.com					
Simpson County School District					
176 W Court St PO Box 127	Mendenhall	MS	39114	601-847-2375	847-2380
Web: www.simpsoncounty.biz					
Skogman Construction Co Inc					
411 1st Ave Suite 500	Cedar Rapids	IA	52401	319-363-8285	366-7257
Web: www.skogman.com					
Smith Bros Construction PO Box 1068	Solana Beach	CA	92075	858-350-1445	
Web: www.smithbrothersconstruction.com					
Southern California Boiler Inc					
5331 Business Dr	Huntington Beach	CA	92649	714-891-0701	891-4320
TF: 800-775-2645 ■ *Web:* www.socalboiler.com					
SS Steele & Co Inc 4951 Government Blvd	Mobile	AL	36693	251-661-9600	
Web: www.steelehomes.cc					
Stabile Cos Inc 20 Cotton Rd Suite 200	Nashua	NH	03063	603-889-0318	595-2571
TF: 800-432-4892 ■ *Web:* www.stabilecompanies.com					
Standard Pacific Corp 26 Technology Dr	Irvine	CA	92618	949-789-1600	789-1609
NYSE: SPF ■ *Web:* www.standardpacifichomes.com					
Stanmar Inc 130 Boston Post Rd	Sudbury	MA	01776	978-443-9922	443-0479
Web: www.stanmar-inc.com					
Staples Construction Co Inc 1501 Eastman Ave	Ventura	CA	93003	805-658-8786	658-8785
TF: 800-881-4650 ■ *Web:* www.staplesconstruction.com					
Structural Component Systems Inc (SCS)					
1255 Front St	Fremont	NE	68026	402-721-5622	721-6170
TF: 800-844-5622 ■ *Web:* www.scstruss.com					
Sunset Development Co					
1 Annabel Ln Suite 201	San Ramon	CA	94583	925-866-0100	866-1330
Web: www.bishopranch.com					
T&g Constructors Inc 8623 Commodity Cir	Orlando	FL	32819	407-352-4443	352-0778
Web: www.t-and-g.com					
T. Gerding Construction Co PO Box 1082	Corvallis	OR	97339	541-753-2012	754-6654*
**Fax Area Code:* 547 ■ *Web:* www.tgerding.com					
TH Properties 345 Main St	Harleysville	PA	19438	215-513-4270	513-0700
TF Sales: 800-225-5847 ■ *Web:* www.thproperties.com					
Thompson Realty Corp					
2505 N Plano Rd Suite 3000	Richardson	TX	75082	972-644-2400	
Web: www.thompson-realty.com					
Thor Construction Inc					
5400 Main St NE Suite 203	Minneapolis	MN	55421	763-571-2580	571-2631
Web: www.thorconstructioninc.com					
Tishman Realty & Construction Co Inc					
666 5th Ave	New York	NY	10103	212-399-3600	957-9791
TF: 800-609-8474 ■ *Web:* www.tishman.com					
Tom Johnson Construction 100 Midland Pk Dr	O Fallon	MO	63366	636-887-4120	887-4130
Web: www.tomjohnsonhomes.com					
TOUSA Inc 4000 Hollywood Blvd Suite 400 N	Hollywood	FL	33021	954-364-4000	364-4010
PINK: TOUSQ ■ *TF:* 866-588-9290 ■ *Web:* www.tousa.com					
Town & Country Homes Inc 1806 S Highland Ave	Lombard	IL	60148	630-953-2222	953-1131
Web: www.townandcountryhomes.com					
Traton Corp 720 Kennesaw Ave NW	Marietta	GA	30060	770-427-9064	427-2714
Web: www.tratonhomes.com					
Triple Crown Corp 5351 Jaycee Ave	Harrisburg	PA	17112	717-657-5729	657-8125
TF: 877-822-4663 ■ *Web:* www.triplecrowncorp.com					
Triple Crown Realty of Ocala Inc					
1740 E Silver Springs Blv	Ocala	FL	34470	352-671-2900	671-2901*
**Fax Area Code:* 877 ■ *Web:* www.triplecrownrealty.com					
True Homes LLC					
2649 Breckenridge Ctr Dr Suite 104	Monroe	NC	28110	704-238-1229	238-1150
Web: truehomesusa.com					
Trustmark Construction Corp					
841 Sweetwater Ave	Florence	AL	35630	256-760-9624	760-0902
Web: www.trustmarkcorp.com					
Tuttle Construction Inc 880 Shawnee Rd	Lima	OH	45805	419-228-6262	229-7414
Web: www.tuttlenet.com					
United-Bilt Homes Inc 8500 Line Ave	Shreveport	LA	71106	318-861-4572	869-0132
TF: 800-551-8955 ■ *Web:* www.ubh.com					
Urban Concrete Contractors Ltd					
24114 Blanco Rd	San Antonio	TX	78258	210-490-0090	490-1505
Web: www.urbanconcrete.com					
Vantage Homes Corp					
6215 Corporate Dr	Colorado Springs	CO	80919	719-534-0984	534-0998
TF: 800-650-3300 ■ *Web:* www.vantagehomescolorado.com					
Venture Express Inc 131 Industrial Blvd	La Vergne	TN	37086	615-793-9500	793-9267
Web: www.ventureexpress.com					
Village Green Cos					
30833 Northwestern Hwy Suite 300	Farmington Hills	MI	48334	248-851-9600	851-6161
Web: www.villagegreen.com					
Voorhees International Inc 1656 Headland Dr	St.Louis	MO	63026	636-349-1555	349-5130
Web: www.voorheesintl.com					
Wagoner Construction Co Inc PO Box 1127	Salisbury	NC	28145	704-633-1431	637-7091
TF: 800-222-1027					
Wallick Construction Co Inc PO Box 1023	Columbus	OH	43216	614-863-4640	863-1725
Web: www.wallickcos.com					
Walsh Group Inc 929 W Adams St	Chicago	IL	60607	312-563-5400	563-5466
TF: 800-759-2574 ■ *Web:* www.walshgroup.com					
Walter Toebe Construction Co					
29001 Wall St PO Box 930129	Wixom	MI	48393	248-349-7500	349-4870
Web: www.toebe-construction.com					
Wayne Homes 3777 Boettler Oaks Dr	Uniontown	OH	44685	330-896-7611	
Web: www.wayne-homes.com					
WC & AN Miller Cos					
4701 Sangamore Rd Suite LL-1	Bethesda	MD	20816	301-229-4000	229-4015
TF: 800-599-4711					
Weavertown Environmental Group					
2 Dorrington Rd	Carnegie	PA	15106	724-746-4850	746-9024
TF: 800-746-4850 ■ *Web:* www.weavertown.com					
Wermers Multi-Family Corp					
5120 Shoreham Pl Suite 150	San Diego	CA	92122	858-535-1475	535-0171
Web: www.wermerscompanies.com					
Western Water Constructors Inc					
707 Aviation Blvd	Santa Rosa	CA	95403	707-570-9640	540-9641
Web: www.westernwater.com					
Wexford Homes 135 Keveling Dr	Saline	MI	48176	734-429-5300	429-3358
Web: www.wexfordhomes.com					
Wheeler Construction Inc					
3255 E Gulf to Lake Hwy	Inverness	FL	34453	352-726-0973	637-4959
Web: www.citrusbuilder.com					
Whittaker Builders Inc					
355A Mid Rivers Mall Dr	Saint Peters	MO	63376	636-970-1511	397-4894
Web: www.whittakerhomes.com					
Wildish Land Co Inc					
3600 Wildish Ln PO Box 7428	Eugene	OR	97401	541-485-1700	683-7722
Web: www.wildish.com					
William Lyon Homes 4490 Von Karman Ave	Newport Beach	CA	92660	949-833-3600	476-2178
NYSE: WLS ■ *Web:* www.lyonhomes.com					
Winchester Homes Inc					
6905 Rockledge Dr Suite 800	Bethesda	MD	20817	301-803-4800	474-1609
Web: www.winchesterhomes.com					
Wohlsen Construction Co					
548 Steel Way PO Box 7066	Lancaster	PA	17604	717-299-2500	299-3419
Web: www.wohlsenconstruction.com					
Woodside Homes Corp 39 Eagle Ridge Dr	Salt Lake City	UT	84054	801-299-6700	
Web: www.woodsidegroupinc.com					
World Development Inc 44600 Village Ct	Palm Desert	CA	92260	760-568-2955	568-4335
Web: www.world-development.com					

191 CONSTRUCTION - HEAVY CONSTRUCTION CONTRACTORS

	City	State	Zip	Phone	Fax
Dcr Business Solutions Inc PO Box 297	Mulberry	FL	33860	863-904-1077	428-9027
Web: www.dcrservices.com					
Utilipath Inc 136 Corporate Pk Dr Suite G	Mooresville	NC	28117	704-948-1005	658-3929
Web: www.utilipath.com					

Company	City	State	ZIP	Phone	Fax
Zellner Construction Services LLC 3252 Linda Dr. *Web:* www.zellnerconstruction.com	Memphis	TN	38118	901-794-1100	794-9141

191-1 Communications Lines & Towers Construction

Company	City	State	ZIP	Phone	Fax
Allied Tower Co 4646 Mandale Rd *TF:* 800-207-4623 ■ *Web:* www.alliedtower.com	Alvin	TX	77511	281-331-9627	332-0325
Bechtel Telecommunications 5275 Westview Dr. *Web:* www.bechtel.com	Frederick	MD	21703	301-228-6000	228-2200
Black & Veatch 8400 Ward Pkwy *Web:* www.bv.com	Kansas City	MO	64114	913-458-2000	458-3730
Cellcom Services Inc 11301 W 218th St.	Peculiar	MO	64078	816-779-5660	779-5120
CLS Group 609 S Kelly Ave Suite D *TF:* 800-580-5460 ■ *Web:* www.clsgroup.com	Edmond	OK	73003	405-348-5460	341-6334
CommStructures Inc 101 E Roberts Rd *Web:* www.commstructures.com	Pensacola	FL	32534	850-968-9293	968-9289
Davidson Engineering Co 296 Covered Bridge Rd. *Web:* www.tower-structures.com	Rogue River	OR	97537	541-582-8074	582-0072
Fluor Daniel Inc 3 Polaris Way *Web:* www.fluor.com	Aliso Viejo	CA	92698	949-349-2000	349-2585
Malouf Engineering International Inc 17950 Preston Rd Suite 720 *Web:* www.maloufengineering.com	Dallas	TX	75252	972-783-2578	783-2583
MasTec Inc 800 Douglas Rd 12th Fl *NYSE: MTZ* ■ *Web:* www.mastec.com	Coral Gables	FL	33134	305-599-1800	599-1900
NAT-COM Inc 2622 Audubon Rd *TF:* 800-486-7947 ■ *Web:* www.nat-com.com	Audubon	PA	19403	610-666-7947	666-7136
NEESCom Inc 25 Research Dr *Web:* www.neescom.com	Westborough	MA	01582	508-389-3300	389-3001
Quanta Services Inc 1360 Post Oak Blvd Suite 2100 *NYSE: PWR* ■ *Web:* www.quantaservices.com	Houston	TX	77056	713-629-7600	629-7676
Seacomm Erectors Inc 32527 SR 2 *TF:* 800-497-8320 ■ *Web:* www.seacomm.com	Sultan	WA	98294	360-793-6564	793-4402
Swager Communications Inc 501 E Swager Dr *TF:* 800-968-5601 ■ *Web:* www.swager.com	Fremont	IN	46737	260-495-5165	495-4205
Thoroughbred Technology & Telecommunications Inc 3 Commercial Pl *Web:* www.t3inc.com	Norfolk	VA	23510	757-629-2600	533-4884
Tower 2000 Inc 310 60th St NW *TF:* 877-720-6249 ■ *Web:* www.truenorthtower.com	Sauk Rapids	MN	56379	320-253-5489	654-9226
Tyco Telecommunications 60 Columbia Rd *Web:* www.tycotelecom.com	Morristown	NJ	07960	973-656-8000	656-8990
Utility Services Inc 400 N 4th St *TF:* 800-638-3278 ■ *Web:* www.montana-dakota.com	Bismarck	ND	58501	701-222-7900	222-7607

191-2 Foundation Drilling & Pile Driving

Company	City	State	ZIP	Phone	Fax
Berkel & Co Contractors Inc PO Box 335 *Web:* www.berkelandcompany.com	Bonner Springs	KS	66012	913-422-5125	422-2013
Case Foundation Co 1325 W Lake St. *Web:* www.casefoundation.com	Roselle	IL	60172	630-529-2911	529-2995
Coastal Caisson Corp 12290 US Hwy 19 N *TF:* 800-723-0015 ■ *Web:* www.coastalcaisson.com	Clearwater	FL	33764	727-536-4748	530-1571
LG Barcus & Sons Inc 1430 State Ave *TF:* 800-255-0180 ■ *Web:* www.barcus.com	Kansas City	KS	66102	913-621-1100	621-3288
Malcolm Drilling Co Inc 3503 Breakwater Ct *Web:* www.malcolmdrilling.com	Hayward	CA	94545	510-780-9181	780-9167
WM Brode Co 100 Elizabeth St PO Box 299 *TF:* 800-848-9217 ■ *Web:* www.wmbrode.com	Newcomerstown	OH	43832	740-498-5121	498-8553

191-3 Golf Course Construction

Company	City	State	ZIP	Phone	Fax
Barbaron Inc 107 NE 4th St. *Web:* www.barbaron.com	Crystal River	FL	34429	352-795-9010	
Bruce Co of Wisconsin Inc Golf Div 2830 W Beltline Hwy *Web:* www.brucecompany.com	Middleton	WI	53562	608-836-7041	831-4236
Buky Golf Inc 522 Bethel Church Rd	Mount Washington	KY	40047	502-538-4494	538-3193
DBI Golf 408 6th St. *TF:* 800-328-8949 ■ *Web:* www.dbigolf.com	Prinsburg	MN	56281	320-978-6011	978-4978
Formost Construction Co 41220 Guava St *TF:* 800-247-7532 ■ *Web:* www.formostconstruction.com	Murrieta	CA	92562	951-698-7270	698-6170
Furness Golf Construction Inc PO Box 2752	Kailua Kona	HI	96745	808-930-1361	930-1360
Golf Development Construction Inc PO Box 197249 *Web:* www.golfdev.com	Louisville	KY	40259	502-894-8916	893-1932
Golf Visions LLC 344 E Lyndale Ave	Northlake	IL	60164	708-562-5247	562-7497
Golf Works Inc 3660 Stone Ridge Rd Suite F102 *Web:* www.golfworksinc.com	Austin	TX	78746	512-327-8089	327-8169
Harris Miniature Golf 141 W Burk Ave *TF:* 888-294-6530 ■ *Web:* www.harrisminigolf.com	Wildwood	NJ	08260	609-522-4200	729-0100
Johnson Golf Course Builders 499 Golf Rd	South Sioux City	NE	68776	402-494-4687	494-0816
Landscapes Unlimited Inc 1201 Aries Dr. *Web:* www.landscapesunlimited.com	Lincoln	NE	68512	402-423-6653	423-4487
MacCurrach Golf Construction Inc 3501 Faye Rd *TF:* 800-646-1581 ■ *Web:* www.maccurrachgolf.com	Jacksonville	FL	32226	904-646-1581	
Niebur Golf Inc 1330 Quail Lake Loop Suite 200 *Web:* www.nieburgolf.com	Colorado Springs	CO	80906	719-527-0313	527-0337
Prince Contracting Co Inc 5411 Willis Rd *Web:* www.princeinc.com	Palmetto	FL	34221	941-722-7707	722-4641
Ryan Inc Central 2700 E Racine St. *Web:* www.ryancentral.com	Janesville	WI	53545	608-754-2291	754-3290
Shapemasters Inc 5003 O'Quinn Blvd Suite J *Web:* www.shapemasters.com	Southport	NC	28461	910-278-1434	278-1944
Total Golf Construction Inc 4045 43rd Ave *Web:* www.totalgolfconstruction.com	Vero Beach	FL	32960	772-562-1177	562-2773
Wadsworth Golf Construction Co 13941 Van Dyke Rd *Web:* www.wadsworthgolf.com	Plainfield	IL	60544	815-436-8400	436-8404
Weitz Golf International 11780 US Hwy 1 Suite 302 *Web:* www.weitzgolf.com	North Palm Beach	FL	33408	561-799-7800	799-7850

191-4 Highway, Street, Bridge, Tunnel Construction

Company	City	State	ZIP	Phone	Fax
A Teichert & Son Inc 3500 American River Dr *Web:* www.teichert.com	Sacramento	CA	95864	916-484-3011	484-6506
Ace Asphalt & Paving Co 115 S Averill Ave	Flint	MI	48506	810-238-1737	238-4326
Adams Construction Co 523 Rutherford Ave NE *TF:* 800-523-4417 ■ *Web:* www.adamspaving.com	Roanoke	VA	24016	540-982-2366	982-2942
AFC Enterprises Inc 88-43 76th Ave	Glendale	NY	11385	718-275-1100	275-4602
Ajax Paving Industries Inc PO Box 7058 *Web:* www.ajaxpaving.com	Troy	MI	48007	248-244-3300	244-0800
Allan A Myers Inc 1805 Berks Rd PO Box 98 *Web:* www.americaninfrastructure.com	Worcester	PA	19490	610-584-6020	584-8205
Allen Co Inc 131 Jefferson St. *TF:* 888-744-3361 ■ *Web:* www.theallen.com	Winchester	KY	40391	859-744-3361	744-3961
Alpha Construction Co 1340 W 171st St.	Hazel Crest	IL	60429	708-335-2323	335-0760
American Bridge Co 1000 American Bridge Way **Fax:* Acctg ■ *Web:* www.americanbridge.net	Coraopolis	PA	15108	412-631-1000	631-2000*
American Civil Constructors Inc 4901 S Windemere St. *TF:* 800-725-5699 ■ *Web:* www.accbuilt.com	Littleton	CO	80120	303-795-2582	347-1844
American Paving Co Inc 315 N Thorne Ave *Web:* www.americanpavingco.com	Fresno	CA	93706	559-268-9886	268-0662
Anderson Bros Construction Co Inc 11325 Hwy 210 E PO Box 668 *Web:* www.andersonbrothers.com	Brainerd	MN	56401	218-829-1768	829-7607
Anderson Columbia Co Inc 871 NW Guerdon St PO Box 1829 *Web:* www.andersoncolumbia.com	Lake City	FL	32056	386-752-7585	755-5430
Angelo Iafrate Construction Co 26300 Sherwood Ave **Fax:* Hum Res ■ *Web:* www.iafrate.com	Warren	MI	48091	586-756-1070	756-0467*
APAC Kansas Inc Shears Div 819 W 1st St.	Hutchinson	KS	67501	620-662-2112	662-9505
Arrow Road Construction Co 3401 S Busse Rd *Web:* www.arrowroad.com	Mount Prospect	IL	60056	847-437-0700	437-0779
Austin Bridge & Road Inc 6330 Commerce Dr Suite 150 *Web:* www.austin-ind.com	Irving	TX	75063	214-596-7300	596-7396
Autostrade International of Virginia 45305 Catalina Ct Suite 102 *Web:* www.autostradeint.com	Sterling	VA	20166	703-707-8870	904-8004
Baldwin Contracting Co Inc 1764 Skyway *TF:* 800-682-5726	Chico	CA	95928	530-891-6555	894-6220
Balfour Beatty Inc 999 Peachtree St NE Suite 200 *Web:* www.balfourbeatty.com	Atlanta	GA	30309	404-875-0356	607-1784
Barber Bros Contracting Co LLC 2636 Dougherty Dr. *Web:* www.barber-brothers.com	Baton Rouge	LA	70805	225-355-5611	355-5615
Barnhill Contracting Co 2311 N Main St *Web:* www.barnhillcontracting.com	Tarboro	NC	27886	252-823-1021	823-0137
Barrett Industries Corp 3 Becker Farm Rd *Web:* www.barrettpaving.com	Roseland	NJ	07068	973-533-1001	533-1020
Barriere Construction Co LLC 1 Galleria Blvd Suite 1650 *Web:* www.barriere.com	Metairie	LA	70001	504-581-7283	581-2270
Basic Resources Inc 928 12th St Suite 700 PO Box 3191	Modesto	CA	95353	209-521-9771	579-9502
Bay Cities Paving & Grading Inc 5029 Forni Dr	Concord	CA	94520	925-687-6666	687-2122
Becon Construction Co Inc 3000 Post Oak Blvd *Web:* www.beconconstruction.com	Houston	TX	77056	713-235-2089	235-1699
Bizzack Constructions 3009 Atkinson Ave Suite 200 *TF General:* 800-599-0424	Lexington	KY	40509	859-299-8001	299-0480
Blythe Construction Inc PO Box 31635 *Web:* www.blytheconstruction.com	Charlotte	NC	28231	704-375-8474	375-7814
Boh Bros Construction Co LLC 730 S Tonti St. *TF:* 800-284-3377 ■ *Web:* www.bohbros.com	New Orleans	LA	70119	504-821-2400	821-0714
Border States Paving Inc 4101 N 32nd St	Fargo	ND	58102	701-237-4860	237-0233
Borderland Construction Co Inc 400 E 38 St	Tucson	AZ	85713	520-623-0900	623-0232
BR Amon & Sons Inc W 2950 State Rd 11 *Web:* www.bramon.com	Elkhorn	WI	53121	262-723-2547	723-2666
Branch Highways Inc PO Box 40004 *Web:* www.branchhighways.com	Roanoke	VA	24022	540-982-1678	982-4216
Brechan Enterprises Inc 2705 Mill Bay Rd. *Web:* www.brechanenterprises.com	Kodiak	AK	99615	907-486-3215	486-4889
Brox Industries Inc 1471 Methuen St. *Web:* www.broxindustries.com	Dracut	MA	01826	978-454-9105	805-9720
Brutoco Engineering & Construction Inc PO Box 429 *Web:* www.brutoco.net	Fontana	CA	92334	909-350-3535	822-9661
CA Rasmussen Inc 2320 Shasta Way Suite F *TF:* 800-479-2888	Simi Valley	CA	93065	805-581-2275	581-2265
Cardi Corp 400 Lincoln Ave *Web:* www.cardi.com	Warwick	RI	02888	401-739-8300	736-2977
CC Mangum Co LLC 6105 Chapel Hill Rd.	Raleigh	NC	27607	919-783-5700	783-6072
CC Myers Inc 3286 Fitzgerald Rd.	Rancho Cordova	CA	95742	916-635-9370	635-8961

Company	City	State	ZIP	Phone	Fax
Web: www.ccmyers.com					
Central Allied Enterprises Inc 1243 Raff Rd SW *TF:* 800-862-6011 ■ *Web:* www.central-allied.com	Canton	OH	44710	330-477-6751	477-1660
Cessford Construction Co PO Box 160	Le Grand	IA	50142	641-479-2695	479-2003
Cherry Hill Construction Inc 8211 Washington Blvd *TF:* 800-262-2606 ■ *Web:* www.cherryhillconstruction.com	Jessup	MD	20794	410-799-3577	799-5483
Cianbro Corp 1 Hunnewell Ave *Web:* www.cianbro.com	Pittsfield	ME	04967	207-487-3311	679-2422
Civil Constructors Inc 2283 US Hwy 20 E *Web:* www.helmgroup.com	Freeport	IL	61032	815-235-2200	235-2219
CJ Mahan Construction Co 3400 SW Blvd *Web:* www.cjmahan.com	Grove City	OH	43123	614-875-8200	875-1175
Clark Construction Group LLC 7500 Old Georgetown Rd *TF:* 800-827-4422 ■ *Web:* www.clarkconstruction.com	Bethesda	MD	20814	301-272-8100	272-8414
Clarkson Construction Co 4133 Gardner Ave *Web:* www.clarksonconstruction.com	Kansas City	MO	64120	816-483-8800	241-6823
Colas Inc 10 Madison Ave 4th Fl *Web:* www.colas.com	Morristown	NJ	07960	973-656-4819	290-9088
Collet Construction Co Inc PO Box 2207	Woodland	CA	95776	530-662-9383	661-1554
Concrete General Inc 8000 Beechcraft Ave *Web:* www.concretegeneral.com	Gaithersburg	MD	20879	301-948-4450	948-8273
Concrete Materials Inc 1201 W Russell St *Web:* www.concretematerialscompany.com	Sioux Falls	SD	57118	605-357-6000	334-6221
Constructors Inc 1815 Y St *Web:* www.constructorslincoln.com	Lincoln	NE	68508	402-434-1764	434-1799
Cornejo & Sons Inc 2060 E Tulsa *Web:* www.cornejocorp.com	Wichita	KS	67216	316-522-5100	522-8187
Crowder Construction Co Inc PO Box 30007 *TF:* 800-849-2966 ■ *Web:* www.crowdercc.com	Charlotte	NC	28230	704-372-3541	376-3573
CS McCrossan Inc PO Box 1240	Maple Grove	MN	55311	763-425-4167	425-1255
Cummins Construction Co Inc PO Box 748 *TF:* 800-375-6001	Enid	OK	73702	580-233-6000	233-9858
Curran Contracting Co Inc 7502 S Main St *Web:* www.currancontracting.com	Crystal Lake	IL	60014	815-455-5100	455-7894
Curran Group Inc 7502 S Main St *Web:* www.currangroup.com	Crystal Lake	IL	60014	815-455-5100	455-7894
Cutler Repaving Inc 921 E 27th St *Web:* www.cutlerrepaving.com	Lawrence	KS	66046	785-843-1524	843-3942
CW Matthews Contracting Co Inc 1600 Kenview Dr *Web:* www.cwmatthews.com	Marietta	GA	30061	770-422-7520	422-1068
D & J Enterprises Inc 3495 Lee Rd 10 *Web:* www.dandjenterprises.net	Auburn	AL	36832	334-821-8205	
D'Ambra Construction Co Inc 800 Jefferson Blvd *Web:* www.d-ambra.com	Warwick	RI	02887	401-737-1300	732-4725
DA Collins Construction Co Inc 101 New York 67 *Web:* www.dacollins.com	Mechanicville	NY	12118	518-664-9855	664-9609
David A Bramble Inc 705 Morgnec Rd *Web:* www.davidabrambleinc.com	Chestertown	MD	21620	410-778-3023	778-3427
David Nelson Construction Co 3483 Alternate 19 *Web:* www.nelson-construction.com	Palm Harbor	FL	34683	727-784-7624	786-8894
Dean Word Co Ltd 1245 River Rd PO Box 310330 *TF:* 800-683-3926 ■ *Web:* www.deanword.com	New Braunfels	TX	78131	830-625-2365	606-5008
Delta Cos Inc 114 S Silver Springs Rd *Web:* www.deltacos.com	Cape Girardeau	MO	63703	573-334-5261	334-9576
Delta Railroad Construction Inc 2648 W Prospect Rd PO Box 1398 *Web:* www.deltarr.com	Ashtabula	OH	44004	440-992-2997	992-1311
Dement Construction Co PO Box 1812 *TF:* 800-821-5778 ■ *Web:* www.dementconstruction.com	Jackson	TN	38302	731-424-6306	424-5308
DH Blattner & Sons Inc 400 CR 50 *TF:* 800-877-2866 ■ *Web:* www.dhblattner.com	Avon	MN	56310	320-356-7351	356-7392
Dickerson Florida Inc 3803 Sunrise Blvd *TF:* 800-772-6246	Fort Pierce	FL	34982	772-429-4444	429-4445
Dondlinger & Sons Construction Co Inc PO Box 398 *Web:* www.dondlinger.biz	Wichita	KS	67201	316-945-0555	945-9009
Driggs Co LLC 8700 Ashwood Dr *Web:* www.driggs.net	Capitol Heights	MD	20743	301-336-6700	336-0004
Duininck Bros Inc PO Box 208 *TF:* 800-328-8949 ■ *Web:* www.dbimn.com	Prinsburg	MN	56281	320-978-6011	978-4978
Dunn Roadbuilders LLC 411 West Oak St PO Drawer 6560 *Web:* www.dunnroadbuilders.com	Laurel	MS	39441	601-649-4111	425-4644
ECCO III Enterprises Inc 201 Saw Mill River Rd	Yonkers	NY	10701	914-963-3600	963-3989
Edward Kraemer & Sons Inc 1 Plainview Rd *Web:* www.edkraemer.com	Plain	WI	53577	608-546-2311	546-2130
Elam Construction Inc 1225 S 7th St *Web:* www.elamconstruction.com	Grand Junction	CO	81501	970-242-5370	245-7716
Elmo Greer & Sons Inc PO Box 730	London	KY	40743	606-843-6136	843-7825
English Construction Co Inc 615 Church St *Web:* www.englishconst.com	Lynchburg	VA	24504	434-845-0301	845-0306
Evans & Assoc Construction Co Inc 3320 N 14th St	Ponca City	OK	74601	580-765-6693	765-2298
F H Paschen S N Nielsen Inc 8725 W Higgins Rd Suite 200 *Web:* www.fhpaschen.com	Chicago	IL	60631	773-444-3474	693-0064
Facchina Construction Co Inc 102 Centennial St Suite 201 *Web:* www.facchina.com	La Plata	MD	20646	240-776-7000	776-7001
FCI Constructors Inc 3070 I-70 Business Loop # A *Web:* www.fciol.com	Grand Junction	CO	81504	970-434-9093	434-7583
Flatiron Constructors Inc 10090 E I25 Frontage Rd *TF:* 800-333-1760 ■ *Web:* www.flatironcorp.com	Longmont	CO	80504	303-485-4050	485-3922
Fluor Constructors International Inc 352 Halton Rd Suite 200	Greenville	CA	29607	864-234-7335	234-5476
FNF Construction Inc 115 S 48th St *TF:* 800-542-9490 ■ *Web:* www.fnfinc.com	Tempe	AZ	85281	480-784-2910	829-8607
Fox Contractors Corp 5430 W Ferguson Rd Suite B *Web:* www.foxcontractors.com	Fort Wayne	IN	46809	260-747-7461	747-7717
Francis O Day Construction Co Inc 850 E Gude Dr *Web:* www.foday.com	Rockville	MD	20850	301-652-2400	340-6592
Fred Weber Inc 2320 Creve Coeur Mill Rd *TF:* 800-808-0980 ■ *Web:* www.fredweberinc.com	Maryland Heights	MO	63043	314-344-0070	344-0970
GA & FC Wagman Inc 3290 Susquehanna Trail N *Web:* www.wagman.com/gafc	York	PA	17402	717-764-8521	767-5457
Gallagher & Burk Inc 344 High St	Oakland	CA	94601	510-261-0466	261-3806
Gallagher Asphalt Corp 18100 S Indiana Ave *TF:* 800-536-7160 ■ *Web:* www.gallagherasphalt.com	Thornton	IL	60476	708-877-7160	877-5222
Gary Merlino Construction Co Inc 9125 10th Ave S	Seattle	WA	98108	206-762-9125	763-4178
George & Lynch Inc 150 Lafferty Ln *Web:* www.geolyn.com	Dover	DE	19901	302-736-3031	734-9743
George Harms Construction Co Inc PO Box 817 *Web:* www.ghcci.com	Farmingdale	NJ	07727	732-938-4004	938-2782
Gilbert Southern Corp 3555 Farnam St **Fax:* Hum Res ■ *Web:* www.kiewit.com	Omaha	NE	68131	402-342-2052	271-2829*
Glasgow Inc 104 Willow Grove Ave *TF:* 888-222-7570 ■ *Web:* www.glasgowinc.com	Glenside	PA	19038	215-884-8800	884-1465
Godbersen-Smith Construction Co Inc PO Box 33	Ida Grove	IA	51445	712-364-3388	364-4301
Gohmann Asphalt & Construction Inc 1630 Broadway St *Web:* www.gohmannasphalt.com	Clarksville	IN	47129	812-282-1349	288-2168
Gowan Construction Inc PO Box 228 *Web:* www.gowanconstruction.com	Oslo	MN	56744	701-699-5171	699-3400
Grace Pacific Corp PO Box 78 *Web:* www.gracepacificcorp.com	Honolulu	HI	96810	808-674-8383	674-1040
Granite Construction Inc 585 W Beach St *NYSE: GVA* ■ *Web:* www.graniteconstruction.com	Watsonville	CA	95076	831-724-1011	722-9657
Gray & Sons Inc P430 W Padonia Rd *TF:* 800-254-0752 ■ *Web:* www.graynson.com	Timonium	MD	21093	410-771-4311	771-8125
Great Lakes Construction Co 2608 Great Lakes Way *Web:* www.tglcc.com	Hinckley	OH	44233	330-220-3900	220-7670
Gulf Asphalt Corp 4116 US Hwy 231 *TF:* 800-300-0177 ■ *Web:* www.gaccontractors.com	Panama City	FL	32404	850-785-4675	769-3456
Guy F Atkinson Construction LLC 600 Naches Ave SW Suite 1201 *Web:* www.atkn.com	Renton	WA	98057	425-255-7551	255-7325
H-K Contractors Inc PO Box 51450	Idaho Falls	ID	83405	208-523-6600	524-1426
Halverson Construction Co Inc 620 N 19th St *Web:* www.halversonconstruction.com	Springfield	IL	62702	217-753-0027	753-1904
Hardrives of Delray Inc 2101 S Congress Ave *Web:* www.hardrivespaving.com	Delray Beach	FL	33445	561-278-0456	278-2147
Harper Co 1648 Petersburg Rd	Hebron	KY	41048	859-586-8890	586-8891
Harper Industries Inc 616 Northview St *TF:* 800-669-0077 ■ *Web:* www.harper1.com	Paducah	KY	42001	270-442-2753	443-9154
Hempt Bros Inc 205 Creek Rd	Camp Hill	PA	17011	717-737-3411	761-5019
Herzog Contracting Corp 600 S Riverside Rd *TF:* 800-950-1969 ■ *Web:* www.herzogcompanies.com	Saint Joseph	MO	64507	816-233-9001	233-9881
Hi-Way Paving Inc 4343 Weaver Ct N *Web:* www.hiwaypaving.com	Hilliard	OH	43026	614-876-1700	876-1899
Hinkle Contracting Corp 395 N Middletown Rd *Web:* www.hinklecontracting.com	Paris	KY	40361	859-987-3670	987-0727
Hoover Construction Co Inc PO Box 1007 *Web:* www.hooverconstruction.biz	Virginia	MN	55792	218-741-3280	741-6804
HRI Inc 1750 W College Ave *Web:* www.hrico.com	State College	PA	16801	814-238-5071	238-0131
Hubbard Construction Co 1936 Lee Rd 3rd Fl *TF:* 800-476-1228 ■ *Web:* www.hubbard.com	Winter Park	FL	32789	407-645-5500	623-3865
Hudson River Construction Co 1800 Church *Web:* www.hudsonriverconstruction.com	Albany	NY	12202	518-434-6677	434-8638
Hughes Group Inc 6200 E HWY 62 #100	Jeffersonville	IN	47130	812-282-4393	283-0142
Hunter Contracting Co 701 N Cooper Rd *Web:* www.huntercontracting.com	Gilbert	AZ	85233	480-892-0521	892-4932
Hutchens Construction Co 1007 Main St *TF:* 888-728-3482 ■ *Web:* www.hutchensconstruction.com	Cassville	MO	65625	417-847-2489	847-5561
IA Construction Corp 158 Lindsay Rd *Web:* www.iaconstruction.com	Zelienople	PA	16063	724-452-8621	452-0514
India Globalization Capital Inc 4336 Montgomery Ave *AMEX: IGC* ■ **Fax Area Code: 240* ■ *Web:* www.indiaglobalcap.com	Bethesda	MD	20814	301-983-0998	465-0273*

Company	City	State	ZIP	Phone	Fax
Interstate Highway Construction Inc PO Box 4356 — Web: www.ihcquality.com	Englewood	CO	80155	303-790-9100	790-8524
J Reese Construction Inc 10805 Thornmint Rd 2nd Fl PO Box 503906 — Web: www.debinc.com	San Diego	CA	92127	858-592-6500	592-1410
Jack B Parson Cos 2350 S 1900 W — TF: 888-672-7766 ■ Web: www.jbparson.com	Ogden	UT	84401	801-731-1111	731-8800
James D Morrissey Inc 9119 Frankford Ave. — Web: www.jdm-inc.com	Philadelphia	PA	19114	215-333-8000	624-3308
James H Drew Corp 8701 Zionsville Rd — TF: 800-772-7342	Indianapolis	IN	46268	317-876-3739	876-3829
James Julian Inc 405 S DuPont Rd	Wilmington	DE	19805	302-999-0271	998-8385
James McHugh Construction Co 1737 S Michigan Ave — Web: www.mchughconstruction.com	Chicago	IL	60616	312-986-8000	431-8518
James W Glover Ltd 248 Sand Island Access Rd	Honolulu	HI	96819	808-591-8977	591-9174
Jay Dee Contractors Inc 38881 Schoolcraft Rd — Web: www.jaydeecontr.com	Livonia	MI	48150	734-591-3400	464-6868
JB Coxwell Contracting Inc 6741 Lloyd Rd W — Web: www.jbcoxwell.com	Jacksonville	FL	32254	904-786-1120	783-2970
JD Abrams LP 111 Congress Ave Suite 2400 — Web: www.jdabrams.com	Austin	TX	78701	512-322-4000	322-4018
JD Posillico Inc 1610 New Hwy — Web: www.jdposillico.com	Farmingdale	NY	11735	631-249-1872	249-8124
Jensen Construction Co Inc PO Box 3345	Des Moines	IA	50316	515-266-5173	266-9857
JF Shea Construction Inc 655 Brea Canyon Rd — TF: 800-755-7432 ■ Web: www.jfshea.com	Walnut	CA	91789	909-594-9500	594-0935
JF White Contracting Co 10 Burr St — *Fax Area Code: 617 ■ TF: 866-539-4400 ■ Web: www.jfwhite.com	Framingham	MA	01701	508-879-4700	558-0460*
JH Lynch & Sons Inc 50 Lynch Pl — Web: www.jhlynch.com	Cumberland	RI	02864	401-333-4300	333-2659
JLB Contracting LP 7151 Randol Mill Rd	Fort Worth	TX	76120	817-261-2991	261-3044
John Carlo Inc 45000 River Ridge Dr — TF: 800-465-6234 ■ Web: www.carlocompanies.com	Clinton Township	MI	48038	586-416-4500	226-5664
John R Jurgensen Co 11641 Mosteller Rd — TF: 800-686-9725 ■ Web: www.jrjnet.com	Cincinnati	OH	45241	513-771-0820	771-2678
Johnson Bros Corp 5476 Lithia Pinecrest Rd — Web: www.johnson-bros.com	Lithia	FL	33547	813-685-5101	685-5939
K-Five Construction Corp 13769 Main St — Web: www.k-five.net	Lemont	IL	60439	630-257-5600	257-6788
Kaikor Construction Co Inc PO Box 30162 — Web: www.kaikor.com	Honolulu	HI	96820	808-841-3110	841-9511
Kamminga & Roodvoets Inc 3435 Broadmoor Ave SE — TF: 800-632-9755	Grand Rapids	MI	49512	616-949-0800	949-1894
Kankakee Valley Construction Co Inc 4356 W SR 17 — Web: www.kvcci.com	Kankakee	IL	60901	815-937-8700	937-0402
KF Jacobsen & Co PO Box 82245	Portland	OR	97282	503-239-5532	235-1350
Kiewit Corp 3555 Farnam St — *Fax: Hum Res ■ Web: www.kiewit.com	Omaha	NE	68131	402-342-2052	271-2829*
Kiska Construction Corp USA 10-34 44th Dr — Web: www.kiskagroup.com	Long Island City	NY	11101	718-943-0400	943-0401
Knife River Corp 1150 W Century Ave — TF: 800-982-5339 ■ Web: www.kniferiver.com	Bismarck	ND	58503	701-530-1400	530-1451
Kokosing Construction Co Inc 17531 Waterford Rd PO Box 226 — TF: 800-800-6315 ■ Web: www.kokosing.biz	Fredericktown	OH	43019	740-694-6315	694-1481
Koss Construction Co 5830 SW Drury Ln — Web: www.kossconstruction.com	Topeka	KS	66604	785-228-2928	228-2927
Lake Erie Construction Co Inc 25 S Norwalk Rd	Norwalk	OH	44857	419-668-3302	668-3314
Lakeside Industries Inc 6505 226th Pl SE # 200 — Web: www.lakesideind.com	Issaquah	WA	98027	425-313-2600	313-2620
Lane Construction Co Inc 1 Indian Rd — Web: www.thelanegroup.us	Denville	NJ	07834	973-586-2700	586-2965
Lane Construction Corp 965 E Main St — Web: www.laneconstruct.com	Meriden	CT	06450	203-235-3351	237-4260
Las Vegas Paving Corp 4420 S Decatur Blvd — Web: www.lasvegaspaving.com	Las Vegas	NV	89103	702-251-5800	251-1968
Lasiter Construction Inc 505 W Dixon Rd — TF: 800-264-1557 ■ Web: www.redstone-cg.com	Little Rock	AR	72206	501-374-1557	374-8314
Lawrence Construction Co Inc 9002 N Moore Rd	Littleton	CO	80125	303-791-5642	791-5647
LC Whitford Co Inc 164 N Main St — Web: www.lcwhitford.com	Wellsville	NY	14895	585-593-3601	593-1876
Lee Construction Co PO Box 7667 — TF: 800-849-5272 ■ Web: www.leecarolinas.com	Charlotte	NC	28241	704-588-5272	588-1535
LeGrand Johnson Construction Co Inc PO Box 248 — TF: 800-286-6820	Logan	UT	84323	435-752-2000	752-2968
Lehigh Asphalt Paving & Construction Co Inc PO Box 549	Tamaqua	PA	18252	570-668-4303	668-5910
LH Lacy Co 1880 Crown Dr — TF: 800-280-2885 ■ Web: www.lhlacy.com	Dallas	TX	75234	214-357-0146	350-0662
Lunda Construction Co Inc 620 Gebhardt Rd — Web: www.lundaconstruction.com	Black River Falls	WI	54615	715-284-9491	284-9146
Madden Contracting Co Inc PO Box 856	Minden	LA	71058	318-377-0928	377-9065
Manatt's Inc 1771 Old 6 Rd — TF: 800-877-1258 ■ Web: www.manatts.com	Brooklyn	IA	52211	641-522-9206	522-5594
Markham Contracting Co Inc 22820 N 19th Ave — Web: www.markhamcontracting.com	Phoenix	AZ	85027	623-869-9100	869-9400
Martin K. Eby Construction Co 610 N Main Suite 500 PO Box 1679 — Web: www.ebycorp.com	Wichita	KS	67203	316-268-3500	268-3649
Mashuda Corp 21101 Rt 19	Cranberry Township	PA	16066	724-452-8330	452-5272
Mathy Construction Co Inc 920 10th Ave N	Onalaska	WI	54650	608-783-6411	783-4311
Matich Corp PO Box 50000 — TF: 800-404-4975 ■ Web: www.matichicm.com	San Bernardino	CA	92412	909-382-7400	382-0169
Maymead Inc PO Box 911 — Web: www.maymead.com	Mountain City	TN	37683	423-727-2000	727-2025
MCC Inc PO Box 1137 — TF: 800-236-8132 ■ Web: www.mcc-inc.bz	Appleton	WI	54912	920-749-3360	749-3384
McCarthy Improvement Co Inc 5401 Victoria Ave — TF: 800-728-0322 ■ Web: www.mccarthyimprovement.com	Davenport	IA	52807	563-359-0321	344-3740
McCourt Equipment Co Inc 60 K St Suite 2 — Web: www.mccourtconstruction.com	Boston	MA	02127	617-269-2330	269-2331
MCM Construction Inc 6413 32nd St — Web: www.mcmconstructioninc.com	North Highlands	CA	95660	916-334-1221	334-0562
McMurry Ready Mix Co 5684 Old W Yellowstone Hwy — Web: www.mcmurryreadymix.com	Casper	WY	82604	307-473-9581	235-0144
Meadow Valley Corp 4602 E Thomas — TF: 800-428-4119 ■ Web: www.meadowvalley.com	Phoenix	AZ	85018	602-437-5400	437-1681
Merco Inc 1117 Rt 31 S — Web: www.mercoinc.com	Lebanon	NJ	08833	908-730-8622	730-6472
Mica Corp 5750 N Riverside Dr — Web: www.micacorporation.com	Fort Worth	TX	76137	817-847-6121	847-6831
Michael Baker Corp 100 Airsite Dr Airsite Business Pk — AMEX: BKR ■ TF: 800-553-1153 ■ Web: www.mbakercorp.com	Moon Township	PA	15108	412-269-6300	375-3977
Michigan Paving & Materials Co 2575 S Haggerty Rd Suite 100 — Web: www.thompsonmccully.com	Canton	MI	48188	734-397-2050	397-8480
Mid Valley School District 52 Underwood Rd — Web: www.mvsd.us	Throop	PA	18512	570-307-1150	307-1107
Milestone Contractors LP 3410 S 650 E — Web: www.milestonelp.com	Columbus	IN	47203	812-579-5248	579-6703
Modern Continental Construction Co 175 Purchase St — TF: 800-833-6307 ■ Web: www.moderncontinental.com	Boston	MA	02110	617-864-6300	864-8766
Mountain States Constructors Inc 3601 Pan American Rd NE	Albuquerque	NM	87107	505-292-0108	292-5311
NAB Construction Corp 112-20 14th Ave — Web: www.nabconstruction.com	College Point	NY	11356	718-762-0001	961-3789
Nagle Paving Co 39525 W 13 Mile Rd 300 — Web: www.naglepaving.com	Novi	MI	48377	248-553-0600	553-0669
National Engineering & Contracting Co Inc 8150 E Dow Cir Suite 200 — Web: www.natlengr.com	Strongsville	OH	44136	440-243-8533	243-8561
Nesbitt Contracting Co Inc 100 S Price Rd — Web: www.nesbitts.com	Tempe	AZ	85281	480-894-2831	423-7680
Newell Roadbuilders Inc 13266 US Hwy 31	Hope Hull	AL	36043	334-288-2702	288-2721
Northern Improvement Co 4000 12th Ave NW — Web: www.nicnd.com/NIC/NIC1.html	Fargo	ND	58102	701-277-1225	277-1516
Oakgrove Construction Inc 6900 Seneca St — Web: www.oakgroveconst.com	Elma	NY	14059	716-652-2200	655-3919
Odebrecht Construction Inc 201 Alhambra Cir Suite 1400 — Web: www.odebrecht.com.br	Coral Gables	FL	33134	305-341-8800	569-1500
Oldcastle Materials Inc 900 Ashwood Pkwy Suite 700 — TF: 800-241-7074 ■ Web: www.apac.com	Atlanta	GA	30338	770-552-5600	522-5008
Overstreet Paving Inc 17728 US Hwy 41 — TF: 800-741-1631	Spring Hill	FL	34610	352-796-1631	799-6435
P Flanigan & Sons Inc 2444 Loch Raven Rd — Web: www.pflanigan.com	Baltimore	MD	21218	410-467-5900	467-3127
Palmer Paving Corp PO Box 47 — TF: 800-266-5859 ■ Web: www.palmerpaving.com	Palmer	MA	01069	413-283-8354	289-1939
Parsons Corp 100 W Walnut St — TF: 800-883-7300 ■ Web: www.parsons.com	Pasadena	CA	91124	626-440-2000	440-2630
Pavex Inc 4400 Gettysburg Rd	Camp Hill	PA	17011	717-761-1502	761-0329
Peckham Industries Inc 20 Haarlem Ave — Web: www.peckham.com	White Plains	NY	10603	914-949-2000	949-2075
Perini Corp 73 Mt Wayte Ave PO Box 9160 — NYSE: TPC ■ Web: www.tutorperini.com	Framingham	MA	01701	508-628-2000	628-2821
Perry Engineering Co Inc 1945 Millwood Pike — TF: 800-272-4310 ■ Web: www.perryeng.com	Winchester	VA	22602	540-667-4310	667-7618
Peter Baker & Son Co 1349 Rockland Rd PO Box 187 — Web: www.peterbaker.com	Lake Bluff	IL	60044	847-362-3663	362-0707
Peterson Contractors Inc 104 Blackhawk St PO Box A — Web: www.petersoncontractors.com	Reinbeck	IA	50669	319-345-2713	345-2991
Petracca & Sons Inc 1802 Petracca Pl	Whitestone	NY	11357	718-746-8000	321-8476
Petricca Industries Inc 550 Cheshire Rd	Pittsfield	MA	01201	413-442-6926	499-9930
Phillips Contracting Co PO Box 2069 — Web: www.phillipscontracting.com	Columbus	MS	39704	662-328-6250	329-3291
Pike Industries Inc 3 Eastgate Pk Rd — TF: 800-283-7453 ■ Web: www.pikeindustries.com	Belmont	NH	03220	603-527-5100	527-5101
PJ Keating Co 998 Reservoir Rd — TF: 800-441-4119 ■ Web: www.pjkeating.com	Lunenburg	MA	01462	978-582-9931	582-7130
PKF-Mark III Inc 170 Pheasant Run PO Box 390 — Web: www.pkfmarkiii.com	Newtown	PA	18940	215-968-5031	968-3829
Plote Inc 1100 Brandt Dr — Web: www.plote.com	Hoffman Estates	IL	60192	847-695-9300	695-9317
Prince Contracting Co Inc 5411 Willis Rd — Web: www.princeinc.com	Palmetto	FL	34221	941-722-7707	722-4641
Professional Construction Services Inc PO Box 2005 — TF: 800-562-4318 ■ Web: www.professionalconstruction.com	Prairieville	LA	70769	225-744-4016	744-4938
Progressive Contractors Inc 14123 42nd St NE — TF: 888-549-1820 ■ Web: www.pciroads.com	Saint Michael	MN	55376	763-497-6100	497-6101
Pulice Construction Inc 2033 W Mountain View Rd — Web: www.pulice.com	Phoenix	AZ	85021	602-944-2241	870-3395

Phone Fax

Ranger Construction Industries Inc
101 Sansbury's Way .... West Palm Beach FL 33411 561-793-9400 790-4332
TF: 800-969-9402 ■ *Web:* www.rangerconstruction.com

Ray Bell Construction Co Inc
255 Wilson Pake Cir PO Box 363 .... Brentwood TN 37027 615-373-4343 373-9224

Rea Contracting LLC 6135 Pk S Dr Suite 400 .... Charlotte NC 28210 704-553-6500 553-6599
Web: www.reaconst.com

Reeves Construction Co Inc
4931 Riverside Dr Bldg 200 PO Box 13 .... Macon GA 31210 478-474-9092 474-9192
Web: www.reevescc.com

Reilly Construction Co Inc PO Box 99 .... Ossian IA 52161 563-532-9211 532-9759
Web: www.reilly-construction.com

Reliable Contracting Co Inc
1 Church View Rd .... Millersville MD 21108 410-987-0313 987-8020
Web: www.reliablecontracting.com

Richard F Kline Inc 7700 Grove Rd .... Frederick MD 21704 301-662-8211 662-0041
Web: www.rfkline.com

Rieth-Riley Construction Co Inc PO Box 477 .... Goshen IN 46527 574-875-5183 875-8405
Web: www.rieth-riley.com

Rifenburg Construction Inc 159 Brick Church Rd .... Troy NY 12180 518-279-3265 279-4260
Web: www.rifenburg.com

Rogers Group Inc 421 Great Cir Rd .... Nashville TN 37228 615-242-0585
Web: www.rogersgroupinc.com

Royal Contracting Co Ltd 677 Ahua St .... Honolulu HI 96819 808-839-9006 839-7571
Web: www.royalcontracting.com

RS Audley Inc 609 Rt 3A .... Bow NH 03304 603-224-7724 225-7614

Ruhlin Co Inc PO Box 190 .... Sharon Center OH 44274 330-239-2800 239-1828
Web: www.ruhlin.com

Sargent Corp 378 Bennoch Rd .... Stillwater ME 04489 207-827-4435 827-6150
TF: 800-533-1812 ■ *Web:* www.sargent-corp.com

Schiavone Construction Co Inc
150 Meadowlands Pkwy 3rd Fl .... Secaucus NJ 07094 201-867-5070 866-6132
Web: www.schiavoneconstruction.com

Scott Construction Inc 560 Munroe Ave .... Lake Delton WI 53940 608-254-2555 254-2249
TF: 800-843-1556 ■ *Web:* www.scottconstruct.com

Scruggs Co Inc PO Box 2065 .... Valdosta GA 31604 229-242-2388 242-7109
TF: 800-230-7263

Shelly Co 80 Pk Dr .... Thornville OH 43076 740-246-6315 246-4715
Web: www.shellyco.com

Sherwood Construction Co Inc 3219 W May St .... Wichita KS 67213 316-943-0211 943-3772
TF: 800-852-6038 ■ *Web:* www.sherwoodcompanies.com

Shirley Contracting Corp 8435 Backlick Rd .... Lorton VA 22079 703-550-8100 550-7897
Web: www.shirleycontracting.com

Sioux Falls Construction Co Inc
800 S 7th Ave .... Sioux Falls SD 57101 605-336-1640 334-9342
TF: 800-888-1640 ■ *Web:* www.sfconst.com

Skanska USA Inc 16-16 Whitestone Expy .... Whitestone NY 11357 718-767-2600 767-2663
Web: www.skanska.com

Sletten Construction Co Inc
1000 25th St N .... Great Falls MT 59401 406-761-7920 761-0923
Web: www.slettencompanies.com

Sloan Construction Co Inc 250 Plemmons Rd .... Duncan SC 29334 864-416-0200 416-0201
Web: www.sloan-construction.com

Staker Parson Cos 2350 S 1900 W .... Ogden UT 84401 801-731-1111 731-8800
TF: 888-672-7766 ■ *Web:* stakerparson.com

Standard Concrete Products 945 Broadway .... Columbus GA 31901 706-322-3274 576-2669
Web: www.standardconcrete.net

Steve P Rados Inc
2002 E McFadden Ave Suite 200 PO Box 15128 .... Santa Ana CA 92705 714-835-4612 835-2186
Web: www.radoscompanies.com

Suburban Grading & Utilities Inc
1190 Harmony Rd .... Norfolk VA 23502 757-461-1800 461-0989
Web: www.suburbangrading.com

Sukut Construction Inc 4010 W Chandler Ave .... Santa Ana CA 92704 714-540-5351 545-2438
TF: 888-785-8801 ■ *Web:* www.sukut.com

Sully-Miller Contracting Co Inc
135 S State Collage Blvd Suite 400 .... Brea CA 92821 714-578-9600 578-2850*
**Fax: Hum Res* ■ *TF:* 800-431-9842 ■ *Web:* www.sullymiller.com

Summers-Taylor Inc 300 W Elk Ave .... Elizabethton TN 37643 423-543-3181 543-6189

Sundt Construction Inc 4101 E Irvington Rd .... Tucson AZ 85714 520-748-7555 750-6266*
**Fax: Mktg* ■ *TF:* 800-467-5544 ■ *Web:* www.sundt.com

Superior Construction Co Inc
2045 E Dunes Hwy PO Box 64888 .... Gary IN 46401 219-886-3728 885-4328
Web: www.superior-construction.com

Sweeping Services Of Texas LP
3324 Roy Orr Blvd .... Grand Prairie TX 75050 817-268-4100
Web: www.mrdirtusa.com

Tidewater Skanska Inc PO Box 57 .... Norfolk VA 23501 757-420-4140 420-3551
TF: 877-263-1119 ■ *Web:* www.usacivil.skanska.com

TJ Lambrecht Construction Inc 10 Gougar Rd .... Joliet IL 60432 815-727-9211 727-6421
Web: www.tjlambrecht.com

Tony Angelo Cement Construction Co
46850 Grand River Ave .... Novi MI 48374 248-344-4000 344-4048
Web: www.tonyangelo.com

Traylor Bros Inc 835 N Congress Ave .... Evansville IN 47715 812-477-1542 474-3223
Web: www.traylor.com

Trumbull Corp 1020 Lebanon Rd .... West Mifflin PA 15122 412-462-9300 462-1074
Web: www.trumbullcorp.com

United Contractors Midwest Inc
PO Box 13420 .... Springfield IL 62791 217-546-6192 546-1904
Web: www.ucm.biz

Utility Contractors Inc 659 N Market St .... Wichita KS 67214 316-265-9506 265-8314
TF: 888-766-2576 ■ *Web:* www.ucict.com

Vecellio & Grogan Inc 2251 Robert C Byrd Dr .... Beckley WV 25802 304-252-6575 252-4131
TF: 800-255-6575 ■ *Web:* www.vecelliogrogan.com

Viasys Services Inc 2944 Drane Field Rd .... Lakeland FL 33811 863-607-9988 607-9955
Web: www.viasyscorp.com

Walsh Group Inc 929 W Adams St .... Chicago IL 60607 312-563-5400 563-5466
TF: 800-759-2574 ■ *Web:* www.walshgroup.com

Washington Corp PO Box 16630 .... Missoula MT 59808 406-523-1300 523-1399
TF: 800-832-7329 ■ *Web:* www.washcorp.com

Waterland Trucking Service PO Box 9320335 .... Wixom MI 48393 248-349-1582 349-5385

WE Blain & Sons Inc PO Box 1208 .... Mount Olive MS 39119 601-797-4551 797-4777

WG Yates & Sons Construction Co Inc
1 Gulley Ave PO Box 456 .... Philadelphia MS 39350 601-656-5411 656-8958
Web: www.wgyates.com

Wilder Construction Co Inc
1525 E Marine View Dr .... Everett WA 98201 425-551-3100 551-3116
TF: 800-377-0954 ■ *Web:* www.wilderconstruction.com

Williams Bros Construction Co Inc
3800 Milam St .... Houston TX 77006 713-522-9821 520-5247
Web: www.wbctx.com

Windsor Service 2415 Kutztown Rd .... Reading PA 19605 610-929-0716 929-4825

Winzinger Inc 1704 Marne Hwy PO Box 537 .... Hainesport NJ 08036 609-267-8600 267-4079
Web: www.winzinger.com

WM Brode Co 100 Elizabeth St PO Box 299 .... Newcomerstown OH 43832 740-498-5121 498-8553
TF: 800-848-9217 ■ *Web:* www.wmbrode.com

Woodworth & Co Inc 1200 E 'D' St .... Tacoma WA 98421 253-383-3585 572-8648
Web: www.woodworthandcompany.com

Yantis Co PO Box 17045 .... San Antonio TX 78217 210-655-3780 655-8526
Web: www.yantiscompany.com

Yonkers Contracting Co Inc 969 Midland Ave .... Yonkers NY 10704 914-965-1500 378-8885
Web: www.mrm.yonkerscontractingco.com

Zachry Holdings Inc PO Box 240130 .... San Antonio TX 78224 210-475-8000 588-5060
Web: www.zachry.com

191-5 Marine Construction

Phone Fax

Andrie Inc 561 E Western Ave PO Box 1548 .... Muskegon MI 49442 231-728-2226 726-6747
Web: www.andrie.com

Atlantic Meeco Inc 1501 E Gene Stipe Blvd .... McAlester OK 74501 918-423-6833 423-3215
TF: 800-627-4621 ■ *Web:* www.atlantic-meeco.com

Bellingham Marine Industries Inc
1001 C St .... Bellingham WA 98225 360-676-2800 734-2417
TF: 800-733-5679 ■ *Web:* www.bellingham-marine.com

Choctaw Transportation Co Inc PO Box 585 .... Dyersburg TN 38025 731-285-4664 285-4668

Civil Constructors Inc 2283 US Hwy 20 E .... Freeport IL 61032 815-235-2200 235-2219
Web: www.helmgroup.com

Corey Delta Inc 610 Industrial Way PO box 637 .... Benicia CA 94510 707-747-7500 745-5619
TF: 800-707-2260 ■ *Web:* www.coreydelta.com

DeSilva Gates Construction Inc
11555 Dublin Blvd .... Dublin CA 94568 925-829-9220 803-4268
Web: www.desilvagates.com

Dot-Line Transportation PO Box 8739 .... Fountain Valley CA 92728 323-780-9010 780-1552
TF: 800-423-3780 ■ *Web:* www.dotline.net

Frontier-Kemper Constructors Inc
1695 Allen Rd .... Evansville IN 47710 812-426-2741 428-0337
Web: www.frontierkemper.com

General Construction Co 19472 Powder Hill Pl .... Poulsbo WA 98370 360-779-3200 779-3132
Web: www.generalconstructionco.com

Granite Construction Inc 585 W Beach St .... Watsonville CA 95076 831-724-1011 722-9657
NYSE: GVA ■ *Web:* www.graniteconstruction.com

Great Lakes Dredge & Dock Co
2122 York Rd Suite 200 .... Oak Brook IL 60523 630-574-3000 574-2981
TF: 800-323-7100 ■ *Web:* www.gldd.com

Hawaiian Dredging & Construction Co
201 Merchant St .... Honolulu HI 96813 808-735-3211 735-7416
Web: www.hdcc.com

Horizon Offshore Inc
2500 Citywest Blvd Suite 2200 .... Houston TX 77042 713-361-2600 361-2690
TF: 877-361-2600 ■ *Web:* www.horizonoffshore.com

James Steele Construction Co
1410 Sylvan St .... Saint Paul MN 55117 651-488-6755 488-4787
Web: www.jamessteeleconstruction.com

JR Filanc Construction Co Inc
740 N Andreasen Dr .... Escondido CA 92029 760-941-7130 941-3969
TF: 877-225-5428 ■ *Web:* www.filanc.com

King Fisher Marine Services Inc
159 Hwy 316 PO Box 108 .... Port Lavaca TX 77979 361-552-6751 552-1200
TF: 888-553-6751 ■ *Web:* www.orionmarinegroup.com

Lane Construction Corp 965 E Main St .... Meriden CT 06450 203-235-3351 237-4260
Web: www.laneconstruct.com

Luhr Bros Inc 250 W Sand Bank Rd .... Columbia IL 62236 618-281-4106 281-4288
Web: www.luhr.com

Manson Construction Co 5209 E Marginal Way S .... Seattle WA 98134 206-762-0850 764-8595
TF: 800-262-6766 ■ *Web:* www.mansonconstruction.com

Massman Construction Co
8901 State Line Rd Suite 240 PO Box 8458 .... Kansas City MO 64114 816-523-1000 333-2109
Web: www.massman.net

McDermott International Inc
757 N Eldridge Pkwy .... Houston TX 77079 281-870-5000 870-5095
NYSE: MDR ■ *Web:* www.mcdermott.com

Misener Marine Construction Inc
5600 W Commerce St .... Tampa FL 33616 813-839-8441 831-7498
TF: 866-211-9742 ■ *Web:* www.orionmarinegroup.com/misener.htm

Modern Continental Construction Co
175 Purchase St .... Boston MA 02110 617-864-6300 864-8766
TF: 800-833-6307 ■ *Web:* www.moderncontinental.com

Norris School District 6940 Calloway Dr .... Bakersfield CA 93312 661-387-7000 399-9750
Web: www.norris.k12.ca.us

P Gioioso & Sons Inc 50 Sprague St .... Hyde Park MA 02136 617-364-5800 364-9462
Web: www.pgioioso.com

Patton-Tully Transportation LLC
1242 N 2nd St .... Memphis TN 38107 901-576-1400 576-1486

Tg Construction Inc 119 Standard St .... El Segundo CA 90245 310-640-0220 640-2907
Web: www.tgconst.com

Tidewater Skanska Inc PO Box 57 .... Norfolk VA 23501 757-420-4140 420-3551
TF: 877-263-1119 ■ *Web:* www.usacivil.skanska.com

Washington Corp PO Box 16630 .... Missoula MT 59808 406-523-1300 523-1399
TF: 800-832-7329 ■ *Web:* www.washcorp.com

Weeks Marine Inc 4 Commerce Dr .... Cranford NJ 07016 908-272-4010 272-4740
Web: www.weeksmarine.com

191-6 Mining Construction

Company	City	State	ZIP	Phone	Fax
AME Inc 2467 Coltharp Rd *TF:* 800-849-7766 ■ *Web:* www.ameonline.com	Fort Mill	SC	29715	803-548-7766	548-7448
Frontier-Kemper Constructors Inc 1695 Allen Rd *Web:* www.frontierkemper.com	Evansville	IN	47710	812-426-2741	428-0337
Sundt Construction Inc 4101 E Irvington Rd **Fax:* Mktg ■ *TF:* 800-467-5544 ■ *Web:* www.sundt.com	Tucson	AZ	85714	520-748-7555	750-6266*
TIC - the Industrial Co 2211 Elk River Rd *TF:* 888-810-9367 ■ *Web:* www.tic-inc.com	Steamboat Springs	CO	80487	970-879-2561	879-2998

191-7 Plant Construction

Company	City	State	ZIP	Phone	Fax
Angelo Iafrate Construction Co 26300 Sherwood Ave **Fax:* Hum Res ■ *Web:* www.iafrate.com	Warren	MI	48091	586-756-1070	756-0467*
Atomic Energy of Canada Ltd 2251 Speakman Dr *Web:* www.aecl.ca	Mississauga	ON	L5K1B2	905-823-9040	823-6120
Bancroft Construction Co 1300 N Grant Ave Suite 110 *Web:* www.bancroftconstruction.com	Wilmington	DE	19806	302-655-3434	655-4599
Barton Malow Enterprises Inc 26500 American Dr *Web:* www.bmco.com	Southfield	MI	48034	248-436-5000	436-5001
Bechtel North America 3000 Post Oak Blvd *Web:* www.bechtel.com	Houston	TX	77056	713-235-2000	960-9031
Bechtel Petroleum & Chemical 3000 Post Oak Blvd *Web:* www.bechtel.com	Houston	TX	77056	713-235-2000	235-4494
Big-D Construction Corp 404 W 400 S *TF:* 877-415-6009 ■ *Web:* www.big-d.com	Salt Lake City	UT	84101	801-415-6000	415-6900
Black & Veatch 8400 Ward Pkwy *Web:* www.bv.com	Kansas City	MO	64114	913-458-2000	458-3730
Bowen Engineering Corp 10315 Allisonville Rd *TF:* 800-377-2580 ■ *Web:* www.bowenengineering.com	Fishers	IN	46038	317-842-2616	841-4257
Brasfield & Gorrie LLC 729 30th St S *TF:* 800-239-8017 ■ *Web:* www.brasfieldgorrie.com	Birmingham	AL	35233	205-328-4000	251-1304
Brinderson 3330 Harbor Blvd Suite 100 *Web:* www.brinderson.com	Costa Mesa	CA	92626	714-466-7100	466-7320
Burns & Roe Enterprises Inc 800 Kinderkamack Rd *Web:* www.roe.com	Oradell	NJ	07649	201-265-2000	986-4459
Cajun Constructors Inc 15635 Airline Hwy *Web:* www.cajunusa.com	Baton Rouge	LA	70817	225-753-5857	751-9777
CCC Group Inc 5797 Dietrich Rd *Web:* www.cccgroupinc.com	San Antonio	TX	78219	210-661-4251	662-1662
Cianbro Corp 1 Hunnewell Ave *Web:* www.cianbro.com	Pittsfield	ME	04967	207-487-3311	679-2422
Cives Corp 1825 Old Alabama Rd Suite 200 *Web:* www.cives.com	Roswell	GA	30076	770-993-4424	998-2361
Civil Constructors Inc 2283 US Hwy 20 E *Web:* www.helmgroup.com	Freeport	IL	61032	815-235-2200	235-2219
Clark Construction Co 3535 Moores River Dr *Web:* www.clarkconstructionco.com	Lansing	MI	48911	517-372-0940	372-0668
Clark Construction Group LLC 7500 Old Georgetown Rd *TF:* 800-827-4422 ■ *Web:* www.clarkconstruction.com	Bethesda	MD	20814	301-272-8100	272-8414
Clayco Construction Co 2199 Innerbelt Business Ctr Dr *TF:* 888-429-3330 ■ *Web:* www.claycorp.com	Saint Louis	MO	63114	314-429-5100	429-3137
Day & Zimmermann Group Inc 1818 Market St *TF:* 800-523-0786 ■ *Web:* www.dayzim.com	Philadelphia	PA	19103	215-299-8000	299-8030
English Construction Co Inc 615 Church St *Web:* www.englishconst.com	Lynchburg	VA	24504	434-845-0301	845-0306
Fluor Daniel Inc 3 Polaris Way *Web:* www.fluor.com	Aliso Viejo	CA	92698	949-349-2000	349-2585
Forcum Lannom Contractors LLC 350 US Hwy 51 Bypass S *Web:* www.forcumlannom.com	Dyersburg	TN	38025	731-287-4700	287-4701
ForeRunner Corp 3900 S Wadsworth Blvd Suite 600 *Web:* www.forerunnercorp.com	Lakewood	CO	80235	303-969-0223	696-0230
Foster Wheeler Constructors Inc 53 Frontage Rd Perryville Corporate Pk *Web:* www.fwc.com	Clinton	NJ	08809	908-730-4000	730-5315
Foster Wheeler North America Corp 53 Frontage Rd Perryville Corporate Pk *Web:* www.fwc.com	Clinton	NJ	08809	908-730-4000	730-5315
Geupel DeMars Hagerman Inc 7930 Castleway Dr *Web:* www.hagermangc.com/geupel_demars_manage.htm	Indianapolis	IN	46250	317-713-0632	713-0641
Gilbane Bldg Co 7 Jackson Walkway *TF:* 800-445-2263 ■ *Web:* www.gilbaneco.com	Providence	RI	02903	800-445-2263	
Gray Construction 10 Quality St *TF:* 800-950-4729 ■ *Web:* www.gray.com	Lexington	KY	40507	859-281-5000	252-5300
H & M Construction Co Inc 50 Security Dr *Web:* www.hmcompany.com	Jackson	TN	38305	731-664-6300	664-1358
Haskell Co 111 Riverside Ave *TF:* 800-733-4275 ■ *Web:* www.thehaskellco.com	Jacksonville	FL	32202	904-791-4500	791-4699
Hoffman Construction Corp 805 SW Broadway Suite 2100 *Web:* www.hoffmancorp.com	Portland	OR	97205	503-221-8811	221-8934
Hunt Construction Group 2450 S Tibbs Ave *TF:* 800-223-6301 ■ *Web:* www.huntconstructiongroup.com	Indianapolis	IN	46241	317-227-7800	227-7810
Hunter Contracting Co 701 N Cooper Rd *Web:* www.huntercontracting.com	Gilbert	AZ	85233	480-892-0521	892-4932
JF White Contracting Co 10 Burr St **Fax Area Code:* 617 ■ *TF:* 866-539-4400 ■ *Web:* www.jfwhite.com	Framingham	MA	01701	508-879-4700	558-0460*
Johnson Bros Corp 5476 Lithia Pinecrest Rd *Web:* www.johnson-bros.com	Lithia	FL	33547	813-685-5101	685-5939
Kimmins Corp 1501 2nd Ave E *Web:* www.kimmins.com	Tampa	FL	33605	813-248-3878	247-0183
Koch Specialty Plant Services 12221 E Sam Houston Pkwy N *TF:* 800-497-1789 ■ *Web:* www.kochservices.com	Houston	TX	77044	713-427-7700	427-7748
Louis P Ciminelli Construction Corp 369 Franklin St *Web:* www.lpciminelli.com	Buffalo	NY	14202	716-855-1200	854-6655
MB Kahn Construction Co Inc PO Box 1179 *Web:* www.mbkahn.com	Columbia	SC	29202	803-736-2950	699-6413
MECS Inc 14522 S Outer 40 Rd *Web:* www.mecsglobal.com	Chesterfield	MO	63017	314-275-5700	275-5701
Modern Continental Construction Co 175 Purchase St *TF:* 800-833-6307 ■ *Web:* www.moderncontinental.com	Boston	MA	02110	617-864-6300	864-8766
Northeast Remsco Construction Inc Rt 34 Bldg B *TF:* 800-879-8204 ■ *Web:* www.northeastconstruction.org	Farmingdale	NJ	07727	732-557-6100	736-8913
Parsons Corp 100 W Walnut St *TF:* 800-883-7300 ■ *Web:* www.parsons.com	Pasadena	CA	91124	626-440-2000	440-2630
Performance Contractors Inc 9901 Pecu Ln *Web:* www.performance-br.com	Baton Rouge	LA	70810	225-751-4156	751-8409
Pizzagalli Construction Co 50 Joy Dr *TF:* 800-760-7607 ■ *Web:* www.pizzagalli.com	South Burlington	VT	05403	802-658-4100	651-1360
Powell Construction Co Inc 3622 Bristol Hwy	Johnson City	TN	37601	423-282-0111	282-1541
Rudolph & Sletten Inc 1600 Seaport Blvd Suite 350 *Web:* www.rsconstruction.com	Redwood City	CA	94063	650-216-3600	599-9030
Rudolph/Libbe Inc 6494 Latcha Rd *Web:* www.rlcos.com	Walbridge	OH	43465	419-241-5000	837-9373
Sargent Corp 378 Bennoch Rd *TF:* 800-533-1812 ■ *Web:* www.sargent-corp.com	Stillwater	ME	04489	207-827-4435	827-6150
Shook Construction 4977 Northcutt Pl *TF:* 800-664-1844 ■ *Web:* www.shookconstruction.com	Dayton	OH	45414	937-276-6666	276-6676
SJ Amoroso Construction Co Inc 390 Bridge Pkwy *Web:* www.sjamoroso.com	Redwood Shores	CA	94065	650-654-1900	654-9002
Skanska USA Bldg Inc 1633 Littleton Rd *Web:* www.skanskausa.com	Parsippany	NJ	07054	973-753-3500	334-5376
Skanska USA Inc 16-16 Whitestone Expy *Web:* www.skanska.com	Whitestone	NY	11357	718-767-2600	767-2663
T E Ibberson Co 828 5th St S *Web:* www.ibberson.com	Hopkins	MN	55343	952-938-7007	939-0451
Technip USA Corp 11700 Katy Fwy Suite 150 *Web:* www.technip.com	Houston	TX	77079	281-249-1111	452-2664
TIC - the Industrial Co 2211 Elk River Rd *TF:* 888-810-9367 ■ *Web:* www.tic-inc.com	Steamboat Springs	CO	80487	970-879-2561	879-2998
Todd & Sargent Inc 2905 SE 5th St *Web:* www.tsargent.com	Ames	IA	50010	515-232-0442	232-0682
Turner Industries Group LLC 8687 United Plaza Blvd Suite 500 **Fax:* Mail Rm ■ *TF:* 800-288-6503 ■ *Web:* www.turner-industries.com	Baton Rouge	LA	70809	225-922-5050	922-5055*
US Contractors Inc 622 Commerce St *TF:* 800-897-9882 ■ *Web:* www.us-contractors.com	Clute	TX	77531	979-265-7451	265-4229
Ventech Engineers Inc 1149 Ellsworth Dr PO Box 4261 *Web:* www.ventech-eng.com	Pasadena	TX	77506	713-477-0201	477-2420
Walbridge Aldinger Co 777 Woodward Ave #300 *Web:* www.walbridge.com	Detroit	MI	48226	313-963-8000	963-8129
Walsh Group Inc 929 W Adams St *TF:* 800-759-2574 ■ *Web:* www.walshgroup.com	Chicago	IL	60607	312-563-5400	563-5466
WG Yates & Sons Construction Co Inc 1 Gulley Ave PO Box 456 *Web:* www.wgyates.com	Philadelphia	MS	39350	601-656-5411	656-8958
Whiting-Turner Contracting Co 300 E Joppa Rd 8th Fl *TF:* 800-638-4279 ■ *Web:* www.whiting-turner.com	Baltimore	MD	21286	410-821-1100	337-5770
Zachry Holdings Inc PO Box 240130 *Web:* www.zachry.com	San Antonio	TX	78224	210-475-8000	588-5060

191-8 Railroad Construction

Company	City	State	ZIP	Phone	Fax
Acme Construction Co Inc 7695 Bond St *TF:* 800-938-2263	Cleveland	OH	44139	440-232-7474	232-7477
Atlas Railroad Construction Co 1253 Pennsylvania 519 *TF:* 800-245-4980 ■ *Web:* www.atlasrailroad.com	Eighty Four	PA	15330	724-228-4500	228-3183
Healey Railroad Corp PO Box 190 *Web:* www.railsource.com	Midlothian	VA	23113	804-379-3904	379-3907
Parsons Corp 100 W Walnut St *TF:* 800-883-7300 ■ *Web:* www.parsons.com	Pasadena	CA	91124	626-440-2000	440-2630
RailWorks Corp 5 Penn Plaza *Web:* www.railworks.com	New York	NY	10001	212-502-7900	
RW Summers Railroad Contractor Inc 3693 E Gandy Rd *Web:* www.rwsummers.net	Bartow	FL	33830	863-533-8107	533-8100

Company / Address	City	State	ZIP	Phone	Fax
Snelson Co Inc 601 W State St	Sedro Woolley	WA	98284	360-856-6511	856-5816
TF: 800-624-6536 ■ *Web:* www.snelsonco.com					
Swanson Contracting Co 11701 S Mayfield Ave	Alsip	IL	60803	708-388-0623	388-9986
TF: 800-622-6850 ■ *Web:* www.swansoncontracting.com					
Trac-Work Inc 3801 I-45 PO Box 550	Ennis	TX	75120	972-875-6565	875-9552
Tutor-Saliba Corp 15901 Olden St	Sylmar	CA	91342	818-362-8391	367-5379
Web: www.tutorsaliba.com					
WE Yoder Inc 41 S Maple St	Kutztown	PA	19530	610-683-7383	683-8638
TF: 800-889-5149 ■ *Web:* www.weyoderinc.com					
William A Smith Construction Co Inc 6060 Armour Dr	Houston	TX	77020	713-673-6208	672-9614
TF: 800-925-5011					

191-9 Refinery (Petroleum or Oil) Construction

Company / Address	City	State	ZIP	Phone	Fax
ARB Inc 26000 Commercentre Dr	Lake Forest	CA	92630	949-598-9242	454-7190
TF: 800-622-2699 ■ *Web:* www.arbinc.com					
Austin Industrial Inc 8031 Airport Blvd	Houston	TX	77061	713-641-3400	641-2424
TF: 800-460-3402 ■ *Web:* www.austin-ind.com					
Bechtel North America 3000 Post Oak Blvd	Houston	TX	77056	713-235-2000	960-9031
Web: www.bechtel.com					
Bechtel Petroleum & Chemical 3000 Post Oak Blvd	Houston	TX	77056	713-235-2000	235-4494
Web: www.bechtel.com					
Fluor Daniel Inc 3 Polaris Way	Aliso Viejo	CA	92698	949-349-2000	349-2585
Web: www.fluor.com					
Foster Wheeler Constructors Inc 53 Frontage Rd Perryville Corporate Pk	Clinton	NJ	08809	908-730-4000	730-5315
Web: www.fwc.com					
McDermott International Inc 757 N Eldridge Pkwy	Houston	TX	77079	281-870-5000	870-5095
NYSE: MDR ■ *Web:* www.mcdermott.com					
Miller & Lents Ltd 1100 Louisiana St 27th Fl	Houston	TX	77002	713-651-9455	654-9914
Oscar J Boldt Construction Co 2525 N Roemer Rd	Appleton	WI	54911	920-739-6321	739-4409
Web: www.theboldtcompany.com					
Parsons Corp 100 W Walnut St	Pasadena	CA	91124	626-440-2000	440-2630
TF: 800-883-7300 ■ *Web:* www.parsons.com					
Ref-Chem LP 1128 S Grandview PO Box 2588	Odessa	TX	79761	432-332-8531	332-3325
Web: www.ref-chem.com					
Snelson Co Inc 601 W State St	Sedro Woolley	WA	98284	360-856-6511	856-5816
TF: 800-624-6536 ■ *Web:* www.snelsonco.com					
TIC - the Industrial Co 2211 Elk River Rd	Steamboat Springs	CO	80487	970-879-2561	879-2998
TF: 888-810-9367 ■ *Web:* www.tic-inc.com					
Turner Industries Group LLC 8687 United Plaza Blvd Suite 500	Baton Rouge	LA	70809	225-922-5050	922-5055*
**Fax:* Mail Rm ■ *TF:* 800-288-6503 ■ *Web:* www.turner-industries.com					
Underground Construction Co Inc 5145 Industrial Way	Benicia	CA	94510	707-746-8800	746-1314
TF: 800-227-2314 ■ *Web:* www.undergrnd.com					
Zachry Holdings Inc PO Box 240130	San Antonio	TX	78224	210-475-8000	588-5060
Web: www.zachry.com					

191-10 Water & Sewer Lines, Pipelines, Power Lines Construction

Company / Address	City	State	ZIP	Phone	Fax
AFC Enterprises Inc 88-43 76th Ave	Glendale	NY	11385	718-275-1100	275-4602
Amzak Corp 1 N Federal Hwy Suite 400	Boca Raton	FL	33432	561-953-4164	338-7677
Web: www.amzak.com					
Angelo Iafrate Construction Co 26300 Sherwood Ave	Warren	MI	48091	586-756-1070	756-0467*
**Fax:* Hum Res ■ *Web:* www.iafrate.com					
Argonaut Constructors Inc 1236 Central Ave	Santa Rosa	CA	95401	707-542-4862	542-3210
Web: www.argonautconstructors.com					
Arthur Bros Inc 29 Vista Ave	San Mateo	CA	94403	650-345-3591	572-8522
Aubrey Silvey Enterprises Inc 371 Hamp Jones Rd	Carrollton	GA	30117	770-834-0738	834-1055
TF: 800-206-3815 ■ *Web:* www.silvey.com					
B Frank Joy LLC 5355 Kilmer Pl	Hyattsville	MD	20781	301-779-9400	699-6013
TF: 800-992-3569 ■ *Web:* www.bfjoy.com					
Balfour Beatty Inc 999 Peachtree St NE Suite 200	Atlanta	GA	30309	404-875-0356	607-1784
Web: www.balfourbeatty.com					
Bancker Construction Corp 218 Blydenburgh Rd	Islandia	NY	11749	631-582-8880	582-3698
Barnard Construction Co Inc PO Box 99	Bozeman	MT	59771	406-586-1995	586-3530
Web: www.barnard-inc.com					
Bechtel North America 3000 Post Oak Blvd	Houston	TX	77056	713-235-2000	960-9031
Web: www.bechtel.com					
Bechtel Pipeline 3000 Post Oak Blvd	Houston	TX	77056	713-235-2000	960-9031
Web: www.bechtel.com					
Bechtel Power Corp 5275 W View Dr	Frederick	MD	21703	301-228-6000	228-2200
Web: www.bechtel.com					
Bechtel Telecommunications 5275 Westview Dr	Frederick	MD	21703	301-228-6000	228-2200
Web: www.bechtel.com					
BRB Contractors Inc 3805 N W Curtis St	Topeka	KS	66608	785-232-1245	235-8045
Web: www.brbcontractors.com					
Cajun Constructors Inc 15635 Airline Hwy	Baton Rouge	LA	70817	225-753-5857	751-9777
Web: www.cajunusa.com					
Callas Contractors Inc 10549 Downsville Pike	Hagerstown	MD	21740	301-739-8400	739-7065
Web: www.callascontractors.com					
Cianbro Corp 1 Hunnewell Ave	Pittsfield	ME	04967	207-487-3311	679-2422
Web: www.cianbro.com					
Cives Corp 1825 Old Alabama Rd Suite 200	Roswell	GA	30076	770-993-4424	998-2361
Web: www.cives.com					
Contractors Northwest Inc 3731 N Ramsey Rd	Coeur d'Alene	ID	83815	208-667-2456	667-6388
Web: www.contractorsnorthwest.com					
Cullum Construction Co Inc PO Box 550489	Dallas	TX	75355	972-271-9333	271-4881
CW Wright Construction Co Inc PO Box 3810	Chester	VA	23831	804-768-1054	768-6057
Dillard Smith Construction Co 4001 Industry Dr	Chattanooga	TN	37416	423-894-4336	490-2219
Web: www.dillardsmith.com					
E Sambol Corp PO Box 5110	Toms River	NJ	08754	732-349-2900	505-1783
Web: www.esambol.com					
Eatherly Constructors Inc PO Box 756	Garden City	KS	67846	620-276-6611	276-4351
EE Cruz & Co Inc 943 Holmdel Rd	Holmdel	NJ	07733	732-946-9700	946-7592
Web: www.eecruz.com					
Elkins Constructors Inc 701 W Adams St	Jacksonville	FL	32204	904-353-6500	387-1303
Web: www.elkinsconstructors.com					
Facchina Construction Co Inc 102 Centennial St Suite 201	La Plata	MD	20646	240-776-7000	776-7001
Web: www.facchina.com					
FCI Constructors Inc 3070 I-70 Business Loop # A	Grand Junction	CO	81504	970-434-9093	434-7583
Web: www.fciol.com					
Fishel Co 1810 Arlingate Ln	Columbus	OH	43228	614-274-8100	274-6794
TF: 800-347-4351 ■ *Web:* www.teamfishel.com					
Flint Energy Services Inc 7633 E 63rd Pl Suite 500	Tulsa	OK	74133	918-294-3030	307-8960
TF: 800-580-7641 ■ *Web:* www.flintenergy.com					
Frontier-Kemper Constructors Inc 1695 Allen Rd	Evansville	IN	47710	812-426-2741	428-0337
Web: www.frontierkemper.com					
Future Telecom Inc PO Box 852728	Mesquite	TX	75185	972-329-6400	
Web: www.futuretelco.com					
Garney Cos Inc 1333 NW Vivion Rd	Kansas City	MO	64118	816-741-4600	741-4488
Web: www.garney.com					
Global Industries Ltd 8000 Global Dr	Carlyss	LA	70665	337-583-5000	583-5100
NASDAQ: GLBL ■ *TF:* 800-525-3483 ■ *Web:* www.globalind.com					
Granite Construction Inc 585 W Beach St	Watsonville	CA	95076	831-724-1011	722-9657
NYSE: GVA ■ *Web:* www.graniteconstruction.com					
GSE Construction Co Inc 1020 Shannon Ct	Livermore	CA	94550	925-447-0292	447-0962
Web: www.gseconstruction.com					
Hall Contracting Corp 6415 Lakeview Rd	Charlotte	NC	28269	704-598-0818	598-3855
TF: 800-741-2117 ■ *Web:* www.hallcontracting.com					
Henkels & McCoy Inc 985 Jolly Rd	Blue Bell	PA	19422	215-283-7600	283-7659
TF: 800-523-2568 ■ *Web:* www.henkelsandmccoy.com					
Hood Corp 3166 Horseless Carriage Rd	Norco	CA	92860	951-520-4282	520-4385
Web: www.hoodcorp.com					
Hubbard Construction Co 1936 Lee Rd 3rd Fl	Winter Park	FL	32789	407-645-5500	623-3865
TF: 800-476-1228 ■ *Web:* www.hubbard.com					
Insituform Technologies Inc 17988 Edison Ave	St. Louis	MO	63005	636-530-8000	519-8010
NASDAQ: INSU ■ *TF Cust Svc:* 800-234-2992 ■ *Web:* www.insituform.com					
Irby Construction Co Inc 815 S State St	Jackson	MS	39201	601-709-4729	960-7231
TF: 800-872-0615 ■ *Web:* www.irby.com					
Irish Construction Inc 2641 River Ave	Rosemead	CA	91770	626-288-8530	573-5136
Web: www.irishteam.com					
James White Construction Co Inc 4156 Freedom Way	Weirton	WV	26062	304-748-8181	748-8183
Jay Dee Contractors Inc 38881 Schoolcraft Rd	Livonia	MI	48150	734-591-3400	464-6868
Web: www.jaydeecontr.com					
JC Evans Construction Co Inc 8660 183 A Toll Rd	Leander	TX	78641	512-244-1400	244-1900
Web: www.jcevans.com					
JF Shea Construction Inc 655 Brea Canyon Rd	Walnut	CA	91789	909-594-9500	594-0935
TF: 800-755-7432 ■ *Web:* www.jfshea.com					
JF White Contracting Co 10 Burr St	Framingham	MA	01701	508-879-4700	558-0460*
**Fax Area Code:* 617 ■ *TF:* 866-539-4400 ■ *Web:* www.jfwhite.com					
JH Berra Construction Co Inc 5091 Baumgartner Rd	Saint Louis	MO	63129	314-487-5617	487-5817
Web: www.jhberra.com					
John F Otto Inc 1717 2nd St	Sacramento	CA	95814	916-441-6870	441-6138
Web: www.ottoconstruction.com					
Johnson Bros Corp 5476 Lithia Pinecrest Rd	Lithia	FL	33547	813-685-5101	685-5939
Web: www.johnson-bros.com					
JR Filanc Construction Co Inc 740 N Andreasen Dr	Escondido	CA	92029	760-941-7130	941-3969
TF: 877-225-5428 ■ *Web:* www.filanc.com					
Kankakee Valley Construction Co Inc 4356 W SR 17	Kankakee	IL	60901	815-937-8700	937-0402
Web: www.kvcci.com					
Kearney Development Co Inc 5115 Joanne Kearney Blvd	Tampa	FL	33619	813-621-0855	620-0001
Web: www.kearneydev.com					
Kimmins Contracting Corp 1501 2nd Ave	Tampa	FL	33605	813-248-3878	247-0183
Web: www.kimmins.com					
Kip Inc 25740 Washington Ave	Murrieta	CA	92562	951-698-7890	
Web: www.kipincorporated.com					
Kiska Construction Corp USA 10-34 44th Dr	Long Island City	NY	11101	718-943-0400	943-0401
Web: www.kiskagroup.com					
Koch Specialty Plant Services 12221 E Sam Houston Pkwy N	Houston	TX	77044	713-427-7700	427-7748
TF: 800-497-1789 ■ *Web:* www.kochservices.com					
Landmark Structures LP 1665 Harmon Rd	Fort Worth	TX	76177	817-439-8888	439-9001
TF: 800-888-6816 ■ *Web:* www.teamlandmark.com					
Lane Construction Corp 965 E Main St	Meriden	CT	06450	203-235-3351	237-4260
Web: www.laneconstruct.com					
Latex Construction Co Inc PO Box 917	Conyers	GA	30012	770-760-0820	760-0852
TF: 800-241-1101 ■ *Web:* www.latexconstruction.com					
MasTec Energy Services Inc 209 Art Bryan Dr PO Box 1	Asheboro	NC	27204	336-672-1244	672-3025
TF: 800-672-5853 ■ *Web:* www.mastec.com					
MasTec Inc 800 Douglas Rd 12th Fl	Coral Gables	FL	33134	305-599-1800	599-1900
NYSE: MTZ ■ *Web:* www.mastec.com					

Company	City	State	ZIP	Phone	Fax
McLean Contracting Co 6700 McLean Way *Web:* www.mcleancont.com	Glen Burnie	MD	21060	410-553-6700	553-6718
Mears Group Inc 4500 N Mission Rd *TF:* 800-632-7727 ■ *Web:* www.mears.net	Rosebush	MI	48878	989-433-2929	433-2199
Michels Corp 817 W Main St *Web:* www.michels-usa.com	Brownsville	WI	53006	920-583-3132	583-3429
Miller Pipeline Corp 8850 Crawfordsville Rd *TF:* 800-428-3742 ■ *Web:* www.millerpipeline.com	Indianapolis	IN	46234	317-293-0278	293-8502
Miron Construction Co Inc 1471 McMahon Dr *Web:* www.mironconst.com	Neenah	WI	54956	920-969-7000	969-7393
Montana Construction Corp Inc 80 Contant Ave *Web:* www.montanaconstructioninc.com	Lodi	NJ	07644	973-478-5200	478-7604
Mountain Cascade Inc PO Box 5050 *Web:* www.mountaincascade.com	Livermore	CA	94551	925-373-8370	638-1962
New River Electrical Corp PO Box 70 *Web:* www.newriverelectrical.com	Cloverdale	VA	24077	540-966-1650	966-1699
Northeast Remsco Construction Inc Rt 34 Bldg B *TF:* 800-879-8204 ■ *Web:* www.northeastconstruction.org	Farmingdale	NJ	07727	732-557-6100	736-8913
Northern Pipeline Construction Co Inc 2355 W Utopia Rd # 3 *Web:* www.nplcc.com	Phoenix	AZ	85027	623-582-1235	582-6853
O'Brien & Gere Technical Services Inc 333 W Washington St *Web:* www.obg.com	Syracuse	NY	13202	315-956-6100	463-7554
Oldcastle Materials Inc 900 Ashwood Pkwy Suite 700 *TF:* 800-241-7074 ■ *Web:* www.apac.com	Atlanta	GA	30338	770-552-5600	522-5008
P Gioioso & Sons Inc 50 Sprague St *Web:* www.pgioioso.com	Hyde Park	MA	02136	617-364-5800	364-9462
Penn Line Service Inc PO Box 462 *TF:* 800-448-9110 ■ *Web:* www.pennline.com	Scottdale	PA	15683	724-887-9110	887-0545
Phylway Construction LLC 1074a Hwy 1 *Web:* www.phylway.com	Thibodaux	LA	70301	985-446-9644	
Quanta Services Inc 1360 Post Oak Blvd Suite 2100 *NYSE:* PWR ■ *Web:* www.quantaservices.com	Houston	TX	77056	713-629-7600	629-7676
R & L Brosamer Co Inc 1777 Oakland Blvd Suite 300 *Web:* www.brosamer.com	Walnut Creek	CA	94591	925-837-5600	627-1700
Reynolds Inc 4520 N State Rd 37 *TF:* 888-891-8009 ■ *Web:* www.reynoldsinc.com	Orleans	IN	47452	812-865-3232	865-3075
RH White Construction Co Inc 41 Central St *TF:* 800-922-8182 ■ *Web:* www.rhwhite.com	Auburn	MA	01501	508-832-3295	832-7084
River City Construction LLC 101 Hoffer Ln *Web:* www.rccllc.com	East Peoria	IL	61611	309-694-3120	435-2457
Satellite Store 7412 Preston Hwy *TF:* 800-693-9393 ■ *Web:* www.thesatellitestore.com	Louisville	KY	40219	502-964-3474	969-3499
Shaw Constructors Inc 36445 Perkins Rd	Prairieville	LA	70769	225-673-4606	744-6202
Sheehan Pipe Line Construction Co 2431 E 61st St Suite 700 *Web:* www.sheehanpipeline.com	Tulsa	OK	74136	918-747-3471	747-9888
Siciliano Inc 3601 Winchester Rd *Web:* www.sicilianoinc.com	Springfield	IL	62707	217-585-1200	585-1211
Sletten Construction Co Inc 1000 25th St N *Web:* www.slettencompanies.com	Great Falls	MT	59401	406-761-7920	761-0923
Snelson Co Inc 601 W State St *TF:* 800-624-6536 ■ *Web:* www.snelsonco.com	Sedro Woolley	WA	98284	360-856-6511	856-5816
Spiniello Cos 12 E Daniel Rd *TF:* 800-227-8384 ■ *Web:* www.spiniello.com	Fairfield	NJ	07004	973-808-8383	808-9591
Stacy & Witbeck Inc 1320 Harbor Bay Pkwy Suite 240 *Web:* www.stacywitbeck.com	Alameda	CA	94502	510-748-1870	748-1205
Suburban Grading & Utilities Inc 1190 Harmony Rd *Web:* www.suburbangrading.com	Norfolk	VA	23502	757-461-1800	461-0989
Sumter Utilities Inc 1151 N Pike W *TF:* 800-678-8665 ■ *Web:* www.sumter-utilities.com	Sumter	SC	29153	803-469-8585	469-4600
TA Loving Co Inc 400 Patetown Rd PO Box 919 *Web:* www.taloving.com	Goldsboro	NC	27530	919-734-8400	731-7538
TJ Lambrecht Construction Inc 10 Gougar Rd *Web:* www.tjlambrecht.com	Joliet	IL	60432	815-727-9211	727-6421
Tri Dal Ltd 540 Commerce St *Web:* www.tridal.com	Southlake	TX	76092	817-481-2886	481-8195
Underground Construction Co Inc 5145 Industrial Way *TF:* 800-227-2314 ■ *Web:* www.undergrnd.com	Benicia	CA	94510	707-746-8800	746-1314
Utility Contractors Inc 659 N Market St *TF:* 888-766-2576 ■ *Web:* www.ucict.com	Wichita	KS	67214	316-265-9506	265-8314
Utility Services Inc 400 N 4th St *TF:* 800-638-3278 ■ *Web:* www.montana-dakota.com	Bismarck	ND	58501	701-222-7900	222-7607
UTILX Corp 22820 Russell Rd *TF:* 800-829-3039 ■ *Web:* www.utilx.com	Kent	WA	98032	253-395-0200	395-1040
Walbridge Aldinger Co 777 Woodward Ave #300 *Web:* www.walbridge.com	Detroit	MI	48226	313-963-8000	963-8129
Welded Construction LP 26933 Eckel Rd *TF:* 800-874-3548 ■ *Web:* www.welded-construction.com	Perrysburg	OH	43551	419-874-3548	874-4883
West Valley Construction Co Inc 580 McGlincey Ln *TF:* 800-588-5510 ■ *Web:* www.westvalleyconstruction.com	Campbell	CA	95008	408-371-5510	371-3604
Wharton-Smith Inc PO Box 471028 *TF:* 888-393-0068 ■ *Web:* www.whartonsmith.com	Lake Monroe	FL	32747	407-321-8410	323-1236
Whitesell-Green Inc 3881 N Palafox St *Web:* www.whitesell-green.com	Pensacola	FL	32505	850-434-5311	434-5315
Willbros Engineers Inc 2087 E 71st St *TF:* 800-434-8970 ■ *Web:* www.willbros.com	Tulsa	OK	74136	918-496-0400	491-9436
WL Hailey & Co Inc 2971 Kraft Dr *Web:* www.wlhailey.com	Nashville	TN	37204	615-255-3161	256-1316
WM Lyles Co 1210 W Olive Ave *Web:* www.wmlyles.com	Fresno	CA	93728	559-441-1900	441-1290
Yantis Co PO Box 17045 *Web:* www.yantiscompany.com	San Antonio	TX	78217	210-655-3780	655-8526
Yates Construction Co Inc 9220 NC Hwy 65 *Web:* www.yatesconstruction.com	Stokesdale	NC	27357	336-548-9621	

192 CONSTRUCTION - SPECIAL TRADE CONTRACTORS

SEE ALSO Swimming Pools p. 2680

192-1 Building Equipment Installation or Erection

Company	City	State	ZIP	Phone	Fax
APi Group Inc Specialty Construction Services Group 1100 Old Hwy 8 NW *TF:* 800-223-4922 ■ *Web:* www.apigroupinc.com/ind_spec_profiles.php	New Brighton	MN	55112	651-636-4320	636-0312
AWC Commercial Window Coverings Inc 825 Williamson Ave *TF:* 800-252-2280 ■ *Web:* www.awc-cwc.com	Fullerton	CA	92832	714-879-3880	879-8419
Aycock LLC 8261 Derry St *TF:* 800-772-5066 ■ *Web:* www.aycockrigging.com	Hummelstown	PA	17036	717-566-5066	566-5077
Baltimore Rigging Co Inc 7475 Lake Dr *TF:* 800-626-2150 ■ *Web:* www.baltimorerigging.com	Baltimore	MD	21237	410-866-6701	866-6807
Bigge Crane & Rigging Co Inc 10700 Bigge St PO Box 1657 *TF:* 888-337-2444 ■ *Web:* www.bigge.com	San Leandro	CA	94577	510-638-8100	639-4053
Chicago Elevator Co 3260 W Grand Ave	Chicago	IL	60651	773-227-0737	645-7581
Columbia Elevator Products Co Inc 175 N Main St *TF:* 877-265-3538 ■ *Web:* www.columbiaelevator.com	Port Chester	NY	10573	914-937-7100	937-9181
Commercial Contracting Corp 4260 N Atlantic Blvd *TF:* 800-521-4386 ■ *Web:* www.cccnetwork.com	Auburn Hills	MI	48326	248-209-0500	209-0501
Don R Fruchey Inc 5608 Old Maumee Rd *Web:* www.donrfruchey.com	Fort Wayne	IN	46803	260-749-8502	749-6337
DW Nicholson Corp 24747 Clawiter Rd *Web:* www.dwnicholson.com	Hayward	CA	94545	510-887-0900	783-9948
Elward Construction Co 680 Harlan St *TF:* 800-933-5339 ■ *Web:* www.elward.com	Lakewood	CO	80214	303-239-6303	239-8719
Fenton Rigging & Contracting Inc 2150 Langdon Farm Rd *Web:* www.fentonrigging.com	Cincinnati	OH	45237	513-631-5500	631-4361
George W Auch Co 735 S Paddock St PO Box 430719 *Web:* www.auchconstruction.com	Pontiac	MI	48341	248-334-2000	334-3404
Hite Crane & Rigging Inc 4323 E Broadway Ave	Spokane	WA	99212	509-535-7738	535-7730
Hoffman Corp 805 SW Broadway Suite 2100 *Web:* www.hoffmancorp.com	Portland	OR	97205	503-221-8811	221-8934
Integral Automation Inc 16w171 Shore Ct *Web:* www.premiertool.com	Burr Ridge	IL	60527	630-654-4300	654-8519
International Industrial Contracting Corp 35900 Mound Rd *Web:* www.iiccusa.com	Sterling Heights	MI	48310	586-264-7070	264-7088
James Machine Works LLC 1521 Adams St *TF:* 800-259-6104 ■ *Web:* www.jmwinc.net	Monroe	LA	71201	318-322-6104	388-4245
Mainco Elevator Services Inc 5-25 51st Ave *TF:* 800-464-6487 ■ *Web:* www.mainco-elevator.com	Long Island City	NY	11101	718-786-3301	729-7640
PS Marcato Elevator Co Inc 44-11 11th St *Web:* www.psmarcato.com	Long Island City	NY	11101	718-392-6400	392-6445
Rigging International PO Box 1285 *Web:* www.rigginginternational.com	Alameda	CA	94501	510-865-2400	
Sand Steel Bldg Co 101 Browell St PO Box 129	Emerado	ND	58228	701-594-4435	594-4438
Schindler Elevator Corp 20 Whippany Rd **Fax:* Mail Rm ■ *TF:* 800-225-3123 ■ *Web:* www.us.schindler.com	Morristown	NJ	07960	973-397-6500	397-6485*
SCI Global Structural Contours Inc PO Box 4970 *Web:* www.sciglobal.com	Greenwich	CT	06830	203-531-4400	531-4403
Thyssen Elevator Co 15141 E Whittier Blvd Suite 505 *TF:* 800-288-3538	Whittier	CA	90603	562-693-9491	693-0028
W & H Systems Inc 120 Asia Pl *TF:* 800-966-6993 ■ *Web:* www.whsystems.com	Carlstadt	NJ	07072	201-933-7840	933-2144
Wales Industrial Service Inc PO Box 21628 *Web:* www.walesindustrial.com	Waco	TX	76702	254-772-3310	772-3420
Wyatt Field Services Co 10810 W Little York St Suite 130-A *TF:* 800-324-3000 ■ *Web:* www.wyattfieldservice.com	Houston	TX	77241	713-570-2000	937-1617

192-2 Carpentry & Flooring Contractors

Company	City	State	ZIP	Phone	Fax
ACMAT Corp 233 Main St *Web:* www.acmatcorp.com	New Britain	CT	06050	860-229-9000	229-1111
Airtite Contractors Inc 343 W Carol Ln *Web:* www.air-tite.net	Elmhurst	IL	60126	630-530-9001	530-9034
Archadeck 2924 Emerywood Pkwy # 101 *TF:* 800-722-4668 ■ *Web:* www.archadeck.com	Richmond	VA	23294	804-353-6999	353-2364
Associated Acc International Ltd 306 Main St **Fax Area Code:* 212 ■ *TF:* 800-800-4320 ■ *Web:* www.assocint.com	Millburn	NJ	07041	908-686-6011	633-0626*
Bonitz Contracting Co Inc 645 Rosewood Dr *TF:* 800-452-7281 ■ *Web:* www.bonitz.com	Columbia	SC	29201	803-799-0181	748-9223

Company	City	State	ZIP	Phone	Fax
Carpenter Contractors of America 941 SW 12th Ave *TF:* 800-959-8805 ■ *Web:* www.carpentercontractors.com	Pompano Beach	FL	33069	954-781-2660	786-9016
Cincinnati Floor Co Inc 5162 Broerman Ave *TF:* 800-886-4501 ■ *Web:* www.cincifloor.com	Cincinnati	OH	45217	513-641-4500	482-4204
Conklin Bros of San Leandro Inc 2999 Teagarden St	San Leandro	CA	94577	510-357-1090	357-3554
Covington Flooring Co Inc 288-A Oxmore Ct *TF:* 800-824-1229 ■ *Web:* www.covington.com	Birmingham	AL	35209	205-328-2330	328-2496
Frank Novak & Sons Inc 23940 Miles Rd	Cleveland	OH	44128	216-475-5440	475-2802
Interior Construction Services Ltd 2930 Market St *Web:* www.ics-stl.com	Saint Louis	MO	63103	314-534-6664	534-6663
John H Hampshire Inc 320 W 24th St *TF:* 800-638-0076 ■ *Web:* www.jhhampshire.com	Baltimore	MD	21211	410-366-8900	467-7391
Kalman Floor Co Inc 1202 Bergen Pkwy Suite 110 *TF:* 800-525-7840 ■ *Web:* www.kalmanfloor.com	Evergreen	CO	80439	303-674-2290	674-1238
Kesseli & Morse Co Inc 242 Canterbury St *Web:* www.kesseliandmorse.com	Worcester	MA	01603	508-752-1901	753-7078
M & H Bldg Specialties Inc 3084 S Highland Dr Suite E *Web:* www.mhbsinc.com	Las Vegas	NV	89109	702-385-3168	385-9042
Meyer & Lundahl 2345 W Lincoln St *TF:* 800-264-9286 ■ *Web:* www.meyerandlundahl.com	Phoenix	AZ	85009	602-254-9286	258-6943
Overhead Door Co of Sacramento Inc 6756 Franklin Blvd *TF:* 800-929-3667 ■ *Web:* www.overheaddoor.com	Sacramento	CA	95823	916-421-3747	399-9485
Partition Specialties Inc 714 C St Suite 3 *TF:* 800-982-9255 ■ *Web:* www.partitionspecialties.com	San Rafael	CA	94901	415-721-1040	721-1053
RL Dresser Inc 4100 Atlantic Ave PO Box 17806 *Web:* www.rldresserinc.com	Raleigh	NC	27604	919-876-4141	876-4300
Rock-Tred Corp 3415 W Howard St *TF:* 800-762-8733 ■ *Web:* www.rocktred.com	Skokie	IL	60076	847-673-8200	679-6665
Schuck Component Systems Inc 8205 N 67th Ave *TF Cust Svc:* 866-991-3661 ■ *Web:* www.schuckaz.com	Glendale	AZ	85302	623-931-3661	937-3435
Tribco Construction Services 200 S Michigan Ave Suite 200	Chicago	IL	60604	312-341-0303	341-1534
Turner-Brooks Inc 28811 John R Rd *TF:* 800-560-7003	Madison Heights	MI	48071	248-548-3400	548-9213

192-3 Concrete Contractors

Company	City	State	ZIP	Phone	Fax
Ahal Contracting Co Inc 3746 Pennridge Dr *Web:* www.ahal.com	Bridgeton	MO	63044	314-739-1142	739-5968
Alex E. Paris Contracting Co 1595 Smith Township State *Web:* www.alexparis.com	Atlasburg	PA	15004	724-947-2235	947-3820
Allied Contractors Inc 204 E Preston St	Baltimore	MD	21202	410-539-6727	332-4594
Asphalt Specialists Inc 1780 Highwood E *Web:* www.asipaving.com	Pontiac	MI	48340	248-334-4570	334-0134
Aurora Blacktop Inc 1065 Sard Ave	Montgomery	IL	60538	630-892-9389	892-3481
B Gentle Concrete Construction Co 5241 NE 89th Ave	Portland	OR	97220	503-236-3902	255-0417
Baker Concrete Construction Inc 900 N Garver Rd *TF:* 800-359-3935 ■ *Web:* www.bakerconcrete.com	Monroe	OH	45050	513-539-4000	539-4380
Barnard Construction Co Inc PO Box 99 *Web:* www.barnard-inc.com	Bozeman	MT	59771	406-586-1995	586-3530
Berglund Construction 8410 S Chicago Ave *Web:* www.berglundco.com	Chicago	IL	60617	773-374-1000	374-0701
Bi-Con Services Inc 10901 Clay Pike Rd *Web:* www.bsicos.com	Derwent	OH	43733	740-685-2542	685-3863
Blair Concrete Services Inc 6336 Oleander Dr Suite 1 *TF:* 800-815-7395 ■ *Web:* www.blairconcrete.com	Wilmington	NC	28403	910-343-4307	
Bomel Construction Co Inc 8195 E Kaiser Blvd *Web:* www.bomelconstruction.com	Anaheim Hills	CA	92808	714-921-1660	921-1943
Bowen Engineering Corp 10315 Allisonville Rd *TF:* 800-377-2580 ■ *Web:* www.bowenengineering.com	Fishers	IN	46038	317-842-2616	841-4257
Capform Inc PO Box 111130	Carrollton	TX	75011	972-245-7292	242-5096
Ceco Concrete Construction LLC 10100 NW Ambassador Dr Suite 400 *TF:* 800-237-7096 ■ *Web:* www.cecoconcrete.com	Kansas City	MO	64153	816-459-7000	459-7735
Cleveland Cement Contractors Inc 4823 Van Epps Rd *Web:* www.clevelandcement.com	Brooklyn Heights	OH	44131	216-741-3954	741-9278
Colasanti Cos 24500 Wood Ct *Web:* www.colasantigroup.com	Macomb Township	MI	48042	586-598-9700	598-9661
Colorado Asphalt Services Inc PO Box 329 *Web:* www.coloradoasphalt.com	Commerce City	CO	80037	303-292-3434	292-6267
Concrete Contractors Interstate Inc 995 Hwy 85 PO Box 8	Brighton	CO	80601	303-659-2383	659-2387
Culbertson Enterprises Inc 600A Snyder Ave	West Chester	PA	19382	610-436-6400	436-6309
Daisy Construction Co Inc 3128 New Castle Ave *Web:* www.daisyconstruction.com	New Castle	DE	19720	302-658-4417	658-0618
Damon G Douglas Co Inc 245 Birchwood Ave PO Box 1030 *TF:* 800-724-1759 ■ *Web:* www.dgdco.com	Cranford	NJ	07016	908-272-0100	272-3949
Dance Bros Inc 825C Hammonds Ferry Rd	Linthicum	MD	21090	410-789-8200	636-3663
Donley's Inc 5430 Warner Rd *Web:* www.donleyinc.com	Cleveland	OH	44125	216-524-6800	642-3216
Dywidag Systems International 320 Marmon Dr *Web:* www.dywidag-systems.com	Bolingbrook	IL	60440	630-739-1100	739-5517
Egizii Electric Inc 700 N MacArthur Blvd *Web:* www.eeiholding.com	Springfield	IL	62702	217-528-4001	528-1677
Francis O Day Construction Co Inc 850 E Gude Dr *Web:* www.foday.com	Rockville	MD	20850	301-652-2400	340-6592
Fricks Co Inc 3000 W Loop 820 S *Web:* www.thefrickscompany.com	Fort Worth	TX	76116	817-560-8281	560-8137
Harris Cos Inc 909 Montreal Cir *Web:* www.hmcc.com	Saint Paul	MN	55102	651-602-6500	602-6699
Healy Long & Jevin Inc 2000 Rodman Rd *Web:* www.healylongjevin.com	Wilmington	DE	19805	302-654-8039	654-8153
Hubbard Construction Co 1936 Lee Rd 3rd Fl *TF:* 800-476-1228 ■ *Web:* www.hubbard.com	Winter Park	FL	32789	407-645-5500	623-3865
John Rohrer Contracting Co Inc 2820 Roe Ln Bldg S *TF:* 800-255-6119 ■ *Web:* www.johnrohrercontracting.com	Kansas City	KS	66103	913-236-5005	236-7291
Kalman Floor Co Inc 1202 Bergen Pkwy Suite 110 *TF:* 800-525-7840 ■ *Web:* www.kalmanfloor.com	Evergreen	CO	80439	303-674-2290	674-1238
Kent Cos Inc 130 60th St SW *TF:* 800-968-2345 ■ *Web:* www.kentcompanies.com	Grand Rapids	MI	49548	616-534-4909	534-4890
Landavazo Bros Inc 29280 Pacific St	Hayward	CA	94544	510-581-7104	581-7423
Larson Contracting Inc PO Box 68 *TF:* 800-765-1426 ■ *Web:* www.larsoncontracting.com	Lake Mills	IA	50450	641-592-5800	592-8610
Lindblad Construction Co 717 E Cass St *Web:* www.lindbladconstruction.com	Joliet	IL	60432	815-726-6251	723-4907
Manafort Bros Inc 414 New Britain Ave *TF:* 888-626-2367 ■ *Web:* www.manafort.com	Plainville	CT	06062	860-229-4853	229-1878
Miller & Long Concrete Construction Inc 4824 Rugby Ave *Web:* www.millerandlong.com	Bethesda	MD	20814	301-657-8000	652-9242
Oldcastle Precast Bldg Systems Div 1401 Trimble Rd *TF:* 800-523-9144 ■ *Web:* www.oldcastle-precast.com	Edgewood	MD	21040	410-612-1213	612-1214
Otto Baum Co Inc 866 N Main St PO Box 161 *Web:* www.ottobaum.com	Morton	IL	61550	309-266-7114	263-1050
Proshot Concrete Inc 4158 Musgrove Dr PO Box 1636 *TF:* 800-633-3141 ■ *Web:* www.proshotconcrete.com	Florence	AL	35631	256-764-5941	764-5946
Richard Goettle Inc 12071 Hamilton Ave *TF:* 800-248-8661 ■ *Web:* www.goettle.com	Cincinnati	OH	45231	513-825-8100	825-8107
SB Ballard Construction Co 2828 Shipps Corner Rd *TF:* 800-296-0209 ■ *Web:* www.sbballard.com	Virginia Beach	VA	23453	757-440-5555	451-2873
Seretta Construction Inc 2604 Clark St *Web:* www.seretta.com	Apopka	FL	32703	407-290-9440	290-9372
Smock Fansler Corp 2910 W Minnesota St *TF:* 800-281-6605 ■ *Web:* www.smockfansler.com	Indianapolis	IN	46241	317-248-8371	244-4507
Structural Preservation Systems Inc 7455 New Ridge Rd Suite T *TF:* 800-899-1016 ■ *Web:* www.structural.net	Hanover	MD	21076	410-850-7000	850-4111
Suncoast Post-Tension LP 654 N Sam Houston Pkwy E Suite 110 *TF:* 866-838-3281 ■ *Web:* www.suncoast-pt.com	Houston	TX	77060	281-668-1840	931-6645
Superior Gunite Inc 12306 Van Nuys Blvd *Web:* www.shotcrete.com	Lakeview Terrace	CA	91342	818-896-9199	896-6699
TAS Commercial Concrete Construction Inc 20105 Krahn Rd *TF:* 800-652-2227 ■ *Web:* www.tasconcrete.com	Spring	TX	77388	281-350-0832	350-6664
Treviicos Corp 273 Summer St *Web:* www.treviicos.com	Boston	MA	02210	617-737-1453	737-5810
UBM Inc 330 S Wells St	Chicago	IL	60606	312-939-0505	939-0483
Weaver-Bailey Contractors Inc PO Box 60 *TF:* 800-253-3385 ■ *Web:* www.weaverbailey.com	El Paso	AR	72045	501-796-2301	796-2372
Western Construction Group 1637 N Warson Rd *TF Cust Svc:* 800-325-2801 ■ *Web:* www.westerngroup.com	Saint Louis	MO	63132	314-427-6733	427-6199

192-4 Electrical Contractors

Company	City	State	ZIP	Phone	Fax
A E C Group Inc The 1735 5TH Ave *Web:* www.aecgroup.com	McKeesport	PA	15132	412-678-1440	
A. M. Ortega Construction Inc 10125 Ch Rd *TF:* 800-909-1988 ■ *Web:* www.amortega.com	Lakeside	CA	92040	619-390-1988	390-1941
AC Corp 301 Creek Ridge Rd *TF:* 800-582-3073 ■ *Web:* www.accorporation.com	Greensboro	NC	27406	336-273-4472	274-6035
AC Electric Co 2921 Hangar Way PO Box 81977 *Web:* www.a-celectric.com	Bakersfield	CA	93308	661-410-0000	410-0400
Acme Electric Inc 412 E Gowan Rd	North Las Vegas	NV	89032	702-876-1116	642-9936
Alabama Electric Co Inc of Dothan PO Box 8277 *Web:* www.alaelectric.com	Dothan	AL	36304	334-792-5164	702-4504
Aldridge Electric Inc 844 E Rockland Rd *Web:* www.aldridge-electric.com	Libertyville	IL	60048	847-680-5200	680-5298
Allan Briteway Electrical Contractors Inc 130 Algonquin Pkwy *Web:* www.allanbriteway.com	Whippany	NJ	07981	973-781-0022	781-1744
Allison-Smith Co Inc 2284 Marietta Blvd *Web:* www.allison-smith.com	Atlanta	GA	30318	404-351-6430	350-1065
Althoff Industries Inc 8001 S Rt 31 *Fax: Sales ■ *TF:* 800-225-2443 ■ *Web:* www.althoffind.com	Crystal Lake	IL	60014	815-455-7000	455-9375*
Anderson Electric Inc 3501 6th St Hwy W # 1 *Web:* www.anderson-electric.com	Springfield	IL	62703	217-529-5471	529-8946
Anixter Inc 2301 Patriot Blvd *TF:* 800-323-8166 ■ *Web:* www.anixter.com	Glenview	IL	60026	224-521-8000	521-8100
APi Electric 4330 W 1st St Suite B *TF:* 866-624-0064 ■ *Web:* www.apielectric.com	Duluth	MN	55807	218-628-3323	624-7485

Company	City	State	ZIP	Phone	Fax
Arc Electric Inc PO Box 1667 TF: 800-989-1053 ■ Web: www.arcelectricinc.com	Chesapeake	VA	23327	757-424-5164	424-7145
Arc Electrical Construction Co Inc 739 2nd Ave	New York	NY	10016	212-573-9600	682-0650
Arrow Electric Co Inc 317 Wabasso Ave TF: 888-999-5591 ■ Web: www.arrowelectric.com	Louisville	KY	40209	502-367-0141	361-8613
Aschinger Electric Co 877 Horan Dr TF: 800-280-4061 ■ Web: www.aschinger.com	Fenton	MO	63026	636-343-1211	343-9658
Athena Engineering Inc 456 E Foothill Blvd TF: 877-777-4778 ■ Web: www.athenaengineering.net	San Dimas	CA	91773	909-599-0947	599-5018
B & I Contractors Inc 2701 Prince St Web: www.bandicontractors.com	Fort Myers	FL	33916	239-332-4646	332-5928
Baker Electric Inc 111 Jackson Ave TF: 800-779-6774 ■ Web: www.bakerelectric.com	Des Moines	IA	50315	515-288-6774	288-2226
Barth Electric Co Inc 1934 N Illinois St TF: 800-666-6226 ■ Web: www.barthelectric.com	Indianapolis	IN	46202	317-924-6226	923-6938
Bell Electrical Contractors Inc 128 Millwell Dr TF: 800-717-2355 ■ Web: www.bellelectrical.com	Maryland Heights	MO	63043	314-739-7744	739-0717
Bergelectric Corp 5650 W Centinela Ave TF: 800-734-2374 ■ Web: www.bergelectric.com	Los Angeles	CA	90045	310-337-1377	337-2663
Berger Engineering Co 10900 Shady Trail Web: www.berger-engr.com	Dallas	TX	75220	214-358-4451	351-2954
Berwick Electric Co 3450 N Nevada Ave Suite 100 Web: www.berwickelectric.com	Colorado Springs	CO	80907	719-632-7683	471-9660
BK Truland 10233 S Dolfield Rd TF: 800-238-8012 ■ Web: www.bktruland.com	Owings Mills	MD	21117	410-363-1200	363-1215
Bodine Electric of Decatur Inc PO Box 976 TF: 800-252-3369 ■ Web: www.bodineelectricofdecatur.com	Decatur	IL	62525	217-423-2593	423-4658
Brink Constructors Inc 2950 N Plaza Dr PO Box 1186 Web: www.brinkred.com	Rapid City	SD	57702	605-342-6966	342-5905
Broadway Electrical Co Inc 295 Freeport St Web: www.broadelec.com	Boston	MA	02122	617-288-7900	288-4169
Broadway Electrical Service Co Inc 1800 N Central St TF: 800-516-6992	Knoxville	TN	37917	865-524-1851	546-2104
Brothers Inc 1000 Sussex Blvd TF: 866-276-7462 ■ Web: www.brotherselectric.com	Broomall	PA	19008	610-328-0670	328-6218
Bruce & Merrilees Electric Co 930 Cass St TF: 800-652-5560 ■ Web: www.bruceandmerrilees.com	New Castle	PA	16101	724-652-5566	652-8290
Budget Electrical Contractors Inc 25051 5th St Web: www.becelectric.com	San Bernardino	CA	92410	909-381-2646	888-5431
Cache Valley Electric Inc 875 N 1000 W TF: 800-735-9345 ■ Web: www.cvelectric.com	Logan	UT	84321	435-752-6405	787-0534
Campbell Alliance Group Inc 8045 Arco Corporate Dr Suite 500 TF: 888-297-2001 ■ Web: www.campbellalliance.com	Raleigh	NC	27617	919-844-7100	844-7560
Cannon & Wendt Electric Co 4020 N 16th St Web: www.cannon-wendt.com	Phoenix	AZ	85016	602-279-1681	230-8464
Capital Electric Construction Co Inc 600 Broadway Suite 600 Web: www.capitalelectric.com	Kansas City	MO	64105	816-472-9500	421-4244
Center Line Electric Inc 26554 Lawrence Web: www.centerline-elec.com	Center Line	MI	48015	586-757-5505	759-2453
Church & Murdock Electric Inc 5709 Wattsburg Rd TF: 800-638-4313 ■ Web: www.churchandmurdock.com	Erie	PA	16509	814-825-3456	825-4043
Cleveland Electric Co Inc 1281 Fulton Industrial Blvd NW TF: 800-282-7150 ■ Web: www.clevelectric.com	Atlanta	GA	30336	404-696-4550	696-2849
Cleveland Group Inc 1281 Fulton Industrial Blvd TF: 800-282-7150 ■ Web: www.clevelectric.com	Atlanta	GA	30336	404-696-4550	505-7792
Cochran Electric Co Inc PO Box 33524 Web: www.cochraninc.com	Seattle	WA	98133	206-367-1900	368-3262
Collins Electric Co Inc 53 2nd Ave TF: 800-321-4459 ■ Web: www.collinselectricco.com	Chicopee	MA	01020	413-592-9221	592-4157
Collins Electrical Co Inc 611 W Fremont St Web: www.collinselectric.com	Stockton	CA	95203	209-466-3691	466-3146
Commander Electric Inc PO Box 526 Web: www.commanderelectric.com	Bohemia	NY	11716	631-563-3223	563-8322
Commonwealth Electric Co of Midwest PO Box 80638 Web: www.commonwealthelectric.com	Lincoln	NE	68501	402-474-1341	474-0114
Compel Corp 10410 Pioneer Blvd Suite 7 TF: 800-553-1162	Santa Fe Springs	CA	90670	562-946-8321	944-9905
Contemporary Electrical Services Inc 112 Glyndon St Ne Suite 200 Web: www.cont-elec.com	Vienna	VA	22180	703-255-9226	
Continental Electric Co Inc 9501 E 5th Ave PO Box 2710 Web: www.continentalelectric.com	Gary	IN	46403	219-938-3460	938-3469
Cupertino Electric Inc 1132 N 7th St Web: www.cei.com	San Jose	CA	95112	408-808-8000	275-8575
Custom Cable Industries Inc 3221 Cherry Palm Dr Web: www.customcable.com	Tampa	FL	33619	813-623-2232	623-3534
Daidone Electric Inc 200 Raymond Blvd	Newark	NJ	07105	973-690-5216	344-3645
Dashiell Corp PO Box 1300 TF: 800-736-6400 ■ Web: www.dashiellcorp.com	Deer Park	TX	77536	281-479-7407	479-1815
Davis Electrical Constructors Inc PO Box 1907 TF: 800-849-3284 ■ Web: www.daviselectrical.com	Greenville	SC	29602	864-250-2500	250-2555
Davis H Elliot Co Inc 1920 Progress Dr SE Web: www.davishelliot.com	Roanoke	VA	24013	540-992-2865	992-1495
Decker Electric Co Inc 1282 Folsom St TF: 800-755-1622	San Francisco	CA	94103	415-552-1622	861-4257
Del Monte Electric Co Inc 6998 Sierra Ct Web: www.delmonteelectric.com	Dublin	CA	94568	925-829-6000	829-6033

Company	City	State	ZIP	Phone	Fax
Divane Bros Electric Co 2424 Rose St Web: www.divanebros.com	Franklin Park	IL	60131	847-455-7143	455-7899
Dorey Electric Co PO Box 10158 Web: www.doreyelectric.com	Norfolk	VA	23513	757-855-3381	857-7835
Ducci Electrical Contractors Inc 427 Goshen Rd	Torrington	CT	06790	860-489-9267	489-7980
Dycom Industries Inc 11770 US Hwy 1 Suite 101 NYSE: DY ■ TF: 877-210-0347 ■ Web: www.dycomind.com	Palm Beach Gardens	FL	33408	561-627-7171	627-7709
Dynalectric Corp 4462 Corporate Ctr Dr *Fax: Acctg ■ TF: 800-729-0444 ■ Web: www.kdc-systems.com	Los Alamitos	CA	90720	714-828-7000	484-2387*
E-J Electric Installation Co 4641 Vernon Blvd TF: 800-660-8658 ■ Web: www.ej1899.com	Long Island City	NY	11101	718-786-9400	937-9120
EC Co PO Box 10286 TF: 800-462-3370 ■ Web: www.e-c-co.com	Portland	OR	97296	503-224-3623	241-0807
EC Ernst Inc 1420 Ritchie Marlboro Rd TF: 800-683-7770 ■ Web: www.ecernst.com	Capitol Heights	MD	20743	301-350-7770	499-0933
Edwin L Heim Co 1918 Greenwood St TF: 800-692-7317 ■ Web: www.elheim.com	Harrisburg	PA	17104	717-233-8711	233-8619
Egizii Electric Inc 700 N MacArthur Blvd Web: www.eeiholding.com	Springfield	IL	62702	217-528-4001	528-1677
ElDeCo Inc 5751 Augusta Rd Web: www.eldecoinc.com	Greenville	SC	29605	864-277-9088	277-2811
Electric Resource Contractors Inc 4024 Washington Ave N Web: www.electricresource.com	Minneapolis	MN	55412	612-522-6511	522-4134
Electrical Contractors Inc 3510 Main St Web: www.ecincorporated.com	Hartford	CT	06120	860-549-2822	549-7948
Electrical Corp of America 7320 Arlington Ave TF: 800-426-9453	Raytown	MO	64133	816-737-3206	356-0731
Electronic Contracting Co PO Box 29195 TF: 800-366-5320 ■ Web: www.eccoinc.com	Lincoln	NE	68529	402-466-8274	466-0819
EMCOR Construction Services Inc 1420 Spring Hill Rd Suite 500 Web: www.emcorgroup.com	McLean	VA	22102	703-556-8000	556-0890
EMCOR Group Inc 301 Merritt 7 6th Fl NYSE: EME ■ TF: 866-890-7794 ■ Web: www.emcorgroup.com	Norwalk	CT	06851	203-849-7800	849-7900
EMCOR Hyre Electric Co 2655 Garfield Ave TF: 800-272-9659 ■ Web: www.emcorhyre.com	Highland	IN	46322	219-923-6100	838-3631
Engineered Protection Systems Inc 750 Front Ave NW Suite 300 TF: 800-966-9199 ■ Web: www.epssecurity.com	Grand Rapids	MI	49504	616-459-0281	459-0553
Enterprise Electric Co 4204 Shannon Dr Web: www.eecompany.com	Baltimore	MD	21213	410-488-8200	488-6639
Ermco Inc 1625 W Thompson Rd TF: 800-380-2923 ■ Web: www.ermco.com	Indianapolis	IN	46217	317-780-2923	780-2853
ESI Inc 3400 Kettering Blvd Web: www.esielectrical.com	Dayton	OH	45439	937-293-6138	293-6301
Evelyn Baird Gentry Corp 4303 Glebe Rd Web: www.cappelectric.com	Houston	TX	77018	713-681-7339	
Faith Technologies 2662 American Dr TF: 800-274-2345 ■ Web: www.faithtechnologies.com	Appleton	WI	54915	920-738-1500	738-1515
Ferguson Electric Construction Co Inc 333 Ellicott St	Buffalo	NY	14203	716-852-2010	852-4887
Ferndale Electric Co Inc 915 E Drayton Ave Web: www.ferndale-electric.com	Ferndale	MI	48220	248-545-4404	545-8140
Ferran Services & Contracting 525 Indiana St Web: www.ferran-services.com	Orlando	FL	32805	407-422-3551	648-0961
Fisk Electric Co 111 TC Jester Blvd Web: www.fiskcorp.com	Houston	TX	77007	713-868-6111	868-3749
Forest Electric Corp 45 Rockefeller Plaza # 630 Web: www.forestelectric.net	New York	NY	10111	212-318-1500	318-1791
Foshay Electric Co Inc 7676 Engineer Rd Web: www.foshayelectric.com	San Diego	CA	92111	858-277-7676	277-2629
Fox Electric Ltd 1104 Colorado Ln Web: www.foxelectric.com	Arlington	TX	76015	817-461-2571	261-7311
Fox Valley Fire & Safety Co Inc 2730 Pinnacle Dr Web: www.foxvalleyfire.com	Elgin	IL	60124	847-695-5990	695-3699
Fuellgraf Electric Co 600 S Washington St Web: www.fuellgraf.com	Butler	PA	16001	724-282-4800	282-1926
G & M Electrical Contractors Co 1746 N Richmond St TF: 800-546-8050	Chicago	IL	60647	773-278-8200	278-8038
Gardner-Zemke Co Inc 6100 Indian School Rd NE	Albuquerque	NM	87110	505-881-0555	888-1536
Gaylor Electric 11711 N College Ave Suite 150 TF: 800-878-0577 ■ Web: www.gaylor.com	Carmel	IN	46032	317-843-0577	848-0364
GEM Industrial Inc 6842 Commodore Dr TF: 800-837-5909 ■ Web: www.gemindustrial.com	Walbridge	OH	43465	419-666-6554	666-7004
Gibson Electric Co Inc 3100 Woodcreek Dr Web: www.gibsonelec.com	Downers Grove	IL	60515	630-288-3800	572-6261
Gill-Simpson Inc 1119 E 30th St Web: www.gill-simpson.com	Baltimore	MD	21218	410-467-3335	366-4557
Goldfield Corp 1684 W Hibiscus Blvd AMEX: GV ■ Web: www.goldfieldcorp.com	Melbourne	FL	32901	321-724-1700	724-1163
GR Sponaugle & Sons Inc 4391 Chambers Hill Rd TF: 800-866-7036 ■ Web: www.grsponaugle.com	Harrisburg	PA	17111	717-564-1515	564-3675
Grand-Kahn Electric 16760 Richmond Ave Web: www.grandkahn.com	Hazel Crest	IL	60429	708-333-4900	596-2280
Gregory Electric Co Inc 2124 College St Web: www.gregoryelectric.com	Columbia	SC	29205	803-748-1122	748-1102
GSL Electric Inc 8540 S Sandy Pkwy TF: 800-221-4135 ■ Web: www.gslelectric.com	Sandy	UT	84070	801-565-0088	565-0099
Guarantee Electrical Co 3405 Bent Ave TF: 800-854-4326 ■ Web: www.geco.com	Saint Louis	MO	63116	314-772-5400	772-9261

				Phone	Fax
Gulf Electric Co Inc of Mobile PO Box 2385	Mobile	AL	36652	251-666-0654	666-6323
Web: www.gulfelec.com					
Gulf States Inc 6711 E Hwy 332	Freeport	TX	77541	979-233-5555	233-3050
TF: 800-231-9849					
H & H Group Inc 2801 Syene Rd	Madison	WI	53713	608-273-3434	273-9654
Web: www.h-hgroup.com					
Hargrove Electric Co Inc 1522 Market Ctr Blvd	Dallas	TX	75207	214-742-8665	744-0846
Web: www.hargroveelectric.com					
Harlan Electric Co 2695 Crooks Rd	Rochester Hills	MI	48309	248-853-4601	853-4603
Web: www.myrgroup.com					
Harry F Ortlip Co Inc 780 Lancaster Ave	Bryn Mawr	PA	19010	610-527-7000	527-7437
Hatzel & Buehler Inc PO Box 7499	Wilmington	DE	19803	302-478-4200	478-2750
Web: www.hatzelandbuehler.com					
HB Frazer Co 514 Shoemaker Rd	King of Prussia	PA	19406	610-992-5060	992-5070
Web: www.hbfrazer.com					
Helix Electric Inc					
8260 Camino Santa Fe Suite A	San Diego	CA	92121	858-535-0505	623-1241
TF: 800-554-3549 ■ *Web:* www.helixelectric.com					
Herre Bros Inc 4417 Valley Rd	Enola	PA	17025	717-732-4454	732-8208
Web: www.herrebros.com					
Hi-Tech Electric Inc					
11116 W Little York Rd Bldg 8	Houston	TX	77041	832-243-0345	467-0132
TF: 800-315-6041 ■ *Web:* www.hitechelectric.com					
Highlines Construction Co Inc					
701 Bridge City Ave PO Box 408	Westwego	LA	70096	504-436-3961	436-4939
TF: 800-762-8860 ■ *Web:* www.highlines.com					
Hilscher Clarke Electric Co 519 4th St NW	Canton	OH	44703	330-452-9806	452-5867
Web: www.hilscher-clarke.com					
Hoffman Corp 805 SW Broadway Suite 2100	Portland	OR	97205	503-221-8811	221-8934
Web: www.hoffmancorp.com					
Honshy Electric Co Inc 7345 SW 41st St	Miami	FL	33155	305-264-5500	266-3159
Web: www.honshyelectric.com					
Hooper Corp 2030 Pennsylvania Ave	Madison	WI	53704	608-249-0451	249-7360
TF: 800-999-0451 ■ *Web:* www.hoopercorp.com					
Howe Electric Inc 4682 E Olive Ave	Fresno	CA	93702	559-255-8992	255-9745
Hunt Electric Corp 2300 Territorial Rd	Saint Paul	MN	55114	651-646-2911	643-6575
TF: 800-989-4432 ■ *Web:* www.huntelec.com					
Hyre Electric Co Inc 2320 W Ogden Ave	Chicago	IL	60608	312-738-7200	738-4090
Web: www.hyreelectric.com					
Industrial Contractors Inc 701 Ch Dr	Bismarck	ND	58501	701-258-9908	258-9988
Web: www.icinorthdakota.com					
Industrial Power & Lighting Corp					
701 Seneca St Suite 500	Buffalo	NY	14210	716-854-1811	854-1828
TF: 800-639-3702 ■ *Web:* www.iplcorp.com					
Industrial Specialty Contractors LLC					
20480 Highland Rd	Baton Rouge	LA	70817	225-756-8001	756-8586
Web: www.iscgrp.com					
Inglett & Stubbs LLC 5200 Riverview Rd	Mableton	GA	30126	404-881-1199	872-3101
Web: www.inglett-stubbs.com					
Integrated Electrical Services Inc					
4801 Woodway Dr Suite 200E	Houston	TX	77056	713-860-1500	860-1599
NASDAQ: IESC ■ *TF:* 877-437-6285 ■ *Web:* www.ielectric.com					
Intermountain Electric Inc 602 S Lipan St	Denver	CO	80223	303-733-7248	722-2410
Interstates Construction Services Inc					
1520 N Main Ave	Sioux Center	IA	51250	712-722-1662	722-1667
TF: 800-827-1662 ■ *Web:* www.interstates.com					
J & M Brown Co Inc 267 Amory St	Jamaica Plain	MA	02122	617-522-6800	522-6424
Web: www.jmbco.com					
J.f. Electric Inc					
100 Lakefront Pkwy PO Box 570	Edwardsville	IL	62025	618-797-5353	797-5354
TF: 800-339-8383 ■ *Web:* www.jfelectric.com					
John A Penney Co Inc 270 Sidney St	Cambridge	MA	02139	617-547-7744	547-4332
Jordano Electric Co Inc 200 Hudson St	Hackensack	NJ	07601	201-489-4800	489-5071
Web: www.jordanoelectric.com					
Kearney Electric Inc 3609 E Superior Ave	Phoenix	AZ	85040	602-437-0235	437-2914
Web: www.kearneyelectric.com					
Kelly Electric LLC					
2100 Consulate Dr Suite 100	Orlando	FL	32837	407-859-8801	240-1290
Web: www.kellyelectricllc.com					
Kelso-Burnett Co 5200 Newport Dr	Rolling Meadows	IL	60008	847-259-0720	259-0839
Web: www.kelso-burnett.com					
Kirby Electric Inc 170 Thorn Hill Rd	Warrendale	PA	15086	724-772-1800	772-2227
Web: www.kirbyelectricinc.com					
Kleinknecht Electric Co Inc					
252 W 37th St 9th Fl	New York	NY	10018	212-728-1800	765-2721
Web: www.kecny.com					
Koontz-Wagner Electric Co Inc					
3801 Voorde Dr	South Bend	IN	46628	574-232-2051	288-8510
TF: 800-345-2051 ■ *Web:* www.koontz-wagner.com					
Lake Erie Electric Inc 25730 First St	Westlake	OH	44145	440-835-5565	835-5688
Web: www.lakeerieelectric.com					
Linder & Assoc Inc 840 N Main St PO Box 1202	Wichita	KS	67201	316-265-6691	265-8097
Web: www.linderandassociates.com					
LK Comstock & Co Inc 5 Penn Plaza 12th Fl	New York	NY	10001	212-502-7900	502-1865
Web: www.railworks.com					
Long Electric Co Inc 1310 S Franklin Rd	Indianapolis	IN	46239	317-356-2455	356-0630
TF: 800-356-2450					
Ludvik Electric Co 3900 S Teller St	Lakewood	CO	80235	303-781-9601	783-6320
Web: www.ludvik.com					
Magaw Electric Inc 16055 W Ryerson Rd	New Berlin	WI	53151	262-782-7400	797-7550
Web: www.h-hgroup.com					
Marathon Electrical Contractors Inc					
PO Box 320067	Birmingham	AL	35232	205-323-8500	323-8501
Web: www.marathonelectrical.com					
Marine Electric Co 110 S 1st St	Louisville	KY	40202	502-587-6514	584-1656
Web: www.marine-electric.com					
Marrs Electric Inc PO Box 690296	Tulsa	OK	74169	918-437-5802	438-3563
Web: www.marrselectric.com					
Mass Electric Construction Co 180 Guest St	Boston	MA	02135	617-254-1015	254-0706
TF: 800-933-6322 ■ *Web:* www.masselec.com					
Matco Electric Corp 320 N Jensen Rd	Vestal	NY	13850	607-729-4921	729-0932
Web: www.matcoelectric.com					
Mayers Electric Co Inc 4004 Erie Ct	Cincinnati	OH	45227	513-272-2900	272-2904
Web: www.mayerselectric.com					
Mcs Of Tampa Inc 3926 W S Ave	Tampa	FL	33614	813-872-0217	876-6317
Web: www.mcsoftampa.com					
Meade Electric Co Inc 9550 W 55th St Suite A	McCook	IL	60525	708-588-2500	588-2501
Web: www.meadeelectric.com					
Meisner Electric Inc 220 NE 1st St	Delray Beach	FL	33444	561-278-8362	278-8397
Web: www.mei.cc					
Merit Electric Co Inc 6520 125th Ave N	Largo	FL	33773	727-536-5945	536-9014
TF: 800-539-3900 ■ *Web:* www.meritelectricco.com					
Merit Electrical Inc 17723 Airline Hwy	Prairieville	LA	70769	225-673-8850	673-8838
Web: www.merit-electrical.com					
Metropower Inc PO Box 5228	Albany	GA	31706	229-432-7345	436-3869
Web: www.metropower.com					
Mid-City Electrical Construction					
1099 Sullivant Ave	Columbus	OH	43223	614-221-5153	221-2225
Web: www.midcityelectric.com					
Miller Electric Co 2251 Rosselle St	Jacksonville	FL	32204	904-388-8000	389-8653
TF Sales: 800-554-4761 ■ *Web:* www.mecojax.com					
Miller Engineering Co 1616 S Main St	Rockford	IL	61102	815-963-4878	963-0823
MJ Electric Inc PO Box 686	Iron Mountain	MI	49801	906-774-8000	779-4217
Web: www.mjelectric.com					
MMR Group Inc 15961 Airline Hwy	Baton Rouge	LA	70817	225-756-5090	753-7012
Web: www.mmrgrp.com					
Mojave Electric Inc 3755 W Hacienda Ave	Las Vegas	NV	89118	702-798-2970	798-3740
Mona Electric Group Inc					
7915 Malcolm Rd Suite 102	Clinton	MD	20735	301-868-8400	868-9769
TF: 800-438-6662 ■ *Web:* www.monaelectric.com					
Morrow-Meadows Corp 231 Benton Ct	Walnut	CA	91789	909-598-7700	598-3907
TF: 800-438-6366 ■ *Web:* www.morrow-meadows.com					
Morse Electric Inc 500 W S St	Freeport	IL	61032	815-266-4200	266-8900
Web: www.morselec.com					
Motor City Electric Co 9440 Grinnell St	Detroit	MI	48213	313-921-5300	921-5310
TF: 800-860-8020 ■ *Web:* www.mceco.com					
Mr Electric Corp 1010 N University Parks Dr	Waco	TX	76707	800-253-9151	745-5068*
**Fax Area Code: 254* ■ *TF:* 800-253-9151 ■ *Web:* www.mrelectric.com					
Msf Electric Inc 13003 SW Fwy	Stafford	TX	77477	281-494-4700	
TF: 866-366-7943 ■ *Web:* www.msfelectric.com					
Muska Electric Co 1985 Oakcrest Ave	Roseville	MN	55113	651-636-5820	636-0916
Web: www.muskaelectric.com					
Muth Electric Inc 1717 N Sanborn PO Box 1400	Mitchell	SD	57301	605-996-3983	996-2203
Web: www.muthelec.com					
Mutual Telecom Services Inc					
250 1st Ave Suite 301	Needham	MA	02494	781-449-1900	449-1996
Web: www.mutualtelecom.com					
MYR Group					
1701 W Golf Rd Tower 3 Suite 1012	Rolling Meadows	IL	60008	847-290-1891	290-1892
Web: www.myrgroup.com					
Nathan Alterman Electric Co					
14703 Jones Maltsberger St	San Antonio	TX	78247	210-496-6888	496-7349
Web: www.nalterman.com					
Network Infrastructure Corp					
1131 W Warner Rd Suite 111	Tempe	AZ	85284	480-850-5050	850-5051
TF: 866-642-6878 ■ *Web:* www.nicweb.com					
Newkirk Electric Assoc Inc 1875 Roberts St	Muskegon	MI	49442	231-722-1691	722-1690
Web: www.newkirk-electric.com					
Newtron Group Inc 8232 W Darryl Dr	Baton Rouge	LA	70815	225-927-8921	927-8921
TF: 800-644-2752 ■ *Web:* www.thenewtrongroup.com					
Nikkel & Assoc Inc 728 E Lincoln Way	Ames	IA	50010	515-232-8606	232-4012
TF: 800-765-1790 ■ *Web:* www.nai-ames.com					
O'Connell Electric Co 830 Phillips Rd	Victor	NY	14564	585-924-2176	924-4973
Web: www.oconnellelectric.com					
Operational Security Systems Inc					
1231 Collier Rd NW Suite D	Atlanta	GA	30318	404-352-0025	350-0815
TF: 866-677-5677 ■ *Web:* www.ossatl.com					
Ostrow Electric Co Inc 9 Mason St	Worcester	MA	01609	508-754-2641	757-1645
TF: 800-922-8289					
Palmer Electric & Showcase Lighting					
875 Jackson Ave	Winter Park	FL	32789	407-646-8700	647-8951
Web: www.palmer-electric.com					
Parsons Electric LLC 5960 Main St NE	Minneapolis	MN	55432	763-571-8000	571-7210
Web: www.parsons-electric.com					
PayneCrest Electric & Communications					
10411 Baur Blvd	Saint Louis	MO	63132	314-996-0400	996-0500
Web: www.payneelectric.com					
Peoples Electric Co Inc					
277 E Fillmore Ave	Saint Paul	MN	55107	651-227-7711	227-9684
TF: 888-777-3409 ■ *Web:* www.peoplesco.com					
Perlectric Inc 2711 Prosperity Ave	Fairfax	VA	22031	703-352-5151	352-5155
Web: www.perlectric.com					
Perreca Electric Co 520 Broadway	Newburgh	NY	12550	845-562-4080	562-0801
TF: 800-973-7732 ■ *Web:* www.perreca.com					
Petrocelli Electric Co Inc					
2209 Queens Plaza N	Long Island City	NY	11101	718-752-2200	756-0695
TF: 800-253-2721 ■ *Web:* www.petrocelli.com					
Phillips Bros Electrical Contractors Inc					
235 Sweet Spring Rd	Glenmoore	PA	19343	610-458-8578	458-8438
TF: 800-220-5051					
Pieper Electric Inc 5070 N 35th St	Milwaukee	WI	53209	414-462-7700	462-7711
Web: www.pieperpower.com					
Pike Electric Corp 100 Pike Way PO Box 868	Mount Airy	NC	27030	336-789-2171	719-7453
NYSE: PEC ■ *TF:* 800-424-7453 ■ *Web:* www.pikeelectric.com					
Power City Electric Inc 3327 E Olive Ave	Spokane	WA	99202	509-535-8500	535-4665
TF: 800-877-8549 ■ *Web:* www.callsesco.com/powercity.html					
Premier Electrical Corp					
4401 85th Ave N	Brooklyn Park	MN	55443	763-424-6551	424-5225
TF: 800-466-8818					
Pritchard Electric Co Inc 2425 8th Ave	Huntington	WV	25703	304-529-2566	529-2567
TF: 877-457-8904 ■ *Web:* www.pritchardelectric.com					
Professional Construction Services Inc					
PO Box 2005	Prairieville	LA	70769	225-744-4016	744-4938
TF: 800-562-4318 ■ *Web:* www.professionalconstruction.com					
Qn Electric Inc PO Box 129	Kailua	HI	96734	808-263-9813	262-6281
Web: www.qnelectric.com					
R K Electric Inc 42021 Osgood Rd	Fremont	CA	94539	510-770-5660	770-5684
TF: 800-400-4418 ■ *Web:* www.rkelectric.com					
R2w Inc 5957 McLeod Dr	Las Vegas	NV	89120	702-434-6500	
TF: 800-488-1811 ■ *Web:* www.r2west.com					
Ready Electric Co Inc					
3300 Gilmore Industrial Blvd	Louisville	KY	40213	502-893-2511	893-2519
Web: www.readyelec.com					
Regency Electric					

				Phone	Fax
4348 Southpoint Blvd Suite 400 *TF:* 877-309-0204	Jacksonville	FL	32216	904-281-0600	281-0599
Rex Moore Electrical Contractors & Engineers 3601 Pkwy Pl *TF:* 800-266-1922 ■ *Web:* www.rexmoore.com	West Sacramento	CA	95691	916-372-1300	372-4013
RFI Communications & Security Systems 360 Turtle Creek Ct *TF:* 800-341-9292 ■ *Web:* www.rfi.com	San Jose	CA	95125	408-298-5400	882-4401
Riggs Distler Co Inc 9411 Philadelphia Rd Unit P *Web:* www.riggsdistler.com	Baltimore	MD	21237	410-633-0300	633-2119
Riviera Electric 5001 S Zuni St *TF:* 800-765-5767 ■ *Web:* www.riviera-electric.com	Littleton	CO	80120	303-937-9300	922-1421
Roman Electric Co Inc PO Box 14396 *TF:* 877-772-7760 ■ *Web:* www.romanelectric.com	Milwaukee	WI	53214	414-771-5400	471-8693
Romanoff Electric Co LLC 5570 Enterprise Blvd *TF:* 800-866-2627	Toledo	OH	43612	419-726-2627	726-5406
Ronco Communications & Electronics Inc 595 Sheridan Dr *TF:* 888-879-8011 ■ *Web:* www.ronconet.com	Tonawanda	NY	14150	716-873-0760	879-8150
Rosendin Electric Inc 880 N Mabury Rd *Fax: Hum Res ■ *TF:* 800-540-4734 ■ *Web:* www.rosendin.com	San Jose	CA	95133	408-286-2800	793-5019*
Rydalch Electric Inc 250 Plymouth Ave *Web:* www.rydalch-electric.com	Salt Lake City	UT	84115	801-265-1813	265-2166
Salem Electric Co Inc 3933 Westpoint Blvd PO Box 26784 *Web:* www.salemelectriccoinc.com	Winston-Salem	NC	27114	336-765-0221	765-7286
Sargent Electric Co 2801 Liberty Ave *Web:* www.sargent.com	Pittsburgh	PA	15222	412-391-0588	394-7535
SASCO Electric 12900 Alondra Blvd *TF:* 800-477-4422 ■ *Web:* www.sasco.com	Cerritos	CA	90703	562-926-0900	926-1399
Schenectady Hardware & Electric Co Inc PO Box 338 *Web:* www.sheinc.com	Schenectady	NY	12301	518-346-2369	372-7549
Schmidt Electric Coy L P 9701 FM 1625 *TF:* 800-833-3649 ■ *Web:* www.schmidt-electric.com	Austin	TX	78747	512-243-1450	243-0601
Sesco Lighting Inc 1133 W Morse Blvd Suite 100 *Web:* www.sescolighting.com	Winter Park	FL	32789	407-629-6100	629-6168
Shambaugh & Son LP 7614 Opportunity Dr *TF:* 800-234-9988 ■ *Web:* www.shambaugh.com	Fort Wayne	IN	46825	260-487-7777	487-7701
Shaw Electric Co 33200 Schoolcraft Rd *Web:* www.shawelectric.com	Livonia	MI	48150	734-425-6800	425-6824
Shawver & Son Inc 144 NE 44th St *TF:* 800-320-5121 ■ *Web:* www.shawver.net	Oklahoma City	OK	73105	405-525-9451	525-6136
Shelley Electric Inc PO Box 12124 *Web:* www.shelleyelectric.com	Wichita	KS	67277	316-945-8311	945-2604
Smith & Keene Electric Service Inc 833 Live Oak Dr *Web:* www.smithandkeene.com	Chesapeake	VA	23320	757-420-1231	420-5340
Southern Air Inc 2655 Lakeside Dr *TF:* 800-743-1214 ■ *Web:* www.southern-air.com	Lynchburg	VA	24501	434-385-6200	385-9081
Spg Solar Inc 20 Leveroni Ct *TF:* 800-815-5562 ■ *Web:* www.spgsolar.com	Novato	CA	94949	415-883-7657	
Sprig Electric Co 1860 S 10th St *Web:* www.sprigelectric.com	San Jose	CA	95112	408-298-3134	298-2132
Staff Electric Co Inc W 133 N 5030 Campbell Dr	Menomonee Falls	WI	53051	262-781-8230	781-1680
Staley Inc 3400 Je Davis Dr *TF:* 877-616-0661 ■ *Web:* www.staleyinc.com	Little Rock	AR	72209	501-565-3006	565-9674
Starr Electric Co Inc PO Box 9298 *TF:* 800-732-0241 ■ *Web:* www.starrelectric.net	Greensboro	NC	27429	336-275-0241	273-0734
Steiny & Co Inc 221 N Ardmore Ave PO Box 74901 *TF:* 800-350-2331 ■ *Web:* www.steinyco.com	Los Angeles	CA	90004	213-382-2331	381-6781
Stoner Electric Inc 1904 SE Ochoco St *Web:* www.stonergroup.com	Milwaukie	OR	97222	503-462-6500	659-6529
Sturgeon Electric Co Inc 12150 E 112th Ave *TF:* 800-288-5155 ■ *Web:* www.sturgeonelectric.com	Henderson	CO	80640	303-286-8000	286-1887
Sunwest Electric Inc 3064 E Miraloma Ave *Web:* www.sunwestelectric.net	Anaheim	CA	92806	714-630-8700	630-8740
Super Electric Construction Co 4300 W Chicago Ave *TF:* 800-344-1936 ■ *Web:* www.superelec.com	Chicago	IL	60651	773-489-4400	235-1455
Syracuse Merit Electric Inc 301 Stoutenger St *Web:* www.syracusemerit.com	East Syracuse	NY	13057	315-437-1453	437-7431
System Electric Co 1278 Montalvo Way *TF:* 800-998-9017 ■ *Web:* www.systemelectric.com	Palm Springs	CA	92262	760-327-7847	323-7247
T & J Electrical Corp 636 2nd Ave *Web:* www.tandjelectric.com	Troy	NY	12182	518-237-1893	237-3195
Taft Electric Co 1694 Eastman Ave	Ventura	CA	93003	805-642-0121	650-9015
TEC Corp PO Box 207 *TF:* 800-832-2936 ■ *Web:* www.tec-corp.com	Sioux City	IA	51102	712-252-4275	252-5344
Teknon Corp 15443 NE 95th St *TF:* 800-338-6142 ■ *Web:* www.teknon.com	Redmond	WA	98052	425-895-8535	895-0535
Telaid Industries Inc 13 W Main St *TF:* 800-205-5556 ■ *Web:* www.telaid.com	Niantic	CT	06357	860-739-4461	739-9913
Tennessee Associated Electric Inc 312 W Jackson Ave	Knoxville	TN	37902	865-524-3686	522-1553
Terry's Electric Inc 600 N Thacker Ave Suite A *TF:* 888-278-3779 ■ *Web:* www.terryselectric.com	Kissimmee	FL	34741	407-846-4252	846-6607
Totem Electric of Tacoma Inc 2332 Jefferson Ave *TF:* 800-562-8478 ■ *Web:* www.totemelectric.com	Tacoma	WA	98402	253-383-5022	272-5214
Tri-City Electrical Contractors Inc 430 W Dr *TF:* 800-768-2489 ■ *Web:* www.tcelectric.com	Altamonte Springs	FL	32714	407-788-3500	682-7353
Triangle Electric Co 29787 Stephenson Hwy *Web:* www.trielec.com	Madison Heights	MI	48071	248-399-2200	399-2612
Truland Systems Corp 1900 Oracle Way Suite 700 *TF:* 800-878-5263 ■ *Web:* www.truland.com	Reston	VA	20190	703-464-3000	796-1718
Van Ert Electric Co Inc 7019 Stewart Ave *Web:* www.vanert.com	Wausau	WI	54401	715-845-4308	848-3671
Vaughn Industries LLC 1201 E Findlay St *Web:* www.vaughnindustries.com	Carey	OH	43316	419-396-3900	
WA Chester LLC 4390 Parliament Pl Suite Q *Web:* www.wachester.com	Lanham	MD	20706	240-487-1940	487-1941
Wagner Industrial Electric Inc PO Box 55 *TF:* 800-775-7799 ■ *Web:* www.wagner-ind.com	Dayton	OH	45401	937-298-7481	298-0268
Wasatch Electric 2455 W 1500 S # A *TF:* 800-999-4511 ■ *Web:* www.wasatchelectric.com	Salt Lake City	UT	84104	801-487-4511	487-5032
Watson Electrical 1500 Charleston St *Web:* www.watsonelec.com	Wilson	NC	27893	252-237-7511	243-1607
Wayne J Griffin Electric Inc 116 Hopping Brook Rd *TF:* 800-421-0151 ■ *Web:* www.waynejgriffin.com	Holliston	MA	01746	508-429-8830	429-7825
Wellington Power Corp 40th & Butler Sts *TF:* 800-540-0017 ■ *Web:* www.wellingtonpower.com	Pittsburgh	PA	15201	412-681-0103	681-0109
Welsbach Electric Corp 111-01 14th Ave *Web:* www.welsbachelectric.com	College Point	NY	11356	718-670-7900	670-7999
West Virginia Electric Corp PO Box 1587 *TF:* 800-982-3532 ■ *Web:* www.wvelectric.com	Fairmont	WV	26554	304-363-6900	366-6356
West-Fair Electric Contractors Inc 200 Brady Ave *TF:* 800-525-0585	Hawthorne	NY	10532	914-769-8050	769-7451
White Electrical Construction Co 1730 Chattahoochee Ave *TF:* 888-519-4483 ■ *Web:* www.whitelectric.com	Atlanta	GA	30318	404-351-5740	355-5823
Williard Limbach 175 Titus Ave Suite 100 *Fax: Cust Svc ■ *TF:* 800-827-5030 ■ *Web:* www.limbachinc.com	Warrington	PA	18976	215-488-9700	488-9699*
Windemuller Electric Inc 1176 Electric Ave *TF:* 800-333-3641 ■ *Web:* www.windemullerelectric.com	Wayland	MI	49348	616-877-8770	877-8700
York River Electric Inc 3201 Old Williamsburg Rd *Web:* www.yorkriverelectric.com	Yorktown	VA	23690	757-369-3673	369-3680
Zwicker Electrical Co Inc 360 Pk Ave S 4th Fl *Web:* www.zwicker-electric.com	New York	NY	10010	212-477-8400	995-8469

192-5 Excavation Contractors

				Phone	Fax
Allied Contractors Inc 204 E Preston St	Baltimore	MD	21202	410-539-6727	332-4594
Aman Environmental Construction Inc 614 E Edna Pl *Web:* www.amanenvironmental.com	Covina	CA	91723	626-967-4287	332-1877
Anastasi Trucking & Paving Inc 4430 Walden St *Web:* www.anastasitrucking.com	Lancaster	NY	14086	716-683-5003	683-5045
Andrews Excavating Inc 5 W Willow Rd	Willow Street	PA	17584	717-464-3329	464-4963
B & B Wrecking & Excavating Inc 5801 Train Ave *Web:* www.bbwrecking.com	Cleveland	OH	44102	216-651-9090	651-9095
Barnard Construction Co Inc PO Box 99 *Web:* www.barnard-inc.com	Bozeman	MT	59771	406-586-1995	586-3530
Beaver Excavating Co Inc 4650 Southway St SW *TF:* 800-255-3767 ■ *Web:* www.beaverexcavating.com	Canton	OH	44706	330-478-2151	478-2122
Berkel & Co Contractors Inc PO Box 335 *Web:* www.berkelandcompany.com	Bonner Springs	KS	66012	913-422-5125	422-2013
Bi-Con Services Inc 10901 Clay Pike Rd *Web:* www.bsicos.com	Derwent	OH	43733	740-685-2542	685-3863
Borderland Construction Co Inc 400 E 38 St	Tucson	AZ	85713	520-623-0900	623-0232
BR Kreider & Son Inc 63 Kreider Ln *TF:* 800-689-7651 ■ *Web:* www.brkreider.com	Manheim	PA	17545	717-898-7651	898-0759
Branscome Inc 4551 John Tyler Hwy *TF:* 888-229-2504 ■ *Web:* www.branscome.com	Williamsburg	VA	23185	757-229-2504	220-0390
Carl Bolander & Sons Co Inc 251 Starkey St *TF:* 800-676-6504 ■ *Web:* www.bolander.com	Saint Paul	MN	55107	651-224-6299	223-8197
Case Foundation Co 1325 W Lake St *Web:* www.casefoundation.com	Roselle	IL	60172	630-529-2911	529-2995
Corrado American Inc 200 Marsh Ln *Web:* www.corrado.com	New Castle	DE	19720	302-655-6501	655-3214
CP Ward Inc PO Box 900 *Web:* www.cpward.com	Scottsville	NY	14546	585-889-8800	889-6008
Daisy Construction Co Inc 3128 New Castle Ave *Web:* www.daisyconstruction.com	New Castle	DE	19720	302-658-4417	658-0618
Dywidag Systems International 320 Marmon Dr *Web:* www.dywidag-systems.com	Bolingbrook	IL	60440	630-739-1100	739-5517
Feutz Contractors Inc 1120 N Main St PO Box 130 *TF:* 800-252-0273 ■ *Web:* www.feutzcontractors.com	Paris	IL	61944	217-465-8402	463-2256
Fisher Contracting Co 614 Jefferson Ave	Midland	MI	48640	989-835-7771	835-8461
Foundation Constructors Inc 81 Big Break Rd PO Box 97 *TF:* 800-841-8740 ■ *Web:* www.foundationpile.com	Oakley	CA	94561	925-625-4455	625-5783
Francis O Day Construction Co Inc 850 E Gude Dr *Web:* www.foday.com	Rockville	MD	20850	301-652-2400	340-6592
Geo-Con Inc 4075 Monroeville Blvd Suite 400 Bldg 2 *Web:* www.geocon.net	Monroeville	PA	15146	412-856-7700	373-3357
George J Igel & Co Inc 2040 Alum Creek Dr *TF:* 800-345-4435 ■ *Web:* www.igelco.com	Columbus	OH	43207	614-445-8421	445-8205
Glenn Rehbein Cos 8651 Naples St NE *Web:* www.rehbein.com	Blaine	MN	55449	763-784-0657	784-6001

	City	State	ZIP	Phone	Fax
Harry C. Crooker & Sons Inc PO Box 5001	Topsham	ME	04086	207-729-5511	725-4025
Web: www.crooker.com					
Hayward Baker Inc 1130 Annapolis Rd Suite 202	Odenton	MD	21113	410-551-8200	551-1900
TF: 800-456-6548 ■ *Web:* www.haywardbaker.com					
HT Sweeney & Son Inc 308 Dutton Mill Rd	Brookhaven	PA	19015	610-872-8896	874-6730
Independence Excavating Inc 5720 Schaaf Rd	Independence	OH	44131	216-524-1700	524-1701
TF: 800-524-3478 ■ *Web:* www.indexc.com					
J Fletcher Creamer & Son Inc 101 E Broadway	Hackensack	NJ	07601	201-488-9800	488-2901
TF: 800-835-9801 ■ *Web:* www.jfcson.com					
JH Beers Inc PO Box 669	Wind Gap	PA	18091	610-759-7628	863-8270
Kamminga & Roodvoets Inc 3435 Broadmoor Ave SE	Grand Rapids	MI	49512	616-949-0800	949-1894
TF: 800-632-9755					
Luburgh Inc 4174 E Pike	Zanesville	OH	43701	740-452-3668	454-7225
M Rondano Inc 49 East Ave.	Norwalk	CT	06851	203-846-1577	846-9564
Web: www.rondano.com					
Manafort Bros Inc 414 New Britain Ave	Plainville	CT	06062	860-229-4853	229-1878
TF: 888-626-2367 ■ *Web:* www.manafort.com					
Mann Bros Inc 1950 N Wisconsin St.	Elkhorn	WI	53121	262-723-5500	723-3463
Web: www.mannbrosinc.com					
Markham Contracting Co Inc 22820 N 19th Ave	Phoenix	AZ	85027	623-869-9100	869-9400
Web: www.markhamcontracting.com					
McAninch Corp 6800 Lake Dr Suite 125	West Des Moines	IA	50266	515-267-2500	267-2550
TF: 800-383-3201 ■ *Web:* www.mcaninchcorp.com					
McGowan-Stauffer Inc PO Box 524	Carnegie	PA	15106	412-279-8846	279-8848
Web: www.mcgowan-stauffer.com					
Merlyn Contractors Inc PO Box 917	Novi	MI	48376	248-349-3800	347-2966
Web: www.merlyn.us					
Moretrench American Corp 100 Stickle Ave PO Box 316	Rockaway	NJ	07866	973-627-2100	627-6078
TF: 800-394-6673 ■ *Web:* www.moretrench.com					
Nicholson Construction Co 12 McClane St	Cuddy	PA	15031	412-221-4500	221-3127
TF: 800-388-2340 ■ *Web:* www.nicholson-rodio.com					
Noralco Corp 1920 Lincoln Rd.	Pittsburgh	PA	15235	412-361-6678	361-6535
Web: www.noralco.com					
Oldcastle Materials Inc 900 Ashwood Pkwy Suite 700	Atlanta	GA	30338	770-552-5600	522-5008
TF: 800-241-7074 ■ *Web:* www.apac.com					
Ortiz Enterprises Inc 6 Cushing Way Suite 200	Irvine	CA	92618	949-753-1414	753-1477
Web: www.ortizent.com					
Park Construction Co Inc 500 73rd Ave NE Suite 123	Minneapolis	MN	55432	763-786-9800	786-2952
TF: 800-328-2556					
Pavex Inc 4400 Gettysburg Rd	Camp Hill	PA	17011	717-761-1502	761-0329
Perry Engineering Co Inc 1945 Millwood Pike	Winchester	VA	22602	540-667-4310	667-7618
TF: 800-272-4310 ■ *Web:* www.perryeng.com					
Phillips & Jordan Inc 6621 Wilbanks Rd	Knoxville	TN	37912	865-688-8342	688-8369
TF: 800-955-0876 ■ *Web:* www.pandj.com					
Pleasant Excavating Co Inc 24024 Frederick Rd Suite 200	Clarksburg	MD	20871	301-428-0800	428-1736
TF: 800-842-1180					
Power & Construction Group Inc PO Box 196	Scottsville	NY	14546	585-889-6016	
Web: www.pandcg.com					
Professional Construction Services Inc PO Box 2005	Prairieville	LA	70769	225-744-4016	744-4938
TF: 800-562-4318 ■ *Web:* www.professionalconstruction.com					
PT Ferro Construction Co 700 Rowell Ave	Joliet	IL	60433	815-726-6284	726-5614
Web: www.ptferro.com					
Raymond Excavating Co Inc 800 Gratiot Blvd	Marysville	MI	48040	810-364-6881	364-6450
TF: 888-837-6770 ■ *Web:* www.raymondexcavating.com					
Richard Goettle Inc 12071 Hamilton Ave.	Cincinnati	OH	45231	513-825-8100	825-8107
TF: 800-248-8661 ■ *Web:* www.goettle.com					
Ruttura & Sons Construction Co Inc 165 Sherwood Ave	Farmingdale	NY	11735	631-454-0291	454-8804
Web: www.ruttura.com					
Ryan Inc Central 2700 E Racine St.	Janesville	WI	53545	608-754-2291	754-3290
Web: www.ryancentral.com					
Seubert Excavators Inc PO Box 57	Cottonwood	ID	83522	208-962-3314	962-3392
Shoosmith Bros Inc 11800 Lewis Rd	Chester	VA	23831	804-748-5823	748-8482
Web: www.shoosmith.com					
Sierrita Mining & Ranching Co Inc HC-70 PO Box 4260	Sahuarita	AZ	85629	520-625-1204	625-3234
Soil Engineering Construction Inc 927 Arguello St.	Redwood City	CA	94063	650-367-9595	367-8139
Stevens Painton Corp 7850 Fwy Cir Suite 100	Middleburg Heights	OH	44130	440-234-7888	234-1967
Web: www.spcdmg.com					
Stroer & Graff Inc 1830 Phillips Ln	Antioch	CA	94509	925-778-0200	778-6766
Subsurface Constructors Inc 110 Angelica St	Saint Louis	MO	63147	314-421-2460	421-2479
Web: www.subsurfaceconstructors.com					
Super Excavators Inc N 59 W 14601 Bobolink Ave.	Menomonee Falls	WI	53051	262-252-3200	252-8079
Web: www.superexcavators.com					
Terra Engineering & Construction Corp 2201 Vondron Rd	Madison	WI	53718	608-221-3501	221-4075
TJ Lambrecht Construction Inc 10 Gougar Rd	Joliet	IL	60432	815-727-9211	727-6421
Web: www.tjlambrecht.com					
Union Engineering Co Inc PO Box 1000	Ventura	CA	93002	805-648-3373	648-6634
Urban Foundation/Engineering LLC PO Box 158	East Elmhurst	NY	11369	718-478-3021	397-1917
Velting Contractors Inc 3060 Breton Rd SE	Kentwood	MI	49512	616-949-6660	949-8168
Web: www.velting.com					

192-6 Glass & Glazing Contractors

	City	State	ZIP	Phone	Fax
Benson Industries Inc 1650 NW Naito Pkwy Suite 250	Portland	OR	97209	503-226-7611	226-0070
TF: 800-999-5113 ■ *Web:* www.bensonglobal.com					
Builders Architectural Products Inc 430 Lake Cook Rd Suite C	Deerfield	IL	60015	847-945-9200	945-9210
Web: www.buildersarch.com					
Carter Glass Co Inc 1608 Locust St	Kansas City	MO	64108	816-471-8288	471-0174
TF: 866-471-8287 ■ *Web:* www.carterglass.net					
Cartner Glass Systems Inc 2508 Westinghouse Blvd PO Box 7744	Charlotte	NC	28241	704-588-1976	588-9440
TF: 800-968-2818					
Culbertson Enterprises Inc 600A Snyder Ave	West Chester	PA	19382	610-436-6400	436-6309
Enclos Corp 2770 Blue Water Rd	Eagan	MN	55121	651-796-6100	994-6360
TF: 800-831-1108 ■ *Web:* www.enclos.com					
General Glass Co Inc 5797 MacCorkle Ave SE	Charleston	WV	25304	304-925-2171	925-8915
Giroux Glass Inc 850 W Washington Blvd.	Los Angeles	CA	90015	213-747-7406	747-8778
TF: 800-684-5277 ■ *Web:* www.girouxglass.com					
Karas & Karas Glass Co Inc 455 Dorchester Ave	Boston	MA	02127	617-268-8800	269-0536
TF: 800-888-1235 ■ *Web:* www.karasglass.com					
Lafayette Glass Co Inc 2841 Teal Rd.	Lafayette	IN	47905	765-474-1402	474-3382
TF Cust Svc: 800-382-7862 ■ *Web:* www.lafayetteglass.com					
Lee & Cates Glass Inc 142 Madison St.	Jacksonville	FL	32203	904-354-4643	355-0131
Web: www.leeandcatesglass.com					
Lynbrook Glass & Architectural Metals Corp 941 Motor Pkwy	Hauppauge	NY	11788	631-582-3060	582-3974
Web: www.lynbrookglass.com					
Masonry Arts Inc 2105 3rd Ave N.	Bessemer	AL	35020	205-428-0780	424-1931
Web: www.masonryarts.com					
MTH Industries 1 MTH Plaza	Hillside	IL	60162	708-498-1100	498-1101
TF: 800-231-9711 ■ *Web:* www.mthindustries.com					
National Glass & Metal Co Inc 1424 Easton Rd Suite 400	Horsham	PA	19044	215-938-8880	938-7028
Web: www.ngmco.com					
Sashco Inc 720 S Rochester Ave Suite D	Ontario	CA	91761	909-937-8222	937-8223
TF: 800-600-3232 ■ *Web:* www.sashcoinc.com					
Sound Glass Sales Inc 5501 75th St W	Tacoma	WA	98499	253-473-7477	473-0849
TF: 800-468-9949 ■ *Web:* www.soundglass.com					
Waltek & Co Ltd 2130 Waycorss Rd	Cincinnati	OH	45240	513-577-7980	577-7990
Web: www.waltekltd.com					
Walters & Wolf 41450 Boscell Rd.	Fremont	CA	94538	510-490-1115	651-7172
TF: 800-969-9653 ■ *Web:* www.waltersandwolf.com					

192-7 Masonry & Stone Contractors

	City	State	ZIP	Phone	Fax
Brisk Waterproofing Co Inc 720 Grand Ave	Ridgefield	NJ	07657	201-945-0210	945-7841
TF: 800-942-9228 ■ *Web:* www.briskwaterproofing.com					
Bruns-Gutzwiller Inc 305 John St	Batesville	IN	47006	812-934-2105	934-2107
Web: www.bruns-gutzwiller.com					
Caretti Inc 4590 Industrial Pk Rd PO Box 331	Camp Hill	PA	17011	717-737-6759	737-6880
Web: www.carettimasonry.com					
Culbertson Enterprises Inc 600A Snyder Ave	West Chester	PA	19382	610-436-6400	436-6309
Dee Brown Inc (DBI) 4101 S Shiloh Rd PO Box 570335	Dallas	TX	75041	214-321-6443	328-1039*
**Fax: Tech Supp ■ *Web:* www.deebrown.com					
Design Masonry Inc 20703 Santa Clara St	Santa Clarita	CA	91351	661-298-1013	
Web: www.designmasonry.com					
Edgar Boettcher Mason Contractors Inc 1616 S Airport Rd.	Traverse City	MI	49686	231-941-5802	941-7627
TF: 800-562-3827 ■ *Web:* www.boettchermasonry.com					
Evans-Mason Inc 1021 S Grand Ave E	Springfield	IL	62703	217-522-3396	522-3190
Fred A Kinateder Masonry Inc 2307 Badger Dr.	Waukesha	WI	53188	262-548-9876	548-0102
Web: www.fkmi.com					
Gallegos Corp PO Box 821	Vail	CO	81658	970-926-3737	926-3727
TF: 800-425-5346 ■ *Web:* www.gallegoscorp.com					
International Chimney Corp 55 S Long St.	Williamsville	NY	14221	716-634-3967	634-3983
TF: 800-828-1446 ■ *Web:* www.internationalchimney.com					
JD Long Masonry Inc 8253 Backlick Rd Suite J	Lorton	VA	22079	703-550-8880	550-9567
Web: www.jdlongmasonry.com					
John J Smith Masonry Co 9200 Green Pk Rd	Saint Louis	MO	63123	314-894-9500	894-1172
Web: www.smithmasonry.com					
Kauai Builders Ltd 3988 Halau St	Lihue	HI	96766	808-245-2911	245-1769
Kretschmar & Smith Inc 6293 Pedley Rd	Riverside	CA	92509	951-361-1405	361-1381
Leonard Masonry Inc 5925 Fee Fee Rd	Hazelwood	MO	63042	314-731-5500	731-3366
Web: www.leonardmasonry.com					
Lindblad Construction Co 717 E Cass St	Joliet	IL	60432	815-726-6251	723-4907
Web: www.lindbladconstruction.com					
Manganaro Corp New England 52 Cummings Pk	Woburn	MA	01801	781-937-8880	937-8882
Masonry Arts Inc 2105 3rd Ave N.	Bessemer	AL	35020	205-428-0780	424-1931
Web: www.masonryarts.com					
MB Haynes Corp 187 Deaverview Rd	Asheville	NC	28806	828-254-6141	253-8136
Web: www.mbhaynes.com					
Mid-Continental Restoration Co Inc 401 E Hudson Rd PO Box 429	Fort Scott	KS	66701	620-223-3700	223-5052
TF: 800-835-3700 ■ *Web:* www.midcontinental.com					

				Phone	Fax
Montana Stone Gallery LLC 6900 Kestrel Dr Suite 17 *Web:* www.montanastonegallery.com	Missoula	MT	59808	406-541-7625	
Otto Baum Co Inc 866 N Main St PO Box 161 *Web:* www.ottobaum.com	Morton	IL	61550	309-266-7114	263-1050
Pettit Construction Inc 450 Partners Ln PO Box 307 *Web:* www.pettitconstruction.com	Roebuck	SC	29376	864-576-4762	576-4766
Pompano Masonry Corp 880 S Andrews Ave *TF:* 800-762-7425 ■ *Web:* www.pompanomasonry.com	Pompano Beach	FL	33069	954-946-3033	941-4857
Pyramid Masonry Contractors Inc 2330 Mellon Ct *TF:* 800-345-4750	Decatur	GA	30035	770-987-4750	981-7142
Rock & Waterscape Systems Inc 24400 Sinacola Dr **Fax Area Code:* 949 ■ *TF:* 800-328-9762 ■ *Web:* www.rockandwaterscape.com	Farmington Hills	MI	48335	248-473-0500	458-6331*
Ron Kendall Masonry Inc 101 Benoist Farms Rd *Web:* www.ronkendallmasonry.com	West Palm Beach	FL	33411	561-793-5924	795-2621
RP Carbone Construction Co 5910 Landerbrook Dr # 230 *Web:* www.rpcarbone.com	Cleveland	OH	44124	440-449-6750	449-5717
Schiffer Mason Contractors Inc 2190 Delhi NE PO Box 250 *Web:* www.schiffermasonry.com	Holt	MI	48842	517-694-2566	694-1936
Seedorff Masonry Inc 408 W Mission St *Web:* www.seedorff.com	Strawberry Point	IA	52076	563-933-2296	933-4114
Snow Jr & King Inc 2415 Church St *Web:* www.snowjrandking.com	Norfolk	VA	23504	757-627-8621	622-3883
Sun Valley Masonry Inc 10828 N Cave Creek Rd *Web:* www.svmasonry.com	Phoenix	AZ	85020	602-943-6106	997-6857
Treviicos Corp 273 Summer St *Web:* www.treviicos.com	Boston	MA	02210	617-737-1453	737-5810
WASCO Inc 1138 2nd Ave N *TF:* 800-952-8631	Nashville	TN	37208	615-244-9090	726-2643
Western Construction Group 1637 N Warson Rd *TF Cust Svc:* 800-325-2801 ■ *Web:* www.westerngroup.com	Saint Louis	MO	63132	314-427-6733	427-6199

192-8 Painting & Paperhanging Contractors

				Phone	Fax
Ascher Bros Co Inc 3033 W Fletcher St *Web:* www.ascherbrothers.com	Chicago	IL	60618	773-588-0001	588-5350
Avalotis Corp 400 Jones St *Web:* www.avalotis.com	Verona	PA	15147	412-242-5825	828-6599
Benise-Dowling & Assoc Inc 5068 Snapfinger Woods Dr *Web:* www.benise-dowling.com	Decatur	GA	30035	770-981-4237	593-0342
Borbon Inc 7312 Walnut Ave *TF:* 800-929-1467	Buena Park	CA	90620	714-994-0170	994-0641
Brock Services Ltd 1670 E Cardinal Dr *TF:* 800-537-7479	Beaumont	TX	77705	409-833-7571	833-3279
Cannon Sline Industrial Inc 10 Industrial Hwy MS 38 *TF:* 800-729-4600 ■ *Web:* www.cannonsline.com	Lester	PA	19113	610-521-2100	521-2178
CB Askins & Co Inc 208 S Blanding St	Lake City	SC	29560	843-394-8555	394-8333
CertaPro Painters Ltd 150 Green Tree Rd Suite 1003 *TF:* 800-462-3782 ■ *Web:* www.certapro.com	Oaks	PA	19456	610-983-9411	650-9997
E Caligari & Son Inc 1333 Ingleside Rd *Web:* www.ecaligariandson.com	Norfolk	VA	23502	757-853-4511	855-9424
F D Thomas Inc PO Box 4663 *Web:* www.fdthomas.com	Medford	OR	97501	541-664-3010	664-1105
George E Masker Inc 887 71st Ave *Web:* www.maskerpainting.com	Oakland	CA	94621	510-568-1206	638-2530
Goodman Decorating Co 2270 Marietta Blvd NW *Web:* www.goodman-decorating.com	Atlanta	GA	30318	404-965-3626	965-2558
Hartman-Walsh Painting Co 7144 N Market St *TF:* 800-899-3535 ■ *Web:* www.hartmanwalsh.com	Saint Louis	MO	63133	314-863-1800	863-6964
Hess Sweitzer Inc 2805 S 160th St *TF:* 800-491-4377 ■ *Web:* www.hesssweitzer.com	New Berlin	WI	53151	262-641-9100	641-6362
JP Carroll Co Inc 310 N Madison Ave *TF:* 800-660-0162	Los Angeles	CA	90004	323-660-9230	660-9238
K2 Industrial Services 5233 Hohman Ave *Web:* www.k2industrial.com	Hammond	IN	46320	219-933-5300	933-5301
Long Painting Co 21414 68th Ave S *TF:* 800-678-5664 ■ *Web:* www.longpainting.com	Kent	WA	98032	253-234-8050	234-0034
Madias Bros Inc 12850 Evergreen Rd	Detroit	MI	48223	313-272-5330	272-5345
Midwest Pro Painting Inc 12845 Farmington Rd *TF:* 800-860-6757 ■ *Web:* www.mpp-inc.com	Livonia	MI	48150	734-427-1040	427-0209
ML McDonald Co 50 Oakland St PO Box 315 *TF:* 800-733-6243 ■ *Web:* www.mlmcdonald.com	Watertown	MA	02471	617-923-0900	923-0597
National Services Group Inc 1682 Langley Ave *TF:* 800-394-6000 ■ *Web:* www.nationalservicesgroup.com	Irvine	CA	92614	714-564-7900	564-8725
NLP Enterprises Inc 11422 Reisterstown Rd *TF:* 800-962-9380 ■ *Web:* www.nlpentinc.com	Owings Mills	MD	21117	410-356-7500	356-7525
Partition Specialties Inc 714 C St Suite 3 *TF:* 800-982-9255 ■ *Web:* www.partitionspecialties.com	San Rafael	CA	94901	415-721-1040	721-1053
Peter King Corp 11040 N 19th Ave	Phoenix	AZ	85029	602-944-4441	943-4876
Redwood Painting Co Inc 620 W 10th St *TF:* 800-227-0622 ■ *Web:* www.redwoodptg.com	Pittsburg	CA	94565	925-432-4500	432-6129
Specialty Finishes Inc 1545 Marietta Blvd NW *TF:* 800-864-7706 ■ *Web:* www.specialtyfinishes.com	Atlanta	GA	30318	404-351-1062	351-0535
Swanson & Youngdale Inc 6565 W 23rd St *TF:* 800-486-7824 ■ *Web:* www.swansonyoungdale.com	Saint Louis Park	MN	55426	952-545-2541	545-4435
TMI Coatings Inc 3291 Terminal Dr *TF:* 800-328-0229 ■ *Web:* www.tmicoatings.com	Saint Paul	MN	55121	651-452-6100	452-0598
Vulcan Painters Inc 2400 Woodward Rd *Web:* www.vulcan-group.com	Bessemer	AL	35020	205-428-0556	424-2267
Whitehouse-PMC LLC 121 Locus St PO Box 368 *TF:* 800-626-5859 ■ *Web:* www.whitehousepmc.com	Charlestown	IN	47111	812-256-1300	256-1303

192-9 Plastering, Drywall, Acoustical, Insulation Contractors

				Phone	Fax
Acousti Engineering Co of Florida Inc 4656 34th St SW *Web:* www.acousti.com	Orlando	FL	32811	407-425-3467	422-6502
Airtite Contractors Inc 343 W Carol Ln *Web:* www.air-tite.net	Elmhurst	IL	60126	630-530-9001	530-9034
Allied Construction Services & Color Inc 2122 Fleur Dr PO Box 937 *TF:* 800-365-4855 ■ *Web:* www.alliedconst.com	Des Moines	IA	50304	515-288-4855	288-2069
Anning Johnson Co Inc 1959 Anson Dr *Web:* www.anningjohnson.com	Melrose Park	IL	60160	708-681-1300	681-1310
APi Construction Co 1100 Old Hwy 8 NW *TF:* 800-223-4922 ■ *Web:* www.apiconst.com	New Brighton	MN	55112	651-636-4320	604-2822
Baker Drywall Co Inc 415 E Hwy 80 PO Box 38299 *TF:* 800-458-3480 ■ *Web:* www.bakerdrywall.com	Dallas	TX	75238	972-289-5534	289-4580
Bayside Interiors Inc 3220 Darby Common *Web:* www.baysideinteriors.com	Fremont	CA	94539	510-438-9171	438-9375
BHN Corp 435 Madison Ave *TF:* 800-238-9046 ■ *Web:* www.bhncorp.com	Memphis	TN	38103	901-521-9500	521-9507
Bouma Corp 4101 Roger B Chaffee Memorial Blvd SE *TF:* 800-813-9208 ■ *Web:* www.boumacorp.com	Grand Rapids	MI	49548	616-538-3600	538-0143
Burnham Industrial Contractors Inc 3229 Babcock Blvd *Web:* www.burnhamins.com	Pittsburgh	PA	15237	412-366-6622	366-7540
Cannon Constructors Inc 17000 Ventura Blvd Suite 301 *Web:* www.cannongroup.com	Encino	CA	91316	818-906-6200	906-6220
CE Thurston & Sons Inc 3335 Croft St *TF Cust Svc:* 800-444-7713 ■ *Web:* www.cethurston.com	Norfolk	VA	23513	757-855-7700	855-1214
Central Ceilings Inc 36 Norfolk Ave *TF:* 800-442-2115 ■ *Web:* www.centralceilings.com	South Easton	MA	02375	508-238-6985	238-2191
Chempower Inc 1501 Raff Rd SW *TF:* 800-442-4299 ■ *Web:* www.chempower.com	Canton	OH	44710	330-479-4202	479-1866
Circle B Co Inc 5636 S Meridian St *TF:* 800-775-5640	Indianapolis	IN	46217	317-787-5746	780-2654
Circle Group The 1275 Alderman Dr *Web:* www.thecirclegroup.com	Alpharetta	GA	30005	678-356-1000	
Cleveland Construction Inc 8620 Tyler Blvd *Web:* www.clevelandconstruction.com	Mentor	OH	44060	440-255-8000	205-1138
Davenport Insulation Inc 7400 Gateway Ct *TF:* 800-328-9485	Manassas	VA	20109	703-631-7744	631-8730
Daw Technologies Inc 1600 W 2200 S Suite 201 *Web:* www.dawtech.com	Salt Lake City	UT	84119	801-977-3100	973-6640
Drywall Contractors Inc 2920 N Arlington Ave *Web:* www.drywallpartners.com	Indianapolis	IN	46218	317-546-6605	
EL Thompson & Assoc LLC 600 Virginia Ave NE *Web:* www.elta-ga.com	Atlanta	GA	30306	404-872-4726	876-4299
Eliason & Knuth Cos Inc 13324 Chandler Rd *TF:* 800-365-5760 ■ *Web:* www.e-kco.com	Omaha	NE	68138	402-896-1614	896-4058
Entrx Corp 800 Nicollet Mall Suite 2690	Minneapolis	MN	55402	612-333-0614	338-7332
FL Crane & Sons Inc 508 S Spring St PO Box 428 *TF:* 800-748-9523 ■ *Web:* www.flcrane.com	Fulton	MS	38843	662-862-2172	862-2649
Group Builders Inc 2020 Democrat St	Honolulu	HI	96819	808-832-0888	832-0890
Henderson-Johnson Co Inc 918 Canal St PO Box 6964 *Web:* www.henderson-johnson.com	Syracuse	NY	13217	315-479-5561	479-5585
Hoge-Warren-Zimmermann Co 40 W Cresentville Rd *TF:* 800-322-3521	Cincinnati	OH	45246	513-671-3300	671-3514
Interior Construction Services Ltd 2930 Market St *Web:* www.ics-stl.com	Saint Louis	MO	63103	314-534-6664	534-6663
Irex Contracting Group 120 N Lime St *TF:* 800-487-7255 ■ *Web:* www.irexcontracting.com	Lancaster	PA	17608	717-397-3633	399-5135
ISI Insulation Specialties Inc 2142 Rheem Dr Suite A *Web:* www.insulspec.com	Pleasanton	CA	94588	925-846-7990	846-7490
Jacobson & Co Inc 1079 E Grand Ave PO Box 511 *TF:* 800-352-2627 ■ *Web:* www.jacobsoncompany.com	Elizabeth	NJ	07207	908-355-5200	355-8680
KHS & S Contractors Inc 5422 Bay Ctr Dr Suite 200 *Web:* www.khss.com	Tampa	FL	33609	813-628-9330	628-4339
Kramig Insulation 323 S Wayne Ave *TF:* 888-579-0079 ■ *Web:* www.kramiginsulation.com	Cincinnati	OH	45215	513-761-4010	761-0362
Land Coast Insulation Inc 4017 2nd St *TF:* 800-333-9424 ■ *Web:* www.landcoast.com	New Iberia	LA	70560	337-367-7741	367-7744
Lotspeich Co 16101 NW 54th Ave *Web:* www.lotspeich.com	Miami	FL	33014	305-624-7777	624-4517
Luse-Stevenson Co 3990 Enterprise Ct *Web:* www.luse.com	Aurora	IL	60504	630-862-2600	862-2674
M Ecker & Co 9525 W Bryn Mawr Ave Suite 900 *Web:* www.eckerusa.com	Rosemont	IL	60018	847-994-6000	233-9710
Mader Southeast Inc 8150 Presidents Dr *Web:* www.madersoutheast.com	Orlando	FL	32809	407-877-8818	
Manganaro Corp New England 52 Cummings Pk	Woburn	MA	01801	781-937-8880	937-8882
Marek Bros Co 3701 Piney Woods *Web:* www.marekbros.com	Houston	TX	77018	713-681-9213	681-0446

			Phone	Fax
Midwest Drywall Co Inc 1351 S Reca Ct. .... Wichita *TF:* 888-722-9559 ■ *Web:* www.mwdw.com	KS	67209	316-722-9559	722-9682
ML McDonald Co 50 Oakland St PO Box 315 .... Watertown *TF:* 800-733-6243 ■ *Web:* www.mlmcdonald.com	MA	02471	617-923-0900	923-0597
Nastasi & Assoc Inc 147 Herricks Rd .... Garden City Park *TF:* 800-353-0990	NY	11040	516-746-1800	746-6796
National Acoustics Inc 515 W 36th St .... New York	NY	10018	212-695-1252	695-4539
National Construction Enterprises Inc 5075 Carpenter Rd .... Ypsilanti *Web:* www.nceusa.com	MI	48197	734-434-1600	434-6699
Niehaus Construction Services Inc 4151 Sarpy Ave. .... Saint Louis *Web:* www.ncs-stl.com	MO	63110	314-533-8434	533-1448
P & P Contractors Inc 19544 Amaranth Dr .... Germantown *Web:* www.pandpcontractors.com	MD	20874	301-251-6750	251-6777
Padilla Construction Co 1605 N O'Donnell Way .... Orange	CA	92867	714-685-8500	685-8500
Partition Specialties Inc 714 C St Suite 3 .... San Rafael *TF:* 800-982-9255 ■ *Web:* www.partitionspecialties.com	CA	94901	415-721-1040	721-1053
Paul J Krez Co 7831 N Nagle Ave .... Morton Grove *Web:* www.krezgroup.com	IL	60053	847-581-0017	965-7841
Precision Walls Inc 1230 NE Maynard Rd .... Cary *TF:* 800-849-9255 ■ *Web:* www.precisionwalls.com	NC	27513	919-832-0380	839-1402
Professional Construction Services Inc PO Box 2005 .... Prairieville *TF:* 800-562-4318 ■ *Web:* www.professionalconstruction.com	LA	70769	225-744-4016	744-4938
Shields Inc 2625 Hope Church Rd .... Winston-Salem *Web:* www.shieldsinc.com	NC	27103	336-765-9040	765-3715
South Valley Drywall Inc 12362 Dumont Way .... Littleton *Web:* www.southvalleydrywall.com	CO	80125	303-791-7212	470-0116
Spectrum Interiors Inc 2652 Crescent Springs Rd .... Crescent Springs *TF:* 888-353-2696 ■ *Web:* www.spectruminterior.com	KY	41017	859-331-2696	331-4322
SSI Services LLC 308 S State Ave .... Indianapolis *Web:* www.ssiweb.com	IN	46201	317-269-2120	269-3608
Tailored Foam Inc PO Box 4186 .... Hickory *TF:* 800-627-1687 ■ *Web:* www.core-fill500.com	NC	28603	828-322-6515	322-7688
Thorne Assoc Inc 1450 W Randolph St .... Chicago *Web:* www.thorneassociates.com	IL	60607	312-738-5230	738-5249
TJ McCartney Inc 3 Capitol St Suite 1 .... Nashua *TF:* 800-889-6380 ■ *Web:* www.tjminc.com	NH	03063	603-889-6380	880-0770
Turner-Brooks Inc 28811 John R Rd .... Madison Heights *TF:* 800-560-7003	MI	48071	248-548-3400	548-9213
United/Anco Industries Inc 16055 Airline Hwy .... Baton Rouge *TF:* 800-999-8479 ■ *Web:* www.unitedanco.com	LA	70817	225-752-2000	756-7686
Waco Inc 5450 Lewis Rd PO Box 829 .... Sandston *Web:* www.wacoinc.net	VA	23150	804-222-8440	226-3241
Walldesign Inc 2350 SE Bristol St .... Newport Beach *Web:* www.walldesigninc.com	CA	92660	949-474-0285	251-9960
Western Partitions Inc 8300 SW Hunziker Rd .... Tigard *Web:* www.westernpartitions.com	OR	97223	503-620-1600	624-5781
Wyatt Inc 4545 Campbells Run Rd .... Pittsburgh *TF:* 800-966-5801 ■ *Web:* www.wyattinc.com	PA	15205	412-787-5800	787-5845

192-10 Plumbing, Heating, Air Conditioning Contractors

			Phone	Fax
AC Corp 301 Creek Ridge Rd. .... Greensboro *TF:* 800-582-3073 ■ *Web:* www.accorporation.com	NC	27406	336-273-4472	274-6035
ACCO Engineered Systems 6265 San Fernando Rd. .... Glendale *TF Cust Svc:* 800-998-2226 ■ *Web:* www.accoair.com	CA	91201	818-244-6571	247-6533
AD Jacobson Co Inc 16210 W 108th St .... Lenexa	KS	66219	913-529-5000	529-5020
Advance Mechanical Contractors Inc 1456 E Hill St .... Signal Hill	CA	90755	562-426-1725	424-7251
Advance Mechanical Systems Inc 2080 S Carboy Rd .... Mount Prospect *Web:* www.jfahern.com	IL	60056	847-593-2510	593-2536
Air Comfort Corp 2550 Braga Dr. .... Broadview *TF:* 800-466-3779 ■ *Web:* www.aircomfort.com	IL	60155	708-345-1900	345-2730
Air Con Refrigeration & Heating Inc 123 Lake St. .... Waukegan	IL	60085	847-336-4128	336-4949
Air Engineering Co Inc 2308 Pahounui Dr. .... Honolulu	HI	96819	808-848-1040	841-5193
Aire Serv Heating & Air Conditioning Inc 1020 N University Parks Dr .... Waco **Fax Area Code:* 254 ■ *TF:* 800-583-2662 ■ *Web:* www.aireserv.com	TX	76707	800-583-2662	745-5098*
Airtrol Inc 3960 N St .... Baton Rouge	LA	70806	225-383-2617	343-7986
Alaka'i Mechanical Corp 2655 Waiwai Loop .... Honolulu *TF:* 800-600-1085 ■ *Web:* www.alakaimechanical.com	HI	96819	808-834-1085	834-1800
Aldag Honold Mechanical Inc 3509 S Business Dr .... Sheboygan *TF:* 800-967-1712 ■ *Web:* www.aldaghonold.com	WI	53082	920-458-5558	458-3750
Allied Fire Protection LP PO Box 2842 .... Pearland *TF:* 800-604-2600 ■ *Web:* www.alliedfireprotection.com	TX	77588	281-485-6803	412-9668
Allied Mechanical Services Inc 5688 E MI Ave # A .... Kalamazoo *TF:* 888-237-3017 ■ *Web:* www.alliedmechanical.com	MI	49048	269-344-0191	344-0196
Althoff Industries Inc 8001 S Rt 31 .... Crystal Lake **Fax:* Sales ■ *TF:* 800-225-2443 ■ *Web:* www.althoffind.com	IL	60014	815-455-7000	455-9375*
American Leak Detection 888 Research Dr Suite 100 .... Palm Springs *TF:* 800-755-6697 ■ *Web:* www.americanleakdetection.com	CA	92262	760-320-9991	320-1288
American Mechanical Services 13300 Mid Atlantic Blvd .... Laurel *TF:* 888-805-4267 ■ *Web:* www.amsofusa.com	MD	20708	301-206-5070	206-2520
American Residential Services LLC 9010 Maier Rd Suite 105 .... Laurel *TF:* 800-822-7332 ■ *Web:* www.ars.com	MD	20723	301-470-1212	470-3724
Anderson Rowe & Buckley Inc 2833 3rd St. .... San Francisco	CA	94107	415-282-1625	282-0752
Anron Heating & Air Conditioning Inc 440 Wyandanch Ave .... North Babylon *TF:* 800-924-3336	NY	11704	631-643-3433	491-6983
Anthony Mechanical Inc 525 E 40th St .... Lubbock	TX	79404	806-747-4151	747-7733
AO Reed & Co 4777 Ruffner St. .... San Diego *Web:* www.aoreed.com	CA	92111	858-565-4131	292-6958
Arden Engineering Constructors LLC 505 Narragansett Pk Dr. .... Pawtucket *Web:* www.ardeneng.com	RI	02861	401-727-3500	727-3540
Armistead Mechanical Inc 168 Hopper Ave. .... Waldwick *Web:* www.armisteadmechanical.com	NJ	07463	201-447-6740	447-6744
Armon Inc 2265 Carlson Dr .... Northbrook *Web:* www.femoran.com	IL	60062	847-498-4800	498-9091
Atlantic Constructors Inc 3800 Deepwater Terminal Rd .... Richmond *Web:* www.atlanticconstructors.com	VA	23234	804-233-7671	233-5970
Atlas Comfort Systems USA LP 4133 Southerland Rd .... Houston *TF:* 800-460-9973 ■ *Web:* www.atlas-air.com	TX	77092	713-460-7300	460-7301
Atlas Welding & Boiler Repair 2960 Webster Ave .... Bronx *TF:* 800-476-0556	NY	10458	718-365-6600	367-5658
August Arace & Sons Inc 642 3rd Ave .... Elizabeth *Web:* www.augustarace.com	NJ	07202	908-354-1626	354-9124
Azco Inc PO Box 567 .... Appleton *Web:* www.azco-inc.com	WI	54912	920-734-5791	734-7432
B & I Contractors Inc 2701 Prince St .... Fort Myers *Web:* www.bandicontractors.com	FL	33916	239-332-4646	332-5928
B-G Mechanical Service Inc 12 2nd Ave .... Chicopee *TF:* 800-992-7386 ■ *Web:* www.bgmechanical.com	MA	01020	413-888-1500	594-2983
Baker Group 4224 Hubbell Ave .... Des Moines *TF:* 800-262-5565 ■ *Web:* www.thebakergroup.com	IA	50317	515-262-4000	266-1025
Bay Mechanical Inc 2696 Reliance Dr Suite 200 .... Virginia Beach *TF:* 888-229-6324 ■ *Web:* www.baymechanical.com	VA	23452	757-468-6700	468-0377
Bch Mechanical Inc 6354 118th Ave N .... Largo *Web:* www.bchmechanical.com	FL	33773	727-546-3561	545-1801
Berg Inc 531 W 61st St. .... Shreveport *Web:* www.bergind.com	LA	71106	318-868-8884	868-7408
Bernhard Mechanical Contractors Inc 10321 Airline Hwy .... Baton Rouge *TF:* 888-773-2791 ■ *Web:* www.bernhardmechanical.com	LA	70816	225-293-2791	296-0931
Beutler Air Conditioning Service 1961 Optisolar Ln .... McClellan *TF:* 800-238-8537 ■ *Web:* www.beutler.com	CA	95652	916-646-2222	646-2200
BMW Constructors Inc 1740 W Michigan St. .... Indianapolis *Web:* www.bmwcnstrs.com	IN	46222	317-267-0400	267-0572
Bogot Cos 8137 Austin Ave .... Morton Grove *Web:* www.bogot.com	IL	60053	847-965-8800	965-8805
Bolton Corp 919 W Morgan St. .... Raleigh *TF:* 800-438-1098	NC	27603	919-828-9021	828-8574
Boone & Darr Inc PO Box 1718 .... Ann Arbor *Web:* www.boone-darr.com	MI	48106	734-665-0648	665-9731
Bosch Mechanical Contractors Inc 3325 Three-Mile Rd NW .... Grand Rapids *Web:* www.boschmechanical.com	MI	49534	616-453-5483	453-7111
Brandt Engineering Co Inc 11245 Indian Trail .... Dallas *Web:* www.brandteng.com	TX	75229	972-241-9411	484-6013
Brewer-Garrett Co (inc) 6800 Eastland Rd .... Cleveland *Web:* www.brewer-garrett.com	OH	44130	440-243-3535	243-9993
Brown Sprinkler Corp 4705 Pinewood Rd .... Louisville *Web:* www.brownsprinkler.com	KY	40218	502-968-6274	968-6278
Butters-Fetting Co Inc 1669 S 1st St .... Milwaukee *Web:* www.buttersfetting.com	WI	53204	414-645-1535	645-7622
C & R Mechanical 12825 Pennridge Dr .... Bridgeton *TF:* 800-233-3828 ■ *Web:* www.crmechanical.com	MO	63044	314-739-1800	739-1721
Calvert-Jones Co Inc 5703 Edsall Rd .... Alexandria *Web:* www.calvertjones.com	VA	22304	703-370-5850	370-6515
Campito Plumbing & Heating Inc 3 Hemlock St .... Latham	NY	12110	518-785-0994	785-0769
CCI Mechanical Inc 758 S Redwood Rd .... Salt Lake City *TF:* 800-521-7600 ■ *Web:* www.ccimech.com	UT	84104	801-973-9000	975-7204
Central Air Conditioning Inc 3435 W Harry St. .... Wichita *Web:* www.centralairco.com	KS	67213	316-945-0797	945-3174
Central Mechanical Construction Co Inc 631 Pecan Cir. .... Manhattan *TF:* 800-631-6999 ■ *Web:* www.centralmechanical.com	KS	66502	785-537-2437	537-2491
Champion Industrial Contractors Inc 1420 Coldwell Ave .... Modesto *Web:* www.championindustrial.com	CA	95350	209-524-6601	524-6931
Chapman Corp 331 S Main St .... Washington *Web:* www.chapmancorporation.com	PA	15301	724-228-1900	228-4311
Charles P. Blouin Inc 203 New Zealand Rd .... Seabrook *Web:* www.cpblouin.com	NH	03874	603-474-3400	474-7118
Chas Roberts Heating & Air Conditioning Inc 9828 N 19th Ave .... Phoenix *Web:* www.chasroberts.com	AZ	85021	602-331-2686	997-0068
Christianson Air Conditioning & Plumbing 1950 Louis Henna Blvd .... Round Rock *Web:* www.christiansonco.com	TX	78664	512-246-5200	246-5201
Cinfab Mechanical Inc 5240 Lester Rd. .... Cincinnati *Web:* www.cinfab.com	OH	45213	513-396-6100	396-7574
Coastal Mechanical Services LLC 394 E Dr .... Melbourne *TF:* 800-391-5757 ■ *Web:* www.coastalmechanical.com	FL	32904	321-725-3061	984-0718
Cobb Mechanical Contractors Inc PO Box 6729 .... Colorado Springs *TF:* 800-808-2622 ■ *Web:* www.cobbmechanical.com	CO	80934	719-471-8958	389-0127
ColonialWebb Contractors Co 2820 Ackley Ave ...... Richmond *TF:* 800-849-5504 ■ *Web:* www.colonialwebb.com	VA	23228	804-916-1400	264-5083
Comfort Engineers Inc 4008 Comfort Ln. .... Durham *Web:* www.comfortengineers.com	NC	27705	919-383-2502	383-2507
Comfort Group Inc The 659 Thompson Ln .... Nashville *Web:* www.thecomfortgroup.com	TN	37204	615-263-2900	263-2939
Comfort Systems USA 6875 W Galveston St .... Chandler *Web:* www.tricitymechanical.com	AZ	85226	480-940-8400	961-7201

Company	City	State	Zip	Phone	Fax
Comfort Systems USA Inc 675 Bering Suite 400	Houston	TX	77057	713-830-9600	830-9696
NYSE: FIX ■ *TF:* 800-723-8431 ■ *Web:* www.comfortsystemsusa.com					
Corrigan Co 3545 Gratiot St	Saint Louis	MO	63103	314-771-6200	771-8537
Web: www.corriganco.com					
Cox Engineering Co 35 Industrial Dr	Canton	MA	02021	781-302-3300	302-3444
TF: 800-538-0027					
Critchfield Mechanical Inc 1901 Junction Ave	San Jose	CA	95131	408-437-7000	437-7199
Web: www.cmihvac.com					
Cullum Mechanical Construction Inc 3325 Pacific Ave	North Charleston	SC	29418	843-554-6645	747-9964
Web: www.culluminc.com					
Dauenhauer & Son Plumbing & Piping Co Inc 3416 Robards Ct	Louisville	KY	40218	502-451-2233	558-8139
Web: www.dauenhauerplumbing.com					
DeBra-Kuempel 3976 Southern Ave	Cincinnati	OH	45227	513-271-6500	271-4676
TF: 800-395-5741 ■ *Web:* www.debra-kuempel.com					
Dmi Corp PO Box 53	Cedar Hill	TX	75106	972-291-9907	299-6437
Web: www.deckermechanical.com					
Doody Mechanical Inc 1301 L'Orient St	Saint Paul	MN	55117	651-487-1061	487-2637
Web: www.doody-united.com					
Dorvin D Leis Co Inc 202 Lalo St	Kahului	HI	96732	808-877-3902	877-5168
Web: www.leisinc.com					
Downey Inc 2203 W Michigan St	Milwaukee	WI	53233	414-933-3123	933-1552
Web: www.downeyinc.com					
Dunbar Mechanical Inc 2806 N Reynolds Rd	Toledo	OH	43615	419-537-1900	537-8840
TF: 800-719-2201 ■ *Web:* www.dunbarmechanical.com					
Dupree Plumbing Co Inc 869 Worley Dr	Marietta	GA	30066	770-428-2291	
Web: www.dupreeplumbing.com					
Egan Cos Inc 7625 Boone Ave N	Brooklyn Park	MN	55428	763-544-4131	591-5532
TF: 800-275-3426 ■ *Web:* www.eganco.com					
EM Duggan Inc 140 Will Dr	Canton	MA	02021	781-828-2292	828-0991
EMCOR Group Inc 301 Merritt 7 6th Fl	Norwalk	CT	06851	203-849-7800	849-7900
NYSE: EME ■ *TF:* 866-890-7794 ■ *Web:* www.emcorgroup.com					
Engineering & Refrigeration Inc 56 Baldwin Ave	Jersey City	NJ	07306	201-333-4200	333-3051
TF Cust Svc: 800-631-3000					
EW Tompkins Co Inc 126 Sheridan Ave	Albany	NY	12210	518-462-6577	462-6570
Web: www.thetompkinsgroup.com					
Fagan Co 3125 Brinkerhoff Rd	Kansas City	KS	66115	913-621-4444	621-3626
TF: 800-966-1178 ■ *Web:* www.faganco.com					
Farmer & Irwin Corp 3300 Ave K	Riviera Beach	FL	33404	561-842-5316	842-5999
TF: 800-883-8229 ■ *Web:* www.fandicorp.com					
FE Moran Inc 2265 Carlson Dr	Northbrook	IL	60062	847-498-4800	498-9091
Web: www.femoran.com					
Ferran Services & Contracting 525 Indiana St	Orlando	FL	32805	407-422-3551	648-0961
Web: www.ferran-services.com					
Fisher Container Corp 1111 Busch Pkwy	Buffalo Grove	IL	60089	847-541-0000	541-0075
TF: 800-837-2247 ■ *Web:* www.fishercontainer.com					
Fitzgerald Contractors Inc PO Box 6600	Shreveport	LA	71136	318-869-3262	865-9640
Web: www.fitzgeraldcontractors.com					
Fountain Construction Co 5655 Hwy 18 W	Jackson	MS	39209	601-373-4162	373-4300
Web: www.fountainconstruction.com					
Fox Service Co PO Box 19047	Austin	TX	78760	512-442-6782	
TF: 866-668-4749 ■ *Web:* www.foxservice.com					
Frank Lill & Son Inc 656 Basket Rd	Webster	NY	14580	585-265-0490	265-1842
TF: 800-756-0490 ■ *Web:* www.franklillandson.com					
Frank M Booth Inc 222 3rd St	Marysville	CA	95901	530-742-7134	742-8109
TF: 800-540-9369 ■ *Web:* www.frankbooth.com					
Fujikawa Assoc 2146 Puuhale Pl	Honolulu	HI	96819	808-845-5936	846-4218
Web: www.contmech.com					
FW Spencer & Son Inc 99 S Hill Dr	Brisbane	CA	94005	415-468-5000	468-4579
Web: www.fwspencersoninc.com					
Gay WW Mechanical Contractor Inc 524 Stockton St	Jacksonville	FL	32204	904-388-2696	389-4901
Web: www.wwgmc.com					
GEM Industrial Inc 6842 Commodore Dr	Walbridge	OH	43465	419-666-6554	666-7004
TF: 800-837-5909 ■ *Web:* www.gemindustrial.com					
George H Wilson Inc 250 Harvey W Blvd	Santa Cruz	CA	95060	831-423-9522	423-9903
GF Connelly Mechanical Contractors Inc 2515 S Wabash Ave	Chicago	IL	60616	312-326-4100	326-3780
Gillette Air Conditioning Co Inc 1215 San Francisco	San Antonio	TX	78201	210-735-9235	736-1932
Web: www.gillette-ac.com					
Gowan Inc 5550 Airline Dr	Houston	TX	77076	713-696-5400	695-1726
TF: 888-724-6926 ■ *Web:* www.gowaninc.com					
Goyette Mechanical Co 3842 Gorey Ave	Flint	MI	48501	810-743-6883	743-9090
TF: 877-469-3883 ■ *Web:* www.goyettemechanical.com					
GR Sponaugle & Sons Inc 4391 Chambers Hill Rd	Harrisburg	PA	17111	717-564-1515	564-3675
TF: 800-866-7036 ■ *Web:* www.grsponaugle.com					
Griesemer RE Inc 440 S Hancock St	Indianapolis	IN	46222	317-638-4344	264-1165
Griffith ID Inc 735 S Market St	Wilmington	DE	19801	302-656-8253	656-8268
Web: www.idgriffith.com					
Gross Mechanical Contractors Inc 7525 Sussex Ave	Saint Louis	MO	63143	314-645-0077	645-0098
TF: 800-641-0071 ■ *Web:* www.grossmechanical.com					
Grunau Co Inc 1100 W Anderson Ct	Oak Creek	WI	53154	414-216-6900	768-7950
TF: 800-365-1920 ■ *Web:* www.grunau.com					
Gulf States Inc 6711 E Hwy 332	Freeport	TX	77541	979-233-5555	233-3050
TF: 800-231-9849					
H & H Group Inc 2801 Syene Rd	Madison	WI	53713	608-273-3434	273-9654
Web: www.h-hgroup.com					
HACI Mechanical Contractors Inc 2108 W Shangri La Rd	Phoenix	AZ	85029	602-944-1555	678-0266
Web: www.hacimechanical.com					
Hampshire Fire Protection Co Inc 8 N Wentworth Ave	Londonderry	NH	03053	603-432-8221	
Web: www.hampshirefire.com					
Hansen Mechanical Contractors Inc 6325 S Valley View Blvd	Las Vegas	NV	89118	702-361-5111	361-6753
Har-Con Corp 9009 W Little York Rd	Houston	TX	77040	713-869-8451	864-1837
TF: 800-438-0536 ■ *Web:* www.har-con.com					
Harder Mechanical Contractors Inc 2148 NE M L King Blvd	Portland	OR	97212	503-281-1112	287-5284
TF: 800-392-3729 ■ *Web:* www.hardercompanies.com					
Hardy Corp 430 12th St S	Birmingham	AL	35233	205-252-7191	326-6268
TF: 800-289-4822 ■ *Web:* www.hardycorp.com					
Harold G Butzer Inc 730 Wicker Ln	Jefferson City	MO	65109	573-636-4115	636-7053
Harris Mechanical Contracting Co 909 Montreal Cir	Saint Paul	MN	55102	651-602-6500	602-6699
Harry Grodsky & Co Inc 33 Shaws Ln	Springfield	MA	01104	413-785-1947	737-9870
Web: www.grodsky.com					
HE Neumann Inc 2100 Middle Creek Rd	Triadelphia	WV	26059	304-232-3040	232-7858
TF: 800-627-5312 ■ *Web:* www.heneumann.com					
Heating & Plumbing Engineers Inc 407 Fillmore Pl	Colorado Springs	CO	80907	719-633-5414	633-4031
TF: 800-530-8592 ■ *Web:* www.hpeinc.com					
Heide & Cook Ltd 1714 Kanakanui St	Honolulu	HI	96819	808-841-6161	841-4889
Web: www.heide-cook.com					
Heritage Mechanical Services Inc 305 Suburban Ave	Deer Park	NY	11729	631-667-1044	667-8613
TF: 800-734-0384 ■ *Web:* www.heritagemech.com					
Herman Goldner Co Inc 7777 Brewster Ave	Philadelphia	PA	19153	215-365-5400	492-6274
TF: 800-355-5997 ■ *Web:* www.goldner.com					
Herre Bros Inc 4417 Valley Rd	Enola	PA	17025	717-732-4454	732-8208
Web: www.herrebros.com					
High Purity Systems Inc 8432 Quarry Rd	Manassas	VA	20110	703-330-5094	
Web: www.highpurity.com					
Hill Mechanical Group 11045 Gage Ave	Franklin Park	IL	60131	847-451-5000	451-5011
Web: www.hillmech.com					
Hill York Corp 2125 S Andrews Ave	Fort Lauderdale	FL	33316	954-525-2971	525-2973
TF: 800-777-2971 ■ *Web:* www.hillyork.com					
HiMEC Mechanical 1400 7th St NW	Rochester	MN	55901	507-281-4000	281-5206
TF: 888-454-4632 ■ *Web:* www.himec.com					
Hoffman Corp 805 SW Broadway Suite 2100	Portland	OR	97205	503-221-8811	221-8934
Web: www.hoffmancorp.com					
Holaday-Parks Inc 4600 S 134 Pl PO Box 69208	Seattle	WA	98168	206-248-9700	248-8700
Web: www.holadayparks.com					
Hooper Corp 2030 Pennsylvania Ave	Madison	WI	53704	608-249-0451	249-7360
TF: 800-999-0451 ■ *Web:* www.hoopercorp.com					
Horwitz/NSI 4401 Quebec Ave N	New Hope	MN	55428	763-533-1900	235-9810
Web: www.horwitzinc.com					
Hubbard & Drake General Mechanical Contractors Inc PO Box 1867	Decatur	AL	35602	256-353-9244	350-5043
TF: 800-353-9245 ■ *Web:* www.hubbarddrake.com					
Humphrey Co Ltd 4439 W 12th St	Houston	TX	77055	713-686-8606	686-7619
Web: www.humphreyltd.com					
Hurckman Mechanical Industries Inc PO Box 10977	Green Bay	WI	54307	920-499-8771	499-6769
Web: www.hurckman.com					
IHP Industrial Inc 1701 S 8th St	Saint Joseph	MO	64503	816-364-1581	232-4473
IMCOR-Interstate Mechanical Corp 1841 E Washington St	Phoenix	AZ	85034	602-257-1319	271-0674
TF: 800-628-0211 ■ *Web:* www.imcor-az.com					
Independent Mechanical Industries Inc 4155 N Knox Ave	Chicago	IL	60641	773-282-4500	282-2046
Web: www.independentmech.com					
Industrial Air Inc 428 Edwardia Dr PO Box 8769	Greensboro	NC	27419	336-292-1030	855-7763
Web: www.industrialairinc.com					
Industrial Contractors Inc 701 Ch Dr	Bismarck	ND	58501	701-258-9908	258-9988
Web: www.icinorthdakota.com					
Industrial Piping & Engineering Corp 2215 Meyer Rd	Fort Wayne	IN	46803	260-422-8402	426-0441
TF: 800-422-8405 ■ *Web:* www.ipecorp.net					
Industrial Piping Inc 800 Culp Rd	Pineville	NC	28134	704-588-1100	588-5614
TF: 800-951-0988 ■ *Web:* www.goipi.com					
Interstate Mechanical Contractors Inc 3200 Henson Rd	Knoxville	TN	37921	865-588-0180	602-4124
TF: 800-556-7072 ■ *Web:* www.interstatemechanical.com					
Jackson & Blanc Inc 7929 Arjons Dr	San Diego	CA	92126	858-831-7900	527-1502
TF: 800-236-1121 ■ *Web:* www.jacksonandblanc.com					
Jamar Co 4701 Mike Colalillo Dr	Duluth	MN	55807	218-628-1027	628-1174
Web: www.jamarcompany.com					
James Craft & Son Inc 2780 York Haven Rd PO Box 8	York Haven	PA	17370	717-266-6629	266-6623
TF: 800-673-2519 ■ *Web:* www.jamescraftson.com					
Janazzo Services Corp 140 Norton St Rt 10 PO Box 469	Milldale	CT	06467	860-621-7381	621-7529
Web: www.janazzo.com					
JC Higgins Corp 70 Hawes Way	Stoughton	MA	02072	781-341-1500	344-6075
Web: www.jchigginscorp.com					
JF Ahern Co 855 Morris St	Fond du Lac	WI	54935	920-921-9020	921-8632
TF: 800-532-0155 ■ *Web:* www.jfahern.com					
JH Kelly 821 3rd Ave	Longview	WA	98632	360-423-5510	423-9170
Web: www.jhkelly.com					
John Bouchard & Sons Co 1024 Harrison St	Nashville	TN	37203	615-256-0112	256-2427
TF: 800-842-9156 ■ *Web:* www.jbouchard.com					
John E Green Co 220 Victor Ave	Highland Park	MI	48203	313-868-2400	868-0011
Web: www.johnegreen.com					
John W Danforth Co 300 Colvin Woods Pkwy	Tonawanda	NY	14150	716-832-1940	832-2388
TF: 800-888-6119 ■ *Web:* www.jwdanforth.com					
Johnson Contracting Co Inc 2750 Morton Dr	East Moline	IL	61244	309-755-0601	752-7056
Web: www.jccinc.com					
Johnson Controls Inc 12393 Slauson Ave	Whittier	CA	90606	562-698-8301	693-4375
TF: 800-222-5247 ■ *Web:* www.johnsoncontrols.com					
Kaelber Co 2925 61st St	Kenosha	WI	53143	262-654-3589	654-2730
Kinetics Systems Inc 26055 SW Canyon Creek Rd	Wilsonville	OR	97070	503-224-5200	224-8521
TF: 800-888-7597 ■ *Web:* www.kineticsgroup.com					

Company / Address	City	State	ZIP	Phone	Fax
Kuhlman Inc N 56 W 16865 Ridgewood Dr	Menomonee Falls	WI	53051	262-252-9400	252-9401
TF: 800-781-9229 ■ *Web:* www.kuhlmaninc.com					
Lawman Heating & Cooling Inc PO Box 599	Sackets Harbor	NY	13685	315-646-2919	
Web: www.lawmanhc.com					
Lawson Mechanical Contractors 6090 S Watt Ave	Sacramento	CA	95829	916-381-5000	381-5073
Web: www.lawsonmechanical.com					
Lee Co Inc 331 Mallory Stn Rd	Franklin	TN	37067	615-567-1000	567-1027
TF: 888-567-7747 ■ *Web:* www.leecompany.com					
Limbach Facility Services LLC 31 35th St	Pittsburgh	PA	15201	412-359-2200	359-2235
Web: www.limbachinc.com					
Linc Mechanical LLC 37695 Interchange Dr	Farmington Hills	MI	48335	248-471-0600	442-6219
Lutz Frey Corp 1195 Ivy Dr	Lancaster	PA	17601	717-394-4635	898-3421
TF: 800-280-6794 ■ *Web:* www.freylutz.com					
MacDonald-Miller Facility Solutions Inc 7717 Detroit Ave SE	Seattle	WA	98106	206-763-9400	767-6773
TF: 800-962-5979 ■ *Web:* www.macmiller.com					
Mallory & Evans Inc 646 Kentucky St	Scottdale	GA	30079	404-297-1000	297-1075
Web: www.malloryandevans.com					
Martin Petersen Co Inc 9800 55th St	Kenosha	WI	53144	262-658-1326	658-1048
TF: 800-677-1326 ■ *Web:* www.martin-petersen.com					
Masters Inc 7891 Beechcraft Ave	Gaithersburg	MD	20879	301-948-8950	258-7368
TF: 800-257-2871					
McCarl's Inc 1413 9th Ave	Beaver Falls	PA	15010	724-843-5660	843-3180
TF: 800-643-5660 ■ *Web:* www.mccarl.com					
McClure Co 4101 N 6th St	Harrisburg	PA	17110	717-232-9743	236-5239
TF: 800-382-1319 ■ *Web:* www.mcclureco.com					
McCrea Equipment Co Inc 4463 Beech Rd	Temple Hills	MD	20748	301-423-4585	899-9476
TF: 800-597-0091 ■ *Web:* www.mccreaway.com					
McKenney's Inc 1056 Moreland Industrial Blvd SE	Atlanta	GA	30316	404-622-5000	624-8665
TF: 800-489-5000 ■ *Web:* www.mckenneys.com					
McKinstry Co 5005 3rd Ave S	Seattle	WA	98134	206-762-3311	768-7741
TF: 800-669-6223 ■ *Web:* www.mckinstry.com					
McNutt Service Group Inc 110 Vista Blvd	Arden	NC	28704	828-693-0933	
Web: www.mcnuttservicegroup.com					
Meccon Industries Inc 2703 Bernice Rd	Lansing	IL	60438	708-474-8300	474-9550
Web: www.meccon.com					
Mechanical Construction Co LLC 3001 17th St	Metairie	LA	70002	504-833-8291	831-4760
Web: www.mccgroup.com					
Mechanical Inc 2279 Rt 20 E	Freeport	IL	61032	815-962-8050	235-1940
TF: 800-747-1955 ■ *Web:* www.helmgroup.com					
Merit Electrical Inc 17723 Airline Hwy	Prairieville	LA	70769	225-673-8850	673-8838
Web: www.merit-electrical.com					
Metropolitan Mechanical Contractors Inc 7340 Washington Ave S	Eden Prairie	MN	55344	952-941-7010	941-9118
Web: www.metromech.com					
Mid-State Contracting LLC 2001 County Hwy U	Wausau	WI	54402	715-675-2388	675-6971
TF: 866-644-6722 ■ *Web:* www.midstatecontracting.com					
Midwest Mechanical Group 540 Executive Dr	Willowbrook	IL	60527	630-655-4200	655-4201
TF Svc: 800-600-4047 ■ *Web:* www.midwestmech.com					
Miller Engineering Co 1616 S Main St	Rockford	IL	61102	815-963-4878	963-0823
Miscor Group Ltd 800 Nave Rd SE	Massillon	OH	44646	574-234-8131	232-7648
PINK: MIGL ■ *Web:* www.miscor.com					
MJ Flaherty Co 1 Gateway Ctr Suite 450	Newton	MA	02458	617-969-1492	964-0176
TF: 800-370-2280 ■ *Web:* www.mjflaherty-hvac.com					
MMC Corp 10955 Lowell Suite 350	Overland Park	KS	66210	913-469-0101	469-8780
Mock Plumbing & Mechanical Inc PO Box 22456	Savannah	GA	31403	912-232-1104	232-6284
Web: www.mocksavannah.com					
Modern Piping Inc 210 33rd St Dr SE	Cedar Rapids	IA	52403	319-364-0131	364-8368
Web: www.modernpiping.com					
Mollenberg-Betz Inc 300 Scott St	Buffalo	NY	14204	716-614-7473	614-7465
TF: 800-368-4998 ■ *Web:* www.mollenbergbetz.com					
Monterey Mechanical Co 8275 San Leandro St	Oakland	CA	94621	510-632-3173	632-0732
Web: www.montmech.com					
Moore J & Co 118 Naylon Ave	Livingston	NJ	07039	973-992-6970	992-8860
TF: 877-456-6673 ■ *Web:* www.jmoore.com					
Morrison Construction Co 1834 Summer St	Hammond	IN	46320	219-932-5036	933-7302
Web: www.morrisonconst.com					
Mr Rooter Corp 1010 N University Parks Dr	Waco	TX	76707	800-583-8003	745-2501*
*Fax Area Code: 254 ■ *TF:* 800-583-8003 ■ *Web:* www.mrrooter.com					
Murphy & Miller Inc 600 W Taylor St	Chicago	IL	60607	312-427-8900	427-0324
Web: www.murphymiller.com					
Murphy Co Mechanical Contractors & Engineers 1233 N Price Rd	Saint Louis	MO	63132	314-997-6600	997-4536
TF: 800-992-6601 ■ *Web:* www.murphynet.com					
MYR Group 1701 W Golf Rd Tower 3 Suite 1012	Rolling Meadows	IL	60008	847-290-1891	290-1892
Web: www.myrgroup.com					
Nagelbush Mechanical Inc 1800 NW 49th St Suite 110	Fort Lauderdale	FL	33309	954-736-3000	748-7881
TF: 800-354-3111 ■ *Web:* www.nagelbush.com					
New England Insulation Co 55 N St	Canton	MA	02021	781-828-6600	828-6749
TF: 800-346-6307					
NewMech Cos Inc 1633 Eustis St	Saint Paul	MN	55108	651-645-0451	642-5591
TF: 800-942-4444 ■ *Web:* www.newmech.com					
Nitro Electric Co LLC 500 Corporate Ctr Dr 2nd Fl Suite 520	Scott Depot	WV	25560	304-722-7701	757-1213*
*Fax: Acctg ■ *Web:* www.nitro-electric.com					
Northern Peabody LLC 25 Depot St	Manchester	NH	03101	603-669-3601	669-2285
NV Heathorn Co 1155 Beecher St	San Leandro	CA	94577	510-569-9100	569-9106
Web: www.nvheathorn.com					
P1 Group Inc 2151 Haskell Ave Bldg 1	Lawrence	KS	66046	785-843-2910	843-2884
TF: 800-376-2911 ■ *Web:* www.p1group.com					
Pace Mechanical Services Inc 301 Merritt Seven	Norwalk	CT	06851	203-849-7800	849-7900
TF: 866-890-7794 ■ *Web:* www.emcorgroup.com					
Pacific Mechanical Corp 2501 Anna Lisa Dr	Concord	CA	94520	925-827-4940	827-0519
TF: 800-362-2202					
Palmer & Sicard Inc 140 Epping Rd	Exeter	NH	03833	603-778-1841	778-0119
Par Plumbing Co Inc 60 N Prospect Ave	Lynbrook	NY	11563	516-887-4000	593-9089
TF: 800-660-4000 ■ *Web:* www.parplumbing.com					
PC Godfrey Inc 1816 Rozzells Ferry Rd	Charlotte	NC	28208	704-334-8604	376-5186
Penguin Air Conditioning Corp 26 West St	Brooklyn	NY	11222	718-706-6500	706-2536
Web: www.penguinac.com					
Performance Contracting Group Inc 16400 College Blvd	Lenexa	KS	66219	913-888-8600	492-8723
TF: 800-255-6866 ■ *Web:* www.pcg.com					
Petersburg Plumbing & Heating Co Inc 117 N 7th St	Petersburg	IL	62675	217-632-2221	632-3117
Piedmont Mechanical Inc 116 John Dodd Rd	Spartanburg	SC	29303	864-578-9114	578-5314
TF: 800-849-5724 ■ *Web:* www.piedmontmechanical.com					
Pierce Assoc Inc 4216 Wheeler Ave Po Box 9050	Alexandria	VA	22304	703-751-2400	751-2479
Web: www.pierceassociates.com					
Plyler Construction 3505 Texoma Pkwy PO Box 912406	Sherman	TX	75091	903-893-6393	892-3523
Web: www.plylerbuilds.com					
Poole & Kent Corp 4530 Hollins Ferry Rd	Baltimore	MD	21227	410-247-2200	247-2331
Web: www.poole-kent.com					
Postler & Jaeckle Corp 615 S Ave	Rochester	NY	14620	585-546-7450	546-4316
TF: 800-724-4252 ■ *Web:* www.postlerandjaeckle.com					
Power Piping Co 436 Butler St	Pittsburgh	PA	15223	412-323-6200	323-6334
Power Process Piping Inc 45780 Port St PO Box 8100-C	Plymouth	MI	48170	734-451-0130	451-0763
Web: www.powerprocesspiping.com					
Precision Piping & Mechanical Inc 5201 Middle Mt Vernon Rd	Evansville	IN	47712	812-425-5052	425-5067
Web: www.ppmiconstruction.com					
Process Construction Inc 1421 Queen City Ave	Cincinnati	OH	45214	513-251-2211	251-2267
TF: 888-251-2211 ■ *Web:* www.processconstruction.com					
PSF Industries Inc 65 S Horton St	Seattle	WA	98134	206-622-1252	682-1070
TF: 800-426-1204 ■ *Web:* www.psfindustries.com					
Quality Mechanical Contractors 3175 Westwood Dr	Las Vegas	NV	89109	702-732-2545	731-5661
Web: www.qualitymechanical.com					
R. A. Walton & Co Inc 1800 Industrial Hwy	York	PA	17402	717-755-9030	755-6919
TF: 800-839-1848 ■ *Web:* www.waltonco.com					
Ray L Hellwig Plumbing & Heating Inc 1301 Laurelwood Rd	Santa Clara	CA	95054	408-727-5612	727-4382
Web: www.rlhellwig.com					
Reedy Industries Inc 2440 Ravine Way Suite 200	Glenview	IL	60025	847-729-9450	729-0558
Web: www.reedyindustries.com					
Riggs Distler Co Inc 9411 Philadelphia Rd Unit P	Baltimore	MD	21237	410-633-0300	633-2119
Web: www.riggsdistler.com					
RK Mechanical Inc 9300 E Smith Rd	Denver	CO	80207	303-355-9696	355-8666
TF: 800-783-0075 ■ *Web:* www.rkmi.com					
Robert Gibb & Sons Inc 205 SW 40th St	Fargo	ND	58103	701-282-5900	281-0819
TF: 800-842-7366 ■ *Web:* www.robertgibb.com					
Rock Hill Mechanical Corp 524 Clark Ave	St. Louis	MO	63122	314-966-0600	966-3679
Web: www.rhmcorp.com					
Ross Bros Construction Co Inc 7201 SR 168	Catlettsburg	KY	41129	606-739-5139	739-8315
TF: 800-910-7222					
Roth Bros Inc PO Box 4209	Youngstown	OH	44515	330-793-5571	793-4155
TF: 800-872-7684 ■ *Web:* www.rothbros.com					
Roto-Rooter Inc 255 E 5th St 2500 Chemed Ctr	Cincinnati	OH	45202	513-762-6690	762-6590
TF: 800-768-6911 ■ *Web:* www.rotorooter.com					
RW Warner Inc 217 Monroe Ave	Frederick	MD	21701	301-662-5387	698-0451
TF: 800-854-5387 ■ *Web:* www.rwwarner.com					
Sauer Inc 30 51st St	Pittsburgh	PA	15201	412-687-4100	687-3576
Web: www.sauer-inc.com					
SB Ballard Construction Co 2828 Shipps Corner Rd	Virginia Beach	VA	23453	757-440-5555	451-2873
TF: 800-296-0209 ■ *Web:* www.sbballard.com					
Schweizer Dipple Inc 7227 Division St	Oakwood Village	OH	44146	440-786-8090	786-8099
Web: www.schweizer-dipple.com					
Service Experts Inc 2140 Lake Pk Blvd	Richardson	TX	75080	972-497-5000	497-6948
TF: 877-536-8580 ■ *Web:* www.serviceexperts.com					
Shambaugh & Son LP 7614 Opportunity Dr	Fort Wayne	IN	46825	260-487-7777	487-7701
TF: 800-234-9988 ■ *Web:* www.shambaugh.com					
Shook & Fletcher Mechanical Contractors Inc 2915 Richard Arrington Jr Blvd N PO Box 10803	Birmingham	AL	35202	205-252-9400	252-9407
Web: shook-fletcher.com					
SI Goldman Co Inc 799 Bennett Dr	Longwood	FL	32750	407-830-5000	830-4599
Web: www.sigoldmanco.com					
Smith & Oby Co 6107 Carnegie Ave	Cleveland	OH	44103	216-361-5121	361-1635
Web: www.smithandoby.com					
Southeast Mechanical Contractors Inc 2120 SW 57th Terr	Hollywood	FL	33023	954-981-3600	962-8630
Web: www.semechanical.com					
Southern Air Inc 2655 Lakeside Dr	Lynchburg	VA	24501	434-385-6200	385-9081
TF: 800-743-1214 ■ *Web:* www.southern-air.com					
Southern Industrial Constructors Inc 6101 Triangle Dr	Raleigh	NC	27617	919-782-4600	782-2935
TF: 800-851-0868 ■ *Web:* www.southernindustrial.com					
Southland Industries 7421 Orangewood Ave	Garden Grove	CA	92841	714-901-5800	901-5811
Web: www.southlandind.com					
Speer Mechanical 600 Oakland Pk Ave	Columbus	OH	43214	614-261-6331	261-6330
TF: 800-282-6017 ■ *Web:* www.speermechanical.com					
Stanley-Carter Co 28702 Wall St	Wixom	MI	48393	248-349-4944	349-4955
Stromberg Sheet Metal Works Inc 6701 Distribution Dr	Beltsville	MD	20705	301-931-1000	931-1020
TF: 800-348-5778 ■ *Web:* www.strombergmetals.com					

Company	City	State	Zip	Phone	Fax
SubZero Constructors Inc 30055 Comercio *Web:* www.szero.com	Rancho Santa Margarita	CA	95000	949-216-9500	216-9539
Superior Air Handling Corp 200 E 700 S *Web:* www.sahco.com	Clearfield	UT	84015	801-776-1997	825-8967
TA Caid Industries Inc 2275 E Ganley Rd *Web:* www.tacaid.com	Tucson	AZ	85706	520-294-3126	294-8180
TDIndustries 13850 Diplomat Dr *Web:* www.tdindustries.com	Dallas	TX	75234	972-888-9500	888-9338
Telgian Corp 11230 Sorrento Valley Rd *Web:* www.telgian.com	San Diego	CA	92121	858-795-1000	795-1001
Tougher Industries Inc 47 Broadway *TF:* 800-836-0752 ■ *Web:* www.tougher.net	Albany	NY	12204	518-465-3426	465-1030
Trautman & Shreve Inc 4406 Race St *Web:* www.trautman-shreve.com	Denver	CO	80216	303-295-1414	295-0324
Triad Mechanical Inc 1419 NE Lombard Pl *TF:* 800-308-7423 ■ *Web:* www.triadpdx.com	Portland	OR	97211	503-289-9000	289-0316
United Industrial Piping Inc 9740 Near Dr *TF:* 800-633-9690 ■ *Web:* www.unitedpiping.com	Cincinnati	OH	45246	513-874-2004	874-7473
University Mechanical & Engineering Contractors Inc 1168 Fesler St *Web:* www.umec.com	El Cajon	CA	92020	619-956-2500	956-2300
US Engineering Co 3433 Roanoke Rd *Web:* www.usengineering.com	Kansas City	MO	64111	816-753-6969	931-5773
US Home Services 7813 N Dixie Dr	Dayton	OH	45414	937-898-0826	898-7166
Vermont Heating & Ventilating Co Inc 16 Tigan St Suite A *Web:* www.vhv.com	Winooski	VT	05404	802-655-8805	655-8809
Walter N Yoder & Sons Inc 16200 McMullen Hwy SW PO Box 1337	Cumberland	MD	21501	301-729-0610	729-1517
Warwick Plumbing & Heating Corp 11048 Warwick Blvd *TF:* 800-423-6111 ■ *Web:* www.wphcorp.com	Newport News	VA	23601	757-599-6111	595-9739
Way Engineering Ltd 5308 Ashbrook Dr *Web:* www.wayholding.com/wayeng	Houston	TX	77081	713-666-3541	666-8455
Wayne Crouse Inc 3370 Stafford St *Web:* www.waynecrouse.com	Pittsburgh	PA	15204	412-771-5176	771-2357
WB Guimarin & Co Inc 1124 Bluff Industrial Blvd *Web:* www.wbguimarin.com	Columbia	SC	29202	803-256-0515	988-0733
WD Manor Mechanical Contractors Inc 1838 N 23rd Ave *Web:* www.wdmanor.com	Phoenix	AZ	85009	602-253-0703	253-3659
Wellington Power Corp 40th & Butler Sts *TF:* 800-540-0017 ■ *Web:* www.wellingtonpower.com	Pittsburgh	PA	15201	412-681-0103	681-0109
Western Air Limbach LP 15914 S Avalon Blvd *TF:* 800-927-1331 ■ *Web:* www.limbachinc.com	Compton	CA	90220	310-327-4400	329-1815
Western Allied Corp 12046 E Florence Ave *Web:* www.westernallied.com	Santa Fe Springs	CA	90670	562-944-6341	944-7092
WG Tomko Inc 2559 Rt 88 *Web:* www.wgtomko.com	Finleyville	PA	15332	724-348-2000	348-7001
William E Walter Inc 1917 Howard Ave *TF:* 800-681-3320 ■ *Web:* www.williamewalter.com	Flint	MI	48503	810-232-7459	232-8698
Williard Limbach 175 Titus Ave Suite 100 **Fax:* Cust Svc ■ *TF:* 800-827-5030 ■ *Web:* www.limbachinc.com	Warrington	PA	18976	215-488-9700	488-9699*
Worth & Co Inc 6263 Kellers Church Rd *TF:* 800-220-5130 ■ *Web:* www.worthandcompany.com	Pipersville	PA	18947	267-362-1100	362-1130
Yale Mechanical Inc 9649 Girard Ave S *Web:* www.yalemech.com	Minneapolis	MN	55431	952-884-1661	884-0295
Yearout Mechanical & Engineering Inc 8501 Washington St Ne *Web:* www.yearout.com	Albuquerque	NM	87113	505-884-0994	883-5073
Young Plumbing & Heating Co 750 S Hackett Rd *Web:* www.youngphc.com	Waterloo	IA	50701	319-234-4411	234-4540

192-11 Remodeling, Refinishing, Resurfacing Contractors

Company	City	State	Zip	Phone	Fax
A J Johns Inc 3225 Anniston Rd *Web:* www.ajjohns.com	Jacksonville	FL	32246	904-641-2055	641-2102
Bathcrest Inc 5195 W 4700 S *TF:* 877-848-9144 ■ *Web:* www.bathcrest.com	Salt Lake City	UT	84118	801-957-1400	955-6499
California Closet Co 1000 4th St Suite 800 *TF:* 800-873-4264 ■ *Web:* www.calclosets.com	San Rafael	CA	94901	415-256-8500	256-8501
Closet Factory 12800 S Broadway *TF:* 800-318-8800 ■ *Web:* www.closetfactory.com	Los Angeles	CA	90061	310-516-7000	516-8065
DreamMaker Bath & Kitchen by Worldwide 1020 N University Parks Dr *TF:* 800-583-9099 ■ *Web:* www.dreammaker-remodel.com	Waco	TX	76707	254-745-2477	745-2588
Handyman Connection Inc 9403 Kenwood Rd Suite D-207 *TF:* 800-466-5530 ■ *Web:* www.handymanconnection.com	Cincinnati	OH	45242	513-771-1122	771-2030
Home Solutions of America Inc 1500 Dragon St Suite B *AMEX:* HOM	Dallas	TX	75207	214-623-8446	333-9435
Kitchen Tune-Up Inc 813 Cir Dr *TF:* 800-333-6385 ■ *Web:* www.kitchentuneup.com	Aberdeen	SD	57401	605-225-4049	225-1371
Miracle Method US Corp 4239 N Nevada Ave Suite 115 *TF:* 800-444-8827 ■ *Web:* www.miraclemethod.com	Colorado Springs	CO	80907	719-594-9091	594-9282
Perma-Glaze Inc 1638 Research Loop Rd Suite 160 *TF:* 800-332-7397 ■ *Web:* www.permaglaze.com	Tucson	AZ	85710	520-722-9718	296-4393
Re-Bath LLC 1055 S Country Club Dr *TF:* 800-426-4573 ■ *Web:* www.re-bath.com	Mesa	AZ	85210	480-844-1575	833-7199

192-12 Roofing, Siding, Sheet Metal Contractors

Company	City	State	Zip	Phone	Fax
A Zahner Sheet Metal Co Inc 1400 E 9th St *Web:* www.azahner.com	Kansas City	MO	64106	816-474-8882	474-7994
AC Dellovade Inc 108 Cavasina Dr *TF:* 800-245-1556 ■ *Web:* www.acdel.com	Canonsburg	PA	15317	724-873-8190	873-8186
All-South Subcontractors Inc 2678 Queenstown Rd *Web:* www.allsouthsub.com	Birmingham	AL	35210	205-836-8111	836-4227
Anson Industries Inc 1959 Anson Dr *Web:* www.ansonindustries.com	Melrose Park	IL	60160	708-681-1300	681-1310
B & M Roofing of Colorado Inc 3768 Eureka Way *Web:* www.bmroofing.com	Frederick	CO	80516	303-443-5843	938-9642
Baker Roofing Co 517 Mercury St *TF:* 800-849-4096 ■ *Web:* www.bakerroofing.com	Raleigh	NC	27603	919-828-2975	828-9352
Beldon Enterprises Inc PO Box 13380 *TF:* 888-612-8023 ■ *Web:* www.beldon.com	San Antonio	TX	78213	210-341-3100	341-2959
BHW Sheet Metal Co 113 Johnson St	Jonesboro	GA	30236	770-471-9303	478-7923
Birdair Inc 65 Lawrence Bell Dr *TF:* 800-622-2246 ■ *Web:* www.birdair.com	Amherst	NY	14221	716-633-9500	633-9850
BL Dalsin Roofing Inc 8824 Wentworth Ave S *Web:* www.bldalsinroofing.com	Bloomington	MN	55420	952-884-5244	884-4342
Bonland Industries Inc 50 Newark-Pompton Tpke *TF:* 800-289-7482 ■ *Web:* www.bonlandhvac.com	Wayne	NJ	07474	973-694-3211	628-1120
Brazos Urethane Inc 1031 6th St N *TF:* 866-527-2967 ■ *Web:* www.brazosurethane.com	Texas City	TX	77590	409-965-0011	
BT Mancini Co Inc 876 S Milpitas Blvd *TF:* 800-488-4286 ■ *Web:* www.btmancini.com	Milpitas	CA	95036	408-942-7900	945-1360
Centimark Corp 12 Grandview Cir *TF:* 800-558-4100 ■ *Web:* www.centimark.com	Canonsburg	PA	15317	724-743-7777	743-7770
CG Bostwick Co 41 Francis Ave *Web:* www.bostwickroofing.com	Hartford	CT	06106	860-523-5249	523-5938
Charles F Evans Co Inc 800 Canal St *Web:* www.evans-roofing.com	Elmira	NY	14901	607-734-8151	733-5422
Commercial Siding & Maintenance Co The 8059 Crile Rd *Web:* www.commercialsiding.com	Painesville	OH	44077	440-352-7800	352-7048
Construction Services Inc 2214 S Lincoln St	Amarillo	TX	79109	806-373-1732	373-9472
Crown Corr Inc 7100 W 21st Ave *Web:* www.crowncorr.com	Gary	IN	46406	219-949-8080	944-9922
DC Taylor Co 312 29th St NE *TF:* 800-333-7763 ■ *Web:* www.dctaylorco.com	Cedar Rapids	IA	52402	319-363-2073	363-8311
Dee Cramer Inc 4221 E Baldwin Rd *TF:* 888-342-6995 ■ *Web:* www.deecramer.com	Holly	MI	48442	810-238-2664	579-2664
Dix Corp 4024 S Grove Rd *TF:* 800-827-8548 ■ *Web:* www.dixcorp.com	Spokane	WA	99224	509-838-4455	838-4464
Earl F Douglass Roofing Co Inc 7281 E 54th Pl *Web:* www.douglassroofing.com	Commerce City	CO	80022	303-288-2635	288-8602
Elmsford Sheet Metal Work Inc 23 Arlo Ln *Web:* www.elmsfordsheetmetal.com	Cortlandt Manor	NY	10567	914-739-6300	739-1285
Enterprise Roofing & Sheet Metal Co 1021 Irving St *Web:* www.enterpriserfg.com	Dayton	OH	45419	937-298-8664	298-4516
Flynn Canada Ltd 1390 Spruce St *TF:* 800-304-8751 ■ *Web:* www.flynn.ca	Winnipeg	MB	R3E2V7	204-786-6951	788-4584
Fort Roofing & Sheet Metal Works Inc 4230 Domino Ave *TF:* 800-356-6716 ■ *Web:* www.fortroofing.com	North Charleston	SC	29405	843-554-9711	554-9708
Gowan Inc 5550 Airline Dr *TF:* 888-724-6926 ■ *Web:* www.gowaninc.com	Houston	TX	77076	713-696-5400	695-1726
Hahnel Bros Co 46 Strawberry Ave *Web:* www.hahnelbrosco.com	Lewiston	ME	04243	207-784-6477	782-9859
Heidler Roofing Services Inc 1345 Spahn Ave *TF:* 866-792-3549 ■ *Web:* www.heidlerroofing.com	York	PA	17403	717-843-9986	848-5363
Henry C Smither Roofing Co Inc 6850 E 32nd St PO Box 26057 *Web:* www.smitherroofing.com	Indianapolis	IN	46226	317-545-1304	546-4764
Industrial First Inc 16400 Miles Ave *Web:* www.industrialfirst.com	Cleveland	OH	44128	216-991-8600	991-2139
Industrial Gasket Inc (IG) 720 S Sara Rd *TF:* 800-654-8433 ■ *Web:* www.igok.com	Mustang	OK	73137	405-376-9393	376-3933
Jamar Co 4701 Mike Colalillo Dr *Web:* www.jamarcompany.com	Duluth	MN	55807	218-628-1027	628-1174
John J Campbell Co Inc 6012 Resources Dr *TF:* 800-274-7663 ■ *Web:* www.campbellroofing.com	Memphis	TN	38134	901-372-8400	372-8404
Johnson Contracting Co Inc 2750 Morton Dr *Web:* www.jccinc.com	East Moline	IL	61244	309-755-0601	752-7056
Jottan Inc PO Box 166 *TF:* 800-364-4234 ■ *Web:* www.jottan.com	Florence	NJ	08518	609-291-8700	447-6200
JP Patti Co Inc 365 Jefferson St PO Box 539 *Web:* www.jppatti.com	Saddle Brook	NJ	07663	973-478-6200	478-2175
Kalkreuth Roofing & Sheet Metal Inc PO Box 6399 *Web:* www.krsm.net	Wheeling	WV	26003	304-232-8540	233-5305
Ketcher & Co Inc 1717 E 5th	North Little Rock	AR	72119	501-372-5216	372-0949
Kirk & Blum Mfg Co Inc 3120 Forrer St *TF:* 800-333-5475 ■ *Web:* www.kirkblum.com	Cincinnati	OH	45209	513-458-2600	351-5475
LE Schwartz & Son Inc 279 Reid St *Web:* www.leschwartz.com	Macon	GA	31206	478-745-6563	745-2711
M Gottfried Inc 89 Research Dr *Web:* www.mgottfried.com	Stamford	CT	06906	203-323-8173	359-2498
Midland Engineering Co 52369 US 33 N *Web:* www.midlandengineering.com	South Bend	IN	46637	574-272-0200	272-7400
Miller-Thomas-Gyekis Inc 3341 Stafford St	Pittsburgh	PA	15204	412-331-4610	331-8871
Mountain Co 166 60th St	Vienna	WV	26105	304-295-3311	295-6991

Company	City	State	Zip	Phone	Fax
National International Roofing Corp 11317 Smith Dr *TF:* 800-221-7663 ■ *Web:* www.nir.com	Huntley	IL	60142	847-669-3444	669-3173
North American Roofing Services Inc 6151 W 80th St *TF:* 800-876-5602 ■ *Web:* www.naroofing.com	Indianapolis	IN	46278	317-875-5434	872-8253
Olsson Roofing Co Inc 740 S Lake St *TF:* 888-766-3967 ■ *Web:* www.olssonroofing.com	Aurora	IL	60506	630-892-0449	892-1556
Orndorff & Spaid Inc 11722 Old Baltimore Pike *TF:* 800-278-7663 ■ *Web:* www.osroofing.com	Beltsville	MD	20705	301-937-5911	937-0310
Pegnato & Pegnato Roof Management Inc 310 Wash Blvd P205 *TF:* 800-435-8216 ■ *Web:* www.pegnato.com	Marina Del Rey	CA	90292	310-574-3820	
R.A. Smith National Inc 16745 W Bluemound Rd Suite 200 *Web:* www.rasmith.com	Brookfield	WI	53005	262-786-1777	786-0826
RD Herbert & Sons Co Inc 1407 3rd Ave N *Web:* www.rdherbert.com	Nashville	TN	37208	615-242-3501	256-4056
Sbb Roofing Inc 3310 Verdugo Rd *TF:* 800-346-7663 ■ *Web:* www.biltwell.com	Los Angeles	CA	90065	323-254-2888	254-3000
Schreiber Corp 2239 Fenkell St *TF:* 800-275-3024 ■ *Web:* www.schreiberroofing.com	Detroit	MI	48238	313-864-4900	864-3016
Schust Engineering Inc 2520 Charleston Pl *Web:* www.schustengineering.com	Fort Wayne	IN	46808	260-482-4820	482-9291
Sechrist-Hall Co 102 Omaha	Corpus Christi	TX	78465	361-884-5264	883-3915
Silktown Roofing Inc 27 Pleasant St *Web:* www.silktownroofing.com	Manchester	CT	06040	860-647-0198	
SingleSource Roofing Corp 24 Summit Pk Dr *TF:* 800-777-6610 ■ *Web:* www.singlesourceroofing.com	Pittsburgh	PA	15275	412-249-6800	249-6950
Snyder Roofing & Sheet Metal Inc 12650 SW Hall Blvd *Web:* www.snyderroofing.com	Tigard	OR	97223	503-620-5252	684-3310
Standard Roofing Co 516 N McDonough St PO Box 1309 *TF:* 800-239-5705 ■ *Web:* www.standardtaylor.com	Montgomery	AL	36102	334-834-3000	834-3004
Superior Roofing & Sheet Metal Co Inc 3405 S 500 W	Salt Lake City	UT	84115	801-266-1473	266-1522
TDIndustries 13850 Diplomat Dr *Web:* www.tdindustries.com	Dallas	TX	75234	972-888-9500	888-9338
Tecta America Co 15002 Wicks Blvd *Web:* www.tectaamerica.com	San Leandro	CA	94577	510-686-4951	
Tom Beattie Inc 1144 N Armando St **Fax Area Code:* 714 ■ *TF:* 800-400-7692 ■ *Web:* www.royalroof.com	Anaheim	CA	92806	800-400-7692	279-2710*
Tri-State Roofing & Sheet Metal Group PO Box 5310 *Web:* www.tri-stateservicegroup.com	Vienna	WV	26105	304-295-3311	295-6991
Turner Roofing & Sheet Metal Inc 1200 E Memphis St *Web:* www.turnerroofing.com	Broken Arrow	OK	74012	918-258-2585	251-9913
US Industries Inc 1701 1st Ave *TF:* 800-264-1501	Evansville	IN	47710	812-425-2428	421-4443
Western Fireproofing Co of Kansas Inc 1501 Westport Rd *Web:* www.westernfireproofing.com	Kansas City	MO	64111	816-561-7667	
Young Group Ltd 1054 Central Industrial Dr *TF:* 800-331-3080	Saint Louis	MO	63110	314-771-3080	771-4597
Zero-Breese Co 4120 Clifton Ave *Web:* www.zerobreese.com	Cincinnati	OH	45232	513-541-1221	541-1918

192-13 Sprinkler System Installation (Fire Sprinklers)

Company	City	State	Zip	Phone	Fax
Active Fire Sprinkler Corp 63 Flushing Ave	Brooklyn	NY	11205	718-834-8300	718-4887
Advance Fire Protection Co Inc 1451 W Lambert Rd	La Habra	CA	90631	562-691-0918	691-5482
All-South Subcontractors Inc 2678 Queenstown Rd *Web:* www.allsouthsub.com	Birmingham	AL	35210	205-836-8111	836-4227
APi Group Inc Fire Protection Group 1100 Old Hwy 8 NW *TF:* 800-223-4922 ■ *Web:* www.apigroupinc.com/fire_protection_profiles.php	New Brighton	MN	55112	651-636-4320	636-0312
Armon Inc 2265 Carlson Dr *Web:* www.femoran.com	Northbrook	IL	60062	847-498-4800	498-9091
August Winter & Sons Inc 2323 N Roemer Rd *TF:* 800-236-8882 ■ *Web:* www.augustwinter.com	Appleton	WI	54911	920-739-8881	739-2230
Brendle Sprinkler Co Inc PO Box 210609 *TF:* 800-392-8021	Montgomery	AL	36121	334-270-8571	277-7967
Cosco Fire Protection Inc 321 E Gardena Blvd **Fax Area Code:* 310 ■ *TF:* 800-827-5612 ■ *Web:* www.coscofire.com	Gardena	CA	90248	323-321-5155	323-0761*
Fire Protection Co 12828 S Ridgeway Ave	Alsip	IL	60803	708-371-4300	371-4340
Fire Protection Systems Inc 22 Industrial Pk Dr *Web:* www.fireprotectionsys.com	Hendersonville	TN	37075	615-822-3600	822-3427
Firetrol Protection Systems Inc 3696 W 900 S Suite A *Web:* www.firetrol.net	Salt Lake City	UT	84104	801-485-6900	485-6902
Geo M Robinson & Co 852 85th Ave *TF:* 800-894-8942	Oakland	CA	94621	510-632-7017	638-5466
High Point Sprinkler Inc 2 Regency Industrial Blvd	Thomasville	NC	27360	336-475-6181	475-4613
JF Ahern Co 855 Morris St *TF:* 800-532-0155 ■ *Web:* www.jfahern.com	Fond du Lac	WI	54935	920-921-9020	921-8632
John E Green Co 220 Victor Ave *Web:* www.johnegreen.com	Highland Park	MI	48203	313-868-2400	868-0011
Ladew Fire Protection Inc 10440 Markison Rd	Dallas	TX	75238	214-349-1927	341-9553
Martin Fireproofing Corp 2200 Military Rd *TF:* 800-766-3969 ■ *Web:* www.martinfireproofing.com	Tonawanda	NY	14150	716-692-3680	693-3402
McDaniel Fire Systems 1055 W Joliet Rd **Fax Area Code:* 800 ■ *TF:* 800-348-2632 ■ *Web:* www.mcdanielfire.com	Valparaiso	IN	46385	219-462-0571	611-2907*
MJ Daly & Sons Inc 110 Mattatuck Heights *TF:* 800-992-3603 ■ *Web:* www.mjdalyinc.com	Waterbury	CT	06705	203-753-5131	597-0227
National Automatic Sprinkler Industries 8000 Corporate Dr *TF:* 800-638-2603 ■ *Web:* www.nasifund.org	Landover	MD	20785	301-577-1700	429-4709
Oliver Sprinkler Co Inc 501 Feheley Dr *Web:* www.oliversprinkler.com	King of Prussia	PA	19406	610-277-1331	277-2837
Patti & Sons Inc 8 Berry St	Brooklyn	NY	11211	718-963-3700	388-8671
SA Comunale Co Inc 2900 Newpark Dr *TF:* 800-776-7181 ■ *Web:* www.comunale.com	Barberton	OH	44203	330-706-3040	861-0860
Security Fire Protection Co Inc 4495 Mendenhall Rd S *TF:* 800-362-6256 ■ *Web:* www.securityfire.com	Memphis	TN	38141	901-362-6250	366-7869
Tyco Fire & Security 301 NE 51st St *Web:* www.tycofireandsecurity.com	Boca Raton	FL	33431	561-988-7200	
VFP Fire Systems 1301 L'Orient St *TF:* 800-229-6263 ■ *Web:* www.vfpfire.com	Saint Paul	MN	55117	651-558-3300	558-3310
VFS Fire Protection Systems 1011 E Lacy Ave	Anaheim	CA	92805	714-778-6070	778-6090
Viking Automatic Sprinkler Co 301 York Ave *Web:* www.vikingsprinkler.com	Saint Paul	MN	55130	651-558-3300	558-3310
Wayne Automatic Fire Sprinklers Inc 222 Capital Ct *Web:* www.waynefire.com	Ocoee	FL	34761	407-656-3030	656-8026
Western States Fire Protection Co 12150 E Briarwood Ave Suite 202 *Web:* www.wsfp.com	Centennial	CO	80112	303-768-0456	790-3875
Wiginton Fire Systems 450 S County Rd 427 *Web:* www.wigintonfiresystems.com	Longwood	FL	32750	407-831-3414	831-5740

192-14 Structural Steel Erection

Company	City	State	Zip	Phone	Fax
Adams & Smith Inc 1380 W Ctr St *Web:* www.adamsmithinc.com	Lindon	UT	84042	801-785-6900	785-6400
Advance Tank & Construction Co 3700 E County Rd 64 PO Box 219 *Web:* www.advancetank.com	Wellington	CO	80549	970-568-3444	568-3435
Albach Co Inc 301 E Prosper St PO Box 1159 *Web:* www.albachco.com	Chalmette	LA	70044	504-271-1113	271-1032
Albany Steel Inc 566 Broadway *TF:* 800-342-9317 ■ *Web:* www.albanysteel.net	Albany	NY	12204	518-436-4851	436-1458
Allstate Steel Co Inc 130 S Jackson Ave *TF:* 888-781-6040 ■ *Web:* www.allstatesteel.com	Jacksonville	FL	32220	904-781-6040	693-0255
Arben Corp 175 Marble Ave	Pleasantville	NY	10570	914-741-5459	741-2923
Area Erectors Inc 2323 Harrison Ave *Web:* www.areaerectors.com	Rockford	IL	61104	815-398-6700	398-6787
Ben Hur Construction Co 3783 Rider Trail S *Web:* www.benhurconstruction.com	Saint Louis	MO	63045	314-298-8007	298-8565
Bosworth Steel Erectors Inc 4001 Jaffee St *Web:* www.bosworthsteel.com	Dallas	TX	75216	214-371-3700	371-1020
Bratton Corp 2801 E 85th St *Web:* www.brattonsteel.com	Kansas City	MO	64132	816-363-1014	361-8021
Brunton Enterprises Inc 8815 Sorensen Ave *Web:* www.plas-tal.com	Santa Fe Springs	CA	90670	562-945-0013	696-7620
Canron Construction Inc 4600 NE 138th Ave *Web:* www.supremesteel.com	Portland	OR	97230	503-255-8634	253-3907
CBI Services Inc 24 Read's Way *TF:* 800-642-8675 ■ *Web:* www.cbi.com	New Castle	DE	19720	302-325-8400	323-0788
CE Toland & Son 5300 Industrial Way *TF:* 800-675-1166	Benicia	CA	94510	707-747-1000	747-5300
Central Maintenance & Welding Inc 2620 E Keysville Rd PO Drawer 777 *TF:* 877-704-7411 ■ *Web:* www.cmw.cc	Lithia	FL	33547	813-737-1402	737-1820
Century Steel Erectors Co 210 Washington Ave PO Box 490 *TF:* 888-601-8801 ■ *Web:* www.centurysteel.com	Dravosburg	PA	15034	412-469-8800	469-0813
Chicago Bridge & Iron Co 6001 Rogerdale Rd *NYSE:* CBI ■ *TF:* 866-235-5687 ■ *Web:* www.cbi.com	Houston	TX	77072	713-485-1000	485-1005
CP Buckner Steel Erection Inc 4732 NC 54 E PO Box 598 *TF:* 800-848-6234 ■ *Web:* www.bucknersteel.com	Graham	NC	27253	336-376-8888	376-8855
Derr Construction Co 13400 Trinity Blvd PO Box 637 *Web:* www.derrsteel.com	Euless	TX	76039	817-571-4044	571-4544
Dix Corp 4024 S Grove Rd *TF:* 800-827-8548 ■ *Web:* www.dixcorp.com	Spokane	WA	99224	509-838-4455	838-4464
Fenton Rigging & Contracting Inc 2150 Langdon Farm Rd *Web:* www.fentonrigging.com	Cincinnati	OH	45237	513-631-5500	631-4361
Fontana Steel Inc 12451 Arrow Rt PO Box 2219 *TF:* 800-877-8758	Rancho Cucamonga	CA	91729	909-899-9993	899-9799
Fought & Co Inc PO Box 23759 *Web:* www.fought.org	Tigard	OR	97281	503-639-3141	620-3279
Havens National Riggers & Erectors Inc 14650 Jib St	Plymouth	MI	48170	734-459-9515	459-9543
Higgins Erectors & Haulers Inc 7715 Lockport Rd	Niagara Falls	NY	14304	716-297-2600	205-0159
High Industries Inc 1853 William Penn Way *Web:* www.high.net	Lancaster	PA	17601	717-293-4444	293-4416
High Steel Structures Inc 1915 Old Philadelphia Pike *Web:* www.highsteel.com	Lancaster	PA	17602	717-299-5211	293-4416
Highland Tank & Mfg Co 1 Highland Rd *Web:* www.highlandtank.com	Stoystown	PA	15563	814-893-5701	893-6126
JL Davidson Co Inc 8663 N Magnolia Ave Suite H	Santee	CA	92071	619-562-2002	562-8453

Company	City	State	Zip	Phone	Fax
Keller-Hall Inc 1247 Eastwood Ave *TF:* 800-831-6147 ■ *Web:* www.kellerrigging.com	Tallmadge	OH	44278	330-633-6160	633-5773
Kelly Steel Erectors Inc 7220 Division St.	Bedford	OH	44146	440-232-9595	232-0272
Koch Skanska Inc 400 Roosevelt Ave.	Carteret	NJ	07008	732-969-1700	969-0197
Lafayette Steel Erector Inc 313 Westgate Rd. *Web:* www.l-s-e.com	Lafayette	LA	70506	337-234-9435	234-0217
Mansfield Structural & Erecting Co 429 Pk Ave E.	Mansfield	OH	44905	419-522-5911	525-4948
Midwest Steel & Equipment Co Inc 9825 Moers Rd. *Web:* www.midwest-steel.com	Houston	TX	77075	713-991-7843	991-4745
Midwest Steel Inc 2525 E Grand Blvd *TF:* 800-578-7880 ■ *Web:* www.midweststeel.com	Detroit	MI	48211	313-873-2220	873-2222
Pittsburg Tank & Tower Co Inc 1 Watertank Pl. **Fax:* Sales ■ *TF:* 800-499-8265 ■ *Web:* www.watertank.com	Henderson	KY	42420	270-826-9000	826-1970*
Rebar Engineering Inc 10706 Painter Ave.	Santa Fe Springs	CA	90670	562-946-2461	941-7740
Ryan Iron Works Inc 1830 Broadway *Web:* www.ryanironworks.net	Raynham	MA	02767	508-822-8001	823-1359
Schuff Steel Co 420 S 19th Ave *TF:* 800-528-0513 ■ *Web:* www.schuff.com	Phoenix	AZ	85009	602-252-7787	452-4466
Shurtleff & Andrews Corp 1875 W 500 S. *Web:* www.shurtleff-slc.com	Salt Lake City	UT	84104	801-973-9096	973-2248
Southeastern Construction & Maintenance Co Inc 1150 Pebbledale Rd PO Box 1055 *TF:* 800-511-1600 ■ *Web:* www.southeasternconst.com	Mulberry	FL	33860	863-428-1511	428-1110
Sowles Co 3045 Sibley Memorial Hwy # 100 *TF:* 888-376-9537 ■ *Web:* www.sowles.com	Eagan	MN	55121	651-287-9700	287-9710
Steel City Inc 2563 Commerce Clr *TF:* 800-264-5075 ■ *Web:* www.steelcitysafe.com	Birmingham	AL	35217	205-426-3807	426-3814
Sure Steel Inc 9632 S 500 W *Web:* www.suresteel.com	Sandy	UT	84070	801-255-0578	255-8977
Tampa Steel Erecting Co 5127 Bloomingdale Ave	Tampa	FL	33619	813-677-7184	677-8364
Walden Structures Inc 801 Opal Ave. *Web:* www.waldenstructures.com	Mentone	CA	92359	909-389-9100	
Waldinger Corp 2601 Bell Ave *TF:* 800-225-0638 ■ *Web:* www.waldinger.com	Des Moines	IA	50321	515-284-1911	323-5150
Washington Ornamental Iron Works Inc 17926 S Broadway *TF:* 800-332-4766	Gardena	CA	90248	310-327-8660	329-4180
Williams Industries Inc 8624 JD Reading Dr *NASDAQ: WMSI* ■ *Web:* www.wmsi.com	Manassas	VA	20109	703-335-7800	335-7802
WO Grubb Steel Erection Inc 5120 Jefferson Davis Hwy *TF:* 800-344-6824 ■ *Web:* www.wogrubb.com	Richmond	VA	23234	804-271-9471	271-2539
Zimkor Industries Inc 7011 W Titan Rd *Web:* www.zimkor.com	Littleton	CO	80125	303-791-1333	791-1340

192-15 Terrazzo, Tile, Marble, Mosaic Contractors

Company	City	State	Zip	Phone	Fax
Belfi Bros & Co Inc 4310 Josephine St PO Box 9582 *Web:* www.belfibrothers.com	Philadelphia	PA	19124	215-289-2766	289-9208
DMI Tile & Marble Inc 3012 5th Ave S *TF:* 800-322-8449 ■ *Web:* www.dmi-tmt.com	Birmingham	AL	35233	205-322-8473	251-9611
Marblelife Inc 300 Northstar Ct *TF:* 800-627-4569 ■ *Web:* www.marblelife.com	Sanford	FL	32771	407-302-9297	302-9311
Tile Trends 1311 Lawrence Dr	Newbury Park	CA	91320	805-497-7471	498-7460

192-16 Water Well Drilling

Company	City	State	Zip	Phone	Fax
Alsay Inc 6615 Gant St. *TF:* 800-833-5969 ■ *Web:* www.alsayinc.com	Houston	TX	77066	281-444-6960	444-7081
Cascade Drilling Inc-California 555 S Harbor Blvd *Web:* www.cascadedrilling.com	La Habra	CA	90631	562-929-8176	863-9534
Kelley Dewatering & Construction Co 5175 Clay Ave SW *Web:* www.kelleydewatering.com	Wyoming	MI	49548	616-538-8010	538-0708
Layne Christensen Co 1900 Shawnee Mission Pkwy *NASDAQ: LAYN* ■ *Web:* www.laynechristensen.com	Mission Woods	KS	66205	913-362-0510	362-0133
Ohio Drilling Co 2405 Bostic Blvd SW *TF:* 800-860-2285	Massillon	OH	44647	330-832-1521	832-5302
Ots-Nj LLC (OTS) 340 Bismark Rd *TF:* 800-533-4687 ■ *Web:* www.otstel.com	Jackson	NJ	08527	732-833-0600	833-1169
Raba-Kistner Consultants Inc 12821 W Golden Ln *TF:* 866-722-2547 ■ *Web:* www.rkci.com	San Antonio	TX	78249	210-699-9090	699-6426
Rosencrantz-Bemis Enterprises Inc 1105 281 Bypass *TF:* 800-466-2467	Great Bend	KS	67530	620-793-5512	793-5176
Sargent Irrigation Co W Old Hwy 2 PO Box 627 *Web:* www.sargentirrigation.com	Broken Bow	NE	68822	308-872-6451	872-6912
Tri-State Drilling Inc 16940 Hwy 55 W *TF:* 800-383-1033 ■ *Web:* www.tristatedrilling.com	Plymouth	MN	55446	763-553-1234	553-9778
Water Resources International Inc 1100 Alakea St Suite 2900 *Web:* www.brninc.com	Honolulu	HI	96813	808-531-8422	531-7181

192-17 Wrecking & Demolition Contractors

Company	City	State	Zip	Phone	Fax
Allied Erecting & Dismantling Co Inc 2100 Poland Ave. *TF:* 800-624-2867 ■ *Web:* www.aed.cc	Youngstown	OH	44502	330-744-0808	744-3218
Barnard Construction Co Inc PO Box 99 *Web:* www.barnard-inc.com	Bozeman	MT	59771	406-586-1995	586-3530
Bi-Con Services Inc 10901 Clay Pike Rd *Web:* www.bsicos.com	Derwent	OH	43733	740-685-2542	685-3863
Bierlein Cos Inc 2000 Bay City Rd *TF:* 800-336-6626 ■ *Web:* www.bierlein.com	Midland	MI	48642	989-496-0066	496-0144
Cherry Demolition 6131 Selinsky Rd *TF:* 800-444-1123 ■ *Web:* www.cherrydemolition.com	Houston	TX	77048	713-987-0000	987-0629
Dustrol Inc 1200 E Main PO Box 309 *Web:* www.dustrol.com	Towanda	KS	67144	316-536-2262	536-2789
Edgerton Contractors Inc 545 W Ryan Rd PO Box 901 *Web:* www.edgertoncontractors.com	Oak Creek	WI	53154	414-764-4443	764-9788
Ferma Corp 1265 Montecito Ave *TF:* 877-337-6211 ■ *Web:* www.fermacorp.com	Mountain View	CA	94043	650-961-2742	968-3945
Gateway Demolition Corp 134-22 32nd Ave. *Web:* www.gatewaydemolition.com	Flushing	NY	11354	718-359-1400	461-6558
James White Construction Co Inc 4156 Freedom Way	Weirton	WV	26062	304-748-8181	748-8183
Kimmins Contracting Corp 1501 2nd Ave *Web:* www.kimmins.com	Tampa	FL	33605	813-248-3878	247-0183
Kipin Industries Inc 4194 Green Garden Rd. *Web:* www.kipin.com	Aliquippa	PA	15001	724-495-6200	495-2219
Manafort Bros Inc 414 New Britain Ave *TF:* 888-626-2367 ■ *Web:* www.manafort.com	Plainville	CT	06062	860-229-4853	229-1878
Mercer Wrecking Recycling Corp 4 Beakes St. *Web:* www.demolitionrecycle.com	Trenton	NJ	08638	609-394-9494	394-6839
Midwest Steel & Equipment Co Inc 9825 Moers Rd. *Web:* www.midwest-steel.com	Houston	TX	77075	713-991-7843	991-4745
National Wrecking Co 2441 N Leavitt St *Web:* www.nationalwrecking.com	Chicago	IL	60647	773-384-2800	384-0403
Noralco Corp 1920 Lincoln Rd. *Web:* www.noralco.com	Pittsburgh	PA	15235	412-361-6678	361-6535
Nuprecon Inc 35131 SE Ctr St. *TF:* 800-442-2072 ■ *Web:* www.nuprecon.com	Snoqualmie	WA	98065	425-881-0623	881-5935
O'Rourke Wrecking Co 660 Lunken Pk Dr. *TF:* 800-354-9850 ■ *Web:* www.orourkewrecking.com	Cincinnati	OH	45226	513-871-1400	871-1313
Patuxent Cos 2124 Priest Bridge Dr Suite 18 *TF:* 800-628-4942 ■ *Web:* www.patuxentcompanies.com	Crofton	MD	21114	410-793-0181	
Penhall International Inc 1801 Penhall Way *TF:* 800-736-4255 ■ *Web:* www.penhall.com	Anaheim	CA	92803	714-778-6677	778-8437
Plant Reclamation 912 Harbour Way S *TF:* 800-637-0339 ■ *Web:* www.plantreclamation.com	Richmond	CA	94804	510-233-6552	237-6739
Robinette Demolition Inc 0 S 560 Hwy 83 *Web:* www.rdidemolition.com	Oakbrook Terrace	IL	60181	630-833-7997	833-8047
Siciliano Inc 3601 Winchester Rd *Web:* www.sicilianoinc.com	Springfield	IL	62707	217-585-1200	585-1211
US Dismantlement LLC 2600 S Throop St *TF:* 800-648-3801 ■ *Web:* www.usdllc.com	Chicago	IL	60608	312-328-1400	328-1477

193 CONSTRUCTION MACHINERY & EQUIPMENT

SEE ALSO Industrial Machinery, Equipment, & Supplies p. 2107; Material Handling Equipment p. 2221

Company	City	State	Zip	Phone	Fax
Allied Bldg Stores Inc PO Box 8030 *Web:* www.absweb.biz	Monroe	LA	71211	318-699-9100	699-9201
Allied Construction Products LLC 3900 Kelley Ave *TF Cust Svc:* 800-321-1046 ■ *Web:* www.alliedcp.com	Cleveland	OH	44114	216-431-2600	431-2601
Altec Industries Inc 210 Inverness Ctr Dr *Web:* www.altec.com	Birmingham	AL	35242	205-991-7733	991-9993
American Alloy Corp 9501 Allen Dr. *Web:* www.pyramidparts.com	Cleveland	OH	44125	216-642-9600	642-9677
Asphalt Drum Mixers Inc 1 ADM Pkwy. *Web:* www.admasphaltplants.com	Huntertown	IN	46748	260-637-5729	637-3164
Astec Industries Inc 1725 Shepherd Rd *NASDAQ: ASTE* ■ *TF:* 800-468-5938 ■ *Web:* www.astecindustries.com	Chattanooga	TN	37421	423-899-5898	899-4456
Atlantic Construction Fabrics Inc 2831 Cardwell Rd *TF:* 800-448-3636 ■ *Web:* www.acfenvironmental.com	Richmond	VA	23234	804-271-2363	743-7779
Bandit Industries Inc 6750 W Millbrook Rd *TF:* 800-952-0178 ■ *Web:* www.banditchippers.com	Remus	MI	49340	989-561-2270	561-2273
Bay Shore Systems Inc 14206 N Ohio St. *TF:* 888-569-3745 ■ *Web:* www.bayshoresystems.com	Rathdrum	ID	83858	208-687-3311	687-4153
Bid-Well Corp 430 S Main St. *TF:* 800-843-9824 ■ *Web:* www.bid-well.com	Canton	SD	57013	605-987-2603	987-2605
Bihler Of America Inc 85 Industrial Rd *Web:* www.bihler.com	Phillipsburg	NJ	08865	908-213-9001	329-9111
Boart Longyear Co 2640 W 1700 S *TF:* 800-453-8740 ■ *Web:* www.boartlongyear.com	Salt Lake City	UT	84104	801-972-6430	977-3376
Bomag Americas Inc 2000 Kentville Rd. *TF:* 800-782-6624 ■ *Web:* www.bomag.com	Kewanee	IL	61443	309-853-3571	852-0350
BradenCarco Gearmatic Paccar Winch Div 800 E Dallas St. *Web:* www.paccarwinch.com	Broken Arrow	OK	74012	918-251-8511	259-1575
Bucyrus Blades Inc 260 E Beal Ave *TF:* 800-532-5233 ■ *Web:* www.escocorp.com	Bucyrus	OH	44820	419-562-6015	562-8360
Bucyrus International Inc 1100 Milwaukee Ave. *NASDAQ: BUCY* ■ *Web:* www.bucyrus.com	South Milwaukee	WI	53172	414-768-4000	768-4006
Caron Compactor Co 1204 Ullrey Ave *TF:* 800-542-2766 ■ *Web:* www.caroncompactor.com	Escalon	CA	95320	209-838-2062	838-1404

Company	City	State	ZIP	Phone	Fax
Caterpillar Inc 100 NE Adams St *NYSE:* CAT ■ **Fax:* PR ■ *Web:* www.cat.com	Peoria	IL	61629	309-675-1000	675-4332*
Cemen Tech Inc 1700 N 14th St *TF:* 800-247-2464 ■ *Web:* www.cementech.com	Indianola	IA	50125	515-961-7407	961-7409
Central Mine Equipment Co Inc 4215 Rider Trail N *TF:* 800-325-8827 ■ *Web:* www.cmeco.com	Earth City	MO	63045	314-291-7700	291-4880
Centurion Industries Inc 1107 N Taylor Rd *TF:* 888-832-4466 ■ *Web:* www.centurionind.com	Garrett	IN	46738	260-357-6665	357-6761
Charles Machine Works Inc PO Box 66 *TF Cust Svc:* 800-654-6481 ■ *Web:* www.ditchwitch.com	Perry	OK	73077	580-336-4402	
Chemgrout Inc 805 E 31st St *Web:* www.chemgrout.com	La Grange Park	IL	60526	708-354-7125	354-3881
CRC Evans Pipeline International Inc 10700 E Independence St *TF:* 800-395-5192 ■ *Web:* www.crc-evans.com	Tulsa	OK	74116	918-438-2100	438-6237
Deere & Co John Deere Construction & Forestry Div 1515 5th Ave	Moline	IL	61265	309-765-0227	748-0117*
Demag Cranes & Components 29201 Aurora Rd *TF:* 800-321-6560 ■ *Web:* www.demagcranes.us	Cleveland	OH	44139	440-248-2400	248-3036
Derr & Gruenewald Construction Co (DGCC) PO Box 218 *Web:* www.dgccsteel.com	Henderson	CO	80640	303-287-3456	287-3459
Eagle Iron Works 129 E Holcomb Ave *Web:* www.eagleironworks.com	Des Moines	IA	50313	515-243-1123	243-8214
ED Etnyre & Co 1333 S Daysville Rd *TF:* 800-995-2116 ■ *Web:* www.etnyre.com	Oregon	IL	61061	815-732-2116	732-7400
Egging Co The 12145 Rd 38 *Web:* www.egging.com	Gurley	NE	69141	308-884-2233	884-2437
Elgin National Industries Inc 2001 Butterfield Rd Suite 1020 *Web:* www.eni.com	Downers Grove	IL	60515	630-434-7200	434-7246
Erie Strayer Co 1851 Rudolph Ave *Web:* www.eriestrayer.com	Erie	PA	16502	814-456-7001	452-3422
Esco Corp 2141 NW 25th Ave *TF:* 800-523-3795 ■ *Web:* www.escocorp.com	Portland	OR	97210	503-228-2141	778-6330
F&m Mafco Inc PO Box 11013 *TF:* 800-333-2151 ■ *Web:* www.fmmafco.com	Cincinnati	OH	45211	513-367-2151	367-0363
Fairchild International 200 Fairchild Ln *Web:* www.fairchildint.com	Glen Lyn	VA	24093	540-726-2380	726-2388
Gencor Industries Inc 5201 N Orange Blossom Trail **Fax:* Sales ■ *TF:* 800-234-3626 ■ *Web:* www.gencor.com	Orlando	FL	32810	407-290-6000	578-0577*
Gradall Industries Inc 406 Mill Ave SW *Web:* www.gradall.com	New Philadelphia	OH	44663	330-339-2211	339-8468
H & E Equipment Services Inc 11100 Mead Rd Suite 200 *NASDAQ:* HEES ■ *TF:* 877-700-7368 ■ *Web:* www.he-equipment.com	Baton Rouge	LA	70816	225-298-5200	298-5377
Hendrix Mfg Co Inc 816 Jenkins St	Mansfield	LA	71052	318-872-1660	872-1508
Hensley Industries Inc 2108 Joe Field Rd PO Box 29779 **Fax:* Cust Svc ■ *TF:* 888-406-6262 ■ *Web:* www.hensleyind.com	Dallas	TX	75229	972-241-2321	241-0915*
Highway Equipment Co Inc 1330 County Hwy E66 *Web:* www.highwayequipment.com	Cedar Rapids	IA	52404	319-363-8281	632-3084
Hydralift AmClyde Inc 240 E Plato Blvd *Web:* www.nov.com	Saint Paul	MN	55107	651-293-4710	293-4648
Jennmar Corp 258 Kappa Dr *Web:* www.jennmar.com	Pittsburgh	PA	15238	412-963-9071	963-6809
JH Fletcher & Co Inc 402 High St *Web:* www.jhfletcher.com	Huntington	WV	25705	304-525-7811	525-3770
JLG Industries Inc 1 JLG Dr *Web:* www.jlg.com	McConnellsburg	PA	17233	717-485-5161	485-6417
John Henry Foster Co 4700 LeBourget Dr *TF:* 800-444-0522 ■ *Web:* www.jhf.com	St. Louis	MO	63134	314-427-0600	427-3502
Joy Mining Machinery 177 Thorn Hill Rd *Web:* www.joyglobal.com	Warrendale	PA	15086	724-779-4500	779-4509
Kress Corp 227 W Illinois St *Web:* www.kresscarrier.com	Brimfield	IL	61517	309-446-3395	446-9625
LeTourneau Inc PO Box 2307 *Web:* www.letourneau-inc.com	Longview	TX	74606	903-237-7000	237-7032
Liebherr-America Inc 4100 Chestnut Ave	Newport News	VA	23607	757-245-5251	928-8700
Link-Belt Construction Equipment Co 2651 Palumbo Dr **Fax:* Sales ■ *Web:* www.linkbelt.com	Lexington	KY	40583	859-263-5200	263-5260*
Manitowoc Co Inc 2400 S 44th St *NYSE:* MTW ■ *Web:* www.manitowoc.com	Manitowoc	WI	54220	920-684-4410	652-9778
Manitowoc Co The 2400 S 44th St PO Box 70 *Web:* www.manitowoccranes.com	Manitowoc	WI	54221	920-684-4410	683-6277
Mayville Engineering Co Inc 715 S St *Web:* www.mayvl.com	Mayville	WI	53050	920-387-4500	387-2682
McLellan Equipment Inc 251 Shaw Rd *TF:* 800-848-8449	South San Francisco	CA	94080	650-873-8100	589-7398
Metso Dynapac Inc 16435 I-H 35 N PO Box 615 *TF:* 800-867-6060 ■ *Web:* www.dynapac.com	Selma	TX	78154	210-474-5770	474-5780
Meyer Products 18513 Euclid Ave **Fax:* Sales ■ *Web:* www.meyerproducts.com	Cleveland	OH	44112	216-486-1313	486-1321*
Midland Machinery Co Inc 101 Cranbrook Ext *Web:* www.midlandmachinery.com	Tonawanda	NY	14150	716-692-1200	692-1206
Midwestern Industries Inc 915 Oberlin Rd SW *TF Cust Svc:* 877-474-9464 ■ *Web:* www.midwesternind.com	Massillon	OH	44647	330-837-4203	837-4210
Millcraft Industries Inc 400 Southpointe Blvd Plaza 1 Suite 400 *Web:* www.millcraftindustries.com	Canonsburg	PA	15317	724-743-3400	745-2400
Nexgen Enterprises Inc PO Box 1036 *Web:* www.nexgenbuildingsupply.com	West Chester	OH	45071	513-618-0300	618-0301
Nordco Inc 245 W Forest Hill Ave *Web:* www.nordco.com	Oak Creek	WI	53154	414-766-2180	766-2260
Pengo Corp 500 E Hwy 10 *TF Cust Svc:* 800-599-0211 ■ *Web:* www.pengoattachments.com	Laurens	IA	50554	712-845-2540	845-2497
Pennsylvania Crusher Corp 600 Abbott Dr *Web:* www.penncrusher.com	Broomall	PA	19008	610-544-7200	543-0190
Pettibone Corp 2626 Warrenville Rd Suite 300	Downers Grove	IL	60515	630-353-5000	353-5026
Pierce Pacific Mfg Inc 4424 NE 158th PO Box 30509 *TF:* 800-760-3270 ■ *Web:* www.piercepacific.com	Portland	OR	97294	503-808-9110	808-9111
Precision Husky Corp 850 Markeeta Spur Rd *Web:* www.precisionhusky.com	Moody	AL	35004	205-640-5181	640-1147
Putzmeister America 1733 90th St *TF:* 800-884-7210 ■ *Web:* www.putzmeister.com	Sturtevant	WI	53177	262-886-3200	886-3212
R. F. Morse & Courtyard Gardens 22 Cranberry Hwy *Web:* www.rfmorse.com	West Wareham	MA	02576	508-295-1553	295-8187
Racine Federated Inc 8635 Washington Ave *Web:* www.racinefederated.com	Racine	WI	53406	262-639-6770	639-2267
Ramsey Winch Co Inc 1600 N Garnett Rd *TF:* 800-777-2760 ■ *Web:* www.ramsey.com	Tulsa	OK	74116	918-438-2760	438-6688
Reco Equipment Inc 66420 Belmont-Morristown Rd *TF:* 800-686-7326 ■ *Web:* www.recoequip.com	Morristown	OH	43759	740-782-1314	782-1020
RKI Inc 2301 Central Pkwy *Web:* www.rki-us.com	Houston	TX	77092	713-688-4414	688-5776
Roadtec Inc 800 Manufacturers Rd PO Box 180515 *TF:* 800-272-7100 ■ *Web:* www.roadtec.com	Chattanooga	TN	37405	423-265-0600	267-7104
Robertson Transformer Co 13611 Thornton Rd *TF:* 800-323-5633 ■ *Web:* www.robertsontransformer.com	Blue Island	IL	60406	708-388-2315	388-2420
Shelby Industries Inc 175 McDaniels Rd *Web:* www.shelbyindustries.com	Shelbyville	KY	40065	502-633-2040	633-2186
Simco Drilling Equipment Inc PO Box 448 *TF:* 855-222-8570 ■ *Web:* www.simcodrill.com	Osceola	IA	50213	641-342-2166	342-6764
Stone Construction Equipment Inc 8662 Main St *TF:* 800-888-9926 ■ *Web:* www.stone-equip.com	Honeoye	NY	14471	585-229-5141	229-2363
Superwinch Inc 359 Lake Rd *TF:* 800-323-2031 ■ *Web:* www.superwinch.com	Dayville	CT	06241	860-928-7787	928-1143
Swenson Spreader Co 127 Walnut St *TF:* 888-825-7323 ■ *Web:* www.swensonproducts.com	Lindenwood	IL	61049	815-393-4455	393-4964
Terex Corp 200 Nyala Farm Rd *NYSE:* TEX ■ *Web:* www.terex.com	Westport	CT	06880	203-222-7170	222-7976
Terex Roadbuilding 40 Morgan Rd *Web:* www.terexrb.com	Oklahoma City	OK	73102	405-787-6020	491-2417
Thrustmaster of Texas Inc PO Box 840189 *Web:* www.thrustmastertexas.com	Houston	TX	77284	713-937-6295	937-7962
Triad Machinery Inc 4530 NE 148th Ave *TF:* 800-221-8512 ■ *Web:* www.triadmachinery.com	Portland	OR	97230	503-254-5100	254-8578
Tulsa Winch Group 11135 S James Ave *Web:* www.team-twg.com	Jenks	OK	74037	918-298-8300	298-8301
Varel International 1625 W Crosby Dr Suite 124 *TF:* 800-827-3526 ■ *Web:* www.varelintl.com	Carrollton	TX	75006	972-242-1160	242-3369
Volvo Construction Equipment of North America Inc 1 Volvo Dr *Web:* www.volvo.com/constructionequipment	Asheville	NC	28803	828-650-2000	650-2501
Wacker Neuson N 92 W 15000 Anthony Ave **Fax Area Code:* 800 ■ *TF:* 800-770-0957 ■ *Web:* products.wackerneuson.com	Menomonee Falls	WI	53051	262-255-0500	822-0710*
Western Products Inc 7777 N 73rd St **Fax:* Cust Svc ■ *Web:* www.westernplows.com	Milwaukee	WI	53223	414-354-2310	354-2310*
Young Corp 3231 Utah Ave S *TF:* 800-321-9090 ■ *Web:* www.youngcorp.com	Seattle	WA	98134	206-624-1071	682-6881

194 CONSTRUCTION MATERIALS

SEE ALSO Home Improvement Centers p. 2024

194-1 Brick, Stone, Related Materials

Company	City	State	ZIP	Phone	Fax
Ahi Supply Inc PO Box 884 *TF:* 800-873-5794 ■ *Web:* www.ahi-supply.com	Friendswood	TX	77549	281-331-0088	331-9813
Allen Refractories Co (inc) 131 Shackelford Rd *Web:* www.allenrefractories.com	Pataskala	OH	43062	740-927-8000	927-9404
Alley-Cassetty Cos Inc 2 Oldham St *Web:* www.alley-cassetty.com	Nashville	TN	37213	615-244-0440	254-4553
Architectural Ceramics Inc 800 E Gude Dr Suite F *Web:* www.architecturalceramics.net	Rockville	MD	20850	301-762-4140	762-2497
Arizona Portland Cement Co 2400 N Central Ave *TF:* 800-462-2475	Phoenix	AZ	85004	602-271-0069	254-9027
Atlas Construction Supply Inc 4640 Brinnell St *TF:* 877-588-2100 ■ *Web:* www.atlasform.com	San Diego	CA	92111	858-277-2100	277-0585
Bierschbach Equipment & Supply Co PO Box 1444 *TF:* 800-843-3707 ■ *Web:* www.bierschbach.com	Sioux Falls	SD	57101	605-332-4466	332-4522
Block USA 327 Fiberglass Rd *TF:* 888-942-5625 ■ *Web:* www.specblockusa.com	Jackson	TN	38301	731-421-4624	421-4625
Breckenridge Material 2833 Breckenridge Industrial Ct PO Box 19918 *Web:* www.breckenridgematerial.com	Saint Louis	MO	63144	314-962-1234	962-1540

	City	State	Zip	Phone	Fax
Castelli Marble Inc 3958 Superior Ave E *Web:* www.castellimarble.com	Cleveland	OH	44114	216-361-1222	361-1797
Clay Ingels Co Inc 914 Delaware Ave *TF:* 800-282-9064 ■ *Web:* www.clay-ingels.com	Lexington	KY	40505	859-252-0836	259-0938
Commercial Ready Mix Products Inc PO Box 189 *Web:* www.crmpinc.com	Winton	NC	27986	252-358-5561	358-4912
Corriveau-Routhier Inc 266 Clay St *Web:* www.corriveaurouthier.com	Manchester	NH	03103	603-627-3805	627-3805
E Stewart Mitchell Inc 1250 Benhill Ave PO Box 2799 *TF:* 800-870-6365 ■ *Web:* www.esm.com	Baltimore	MD	21226	410-354-0600	354-3029
Franklin Industries Inc 612 10th Ave N *TF:* 800-626-8147 ■ *Web:* www.frankmin.com	Nashville	TN	37203	615-259-4222	726-2693
Fullen Dock & Warehouse Inc 382 Klinke Ave *TF:* 800-467-7104 ■ *Web:* www.fullendock.com	Memphis	TN	38127	901-358-9544	357-2879
Georgeco Inc 2609 Willowbrook Rd *Web:* www.barnsco.com	Dallas	TX	75220	214-352-9091	352-7020
Granite Construction Inc 585 W Beach St *NYSE:* GVA ■ *Web:* www.graniteconstruction.com	Watsonville	CA	95076	831-724-1011	722-9657
Graniterock Co 350 Technology Dr PO Box 50001 *TF:* 800-327-1711 ■ *Web:* www.graniterock.com	Watsonville	CA	95077	831-768-2000	768-2201
Hanson Bldg Products North America 3500 Maple Ave *TF:* 800-527-2362 ■ *Web:* www.heidelbergcement.com	Dallas	TX	75219	214-525-5500	525-5563
Henry Products Inc 302 S 23rd Ave *TF:* 800-525-5533 ■ *Web:* www.henryproducts.com	Phoenix	AZ	85009	602-253-3191	254-2325
Hudson Liquid Asphalts Inc 89 Ship St *TF:* 800-556-3406 ■ *Web:* www.hudsoncompanies.com	Providence	RI	02903	401-274-2200	274-2220
Iberia Tiles Corp 2975 NW 77 Ave *Web:* www.iberiatiles.com	Miami	FL	33122	305-591-3880	591-4341
International Wholesale Tile Inc PO Box 2267 **Fax Area Code:* 888 ■ *TF:* 800-340-8453 ■ *Web:* www.internationalwholesaletile.com	Palm City	FL	34991	772-223-5151	765-8453*
Intrepid Enterprises Inc 1848 Industrial Blvd	Harvey	LA	70058	504-348-2861	340-7018
Jaeckle Wholesale Inc 4101 Owl Creek Dr **Fax Area Code:* 800 ■ *TF:* 800-236-7225 ■ *Web:* www.jaeckledistributors.com	Madison	WI	53718	608-838-5400	523-2553*
Kobrin Builders Supply Inc 1924 W Princeton St *TF:* 800-273-5511 ■ *Web:* www.kobrinbuilderssupply.com	Orlando	FL	32804	407-843-1000	649-8600
L Thorn Co Inc 6000 Grant Line Rd PO Box 198 *TF:* 800-662-4594 ■ *Web:* www.lthorn.com	New Albany	IN	47151	812-246-4461	246-2678
Lyman-Richey Corp 4315 Cuming St *TF:* 800-727-8432 ■ *Web:* www.lymanrichey.com	Omaha	NE	68131	402-558-2727	556-5171
Nu Way Concrete Forms Inc 4190 Hoffmeister Ave *Web:* www.nuwayinc.com	Saint Louis	MO	63125	314-544-1214	544-1656
Ontario Stone Corp Whiskey Island *Web:* www.ontariostone.com	Cleveland	OH	44113	216-631-3645	
Reimers-kaufman Concrete Prods 6200 Cornhusker Hwy *Web:* www.reimerskaufman.com	Lincoln	NE	68507	402-434-1855	434-1877
Rio Grande Co 201 Santa Fe Dr *TF:* 800-864-4280 ■ *Web:* www.riograndeco.com	Denver	CO	80223	303-825-2211	629-0417
Ross Island Sand & Gravel Co 4315 SE McLoughlin Blvd PO Box 82249 *TF:* 800-543-0230	Portland	OR	97282	503-239-5504	235-1350
Saf-t-co Supply 1300 E Normandy Pl *Web:* www.saftco.com	Santa Ana	CA	92705	714-547-9975	667-7985
Stone Source LLC 215 Pk Ave S *Web:* www.stonesource.com	New York	NY	10003	212-979-6400	979-6989
Terrazzo & Marble Supply Co of Illinois 77 Wheeling Rd *Web:* www.tmsupply.com	Wheeling	IL	60090	847-353-8000	353-8001
Tile Imports LLC 5800 E Jewell Ave *TF:* 800-727-2272 ■ *Web:* www.capcotile.com	Denver	CO	80224	303-759-1919	756-3416
Tri-State Brick & Stone of New York Inc 333 7th Ave 5th Fl *Web:* www.tristatebrick.com	New York	NY	10001	212-686-3939	686-4387
Vimco Concrete Accessories Inc 300 Hansen Access Rd *TF Cust Svc:* 888-468-4626 ■ *Web:* www.vimcoinc.com	King of Prussia	PA	19406	610-768-0500	768-0586
Western Brick Co 7620 Washington Ave *Web:* www.western-brick.com	Houston	TX	77007	713-861-1751	864-1231
WF Saunders & Sons Inc PO Box A *Web:* www.saundersconcrete.com	Nedrow	NY	13120	315-469-3217	469-3940

194-2 Construction Materials (Misc)

	City	State	Zip	Phone	Fax
Acoustical Material Services Inc 1620 S Maple Ave *TF:* 800-486-3517 ■ *Web:* www.a-m-s.com	Montebello	CA	90640	323-721-9011	721-2476
Alliance Wood Group Engineering LP 330 Barker Cypress Rd *Web:* www.alliance-engineering.com	Houston	TX	77094	281-828-6000	647-9701
American Fence Inc 2502 N 27th Ave *TF:* 888-691-4565 ■ *Web:* www.americanfence.com	Phoenix	AZ	85009	602-734-0500	734-0573
APi Group Inc Materials Distribution Group 1100 Old Hwy 8 NW *TF:* 800-223-4922 ■ *Web:* web.apigroupinc.com/materials.html	New Brighton	MN	55112	651-636-4320	636-0312
Arabel Inc 16301 NW 49th Ave *TF Sales:* 800-759-5959 ■ *Web:* www.arabel.com	Hialeah	FL	33014	305-623-8302	624-0714
Basic Components Inc 1201 S 2nd Ave *TF:* 800-452-1780 ■ *Web:* www.basiccomp.com	Mansfield	TX	76063	817-473-7224	473-3388
Brooks Construction Co Inc 6525 Ardmore Ave *Web:* www.brooks1st.com	Fort Wayne	IN	46809	260-478-1990	747-7086
Buchheit Inc 33 Perry County Rd 540 *Web:* www.buchheitonline.com	Perryville	MO	63775	573-547-1010	547-1689
Builders Hardware & Specialty Co Inc 2002 W 16th St **Fax Area Code:* 412 ■ *TF:* 866-455-4799 ■ *Web:* www.builders-hardware.net	Erie	PA	16505	814-453-4736	488-8909*
Cast Products Corp 58263 Charlotte Ave PO Box 1368 *TF:* 800-621-2278 ■ *Web:* www.castproductscorp.com	Elkhart	IN	46515	574-294-2684	295-6921
Chemung Supply Corp PO Box 527 *TF:* 800-733-5508 ■ *Web:* www.chemungsupply.com	Elmira	NY	14902	607-733-5506	732-5379
Clyde Cos Inc 730 N 1500 W *Web:* www.clydeinc.com	Orem	UT	84057	801-802-6900	802-6906
Concrete Materials Inc 1201 W Russell St *Web:* www.concretematerialscompany.com	Sioux Falls	SD	57118	605-357-6000	334-6221
CR Laurence Co Inc 2503 E Vernon Ave PO Box 58923 **Fax Area Code:* 800 ■ *TF:* 800-421-6144 ■ *Web:* www.crlaurence.com	Los Angeles	CA	90058	323-588-1281	262-3299*
Dmg Equipment Co Ltd 1572 FM 1485 PO Box 691	Conroe	TX	77305	936-756-6960	760-1625
DS Brown Co 300 E Cherry St *TF:* 800-848-1730 ■ *Web:* www.dsbrown.com	North Baltimore	OH	45872	419-257-3561	257-2200
Eastern Wholesale Fence Co Inc 274 Middle Island Rd *Web:* www.easternfence.com	Medford	NY	11763	631-698-0975	698-1193
Empire Bldg Materials Inc PO Box 220 *TF:* 800-332-4577 ■ *Web:* www.empireinc.com	Bozeman	MT	59771	406-587-3191	587-3144
Fargo Glass & Paint Co Inc 1801 7th Ave N *TF:* 800-437-4612	Fargo	ND	58102	701-235-4441	235-3435
Gossen /corp 2030 W Bender Rd *TF:* 800-558-8984 ■ *Web:* www.gossencorp.com	Milwaukee	WI	53209	414-228-9800	228-9077
H Myers John & Son Inc 2200 Monroe St *Web:* www.jhmson.com	York	PA	17404	717-792-2500	792-5115
J O Galloup Co 135 Manufacturers Dr *TF:* 888-755-3110 ■ *Web:* www.galloup.com	Holland	MI	49424	269-965-4005	965-3263
Kuriyama of America Inc 360 E State Pkwy *TF:* 800-800-0320 ■ *Web:* www.kuriyama.com	Schaumburg	IL	60173	847-755-0360	885-0996
Lummus Supply Co 1554 Bolton Rd NW *Web:* www.lummus-supply.com	Atlanta	GA	30331	404-794-1501	794-4519
Oldcastle Glass Group 2425 Olympic Blvd Suite 525E *TF:* 866-653-2278 ■ *Web:* www.oldcastlebe.com	Santa Monica	CA	90404	310-264-4700	264-4703
Penrod Co 2809 S Lynnhaven Rd Suite 350 *TF:* 800-537-3497 ■ *Web:* www.thepenrodcompany.com	Virginia Beach	VA	23452	757-498-0186	498-1075
Powers Products Co PO Box 1187 *Web:* www.powersproducts.com	Cheyenne	WY	82003	307-632-5521	632-2335
Robert N Karpp Co Inc 480 E First St *TF:* 800-244-5886 ■ *Web:* www.karpp.com	Boston	MA	02127	617-269-5880	269-2387
Rose & Walker Supply Lafayette Inc (RWS) 3565 US Hwy 52 S *TF:* 888-447-1275 ■ *Web:* www.roseandwalkersupply.com	Lafayette	IN	47905	765-471-7070	474-7507
Southeastern Energy Corp 700 Military Cutoff Rd Suite 235 PO Box 9309 *Web:* www.southeasternenergycorp.com	Wilmington	NC	28405	910-332-4157	
Spates Fabricators 85435 Middleton *Web:* www.spates.com	Thermal	CA	92274	760-397-4122	397-4724
Star Sales & Distributing Corp 29 Commerce Way *TF:* 800-222-8118 ■ *Web:* www.starsales.com	Woburn	MA	01801	781-933-8830	933-2145
T H Rogers Lumber Co The PO Box 5770 *Web:* www.throgers.com	Edmond	OK	73083	405-330-2181	330-2186

194-3 Lumber & Building Supplies

	City	State	Zip	Phone	Fax
84 Lumber Co 1019 Rt 519 *TF:* 800-664-1984 ■ *Web:* www.84lumber.com	Eighty Four	PA	15330	724-228-8820	
AC Houston Lumber Co 5555 Arville St *Web:* www.houstonlumber.com	Las Vegas	NV	89118	702-633-5100	633-5111
Alamo Lumber Co 10800 Sentinel Dr *Web:* www.alamo.doitbest.com	San Antonio	TX	78217	210-352-1300	590-1438
Allied Bldg Products Corp 15 E Union Ave *TF:* 800-541-2198 ■ *Web:* www.alliedbuilding.com	East Rutherford	NJ	07073	201-507-8400	507-3855
Alpine Lumber Co 1120 W 122nd Ave Suite 301 *TF:* 800-275-2365 ■ *Web:* www.alpinelumber.com	Westminster	CO	80234	303-451-8001	451-5232
American Direct Procurement Inc 11000 Lakeview Ave *Web:* www.americandirectco.com	Lenexa	KS	66219	913-677-5588	
American International Forest Products LLC 5560 SW 107th St *TF:* 800-366-1611 ■ *Web:* www.lumber.com	Beaverton	OR	97005	503-641-1611	641-2800
Ar-Jay Bldg Products Inc PO Box 10017 *Web:* www.ar-jay.com	Cedar Rapids	IA	52410	319-393-5885	393-5638
Arnold Lumber Co 251 Fairgrounds Rd *TF:* 800-339-0116 ■ *Web:* www.arnold.myeshowroom.com	West Kingston	RI	02892	401-783-2266	792-3610
Ashe Industries Inc 4505 Transport Dr *TF:* 800-780-2743 ■ *Web:* www.asheindustries.com	Tampa	FL	33605	813-247-2743	247-2809
Auburn Corp 10490 164th Pl *TF:* 800-393-1826 ■ *Web:* www.auburncorp.com	Orland Park	IL	60467	708-349-7676	349-9461
Babcock Lumber Co Inc 2220 Palmer St PO Box 8348 *TF:* 800-553-4441 ■ *Web:* www.babcocklumber.com	Pittsburgh	PA	15218	412-351-3515	351-1522
Baille Lumber Co 4002 Legion Dr PO Box 6 *TF:* 800-950-2850 ■ *Web:* www.baillie.com	Hamburg	NY	14075	716-649-2850	649-2811
Banner Supply Co 7195 NW 30th St *TF:* 888-511-4004 ■ *Web:* www.bannersupply.com	Miami	FL	33122	305-593-2946	477-2775
Bayer Built Woodworks Inc 24614 Hwy 71 *Web:* www.bayerbuilt.com	Belgrade	MN	56312	320-254-3651	254-3601
Beavertooth Oak Inc 401 S Fir St *TF:* 800-306-1942 ■ *Web:* www.beavertooth.net	Medford	OR	97501	541-779-1942	776-0944

Company	City	State	Zip	Phone	Fax
Bender Lumber Co Inc 3120 Brock Ln *Web:* www.benderlumber.com	Bedford	IN	47421	812-279-9737	279-1659
Big C Lumber Inc 50860 Princess Way PO Box 176 *TF:* 888-297-0010 ■ *Web:* www.bigclumber.com	Granger	IN	46530	574-277-4550	271-3823
Big Creek Lumber 3564 Hwy 1 *Web:* www.big-creek.com	Davenport	CA	95017	831-457-5015	423-2800
Birmingham International Forest Products LLC 300 Riverhills Business Pk *TF:* 800-767-2437 ■ *Web:* www.bifp.com	Birmingham	AL	35242	205-972-1500	972-1461
Bison Bldg Materials Ltd 1445 W Sam Houston Pkwy N *Web:* www.bisonbuilding.com	Houston	TX	77043	713-467-6700	935-1212
Bloch Lumber Co 123 N Wacker Dr Suite 1350 *TF:* 800-621-2107 ■ *Web:* www.blochlumber.com	Chicago	IL	60606	312-466-4500	466-4800
BlueLinx Holdings Inc 4300 Wildwood Pkwy *NYSE: BXC* ■ **Fax Area Code:* 800 ■ *TF:* 888-502-2583 ■ *Web:* www.bluelinxco.com	Atlanta	GA	30339	770-953-7000	203-3780*
Boise Cascade Bldg Materials Distribution Div 1111 W Jefferson St Suite 300 PO Box 50 *Web:* www.bc.com/bmd/index.jsp	Boise	ID	83728	208-384-6354	384-7291
Bradco Supply Corp 13 Production Way *TF:* 877-427-2320 ■ *Web:* www.bradcosupply.com	Avenel	NJ	07001	732-382-3400	382-6577
Britton Lumber Co Inc 7 Ely Rd PO Box 389 *TF:* 800-343-5300 ■ *Web:* www.brittonlumber.com	Fairlee	VT	05045	802-333-4388	333-4295
Brookside Lumber & Supply Co PO Box 327 *Web:* www.brooksidelumber.com	Bethel Park	PA	15102	412-835-7610	835-8672
Buckeye Pacific LLC 4386 SW Macadam Ave Suite 200 *TF:* 800-767-9191 ■ *Web:* www.buckeyepacific.com	Portland	OR	97207	503-228-3330	274-1039
Builders FirstSource Inc 2001 Bryan St Suite 1600 *NASDAQ: BLDR* ■ *Web:* www.bldr.com	Dallas	TX	75201	214-880-3500	880-3599
Builders General Supply Co 15 Sycamore Ave *TF:* 800-570-7227 ■ *Web:* www.buildersgeneral.com	Little Silver	NJ	07739	732-747-0808	741-1095
Campbellsport Bldg Supply Inc 227 W Main St PO Box 510 *Web:* www.furnishanddesign.com	Campbellsport	WI	53010	920-533-4412	533-4333
Canfor USA Corp 4395 Curtis Rd	Bellingham	WA	98226	360-647-2434	647-2437
Carolina Holdings Inc 4403 Bland Rd *TF:* 877-734-6365 ■ *Web:* www.carolinaholdings.com	Raleigh	NC	27609	919-431-1000	431-1199
Causeway Lumber Co 2627 S Andrews Ave *TF:* 800-375-5050 ■ *Web:* www.causewaylumber.com	Fort Lauderdale	FL	33316	954-763-1224	768-5921
Champion Lumber Co 1313 Chicago Ave Suite 100 *Web:* www.championlumber.net	Riverside	CA	92507	951-684-5670	275-0825
Chelsea Lumber Co 1 Old Barn Cir *TF:* 800-875-9126 ■ *Web:* www.chelsealumber.com	Chelsea	MI	48118	734-475-9126	475-7320
Chicago Lumber Co of Omaha The 1324 Pierce St PO Box 3487 *TF:* 800-642-8210 ■ *Web:* www.chicagolumbercompany.com	Omaha	NE	68103	402-342-0840	344-8323
Cleary Millwork Co Inc 235 Dividend Rd *TF:* 800-486-7600 ■ *Web:* www.clearymillwork.com	Rocky Hill	CT	06067	860-721-0520	
Clem Lumber Distributing Co Inc PO Box 2238 *TF:* 800-362-9831 ■ *Web:* www.clemlumber.com	Alliance	OH	44601	330-821-2130	821-6143
Cnc Assoc Ny Inc 101 Kentile Rd *Web:* www.cncassociates.com	South Plainfield	NJ	07080	718-416-3853	475-3900
Counter Pro Inc 210 Lincoln St *TF:* 800-899-2444 ■ *Web:* www.counterproinc.com	Manchester	NH	03103	603-647-2444	647-6770
Coventry Lumber Inc 2030 Nooseneck Hill Rd *TF:* 800-390-0919 ■ *Web:* www.coventrylumber.com	Coventry	RI	02816	401-821-2800	828-2870
Creative Pultrusions Inc 214 Industrial Ln *TF:* 888-274-7855 ■ *Web:* www.pultrude.com	Alum Bank	PA	15521	814-839-4186	839-4276
Custom Builder Supply Co Inc PO Box 413 *Web:* www.custombuildersupply.com	Williamsburg	VA	23187	757-229-5150	253-7568
DeGol Organization LP The 3229 Pleasant Valley Blvd c/o Marketing Dept *TF:* 800-800-5881 ■ *Web:* www.degol.com	Altoona	PA	16602	814-941-7777	941-5377
Delmarva Millwork Corp PO Box 4068 *Web:* www.d-m-c.com	Lancaster	PA	17604	717-299-2364	293-9249
Doka USA Ltd 214 Gates Rd *TF:* 877-365-2872 ■ *Web:* www.doka.com	Little Ferry	NJ	07643	201-329-7839	641-6254
Door Systems Inc PO Box 511 *TF:* 800-545-3667 ■ *Web:* www.doorsys.com	Framingham	MA	01704	508-875-3508	
EC Barton & Co 2929 Browns Ln *Web:* www.ecbarton.com	Jonesboro	AR	72403	870-932-6673	972-1304
Edward Hines Lumber Co 1000 Corporate Grove Dr **Fax Area Code:* 847 ■ *TF:* 888-334-4637 ■ *Web:* www.hineslumber.com	Buffalo Grove	IL	60089	888-334-4637	353-7891*
Eldredge Lumber & Hardware Inc PO Box 69 *Web:* www.eldredgelumber.com	Cape Neddick	ME	03902	207-363-2004	363-7453
Falmouth Lumber Inc 670 Teaticket Hwy *Web:* www.falmouthlumber.com	East Falmouth	MA	02536	508-548-6868	457-0649
FE Wheaton & Co 204 W Wheaton Ave *Web:* www.fewheaton.com	Yorkville	IL	60560	630-553-8300	553-8320
Forest City Trading Group LLC 10250 SW Greenburg Rd Suite 200 PO Box 4209 *TF:* 800-767-3284 ■ *Web:* www.fctg.com	Portland	OR	97208	503-246-8500	246-1116
Forest Products Group Inc The 1033 Dublin Rd *Web:* www.forestproductsgroup.com	Columbus	OH	43215	614-488-9743	
Foxworth-Galbraith Lumber Co 4965 Preston Pk Blvd Suite 400 *TF:* 800-688-8082 ■ *Web:* www.foxgal.com	Plano	TX	75093	972-665-2400	454-4238
Frank Miller Lumber Co Inc 1690 Frank Miller Rd *Web:* www.frankmiller.com	Union City	IN	47390	765-964-3196	964-6618
Frank Paxton Lumber Co 7455 Dawson Rd **Fax:* Sales ■ *TF:* 800-325-9800 ■ *Web:* www.paxtonwood.com	Cincinnati	OH	45243	513-984-8200	984-9060*
Genesee Reserve Supply Inc 200 Jefferson Rd PO Box 20619 *Web:* www.geneseereserve.com	Rochester	NY	14602	585-292-7040	292-7046
Gerretsen Bldg Supply Co 1900 NE Airport Rd *Web:* www.gerretsen.com	Roseburg	OR	97470	541-672-2636	464-6230
Gold & Reiss Corp 254 Bay Ridge Ave *Web:* www.goldnreisskitchens.com	Brooklyn	NY	11220	718-680-2600	435-2523
Great Lakes Veneer Inc 222 S Parkview Ave PO Box 476 *Web:* www.greatlakesveneer.com	Marion	WI	54950	715-754-2501	754-2582
Guardian Bldg Products Distribution (GBPD) 979 Batesville Rd *TF:* 800-569-4262 ■ *Web:* www.guardianbp.com	Greer	SC	29651	864-297-6101	
H. W. Culp Lumber Co PO Box 235 *Web:* www.culplumber.com	New London	NC	28127	704-463-7311	463-4100
Hagle Lumber Co Inc 3100 Somis Rd PO Box 120 *Web:* www.haglelumber.com	Somis	CA	93066	805-987-3887	987-7564
Hallmark Bldg Supplies Inc 2120 Pewaukee Rd Suite 100 **Fax Area Code:* 414 ■ *TF:* 800-642-2246 ■ *Web:* www.hllmark.com	Waukesha	WI	53188	262-408-4200	688-7842*
Hatch & Bailey Co Inc 1 Meadow St Ext *Web:* www.hatchandbailey.com	Norwalk	CT	06854	203-866-5515	854-1712
Hawaii Planing Mill Ltd (HPM) 16-166 Melekahiwa St *Web:* www.hpmhawaii.com	Keaau	HI	96749	808-966-5662	966-7564
Holt & Bugbee Co 1600 Shawsheen St *TF:* 800-325-6010 ■ *Web:* www.holtandbugbee.com	Tewksbury	MA	01876	978-851-7201	851-3941
Hood Distribution McQuesten Group 600 Iron Horse Pk *TF:* 800-752-0129 ■ *Web:* www.hooddistribution.com/products/mcquesten	North Billerica	MA	01862	978-663-3435	667-0934
Hope Lumber & Supply Co 12213 E 61st St *Web:* www.hopelumber.com	Broken Arrow	OK	74012	918-250-9766	252-0727
Howard Lumber Co 475 Columbia Industrial Blvd PO Box 1039 *TF:* 800-868-3227 ■ *Web:* www.howardlumber.net	Evans	GA	30809	706-868-8400	868-9989
Hutchison Inc 7460 Hwy 85 PO Box 1158 *TF:* 800-525-0121 ■ *Web:* www.hutchison-inc.com	Adams City	CO	80022	303-287-2826	289-3286
Huttig Bldg Products Inc (HBP) 555 Maryville University Dr Suite 400 *NYSE: HBP* ■ *TF:* 800-325-4466 ■ *Web:* www.huttig.com	Saint Louis	MO	63141	314-216-2600	216-2601
Idaho Pacific Lumber Co (IdaPac) 7255 Franklin Rd *TF:* 800-231-2310 ■ *Web:* www.idapac.com	Boise	ID	83704	208-375-8052	375-3054
Jb Wholesale Roofing & Bldg Supplies Inc 21544 Nordhoff St PO Box 5289 *Web:* www.jbroofing.com	Chatsworth	CA	91313	818-998-0440	998-7895
JE Higgins Lumber Co 6999 S Front Rd *TF:* 800-241-1883 ■ *Web:* www.higlum.com	Livermore	CA	94551	925-245-4300	245-4343
Jewett-Cameron Trading Co Ltd 32275 NW Hillcrest PO Box 1010 *NASDAQ: JCTCF* ■ *TF:* 800-547-5877 ■ *Web:* www.jewettcameron.com	North Plains	OR	97133	503-647-0110	647-2272
JM Thomas Forest Products PO Box 12668 *TF Sales:* 800-962-8780 ■ *Web:* www.thomasforest.com	Ogden	UT	84412	801-782-8090	
Kight Home Ctr 5521 Oak Grove Rd *Web:* www.kighthomecenter.com	Evansville	IN	47715	812-479-8281	473-7763
Kimal Lumber Co 400 Riverview Dr *Web:* www.kimallumber.com	Nokomis	FL	34275	941-484-9721	484-9593
Kleet Lumber Co Inc 777 Pk Ave *TF:* 800-696-5533 ■ *Web:* www.kleet.com	Huntington	NY	11743	631-427-7060	427-4384
Livonia Bldg Materials Co 33900 Concord Rd	Livonia	MI	48150	734-421-1170	421-5237
Louis & Co 895 Columbia St *TF:* 800-422-4389 ■ *Web:* www.louisandcompany.com	Brea	CA	92821	714-529-1771	990-6184
Lumbermen's Merchandising Corp 137 W Wayne Ave *Web:* www.lmc.net	Wayne	PA	19087	610-293-7000	293-7924
Lyman Lumber Co 300 Morse Ave PO Box 40 *Web:* www.lymanlumber.com	Excelsior	MN	55331	952-470-3600	470-3670
Lyon & Billard Co The 38 Gypsy Ln *Web:* www.lyon-billard.com	Meriden	CT	06451	203-235-4487	235-9736
Magbee Contractors Supply 1065 Bankhead Hwy *Web:* www.magbee.com	Winder	GA	30680	678-425-2600	425-2602
Magnolia Forest Products Inc 13252 I- 55 S PO Box 99 **Fax Area Code:* 601 ■ *TF:* 800-366-6374 ■ *Web:* www.magnoliaforest.com	Terry	MS	39170	800-366-6374	878-2590*
Markraft Cabinets Inc 2705 Castle Creek Ln *Web:* www.markraft.com	Wilmington	NC	28401	910-762-1986	762-1985
Matheus Lumber Co Inc 15800 Woodinville-Redmond Rd NE PO Box 2260 *TF:* 800-284-7501 ■ *Web:* www.matheuslumber.com	Woodinville	WA	98072	425-489-3000	822-4028
Matt's Building Materials 404 E Expy 83 *Web:* www.mattsbuildingmaterials.com	Pharr	TX	78577	956-787-5561	787-7096
Mattingly Lumber & Millwork Inc 410 E St *Web:* www.mattinglylumber.com	Madison	IL	62040	636-343-3877	343-4141
McCray Lumber Co 10741 El Monte Ln *Web:* www.mccraylumber.com	Overland Park	KS	66211	913-341-6900	341-1881
Mead Clark Lumber Co Hearn Ave & Dowd Dr PO Box 529 *TF:* 800-585-9663 ■ *Web:* www.meadclark.com	Santa Rosa	CA	95402	707-576-3333	523-0350
MID-AM Bldg Supply Inc 1615 Omar Bradley Dr PO Box 645 *TF:* 800-892-5850 ■ *Web:* www.midambuilding.com	Moberly	MO	65270	660-263-2140	263-7892
Mid-South Bldg Supply Inc 7940 Woodruff Ct *Web:* www.msbs.net	Springfield	VA	22151	703-321-8500	321-9308
Mill Creek Lumber & Supply Co 6201 S 129th E Ave PO Box 4770 *TF:* 800-364-6455 ■ *Web:* www.millcreeklumber.com	Tulsa	OK	74012	918-461-9090	461-2445
Millard Lumber Inc 12900 I St PO Box 45445 *Web:* www.millardlumber.com	Omaha	NE	68145	402-896-2800	896-2865
Musser Lumber Co Inc 200 Shoal Ridge Dr *Web:* www.musserlumber.com	Rural Retreat	VA	24368	276-686-5113	686-5169

	City	State	ZIP	Phone	Fax
N A Mans & Sons Inc 3300 W Jefferson *Web:* www.namans.com	Trenton	MI	48183	734-676-3000	676-7319
Nassau Suffolk Lumber & Supply Corp 2000 Ocean Ave *Web:* www.nassausuffolklumber.com	Ronkonkoma	NY	11779	631-467-2020	467-2720
National Lumber Co 24595 Groesbeck Hwy *TF:* 800-462-9712	Warren	MI	48089	586-775-8200	775-4110
North Pacific 2419 Science Pkwy *TF:* 800-942-8220 ■ *Web:* www.northpacific.com	Okemos	MI	48864	517-349-8220	349-8377
North Pacific Group Inc (NORPAC) 815 NE Davis St **Fax:* Hum Res ■ *TF:* 800-547-8440	Portland	OR	97232	503-231-1166	238-2646*
Ohio Valley Supply Co 3512 Spring Grove Ave *TF:* 800-696-5608 ■ *Web:* www.ovsco.com	Cincinnati	OH	45223	513-681-8300	853-3307
Omega Products Intl 1681 California Ave *Web:* www.omega-products.com	CORONA	CA	92881	951-737-7447	520-2594
Orgain Building Supply Co 65 Commerce St *Web:* www.orgainbuilding.com	Clarksville	TN	37040	931-647-1567	648-4482
Pacific Source Inc PO Box 2323 *TF:* 800-343-1515 ■ *Web:* www.pacsource.com	Woodinville	WA	98072	425-483-5511	486-1445
Pacific Wood Laminates Inc 885 Railroad Ave PO Box 820 *Web:* www.pacificwoodlaminates.com	Brookings	OR	97415	541-469-4177	469-9105
Palmer-Donavin Mfg Co 1200 Steelwood Rd *TF:* 800-589-4412 ■ *Web:* www.palmerdonavin.com	Columbus	OH	43212	614-486-9657	486-5073
Park Avenue Building & Roofing Supplies LLC 2120 Atlantic Ave *Web:* www.parkavebenmoore.com	Brooklyn	NY	11233	718-403-0100	596-5085
Parker Lumber Co Inc 2192 Eastex Fwy *Web:* www.parkerlumber.com	Bremerton	TX	77703	409-898-7000	347-0942
Parker Lumber Co of Port Arthur Inc 2948 Gulfway DR *Web:* www.parkerlumber.net	Port Arthur	TX	77642	409-983-2745	983-3993
Parksite Inc 1563 Hubbard Ave *TF:* 800-338-3355 ■ *Web:* www.parksite.com	Batavia	IL	60510	630-761-9490	761-6820
PrimeSource Bldg Products Inc 2115 E Beltline Rd *TF:* 800-745-3341 ■ *Web:* www.primesourcebp.com	Carrollton	TX	75006	972-416-1976	416-8331
ProBuild 7595 Technology Way *TF:* 800-211-2571 ■ *Web:* www.homelumber.com	Denver	CO	80237	303-262-8500	791-4352
Product Distributors Inc 4200 Beach Dr Suite 2 PO Box 8088 *Web:* www.forpd.com	Rapid City	SD	57702	605-341-6500	341-1976
Pyramid Interiors Distributors Inc PO Box 181058 *TF:* 800-456-0592 ■ *Web:* www.pyramidinteriors.com	Memphis	TN	38181	901-375-4197	
Quality Plywood Specialties Inc 4500 110th Ave N *TF:* 888-722-1181 ■ *Web:* www.qualityplywoodspec.com	Clearwater	FL	33762	727-572-0500	571-3623
Quality Wholesale Bldg Products Inc 11701 Kinard Rd	North Little Rock	AR	72117	501-945-3442	945-0506
R & K Bldg Supplies Inc PO Box 4740 *Web:* www.randkbuildingsupplies.com	Mesa	AZ	85211	480-892-0025	926-3866
Raymond Bldg Supply Corp 7751 Bayshore Rd *TF:* 877-731-7272 ■ *Web:* www.rbsc.net	North Fort Myers	FL	33917	239-731-8300	731-3299
Reliable Wholesale Lumber Inc 7600 Redondo Cir *Web:* www.rwli.net	Huntington Beach	CA	92648	714-848-8222	847-1605
Richard G. Jennings III Enterprises Inc PO Box 1459	Cashiers	NC	28717	828-743-3684	743-9061
Richmond International Forest Products Inc 4050 Innslake Dr Suite 100 *TF:* 800-767-0111 ■ *Web:* www.rifp.com	Glen Allen	VA	23060	804-747-0111	270-4547
Ridout Lumber Co Inc 125 Henry Farrar Dr *Web:* www.ridoutlumber.com	Searcy	AR	72143	501-268-3929	268-0678
Rigidply Rafters Inc 701 E Linden St *Web:* www.rigidply.com	Richland	PA	17087	717-866-6581	
Riverhead Bldg Supply Corp 1093 Pulaski St *TF:* 800-378-3650 ■ *Web:* www.rbscorp.com	Riverhead	NY	11901	631-727-3650	727-7713
Riverside Forest Products Inc 2912 Professional Pkwy *TF:* 888-855-8733 ■ *Web:* www.riversideforest.com	Augusta	GA	30907	706-855-5500	863-3362
RP Lumber Co Inc 514 E Vandalia St *Web:* www.rplumber.com	Edwardsville	IL	62025	618-656-1514	656-6785
Russin Lumber Corp 21 Leonards Dr *TF:* 800-724-0010 ■ *Web:* www.russinlumber.com	Montgomery	NY	12549	845-457-4000	457-4010
Saxonville USA 96 Springfield Rd *TF:* 800-882-2106 ■ *Web:* www.saxonville.com	Charlestown	NH	03603	603-826-4024	826-5205
Schoeneman Bros Co 4000 S Western Ave *Web:* www.schoenemans.com	Sioux Falls	SD	57103	605-336-2441	336-2529
Seaboard International Forest Products LLC 22 Cotton Rd Suite F PO Box 6059 *TF:* 800-669-6800 ■ *Web:* www.sifp.com	Nashua	NH	03063	603-881-3700	598-2280
Seigle's 1331 Davis Rd *Web:* www.seigles.com	Elgin	IL	60123	847-742-2000	697-6521
Service Construction Supply Inc PO Box 13405 *TF:* 866-729-4968 ■ *Web:* www.serviceconstructionsupply.com	Birmingham	AL	35202	205-252-3158	252-5720
Solar Industries Inc PO Box 27337 *TF:* 800-449-2323 ■ *Web:* www.solarindustriesinc.com	Tucson	AZ	85726	520-790-8989	294-6804
Spellman Hardwoods Inc 4645 N 43rd Ave **Fax Area Code:* 623 ■ *TF:* 800-624-5401 ■ *Web:* www.spellmanhardwoods.com	Phoenix	AZ	85031	602-272-2313	930-7668*
Sprenger Midwest Inc 700 S 4th Ave *Web:* www.sprengermidwest.com	Sioux Falls	SD	57104	605-334-7705	334-5205
STAN'S LUMBER INC 202 E Main St **Fax Area Code:* 262 ■ *Web:* www.stanslumber.com	Twin Lakes	WI	53181	800-763-9327	723-3472*
Standard Supplies Inc 4 Meem Ave *TF:* 800-627-8775 ■ *Web:* www.standardsupplies.com	Gaithersburg	MD	20877	301-948-2690	590-1789
Stevenson Lumber 1585 Monroe Tpke PO Box 123 *TF:* 800-972-4260	Stevenson	CT	06468	203-261-2555	261-8046
Stock Bldg Supply 8020 Arco Corporate Dr *TF:* 877-734-6365 ■ *Web:* www.stockbuildingsupply.com	Raleigh	NC	27617	919-431-1000	431-1199
Sunderland Bros Co 9700 J St *Web:* www.sunderlands.com	Omaha	NE	68127	402-339-2220	339-4455
Timber Products Co 305 S 4th St PO Box 269 *TF:* 800-547-9520 ■ *Web:* www.timberproducts.com	Springfield	OR	97477	541-747-4577	744-4296
Timberline Forest Products LLC PO Box 1568 *Web:* www.timberlineforestproducts.com	Sherwood	OR	97140	503-590-5485	590-7421
Tischler Und Sohn 6 Suburban Ave *Web:* www.tischlerwindows.com	Stamford	CT	06901	203-674-0600	674-0601
Tri-state Forest Products Inc 2105 Sheridan Ave *TF:* 800-949-6325 ■ *Web:* www.tsfpi.com	Springfield	OH	45505	937-323-6325	323-6888
Tulnoy Lumber Inc 1620 Webster Ave *Web:* www.tulnoylumber.com	Bronx	NY	10457	718-901-1700	299-8920
US Lumber Group Inc 2160 Satellite Blvd Suite 450 *Web:* www.uslumber.com	Duluth	GA	30097	678-474-4577	474-4575
Verhalen Inc 500 Pilgrim Way PO Box 11968 *TF:* 800-236-8646 ■ *Web:* www.verhaleninc.com	Green Bay	WI	54307	920-431-8900	431-8901
Viking Forest Products LLC 7615 Smetana Ln *TF:* 800-733-3801 ■ *Web:* www.vikingforest.com	Eden Prairie	MN	55344	952-941-6512	941-4633
Vns Corp 325 Commerce Loop PO Box 1659 *Web:* www.vnscorp.com	Vidalia	GA	30475	912-537-8964	537-4839
Vytex Corp 9425 Washington Blvd N *TF:* 877-747-8735 ■ *Web:* www.vytexwindows.com	Laurel	MD	20723	301-362-1000	
Warren Trask CO 1481 Central St *Web:* www.wtrask.com	Stoughton	MA	02072	781-341-2426	341-3522
West Elizabeth Lumber Co 1 Chicago Ave *TF:* 800-289-9352	Elizabeth	PA	15037	412-384-3900	384-3955
Western Lumber Cy LLC 2240a Tower E Suite 200 *TF:* 800-633-5554 ■ *Web:* www.westernlumber.com	Medford	OR	97504	541-779-5121	779-0155
Weyrick Cos Inc 626 N Main St *Web:* www.weyrick.com	Templeton	CA	93465	805-434-4800	434-3770
Wheeler Lumber LLC 9330 James Ave S *TF:* 800-328-3986 ■ *Web:* www.wheeler-con.com	Bloomington	MN	55431	952-929-7854	929-2909
Wheeler's Corp 550 Riverside Pkwy NE *Web:* www.wheelers.com	Rome	GA	30161	706-232-2400	
White Cap Industries Inc 1723 S Ritchie St *TF:* 800-922-9922 ■ *Web:* www.whitecap.com	Santa Ana	CA	92705	714-258-3300	258-3289
Wilson Lumber Co Inc 4818 Meridian St PO Box 3159 *Web:* www.wilsonlumber.net	Huntsville	AL	35811	256-852-7411	464-7266
Window Rama Enterprises Inc 71 Heartland Blvd *Web:* www.windowrama.com	Edgewood	NY	11717	631-667-2555	
Woodinville Lumber Inc 15900 Wdnville Redmond Rd *Web:* www.woodinvillelumber.com	Woodinville	WA	98072	425-488-1818	402-6870
Wright Do-it center 1306 N Market *Web:* www.wrightdoit.com	SPARTA	IL	62286	618-443-5335	687-1030
WT Harvey Lumber Co 800 15th St PO Box 310 *Web:* www.harveylumber.com	Columbus	GA	31902	706-322-8204	323-2433
Zeeland Lumber & Supply Co 146 E Washington *Web:* www.zeelandlumber.com	Zeeland	MI	49464	616-772-2119	772-6409

194-4 Roofing, Siding, Insulation Materials

	City	State	ZIP	Phone	Fax
ABC Seamless 3001 Fiechtner Dr *TF:* 800-732-6577 ■ *Web:* www.abcseamless.com	Fargo	ND	58103	701-293-5952	293-3107
ABC Supply Co Inc 1 ABC Pkwy *TF:* 800-366-2227 ■ *Web:* www.abc-supply.com	Beloit	WI	53511	608-362-7777	362-6215
Aluminum Service Corp 4720 E Adamo Dr *TF:* 877-693-5442 ■ *Web:* www.asibp.com	Tampa	FL	33605	813-247-4667	248-2409
Austin Roofer's Supply Inc 8319 N Lamar Blvd *Web:* www.roofingsupplygroup.com	Austin	TX	78753	512-834-4347	834-4352
B & L Wholesale Supply Inc 70 Hartford St *Web:* www.blwholesale.com	Rochester	NY	14605	585-546-6616	546-7326
Beacon Roofing Supply Inc One Lakeland Pk Dr *NASDAQ: BECN* ■ *TF:* 877-645-7663 ■ *Web:* www.beaconroofingsupply.com	Peabody	MA	01960	978-535-7668	535-7358
Best Distributing Co Inc PO Box 128 *Web:* www.bestdist.com	Goldsboro	NC	27533	919-735-1651	
Bradco Supply Corp 13 Production Way *TF:* 877-427-2320 ■ *Web:* www.bradcosupply.com	Avenel	NJ	07001	732-382-3400	382-6577
Burbank Roofing Supply Inc 700 N Victory Blvd *Web:* www.roofingdealer.com	Burbank	CA	91502	818-840-8851	840-8234
Carlisle Cos Inc 13925 Ballantyne Corporate Pl Suite 400 *NYSE: CSL* ■ *Web:* www.carlisle.com	Charlotte	NC	28277	704-501-1100	501-1190
Carlisle SynTec 1285 Ritner Hwy PO Box 7000 *TF:* 800-479-6832 ■ *Web:* www.carlisle-syntec.com	Carlisle	PA	17013	717-245-7000	245-7053
Crane Composites Inc 23525 W Eames St **Fax:* Hum Res ■ *TF:* 800-435-0080 ■ *Web:* www.cranecomposites.com	Channahon	IL	60410	815-467-8600	467-8666*
E O Wood Co Inc PO Box 7416 *Web:* www.eowood.com	Fort Worth	TX	76111	817-834-8811	831-0834
EJ Bartells Co 700 Powell Ave SW PO Box 4160 *TF:* 800-468-9528 ■ *Web:* www.ejbartells.com	Renton	WA	98057	425-228-4111	228-8807
Frank Roberts & Sons Inc 1130 Robertsville Rd *TF:* 800-262-8955 ■ *Web:* www.roberts-sons.com	Punxsutawney	PA	15767	814-938-5000	938-0880
General Insulation Co Inc 278 Mystic Ave Suite 209 *TF:* 800-442-6662 ■ *Web:* www.generalinsulation.com	Medford	MA	02155	781-391-2070	391-3094
Gulfeagle Supply 501 N Reo St	Tampa	FL	33609	813-636-9808	
H Verby Co Inc 186-14 Jamaica Ave *Web:* www.hverby.com	Jamaica	NY	11423	718-454-5522	454-6609

	City	State	Zip	Phone	Fax
Harvey Industries Inc 1400 Main St *Fax Area Code: 781 ■ TF: 800-598-5400 ■ Web: www.harveybp.com	Waltham	MA	02451	800-598-5400	398-7715*
Howred Corp 7887 San Felipe St Suite 122 Web: www.howred.com	Houston	TX	77063	713-781-3980	784-3985
Ib Roof Systems Inc 2877 Chad Dr *Fax Area Code: 888 ■ TF: 800-426-1626 ■ Web: www.ibroof.com	Eugene	OR	97408	800-426-1626	741-1160*
Intermountain Supply Inc 7011 E Mission Ave Web: www.intermountainsupply.com	Spokane	WA	99212	509-891-8802	891-8725
James Hardie Bldg Products 26300 La Alameda Ave Suite 400 TF: 888-542-7343 ■ Web: www.jameshardie.com	Mission Viejo	CA	92691	949-348-1800	367-1294
JPS Industries Inc 55 Beattie Pl # 1510	Greenville	SC	29601	864-239-3900	271-9939
Lansing Bldg Products 8501 Sanford Dr TF: 800-768-5762 ■ Web: www.tedlansing.com	Richmond	VA	23228	804-266-8771	266-0166
MacArthur Co 2400 Wycliff St TF: 800-777-7507 ■ Web: www.macarthurco.com	Saint Paul	MN	55114	651-646-2773	642-9630
McClure-Johnston Co 201 Corey Ave TF: 800-232-0018 ■ Web: www.mcclurejohnston.com	Braddock	PA	15104	412-351-4300	351-1480
Norandex Bldg Materials Distribution Inc 300 Executive Pkwy W Suite 100 TF: 800-528-0942 ■ Web: www.norandex.com	Hudson	OH	44236	800-528-0942	
North Carolina Foam Industries Inc 1515 Carter St TF: 800-346-8229 ■ Web: www.ncfi.com	Mount Airy	NC	27030	336-789-9161	789-9586
OFIC North America Inc 4900 Ondura Dr TF: 800-777-7663 ■ Web: www.ondura.com	Fredericksburg	VA	22407	540-898-7000	898-4991
Owens Corning 1 Owens Corning Pkwy Web: www.owenscorning.com	Toledo	OH	43659	419-248-8000	325-1538
Pacific Coast Bldg Products Inc 10600 White Rock Rd Bldg B Suite 100 Web: www.paccoast.com	Rancho Cordova	CA	95670	916-631-6500	631-6685
Philadelphia Reserve Supply Co 200 Mack Dr TF: 800-347-7726 ■ Web: www.prsco.org	Croydon	PA	19021	215-785-3141	785-5806
Plastatech Engineering Ltd 725 W Morley Dr TF: 800-892-9358 ■ Web: www.plastatech.com	Saginaw	MI	48601	989-754-6500	754-1626
Roofing & Insulation Supply Inc 12221 Merit Dr Suite 1015 Web: www.risris.com	Dallas	TX	75251	972-239-8309	239-8310
Roofing Products & Bldg Supply Co Inc 4955 River Rd Web: www.rfgproducts.com	Jefferson	LA	70121	504-733-0404	733-0360
Roofing Wholesale Co Inc 1918 W Grant St TF Cust Svc: 800-628-5864 ■ Web: www.rwc.org	Phoenix	AZ	85009	602-258-3794	256-0932
SG Wholesale Roofing Supplies Inc 1101 E 6th St TF Cust Svc: 888-747-8500 ■ Web: www.sgroof.com	Santa Ana	CA	92701	714-568-1906	568-1915
Shelter Distribution Inc 1602 Lavon Dr Web: www.shelterdistribution.com	McKinney	TX	75069	972-369-8000	369-8040
Shook & Fletcher Insulation Co 4625 Valleydale Rd TF: 888-829-2575 ■ Web: www.shookandfletcher.com	Birmingham	AL	35242	205-991-7606	991-7745
Spec Bldg Materials Inc 4300 W Ave TF: 800-588-3892	San Antonio	TX	78213	210-342-2727	340-0688
Specialty Products & Insulation Co (SPI) 1650 Manheim Pike Suite 202 TF: 800-788-7764 ■ Web: www.spi-co.com	Lancaster	PA	17601	717-569-3900	519-4046
Standard Roofings Inc 100 Pk Rd TF: 800-624-0036	Tinton Falls	NJ	07724	732-542-3300	542-3807
Sunniland Corp 1721 Hwy 1735 TF: 800-432-1130 ■ Web: www.sunniland.com	Sanford	FL	32773	407-322-2421	324-5784
Variform Inc 303 W Major St PO Box 559 TF: 800-800-2244 ■ Web: www.variform.com	Kearney	MO	64060	816-903-6400	903-6942
Warko Roofing Co Inc 18 Morgan Dr Web: www.thewarkogroup.com	Reading	PA	19608	610-796-4545	796-4547
Wesco Cedar Inc 105 E Hilliard Ln PO Box 40847 TF: 800-547-2511 ■ Web: www.wescocedar.com	Eugene	OR	97404	541-688-5020	688-5024

195 CONSULTING SERVICES - ENVIRONMENTAL

SEE ALSO Recyclable Materials Recovery p. 2530; Remediation Services p. 2533; Waste Management p. 2771

	City	State	Zip	Phone	Fax
A G Miller Co Inc 53 Batavia St Web: www.agmiller.com	Springfield	MA	01109	413-732-9297	734-1236
Aadfw Inc 2161 Regal Pkwy Web: www.aadfwinc.com	Euless	TX	76040	817-540-0153	540-0886
Ameresco Inc 111 Speen St Suite 410 TF: 800-263-7372 ■ Web: www.ameresco.com	Framingham	MA	01701	508-661-2200	661-2201
Arcadis 630 Plaza Dr Suite 200 Web: www.arcadis-us.com	Highlands Ranch	CO	80129	720-344-3500	344-3535
Architectural Energy Corp 2540 Frontier Ave Suite 201 TF: 800-450-4454 ■ Web: www.archenergy.com	Boulder	CO	80301	303-444-4149	444-4304
ATC Assoc Inc 104 E 25th St 10th Fl TF: 800-725-3282 ■ Web: www.atc-enviro.com	New York	NY	10010	212-353-8280	353-8306
Badger Express LLC 181 Quality Ct TF: 800-972-0084 ■ Web: www.badgerexpress.com	Fall River	WI	53932	920-484-5808	484-5818
Blade Energy Partners Ltd 2600 Network Blvd Suite 550 TF: 800-849-1545 ■ Web: www.blade-energy.com	Frisco	TX	75034	972-712-8407	712-8408
CH2M Hill Cos Ltd 9191 S Jamica St *Fax Area Code: 720 ■ Web: www.ch2m.com	Englewood	CO	80112	303-771-0900	286-9250*
Chicanos Por La Causa Inc 1112 E Buckeye Rd Web: www.cplc.org	Phoenix	AZ	85034	602-257-0700	256-2740
Conti Cos 3001 S Clinton Ave Web: www.conticorp.com	South Plainfield	NJ	07080	908-561-7600	754-3283
Covino Environmental Assoc Inc 300 Wildwood Ave Web: www.covinoinc.com	Woburn	MA	01801	781-933-2555	932-9402
Direct Supply Inc 6767 N Industrial Rd Web: www.directsupplycareers.com	Milwaukee	WI	53223	414-358-2805	358-7411
DPRA Inc 200 Research Dr Web: www.dpra.com	Manhattan	KS	66503	785-539-3565	539-5353
Draper Aden Assoc Inc 2206 S Main St Suite A Web: www.daa.com	Blacksburg	VA	24060	540-552-0444	552-0291
Earth Systems Inc 895 Aerovista Pl Suite 102 TF: 866-781-0112 ■ Web: www.earthsystems.com	San Luis Obispo	CA	93401	805-781-0112	781-0180
Ecology & Environment Inc 368 Pleasant View Dr AMEX: EEI ■ Web: www.ene.com	Lancaster	NY	14086	716-684-8060	684-0844
Ehs-International Inc 13228 NE 20th St Suite 100 Web: www.ehsintl.com	Bellevue	WA	98005	425-455-2959	646-7247
Energy & Environmental Analysis Inc 1655 N Fort Myer Dr Suite 600 Web: www.eea-inc.com	Arlington	VA	22209	703-528-1900	528-5106
Entact LLC 3129 Bass Pro Dr Web: www.entact.com	Irving	TX	75063	972-580-1323	550-7464
ENVIRON International Corp 4350 N Fairfax Dr Suite 300 Web: www.environcorp.com	Arlington	VA	22203	703-516-2300	516-2345
Environmental & Safety Designs Inc 5724 Summer Trees Dr TF: 800-588-7962 ■ Web: www.ensafe.com	Memphis	TN	38134	901-372-7962	372-2454
ERM Group Inc 350 Eagle View Blvd TF: 800-662-1124 ■ Web: www.erm.com	Exton	PA	19341	610-524-3500	524-7335
Evans Environmental & Geosciences 14505 Commerce Way Suite 400 TF: 800-486-7458 ■ Web: www.eeandg.com	Miami Lakes	FL	33016	305-374-8300	374-9004
Evergreen Energy 1225 17th St Suite 1300 NYSE: EEE ■ TF: 800-590-4180 ■ Web: www.evgenergy.com	Denver	CO	80202	303-293-2992	293-8430
Fauske & Assoc LLC 16w070 83rd St TF: 877-328-7531 ■ Web: www.fauske.com	Burr Ridge	IL	60527	630-323-8750	986-5481
First Environment Inc 91 Fulton St TF: 800-486-5869 ■ Web: www.firstenvironment.com	Boonton	NJ	07005	973-334-0003	334-0928
Gilman & Pastor LLP 63 Atlantic Ave 3rd Fl *Fax Area Code: 508 ■ TF: 877-428-7374 ■ Web: www.gilmanpastor.com	Boston	MA	02110	617-742-9700	291-3258*
GZA GeoEnvironmental Inc 1 Edgewater Dr Web: www.gza.com	Norwood	MA	02062	781-278-3700	278-5701
Heath Consultants Inc 9030 Monroe Rd TF: 800-432-8487 ■ Web: www.heathus.com	Houston	TX	77061	713-844-1300	844-1309
Kemron Environmental Services Inc 8150 Leesburg Pike Suite 1410 TF: 800-777-1042 ■ Web: www.kemron.com	Vienna	VA	22182	703-893-4106	893-5636
Kingston Environmental Services Inc 15450 Hangar Rd Web: www.kingstonenv.com	Kansas City	MO	64147	816-524-8811	525-5027
Los Alamos Technical Assoc Inc 999 Central Ave Suite 300 TF: 800-888-1745 ■ Web: www.lata.com	Los Alamos	NM	87544	505-662-9080	662-1757
MACTEC Inc 1105 Lakewood Dr Suite 300 Web: www.mactec.com	Alpharetta	GA	30004	770-360-0600	
Maxymillian Technologies Inc 1801 E St *Fax Area Code: 781 ■ Web: www.maxymillian.com	Pittsfield	MA	01201	413-499-3050	890-8672*
Medallion Laboratories 9000 Plymouth Ave N TF: 800-245-5615 ■ Web: www.medallionlabs.com	Minneapolis	MN	55427	763-764-4453	764-4010
Micah Group LLC 746 Westland Dr #110 Web: www.micahgroup.com	Lexington	KY	40504	859-260-7760	260-1256
Miralles Assoc Inc 729 W Woodbury Rd Web: www.maiarchitects.com	Altadena	CA	91001	626-791-7691	791-0901
MPS Group Inc 2920 Scotten St TF: 800-741-8779 ■ Web: www.mpsgrp.com	Detroit	MI	48210	313-841-7588	843-1479
Mwh Global Inc 380 Interlocken Crescent Suite 200 Web: www.mw.com	Broomfield	CO	80021	303-533-1900	533-1901
Navarro Research & Engineering Inc 669 Emory Valley Rd Web: www.navarro-inc.com	Oak Ridge	TN	37830	865-220-9650	220-9651
Neo Corp PO Box 646 TF: 800-822-1247 ■ Web: www.neocorporation.com	Waynesville	NC	28786	800-822-1247	
Norman Scott Co Inc 126 29th St Dr SE Web: www.in-tolerance.com	Cedar Rapids	IA	52403	319-363-8561	363-2106
Normandeau Assoc Inc 25 Nashua Rd Web: www.normandeau.com	Bedford	NH	03110	603-472-5191	472-7052
Operations Management International Inc (OMI) 9193 S Jamaica St Suite 400 Web: www.omiinc.com	Englewood	CO	80112	303-740-0019	740-7061
Outotec Oyj 6100 Philips Hwy Web: www.outotec.com	Jacksonville	FL	32216	904-353-3681	353-8705
P E La Moreaux & Assoc Inc PO Box 2310 Web: www.pela.com	Tuscaloosa	AL	35403	205-752-5543	752-4043
Parsons Infrastructure & Technology 100 W Walnut St TF: 800-883-7300 ■ Web: www.parsons.com	Pasadena	CA	91124	626-440-4000	440-6200
Perma-Fix Environmental Services Inc 8302 Dunwoody Pl Suite 250 NASDAQ: PESI ■ TF: 800-365-6066 ■ Web: www.perma-fix.com	Atlanta	GA	30350	770-587-9898	587-9937
Philip Services Corp (PSC) 51 San Felipe Rd Suite 1600 TF: 800-726-1300 ■ Web: www.pscnow.com	Houston	TX	77056	713-623-8777	625-7185
Portage Inc 1075 S Utah Ave Suite 200 Web: www.portageinc.com	Idaho Falls	ID	83402	208-528-6608	523-8860
R E I Consultants Inc PO Box 286 Web: www.reiclabs.com	Beaver	WV	25813	304-255-2500	255-2572
Randys Environmental Services 4351 US Hwy 12 SE PO Box 169 Web: www.randyssanitation.com	Delano	MN	55328	763-972-3335	972-6042

	City	State	Zip	Phone	Fax
RJN Group Inc 200 W Front St *TF:* 800-227-7838 ■ *Web:* www.rjn.com	Wheaton	IL	60187	630-682-4700	682-4754
RW Beck Inc 1001 4th Ave Suite 2500 *TF:* 800-285-2325 ■ *Web:* www.rwbeck.com	Seattle	WA	98154	206-695-4700	695-4701
S & ME Inc 3201 Spring Forest Rd *TF Cust Svc:* 800-849-2517 ■ *Web:* www.smeinc.com	Raleigh	NC	27616	919-872-2660	876-3958
Shaw Environmental & Infrastructure Inc 4171 Essen Ln *TF:* 800-747-3322 ■ *Web:* www.shawgrp.com	Baton Rouge	LA	70809	225-932-2500	
Spherix Inc 6430 Rockledge Dr Suite 503 *NASDAQ: SPEX* ■ *TF:* 866-774-3749 ■ *Web:* www.spherix.com	Bethesda	MD	20817	301-897-2540	897-2567
Sullivan International Group Inc 4750 Womble Rd *TF:* 888-744-1432 ■ *Web:* www.onesullivan.com	San Diego	CA	92106	619-260-1432	260-1421
SWCA Inc 3033 N Central Ave # 145 *TF:* 800-828-8517 ■ *Web:* www.swca.com	Phoenix	AZ	85012	602-274-3831	274-3958
Tetra Tech EC Inc 1000 the American Rd *TF:* 800-580-3765 ■ *Web:* www.tteci.com	Morris Plains	NJ	07950	973-630-8000	630-8165
Tetra Tech Geo 21335 Signal Hill Plaza Suite 100 *Web:* www.geotransinc.com	Sterling	VA	20166	703-444-7000	444-1685
Tetra Tech Inc 3475 E Foothill Blvd *NASDAQ: TTEK* ■ *Web:* www.tetratech.com	Pasadena	CA	91107	626-351-4664	351-5291
TRC Cos Inc 21 Griffin Rd N *NYSE: TRR* ■ *TF:* 800-365-8254 ■ *Web:* www.trcsolutions.com	Windsor	CT	06095	860-289-8631	298-6399
TRC Environmental Corp 21 Griffin Rd N *TF:* 800-365-8254 ■ *Web:* www.trcsolutions.com	Windsor	CT	06095	860-289-8631	298-6399
Vertex Engineering Services Inc 400 Libbey Pkwy *TF:* 888-298-5162 ■ *Web:* www.vertexeng.com	Weymouth	MA	02189	781-952-6000	335-3543
Western Technologies Inc 3737 E Broadway Rd *TF:* 800-580-3737 ■ *Web:* www.wt-us.com	Phoenix	AZ	85040	602-437-3737	470-1341
Winston Co Inc 7704 E 38th St *Web:* www.winstoncompany.com	Tulsa	OK	74145	918-610-1006	610-1010
Woolpert Inc 4454 IBA Central Blvd *Web:* www.woolpert.com	Dayton	OH	45430	937-461-5660	461-0743
WorleyParsons Corp 6330 W Loop S *Web:* www.worleyparsons.com	Bellaire	TX	77401	713-407-5000	350-1300
Zerowait Corp 707 Kirkwood Hwy *TF:* 888-811-0808 ■ *Web:* www.zerowait.com	Wilmington	DE	19805	302-266-9408	738-4302

196 CONSULTING SERVICES - HUMAN RESOURCES

SEE ALSO Professional Employer Organizations (PEOs) p. 2455

	City	State	Zip	Phone	Fax
Acrt Inc 1333 Home Ave *TF:* 800-622-2562 ■ *Web:* www.acrtinc.com	Akron	OH	44310	330-945-7500	945-7200
Administrate Concept Inc 406 43rd St W *TF:* 800-952-7758 ■ *Web:* www.accpeo.com	Bradenton	FL	34209	941-744-1317	744-1487
Administrative Resource Options Inc 200 W Adams St Suite 2000 *Web:* www.aroptions.com	Chicago	IL	60606	312-634-0300	
Advantage Sci LLC 2321 Rosecrans Ave *TF:* 866-348-9876 ■ *Web:* www.advantagesci.com	El Segundo	CA	90245	310-536-9876	
Alliance For Employee Growth & Development Inc The 80 Cottontail Ln Suite 320 *TF:* 800-323-3436 ■ *Web:* www.employeegrowth.com	Somerset	NJ	08873	732-563-0028	
Alpine Access Inc 1120 Lincoln St Suite 1400 *TF:* 888-466-2749 ■ *Web:* www.alpineaccess.com	Denver	CO	80203	303-279-0585	279-0584
Arthur J Gallagher & Co 2 Pierce Pl *NYSE: AJG* ■ *Web:* www.ajg.com	Itasca	IL	60143	630-773-3800	285-4000
Ascentis 150 120th Ave NE Suite 400 *Web:* www.ascentis.com	Bellevue	WA	98005	425-462-7171	462-1313
Ashtead Technology Inc 19407 Pk Row Suite 160 *TF:* 800-242-3910 ■ *Web:* www.ashtead-technology.com	Houston	TX	77084	281-398-9533	
Behre Dolbear & Co Inc 999 18th St Suite 1500 *Web:* www.dolbear.com	Denver	CO	80202	303-620-0020	620-0024
BH Careers International 192 Lexington Ave Suite 804 *Web:* www.bhcareers.com	New York	NY	10016	212-679-3360	532-0059
Blackwell Consulting Services Inc 100 S Wacker Dr Suite 800 *Web:* www.bcsinc.com	Chicago	IL	60606	312-553-0730	553-0745
Cadmus Group Inc 57 Water St *Web:* www.cadmusgroup.com	Watertown	MA	02472	617-673-7000	673-7001
Cambridge Human Resource Group Inc 65 W Jackson Blvd PO Box 108 *Web:* www.cambridgehr.com	Chicago	IL	60604	312-420-8880	251-0455
Carnow Conibear & Assoc Ltd 300 W Adams St Suite 1200 *TF:* 800-860-4486 ■ *Web:* www.ccaltd.com	Chicago	IL	60606	312-782-4486	782-5145
Cascade Disability Management Inc 4601 NE 77th Ave Suite 250 **Fax Area Code:* 888 ■ *Web:* www.cascadedisability.com	Vancouver	WA	98662	360-713-5118	324-4621*
Casco International Inc 7221 Pineville Matthews Rd Suite 600 *TF:* 800-535-5690 ■ *Web:* www.cashort.com	Charlotte	NC	28226	704-752-0119	752-9698
Challenger Gray & Christmas Inc 150 S Wacker Dr Suite 2700 *Web:* www.challengergray.com	Chicago	IL	60606	312-332-5790	332-4843
Clark Consulting 2100 Ross Ave Suite 2200 *TF:* 800-999-3125 ■ *Web:* www.clarkconsulting.com	Dallas	TX	75201	214-871-8717	720-6050
Collaborative Consulting LLC 70 Blanchard Rd Suite 500 *Web:* www.collaborativeconsulting.com	Burlington	MA	01803	781-565-2600	565-2700
Crown Partners LLC 7750 Paragon Rd *TF:* 866-210-8809 ■ *Web:* www.crownpartners.com	Dayton	OH	45459	937-723-2300	
Db Consulting Group Inc 8403 Colesville Rd *Web:* www.dbconsultinggroup.com	Silver Spring	MD	20910	301-589-4020	
Development Dimensions International 1225 Washington Pike *TF Mktg:* 800-933-4463 ■ *Web:* www.ddiworld.com	Bridgeville	PA	15017	412-257-0600	257-3916
Drake Beam Morin Inc 100 Pk Ave 11th Fl *Web:* www.dbm.com	New York	NY	10017	212-692-7700	297-0426
Engineering Services Network Inc 2450 Crystal Dr Suite 1015 *Web:* www.esncc.com	Arlington	VA	22202	703-412-3640	
Ensynch Inc 125 S 52nd St *TF:* 866-367-9624 ■ *Web:* www.ensynch.com	Tempe	AZ	85281	480-894-3501	894-3525
Entrix Inc 5252 Westchester St *TF:* 800-368-7511 ■ *Web:* www.entrix.com	Houston	TX	77005	713-666-6223	666-5227
Findley Davies 1 Seagate # 2050 *Web:* www.findleydavies.com	Toledo	OH	43604	419-255-1360	259-5685
Floyd Browne Group PO Box 8016 *TF:* 800-325-7647 ■ *Web:* www.floydbrowne.com	Delaware	OH	43015	740-363-6792	382-1420
FPMI Solutions Inc 101 Quality Cir NW # 110 *Web:* www.fpmisolutions.com	Huntsville	AL	35806	256-539-1850	539-0911
Frederic W Cook & Co 90 Pk Ave 35th Fl *Web:* www.fwcook.com	New York	NY	10016	212-986-6330	986-3836
Gabriel Roeder Smith & Co 1 Towne Sq Suite 800 *TF:* 800-521-0498 ■ *Web:* www.gabrielroeder.com	Southfield	MI	48076	248-799-9000	799-9020
Gaming Laboratories International Inc 600 Airport Rd *Web:* www.gaminglabs.com	Lakewood	NJ	08701	732-942-3999	942-0043
Geomet Technologies LLC 20251 Century Blvd *TF:* 800-296-9898 ■ *Web:* www.geomet.com	Germantown	MD	20874	301-428-9898	428-9482
Globe Consultants Inc 3112 Porter St Suite D *TF:* 800-208-0663 ■ *Web:* www.globeconsultants.com	Soquel	CA	95073	831-464-9243	
Goodwill Industries of Akron Ohio Inc The 570 E Waterloo Rd *TF:* 800-989-8428 ■ *Web:* www.goodwillakron.org	Akron	OH	44319	330-724-6995	
Hanley Wood Market Intelligence 555 Anton Blvd Suite 950 **Fax Area Code:* 949 ■ *TF:* 800-639-3777 ■ *Web:* www.hwmarketintelligence.com	Costa Mesa	CA	92626	714-540-8500	540-8555*
Hay Group Inc 100 E Penn Sq # 10 *TF:* 800-776-1774 ■ *Web:* www.haygroup.com	Philadelphia	PA	19107	215-861-2000	861-2111
Hudson Highland Group Inc 622 3rd Ave *NASDAQ: HHGP* ■ **Fax Area Code:* 917 ■ *Web:* www.ir.hhgroup.com	New York	NY	10017	212-351-7300	256-8546*
Huthwaite Inc 901 N Glebe Rd Suite 200 *TF:* 800-851-3842 ■ *Web:* www.huthwaite.com	Arlington	VA	22203	703-467-3800	467-3801
Impact Science & Technology Inc 85 NW Blvd *Web:* www.iiw.itt.com	Nashua	NH	03063	603-459-2200	
Independent Roofing Consultants 1761 E Garry Ave Suite 100 *Web:* www.irctech.com	Santa Ana	CA	92705	949-476-8626	476-9810
Insight Global Inc (IGI) 4170 Ashford Dunwoody Rd Suite 580 *Web:* www.insightglobal.net	Atlanta	GA	30319	404-257-7900	257-1004
Jwc Environmental Inc 290 Paularino Ave *TF:* 800-331-2277 ■ *Web:* www.jwce.com	Costa Mesa	CA	92626	949-833-3888	833-8858
Kazak Composites Inc 10f Gill St *Web:* www.kazakcomposites.com	Woburn	MA	01801	781-932-5667	932-5671
Kenexa Corp 650 Swedesford Rd 2nd Fl *NASDAQ: KNXA* ■ *Web:* www.kenexa.com	Wayne	PA	19087	610-971-9171	971-9181
Lee Hecht Harrison LLC 50 Tice Blvd *TF:* 800-611-4544 ■ *Web:* www.lhh.com	Woodcliff Lake	NJ	07677	201-782-3704	505-1428
Lsa Assoc Inc 20 Executive Pk Suite 200 *Web:* www.lsa-assoc.com	Irvine	CA	92614	949-553-0666	553-8076
Mid-Michigan Industries Inc (MMI) 2426 Pkwy Dr *Web:* www.mmionline.com	Mount Pleasant	MI	48858	989-773-6918	773-1317
Modern Management Inc 253 Commerce Dr Suite 105 *TF:* 800-323-1331 ■ *Web:* www.modernmanagement.com	Grayslake	IL	60030	847-945-7400	543-7710
Montgomery County Intermediate Unit 23 1605 W Main St Suite B *TF:* 866-461-9159 ■ *Web:* www.mciu.org	Norristown	PA	19403	610-539-8550	
National Center for Retirement Benefits Inc 666 Dundee Rd Suite 1200 *TF:* 800-666-1000 ■ *Web:* www.ncrb.com	Northbrook	IL	60062	847-564-1111	564-4944
Optimance 3608 Preston Rd Suite 220 *Web:* www.optimance.com	Plano	TX	75093	469-467-2800	467-2880
ORC Worldwide 500 5th Ave 5th Fl *Web:* www.orcworldwide.com	New York	NY	10110	212-719-3400	398-1358
Pacific Rim Partners Ltd PO Box 1729 **Fax Area Code:* 864 ■ *Web:* www.prpltd.com	Taylors	SC	29687	775-348-7008	322-0070*
Pembrooke Occupational Health Inc 2307 N Parham Rd *TF:* 800-733-1676 ■ *Web:* www.pembrooke.com	Richmond	VA	23229	804-346-1010	346-5050
Personnel Decisions International Corp 33 S 6th St Suite 4900 *TF:* 800-344-2415 ■ *Web:* www.personneldecisions.com	Minneapolis	MN	55402	612-339-0927	337-8217
Ricklin-Echikson Assoc 374 Millburn Ave *TF:* 800-544-2317 ■ *Web:* www.r-e-a.com	Millburn	NJ	07041	973-376-2020	376-2072
Right Management Consultants Inc 1818 Market St 33rd Fl *TF:* 800-237-4448 ■ *Web:* www.right.com	Philadelphia	PA	19103	215-988-1588	988-9112
Roux Assoc Inc 209 Shafter St *TF:* 800-322-7689 ■ *Web:* www.rouxinc.com	Islandia	NY	11749	631-232-2600	232-9898
Runzheimer International Runzheimer Pk *TF:* 800-558-1702 ■ *Web:* www.runzheimer.com	Rochester	WI	53167	262-971-2200	971-2254
Segal Co 1 Pk Ave *Web:* www.segalco.com	New York	NY	10016	212-251-5000	251-5490
Source Group Inc The 3451 Vincent Rd Suite C *Web:* www.thesourcegroup.net	Pleasant Hill	CA	94523	925-944-2856	

			Phone	Fax
Stanley Hunt DuPree & Rhine Inc PO Box 14967 . . . . Greensboro *TF:* 888-999-4701 ■ *Web:* www.shdr.com	NC	27415	336-273-9492	273-9491
Superior Environmental Corp 1128 Franklin Ct . . . . . . Marne *TF:* 877-667-4142 ■ *Web:* www.superiorenvironmental.com	MI	49435	616-667-4000	667-3668
Synechron Inc 15 Corporate Pl S Suite 400 . . . . . . Piscataway *Web:* www.synechron.com	NJ	08854	732-562-0088	562-1414
TerraFirma 600 Grant St Suite 700 . . . . . . Denver *Web:* www.exposonline.com	CO	80203	303-861-0388	861-0377
Total Resource Management Inc 510 King St Suite 300 . . . . . . Alexandria *TF:* 877-548-5100 ■ *Web:* www.trmnet.com	VA	22314	703-548-4285	548-3641
United Way Of Central Md Inc The 100 S Charles St PO Box 1576 . . . . . . Baltimore *Web:* www.uwcm.org	MD	21203	410-547-8000	547-8289
Walsh Environmental Scientists & Engineers LLC 4888 Pearl E Cir . . . . . . Boulder *TF:* 877-941-4636 ■ *Web:* www.walshenv.com	CO	80301	303-443-3282	443-0367
Webgen Systems Inc 41 Linskey Way . . . . . . Cambridge *TF:* 866-349-0724 ■ *Web:* www.webgensystems.com	MA	02142	617-349-0724	349-3612

197 CONSULTING SERVICES - MANAGEMENT

SEE ALSO Association Management Companies p. 1404; Management Services p. 2216

			Phone	Fax
1 Source Consulting Inc 1250 H St NW Suite 575 . . . . . . Washington *Web:* www.1-sc.com	DC	20005	202-624-0800	624-0810
Abba Technologies Inc 1501 San Pedro Dr Ne . . . . . . Albuquerque *TF:* 888-222-2832 ■ *Web:* www.abbatech.com	NM	87110	505-889-3337	889-3338
Addx Corp 4900 Seminary Rd Suite 570 . . . . . . Alexandria *Web:* www.addxcorp.com	VA	22311	703-933-7637	933-7638
ADS Financial Services Solutions 1 Batterymarch Pk . . . . . . Quincy *TF:* 800-729-3334 ■ *Web:* www.adsfs.com	MA	02169	617-770-3333	689-1103
Advantage Performance Group Inc 700 Larkspur Landing Cir . . . . . . Larkspur *TF:* 800-494-6646 ■ *Web:* www.advantageperformance.com	CA	94939	415-925-6832	925-9512
Advisory Board Co The 2445 M St NW . . . . . . Washington *NASDAQ:* ABCO ■ *TF:* 800-672-6620 ■ *Web:* www.advisoryboardcompany.com	DC	20037	202-672-5600	672-5700
Affinitas Corp 1015 N 98th St Suite 100 . . . . . . Omaha *TF:* 800-369-6495 ■ *Web:* www.affinitas.net	NE	68114	402-505-5000	
Agency.com Ltd 488 Madison Ave 4th Fl . . . . . . New York *TF:* 800-736-4644 ■ *Web:* www.agency.com	NY	10022	212-358-2600	358-2604
Ai Solutions Inc 10001 Derekwood Ln Suite 215 . . . . . . Lanham *Web:* www.ai-solutions.com	MD	20706	301-306-1756	306-1754
AIG Consultants Inc 70 Pine St 10th Fl . . . . . . New York	NY	10270	212-770-5038	742-1564
Airbus North America Holdings 198 Van Buren St # 300 . . . . . . Herndon *TF:* 800-235-9234 ■ *Web:* www.airbus.com	VA	20170	703-834-3400	834-3340
Aldon Computer Group 6001 Shellmound St Suite 600 . . . . . . Emeryville *Web:* www.aldon.com	CA	94608	510-839-3535	839-2894
Allant Group Inc The 2056 Westings Ave Suite 500 . . . . . . Naperville **Fax Area Code:* 630 ■ *Web:* www.allantgroup.com	IL	60563	800-367-7311	355-3090*
Allsup Inc 300 Allsup Pl . . . . . . Belleville *TF:* 800-854-1418 ■ *Web:* www.allsup.com	IL	62223	618-234-8434	236-5778
Alpha Corp 21351 Ridgetop Cir Suite 200 . . . . . . Dulles *Web:* www.alphacorporation.com	VA	20166	703-450-0800	450-0043
Altair Engineering Inc 1820 E Big Beaver Rd . . . . . . Troy *TF:* 888-222-7822 ■ *Web:* www.altair.com	MI	48083	248-614-2400	614-2411
Altman Weil Inc PO Box 625 . . . . . . Newtown Square *TF:* 800-947-2875 ■ *Web:* www.altmanweil.com	PA	19073	610-359-9900	359-0467
Alvarez & Marsal Holdings LLC 600 Lexington Ave 6th Fl . . . . . . New York *Web:* www.alvarezandmarsal.com	NY	10022	212-759-4433	759-5532
American Cybersystems Inc (ACS) 2400 Meadowbrook Pkwy . . . . . . Duluth **Fax Area Code:* 877 ■ *Web:* www.acsicorp.com	GA	30096	770-493-5588	270-6248*
Analysis Group Inc 111 Huntington Ave 10th Fl . . . . . . Boston *Web:* www.analysisgroup.com	MA	02199	617-425-8400	425-8401
Andrews Logistics Inc 1431 Greenway Dr Suite 300 . . . . . . Irving *Web:* www.andrewslogistics.com	TX	75038	972-871-2898	
Answerthink Inc 1001 Brickell Bay Dr 30th Fl . . . . . . Miami *TF:* 866-442-2538 ■ *Web:* www.answerthink.com	FL	33131	305-375-8005	379-8810
APEX Management Group Inc 125-310 Village Blvd . . . . . . Princeton *Web:* www.apexmgmt.com	NJ	08540	609-452-2488	452-2668
Apparel Business Systems Inc (ABS) 2 W Lafayette St Suite 300 . . . . . . Norristown *TF:* 800-426-7880 ■ *Web:* www.apparelbusiness.com	PA	19401	610-592-0880	592-0890
APS Consulting Inc 6360 I 55 N Suite 330 . . . . . . Jackson *TF:* 800-838-0663 ■ *Web:* www.eco-systemsinc.com	MS	39211	601-936-4440	936-4463
Arthur D. Little 125 High St, High St Tower 28th Fl . . . . . . Boston *Web:* www.adl.com	MA	02210	617-532-9550	261-6630
AT Kearney Inc 222 W Adams St Suite 2500 . . . . . . Chicago *Web:* www.atkearney.com	IL	60606	312-648-0111	223-6200
Austin Co Austin Consulting Div 303 E Wacker Dr Suite 900 . . . . . . Chicago *Web:* www.theaustin.com	IL	60601	312-373-7700	373-7710
Austin Ribbon & Computer Supplies Inc (ARC) 9211 Waterford Centre Blvd Suite 202 . . . . . . Austin *TF:* 800-783-7459 ■ *Web:* www.arc-texas.com	TX	78758	512-681-6200	452-0691
Bain & Co 131 Dartmouth St . . . . . . Boston *TF:* 800-800-8338 ■ *Web:* www.bain.com	MA	02116	617-572-2000	572-2427
Banta Global Turnkey Group 6315 W by NW Blvd . . . . . . Houston	TX	77040	713-354-1300	354-1365
Barnett International 1400 N Providence Rd Rose Tree Corporate Ctr Suite 1050 . . . . . . Media *TF:* 800-856-2556 ■ *Web:* www.barnettinternational.com	PA	19063	610-565-9400	565-5223
Beacon Occupational Health & Safety Services Inc 800 Cordova St . . . . . . Anchorage *Web:* www.beaconohss.com	AK	99501	907-222-7612	
Booz Allen Hamilton Inc 8283 Greensboro Dr . . . . . . McLean *TF:* 800-862-4511 ■ *Web:* www.boozallen.com	VA	22102	703-902-5000	902-3333
Bortz Media & Sports Group Inc 4582 S Ulster St Suite 1450 . . . . . . Denver *Web:* www.bortz.com	CO	80237	303-893-9902	893-9913
Boston Consulting Group Inc 53 State St 6th Fl . . . . . . Boston *TF:* 800-367-1989 ■ *Web:* www.bcg.com	MA	02109	617-973-1200	973-1399
Boundless Network Inc 200 E 6th St Suite 300 . . . . . . Austin *Web:* www.boundlessnetwork.com	TX	78701	512-472-9200	
Bowne Global Solutions 6500 Wilshire Blvd Suite 700 . . . . . . Los Angeles **Fax Area Code:* 310 ■ *TF:* 800-628-4808 ■ *Web:* www.bowne.com	CA	90048	917-339-4700	395-0983*
Brooks Group 4731 W Atlantic Ave Suite B10 . . . . . . Delray Beach *Web:* www.tbrooksgroup.com	FL	33445	561-865-3800	865-3700
Bts USA Inc 300 Stamford Pl Suite 425 . . . . . . Stamford *TF:* 800-445-7089 ■ *Web:* www.bts.com	CT	06902	203-316-2740	
Business Resource Group 8080 Pk Ln Suite 770 . . . . . . Dallas *Web:* www.brg.com	TX	75231	214-777-5100	777-5101
California MedTech 15870 Bernardo Ctr Dr . . . . . . San Diego *Web:* www.paragonmedsystems.com	CA	92127	858-613-1200	613-1201
Calnet Inc 12359 Sunrise Valley Dr Suite 270 . . . . . . Reston *TF:* 877-322-5638 ■ *Web:* www.calnet.com	VA	20191	703-547-6800	547-6806
Cape Fox Corp PO Box 8558 . . . . . . Ketchikan *Web:* www.capefoxcorp.com	AK	99901	907-225-5163	
Carana Corp 4350 Fairfax Dr Suite 900 . . . . . . Arlington *Web:* www.carana.com	VA	22203	703-243-1701	243-0471
Carmody & Bloom Inc 600 Lake St Suite 600B . . . . . . Ramsey *Web:* www.carmodyandbloom.com	NJ	07446	201-670-1700	670-1771
CartwrightDownes Inc 650 Busse Hwy . . . . . . Park Ridge *TF:* 800-323-2049 ■ *Web:* www.cartwrightdownes.com	IL	60068	847-685-2700	685-2727
Cato Research Ltd 4364 S Alston Ave . . . . . . Durham *TF:* 800-455-2286 ■ *Web:* www.cato.com	NC	27713	919-361-2286	361-2290
CFI Group 625 Avis Dr . . . . . . Ann Arbor *Web:* www.cfigroup.com	MI	48108	734-930-9090	930-0911
Cgn & Assoc Inc 415 SW Washington St . . . . . . Peoria *TF:* 888-746-4246 ■ *Web:* www.cgn.net	IL	61602	309-672-6400	495-2370
Channel Marketing Corp 5200 Keller Springs Rd . . . . . . Dallas *Web:* www.cmcus.com	TX	75248	972-960-0800	960-0801
Checchi & Co Consulting Inc 1899 L St NW Suite 800 . . . . . . Washington *Web:* www.checchiconsulting.com	DC	20036	202-452-9700	466-9070
Chp & Assoc Consulting Engineers Inc 7660 Woodway Dr Suite 400 . . . . . . Houston *Web:* www.chpengr.com	TX	77063	713-977-3430	977-3828
Cipher Systems LLC 2661 Riva Rd Suite 1000 . . . . . . Annapolis *TF:* 888-899-1523 ■ *Web:* www.cipher-sys.com	MD	21401	410-412-3326	897-1066
CipherMax Inc 3 Results Way . . . . . . Cupertino *Web:* www.ciphermaxinc.com	CA	95014	408-861-3697	861-3650
Circadian Technologies Inc 2 Main St Suite 310 . . . . . . Stoneham *TF:* 800-284-5001 ■ *Web:* www.circadian.com	MA	02180	781-439-6300	439-6399
Clinical Marketing Consortium Inc 777 Old Saw Mll Rv Rd 2 . . . . . . Tarrytown *TF:* 800-253-6140 ■ *Web:* www.clinicalmkt.com	NY	10591	914-345-9009	347-2847
Cohen Rutherford Blum & Knight Pc 6903 Rockledge Dr Suite 500 . . . . . . Bethesda *Web:* www.crkcpa.com	MD	20817	301-828-1000	530-3625
Compliance Corp 21617 S Essex Dr Suite 34 . . . . . . Lexington Park *Web:* www.compliancecorporation.com	MD	20653	301-863-8070	863-8290
Comprehensive Pharmacy Services Inc (CPS) 6409 N Quail Hollow Rd . . . . . . Memphis *TF:* 800-968-6962 ■ *Web:* www.cpspharm.com	TN	38120	901-748-0470	748-4062
Computer Management Technologies Inc 731 Gratiot Ave . . . . . . Saginaw *Web:* www.cmtonline.com	MI	48602	989-791-4860	791-4928
Concours Group 800 Rockmead Dr Suite 151 . . . . . . Kingwood	TX	77339	281-359-3464	359-3443
Condor Earth Technologies Inc PO Box 3905 . . . . . . Sonora *TF:* 800-800-0490 ■ *Web:* www.condorearth.com	CA	95370	209-532-0361	532-0773
Continental Shelf Assoc Inc 8502 SW Kansas Ave . . . . . . Stuart *Web:* www.conshelf.com	FL	34997	772-219-3000	219-3010
Contract Land Staff LLC 2245 Texas Dr Suite 200 . . . . . . Sugar Land *TF:* 800-874-4519 ■ *Web:* www.contractlandstaff.com	TX	77479	281-240-3370	240-5009
CoreTech 500 N Gulph Rd Suite 110 . . . . . . King of Prussia *TF:* 800-220-3337 ■ *Web:* www.coretech.com	PA	19406	800-220-3337	649-1814
Coreval Consulting 6161 Oak Tree Blvd Suite 450 . . . . . . Independence *Web:* www.corevalconsulting.com	OH	44131	216-520-3600	
Corporate Dynamics Inc 1560 Wall St Suite 222 . . . . . . Naperville *TF:* 888-267-7396 ■ *Web:* www.corpdyn.com	IL	60563	630-778-9991	778-9915
Corporate Executive Board Co 1919 N Lynn St . . . . . . Arlington *NYSE:* EXBD ■ *TF:* 866-913-2632 ■ *Web:* www.executiveboard.com	VA	22209	571-303-3000	303-3100
Counter Point Language Consultants Inc PO Box 6184 . . . . . . Bridgewater *Web:* www.counterpointlanguage.com	NJ	08807	908-231-0991	231-8266
Covente Inc 3200 Cobb Galleria Pkwy Suite 205 . . . . . . Atlanta **Fax Area Code:* 678 ■ *Web:* www.covente.com	GA	30339	404-287-3400	829-0740*
CRA International Inc 200 Clarendon St Suite T-33 . . . . . . Boston *NASDAQ:* CRAI ■ *Web:* www.crai.com	MA	02116	617-425-3000	425-3132

	City	State	Zip	Phone	Fax
Cradlerock Group LLC The 65 High St 402 *Web:* www.cradlerock.com	Stamford	CT	06905	203-324-0088	547-7778
Creative Advantage Inc 41 Union Sqr W Suite 504 **Fax Area Code:* 888 ■ *Web:* www.creativeadvantage.com	New York	NY	10003	212-475-9300	467-7684*
Creative Assoc International Inc 5301 Wisconsin Ave NW Suite 700 *Web:* www.creativeassociatesinternational.com	Washington	DC	20015	202-966-5804	363-4771
CTI Consulting 20410 Observation Dr Suite 203 *TF:* 800-783-4284 ■ *Web:* www.countertech.com	Germantown	MD	20876	301-528-8591	528-2037
Cyon Research Corp 8220 Stone Trail Dr *Web:* www.cyonresearch.com	Bethesda	MD	20817	301-365-9085	365-4586
Davies Consulting Inc 6935 Wisconsin Ave Suite 600 *TF:* 800-535-6470 ■ *Web:* www.daviescon.com	Chevy Chase	MD	20815	301-652-4535	907-9355
Dean & Co 8065 Leesburg Pike Suite 500 *Web:* www.dean.com	Vienna	VA	22182	703-506-3900	506-3905
Dechert-Hampe & Co (DHC) 33332 Valle Rd *Web:* www.dechert-hampe.com	San Juan Capistrano	CA	92675	949-429-1999	
Deloitte Consulting LLP 25 Broadway Cunard Bldg *Web:* www.deloitte.com	New York	NY	10004	212-618-4000	
Demos Solutions 600 Cordwainer Dr *TF:* 800-434-4924 ■ *Web:* www.demossolutions.com	Norwell	MA	02061	781-681-1400	681-1499
Deprince Race & Zollo Inc 250 Pk Ave S Suite 250 PO Box 2231 *Web:* www.drz-inc.com	Winter Park	FL	32790	407-420-9903	841-8778
DevTech Systems Inc 1700 N Moore St Suite 1720 *Web:* www.devtechsys.com	Arlington	VA	22209	703-312-6038	312-6039
Dm Transportation Management Services Inc PO Box 621 *TF:* 888-399-0162 ■ *Web:* www.dmtrans.com	Boyertown	PA	19512	610-367-0162	369-0270
Earning Performance Group 830 Morris Tpke Suite 204	Short Hills	NJ	07078	973-379-7772	379-3639
ECG Management Consultants Inc 1111 3rd Ave Suite 2700 *TF:* 800-729-7635 ■ *Web:* www.ecgmc.com	Seattle	WA	98101	206-689-2200	689-2209
Eckler Ltd 110 Sheppard Ave E Suite 900 *Web:* www.eckler.ca	Toronto	ON	M2N7A3	416-429-3330	429-3713
Eltrex Industries 65 Sullivan St *Web:* www.eltrex.com	Rochester	NY	14605	585-454-6100	263-7766
EMC Corp Documentum Div 6801 Koll Ctr Pkwy *Web:* www.emc.com	Pleasanton	CA	94566	925-600-6800	600-6850
EnerVision Inc 2100 E Exchange Pl *TF:* 888-999-8840 ■ *Web:* www.enervision-inc.com	Tucker	GA	30084	770-270-7900	270-7535
Evergreen Healthcare Management LLC (EHC) 4601 NE 77th Ave Suite 300 *Web:* www.evergreenhealthcare.com	Vancouver	WA	98662	360-892-6628	882-5793
Faulk & Winkler LLC 6811 Jefferson Hwy *Web:* www.fw-cpa.com	Baton Rouge	LA	70806	225-927-6811	932-0000
First Manhattan Consulting Group 90 Pk Ave 18th Fl *Web:* www.fmcg.com	New York	NY	10016	212-557-0500	338-9296
Fisher International Inc 50 Water St *Web:* www.fisheri.com	Norwalk	CT	06854	203-854-5390	854-5070
Fluor Corp 6700 Las Colinas Blvd *TF:* 800-405-6637 ■ *Web:* www.fluor.com	Irving	TX	75039	469-398-7000	398-7255
FMI Corp 5171 Glenwood Ave Suite 200 *TF:* 800-669-1364 ■ *Web:* www.fminet.com	Raleigh	NC	27612	919-787-8400	785-9320
Foodbuy LLC 1105 Lakewood Pkwy Suite 400 *TF:* 800-896-4442 ■ *Web:* www.foodbuy.com	Alpharetta	GA	30009	678-256-8000	256-8100
Franchoice Inc 7500 Flying Cloud Dr *TF:* 877-396-4238 ■ *Web:* www.franchoice.com	Eden Prairie	MN	55344	952-345-8400	942-5793
Fry Consultants 2100 Powers Ferry Rd Suite 125 *Web:* www.fryconsultants.com	Atlanta	GA	30339	770-226-8888	226-8899
Gavin de Becker & Assoc 11684 Ventura Blvd Suite 440 *Web:* www.gavindebecker.com	Studio City	CA	91604	818-505-0177	506-0426
Genex Services Inc 440 E Swedesford Rd Suite 1000 *TF:* 888-464-3639 ■ *Web:* www.genexservices.com	Wayne	PA	19087	610-964-5100	964-1919
George S May International Co 303 S NW Hwy *TF:* 800-999-3020	Park Ridge	IL	60068	847-825-8806	825-7937
Glass & Assoc Inc 4571 Stephen Cir NW Suite 130 *Web:* www.glass-consulting.com	Canton	OH	44718	330-494-3252	494-2420
Golden Cos Inc 107 N Murrow Blvd Suite 204 PO Box 2120 *Web:* www.goldencompanies.com	Greensboro	NC	27402	336-274-6700	274-7020
Goodman Networks Inc 6400 International Suite 1000 *Web:* www.goodmannetworks.com	Plano	TX	75093	972-406-9692	406-9291
GP Deltapoint 6095 Marshalee Dr Suite 300 *TF:* 800-727-6677 ■ *Web:* www.gpworldwide.com	Elkridge	MD	21075	410-379-3600	540-5311
Gradient Corp 20 University Rd *Web:* www.gradientcorp.com	Cambridge	MA	02138	617-395-5000	395-5001
Grant Thornton LLP 175 W Jackson Blvd 20th Fl *Web:* www.grantthornton.com	Chicago	IL	60604	312-856-0001	602-8099
Greenwich Assoc LLC 6 High Ridge Pk *Web:* www.greenwich.com	Stamford	CT	06905	203-629-1200	629-1229
Hatch Ltd 2800 Speakman Dr *Web:* www.hatch.ca	Mississauga	ON	L5K2R7	905-855-7600	855-8270
Hay Group Inc 100 E Penn Sq # 10 *TF:* 800-776-1774 ■ *Web:* www.haygroup.com	Philadelphia	PA	19107	215-861-2000	861-2111
Hazmat Environmental Group Inc 60 Commerce Dr *Web:* www.hazmatinc.com	Buffalo	NY	14218	716-827-7200	827-7217
Healthforce Partners Inc 18323 Bothell Everett Hwy *TF:* 877-437-2497 ■ *Web:* www.healthforcepartners.com	Bothell	WA	98012	425-806-5700	806-5701
Hildebrandt International 200 Cottontail Ln *Web:* www.hbrconsulting.com	Somerset	NJ	08873	732-560-8888	560-2566
Hitachi Consulting Corp 2001 Bryan St Suite 3600 *TF:* 877-664-0010 ■ *Web:* www.hitachiconsulting.com	Dallas	TX	75201	214-665-7000	665-7010
HRB Business Services Inc 4400 Main St	Kansas City	MO	64111	816-753-6900	504-1160
Hughes Assoc Inc 3610 Commerce Dr Suite 817 *Web:* www.haifire.com	Baltimore	MD	21227	410-737-8677	737-8688
Huron Consulting Group Inc 550 W Van Buren St *NASDAQ: HURN* ■ *Web:* www.huronconsultinggroup.com	Chicago	IL	60607	312-583-8700	583-8701
IBT Enterprises LLC 1770 Indian Trail Rd Suite 300 *Web:* www.ibtenterprises.com	Norcross	GA	30093	770-381-2023	381-2123
ICF International Inc 9300 Lee Hwy *NASDAQ: ICFI* ■ *TF:* 800-532-4783 ■ *Web:* www.icfi.com	Fairfax	VA	22031	703-934-3603	934-3740
Ideal Innovations Inc 950 N Glebe Rd Suite 800 *Web:* www.idealinnovations.com	Arlington	VA	22203	703-528-9101	528-1913
Inca Engineers Inc 400 112th Ave Ne Suite 400 *TF:* 800-825-4622 ■ *Web:* www.incainc.com	Bellevue	WA	98004	425-635-1000	635-1150
Infodata Corp 3801 W Lake Ave Suite 100 *Web:* www.infodatacorp.com	Glenview	IL	60026	847-486-0000	486-1484
Innovative Resources Consultant Group Inc 1 Pk Plaza Suite 600 *TF:* 800-945-4724 ■ *Web:* www.ircginc.com	Irvine	CA	92614	949-252-0590	252-0592
Institute For Intergovernmental Research In The PO Box 12729 *TF:* 800-320-5744 ■ *Web:* www.iir.com	Tallahassee	FL	32317	850-385-0600	
Integrated Decisions & Systems Inc 8500 Normandale Lake Blvd Suite 1200 *Web:* www.ideas.com	Minneapolis	MN	55437	952-698-4200	698-4299
Interaction Assoc 625 Mt Auburn St *TF:* 888-441-8283 ■ *Web:* www.interactionassociates.com	Cambridge	MA	02138	617-234-2700	234-2727
International Profit Assoc Inc (IPA) 1250 Barclay Blvd *TF:* 800-531-7100	Buffalo Grove	IL	60089	847-808-5590	808-5599
Irvine Technology Corp 201 E Sandpointe Ave Suite 300 **Fax Area Code:* 714 ■ *TF:* 866-322-4482 ■ *Web:* www.irvinetechcorp.com	Santa Ana	CA	92707	866-322-4482	434-8869*
iWay Software 2 Penn Plaza *TF:* 800-736-6130 ■ *Web:* www.iwaysoftware.com	New York	NY	10121	212-736-4433	967-6406
Jacobs-Sirrine Consultants 1 Concourse Pkwy Suite 600	Atlanta	GA	30328	770-673-6700	673-6681
Jax Kneppers Assoc 4100 Macarthur Blvd *Web:* www.jaxkneppers.com	Newport Beach	CA	92660	925-933-3914	933-9370
John Snow Inc 44 Farnsworth St *Web:* www.jsi.com	Boston	MA	02210	617-482-9485	482-0617
Julie Morgenstern Enterprises LLC 850 7th Ave *Web:* www.juliemorgenstern.com	New York	NY	10019	212-586-8084	544-0755
Kaiser Assoc 1747 Pennslvania Ave NW	Washington	DC	20006	202-530-0967	454-2001
Kaya Assoc Inc 101 Quality Cir NW *Web:* www.kayacorp.com	Huntsville	AL	35806	256-382-8084	
KEMA Consulting 67 S Bedford St Suite 201 E *TF:* 800-892-2006 ■ *Web:* www1.kemaconsulting.com	Burlington	MA	01803	781-273-5700	229-4867
Kepner-Tregoe Inc PO Box 704 *TF:* 800-537-6378 ■ *Web:* www.kepner-tregoe.com	Princeton	NJ	08542	609-921-2806	497-0130
Kessler & Assoc Inc 31800 Northwestern Hwy *Web:* www.kesslercpa.com	Farmington Hills	MI	48334	248-855-4224	855-4405
Keystone Fruit Marketing Inc 11 N Carlisle St, Suite 102 PO Box 189 *Web:* www.keystonefruit.com	Greencastle	PA	17225	717-597-2112	597-4096
King Chapman & Broussard Consulting Group Inc 700 Louisiana St Suite 4550 *Web:* www.kcbcg.com	Houston	TX	77002	713-223-7230	223-7260
Kipp Foundation 135 Main St Suite 1700 *TF:* 866-345-5477 ■ *Web:* www.kipp.org	San Francisco	CA	94105	415-399-1556	
Kline & Co Inc 150 Clove Rd 7th Fl *TF:* 800-290-5214 ■ *Web:* www.klinegroup.com	Little Falls	NJ	07424	973-435-6262	435-6291
Knight Facilities Management Inc 5360 Hampton Pl *Web:* www.knightfm.com	Saginaw	MI	48604	989-793-8820	399-9093
KnowledgePlanet.com 5095 Ritter Rd Suite 400 *TF:* 800-869-5763 ■ *Web:* www.knowledgeplanet.com	Mechanicsburg	PA	17055	717-790-0400	790-0401
KPMG LLP 333 Base St Suite 4600 *Web:* www.kpmg.ca	Toronto	ON	M5H2S5	416-777-8500	777-8818
KPMG LLP US 3 Chestnut Ridge Rd *Web:* www.kpmg.com	Montvale	NJ	07645	201-307-7000	307-7575
Kroll Inc 600 Third Ave *TF:* 888-209-9526 ■ *Web:* www.kroll.com	New York	NY	10016	212-593-1000	593-2631
Kurt Salmon Assoc Inc 1355 Peachtree St NE Suite 900 *TF:* 800-637-7403 ■ *Web:* www.kurtsalmon.com	Atlanta	GA	30309	404-892-0321	898-9590
L E Peabody & Assoc Inc 1501 Duke St Suite 200 *Web:* www.lepeabody.com	Alexandria	VA	22314	703-836-0100	836-0285
Lamont Engineers 1 Main St *Web:* www.lamontengineers.com	Cobleskill	NY	12043	518-234-4028	234-4613
Lang Asset Management Inc 5605 Glenridge Dr NE Suite 1080 *Web:* www.langasset.com	Atlanta	GA	30342	404-256-4100	256-1473
LEK Consulting 28 State St 16th Fl *TF:* 800-929-4535 ■ *Web:* www.lek.com	Boston	MA	02109	617-951-9500	951-9392

	City	State	Zip	Phone	Fax
Leopard Communications Inc 555 17th St Suite 300 *Web:* www.leopard.com	Denver	CO	80202	303-527-2900	530-3480
Lewin Group 3130 Fairview Pk Dr Suite 800 *TF:* 877-227-5030 ■ *Web:* www.lewin.com	Falls Church	VA	22042	703-269-5500	269-5501
Lewtan Technologies Inc 300 5th Ave Suite 1 *Web:* www.lewtan.com	Waltham	MA	02451	781-895-9800	890-3684
LifePlans Inc 51 Sawyer Rd Suite 340 *Web:* www.lifeplansinc.com	Waltham	MA	02453	781-893-7600	647-3552
Liquidhub Inc 500 E Swedesford Rd Suite 300 *Web:* www.liquidhub.com	Wayne	PA	19087	484-654-1400	654-1401
LLoyd Staffing Inc 445 Broadhollow Rd Suite 119 *Fax Area Code: 800 ■ *Web:* www.lloydstaffing.com	Melville	NY	11747	631-777-7600	622-9234*
Lochridge Group 275 Grove St Suite 2-400 *Web:* www.lochridge.com	Newton	MA	02466	617-267-5959	267-8438
Long International 10029 Whistling Elk Dr *Web:* www.long-intl.com	Littleton	CO	80127	303-972-2443	972-6980
LTD Management 1230 Pottstown Pike Suite 6 *Web:* www.ltdmgmt.com	Glenmoore	PA	19343	610-458-3636	458-8039
Lucidity Consulting Group LP 1300 E Lookout Dr Suite 225 *Fax Area Code: 972 ■ *Web:* www.luciditycg.com	Richardson	TX	75082	866-414-2901	608-4901*
Lynda.com Inc PO Box 789 *TF:* 888-335-9632 ■ *Web:* www.lynda.com	Ojai	CA	93024	805-477-3900	
M Floyd John & Assoc Inc 125 N Burnett Dr Bay Dr *TF:* 800-809-2307 ■ *Web:* www.jmfa.com	Baytown	TX	77520	281-424-3800	354-3085
Marakon Assoc 245 Pk Ave 44th Fl *TF:* 800-264-3000 ■ *Web:* www.marakon.com	New York	NY	10167	212-377-5000	377-6000
Marketing Werks Inc 130 E Randolph St *Web:* www.marketingwerks.com	Chicago	IL	60601	312-228-0800	228-0801
Mars & Co 124 Mason St *Web:* www.marsandco.com	Greenwich	CT	06830	203-629-9292	629-9432
Marshall & Stevens Inc 355 S Grand Ave Suite 1750 *TF:* 800-950-9588 ■ *Web:* www.marshall-stevens.com	Los Angeles	CA	90071	213-612-8000	612-8010
Masterplan Inc 21540 Plummer St *Web:* www.masterplan-inc.com	Chatsworth	CA	91311	818-773-2647	341-9895
MAXIMUS Inc 11419 Sunset Hills Rd *NYSE: MMS* ■ *TF:* 800-629-4687 ■ *Web:* www.maximus.com	Reston	VA	20190	703-251-8500	251-8240
McBee Assoc Inc 997 Old Eagle School Rd Suite 205 *Web:* www.mcbeeassociates.com	Wayne	PA	19087	610-964-9680	964-7987
McKinsey & Co Inc 55 E 52nd St *TF:* 800-221-1026 ■ *Web:* www.mckinsey.com	New York	NY	10022	212-446-7000	446-8575
Media Breakaway LLC 1490 W 121st Ave Suite 201 *Web:* www.mediabreakaway.com	Westminster	CO	80234	303-464-8164	464-8218
Medical Business Consultants Inc 6800 Pk 10 Blvd Suite 110 N *TF:* 888-332-5622 ■ *Web:* www.mbcsatx.com	San Antonio	TX	78213	210-734-4358	734-4329
Medical Doctor Assoc Inc 145 Technology Pkwy NW *TF:* 800-780-3500 ■ *Web:* www.mdainc.com	Norcross	GA	30092	770-246-9191	246-0882
Medifit Corporate Services Inc 25 Hanover Rd Suite 6 *Web:* www.medifit.com	Florham Park	NJ	07932	973-593-9000	593-9007
Mercer Inc 1166 Avenue of the Americas *Web:* www.mercer.com	New York	NY	10036	212-345-5000	345-7415
MGT of America Inc 2123 Centre Pt Blvd *TF:* 800-326-9132 ■ *Web:* www.mgtamer.com	Tallahassee	FL	32308	850-386-3191	385-4501
Milliman USA 1301 5th Ave Suite 3800 *Fax: Mktg ■ *Web:* www.milliman.com	Seattle	WA	98101	206-624-7940	340-1380*
Mindlance Inc 80 River St Suite 4b *Web:* www.mindlance.com	Hoboken	NJ	07030	201-386-5400	386-0553
Miratek Corp Inc 8201 Lockheed Dr Suite 218 *Web:* www.miratekcorporation.com	El Paso	TX	79925	915-772-2852	772-1764
Mitsubishi Power Systems Inc 100 Colonial Ctr Pky *Web:* www.mpshq.com	Lake Mary	FL	32746	407-688-6201	688-6481
Mobile Video Services Ltd 1620 I St NW Suite 1000 10th Fl *Web:* www.mobilevideo.net	Washington	DC	20006	202-331-8882	331-9064
Monitor Group 2 Canal Pk *Web:* www.monitor.com	Cambridge	MA	02141	617-252-2000	252-2100
Moody International Inc 24900 Pitkin Rd Suite 200 *Web:* www.moodyint.com	The Woodlands	TX	77386	281-367-8764	367-3496
Morley Cos Inc 2717 Schust *Web:* www.morleytravel.com	Saginaw	MI	48603	989-791-2565	497-1874
Nathan Assoc Inc 2101 Wilson Blvd Suite 1200 *Web:* www.nathanassoc.com	Arlington	VA	22201	703-516-7700	351-6162
National Economic Research Assoc Inc 50 Main St 14th Fl *Web:* www.nera.com	White Plains	NY	10606	914-448-4000	448-4040
Navigant Consulting Inc 30 S Wacker Dr Suite 3100 *NYSE: NCI* ■ *Fax: Mktg ■ *TF:* 800-621-8390 ■ *Web:* www.navigant.com	Chicago	IL	60606	312-583-5700	583-5701*
Navis Corp 1000 Broadway Suite 150 *Web:* www.navis.com	Oakland	CA	94607	510-267-5000	267-5100
Navitaire Inc 333 S Seventh St Suite 500 *TF:* 877-216-6787 ■ *Web:* www.navitaire.com	Minneapolis	MN	55402	612-317-7000	317-7575
Neace Lukens Inc 2305 River Rd *TF:* 877-632-2358 ■ *Web:* www.neacelukens.com	Louisville	KY	40206	502-894-2100	894-8602
Network Engineering Inc 2041 Martin Luther King Jr Ave SE *Web:* www.netengr.com	Washington	DC	20020	202-610-9980	610-9982
Nexant Inc 44 S Broadway 5th Fl *Web:* www.nexant.com	White Plains	NY	10601	914-609-0300	609-0399
Nielsen-Wurster Group Inc The 1060 State Rd Suite 2 *Web:* www.nielsen-wurster.com	Princeton	NJ	08540	609-497-2260	497-3412
North Central Pennsylvania Regional Planning & Development Commission 651 Montmorenci Rd *Web:* www.ncentral.com	Ridgway	PA	15853	814-773-3162	772-7045
O M V Medical Inc 6940 Carroll Ave *TF:* 800-773-3105 ■ *Web:* www.omvmedical.com	Takoma Park	MD	20912	301-270-9212	270-9335
Oak Creek Energy Systems Inc 14633 Willow Springs Rd *Web:* www.oces.com	Mojave	CA	93501	661-822-6853	822-5991
Omniture Inc 250 Brannan St *Web:* www.omniture.com	San Francisco	CA	94107	415-957-8767	615-0741
Optimum Solutions Group LLC 2 Embarcadero Ctr Suite 1660 *Web:* www.optimumsolutions.com	San Francisco	CA	94111	415-362-8200	651-8881
Organization Consultants Inc 1949 Pk Rd *Web:* www.ociofcharlotte.com	Charlotte	NC	28203	704-375-6262	375-2217
Organizational Dynamics Inc 790 Boston Rd Suite 201 *TF:* 800-634-4636 ■ *Web:* www.orgdynamics.com	Billerica	MA	01821	978-671-5454	671-5005
Orion Mobility LLC 88 Danbury Rd *TF:* 800-476-7787 ■ *Web:* www.orionmobility.com	Wilton	CT	06897	203-762-0365	834-9625
Ortloff Engineers Ltd 415 W Wall Ave Suite 2000 *Web:* www.ortloff.com	Midland	TX	79701	432-685-0277	685-0258
Osi Consulting Inc 5950 Canoga Ave Suite 300 *Web:* www.osius.com	Woodland Hills	CA	91367	818-992-2700	992-8700
Osp Consultants Inc 4315 Metro Pkwy *Web:* www.rjetelecom.com	Fort Myers	FL	33916	800-444-1400	677-6078
PA Consulting Group 4601 N Fairfax Dr Suite 600 *Web:* www.paconsulting.com	Arlington	DC	22203	571-227-9000	227-9001
Palladium Group Inc 55 Old Bedford Rd Suite 100 *TF:* 800-773-2399 ■ *Web:* www.thepalladiumgroup.com	Lincoln	MA	01773	781-259-3737	259-3389
Paradigm Learning Inc 2701 N Rocky Pt Dr *Web:* www.paradigmlearning.com	Tampa	FL	33607	813-287-9330	287-9331
Parthenon Group 200 State St 14th Fl *Web:* www.parthenon.com	Boston	MA	02109	617-478-2550	478-2555
Peer Group Inc The 379 Thornall St 12th Fl *Web:* www.peergroupinc.com	Edison	NJ	08837	732-321-3670	321-0390
Pegasus Consulting Group Inc 100 Matawan Rd Suite 410 *Web:* www.pegasusconsultinggroup.com	Matawan	NJ	07747	732-203-2600	203-2601
Pencor Inc 1361 13th Ave S Suite 250 *Web:* www.pencor-inc.com	Jacksonville Beach	FL	32250	904-242-4245	242-0521
Perficient Inc 520 Maryville Centre Dr Suite 400 *NASDAQ: PRFT* ■ *Web:* www.perficient.com	Saint Louis	MO	63141	314-529-3600	529-3640
Perot Systems Corp Government Services Group 8270 Willow Oaks Corporate Dr Suite 300 *TF:* 888-560-9477	Fairfax	VA	22031	703-289-8000	289-8099
Philip Crosby Assoc 306 Dartmouth St *Fax: Hum Res ■ *TF:* 877-276-7295 ■ *Web:* www.philipcrosby.com	Boston	MA	02116	617-716-0218	716-0223*
Pinnacle Consulting Group Inc 71 Moore Rd *TF:* 800-693-7466 ■ *Web:* www.pinnaclecg.com	Wayland	MA	01778	508-358-8070	358-8071
Pinnacle Management Systems Inc 320 Decker Dr Suite 100 *Fax Area Code: 866 ■ *TF:* 888-975-1119 ■ *Web:* www.pinnaclemanagement.com	Irving	TX	75062	703-382-9161	975-9991*
Pinney Assoc Inc 3 Bethesda Metro Ctr *Web:* www.pinneyassociates.com	Bethesda	MD	20814	301-718-8440	718-0034
Pittiglio Rabin Todd & McGrath 1050 Winter St *Web:* www.prtm.com	Waltham	MA	02451	781-647-2800	647-2804
Platinum Systems Specialists Inc 4715 Yender Ave *Web:* www.platinum-universe.com	Lisle	IL	60532	630-375-6800	375-9069
Pma Consultants LLC 1 Woodward Ave Suite 1400 *Web:* www.pmaconsultants.com	Detroit	MI	48226	313-963-8863	963-8918
Porter Henry & Co Inc 455 E 86th St *Web:* www.porterhenry.com	New York	NY	10028	212-953-5544	953-5899
Pragmatek Consulting Group 8500 Normandale Lake Blvd Suite 1060 *Fax Area Code: 952 ■ *TF:* 800-833-3164 ■ *Web:* www.pragmatek.com	Bloomington	MN	55437	612-333-3164	844-5201*
Preferred Health Strategies 2 Bellesair Blvd *Web:* www.phsconsult.com	Rye Brook	NY	10573	914-937-1072	206-4129
PricewaterhouseCoopers LLP 77 King St W Royal Trust Tower 25th Fl *Web:* www.secure.ca.pwc.com	Toronto	ON	M5C1G3	416-863-1133	365-8215
Primesource Staffing LLC 400 S Colorado Blvd Suite 400 *Web:* www.primesourcestaffing.com	Denver	CO	80246	303-869-2990	869-2997
Pritchett LLC 13355 Noel Rd Suite 1650 *TF:* 800-992-5922 ■ *Web:* www.pritchettnet.com	Dallas	TX	75240	214-239-9600	239-9650
Pro2Serve Professional Project Services Inc 545 Oakridge Tpke Suite 101 *TF:* 888-243-4150 ■ *Web:* www.p2s.com	Oak Ridge	TN	37830	865-483-2030	483-2660
Professional & Scientific Assoc 2100 Reston Pkwy Suite 300 *TF:* 800-546-9184 ■ *Web:* www.psava.com	Reston	VA	20191	703-234-1700	
Professional Bank Services Inc 6200 Dutchmans Ln Suite 305 *TF:* 800-523-4778 ■ *Web:* www.probank.com	Louisville	KY	40205	502-451-6633	451-6755
Professional Research Consultants Inc 11326 P St *TF:* 800-428-7455 ■ *Web:* www.prconline.com	Omaha	NE	68137	402-592-5656	592-3019

				Phone	Fax
Progeny Marketing Innovations 801 Crescent Ctr Dr Suite 200 TF: 800-251-2148 ■ Web: www.progenymarketing.com	Franklin	TN	37067	800-251-2148	
Program Planning Professionals 1340 Eisenhower Pl TF: 888-364-1182 ■ Web: www.pcubed.com	Ann Arbor	MI	48108	734-741-7770	741-1343
Projects Plus Inc 145 W 45th St Suite 300 Web: www.projectsplusinc.com	New York	NY	10036	212-997-0100	997-0188
Public Consulting Group Inc 148 State St *Fax Area Code: 617 ■ TF: 800-210-6113 ■ Web: www.publicconsultinggroup.com	Boston	MA	02109	800-210-6113	426-4632*
Q Analysts LLC 5201 Great America Pkwy TF: 866-492-8500 ■ Web: www.qanalysts.com	Santa Clara	CA	95054	408-907-8500	
Q1 Labs Inc 890 Winter St Suite 230 Web: www.q1labs.com	Waltham	MA	02451	781-250-5800	
Qek Global Solutions Inc 7047 Murthum Web: www.qekglobalsolutions.com	Warren	MI	48092	248-729-5400	
Quadel Consulting 1200 G St NW Suite 700 TF: 866-640-1019 ■ Web: www.quadel.com	Washington	DC	20005	202-789-2500	898-0632
Quality Business Solutions Inc 12701 Whitewater Dr Suite 180 Web: www.qbs.com	Minnetonka	MN	55343	952-564-3088	
Questor 700 E Maple Rd 4th Fl Web: www.questor.com	Birmingham	MI	48009	248-593-1930	723-3907
R2H Engineering Inc 840 Grier Dr Suite 320 Web: www.r2h.com	Las Vegas	NV	89119	702-260-7000	260-7070
Rath & Strong Inc 1666 Massachusetts Ave # 17 TF: 800-622-2025 ■ Web: www.rathstrong.com	Lexington	MA	02420	781-861-1700	861-1424
Rawle-Murdy Assoc Inc PO Box 1117 Web: www.rawle-murdy.com	Charleston	SC	29401	843-577-7327	722-3960
Raytheon Professional Services LLC 1200 S Jupiter Rd Web: www.raytheon.com/businesses/rps	Garland	TX	75042	972-205-5100	344-5369
Rci Consultants Inc 17314 State Hwy 249 Suite 350 Web: www.rcigroup.us	Houston	TX	77064	281-970-4221	970-4241
Reed Group Ltd 10155 Westmoor Dr Suite 210 Web: www.reedgroup.com	Westminster	CO	80021	303-247-1860	247-1863
Resource Dynamics International Inc 500 N Michigan Ave Suite 300 TF: 888-999-1623 ■ Web: www.resourcedynamics.com	Chicago	IL	60611	888-999-1623	999-1624
Revere Group The 325 N LaSalle Suite 325 TF: 888-473-8373 ■ Web: www.reveregroup.com	Chicago	IL	60610	312-873-3400	873-3500
Revolution Technologies LLC 1676 W Hibiscus Blvd Suite 102 TF: 877-738-8324 ■ Web: www.revolutiontechnologies.com	Melbourne	FL	32901	321-409-4949	768-2629
RHR International LLP 233 S Wacker Dr Suite 9500 *Fax Area Code: 630 ■ TF: 800-892-4496 ■ Web: www.rhrinternational.com	Chicago	IL	60606	312-924-0800	766-9037*
Risk Management Services Co (RMSC) 9100 Marksfield Rd Web: www.rmsc.com	Louisville	KY	40222	502-326-5900	326-5909
Robbins-Gioia 11 Canal Ctr Plaza Suite 200 Web: www.rgalex.com	Alexandria	VA	22314	703-548-7006	684-5189
Robert E Nolan Co Inc 92 Hopmeadow St TF: 800-653-1941 ■ Web: www.renolan.com	Weatogue	CT	06089	860-658-1941	651-3465
Robert H Schaffer & Assoc 30 Oak St 3rd Fl Web: www.rhsa.com	Stamford	CT	06905	203-322-1604	322-3599
Robert Half Management Resources (RHIMR) 2884 Sand Hill Rd Suite 200 TF: 888-400-7474 ■ Web: www.roberthalfmr.com	Menlo Park	CA	94025	650-234-6000	234-6999
Robinson & Maites Inc 35 E Wacker Dr Suite 3500 Web: www.robinsonmaites.com	Chicago	IL	60601	312-372-9333	372-0682
Robson Forensic Inc 354 N Prince St TF: 800-813-6736 ■ Web: www.robsonforensic.com	Lancaster	PA	17603	717-293-9050	
Roland Berger & Partners 230 Pk Ave 10th Fl Web: www.rolandberger.com	New York	NY	10169	212-651-9660	756-8750
Royal Paper Corp 15050 Shoemaker Ave Web: www.royal-paper.com	Santa Fe Springs	CA	90670	562-903-9030	944-6000
Ryan Group Inc 14110 Dallas Pkwy Suite 270 Web: www.ryangroupinc.com	Dallas	TX	75254	972-385-7781	385-7884
Sandy Corp 300 E Big Beaver Rd Suite 500 TF: 800-733-4739 ■ Web: www.sandycorp.com	Troy	MI	48083	248-649-0800	729-4701
Sapient Corp 131 Dartmouth St 3rd Fl NASDAQ: SAPE ■ Web: www.sapient.com	Boston	MA	02116	617-621-0200	621-1300
Schahet Hotels Inc 9333 N Meridian St TF: 800-426-7866 ■ Web: www.schahethotels.com	Indianapolis	IN	46260	317-848-9000	
Scott Madden & Assoc Inc 2626 Glenwood Ave Suite 480 TF: 800-321-9774 ■ Web: www.scottmadden.com	Raleigh	NC	27608	919-781-4191	781-2537
Secova Inc 5000 Birch St E Tower Suite 300 TF: 800-257-0011 ■ Web: www.ultralink.com	Newport Beach	CA	92660	714-384-0530	384-0600
Sedlak Management Consultants Inc Metropolitan Plaza 22901 Millcreek Blvd Suite 600 Web: www.jasedlak.com	Highland Hills	OH	44122	216-206-4700	206-4840
Selling Source LLC 325 E Warm Springs Rd Suite 200 TF: 800-397-7706 ■ Web: www.sellingsource.com	Las Vegas	NV	89119	702-407-0707	407-0711
Sequent Energy Management LP 1200 Smith St # 900 Web: www.sequentenergy.com	Houston	TX	77002	832-397-1700	397-1722
Sirius Solution LLC 1233 W Loop S TF: 800-585-1085 ■ Web: www.sirsol.com	Houston	TX	77027	713-888-0488	888-0235
Smith Consulting Architects 12220 El Camino Real Suite 200 Web: www.sca-sd.com	San Diego	CA	92130	858-793-4777	793-4787
Smith Elliott Kearns & Co LLC PO Box 947 TF: 800-841-9463 ■ Web: www.sek.com	Hagerstown	MD	21741	301-733-5020	733-1864
Solving International 1755 The Exchange Suite 380 TF: 800-637-4887 ■ Web: www.solving-int.com	Atlanta	GA	30339	770-988-2600	988-2626
Spectrum Financial System Inc 163 McKenzie Rd TF: 800-525-0555 ■ Web: www.spectrumfinancialinc.com	Mooresville	NC	28115	704-663-4466	663-0611
Ssci 3065 Kent Ave Web: www.ssci-inc.com	West Lafayette	IN	47906	765-463-0112	463-4722
State Street Consultants Inc 22 Batterymarch St Web: www.statestreetconsultants.com	Boston	MA	02109	617-482-1234	482-2060
Stem International Inc 4692 Millennium Dr Suite 400 Web: www.stemint.com	Belcamp	MD	21017	410-272-9080	272-9085
Stockbridge Risk Management Inc 40 Cutter Mill Rd Web: www.stockbridgegroup.com	Great Neck	NY	11021	516-487-1700	487-1146
Strategic Decisions Group 745 Emerson St Web: www.sdg.com	Palo Alto	CA	94301	650-475-4400	475-4401
Strategic Employee Services Inc 11410 Kingston Pike Suite 100 Web: www.seshr.com	Knoxville	TN	37934	865-671-0534	675-0186
Strategic Resources Inc 7927 Jones Branch Dr Web: www.sri-hq.com	McLean	VA	22102	703-749-3040	749-3046
Stromberg Consulting 1285 Avenue of the Americas Web: www.scny.com	New York	NY	10019	646-935-4300	935-4368
Sunrise Labs Inc 5 Dartmouth Dr Web: www.sunriselabs.com	Auburn	NH	03032	603-644-4500	622-9797
Synergy Global Solutions Inc 1100 Pittsford-Victor Rd Web: www.synergy.gs	Pittsford	NY	14534	585-381-4120	246-6073
Sysorex Consulting Inc 405 Clyde Ave Web: www.sysorex.com	Mountain View	CA	94043	650-967-2200	967-9327
Systech Solutions Inc 700 N Brand Blvd Suite 800 Web: www.systechusa.com	Glendale	CA	91203	818-550-9690	550-9692
System Planning Corp (SPC) 3601 Wilson Blvd Web: www.sysplan.com	Arlington	VA	22201	703-351-8200	
Target Rx Inc 220 Gibraltar Rd 2nd Fl Web: www.targetrx.com	Horsham	PA	19044	215-444-8700	444-8701
Tata Consultancy Services 115 Perimeter Ctr Pl Suite 1099 Web: www.tcs.com	Atlanta	GA	30346	770-396-1223	396-1239
Tbm Consulting Group Inc 4400 Ben Franklin Blvd Web: www.tbmcg.com	Durham	NC	27704	919-471-5535	471-5135
Tech Usa Inc 8334 Veterans Hwy TF: 888-584-8181 ■ Web: www.techusa.net	Millersville	MD	21108	410-729-4328	987-9080
Technology & Business Integrators 275 N Franklin Tpke TF: 800-676-9470 ■ Web: www.tbicentral.com	Ramsey	NJ	07446	201-573-0400	573-9191
Technomic Inc 300 S Riverside Plaza Suite 1200 Web: www.technomic.com	Chicago	IL	60606	312-876-0004	876-1158
Tel-Adjust Inc 29000 Inkster Rd Suite 115 Web: www.teladjust.com	Southfield	MI	48034	248-208-1600	208-0805
Telesoft Corp 1661 E Camelback Rd Suite 300 Web: www.telesoft.com	Phoenix	AZ	85016	602-308-2100	308-1300
Tenera Environmental 971 Dewing Ave Suite 101 TF: 800-447-9388 ■ Web: www.tenera.com	Lafayette	CA	94549	925-962-9769	
Termnet Merchant Services Inc 2727 Paces Ferry Rd Suite 1600 TF: 800-344-8472 ■ Web: www.termnetinc.com	Atlanta	GA	30339	770-431-3022	431-3012
Terrahealth Inc 5710 Hausman Rd W Suite 108 Web: www.thi-terra.com	San Antonio	TX	78249	210-475-9881	475-9397
Thomas Group Inc 5221 N O'Connor Blvd Suite 500 NASDAQ: TGIS ■ TF: 800-826-2057 ■ Web: www.thomasgroup.com	Irving	TX	75039	972-869-3400	443-1701
Thyssen Krupp Hearn 59 I- Dr TF: 877-977-8420 ■ Web: www.thyssenkrupphearn.com	Wentzville	MO	63385	636-332-1772	639-1572
Tom McCall & Assoc Inc 20180 Governors Hwy Suite 100 Web: www.tmccall.com	Olympia Fields	IL	60461	708-747-5707	747-5890
Tompkins Assoc Inc 6870 Perry Creek Rd TF: 800-789-1257 ■ Web: www.tompkinsinc.com	Raleigh	NC	27616	919-876-3667	872-9666
Towers Perrin Inc 175 Bloor St E S Tower Suite 1701 Web: www.towerswatson.com	Toronto	ON	M4W3T6	416-960-2700	960-2819
Travelclick Inc 1211 Avenue of the Americas 38th Fl Web: www.travelclick.net	New York	NY	10036	847-585-5000	
Triage Consulting Group 221 Main St Suite 1100 Web: www.triageconsulting.com	San Francisco	CA	94105	415-512-9400	512-9404
Tritech Marketing LLC 7020 High Grove Blvd *Fax Area Code: 630 ■ Web: www.market-sense.com	Burr Ridge	IL	60527	800-827-0170	654-0302*
Trout & Partners Ltd 8 Wahneta Rd Web: www.troutandpartners.com	Old Greenwich	CT	06870	203-637-7001	637-7071
Tunnell Consulting 900 E 8th Ave Suite 106 TF: 800-532-2483 ■ Web: www.tunnellconsulting.com	King of Prussia	PA	19406	610-337-0820	337-1884
Tunstall Consulting Inc 13153 N Dale Mabry Hwy Suite 200 Web: www.tunstallconsulting.com	Tampa	FL	33618	813-968-4461	961-2315
UMS Group Inc 20 Waterview Blvd Web: www.umsgroup.com	Parsippany	NJ	07054	973-335-3555	335-7738
University Research Co LLC 7200 Wisconsin Ave Suite 600 Web: www.urc-chs.com	Bethesda	MD	20814	301-654-8338	941-8427

Phone | Fax

Urban Science 200 Renaissance Ctr Suite 1800 .... Detroit MI 48243 313-259-9900 259-9901
Web: www.urbanscience.com

VDC Research Group Inc
679 Worcester Rd Suite 2 .... Natick MA 01760 508-653-9000 653-9836
Web: www.vdcresearch.com

Velocity Solutions Inc 1710 Dawson St .... Wilmington NC 28403 910-254-9383 245-4739
Web: www.myvelocity.com

Vermont Composites Inc 25 Performance Dr .... Bennington VT 05201 802-442-9964 445-2921
Web: www.vtcomposites.com

VerticalResponse Inc
501 2nd St Suite 700 .... San Francisco CA 94107 415-905-6880 808-2480
TF: 866-683-7842 ■ Web: www.verticalresponse.com

Viatech Systems Inc
7901 Jones Branch Dr Suite 120 .... Mc Lean VA 22102 703-917-0550 917-0558
Web: www.viatech-systems.net

Viccs Inc 11821 Parklawn Dr Suite 224 .... Rockville MD 20852 301-984-1355 984-1360
Web: www.viccs.com

Virginia Braswell PO Box 3610 .... Albany GA 31706 229-883-0505 883-0515
Web: www.fwforestry.com

Wakely Consulting Group Inc
19321 US Hwy 19 N Suite 515 .... Clearwater FL 33764 727-507-9858 507-9658
Web: www.wakelyconsulting.com

Washington Group Consultants LLC PO Box A .... Fairfax VA 22031 703-591-6600 591-6602
Web: www.washingtongroup.com

Welocalize Inc 241 E 4th St Suite 207 .... Frederick MD 21701 301-668-0330 668-0335
TF: 800-370-9515 ■ Web: www.welocalize.com

West Monroe Partners LLC 175 W Jackson Blvd .... Chicago IL 60604 312-602-4000
TF: 800-828-6708 ■ Web: www.westmonroepartners.com

Windmill International Inc 2 Robinson Rd .... Nashua NH 03060 603-888-5502 888-5512
TF: 877-862-5478 ■ Web: www.windmill-intl.com

Wk Dickson & Co Inc 616 Colonnade Dr .... Charlotte NC 28205 704-334-5348 334-0078
Web: www.wkdickson.com

Zeiders Enterprises Inc
2750 Killarney Dr Suite 100 .... Woodbridge VA 22192 703-496-9000 497-0494
Web: www.zeiders.com

198 CONSULTING SERVICES - MARKETING

Phone | Fax

4Kids Entertainment Licensing Inc
53 W 23rd St 11 Fl .... New York NY 10010 212-758-7666 727-8933
Web: www.4kidsentertainment.com

Acosta Sales & Marketing Co
665 W N Ave Suite 300 .... Lombard IL 60148 630-620-7600 620-7698
TF: 800-843-2750 ■ Web: www.acosta.com

ANALYTICi 100 W 33rd St 6th Fl .... New York NY 10001 877-568-8032 907-7490*
*Fax Area Code: 212 ■ TF: 877-568-8032 ■ Web: www.analytici.com

Band Digital Inc 150 N Michigan Ave Suite 300 .... Chicago IL 60661 312-981-6000 981-6100
Web: www.whittmanhart.com

Beverage Marketing Corp 850 3rd Ave 18th Fl .... New York NY 10022 212-688-7640 826-1255
TF: 800-275-4630 ■ Web: www.beveragemarketing.com

Boomers & Beyond Inc
1998 Ruffin Mill Rd .... Colonial Heights VA 23834 804-524-9888 524-9889
Web: www.firststreetonline.com

Business-to-Business Marketing Communications Inc
900 Ridgefield Dr Suite 270 .... Raleigh NC 27609 919-872-8172 872-8875
Web: www.btbmarketing.com

Cargill AgHorizons PO Box 9300 .... Minneapolis MN 55440 952-742-7575 742-7313
TF: 800-227-4455 ■ Web: www.CargillAg.com

CMGI Inc
ModusLink Global Solutions Inc
1100 Winter St Suite 4600 .... Waltham MA 02451 781-663-5000 663-5100
NASDAQ: MLNK ■ Web: www.moduslink.com

Collegiate Licensing Co
290 I- N Cir Suite 200 .... Atlanta GA 30339 770-956-0520 955-4491
Web: www.clc.com

Competitive Technologies Inc
1375 Kings Hwy .... Fairfield CT 06824 203-368-6044 368-5399
Web: www.competitivetech.net

Corporate Branding 470 W Ave .... Stamford CT 06902 203-327-6333 353-8180
TF: 888-969-2726 ■ Web: www.corebrand.com

Creative Good Inc 307 W 38th St Suite 1701 .... New York NY 10018 212-736-2075 736-0697
Web: www.creativegood.com

Crimson Consulting Group
4970 El Camino Real Suite 200 .... Los Altos CA 94022 650-960-3600 960-3737
Web: www.crimson-consulting.com

Crossmark Inc 5100 Legacy Dr .... Plano TX 75024 469-814-1000 814-1355
TF: 888-695-6733 ■ Web: www.crossmark.com

Daymon Assoc Inc 700 Fairfield Ave .... Stamford CT 06902 203-352-7500 352-7947
Web: www.daymon.com

DCI Marketing Inc 2727 W Good Hope Rd .... Milwaukee WI 53209 414-228-7000 228-3421
TF: 800-778-4805 ■ Web: www.dcimarketing.com

EBSCO Professional Partnership Group
5724 Hwy 280 E .... Birmingham AL 35242 205-991-1188 980-6766
TF: 800-528-3476 ■ Web: www.ebscodas.com

Economic Consulting Services LLC
2001 L St NW .... Washington DC 20036 202-466-7720 466-2710
Web: www.economic-consulting.com

Ernst-Van Praag Inc
4800 N Federal Hwy Suite E 207 .... Boca Raton FL 33431 561-447-0557 447-0527
Web: www.evpconsulting.com

Excellence in Motivation Inc (EIM)
6 N Main St Suite 370 .... Dayton OH 45402 937-222-2900 824-8393
TF: 800-963-9235 ■ Web: www.eim-inc.com

Eze Castle Integration Inc
260 Franklin St 12th Fl .... Boston MA 02110 617-217-3000 217-3001
Web: www.eci.com

Faith Popcorn's BrainReserve
1 Dag hammarskjold Plaza 16th Fl .... New York NY 10017 212-772-7778 772-7787
TF: 800-873-6337 ■ Web: www.faithpopcorn.com

Phone | Fax

Fitch Inc 1266 Manning Pkwy .... Powell OH 43065 614-885-3453 885-4289
Web: www.fitch.com

Frank Lynn & Assoc Inc
150 S Wacker Dr 17th Fl .... Chicago IL 60606 312-263-7888 263-1117
TF: 800-245-5966 ■ Web: www.franklynn.com

Frost & Sullivan 7550 W I-10 Suite 400 .... San Antonio TX 78229 210-348-1000 348-1003
TF: 877-463-7678 ■ Web: www.frost.com

Fulcrum Analytics Inc 70 W 40th St 10th Fl .... New York NY 10018 212-651-7000 651-7049
TF: 888-245-9450 ■ Web: www.fulcrum-mktg.com

Gannett Offset 6883 Commercial Dr .... Springfield VA 22159 703-750-8643 750-8717
TF: 800-255-1457 ■ Web: www.gannettoffset.com

Harte-Hanks Market Intelligence
9980 Huennekens St .... San Diego CA 92121 858-450-1667 452-7491
TF: 800-854-8409 ■ Web: www.hartehanksmi.com

Hcpro Inc 75 Sylvan St Suite A-10 .... Danvers MA 01923 800-650-6787
TF: 800-650-6787 ■ Web: www.hcpro.com

Hunter Business Group LLC
4650 N Port Washington Rd PO Box 12970 .... Milwaukee WI 53212 414-203-8060 203-8225
TF: 800-423-4010 ■ Web: www.hunterbusiness.com

I-F Consulting 28 State St 11th Fl .... Boston MA 02109 617-232-8880 232-2525
Web: www.i-f.com

IdentityWEB Inc
2999 Overland Ave Suite 2112 .... Los Angeles CA 90064 310-559-2476 559-2485
Web: www.identityweb.com

Impact Planning Group 10 Winfield St .... Norwalk CT 06855 203-854-1011 854-4888
Web: www.impactplan.com

Innotrac Corp 6465 E Johns Crossing .... Johns Creek GA 30097 678-584-4000 475-5840
NASDAQ: INOC ■ TF: 800-827-4666 ■ Web: www.innotrac.com

Intellimar Inc 7560 Main St .... Sykesville MD 21784 410-552-9940 552-9939
Web: www.intellimar.com

Kahler Slater Inc 111 W Wisconsin Ave .... Milwaukee WI 53203 414-272-2000
Web: www.kahlerslater.com

Khong Guan Corp 30068 Eigenbrodt Way .... Union City CA 94587 510-487-7800 487-0301
TF: 877-889-8968 ■ Web: khongguan.com

Kuczmarski & Assoc 1165 N Clark St Suite 700 .... Chicago IL 60610 312-988-1500 988-9393
Web: www.kuczmarski.com

Landor Assoc Ltd 1001 Front St .... San Francisco CA 94111 415-365-1700 365-3190
TF: 888-252-6367 ■ Web: www.landor.com

Lexicon Branding Inc
30 Liberty Ship Way Suite 3360 .... Sausalito CA 94965 415-332-1811 332-2528
TF: 800-783-9713 ■ Web: www.lexiconbranding.com

Lippincott Mercer Inc 499 Pk Ave .... New York NY 10022 212-521-0000 308-8952
Web: www.lippincottmercer.com

MarketBridge Inc 4350 East-West Hwy 6th Fl .... Bethesda MD 20814 240-752-1800 907-3282*
*Fax Area Code: 301 ■ TF: 888-468-6658 ■ Web: www.market-bridge.com

Massini Group
1323 NE Orenco Stn Pkwy Suite 300 .... Hillsboro OR 97124 503-640-9800 640-9888
Web: www.massini-group.com

Mattson Jack Group
11960 Westline Industrial Dr Suite 180 .... Saint Louis MO 63146 314-469-7600 469-6794
Web: www.mattsonjack.com

Membership Marketing Services
1280 Perimeter Pkwy .... Virginia Beach VA 23454 757-430-1600 430-2901
Web: www.mms-va.com

Military Sales & Service Co
5301 S Westmoreland Rd .... Dallas TX 75237 469-221-4224
Web: www.mssco.com

Millstone Medical Outsourcing LLC
580 Commerce Dr .... Fall River MA 02720 508-679-8384 679-8414
Web: www.millstonemedical.com

Morgan Anderson Consulting 4 Pk Ave 22nd Fl .... New York NY 10016 212-741-0777 851-4883*
*Fax Area Code: 866 ■ TF: 800-850-3550 ■ Web: www.morgananderson.com

Morrison Agency Inc The
3365 Piedmont Rd Suite 1400
Tower Walk at Tower Pl .... Atlanta GA 30305 404-233-3405 261-8384
Web: www.morrisonagency.com

National Food Laboratory Inc 6363 Clark Ave .... Dublin CA 94568 925-828-1440 833-9239
Web: www.thenfl.com

Niven Marketing Group The
955 Kimberly Dr .... Carol Stream IL 60188 630-580-6000 580-5690
Web: www.niven.net

PDI Inc
Bui 300 Interpace Pkwy
Morris Corporate Ctr 1 .... Parsippany NJ 07054 862-207-7800 207-7820
NASDAQ: PDII ■ TF: 800-242-7494 ■ Web: www.pdi-inc.com

Peppers & Rogers Group 901 Main Ave # 212 .... Norwalk CT 06851 203-642-5121 642-5126
Web: www.1to1.com

Populus Group LLC 850 Stephenson Hwy Suite 500 .... Troy MI 48083 248-581-1100 350-3462
Web: www.populusgroup.com

Rainmaker Systems Inc 900 E Hamilton Ave .... Campbell CA 95008 408-626-3800 369-0910
NASDAQ: RMKR ■ TF: 800-631-1545 ■ Web: www.rmkr.com

RedF 14120 Ballantyne Corp Pl Suite 200 .... Charlotte NC 28277 704-971-2300 971-2303
Web: www.redf.com

Richmark Group 39 S LaSalle St 5th Fl .... Chicago IL 60603 312-368-0800 368-0832
Web: www.richmark.com

Ries & Ries 2195 River Cliff Dr .... Roswell GA 30076 770-643-0880 643-0051
Web: www.ries.com

Ronin Corp 2 Research Way 2nd Fl .... Princeton NJ 08540 609-452-0060 452-0091
TF: 800-352-2926 ■ Web: www.ronin.com

Starmark International Inc
1815 Griffin Rd .... Dania Beach FL 33004 954-874-9000 874-9010
Web: www.starmark.com

Suarez Corp Industries
7800 Whipple Ave NW .... North Canton OH 44767 330-494-5504 497-6802
TF: 800-764-0008 ■ Web: www.suarez.com

Suss Consulting
801 Old York Rd Noble Plaza Suite 305 .... Jenkintown PA 19046 215-884-5900 884-1637
TF: 888-984-5900 ■ Web: www.sussconsulting.com

Tasc Technical Services LLC 73 Newton Rd .... Plaistow NH 03865 877-304-8272
Web: www.tasctech.com

Phone Fax

Technical Communities Inc
1000 Cherry Ave Suite 100........................San Bruno CA 94066 650-624-0525 624-0535
TF: 888-665-2765 ■ Web: www.technicalcommunities.com
Thobe Group Inc 2727 Raintree Dr..................Carrollton TX 75006 972-245-9444 418-5195
TF: 888-462-3477 ■ Web: www.thobe.com
United Marketing Group LLC
929 N Plum Grove Rd...........................Schaumburg IL 60173 847-240-2005 240-2022
TF: 800-513-9000 ■ Web: www.unitedmarket.com
Ventiv Health Inc 200 Cottontail Ln..................Somerset NJ 08873 800-416-0555 537-4912*
NASDAQ: VTIV ■ *Fax Area Code: 732 ■ TF: 800-416-0555 ■ Web: www.ventiv.com
Walter Karl Inc 2 Blue Hill Plaza 3rd Fl...............Pearl River NY 10965 845-620-0700 620-1885
TF: 877-955-4787 ■ Web: www.walterkarl.com
Weller Co PO Box 8637..............................Tucson AZ 85738 520-818-7797
Wellness International Network Ltd
5800 Democracy Dr.................................Plano TX 75024 972-312-1100 943-5260
Web: web.winltd.com
WSI Internet 5580 Explorer Dr Suite 600............Mississauga ON L4W4Y1 905-678-7588 678-7242
TF: 888-678-7588 ■ Web: www.wsicorporate.com
Wunderman 285 Madison Ave........................New York NY 10017 212-941-3000
Web: www.wunderman.com
Young & Assoc Ltd
2625 Butterfield Rd Suite 216 S....................Oak Brook IL 60523 630-573-2500 573-2522
TF: 800-553-2503 ■ Web: www.youngltd.com
ZS Assoc 1800 Sherman Ave Suite 700................Evanston IL 60201 847-492-3600 864-6280
Web: www.zsassociates.com

199 CONSULTING SERVICES - TELECOMMUNICATIONS

Phone Fax

Ajilon Communications
970 Peachtree Industrial Blvd Suite 200...............Suwanee GA 30024 678-482-5103 215-4910*
*Fax Area Code: 800 ■ TF: 800-843-6910 ■ Web: www.ajiloncom.com
Angus TeleManagement Group Inc
8 Old Kingston Rd.....................................Ajax ON L1T2Z7 905-686-5050 686-2655
Associated Communications & Research Services Inc (ACRS)
817 NE 63rd St..............................Oklahoma City OK 73105 405-843-9966 843-9852
Web: www.acrsokc.com
Atcom Business Telecom Solutions
PO Box 13476........................Research Triangle Park NC 27709 919-314-1001 314-1010
TF: 800-891-3917 ■ Web: www.atcombts.com
Atrion Networking Corp 30 Service Ave..............Warwick RI 02886 401-736-6400 736-6440
TF: 800-890-4526 ■ Web: www.atrion.net
ComSci LLC 485B Rt 1 S Suite 100.....................Iselin NJ 08830 732-632-8000 632-1830
Web: www.comsci.com
DIGICON Corp 9601 Blackwell Rd Suite 250.............Rockville MD 20850 301-721-6300 869-8081
Web: www.digicon.com
First Communications Inc 3340 W Market St.............Akron OH 44333 330-835-2323 835-2330
TF: 800-860-1261 ■ Web: www.firstcommunications.com
GLA Integrated Network Solutions LLC
17 Research Pk Dr Suite 200....................Saint Charles MO 63304 636-720-0900 720-0913
TF: 800-896-3355 ■ Web: www.glai.com
Infotrends/CAP Ventures Inc
97 Libbey Industrial Pkwy Suite 300................Weymouth MA 02189 781-616-2100 616-2121
Web: www.capv.com
Ipc Technologies Inc
7200 Glen Forest Dr Suite 100.....................Richmond VA 23226 804-622-7288
Web: www.ipctech.com
Lawrence Behr Assoc Inc
3400 Tupper Dr PO Box 8026......................Greenville NC 27834 252-757-0279 752-9155
TF: 800-522-4464 ■ Web: www.lbagroup.com/associates
Management Network Group Inc (TMNG)
7300 College Blvd Suite 302....................Overland Park KS 66210 913-345-9315 451-1845
NASDAQ: TMNG ■ TF: 888-480-8664 ■ Web: www.tmng.com
Patient Portal Technologies Inc
8276 Willett Pkwy............................Baldwinsville NY 13027 315-638-6708 638-4585
PINK: PPRG ■ TF: 888-774-3579 ■ Web: www.patientportal.com
QuBX Consulting Inc 660 First Bank Dr................Palatine IL 60067 847-776-3400 776-3406
Web: www.qubxconsulting.com
Superior Communications Inc 704 E Gude Dr.........Rockville MD 20850 301-762-7878 762-6870
Web: www.scicommo.com
Technology Futures Inc 10323 Lake Creek Pkwy.........Austin TX 78750 512-258-8898 258-0087
TF: 800-835-3887 ■ Web: www.tfi.com
Telcordia Technologies Inc 1 Telcordia Dr...........Piscataway NJ 08854 732-699-2000
TF: 800-521-2673 ■ Web: www.telcordia.com
Telwares Inc 7901 Stoneridge Dr....................Pleasanton CA 94588 925-224-7800
TF: 888-835-9273 ■ Web: www.telwares.com
Vectren Communications Services Inc
421 John St.....................................Evansville IN 47713 812-437-6700 437-6781
TF: 888-326-6782
Windfall Assoc 981 Chestnut St.............Newton Upper Falls MA 02464 617-969-1790 969-1777
TF: 877-946-3325 ■ Web: www.windfall-assoc.com
Wireless Facilities Inc (WFI)
4800 Westfields Blvd Suite 200......................Chantilly VA 20151 703-563-7100 563-7200
NASDAQ: WFII ■ Web: www.wfinet.com

200 CONSUMER INFORMATION RESOURCES - GOVERNMENT

Phone Fax

Afterschool.gov 370 L'Enfant Promenade............Washington DC 20447 202-401-9215 401-5450
Web: www.afterschool.gov
Alzheimer's Disease Education & Referral Ctr
PO Box 8250..................................Silver Spring MD 20907 301-495-1080 495-3334
TF: 800-438-4380 ■ Web: www.nia.nih.gov/alzheimers
National Center for Immunization & Respiratory Diseases
1600 Clifton Rd NE MS E-05.........................Atlanta GA 30333 800-232-4636
TF: 800-232-4636 ■ Web: www.cdc.gov/vaccines
National Prevention Information Network
PO Box 6003.....................................Rockville MD 20849 404-679-3860 282-7681*
*Fax Area Code: 888 ■ TF: 800-458-5231 ■ Web: www.cdcnpin.org

Phone Fax

Travelers' Health 1600 Clifton Rd NE..................Atlanta GA 30333 800-232-4636 232-3299*
*Fax Area Code: 888 ■ TF: 800-232-4636 ■ Web: wwwnc.cdc.gov/travel
Consumer Product Safety Commission (CPSC)
4340 E W Hwy # 502..............................Bethesda MD 20814 301-504-7923 504-0051
TF: 800-638-0127 ■ Web: www.cpsc.gov
Corp for National & Community Service
AmeriCorps USA 1201 New York Ave NW...........Washington DC 20525 202-606-5000
TF: 800-833-3722 ■ Web: www.americorps.gov
Learn & Serve America
1201 New York Ave NW.......................Washington DC 20525 202-606-5000
TF: 800-942-2677 ■ Web: www.learnandserve.org
Education Resource Information Ctr (ERIC)
655 15th St NW Suite 500.......................Washington DC 20005 800-538-3742
TF: 800-538-3742 ■ Web: www.eric.ed.gov
Eldercare Locator
1730 Rhode Island Ave NW Suite 1200.............Washington DC 20036 202-872-0888 872-0057
TF: 800-677-1116 ■ Web: www.eldercare.gov
Energy Efficiency & Renewable Energy Information Ctr
1000 Independence Ave SW......................Washington DC 20585 877-337-3463 236-2023*
*Fax Area Code: 360 ■ TF: 877-337-3463 ■ Web: www.eere.energy.gov/consumer
FedWorld.gov
National Technical Information Service
5285 Port Royal Rd..............................Alexandria VA 22312 703-605-6000
TF: 800-553-6847 ■ Web: www.fedworld.gov
Foster Grandparent Program
c/o Senior Corps 1201 New York Ave NW...........Washington DC 20525 202-606-5000 561-3479
TF: 800-424-8867 ■ Web: www.seniorcorps.gov/about/programs/fg.asp
Grants.gov
Dept of Health & Human Services
200 Independence Ave SW HHH Bldg............Washington DC 20201 800-518-4726
TF: 800-518-4726 ■ Web: www.grants.gov
Healthfinder PO Box 1133.......................Washington DC 20013 301-565-4167 984-4256
TF: 800-336-4797 ■ Web: www.healthfinder.gov
Homeland Security Information Ctr
National Technical Information Service
5301 Shawnee Rd................................Alexandria VA 22312 703-605-6040 487-4639
Web: www.ntis.gov/hs
National Clearinghouse for Alcohol & Drug Information
11426 Rockville Pk PO Box 2345....................Rockville MD 20847 800-729-6686
TF: 800-729-6686 ■ Web: www.ncadi.samhsa.gov
National Institute for Literacy (NIFL)
1775 'I' St NW Suite 730.........................Washington DC 20006 202-233-2025 233-2050
TF: 800-228-8813 ■ Web: www.lincs.ed.gov
National Cancer Institute - Cancer Information Service
6116 Executive Blvd Suite 300...................Bethesda MD 20892 800-422-6237
TF: 800-422-6237 ■ Web: www.cancer.gov
National Mental Health Information Ctr
PO Box 42557...................................Washington DC 20015 240-747-5484 747-5470
TF: 800-789-2647 ■ Web: www.samhsa.gov
National Women's Health Information Ctr
8270 Willow Oaks Corporate Dr.......................Fairfax VA 22031 800-994-9662
TF: 800-994-9662 ■ Web: www.womenshealth.gov
President's Council on Physical Fitness Sports & Nutrition
1101 Wootton Pkwy..............................Rockville MD 20852 240-276-9567 276-9860
Web: www.fitness.gov
Project Safe Neighborhoods
Office of Justice Programs 810 7th St NW...........Washington DC 20531 800-458-0786
TF: 800-458-0786 ■ Web: www.psn.gov
PubMed
US National Library of Medicine
8600 Rockville Pike..............................Bethesda MD 20894 301-594-5983 402-1384
TF: 888-346-3656 ■ Web: www.ncbi.nlm.nih.gov
Recreation.gov 1849 C St NW...................Washington DC 20240 202-208-6416
TF: 877-444-6777 ■ Web: www.recreation.gov
Retired & Senior Volunteer Program (RSVP)
c/o Senior Corps 1201 New York Ave NW...........Washington DC 20525 202-606-5000
TF: 800-424-8867 ■
Web: www.seniorcorps.gov/about/sc/history_timeline.asp
Senior Corp 1201 New York Ave NW...............Washington DC 20525 202-606-5000 832-0127
TF: 800-833-3722 ■ Web: www.seniorcorps.gov/home/site_map/index.asp
Tobacco Information & Prevention Source (TIPS)
NCCDPHP 4770 Buford Hwy NE MS K-40...............Atlanta GA 30341 800-232-4636
TF: 800-232-4636 ■ Web: www.cdc.gov/tobacco
US Dept of Labor Women's Bureau
200 Constitution Ave NW Rm S-3002...............Washington DC 20210 202-693-6710
TF: 800-827-5335 ■ Web: www.dol.gov/wb
US General Services Administration
1800 F St NW...................................Washington DC 20405 800-488-3111
TF: 800-333-4636 ■ Web: www.usa.gov
USA Freedom Corps
1600 Pennsylvania Ave NW.......................Washington DC 20500 877-872-2677
TF: 877-872-2677 ■ Web: www.usafreedomcorps.gov
USAJOBS 1900 E St NW..........................Washington DC 20415 202-606-1800
Web: www.usajobs.opm.gov
USDA Center for Nutrition Policy & Promotion
3101 Pk Ctr Dr..................................Alexandria VA 22302 703-305-7600 305-3300
TF: 888-779-7264 ■ Web: www.choosemyplate.gov
White House Office
1600 Pennsylvania Ave NW.......................Washington DC 20500 202-456-1414
Web: www.whitehouse.gov

201 CONTAINERS - METAL (BARRELS, DRUMS, KEGS)

Phone Fax

Actron Steel Inc PO Box 966.....................Traverse City MI 49685 231-947-3981 947-2961
Berenfield Containers Inc 1229 Castle Dr..............Mason OH 45040 513-398-1300 398-3457
Web: www.berenfield.com
Champion Co 400 Harrison St......................Springfield OH 45505 937-324-5681 324-2397
TF Sales: 800-328-0115 ■ Web: www.championspd.com

Phone Fax

Champion Container Corp
180 Essex Ave PO Box 90 ... Avenel NJ 07001 732-636-6700 855-8663
Web: www.championcontainer.com
Chicago Steel Container Corp
1846 S Kilbourn Ave ... Chicago IL 60623 773-277-2244 277-1585
Conco Inc 4000 Oaklawn Dr ... Louisville KY 40219 502-969-1333 962-2190
Web: www.conco.org
Container Research Corp PO Box 159 ... Glen Riddle PA 19037 610-459-2160 358-9297
Web: www.crc-flex.com
CP Louisiana Inc 6000 Jefferson Hwy ... Harahan LA 70123 504-733-6644 733-4412
CSI Fabricated Metal Bins Inc
6910 W Ridge Rd ... Fairview PA 16415 814-474-9353 474-5797
TF: 800-937-9033 ■ *Web:* www.flo-bin.com
Erie Engineered Products Inc
908 Niagara Falls Blvd ... North Tonawanda NY 14120 716-694-2020 694-4339
Web: www.containers-cases.com
Evans Industries Inc 1255 Peters Rd ... Harvey LA 70058 504-374-6000 374-6001
TF: 800-749-6012 ■ *Web:* www.evansind.com
Fiba Technologies Inc
1535 Grafton Rd PO Box 360 ... Millbury MA 01527 508-887-7100 754-2254
Web: www.fibatech.com
Greif Inc 425 Winter Rd ... Delaware OH 43015 740-549-6000 549-6100
NYSE: GEF ■ *TF:* 800-354-7343 ■ *Web:* www.greif.com
Imperial Industries Inc
505 Industrial Pk Ave ... Rothschild WI 54474 715-359-0200 355-5349
TF: 800-558-2945 ■ *Web:* www.imperialind.com
Industrial Container Services 7152 1st Ave S ... Seattle WA 98108 206-763-2345 763-2699
TF: 800-451-3471 ■ *Web:* www.iconserv.com
Innovative Fluid Handling Systems Inc
200 E 3rd St ... Rock Falls IL 61071 815-626-1018 626-1438
TF: 800-435-7003 ■ *Web:* www.ifhgroup.com
Justrite Mfg Co 2454 E Dempster St # 300 ... Des Plaines IL 60016 847-298-9250 298-3429
TF: 800-469-5382 ■ *Web:* www.justritemfg.com
Lebus International Inc 215 Industrial Dr ... Longview TX 75602 903-758-5521 757-7782
Web: www.lebus-intl.com
Meyer Steel Drum Inc 3201 S Millard Ave ... Chicago IL 60623 773-376-8376 376-7060
Web: www.meyersteeldrum.com
Mid-America Steel Drum Co Inc
8570 S Chicago Rd ... Oak Creek WI 53154 414-762-1114 762-1623
Web: www.midamericasteeldrum.com
Myers Container Corp
5801 Christie Ave Suite 255 ... Emeryville CA 94608 510-652-6847 271-6280
TF: 800-228-7269 ■ *Web:* www.myerscontainer.com
North Coast Container Corp 8806 Crane Ave ... Cleveland OH 44105 216-441-6214 441-6239
Web: www.ncc-corp.com
Norton Packaging Inc 20670 Cosair Blvd ... Hayward CA 94545 510-786-3445 782-5329
Web: www.nortonpackaging.com
Packaging Specialties Inc 300 Lake Rd ... Medina OH 44256 330-723-6000 725-8180
TF: 800-344-9271 ■ *Web:* www.packspec.com
Queen City Barrel Co 1937 S St ... Cincinnati OH 45204 513-921-8811 921-3684
Russell-Stanley Corp 685 Rt 202/206 ... Bridgewater NJ 08807 908-203-9500 203-1940
Web: www.russell-stanley.com
Self Industries Inc 3491 Mary Taylor Rd ... Birmingham AL 35235 205-655-3284 655-3288
Southline Metal Products Co 3777 W 12th St ... Houston TX 77055 713-869-4343 869-5650
Stackbin Corp 29 Powderhill Rd ... Lincoln RI 02865 401-333-1600 333-1952
TF Sales: 800-333-1603 ■ *Web:* www.stackbin.com
Stainless Metals Inc 4349 10th St ... Long Island City NY 11101 718-784-1454 784-4719
Web: www.stainlessmetals.com
Textainer Equipment Management Ltd
650 California St Fl 16 ... San Francisco CA 94108 415-434-0551 434-0599
Web: www.textainer.com
Trilla-Nesco Corp 2391 Cassens Dr ... Fenton MO 63026 636-343-7333 326-2891
TF: 800-966-3786 ■ *Web:* www.trilla-nesco.com

202 CONTAINERS - PLASTICS (DRUMS, CANS, CRATES, BOXES)

Phone Fax

Akro-Mils Inc 250 County Hwy 16 ... Wadsworth OH 44281 330-336-6621 334-7100
Web: www.akro-mils.com
Amherst-Merritt International
5565 Red Bird Ctr Dr Suite 150 ... Dallas TX 75237 214-339-0753 339-1313
TF: 800-627-7752
B & R Specialties Inc 2092 Rt 9G ... Staatsburg NY 12580 845-889-4000 889-4002
Web: www.unifuse.com
Beden-Baugh Products Inc 105 Lisbon Rd ... Laurens SC 29360 864-682-3136 682-9302
TF: 866-598-5794 ■ *Web:* www.naclsolutions.com
Belco Mfg Co Inc 2303 Taylors Valley Rd ... Belton TX 76513 254-933-9000 939-2644
TF: 800-251-8265 ■ *Web:* www.belco-mfg.com
Berry Plastics Corp 101 Oakley St ... Evansville IN 47710 812-424-2904 424-0128
TF: 800-234-1930 ■ *Web:* www.berryplastics.com
Brentwood Industries Inc 610 Morgantown Rd ... Reading PA 19611 610-374-5109* 376-6022
Web: www.brentw.com
Buckhorn Inc 55 W TechneCenter Dr ... Milford OH 45150 513-831-4402 831-5474
TF: 800-543-4454 ■ *Web:* www.buckhorninc.com
Captive Plastics Inc 251 Cir Dr N ... Piscataway NJ 08854 732-469-7900 271-5200
Web: www.caplas.com
Case Design Corp 333 N School Ln ... Telford PA 18969 215-703-0130 703-0139
TF: 800-847-4176 ■ *Web:* www.casedesigncorp.com
Champion Container Corp
180 Essex Ave PO Box 90 ... Avenel NJ 07001 732-636-6700 855-8663
Web: www.championcontainer.com
Chem-Tainer Industries Inc
361 Neptune Ave ... North Babylon NY 11704 631-661-8300 661-8209
TF: 800-275-2436 ■ *Web:* www.chemtainer.com
Comar Inc 1 Comar Pl ... Buena NJ 08310 856-692-6100 692-9251
Web: www.comar.com
Custom-Pak Inc 1131 Roosevelt St ... Clinton IA 52732 563-242-1801 244-5362
Web: www.custom-pak.com
EarthShell Corp 1301 York Rd Suite 200 ... Lutherville MD 21093 410-847-9420 847-9431
ECS Composites Inc 3560 Rogue River Hwy ... Grants Pass OR 97527 541-476-8871 474-2479
Web: www.ecscase.com

Phone Fax

Fibrenetics Inc 2 Cutters Dock Rd ... Woodbridge NJ 07095 732-636-5670 636-6624
Web: www.fibglass.com
Fort Recovery Industries Inc
2440 Ohio 49 ... Fort Recovery OH 45846 419-375-4121 375-4150
TF Sales: 800-445-5695 ■ *Web:* www.fortrecoveryindustries.com
Gatekeeper Systems Inc 8 Studebaker ... Irvine CA 92618 949-453-1940 453-8148
TF: 888-808-9433 ■ *Web:* www.gatekeepersystems.com
Handley Industries Inc 2101 Brooklyn Rd ... Jackson MI 49203 517-787-8821 787-3946
TF: 800-870-5088 ■ *Web:* www.handleyind.com
Hardigg Industries Inc 147 N Main St ... South Deerfield MA 01373 413-665-2163 665-4801
TF: 800-542-7344 ■ *Web:* www.hardigg.com
Hedwin Corp 1600 Roland Heights Ave ... Baltimore MD 21211 410-467-8209 889-5189*
*Fax: Cust Svc ■ *TF:* 800-638-1012 ■ *Web:* www.hedwin.com
HGI Skydyne 100 River Rd ... Port Jervis NY 12771 845-856-6655 856-8378
TF: 800-428-2273 ■ *Web:* www.skydyne.com
Iroquois Products of Chicago 2220 W 56th St ... Chicago IL 60636 773-436-3900 436-4908
TF: 800-453-3355 ■ *Web:* www.iroquoisproducts.com
Jewel Case Corp 110 Dupont Dr ... Providence RI 02907 401-943-1400 943-1426
TF: 800-441-4447 ■ *Web:* www.jewelcase.com
McConkey Co 1615 Puyallup St PO Box 1690 ... Sumner WA 98390 253-863-8111 863-5833
TF: 800-426-8124 ■ *Web:* www.mcconkeyco.com
Meese Orbitron Dunne Co 4902 State Rd ... Ashtabula OH 44004 440-998-1202
TF: 800-829-3230 ■ *Web:* www.meeseinc.com
Menasha Corp 1645 Bergstrom Rd ... Neenah WI 54956 920-751-1000 751-1236
TF: 800-558-5073 ■ *Web:* www.menasha.com
Molded Fiber Glass Tray Co 6175 US Hwy 6 ... Linesville PA 16424 814-683-4500 683-4504
TF Sales: 800-458-6050 ■ *Web:* www.mfgtray.com
Myers Industries Inc 1293 S Main St ... Akron OH 44301 330-253-5592 761-6156*
NYSE: MYE ■ *Fax: Acctg ■ *Web:* www.myersindustries.com
ORBIS Corp 1055 Corporate Ctr Dr ... Oconomowoc WI 53066 262-560-5000 560-5841
TF: 800-999-8683 ■ *Web:* www.orbiscorporation.com
Owens-Illinois Inc One Michael Owens Way ... Perrysburg OH 43551 567-336-5000 247-1132*
NYSE: OI ■ *Fax Area Code: 419 ■ *Web:* www.o-i.com
Paragon Mfg Co Inc 2001 N 15th Ave ... Melrose Park IL 60160 708-345-1717 345-1721
Web: www.paragonmanufacturing.com
Plano Molding Co 431 E S St ... Plano IL 60545 630-552-3111 552-8989
TF: 800-451-2122 ■ *Web:* www.planomolding.com
Plas-Tanks Industries Inc 39 Standen Dr ... Hamilton OH 45015 513-942-3800 942-3993
Web: www.plastanks.com
Plastic Enterprises Co Inc
401 SE Thomson Dr ... Lee's Summit MO 64082 816-246-8200 246-8119
Web: www.plasticenterprises.com
Plastic Forming Co Inc 20 S Bradley Rd ... Woodbridge CT 06525 203-397-1338 389-0420
TF: 800-732-2060 ■ *Web:* www.pfccases.com
Plastic Packaging Corp
1227 Union St ... West Springfield MA 01090 413-785-1553 731-5952
TF Cust Svc: 800-342-2011 ■ *Web:* www.plasticpkg.com
Plastican Inc 196 Industrial Rd PO Box 868 ... Leominster MA 01453 978-537-4911 466-6073
Web: www.plastican.com
Plastics Research Corp 1400 S Campus Ave ... Ontario CA 91761 909-391-2006 391-2205
Web: www.prccal.com
Rehrig Pacific Co 4010 E 26th St ... Los Angeles CA 90023 323-262-5145 269-8506
TF: 800-421-6244 ■ *Web:* www.rehrigpacific.com
River Bend Industries 2421 16th Ave S ... Moorhead MN 56560 218-236-1818 236-6168
TF: 800-365-3070 ■ *Web:* www.riverbendind.com
Rocket Box Inc 125 E 144th St ... Bronx NY 10451 718-292-5370 402-2021
TF: 800-762-5521 ■ *Web:* www.rocketbox.com
Rotonics Mfg Inc 6770 Brighton Blvd ... Commerce City CO 90248 303-952-2803 227-9308
Web: www.rotonics.com
RPM Industries Inc 26 Aurelius Ave ... Auburn NY 13021 315-255-1105 252-1167
TF: 800-669-3676 ■ *Web:* www.rpmindustriesinc.com
Schaefer Systems International Inc
10021 Westlake Dr ... Charlotte NC 28273 704-944-4500 588-1862
TF: 800-876-6000 ■ *Web:* www.ssi.schaefer-us.com
Setco Inc 4875 E Hunter Ave ... Anaheim CA 92807 714-777-5200 777-5234
Web: www.setcobottle.com
Shaw-Clayton Corp 123 Carlos Dr ... San Rafael CA 94903 415-472-1522 472-1599
TF Cust Svc: 800-537-6712
Snyder Industries Inc 4700 Fremont St ... Lincoln NE 68504 402-467-5221 465-1210
Web: www.snydernet.com
Specialty Plastic Fabricators Inc
9658 196th St ... Mokena IL 60448 708-479-5501 479-5598
TF: 800-747-9509 ■ *Web:* www.spfinc.com
Stack-On Products Co 1360 N Old Rand Rd ... Wauconda IL 60084 847-526-1611 526-6599
TF: 800-323-9601 ■ *Web:* www.stack-on.com
Toter Inc PO Box 5338 ... Statesville NC 28687 704-872-8171 878-0734
TF: 800-424-0422 ■ *Web:* www.toter.com
Tulip Corp 714 E Keefe Ave ... Milwaukee WI 53212 414-963-3120 962-1825
Web: www.tulipproducts.com
Tulip Corp 3125 Highland Ave ... Niagara Falls NY 14305 716-282-1261 285-6075
Web: www.tulipcorp.com
US Plastic Corp 1390 Newbrecht Rd ... Lima OH 45801 419-228-2242 228-5034
TF: 800-537-9724 ■ *Web:* www.usplastic.com
Xerxes Corp 7901 Xerxes Ave S Suite 201 ... Minneapolis MN 55431 952-887-1890 887-1870
Web: www.xerxescorp.com
Zarn LLC 12700 General Dr ... Charlotte NC 28273 704-588-9191 588-5250
TF: 800-227-5885 ■ *Web:* www.zarn.com

203 CONTAINERS - WOOD

SEE ALSO Pallets & Skids p. 2334

Phone Fax

Abbot & Abbot Box Corp
37-11 10th St ... Long Island City NY 11101 718-392-2600 392-8439
TF: 800-377-0037 ■ *Web:* www.abbotbox.com
Carter Mfg Co Inc 346 S Church St ... Lake City SC 29560 843-394-8123 394-3069
Container Systems Inc 6863 Hwy 56 E ... Franklinton NC 27525 919-496-6133 496-2873
Demptos Napa Cooperage 1050 Soscol Ferry Rd ... Napa CA 94558 707-257-2628 257-1622
Web: www.demptos.fr

Company / Address	City	State	ZIP	Phone	Fax
Elberta Crate & Box Co					
606 Dothan Hwy PO Box 760	Bainbridge	GA	39818	229-246-2266	246-0387
Web: www.elberta.net					
Franklin Crates Inc PO Box 279	Micanopy	FL	32667	352-466-3141	466-0708
Web: www.franklincrates.com					
Greif Inc 425 Winter Rd	Delaware	OH	43015	740-549-6000	549-6100
NYSE: GEF ■ *TF:* 800-354-7343 ■ *Web:* www.greif.com					
Independent Stave Co Inc					
1078 S Jefferson PO Box 104	Lebanon	MO	65536	417-588-4151	588-3344
Johnston's Trading Inc					
11 N Pioneer Ave Suite 101	Woodland	CA	95776	530-661-6152	661-0566
Mautner Enterprises 155 E 76 St	New York	NY	10021	212-452-1871	
TF: 800-628-8637					
McGraw Box Co Inc PO Box 547	McGraw	NY	13101	607-836-6465	836-6413
Mele Enterprises Inc 2007 Beechgrove Pl	Utica	NY	13501	315-733-4600	733-3183
TF: 800-635-6353 ■ *Web:* www.melejewelrybox.com					
Monte Package Co Inc 3752 Riverside Rd	Riverside	MI	49084	269-849-1722	849-0185
TF: 800-653-2807 ■ *Web:* www.montepkg.com					
Peacock Crate Factory 225 Cash St	Jacksonville	TX	75766	903-586-5321	586-7476
TF Orders: 800-666-5647					
Pomona Box Co 301 W Imperial Hwy	La Habra	CA	90631	562-697-6728	871-3483*
**Fax Area Code:* 310					
Quality Woodworking Corp 255 Douglass St	Brooklyn	NY	11217	718-875-3437	875-0036
Stearnswood Inc 320 3rd Ave NW	Hutchinson	MN	55350	320-587-2137	587-7646
TF: 800-657-0144 ■ *Web:* www.stearnswood.com					
Texas Basket Co 100 Myrtle Dr	Jacksonville	TX	75766	903-586-8014	586-0988
TF: 800-657-2200 ■ *Web:* www.texasbasket.com					
TKV Containers Inc 4582 E Harvey Ave	Fresno	CA	93702	559-251-5551	255-8090
Web: www.tkvcontainers.com					
Wisconsin Box Co Inc 929 Townline Rd	Wausau	WI	54402	715-842-2248	842-2240
TF: 800-876-6658 ■ *Web:* www.wisconsinbox.com					

204 CONTROLS - INDUSTRIAL PROCESS

Company / Address	City	State	ZIP	Phone	Fax
ADA-ES Inc 8100 Southpark Way Suite B	Littleton	CO	80120	303-734-1727	734-0330
NASDAQ: ADES ■ *TF:* 888-822-8617 ■ *Web:* www.adaes.com					
ADS Corp 4940 Research Dr	Huntsville	AL	35805	256-430-3366	430-6633
TF: 800-633-7246 ■ *Web:* www.adsenv.com					
AeroControlex Group 313 Gillett St	Painesville	OH	44077	440-352-6182	354-2912
Web: www.aerocontrolex.com					
Alpha Technologies Services LLC					
3030 Gilchrist Rd	Akron	OH	44305	330-745-1641	848-7326
TF: 800-356-9886 ■ *Web:* www.alpha-technologies.com					
AMETEK Automation & Process Technologies					
1080 N Crooks Rd	Clawson	MI	48017	248-435-0700	435-8120
TF: 800-635-0289 ■ *Web:* www.ametekapt.com					
AMETEK Power Instruments 50 Fordham Rd	Wilmington	MA	01887	978-988-4101	988-4944*
**Fax:* Cust Svc ■ *Web:* www.ametekpower.com					
AMETEK Power Instruments Rochester Instruments Products Div					
255 N Union St	Rochester	NY	14605	585-263-7700	262-4777
AMETEK Process & Analytical Instruments THERMOX Div					
150 Freeport Rd	Pittsburgh	PA	15238	412-828-9040	826-0399
Web: www.thermox.com					
Amot Controls Corp 8824 Fallbrook Dr	Houston	TX	77064	281-940-1800	668-8808
Web: www.amotusa.com					
Anderson Instrument Co					
156 Auriesville Rd	Fultonville	NY	12072	518-922-5315	922-8997
TF: 800-833-0081 ■ *Web:* www.andinst.com					
Athena Controls Inc 5145 Campus Dr	Plymouth Meeting	PA	19462	610-828-2490	828-7084
TF: 800-782-6776					
Ati Industrial Automation Export Co					
1031 Goodworth Dr	Apex	NC	27539	919-772-0115	772-8259
Web: www.ati-ia.com					
Automation Products Group Inc 2005 N 600 W	Logan	UT	84321	435-753-7300	753-7490
TF: 888-525-7300 ■ *Web:* www.apgsensors.com					
Azonix Corp 900 Middlesex Tpke Bldg 6	Billerica	MA	01821	978-670-6300	670-8855
TF: 800-967-5558 ■ *Web:* www.azonix.com					
Bacharach Inc 621 Hunt Valley Cir	New Kensington	PA	15068	724-334-5000	334-5001
TF: 800-736-4666 ■ *Web:* www.bacharach-inc.com					
Barksdale Inc 3211 Fruitland Ave	Los Angeles	CA	90058	323-589-6181	589-3463
TF: 800-835-1060 ■ *Web:* www.barksdale.com					
Blue-White Industries Ltd					
5422 Business Dr	Huntington Beach	CA	92649	714-893-8529	894-9492
Web: www.bluwhite.com					
Brookfield Engineering Lab Inc					
11 Commerce Blvd	Middleboro	MA	02346	508-946-6200	946-6262
TF: 800-628-8139 ■ *Web:* www.brookfieldengineering.com					
Buhler Inc 13105 12th Ave N	Plymouth	MN	55441	763-847-9900	847-9911
Web: www.buhlergroup.com/us					
Campbell Scientific Inc 815 W 1800 N	Logan	UT	84321	435-753-2342	750-9540
Web: www.campbellsci.com					
Cec Controls Co Inc 14555 Barber Ave	Warren	MI	48088	586-779-0222	779-0266
Web: www.ceccontrols.com					
Cincinnati Test Systems Inc 5555 Dry Fork Rd	Cleves	OH	45002	513-367-6699	367-5426
Web: www.cincinnati-test.com					
Compressor Controls Corp 4725 121st St	Des Moines	IA	50323	515-270-0857	270-1331
Web: www.cccglobal.com					
Conax Buffalo Technologies LLC					
2300 Walden Ave	Buffalo	NY	14225	716-684-4500	684-7433
TF: 800-223-2389 ■ *Web:* www.conaxbuffalo.com					
Cooper Atkins Corp 33 Reeds Gap Rd	Middlefield	CT	06455	860-349-3473	349-8994
TF Sales: 800-835-5011 ■ *Web:* www.cooperinstrument.com					
CPM Beta Raven 40 S Corporate Hills Dr	Saint Charles	MO	63301	314-291-4504	255-0299*
**Fax Area Code:* 636 ■ *Web:* www.betaraven.com					
Crane Co Dynalco Controls Div					
3690 NW 53rd St	Fort Lauderdale	FL	33309	954-739-4300	484-3376
TF: 800-368-6666 ■ *Web:* www.dynalco.com					
Custom Control Sensors Inc					
21111 Plummer St	Chatsworth	CA	91311	818-341-4610	709-0426
Web: www.ccsdualsnap.com					
Custom Sensors & Technologies					
14501 Princeton Avew	Moorpark	CA	93021	805-552-3599	552-3577
Web: www.cst.schneider-electric.com					
Daniel Measurement & Control Inc					
5650 Brittmoore Rd	Houston	TX	77041	713-467-6000	827-3880
Web: www.emersonprocess.com					
Davis Inotek Instruments LLC					
4701 Mt Hope Dr Suite J	Baltimore	MD	21215	410-358-3900	358-0252
TF: 800-358-5545 ■ *Web:* www.davis.com					
DICKEY-john Corp 5200 County Rd 15 S	Auburn	IL	62615	217-438-3371	438-6012
TF: 800-637-2952 ■ *Web:* www.dickey-john.com					
Dickson Co 930 S Westwood Ave	Addison	IL	60101	630-543-3747	543-0498
TF: 800-757-3747 ■ *Web:* www.dicksondata.com					
Dwyer Instruments Inc					
102 Indiana Hwy 212 PO Box 373	Michigan City	IN	46360	219-879-8000	872-9057
Web: www.dwyer-inst.com					
Electro Optical Industries Inc					
859 Ward Dr	Santa Barbara	CA	93111	805-964-6701	967-8590
Web: www.electro-optical.com					
Emerson Process Management					
8100 W Florissant Bldg K-Annex					
PO Box 36911	Saint Louis	MO	63136	314-553-1900	553-1880
Web: www.emersonprocess.com					
Encoder Products Co 464276 Hwy 95 S PO Box 249	Sagle	ID	83860	208-263-8541	263-0541
TF: 800-366-5412 ■ *Web:* www.encoder.com					
Endress+Hauser Inc 2350 Endress Pl	Greenwood	IN	46143	317-535-7138	535-8498
TF: 800-428-4344 ■ *Web:* www.us.endress.com					
Environmental Systems Corp 200 Tech Ctr Dr	Knoxville	TN	37912	865-688-7900	687-8977
Web: www.envirosys.com					
Fairchild Industrial Products Co					
3920 W Pt Blvd	Winston-Salem	NC	27103	336-659-3400	659-9323*
**Fax:* Sales ■ *TF:* 800-423-1093 ■ *Web:* www.fairchildproducts.com					
Fast Heat Inc 776 Oaklawn Ave	Elmhurst	IL	60126	630-833-5400	833-2040
TF: 800-982-4328 ■ *Web:* www.fastheat.com					
Fluid Components International					
1755 La Costa Meadows Dr	San Marcos	CA	92078	760-744-6950	736-6250
TF: 800-863-8703 ■ *Web:* www.fluidcomponents.com					
Forney Corp 3405 Wiley Post Rd	Carrollton	TX	75006	972-458-6100	458-6650
TF Cust Svc: 800-356-7740 ■ *Web:* www.forneycorp.com					
FW Murphy 5311 S 122nd E Ave PO Box 470248	Tulsa	OK	74146	918-317-4100	317-4266
Web: www.fwmurphy.com					
GE Infrastructure Sensing					
1100 Technology Pk Dr	Billerica	MA	01821	978-437-1000	437-1031
TF: 800-833-9438 ■ *Web:* www.ge-mcs.com					
Gems Sensors Inc 1 Cowles Rd	Plainville	CT	06062	860-747-3000	747-4244
TF: 800-378-1600 ■ *Web:* www.gemssensors.com					
Geotech Environmental Equipment Inc					
2650 E 40th Ave	Denver	CO	80205	303-320-4764	322-7242
TF: 800-833-7958 ■ *Web:* www.geotechenv.com					
Harco Laboratories Inc 186 Cedar St	Branford	CT	06405	203-483-3700	483-0391
Web: www.harcolabs.com					
Hart Scientific Inc					
799 E Utah Valley Dr	American Fork	UT	84003	801-763-1600	763-1010
TF: 800-438-4278 ■ *Web:* www.hartscientific.com					
Heraeus Electro-Nite Co					
1 Summit Sq Suite 100	Langhorne	PA	19047	215-944-9000	944-9000
Web: www.heraeus-electro-nite.com					
HO Trerice Co 12950 W Eight-Mile Rd	Oak Park	MI	48237	248-399-8000	399-7246
TF: 888-873-7423 ■ *Web:* www.trerice.com					
Hoffland Environmental Inc					
10391 Silver Springs Rd	Conroe	TX	77303	936-856-4515	856-4589
Web: www.hoffland.net					
Honeywell Automation & Control Solutions					
11 W Spring St	Freeport	IL	61032	815-235-5500	
Web: www.honeywell.com					
HSQ Technology 26227 Research Rd	Hayward	CA	94545	510-259-1334	259-1391
TF: 800-486-6684 ■ *Web:* www.hsq.com					
Industrial Scientific Corp					
7848 Steubenville Pike	Oakdale	PA	15071	412-788-4353	788-8353
TF: 800-338-3287 ■ *Web:* www.indsci.com					
INFICON Inc 2 Technology Pl	East Syracuse	NY	13057	315-434-1100	437-3803
Web: www.inficon.com					
Intelligent Instrumentation Inc					
3000 E Valencia Rd	Tucson	AZ	85706	520-573-0887	573-0522
TF: 800-685-9911 ■ *Web:* www.instrument.com					
Isco Inc 4700 Superior St PO Box 82531	Lincoln	NE	68501	402-464-0231	465-3022*
**Fax:* Cust Svc ■ *TF:* 800-228-4250 ■ *Web:* www.isco.com					
ITT Conoflow 5154 Hwy 78 PO Box 768	Saint George	SC	29477	843-563-9281	563-2131*
**Fax:* Cust Svc ■ *Web:* www.ittconoflow.com					
ITT Industries Inc 1133 Westchester Ave	White Plains	NY	10604	914-641-2000	696-2950
NYSE: ITT ■ *Web:* www.itt.com					
Kistler-Morse Corp 150 Venture Blvd	Spartanburg	SC	29306	864-574-2763	574-8063
TF: 800-426-9010 ■ *Web:* www.kistlermorse.com					
Lake Monitors Inc 8809 Industrial Dr	Franksville	WI	53126	262-884-9800	884-9810
TF: 800-850-6110 ■ *Web:* www.lakemonitors.com					
Lake Shore Cryotronics 575 McCorkle Blvd	Westerville	OH	43082	614-891-2243	818-1600
TF: 800-394-2243 ■ *Web:* www.lakeshore.com					
LaMotte Co 802 Washington Ave	Chestertown	MD	21620	410-778-3100	778-6394
TF: 800-344-3100 ■ *Web:* www.lamotte.com					
Linear Laboratories 42025 Osgood Rd	Fremont	CA	94539	510-226-0488	226-1112
Web: www.linearlabs.com					
Magnetrol International Inc					
5300 Belmont Rd	Downers Grove	IL	60515	630-969-4000	969-9489
TF: 800-624-8765					
Mahr Federal Inc 1144 Eddy St	Providence	RI	02905	401-784-3100	784-3246
TF Orders: 800-343-2050 ■ *Web:* www.mahrfederal.com					
Malema Engineering Corp 1060 S Rogers Cir	Boca Raton	FL	33487	561-995-0595	982-8608
TF: 800-637-6418 ■ *Web:* www.malema.com					
Marsh Bellofram Corp 8019 Ohio River Blvd	Newell	WV	26050	304-387-1200	387-1212
TF: 800-727-5646 ■ *Web:* www.marshbellofram.com					
Maxitrol Co 23555 Telegraph Rd PO Box 2230	Southfield	MI	48034	248-356-1400	356-0829
Web: www.maxitrol.com					

Company	City	State	Zip	Phone	Fax
McCrometer Inc 3255 W Stetson Ave *TF:* 800-220-2279 ■ *Web:* www.mccrometer.com	Hemet	CA	92545	951-652-6811	652-3078
Metron Inc 1505 W 3rd Ave *Web:* www.metroninc.com	Denver	CO	80223	303-592-1903	534-1947
Micro Lithography Inc 1257 Elko Dr *Web:* www.mliusa.com	Sunnyvale	CA	94089	408-747-1769	
Micro Motion Inc 7070 Winchester Cir *Web:* www.emersonprocess.com/micromotion	Boulder	CO	80301	303-530-8400	530-8242
Minco Products Inc 7300 Commerce Ln NE **Fax:* Sales ■ *Web:* www.minco.com	Minneapolis	MN	55432	763-571-3121	571-0927*
MKS Instruments Inc 2 Tech Dr Suite 201 *Web:* www.mksinst.com	Andover	MA	01810	978-645-5500	557-5100
Mocon Inc 7500 Boone Ave N Suite 111 *NASDAQ: MOCO* ■ *Web:* www.mocon.com	Minneapolis	MN	55428	763-493-6370	493-6358
Moore Industries International Inc 16650 Schoenborn St *TF:* 800-999-2900 ■ *Web:* www.miinet.com	North Hills	CA	91343	818-894-7111	891-2816
NDC Infrared Engineering 5314 N Irwindale Ave *Web:* www.ndcinfrared.com	Irwindale	CA	91706	626-939-3887	939-3870
Noren Products Inc 1010 Obrien Dr *TF:* 866-936-6376 ■ *Web:* www.norenproducts.com	Menlo Park	CA	94025	650-322-9500	324-1348
Noshok Inc 1010 W Bagley Rd *Web:* www.noshok.com	Berea	OH	44017	440-243-0888	243-3472
NRD LLC 2937 Alt Blvd PO Box 310 *TF:* 800-525-8076 ■ *Web:* www.nrdstaticcontrol.com	Grand Island	NY	14072	716-773-7634	773-7744
Omega Engineering Inc 1 Omega Dr PO Box 4047 **Fax:* Cust Svc ■ *TF:* 800-826-6342 ■ *Web:* www.omega.com	Stamford	CT	06907	203-359-1660	359-7700*
Onset Computer Corp PO Box 3450 *TF:* 800-564-4377 ■ *Web:* www.onsetcomp.com	Pocasset	MA	02559	508-759-9500	759-9100
OPW Fuel Management Systems 6900 Santa Fe Dr **Fax:* Cust Svc ■ *Web:* www.opwglobal.com	Hodgkins	IL	60525	708-485-4200	485-4630*
Parker Climate & Industrial Controls Group 6035 Parkland Blvd *Web:* www.parker.com/cig	Cleveland	OH	44124	216-896-3000	896-4007
Parker Hannifin Corp Veriflo Div 250 Canal Blvd *TF:* 800-962-4074 ■ *Web:* www.parker.com/veriflo	Richmond	CA	94804	510-235-9590	232-7396
Portage Electric Products Inc 7700 Freedom Ave NW *TF:* 888-464-7374 ■ *Web:* www.pepiusa.com	North Canton	OH	44720	330-499-2727	499-1853
Porter Instrument Co Inc 245 Township Line Rd PO Box 907 *TF:* 800-457-2001 ■ *Web:* www.porterinstrument.com	Hatfield	PA	19440	215-723-4000	723-2199
Potter Electric Signal Co Inc 5757 Phantom Dr Suite 125 *TF:* 800-325-3936 ■ *Web:* www.pottersignal.com	Hazelwood	MO	63042	314-878-4321	595-6999
Pyromation Inc 5211 Industrial Rd *Web:* www.pyromation.com	Fort Wayne	IN	46825	260-484-2580	482-6805
Qualitrol Co LLC 1385 Fairport Rd *Web:* www.qualitrolcorp.com	Fairport	NY	14450	585-586-1515	377-0220
Racine Federated Inc 8635 Washington Ave *Web:* www.racinefederated.com	Racine	WI	53406	262-639-6770	639-2267
RAE Systems 3775 N 1st St *AMEX: RAE* ■ *TF:* 877-723-2878 ■ *Web:* www.raesystems.com	San Jose	CA	95134	408-952-8200	952-8480
Raven Industries Inc 205 E 6th St *NASDAQ: RAVN* ■ *TF:* 800-227-2836 ■ *Web:* www.ravenind.com	Sioux Falls	SD	57104	605-336-2750	335-0268
Raytheon Commercial Infrared 13532 N Central Expy MS 37 *TF:* 800-990-3275 ■ *Web:* www.raytheoninfrared.com	Dallas	TX	75243	972-344-4000	344-4004
Raytheon Network Centric Systems 2501 W University	McKinney	TX	75071	972-952-2000	
Renco Encoders Inc 26 Coromar Dr *TF:* 800-248-6044 ■ *Web:* www.renco.com	Goleta	CA	93117	805-968-1525	685-7965
Research Inc 7128 Shady Oak Rd *Web:* www.researchinc.com	Eden Prairie	MN	55344	952-941-3300	941-3628
Robertshaw Industrial Products 1602 Mustang Dr *TF:* 800-228-7429 ■ *Web:* www.robertshawindustrial.com	Maryville	TN	37801	865-981-3100	981-3168
Rochester Gauges Inc of Texas 11616 Harry Hines Blvd *TF:* 800-821-1829 ■ *Web:* www.rochestergauges.com	Dallas	TX	75229	972-241-2161	620-1403
Ronan Engineering Co 21200 Oxnard St *TF:* 800-327-6626 ■ *Web:* www.ronan.com	Woodland Hills	CA	91367	818-883-5211	992-6435
Roper Industries Inc 6901 Professional Pkwy Suite 200 *NYSE: ROP* ■ *Web:* www.roperind.com	Sarasota	FL	34240	941-556-2601	556-2670
Rosemount Analytical Inc Process Analytical Div 6565 P Davis Industrial Pkwy *TF:* 800-433-6076 ■ *Web:* www.emersonprocess.com	Solon	OH	44139	330-682-9010	684-4434
Rosemount Analytical Inc Uniloc Div 2400 Barranca Pkwy *TF:* 800-854-8257 ■ *Web:* www.emersonprocess.com/raihome/liquid	Irvine	CA	92606	949-863-1181	474-7250
RTP Corp 1834 SW 2nd St *Web:* www.rtpcorp.com	Pompano Beach	FL	33069	954-974-5500	975-9815
Sabina Motors & Controls Inc 1440 N Burton Pl *Web:* www.sabinamotors.com	Anaheim	CA	92806	714-956-0480	956-0486
Scully Signal Co 70 Industrial Way *TF:* 800-272-8559 ■ *Web:* www.scully.com	Wilmington	MA	01887	617-692-8600	692-8620
See Water Inc 121 N Dillon St *TF:* 888-733-9283 ■ *Web:* www.seewaterinc.com	San Jacinto	CA	92583	951-487-8073	487-0557
Sensidyne Inc 16333 Bay Vista Dr *TF:* 800-451-9444 ■ *Web:* www.sensidyne.com	Clearwater	FL	33760	727-530-3602	539-0550
Sierra Instruments Inc 5 Harris Ct Bldg L *TF:* 800-866-0200 ■ *Web:* www.sierrainstruments.com	Monterey	CA	93940	831-373-0200	373-4402
Signet Scientific Co Inc 3401 Aero Jet Ave *Web:* www.gfsignet.com	El Monte	CA	91731	626-571-2770	573-2057
SJE-Rhombus 22650 County Hwy 6 PO Box 1708 *TF:* 800-746-6287 ■ *Web:* www.sjerhombus.com	Detroit Lakes	MN	56502	218-847-1317	847-4617
SOR Inc 14685 W 105th St *TF:* 800-676-6794 ■ *Web:* www.sorinc.com	Lenexa	KS	66215	913-888-2630	888-0767
Spectronics Corp 956 Brush Hollow Rd *TF:* 800-274-8888 ■ *Web:* www.spectroline.com	Westbury	NY	11590	800-274-8888	491-6868
Spectrum Controls Inc PO Box 5533 *Web:* www.spectrumcontrols.com	Bellevue	WA	98006	425-746-9481	641-9473
Spirax Sarco Inc 1150 Northpoint Blvd *TF:* 800-883-4411 ■ *Web:* www.spiraxsarco.com/us	Blythewood	SC	29016	803-714-2000	714-2222
Sterling Inc 2900 S 160th St *TF Cust Svc:* 800-783-7835 ■ *Web:* www.sterlco.com	New Berlin	WI	53151	262-641-8600	641-8654
Sutron Corp 22400 Davis Dr *NASDAQ: STRN* ■ *Web:* www.sutron.com	Sterling	VA	20164	703-406-2800	406-2801
Taylor Precision Products LLC 2311 W 22nd St Suite 200 *TF:* 800-289-0944 ■ *Web:* www.taylorusa.com	Oak Brook	IL	60523	630-954-1250	954-1275
Teledyne Advanced Pollution Instrumentation 9480 Carroll Pk Dr *TF:* 800-324-5190 ■ *Web:* www.teledyne-api.com	San Diego	CA	92121	858-657-9800	657-9816
Teledyne Monitor Labs Inc (TML) 35 Inverness Dr E *TF:* 800-422-1499 ■ *Web:* www.monitorlabs.com	Englewood	CO	80112	303-792-3300	799-4853
Test Automation & Controls 1036 Destrehan Ave *TF:* 800-861-6792	Harvey	LA	70058	504-371-3000	371-3001
Thermo Fisher Scientific 81 Wyman St PO Box 9046 *NYSE: TMO* ■ *TF:* 800-678-5599 ■ *Web:* www.thermofisher.com	Waltham	MA	02454	781-622-1000	622-1207
Transcat Inc 35 Vantage Pt Dr *NASDAQ: TRNS* ■ *TF:* 800-800-5001 ■ *Web:* www.transcat.com	Rochester	NY	14624	585-352-9460	352-1486
Troxler Electronic Laboratories Inc 3008 E Cornwallis Rd PO Box 12057 *TF:* 877-876-9537 ■ *Web:* www.troxlerlabs.com	Research Triangle Park	NC	27709	919-549-8661	549-0761
TSI Inc 500 Cardigan Rd *TF:* 800-874-2811 ■ *Web:* www.tsi.com	Shoreview	MN	55126	651-483-0900	490-3824
Tyco Thermal Controls 2415 Bay Rd **Fax Area Code:* 800 ■ *TF:* 800-545-6258 ■ *Web:* www.tycothermal.com	Redwood City	CA	94063	650-216-1526	827-5703*
United Electric Controls Co 180 Dexter Ave *TF:* 800-545-1416 ■ *Web:* www.ueonline.com	Watertown	MA	02472	617-926-1000	926-2568
Uson LP 8640 N Eldridge Pkwy *Web:* www.uson.com	Houston	TX	77041	281-671-2000	671-2001
Veeder-Root 125 Powder Forest Dr *TF:* 800-879-0301 ■ *Web:* www.veeder.com	Simsbury	CT	06070	860-651-2700	651-2704
Venture Measurement Co LLC 150 Venture Blvd *Web:* www.venturemeasurement.com	Spartanburg	SC	29306	864-574-8960	578-7308
Wika Instrument Corp 1000 Wiegand Blvd *TF:* 888-945-2872 ■ *Web:* www.wika.us	Lawrenceville	GA	30043	770-513-8200	338-5118
Winland Electronics Inc 1950 Excel Dr *AMEX: WEX* ■ *TF:* 800-635-4269 ■ *Web:* www.winland.com	Mankato	MN	56001	507-625-7231	387-2488
Yokogawa Corp of America 12530 W Airport Blvd *TF:* 800-888-6400 ■ *Web:* www.yokogawa.com/us	Sugar Land	TX	30265	281-340-3800	340-3838
YSI Inc 1700-1725 Brannum Ln *TF Cust Svc:* 800-765-4974 ■ *Web:* www.ysi.com	Yellow Springs	OH	45387	937-767-7241	767-9353

205 CONTROLS - TEMPERATURE - RESIDENTIAL & COMMERCIAL

Company	City	State	Zip	Phone	Fax
APCOM Inc 125 SE Pkwy *TF:* 800-251-3535 ■ *Web:* www.apcom-inc.com	Franklin	TN	37064	615-794-5574	791-0660
Automated Logic Corp 1150 Roberts Rd N *Web:* www.automatedlogic.com	Kennesaw	GA	30144	770-429-3000	429-3001
Azonix Corp 900 Middlesex Tpke Bldg 6 *TF:* 800-967-5558 ■ *Web:* www.azonix.com	Billerica	MA	01821	978-670-6300	670-8855
CAPP/USA 201 Marple Ave **Fax Area Code:* 800 ■ **Fax:* Sales ■ *TF:* 800-356-8000 ■ *Web:* www.cappusa.com	Clifton Heights	PA	19018	610-394-1100	237-3292*
Channel Products Inc 7100 Wilson Mills Rd *Web:* www.channelproducts.com	Chesterland	OH	44026	440-423-0113	423-1502
Columbus Electric Mfg Co PO Box 4973 *TF Cust Svc:* 800-682-3398	Johnson City	TN	37602	423-477-4131	477-0084
Cooper Atkins Corp 33 Reeds Gap Rd *TF Sales:* 800-835-5011 ■ *Web:* www.cooperinstrument.com	Middlefield	CT	06455	860-349-3473	349-8994
DeltaTRAK Inc PO Box 398 *TF:* 800-962-6776 ■ *Web:* www.deltatrak.com	Pleasanton	CA	94566	925-249-2250	249-2251
Emerson Climate Technologies - Retail Solutions 3240 Town Pt Dr *TF:* 800-829-2724 ■ *Web:* www.emersonclimate.com	Kennesaw	GA	30144	770-425-2724	425-9319
Emerson Electric Co White-Rodgers Div 8100 W Florissant Ave *Web:* www.white-rodgers.com	Saint Louis	MO	63136	314-553-3600	553-3706
Eurotherm USA 44621 Guilford Dr Suite 100 *Web:* www.eurotherm.com	Ashburn	VA	20147	703-724-7300	724-7301
Food Automation-Service Techniques Inc (FAST) 905 Honeyspot Rd *TF:* 800-327-8766 ■ *Web:* www.fastinc.com	Stratford	CT	06615	203-377-4414	377-8187
Hallcrest Inc 1820 Pickwick Ln *TF:* 800-527-1419 ■ *Web:* www.hallcrest.com	Glenview	IL	60026	847-998-8580	998-6866
Hansen Technologies Corp 6827 High Grove Blvd *TF:* 800-426-7368 ■ *Web:* www.hantech.com	Burr Ridge	IL	60527	630-325-1565	325-1572
Honeywell International Inc 6670 185th Ave NE *Web:* www.alerton.com	Redmond	WA	98052	425-869-8400	869-8445
HSQ Technology 26227 Research Rd *TF:* 800-486-6684 ■ *Web:* www.hsq.com	Hayward	CA	94545	510-259-1334	259-1391
Invensys Controls 191 E N Ave *TF Cust Svc:* 800-304-6563 ■ *Web:* www.invensyscontrols.com	Carol Stream	IL	60188	630-260-3400	260-7294
Ircon Inc 7300 N Natchez Ave *TF:* 800-323-7660 ■ *Web:* www.ircon.com	Niles	IL	60714	847-967-5151	647-0948

Company	City	State	ZIP	Phone	Fax
ITT McDonnell & Miller 8200 N Austin Ave *Web:* www.completewatersystems.com	Morton Grove	IL	60053	847-966-3700	983-5954
Johnson Controls Inc 5757 N Green Bay Ave *NYSE: JCI* ■ *TF:* 800-972-8040 ■ *Web:* www.johnsoncontrols.com	Milwaukee	WI	53209	414-524-1200	524-3232
Johnson Controls Systems 9410 Bunsen Pkwy Suite 100-B *TF:* 800-765-7773 ■ *Web:* www.johnsoncontrols.com	Louisville	KY	40220	502-671-7300	499-2135
Kidde-Fenwal Inc 400 Main St *TF:* 800-872-6527 ■ *Web:* www.kidde-fenwal.com	Ashland	MA	01721	508-881-2000	881-6729
KMC Controls Inc 19476 Industrial Dr *TF:* 877-444-5622 ■ *Web:* www.kmc-controls.com	New Paris	IN	46553	574-831-5250	831-5252
Nailor Industries of Texas Inc 4714 Winfield Rd *Web:* www.nailor.com	Houston	TX	77039	281-590-1172	590-3086
Nexus Custom Electronics Inc PO Box 250	Brandon	VT	05733	802-247-6811	247-6811
Novar Controls Corp 6060 Rockside Woods Blvd Suite 400 *TF:* 800-348-1235 ■ *Web:* www.novar.com	Cleveland	OH	44118	216-682-1600	682-1614
PECO Mfg Co Inc PO Box 82189 *Web:* www.pecomanufacturing.com	Portland	OR	97282	503-233-6401	233-6407
Phoenix Controls Corp 75 Discovery Way *Web:* www.phoenixcontrols.com	Acton	MA	01720	978-795-1285	795-1111
Portage Electric Products Inc 7700 Freedom Ave NW *TF:* 888-464-7374 ■ *Web:* www.pepiusa.com	North Canton	OH	44720	330-499-2727	499-1853
Prentke Romich Co 1022 Heyl Rd *TF:* 800-848-8008 ■ *Web:* www.prentrom.com	Wooster	OH	44691	330-262-1984	263-4829
Residential Control Systems 11481 Sunrise Gold Cir Suite 1 *TF:* 888-727-4822 ■ *Web:* www.resconsys.com	Rancho Cordova	CA	95742	916-635-6784	635-7668
Sabine River Authority of Texas PO Box 579 *Web:* www.sra.dst.tx.us	Orange	TX	77631	409-746-2192	746-3780
Siemens Bldg Technologies Inc 1000 Deerfield Pkwy *TF:* 800-877-7545 ■ *Web:* www.buildingtechnologies.siemens.com	Buffalo Grove	IL	60089	847-215-1000	215-1093
SPX Corp Robinair Div 655 Eisenhower Dr *TF:* 800-628-6496 ■ *Web:* www.robinair.com	Owatonna	MN	55060	507-455-7000	
Taylor Precision Products LLC 2311 W 22nd St Suite 200 *TF:* 800-289-0944 ■ *Web:* www.taylorusa.com	Oak Brook	IL	60523	630-954-1250	954-1275
Therm-O-Disc Inc 1320 S Main St **Fax:* Sales ■ *Web:* www.tod.com	Mansfield	OH	44907	419-525-8500	525-8344*
WAKO Electronics 3600 Chamberlain Ln Suite 500 *Web:* www.wako-usa.com	Louisville	KY	40241	502-429-8866	429-8869
Watlow Winona 1241 Bundy Blvd *TF:* 800-833-7492 ■ *Web:* www.watlow.com	Winona	MN	55987	507-454-5300	452-4507
Weiss Instruments Inc 905 Waverly Ave *Web:* www.weissinstruments.com	Holtsville	NY	11742	631-207-1200	207-0900

206 CONTROLS & RELAYS - ELECTRICAL

Company	City	State	ZIP	Phone	Fax
ABB SSAC 8242 Loop Rd *TF Tech Supp:* 800-377-7722 ■ *Web:* www.ssac.com	Baldwinsville	NY	13027	315-638-1300	638-0333
Alcoa Fujikura Ltd 830 Crescent Ctr Dr Suite 600 *TF:* 800-627-7854 ■ *Web:* www.alcoa.com	Franklin	TN	37067	615-778-6000	778-5927
Allied Controls Inc 150 E Aurora St *TF:* 800-648-8871 ■ *Web:* www.alliedcontrols.com	Waterbury	CT	06708	203-757-4200	757-4202
American Relays Inc 10306 Norwalk Blvd *Web:* www.americanrelays.com	Santa Fe Springs	CA	90670	562-944-0447	944-0590
American Zettler Inc 75 Columbia *Web:* www.azettler.com	Aliso Viejo	CA	92656	949-831-5000	831-8642
AMETEK National Controls Corp 1725 Western Dr *TF:* 800-323-2593 ■ *Web:* www.nationalcontrols.com	West Chicago	IL	60185	630-231-5900	231-1377
AMX Corp 3000 Research Dr *TF:* 800-222-0193 ■ *Web:* www.amx.com	Richardson	TX	75082	469-624-8000	624-7153
Anaheim Automation 910 E Orangefair Ln *TF Sales:* 800-345-9401 ■ *Web:* www.anaheimautomation.com	Anaheim	CA	92801	714-992-6990	992-0471
Arens Controls Co LLC 855 Commerce Pkwy *Web:* www.arenscontrols.com	Carpentersville	IL	60110	847-844-4700	844-4790
Basler Electric Co 12570 SR- 143 PO Box 269 *Web:* www.basler.com	Highland	IL	62249	618-654-2341	654-2351
Beckwood Services Inc 27 Hale Spring Rd *Web:* www.beckwood.com	Plaistow	NH	03865	603-382-3840	382-3852
Bright Image Corp 2830 S18th Ave *TF:* 800-733-5656 ■ *Web:* www.touchandglow.com	Broadview	IL	60155	708-449-5656	449-1155
Bus-tech Inc 129 Middlesex Tpke *TF:* 800-284-3172 ■ *Web:* www.bustech.com	Burlington	MA	01803	781-272-8200	272-0342
Cim Products Inc 21360 Gateway Ct *Web:* www.engspec.com	Brookfield	WI	53045	262-790-8000	790-8001
Cleveland Motion Controls Inc 7550 Hub Pkwy *TF:* 800-321-8072 ■ *Web:* www.cmccontrols.com	Cleveland	OH	44125	216-524-8800	642-2199
Control Masters Inc 5235 Katrine Ave *Web:* www.controlmasters.com	Downers Grove	IL	60515	630-968-2390	968-3260
Converteam Inc 610 Epsilon Dr *Web:* www.converteam.com	Pittsburgh	PA	15238	412-967-6900	967-7660
Coto Technology USA 66 Whitecap Dr *Web:* www.cotorelay.com	North Kingstown	RI	02852	401-943-2686	942-0920
Digi-Data Corp 7165 Columbia Gateway Dr # G *Web:* www.digidata.com	Columbia	MD	21046	410-730-6880	730-7708
DST Controls 651 Stone Rd *TF:* 800-251-0773 ■ *Web:* www.dstcontrols.com	Benicia	CA	94510	707-745-5117	745-8952
Ducommun Inc 23301 Wilmington Ave *TF:* 800-421-5032 ■ *Web:* www.ducommun.com	Carson	CA	90745	310-513-7280	513-7279
Duct-O-Wire Co 345 Adams Cir *TF:* 800-752-6001 ■ *Web:* www.ductowire.com	Corona	CA	92882	951-735-8220	735-2372
Durex Industries Inc 190 Detroit St *Web:* www.durexindustries.com	Cary	IL	60013	847-639-5600	639-2199
Eaton Corp 1111 Superior Ave Eaton Ctr *NYSE: ETN* ■ *Web:* www.eaton.com	Cleveland	OH	44114	216-523-5000	523-4787
Electric Motor & Contracting Co Inc 3703 Cook Blvd *Web:* www.emc-co.com	Chesapeake	VA	23323	757-487-2121	487-5983
Electric Regulator Corp 6189 El Camino Real *TF:* 800-458-6566 ■ *Web:* www.electricregulator.com	Carlsbad	CA	92009	760-438-7873	438-0437
Electrical & Electronics 3881 Danbury Rd *Web:* www.eecontrols.com	Brewster	NY	10509	914-769-5000	769-3641
Electrical Design & Control Co 2200 Stephenson Hwy *Web:* www.edandc.com	Troy	MI	48083	248-743-2400	743-2401
Electro-Matic Products Co 2235 N Knox Ave *Web:* www.em-chicago.com	Chicago	IL	60639	773-235-4010	235-7317
Electroid Co 45 Fadem Rd *TF:* 800-242-7184 ■ *Web:* www.electroid.com	Springfield	NJ	07081	973-467-8100	467-2606
Electronic Theatre Controls Inc 3031 Pleasantview Rd *TF:* 800-688-4116 ■ *Web:* www.etcconnect.com	Middleton	WI	53562	608-831-4116	836-1736
Enercon Engineering Inc 1 Altorfer Ln *TF:* 800-218-8831 ■ *Web:* www.enercon-eng.com	East Peoria	IL	61611	309-694-1418	694-3703
Entron Controls LLC 601 High Tech Port *Web:* www.entroncontrols.com	Greer	SC	29650	864-416-0190	416-0195
Fife Corp 222 W Memorial Rd PO Box 26508 *TF:* 800-333-3433 ■ *Web:* www.fife.com	Oklahoma City	OK	73126	405-755-1600	755-8425
FSI/Fork Standards Inc 668 E Western Ave *TF:* 800-468-6009 ■ *Web:* www.fsinet.com	Lombard	IL	60148	630-932-9380	932-0016
Fujitsu Components America Inc 250 E Caribbean Dr *Web:* www.fujitsu.com	Sunnyvale	CA	94089	408-745-4900	745-4970
FXC Corp 3410 S Susan St *Web:* www.pia.com	Santa Ana	CA	92704	714-556-7400	641-5093
GE Multilin 215 Anderson Ave *TF:* 800-547-8629 ■ *Web:* www.geindustrial.com/multilin	Markham	ON	L6E1B3	905-294-6222	201-2098
GET Engineering Corp 9350 Bond Ave *Web:* www.getntds.com	El Cajon	CA	92021	619-443-8295	443-8613
Glendinning Marine Products 740 Century Cir *TF:* 800-500-2380 ■ *Web:* www.glendinningprods.com	Conway	SC	29526	843-399-6146	399-5005
Globe Electronic Hardware Inc 34-24 56th St *TF:* 800-221-1505 ■ *Web:* www.globelectronics.com	Woodside	NY	11377	718-457-0303	457-7493
Guardian Electric Mfg Co Inc 1425 Lake Ave *TF:* 800-762-0369 ■ *Web:* www.guardian-electric.com	Woodstock	IL	60098	815-334-3600	337-0377
Hamlin Electronics Inc 612 E Lake St *Web:* www.hamlin.com	Lake Mills	WI	53551	920-648-3000	648-3001
Honeywell Automation & Control Solutions 11 W Spring St *Web:* www.honeywell.com	Freeport	IL	61032	815-235-5500	
Honeywell Sensing & Control 11 W Spring St *TF Cust Svc:* 800-537-6945 ■ *Web:* www.honeywell.com	Freeport	IL	61032	815-235-5500	235-5574
Hubbell Industrial Controls 4301 Cheyenne Dr *TF:* 800-828-4032 ■ *Web:* www.hubbell-icd.com	Archdale	NC	27263	336-434-2800	434-2803
Icm Controls Corp 7313 William Barry Blvd *TF:* 800-365-5525 ■ *Web:* www.icmcontrols.com	North Syracuse	NY	13212	315-233-5266	233-5276
IDEC Corp 1175 Elko Dr *TF:* 800-262-4332 ■ *Web:* www.idec.com	Sunnyvale	CA	94089	408-747-0550	744-9055
Imperial Irrigation District (IID) PO Box 937 *Web:* www.iid.com	Imperial	CA	92251	760-482-9600	482-9611
Inertia Dynamics Inc 31 Industrial Pk Rd *TF:* 800-800-6445 ■ *Web:* www.idicb.com	New Hartford	CT	06057	860-482-4444	693-6463
Intermatic Inc 7777 Winn Rd *Web:* www.intermatic.com	Spring Grove	IL	60081	815-675-7000	675-7001
J & A.k Inc 5350 Campbells Run Rd *TF:* 800-888-9750 ■ *Web:* www.tmi-pvc.com	Pittsburgh	PA	15205	412-787-9750	
Jennings Technology Co 970 McLaughlin Ave *Web:* www.jenningstech.com	San Jose	CA	95122	408-292-4025	286-1789
Johnson Controls Inc 5757 N Green Bay Ave *NYSE: JCI* ■ *TF:* 800-972-8040 ■ *Web:* www.johnsoncontrols.com	Milwaukee	WI	53209	414-524-1200	524-3232
Joslyn Clark Corp 2100 W Broad St **Fax Area Code:* 803 ■ *TF:* 800-476-6952 ■ *Web:* www.joslynclark.com	Elizabethtown	NC	28337	800-476-6952	285-0885*
K/E Electric Supply Co 146 N Groesbeck Hwy *Web:* www.keelectric.com	Mount Clemens	MI	48043	586-469-3005	469-3006
KB Electronics Inc 12095 NW 39th St *TF:* 800-221-6570 ■ *Web:* www.kbelectronics.com	Coral Springs	FL	33065	954-346-4900	346-3377
Keyence Corp of America 50 Tice Blvd *TF:* 888-539-3623 ■ *Web:* www.keyence.com	Woodcliff Lake	NJ	07677	201-930-0100	930-0099
Leach International Corp 6900 Orangethorpe Ave *Web:* www.esterline.com	Buena Park	CA	90622	714-736-7598	739-1713
Lutron Electronics Co Inc 7200 Suter Rd *TF Tech Supp:* 800-523-9466 ■ *Web:* www.lutron.com	Coopersburg	PA	18036	610-282-6280	282-6253
Mac Products Inc 60 Pennsylvania Ave PO Box 469 *Web:* www.macproducts.net	Kearny	NJ	07032	973-344-0700	344-5368
Magnet Schultz of America Inc 401 Plaza Dr *TF Cust Svc:* 800-635-3778 ■ *Web:* www.magnet-schultz.com	Westmont	IL	60559	630-789-0600	789-0614
MagneTek Inc N49 W13650 Campbell Dr *NYSE: MAG* ■ **Fax Area Code:* 800 ■ *TF:* 800-288-8178 ■ *Web:* www.magnetek.com	Menomonee Falls	WI	53051	262-783-3500	298-3503*
Marquardt Switches Inc 2711 US Rt 20 *Web:* www.switches.com	Cazenovia	NY	13035	315-655-8050	655-8042
Martin Automatic Inc 1661 Northrock Ct *Web:* www.martinauto.com	Rockford	IL	61103	815-654-4800	654-4810

Company	City	State	ZIP	Phone	Fax
McDade-Woodcock Inc					
2404 Claremont Ave NE PO Box 11592	Albuquerque	NM	87107	505-884-0155	884-6073
Web: www.mwieic.com					
Moog Inc Jamison Rd.	East Aurora	NY	14052	716-652-2000	687-4457
NYSE: MOG.A ■ *Web:* www.moog.com					
Networks Electronic Co 9750 De Soto Ave.	Chatsworth	CA	91311	818-341-0440	718-7133
Web: www.networkselectronic.com					
Novaspect Inc 1124 Tower Rd.	Schaumburg	IL	60173	847-956-8020	885-8200
Web: www.novaspect.com					
OEM Controls Inc 12 Controls Dr	Shelton	CT	06484	203-929-8431	929-3867
Web: www.oemcontrols.com					
OMRON Corp 1 Commerce Dr.	Schaumburg	IL	60173	847-843-7900	843-7787
TF: 800-556-6766 ■ *Web:* www.omron247.com					
OMRON Scientific Technologies Inc					
6550 Dumbarton Cir.	Fremont	CA	94555	510-608-3400	744-1440
TF: 888-510-4357 ■ *Web:* www.sti.com					
Ormec Systems Corp 19 Linden Pk	Rochester	NY	14625	585-385-3520	385-5999
TF: 800-656-7632 ■ *Web:* www.ormec.com					
Panasonic Electric Works Corp of America					
629 Central Ave	New Providence	NJ	07974	908-464-3550	464-8513
TF: 800-276-6289 ■ *Web:* www.pewa.panasonic.com					
Parker Hannifin Corp Electromechanical Automation Div					
5500 Business Pk Dr	Rohnert Park	CA	94928	707-584-7558	584-8015
TF: 800-358-9068 ■ *Web:* www.parkermotion.com					
Parker McCrory Mfg Co 2000 Forest Ave	Kansas City	MO	64108	816-221-2000	221-9879
TF: 800-662-1038 ■ *Web:* www.parmakusa.com					
Payne Engineering Co					
Rt 29 Rocky Step Rd PO Box 70	Scott Depot	WV	25560	304-757-7353	757-7305
TF Orders: 800-331-1345 ■ *Web:* www.payneng.com					
Peerless Instrument Co Inc					
1966-D Broadhollow Rd	Farmingdale	NY	11735	631-396-6500	396-6555
Web: www.peerless.cwfc.com					
Pepperl Fuchs Inc 1600 Enterprise Pkwy.	Twinsburg	OH	44087	330-425-3555	425-4607
Web: www.pepperl-fuchs.us					
Pine Instrument Co 101 Industrial Dr.	Grove City	PA	16127	724-458-6391	458-4648
Web: www.pineinst.com					
Polytron Corp 4400 Wyland Dr	Elkhart	IN	46516	574-522-0246	522-0457
TF: 888-228-0246 ■ *Web:* www.polytron-corp.com					
Precision Multiple Controls Inc					
33 Greenwood Ave	Midland Park	NJ	07432	201-444-0600	445-8575
Web: www.precisionmulticontrols.com					
Premier System Integrators Inc					
140 Weakley Ln PO Box 329	Smyrna	TN	37167	615-355-7200	355-7210
Web: www.premier-system.com					
Pva Tepla America Inc 251 Corporate Terr	Corona	CA	92879	951-371-2500	371-9792
TF Sales: 800-527-5667 ■ *Web:* www.plasmapen.com					
Rci Custom Products 801 N E St Suite 2A	Frederick	MD	21701	301-620-9130	620-9103
TF: 800-546-4724 ■ *Web:* www.rcicustom.com					
Rockford Systems Inc 4620 Hydraulic Rd	Rockford	IL	61109	815-874-7891	874-6144*
**Fax:* Sales ■ *TF Cust Svc:* 800-922-7533 ■ *Web:* www.rockfordsystems.com					
Rockwell Collins Electromechanical Systems					
17000 Red Hill Ave.	Irvine	CA	92614	949-250-1015	250-0497
TF: 800-866-5775 ■ *Web:* www.rockwellcollins.com					
Saftronics Inc 5580 Enterprise Pkwy.	Fort Myers	FL	33905	239-693-7200	693-2431
TF: 800-893-2321 ■ *Web:* www.saftronics.com					
Saia-Burgess Inc 801 Scholz Dr.	Vandalia	OH	45377	937-454-2345	898-8624
Web: www.saia-burgess.com					
Sendec Corp 72 Perinton Pkwy	Fairport	NY	14450	585-425-3390	425-3392
TF: 800-295-8000 ■ *Web:* www.sendec.com					
SOR Inc 14685 W 105th St	Lenexa	KS	66215	913-888-2630	888-0767
TF: 800-676-6794 ■ *Web:* www.sorinc.com					
South/Shore Controls Inc 4823 N Ridge Rd	Perry	OH	44081	440-259-2500	259-2500
Web: www.southshorecontrols.com					
Sprecher & Schuh 15910 International Plaza	Houston	TX	77032	281-442-9000	442-1570
Web: www.ssusa.cc					
Statek Corp 512 N Main St	Orange	CA	92868	714-639-7810	997-1256
Web: www.statek.com					
Static Controls Corp 30460 S Wixom Rd.	Wixom	MI	48393	248-926-4400	926-4412
Web: www.scccontrols.com					
Struthers-Dunn 407 E Smith St Suite B	Timmonsville	SC	29161	843-346-4427	346-4465
Web: www.struthers-dunn.com					
Sturdy Corp 1822 Carolina Beach Rd	Wilmington	NC	28401	910-763-8261	763-2650
TF: 800-721-3282 ■ *Web:* www.sturdycorp.com					
Syron Engineering & Mfg LLC 1325 Woodland Dr	Saline	MI	48176	734-429-4989	429-7764
TF: 800-272-4511 ■ *Web:* www.syron.com					
Systems Machines Automation Components Corp					
5807 Van Allen Way	Carlsbad	CA	92008	760-929-7575	929-7588
Web: www.smac-mca.com					
Tech/Ops Sevcon Inc 155 Northboro Rd	Southborough	MA	01772	508-281-5510	281-5520
AMEX: TO ■ *Web:* www.techopssevcon.com					
Time Mark Corp 11440 E Pine St	Tulsa	OK	74116	918-438-1220	437-7584
TF: 800-862-2875 ■ *Web:* www.time-mark.com					
Time-O-Matic Inc 1015 Maple St.	Danville	IL	61832	217-442-0611	442-1020
TF: 800-637-2645 ■ *Web:* www.timeomatic.com					
Transdyn Inc 4256 Hacienda Dr # 100	Pleasanton	CA	94588	925-225-1600	225-1610
Web: www.transdyn.com					
Triumph Controls Inc 205 Church Rd	North Wales	PA	19454	215-699-4861	699-2595
Tyco Electronics Corp Hartman Div					
175 N Diamond St	Mansfield	OH	44902	419-521-9500	526-2749
Tympanium Corp 197 Commercial St	Malden	MA	02148	781-324-8752	
Web: www.tympanium.com					
Unico Inc 3725 Nicholson Rd.	Franksville	WI	53126	262-886-5678	504-7396
TF: 800-245-1859 ■ *Web:* www.unicous.com					
Wago Corp N120 W19129 Freistadt Rd	Germantown	WI	53022	800-346-7245	255-3232*
**Fax Area Code:* 262 ■ *TF:* 800-346-7245 ■ *Web:* www.wago.us					
Wescon Products Co 2533 S W St.	Wichita	KS	67217	316-942-7266	942-5114
TF: 800-835-0160 ■ *Web:* www.wesconproducts.com					
Whitepath Fab Tech Inc 16402 Hwy 515 N.	Ellijay	GA	30540	706-276-2511	276-2524
Web: www.whitepath.com					
Whittaker Controls Inc					
12838 Saticoy St	North Hollywood	CA	91605	818-765-8160	759-2190
Web: www.whittakercontrols.com					
Yaskawa America Inc 2121 Norman Dr S	Waukegan	IL	60085	847-887-7000	887-7310*
**Fax:* Mktg ■ *TF:* 800-927-5292 ■ *Web:* www.yaskawa.com					

207 CONVENIENCE STORES

SEE ALSO Gas Stations p. 1902; Grocery Stores p. 2000

Company	City	State	ZIP	Phone	Fax
7-Eleven Canada Inc 13450 2Nnd Ave Suite 2400	Surrey	BC	V3T0C3	604-299-0711	586-1511
TF: 800-255-0711 ■ *Web:* www.7-eleven.com					
7-Eleven Inc 2711 N Haskell Ave PO Box 711	Dallas	TX	75221	214-828-7011	828-7848
TF: 800-255-0711 ■ *Web:* www.7-eleven.com					
A & E Stores Inc 1000 Huyler St	Teterboro	NJ	07608	201-393-0600	393-0233
Web: www.aestores.com					
Alimentation Couche-Tard Inc					
1600 Boul St Martin E	Laval	QC	H7G4S8	450-662-3272	662-7537
TSX: ATD ■ *TF:* 800-361-2612 ■ *Web:* www.couche-tard.com					
Bull Bros Inc 401 Herkimer Rd	Utica	NY	13503	315-797-7760	797-1174
Cafepress.com Inc					
1850 Gateway Dr Suite 300	Foster City	CA	94404	650-655-3120	240-0260
Web: www.cafepress.com					
Casey's General Stores Inc 1 Convenience Blvd	Ankeny	IA	50021	515-965-6100	965-6160
NASDAQ: CASY ■ *Web:* www.caseys.com					
Convenient Food Mart Inc 467 N State St	Painesville	OH	44077	800-860-4844	639-6526*
**Fax Area Code:* 440 ■ *TF:* 800-860-4844 ■ *Web:* www.convenientfoodmart.com					
Cracker Barrel Convenience Stores Inc					
12221 Industriplex Blvd	Baton Rouge	LA	70809	225-753-3200	753-3200
Dairy Barn Stores Inc 544 Elwood Rd	East Northport	NY	11731	631-368-8050	266-2547
TF: 888-320-0246 ■ *Web:* www.dairybarn.com					
Deweese Enterprises Inc 5625 Old Hwy 80 W	Meridian	MS	39307	601-483-8291	693-5410
E-Z Mart Stores Inc 602 Falvey Ave	Texarkana	TX	75501	903-832-6502	832-7903
TF: 800-234-6502 ■ *Web:* www.ezmart.com					
FFP Marketing Co Inc 2801 Glenda Ave	Fort Worth	TX	76117	817-838-4700	838-4700
TF: 800-695-3282					
Fkg Oil Co 721 W Main	Belleville	IL	62220	618-233-6754	233-1327
TF: 800-873-3546 ■ *Web:* www.motomart.net					
Gibbs Oil Co LP 90 Everett Ave PO Box 9151	Chelsea	MA	02150	617-889-9000	884-6075
TF: 800-352-3558 ■ *Web:* www.gibbsoil.com					
Heritage Dairy Stores Inc 376 Jessup Rd.	Thorofare	NJ	08086	856-845-2855	845-8392
Web: www.heritages.com					
Holiday Stationstores					
4567 American Blvd W	Bloomington	MN	55437	952-830-8700	
TF: 800-745-7411 ■ *Web:* www.holidaystationstores.com					
Hollar Co 2012 Rainbow Dr	Gadsden	AL	35901	256-547-1644	547-1494
Jet Food Stores of Georgia					
1106 S Harris St	Sandersville	GA	31082	478-552-2588	552-8758
TF: 800-277-1168					
JFM Inc 4276 Lakeland Dr	Flowood	MS	39232	601-664-7177	664-7272
Johnny Quick Food Stores Inc					
96 Shaw Ave Suite 240	Clovis	CA	93612	559-297-6830	297-7519
Junior Food Stores of West Florida Inc					
619 8th Ave.	Crestview	FL	32536	850-682-5171	689-1055
TF: 800-682-8486 ■ *Web:* www.tomt.com					
Krause Gentle Corp 6400 Westown Pkwy	West Des Moines	IA	50266	515-226-0128	226-0995
Web: www.kumandgo.com					
Kwik Trip Inc 1626 Oak St PO Box 2107	La Crosse	WI	54602	608-781-8988	781-8950
Web: www.kwiktrip.com					
Kwik-Way Inc 509 N 24 St W	Billings	MT	59102	406-656-6310	656-0244
Lassus BROS Handy Dandy 1800 Magnavox Way	Fort Wayne	IN	46804	260-436-1415	436-0340
TF: 800-686-2836 ■ *Web:* www.lassus.com					
Li'l Thrift Food Marts Inc					
3563 Gillispie St.	Fayetteville	NC	28306	910-433-4490	
Web: www.shortstopfoodmarts.com					
Loaf N' Jug Mini Mart 442 Keeler Pkwy.	Pueblo	CO	81001	719-948-3071	948-2602
NASDAQ: KRO ■ *TF:* 866-562-3658 ■ *Web:* www.loafnjug.com					
Love's Travel Stops & Country Stores Inc					
10601 N Pennsylvania Ave	Oklahoma City	OK	73120	405-751-9000	749-9110
TF: 800-388-0983 ■ *Web:* www.loves.com					
Mac's Convenience Stores Inc					
305 Milner Ave Suite 300 4th Fl	Toronto	ON	M1B3V4	800-268-5574	291-4947*
**Fax Area Code:* 416 ■ *TF:* 800-424-2403 ■ *Web:* www.macs.ca					
Maverik Country Stores Inc					
1014 S Washington St PO Box 288	Afton	WY	83110	307-885-9412	885-3832
Web: www.maverik.com					
Open Pantry Food Marts					
10505 Corporate Dr Suite 101	Pleasant Prairie	WI	53158	262-857-1156	857-9667
Web: www.openpantry.com					
Pantry Inc 305 Gregson Dr	Cary	NC	27511	919-774-6700	776-5303
NASDAQ: PTRY ■ *TF:* 877-798-4792 ■ *Web:* www.thepantry.com					
Plaid Pantries Inc 10025 SW Allen Blvd	Beaverton	OR	97005	503-646-4246	646-3071
TF: 800-677-5243 ■ *Web:* www.plaidpantry.com					
Presto Food Stores Inc 2009 N Airport Rd	Plant City	FL	33563	813-754-3511	752-5494
TF: 800-881-3511					
Quick Chek Food Stores					
3 Old Hwy 28	Whitehouse Station	NJ	08889	908-534-2200	534-7216
Web: www.qchek.com					
Quik Stop Markets Inc 4567 Enterprise St.	Fremont	CA	94538	510-657-8500	657-1544
QuikTrip Corp 4705 S 129th E Ave.	Tulsa	OK	74134	918-615-7700	615-7615
TF: 800-544-5749 ■ *Web:* www.quiktrip.com					
Red Apple Group Inc 823 11th Ave	New York	NY	10019	212-956-5803	247-4509
Rosenberger's Dairies Inc					
847 Forty Foot Rd PO Box 901	Hatfield	PA	19440	215-855-9074	855-6486
TF: 800-355-9074					
Sheetz Inc 5700 6th Ave.	Altoona	PA	16602	814-946-3611	946-4375
TF: 800-487-5444 ■ *Web:* www.sheetz.com					
Speedway SuperAmerica LLC 500 Speedway Dr	Enon	OH	45323	937-864-3000	
TF Cust Svc: 800-643-1948 ■ *Web:* www.speedway.com					
Susser Holdings LLC 4433 Baldwin Blvd	Corpus Christi	TX	78408	361-693-3600	884-2494
TF: 800-569-3585 ■ *Web:* www.susser.com					
Tedeschi Food Shops Inc 14 Howard St	Rockland	MA	02370	781-878-8210	878-0476
Web: www.tedeschifoodshops.com					

				Phone	Fax
Tom Thumb Food Stores Inc 97 W Okeechobee Rd *Web:* www.tomthumbfla.com	Hialeah	FL	33010	305-885-5451	885-0144
Uppy's Convenience Stores Inc 1011 Boulders Spring Dr *Web:* www.uppys.com	Richmond	VA	23225	804-706-4702	748-4703
Valdak Corp 1149 36th Ave S *Web:* www.valleydairy.com	Grand Forks	ND	58201	701-746-8371	780-9286
Wawa Inc 260 W Baltimore Pike **Fax:* Hum Res ■ *TF:* 800-283-9292 ■ *Web:* www.wawa.com	Media	PA	19063	610-358-8000	358-8878*
Worsley Cos Inc 1410 Commonwealth Dr # 202 *TF:* 800-348-3429 ■ *Web:* www.scotchmanstores.com	Wilmington	NC	28403	910-395-5300	395-6691
Xtramart 221 Quinebaug Rd *TF:* 800-243-6366 ■ *Web:* www.xtramart.com	North Grosvenordale	CT	06255	860-935-5200	

208 CONVENTION CENTERS

SEE ALSO Performing Arts Facilities p. 2392; Stadiums & Arenas p. 2671

Listings Are Alphabetized By City Names Within State Groupings.

ALABAMA

				Phone	Fax
Birmingham-Jefferson Convention Complex 2100 Richard Arrington Jr Blvd N *TF:* 877-843-2522 ■ *Web:* www.bjcc.org	Birmingham	AL	35203	205-458-8400	458-8437
Von Braun Ctr 700 Monroe St *Web:* www.vonbrauncenter.com	Huntsville	AL	35801	256-533-1953	551-2203
Arthur R Outlaw Mobile Convention Ctr 1 S Water St *TF:* 800-566-2453 ■ *Web:* www.mobileconventions.com	Mobile	AL	36602	251-208-2100	208-2150

ALASKA

				Phone	Fax
William A Egan Civic & Convention Ctr 555 W 5th Ave *Web:* www.anchorageconventioncenters.com	Anchorage	AK	99501	907-263-2800	263-2858
Carlson Ctr 2010 2nd Ave *Web:* www.carlson-center.com	Fairbanks	AK	99701	907-451-7800	451-1195
Centennial Hall Convention Ctr 101 Egan Dr *Web:* www.juneau.org	Juneau	AK	99801	907-586-5283	586-1135

ARIZONA

				Phone	Fax
Glendale Civic Ctr 5750 W Glenn Dr *Web:* www.glendaleciviccenter.com	Glendale	AZ	85301	623-930-4300	930-4319
Mesa Convention Ctr 263 N Ctr St *Web:* www.mesaconventioncenter.com	Mesa	AZ	85201	480-644-2178	644-2617
Phoenix Convention Ctr 100 N 3rd St *TF:* 800-282-4842 ■ *Web:* www.phoenixconventioncenter.com	Phoenix	AZ	85004	602-262-6225	495-3642
Tucson Convention Ctr 260 S Church Ave *Web:* www.tucsonaz.gov/tcc	Tucson	AZ	85701	520-791-4101	791-5572
Yuma Civic Ctr 1440 W Desert Hills Dr *Web:* www.yumaconventioncenter.com	Yuma	AZ	85365	928-373-5040	344-9121

ARKANSAS

				Phone	Fax
Fort Smith Convention Ctr 55 S 7th St *Web:* www.fortsmith.org	Fort Smith	AR	72901	479-788-8932	788-8930
Hot Springs Convention Ctr (HSCVB) 134 Convention Blvd PO Box 6000 *TF:* 800-543-2284 ■ *Web:* www.hotsprings.org	Hot Springs	AR	71902	501-321-2277	321-2136
Statehouse Convention Ctr Markham & Main # 1 1 Statehouse Plaza *TF:* 800-844-4781 ■ *Web:* www.littlerockmeetings.com/conv-centers/Statehouse	Little Rock	AR	72201	501-376-4781	376-7833
Pine Bluff Convention Ctr 1 Convention Ctr Plaza *TF:* 800-536-7660 ■ *Web:* www.pinebluffcvb.org	Pine Bluff	AR	71601	870-536-7600	535-4867

BRITISH COLUMBIA

				Phone	Fax
Vancouver Convention & Exposition Centre (VCEC) 1055 Canada Pl *TF:* 866-785-8232 ■ *Web:* www.vancouverconventioncentre.com	Vancouver	BC	V6C3T4	604-689-8232	647-7232

CALIFORNIA

				Phone	Fax
Anaheim Convention Ctr 800 W Katella Ave *Web:* www.anaheimconventioncenter.com	Anaheim	CA	92802	714-765-8900	765-8965
Rabobank Arena Theater & Convention Ctr 1001 Truxtun Ave	Bakersfield	CA	93301	661-852-7300	861-9904
Carson Ctr 801 E Carson St *Web:* www.carsoncenter.com	Carson	CA	90745	310-835-0212	835-0160
Cow Palace 2600 Geneva Ave *Web:* www.cowpalace.com	Daly City	CA	94014	415-404-4100	404-4111
Fresno Convention Ctr 848 M St *Web:* www.fresnoconventioncenter.com	Fresno	CA	93721	559-445-8100	445-8110
Bren Events Ctr 100 Bren Events Ctr *Web:* www.bren.uci.edu	Irvine	CA	92697	949-824-5050	824-5097
Long Beach Convention & Entertainment Ctr 300 E Ocean Blvd *Web:* www.longbeachcc.com	Long Beach	CA	90802	562-436-3636	436-9491
California Market Ctr 110 E 9th St *TF:* 800-225-6278 ■ *Web:* www.californiamarketcenter.com	Los Angeles	CA	90079	213-630-3600	630-3708
Los Angeles Convention Ctr 1201 S Figueroa St *TF:* 800-448-7775 ■ *Web:* www.lacclink.com	Los Angeles	CA	90015	213-741-1151	765-4266
Shrine Auditorium & Exposition Ctr 665 W Jefferson Blvd *Web:* www.shrineauditorium.com	Los Angeles	CA	90007	213-748-5116	742-9922
Modesto Centre Plaza 1000 L St *Web:* www.modestogov.com/prnd/facilities/cplaza	Modesto	CA	95354	209-577-6444	544-6729
Monterey Conference Ctr 1 Portola Plaza *TF Sales:* 800-742-8091 ■ *Web:* www.montereyconferencecenter.com	Monterey	CA	93940	831-646-3770	646-3777
Oakland Convention Ctr 1001 Broadway *TF:* 800-228-9290	Oakland	CA	94607	510-451-4000	835-3466
Ontario Convention Ctr 2000 E Convention Ctr Way *TF:* 800-455-5755 ■ *Web:* www.ontariocc.com	Ontario	CA	91764	909-937-3000	937-3080
Palm Springs Convention Ctr 277 N Avenida Caballeros *TF:* 800-333-7535 ■ *Web:* www.palmspringscc.com	Palm Springs	CA	92262	760-325-6611	778-4102
Sacramento Convention Ctr 1400 J St *Web:* www.sacramentoconventioncenter.com	Sacramento	CA	95814	916-808-5291	808-7687
NOS Events Ctr 689 S E St *Web:* www.nosevents.com	San Bernardino	CA	92408	909-888-6788	889-7666
San Diego Convention Ctr 111 W Harbor Dr *TF:* 800-525-7322 ■ *Web:* www.sdccc.org	San Diego	CA	92101	619-525-5000	525-5005
Concourse Exhibition Ctr 635 8th St *TF:* 800-877-8522 ■ *Web:* www.sfdesigncenter.com	San Francisco	CA	94103	415-864-1500	490-5885
Moscone Ctr 747 Howard St *Web:* www.moscone.com	San Francisco	CA	94103	415-974-4000	974-4073
Nob Hill Masonic Ctr 1111 California St *Web:* www.sfmasoniccenter.com	San Francisco	CA	94108	415-776-4702	776-3945
San Jose Convention & Cultural Facilities (SJC) 150 W San Carlos St *TF:* 800-726-5673 ■ *Web:* www.sanjose.org/plan-a-meeting-event/venues/convention-center	San Jose	CA	95110	408-792-4194	277-3535
San Mateo County Event Ctr 2495 S Delaware St *TF:* 800-338-3976 ■ *Web:* www.smeventcenter.com	San Mateo	CA	94403	650-574-3247	574-3985
Santa Clara Convention Ctr 5001 Great America Pkwy *Web:* www.santaclara.org	Santa Clara	CA	95054	408-748-7000	748-7013
Santa Monica Civic Auditorium 1855 Main St *Web:* www.santamonicacivic.org	Santa Monica	CA	90401	310-458-8551	394-3411
Visalia Convention Ctr 303 E Acequia Ave *TF:* 800-640-4888 ■ *Web:* www.ci.visalia.ca.us	Visalia	CA	93291	559-713-4000	713-4804

COLORADO

				Phone	Fax
Colorado Springs City Auditorium 221 E Kiowa St *Web:* www.springsgov.com	Colorado Springs	CO	80903	719-385-5969	385-6584
Colorado Convention Ctr 700 14th St *Web:* www.denverconvention.com	Denver	CO	80202	303-228-8000	228-8104
Two Rivers Convention Ctr 159 Main St *Web:* www.tworiversconvention.com	Grand Junction	CO	81501	970-263-5700	263-5720

CONNECTICUT

				Phone	Fax
XL Ctr 1 Civic Ctr Plaza *Web:* www.xlcenter.com	Hartford	CT	06103	860-249-6333	241-4226

DISTRICT OF COLUMBIA

				Phone	Fax
Washington Convention Center Authority 801 Mt Vernon Pl NW *TF:* 800-368-9000 ■ *Web:* www.dcconvention.com	Washington	DC	20001	202-249-3000	

FLORIDA

				Phone	Fax
Harborview Ctr 300 Cleveland St *Web:* www.harborv.com	Clearwater	FL	33755	727-462-6778	462-6798
Ocean Ctr 101 N Atlantic Ave *TF:* 800-858-6444 ■ *Web:* www.oceancenter.com	Daytona Beach	FL	32118	386-254-4500	254-4512
Greater Fort Lauderdale-Broward County Convention Ctr 1950 Eisenhower Blvd *Web:* www.ftlauderdalecc.com	Fort Lauderdale	FL	33316	954-765-5900	763-9551
Harborside Event Ctr 1375 Monroe St *TF:* 800-294-9516 ■ *Web:* www.fmharborside.com	Fort Myers	FL	33901	239-332-6888	332-6683
Prime Osborn Convention Ctr 1000 Water St *Web:* www.jaxevents.com/primeosbornconventioncenter	Jacksonville	FL	32204	904-630-4000	630-4029
Lakeland Ctr 701 W Lime St *Web:* www.thelakelandcenter.com	Lakeland	FL	33815	863-834-8100	834-8101
Miami Beach Convention Ctr 1901 Convention Ctr Dr *Web:* www.miamibeachconvention.com	Miami Beach	FL	33139	305-673-7311	673-7435

				Phone	Fax
Orange County Convention Ctr (OCCC) 9800 International Dr *TF:* 800-345-9845 ■ *Web:* www.occc.net	Orlando	FL	32819	407-685-9800	685-9876
Manatee Convention Ctr 1 Haben Blvd. *Web:* www.manateeconventioncenter.com	Palmetto	FL	34221	941-722-3244	729-1820
Sarasota Bradenton International Convention Ctr 8005 15th St E *TF:* 800-355-9161 ■ *Web:* www.sbicc.net	Sarasota	FL	34243	941-355-9161	355-9163
Tallahassee-Leon County Civic Ctr (TLCCC) 505 W Pensacola St PO Box 10604 *TF:* 800-322-3602 ■ *Web:* www.tlccc.org	Tallahassee	FL	32301	850-487-1691	222-6947
Turnbull Conference Ctr 555 W Pensacola St FSU Ctr for Professional Development *Web:* learningforlife.fsu.edu	Tallahassee	FL	32306	850-644-3801	644-2589
Tampa Convention Ctr 333 S Franklin St. *TF:* 800-426-5630 ■ *Web:* www.tampagov.net	Tampa	FL	33602	813-274-8511	274-7430
Palm Beach County Convention Ctr 650 Okeechobee Blvd *Web:* www.palmbeachfl.com	West Palm Beach	FL	33401	561-366-3000	366-3001

GEORGIA

				Phone	Fax
AmericasMart 240 Peachtree St NW Suite 2200 *TF:* 800-285-6278 ■ *Web:* www.americasmart.com	Atlanta	GA	30303	404-220-3000	220-3030
Cobb Galleria Centre 2 Galleria Pkwy *Web:* www.cobbgalleria.com	Atlanta	GA	30339	770-955-8000	955-7719
Georgia World Congress Ctr 285 Andrew Young International Blvd NW *Web:* www.gwcc.com	Atlanta	GA	30313	404-223-4200	223-4211
Georgia International Convention Ctr 2000 Convention Ctr Concourse *TF:* 888-331-4422 ■ *Web:* www.gicc.com	College Park	GA	30337	770-997-3566	994-8559
Columbus Georgia Convention & Trade Ctr 801 Front Ave *Web:* www.columbusga.org/TradeCenter	Columbus	GA	31901	706-327-4522	327-0162
Northwest Georgia Trade & Convention Ctr 2211 Dug Gap Battle Rd *TF:* 800-824-7469 ■ *Web:* www.nwgtcc.com	Dalton	GA	30720	706-272-7676	278-5811
Gwinnett Ctr 6400 Sugarloaf Pkwy *TF:* 800-224-6422 ■ *Web:* www.gwinnettcenter.com	Duluth	GA	30097	770-813-7500	813-7501
Georgia Mountains Ctr 301 Main St SW PO Box 2496 *Web:* www.gainesville.org	Gainesville	GA	30503	770-534-8420	534-8425
Jekyll Island Convention Ctr 1 N Beachview Dr *TF:* 877-453-5955 ■ *Web:* www.jekyllisland.com	Jekyll Island	GA	31527	912-635-3400	635-4106
Savannah International Trade & Convention Ctr 1 International Dr **Fax:* Sales ■ *TF:* 888-644-6822 ■ *Web:* www.savtcc.com	Savannah	GA	31421	912-447-4000	447-4722*

HAWAII

				Phone	Fax
Hawaii Convention Ctr 1801 Kalakaua Ave *TF:* 800-295-6603 ■ *Web:* www.hawaiiconvention.com	Honolulu	HI	96815	808-943-3500	943-3599
Neal S Blaisdell Ctr 777 Ward Ave. *Web:* www.blaisdellcenter.com	Honolulu	HI	96814	808-527-5400	527-5433

IDAHO

				Phone	Fax
Boise Centre on the Grove 850 W Front St. *Web:* www.boisecentre.com	Boise	ID	83702	208-336-8900	336-8803

ILLINOIS

				Phone	Fax
McCormick Place 2301 S Lake Shore Dr *TF:* 800-263-9170 ■ *Web:* www.mccormickplace.com	Chicago	IL	60616	312-791-7000	791-6543
Merchandise Mart 320 N Wells St. *TF:* 800-677-6278 ■ *Web:* www.merchandisemart.com/mmart	Chicago	IL	60654	312-527-7902	527-7998
Navy Pier 600 E Grand Ave. *TF:* 800-595-7437 ■ *Web:* www.navypier.com	Chicago	IL	60611	312-595-7437	
Gateway Ctr 1 Gateway Dr *TF:* 800-289-2388 ■ *Web:* www.gatewaycenter.com	Collinsville	IL	62234	618-345-8998	345-9024
Exposition Gardens 1601 W Northmoor Rd *Web:* www.expogardensinc.com	Peoria	IL	61614	309-691-6332	691-2372
Oakley-Lindsay Ctr 300 Civic Ctr Plaza Suite 237 *Web:* www.quincyciviccenter.com	Quincy	IL	62301	217-223-1000	223-1330
Quad City Conservation Alliance Expo Ctr 2621 4th Ave. *TF:* 877-734-1565 ■ *Web:* www.qccaexpocenter.com	Rock Island	IL	61201	309-788-5912	788-9619
Donald E Stephens Convention Ctr 5555 N River Rd *Web:* www.rosemont.com	Rosemont	IL	60018	847-692-2220	696-9700
Prairie Capital Convention Ctr (PC3) 1 Convention Ctr Plaza *Web:* www.springfield-pccc.com	Springfield	IL	62701	217-788-8800	788-0811

INDIANA

				Phone	Fax
Bloomington Monroe County Convention Ctr 302 S College Ave *Web:* www.bloomingtonconvention.com	Bloomington	IN	47403	812-336-3681	349-2981
Evansville Auditorium & Convention Ctr 715 Locust St *Web:* www.smgevansville.com/centre/centre.html	Evansville	IN	47708	812-435-5770	435-5500
Grand Wayne Convention Ctr 120 W Jefferson Blvd *Web:* www.grandwayne.com	Fort Wayne	IN	46802	260-426-4100	420-9080
Genesis Convention Ctr 1 Genesis Ctr Plaza. *Web:* www.genesisarena.com	Gary	IN	46402	219-882-5505	885-3133
Indiana Convention Center & Lucas Oil Stadium (ICCLOS) 100 S Capitol Ave. *Web:* www.icclos.com	Indianapolis	IN	46225	317-262-3400	262-3685
Horizon Convention Ctr 401 S High St *TF:* 888-288-8860 ■ *Web:* www.horizonconvention.com	Muncie	IN	47305	765-288-8860	751-9190
Century Ctr 120 S St Joseph St *Web:* www.centurycenter.org	South Bend	IN	46601	574-235-9711	235-9185

IOWA

				Phone	Fax
US Cellular Ctr 370 1st Ave E *Web:* www.uscellularcenter.com	Cedar Rapids	IA	52401	319-398-5211	362-2102
RiverCenter Adler Theatre 136 E 3rd St. *Web:* www.riverctr.com	Davenport	IA	52801	563-326-8500	326-8505
Polk County Convention Complex 501 Grand Ave *Web:* www.iowaeventscenter.com	Des Moines	IA	50309	515-242-2500	564-8140
Veterans Memorial Auditorium 833 5th Ave *Web:* www.iowaeventscenter.com	Des Moines	IA	50309	515-323-5400	564-8001
Sioux City Convention Ctr 801 4th St *TF:* 800-593-2228 ■ *Web:* www.visitsiouxcity.org/convention-center	Sioux City	IA	51101	712-279-4800	279-4900
Tyson Events Ctr 401 Gordon Dr *Web:* www.tysoncenter.com	Sioux City	IA	51101	712-279-4850	279-4903

KANSAS

				Phone	Fax
Kansas Expocentre 1 Expocentre Dr *TF:* 800-745-3000 ■ *Web:* www.ksexpo.com	Topeka	KS	66612	785-235-1986	235-2967
Century II Performing Arts & Convention Ctr 225 W Douglas Ave *Web:* www.century2.org	Wichita	KS	67202	316-264-9121	303-8688

KENTUCKY

				Phone	Fax
Frankfort Convention Ctr 405 Mero St. *Web:* www.frankfortconventioncenter.com	Frankfort	KY	40601	502-564-5335	564-3310
Lexington Convention Ctr 430 W Vine St *Web:* www.lexingtoncenter.com	Lexington	KY	40507	859-233-4567	253-2718
Kentucky International Convention Ctr 221 S 4th St *TF:* 800-701-5831 ■ *Web:* www.kyconvention.org	Louisville	KY	40202	502-595-4381	584-9711

LOUISIANA

				Phone	Fax
Baton Rouge River Ctr 275 S River Rd *Web:* www.brrivercenter.com	Baton Rouge	LA	70802	225-389-3030	389-4954
Bossier Civic Ctr 620 Benton Rd *TF:* 800-522-4842 ■ *Web:* www.bossiercity.org	Bossier City	LA	71111	318-741-8900	741-8910
Pontchartrain Ctr 4545 Williams Blvd *Web:* www.pontchartraincenter.com	Kenner	LA	70065	504-465-9985	468-6692
Cajundome & Convention Ctr 444 Cajundome Blvd *Web:* www.cajundome.com	Lafayette	LA	70506	337-265-2100	265-2311
Monroe Civic Ctr 401 Lea Joyner Expy. 	Monroe	LA	71201	318-329-2225	329-2548
Ernest N Morial Convention Ctr 900 Convention Ctr Blvd *Web:* www.mccno.com	New Orleans	LA	70130	504-582-3023	582-3088
SPAR Event Services 101 Crockett St Suite A.	Shreveport	LA	71101	318-673-5100	673-5105

MAINE

				Phone	Fax
Augusta Civic Ctr 16 Cony St. *Web:* www.augustamaine.gov	Augusta	ME	04330	207-626-2405	626-5968
Bangor Civic Ctr 100 Dutton St. *Web:* www.bangorciviccenter.com	Bangor	ME	04401	207-947-5555	947-5105

MARYLAND

				Phone	Fax
Baltimore Convention Ctr 1 W Pratt St. *Web:* www.bccenter.org	Baltimore	MD	21201	410-649-7000	649-7008
Roland E Powell Convention Ctr 4001 Coastal Hwy. *TF:* 800-626-2326 ■ *Web:* www.ocean-city.com/convention	Ocean City	MD	21842	410-289-8311	289-0058

MASSACHUSETTS

				Phone	Fax
Bayside Expo Ctr 200 Mt Vernon St *Web:* www.baysideexpo.com	Boston	MA	02125	617-474-6000	265-8434
Boston Convention & Exhibition Ctr 415 Summer St. *TF:* 800-845-8800 ■ *Web:* www.mccahome.com	Boston	MA	02210	617-954-2000	954-2299
Exchange Conference Ctr 212 Northern Ave *Web:* www.exchangeconferencecenter.com	Boston	MA	02210	617-790-1900	790-1922

	City	State	ZIP	Phone	Fax
John B Hynes Veterans Memorial Convention Ctr 900 Boylston St *TF:* 800-845-8800 ■ *Web:* www.mccahome.com	Boston	MA	02115	617-954-2000	954-2299
MassMutual Ctr 1277 Main St *TF:* 800-639-8602 ■ *Web:* www.massmutualcenter.com	Springfield	MA	01103	413-787-6610	787-6645
DCU Ctr 50 Foster St *Web:* www.dcucenter.com	Worcester	MA	01608	508-755-6800	929-0111

MICHIGAN

	City	State	ZIP	Phone	Fax
Cobo Conference & Exhibition Ctr 1 Washington Blvd *Web:* www.cobocenter.com	Detroit	MI	48226	313-877-8777	877-8577
DeVos Place 303 Monroe Ave *Web:* www.devosplace.org	Grand Rapids	MI	49503	616-742-6600	742-6590
Lansing Ctr 333 E Michigan Ave *Web:* www.lepfa.com	Lansing	MI	48933	517-483-7400	483-7439
Horizons Conference Ctr 6200 State St *Web:* www.horizonscenter.com	Saginaw	MI	48603	989-799-4122	799-4188

MINNESOTA

	City	State	ZIP	Phone	Fax
Earle Brown Heritage Ctr 6155 Earle Brown Dr *TF:* 800-524-0239 ■ *Web:* www.earlebrown.com	Brooklyn Center	MN	55430	763-569-6300	569-6320
Duluth Entertainment Convention Ctr 350 Harbor Dr *TF:* 800-628-8385 ■ *Web:* www.decc.org	Duluth	MN	55802	218-722-5573	722-4247
Minneapolis Convention Ctr 1301 2nd Ave S *Web:* www.minneapolisconventioncenter.com	Minneapolis	MN	55403	612-335-6000	335-6757
Mayo Civic Ctr 30 Civic Ctr Dr SE *TF:* 800-422-2199 ■ *Web:* www.mayociviccenter.com	Rochester	MN	55904	507-328-2220	328-2221
Saint Cloud Civic Ctr 10 4th Ave S *TF:* 800-450-7272 ■ *Web:* www.ci.stcloud.mn.us/CivicCenter	Saint Cloud	MN	56301	320-255-7272	255-9863
Saint Paul RiverCentre 175 W Kellogg Blvd *Web:* www.rivercentre.org	Saint Paul	MN	55102	651-265-4800	265-4899

MISSISSIPPI

	City	State	ZIP	Phone	Fax
Mississippi Coast Coliseum & Convention Ctr 2350 Beach Blvd *TF:* 800-726-2781	Biloxi	MS	39531	228-594-3700	594-3812
James M Trotter Convention Ctr 402 2nd Ave N	Columbus	MS	39701	662-328-4164	329-5166
Natchez Convention Ctr 211 Main St *TF:* 888-475-9144 ■ *Web:* www.natchezconventioncenter.org	Natchez	MS	39120	601-442-5850	

MISSOURI

	City	State	ZIP	Phone	Fax
Jack Lawton Webb Convention Ctr 5300 S Range Line Rd	Joplin	MO	64804	417-781-4000	623-7400
Kansas City Convention & Entertainment Centers 301 W 13th St *TF:* 800-821-7060 ■ *Web:* www.kcconvention.com	Kansas City	MO	64105	816-513-5000	513-5001
America's Center Convention Ctr 701 Convention Plaza *Web:* www.explorestlouis.com/americasCenter/public.asp	Saint Louis	MO	63101	314-342-5036	342-5040
Saint Louis Executive Conference Ctr 701 Convention Plaza *TF:* 800-325-7962 ■ *Web:* www.explorestlouis.com	Saint Louis	MO	63101	314-342-5050	342-5053
Springfield Exposition Ctr 635 E St Louis St *Web:* www.upspringfield.com	Springfield	MO	65806	417-522-3976	864-3077

MONTANA

	City	State	ZIP	Phone	Fax
MetraPark PO Box 2514 *TF:* 800-366-8538 ■ *Web:* www.metrapark.com	Billings	MT	59103	406-256-2400	256-2479
Mansfield Convention Ctr 2 Pk Dr S Great Falls Civic Ctr *Web:* www.greatfallsmt.net	Great Falls	MT	59401	406-455-8495	
Helena Civic Ctr 340 Neill Ave *Web:* www.ci.helena.mt.us/index.php?id=279	Helena	MT	59601	406-447-8481	447-8480

NEBRASKA

	City	State	ZIP	Phone	Fax
Pershing Ctr 226 Centennial Mall S *Web:* www.pershingcenter.com	Lincoln	NE	68508	402-441-8744	441-7913

NEVADA

	City	State	ZIP	Phone	Fax
Elko Convention & Visitors Authority 700 Moren Way *TF:* 800-248-3556 ■ *Web:* www.elkocva.com	Elko	NV	89801	775-738-4091	738-2420
Henderson Convention Ctr 200 S Water St *TF:* 877-775-5252 ■ *Web:* www.visithenderson.com	Henderson	NV	89015	702-267-2171	267-2177
Las Vegas Convention Ctr 3150 Paradise Rd **Fax:* Mktg ■ *TF:* 800-332-5333 ■ *Web:* www.lvcva.com	Las Vegas	NV	89109	702-892-0711	892-2824*
Sands Expo & Convention Ctr 201 Sands Ave *Web:* www.sandsexpo.com	Las Vegas	NV	89169	702-733-5556	733-5568
Reno-Sparks Convention Ctr 4590 S Virginia St *TF:* 800-367-7366 ■ *Web:* www.visitrenotahoe.com	Reno	NV	89502	775-827-7600	827-7701

NEW JERSEY

	City	State	ZIP	Phone	Fax
Atlantic City Convention Ctr 1 Miss America Way *Web:* www.accenter.com	Atlantic City	NJ	08401	609-449-2000	449-2090
New Jersey Convention & Exposition Ctr 97 Sunfield Ave Raritan Ctr *Web:* www.njexpocenter.com	Edison	NJ	08837	732-417-1400	417-1414
Meadowlands Exposition Ctr 355 Plaza Dr *TF:* 888-400-3976 ■ *Web:* www.mecexpo.com	Secaucus	NJ	07094	201-330-7773	330-1172
Garden State Exhibit Ctr 50 Atrium Dr *Web:* www.gsec.com	Somerset	NJ	08873	732-469-4000	563-4500
Wildwoods Convention Ctr 4501 Boardwalk *TF:* 800-992-9732 ■ *Web:* www.wildwoodsnj.com	Wildwood	NJ	08260	609-729-9000	846-2631

NEW MEXICO

	City	State	ZIP	Phone	Fax
Albuquerque Convention Ctr 401 2nd St NW *Web:* www.albuquerquecc.com	Albuquerque	NM	87102	505-768-4575	768-3239
LifeWay Glorieta Conference Ctr PO Box 8 *TF:* 800-797-4222 ■ *Web:* www.lifeway.com/glorieta	Glorieta	NM	87535	505-757-6161	757-6149
Santa Fe Convention Ctr 201 W Marcy St *TF:* 800-777-2489 ■ *Web:* www.santafe.org	Santa Fe	NM	87501	505-955-6200	955-6222

NEW YORK

	City	State	ZIP	Phone	Fax
Office of General Services Corning Tower 41st Fl, Empire State Plaza *TF:* 877-659-4377 ■ *Web:* www.ogs.state.ny.us	Albany	NY	12242	518-474-3899	457-3081
Buffalo Niagara Convention Ctr 153 Franklin St Convention Ctr Plaza *TF:* 800-995-7570 ■ *Web:* www.buffaloconvention.com	Buffalo	NY	14202	716-855-5555	855-3158
Jacob K Javits Convention Ctr 655 W 34th St *Web:* www.javitscenter.com	New York	NY	10001	212-216-2000	216-2588
Rochester Riverside Convention Ctr 123 E Main St *Web:* www.rrcc.com	Rochester	NY	14604	585-232-7200	232-1510
Saratoga Springs City Ctr 522 Broadway	Saratoga Springs	NY	12866	518-584-0027	584-0117
Oncenter Complex 800 S State St *TF:* 888-797-6623 ■ *Web:* www.oncenter.org	Syracuse	NY	13202	315-435-8000	435-8099

NORTH CAROLINA

	City	State	ZIP	Phone	Fax
Asheville Civic Ctr 87 Haywood St *Web:* www.ashevillenc.gov	Asheville	NC	28801	828-259-5743	259-5777
Charlotte Convention Ctr 501 S College St *Web:* www.charlotteconventionctr.com	Charlotte	NC	28202	704-339-6000	339-6024
Charlotte Merchandise Mart 2500 E Independence Blvd *Web:* www.carolinasmart.com	Charlotte	NC	28205	704-333-7709	375-9410
Metrolina Expo Trade Ctr 7100 Statesville Rd PO Box 26668 *Web:* www.metrolinatradeshowexpo.com	Charlotte	NC	28269	704-596-4650	295-1983
Crown Ctr 1960 Coliseum Dr *Web:* www.crowncoliseum.com	Fayetteville	NC	28306	910-438-4100	323-0489
Greensboro Coliseum Complex 1921 W Lee St *Web:* www.greensborocoliseum.com	Greensboro	NC	27403	336-373-7400	373-2170
International Home Furnishings Ctr 210 E Commerce Ave *Web:* www.ihfc.com	High Point	NC	27260	336-888-3700	882-1873
Raleigh Convention Ctr 500 S Salisbury St *Web:* www.raleighconvention.com	Raleigh	NC	27601	919-831-6011	831-6013
Benton Convention Ctr 301 W 5th St *Web:* www.twincityquarter.com/benton.html	Winston-Salem	NC	27101	336-727-2976	727-2879

NORTH DAKOTA

	City	State	ZIP	Phone	Fax
Bismarck Civic Ctr 315 S 5th St *Web:* www.bismarckciviccenter.com	Bismarck	ND	58504	701-355-1370	222-6599
Fargo Civic Ctr 207 N 4th St *Web:* www.cityoffargo.com	Fargo	ND	58102	701-241-1480	241-1483
Alerus Ctr 1200 42nd St S *Web:* www.aleruscenter.com	Grand Forks	ND	58201	701-792-1200	746-6511

OHIO

	City	State	ZIP	Phone	Fax
John S Knight Ctr 77 E Mill St *TF:* 800-245-4254 ■ *Web:* www.johnsknightcenter.org	Akron	OH	44308	330-374-8900	374-8971
Duke Energy Ctr 525 Elm St *Web:* www.duke-energycenter.com	Cincinnati	OH	45202	513-419-7300	419-7327
Cleveland Convention Ctr 500 Lakeside Ave *TF:* 800-543-2489	Cleveland	OH	44114	216-348-2200	348-2200
International Exposition Ctr 1-X Ctr Dr *TF:* 800-492-3683 ■ *Web:* www.ixcenter.com	Cleveland	OH	44135	216-676-6000	265-7300
Franklin County Veterans Memorial 300 W Broad St *Web:* www.fcvm.com	Columbus	OH	43215	614-221-4341	221-8422
Greater Columbus Convention Ctr 400 N High St *TF:* 800-626-0241 ■ *Web:* www.columbusconventions.com	Columbus	OH	43215	614-827-2500	221-7239

				Phone	Fax
Dayton Convention Ctr 22 E 5th St *TF:* 800-822-3498 ■ *Web:* www.daytonconventioncenter.com	Dayton	OH	45402	937-333-4700	333-4711
Veterans Memorial Civic & Convention Ctr 7 Town Sq. *Web:* www.limaciviccenter.com	Lima	OH	45801	419-224-5222	224-6964
Eastwood Expo Ctr 5555 Youngstown Warren Rd Unit 700 *Web:* www.eastwoodexpo.com	Niles	OH	44446	330-652-6980	743-2902
Sharonville Convention Ctr 11355 Chester Rd. *Web:* www.sharonvilleconventioncenter.com	Sharonville	OH	45246	513-771-7744	772-5745
SeaGate Convention Centre 401 Jefferson Ave *TF:* 800-243-4667 ■ *Web:* www.toledo-seagate.com	Toledo	OH	43604	419-255-3300	255-7731

OKLAHOMA

				Phone	Fax
Cherokee Strip Conference Ctr 123 W Maine St. *Web:* www.csccenid.com	Enid	OK	73701	580-234-1919	242-8975
Cox Business Services Convention Ctr 1 Myriad Gardens *Web:* www.coxconventioncenter.com	Oklahoma City	OK	73102	405-602-8500	602-8505
Expo Square 4145 E 21st St. *Web:* www.exposquare.com	Tulsa	OK	74114	918-744-1113	744-8725
Tulsa Convention Ctr 100 Civic Ctr *TF:* 800-678-7177 ■ *Web:* www.tulsaconvention.com	Tulsa	OK	74103	918-596-7177	596-7155

ONTARIO

				Phone	Fax
Metro Toronto Convention Centre 255 Front St W **Fax:* Hum Res ■ *Web:* www.mtccc.com	Toronto	ON	M5V2W6	416-585-8000	585-8262*

OREGON

				Phone	Fax
Lane Events Ctr 796 W 13th Ave. *Web:* www.atthefair.com	Eugene	OR	97402	541-682-4292	682-3614
Florence Events Ctr 715 Quince St *TF:* 888-968-4086 ■ *Web:* www.eventcenter.org	Florence	OR	97439	541-997-1994	902-0991
Pendleton Convention Ctr 1601 Westgate *TF:* 800-863-9358 ■ *Web:* www.pendleton.or.us	Pendleton	OR	97801	541-276-6569	278-1317
Oregon Convention Ctr 777 NE Martin Luther King Jr Blvd *TF:* 800-791-2250 ■ *Web:* www.oregoncc.org	Portland	OR	97232	503-235-7575	235-7417
Portland Metropolitan Exposition Ctr 2060 N Marine Dr. *Web:* www.expocenter.org	Portland	OR	97217	503-736-5200	736-5201
Oregon State Fair & Expo Ctr 2330 17th St NE *Web:* www.oregonstatefair.org/expo/index.htm	Salem	OR	97301	503-947-3247	947-3206
Salem Conference Ctr 200 Commercial St SE. *TF Sales:* 877-589-1700 ■ *Web:* www.salemconferencecenter.org	Salem	OR	97301	503-589-1700	589-1715
Seaside Civic & Convention Ctr 415 1st Ave *TF:* 800-394-3303 ■ *Web:* www.seasideconvention.com	Seaside	OR	97138	503-738-8585	738-0198

PENNSYLVANIA

				Phone	Fax
Valley Forge Convention Ctr 1210 First Ave. *Web:* www.vfconventioncenter.com	King of Prussia	PA	19406	610-354-8212	992-2884
Hampton Inn Philadelphia Center City-Convention Ctr 1301 Race St *TF:* 800-426-7866 ■ *Web:* www.hamptoninn1.hilton.com	Philadelphia	PA	19107	215-665-9100	665-9200
Pennsylvania Convention Ctr 1101 Arch St. *TF:* 800-428-9000 ■ *Web:* www.paconvention.com	Philadelphia	PA	19107	215-418-4700	418-4747
David L Lawrence Convention Ctr 1000 Fort Duquesne Blvd *Web:* www.pittsburghcc.com	Pittsburgh	PA	15222	412-565-6000	565-6008
Stetson Convention Services Inc 2900 Stayton St *Web:* www.stetsonexpo.com	Pittsburgh	PA	15212	412-223-1090	223-1094

QUEBEC

				Phone	Fax
Palais des Congres de Montreal-Convention Centre 159 St Antoine St W 9th Fl *TF:* 800-268-8122 ■ *Web:* www.congresmtl.com	Montreal	QC	H2Z1H2	514-871-8122	871-3188

RHODE ISLAND

				Phone	Fax
Rhode Island Convention Ctr 1 Sabin St *Web:* www.riconvention.com	Providence	RI	02903	401-458-6000	458-6500

SOUTH CAROLINA

				Phone	Fax
Charleston Area Convention Center Complex (CACC) 5001 Coliseum Dr *Web:* www.charlestonconvention.com	Charleston	SC	29418	843-529-5000	529-5010
Carolina First Ctr 1 Exposition Dr *Web:* www.carolinafirstcenter.com	Greenville	SC	29607	864-233-2562	255-8600
Myrtle Beach Convention Ctr 2101 N Oak St *TF:* 800-537-1690 ■ *Web:* www.myrtlebeachconventioncenter.com	Myrtle Beach	SC	29577	843-918-1225	918-1243

SOUTH DAKOTA

				Phone	Fax
Rushmore Plaza Civic Ctr 444 Mt Rushmore Rd N *TF:* 800-468-6463 ■ *Web:* www.gotmine.com	Rapid City	SD	57701	605-394-4115	394-4119

TENNESSEE

				Phone	Fax
Chattanooga Convention Ctr 1150 Carter St PO Box 6008 *TF:* 800-962-5213 ■ *Web:* www.chattconvention.org	Chattanooga	TN	37402	423-756-0001	267-5291
Gatlinburg Convention Ctr 303 Reagan Dr *TF:* 800-343-1475 ■ *Web:* www.gatlinburg-tennessee.com	Gatlinburg	TN	37738	865-436-2392	436-3704
Carl Perkins Civic Ctr 400 S Highland Ave *Web:* www.cityofjackson.net	Jackson	TN	38301	731-425-8580	425-8589
Knoxville Convention Ctr 701 Henley St. *Web:* www.kccsmg.com	Knoxville	TN	37902	865-522-5669	329-0422
Memphis Cook Convention Ctr 3205 Elvis Presley Blvd *Web:* www.memphisconvention.com	Memphis	TN	38116	901-543-5333	
Nashville Convention Ctr 601 Commerce St. *Web:* www.nashvilleconventionctr.com	Nashville	TN	37203	615-742-2000	742-2014

TEXAS

				Phone	Fax
Amarillo Civic Ctr 401 S Buchanan St *Web:* www.civicamarillo.com	Amarillo	TX	79101	806-378-4297	378-4234
Arlington Convention Ctr 1200 Ballpark Way *Web:* www.arlingtontx.gov	Arlington	TX	76011	817-459-5000	459-5091
Austin Convention Ctr 500 E Cesar Chavez St. *Web:* www.austinconventioncenter.com	Austin	TX	78701	512-404-4000	404-4416
Palmer Events Ctr 900 Barton Springs Rd *Web:* www.austinconventioncenter.com	Austin	TX	78704	512-404-4500	404-4422
Beaumont Civic Center Complex 701 Main St *TF:* 800-782-3081 ■ *Web:* www.beaumont-tx-complex.com	Beaumont	TX	77701	409-838-3435	838-3715
Bell County Expo Ctr 301 W Loop 121. *Web:* www.bellcountyexpo.com	Belton	TX	76513	254-933-5353	933-5354
American Bank Ctr 1901 N Shoreline Blvd *Web:* www.americanbankcenter.com	Corpus Christi	TX	78401	361-826-4700	826-4905
Dallas Convention Ctr 650 S Griffin St *TF:* 877-850-2100 ■ *Web:* www.dallasconventioncenter.com	Dallas	TX	75202	214-939-2700	939-2700
Dallas Market Ctr 2100 Stemmons Fwy Suite MS 150 *TF:* 800-325-6587 ■ *Web:* www.dallasmarketcenter.com	Dallas	TX	75207	214-655-6100	749-5479
Fair Park 1300 Robert B Cullum Blvd. *Web:* www.fairparkdallas.com	Dallas	TX	75210	214-670-8400	670-8907
El Paso Convention & Performing Arts Ctr 1 Civic Ctr Plaza *TF:* 800-351-6024 ■ *Web:* www.visitelpaso.com/cpac_index.sstg	El Paso	TX	79901	915-534-0600	534-0687
Fort Worth Convention Ctr 1201 Houston St *TF:* 866-630-2588 ■ *Web:* www.fortworthgov.org	Fort Worth	TX	76102	817-392-6338	392-2756
Moody Gardens Convention Ctr 7 Hope Blvd *TF:* 888-388-8484 ■ *Web:* www.moodygardenshotel.com	Galveston	TX	77554	409-741-8484	683-4928
Grapevine Convention Ctr The 1209 S Main St. *Web:* www.grapevinetexasusa.com	Grapevine	TX	76051	817-410-3459	410-3090
George R Brown Convention Ctr 1001 Avenida de Las Americas *TF:* 800-427-4697 ■ *Web:* www.houstonconventionctr.com	Houston	TX	77010	713-853-8000	853-8090
Maude Cobb Convention Ctr 100 Grand Blvd. *Web:* www.longviewtexas.co	Longview	TX	75604	903-237-1230	236-7845
Lubbock Memorial Civic Ctr 1501 MacDavis Ln *Web:* lmcc.ci.lubbock.tx.us	Lubbock	TX	79401	806-775-2242	775-3240
Plano Centre 2000 E Springcreek Pkwy. *TF:* 800-817-5266 ■ *Web:* www.plano.gov/departments/PlanoCentre	Plano	TX	75074	972-422-0296	424-0002
Robert A "Bob" Bowers Civic Ctr 3401 Cultural Ctr Dr *Web:* www.portarthur.net	Port Arthur	TX	77642	409-985-8801	985-3125
San Angelo Convention Center Coliseum & Auditorium 500 Rio Concho Dr. *Web:* www.sanangelotexas.org	San Angelo	TX	76903	325-653-9577	659-0900
Henry B Gonzalez Convention Ctr 200 E Market St *TF:* 877-504-8895 ■ *Web:* www.ci.sat.tx.us	San Antonio	TX	78205	210-207-8500	223-1495
South Padre Island Convention Centre 7355 Padre Blvd *TF:* 800-657-2373 ■ *Web:* www.sopadre.com	South Padre Island	TX	78597	956-761-3000	761-3024
Frank W Mayborn Civic & Convention Ctr 3303 N 3rd St	Temple	TX	76501	254-298-5720	298-5388
Oil Palace The 10408 Hwy 64 E *Web:* www.oilpalace.com	Tyler	TX	75707	903-566-2122	566-4206
MPEC (Multi-Purpose Events Center) 1000 5th St. *TF:* 800-799-6732 ■ *Web:* www.wfmpec.com	Wichita Falls	TX	76301	940-716-5500	716-5509

UTAH

				Phone	Fax
Golden Spike Event Ctr 1000 N 1200 W *TF:* 800-442-7362 ■ *Web:* www.goldenspikeeventcenter.com	Ogden	UT	84404	801-399-8544	392-1995
Ogden Eccles Conference Ctr 2415 Washington Blvd *Web:* www.oecenter.com	Ogden	UT	84401	801-689-8600	689-8651

				Phone	Fax
Salt Palace Convention Ctr 100 S W Temple *TF:* 877-547-4656 ■ *Web:* www.saltpalace.com	Salt Lake City	UT	84101	801-534-4777	534-6391

VIRGINIA

				Phone	Fax
Greater Richmond Convention Ctr 403 N 3rd St *TF:* 800-370-9004 ■ *Web:* www.richmondcenter.com	Richmond	VA	23219	804-783-7300	780-2577

WASHINGTON

				Phone	Fax
Meydenbauer Ctr 11100 NE 6th St *Web:* www.meydenbauer.com	Bellevue	WA	98004	425-637-1020	637-0166
Three Rivers Convention Center & Coliseum 7016 W Grandbridge Blvd *Web:* www.threeriversconventioncenter.com	Kennewick	WA	99336	509-735-9400	735-9431
Ocean Shores Convention Ctr 120 W Chance a La Mer NW *TF:* 800-874-6737 ■ *Web:* www.oceanshoresconventioncenter.com	Ocean Shores	WA	98569	360-289-4411	289-4412
Bell Harbor International Conference Ctr 2203 Alaskan Way *TF:* 888-772-4422 ■ *Web:* www.bellharbor.org	Seattle	WA	98121	206-441-6666	269-4159
Washington State Convention 800 Convention Pl *Web:* www.wsctc.com	Seattle	WA	98101	206-694-5000	694-5399
Spokane Ctr 720 W Mallon Ave *Web:* www.spokanecenter.com	Spokane	WA	99201	509-279-7000	279-7050
Greater Tacoma Convention & Trade Ctr 1500 Broadway *TF:* 888-227-3705 ■ *Web:* www.tacomaconventioncenter.com	Tacoma	WA	98402	253-830-6601	573-2363
Yakima Convention Ctr 10 N 8th St *TF:* 800-221-0751 ■ *Web:* www.yakimacenter.com	Yakima	WA	98901	509-575-6062	575-6252

WEST VIRGINIA

				Phone	Fax
Charleston Civic Center & Coliseum 200 Civic Ctr Dr *Web:* www.charlestonwvciviccenter.com	Charleston	WV	25301	304-345-1500	345-3492

WISCONSIN

				Phone	Fax
La Crosse Ctr 300 Harborview Plaza *Web:* www.lacrossecenter.com	La Crosse	WI	54601	608-789-7400	789-7444
Alliant Energy Center of Dane County 1919 Alliant Energy Ctr Way *Web:* www.alliantenergycenter.com	Madison	WI	53713	608-267-3976	267-0146
Monona Terrace Community & Convention Ctr 1 John Nolen Dr *Web:* www.mononaterrace.com	Madison	WI	53703	608-261-4000	261-4049
Frontier Airlines Ctr 400 W Wisconsin Ave *Web:* www.midwestexpresscenter.com	Milwaukee	WI	53203	414-908-6000	908-6010

WYOMING

				Phone	Fax
Casper Events Ctr 1 Events Dr *TF:* 800-442-2256 ■ *Web:* www.casperwy.gov	Casper	WY	82601	307-235-8441	235-8445

209 CONVENTION & VISITORS BUREAUS

SEE ALSO Travel & Tourism Information - Canadian p. 2732; Travel & Tourism Information - Foreign Travel p. 2732

Listings Are Alphabetized By City Names.

				Phone	Fax
Aberdeen Convention & Visitors Bureau 10 Railroad Ave SW PO Box 78 *TF:* 800-645-3851 ■ *Web:* www.visitaberdeensd.com	Aberdeen	SD	57401	605-225-2414	225-3573
Abilene Convention & Visitors Bureau 1101 N 1st St *TF:* 800-727-7704 ■ *Web:* www.abilenevisitors.com	Abilene	TX	79601	325-676-2556	676-1630
Abilene Convention & Visitors Bureau 201 NW 2nd St *TF:* 800-569-5915 ■ *Web:* www.abilenecityhall.com	Abilene	KS	67410	785-263-2231	263-4125
Abingdon Convention & Visitors Bureau 335 Cummings St *TF:* 800-435-3440 ■ *Web:* www.abingdon.com/tourism	Abingdon	VA	24210	276-676-2282	676-3076
Akron/Summit County Convention & Visitors Bureau 77 E Mill St *TF:* 800-245-4254 ■ *Web:* www.visitakron-summit.org	Akron	OH	44308	330-374-7560	374-7626
Albany County Convention & Visitors Bureau 25 Quackenbush Sq *TF:* 800-258-3582 ■ *Web:* www.albany.org	Albany	NY	12207	518-434-1217	434-0887
Albany Visitors Assn 300 2nd Ave SW *TF:* 800-526-2256 ■ *Web:* www.albanyvisitors.com	Albany	OR	97321	541-928-0911	926-1500
Albuquerque Convention & Visitors Bureau 20 First Plaza Suite 601 *TF:* 800-733-9918 ■ *Web:* www.itsatrip.org	Albuquerque	NM	87102	505-842-9918	247-9101
Alexandria Convention & Visitors Assn 221 King St *TF:* 800-388-9119 ■ *Web:* www.visitalexandriava.com	Alexandria	VA	22314	703-746-3301	838-4683
Alexandria/Pineville Area Convention & Visitors Bureau (APACVB) 707 Main St PO Box 1070 *TF:* 800-551-9546 ■ *Web:* www.theheartoflouisiana.com	Alexandria	LA	71301	318-442-9546	443-1617
Allegan County Tourist & Recreational Council 3255 122nd Ave Suite 102 *TF:* 888-425-5342 ■ *Web:* www.visitallegancounty.com	Allegan	MI	49010	269-686-9088	673-0454
Lehigh Valley Convention & Visitors Bureau 840 Hamilton St Suite 200 PO Box 20785 *TF:* 800-747-0561	Allentown	PA	18101	610-882-9200	882-0343
Alpena Area Convention & Visitors Bureau 235 W Chisholm St *TF:* 800-425-7362 ■ *Web:* www.alpenacvb.com	Alpena	MI	49707	989-354-4181	356-3999
Alton Regional Convention & Visitors Bureau (ARCVB) 200 Piasa St *TF:* 800-258-6645 ■ *Web:* www.visitalton.com	Alton	IL	62002	618-465-6676	465-6151
Alvin Convention & Visitors Bureau 121 E Willis St *TF:* 800-331-4063 ■ *Web:* www.alvintexas.org	Alvin	TX	77511	281-585-3359	585-8662
Amana Colonies Convention & Visitors Bureau 622 46th Ave *TF:* 800-579-2294 ■ *Web:* www.amanacolonies.com	Amana	IA	52203	319-622-7622	622-6395
Amarillo Convention & Visitor Council 1000 S Polk St PO Box 9480 *TF:* 800-692-1338 ■ *Web:* www.visitamarillotx.com	Amarillo	TX	79105	806-374-1497	373-3909
Lorain County Visitors Bureau 8025 Leavitt Rd *TF:* 800-334-1673 ■ *Web:* www.visitloraincounty.com	Amherst	OH	44001	440-984-5282	984-7363
Anaheim/Orange County Visitor & Convention Bureau 800 W Katella Ave PO Box 4270 *TF:* 888-598-3200 ■ *Web:* www.anaheimoc.org	Anaheim	CA	92802	714-765-8888	991-8963
Anchorage Convention & Visitors Bureau 524 W 4th Ave *TF:* 800-478-1255 ■ *Web:* www.anchorage.net	Anchorage	AK	99501	907-276-4118	278-5559
Anderson/Madison County Visitors & Convention Bureau 6335 S Scatterfield Rd *TF:* 800-533-6568 ■ *Web:* www.heartlandspirit.com	Anderson	IN	46013	765-643-5633	643-9083
Steuben County Tourism Bureau 430 N Wayne St Suite 1B *TF:* 800-525-3101 ■ *Web:* www.lakes101.org	Angola	IN	46703	260-665-5386	665-5461
Ann Arbor Area Convention & Visitors Bureau 120 W Huron St *TF:* 800-888-9487 ■ *Web:* www.visitannarbor.org	Ann Arbor	MI	48104	734-995-7281	995-7283
Southernmost Illinois Tourism Bureau 1000 N Main St PO Box 378 *TF:* 800-248-4373 ■ *Web:* www.southernmostillinois.com	Anna	IL	62906	618-833-9928	833-9924
Annapolis & Anne Arundel County Conference & Visitors Bureau (AAACCVB) 26 W St *TF:* 888-302-2852 ■ *Web:* www.visitannapolis.org	Annapolis	MD	21401	410-280-0445	263-9591
Fox Cities Convention & Visitors Bureau 3433 W College Ave *TF:* 800-236-6673 ■ *Web:* www.foxcities.org	Appleton	WI	54914	920-734-3358	734-1080
Arkansas City Convention & Visitors Bureau 106 S Summit St PO Box 795 *Web:* www.arkcity.org	Arkansas City	KS	67005	620-442-0230	441-0048
Arlington Convention & Visitors Bureau 1905 E Randol Mill Rd *TF:* 800-433-5374 ■ *Web:* www.arlington.org	Arlington	TX	76011	817-265-7721	265-5640
Arlington Convention & Visitors Service 1100 N Glebe Rd Suite 1500 *TF:* 800-296-7996 ■ *Web:* www.stayarlington.com	Arlington	VA	22201	703-228-0888	228-0806
Asheville Area Convention & Visitors Bureau 36 Montford Ave *TF:* 800-257-5583 ■ *Web:* www.exploreasheville.com	Asheville	NC	28801	828-258-6101	
Athens Convention & Visitors Bureau 300 N Thomas St *TF:* 800-653-0603 ■ *Web:* www.visitathensga.com	Athens	GA	30601	706-357-4430	546-8040
Athens County Convention & Visitors Bureau 667 E State St *TF:* 800-878-9767 ■ *Web:* www.athensohio.com	Athens	OH	45701	740-592-1819	593-7365
Atlanta Convention & Visitors Bureau 233 Peachtree St NE Suite 1400 **Fax:* Sales ■ *TF:* 800-285-2682 ■ *Web:* www.atlanta.net	Atlanta	GA	30303	404-521-6600	584-6331*
Cobb County Convention & Visitors Bureau 1 Galleria Pkwy *TF:* 800-451-3480 ■ *Web:* www.cobbcvb.com	Atlanta	GA	30339	678-303-2622	303-2625
Atlantic City Convention & Visitors Authority 2314 Pacific Ave *TF:* 888-228-4748 ■ *Web:* www.atlanticcitynj.com	Atlantic City	NJ	08401	609-348-7100	345-7287
Auburn-Opelika Tourism Bureau 714 E Glenn Ave *TF:* 866-880-8747 ■ *Web:* www.aotourism.com	Auburn	AL	36830	334-887-8747	821-5500
Augusta Metropolitan Convention & Visitors Bureau 1450 Greene St Suite 110 *TF:* 800-726-0243 ■ *Web:* www.augustaga.org	Augusta	GA	30901	706-823-6600	823-6609
Aurora Area Convention & Visitors Bureau 43 W Galena Blvd *TF:* 800-477-4369 ■ *Web:* www.enjoyaurora.com	Aurora	IL	60506	630-897-5581	897-5589
Austin Convention & Visitors Bureau 301 Congress Ave Suite 200 *TF:* 800-926-2282 ■ *Web:* www.austintexas.org	Austin	TX	78701	512-474-5171	583-7282
Catalina Island Visitors Bureau 1 Green Pier PO Box 217 *Web:* www.catalinachamber.com	Avalon	CA	90704	310-510-1520	510-7607
Baker County Visitors & Convention Bureau 490 Campbell St *TF:* 800-523-1235 ■ *Web:* www.visitbaker.com	Baker City	OR	97814	541-523-3356	523-9187
Greater Bakersfield Convention & Visitors Bureau 515 Truxtun Ave *TF:* 866-425-7353 ■ *Web:* www.visitbakersfield.com	Bakersfield	CA	93301	661-852-7282	325-7074
Baltimore Area Convention & Visitors Assn (BACVA) 100 Light St 12th Fl *TF:* 877-225-8466 ■ *Web:* www.baltimore.org	Baltimore	MD	21202	410-659-7300	727-2308
Bandera County Convention & Visitors Bureau 126 State Hwy 16 S PO Box 171 *TF:* 800-364-3833 ■ *Web:* www.banderacowboycapital.com	Bandera	TX	78003	830-796-3045	796-4121

Phone | Fax

Greater Bangor Convention & Visitors Bureau
40 Harlow St. ... Bangor ME 04401 — Phone 207-947-5205 — Fax 942-2146
TF: 800-916-6673 ■ Web: www.bangorcvb.org

Bardstown-Nelson County Tourist & Convention Commission
1 Ct Sq PO Box 867 ... Bardstown KY 40004 — Phone 502-348-4877 — Fax 349-0804
TF: 800-638-4877 ■ Web: www.visitbardstown.com

Clermont County Convention & Visitors Bureau (CCCVB)
410 E Main St PO Box 100 ... Batavia OH 45103 — Phone 513-732-3600 — Fax 732-2244
TF: 800-796-4282 ■ Web: www.visitclermontohio.com

Baton Rouge Convention & Visitors Bureau
359 3rd St. ... Baton Rouge LA 70801 — Phone 225-383-1825 — Fax 346-1253
TF: 800-527-6843 ■ Web: www.visitbatonrouge.com

Battle Creek/Calhoun County Convention & Visitors Bureau
77 E Michigan Ave Suite 100 ... Battle Creek MI 49017 — Phone 269-962-2240 — Fax 962-6917
TF: 800-397-2240 ■ Web: www.battlecreekvisitors.org

Beaumont Convention & Visitors Bureau
505 Willow St. ... Beaumont TX 77701 — Phone 409-880-3749 — Fax 880-3750
TF: 800-392-4401 ■ Web: www.beaumontcvb.com

Greene County Convention & Visitors Bureau
1221 Meadowbridge Dr ... Beavercreek OH 45434 — Phone 937-429-9100 — Fax 429-7726
TF: 800-733-9109 ■ Web: www.greenecountyohio.org

Washington County Visitors Assn
11000 SW Stratus St Suite 1707 ... Beaverton OR 97008 — Phone 503-644-5555 — Fax 644-9784
TF: 800-537-3149 ■ Web: www.visitwashingtoncountyoregon.com

Southern West Virginia Convention & Visitors Bureau
1406 Harper Rd ... Beckley WV 25801 — Phone 304-252-2244 — Fax 252-2252
TF: 800-847-4898 ■ Web: www.visitwv.com

Bedford County Visitors Bureau
131 S Juliana St ... Bedford PA 15522 — Phone 814-623-1771 — Fax 623-1671
TF: 800-765-3331 ■ Web: www.bedfordcounty.net

Bellevue Area Tourism & Visitors Bureau
110 W Main St ... Bellevue OH 44811 — Phone 419-483-5359
Web: www.bellevuetourism.org

Gaston County Travel & Tourism 620 N Main St. ... Belmont NC 28012 — Phone 704-825-4044 — Fax 825-4029
TF: 800-849-9994 ■ Web: www.gastontourism.com

Beloit Convention & Visitors Bureau
500 Public Ave ... Beloit WI 53511 — Phone 608-365-4838 — Fax 365-6850
TF: 800-423-5648 ■ Web: www.visitbeloit.com

Northern Illinois Tourism Development Office
419 1/2 S State St. ... Belvidere IL 61008 — Phone 815-547-3740 — Fax 547-3749
Web: www.visitnorthernillinois.com

Bucks County Conference & Visitors Bureau (BCCVB)
3207 St Rd ... Bensalem PA 19020 — Phone 215-639-0300 — Fax 642-3277
TF: 800-836-2825 ■ Web: www.visitbuckscounty.com

Franklin County Tourism Bureau (FCTB)
209 W Main St ... Benton IL 62812 — Phone 618-439-0608 — Fax 435-4054
TF: 800-661-9998 ■ Web: www.fctb.com

Southwestern Michigan Tourism Council
2300 Pipestone Rd ... Benton Harbor MI 49022 — Phone 269-925-6301 — Fax 925-7540
Web: www.swmichigan.org

Beverly Hills Conference & Visitors Bureau
239 S Beverly Dr. ... Beverly Hills CA 90212 — Phone 310-248-1000 — Fax 248-1020
TF: 800-345-2210 ■ Web: www.beverlyhillscvb.com

Greater Big Rapids Convention & Visitors Bureau
246 N State St. ... Big Rapids MI 49307 — Phone 231-796-7640 — Fax 796-0832
TF: 888-229-4386 ■ Web: www.bigrapids.org

Big Spring Convention & Visitor Bureau
310 Nolan St. ... Big Spring TX 79720 — Phone 432-263-8235 — Fax 264-8310
TF: 866-430-7100 ■ Web: www.bigspringtx.com

Billings Convention & Visitors Bureau
815 S 27th St PO Box 31177 ... Billings MT 59107 — Phone 406-245-4111 — Fax 245-7333
TF: 800-735-2635 ■ Web: www.visitbillings.com

Greater Binghamton Convention & Visitors Bureau
49 Ct St 2nd Fl PO Box 995 ... Binghamton NY 13902 — Phone 607-772-8860 — Fax 722-4513
TF: 800-836-6740 ■ Web: www.binghamtoncvb.com

Greater Birmingham Convention & Visitors Bureau
2200 9th Ave N ... Birmingham AL 35203 — Phone 205-458-8000 — Fax 458-8086
TF: 800-458-8085 ■ Web: www.birminghamal.org

Bismarck-Mandan Convention & Visitors Bureau
1600 Burnt Boat Dr ... Bismarck ND 58503 — Phone 701-222-4308 — Fax 222-0647
TF: 800-767-3555 ■ Web: www.discoverbismarckmandan.com

Bloomington Convention & Visitors Bureau (BCVB)
7900 International Dr Suite 990 ... Bloomington MN 55425 — Phone 952-858-8500 — Fax 858-8854
TF: 800-346-4289 ■ Web: www.bloomingtonmn.org

Bloomington-Normal Area Convention & Visitors Bureau
3201 CIRA Dr Suite 201 ... Bloomington IL 61704 — Phone 309-665-0033 — Fax 661-0743
TF: 800-433-8226 ■ Web: www.bloomingtonnormalcvb.org

Bloomington/Monroe County Convention & Visitors Bureau
2855 N Walnut St ... Bloomington IN 47404 — Phone 812-334-8900 — Fax 334-2344
TF: 800-800-0037 ■ Web: www.visitbloomington.com

Columbia-Montour Visitors Bureau
121 Papermill Rd ... Bloomsburg PA 17815 — Phone 570-784-8279 — Fax 784-1166
TF: 800-847-4810 ■ Web: www.itourcolumbiamontour.com

Mercer County Convention & Visitors Bureau
704 Bland St PO Box 4088 ... Bluefield WV 24701 — Phone 304-325-8438 — Fax 324-8483
TF: 800-221-3206 ■ Web: www.visitmercercounty.com

Boise Convention & Visitors Bureau
1199 Main St ... Boise ID 83702 — Phone 208-344-7777 — Fax 344-6236
TF: 800-635-5240 ■ Web: www.boise.org

North Carolina High Country Host
1700 Blowing Rock Rd ... Boone NC 28607 — Phone 828-264-1299 — Fax 265-0550
TF: 800-438-7500 ■ Web: www.highcountryhost.com

Greater Boston Convention & Visitors Bureau (GBCVB)
2 Copley Pl Suite 105 ... Boston MA 02116 — Phone 617-536-4100 — Fax 424-7664
TF: 888-733-2678 ■ Web: www.bostonusa.com

Bottineau Convention & Visitor Bureau
519 Main St ... Bottineau ND 58318 — Phone 701-228-3849 — Fax 228-5130
TF: 800-735-6932 ■ Web: www.bottineau.com

Boulder Convention & Visitors Bureau
2440 Pearl St ... Boulder CO 80302 — Phone 303-442-2911 — Fax 938-2098
TF: 800-444-0447 ■ Web: www.bouldercoloradousa.com

Bradenton Area Convention & Visitors Bureau
1 Haven Blvd PO Box 1000 ... Bradenton FL 34206 — Phone 941-729-9177 — Fax 729-1820
TF: 800-822-2017 ■ Web: www.annamariaisland-longboatkey.com

Brainerd Lakes Area Convention & Visitors Bureau
7393 State Hwy 371 S ... Brainerd MN 56401 — Phone 218-829-2838 — Fax 822-7116
TF: 800-450-2838 ■ Web: www.explorebrainerdlakes.com

Branson Lakes Area Chamber of Commerce
269 State Hwy 248 PO Box 1897 ... Branson MO 65615 — Phone 417-334-4084 — Fax 334-4139
TF: 800-214-3661 ■ Web: www.bransonchamber.com

Brenham/Washington County Convention & Visitor Bureau
314 S Austin St. ... Brenham TX 77833 — Phone 979-836-3695 — Fax 836-2540
TF: 800-225-3695 ■ Web: www.brenhamtexas.com

Greater Bridgeport Conference & Vistors Ctr
164 W Main St ... Bridgeport WV 26330 — Phone 304-842-7272 — Fax 842-1941
TF: 800-368-4324 ■ Web: www.greater-bridgeport.com

Northwest Pennsylvania's Great Outdoors Visitors Bureau
2801 Maplevale Rd ... Brookville PA 15825 — Phone 814-849-5197 — Fax 849-1969
TF: 800-348-9393 ■ Web: www.visitpago.com

Brownsville Convention & Visitors Bureau
2305 N Expy ... Brownsville TX 78520 — Phone 956-546-3721 — Fax 546-3972
TF: 800-626-2639 ■ Web: www.brownsville.org

Brunswick & The Golden Isles of Georgia Visitors Bureau
4 Glynn Ave ... Brunswick GA 31520 — Phone 912-265-0620 — Fax 265-0629
TF: 800-933-2627 ■ Web: www.comecoastawhile.com

Buckhannon/Upshur Convention & Visitor Bureau
16 Kanawha St PO Box 442 ... Buckhannon WV 26201 — Phone 304-472-1722 — Fax 472-4938
Web: www.buchamber.com

Buena Park Convention & Visitors Office
6601 Beach Blvd Suite 200 ... Buena Park CA 90621 — Phone 714-562-3560 — Fax 562-3569
TF: 800-541-3953 ■ Web: www.visitbuenapark.com

Buffalo Niagara Convention & Visitors Bureau
617 Main St Suite 200 ... Buffalo NY 14203 — Phone 716-852-2356 — Fax 852-0131
TF: 800-283-3256 ■ Web: www.visitbuffaloniagara.com

San Mateo County Convention & Visitors Bureau
111 Anza Blvd Suite 410 ... Burlingame CA 94010 — Phone 650-348-7600 — Fax 348-7687
TF: 800-288-4748 ■ Web: www.sanmateocountycvb.com

Burlington/Alamance County Convention & Visitors Bureau
610 S Lexington Ave PO Drawer 519 ... Burlington NC 27216 — Phone 336-570-1444 — Fax 228-1330
TF: 800-637-3804 ■ Web: www.visitalamance.com

Vermont Convention Bureau
60 Main St Suite 100 ... Burlington VT 05401 — Phone 802-863-3489 — Fax 863-1538
TF: 877-264-3503 ■ Web: www.vermontmeetings.org

Cadillac Area Visitors Bureau 222 N Lake St ... Cadillac MI 49601 — Phone 231-775-0657 — Fax 775-1440
TF: 800-225-2537 ■ Web: www.cadillacmichigan.com

Tourism Calgary 200, 238 11th Ave SE ... Calgary AB T2G0X8 — Phone 403-263-8510 — Fax 262-3809
TF: 800-661-1678 ■ Web: www.visitcalgary.com

Finger Lakes Visitors Connection
25 Gorham St ... Canandaigua NY 14424 — Phone 585-394-3915 — Fax 394-4067
TF: 877-386-4669 ■ Web: www.visitfingerlakes.com

Canton/Stark County Convention & Visitors Bureau
222 Market Ave N ... Canton OH 44702 — Phone 330-454-1439 — Fax 456-3600
TF: 800-552-6051 ■ Web: www.visitcantonstark.com

Cape Girardeau Convention & Visitors Bureau
400 Broadway Suite 100 ... Cape Girardeau MO 63701 — Phone 573-335-1631 — Fax 334-6702
TF: 800-777-0068 ■ Web: www.visitcape.com

Carbondale Convention & Tourism Bureau
1185 E Main St Suite 1046 ... Carbondale IL 62901 — Phone 618-529-4451 — Fax 529-5590
TF: 800-526-1500 ■ Web: www.cctb.org

Carlsbad Convention & Visitors Bureau
400 Carlsbad Village Dr ... Carlsbad CA 92008 — Phone 760-434-6093 — Fax 434-6056
TF: 800-227-5722 ■ Web: www.visitcarlsbad.com

Hamilton County Convention & Visitors Bureau Inc
37 E Main St. ... Carmel IN 46032 — Phone 317-848-3181 — Fax 848-3191
TF: 800-776-8687 ■ Web: 8greattowns.com

Carrington Convention & Visitors Bureau
871 Main St PO Box 439 ... Carrington ND 58421 — Phone 701-652-2524 — Fax 652-2391
TF: 800-641-9668 ■ Web: www.cgtn-nd.com

Carson City Convention & Visitors Bureau
1900 S Carson St Suite 100 ... Carson City NV 89701 — Phone 775-687-7410 — Fax 687-7416
TF: 800-638-2321 ■ Web: www.visitcarsoncity.com

Cartersville Bartow County Convention & Visitors Bureau
1 Friendship Plaza Suite 1
PO Box 200397 ... Cartersville GA 30120 — Phone 770-387-1357 — Fax 607-3104
TF: 800-733-2280 ■ Web: www.notatlanta.org

Casper Area Convention & Visitors Bureau
992 N Poplar St ... Casper WY 82601 — Phone 307-234-5362 — Fax 261-9928
TF: 800-852-1889 ■ Web: www.casperwyoming.info

Cedar City-Brian Head Tourism & Convention Bureau
581 N Main St Suite A ... Cedar City UT 84721 — Phone 435-586-5124 — Fax 586-4022
TF: 800-354-4849 ■ Web: www.scenicsouthernutah.com

Cedar Rapids Area Convention & Visitors Bureau
119 1st Ave SE PO Box 5339 ... Cedar Rapids IA 52401 — Phone 319-398-5009 — Fax 398-5089
TF: 800-735-5557 ■ Web: www.cedar-rapids.com

Brandywine Conference & Visitors Bureau
1 Beaver Valley Rd ... Chadford PA 19317 — Phone 610-565-3679 — Fax 565-0833
TF: 800-343-3983 ■ Web: www.brandywinecvb.org

Champaign County Convention & Visitors Bureau
108 S Neil St ... Champaign IL 61820 — Phone 217-351-4133 — Fax 359-1809
TF: 800-369-6151 ■ Web: www.visitchampaigncounty.org

Chapel Hill/Orange County Visitors Bureau
501 W Franklin St. ... Chapel Hill NC 27516 — Phone 919-968-2060 — Fax 968-2062
TF: 888-968-2060 ■ Web: www.chocvb.org

Charleston Area Convention & Visitors Bureau
423 King St. ... Charleston SC 29403 — Phone 843-853-8000 — Fax 853-0444
TF: 800-868-8118 ■ Web: www.charlestoncvb.com

Charleston Convention & Visitors Bureau
200 Civic Ctr Dr ... Charleston WV 25301 — Phone 304-344-5075 — Fax 344-1241
TF: 800-733-5469 ■ Web: www.charlestonwv.com

Charlotte Convention & Visitors Bureau
500 S College St Suite 300 ... Charlotte NC 28202 — Phone 704-334-2282 — Fax 342-3972
TF: 800-722-1994 ■ Web: www.charlottesgotalot.com

Chattanooga Area Convention & Visitors Bureau
215 Broad St. ... Chattanooga TN 37402 — Phone 423-756-8687 — Fax 265-1630
TF: 800-322-3344 ■ Web: www.chattanoogafun.com

Name / Address	City	State	ZIP	Phone	Fax
Chautauqua County Visitors Bureau Chautauqua Main Gate Rt 394 PO Box 1441 *TF:* 800-242-4569 ■ *Web:* www.tourchautauqua.com	Chautauqua	NY	14722	716-357-4569	357-2284
Lewis County Convention & Visitor Bureau 500 NW Chamber Way *TF:* 800-525-3323 ■ *Web:* www.tourlewiscounty.com	Chehalis	WA	98532	360-748-8885	748-8763
Cherokee Tribal Travel & Promotions 498 Tsali Blvd PO Box 460 *TF:* 800-438-1601 ■ *Web:* www.cherokee-nc.com	Cherokee	NC	28719	828-497-9195	497-2505
Chesapeake Conventions & Tourism Bureau (CCT) 860 Greenbrier Cir Suite 101 *TF:* 888-889-5551 ■ *Web:* www.visitchesapeake.com	Chesapeake	VA	23320	757-502-4898	502-8016
Randolph County Tourism Committee 1 Taylor St Rm 104 Randolph County Courthouse *Web:* www.randolphco.org	Chester	IL	62233	618-826-5000	826-3750
Cheyenne Area Convention & Visitors Bureau 121 W 15th St Suite 202 *TF:* 800-426-5009 ■ *Web:* www.cheyenne.org	Cheyenne	WY	82001	307-778-3133	778-3190
Chicago Convention & Tourism Bureau 2301 S Lake Shore Dr McCormick Complex Lakeside Ctr *Web:* www.choosechicago.com	Chicago	IL	60616	312-567-8500	567-8533
Chicago Office of Tourism & Culture 78 E Washington St 4th Fl *TF:* 877-244-2246 ■ *Web:* www.explorechicago.org	Chicago	IL	60602	312-744-2400	744-2359
Chula Vista Convention & Visitors Bureau 233 4th Ave. *Web:* www.chulavistaconvis.com	Chula Vista	CA	91910	619-426-2882	420-1269
Greater Cincinnati Convention & Visitors Bureau 525 Vine St Suite 1500 *TF:* 800-543-2613 ■ *Web:* www.cincyusa.com	Cincinnati	OH	45202	513-621-2142	621-5020
Pickaway County Visitors Bureau 325 W Main St *TF:* 888-770-7425 ■ *Web:* www.pickaway.com	Circleville	OH	43113	740-474-3636	477-6800
Clarksville/Montgomery County Tourist Commission 25 Jefferson St Suite 300 *TF:* 800-530-2487 ■ *Web:* www.clarksvillepartnership.com	Clarksville	TN	37040	931-647-2331	645-1574
Clear Lake Convention & Visitors Bureau 205 Main Ave PO Box 188 *TF:* 800-285-5338 ■ *Web:* www.clearlakeiowa.com	Clear Lake	IA	50428	641-357-2159	357-8141
Saint Petersburg/Clearwater Area Convention & Visitors Bureau 13805 58th St N Suite 2-200 *TF:* 877-352-3224 ■ *Web:* www.visitstpeteclearwater.com	Clearwater	FL	33760	727-464-7200	464-7222
Cleveland/Bradley Convention & Visitors Bureau 225 Keith St PO Box 2275 *TF:* 800-472-6588 ■ *Web:* www.clevelandchamber.com	Cleveland	TN	37320	423-472-6587	472-2019
Positively Cleveland Visitors Ctr 100 Public Sq Suite 100 *TF:* 800-321-1004 ■ *Web:* www.positivelycleveland.com	Cleveland	OH	44113	216-875-6680	621-5967
Clinton Convention & Visitors Bureau 721 S 2nd St. *Web:* www.clintoniowatourism.com	Clinton	IA	52732	563-242-5702	242-5803
Florida's Space Coast Office of Tourism 430 Brevard Ave Suite 150 *TF:* 877-572-3224 ■ *Web:* www.space-coast.com	Cocoa Village	FL	32922	321-433-4470	433-4476
Park County Travel Council (PCTC) 836 Sheridan Ave PO Box 2454 *TF:* 800-393-2639 ■ *Web:* www.yellowstonecountry.org	Cody	WY	82414	307-587-2297	527-6228
Coffeyville Area Chamber of Commerce The 807 Walnut St PO Box 457 *TF:* 800-626-3357 ■ *Web:* www.coffeyvillechamber.org	Coffeyville	KS	67337	620-251-2250	251-5448
Colby Convention & Visitors Bureau 350 S Range Suite 10 *TF:* 800-611-8835 ■ *Web:* www.oasisontheplains.com	Colby	KS	67701	785-460-7643	460-4509
Bryan/College Station Convention & Visitors Bureau (BCSCVB) 715 University Dr E. *TF:* 800-777-8292 ■ *Web:* www.visitaggieland.com	College Station	TX	77840	979-260-9898	260-9800
Colorado Springs Convention & Visitors Bureau 515 S Cascade Ave. *TF:* 800-368-4748 ■ *Web:* www.visitcos.com	Colorado Springs	CO	80903	719-635-7506	635-4968
Columbia Convention & Visitors Bureau 300 S Providence Rd *TF:* 800-652-0987 ■ *Web:* www.visitcolumbiamo.com	Columbia	MO	65203	573-875-1231	443-3986
Columbia Metropolitan Convention & Visitors Bureau 1101 Lincoln St PO Box 15 *TF:* 800-264-4884 ■ *Web:* www.columbiacvb.com	Columbia	SC	29202	803-545-0000	545-0013
Columbus Area Visitors Ctr 506 5th St. *TF:* 800-468-6564 ■ *Web:* www.columbus.in.us	Columbus	IN	47201	812-378-2622	372-7348
Columbus Convention & Visitors Bureau 900 Front Ave *TF:* 800-999-1613 ■ *Web:* www.visitcolumbusga.com	Columbus	GA	31901	706-322-1613	322-0701
Columbus Convention & Visitors Bureau 318 7th St N *TF:* 800-327-2686 ■ *Web:* www.columbus-ms.info	Columbus	MS	39701	662-329-1191	329-8969
Greater Columbus Convention & Visitors Bureau 277 W Nationwide Blvd Suite 125 *TF:* 866-397-2657 ■ *Web:* www.experiencecolumbus.com	Columbus	OH	43215	614-221-6623	221-5618
Polk County Travel & Tourism 20 E Mills St PO Box 308 *TF:* 800-440-7848 ■ *Web:* www.nc-mountains.org	Columbus	NC	28722	828-894-2324	894-6142
New Hampshire Div of Travel & Tourism Development 172 Pembroke Rd PO Box 1856 *TF:* 800-262-6660 ■ *Web:* www.visitnh.gov	Concord	NH	03302	603-271-2665	271-6870
Coos Bay-North Bend Visitor & Convention Bureau 50 Central Ave *TF:* 800-824-8486 ■ *Web:* www.oregonsadventurecoast.com	Coos Bay	OR	97420	541-269-0215	269-2861
Iowa City/Coralville Area Convention & Visitors Bureau 900 1st Ave Hayden Fry Way *TF:* 800-283-6592 ■ *Web:* www.iowacitycoralville.org	Coralville	IA	52241	319-337-6592	337-9953
Corinth Area Convention & Visitors Bureau 215 N Fillmore St *TF:* 800-748-9048 ■ *Web:* www.corinth.net	Corinth	MS	38834	662-287-8300	286-0102
Corpus Christi Convention & Visitors Bureau 101 N Shoreline Blvd Suite 430 *TF:* 800-678-6232 ■ *Web:* www.visitcorpuschristitx.org	Corpus Christi	TX	78401	361-881-1888	887-9023
Corvallis Tourism 553 NW Harrison Blvd *TF:* 800-334-8118 ■ *Web:* www.visitcorvallis.com	Corvallis	OR	97330	541-757-1544	753-2664
Council Grove/Morris County Chamber of Commerce & Tourism 207 W Main St *TF:* 800-732-9211 ■ *Web:* www.councilgrove.com	Council Grove	KS	66846	620-767-5413	767-5553
Northern Kentucky Convention & Visitors Bureau (NKYCVB) 50 E RiverCenter Blvd Suite 200 *TF:* 877-659-8474 ■ *Web:* www.nkycvb.com	Covington	KY	41011	859-261-4677	261-5135
Montgomery County Visitors & Convention Bureau 218 E Pike St *TF:* 800-866-3973 ■ *Web:* www.crawfordsville.org	Crawfordsville	IN	47933	765-362-5200	362-5215
Crescent City-Del Norte County Chamber of Commerce (CCDNCVB) 1001 Front St *TF:* 800-343-8300 ■ *Web:* www.exploredelnorte.com	Crescent City	CA	95531	707-464-3174	464-9676
Dallas Convention & Visitors Bureau 325 N St Paul St Suite 700 *TF:* 800-232-5527 ■ *Web:* www.visitdallas.com	Dallas	TX	75201	214-571-1000	571-1000
Central Florida Visitors & Convention Bureau 101 Adventure Ct *TF:* 800-828-7655 ■ *Web:* www.visitcentralflorida.org	Davenport	FL	33837	863-420-2586	420-2593
Tucker County Convention & Visitors Bureau 410 William Ave *TF:* 800-782-2775 ■ *Web:* www.canaanvalley.org	Davis	WV	26260	304-259-5315	259-4210
Dayton/Montgomery County Convention & Visitors Bureau 1 Chamber Plaza Suite A *TF:* 800-221-8235 ■ *Web:* www.daytoncvb.com	Dayton	OH	45402	937-226-8211	226-8294
Daytona Beach Area Convention & Visitors Bureau 126 E Orange Ave *TF:* 800-544-0415 ■ *Web:* www.daytonabeachcvb.org	Daytona Beach	FL	32114	386-255-0415	255-5478
Decatur Area Convention & Visitors Bureau 202 E N St *TF:* 800-331-4479 ■ *Web:* www.decaturcvb.com	Decatur	IL	62523	217-423-7000	423-7455
Decatur/Morgan County Convention & Visitors Bureau (DMCCVB) 719 6th Ave SE PO Box 2349 *TF:* 800-232-5449 ■ *Web:* www.decaturcvb.org	Decatur	AL	35602	256-350-2028	350-2054
Wicomico County Convention & Visitors Bureau 8480 Ocean Hwy. *TF:* 800-332-8687 ■ *Web:* www.wicomicotourism.org	Delmar	MD	21875	410-548-4914	548-0490
Denver Metro Convention & Visitors Bureau 1555 California St Suite 300 *TF:* 800-480-2010 ■ *Web:* www.denver.org	Denver	CO	80202	303-892-1112	892-1636
Greater Des Moines Convention & Visitors Bureau 400 Locust St Suite 265 *TF:* 800-451-2625 ■ *Web:* www.seedesmoines.com	Des Moines	IA	50309	515-286-4960	244-9757
Detroit Metropolitan Convention & Visitors Bureau 211 W Fort St Suite 1000 *TF:* 800-225-5389 ■ *Web:* www.visitdetroit.com	Detroit	MI	48226	313-202-1800	202-1808
Dickinson Convention & Visitors Bureau 72 E Museum Dr. *TF:* 800-279-7391 ■ *Web:* www.visitdickinson.com	Dickinson	ND	58601	701-483-4988	483-9261
Dothan Area Convention & Visitors Bureau 3311 Ross Clark Cir PO Box 8765 *TF:* 888-449-0212 ■ *Web:* www.dothanalcvb.com	Dothan	AL	36301	334-794-6622	712-2731
Kent County & Greater Dover Delaware Convention & Visitors Bureau 435 N DuPont Hwy *TF:* 800-233-5368 ■ *Web:* www.visitdover.com	Dover	DE	19901	302-734-1736	734-0167
Downers Grove Tourism & Events 2001 Butterfield Rd Suite 120 *TF:* 800-934-0615 ■ *Web:* www.visitdownersgrove.com	Downers Grove	IL	60515	630-729-0380	729-0381
Drummond Island Tourism Assn PO Box 200 *TF:* 800-737-8666 ■ *Web:* www.drummondislandchamber.com	Drummond Island	MI	49726	906-493-5245	493-6362
Dublin Convention & Visitors Bureau 9 S High St *TF:* 800-245-8387 ■ *Web:* www.irishisanattitude.com	Dublin	OH	43017	614-792-7666	760-1818
Atlanta's Gwinnett Convention & Visitors Bureau (GCVB) 6500 Sugarloaf Pkwy Suite 200 *TF:* 888-494-6638 ■ *Web:* www.gcvb.org	Duluth	GA	30097	770-623-3600	623-1667
Duluth Convention & Visitors Bureau 21 W Superior St Suite 100 *TF:* 800-438-5884 ■ *Web:* www.visitduluth.com	Duluth	MN	55802	218-722-4011	722-1322
DuQuoin Tourism Commission 20 N Chestnut St PO Box 1037 *TF:* 800-455-9570 ■ *Web:* www.duquointourism.org	DuQuoin	IL	62832	618-542-8338	542-2098
Durango Area Tourism Office 111 S Camino del Rio *TF:* 800-525-8855 ■ *Web:* www.durango.org	Durango	CO	81301	970-247-3500	385-7884
Durham Convention & Visitors Bureau 101 E Morgan St. *TF:* 800-446-8604 ■ *Web:* www.durham-nc.com	Durham	NC	27701	919-687-0288	683-9555
Eagan Convention & Visitors Bureau 1501 Central Pkwy *TF:* 800-324-2620 ■ *Web:* www.eaganmn.com	Eagan	MN	55121	651-675-5546	675-5545
Talbot County Tourism Office 11 S Harrison St *Web:* www.tourtalbot.org	Easton	MD	21601	410-770-8000	770-8057
Visit Eau Claire 4319 Jeffers Rd Suite 201 *TF:* 888-523-3866 ■ *Web:* www.visiteauclaire.com	Eau Claire	WI	54703	715-831-2345	831-2340
Effingham Convention & Visitors Bureau 201 E Jefferson Ave *TF:* 800-772-0750 ■ *Web:* www.effinghamil.com	Effingham	IL	62401	217-342-5305	342-2746
El Paso Convention & Visitors Bureau 1 Civic Ctr Plaza *TF:* 800-351-6024 ■ *Web:* www.visitelpaso.com	El Paso	TX	79901	915-534-0600	534-0600
Elgin Area Convention & Visitors Bureau 77 S Riverside Dr # 1 *TF:* 800-217-5362 ■ *Web:* www.enjoyelgin.com	Elgin	IL	60120	847-695-7540	695-7668

				Phone	Fax
Elkhart County Convention & Visitors Bureau 219 Caravan Dr. *TF:* 800-250-4827 ■ *Web:* www.amishcountry.org	Elkhart	IN	46514	574-262-8161	262-3925
Howard County Tourism Council 8267 Main St Side Entrance *TF:* 800-288-8747 ■ *Web:* www.howardcountymd.gov	Ellicott City	MD	21043	410-313-1900	313-1902
Grays Harbor Tourism PO Box 1229 *TF:* 800-621-9625 ■ *Web:* www.visitgraysharbor.com	Elma	WA	98541	360-482-2651	482-3297
VisitErie 208 E Bayfront Pkwy Suite 103 *TF:* 800-524-3743 ■ *Web:* www.visiteriepa.com	Erie	PA	16507	814-454-1000	459-0241
Travel Lane County PO Box 10286 *TF:* 800-547-5445 ■ *Web:* www.travellanecounty.org	Eugene	OR	97440	541-484-5307	343-6335
Humboldt County Convention & Visitors Bureau 1034 2nd St *TF:* 800-346-3482 ■ *Web:* www.redwoods.info	Eureka	CA	95501	707-443-5097	443-5115
Evansville Convention & Visitors Bureau 401 SE Riverside Dr *TF:* 800-433-3025 ■ *Web:* www.evansvillecvb.org	Evansville	IN	47713	812-421-2200	421-2207
Fairbanks Convention & Visitors Bureau 101 Dunkel St Suite 111 *TF:* 800-327-5774 ■ *Web:* www.explorefairbanks.com	Fairbanks	AK	99701	907-456-5774	459-3757
Jefferson County Visitor's Bureau PO Box 274 *Web:* www.visitoregontrail.org	Fairbury	NE	68352	402-729-3000	729-3076
Fairmont Convention & Visitors Bureau 323 E Blue Earth Ave *TF:* 800-657-3280 ■ *Web:* www.fairmontcvb.com	Fairmont	MN	56031	507-235-8585	235-8411
Tourism Bureau Southwestern Illinois 10950 Lincoln Trail *TF:* 800-442-1488 ■ *Web:* www.thetourismbureau.org	Fairview Heights	IL	62208	618-397-1488	397-1945
Fargo-Moorhead Convention & Visitors Bureau 2001 44th St S *TF:* 800-235-7654 ■ *Web:* www.fargomoorhead.org	Fargo	ND	58103	701-282-3653	282-4366
Farmington Convention & Visitors Bureau 3041 E Main St *TF:* 800-448-1240 ■ *Web:* www.farmingtonnm.org	Farmington	NM	87402	505-326-7602	327-0577
Fayetteville Area Convention & Visitors Bureau (FACVB) 245 Person St *TF:* 800-255-8217 ■ *Web:* www.visitfayettevillenc.com	Fayetteville	NC	28301	910-483-5311	484-6632
Flagstaff Convention & Visitors Bureau 323 W Aspen Ave *TF:* 800-217-2367 ■ *Web:* www.flagstaffarizona.org	Flagstaff	AZ	86001	928-779-7611	556-1305
Flint Area Convention & Visitors Bureau 502 Church St *TF Sales:* 800-253-5468 ■ *Web:* www.flint.travel	Flint	MI	48502	810-232-8900	232-1515
Florence Convention & Visitors Bureau 3290 W Radio Dr *TF:* 800-325-9005 ■ *Web:* www.visitflow.com	Florence	SC	29501	843-664-0330	665-9480
Tropical Everglades Visitor Assn 160 US Hwy 1 *TF:* 800-388-9669 ■ *Web:* www.tropicaleverglades.com	Florida City	FL	33034	305-245-9180	247-4335
Fond du Lac Convention & Visitors Bureau 171 S Pioneer Rd *TF:* 800-937-9123 ■ *Web:* www.fdl.com	Fond du Lac	WI	54935	920-923-3010	929-6846
Fort Collins Convention & Visitors Bureau 19 Old Town Sq Suite 137 *TF:* 800-274-3678 ■ *Web:* www.ftcollins.com	Fort Collins	CO	80524	970-232-3840	232-3841
Greater Fort Lauderdale Convention & Visitors Bureau 100 E Broward Blvd Suite 200 *TF:* 800-227-8669 ■ *Web:* www.sunny.org	Fort Lauderdale	FL	33301	954-765-4466	765-4467
Fort Madison Convention & Visitors Bureau 614 9th St *TF:* 800-210-8687 ■ *Web:* www.visitfortmadison.com	Fort Madison	IA	52627	319-372-5472	372-3039
Lee County Visitors & Convention Bureau 12800 University Dr Suite 550 *TF:* 800-237-6444 ■ *Web:* www.fortmyers-sanibel.com	Fort Myers	FL	33907	239-338-3500	334-1106
Saint Lucie County Tourist Development Council 2300 Virginia Ave *TF:* 800-344-8443 ■ *Web:* www.visitstluciefla.com	Fort Pierce	FL	34982	772-462-1535	462-2131
Fort Smith Convention & Visitors Bureau 2 N 'B' St *TF:* 800-637-1477 ■ *Web:* www.fortsmith.org	Fort Smith	AR	72901	479-783-8888	784-2421
Fort Wayne/Allen County Convention & Visitors Bureau 927 S Harrison St *TF:* 800-767-7752 ■ *Web:* www.visitfortwayne.com	Fort Wayne	IN	46802	260-424-3700	424-3914
Fort Worth Convention & Visitors Bureau 111 W 4th St Suite 200 *TF:* 800-433-5747 ■ *Web:* www.fortworth.com	Fort Worth	TX	76102	817-336-8791	336-3282
Frankenmuth Convention & Visitors Bureau 635 S Main St *TF:* 800-386-8696 ■ *Web:* www.frankenmuth.org	Frankenmuth	MI	48734	989-652-6106	652-3841
Frankfort/Franklin County Tourist & Convention Commission 100 Capitol Ave *TF:* 800-960-7200 ■ *Web:* www.visitfrankfort.com	Frankfort	KY	40601	502-875-8687	227-2604
Williamson County Convention & Visitors Bureau 108 4th Ave S Suite 203 *TF:* 866-253-9207 ■ *Web:* www.visitwilliamson.com	Franklin	TN	37064	615-791-7554	550-2707
Fredericksburg Chamber of Commerce 302 E Austin St *TF:* 888-997-3600 ■ *Web:* www.fredericksburg-texas.com	Fredericksburg	TX	78624	830-997-6523	997-8588
Dodge County Convention & Visitors Bureau 1420 E Military Ave *TF:* 800-727-8323	Fremont	NE	68025	402-753-6414	753-6482
Fremont/Sandusky County Convention & Visitors Bureau 712 N St Suite 102 *TF:* 800-255-8070 ■ *Web:* www.lakeeriesfavoriteneighbor.com	Fremont	OH	43420	419-332-4470	332-4359
Fresno City & County Convention & Visitors Bureau 848 M St 3rd Fl *TF:* 800-788-0836 ■ *Web:* www.playfresno.org	Fresno	CA	93721	559-445-8300	445-0122
Alachua County Visitors & Convention Bureau 30 E University Ave *TF:* 866-778-5002 ■ *Web:* www.visitgainesville.com	Gainesville	FL	32601	352-374-5260	338-3213

				Phone	Fax
Galena/Jo Daviess County Convention & Visitors Bureau (GJDCCVB) 101 Bouthillier St *TF:* 800-464-2536 ■ *Web:* www.galena.org	Galena	IL	61036	815-777-3557	777-3566
Galesburg Area Convention & Visitors Bureau 2163 E Main St *TF:* 800-916-3330 ■ *Web:* www.visitgalesburg.com	Galesburg	IL	61401	309-343-2485	343-2521
Finney County Convention & Visitors Bureau 1511 E Fulton Terr *TF:* 800-879-9803 ■ *Web:* www.gardencity.net	Garden City	KS	67846	620-276-3264	276-3290
Garden Grove Visitors Bureau 12866 Main St Suite 102 *TF:* 800-959-5560 ■ *Web:* www.gardengrovechamber.org	Garden Grove	CA	92840	714-638-7950	636-6672
Gatlinburg Dept of Tourism & Convention Ctr 303 Reagan Dr *TF:* 800-343-1475 ■ *Web:* www.gatlinburg-tennessee.com	Gatlinburg	TN	37738	865-436-2392	436-3704
Georgetown Convention & Visitors Bureau 101 W 7th St *TF:* 800-436-8696 ■ *Web:* www.visit.georgetown.org	Georgetown	TX	78626	512-930-3545	930-3697
Gettysburg Convention & Visitors Bureau 571 W Middle St PO Box 4117 *TF:* 800-337-5015 ■ *Web:* www.gettysburg.travel	Gettysburg	PA	17325	717-334-6274	334-1166
Greater Grand Forks Convention & Visitors Bureau 4251 Gateway Dr *TF:* 800-866-4566 ■ *Web:* www.visitgrandforks.com	Grand Forks	ND	58203	701-746-0444	746-0775
Grand Junction Visitors & Convention Bureau 740 Horizon Dr *TF:* 800-962-2547 ■ *Web:* www.visitgrandjunction.com	Grand Junction	CO	81506	970-244-1480	243-7393
Grand Rapids Area Convention & Visitors Bureau 501 S Tokegama Ave Suite 3 *TF:* 800-355-9740 ■ *Web:* www.visitgrandrapids.com	Grand Rapids	MN	55744	218-326-9607	326-8219
Grand Rapids/Kent County Convention & Visitors Bureau 171 Monroe Ave NW Suite 700 *TF:* 800-678-9859 ■ *Web:* www.experiencegr.com	Grand Rapids	MI	49503	616-459-8287	459-7291
Grants Pass Visitors & Convention Bureau 1995 NW Vine St *TF:* 800-547-5927 ■ *Web:* www.visitgrantspass.org	Grants Pass	OR	97526	541-476-5510	476-9574
Grapevine Convention & Visitors Bureau 1 Liberty Pk Plaza *TF:* 800-457-6338 ■ *Web:* www.grapevinetexasusa.com	Grapevine	TX	76051	817-410-3185	410-3038
Houma Area Convention & Visitors Bureau 114 Tourist Dr *TF:* 800-688-2732 ■ *Web:* www.houmatourism.com	Gray	LA	70359	985-868-2732	868-7170
Grayling Visitors Bureau PO Box 217 *TF:* 800-937-8837 ■ *Web:* www.grayling-mi.com	Grayling	MI	49738	989-348-4945	348-9168
Greeley Convention & Visitors Bureau 902 7th Ave *TF:* 800-449-3866 ■ *Web:* www.greeleycvb.com	Greeley	CO	80631	970-352-3567	352-3572
Packer Country Visitor & Convention Bureau 1901 S Oneida St *TF:* 888-867-3342 ■ *Web:* www.greenbay.com	Green Bay	WI	54304	920-494-9507	405-1271
Putnam County Convention & Visitors Bureau 12 W Washington St *TF:* 800-829-4639 ■ *Web:* www.coveredbridgecountry.com	Greencastle	IN	46135	765-653-8743	653-0851
Greensboro Area Convention & Visitors Bureau 2200 Pinecroft Rd Suite 200 *TF:* 800-344-2282 ■ *Web:* www.greensboronc.org	Greensboro	NC	27407	336-274-2282	230-1183
Greater Greenville Convention & Visitors Bureau 148 River St Suite 222 *TF:* 800-351-7180 ■ *Web:* www.greenvillecvb.com	Greenville	SC	29601	864-421-0000	421-0005
Greenville-Pitt County Convention & Visitors Bureau (GPCCVB) 303 SW Greenville Blvd PO Box 8027 *TF:* 800-537-5564 ■ *Web:* www.visitgreenvillenc.com	Greenville	NC	27835	252-329-4200	329-4205
Greenwood Convention & Visitors Bureau 111 E Market St *TF:* 800-748-9064 ■ *Web:* www.gcvb.com	Greenwood	MS	38930	662-453-9197	453-5526
Alabama Gulf Coast Convention & Visitors Bureau 3150 Gulf Shores Pkwy PO Drawer 457 *TF:* 800-745-7263 ■ *Web:* www.gulfshores.com	Gulf Shores	AL	36547	251-968-7511	968-6095
Mississippi Gulf Coast Convention & Visitors Bureau PO Box 6128 *TF:* 888-467-4853 ■ *Web:* www.gulfcoast.org	Gulfport	MS	39506	228-896-6699	896-6788
Lake County Convention & Visitors Bureau 5465 W Grand Ave Suite 100 *TF:* 800-525-3669 ■ *Web:* www.lakecounty.org	Gurnee	IL	60031	847-662-2700	662-2702
Hagerstown/Washington County Convention & Visitors Bureau 16 Public Sq *TF:* 888-257-2600 ■ *Web:* www.marylandmemories.org	Hagerstown	MD	21740	301-791-3246	791-2601
Haines Visitors Bureau 122 2nd Ave PO Box 530 *TF:* 800-458-3579 ■ *Web:* www.haines.ak.us	Haines	AK	99827	907-766-2234	766-3155
Hampton Conventions & Visitors Bureau 1919 Commerce Dr Suite 290 *TF:* 800-487-8778 ■ *Web:* www.hamptoncvb.com	Hampton	VA	23666	757-722-1222	896-4600
Hannibal Convention & Visitors Bureau 505 N 3rd St *TF:* 866-263-4825 ■ *Web:* www.visithannibal.com	Hannibal	MO	63401	573-221-2477	221-6999
Jefferson County Convention & Visitors Bureau 37 Washington Ct *TF:* 866-435-5698 ■ *Web:* www.wveasterngateway.com	Harpers Ferry	WV	25425	304-535-2627	535-2131
Hershey Harrisburg Region Visitors Bureau 17 S 2nd St *TF:* 877-727-8573 ■ *Web:* www.visithersheyharrisburg.org	Harrisburg	PA	17101	717-231-7788	231-2808
Greater Hartford Convention & Visitors Bureau 31 Pratt St 4th Fl *TF:* 800-446-7811 ■ *Web:* www.enjoyhartford.com	Hartford	CT	06103	860-728-6789	293-2365
Long Island Convention & Visitors Bureau & Sports Commission 330 Motor Pkwy Suite 203 **Fax Area Code:* 631 ■ *TF:* 800-441-4601 ■ *Web:* www.discoverlongisland.com	Hauppauge	NY	11788	877-386-6654	951-3439*
Hays Convention & Visitors Bureau 2700 Vine St *TF:* 800-569-4505 ■ *Web:* www.haysusa.net	Hays	KS	67601	785-628-8202	628-1471
Seminole County Convention & Visitors Bureau 1000 AAA Dr Suite 200 *TF:* 800-800-7832 ■ *Web:* www.visitseminole.com	Heathrow	FL	32746	407-665-2900	665-2920

				Phone	Fax
Alpine Helen/White County Convention & Visitors Bureau 726 Bruckenstrasse PO Box 730	Helen	GA	30545	706-878-2181	878-4032
TF: 800-858-8027 ■ *Web:* www.helenga.org					
Helena Convention & Visitors Bureau 225 Cruse Ave	Helena	MT	59601	406-447-1530	447-1532
TF: 800-743-5362 ■ *Web:* www.gohelena.com					
Henderson County Tourist Commission 101 N Water St Suite B	Henderson	KY	42420	270-826-3128	826-0234
TF: 800-648-3128 ■ *Web:* www.hendersonky.org					
Henderson County Travel & Tourism 201 S Main St	Hendersonville	NC	28792	828-693-9708	697-4996
TF: 800-828-4244 ■ *Web:* www.historichendersonville.org					
Huntingdon County Visitors Bureau 6993 Seven Pt Rd Suite 2	Hesston	PA	16647	814-658-0060	658-0068
TF: 888-729-7869 ■ *Web:* www.raystown.org					
Hickory Metro Convention & Visitors Bureau 1960 13th Ave Dr SE	Hickory	NC	28602	828-322-1335	322-8983
TF: 800-509-2444 ■ *Web:* www.hickorymetro.com					
High Point Convention & Visitors Bureau 300 S Main St	High Point	NC	27260	336-884-5255	884-5256
TF: 800-720-5255 ■ *Web:* www.highpoint.org					
Hilton Head Island Visitors & Convention Bureau 1 Chamber Dr PO Box 5647	Hilton Head Island	SC	29938	843-785-3673	785-7110
TF: 800-523-3373 ■ *Web:* www.hiltonheadisland.org					
Holland Area Convention & Visitors Bureau 76 E 8th St	Holland	MI	49423	616-394-0000	394-0122
TF: 800-506-1299 ■ *Web:* www.holland.org					
Hawaii Visitors & Convention Bureau 2270 Kalakaua Ave Suite 804	Honolulu	HI	96815	808-923-1811	924-0290
TF: 800-464-2924 ■ *Web:* www.gohawaii.com					
Hot Springs Convention & Visitors Bureau 134 Convention Blvd	Hot Springs	AR	71901	501-321-2277	321-2136
TF: 800-543-2284 ■ *Web:* www.hotsprings.org					
Houghton Lake Area Tourism & Convention Bureau PO Box 1	Houghton Lake	MI	48629	989-366-8474	366-8395
TF: 800-676-5330 ■ *Web:* www.visithoughtonlake.com					
Greater Houston Convention & Visitors Bureau 901 Bagby St Suite 100	Houston	TX	77002	713-437-5200	227-6336
TF: 800-446-8786 ■ *Web:* www.visithoustontexas.com					
Cabell-Huntington Convention & Visitors Bureau PO Box 347	Huntington	WV	25708	304-525-7333	525-7345
TF: 800-635-6329 ■ *Web:* www.wvvisit.org					
Huntington County Visitors & Convention Bureau 407 N Jefferson St	Huntington	IN	46750	260-359-8687	359-9754
TF: 800-848-4282 ■ *Web:* www.visithuntington.org					
Huntington Beach Marketing & Visitors Bureau 301 Main St Suite 208	Huntington Beach	CA	92648	714-969-3492	969-5592
TF: 800-729-6232 ■ *Web:* www.surfcityusa.com					
Huntsville/Madison County Convention & Visitor's Bureau 500 Church St Suite 1	Huntsville	AL	35801	256-551-2230	551-2324
TF: 800-843-0468 ■ *Web:* www.huntsville.org					
Huron Chamber & Visitors Bureau 1725 Dakota Ave S	Huron	SD	57350	605-352-0000	352-8321
TF: 800-487-6673 ■ *Web:* www.huronsd.com					
Hurricane Convention & Visitors Bureau 3255 Teays Valley Rd PO Box 1086	Hurricane	WV	25526	304-562-5896	562-5858
TF: 877-487-7982 ■ *Web:* www.hurricanewv.com					
Greater Hutchinson Convention & Visitors Bureau 117 N Walnut St PO Box 519	Hutchinson	KS	67504	620-662-3391	662-2168
TF: 800-691-4282 ■ *Web:* www.hutchchamber.com					
Incline Village/Crystal Bay Visitors Bureau 969 Tahoe Blvd	Incline Village	NV	89451	775-832-1606	832-1605
TF: 800-468-2463 ■ *Web:* www.gotahoenorth.com					
Indiana County Tourist Bureau 2334 Oakland Ave Suite 68	Indiana	PA	15701	724-463-7505	465-3819
TF: 877-746-3426 ■ *Web:* www.visitindianacountypa.org					
Indianapolis Convention & Visitors Assn 30 S Meridian St Suite 410	Indianapolis	IN	46204	317-639-4282	639-5273
TF: 800-323-4639 ■ *Web:* www.visitindy.com					
Tourism Assn of the Dickinson County Area 600 S Stephenson Ave	Iron Mountain	MI	49804	906-774-2945	774-2005
TF: 800-236-2447 ■ *Web:* www.ironmountain.org					
Western Upper Peninsula Convention & Visitor Bureau 648 W Cloverland Dr PO Box 706	Ironwood	MI	49938	906-932-4850	932-3455
TF: 800-522-5657 ■ *Web:* www.westernup.info					
Irving Convention & Visitors Bureau 222 W Las Colinas Blvd Suite 1550	Irving	TX	75039	972-252-7476	257-3153
TF: 800-247-8464 ■ *Web:* www.irvingtexas.com					
Ithaca/Tompkins County Convention & Visitors Bureau 904 E Shore Dr	Ithaca	NY	14850	607-272-1313	272-7617
TF: 800-284-8422 ■ *Web:* www.visitithaca.com					
East Feliciana Parish Tourist Commission 1752 High St PO Box 667	Jackson	LA	70748	225-634-7155	634-7155
Web: www.felicianatourism.org					
Jackson County Convention & Visitors Bureau 141 S Jackson St	Jackson	MI	49201	517-764-4440	780-3688
TF: 800-245-5282 ■ *Web:* www.visitjacksonmi.com					
Metro Jackson Convention & Visitors Bureau 111 E Capitol St Suite 102	Jackson	MS	39202	601-960-1891	960-1827
TF: 800-354-7695 ■ *Web:* www.visitjackson.com					
Jacksonville Convention & Visitors Bureau 310 E State St	Jacksonville	IL	62650	217-243-5678	
TF: 800-593-5678 ■ *Web:* www.jacksonvilleil.org					
Onslow County Tourism 1099 Gum Branch Rd	Jacksonville	NC	28540	910-455-1113	347-4705
TF: 800-932-2144 ■ *Web:* www.onslowcountytourism.com					
Visit Jacksonville 208 N Laura St # 1	Jacksonville	FL	32202	904-798-9111	798-9103
TF: 800-733-2668 ■ *Web:* www.visitjacksonville.com					
Jamestown Promotions & Tourism Ctr 404 Louis L'Amour Ln	Jamestown	ND	58401	701-251-9145	251-9146
TF: 800-222-4766 ■ *Web:* www.tourjamestown.com					
Jefferson City Convention & Visitors Bureau 100 E High St PO Box 2227	Jefferson City	MO	65101	573-632-2820	638-4892
TF: 800-769-4183 ■ *Web:* www.visitjeffersoncity.com					
Clark-Floyd Counties Convention & Tourism Bureau 315 Southern Indiana Ave	Jeffersonville	IN	47130	812-282-6654	282-1904
TF: 800-552-3842 ■ *Web:* www.sunnysideoflouisville.org					
Johnson City Convention & Visitors Bureau 601 E Main St	Johnson City	TN	37601	423-461-8000	461-8047
TF: 800-852-3392 ■ *Web:* www.johnsoncitytn.org					
Greater Johnstown/Cambria County Convention & Visitors Bureau 416 Main St Suite 100	Johnstown	PA	15901	814-536-7993	539-3370
TF: 800-237-8590 ■ *Web:* www.visitjohnstownpa.com					
Heritage Corridor Convention & Visitors Bureau 339 W Jefferson St	Joliet	IL	60435	815-727-2323	727-2324
TF: 800-926-2262 ■ *Web:* www.heritagecorridorcvb.com					
Joplin Convention & Visitors Bureau 222 W 3rd St	Joplin	MO	64801	417-625-4789	624-7948
TF: 800-657-2534 ■ *Web:* www.joplincvb.com					
Juneau Convention & Visitors Bureau 101 Egan Dr	Juneau	AK	99801	907-586-1737	586-6304
TF: 800-581-2201 ■ *Web:* www.traveljuneau.com					
Kalamazoo County Convention & Visitors Bureau 141 E Michigan Ave Suite 100	Kalamazoo	MI	49007	269-488-9000	488-0050
TF: 800-888-0509 ■ *Web:* www.discoverkalamazoo.com					
Flathead Convention & Visitors Bureau 15 Depot Pk	Kalispell	MT	59901	406-756-9091	257-2500
TF: 800-543-3105 ■ *Web:* www.fcvb.org					
Cabarrus County Convention & Visitors Bureau 3003 Dale Earnhardt Blvd	Kannapolis	NC	28083	704-782-4340	782-4333
TF: 800-848-3740 ■ *Web:* www.visitcabarrus.com					
Kansas City Convention & Visitors Assn 1100 Main St Suite 2200	Kansas City	MO	64105	816-221-5242	691-3805
TF: 800-767-7700 ■ *Web:* www.visitkc.com					
Kansas City Kansas Convention & Visitors Bureau Inc 901 N 8th St PO Box 171517	Kansas City	KS	66117	913-321-5800	371-3732
TF: 800-264-1563 ■ *Web:* www.visitkansascityks.com					
Cowlitz County Tourism 105 N Minor Rd	Kelso	WA	98626	360-577-3137	578-2660
Web: www.visitmtsthelens.com					
Chester County Tourist Bureau 300 Greenwood Rd	Kennett Square	PA	19348	610-388-2900	388-6241
TF: 800-228-9933 ■ *Web:* www.brandywinevalley.com					
Tri-Cities Visitor & Convention Bureau 7130 W Grandridge Blvd Suite B	Kennewick	WA	99336	509-735-8486	783-9005
TF: 800-254-5824 ■ *Web:* www.visittri-cities.com					
Kenosha Area Convention & Visitors Bureau 812 56th St	Kenosha	WI	53140	262-654-7307	654-0882
TF: 800-654-7309 ■ *Web:* www.kenoshacvb.com					
Kerrville Convention & Visitors Bureau 2108 Sidney Baker St	Kerrville	TX	78028	830-792-3535	792-3230
TF: 800-221-7958 ■ *Web:* www.kerrvilletexascvb.com					
Ketchikan Visitors Bureau 131 Front St	Ketchikan	AK	99901	907-225-6166	225-4250
TF: 800-770-3300 ■ *Web:* www.visit-ketchikan.com					
Key West Visitors Ctr 402 Wall St	Key West	FL	33040	305-294-2587	294-7806
TF: 800-648-6269 ■ *Web:* www.keywestchamber.org					
Monroe County Tourist Development Council 1201 White St Suite 102	Key West	FL	33040	305-296-1552	296-0788
TF: 800-648-5510 ■ *Web:* www.fla-keys.com					
Killeen Civic & Conference Center & Visitors Bureau 3601 S WS Young Dr PO Box 1329	Killeen	TX	76543	254-501-3888	554-3219
Web: www.killeen-cvb.com					
Valley Forge Convention & Visitors Bureau 1000 First Ave Suite 101	King of Prussia	PA	19406	610-834-1550	834-0202
TF: 800-441-3549 ■ *Web:* www.valleyforge.org					
Kingsport Convention & Visitors Bureau 151 E Main St	Kingsport	TN	37660	423-392-8820	392-8803
TF: 800-743-5282 ■ *Web:* www.kcvb.org					
Kinston Convention & Visitors Bureau 301 N Queen St	Kinston	NC	28501	252-523-2500	527-1914
TF: 800-869-0032 ■ *Web:* www.visitkinston.com					
Kissimmee Convention & Visitors Bureau 1925 E Irlo Bronson Memorial Hwy	Kissimmee	FL	34744	407-742-8200	847-0878
TF: 800-327-9159 ■ *Web:* www.visitkissimmee.com					
Armstrong County Tourist Bureau 125 Market St Suite 2	Kittanning	PA	16201	724-548-3226	545-3119
TF: 888-265-9954 ■ *Web:* www.armstrongcounty.com					
Discover Klamath 205 Riverside Dr # B	Klamath Falls	OR	97601	541-882-1501	850-0125
TF: 800-445-6728 ■ *Web:* www.discoverklamath.com					
Knoxville Tourism & Sports Corp 301 S Gay St	Knoxville	TN	37902	865-523-7263	673-4400
TF: 800-727-8045 ■ *Web:* www.knoxville.org					
Lake Barkley Tourist Commission 82 Days Inn Dr	Kuttawa	KY	42055	270-388-5300	388-5301
TF: 800-355-3885 ■ *Web:* www.lakebarkley.org					
La Crosse Area Convention & Visitors Bureau 410 Veterans Memorial Dr	La Crosse	WI	54601	608-782-2366	782-4082
TF: 800-658-9424 ■ *Web:* www.explorelacrosse.com					
Lafayette Convention & Visitors Commission 1400 NW Evangeline Thwy	Lafayette	LA	70501	337-232-3737	232-0161
TF: 800-346-1958 ■ *Web:* www.lafayettetravel.com					
Lafayette-West Lafayette Convention & Visitors Bureau 301 Frontage Rd	Lafayette	IN	47905	765-447-9999	447-5062
TF: 800-872-6648 ■ *Web:* www.homeofpurdue.com					
Laguna Beach Visitors & Conference Bureau 381 Forest Ave	Laguna Beach	CA	92651	949-497-9229	376-0558
TF: 800-877-1115 ■ *Web:* www.lagunabeachinfo.org					
Southwest Louisiana Convention & Visitors Bureau 1205 N Lakeshore Dr	Lake Charles	LA	70601	337-436-9588	494-7952
TF: 800-456-7952 ■ *Web:* www.visitlakecharles.org					
Lake Placid Convention & Visitors Bureau 49 Parkside Dr	Lake Placid	NY	12946	518-523-2445	523-2605
TF: 800-447-5224 ■ *Web:* www.lakeplacid.com					
Pennsylvania Dutch Convention & Visitors Bureau 501 Greenfield Rd	Lancaster	PA	17601	717-299-8901	299-0470
TF: 800-723-8824 ■ *Web:* www.padutchcountry.com					

			Phone	Fax
Chicago Southland Convention & Visitors Bureau 2304 173rd St. . . . . Lansing *TF:* 888-895-8233 ■ *Web:* www.cscvb.com	IL	60438	708-895-8200	895-8288
Greater Lansing Convention & Visitors Bureau 500 E Michigan Ave Suite 180 . . . . . Lansing *TF:* 888-252-6746 ■ *Web:* www.lansing.org	MI	48912	517-487-0077	487-5151
Prince George's County Conference & Visitors Bureau 9200 Basil Ct Suite 101 . . . . . Largo *TF:* 888-925-8300 ■ *Web:* www.visitprincegeorges.com	MD	20774	301-925-8300	925-2053
Las Cruces Convention & Visitors Bureau 211 N Water St. . . . . Las Cruces *TF:* 800-343-7827 ■ *Web:* www.lascrucescvb.org	NM	88001	575-541-2444	541-2164
Las Vegas Convention & Visitors Authority 3275 Paradise Rd. . . . . Las Vegas *TF:* 877-847-4858 ■ *Web:* www.lvcva.com	NV	89109	702-892-0711	892-2824
Lawrence Visitor Information Ctr 402 N 2nd St . . . . . Lawrence *Web:* www.visitlawrence.com	KS	66044	785-865-4499	865-4488
Leavenworth Convention & Visitors Bureau 518 Shawnee St PO Box 44 . . . . . Leavenworth *TF:* 800-844-4114 ■ *Web:* www.visitleavenworthks.com	KS	66048	913-682-4113	682-8170
Boone County Convention & Visitors Bureau 101 E Main St. . . . . Lebanon *TF:* 800-852-9506 ■ *Web:* www.boonecvb.com	IN	46052	765-484-8572	
Lenexa Convention & Visitors Bureau 11180 Lackman Rd. . . . . Lenexa *TF:* 800-950-7867 ■ *Web:* www.lenexa.org	KS	66219	913-888-1414	888-3770
Greenbrier County Convention & Visitors Bureau 540 N Jefferson St Suite N . . . . . Lewisburg *TF:* 800-833-2068 ■ *Web:* www.greenbrierwv.com	WV	24901	304-645-1000	647-3001
Juniata River Valley Visitors Bureau (JRVVB) Historic Courthouse 1 W Market St Suite 103. . . . . Lewistown *TF:* 877-568-9739 ■ *Web:* www.juniatarivervalley.org	PA	17044	717-248-6713	248-6714
Lexington Convention & Visitors Bureau 301 E Vine St . . . . . Lexington *TF:* 800-845-3959 ■ *Web:* www.visitlex.com	KY	40507	859-233-7299	254-4555
Laurel Highlands Visitors Bureau 120 E Main St. . . . . Ligonier *TF:* 800-333-5661 ■ *Web:* www.laurelhighlands.org	PA	15658	724-238-5661	238-3673
Lima/Allen County Convention & Visitors Bureau 144 S Main St Suite 101. . . . . Lima *TF:* 888-222-6075 ■ *Web:* www.lima-allencvb.com	OH	45801	419-222-6075	222-0134
Abraham Lincoln Tourism Bureau of Logan County 1555 5th St. . . . . Lincoln	IL	62656	217-732-8687	735-9205
Lincoln Convention & Visitors Bureau 1135 M St Suite 300. . . . . Lincoln *TF:* 800-423-8212 ■ *Web:* www.lincoln.org	NE	68508	402-434-5335	436-2360
Lincoln City Visitor & Convention Bureau 801 SW Hwy 101 Suite 401 . . . . . Lincoln City *TF:* 800-452-2151 ■ *Web:* www.oregoncoast.org	OR	97367	541-996-4274	994-2408
Lisle Convention & Visitors Bureau 4746 Main St . . . . . Lisle *TF:* 800-733-9811 ■ *Web:* www.lislecvb.com	IL	60532	630-769-1000	769-1006
Western CT Convention & Visitors Bureau PO Box 968 . . . . . Litchfield *Web:* www.northwestct.com	CT	06759	860-567-4506	567-5214
Little Rock Convention & Visitors Bureau 426 W Markham St PO Box 3232. . . . . Little Rock *TF:* 800-844-4781 ■ *Web:* www.littlerock.com	AR	72203	501-376-4781	374-2255
Lodi Conference & Visitors Bureau 115 S School St Suite 9 . . . . . Lodi *TF:* 800-798-1810 ■ *Web:* www.visitlodi.com	CA	95240	209-365-1195	365-1191
London/Laurel County Tourist Commission 140 Faith Assembly Church Rd . . . . . London *TF:* 800-348-0095 ■ *Web:* www.laurelkytourism.com	KY	40741	606-878-6900	877-1689
Long Beach Convention & Visitors Bureau 301 E Ocean Blvd . . . . . Long Beach *TF:* 800-452-7829 ■ *Web:* www.visitlongbeach.com	CA	90802	562-436-3645	435-5653
Los Angeles Convention & Visitors Bureau 333 S Hope St 18th Fl . . . . . Los Angeles *TF:* 800-228-2452 ■ *Web:* www.discoverlosangeles.com	CA	90071	213-624-7300	452-1403
Louisville & Jefferson County Convention & Visitors Bureau 401 W Main St Suite 2300 . . . . . Louisville *TF:* 800-626-5646 ■ *Web:* www.gotolouisville.com	KY	40202	502-584-2121	584-6697
Greater Merrimack Valley Convention & Visitors Bureau 40 French St 2nd Fl . . . . . Lowell *TF:* 800-443-3332 ■ *Web:* www.merrimackvalley.org	MA	01852	978-459-6150	459-4595
Lubbock Convention & Visitors Bureau 1500 Broadway St 6th Fl. . . . . Lubbock *TF:* 800-692-4035 ■ *Web:* www.visitlubbock.org	TX	79401	806-747-5232	747-1419
Lufkin Visitor & Convention Bureau 1615 S Chestnut St PO Box 1606. . . . . Lufkin *TF:* 800-409-5659 ■ *Web:* www.visitlufkin.com	TX	75901	936-634-6305	634-8726
Lumberton Area Visitors Bureau 3431 Lackey St. . . . . Lumberton *TF:* 800-359-6971 ■ *Web:* www.lumberton-nc.com	NC	28360	910-739-9999	739-9777
Mackinaw Area Visitors Bureau 10800 US 23 . . . . . Mackinaw City *TF:* 800-666-0160 ■ *Web:* www.mackinawcity.com	MI	49701	231-436-5664	436-5991
Macomb Area Convention & Visitors Bureau 201 S Lafayette St. . . . . Macomb *Web:* www.makeitmacomb.com	IL	61455	309-833-1315	833-3575
Macon-Bibb County Convention/Visitors Bureau 450 Martin Luther King Jr Blvd. . . . . Macon *TF:* 800-768-3401 ■ *Web:* www.maconga.org	GA	31201	478-743-1074	745-2022
Greater Madison Convention & Visitors Bureau 615 E Washington Ave . . . . . Madison *TF:* 800-373-6376 ■ *Web:* www.visitmadison.com	WI	53703	608-255-2537	258-4950
Madison Convention & Visitors Bureau 115 E Jefferson St. . . . . Madison *TF:* 800-709-7406 ■ *Web:* www.madisonga.org	GA	30650	706-342-4454	342-4455
Maggie Valley Area Convention & Visitors Bureau 2511 Soco Rd PO Box 279. . . . . Maggie Valley *TF:* 800-624-4431 ■ *Web:* www.maggievalley.org	NC	28751	828-926-1686	926-9398
Saint Tammany Parish Tourist & Convention Commission 68099 Hwy 59 . . . . . Mandeville *TF:* 800-634-9443 ■ *Web:* www.louisiananorthshore.com	LA	70471	985-892-0520	892-1441
Manhattan Convention & Visitors Bureau 501 Poyntz Ave. . . . . Manhattan *TF:* 800-759-0134 ■ *Web:* www.manhattancvb.org	KS	66502	785-776-8829	776-0679
Manitowoc Visitor & Convention Bureau 4221 Calumet Ave. . . . . Manitowoc *TF:* 800-627-4896 ■ *Web:* www.manitowoc.org	WI	54220	920-683-4388	683-4876
Greater Mankato Growth 1961 Premier Dr. . . . . Mankato *TF:* 800-657-4733 ■ *Web:* www.greatermankato.com	MN	56001	507-385-6640	345-4451
Mansfield/Richland County Convention & Visitors Bureau 124 N Main St . . . . . Mansfield *TF:* 800-642-8282 ■ *Web:* www.mansfieldtourism.com	OH	44902	419-525-1300	524-7722
Outer Banks Visitors Bureau 1 Visitor Ctr Cir . . . . . Manteo *TF:* 877-629-4386 ■ *Web:* www.outerbanks.org	NC	27954	252-473-2138	473-5777
Marion-Grant County Convention & Visitors Bureau 428 S Washington St Suite 261 . . . . . Marion *TF:* 800-662-9474 ■ *Web:* www.showmegrantcounty.com	IN	46953	765-668-5435	668-5424
Williamson County Tourism Bureau 1602 Sioux Dr . . . . . Marion *TF:* 800-433-7399 ■ *Web:* www.visitsi.com	IL	62959	618-997-3690	997-1874
Marquette Country Convention & Visitors Bureau 337 W Washington St. . . . . Marquette *TF:* 800-544-4321 ■ *Web:* www.marquettecountry.org	MI	49855	906-228-7749	228-3642
Marshall Area Convention & Visitors Bureau 317 W Main St . . . . . Marshall *Web:* www.marshall-mn.org	MN	56258	507-532-4484	532-4485
Marshfield Convention & Visitors Bureau 700 S Central Ave. . . . . Marshfield *TF:* 800-422-4541 ■ *Web:* www.marshfieldchamber.com	WI	54449	715-384-3454	387-8925
Mason City Convention & Visitors Bureau 25 W State St . . . . . Mason City *TF:* 800-423-5724 ■ *Web:* www.visitmasoncityiowa.com	IA	50401	641-422-1663	423-5725
Fairfax County Convention & Visitors Bureau (FXVA) 7927 Jones Branch Dr Suite S-100 . . . . . McLean *TF:* 800-732-4732 ■ *Web:* www.fxva.com	VA	22102	703-790-0643	790-5097
Melbourne Regional Chamber of East Central Florida 1005 E Strawbridge Ave . . . . . Melbourne *TF:* 800-771-9922 ■ *Web:* www.melpb-chamber.org	FL	32901	321-724-5400	725-2093
Memphis Convention & Visitors Bureau 47 Union Ave . . . . . Memphis *TF:* 888-633-9099 ■ *Web:* www.memphistravel.com	TN	38103	901-543-5300	543-5350
Merced Conference & Visitors Bureau (MCVB) 710 W 16th St. . . . . Merced *TF:* 800-446-5353 ■ *Web:* www.yosemite-gateway.org	CA	95340	209-384-2791	384-2793
Meridian/Lauderdale County Tourism Bureau 212 Constitution Ave PO Box 5313 . . . . . Meridian *TF:* 888-868-7720 ■ *Web:* www.visitmeridian.com	MS	39302	601-482-8001	486-4988
Mesa Convention & Visitors Bureau 120 N Ctr St . . . . . Mesa *TF:* 800-283-6372 ■ *Web:* www.visitmesa.com	AZ	85201	480-827-4700	827-4704
Greater Miami Convention & Visitors Bureau 701 Brickell Ave Suite 2700 . . . . . Miami *TF:* 800-933-8448 ■ *Web:* www.miamiandbeaches.com	FL	33131	305-539-3000	530-5859
Puerto Rico Convention Bureau 10544 NW 26th St Suite E-203. . . . . Miami *TF:* 800-875-4765 ■ *Web:* www.meetpuertorico.com	FL	33172	305-471-0202	
LaPorte County Convention & Visitors Bureau 4073 S Franklin St . . . . . Michigan City *TF:* 800-634-2650 ■ *Web:* www.michigancitylaporte.com	IN	46360	219-872-5055	872-3660
Middletown Convention & Visitors Bureau (MCVB) PO Box 1245 . . . . . Middletown *TF:* 888-462-2282 ■ *Web:* www.mcvbcorporate.org	OH	45042	513-860-4194	860-4195
Midland County Convention & Visitors Bureau 300 Rodd St Suite 101 . . . . . Midland *TF:* 888-464-3526 ■ *Web:* www.visitgreatlakesbay.org	MI	48640	989-839-0340	835-3701
Milledgeville-Baldwin County Convention & Visitors Bureau 200 W Hancock St . . . . . Milledgeville *TF:* 800-653-1804 ■ *Web:* www.visitmilledgeville.org	GA	31061	478-452-4687	453-4440
Greater Milwaukee Convention & Visitors Bureau 648 N Plankinton Ave Suite 425. . . . . Milwaukee *TF:* 800-554-1448 ■ *Web:* www.visitmilwaukee.org	WI	53203	414-273-7222	273-5596
Meet Minneapolis 250 Marquette Ave Suite 1300. . . . . Minneapolis *TF:* 800-445-7412 ■ *Web:* www.minneapolis.org	MN	55401	612-767-8000	335-5839
Minneapolis Northwest 6200 Shingle Creek Pkwy. . . . . Minneapolis *TF:* 800-541-4364 ■ *Web:* www.minneapolisnorthwest.com	MN	55430	763-566-7722	566-6526
Minot Convention & Visitors Bureau 1020 S Broadway . . . . . Minot *TF:* 800-264-2626 ■ *Web:* www.visitminot.org	ND	58701	701-857-8206	857-8228
Missoula Convention & Visitors Bureau 1121 E Broadway Suite 103 . . . . . Missoula *TF:* 800-526-3465 ■ *Web:* www.missoulacvb.org	MT	59802	406-532-3250	532-3252
Mobile Bay Convention & Visitors Bureau PO Box 204 . . . . . Mobile *TF:* 800-566-2453 ■ *Web:* www.mobile.org	AL	36601	251-208-2000	208-2060
Modesto Convention & Visitors Bureau 1150 9th St Suite C . . . . . Modesto *TF:* 888-640-8467 ■ *Web:* www.visitmodesto.com	CA	95354	209-526-5588	526-5586
Quad Cities Convention & Visitors Bureau 1601 River Dr Suite 110. . . . . Moline *TF:* 800-747-7800 ■ *Web:* www.visitquadcities.com	IL	61265	309-277-0937	764-9443
Monterey County Convention & Visitors Bureau PO Box 1770 . . . . . Monterey *TF:* 888-221-1010 ■ *Web:* www.seemonterey.com	CA	93942	831-657-6400	648-5373
Montgomery Area Chamber of Commerce Convention & Visitor Bureau 300 Water St. . . . . Montgomery *TF:* 800-240-9452 ■ *Web:* www.visitingmontgomery.com	AL	36104	334-261-1100	261-1111

			Phone	Fax
Greater Montreal Convention & Tourism Bureau PO Box 979 . . . . Montreal *TF:* 800-051-7055 ■ *Web:* www.tourisme-montreal.org	QC	H3C2W3	514-873-2015	864-3838
Montrose Visitor & Convention Bureau 1519 E Main St. Montrose *TF:* 800-873-0244 ■ *Web:* www.visitmontrose.com	CO	81401	970-252-0505	249-2907
Greater Morgantown Convention & Visitors Bureau 68 Donley St. Morgantown *TF:* 800-458-7373 ■ *Web:* www.tourmorgantown.com	WV	26501	304-292-5081	291-1354
Knox County Convention & Visitors Bureau 107 S Main St. Mount Vernon *TF:* 800-837-5282 ■ *Web:* www.visitknoxohio.org	OH	43050	740-392-6102	392-7840
Mount Vernon Convention & Visitors Bureau 200 Potomac Blvd . . . . Mount Vernon *TF:* 800-252-5464 ■ *Web:* www.mtvernon.com	IL	62864	618-242-3151	242-6849
Muncie Visitors Bureau 425 N High St. . . . . Muncie *TF:* 800-568-6862 ■ *Web:* www.munciecvb.org	IN	47305	765-284-2700	284-3002
Muskegon County Convention & Visitors Bureau 610 W Western Ave. Muskegon *TF:* 800-250-9283 ■ *Web:* www.visitmuskegon.org	MI	49440	231-724-3100	724-1398
Myrtle Beach Area Convention Bureau 1200 N Oak St . . . . Myrtle Beach *TF:* 800-356-3016 ■ *Web:* www.visitmyrtlebeach.com	SC	29577	843-626-7444	448-3010
Connecticut's Mystic & More! 27 Coogan Blvd Bldg 3A . . . . Mystic *TF:* 800-863-6569 ■ *Web:* www.mystic.org	CT	06355	860-536-8822	536-8855
Nacogdoches Convention & Visitors Bureau 200 E Main St. Nacogdoches *TF:* 888-653-3788 ■ *Web:* www.visitnacogdoches.org	TX	75961	936-564-7351	462-7688
Napa Valley Conference & Visitors Bureau 600 Main St . . . . Napa *Web:* www.legendarynapavalley.com	CA	94559	707-251-5895	
Greater Naples Marco Island Everglades Convention & Visitors Bureau 2800 Horseshoe Dr. Naples *TF:* 800-688-3600 ■ *Web:* www.paradisecoast.com	FL	34104	239-252-2384	252-2404
Brown County Convention & Visitors Bureau 10 N Van Buren St PO Box 840 . . . . Nashville *TF:* 800-753-3255 ■ *Web:* www.browncounty.com	IN	47448	812-988-7303	988-1070
Nashville Convention & Visitors Bureau (NCVB) 150 4th Ave N Suite G250 . . . . Nashville *TF:* 800-657-6910 ■ *Web:* www.visitmusiccity.com	TN	37219	615-259-4730	259-4126
Natchez Convention & Visitors Bureau 640 S Canal St . . . . Natchez *TF:* 800-647-6724 ■ *Web:* www.visitnatchez.org	MS	39120	601-446-6345	442-0814
Craven County Convention & Visitors Bureau 203 S Front St . . . . New Bern *TF:* 800-437-5767 ■ *Web:* www.visitnewbern.com	NC	28560	252-637-9400	637-0250
Greater New Braunfels Chamber of Commerce Inc The 390 S Seguin Ave PO Box 311417. . . . . New Braunfels *TF:* 800-572-2626 ■ *Web:* www.nbcham.org	TX	78130	830-625-2385	625-7918
Convention & Visitors Bureau of Henry County 2020 S Memorial Dr Suite I . . . . New Castle *TF:* 888-676-4302 ■ *Web:* www.henrycountyin.org	IN	47362	765-593-0764	593-0766
Lawrence County Tourist Promotion Agency 229 S Jefferson St . . . . New Castle *TF:* 888-284-7599 ■ *Web:* www.visitlawrencecounty.com	PA	16101	724-654-8408	654-2044
Greater New Haven Convention & Visitors Bureau 169 Orange St. New Haven	CT	06510	203-777-8550	782-7755
Jefferson Convention & Visitors Bureau 1221 Elmwood Pk Blvd Suite 411. . . . . New Orleans *TF:* 877-572-7474 ■ *Web:* www.experiencejefferson.com	LA	70123	504-731-7083	731-7089
New Orleans Metropolitan Convention & Visitors Bureau 2020 St Charles Ave. New Orleans *TF:* 800-672-6124 ■ *Web:* www.neworleanscvb.com	LA	70130	504-566-5011	566-5046
NYC & Co 810 7th Ave 3rd Fl . . . . New York *Web:* www.nycgo.com	NY	10019	212-484-1200	397-1931
Newberry Area Tourism Assn 4947 E County Rd 460 . . . . Newberry *TF:* 800-831-7292 ■ *Web:* www.exploringthenorth.com	MI	49868	906-293-5739	293-5739
Newport County Convention & Visitors Bureau 23 America's Cup Ave. Newport *TF:* 800-976-5122 ■ *Web:* www.gonewport.com	RI	02840	401-849-8048	849-0291
Newport Beach Conference & Visitors Bureau 1200 Newport Ctr Dr Suite 120. . . . . Newport Beach *TF:* 800-942-6278 ■ *Web:* www.visitnewportbeach.com	CA	92660	949-719-6100	719-6101
Newport News Tourism Development Office 700 Town Ctr Dr Suite 320. . . . . Newport News *TF:* 888-493-7386 ■ *Web:* www.newport-news.org	VA	23606	757-926-1400	926-1441
Newton Convention & Visitor Bureau 113 1st Ave W. Newton *TF:* 800-798-0299 ■ *Web:* www.visitnewton.com	IA	50208	641-792-0299	791-0879
Niagara Tourism & Convention Corp 10 Rainbow Blvd. Niagara Falls *TF:* 800-338-7890 ■ *Web:* www.niagara-usa.com	NY	14303	716-282-8992	285-0809
Four Flags Area Council on Tourism 404 E Main St. Niles *Web:* www.fourflagsarea.org	MI	49120	269-684-7444	683-3722
Nome Convention & Visitors Bureau 301 Front St PO Box 240 HP-N . . . . Nome *Web:* www.visitnomealaska.com	AK	99762	907-443-6624	443-5832
Norfolk Area Chamber of Commerce 405 Madison Ave . . . . Norfolk *TF:* 888-371-2932 ■ *Web:* www.norfolk.ne.us	NE	68701	402-371-4862	371-0182
Norfolk Convention & Visitors Bureau 232 E Main St. Norfolk *TF:* 800-368-3097 ■ *Web:* www.visitnorfolktoday.com	VA	23510	757-664-6620	622-3663
Norman Convention & Visitors Bureau 223 E Main St. Norman *TF:* 800-767-7260 ■ *Web:* www.visitnorman.com	OK	73069	405-366-8095	366-8096
Lincoln County Convention & Visitor's Bureau 219 S Dewey. North Platte *Web:* www.visitnorthplatte.com	NE	69101	308-532-4729	532-5914
North Ridgeville Visitors Bureau 34845 Lorain Rd. North Ridgeville *Web:* www.nrchamber.com	OH	44039	440-327-3737	327-1474
DuPage Convention & Visitors Bureau 915 Harger Rd Suite 240 . . . . Oak Brook *TF:* 800-232-0502 ■ *Web:* www.dupagecvb.com	IL	60523	630-575-8070	575-8078
Oak Park Area Convention & Visitors Bureau 1118 Westgate . . . . Oak Park *TF:* 888-625-7275 ■ *Web:* www.visitoakpark.com	IL	60301	708-524-7800	524-7473
Oak Ridge Convention & Visitors Bureau 102 Robertsville Rd Suite C . . . . Oak Ridge *TF:* 800-887-3429 ■ *Web:* www.oakridgevisitor.com	TN	37830	865-482-7821	481-3543
Yosemite Sierra Visitors Bureau 40637 Hwy 41 . . . . Oakhurst *Web:* www.yosemitethisyear.com	CA	93644	559-683-4636	683-5697
Oakland Convention & Visitors Bureau 463 11th St. Oakland *Web:* www.visitoakland.org	CA	94607	510-839-9000	839-5924
Ocean City Convention & Visitors Bureau 4001 Coastal Hwy. Ocean City *TF:* 800-626-2326 ■ *Web:* www.ococean.com	MD	21842	410-289-8181	723-8655
Oconomowoc Convention & Visitors Bureau 174 E Wisconsin Ave . . . . Oconomowoc *TF:* 800-524-3744 ■ *Web:* www.oconomowocusa.com	WI	53066	262-569-2186	569-3238
Odessa Convention & Visitors Bureau 700 N Grant Ave Suite 200 . . . . Odessa *TF:* 800-780-4678 ■ *Web:* www.odessacvb.com	TX	79761	432-333-7871	333-7858
Ogden/Weber Convention & Visitors Bureau 2438 Washington Blvd . . . . Ogden *TF:* 800-255-8824 ■ *Web:* www.ogdencvb.org	UT	84401	801-778-6250	399-0783
Oklahoma City Convention & Visitors Bureau 123 Pk Ave . . . . Oklahoma City *TF:* 800-225-5652 ■ *Web:* www.visitokc.com	OK	73102	405-297-8912	297-8888
McDowell County Tourism Development Authority 25 W Main St . . . . Old Fort *TF:* 888-233-6111 ■ *Web:* www.mcdowellnc.org	NC	28762	828-668-4282	668-4924
Olympia Lacey Tumwater Visitor & Convention Bureau 103 Sid Snyder Ave SW . . . . Olympia *TF:* 877-704-7500 ■ *Web:* www.visitolympia.com	WA	98501	360-704-7544	704-7533
Greater Omaha Convention & Visitors Bureau 1001 Farnam St Suite 200 . . . . Omaha *TF:* 866-937-6624 ■ *Web:* www.visitomaha.com	NE	68102	402-444-4660	444-4511
Onalaska Center for Commerce & Tourism 1101 Main St . . . . Onalaska *TF:* 800-873-1901 ■ *Web:* www.discoveronalaska.com	WI	54650	608-781-9570	781-9572
Ontario Convention & Visitors Bureau 2000 E Convention Ctr Way . . . . Ontario *TF:* 800-455-5755 ■ *Web:* www.ontariocc.com	CA	91764	909-937-3000	937-3080
Ontario Convention & Visitors Bureau 876 SW 4th Ave . . . . Ontario *TF:* 866-989-8012 ■ *Web:* www.ontariochamber.com	OR	97914	541-889-8012	889-8331
Orlando/Orange County Convention & Visitors Bureau Inc 6700 Forum Dr Suite 100. . . . . Orlando *TF:* 800-972-3304 ■ *Web:* www.visitorlando.com	FL	32821	407-363-5872	370-5000
Lake of the Ozarks Convention & Visitors Bureau 5815 Hwy 54 PO Box 1498. . . . . Osage Beach *TF:* 800-386-5253 ■ *Web:* www.funlake.com	MO	65065	573-348-1599	348-2293
Ottawa Tourism & Convention Authority 130 Albert St Suite 1800. . . . . Ottawa *TF:* 800-363-4465 ■ *Web:* www.ottawatourism.ca	ON	K1P5G4	613-237-5150	237-7339
Ottawa Visitors Ctr 106 W Lafayette St . . . . Ottawa *TF:* 888-688-2924 ■ *Web:* www.experienceottawa.com	IL	61350	815-434-2737	434-5477
Overland Park Convention & Visitors Bureau 9001 W 110th St Suite 100. . . . . Overland Park *TF:* 800-262-7275 ■ *Web:* www.visitoverlandpark.com	KS	66210	913-491-0123	491-0015
Owensboro-Davies County Tourist Commission 215 E 2nd St. Owensboro *TF:* 800-489-1131 ■ *Web:* www.visitowensboro.com	KY	42303	270-926-1100	926-1161
Oxford Convention & Visitors Bureau 102 Ed Perry Blvd. Oxford *TF:* 800-758-9177 ■ *Web:* www.oxfordcvb.com	MS	38655	662-232-2367	
Oxnard Convention & Visitors Bureau 1000 Town Ctr Dr Suite 130 . . . . Oxnard *TF:* 800-269-6273 ■ *Web:* www.visitoxnard.com	CA	93036	805-385-7545	385-7571
Panama City Beach Convention & Visitors Bureau 17001 Panama City Beach Pkwy. . . . . Panama City Beach *TF:* 800-722-3224 ■ *Web:* www.visitpanamacitybeach.com	FL	32413	850-233-5070	233-5072
Paris Convention & Visitors Bureau 8 W Plaza . . . . Paris *TF:* 800-727-4789 ■ *Web:* www.paristexas.com	TX	75460	903-784-2501	784-2503
Park City Chamber of Commerce/Convention & Visitors Bureau 1910 Prospector Ave PO Box 1630. . . . . Park City *TF:* 800-453-1360 ■ *Web:* www.parkcityinfo.com	UT	84060	435-649-6100	649-4132
Greater Parkersburg Convention & Visitors Bureau 350 7th St. Parkersburg *TF:* 800-752-4982 ■ *Web:* www.greaterparkersburg.com	WV	26101	304-428-1130	428-8117
Pasadena Convention & Visitors Bureau 300 E Green St . . . . Pasadena *TF:* 800-307-7977 ■ *Web:* www.visitpasadena.com	CA	91101	626-795-9311	795-9656
Pensacola Convention & Visitors Bureau 1401 E Gregory St . . . . Pensacola *TF:* 800-874-1234 ■ *Web:* www.visitpensacola.com	FL	32502	850-434-1234	432-8211
Peoria Area Convention & Visitors Bureau 456 Fulton St Suite 300 . . . . Peoria *TF:* 800-747-0302 ■ *Web:* www.peoria.org	IL	61602	309-676-0303	676-8470
Perry Area Convention & Visitors Bureau 101 Gen Courtney Hodges Blvd PO Box 1609 . . . . Perry *Web:* www.perryga.com	GA	31069	478-988-8000	988-8005
Petoskey Area Visitors Bureau 401 E Mitchell St . . . . Petoskey *TF:* 800-845-2828 ■ *Web:* www.petoskeyarea.com	MI	49770	231-348-2755	348-1810
Philadelphia Convention & Visitors Bureau 1700 Market St Suite 3000. . . . . Philadelphia *TF:* 800-225-5745 ■ *Web:* www.philadelphiausa.travel	PA	19103	215-636-3300	636-3327

	City	State	Zip	Phone	Fax
Greater Phoenix Convention & Visitors Bureau 400 E Van Buren St Suite 600 *TF:* 877-225-5749 ■ *Web:* www.visitphoenix.com	Phoenix	AZ	85004	602-254-6500	253-4415
Pierre Convention & Visitors Bureau 800 W Dakota Ave *TF:* 800-962-2034 ■ *Web:* www.pierre.org	Pierre	SD	57501	605-224-7361	224-6485
Pigeon Forge Dept of Tourism 2450 Pkwy *TF:* 800-251-9100 ■ *Web:* www.mypigeonforge.com	Pigeon Forge	TN	37863	865-453-8574	429-7362
Pine Bluff Convention & Visitors Bureau (PBCVB) 1 Convention Ctr Plaza *TF:* 800-536-7660 ■ *Web:* www.pinebluffcvb.org	Pine Bluff	AR	71601	870-536-7600	850-2105
Greater Pittsburgh Convention & Visitors Bureau 425 6th Ave 30th Fl *TF:* 800-359-0758 ■ *Web:* www.visitpittsburgh.com	Pittsburgh	PA	15219	412-281-7711	644-5512
Plano Convention & Visitors Bureau 2000 E Spring Creek Pkwy *TF:* 800-817-5266 ■ *Web:* www.planocvb.com	Plano	TX	75074	972-941-5840	424-0002
Pocatello Convention & Visitors Bureau 324 S Main St Suite B *TF:* 877-922-7659 ■ *Web:* www.pocatellocvb.com	Pocatello	ID	83204	208-235-7659	233-1527
Ponca City Tourism 420 E Grand Ave *TF:* 866-763-8092 ■ *Web:* www.poncacitytourism.com	Ponca City	OK	74602	580-765-4400	765-2798
North Olympic Peninsula Visitor & Convention Bureau 338 W 1st St Suite 104 *TF:* 800-942-4042 ■ *Web:* www.olympicpeninsula.org/vcb	Port Angeles	WA	98362	360-452-8552	452-7383
Port Arthur Convention & Visitors Bureau 3401 Cultural Ctr Dr *TF:* 800-235-7822 ■ *Web:* www.portarthurtexas.com	Port Arthur	TX	77642	409-985-7822	985-5584
Lake Erie Shores & Islands Welcome Ctr 770 SE Catawba Rd *TF:* 800-441-1271 ■ *Web:* www.lake-erie.com	Port Clinton	OH	43452	419-734-4386	734-9798
Blue Water Area Convention & Visitors Bureau 520 Thomas Edison Pkwy *TF:* 800-852-4242 ■ *Web:* www.bluewater.org	Port Huron	MI	48060	810-987-8687	987-1441
Indiana Dunes the Casual Coast 1215 N State Rd 49 *TF:* 800-283-8687 ■ *Web:* www.indianadunes.com	Porter	IN	46304	219-926-2255	929-5395
Greater Portland Convention & Visitors Bureau 94 Commercial St Suite 300 *Web:* www.visitportland.com	Portland	ME	04101	207-772-4994	874-9043
Travel Portland 1000 SW Broadway Suite 2300 *TF:* 800-962-3700 ■ *Web:* www.travelportland.com	Portland	OR	97205	503-275-9750	275-9284
Portsmouth Convention & Visitors Bureau 6 Crawford Pkwy *TF:* 800-767-8782 ■ *Web:* www.portsmouthva.gov	Portsmouth	VA	23704	757-393-5111	393-5330
Providence Warwick Convention & Visitors Bureau 144 Westminster St *TF:* 800-233-1636 ■ *Web:* www.goprovidence.com	Providence	RI	02903	401-456-0200	351-2090
Utah Valley Convention & Visitors Bureau 111 S University Ave *TF:* 800-222-8824 ■ *Web:* www.utahvalley.com	Provo	UT	84601	801-851-2100	851-2109
Greater Pueblo Chamber of Commerce & Visitors Council 302 N Santa Fe Ave *TF:* 800-233-3446 ■ *Web:* www.pueblochamber.org	Pueblo	CO	81003	719-542-1704	542-1624
Quebec City Tourism 399 St Joseph St E *TF:* 877-783-1608 ■ *Web:* www.quebecregion.com/en	Quebec	QC	G1K8E2	418-641-6654	641-6578
Plumas County Visitors Bureau 550 Crescent St *TF:* 800-326-2247 ■ *Web:* www.plumascounty.org	Quincy	CA	95971	530-283-6345	283-5465
Quincy Convention & Visitors Bureau 532 Gardner Expy *TF:* 800-978-4748 ■ *Web:* www.quincy-cvb.org	Quincy	IL	62301	217-214-3700	214-2721
Greater Raleigh Convention & Visitors Bureau 421 Fayetteville St Mall Suite 1505 *TF:* 800-849-8499 ■ *Web:* www.visitraleigh.com	Raleigh	NC	27602	919-834-5900	831-2887
Palm Springs Desert Resorts Convention & Visitors Authority 70-100 Hwy 111 *TF:* 800-967-3767 ■ *Web:* www.palmspringsusa.com	Rancho Mirage	CA	92270	760-770-9000	770-3029
Rapid City Convention & Visitors Bureau 444 Mt Rushmore Rd N *TF:* 800-487-3223 ■ *Web:* www.visitrapidcity.com	Rapid City	SD	57701	605-718-8484	348-9217
Reading & Berks County Visitors Bureau 2525 N 12th St Suite 101 *TF:* 800-443-6610 ■ *Web:* www.readingberkspa.com	Reading	PA	19605	610-375-4085	375-9606
Redding Convention & Visitors Bureau 840 Sundial Bridge Dr *TF:* 888-225-4130 ■ *Web:* www.reddingconventioncenter.com	Redding	CA	96001	530-225-4100	225-4354
Rehoboth Beach Convention Ctr 229 Rehoboth Ave *Web:* www.cityofrehoboth.com	Rehoboth Beach	DE	19971	302-227-4641	227-4643
Reno-Sparks Convention & Visitors Authority PO Box 837 *TF:* 800-443-1482 ■ *Web:* www.visitrenotahoe.com	Reno	NV	89504	775-827-7600	827-7678
Richardson Convention & Visitors Bureau 411 W Arapaho Rd Suite 105 *TF:* 888-690-7287 ■ *Web:* www.richardsontexas.org	Richardson	TX	75080	972-744-4034	744-5834
Richmond Metropolitan Convention & Visitors Bureau 401 N 3rd St *TF:* 800-370-9004 ■ *Web:* www.visit.richmond.com	Richmond	VA	23219	804-782-2777	780-2577
Richmond/Wayne County Convention & Tourism Bureau 5701 National Rd E *TF:* 800-828-8414 ■ *Web:* www.visitrichmond.org	Richmond	IN	47374	765-935-8687	935-0440
Ridgecrest Area Convention & Visitors Bureau (RACVB) 139 Balsam St Suite 1700 *TF:* 800-847-4830 ■ *Web:* www.visitdeserts.com	Ridgecrest	CA	93555	760-375-8202	375-9850
Rising Sun/Ohio County Convention Tourism & Visitors Commission 120 N Walnut St PO Box 112 *TF:* 888-776-4786 ■ *Web:* www.enjoyrisingsun.com	Rising Sun	IN	47040	812-438-4933	438-4932
Riverside Convention & Visitors Bureau 3750 University Ave Suite 175 *TF:* 888-748-7733 ■ *Web:* www.riversidecvb.com	Riverside	CA	92501	951-222-4700	222-4712
Roanoke Valley Convention & Visitors Bureau 101 Shenandoah Ave NE *TF:* 800-635-5535 ■ *Web:* www.visitroanokeva.com	Roanoke	VA	24016	540-342-6025	342-7119
Rochester Convention & Visitors Bureau 30 Civic Ctr Dr SE Suite 200 *TF:* 800-634-8277 ■ *Web:* www.rochestercvb.org	Rochester	MN	55904	507-288-4331	288-9144
Visit Rochester 45 E Ave Suite 400 *TF:* 800-677-7282 ■ *Web:* www.visitrochester.com	Rochester	NY	14604	585-279-8300	232-4822
Rockhill-York County Convention & Visitors Bureau 452 S Anderson Rd *TF:* 800-702-1320 ■ *Web:* www.visityorkcounty.com	Rock Hill	SC	29730	803-329-5200	329-0145
Rockford Area Convention & Visitors Bureau 102 N Main St *TF:* 800-521-0849 ■ *Web:* www.gorockford.com	Rockford	IL	61101	815-963-8111	963-4298
Conference & Visitors Bureau of Montgomery County MD Inc 111 Rockville Pike Suite 800 *TF:* 877-789-6904 ■ *Web:* www.visitmontgomery.com	Rockville	MD	20850	240-777-2060	777-2065
Nash County Visitors Bureau 107 Gateway Blvd PO Box 7637 *TF:* 800-849-6825 ■ *Web:* www.rockymounttravel.com	Rocky Mount	NC	27804	252-972-5080	972-5090
Greater Rome Convention & Visitors Bureau 402 Civics Ctr Dr *TF:* 800-444-1834 ■ *Web:* www.romegeorgia.org	Rome	GA	30161	706-295-5576	236-5029
Rosemont Convention Bureau 9301 Bryn Mawr Ave *Web:* www.rosemont.com	Rosemont	IL	60018	847-823-2100	696-9700
Historic Roswell Convention & Visitors Bureau 617 Atlanta St *TF:* 800-776-7935 ■ *Web:* www.visitroswellga.com	Roswell	GA	30075	770-640-3253	640-3252
Wausau Central Wisconsin Convention & Visitors Bureau (CWCVB) 10204 Pk Plaza Suite B *TF:* 888-948-4748 ■ *Web:* www.visitwausau.com	Rothschild	WI	54474	715-355-8788	359-2306
Greater Rugby Area Convention & Visitors Bureau 224 Hwy 2 SW *Web:* www.rugbynothdakota.com	Rugby	ND	58368	701-776-5846	776-6390
Rutherford County Tourism Development Authority 117 W Ct St *TF:* 800-849-5998 ■ *Web:* www.rutherfordtourism.com	Rutherfordton	NC	28139	828-287-6113	247-0499
Sacramento Convention & Visitors Bureau 1608 'I' St *TF:* 800-292-2334 ■ *Web:* www.discovergold.org	Sacramento	CA	95814	916-808-7777	808-7788
Saginaw County Convention & Visitors Bureau 901 S Washington Ave *TF:* 800-444-9979	Saginaw	MI	48607	989-752-7164	752-6642
Saint Johns County Convention & Visitors Bureau 500 San Sebastian View *TF:* 800-653-2489	Saint Augustine	FL	32084	904-829-1711	829-6149
Greater Saint Charles Convention & Visitors Bureau 230 S Main St *TF:* 800-366-2427 ■ *Web:* www.historicstcharles.com	Saint Charles	MO	63301	636-946-7776	949-3217
Saint Cloud Area Convention & Visitors Bureau 525 Hwy 10 S Suite 1 *TF:* 800-264-2940 ■ *Web:* www.granitecountry.com	Saint Cloud	MN	56304	320-251-4170	656-0401
Saint Joseph Convention & Visitors Bureau 109 S 4th St *TF:* 800-785-0360 ■ *Web:* www.stjomo.com	Saint Joseph	MO	64501	816-233-6688	233-9120
Saint Louis Convention & Visitors Commission 701 Convention Plaza Suite 300 *TF:* 800-916-8938 ■ *Web:* www.explorestlouis.com	Saint Louis	MO	63101	314-421-1023	421-0039
Auglaize & Mercer Counties Convention & Visitors Bureau 900 Edgewater Dr *TF:* 800-860-4726 ■ *Web:* www.seemore.org	Saint Marys	OH	45885	419-394-1294	394-1642
Saint Paul RiverCentre Convention & Visitors Authority 175 W Kellogg Blvd Suite 502 *TF:* 800-627-6101 ■ *Web:* www.stpaulcvb.org	Saint Paul	MN	55102	651-265-4900	265-4999
City Of Salem 101 S Broadway *Web:* www.salemil.us	Salem	IL	62881	618-548-2222	548-5330
Salem Convention & Visitors Assn 181 High St NE *TF:* 800-874-7012 ■ *Web:* www.travelsalem.com	Salem	OR	97301	503-581-4325	581-4540
North of Boston Convention & Visitors Bureau (NBCVB) I-95 Southbound Exit 60 PO Box 5193 *TF:* 877-662-9299 ■ *Web:* www.northofboston.org	Salisbury	MA	01952	978-465-6555	977-7758
Rowan County Convention & Visitors Bureau 204 E Innes St Suite 120 *TF:* 800-332-2343 ■ *Web:* www.visitsalisburync.com	Salisbury	NC	28144	704-638-3100	642-2011
Salt Lake Convention & Visitors Bureau 90 S W Temple **Fax Area Code:* 800 ■ *TF:* 800-541-4955 ■ *Web:* www.visitsaltlake.com	Salt Lake City	UT	84101	801-534-4900	541-4955*
San Angelo Chamber of Commerce 418 W Ave B *TF:* 800-375-1206 ■ *Web:* www.sanangelo.org	San Angelo	TX	76903	325-655-4136	658-1110
San Antonio Convention & Visitors Bureau 203 S St Marys St Suite 200 *TF:* 800-447-3372 ■ *Web:* www.visitsanantonio.com	San Antonio	TX	78205	210-207-6700	207-6768
San Bernardino Convention & Visitors Bureau 1955 Hunts Ln Suite 102 *TF:* 800-867-8366 ■ *Web:* www.san-bernardino.org	San Bernardino	CA	92408	909-891-1151	891-1873
San Diego Convention & Visitors Bureau 2215 India St *Web:* www.sandiego.org	San Diego	CA	92101	619-232-3101	696-9371
San Francisco Convention & Visitors Bureau 201 3rd St Suite 900 *Web:* www.sanfrancisco.travel	San Francisco	CA	94103	415-974-6900	227-2602
San Jose Convention & Visitors Bureau 408 Almaden Blvd *TF:* 800-726-5673 ■ *Web:* www.sanjose.org	San Jose	CA	95110	408-295-9600	277-3535
Puerto Rico Convention Bureau 100 Convention Blvd *TF:* 800-214-0420 ■ *Web:* www.prconvention.com	San Juan	PR	00907	787-725-2110	725-2133
Marin Convention & Visitors Bureau 1 Mitchell Blvd Suite B-112 *TF:* 866-925-2060 ■ *Web:* www.visitmarin.org	San Rafael	CA	94903	415-925-2060	925-2063
Santa Barbara Visitors Bureau & Film Commission 1601 Anacapa St *TF:* 800-676-1266 ■ *Web:* www.santabarbaraca.com	Santa Barbara	CA	93101	805-966-9222	966-1728

Organization / Address	City	State	Zip	Phone	Fax
Santa Clara Convention/Visitors Bureau 1850 Warburton Ave *TF:* 800-272-6822 ■ *Web:* www.santaclara.org	Santa Clara	CA	95050	408-244-9660	244-9202
Santa Cruz County Conference & Visitors Council 303 Water St Suite 100 *TF:* 800-833-3494 ■ *Web:* www.santacruz.org	Santa Cruz	CA	95060	831-425-1234	425-1260
Santa Fe Convention & Visitors Bureau 201 W Marcy St *TF:* 800-777-2489 ■ *Web:* www.santafe.org	Santa Fe	NM	87501	505-955-6200	955-6222
Santa Maria Valley Convention & Visitors Bureau 614 S Broadway *TF:* 800-331-3779 ■ *Web:* www.santamaria.com	Santa Maria	CA	93454	805-925-2403	928-7559
Santa Monica Convention & Visitors Bureau 1920 Main St Suite B *TF:* 800-544-5319 ■ *Web:* www.santamonica.com	Santa Monica	CA	90405	310-319-6263	319-6273
Beaches of South Walton Tourist Development Council PO Box 1248 *TF:* 800-822-6877 ■ *Web:* www.beachesofsouthwalton.com	Santa Rosa Beach	FL	32459	850-267-1216	267-3943
Sarasota Convention & Visitors Bureau 766 Hudson Ave # A *TF:* 800-522-9799 ■ *Web:* www.sarasotafl.org	Sarasota	FL	34236	941-957-1877	951-2956
Saratoga Convention & Tourism Bureau 60 Railroad Pl Suite 100 *Web:* www.discoversaratoga.org	Saratoga Springs	NY	12866	518-584-1531	584-2969
Sault Sainte Marie Convention & Visitors Bureau 536 Ashman St *TF:* 800-647-2858 ■ *Web:* www.saultstemarie.com	Sault Sainte Marie	MI	49783	906-632-3366	632-6161
Hardin County Convention & Visitors Bureau 495 Main St *TF:* 800-552-3866 ■ *Web:* www.tourhardincounty.org	Savannah	TN	38372	731-925-8181	925-6987
Savannah Area Convention & Visitors Bureau 101 E Bay St *TF:* 877-728-2662 ■ *Web:* www.savannahvisit.com	Savannah	GA	31401	912-644-6401	644-6499
Greater Woodfield Convention & Visitors Bureau 1375 E Woodfield Rd Suite 120 *TF:* 800-847-4849 ■ *Web:* www.chicagonorthwest.com	Schaumburg	IL	60173	847-490-1010	490-1212
Scottsdale Convention & Visitors Bureau 4343 N Scottsdale Rd Suite 170 *TF:* 800-782-1117 ■ *Web:* www.scottsdalecvb.com	Scottsdale	AZ	85251	480-421-1004	421-9733
Lackawanna County Convention & Visitors Bureau 99 Glenmaura National Blvd *TF:* 800-229-3526 ■ *Web:* www.visitnepa.org	Scranton	PA	18507	570-496-1701	
Seattle's Convention & Visitors Bureau 701 Pike St Suite 800 *TF:* 866-732-2695 ■ *Web:* www.visitseattle.org	Seattle	WA	98101	206-461-5800	461-5855
Seward Convention & Visitors Bureau PO Box 749 *Web:* www.directory.seward.com	Seward	AK	99664	907-224-8051	224-5353
Southeastern Welcome Ctr 394 Whiteville Rd NW	Shallotte	NC	28459	910-754-2505	754-3670
Visit MercerCounty PA 50 N Water Ave *TF:* 800-637-2370 ■ *Web:* www.visitmercercountypa.com	Sharon	PA	16146	724-346-3771	346-0575
Shelby County Office of Tourism 315 E Main St *TF:* 800-874-3529 ■ *Web:* www.lakeshelbyville.com	Shelbyville	IL	62565	217-774-2244	774-2224
Shepherdsville-Bullitt County Tourist & Convention Commission 395 Paroquet Springs Dr *TF:* 800-526-2068 ■ *Web:* www.travelbullitt.org	Shepherdsville	KY	40165	502-543-8687	543-4889
Sherman Convention & Visitors Council 307 W Washington Suite 100 *TF:* 888-893-1188 ■ *Web:* www.shermantexas.com	Sherman	TX	75090	903-893-1184	893-4266
Shipshewana/LaGrange County Convention & Visitors Bureau 780 S Van Buren St *TF:* 800-254-8090 ■ *Web:* www.backroads.org	Shipshewana	IN	46565	260-768-4008	768-4091
Shreveport-Bossier Convention & Tourist Bureau 629 Spring St *TF:* 800-551-8682 ■ *Web:* www.shreveport-bossier.org	Shreveport	LA	71101	318-222-9391	222-0056
Sioux City Tourism Bureau 801 4th St *TF:* 800-593-2228 ■ *Web:* www.visitsiouxcity.org	Sioux City	IA	51101	712-279-4800	279-4900
Sioux Falls Convention & Visitors Bureau 200 N Phillips Ave Suite 102 *TF:* 800-333-2072 ■ *Web:* www.siouxfallscvb.com	Sioux Falls	SD	57104	605-336-1620	336-6499
Sitka Convention & Visitors Bureau 303 Lincoln St Suite 4 *TF:* 800-557-4852 ■ *Web:* www.sitka.org	Sitka	AK	99835	907-747-5940	747-3739
Skagway Convention & Visitors Bureau 245 Broadway PO Box 1029 *TF:* 888-762-1898 ■ *Web:* www.skagway.com	Skagway	AK	99840	907-983-2854	983-3854
Johnston County Convention & Visitors Bureau 1535-A Booker Dairy Rd *TF:* 800-441-7829 ■ *Web:* www.johnstonco-cvb.org	Smithfield	NC	27577	919-989-8687	989-6295
South Bend/Mishawaka Convention & Visitors Bureau 401 E Colfax Ave Suite 310 *TF:* 800-519-0577 ■ *Web:* www.visitsouthbend.com	South Bend	IN	46617	574-400-4022	289-0358
Lake Tahoe Visitors Authority 3066 Lake Tahoe Blvd *TF:* 800-288-2463 ■ *Web:* www.tahoesouth.com	South Lake Tahoe	CA	96150	530-544-5050	541-7121
South Padre Island Convention & Visitors Bureau 7355 Padre Blvd *TF:* 800-767-2373 ■ *Web:* www.sopadre.com	South Padre Island	TX	78597	956-761-6433	761-9462
South Sioux City Convention & Visitors Bureau 3900 Dakota Ave Suite 11 *TF:* 866-494-1307 ■ *Web:* www.visitsouthsioucity.com	South Sioux City	NE	68776	402-494-1307	494-5010
Convention & Visitors Bureau-Village of Pinehurst Southern Pines Aberdeen Area 10677 Hwy 15-501 *TF:* 800-346-5362 ■ *Web:* www.homeofgolf.com	Southern Pines	NC	28387	910-692-3330	692-2493
Spokane Convention & Visitors Bureau 801 W Riverside Suite 301 *TF:* 800-662-0084 ■ *Web:* www.visitspokane.com	Spokane	WA	99201	509-624-1341	623-1297
Central Illinois Tourism Development Office 700 E Adams St *Web:* www.visitcentralillinois.com	Springfield	IL	62701	217-525-7980	525-8004
Greater Springfield Convention & Visitors Bureau 1441 Main St *TF:* 800-723-1548 ■ *Web:* www.valleyvisitor.com	Springfield	MA	01103	413-787-1548	781-4607
Greater Springfield Convention & Visitors Bureau 20 S Limestone St Suite 100 *TF:* 800-803-1553 ■ *Web:* www.greaterspringfield.com	Springfield	OH	45502	937-325-7621	325-8765
Springfield Convention & Visitors Bureau 109 N 7th St *TF:* 800-545-7300 ■ *Web:* www.visitspringfieldillinois.com	Springfield	IL	62701	217-789-2360	544-8711
Springfield Missouri Convention & Visitors Bureau 815 E St Louis St Suite 100 *TF:* 800-678-8767 ■ *Web:* www.springfieldmo.org	Springfield	MO	65806	417-881-5300	881-2231
Centre County Convention & Visitors Bureau 800 E Pk Ave *TF:* 800-358-5466 ■ *Web:* www.visitpennstate.org	State College	PA	16803	814-231-1400	231-8123
Stevens Point Area Convention & Visitors Bureau 340 Division St N *TF:* 800-236-4636 ■ *Web:* www.spacvb.com	Stevens Point	WI	54481	715-344-2556	344-5818
Pocono Mountains Vacation Bureau 1004 Main St *TF:* 800-722-9199 ■ *Web:* www.800poconos.com	Stroudsburg	PA	18360	570-421-5791	421-6927
Racine County Convention & Visitors Bureau 14015 Washington Ave *TF:* 800-272-2463 ■ *Web:* www.racine.org	Sturtevant	WI	53177	262-884-6400	884-6404
Superior/Douglas County Convention & Visitors Bureau 305 Harborview Pkwy *TF:* 800-942-5313 ■ *Web:* www.superiorchamber.org	Superior	WI	54880	715-392-7151	392-3810
Syracuse Convention & Visitors Bureau 572 S Salina St *TF:* 800-234-4797 ■ *Web:* www.visitsyracuse.org	Syracuse	NY	13202	315-470-1910	471-8545
Tacoma Regional Convention & Visitor Bureau 1516 Pacific Ave Suite 500 *TF:* 800-272-2662 ■ *Web:* www.traveltacoma.com	Tacoma	WA	98402	253-627-2836	627-8783
North Lake Tahoe Resort Assn 100 N Lake Blvd *TF:* 800-824-6348 ■ *Web:* www.gotahoenorth.com	Tahoe City	CA	96145	530-581-6900	581-1686
North Lake Tahoe Visitors & Convention Bureau PO Box 1757 *TF:* 800-462-5196 ■ *Web:* www.gotahoenorth.com	Tahoe City	CA	96145	530-581-8700	581-1686
Chambers of Commerce / Tourism 106 E Jefferson St *TF:* 800-628-2866 ■ *Web:* www.visittallahassee.com	Tallahassee	FL	32301	850-606-2305	606-2301
Tampa Bay & Co 401 E Jackson St Suite 2100 *TF:* 800-448-2672 ■ *Web:* www.visittampabay.com	Tampa	FL	33602	813-223-1111	229-6616
Tawas Bay Convention & Visitors Bureau PO Box 10 *TF:* 877-868-2927 ■ *Web:* www.tawasbay.com	Tawas City	MI	48764	989-876-6018	
Tempe Convention & Visitors Bureau 51 W 3rd St Suite 105 *TF:* 866-914-1052 ■ *Web:* www.tempetourism.com	Tempe	AZ	85281	480-894-8158	968-8004
Terre Haute Convention & Visitors Bureau 5353 E Margaret Dr *TF:* 800-366-3043 ■ *Web:* www.terrehaute.com	Terre Haute	IN	47803	812-234-5555	234-6750
Thief River Falls Convention & Visitors Bureau (TRFCVB) 2042 St Hwy 1 NE PO Box 176 *TF:* 800-827-1629 ■ *Web:* www.visitthiefriverfalls.com	Thief River Falls	MN	56701	218-686-9785	683-5107
City of Thomasville Tourism Authority 144 E Jackson St *TF:* 866-577-3600 ■ *Web:* www.thomasvillega.com	Thomasville	GA	31792	229-228-7977	228-4188
Three Lakes Information Bureau 1704 Superior St PO Box 268 *TF:* 800-972-6103 ■ *Web:* www.threelakes.com	Three Lakes	WI	54562	715-546-3344	546-2103
River Country Tourism Bureau PO Box 214 **Fax Area Code:* 269 ■ *TF:* 800-447-2821 ■ *Web:* www.rivercountry.com	Three Rivers	MI	49093	800-447-2821	651-4342*
Seneca County Convention & Visitors Bureau 114 S Washington St *TF:* 888-736-3221 ■ *Web:* www.senecacounty.com	Tiffin	OH	44883	419-447-5866	447-6628
Greater Toledo Convention & Visitors Bureau 401 Jefferson Ave *TF:* 800-243-4667 ■ *Web:* www.dotoledo.org	Toledo	OH	43604	419-321-6404	255-7731
Tomah Convention & Visitors Bureau 901 Kilbourn Ave PO Box 625 *TF:* 800-948-6624 ■ *Web:* www.tomahwisconsin.com	Tomah	WI	54660	608-372-2166	372-2167
Travel Industry Assn of Kansas 919 S Kansas Ave *Web:* www.tiak.org	Topeka	KS	66612	785-233-9465	232-5705
Visit Topeka Inc 1275 SW Topeka Blvd *TF:* 800-235-1030 ■ *Web:* www.visittopeka.travel	Topeka	KS	66612	785-234-1030	234-8282
Toronto Convention & Visitors Assn 207 Queen's Quay W Suite 405 PO Box 126 *TF:* 800-499-2514 ■ *Web:* www.seetorontonow.com	Toronto	ON	M5J1A7	416-203-2600	203-6753
Smoky Mountain Visitors Bureau 7906 E Lamar Alexander Pkwy *TF:* 800-525-6834 ■ *Web:* www.smokymountains.org	Townsend	TN	37882	865-448-6134	448-9806
Baltimore County Visitor Ctr 44 W Chesapeake Ave *TF:* 800-570-2836 ■ *Web:* www.enjoybaltimorecounty.com	Towson	MD	21204	410-296-4886	296-8618
Traverse City Convention & Visitors Bureau 101 W Grandview Pkwy *TF:* 800-940-1120 ■ *Web:* www.mytraversecity.com	Traverse City	MI	49684	231-947-1120	947-2621
Atlanta's DeKalb Convention & Visitors Bureau 1957 Lakeside Pkwy Suite 510 *TF:* 800-999-6055 ■ *Web:* www.dcvb.org	Tucker	GA	30084	770-492-5000	492-5033
Metropolitan Tucson Convention & Visitors Bureau 100 S Church Ave *TF:* 800-638-8350 ■ *Web:* www.visittucson.org	Tucson	AZ	85701	520-624-1817	884-7804
Tulsa Convention & Visitors Bureau 2 W 2nd St Suite 150 *TF:* 800-558-3311 ■ *Web:* www.visittulsa.com	Tulsa	OK	74103	918-585-1201	592-6244
Tunica County Convention & Visitors Bureau 13625 Hwy 61 N *TF:* 888-488-6422 ■ *Web:* www.tunicatravel.com	Tunica Resorts	MS	38664	662-363-3800	363-1493

Listing	City	State	ZIP	Phone	Fax
Tupelo Convention & Visitors Bureau 399 E Main St. *TF:* 800-533-0611 ■ *Web:* www.tupelo.net	Tupelo	MS	38804	662-841-6521	841-6558
Turlock Convention & Visitors Bureau 115 S Golden State Blvd *Web:* www.visitturlock.org	Turlock	CA	95380	209-632-2221	632-5289
Tuscaloosa Convention & Visitors Bureau 1305 Greensboro Ave PO Box 3167 *TF:* 800-538-8696 ■ *Web:* www.tcvb.org	Tuscaloosa	AL	35403	205-391-9200	759-9002
Colbert County Tourism & Convention Bureau 719 Hwy 72 W PO Box 740425 *TF:* 800-344-0783 ■ *Web:* www.colbertcountytourism.org	Tuscumbia	AL	35674	256-383-0783	383-2080
Tyler Convention & Visitors Bureau (TCVB) 315 N Broadway *TF:* 800-235-5712 ■ *Web:* www.visittyler.com	Tyler	TX	75702	903-592-1661	592-1268
Oneida County Convention & Visitors Bureau PO Box 551 *TF:* 800-426-3132 ■ *Web:* www.oneidacountycvb.com	Utica	NY	13503	315-724-7221	724-7335
Vail Valley Tourism Bureau PO Box 1130 *TF:* 800-525-3875 ■ *Web:* www.visitvailvalley.com	Vail	CO	81658	970-476-1000	476-6008
Vallejo Convention & Visitors Bureau 289 Mare Island Way *TF:* 800-482-5535 ■ *Web:* www.visitvallejo.com	Vallejo	CA	94590	707-642-3653	644-2206
Greater Vancouver Convention & Visitors Bureau 200 Burrard St *Web:* www.tourismvancouver.com	Vancouver	BC	V6C3L6	604-682-2222	682-1717
Southwest Washington Convention & Visitors Bureau 101 E 8th St Suite 240 *TF:* 877-600-0800 ■ *Web:* www.visitvancouverusa.com	Vancouver	WA	98660	360-750-1553	750-1553
Ventura Visitors & Convention Bureau 101 S California St *TF:* 800-333-2989 ■ *Web:* www.ventura-usa.com	Ventura	CA	93001	805-648-2075	648-2150
Vicksburg Convention & Visitors Bureau 3300 Clay St PO Box 110 *TF:* 800-221-3536 ■ *Web:* www.visitvicksburg.com	Vicksburg	MS	39181	601-636-9421	636-9475
Iron Range Tourism Bureau 403 N 1st St *TF:* 800-777-8497 ■ *Web:* www.ironrange.org	Virginia	MN	55792	218-749-8161	749-8055
Virginia Beach Convention & Visitor Bureau (VBCVB) 2101 Parks Ave Suite 500 *TF:* 800-700-7702 ■ *Web:* www.visitvirginiabeach.com	Virginia Beach	VA	23451	757-385-4700	437-4747
Visalia Convention & Visitors Bureau PO Box 2734 *TF:* 800-524-0303 ■ *Web:* www.visitvisalia.org	Visalia	CA	93279	559-334-0141	713-4800
Waco Convention & Visitors Bureau 100 Washington Ave *TF:* 800-321-9226 ■ *Web:* www.wacocvb.com	Waco	TX	76701	254-750-5810	750-5801
Wahpeton Visitors Bureau 118 N 6th St *TF:* 800-892-6673 ■ *Web:* www.wahpchamber.com	Wahpeton	ND	58075	701-642-8744	642-8745
Warren County Visitors Bureau 2883 Pennsylvania Ave W *TF:* 800-624-7802 ■ *Web:* www.wcvb.net	Warren	PA	16365	814-726-1222	726-7266
Kosciusko County Convention & Visitors Bureau (KOSCVB) 111 Capital Dr *TF:* 800-800-6090 ■ *Web:* www.koscvb.org	Warsaw	IN	46582	574-269-6090	269-2405
Washington DC Convention & Tourism Corp 901 7th St NW 4th Fl *TF:* 800-422-8644 ■ *Web:* www.washington.org	Washington	DC	20001	202-789-7000	789-7037
Waterloo Convention & Visitor Bureau 500 Jefferson St *TF:* 800-728-8431 ■ *Web:* www.waterloocvb.org	Waterloo	IA	50701	319-233-8350	233-2733
Tioga County Visitors Bureau 2053 Rt 660 PO Box 139 *TF:* 888-846-4228 ■ *Web:* www.visittiogapa.com	Wellsboro	PA	16901	570-724-0635	723-1016
West Branch Visitors Bureau 422 W Houghton Ave *TF:* 800-755-9091	West Branch	MI	48661	989-345-2821	345-9075
West Hollywood Convention & Visitors Bureau 8687 Melrose Ave Suite M38 *TF:* 800-368-6020 ■ *Web:* www.visitwesthollywood.com	West Hollywood	CA	90069	310-289-2525	289-2529
Monroe-West Monroe Convention & Visitors Bureau 601 Constitution Dr PO Box 1436 *TF:* 800-843-1872 ■ *Web:* www.monroe-westmonroe.org	West Monroe	LA	71292	318-387-5691	324-1752
Palm Beach County Convention & Visitors Bureau 1555 Palm Beach Lakes Blvd Suite 800 *TF:* 800-554-7256 ■ *Web:* www.palmbeachfl.com	West Palm Beach	FL	33401	561-233-3000	233-3009
Wheeling Convention & Visitors Bureau 1401 Main St *TF:* 800-828-3097 ■ *Web:* www.wheelingcvb.com	Wheeling	WV	26003	304-233-7709	233-1470
Convention & Visitors Bureau of Marion County 2 Mountain Pk Dr *TF:* 800-834-7365 ■ *Web:* www.marioncvb.com	White Hall	WV	26554	304-368-1123	333-0155
Westchester County Tourism & Film 148 Martine Ave Suite 104 *TF:* 800-833-9282 ■ *Web:* www.thewestchesterway.com	White Plains	NY	10801	914-995-8500	995-8505
Wichita Convention & Visitors Bureau 515 Main St Suite 115 *TF:* 800-288-9424 ■ *Web:* www.gowichita.com	Wichita	KS	67202	316-265-2800	265-0162
Wichita Falls Convention & Visitors Bureau 1000 5th St *TF:* 800-799-6732 ■ *Web:* www.wichitafalls.org	Wichita Falls	TX	76301	940-716-5500	716-5509
Williamsburg Destination Marketing Committee 421 N Boundary St PO Box 3495 *TF:* 800-368-6511 ■ *Web:* www.visitwilliamsburg.com	Williamsburg	VA	23187	757-229-6511	229-2047
Martin County Travel & Tourism Authority 100 E Church St PO Box 382 *TF:* 800-776-8566 ■ *Web:* www.visitmartincounty.com	Williamston	NC	27892	252-792-6605	792-8710
Cape Fear Coast Convention & Visitors Bureau 505 Nutt St Unit A *TF:* 877-406-2356 ■ *Web:* www.capefearcoast.com	Wilmington	NC	28401	910-341-4030	341-4029
Greater Wilmington Convention & Visitors Bureau 100 W 10th St Suite 20 *TF:* 800-489-6664 ■ *Web:* www.visitwilmingtonde.com	Wilmington	DE	19801	302-295-2210	652-4726
Wilson Visitors Bureau 4916 Hayes Pl # E *TF:* 800-497-7398 ■ *Web:* www.wilson-nc.com	Wilson	NC	27893	252-243-8440	243-7550
Winnemucca Convention & Visitors Authority 50 W Winnemucca Blvd *TF:* 800-962-2638 ■ *Web:* www.winnemucca.nv.us	Winnemucca	NV	89445	775-623-5071	623-5087
Winona Convention & Visitors Bureau 160 Johnson St *TF:* 800-657-4972 ■ *Web:* www.visitwinona.com	Winona	MN	55987	507-452-0735	454-0006
Winston-Salem Convention & Visitors Bureau 200 Brookstown Ave *TF:* 800-331-7018 ■ *Web:* www.visitwinstonsalem.com	Winston-Salem	NC	27101	336-728-4200	728-4220
Wisconsin Dells Visitors & Convention Bureau 115 La Crosse St PO Box 390 *TF:* 800-223-3557 ■ *Web:* www.wisdells.com	Wisconsin Dells	WI	53965	608-254-8088	254-4293
Wayne County Convention & Visitors Bureau 428 W Liberty St *TF:* 800-362-6474 ■ *Web:* www.waynecountycvb.org	Wooster	OH	44691	330-264-1800	264-1141
Worcester County Convention & Visitors Bureau 30 Elm St 2nd Fl *TF:* 866-755-7439 ■ *Web:* www.centralmass.org	Worcester	MA	01609	508-755-7400	754-2703
York County Convention & Visitors Bureau 149 W Market St *TF:* 888-858-9675 ■ *Web:* www.yorkpa.org	York	PA	17401	717-852-9675	854-5095
Mahoning County Convention & Visitors Bureau 21 W Boardman St *TF:* 800-447-8201 ■ *Web:* www.youngstownlive.com	Youngstown	OH	44503	330-740-2130	740-2144
Ypsilanti Area Convention & Visitors Bureau 106 W Michigan Ave *TF:* 800-265-9045 ■ *Web:* www.ypsilanti.org	Ypsilanti	MI	48197	734-483-4444	483-0400
Yuma Convention & Visitors Bureau 201 N 4th Ave *TF:* 800-293-0071 ■ *Web:* www.visityuma.com	Yuma	AZ	85364	928-783-0071	783-1897
Zanesville-Muskingum County Convention & Visitors Bureau 205 N 5th St *TF:* 800-743-2303 ■ *Web:* www.zmchamber.com	Zanesville	OH	43701	740-455-8282	454-2963
Aspen Chamber Resort Assn 425 Rio Grande Pl *TF:* 800-670-0792 ■ *Web:* www.aspenchamber.org	Aspen	CO	81611	970-925-1940	920-1173

210 CONVEYORS & CONVEYING EQUIPMENT

SEE ALSO Material Handling Equipment p. 2221

Listing	City	State	ZIP	Phone	Fax
Airfloat LLC 2230 Brush College Rd *TF:* 800-888-0018 ■ *Web:* www.airfloat.com	Decatur	IL	62526	217-423-6001	422-1049
Allor Mfg Inc 12534 Emerson Dr *TF:* 888-244-4028 ■ *Web:* www.allor.com	Brighton	MI	48116	248-486-4500	486-4040
AMF Bakery Systems 2115 W Laburnum Ave *TF:* 800-225-3771 ■ *Web:* www.amfbakery.com	Richmond	VA	23227	804-355-7961	355-1074
Arrowhead Conveyor Corp Inc 3255 Medalist Dr PO Box 2408 *Web:* www.arrowheadconveyor.com	Oshkosh	WI	54903	920-235-5562	235-3638
Automated Conveyor Systems Inc 3850 Southland Dr *Web:* www.automatedconveyors.com	West Memphis	AR	72301	870-732-5050	732-5191
Automatic Systems Inc 9230 E 47th St *TF:* 800-366-3488 ■ *Web:* www.asi.com	Kansas City	MO	64133	816-356-0660	356-5730
Automotion Inc 11000 Lavergne Ave *Web:* www.automotionconveyors.com	Oak Lawn	IL	60453	708-229-3700	229-3702
Beltservice Corp 4143 Rider Trail N *TF:* 800-727-2358 ■ *Web:* www.beltservice.com	Earth City	MO	63045	314-344-8500	344-8511
Bilt-Rite Conveyors Inc 141 Lanza Ave *Web:* www.bilt-rite.com	Garfield	NJ	07026	973-546-1000	546-2539
C & M Conveyor 4598 SR 37 *TF:* 800-551-3195 ■ *Web:* www.cmconveyor.com	Mitchell	IN	47446	812-849-5647	849-6126
Caddy Corp of America 509 Sharptown Rd *Web:* www.caddycorp.com	Bridgeport	NJ	08014	856-467-4222	467-5511
Cambelt International Corp 2820 Directors Row *Web:* www.cambelt.com	Salt Lake City	UT	84104	801-972-5511	
Cambridge Inc 105 Goodwill Rd PO Box 399 *TF:* 877-649-7492 ■ *Web:* www.cambridge-intl.com	Cambridge	MD	21613	410-228-3000	901-4905
Can Lines Engineering 9839 Downey Norwalk Rd PO Box 7039 **Fax Area Code:* 562 ■ *TF:* 800-233-4597 ■ *Web:* www.canlines.com	Downey	CA	90241	323-773-5676	869-5293*
Carman Industries Inc 133 E Riverside Dr *TF:* 800-456-7560 ■ *Web:* www.carmanindustries.com	Jeffersonville	IN	47130	812-288-4700	288-4707
Carrier Vibrating Equipment Inc 3400 Fern Valley Rd *TF:* 800-547-7278 ■ *Web:* www.carriervibrating.com	Louisville	KY	40213	502-969-3171	969-3172
Chantland-Pvs Co The PO Box 69 *Web:* www.chantlandpulley.com	Humboldt	IA	50548	515-332-4040	332-4923
Christianson Systems Inc 20421 15th St SE PO Box 138 *TF:* 800-328-8896 ■ *Web:* www.christianson.com	Blomkest	MN	56216	320-995-6141	995-6145
CIGNYS 68 Williamson St *TF:* 888-424-4697 ■ *Web:* www.cignys.com	Saginaw	MI	48601	989-753-1411	753-4386
Cinetic Sorting Corp 500 E Burnett Ave *TF:* 800-926-6839 ■ *Web:* www.sorting.com	Louisville	KY	40217	502-636-1414	636-1491
Con-Vey Keystone Inc 526 NE Chestnut St PO Box 1399 *TF:* 800-668-1425 ■ *Web:* www.con-vey.com	Roseburg	OR	97470	541-672-5506	672-2513
Conveyor Components Co 130 Seltzer Rd *TF Cust Svc:* 800-233-3233 ■ *Web:* www.conveyorcomponents.com	Croswell	MI	48422	810-679-4211	679-4510
Conveyors Inc 620 S 4th Ave *Web:* www.conveyorsinc.net	Mansfield	TX	76063	817-473-4645	473-3024
Cyclonaire Corp PO Box 366 *Web:* www.cyclonaire.com	York	NE	68467	402-362-2000	362-2001
Daifuku America Corp 6700 Tussing Rd *TF:* 800-531-1888 ■ *Web:* www.daifukuamerica.com	Reynoldsburg	OH	43068	614-863-1888	863-9997

Company	City	State	Zip	Phone	Fax
Dearborn Mid-West Conveyor Co (DMWCC)					
20334 Superior Rd	Taylor	MI	48180	734-288-4400	288-1916
TF: 800-655-5105 ■ *Web:* www.dmwcc.com					
Dematic 507 Plymouth Ave NE	Grand Rapids	MI	49505	616-913-6200	913-7701
TF Cust Svc: 800-530-9153 ■ *Web:* www.dematic.us					
Dynamic Air Inc 1125 Wolters Blvd	Saint Paul	MN	55110	651-484-2900	484-7015
Web: www.dynamicair.com					
Engineered Products Inc					
500 Furman Hall Rd	Greenville	SC	29609	864-234-4888	234-4860
TF: 888-301-1421 ■ *Web:* www.engprod.com					
Essmueller Co 334 Ave A PO Box 1966	Laurel	MS	39440	601-649-2400	649-4320
TF: 800-325-7175 ■ *Web:* www.essmueller.com					
Evana Tool & Engineering Inc					
5825 Old Boonville Hwy	Evansville	IN	47715	812-479-8246	474-3138
TF: 800-468-6774 ■ *Web:* www.evana-online.com					
Fame Industries Inc 51100 Grand River Ave	Wixom	MI	48393	248-348-7760	348-2120
Web: www.fameind.com					
Feeco International Inc 3913 Algoma Rd	Green Bay	WI	54311	920-468-1000	469-5110
TF: 800-373-9347 ■ *Web:* www.feeco.com					
Fleetwood Inc 1305 Lakeview Dr	Romeoville	IL	60446	630-759-6800	759-2299
TF: 800-824-6609 ■ *Web:* www.fleetinc.com					
Flexible Steel Lacing Co					
2525 Wisconsin Ave	Downers Grove	IL	60515	562-944-9450	971-1180*
**Fax Area Code:* 630 ■ *TF:* 800-323-3444 ■ *Web:* www.flexco.com					
Fred D Pfening Co 1075 W 5th Ave	Columbus	OH	43212	614-294-5361	294-1633
Web: www.pfening.com					
Frost Inc 2020 Bristol Ave NW	Grand Rapids	MI	49504	616-453-7781	453-2161
TF Cust Svc: 800-783-6633 ■ *Web:* www.frostinc.com					
Garvey Corp 208 S Rt 73	Blue Anchor	NJ	08037	609-561-2450	561-2328
TF: 800-257-8581 ■ *Web:* www.garvey.com					
General Kinematics Corp 5050 Rickert Rd	Crystal Lake	IL	60014	815-455-3222	455-2285
Web: www.generalkinematics.com					
Grasan Equipment Co 440 S Illinois Ave	Mansfield	OH	44907	419-526-4440	524-2176
TF: 800-526-4602 ■ *Web:* www.grasan.com					
Hansen Mfg Corp 5100 W 12th St	Sioux Falls	SD	57107	605-332-3200	
TF: 800-328-1785 ■ *Web:* www.hiroller.com					
Hapman 6002 E N Ave	Kalamazoo	MI	49048	269-343-1675	349-2477
TF: 800-427-6260 ■ *Web:* www.hapman.com					
Hohl Machine & Conveyor Co Inc					
1580 Niagara St	Buffalo	NY	14213	716-882-7210	882-9575
Web: www.hohl.com					
Hytrol Conveyor Co Inc 2020 Hytrol St	Jonesboro	AR	72401	870-935-3700	852-3233*
**Fax Area Code:* 800 ■ *Web:* www.hytrol.com					
Intelligrated Products					
475 E High St PO Box 899	London	OH	43140	740-490-0300	490-0281
TF: 888-239-1167 ■ *Web:* www.intelligrated.com					
Interroll Corp 3000 Corporate Dr	Wilmington	NC	28405	910-799-1100	830-9679*
**Fax Area Code:* 800 ■ *TF Sales:* 800-830-9680 ■ *Web:* www.interroll.com					
Intralox LLC 8715 Bollman Pl	Savage	MD	20763	301-575-2200	575-2266
Web: www.intralox.com					
Jervis B Webb Co 34375 W 12-Mile Rd	Farmington Hills	MI	48331	248-553-1220	553-1200
TF: 800-526-9322 ■ *Web:* www.jervisbwebb.com					
Jorgensen Conveyors Inc 10303 N Baehr Rd	Mequon	WI	53092	262-242-3089	242-4382
TF: 800-325-7705 ■ *Web:* www.jorgensenconveyors.com					
Kice Industries Inc 5500 N Mill Heights Dr	Wichita	KS	67219	316-744-7151	744-7355
Web: www.kice.com					
Knight Global 1140 Centre Rd	Auburn Hills	MI	48326	248-377-4950	377-2135
Web: www.knight-ind.com					
KWS Mfg Co Ltd 3041 Conveyor Dr	Burleson	TX	76028	817-295-2247	447-8528
TF: 800-543-6558 ■ *Web:* www.kwsmfg.com					
Laitram LLC 200 Laitram Ln	Harahan	LA	70123	504-733-6000	733-2143
TF: 800-533-8253 ■ *Web:* www.laitram.com					
Lipe Automation Equipment					
7645 Henry Clay Blvd	Liverpool	NY	13088	315-457-1052	457-1678
TF: 800-448-7822 ■ *Web:* www.lipeautomation.com					
Mac Equipment Inc 7901 NW 107th Terr	Kansas City	MO	64153	816-891-9300	891-8978
TF: 800-821-2476 ■ *Web:* www.macequipment.com					
Martin Engineering 1 Martin Pl	Neponset	IL	61345	309-594-2384	594-2432
TF: 800-544-2947 ■ *Web:* www.martin-eng.com					
Mayfran International Inc 6650 Beta Dr	Cleveland	OH	44143	440-461-4100	461-5565
TF: 800-321-6988 ■ *Web:* www.mayfran.com					
Metzgar Conveyor Co Inc					
901 Metzgar Dr NW	Comstock Park	MI	49321	616-784-0930	784-4100
Web: www.metzgarconveyors.com					
Montague Industrial Inc 1236-A Wilson Hall Rd	Sumter	SC	29150	803-905-7676	905-7683
Nercon Engineering & Mfg Inc					
3972 S US Hwy 45	Oshkosh	WI	54902	920-233-3268	233-3159
Web: www.nercon.com					
Nim-Cor Inc 575 Amherst St	Nashua	NH	03063	603-889-2153	883-6980
TF: 888-464-6267 ■ *Web:* www.nimcor.com					
NKC of America Inc 1584 E Brooks Rd	Memphis	TN	38116	901-396-5353	396-2339
TF: 800-532-6727					
Nol-tec Systems Inc 425 Apollo Dr	Circle Pines	MN	55014	651-780-8600	780-4400
Web: www.nol-tec.com					
Novi Precision Products Inc					
11777 E Grand River Ave	Brighton	MI	48116	810-227-1024	227-6160
Web: www.noviprecision.com					
Overhead Conveyor Co 1330 Hilton Rd	Ferndale	MI	48220	248-547-3800	547-8344
TF: 800-396-2554 ■ *Web:* www.occ-conveyor.com					
Prab Inc 5944 E Kilgore Rd	Kalamazoo	MI	49048	269-382-8200	349-2477
TF: 800-968-7722 ■ *Web:* www.prab.com					
Railex Corp 89-02 Atlantic Ave	Ozone Park	NY	11416	718-845-5454	738-1020
TF: 800-352-3244 ■ *Web:* www.railexcorp.com					
Rapat Corp 919 Odonnel St	Hawley	MN	56549	218-483-3344	483-3535
Web: www.rapat.com					
Rapid Industries Inc 4003 Oaklawn Dr	Louisville	KY	40219	502-968-3645	968-6331
TF: 800-727-4381 ■ *Web:* www.rapidi.com					
Renold Jeffrey 2307 Maden Dr	Morristown	TN	37813	423-586-1951	581-2399
TF: 800-251-9012 ■ *Web:* www.renoldjeffrey.com					
Richards-Wilcox Inc 600 S Lake St	Aurora	IL	60506	630-897-6951	897-6994
TF: 800-253-5668 ■ *Web:* www.richardswilcox.com					
Roll-A-Way Conveyor Inc 2335 N Delaney Rd	Gurnee	IL	60031	847-336-5033	336-6542
Web: www.roll-away.com					
Ryson International Inc 300 Newsome Dr	Yorktown	VA	23692	757-898-1530	898-1580
Web: www.ryson.com					
Schroeder Industries LLC 580 W Pk Rd	Leetsdale	PA	15056	724-318-1100	318-1200
TF: 800-722-4810 ■ *Web:* www.schroederindustries.com					
Screw Conveyor Corp 700 Hoffman St	Hammond	IN	46327	219-931-1450	931-0209
Web: www.screwconveyor.com					
Shick Tube Veyor Corp 4346 Clary Blvd	Kansas City	MO	64130	816-861-7224	921-1901
Web: www.shickusa.com					
Shuttleworth Inc 10 Commercial Rd	Huntington	IN	46750	260-356-8500	359-7810
TF: 800-444-7412 ■ *Web:* www.shuttleworth.com					
Southern Systems Inc 4101 Viscount Ave	Memphis	TN	38118	901-362-7340	360-8002
Web: www.ssiconveyors.com					
Spar Aerospace Ltd					
7th Ave & Airport Service Rd PO Box 9864	Edmonton	AB	T5J2T2	780-890-6300	890-6547
Web: www.dougalco.com					
Stewart Systems 808 Stewart Ave	Plano	TX	75074	972-422-5808	424-5041
TF: 800-966-5808 ■ *Web:* www.stewart-systems.com					
Sweet Mfg Co Inc 2000 E Leffel Ln	Springfield	OH	45505	937-325-1511	322-1963
TF Cust Svc: 800-334-7254 ■ *Web:* www.sweetmfg.com					
Swisslog 10825 E 47th Ave	Denver	CO	80239	303-371-7770	373-7870
TF: 800-525-1841 ■ *Web:* www.swisslog.com					
TGW-Ermanco Inc 6870 Grand Haven Rd	Spring Lake	MI	49456	231-798-4547	798-8322
Web: www.tgw-group.com					
Thomas Conveyor Co 555 Burleson Blvd	Burleson	TX	76028	817-295-7151	447-3840
TF: 800-433-2217 ■ *Web:* www.thomasconveyor.com					
Transco Industries Inc					
5534 NE 122nd Ave PO Box 20429	Portland	OR	97230	503-256-1955	256-0723
TF: 800-545-9991 ■ *Web:* www.transco-ind.com					
Unex Mfg Inc 50 Progress Pl	Jackson	NJ	08527	732-928-2800	928-2828
TF Cust Svc: 800-695-7726 ■ *Web:* www.unex.com					
Uni-Pak Corp 1015 N Ronald Reagan Blvd	Longwood	FL	32750	407-830-9300	830-4106
Web: www.unipak.com					
United Conveyor Corp 2100 Norman Dr W	Waukegan	IL	60085	847-473-5900	473-5959
Web: www.unitedconveyor.com					
Universal Industries Inc 5800 Nordic Dr	Cedar Falls	IA	50613	319-277-7501	277-2318
TF: 800-553-4446 ■ *Web:* www.universalindustries.com					
W & H Systems Inc 120 Asia Pl	Carlstadt	NJ	07072	201-933-7840	933-2144
TF: 800-966-6993 ■ *Web:* www.whsystems.com					
Wasp Inc PO Box 249	Glenwood	MN	56334	320-634-5126	634-5881
Web: www.waspinc.com					
Webb-Stiles Co					
675 Liverpool Dr PO Box 464	Valley City	OH	44280	330-225-7761	225-5532
Web: www.webb-stiles.com					
Webster Industries Inc 325 Hall St	Tiffin	OH	44883	419-447-8232	448-1618
TF: 800-243-9327 ■ *Web:* www.websterchain.com					
Western Pneumatics Inc PO Box 21340	Eugene	OR	97402	541-461-2600	461-2606
Web: www.westernp.com					
Westfalia Technologies Inc 3655 Sandhurst Dr	York	PA	17406	717-764-1115	764-1118
TF: 800-673-2522 ■ *Web:* www.westfaliausa.com					
Westmont Industries					
10805 Painter Ave	Santa Fe Springs	CA	90670	562-944-6137	946-5299
Web: www.westmont.com					
Whirl Air Flow Corp 20055 177th St	Big Lake	MN	55309	763-262-1200	262-1212
TF: 800-373-3461 ■ *Web:* www.whirlair.com					
Wire Belt Co of America 154 Harvey Rd	Londonderry	NH	03053	603-644-2500	644-3600
TF Cust Svc: 800-922-2637 ■ *Web:* www.wirebelt.com					
Young Industries Inc 16 Painter St	Muncy	PA	17756	570-546-3165	546-1888
TF: 800-546-3165 ■ *Web:* www.younginds.com					

211 CORD & TWINE

Company	City	State	Zip	Phone	Fax
40-Up Tackle Co 16 Union Ave PO Box 442	Westfield	MA	01086	413-562-0385	
Web: www.40uptackleco.com					
Algoma Net Co 1525 Mueller St	Algoma	WI	54201	920-487-5577	487-2852
Web: www.algomanet.com					
All Line Inc 31 W 310 91st St	Naperville	IL	60564	630-820-1800	820-1830
TF: 800-843-5733 ■ *Web:* www.alllinerope.com					
Ashaway Line & Twine Mfg Co 24 Laurel St	Ashaway	RI	02804	401-377-2221	377-9091
TF: 800-556-7260 ■ *Web:* www.ashawayusa.com					
Atkins & Pearce Inc 1 Braid Way	Covington	KY	41017	859-356-2001	356-2395
TF: 800-837-7477 ■ *Web:* www.braidway.com					
Bridon Cordage LLC 909 E 16th St	Albert Lea	MN	56007	507-377-1601	377-7221
TF: 800-533-6002 ■ *Web:* www.bridoncordage.com					
Brownell & Co Inc 423 E Haddam-Moodus Rd	Moodus	CT	06469	860-873-8625	873-1944
Web: www.brownellco.com					
Carron Net Co Inc 1623 17th St PO Box 177	Two Rivers	WI	54241	920-793-2217	793-2122
TF: 800-558-7768 ■ *Web:* www.carronnet.com					
Cordage Inc 1140 Monticello Hwy PO Box 244	Madison	GA	30650	706-342-1916	343-1720
TF: 800-221-5054 ■ *Web:* www.wellingtoninc.com					
Cordage Source The					
Bridgeline Ltd 70 Dundas St	Deseronto	ON	K0K1X0	613-396-9990	396-9996
Web: www.bridgeline.ca					
Cortland Line Co Inc 3736 Kellogg Rd	Cortland	NY	13045	607-756-2851	753-8835
TF: 800-847-6787 ■ *Web:* www.cortlandline.com					
Flow Tek Inc PO Box 2018	Boulder	CO	80306	303-530-3050	
Web: www.monic.com					
Gladding Braided Products LLC					
1 Gladding St	South Otselic	NY	13155	315-653-7211	653-4492
I & I Sling Inc PO Box 2423	Aston	PA	19014	610-485-8500	494-5835
Web: www.slingmax.com					
James Thompson & Co Inc 381 Pk Ave S # 718	New York	NY	10016	212-686-4242	686-9528
Web: www.jamesthompson.com					
Lehigh Group 2834 Shoeneck Rd	Macungie	PA	18062	610-966-9702	966-3529
TF: 800-523-9382 ■ *Web:* www.lehighgroup.com					
New England Ropes Inc 848 Airport Rd	Fall River	MA	02720	508-678-8200	679-2363
TF: 800-333-6679 ■ *Web:* www.neropes.com					
Pacific Fibre & Rope Co Inc					
903 Flint Ave Suite 27	Wilmington	CA	90748	310-834-4567	835-6781
TF Cust Svc: 800-825-7673 ■ *Web:* www.pacificfibre.com					

Phone | Fax

Pelican Rope Works Inc 4001 W Carriage Dr......... Santa Ana CA 92704 714-545-0116 545-7673
TF: 800-464-7673 ■ Web: www.pelicanrope.com
PlymKraft Inc 479 Export Cir...................Newport News VA 23601 757-595-0364 595-3993
TF: 800-992-0854 ■ Web: www.plymkraft.com
Puget Sound Rope Corp 1012 2nd St............... Anacortes WA 98221 360-293-8488 293-8480
TF: 888-525-8488 ■ Web: www.cortlandcompany.com
Rockford Mfg Co 3901 Little River Rd .... Rockford TN 37853 865-970-3131
Rocky Mount Cord Co 381 N Grace St.............Rocky Mount NC 27804 252-977-9130 977-9123
TF Orders: 800-342-9130 ■ Web: www.rmcord.com
Samson Rope Technologies Inc
2090 Thornton Rd............................... Ferndale WA 98248 360-384-4669 299-9246*
*Fax Area Code: 800 ■ TF Cust Svc: 800-227-7673 ■ Web: www.samsonrope.com

212 CORK & CORK PRODUCTS

SEE ALSO Office & School Supplies p. 2321

Phone | Fax

American Star Cork Co 33-53 62nd St .... Woodside NY 11377 718-335-3000 335-3037
TF: 800-338-3581 ■ Web: www.amstarcork.com
Amorim Cork Composites 26112 110th St.............. Trevor WI 53179 262-862-2311 862-2500
TF: 800-558-3206 ■ Web: www.amorim.com
Expanko Cork Co Inc 1129 W Lincoln Hwy ....Coatesville PA 19320 610-593-3000 380-0302
TF: 800-345-6202 ■ Web: www.expanko.com
Manton Industrial Cork Products Inc
415 Oser Ave Unit U........................... Hauppauge NY 11788 631-273-0700 273-0038
TF: 800-663-1921 ■ Web: www.mantoncork.com
Maryland Cork Co Inc
190 Triumph Industrial Pk PO Box 126................. Elkton MD 21922 410-398-2955 392-9433
TF: 800-662-2675 ■ Web: www.marylandcork.com

213 CORPORATE HOUSING

Phone | Fax

Alikar Gardens Resort The
1123 Verde Dr........................... Colorado Springs CO 80910 719-475-2564 471-5835
TF: 800-456-1123 ■ Web: www.alikar.com
Cabernet Corporate Housing
PO Box 18281 ....Oklahoma City OK 73154 405-236-0066 285-4379
TF: 888-413-3463 ■ Web: www.cabernetsuites.com
Churchill Corporate Services 56 Utter Ave ....Hawthorne NJ 07506 973-636-9400 636-0179
TF: 800-941-7458 ■ Web: www.furnishedhousing.com
Cincinnati Metropolitan Housing Authority
16 W Central Pkwy.............................. Cincinnati OH 45202 513-977-5610
Web: www.cintimha.com
Coast to Coast Corporate Housing PO Box 1597.......Cypress CA 90630 562-795-0250 795-0251
TF: 800-451-9466 ■ Web: www.ctchousing.com
ExecSuite 3rd Ave SW Suite 702......................... Calgary AB T2P3B4 403-294-5800 294-5959
TF: 866-489-2451 ■ Web: www.execsuite.ca
K & M Corporate Housing Inc
16060 Caputo Dr Suite 120 ....Morgan Hill CA 95037 408-782-1212 782-8744
TF: 800-646-0907 ■ Web: www.kmrelo.com
Klein & Co Corporate Housing Services Inc
914 Washington Ave..................................Golden CO 80401 303-796-2100 796-2101
TF: 800-208-9826 ■ Web: www.kleinandcompany.com
ExecuStay Corp 1 Marriott Dr ....Washington DC 20058 301-212-9660 778-1113*
*Fax Area Code: 888 ■ TF: 888-840-7829 ■ Web: www.execustay.com
Oakwood Crystal City 400 15th St S................Arlington VA 22202 703-920-9550 271-0190
TF: 877-969-5142 ■ Web: www.oakwood.com
Oakwood Worldwide 2222 Corinth Ave.............Los Angeles CA 90064 310-478-1021 444-2210
TF: 800-888-0808 ■ Web: www.oakwood.com
Preferred Living 8258 Spyglass Dr............West Palm Beach FL 33412 800-343-2177 630-8776*
*Fax Area Code: 561 ■ TF: 800-343-2177 ■ Web: www.preferred-living.com
SuiteAmerica
4970 Windplay Dr Suite C-1.................. El Dorado Hills CA 95762 916-363-9700 941-7989
TF: 800-363-9779 ■ Web: www.suiteamerica.com
US Suites 8301 Washington St.................... Albuquerque NM 87113 505-292-1896 294-2588
TF: 800-877-8483 ■ Web: www.ussuites.com
Windsor Corporate Suites
3516 Stearns Hills Rd................................. Waltham MA 02451 781-899-5100 893-0046
Web: www.windsorcommunities.com
Wynne Residential Corporate Housing
2214 Westwood Ave............................ Richmond VA 23230 804-359-8534 355-7931
TF: 800-338-8534

214 CORRECTIONAL & DETENTION MANAGEMENT (PRIVATIZED)

SEE ALSO Correctional Facilities - Federal p. 1764; Correctional Facilities - State p. 1764; Juvenile Detention Facilities p. 2136

Phone | Fax

Avalon Correctional Services Inc
13401 Railway Dr...........................Oklahoma City OK 73114 405-752-8802 752-8852
TF: 800-919-9113 ■ Web: www.avaloncorrections.com
Colorado Correctional Industries
2862 S Cir Dr.......................... Colorado Springs CO 80906 719-226-4206 226-4220
TF Cust Svc: 800-685-7891 ■ Web: www.coloradoci.com
Corrections Corp of America
10 Burton Hills Blvd..............................Nashville TN 37215 615-263-3000 263-3000
NYSE: CXW ■ TF: 800-624-2931 ■ Web: www.cca.com
GEO Group Inc 621 NW 53rd St Suite 700.......... Boca Raton FL 33487 561-893-0101 999-7635
NYSE: GGI ■ TF: 866-301-4436 ■ Web: www.thegeogroupinc.com
Youth Services International Inc
1819 Main St Suite 1000 .... Sarasota FL 34236 941-953-9199 953-9198
TF: 800-275-3766 ■ Web: www.youthservices.com

215 CORRECTIONAL FACILITIES - FEDERAL

SEE ALSO Correctional & Detention Management (Privatized) p. 1764; Correctional Facilities - State p. 1764; Juvenile Detention Facilities p. 2136

Phone | Fax

Federal Bureau of Prisons 320 1st St NW ....Washington DC 20534 202-307-3250 514-6620
Web: www.bop.gov
Administrative-Maximum US Penitentiary
Florence PO Box 8500.......................... Florence CO 81226 719-784-9464 784-5290
Federal Correctional Complex
Beaumont PO Box 26015........................ Beaumont TX 77720 409-727-8187 626-3401
Coleman 846 NE 54th Terr......................... Coleman FL 33521 352-689-5000 689-3013
Federal Correctional Institution
Bastrop 1341 Hwy 95 N PO Box 730................. Bastrop TX 78602 512-321-3903 304-0117
Web: www.bop.gov
Big Spring 1900 Simler Ave ....Big Spring TX 79720 432-263-2300 466-2756
Web: www.bop.gov/locations/institutions/big/index.jsp
Butner PO Box 1000 .... Butner NC 27509 919-575-4541 575-6341
Cumberland 14601 Burbridge Rd SE...............Cumberland MD 21502 301-784-1000 784-1008*
Danbury Rt 37 33 1/2 Pembroke Rd ....Danbury CT 06811 203-743-6471 312-5110
Edgefield 501 Gary Hill Rd PO Box 723.............. Edgefield SC 29824 803-637-1500 637-9840
El Reno PO Box 1000 .... El Reno OK 73036 405-262-4875 262-6266
Englewood 9595 W Quincy Ave..................... Littleton CO 80123 303-985-1566 763-2553
Web: www.bop.gov
Fairton PO Box 280.................................Fairton NJ 08320 856-453-1177 453-4186
Florence 5880 State Hwy 67 S..................... Florence CO 81226 719-784-9100 784-9504
Forrest City PO Box 7000 ....Forrest City AR 72336 870-630-6000 630-6250
Jesup 2600 Hwy 301 S...............................Jesup GA 31599 912-427-0870 427-1125
Loretto PO Box 1000...............................Loretto PA 15940 814-472-4140 472-6046
Web: www.bop.gov
Manchester PO Box 3000 .... Manchester KY 40962 606-598-1900 599-4115
Marianna 3625 FCI Rd............................ Marianna FL 32446 850-526-2313 718-2014
McKean PO Box 5000............................. Bradford PA 16701 814-362-8900 363-6821
Milan PO Box 9999...................................Milan MI 48160 734-439-1511 439-0949
Morgantown 446 Greenbag Rd .... Morgantown WV 26505 304-296-4416 284-3613
Web: www.bop.gov
Oxford PO Box 500 .... Oxford WI 53952 608-584-5511 584-6371
Web: www.bop.gov
Pekin 2600 S 2nd St ....Pekin IL 61554 309-346-8588 477-4685
Phoenix 37900 N 45th Ave ....Phoenix AZ 85086 623-465-9757 465-5199
Ray Brook 128 Ray Brook Rd PO Box 300........... Ray Brook NY 12977 518-897-4000 897-4216
Web: www.bop.gov/locations/institutions/rbk/index.jsp
Safford PO Box 820.................................Safford AZ 85548 928-428-6600 348-1331
Talladega 565 E Renfroe Rd....................... Talladega AL 35160 256-315-4100 315-4495
Tallahassee 501 Capital Cir NE .... Tallahassee FL 32301 850-878-2173 216-1299
Terminal Island 1299 Seaside Ave............. Terminal Island CA 90731 310-831-8961 732-5335
Web: www.bop.gov
Waseca 1000 University Dr SW PO Box 1731.......... Waseca MN 56093 507-835-8972 837-4547
Yazoo City
2225 Haley Barbour Pkwy PO Box 5050 ....Yazoo City MS 39194 662-751-4800 751-4958
Web: www.bop.gov
Federal Detention Ctr
Honolulu 351 Elliot St PO Box 30547...............Honolulu HI 96820 808-838-4200 838-4510
Houston 1200 Texas Ave PO Box 52645..............Houston TX 77052 713-221-5400 229-4200
Miami 33 NE 4th St PO Box 019120.................. Miami FL 33101 305-577-0010 536-7368
Oakdale PO Box 5060 ....Oakdale LA 71463 318-335-4466 215-2046
Web: www.bop.gov
Philadelphia PO Box 572........................ Philadelphia PA 19106 215-521-4000 521-7220
Web: www.bop.gov
SeaTac PO Box 13901............................... Seattle WA 98198 206-870-5700 870-5717
Federal Medical Ctr
Butner PO Box 1500 .... Butner NC 27509 919-575-3900 575-4801
Lexington 3301 Leestown Rd......................... Lexington KY 40511 859-255-6812 253-8821
Rochester 2110 E Ctr St PO Box 4600............... Rochester MN 55903 507-287-0674 287-9601
Federal Prison Camp
Bryan 1100 Ursuline Ave PO Box 2147................Bryan TX 77805 979-823-1879 821-3316*
Duluth 6902 Airport Rd PO Box 1400 .... Duluth MN 55814 218-722-8634 733-4701
Web: www.bop.gov
Montgomery Maxwell AFB .... Montgomery AL 36112 334-293-2100 293-2326
Pensacola 110 Raby Ave .... Pensacola FL 32509 850-457-1911 458-7295
Medical Center for Federal Prisoners Springfield
1900 W Sunshine St PO Box 4000.................Springfield MO 65801 417-862-7041 837-1711
Metropolitan Correctional Ctr
Chicago 71 W Van Buren St ....Chicago IL 60605 312-322-0567 322-1120
Web: www.bop.gov
New York 150 Pk Row............................New York NY 10007 646-836-6300 836-7751
US Penitentiary
Allenwood PO Box 3500 ....White Deer PA 17887 570-547-0963 547-9201
Atwater 1 Federal Way PO Box 019000................ Atwater CA 95301 209-386-4620 386-4719
Leavenworth 1300 Metropolitan Ave............. Leavenworth KS 66048 913-682-8700 578-1026
Lee PO Box 900.................................. Jonesville VA 24263 276-546-0150 546-9115
Lewisburg 2400 Robert Miller Dr.................. Lewisburg PA 17837 570-523-1251 522-7745
Pollock 1000 Airbase Rd PO Box 1000................ Pollock LA 71467 318-561-5300 561-5391

216 CORRECTIONAL FACILITIES - STATE

SEE ALSO Correctional & Detention Management (Privatized) p. 1764; Correctional Facilities - Federal p. 1764; Juvenile Detention Facilities p. 2136

ALABAMA

Phone | Fax

Bibb Correctional Facility 565 Bibb Ln................ Brent AL 35034 205-926-5252 926-9928
Bullock County Correctional Facility
104 Bullock Dr PO Box 5107 ....Union Springs AL 36089 334-738-5625 738-5020
Donaldson Correctional Facility
100 Warrior Ln................................Bessemer AL 35023 205-436-3681 436-3399

Facility	City	State	Zip	Phone	Fax
Draper Correctional Facility 2828 Hwy 143 PO Box 1107	Elmore	AL	36025	334-567-2221	567-1519
Elmore Correctional Ctr 3520 Marion Spillway Rd *Web:* www.doc.state.al.us	Elmore	AL	36025	334-567-1460	567-1804
Holman Correctional Facility PO Box 3700	Atmore	AL	36503	251-368-8173	368-1095
Kilby Correctional Facility PO Box 150	Mount Meigs	AL	36057	334-215-6600	
Limestone Correctional Facility 28779 Nick Davis Rd	Harvest	AL	35749	256-233-4600	233-1930
Saint Clair Correctional Facility 1000 St Clair Rd	Springville	AL	35146	205-467-6111	467-2474
Staton Correctional Facility PO Box 56	Elmore	AL	36025	334-567-2221	567-0704
Tutwiler Prison for Women 8966 US Hwy 231	Wetumpka	AL	36092	334-567-4369	514-6576
Ventress Correctional Facility PO Box 767	Clayton	AL	36016	334-775-3331	775-8905

ALASKA

Facility	City	State	Zip	Phone	Fax
Anchorage Correctional Complex 1400 E 4th Ave *Web:* www.correct.state.ak.us	Anchorage	AK	99501	907-269-4100	269-4208
Anvil Mountain Correctional Ctr 1810 Ctr Creek Rd PO Box 730 *Web:* www.correct.state.ak.us	Nome	AK	99762	907-443-2241	443-5195
Fairbanks Correctional Ctr 1931 Eagan Ave	Fairbanks	AK	99701	907-458-6700	458-6751
Hiland Mountain Correctional Ctr 9101 Hesterberg Rd	Eagle River	AK	99577	907-694-9511	694-4507
Ketchikan Correctional Ctr 1201 Schoenbar Rd *Web:* www.correct.state.ak.us	Ketchikan	AK	99901	907-225-9429	225-7031
Lemon Creek Correctional Ctr 2000 Lemon Creek Rd *Web:* www.correct.state.ak.us	Juneau	AK	99801	907-465-6200	465-6224
Palmer Correctional Ctr PO Box 919	Palmer	AK	99645	907-745-5054	746-1574
Spring Creek Correctional Ctr Mile 5 Nash Rd PO Box 2109 *Web:* www.correct.state.ak.us/corrections	Seward	AK	99664	907-224-8200	224-8062
Wildwood Correctional Ctr 10 Chugach Ave *Web:* www.correct.state.ak.us	Kenai	AK	99611	907-260-7200	260-7208
Yukon-Kuskokwim Correctional Center 1000 Chief Eddie Hoffman Hwy PO Box 400 *Web:* www.correct.state.ak.us	Bethel	AK	99559	907-543-5245	543-3097

ARIZONA

Facility	City	State	Zip	Phone	Fax
Arizona State Prison Complex-Douglas 6911 N BDI Blvd PO Box 3867 *Web:* www.adc.state.az.us	Douglas	AZ	85607	520-364-7521	364-7445
Arizona State Prison Complex-Eyman 4374 E Butte Ave PO Box 3500 *Web:* www.azcorrections.gov/prisons/Jeff_Florence.aspx	Florence	AZ	85132	520-868-0201	868-0276
Arizona State Prison Complex-Florence 1305 E Butte Ave PO Box 629 *Web:* www.azcorrections.gov/prisons/Jeff_Florence.aspx	Florence	AZ	85132	520-868-4011	868-5333
Arizona State Prison Complex-Lewis 26700 S Hwy 85 PO Box 70 *Web:* www.adc.state.az.us	Buckeye	AZ	85326	623-386-6160	386-7332
Arizona State Prison Complex-Perryville 2105 N Citrus Rd *Web:* www.adc.state.az.us	Goodyear	AZ	85395	623-853-0304	853-0425
Arizona State Prison Complex-Phoenix 2500 E Van Buren PO Box 52109 *Web:* www.adc.state.az.us	Phoenix	AZ	85072	602-685-3100	685-3124
Arizona State Prison Complex-Safford 896 S Crook Rd PO Box 2222 *Web:* www.azcorrections.gov	Safford	AZ	85546	928-428-4698	428-3235
Arizona State Prison Complex-Winslow 2100 S Hwy 87 *Web:* www.adc.state.az.us	Winslow	AZ	86047	928-289-9551	289-2951
Arizona State Prison Complex-Yuma 7125 E Juan Sanchez Blvd *Web:* www.azcorrections.gov	San Luis	AZ	85349	928-627-8871	627-6703

ARKANSAS

Facility	City	State	Zip	Phone	Fax
Arkansas Dept of Corrections Cummins Unit Hwy 388 PO Box 500 *Web:* adc.arkansas.gov	Grady	AR	71644	870-850-8899	850-8861
Arkansas Dept of Corrections Delta Regional Unit 880 E Gaines St *Web:* www.arkansas.gov	Dermott	AR	71638	870-538-2000	538-2027
Arkansas Dept of Corrections East Arkansas Regional Unit 326 Lee St PO Box 180 *Web:* adc.arkansas.gov/Pages/default.aspx	Brickeys	AR	72320	870-295-4700	295-6564
Arkansas Dept of Corrections Maximum Security Unit 2501 State Farm Rd *Web:* www.arkansas.gov	Tucker	AR	72168	501-842-3800	842-1977
Arkansas Dept of Corrections North Central Unit 10 Prison Cir HC 62 PO Box 300 *Web:* adc.arkansas.gov	Calico Rock	AR	72519	870-297-4311	297-4322
Arkansas Dept of Corrections Tucker Unit 2400 State Farm Rd PO Box 240 *Web:* www.arkansas.gov/doc	Tucker	AR	72168	501-842-2519	842-3958
Arkansas Dept of Corrections Varner Unit Hwy 388 PO Box 600 *Web:* adc.arkansas.gov	Grady	AR	71644	870-575-1800	479-3803
Arkansas Dept of Corrections Wrightsville Unit PO Box 1000 *Web:* adc.arkansas.gov	Wrightsville	AR	72183	501-897-5806	897-5716
Ronald McPherson Correctional Facility 302 Wackenhut Way *Web:* www.adc.arkansas.gov	Newport	AR	72112	870-523-2639	523-6202
Scott Grimes Correctional Facility 300 Wackenhut Way	Newport	AR	72112	870-523-5877	523-8302
Texarkana Regional Correction Ctr 305 E 5th St	Texarkana	AR	71854	870-779-3939	779-1616

CALIFORNIA

Facility	City	State	Zip	Phone	Fax
Avenal State Prison 1 Kings Hwy PO Box 39	Avenal	CA	93204	559-386-0587	386-0907
California Correctional Institution 24900 Highway 202 PO Box 1031 *Web:* www.cdcr.ca.gov	Tehachapi	CA	93581	661-822-4402	823-5020
California Men's Colony Hwy 1 PO Box 8101	San Luis Obispo	CA	93409	805-547-7900	547-7529
California State Prison Corcoran 4001 King Ave PO Box 8800	Corcoran	CA	93212	559-992-8800	992-7354
California State Prison Los Angeles County 44750 60th St W	Lancaster	CA	93536	661-729-2000	729-6930
California State Prison Sacramento 100 Prison Rd	Folsom	CA	95630	916-985-8610	294-3001
California State Prison Solano 2100 Peabody Rd PO Box 4000	Vacaville	CA	95696	707-451-0182	454-3200
Calipatria State Prison 7018 Blair Rd	Calipatria	CA	92233	760-348-7000	348-7188
Centinela State Prison 2302 Brown Rd PO Box 731	Imperial	CA	92251	760-337-7900	337-7692
Central California Women's Facility PO Box 1501	Chowchilla	CA	93610	559-665-5531	665-7158*
Chuckawalla Valley State Prison PO Box 2289 *Web:* www.corr.ca.gov	Blythe	CA	92226	760-922-5300	922-6855
Folsom State Prison 300 Prison Rd	Represa	CA	95671	916-985-2561	351-3010
High Desert State Prison PO Box 750	Susanville	CA	96127	530-251-5100	
Ironwood State Prison PO Box 2229	Blythe	CA	92226	760-921-3000	921-3106
Mule Creek State Prison 4001 Hwy 104	Ione	CA	95640	209-274-4911	274-4861
Pelican Bay State Prison PO Box 7000	Crescent City	CA	95532	707-465-1000	465-4376
Pleasant Valley State Prison PO Box 8500	Coalinga	CA	93210	559-935-4900	935-4903
RJ Donovan Correctional Facility at Rock Mountain 480 Alta Rd	San Diego	CA	92179	619-661-6500	661-6253
Salinas Valley State Prison 31625 Hwy 101 N	Soledad	CA	93960	831-678-5500	678-5503
San Quentin State Prison 13 Main St *Web:* www.cdcr.ca.gov	San Quentin	CA	94974	415-454-1460	454-6288
Valley State Prison for Women PO Box 99	Chowchilla	CA	93610	559-665-6100	665-6102

COLORADO

Facility	City	State	Zip	Phone	Fax
Arkansas Valley Correctional Facility 5501 County Ln 13 *Web:* www.doc.state.co.us	Crowley	CO	81034	719-267-3520	267-5024
Buena Vista Correctional Complex 15125 Hwy 24 & 285 PO Box 2017 *Web:* www.doc.state.co.us	Buena Vista	CO	81211	719-395-2404	395-7214
Centennial Correctional Facility E US Hwy 50 Evans Blvd PO Box 600 *Web:* www.doc.state.co.us/facility/ccf-centennial-correctional-facility	Canon City	CO	81215	719-269-5510	269-5545
Colorado Correctional Ctr 15445 S Old Golden Rd PO Box 4020 *Web:* www.doc.state.co.us	Golden	CO	80401	303-273-1620	
Colorado State Penitentiary E US Hwy 50 Evans Blvd PO Box 777 *Web:* www.doc.state.co.us	Canon City	CO	81212	719-269-5120	
Colorado Territorial Correctional Facility 275 W Hwy 50	Canon City	CO	81212	719-275-4181	269-4129
Delta Correctional Ctr 4102 Saw Mill Mesa Rd	Delta	CO	81416	970-874-7614	874-7614
Denver Women's Correctional Facility 3600 Havana St PO Box 392005 *Web:* www.doc.state.co.us/facility/dwcf-denver-womens-correctional-facility	Denver	CO	80239	303-371-4804	
Fremont Correctional Facility E US Hwy 50 Evans Blvd PO Box 999 *Web:* www.doc.state.co.us	Canon City	CO	81215	719-269-5002	269-5020
Limon Correctional Facility 49030 State Hwy 71	Limon	CO	80826	719-775-9221	775-7607
Rifle Correctional Ctr 200 County Rd 219	Rifle	CO	81650	970-625-1700	625-1706
Sterling Correctional Facility PO Box 6000	Sterling	CO	80751	970-521-5010	521-8225

CONNECTICUT

Facility	City	State	Zip	Phone	Fax
Bridgeport Correctional Ctr 1106 N Ave *Web:* www.ccdlc.gov	Bridgeport	CT	06606	203-579-6131	579-6693
Brooklyn Correctional Institution 59 Hartford Rd	Brooklyn	CT	06234	860-779-2600	779-2394

Facility / Address	City	State	Zip	Phone	Fax
Corrigan Correctional Institution 982 Norwich-New London Tpke	Uncasville	CT	06382	860-848-5700	848-5762
Enfield Correctional Institution 289 Shaker Rd	Enfield	CT	06082	860-763-7310	763-7300
Garner Correctional Institution 50 Nunnawauk Rd	Newtown	CT	06470	203-270-2800	270-1826
Gates Correctional Institution 131 N Bridebrook Rd	Niantic	CT	06357	860-691-4700	691-4745
Hartford Correctional Ctr 177 Weston St	Hartford	CT	06120	860-240-1800	566-2725
MacDougall Correctional Institution 1153 E St S	Suffield	CT	06080	860-627-2100	627-2144
New Haven Correctional Ctr 245 Whalley Ave	New Haven	CT	06511	203-789-7111	974-4153
Northern Correctional Institution 287 Bilton Rd	Somers	CT	06071	860-763-8600	763-8651
Radgowski Correctional Institution 982 Norwich-New London Tpke	Uncasville	CT	06382	860-848-5000	848-5020
Webster Correctional Institution 111 Jarvis St	Cheshire	CT	06410	203-271-5900	271-5909
Willard-Cybulski Correctional Institution 391 Shaker Rd	Enfield	CT	06082	860-763-6100	763-6111
York Correctional Institution 201 W Main St	Niantic	CT	06357	860-691-6700	691-6800

DELAWARE

Facility / Address	City	State	Zip	Phone	Fax
Delores J Baylor Women's Correctional Institution 660 Baylor Blvd	New Castle	DE	19720	302-577-3004	577-7099
John L Webb Correctional Facility 200 Greenbank Rd	Wilmington	DE	19808	302-995-6120	995-8596
Multi-Purpose Criminal Facility 1301 E 12th St	Wilmington	DE	19801	302-429-7700	429-7707
Sussex Correctional Institution PO Box 500	Georgetown	DE	19947	302-856-5280	856-5103

FLORIDA

Facility / Address	City	State	Zip	Phone	Fax
Apalachee Correctional Institution 35 Apalachee Dr *Web:* www.dc.state.fl.us/facilities	Sneads	FL	32460	850-718-0688	593-6445
Avon Park Correctional Institution Hwy 64 E PO Box 1100	Avon Park	FL	33826	863-453-3174	453-1511
Baker Correctional Institution 20706 US Hwy 90 *Web:* www.dc.state.fl.us	Sanderson	FL	32087	386-719-4500	758-5759
Bay Correctional Facility 5400 Bayline Dr *Web:* www.correctionscorp.com	Panama City	FL	32404	850-769-1455	769-1942
Brevard Correctional Institution 855 Camp Rd	Cocoa	FL	32927	321-634-6000	634-6066
Broward Correctional Institution 20421 Sheridan St *Web:* www.dc.state.fl.us	Fort Lauderdale	FL	33332	954-252-6400	680-4168
Calhoun Correctional Institution 19562 SE Institutional Dr Unit 1 *Web:* www.dc.state.fl.us	Blountstown	FL	32424	850-237-6500	237-6508
Charlotte Correctional Institution 33123 Oil Well Rd *Web:* www.dc.state.fl.us	Punta Gorda	FL	33955	941-833-2300	575-5747
Columbia Correctional Institution 216 SE Corrections Way	Lake City	FL	32055	386-754-7600	754-7602
Cross City Correctional Institution 568 NE 255 St *Web:* www.dc.state.fl.us	Cross City	FL	32628	352-498-4444	498-1265
Desoto Correctional Institution 13617 SE Hwy 70	Arcadia	FL	34266	863-494-3727	494-1740
Everglades Correctional Institution 1599 SW 187th Ave	Miami	FL	33194	305-228-2000	228-2039
Florida State Prison 7819 NW 228 St	Raiford	FL	32026	904-368-2500	368-2732
Gadsden Correctional Facility 6044 Greensboro Hwy *Web:* www.correctionscorp.com	Quincy	FL	32351	850-875-9701	875-9710
Gainesville Correctional Institution 2845 NE 39th Ave	Gainesville	FL	32609	352-955-2001	334-1675
Glades Correctional Institution 500 Orange Ave Cir	Belle Glade	FL	33430	561-829-1400	992-1355
Gulf Correctional Institution 500 Ike Steele Rd	Wewahitchka	FL	32465	850-639-1000	639-1182
Hamilton Correctional Institution 10650 SW 46th St *Web:* www.dc.state.fl.us	Jasper	FL	32052	386-792-5151	792-5159
Hamilton Correctional Institution Annex 10650 SW 46th St *Web:* www.dc.state.fl.us	Jasper	FL	32052	386-792-5151	792-5159
Hendry Correctional Institution 12551 Wainwright Dr *Web:* www.dc.state.fl.us/facilities/region4	Immokalee	FL	34142	239-867-2100	867-2255
Hernando Correctional Institution 16415 Spring Hill Dr	Brooksville	FL	34604	352-754-6715	544-2307
Hillsborough Correctional Institution 11150 County Rd 672	Riverview	FL	33569	813-671-5022	671-5037
Indian River Correctional Institution 7625 17th St SW *Web:* www.myflorida.com	Vero Beach	FL	32968	772-564-2812	564-2880
Jackson Correctional Institution 5563 10th St	Malone	FL	32445	850-569-5260	482-9969
Lake City Correctional Facility 7906 E US Hwy 90 *Web:* www.cca.com	Lake City	FL	32055	386-755-3379	752-7202
Lake Correctional Institution 19225 US Hwy 27	Clermont	FL	34711	352-394-6146	394-3504
Lancaster Correctional Institution 3449 SW SR 26	Trenton	FL	32693	352-463-4100	463-3476
Lawtey Correctional Institution 7819 NW 228 St	Raiford	FL	32026	904-782-2000	782-1388
Liberty Correctional Institution 11064 NW Dempsey Barron Rd *Web:* www.dc.state.fl.us	Bristol	FL	32321	850-643-9400	643-9412
Lowell Correctional Institution-Men's Unit PO Box 158	Lowell	FL	32663	352-401-6400	840-5657
Lowell Correctional Institution-Women's Unit 11120 NW Gainesville Rd	Ocala	FL	34482	352-401-5301	401-5331
Madison Correctional Institution 382 SW MCI Way	Madison	FL	32340	850-973-5300	973-3666
Mayo Correctional Institution 8784 W US 27 **Fax Area Code:* 904	Mayo	FL	32066	386-294-4500	829-4534*
Moore Haven Correctional Facility 1990 E SR 78 NW PO Box 718501	Moore Haven	FL	33471	863-946-2420	946-2481
New River East Correctional Institution 7819 NW 228th St	Raiford	FL	32028	904-368-3000	368-3205
New River West Correctional Institution 7819 NW 228th St	Raiford	FL	32028	904-368-3000	368-3205
Okaloosa Correctional Institution 3189 Little Silver Rd	Crestview	FL	32539	850-682-0931	689-7803
Okeechobee Correctional Institution 3420 NE 168th St *Web:* www.floridadepartmentofcorrections.com	Okeechobee	FL	34972	863-462-5400	462-5402
Polk Correctional Institution 10800 Evans Rd	Polk City	FL	33868	863-984-2273	984-3072
Putnam Correctional Institution 128 Yelvington Rd *Web:* www.floridadepartmentofcorrections.com	East Palatka	FL	32131	386-326-6800	312-2219
Quincy Correctional Institution 2225 Pat Thomas Pkwy	Quincy	FL	32351	850-627-5400	875-3572
Santa Rosa Correctional Institution 5850 E Milton Rd	Milton	FL	32583	850-983-5800	983-5907
South Bay Correctional Facility 600 US Hwy 27 S	South Bay	FL	33493	561-992-9505	992-9551
Sumter Correctional Institution 9544 County Rd 476 B	Bushnell	FL	33513	352-793-2525	793-3542
Taylor Correctional Institution 8501 Hampton Springs Rd	Perry	FL	32348	850-838-4136	838-4024
Tomoka Correctional Institution 3950 Tiger Bay Rd	Daytona Beach	FL	32124	386-323-1072	323-1006
Union Correctional Institution 7819 NW 228th St	Raiford	FL	32026	386-431-2000	431-2010
Walton Correctional Institution 691 Institution Rd	De Funiak Springs	FL	32433	850-951-1300	951-1750
Washington Correctional Institution 4455 Sam Mitchell Dr	Chipley	FL	32428	850-773-6100	773-6252
Zephyrhills Correctional Institution 2739 Gall Blvd	Zephyrhills	FL	33540	813-782-5521	780-0134

GEORGIA

Facility / Address	City	State	Zip	Phone	Fax
Autry State Prison 3178 Mt Zion Church Rd	Pelham	GA	31779	229-294-2940	294-6691
Baldwin State Prison Laying Farm Rd PO Box 218	Hardwick	GA	31034	478-445-5218	445-6507
Bostick State Prison Bostick Cir PO Box 1700	Hardwick	GA	31034	478-445-4623	445-4623
Calhoun State Prison 823 Main St PO Box 24927	Morgan	GA	39866	229-849-5000	849-5017
Central State Prison 4600 Fulton Mill Rd	Macon	GA	31208	478-471-2906	471-2068
Coastal State Prison 200 Gulfstream Rd	Garden City	GA	31418	912-965-6330	966-6799
Dodge State Prison 2971 Old Bethel Church Rd PO Box 276	Chester	GA	31012	478-358-7200	358-7310
Dooly State Prison 1412 Plunkett Rd PO Box 750	Unadilla	GA	31091	478-627-2000	627-2140
Georgia State Prison 300 1st Ave S	Reidsville	GA	30453	912-557-7301	557-7341
Hancock State Prison 701 Prison Blvd PO Box 339	Sparta	GA	31087	706-444-1000	444-1137
Hays State Prison PO Box 668	Trion	GA	30753	706-857-0400	857-0624
Lee Arrendale State Prison PO Box 709	Alto	GA	30510	706-776-4700	776-4998
Lee State Prison 153 Pinewood Rd	Leesburg	GA	31763	229-759-6453	759-3065
Macon State Prison PO Box 426	Oglethorpe	GA	31068	478-472-3400	472-3524
Metro State Prison 1301 Constitution Rd	Atlanta	GA	30316	404-624-2200	624-2235
Phillips State Prison 2989 W Rock Quarry Rd	Buford	GA	30519	770-932-4500	932-4544
Pulaski State Prison PO Box 839	Hawkinsville	GA	31036	478-783-6000	783-6008
Rivers State Prison PO Box 1500	Hardwick	GA	31034	478-445-4591	445-1391
Rogers State Prison 1978 Georgia Hwy 147	Reidsville	GA	30453	912-557-7771	557-7051
Rutledge State Prison 7175 Manor Rd	Columbus	GA	31907	706-568-2340	568-2126
Smith State Prison PO Box 726	Glennville	GA	30427	912-654-5000	654-5131
Telfair State Prison 201 Long Bridge Rd	Helena	GA	31037	229-868-7721	868-6509
Valdosta State Prison PO Box 310	Valdosta	GA	31601	229-333-7900	333-5387
Walker State Prison PO Box 98	Rock Spring	GA	30739	706-764-3600	764-3613
Ware State Prison 3620 N Harris Rd	Waycross	GA	31501	912-285-6400	287-6520
West Central State Prison PO Box 589	Zebulon	GA	30295	770-567-0531	567-0257
Wilcox State Prison 470 S Broad St	Abbeville	GA	31001	229-467-3000	467-3017

HAWAII

Facility / Address	City	State	Zip	Phone	Fax
Waiawa Correctional Facility PO Box 1839	Pearl City	HI	96782	808-677-6150	677-6155

IDAHO

Facility / Address	City	State	Zip	Phone	Fax
Idaho Correctional Institution-Orofino 23 N Hospital Dr	Orofino	ID	83544	208-476-3655	476-4050
Idaho Maximum Security Institution PO Box 51	Boise	ID	83707	208-338-1635	344-9826
Idaho State Correctional Institution PO Box 14	Boise	ID	83707	208-336-0740	334-2748
North Idaho Correctional Institution 236 Radar Rd	Cottonwood	ID	83522	208-962-3276	962-7119
Pocatello Women's Correctional Ctr 1451 Fore Rd	Pocatello	ID	83204	208-236-6360	236-6362

ILLINOIS

Facility	City	State	ZIP	Phone	Fax
Big Muddy River Correctional Ctr 251 N Hwy 37 PO Box 1000	Ina	IL	62846	618-437-5300	437-5627
Centralia Correctional Ctr 9330 Shattuc Rd PO Box 1266	Centralia	IL	62801	618-533-4111	533-4112
Web: www.idoc.state.il.us/subsections/facilities/information.asp?instchoice=cen					
Danville Correctional Ctr 3820 E Main St	Danville	IL	61834	217-446-0441	446-5347
Web: www.idoc.state.il.us					
Dixon Correctional Ctr 2600 N Brinton Ave.	Dixon	IL	61021	815-288-5561	288-0118
Dwight Correctional Ctr 23813 E 3200 N Rd PO Box 5001	Dwight	IL	60420	815-584-2806	584-2889
East Moline Correctional Ctr 100 Hillcrest Rd	East Moline	IL	61244	309-755-4511	755-2589
Graham Correctional Ctr PO Box 499	Hillsboro	IL	62049	217-532-6961	532-6799
Hill Correctional Ctr PO Box 1327	Galesburg	IL	61401	309-343-4212	343-3812
Illinois River Correctional Ctr Rt 9 W PO Box 999	Canton	IL	61520	309-647-7030	647-0353
Jacksonville Correctional Ctr 2268 E Morton Ave.	Jacksonville	IL	62650	217-245-1481	
Lincoln Correctional Ctr PO Box 549	Lincoln	IL	62656	217-735-5411	735-5381
Logan Correctional Ctr 1096 1350th St	Lincoln	IL	62656	217-735-5581	735-2339
Menard Correctional Ctr 711 Kaskaskia St.	Menard	IL	62259	618-826-5071	826-4915
Pinckneyville Correctional Ctr 5835 SR- 154	Pinckneyville	IL	62274	618-357-9722	357-2083
Pontiac Correctional Ctr 700 W Lincoln St	Pontiac	IL	61764	815-842-2816	842-3420
Robinson Correctional Ctr PO Box 1000	Robinson	IL	62454	618-546-5659	544-2166
Web: www.idoc.state.il.us					
Shawnee Correctional Ctr 6665 SR 146 E	Vienna	IL	62995	618-658-8331	658-8822
Southwestern Correctional Ctr 950 Kings Hwy	East Saint Louis	IL	62203	618-394-2200	394-2228
Stateville Correctional Ctr PO Box 112	Joliet	IL	62434	815-727-3607	727-5511
Tamms Correctional Ctr 200 E Supermax Rd	Tamms	IL	62988	618-747-2042	747-2062
Taylorville Correctional Ctr PO Box 1000	Taylorville	IL	62568	217-824-4004	824-4371
Vandalia Correctional Ctr PO Box 500	Vandalia	IL	62471	618-283-4170	283-9147
Vienna Correctional Ctr 6695 SR 146 E	Vienna	IL	62995	618-658-8371	658-3609
Western Illinois Correctional Ctr RR 4 PO Box 196	Mount Sterling	IL	62353	217-773-4441	773-2202

INDIANA

Facility	City	State	ZIP	Phone	Fax
Edinburgh Correctional Facility 23 & Schoolhouse Rd.	Edinburgh	IN	46124	812-526-8434	526-0406
Henryville Correctional Facility PO Box 148	Henryville	IN	47126	812-294-4372	294-1523
Web: www.in.gov/idoc/2398.htm					
Indiana State Prison 1 Pk Row	Michigan City	IN	46360	219-874-7258	878-5825
Indiana Women's Prison 2596 N Girls School Rd	Indianapolis	IN	46214	317-244-3387	244-4670
Madison Correctional Facility 800 MSH Busstop Dr	Madison	IN	47250	812-265-6154	265-2142
Miami Correctional Facility 3038 W 850 S	Bunker Hill	IN	46914	765-689-8920	689-7479
Pendleton Correctional Facility 4490 W Reformatory Rd	Pendleton	IN	46064	765-778-2107	778-3395
Plainfield Correctional Facility 727 Moon Rd	Plainfield	IN	46168	317-839-2513	837-1875
Putnamville Correctional Facility 1946 W Hwy 40	Greencastle	IN	46135	765-653-8441	653-7461*
Rockville Correctional Facility 811 W 50 N	Rockville	IN	47872	765-569-3178	569-3178
Wabash Valley Correctional Facility PO Box 1111	Carlisle	IN	47838	812-398-5050	398-5065*

IOWA

Facility	City	State	ZIP	Phone	Fax
Anamosa State Penitentiary 406 N High St PO Box 10	Anamosa	IA	52205	319-462-3504	462-4962
Clarinda Correctional Facility 1800 N 16th St # 1	Clarinda	IA	51632	712-542-5634	542-4844
Web: www.doc.state.ia.us					
Fort Dodge Correctional Facility 1550 L St	Fort Dodge	IA	50501	515-574-4700	574-4752
Iowa Correctional Institution for Women 300 Elm Ave SW PO Box 700	Mitchellville	IA	50169	515-967-4236	967-5347
Iowa State Penitentiary PO Box 316	Fort Madison	IA	52627	319-372-5432	372-6967
Newton Correctional Facility 307 S 50th Ave W PO Box 218	Newton	IA	50208	641-792-7552	791-1683
North Central Correctional Facility 313 Lanedale St	Rockwell City	IA	50579	712-297-7521	297-7875

KANSAS

Facility	City	State	ZIP	Phone	Fax
El Dorado Correctional Facility 1737 SE Hwy 54 PO Box 311	El Dorado	KS	67042	316-321-7284	321-5349
Web: www.docnet.dc.state.ks.us					
Hutchinson Correctional Facility PO Box 1568	Hutchinson	KS	67504	620-662-2321	662-8662
Web: www.doc.ks.gov/facilities/hcf					
Lansing Correctional Facility PO Box 2	Lansing	KS	66043	913-727-3235	727-2675
Web: www.accesskansas.org					
Topeka Correctional Facility 815 SE Rice Rd	Topeka	KS	66607	785-296-3432	559-5112
Winfield Correctional Facility 1806 Pine Crest Cir	Winfield	KS	67156	620-221-6660	221-0068

KENTUCKY

Facility	City	State	ZIP	Phone	Fax
Blackburn Correctional Complex 3111 Spurr Rd	Lexington	KY	40511	859-246-2366	246-2376
Eastern Kentucky Correctional Complex 200 Rd to Justice	West Liberty	KY	41472	606-743-2800	743-2811
Web: www.corrections.ky.gov					
Green River Correctional Complex 1200 River Rd PO Box 9300	Central City	KY	42330	270-754-5415	754-2732
Kentucky Correctional Institution for Women PO Box 337	Pewee Valley	KY	40056	502-241-8454	241-0372
Kentucky State Penitentiary PO Box 128	Eddyville	KY	42038	270-388-2211	388-7753
Kentucky State Reformatory 3001 W Hwy 146	LaGrange	KY	40032	502-222-9441	222-8115
Luther Luckett Correctional Complex PO Box 6	LaGrange	KY	40031	502-222-0363	222-2043
Western Kentucky Correctional Complex 374 New Bethel Rd	Ferdonia	KY	42411	270-388-9781	388-0031

LOUISIANA

Facility	City	State	ZIP	Phone	Fax
Allen Correctional Ctr 3751 Lauderdale Woodyard Rd.	Kinder	LA	70648	337-639-2942	639-2944
Avoyelles Correctional Ctr 1630 Prison Rd	Cottonport	LA	71327	318-876-2891	876-4220
C Paul Phelps Correctional Ctr 14925 Hwy 27 N PO Box 1056	Dequincy	LA	70633	337-786-7963	786-4524
Catahoula Correctional Ctr 499 Columbia Rd	Harrisonburg	LA	71340	318-744-2121	744-2126
David Wade Correctional Ctr 670 Bell Hill Rd	Homer	LA	71040	318-927-9631	927-0443
Dixon Correctional Institute 5568 Hwy 68	Jackson	LA	70748	225-634-1200	634-4543
Elayn Hunt Correctional Ctr 6925 Hwy 74 PO Box 174	Saint Gabriel	LA	70776	225-642-3306	319-4596
Web: www.floridadepartmentofcorrections.com					
Louisiana State Penitentiary Hwy 66	Angola	LA	70712	225-655-4411	655-2319
Vernon Correctional Facility 2294 Slagle Rd	Leesville	LA	71446	337-238-4522	238-4208

MAINE

Facility	City	State	ZIP	Phone	Fax
Charleston Correctional Facility 1202 Dover Rd	Charleston	ME	04422	207-285-0800	285-0815
Downeast Correctional Facility 64 Base Rd	Machiasport	ME	04655	207-255-1100	255-1176
Maine Correctional Ctr 17 Mallison Falls Rd	Windham	ME	04062	207-893-7000	893-7001

MARYLAND

Facility	City	State	ZIP	Phone	Fax
Eastern Correctional Institution 30420 Revells Neck Rd.	Westover	MD	21890	410-845-4000	845-4055
Web: www.dpscs.state.md.us					
Jessup Correctional Institution PO Box 534	Jessup	MD	20794	410-799-0100	799-4607
Maryland Correctional Adjustment Ctr 401 E Madison St	Baltimore	MD	21202	410-539-5445	332-4561
Maryland Correctional Institution for Women PO Box 535	Jessup	MD	20794	410-799-5550	799-6146
Maryland Correctional Institution-Hagerstown 18601 Roxbury Rd	Hagerstown	MD	21746	301-733-2800	797-2872
Maryland Correctional Institution-Jessup PO Box 549	Jessup	MD	20794	410-799-7610	799-7527
Web: www.dpscs.maryland.gov					
Maryland Correctional Training Ctr 18800Roxbury Rd	Hagerstown	MD	21746	240-420-1601	797-8574*
**Fax Area Code:* 301 ■ *Web:* www.dpscs.state.md.us					
Roxbury Correctional Institution 18701 Roxbury Rd	Hagerstown	MD	21746	240-420-3000	797-0795*
**Fax Area Code:* 301					
Western Correctional Institution 13800 McMullen Hwy	Cumberland	MD	21502	301-729-7000	729-7063

MASSACHUSETTS

Facility	City	State	ZIP	Phone	Fax
Bay State Correctional Ctr 28 Clark St.	Norfolk	MA	02056	508-668-1687	668-1687
Massachusetts Correctional Institution-Cedar Junction Rt 1 PO Box 100	South Walpole	MA	02071	508-668-2100	660-8008
Massachusetts Correctional Institution-Concord PO Box 9106	Concord	MA	01742	978-405-6100	405-6133
Massachusetts Correctional Institution-Framingham PO Box 9007	Framingham	MA	01704	508-532-5100	532-5104
Massachusetts Correctional Institution-Plymouth PO Box 207	South Carver	MA	02366	508-291-2441	727-3005
North Central Correctional Institution at Gardner 500 Colony Rd	Gardner	MA	01440	978-632-2000	630-6040
Old Colony Correctional Ctr 1 Administration Rd	Bridgewater	MA	02324	508-279-6000	279-6754
Pondville Correctional Ctr PO Box 146	Norfolk	MA	02056	508-660-3924	660-7963
South Middlesex Correctional Ctr 135 Western Ave.	Framingham	MA	01701	508-879-1241	
Souza-Baranowski Correctional Ctr PO Box 8000	Shirley	MA	01464	978-514-6500	514-6529
Web: www.mass.gov					

MICHIGAN

Facility	City	State	ZIP	Phone	Fax
Alger Correctional Facility N 6141 Industrial Pk Dr PO Box 600	Munising	MI	49862	906-387-5000	387-5033
Web: www.michigan.gov/corrections					
Baraga Correctional Facility 13924 Wadaga Rd	Baraga	MI	49908	906-353-7070	353-8246
Web: www.michigan.gov/corrections					

Facility / Address	City	State	ZIP	Phone	Fax
Carson City Correctional Facility 10274 Boyer Rd; *Web:* www.michigan.gov/corrections	Carson City	MI	48811	989-584-3941	
Central Michigan Correctional Facility 320 N Hubbard; *Web:* www.michigan.gov/corrections	Saint Louis	MI	48880	989-681-6668	
Charles E Egeler Correctional Facility 3855 Cooper St; *Web:* www.michigan.gov/corrections	Jackson	MI	49201	517-780-5600	780-5814
Chippewa Correctional Facility 4269 W M-80; *Web:* www.michigan.gov/corrections	Kincheloe	MI	49784	906-495-2275	495-5787
Cooper Street Correctional Facility 3100 Cooper St; *Web:* www.michigan.gov/corrections	Jackson	MI	49201	517-780-6175	780-6179
Earnest C Brooks Correctional Facility 2500 S Sheridan Dr; *Web:* www.michigan.gov/corrections	Muskegon Heights	MI	49444	231-773-9200	777-2097
G Robert Cotton Correctional Facility 3500 N Elm Rd; *Web:* www.michigan.gov/corrections	Jackson	MI	49201	517-780-5000	780-5100
Gus Harrison Correctional Facility 2727 E Beecher St; *Web:* www.michigan.gov	Adrian	MI	49221	517-265-3900	263-4401
Hiawatha Correctional Facility 4533 W Industrial Pk Dr; *Web:* www.michigan.gov	Kincheloe	MI	49786	906-495-5661	495-5291
Huron Valley Correctional Facility 3201 Bemis Rd; *Web:* www.michigan.gov	Ypsilanti	MI	48197	734-572-9900	572-9499
Ionia Maximum Correctional Facility 1576 W Bluewater Hwy; *Web:* www.michigan.gov/corrections	Ionia	MI	48846	616-527-6331	527-6863
Kinross Correctional Facility 16770 S Watertower Dr; *Web:* www.michigan.gov/corrections	Kincheloe	MI	49788	906-495-2282	495-5837
Lakeland Correctional Facility 141 1st St; *Web:* www.michigan.gov/corrections	Coldwater	MI	49036	517-278-6942	279-0327
Macomb Correctional Facility 34625 26th Mile Rd	New Haven	MI	48048	586-749-4900	749-4927
Marquette Branch Prison 1960 US Hwy 41 S; *Web:* www.michigan.gov/corrections	Marquette	MI	49855	906-226-6531	226-6557
Michigan Reformatory 1727 Bluewater Hwy; *Web:* www.michigan.gov/corrections	Ionia	MI	48846	616-527-2500	527-7155
Mound Correctional Facility 17601 Mound Rd; *Web:* www.michigan.gov/corrections	Detroit	MI	48212	313-368-8300	368-8972
Muskegon Correctional Facility 2400 S Sheridan Dr; *Web:* www.michigan.gov/corrections	Muskegon	MI	49442	231-773-3201	773-3657
Newberry Correctional Facility 3001 S Newberry Ave; *Web:* www.michigan.gov/corrections	Newberry	MI	49868	906-293-6200	293-0011
Oaks Correctional Facility 1500 Caberfae Hwy; *Web:* www.michigan.gov/corrections	Manistee	MI	49660	231-723-8272	728-4278
Richard A Handlon Correctional Facility 1728 Bluewater Hwy; *Web:* www.michigan.gov/corrections	Ionia	MI	48846	616-527-3100	527-2991
Riverside Correctional Facility 777 W Riverside Dr; *Web:* www.michigan.gov	Ionia	MI	48846	616-527-0110	527-2936
Saginaw Correctional Facility 9625 Pierce Rd; *Web:* www.michigan.gov	Freeland	MI	48623	989-695-9880	695-6662
Saint Louis Correctional Facility 8585 N Croswell Rd; *Web:* www.michigan.gov	Saint Louis	MI	48880	989-681-6444	681-2425
Thumb Correctional Facility 3225 John Conley Dr; *Web:* www.michigan.gov	Lapeer	MI	48446	810-667-2045	667-2048

MINNESOTA

Facility / Address	City	State	ZIP	Phone	Fax
Minnesota Correctional Facility-Fairbault 1101 Linden Ln; *Fax: Warden ■ *Web:* www.doc.state.mn.us	Faribault	MN	55021	507-334-0700	332-4538*
Minnesota Correctional Facility-Lino Lakes 7525 4th Ave.	Lino Lakes	MN	55014	651-717-6100	
Minnesota Correctional Facility-Moose Lake 1000 Lake Shore Dr	Moose Lake	MN	55767	218-485-5000	485-5010
Minnesota Correctional Facility-Park Heights 5329 Osgood Ave N	Stillwater	MN	55082	651-779-1400	779-1385
Minnesota Correctional Facility-Rush City 7600 525th St.	Rush City	MN	55069	320-358-0400	358-0538
Minnesota Correctional Facility-Shakopee 1010 W 6th Ave; *Web:* www.doc.state.mn.us	Shakopee	MN	55379	952-496-4440	496-4476
Minnesota Correctional Facility-Stillwater 970 Picket St N.	Bayport	MN	55003	651-779-2700	351-3603

MISSISSIPPI

Facility / Address	City	State	ZIP	Phone	Fax
Central Mississippi Correctional Facility 3794 Hwy 468	Pearl	MS	39208	601-932-2880	932-6201
Issaquena County Correctional Facility PO Box 220	Mayersville	MS	39113	662-873-2153	873-2956
Jefferson/Franklin Correctional Facility 279 Hwy 33	Fayette	MS	39069	601-786-2284	786-2289
Leake County Correctional Facility 399 CO Brooks St.	Carthage	MS	39051	601-298-9003	298-9006
Marion/Walthall Correctional Facility 503 S Main St.	Columbia	MS	39429	601-736-3621	736-4473
Marshall County Correctional Facility PO Box 5188	Holly Springs	MS	38634	662-252-7111	252-5777
Mississippi State Penitentiary PO Box 1057	Parchman	MS	38738	662-745-6611	745-8912
South Mississippi Correctional Institution PO Box 1419	Leakesville	MS	39451	601-394-5600	394-6433
Wilkinson County Correctional Ctr PO Box 1079	Woodville	MS	39669	601-888-3199	888-3235
Winston County Correctional Facility PO Drawer 928	Louisville	MS	39339	662-773-2528	773-4989

MISSOURI

Facility / Address	City	State	ZIP	Phone	Fax
Algoa Correctional Ctr 8501 No More Victims Rd PO Box 538	Jefferson City	MO	65102	573-751-3911	526-1385*
Boonville Correctional Ctr 1216 E Morgan St.	Boonville	MO	65233	660-882-6521	882-7825*
Camp Hawthorn 413 Camp Hawthorn Dr PO Box 140	Kaiser	MO	65047	573-348-3194	348-4679
Central Missouri Correctional Ctr 2600 Hwy 179 PO Box 539	Jefferson City	MO	65102	573-751-2053	751-9037
Chillicothe Correctional Ctr 3151 Litton Rd	Chillicothe	MO	64601	660-646-4032	646-1217
Farmington Correctional Ctr 1012 W Columbia St	Farmington	MO	63640	573-218-7100	
Jefferson City Correctional Ctr 8200 No More Victims Rd	Jefferson City	MO	65101	573-751-3224	751-0355
Missouri Eastern Correctional Ctr 18701 Old Hwy 66	Pacific	MO	63069	636-257-3322	257-5296
Moberly Correctional Ctr 201 S Morley St PO Box 7	Moberly	MO	65270	660-263-3778	263-0377
Northeast Correctional Ctr 13698 County Rd 46	Bowling Green	MO	63334	573-324-9975	324-5183
Ozark Correctional Ctr 929 Honor Camp Ln	Fordland	MO	65652	417-767-4491	738-2400
Potosi Correctional Ctr 11593 State Hwy O	Mineral Point	MO	63660	573-438-6000	438-6006
Tipton Correctional Ctr 619 N Osage Ave	Tipton	MO	65081	660-433-2031	433-2613
Western Missouri Correctional Ctr 609 E Pence Rd	Cameron	MO	64429	816-632-1390	632-2562

MONTANA

Facility / Address	City	State	ZIP	Phone	Fax
Montana State Prison 400 Conley Lake Rd	Deer Lodge	MT	59722	406-846-1320	846-2951
Montana Women's Prison 701 S 27th St	Billings	MT	59101	406-247-5100	247-5161

NEBRASKA

Facility / Address	City	State	ZIP	Phone	Fax
Lincoln Correctional Ctr PO Box 22800	Lincoln	NE	68542	402-471-2861	479-6100
Nebraska Correctional Center for Women 1107 Recharge Rd; *Web:* www.corrections.nebraska.gov	York	NE	68467	402-362-3317	362-3892
Nebraska State Penitentiary 4201 S 14th St; *Web:* www.corrections.nebraska.gov	Lincoln	NE	68502	402-471-3161	471-4326
Omaha Correctional Ctr 2323 Ave J PO Box 11099	Omaha	NE	68111	402-595-3964	595-2227

NEVADA

Facility / Address	City	State	ZIP	Phone	Fax
Ely State Prison 4569 N SR 590	Ely	NV	89301	775-289-8800	289-1263
Lovelock Correctional Ctr 1200 Prison Rd.	Lovelock	NV	89419	775-273-1300	273-4277
Nevada State Prison 3301 E 5th St	Carson City	NV	89702	775-887-3406	887-3420
Northern Nevada Correctional Ctr 1721 Snyder Dr PO Box 7000; *Web:* www.doc.nv.gov/nncc	Carson City	NV	89702	775-887-9297	
Southern Desert Correctional Ctr 1 Cold Creek Rd PO Box 208	Indian Springs	NV	89072	702-486-3888	486-3398
Southern Nevada Women's Correctional Facility 4370 Smiley Rd	Las Vegas	NV	89115	702-651-8866	651-0978
Warm Springs Correctional Ctr PO Box 7007	Carson City	NV	89702	775-684-3000	684-3051

NEW HAMPSHIRE

Facility / Address	City	State	ZIP	Phone	Fax
New Hampshire State Prison 281 N State St PO Box 14; *Web:* www.nh.gov/nhdoc/facilities/concord.html	Concord	NH	03302	603-271-1801	271-4092
New Hampshire State Prison for Women 317 Mast Rd	Goffstown	NH	03045	603-668-6137	666-7109
Northern New Hampshire Correctional Facility 138 E Milan Rd	Berlin	NH	03570	603-752-2906	752-0405

NEW JERSEY

Facility / Address	City	State	ZIP	Phone	Fax
Bayside State Prison 4293 Rt 47	Leesburg	NJ	08327	856-785-0040	785-2559
East Jersey State Prison 1100 Woodbridge Ave Lock Bag R	Rahway	NJ	07065	732-499-5010	499-5022
Edna Mahan Correctional Facility for Women 30 County Rd 513 PO Box 4004	Clinton	NJ	08809	908-735-7111	735-5246
Mid-State Correctional Facility PO Box 866	Wrightstown	NJ	08562	609-723-4221	723-1091
New Jersey State Prison PO Box 861	Trenton	NJ	08625	609-292-9700	777-1203
Riverfront State Prison PO Box 9104	Camden	NJ	08101	856-225-5700	225-5998
South Woods State Prison 215 Burlington Rd S	Bridgeton	NJ	08302	856-459-7000	459-7140
Southern State Correctional Facility 4295 Rt 47 PO Box 150	Delmont	NJ	08314	856-785-1300	785-1236

NEW MEXICO

Facility	City	State	Zip	Phone	Fax
Central New Mexico Correctional Facility 1525 Morris Rd	Los Lunas	NM	87031	505-865-1622	865-2316
Guadalupe County Correctional Facility 261 Hwy 54 PO Box 520	Santa Rosa	NM	88435	575-472-1159	472-1006*
**Fax Area Code: 505*					
New Mexico Women's Correctional Facility PO Box 800	Grants	NM	87020	505-287-2941	285-6828
Penitentiary of New Mexico 4311 Hwy 14	Santa Fe	NM	87505	505-827-8205	827-8220
Roswell Correctional Ctr 578 W Chickasaw Rd	Hagerman	NM	88232	505-625-3100	625-3190
Web: www.corrections.state.nm.us					
Southern New Mexico Correctional Facility 1983 Joe R Silva Blvd	Las Cruces	NM	88004	575-523-3200	523-3349
Torrance County Detention Ctr PO Box 837	Estancia	NM	87016	505-384-2711	384-5184

NEW YORK

Facility	City	State	Zip	Phone	Fax
Adirondack Correctional Facility Old Ray Brooks Rd PO Box 110	Ray Brook	NY	12977	518-891-1343	
Albion Correctional Facility 3595 State School Rd	Albion	NY	14411	585-589-5511	
Altona Correctional Facility 555 Devil Den Rd	Altona	NY	12910	518-236-7841	
Arthur Kill Correctional Facility 2911 Arthur Kill Rd	Staten Island	NY	10309	718-356-7333	
Attica Correctional Facility 639 Exchange St PO Box 149	Attica	NY	14011	585-591-2000	
Auburn Correctional Facility 135 State St PO Box 618	Auburn	NY	13021	315-253-8401	253-8401
Bare Hill Correctional Facility 181 Brand Rd	Malone	NY	12953	518-483-8411	483-8411
Bayview Correctional Facility 550 W 20th St	New York	NY	10011	212-255-7590	
Beacon Correctional Facility 50 Camp Beacon Rd PO Box 780	Beacon	NY	12508	845-831-4200	
Bedford Hills Correctional Facility 247 Harris Rd	Bedford Hills	NY	10507	914-241-3100	
Buffalo Correctional Facility 3052 Wende Rd PO Box 300	Alden	NY	14004	716-937-3786	937-3789
Camp Gabriels Correctional Facility Rt 86 PO Box 100	Gabriels	NY	12939	518-327-3111	
Camp Georgetown Correctional Facility 3191 Crumbhill Rd	Georgetown	NY	13072	315-837-4446	847-2099
Camp Pharsalia Correctional Facility 496 Ctr Rd	South Plymouth	NY	13844	607-334-2264	
Cape Vincent Correctional Facility Rt 12E PO Box 599	Cape Vincent	NY	13618	315-654-4100	654-4103
Cayuga Correctional Facility Rt 38 A PO Box 1150	Moravia	NY	13118	315-497-1110	
Chateaugay Correctional Facility 7874 SR 11 PO Box 320	Chateaugay	NY	12920	518-497-3300	
Clinton Correctional Facility 1156 Cook St PO Box 2000	Dannemora	NY	12929	518-492-2511	
Collins Correctional Facility Middle Rd PO Box 490	Collins	NY	14034	716-532-4588	
Coxsackie Correctional Facility Rt 9 W PO Box 200	Coxsackie	NY	12051	518-731-2781	
Downstate Correctional Facility 121 Red School House Rd	Fishkill	NY	12524	845-831-6600	
Eastern Correctional Facility Institution Rd PO Box 338	Napanoch	NY	12458	845-647-7400	
Edgecombe Correctional Facility 611 Edgecombe Ave	New York	NY	10032	212-923-2575	
Elmira Correctional Facility 1879 Davis St	Elmira	NY	14902	607-734-3901	
Fishkill Correctional Facility 271 Matteawan Rd	Beacon	NY	12508	845-831-4800	
Franklin Correctional Facility 62 Bare Hill Rd PO Box 10	Malone	NY	12953	518-483-6040	
Fulton Correctional Facility 1511 Fulton Ave	Bronx	NY	10457	718-583-8000	
Gouverneur Correctional Facility 112 Scotch Settlement Rd	Gouverneur	NY	13642	315-287-7351	287-7351
Gowanda Correctional Facility PO Box 350	Gowanda	NY	14070	716-532-0177	
Great Meadow Correctional Facility 11739 SR 22 PO Box 51	Comstock	NY	12821	518-639-5516	
Green Haven Correctional Facility Rt 554	Stormville	NY	12582	845-221-2711	
Greene Correctional Facility Rt 9 W PO Box 975	Coxsackie	NY	12051	518-731-2741	
Groveland Correctional Facility 7000 Sonyea Rd	Sonyea	NY	14556	585-658-2871	
Hudson Correctional Facility 50 E Ct St PO Box 576	Hudson	NY	12534	518-828-4311	
Lakeview Correctional Facility PO Box T	Brocton	NY	14716	716-792-7100	792-3099
Lincoln Correctional Facility 31-33 W 110th St	New York	NY	10026	212-860-9400	860-2099
Livingston Correctional Facility Sonyea Rd Rt 36 PO Box 49	Sonyea	NY	14556	585-658-3710	658-3710
Lyon Mountain Correctional Facility 3864 SR 374	Lyon Mountain	NY	12952	518-735-4546	
Marcy Correctional Facility PO Box 5000	Marcy	NY	13403	315-768-1400	
Mid-Orange Correctional Facility 900 Kings Hwy	Warwick	NY	10990	845-986-2291	
Mid-State Correctional Facility PO Box 216	Marcy	NY	13403	315-768-8581	
Mohawk Correctional Facility 6100 School Rd PO Box 8450	Rome	NY	13440	315-339-5232	
Monterey Shock Incarceration Correctional Facility 2150 Evergreen Hill Rd	Beaver Dams	NY	14812	607-962-3184	
Moriah Shock Incarceration Correctional Facility PO Box 999	Mineville	NY	12956	518-942-7561	
Mount McGregor Correctional Facility 1000 Mt McGregor Rd PO Box 2071	Wilton	NY	12831	518-587-3960	
Ogdensburg Correctional Facility 1 Correctional Way	Ogdensburg	NY	13669	315-393-0281	
Oneida Correctional Facility 6100 School Rd	Rome	NY	13440	315-339-6880	
Orleans Correctional Facility 3531 Gaines Basin Rd	Albion	NY	14411	585-589-6820	
Otisville Correctional Facility PO Box 8	Otisville	NY	10963	845-386-1490	
Queensboro Correctional Facility 47-04 Van Dam St	Long Island City	NY	11101	718-361-8920	
Riverview Correctional Facility PO Box 158	Ogdensburg	NY	13669	315-393-8400	
Rochester Correctional Facility 470 Ford St	Rochester	NY	14608	585-454-2280	454-3412
Shawangunk Correctional Facility 750 Prison Rd	Wallkill	NY	12589	845-895-2081	
Sing Sing Correctional Facility 354 Hunter St	Ossining	NY	10562	914-941-0108	
Southport Correctional Facility PO Box 2000	Pine City	NY	14871	607-737-0850	
Sullivan Correctional Facility 325 Riverside Dr	Fallsburg	NY	12733	845-434-2080	
Summit Shock Incarceration Correctional Facility 137 Eagle Heights Rd	Summit	NY	12175	518-287-1721	
Taconic Correctional Facility 250 Harris Rd	Bedford Hills	NY	10507	914-241-3010	
Ulster Correctional Facility 750 Berme Rd PO Box 800	Napanoch	NY	12458	845-647-1670	
Upstate Correctional Facility PO Box 2000	Malone	NY	12953	518-483-6997	
Wallkill Correctional Facility PO Box G	Wallkill	NY	12589	845-895-2021	
Washington Correctional Facility PO Box 180	Comstock	NY	12821	518-639-4486	
Watertown Correctional Facility 23147 Swan Rd	Watertown	NY	13601	315-782-7490	
Wende Correctional Facility 3040 Wende Rd PO Box 1187	Alden	NY	14004	716-937-4000	
Wyoming Correctional Facility PO Box 501	Attica	NY	14011	585-591-1010	

NORTH CAROLINA

Facility	City	State	Zip	Phone	Fax
Anson Correctional Center 1019 Old Prison Camp Rd PO Box 189	Polkton	NC	28135	704-694-7500	694-9655
Web: www.doc.state.nc.us/dop					
Avery/Mitchell Correctional Ctr Amity Rd PO Box 608	Spruce Pine	NC	28777	828-765-0229	765-0946
Brown Creek Correctional Institution 248 Prison Camp Rd PO Box 310	Polkton	NC	28135	704-694-2622	694-2709
Buncombe Correctional Ctr Hwy 251 N PO Box 18089	Asheville	NC	28814	828-645-7630	658-2494
Cabarrus Correctional Ctr 130 Dutch Rd PO Box 158	Mount Pleasant	NC	28124	704-436-6519	436-2709*
**Fax Area Code: 784*					
Caldwell Correctional Ctr 480 Pleasant Hill Rd	Hudson	NC	28645	828-726-2509	726-2516
Web: www.doc.state.nc.us					
Caledonia Correctional Institution 2787 Caledonia Dr PO Box 137	Tillery	NC	27887	252-826-5621	826-5434
Carteret Correctional Facility 1084 Orange St PO Box 220	Newport	NC	28570	252-223-5100	223-3069
Web: www.doc.state.nc.us					
Caswell Correctional Ctr 444 County Home Rd PO Box 217	Yanceyville	NC	27379	336-694-4531	694-5098
Web: www.doc.state.nc.us					
Catawba Correctional Ctr 1347 Prison Camp Rd	Newton	NC	28658	828-466-5521	466-5523
Central Prison 1300 Western Blvd	Raleigh	NC	27606	919-733-0800	733-6915
Charlotte Correctional Ctr 4100 Meadow Oak Dr	Charlotte	NC	28208	704-357-6030	357-8313
Web: www.doc.state.nc.us					
Cleveland Correctional Ctr 260 Kemper Rd	Shelby	NC	28152	704-480-5428	480-5429
Columbus Correctional Institution 1255 Prison Camp Rd	Brunswick	NC	28424	910-642-3285	642-8456
Craggy Correctional Ctr 2992 Riverside Dr	Asheville	NC	28804	828-645-5315	658-2183
Davidson Correctional Ctr 1400 Thomason St	Lexington	NC	27292	336-249-7528	249-6962
Web: www.doc.state.nc.us					
Duplin Correctional Ctr 364 S Hwy 11 & 903 PO Box 780	Kenansville	NC	28349	910-296-0315	296-0165
Web: www.doc.state.nc.us					
Durham Correctional Ctr 3900 Guess Rd	Durham	NC	27705	919-477-2314	471-2257
Eastern Correctional Institution 2821 Hwy 903 N PO Box 215	Maury	NC	28554	252-747-8101	747-8260
Forsyth Correctional Ctr 307 Craft Dr	Winston-Salem	NC	27105	336-896-7041	896-7045
Web: www.doc.state.nc.us					
Fountain Correctional Center for Women 300 Fountain School Rd PO Box 1435	Rocky Mount	NC	27802	252-442-9712	442-1413
Franklin Correctional Ctr 5918 NC 39 Hwy S PO Box 155	Bunn	NC	27508	919-496-6119	496-6032
Gaston Correctional Ctr 520 Justice Ct	Dallas	NC	28034	704-922-3861	922-1491
Web: www.doc.state.nc.us					
Gates Correctional Ctr 308 US 158 W PO Box 385	Gatesville	NC	27938	252-357-0778	357-2005
Greene Correctional Institution 2699 Hwy 903 N PO Box 39	Maury	NC	28554	252-747-3676	747-4432
Guilford Correctional Ctr 4250 Camp Burton Rd	McLeansville	NC	27301	336-375-5024	375-0382
Harnett Correctional Institution 1210 McNeil St	Lillington	NC	27546	910-893-2751	893-6432
Haywood Correctional Ctr 141 Hemlock St	Waynesville	NC	28786	828-452-5141	456-8473
Hoke Correctional Institution PO Box 700	Raeford	NC	28376	910-944-7612	944-4752
Hyde Correctional Ctr 620 Prison Rd PO Box 278	Swanquarter	NC	27885	252-926-1810	926-2306
Web: www.doc.state.nc.us					
Johnston Correctional Institution 2465 US 70 W	Smithfield	NC	27577	919-934-8386	934-9150
Lincoln Correctional Ctr 464 Roper Dr	Lincolnton	NC	28092	704-735-0485	735-7801
Lumberton Correctional Institution PO Box 1649	Lumberton	NC	28359	910-618-5574	618-5615
Marion Correctional Institution 355 Old Glenwood Rd	Marion	NC	28752	828-659-7810	652-0115
Nash Correctional Institution PO Box 600	Nashville	NC	27856	252-459-4455	459-7728

Facility	City	State	ZIP	Phone	Fax
Neuse Correctional Institution Caller Box 8009	Goldsboro	NC	27533	919-731-2023	731-2033
New Hanover Correctional Ctr PO Box 240	Wilmington	NC	28402	910-251-2666	251-2670
North Carolina Correctional Institution for Women 1034 Bragg St	Raleigh	NC	27610	919-733-4340	733-8031
North Piedmont Correctional Center for Women PO Box 1227	Lexington	NC	27292	336-242-1259	248-6539
Odom Correctional Institution 485 Odom Prison Rd	Jackson	NC	27845	252-534-5611	534-1852
Orange Correctional Ctr 2110 Clarence Walters Rd	Hillsborough	NC	27278	919-732-9301	644-1395
Pasquotank Correctional Institution 527 Commerce Dr	Elizabeth City	NC	27906	252-331-4881	331-4866
Pender Correctional Institution PO Box 1058	Burgaw	NC	28425	910-259-8735	259-8760
Piedmont Correctional Institution 1245 Camp Rd	Salisbury	NC	28147	704-639-7540	639-7610
Raleigh Correctional Center for Women 1201 S State St	Raleigh	NC	27610	919-733-4248	733-9737
Randolph Correctional Ctr 2760 US Hwy 220 PO Box 4128	Asheboro	NC	27203	336-625-2578	625-5717
Robeson Correctional Ctr PO Box 1979	Lumberton	NC	28356	910-618-5535	618-5539
Rowan Correctional Ctr PO Box 1207	Salisbury	NC	28145	704-639-7552	639-7558
Rutherford Correctional Ctr PO Box 127	Spindale	NC	28160	828-286-4121	286-9285
Sampson Correctional Institution PO Box 1109	Clinton	NC	28328	910-592-2151	592-2543
Sanford Correctional Ctr 417 Prison Camp Rd	Sanford	NC	27330	919-776-4325	774-1866
Southern Correctional Institution PO Box 786	Troy	NC	27371	910-572-3784	576-2145
Tillery Correctional Ctr PO Box 222	Tillery	NC	27887	252-826-4165	826-3287
Union Correctional Ctr 200 S Sutherland Ave	Monroe	NC	28112	704-283-6142	283-6832
Wake Correctional Ctr 1000 Rock Quarry Rd	Raleigh	NC	27610	919-733-7988	733-9166
Warren Correctional Institution 379 Collins Rd PO Box 399	Manson	NC	27553	252-456-3400	456-4300
Wilkes Correctional Ctr 404 Statesville Rd	North Wilkesboro	NC	28659	336-667-4533	667-4095

OHIO

Facility	City	State	ZIP	Phone	Fax
Allen Correctional Institution 2238 N W St (*Web:* www.drc.state.oh.us)	Lima	OH	45802	419-224-8000	224-2726
Belmont Correctional Institution 68318 Bannock Rd	Saint Clairsville	OH	43950	740-695-5169	695-6869
Chillicothe Correctional Institution 15802 SR 104 PO Box 5500	Chillicothe	OH	45601	740-774-7080	773-8296
Dayton Correctional Institution 4104 Germantown St	Dayton	OH	45417	937-263-0058	263-9285
Grafton Correctional Institution 2500 S Avon Beldon Rd	Grafton	OH	44044	440-748-1161	748-2521
Lebanon Correctional Institution PO Box 56	Lebanon	OH	45036	513-932-1211	932-5093
London Correctional Institution 1580 SR 56 (*Web:* www.drc.ohio.gov)	London	OH	43140	740-852-2454	852-4854
Lorain Correctional Institution 2075 Avon Belden Rd	Grafton	OH	44044	440-748-1049	748-2191
Madison Correctional Institution PO Box 740	London	OH	43140	740-852-9777	852-2017
Mansfield Correctional Institution PO Box 788	Mansfield	OH	44901	419-525-4455	524-8022
Marion Correctional Institution PO Box 57 (*Web:* www.state.oh.us)	Marion	OH	43302	740-382-5781	382-0595
Noble Correctional Institution 15708 SR 78	Caldwell	OH	43724	740-732-5188	732-2651
North Central Correctional Institution 670 Marion Williamsport	Marion	OH	43302	740-387-7040	387-5587
Ohio Reformatory for Women 1479 Collins Ave	Marysville	OH	43040	937-642-1065	642-7603
Ohio State Penitentiary 878 Coitsville Hubbard Rd	Youngstown	OH	44505	330-743-0700	742-5144
Pickaway Correctional Camp 1171 SR 762 PO Box 209	Orient	OH	43146	614-877-4367	877-1739
Pickaway Correctional Institution PO Box 209 (*Web:* www.drc.ohio.gov)	Orient	OH	43146	614-877-4362	877-4514
Richland Correctional Institution 1001 Olivesburg Rd	Mansfield	OH	44905	419-526-2100	521-2810
Ross Correctional Institution 16149 SR 104 PO Box 7010	Chillicothe	OH	45601	740-774-7050	774-7065
Southeastern Correctional Institution 5900 B I S Rd	Lancaster	OH	43130	740-653-4324	653-0779
Southern Ohio Correctional Facility 1724 SR 728 PO Box 45699	Lucasville	OH	45699	740-259-5544	259-2882
Toledo Correctional Institution 2001 E Central Ave PO Box 80033	Toledo	OH	43608	419-726-7977	726-7157
Trumbull Correctional Institution 5701 Burnett Rd	Leavittsburg	OH	44430	330-898-0820	898-0848
Warren Correctional Institution 5787 SR 63	Lebanon	OH	45036	513-932-3388	932-0312

OKLAHOMA

Facility	City	State	ZIP	Phone	Fax
Charles E Johnson Correctional Ctr 1856 Eastland St	Alva	OK	73717	580-327-8000	327-8010
Cimarron Correctional Facility 3200 S Kings Hwy (*Web:* www.cca.com)	Cushing	OK	74023	918-225-3336	225-3363
Davis Correctional Facility 6888 E 133rd Rd (*Web:* www.correctionscorp.com)	Holdenville	OK	74848	405-379-6400	379-6496
Diamondback Correctional Facility Rt 2 PO Box 336	Watonga	OK	73772	580-614-2000	614-2020
Eddie Warrior Correctional Ctr 400 N Oak St	Taft	OK	74463	918-683-8365	682-4782
Great Plains Correctional Facility 700 Sugar Creek Dr PO Box 1018	Hinton	OK	73047	405-542-3711	542-3710
Howard McLeod Correctional Ctr 1970 E Whippoorwill Ln (*Web:* www.doc.state.ok.us)	Atoka	OK	74525	580-889-6651	889-2264
Jackie Brannon Correctional Ctr PO Box 1999	McAlester	OK	74502	918-421-3399	426-0004
James Crabtree Correctional Ctr Rt 1 PO Box 8	Helena	OK	73741	580-852-3221	852-3695
Jess Dunn Correctional Ctr PO Box 316 (*Web:* www.doc.state.ok.us)	Taft	OK	74463	918-682-7841	682-4372
John Lilley Correctional Ctr PO Box 1908	Boley	OK	74829	918-667-3381	667-3959
Joseph Harp Correctional Ctr PO Box 548	Lexington	OK	73051	405-527-5593	527-4841
Lawton Correctional Facility 8607 SE Flower Mound Rd	Lawton	OK	73501	580-351-2778	351-2641
Mabel Bassett Correctional Center 29501 Kickapoo Rd	McLoud	OK	74851	405-964-3020	964-3014
Mack Alford Correctional Ctr PO Box 220	Stringtown	OK	74569	580-346-7301	346-7214
Northeast Oklahoma Correctional Ctr 442606 E 250th Rd	Vinita	OK	74301	918-256-3392	256-2108
Oklahoma State Penitentiary PO Box 97	McAlester	OK	74502	918-423-4700	423-3862
Oklahoma State Reformatory PO Box 514	Granite	OK	73547	580-480-3700	535-4803

OREGON

Facility	City	State	ZIP	Phone	Fax
Coffee Creek Correctional Facility 24499 SW Grahams Ferry Rd (*Web:* www.oregon.gov)	Wilsonville	OR	97070	503-570-6400	570-6417
Columbia River Correctional Institution 9111 NE Sunderland Ave (*Web:* www.oregon.gov)	Portland	OR	97211	503-280-6646	280-6012
Millcreek Correctional Facility 5465 Turner Rd	Salem	OR	97301	503-378-2600	373-7424
Oregon State Correctional Institution 3405 Deer Pk Dr SE	Salem	OR	97310	503-373-0101	378-8919
Oregon State Penitentiary 2605 State St	Salem	OR	97310	503-378-2453	378-3897
Powder River Correctional Facility 3600 13th St	Baker City	OR	97814	541-523-6680	523-6678
Santiam Correctional Institution 4005 Aumsville Hwy SE	Salem	OR	97301	503-378-5807	378-3261
Shutter Creek Correctional Institution 95200 Shutters Landing Ln	North Bend	OR	97459	541-756-6666	756-6888
Snake River Correctional Institution 777 Stanton Blvd	Ontario	OR	97914	541-881-5000	881-5052
South Fork Forest Camp 48300 Wilson River Hwy	Tillamook	OR	97141	503-842-2811	842-6572
Two Rivers Correctional Institution 82911 Beach Access Rd	Umatilla	OR	97882	541-922-2001	922-2046

PENNSYLVANIA

Facility	City	State	ZIP	Phone	Fax
Quehanna Motivational Boot Camp HC PO Box 32	Karthaus	PA	16845	814-263-4125	263-3901
SCI-Albion 10745 Rt 18	Albion	PA	16475	814-756-5778	756-9737
SCI-Cambridge Springs 451 Fullerton Ave	Cambridge Springs	PA	16403	814-398-5400	398-5413
SCI-Coal Township 1 Kelley Dr	Coal Township	PA	17866	570-644-7890	644-3410
SCI-Cresson PO Box A Old Rt 22	Cresson	PA	16699	814-886-8181	946-6977
SCI-Dallas 1000 Follies Rd	Dallas	PA	18612	570-675-1101	820-4842
SCI-Frackville 1111 Altamont Blvd	Frackville	PA	17931	570-874-4516	794-2013
SCI-Graterford PO Box 246	Graterford	PA	19426	610-489-4151	409-1165
SCI-Greene 169 Progress Dr	Waynesburg	PA	15370	724-852-2902	852-5548
SCI-Greensburg Rt 119 S Rd 10 PO Box 10	Greensburg	PA	15601	724-837-4397	832-5412
SCI-Houtzdale PO Box 1000	Houtzdale	PA	16698	814-378-1000	378-1030
SCI-Huntingdon 1100 Pike St	Huntingdon	PA	16654	814-643-2400	946-7380
SCI-Laurel Highlands PO Box 631	Somerset	PA	15501	814-443-0305	433-0269
SCI-Mahanoy 301 Morea Rd	Frackville	PA	17932	570-773-2158	621-3096
SCI-Muncy PO Box 180	Muncy	PA	17756	570-546-3171	546-8609
SCI-Pine Grove 189 Fyock Rd	Indiana	PA	15701	724-465-9630	464-5139
SCI-Pittsburgh 3001 Beaver Rd	Pittsburgh	PA	15233	412-761-1955	223-2010
SCI-Retreat 660 SR 11	Hunlock Creek	PA	18621	570-735-8754	733-1041
SCI-Rockview PO Box A	Bellefonte	PA	16823	814-355-4874	355-6026
SCI-Smithfield 1120 Pike St	Huntingdon	PA	16652	814-643-6520	946-7339
SCI-Somerset 1590 Walters Mill Rd	Somerset	PA	15510	814-443-8100	443-8137
SCI-Waymart PO Box 256	Waymart	PA	18472	570-488-5811	253-7129

RHODE ISLAND

Facility	City	State	ZIP	Phone	Fax
Donald Price Medium Security Ctr Goddard Rd PO Box 20983	Cranston	RI	02920	401-462-1202	462-1198
Donald W Wyatt Detention Facility 950 High St (*Web:* www.wyattdetention.com)	Central Falls	RI	02863	401-729-1190	729-1194
High Security Ctr PO Box 8200	Cranston	RI	02920	401-462-2028	462-2936
John J Moran Medium Security Ctr PO Box 8274	Cranston	RI	02920	401-462-3774	
Maximum Security Ctr PO Box 8273	Cranston	RI	02920	401-462-2054	
Women's Facility PO Box 8312	Cranston	RI	02920	401-462-2361	462-1842

SOUTH CAROLINA

Facility	City	State	ZIP	Phone	Fax
Allendale Correctional Institution 1057 Revolutionary Trail PO Box 1151	Fairfax	SC	29827	803-632-2561	632-2498
Broad River Correctional Institution 4460 Broad River Rd	Columbia	SC	29210	803-896-2200	896-2192
Evans Correctional Institution 610 Hwy 9 W (**Fax Area Code:* 803)	Bennettsville	SC	29512	843-479-4181	896-4977*
Goodman Correctional Institution 4556 Broad River Rd	Columbia	SC	29210	803-896-8565	896-1216
Kershaw Correctional Institution 4848 Gold Mine Hwy	Kershaw	SC	29067	803-896-3300	896-3310
Kirkland Correctional Institution 4344 Broad River Rd	Columbia	SC	29210	803-896-8572	896-8570
Leath Correctional Institution 2809 Airport Rd (**Fax Area Code:* 803)	Greenwood	SC	29649	864-229-5709	896-1012*

Facility	City	State	ZIP	Phone	Fax
Lee Correctional Institution 990 Wisacky Hwy	Bishopville	SC	29010	803-896-2400	896-2405
Lieber Correctional Institution PO Box 205 *Fax Area Code: 803	Ridgeville	SC	29472	843-875-3332	896-3740*
MacDougall Correctional Institution 1516 Old Gilliard Rd	Ridgeville	SC	29472	843-688-5251	688-4047
McCormick Correctional Institution 386 Redemption Way	McCormick	SC	29899	864-443-2114	443-2114
Northside Correctional Institution PO Box 580	Una	SC	29378	864-594-4915	594-4919
Perry Correctional Institution 430 Oaklawn Rd	Pelzer	SC	29669	864-243-4700	243-4244
Ridgeland Correctional Institution PO Box 2039 *Fax Area Code: 803	Ridgeland	SC	29936	843-726-6888	896-3222*
Stevenson Correctional Institution 4546 Broad River Rd	Columbia	SC	29210	803-896-8575	896-1222
Trenton Correctional Institution 84 Greenhouse Rd	Trenton	SC	29847	803-896-3000	896-3013
Turbeville Correctional Institution PO Box 252 *Fax Area Code: 803	Turbeville	SC	29162	843-659-4800	896-3195*
Walden Correctional Institution 4340 Broad River Rd	Columbia	SC	29210	803-896-8580	896-1225
Wateree River Correctional Institution PO Box 189	Rembert	SC	29128	803-432-6191	896-3408
Women's Correctional Institution 4450 Broad River Rd	Columbia	SC	29210	803-896-8590	896-1226

SOUTH DAKOTA

Facility	City	State	ZIP	Phone	Fax
Jameson Annex PO Box 5911	Sioux Falls	SD	57117	605-367-5120	367-5585
Mike Durfee State Prison 1412 Wood St	Springfield	SD	57062	605-369-2201	369-2813
Redfield Trusty Unit 17262 W 6th St	Redfield	SD	57469	605-472-4424	472-4408
South Dakota State Penitentiary 1600 N Dr PO Box 5911 *Web:* doc.sd.gov	Sioux Falls	SD	57117	605-367-5051	367-5038
Yankton Trusty Unit 176 Micholson Dr	Yankton	SD	57078	605-668-3354	668-3358

TENNESSEE

Facility	City	State	ZIP	Phone	Fax
Hardeman County Correctional Facility 2520 Union Springs Rd PO Box 549 *Web:* www.cca.com	Whiteville	TN	38075	731-254-6000	254-6060
Northeast Correctional Complex PO Box 5000	Mountain City	TN	37683	423-727-7387	727-5415
Northwest Correctional Complex 960 SR 212	Tiptonville	TN	38079	731-253-5000	253-5150
Riverbend Maximum Security Institution 7475 Cockrill Bend Blvd	Nashville	TN	37243	615-350-3100	350-3400
South Central Correctional Facility PO Box 279	Clifton	TN	38425	931-676-5372	676-5104
Tennessee Prison for Women 3881 Stewarts Ln *Web:* www.tenesse.gov	Nashville	TN	37243	615-741-1255	253-5388
Turney Center Industrial Prison & Farm 1499 RW Moore Memorial Hwy	Only	TN	37140	931-729-5161	729-9275
Wayne County Boot Camp PO Box 182	Clifton	TN	38425	931-676-3345	676-5385
West Tennessee State Penitentiary PO Box 1150	Henning	TN	38041	731-738-5044	

TEXAS

Facility	City	State	ZIP	Phone	Fax
Bartlett State Jail 1018 Arnold Dr *Web:* www.correctionscorp.com	Bartlett	TX	76511	254-527-3300	527-4489
Bradshaw State Jail 3900 W Loop 571 N PO Box 9000 *Web:* www.correctionscorp.com	Henderson	TX	75653	903-655-0880	655-0500
Cole State Jail 3801 Silo Rd	Bonham	TX	75418	903-583-1100	583-7903*
Dawson State Jail 106 W Commerce St *Web:* www.correctionscorp.com	Dallas	TX	75207	214-744-4422	744-3113
Dominguez State Jail 6535 Cagnon Rd	San Antonio	TX	78252	210-675-6620	677-0316
Formby State Jail 998 County Rd AA	Plainview	TX	79072	806-296-2448	293-4877
Gist State Jail 3295 FM 3514	Beaumont	TX	77705	409-727-8400	722-9569
Hutchins State Jail 1500 E Langdon Rd *Fax Area Code: 469	Dallas	TX	75241	972-225-1304	941-3613*
Kegans State Jail 707 Top St	Houston	TX	77002	713-224-6584	298-6371
Lindsey State Jail 1620 FM 3344	Jacksboro	TX	76458	940-567-2272	567-2292
Lopez State Jail 1203 El Cibolo Rd	Edinburg	TX	78542	956-316-3810	316-7447
Lychner State Jail 2350 Atascocita Rd	Humble	TX	77396	281-454-5036	454-4163
Plane State Jail 904 FM 686	Dayton	TX	77535	936-258-2476	257-4449
Sanchez State Jail 3901 State Jail Rd	El Paso	TX	79938	915-856-0046	849-4795
Travis County State Jail 8101 FM 969	Austin	TX	78724	512-926-4482	929-8297
Willacy County State Jail 1695 S Buffalo Dr	Raymondville	TX	78580	956-689-4900	689-4001
Woodman State Jail 1210 Coryell City Rd	Gatesville	TX	76528	254-865-9398	865-2940

UTAH

Facility	City	State	ZIP	Phone	Fax
Central Utah Correctional Facility 255 E 300 N	Gunnison	UT	84634	435-528-6000	528-6051
Iron County Utah State Correctional Facility 2136 N Main St	Cedar City	UT	84720	435-867-7555	867-7604
Utah State Prison PO Box 250	Draper	UT	84020	801-576-7000	545-5523

VERMONT

Facility	City	State	ZIP	Phone	Fax
Chittenden Regional Correctional Facility 7 Farrell St *Web:* www.doc.state.vt.us	South Burlington	VT	05403	802-863-7356	863-7473
Marble Valley Regional Correctional Facility 167 State St	Rutland	VT	05701	802-786-5830	786-5843
Northeast Regional Correctional Facility 1270 W Rt 5	Saint Johnsbury	VT	05819	802-748-8151	748-6604
Northern State Correctional Facility 2559 Glen Rd	Newport	VT	05855	802-334-3364	334-3367
Northwest State Correctional Facility 3649 Lower Newton Rd	Swanton	VT	05488	802-524-6771	527-7534
Southeast State Correctional Facility 546 State Farm Rd	Windsor	VT	05089	802-674-6717	674-2243

VIRGINIA

Facility	City	State	ZIP	Phone	Fax
Augusta Correctional Ctr 1821 Estaline Valley Rd	Craigsville	VA	24430	540-997-7000	997-7017
Bland Correctional Ctr 256 Bland Farm Rd *Web:* www.vadoc.state.va.us/facilities/institutions/bland.htm	Bland	VA	24315	276-688-3341	688-3318
Buckingham Correctional Ctr Rt 20 N PO Box 430 *Web:* www.vadoc.state.va.us/facilities/institutions/buckingham.htm	Dillwyn	VA	23936	434-391-5980	983-1752
Coffeewood Correctional Ctr 12352 Coffeewood Dr	Mitchells	VA	22729	540-829-6483	829-7383
Deep Meadow Correctional Ctr 300 Woods Way	State Farm	VA	23160	804-598-5503	403-3406
Deerfield Correctional Ctr 21360 Deerfield Dr	Capron	VA	23829	434-658-4368	658-9302
Greensville Correctional Ctr 901 Corrections Way	Jarratt	VA	23870	434-535-7000	535-7640
Haynesville Correctional Ctr PO Box 129	Haynesville	VA	22472	804-333-3577	333-0192
Keen Mountain Correctional Ctr 3402 Kennel Gap Rd	Oakwood	VA	24631	276-498-7411	498-3396
Lawrenceville Correctional Ctr 1607 Planters Rd	Lawrenceville	VA	23868	434-848-9349	848-0232
Lunenburg Correctional Ctr PO Box 1424	Victoria	VA	23974	434-696-2045	696-2155
Nottoway Correctional Ctr PO Box 488	Burkeville	VA	23922	434-767-5543	767-4685
Red Onion State Prison PO Box 970	Pound	VA	24279	276-796-7510	796-4369
Saint Brides Correctional Ctr PO Box 16482	Chesapeake	VA	23328	757-421-6600	421-2594
Southampton Correctional Ctr 14545 Old Belfield Rd	Capron	VA	23829	434-658-4174	658-3960
Sussex I State Prison 24414 Musselwhite Dr	Waverly	VA	23891	804-834-9967	834-9995
Sussex II State Prison 24427 Musselwhite Dr	Waverly	VA	23891	804-834-2678	834-4073
Virginia Correctional Center for Women 2841 River Rd W PO Box 1	Goochland	VA	23063	804-784-3582	784-5037
Wallens Ridge State Prison PO Box 759	Big Stone Gap	VA	24219	276-523-3310	523-9612

WASHINGTON

Facility	City	State	ZIP	Phone	Fax
Airway Heights Corrections Center 11919 W Sprague Ave PO Box 1899 *Web:* www.doc.wa.gov	Airway Heights	WA	99001	509-244-6700	244-6710
Cedar Creek Correctional Ctr 12200 Bordeaux Rd	Littlerock	WA	98556	360-753-7278	586-5826
Clallam Bay Corrections Ctr 1830 Eagle Crest Way	Clallam Bay	WA	98326	360-963-2000	963-3292
Coyote Ridge Corrections Ctr 1301 N Ephrata St *Web:* www.doc.wa.gov	Connell	WA	99326	509-234-9201	543-5801
Larch Corrections Ctr 15314 NE Dole Valley Rd	Yacolt	WA	98675	360-260-6300	686-3892
McNeil Island Correctional Ctr PO Box 88900	Steilacoom	WA	98388	253-588-5281	512-6603
Olympic Corrections Ctr 11235 Hoh Mainline	Forks	WA	98331	360-374-6181	374-8336
Twin Rivers Corrections Ctr PO Box 888	Monroe	WA	98272	360-794-2400	794-2584
Washington Corrections Center for Women 9601 Bujacich Rd NW	Gig Harbor	WA	98332	253-858-4200	858-4289
Washington State Penitentiary 1313 N 13th Ave	Walla Walla	WA	99362	509-525-3610	526-6326
Washington State Reformatory PO Box 777	Monroe	WA	98272	360-794-2600	794-2569

WEST VIRGINIA

Facility	City	State	ZIP	Phone	Fax
Denmar Correctional Ctr HC 64 PO Box 125	Hillsboro	WV	24946	304-653-4201	653-4855
Huttonsville Correctional Ctr PO Box 1	Huttonsville	WV	26273	304-335-2291	335-4680
Mount Olive Correctional Complex 1 Mountainside Way	Mount Olive	WV	25185	304-442-7213	442-7225
Northern Regional Correctional Facility Rd 2 PO Box 1	Moundsville	WV	26041	304-843-4067	843-4089
Ohio County Correctional Ctr 1501 Eoff St	Wheeling	WV	26003	304-238-1007	238-1009
Pruntytown Correctional Ctr PO Box 159	Grafton	WV	26354	304-265-6112	265-6120
Saint Mary's Correctional Ctr 2880 N Pleasants Hwy	Saint Marys	WV	26170	304-684-5500	684-5506

WISCONSIN

Facility	City	State	ZIP	Phone	Fax
Columbia Correctional Institution 2925 Columbia Dr PO Box 950 *Web:* www.wi-doc.com	Portage	WI	53901	608-742-9100	742-9111
Dodge Correctional Institution 1 W Lincoln St	Waupun	WI	53963	920-324-5577	324-6297
Fox Lake Correctional Institution Lake Emily Rd PO Box 147	Fox Lake	WI	53933	920-928-3151	928-6929
Green Bay Correctional Institution 2833 Riverside Dr	Green Bay	WI	54307	920-432-4877	432-5388
Jackson Correctional Institution PO Box 232	Black River Falls	WI	54615	715-284-4550	284-7335
Kettle Moraine Correctional Institution PO Box 31	Plymouth	WI	53073	920-526-3244	526-3989

	City	State	Zip	Phone	Fax
Oakhill Correctional Institution 5212 Hwy M	Oregon	WI	53575	608-835-3101	835-9196
Oshkosh Correctional Institution PO Box 3530	Oshkosh	WI	54903	920-231-4010	236-2626
Prairie du Chien Correctional Institution 500 E Parrish St — *Web:* www.wi-doc.com	Prairie du Chien	WI	53821	608-326-7828	326-5960
Racine Correctional Institution 2019 Wisconsin St	Sturtevant	WI	53177	262-886-3214	886-3514
Supermax Correctional Institution PO Box 1000	Boscobel	WI	53805	608-375-5656	375-5595
Taycheedah Correctional Institution PO Box 1947	Fond du Lac	WI	54935	920-929-3800	929-2946
Waupun Correctional Institution 200 S Madison St PO Box 351	Waupun	WI	53963	920-324-5571	324-4478

WYOMING

	City	State	Zip	Phone	Fax
Wyoming Honor Conservation Camp & Boot Camp PO Box 160 — *Web:* www.doc.state.wy.us	Newcastle	WY	82701	307-746-4436	746-9316
Wyoming Honor Farm 40 Honor Farm Rd	Riverton	WY	82501	307-856-9578	856-2505
Wyoming State Penitentiary PO Box 400	Rawlins	WY	82301	307-328-1441	328-7424*
Wyoming Women's Ctr PO Box 300	Lusk	WY	82225	307-334-3693	334-2254

217 COSMETICS, SKIN CARE, AND OTHER PERSONAL CARE PRODUCTS

SEE ALSO Perfumes p. 2409

	City	State	Zip	Phone	Fax
AHAVA North America 411 5th Ave 4th Fl — *TF:* 800-366-7254 ■ *Web:* www.ahavaus.com	New York	NY	10016	212-532-7911	696-9789
Aire-Master of America Inc 1821 N State Hwy Cc — *TF:* 800-525-0957 ■ *Web:* www.airemaster.com	Nixa	MO	65714	417-725-2691	725-5737
Alberto-Culver Consumer Products Worldwide 2525 Armitage Ave — *TF:* 800-333-0005 ■ *Web:* www.alberto.com	Melrose Park	IL	60160	708-450-3000	
Alleghany Pharmacal Corp 277 Northern Blvd — *TF:* 800-645-6190 ■ *Web:* www.alleghanypharmacal.com	Great Neck	NY	11022	516-466-0660	482-1525
Almay Inc 1501 Williamsboro St — *TF:* 800-473-8566 ■ *Web:* www.almay.com	Oxford	NC	27565	212-527-4000	527-4995
Aloette Cosmetics Inc 3715 Northside Pkwy NW Bldg 200 — *TF:* 800-256-3883 ■ *Web:* www.aloette.com	Atlanta	GA	30327	678-444-2563	444-2566
American Safety Razor Co 1 Razor Blade Ln — *TF:* 800-445-9284 ■ *Web:* www.asrco.com	Verona	VA	24482	540-248-8000	248-0522
Arizona Natural Resources 2525 E Beardsley Rd — *Web:* www.arizonanaturalresources.com	Phoenix	AZ	85050	602-569-6900	569-9697
At Last Naturals Inc 401 Columbus Ave — *TF:* 800-527-8123 ■ *Web:* www.atlastnaturals.com	Valhalla	NY	10595	914-747-3599	747-3791
Autumn Harp Inc 26 Thompson Dr — *Web:* www.autumnharp.com	Essex Junction	VT	05452	802-857-4600	857-4601
Avalon Natural Cosmetics Inc 1105 Industrial Ave Suite 200 — *TF:* 800-227-5120	Petaluma	CA	94952	707-769-5120	769-0868
Aveda Corp 4000 Pheasant Ridge Dr — *TF:* 800-283-3224 ■ *Web:* www.aveda.com	Blaine	MN	55449	763-783-4000	783-4110
Avon Products Inc 1345 Avenue of the Americas — *NYSE: AVP* ■ *TF Cust Svc:* 800-367-2866 ■ *Web:* www.avon.com	New York	NY	10105	212-282-5000	282-6825
Bath & Body Works 8455 E Broad St — *TF:* 888-856-1616 ■ *Web:* www.bathandbodyworks.com	Reynoldsburg	OH	43068	614-856-6000	856-6313
Bath-and-Body.com 1073 Exchange St — *TF:* 866-667-2284 ■ *Web:* www.bath-and-body.com	Boise	ID	83716	208-345-5136	947-1504
BeautiControl Inc 2121 Midway Rd PO Box 815189 — **Fax: Sales* ■ *TF:* 800-232-8841 ■ *Web:* www.beauticontrol.com	Carrollton	TX	75006	972-458-0601	458-6904*
Beiersdorf North America 187 Danbury Rd — **Fax: Hum Res* ■ *TF:* 800-233-2340 ■ *Web:* www.beiersdorf.com	Wilton	CT	06897	203-563-5800	854-8112*
Belcam Inc Delagar Div 27 Montgomery St — *TF:* 800-328-3006 ■ *Web:* www.belcamshop.com	Rouses Point	NY	12979	518-297-3366	297-3366
BeneFit Cosmetics 685 Market St 7th Fl — *TF Cust Svc:* 800-781-2336 ■ *Web:* www.benefitcosmetics.com	San Francisco	CA	94105	415-781-8153	781-3930
Blissworld LLC 75 Varick St 10th Fl — *TF:* 888-243-8825 ■ *Web:* www.blissworld.com	New York	NY	10013	212-931-6383	931-8257
Blue Cross Laboratories Inc 20950 Ctr Pointe Pkwy — *Web:* www.bc-labs.com	Santa Clarita	CA	91350	661-255-0955	255-3628
Bobbi Brown Professional Cosmetics Inc 767 5th Ave — *TF:* 877-310-9222 ■ *Web:* www.bobbibrowncosmetics.com	New York	NY	10153	877-310-9222	
Body Shop The 5036 One World Way — *TF Cust Svc:* 800-747-4827 ■ *Web:* www.thebodyshop.com	Wake Forest	NC	27587	919-554-4900	554-4361
Bonne Bell Co The 18519 Detroit Ave PO Box 770349 — *TF:* 800-321-1006 ■ *Web:* www.bonnebell.com	Lakewood	OH	44107	216-221-0800	
Borghese Inc 10 E 34th St 3rd Fl — *Web:* www.borghese.com	New York	NY	10016	212-659-5300	659-5301
Bradford Soap Works Inc 200 Providence St — *Web:* www.bradfordsoap.com	West Warwick	RI	02893	401-821-2141	821-1660
Bronner Bros Inc 2141 Powers Ferry Rd — *TF:* 800-241-6151 ■ *Web:* www.bronnerbros.com	Marietta	GA	30067	770-988-0015	953-0848
C B Sullivan Co PO Box 546 — *TF:* 800-321-2889 ■ *Web:* www.cbsullivan.com	Manchester	NH	03105	603-624-4752	624-8621
Caswell-Massey Co Ltd 121 Fieldcrest Ave — *TF:* 800-326-0500 ■ *Web:* www.caswellmassey.com	Edison	NJ	08837	732-225-2181	225-2385
CBI Laboratories 4201 Diplomacy Rd — **Fax Area Code: 800* ■ *TF:* 800-822-7546 ■ *Web:* www.cbiskincare.com	Fort Worth	TX	76155	972-241-7546	352-1094*
CCA Industries Inc 200 Murray Hill Pkwy — *AMEX: CAW* ■ *TF Cust Svc:* 800-524-2720 ■ *Web:* www.ccaindustries.com	East Rutherford	NJ	07073	201-935-3232	
Chattem Inc 1715 W 38th St PO Box 2219 — *NASDAQ: CHTT* ■ *TF:* 800-366-6077 ■ *Web:* www.chattem.com	Chattanooga	TN	37409	423-821-4571	821-0395
Church & Dwight Co Inc 469 N Harrison St — *NYSE: CHD* ■ *Web:* www.churchdwight.com	Princeton	NJ	08543	609-683-5900	
Clarins USA Inc 110 E 59th St 36th Fl — *Web:* www.us.clarins.com	New York	NY	10022	212-980-1800	752-5910
Clinique Laboratories Inc 767 5th Ave 37th Fl — *TF:* 800-723-7310 ■ *Web:* www.clinique.com	New York	NY	10153	212-572-3800	572-4770
Colgate-Palmolive Co 300 Pk Ave — *NYSE: CL* ■ *Web:* www.colgate.com	New York	NY	10022	212-310-2000	310-2595
Color Factory The 11312 Penrose St — *Web:* www.colorfactoryla.com	Sun Valley	CA	91352	818-767-2889	767-4062
Combe Inc 1101 Westchester Ave — *TF:* 800-873-7400 ■ *Web:* www.combe.com	White Plains	NY	10604	914-694-5454	694-6233
Cosmetic Essence Inc 2182 SR-35 — *Web:* www.onex.com	Holmdel	NJ	07733	732-888-7788	888-6086
Cosmolab Inc 1100 Garrett Pkwy — *TF:* 800-359-6254 ■ *Web:* www.cosmolab.com	Lewisburg	TN	37091	931-359-6253	359-8465
Cosmopolitan Cosmetics 909 3rd Ave 20th Fl — *TF:* 800-589-1412 ■ *Web:* www.cosmopolitan-cosmetics.com	New York	NY	10022	212-980-6400	980-6464
Cosrich Group Inc 55 LaFrance Ave — *TF:* 888-898-9176	Bloomfield	NJ	07003	973-566-6240	566-6240
Cover Girl 1 Procter & Gamble Plaza — *Web:* www.covergirl.com	Cincinnati	OH	45202	513-983-1100	
Crabtree & Evelyn Ltd 102 Peake Brook Rd — *TF:* 800-624-5211 ■ *Web:* www.crabtree-evelyn.com	Woodstock	CT	06281	860-928-2761	928-0462
DEB Inc 1100 Hwy 27 S — *TF:* 800-248-7190 ■ *Web:* www.debgroup.com	Stanley	NC	28164	704-263-4240	263-9601
Del Laboratories Inc 726 Reckson Plaza PO Box 9357 — *TF:* 800-952-5080 ■ *Web:* www.dellabs.com	Uniondale	NY	11553	516-844-2020	
Dena Corp 825 Nicholas Blvd	Elk Grove Village	IL	60007	847-593-3041	593-3041
Dudley Products Inc 1080 Old Greensboro Rd — *TF:* 800-334-4150	Kernersville	NC	27284	336-993-8800	993-1768
Estee Lauder Cos Inc The 767 5th Ave — *NYSE: EL* ■ *Web:* www.elcompanies.com	New York	NY	10153	212-572-4200	893-7782
Estee Lauder Inc 767 5th Ave — *Web:* www.esteelauder.com	New York	NY	10153	212-572-4200	572-3941
Farouk Systems Inc 250 Pennbright Dr — *TF:* 800-237-9175 ■ *Web:* www.farouk.com	Houston	TX	77090	281-876-2000	876-1700
Flents Products Co 5401 S Graham Rd — *TF:* 800-262-8221 ■ *Web:* www.flents.com	Saint Charles	MI	48655	989-865-8221	865-8156
Forever Living Products International Inc 7501 E McCormick Pkwy — *TF:* 888-440-2563 ■ *Web:* www.foreverliving.com	Scottsdale	AZ	85258	480-998-8888	905-8451
Fruit Of The Earth Inc 3101 High Rver Rd Suite 175 — *TF:* 800-527-7731 ■ *Web:* www.fote.com	Fort Worth	TX	76155	972-790-0808	790-1322
Gloss.com Inc 767 5th Ave — *TF Orders:* 888-550-4567 ■ *Web:* www.gloss.com	New York	NY	10153	212-572-4200	
GOJO Industries Inc 1 GOJO Plaza Suite 500 — **Fax Area Code: 800* ■ *TF:* 800-321-9647 ■ *Web:* www.gojo.com	Akron	OH	44311	330-255-6000	329-4656*
Goody Products Inc 400 Galleria Pkwy Suite 1100 — *TF:* 800-241-4324 ■ *Web:* www.goody.com	Atlanta	GA	30339	770-615-4700	615-4740
Guest Supply Inc 4301 US Hwy 1 PO Box 902 — *TF Cust Svc:* 800-221-1457 ■ *Web:* www.guestsupply.com	Monmouth Junction	NJ	08852	609-514-9696	514-2692
Gurwitch Products LLC 13259 N Promenade Blvd — *Web:* www.lauramercier.com	Stafford	TX	77477	281-275-7000	275-7094
H2O Plus Inc 845 W Madison St — *TF Cust Svc:* 800-690-2284 ■ *Web:* www.h2oplus.com	Chicago	IL	60607	312-850-9283	633-1440
Hydron Technologies Inc 9843 18th St N # 150 — *TF:* 800-449-3766 ■ *Web:* www.hydron.com	Saint Petersburg	FL	33716	727-342-5050	344-3920
Imperial Distributors Inc 33 Sword St — *Web:* www.imperialdist.com	Auburn	MA	01501	508-756-5156	756-0085
Jafra Cosmetics International 2451 Townsgate Rd — *TF:* 800-551-2345 ■ *Web:* www.jafra.com	Westlake Village	CA	91361	805-449-3000	449-3254
Jan Marini Skin Research Inc 6951 Via Del Oro — *TF:* 800-347-2223 ■ *Web:* www.janmarini.com	San Jose	CA	95119	408-362-0130	362-0140
Jason Natural Cosmetics Inc 5500 W 83rd St — *TF:* 800-527-6605 ■ *Web:* www.jason-natural.com	Los Angeles	CA	90045	310-838-7543	838-9274
John Amico Haircare Products 4731 W 136th St — *TF:* 800-676-5264 ■ *Web:* www.johnamico.com	Crestwood	IL	60445	708-824-4000	824-0413
John Paul Mitchell Systems 9701 Wilshire Blvd Suite 1205 — *TF Cust Svc:* 800-793-8790 ■ *Web:* www.paulmitchell.com	Beverly Hills	CA	90212	310-248-3888	248-2780
Johnson & Johnson Consumer Products Co 199 Grandview Rd — *TF:* 800-526-3967 ■ *Web:* www.johnsonsbaby.com	Skillman	NJ	08558	908-874-1000	
Johnson & Johnson Inc 7101 Notre-Dame E — *TF:* 800-361-8990 ■ *Web:* www.jnjcanada.com	Montreal	QC	H1N2G4	514-251-5100	251-6233
Kao Brands Co 2535 Spring Grove Ave — *TF:* 800-742-8798 ■ *Web:* www.kaobrands.com	Cincinnati	OH	45214	513-421-1400	455-7889
Key West Fragrance & Cosmetics Factory Inc 419 Duval St — *TF:* 800-445-2563 ■ *Web:* www.keywestaloe.com	Key West	FL	33040	305-293-1885	

Phone Fax

Kolmar Laboratories Inc
20 W King St PO Box 1111 .... Port Jervis NY 12771 845-856-5311 856-5831
Web: www.kolmar.com
L'Oreal USA 575 5th Ave .... New York NY 10017 212-818-1500
TF: 800-562-2159 ■ *Web:* www.lorealusa.com
L'Oreal USA Lancome Div 575 5th Ave .... New York NY 10017 212-818-1500 984-4776
Web: www.lancome-usa.com
Lander Co Inc 200 Lenox Dr Suite 202 .... Lawrenceville NJ 08648 609-219-0930 219-1238
TF Orders: 800-452-6337
Lee Pharmaceuticals Inc
1434 Santa Anita Ave .... South El Monte CA 91733 626-442-3141 443-8745
TF: 800-950-5337 ■ *Web:* www.leepharmaceuticals.com
Limited Brands Inc 3 Limited Pkwy .... Columbus OH 43230 614-415-7000 415-2491*
NYSE: LTD ■ **Fax:* Mail Rm ■ *TF:* 800-945-9000 ■ *Web:* www.limitedbrands.com
Luster Products Inc 1104 W 43rd St .... Chicago IL 60609 773-579-1800 579-1912
TF: 800-621-4255 ■ *Web:* www.lusterproducts.com
Luzier Cosmetics 7910-12 Troost Ave .... Kansas City MO 64131 816-531-8338 531-6979
TF: 800-821-6632 ■ *Web:* www.luzier.com
MAC Cosmetics 767 5th Ave .... New York NY 10153 212-572-4200 572-3941
TF: 800-723-7310 ■ *Web:* www.maccosmetics.com
Mana Products Inc 32-02 Queens Blvd .... Long Island City NY 11101 718-361-2550 786-3204
TF Cust Svc: 800-221-3071 ■ *Web:* www.manaproducts.com
Markwins International Corp
22067 Ferrero Pkwy .... City of Industry CA 91789 909-595-8898 595-8820
TF: 800-626-8878 ■ *Web:* www.markwins.com
Mary Kay Inc PO Box 799045 .... Dallas TX 75379 972-687-6300 687-1623*
**Fax:* Cust Svc ■ *TF Cust Svc:* 800-627-9529 ■ *Web:* www.marykay.com
Mary Kay Inc Mfg Group 1330 Regal Row .... Dallas TX 75247 972-687-6300 905-6997*
**Fax Area Code:* 214 ■ **Fax:* Hum Res ■ *TF Cust Svc:* 800-627-9529 ■ *Web:* www.marykay.com
Matrix Essentials Inc 30601 Carter St .... Solon OH 44139 440-248-3700
TF: 800-282-2822 ■ *Web:* www.matrixbeautiful.com
Max Factor 1 Procter & Gamble Plaza .... Cincinnati OH 45202 513-983-1100
TF: 800-526-8787 ■ *Web:* www.maxfactor.com
Maybelline New York 575 5th Ave .... New York NY 10017 212-818-1500 984-4511*
**Fax:* Mail Rm ■ *TF:* 800-944-0730 ■ *Web:* www.maybelline.com
Merle Norman Cosmetics Inc
9130 Bellanca Ave .... Los Angeles CA 90045 310-641-3000 641-7144
TF: 800-421-2060 ■ *Web:* www.merlenorman.com
Neutrogena Corp 5760 W 96th St .... Los Angeles CA 90045 310-642-1150 642-3260
TF: 800-217-1136 ■ *Web:* www.neutrogena.com
Norelco Consumer Products Co
1010 Washington Blvd .... Stamford CT 06912 203-973-0200 351-5717*
**Fax:* Cust Svc ■ *TF:* 800-243-7884
NutraMax Products Inc 51 Blackburn Dr .... Gloucester MA 01930 978-283-1800 282-3794
Web: www.nutramax.com
Obagi Medical Products Inc
3760 Kilroy Airport Way # 500 .... Long Beach CA 90806 562-628-1007 628-1008
TF: 800-636-7546 ■ *Web:* www.obagi.com
Origins Natural Resources Inc 767 5th Ave .... New York NY 10153 212-572-4200
TF Cust Svc: 800-723-7310 ■ *Web:* www.origins.com
Orly International Inc 7710 Haskell Ave .... Los Angeles CA 91406 818-994-1001 994-1144
Web: www.orlybeauty.com
Pacific World Corp 25800 Commercentre Dr .... Lake Forest CA 92630 949-598-2400
Web: www.nailene.com
Paramount Cosmetics Inc 93 Entin Rd Suite 4 .... Clifton NJ 07014 973-472-2323 472-5005
TF: 800-522-9880 ■ *Web:* www.paramountcosmetics.net
Penthouse Mfg Co Inc 225 Buffalo Ave .... Freeport NY 11520 516-379-1300 378-2844
Web: www.thepenthousegroup.com
Person & Covey Inc 616 Allen Ave .... Glendale CA 91201 818-240-1030 547-9821
TF: 800-423-2341 ■ *Web:* www.personandcovey.com
Personal Products Co 199 Grandview Rd .... Skillman NJ 08558 908-874-1000
Web: www.jnj.com/our_company/family_of_companies
Peter Thomas Roth Labs LLC 460 Pk Ave FL 16 .... New York NY 10022 212-581-5800 581-5810
Web: www.peterthomasroth.com
Pfizer Inc 235 E 42nd St .... New York NY 10017 212-733-2323 573-7851
NYSE: PFE ■ *TF:* 800-733-4717 ■ *Web:* www.pfizer.com
Philips Oral Healthcare Inc
35301 SE Ctr St .... Snoqualmie WA 98065 425-396-2000 396-4824
TF: 800-957-9310 ■ *Web:* www.sonicare.com
Philosophy Inc 3809 E Watkins .... Phoenix AZ 85034 602-794-8500 794-8701
TF: 800-568-3151 ■ *Web:* www.philosophy.com
Physicians Formula Holdings Inc 1055 W 8th St .... Azusa CA 91702 626-334-3395 812-9462
NASDAQ: FACE ■ *Web:* www.physiciansformula.com
Prescriptives Inc 767 5th Ave .... New York NY 10153 212-572-4200
TF: 800-723-7310 ■ *Web:* www.prescriptives.com
Prestige Brands International Inc
90 N Broadway .... Irvington NY 10533 914-524-6810 524-6815
NYSE: PBH ■ *Web:* www.prestigebrandsinc.com
Prestige Cosmetics Corp
1441 W Newport Ctr Dr .... Deerfield Beach FL 33442 954-480-9202 480-9220
TF: 800-722-7488 ■ *Web:* www.prestigecosmetics.com
Pro-Line International Inc 2121 Panoramic Cir .... Dallas TX 75212 214-631-4247 634-8155
TF: 800-527-5879
Procter & Gamble Cosmetics 11050 York Rd .... Hunt Valley MD 21030 800-851-8262
TF Cust Svc: 800-638-6204 ■ *Web:* www.pg.com
Qosmedix 95-Q Executive Dr .... Edgewood NY 11717 631-242-3270 242-3291
Web: www.qosmedix.com
Revlon Consumer Products Corp
1501 Williamsboro St .... Oxford NY 27565 212-527-4000 527-4995
TF: 800-473-8566 ■ *Web:* www.revlon.com
Rozelle Cosmetics PO Box 70 .... Westfield VT 05874 802-744-2270 744-2236
TF: 800-451-4216 ■ *Web:* www.rozelle.com
Saint Ives Laboratories Inc
2525 Armitage Ave .... Melrose Park IL 60160 708-450-3000 450-3394
TF: 800-333-6666 ■ *Web:* www.stives.com
Sara Lee Household & Body Care
707 Eagleview Blvd .... Exton PA 19341 610-321-1220 321-1440
TF: 800-879-5494 ■ *Web:* www.saralee.com
Scolding Locks Corp 1520 W Rogers Ave .... Appleton WI 54914 920-733-5561 733-8800
TF: 800-537-9707 ■ *Web:* www.scoldinglocks.com
Sebastian International Inc
6109 DeSoto Ave .... Woodland Hills CA 91367 818-999-5112 712-7770
TF Cust Svc: 800-347-4424

Phone Fax

Sentinel Consumer Products Inc
7750 Tyler Blvd .... Mentor OH 44060 440-974-8144 974-0249
sephora.com Inc
525 Market St
First Market Tower 32nd Fl .... San Francisco CA 94105 415-284-3300
TF Cust Svc: 877-737-4672 ■ *Web:* www.sephora.com
Sheffield Laboratories 170 Broad St .... New London CT 06320 860-442-4451 442-0356
TF: 800-222-1087
SkinMedica Inc 5909 Sea Lion Pl Suite H .... Carlsbad CA 92010 760-448-3600 448-3601
TF: 866-577-3072 ■ *Web:* www.skinmedica.com
Sothys USA Inc 1500 NW 94th Ave .... Miami FL 33172 305-594-4222 592-5785
Web: www.sothys-usa.com
Star Nail Products Inc 29120 Ave Paine .... Valencia CA 91355 661-257-7827 257-5856
TF: 800-762-6245 ■ *Web:* www.starnail.com
Tanning Research Labs Inc
1190 N US Hwy 1 .... Ormond Beach FL 32174 386-677-9559 677-9595
TF: 800-874-4844 ■ *Web:* www.hawaiiantropic.com
Tom's of Maine Inc
302 Lafayette Ctr PO Box 710 .... Kennebunk ME 04043 207-985-2944 985-2196
TF: 888-572-0004 ■ *Web:* www.tomsofmaine.com
Twincraft Inc 2 Tigan St .... Winooski VT 05404 802-655-2200
Web: www.twincraft.com
Ulta3 Inc 1135 Arbor Dr .... Romeoville IL 60446 630-226-0020 226-8210
TF: 866-304-3704 ■ *Web:* www.ulta.com
Urban Decay 729 Farad St .... Costa Mesa CA 92627 949-631-4504 631-5986*
**Fax:* Cust Svc ■ *TF:* 800-784-8722 ■ *Web:* www.urbandecay.com
Vi-Jon Labs Inc 8515 Page Ave .... Saint Louis MO 63114 314-427-1000 427-1010
TF: 800-325-8167 ■ *Web:* www.vijon.com
Victoria Vogue Inc 90 Southland Dr .... Bethlehem PA 18017 610-865-1500 865-6089
TF: 800-967-7833 ■ *Web:* www.victoriavogue.com
Wahl Clipper Corp 2900 Locust St .... Sterling IL 61081 815-625-6525 625-1193
TF: 800-767-9245 ■ *Web:* www.wahlclipper.com
WE Bassett Co 100 Trap Falls Rd Ext .... Shelton CT 06484 203-929-8483 929-8963
TF: 800-394-8746 ■ *Web:* www.trim.com
Wella Corp 6109 DeSoto Ave .... Woodland Hills CA 91367 818-999-5112 712-7770
TF: 800-829-4422 ■ *Web:* www.wella.com
YSL Boutique 855 Madison Ave .... New York NY 10021 212-988-3821 517-4814
Web: www.yslbeautyus.com
Zotos International Inc 100 Tokeneke Rd .... Darien CT 06820 203-655-8911 656-7784
TF: 888-242-4247 ■ *Web:* www.zotos.com

218 CREDIT CARD PROVIDERS & RELATED SERVICES

Companies Listed Here Include Those That Issue Credit Cards As Well As Companies That Provide Services To These Companies (I.E., Rewards Programs, Theft Prevention, Etc.).

Phone Fax

American Express Co Inc
World Financial Ctr 200 Vesey St .... New York NY 10285 212-640-2000 640-0128
NYSE: AXP ■ *TF:* 800-666-1775 ■ *Web:* www.home.americanexpress.com
Applied Card Systems 800 Delaware Ave .... Wilmington DE 19801 302-467-4600 467-4650
TF: 800-334-3180 ■ *Web:* www.appliedcard.com
Bank of America Card Services
1 Commercial Pl 2nd Fl .... Norfolk VA 23510 757-441-4770 441-4780
TF: 800-732-9194
Bloomingdale's Credit Services 9111 Duke Blvd .... Mason OH 45040 513-398-5221 573-2957*
NYSE: M ■ **Fax:* Cust Svc ■ *TF Cust Svc:* 800-235-6229 ■ *Web:* www.macys.com
Capital One Financial Corp
1680 Capital One Dr .... McLean VA 22102 703-448-3747 720-1755
NYSE: COF ■ *TF:* 800-801-1164 ■ *Web:* www.capitalone.com
Chevron Texaco Credit Card Ctr
2001 Diamond Blvd .... Concord CA 94520 925-842-1000 827-7919
TF: 800-243-8766 ■ *Web:* www.chevrontexacocards.com
CompuCredit Corp
Five Concourse Pkwy Suite 400 .... Atlanta GA 30328 770-828-2000 901-5815
NASDAQ: CCRT ■ *Web:* www.compucredit.com
Dillard's Credit Services Inc PO Box 960012 .... Orlando FL 32896 800-643-8278
TF: 800-643-8278 ■ *Web:* www.dillards.com
Diners Club International
8430 W Bryn Mawr Ave .... Chicago IL 60631 773-380-5100 380-5532
TF: 800-234-6377 ■ *Web:* www.dinersclubnorthamerica.com
Intersections Inc
3901 Stonecroft Blvd PO Box 222455 .... Chantilly VA 20151 703-488-6100 488-6223
NASDAQ: INTX ■ *TF:* 800-695-7536 ■ *Web:* www.intersections.com
iPayment Inc 40 Burton Hills Blvd Suite 415 .... Nashville TN 37215 615-665-1858 665-8434
TF: 800-324-9825 ■ *Web:* www.ipaymentinc.com
MasterCard Inc 2000 Purchase St .... Purchase NY 10577 914-249-2000 249-4135*
NYSE: MA ■ **Fax:* Hum Res ■ *TF:* 800-247-4623 ■ *Web:* www.mastercard.com
Rewards Network 2 N Riverside Plaza Suite 950 .... Chicago IL 60606 877-392-7313
OTC: IRNWP ■ *TF:* 877-392-7313 ■ *Web:* www.rewardsnetwork.com
Saks Inc 12 E 49th St .... New York NY 10017 212-753-4000 940-4849
Web: www.saksincorporated.com
TNS Merchant & Credit Card Services
1939 Roland Clarke Pl .... Reston VA 20191 703-453-8338 453-8460
TF: 800-240-2824 ■ *Web:* www.tnsi.com
Vesta Corp 11950 SW Garden PL .... Portland OR 97223 503-790-2500 790-2525
Web: www.trustvesta.com
Visa Inc PO Box 8999 .... San Francisco CA 94128 650-432-3200
TF: 800-847-2911 ■ *Web:* www.visa.com
Wright Express Corp 97 Darling Ave .... South Portland ME 04106 207-773-8171 828-5181
NYSE: WXS ■ *TF:* 800-761-7181 ■ *Web:* www.wrightexpress.com

219 CREDIT & FINANCING - COMMERCIAL

SEE ALSO Banks - Commercial & Savings p. 1506; Credit & Financing - Consumer p. 1775

Phone Fax

Advanta Leasing Services 40 E Clementon Rd .... Gibbsboro NJ 08026 800-255-0022 782-1110*
**Fax Area Code:* 856 ■ *TF:* 800-255-0022 ■ *Web:* www.advantalease.com

	City	State	Zip	Phone	Fax
AFCO Credit Corp 14 Wall St Suite 8A-19 *TF:* 800-288-2313	New York	NY	10005	212-401-4400	401-4436
Ag Georgia Farm Credit PO Box 1820 *Web:* www.aggeorgia.com	Perry	GA	31069	478-272-4603	275-3550
Agricredit Acceptance LLC 8001 Birchwood Ct Suite C PO Box 2000 *TF:* 800-873-2474 ■ *Web:* www.agricredit.com	Johnston	IA	50131	515-251-2800	334-5825
Aimbridge Group Inc The 116 Invrneco Dr E Suite 250 *TF:* 888-400-2865 ■ *Web:* www.aimbridge.com	Englewood	CO	80112	303-306-3220	306-3248
Alexander Capital Corp 900 Castleton Rd Suite 150 *Web:* www.alexandercapital.net	Castle Rock	CO	80109	303-814-0475	
Amada Capital Corp 7025 Firestone Blvd *TF:* 800-626-6612 ■ *Web:* www.amadacapital.com	Buena Park	CA	90621	714-739-2111	739-4099
American AgCredit (ACA) PO Box 1120 *TF:* 800-800-4865 ■ *Web:* www.agloan.com	Santa Rosa	CA	95402	707-545-1200	545-9400
American Capital Strategies Ltd 2 Bethesda Metro Ctr 14th Fl *NASDAQ: ACAS* ■ *Web:* www.americancapital.com	Bethesda	MD	20814	301-951-6122	654-6714
American Express Credit Corp 301 N Walnut St 1 Christina Centre Suite 1002 *TF:* 800-525-5450 ■ *Web:* www.home.americanexpress.com	Wilmington	DE	19801	302-594-3350	571-8073
AMRESCO Commercial Finance LLC 412 E Parkcenter Blvd *Web:* www.amresco.com	Boise	ID	83706	208-333-2000	333-2050
Arkansas Capital Corp Group 200 S Commerce St Suite 400 *TF:* 800-216-7237 ■ *Web:* www.arcapital.com	Little Rock	AR	72201	501-374-9247	374-9425
ATEL Capital Group 600 California St 6th Fl *TF:* 800-543-2835 ■ *Web:* www.atel.com	San Francisco	CA	94108	415-989-8800	989-3796
Athens First Bank & Trust Co (AFB&T) 150 W Hancock Ave *Web:* www.athensfirstbank.com	Athens	GA	30601	706-357-7070	425-3465
Automotive Finance Corp (AFC) 13085 Hamilton Crossing Blvd *TF:* 888-335-6675 ■ *Web:* www.afcdealer.com	Carmel	IN	46032	317-815-9645	815-9650
AutoStar 180 Glastonbury Blvd Suite 201 *Web:* www.autostar.com	Glastonbury	CT	06033	860-815-5900	815-5901
Bank of America Business Capital 200 Glastonbury Blvd *TF:* 866-287-4098 ■ *Web:* www.corp.bankofamerica.com	Glastonbury	CT	06033	860-659-3200	657-7768
Bank of America Leasing & Capital Group 555 California St 4th Fl	San Francisco	CA	94104	415-765-7300	765-1824
Bombardier Capital Group 261 Mountain View Dr 4th Fl **Fax:* Sales ■ *TF:* 800-949-5568 ■ *Web:* www.bombardier.com	Colchester	VT	05446	802-764-5232	764-5244*
BTM Capital Corp 111 Huntington Ave *TF:* 800-343-6597 ■ *Web:* www.btmcapital.com	Boston	MA	02199	617-573-9000	345-5153
Capital Business Credit LLC 1700 Broadway 19th Fl *Web:* www.capfac.com	New York	NY	10019	212-887-7900	887-7968
Capital Lease Funding Inc 1065 Avenue of the Americas 19th Fl *NYSE: LSE* ■ *Web:* www.caplease.com	New York	NY	10018	212-217-6300	217-6301
Capital Trust Inc 410 Pk Ave 14th Fl *NYSE: CT* ■ *Web:* www.capitaltrust.com	New York	NY	10022	212-655-0220	655-0044
Cascade Federal Credit Union 18020 80th Ave S *TF:* 800-562-2853 ■ *Web:* www.cascadefcu.org	Kent	WA	98032	425-251-8888	251-0299
CCO Mortgage Corp 10561 Telegraph Rd *Web:* www.ccomortgage.com	Glen Allen	VA	23059	804-627-4000	
CDC Small Business Finance Corp 2448 Historic Decatur Rd Suite 200 *TF:* 800-611-5170 ■ *Web:* www.cdcloans.com	San Diego	CA	92106	619-291-3594	291-6954
Century Business Credit Corp 100 Pk Ave 3rd Fl 10th Fl *TF Cust Svc:* 800-883-3539 ■ *Web:* www.wellsfargo.com	New York	NY	10017	212-703-3500	703-3520
Church Loans & Investment Trust 5305 W IH- 40 *TF:* 800-692-1111 ■ *Web:* www.churchloans.com	Amarillo	TX	79106	806-358-3666	358-1430
CIT Group Inc 505 5th Ave *NYSE: CIT* ■ *Web:* www.cit.com	New York	NY	10017	212-771-0505	382-6871
CIT Group Inc 1 CIT Dr *NYSE: CIT* ■ *Web:* www.cit.com	Livingston	NJ	07039	973-740-5000	
Co-op Finance Assn Inc 10100 N Ambassador Dr Suite 315 PO Box 901532 *TF:* 877-835-5232 ■ *Web:* www.cfafs.com	Kansas City	MO	64190	816-214-4200	214-4221
Colonial Farm Credit Aca 7104 Mechanicsville Tpke PO Box 727 *TF:* 800-777-8908 ■ *Web:* www.colonialfarmcredit.com	Mechanicsville	VA	23111	804-746-4581	746-3159
Comfort Financial Services PO Box 1140 *TF:* 866-866-1331 ■ *Web:* www.comfortfinancial.com	Evansville	IN	47706	866-866-1331	866-1334
Connell Equipment Leasing Co 200 Connell Dr *Web:* www.connellco.com/CEL.htm	Berkeley Heights	NJ	07922	908-673-3700	673-3800
Connell Finance Co Inc 200 Connell Dr *TF:* 800-233-3240 ■ *Web:* www.connellco.com/CFC.htm	Berkeley Heights	NJ	07922	908-673-3700	673-3800
Connell Technologies Co LLC 350 Lindbergh Ave *TF:* 888-301-0300 ■ *Web:* www.connellco.com	Livermore	CA	94550	925-455-6790	455-6791
ContiInvestments LLC 277 Pk Ave *Web:* www.contigroup.com/2004_business_ci.html	New York	NY	10172	212-207-5142	207-5181
Credit Union 24 Inc 2252 Killearn Ctr Blvd Suite 300 *TF:* 877-570-2824 ■ *Web:* www.cu24.com	Tallahassee	FL	32309	850-701-2824	701-2424
Csa Financial Corp 343 Commercial St *Web:* www.csafinancial.com	Boston	MA	02109	617-357-1700	357-1720
De Lage Landen Financial Services 1111 Old Eagle School Rd *TF:* 800-669-9441 ■ *Web:* www.delagelanden.com	Wayne	PA	19087	610-386-5000	386-5840
Dexia CLF 445 Pk Ave 7th Fl *Web:* www.dexia.com	New York	NY	10022	212-515-7000	753-5522
Dot Group 6223 Constitution Dr	Fort Wayne	IN	46804	260-432-3822	432-0083
Equity Funding 12505 Bel-Red Rd Suite 200 *TF:* 866-332-3863 ■ *Web:* www.equity-funding.com	Bellevue	WA	98005	425-283-1040	283-1054
Farm Credit Leasing (FCL) 600 Hwy 169 S Suite 300 *TF:* 800-444-2929 ■ *Web:* www.farmcreditleasing.com	Minneapolis	MN	55426	952-417-7800	417-7801
Farm Credit Of Central Florida Aca 115 S Missouri Ave Suite 400 PO Box 8009 *Web:* www.farmcreditcfl.com	Lakeland	FL	33815	863-682-4117	688-9364
Farm Credit Of Northwest Florida Aca 5052 Hwy 90 *TF:* 800-527-0647 ■ *Web:* www.farmcredit-fl.com	Marianna	FL	32446	850-526-4910	526-7388
Financial Pacific Co 3455 S 344th Way Suite 300 *TF:* 800-447-7107 ■ *Web:* www.finpac.com	Federal Way	WA	98001	800-447-7107	447-7106
First California Financial Group Inc 3027 Townsgate Rd Suite 300 *NASDAQ: FCAL* ■ *Web:* www.fcalgroup.com	Westlake Village	CA	91361	805-322-9655	
First Carolina Corporate Credit Union 4160 Piedmont Pkwy Suite 200 *TF:* 800-585-4317 ■ *Web:* www.firstcarolina.org	Greensboro	NC	27410	336-299-6286	299-7842
First Community Financial Corp (FCFC) 4000 N Central Ave Suite 100 *TF:* 800-242-3232 ■ *Web:* www.fcfinancial.com	Phoenix	AZ	85012	602-265-7715	265-0631
First Hawaiian Leasing Inc 1580 Kapiolani Blvd PO Box 1240	Honolulu	HI	96807	808-943-4905	943-4975
First South FarmCredit 713 S Pear Orchard Rd Suite 300 *TF:* 800-955-1722 ■ *Web:* www.firstsouthfarmcredit.com	Ridgeland	MS	39158	601-977-8381	977-8358
First Star Bancorp Inc 418 W Broad St PO BOX 4305 *Web:* www.firststarbank.com	Bethlehem	PA	18018	610-691-2233	691-5655
FirstCity Financial Corp 6400 Imperial Dr *NASDAQ: FCFC* ■ **Fax Area Code:* 713 ■ *TF:* 800-247-4274 ■ *Web:* www.fcfc.com	Waco	TX	76712	254-761-2800	751-7648*
Ford Motor Credit Co 1 American Rd PO Box 1732 *TF:* 800-727-7000 ■ *Web:* www.fordcredit.com	Dearborn	MI	48121	313-322-3000	323-2959
GATX Corp 500 W Monroe St *NYSE: GMT* ■ **Fax:* Hum Res ■ *TF:* 800-525-4289 ■ *Web:* www.gatx.com	Chicago	IL	60661	312-621-6200	621-6665*
GATX Specialty Finance 4 Embarcadero Ctr Suite 2200 *TF:* 800-227-4289 ■ *Web:* www.gatx.com	San Francisco	CA	94111	415-955-3200	955-3415
GE Capital Corp 260 Long Ridge Rd **Fax:* PR ■ *Web:* www.gecapital.com	Stamford	CT	06927	203-357-4000	357-6226*
GE Capital Small Business Finance 635 Maryville Ctr Dr Suite 120 **Fax:* Mktg ■ *TF:* 800-447-2025 ■ *Web:* www.ge.com	Saint Louis	MO	63141	314-205-3500	205-3698*
GE Commercial Distribution Finance (GECDF) 2625 S Plaza Dr Suite 201 *TF:* 800-289-4488 ■ *Web:* www.gecdf.com	Tempe	AZ	85282	480-449-7100	829-3963
GE Commercial Finance 260 Long Ridge Rd **Fax Area Code:* 914 ■ *Web:* www.gecapital.com/en	Stamford	CT	06927	203-357-4000	335-8287*
GE Healthcare 540 W NW Hwy *TF Cust Svc:* 800-488-5208 ■ *Web:* www.ge.com/capital/auto	Barrington	IL	60010	847-277-4000	
GE Healthcare Financial Services 500 W Monroe *TF:* 800-598-6201 ■ *Web:* www.gehealthcarefinance.com	Chicago	IL	60661	312-441-7705	441-7770
GE Vendor Financial Services 10 Riverview Dr *TF:* 800-876-2033 ■ *Web:* www.ge.com/capital/vendor	Danbury	CT	06810	203-749-6000	
Grandbridge Real Estate Capital LLC 227 W Trade St Suite 400 *Web:* www.gbrecap.com	Charlotte	NC	28202	704-332-4454	332-5810
Green Tree Servicing LLC 345 St Peter St Suite 600 **Fax:* Hum Res ■ *TF:* 800-423-9527 ■ *Web:* www.gtservicing.com	Saint Paul	MN	55102	651-293-3400	293-3622*
Greenstone Farm Credit Services Aca 1760 Abbey Rd *TF:* 800-968-0061 ■ *Web:* www.greenstonefcs.com	East Lansing	MI	48823	517-318-2290	318-1259
Greystone Metro Financial LP 8144 Walnut Hill Ln Suite 900 *TF:* 800-327-2274 ■ *Web:* www.greystonecs.com	Dallas	TX	75231	214-363-4557	987-7381
IBM Credit Corp 1 N Castle Dr	Armonk	NY	10504	914-499-1900	
Imh Financial Corp 4900 N Scottsdale Rd Suite 5000 *TF:* 800-510-6445 ■ *Web:* www.imhfc.com	Scottsdale	AZ	85251	480-840-8400	
iStar Financial Inc 1114 Avenue of the Americas 39th Fl *NYSE: SFI* ■ *TF:* 888-335-3122 ■ *Web:* www.istarfinancial.com	New York	NY	10036	212-930-9400	930-9494
Jackson Purchase Ag Credit Assn PO Box 309 *Web:* www.jacksonpurchaseaca.com	Mayfield	KY	42066	270-247-5613	247-6043
John Deere Credit Co 6400 NW 86th St *TF:* 800-275-5322 ■ *Web:* www.deere.com/en_US/jdc	Johnston	IA	50131	515-267-3000	267-3292
Key Equipment Finance 1000 S McCaslin Blvd *TF:* 888-301-6238 ■ *Web:* www.kefonline.com	Superior	CO	80027	720-304-1500	
Kraus-Anderson Capital Inc 523 S 8th St Suite 523 *TF:* 888-547-3983 ■ *Web:* www.krausanderson.com/ka-capital.html	Minneapolis	MN	55404	612-305-2934	305-2932
Latin American Agribusiness Development Corp 75 Valencia Ave Suite 1050 *Web:* www.laadsa.com	Coral Gables	FL	33134	305-445-1341	446-8444
Lawfinance Group Inc 1401 Los Gamos Dr Suite 140 *Web:* www.lawfinance.com	San Rafael	CA	94903	415-446-2300	446-2301
M & I Equipment Finance Co 250 E Wisconsin Ave Suite 1400 **Fax:* Mktg ■ *TF:* 800-558-9840 ■ *Web:* www.micorp.com	Milwaukee	WI	53202	414-272-2374	272-1765*
MarCap Corp 200 W Jackson Blvd Suite 2000 *TF:* 800-621-1677	Chicago	IL	60606	312-641-0233	425-2441

Phone Fax

Marquette Commercial Finance Inc
5910 N Central Expy Suite 1900 .... Dallas TX 75206 214-389-5900 389-5901
Web: www.marquettecommercial.com

Marquette Financial Cos
60 S 6th St Suite 3800 .... Minneapolis MN 55402 612-661-3880
Web: www.marquette.com

Medallion Financial Corp
437 Madison Ave 38th Fl .... New York NY 10022 212-328-2100 328-2195*
NASDAQ: TAXI ■ **Fax:* PR ■ *TF:* 877-633-2554 ■ *Web:* www.medallionfinancial.com

MicroFinancial Inc
16 New England Executive Pk Suite 200 .... Burlington MA 01803 781-994-4800 994-4710
NASDAQ: MFI ■ *TF:* 877-868-3800 ■ *Web:* www.microfinancial.com

NAFCO 3907 Aero Pl Suite 1 .... Lakeland FL 33811 863-644-8463 646-1671
TF: 800-999-3712 ■ *Web:* www.airloans.com

New York Business Development Corp (NYBDC)
50 Beaver St 6th Fl .... Albany NY 12207 518-463-2268 463-0240
TF: 800-923-2504 ■ *Web:* www.nybdc.com

Orix Financial Services Inc 600 Town Pk Ln .... Kennesaw GA 30144 770-970-6000 970-6018

ORIX USA Corp 1717 Main St Suite 900 .... Dallas TX 75201 214-237-2000 237-2018
Web: www.orix.com

PACCAR Financial Corp 777 106th Ave NE .... Bellevue WA 98004 425-468-7100 468-8220
Web: www.paccarfinancial.com

Park Community Federal Credit Union
PO Box 18630 .... Louisville KY 40261 502-968-3681 964-6704
TF: 800-626-2870 ■ *Web:* www.parkcommunity.com

PDS Gaming Corp 6280 Annie Oakley Dr .... Las Vegas NV 89120 702-736-0700 740-8692
TF: 800-479-3612 ■ *Web:* www.pdsgaming.com

Philip Morris Capital Corp
225 High Ridge Rd Suite 300-W .... Stamford CT 06902 203-348-1350 335-8287*
**Fax Area Code:* 914 ■ *Web:* www.philipmorriscapitalcorp.com

Phoenix American Inc 2401 Kerner Blvd .... San Rafael CA 94901 415-485-4500 485-4813
TF: 866-895-5050 ■ *Web:* www.phxa.com

Phoenix Growth Capital Corp
2401 Kerner Blvd .... San Rafael CA 94901 415-485-4500 485-4813
TF: 866-895-5050 ■ *Web:* www.phxa.com

Phoenix Leasing Inc 2401 Kerner Blvd .... San Rafael CA 94901 415-485-4500 485-4813
TF: 866-895-5050 ■ *Web:* www.phxa.com

Pinnacle Business Finance Inc PO Box 1817 .... Tacoma WA 98401 253-926-1800 926-1830
TF: 800-566-1993 ■ *Web:* www.pinnaclecap.com

Pioneer Credit Co 1870 Executive Pk NW .... Cleveland TN 37312 423-476-6511 559-8439
Web: www.pioneercredit.net

Pls Financial Services Inc
300 N Elizabeth St 4th Fl .... Chicago IL 60607 312-491-7300
Web: www.plsfinancial.com

PMC Commercial Trust
17950 Preston Rd Suite 600 .... Dallas TX 75252 972-349-3200 349-3265
AMEX: PCC ■ *TF:* 800-486-3223 ■ *Web:* www.pmctrust.com

PNC Leasing LLC 249 5th Ave .... Pittsburgh PA 15222 412-762-4848 762-7575
TF: 800-762-6260 ■ *Web:* www.pnc.com

Presidential Realty Corp
180 S Broadway Suite 400 .... White Plains NY 10605 914-948-1300 948-1327
AMEX: PDL/A ■ *TF:* 800-948-2977

Priority Capital Inc 174 Green St .... Melrose MA 02176 781-321-8778 321-4108
TF: 800-761-2118 ■ *Web:* www.priorityleasing.com

Private Export Funding Corp
280 Pk Ave 4th Fl W .... New York NY 10017 212-916-0300 286-0304
Web: www.pefco.com

PSCU Financial Services Inc
560 Carillon Pkwy .... Saint Petersburg FL 33716 727-572-7723 572-8503
TF: 800-443-7728 ■ *Web:* www.pscufs.com

Public Financial Management Inc (PFM)
One Keystone Plaza Suite 300 .... Harrisburg PA 17101 717-232-2723 233-6073
Web: www.pfm.com

Puerto Rico Farm Credit Aca PO Box 363649 .... San Juan PR 00936 787-753-0587 250-8414
TF: 800-981-3323 ■ *Web:* www.puertoricofarmcredit.com

Relational Technology Solutions Inc
1070 Polaris Pkwy Suite 200 .... Columbus OH 43240 866-222-8895 818-1711*
**Fax Area Code:* 847 ■ *TF:* 866-222-8895 ■ *Web:* www.rts.com

Republic Financial Corp
3300 S Parker Rd Suite 500 .... Aurora CO 80014 303-751-3501 751-4777
Web: www.republic-financial.com

Rockville Financial Inc
1645 Ellington Rd .... South Windsor CT 06074 860-291-3600
NASDAQ: RCKB ■ *Web:* www.rockvillebank.com

Schroder Investment Management North America Inc (SIMNA)
875 3rd Ave 22nd Fl .... New York NY 10022 800-730-2932 632-2954*
**Fax Area Code:* 212 ■ *TF:* 800-730-2932 ■ *Web:* www.schroders.com/us

Siemens Financial Services Inc 170 Wood Ave S .... Iselin NJ 08830 732-590-6500 476-3417
TF: 800-798-7721 ■ *Web:* www.siemensfinancial.com

Snap-on Credit LLC
950 Technology Way Suite 301 .... Libertyville IL 60048 847-782-7700 777-9375*
**Fax Area Code:* 877 ■ *TF:* 877-777-8455 ■ *Web:* www.snaponcredit.com

Southern Community Financial Corp
4605 Country Club Rd PO Box 26134 .... Winston-Salem NC 27104 336-768-8500 768-2437
Web: ir.smallenoughtocare.com

Southgroup & Financial Services Inc
795 Woodlands Pkwy Suite 101 .... Ridgeland MS 39157 601-914-3220 914-3188
Web: www.southgroup.net

Sta International
333 Earle Ovington Blvd Suite 1025 .... Uniondale NY 11553 516-997-2400 997-2632
TF: 866-970-9882 ■ *Web:* www.stacollect.com

Sunrise Credit Services Inc
2600 Airport Plaza .... Farmingdale NY 11735 800-208-8565
Web: www.sunrisecreditservices.com

Taycor LLC 6065 Bristol Pkwy .... Culver City CA 90230 310-895-7704 568-9922
TF: 800-322-9738 ■ *Web:* www.taycor.com

Textron Financial Corp 40 Westminster St .... Providence RI 02903 401-621-4200 621-5037
Web: www.textronfinancial.com
Systran Financial Services Div
4949 SW Meadows Rd Suite 500 .... Oswego OR 97035 800-824-2075 560-1565*
**Fax Area Code:* 678 ■ *TF:* 866-844-8398 ■ *Web:* www.textronfinancial.com

Tyndall Federal Credit Union Inc
PO Box 59760 .... Panama City FL 32412 850-769-9999 747-4215
TF: 888-896-3255 ■ *Web:* www.tyndallfcu.org

Universal Premium Acceptance Corp (UPAC)
8245 Nieman Rd Suite 100 .... Lenexa KS 66214 913-894-6150 894-4988
TF: 800-877-7848 ■ *Web:* www.upac.com

US Bancorp Equipment Finance Inc
13010 SW 68th Pkwy .... Portland OR 97223 503-797-0200 234-4210
TF: 800-253-3468 ■ *Web:* www.usbank.com

Verizon Credit Inc 201 N Franklin St Suite 3300 .... Tampa FL 33602 813-229-6000 229-4883
TF: 800-483-7988 ■ *Web:* www22.verizon.com/credit

Wachovia Capital Finance
1133 Avenue of the Americas .... New York NY 10036 212-840-2000 545-4555*
**Fax:* Mktg ■ *TF:* 800-223-6352 ■ *Web:* www.wachovia.com/corp_inst

Watson Group Financial Corp
6501 Highland Rd .... Waterford MI 48327 248-666-2700 666-1572
TF: 800-666-1572 ■ *Web:* www.watsongrp.com

Wells Fargo Equipment Finance Inc
733 Marquette Ave
Investors Bldg Suite 700 .... Minneapolis MN 55402 612-667-9876 667-9711
TF: 800-322-6220

Wells Fargo Financial Leasing Inc
PO Box 4943 .... Syracuse NY 13221 800-451-3322 887-1950*
**Fax Area Code:* 866 ■ *TF:* 800-451-3322 ■ *Web:* www.wellsfargoleasing.com

Western Agcredit PO Box 95850 .... South Jordan UT 84095 801-571-9200 576-0600
TF: 800-824-9198 ■ *Web:* www.westernagcredit.com

Winthrop Resources Corp
11100 Wayzata Blvd Suite 800 .... Minnetonka MN 55305 952-936-0226 936-0201
TF: 800-843-8264

Xerox Financial Services Inc
800 Long Ridge Rd .... Stamford CT 06904 203-968-3000 420-3402*
**Fax Area Code:* 972 ■ *TF:* 800-822-2502

220 CREDIT & FINANCING - CONSUMER

SEE ALSO Banks - Commercial & Savings p. 1506; Credit & Financing - Commercial p. 1773; Credit Unions p. 1776

Phone Fax

Ameristar Financial Co LLC
1795 N Butterfield Rd Suite 200 .... Libertyville IL 60048 847-247-2600 247-2585
TF: 800-784-1535 ■ *Web:* www.ameristarfinancial.com

AutoNation Financial Services
110 SE 6th St .... Fort Lauderdale FL 33301 954-769-7000 769-8994
TF: 888-825-8929 ■ *Web:* www.autonation.com

Budget Finance Co 1849 Sawtelle Blvd .... Los Angeles CA 90025 310-696-4050
TF: 800-225-6267 ■ *Web:* www.bfcloans.com

Collegiate Funding Services LLC
10304 Spotsylvania Ave Suite 100 .... Fredericksburg VA 22408 540-374-1600 374-1981
TF: 800-762-6441 ■ *Web:* www.cfsloans.com

Comfort Financial Services PO Box 1140 .... Evansville IN 47706 866-866-1331 866-1334
TF: 866-866-1331 ■ *Web:* www.comfortfinancial.com

Continental Currency Services Inc (CCS)
PO Box 27790 .... Santa Ana CA 92799 714-667-6699 569-0882
Web: www.ccurr.com

Credit Acceptance Corp 25505 W 12 Mile Rd .... Southfield MI 48034 248-353-2700
TF: 800-634-1506 ■ *Web:* www.credaccept.com

Dollar Loan Center LLC 6122 W Sahara Ave .... Las Vegas NV 89146 702-364-5626 364-5627
TF: 866-550-4352 ■ *Web:* www.dontbebroke.com

Farm Credit of The Virginias Aca
106 Sangers Ln .... Staunton VA 24401 540-886-3435 886-3437
TF: 800-559-1016 ■ *Web:* www.farmcreditofvirginias.com

Farm Credit West 1478 Stone Pt Dr Suite 450 .... Roseville CA 95661 860-741-4380
Web: www.farmcreditwest.com

Finance Factors Ltd 1164 Bishop St .... Honolulu HI 96813 808-548-3311 548-5148
TF: 800-648-7136 ■ *Web:* www.financefactors.com

First Insurance Funding Corp
450 Skokie Blvd Suite 1000 .... Northbrook IL 60062 800-837-3707 837-3709
TF: 800-837-3707 ■ *Web:* www.firstinsurancefunding.com

Ford Motor Credit Co
1 American Rd PO Box 1732 .... Dearborn MI 48121 313-322-3000 323-2959
TF: 800-727-7000 ■ *Web:* www.fordcredit.com

Franklin Credit Management Corp
101 Hudson St .... Jersey City NJ 07302 201-604-1800 604-4400
NASDAQ: FCMC ■ *TF:* 800-255-5897 ■ *Web:* www.franklincredit.com

GE Healthcare 540 W NW Hwy .... Barrington IL 60010 847-277-4000
TF Cust Svc: 800-488-5208 ■ *Web:* www.ge.com/capital/auto

General Motors Acceptance Corp (GMAC)
200 Renaissance Ctr .... Detroit MI 48265 313-556-5000 556-5108
TF: 800-200-4622 ■ *Web:* www.gmacfs.com

Green Tree Servicing LLC
345 St Peter St Suite 600 .... Saint Paul MN 55102 651-293-3400 293-3622*
**Fax:* Hum Res ■ *TF:* 800-423-9527 ■ *Web:* www.gtservicing.com

Harley-Davidson Financial Services Inc
PO Box 21489 .... Carson City NV 89721 888-691-4337
TF: 888-691-4337 ■ *Web:* www.harley-davidson.com

Imperial Finance & Trading
701 Pk of Commerce Blvd Suite 301 .... Boca Raton FL 33487 888-364-6775 704-0772*
NYSE: IFT ■ **Fax Area Code:* 866 ■ *TF:* 888-364-6775 ■ *Web:* www.imprl.com

Key Corporate Banking & Finance
601 Oakmont Ln Suite 110 .... Westmont IL 60559 630-655-7100
TF: 800-877-2860 ■ *Web:* www.key.com

Mercedes-Benz Financial Services USA LLC
PO Box 685 .... Roanoke TX 76262 800-654-6222 267-6745*
**Fax Area Code:* 877 ■ *TF:* 800-654-6222 ■ *Web:* www.mbfs.com

Nellie Mae Corp
50 Braintree Hill Pk Suite 300 .... Braintree MA 02184 781-849-1325 338-5626*
**Fax Area Code:* 800 ■ *TF Cust Svc:* 800-367-8848 ■ *Web:* www.nelliemae.com

Nelnet Inc 121 S 13th St Suite 201 .... Lincoln NE 68508 402-458-3038 458-2399
NYSE: NNI ■ *TF:* 888-486-4722 ■ *Web:* www.nelnet.com

	City	State	Zip	Phone	Fax
New York City Housing Development Corp 110 William St	New York	NY	10038	212-227-5500	227-6865
Web: www.nychdc.com					
Nicholas Financial Inc 2454 McMullen Booth Rd Bldg C	Clearwater	FL	33759	727-726-0763	726-2140
NASDAQ: NICK ■ *TF:* 800-237-2721 ■ *Web:* www.nicholasfinancial.com					
Prestige Financial Services Inc 1420 S 500 W	Salt Lake City	UT	84115	801-844-2100	844-2600
TF: 888-822-7422 ■ *Web:* www.gopfs.com					
Prime Rate Premium Finance Corp 2141 Enterprise Dr PO Box 100507	Florence	SC	29501	843-669-0937	677-9850*
**Fax Area Code:* 800 ■ *TF Cust Svc:* 800-777-7458 ■ *Web:* www.primeratepfc.com					
Redwood Credit Union PO Box 6104	Santa Rosa	CA	95406	707-545-4000	
TF: 800-479-7928 ■ *Web:* www.redwoodcu.org					
Regional Acceptance Corp 1424 E Fire Tower Rd	Greenville	NC	27858	252-321-7700	353-1852
TF: 877-999-7708 ■ *Web:* www.regionalacceptance.com					
Republic Finance LLC 7031 Commerce Cir Suite 100	Baton Rouge	LA	70809	225-927-0005	927-1063
TF: 800-317-7662 ■ *Web:* www.republicfinance.com					
Sallie Mae 12061 Bluemont Way	Reston	VA	20190	703-810-3000	848-1949*
**Fax Area Code:* 800 ■ *TF Cust Svc:* 888-272-5543 ■ *Web:* www.salliemae.com					
Sears Roebuck Acceptance Corp 3711 Kennett Pike	Greenville	DE	19807	302-434-3100	434-3150
TF: 800-729-7722					
Security Finance Corp 181 Security Pl	Spartanburg	SC	29307	864-582-8193	
TF: 800-395-8195 ■ *Web:* www.security-finance.com					
Select Portfolio Servicing Inc 3815 S W Temple	Salt Lake City	UT	84115	801-293-1883	
TF: 800-258-8602 ■ *Web:* www.spservicing.com					
SLM Corp 12061 Bluemont Way	Reston	VA	20190	703-810-3000	984-5046
NYSE: SLM ■ *TF Cust Svc:* 888-272-5543 ■ *Web:* www.salliemae.com					
Sotheby's Financial Services Inc 1334 York Ave	New York	NY	10021	212-894-1140	894-1141
Web: www.sothebys.com					
Student Loan Corp 701 E 60th St N PO Box 6191	Sioux Falls	SD	57117	605-331-0821	357-2013*
**Fax:* Cust Svc ■ *TF:* 800-967-2400 ■ *Web:* www.studentloan.com					
Toyota Motor Credit Corp 19001 S Western Ave	Torrance	CA	90509	310-787-1310	787-3505
TF Cust Svc: 800-392-2968					
United Finance Co 515 E Burnside St	Portland	OR	97214	503-232-5153	238-6453
Web: www.unitedfinance.com					
United Student Aid Funds Inc 11100 USA Pkwy	Fishers	IN	46037	317-849-6510	594-1974*
**Fax:* Hum Res ■ *TF:* 800-824-7044 ■ *Web:* www.usafunds.org					
Usa Discounters Ltd PO Box 8008	Virginia Beach	VA	23450	757-368-3300	368-3107
TF: 800-400-7291 ■ *Web:* www.usadiscounters.net					
Wells Fargo Education Financial Services PO Box 5185	Sioux Falls	SD	57117	800-658-3567	456-0561
TF: 800-658-3567 ■ *Web:* www.wellsfargo.com					
Wells Fargo Financial Inc 800 Walnut St	Des Moines	IA	50309	515-243-2131	557-5035
Web: www.financial.wellsfargo.com					
Western Funding Inc PO Box 94858	Las Vegas	NV	89193	702-434-1990	434-4286
Web: www.westernfundinginc.com					
WFS Financial Inc 23 Pasteur	Irvine	CA	92618	949-753-3866	
Web: www.wellsfargodealerservices.com					
World Acceptance Corp 108 Frederick St PO Box 6429	Greenville	SC	29606	864-298-9800	298-9810
NASDAQ: WRLD ■ *Web:* www.worldacceptance.com					

221 CREDIT REPORTING SERVICES

	City	State	Zip	Phone	Fax
Coface Services North America Inc 900 Chapel St	New Haven	CT	06510	203-781-3800	929-7779*
**Fax Area Code:* 800 ■ *TF:* 800-929-8374 ■ *Web:* www.coface-usa.com					
Equifax Credit Marketing Services 1525 Windward Concourse	Alpharetta	GA	30005	404-885-8000	885-8030
TF: 888-869-8413 ■ *Web:* www.equifax.com					
Equifax Inc 1550 Peachtree St NW	Atlanta	GA	30309	404-885-8000	888-5043
NYSE: EFX ■ *TF Sales:* 888-202-4025 ■ *Web:* www.equifax.com					
Experian Information Solutions Inc 475 Anton Blvd	Costa Mesa	CA	92626	714-830-7000	
TF Cust Svc: 888-397-3742 ■ *Web:* www.experian.com					
Fitch Ratings Inc 1 State St Plaza	New York	NY	10004	212-908-0500	
TF: 800-753-4824 ■ *Web:* www.fitchratings.com					
Kroll Factual Data Inc 5200 Hahns Peak Dr	Loveland	CO	80538	970-663-5700	929-3297*
**Fax Area Code:* 800 ■ *TF:* 800-929-3400 ■ *Web:* www.krollfactualdata.com					
Merchants Credit Bureau 955 Green St	Augusta	GA	30901	706-823-6246	823-6253
TF: 800-426-5265 ■ *Web:* www.mcbusa.com					
Moody's Corp 250 Greenwich St 7 World Trade Ctr	New York	NY	10007	212-553-0300	553-5376
NYSE: MCO ■ *Web:* www.moodys.com					
Standard & Poor's Ratings Services 55 Water St	New York	NY	10041	212-438-2000	438-6738*
**Fax:* Hum Res ■ *Web:* www.standardandpoors.com					
Tele-Track 155 Technology Pkwy Suite 800	Norcross	GA	30092	770-449-8809	449-6647
TF: 800-729-6981 ■ *Web:* www.teletrack.com					
TransUnion LLC 555 W Adams St	Chicago	IL	60661	312-258-1717	
TF: 800-916-8800 ■ *Web:* www.transunion.com					

222 CREDIT UNIONS

	City	State	Zip	Phone	Fax
49Er Federal Credit Union PO Box 1147	Placerville	CA	95667	530-621-5878	626-6360
Web: www.49erfcu.com					
66 Federal Credit Union PO Box 1358	Bartlesville	OK	74005	918-336-7662	337-7634
TF: 800-897-6991 ■ *Web:* www.66fcu.org					
AEDC Federal Credit Union 520 Airpark Dr PO Box 1210	Tullahoma	TN	37388	931-455-5441	454-1311
TF: 800-342-3086 ■ *Web:* www.aedcfcu.org					
Affinity Federal Credit Union 73 Mountain View Blvd PO Box 621	Basking Ridge	NJ	07920	908-860-7300	
TF: 800-325-0808 ■ *Web:* www.affinityfcu.org					
Air Force Federal Credit Union 1560 Cable Ranch Rd Suite 200	San Antonio	TX	78245	210-673-5610	673-5102
TF: 800-227-5328 ■ *Web:* www.airforcefcu.com					
Alaska USA Federal Credit Union 4000 Credit Union Dr PO Box 196613	Anchorage	AK	99503	907-563-4567	561-0773
TF: 800-525-9094 ■ *Web:* www.alaskausa.org					
Allegacy Federal Credit Union 1691 Westbrook Plaza Dr	Winston-Salem	NC	27103	336-774-3400	844-6464*
**Fax Area Code:* 800 ■ *TF:* 800-782-4670 ■ *Web:* www.allegacyfcu.org					
America First Credit Union 1344 W 4675 S	Riverdale	UT	84405	801-627-0900	778-8079*
**Fax:* Hum Res ■ *TF:* 800-999-3961 ■ *Web:* www.americafirst.com					
American Airlines Employees Federal Credit Union 4151 Amon Carter Blvd PO Box 155489	Fort Worth	TX	76155	817-963-6000	963-6108
TF: 800-533-0035 ■ *Web:* www.aacreditunion.org					
American Eagle Federal Credit Union 417 Main St	East Hartford	CT	06118	860-568-2020	568-2020
TF: 800-842-0145 ■ *Web:* www.americaneagle.org					
Amoco Federal Credit Union PO Box 889	Texas City	TX	77592	409-948-8541	948-3944
TF: 800-541-6249 ■ *Web:* www.amocofcu.org					
Andrews Federal Credit Union (AFCU) 5711 Allentown Rd	Suitland	MD	20746	301-702-5500	702-5330
TF: 800-487-5500 ■ *Web:* www.andrewsfcu.org					
Ang Federal Credit Union PO Box 170204	Birmingham	AL	35217	205-841-4525	841-4545
TF: 800-237-6211 ■ *Web:* www.angfcu.org					
APCO Employees Credit Union 1608 7th Ave N	Birmingham	AL	35203	205-257-3601	257-3787
TF: 800-249-2726 ■ *Web:* www.apcocu.org					
Arizona Federal Credit Union PO Box 60070	Phoenix	AZ	85082	602-683-1000	683-1903
TF: 800-523-4603 ■ *Web:* www.arizonafederal.org					
Atlanta Postal Credit Union 501 Pulliam St SW # 350	Atlanta	GA	30312	404-768-4126	768-0815
TF: 800-849-8431 ■ *Web:* www.apcu.com					
Autotruck Federal Credit Union 3611 Newburg Rd PO Box 18890	Louisville	KY	40261	502-459-8981	458-0371
TF: 800-459-2328 ■ *Web:* www.autotruckfcu.org					
Bank-Fund Staff Federal Credit Union PO Box 27755	Washington	DC	20038	202-458-4300	522-1528
TF: 800-923-7328 ■ *Web:* www.bfsfcu.org					
BayPort Credit Union Inc 3711 Huntington Ave	Newport News	VA	23607	757-928-8850	245-1019
TF: 800-928-8801 ■ *Web:* www.bayportcu.org/home.html					
Beacon Credit Union PO Box 627	Wabash	IN	46992	260-563-7443	
TF: 800-762-3136 ■ *Web:* www.beaconcu.org					
Bellco First Federal Credit Union 7600 E Orchard Rd # 400N	Greenwood Village	CO	80111	303-689-7800	689-7942
TF: 800-235-5261 ■ *Web:* www.bellco.org					
Bethpage Federal Credit Union 899 S Oyster Bay Rd	Bethpage	NY	11714	516-349-6700	349-6765
TF: 800-628-7070 ■ *Web:* www.bethpage.org					
Boeing Employees' Credit Union (BECU) PO Box 97050	Seattle	WA	98124	206-439-5700	439-5806*
**Fax:* Mktg ■ *TF:* 800-233-2328 ■ *Web:* www.becu.org					
Boulder Valley Credit Union Inc 5505 Arapahoe Ave	Boulder	CO	80303	303-442-8850	440-0838
TF: 800-783-8850 ■ *Web:* www.bvcu.org					
California Feminist Federal Credit Union PO Box 16587	San Diego	CA	92176	619-298-7283	
Web: www.feministcu.org					
Campus Federal Credit Union PO Box 98036	Baton Rouge	LA	70898	225-769-8841	381-9474
TF: 877-636-2377 ■ *Web:* www.campusfederal.org					
Campus USA Credit Union PO Box 147029	Gainesville	FL	32614	352-335-9090	
TF: 800-367-6440 ■ *Web:* www.campuscu.com					
Chartway Federal Credit Union 160 Newtown Rd	Virginia Beach	VA	23462	757-552-1000	671-7691*
**Fax:* Hum Res ■ *TF:* 800-678-8765 ■ *Web:* www.chartway.com					
Citizens Equity First Credit Union 5401 W Dirksen Pkwy	Peoria	IL	61607	309-633-7000	633-3621
TF Cust Svc: 800-633-7077 ■ *Web:* www.cefcu.com					
Class Act Federal Credit Union 3620 Fern Valley Rd	Louisville	KY	40219	502-964-7575	966-2061
TF: 800-292-2960 ■ *Web:* www.classact.org					
Coast Central Credit Union Inc 2650 Harrison Ave	Eureka	CA	95501	707-445-8801	442-2532
TF: 800-974-9727 ■ *Web:* www.coastccu.org					
Coastal Federal Credit Union 1000 St Albans Dr	Raleigh	NC	27609	919-420-8000	
TF: 800-868-4262 ■ *Web:* www.coastal24.com					
Commonwealth Credit Union PO Box 978	Frankfort	KY	40602	502-564-4775	
TF: 800-228-6420 ■ *Web:* www.ccuky.org					
Community America Credit Union (CACU) 9777 Ridge Dr	Lenexa	KS	66219	913-905-7000	905-7070
TF: 800-892-7957 ■ *Web:* www.cacu.com					
Community Resource Federal Credit Union 20 Wade Rd	Latham	NY	12110	518-783-2211	783-2266
TF: 888-783-2211 ■ *Web:* www.communityresource.coop					
Communitywide Federal Credit Union 1555 W Western Ave	South Bend	IN	46619	574-239-2700	
Web: www.comwide.com					
Contra Costa Federal Credit Union PO Box 509	Martinez	CA	94553	925-228-7550	
TF: 888-387-8632 ■ *Web:* www.contracostafcu.org					
Coors Credit Union 816 Washington Ave	Golden	CO	80401	303-279-6414	279-6336
TF: 800-770-6414 ■ *Web:* www.coorscu.org					
Coosa Pines Federal Credit Union Hwy 235 N	Childersburg	AL	35044	256-378-7965	378-3881
TF: 800-237-9789 ■ *Web:* www.coosapinesfcu.org					

				Phone	Fax
Credit Union of Southern California PO Box 200 *Fax Area Code: 714 ■ TF: 866-287-6225 ■ Web: www.cusocal.org	Whittier	CA	90608	562-698-8326	990-5492*
Credit Union of Texas PO Box 517028 TF: 800-314-3828 ■ Web: www.cuoftexas.org	Dallas	TX	75251	972-263-9497	301-1980
Ctce Federal Credit Union PO Box 13385 TF: 877-875-8078 ■ Web: www.ctce.org	Reading	PA	19612	610-376-6639	373-5045
Dearborn Federal Credit Union 400 Town Ctr Dr TF: 888-336-2700 ■ Web: www.dfcufinancial.com	Dearborn	MI	48126	313-336-2700	336-2700
Deer Valley Federal Credit Union 15458 N 28th Ave Suite A TF: 800-579-5051 ■ Web: www.dvcu.org	Phoenix	AZ	85053	602-439-2559	375-7333
Delta Employees Credit Union 1025 Virginia Ave TF: 800-544-3328 ■ Web: www.deltacommunitycu.com	Atlanta	GA	30354	404-715-4725	677-4776
Denton Area Teachers Credit Union PO Box 827 TF: 866-387-8585 ■ Web: www.datcu.org	Denton	TX	76202	940-387-8585	
Denver Fire Dept Federal Credit Union (DFDFCU) 2201 Federal Blvd TF: 866-880-7770 ■ Web: www.dfdfcu.com	Denver	CO	80211	303-228-5300	228-5333
Desert Schools Federal Credit Union 148 N 48th St TF: 800-456-9171 ■ Web: www.desertschools.org	Phoenix	AZ	85034	602-433-7000	335-3186
Digital Employees' Federal Credit Union 220 Donald Lynch Blvd TF: 800-328-8797 ■ Web: www.dcu.org	Marlborough	MA	01752	508-263-6700	263-6392
Direct Federal Credit Union PO Box 9123 TF: 800-676-0001 ■ Web: www.direct.com	Needham	MA	02494	781-455-6500	455-9922
Dow Chemical Employees' Credit Union 600 E Lyon Rd TF: 800-835-7794 ■ Web: www.dcecu.org	Midland	MI	48640	989-835-7794	832-2622
Educational Employees Credit Union PO Box 5242 TF: 800-538-3328 ■ Web: www.myeecu.org	Fresno	CA	93755	559-437-7700	451-0198
Educators Credit Union (ECU) 1400 N Newman Rd PO Box 81040 TF: 800-236-5898 ■ Web: www.ecu.com	Racine	WI	53406	262-886-5900	884-7233
Eglin Federal Credit Union 838 Eglin Pkwy NE TF: 800-367-6159 ■ Web: www.eglinfcu.org	Fort Walton Beach	FL	32547	850-862-0111	862-0111
Ent Federal Credit Union 7250 Campus Dr TF: 800-525-9623 ■ Web: www.ent.com	Colorado Springs	CO	80920	719-574-1100	388-9065
ESL Federal Credit Union 100 Kings Hwy S Suite 1200 TF: 800-848-2265 ■ Web: www.esl.org	Rochester	NY	14617	585-336-1000	336-1034
Evansville Teachers Federal Credit Union PO Box 5129 TF: 800-800-9271 ■ Web: www.etfcu.org	Evansville	IN	47716	812-477-9271	473-9704
Faa Credit Union PO Box 26406 TF: 800-448-1990 ■ Web: www.faaecu.org	Oklahoma City	OK	73126	405-682-1990	
Fairwinds Federal Credit Union 3087 N Alafaya Trail *Fax: Acctg ■ TF: 800-443-6887 ■ Web: www.fairwinds.org	Orlando	FL	32826	407-277-5045	658-7937*
Finance Center Federal Credit Union PO Box 26501 TF: 800-473-2328 ■ Web: www.fcfcu.com	Indianapolis	IN	46226	317-916-7700	916-6206
Financial Partners Credit Union PO Box 7005 TF: 800-950-7328 ■ Web: www.fpcu.org	Downey	CA	90241	562-923-0311	904-4285
Firefighters Community Credit Union Inc 2300 St Clair Ave NE TF: 800-621-4644 ■ Web: www.ffcommunity.com	Cleveland	OH	44114	216-621-4644	694-3600
First Community Credit Union (FCCU) PO Box 1030 TF: 800-767-8880 ■ Web: www.firstcommunity.com	Chesterfield	MO	63006	636-728-3333	537-4448
Fort Knox Federal Credit Union PO Box 900 TF: 800-756-3678 ■ Web: www.fkfcu.org	Radcliff	KY	40159	502-942-0254	
Fort Worth City Credit Union PO Box 100099 TF: 888-732-3085 ■ Web: www.fwccu.org	Fort Worth	TX	76185	817-732-2803	377-7966
Fort Worth Community Credit Union 1905 Forest Ridge Dr PO Box 210848 TF: 800-817-8234 ■ Web: www.ftwccu.org	Bedford	TX	76021	817-835-5000	835-5235
Forum Credit Union PO Box 50738 TF: 800-382-5414 ■ Web: www.forumcu.com	Indianapolis	IN	46250	317-558-6000	558-6319
Founders Federal Credit Union 607 N Main St TF Tech Supp: 888-918-7403 ■ Web: www.foundersfcu.com	Lancaster	SC	29720	803-283-5900	283-5919
Georgia Telco Credit Union 1155 Peachtree St NE Suite 400 TF: 800-533-2062 ■ Web: www.gatelco.org	Atlanta	GA	30309	404-874-1166	881-2950
Gesa Credit Union 51 Gage Blvd PO Box 500 TF: 888-946-4372 ■ Web: www.gesa.com	Richland	WA	99352	509-946-1611	628-2498
Golden One Credit Union PO Box 15966 TF: 877-465-3361 ■ Web: www.golden1.com	Sacramento	CA	95852	916-732-2900	451-3053
Government Employees Credit Union of El Paso (GECU) 1225 Airway PO Box 20998 TF: 800-772-4328 ■ Web: www.gecu-ep.org	El Paso	TX	79925	915-778-9221	774-1798
GTE Federal Credit Union PO Box 172599 TF: 800-241-4120 ■ Web: www.gtefcu.org	Tampa	FL	33672	813-871-2690	
Guadalupe Credit Union 3601 Mimbres Ln Web: www.guadalupecu.org	Santa Fe	NM	87507	505-982-8942	216-0497
Hamilton City Employees Federal Credit Union 309 Ct St Web: www.allwealth.org	Hamilton	OH	45011	513-868-5881	867-7339
HarborOne Credit Union 770 Oak St PO Box 720 TF: 800-244-7592 ■ Web: www.harboronecu.com	Brockton	MA	02301	508-895-1000	895-1674
Hawthorne Credit Union 1519 N Naper Blvd TF: 800-848-1697 ■ Web: www.hawthornecu.org	Naperville	IL	60563	630-369-4070	369-4178
Hudson Valley Federal Credit Union 159 Barnegat Rd TF: 800-468-3011 ■ Web: www.hvfcu.org	Poughkeepsie	NY	12601	845-463-3011	463-3613
Hughes Federal Credit Union Inc PO Box 11900 TF: 866-760-3156 ■ Web: www.hughesfcu.org	Tucson	AZ	85734	520-794-8341	
I B M Southeast Employees Federal Credit Union PO Box 5090 TF: 888-567-8688 ■ Web: www.ibmsecu.org	Boca Raton	FL	33431	561-982-4700	
Indiana Members Credit Union PO Box 47769 Web: www.imcu.org	Indianapolis	IN	46247	317-788-4693	780-6716
Island Federal Credit Union 120 Motor Pkwy TF: 866-826-8471 ■ Web: www.islandfcu.org	Hauppauge	NY	11788	631-851-1100	
Keesler Federal Credit Union PO Box 7001 TF: 888-533-7537 ■ Web: www.kfcu.org	Biloxi	MS	39534	228-392-6438	385-5501
Kern Schools Federal Credit Union PO Box 9506 TF: 800-221-3311 ■ Web: www.ksfcu.com	Bakersfield	CA	93389	661-833-7900	833-7989
KeyPoint Credit Union 2805 Bowers Ave TF: 888-255-3637 ■ Web: www.keypointcu.com	Santa Clara	CA	95051	408-731-4100	731-4485
Kinecta Federal Credit Union 1440 Rosecrans Ave PO Box 10003 *Fax: Hum Res ■ TF: 800-854-9846 ■ Web: www.kinecta.org	Manhattan Beach	CA	90266	310-643-5400	643-5473*
L & N Federal Credit Union 9265 Smyrna Pkwy TF: 800-443-2479 ■ Web: www.lnfcu.com	Louisville	KY	40229	502-368-5858	
La Capitol Federal Credit Union PO Box 3398 TF: 800-522-2748 ■ Web: www.lacapfcu.org	Baton Rouge	LA	70821	225-342-5055	342-9135
Lafayette Federal Credit Union (inc) 3535 University Blvd W TF: 800-888-6560 ■ Web: www.lfcu.org	Kensington	MD	20895	301-929-7990	
Landmark Credit Union 5445 S Westridge Dr PO Box 510910 TF: 800-801-1449 ■ Web: www.landmarkcu.com	New Berlin	WI	53151	262-796-4500	549-8230
Langley Federal Credit Union 1055 W Mercury Blvd TF: 800-826-7490 ■ Web: www.langleyfcu.org	Hampton	VA	23666	757-827-7200	825-7557
Leominster Credit Union 20 Adams St TF: 800-649-4646 ■ Web: www.leominstercu.com	Leominster	MA	01453	978-537-8021	
Local Government Federal Credit Union 323 W Jones St Suite 600 TF: 888-732-8562 ■ Web: www.lgfcu.org	Raleigh	NC	27603	919-755-0534	755-0193
Lockheed Federal Credit Union (LFCU) 2340 Hollywood Way TF: 800-328-5328 ■ Web: www.secure.lockheedfcu.org	Burbank	CA	91505	818-565-2020	846-4379
Los Angeles Federal Credit Union PO Box 53032 TF: 877-695-2328 ■ Web: www.lafcu.org	Los Angeles	CA	90053	818-242-8640	242-5812
Los Angeles Police Federal Credit Union PO Box 10188 TF: 877-695-2732 ■ Web: www.lapfcu.org	Van Nuys	CA	91410	818-787-6520	786-9508
MacDill Federal Credit Union PO Box 89909 TF: 800-839-6328 ■ Web: www.growfinancial.org	Tampa	FL	33619	813-837-2451	832-2080
Members Heritage Federal Credit Union 440 Pk Pl TF: 800-359-3466 ■ Web: www.membersheritage.org	Lexington	KY	40511	859-259-3466	455-7281
Meriwest Credit Union PO Box 530953 TF: 877-637-4937 ■ Web: www.meriwest.com	San Jose	CA	95153	408-972-5222	363-3330
Midwest America Federal Credit Union 1104 Medical Pk Dr TF: 800-348-4738 ■ Web: www.mwafcu.org	Fort Wayne	IN	46825	260-482-3334	423-8298
Miramar Federal Credit Union PO Box 261370 TF: 800-640-1228 ■ Web: www.miramarfcu.org	San Diego	CA	92196	858-695-9494	271-1537
Mission Federal Credit Union PO Box 919023 TF: 800-500-6328 ■ Web: www.missionfed.com	San Diego	CA	92121	858-524-2850	546-7637
Mountain America Credit Union PO Box 9001 TF: 800-748-4302 ■ Web: www.macu.com	West Jordan	UT	84084	801-325-6228	325-6395
Municipal Credit Union PO Box 3205 TF: 800-843-1867 ■ Web: www.nymcu.org	New York	NY	10007	212-693-4900	416-7051
Nassau Financial Federal Credit Union 1325 Franklin Ave Suite 500 TF: 888-287-9475 ■ Web: www.nassaufinancial.org	Garden City	NY	11530	516-742-4900	
Neighbors Federal Credit Union PO Box 2831 TF: 866-819-2178 ■ Web: www.neighborsfcu.org	Baton Rouge	LA	70821	225-819-2178	819-8923
New England Federal Credit Union PO Box 527 TF: 800-400-8790 ■ Web: www.nefcu.com	Williston	VT	05495	802-879-8790	879-8557
New Orleans Firemens Federal Credit Union PO Box 689 TF: 800-647-1689 ■ Web: www.noffcu.org	Metairie	LA	70004	504-889-9090	889-9082
North Country Federal Credit Union Inc 69 Swift St Suite 100 TF: 800-660-3258 ■ Web: www.northcountry.org	South Burlington	VT	05403	802-657-6847	864-9849
North Island Financial Credit Union 2300 Boswell Rd TF Cust Svc: 800-752-4419 ■ Web: www.myisland.com/nifcu	Chula Vista	CA	91914	619-656-1600	656-4056
Northeast Arkansas Federal Credit Union (NEAFCU) PO Box 467 Web: www.neafcu.org	Blytheville	AR	72316	870-763-1111	763-2095
NuUnion Credit Union 501 S Capitol Ave TF: 888-267-7200 ■ Web: www.laketrust.org	Lansing	MI	48933	517-267-7200	267-7095
Oklahoma Federal Credit Union 517 NE 36th St Web: www.okfcu.com	Oklahoma City	OK	73105	405-524-6467	524-1067
Orange County's Credit Union PO Box 11777 Web: www.orangecountyscu.org	Santa Ana	CA	92711	714-755-5900	
Owensboro Federal Credit Union 717 Harvard Dr PO Box 1189 TF: 800-264-1054 ■ Web: www.ofcuonline.com	Owensboro	KY	42302	270-683-1054	685-3987
Pacific Marine Credit Union M C X Complex TF: 800-736-4500 ■ Web: www.pmcu.com	Oceanside	CA	92055	760-430-7511	

Name / Address	City	State	ZIP	Phone	Fax
Pacific NW Federal Credit Union (PNWFCU) 12106 NE Marx St — *TF:* 866-692-8669 ■ *Web:* www.pnwfcu.org	Portland	OR	97220	503-256-5858	253-5858
Pacific Service Federal Credit Union 2850 Shadelands Dr — *TF:* 888-858-6878 ■ *Web:* www.pacificservice.org	Walnut Creek	CA	94598	925-296-6200	296-6209
Patelco Credit Union 156 2nd St — *TF:* 800-358-8228 ■ *Web:* www.patelco.org	San Francisco	CA	94105	415-442-6200	442-6248
Pearl Harbor Federal Credit Union (PHFCU) 94-449 Ukee St — *TF:* 800-987-5583 ■ *Web:* www.phfcu.com	Waipahu	HI	96818	808-423-1331	422-1576
Pen-Air Federal Credit Union Inc 1495 E Nine Mile Rd — *TF:* 877-473-6247 ■ *Web:* www.penair.org/webfederal.asp	Pensacola	FL	32514	850-505-3200	458-2367
Pennsylvania State Employees Credit Union 1 Credit Union Pl — *TF:* 800-237-7328 ■ *Web:* www.psecu.com	Harrisburg	PA	17110	717-234-8484	772-2272
Pentagon Federal Credit Union 2930 Eisenhower Ave — *TF:* 800-247-5626 ■ *Web:* www.penfed.org	Alexandria	VA	22314	800-247-5626	253-6589
Pine Bluff Cotton Belt Federal Credit Union 1703 River Pines Blvd — *TF:* 888-249-1904 ■ *Web:* www.pbcottonbeltfcu.coop	Pine Bluff	AR	71601	870-535-6365	535-0765
Police & Fire Federal Credit Union 901 Arch St — *TF:* 800-228-8801 ■ *Web:* www.pffcu.org	Philadelphia	PA	19107	215-931-0300	931-2926
Polish & Slavic Federal Credit Union 140 Greenpoint Ave — *TF:* 800-297-2181	Brooklyn	NY	11222	718-383-6268	389-8210
Portland Teachers Credit Union 2701 NW Vaughn Suite 800 — *TF:* 800-527-3932 ■ *Web:* www.onpointcu.com	Portland	OR	97210	503-228-7077	273-2698
Premier America Credit Union 19867 Prairie St PO Box 2178 — *TF:* 800-772-4000 ■ *Web:* www.premier.org	Chatsworth	CA	91313	818-772-4000	772-4175
Premier Members Federal Credit Union 5495 Arapahoe Ave — *TF:* 800-468-0634 ■ *Web:* www.premiermembers.org	Boulder	CO	80303	303-657-7000	682-7914
Provident Central Credit Union 303 Twin Dolphin Dr — *TF:* 800-632-4600 ■ *Web:* www.providentcu.org	Redwood City	CA	94065	650-508-0300	508-7202
Randolph-Brooks Federal Credit Union PO Box 2097 — *TF:* 800-580-3300 ■ *Web:* www.rbfcu.org	Universal City	TX	78148	210-945-3300	945-3764
Redstone Federal Credit Union 220 Wynn Dr NW — **Fax:* Cust Svc ■ *TF:* 800-234-1234 ■ *Web:* www.redfcu.org	Huntsville	AL	35893	256-837-6110	722-3655*
Rhode Island State Employees Credit Union 160 Francis St — *Web:* www.ricreditunion.org	Providence	RI	02903	401-751-7440	331-5907
Rockland Federal Credit Union 241 Union St — *TF:* 800-562-7328 ■ *Web:* www.rfcu.com	Rockland	MA	02370	781-878-0232	792-3866
RTN Federal Credit Union 600 Main St Suite 3 — *TF:* 800-338-0221 ■ *Web:* www.rtn.org	Waltham	MA	02452	781-736-9900	736-9856
SAC Federal Credit Union (SAFCU) 11515 S 39th St PO Box 1149 — *TF:* 800-228-0392 ■ *Web:* www.sacfcu.com	Bellevue	NE	68123	402-292-8000	829-0149
Sacramento District Postal Employees Credit Union Co 1485 River Pk Dr — *TF:* 800-300-7053 ■ *Web:* www.sacpostalcu.org	Sacramento	CA	95815	916-921-5050	921-0800
Safe 1 Credit Union PO Box 2203 — *TF:* 800-322-4529 ■ *Web:* www.safe1.org	Bakersfield	CA	93303	661-327-3818	
SAFE Credit Union 3720 Madison Ave — *TF:* 800-733-7233 ■ *Web:* www.safecu.org	North Highlands	CA	95660	916-979-7233	331-7125
Safeamerica Credit Union 6001 Gibraltar Dr — *TF:* 800-851-6789 ■ *Web:* www.safeamerica.com	Pleasanton	CA	94588	925-734-4111	
San Antonio Federal Credit Union 6061 IH 10W — *TF:* 800-234-7228 ■ *Web:* www.sacu.com	San Antonio	TX	78201	210-258-1414	258-1543
San Diego County Credit Union 6545 Sequence Dr — **Fax Area Code:* 619 ■ *TF:* 877-732-2848 ■ *Web:* www.sdccu.com	San Diego	CA	92121	877-732-2848	294-9320*
San Francisco Federal Credit Union 770 Golden Gate Ave — *TF:* 800-852-7598 ■ *Web:* www.sanfranciscofcu.com	San Francisco	CA	94102	415-775-5377	775-5340
Santa Clara County Federal Credit Union (inc) (SCCFCU) 1641 N 1st St Suite 170 — *Web:* www.sccfcu.org/ASP/home.asp	San Jose	CA	95112	408-282-0700	287-8687
Sb1 Federal Credit Union PO Box 7480 — *TF:* 800-806-9465 ■ *Web:* www.sb1fcu.org	Philadelphia	PA	19101	215-569-3700	
Schools Financial Credit Union 1485 Response Rd # 126 — *TF:* 800-962-0990 ■ *Web:* www.schools.org	Sacramento	CA	95815	916-569-5400	331-2242
Secure First Credit Union PO Box 170070 — *TF:* 877-520-2115 ■ *Web:* www.securefirstcu.org	Birmingham	AL	35217	205-520-2115	520-2110
Security Service Federal Credit Union 16211 La Cantera Pkwy — *TF:* 800-527-7328 ■ *Web:* www.ssfcu.org	San Antonio	TX	78256	210-476-4000	444-3000
Selco Community Credit Union 299 E 11th Ave — *Web:* www.selco.org	Eugene	OR	97401	541-686-8000	686-4367
Seven Seventeen Credit Union Inc 3181 Larchmont Ave Ne — *Web:* www.sscu.net	Warren	OH	44483	330-372-8100	372-8337
South Carolina Federal Credit Union PO Box 190012 — *TF:* 800-845-0432 ■ *Web:* www.scfederal.org	North Charleston	SC	29419	843-797-8300	
Southwest Corporate Federal Credit Union 6801 Parkwood Blvd — *TF:* 800-442-5763 ■ *Web:* www.swcorp.org	Plano	TX	75024	214-703-7500	703-7906
Space Coast Credit Union 8045 N Wickham Rd PO Box 419001 — *TF:* 800-447-7228 ■ *Web:* www.sccu.com	Melbourne	FL	32941	321-752-2222	723-3716
St Anne's Credit Union of Fall River 286 Oliver St — *Web:* www.stannes.com	Fall River	MA	02724	508-324-7300	673-1542
Stanford Federal Credit Union 1860 Embarcadero Rd — **Fax Area Code:* 866 ■ *TF:* 888-723-7328 ■ *Web:* www.sfcu.org	Palo Alto	CA	94303	650-723-2509	579-9764*
Star One Federal Credit Union 166 8th Ave — *TF:* 800-552-1455 ■ *Web:* www.starone.org	Sunnyvale	CA	94089	408-543-5202	543-5203
State Employees Credit Union of Maryland Inc 971 Corporate Blvd — *TF:* 800-879-7328 ■ *Web:* www.secumd.org	Linthicum	MD	21090	410-487-7328	487-7011
State Employees Federal Credit Union 700 Patroon Creek Blvd Patroon Creek Corporate Ctr — **Fax:* Hum Res ■ *TF:* 800-727-3328 ■ *Web:* www.sefcu.com	Albany	NY	12206	518-452-8234	464-5363*
State Employees' Credit Union 1000 Wade Ave — *TF:* 888-732-8562 ■ *Web:* www.ncsecu.org	Raleigh	NC	27605	919-839-5000	839-5476
Suncoast Schools Federal Credit Union 6804 E Hillsborough Ave — *TF:* 800-999-5887 ■ *Web:* www.suncoastfcu.org	Tampa	FL	33610	813-621-7511	621-2527
Sunstate Federal Credit Union (inc) PO Box 1162 — *Web:* www.sunstatefcu.org	Gainesville	FL	32602	352-381-5200	
Teachers Credit Union (TCU) PO Box 1395 — **Fax:* Hum Res ■ *TF:* 800-552-4745 ■ *Web:* www.tcunet.com	South Bend	IN	46624	574-284-6290	284-6313*
Teachers Federal Credit Union (TFCU) 2410 N Ocean Ave PO Box 9029 — *TF:* 800-341-4333 ■ *Web:* www.teachersfcu.org	Farmingville	NY	11738	631-698-7000	698-7004
Tech Credit Union 10951 Broadway — *TF:* 800-276-8324 ■ *Web:* www.techcu.org	Crown Point	IN	46307	219-663-5120	662-4384
Texans Credit Union 777 E Campbell Rd — *TF:* 800-843-5295 ■ *Web:* www.texanscu.org	Richardson	TX	75081	972-348-2000	348-2200
Texas Dow Employees Credit Union (TDECU) 1001 FM 2004 — *TF:* 800-839-1154 ■ *Web:* www.tdecu.org	Lake Jackson	TX	77566	979-297-1154	299-0212
Tinker Federal Credit Union 4140 W I-40 PO Box 45750 — *TF:* 800-456-4828 ■ *Web:* www.tinkerfcu.org	Oklahoma City	OK	73108	405-732-0324	946-6251
Tower Federal Credit Union 7901 Sandy Spring Rd — **Fax:* Cust Svc ■ *TF:* 800-787-8328 ■ *Web:* www.towerfcu.org	Laurel	MD	20707	301-497-7000	497-8930*
Travis Federal Credit Union 1 Travis Way — *TF:* 800-877-8328 ■ *Web:* www.traviscu.org	Vacaville	CA	95687	707-449-4000	449-9566
Truliant Federal Credit Union 3200 Truliant Way — *TF:* 800-822-0382 ■ *Web:* www.truliantfcu.org	Winston-Salem	NC	27103	336-659-1955	659-3540
Tyco Electronics Federal Credit Union PO Box 3449 — **Fax Area Code:* 800 ■ *TF:* 888-673-3288 ■ *Web:* www.tycocu.org	Redwood City	CA	94064	888-673-3288	280-8926*
U S Employees O C Federal Credit Union PO Box 44000 — *TF:* 800-227-6366 ■ *Web:* www.usecreditunion.org	Oklahoma City	OK	73144	405-685-6200	685-6234
Ukrainian National Federal Credit Union 215 2nd Ave PO Box 160 — *TF:* 866-859-5848 ■ *Web:* www.ukrnatfcu.org	New York	NY	10003	212-533-2980	995-5204
United Nations Federal Credit Union (UNFCU) 24-01 44th Rd Court Sq Pl — *TF:* 800-891-2471 ■ *Web:* www.unfcu.org	Long Island City	NY	11101	347-686-6000	686-6400
Unitus Community Credit Union PO Box 1937 — *TF:* 800-452-0900 ■ *Web:* www.unitusccu.com	Portland	OR	97207	503-227-5571	423-8345
University & State Employees Credit Union 10120 Pacific Heights Blvd Suite 100 — *TF:* 866-873-2448 ■ *Web:* www.usecu.org	San Diego	CA	92121	858-795-6100	795-6007
University of Hawaii Federal Credit Union PO Box 22070 — *TF:* 800-927-3397 ■ *Web:* www.uhfcu.com	Honolulu	HI	96823	808-983-5500	
US Alliance Federal Credit Union 600 Midland Ave — *TF Cust Svc:* 800-431-2754 ■ *Web:* www.usalliance.org	Rye	NY	10580	914-921-0500	881-3464
US Central Credit Union 9701 Renner Blvd — *TF:* 888-872-0440 ■ *Web:* www.uscentral.org	Lenexa	KS	66219	913-227-6000	438-1564
US New Mexico Federal Credit Union (USNMFCU) 3939 Osuna Rd NE Suite 300b PO Box 129 — *TF:* 888-342-8766 ■ *Web:* www.usnmfcu.org	Albuquerque	NM	87109	505-342-8888	342-8975
Valley First Credit Union PO Box 1411 — *TF:* 877-549-4567 ■ *Web:* www.valleyfirstcu.org	Modesto	CA	95353	209-549-8500	524-1741
Vantage Credit Union (VCU) PO Box 4433 — *TF:* 800-522-6009 ■ *Web:* www.vcu.com	Bridgeton	MO	63044	314-298-0055	
Verity Credit Union PO Box 75974 — *TF:* 800-890-6488 ■ *Web:* www.veritycu.com	Seattle	WA	98175	206-440-9000	361-5300
Virginia Credit Union 7500 Boulders View Dr — *TF:* 800-285-5051 ■ *Web:* www.vacu.org	Richmond	VA	23225	804-323-6000	608-8619
Visions Federal Credit Union (VFUC) 24 McKinley Ave — *TF:* 800-242-2120 ■ *Web:* www.visionsfcu.org	Endicott	NY	13760	607-754-7900	786-1718
Vons Employees Federal Credit Union 4455 Arden Dr PO Box 8023 — *Web:* www.vonscu.com	El Monte	CA	91731	626-444-1972	350-5850
Vystar Credit Union 1802 Kernan Blvd S — *TF:* 800-445-6289 ■ *Web:* www.vystarcu.org	Jacksonville	FL	32246	904-777-6000	908-2488
Washington State Employees Credit Union 400 E Union Ave — *TF:* 800-562-0999 ■ *Web:* www.wsecu.org	Olympia	WA	98501	360-943-7911	754-1385
Wescom Credit Union 123 S Marengo Ave PO Box 7058 — *TF:* 888-493-7266 ■ *Web:* www.wescom.org	Pasadena	CA	91101	626-535-1000	
Western Bridge Corporate Federal Credit Union 924 Overland Ct PO Box 9024 — *TF:* 800-442-4366 ■ *Web:* www.wescorp.org	San Dimas	CA	91773	909-394-6300	592-4545
Wings Financial Credit Union 14985 Glazier Ave Suite 100 — *TF:* 800-692-2274 ■ *Web:* www.wingsfinancial.com	Apple Valley	MN	55124	952-997-8000	997-8124

Company	City	State	ZIP	Phone	Fax
Workers' Credit Union 815 Main St PO Box 900 *TF:* 800-221-4020 ■ *Web:* www.wcu.com	Fitchburg	MA	01420	978-345-1021	343-5825
Wright-Patt Credit Union Inc 2455 Executive Pk Blvd PO Box 286 *TF:* 800-762-0047 ■ *Web:* www.wpcu.coop	Fairborn	OH	45324	937-912-7000	912-8002
Y-12 Federal Credit Union 501 Lafayette Dr PO Box 2512 *TF:* 800-482-1043 ■ *Web:* www.y12fcu.org	Oak Ridge	TN	37830	865-482-1043	

223 CRUISE LINES

SEE ALSO Casinos p. 1558; Cruises - Riverboat p. 1779; Ports & Port Authorities p. 2440; Travel Agencies p. 2729

Company	City	State	ZIP	Phone	Fax
Baja Expeditions Inc 3096 Palm St *TF:* 800-843-6967 ■ *Web:* www.bajaex.com	San Diego	CA	92104	858-581-3311	581-6542
Blount Small Ship Adventures 461 Water St *TF:* 800-556-7450 ■ *Web:* blountsmallshipadventures.com	Warren	RI	02885	401-247-0955	247-2350
Blue Lagoon Cruises 2222 Foothill Blvd Suite E-175 *Web:* www.bluelagooncruises.com	La Canada Flintridge	CA	91011	818-424-7550	957-2476
Bluewater Adventures Ltd 252 E 1st St Suite 3 *TF:* 888-877-1770 ■ *Web:* www.bluewateradventures.ca	North Vancouver	BC	V7L1B3	604-980-3800	980-1800
Carnival Cruise Lines 3655 NW 87th Ave *TF:* 888-227-6482 ■ *Web:* www.carnivalcruises.com	Miami	FL	33178	305-599-2600	406-4700
Celebrity Cruises Inc 1050 Caribbean Way *TF:* 800-256-6649 ■ *Web:* www.celebritycruises.com	Miami	FL	33132	305-539-6000	982-4995
China Ocean Shipping Co Americas Inc (COSCO) 100 Lighting Way *Web:* www.cosco-usa.com	Secaucus	NJ	07094	201-422-0500	422-8956
Clipper Cruise Line Inc 11969 Westline Industrial Dr *TF:* 800-325-0010	Saint Louis	MO	63146	314-655-6700	655-6700
Costa Cruise Lines 200 S Pk Rd Suite 200 **Fax:* Hum Res ■ *TF:* 800-462-6782 ■ *Web:* www.costacruises.com	Hollywood	FL	33021	954-266-5645	266-5880*
Cruise West 2301 5th Ave Suite 401 *TF:* 888-851-8133 ■ *Web:* www.cruisewest.com	Seattle	WA	98121	206-441-8687	441-4757
Crystal Cruises Inc 2049 Century Pk E Suite 1400 **Fax:* Hum Res ■ *Web:* www.crystalcruises.com	Los Angeles	CA	90067	310-785-9300	785-0011*
Cunard Line Ltd 24303 Town Ctr Dr Suite 200 *TF:* 800-223-0764 ■ *Web:* www.cunard.com	Valencia	CA	91355	661-753-1000	753-1005
Discovery Cruises Inc 1775 NW 70th Ave *TF:* 800-866-8687 ■ *Web:* www.discoverycruiseline.com	Miami	FL	33126	305-597-0336	477-2867
Great Lakes Cruise Co 3270 Washtenaw Ave *TF:* 888-891-0203 ■ *Web:* www.greatlakescruising.com	Ann Arbor	MI	48104	734-677-0900	677-1428
Holland America Line 300 Elliott Ave W *TF:* 800-426-0327 ■ *Web:* www.hollandamerica.com	Seattle	WA	98119	206-281-3535	281-7110
Hurtigruten 405 Pk Ave *TF:* 866-257-6071 ■ *Web:* www.hurtigruten.us	New York	NY	10022	212-319-1300	319-1390
Lindblad Expeditions 96 Morton St 9th Fl *TF:* 800-397-3348 ■ *Web:* www.expeditions.com	New York	NY	10014	212-765-7740	265-3770
Maine Windjammer Cruises 11 Main St *TF:* 800-736-7981 ■ *Web:* www.mainewindjammercruises.com	Camden	ME	04843	207-236-2938	236-3229
Maui-Molokai Sea Cruises 831 Eha St Suite 101 *TF:* 800-468-1287	Wailuku	HI	96793	808-242-8777	244-5890
MSC Cruises USA Inc 6750 N Andrews Ave Suite 100 *TF:* 800-666-9333 ■ *Web:* www.msccruises.com	Fort Lauderdale	FL	33309	954-772-6262	776-5881
Nekton Diving Cruises 520 SE 32nd St *TF:* 800-899-6753 ■ *Web:* www.nektoncruises.com	Fort Lauderdale	FL	33316	954-463-9324	463-8938
Norwegian Cruise Line Ltd 7665 Corporate Ctr Dr **Fax:* PR ■ *TF:* 866-234-0292 ■ *Web:* www.ncl.com	Miami	FL	33126	305-436-4000	436-4124*
Oceania Cruises Inc 8300 NW 33rd St Suite 308 *TF:* 800-531-5619 ■ *Web:* www.oceaniacruises.com	Miami	FL	33122	305-514-2300	514-2222
Orient Lines Inc 7665 Corporate Ctr Dr *TF:* 800-333-7300 ■ *Web:* www.orientlines.com	Miami	FL	33126	305-468-2000	436-4118
Party Line Cruise Co 301 Broadway Suite 142 *TF:* 866-463-3779	Riviera Beach	FL	33404	561-472-9860	841-0472
Princess Cruises 24844 Rockefeller Ave **Fax:* Sales ■ *TF:* 800-872-6779 ■ *Web:* www.princess.com	Santa Clarita	CA	91355	661-753-0000	284-4771*
Quark Expeditions Inc 1019 Post Rd *TF:* 800-356-5699 ■ *Web:* www.quarkexpeditions.com	Darien	CT	06820	203-656-0499	655-6623
Regent Seven Seas Cruises 1000 Corporate Dr Suite 500 *TF:* 800-477-7500 ■ *Web:* www.rssc.com	Fort Lauderdale	FL	33334	954-776-6123	772-3763
Rockport Schooner Cruises PO Box 272 *TF:* 866-732-2473 ■ *Web:* www.wanderbirdcruises.com	Belfast	ME	04915	207-338-3088	
Royal Caribbean Cruises Ltd 1050 Caribbean Way *NYSE:* RCL ■ *TF:* 800-398-9819 ■ *Web:* www.royalcaribbean.com	Miami	FL	33132	305-539-6000	374-7354
Royal Caribbean International 1050 Caribbean Way **Fax:* Hum Res ■ *TF:* 800-327-6700 ■ *Web:* www.royalcaribbean.com	Miami	FL	33132	305-539-6000	539-6168*
Sea Cloud Cruises Inc 32-40 N Dean St *TF:* 888-732-2568 ■ *Web:* www.seacloud.com	Englewood	NJ	07631	201-227-9404	227-9424
Seabourn Cruise Line 300 Elliott Ave W *TF:* 800-929-9595 ■ *Web:* www.seabourn.com	Seattle	WA	98119	206-626-9100	626-9120
SeaDream Yacht Club 601 Brickell Key Dr Suite 1050 *TF:* 800-707-4911 ■ *Web:* www.seadream.com	Miami	FL	33131	305-631-6110	631-6110
Silversea Cruises 110 E Broward Blvd *TF:* 800-722-9955 ■ *Web:* www.silversea.com	Fort Lauderdale	FL	33301	954-522-4477	522-4499
Star Clippers Inc 7200 NW 19th St Suite 206 *TF:* 800-442-0551 ■ *Web:* www.star-clippers.com	Miami	FL	33126	305-442-0550	442-1611
Star Cruises 7665 Corporate Ctr Dr *TF:* 800-327-9020 ■ *Web:* www.starcruises.com	Miami	FL	33126	305-436-4000	436-4126
Travel Dynamics International 132 E 70th St *TF:* 800-257-5767 ■ *Web:* www.traveldynamicsinternational.com	New York	NY	10021	212-517-7555	774-1545
Windstar Cruises 2101 4th Ave Suite 1150 *TF Resv:* 800-258-7245 ■ *Web:* www.windstarcruises.com	Seattle	WA	98121	206-292-9606	733-2790
world The 14471 Miramar Pkwy Suite 790 *TF:* 800-970-6601 ■ *Web:* www.aboardtheworld.com	Miramar	FL	33027	954-416-3644	431-7151

224 CRUISES - RIVERBOAT

SEE ALSO Casinos p. 1558; Cruise Lines p. 1779

Company	City	State	ZIP	Phone	Fax
American Cruise Lines 741 Boston Post Rd Suite 200 *TF:* 800-814-6880 ■ *Web:* www.americancruiselines.com	Guilford	CT	06437	203-453-6800	453-0417
American Rivers Cruise Lines 2101 4th Ave Suite 2200 *TF:* 800-901-9152	Seattle	WA	98121	206-388-0444	388-0445
Englund Marine & Industrial Supply Co Inc 95 Hamburg Ave PO Box 296 *TF:* 800-228-7051 ■ *Web:* www.englundmarine.com	Astoria	OR	97103	503-325-4341	325-6421
French Country Waterways Ltd PO Box 2195 *TF:* 800-222-1236 ■ *Web:* www.fcwl.com	Duxbury	MA	02331	781-934-2454	934-9048
Gateway Arch Riverfront The 707 N 1st St *TF:* 877-982-1410 ■ *Web:* www.gatewayarch.com	Saint Louis	MO	63102	314-982-1410	923-3069
Gateway Clipper Fleet 350 W Stn Sq Dr *Web:* www.gatewayclipper.com	Pittsburgh	PA	15219	412-355-7980	355-7987
Les Etoiles Barges 3355 Lenox Rd Suite 750 **Fax Area Code:* 404 ■ *TF:* 800-280-1492	Atlanta	GA	30326	770-394-6565	237-1841*
RiverBarge Excursion Lines Inc 201 Opelousas Ave *TF:* 888-462-2743 ■ *Web:* www.riverbarge.com	New Orleans	LA	70114	504-365-0022	365-0000
Riverboat Cruises 110 L St	Sacramento	CA	95814	916-552-2934	552-5900
Spirit of Dubuque 400 E 3rd St Ice Harbor *TF:* 800-747-8093 ■ *Web:* www.spiritofdubuque.com	Dubuque	IA	52001	563-583-8093	585-0634
Uniworld 17323 Ventura Blvd *TF:* 800-733-7820 ■ *Web:* www.uniworld.com	Encino	CA	91316	818-382-7820	382-7829
Victoria Cruises Inc 57-08 39th Ave *TF Cust Svc:* 800-348-8084 ■ *Web:* www.victoriacruises.com	Woodside	NY	11377	212-818-1680	818-9889
Viking River Cruises 5700 Canoga Ave Suite 200 *TF Cust Svc:* 877-668-4546 ■ *Web:* www.vikingrivercruises.com	Woodland Hills	CA	91367	818-227-1234	227-1237
Wings Nile Cruises 11350 McCormick Rd Suite 703 *TF:* 800-869-4647 ■ *Web:* www.wingsegypt.com	Hunt Valley	MD	21031	410-771-0925	771-0928

225 CUTLERY

SEE ALSO Silverware p. 2658

Company	City	State	ZIP	Phone	Fax
American Safety Razor Co 1 Razor Blade Ln *TF:* 800-445-9284 ■ *Web:* www.asrco.com	Verona	VA	24482	540-248-8000	248-0522
Atlanta Cutlery Corp 2147 Gees Mill Rd *TF:* 800-883-0300 ■ *Web:* www.atlantacutlery.com	Conyers	GA	30013	770-922-3700	918-2026
Buck Knives Inc 660 S Lochsa St *TF:* 800-326-2825 ■ *Web:* www.buckknives.com	Post Falls	ID	83854	208-262-0500	262-0555
Crescent Mfg Co 1310 Majestic Dr *TF:* 800-537-1330 ■ *Web:* www.crescentblades.com	Fremont	OH	43420	419-332-6484	332-6564
Cutco Corp 1116 E State St *TF:* 800-828-0448	Olean	NY	14760	716-373-6141	
Dexter-Russell Inc 44 River St *Web:* www.dexter-russell.com	Southbridge	MA	01550	508-765-0201	764-2897
Douglas/Quikut Co 118 E Douglas Rd *TF:* 800-982-5233 ■ *Web:* www.quikut.com	Walnut Ridge	AR	72476	870-886-6774	886-9162
Excel Group 1 Merrick Ave *TF:* 800-252-3390 ■ *Web:* www.lifetimebrands.com	Westbury	NY	11590	516-683-6000	683-6116
Fiskars Brands Inc 2537 Daniels St *TF:* 866-348-5661 ■ *Web:* www.fiskars.com	Madison	WI	53718	608-259-1649	294-4790
Gerber Legendary Blades Inc 14200 SW 72nd Ave **Fax:* Cust Svc ■ *TF:* 800-950-6161	Portland	OR	97224	503-639-6161	403-1102*
KA-BAR Knives Inc 200 Homer St *TF:* 800-282-0130 ■ *Web:* www.kabar.com	Olean	NY	14760	716-372-5952	790-7188
Kai USA Ltd 18600 SW Teton Ave *Web:* www.kershawknives.com	Tualatin	OR	97062	503-682-1966	682-7168
Lamson & Goodnow Mfg Co 45 Conway St *TF:* 800-872-6564 ■ *Web:* www.lamsonsharp.com	Shelburne Falls	MA	01370	413-625-6331	625-9816
Marfione Inc 300 Chestnut St Ext *Web:* www.microtechknives.com	Bradford	PA	16701	814-363-9260	363-9284
Master Cutlery Inc 700 Penhorn Ave *TF:* 888-271-7229 ■ *Web:* www.mastercutlery.com	Secaucus	NJ	07094	201-271-7600	271-7666
Midwest Tool & Cutlery Co Inc 1210 Progress St PO Box 160 *TF:* 800-782-4659 ■ *Web:* www.midwestsnips.com	Sturgis	MI	49091	269-651-2476	651-1811
Millers Forge Inc 1411 Capital Ave *TF:* 800-527-3474 ■ *Web:* www.millersforge.com	Plano	TX	75074	972-422-2145	881-0639
Ontario Knife Co 26 Empire St **Fax Area Code:* 800 ■ *TF:* 800-222-5233 ■ *Web:* www.ontarioknife.com	Franklinville	NY	14737	716-676-5527	299-2618*
Pacific Handy Cutter Inc 2968 Randolph Ave *TF Cust Svc:* 800-229-2233 ■ *Web:* www.pacifichandycutter.com	Costa Mesa	CA	92626	714-662-1033	662-7595
Professional Cutlery Direct LLC 242 Branford Rd *TF:* 800-859-6994 ■ *Web:* www.cookingenthusiast.com	North Branford	CT	06471	800-792-6650	296-8039

				Phone	Fax
Queen Cutlery Co 507 Chestnut St *TF Sales:* 800-222-5233 ■ *Web:* www.queencutlery.com	Titusville	PA	16354	814-827-3673	827-9693
Rada Mfg Co 905 Industrial St *TF:* 800-311-9691 ■ *Web:* www.radamfg.com	Waverly	IA	50677	319-352-5454	352-3947
Swiss Army Brands Inc 1 Research Dr PO Box 874 *TF Cust Svc:* 800-243-4057 ■ *Web:* www.swissarmy.com	Shelton	CT	06484	203-929-6391	929-3786
Taylor Cutlery 1736 N Eastman Rd *TF:* 800-251-0254 ■ *Web:* www.taylorcutlery.com	Kingsport	TN	37664	423-247-2406	247-5371
Wenger North America Inc 15 Corporate Dr *TF Cust Svc:* 800-431-2996 ■ *Web:* www.wengerna.com	Orangeburg	NY	10962	845-365-3500	425-4700
WR Case & Sons Cutlery Co Owens Way PO Box 4000 *TF:* 800-523-6350 ■ *Web:* www.wrcase.com	Bradford	PA	16701	814-368-4123	368-1736
Zippo Mfg Co 33 Barbour St *Web:* www.zippo.com	Bradford	PA	16701	814-368-2700	362-2388

226 CYLINDERS & ACTUATORS - FLUID POWER

SEE ALSO Automotive Parts & Supplies - Mfr p. 1497

				Phone	Fax
Actuant Corp 13000 W Silver Spring Dr *NYSE: ATU* ■ *TF:* 800-624-5242 ■ *Web:* www.actuant.com	Butler	WI	53007	414-352-4160	918-0033
Advance Automation Co Inc 3526 N Elston Ave *Web:* www.advanceautomationco.com	Chicago	IL	60618	773-539-7633	539-7299
American Cylinder Co Inc 481 S Governors Hwy *Web:* www.americancylinder.com	Peotone	IL	60468	708-258-3935	258-3980
Atlas Cylinder Corp 500 S Wolf Rd *Web:* www.parker.com/atlas	Des Plaines	IL	60016	847-298-2400	294-2655
Beaver Aerospace & Defense Inc 11850 Mayfield St *Web:* www.beaver-online.com	Livonia	MI	48150	734-261-9352	853-5043
Best Metal Products Co 3570 Raleigh Dr SE PO Box 888440 *Web:* www.bestmetalproducts.com	Grand Rapids	MI	49588	616-942-7141	942-0949
Bimba Mfg Co PO Box 68 **Fax:* Cust Svc ■ *TF:* 800-323-0445 ■ *Web:* www.bimba.com	Monee	IL	60449	708-534-8544	534-8346*
Bosch Rexroth Corp 5150 Prairie Stone Pkwy *TF:* 800-860-1055 ■ *Web:* www.boschrexroth-us.com	Hoffman Estates	IL	60192	847-645-3600	645-6201
Clippard Instrument Lab 7390 Colerain Ave *TF:* 877-245-6247 ■ *Web:* www.clippard.com	Cincinnati	OH	45239	513-521-4261	521-4464
Columbus Hydraulics Co 1705 12th Ave *Web:* www.columbushydraulics.com	Columbus	NE	68601	402-564-8544	564-0129
Commercial Honing Co Inc 8606 Sultana Ave *Web:* www.commercialhoning.com	Fontana	CA	92335	909-829-1211	829-7631
Cunningham Mfg Co 318 S Webster St *TF:* 800-767-0038 ■ *Web:* www.cunninghamcylinders.com	Seattle	WA	98108	206-767-3713	767-3713
Dynex Rivett Inc 770 Capitol Dr *Web:* www.dynexhydraulics.com	Pewaukee	WI	53072	262-691-0300	691-0312
Eckel Mfg Co Inc 8035 N County Rd W *TF:* 800-654-4779 ■ *Web:* www.eckel.com	Odessa	TX	79764	432-362-4336	362-1827
Energy Mfg Co Inc 204 Plastic Ln *Web:* www.energymfg.com	Monticello	IA	52310	319-465-3537	465-5279
Fabco-Air Inc 3716 NE 49th Ave *Web:* www.fabco-air.com	Gainesville	FL	32609	352-373-3578	375-8024
Flo-Tork Inc 1701 N Main St PO Box 68 **Fax:* Sales ■ *Web:* www.flo-tork.com	Orrville	OH	44667	330-682-0010	683-6857*
Galland Henning Nopak Inc 1025 S 40th St *Web:* www.nopak.com	West Milwaukee	WI	53215	414-645-6000	645-6048
General Engineering Co 26485 Hillman Hwy PO Box 549	Abingdon	VA	24212	276-628-6068	628-4311
Great Bend Industries Inc 8701 6th St *Web:* www.hydrauliccylindergroup.com	Great Bend	KS	67530	620-792-4368	792-3935
Hader/Seitz Inc 15600 W Lincoln Ave PO Box 510260 *TF:* 877-388-2101 ■ *Web:* www.haderind.com/seitz.htm	New Berlin	WI	53151	262-641-6000	641-5310
Hannon Hydraulics Inc 625 N Loop 12 *TF:* 800-333-4266 ■ *Web:* www.hannonhydraulics.com	Irving	TX	75061	972-438-2870	554-4047
Helac Corp 225 Battersby Ave *TF:* 800-327-2589 ■ *Web:* www.helac.com	Enumclaw	WA	98022	360-825-1601	825-1603
Hol-Mac Corp 2730-A Hwy 15 PO Box 349 *TF:* 800-844-3019 ■ *Web:* www.hol-mac.com	Bay Springs	MS	39422	601-764-4121	764-3438
Humphrey Products Co 5070 E N Ave PO Box 2008 *TF:* 800-477-8707 ■ *Web:* www.humphrey-products.com	Kalamazoo	MI	49048	269-381-5500	381-4113
IMI Norgren Inc 325 Carr Dr *Web:* www.iminorgren.com	Brookville	OH	45309	937-833-4033	833-4205
Ingersoll-Rand Co ARO Fluid Products Div 1 Aro Ctr PO Box 151 *TF Cust Svc:* 800-495-0276 ■ *Web:* www.company.ingersollrand.com	Bryan	OH	43506	419-636-4242	633-1674
ITT Industries Inc Engineered Valves Div 33 Centerville Rd *TF:* 800-366-1111 ■ *Web:* www.engvalves.com	Lancaster	PA	17603	717-509-2200	509-2336
Jarp Industries Inc 1051 Pine St PO Box 923 *Web:* www.jarpind.com	Schofield	WI	54476	715-359-4241	355-4960
Kaydon Corp 315 E Eisenhower Pkwy Suite 300 *NYSE: KDN* ■ *Web:* www.kaydon.com	Ann Arbor	MI	48108	734-747-7025	747-6565
Linak Us Inc 2200 Stanley Gault Pkwy *Web:* www.linak-us.com	Louisville	KY	40223	502-253-5595	253-5596
Luxfer Gas Cylinders 3016 Kansas Ave *TF:* 800-764-0366 ■ *Web:* www.luxfercylinders.com	Riverside	CA	92507	951-684-5110	781-6598
Lynair Inc 3515 Scheele Dr *Web:* www.lynair.com	Jackson	MI	49202	517-787-2240	787-4521
Micromatic LLC 525 Berne St *TF:* 800-333-5752 ■ *Web:* www.micromaticllc.com	Berne	IN	46711	260-589-2136	589-8966
Miller Fluid Power Corp 500 S Wolf Rd **Fax Area Code:* 800 ■ *TF:* 800-323-8207	Des Plaines	IL	60016	630-766-3400	892-1008*
Milwaukee Cylinder 5877 S Pennsylvania Ave PO Box 100498 *Web:* www.milwaukeecylinder.com	Cudahy	WI	53110	414-769-9700	769-0157
Motion Systems Corp 600 Industrial Way W *Web:* www.motionsystem.com	Eatontown	NJ	07724	732-222-1800	389-9191
Norris Cylinder Co 1535 FM 1845 *TF:* 800-527-8418 ■ *Web:* www.norriscylinder.com	Longview	TX	75603	903-757-7633	753-3012
Parker Hannifin Corp 6035 Parkland Blvd *NYSE: PH* ■ *TF Cust Svc:* 800-272-7537 ■ *Web:* www.parker.com	Cleveland	OH	44124	216-896-3000	896-4000
Parker Hannifin Corp Automation Actuator Div 135 Quadral Dr *TF:* 866-727-5228 ■ *Web:* www.parker.com	Wadsworth	OH	44281	330-336-3511	334-3335
Parker Hannifin Corp Cylinder Div 500 S Wolf Rd *Web:* www.parker.com/cylinder	Des Plaines	IL	60016	847-298-2400	294-2655
Parker Hannifin Corp Oildyne Div 5520 Hwy 169 N *Web:* www.parker.com/oildyne	Minneapolis	MN	55428	763-533-1600	533-0082
Parker Instrumentation Group 6035 Parkland Blvd *TF:* 800-272-7537 ■ *Web:* www.parker.com/instrumentation	Cleveland	OH	44124	216-896-3000	896-4022
PHD Inc 9009 Clubridge Dr *TF:* 800-624-8511 ■ *Web:* www.phdinc.com	Fort Wayne	IN	46809	260-747-6151	747-6754
Production Engineering Inc 2330 Brooklyn Rd	Jackson	MI	49203	517-788-6800	788-6705
Quincy Ortman Cylinders 3501 Wismann Ln PO Box C-2 *Web:* www.ortmanfluidpower.com	Quincy	IL	62305	217-277-0321	222-1773
Sargent Controls & Aerospace 5675 W Burlingame Rd *TF:* 800-932-5273 ■ *Web:* www.sargentcontrols.com	Tucson	AZ	85743	520-744-1000	744-9494
Seabee Corp 712 First St NW *Web:* www.seabeecylinders.com	Hampton	IA	50441	641-456-4871	456-2387
Sheffer Corp 6990 Cornell Rd **Fax:* Sales ■ *TF Sales:* 800-387-2191 ■ *Web:* www.sheffercorp.com	Cincinnati	OH	45242	513-489-9770	489-3034*
SMC Pneumatics Inc 3011 N Franklin Rd PO Box 26646 *TF:* 800-762-7621 ■ *Web:* www.smcusa.com	Indianapolis	IN	46226	317-899-4440	899-3102
Standex International Corp Custom Hoists Div 771 County Rd 30-A W PO Box 98 *TF:* 800-837-4668 ■ *Web:* www.customhoists.com	Hayesville	OH	44838	419-368-4721	368-4209
Tactair Fluid Controls Inc 4806 W Taft Rd *Web:* www.tactair.com	Liverpool	NY	13088	315-451-3928	451-8919
Texas Hydraulics Inc PO Box 1067 *Web:* www.texashydraulics.com	Temple	TX	76503	254-778-4701	774-9940
Tol-O-Matic Inc 3800 County Rd 116 *TF:* 800-328-2174 ■ *Web:* www.tolomatic.com	Hamel	MN	55340	763-478-8000	478-8080
Wabash Technologies 1375 Swan St PO Box 829 **Fax:* Sales ■ *Web:* www.wabashtech.com	Huntington	IN	46750	260-356-8300	355-4265*
@Road Inc 47200 Bayside Pkwy *TF:* 877-428-7623	Fremont	CA	94538	510-668-1638	353-6021

227 DATA COMMUNICATIONS SERVICES FOR WIRELESS DEVICES

Companies Listed Here Deliver Data Such As Customized News Or Stock Information, Other Personalized Content, And/Or Multimedia, Audio, And Video From The Internet To Wireless Devices (Cellular Phones, Personal Digital Assistants, Pagers, Laptop Computers).

				Phone	Fax
Air2Web Inc 1230 Peachtree St 12th Fl *TF:* 877-238-3637 ■ *Web:* www.air2web.com	Atlanta	GA	30309	404-815-7707	815-7708
Airvana Corp 19 Alpha Rd *TF:* 866-344-7437 ■ *Web:* www.airvana.com	Chelmsford	MA	01824	978-250-3100	250-3910
Antenna Software 111 Town Sq Pl #520 *Web:* www.antennasoftware.com	Jersey City	NJ	07310	201-217-3800	239-2315
Azimuth Systems Inc 35 Nagog Pk *Web:* www.azimuthsystems.com	Acton	MA	01720	978-263-6610	263-5352
BlackBerry 295 Phillip St *TF:* 877-255-2377 ■ *Web:* www.blackberry.net	Waterloo	ON	N2L3W8	519-888-7465	888-7884
Broadcast Microwave Services Inc (BMS) 12367 Crosthwaite Cir *TF:* 800-669-9667 ■ *Web:* www.bms-inc.com	Poway	CA	92064	858-391-3050	391-3049
Carousel Industries of North America Inc 659 S County Trail *TF:* 800-401-0760 ■ *Web:* www.carouselindustries.com	Exeter	RI	02822	401-284-1925	284-1984
Cell-Loc Location Technologies Inc 37th St SW Suite 1600 *Web:* www.cell-loc.com	Calgary	AB	T3C3P1	403-569-5700	569-5701
Champaign Telephone Co The 126 Scioto St *TF:* 877-742-5622 ■ *Web:* www.ctcn.net	Urbana	OH	43078	937-653-4000	653-8082
Dynamic Mobile Data Systems Inc 285 Davidson Ave Suite 501	Somerset	NJ	08873	732-302-1700	302-9558
Everypath Inc 2211 N 1st St Suite 200 *TF Sales:* 800-355-1068 ■ *Web:* www.everypath.com	San Jose	CA	95131	408-562-8000	562-8100
fusionOne Inc 1 Almaden Blvd 11th Fl *Web:* www.fusionone.com	San Jose	CA	95113	408-282-1200	282-1233
Intermec Technologies Corp 6001 36th Ave W *TF Sales:* 800-934-3163 ■ *Web:* www.intermec.com	Everett	WA	98203	425-348-2600	355-9551
Linx Communications Inc 175 Crossing Blvd Suite 300 *TF:* 888-367-5469 ■ *Web:* www.linxcom.com	Framingham	MA	01702	617-747-4200	747-4203
Masergy Communications Inc 2740 N Dallas Pkwy Suite 260 *TF:* 866-588-5885 ■ *Web:* www.masergy.com	Plano	TX	75093	214-442-5700	442-5756
Meteor Communications Corp 1201 SW 7th St *Web:* www.meteorcomm.com	Renton	WA	98057	253-872-2521	872-7662
Metro One Telecommunications Inc 11200 Murray Scholls Pl *NASDAQ: INFO* ■ *TF:* 800-933-4034 ■ *Web:* www.metro1.com	Beaverton	OR	97007	503-643-9500	643-9600
Motricity 601-108th Ave NE Suite 800 *TF:* 800-746-7646 ■ *Web:* www.motricity.com	Bellevue	NC	98004	425-957-6200	957-6201

Phone | Fax

MSN Mobile 1 Microsoft Way — Redmond WA 98052 — 425-882-8080 — 936-7329
Web: www.discovermsn.com

NAVTEQ Corp 425 W Randolph St Suite 900 — Chicago IL 60606 — 312-894-7000 — 894-7050
TF: 888-628-6277 ■ *Web:* www.navteq.com

PacketVideo Corp
10350 Science Ctr Dr Suite 210 — San Diego CA 92121 — 858-731-5300 — 731-5301
TF: 877-308-2500 ■ *Web:* www.packetvideo.com

Remote Dynamics Inc 1155 Kas Dr Suite 100 — Richardson TX 75081 — 972-301-2000 — 301-2588
TF: 800-828-4696

Superheat Fgh Services Inc
680 Industrial Pk Dr — Evans GA 30809 — 888-508-3226
TF: 888-508-3226 ■ *Web:* www.superheatfgh.com

TeleCommunication Systems Inc
275 W St Suite 400 — Annapolis MD 21401 — 410-263-7616 — 263-7617
NASDAQ: TSYS ■ *TF:* 800-810-0827 ■ *Web:* www.telecomsys.com

Traffic.com Inc 851 Duportail Rd Suite 220 — Wayne PA 19087 — 610-725-9700 — 725-0530
Web: www.traffic.com

Yahoo! Mobile 701 1st Ave — Sunnyvale CA 94089 — 408-349-3300 — 349-3301
Web: mobile.yahoo.com

228 DATA PROCESSING & RELATED SERVICES

SEE ALSO Electronic Transaction Processing p. 1815; Payroll Services p. 2391

Phone | Fax

Aci Communications
5115 Douglas Fir Rd Suite A — Calabasas CA 91302 — 818-223-3600 — 223-3609
Web: www.acicommunications.com

ADEC Solutions USA 10 Monument St PO Box 275 — Deposit NY 13754 — 607-467-4600 — 467-4632
Web: www.4dcsi.com

Adva Optical Networking Inc
1 International Blvd Suite 705 — Mahwah NJ 07495 — 201-258-8300 — 684-9200
Web: www.advaoptical.com

Affiliated Computer Services Inc (ACS)
2828 N Haskell Ave — Dallas TX 75204 — 214-841-6111 — 823-9369*
NYSE: ACS ■ **Fax:* Hum Res ■ *Web:* www.acs-inc.com

Ambient Consulting LLC
5500 Wayzata Blvd Suite 1250 — Minneapolis MN 55416 — 763-582-9000 — 582-7901
Web: www.ambientconsulting.com

Apx Power Markets Inc
224 Airport Pkwy Suite 600 — San Jose CA 95110 — 408-517-2100 — 517-2985
Web: www.apx.com

Automatic Data Processing Inc (ADP) 1 ADP Blvd — Roseland NJ 07068 — 973-994-5000 — 974-5390
NASDAQ: ADP ■ *TF:* 800-225-5237 ■ *Web:* www.adp.com

BlueTie Inc 220 Kenneth Dr — Rochester NY 14623 — 585-586-2000 — 586-2268
Web: www.bluetie.com

Capricorn Systems Inc 3569 Habersham At N — Tucker GA 30084 — 678-514-1080 — 514-1081
Web: www.capricornsys.com

Carahsoft Technology Corp
12369 Sunrise Valley Dr Suite D2 — Reston VA 20191 — 703-871-8500 — 871-8505
TF: 888-662-2724 ■ *Web:* www.carahsoft.com

Cass Information Systems Inc
13001 Hollenberg Dr — Bridgeton MO 63044 — 314-506-5500 — 506-5560
NASDAQ: CASS ■ *Web:* www.cassinfo.com

CCC Information Services Inc
222 Merchandise Mart Plaza — Chicago IL 60654 — 312-222-4636 — 527-5379*
**Fax Area Code:* 310 ■ **Fax:* Hum Res ■ *TF:* 800-621-8070 ■ *Web:* www.cccis.com

Central Service Assn 93 S Coley Rd — Tupelo MS 38801 — 662-842-5962 — 840-1329
Web: www.csa1.com

Claimsnet.com Inc 14860 Montfort Dr Suite 250 — Dallas TX 75254 — 972-458-1701 — 458-1737
TF: 800-356-1511 ■ *Web:* www.claimsnet.com

Collective Technologies LLC 9433 Bee Caves Rd — Austin TX 78733 — 512-263-5500 — 263-0606
TF: 800-994-1640 ■ *Web:* www.colltech.com

Commercial Computer Service Inc
2916 W 6th St — Fort Worth TX 76107 — 817-335-6411 — 870-1532

Communication Data Services 1901 Bell Ave — Des Moines IA 50315 — 515-247-7500 — 246-6687
TF: 800-378-9982 ■ *Web:* www.cdsfulfillment.com

Computer Consultants of America Inc
24901 Northwestern Hwy — Southfield MI 48075 — 248-353-0830 — 353-4217
Web: www.computer-consultants.com

Computer Fulfillment 275 Billerica Rd — Chelmsford MA 01824 — 978-256-9040 — 256-6597
Web: www.computerfulfillment.com

Computer Services Inc 3901 Technology Dr — Paducah KY 42001 — 270-442-7361 — 575-9569
TF: 800-545-4274 ■ *Web:* www.csiweb.com

Connecticut On-Line Computer Center Inc
135 Darling Dr — Avon CT 06001 — 860-678-0444 — 677-1169
Web: www.cocc.com

Consulier Engineering Inc
2391 Old Dixie Hwy — Riviera Beach FL 33404 — 561-842-2492 — 845-3237
PINK: CSLR ■ *Web:* www.consulier.com

Continental Graphics Corp
222 N Sepulveda Blvd Suite 300 — El Segundo CA 90245 — 310-662-2300 — 662-2310
TF: 800-862-5691 ■ *Web:* www.cdgnow.com

Crosscom National LLC
900 Deerfield Pkwy — Buffalo Grove IL 60089 — 847-520-9200 — 419-4884
Web: www.crosscomnational.com

Dantom Systems Inc 29241 Beck Rd — Wixom MI 48393 — 248-567-7300 — 567-7301
TF: 866-536-2376 ■ *Web:* www.dantomsystems.com

Data Lab Corp 7333 N Oak Pk Ave — Niles IL 60714 — 847-647-6678 — 647-6821
Web: www.data-lab.com

DataBank 12000 Baltimore Ave — Beltsville MD 20705 — 301-837-0197
TF: 800-873-9426 ■ *Web:* www.databankimx.com

Datamark Inc 43 Butterfield Cir Suite C-1 — El Paso TX 79906 — 915-774-0856 — 778-1988
Web: www.datamark.net

Discovery Research Group
6975 Union Pk Ctr Suite 450 — Midvale UT 84047 — 801-569-0107 — 748-2784
TF: 800-678-3748 ■ *Web:* www.discoveryresearchgroup.com

DPF Data Services Group Inc
1990 Swarthmore Ave — Lakewood NJ 08701 — 732-370-8840 — 370-1751
TF: 800-431-4416 ■ *Web:* www.dpfdata.com

E Ink Holdings Inc 733 Concord Ave — Cambridge MA 02138 — 617-499-6000 — 499-6200
Web: www.eink.com

Equifax Inc 1550 Peachtree St NW — Atlanta GA 30309 — 404-885-8000 — 888-5043
NYSE: EFX ■ *TF Sales:* 888-202-4025 ■ *Web:* www.equifax.com

Examination Management Services Inc
15333 N Pima Rd Suite 330 — Scottsdale AZ 85260 — 214-689-3600 — 689-3644
Web: www.emsinet.com

Fair Isaac Corp
901 Marquette Ave Suite 3200 — Minneapolis MN 55402 — 612-758-5200 — 758-5200
NYSE: FIC ■ *TF Cust Svc:* 877-434-7877 ■ *Web:* www.fico.com

Financial Services Inc 21 Harristown Rd — Glen Rock NJ 07452 — 201-652-6000
Web: www.insidefsi.net

Global Geophysical Services Inc
13927 S Gessner Rd — Missouri City TX 77489 — 713-972-9200 — 972-1008
NYSE: GGS ■ *Web:* www.globalgeophysical.com

Global Health Care Exchange LLC (GHX)
1315 W Century Dr — Louisville CO 80027 — 720-887-7000 — 887-7200
TF: 800-968-7449 ■ *Web:* www.ghx.com

Goold Health Systems Inc PO Box 1090 — Augusta ME 04332 — 207-622-7153
TF: 800-832-9672 ■ *Web:* www.ghsinc.com

Gtess Corp 2435 N Central Expwy Suite 500 — Richardson TX 75080 — 972-792-5500 — 234-5763
Web: www.gtess.com

Hartley Data Service Inc (HDS)
1807 Glenview Rd Suite 201 — Glenview IL 60025 — 847-724-9280 — 729-2199
TF: 800-433-2796 ■ *Web:* hartleydata.com

Health Management Systems Inc 401 Pk Ave S — New York NY 10016 — 212-685-4545 — 857-5004*

Iostudio LLC 565 Marriott Dr Suite 700 — Nashville TN 37214 — 615-256-6282
Web: www.iostudio.com

It Solutions Inc 210 Porter Dr Suite 315 — San Ramon CA 94583 — 925-838-8600 — 241-9507*
**Fax Area Code:* 617

Kelser Corp 111 Roberts St Suite D — East Hartford CT 06108 — 860-528-9819 — 291-9088
Web: www.kelsercorp.com

Lumension Security Inc
8660 E Hartford Dr # 300 — Scottsdale AZ 85255 — 888-725-7828 — 970-6323*
**Fax Area Code:* 480 ■ *TF:* 888-725-7828 ■ *Web:* www.lumension.com

Masterplan Inc 21540 Plummer St — Chatsworth CA 91311 — 818-773-2647 — 341-9895
Web: www.masterplan-inc.com

MIB Inc 160 University Ave — Westwood MA 02090 — 781-329-4500 — 329-3379
Web: www.mib.com

Mid America Computer Corp PO Box 700 — Blair NE 68008 — 402-426-6222 — 533-5369
TF: 800-622-2502 ■ *Web:* www.maccnet.com

Nextpage Inc 13997 S Minuteman Dr Suite 300 — Draper UT 84020 — 801-748-4400 — 748-4401
TF: 800-639-8724 ■ *Web:* www.nextpage.com

Oasis Systems Inc 24 Hartwell Ave — Lexington MA 02421 — 781-676-7333 — 676-7353
Web: www.oasissystems.com

Opinion Access Corp 47-10 32nd Pl — Long Island City NY 11101 — 718-729-2622
Web: www.opinionaccess.com

Pinnacle Business Systems Inc
3824 S Blvd St Suite 200 — Edmond OK 73083 — 800-311-0757 — 444-3439
Web: www.pbsnow.com

Printmail Systems Inc 23 Friends Ln — Newtown PA 18940 — 215-860-4250 — 860-2204
TF: 800-910-4844 ■ *Web:* www.printmailsystems.com

PRWT Services Inc 1835 Market St 8th Fl — Philadelphia PA 19103 — 215-569-8810 — 569-9893
Web: www.prwt.com

Ramco Systems Corp
3150 US Hwy 1 Suite 130 — Lawrenceville NJ 08648 — 609-620-4800 — 620-4860
TF: 800-472-6261 ■ *Web:* www.ramco.com

Reed Technology & Information Services Inc
7 Walnut Grove Dr — Horsham PA 19044 — 215-441-6400
Web: www.reedtech.com

Renew Data Corp 9500 Arboretum Blvd — Austin TX 78759 — 512-276-5500 — 276-5555
TF: 888-811-3789 ■ *Web:* www.renewdata.com

Resolve Corp 85 the E Mall — Toronto ON M8Z5W4 — 416-503-1800 — 503-8899
TF: 866-678-6019 ■ *Web:* www.resolvecorporation.com

Right Systems Inc 2600 Willamette Dr Ne Suite C — Lacey WA 98516 — 360-956-0414 — 956-0336
Web: www.rightsys.com

Riverbed Technology Inc 199 Fremont St — San Francisco CA 94105 — 415-247-8800 — 247-8801
NASDAQ: RVBD ■ *Web:* www.riverbed.com

Rurbanc Data Services Inc 7622 N SR- 66 — Defiance OH 43512 — 419-783-8800 — 784-6542
TF: 888-275-7374 ■ *Web:* www.rdsiweb.com

Scicom Data Services Ltd 10101 Bren Rd E — Minnetonka MN 55343 — 952-933-4200 — 936-4132
TF: 800-488-9087 ■ *Web:* www.scicom.com

Sigma Solutions Inc 422 E Ramsey Rd — San Antonio TX 78216 — 210-348-9876 — 348-9124
Web: www.sigmasolinc.com

Sof Tec Solutions Inc
384 Inverness Pkwy # 211 — Englewood CO 80112 — 303-662-1010 — 662-1060
TF: 888-376-3832 ■ *Web:* www.softecinc.com

Softlayer Technologies Inc 4849 Alpha Rd — Dallas TX 75244 — 214-442-0600 — 442-0601
TF Sales: 866-398-7638 ■ *Web:* www.softlayer.com

Sogeti USA LLC 7735 Paragon Rd — Dayton OH 45459 — 937-291-8100 — 433-4048
Web: www.us.sogeti.com

Standard Data Corp 26 Journal Sq — Jersey City NJ 07306 — 201-533-4433 — 533-8236
Web: www.standarddata.com

SunGard Data Systems Inc 680 E Swedesford Rd — Wayne PA 19087 — 484-582-2000 — 225-1120*
**Fax Area Code:* 610 ■ *TF:* 800-523-4970 ■ *Web:* www.sungard.com

TDEC 8120 Woodmont Ave Suite 550 — Bethesda MD 20814 — 301-718-0703 — 718-1615
TF: 800-424-8332 ■ *Web:* www.tdec.com

Technigraphics Inc 2000 Noble Dr — Wooster OH 44691 — 330-263-6222 — 263-6294
TF: 800-832-8779 ■ *Web:* www.tgstech.com

Teradata Corp 10000 Innovation Dr — Dayton OH 45342 — 866-548-8348 — 445-1682*
NYSE: TDC ■ **Fax Area Code:* 937 ■ *TF:* 866-548-8348 ■ *Web:* www.teradata.com

Travidia Inc 265 Airpark Blvd Suite 500 — Chico CA 95973 — 530-343-6400 — 892-9369
TF: 866-343-6400 ■ *Web:* www.travidia.com

Vangent Inc 4250 N Fairfax Dr Suite 1200 — Arlington VA 22203 — 703-284-5600 — 284-5628
TF: 800-359-1440 ■ *Web:* www.vangent.com

Versatile Systems Inc
100 Sterling Pkwy Suite 307 — Mechanicsburg PA 17050 — 717-796-1936 — 796-9759
Web: www.versatile.com

Vertafore Inc 11724 NE 195th St — Bothell WA 98011 — 425-402-1000 — 402-9569
TF: 800-444-4813 ■ *Web:* www.vertafore.com

				Phone	Fax
Williams Records Management 1925 E Vernon Ave *TF Cust Svc:* 800-207-3267 ■ *Web:* www.williamsrecords.com	Los Angeles	CA	90058	323-234-3453	233-5451
Z57 Internet Solutions 10045 Mesa Rim Rd *TF:* 800-899-8148 ■ *Web:* www.z57.com	San Diego	CA	92121	858-623-5577	869-9931

229 DATING SERVICES

				Phone	Fax
Eharmony.com Inc 300 N Lake Ave Suite 1111 *Web:* www.eharmony.com	Pasadena	CA	91101	626-795-4814	585-4040
Friendfinder Network Inc 445 Sherman Ave Suite C *TF:* 800-388-0760 ■ *Web:* www.friendfinder.com	Palo Alto	CA	94306	650-847-3100	324-9379
Great Expectations 14180 Dallas Pkwy Suite 100 *Web:* www.ge-dating.com	Dallas	TX	75254	972-448-7900	448-7969
It's Just Lunch! Inc 101 W Grand Ave Suite 502 *Web:* www.itsjustlunch.com	Chicago	IL	60610	312-644-9999	644-9474
Match.com Inc PO Box 25472 *TF:* 800-926-2824 ■ *Web:* www.match.com	Dallas	TX	75225	214-576-9352	576-9475
Matchmaker International 1027 Trexlertown Rd *Web:* www.matchmakerintl.com	Allentown	PA	18087	610-395-5222	
Spark Networks PLC 8383 Wilshire Blvd Suite 800 *AMEX: LOV* ■ *Web:* www.spark.net	Beverly Hills	CA	90211	323-836-3000	836-3333
Spring Street Networks PO Box 547 *Web:* www.springstreetnetworks.com	New York	NY	10012	212-929-8890	929-9046

230 DENTAL ASSOCIATIONS - STATE

SEE ALSO Health & Medical Professionals Associations p. 1452

				Phone	Fax
Alabama Dental Assn 836 Washington Ave *Web:* www.aldaonline.org	Montgomery	AL	36104	334-265-1684	262-6218
Alaska Dental Society 9170 Jewel Lake Rd Suite 203 *Web:* www.akdental.org	Anchorage	AK	99502	907-563-3003	563-3009
Arizona Dental Assn 3193 N Drinkwater Blvd *TF:* 800-866-2732 ■ *Web:* www.azda.org	Scottsdale	AZ	85251	480-344-5777	344-1442
Arkansas State Dental Assn 7480 Hwy 107 Suite 205 *Web:* www.arkansasdentistry.org	Sherwood	AR	72120	501-834-7650	834-7657
California Dental Assn 1201 K St *TF:* 800-736-7071 ■ *Web:* www.cda.org	Sacramento	CA	95853	916-443-0505	443-2943
Colorado Dental Assn 3690 S Yosemite St Suite 100 *Web:* www.cdaonline.org	Denver	CO	80237	303-740-6900	740-7989
Delaware State Dental Society 200 Continental Dr Suite 111 *Web:* www.delawarestatedentalsociety.org	Newark	DE	19713	302-368-7634	368-7669
District of Columbia Dental Society 502 C St NE *Web:* www.dcdental.org	Washington	DC	20002	202-547-7613	546-1482
Florida Dental Assn 1111 E Tennessee St *TF:* 800-877-9922 ■ *Web:* www.floridadental.org	Tallahassee	FL	32308	850-681-3629	561-0504
Georgia Dental Assn 7000 Peachtree Dnwdy # 17-200 *TF:* 800-432-4357 ■ *Web:* www.gadental.org	Atlanta	GA	30328	404-636-7553	633-3943
Hawaii Dental Assn 1345 S Beretania St Suite 301 *TF:* 800-359-6725 ■ *Web:* www.hawaiidentalassociation.net	Honolulu	HI	96814	808-593-7956	593-7636
Idaho State Dental Assn 1220 W Hays St *Web:* www.isdaweb.com	Boise	ID	83702	208-343-7543	343-0775
Illinois State Dental Society 1010 S 2nd St *Web:* www.isds.org	Springfield	IL	62704	217-525-1406	525-8872
Indiana Dental Assn 401 W Michigan St *TF:* 800-562-5646 ■ *Web:* www.indental.org	Indianapolis	IN	46202	317-634-2610	634-2612
Iowa Dental Assn 5530 W Pkwy *TF:* 800-828-2181 ■ *Web:* www.iowadental.org	Johnston	IA	50131	515-986-5605	986-5626
Louisiana Dental Assn 7833 Office Pk Blvd *TF:* 800-388-6642 ■ *Web:* www.ladental.org	Baton Rouge	LA	70809	225-926-1986	926-1886
Maine Dental Assn 29 Assn Dr PO Box 215 *Web:* www.medental.org	Manchester	ME	04351	207-622-7900	622-6210
Maryland State Dental Assn 6410 Dobbin Rd *Web:* www.msda.com	Columbia	MD	21045	410-964-2880	964-0583
Massachusetts Dental Society 2 Willow St Suite 200 *TF:* 800-342-8747 ■ *Web:* www.massdental.org	Southborough	MA	01745	508-480-9797	480-0002
Michigan Dental Assn 3657 Okemos Rd Suite 200 **Fax: PR* ■ *TF:* 800-589-2632 ■ *Web:* www.smilemichigan.com	Okemos	MI	48864	517-372-9070	372-0008*
Minnesota Dental Assn 1335 Industrial Blvd Suite 200 *Web:* www.mndental.org	Minneapolis	MN	55413	612-767-8400	767-8500
Mississippi Dental Assn 2630 Ridgewood Rd Suite C *TF:* 866-982-0442 ■ *Web:* www.msdental.org	Jackson	MS	39216	601-982-0442	366-3050
Missouri Dental Assn 3340 American Ave *TF:* 800-688-1907 ■ *Web:* www.modental.org	Jefferson City	MO	65109	573-634-3436	635-0764
Montana Dental Assn 17 1/2 S Last Chance Gulch PO Box 1154 *TF:* 800-257-4988 ■ *Web:* www.mtdental.com	Helena	MT	59624	406-443-2061	443-1546
Nebraska Dental Assn 7160 S 29th St Suite 1 *Web:* www.nedental.org	Lincoln	NE	68516	402-476-1704	476-2641
Nevada Dental Assn 8863 W Flamingo Rd Suite 102 *TF:* 800-962-6710 ■ *Web:* www.nvda.org	Las Vegas	NV	89147	702-255-4211	255-3302
New Hampshire Dental Society 23 S State St *Web:* www.nhds.org	Concord	NH	03301	603-225-5961	226-4880
New Jersey Dental Assn 1 Dental Plaza PO Box 6020 *Web:* www.njda.org	North Brunswick	NJ	08902	732-821-9400	821-1082
New Mexico Dental Assn 9201 Montgomery Blvd NE Suite 601 *Web:* www.nmdental.org	Albuquerque	NM	87111	505-294-1368	294-9958
New York State Dental Assn 20 Corporate Woods Blvd #602 *Web:* www.nysdental.org	Albany	NY	12211	518-465-0044	465-3219
North Carolina Dental Society 1600 Evans Rd *TF:* 800-662-8754 ■ *Web:* www.ncdental.org	Cary	NC	27513	919-677-1396	677-1397
North Dakota Dental Assn PO Box 1332 *Web:* www.nddental.com	Bismarck	ND	58502	701-223-8870	223-0855
Ohio Dental Assn 1370 Dublin Rd *Web:* www.oda.org	Columbus	OH	43215	614-486-2700	486-0381
Oklahoma Dental Assn 317 NE 13th St *TF:* 800-876-8890 ■ *Web:* www.okda.org	Oklahoma City	OK	73104	405-848-8873	848-8875
Oregon Dental Assn PO Box 3710 *TF:* 800-452-5628 ■ *Web:* www.oregondental.org	Portland	OR	97070	503-620-3230	218-2009
Pennsylvania Dental Assn 3501 N Front St *Web:* www.padental.org	Harrisburg	PA	17110	717-234-5941	232-7169
Riverside Dental Group 7251 Magnolia Ave *Web:* www.riversidedentalgroup.com	Riverside	CA	92504	909-689-5031	352-7735
South Carolina Dental Assn 120 Stonemark Ln *Web:* www.scda.org	Columbia	SC	29210	803-750-2277	750-1644
South Dakota Dental Assn 804 N Euclid Ave Suite 103 *Web:* www.sddental.org	Pierre	SD	57501	605-224-9133	224-9168
Tennessee Dental Assn (TDA) 660 Bakers Bridge Ave Suite 300 *Web:* www.tenndental.org	Franklin	TN	37067	615-628-0208	
Texas Dental Assn 1946 S IH-35 Suite 400 *TF:* 800-832-1145 ■ *Web:* www.tda.org	Austin	TX	78704	512-443-3675	443-3031
Utah Dental Assn 1151 E 3900 S Suite 160	Salt Lake City	UT	84124	801-261-5315	261-1235
Vermont State Dental Society 100 Dorset St Suite 18 *Web:* www.vsds.org	South Burlington	VT	05403	802-864-0115	864-0116
Virginia Dental Assn (VDA) 3460 Mayland Ct Suite 110 *TF:* 877-726-0850 ■ *Web:* www.vadental.org	Richmond	VA	23233	804-288-5750	288-1880
Washington State Dental Assn 1001 4th Ave Suite 3800 *TF:* 800-448-3368 ■ *Web:* www.wsda.org	Seattle	WA	98154	206-448-1914	443-9266
West Virginia Dental Assn 2016 1/2 Kanawha Blvd E *Web:* www.wvdental.org	Charleston	WV	25311	304-344-5246	344-5316
Wisconsin Dental Assn 6737 W Washington St Suite 2360 **Fax Area Code: 800* ■ *TF:* 800-364-7646 ■ *Web:* www.wda.org	West Allis	WI	53214	414-276-4520	864-2997*
Wyoming Dental Assn 1637 S Spruce St *Web:* www.wyda.org	Casper	WY	82601	307-237-1186	237-1187

231 DENTAL EQUIPMENT & SUPPLIES - MFR

				Phone	Fax
3M ESPE Dental Products Div 3M Ctr Bldg 0275-02-SE-03 *TF:* 800-634-2249 ■ *Web:* www.3m.com/product/business-units/espe-dental.html	Saint Paul	MN	55144	651-575-5144	733-2481
3M Unitek 2724 Peck Rd *TF:* 800-634-5300 ■ *Web:* www.3m.com	Monrovia	CA	91016	626-445-7960	574-4793
A-dec Inc 2601 Crestview Dr *TF Cust Svc:* 800-547-1883 ■ *Web:* www.in.a-dec.com/en	Newberg	OR	97132	503-538-7478	538-0276
Align Technology Inc 2560 Orchard Pkwy *NASDAQ: ALGN* ■ *Web:* www.aligntech.com	San Jose	CA	95131	408-470-1000	470-1010
American Medical Technologies Inc 5655 Bear Ln *TF:* 800-359-1959 ■ *Web:* www.americanmedicaltech.com	Corpus Christi	TX	78405	361-289-1145	289-5554
American Orthodontics Corp 1714 Cambridge Ave *TF:* 800-558-7687 ■ *Web:* www.americanortho.com	Sheboygan	WI	53081	920-457-5051	457-1485
Barnhardt Mfg Co 1100 Hawthorne Ln *TF:* 800-277-0377 ■ *Web:* www.barnhardt.net	Charlotte	NC	28205	704-376-0380	342-1892
Brasseler USA 1 Brasseler Blvd *TF:* 800-841-4522 ■ *Web:* www.brasselerusa.com	Savannah	GA	31419	912-925-8525	927-8671
Closure Medical Corp 5250 Greens Dairy Rd *Web:* www.closuremed.com	Raleigh	NC	27616	919-876-7800	790-1041
Colgate Oral Pharmaceuticals One Colgate Way *TF:* 800-821-2880 ■ *Web:* www.colgateprofessional.com	Canton	MA	02021	781-821-2880	821-2187
Coltene/Whaledent Inc 235 Ascot Pkwy *Web:* www.coltene.com	Cuyahoga Falls	OH	44223	330-916-8800	916-7077
Darby Group Cos Inc 300 Jericho Quad **Fax Area Code: 800* ■ *TF:* 800-468-1001 ■ *Web:* www.darbygroup.com	Jericho	NY	11753	516-683-1800	957-7362*
Den-Mat Corp 2727 Skyway Dr *TF:* 800-433-6628 ■ *Web:* www.denmat.com	Santa Maria	CA	93455	805-922-8491	922-6933
DEN-TAL-EZ Group Inc 2 W Liberty Blvd # 160 *TF:* 866-383-4636 ■ *Web:* www.dentalez.com	Malvern	PA	19355	610-725-8004	725-9898
DEN-TAL-EZ Inc Equipment Div 2500 Hwy 31 S *TF:* 800-383-4636	Bay Minette	AL	36507	251-937-6781	937-0461
Dentsply Caulk 38 W Clarke Ave **Fax: Acctg* ■ *TF:* 800-532-2855 ■ *Web:* www.caulk.com	Milford	DE	19963	302-422-4511	422-3480*

	City	State	ZIP	Phone	Fax
Dentsply International Inc 221 W Philadelphia St PO Box 872 *NASDAQ:* XRAY ■ *TF:* 800-877-0020 ■ *Web:* www.dentsply.com	York	PA	17405	717-845-7511	849-4762
Dentsply International Inc Rinn Div 1212 Abbott Dr **Fax Area Code:* 800 ■ *TF:* 800-323-0970 ■ *Web:* www.rinncorp.com	Elgin	IL	60123	847-742-1115	544-0787*
Dentsply International Inc Trubyte Div 221 W Philadelphia St PO Box 872 **Fax Area Code:* 800 ■ **Fax:* Cust Svc ■ *TF:* 800-877-0020 ■ *Web:* www.trubyte.com	York	PA	17405	717-845-7511	735-1101*
Dentsply International Inc Tulsa Dental Div 5100 E Skelly Dr Suite 300 *TF:* 800-662-1202 ■ *Web:* www.tulsadental.com	Tulsa	OK	74135	918-493-6598	493-6599
Dentsply Professional 1301 Smile Way **Fax Area Code:* 800 ■ **Fax:* Cust Svc ■ *TF:* 800-989-8825 ■ *Web:* www.professional.dentsply.com	York	PA	17404	717-767-8500	278-4344*
GC America Inc 3737 W 127th St **Fax:* Cust Svc ■ *TF Cust Svc:* 800-323-7063 ■ *Web:* www.gcamerica.com	Alsip	IL	60803	708-597-0900	371-5103*
Heraeus Kulzer Inc 99 Business Pk Dr **Fax Area Code:* 800 ■ **Fax:* Cust Svc ■ *TF:* 800-343-5336 ■ *Web:* www.kulzer.com	Armonk	NY	10504	914-273-8600	522-1545*
Hygenic Corp 1245 Home Ave *TF:* 800-321-2135 ■ *Web:* www.hygenic.com	Akron	OH	44310	330-633-8460	633-9359
Lancer Orthodontics Inc 2330 Cousteau Ct *TF Cust Svc:* 800-854-2896 ■ *Web:* www.lancerortho.com	Vesta	CA	92081	760-744-5585	744-5724
LifeCore Biomedical LLC 3515 Lyman Blvd *TF Cust Svc:* 800-752-2663 ■ *Web:* www.lifecore.com	Chaska	MN	55318	952-368-4300	368-3411
Midwest Dental Equipment Services & Supplies 2700 Commerce St **Fax Area Code:* 888 ■ *TF:* 800-766-2025 ■ *Web:* www.mwdental.com	Wichita Falls	TX	76301	800-766-2025	551-3514*
Nobel Biocare USA Inc 22715 Savi Ranch Pkwy *TF:* 800-993-8100 ■ *Web:* www.nobelbiocare.com	Yorba Linda	CA	92887	714-282-4800	998-9236
ORMCO Corp 1717 W Collins Ave **Fax Area Code:* 800 ■ *TF Cust Svc:* 800-854-1741 ■ *Web:* www.ormco.com	Orange	CA	92867	714-516-7400	317-6012*
Pelton & Crane 11727 Fruehauf Dr *TF Cust Svc:* 800-659-6560 ■ *Web:* www.pelton.net	Charlotte	NC	28273	704-588-2126	587-7204
Premier Dental Products Co 1710 Romano Dr PO Box 4500 *TF:* 888-773-6872 ■ *Web:* www.premusa.com	Plymouth Meeting	PA	19462	610-239-6000	239-6171
Rocky Mountain Orthodontics Inc (RMO Inc) 650 W Colfax Ave **Fax:* Hum Res ■ *TF:* 800-525-6044 ■ *Web:* www.rmortho.com	Denver	CO	80204	303-592-8200	592-8200*
Sunstar Americas Inc 4635 W Foster Ave *TF:* 800-528-8537 ■ *Web:* www.jbutler.com	Chicago	IL	60630	773-777-4000	777-5101
Sybron Dental Specialties Inc (SDS) 1717 W Collins *TF:* 800-537-7824 ■ *Web:* www.sybrondental.com	Orange	CA	92867	714-516-7400	
TP Orthodontics Inc 100 Ctr Plaza *TF:* 800-348-8856 ■ *Web:* www.tportho.com	La Porte	IN	46350	219-785-2591	324-3029
Water Pik Inc 1730 East Prospect Rd *NYSE:* PIK ■ *TF:* 800-525-2774 ■ *Web:* www.waterpik.com	Fort Collins	CO	80553	800-525-2774	

232 DEPARTMENT STORES

	City	State	ZIP	Phone	Fax
Ammar's Inc 710 S College Ave *Web:* www.magicmartstores.com	Bluefield	VA	24605	276-322-4686	326-1060
Ann & Hope Inc 1 Ann & Hope Way *Web:* www.curtainandbathoutlet.com	Cumberland	RI	02864	401-722-1000	495-8218
Apex Inc 100 Main St *TF:* 800-450-2739 ■ *Web:* www.apexstores.com	Pawtucket	RI	02860	401-723-3500	723-9452
Beall's Inc 1806 38th Ave E *Web:* www.beallsinc.com	Bradenton	FL	34208	941-747-2355	746-1171
Belk Inc 2801 W Tyvola Rd *Web:* www.belk.com	Charlotte	NC	28217	704-357-1000	
Bering Home Center Inc 6102 Westheimer Rd *Web:* www.berings.com	Houston	TX	77057	713-785-6400	785-3697
Bloomingdale's 1000 3rd Ave *TF:* 800-950-0047 ■ *Web:* www.bloomingdales.com	New York	NY	10022	212-705-2000	705-2502
Bob's Merchandise Inc 1111 Hudson St *TF:* 800-292-5551 ■ *Web:* www.bobsmerch.com	Longview	WA	98632	360-425-3870	636-4334
Bon-Ton Stores Inc 2801 E Market St *NASDAQ:* BONT ■ *TF:* 800-945-4438 ■ *Web:* www.bonton.com	York	PA	17402	717-757-7660	751-3108
Boscov's Dept Stores 4500 Perkiomen Ave *Web:* www.boscovs.com	Reading	PA	19606	610-779-2000	370-3495
Bracker's Dept Store 68 N Morley Ave *TF:* 800-635-5431	Nogales	AZ	85621	520-287-3631	287-7137
Carson Pirie Scott 331 W Wisconsin Ave **Fax:* Hum Res ■ *Web:* www.carsons.com	Milwaukee	WI	53203	414-347-4141	347-5337*
Century 21 Dept Stores 22 Cortlandt St **Fax:* Hum Res ■ *Web:* www.century21deptstores.com	New York	NY	10007	212-227-9092	267-4271*
Dillard's Inc 1600 Cantrell Rd *NYSE:* DDS ■ **Fax:* Acctg ■ *Web:* www.dillards.com	Little Rock	AR	72201	501-376-5200	399-7271*
Dunlap Co 200 Bailey Ave *TF:* 866-274-0163	Fort Worth	TX	76107	817-336-4985	336-4985
Fred's Inc 4300 New Getwell Rd PO Box 18356 *NASDAQ:* FRED ■ *TF:* 800-374-7417 ■ *Web:* www.fredsinc.com	Memphis	TN	38118	901-365-8880	365-8865
Glik Co 3248 Nameoki Rd *TF:* 800-454-5182 ■ *Web:* www.gliks.com	Granite City	IL	62040	618-876-6717	876-7819
Gordman 12100 W Ctr Rd *TF:* 800-456-7463 ■ *Web:* www.gordmans.com	Omaha	NE	68144	402-691-4000	691-4269
GR Herberger's Inc 600 W St Germain St *TF:* 800-398-7896 ■ *Web:* www.herbergers.com	Saint Cloud	MN	56301	320-251-5351	654-2277
Grigg Enterprises Inc 801 W Columbia St PO Box 2348 *Web:* www.griggsonline.com	Pasco	WA	99301	509-547-0566	547-4387
Halls Merchandising Inc 200 E 25th St *TF:* 888-425-5722 ■ *Web:* www.halls.com	Kansas City	MO	64108	816-274-8111	274-4471
Isetan Mitsu koshi 1411 Broadway Suite 2550 *Web:* www.isetan.co.jp	New York	NY	10018	212-767-0300	767-0307
JC Penney Co Inc 6501 Legacy Dr *NYSE:* JCP ■ **Fax:* Cust Svc ■ *TF Orders:* 800-222-6161 ■ *Web:* www.jcpenney.net	Plano	TX	75024	972-431-1000	431-9140*
Jones & Jones Inc 4500 N 10th St Suite 90	McAllen	TX	78504	956-687-1171	631-3345
Kohl's Corp N 56 W 17000 Ridgewood Dr *NYSE:* KSS ■ *TF:* 800-837-6644 ■ *Web:* www.kohls.com	Menomonee Falls	WI	53051	262-703-7000	
Lancaster Sales Co 1375 Old Logan Rd Rt 33S	Lancaster	OH	43130	740-653-5334	653-2783
Langstons Co 2224 Exchange Ave *TF:* 800-658-2831 ■ *Web:* www.langstons.com	Oklahoma City	OK	73108	405-235-9536	235-1645
Lord & Taylor 424 5th Ave *TF:* 800-223-7440 ■ *Web:* www.lordandtaylor.com	New York	NY	10018	212-391-3344	391-3265
Macy's 400 5th Ave **Fax:* Cust Svc ■ *Web:* www.macys.com	Pittsburgh	PA	15219	412-232-2000	232-9565*
Macy's 111 N State St *Web:* www.macys.com	Chicago	IL	60602	312-781-1000	
Macy's Inc 7 W 7th St *NYSE:* M ■ *TF:* 800-261-5385 ■ *Web:* www.federated-fds.com	Cincinnati	OH	45202	513-579-7000	579-7555
Masters Inc 111 Hempstead Tpke 2nd Fl	West Hempstead	NY	11552	516-292-3710	292-3836
Mervyns 22301 Foothill Blvd **Fax:* Hum Res ■ *TF:* 800-637-8967	Hayward	CA	94541	510-727-3000	727-5760*
MH King Co 1032 Idaho Ave PO Box 669	Burley	ID	83318	208-678-7181	678-7907
Neiman Marcus Group Inc 1618 Main St *TF:* 800-937-9146 ■ *Web:* www.neimanmarcusgroup.com	Dallas	TX	75201	214-757-2954	573-6824
Nordstrom Inc 1617 6th Ave Suite 500 *NYSE:* JWN ■ *TF:* 800-285-5800 ■ *Web:* www.shop.nordstrom.com	Seattle	WA	98101	206-628-2111	628-1795
OW Houts & Sons Inc 120 N Buckhout St *TF Cust Svc:* 800-252-3583 ■ *Web:* www.owhouts.com	State College	PA	16801	814-238-6701	238-6700
Pamida Inc 8800 F St *Web:* www.pamida.com	Omaha	NE	68127	402-339-2400	596-7330
Peebles Inc 1 Peebles St *TF:* 800-723-4548 ■ *Web:* www.peebles.com	South Hill	VA	23970	434-447-5200	447-5474
Phelps Dodge Mercantile Co 172 Plaza Dr *Web:* www.fmi.com	Morenci	AZ	85540	928-865-4121	865-2935
Reitmans (Canada) Ltd 250 Sauve St W *TSE:* RET.A ■ *Web:* www.reitmans.ca	Montreal	QC	H3L1Z2	514-384-1140	
RH Macy & Co Inc 151 W 34th St *TF Cust Svc:* 800-526-1202 ■ *Web:* www.macys.com	New York	NY	10001	212-695-4400	494-1057
RH Reny Inc 731 Rt 1 *Web:* www.renys.com	Newcastle	ME	04553	207-563-3177	563-5681
Richard I Spiece Sales Co Inc 1150 Manchester Ave *TF:* 800-824-9622	Wabash	IN	46992	260-563-8033	563-0358
Saks Fifth Avenue 12 E 49th St *TF:* 877-551-7257 ■ *Web:* www.saksfifthavenue.com	New York	NY	10017	212-940-5305	940-4849
Sav-Mart Co 1729 N Wenatchee Ave	Wenatchee	WA	98801	509-663-1671	662-3788
Sears Canada Inc 290 Yonge St Suite 700 *TSX:* SCC ■ *TF:* 800-973-7579 ■ *Web:* www.sears.ca	Toronto	ON	M5B2C3	416-362-1711	941-2501
Sears Roebuck & Co 3333 Beverly Rd *Web:* www.sears.com	Hoffman Estates	IL	60179	847-286-2500	
Shopko LLC 700 Pilgrim Way *Web:* www.shopko.com	Green Bay	WI	54304	920-429-2211	
Skagway Dept Stores 620 State St *Web:* www.skagwaystores.com	Grand Island	NE	68801	308-384-8222	384-4308
SmartBargains Inc 10 Milk St 10th Fl *Web:* www.smartbargains.com	Boston	MA	02108	617-695-7300	695-7391
Stein Mart Inc 1200 Riverplace Blvd *NASDAQ:* SMRT ■ *TF:* 800-634-6915 ■ *Web:* www.steinmart.com	Jacksonville	FL	32207	904-346-1500	398-4341
Takashimaya Inc 693 5th Ave *TF:* 800-753-2038	New York	NY	10022	212-350-0100	350-0192
Target Corp 1000 Nicollet Mall *NYSE:* TGT ■ **Fax:* Hum Res ■ *TF Cust Svc:* 800-440-0680 ■ *Web:* www.targetcorp.com	Minneapolis	MN	55403	612-304-6073	304-6073*
Target Stores 1000 Nicollet Mall *TF:* 800-440-0680 ■ *Web:* www.target.com	Minneapolis	MN	55403	612-304-6073	307-8870
Tongass Trading Co 201 Dock St *TF:* 800-235-5102 ■ *Web:* www.tongasstrading.com	Ketchikan	AK	99901	907-225-5101	225-0481
Trading Union Inc 401 N Nordic Dr	Petersburg	AK	99833	907-772-3881	772-9309
Value City 7735 Eastern Ave *Web:* www.valuecity.com	Baltimore	MD	21224	410-288-1111	285-2150
Vivre Inc 11 E 26th St 15th Fl **Fax Area Code:* 800 ■ *TF:* 800-411-6515 ■ *Web:* www.vivre.com	New York	NY	10010	212-739-6205	770-3065*
Von Maur Inc 6565 Brady St *Web:* www.vonmaur.com	Davenport	IA	52806	563-388-2200	388-2242
Wal-Mart Stores Inc 702 SW 8th St *NYSE:* WMT ■ **Fax:* PR ■ *TF Cust Svc:* 800-925-6278 ■ *Web:* www.walmartstores.com	Bentonville	AR	72716	479-273-4000	273-4053*
Wal-Mart Stores Inc Supercenter Div 702 SW 8th St *TF:* 800-925-6278 ■ *Web:* walmartstores.com	Bentonville	AR	72716	479-273-4000	273-4053
Walmart.com 7000 Marina Blvd *TF:* 800-966-6546 ■ *Web:* www.walmart.com	Brisbane	CA	94005	650-837-5000	

233 DEVELOPMENTAL CENTERS

Residential Facilities For The Developmentally Disabled.

	City	State	ZIP	Phone	Fax
Altoona Ctr 1515 4th St *TF:* 800-398-3202 ■ *Web:* www.altoonacenter.com	Altoona	PA	16601	814-946-6900	946-6943
Caswell Ctr 2415 W Vernon Ave **Fax:* Acctg ■ *Web:* www.caswellcenter.org	Kinston	NC	28504	252-559-5100	208-4288*
Central Virginia Training Ctr 521 Colony Rd **Fax:* Hum Res ■ *TF:* 866-897-6095 ■ *Web:* www.cvtc.dmhmrsas.virginia.gov	Madison Heights	VA	24572	434-947-6000	947-2459*
Development Counsellors International Ltd (DCI) 215 Pk Ave S Fl 10 *Web:* www.aboutdci.com	New York	NY	10003	212-725-0707	725-2254
Glenwood Resource Ctr 711 S Vine St	Glenwood	IA	51534	712-527-4811	527-2329
Lanterman Developmental Ctr 3530 Pomona Blvd *Web:* www.dds.ca.gov	Pomona	CA	91769	909-595-1221	598-4352
Parsons State Hospital & Training Ctr 2601 Gabriel St	Parsons	KS	67357	620-421-6550	421-3623
Porterville Developmental Ctr (PDC) 26501 Ave 140 PO Box 2000 *Web:* www.dds.ca.gov/Porterville/Index.cfm	Porterville	CA	93258	559-782-2222	784-5630

Phone *Fax*

Productive Alternatives Inc
1205 N Tower Rd ....Fergus Falls MN 56537 218-998-5630 736-2541
TF: 800-477-7246 ■ *Web:* www.paiff.org

Sonoma Developmental Ctr 15000 Arnold Dr ....Eldridge CA 95431 707-938-6000 938-3605*
**Fax:* Admitting ■ *Web:* www.dds.ca.gov

Woodward Resource Ctr 1251 334th St ....Woodward IA 50276 515-438-2600 438-3176*
**Fax:* Hum Res ■ *Web:* www.dhs.state.ia.us

234 DIAGNOSTIC PRODUCTS

SEE ALSO Biotechnology Companies p. 1525; Medicinal Chemicals & Botanical Products p. 2231; Pharmaceutical Companies p. 2414; Pharmaceutical Companies - Generic Drugs p. 2416

Phone *Fax*

Abaxis Inc 3240 Whipple Rd ....Union City CA 94587 510-675-6500 441-6150
NASDAQ: ABAX ■ *TF:* 800-822-2947 ■ *Web:* www.abaxis.com

Abbott Laboratories 100 Abbott Pk Rd ....Abbott Park IL 60064 847-937-6100
NYSE: ABT ■ *TF:* 800-323-9100 ■ *Web:* www.abbott.com

Abbott Laboratories Abbott Diagnostics Div
100 Abbott Pk Rd ....Abbott Park IL 60064 847-937-6100
TF: 800-323-9100 ■ *Web:* www.abbottdiagnostics.com

Accurate Chemical & Scientific Corp
300 Shames Dr..................................Westbury NY 11590 516-333-2221 997-4948
TF: 800-645-6264 ■ *Web:* www.accuratechemical.com

Advanced Biotechnologies Inc (ABI)
9108 Guilford Rd Rivers Pk II.......................Columbia MD 21046 301-470-3220 497-9773
TF: 800-426-0764 ■ *Web:* www.abionline.com

Advanced Magnetics Inc 61 Mooney St.............Cambridge MA 02138 617-497-2070 547-2445
AMEX: AVM

Aero Pharmaceuticals Inc
3848 FAU Blvd Suite 100........................Boca Raton FL 33431 561-208-2200 414-1202*
**Fax Area Code:* 800 ■ *TF:* 800-223-6837 ■ *Web:* www.aeropharmaceuticals.com

Akorn Inc 1925 W Field Ct........................Lake Forest IL 60045 847-279-6100 279-6123
NASDAQ: AKRX ■ *TF:* 800-932-5676 ■ *Web:* www.akorn.com

ALerCHEK Inc 203 Anderson St........................Portland ME 04101 207-775-2574 775-0594
TF: 877-282-9542 ■ *Web:* www.alerchek.com

Alere Inc 51 Sawyer Rd Suite 200 ....Waltham MA 02453 781-647-3900 647-3939
TF: 877-696-2525 ■ *Web:* www.alere.com

Allermed Laboratories Inc 7203 Convoy Ct..........San Diego CA 92111 800-221-2748 292-5934*
**Fax Area Code:* 858 ■ *TF:* 800-221-2748 ■ *Web:* www.allermed.com

Ambion Inc 2130 Woodward St ....Austin TX 78744 512-651-0200 651-0190
Web: www.ambion.com

American Diagnostica Inc 500 W Ave ....Stamford CT 06902 203-602-7777 602-2221
TF: 888-234-4435 ■ *Web:* www.americandiagnostica.com

American Qualex International Inc (AQSP)
920-A Calle Negocio ....San Clemente CA 92673 949-492-8298 492-6790
TF: 800-772-1776 ■ *Web:* www.aqsp.com

Amresco Inc 6681 Cochran Rd ....Solon OH 44139 440-349-1313 349-3255
TF: 800-448-4442 ■ *Web:* www.amresco-inc.com

Anachemia Chemicals Inc 3 Lincoln Blvd ....Rouses Point NY 12979 518-297-4444 297-2960
TF: 800-323-1414 ■ *Web:* www.anachemiachemicals.com

AnaSpec Inc 34801 Campus Dr.......................Fremont CA 94555 510-791-9560 791-9572
TF: 800-452-5530 ■ *Web:* www.anaspec.com

Angus Buffers & Biochemicals
2236 Liberty Dr...............................Niagara Falls NY 14304 716-283-1434 283-1570
TF: 800-648-6689 ■ *Web:* www.dow.com

AntiCancer Inc 7917 Ostrow St.....................San Diego CA 92111 858-654-2555 268-4175
TF: 800-511-2555 ■ *Web:* www.anticancer.com

Armor Forensics
13386 International Pkwy ....Jacksonville FL 32218 904-741-5400 741-5403
TF: 800-654-9943 ■ *Web:* www.armorholdings.com

Athena Diagnostics Inc
377 Plantation St 4 Biotech Pk.......................Worcester MA 01605 508-756-2886 753-5601
TF: 800-394-4493 ■ *Web:* www.athenadiagnostics.com

Bachem-Peninsula Laboratories Inc
305 Old County Rd..............................San Carlos CA 94070 650-801-6090 595-4071
TF: 800-922-1516 ■ *Web:* www.bachem.com

BD Diagnostics 7 Loveton Cir..........................Sparks MD 21152 410-316-4000 316-4066
TF: 800-666-6433 ■ *Web:* www.bd.com

Becton Dickinson & Co 1 Becton Dr............Franklin Lakes NJ 07417 201-847-6800 847-4882*
NYSE: BDX ■ **Fax:* Cust Svc ■ *TF Cust Svc:* 888-237-2762 ■ *Web:* www.bd.com

Berlex Laboratories Inc 6 W Belt ....Wayne NJ 07470 973-694-4100 305-5475
TF: 888-237-2394 ■ *Web:* www.berlex.com

Binax Inc 10 Southgate Rd.......................Scarborough ME 04074 207-730-5700 730-5710
TF: 800-323-3199 ■ *Web:* www.binaxnow.com

Bio-Rad Laboratories 1000 Alfred Nobel Dr ....Hercules CA 94547 510-724-7000 741-5824*
AMEX: BIO ■ **Fax:* Cust Svc ■ *TF:* 800-424-6723 ■ *Web:* www.bio-rad.com

BioGenex Laboratories Inc
4600 Norris Canyon Rd ....San Ramon CA 94583 925-275-0550 275-0580
TF: 800-421-4149 ■ *Web:* www.biogenex.com

Biomeda Corp 1851 Vanderbilt Rd...................Texarkana AR 71854 870-779-8787 216-2299
TF: 800-341-8787 ■ *Web:* www.biomeda.com

Biomedical Technologies Inc 378 Page St ....Stoughton MA 02072 781-344-9942 341-1451
Web: www.btiinc.com

Biomerica Inc 1533 Monrovia Ave ....Newport Beach CA 92663 949-645-2111 722-6674
TF Cust Svc: 800-854-3002 ■ *Web:* www.biomerica.com

BioMerieux Inc 595 Anglum Rd ....Hazelwood MO 63042 314-731-8500 325-1598*
**Fax Area Code:* 800 ■ *TF:* 800-638-4835 ■ *Web:* www.biomerieux.com

Bionostics Inc 7 Jackson Rd..........................Devens MA 01434 978-772-7070 772-7072
TF: 800-533-6162 ■ *Web:* www.bionostics.com

Biosite Inc 9975 Summers Ridge Rd.................San Diego CA 92121 858-455-4808
TF Cust Svc: 888-246-7483 ■ *Web:* www.biosite.com

BioSource International Inc 542 Flynn Rd............Camarillo CA 93012 805-987-0086 383-5379
TF: 800-242-0607 ■ *Web:* www.biosource.com

BiosPacific Inc 5980 Horton St Suite 225 ....Emeryville CA 94608 510-652-6155 652-4531
TF: 800-344-6686 ■ *Web:* www.biospacific.com

Biotest Diagnostics Corp
66 Ford Rd Suite 220...............................Denville NJ 07834 973-625-1300 625-5882
TF: 800-522-0090 ■ *Web:* www.biotest.de

Phone *Fax*

Calypte Biomedical Corp 15875 SW 72nd Ave..........Portland OR 97224 503-726-2227 601-6299
PINK: CBMC ■ *Web:* www.calypte.com

Cedarlane Laboratories Inc
4410 Paletta Ct.................................Burlington ON L7L5R2 905-878-8891 288-0020*
**Fax Area Code:* 289 ■ *TF:* 800-268-5058 ■ *Web:* www.cedarlanelabs.com

Chematics Inc Hwy 13 S PO Box 293............North Webster IN 46555 574-834-2406 834-7427
TF: 800-348-5174 ■ *Web:* www.chematics.com

Cholestech Corp 3347 Investment Blvd ....Hayward CA 94545 510-732-7200 732-7227
TF: 800-733-0404 ■ *Web:* www.cholestech.com

Chromaprobe Inc 378 Fee Fee Rd.............Maryland Heights MO 63043 314-738-0001 738-0001
TF: 888-964-1400 ■ *Web:* www.chromaprobe.com

CST Technologies Inc
55 Northern Blvd Suite 200 ....Great Neck NY 11021 516-482-9001 482-0186
TF: 800-448-4407 ■ *Web:* www.cstti.com

DakoCytomation 6392 Via Real ....Carpinteria CA 93013 805-566-6655 566-6688
TF Cust Svc: 800-400-3256 ■ *Web:* www.dako.com

Diagnostic Systems Laboratories Inc
445 Medical Ctr Blvd ....Webster TX 77598 281-332-9678 338-1895
TF: 800-231-7970 ■ *Web:* www.diagnosticsproductguide.com

Diagnostic Technology Inc
175 Commerce Dr Suite L ....Hauppauge NY 11788 631-582-4949 582-4694

Diagnostics Biochem Canada Inc
1020 Hargrieve Rd Unit 11 ....London ON N6E1P5 519-681-8731 681-8731
Web: www.dbc-labs.com

DiaSorin Inc 1951 Northwestern Ave..................Stillwater MN 55082 651-439-9710 351-5669
TF: 800-328-1482 ■ *Web:* www.diasorin.com

DuPont Qualicon
Henry Clay Rd Bldg 400 Rt 141
PO Box 80357 ....Wilmington DE 19880 302-695-5300 695-8860
TF: 800-863-6842 ■ *Web:* www.qualicon.com

EMD Biosciences Inc 10394 Pacific Ctr Ct ....San Diego CA 92121 858-450-9600 453-3552
TF Cust Svc: 888-854-3417 ■ *Web:* www.emdchemicals.com

Enzo Biochem Inc 527 Madison Ave ....New York NY 10022 212-583-0100 583-0150
NYSE: ENZ ■ *TF:* 800-522-5052 ■ *Web:* www.enzo.com

EXACT Sciences Corp 100 Campus Dr ....Marlborough MA 01752 508-683-1200 683-1201
NASDAQ: EXAS ■ *Web:* www.exactlabs.com

Exalpha Biologicals Inc
5 Clock Tower Pl Suite 255.........................Maynard MA 01754 978-461-0435 461-0436
TF: 800-395-1137 ■ *Web:* www.exalpha.com

Fisher Diagnostics
8365 Valley Pike PO Box 307.....................Middletown VA 22645 540-869-3200 869-8126
TF: 800-528-0494 ■ *Web:* www.thermofisher.com

Fortune Biologicals Inc
18919 Premiere Ct ....Gaithersburg MD 20879 301-330-8547 330-8648

Gen-Probe Inc 10210 Genetic Ctr Dr...............San Diego CA 92121 858-410-8000 410-8625
NASDAQ: GPRO ■ *TF:* 800-523-5001 ■ *Web:* www.gen-probe.com

GenBio 15222 Avenue of Science Suite A..............San Diego CA 92128 858-592-9300 592-9400
TF Tech Supp: 800-288-4368 ■ *Web:* www.genbio.com

Genzyme Corp 500 Kendall St........................Cambridge MA 02142 617-252-7500 252-7600
TF: 800-326-7002 ■ *Web:* www.genzyme.com

Gibson Laboratories Inc 1040 Manchester St..........Lexington KY 40508 859-254-9500 253-1476
TF: 800-477-4763 ■ *Web:* www.gibsonlabs.com

Golden Bridge International Inc
9700 Harbour Pl Suite 129.........................Mukilteo WA 98275 425-493-1801 672-2027
Web: www.gbi-inc.com

Goodwin Biotechnology Inc
1850 NW 69th Ave ....Plantation FL 33313 954-321-5300 587-6378
TF: 800-814-8600 ■ *Web:* www.goodwinbio.com

Harlan Bioproducts for Science Inc (HBPS)
298 S Carroll Rd.................................Indianapolis IN 46229 317-353-8810 898-6400
TF: 800-972-4362 ■ *Web:* www.harlan.com

Helena Laboratories Inc 1530 Lindbergh Dr.......... Beaumont TX 77704 409-842-3714 842-3094
TF: 800-231-5663 ■ *Web:* www.helena.com

Hemagen Diagnostics Inc 9033 Red Branch Rd........Columbia MD 21045 443-367-5500 997-7812*
**Fax Area Code:* 410 ■ *TF:* 800-436-2436 ■ *Web:* www.hemagen.com

Hitachi Chemical Diagnostics
630 Clyde Ct...............................Mountain View CA 94043 650-961-5501 969-2745
TF: 800-233-6278 ■ *Web:* www.hcdiagnostics.com

Home Diagnostics Inc 2400 NW 55th Ct.........Fort Lauderdale FL 33309 954-677-9201 739-8506
TF: 800-342-7226 ■ *Web:* www.homediagnosticsinc.com

Hycor Biomedical Inc 7272 Chapman Ave ....Garden Grove CA 92841 714-933-3000 933-3222
TF Cust Svc: 800-382-2527 ■ *Web:* www.hycorbiomedical.com

IDEXX Laboratories Inc One IDEXX Dr ....Westbrook ME 04092 207-556-0300 556-4346
NASDAQ: IDXX ■ *TF:* 800-932-4399 ■ *Web:* www.idexx.com

ImmucorGamma Inc 3130 Gateway Dr PO Box 5625.....Norcross GA 30091 770-441-2051 441-3807
NASDAQ: BLUD ■ *TF Cust Svc:* 800-829-2553 ■ *Web:* www.immucor.com

Immuno-Mycologics Inc (IMMY) 2700 Technology Pl....Norman OK 73071 405-360-4669 364-1058
TF: 800-654-3639 ■ *Web:* www.immy.com

ImmunoDiagnostics Inc 21 F Olympia Ave ....Woburn MA 01801 781-938-6300 938-7300
TF: 800-573-1700 ■ *Web:* www.immunodx.com

Immunovision Inc 1820 Ford Ave..................Springdale AR 72764 479-751-7005 751-7002
TF: 800-541-0960

Inova Diagnostics Inc 9900 Old Grove Rd............San Diego CA 92131 858-586-9900 586-9911
TF: 800-545-9495 ■ *Web:* www.inovadx.com

InSite Vision Inc 965 Atlantic Ave.....................Alameda CA 94501 510-865-8800 865-5700
OTC: INSV ■ *Web:* www.insitevision.com

Interleukin Genetics Inc 135 Beaver St 3rd Fl ....Waltham MA 02452 781-398-0700 398-0720
PINK: ILIU ■ *TF Cust Svc:* 866-990-4363 ■ *Web:* www.ilgenetics.com

International Immunology Corp
25549 Adams Ave..................................Murrieta CA 92562 951-677-5629 677-6752
TF: 800-843-2853 ■ *Web:* www.iicsera.com

International Isotopes Inc
4137 Commerce Cir...............................Idaho Falls ID 83401 208-524-5300 524-1411
TF: 800-699-3108 ■ *Web:* www.intisoid.com

InVitro International 17751 Sky Pk Cir # G...............Irvine CA 92614 949-851-8356 851-4985
TF: 800-246-8487 ■ *Web:* www.invitrointl.com

Iso-Tex Diagnostics Inc PO Box 909.............Friendswood TX 77549 281-482-1231 482-1070
TF: 800-477-4839 ■ *Web:* www.isotexdiagnostics.com

IVAX Diagnostics Inc 2140 N Miami Ave................Miami FL 33127 305-324-2300 324-2395
AMEX: IVD ■ *TF:* 800-327-4565 ■ *Web:* www.ivaxdiagnostics.com

	City	State	ZIP	Phone	Fax
Jackson ImmunoResearch Laboratories Inc					
872 W Baltimore Pike PO Box 9	West Grove	PA	19390	610-869-4024	869-0171
TF: 800-367-5296 ■ *Web:* www.jacksonimmuno.com					
Kamiya Biomedical Co 12779 Gateway Dr	Seattle	WA	98168	206-575-8068	575-8094
Web: www.kamiyabiomedical.com					
Kirkegaard & Perry Laboratories Inc					
2 Cessna Ct	Gaithersburg	MD	20879	301-948-7755	948-0169
TF: 800-638-3167 ■ *Web:* www.kpl.com					
KMI Diagnostics Inc					
8201 Central Ave NE Suite P	Minneapolis	MN	55432	763-231-3313	780-2988
TF: 888-564-3424 ■ *Web:* www.kmidiagnostics.com					
Life Sciences Inc 2900 72nd St N	Saint Petersburg	FL	33710	727-345-9371	347-2957
TF: 800-237-4323 ■ *Web:* www.lifesci.com					
LifeScan Inc 1000 Gibraltar Dr	Milpitas	CA	95035	408-263-9789	946-6070
TF: 800-227-8862 ■ *Web:* www.lifescan.com					
Lightning Powder Co Inc					
13386 International Pkwy	Jacksonville	FL	32218	904-741-5400	741-5403
Web: www.redwop.com					
LipoScience Inc 2500 Sumner Blvd	Raleigh	NC	27616	919-212-1999	255-3055
TF: 877-547-6837 ■ *Web:* www.liposcience.com					
Maine Biotechnology Services Inc					
1037 R Forest Ave	Portland	ME	04103	207-797-5454	797-5595
TF: 800-925-9476 ■ *Web:* www.mainebiotechnology.com					
Mallinckrodt Inc 675 McDonnell Blvd	Hazelwood	MO	63042	314-654-2000	654-6852*
**Fax:* Hum Res ■ *TF:* 888-744-1414 ■ *Web:* www.pharmaceuticals.covidien.com					
Matritech Inc 330 Nevada St	Newton	MA	02460	617-928-0820	928-0821
Web: www.matritech.com					
Medical Analysis Systems Inc					
46360 Fremont Blvd	Fremont	CA	94538	510-979-5000	979-5002
TF: 800-232-3342 ■ *Web:* www.mas-inc.com					
MEDTOX Diagnostics Inc 1238 Anthony Rd	Burlington	NC	27215	336-226-6311	229-4471
TF: 800-334-1116 ■ *Web:* www.medtox.com					
Meridian Bioscience Inc					
3471 River Hills Dr	Cincinnati	OH	45244	513-271-3700	272-5421
NASDAQ: VIVO ■ *TF Cust Svc:* 800-543-1980 ■ *Web:* www.meridianbioscience.com					
Millipore Corp 290 Concord Rd	Billerica	MA	01821	781-533-6000	645-5439*
**Fax Area Code:* 800 ■ *TF:* 800-645-5476 ■ *Web:* www.millipore.com					
Monobind Inc 100 N Pt Dr	Lake Forest	CA	92630	949-951-2665	951-3539
TF: 800-854-6265 ■ *Web:* www.monobind.com					
Moss Inc 2605 Cab Over Dr Suite 11	Hanover	MD	21076	410-768-3442	768-3971
TF: 800-932-6677 ■ *Web:* www.mosssubstrates.com					
Nabi Biopharmaceuticals 12276 Wilkins Ave	Rockville	MD	20852	301-770-3099	770-3097
NASDAQ: NABI ■ *TF:* 800-685-5579 ■ *Web:* www.nabi.com					
National Diagnostics Inc 305 Patton Dr	Atlanta	GA	30336	404-699-2121	699-2077
TF: 800-526-3867 ■ *Web:* www.nationaldiagnostics.com					
Neogen Corp 620 Lesher Pl	Lansing	MI	48912	517-372-9200	372-2006
NASDAQ: NEOG ■ *TF:* 800-234-5333 ■ *Web:* www.neogen.com					
New Horizons Diagnostics Corp					
9110 Red Branch Rd	Columbia	MD	21045	410-992-9357	992-0328
TF: 800-888-5015 ■ *Web:* www.nhdiag.com					
Novartis Vaccines & Diagnostics					
4560 Horton St	Emeryville	CA	94608	510-655-8730	655-9910
TF: 800-524-4766 ■ *Web:* www.novartis-vaccines.com					
Omega Biologicals Inc 910 Technology Blvd	Bozeman	MT	59718	406-586-3790	586-3792
OraSure Technologies Inc 220 E 1st St	Bethlehem	PA	18015	610-882-1820	882-1830
NASDAQ: OSUR ■ *TF:* 800-869-3538 ■ *Web:* www.orasure.com					
Ortho-Clinical Diagnostics Inc					
1001 US Rt 202 N PO Box 350	Raritan	NJ	08869	908-218-1300	453-3660*
**Fax Area Code:* 585 ■ **Fax:* Cust Svc ■ *TF:* 800-828-6316 ■ *Web:* www.orthoclinical.com					
Oxford Biomedical Research Inc					
2165 Avon Industrial Dr	Rochester Hills	MI	48309	248-852-8815	852-4466
TF: 800-692-4633 ■ *Web:* www.oxfordbiomed.com					
Pacific Biometrics Inc 220 W Harrison St	Seattle	WA	98119	206-298-0068	298-9838
TF: 800-767-9151 ■ *Web:* www.pacbio.com					
Peptides International Inc					
11621 Electron Dr	Louisville	KY	40299	502-266-8787	267-1329
TF: 800-777-4779 ■ *Web:* www.pepnet.com					
PerkinElmer Inc 45 William St	Wellesley	MA	02481	781-237-5100	237-9386
NYSE: PKI ■ *Web:* www.perkinelmer.com					
Pharmaceutical Innovations Inc					
897 Frelinghuysen Ave	Newark	NJ	07114	973-242-2900	242-0578
Web: www.pharminnovations.com					
PML Microbiologicals Inc					
27120 SW 95th Ave	Wilsonville	OR	97070	503-570-2500	570-2501
TF Cust Svc: 800-628-7014 ■ *Web:* www.pmlmicro.com					
Pointe Scientific Inc					
5449 Research Dr PO Box 87188	Canton	MI	48188	734-487-8300	483-1592
TF: 800-445-9853 ■ *Web:* www.pointescientific.com					
Polymedco Inc 510 Furnace Dock Rd	Cortlandt Manor	NY	10567	914-739-5400	739-5890
TF: 800-431-2123 ■ *Web:* www.polymedco.com					
Polysciences Inc 400 Valley Rd	Warrington	PA	18976	215-343-6484	343-0214
TF Cust Svc: 800-523-2575 ■ *Web:* www.polysciences.com					
Promega Corp 2800 Woods Hollow Rd	Madison	WI	53711	608-274-4330	277-2516
TF: 800-356-9526 ■ *Web:* www.promega.com					
Prozyme Inc 3832 Bay Ctr Pl	Hayward	CA	94545	510-638-6900	638-6919
TF: 800-457-9444 ■ *Web:* www.prozyme.com					
Quality Biological Inc					
7581 Lindbergh Dr	Gaithersburg	MD	20879	301-840-9331	840-0743
TF: 800-443-9331 ■ *Web:* www.qualitybiological.com					
Quantimetrix Corp					
2005 Manhattan Beach Blvd	Redondo Beach	CA	90278	310-536-0006	536-9977
TF: 800-624-8380 ■ *Web:* www.4qc.com					
Quidel Corp 10165 McKellar Ct	San Diego	CA	92121	858-552-1100	453-4338
NASDAQ: QDEL ■ *TF:* 800-874-1517 ■ *Web:* www.quidel.com					
R & D Systems Inc 614 McKinley Pl NE	Minneapolis	MN	55413	612-379-2956	656-4400
TF: 800-343-7475 ■ *Web:* www.rndsystems.com					
Radient Pharmaceuticals Corp					
2492 Walnut Ave Suite 100	Tustin	CA	92780	714-505-4461	505-4464
AMEX: RPC ■ *Web:* www.radient-pharma.com					
Remel Inc 12076 Santa Fe Dr PO Box 14428	Lenexa	KS	66215	913-888-0939	621-8251*
**Fax Area Code:* 800 ■ *TF:* 800-255-6730 ■ *Web:* www.remel.com					
Research & Diagnostic Antibodies					
2645 W Cheyenne Ave	North Las Vegas	NV	89032	702-638-7800	638-7801
TF: 800-858-7322 ■ *Web:* www.rdabs.com					
Research Organics Inc 4353 E 49th St	Cleveland	OH	44125	216-883-8025	883-1576
TF: 800-321-0570 ■ *Web:* www.resorg.com					
Roche Diagnostics Corp (RDC)					
9115 Hague Rd PO Box 50457	Indianapolis	IN	46250	317-521-2000	521-2090
TF Cust Svc: 800-428-5076 ■ *Web:* www.roche-diagnostics.us					
Rockland Immunochemicals Inc					
650 Englesville Rd	Boyertown	PA	19512	610-369-1008	367-7825
TF: 800-656-7625 ■ *Web:* www.rockland-inc.com					
Scantibodies Laboratory Inc 9336 Abraham Way	Santee	CA	92071	619-258-9300	258-9366
Web: www.scantibodies.com					
SCIMEDX Corp 100 Ford Rd	Denville	NJ	07834	973-625-8822	625-8796
TF: 800-221-5598 ■ *Web:* www.scimedx.com					
Scripps Laboratories Inc 6838 Flanders Dr	San Diego	CA	92121	858-546-5800	546-5812
Web: www.scrippslabs.com					
Sigma-Aldrich Corp 3050 Spruce St	Saint Louis	MO	63103	314-771-5765	325-5052*
NASDAQ: SIAL ■ **Fax Area Code:* 800 ■ *TF:* 800-325-3010 ■ *Web:* www.sigmaaldrich.com					
Southern Biotechnology Assoc Inc					
160A Oxmoor Blvd	Birmingham	AL	35209	205-945-1774	945-8768
TF: 800-722-2255 ■ *Web:* www.southernbiotech.com					
Strategic Diagnostics Inc 111 Pencader Dr	Newark	DE	19702	302-456-6789	456-6770
NASDAQ: SDIX ■ *TF:* 800-544-8881 ■ *Web:* www.sdix.com					
SurModics Inc 9924 W 74th St	Eden Prairie	MN	55344	952-829-2700	500-7001
NASDAQ: SRDX ■ *TF:* 866-787-6639 ■ *Web:* www.surmodics.com					
Synergent Biochem Inc					
12026 Centralia Rd Suite H	Hawaiian Gardens	CA	90716	562-809-3389	809-6191
TF: 800-585-8580 ■ *Web:* www.synergentbiochem.com					
Techne Corp 614 McKinley Pl NE	Minneapolis	MN	55413	612-379-8854	379-6580
NASDAQ: TECH ■ *TF:* 800-328-2400 ■ *Web:* www.techne-corp.com					
Teco Diagnostics 1268 N Lakeview Ave	Anaheim	CA	92807	714-463-1111	463-1169
TF: 800-222-9880 ■ *Web:* www.tecodiag.com					
Theragenics Corp 5203 Bristol Industrial Way	Buford	GA	30518	770-271-0233	482-4909*
NYSE: TGX ■ **Fax Area Code:* 678 ■ *TF:* 800-458-4372 ■ *Web:* www.theragenics.com					
Thermo Fisher Scientific Inc					
3747 N Meridian Rd	Rockford	IL	61101	815-968-0747	968-7316
TF: 800-874-3723 ■ *Web:* www.piercenet.com					
Trinity Biotech PLC 5919 Farnsworth Ct	Carlsbad	CA	92008	760-929-0500	929-0124
NASDAQ: TRIB ■ *TF:* 800-331-2291 ■ *Web:* www.trinitybiotech.com					
Utak Laboratories Inc 25020 Ave Tibbitts	Valencia	CA	91355	661-294-3935	294-9272
TF: 800-235-3442 ■ *Web:* www.utak.com					
Varian Inc 25200 Commercentre Dr	Lake Forest	CA	92630	949-770-9381	768-1050
TF: 800-854-0277 ■ *Web:* www.varianinc.com					
Wako Chemicals USA Inc 1600 Bellwood Rd	Richmond	VA	23237	804-271-7677	271-7791
TF: 800-992-9256 ■ *Web:* www.wakousa.com					
Worthington Biochemical Corp 730 Vassar Ave	Lakewood	NJ	08701	732-942-1660	942-9270
TF: 800-445-9603 ■ *Web:* www.worthington-biochem.com					
Zepto Metrix Corp 872 Main St	Buffalo	NY	14202	716-882-0920	882-0959
TF Cust Svc: 800-274-5487 ■ *Web:* www.zeptometrix.com					

235 DISPLAYS - EXHIBIT & TRADE SHOW

	City	State	ZIP	Phone	Fax
3D Exhibits Inc 2900 Lively Blvd	Elk Grove Village	IL	60007	847-250-9000	860-8165
TF: 800-471-9617 ■ *Web:* www.3dexhibits.com					
CB Displays International					
5141 S Procyon Ave	Las Vegas	NV	89118	702-739-9301	739-8154
Web: www.cbdisplays.com					
Charles Mayer Studios Inc					
105 E Market St Suite 114	Akron	OH	44308	330-535-6121	434-2016
Derse Exhibits Inc 3800 W Canal St	Milwaukee	WI	53208	414-257-2000	257-1145
TF: 800-562-2300 ■ *Web:* www.derse.com					
Design & Production Inc 7110 Rainwater Pl	Lorton	VA	22079	703-550-8640	339-0296
Web: www.d-and-p.com					
Downing Displays Inc 550 TechneCenter Dr	Milford	OH	45150	513-248-9800	248-2605
TF: 800-883-1800 ■ *Web:* www.downingdisplays.com					
Exhibits & More 7615 Omnitech Pl Suite 4	Victor	NY	14564	585-924-4040	924-4056
Web: www.exhibitsandmore.com					
Expon Exhibits 1902 Ch Dr	West Sacramento	CA	95691	916-371-1600	371-1665
TF: 800-783-9766 ■ *Web:* www.exponexhibits.com					
Gilbert Displays Inc 110 Spagnoli Rd	Melville	NY	11747	631-577-1100	577-1139
TF: 855-577-1100 ■ *Web:* www.gilbertdisplays.com					
Group360 Inc 1227 Washington Ave	Saint Louis	MO	63103	314-260-6360	423-6104
Web: www.group360.com					
Hadley Exhibits Inc 1700 Elmwood Ave	Buffalo	NY	14207	716-874-3666	874-9994
TF: 866-429-3666 ■ *Web:* www.hadleyexhibits.com					
HB Stubbs Co 27027 Mound Rd	Warren	MI	48092	586-574-9700	574-9741
TF: 800-968-2132 ■ *Web:* www.hbstubbs.com					
Lynch Exhibits					
7 Campus Dr Burlington Business Campus	Burlington	NJ	08016	609-387-1600	239-1666
TF: 800-343-1666 ■ *Web:* www.lynchexhibits.com					
Marketechsálnc 3425 Woodbridge Cir	York	PA	17402	717-764-2588	764-2930
Web: www.marketechs.com					
MG Design Assoc Corp 8778 100th St	Pleasant Prairie	WI	53158	262-947-8890	947-8898
TF: 800-643-9442 ■ *Web:* www.mgdesign.com					
Siegel Display Products 300 6th Ave N	Minneapolis	MN	55401	612-340-1493	230-5598*
**Fax Area Code:* 800 ■ *TF:* 800-626-0322 ■ *Web:* www.siegeldisplay.com					
Skyline Displays Inc 3355 Discovery Rd	Eagan	MN	55121	651-234-6000	234-6001
TF: 800-328-2725 ■ *Web:* www.skycorp.com					
Sparks Exhibits & Environments					
10232 Palm Dr	Santa Fe Springs	CA	90670	562-941-0101	941-5551
Web: www.sparksonline.com					
Structural Display Inc					
12-12 33rd Ave	Long Island City	NY	11106	718-274-1136	278-8212
Web: www.sdiny.com					
Tandem Design Inc 1846 W Sequoia Ave	Orange	CA	92868	714-978-7272	978-7273

236 DISPLAYS - POINT-OF-PURCHASE

SEE ALSO Signs p. 2657

Company	City	State	Zip	Phone	Fax
Acrylic Design Assoc 6050 Nathan Ln N *TF:* 800-445-2167 ■ *Web:* www.acrylicdesign.com	Plymouth	MN	55442	763-559-8395	559-2589
Advance Display Co 1657 N Kostner Ave	Chicago	IL	60639	773-235-0686	235-3633
AMD Industries Inc 4620 W 19th St *TF:* 800-367-9999 ■ *Web:* www.amdpop.com	Cicero	IL	60804	708-863-8900	863-2065
Apco Products Inc PO Box 236 *Web:* www.apco-products.com	Essex	CT	06426	860-767-2108	767-7259
Archbold Container Corp 800 W Barre Rd PO Box 10 *TF:* 800-446-2520 ■ *Web:* www.archboldcontainer.com	Archbold	OH	43502	419-445-8865	446-2529
Arlington Display Industries 19303 W Davison St *Web:* www.arlingtondisplay.com	Detroit	MI	48223	313-837-1212	837-3425
Array Marketing 45 Progress Ave *TF:* 800-295-4120 ■ *Web:* www.arraymarketing.com	Toronto	ON	M1P2Y6	416-299-4865	292-9759
Art-Phyl Creations 16250 NW 48th Ave *TF:* 800-327-8318	Hialeah	FL	33014	305-624-2333	621-4093
Artkraft Strauss LLC 1776 Broadway Suite 1810 *Web:* www.artkraft.com	New York	NY	10019	212-265-5155	265-5159
Blitz USA Inc 404 26th Ave NW *TF Cust Svc:* 800-331-3795 ■ *Web:* www.blitzusa.com	Miami	OK	74354	918-540-1515	542-1380
Cannon Equipment Co 15100 Business Pkwy *TF:* 800-825-8501 ■ *Web:* www.cannonequipment.com	Rosemount	MN	55068	651-322-6300	322-1583
Chicago Display Marketing Corp 2021 W St *TF:* 800-681-4340	River Grove	IL	60171	708-842-0001	456-4672
Colony Inc 11419 Smith Dr *TF:* 800-735-1300 ■ *Web:* www.colonydisplay.com	Huntley	IL	60142	847-515-1500	515-1501
Concept Display & Packaging Corp 250 Hudson St 8th Fl *Web:* www.conceptdisplaycorp.com	New York	NY	10013	212-645-3118	645-3979
Display Smart LLC 402 Dakota St *TF:* 888-843-1870 ■ *Web:* www.display-smart.com	Lawrence	KS	66046	785-843-1869	843-1874
Display Technologies LLC 111-01 14th Ave 3rd Fl *TF:* 800-424-4220 ■ *Web:* www.display-technologies.com	College Point	NY	11356	718-321-3100	321-1932
Felbro Inc 3666 E Olympic Blvd *TF:* 800-733-5276 ■ *Web:* www.felbro-inc.com	Los Angeles	CA	90023	323-263-8686	263-8874
Frank Mayer & Assoc Inc 1975 Wisconsin Ave *TF:* 800-225-3987 ■ *Web:* www.frankmayer.com	Grafton	WI	53024	262-377-4700	377-3449
Harbor Industries Inc 14130 172nd Ave *TF:* 800-968-6993 ■ *Web:* www.harbor-ind.com	Grand Haven	MI	49417	616-842-5330	842-1385
Hunter Display 14 Hewlett Ave *TF:* 800-767-2110 ■ *Web:* www.hunterdisplays.com	East Patchogue	NY	11772	631-475-5900	475-5950
IDEAL 4800 S Austin Ave *TF:* 800-287-3104 ■ *Web:* www.idealpop.com	Chicago	IL	60638	708-594-3100	594-3109
Ideal Wire Works Inc 820 S Date Ave *Web:* www.idealwireworks.com	Alhambra	CA	91803	626-282-0886	282-2674
Kay Co Inc The 509 W Barner St	Frankfort	IN	46041	765-659-3388	659-2956
Kosakura & Assoc 2215 S Standard Ave *TF:* 866-511-2587 ■ *Web:* www.kosakura.com	Santa Ana	CA	92707	714-668-3000	668-3010
Lakeshore Display Co Inc 2031 Washington Ave *Web:* www.lakeshoredisplay.com	Sheboygan	WI	53081	920-457-3695	457-5673
Lingo Mfg Co 7400 Industrial Rd *TF Cust Svc:* 800-354-9771 ■ *Web:* www.lingomfg.com	Florence	KY	41042	859-371-2662	371-0283
MCA Industries 6811st St SW *Web:* www.mca-industries.com	Massillon	OH	44646	330-833-3165	832-9771
MDI Worldwide 38271 W 12-Mile Rd **Fax:* Sales ■ *TF Sales:* 800-228-8925 ■ *Web:* www.mdiworldwide.com	Farmington Hills	MI	48331	248-553-1900	488-5700*
Miller Multiplex Inc 512 Stockton St *TF:* 800-757-1112	Richmond	VA	23224	804-232-4551	233-0986
Millrock Div Modular Brand Group LLC 405 W St **Fax Area Code:* 617 ■ *TF:* 800-645-7625 ■ *Web:* www.millrock.com	West Bridgewater	MA	02379	508-584-0084	687-7700*
Mpo Videotronics Inc 5069 Maureen Ln *Web:* www.mpo-video.com	Moorpark	CA	93021	805-499-8513	499-8206
Nashville Display Mfg Co 306 Hartmann Dr *TF:* 800-251-1150 ■ *Web:* www.nashvilledisplay.com	Lebanon	TN	37087	615-743-2900	743-2901
New Dimensions Research Corp 260 Spagnoli Rd *TF:* 800-637-8870 ■ *Web:* www.ndrc.com	Melville	NY	11747	631-694-1356	694-6097
Ovation Instore 57-13 49th Pl *TF:* 800-553-2202 ■ *Web:* www.ovationadvantage.com	Maspeth	NY	11378	718-628-2600	628-2637
Rapid Displays 4300 W 47th St *TF:* 800-356-5775 ■ *Web:* www.rapiddisplays.com	Chicago	IL	60632	773-927-5000	927-1091
Service Products Inc 5248 S Cicero Ave **Fax Area Code:* 708	Chicago	IL	60638	773-767-2360	496-1818*
Thorco Industries Inc 1300 E 12th St *TF:* 800-445-3375 ■ *Web:* www.thorco.com	Lamar	MO	64759	417-682-3375	682-3247
Trans World Marketing Corp 360 Murray Hill Pkwy *Web:* www.transworldmarketing.com	East Rutherford	NJ	07073	201-935-5565	559-1888
United Displaycraft 333 E Touhy Ave *TF:* 877-632-8767 ■ *Web:* www.uniteddisplaycraft.com	Des Plaines	IL	60018	847-375-3800	375-3801
Universal Display & Fixtures Co 726 E Hwy 121 *TF:* 800-235-0701	Lewisville	TX	75057	972-221-5022	221-6624
Visual Marketing Inc 154 W Erie St *TF:* 800-662-8640 ■ *Web:* www.vmichicago.com	Chicago	IL	60610	312-664-9177	664-9473
Vulcan Industries Inc 300 Display Dr *TF:* 888-444-4417 ■ *Web:* www.vulcanind.com	Moody	AL	35004	205-640-2400	640-2412

DOOR & WINDOW GLASS

SEE Glass - Flat, Plate, Tempered p. 1906

237 DOORS & WINDOWS - METAL

SEE ALSO Shutters - Window (All Types) p. 2656

Company	City	State	Zip	Phone	Fax
Aluma-Glass Industries Inc 909 N Orchard St *Web:* www.atkinsonsmirrorandglass.com	Boise	ID	83706	208-375-0326	375-3774
Amsco Windows Inc 1880 S 1045 W **Fax Area Code:* 800 ■ *TF:* 800-748-4661 ■ *Web:* www.amscowindows.com	Salt Lake City	UT	84104	801-978-5000	862-6726*
Anemostat 1220 Watsoncenter Rd PO Box 4938 *TF:* 800-982-9000 ■ *Web:* www.anemostat.com	Carson	CA	90745	310-835-7500	835-0448
Asi Technologies Inc 5848 N 95th Ct *TF:* 800-558-7068 ■ *Web:* www.asidoors.com	Milwaukee	WI	53225	414-464-6200	464-9863
ASSA ABLOY Door Security Solutions 110 Sargent Dr **Fax:* Sales ■ *TF:* 800-377-3948 ■ *Web:* www.assaabloydss.com	New Haven	CT	06511	203-624-5225	777-9042*
Atrium Cos Inc 3890 W NW Hwy Suite 500 *TF:* 800-421-6292 ■ *Web:* www.atriumcompanies.com	Dallas	TX	75220	214-630-5757	630-5001
Babcock-Davis 9300 73rd Ave N *TF:* 888-412-3726 ■ *Web:* www.babcock-davis.com	Brooklyn Park	MN	55428	763-488-9247	488-9248
Ceco Door 9159 Telecom Dr *Web:* www.cecodoor.com	Milan	TN	38358	731-686-8345	686-4211
Champion Aluminum Corp 140 Eileen Way *Web:* www.championwindows.com	Syosset	NY	11791	516-921-6200	921-6370
Clopay Bldg Products Inc 320 10th Ave **Fax Area Code:* 800 ■ *TF:* 800-621-3667 ■ *Web:* www.clopaydoor.com	Baldwin	WI	54002	715-684-3223	545-0664*
Columbia Extrusion Corp 1200 E Washington St *TF:* 800-668-1645 ■ *Web:* www.ccbpwin.com	Rockwall	TX	75087	972-771-5362	722-6033
Columbia Mfg Corp 14400 S San Pedro St *TF:* 800-729-3667 ■ *Web:* www.columbiamfg.com	Gardena	CA	90248	310-327-9300	323-9862
Comprehensive Mfg Services LLC 3044 Lambdin Ave *TF:* 800-533-5760	Saint Louis	MO	63115	314-533-5700	533-5720
Cook & Boardman Inc 9347 D Ducks Ln Suite A *Web:* www.cookandboardman.com	Charlotte	NC	28273	704-334-8683	334-9366
Cookson Co 2417 S 50th Ave *TF:* 800-294-4358 ■ *Web:* www.cooksondoor.com	Phoenix	AZ	85043	602-272-4244	233-2132
Cornell Iron Works Inc 24 Elmwood Rd *TF:* 800-233-8366 ■ *Web:* www.cornelliron.com	Mountain Top	PA	18707	570-474-6773	474-9973
Creation Group Inc 53032 County Rd 13 PO Box 1025 *TF:* 800-862-3131 ■ *Web:* www.creationgroup.com	Elkhart	IN	46515	574-264-3131	264-6268
Curries Co 1502 12th St NW *Web:* www.curries.com	Mason City	IA	50401	641-423-1334	424-8305
Dawson Metal Co Inc 825 Allen St *TF:* 877-732-9766 ■ *Web:* www.dawsonmetal.com	Jamestown	NY	14701	716-664-3815	664-3485
Dent & Ding Appliance Co 4020 W Reno *TF:* 800-785-2620 ■ *Web:* www.dentandding.com	Oklahoma City	OK	73107	405-917-1610	949-5539
Dominion Bldg Products 6949 Fairbanks N Houston Rd *Web:* www.dominionproducts.com	Houston	TX	77040	713-466-6790	466-8177
Door Components Inc 7980 Redwood Ave *TF:* 866-989-3667 ■ *Web:* www.doorcomponents.com	Fontana	CA	92336	909-770-5700	
Drew Industries Inc 200 Mamaroneck Ave Suite 301 *NYSE: DW* ■ *Web:* www.drewindustries.com	White Plains	NY	10601	914-428-9098	428-4581
Dunbarton Corp 868 Murray Rd *TF:* 800-633-7553 ■ *Web:* www.dunbarton.com	Dothan	AL	36303	334-794-0661	793-7022
Eastern Garage Door 417 Canal St *TF:* 800-766-6012 ■ *Web:* www.lawrenceplate.com	Lawrence	MA	01842	978-683-3158	794-0745
EFCO Corp 1000 County Rd *TF:* 800-221-4169 ■ *Web:* www.efcocorp.com	Monett	MO	65708	417-235-3193	235-7313
Elixir Industries Inc 24800 Chrisanta Dr Suite 210 *TF:* 800-421-1942 ■ *Web:* www.elixirind.com	Mission Viejo	CA	92691	949-860-5000	860-5011
Ellison Bronze Co Inc 125 W Main St *TF:* 800-665-6445 ■ *Web:* www.ellison-bronze.com	Falconer	NY	14733	716-665-6522	665-5552
Emco Specialties Inc 2121 E Walnut St *TF Cust Svc:* 800-933-3626 ■ *Web:* www.forever.com	Des Moines	IA	50317	515-265-6101	299-8765
Empire Pacific Industries 10255 SW Spokane Ct PO Box 4210 *TF:* 800-473-7013 ■ *Web:* www.empirepacificwindows.com	Tualatin	OR	97062	503-692-6167	692-3075
Engineered Products Inc 1844 Ardmore Blvd *TF:* 800-245-4814 ■ *Web:* www.epimetal.com	Pittsburgh	PA	15221	412-242-6900	242-5205
Fimbel Architectural Door Specialties LLC PO Box 96 *Web:* www.fimbelarchitecturaldoor.com	Whitehouse	NJ	08888	908-534-1732	
Fleming Door Products Ltd 20 Barr Rd *TF:* 800-263-7515 ■ *Web:* www.flemingdoor.com	Ajax	ON	L1S3X9	905-683-3667	427-1668
General Aluminum Co of Texas LLP 1001 W Crosby Rd *TF:* 800-727-0835 ■ *Web:* www.gactx.com	Carrollton	TX	75006	972-242-5271	242-7322
GlassCraft Door Co 2002 Brittmoore Rd *TF:* 800-766-2196 ■ *Web:* www.gcdoor.com	Houston	TX	77043	713-690-8282	690-2919
Graef Windows Inc 1750 Indian Woods Cir *TF:* 800-877-2911	Youngstown	OH	44512	330-629-2999	629-2999
Graham Architectural Products Corp 1551 Mt Rose Ave **Fax Area Code:* 711 ■ *TF:* 800-755-6274 ■ *Web:* www.grahamwindows.com	York	PA	17403	717-849-8100	813-5344*
Habersham Metal Products Co 264 Stapleton Rd *Web:* www.habershammetal.com	Cornelia	GA	30531	706-778-2212	778-2769
Hehr International Inc 3333 Casitas Ave *Web:* www.hehrintl.com	Los Angeles	CA	90039	323-663-1261	666-9458
Homeshield 7942 N 3350 E Rd *TF:* 800-323-2512 ■ *Web:* www.home-shield.com	Chatsworth	IL	60921	815-635-3171	635-3551
Hope's Windows Inc 84 Hopkins Ave PO Box 580 *Web:* www.hopeswindows.com	Jamestown	NY	14702	716-665-5124	665-3365
Hufcor Inc 2101 Kennedy Rd *TF:* 800-356-6968 ■ *Web:* www.hufcor.com	Janesville	WI	53545	608-756-1241	756-1246
Hygrade Metal Moulding Mfg Corp 1990 Highland Ave *TF:* 800-645-9475 ■ *Web:* www.hygrademetal.com	Bethlehem	PA	18020	610-866-2441	866-3761

Company	City	State	ZIP	Phone	Fax
International Aluminum Corp 767 Monterey Pass Rd *Web:* www.intlalum.com	Monterey Park	CA	91754	323-264-1670	266-3838
International Revolving Door Co 2138 N 6th Ave *TF:* 800-745-4726 ■ *Web:* www.internationalrevolvingdoors.com	Evansville	IN	47710	812-425-3311	426-2682
International Window Corp 5625 E Firestone Blvd *TF:* 800-477-4032 ■ *Web:* www.intlwindow.com	South Gate	CA	90280	562-928-6411	928-3492
J T Walker Industries Inc 1310 N Hercules Ave	Clearwater	FL	33765	727-461-0501	443-7167
Jamison Door Co 55 JV Jamison Dr PO Box 70 *Fax Area Code: 240 ■ *TF:* 800-532-3667 ■ *Web:* www.jamison-door.com	Hagerstown	MD	21740	301-733-3100	329-5155*
Jantek Industries 230 Rt 70	Medford	NJ	08055	609-654-1030	654-1083
Jordan Co PO Box 18377 *TF:* 800-888-8848 ■ *Web:* www.jordancompany.com	Memphis	TN	38181	901-363-2121	362-5051
Kane Mfg Corp 515 N Fraley St *TF:* 800-952-6399 ■ *Web:* www.kanescreens.com	Kane	PA	16735	814-837-6464	837-6230
Kawneer Co Inc 555 Guthridge Ct *Web:* www.kawneer.com	Norcross	GA	30092	770-449-5555	734-1560
Kinro Inc 4381 W Green Oaks Blvd Suite 200 *Web:* www.kinro.com	Arlington	TX	76016	817-483-7791	478-8649
Krieger Specialty Products Co 4880 Gregg Rd *TF:* 866-203-5060 ■ *Web:* www.kriegerproducts.com	Pico Rivera	CA	90660	562-695-0645	692-0146
LaForce Inc 1060 W Mason St *TF:* 800-236-8858 ■ *Web:* www.laforceinc.com	Green Bay	WI	54303	920-497-7100	497-4955
Lausell Inc PO Box 938 *TF:* 800-981-7724 ■ *Web:* www.lausell.com	Bayamon	PR	00960	787-798-7610	740-3415
Lockheed Window Corp Rt 100 PO Box 166 *TF:* 800-537-3061 ■ *Web:* www.lockheedwindow.com	Pascoag	RI	02859	401-568-3061	568-2273
Loxcreen Co Inc The 1630 Old Dunbar Rd PO Box 4004 *TF:* 800-394-8667 ■ *Web:* www.loxcreen.com	West Columbia	SC	29172	803-822-8200	822-8547
M-D Bldg Products Inc 4041 N Santa Fe Ave *TF Cust Svc:* 800-654-8454 ■ *Web:* www.mdteam.com	Oklahoma City	OK	73118	405-528-4411	
Mannix Architectural Window Products 345 Crooked Hill Rd *TF:* 800-752-6483	Brentwood	NY	11717	631-231-0800	231-0571
McKeon Door Co 44 Sawgrass Dr *TF:* 800-266-9392 ■ *Web:* www.mckeondoor.com	Bellport	NY	11713	631-803-3000	803-3030
MI Windows & Doors Inc 650 W Market St *TF:* 800-949-3818 ■ *Web:* www.miwd.com	Gratz	PA	17030	717-365-3300	365-3780
Milgard Mfg 1010 54th Ave E *TF:* 800-562-8444 ■ *Web:* www.milgard.com	Tacoma	WA	98424	253-922-2030	926-0848
Milgo Industrial Inc 68 Lombardi St *Web:* www.milgo-bufkin.com	Brooklyn	NY	11222	718-388-4363	963-0614
MM Systems Corp 50 MM Way *TF:* 800-241-3460 ■ *Web:* www.mmsystemscorp.com	Pendergrass	GA	30567	706-824-7500	824-7501
Moss Supply Co Inc 5001 N Graham St *TF:* 800-438-0770 ■ *Web:* www.mosssupply.com	Charlotte	NC	28269	704-596-8717	598-9012
MW Manufacturers Inc 433 N Main St *Fax Area Code: 800 ■ *TF:* 888-999-8400 ■ *Web:* www.mwwindows.com	Rocky Mount	VA	24151	540-483-0211	950-3220*
Napoleon/Lynx 111 Weires Dr *TF:* 800-338-5399 ■ *Web:* www.lynx-nsw.com	Archbold	OH	43502	419-445-1010	446-2616
National Guard Products Inc 4985 E Raines Rd *Fax Area Code: 800 ■ *TF:* 800-647-7874 ■ *Web:* www.ngpinc.com	Memphis	TN	38118	901-795-6900	255-7874*
Northeast Bldg Products Corp 4280 Aramingo Ave *Web:* www.nbpcorporation.com	Philadelphia	PA	19124	215-535-7110	288-9880
Nu-Air Windows & Doors Inc 107 S 26th St PO Box 569 *Fax Area Code: 866 ■ *TF:* 800-282-6627 ■ *Web:* www.nuair.com	Gadsden	AL	35904	800-282-6627	521-3391*
Nystrom Inc 9300 73rd Ave N *Fax Area Code: 800 ■ *TF:* 800-547-2635 ■ *Web:* www.nystrom.com	Brooklyn Park	MN	55428	763-488-9200	317-8770*
O'Keeffe's Inc 325 Newhall St *TF:* 888-653-3333 ■ *Web:* www.okeeffes.com	San Francisco	CA	94124	415-822-4222	822-5222
Overhead Door Corp 2501 S State Hwy 121 Bus Suite 200 *TF:* 800-275-3290 ■ *Web:* www.overheaddoor.com	Louisville	TX	75067	469-549-7100	549-7281
Overly Mfg Co 574 W Otterman St *TF:* 800-979-7300 ■ *Web:* www.overly.com	Greensburg	PA	15601	724-834-7300	830-2871
Peachtree Doors & Windows Inc 2744 Ramsey Rd *TF:* 800-443-5692 ■ *Web:* www.peachtreedoor.com	Gainesville	GA	30501	770-534-8070	538-5331
Peelle Co 373 Smithtown Byp # 311 *TF:* 800-645-1056 ■ *Web:* www.peelledoor.com	Hauppauge	NY	11788	631-231-6000	231-6059
Peerless Products Inc 2403 S Main St *TF:* 800-279-9999 ■ *Web:* www.peerlessproducts.com	Fort Scott	KS	66701	620-223-4610	224-3107
PGT Industries 1070 Technology Dr *TF:* 800-282-6019 ■ *Web:* www.pgtindustries.com	Nokomis	FL	34275	941-480-1600	480-2755
Pioneer Industries Inc 171 S Newman St *Web:* www.pioneerindustries.com	Hackensack	NJ	07601	201-933-1900	933-9580
Portal Inc 10 Tracy Dr *TF:* 800-966-3030 ■ *Web:* www.portal-national.com	Avon	MA	02322	508-588-3030	580-9943
Public Supply Co Inc 1236 NW 4th St *TF:* 800-259-6355 ■ *Web:* www.publicsupply.com	Oklahoma City	OK	73106	405-272-9621	272-9835
Pyramid Mouldings Inc 300 S Magnolia Ave *Web:* www.pyramidmouldings.com	Green Cove Springs	FL	32043	904-284-5611	284-1705
Quaker Window Products Inc 504 S Hwy 63 PO Box 128 *TF:* 800-347-0438 ■ *Web:* www.quakerwindows.com	Freeburg	MO	65035	573-744-5211	744-5586
Raynor Garage Doors 1101 E River Rd *Fax: Cust Svc ■ *TF:* 800-472-9667 ■ *Web:* www.raynor.com	Dixon	IL	61021	815-288-1431	288-3720*
RC Aluminum Industries Inc 2805 NW 75th Ave *Web:* www.rcalum.com	Miami	FL	33122	305-592-1515	592-2184
Rebco Inc 1171-1225 Madison Ave *TF:* 800-777-0787 ■ *Web:* www.rebcoinc.com	Paterson	NJ	07509	973-684-0200	684-0118
Reese Enterprises Inc 16350 Asher Ave *TF:* 800-328-0953 ■ *Web:* www.reeseusa.com	Rosemount	MN	55068	651-423-1126	423-2662
Richards-Wilcox Inc 600 S Lake St *TF:* 800-253-5668 ■ *Web:* www.richardswilcox.com	Aurora	IL	60506	630-897-6951	897-6994
Sellmore Industries Inc 815 Smith St *Web:* www.sellmoreind.com	Buffalo	NY	14206	716-854-1600	856-4509
Silver Line Bldg Products 1 Silver Line Dr *TF Sales:* 800-234-4228 ■ *Web:* www.silverlinewindow.com	North Brunswick	NJ	08902	732-435-1000	418-0190
Southeastern Aluminum Products Inc 6701 Suemac Pl *TF Sales:* 800-243-8200 ■ *Web:* www.southeasternaluminum.com	Jacksonville	FL	32254	904-781-8200	224-8068
Southeastern Metals Mfg Co Inc 11801 Industry Dr *TF:* 800-874-2335 ■ *Web:* www.semetals.com	Jacksonville	FL	32218	904-757-4200	696-7542
Special-Lite Inc PO Box 6 *TF:* 800-821-6531 ■ *Web:* www.special-lite.com	Decatur	MI	49045	269-423-7068	423-7610
Stanley Access Technologies 65 Scott Swamp Rd *Fax Area Code: 877 ■ *Fax: Cust Svc ■ *TF:* 800-722-2377 ■ *Web:* www.stanleyaccesstechnologies.com	Farmington	CT	06032	860-677-2861	339-7923*
Stanley Home Decor 480 Myrtle St *TF:* 800-782-6539	New Britain	CT	06053	860-225-5111	827-3895
Steelcraft Mfg Co 9017 Blue Ash Rd *TF Cust Svc:* 800-930-8585 ■ *Web:* www.steelcraft.com	Cincinnati	OH	45242	513-745-6400	745-6300
Steves & Sons Inc 203 Humble Ave *Fax: Sales ■ *TF Sales:* 800-627-5111 ■ *Web:* www.stevesdoors.com	San Antonio	TX	78225	210-924-5111	924-0470*
Super Sky Products Inc 10301 N Enterprise Dr *TF:* 800-558-0467 ■ *Web:* www.supersky.com	Mequon	WI	53092	262-242-2000	242-7409
Taylor Bldg Products 631 N 1st St *TF:* 800-248-3600 ■ *Web:* www.taylordoor.com	West Branch	MI	48661	989-345-5110	345-5116
Therma-Tru Corp 1750 Indian Wood Cir *TF:* 800-537-8827 ■ *Web:* www.thermatru.com	Maumee	OH	43537	419-891-7400	891-7411
Thermo-Twin Industries Inc 1155 Allegheny Ave *TF:* 800-641-2211 ■ *Web:* www.thermotwin.com	Oakmont	PA	15139	412-826-1000	435-0388
TKO Dock Doors N56 W24701 N Corporate Cir Suite A *TF:* 800-575-3366 ■ *Web:* www.tkodoors.com	Sussex	WI	53089	262-820-1217	820-1273
TM Window & Door 601 NW 12th Ave *TF:* 800-511-1746 ■ *Web:* www.floridasbestwindow.com	Pompano Beach	FL	33069	954-781-4430	781-3595
TRACO 71 Progress Ave *TF:* 800-468-7226 ■ *Web:* www.alcoa.com	Cranberry Township	PA	16066	724-776-7000	776-7014
Trussbilt LLC 2112 Old Hwy 8 NW *Web:* www.trussbilt.com	New Brighton	MN	55112	651-633-6100	633-7100
Tubelite Inc 4878 Mackinaw Trail *TF:* 800-866-2227 ■ *Web:* www.tubeliteinc.com	Reed City	MI	49677	231-832-2211	832-4392
Wayne-Dalton Corp 1 Door Dr PO Box 67 *TF:* 800-827-3667 ■ *Web:* www.wayne-dalton.com	Mount Hope	OH	44660	330-674-7015	763-8047
West Window Corp 226 Industrial Pk Dr *TF:* 800-446-4167 ■ *Web:* www.westwindow.com	Martinsville	VA	24112	276-638-2394	638-2300
Western Window Systems 5621 S 25th St *TF:* 877-268-1300 ■ *Web:* www.westernwindowsystems.com	Phoenix	AZ	85040	602-268-1300	243-3119
Willo Products Co Inc 714 Willo Industrial Dr SE *TF:* 800-633-3276 ■ *Web:* www.willoproducts.com	Decatur	AL	35601	256-353-7161	350-8436
Winco Window Co Inc 6200 Maple Ave *TF:* 800-525-8089 ■ *Web:* www.wincowindow.com	Saint Louis	MO	63130	314-725-8088	725-1419
Window Mart Inc PO Box 570 *TF:* 888-283-6278 ■ *Web:* www.windowmart.com	Royal	AR	71968	501-760-4730	760-4725
Won-Door Corp 1865 S 3480 W *TF:* 800-453-8494 ■ *Web:* www.wondoor.com	Salt Lake City	UT	84104	801-973-7500	974-5273
Yale Ogron Mfg Co Inc 671 W 18th St	Hialeah	FL	33010	305-887-2646	883-1309
Young Windows Inc 680 Colwell Ln *Web:* www.youngwindows.com	Conshohocken	PA	19428	610-828-5422	828-2144

238 DOORS & WINDOWS - VINYL

Company	City	State	ZIP	Phone	Fax
Alenco Window Holding LLC 615 Carson St *Web:* www.alenco.com	Bryan	TX	77801	979-779-7770	822-3259
American Exteriors LLC 1169 W Littleton Blvd *TF:* 800-794-6369 ■ *Web:* www.800-7window.com	Littleton	CO	80120	303-794-6369	730-5744
Amerimax Bldg Products Inc 5208 Tennyson Pkwy Suite 100 *TF:* 800-258-6295 ■ *Web:* www.amerimaxbp.com	Plano	TX	75024	469-366-3200	366-3260
Associated Materials Inc Alside Div PO Box 2010 *TF Cust Svc:* 800-922-6009 ■ *Web:* www.alside.com	Akron	OH	44309	330-929-1811	922-2354
Benjamin F Rich Co PO Box 6031 *TF:* 800-237-4241 ■ *Web:* www.bfrich.com	Newark	DE	19714	302-894-0498	894-0499
CertainTeed Corp 750 E Swedesford Rd *TF Prod Info:* 800-782-8777 ■ *Web:* www.certainteed.com	Valley Forge	PA	19482	610-341-7000	341-7797
Champion Window Mfg Inc 12121 Champion Way *TF:* 888-653-8479 ■ *Web:* www.championwindow.com	Cincinnati	OH	45241	513-346-4600	346-4614
Chelsea Bldg Products 565 Cedar Way *Web:* www.chelseabuildingproducts.com	Oakmont	PA	15139	412-826-8077	826-1598
Fortune Brands Home & Hardware Inc 520 Lake Cook Rd *Web:* www.fortunebrands.com	Deerfield	IL	60015	847-484-4400	
Great Lakes Window Inc 30499 Tracy Rd *Fax: Hum Res ■ *Web:* www.greatlakeswindow.com	Walbridge	OH	43465	419-666-5555	661-2923*
Harry G Barr Co 6500 S Zero St *TF:* 800-829-2277 ■ *Web:* www.weatherbarr.com	Fort Smith	AR	72903	479-646-7891	646-8591
Larson Mfg Co 2333 Eastbrook Dr *TF Cust Svc:* 800-352-3360 ■ *Web:* www.larsondoors.com	Brookings	SD	57006	605-692-6115	696-6403
Mikron Industries Inc 1034 6th Ave N *TF Cust Svc:* 800-456-8020 ■ *Web:* www.mikronvinyl.com	Kent	WA	98032	253-854-8020	852-3769
Moss Supply Co Inc 5001 N Graham St *TF:* 800-438-0770 ■ *Web:* www.mosssupply.com	Charlotte	NC	28269	704-596-8717	598-9012
PGT Industries 1070 Technology Dr *TF:* 800-282-6019 ■ *Web:* www.pgtindustries.com	Nokomis	FL	34275	941-480-1600	480-2755

Company	City	State	Zip	Phone	Fax
Polybau Windows & Doors 1851 E Paradise Rd *TF:* 877-765-9228 ■ *Web:* www.polybau.com	Tracy	CA	95304	209-830-5170	830-5175
Provia Door Inc 2150 SR- 39 *TF:* 877-389-0835 ■ *Web:* www.proviadoor.com	Sugarcreek	OH	44681	330-852-4711	852-2107
Rehau Inc 1501 Edwards Ferry Rd NE *TF:* 800-247-9445 ■ *Web:* www.na.rehau.com	Leesburg	VA	20176	703-777-5255	777-3053
Royal Group The 30âRoyal Group Crescent *NYSE:* RYG ■ *Web:* www.royalbuildingproducts.com	Woodbridge	ON	L4H1X9	905-264-0701	850-9184
RubbAir Door Div Eckel Industries Inc 100 Groton Shirley Rd *TF:* 800-966-7822 ■ *Web:* www.rubbair.com	Ayer	MA	01432	978-772-0480	772-7114
Slocomb Industries Inc 801 Pencader Dr *TF:* 800-348-6233	Newark	DE	19702	302-266-7101	266-7209
Soft-Lite LLC 10250 Philipp Pkwy *TF:* 800-551-1953 ■ *Web:* www.softlitewindows.com	Streetsboro	OH	44241	330-528-3400	528-3501
Statewide Remodeling Inc 2940 N Hwy 360 Suite 300 *TF:* 800-317-8283 ■ *Web:* www.statewideremodeling.com	Grand Prairie	TX	75050	214-677-9000	
Superseal Mfg Co Inc PO Box 795 *Web:* www.supersealwindows.com	South Plainfie	NJ	07080	908-561-5910	561-7885
Thermal Industries Inc 5450 Second Ave *TF:* 800-245-1540 ■ *Web:* www.thermalindustries.com	Pittsburgh	PA	15207	412-244-6400	395-1999
Veka Inc 100 Veka Dr *TF:* 800-654-5589 ■ *Web:* www.vekainc.com	Fombell	PA	16123	724-452-1000	452-1007
VINYLMAX LLC 2921 McBride Ct *Web:* www.vinylmax.com	Hamilton	OH	45011	513-772-2247	772-3248
Weather Shield Mfg Inc 1 Weather Shield Plaza PO Box 309 **Fax Area Code:* 800 ■ *TF:* 800-222-2995 ■ *Web:* www.weathershield.com	Medford	WI	54451	715-748-2100	222-2146*
West Window Corp 226 Industrial Pk Dr *TF:* 800-446-4167 ■ *Web:* www.westwindow.com	Martinsville	VA	24112	276-638-2394	638-2300
Wilmes Window Mfg Co 234 W 23rd St *TF:* 800-477-1811	Ferdinand	IN	47532	812-367-1811	
Windsor Windows & Doors 900 S 19th St **Fax:* Cust Svc ■ *TF:* 800-218-6186 ■ *Web:* www.windsorwindows.com	West Des Moines	IA	50265	515-223-6660	224-1938*

239 DOORS & WINDOWS - WOOD

SEE ALSO Millwork p. 2248; Shutters - Window (All Types) p. 2656

Company	City	State	Zip	Phone	Fax
Algoma Hardwoods Inc 1001 Perry St *TF:* 800-678-8910 ■ *Web:* www.algomahardwoods.com	Algoma	WI	54201	920-487-5221	487-3636
Allwood Door Co Inc 6000 3rd St	San Francisco	CA	94124	415-822-8900	822-5832
Andersen Corp 100 4th Ave N **Fax:* Hum Res ■ *TF:* 888-888-7020 ■ *Web:* www.andersencorp.com	Bayport	MN	55003	651-264-5150	264-5526*
Burton Lumber Corp 835 Wilson Rd	Chesapeake	VA	23324	757-545-4613	545-8852
Combination Door Co 1000 Morris St *Web:* www.combinationdoor.com	Fond du Lac	WI	54935	920-922-2050	922-2917
Donlin Co Inc 3405 Energy Dr PO Box 8 *TF:* 800-892-7015 ■ *Web:* www.donlin.com	Saint Cloud	MN	56302	320-251-3680	251-3680
General Doors Corp 1 Monroe St PO Box 205 *Web:* www.general-doors.com	Bristol	PA	19007	215-788-9277	788-9450
Haley Bros Inc 6291 Orangethorpe Ave *TF:* 800-848-3240 ■ *Web:* www.haleybros.com	Buena Park	CA	90620	714-670-2112	994-6971
Industrial Door Co Inc 360 Coon Rapids Blvd *TF:* 888-798-0199 ■ *Web:* www.idcdoors.com	Minneapolis	MN	55433	763-786-4730	786-9186
Jenkins Mfg Co Inc PO Box 249 **Fax Area Code:* 800 ■ *TF:* 800-633-2323	Anniston	AL	36202	256-831-7000	261-6116*
King Sash & Door Inc PO Box 1029 *Web:* www.kingsashanddoor.com	Mocksville	NC	27028	336-768-4650	
Larson Mfg Co 2333 Eastbrook Dr *TF Cust Svc:* 800-352-3360 ■ *Web:* www.larsondoors.com	Brookings	SD	57006	605-692-6115	696-6403
Lincoln Wood Products Inc 701 N State St *TF:* 800-967-2461 ■ *Web:* www.lincolnwindows.com	Merrill	WI	54452	715-536-2461	536-7090
Marvin Windows & Doors 104 State Ave N PO Box 100 *TF:* 800-346-5044 ■ *Web:* www.marvin.com	Warroad	MN	56763	218-386-1430	386-1904
Masonite International Corp 1 Tampa City Ctr 201 N Franklin St Suite 300 *TF:* 800-895-2723 ■ *Web:* www.masonite.com	Tampa	FL	33602	813-877-2726	739-0204
Mathews Bros Co 22 Perkins Rd PO Box 345 *TF:* 800-639-7203 ■ *Web:* www.mathewsbrothers.com	Belfast	ME	04915	207-338-3360	338-6300
McPhillips Mfg Co Inc PO Box 169 *TF:* 800-348-6274	Mobile	AL	36601	251-438-1681	438-1338
Mohawk Flush Doors Inc 980 Pt Township Dr PO Box 112 *Web:* www.mohawkdoors.com	Northumberland	PA	17857	570-473-3557	473-3737
Peachtree Doors & Windows Inc 2744 Ramsey Rd *TF:* 800-443-5692 ■ *Web:* www.peachtreedoor.com	Gainesville	GA	30501	770-534-8070	538-5331
Pella Corp 102 Main St *TF Cust Svc:* 800-288-7281 ■ *Web:* www.pella.com	Pella	IA	50219	641-628-1000	628-6070
Quaker Window Products Inc 504 S Hwy 63 PO Box 128 *TF:* 800-347-0438 ■ *Web:* www.quakerwindows.com	Freeburg	MO	65035	573-744-5211	744-5586
Semling-Menke Co Inc PO Box 378 *TF:* 800-333-2206 ■ *Web:* www.semcowindows.com	Merrill	WI	54452	715-536-9411	536-3067
SNE Enterprises Inc 880 Southview Dr **Fax:* Hum Res ■ *TF:* 800-826-1707	Mosinee	WI	54455	715-693-7000	693-8505*
Steves & Sons Inc 203 Humble Ave **Fax:* Sales ■ *TF Sales:* 800-627-5111 ■ *Web:* www.stevesdoors.com	San Antonio	TX	78225	210-924-5111	924-0470*
Trustile Doors LLC 1780 E 66th Ave *TF:* 866-442-5302 ■ *Web:* www.trustile.com	Denver	CO	80229	303-286-3931	288-6521
Vancouver Door Co Inc 203 5th St NW *TF:* 800-999-3667 ■ *Web:* www.vancouverdoorco.com	Puyallup	WA	98371	253-845-9581	845-3364
Weather Shield Mfg Inc 1 Weather Shield Plaza PO Box 309 **Fax Area Code:* 800 ■ *TF:* 800-222-2995 ■ *Web:* www.weathershield.com	Medford	WI	54451	715-748-2100	222-2146*
WIL-C-MEEK Corp 1311 E Woodhurst Dr PO Box 1746 *Web:* midwest.meeks.com	Springfield	MO	65804	417-521-2801	521-2870
Windsor Windows & Doors 900 S 19th St **Fax:* Cust Svc ■ *TF:* 800-218-6186 ■ *Web:* www.windsorwindows.com	West Des Moines	IA	50265	515-223-6660	224-1938*

240 DRUG STORES

SEE ALSO Health Food Stores p. 2009

Company	City	State	Zip	Phone	Fax
Assured Pharmacy Inc 17935 Sky Pk Cir Suite F *PINK:* APHY	Irvine	CA	92624	949-222-9971	222-0978
Bartell Drug Co 4727 Denver Ave S *TF:* 877-227-8355 ■ *Web:* www.bartelldrugs.com	Seattle	WA	98134	206-763-2626	763-2062
CVS Corp 1 CVS Dr *NYSE:* CVS ■ **Fax:* Cust Svc ■ *TF Cust Svc:* 888-607-4287 ■ *Web:* www.cvs.com	Woonsocket	RI	02895	401-765-1500	765-1500*
CVS ProCare Pharmacy 695 George Washington Hwy *Web:* www.cvsprocare.com	Lincoln	RI	02865	401-334-0069	
Diamond Drugs Inc 645 Kolter Dr *Web:* www.diamondpharmacy.com	Indiana	PA	15701	724-349-1111	349-2945
Discount Drug Mart Inc 211 Commerce Dr *Web:* www.discount-drugmart.com	Medina	OH	44256	330-725-2340	722-2990
Doc's Drugs 230 Comet Dr *Web:* www.docsdrugs.com	Braidwood	IL	60408	815-458-6104	458-6158
Drugstore.com Inc 411 108th Ave NE Suite 1400 *NASDAQ:* DSCM ■ *TF:* 800-378-4786 ■ *Web:* www.drugstore.com	Bellevue	WA	98004	425-372-3200	372-3800
Duane Reade Inc 42 W Broad St *Web:* www.duanereade.com	Mount Vernon	NY	10552	914-664-3900	664-7580
Fagen Pharmacy 915 S Halleck St PO Box 662 *Web:* www.fagenpharmacy.com	Demotte	IN	46310	219-987-6468	987-7226
Feelbest.com 778 Bank St *TF:* 888-689-9890 ■ *Web:* www.feelbest.com	Ottawa	ON	K1S3V6	613-234-4643	234-8432
Fruth Pharmacy Inc Rt 62 N *Web:* www.fruthpharmacy.com	Point Pleasant	WV	25550	304-675-1612	675-7338
Gemmel Pharmacy Group Inc 143 N Euclid Ave *Web:* www.gemmelrx.com	Ontario	CA	91762	909-988-5805	983-2737
Graymark Healthcare Inc 210 Pk Ave Suite 1350 *NASDAQ:* GRMH ■ *Web:* www.graymarkhealthcare.com	Oklahoma City	OK	73102	405-601-5300	601-4550
Harmon Stores Inc 650 Liberty Ave *TF:* 866-427-6661 ■ *Web:* www.facevaluesonline.com	Union	NJ	07083	908-688-7023	688-4876
Hartig Drug Co 703 Main St PO Box 709 *Web:* www.hartigdrug.com	Dubuque	IA	52004	563-588-8700	588-8750
Hi-School Pharmacy Inc 915 W 11th St *Web:* www.hi-schoolpharmacy.com	Vancouver	WA	98660	360-693-5879	694-5161
Hy-Vee Drug Stores 5820 Westown Pkwy *Web:* www.hy-vee.com/pharmacy/pharmacy.asp	West Des Moines	IA	50266	515-267-2800	327-2162
Jean Coutu Group (PJC) Inc 530 Rue Beriault *TSE:* PJC.A ■ **Fax:* PR ■ *TF:* 877-695-6175 ■ *Web:* www.jeancoutu.com	Longueuil	QC	J4G1S8	450-646-9760	646-5649*
Katz Group 10104 103rd Ave Suite 1702 Bell Tower *TF:* 877-378-4100 ■ *Web:* www.katzgroup.ca	Edmonton	AB	T5J0H8	780-990-0505	
Keltsch Pharmacy Inc 4118 N Clinton St	Fort Wayne	IN	46805	260-483-9537	484-5034
Kerr Drug Stores Inc 3220 Spring Forest Rd *TF:* 800-494-3053 ■ *Web:* www.kerrdrug.com	Raleigh	NC	27616	919-544-3896	544-3796
Kinney Drugs Inc 520 E Main St *Web:* www.kinneys.com	Gouverneur	NY	13642	315-287-3600	
Lewis Drug Inc 4409 E 26th St *TF:* 800-658-3620 ■ *Web:* www.lewisdrug.com	Sioux Falls	SD	57103	605-367-2000	367-2876
Liberty Drug & Surgical Inc 195 Main St *Web:* www.libertydrug.com	Chatham	NJ	07928	973-635-6200	635-6208
Love Stores 144 W 72nd St	New York	NY	10023	212-877-5351	877-5135
Mast Drug Co Inc 1910 Ross Mill Rd *Web:* www.mastdrug.com	Henderson	NC	27537	252-438-3112	492-4096
Medicap Pharmacies Inc 4350 Westown Pkwy Suite 400 *TF Cust Svc:* 800-445-2244 ■ *Web:* www.medicaprx.com	West Des Moines	IA	50266	515-224-8400	224-8415
Medicine Shoppe International Inc 7000 Cardinal Pl *TF Cust Svc:* 800-325-1397 ■ *Web:* www.medicineshoppe.com	Dublin	OH	43017	314-993-6000	872-5500
MediServ Inc 3684 Trabue Rd	Columbus	OH	43228	614-481-4272	481-7580
Navarro Discount Pharmacies 9400 *Web:* www.navarro.com	Miami	FL	33142	305-633-3000	633-7555
Osco Drugs 250 E Pk Ctr Blvd *TF:* 800-541-2863 ■ *Web:* www.supervalu-pharmacies.com	Boise	ID	83706	208-395-6200	395-6225
Ralston Drug & Discount Liquor 3147 Southmore Blvd	Houston	TX	77004	713-524-3045	524-5981
Rite Aid Corp 30 Hunter Ln *NYSE:* RAD ■ *TF:* 800-748-3243 ■ *Web:* www.riteaid.com	Camp Hill	PA	17011	717-761-2633	975-3754
Ritzman Pharmacies Inc 8614 Hartman Rd	Wadsworth	OH	44281	330-335-2318	335-3222
Rodman's Discount Food & Drugs 4301 Randolph Rd *Web:* www.rodmans.com	Silver Spring	MD	20906	301-230-8930	946-8329
RXD Pharmacies Inc 724 Haddon Ave	Collingswood	NJ	08108	856-858-9292	858-7286
Rxusa Inc 81 Seaview Blvd *TF:* 800-764-3648 ■ *Web:* www.rxusa.com	Port Washington	NY	11050	516-467-2500	467-2539
Sav-Mor Drug Stores 43155 W Nine-Mile Rd *Web:* www.sav-mor.com	Novi	MI	48376	248-348-1570	348-4316
Sav-on Drugs Inc 21118 Bridge St	Southfield	MI	48034	248-357-4550	357-2332
Schwieterman's Drug Store Inc 2 N Washington St *TF:* 800-311-1612 ■ *Web:* www.schwietermanpharmacy.com	New Bremen	OH	45869	419-629-2336	
Shoppers Drug Mart Inc 243 Consumers Rd *TSX:* SC ■ *Web:* www1.shoppersdrugmart.ca	Toronto	ON	M2J4W8	416-493-1220	

	Phone	Fax
Stephen L LaFrance Pharmacy Inc 3017 N Midland Dr . . . Pine Bluff AR 71603 *Web:* www.usadrug.com	870-535-2411	535-5601
Thrifty White Stores 6901 E Fish Lake Rd Suite 118 . . . Maple Grove MN 55369 *Fax Area Code: 800 ■ *TF:* 800-816-2887 ■ *Web:* www.thriftywhite.com	763-513-4300	816-2823*
Value Drugs 17 Green St . . . Huntington NY 11743	631-271-6663	271-5267
Vitacost.com Inc 5400 Broken Sound Blvd NW Suite 500 . . . Boynton Beach FL 33487 *TF:* 800-793-2601 ■ *Web:* www.vitacost.com	561-752-8888	443-7721
Vitamin Shoppe Inc 2101 91st St . . . North Bergen NJ 07047 *Fax Area Code: 800 ■ *TF:* 800-223-1216 ■ *Web:* www.vitaminshoppe.com	201-868-5959	852-7153*
Walgreen Co 200 Wilmot Rd . . . Deerfield IL 60015 *NYSE:* WAG ■ *TF Cust Svc:* 800-289-2273 ■ *Web:* www.walgreens.com	847-940-2500	236-0862

DRUGS - MFR

SEE Biotechnology Companies p. 1525; Diagnostic Products p. 1784; Medicinal Chemicals & Botanical Products p. 2231; Pharmaceutical Companies p. 2414; Pharmaceutical Companies - Generic Drugs p. 2416; Pharmaceutical & Diagnostic Products - Veterinary p. 2417; Vitamins & Nutritional Supplements p. 2762

241 DRUGS & PERSONAL CARE PRODUCTS - WHOL

Companies Listed Here Distribute Pharmaceuticals, Over-The-Counter (Otc) Drugs, And/Or Personal Care Products Typically Found In Drug Stores.

	Phone	Fax
Agion Technologies Inc 60 Audubon Rd . . . Wakefield MA 01880 *Web:* www.agion-tech.com	781-224-7100	246-3340
American Herbal Products 1440 JFK Cswy Suite 400 . . . North Bay Village FL 33141 *TF Cust Svc:* 888-446-6884 ■ *Web:* www.immuvit.com	305-865-2919	865-1538
AmerisourceBergen Corp 1300 Morris Dr Suite 100 PO Box 959 . . . Chesterbrook PA 19087 *NYSE:* ABC ■ *TF:* 800-829-3132 ■ *Web:* www.amerisourcebergen.net	610-727-7000	727-3600
Anderson Wholesale Co PO Box 69 . . . Muskogee OK 74402 *TF:* 800-324-9656 ■ *Web:* www.andersonwholesale.com	918-682-5568	687-9567
Bellco Health Corp 5500 New Horizons Blvd . . . North Amityville NY 11701 *TF:* 800-645-5314 ■ *Web:* www.bellcoonline.com	631-789-6300	841-6185
Cadeau Express Inc 3494 E Sunset Rd . . . Las Vegas NV 89120 *TF:* 800-240-0301 ■ *Web:* www.cadeauexpress.com	702-433-1333	
Camphor Technologies Inc 183 Providence New London . . . North Stonington CT 06359 *TF:* 888-608-8884 ■ *Web:* www.camphortech.com	860-535-0241	535-0341
Cardinal Health Distribution 7000 Cardinal Pl . . . Dublin OH 43017 *TF:* 800-234-8701 ■ *Web:* www.cardinal.com	614-757-5000	757-6000
Cardinal Health Nuclear Pharmacy Services 7000 Cardinal Pl . . . Dublin OH 43017 *TF:* 800-999-9098 ■ *Web:* www.nps.cardinal.com	614-757-5000	757-6000
Charles Bowman & Co Inc 3328 John F Donnelly Dr . . . Holland MI 49424 *Web:* www.charlesbowman.com	616-786-4000	786-2864
Connie Stevens Forever Spring 426 S Robertson Blvd . . . Los Angeles CA 90048 *Web:* www.foreverspring.com	310-657-5910	288-3042
Contract Pharmacy Services Inc 125 Titus Ave . . . Warrington PA 18976 *TF:* 800-555-8062 ■ *Web:* www.contractrx.com	267-487-9000	487-9050
Dakota Drug Inc 28 Main St N . . . Minot ND 58703 *TF:* 800-437-2018 ■ *Web:* www.dakdrug.com	701-852-2141	857-1134
Esscentual Brands LLC 4835 E Cactus Rd Suite 245 . . . Scottsdale AZ 85254 *Web:* www.esscentualbrands.com	602-889-4800	889-4837
HD Smith Wholesale Drug Co 4650 Industrial Dr . . . Springfield IL 62703 *TF:* 800-252-8090 ■ *Web:* www.hdsmith.com	217-529-0211	529-1546
Iredale Mineral Cosmetics Ltd 28 Church St . . . Great Barrington MA 01230 *TF:* 800-762-1132 ■ *Web:* www.janeiredale.com	413-644-9900	644-9105
JM Smith Corp 9098 Fairforest Rd . . . Spartanburg SC 29301 *Web:* www.cornerdrugstore.com	864-582-1216	591-0333
Kinray Inc 152-35 10th Ave . . . Whitestone NY 11357 *TF:* 800-854-6729 ■ *Web:* www.kinray.com	718-767-1234	767-4706
Majestic Sales Corp 1 Propritors Dr 2nd Fl PO Box 1067 . . . Marshfield MA 02050 *Web:* www.majesticsales.com	781-829-8884	829-8886
McKesson Canada 8625 TransCanada Hwy . . . Saint-Laurent QC H4S1Z6 *TF:* 800-363-7139 ■ *Web:* www.mckesson.ca	514-745-2100	745-2300
Mechanical Servants Inc 2755 Thomas St . . . Melrose Park IL 60160 *TF:* 800-351-2000 ■ *Web:* www.cvalet.com	708-486-1500	486-1501
Millbrook Distribution Services 88 Huntoon Memorial Hwy . . . Leicester MA 01524 *TF:* 800-225-7398 ■ *Web:* www.millbrookds.com	508-892-8171	892-4827
Morris & Dickson Co Ltd PO Box 51367 . . . Shreveport LA 71135 *TF:* 800-388-3833 ■ *Web:* www.morrisdickson.com	318-797-7900	798-6007
Natural Health Trends Corp 751 Canyon Dr Suite 150 . . . Coppell TX 75019 *PINK:* NHTC ■ *Web:* www.naturalhealthtrendscorp.com	972-241-4080	
North Carolina Mutual Wholesale Drug Co 816 Ellis Rd . . . Durham NC 27703 *TF:* 800-800-8551 ■ *Web:* www.mutualdrugcompany.com/?page_id=26	919-596-2151	596-1453
Parmed Pharmaceuticals Inc 4220 Hyde Pk Blvd . . . Niagara Falls NY 14305 *Fax Area Code: 800 ■ *TF:* 800-727-6331 ■ *Web:* www.parmed.com	716-284-5666	727-6330*
Pharmed Group Corp 3075 NW 107th Ave . . . Miami FL 33172	305-592-2324	591-0221
Plant Sciences Inc 342 Green Valley Rd . . . Watsonville CA 95076 *Web:* www.plantsciences.com	831-728-7771	728-4967
Procter & Gamble 1 or 2 Procter & Gamble Plaza . . . Cincinnati OH 45201	513-983-1100	983-1100
Quality King Distributors Inc 2060 9th Ave . . . Ronkonkoma NY 11779 *TF:* 800-676-5554	631-439-2000	439-2222
Reese Pharmaceutical Co 10617 Frank Ave . . . Cleveland OH 44106 *TF:* 800-321-7178 ■ *Web:* www.reesechemical.com	216-231-6441	231-6444
Respiratory Distributors Inc 110 E Azalea Ave . . . Foley AL 36535 *Fax Area Code: 800 ■ *TF:* 800-872-8672 ■ *Web:* www.rdiworld.com	251-943-5844	891-8671*
RG Shakour Inc 254 Tpke Rd . . . Westborough MA 01581 *TF:* 800-262-9090	508-366-8282	898-3212
Rochester Drug Co-op Inc 50 Jet View Dr . . . Rochester NY 14624 *TF:* 800-333-0538 ■ *Web:* www.rdcdrug.com	585-271-7220	271-3551
Sothys USA Inc 1500 NW 94th Ave . . . Miami FL 33172 *Web:* www.sothys-usa.com	305-594-4222	592-5785
Sun Healthcare Group Inc Pharmaceutical Services 101 Sun Ave NE . . . Albuquerque NM 87109 *TF:* 800-729-6600 ■ *Web:* www.sunh.com	505-468-4168	468-4344
Victory Pharma Inc 11682 El Camino Real . . . San Diego CA 92130 *TF:* 866-427-6819 ■ *Web:* www.victorypharma.com	858-720-4500	720-4501

242 DUDE RANCHES

SEE ALSO Resorts & Resort Companies p. 2542

	Phone	Fax
63 Ranch PO Box 979 . . . Livingston MT 59047 *TF:* 888-395-5151 ■ *Web:* www.sixtythree.com	406-222-0570	222-6363
7 D Ranch 7D Ranch PO Box 100 . . . Cody WY 82414 *TF:* 888-587-9885 ■ *Web:* www.7dranch.com	307-587-9885	587-9885
Absaroka Ranch PO Box 929 . . . Dubois WY 82513 *Web:* www.absarokaranch.com	307-455-2275	455-2275
Aspen Canyon Ranch 13206 County Rd 3 . . . Parshall CO 80468 *TF:* 800-321-1357 ■ *Web:* www.aspencanyon.com	970-725-3600	725-0040
Averill's Flathead Lake Lodge PO Box 248 . . . Bigfork MT 59911	406-837-4391	837-6977
Bar Lazy J Guest Ranch 447 County Rd 3 PO Box N . . . Parshall CO 80468 *TF:* 800-396-6279 ■ *Web:* www.barlazyj.com	970-725-3437	725-0121
Bar M Dude Ranch 58840 Bar M Ln . . . Adams OR 97810 *TF:* 888-824-3381 ■ *Web:* www.barmranch.com	541-566-3381	566-0100
Bellota Ranch 14301 E Speedway . . . Tucson AZ 85748 *Web:* www.bellotaranch.com	520-623-0203	721-9426
Black Mountain Ranch 4000 Conger Mesa Rd . . . McCoy CO 80463 *TF:* 800-967-2401 ■ *Web:* www.blackmtnranch.com	970-653-4226	653-4227
Bonanza Creek Country Guest Ranch 523 Bonanza Creek Rd . . . Martinsdale MT 59053 *TF:* 800-476-6045 ■ *Web:* www.bonanzacreekcountry.com	406-572-3366	572-3366
Brooks Lake Lodge & Guest Ranch 458 Brooks Lake Rd . . . Dubois WY 82513 *Web:* www.brookslake.com	307-455-2121	455-2221
Brush Creek Ranch 66 Brush Creek Ranch Rd . . . Saratoga WY 82331 *Web:* www.brushcreekranch.com	307-327-5284	327-5970
Buffalo Horn Ranch 13825 County Rd 7 . . . Meeker CO 81641 *TF:* 877-878-5450 ■ *Web:* www.buffalohorn.com	970-878-5450	
Cherokee Park Ranch 436 Cherokee Hills Dr . . . Livermore CO 80536 *TF:* 800-628-0949 ■ *Web:* www.cherokeeparkranch.com	970-493-6522	493-5802
Circle Z Ranch PO Box 194 . . . Patagonia AZ 85624 *TF:* 888-854-2525 ■ *Web:* www.circlez.com	520-394-2525	394-2058
CM Ranch 167 Fish Hatchery Rd PO Box 217 . . . Dubois WY 82513 *TF:* 800-455-0721 ■ *Web:* www.cmranch.com	307-455-2331	455-3984
Colorado Cattle Co & Guest Ranch 70008 County Rd 132 . . . New Raymer CO 80742 *Web:* www.coloradocattlecompany.com	970-437-5345	437-5432
Colorado Trails Ranch 12161 County Rd 240 . . . Durango CO 81301 *TF:* 800-323-3833 ■ *Web:* www.coloradotrails.com	970-247-5055	385-7372
Coulter Lake Guest Ranch 80 County Rd 273 . . . Rifle CO 81650 *TF:* 800-858-3046 ■ *Web:* www.coulterlake.com	970-625-1473	625-2781
Crossed Sabres Ranch 829 N Fork Hwy . . . Cody WY 82414 *TF:* 888-587-3750 ■ *Web:* www.crossedsabresranch.com	307-587-3750	587-5451
David Ranch PO Box 5 . . . Daniel WY 83115 *Web:* www.davidranch.com	307-859-8228	
Deer Valley Ranch 16825 County Rd 162 . . . Nathrop CO 81236 *TF:* 800-284-1708 ■ *Web:* www.deervalleyranch.com	719-395-2353	395-2394
Diamond J Ranch PO Box 577 . . . Ennis MT 59729 *TF:* 877-929-4867 ■ *Web:* www.ranchweb.com	406-682-4867	682-4106
Drowsy Water Ranch PO Box 147 . . . Granby CO 80446 *TF:* 800-845-2292 ■ *Web:* www.drowsywater.com	970-725-3456	725-3611
Dryhead Schively Ranch 1062 Rd 15 . . . Lovell WY 82431 *Web:* www.dryheadranch.com	307-548-6688	548-2322
Eatons' Ranch 270 Eatons' Ranch Rd . . . Wolf WY 82844 *TF:* 800-210-1049 ■ *Web:* www.eatonsranch.com	307-655-9285	655-9269
Echo Canyon Guest Ranch 12507 Echo Canyon Creek Rd PO Box 328 . . . La Veta CO 81055 *TF:* 800-341-6603 ■ *Web:* www.guestecho.com	719-742-5524	742-5525
Elk Mountain Ranch PO Box 910 . . . Buena Vista CO 81211 *TF:* 800-432-8812 ■ *Web:* www.elkmtn.com	719-539-4430	
Elkhorn Ranch HC 1 PO Box 97 . . . Tucson AZ 85736 *Web:* www.guestranches.com/elkhorn	520-822-1040	
Elkhorn Ranch Montana 33133 Gallatin Rd . . . Gallatin Gateway MT 59730 *Web:* www.elkhornranchmt.com	406-995-4291	
Flying A Ranch 771 Flying A Ranch Rd . . . Pinedale WY 82941 *TF:* 888-833-3348 ■ *Web:* www.flyinga.com	307-367-2385	
Flying E Ranch 2801 W Wickenburg Way . . . Wickenburg AZ 85390 *TF:* 888-684-2650 ■ *Web:* www.flyingeranch.com	928-684-2690	684-5304
Focus Ranch 76143 County Rd 129 . . . Slater CO 81653 *Web:* www.focusranch.com	970-583-2410	
G Bar M Ranch PO Box 29 . . . Clyde Park MT 59018 *Web:* www.gbarm.com	406-686-4423	686-4423
Grapevine Canyon Ranch Inc PO Box 302 . . . Pearce AZ 85625 *TF:* 800-245-9202 ■ *Web:* www.gcranch.com	520-826-3185	826-3636
Greenhorn Creek Guest Ranch 2116 Greenhorn Ranch Rd . . . Quincy CA 95971 *TF:* 800-334-6939 ■ *Web:* www.greenhornranch.com	530-283-0930	283-4401
Gros Ventre River Ranch PO Box 151 . . . Moose WY 83012 *Web:* www.grosventreriverranch.com	307-733-4138	733-4272

				Phone	Fax
Hawley Mountain Guest Ranch PO Box 4 *TF:* 877-496-7848 ■ *Web:* www.hawleymountain.com	McLeod	MT	59052	406-932-5791	932-5715
Heart Six Ranch 16985 Buffalo Valley Rd PO Box 70 *TF:* 888-543-2477 ■ *Web:* www.heartsix.com	Moran	WY	83013	307-543-2477	543-0918
Hidden Creek Ranch 11077 E Blue Lake Rd *TF:* 800-446-3833	Harrison	ID	83833	208-689-3209	689-9115
Hideout at Flitner Ranch Resort PO Box 206 *TF:* 800-354-8637 ■ *Web:* www.thehideout.com	Shell	WY	82441	307-765-2080	765-2681
High Island Ranch & Cattle Co 346 Amoretti St Suite 10 *Web:* www.highislandranch.com	Thermopolis	WY	82443	307-867-2374	867-2374
Historic Pines Ranch PO Box 311 *TF:* 800-446-9462	Westcliffe	CO	81252	719-783-9261	783-2977
Home Ranch PO Box 822 *TF:* 800-688-2982 ■ *Web:* www.homeranch.com	Clark	CO	80428	970-879-1780	879-1795
Homeplace Ranch RR 1 Site 2 PO Box 6 *TF:* 877-931-3245 ■ *Web:* www.homeplaceranch.com	Priddis	AB	T0L1W0	403-931-3245	931-3245
Horse Prairie Ranch 3300 Bachelor Mountain Rd **Fax Area Code:* 775 ■ *TF:* 888-726-2454 ■ *Web:* www.ranchlife.com	Dillon	MT	59725	406-681-3155	719-5312*
Hunewill Circle H Ranch 1110 Hunewill Ranch Rd *Web:* www.hunewillranch.com	Bridgeport	CA	93517	760-932-7710	932-1933
Kay El Bar Guest Ranch PO Box 2480 *TF:* 800-684-7583 ■ *Web:* www.kayelbar.com	Wickenburg	AZ	85358	928-684-7593	684-4497
King Mountain Ranch 11845 Hwy 125 N PO Box 497 *TF:* 800-476-5464	Granby	CO	80446	970-887-2511	887-9511
Lake Mancos Ranch 42688 Rd N *TF:* 800-325-9462 ■ *Web:* www.majesticduderanch.com	Mancos	CO	81328	970-533-7900	533-7858
Laramie River Dude Ranch 25777 County Rd 103 *TF:* 800-551-5731 ■ *Web:* www.lrranch.com	Jelm	WY	82063	970-435-5716	435-5731
Latigo Ranch PO Box 237 *TF:* 800-227-9655 ■ *Web:* www.latigotrails.com	Kremmling	CO	80459	970-724-9008	
Laughing Water Guest Ranch PO Box 157 *TF:* 800-847-5095 ■ *Web:* www.lwranch.com	Fortine	MT	59918	406-882-4680	882-4880
Lazy K Bar Guest Ranch 8401 N Scenic Dr *Web:* www.lazykbarranch.com	Tucson	AZ	85743	520-299-7433	579-9164
Lazy K Bar Ranch PO Box 1550 *Web:* www.lazykbar.net	Big Timber	MT	59011	406-537-4404	537-4593
Lazy L & B Ranch 1072 E Fork Rd *TF Cust Svc:* 800-453-9488 ■ *Web:* www.lazylb.com	Dubois	WY	82513	307-455-2839	455-2849
Lone Mountain Ranch 750 Lone Mountain Ranch Rd PO Box 160069 *TF:* 800-514-4644 ■ *Web:* www.lmranch.com	Big Sky	MT	59716	406-995-4644	995-4670
Long Hollow Ranch 71105 Holmes Rd *TF:* 877-923-1901 ■ *Web:* www.lhranch.com	Sisters	OR	97759	541-923-1901	610-1993
Lost Valley Ranch 29555 Goose Creek Rd *Web:* www.ranchweb.com/lost	Sedalia	CO	80135	303-647-2311	647-2315
Lozier's Box R Ranch 552 Willow Creek Rd PO Box 100 *TF:* 800-822-8466 ■ *Web:* www.boxr.com	Cora	WY	82925	307-367-4868	367-6260
McGinnis Meadows Cattle & Guest Ranch 6220 Mcginnis Meadows Rd *Web:* www.mmgranch.com	Libby	MT	59923	406-293-5000	293-5005
Moose Head Ranch Hwy 89 N	Moose	WY	83012	307-733-3141	
Mountain Sky Guest Ranch PO Box 1219 *TF:* 800-548-3392 ■ *Web:* www.mtnsky.com	Emigrant	MT	59027	406-333-4911	333-4537
Nine Quarter Circle Ranch 5000 Taylor Fork Rd *Web:* www.ninequartercircle.com	Gallatin Gateway	MT	59730	406-995-4276	995-4276
North Fork Ranch (NFR) 55395 Hwy 285 PO Box B *TF:* 800-843-7895 ■ *Web:* www.northforkranch.com	Shawnee	CO	80475	303-838-9873	838-1549
Paradise Guest Ranch 282 Hunter Creek Rd **Fax Area Code:* 720 ■ *Web:* www.paradiseranch.com	Buffalo	WY	82834	307-684-7876	862-2126*
Peaceful Valley Ranch 475 Peaceful Valley Rd *TF:* 800-955-6343 ■ *Web:* www.peacefulvalley.com	Lyons	CO	80540	303-747-2881	747-2167
Pine Butte Guest Ranch 351 S Fork Rd *Web:* www.nature.org	Choteau	MT	59422	406-466-2158	466-5462
Price Canyon Ranch PO Box 39 *TF:* 800-727-0065 ■ *Web:* www.pricecanyon.com	Rodeo	NM	88056	520-558-2383	731-9453
R Lazy S Ranch PO Box 308 *Web:* www.rlazys.com	Teton Village	WY	83025	307-733-2655	734-1120
Rainbow Trout Ranch (RTR) 1484 FDR 250 PO Box 458 *TF:* 800-633-3397 ■ *Web:* www.rainbowtroutranch.com	Antonito	CO	81120	719-376-5659	376-5659
Rancho de la Osa Guest Ranch PO Box 1 *TF:* 800-872-6240 ■ *Web:* www.ranchodelaosa.com	Sasabe	AZ	85633	520-823-4257	823-4238
Ranger Creek Guest Ranch PO Box 47 *TF:* 888-817-7787 ■ *Web:* www.rangercreekranch.net	Shell	WY	82441	307-272-5107	
Rawah Ranch 11447 N County Rd 103 **Fax Area Code:* 970 ■ *TF:* 800-820-3152 ■ *Web:* www.rawahranch.com	Glendevey	CO	82063	800-820-3152	435-5705*
Red Rock Ranch The PO Box 38 *Web:* www.theredrockranch.com	Kelly	WY	83011	307-733-6288	733-6287
Rich Ranch 939 Cottonwood Lakes Rd *TF:* 800-532-4350 ■ *Web:* www.richranch.com	Seeley Lake	MT	59868	406-677-2317	677-3530
Rimrock Dude Ranch 2728 Northfork Rt *TF:* 800-208-7468 ■ *Web:* www.rimrockranch.com	Cody	WY	82414	307-587-3970	527-5014
Rock Springs Guest Ranch 64201 Tyler Rd *TF:* 800-225-3833 ■ *Web:* www.rocksprings.com	Bend	OR	97701	541-382-1957	382-7774
Scott Valley Resort & Guest Ranch 223 Scott Valley Trail PO Box 1447 *TF:* 888-855-7747	Mountain Home	AR	72653	870-425-5136	
Seven Lazy P Guest Ranch PO Box 178 *Web:* www.sevenlazyp.com	Choteau	MT	59422	406-466-2044	466-2903
Smith Fork Ranch 45362 Needle Rock Rd *Web:* www.smithforkranch.com	Crawford	CO	81415	970-921-3454	921-3475
Sundance Trail Guest Ranch 17931 Red Feather Lakes Rd *TF:* 800-357-4930 ■ *Web:* www.sundancetrail.com	Red Feather Lakes	CO	80545	970-224-1222	224-1222
Sweet Grass Ranch 460 Rein Ln *Web:* www.sweetgrassranch.com	Big Timber	MT	59011	406-537-4477	537-4477
Sylvan Dale Guest Ranch 2939 N County Rd 31 D *TF:* 877-667-3999 ■ *Web:* www.sylvandale.com	Loveland	CO	80538	970-667-3915	635-9336
T Cross Ranch LLC 82 Parque Creek Rd PO Box 638 *TF:* 877-827-6770 ■ *Web:* www.tcross.com	Dubois	WY	82513	307-455-2206	455-2720
Tarryall River Ranch 27001.5 County Rd 77 *TF:* 800-408-8407 ■ *Web:* www.tarryallriverranch.com	Lake George	CO	80827	719-748-1214	748-1319
Three Bars Cattle & Guest Ranch 9500 Wycliffe Perry Creek Rd *TF:* 877-426-5230 ■ *Web:* www.threebarsranch.com	Cranbrook	BC	V1C7C7	250-426-5230	426-8240
Trail Creek Ranch 7100 W Trail Creek Rd PO Box 10 *Web:* www.jacksonholetrailcreekranch.com	Wilson	WY	83014	307-733-2610	
Triangle C Ranch 3737 Hwy 26 *TF:* 800-661-4928 ■ *Web:* www.trianglec.com	Dubois	WY	82513	307-455-2225	455-2031
Triangle X Ranch 2 Triangle X Ranch Rd *TF:* 888-860-0005 ■ *Web:* www.trianglex.com	Moose	WY	83012	307-733-2183	733-8685
Triple J Wilderness Ranch 80 Mortimer Rd PO Box 310 *Web:* www.triplejranch.com	Augusta	MT	59410	406-562-3653	562-3836
Triple R Ranch PO Box 124 *TF:* 888-777-2624 ■ *Web:* www.rrrranch.com	Keystone	SD	57751	605-666-4605	
Tumbling River Ranch 3715 Pk County Rd 62 PO Box 30 *TF:* 800-654-8770 ■ *Web:* www.tumblingriver.com	Grant	CO	80448	303-838-5981	838-5133
Twin Peaks Ranch PO Box 774 *TF:* 800-659-4899 ■ *Web:* www.twinpeaksranch.com	Salmon	ID	83467	208-894-2290	894-2429
Two Bars Seven Ranch PO Box 67 *Web:* www.twobarssevenranch.com	Tie Siding	WY	82084	307-742-6072	
UXU Ranch 1710 Yellowstone Hwy *TF:* 800-373-9027 ■ *Web:* www.uxuranch.com	Wapiti	WY	82450	307-587-2143	587-7390
Vee Bar Guest Ranch 2091 Wyoming 130 *TF:* 800-483-3227 ■ *Web:* www.veebar.com	Laramie	WY	82070	307-745-7036	745-7433
Vista Verde Guest & Ski Ranch PO Box 770465 *TF:* 800-526-7433 ■ *Web:* www.vistaverde.com	Steamboat Springs	CO	80477	970-879-3858	879-6814
Wapiti Meadow Ranch 1667 Johnson Creek Rd *Web:* www.wapitimeadowranch.com	Cascade	ID	83611	208-633-3217	633-3219
Waunita Hot Springs Ranch 8007 County Rd 887 PO Box 7 D *Web:* www.waunita.com	Gunnison	CO	81230	970-641-1266	641-0650
Whistling Acres Guest Ranch 44325 Minnesota Creek Rd PO Box 88 *TF:* 800-346-1420 ■ *Web:* www.whistlingacres.com	Paonia	CO	81428	970-527-4560	527-6397
White Stallion Ranch 9251 W Twin Peaks Rd *TF:* 888-977-2624 ■ *Web:* www.wsranch.com	Tucson	AZ	85743	520-297-0252	744-2786
Wild Rose Ranch PO Box 181 *TF:* 800-324-6188 ■ *Web:* www.wildrose-ranch.com	Kimberley	BC	V1A2Y6	250-422-3403	422-3149
Wilderness Trails Ranch 1766 County Rd 302 *TF:* 800-527-2624 ■ *Web:* www.wildernesstrails.com	Durango	CO	81303	970-247-0722	247-1006
Wind River Ranch PO Box 3410 *TF:* 800-523-4212 ■ *Web:* www.windriverranch.com	Estes Park	CO	80517	970-586-4212	586-2255
Wind Walker Guest Ranch 11550 N 6400 E *TF:* 888-606-9463 ■ *Web:* www.windwalker.org	Spring City	UT	84662	435-462-0282	462-9212
Echo Valley Ranch & Spa Clinton PO Box 16 **Fax Area Code:* 778 ■ *TF:* 800-253-8831 ■ *Web:* www.evranch.com	Jesmond	BC	V0K1K0	604-988-3230	340-1077*
C Lazy U Ranch 3640 Colorado Hwy 125 PO Box 379 *Web:* www.clazyu.com	Granby	CO	80446	970-887-3344	887-3917

243 DUPLICATION & REPLICATION SERVICES

				Phone	Fax
Andrew T Johnson Co Inc 15 Tremont Pl *Web:* www.andrewtjohnson.com	Boston	MA	02108	617-742-1610	523-0719
ARC 1981 N Broadway Suite 385 *NYSE:* ARC ■ *Web:* www.e-arc.com	Walnut Creek	CA	94596	925-949-5100	949-5101
Avery Dennison Microreplication Div 150 N Orange Grove Blvd *Web:* www.averydennison.com	Pasadena	CA	91103	626-304-2000	304-2192
Blair Graphics Inc 1740 Stanford St *Web:* www.blairgfx.com	Santa Monica	CA	90404	310-829-4621	453-0868
BPS Reprographic Services Inc 945 Bryant St *Web:* www.bps.com	San Francisco	CA	94103	415-495-8700	495-2773
Campbell Blueprint & Supply Co Inc 3124 Broad Ave *TF:* 800-238-7564 ■ *Web:* www.campbellblueprint.com	Memphis	TN	38112	901-327-7385	327-0917
Color Film Media Group LLC 28 Thorndale Cir *TF:* 800-882-1120 ■ *Web:* www.colorfilm.com	Darien	CT	06820	203-866-2711	854-3526
Consolidated Reprographics 1181 N Kraemer Blvd *Web:* www.consrepro.com	Anaheim	CA	92806	714-526-0905	871-8129
Corporate Disk Co 4610 Crime Pkwy *TF:* 800-634-3475 ■ *Web:* www.disk.com	McHenry	IL	60050	815-331-6000	333-6030
Denon Digital LLC 1380 Monticello Rd	Madison	GA	30650	706-342-3425	342-3425
Dering Corp The 1702 Hempstead Rd *TF:* 877-433-7464 ■ *Web:* www.dering.com	Lancaster	PA	17601	717-394-4200	394-4276
Digital Video Services 4592 40th St SE *TF:* 800-747-8273 ■ *Web:* www.digivid.com	Grand Rapids	MI	49512	616-975-9911	975-9696
Eva-Tone Soundsheets Inc 4801 Ulmerton Rd *TF Sales:* 800-382-8663	Clearwater	FL	33762	727-572-7000	572-7000
Ford Graphics-Northwest 1431 NW 17th Ave *Web:* www.fordgraphics.com	Portland	OR	97209	503-227-3424	223-4254
GlobalWare Solutions Inc 200 Ward Hill *TF:* 800-224-6326 ■ *Web:* www.globalwaresolutions.com	Haverhill	MA	01835	978-469-7500	469-7373
Illinois Blueprint Corp 800 SW Jefferson Ave *Web:* www.illinoisblue.com	Peoria	IL	61605	309-676-1300	676-1310
Infodisc Technology USA Inc 3535 Hayden Ave *Web:* www.infodisc.com	Culver City	CA	90232	310-280-1200	280-1222
MerX City 608 2nd Ave S Suite 167 *TF:* 800-356-6826 ■ *Web:* www.merxcity.com	Minneapolis	MN	55402	612-332-2555	333-4080
Online Copy Corp 48815 Kato Rd *TF:* 800-833-4460 ■ *Web:* www.wecopycds.com	Fremont	CA	94539	510-226-6810	226-7543
Producers & Quantity Photos Inc 6660 Santa Monica Blvd *TF Cust Svc:* 800-843-9259 ■ *Web:* www.pqphoto.com	Hollywood	CA	90038	323-467-4500	466-0939
Reproduction Systems Inc 1828 Walnut St Suite 900 *TF Cust Svc:* 800-633-6125 ■ *Web:* www.rsi-kc.com	Kansas City	MO	64108	816-471-1414	472-7155
Standard Digital Imaging 4426 S 108th St *TF:* 800-642-8062 ■ *Web:* www.standardshare.com	Omaha	NE	68137	402-592-1292	592-8003
T-Square Miami Blueprint Co 3946 N Miami Ave *TF:* 800-432-3360 ■ *Web:* www.t-square.com	Miami	FL	33127	305-324-1234	547-1556
Thomas Reprographics 600 N Central Expy *TF:* 800-877-3776 ■ *Web:* www.thomasrepro.com	Richardson	TX	75080	972-231-7227	231-0623
Triangle Blueprint Co 3175 Princeton Pike *TF:* 800-792-8800 ■ *Web:* www.triangleart.com	Lawrenceville	NJ	08648	609-896-4100	896-2250
Victory Studios 2247 15th Ave W *TF:* 888-282-1776 ■ *Web:* www.victorystudios.com	Seattle	WA	98119	206-282-1776	282-3535

244 DUTY-FREE SHOPS

SEE ALSO Gift Shops p. 1905

	City	State	ZIP	Phone	Fax
Ambassador Duty Free Store 707 Patricia St *Web:* www.ambassadordutyfree.com	Windsor	ON	N9B3B8	519-977-9100	977-7811
Ammex Tax & Duty Free Shops 6100 Hollywood Blvd 7th Fl *Web:* www.dutyfreeamericas.com	Hollywood	FL	33024	954-986-7700	965-6800
Baja Duty Free (BDF) 4590 Border Village Rd *TF:* 877-438-8937 ■ *Web:* www.bajadutyfree.com	San Ysidro	CA	92173	619-428-6671	428-6673
Colombian Emeralds International PO Box 5868 *TF:* 800-666-3889 ■ *Web:* www.colombianemeralds.com	Fort Lauderdale	FL	33310	954-917-2547	971-7693
DFS Group Ltd 525 Market St 31st Fl *Web:* www.dfsgalleria.com	San Francisco	CA	94105	415-977-2700	977-2700
Duty Free Americas Inc 6100 Hollywood Blvd 7th Fl *Web:* www.dutyfreeamericas.com	Hollywood	FL	33024	954-986-7700	965-6800
DUTYFREE.COM 300 Terminal Dr *TF:* 800-666-3889 ■ *Web:* www.dutyfree.com	Fort Lauderdale	FL	33310	954-359-5272	
Niagara Duty Free Shop 5726 Falls Ave *TF:* 877-612-4337 ■ *Web:* www.niagaradutyfree.com	Niagara Falls	ON	L2G7T5	905-374-3700	374-7503
Peace Bridge Duty Free Inc Peace Bridge Plaza PO Box 339 *TF:* 800-361-1302 ■ *Web:* www.dutyfree.ca	Fort Erie	ON	L2A5N1	905-871-5400	871-6335
Starboard Cruise Services Inc 8400 NW 36th St *TF:* 800-547-4785 ■ *Web:* www.starboardcruise.com	Miami	FL	33166	786-845-7300	845-1111
Tunnel Duty Free Shop Inc 465 Goyeau St *TF:* 800-669-2105 ■ *Web:* www.tunneldutyfree.com	Windsor	ON	N9A1H1	519-252-2713	252-1688

EDUCATIONAL INSTITUTIONS

SEE Children's Learning Centers p. 1604; Colleges - Bible p. 1617; Colleges - Community & Junior p. 1618; Colleges - Culinary Arts p. 1634; Colleges - Fine Arts p. 1634; Colleges - Tribal p. 1635; Colleges - Women's (Four-Year) p. 1636; Colleges & Universities - Christian p. 1636; Colleges & Universities - Four-Year p. 1638; Colleges & Universities - Graduate & Professional Schools p. 1659; Colleges & Universities - Historically Black p. 1666; Colleges & Universities - Jesuit p. 1668; Military Service Academies p. 2248; Preparatory Schools - Boarding p. 2445; Preparatory Schools - Non-boarding p. 2449; Universities - Canadian p. 2746; Vocational & Technical Schools p. 2763

245 EDUCATIONAL INSTITUTION OPERATORS & MANAGERS

	City	State	ZIP	Phone	Fax
Apollo Group Inc 4025 E Elwood St *NASDAQ: APOL* ■ **Fax:* Hum Res ■ *TF:* 800-990-2765 ■ *Web:* www.apollogrp.edu	Phoenix	AZ	85040	480-966-5394	929-7417*
Argosy Education Group 20 S Clark St Suite 2800	Chicago	IL	60603	312-424-7282	201-1907
Bridgepoint Education Inc 13500 Evening Creek Dr N Suite 600 *NYSE: BPI* ■ *TF:* 866-475-0317 ■ *Web:* www.bridgepointeducation.com	San Diego	CA	92128	858-668-2586	408-2903
Capella Education Co 225 S 6th St 9th Fl *NASDAQ: CPLA* ■ *TF Cust Svc:* 888-227-3552 ■ *Web:* www.capella.edu	Minneapolis	MN	55402	612-977-5100	977-5058
Career Education Corp (CEC) 2895 Greenspoint Pkwy Suite 600 *NASDAQ: CECO* ■ *TF:* 877-559-9222 ■ *Web:* www.careered.com	Hoffman Estates	IL	60196	847-781-3600	781-3610
Charter Schools USA 6245 N Federal Hwy 5th Fl *Web:* www.charterschoolsusa.com	Fort Lauderdale	FL	33308	954-202-3500	202-3512
Corinthian Colleges Inc 6 Hutton Centre Dr Suite 400 *NASDAQ: COCO* ■ *TF:* 800-611-2101 ■ *Web:* www.cci.edu	Santa Ana	CA	92707	714-427-3000	427-3013
DeVRY Inc 3005 Highland Pkwy *NYSE: DV* ■ *Web:* www.devryinc.com	Downers Grove	IL	60515	630-515-7700	
Edison Schools Inc 485 Lexington Ave 2nd Fl *TF:* 877-276-3375 ■ *Web:* www.edisonlearning.com	New York	NY	10017	212-419-1600	419-1764
Education Management Corp (EDMC) 210 6th Ave 33rd Fl *NASDAQ: EDMC* ■ *TF:* 800-275-2440 ■ *Web:* www.edmc.edu	Pittsburgh	PA	15222	412-562-0900	562-0598
Excel Education Centers 1040 Whipple St Suite 324 *TF:* 800-417-9036 ■ *Web:* www.exceleducationcenters.org	Prescott	AZ	86305	928-778-5764	445-2989
Holy Family Institute 8235 Ohio River Blvd *Web:* www.hfi-pgh.org	Pittsburgh	PA	15202	412-766-4030	
Imagine Schools 1005 N Glebe Rd Suite 610 *Web:* www.imagineschools.com	Arlington	VA	22201	703-527-2600	527-0038
ITT Educational Services Inc 13000 N Meridian St *NYSE: ESI* ■ *TF:* 800-388-3368 ■ *Web:* www.ittesi.com	Carmel	IN	46032	317-706-9200	706-9327
Kaplan Higher Education 1400 Hembree Rd Suite 100 *Web:* www.khec.com	Roswell	GA	30076	770-510-2000	510-2001
Lake County Educational Service Ctr 382 Blackbrook Rd *Web:* www.lcesc.k12.oh.us	Painesville	OH	44077	440-350-2563	350-2566
Laureate Education Inc 1001 Fleet St *NASDAQ: LAUR* ■ *TF:* 866-367-5287 ■ *Web:* www.laureate.net	Baltimore	MD	21202	410-843-6394	880-8065
Leona Group LLC 4660 S Hagadorn Rd Suite 500 *TF:* 800-656-6763 ■ *Web:* www.leonagroup.com	East Lansing	MI	48823	517-333-9030	333-4559
Lincoln Educational Services 200 Executive Dr *NASDAQ: LINC* ■ *TF:* 877-693-8887 ■ *Web:* www.lincolnedu.com	West Orange	NJ	07052	973-736-9340	736-1750
National Heritage Academies 3850 Broadmoor Ave SE Suite 201 *TF:* 800-699-9235 ■ *Web:* www.heritageacademies.com	Grand Rapids	MI	49512	616-222-1700	222-1701
Nobel Learning Communities Inc 1615 W Chester Pike Suite 200 *NASDAQ: NLCI* ■ *Web:* www.nobellearning.com	West Chester	PA	19382	484-947-2000	947-2006
SABIS Educational Systems Inc 6385 Beach Rd *Web:* www.sabis.net	Eden Prairie	MN	55344	952-918-1850	918-1851
Strayer Education Inc 1100 Wilson Blvd Suite 2500 *NASDAQ: STRA* ■ *TF:* 877-892-5100 ■ *Web:* www.strayereducation.com	Arlington	VA	22209	703-247-2500	527-0112
Sylvan Learning Centers 1001 Fleet St *Web:* www.tutoring.sylvanlearning.com	Baltimore	MD	21202	410-843-8000	880-8717
UNext.com 111 N Canal St Suite 455 *TF:* 877-405-4500 ■ *Web:* www.unext.com	Chicago	IL	60606	312-669-5000	669-5005

246 EDUCATIONAL MATERIALS & SUPPLIES

SEE ALSO Educational & Reference Software p. 1683; Office & School Supplies p. 2321

	City	State	ZIP	Phone	Fax
American Educational Products Inc 401 Hickory St PO Box 2121 *TF:* 800-289-9299 ■ *Web:* www.amep.com	Fort Collins	CO	80522	970-484-7445	484-1198
American Educational Products LLC Hubbard Scientific Div (AMEP) 401 Hickory St *TF:* 800-289-9299 ■ *Web:* www.amep.com	Fort Collins	CO	80522	970-484-7445	484-1198
Carolina Biological Supply Co 2700 York Rd *TF:* 800-334-5551 ■ *Web:* www.carolina.com	Burlington	NC	27215	336-584-0381	584-3399
Carson-Dellosa Publishing Co Inc 7027 Albert Pick Rd *TF:* 800-321-0943 ■ *Web:* www.carsondellosa.com	Greensboro	NC	27409	336-632-0084	808-3271
Center Enterprises Inc 30 Shield St *TF Orders:* 800-542-2214 ■ *Web:* www.centerenterprises.com	West Hartford	CT	06110	860-953-4423	953-2948
Chenille Kraft Co 65 Ambrogio Dr *TF:* 800-621-1261 ■ *Web:* www.chenillekraft.com	Gurnee	IL	60031	847-249-2900	249-2906
Claridge Products & Equipment Inc 601 Hwy 62 65 *Web:* www.claridgeproducts.com	Harrison	AR	72601	870-743-2200	743-1908
Classroom Connect Inc 8000 Marina Blvd Suite 400 **Fax Area Code:* 888 ■ *TF:* 800-638-1639 ■ *Web:* www.corporate.classroom.com	Brisbane	CA	94005	800-638-1639	801-8299*
Creative Teaching Press Inc 15342 Graham St *TF:* 800-444-4287 ■ *Web:* www.creativeteaching.com	Huntington Beach	CA	92649	714-895-5047	895-6547
Delta Education LLC 80 NW Blvd *TF:* 800-258-1302 ■ *Web:* www.delta-education.com	Nashua	NH	03063	603-889-8899	880-6520
Didax Inc 395 Main St *TF:* 800-458-0024 ■ *Web:* www.didax.com	Rowley	MA	01969	978-948-2340	948-2813
Edcon/Imperial/AV 30 Montauk Blvd *TF:* 888-553-3266 ■ *Web:* www.edconpublishing.com	Oakdale	NY	11769	631-567-7227	567-8745
Education Center Inc 3515 W Market St Suite 200 *TF:* 800-714-7991 ■ *Web:* www.theeducationcenter.com	Greensboro	NC	27403	336-854-0309	547-1587
Educational Insights Inc 380 N Fairway Dr *TF:* 888-800-7893 ■ *Web:* www.educationalinsights.com	Vernon Hills	IL	60061	800-995-4436	995-0506
Educational Resources 1550 Executive Dr **Fax:* Orders ■ *TF Orders:* 800-624-2926 ■ *Web:* www.edresources.com	Elgin	IL	60123	847-888-8300	888-8499*
Educational Supplies Inc 1506 S Salisbury Blvd *TF:* 800-797-8775 ■ *Web:* www.educationalsuppliesinc.com	Salisbury	MD	21801	410-543-2519	860-0584
Educators Resource Inc 2575 Schillingers Rd **Fax:* Cust Svc ■ *TF Cust Svc:* 800-868-1588 ■ *Web:* www.erdealer.com	Semmes	AL	36575	800-868-2368	868-6212*
Edupress Inc W 5527 Hwy 106 *TF:* 800-835-7978 ■ *Web:* www.highsmith.com	Fort Atlinson	WI	53538	920-563-9571	563-7395
Evan-Moor Educational Publishers Inc 18 Lower Ragsdale Dr *TF:* 800-777-4489 ■ *Web:* www.evan-moor.com	Monterey	CA	93940	831-649-5901	649-6256
Excelligence Learning Corp 2 Lower Ragsdale Dr Suite 200 **Fax Area Code:* 800 ■ *TF:* 800-627-2829 ■ *Web:* www.excelligencelearning.com	Monterey	CA	93940	831-333-2000	879-3753*
Films for the Humanities & Sciences PO Box 2053 *TF:* 800-257-5126 ■ *Web:* www.ffh.films.com	Princeton	NJ	08543	609-671-1000	671-0266
Fisher Science Education 4500 Turnberry Dr **Fax Area Code:* 800 ■ *TF Cust Svc:* 800-955-1177 ■ *Web:* www.fisheredu.com	Hanover Park	IL	60133	630-259-1200	955-0740*
Frank Schaffer Publications PO Box 141487 **Fax Area Code:* 888 ■ *TF:* 800-253-5469 ■ *Web:* www.schoolspecialtypublishing.com/Frank_Schaffer/?start=0	Grand Rapids	NC	49514	800-417-3261	203-9361*

Company / Address	City	State	Zip	Phone	Fax
Frog Street Press Inc 800 Industrial Blvd Suite 100 *TF:* 800-884-3764 ■ *Web:* www.fsp3.com	Grapevine	TX	76051	800-884-3764	759-3828
Ghent Mfg Inc 2999 Henkle Dr *TF:* 800-543-0550 ■ *Web:* www.ghent.com	Lebanon	OH	45036	513-932-3445	932-9252
Great Source Education Group 181 Ballardvale St. **Fax Area Code:* 800 ■ *TF:* 800-289-4490 ■ *Web:* www.greatsource.com	Wilmington	MA	01887	978-661-1500	289-3994*
Guidecraft USA 66 Grand Ave Suite 207 *TF:* 800-544-6526 ■ *Web:* www.guidecraft.com	Englewood	NJ	07631	201-894-5401	894-5405
Hayes School Publishing Co Inc 321 Pennwood Ave. **Fax Area Code:* 800 ■ *TF:* 800-245-6234 ■ *Web:* www.hayespub.com	Pittsburgh	PA	15221	412-371-2373	543-8771*
Highsmith Inc PO Box 7820 *TF:* 800-558-2110 ■ *Web:* www.highsmith.com	Madison	WI	53707	920-563-9571	563-7395
Holcomb's Education Resource 3205 Harvard Ave. *TF:* 800-362-9907	Newburgh Heights	OH	44105	216-341-3000	341-5151
Incentive Publications Inc 2400 Crestmoor Dr Suite 211 *TF Mktg:* 800-421-2830 ■ *Web:* www.incentivepublications.com	Nashville	TN	37215	615-385-2934	385-2967
JR Holcomb & Co Inc 3205 Harvard Ave PO Box 94636	Cleveland	OH	44105	216-341-3000	341-5151
Kaplan Early Learning Co 1310 Lewisville-Clemmons Rd. *TF:* 800-334-2014 ■ *Web:* www.kaplanco.com	Lewisville	NC	27023	336-766-7374	766-6960
Kimbo Educational 10 N 3rd Ave PO Box 477 *TF:* 800-631-2187 ■ *Web:* www.kimboed.com	Long Branch	NJ	07740	732-229-4949	870-3340
Learning Resources 380 N Fairway Dr. *TF:* 800-222-3909 ■ *Web:* www.learningresources.com	Vernon Hills	IL	60061	847-573-8400	573-8425
Learning Works 181 Brackett St *Web:* www.learningworks.me	Portland	ME	04102	207-775-0105	780-1701
Learning Wrap-Ups Inc 1660 W Gordon Ave Suite 4 *TF:* 800-992-4966 ■ *Web:* www.learningwrapups.com	Layton	UT	84041	801-497-0050	497-0063
McDonald Publishing 567 Hanley Industrial Ct *TF:* 800-722-8080 ■ *Web:* www.mcdonaldpublishing.com	Saint Louis	MO	63144	314-781-7400	781-7480
McGraw-Hill Cos Inc Macmillan/McGraw-Hill Div 2 Penn Plaza **Fax:* Mktg ■ *TF:* 800-442-9685 ■ *Web:* www.mhschool.com	New York	NY	10121	212-512-2000	904-6633*
McGraw-Hill Cos Inc SRA/McGraw-Hill Div 8787 Orion Pl *TF:* 800-468-4850 ■ *Web:* www.mheonline.com/segment/view/1	Columbus	OH	43240	614-430-4000	430-6621
McGraw-Hill Everyday Learning 1 Prudential Plaza Suite 400 *Web:* www.sraonline.com	Chicago	IL	60601	312-233-7820	233-6730
Milliken Publishing Co Inc 3190 Rider Trail S *TF:* 800-325-4136 ■ *Web:* www.millikenpub.com	Earth City	MO	63045	314-991-4220	991-4807
Monday Morning Books 150 Bayview Dr PO Box 1134 *TF:* 800-255-6049 ■ *Web:* www.mondaymorningbooks.com	Palo Alto	CA	94301	800-255-6049	255-6048
National School Products 101 E Broadway **Fax Area Code:* 800 ■ *TF:* 800-627-9393 ■ *Web:* www.nationalschoolproducts.com	Maryville	TN	37804	865-984-3960	289-3960*
Paper Magic Group Inc Eureka School Div 401 Adams Ave. *TF Cust Svc:* 800-258-1044 ■ *Web:* www.papermagic.com	Scranton	PA	18510	570-961-3863	961-2628
Replogle Globes Inc 2801 S 25th Ave *TF:* 800-275-4452 ■ *Web:* www.replogleglobes.com	Broadview	IL	60155	708-343-0900	343-0923
Rock 'N Learn Inc 105 Commercial Cir *TF:* 800-348-8445 ■ *Web:* www.rocknlearn.com	Conroe	TX	77304	936-539-2731	539-2659
Roylco Inc 3251 Abbeville Hwy PO Box 13409 *TF:* 800-362-8656 ■ *Web:* www.roylco.com	Anderson	SC	29624	864-296-0043	296-6736
Scholastic News 557 Broadway **Fax:* PR ■ *TF Orders:* 800-724-6527 ■ *Web:* www.scholastic.com/scholasticnews	New York	NY	10012	212-343-6100	343-6930*
School Specialty Inc PO Box 1579 *NASDAQ: SCHS* ■ *TF:* 888-388-3224 ■ *Web:* www.schoolspecialty.com	Appleton	WI	54912	920-734-5712	882-5603
School Stuff Inc 7440 Calumet Ave *TF:* 877-931-6767	Hammond	IN	46324	219-931-6767	931-6727
Teacher Created Resources 6421 Industry Way **Fax Area Code:* 800 ■ *TF:* 888-343-4335 ■ *Web:* www.teachercreated.com	Westminster	CA	92683	714-891-7895	525-1254*
Teaching & Learning Co 1204 Buchanan St *TF:* 800-852-1234 ■ *Web:* www.teachinglearning.com	Carthage	IL	62321	217-357-2591	357-6789
Touchstone Applied Science Assoc Inc 4 Hardscrabble Heights PO Box 382 *TF Cust Svc:* 800-800-2598 ■ *Web:* www.tasa.com	Brewster	NY	10509	845-277-8100	277-3548
TREND Enterprises Inc 300 9th Ave SW *TF Cust Svc:* 800-328-0818 ■ *Web:* www.trendenterprises.com	New Brighton	MN	55112	651-631-2850	582-3500
Weekly Reader Corp 200 First Stamford Pl 2nd Fl *TF:* 800-446-3355 ■ *Web:* www.weeklyreader.com	Stamford	CT	06912	203-705-3500	705-1665
World*Class Learning Materials 53 Rutherford Rd PO Box 639 *TF:* 800-638-6470 ■ *Web:* www.wclm.com	Candler	NC	28715	800-638-6470	638-6499

247 EDUCATIONAL TESTING SERVICES - ASSESSMENT & PREPARATION

Company / Address	City	State	Zip	Phone	Fax
ACT Inc 500 ACT Dr PO Box 168 *Web:* www.act.org	Iowa City	IA	52243	319-337-1000	339-3020
Alpine Testing INC 51 W Centre *Web:* www.alpinetesting.com	Orem	UT	84057	801-226-4283	224-7599
Applied Measurement Professionals Inc (AMP) 18000 W 105th St. *Web:* www.goamp.com	Olathe	KS	66061	913-895-4600	895-4650
Barron's Educational Series Inc 250 Wireless Blvd. *TF:* 800-645-3476 ■ *Web:* www.barronseduc.com	Hauppauge	NY	11788	631-434-3311	434-3723
Castle Worldwide Inc 900 Perimeter Pk Rd Suite G *TF:* 866-422-7853 ■ *Web:* www.castleworldwide.com	Morrisville	NC	27560	919-572-6880	361-2426
College Board 45 Columbus Ave. **Fax:* PR ■ *TF:* 800-927-4302 ■ *Web:* www.collegeboard.com	New York	NY	10023	212-713-8000	713-8184*
Educational Testing Service Rosedale Rd *Web:* www.ets.org	Princeton	NJ	08541	609-921-9000	734-5410
General Educational Development Testing Service *American Council on Education* 1 Dupont Cir NW *Web:* www.acenet.edu/calec/ged/home.html	Washington	DC	20036	202-939-9300	659-8875
H & H Publishing Co Inc 1231 Kapp Dr. *TF:* 800-366-4079 ■ *Web:* www.hhpublishing.com	Clearwater	FL	33765	727-442-7760	442-2195
Human Resources Research Organization (HumRRO) 66 Canal Ctr Plaza Suite 400 *TF:* 800-301-1508 ■ *Web:* www.humrro.org	Alexandria	VA	22314	703-549-3611	549-9025
Kaplan Inc 888 7th Ave 21st Fl *TF Cust Svc:* 800-527-5268 ■ *Web:* www.kaplan.com	New York	NY	10106	212-492-5800	
Kaplan Inc Test Preparation & Admissions Div 888 7th Ave 21st Fl. *TF:* 888-527-8378 ■ *Web:* www.kaptest.com	New York	NY	10106	212-492-5800	
Law School Admission Council Inc (LSAC) PO Box 40 *Web:* www.lsac.org	Newtown	PA	18940	215-968-1101	968-1169
McGraw-Hill Cos Inc CTB/McGraw-Hill Div 20 Ryan Ranch Rd *TF:* 800-538-9547 ■ *Web:* www.ctb.com	Monterey	CA	93940	831-393-0700	393-6528
NCS Pearson Inc 5601 Green Valley Dr Suite 220 *TF:* 800-431-1421 ■ *Web:* www.ncspearson.com	Bloomington	MN	55437	952-681-3000	681-3580
Pearson Vue 3 Bala Plaza W Suite 300 **Fax:* Cust Svc ■ *TF:* 888-204-6231 ■ *Web:* www.pearsonvue.com	Bala Cynwyd	PA	19004	610-617-5093	617-9329*
Praxis Series Online Educational Testing Service Teaching & Learning Div Rosedale Rd *TF:* 800-772-9476 ■ *Web:* www.ets.org/praxis	Princeton	NJ	08541	609-771-7395	530-0581
Princeton Review Inc The 2315 Broadway *NASDAQ: REVU* ■ *TF:* 800-333-0369 ■ *Web:* www.princetonreview.com	New York	NY	10024	212-874-8282	874-0775
Professional Examination Service 475 Riverside Dr 6th Fl. *Web:* www.proexam.org	New York	NY	10115	212-367-4200	367-4266
Promissor Inc 1007 Church St Suite 314 *TF:* 800-255-1312 ■ *Web:* www.promissor.com	Evanston	IL	60201	847-866-2001	866-2002
Riverside Publishing Co 3800 Golf Rd Suite 200 *TF Cust Svc:* 800-323-9540 ■ *Web:* www.riversidepublishing.com	Rolling Meadows	IL	60008	630-467-7000	467-7192
TestTakers 1 Plaza Rd Suite 204 *Web:* www.ttprep.com	Greenvale	NY	11548	516-626-6100	626-6182
Thomson Prometric 1000 Lancaster St **Fax Area Code:* 443 ■ *TF:* 866-776-6387 ■ *Web:* www.prometric.com	Baltimore	MD	21202	800-616-3926	923-8695*

248 ELECTRIC COMPANIES - COOPERATIVES (RURAL)

SEE ALSO Utility Companies p. 2748

Companies Listed Here Are Members Of The National Rural Electric Cooperative Association; Most Are Consumer-Owned, But Some Are Public Power Districts. In Addition, The Companies Listed Are Electricity Distribution Cooperatives. Companies That Generate And/Or Transmit Electricity, But Do Not Distribute It, Are Not Included.

ALABAMA

Company / Address	City	State	Zip	Phone	Fax
Baldwin County Electric Membership Corp 19600 Hwy 59 *TF:* 800-837-3374 ■ *Web:* www.baldwinemc.org	Summerdale	AL	36580	251-989-6247	989-0133
Central Alabama Electric Co-op 1802 Hwy 31 N. *TF:* 800-545-5735	Prattville	AL	36067	334-365-6762	365-6148
Cherokee Electric Co-op 1550 Clarence Chestnut Bypass PO Box O *TF:* 800-952-2667 ■ *Web:* www.cherokee.coop	Centre	AL	35960	256-927-5524	927-2278
Clarke-Washington Electric Membership Corp 1307 College Ave *TF:* 800-323-9081 ■ *Web:* www.cwemc.com	Jackson	AL	36545	251-246-9081	246-9822
Coosa Valley Electric Co-op 69220 Alabama Hwy 77 PO Box 837 *TF:* 800-273-7210 ■ *Web:* www.coosavalleyec.com	Talladega	AL	35160	256-362-4180	761-2615
Covington Electric Co-op Inc 18836 US Hwy 84. *TF:* 800-239-4121 ■ *Web:* www.cov-elect.com	Andalusia	AL	36420	334-222-4121	222-1546
Cullman Electric Co-op 1749 Eva Rd NE PO Box 1168 *TF:* 800-242-1806 ■ *Web:* www.cullmanec.com	Cullman	AL	35055	256-737-3200	737-3218
Dixie Electric Co-op 402 Blackmon Ave E. *TF:* 888-349-4332 ■ *Web:* www.dixieec.com	Union Springs	AL	36089	334-738-2500	738-2527
Franklin Electric Co-op Inc 225 Franklin St NW *TF:* 800-451-1505	Russellville	AL	35653	256-332-2730	332-2753
Joe Wheeler Electric Membership Corp PO Box 460 *TF:* 800-239-6518 ■ *Web:* www.jwemc.org	Trinity	AL	35673	256-552-2300	355-0631
Marshall DeKalb Electric Co-op 201 W Mill Ave *TF:* 800-239-3692 ■ *Web:* www.mdec.org	Boaz	AL	35957	256-593-4262	840-2211
North Alabama Electric Co-op 41103 US Hwy 72. *TF:* 800-572-2900	Stevenson	AL	35772	256-437-2281	437-2286

	City	State	ZIP	Phone	Fax
Pea River Electric Co-op 1311 W Roy Parker Rd PO Box 969	Ozark	AL	36361	334-774-2545	774-2548
TF: 800-264-7732					
Pioneer Electric Co-op 300 Herbert St	Greenville	AL	36037	334-382-6636	382-8641
TF: 800-239-3092 ■ *Web:* www.pioneerelectric.com					
Sand Mountain Electric Co-op 402 Main St W	Rainsville	AL	35986	256-638-2153	638-4957
TF: 877-843-2512 ■ *Web:* www.smec.coop					
South Alabama Electric Co-op 13192 US Hwy 231	Troy	AL	36081	334-566-2060	566-8949
TF: 800-556-2060 ■ *Web:* www.southaec.com					
Southern Pine Electric Co-op 2134 S Blvd PO Box 528	Brewton	AL	36427	251-867-5415	867-5219
Web: www.southernpine.org					
Tallapoosa River Electric Co-op 15163 US Hwy 431 S PO Box 675	Lafayette	AL	36862	334-864-9331	864-0817
TF: 800-332-8732 ■ *Web:* www.trec.coop					
Tombigbee Electric Co-op Inc 7686 US Hwy PO Box 610	Guin	AL	35563	205-468-3325	468-3338
TF: 800-621-8069 ■ *Web:* www.tombigbee.net					
Wiregrass Electric Co-op Inc 509 N State Hwy 167 PO Box 158	Hartford	AL	36344	334-588-2223	588-0683
TF: 800-239-4602 ■ *Web:* www.wiregrass.coop					

ALASKA

	City	State	ZIP	Phone	Fax
Alaska Village Electric Co-op Inc 4831 Eagle St	Anchorage	AK	99503	907-561-1818	562-4086
Web: www.avec.org					
Barrow Utilities & Electric Coop Inc (BUECI) 1295 Agvik St PO Box 449	Barrow	AK	99723	907-852-6166	852-6372
Web: www.bueci.org					
Chugach Electric Assn Inc 5601 Electron Dr	Anchorage	AK	99518	907-563-7494	562-0027
TF: 800-478-7494 ■ *Web:* www.chugachelectric.com					
Copper Valley Electric Assn Inc (CVEA) Mile 187 Glenn Hwy PO Box 45	Glennallen	AK	99588	907-822-3211	822-5586
TF: 866-835-2832 ■ *Web:* www.cvea.org					
Cordova Electric Co-op Inc 705 2nd St PO Box 20	Cordova	AK	99574	907-424-5555	424-5527
Web: www.cordovaelectric.com					
Golden Valley Electrical Assn Inc 758 Illinois St	Fairbanks	AK	99701	907-452-1151	451-5633
TF: 800-770-4832 ■ *Web:* www.gvea.com					
Homer Electric Assn Inc 3977 Lake St	Homer	AK	99603	907-235-8551	235-3313
TF: 800-478-8551 ■ *Web:* www.homerelectric.com					
Kodiak Electric Assn Inc 515 E Marine Way	Kodiak	AK	99615	907-486-7700	486-7717
Web: www.kodiakelectric.com					
Kotzebue Electric Assn Inc PO Box 44	Kotzebue	AK	99752	907-442-3491	442-2482
Web: www.kea.coop					
Naknek Electric Assn Inc 1 School Rd	Naknek	AK	99633	907-246-4261	246-6242
Web: www.nea.coop					
Nushagak Electric & Telephone Co-op Inc 557 Kenny Wren Rd	Dillingham	AK	99576	907-842-5251	842-2799
TF: 800-478-5296 ■ *Web:* www.nushtel.com					
Unalakleet Valley Electric Co-op PO Box 186	Unalakleet	AK	99684	907-624-3474	624-3009
Yakutat Power Inc PO Box 129	Yakutat	AK	99689	907-784-3248	784-3922

ARIZONA

	City	State	ZIP	Phone	Fax
Duncan Valley Electric Co-op Inc PO Box 440	Duncan	AZ	85534	928-359-2503	359-2370
TF: 800-669-2503 ■ *Web:* www.dvec.org					
Farmers Electric Co-op Inc PO Box 80094	Prescott	AZ	86304	903-455-1715	455-8125
TF: 800-541-2662 ■ *Web:* www.fecelectric.com					
Graham County Electric Co-op Inc PO Drawer B	Pima	AZ	85543	928-485-2451	485-9491
TF: 800-577-9266					
Mohave Electric Co-op Inc 1509 Goldrush Rd	Bullhead City	AZ	86442	928-763-4115	763-6094
TF: 800-685-4251 ■ *Web:* www.mohaveaz.com					
Navopache Electric Co-op Inc 1878 W White Mountain Blvd	Lakeside	AZ	85929	928-368-5118	368-6038
TF: 800-543-6324 ■ *Web:* www.navopache.org					
Sulphur Springs Valley Electric Co-op Inc PO Box 820	Willcox	AZ	85644	520-384-2221	384-5223
TF: 800-422-9288 ■ *Web:* www.ssvec.org					
Tohono O'odham Utility Authority PO Box 816	Sells	AZ	85634	520-383-2236	383-2218
Web: www.toua.net					
Trico Electric Co-op Inc 8600 W Tangerine Rd	Marana	AZ	85653	520-744-2944	744-2329
Web: www.trico.org					

ARKANSAS

	City	State	ZIP	Phone	Fax
Arkansas Valley Electric Co-op Corp 1811 W Commercial St PO Box 47	Ozark	AR	72949	479-667-2176	667-5238
TF: 800-468-2176 ■ *Web:* www.avecc.com					
Ashley-Chicot Electric Co-op Inc 307 E Jefferson St	Hamburg	AR	71646	870-853-5212	853-2531
TF: 800-281-5212 ■ *Web:* www.ashley-chicot.com					
C & L Electric Co-op Corp 900 Church St PO Box 9	Star City	AR	71667	870-628-4221	628-4676
Web: www.clelectric.com					
Carroll Electric Co-op Corp 920 Hwy 62 Spur	Berryville	AR	72616	870-423-2161	423-4815
TF: 800-432-9720 ■ *Web:* www.carrollecc.com					
Clay County Electric Co-op Corp 300 N Missouri Ave	Corning	AR	72422	870-857-3521	857-3523
TF: 800-521-2450 ■ *Web:* www.claycountyelectric.com					
Craighead Electric Co-op Corp 4314 Stadium Blvd PO Box 7503	Jonesboro	AR	72403	870-932-8301	972-5674
TF: 800-794-5012 ■ *Web:* www.craigheadelectric.coop					
Farmers Electric Co-op Corp 300 Hwy 367 N	Newport	AR	72112	870-523-3691	523-6853
TF: 800-834-9055 ■ *Web:* www.farmersecc.com					
First Electric Co-op Corp 1000 S JP Wright Loop Rd	Jacksonville	AR	72076	501-982-4545	982-8450
TF: 800-489-7405 ■ *Web:* www.firstelectric.coop					
Mississippi County Electric Co-op 510 N Broadway St	Blytheville	AR	72315	870-763-4563	763-0513
TF: 800-439-4563 ■ *Web:* www.mceci.com					
North Arkansas Electric Co-op Inc 225 S Main St	Salem	AR	72576	870-895-3221	895-6279
Web: www.naeci.com					
Ouachita Electric Co-op Corp 700 Bradley Ferry Rd PO Box 877	Camden	AR	71711	870-836-5791	836-5794
Web: www.oecc.com					
Ozarks Electric Co-op Corp 3641 W Wedington Dr	Fayetteville	AR	72704	479-521-2900	444-0943
TF: 800-521-6144 ■ *Web:* www.ozarksecc.com					
Petit Jean Electric Co-op 270 Quality Dr PO Box 37	Clinton	AR	72031	501-745-2493	745-4150
TF: 800-786-7618 ■ *Web:* www.pjecc.com					
Rich Mountain Electric Co-op Inc 515 Janssen PO Box 897	Mena	AR	71953	479-394-4140	394-1211
TF: 877-828-4074 ■ *Web:* www.rmec.com					
South Central Arkansas Electric Co-op 1140 Main St	Arkadelphia	AR	71923	870-246-6701	246-8223
TF: 800-814-2931 ■ *Web:* www.scaec.com					
Southwest Arkansas Electric Co-op 2904 E 9th St	Texarkana	AR	71854	870-772-2743	773-2161
Web: www.swrea.com					
Woodruff Electric Co-op PO Box 1619	Forrest City	AR	72336	870-633-2262	633-0629
Web: www.woodruffelectric.com					

CALIFORNIA

	City	State	ZIP	Phone	Fax
Anza ElectricCo-op Inc 58470 Hwy 371 PO Box 391909	Anza	CA	92539	951-763-4333	763-5297
Web: www.anzaelectric.org					
Brightsource Energy Inc 1999 Harrison St Suite 2150	Oakland	CA	94612	510-550-8161	550-8165
Web: www.brightsourceenergy.com					
Plumas-Sierra Rural Electric Co-op 73233 SR 70 Suite A	Portola	CA	96122	530-832-4261	832-5761
TF: 800-555-2207 ■ *Web:* www.psrec.coop					
Surprise Valley Electric Co-op PO Box 691	Alturas	CA	96101	530-233-3511	233-2190
TF: 866-843-2667					
Trinity Public Utility District 26 pondersoa Ln PO Box 1216	Weaverville	CA	96093	530-623-5536	623-5549*
**Fax:* Admin ■ *TF local county:* 800-968-7783					
Truckee Donner Public Utility District (TDPUD) 11570 Donner Pass Rd PO Box 309	Truckee	CA	96160	530-587-3896	587-5056
Web: www.tdpud.org					
Yuba County Water Agency 1220 F St	Marysville	CA	95901	530-741-6278	741-6541
Web: www.ycwa.com					

COLORADO

	City	State	ZIP	Phone	Fax
Delta-Montrose Electric Assn 11925 6300 Rd	Montrose	CO	81401	970-249-4572	240-6801
Web: www.dmea.com					
Empire Electric Assn Inc 801 N Broadway	Cortez	CO	81321	970-565-4444	565-9198
TF: 800-709-3726 ■ *Web:* www.eea.coop					
Grand Valley Rural Power Lines Inc 845 22 Rd	Grand Junction	CO	81505	970-242-0040	242-0612
Web: www.gvp.org					
Gunnison County Electric Assn Inc 37250 W Hwy 50 PO Box 180	Gunnison	CO	81230	970-641-3520	641-5302
TF: 800-726-3523 ■ *Web:* www.gcea.coop					
Highline Electric Assn 1300 S Interocean Ave	Holyoke	CO	80734	970-854-2236	854-3652
Web: www.hea.coop					
Holy Cross Energy PO Box 2150	Glenwood Springs	CO	81602	970-945-5491	945-4081
TF: 888-347-4425 ■ *Web:* www.holycross.com					
Intermountain Rural Electric Assn 5496 Hwy 85	Sedalia	CO	80135	303-688-3100	688-7431
TF: 800-332-9540 ■ *Web:* www.intermountain-rea.com					
KC Electric Assn 422 3rd Ave	Hugo	CO	80821	719-743-2431	743-2396
TF: 800-700-3123					
La Plata Electric Assn Inc 45 Stewart St	Durango	CO	81303	970-247-5786	247-2674
TF: 888-839-5732 ■ *Web:* www.lpea.com					
Morgan County Rural Electric Assn 20169 US Hwy 34	Fort Morgan	CO	80701	970-867-5688	867-3277
Web: www.mcrea.org					
Mountain Parks Electric Inc 321 W Agate Ave	Granby	CO	80446	970-887-3378	887-3996
TF: 877-887-3378 ■ *Web:* www.mpei.com					
Mountain View Electric Assn Inc 1655 5th St	Limon	CO	80828	719-775-2861	775-9513
TF: 800-388-9881 ■ *Web:* www.mvea.org					
Poudre Valley Rural Electric Assn Inc 7649 Rea Pkwy	Fort Collins	CO	80528	970-226-1234	226-2123
TF: 800-432-1012 ■ *Web:* www.pvrea.com					
San Isabel Electric 893 E Enterprise Dr	Pueblo West	CO	81007	719-547-2160	547-2229
TF: 800-279-7432 ■ *Web:* www.siea.com					
San Luis Valley Rural Electric Co-op 3625 US Hwy 160 W	Monte Vista	CO	81144	719-852-3538	852-4333
TF: 800-332-7634 ■ *Web:* www.slvrec.com					
San Miguel Power Assn Inc 170 W 10th Ave	Nucla	CO	81424	970-864-7311	864-7257
TF: 800-864-7256 ■ *Web:* www.smpa.com					
Sangre de Cristo Electric Assn 29780 US Hwy 24	Buena Vista	CO	81211	719-395-2412	395-8742
TF: 800-933-3823 ■ *Web:* www.sdcea.com					

	City	State	Zip	Phone	Fax
Southeast Colorado Power Assn (SECPA) 901 W 3rd *TF:* 800-332-8634 ■ *Web:* www.secpa.com	La Junta	CO	81050	719-384-2551	384-7320
United Power Inc 500 Co-op Way *TF:* 800-468-8809 ■ *Web:* www.unitedpower.com	Brighton	CO	80603	303-659-0551	659-2172
White River Electric Assn Inc 233 6th St *Web:* www.wrea.org	Meeker	CO	81641	970-878-5041	878-5766
Y-W Electric Assn Inc 250 Main Ave *TF:* 800-660-2291 ■ *Web:* www.ywelectric.com	Akron	CO	80720	970-345-2291	345-2154
Yampa Valley Electric Assn Inc 32 10th St *TF:* 888-873-9832 ■ *Web:* www.yvea.com	Steamboat Springs	CO	80487	970-879-1160	879-7270

CONNECTICUT

	City	State	Zip	Phone	Fax
Alstom Inc 2000 Day Hill Rd *TF:* 866-257-8664 ■ *Web:* www.apcompower.com	Windsor	CT	06095	860-285-5400	285-5062

DELAWARE

	City	State	Zip	Phone	Fax
Delaware Electric Co-op Inc PO Box 600 *TF:* 800-282-8595 ■ *Web:* www.delaware.coop	Greenwood	DE	19950	302-349-3147	349-3147

FLORIDA

	City	State	Zip	Phone	Fax
Central Florida Electric Co-op Inc 1124 N Young Blvd *TF:* 800-227-1302 ■ *Web:* www.cfec.com	Chiefland	FL	32644	352-493-2511	493-4499
Choctawhatchee Electric Co-op Inc 1350 W Baldwin Ave *TF:* 800-342-0990 ■ *Web:* www.chelco.com	De Funiak Springs	FL	32435	850-892-2111	892-9243
Clay Electric Co-op Inc 7450 State Rd 100 *TF:* 800-224-4917 ■ *Web:* www.clayelectric.com	Keystone Heights	FL	32656	352-473-8000	473-1403
Escambia River Electric Co-op Inc 3425 Florida 4 *TF:* 800-235-3848 ■ *Web:* www.erec.net	Jay	FL	32565	850-675-4521	675-8415
Florida Keys Electric Co-op Assn 91630 Overseas Hwy *TF:* 800-858-8845 ■ *Web:* www.fkec.com	Tavernier	FL	33070	305-852-2431	853-5381
Glades Electric Co-op Inc 1190 S U S Hwy 27 *TF:* 800-226-4024 ■ *Web:* www.gladesec.com	Moore Haven	FL	33471	863-946-0061	946-0824
Gulf Coast Electric Co-op Inc 722 Florida 22 *TF:* 800-333-9392 ■ *Web:* www.gcec.com	Wewahitchka	FL	32465	850-639-2216	639-5061
Lee County Electric Co-op Inc 4980 Bayline Dr PO Box 3455 *TF:* 800-282-1643 ■ *Web:* www.lcec.net	North Fort Myers	FL	33917	239-995-2121	995-7904
Peace River Electric Co-op Inc 210 Metheny Rd PO Box 1310 **Fax Area Code:* 863 ■ *TF:* 800-282-3824 ■ *Web:* www.preco.org	Wauchula	FL	33873	800-282-3824	773-3737*
Seminole Electricco-op Inc 16313 N Dale Mabry Hwy *Web:* www.seminole-electric.com	Tampa	FL	33618	813-963-0994	264-7906
Sumter Electric Co-op Inc PO Box 301 **Fax:* Mktg ■ *Web:* www.secoenergy.com	Sumterville	FL	33585	352-793-3801	793-6603*
Suwannee Valley Electric Co-op PO Box 160 *TF:* 800-752-0025 ■ *Web:* www.svec-coop.com	Live Oak	FL	32064	386-362-2226	364-5008
Talquin Electric Co-op Inc 1640 W Jefferson St *Web:* www.talquinelectric.com	Quincy	FL	32351	850-627-7651	627-2553
Tri-County Electric Co-op Inc 2862 W US Hwy 90 *TF:* 800-999-2285 ■ *Web:* www.tcec.com	Madison	FL	32340	850-973-2285	973-1209
West Florida Electric Co-op 5282 Peanut Rd *TF:* 800-342-7400 ■ *Web:* www.wfeca.net	Graceville	FL	32440	850-263-3231	263-3726
Withlacoochee River Electric Co-op PO Box 278 *Web:* www.wrec.net	Dade City	FL	33526	352-567-5133	521-5971

GEORGIA

	City	State	Zip	Phone	Fax
Altamaha Electric Membership Corp 611 W Liberty St *TF:* 800-822-4563 ■ *Web:* www.altamahaemc.com	Lyons	GA	30436	912-526-8181	526-4235
Amicalola Electric Membership Corp 544 Hwy 515 S *TF:* 800-992-6471 ■ *Web:* www.amicalolaemc.com	Jasper	GA	30143	706-253-5200	253-5251
Blue Ridge Mountain Electric Membership Corp 1360 Main St *TF:* 800-292-6456 ■ *Web:* www.brmemc.com	Young Harris	GA	30582	706-379-3121	379-4834
Canoochee Electric Membership Corp 342 E Brazell St *TF:* 800-342-0134 ■ *Web:* www.canoocheeemc.com	Reidsville	GA	30453	800-342-0134	
Carroll Electric Membership Corp 155 N Hwy 113 *Web:* www.cemc.com	Carrollton	GA	30117	770-832-3552	832-0240
Central Georgia Electric Membership Corp 923 S Mulberry St **Fax:* Cust Svc ■ *TF:* 800-222-4877 ■ *Web:* www.cgemc.com	Jackson	GA	30233	770-775-7857	504-7877*
Coastal Electric Co-op 1265 S Coastal Hwy PO Box 109 *TF:* 800-421-2343 ■ *Web:* www.coastalemc.com	Midway	GA	31320	912-884-3311	884-2362
Cobb Electric Membership Corp 1000 EMC Pkwy PO Box 369 **Fax Area Code:* 678 ■ **Fax:* Hum Res ■ *Web:* www.cobbemc.com	Marietta	GA	30061	770-429-2100	355-3363*
Colquitt Electric Membership Corp 15 Rowland Dr *TF:* 800-342-8694 ■ *Web:* www.colquittemc.com	Moultrie	GA	31768	229-985-3620	985-6705
Coweta-Fayette Electric Membership Corp 807 Collinsworth Rd *TF:* 877-746-4362 ■ *Web:* www.utility.org	Palmetto	GA	30268	770-502-0226	251-9788
Crisp County Power Commission Inc PO Box 1218 *Web:* www.crispcountypower.com	Cordele	GA	31010	229-273-3811	
Diverse Power Inc 1400 S Davis Rd *TF:* 800-845-8362 ■ *Web:* www.diversepower.com	LaGrange	GA	30241	706-845-2000	845-2020
Excelsior Electric Membership Corp 986 SE Broad St *Web:* www.excelsioremc.com	Metter	GA	30439	912-685-2115	685-5782
Flint Energies 103 Macon Rd *TF:* 800-342-3616 ■ *Web:* www.flintenergies.com	Reynolds	GA	31076	478-847-3415	847-5181
Grady Electric Membership Corp 1499 US Hwy 84 W *TF:* 800-942-4362 ■ *Web:* www.gradyemc.com	Cairo	GA	39828	229-377-4182	377-7176
Greystone Power Corp 4040 Bankhead Hwy *Web:* www.greystonepower.com	Douglasville	GA	30134	770-942-6576	489-0940
Habersham Electric Membership Corp 6135 Georgia 115 **Fax Area Code:* 800 ■ *TF:* 800-640-6812 ■ *Web:* www.habershamemc.com	Clarkesville	GA	30523	706-754-2114	640-6813*
Hart Electric Membership Corp 1071 Elberton Hwy **Fax Area Code:* 800 ■ *TF:* 800-241-4109 ■ *Web:* www.hartemc.com	Hartwell	GA	30643	706-376-4714	486-3277*
Irwin Electric Membership Corp 915 Jefferson Davis Memorial Hwy *TF:* 800-237-3745 ■ *Web:* www.irwinemc.com	Ocilla	GA	31774	229-468-7415	468-7009
Jackson Electric Membership Corp 850 Commerce Rd *TF:* 800-462-3691 ■ *Web:* www.jacksonemc.com	Jefferson	GA	30549	706-367-5281	367-6102
Jefferson Energy Co-op 3077 Hwy 17 PO Box 457 *TF:* 800-342-0322 ■ *Web:* www.jeffersonenergy.com	North Wrens	GA	30833	706-547-2167	547-5075
Lamar Electric Membership Corp 1367 Hwy 341 S PO Box 40 *TF:* 877-358-1383 ■ *Web:* www.lamaremc.com	Barnesville	GA	30204	770-358-1383	358-6078
Little Ocmulgee Electric Membership Corp 163 W Railroad Ave *Web:* www.littleocmulgeeemc.com	Alamo	GA	30411	912-568-7171	568-7174
Middle Georgia Electric Membership Corp 600 Tippettville Rd *TF:* 800-342-0144 ■ *Web:* www.mgemc.com	Vienna	GA	31092	229-268-2671	268-7215
Mitchell Electric Membership Corp 475 Cairo Rd *TF:* 800-479-6034 ■ *Web:* www.mitchellemc.com	Camilla	GA	31730	229-336-5221	336-7088
North Georgia Electric Membership Corp 1850 Cleveland Hwy *TF:* 800-282-4022 ■ *Web:* www.ngemc.com	Dalton	GA	30722	706-259-9441	259-9625
Ocmulgee Electric Membership Corp 5722 Eastman St *TF:* 800-342-5509 ■ *Web:* www.ocmulgeeemc.com	Eastman	GA	31023	478-374-7001	374-0759
Oconee Electric Membership Corp 3445 US Hwy 80 W *TF:* 800-522-2930 ■ *Web:* www.oconeeemc.com	Dudley	GA	31022	478-676-3191	676-4200
Okefenoke Rural Electric Membership Corp 174 E Cleveland St *TF:* 800-262-5131 ■ *Web:* www.oremc.com	Nahunta	GA	31553	912-462-5131	462-6100
Pataula Electric Membership Corp 925 Barkley St PO Box 289 *TF:* 888-631-9757 ■ *Web:* www.pataulaemc.com	Cuthbert	GA	31740	229-732-3171	732-5191
Planters Electric Membership Corp 1740 Hwy 25 N *TF:* 800-324-4722 ■ *Web:* www.plantersemc.com	Millen	GA	30442	478-982-4722	982-4798
Rayle Electric Membership Corp 616 Lexington Ave *Web:* www.rayleemc.com	Washington	GA	30673	706-678-2116	678-5381
Sawnee Electric Membership Corp 543 Atlantic Hwy *TF:* 800-635-9131	Cumming	GA	30028	770-887-2363	886-8119
Slash Pine Electric Membership Corp 794 W Dame Ave	Homerville	GA	31634	912-487-5201	487-2948
Snapping Shoals Electric Membership Corp 14750 Brown Bridge Rd	Covington	GA	30016	770-786-3484	385-2720
Sumter Electric Membership Corp 1120 Felder St *TF:* 800-342-6978 ■ *Web:* www.sumteremc.com	Americus	GA	31709	229-924-8041	924-4982
Three Notch Electric Membership Corp PO Box 367 *TF:* 800-239-5377 ■ *Web:* www.threenotchemc.com	Donalsonville	GA	39845	229-524-5377	524-8046
Tri-County Electric Membership Corp PO Box 487 *TF:* 866-254-8100 ■ *Web:* www.tri-countyemc.com	Gray	GA	31032	478-986-8100	986-4733
Tri-State Electric Membership Corp PO Box 68	McCaysville	GA	30555	706-492-3251	492-7617
Upson County Electric Membership Corp 607 E Main St *Web:* www.upsonemc.com	Thomaston	GA	30286	706-647-5475	647-8545
Walton EMC 842 Hwy 78 NW PO Box 260 *Web:* www.waltonemc.com	Monroe	GA	30655	770-267-2505	267-1223
Washington Electric Membership Corp 258 N Harris St *TF:* 800-552-2577 ■ *Web:* www.washingtonemc.com	Sandersville	GA	31082	478-552-2577	552-5552

IDAHO

	City	State	Zip	Phone	Fax
Clearwater Power Co 4230 Hatwai Rd PO Box 997 *TF:* 888-743-1501 ■ *Web:* www.clearwaterpower.com	Lewiston	ID	83501	208-743-1501	746-3902

	City	State	Zip	Phone	Fax
Fall River Rural Electric Co-op Inc 1150 N 3400 E *TF:* 800-632-5726 ■ *Web:* www.frrec.com	Ashton	ID	83420	208-652-7431	652-7825
Idaho County Light & Power Co-op 1065 Idaho 13 Scenic *TF:* 877-212-0424 ■ *Web:* www.iclp.coop	Grangeville	ID	83530	208-983-1610	983-1432
Kootenai Electric Co-op Inc 2451 W Dakota Ave *Web:* www.kec.com	Hayden	ID	83835	208-765-1200	772-5858
Lost River Electric Co-op Inc 305 Pine St PO Box 420 *Web:* www.lrecoop.com	Mackay	ID	83251	208-588-3311	588-3038
Northern Lights Inc 421 Cherry St PO Box 269 *TF:* 800-326-9594 ■ *Web:* www.norlight.org	Sagle	ID	83860	208-263-5141	263-7412
Raft River Rural Electric Co-op Inc 155 N Main St PO Box 617 *TF:* 800-342-7732 ■ *Web:* www.rrelectric.com	Malta	ID	83342	208-645-2211	645-2300
Salmon River Electric Co-op Inc 1130 Main St PO Box 384 *TF:* 877-806-2283 ■ *Web:* www.srec.org	Challis	ID	83226	208-879-2283	879-2596
South Side Electric Lines Inc PO Box 69	Declo	ID	83323	208-654-2313	
United Electric Co-op 1330 21st St *Web:* www.unitedelectric.org	Heyburn	ID	83336	208-679-2222	679-3333

ILLINOIS

	City	State	Zip	Phone	Fax
Adams Electric Co-op 700 Eastwood St PO Box 247 *TF:* 800-232-4797 ■ *Web:* www.adamselectric.coop	Camp Point	IL	62320	217-593-7701	593-7120
Clinton County Electric Co-op Inc 475 N Main St PO Box 40 *TF:* 800-526-7282 ■ *Web:* www.cceci.com	Breese	IL	62230	618-526-7282	526-4561
Coles-Moultrie Electric Co-op 104 DeWitt Ave E PO Box 709 *TF:* 888-661-2632 ■ *Web:* www.cmec.coop	Mattoon	IL	61938	217-235-0341	234-8342
Corn Belt Energy Corp 1 Energy Way *TF:* 800-879-0339 ■ *Web:* www.cornbeltenergy.com	Bloomington	IL	61705	309-662-5330	663-4516
Eastern Illini Electric Co-op 330 W Ottawa PO Box 96 *TF:* 800-824-5102 ■ *Web:* www.eiec.org	Paxton	IL	60957	217-379-2131	379-2936
Egyptian Electric Co-op Assn PO Box 38 *TF:* 800-606-1505 ■ *Web:* www.eeca.coop	Steeleville	IL	62288	618-965-3434	965-3111
EnerStar Electric Co-op 11597 Illinois Hwy 1 *TF:* 800-635-4145 ■ *Web:* www.enerstar.com	Paris	IL	61944	217-463-4145	465-5801
Illinois Rural Electric Co-op 2 S Main St *Web:* www.e-co-op.com	Winchester	IL	62694	217-742-3128	742-3831
Jo-Carroll Energy 793 US Hwy 20 W *TF:* 800-858-5522 ■ *Web:* www.jocarroll.com	Elizabeth	IL	61028	815-858-2207	858-3731
McDonough Power Co-op 1210 W Jackson St	Macomb	IL	61455	309-833-2101	833-2104
Menard Electric Co-op 122 S 6th St *TF:* 800-872-1203 ■ *Web:* www.menard.com	Petersburg	IL	62675	217-632-7746	632-2578
MJM Electric Co-op Inc (MJMEC) 264 N E St PO Box 80 *TF:* 800-648-4729 ■ *Web:* www.mjmec.coop	Carlinville	IL	62626	217-854-3137	854-3918
Norris Electric Co-op 8543 N State Hwy 130 PO Box 6000 *TF:* 877-783-8765 ■ *Web:* www.norriselectric.com	Newton	IL	62448	618-783-8765	783-3673
Rural Electric Convenience Co-op Co 3973 W SR 104 PO Box 19 *TF:* 800-245-7322 ■ *Web:* www.recc.coop	Auburn	IL	62615	217-438-6197	438-3212
Shelby Electric Co-op (SEC) Rt 128 N 6th St PO Box 560 *TF:* 800-677-2612 ■ *Web:* www.shelbyelectric.coop	Shelbyville	IL	62565	217-774-3986	774-3330
SouthEastern Illinois Electric Co-op 585 Hwy 142 S PO Box 251 *TF:* 800-833-2611 ■ *Web:* www.seiec.com	Eldorado	IL	62930	618-273-2611	273-3886
Southern Illinois Electric Co-op 7420 US Hwy 51 S *TF:* 800-762-1400 ■ *Web:* www.siec.coop	Dongola	IL	62926	618-827-3555	827-3585
Southwestern Electric Co-op Inc 525 US Rt 40 PO Box 549 *TF:* 800-637-8667 ■ *Web:* www.sweci.com	Greenville	IL	62246	618-664-1025	664-4179
Spoon River Electric Co-op Inc (SREC) 930 S 5th Ave PO Box 340 *TF:* 877-404-2572 ■ *Web:* www.srecoop.org	Canton	IL	61520	309-647-2700	647-7354
Tri-County Electric Co-op Inc 3906 Broadway St *TF:* 800-244-5151 ■ *Web:* www.tricountycoop.com	Mount Vernon	IL	62864	618-244-5151	244-1496
Wayne-White Counties Electric Co-op PO Drawer E *TF:* 888-871-7695 ■ *Web:* www.wwcec.com	Fairfield	IL	62837	618-842-2196	842-4497
Western Illinois Electrical Co-op 524 N Madison St *Web:* www.wiec.net	Carthage	IL	62321	217-357-3125	357-3127

INDIANA

	City	State	Zip	Phone	Fax
Bartholomew County Rural Electric Membership Corp 801 2nd St *TF:* 800-927-5672 ■ *Web:* www.bcremc.com	Columbus	IN	47201	812-372-2546	372-2112
Boone County Rural Electric Membership Corp 1207 Indianapolis Ave *TF:* 800-897-7362 ■ *Web:* www.bremc.com	Lebanon	IN	46052	765-482-2390	482-7869
Carroll County Rural Electric Membership Corp 119 W Franklin St PO Box 298 *TF:* 800-506-7362 ■ *Web:* www.remconline.net	Delphi	IN	46923	765-564-2057	564-4461
Clark County REMC 7810 State Rd 60 PO Box 411 *TF:* 800-462-6988 ■ *Web:* www.theremc.com	Sellersburg	IN	47172	812-246-3316	246-3947
Crawfordsville Electric Light & Power PO Box 428 *Web:* www.accelplus.net	Crawfordsville	IN	47933	765-362-1900	
Daviess-Martin County REMC 12628 E 75 N PO Box 430 *TF:* 800-762-7362 ■ *Web:* www.dmremc.com	Loogootee	IN	47553	812-295-4200	295-4216
Decatur County Rural Electric Membership Corp 1430 W Main St PO Box 46 *TF:* 800-844-7362 ■ *Web:* www.dcremc.com	Greensburg	IN	47240	812-663-3391	663-8572
Dubois Rural Electric Co-op Inc 458 3rd Ave *Web:* www.duboisrec.com	Jasper	IN	47546	812-482-5454	482-7015
Fulton County Rural Electric Membership Corp 1448 W State Rd 14 *Web:* www.fultoncountyremc.com	Rochester	IN	46975	574-223-3156	223-4353
Harrison County Rural Electric Membership Corp 1165 Old Forest Rd NW *Web:* www.theremc.com	Corydon	IN	47112	812-738-4115	738-2378
Hendricks Power Co-op 86 N County Rd 500 E *TF:* 800-876-5473 ■ *Web:* www.hendrickspower.com	Avon	IN	46123	317-745-5473	745-6865
Jackson County Rural Electric Membership Corp 274 E Base Rd *TF:* 800-288-4458 ■ *Web:* www.jacksonremc.com	Brownstown	IN	47220	812-358-4458	358-5719
Jasper County Rural Electric Membership Corp 280 E 400 S *TF:* 888-866-7362 ■ *Web:* www.jasperremc.com	Rensselaer	IN	47978	219-866-4601	866-2199
Jay County Rural Electric Membership Corp 484 S 200 W PO Box 904 *TF:* 800-835-7362 ■ *Web:* www.jayremc.com	Portland	IN	47371	260-726-7121	726-6240
Johnson County Rural Electric Membership Corp 750 International Dr *Web:* www.jcremc.com	Franklin	IN	46131	317-736-6174	736-8185
Kankakee Valley Rural Electric Membership Corp 114 S Main St *TF:* 800-552-2622 ■ *Web:* www.kvremc.com	Wanatah	IN	46390	219-733-2511	733-2991
Kosciusko County Rural Electric Membership Corp 370 S 250 E *TF:* 800-790-7362 ■ *Web:* www.kosciuskoremc.com	Warsaw	IN	46582	574-267-6331	267-7273
LaGrange County Rural Electric Membership Corp 1995 E US Hwy 20 *TF:* 877-463-7165 ■ *Web:* www.lagrangeremc.com	LaGrange	IN	46761	260-463-7165	463-4329
Marshall County REMC 11299 12th Rd PO Box 250 *Web:* www.marshallcoremc.com	Plymouth	IN	46563	574-936-3161	935-4162
Miami-Cass County Rural Electric Membership Corp PO Box 168 *TF:* 800-844-6668 ■ *Web:* www.miami-cassremc.com	Peru	IN	46970	765-473-6668	473-8770
Newton County Rural Electric Membership Corp 207 E Goss St	Kentland	IN	47951	219-474-6224	474-6290
Noble REMC 300 Weber Rd PO Box 137 *TF:* 800-933-7362 ■ *Web:* www.nobleremc.com	Albion	IN	46701	260-636-2113	636-3319
Northeastern REMC 4901 E Pk 30 Dr *Web:* www.nremc.com	Columbia City	IN	46725	260-244-6111	625-3407
Orange County Rural Electric Membership Corp 7133 N State Rd 337 PO Box 208 *TF:* 888-337-5900 ■ *Web:* www.myremc.coop	Orleans	IN	47452	812-865-2229	865-2061
Parke County Rural Electric Membership Corp 119 W High St *TF:* 800-537-3913 ■ *Web:* www.parkecountyremc.com	Rockville	IN	47872	765-569-3133	569-3360
Rush Shelby Energy Inc 2777 S 840 W PO Box 55 *TF:* 800-706-7362 ■ *Web:* www.rse.coop	Manilla	IN	46150	765-544-2600	544-2620
South Central Indiana Rural Electric Membership Corp 300 Morton Ave PO Box 3100 *TF:* 800-264-7362 ■ *Web:* www.sciremc.com	Martinsville	IN	46151	765-342-3344	342-1335
Southeastern Indiana Rural Electric Membership Corp 712 S Buckeye St *TF:* 800-737-4111 ■ *Web:* www.seiremc.com	Osgood	IN	47037	812-689-4111	689-6987
Southern Indiana Rural Electric Co-op Inc 1776 10th St PO Box 219 *TF:* 800-323-2316 ■ *Web:* www.sirec.com	Tell City	IN	47586	812-547-2316	547-6853
Steuben County Rural Electric Membership Corp 1212 S Wayne St *TF:* 888-233-9088 ■ *Web:* www.remcsteuben.com	Angola	IN	46703	260-665-3563	665-7495
Tipmont Rural Electric Membership Corp 403 S Main St *TF:* 800-726-3953 ■ *Web:* www.tipmont.org	Linden	IN	47955	765-339-7211	339-4865
UDWI Rural Electric Membership Corp PO Box 427 *TF:* 800-489-7362 ■ *Web:* www.hepn.com	Bloomfield	IN	47424	812-384-4446	384-3127
United Rural Electric Membership Corp 4563 E Markle Rd *TF:* 800-542-6339 ■ *Web:* www.unitedremc.com	Markle	IN	46770	260-758-3155	758-3157
Wabash County Rural Electric Membership Corp 350 Wedcor Ave *TF:* 800-563-2146	Wabash	IN	46992	260-563-2146	563-1523
Wabash Valley Power Assn Inc 722 N High School Rd *Web:* www.wvpa.com	Indianapolis	IN	46214	317-481-2800	243-6416
Warren County Rural Electric Membership Corp 15 Midway St *TF:* 800-872-7319	Williamsport	IN	47993	765-762-6114	762-6117
White County Rural Electric Membership Corp 302 N 6th St *TF:* 800-844-7161 ■ *Web:* www.whitecountyremc.com	Monticello	IN	47960	574-583-7161	583-4156
Whitewater Valley Rural Electric Membership Corp 101 Brownsville Ave *TF:* 800-529-5557 ■ *Web:* www.wwvremc.com	Liberty	IN	47353	765-458-5171	458-5938
WIN Energy Rural Electric Membership Corp 3981 S US Hwy 41 *TF:* 800-882-5140 ■ *Web:* www.winenergyremc.com	Vincennes	IN	47591	812-882-5140	886-0306

IOWA

	City	State	Zip	Phone	Fax
Access Energy Co-op 1800 W Washington St *TF:* 866-242-4232 ■ *Web:* www.accessenergycoop.com	Mount Pleasant	IA	52641	319-385-1577	385-6873

Company / Address	City	State	Zip	Phone	Fax
Allamakee-Clayton Electric Co-op Inc 228 W Greene St — *Web:* www.acrec.com	Postville	IA	52162	563-864-7611	864-7820
Butler County Rural Electric Co-op 521 N Main St — *TF:* 888-267-2726 ■ *Web:* www.butlerrec.com	Allison	IA	50602	319-267-2726	267-2566
Calhoun County Electric Co-op Assn 1015 Tonawanda St PO Box 312 — *Web:* www.calhounrec.coop	Rockwell City	IA	50579	712-297-7112	297-7211
Chariton Valley Electric Co-op 2090 Hwy 5 PO Box 486 — *Web:* www.cvrec.com	Albia	IA	52531	641-932-7126	932-2534
Clarke Electric Co-op Inc 1103 N Main St — *TF:* 800-362-2154 ■ *Web:* www.cecnet.net	Osceola	IA	50213	641-342-2173	342-6292
Consumers Energy 2074 242nd St — *TF:* 800-696-6552 ■ *Web:* www.consumersenergy.net	Marshalltown	IA	50158	641-752-1593	752-5738
Corn Belt Power Co-op 1300 13th St N PO Box 508 — *Web:* www.cbpower.coop	Humboldt	IA	50548	515-332-2571	332-1375
East-Central Iowa Rural Electric Co-op 2400 Bing Miller Ln — *TF:* 877-850-4343 ■ *Web:* www.ecirec.com	Urbana	IA	52345	319-443-4343	443-4359
Eastern Iowa Light & Power Co-op 600 E 5th St Po Box 3003 — *TF:* 800-728-1242 ■ *Web:* www.easterniowa.com	Wilton	IA	52778	563-732-2211	732-2219
Farmers Electric Co-op Inc 1959 Yoder Ave SW — *TF:* 877-426-6540 ■ *Web:* www.feckalona.com	Kalona	IA	52247	319-683-2510	683-2506
Farmers Rural Electric Co-op Inc 102 SE 6th St — *TF:* 800-397-4821 ■ *Web:* www.farmersrec.com	Greenfield	IA	50849	641-743-6146	343-7187
Franklin Rural Electric Co-op 1560 Hwy 65 — *TF:* 800-750-3557 ■ *Web:* www.franklinrec.com	Hampton	IA	50441	641-456-2557	456-5183
Grundy County Rural Electric Co-op 102 E 'G' Ave — *TF:* 800-390-7605 ■ *Web:* www.grundycountyrecia.org	Grundy Center	IA	50638	319-824-5251	824-3118
Guthrie County Rural Electric Co-op Assn PO Box 7 — *TF:* 888-747-2206	Guthrie Center	IA	50115	641-747-2206	747-3701
Harrison County Rural Electric Co-op 61 4th St — *Web:* www.hcrec.coop	Woodbine	IA	51579	712-647-2727	647-2242
Hawkeye REC 24049 Iowa 9 — *TF:* 800-658-2243 ■ *Web:* www.hawkeyerec.com	Cresco	IA	52136	563-547-3801	547-4033
Heartland Power Co-op 216 Jackson St PO Box 65 — *TF:* 888-584-9732 ■ *Web:* www.heartlandpower.com	Thompson	IA	50478	641-584-2251	584-2253
Humboldt County Rural Electric Co-op (HCREC) 1210 13th St N — *TF:* 800-994-3532 ■ *Web:* www.humboldtrec.coop	Humboldt	IA	50548	515-332-1616	332-3007
Iowa Lakes Electric Co-op 702 S 1st St — *TF:* 800-225-4532 ■ *Web:* www.ilec.coop	Estherville	IA	51334	712-362-7870	362-2819
Linn County Rural Electric Co-op 5695 Rec Dr — *Web:* www.linncountyrec.com	Marion	IA	52302	319-377-1587	377-5875
Lyon Rural Electric Co-op 116 S Marshall St — *TF:* 800-658-3976 ■ *Web:* www.lyonrec.coop	Rock Rapids	IA	51246	712-472-2506	472-3925
Maquoketa Valley Rural Electric Co-op 109 N Huber St — *TF:* 800-927-6068 ■ *Web:* www.mvec.com	Anamosa	IA	52205	319-462-3542	462-3217
Midland Power Co-op 1005 135th St — *Web:* www.midlandpower.com	Jefferson	IA	50129	515-386-4111	386-2385
Nishnabotna Valley Rural Electric Co-op 1317 Chatburn Ave — *TF:* 800-234-5122 ■ *Web:* www.nvrec.com	Harlan	IA	51537	712-755-2166	755-2351
North West REC 1505 Albany Pl SE PO Box 435 — *TF:* 800-383-0476 ■ *Web:* www.nwrec.com	Orange City	IA	51041	712-707-4935	707-4934
Northwest Iowa Power Co-op (NIPCO) 31002 County Rd C38 PO Box 240 — *Web:* www.nipco.coop	Le Mars	IA	51031	712-546-4141	546-8795
Osceola Electric Co-op Inc 204 8th St — *TF:* 888-754-2519	Sibley	IA	51249	712-754-2519	754-2510
Pella Co-op Electric Assn 2615 Washington St — *TF:* 800-619-1040 ■ *Web:* www.pella-cea.org	Pella	IA	50219	641-628-1040	628-4856
Raccoon Valley Electric Co-op 28725 Hwy 30 PO Box 486 — *TF:* 800-253-6211 ■ *Web:* www.gliddenrec.com	Glidden	IA	51443	712-659-3649	659-3716
Sac County Rural Electric Co-op 601 E Main St PO Box 397 — *TF:* 866-722-6732 ■ *Web:* www.sacrec.com	Sac City	IA	50583	712-662-4275	662-4538
Southern Iowa Electric Co-op Inc 22458 Hwy 2 PO Box 70 — *TF:* 800-607-2027 ■ *Web:* www.sie.coop	Bloomfield	IA	52537	641-664-2277	664-3502
Southwest Iowa Rural Electric Co-op 1801 grove Ave — *TF:* 888-591-1261 ■ *Web:* www.swiarec.coop	Corning	IA	50841	641-322-3165	322-5274
TIP Rural Electric Co-op 612 W Des Moines St PO Box 534 — *TF:* 800-934-7976 ■ *Web:* www.tiprec.com	Brooklyn	IA	52211	641-522-9221	522-9271
Western Iowa Power Co-op 809 Iowa 39 — *TF:* 800-253-5189 ■ *Web:* www.wipco.com	Denison	IA	51442	712-263-2943	263-8655
Woodbury County Rural Electric Co-op Assn 1495 Humboldt Ave — *TF:* 800-469-3125 ■ *Web:* www.showcase.netins.net/web/wdbyrec	Moville	IA	51039	712-873-3125	873-5377

KANSAS

Company / Address	City	State	Zip	Phone	Fax
Ark Valley Electric Co-op Assn 10 E 10th St — *TF:* 888-297-9212 ■ *Web:* www.arkvalley.com	South Hutchinson	KS	67504	620-662-6661	665-0148
Bluestem Electric Co-op Inc 614 E Hwy 24 PO Box 5 — *TF:* 800-558-1580 ■ *Web:* www.bluestemelectric.com	Wamego	KS	66547	785-456-2212	456-2003
Brown-Atchison Electric Co-op Assn Inc 1712 Central Ave — *Web:* www.baelectric.com	Horton	KS	66439	785-486-2117	486-3910
Butler Rural Electric Co-op Assn Inc 216 S Vine St PO Box 1242 — *TF:* 800-464-0060 ■ *Web:* www.butler.coop	El Dorado	KS	67042	316-321-9600	321-9980
Caney Valley Electric Co-op Assn Inc The 401 Lawrence St PO Box 308 — *TF:* 800-310-8911 ■ *Web:* www.caneyvalley.com	Cedar Vale	KS	67024	620-758-2262	758-2926
CMS Electric Co-op Inc 509 E Carthage St — *TF:* 800-794-2353 ■ *Web:* www.cmselectric.com	Meade	KS	67864	620-873-2184	873-5303
Doniphan Electric Co-op Assn Inc 101 N Main St — *TF:* 800-699-0810 ■ *Web:* www.donrec.org	Troy	KS	66087	785-985-3523	985-2298
DS & O Rural Electric Co-op Assn 129 W Main St PO Box 286 — *TF:* 800-376-3533 ■ *Web:* www.dsoelectric.com	Solomon	KS	67480	785-655-2011	655-2805
Flint Hills Rural Electric Co-op Assn Inc 1564 S 1000 Rd — *Web:* www.flinthillsrec.com	Council Grove	KS	66846	620-767-5144	767-6311
Heartland Rural Electric Co-op 110 Enterprise St — *TF:* 888-835-9585 ■ *Web:* www.heartland-rec.com	Girard	KS	66743	620-724-8251	724-8253
Kaw Valley Electric Co-op Inc 1100 SW Auburn Rd — *TF:* 800-794-2011 ■ *Web:* www.kawvalleyelectric.coop	Topeka	KS	66615	785-478-3444	478-1088
Lane-Scott Electric Co-op Inc 410 S High — *TF:* 800-407-2217 ■ *Web:* www.lanescott.coop	Dighton	KS	67839	620-397-5327	397-5997
Leavenworth-Jefferson Electric Co-op Inc 507 N Union St — *TF:* 888-796-6111 ■ *Web:* www.ljec.coop	McLouth	KS	66054	913-796-6111	796-6164
Lyon-Coffey Electric Co-op Inc 1013 N 4th PO Box 229 — *TF:* 800-748-7395 ■ *Web:* www.lyon-coffey.coop	Burlington	KS	66839	620-364-2116	364-5122
Midwest Energy Inc 1330 Canterbury Dr — *TF:* 800-222-3121 ■ *Web:* www.mwenergy.com	Hays	KS	67601	785-625-3437	625-1494
Nemaha-Marshall Electric Co-op PO Box O — *TF Cust Svc:* 866-736-2347	Axtell	KS	66403	785-736-2345	736-2348
Pioneer Electric Co-op Inc 1850 W Oklahoma St PO Box 368 — *TF:* 800-794-9302 ■ *Web:* www.pioneerelectric.coop	Ulysses	KS	67880	620-356-1211	356-1669
Prairie Land Electric Co-op Inc 14935 US HWY 36 — *TF:* 800-577-3323 ■ *Web:* www.prairielandelectric.com	Norton	KS	67654	785-877-3323	877-3572
Radiant Electric Co-op Inc 100 N 15th St — *TF:* 800-821-0956	Fredonia	KS	66736	620-378-2161	378-3164
Rolling Hills Electric Co 122 W Main St — *TF:* 877-906-5903	Mankato	KS	66956	785-378-3151	378-3219
Sedgwick County Electric Co-op 1355 S 383rd St W PO Box 220 — *TF:* 866-542-4732 ■ *Web:* www.sedgwickcountyelectric.coop	Cheney	KS	67025	316-542-3131	542-3943
Sumner-Cowley Electric Co-op Inc 2223 N A St PO Box 220 — *TF:* 888-326-3356 ■ *Web:* www.sucocoop.com	Wellington	KS	67152	620-326-3356	326-6579
Twin Valley Electric Co-op PO Box 385 — *TF:* 866-784-5500	Altamont	KS	67330	620-784-5500	784-2464
Victory Electric Co-op Assn Inc 3230 N 14th Ave — *TF:* 800-279-7915 ■ *Web:* www.victoryelectric.net	Dodge City	KS	67801	620-227-2139	227-8819
Western Co-op Electric Assn Inc 635 S 13th St — *Web:* www.westerncoop.com	WaKeeney	KS	67672	785-743-5561	743-2717
Wheatland Electric Co-op Inc 101 S Main St — *TF:* 800-762-0436 ■ *Web:* www.weci.net	Scott City	KS	67871	620-872-5885	872-7170

KENTUCKY

Company / Address	City	State	Zip	Phone	Fax
Big Sandy Rural Electric Co-op Corp 504 11th St — *TF:* 800-789-7322 ■ *Web:* www.bigsandyrecc.com	Paintsville	KY	41240	606-789-4095	789-5454
Blue Grass Energy Co-op Corp 1201 Lexington Rd — *TF:* 888-546-4243 ■ *Web:* www.bgenergy.com	Nicholasville	KY	40356	859-885-4191	885-2854
Clark Energy Co-op Inc 2640 Ironworks Rd — *TF:* 800-992-3269 ■ *Web:* www.clarkenergy.com	Winchester	KY	40391	859-744-4251	744-4218
Cumberland Valley Electric Inc Cumberland Gap Pkwy PO Box 440 — *TF:* 800-513-2677	Gray	KY	40734	606-528-2677	528-8458
Farmers Rural Electric Co-op Corp 504 S Broadway St — *TF:* 800-253-2191	Glasgow	KY	42141	270-651-2191	651-7332
Fleming Mason Energy Co-op 1449 Elizaville Rd — *TF:* 800-464-3144 ■ *Web:* www.fmenergy.com	Flemingsburg	KY	41041	606-845-2661	845-1008
Grayson Rural Electric Co-op Corp 109 Bagby Pk — *Web:* www.graysonrecc.com	Grayson	KY	41143	606-474-5136	474-5862
Hickman-Fulton Counties Rural Electric Co-op Corp PO Box 190	Hickman	KY	42050	270-236-2521	236-3028
Inter-County Energy Co-op 1009 Hustonville Rd — *TF:* 888-266-7322 ■ *Web:* www.intercountyenergy.net	Danville	KY	40422	859-236-4561	236-3627
Jackson Energy Co-op 115 Jackson Energy Ln — *TF:* 800-262-7480 ■ *Web:* www.jacksonenergy.com	McKee	KY	40447	606-364-1000	364-1007
Jackson Purchase Energy Corp 2900 Irvin Cobb Dr — *TF:* 800-633-4044 ■ *Web:* www.jpenergy.com	Paducah	KY	42002	270-442-7321	442-5337

				Phone	Fax
Kenergy Corp 6402 Old Corydon Rd *Web:* www.kenergycorp.com	Henderson	KY	42420	270-826-3991	826-3999
Licking Valley Rural Electric Co-op Corp 271 Main St	West Liberty	KY	41472	606-743-3179	743-2415
Meade County Rural Electric Co-op Corp 1351 Kentucky 79 *Web:* www.mcrecc.coop	Brandenburg	KY	40108	270-422-2162	422-4705
Nolin Rural Electric Co-op Corp 411 Ring Rd *Web:* www.nolinrecc.com	Elizabethtown	KY	42701	270-765-6153	735-1053
Owen Electric Co-op Inc 8205 Hwy 127 N PO Box 400 *TF:* 800-372-7612 ■ *Web:* www.owenelectric.com	Owenton	KY	40359	502-484-3471	484-2661
Pennyrile Rural Electric Co-op Corp 2000 Harrison St PO Box 2900 *TF Cust Svc:* 800-297-4710 ■ *Web:* www.precc.com	Hopkinsville	KY	42241	270-886-2555	885-6469
Salt River Electric Co-op Corp 111 W Brashear Ave *TF:* 800-221-7465 ■ *Web:* www.srelectric.com	Bardstown	KY	40004	502-348-3931	348-1993
Shelby Energy Co-op Inc 620 Old Finchville Rd *TF:* 800-292-6585 ■ *Web:* www.shelbyenergy.com	Shelbyville	KY	40065	502-633-4420	633-2387
South Kentucky Rural Electrical Co-op 925 N Main St PO Box 910 *TF:* 800-264-5112 ■ *Web:* www.skrecc.com	Somerset	KY	42502	606-678-4121	679-8279
Taylor County Rural Electric Corp PO Box 100	Campbellsville	KY	42719	270-465-4101	789-3625
Warren Rural Electric Co-op Corp 951 Fairview Ave *Web:* www.wrecc.com	Bowling Green	KY	42101	270-842-6541	781-3299
West Kentucky Rural Electric Co-op Corp PO Box 589 *TF:* 877-495-7322 ■ *Web:* www.wkrecc.com	Mayfield	KY	42066	270-247-1321	247-8496

LOUISIANA

				Phone	Fax
Beauregard Electric Co-op Inc 1010 E 1st St *TF:* 800-367-0275 ■ *Web:* www.beci.org	DeRidder	LA	70634	337-463-6221	463-2809
Claiborne Electric Co-op 12525 Hwy 9 PO Box 719 *TF:* 800-929-3504 ■ *Web:* www.claiborneelectric.org	Homer	LA	71040	318-927-3504	368-3011
Concordia Electric Co-op Inc 1865 Hwy 84 W *TF:* 800-617-6282	Jonesville	LA	71343	318-339-7969	339-7462
Dixie Electric Membership Corp (DEMCO) PO Box 15659 *TF:* 800-262-0221 ■ *Web:* www.demco.org	Baton Rouge	LA	70895	225-261-1221	261-1383
Jefferson Davis Electric Co-op 906 N Lake Arthur Ave *TF:* 800-256-5332	Jennings	LA	70546	337-824-4330	824-8936
Northeast Louisiana Power Co-op Inc 1411 Landis St	Winnsboro	LA	71295	318-435-4523	435-3887
Pointe Coupee Electric Membership Corp 2506 False River Dr PO Box 160 *TF:* 800-738-7232 ■ *Web:* www.pcemc.org	New Roads	LA	70760	225-638-3751	638-8124
Southwest Louisiana Electric Membership Corp 3420 Hwy 167 N *TF:* 888-275-3626 ■ *Web:* www.slemco.com	Lafayette	LA	70509	337-896-5384	896-2533
Washington-Saint Tammany Electric Co-op 950 Pearl St PO Box N *Web:* www.wste.coop	Franklinton	LA	70438	985-839-3562	839-4315

MAINE

				Phone	Fax
Eastern Maine Electric Co-op Inc 21 Union St *TF:* 800-696-7444 ■ *Web:* www.emec.com	Calais	ME	04619	207-454-7555	454-8376
Fox Islands Electric Co-op 66 Main St *Web:* www.foxislands.net	Vinalhaven	ME	04863	207-863-4636	863-4526

MARYLAND

				Phone	Fax
Choptank Electric Co-op Inc 24820 Meeting House Rd PO Box 430 *TF:* 877-892-0001 ■ *Web:* www.choptankelectric.com	Denton	MD	21629	410-479-0380	479-3516
Southern Maryland Electric Co-op PO Box 1937 *TF:* 888-440-3311 ■ *Web:* www.smeco.com	Hughesville	MD	20637	301-274-3111	274-0086

MASSACHUSETTS

				Phone	Fax
Intergen 15 Wayside Rd *Web:* www.intergen.com	Burlington	MA	01803	781-993-3000	
Taunton Municipal Lighting Plant PO Box 870 *Web:* www.tmlp.com	Taunton	MA	02780	508-824-5844	

MICHIGAN

				Phone	Fax
Alger Delta Co-op Electric Assn 426 N 9th St *TF:* 800-562-0950 ■ *Web:* www.algerdelta.com	Gladstone	MI	49837	906-428-4141	428-3840
Cherryland Electric Co-op 5930 US Hwy 31 *TF:* 800-442-8616 ■ *Web:* www.cecelec.com	Grawn	MI	49637	231-486-9200	943-8204
Cloverland Electric Co-op 2916 W Hwy M-28 *TF:* 800-562-4953 ■ *Web:* www.cloverland.com	Dafter	MI	49724	906-635-6800	635-6815
Grand Haven Board of Lightand & Power (GHBLP) 1700 Eaton Dr *Web:* www.ghblp.org	Grand Haven	MI	49417	616-846-6250	846-3114
Great Lakes Energy Co-op 1323 Boyne Ave *Fax Area Code:* 231 ■ *Fax:* Cust Svc ■ *TF:* 888-485-2537 ■ *Web:* www.gtlakes.com	Boyne City	MI	49712	888-485-2537	582-6213*
HomeWorks Tri-County Electric Co-op 7973 E Grand River Ave PO Box 350 *TF:* 800-848-9333 ■ *Web:* www.homeworks.org	Portland	MI	48875	517-647-7554	647-4856
Midwest Energy Co-op 901 E State St *TF:* 800-492-5989 ■ *Web:* www.teammidwest.com	Cassopolis	MI	49031	269-445-1000	445-3792
Ontonagon County Rural Electric Assn 500 James K Paul St *TF:* 800-562-7128	Ontonagon	MI	49953	906-884-4151	884-6247
Presque Isle Electric & Gas Co-op PO Box 308 *TF:* 800-423-6634 ■ *Web:* www.pieg.com	Onaway	MI	49765	989-733-8515	733-2247
Thumb Electric Co-op Inc 2231 E Main St *Web:* www.tecmi.com	Ubly	MI	48475	989-658-8571	658-2571

MINNESOTA

				Phone	Fax
Agralite Electric Co-op 320 Hwy 12 SE *TF:* 800-950-8375 ■ *Web:* www.agralite.coop	Benson	MN	56215	320-843-4150	843-3738
Arrowhead Electric Co-op Inc 5401 W Hwy 61 PO Box 39 *TF:* 800-864-3744 ■ *Web:* www.aecimn.com	Lutsen	MN	55612	218-663-7239	663-7850
Beltrami Electric Co-op Inc 4111 Technology Dr NW *TF:* 800-955-6083 ■ *Web:* www.beltramielectric.com	Bemidji	MN	56601	218-444-2540	444-3676
Benco Electric Co-op 20946 549 Ave PO Box 8 *TF:* 888-792-3626 ■ *Web:* www.benco.org	Mankato	MN	56002	507-387-7963	387-1269
Brown County Rural Electric Assn 24386 State Hwy 4 PO Box 529 *TF:* 800-658-2368 ■ *Web:* www.browncountyrea.coop	Sleepy Eye	MN	56085	507-794-3331	794-4282
Clearwater-Polk Electric Co-op 315 Main Ave N *TF:* 888-694-3833 ■ *Web:* www.clearwater-polk.com	Bagley	MN	56621	218-694-6241	694-6245
Connexus Energy Co-op 14601 Ramsey Blvd *TF:* 800-642-1672 ■ *Web:* www.connexusenergy.com	Ramsey	MN	55303	763-323-2650	323-2603
Crow Wing Co-op Power & Light Co Hwy 371 N PO Box 507 *TF:* 800-648-9401 ■ *Web:* www.cwpower.com	Brainerd	MN	56401	218-829-2827	825-2209
Dakota Electric Assn 4300 220th St W *TF:* 800-874-3409 ■ *Web:* www.dakotaelectric.com	Farmington	MN	55024	651-463-6144	463-6144
East Central Energy PO Box 39 *Fax Area Code:* 320 ■ *TF:* 800-254-7944 ■ *Web:* www.eastcentralenergy.com	Braham	MN	55006	800-254-7944	396-4114*
Federated Rural Electric Assn 77100 US Hwy 71 PO Box 69 *TF:* 800-321-3520 ■ *Web:* www.federatedrea.com	Jackson	MN	56143	507-847-3520	728-8366
Freeborn-Mower Co-op Services 2501 E Main St *Web:* www.fmcs.coop	Albert Lea	MN	56007	507-373-6421	377-7145
Goodhue County Co-op Electric Assn 1410 Northstar Dr *TF:* 800-927-6864 ■ *Web:* www.gccea.com	Zumbrota	MN	55992	507-732-5117	732-5110
Great River Energy 12300 Elm Creek Blvd *TF:* 888-521-0130 ■ *Web:* www.greatriverenergy.com	Maple Grove	MN	55369	763-445-5000	445-5050
Itasca-Mantrap Co-op Electrical Assn 16930 Henrietta Ave S *Web:* www.itasca-mantrap.com	Park Rapids	MN	56470	218-732-3377	732-5890
Lake Country Power 2810 Elida Dr *Fax Area Code:* 218 ■ *TF:* 800-421-9959 ■ *Web:* www.lakecountrypower.com	Grand Rapids	MN	55744	800-421-9959	326-8136*
Lake Region Co-op Electrical Assn 1401 S Broadway PO Box 643 *TF:* 800-552-7658 ■ *Web:* www.lrec.coop	Pelican Rapids	MN	56572	218-863-1171	863-1172
Lyon-Lincoln Electric Co-op Inc (LLEC) 205 W Hwy 14 PO Box 639 *TF:* 800-927-6276 ■ *Web:* www.llec.coop	Tyler	MN	56178	507-247-5505	247-5508
McLeod Co-op Power Assn 1231 Ford Ave N *TF:* 800-494-6272 ■ *Web:* www.mcleodcoop.com	Glencoe	MN	55336	320-864-3148	864-4850
Meeker Co-op Light & Power Assn 1725 E US Hwy 12 # 100 *TF:* 800-232-6257 ■ *Web:* www.meekercoop.com	Litchfield	MN	55355	320-693-3231	693-2980
Mille Lacs Electric Co-op PO Box 230 *TF:* 800-450-2191 ■ *Web:* www.mlecmn.net	Aitkin	MN	56431	218-927-2191	927-6822
Minnesota Valley Co-op Light & Power Assn 501 S 1st St *TF:* 800-247-5051 ■ *Web:* www.mnvalleyrec.com	Montevideo	MN	56265	320-269-2163	269-2302
Minnesota Valley Electric Co-op 125 Minnesota Valley Electric Dr PO Box 77024 *TF:* 800-282-6832 ■ *Web:* www.mvec.net	Jordan	MN	55352	952-492-2313	492-8281
Nobles Co-op Electric 22636 US Hwy 59 *TF:* 800-776-0517 ■ *Web:* www.noblesce.com	Worthington	MN	56187	507-372-7331	372-5148
North Itasca Electric Co-op Inc 301 Main Ave PO Box 227 *TF:* 800-762-4048 ■ *Web:* www.northitascaelectric.com	Bigfork	MN	56628	218-743-3131	743-3644
North Star Electric Co-op 441 State Hwy 172 NW PO Box 719 *TF:* 888-634-2202 ■ *Web:* www.northstarelectric.coop	Baudette	MN	56623	218-634-2202	634-2203
People's Co-op Services 3935 Hwy 14 PO Box 339 *TF:* 800-214-2694 ■ *Web:* www.peoplesrec.com	Rochester	MN	55903	507-288-4004	288-9438
PKM Electric Co-op Inc 406 N Minnesota St *TF:* 800-552-7366 ■ *Web:* www.pkmcoop.com	Warren	MN	56762	218-745-4711	745-4713
Red Lake Electric Co-op Inc 412 International Dr *TF:* 800-245-6068	Red Lake Falls	MN	56750	218-253-2168	253-2630
Red River Valley Co-op Power Assn 109 2nd Ave E *TF:* 800-788-7784 ■ *Web:* www.rrvcoop.com	Halstad	MN	56548	218-456-2139	456-2102
Redwood Electric Co-op 60 Pine St PO Box 15 *TF:* 888-251-5100	Clements	MN	56224	507-692-2214	692-2211
Renville-Sibley Co-op Power Assn 103 Oak St PO Box 68 *TF:* 800-826-2593 ■ *Web:* www.renville-sibley.coop	Danube	MN	56230	320-826-2593	826-2679

Name / Address	City	State	Zip	Phone	Fax
Roseau Electric Co-op Inc 1107 3rd St NE *TF:* 888-847-8840 ■ *Web:* www.roseauelectric.coop	Roseau	MN	56751	218-463-1543	463-3713
South Central Electric Assn 71176 Tiell Dr PO Box 150 *TF:* 888-805-7232 ■ *Web:* www.southcentralelectric.com	Saint James	MN	56081	507-375-3164	375-3166
Southern Minnesota Municipal Power Agency 500 1st Ave SW *TF:* 800-824-0488 ■ *Web:* www.smmpa.com	Rochester	MN	55902	507-285-0478	292-6414
Stearns ElectricAssn 900 E Kraft Dr *TF:* 800-962-0655 ■ *Web:* www.stearnselectric.org	Melrose	MN	56352	320-256-4241	256-3618
Steele-Waseca Co-op Electric (SWCE) 2411 W Bridge St PO Box 485 *TF:* 800-526-3514 ■ *Web:* www.swce.com	Owatonna	MN	55060	507-451-7340	446-4242
Todd-Wadena Electric Co-op 550 Ash Ave NE *TF:* 800-321-8932 ■ *Web:* www.toddwadena.com	Wadena	MN	56482	218-631-3120	631-4188
Traverse Electric Co-op Inc 1618 Broadway PO Box 66 *TF:* 800-927-5443 ■ *Web:* www.traverseelectric.com	Wheaton	MN	56296	320-563-8616	563-4863
Tri-County Electric Co-op 31110 Co-op Way PO Box 626 *TF:* 800-432-2285 ■ *Web:* www.tec.coop	Rushford	MN	55971	507-864-7783	864-2871
Wild Rice Electric Co-op Inc 502 N Main PO Box 438 *TF:* 800-244-5709 ■ *Web:* www.wildriceelectric.com	Mahnomen	MN	56557	218-935-2517	935-2519
Wright-Hennepin Co-op Electric Assn 6800 Electric Dr PO Box 330 *TF:* 800-943-2667 ■ *Web:* www.whe.org	Rockford	MN	55373	763-477-3000	477-3054

MISSISSIPPI

Name / Address	City	State	Zip	Phone	Fax
Alcorn County Electric Power Assn 1909 S Tate St	Corinth	MS	38834	662-287-4402	287-4088
Central Electric Power Assn 104 E Main St *Web:* www.centralepa.com	Carthage	MS	39051	601-267-5671	267-6032
Coahoma Electric Power Assn 340 Hopson St	Lyon	MS	38645	662-624-8321	624-8327
Coast Electric Power Assn 302 Hwy 90 *TF Cust Svc:* 800-624-3348 ■ *Web:* www.coastepa.com	Bay Saint Louis	MS	39521	228-467-6535	467-7066
Delta Electric Power Assn 1700 Hwy 82 W	Greenwood	MS	38930	662-453-6352	453-6359
Dixie Electric Power Assn PO Box 88 *Web:* www.dixieepa.com	Laurel	MS	39441	601-425-2535	425-2535
East Mississippi Electric Power Assn (EMEPA) 2128 Hwy 39 N PO Box 5517 *Web:* www.emepa.com	Meridian	MS	39302	601-581-8600	482-0701
Four County Electric Power Assn 5265 S Frontage Rd *Web:* www.4county.org	Columbus	MS	39701	662-327-8900	327-8790
Magnolia Electric Power Assn PO Box 747	McComb	MS	39649	601-684-4011	684-5535
Monroe County Electric Power Assn PO Box 300	Amory	MS	38821	662-256-2962	257-9909
Natchez Trace Electric Power 551 E Madison St *Web:* www.ntepa.com	Houston	MS	38851	662-456-3037	456-2086
North East Mississippi Electric Power Assn 10 County Rd 2050 *TF:* 877-234-6331	Oxford	MS	38655	662-234-6331	234-0046
Northcentral Mississippi Electric Power Assn 225 Hwy 309 S PO Box 405	Byhalia	MS	38611	662-838-2151	838-4751
Pearl River Valley Electric Power Assn 1422 Hwy 13 N PO Box 1217 *TF:* 800-320-0312 ■ *Web:* www.prvepa.com	Columbia	MS	39429	601-736-2666	736-9702
Pontotoc Electric Power Assn 12 S Main St	Pontotoc	MS	38863	662-489-3211	489-5156
Prentiss County Electric Power Assn 302 W Church St *Web:* www.pcepa.com	Booneville	MS	38829	662-728-4433	728-4059
Singing River Electric Power Assn Inc 11187 Old Hwy 63 PO Box 767 *Web:* www.singingriver.com	Lucedale	MS	39452	601-947-4211	947-6548
South Mississippi Electric Power Assn (SMEPA) 7037 US Hwy 49 *Web:* www.smepa.coop	Hattiesburg	MS	39402	601-268-2083	
Southern Pine Electric Power Assn 110 Risher St PO Box 60 *TF:* 800-231-5240 ■ *Web:* www.spepa.com	Taylorsville	MS	39168	601-785-6511	785-4980
Southwest Mississippi Electric Power Assn 18671 Hwy 61 *TF:* 800-287-8564 ■ *Web:* www.southwestepa.com	Lorman	MS	39096	601-437-3611	437-8736
Tallahatchie Valley Electric Power Assn 250 Power Dr *Web:* www.tvepa.com	Batesville	MS	38606	662-563-4742	563-8615
Tombigbee Electric Power Assn Co-op 1906 N Gloster St	Tupelo	MS	38801	662-842-7635	842-0369
Twin County Electric Power Assn 900 E Ave N	Hollandale	MS	38748	662-827-2262	827-2832
Yazoo Valley Electric Power Assn PO Box 8	Yazoo City	MS	39194	662-746-4251	751-1060

MISSOURI

Name / Address	City	State	Zip	Phone	Fax
Associated ElectricCo-op Inc 2814 S Golden PO Box 754 *Web:* www.aeci.org	Springfield	MO	65801	417-881-1204	885-9252
Atchison-Holt Electric Co-op 18585 Industrial Rd *TF:* 888-744-5366 ■ *Web:* www.ahec.coop	Rock Port	MO	64482	660-744-5344	744-5880
Barry Electric Co-op 4015 Main St PO Box 307 *TF:* 866-847-2333 ■ *Web:* www.barryelectric.com	Cassville	MO	65625	417-847-2131	847-5524
Barton County Electric Co-op 91 W Hwy 160 PO Box 459 *TF:* 800-286-5636 ■ *Web:* www.bartonelectric.com	Lamar	MO	64759	417-682-5636	682-5276
Black River Electric Co-op 2600 Hwy 67 PO Box 31 *TF:* 800-392-4711 ■ *Web:* www.blackriverelectric.com	Fredericktown	MO	63645	573-783-3381	783-7343
Boone Electric Co-op 1413 Rangeline St PO Box 797 *TF:* 800-225-8143 ■ *Web:* www.booneelectric.coop	Columbia	MO	65205	573-449-4181	441-7226
Callaway Electric Co-op 503 Truman Rd *TF:* 888-642-4840 ■ *Web:* www.callawayelectric.com	Fulton	MO	65251	573-642-3326	642-3328
Central Missouri ElectricCo-op Inc 22702 Hwy 65 PO Box 939 *Web:* www.cmecinc.com	Sedalia	MO	65302	660-826-2900	826-7180
Citizens Electric Corp 150 Merchant St PO Box 311 *TF:* 877-876-3511 ■ *Web:* www.citizenselectriccorp.com	Sainte Genevieve	MO	63670	573-883-5339	883-3381
Co-Mo Electric Co-op Inc 29868 Hwy 5 PO Box 220 *TF:* 800-781-0157 ■ *Web:* www.co-mo.coop	Tipton	MO	65081	660-433-5521	433-5631
Consolidated Electric Co-op 3940 E Liberty St *TF:* 800-621-0091 ■ *Web:* www.consolidatedelectric.com	Mexico	MO	65265	573-581-3630	581-0990
Crawford Electric Co-op Inc 10301 N Service Rd PO Box 10 *TF:* 800-677-2667 ■ *Web:* www.crawfordelec.com	Bourbon	MO	65441	573-732-4415	732-5409
Cuivre River Electric Co-op 1112 E Cherry St *TF:* 800-392-3709 ■ *Web:* www.cuivre.com	Troy	MO	63379	636-528-8261	528-7696
Farmers' Electric Co-op 201 W Business 36 PO Box 680 *TF:* 800-279-0496 ■ *Web:* www.fec-co.com	Chillicothe	MO	64601	660-646-4281	646-3569
Gascosage Electric Co-op 803 S Hwy 28 PO Drawer G *TF:* 866-568-8243 ■ *Web:* www.gascosage.com	Dixon	MO	65459	573-759-7146	759-6020
Grundy Electric Co-op Inc 4100 Oklahoma Ave *TF:* 800-279-2249 ■ *Web:* www.grundyec.com	Trenton	MO	64683	660-359-3941	359-6030
Howard Electric Co-op 205 Hwy 5 & 240 N PO Box 391 *TF:* 877-352-0122 ■ *Web:* www.howardelectric.com	Fayette	MO	65248	660-248-3311	248-3543
Howell-Oregon Electric Co-op Inc 6327 N US Hwy 63 PO Box 649 *TF:* 888-463-7693 ■ *Web:* www.hoecoop.org	West Plains	MO	65775	417-256-2131	256-4571
Intercounty Electric Co-op 102 Maple Ave *TF:* 866-621-3679 ■ *Web:* www.intercoelec.com	Licking	MO	65542	573-674-2211	674-2888
Laclede Electric Co-op 1400 E Rt 66 *TF:* 800-299-3164 ■ *Web:* www.lacledeelectric.com	Lebanon	MO	65536	417-532-3164	532-8321
Lewis County Rural Electric Co-op 18256 Hwy 16 PO Box 68 *TF:* 888-454-4485 ■ *Web:* www.lewiscountyrec.org	Lewistown	MO	63452	573-215-4000	215-4004
Macon Electric Co-op 31571 Bus Hwy 36 E PO Box 157 *TF:* 800-553-6901 ■ *Web:* www.maconelectric.com	Macon	MO	63552	660-385-3157	385-3334
N W Electric Power Coop PO Box 565 *Web:* www.nwepc.com	Cameron	MO	64429	816-632-2121	632-3114
New-Mac Electric Co-op Inc 12105 E Hwy 86 *Web:* www.newmac.com	Neosho	MO	64850	417-451-1515	451-9042
North Central Electric Co-op Inc Hwy E W PO Box 220 *TF:* 800-279-2264 ■ *Web:* www.northcentralelectric.com	Milan	MO	63556	660-265-4404	265-4311
Northeast Missouri Electric Power Co-op 3705 Business 61 PO Box 191 *Web:* www.northeast-power.coop	Palmyra	MO	63461	573-769-2107	769-4358
Osage Valley Electric Co-op Assn 1321 N Orange St *TF:* 800-889-6832 ■ *Web:* www.osagevalley.com	Butler	MO	64730	660-679-3131	679-3142
Ozark Border Electric Co-op 3281 S Westwood *TF:* 800-392-0567 ■ *Web:* www.ozarkborder.org	Poplar Bluff	MO	63901	573-785-4631	785-1853
Ozark Electric Co-op 10943 Missouri 39 *TF:* 800-947-6393 ■ *Web:* www.ozarkelectric.com	Mount Vernon	MO	65712	417-466-2144	466-7239
Pemiscot-Dunklin Electric Co-op PO Box 657 *TF:* 800-558-6641 ■ *Web:* www.pemdunk.com	Hayti	MO	63851	573-757-6641	757-6656
Platte-Clay Electric Co-op Inc 1000 W Hwy 92 PO Box 100 *TF:* 800-431-2131 ■ *Web:* www.pcec.coop	Kearney	MO	64060	816-628-3121	628-3141
Ralls County Electric Co-op 17594 Hwy 19 PO Box 157 *TF:* 877-985-8711	New London	MO	63459	573-985-8711	985-3658
Sac Osage Electric Co-op Inc 4815 E Hwy 54 PO Box 111 *TF:* 800-876-2701 ■ *Web:* www.sacosage.com	El Dorado Springs	MO	64744	417-876-2721	876-5368
Se-Ma-No Electric Co-op 601 N Business 60	Mansfield	MO	65704	417-924-3243	924-8215
Three Rivers Electric Co-op 1324 E Main St PO Box 918 *Web:* www.threeriverselectric.com	Linn	MO	65051	573-897-2251	897-3511
Tri-County Electric Co-op Assn PO Box 159 *TF:* 888-457-3734	Lancaster	MO	63548	660-457-3733	457-3736
United Electric Co-op Inc 401 N Hwy 71 PO Box 319 *TF:* 800-748-1488 ■ *Web:* www.ueci.org	Savannah	MO	64485	816-324-3155	324-3157
Webster Electric Co-op 1240 Spur Dr *TF:* 800-643-4305 ■ *Web:* www.websterec.com	Marshfield	MO	65706	417-859-2216	859-4579
West Central Electric Co-op Inc PO Box 452 *Web:* www.westcentralelectric.com	Higginsville	MO	64037	660-584-2131	584-6286
White River Valley Electric Co-op Inc 2449 State Hwy 76 E *TF:* 800-879-4056 ■ *Web:* www.whiteriver.org	Branson	MO	65616	417-335-9335	335-9250

MONTANA

Name / Address	City	State	Zip	Phone	Fax
Beartooth Electric Co-op Inc 1306 N Broadway St PO Box 1110 *TF:* 800-472-9821	Red Lodge	MT	59068	406-446-2310	446-3934
Big Flat Electric Co-op Inc 333 S 7th St *TF:* 800-242-2040 ■ *Web:* www.bigflatelectric.com	Malta	MT	59538	406-654-2040	654-2292

			Phone	Fax
Big Horn County Electric Co-op Inc 303 S Mitchell St . . . . . Hardin	MT	59034	406-665-2830	665-2644
Fergus Electric Co-op Inc 84423 US Hwy 87 . . . . . Lewistown *Web:* www.ferguselectric.coop	MT	59457	406-538-3465	538-7391
Flathead Electric Co-op Inc 2510 Hwy 2 E . . . . . Kalispell *TF:* 800-735-8489 ■ *Web:* www.flatheadelectric.com	MT	59901	406-752-4483	752-4283
Glacier Electric Co-op Inc 410 E Main St. . . . . Cut Bank *TF:* 800-347-6795 ■ *Web:* www.glacierelectric.com	MT	59427	406-873-5566	873-2071
Goldenwest Electric Co-op Inc 119 1 Ave. . . . . Wibaux	MT	59353	406-796-2423	796-2445
Hill County Electric Co-op Inc PO Box 2330. . . . . Havre *TF:* 877-394-7804 ■ *Web:* www.hcelectric.com	MT	59501	406-394-7802	394-7801
Lincoln Electric Co-op Inc (LEC) 500 Osloski Rd PO Box 628 . . . . . Eureka *TF:* 800-442-2994 ■ *Web:* www.lincolnelectric.coop	MT	59917	406-889-3301	889-3874
Lower Yellowstone Rural Electric Assn Inc Hwy 16 NW PO Box 1047. . . . . Sidney *Web:* www.lyrec.com	MT	59270	406-488-1602	488-6524
Marias River Electric Co-op Inc PO Box 729 . . . . . Shelby *Web:* www.mariasriverec.com	MT	59474	406-434-5575	434-2531
McCone Electric Co-op Inc 110 Main St . . . . . Circle *TF:* 800-684-3605 ■ *Web:* www.mcconeelectric.coop	MT	59215	406-485-3430	485-3397
Mid-Yellowstone Electric Co-op PO Box 386. . . . . Hysham	MT	59038	406-342-5521	342-5511
Missoula Electric Co-op Inc 1700 W Broadway. . . . . Missoula *TF:* 800-352-5200 ■ *Web:* www.missoulaelectric.com	MT	59808	406-541-4433	541-6318
Park Electric Co-op Inc 5706 US Hwy 89 S PO Box 1119 . . . . . Livingston *TF:* 888-298-0657 ■ *Web:* www.parkelectric.coop	MT	59047	406-222-3100	222-3418
Ravalli County Electric Co-op Inc 1051 Eastside Hwy. . . . . Corvallis *Web:* www.ravallielectric.com	MT	59828	406-961-3001	961-3230
Sheridan Electric Co-op Inc 6408 Hwy 16 S. . . . . Medicine Lake	MT	59247	406-789-2231	789-2234
Southeast Electric Co-op Inc 110 S Main St. . . . . Ekalaka *TF:* 888-485-8762 ■ *Web:* www.midrivers.com/~seco	MT	59324	406-775-8762	775-8763
Sun River Electric Co-op Inc 310 1st Ave S PO Box 309 . . . . . Fairfield *TF:* 800-452-7516 ■ *Web:* www.sunriverelectric.coop	MT	59436	406-467-2527	467-3108
Vigilante Electric Co-op Inc 225 E Bannack St . . . . . Dillon *Web:* www.vec.coop	MT	59725	406-683-2327	683-4328
Yellowstone Valley Electric Co-op 150 Co-op Way. . . . . Huntley *TF:* 800-736-5323 ■ *Web:* www.yvec.com	MT	59037	406-348-3411	348-3414

NEBRASKA

			Phone	Fax
Burt County Public Power District 613 N 13th St PO Box 209 . . . . . Tekamah *TF:* 888-835-1620 ■ *Web:* www.burtcoppd.com	NE	68061	402-374-2631	374-1605
Butler County Rural Public Power District 1331 N 4th St. . . . . David City *TF:* 800-230-0569 ■ *Web:* www.butlerppd.com	NE	68632	402-367-3081	367-6114
Cedar-Knox Public Power District 56272 W Hwy 84 PO Box 947 . . . . . Hartington *Web:* www.cedarknoxppd.com	NE	68739	402-254-6291	254-6991
Chimney Rock Public Power District 805 W 8th St PO Box 608. . . . . Bayard *TF:* 877-773-6300 ■ *Web:* www.crppd.com	NE	69334	308-586-1824	586-2511
Cornhusker Public Power District 23169 235th Ave PO Box 9. . . . . Columbus *Web:* www.cornhusker-power.com	NE	68601	402-564-2821	564-9907
Cuming County Public Power District 500 S Main St. . . . . West Point *TF:* 877-572-2463 ■ *Web:* www.ccppd.com	NE	68788	402-372-2463	372-5832
Custer Public Power District 625 E S E St PO Box 10 . . . . . Broken Bow *TF:* 888-749-2453 ■ *Web:* www.custerpower.com	NE	68822	308-872-2451	
Dawson Public Power District 75191 Rd 433 . . . . . Lexington *TF:* 800-752-8305 ■ *Web:* www.dawsonpower.com	NE	68850	308-324-2386	324-2907
Elkhorn Rural Public Power District 206 N 4th St. . . . . Battle Creek *TF:* 800-675-2185 ■ *Web:* www.erppd.com	NE	68715	402-675-2185	675-6275
Howard Greeley Rural Public Power District 422 Howard Ave . . . . . Saint Paul *TF:* 800-280-4962	NE	68873	308-754-4457	754-4230
KBR Rural Public Power District 374 N Pine St. . . . . Ainsworth *TF:* 800-672-0009	NE	69210	402-387-1120	387-1033
Loup Public Power District (LPPD) 2404 15th St PO Box 988. . . . . Columbus *TF:* 888-564-3172 ■ *Web:* www.loup.com	NE	68602	402-564-3171	564-0970
McCook Public Power District PO Box 1147 . . . . . McCook *TF:* 800-658-4285	NE	69001	308-345-2500	345-4772
Midwest Electric Co-op Corp 104 Washington Ave. . . . . Grant *TF:* 800-451-3691 ■ *Web:* www.midwestecc.com	NE	69140	308-352-4356	352-4957
Nebraska Public Power District 1414 15th St PO Box 499. . . . . Columbus *TF:* 877-275-6773 ■ *Web:* www.nppd.com	NE	68602	402-564-8561	563-5551
Niobrara Valley Electric Membership Corp 427 N 4th St. . . . . O'Neill *Web:* www.nvemc.org	NE	68763	402-336-2803	336-4858
Norris Public Power District 606 Irving St PO Box 399. . . . . Beatrice *TF:* 800-858-4707 ■ *Web:* www.norrisppd.com	NE	68310	402-223-4038	228-2895
North Central Public Power District 1409 Main St PO Box 90 . . . . . Creighton *TF:* 800-578-1060 ■ *Web:* www.ncppd.com	NE	68729	402-358-5112	358-5129
Northeast Nebraska Public Power District 303 Logan St PO Box 350 . . . . . Wayne *TF:* 800-750-9277	NE	68787	402-375-1360	375-1233
Northwest Rural Public Power District 5613 State Hwy 87 PO Box 249 . . . . . Hay Springs *TF:* 800-847-0492 ■ *Web:* www.nrppd.com	NE	69347	308-638-4445	638-4448
Perennial Public Power District 2122 S Lincoln Ave. . . . . York *TF:* 800-289-0288 ■ *Web:* www.perennialpower.com	NE	68467	402-362-3355	362-3623
Polk County Rural Public Power District 120 W 4th St PO Box 465. . . . . Stromsburg *TF:* 888-242-5265 ■ *Web:* www.pcrppd.com	NE	68666	402-764-4381	764-4382
Seward County Rural Public Power District 1363 Progressive Rd PO Box 69. . . . . Seward	NE	68434	402-643-2951	646-4695
South Central Public Power District (SCPPD) 275 S Main St PO Box 406. . . . . Nelson *TF:* 800-557-5254 ■ *Web:* www.southcentralppd.com	NE	68961	402-225-2351	225-2353
Southern Public Power District (SPPD) 4550 W Husker Hwy PO Box 1687 . . . . . Grand Island *TF:* 800-652-2013 ■ *Web:* www.southernpd.com	NE	68801	308-384-2350	384-5018
Southwest Public Power District 221 N Main St . . . . . Palisade *TF:* 800-379-7977 ■ *Web:* www.swppd.com	NE	69040	308-285-3295	285-3811
Stanton County Public Power District 807 Douglas St. . . . . Stanton *TF:* 877-439-2300	NE	68779	402-439-2228	439-7000
Twin Valleys Public Power District 1145 Nasby St . . . . . Cambridge *TF:* 800-658-4266 ■ *Web:* www.twinvalleysppd.com	NE	69022	308-697-3315	697-4877
Wheat Belt Public Power District 2104 Illinois St. . . . . Sidney *TF:* 800-261-7114 ■ *Web:* www.wheatbelt.com	NE	69162	308-254-5871	254-2384

NEVADA

			Phone	Fax
Mount Wheeler Power Inc PO Box 15000 . . . . . Ely *TF:* 800-977-6937 ■ *Web:* www.mwpower.net	NV	89315	775-289-8981	289-8987
Overton Power District # 5 615 N Moapa Valley Blvd PO Box 395 . . . . . Overton *TF:* 888-409-6735 ■ *Web:* www.opd5.com	NV	89040	702-397-2512	
Valley Electric Assn Inc 800 E Hwy 372 PO Box 237 . . . . . Pahrump *TF:* 800-742-3330 ■ *Web:* www.vea.coop	NV	89048	775-727-5312	727-6320
Wells Rural Electric Co 1451 Humboldt Ave. . . . . Wells *Web:* www.wellsrec.com	NV	89835	775-752-3328	752-3407

NEW HAMPSHIRE

			Phone	Fax
New Hampshire Electric Co-op 579 Tenney Mountain Hwy . . . . . Plymouth *TF:* 800-698-2007 ■ *Web:* www.nhec.com	NH	03264	603-536-1800	536-8682

NEW JERSEY

			Phone	Fax
Sussex Rural Electric Co-op 64 County Rt 639 PO Box 346 . . . . . Sussex *TF:* 877-504-6463 ■ *Web:* www.sussexrec.com	NJ	07461	973-875-5101	875-4114

NEW MEXICO

			Phone	Fax
Central Valley Electric Co-op Inc 1505 N 13th St PO Box 230 . . . . . Artesia *Web:* www.cvecoop.org	NM	88211	505-746-3571	746-4219
Columbus Electric Co-op Inc 900 N Gold St PO Box 631. . . . . Deming *TF:* 800-950-2667 ■ *Web:* www.columbusco-op.org	NM	88031	505-546-8838	546-3128
Continental Divide ElectricCo-op Inc (CDEC) 200 E High St PO Box 1087 . . . . . Grants *Web:* www.cdec.coop	NM	87020	505-285-6656	287-2234
Farmers Electric Co-op Inc 3701 Thornton PO Box 550 . . . . . Clovis **Fax Area Code:* 505 ■ *TF:* 800-445-8541 ■ *Web:* www.farmerselectric.org	NM	88101	575-762-4466	769-2118*
Jemez Mountains Electric Co-op PO Box 128 . . . . . Espanola *TF:* 888-755-2105 ■ *Web:* www.jemezcoop.org	NM	87532	505-753-2105	753-6958
Kit Carson Electric Co-op Inc 118 Cruz Alta Rd PO Box 578. . . . . Taos **Fax Area Code:* 575 ■ *TF:* 800-688-6780 ■ *Web:* www.kitcarson.com	NM	87571	505-758-2258	758-4611*
Lea County Electric Co-op Inc (LCEC) 1300 W Ave D Lovington . . . . . Lovington *TF:* 800-510-5232 ■ *Web:* www.leacountyelectric.coop	NM	88260	505-396-3631	396-3634
Mora-San Miguel Electric Co-op PO Box 240 . . . . . Mora *TF:* 800-421-6773 ■ *Web:* www.moraelectric.org	NM	87732	505-387-2205	387-5975
Northern Rio Arriba Electric Co-op 1135 Camino Escondido PO Box 217. . . . . Chama *Web:* www.noraelectric.org	NM	87520	505-756-2181	756-2200
Otero County Electric Co-op Inc 202 Burro Ave PO Box 227. . . . . Cloudcroft *TF:* 800-548-4660 ■ *Web:* www.ocec-inc.com	NM	88317	505-682-2521	682-3109
Roosevelt County Electric Co-op Inc (RCEC) 121 N Main St PO Box 389. . . . . Portales *Web:* www.rcec.org	NM	88130	505-356-4491	359-1651
Sierra Electric Co-op 610 Hwy 195 PO Box 290. . . . . Elephant Butte *Web:* www.sierraelectric.org	NM	87935	505-744-5231	744-5819
Socorro Electric Co-op Inc 215 E Manazannez St PO Box H . . . . . Socorro *TF:* 800-351-7575 ■ *Web:* www.socorroelectric.com	NM	87801	505-835-0560	835-4449
Springer Electric Co-op Inc 408 Maxwell Ave PO Box 698. . . . . Springer *TF:* 800-288-1353 ■ *Web:* www.springercoop.com	NM	87747	505-483-2421	483-2692

NEW YORK

Company	City	State	Zip	Phone	Fax
1st Rochdale Co-op Group Ltd 465 Grand St 2nd Fl *TF:* 877-624-3253 ■ *Web:* www.1strochdalenyc.net	New York	NY	10002	212-673-3900	673-3902
Delaware County Electric Co-op (DCEC) 39 Elm St PO Box 471 *Web:* www.dce.coop	Delhi	NY	13753	607-746-2341	746-7548
Oneida-Madison Electric Co-op Inc 15630 Rt 20 PO Box 27 *Web:* www.oneida-madison.coop	Bouckville	NY	13310	315-893-1851	893-1857
Otsego ElectricCo-op Inc (OEC) 3192 County Hwy 11 PO Box 128 *Web:* www.otsegoec.coop	Hartwick	NY	13348	607-293-6622	293-6624
Steuben Rural Electric Co-op Inc 9 Wilson Ave *TF:* 800-843-3414 ■ *Web:* www.steubenrec.com	Bath	NY	14810	607-776-4161	776-2293

NORTH CAROLINA

Company	City	State	Zip	Phone	Fax
Albemarle Electric Membership Corp 159 Creek Dr *TF:* 800-215-9915 ■ *Web:* www.albemarle-emc.com	Hertford	NC	27944	252-426-5735	426-8270
Blue Ridge Electric Membership Corp 1216 Blowing Rock Blvd. *TF:* 800-451-5474	Lenoir	NC	28645	828-758-2383	758-2699
Brunswick Electric Membership Corp 795 Ocean Hwy PO Box 226 *TF:* 800-842-5871 ■ *Web:* www.bemc.org	Shallotte	NC	28459	910-754-4391	755-4299
Cape Hatteras Electric Co-op 47109 Light Plant Rd PO Box 9 *TF:* 800-454-5616 ■ *Web:* www.chec.coop	Buxton	NC	27920	252-995-5616	995-4088
Carteret-Craven Electric Co-op (CCEC) 1300 Hwy 24 W PO Box 1490 *TF:* 800-682-2217 ■ *Web:* www.carteretcravenelectric.coop	Newport	NC	28570	252-247-3107	247-0235
Central Electric Membership Corp 128 Wilson Rd *TF:* 800-446-7752 ■ *Web:* www.centralelectriconline.com	Sanford	NC	27331	919-774-4900	774-1860
Cogentrix Energy Inc 9405 Arrowpoint Blvd *Web:* www.cogentrix.com	Charlotte	NC	28273	704-525-3800	529-5313
Edgecombe-Martin County Electric Membership Corp 679 Nc Hwy 33 E *TF:* 800-445-6486	Tarboro	NC	27886	252-823-2171	823-4535
EnergyUnited Electric Membership Corp PO Box 1831 *TF:* 800-522-3793 ■ *Web:* www.energyunited.com	Statesville	NC	28687	704-873-5241	878-0161
Four County Electric Membership Corp 1822 NC Hwy 53 W PO Box 667 *TF:* 888-368-7289 ■ *Web:* www.fourcty.org	Burgaw	NC	28425	910-259-2171	259-1860
French Broad Electric Membership Corp 3043 Nc 213 Hwy *Web:* www.frenchbroademc.com	Marshall	NC	28753	828-649-2051	649-2989
Halifax Electric Membership Corp 208 Whitfield St *Web:* www.halifaxemc.com	Enfield	NC	27823	252-445-5111	445-2398
Haywood Electric Membership Corp 376 Grindstone Rd *TF:* 800-951-6088 ■ *Web:* www.haywoodemc.com	Waynesville	NC	28785	828-452-2281	456-8803
Jones-Onslow Electric Membership Corp 259 Western Blvd *TF:* 800-682-1515 ■ *Web:* www.joemc.com	Jacksonville	NC	28546	910-353-1940	353-8000
Lumbee River Electric Membership Corp PO Box 830 *TF:* 800-683-5571 ■ *Web:* www.lumbeeriver.com	Red Springs	NC	28377	910-843-4131	843-5035
Pee Dee Electric Membership Corp (PDEMC) 575 US Hwy 52 S *TF:* 800-992-1626 ■ *Web:* www.pdemc.com	Wadesboro	NC	28170	704-694-2114	694-9636
Piedmont Electric Membership Corp 2500 Nc Hwy 86 S *Web:* www.pemc.org	Hillsborough	NC	27278	919-732-2123	644-1030
Randolph Electric Membership Corp 879 McDowell Rd PO Box 40 *TF:* 800-672-8212 ■ *Web:* www.randolphemc.com	Asheboro	NC	27204	336-625-5177	626-1551
Roanoke Electric Co-op 518 NC 561 W *TF:* 800-433-2236 ■ *Web:* www.ncelectriccooperatives.com	Aulander	NC	27805	252-539-2236	539-3021
Rutherford Electric Membership Corp 186 Hudlow Rd PO Box 1569 *TF:* 800-521-0920 ■ *Web:* www.remc.com	Forest City	NC	28043	828-245-1621	248-2319
South River Electric Membership Corp 17494 US 421 S PO Box 931 *TF:* 800-338-5530 ■ *Web:* www.sremc.com	Dunn	NC	28335	910-892-8071	891-7189
Surry-Yadkin Electric Membership Corp 510 S Main St. *TF:* 800-682-5903 ■ *Web:* www.syemc.com	Dobson	NC	27017	336-386-8241	386-9744
Tideland Electric Membership Corp 25831 Hwy 264 E *TF:* 800-637-1079 ■ *Web:* www.tidelandemc.com	Pantego	Nc	27860	252-943-3046	943-3510
Tri-County Electric Membership Corp 4255 Us Hwy 117 S Alt.	Dudley	NC	28333	919-735-2611	734-6277
Union Power Co-op PO Box 5014 *TF:* 800-922-6840 ■ *Web:* www.union-power.com	Monroe	NC	28111	704-289-3145	296-0408
Wake Electric 414 E Wait Ave PO Box 1229 *TF:* 800-474-6300 ■ *Web:* www.wemc.com	Wake Forest	NC	27588	919-863-6300	863-6379

NORTH DAKOTA

Company	City	State	Zip	Phone	Fax
Basin Electric Power Co-op 1717 E IH- Ave *Web:* www.basinelectric.com	Bismarck	ND	58501	701-223-0441	224-5336
Burke-Divide Electric Co-op Inc (BDEC) 9549 Hwy 5 W *Web:* www.bdec.coop	Columbus	ND	58727	701-939-6671	939-6666
Capital Electric Co-op Inc 4111 State St *Web:* www.capitalelec.com	Bismarck	ND	58503	701-223-1513	223-1557
Cass County Electric Co-op Inc 4100 32nd Ave SW *TF:* 800-248-3292 ■ *Web:* www.kwh.com	Fargo	ND	58104	701-356-4400	356-4500
Cavalier Rural Electric Co-op Inc 1111 9th Ave.	Langdon	ND	58249	701-256-5511	256-5513
Central Power Electric Co-op 525 20th Ave SW *Web:* www.centralpwr.com	Minot	ND	58701	701-852-4407	852-3847
Dakota Valley Electric Co-op 7296 Hwy 281 *TF:* 800-342-4671 ■ *Web:* www.dakotavalley.com	Edgeley	ND	58433	701-493-2281	493-2454
KEM Electric Co-op Inc 107 S Broadway *TF:* 800-472-2673 ■ *Web:* www.kemelectric.com	Linton	ND	58552	701-254-4666	254-4975
McKenzie Electric Co-op Inc 908 4th Ave NE *Web:* www.mckenzieelectric.com	Watford City	ND	58854	701-444-9288	444-3002
McLean Electric Co-op Inc 4031 Hwy 37 Bypass NW *TF:* 800-263-4922 ■ *Web:* www.mcleanelectric.com	Garrison	ND	58540	701-463-2291	337-5303
Mor-Gran-Sou Electric Co-op Inc 202 6th Ave W *TF:* 800-750-8212 ■ *Web:* www.morgransou.com	Flasher	ND	58535	701-597-3301	597-3915
Mountrail-Williams Electric Co-op 218 58th St W PO Box 1346 *TF:* 800-279-2667 ■ *Web:* www.mwec.com	Williston	ND	58802	701-577-3765	577-3777
Nodak Electric Co-op Inc 4000 32nd Ave S *TF:* 800-732-4373 ■ *Web:* www.nodakelectric.com	Grand Forks	ND	58201	701-746-4461	795-6701
North Central Electric Co-op Inc 538 11th St W *TF:* 800-247-1197 ■ *Web:* www.nceci.com	Bottineau	ND	58318	701-228-2202	228-2592
Northern Plains Electric Co-op 1515 W Main St *TF:* 800-882-2500 ■ *Web:* www.nplains.com	Carrington	ND	58421	701-652-3156	652-1848
Oliver-Mercer Electric Co-op Inc 800 Hwy Dr *TF:* 800-748-5533 ■ *Web:* www.roughriderelectric.com	Hazen	ND	58545	701-748-2293	748-6500
Slope Electric Co-op Inc 116 E 12th St PO Box 338 *TF:* 800-559-4191 ■ *Web:* www.slopeelectric.coop	New England	ND	58647	701-579-4191	579-4193
Verendrye Electric Co-op Inc 615 Hwy 52 *TF:* 800-472-2141 ■ *Web:* www.verendrye.com	Velva	ND	58790	701-338-2855	624-0353
West Plains Electric Co-op Inc PO Box 1038 *TF:* 800-627-8470 ■ *Web:* www.wpec.net	Dickinson	ND	58602	701-483-5111	483-6057

OHIO

Company	City	State	Zip	Phone	Fax
Adams Rural Electric Co-op Inc 4800 SR 125 *TF:* 800-283-1846 ■ *Web:* www.adamsrec.com	West Union	OH	45693	937-544-2305	544-3877
Buckeye Rural Electric Co-op Inc 4848 SR 325 S *TF:* 800-231-2732 ■ *Web:* www.buckeyerec.com	Patriot	OH	45658	740-379-2025	379-2048
Butler Rural Electric Co-op Inc (BREC) 3888 Still-Beckett Rd *TF:* 800-255-2732 ■ *Web:* www.butlerrural.coop	Oxford	OH	45056	513-867-4400	867-4422
Carroll Electric Co-op Inc 350 Canton Rd NW *TF:* 800-232-7697 ■ *Web:* www.carrollelectriccoop.com	Carrollton	OH	44615	330-627-2116	627-7050
Darke Rural Electric Co-op Inc 1120 Fort Jefferson Rd *TF:* 800-776-5612	Greenville	OH	45331	937-548-4114	548-0446
Denier Electric Co Inc 10891 SR- 128 *TF:* 800-676-3282 ■ *Web:* www.denier.com	Harrison	OH	45030	513-738-2641	738-2492
Firelands Electric Co-op Inc 1 Energy Pl PO Box 32 *TF:* 800-533-8658 ■ *Web:* www.firelandsec.com	New London	OH	44851	419-929-1571	929-8550
Frontier Power Co 770 S 2nd St. *TF:* 800-624-8050 ■ *Web:* www.frontier-power.com	Coshocton	OH	43812	740-622-6755	622-0711
Guernsey-Muskingum Electric Co-op 17 S Liberty St *Web:* www.gmenergy.com	New Concord	OH	43762	740-826-7661	826-7171
Hancock-Wood Electric Co-op Inc 1399 Business Pk Dr S *TF:* 800-445-4840 ■ *Web:* www.hwelectric.com	North Baltimore	OH	45872	419-257-3241	257-3024
Holmes-Wayne Electric Co-op Inc 6060 Ohio 83 *TF:* 877-520-1055 ■ *Web:* www.hwecoop.com	Millersburg	OH	44654	330-674-1055	674-1869
Logan County Co-op Power & Light Assn Inc 1587 County Rd 32 N *Web:* www.loganrec.com	Bellefontaine	OH	43311	937-592-4781	592-5746
Lorain-Medina Rural Electric Co-op Inc 22898 W Rd *TF:* 800-222-5673 ■ *Web:* www.lmre.org	Wellington	OH	44090	440-647-2133	647-4870
Mid Ohio Energy Co-op Inc 555 W Franklin St *TF:* 888-382-6732 ■ *Web:* www.midohioenergy.com	Kenton	OH	43326	419-673-7289	673-8388
Midwest Electric Inc 6029 County Rd 33A *TF:* 800-962-3830 ■ *Web:* www.midwestrec.com	Saint Marys	OH	45885	419-394-4110	394-8333
North Central Electric Co-op Inc 13978 E County Rd 56 *TF:* 800-426-3072 ■ *Web:* www.ncelec.org	Attica	OH	44807	419-426-3072	426-1245
North Western Electric Co-op Inc 04125 SR 576 *TF:* 800-647-6932 ■ *Web:* www.nwec.com	Bryan	OH	43506	419-636-5051	636-0194
Paulding-Putman Electric Co-op 910 N Williams St. *TF:* 800-686-2357 ■ *Web:* www.ppec.coop	Paulding	OH	45879	419-399-5015	399-3026
Pioneer Electric Co-op 344 W US Rt 36 PO Box 604 *TF:* 800-762-0997 ■ *Web:* www.pioneerec.com	Piqua	OH	45356	937-773-2523	773-7549

Company / Address	City	State	Zip	Phone	Fax
South Central Power Co Inc 2780 Coon Path Rd *TF:* 800-282-5064 ■ *Web:* www.southcentralpower.com	Lancaster	OH	43130	740-653-4422	681-4488
Tri-County Rural Electric Co-op Inc 8200 Township Rd K2	Malinta	OH	43535	419-256-7900	256-6581
Union Rural Electric Co-op Inc 15461 US 36E *TF:* 800-642-1826 ■ *Web:* www.ure.com	Marysville	OH	43040	937-642-1826	644-4239
Washington Electric Co-op Inc 406 Colegate Dr *TF:* 877-594-9324 ■ *Web:* www.weci.org	Marietta	OH	45750	740-373-2141	373-2941

OKLAHOMA

Company / Address	City	State	Zip	Phone	Fax
Alfalfa Electric Co-op Inc 121 E Main St *TF:* 888-736-3837 ■ *Web:* www.alfalfaelectric.com	Cherokee	OK	73728	580-596-3333	596-2464
Caddo Electric Co-op PO Box 70 *Web:* www.caddoelectric.com	Binger	OK	73009	405-656-2322	656-2327
Canadian Valley Electric Co-op I-40 & US 377 PO Box 751 *TF:* 877-382-3680 ■ *Web:* www.canadianvalley.org	Seminole	OK	74868	405-382-3680	382-8808
Central Rural Electric Co-op 3304 S Boomer Rd PO Box 1809 *TF:* 800-375-2884 ■ *Web:* www.crec.coop	Stillwater	OK	74076	405-372-2884	372-8559
Choctaw Electric Co-op Inc 1033 N 4250 Rd *TF:* 800-780-6486 ■ *Web:* www.choctawelectric.com	Hugo	OK	74743	580-326-6486	326-2492
Cimarron Electric Co-op PO Box 299 *TF:* 800-375-4121 ■ *Web:* www.cimarronelectric.com	Kingfisher	OK	73750	405-375-4121	375-4209
Cookson Hills Electric Co-op Inc 1002 E Main St *TF:* 800-328-2368 ■ *Web:* www.cooksonhills.com	Stigler	OK	74462	918-967-4614	967-1200
Cotton Electric Co-op Inc 226 N Broadway *TF:* 800-522-3520 ■ *Web:* www.cottonelectric.com	Walters	OK	73572	580-875-3351	875-3101
East Central Oklahoma Electric Co-op Inc 2001 S Wood Dr PO Box 1178 *TF:* 800-783-9317 ■ *Web:* www.ecoec.com	Okmulgee	OK	74447	918-756-0833	756-6347
Harmon Electric Assn Inc (HEA) 114 N 1st St PO Box 393 *TF:* 800-643-7769 ■ *Web:* www.harmonelectric.com	Hollis	OK	73550	580-688-3342	688-2981
Indian Electric Co-op Inc 2506 E Hwy 64 *TF:* 800-482-2750 ■ *Web:* www.iecok.com	Cleveland	OK	74020	918-358-2514	358-2518
Kamo ElectricCo-op Inc 500 S Kamo Dr PO Box 577 *Web:* www.kamopower.com	Vinita	OK	74301	918-256-5551	256-8023
Kay Electric Co-op 300 W Doolin Ave *TF:* 800-535-1079 ■ *Web:* www.kayelectric.com	Blackwell	OK	74631	580-363-1260	363-2308
Kiamichi Electric Co-op Inc (KEC) 966 SW Hwy 2 PO Box 340 *TF:* 800-888-2731 ■ *Web:* www.kiamichielectric.org	Wilburton	OK	74578	918-465-2338	465-2405
Kiwash Electric Co-op Inc 120 W 1st St *TF:* 888-832-3362 ■ *Web:* www.kiwash.coop	Cordell	OK	73632	580-832-3361	832-5174
Lake Region Electric Co-op Inc 516 S Lake Region Rd *Web:* www.lrecok.coop	Hulbert	OK	74441	918-772-2526	772-2528
Northeast Oklahoma Electric Co-op Inc 443857 E Hwy 60 PO Box 948 *TF:* 800-256-6405 ■ *Web:* www.neelectric.com	Vinita	OK	74301	918-256-6405	256-9380
Northfork Electric Co-op 311 E Madden St PO Box 400 *Web:* www.nfecoop.com	Sayre	OK	73662	580-928-3366	928-3105
Northwestern Electric Co-op Inc 2925 William Ave *TF:* 800-375-7423 ■ *Web:* www.nwecok.coop	Woodward	OK	73802	580-256-7425	254-2858
Oklahoma Electric Co-op 242 24th Ave NW *Web:* www.okcoop.org	Norman	OK	73069	405-321-2024	217-6900
People's Electric Co-op 1600 N Country Club Rd *TF:* 877-455-3031 ■ *Web:* www.peoplesec.com	Ada	OK	74821	580-332-3031	436-0229
Red River Valley Rural Electric Co-op (REA) 1003 Memorial Dr PO Box 220 *TF:* 800-749-3364 ■ *Web:* www.rrvrea.com	Marietta	OK	73448	580-276-3364	276-3828
Rural Electric Co-op Inc (REC) 801 N Industrial Heights PO Box 609 *TF:* 800-259-3504 ■ *Web:* www.recok.coop	Lindsay	OK	73052	405-756-3104	756-8957
Southeastern Electric Co-op Inc 1514 E Hwy 70 PO Box 1370 *TF:* 866-924-1315 ■ *Web:* www.se-coop.com	Durant	OK	74702	580-924-2170	924-6402
Southwest Rural Electric Assn 700 N Broadway PO Box 310 *TF:* 800-256-7973 ■ *Web:* www.swre.com	Tipton	OK	73570	580-667-5281	667-5284
Stillwater Utilities Authority PO Box 1449 *Web:* www.stillwater.org	Stillwater	OK	74076	405-372-0025	
Tri-County Electric 302 E Glaydas St PO Box 880 *TF:* 800-522-3315 ■ *Web:* www.tri-countyelectric.coop	Hooker	OK	73945	580-652-2418	652-3151
Verdigris Valley Electric Co-op 8901 E 146th St N *TF:* 800-870-5948 ■ *Web:* www.vvec.com	Collinsville	OK	74021	918-371-2584	371-9873
Western Farmers Electric Co-op 701 NE 7th St *Web:* www.wfec.com	Anadarko	OK	73005	405-247-3351	247-4451

OREGON

Company / Address	City	State	Zip	Phone	Fax
Blachly-Lane Inc PO Box 70 *TF:* 800-446-8418 ■ *Web:* www.blachlylane.coop	Junction City	OR	97448	541-688-8711	688-8958
Central ElectricCo-op Inc (CEC) 2098 Hwy 97 N PO Box 846 *Web:* www.cec-co.com	Redmond	OR	97756	541-548-2144	548-0366
Columbia Basin Electric Co-op 171 W Linden Way *Web:* www.rapidserve.net	Heppner	OR	97836	541-676-9146	676-5159
Columbia Power Co-op Assn 311 Wilson St PO Box 97	Monument	OR	97864	541-934-2311	934-2312
Consumers Power Inc (CPI) 6990 W Hills Rd PO Box 1180 *TF:* 800-872-9036 ■ *Web:* www.cpi.coop	Philomath	OR	97370	541-929-3124	929-8673
Coos-Curry Electric Co-op Inc 43050 Hwy 101 PO Box 1268 *Web:* www.ccec.coop	Port Orford	OR	97465	541-332-3931	332-3501
Harney Electric Co-op Inc 1326 Hines Blvd *Web:* www.harneyelectric.org	Burns	OR	97720	541-573-2061	
Lane Electric Co-op 787 Bailey Hill Rd PO Box 21410 *Web:* www.laneelectric.com	Eugene	OR	97402	541-484-1151	484-7316
Midstate Electric Co-op Inc 16755 Finley Butte Rd *TF:* 800-722-7219 ■ *Web:* www.midstateelectric.coop	La Pine	OR	97739	541-536-2126	536-1423
Northern Wasco County People's Utility District 2345 River Rd	The Dalles	OR	97058	541-296-2226	298-3320
Oregon Trail Electric ConsumersCo-op Inc (OTEC) 4005 23rd St PO Box 226 *Web:* www.otecc.com	Baker City	OR	97814	541-523-3616	524-2865
Salem Electric 633 7th St NW *Web:* www.salemelectric.com	Salem	OR	97304	503-362-3601	371-2956
Tillamook People's Utility District 1115 Pacific Ave *TF:* 800-422-2535 ■ *Web:* www.tpud.org	Tillamook	OR	97141	503-842-2535	842-4161
Umatilla Electric Co-op Assn 750 W Elm Ave *Web:* www.ueinet.com	Hermiston	OR	97838	541-567-6414	567-8142
Wasco Electric Co-op Inc 105 E 4th St *Web:* www.wascoelectric.com	The Dalles	OR	97058	541-296-2740	296-7781
West Oregon Electric Co-op Inc 715 Maple St PO Box 69 *TF:* 800-777-1276 ■ *Web:* www.westoregon.com	Vernonia	OR	97064	503-429-3021	429-8440

PENNSYLVANIA

Company / Address	City	State	Zip	Phone	Fax
Adams Electric Co-op Inc 1338 Biglerville Rd PO Box 1055 *TF:* 888-232-6732 ■ *Web:* www.adamsec.coop	Gettysburg	PA	17325	717-334-2171	334-3980
Bedford Rural Electric Co-op Inc 8846 Lincoln Hwy *TF:* 800-808-2732 ■ *Web:* www.bedfordrec.com	Bedford	PA	15522	814-623-5101	623-7983
Citizens' Electric Co 1775 Industrial Blvd PO Box 551 *Web:* www.citizenselectric.com	Lewisburg	PA	17837	570-524-2231	524-5887
Claverack Rural Electric Co-op Inc 32750 W US 6 *TF:* 800-326-9799 ■ *Web:* www.claverack.com	Wysox	PA	18854	570-265-2167	265-6019
New Enterprise Rural Electric Co-op Inc 3596 Brumbaugh Rd *TF:* 800-270-3177 ■ *Web:* www.newenterpriserec.com	New Enterprise	PA	16664	814-766-3221	766-3319
Northwestern Rural Electric Co-op Assn Inc PO Box 207 **Fax Area Code:* 814 ■ *TF:* 800-352-0014 ■ *Web:* www.northwesternrec.com	Cambridge Springs	PA	16403	800-352-0014	398-8064*
REA Energy Co-op Inc 75 Airport Rd *TF:* 800-211-5667 ■ *Web:* www.reaenergy.com	Indiana	PA	15701	724-349-4800	349-7151
Somerset Rural Electric Co-op 223 Industrial Pk Rd PO Box 270 *TF:* 800-443-4255 ■ *Web:* www.somersetrec.com	Somerset	PA	15501	814-445-4106	445-5526
Sullivan County Rural Electric Co-op Inc (SCREC) 5675 Rt 87 PO Box 65 *TF:* 800-570-5081 ■ *Web:* www.screc.com	Forksville	PA	18616	570-924-3381	924-3383
Tri-County Rural Electric Co-op Inc 22 N Main St PO Box 526 *TF:* 800-343-2559 ■ *Web:* www.tri-countyrec.com	Mansfield	PA	16933	570-662-2175	662-2142
United Electric Co-op Inc 29 United Rd PO Box 688 *TF:* 888-581-8969 ■ *Web:* www.unitedpa.com	Du Bois	PA	15801	814-371-8570	371-2594
Valley Rural Electric Co-op Inc 11375 Standing Stone Rd PO Box 477 *TF:* 800-432-0680 ■ *Web:* www.valleyrec.com	Huntingdon	PA	16652	814-643-2650	643-1678
Warren Electric Co-op Inc (WEC) 320 E Main St PO Box 208 *TF:* 800-364-8640 ■ *Web:* www.warrenec.coop	Youngsville	PA	16371	814-563-7548	563-7012

SOUTH CAROLINA

Company / Address	City	State	Zip	Phone	Fax
Aiken Electric Co-op Inc 2790 Wagener Rd *TF Tech Supp:* 877-264-5368 ■ *Web:* www.aikenelectric.net	Aiken	SC	29802	803-649-6245	641-8310
Berkeley Electric Co-op Inc 551 Rembert C Dennis Blvd *Web:* www.becsc.com	Moncks Corner	SC	29461	843-761-8200	572-1280
Black River Electric Co-op Inc 1121 N Pike Rd W *Web:* www.blackriver.net	Sumter	SC	29153	803-469-8060	469-8320
Broad River Electric Co-op Inc 811 Hamrick St *TF:* 866-687-2667 ■ *Web:* www.broadriverelectric.com	Gaffney	SC	29342	864-489-5737	487-7808
Coastal Electric Co-op Inc 2269 Jefferies Hwy *TF:* 877-538-5700 ■ *Web:* www.coastal.coop	Walterboro	SC	29488	843-538-5700	538-5081
Edisto Electric Co-op Inc 896 Calhoun St *TF:* 800-433-3292 ■ *Web:* www.edistoelectric.com	Bamberg	SC	29003	803-245-5141	245-0188
Horry Electric Co-op Inc 2774 Cultra Rd *Web:* www.horryelectric.com	Conway	SC	29526	843-369-2211	369-6040

	City	State	Zip	Phone	Fax
Laurens Electric Co-op Inc 2254 S Carolina 14	Laurens	SC	29360	864-682-3141	683-5178
TF: 800-942-3141 ■ Web: www.laurenselectric.com					
Little River Electric Co-op Inc (LRECI) PO Box 220	Abbeville	SC	29620	864-366-2141	366-4524
TF: 800-459-2141 ■ Web: www.lreci.coop					
Lynches River Electric Co-op Inc 1104 W McGregor St	Pageland	SC	29728	843-672-6111	672-6118
TF: 800-922-3486 ■ Web: www.lynchesriver.com					
Marlboro Electric Co-op Inc PO Box 1057	Bennettsville	SC	29512	843-479-3855	479-8990
TF: 800-922-9174 ■ Web: www.web.marlboroelectric.net					
Mid-Carolina Electric Co-op Inc PO Box 669	Lexington	SC	29071	803-749-6555	749-6466
TF Cust Svc: 888-813-8000 ■ Web: www.mcecoop.com					
Newberry Electric Co-op Inc 882 Wilson Rd	Newberry	SC	29108	803-276-1121	276-4121
TF: 800-479-8838 ■ Web: www.nec.coop					
Palmetto Electric Co-op 4063 Grays Hwy PO Box 820	Ridgeland	SC	29936	843-726-5551	726-5632
TF: 800-922-5551 ■ Web: www.palelec.com					
Pee Dee Electric Co-op Inc PO Box 491	Darlington	SC	29540	843-665-4070	669-7931
Web: www.peedeeelectric.com					
Santee Electric Co-op Inc 424 Sumter Hwy	Kingstree	SC	29556	843-355-6187	355-0609
TF: 800-922-1604 ■ Web: www.santee.org					
Tri-County Electric Co-op Inc PO Box 217	Saint Matthews	SC	29135	803-874-1215	874-3888
TF: 877-874-1215					
York Electric Co-op Inc PO Box 150	York	SC	29745	803-684-4247	684-6306
TF: 800-582-8810 ■ Web: www.yorkelectric.net					

SOUTH DAKOTA

	City	State	Zip	Phone	Fax
Black Hills Electric Co-op Inc 25178 Co-op Way	Custer	SD	57730	605-673-4461	673-3147
TF: 800-742-0085 ■ Web: www.bhec.com					
Bon Homme Yankton Electric Assn 134 N Lidice Ave	Tabor	SD	57063	605-463-2507	463-2419
Web: www.byelectric.com					
Butte Electric Co-op Inc 109 S Dartmouth Ave	Newell	SD	57760	605-456-2494	456-2496
TF: 800-928-8839 ■ Web: www.butteelectric.com					
Cam-Wal Electric Co-op Inc 404 W Scranton St	Selby	SD	57472	605-649-7676	649-7031
Web: www.cam-walnet.com					
Central Electric Co-op 1420 N Main St PO Box 846	Mitchell	SD	57301	605-996-7516	996-0869
TF: 800-477-2892 ■ Web: www.centralec.com					
Charles Mix Electric Assn Inc 440 Lake St	Lake Andes	SD	57356	605-487-7321	487-7868
TF: 800-208-8587 ■ Web: www.charles-mix.com					
Cherry-Todd Electric Co-op Inc Hwy 18 PO Box 169	Mission	SD	57555	605-856-4416	856-4268
TF: 800-856-4417					
Clay-Union Electric Corp 1410 E Cherry St PO Box 317	Vermillion	SD	57069	605-624-2673	624-5526
TF: 800-696-2832 ■ Web: www.clayunionelectric.coop					
Codington-Clark Electric Co-op 3520 9th Ave SW	Watertown	SD	57201	605-886-5848	886-5934
TF: 800-463-8938					
Dakota Energy Co-op Inc 40294 US Hwy 14 PO Box 830	Huron	SD	57350	605-352-8591	352-8578
TF: 800-353-8591					
Douglas Electric Co-op Inc PO Box 370	Armour	SD	57313	605-724-2323	724-2972
East River Electric PowerCo-op Inc 211 S Harth Ave PO Box 227	Madison	SD	57042	605-256-4536	256-8058
Web: www.eastriver.coop					
FEM Electric Assn Inc PO Box 468	Ipswich	SD	57451	605-426-6891	426-6791
TF: 800-587-5880 ■ Web: www.femelectric.coop					
Grand Electric Co-op Inc 801 Coleman Ave PO Box 39	Bison	SD	57620	605-244-5211	244-7288
TF: 800-592-1803 ■ Web: www.grandelectric.coop					
H-D Electric Co-op Inc 423 3rd Ave S	Clear Lake	SD	57226	605-874-2171	874-8173
Kingsbury Electric Co-op Inc 511 Us Hwy 14	De Smet	SD	57231	605-854-3522	854-3465
Lake Region Electric Assn Inc 1212 Main St	Webster	SD	57274	605-345-3379	345-4442
TF: 800-657-5869 ■ Web: www.lakeregion.coop					
Moreau-Grand Electric Co-op Inc 405 9th St	Timber Lake	SD	57656	605-865-3511	865-3340
TF: 800-952-3158 ■ Web: www.mge.coop					
Northern Electric Co-op Inc 39456 133nd St	Bath	SD	57427	605-225-0310	225-1684
TF: 800-529-0310 ■ Web: www.northernelectric.coop					
Oahe Electric Co-op Inc 102 S Cranford St PO Box 216	Blunt	SD	57522	605-962-6243	962-6306
TF: 800-640-6243 ■ Web: www.oaheelectric.com					
Rosebud Electric Co-op Inc 512 Rosebud Ave PO Box 439	Gregory	SD	57533	605-835-9624	835-9649
Web: www.rosebudelectric.com					
Sioux Valley-Southwestern Electric Co-op Inc 47092 SD Hwy 34 PO Box 216	Colman	SD	57017	605-534-3535	256-1693
TF: 800-234-1960 ■ Web: www.siouxvalleyenergy.com					
Union County Electric Co-op Inc 122 W Main St	Elk Point	SD	57025	605-356-3395	356-3397
West Central Electric Co-op Inc 204 Main St PO Box 17	Murdo	SD	57559	605-669-2472	669-2358
TF: 800-242-9232 ■ Web: www.wce.coop					
West River Electric Assn Inc 1200 W Fourth Ave PO Box 412	Wall	SD	57790	888-279-2135	279-2630*
*Fax Area Code: 605 ■ TF: 888-279-2135 ■ Web: www.westriver.com					
Whetstone Valley Electric Co-op 1101 E 4th Ave	Milbank	SD	57252	605-432-5331	432-5951
TF: 800-568-6631 ■ Web: www.whetstoneelectric.com					

TENNESSEE

	City	State	Zip	Phone	Fax
Appalachian Electric Co-op 1109 Hill Dr	New Market	TN	37820	865-475-2032	475-0888
Web: www.appalachianelectric.coop					
Caney Fork Electric Co-op Inc 920 Smithville Hwy PO Box 272	McMinnville	TN	37110	931-473-3116	473-4939
TF: 888-505-3030 ■ Web: www.caneyforkec.com					
Chickasaw Electric Co-op 17970 US Hwy 64	Somerville	TN	38068	901-465-3591	465-5392
TF: 866-465-3591					
Cumberland Electric Membership Corp 1940 Madison St	Clarksville	TN	37043	931-645-2481	542-9445
Web: www.cemc.org					
Duck River Electric Membership Corp 305 Learning Way PO Box 89	Shelbyville	TN	37160	931-684-4621	685-0013
Web: www.dremc.com					
Fayetteville Public Utilities 408 W College St	Fayetteville	TN	37334	931-433-1522	433-0646
TF: 800-379-2534 ■ Web: www.fayelectric.com					
Forked Deer Electric Co-op Inc 1135 N Church St	Halls	TN	38040	731-836-7508	836-5070
Fort Loudoun Electric Co-op PO Box 1030	Vonroe	TN	37885	423-442-2487	442-6689
Web: www.flec.org					
Gibson Electric Membership Corp 1207 S College St PO Box 47	Trenton	TN	38382	731-855-4740	855-3944
Web: www.gibsonemc.com					
Greeneville Light & Power System PO Box 1690	Greeneville	TN	37744	423-636-6200	636-6206
Web: www.glps.net					
Holston Electric Co-op Inc 1200 W Main St	Rogersville	TN	37857	423-272-8821	272-6051
Web: www.holstonelectric.com					
La Follette Utilities Board 302 N Tennessee Ave PO Box 1411	La Follette	TN	37766	423-562-3316	566-0580
TF: 800-352-1340 ■ Web: www.lub.org					
Middle Tennessee Electric Membership Corp 555 New Salem Rd	Murfreesboro	TN	37129	615-890-9762	895-3594
Web: www.mtemc.com					
Mountain Electric Co-op Inc PO Box 180	Mountain City	TN	37683	423-727-1800	727-1822
TF: 888-721-9111 ■ Web: www.mountainelectric.com					
Newport Utilities Board Inc PO Box 519	Newport	TN	37822	423-625-2800	623-5767
Web: www.newportutilities.com					
Pickwick Electric Co-op 530 Mulberry Ave	Selmer	TN	38375	731-645-3411	645-7167
TF: 800-372-8258 ■ Web: www.pickwick-electric.com					
Plateau Electric Co-op 16200 Scott Hwy PO Box 4669	Oneida	TN	37841	423-569-8591	569-5726
Web: www.plateauelectric.com					
Powell Valley Electric Co-op 325 Straight Creek Rd PO Box 1528	New Tazewell	TN	37824	423-626-5204	626-0711
Web: www.pve.coop					
Sequachee Valley Electric Co-op 512 Cedar Ave PO Box 31	South Pittsburg	TN	37380	423-837-8605	837-9836
TF: 800-923-2203 ■ Web: www.svalleyec.com					
Southwest Tennessee Electric Membership Corp PO Box 989	Brownsville	TN	38012	731-772-1322	772-1037
TF: 800-772-0472 ■ Web: www.stemc.com					
Tennessee Valley Electric Co-op 590 Florence Rd	Savannah	TN	38372	731-925-4916	925-4919
TF: 866-925-4916 ■ Web: www.tvec.com					
Tri-County Electric Membership Corp 405 College St	Lafayette	TN	37083	615-666-2111	688-2141
TF: 800-369-2111 ■ Web: www.tcemc.org					
Upper Cumberland Electric Membership Corp 138 Gordonsville Hwy	South Carthage	TN	37030	615-735-2940	735-2603
TF: 800-261-2940 ■ Web: www.ucemc.com					
Volunteer Energy Co-op (VEC) PO Box 277	Decatur	TN	37322	423-334-5721	334-7003
Web: www.vec.org					

TEXAS

	City	State	Zip	Phone	Fax
Bailey County Electric Co-op Inc 305 E Ave B PO Drawer 1013	Muleshoe	TX	79347	806-272-4504	272-4509
TF: 800-869-7049 ■ Web: www.bcecoop.com					
Bandera Electric Co-op Inc 3172 State Hwy 16 N	Bandera	TX	78003	830-796-3741	460-3030
TF: 866-226-3372 ■ Web: www.bandera-ec.com					
Bartlett Electric Co-op Inc 27492 Texas 95	Bartlett	TX	76511	254-527-3551	527-3221
Web: www.bartlettec.coop					
Big Country Electric Co-op 1010 W S 1st St PO Box 518	Roby	TX	79543	325-776-2244	776-2246
TF: 888-662-2232 ■ Web: www.bigcountry.net					
Bluebonnet Electric Co-op Inc 3186 E Austin St	Giddings	TX	78942	979-542-3151	542-1187
TF: 800-842-7708 ■ Web: www.bluebonnet.com					
Bowie-Cass Electric Co-op Inc 117 N St	Douglassville	TX	75560	903-846-2311	846-2406
TF: 800-794-2919 ■ Web: www.bcec.com					
Central Texas Electric Co-op Inc 386 Friendship Ln	Fredericksburg	TX	78624	830-997-2126	997-9034
TF: 800-900-2832 ■ Web: www.centexec.com					
Coleman County Electric Co-op Inc 3300 N Hwy 84 PO Box 860	Coleman	TX	76834	325-625-2128	625-4600
TF: 800-560-2128 ■ Web: www.colemancountyelectcoop.org					
Comanche Electric Co-op Assn 201 W Wrights Ave	Comanche	TX	76442	325-356-2533	356-3038
TF: 800-915-2533 ■ Web: www.ceca.coop					
Concho Valley Electric Co-op Inc 2530 Bus US Hwy 67-J	San Angelo	TX	76905	325-655-6957	655-6950
Web: www.cvec.coop					
Cooke County Electric Co-op 11799 W US Hwy 82 PO Box 530	Muenster	TX	76252	940-759-2211	759-4122*
*Fax: Cust Svc ■ TF: 800-962-0296 ■ Web: www.cceca.com					
CoServ Electric 7701 S Stemmons Fwy	Corinth	TX	76210	940-321-7800	270-6640
TF: 800-274-4014 ■ Web: www.coserv.com					
Deaf Smith Electric Co-op Inc 1501 E 1st St	Hereford	TX	79045	806-364-1166	364-5481
TF: 800-687-8189 ■ Web: www.dsec.org					

Name / Address	City	State	Zip	Phone	Fax
Deep East Texas Electric Co-op Inc 880 State Hwy 21 E *TF:* 800-392-5986 ■ *Web:* www.deepeast.com	San Augustine	TX	75972	936-275-2314	275-2135
DeWitt Electric Co-op Inc PO Box 118	Gonzales	TX	78629	361-275-2334	275-5662
Fannin County Electric Co-op Inc 1530 Silo Rd *TF:* 800-695-9020 ■ *Web:* www.fcec.coop	Bonham	TX	75418	903-583-2117	583-7384
Fayette Electric Co-op Inc 357 N Washington St *TF:* 800-874-8290 ■ *Web:* www.fayette.coop	La Grange	TX	78945	979-968-3181	968-6752
Fort Belknap Electric Co-op Inc 1302 W Main PO Box 486 *Web:* www.fortbelknapec.com	Olney	TX	76374	940-564-2343	564-3247
Grayson-Collin Electric Co-op (GCEC) PO Box 548 *TF:* 800-967-5235 ■ *Web:* www.gcec.net	Van Alstyne	TX	75495	903-482-7100	482-5906
Greenbelt Electric Co-op Inc PO Box 948 *TF:* 800-527-3082 ■ *Web:* www.greenbeltelectric.coop	Wellington	TX	79095	806-447-2536	447-2434
Guadalupe Valley Electric Co-op Inc 825 E Sarah Dewitt Dr *TF:* 800-223-4832 ■ *Web:* www.gvec.org	Gonzales	TX	78629	830-857-1200	857-1205
Guadalupe-Blanco River Authority (GBRA) 933 E Ct St *Web:* www.gbra.org	Seguin	TX	78155	830-379-5822	379-9718
Hamilton County Electric Co-op Assn 420 N Rice St *TF:* 800-595-3401	Hamilton	TX	76531	254-386-3123	386-8757
Hilco Electric Co-op Inc 115 E Main PO Box 127 *TF:* 800-338-6425 ■ *Web:* www.hilco.org	Itasca	TX	76055	254-687-2331	687-2428
Houston County Electric Co-op Inc PO Box 52 *TF:* 800-657-2445	Crockett	TX	75835	936-544-5641	544-4628
J-A-C Electric Co-op Inc PO Box 278 *Web:* www.jacelectric.com	Bluegrove	TX	76352	940-895-3311	895-3321
Jackson ElectricCo-op Inc 8925 State Hwy 111 S *Web:* www.jecec.com	Ganado	TX	77962	361-771-4400	771-4406
Jasper-Newton Electric Co-op Inc 812 S Margaret Ave *TF:* 800-231-9340 ■ *Web:* www.jnec.com	Kirbyville	TX	75956	409-423-2241	423-3648
Karnes Electric Co-op Inc 1007 N Hwy 123 *TF:* 888-807-3952 ■ *Web:* www.karnesec.org	Karnes City	TX	78118	830-780-3952	780-2347
Lamar County Electric Co-op Assn 1485 N Main St *TF:* 800-782-9010 ■ *Web:* www.lamarelectric.com	Paris	TX	75460	903-784-4303	784-7084
Lamb County Electric Co-op Inc 2415 S Phelps Ave *TF:* 800-365-9000 ■ *Web:* www.lcec.coop	Littlefield	TX	79339	806-385-5191	385-5197
Lighthouse Electric Co-op Inc 70 E Matador Hwy *TF:* 800-657-7192 ■ *Web:* www.lighthouse.coop	Floydada	TX	79235	806-983-2814	983-2804
Lyntegar Electric Co-op Inc PO Box 970	Tahoka	TX	79373	806-561-4588	561-4724
Magic Valley Electric Co-op Inc 1 3/4 Mile W Hwy 83 PO Box 267 **Fax Area Code:* 956 ■ *TF:* 800-880-6832 ■ *Web:* www.magval.com	Mercedes	TX	78570	866-225-5683	565-4182*
McLennan County Electric Co-op PO Box 357 *TF:* 800-840-2957 ■ *Web:* www.mclennanelectric.com	McGregor	TX	76657	254-840-2871	840-4250
Medina Electric Co-op Inc PO Box 370 *TF:* 866-632-3532 ■ *Web:* www.medinaec.org	Hondo	TX	78861	830-741-4384	426-2796
Mid-South Electric Co-op Assn 7625 Texas 6 *TF:* 888-525-6677 ■ *Web:* www.midsouthsynergy.com	Navasota	TX	77868	936-825-5100	825-5166
Navarro County Electric Co-op Inc 3800 Texas 22 *TF:* 800-771-9095	Corsicana	TX	75110	903-874-7411	874-8422
Navasota Valley Electric Co-op Inc 2281 E US Hwy 79 PO Box 848 *TF:* 800-443-9462 ■ *Web:* www.navasotavalley.com	Franklin	TX	77856	979-828-3232	828-5563
North Plains Electric Co-op Inc 14585 Hwy 83 N PO Box 1008 *TF:* 800-272-5482 ■ *Web:* www.npec.org	Perryton	TX	79070	806-435-5482	435-7225
Nueces Electric Co-op 709 E Main St *TF:* 800-632-9288 ■ *Web:* www.nueceselectriccoop.com	Robstown	TX	78380	361-387-2581	387-4139
Panola-Harrison Electric Co-op 410 E Houston St *TF:* 800-972-1093	Marshall	TX	75670	903-935-7936	935-3361
Pedernales Electric Co-op Inc 300 Haley Rd PO Box 1 **Fax:* Cust Svc ■ *TF:* 888-554-4732 ■ *Web:* www.lcra.org/pec	Johnson City	TX	78636	830-868-7155	868-4767*
Rio Grande Electric Co-op Inc Hwy 90 & State Hwy 131 PO Box 1509 *TF:* 800-749-1509 ■ *Web:* www.riogrande.coop	Brackettville	TX	78832	830-563-2444	563-2450
Rusk County ElectricCo-op Inc 3162 State Hwy 43 E PO Box 1169 *Web:* www.rcelectric.org	Henderson	TX	75653	903-657-4571	657-5377
Sam Houston Electric Co-op Inc 1157 E Church St *TF:* 800-458-0381 ■ *Web:* www.samhouston.net	Livingston	TX	77351	936-327-5711	328-1244
San Bernard Electric Co-op Inc 309 W Main St *TF:* 800-364-3171 ■ *Web:* www.sbec.org	Bellville	TX	77418	979-865-3171	865-9706
San Patricio Electric Co-op Inc 402 E Sinton St *TF:* 888-740-2220 ■ *Web:* www.sanpatricioelectric.org	Sinton	TX	78387	361-364-2220	364-3467
South Plains Electric Co-op Inc PO Box 1830 *TF:* 800-658-2655 ■ *Web:* www.spec.coop	Lubbock	TX	79408	806-775-7766	775-7796
Southwest Texas Electric Co-op Inc 101 E Gillis St PO Box 677 *TF:* 800-643-3980 ■ *Web:* www.swtec.com	Eldorado	TX	76936	325-853-2544	853-3141
Swisher Electric Co-op Inc 401 SW 2nd St PO Box 67 *TF:* 800-530-4344 ■ *Web:* www.swisherelectric.org	Tulia	TX	79088	806-995-3567	995-2249
Taylor Electric Co-op Inc (TEC) 226 County Rd 287 Bldg A PO Box 250 *TF:* 800-992-0086 ■ *Web:* www.taylorelectric.com	Merkel	TX	79536	325-793-8500	793-8520
Texas Electric Co-ops Inc 1122 Colorado St 24th Fl *TF:* 800-301-2860 ■ *Web:* www.texas-ec.org	Austin	TX	78701	512-454-0311	486-6237
Tri-County Electric Co-op Inc 600 NW Pkwy *TF:* 800-367-8232 ■ *Web:* www.tcectexas.com	Azle	TX	76020	817-444-3201	444-3542
Trinity Valley Electric Co-op Inc (TVEC) 1800 Hwy 243 E PO Box 888 *TF:* 800-766-9576 ■ *Web:* www.tvec.net	Kaufman	TX	75142	972-932-2214	932-6466
United Co-op Services 3309 N Main St *Web:* www.united-cs.com	Cleburne	TX	76033	817-556-4000	556-4068
Upshur Rural Electric Co-op Corp PO Box 70 *Web:* www.urecc.com	Gilmer	TX	75644	903-843-2536	843-2736
Victoria Electric Co-op Inc 102 S Ben Jordan St *Web:* www.vicec.org	Victoria	TX	77901	361-573-2428	573-5753
Wharton County Electric Co-op Inc 1701 E Jackson St *TF:* 800-460-6271 ■ *Web:* www.wcecnet.net	El Campo	TX	77437	979-543-6271	543-6259
Wise Electric Co-op Inc 1900 N Trinity St *TF:* 888-627-9326 ■ *Web:* www.wiseec.com	Decatur	TX	76234	940-627-2167	627-6540
Wood County Electric Co-op Inc 501 S Main St *TF:* 800-762-2203 ■ *Web:* www.wcec.org	Quitman	TX	75783	903-763-2203	763-5693

UTAH

Name / Address	City	State	Zip	Phone	Fax
Dixie-Escalante Rural Electric Assn 71 E Hwy 56	Beryl	UT	84714	435-439-5311	439-5352
Flowell Electric Assn Inc 495 N 3200 W	Fillmore	UT	84631	435-743-6214	743-5722
GarKane Energy Inc 120 W 300 S *TF:* 800-747-5403 ■ *Web:* www.garkaneenergy.com	Loa	UT	84747	435-836-2795	836-2497
Moon Lake Electric Assn Inc 188 W 200 N PO Box 278 *Web:* www.mleainc.com/index.html	Roosevelt	UT	84066	435-722-5400	722-3752

VERMONT

Name / Address	City	State	Zip	Phone	Fax
Vermont Electric Co-op Inc 42 Wescom Rd *TF:* 800-832-2667 ■ *Web:* www.vermontelectric.coop	Johnson	VT	05656	802-635-2331	635-7645
Washington Electric Co-op PO Box 8 Rt 14 *TF:* 800-932-5245 ■ *Web:* www.washingtonelectric.coop	East Montpelier	VT	05651	802-223-5245	223-6780

VIRGINIA

Name / Address	City	State	Zip	Phone	Fax
A & N Electric Co-op 21275 Co-op Way PO Box 290 *TF:* 800-431-2632 ■ *Web:* www.anecop.com	Tasley	VA	23441	757-787-9750	787-9780
BARC Electric Co-op 100 High St PO Box 264 *TF:* 800-846-2272 ■ *Web:* www.barcelectric.com	Millboro	VA	24460	540-997-9124	997-9011
Central Virginia Electric Co-op 800 Co-op Way PO Box 247 *TF:* 800-367-2832 ■ *Web:* www.forcvec.com	Lovingston	VA	22949	434-263-8336	263-8339
Community Electric Co-op 52 W Windsor Blvd *Web:* www.comelec.coop	Windsor	VA	23487	757-242-6181	242-3923
Craig-Botetourt Electric Co-op PO Box 265 *TF Cust Svc:* 800-760-2232	New Castle	VA	24127	540-864-5121	864-5461
Mecklenburg Electric Co-op 11633 Hwy Ninety Two *TF:* 800-989-4161 ■ *Web:* www.meckelec.org	Chase City	VA	23924	434-372-6100	372-6102
Northern Neck Electric Co-op Inc 85 St Johns St PO Box 288 *TF:* 800-243-2860 ■ *Web:* www.nnec.com	Warsaw	VA	22572	804-333-3621	333-5581
Northern Virginia Electric Co-op PO Box 2710 *TF:* 888-335-0500 ■ *Web:* www.novec.com	Manassas	VA	22110	703-335-0500	392-1546
Old Dominion Electric Co-op (ODEC) 4201 Dominion Blvd *Web:* www.odec.com	Glen Allen	VA	23060	804-747-0592	747-3742
Prince George Electric Co-op 7103 General Mahone Hwy PO Box 168 *Web:* www.pgec.coop	Waverly	VA	23890	804-834-2424	834-3544
Shenandoah Valley Electric Co-op PO Box 236 *TF:* 800-234-7832 ■ *Web:* www.shenvalleyelectric.com	Mount Crawford	VA	22841	540-434-2200	434-2227
Southside Electric Co-op Inc 2000 W Virgina Ave *TF:* 800-552-2118 ■ *Web:* www.sec.coop	Crewe	VA	23930	434-645-7721	645-1147

WASHINGTON

Name / Address	City	State	Zip	Phone	Fax
Benton Rural Electric Assn (BREA) 402 7th St PO Box 1150 *TF:* 800-221-6987 ■ *Web:* www.bentonrea.org	Prosser	WA	99350	509-786-2913	786-0291
Big Bend Electric Co-op 1373 N Hwy 261 PO Box 348 *TF:* 866-844-2363 ■ *Web:* www.bbec.org	Ritzville	WA	99169	509-659-1700	659-1404
Columbia Rural Electric Assn Inc 115 E Main St *TF:* 800-642-1231 ■ *Web:* www.columbiarea.com	Dayton	WA	99328	509-382-2578	382-2736
Elmhurst Mutual Power & Light Co 120 132nd St S *Web:* www.elmhurstmutual.org	Tacoma	WA	98444	253-531-4646	531-8969
Energy Northwest 76 N Power Plant Loop *TF:* 800-468-6883 ■ *Web:* www.energy-northwest.com	Richland	WA	99354	509-372-5000	372-5205
Inland Power & Light Co Inc 10110 W Hallett Rd *TF:* 800-747-7151 ■ *Web:* www.inlandpower.com	Spokane	WA	99224	509-747-7151	747-7987

				Phone	Fax
Nespelem Valley Electric Co-op Inc 1009 F St *Web:* www.nvec.org	Nespelem	WA	99155	509-634-4571	634-8138
OHOP Mutual Light Co 34014 Mountain Hwy E	Eatonville	WA	98328	253-847-4364	847-2877
Okanogan County Electric Co-op 93 W Chewuch Rd	Winthrop	WA	98862	509-996-2228	996-2241
Orcas Power & Light Co-op 183 Mt Baker Rd. *Web:* www.opalco.com	Eastsound	WA	98245	360-376-3500	376-3505
Parkland Light & Water Co 12918 Pk Ave *Web:* www.plw.coop	Tacoma	WA	98444	253-531-5666	531-2684
Peninsula Light Co 13315 Goodnough Dr NW *TF:* 888-809-8021 ■ *Web:* www.penlight.org	Gig Harbor	WA	98332	253-857-5950	857-3100
Public Utility District #1 of Ferry County 686 S Clark Ave PO Box 1039 *Web:* www.fcpud.com	Republic	WA	99166	509-775-3325	775-3326
Tanner Electric Co PO Box 1426 *TF:* 800-472-0208	North Bend	WA	98045	425-888-0623	888-5688

WEST VIRGINIA

				Phone	Fax
Harrison Rural Electrification Assn Inc Rt 6 PO Box 502 *TF:* 800-540-4732 ■ *Web:* www.harrisonrea.com	Clarksburg	WV	26301	304-624-6365	624-6366

WISCONSIN

				Phone	Fax
Adams-Columbia Electric Co-op 401 E Lake St *TF:* 800-831-8629	Friendship	WI	53934	608-339-3346	339-7756
Barron Electric Co-op 1434 State Hwy 25 N *TF:* 800-322-1008 ■ *Web:* www.barronelectric.com	Barron	WI	54812	715-537-3171	537-5146
Bayfield Electric Co-op Inc 7400 Iron River Dam Rd *TF:* 800-278-0166 ■ *Web:* www.bayfieldelectric.com	Iron River	WI	54847	715-372-4287	372-4318
Chippewa Valley Electric Co-op 317 S 8th St. *TF:* 800-300-6800 ■ *Web:* www.cvecoop.com	Cornell	WI	54732	715-239-6800	239-6160
Clark Electric Co-op 124 N Main St PO Box 190 *TF:* 800-272-6188 ■ *Web:* www.cecoop.com	Greenwood	WI	54437	715-267-6188	267-7355
Dairyland Power Coop 3200 E Ave S *Web:* www.dairynet.com	La Crosse	WI	54601	608-788-4000	787-1420
Dunn Energy Co-op PO Box 220 *TF:* 800-924-0630 ■ *Web:* www.dunnenergy.com	Menomonie	WI	54751	715-232-6240	232-6244
Eau Claire Electric Co-op 8214 Us Hwy 12 *TF:* 800-927-5090 ■ *Web:* www.ecec.com	Fall Creek	WI	54742	715-832-1603	832-2055
Jackson Electric Co-op N6868 County Rd F PO Box 546 *TF:* 800-370-4607 ■ *Web:* www.jackelec.com	Black River Falls	WI	54615	715-284-5385	284-7143
Jump River Electric Co-op 1102 W 9th St N. *Web:* www.jrec.com	Ladysmith	WI	54848	715-532-5524	532-3065
Oakdale Electric Co-op PO Box 128 *TF:* 800-241-2468 ■ *Web:* www.oakdalerec.com	Oakdale	WI	54649	608-372-4131	372-5173
Oconto Electric Co-op 7478 Rea Rd PO Box 168 *TF:* 800-472-8410 ■ *Web:* www.ocontoelectric.com	Oconto Falls	WI	54154	920-846-2816	846-4327
Pierce Pepin Co-op Services W7725 US Hwy 10 PO Box 420 *TF:* 800-924-2133 ■ *Web:* www.piercepepin.com	Ellsworth	WI	54011	715-273-4355	273-4476
Polk-Burnett Electric Co-op (PBEC) 1001 State Rd 35 *TF:* 800-421-0283 ■ *Web:* www.polkburnett.com	Centuria	WI	54824	715-646-2191	646-2404
Price Electric Co-op 508 N Lake Ave PO Box 110 *TF:* 800-884-0881 ■ *Web:* www.price-electric.com	Phillips	WI	54555	715-339-2155	339-2921
Richland Electric Co-op 1027 N Jefferson St *Web:* www.richec.com	Richland Center	WI	53581	608-647-3173	647-4265
Riverland Energy Co-op 625 W Main St PO Box 277 *TF:* 800-411-9115 ■ *Web:* www.riverlandenergy.com	Arcadia	WI	54612	608-323-3381	323-3014
Rock County Electric Co-op Assn 2815 Kennedy Rd PO Box 1758 *TF:* 888-236-0665 ■ *Web:* www.rceca.com	Janesville	WI	53547	608-752-4550	752-6620
Saint Croix Electric Co-op 1925 Ridgeway St. *TF:* 800-924-3407 ■ *Web:* www.scecnet.net	Hammond	WI	54015	715-796-7000	796-7070
Scenic Rivers Energy Co-op 231 N Sheridan St *TF:* 800-236-2141 ■ *Web:* www.scenicriversenergy.com	Lancaster	WI	53813	608-723-2121	723-2688
Taylor Electric Co-op N1831 State Hwy 13 *TF:* 800-862-2407 ■ *Web:* www.taylorelectric.org	Medford	WI	54451	715-678-2411	678-2555
Vernon Electric Co-op 110 N Main St *TF:* 800-447-5051 ■ *Web:* www.vernonelectric.org	Westby	WI	54667	608-634-3121	634-7452

WYOMING

				Phone	Fax
Big Horn Rural Electric Co-op 208 S 5th St PO Box 270 *TF:* 800-564-2419	Basin	WY	82410	307-568-2419	568-2402
Bridger Valley Electric Assn Inc 40014 Business Loop 1-80 PO Box 399 *TF:* 800-276-3481 ■ *Web:* www.bvea.net	Mountain View	WY	82939	307-786-2800	786-4362
Carbon Power & Light Inc 110 E Spring St. *TF:* 800-359-0249 ■ *Web:* www.carbonpower.com	Saratoga	WY	82331	307-326-5206	326-5934
Garland Light & Power Co 755 Hwy 14A	Powell	WY	82435	307-754-2881	754-5320
High Plains Power Inc 230 W Main St. *TF:* 800-445-0613 ■ *Web:* www.highplainspower.org	Riverton	WY	82501	307-856-9426	856-4207
High West Energy Inc (HWE) 6270 County Rd 212 PO Box 519 *TF:* 888-834-1657 ■ *Web:* www.highwest-energy.com	Pine Bluffs	WY	82082	307-245-3261	245-9292
Lower Valley Energy 236 N Washington PO Box 188 *TF:* 800-882-5875 ■ *Web:* www.lvenergy.com	Afton	WY	83110	307-885-3175	885-5787
Niobrara Electric Assn Inc 3947 Us Hwy 20 *TF:* 800-322-0544 ■ *Web:* www.tristategt.org	Lusk	WY	82225	307-334-3221	334-2620
Powder River Energy Corp (PRE) 221 Main St PO Box 930 *TF:* 800-442-3630 ■ *Web:* www.precorp.coop	Sundance	WY	82729	307-283-3531	283-3527
Wheatland Rural Electric Assn 2154 S St. *TF:* 800-344-3351 ■ *Web:* www.wheatlandrea.com	Wheatland	WY	82201	307-322-2125	322-5340
Wyrulec Co 500 Main St *TF:* 800-628-5266	Lingle	WY	82223	307-837-2225	837-2115

249 ELECTRICAL & ELECTRONIC EQUIPMENT & PARTS - WHOL

				Phone	Fax
AAAA World Import-Export Inc 7800 NW 29th St *Web:* www.aaaaworld.com	Miami	FL	33122	305-688-1000	644-8957
ACF Components & Fasteners Inc 31012 Huntwood Ave *TF Cust Svc:* 800-227-2901 ■ *Web:* www.acfcom.com	Hayward	CA	94544	510-487-2100	471-7018
ADDvantage Technologies Group Inc 1221 E Houston *NASDAQ: AEY* ■ *Web:* www.addvantagetech.com	Broken Arrow	OK	74012	918-251-9121	251-0792
Adi American Distributors Inc 2 Emery Ave Suite 1 *TF:* 800-877-0510 ■ *Web:* www.americandistr.com	Randolph	NJ	07869	973-328-1181	328-2302
Advance Electrical Supply Co 263 N Oakley Blvd *Web:* www.advanceelectrical.com	Chicago	IL	60612	312-421-2300	421-0926
Advanced MP Technology 1010 Calle Sombra *TF:* 800-492-3113 ■ *Web:* www.advancedmp.com	San Clemente	CA	92673	949-492-3113	492-6480
AE Petsche Co Inc 2112 W Division St *TF:* 800-777-9280 ■ *Web:* www.aepetsche.com	Arlington	TX	76012	817-461-9473	277-2887
Aee Solar Inc 1271 Evergreen Rd PO Box 339 *TF:* 800-777-6609 ■ *Web:* www.aeesolar.com	Redway	CA	95560	707-923-2277	923-3009
Aesco Electronics Inc 2230 Picton Pkwy *TF:* 877-442-6987 ■ *Web:* www.aesco.com	Akron	OH	44312	330-245-2630	245-2631
All American Semiconductor Inc 16115 NW 52nd Ave *NASDAQ: SEMI* ■ **Fax:* Hum Res ■ *TF:* 800-762-2095 ■ *Web:* www.allamerican.com	Miami	FL	33014	305-621-8282	620-7831*
Allied Electronics Inc 7151 Jack Newell Blvd S *TF:* 866-433-5722 ■ *Web:* www.alliedelec.com	Fort Worth	TX	76118	817-595-3500	595-6404
Allstar Magnetics LLC 6205 NE 63rd St *Web:* www.allstarmagnetics.com	Vancouver	WA	98661	360-693-0213	693-0639
America II Electronics Inc 2600 118th Ave N *TF:* 800-767-2637 ■ *Web:* www.americaii.com	Saint Petersburg	FL	33716	727-573-0900	572-9696
American Electric Supply Inc 1872 W Pomona Rd *TF:* 800-877-8346 ■ *Web:* www.amelect.com	Corona	CA	92880	951-734-7910	737-9906
American Technology Corp 15378 Avenue of Science Suite 100 *NASDAQ: LRAD* ■ *Web:* www.lradx.com	San Diego	CA	92128	858-676-1112	676-1120
Anixter International Inc 2301 Patriot Blvd *NYSE: AXE* ■ *TF:* 800-264-9837 ■ *Web:* www.anixter.com	Glenview	IL	60025	224-521-8000	323-8166
Apollo Display Technologies Inc 85 Remington Blvd *TF:* 800-523-7862 ■ *Web:* www.apollodisplays.com	Ronkonkoma	NY	11779	631-580-4360	580-4370
Area 51 Esg Inc 51 Post *TF:* 877-476-8751 ■ *Web:* www.area51esg.com	Irvine	CA	92618	949-387-0051	
Argo International Corp 140 Franklin St. *TF:* 877-274-6468 ■ *Web:* www.argointl.com	New York	NY	10013	212-431-1700	226-9072
Arizona Components Co Inc 2901 W McDowell Rd *TF:* 800-255-5420 ■ *Web:* www.azcompco.com	Phoenix	AZ	85009	602-269-5655	278-6375
Arrow Electronics Inc 50 Marcus Dr *NYSE: ARW* ■ *TF Sales:* 800-777-2776 ■ *Web:* www.arrow.com	Melville	NY	11747	631-847-2000	847-2222
Astrex Inc 205 Express St *TF:* 800-633-6360 ■ *Web:* www.astrex.net	Plainview	NY	11803	516-433-1700	433-1796
Audio-technica Us Inc 1221 Commerce Dr. *TF:* 888-918-2244 ■ *Web:* www.audio-technica.com	Stow	OH	44224	330-686-2600	688-3752
Avnet Inc 2211 S 47th St *NYSE: AVT* ■ *TF:* 888-822-8638 ■ *Web:* www.avnet.com	Phoenix	AZ	85034	480-643-2000	
Barbey Electronics Corp 210 Corporate Dr PO Box 2 *TF:* 800-822-2251 ■ *Web:* www.barbeyele.com	Reading	PA	19605	610-916-7955	916-1975
Barnett Inc 801 W Bay St. **Fax:* Mktg ■ *TF:* 800-288-2000 ■ *Web:* www.e-barnett.com	Jacksonville	FL	32204	904-384-6530	388-2723*
Beacon Electric Supply 9630 Chesapeake Dr. *Web:* www.beaconelectric.com	San Diego	CA	92123	858-279-9770	279-9908
Bearcom Inc 4009 Distribution Dr Suite 200 *TF Sales:* 800-527-1670 ■ *Web:* www.bearcom.com	Garland	TX	75041	214-340-8876	
Becker Electric Supply Inc 1341 E 4th St *TF:* 800-762-9515 ■ *Web:* www.beckerelectric.com	Dayton	OH	45402	937-226-1341	226-1790
Benfield Electric Supply Co Inc 25 Lafayette Ave *Web:* www.benfieldelectric.com	North White Plains	NY	10603	914-948-6660	993-0558
Bertech-Kelex 640 Maple Ave. *Web:* www.bertech.com	Torrance	CA	90503	310-787-0337	787-0854
Beyond Components 5 Carl Thompson Rd. *Web:* www.beyondcomponents.com	Westford	MA	01886	978-392-9191	392-1199
Billows Electric Supply Co 9100 State Rd *Web:* www.billows.com	Philadelphia	PA	19136	215-332-9700	338-8320
Bisco Industries Inc 1500 N Lakeview Ave *TF:* 800-323-1232 ■ *Web:* www.biscoind.com	Anaheim	CA	92807	714-693-3670	693-9470
Bliley Technologies Inc PO Box 3428 *Web:* www.bliley.com	Erie	PA	16508	814-838-3571	833-2712

Company	City	State	Zip	Phone	Fax
Boggis-Johnson Electric Co 2900 N 112th St PO Box 26068 *TF:* 800-333-7650	Milwaukee	WI	53226	414-475-6900	475-6607
Border States Electric Supply 105 25th St N *TF:* 800-676-5834 ■ *Web:* www.bseweb.com	Fargo	ND	58102	701-293-5834	237-9488
Brightpoint Inc 7635 Interactive way Suit 200 *NASDAQ: CELL* ■ *TF:* 800-952-2355 ■ *Web:* www.brightpoint.com	Indianapolis	IN	46278	317-707-2355	707-2512
Brightstar Corp 9725 NW 117th Ave Suite 300 *TF Cust Svc:* 800-381-8402 ■ *Web:* www.brightstarcorp.com	Miami	FL	33178	305-477-8676	477-9072
Broadfield Distributing Inc 67A Glen Cove Ave *TF:* 800-634-5178 ■ *Web:* www.broadfield.com	Glen Cove	NY	11542	516-676-2378	671-3092
Broken Arrow Electric Supply Inc 2350 W Vancouver *TF:* 877-999-2237 ■ *Web:* www.baes.com	Broken Arrow	OK	74012	918-258-3581	251-3799
Buckles-Smith 801 Savaker Ave *TF:* 800-833-7362 ■ *Web:* www.buckles-smith.com	San Jose	CA	95126	408-280-7777	280-0729
Burst Communication Inc 8200 S Akron St Suite 108 *Web:* www.burstvideo.com	Centennial	CO	80112	303-649-9600	649-9890
Butler Supply Inc 965 Horan Dr *Web:* www.butlersupply.com	Fenton	MO	63026	636-349-9000	349-7877
Cabletel Communications Corp 55 Valleywood Dr *TF:* 800-268-3231 ■ *Web:* www.cabletelgroup.com	Markham	ON	L3R5L9	905-475-1030	475-9571
California Eastern Laboratories Inc (CEL) 4590 Patrick Henry Dr *Web:* www.cel.com	Santa Clara	CA	95054	408-988-3500	988-0279
Capital Electric Supply Co 7310 W Roosevelt Suite 2 *Web:* www.capitalelectricsupplyco.com	Phoenix	AZ	85043	623-936-6789	936-6262
Cardello Electric Supply Co 701 N Pt Dr *TF:* 800-333-0454 ■ *Web:* www.cardello.com	Pittsburgh	PA	15233	412-322-8031	322-9121
Carlton Bates Co 3600 W 69th St *TF:* 800-482-9313 ■ *Web:* www.carlton-bates.com	Little Rock	AR	72209	501-562-9100	562-4931
Cell-Tel Government Systems Inc 8226-B Phillips Hwy Suite 290 *TF:* 800-737-7545 ■ *Web:* www.cell-tel.com	Jacksonville	FL	32256	904-363-1111	363-0032
Central Wholesale Electrical Distributors Inc 6611 Preston Ave Suite E *TF:* 800-834-8122 ■ *Web:* www.cwed.com	Livermore	CA	94551	925-245-9310	245-9292
Century Fasteners Corp 50-20 Ireland St *TF:* 800-221-0769 ■ *Web:* www.centuryfasteners.com	Elmhurst	NY	11373	718-446-5000	426-8119
Codale Electric Supply Inc 3150 S 900 W *TF:* 800-300-6634 ■ *Web:* www.codale.com	Salt Lake City	UT	84119	801-975-7300	977-8833
Coghlin Electric/Electronics PO Box 5100 *TF:* 800-343-1201 ■ *Web:* www.ceewesco.com	Westborough	MA	01581	508-870-5000	870-5150
Commodity Components International Inc 100 Summit St *TF:* 800-424-7364 ■ *Web:* www.cci-inc.com	Peabody	MA	01960	978-538-0020	538-3633
Communications Supply Corp (CSC) 200 E Lies Rd *TF:* 800-468-2121 ■ *Web:* www.gocsc.com	Carol Stream	IL	60188	630-221-6400	221-6420
Components Distributors Inc 1748 Platte St **Fax Area Code:* 954 ■ *Web:* www.cdiweb.com	Denver	CO	80202	303-861-2872	973-6915*
Comtel Corp 39810 Grand River Ave Suite 180 *Web:* www.comtel.com	Novi	MI	48375	248-888-4730	888-4743
Consolidated Electrical Distributors Inc 31356 Via Colinas Suite 107 *Web:* www.ced-aec.com	Westlake Village	CA	91362	818-991-9000	991-6858
Corporate Telephone 184 W 2nd St *TF:* 800-274-1211 ■ *Web:* www.corporatetelephone.com	Boston	MA	02127	617-625-1200	625-1201
Cortelco Inc 1703 Sawyer Rd *TF:* 800-288-3132 ■ *Web:* www.cortelco.com	Corinth	MS	38834	662-287-5281	287-3889
Crescent Electric Supply Co 7750 Timmerman Dr *Web:* www.cesco.com	East Dubuque	IL	61025	815-747-3145	747-7720
Cross Automation Inc 2001 Oak Pkwy PO Box 1026 *TF:* 800-866-4568 ■ *Web:* www.cross-automation.com	Belmont	NC	28012	704-523-2222	523-6500
Crum Electric Supply Co 1165 W English Ave *TF:* 800-726-2239 ■ *Web:* www.crum.com	Casper	WY	82601	307-266-1278	577-1312
Dakota Supply Group 2601 3rd Ave N *TF:* 800-437-4702 ■ *Web:* www.dakotasupplygroup.com	Fargo	ND	58102	701-237-9440	237-6504
Dee Electronics Inc 2500 16th Ave SW *TF:* 800-747-3331 ■ *Web:* www.dee-inc.com	Cedar Rapids	IA	52404	319-365-7551	365-8506
Dependable Component Supply Corp 1003 E Newport Ctr Dr *TF:* 800-336-7100 ■ *Web:* www.dependonus.com	Deerfield Beach	FL	33442	954-283-5800	283-5802
Desco Inc 1205 Lincolnton Rd PO Box 1809 *TF:* 800-222-2140 ■ *Web:* www.descoinc.com	Salisbury	NC	28145	704-633-6331	637-6966
DH Supply Co 6915 NE Expy Access Rd NW	Doraville	GA	30340	770-409-0500	409-0403
Digi-Key Corp 701 Brooks Ave S *TF:* 800-344-4539 ■ *Web:* www.digikey.com	Thief River Falls	MN	56701	218-681-6674	681-3380
Diversified Electronics Co Inc PO Box 566 *Web:* www.diversifiedelectronics.com	Forest Park	GA	30298	404-361-4840	361-6327
Dominion Electric Supply Co Inc 5053 Lee Hwy *TF:* 800-525-5006 ■ *Web:* www.dominionelectric.com	Arlington	VA	22207	703-536-4400	241-9047
Don Blackburn & Co Inc 21251 Ryan Rd *TF:* 800-882-3426 ■ *Web:* www.donblackburn.com	Warren	MI	48091	586-755-0200	755-5464
Dow Electronics Inc 8603 E Adamo Dr *TF:* 800-627-2900 ■ *Web:* www.dowelectronics.com	Tampa	FL	33619	813-626-5195	628-4990
E Sam Jones Distributor Inc 4898 S Atlanta Rd *TF:* 800-624-9849 ■ *Web:* www.esamjones.com	Smyrna	GA	30080	404-351-3250	351-4140
Earl & Brown Co Inc 9700 SW Harvest Ct *Web:* www.earlbrown.com	Beaverton	OR	97005	503-670-1170	684-2001
Eck Supply Co 1405 W Main St *Web:* www.ecksupply.com	Richmond	VA	23220	804-359-5781	358-1353
Eforcity Corp 12339 Denholm Dr *Web:* www.eforcity.com	El Monte	CA	91732	626-442-3168	
EIS Inc 2018 Powers Ferry Rd Suite 500 *Web:* www.eis-inc.com	Atlanta	GA	30339	678-255-3600	255-3725
EIS Inc 13200 10th Ave N Suite E *TF:* 800-328-4662	Plymouth	MN	55441	763-513-7300	513-7351
Electric Supply & Equipment Co 1812 E Wendover Ave *TF:* 800-632-0268 ■ *Web:* www.ese-co.com	Greensboro	NC	27405	336-272-4123	274-4632
Electric Supply Inc 4407 N Manhattan Ave *TF:* 800-678-1894 ■ *Web:* www.electricsupplyinc.com	Tampa	FL	33614	813-872-1894	874-1680
Electrical Wholesale Supply Co of Utah 158 E 4500 S *Web:* www.ewsutah.com	Salt Lake City	UT	84107	801-268-2555	268-2555
Electro Brand Inc 1127 S Mannheim Rd Suite 305 *TF:* 800-982-3954	Westchester	IL	60154	773-261-5000	261-5000
Electro Sonic Inc 55 rensrew Dr Suite 100 **Fax Area Code:* 905 ■ *TF:* 800-567-6642 ■ *Web:* www.e-sonic.com	markham	ON	L3RHH3	416-494-1666	946-1900*
Electro-Matic Products Inc 23409 Industrial Pk Ct *TF:* 888-879-1088 ■ *Web:* www.electro-matic.com	Farmington Hills	MI	48335	248-478-1182	478-1472
ElectroTech Inc 3268 Winpark Dr *TF:* 800-544-4288 ■ *Web:* www.electrotech-inc.com	Minneapolis	MN	55427	763-544-4288	542-8102
Elliott Electric Supply Co 2526 N Stallings Dr PO Box 630610 *TF:* 877-777-0242 ■ *Web:* www.elliottelectric.com	Nacogdoches	TX	75963	936-569-1184	569-1836
Emergency Radio Service Inc PO Box 110 *Web:* www.ers2way.com	Ligonier	IN	46767	260-894-4145	894-7581
Englewood Electrical Supply 716 Belvedere Dr *TF:* 800-589-8886	Kokomo	IN	46901	765-452-4087	454-5138
Equity Utility Service Co Inc 1060-D Triad Ct *TF:* 800-282-9695	Marietta	GA	30062	770-422-1005	427-8455
Eric Electronics 2220 Lundy Ave *TF:* 800-406-3742 ■ *Web:* www.ericnet.com	San Jose	CA	95131	408-432-1111	433-0570
Essco Wholesale Electric Inc 175 E Corporate Pl *TF:* 888-812-3698 ■ *Web:* www.esscous.com	Chandler	AZ	85225	480-497-8000	497-9100
Evans Enterprises Inc 1536 S Western Ave *TF:* 800-423-8267 ■ *Web:* www.goevans.com	Oklahoma City	OK	73109	405-631-1344	631-8948
Facility Solutions Group (FSG) 4401 Westgate Blvd Suite 310 *TF:* 800-854-6465 ■ *Web:* www.fsgconnect.com	Austin	TX	78745	512-440-7985	440-0399
FD Lawrence Electric Co Inc 3450 Beekman St *TF Cust Svc:* 800-582-4490 ■ *Web:* www.fdlawrence.com	Cincinnati	OH	45223	513-542-1100	542-2422
Feldman Bros Electrical Supply Co 26 Maryland Ave *Web:* www.feldmanbros.com	Paterson	NJ	07503	973-742-7329	742-2220
Fiber Instruments Sales Inc 161 Clear Rd *TF Sales:* 800-500-0347 ■ *Web:* www.fiberinstrumentsales.com	Oriskany	NY	13424	315-736-2206	736-2285
Fidelitone Inc 1260 Karl Ct *TF Cust Svc:* 800-342-2112 ■ *Web:* www.fidelitone.com	Wauconda	IL	60084	847-487-3300	487-2681
Fitzpatrick Electric Supply Co 1699 Wierengo Dr *TF:* 800-968-6621 ■ *Web:* www.fitzpatrick.com	Muskegon	MI	49442	231-723-6621	773-5523
Flame Enterprises Inc 21500 Gledhill St *TF:* 800-854-2255 ■ *Web:* www.flamecorp.com	Chatsworth	CA	91311	818-700-2905	700-9168
Foxcom Inc 136 Main St Suite 300b *Web:* www.foxcom.com	Princeton	NJ	08540	609-514-1800	514-1881
Friedman Electric 1321 Wyoming Ave *TF:* 800-545-5517 ■ *Web:* www.friedmanelectric.com	Exeter	PA	18643	570-654-3371	655-6194
Fromm Electric Supply Corp 2101 Centre Ave PO Box 15147 *TF:* 800-360-4441 ■ *Web:* www.frommelectric.com	Reading	PA	19605	610-374-4441	374-8756
FSG Lighting 4401 Westgate Blvd Suite 310 *TF:* 800-854-6465 ■ *Web:* www.fsgi.com	Austin	TX	78745	512-440-7985	440-0399
FTG Inc 725 Marshall Phelps Rd *TF:* 888-610-6020 ■ *Web:* www.farmstead.com	Windsor	CT	06095	860-610-6000	610-6001
Future Electronics 237 Hymus Blvd *TF Cust Svc:* 800-675-1619 ■ *Web:* www.futureelectronics.com	Pointe-Claire	QC	H9R5C7	514-694-7710	695-3707
Galco Industrial Electronics Inc 26010 Pinehurst Dr *TF:* 888-783-4611 ■ *Web:* www.galco.com	Madison Heights	MI	48071	248-542-9090	542-8031
George R Peters Assoc Inc PO Box 850 *TF:* 800-929-5972 ■ *Web:* www.grpeters.com	Troy	MI	48099	248-524-2211	524-1758
Graybar Electric Co Inc 34 N Meramec Ave *TF:* 800-472-9227 ■ *Web:* www.graybar.com	Saint Louis	MO	63105	314-573-9200	573-9216
Gross Electric Inc 2807 N Reynolds Rd *TF:* 800-824-7268 ■ *Web:* www.grosselectric.com	Toledo	OH	43615	419-537-1818	537-6627
Grove-Madsen Industries 390 E 6th St *Web:* www.g-m-i.com	Reno	NV	89512	775-322-3400	322-3495
Hagemeyer North America 12117 Insurance Way **Fax:* Cust Svc ■ *TF:* 800-638-3552 ■ *Web:* www.hagemeyer.com	Hagerstown	MD	21740	301-733-1212	790-2423*
Hammond Electronics Inc 1230 W Central Blvd *TF Sales:* 800-929-3672 ■ *Web:* www.hammondelec.com	Orlando	FL	32805	407-849-6060	872-0826
Hardware Specialty Co Inc 48-75 36th St *Web:* www.hardwarespecialty.com	Long Island City	NY	11101	718-361-9393	706-0238
Hartford Electric Supply Co (HESCO) 30 Inwood Rd Suite 1 *TF:* 800-969-5444 ■ *Web:* www.hesconet.com	Rocky Hill	CT	06067	860-236-6363	236-0233
Heartland Label Printers Inc PO Box 347 *TF:* 800-236-7914 ■ *Web:* www.hbs.net	Little Chute	WI	54140	920-788-7720	788-7739
Heilind Electronics Inc 58 Jonspin Rd *TF:* 800-400-7041 ■ *Web:* www.heilind.com	Wilmington	MA	01887	978-657-4870	658-0278
Hite Co 3101 Beale Ave *Web:* www.hiteco.com	Altoona	PA	16601	814-944-6121	944-3052

Company	City	State	Zip	Phone	Fax
Hitec Group International Inc 8160 S Madison St *TF:* 800-288-8303 ■ *Web:* www.hitec.com	Burr Ridge	IL	60527	630-654-9200	654-9219
HL Dalis Inc 35-35 24th St *TF:* 800-453-2547 ■ *Web:* www.hldalis.com	Long Island City	NY	11106	718-361-1100	392-7654
Houston Wire & Cable Co (HWC) 10201 N Loop E *TF:* 800-468-9473 ■ *Web:* www.houwire.com	Houston	TX	77029	713-609-2230	609-2236
Hutton Communications Inc 2520 Marsh Ln *Web:* www.hol4g.com	Carrollton	TX	75006	972-417-0100	417-0180
IBS Electronics Inc 3506 W Lake Ctr Dr # D *TF:* 800-527-2888 ■ *Web:* www.ibselectronics.com	Santa Ana	CA	92704	714-751-6633	751-8159
ICO RALLY 2575 E Bayshore Rd *TF:* 800-856-9909 ■ *Web:* www.icorally.com	Palo Alto	CA	94303	650-856-9900	856-8378
ICS Telecom Inc Larkin at Exchange Suite 820 **Fax Area Code:* 585 ■ *TF:* 800-836-8677 ■ *Web:* www.icstelecom.com	Buffalo	NY	14210	716-633-8200	427-0863*
IMS Inc 340 Progress Dr *TF:* 800-666-1626 ■ *Web:* www.imswire.com	Manchester	CT	06040	860-649-4415	649-0806
Independent Electric Supply Inc 1370 Bayport Ave *Web:* www.iesupply.com	San Carlos	CA	94070	650-594-9440	594-0484
Industrial Electric Wire & Cable Inc (IEWC) 5001 S Towne Dr *TF:* 800-344-2323 ■ *Web:* www.iewc.com	New Berlin	WI	53151	262-782-2323	957-1600
InfoSonics Corp 4350 Executive Dr Suite 100 *NASDAQ: IFON* ■ *TF:* 800-519-1599 ■ *Web:* www.infosonics.com	San Diego	CA	92121	858-373-1600	373-1503
Insulectro 20362 Windrow Dr *Web:* www.insulectro.com	Lake Forest	CA	92630	949-587-3200	454-0066
Integrated Components Source (ICS) 3977 Camino Ranchero *Web:* www.yourdrive.com	Camarillo	CA	93012	805-822-5100	483-1300
Integrated Electronics Corp 420 E 58th Ave *TF Cust Svc:* 800-876-8686	Denver	CO	80216	303-292-5537	296-1528
Inter-Technical LLC PO Box 535 *Web:* www.inter-technical.com	Elmsford	NY	10523	914-347-2474	347-7230
International Electrical Sales Corp (IESCO) 7540 NW 66th St *Web:* www.iescomia.com	Miami	FL	33166	305-591-8390	591-3294
Interstate Connecting Components Inc 120 Mt Holly By Pass **Fax Area Code:* 856 ■ *TF:* 888-899-1990 ■ *Web:* www.connecticc.com	Lumberton	NJ	08048	888-899-1990	722-9425*
Interstate Electrical Supply Inc 2300 2nd Ave *TF:* 800-903-4409 ■ *Web:* www.interstate-electrical.com	Columbus	GA	31901	706-324-1000	576-5821
Jaco Electronics Inc 145 Oser Ave *PINK: JACO* ■ *TF:* 800-966-5226	Hauppauge	NY	11788	631-273-5500	273-5799
Janesway Electronic Corp 404 N Terr Ave *TF:* 800-431-1348 ■ *Web:* www.janesway.com	Mount Vernon	NY	10552	914-699-6710	699-6969
Jasco Products Inc 10 E Memorial Rd *TF:* 800-654-8483 ■ *Web:* www.jascoproducts.com	Oklahoma City	OK	73114	405-752-0710	752-1537
JH Larson Co 10200 51st Ave N *TF:* 800-292-7970 ■ *Web:* www.jhlarson.com	Plymouth	MN	55442	763-545-1717	545-1144
Justin Electronics Corp 400 Oser Ave Suite 800 *Web:* www.justinelectronics.com	Hauppauge	NY	11788	631-951-4900	951-4747
K & M Electric Supply Inc 7641 Central Industrial Dr *Web:* www.kmelectric.com	Riviera Beach	FL	33404	561-842-4911	842-3834
Kansas City Electrical Supply Co (KCES) 10900 MidAmerica Ave *Web:* www.kcelectricalsupply.com	Lenexa	KS	66219	913-563-7002	563-7052
Keltron Connector Corp Div 2000 Artic Ave *TF:* 800-346-3532 ■ *Web:* www.keltronconnectors.com	Bohemia	NY	11716	631-567-6300	567-6363
Kendall Electric Inc 131 Grand Trunk Ave *TF:* 800-632-5422 ■ *Web:* www.kendallelectric.com	Battle Creek	MI	49015	269-963-5585	963-5606
Kimball Electronics Inc 2233 S 300 E *Web:* www.kimballinc.com	Salt Lake City	UT	84115	801-466-0569	466-8636
King Wire Inc 2500 Commonwealth Ave *TF:* 800-453-5464 ■ *Web:* www.kingwire.com	North Chicago	IL	60064	847-688-1100	688-0244
Kirby Risk Corp 1815 Sagamore Pkwy N **Fax:* Sales ■ *Web:* www.kirbyrisk.com	Lafayette	IN	47904	765-448-4567	448-1342*
Kovalsky-Carr Electric Supply Co Inc 208 St Paul St *Web:* www.kovalskycarr.com	Rochester	NY	14604	585-325-1950	546-6904
Ladd Industries LLC 4849 Hempstead Stn Dr *TF:* 800-223-1236 ■ *Web:* www.laddinc.com	Kettering	OH	45429	937-438-2646	438-9755
Leff H Electric Co Inc 4700 Spring Rd *TF:* 800-686-5333 ■ *Web:* www.leffelectric.com	Cleveland	OH	44131	216-432-3000	432-0051
Lester Sales Co Inc 4312 W Minnesota St PO Box 42407 *TF:* 800-243-7811 ■ *Web:* www.lestersalesco.com	Indianapolis	IN	46242	317-244-7811	248-2369
Lewis Electric Supply Co Inc 1306 2nd St PO Box 2237 *TF:* 800-239-0681 ■ *Web:* www.lesupply.com	Muscle Shoals	AL	35662	256-383-0681	383-0834
Loeb Electric Co 915 Williams Ave *TF:* 800-837-2852 ■ *Web:* www.loebelectric.com	Columbus	OH	43212	614-294-6351	294-7640
Lowe Electric Supply Co 1525 Forsyth St PO Box 4767 *TF:* 800-868-8661 ■ *Web:* www.loweelectric.com	Macon	GA	31208	478-743-8661	742-3374
Loyd's Electric Supply Inc (LES) 838 Stonetree Dr PO Box 1169 *TF:* 800-492-4030 ■ *Web:* www.loydselectric.com	Branson	MO	65615	417-334-2171	334-6635
Madison Electric Co 31855 Van Dyke Ave *Web:* www.madisonelectric.com	Warren	MI	48093	586-825-0200	825-0225
Main Electric Supply Co 6700 S Main St *Web:* www.mainelectricsupply.com	Los Angeles	CA	90003	323-753-5131	753-7750
Maltby Electric Supply Co Inc 336 7th St *TF:* 800-339-0668 ■ *Web:* www.maltbyelec.com	San Francisco	CA	94103	415-863-5000	863-5011
Marcone Supply 1 City Pl Dr Suite 400 *TF:* 877-993-9196 ■ *Web:* www.marcone.com	Saint Louis	MO	63141	877-993-9196	
Mars Electric Co 38868 Mentor Ave *TF:* 800-288-6277 ■ *Web:* www.mars-electric.com	Willoughby	OH	44094	440-946-2250	946-3214
Marsh Electronics Inc 1563 S 101st St *TF Cust Svc:* 800-558-1238 ■ *Web:* www.marshelectronics.com	Milwaukee	WI	53214	414-475-6000	771-2847
Maurice Electrical Supply Co 500 Penn St NE *Web:* www.mauriceelectric.com	Washington	DC	20002	202-675-9400	547-1956
Mayer Electric Supply Co 3405 4th Ave S PO Box 1328 *TF:* 800-444-8524 ■ *Web:* www.mayerelectric.com	Birmingham	AL	35222	205-583-3500	322-2625
McNaughton-McKay Electric Co Inc 1357 E Lincoln Ave *TF:* 888-626-2785 ■ *Web:* www.mc-mc.com	Madison Heights	MI	48071	248-399-7500	399-6828
Mercedes Electric Supply Inc 8550 NW S River Dr *TF:* 800-636-5550 ■ *Web:* www.mercedeselectric.com	Miami	FL	33166	305-887-5550	887-8761
Metro Wire & Cable Co 6636 Metropolitan Pkwy *TF:* 800-633-1432 ■ *Web:* www.metrowire.net	Sterling Heights	MI	48312	586-264-3050	264-7390
Michigan Chandelier Co Inc 20855 Telegraph Rd *Web:* www.michand.com	Southfield	MI	48033	248-353-0510	353-0973
Mid-Coast Electric Supply Inc (MCESI) 1801 Stolz St PO Box 2505 *Web:* www.mcesi.com	Victoria	TX	77902	361-575-6311	575-5515
Mid-Island Electrical Supply 59 Mall Dr *TF:* 877-324-2636 ■ *Web:* www.mid-island.com	Commack	NY	11725	631-864-4242	864-6644
Mid-South Electronics Inc (MSI) 2620 E Meighan Blvd PO Box 322 *TF:* 800-223-5059 ■ *Web:* www.msi-mfg.com	Gadsden	AL	35903	256-494-3265	492-0625
Midtown Electric Supply Corp 157 W 18th St *Web:* www.midtownelectric.com	New York	NY	10011	212-255-3388	255-3177
Minnesota Electric Supply Co 1209 E Hwy 12 *TF:* 800-992-8830	Willmar	MN	56201	320-235-2255	214-4242
Mouser Electronics Corp 1000 N Main St *TF:* 800-346-6873 ■ *Web:* www.mouser.com	Mansfield	TX	76063	817-804-3888	804-3899
Murdock Industrial Supply 1111 E 1st *TF:* 800-362-2422 ■ *Web:* www.mcos.com	Wichita	KS	67202	316-262-4476	263-8100
Music People Inc 154 Woodlawn Rd Suite C *Web:* www.musicpeopleinc.com	Berlin	CT	06037	860-829-9229	828-1353
Nedco Electronics 594 American Way **Fax Area Code:* 800 ■ *TF:* 800-605-2323 ■ *Web:* www.nedcoelectronics.com	Payson	UT	84651	801-465-1790	605-3836*
Nedco Supply Inc 4200 W Spring Mountain Rd *Web:* www.nedco.com	Las Vegas	NV	89102	702-367-0400	362-8365
Nelson Electric Supply Co Inc 926 State St *TF:* 800-806-3576 ■ *Web:* www.nelson-electric.com	Racine	WI	53404	262-635-5050	637-2465
Nep Electronics Inc 805 Mittel Dr *TF:* 800-284-7470 ■ *Web:* www.nepelectronics.com	Wood Dale	IL	60191	630-595-8500	595-8706
Newark In One 4801 N Ravenswood Ave **Fax Area Code:* 888 ■ **Fax:* Sales ■ *TF:* 800-463-9275 ■ *Web:* www.newark.com	Chicago	IL	60640	800-463-9275	551-4801*
NF Smith & Assoc LP 5306 Hollister Rd *TF:* 800-468-7866 ■ *Web:* www.smithweb.com	Houston	TX	77040	713-430-3000	430-3099
Nora Lighting Inc 6505 Gayhart St **Fax Area Code:* 800 ■ *TF:* 800-686-6672 ■ *Web:* www.noralighting.com	Commerce	CA	90040	323-767-2600	500-9955*
Northern Video Systems Inc 3625 Cincinnati Ave *TF:* 800-366-4472 ■ *Web:* www.tri-ed.com	Rocklin	CA	95765	916-543-4000	543-4020
Norvac Electronics Inc 7940 SW Nimbus Ave Suite 8 *Web:* www.norvac.net	Beaverton	OR	97075	503-644-1025	644-9298
Norvell Electronics Inc PO Box 701027 *TF:* 800-477-0021 ■ *Web:* www.norvell.com	Dallas	TX	75370	972-858-3713	490-7245
Nu Horizons Electronics Corp 70 Maxess Rd *TF:* 888-747-6846 ■ *Web:* www.nuhorizons.com	Melville	NY	11747	631-396-5000	396-5050
Nu-Lite Electrical Wholesalers 850 Edwards Ave *TF:* 800-256-1603 ■ *Web:* www.nulite.com	Harahan	LA	70123	504-733-3300	736-1617
Omni Cable Corp 2 Hagerty Blvd *TF:* 800-292-6664 ■ *Web:* www.omnicable.com	West Chester	PA	19382	610-701-0100	701-9870
OneSource Distributors Inc 3951 Oceanic Dr *Web:* www.1sourcedist.com	Oceanside	CA	92056	760-966-4500	966-4599
P D Circuits Inc 10 Starwood Dr *Web:* www.pdcircuits.com	Hampstead	NH	03841	603-329-4551	329-5033
Paige Electric Co LP 1160 Springfield Rd *TF:* 800-327-2443 ■ *Web:* www.paigeelectric.com	Union	NJ	07083	908-687-7810	687-2722
Parrish-Hare Electrical Supply LP 1211 Regal Row PO Box 560547 *Web:* www.parrish-hare.com	Dallas	TX	75356	214-905-1001	951-8101
Path Master Inc 1960 Midway Dr *Web:* www.pathmasterinc.com	Twinsburg	OH	44087	330-425-4994	425-9338
Peerless Electronics Inc 700 Hicksville Rd *TF:* 800-285-2121 ■ *Web:* www.peerlesselectronics.com	Bethpage	NY	11714	516-594-3500	593-2179
PEI-Genesis 2180 Hornig Rd *TF:* 800-675-1214 ■ *Web:* www.pei-genesis.com	Philadelphia	PA	19116	215-673-0400	552-8022
Platt Electric Supply 10605 SW Allen Blvd *TF:* 800-257-5288 ■ *Web:* www.platt.com	Beaverton	OR	97005	503-641-6121	277-7494
Pool & Electrical Products Inc Norcal 1250 E Francis St **Fax Area Code:* 877 ■ *TF:* 800-320-8050 ■ *Web:* www.poolelectrical.com	Ontario	CA	91761	800-320-8050	320-8885*
Powell Electronics Inc 200 Commodore Dr *TF:* 800-235-7880 ■ *Web:* www.powell.com	Swedesboro	NJ	68085	856-241-8000	241-8630
Power & Telephone Supply Co Inc 2673 Yale Ave *TF Cust Svc:* 800-238-7514 ■ *Web:* www.ptsupply.com	Memphis	TN	38112	901-324-6116	320-3082
Priority Wire & Cable Inc 8200 E Roosevelt Rd *TF:* 800-945-5542 ■ *Web:* www.prioritywire.com	North Little Rock	AR	72206	501-372-5444	372-3988
Professional Electric Products Co (PEPCO) 33210 Lakeland Blvd *TF:* 800-872-7000 ■ *Web:* www.pepconet.com	Eastlake	OH	44095	440-946-3790	942-5883
Projections Unlimited Inc 15311 VARRENCA PKWY *TF Cust Svc:* 800-551-4405 ■ *Web:* www.gopui.com	Irvinine	CA	92618	714-544-2700	544-8711

Company	City	State	ZIP	Phone	Fax
QED Inc 1661 W 3rd Ave *TF:* 800-700-5011 ■ *Web:* www.qedelectric.com	Denver	CO	80223	303-825-5011	893-5019
Quality Transmission Component (QTC) 125 Railroad Ave *Web:* www.qtcgears.com	New Hyde Park	NY	11040	516-437-6700	328-3343
Queen City Electrical Supply Co Inc 3rd & Walnut St PO Box 1288 *Web:* www.queencityelec.com	Allentown	PA	18105	610-439-0525	439-8637
Ralph Pill Electrical Supply Co 307 Dorchester Ave *TF:* 800-879-7455	Boston	MA	02127	617-269-8200	269-6392
Rawson & Co Inc PO Box 924288 **Fax:* Sales ■ *TF:* 800-779-1414 ■ *Web:* www.rawson.net	Houston	TX	77292	713-684-1400	684-1409*
Reagan Wireless Corp 3390 SW 15th St *TF:* 877-724-3266 ■ *Web:* www.reaganwireless.com	Deerfield Beach	FL	33442	954-596-2355	596-0070
Red Peacock International Inc 1945 Gardena Ave *Web:* www.redpeacock.com	Glendale	CA	91204	818-265-7722	265-7750
Regency Lighting Co 9261 Jordan Ave *TF:* 800-284-2024 ■ *Web:* www.regencylighting.com	Chatsworth	CA	91311	818-901-0255	901-0118
Renco Electronics Inc 595 International Pl *Web:* www.rencousa.com	Rockledge	FL	32955	321-637-1000	637-1600
Rexel Canada Inc 5600 Keaton Crescent *Web:* www.rexel.ca	Mississauga	ON	L5R3G3	905-712-4004	712-4024
Rexel Inc 14951 Dallas Pkwy PO Box 9085 *Web:* www.rexelusa.com	Dallas	TX	75254	972-387-3600	991-1831
Rexel Ryall Electrical Supplies 11775 E 45th Ave *TF:* 800-759-2728 ■ *Web:* www.rexelusa.com	Denver	CO	80239	303-629-7721	825-7608
Reynolds Co 2861 Merrell Rd *TF:* 800-851-0304 ■ *Web:* www.reynco.com	Dallas	TX	75229	214-630-9000	438-4617
RF Monolithics Inc 4441 Sigma Rd *NASDAQ: RFMI* ■ *TF:* 800-704-6079 ■ *Web:* www.rfm.com	Dallas	TX	75244	972-233-2903	387-8148
Richardson Electronics Ltd 40 W 267 Keslinger Rd PO Box 393 *NASDAQ: RELL* ■ *TF Sales:* 800-348-5580 ■ *Web:* www.rell.com	LaFox	IL	60147	630-208-2200	208-2550
Richmar Electronics Corp 1307 Butterfield Rd Suite 418 *Web:* www.richmarcorp.com	Downers Grove	IL	60515	630-968-0118	968-0197
Rochester Electronics Inc 16 Malcolm Hoyt Dr *Web:* www.rocelec.com	Newburyport	MA	01950	978-462-9332	462-9512
Roden Electrical Supply Co 170 Mabry Hood Rd *TF:* 800-532-8742 ■ *Web:* www.rodenelectric.com	Knoxville	TN	37922	865-546-8755	546-6076
Rohm Electronics USA LLC *ROHM Semiconductor USA LLC* 6815 Flanders Dr Suite 150 *TF:* 800-955-7646 ■ *Web:* www.rohm.com	San Diego	CA	92121	858-625-3600	625-3640
Rondout Electric Inc 33 Arlington Ave	Poughkeepsie	NY	12603	845-471-4810	471-1903
RS Electronics Inc 34443 Schoolcraft Rd *TF:* 800-366-7750 ■ *Web:* www.rselectronics.com	Livonia	MI	48150	734-525-1155	525-1184
Rumsey Electric Co 15 Colwell Ln *TF:* 800-462-2402 ■ *Web:* www.rumsey.com	Conshohocken	PA	19428	610-832-9000	941-8181
S K C Communication Products Inc 8320 Hedge Ln Ter *TF:* 800-882-7779 ■ *Web:* www.skccom.com	Shawnee Mission	KS	66227	913-422-4222	454-4752
Sager Electronics Inc 19 Lorena Dr **Fax Area Code:* 508 ■ *TF:* 800-541-9371 ■ *Web:* www.sager.com	Middleboro	MA	02346	800-541-9371	923-6797*
Sandusky Electric Inc 1513 Sycamore Line PO Box 2353 *TF:* 800-589-5959 ■ *Web:* www.sanduskyelectric.com	Sandusky	OH	44870	419-625-4915	625-9438
Schuster Electronics Inc 11320 Grooms Rd *TF:* 800-877-6875 ■ *Web:* www.schusterusa.com	Cincinnati	OH	45242	513-489-1400	489-8686
Scott Electric 1000 S Main St PO Box S **Fax Area Code:* 800 ■ *TF:* 800-442-8045 ■ *Web:* www.scottelectricusa.com	Greensburg	PA	15601	724-834-4321	426-9598*
Secured Digital Applications Inc 230 Pk Ave 10th Fl *Web:* www.digitalapps.net	New York	NY	10169	212-551-1747	808-3020
SED International Inc 4916 N Royal Atlanta Dr *TF Sales:* 800-444-8962 ■ *Web:* www.sedonline.com	Tucker	GA	30084	770-491-8962	938-2814
Semi Dice Inc PO Box 3002 *Web:* www.semidice.com	Los Alamitos	CA	90720	562-594-4631	430-5942
Sennheiser Electronics Corp 1 Enterprise Dr *TF:* 877-736-6434 ■ *Web:* www.sennheiserusa.com	Old Lyme	CT	06371	860-434-9190	434-1759
Service Electric Supply Inc 15424 Oakwood Dr *Web:* www.servelectric.com	Romulus	MI	48174	734-229-9100	229-9101
Shanor Electric Supply Inc 285 Hinman Ave *Web:* www.shanorelectric.com	Buffalo	NY	14216	716-876-0711	876-7375
Shealy Electrical Wholesalers Inc 422 Fairforest Way *Web:* www.shealyelectrical.com	Greenville	SC	29607	864-242-6880	235-6097
Shearer Equipment 7762 Cleveland Rd *Web:* www.shearerequipment.com	Wooster	OH	44691	330-345-9023	345-9348
Shepherd Electric Supply 7401 Pulaski Hwy *TF Sales:* 800-253-1777 ■ *Web:* www.shepherdelec.com	Baltimore	MD	21237	410-866-6000	866-6001
Singing Machine Co Inc The 6601 Lyons Rd Bldg A-7 *OTC: SMDM* ■ *TF:* 866-670-6888 ■ *Web:* www.singingmachine.com	Coconut Creek	FL	33073	954-596-1000	596-2000
Skywalker Communications Inc 9390 Veterans Memorial Pkwy *TF:* 800-844-9555 ■ *Web:* www.skywalker.com	O'Fallon	MO	63366	636-272-8025	272-8214
Sommer Electric Corp 818 3rd St NE *TF:* 800-766-6373 ■ *Web:* www.sommerelectric.com	Canton	OH	44704	330-455-9454	455-6561
Sonepar USA 510 Walnut St Suite 400 *Web:* www.sonepar-usa.com	Philadelphia	PA	19106	215-399-5900	
Sound Inc 1550 Shore Rd *Web:* www.soundinc.com	Naperville	IL	60563	630-369-2900	
South Dade Electrical Supply 13100 SW 87th Ave *Web:* www.south-dade.com	Miami	FL	33176	305-238-7131	251-5254
Southern Controls Inc 3511 Wetumpka Hwy *TF:* 800-633-8796 ■ *Web:* southerncontrols.vpweb.com	Montgomery	AL	36110	334-277-5030	272-4988
Spectra Integrated Systems Inc 8100 Arrowridge Blvd *TF:* 800-443-7561 ■ *Web:* www.spectra-is.com	Charlotte	NC	28273	704-525-7099	523-8558
Springfield Electric Supply Co 700 N 9th St *TF:* 800-757-2101 ■ *Web:* www.springfieldelectric.com	Springfield	IL	62708	217-788-2100	788-2133
Sprint North Supply Co Inc 600 New Century Pkwy **Fax Area Code:* 800 ■ **Fax:* Sales ■ *TF:* 800-755-3004	New Century	KS	66031	913-791-7000	755-9023*
Standard Electric Co 2650 Trautner Dr PO Box 5289 *TF:* 800-322-0215 ■ *Web:* www.standardelectricco.com	Saginaw	MI	48603	989-497-2100	497-2101
Standard Electric Supply Co 222 N Emmber Ln PO Box 651 *TF:* 800-776-8222 ■ *Web:* www.sescowi.com	Milwaukee	WI	53233	414-272-8100	272-8111
Stanion Wholesale Electric Co 812 S Main St PO Box F *TF:* 800-880-2008 ■ *Web:* www.stanion.com	Pratt	KS	67124	620-672-5678	672-6220
State Electric Supply Co Inc 2010 2nd Ave *TF Cust Svc:* 800-624-3417 ■ *Web:* www.stateelectric.com	Huntington	WV	25703	304-523-7491	525-8917
Steiner Electric Co 1250 Touhy Ave *TF:* 800-783-4637 ■ *Web:* www.stnr.com	Elk Grove Village	IL	60007	847-228-0400	228-1352
Stereo Advantage Co 1955 Wehrle Dr *Web:* www.theadvantage.com	Williamsville	NY	14221	716-204-2340	
Steven Engineering Inc 230 Ryan Way **Fax Area Code:* 888 ■ *TF:* 800-258-9200 ■ *Web:* www.stevenengineering.com	South San Francisco	CA	94080	650-588-9200	258-9200*
Stokes Electric Co Inc 1701 McCalla Ave *TF:* 800-999-0351 ■ *Web:* www.stokeselec.com	Knoxville	TN	37915	865-525-0351	971-4149
Stoneway Electric Supply Co 402 N Perry St *TF:* 800-841-1408 ■ *Web:* www.stoneway.com	Spokane	WA	99202	509-535-2933	534-4512
Storage Battery Systems Inc (SBS) N56 W16665 Ridgewood Dr *TF:* 800-554-2243 ■ *Web:* www.sbsbattery.com	Menomonee Falls	WI	53051	262-703-5800	703-3073
Stuart C Irby Co 815 S State St PO Box 1819 *TF:* 800-844-1811 ■ *Web:* www.irby.com	Jackson	MS	39215	601-969-1811	960-7277
Summit Electric Supply Co 2900 Stanford NE *TF:* 800-824-4400 ■ *Web:* www.summit.com	Albuquerque	NM	87107	505-884-4400	346-1616
Surface Mount Distribution Inc 1 Oldfield Rd *TF:* 800-229-7634 ■ *Web:* www.smdinc.com	Irvine	CA	92618	949-470-7700	470-7777
Swift Electrical Supply Co 100 Hollister Rd Unit 5 *Web:* www.swiftelectrical.com	Teterboro	NJ	07608	201-462-0900	462-1030
Syn-Tech Inc 3100 Ridgelake Dr Suite 101 *TF:* 800-535-7619 ■ *Web:* www.syntech-inc.com	Metairie	LA	70002	504-835-7825	835-7853
Tacoma Electric Supply Inc 1311 S Tacoma Way *TF:* 800-422-0540 ■ *Web:* www.tacomaelectric.com	Tacoma	WA	98409	253-475-0540	475-0707
Taitron Components Inc 28040 W Harrison Pkwy *NASDAQ: TAIT* ■ *TF:* 800-247-2232 ■ *Web:* www.taitroncomponents.com	Valencia	CA	91355	661-257-6060	257-6415
Tele-Communications Inc 5125 W 140th St *TF:* 877-841-8914 ■ *Web:* www.tci-telecom.com	Cleveland	OH	44142	216-267-0800	267-3974
Teleco Inc 430 Woodruff Rd Suite 300 *TF:* 800-800-6159 ■ *Web:* www.teleco.com	Greenville	SC	29607	864-297-4400	297-9983
Telesource Services LLC 1450 Highwood E *TF:* 800-525-4300 ■ *Web:* www.telesourcenet.com	Pontiac	MI	48340	248-335-3000	335-0470
Telmar Technology 6410 Via Real *TF:* 800-761-1206 ■ *Web:* www.telmarnt.com	Carpinteria	CA	93013	805-681-3322	681-3325
Terry-Durin Co 409 7th Ave SE *TF:* 800-332-8114 ■ *Web:* www.terrydurin.com	Cedar Rapids	IA	52401	319-364-4106	364-2562
TESSCO Technologies Inc 11126 McCormick Rd *NASDAQ: TESS* ■ *TF:* 800-472-7373 ■ *Web:* www.tessco.com	Hunt Valley	MD	21031	410-229-1000	527-0005
Thalner Electronics Laboratory Inc 7235 Jackson Rd *TF:* 800-686-7235 ■ *Web:* www.thalner.com	Ann Arbor	MI	48103	734-761-4506	761-9776
Thorpe Electric Supply Co 27 Washington St *Web:* www.thorpeelectric.com	Rensselaer	NY	12144	518-462-5496	462-3891
Total Communications Inc 333 Burnham St *TF:* 800-300-0824 ■ *Web:* www.totalcomm.com	East Hartford	CT	06108	860-282-9999	528-1904
Total Fire & Safety Inc 7909 Carr St *TF:* 800-303-6116 ■ *Web:* www.totalfire.com	Dallas	TX	75227	214-381-6116	381-4633
Trembly Assoc Inc 119 Quincy St Ne *Web:* www.trembly.com	Albuquerque	NM	87108	505-266-8616	255-0635
Tri-Ed Distribution Inc 100 Crossways Pk Dr W *TF:* 888-874-3336 ■ *Web:* www.tri-ed.com	Woodbury	NY	11797	516-941-2800	
Tri-State Armature & Electrical Works Inc 330 GE Patterson PO Box 466 *TF:* 800-238-7654 ■ *Web:* www.tristatearmature.com	Memphis	TN	38126	901-527-8412	521-1065
Tri-State Utility Products Inc 1030 Atlanta Industrial Dr *TF:* 800-282-7985 ■ *Web:* www.tristateutility.com	Marietta	GA	30066	770-427-3119	427-3945
Tronicom Corp 6437 Manchester Ave *Web:* www.techelectronics.com	Saint Louis	MO	63139	314-645-6200	951-1274
TTI Inc 2441 NE Pkwy **Fax:* Hum Res ■ *TF Sales:* 800-845-5119 ■ *Web:* www.ttiinc.com	Fort Worth	TX	76106	817-740-9000	740-1622*
Turtle & Hughes Inc 1900 Lower Rd *Web:* www.turtle.com	Linden	NJ	07036	732-574-3600	574-3723
Unique Communications Inc 3650 Coral Ridge Dr *TF:* 800-881-8182 ■ *Web:* www.uniquecommunications.com	Coral Springs	FL	33065	954-735-4002	735-2612
United Electrical Sales Ltd 4496 36th St *TF:* 800-432-5126 ■ *Web:* www.uesfl.com	Orlando	FL	32811	407-246-1992	246-1588
United Lighting & Supply Co 121 Chestnut Ave SE PO Box 307 *Web:* www.unitedlighting.com	Fort Walton Beach	FL	32548	850-244-8155	244-5629
United Utility Supply Co-op Inc 4515 Bishop Ln *TF:* 800-357-5232 ■ *Web:* www.uus.org	Louisville	KY	40218	502-459-4011	815-6378

Phone / Fax

Upchurch Electrical Supply Co
2355 N Gregg St PO Box 8340 ... Fayetteville AR 72703 479-521-2823 521-6673
Web: www.upchurchelectrical.com

Utility Lines Inc 206 W Walnut St ... Davidson NC 28036 704-896-8866 896-8868
Web: www.utilitylines.com

Valley Electric Supply Corp
1361 N State Rd PO Box 724 ... Vincennes IN 47591 812-882-7860 882-7893
TF: 800-825-7877 ■ *Web:* www.vesupply.com

Van Meter Industrial Inc
850 32nd Ave SW ... Cedar Rapids IA 52404 319-366-5301 366-4709
TF: 800-332-8468 ■ *Web:* www.vanmeterindustrial.com

Venkel Ltd 5900 Shepherd Mountain Cove ... Austin TX 78730 512-794-0081 794-0087
TF: 800-950-8365 ■ *Web:* www.venkel.com

Versa Electronics 3943 Quebec Ave N ... Minneapolis MN 55427 763-557-6737 557-8073
Web: www.versaelectronics.com

Viking Electric Supply Inc
451 Industrial Blvd W ... Minneapolis MN 55413 612-627-1300 627-1313
TF: 800-435-3345 ■ *Web:* www.vikingelectric.com

Virginia West Electric Supply Co (WVES)
250 12-th St W ... Huntington WV 25704 304-525-0361 525-2726
TF: 800-624-3433 ■ *Web:* www.wvesco.com

Voss Lighting 1601 Cushman Dr ... Lincoln NE 68512 402-328-2281 421-2282
TF: 800-828-8677

Vsa Inc 6929 Seward Ave ... Lincoln NE 68507 402-467-3668 467-3780
TF: 800-888-2140 ■ *Web:* www.vsa1.com

Wabash Electric Supply Inc 1400 S Wabash St ... Wabash IN 46992 260-563-4146 563-4140
TF: 800-552-7777 ■ *Web:* www.wabashelectric.com

Walters Wholesale Electric Co
2825 Temple Ave ... Signal Hill CA 90755 562-988-3100 988-3150
Web: www.walterswholesale.com

Warshauer Electric Supply Co
800 Shrewsbury Ave ... Tinton Falls NJ 07724 732-741-6400 741-3866*
**Fax:* Sales ■ *Web:* www.warshauerelectric.com

Weinstock Lamp Co Inc
34-30 Steinway St ... Long Island City NY 11101 718-729-4848 729-4848
Web: www.weinstocklighting.com

Weldylamont Assoc Inc 1008 E NW Hwy ... Mount Prospect IL 60056 847-398-4510 398-0597
Web: www.weldy-lamont.com

Werner Electric Supply Co 2341 Industrial Dr ... Neenah WI 54956 920-729-4500 729-4484
TF: 800-236-5026 ■ *Web:* www.wernerelectric.com

Wes-Garde Components Group Inc
190 Elliott St ... Hartford CT 06114 860-525-6907 527-6047
TF: 800-554-8866 ■ *Web:* www.wesgarde.com

WESCO Distribution Inc
225 W Stn Sq Dr Suite 700 ... Pittsburgh PA 15219 412-454-2200 454-2505
Web: www.wesco.com

West-Lite Supply Co Inc 12951 166th St ... Cerritos CA 90703 562-802-0224 802-0154
TF: 800-660-6678 ■ *Web:* www.west-lite.com

Western Electrical Sales Inc (WES)
521 Glide Ave Unit A ... West Sacramento CA 95691 916-372-1001 372-1172
Web: www.wesisales.com

Western Extralite Co 1470 Liberty St ... Kansas City MO 64102 816-421-8404 421-6211
TF: 800-279-8833 ■ *Web:* www.westernextralite.com

Whitlock Group 12820 W Creekk Pkwy Suite M ... Richmond VA 23238 804-273-9100 273-9380
TF: 800-726-9843 ■ *Web:* www.whitlock.com

Wholesale Electric Supply Co LP
4040 Guls Fwy ... Houston TX 77004 713-748-6100 749-8415
TF: 800-486-8563 ■ *Web:* www.wholesaleelectric.com

Wholesale Electric Supply Inc
1400 Waterall St ... Texarkana TX 75501 903-794-3404 792-2720
TF: 800-869-8672 ■ *Web:* www.netwes.com

Wieland Electric Inc (WEI) 49 International Rd ... Burgaw NC 28425 910-259-5050 259-3691
TF: 800-943-5263 ■ *Web:* www.wielandinc.com

Williams Supply Inc 210 7th St ... Roanoke VA 24016 540-343-9333 342-3254
TF: 800-533-6969 ■ *Web:* www.williams-supply.com

Willow Electrical Supply Inc
3828 River Rd ... Schiller Park IL 60176 847-801-5010 801-5020
Web: www.willowelectric.com

Winncom Technologies Corp
30700 Carter St Suite A ... Solon OH 44139 440-498-9510 498-9511
Web: www.winncom.com

Wiremasters Inc 1788 N Pointe Rd ... Columbia TN 38401 615-791-0281 791-6182
TF: 800-635-5342 ■ *Web:* www.wiremasters.net

Womack Electric Supply Co 518 Newton St ... Danville VA 24541 434-793-5134 792-8256
Web: www.womackelectric.com

World Electric Supply Orlando Inc
4501 SW 34th St ... Orlando FL 32811 407-447-2000 447-2008
Web: www.worldelectricsupply.com

WW Grainger Inc 100 Grainger Pkwy ... Lake Forest IL 60045 847-535-1000
NYSE: GWW ■ *TF:* 888-361-8649 ■ *Web:* www.grainger.com

XP Power 990 Benicia Ave ... Sunnyvale CA 94085 408-732-7777 522-8227
TF: 800-276-9378 ■ *Web:* www.xppower.com

Zack Electronics Inc 1070 Hamilton Rd ... Duarte CA 91010 626-303-0655 303-8694
TF: 800-466-0449 ■ *Web:* www.zackelectronics.com

250 ELECTRICAL EQUIPMENT FOR INTERNAL COMBUSTION ENGINES

SEE ALSO Automotive Parts & Supplies - Mfr p. 1497; Motors (Electric) & Generators p. 2263

Phone / Fax

Altronic Inc 712 Trumbull Ave ... Girard OH 44420 330-545-9768 545-9005
Web: www.altronicinc.com

American Electronic Components
1101 Lafayette St ... Elkhart IN 46516 574-295-6330 293-8013
TF: 888-847-6552 ■ *Web:* www.aecsensors.com

Andover Inc PO Box 4848 ... Lafayette IN 47903 765-447-1157 447-1150
Web: www.andovercoils.com

Autotronic Controls Corp
1490 Henry Brennan Dr ... El Paso TX 79936 915-857-5200 857-3344
Web: www.msdignition.com

CE Niehoff & Co 2021 Lee St ... Evanston IL 60202 847-866-6030 492-1242
TF Tech Supp: 800-643-4633 ■ *Web:* www.ceniehoff.com

CPX Inc 410 Kent St ... Kentland IN 47951 812-718-5335 569-0909*
**Fax Area Code:* 317 ■ *Web:* www.cpxinc.com

Edge Products 1080 S Depot Dr ... Ogden UT 84404 801-476-3343 476-3348
TF: 888-360-3343 ■ *Web:* www.edgeproducts.com

Electricfil Corp 11880 Belden Ct ... Livonia MI 48150 734-425-2774 425-3669

EMB Corp 1203 Hawkins Dr ... Elizabethtown KY 42701 270-737-1996 737-1909
Web: www.embcorp.com

ETCO Inc Automotive Products Div
3004 62nd Ave E ... Bradenton FL 34203 941-756-8426 758-7195
Web: www.etco.com

Fargo Assembly of Pennsylvania Inc
800 W Washington St PO Box 550 ... Norristown PA 19404 610-272-6850 272-6858
Web: www.fargopa.com

Fisher Electric Technology
2801 72nd St N ... Saint Petersburg FL 33710 727-345-9122 345-2904
TF: 800-789-2347 ■ *Web:* www.fisherelectric.com

Flight Systems Inc 505 Fishing Creek Rd ... Lewisberry PA 17339 717-932-7000 932-9925
TF: 800-403-3728 ■ *Web:* www.flightsystems.com

Goodall Mfg Co 7558 Washington Ave S ... Eden Prairie MN 55344 952-941-6666 941-2617
TF: 800-328-7730 ■ *Web:* www.goodallmfg.com

Hitachi Automotive Systems Americas Inc
955 Warwick Rd ... Harrodsburg KY 40330 859-734-9451 734-5309
Web: www.hap.com

Hood Cable Co 8 Industrial Rd PO Box 1253 ... Prentiss MS 39474 601-792-0375 792-4309

Ignition Systems & Controls LP 6300 W Hwy 80 ... Midland TX 79706 432-697-6472 697-0563
Web: www.ignition-systems.com

Interconnect Wiring Harnesses Inc
5024 W Vickery Blvd ... Fort Worth TX 76107 817-377-9473 732-8667
Web: www.interconnect-wiring.com

Interstate Industries Inc PO Box 1285 ... Kosciusko MS 39090 662-289-3877 289-7439

Kelly Aerospace 1404 E S Blvd ... Montgomery AL 36116 334-286-8551 227-8596
Web: www.kellyaerospace.com

KEM Mfg Co 18-35 River Rd ... Fair Lawn NJ 07410 201-796-8000 796-3277
TF: 800-289-5362

Kongsberg Automotive 90 28th St ... Grand-Mere QC G9T5Z8 819-533-3201 533-3901
Web: www.kongsbergautomotive.com

KRA International LLC 1810 Clover Rd ... Mishawaka IN 46545 574-259-3550 255-1079
Web: www.krainternational.com

M & G Electronics Corp
889 Seahawk Cir ... Virginia Beach VA 23452 757-468-6000 468-5442
Web: www.mgelectronic.com

Mitsubishi Electric Automotive America Inc
4773 Bethany Rd ... Mason OH 45040 513-398-2220 398-1121
Web: www.meaa-mea.com

Motorcar Parts & Accessories
2929 California St ... Torrance CA 90503 310-212-7910 212-7581
Web: www.motorcarparts.com

N/C Electronics Inc
42820 Port Orford Loop Rd ... Port Orford OR 97465 541-332-7004

NGK Spark Plugs Inc 46929 Magellan ... Wixom MI 48393 248-926-6900 926-6910
TF: 877-473-6767 ■ *Web:* www.ngksparkplugs.com

Precision Parts & Remanufacturing Co
4411 SW 19th St ... Oklahoma City OK 73108 405-681-2592 681-2596
TF: 800-654-3846 ■ *Web:* www.pprok.com

Prestolite Wire Corp
200 Galleria Officentre Suite 212 ... Southfield MI 48034 248-355-4422 386-4462
TF: 800-498-3132 ■ *Web:* www.prestolitewire.com

Prettl Electric Corp 1721 White Horse Rd ... Greenville SC 29605 864-220-1010 220-1020
Web: www.prettl.com

RE Phelon Co Inc 2063 University Pkwy ... Aiken SC 29801 803-649-1381 648-7309
Web: www.phelon.com

Remy International Inc 600 Corp Dr ... Pendleton IN 46064 765-778-6499
TF: 800-372-3555 ■ *Web:* www.remyinc.com

Standard Motor Products Inc
37-18 Northern Blvd ... Long Island City NY 11101 718-392-0200 729-4549
NYSE: SMP ■ *Web:* www.smpcorp.com

Syncro Corp PO Box 890 ... Arab AL 35016 256-931-7800 931-7920
Web: www.syncrocorp.com

Transpo Electronics Inc 2150 Brengle Ave ... Orlando FL 32808 407-298-4563 298-4519
TF: 800-327-7792 ■ *Web:* www.transpo-usa.com

Unison Industries Inc
7575 Baymeadows Way ... Jacksonville FL 32256 904-739-4000 739-4006
Web: www.unisonindustries.com

Unit Parts Co Inc PO Box 6068 ... Edmond OK 73083 405-677-3361 672-9979

Van Bergen & Greener Inc 1818 Madison St ... Maywood IL 60153 708-343-4700 343-9425
TF: 800-621-3889 ■ *Web:* www.starterdrives.com

251 ELECTRICAL SIGNALS MEASURING & TESTING INSTRUMENTS

Phone / Fax

3M Telecommunications Div 6801 River Pl Blvd ... Austin TX 78726 651-733-1110 733-9973
Web: www.3m.com/market/telecom/index.jhtml

Advanced Measurement Technology
801 S Illinois Ave ... Oak Ridge TN 37831 865-482-4411 483-0396
TF: 800-251-9750 ■ *Web:* www.ametek-online.com

Advantest America Inc (ATE) 3201 Scott Blvd ... Santa Clara CA 95054 408-988-7700 987-0680
NYSE: ATE ■ *Web:* www.advantest.com/aai.htm

Aeroflex 400 New Century Pkwy ... New Century KS 66031 913-764-2452 782-5104*
**Fax:* Cust Svc ■ *TF:* 800-316-4981 ■ *Web:* www.aeroflex.com

Aetrium Inc 2350 Helen St ... North Saint Paul MN 55109 651-770-2000 770-7975
NASDAQ: ATRM ■ *TF:* 800-274-3500 ■ *Web:* www.aetrium.com

Agilent Technologies Inc
5301 Stevens Creek Blvd ... Santa Clara CA 95051 877-424-4536 345-8474*
NYSE: A ■ **Fax Area Code:* 408 ■ *TF:* 877-424-4536 ■ *Web:* www.home.agilent.com

Allied Motion Technologies Inc
23 Inverness Way E Suite 150 ... Englewood CO 80112 303-799-8520 799-8521
NASDAQ: AMOT ■ *TF:* 888-392-5543 ■ *Web:* www.alliedmotion.com

Company	City	State	ZIP	Phone	Fax
Analog Devices Inc 3 Technology Way *NYSE: ADI* ■ *TF:* 800-262-5643 ■ *Web:* www.analog.com	Norwood	MA	02062	781-329-4700	461-3113
Anritsu Co 490 Jarvis Dr *TF:* 800-267-4878 ■ *Web:* www.anritsu.com	Morgan Hill	CA	95037	408-778-2000	776-1744
Associated Equipment Corp 5043 Farlan Ave *TF:* 800-949-1472 ■ *Web:* www.associatedequip.com	Saint Louis	MO	63115	314-385-5178	385-3254
Avtron Mfg Inc 7900 E Pleasant Valley Rd *TF:* 800-922-9751 ■ *Web:* www.avtron.com	Independence	OH	44131	216-573-7600	642-6037
B & K Corp 5675 Dixie Hwy *TF:* 800-977-3775	Saginaw	MI	48601	989-777-2111	777-5620
Beede Electrical Instrument Co 88 Village St *Web:* www.beede.com	Penacook	NH	03303	603-753-6362	753-6201
BEI Technologies Inc Precision Systems & Space Div 1100 Murphy Dr *Web:* www.beissd.com	Maumelle	AR	72113	501-851-4000	851-5476
BI Technologies Corp 4200 Bonita Pl *Web:* www.bitechnologies.com	Fullerton	CA	92835	714-447-2300	447-2745
Bird Electronic Corp 30303 Aurora Rd *TF:* 866-695-4569 ■ *Web:* www.bird-technologies.com	Solon	OH	44139	440-248-1200	248-5426
Bird Technologies Group Inc 30303 Aurora Rd *TF:* 866-695-4569 ■ *Web:* www.bird-technologies.com	Solon	OH	44139	440-519-2050	248-3790
Bruel & Kjaer Instruments Inc 2815 Colonnades Ct # A *TF:* 800-241-9188 ■ *Web:* www.bkhome.com	Norcross	GA	30071	770-209-6907	448-3246
Cascade Microtech Inc 2430 NW 206th Ave *NASDAQ: CSCD* ■ *TF:* 800-854-8400 ■ *Web:* www.cmicro.com	Beaverton	OR	97006	503-601-1000	601-1010
Chatsworth Data Corp 9735 Lurline Ave **Fax Area Code:* 877 ■ *TF:* 877-380-6855 ■ *Web:* www.chatsworthdata.com	Chatsworth	CA	91311	818-350-5072	380-6855*
Cohu Inc 12367 Crosthwaite Cir *NASDAQ: COHU* ■ *Web:* www.cohu.com	Poway	CA	92064	858-848-8100	848-8185
Communications Mfg Co 2239 Colby Ave *TF:* 800-462-5532 ■ *Web:* www.gotocmc.com	Los Angeles	CA	90064	310-828-3200	481-0965
Curtis Instruments Inc 200 Kisco Ave *Web:* www.curtisinstruments.com	Mount Kisco	NY	10549	914-666-2971	666-2971
CXR Larus Corp 894 Faulstich Ct *TF:* 800-999-9946 ■ *Web:* www.cxrlarus.com	San Jose	CA	95112	408-573-2700	573-2708
CyberOptics Corp 5900 Golden Hills Dr *NASDAQ: CYBE* ■ *TF Cust Svc:* 800-746-6315 ■ *Web:* www.cyberoptics.com	Golden Valley	MN	55416	763-542-5000	542-5100
Delta Design Inc 12367 Crosthwaite Cir **Fax:* Sales ■ *TF:* 800-776-0697 ■ *Web:* www.deltad.com	Poway	CA	92064	858-848-8000	848-8180*
Desco Industries Inc 3651 Walnut Ave *Web:* www.desco.com	Chino	CA	91710	909-627-8178	627-7449
DIT-MCO International Corp 5612 Brighton Terr *TF:* 800-821-2168 ■ *Web:* www.ditmco.com	Kansas City	MO	64130	816-444-9700	444-6843
Doble Engineering Co Inc 85 Walnut St *Web:* www.doble.com	Watertown	MA	02472	617-926-4900	926-0528
Dranetz-BMI 1000 New Durham Rd *TF:* 800-372-6832 ■ *Web:* www.dranetz.com	Edison	NJ	08818	732-287-3680	287-3680
DRS Test & Energy Management Inc 110 Wynn Dr *Web:* www.drs-tem.com	Huntsville	AL	35805	256-895-2000	895-2064
EADS North American Defense Test & Services Inc 4 Goodyear **Fax:* Sales ■ *TF Cust Svc:* 800-722-2528 ■ *Web:* www.eads-nadefense.com	Irvine	CA	92618	949-859-8999	859-7139*
EDAC Technologies Corp 1806 New Britain Ave *Web:* www.edactechnologies.com	Farmington	CT	06032	860-678-8140	674-2718
Electro-Metrics Corp 231 Enterprise Rd *Web:* www.electro-metrics.com	Johnstown	NY	12095	518-762-2600	762-2812
Everett Charles Technologies (ECT) 700 E Harrison Ave *Web:* www.ectinfo.com	Pomona	CA	91767	909-625-5551	624-9746
Everett Charles Technologies Inc Test Equipment Div 700 E Harrison Ave *Web:* www.ectinfo.com	Pomona	CA	91767	909-625-5551	624-9746
EXFO Electro-Optical Engineering Inc 400 Godin Ave *NASDAQ: EXFO* ■ *TF:* 800-663-3936 ■ *Web:* www.exfo.com	Vanier	QC	G1M2K2	418-683-0211	683-2170
Fluke Biomedical 6920 Seaway Blvd *TF:* 800-443-5853 ■ *Web:* www.flukebiomedical.com	Everett	WA	98203	425-446-6945	446-5716
Fluke Corp 6920 Seaway Blvd *TF:* 800-753-5853 ■ *Web:* www.fluke.com	Everett	WA	98203	425-446-6100	446-5116
Fluke Networks Inc 6920 Seaway Blvd *TF:* 800-283-5853 ■ *Web:* www.flukenetworks.com	Everett	WA	98203	425-446-4519	446-5043
Frequency Electronics Inc 55 Charles Lindbergh Blvd *NASDAQ: FEIM* ■ *Web:* www.freqelec.com	Mitchel Field	NY	11553	516-794-4500	794-4340
Giga-Tronics Inc 4650 Norris Canyon Rd *NASDAQ: GIGA* ■ *TF:* 800-726-4442 ■ *Web:* www.gigatronics.com	San Ramon	CA	94583	925-328-4650	328-4700
Gleason M & M Precision Systems Corp 300 Progress Rd *Web:* www.gleason.com	Dayton	OH	45449	937-859-8273	859-4452
Gold Line Connector Inc PO Box 500 *Web:* www.gold-line.com	West Redding	CT	06896	203-938-2588	938-8740
Hickok Inc 10514 Dupont Ave *TF:* 800-342-5080 ■ *Web:* www.hickok-inc.com	Cleveland	OH	44108	216-541-8060	761-9879
Hipotronics Inc 1650 Rt 22 PO Box 414 *TF:* 800-727-4476 ■ *Web:* www.hipotronics.com	Brewster	NY	10509	845-279-8091	279-2467
Hughes Corp Weschler Instruments Div 16900 Foltz Pkwy *TF:* 800-557-0064 ■ *Web:* www.weschler.com	Cleveland	OH	44149	440-238-2550	238-0660
ILX Lightwave Corp 31950 E Frontage Rd *TF:* 800-459-9459 ■ *Web:* www.ilxlightwave.com	Bozeman	MT	59715	406-586-1244	586-9405
IMPulse NC Inc 100 IMPulse Way *Web:* www.impulsenc.com	Mount Olive	NC	28365	919-658-2200	658-2268
ISEC Inc 33 Inverness Dr E *Web:* www.iseinc.com	Englewood	CO	80112	303-790-1444	799-8652
Itron Inc 2111 N Molter Rd *NASDAQ: ITRI* ■ *TF:* 800-635-5461 ■ *Web:* www.itron.com	Liberty Lake	WA	99019	509-924-9900	891-3355

Company	City	State	ZIP	Phone	Fax
Ixia 26601 W Agoura Rd *NASDAQ: XXIA* ■ *TF:* 877-367-4942 ■ *Web:* www.ixiacom.com	Calabasas	CA	91302	818-871-1800	871-1805
JDS Uniphase Corp 430 N McCarthy Blvd *NASDAQ: JDSU* ■ *TF:* 800-543-1550 ■ *Web:* www.jdsu.com	Milpitas	CA	95035	408-546-5000	546-4300
Keithley Instruments Inc 28775 Aurora Rd *NYSE: KEI* ■ *TF:* 800-552-1115 ■ *Web:* www.keithley.com	Cleveland	OH	44139	440-248-0400	498-2664
KLA-Tencor Corp One Technology Dr *NASDAQ: KLAC* ■ *TF:* 800-600-2829 ■ *Web:* www.kla-tencor.com	Milpitas	CA	95035	408-875-3000	875-4144
Knopp Inc 1307 66th St *TF:* 800-227-1848 ■ *Web:* www.knoppinc.com	Emeryville	CA	94608	510-653-1661	653-2202
L-3 Electrodynamics Inc 1200 Hicks Rd *Web:* www.l-3com.com/edi	Rolling Meadows	IL	60008	847-660-1750	660-1751
Landis gyr Inc 2800 Duncan Rd *TF:* 888-390-5733 ■ *Web:* www.landisgyr.com	Lafayette	IN	47904	765-742-1001	742-0936
LeCroy Corp 700 Chestnut Ridge Rd *NASDAQ: LCRY* ■ *TF:* 800-553-2769 ■ *Web:* www.lecroy.com	Chestnut Ridge	NY	10977	845-425-2000	425-8967
LTS Corp 7250 Woodmont Ave Suite 340 *Web:* www.ltscorporation.com	Bethesda	MD	20814	301-652-2121	951-9624
LTX-Credence Corp 1355 California Cir *NASDAQ: LTXC* ■ *Web:* www.ltx.com	Milpitas	CA	95035	408-635-4300	635-4985
Megger 4271 Bronze Way *TF:* 800-723-2861 ■ *Web:* www.megger.com	Dallas	TX	75237	214-333-3201	331-7399
Micro Control Co 7956 Main St Ne *TF:* 800-328-9923 ■ *Web:* www.microcontrol.com	Minneapolis	MN	55432	763-786-8750	786-6543
Micromanipulator Co Inc 1555 Forrest Way *TF Cust Svc:* 800-654-5659 ■ *Web:* www.micromanipulator.com	Carson City	NV	89706	775-882-7377	882-7694
Monroe Electronics Inc 100 Housel Ave *TF:* 800-821-6001 ■ *Web:* www.monroe-electronics.com	Lyndonville	NY	14098	585-765-2254	765-9330
Nartron Corp 5000 N US 131 *Web:* www.nartron.com	Reed City	MI	49677	231-832-5513	832-3876
National Instruments Corp 11500 N Mopac Expy *NASDAQ: NATI* ■ *TF Cust Svc:* 800-433-3488 ■ *Web:* www.ni.com	Austin	TX	78759	512-794-0100	683-8411
Newport Electronics Inc 2229 S Yale St *TF Cust Svc:* 800-639-7678 ■ *Web:* www.newportinc.com	Santa Ana	CA	92704	714-540-4914	546-3022
NH Research Inc 16601 Hale Ave *Web:* www.nhresearch.com	Irvine	CA	92606	949-474-3900	474-7062
PerkinElmer Inc 45 William St *NYSE: PKI* ■ *Web:* www.perkinelmer.com	Wellesley	MA	02481	781-237-5100	237-9386
Phase Matrix Inc 109 Bonaventura Dr *TF:* 877-447-2736 ■ *Web:* www.phasematrix.com	San Jose	CA	95134	408-428-1000	428-1500
Phenix Technologies Inc 75 Speicher Dr *Web:* www.phenixtech.com	Accident	MD	21520	301-746-8118	895-5570
Precision Flow Technologies Inc PO Box 149 *Web:* www.precisionflowtechnologies.com	Saugerties	NY	12477	845-247-0810	247-8764
Prime Technology LLC 344-352 Twin Lakes Rd PO Box 185 *Web:* www.primetechnology.com	North Branford	CT	06471	203-481-5721	481-8937
Prominent Fluid Controls Inc 136 Industry Dr *Web:* www.prominent.us	Pittsburgh	PA	15275	412-787-2484	787-0704
Radiodetection Corp 154 Portland Rd *TF:* 877-247-3797 ■ *Web:* www.radiodetection.com	Bridgton	ME	04009	207-647-9495	647-9496
Reliability Inc 15720 Pk Row *Web:* www.relinc.com	Houston	TX	77084	281-492-0550	492-0615
Rodale Electronics Inc 20 Oser Ave *Web:* www.rodaleelectronics.com	Hauppauge	NY	11788	631-231-0044	231-1345
Schlumberger Ltd 5599 San Felipe Suite 100 *NYSE: SLB* ■ *Web:* www.slb.com	Houston	TX	77056	713-513-2000	513-2006
Schweitzer E O Mfg Co Inc 450 Enterprise Pkwy *TF:* 888-870-7350 ■ *Web:* www.eosmfg.com	Lake Zurich	IL	60047	847-362-8304	362-8396
Sencore Inc 3200 W Sencore Dr *TF:* 800-736-2673 ■ *Web:* www.sencore.com	Sioux Falls	SD	57107	605-339-0100	335-6379
Simpson Electric Co 520 Simpson Ave *Web:* www.simpsonelectric.com	Lac Du Flambeau	WI	54538	715-588-3311	588-1248
Snap-on Diagnostics 420 Barclay Blvd *TF:* 800-424-7226 ■ *Web:* www1.snapon.com	Lincolnshire	IL	60069	847-478-0700	478-7311
TEGAM Inc 10 Tegam Way *TF:* 800-666-1010 ■ *Web:* www.tegam.com	Geneva	OH	44041	440-466-6100	466-6110
Tektronix Inc 14150 SW Karl Braun Dr PO Box 500 *NYSE: TEK* ■ **Fax:* Sales ■ *TF:* 800-833-9200 ■ *Web:* www.tek.com	Beaverton	OR	97077	503-627-7111	627-3247*
Tempo Research Corp 1390 Aspen Way *TF:* 800-642-2155 ■ *Web:* www.tempo.textron.com	Vista	CA	92083	760-598-8900	598-5634
Teradyne Inc 600 Riverpark Dr *NYSE: TER* ■ *Web:* www.teradyne.com	North Reading	MA	01864	978-370-2700	
Teradyne Inc Assembly Test Div 600 Riverpark Dr	North Reading	MA	01864	978-370-2700	
Teradyne Inc Industrial/Consumer Div 600 Riverpark Dr	North Reading	MA	01864	978-370-2700	
Teradyne Inc Semiconductor Test Div 30701 Agoura Rd **Fax:* Hum Res ■ *Web:* www.teradyne.com/prods/prodserv.html	Agoura Hills	CA	91301	818-991-2900	735-5611*
Test Electronics 821 Smith Rd *Web:* www.testelectronics.com	Watsonville	CA	95076	831-763-2000	763-2085
Trek Inc 11601 Maple Ridge Rd **Fax:* Sales ■ *TF:* 800-367-8735 ■ *Web:* www.trekinc.com	Medina	NY	14103	585-798-3140	798-3106*
Trilithic Inc 9710 Pk Davis Dr *TF:* 800-344-2412 ■ *Web:* www.trilithic.com	Indianapolis	IN	46235	317-895-3600	423-7604
Trio-Tech International 14731 Califa St *AMEX: TRT* ■ *Web:* www.triotech.com	Van Nuys	CA	91411	818-787-7000	787-9130
Tyco Electronics Corp Corcom Div 62 S Butterfield Rd *Web:* www.corcom.com	Mundelein	IL	60060	847-680-7400	680-8169
Wems Electronics Inc 4650 W Rosecrans Ave *Web:* www.wems.com	Hawthorne	CA	90250	310-644-0251	644-5334
Wenzel Assoc Inc PO Box 80289 *Web:* www.wenzel.com	Austin	TX	78708	512-835-2038	719-4086
Wireless Telecom Group Inc 25 Eastmans Rd *AMEX: WTT* ■ *Web:* www.wirelesstelecomgroup.com	Parsippany	NJ	07054	973-386-9696	386-9191
Yokogawa Corp of America 12530 W Airport Blvd *TF:* 800-888-6400 ■ *Web:* www.yokogawa.com/us	Sugar Land	TX	30265	281-340-3800	340-3838
Zetec Inc 8226 Bracken Pl SE Suite 100 *TF:* 800-643-1771 ■ *Web:* www.zetec.com	Snoqualmie	WA	98065	425-974-2739	974-2621

252 ELECTRICAL SUPPLIES - PORCELAIN

Company	City	State	Zip	Phone	Fax
American Technical Ceramics Corp 1 Norden Ln *Web:* www.atceramics.com	Huntington Station	NY	11746	631-622-4700	622-4748
Associated Ceramics & Technology Inc 400 N Pike Rd *Web:* www.associatedceramics.com	Sarver	PA	16055	724-353-1585	353-1050
Ceradyne Inc 3169 Redhill Ave *NASDAQ: CRDN* ■ **Fax:* Sales ■ *TF:* 800-839-2189 ■ *Web:* www.ceradyne.com	Costa Mesa	CA	92626	714-549-0421	549-5787*
CeramTec North America 1 Technology Pl *TF:* 800-845-9761 ■ *Web:* www.ceramtec.com	Laurens	SC	29360	864-682-3215	682-1121
CeramTec North America Corp 1 Technology Pl *TF:* 800-845-9761 ■ *Web:* www.ceramtec.com	Laurens	SC	29360	864-682-3215	682-1140
CoorsTek Inc 600 9th St *TF:* 800-821-6110 ■ *Web:* www.coorstek.com	Golden	CO	80401	303-278-4000	277-4574
Cps Technologies Corp 111 S Worcester St *OTC: CPSH* ■ *Web:* www.alsic.com	Norton	MA	02766	508-222-0614	222-0220
Custom Technical Ceramics Inc 8041 N I-70 Unit 6 *Web:* www.customtechceramics.com	Arvada	CO	80002	303-431-7798	431-6168
Du-Co Ceramics Co Inc 155 S Rebecca St PO Box 568 *Web:* www.ceramics.com	Saxonburg	PA	16056	724-352-1511	352-1266
Electrical Distributors Co 1135 Auzerais Ave *Web:* www.electdist.com	San Jose	CA	95126	408-293-5818	287-1152
Evergreen Oak Electric Supply and Sales Co 13400 S Cicero Ave PO Box 549 *TF:* 888-273-7848 ■ *Web:* www.evergreenoak.com	Crestwood	IL	60445	708-597-4220	597-1827
Fair-Rite Products Corp 1 Commerical Row PO Box J *TF:* 888-324-7748 ■ *Web:* www.fair-rite.com	Wallkill	NY	12589	845-895-2055	895-2629
Ferronics Inc 45 O'Connor Rd *Web:* www.ferronics.com	Fairport	NY	14450	585-388-1020	388-0036
International Ceramic Engineering 235 Brooks St *TF:* 800-779-3321 ■ *Web:* www.intlceramics.com	Worcester	MA	01606	508-853-4700	852-4101
Kyocera Industrial Ceramics Corp 5713 E Fourth Plain Rd *TF:* 800-826-0527 ■ *Web:* www.americas.kyocera.com/KICC	Vancouver	WA	98661	360-696-8950	696-9804
Lapp Insulator Co 130 Gilbert St **Fax:* Cust Svc ■ *Web:* www.lappinsulator.com	Le Roy	NY	14482	585-768-6221	768-6219*
LTD Ceramics Inc 7411 Central Ave *Web:* www.ltdceramics.com	Newark	CA	94560	510-789-2222	789-2231
Maryland Ceramic & Steatite Co Inc PO Box 527 *Web:* www.marylandceramic.com	Bel Air	MD	21014	410-838-4114	457-4333
Medler Eelectric Co Inc 2155 Redman Dr **Fax Area Code:* 989 ■ *TF:* 800-229-5740 ■ *Web:* www.medlerelectric.com	Alma	MI	48801	800-229-5740	463-4522*
Morgan Advanced Ceramics Inc Alberox Div 225 Theodore Rice Blvd *Web:* www.alberox.com	New Bedford	MA	02745	508-995-1725	995-6954
Power & Composite Technologies LLC (PCT) 200 Wallins Corners Rd *Web:* www.pactinc.com	Amsterdam	NY	12010	518-843-6825	843-6723
Precision Engineered Ceramics 812 Tradesman Pk Loop PO Box 938	Hutto	TX	78634	512-759-2994	846-2903
Revere Electric Supply Co 2501 W Washington Blvd *Web:* www.revereelectric.com	Chicago	IL	60612	312-738-3636	738-2725
Saint-Gobain Advanced Ceramics Latrobe 4702 Rt 982 *TF:* 800-438-7237 ■ *Web:* www.wrt.saint-gobain.com	Latrobe	PA	15650	724-539-6000	539-6070
Saxonburg Ceramics Inc 100 N Isabella St PO Box 688 *TF:* 800-245-1270 ■ *Web:* www.saxonburgceramics.com	Saxonburg	PA	16056	724-352-1561	352-3580
Sunbelt Transfomer Ltd 1922 S Martin Luther King Jr Dr *TF:* 800-433-3128 ■ *Web:* www.sunbeltusa.com	Temple	TX	76504	254-771-3777	771-5719
Superior Technical Ceramics Corp 600 Industrial Pk Rd *Web:* www.ceramics.net	Saint Albans	VT	05478	802-527-7726	527-1181
Trans-Tech Inc 5520 Adamstown Rd *Web:* www.trans-techinc.com	Adamstown	MD	21710	301-695-9400	695-7065
Victor Insulators Inc 280 Maple Ave *Web:* www.victorinsulators.com	Victor	NY	14564	585-924-2127	924-7906
Wesgo Ceramics 2425 Whipple Rd *Web:* www.wesgo.com	Hayward	CA	94544	510-491-1100	491-1175

253 ELECTROMEDICAL & ELECTROTHERAPEUTIC EQUIPMENT

SEE ALSO Medical Instruments & Apparatus - Mfr p. 2227

Company	City	State	Zip	Phone	Fax
ABIOMED Inc 22 Cherry Hill Dr *NASDAQ: ABMD* ■ *TF:* 800-422-8666 ■ *Web:* www.abiomed.com	Danvers	MA	01923	978-777-5410	777-8411
Affymetrix Inc 3420 Central Expy *NASDAQ: AFFX* ■ *TF:* 888-362-2447 ■ *Web:* www.affymetrix.com	Santa Clara	CA	95051	408-731-5000	731-5380
Alere Medical Inc 595 Double Eagle Ct Suite 1000 *Web:* www.alere.com	Reno	NV	89521	775-829-8885	829-8637
Angeion Corp 350 Oak Grove Pkwy *NASDAQ: ANGN* ■ *Web:* www.angeion.com	Saint Paul	MN	55127	651-484-4874	379-8227
Arrhythmia Research Technology Inc 25 Sawyer Passway *AMEX: HRT* ■ *Web:* www.arthrt.com	Fitchburg	MA	01420	978-345-0181	342-0168
ArthroCare Corp 7500 Rialto Blvd Bldg Two Suite 100 *NASDAQ: ARTC* ■ *TF:* 800-348-8929 ■ *Web:* www.arthrocare.com	Austin	TX	78735	512-391-3900	391-3901
Astro-Med Inc 600 E Greenwich Ave *NASDAQ: ALOT* ■ *TF:* 877-757-7978 ■ *Web:* www.astro-medinc.com	West Warwick	RI	02893	401-828-4000	822-2430
Beacon Medaes 1800 Overview Dr *Web:* www.beaconmedaes.com	Rock Hill	SC	29730	803-817-5600	817-5750
Bovie Medical Corp 734 Walt Whitman Rd Suite 207 *AMEX: BVX* ■ *TF:* 800-888-4999 ■ *Web:* www.boviemedical.com	Melville	NY	11747	631-421-5452	421-5821
BSD Medical Corp (BSDM) 2188 W 2200 S *NASDAQ: BSDM* ■ *Web:* www.bsdmc.com	Salt Lake City	UT	84119	801-972-5555	972-5930
Cardiac Science Corp 3303 Monte Villa Pkwy **Fax:* Cust Svc ■ *TF Cust Svc:* 800-426-0337 ■ *Web:* www.cardiacscience.com	Bothell	WA	98021	425-402-2000	402-2001*
CAS Medical Systems Inc 44 E Industrial Rd *NASDAQ: CASM* ■ *TF:* 800-227-4414 ■ *Web:* www.casmed.com	Branford	CT	06405	203-488-6056	488-9438
Compumedics USA Ltd 7850 Paseo del Norte *TF:* 877-717-3975 ■ *Web:* www.compumedics.com	El Paso	TX	79912	915-845-5600	845-2965
Computerized Thermal Imaging Inc (CTI) 1719 W 2800 S *Web:* www.cti-net.com	Ogden	UT	84401	801-776-4700	776-6440
Conmed Corp 525 French Rd *NASDAQ: CNMD* ■ **Fax Area Code:* 800 ■ **Fax:* Cust Svc ■ *TF:* 800-448-6506 ■ *Web:* www.conmed.com	Utica	NY	13502	315-797-8375	438-3051*
Cook Vascular Inc 1186 Montgomery Ln *TF:* 800-245-4715 ■ *Web:* www.cookvascular.com	Vandergrift	PA	15690	724-845-8621	845-2848
Covidien 5920 Longbow Dr *TF:* 800-255-8522 ■ *Web:* www.covidien.com	Boulder	CO	80301	303-530-2300	
Criticare Systems Inc N7W22025 Johnson Dr *TF:* 800-458-4615 ■ *Web:* www.csiusa.com	Waukesha	WI	53186	262-798-8282	798-8290
Draeger Medical Inc 3135 Quarry Rd **Fax Area Code:* 215 ■ *TF:* 800-437-2437 ■ *Web:* www.draeger.com	Telford	PA	18969	800-437-2437	723-5935*
Dynatronics Corp 7030 Pk Centre Dr *NASDAQ: DYNT* ■ **Fax Area Code:* 800 ■ *TF:* 800-874-6251 ■ *Web:* www.dynatronics.com	Salt Lake City	UT	84121	801-568-7000	221-1919*
Fisher & Paykel Healthcare Inc 15365 Barranca Pkwy *TF:* 800-446-3908 ■ *Web:* www.fphcare.co.nz	Irvine	CA	92618	949-453-4000	453-4001
Gambro Renal Products 14143 Denver W Pkwy *TF:* 800-525-2623 ■ *Web:* www.gambro.com	Lakewood	CO	80401	303-232-6800	222-6810
GE Healthcare 3000 N Grandview Blvd *TF:* 800-558-5102 ■ *Web:* www.gehealthcare.com	Waukesha	WI	53188	262-544-3011	548-2443
GE Healthcare Information Technologies 8200 W Tower Ave *TF:* 800-558-5102	Milwaukee	WI	53223	414-355-5000	
HealthTronics Inc 9825 Spectrum Dr Bldg 3 *TF:* 888-252-6575 ■ *Web:* www.healthtronics.com	Austin	TX	78717	512-328-2892	439-8303
Hillenbrand Industries Inc 1 Batesville Blvd *NYSE: HI* ■ *Web:* www.hillenbrand.com	Batesville	IN	47006	812-934-7500	934-7613
Inovio Pharmaceuticals Inc 1787 Sentry PkwyW Bldg 18 *AMEX: INO* ■ *TF:* 877-446-6846 ■ *Web:* www.inovio.com	Blue Bell	PA	19422	267-440-4200	
IVY Biomedical Systems Inc 11 Business Pk Dr *TF:* 800-247-4614 ■ *Web:* www.ivybiomedical.com	Branford	CT	06405	203-481-4183	481-8734
MAQUET Cardiac Assist 15 Law Dr **Fax Area Code:* 201 ■ *TF:* 800-777-4222 ■ *Web:* www.ca.maquet.com	Fairfield	NJ	07004	973-244-6100	307-5400*
Masimo Corp 40 Parker *TF:* 800-326-4890 ■ *Web:* www.masimo.com	Irvine	CA	92618	949-297-7000	297-7001
Medical Education Technologies Inc (METI) 6300 Edgelake Dr *Web:* www.meti.com	Sarasota	FL	34240	941-377-5562	377-5590
Medical Graphics Corp 350 Oak Grove Pkwy *TF:* 800-333-4137 ■ *Web:* www.medgraph.com	Saint Paul	MN	55127	651-484-4874	484-8941
Medtronic Inc 710 Medtronic Pkwy NE *NYSE: MDT* ■ *TF Cust Svc:* 800-328-2518 ■ *Web:* www.medtronic.com	Minneapolis	MN	55432	763-514-4000	514-4879
Medtronic of Canada Ltd 6733 Kitimat Rd *TF:* 800-268-5346 ■ *Web:* www.medtronic.com	Mississauga	ON	L5N1W3	905-826-6020	826-6620
Medtronic Perfusion Systems 7611 Northland Dr *TF:* 800-328-3320 ■ *Web:* www.medtronic.com	Brooklyn Park	MN	55428	763-391-9000	391-9100
Mennen Medical Corp 950 Industrial Hwy *TF:* 800-223-2201 ■ *Web:* www.mennenmedical.com	SouthHampton	PA	18966	215-259-1020	675-6212
Meridian Medical Technologies Inc 6350 Stevens Forest Rd Suite 301 *TF:* 800-638-8093 ■ *Web:* www.meridianmeds.com	Columbia	MD	21046	443-259-7800	259-7801
MicroMed Technology Inc 8965 Interchange Dr *Web:* www.micromedtech.com	Houston	TX	77054	713-838-9210	838-9214
Mortara Instrument Inc 7865 N 86th St *TF:* 800-231-7437 ■ *Web:* www.mortara.com	Milwaukee	WI	53224	414-354-1600	354-4760
Natus Medical Inc 1501 Industrial Rd *NASDAQ: BABY* ■ *TF:* 800-255-3901 ■ *Web:* www.natus.com	San Carlos	CA	94070	650-802-0400	802-0401
NeuroMetrix 62 4th Ave *NASDAQ: NURO* ■ *TF:* 888-786-7287 ■ *Web:* www.neurometrix.com	Waltham	MA	02451	781-890-9989	890-1556
Oscor Inc 3816 DeSoto Blvd **Fax:* Cust Svc ■ *TF Cust Svc:* 800-726-7267 ■ *Web:* www.oscor.com	Palm Harbor	FL	34683	727-937-2511	934-9835*
OSI Systems Inc 12525 Chadron Ave *NASDAQ: OSIS* ■ *Web:* www.osi-systems.com	Hawthorne	CA	90250	310-978-0516	644-1727
Paradigm Medical Industries Inc 4273 S 590 W *TF:* 800-742-0671 ■ *Web:* www.paradigm-medical.com	Salt Lake City	UT	84123	801-977-8970	977-8973
Philips Respironics Georgia Inc 175 Chastain Meadows Ct *Web:* www.global.respironics.com	Kennesaw	GA	30144	770-499-1212	499-1139
Physio-Control Inc 11811 Willows Rd NE **Fax:* Acctg ■ *TF:* 800-442-1142 ■ *Web:* www.physio-control.com	Redmond	WA	98052	425-867-4000	881-2405*
QMed Inc 25 Christopher Way *PINK: QMED*	Eatontown	NJ	07724	732-544-5544	544-5404

	City	State	Zip	Phone	Fax
Respironics Novametrix LLC 5 Technology Dr *TF:* 800-345-6443 ■ *Web:* www.respironics.com	Wallingford	CT	06492	724-387-4000	
Richard Wolf Medical Instruments Corp 353 Corporate Woods Pkwy *TF:* 800-323-9653 ■ *Web:* www.richardwolfusa.com	Vernon Hills	IL	60061	847-913-1113	913-1488
Rockwell Medical Inc 30142 Wixom Rd *NASDAQ: RMTI* ■ *TF:* 800-449-3353 ■ *Web:* www.rockwellmed.com	Wixom	MI	48393	248-960-9009	960-9119
Saint Jude Medical Inc Cardiac Rhythm Management Div 1 St jude *Web:* www.sjm.com	Sylmar	CA	91342	818-362-6822	364-5814
Saint Jude Medical Inc Heart Valve Div 1 Lillehei Plaza *TF:* 800-328-9634 ■ *Web:* www.sjm.com	Saint Paul	MN	55117	651-483-2000	482-8318
SensorMedics Corp 22745 Savi Ranch Pkwy **Fax:* Mktg ■ *TF:* 800-231-2466 ■ *Web:* www.sensormedics.com	Yorba Linda	CA	92887	714-283-2228	283-8439*
Siemens Medical Solutions Inc 51 Valley Stream Pkwy *TF:* 866-872-9745 ■ *Web:* www.medical.siemens.com	Malvern	PA	19355	610-448-6300	219-3124
Somanetics Corp 2600 Troy Ctr Dr *NASDAQ: SMTS* ■ *TF:* 800-359-7662 ■ *Web:* www.somanetics.net	Troy	MI	48084	248-244-1400	244-0978
Spacelabs Health Care 5150 220th Ave SE *TF:* 800-522-7025 ■ *Web:* www.spacelabshealthcare.com	Issaquah	WA	98029	425-657-7200	657-7212
Thoratec Corp 6035 Stoneridge Dr *NASDAQ: THOR* ■ *TF:* 800-528-2577 ■ *Web:* www.thoratec.com	Pleasanton	CA	94588	925-847-8600	847-8574
Vasomedical Inc 180 Linden Ave *PINK: VASO* ■ *TF:* 800-455-3327 ■ *Web:* www.vasomedical.com	Westbury	NY	11590	516-997-4600	997-2299
Viasys Respiratory Care 1100 Bird Ctr Dr **Fax:* Cust Svc ■ *Web:* www.viasyshealthcare.com	Palm Springs	CA	92262	760-778-7200	778-7274*
Welch Allyn Medical Products 4341 State St Rd *TF:* 800-535-6663 ■ *Web:* www.welchallyn.com/medical	Skaneateles Falls	NY	13153	315-685-4100	685-3361
Welch Allyn Monitoring Inc 8500 SW Creekside Pl **Fax:* Cust Svc ■ *TF Cust Svc:* 800-289-2500 ■ *Web:* www.monitoring.welchallyn.com	Beaverton	OR	97008	503-530-7500	526-4200*
World Heart Inc 7799 Pardee Ln *NASDAQ: WHRT* ■ *TF:* 888-843-5827 ■ *Web:* www.worldheart.com	Oakland	CA	94621	510-563-5000	563-5005
ZOLL Medical Corp 269 Mill Rd *NASDAQ: ZOLL* ■ *TF:* 800-348-9011 ■ *Web:* www.zoll.com	Chelmsford	MA	01824	978-421-9655	421-0025

254 ELECTRONIC BILL PRESENTMENT & PAYMENT SERVICES

SEE ALSO Application Service Providers (ASPs) p. 1398

	City	State	Zip	Phone	Fax
Alpha Card Services Inc 475 Veit Rd *TF:* 866-253-2227 ■ *Web:* www.alphacardservices.com	Huntingdon Valley	PA	19006	866-253-2227	
CheckFree Corp 4411 E Jones Bridge Rd *NASDAQ: CKFR* ■ *TF Cust Svc:* 800-305-3716 ■ *Web:* www.checkfree.com	Norcross	GA	30092	678-375-3000	
Crosscheck Inc 6119 State Farm Dr *TF:* 888-937-2249 ■ *Web:* www.cross-check.com	Rohnert Park	CA	94928	707-586-0551	586-1024
Harbor Payments Inc 400 Galleria Pkwy SE # 700 *Web:* www.harborpayments.com	Atlanta	GA	30339	404-267-5000	267-5200
Heartland Payment Systems Inc 90 Nassau St 2nd Fl *NYSE: HPY* ■ *TF:* 888-798-3131 ■ *Web:* www.heartlandpaymentsystems.com	Princeton	NJ	08542	609-683-3831	683-3815
LML Payment Systems Inc 1140 W Pender St Suite 1680 *NASDAQ: LMLP* ■ **Fax Area Code:* 604 ■ *TF:* 800-888-2260 ■ *Web:* www.lmlpayment.com	Vancouver	BC	V6E4G1	800-888-2260	689-4413*
Metavante Corp 4900 W Brown Deer Rd *TF:* 800-236-3282 ■ *Web:* www.metavante.com	Brown Deer	WI	53223	414-357-2290	357-9606
PayPal Inc PO Box 45950 *Web:* www.paypal.com	Omaha	NE	68145	402-935-2050	537-5734
TPi Billing Solutions PO Box 472330 *TF:* 800-332-0023 ■ *Web:* www.tpibillingsolutions.com	Tulsa	OK	74147	918-664-0144	665-6677

255 ELECTRONIC COMMUNICATIONS NETWORKS (ECNS)

SEE ALSO Securities Brokers & Dealers p. 2646; Securities & Commodities Exchanges p. 2648

Ecns Are Computerized Trade-Matching Systems That Unite Best Bid And Offer Prices And Provide Anonymity To Investors.

	City	State	Zip	Phone	Fax
Acme Packet Inc 100 Crosby Dr *NASDAQ: APKT* ■ *Web:* www.acmepacket.com	Burlington	MA	01803	781-328-4400	275-8800
Archipelago Holdings LLC 100 S Wacker Dr Suite 1800 *TF:* 888-514-7284 ■ *Web:* www.tradearca.com	Chicago	IL	60606	312-960-1696	960-1369
Bloomberg Tradebook LLC 731 Lexington Ave *Web:* www.tradebook.bloomberg.com	New York	NY	10022	212-893-5555	
Bluesocket Inc 52 2nd Ave *Web:* www.bluesocket.com	Burlington	MA	01803	781-328-0888	328-0899
Comm-Works Holdings LLC 1405 Xenium Ln N Suite 120 *TF:* 800-853-8090 ■ *Web:* www.comm-works.com	Minneapolis	MN	55441	763-258-5800	475-6656
Entropic Communications Inc 6290 Sequence Dr *NASDAQ: ENTR* ■ *Web:* www.entropic.com	San Diego	CA	92121	858-768-3600	768-3601
Instinet Group Inc 3 Times Sq *TF:* 888-819-5236 ■ *Web:* www.instinet.com	New York	NY	10036	212-310-9500	
Javelin Technologies 100 Wall St 26th Fl *Web:* www.javtech.com	New York	NY	10005	212-525-3000	809-1013
Layer 3 Communications LLC 1555 Oakbrook Dr Suite 100 *TF:* 866-535-3924 ■ *Web:* www.layer3com.com	Norcross	GA	30093	770-225-5300	225-5298
Network Telephone Services Inc 21135 Erwin St *TF:* 800-742-5687 ■ *Web:* www.nts.net	Woodland Hills	CA	91367	800-742-5687	
NexTrade 301 S Missouri Ave *Web:* www.nextrade.com	Clearwater	FL	33756	727-446-6660	441-8880
NYFIX Inc 11 Wall St *Web:* www.nyfix.com	New York	NY	10005	212-656-3000	
OTC Markets Group Inc 304 Hudson St 2nd Fl *Web:* www.otcmarkets.com	New York	NY	10013	212-896-4400	868-3848
Vector Resources Inc 3530 Voyager St *Web:* www.vectorusa.com	Torrance	CA	90503	310-436-1000	436-1060

256 ELECTRONIC COMPONENTS & ACCESSORIES - MFR

SEE ALSO Printed Circuit Boards p. 2449; Semiconductors & Related Devices p. 2651

	City	State	Zip	Phone	Fax
3M Electrical Products Div 6801 River Pl Blvd 3M Austin Ctr **Fax Area Code:* 800 ■ *TF:* 800-245-3573 ■ *Web:* www.3m.com/elpd	Austin	TX	78726	512-984-1800	245-0329*
3M Electronic Handling & Protection Div 6801 River Pl Blvd *TF:* 800-328-1368 ■ *Web:* www.3m.com/ehpd	Austin	TX	78726	800-328-1368	858-9136
3M Interconnect Solutions Div 6801 River Pl Blvd *TF:* 800-225-5373 ■ *Web:* www.3m.com	Austin	TX	78726	512-984-1800	984-3417
Aavid Thermalloy LLC 70 Commercial St Suite 200 *TF:* 855-322-2843 ■ *Web:* www.aavidthermalloy.net	Concord	NH	03301	603-224-9988	223-1790
Actown-Electrocoil Inc 2414 Highview St *TF:* 800-531-6366 ■ *Web:* www.actown.com	Spring Grove	IL	60081	815-675-6641	675-2050
Adco Circuits 2868 Bond St *Web:* www.adcocircuits.com	Rochester Hills	MI	48309	248-853-6620	853-6698
Advanced Bionics LLC 28515 Westinghouse Pl *TF:* 877-829-0026 ■ *Web:* www.advancedbionics.com	Valencia	CA	91355	661-362-1400	362-1503
AEM Inc 11525 Sorrento Valley Rd *TF:* 888-323-6462 ■ *Web:* www.aem-usa.com	San Diego	CA	92121	858-481-0210	481-1123
Aeroflex Inc 35 S Service Rd PO Box 6022 *NASDAQ: ARX* ■ *TF:* 800-843-1553 ■ *Web:* www.aeroflex.com	Plainview	NY	11803	516-694-6700	694-0658
Aerovox Inc 167 John Vertente Blvd *TF:* 800-343-3348 ■ *Web:* www.aerovox.com	New Bedford	MA	02745	508-994-9661	999-1000
AESP Inc 16295 NW 13th Ave *TF:* 800-446-2377 ■ *Web:* www.aesp.com	Miami	FL	33169	305-944-7710	949-4483
Alliance Fiber Optic Products Inc 275 Gibralter Dr *NASDAQ: AFOP* ■ *Web:* www.afop.com	Sunnyvale	CA	94089	408-736-6900	736-2466
Alpha Group The 3767 Alpha Way **Fax:* Sales ■ *TF:* 800-322-5742 ■ *Web:* www.alpha.com	Bellingham	WA	98226	360-647-2360	671-4936*
American International Inc 1040 Avendia Acaso *TF:* 800-336-6500 ■ *Web:* www.aius.net	Camarillo	CA	93012	805-388-6800	388-7950
American Power Conversion Corp (APC) 132 Fairgrounds Rd *TF Cust Svc:* 800-788-2208 ■ *Web:* www.apc.com	West Kingston	RI	02892	401-789-5735	789-3710
AMETEK Automation & Process Technologies 1080 N Crooks Rd *TF:* 800-635-0289 ■ *Web:* www.ametekapt.com	Clawson	MI	48017	248-435-0700	435-8120
Ametek HDR Power Systems Inc 3563 Interchange Rd *TF:* 888-797-2685 ■ *Web:* www.hdrpower.com	Columbus	OH	43204	614-308-5500	308-5506
AMETEK Prestolite Power & Switch 2220 Corporate Dr *TF:* 800-367-2002 ■ *Web:* www.prestolitepower.com	Troy	OH	45373	937-440-0800	440-0893
AMETEK Solidstate Controls 875 Dearborn Dr *TF:* 800-635-7300 ■ *Web:* www.solidstatecontrolsinc.com	Columbus	OH	43085	614-846-7500	885-3990
Amphenol Aerospace 40-60 Delaware Ave *TF:* 800-678-0141 ■ *Web:* www.amphenol-aerospace.com	Sidney	NY	13838	607-563-5011	563-5157
Amphenol Interconnect Products Corp (AIPC) 20 Valley St **Fax:* Hum Res ■ *TF:* 888-275-2473 ■ *Web:* www.amphenol-aipc.com	Endicott	NY	13760	607-754-4444	786-4234*
Amphenol PCD 72 Cherry Hill Dr **Fax:* Sales ■ *Web:* www.amphenolpcd.com	Beverly	MA	01915	978-624-3400	972-1513*
Amphenol RF 4 Old Newtown Rd *TF:* 800-627-7100 ■ *Web:* www.amphenolrf.com	Danbury	CT	06810	203-743-9272	796-2032
Amphenol Sine Systems 44724 Morley Dr *Web:* www.sineco.com	Clinton Township	MI	48036	586-465-3131	
Amphenol Spectra-Strip 720 Sherman Ave *TF:* 800-846-6400 ■ *Web:* www.spectra-strip.com	Hamden	CT	06514	203-281-3200	281-5872
Amphenol-Tuchel Electronics 6900 Haggerty Rd Suite 200 *TF:* 800-380-8052 ■ *Web:* www.amphenol.info	Canton	MI	48187	734-451-6400	451-7197
AmRad Engineering Inc 32 Hargrove Grade *TF:* 800-445-6033 ■ *Web:* www.amradcapacitors.com	Palm Coast	FL	32137	386-445-6000	445-6871
Anaren Microwave Inc 6635 Kirkville Rd *NASDAQ: ANEN* ■ *TF:* 800-544-2414 ■ *Web:* www.anaren.com	East Syracuse	NY	13057	315-432-8909	432-9121
Antec Inc 47900 Fremont Blvd *TF Cust Svc:* 888-542-6832 ■ *Web:* www.antec-inc.com	Fremont	CA	94538	510-770-1200	770-1288
API Delevan 270 Quaker Rd *Web:* www.delevan.com	East Aurora	NY	14052	716-652-3600	652-4814
Aries Electronics Inc 62-A Trenton Ave PO Box 130 *Web:* www.arieselec.com	Frenchtown	NJ	08825	908-996-6841	996-3891
ASC Capacitors 301 W O St *Web:* www.ascapacitor.com	Ogallala	NE	69153	308-284-3611	284-8324
Astec America Inc 5810 Van Allen Way *TF:* 888-412-7832	Carlsbad	CA	92008	760-930-4600	930-0698
Atotech USA Inc 1750 Overview Dr *Web:* www.atotech.com/en	Rock Hill	SC	29730	803-817-3500	817-3666
AVG Automation 4140 Utica St **Fax Area Code:* 563 ■ *TF:* 800-711-5109 ■ *Web:* www.avg.net/avgautomation	Battendorf	IA	52722	630-462-5906	359-9094*

Company	City	State	Zip	Phone	Fax
Avionic Instruments Inc 1414 Randolph Ave *Web:* www.avionicinstruments.com	Avenel	NJ	07001	732-388-3500	382-4996
Avnet Electronics Marketing 2211 S 47th St *TF:* 888-822-8638 ■ *Web:* avnetexpress.avnet.com	Phoenix	AZ	85034	480-643-2000	
AVX Corp 801 17th Ave S *NYSE: AVX* ■ *Web:* www.avxcorp.com	Myrtle Beach	SC	29577	843-448-9411	444-0424
Ballard Power Systems Inc 9000 Glenlyon Pkwy *NASDAQ: BLDP* ■ *Web:* www.ballard.com	Burnaby	BC	V5J5J8	604-454-0900	412-4700
Banner Engineering Corp 9714 10th Ave N *TF:* 888-373-6767 ■ *Web:* www.bannerengineering.com	Minneapolis	MN	55441	763-544-3164	544-3213
Beacon Power Corp 65 Middlesex Rd *NASDAQ: BCON* ■ *TF:* 888-938-9112 ■ *Web:* www.beaconpower.com	Tyngsboro	MA	01879	978-694-9121	694-9127
BEI Technologies Inc Industrial Encoder Div 7230 Hollister Ave *TF Sales:* 800-350-2727 ■ *Web:* www.beiied.com	Goleta	CA	93117	805-968-0782	968-3154
Bel Stewart Connector 11118 Susquehanna Trail S *Web:* www.belfuse.com	Glen Rock	PA	17327	717-235-7512	235-7954
Bergquist Co 18930 W 78th St *TF:* 800-347-4572 ■ *Web:* www.bergquistcompany.com	Chanhassen	MN	55317	952-835-2322	835-4156
BH Electronics Inc 12219 Wood Lake Dr *Web:* www.bhelectronics.com	Burnsville	MN	55337	952-894-9590	894-9380
C & D Technologies Inc 1400 Union Meeting Rd PO Box 3053 *NYSE: CHP* ■ *TF:* 800-543-8630 ■ *Web:* www.cdtechno.com	Blue Bell	PA	19422	215-619-2700	619-7899
C&D Technologies 11 Cabot Blvd *TF:* 800-233-2765 ■ *Web:* www.cd4power.com	Mansfield	MA	02048	508-339-3000	339-6356
Califone International Inc 1145 Arroyo St Suite A *TF:* 800-722-0500 ■ *Web:* www.califone.com	San Fernando	CA	91340	818-407-2400	407-2405
Celestica Inc 844 Don Mills Rd *NYSE: CLS* ■ *TF:* 888-899-9998 ■ *Web:* www.celestica.com	Toronto	ON	M3C1V7	416-448-5800	448-4810
CeramTec North America 1 Technology Pl *TF:* 800-845-9761 ■ *Web:* www.ceramtec.com	Laurens	SC	29360	864-682-3215	682-1121
Circuit Assembly Corp 18 Thomas St *Web:* www.circuitassembly.com	Irvine	CA	92618	949-855-7887	855-4298
Clary Corp 150 E Huntington Dr *TF:* 800-551-6111 ■ *Web:* www.clary.com	Monrovia	CA	91016	626-359-4486	305-0254
Coilcraft Inc 1102 Silver Lake Rd *TF:* 800-323-5045 ■ *Web:* www.coilcraft.com	Cary	IL	60013	847-639-2361	639-1469
Coils Inc 11716 Algonquin Rd PO Box 247	Huntley	IL	60142	847-669-5115	669-5115
Comdel Inc 11 Kondelin Rd *TF:* 800-468-3144 ■ *Web:* www.comdel.com	Gloucester	MA	01930	978-282-0620	282-4980
Communications & Power Industries Inc EIMAC Div (CPII) 301 Industrial Rd *TF:* 800-423-4622 ■ *Web:* www.cpii.com/eimac	San Carlos	CA	94070	650-592-1221	592-9988
Communications & Power Industries LLC 607 Hansen Way **Fax:* PR ■ *TF:* 800-231-4818 ■ *Web:* www.cpii.com	Palo Alto	CA	94303	650-846-2900	846-3276*
Cooper Industries 600 Travis St Suite 5800 *NYSE: CBE* ■ *TF:* 866-853-4293 ■ *Web:* www.cooperindustries.com	Houston	TX	77002	713-209-8400	209-8995
Corning Gilbert Inc 5310 W Camelback Rd *TF Cust Svc:* 800-528-0199 ■ *Web:* www.corning.com	Glendale	AZ	85301	623-245-1050	934-5160
Cornucopia Tool & Plastics Inc 448 Sherwood Rd PO Box 1915 *TF:* 800-235-4144 ■ *Web:* www.cornucopiaplastics.com	Paso Robles	CA	93447	805-369-0030	369-0033
Cougar Components Corp 927 Thompson Pl *Web:* www.cougarcorp.com	Sunnyvale	CA	94085	408-522-3838	522-3839
Crystek Crystals Corp 12730 Commonwealth Dr *TF:* 800-237-3061 ■ *Web:* www.crystek.com	Fort Myers	FL	33913	239-561-3311	561-3311
CTS Corp 905 W Blvd N *NYSE: CTS* ■ *TF:* 800-757-6686 ■ *Web:* www.ctscorp.com	Elkhart	IN	46514	574-293-7511	293-6146
Cyber Power Systems Inc 4241 12th Ave E Suite 400 *Web:* www.cyberpowersystems.com	Shakopee	MN	55379	952-403-9500	403-0009
Cyberex 5900 Eastport Blvd *TF:* 800-238-5000 ■ *Web:* www.tnbpowersolutions.com	Richmond	VA	23231	804-236-3300	236-3300
Data Device Corp 105 Wilbur Pl *TF Cust Svc:* 800-332-5757 ■ *Web:* www.ddc-web.com	Bohemia	NY	11716	631-567-5600	567-6015
Dekko Technologies LLC 2505 Dekko Dr *TF:* 800-829-3101 ■ *Web:* www.dekko.com	Garrett	IN	46738	260-357-3621	357-3399
Delta Electronics Mfg Corp 416 Cabot St *Web:* www.deltarf.com	Beverly	MA	01915	978-927-1060	922-6430
Delta Group Inc 4801 Lincoln Rd Ne *Web:* www.deltagroupinc.com	Albuquerque	NM	87109	505-883-7674	888-5460
Delta Products Corp 4405 Cushing Pkwy *Web:* www.delta-americas.com	Fremont	CA	94538	510-668-5100	668-0680
Diamond Antenna & Microwave Corp 59 Porter Rd *Web:* www.diamondantenna.com	Littleton	MA	01460	978-486-0039	486-0079
Dielectric Laboratories Inc 2777 US Rt 20 *TF:* 800-656-9499 ■ *Web:* www.dilabs.com	Cazenovia	NY	13035	315-655-8710	655-8179
Digital Power Corp 41324 Christy St *AMEX: DPW* ■ *TF:* 866-344-7697 ■ *Web:* www.digipwr.com	Fremont	CA	94538	510-353-4023	657-2635
Distributed Energy Systems Corp 10 Technology Dr *NASDAQ: DESC* ■ *Web:* www.distributed-energy.com	Wallingford	CT	06492	203-678-2000	949-8016
Dow-Key Microwave Corp 4822 McGrath St *TF:* 800-266-3695 ■ *Web:* www.dowkey.com	Ventura	CA	93003	805-650-0260	650-1734
DRS Laurel Technologies 246 Airport Rd *Web:* www.drs.com	Johnstown	PA	15904	814-534-8900	534-8815
Dynalloy Inc 14762 Bentley Cir *Web:* www.dynalloy.com	Tustin	CA	92780	714-436-1206	436-0511
Eby Co 4300 H St *TF:* 800-329-3430 ■ *Web:* www.ebycompany.com	Philadelphia	PA	19124	215-537-4700	537-4780
Electrex Inc PO Box 948 *TF:* 800-319-3676 ■ *Web:* www.electrexinc.com	Hutchinson	KS	67504	620-669-9966	669-9988
Electro-Mechanical Corp 1 Goodson St *Web:* www.electro-mechanical.com	Bristol	VA	24201	276-466-8200	466-6931
Electrocube Inc 3366 Pomona Blvd **Fax Area Code:* 626 ■ *Web:* www.electrocube.com	Pomona	CA	91768	909-595-4037	357-8099*
Electronic Instrumentation & Technology Inc (EIT) 108 Carpenter Dr *Web:* www.eit.com	Sterling	VA	20164	703-478-0700	478-0291
Electroswitch Corp 180 King Ave *Web:* www.electroswitch.com	Weymouth	MA	02188	781-335-5200	335-4253
Elgar Electronics Corp 9250 Brown Deer Rd **Fax:* Sales ■ *TF:* 800-733-5427 ■ *Web:* www.elgar.com	San Diego	CA	92121	858-450-0085	458-0267*
Ellanef Mfg Corp 97-11 50th Ave *Web:* www.ellanef.com	Corona	NY	11368	718-699-4000	592-0722
Elma Electronic Inc 44350 Grimmer Blvd *Web:* www.elma.com	Fremont	CA	94538	510-656-3400	656-3783
Emerson Network Power Connectivity Solutions 300 Lakeside Dr Suite 308-N *Web:* emersonnetworkpower.com	Bannockburn	IL	60015	847-739-0300	739-0301
Energy Conversion Devices Inc 2956 Waterview Dr *NASDAQ: ENER* ■ *TF:* 800-528-0617 ■ *Web:* www.energyconversiondevices.com	Rochester Hills	MI	48309	248-293-7002	299-4228
EPCOS Inc 485-B Rt 1 S Suite 200 *NYSE: EPC* ■ *TF:* 800-689-3717 ■ *Web:* www.epcos.com	Iselin	NJ	08830	732-906-4300	906-4395
eSilicon Corp 501 Macara Ave *Web:* www.esilicon.com	Sunnyvale	CA	94085	408-616-4600	991-9567
Espey Mfg & Electronics Corp 233 Ballston Ave *AMEX: ESP* ■ *Web:* www.espey.com	Saratoga Springs	NY	12866	518-245-4400	245-4421
Evolve Mfg Technologies 960 Linda Vista Ave *Web:* www.evolvemfg.com	Mountain View	CA	94043	650-968-9292	968-9299
Fawn Industries Inc 1920 Greenspring Dr Suite 140 *Web:* www.fawn-ind.com	Timonium	MD	21093	410-308-9200	308-9201
Filnor Inc 227 N Freedom Ave PO Box 2328 *Web:* www.filnor.com	Alliance	OH	44601	330-821-7667	829-3175
Flextronics International Ltd 2090 Fortune Dr *NASDAQ: FLEX* ■ *Web:* www.flextronics.com	San Jose	CA	95131	408-428-1300	576-7988
Foxlink International Inc 925 W Lambert Rd Suite C *Web:* www.foxlink.com	Brea	CA	92821	714-256-1777	256-1700
Framatome Connectors USA Inc (FCI) 47 E Industrial Pk Dr **Fax:* Cust Svc ■ *TF:* 800-346-4175 ■ *Web:* www.fciconnect.com	Manchester	NH	03109	603-672-1679	672-5205*
FuelCell Energy Inc 3 Great Pasture Rd *NASDAQ: FCEL* ■ *Web:* www.fuelcellenergy.com	Danbury	CT	06810	203-825-6000	825-6100
Fujitsu Components America Inc 250 E Caribbean Dr *Web:* www.fujitsu.com	Sunnyvale	CA	94089	408-745-4900	745-4970
G & H Technology Inc 750 W Ventura Blvd *Web:* www.ghtech.com	Camarillo	CA	93010	805-484-0543	987-5062
GE Aviation Electrical Power Systems 2855 W McNab Rd **Fax:* Sales ■ *TF:* 800-952-6909 ■ *Web:* www.geaviation.com	Pompano Beach	FL	33069	954-984-7000	984-2479*
General Microcircuits Inc 1133 N Main St PO Box 748 *Web:* www.gmimfg.com	Mooresville	NC	28115	704-663-5975	663-6569
Greatbatch Inc 9645 Wehrle Dr *NYSE: GB* ■ *Web:* www.greatbatch.com	Clarence	NY	14031	716-759-5600	759-5654
GW Lisk Co Inc 2 S St *Web:* www.gwlisk.com	Clifton Springs	NY	14432	315-462-2611	462-7661
Harco Laboratories Inc 186 Cedar St *Web:* www.harcolabs.com	Branford	CT	06405	203-483-3700	483-0391
HCC Industries Inc 4232 Temple City Blvd *Web:* www.hccindustries.com	Rosemead	CA	91770	626-443-8933	575-2437
HCC Industries Inc Glasseal Div 485 Oberlin Ave S *Web:* www.hccindustries.com	Lakewood	NJ	08701	732-370-9100	370-7107
HCC Industries Inc Sealtron Div 9705 Reading Rd *Web:* www.hccindustries.com	Cincinnati	OH	45215	513-733-8400	733-0131
Heraeus Shin-Etsu America Inc 4600 NW Pacific Rim Blvd	Camas	WA	98607	360-834-4004	834-3115
Herley New England 10 Sonar Dr *Web:* www.herley.com	Woburn	MA	01801	781-729-9450	729-9547
Herley-CTI Inc 9 Whippany Rd *Web:* www.herley.com	Whippany	NJ	07981	973-884-2580	887-6245
Hilby-yates Inc 282 Brokaw Rd	Santa Clara	CA	95050	408-988-0700	970-9860
HiRel Systems 11100 Wayzata Blvd Suite 501 *Web:* www.hirelsystems.com	Minnetonka	MN	55305	952-544-1344	544-1345
Hirose Electric (USA) Inc 2688 Westhills Ct *Web:* www.hirose.com	Simi Valley	CA	93065	805-522-7958	522-3217
Hitachi Canada Ltd 5750 Explore Dr Suit 301 *TF:* 800-906-4482 ■ *Web:* www.hitachi.ca	Mississauga	ON	L4W0A9	905-821-4545	290-0141
Hitachi Electronic Devices (USA) Inc 208 Fairforest Way *Web:* www.hedus.com	Greenville	SC	29607	864-299-2600	299-2700
Hitachi High Technologies America Inc 10 N Martingale Rd Suite 500 *Web:* www.hii-hitachi.com	Schaumburg	IL	60173	847-273-4141	273-4407
Honeywell Electronic Materials 1349 Moffett Pk Dr *Web:* www.honeywell.com/sites/sm/em	Sunnyvale	CA	94089	408-962-2000	980-1430
Hubbell Power Systems Inc 210 N Allen St *TF:* 800-482-2355 ■ *Web:* www.hubbellpowersystems.com	Centralia	MO	65240	573-682-5521	682-8714
Hunting Innova 8383 N Sam Houston Pkwy W *TF:* 800-203-1653 ■ *Web:* www.innovaelec.com	Houston	TX	77064	281-653-5500	653-5501
Hutchinson Technology Inc 40 W Highland Pk Dr *NASDAQ: HTCH* ■ *Web:* www.htch.com	Hutchinson	MN	55350	320-587-3797	587-1810
Illinois Capacitor Inc 3757 W Touhy Ave *TF:* 800-323-5420 ■ *Web:* www.illinoiscapacitor.com	Lincolnwood	IL	60712	847-675-1760	673-2850

	City	State	Zip	Phone	Fax
Imaging & Sensing Technology Corp 315 Daniel Zenker Dr *Web:* www.istcorp.com	Horseheads	NY	14845	607-562-4300	562-4499
Integrated Microwave Corp 11353 Sorrento Valley Rd *Web:* www.imcsd.com	San Diego	CA	92121	858-259-2600	755-8679
Interconnect Devices Inc (IDI) 5101 Richland Ave *Web:* www.idinet.com	Kansas City	KS	66106	913-342-5544	342-7043
International Resistive Co Inc (IRC) 736 Greenway Rd *TF:* 800-472-6467 ■ *Web:* www.irctt.com	Boone	NC	28607	828-264-8861	264-8865
Interpoint Corp PO Box 97005 *TF:* 800-822-8782 ■ *Web:* www.interpoint.com	Redmond	WA	98073	425-882-3100	882-1990
inTEST Corp 804 E Gate Dr Suite 200 *NASDAQ: INTT* ■ *TF:* 800-501-6886 ■ *Web:* www.intest.com	Mount Laurel	NJ	08054	856-505-8800	505-8801
Isis Surface Mounting Inc 2530 Zanker Rd *Web:* www.isissm.com	San Jose	CA	95131	408-953-7700	434-5937
ITT Defense 1650 Tysons Blvd Suite 1700 *Web:* www.defense.itt.com	McLean	VA	22102	703-790-6300	790-6360
ITT Industries Inc 1133 Westchester Ave *NYSE: ITT* ■ *Web:* www.itt.com	White Plains	NY	10604	914-641-2000	696-2950
ITT Power Solutions 11 IH- Dr. *TF:* 800-442-4334 ■ *Web:* www.ittpowersolutions.com	West Springfield	MA	01089	413-263-6200	737-0608
ITW Paktron 1205 McConville Rd PO Box 4539 *TF:* 888-227-7845 ■ *Web:* www.paktron.com	Lynchburg	VA	24502	434-239-6941	239-4730
JAE Electronics Inc 142 Technology Dr Suite 100 *TF:* 800-523-7278 ■ *Web:* www.jae.com	Irvine	CA	92618	949-753-2600	753-2699
Jewell Instruments LLC 850 Perimeter Rd *TF:* 800-227-5955 ■ *Web:* www.jewellinstruments.com	Manchester	NH	03103	603-669-6400	669-5962
Johanson Mfg Corp 301 Rockaway Valley Rd. **Fax:* Sales ■ *Web:* www.johansonmfg.com	Boonton	NJ	07005	973-334-2676	334-2954*
K & L Microwave Inc 2250 Northwood Dr *Web:* www.klmicrowave.com	Salisbury	MD	21801	410-749-2424	749-1598
Kaiser Systems Inc 126 Sohier Rd. *Web:* www.kaisersys.com	Beverly	MA	01915	978-922-9300	922-8374
Kay Pentax 2 Bridgewater Ln *TF:* 800-289-5297 ■ *Web:* www.kaypentax.com	Lincoln Park	NJ	07035	973-628-6200	628-6363
KEMET Corp PO Box 5928 *NYSE: KEM* ■ *Web:* www.kemet.com	Greenville	SC	29606	864-963-6300	963-6322
Kepco Inc 131-38 Sanford Ave. *Web:* www.kepcopower.com	Flushing	NY	11355	718-461-7000	767-1102
Key Tronic Corp 4424 N Sullivan Rd. *NASDAQ: KTCC* ■ *Web:* www.keytronic.com	Spokane	WA	99214	509-928-8000	927-5555
Knowles Electronics Inc 1151 Maplewood Dr *Web:* www.knowlesinc.com	Itasca	IL	60143	630-250-5100	250-0575
L-3 Communications Corp Display Systems Div 1355 Bluegrass Lakes Pkwy *Web:* www.l-3com.com	Alpharetta	GA	30004	770-752-7000	752-5525
L-3 Communications Narda Microwave West 107 Woodmere Rd *Web:* www.nardamicrowave.com	Folson	CA	95630	916-351-4500	351-4550
La Marche Mfg Co 106 Bradrock Dr. *Web:* www.lamarchemfg.com	Des Plaines	IL	60018	847-299-1188	299-3061
LaBarge Inc 9900 Clayton Rd *AMEX: LB* ■ *Web:* www.labarge.com	Saint Louis	MO	63124	314-997-0800	812-9438
Larco 210 NE 10th Ave PO Box 547 *TF Cust Svc:* 800-523-6996 ■ *Web:* www.larcomfg.com	Brainerd	MN	56401	218-829-9797	829-0139
Lexel Imaging Systems Inc 1501 Newtown Pike *Web:* www.lexelimaging.com	Lexington	KY	40511	859-243-5500	243-5555
Linear LLC 1950 Camino Vida Roble Suite 150 *TF Cust Svc:* 800-421-1587 ■ *Web:* www.linearcorp.com	Carlsbad	CA	92008	760-438-7000	931-1340
Lippert Components Inc 2703 College Ave. *TF:* 866-524-7821 ■ *Web:* www.lci1.com	Goshen	IN	46528	574-535-1125	535-2086
Logitek Inc 110 Wilbur Pl *Web:* www.naii.com	Bohemia	NY	11716	631-567-1100	567-1823
Lumex Inc 290 E Helen Rd *TF:* 800-278-5666 ■ *Web:* www.lumex.com	Palatine	IL	60067	847-359-2790	359-8904
MagneTek Inc N49 W13650 Campbell Dr. *NYSE: MAG* ■ **Fax Area Code:* 800 ■ *TF:* 800-288-8178 ■ *Web:* www.magnetek.com	Menomonee Falls	WI	53051	262-783-3500	298-3503*
Maida Development Co 201 S Mallory St. *Web:* www.maida.com	Hampton	VA	23663	757-723-0785	722-1194
Marlow Industries Inc 10451 Vista Pk Rd. *TF:* 877-627-5691 ■ *Web:* www.marlow.com	Dallas	TX	75238	214-340-4900	340-7728
Maxwell Technologies Inc 5271 Viewridge Ct Suite 100 *NASDAQ: MXWL* ■ *TF:* 877-511-4324 ■ *Web:* www.maxwell.com	San Diego	CA	92123	858-503-3300	503-3301
McDonald Technologies International Inc 1920 Diplomat Dr. *TF:* 800-678-7046 ■ *Web:* www.mcdonald-tech.com	Farmers Branch	TX	75234	972-243-6767	241-2643
Meggitt Safety Systems Inc 1915 Voyager Ave. *Web:* www.meggitt.com	Simi Valley	CA	93063	805-584-4100	578-3400
Melcor 1040 Spruce St.	Trenton	NJ	08648	609-393-4178	393-9461
Merrimac Industries Inc 41 Fairfield Pl *NYSE: MRM* ■ **Fax:* Sales ■ *TF:* 800-575-1301 ■ *Web:* www.merrimacind.com	West Caldwell	NJ	07006	973-575-1300	575-0531*
Methode Electronics Inc 7401 W Wilson Ave *NYSE: MEI* ■ *TF:* 877-316-7700 ■ *Web:* www.methode.com	Chicago	IL	60706	708-867-6777	867-6999
Micro-coax Inc 206 Jones Blvd *TF:* 800-223-2629 ■ *Web:* www.micro-coax.com	Pottstown	PA	19464	610-495-0110	495-6656
Microwave Engineering Corp 1551 Osgood St *Web:* www.microwaveeng.com	North Andover	MA	01845	978-685-2776	975-4363
Millennia Group The 1105 Pittsburgh St *Web:* www.the-millennia-group.com	Cheswick	PA	15024	724-274-7741	274-2234
Miteq Inc 100 Davids Dr *Web:* www.miteq.com	Hauppauge	NY	11788	631-436-7400	436-7430
Mitsubishi Electric & Electronics USA Inc *Elevator & Escalator Div* 5665 Plaza Dr. *Web:* www.mitsubishi-elevator.com	Cypress	CA	90630	714-220-4822	220-4812
Molex Inc 2222 Wellington Ct *NASDAQ: MOLX* ■ *TF Cust Svc:* 800-786-6539 ■ *Web:* www.molex.com	Lisle	IL	60532	630-969-4550	969-1352
Morey Corp 100 Morey Dr *Web:* www.moreycorp.com	Woodridge	IL	60517	630-754-2300	754-2001
MS Kennedy Corp 4707 Dey Rd *Web:* www.mskennedy.com	Liverpool	NY	13088	315-701-6751	701-6752
MtronPTI 1703 E Hwy 50 *TF:* 800-762-8800 ■ *Web:* www.mtronpti.com	Yankton	SD	57078	605-665-9321	665-1709
Multi-Fineline Electronix Inc (Mflex) 3140 E Coronado St *NASDAQ: MFLX* ■ *Web:* www.mflex.com	Anaheim	CA	92806	714-238-1488	996-3834
Murata Electronics North America Inc 2200 Lake Pk Dr *TF:* 800-241-6574 ■ *Web:* www.murata.com	Smyrna	GA	30080	770-436-1300	436-3030
Namco Controls Corp 201 W Meeting St **Fax Area Code:* 910 ■ *TF Cust Svc:* 800-626-8324 ■ *Web:* www.namcocontrols.com	Elizabethtown	SC	28337	800-476-6952	879-5486*
Netcom Inc 599 S Wheeling Rd *Web:* www.netcominc.com	Wheeling	IL	60090	847-537-6300	537-2700
Newport Corp 1791 Deere Ave. *NASDAQ: NEWP* ■ **Fax:* Sales ■ *TF Sales:* 800-222-6440 ■ *Web:* www.newport.com	Irvine	CA	92606	949-863-3144	253-1680*
Niles Audio Corp 1969 Kellog Ave *TF:* 800-289-4434 ■ *Web:* www.nilesaudio.com	Carlsbad	CA	92008	760-710-0992	
Nortech Systems Inc 1120 Wayzata Blvd E Suite 201 *NASDAQ: NSYS* ■ *TF:* 800-808-8281 ■ *Web:* www.nortechsys.com	Wayzata	MN	55391	952-345-2244	449-0442
Novacap Inc 25111 Anza Dr. *Web:* www.novacap.com	Valencia	CA	91355	661-295-5920	295-5928
Novacentrix Corp 200-B Parker Dr Suite 580 *Web:* www.novacentrix.com	Austin	TX	78728	512-491-9500	491-0002
NWL Transformers Inc 312 Rising Sun Rd. *TF:* 800-742-5695 ■ *Web:* www.nwl.com	Bordentown	NJ	08505	609-298-7300	298-1982
O M Jones Inc PO Box 4375 *Web:* www.micro-tronics.net	Sonora	CA	95370	209-532-1008	532-1009
Oeco LLC 4607 SE International Way *Web:* www.oeco.com	Milwaukie	OR	97222	503-659-7932	653-6310
OEM Worldwide Inc 2920 13th Ave SE. *TF:* 800-258-7989 ■ *Web:* www.oemworldwide.com	Watertown	SD	57201	605-886-2519	886-5123
Ohmite Mfg Co 1600 Golf Rd Suite 850 *TF:* 866-964-6483 ■ *Web:* www.ohmite.com	Rolling Meadows	IL	60008	847-258-0300	574-7501
OK International 12151 Monarch St. *Web:* www.okinternational.com	Garden Grove	CA	92841	714-799-9910	799-9533
Omron Corp 55 Commerce Dr *Web:* www.omron.com	Schaumburg	IL	60173	224-520-7650	520-7680
Oppenheimer Precision Products 173 Gibraltar Rd *Web:* www.oppiprecision.com	Horsham	PA	19044	215-674-9100	675-5139
Oren Elliott Products Inc 128 W Vine St. *Web:* www.orenelliottproducts.com	Edgerton	OH	43517	419-298-2306	298-3545
OSI Systems Inc 12525 Chadron Ave *NASDAQ: OSIS* ■ *Web:* www.osi-systems.com	Hawthorne	CA	90250	310-978-0516	644-1727
OSRAM Sylvania Inc 100 Endicott St *Web:* www.sylvania.com	Danvers	MA	01923	978-777-1900	750-2152
Panamax Inc 1690 Corporate Cir. *TF:* 800-472-5555 ■ *Web:* www.panamax.com	Petaluma	CA	94954	707-283-5900	283-5901
Para Systems Inc *Minuteman UPS* 1455 LeMay Dr. *TF:* 800-238-7272 ■ *Web:* www.minutemanups.com	Carrollton	TX	75007	972-446-7363	446-9011
Pcb Group Inc 3425 Walden Ave *TF:* 800-828-8840 ■ *Web:* www.pcb.com	Depew	NY	14043	716-684-0001	684-0987
PECO II Inc 1376 SR 598 PO Box 910 *TF:* 800-999-7326 ■ *Web:* www.peco2.com	Galion	OH	44833	419-468-7600	468-3688
PerkinElmer Inc 45 William St *NYSE: PKI* ■ *Web:* www.perkinelmer.com	Wellesley	MA	02481	781-237-5100	237-9386
Piller Inc 45 Turner Rd *TF:* 800-597-6937 ■ *Web:* www.piller.com	Middletown	NY	10941	845-695-5300	692-0295
Plastronics Socket Co Inc 2601 Texas Dr *TF Cust Svc:* 800-582-5822 ■ *Web:* www.locknest.com	Irving	TX	75062	972-258-1906	258-6771
Plug Power Inc 968 Albany-Shaker Rd *NASDAQ: PLUG* ■ *Web:* www.plugpower.com	Latham	NY	12110	518-782-7700	782-9060
Polyflon Co 1 Willard Rd *Web:* www.polyflon.com	Norwalk	CT	06851	203-840-7555	840-7565
Positronic Industries Inc 423 N Campbell Ave PO Box 8247 *TF:* 800-641-4054 ■ *Web:* www.connectpositronic.com	Springfield	MO	65801	417-866-2322	866-0210
Post Glover LifeLink Inc 167 Gap Way *TF:* 800-287-4123 ■ *Web:* www.postgloverhalsey.com	Erlanger	KY	41018	859-283-5900	372-6272
Post Glover Resistors Inc 4750 Olympic Blvd Bldg B *TF Cust Svc:* 800-537-6144 ■ *Web:* www.postglover.com	Erlanger	KY	41018	859-283-0778	283-2978
Power-One Inc 740 Calle Plano *NASDAQ: PWER* ■ *TF:* 800-678-9445 ■ *Web:* www.power-one.com	Camarillo	CA	93012	805-987-8741	987-5212
Precision Cable Assemblies LLC 16830 Pheasant Dr *Web:* www.pca-llc.com	Brookfield	WI	53005	262-784-7887	784-5907
Precision Devices Inc 8840 N Greenview Dr. *TF:* 800-274-9825 ■ *Web:* www.pdixtal.com	Middleton	WI	53562	608-831-4445	831-3343
Precision Interconnect Corp 10025 SW Freeman Ct *Web:* www.precisionint.com	Wilsonville	OR	97070	503-685-9300	685-9305
Progressive Dynamics Inc 507 Industrial Rd *Web:* www.progressivedyn.com	Marshall	MI	49068	269-781-4241	781-7802
Pulse Engineering Inc 12220 World Trade Dr *Web:* www.pulseelectronics.com	San Diego	CA	92128	858-674-8100	674-8262
Q P Semiconductor 2945 Oakmead Village Ct *Web:* www.qpsemi.com	Santa Clara	CA	95051	408-737-0992	736-8708
Q-tech Corp 10150 Jefferson Blvd *Web:* www.q-tech.com	Culver City	CA	90232	310-836-7900	836-2157
Q-tran Inc 304 Bishop Ave *Web:* www.q-tran.com	Bridgeport	CT	06610	203-367-8777	367-8771
Qual-Tron Inc (QTI) 9409 E 55th Pl. *Web:* www.qual-tron.com	Tulsa	OK	74145	918-622-7052	664-8557

Company / Address	City	State	ZIP	Phone	Fax
QualiTau Inc 915 Walsh Ave *Web:* www.qualitau.com	Santa Clara	CA	95050	408-522-9200	522-8110
Qualitel Corp 11831 Beverly Pk Rd *Web:* www.qualitelcorp.com	Everett	WA	98204	425-423-8388	702-8885
Quartzdyne Inc 4334 W Links Dr. *TF:* 888-353-7956 ■ *Web:* www.quartzdyne.com	Salt Lake City	UT	84120	801-266-6958	266-7985
Quvis Inc 900 SW 39th St Suite N *TF:* 800-554-8116 ■ *Web:* www.quvis.com	Topeka	KS	66609	785-272-3656	272-3657
Raritan Computer Inc 400 Cottontail Ln *TF:* 800-724-8090 ■ *Web:* www.raritan.com	Somerset	NJ	08873	732-764-8886	764-8887
Record USA 4324 Phil Hargett Ct *TF Sales:* 800-438-1937 ■ *Web:* www.record-usa.com	Monroe	NC	28220	704-289-9212	289-2024
Regal Research & Mfg Co Inc PO Box 940529 *Web:* www.regalresearch.com	Plano	TX	75094	972-494-0359	272-0220
RF Industries 7610 Miramar Rd Bldg 6000 *NASDAQ: RFIL* ■ *TF:* 800-233-1728 ■ *Web:* www.rfindustries.com	San Diego	CA	92126	858-549-6340	549-6345
Rovi Corp 2830 De La Cruz Blvd. *NASDAQ: ROVI* ■ *Web:* www.rovicorp.com	Santa Clara	CA	95050	408-562-8400	743-8610
Ruhle Cos Inc 99 Wall St. *Web:* www.ruhle.com	Valhalla	NY	10595	914-761-2600	761-0405
S & K Electronics Inc 56301 US Hwy 93 *Web:* www.skecorp.com	Ronan	MT	59864	406-883-6241	883-6228
S V Microwave Inc 2400 Centre Pk W Dr *Web:* www.svmicrowave.com	West Palm Beach	FL	33409	561-840-1800	842-6277
Samtec Inc 520 Parkeast Blvd *TF:* 800-726-8329 ■ *Web:* www.samtec.com	New Albany	IN	47150	812-944-6733	948-5047
SatCon Technology Corp 27 Dry Dock Ave *NASDAQ: SATC* ■ *TF:* 888-728-2760 ■ *Web:* www.satcon.com	Boston	MA	02210	617-897-2400	897-2401
Schott Corp 1401 Air Wing Rd. *Web:* www.schottcorp.com	San Diego	CA	92154	507-223-5572	223-5055
Schumacher Electric Corp 801 E Business Ctr Dr *TF:* 800-621-5485 ■ *Web:* www.batterychargers.com	Mount Prospect	IL	60056	847-385-1600	298-1698
Scosche Industries Inc PO Box 2901 *Web:* www.scosche.com	Oxnard	CA	93034	805-486-4450	486-9996
Seiko Instruments USA Inc 1309 Rutherford Ln *TF:* 800-358-0880 ■ *Web:* www.seikoinstruments.com	Austin	TX	78753	512-349-3800	349-3000
Semicon Assoc 695 Laco Dr *Web:* www.semiconassociates.com	Lexington	KY	40510	859-255-3664	255-6829
Semiconductor Circuits Inc 49 Range Rd *Web:* www.dcdc.com	Windham	NH	03087	603-893-2330	893-6280
Sendec Corp 72 Perinton Pkwy *TF:* 800-295-8000 ■ *Web:* www.sendec.com	Fairport	NY	14450	585-425-3390	425-3392
Sharp Microelectronics of the Americas 5700 NW Pacific Rim Blvd *Web:* www.sharpsma.com	Camas	WA	98607	360-834-2500	834-8903
Shelly Assoc Inc 17171 Murphy Ave *TF:* 888-669-9850 ■ *Web:* www.shellyinc.com	Irvine	CA	92614	949-417-8070	417-8075
Shogyo International Corp 6851 Jericho Tpke *Web:* www.shogyo.com	Syosset	NY	11791	516-921-9111	921-3777
Siemens Intelligent Transportation Systems 8004 Cameron Rd. *TF:* 800-388-6882 ■ *Web:* www.itssiemens.com	Austin	TX	78754	512-837-8310	837-0196
Sierra Nevada Corp (SNC) 444 Salomon Cir *Web:* www.sncorp.com	Sparks	NV	89434	775-331-0222	331-0370
Sigma Electronics Inc 1027 Commercial Ave. *TF:* 866-569-2681 ■ *Web:* www.sigmatechsys.com	East Petersburg	PA	17520	717-569-2926	569-4056
Signal Transformer Co Inc 500 Bayview Ave *TF:* 866-239-5777 ■ *Web:* www.signaltransformer.com	Inwood	NY	11096	516-239-5777	239-7208
Simclar Inc 2230 W 77th St. *NASDAQ: SIMC* ■ *Web:* www.simclar.com	Hialeah	FL	33016	305-556-9210	827-5209
Simplex Inc 5300 Rising Moon Rd. *TF:* 800-637-8603 ■ *Web:* www.simplexdirect.com	Springfield	IL	62711	217-483-1600	483-1616
SL Power Electronics Inc 6050 King Dr Bldg A **Fax Area Code:* 858 ■ *Web:* www.slpower.com	Ventura	CA	93003	805-486-4565	712-2040*
Smart Power Systems Inc 1760 Stebbins Dr *TF:* 800-241-6880 ■ *Web:* www.smartpowersystems.com	Houston	TX	77043	713-464-8000	
SMK Electronics Corp USA 1055 Tierra Del Rey *Web:* www.smk.co.jp	Chula Vista	CA	91910	619-216-6400	216-6498
SMTC Corp 635 Hood Rd *NASDAQ: SMTX* ■ *Web:* www.smtc.com	Markham	ON	L3R4N6	905-479-1810	479-1877
SNC Mfg Co Inc 101 W Waukau Ave *TF:* 800-558-3325 ■ *Web:* www.sncmfg.com	Oshkosh	WI	54902	920-231-7370	231-1090
Sorenson Communications Inc 4192 Riverboat Rd Suite 100 *Web:* www.sorenson.com	Salt Lake City	UT	84123	801-287-9400	287-9401
Spang & Co 110 Delta Dr *Web:* www.spang.com	Pittsburgh	PA	15238	412-963-9363	696-0333
Spectrum Control Inc 8031 Avonia Rd *Web:* www.spectrumcontrol.com	Fairview	PA	16415	814-474-2207	474-2208
Spellman High Voltage Electronics Corp 475 Wireless Blvd. **Fax:* Sales ■ *Web:* www.spellmanhv.com	Hauppauge	NY	11788	631-435-1600	435-1620*
Spinnaker Microwave Inc 3281 Kifer Rd *Web:* www.spinnakermicrowave.com	Santa Clara	CA	95051	408-732-9828	
Standex Electronics Inc 4538 Camberwell Rd *TF:* 866-782-6339 ■ *Web:* www.standexelectronics.com	Cincinnati	OH	45209	513-871-3777	871-3779
STATS ChipPAC Test Services Inc 1768 McCandless Dr *Web:* www.statschippac.com	Milpitas	CA	95035	408-586-0600	586-0601
Stellar Microelectronics Inc 28575 Livingston Ave. *Web:* www.stellarmicro.com	Valencia	CA	91355	661-775-3500	775-3522
Stevens Water Monitoring Systems 12067 NE Glenn Widing Dr Suite 106 *TF:* 800-452-5272 ■ *Web:* www.stevenswater.com	Portland	OR	97220	503-469-8000	469-8100
Strax Americas Inc 1869 SW 97th Ave *Web:* www.strax.com	Miami	FL	33172	305-468-1770	468-1771
Sumida America Inc 1251 N Plum Grove Rd Suite 150 *Web:* www.sumida.com	Schaumburg	IL	60173	847-545-6700	545-6721
Superconductor Technologies Inc (STI) 460 Ward Dr *NASDAQ: SCON* ■ *TF:* 800-727-3648 ■ *Web:* www.suptech.com	Santa Barbara	CA	93111	805-690-4500	967-0342
Switchcraft Inc 5555 N Elston Ave *Web:* www.switchcraft.com	Chicago	IL	60630	773-792-2700	792-2129
SynQor Inc 155 Swanson Rd *Web:* www.synqor.com	Boxborough	MA	01719	978-849-0600	849-0601
Sypris Electronics LLC 10901 N McKinley Dr *Web:* www.sypris.com	Tampa	FL	33612	813-972-6000	972-6704
Sypris Solutions Inc 101 Bullitt Ln Suite 450 *NASDAQ: SYPR* ■ *Web:* www.sypris.com	Louisville	KY	40222	502-329-2000	329-2050
System Sensor 3825 Ohio Ave *TF Tech Supp:* 800-736-7672 ■ *Web:* www.systemsensor.com	St. Charles	IL	60174	630-377-6580	377-6495
Taiyo Yuden (USA) Inc 1930 N Thoreau Dr Suite 190 *TF:* 800-348-2496 ■ *Web:* www.t-yuden.com	Schaumburg	IL	60173	847-925-0888	925-0899
TDI-Transistor Devices Inc 85 Horsehill Rd. *Web:* www.tdipower.com	Cedar Knolls	NJ	07927	973-267-1900	267-2047
TDK Corp of America 475 Hathway Rd. *Web:* www.component.tdk.com	Lincolnshire	IL	60056	847-803-6100	390-4370
TDK-Lambda Americas Inc 405 Essex Rd. *Web:* www.us.tdk-lambda.com/hp	Neptune	NJ	07753	732-922-9300	922-1441
Techneglas 707 E Jenkins Ave. *Web:* www.techneglas.com	Columbus	OH	43207	614-443-6551	445-1900
Technical Services for Electronics Inc 108 5th Ave NW PO Box 616 *Web:* www.tseinc.net	Arlington	MN	55307	507-964-2237	964-2465
Teledyne Electronic Safety Products 19735 Dearborn St *Web:* www.teledynesafetyproducts.com	Chatsworth	CA	91311	818-718-6640	998-3312
Telonic Berkeley Inc 2825 Laguna Canyon Rd *TF:* 800-854-2436 ■ *Web:* www.telonicberkeley.com	Laguna Beach	CA	92651	949-494-9401	497-7331
Tempo Research Corp 1390 Aspen Way *TF:* 800-642-2155 ■ *Web:* www.tempo.textron.com	Vista	CA	92083	760-598-8900	598-5634
Times Microwave Systems Inc PO Box 5039 *TF:* 800-867-2629 ■ *Web:* www.timesmicrowave.com	Wallingford	CT	06492	203-949-8400	949-8423
Toshiba America Inc 1251 Avenue of the Americas Suite 4100 *TF:* 800-457-7777 ■ *Web:* www.toshiba.com	New York	NY	10020	212-596-0600	593-3875
Total Technologies Ltd 9 Studebaker *TF:* 800-669-4885 ■ *Web:* www.total-technologies.com	Irvine	CA	92618	949-465-0200	465-0212
TRAK Microwave Corp 4726 Eisenhower Blvd. *TF:* 888-283-8444 ■ *Web:* www.trak.com	Tampa	FL	33634	813-901-7200	901-7490
Tri Source Inc 84 Platt Rd *Web:* www.trisourceinc.com	Shelton	CT	06484	203-926-9460	567-8181
Tri-Star Electronics International Inc 2201 Rosecrans Ave *Web:* www.tri-starelectronics.com	El Segundo	CA	90245	310-536-0444	536-9322
Triana Industries Inc 511 6th St	Madison	AL	35756	256-772-9304	258-0411
TSI Power Corp 1103 W Pierce Ave. *TF:* 800-874-3160 ■ *Web:* www.tsipower.com	Antigo	WI	54409	715-623-0636	623-2426
Tyco Electronics Corp 1050 Westlakes Dr. *Web:* www.tycoelectronics.com	Berwyn	PA	19312	610-893-9800	
Unisar Inc 51-02 21st St 7th Fl **Fax Area Code:* 800 ■ *TF:* 877-736-6760 ■ *Web:* www.unisar.com	Long Island City	NY	11101	877-736-6760	428-4729*
United Chemi-Con Inc 9801 W Higgins Rd *Web:* www.chemi-con.com	Rosemont	IL	60018	847-696-2000	696-9278
Usi Electronics Inc 2775 W Cypress Creek Rd *TF:* 800-874-8111 ■ *Web:* www.usielectronics.com	Fort Lauderdale	FL	33309	954-493-8111	493-8212
UTC Power 195 Governors Hwy *TF:* 866-383-5235 ■ *Web:* www.utcfuelcells.com	South Windsor	CT	06074	860-727-2200	727-2319
Valberg LLC 14286 169th Dr SE Suite 1 *TF:* 800-487-2206 ■ *Web:* www.valbergllc.com	Monroe	WA	98272	360-794-9885	794-9885
Valpey Fisher Corp 75 S St *AMEX: VPF* ■ *TF:* 800-982-5737 ■ *Web:* www.valpeyfisher.com	Hopkinton	MA	01748	508-435-6831	435-5289
Vectron International 267 Lowell Rd **Fax Area Code:* 603 ■ **Fax:* Cust Svc ■ *TF:* 888-328-7661 ■ *Web:* www.vectron.com	Hudson	NH	03051	888-328-7661	598-0075*
Viasystems Group Inc 101 S Hanley Rd Suite 400 *Web:* www.viasystems.com	Saint Louis	MO	63105	314-727-2087	746-2233
Viatran Corp 3829 Forest Pkwy Suite 500 *TF:* 800-688-0030 ■ *Web:* www.viatran.com	Wheatfield	NY	14120	716-629-3800	693-9162
Vicor Corp 25 Frontage Rd *NASDAQ: VICR* ■ *TF:* 800-869-5300 ■ *Web:* www.vicorpower.com	Andover	MA	01810	978-470-2900	475-6715
Viking Technologies Group Ltd 80 E Montauk Hwy *Web:* www.cardwellcondenser.com	Lindenhurst	NY	11757	631-957-7200	957-7203
Vishay Intertechnology Inc 63 Lancaster Ave *NYSE: VSH* ■ *Web:* www.vishay.com	Malvern	PA	19355	610-644-1300	296-0657
Wakefield Thermal Solutions Inc 33 Bridge St *TF:* 800-325-1426 ■ *Web:* www.wakefield.com	Pelham	NH	03076	603-635-2800	635-1900
Wellex Corp 551 Brown Rd *Web:* www.wellex.com	Fremont	CA	94539	510-743-1818	743-1899
Western Electronics LLC 1550 S Tech Ln *TF:* 888-857-5775 ■ *Web:* www.westernelectronics.com	Meridian	ID	83642	208-955-9700	955-9752
Wilmore Electronics Co Inc 607 US 70-A E PO Box 1329 *Web:* www.wilmoreelectronics.com	Hillsborough	NC	27278	919-732-9351	732-9359
Wireless Xcessories Group Inc 1840 County Line Rd Suite 301 *AMEX: XWG* ■ **Fax Area Code:* 888 ■ *TF:* 800-233-0013 ■ *Web:* www.wirexgroup.com	Huntingdon Valley	PA	19006	215-322-4600	233-0220*
World Electronics Sales & Service Inc 3000 Kutztown Rd. *TF:* 800-523-0427 ■ *Web:* www.world-electronics.com	Reading	PA	19605	610-939-9800	939-9895

				Phone	Fax
Xantrex Technology Inc 3700 Gilmore Way *TF:* 800-670-0707 ■ *Web:* www.xantrex.com	Burnaby	BC	V5G4M1	604-422-8595	420-1591
Yazaki North America Inc 6801 N Haggerty Rd *Web:* www.yazaki-na.com	Canton	MI	48187	734-983-1000	
Z Communications Inc 9939 Via Pasar *Web:* www.zcomm.com	San Diego	CA	92126	858-621-2700	
Ziptronix Inc 800 Perimeter Pk Dr Suite B *Web:* www.ziptronix.com	Morrisville	NC	27560	919-459-2400	459-2401

257 ELECTRONIC ENCLOSURES

				Phone	Fax
A & J Mfg Co 14831 Franklin Ave *Web:* www.aj-racks.com	Tustin	CA	92780	714-544-9570	544-4215
American Electric Technologies Inc (AETI) 6410 Long Dr *NASDAQ: AETI* ■ *Web:* www.aeti.com	Houston	TX	77087	713-644-8182	
APW Ltd N 22 W 23685 Ridgeview Pkwy W *TF:* 800-599-5556 ■ *Web:* www.apw.com	Waukesha	WI	53188	262-523-7600	523-7588
Buckeye ShapeForm 555 Marion Rd *TF:* 800-728-0776 ■ *Web:* www.buckeyeshapeform.com	Columbus	OH	43207	614-445-8433	445-8224
Bud Industries Inc 4605 E 355th St *Web:* www.budind.com	Willoughby	OH	44094	440-946-3200	951-4015
Commercial Sheet Metal Co 465 Tpke St *Web:* www.commercialsheetmetal.net	Canton	MA	02021	781-828-7900	828-3565
Crenlo LLC 1600 4th Ave NW **Fax:* Sales ■ *Web:* www.crenlo.com	Rochester	MN	55901	507-289-3371	287-3405*
Dawson Metal Co Inc 825 Allen St *TF:* 877-732-9766 ■ *Web:* www.dawsonmetal.com	Jamestown	NY	14701	716-664-3815	664-3485
Electrol Specialties Co 441 Clark St PO Box 7 *Web:* www.esc4cip.com	South Beloit	IL	61080	815-389-2291	389-2294
Emcor Enclosures 1600 4th Ave NW **Fax:* Sales ■ *Web:* www.emcorenclosures.com	Rochester	MN	55901	507-289-3371	287-3405*
Equipto Electronics Corp 351 Woodlawn Ave *TF:* 800-204-7225 ■ *Web:* www.equiptoelec.com	Aurora	IL	60506	630-897-4691	897-5314
Gerome Mfg Co Inc 135 Oliver Plaza *Web:* www.geromemfg.com	Uniontown	PA	15401	724-438-8544	437-5608
Global MetalForm LP 733 Davis St	Scranton	PA	18505	570-346-3871	346-1612
I-Bus Corp 3350 Scott Blvd Bldg 54 *TF:* 877-777-4287 ■ *Web:* www.ibus.com	Santa Clara	CA	95054	408-450-7880	450-7881
JMR Electronics Inc 8968 Fullbridht Ave **Fax:* Hum Res ■ *Web:* www.jmr.com	Chatsworth	CA	91311	818-993-4801	727-2248*
Macase Industrial Corp 3005 Ctr Pl Suite 100 *Web:* www.macase.com/macase	Norcross	GA	30093	770-840-8840	840-7006
National Mfg Co Inc 12 River Rd *Web:* www.natlmfg.com	Chatham	NJ	07928	973-635-8846	635-7810
Omega Tool 308 S Mountain View Ave	San Bernardino	CA	92408	909-888-0440	889-8740
Optima Electronic Packaging Systems 1775 MacLeod Dr **Fax:* Sales ■ *Web:* www.optimaeps.com	Lawrenceville	GA	30043	770-496-4000	496-4041*
Pentair Inc 5500 Wayzata Blvd Suite 800 *NYSE: PNR* ■ *TF:* 800-328-9626 ■ *Web:* www.pentair.com	Golden Valley	MN	55416	763-545-1730	656-5400
Stahlin Enclosures 505 W Maple St *Web:* www.stahlin.com	Belding	MI	48809	616-794-0700	794-3378
TRI MAP International Inc 111 Val Dervin Pkwy *TF:* 888-687-4627 ■ *Web:* www.trimapintl.com	Stockton	CA	95206	209-234-0100	234-5990
Universal Enclosure Systems 1146 S Cedar Ridge Dr *Web:* www.universalenclosures.com	Duncanville	TX	75137	972-298-0531	298-0614
Zendex Corp 6780 Sierra Ct Suite A *Web:* www.zendex.com	Dublin	CA	94568	925-828-3000	828-1574
Zero Mfg Inc 500 W 200 N *TF:* 800-545-1030 ■ *Web:* www.zerocases.com	North Salt Lake	UT	84054	801-298-5900	292-9450

258 ELECTRONIC TRANSACTION PROCESSING

				Phone	Fax
Alliance Data Systems Corp 17655 Waterview Pkwy *NYSE: ADS* ■ **Fax:* Hum Res ■ *TF:* 866-595-4896 ■ *Web:* www.alliancedata.com	Dallas	TX	75252	972-348-5100	348-5335*
Automated License Systems Inc 3055 Lebanon Pike Bldg 2 Suite 2301 *Web:* www.als-xtn.com	Nashville	TN	37214	615-263-4257	263-4271
Avid Payment Solutions 950 S Old Woodward Suite 220 **Fax Area Code:* 866 ■ *TF:* 888-855-8644 ■ *Web:* www.avidpays.com	Birmingham	MI	48009	248-723-5760	671-9773*
BA Merchant Services LLC 1231 Durrett Ln *TF:* 800-949-7379 ■ *Web:* www.npc.net	Louisville	KY	40213	502-315-2000	315-5739
Ceridian Corp 3311 E Old Shakopee Rd *TF:* 800-767-4969 ■ *Web:* www.ceridian.com	Minneapolis	MN	55425	952-853-8100	
Chase Paymentech Solutions LLC 14221 Dallas Pkwy *TF Cust Svc:* 800-934-7717 ■ *Web:* www.chasepaymentech.com	Dallas	TX	75254	800-708-3740	
Covera Card Solutions 19 British American Blvd *TF:* 866-526-8372 ■ *Web:* www.coverasolutions.com	Latham	NY	12110	518-437-8100	437-8500
Elavon 1 Concourse Pkwy Suite 300 **Fax Area Code:* 865 ■ *TF:* 800-725-1243 ■ *Web:* www.elavon.com	Atlanta	GA	30328	678-731-5000	577-0661*
Electracash 2501 Cherry Ave Suite 360 *TF Cust Svc:* 800-444-6952 ■ *Web:* www.electracash.com	Signal Hill	CA	90755	562-498-5877	424-6481
Electronic Clearing House Inc (ECHO) 600 W Chicago Ave Suite 725 *NASDAQ: ECHO* ■ **Fax Area Code:* 888 ■ *TF:* 800-354-7993 ■ *Web:* www.echo.com	Chicago	IL	60654	800-354-7993	796-4445*
Euronet Worldwide Inc 3500 College Blvd *NASDAQ: EEFT* ■ *Web:* www.euronetworldwide.com	Leawood	KS	66211	913-327-4200	327-1921
Global Payments Inc 10 Glenlake Pkwy N Tower *NYSE: GPN* ■ *TF:* 800-560-2960 ■ *Web:* www.globalpaymentsinc.com	Atlanta	GA	30328	770-829-8000	
Litle & Co 900 Chelmsford St *Web:* www.litle.com	Lowell	MA	01851	978-275-6500	937-7250
National Bankcard Systems 2600 Via Fortuna Suite 240 *TF:* 800-823-6835 ■ *Web:* www.enbs.com	Austin	TX	78749	512-494-9200	344-2979
Pershing LLC 95 Christopher Columbus Dr **Fax:* Hum Res ■ *TF:* 800-443-4342 ■ *Web:* www.pershing.com	Jersey City	NJ	07302	201-413-2000	413-3103*
Protegrity USA Inc 5 High Ridge Pk *Web:* www.protegrity.com	Stamford	CT	06905	203-326-7200	348-1251
Total System Services Inc 1600 1st Ave PO Box 2567 *NYSE: TSS* ■ *TF:* 800-686-1999 ■ *Web:* www.tsys.com	Columbus	GA	31901	706-644-3110	649-4266

259 ELEVATORS, ESCALATORS, MOVING WALKWAYS

				Phone	Fax
CemcoLift Inc 2801 Township Line Rd *TF Sales:* 800-962-3626 ■ *Web:* www.cemcolift.com	Hatfield	PA	19440	215-799-2900	703-0343
Elevator Equipment Corp 4035 Goodwin Ave *TF:* 888-577-3326 ■ *Web:* www.elevatorequipment.com	Los Angeles	CA	90039	323-245-0147	245-9771
Fujitec America Inc 7258 Innovation Way *Web:* www.fujitecamerica.com	Mason	OH	45040	513-932-8000	
Hollister-Whitney Elevator Corp 2603 N 24th St *Web:* www.hollisterwhitney.com	Quincy	IL	62305	217-222-0466	222-0493
Lifeport Inc 1610 Heritage St *Web:* www.lifeport.com	Woodland	WA	98674	360-225-1212	225-1214
Matot Inc 2501 Van Buren St *TF:* 800-369-1070 ■ *Web:* www.matot.com	Bellwood	IL	60104	708-547-1888	547-1608
Minnesota Elevator Inc 19336 607th Ave *Web:* www.minnesotaelevator.com	Mankato	MN	56001	507-245-3060	245-3956
Mitsubishi Electric & Electronics USA Inc *Elevator & Escalator Div* 5665 Plaza Dr *Web:* www.mitsubishi-elevator.com	Cypress	CA	90630	714-220-4822	220-4812
Motion Control Engineering Inc 11380 White Rock Rd *TF:* 800-444-7442 ■ *Web:* www.mceinc.com	Rancho Cordova	CA	95742	916-463-9200	638-0324
Otis Elevator Co 10 Farm Springs Rd *Web:* www.otisworldwide.com	Farmington	CT	06032	860-676-6000	676-6970
Ricon Corp 7900 Nelson Rd *TF:* 800-322-2884 ■ *Web:* www.riconcorp.com	Panorama City	CA	91402	818-267-3000	267-3001
Schindler Elevator Corp 20 Whippany Rd **Fax:* Mail Rm ■ *TF:* 800-225-3123 ■ *Web:* www.us.schindler.com	Morristown	NJ	07960	973-397-6500	397-6485*
Schumacher Elevator Co 111 Commercial St *Web:* www.schumacherelevator.com	Denver	IA	50622	319-984-5676	984-6316
Sematic USA 6161 Halle Dr	Valley View	OH	44125	216-524-0100	524-9710
ThyssenKrupp Access Inc 4001 E 138th St *TF:* 800-669-9047 ■ *Web:* www.tkaccess.com	Grandview	MO	64030	816-763-3100	763-4467
Waupaca Elevator Co Inc 1726 N Ballard Rd *Web:* www.waupacaelevator.com	Appleton	WI	54911	920-991-9082	991-9087

260 EMBASSIES & CONSULATES - FOREIGN, IN THE US

SEE ALSO Travel & Tourism Information - Foreign Travel p. 2732

Foreign Embassies In The U.S. Generally Include Consular Services Among Their Functions. These Embassy-Based Consulates Are Listed Here Only If Their Address Differs From The Embassy's.

				Phone	Fax
Afghanistan Embassy 2341 Wyoming Ave NW *Web:* www.embassyofafghanistan.org	Washington	DC	20008	202-483-6410	483-6488
Albania Embassy 2100 S St NW	Washington	DC	20008	202-223-4942	628-7342
Algeria Embassy 2118 Kalorama Rd NW	Washington	DC	20008	202-265-2800	667-2174
Andorra Embassy 2 United Nations Plaza 27th Fl *Web:* www.andorra.ad	New York	NY	10017	212-750-8064	750-6630
Angola Embassy 2108 16th St NW *Web:* www.angola.org	Washington	DC	20009	202-785-1156	822-9049
Antigua & Barbuda					
Consulate General 25 SE 2nd Ave Suite 300	Miami	FL	33131	305-381-6762	381-7908
Embassy 3216 New Mexico Ave NW *Web:* www.antigua-barbuda.org	Washington	DC	20016	202-362-5122	362-5225
Argentina					
Consulate General 5055 Wilshire Blvd Suite 210	Los Angeles	CA	90036	323-954-9155	934-9076
Consulate General 2200 W Loop S Suite 1025 *Web:* www.consuladoarhouston.com	Houston	TX	77027	713-871-8935	871-0639
Consulate General 12 W 56th St *Web:* www.congenargentinany.com	New York	NY	10019	212-603-0400	541-7746
Consulate General 245 Peachtree Ctr Ave Suite 2101	Atlanta	GA	30303	404-880-0805	880-0806
Embassy 1600 New Hampshire Ave NW *Web:* www.embassyofargentina.us	Washington	DC	20009	202-238-6400	332-3171
Armenia Embassy 2225 R St NW *Web:* www.armeniaemb.org	Washington	DC	20008	202-319-1976	319-2982
Australia					
Consulate General 150 E 42nd St 34th Fl *Web:* www.australia.visahq.com	New York	NY	10017	212-351-6500	351-6501
Consulate General 2049 Century Pk E Century Plaza Towers 19th Fl *Web:* www.australia.visahq.com	Los Angeles	CA	90067	310-229-4800	277-2258
Consulate General 1000 Bishop St PH *Web:* www.austemb.org/honolulu.html	Honolulu	HI	96813	808-524-5050	531-5142
Embassy 2005 Massachusetts Ave NW *TF:* 800-345-6541 ■ *Web:* www.visahq.com	Washington	DC	20036	202-558-2216	318-0771

				Phone	Fax
Australian Consulate General					
Consulate General 123 N Wacker Dr Suite 1330	Chicago	IL	60606	312-419-1480	419-1499
Web: www.austemb.org/chicago.html					
Austria					
Consulate General 31 E 69th St	New York	NY	10021	212-933-5140	585-1992
Web: www.austria-ny.org					
Consulate General 400 N Michigan Ave Suite 707	Chicago	IL	60611	312-222-1515	222-4113
Web: www.austria.org					
Consulate General 11859 Wilshire Blvd Suite 501	Los Angeles	CA	90025	310-444-9310	477-9897
Web: www.austria.org					
Embassy 3524 International Ct NW	Washington	DC	20008	202-895-6700	895-6750
Web: www.austria.org					
Azerbaijan Embassy 2741 34th St NW	Washington	DC	20008	202-337-3500	337-5911
Web: www.azembassy.com					
Bahamas					
Consulate General 25 SE 2nd Ave	Miami	FL	33131	305-373-6295	373-6312
Consulate General 231 E 46th St	New York	NY	10017	212-421-6420	688-5926
Web: www.bahamasny.net					
Embassy 2220 Massachusetts Ave NW	Washington	DC	20008	202-319-2660	319-2668
Bahrain					
Consulate General 866 2nd Ave 14th Fl	New York	NY	10017	212-223-6200	223-6206
Web: www.un.int/bahrain/consulate.html					
Embassy 3502 International Dr NW	Washington	DC	20008	202-342-1111	362-2192
Web: www.bahrainembassy.org					
Bangladesh Consulate General					
4201 Wilshire Blvd Suite 605	Los Angeles	CA	90010	323-932-0100	932-9703
Web: www.bangladeshconsulatela.com					
Barbados Consulate General					
2121 Poncedaleon Blvd Suite 1300	Coral Gables	FL	33134	305-442-1994	455-7975
Web: www.foreign.gov.bb					
Belarus Embassy 1619 New Hampshire Ave NW	Washington	DC	20009	202-986-1604	986-1805
Web: www.usa.belembassy.org					
Belgium					
Consulate General 1065 Avenue of the Americas 22nd Fl	New York	NY	10018	212-586-5110	582-9657
Web: www.diplomatie.be/newyork					
Consulate General 6100 Wilshire Blvd Suite 1200	Los Angeles	CA	90048	323-857-1244	936-2564
Consulate General 230 Peachtree St NW Suite 2710	Atlanta	GA	30303	404-659-2150	659-8474
Embassy 3330 Garfield St NW	Washington	DC	20008	202-333-6900	333-3079
Web: www.diplobel.us					
Belize Embassy 2535 Massachusetts Ave NW	Washington	DC	20008	202-332-9636	332-6888
Web: www.embassyofbelize.org					
Benin Embassy 2124 Kalorama Rd NW	Washington	DC	20008	202-232-6656	265-1996
Web: www.beninembassy.us					
Bolivia					
Consulate General 211 E 43rd St Suite 702	New York	NY	10017	212-687-0530	687-0532
Web: www.consulatebolivianonewyork.com					
Embassy 3014 Massachusetts Ave NW	Washington	DC	20008	202-483-4410	328-3712
Web: www.bolivia-usa.org					
Bosnia & Herzegovina					
Consulate General 2109 E St NW	Washington	DC	20037	202-337-1500	337-2909
Web: www.bhembassy.org					
Embassy 2109 E St NW	Washington	DC	20037	202-337-1500	337-1502
Web: www.bhembassy.org					
Botswana Embassy					
1531 New Hampshire Ave NW	Washington	DC	20036	202-244-4990	244-4164
Web: www.botswanaembassy.org					
Brazil					
Consulate General 80 SW 8th St 26th Fl	Miami	FL	33130	305-285-6200	285-6240
Web: www.brazilmiami.org					
Consulate General 300 Montgomery St Suite 900	San Francisco	CA	94104	415-981-8170	986-4625
Web: www.brazilsf.org					
Consulate General 20 Pk Plaza Suite 810	Boston	MA	02116	617-542-4000	542-4318
Web: www.consulatebrazil.org					
Consulate General 1233 W Loop S Suite 1150	Houston	TX	77027	713-961-3063	961-3070
Web: www.brazilhouston.org					
Consulate General 8484 Wilshire Blvd Suite 711	Beverly Hills	CA	90211	323-651-2664	651-1274
Web: www.brazilian-consulate.org					
Consulate General 1185 6th Ave	New York	NY	10036	917-777-7777	827-0225*
**Fax Area Code: 212* ■ *Web:* www.novayork.itamaraty.gov.br					
Embassy 3006 Massachusetts Ave NW	Washington	DC	20008	202-238-2700	238-2827
TF: 800-727-2945 ■ *Web:* www.brasilemb.org					
Embassy - Consular Section 3006 Massachusetts Ave NW	Washington	DC	20008	202-238-2805	238-2827
Web: www.brasilemb.org					
Brunei Darussalam					
Embassy 3520 International Ct NW	Washington	DC	20008	202-237-1838	885-0560
Web: www.bruneiembassy.org					
Bulgaria					
Consulate General 121 E 62nd St	New York	NY	10021	212-935-4646	319-5955
Web: www.consulbulgaria-ny.org					
Embassy 1621 22nd St NW	Washington	DC	20008	202-387-0174	234-7973
Web: www.bulgaria-embassy.org					
Burkina Faso Embassy					
2005 Massachusetts Ave NW	Washington	DC	20008	202-332-5577	667-1882
Web: www.visahq.com					
Burundi Embassy					
2233 Wisconsin Ave NW Suite 212	Washington	DC	20007	202-342-2574	342-2578
Web: www.burundiembassy-usa.org					
Cambodia Embassy 4530 16th St NW	Washington	DC	20011	202-726-7742	726-8381
Web: www.embassyofcambodia.org					
Cameroon Embassy					
2349 Massachusetts Ave NW	Washington	DC	20008	202-265-8790	387-3826
Canada					
Consulate General 500 N Akard St Suite 2900	Dallas	TX	75201	214-922-9806	922-9815
Web: www.canadainternational.gc.ca					
Consulate General 200 S Biscayne Blvd Suite 1600	Miami	FL	33131	305-579-1600	374-6774
Consulate General 600 Renaissance Ctr Suite 1100	Detroit	MI	48243	313-567-2340	567-2164
Web: www.canadainternational.gc.ca					
Consulate General 550 S Hope St Fl 9	Los Angeles	CA	90071	213-346-2700	346-2767
Web: www.canadainternational.gc.ca					
Consulate General 1251 Avenue of the Americas Concourse Level	New York	NY	10020	212-596-1628	596-1790
Web: www.canadainternational.gc.ca					
Consulate General 180 N Stetson Ave Suite 2400	Chicago	IL	60601	312-616-1860	616-1877
Web: www.geo.international.gc.ca					
Consulate General 701 4th Ave S Suite 900	Minneapolis	MN	55415	612-332-7486	332-4061
Web: www.geo.international.gc.ca					
Consulate General 1501 4th Ave Suite 600	Seattle	WA	98101	206-443-1777	443-9662
Web: geo.international.gc.ca/can-am/seattle					
Consulate General 1175 Peachtree St NE 100 Colony Sq Suite 1700	Atlanta	GA	30361	404-532-2000	532-2050
Web: geo.international.gc.ca/can-am/atlanta					
Consulate General 3 Copley Pl Suite 400	Boston	MA	02116	617-262-3760	262-3415
Web: www.geo.international.gc.ca/can-am/boston					
Consulate General 3000 HSBC Ctr	Buffalo	NY	14203	716-858-9500	852-2477
Web: www.geo.international.gc.ca/can-am/buffalo					
Embassy 501 Pennsylvania Ave NW	Washington	DC	20001	202-682-1740	682-7726
Web: www.canadianembassy.org					
Cape Verde					
Consulate General 607 Boylston St 4th Fl	Boston	MA	02116	617-353-0014	859-9798
Embassy 3415 Massachusetts Ave NW	Washington	DC	20007	202-965-6820	965-1207
Chad Embassy 2002 R St	Washington	DC	20009	202-462-4009	265-1937
Web: www.chadembassy.org					
Consulate General 6th & Chestnut St Public Ledger Bldg Suite 1030	Philadelphia	PA	19106	215-829-9520	829-0594
Consulate General 866 UN Plaza Suite 601	New York	NY	10017	212-980-3366	888-5288
Web: www.chileny.com					
Consulate General 870 Market St Suite 1058	San Francisco	CA	94102	415-982-7662	982-2384
Web: www.consuladochilesfo.com					
Embassy 1732 Massachusetts Ave NW	Washington	DC	20036	202-785-1746	887-5579
Web: www.chile-usa.org					
China					
Consulate General 3417 Montrose Blvd	Houston	TX	77006	713-520-1462	521-3064
Web: www.houston.china-consulate.org					
Consulate General 1450 Laguna St	San Francisco	CA	94115	415-674-2900	563-0494
Web: www.chinaconsulatesf.org					
Consulate General 100 W Erie St	Chicago	IL	60654	312-803-0095	803-0110
Web: www.chinaconsulatechicago.org					
Consulate General 520 12th Ave	New York	NY	10036	212-244-9456	
Web: www.nyconsulate.prchina.org					
Consulate General 443 Shatto Pl	Los Angeles	CA	90020	213-807-8088	807-1961
Web: www.china.visahq.com					
Embassy 2201 Wisconsin Ave NW Suite 1100	Washington	DC	20007	202-337-1956	588-9760
Web: www.china-embassy.org					
Colombia					
Consulate General 5851 San Felipe Suite 300	Houston	TX	77057	713-527-8919	529-3395
Web: www.colhouston.org					
Consulate General 500 N Michigan Ave Suite 2040	Chicago	IL	60611	312-923-1196	923-1197
Embassy 2118 Leroy Pl NW	Washington	DC	20008	202-387-8338	232-8643
Web: www.colombiaemb.org					
Embassy - Consular Section 1101 17th St NW Suite 1007	Washington	DC	20036	202-332-7573	332-7180
Web: www.colombiaemb.org					
Comoros Embassy					
866 United Nations Plaza Suite 418	New York	NY	10017	212-750-1637	750-1657
Consulate General of Argentina					
205 N Michigan Ave Suite 4208	Chicago	IL	60601	312-819-2610	819-2612
Web: www.chicago.argentinaconsul.ar					
Consulate General of Paraguay					
211 E 43rd St Suite 400	New York	NY	10017	212-682-9441	682-9443
Web: www.consulparny.com					
Consulate General of Switzerland					
633 3rd Ave 30th Fl	New York	NY	10017	212-599-5700	212-4266
Web: www.eda.admin.ch/newyork					
Consulate General of the Republic of Suriname					
6303 Blue Lagoon Dr Suite 325	Miami	FL	33126	305-265-4655	265-4599
Web: www.scgmia.com					
Costa Rica					
Consulate General 1605 W Olympic Blvd Suite 400	Los Angeles	CA	90015	213-380-7915	380-5639
Web: www.costarica-embassy.org					

	City	State	Zip	Phone	Fax
Consulate General 203 N Wabash Ave Suite 702	Chicago	IL	60601	312-263-2772	263-5807
Web: www.costarica-embassy.org					
Consulate General 3000 Wilcrest Dr Suite 112	Houston	TX	77042	713-266-0484	266-1527
Web: www.costarica-embassy.org/consular/consulates					
Consulate General 1101 Brickell Ave Suite 401 N Tower	Miami	FL	33131	305-871-7485	871-0860
Web: www.costarica-embassy.org					
Consulate General 225 W 34th St Suite 1203 Penn Plaza Blvd	New York	NY	10122	212-509-3066	509-3068
Web: www.costarica-embassy.org					
Consulate General 2114 S St NW	Washington	DC	20008	202-480-2200	265-4795
Web: www.costarica-embassy.org					
Consulate General 2112 S St NW	Washington	DC	20008	202-328-6628	265-4795
Web: www.costarica-embassy.org					
Embassy 2114 S St NW	Washington	DC	20008	202-234-2945	265-4795
Web: www.costarica-embassy.org					
Cote d'Ivoire Embassy 2424 Massachusetts Ave	Washington	DC	20008	202-797-0300	462-9444
Web: www.embaci.com					
Croatia					
Consulate General 737 N Michigan Ave Suite 1030	Chicago	IL	60611	312-482-9902	482-9987
Web: www.croatiaemb.org					
Consulate General 369 Lexington Ave	New York	NY	10017	212-599-3066	599-3106
Consulate General 11766 Wilshire Blvd Suite 1250	Los Angeles	CA	90025	310-477-1009	477-1866
Web: www.croatiaemb.org					
Embassy 2343 Massachusetts Ave NW	Washington	DC	20008	202-588-5899	588-8936
Web: www.croatiaemb.org					
Cyprus					
Consulate General 13 E 40th St	New York	NY	10016	212-686-6016	686-3660
Embassy 2211 R St NW	Washington	DC	20008	202-462-5772	483-6710
Web: www.cyprusembassy.net					
Czech Republic					
Consulate General 1109-1111 Madison Ave	New York	NY	10028	646-981-4001	981-4099
Web: www.mzv.cz/newyork					
Consulate General 10990 Wilshire Blvd Suite 1100	Los Angeles	CA	90024	310-473-0889	473-9813
Web: www.mzv.cz/losangeles					
Embassy 3900 Spring of Freedom St NW	Washington	DC	20008	202-274-9100	966-8540
Web: www.mzv.cz					
Democratic & Popular Republic of Algeria The					
Embassy - Consular Section 2118 Kalorama Rd NW	Washington	DC	20008	202-265-2800	667-2174
Web: www.embassy.org					
Denmark					
Consulate General 211 E Ontario St Suite 1800	Chicago	IL	60611	312-787-8780	787-8744
Web: www.consulatedk.org					
Consulate General 1 Dag Hammarskjold Plaza 18th Fl 885 2nd Ave	New York	NY	10017	212-223-4545	754-1904
Web: www.denmark.org					
Embassy 3200 Whitehaven St NW	Washington	DC	20008	202-234-4300	328-1470
Web: www.ambwashington.um.dk					
Dominica Embassy 3216 New Mexico Ave NW	Washington	DC	20016	202-364-6781	364-6791
Dominican Republic					
Consulate General 1715 22nd St NW	Washington	DC	20008	202-332-6280	387-2459
Web: www.domrep.org					
Consulate General 8770 W Bryn Mawr Ave Triangle Plaza	Chicago	IL	60631	773-714-4924	
Web: www.domrep.org					
Consulate General 20 Pk Plaza Statler Bldg Suite 601	Boston	MA	02116	617-482-2101	482-8133
Web: www.domrep.org					
Consulate General 1038 Brickell Ave	Miami	FL	33131	305-358-3220	358-2318
Web: www.domrep.org					
Consulate General 1501 Broadway Suite 410	New York	NY	10036	212-768-2480	768-2677
Web: www.domrep.org					
Consulate General 1516 Oak St Suite 321	Alameda	CA	94501	510-864-7777	504-6617*
**Fax Area Code: 818* ■ *Web:* www.domrep.org					
Embassy 1715 22nd St NW	Washington	DC	20008	202-332-6280	265-8057
Web: www.domrep.org					
Ecuador					
Consulate General 800 2nd Ave Suite 600	New York	NY	10017	212-808-0170	808-0188
Web: www.consulecuadornewyork.com					
Consulate General 8484 Wilshire Blvd Suite 540	Beverly Hills	CA	90211	323-658-5146	658-1198
Web: www.ecuador.org/consulates.htm					
Consulate General 400 Market St 4th Fl	Newark	NJ	07105	973-344-6900	344-0008
Web: www.consuladoecuadornj.com					
Consulate General 235 Montgomery St Suite 944	San Francisco	CA	94104	415-982-1819	982-1833
Web: www.ecuador.org/consulates.htm					
Consulate General 30 S Michigan Ave Suite 204	Chicago	IL	60603	312-338-1002	338-1502
Web: www.mmrree.gop.ec					
Consulate General 4200 Westheimer Rd Suite 218	Houston	TX	77027	713-572-8731	572-8732
Web: www.ecuador.org/consulates.htm					
Consulate General 1101 Brickell Ave Suite M102	Miami	FL	33131	305-539-8214	539-8313
Web: www.ecuador.org					
Embassy 2535 15th St NW	Washington	DC	20009	202-234-7200	234-3429
Web: www.ecuador.org					
Egypt					
Consulate General 1110 2nd Ave Suite 201	New York	NY	10022	212-759-7120	308-7643
Web: www.egyptnyc.net					
Consulate General 500 N Michigan Ave Suite 1900	Chicago	IL	60611	312-828-9162	828-9167
Web: www.eg2002.net					
Consulate General 3001 Pacific Ave	San Francisco	CA	94115	415-346-9700	346-9480
Web: www.egy2000.com					
Embassy 3521 International Ct NW	Washington	DC	20008	202-895-5400	244-4319
Web: www.egyptembassy.net					
El Salvador					
Consulate General 46 Pk Ave	New York	NY	10016	212-889-3608	679-2835
Web: www.elsalvador.org					
Consulate General 3450 Wilshire Blvd Suite 250	Los Angeles	CA	90010	213-383-8580	383-8599
Web: www.elsalvador.org					
Consulate General 1555 W Mockingbird Ln Suite 216	Dallas	TX	75235	214-637-0732	637-1106
Web: www.elsalvador.org					
Consulate General 1702 Hillendahl Blvd	Houston	TX	77055	713-270-6239	270-9683
Web: www.elsalvador.org					
Consulate General 2600 Douglas Rd Suite 104	Coral Gables	FL	33134	305-774-0840	774-0850
Web: www.elsalvador.org					
Consulate General 507 Polk St Suite 280	San Francisco	CA	94102	415-771-8524	771-8522
Embassy 1400 16th St NW Suite 100	Washington	DC	20036	202-595-7500	232-3763
Web: www.elsalvador.org					
Embassy of Hungary 3910 Shoemaker St NW	Washington	DC	20008	202-362-6730	966-8135
Web: www.huembwas.org					
Embassy of Syria 2215 Wyoming Ave NW	Washington	DC	20008	202-232-6316	265-4585
Web: www.syrianembassy.us					
Equatorial Guinea					
Embassy 2020 16th St NW	Washington	DC	20009	202-518-5700	518-5252
Eritrea Embassy 1708 New Hampshire Ave NW	Washington	DC	20009	202-319-1991	319-1304
Web: www.embassyoferitrea.com					
Estonia					
Consulate General 305 E 47th St 3 Dag Hammarskjold Pl Suite 6B	New York	NY	10016	212-883-0636	883-0648
Web: www.nyc.estemb.org					
Embassy 2131 Massachusetts Ave NW	Washington	DC	20008	202-588-0101	588-0108
Web: www.estemb.org					
Ethiopia Embassy 3506 International Dr NW	Washington	DC	20008	202-364-1200	587-0195
Web: www.ethiopianembassy.org					
Fiji Embassy 2000 M St NW Suite 710	Washington	DC	20036	202-337-8320	466-8325
Web: www.fijiembassydc.com					
Finland					
Consulate General 1801 Century Pk E Suite 2100	Los Angeles	CA	90067	310-203-9903	203-9186
Web: www.finland.org					
Consulate General 866 UN Plaza Suite 250	New York	NY	10017	212-750-4400	750-4418
Web: www.finland.org					
Embassy 3301 Massachusetts Ave NW	Washington	DC	20008	202-298-5800	298-6030
Web: www.finland.org					
France					
Consulate General 205 N Michigan Ave Suite 3700	Chicago	IL	60601	312-327-5200	327-5201
Web: www.consulfrance-chicago.org					
Consulate General 1340 Poydras St Suite 1710	New Orleans	LA	70112	504-569-2870	569-2871
Web: www.consulfrance-nouvelleorleans.org					
Consulate General 1395 Brickell Ave Suite 1050	Miami	FL	33131	305-403-4185	403-4187
Web: www.consulfrance-miami.org					
Consulate General 777 Post Oak Blvd Suite 600	Houston	TX	77056	713-572-2799	572-2911
Web: www.consulfrance-houston.org					
Consulate General 10990 Wilshire Blvd Suite 300	Los Angeles	CA	90024	310-235-3200	312-0704
Web: www.consulfrance-losangeles.org					
Consulate General 934 5th Ave	New York	NY	10021	212-606-3680	606-3614
Web: www.consulfrance-newyork.org					
Consulate General 540 Bush St	San Francisco	CA	94108	415-397-4330	433-8357
Web: www.consulfrance-sanfrancisco.org					
Consulate General 3475 Piedmont Rd NE Suite 1840	Atlanta	GA	30305	404-495-1660	495-1661
Web: www.consulfrance-atlanta.org					
Consulate General 31 St James Ave Suite 750	Boston	MA	02116	617-832-4400	
Web: www.consulfrance-boston.org					
Embassy 4101 Reservoir Rd NW	Washington	DC	20007	202-944-6000	944-6175
Web: www.ambafrance-us.org					
Gabon Embassy 2034 20th St NW	Washington	DC	20009	202-797-1000	332-0668
Gambia Embassy 1156 15th St NW Suite 905	Washington	DC	20005	202-785-1399	785-1430
Web: www.gambiaembassy.us					
Georgia Embassy 1101 15th St NW Suite 602	Washington	DC	20005	202-387-2390	393-4537
Web: www.georgiaemb.org					
Germany					
Consulate General 100 Biscayne Blvd # 2200	Miami	FL	33132	305-358-0290	358-0307
Web: www.germany.info\miami					
Consulate General 3 Copley Pl Suite 500	Boston	MA	02116	617-536-4414	536-8573
Web: www.germany.info\boston					

Name / Address	City	State	Zip	Phone	Fax
Consulate General 1330 Post Oak Blvd Suite 1850	Houston	TX	77056	713-627-7770	627-0506
Web: www.germany.info/Vertretung/usa/en/03__Consulates/Houston/00/__Home.html					
Consulate General 1960 Jackson St	San Francisco	CA	94109	415-775-1061	775-0187
Web: www.germany.info					
Consulate General 676 N Michigan Ave Suite 3200	Chicago	IL	60611	312-202-0480	202-0466
Web: www.germany.info\chicago					
Consulate General 285 Peachtree Ctr Ave NE Suite 901	Atlanta	GA	30303	404-659-4760	659-1280
Web: www.germany.info\atlanta					
Consulate General 6222 Wilshire Blvd Suite 500	Los Angeles	CA	90048	323-930-2703	930-2805
Web: www.germany.info\losangeles					
Consulate General 871 UN Plaza	New York	NY	10017	212-610-9700	610-9702
Web: www.germany.info\newyork					
Embassy 4645 Reservoir Rd NW	Washington	DC	20007	202-298-4000	298-4249
Web: www.germany-info.org					
Ghana					
Consulate General 19 E 47th St	New York	NY	10017	212-832-1300	751-6743
Embassy 3512 International Dr NW	Washington	DC	20008	202-686-4520	686-4527
Web: www.ghanaembassy.org					
Greece					
Consulate General 12424 Wilshire Blvd Suite 800	Los Angeles	CA	90025	310-826-5555	826-8670
Web: www.greekembassy.org/consular/los_angeles					
Consulate General 650 N St Clair St	Chicago	IL	60611	312-335-3915	335-3958
Web: www.greekembassy.org					
Consulate General 86 Beacon St	Boston	MA	02108	617-523-0100	523-0511
Web: www.greekembassy.org					
Consulate General 69 E 79th St	New York	NY	10021	212-988-5500	734-8492
Web: www.greekembassy.org					
Consulate General 2441 Gough St	San Francisco	CA	94123	415-775-2102	776-6815
Web: www.greekembassy.org					
Embassy 2219 Massachusetts Ave NW	Washington	DC	20008	202-939-1300	939-1324
Web: www.greekembassy.org					
Grenada					
Consulate General 800 2nd Ave Suite 400-K	New York	NY	10017	212-599-0301	599-1540
Web: www.grenadaconsulate.org					
Embassy 1701 New Hampshire Ave NW	Washington	DC	20009	202-265-2561	265-2468
Web: www.grenadaembassyusa.org					
Guatemala					
Consulate General 203 N Wabash Ave Suite 910	Chicago	IL	60601	312-332-1587	332-4256
Consulate General 3013 Fountain View Dr Suite 210	Houston	TX	77057	713-953-9531	953-9383
Consulate General 1101 Brickell Ave Suite 1003-S	Miami	FL	33131	305-679-9945	679-9983
Consulate General 57 Pk Ave	New York	NY	10016	212-686-3837	447-6947
Embassy 2220 R St NW	Washington	DC	20008	202-745-4952	745-1908
Web: www.guatemala-embassy.org					
Guinea Embassy 2112 Leroy Pl NW	Washington	DC	20008	202-986-4300	986-4800
Guyana					
Consulate General 370 7th Ave Suite 402	New York	NY	10001	212-947-5110	947-5163
Web: www.guyana.org					
Embassy 2490 Tracy Pl NW	Washington	DC	20008	202-265-6900	232-1297
Web: www.georgetown.usembassy.gov					
Haiti					
Consulate General 259 SW 13th St	Miami	FL	33130	305-859-2003	854-7441
Consulate General 271 Madison Ave 5th Fl	New York	NY	10016	212-697-9767	681-6991
Web: www.haitianconsulate-nyc.org					
Consulate General 220 S State St Suite 2110	Chicago	IL	60604	312-922-4004	922-7122
Web: www.haitianconsulate.org					
Consulate General 545 Boylston St Rm 201	Boston	MA	02116	617-266-3660	778-6898
Embassy 2311 Massachusetts Ave NW	Washington	DC	20008	202-332-4090	745-7215
Web: www.haiti.org					
Honduras					
Consulate General 4439 W Fullerton Ave	Chicago	IL	60639	773-342-8281	342-8293
Consulate General World Trade Ctr 2 Canal St Suite 2340	New Orleans	LA	70130	504-522-3118	523-0544
Consulate General 7400 harwin Dr Suite 200	Houston	TX	77036	713-785-5932	785-5931
Web: www.consulate@consuladohonduras.org					
Consulate General 3550 Wilshire Blvd Suite 410	Los Angeles	CA	90010	213-383-9244	383-9309
Web: www.consuladodehonduras.com					
Consulate General 870 Market St Suite 449	San Francisco	CA	94102	415-392-0076	392-6726
Embassy 3007 Tilden St NW Suite 4M	Washington	DC	20008	202-966-7702	966-9751
Web: www.hondurasemb.org					
Hungary Consulate General 223 E 52nd St	New York	NY	10022	212-752-0662	755-5986
Iceland					
Consulate General 800 3rd Ave 36th Fl	New York	NY	10022	212-593-2700	282-9369*
**Fax Area Code: 646* ■ *Web:* www.iceland.org					
Embassy 1156 15th St NW Suite 1200	Washington	DC	20005	202-265-6653	265-6656
Web: www.iceland.org/us					
India					
Consulate General 3 E 64th St	New York	NY	10021	212-774-0600	861-3788
Web: www.indiacgny.org					
Consulate General 540 Arguello Blvd	San Francisco	CA	94118	415-668-0662	668-9764
Web: www.cgisf.org					
Consulate General 1990 Post Oak Blvd Suite 600	Houston	TX	77056	713-626-2148	626-2450
Web: www.cgihouston.org					
Consulate General 455 N Cityfront Plaza Dr Suite 850	Chicago	IL	60611	312-595-0405	595-0417
Web: www.indianconsulate.com					
Embassy 2107 Massachusetts Ave NW	Washington	DC	20008	202-939-7000	265-4351
Web: www.indianembassy.org					
Embassy - Consular Wing 2536 Massachusetts Ave NW	Washington	DC	20008	202-939-9806	
Web: www.indianembassy.org					
Indonesia					
Consulate General 211 W Wacker Dr 8th Fl	Chicago	IL	60606	312-920-1880	920-1881
Web: www.indonesiachicago.org					
Consulate General 5 E 68th St	New York	NY	10021	212-879-0600	570-6206
Web: www.indonesianewyork.org					
Embassy 2020 Massachusetts Ave NW	Washington	DC	20036	202-775-5200	775-5365
Web: www.embassyofindonesia.org					
Iran Interests Section					
Embassy of Pakistan 2209 Wisconsin Ave NW	Washington	DC	20007	202-965-4990	965-1073
Web: www.daftar.org					
Ireland					
Consulate General 400 N Michigan Ave Suite 911	Chicago	IL	60611	312-337-1868	337-1954
Consulate General 100 Pine St 33rd Fl	San Francisco	CA	94111	415-392-4214	392-0885
Embassy 2234 Massachusetts Ave NW	Washington	DC	20008	202-462-3939	232-5993
Web: www.embassyofireland.org					
Israel					
Consulate General 1100 Spring St NW Suite 440	Atlanta	GA	30309	404-487-6500	487-6555
Web: www.israelemb.org					
Consulate General 456 Montgomery St Suite 2100	San Francisco	CA	94104	415-844-7500	844-7555
Web: www.israelemb.org					
Consulate General 111 E Wacker Dr Suite 1308	Chicago	IL	60601	312-297-4800	297-4855
Web: www.israelemb.org					
Consulate General 24 Greenway Plaza Suite 1500	Houston	TX	77046	713-627-3780	627-0149
Web: www.israelemb.org					
Consulate General 6380 Wilshire Blvd Suite 1700	Los Angeles	CA	90048	323-852-5500	852-5555
Web: www.israelemb.org					
Consulate General 100 Biscayne Blvd # 1800	Miami	FL	33132	305-925-9400	925-9451
Web: www.israelemb.org					
Consulate General 800 2nd Ave	New York	NY	10017	212-499-5300	499-5455
Web: www.israelemb.org					
Consulate General 230 S 15th St	Philadelphia	PA	19102	215-546-5556	545-3986
Web: www.israelemb.org					
Embassy 3514 International Dr NW	Washington	DC	20008	202-364-5500	364-5429
Web: www.israelemb.org					
Italy					
Consulate General 4000 Ponce de Leon Blvd Suite 590	Coral Gables	FL	33146	305-374-6322	374-7945
Web: www.consmiami.esteri.it					
Consulate General 2590 Webster St	San Francisco	CA	94115	415-292-9200	931-7205
Web: www.conssanfrancisco.esteri.it					
Consulate General 150 S Independence Mall W Public Ledger Bldg Suite 1026	Philadelphia	PA	19106	215-592-7329	592-9808
Web: www.consfiladelfia.esteri.it					
Consulate General 1300 Post Oak Blvd Suite 660	Houston	TX	77056	713-850-7520	850-9113
Web: www.conshouston.esteri.it					
Consulate General 12400 Wilshire Blvd Suite 300	Los Angeles	CA	90025	310-820-0622	820-0727
Web: www.conslosangeles.esteri.it					
Consulate General 690 Pk Ave	New York	NY	10021	212-737-9100	249-4945
Web: www.consnewyork.esteri.it					
Consulate General 600 Atlantic Ave 17th Fl	Boston	MA	02210	617-722-9201	722-9407
Web: www.consboston.esteri.it					
Embassy 3000 Whitehaven St NW	Washington	DC	20008	202-612-4400	518-2154
Web: www.ambwashingtondc.esteri.it					
Vice Consulate 1 Gateway Ctr Suite 100	Newark	NJ	07102	973-643-1448	643-3043
Web: www.consnewark.esteri.it/Consolato_Newark					
Jamaica Embassy 1520 New Hampshire Ave NW	Washington	DC	20036	202-452-0660	452-0081
Web: www.jamaicaembassy.org					
Japan					
Consulate General 350 S Grand Ave Suite 1700	Los Angeles	CA	90071	213-617-6700	617-6727
Web: www.la.us.emb-japan.go.jp					
Consulate General 3601 C St Suite 1300	Anchorage	AK	99503	907-562-8424	562-8434
Web: www.anchorage.us.emb-japan.go.jp					
Consulate General 1 Alliance Ctr 3500 Lenox Rd Suite 1600	Atlanta	GA	30326	404-240-4300	240-4311
Web: www.japanatlanta.org					
Consulate General 1742 Nuuanu Ave	Honolulu	HI	96817	808-543-3111	543-3170
Web: www.honolulu.us.emb-japan.go.jp					
Consulate General 737 N Michigan Ave Suite 1100	Chicago	IL	60611	312-280-0400	280-9568
Web: www.chicago.us.emb-japan.go.jp					
Consulate General 50 Fremont St Suite 2300	San Francisco	CA	94105	415-777-3533	974-3660
Web: www.sf.us.emb-japan.go.jp					
Consulate General 1801 W End Ave Suite 900	Nashville	TN	37203	615-340-4300	340-4311
Web: www.nashville.us.emb-japan.go.jp					

				Phone	Fax
Consulate General 400 Renaissance Ctr Suite 1600	Detroit	MI	48243	313-567-0120	567-0274
Web: www.detroit.us.emb-japan.go.jp					
Consulate General Wells Fargo Ctr 1300 SW 5th Ave Suite 2700	Portland	OR	97201	503-221-1811	224-8936
Web: www.portland.us.emb-japan.go.jp					
Consulate General 1225 17th St Suite 3000	Denver	CO	80202	303-534-1151	534-3393
Web: www.denver.us.emb-japan.go.jp					
Consulate General 909 Fannin St Suite 3000 2 Houston Ctr	Houston	TX	77010	713-652-2977	651-7822
Web: www.houston.us.emb-japan.go.jp					
Consulate General 299 Pk Ave 18th Fl	New York	NY	10171	212-371-8222	319-6357
Web: www.ny.us.emb-japan.go.jp					
Consulate General 601 Union St Suite 500	Seattle	WA	98101	206-682-9107	624-9097
Web: www.seattle.us.emb-japan.go.jp					
Consulate General 80 SW 8th St Brickell Bay View Ctr Suite 3200	Miami	FL	33130	305-530-9090	530-0950
Web: www.miami.us.emb-japan.go.jp					
Consulate General 600 Atlantic Ave Federal Reserve Plaza 14th Fl	Boston	MA	02210	617-973-9772	542-1329
Web: www.boston.us.emb-japan.go.jp					
Embassy 2520 Massachusetts Ave NW	Washington	DC	20008	202-238-6700	328-2187
Web: www.us.emb-japan.go.jp					
Jordan					
Embassy 3504 International Dr NW	Washington	DC	20008	202-966-2664	966-3110
Web: www.jordanembassyus.org					
Kazakhstan					
Consulate 305 E 47th St 3rd Fl	New York	NY	10017	212-888-3024	888-3025
Web: www.kazconsulny.org					
Embassy 1401 16th St NW	Washington	DC	20036	202-232-5488	232-5845
Web: www.kazakhembus.com					
Kenya Embassy 2249 R St NW	Washington	DC	20008	202-387-6101	462-3829
Web: www.kenyaembassy.com					
Korea Republic of					
Consulate General 335 E 45th St 4th Fl	New York	NY	10017	646-674-6000	674-6023
Web: www.usa-newyork.mofat.go.kr/eng/am/usa-newyork/main/index.jsp					
Consulate General 2320 Massachusetts Ave NW	Washington	DC	20008	202-939-5661	342-1597
Web: www.koreanembassy.com					
Consulate General 3500 Clay St	San Francisco	CA	94118	415-921-2251	921-5946
Web: www.usa-sanfranciscomofat.go.kr					
Consulate General 455 N City Front Plaza Dr NBC Tower Suite 2700	Chicago	IL	60611	312-822-9485	822-9849
Web: www.chicagoconsulate.org					
Consulate General 1990 Post Oak Blvd Suite 1250	Houston	TX	77056	713-961-0186	961-3340
Consulate General 3243 Wilshire Blvd	Los Angeles	CA	90010	213-385-9300	385-1849
Web: www.usa-losangeles.mofat.go.kr/eng/am/usa-losangeles/main/index.jsp					
Consulate General 2033 6th Ave Suite 1125	Seattle	WA	98121	206-441-1011	441-7912
Web: www.usa-seattle.mofat.go.kr/eng/am/usa-seattle/main/index.jsp					
Consulate General 229 Peachtree St NE Suite 2100 International Tower	Atlanta	GA	30303	404-522-1611	521-3169
Web: www.koreancosul.org					
Consulate General 2756 Pali Hwy	Honolulu	HI	96817	808-595-6109	595-3046
Consulate General 1 Gateway Ctr Suite 251	Newton	MA	02458	617-641-2830	641-2831
TF: 866-549-1607 ■ *Web:* www.usa-boston.mofat.go.kr					
Embassy 2320 Massachusetts Ave NW	Washington	DC	20008	202-939-5600	342-1597
Web: www.dynamic-korea.com					
Kuwait Embassy 2940 Tilden St NW	Washington	DC	20008	202-966-0702	966-0517
Kyrgyzstan Embassy 2360 Massachusetts Ave NW	Washington	DC	20008	202-449-9822	386-7550
Web: www.kyrgyzstan.org					
Lao People's Democratic Republic Embassy 2222 S St NW	Washington	DC	20008	202-332-6416	332-4923
Web: www.laoembassy.com					
Latvia Embassy 2306 Massachusetts Ave NW	Washington	DC	20008	202-328-2840	328-2860
Web: www.latvia-usa.org					
Lebanon					
Consulate General 3031 W Grand Blvd Suite 560	Detroit	MI	48202	313-758-0753	758-0756
Web: www.lebconsdet.org					
Consulate General 9 E 76th St	New York	NY	10021	212-744-7905	794-1510
Web: www.lebconsny.org					
Embassy 2560 28th St NW	Washington	DC	20008	202-939-6300	939-6324
Web: www.lebanonembassyus.org					
Lesotho Embassy 2511 Massachusetts Ave NW	Washington	DC	20008	202-797-5533	234-6815
Web: www.lesothoemb-usa.gov.ls					
Liberia					
Consulate General 866 United Nations Plaza Suite 478	New York	NY	10017	212-687-1025	599-3189
Web: www.liberiaconsulate.com					
Embassy 5201 16th St NW	Washington	DC	20011	202-723-0437	723-0436
Web: www.liberianembassyus.org					
Liechtenstein Embassy 888 17th St NW Suite 1250	Washington	DC	20006	202-331-0590	331-3221
Web: www.liechtenstein.li					
Lithuania					
Consulate General 420 5th Ave 3rd Fl	New York	NY	10018	212-354-7840	354-7911
Web: www.ltembassyus.org					
Consulate General 211 E Ontario St Suite 1500	Chicago	IL	60611	312-397-0382	397-0385
Web: www.usa.mfa.lt					
Embassy 4590 MacArthur Blvd NW Suite 200	Washington	DC	20009	202-234-5860	328-0466
Luxembourg					
Consulate General 1 Sansome St Suite 830	San Francisco	CA	94104	415-788-0816	788-0985
Web: www.luxembourgsf.org					
Consulate General 17 Beekman Pl	New York	NY	10022	212-888-6664	888-6116
Web: www.newyork-cg.mae.lu/en					
Embassy 2200 Massachusetts Ave NW	Washington	DC	20008	202-265-4171	328-8270
Web: www.luxembourg-usa.org					
Macedonia Embassy 2129 Wyoming Ave	Washington	DC	20008	202-667-0501	667-2131
Web: www.macedoniaembassy.org					
Madagascar Embassy 2374 Massachusetts Ave NW	Washington	DC	20008	202-265-5525	265-3034
Malawi Embassy 1156 15th St NW Suite 320	Washington	DC	20005	202-721-0270	721-0288
Malaysia					
Consulate General 313 E 43rd St	New York	NY	10017	212-490-2722	490-2049
Web: www.kln.gov.my/web/usa_new-york/home					
Consulate General 550 S Hope St Suite 400	Los Angeles	CA	90071	213-892-1238	892-9031
Web: www.malaysianconsulatela.com					
Embassy 3516 International Ct NW	Washington	DC	20008	202-572-9700	572-9882
Mali Embassy 2130 R St NW	Washington	DC	20008	202-332-2249	332-6603
Web: www.maliembassy.us					
Malta Embassy 2017 Connecticut Ave NW	Washington	DC	20008	202-462-3611	387-5470
Marshall Islands Embassy 2433 Massachusetts Ave NW	Washington	DC	20008	202-234-5414	232-3236
Web: www.rmiembassyus.org					
Mauritania Embassy 2129 Leroy Pl NW	Washington	DC	20008	202-232-5700	319-2623
Mauritius Embassy 1709 N St NW Suite 441	Washington	DC	20008	202-244-1491	966-0983
Web: www.maurinet.com/embasydc.html					
Mexico					
Consulate General 4506 Carolinas St	Houston	TX	77004	713-271-6800	271-3201
Web: www.sre.gob.mx					
Consulate General 1700 Chantilly Dr NE	Atlanta	GA	30324	404-266-2233	266-2302
Web: www.portal.sre.gob.mx/atlanta					
Consulate General 20 Pk Plaza Suite 506	Boston	MA	02116	617-426-4942	695-1957
TF: 800-601-1289 ■ *Web:* www.sre.gob.mx/boston					
Consulate General 571 N Grand Ave	Nogales	AZ	85621	520-287-2521	287-3175
Web: www.sre.gob.mx					
Consulate General 800 Brazos St Suite 330	Austin	TX	78701	512-478-2866	478-8008
Web: www.sre.gob.mx					
Consulate General 1010 8th St	Sacramento	CA	95814	916-441-3287	441-3176
Web: www.mexico.us/consulate.htm					
Consulate General 1549 India St	San Diego	CA	92101	619-231-8414	
Web: www.mexico.us/consulate.htm					
Consulate General 910 E San Antonio St	El Paso	TX	79901	915-533-3644	532-7163
Web: www.sre.gob.mx					
Consulate General 127 Navarro St	San Antonio	TX	78205	210-227-9145	227-9817
Web: www.consulmexsat.org					
Consulate General 1612 Farragut St	Laredo	TX	78040	956-723-0990	723-1741
Web: www.sre.gob.mx					
Consulate General 1990 W Camelback Rd Suite 110	Phoenix	AZ	85015	602-242-7398	242-2957
Web: www.sre.gob.mx					
Consulate General 540 N 1st St	San Jose	CA	95112	408-294-3414	294-4506
Web: www.consulmexsj.com					
Consulate General 5350 Leesdale Dr	Denver	CO	80246	303-331-1110	331-1872
Web: www.consulmex-denver.com					
Consulate General 204 S Ashland Ave	Chicago	IL	60607	312-855-1380	
Web: www.consulmexchicago.com					
Consulate General 27 E 39th St	New York	NY	10016	212-217-6400	217-6493
Web: www.consulmexny.org					
Consulate General 5975 SW 72nd St Suite 101	Miami	FL	33143	786-268-4900	268-4875
Web: www.sre.gob.mx					
Consulate General 532 Folsom St	San Francisco	CA	94105	415-392-5554	495-3971
Consulate General 2401 W 6th St	Los Angeles	CA	90057	213-351-6800	
Web: www.sre.gob.mx/losangeles					
Embassy 1911 Pennsylvania Ave NW	Washington	DC	20006	202-728-1600	728-1766
Web: portal.sre.gob.mx/usa					
Micronesia					
Consulate 3049 Ualena St Suite 910	Honolulu	HI	96819	808-836-4775	836-6896
Embassy 1725 N St NW	Washington	DC	20036	202-223-4383	223-4391
Moldova Embassy 2101 S St NW	Washington	DC	20008	202-667-1130	667-1204
Web: www.embassy.org					
Mongolia Embassy 2833 M St NW	Washington	DC	20007	202-333-7117	298-9227
Web: www.mongolianembassy.us					
Montenegro					
Consulate General 801 2nd Ave 7th Fl	New York	NY	10017	212-661-5400	661-5466
Morocco					
Consulate General 10 E 40th St 24th Fl	New York	NY	10016	212-758-2625	779-7441
Web: www.moroccanconsulate.com					
Embassy 1601 21st St NW	Washington	DC	20009	202-462-7980	462-7643
Web: www.dcusa.themoroccanembassy.com					
Mozambique Embassy 1525 New Hampshire Ave NW	Washington	DC	20036	202-293-7146	835-0245
Web: www.embamoc-usa.org					
Myanmar Embassy 2300 S St NW	Washington	DC	20008	202-332-3344	332-4351
Web: www.mewashingtondc.com					
Nepal					
Consulate General 820 2nd Ave Suite 17B	New York	NY	10017	212-370-3988	953-2038
Embassy 2131 Leroy Pl NW	Washington	DC	20008	202-667-4550	667-5534
Web: www.nepalembassyusa.org					

	City	State	ZIP	Phone	Fax
Netherlands					
Consulate General 1 Rockefeller Plaza 11th Fl	New York	NY	10020	212-246-1429	333-3603
TF: 877-388-2443 ■ *Web:* www.ny.the-netherlands.org					
Consulate General 701 Brickell Ave 5th Fl	Miami	FL	33131	786-866-0480	866-0497
TF: 877-388-2443 ■ *Web:* www.miami.the-netherlands.org					
Consulate General 303 E Wacker Dr Suite 2600	Chicago	IL	60601	312-856-0110	856-9218
TF: 877-388-2443 ■ *Web:* www.chicago.the-netherlands.org					
Embassy 4200 Linnean Ave NW	Washington	DC	20008	877-388-2443	362-3430*
**Fax Area Code:* 202 ■ *TF:* 877-388-2443 ■ *Web:* www.netherlands-embassy.org					
New Zealand					
Consulate General 222 E 41st St Suite 2510	New York	NY	10017	212-832-4038	832-7602
Consulate General 2425 Olympic Blvd Suite 600-E	Santa Monica	CA	90404	310-566-6555	566-6556
Web: www.nzcgla.com					
Embassy 37 Observatory Cir NW	Washington	DC	20008	202-328-4800	667-5227
Web: www.nzembassy.com					
Nicaragua					
Consulate General 8989 Westheimer St Suite 103	Houston	TX	77063	713-789-2762	789-3164
Consulate General 8532 SW 8th St Suite 270	Miami	FL	33144	305-265-1415	265-1780
Consulate General 820 2nd Ave Suite 802	New York	NY	10017	212-986-6562	983-2646
Embassy 1627 New Hampshire Ave NW	Washington	DC	20009	202-939-6570	939-6542
Niger Embassy 2204 R St NW	Washington	DC	20008	202-483-4224	483-3169
Nigeria					
Consulate General 828 2nd Ave	New York	NY	10017	212-850-2200	687-1476
Web: www.nigeriahouse.com					
Embassy 3519 International Ct NW	Washington	DC	20008	202-986-8400	362-6981
Web: www.nigeriaembassyusa.org					
Norway					
Consulate General 3410 W Dallas St	Houston	TX	77019	713-620-4200	620-4290
Web: www.norway.org/Embassy					
Consulate General 20 California St 6th Fl	San Francisco	CA	94111	415-986-0766	986-3318
Web: www.norway.org/embassy					
Consulate General 901 Marquette Ave Suite 2750	Minneapolis	MN	55402	612-332-3338	332-1386
Web: www.norway.org					
Consulate General 825 3rd Ave 38th Fl	New York	NY	10022	212-421-7333	754-0583
Web: www.norway.org/embassy					
Embassy 2720 34th St NW	Washington	DC	20008	202-333-6000	337-0870
Web: www.norway.org					
Oman Embassy 2535 Belmont Rd NW	Washington	DC	20008	202-387-1980	745-4933
Pakistan					
Consulate General 10850 Wilshire Blvd Suite 1250	Los Angeles	CA	90024	310-441-5114	441-9256
Web: www.pakconsulatela.org					
Consulate General 12 E 65th St	New York	NY	10065	212-879-5800	517-6987
Web: www.pakistanconsulateny.org					
Embassy 3517 International Ct NW	Washington	DC	20008	202-243-6500	686-1534
Web: www.embassyofpakistanusa.org					
Palau Embassy 1700 Pennsylvania Ave NW Suite 400	Washington	DC	20006	202-349-8598	349-8597
Panama					
Consulate General 2424 World Trade Ctr 1100 Poydras St	New Orleans	LA	70163	504-525-3458	524-8960
Web: www.consulateofpanama.com					
Consulate General 5775 Blue Lagoon Dr Suite 200	Miami	FL	33126	305-447-3700	447-4142
Embassy 2862 McGill Terr NW	Washington	DC	20008	202-483-1407	483-8413
Web: www.embassyofpanama.org/cms/index3.php					
Papua New Guinea Embassy 1779 Massachusetts Ave NW Suite 805	Washington	DC	20036	202-745-3680	745-3679
Web: www.pngembassy.org					
Paraguay					
Consulate General 25 SE 2nd Ave Ingraham Bldg Suite 705	Miami	FL	33131	305-374-9090	374-5522
Web: www.paraguaymiami.org					
Embassy 2400 Massachusetts Ave NW	Washington	DC	20008	202-483-6960	234-4508
Web: www.paraguayembassy.in					
Peru					
Consulate General 100 Hamilton Plaza Suite 1221	Paterson	NJ	07505	973-278-3324	278-0254
Web: www.consuladoperu.com					
Consulate General 870 Market St Suite 1067	San Francisco	CA	94102	415-362-7136	362-2836
Web: www.consuladoperu.com					
Consulate General 1001 S Monaco Pkwy Suite 210	Denver	CO	80224	303-355-8555	355-8555
Web: www.consuladoperu.com					
Consulate General 20 Pk Plaza Suite 511	Boston	MA	02116	617-338-2227	338-2742
Web: www.consuladoperu.com					
Consulate General 5177 Richmond Ave Suite 695	Houston	TX	77056	713-355-9517	355-9377
Web: www.consuladoperu.com					
Consulate General 3450 Wilshire Blvd Suite 800	Los Angeles	CA	90010	213-252-5910	252-8130
Web: www.consuladoperu.com					
Consulate General 444 Brickell Ave Suite M135	Miami	FL	33131	305-374-1305	381-6027
Web: www.consuladoperu.com					
Consulate General 180 N Michigan Ave Suite 1830	Chicago	IL	60601	312-782-1599	704-6969
Web: www.consuladoperu.com					
Consulate General 241 E 49th St	New York	NY	10017	646-735-3828	735-3866
Web: www.consuladoperu.com					
Embassy 1700 Massachusetts Ave NW	Washington	DC	20036	202-833-9860	659-8124
Web: www.peruvianembassy.us					
Philippines					
Consulate General 30 N Michigan Ave Suite 2100	Chicago	IL	60602	312-332-6458	332-3657
Web: www.chicagopcg.com					
Consulate General 447 Sutter St 6th Fl Philippine Ctr Bldg	San Francisco	CA	94108	415-433-6666	421-2641
Web: www.philippines.visahq.com					
Consulate General 3600 Wilshire Blvd Suite 500	Los Angeles	CA	90010	213-639-0980	639-0990
Web: www.pcgenla.org					
Consulate General 556 5th Ave	New York	NY	10036	212-764-1330	382-1146
Web: www.pcgny.net					
Embassy 1600 Massachusetts Ave NW	Washington	DC	20036	202-467-9300	328-9417
Web: www.philippineembassy-usa.org					
Poland					
Consulate General 233 Madison Ave	New York	NY	10016	212-561-8160	237-2105*
**Fax Area Code:* 646 ■ *Web:* www.polandconsulateny.com					
Consulate General 820 N Orleans St Suite 335	Chicago	IL	60610	312-337-8166	337-7841
Web: www.polishconsulatechicago.org					
Consulate General 12400 Wilshire Blvd Suite 555	Los Angeles	CA	90025	310-442-8500	442-8515
Web: www.polishconsulatela.com					
Embassy 2640 16th St NW	Washington	DC	20009	202-234-3800	328-6271
Web: www.polandembassy.org					
Qatar					
Consulate General 1990 Post Oak Blvd Suite 810	Houston	TX	77056	713-355-8221	355-8184
Embassy 2555 M St NW	Washington	DC	20037	202-274-1600	237-0061
Web: www.qatarembassy.net					
Romania					
Consulate General 11766 Wilshire Blvd Suite 560	Los Angeles	CA	90025	310-444-0043	445-0043
Web: www.consulateromania.org					
Consulate General 200 E 38th St	New York	NY	10016	212-682-9122	972-8463
Web: www.newyork.mae.ro					
Embassy 1607 23rd St NW	Washington	DC	20008	202-332-2879	232-4748
Web: www.washington.mae.ro					
Russia					
Consulate General 2790 Green St	San Francisco	CA	94123	415-928-6878	929-0306
Web: www.consulrussia.org					
Consulate General 2001 6th Ave Westin Bldg Suite 1705	Seattle	WA	98121	206-441-1106	441-1164
Web: www.netconsul.org					
Consulate General 9 E 91st St	New York	NY	10128	212-348-0926	831-9162
Embassy 2650 Wisconsin Ave NW	Washington	DC	20007	202-298-5700	298-5735
Web: www.russianembassy.org					
Rwanda Embassy 1714 New Hampshire Ave NW	Washington	DC	20009	202-232-2882	232-4544
Web: www.rwandaembassy.org					
Saint Kitts & Nevis Embassy 3216 New Mexico Ave NW	Washington	DC	20016	202-686-2636	686-5740
Web: www.stkittsnevis.org					
Saint Lucia					
Consulate General 800 2nd Ave 9th Fl	New York	NY	10017	212-697-9360	697-4993
Web: www.un.int/stlucia/consulate.htm					
Embassy 3216 New Mexico Ave NW	Washington	DC	20016	202-364-6792	364-6723
Saint Vincent & the Grenadines					
Consulate General 801 2nd Ave 21st Fl	New York	NY	10017	212-687-4490	949-5946
Embassy 3216 New Mexico Ave NW	Washington	DC	20016	202-364-6730	364-6736
Web: www.embsvg.com					
Saudi Arabia					
Consulate General 5718 Westheimer Rd Suite 1500	Houston	TX	77057	713-785-5577	273-6937
Web: www.saudiembassy.net					
Consulate General 866 2nd Ave 5th Fl	New York	NY	10017	212-752-2740	688-2719
Web: www.saudiembassy.net					
Embassy 601 New Hampshire Ave NW	Washington	DC	20037	202-342-3800	944-5983
Web: www.saudiembassy.net					
Senegal Embassy 2112 Wyoming Ave NW	Washington	DC	20008	202-234-0540	332-6315
Web: www.senegalembassy-us.org					
Serbia					
Consulate General 201 E Ohio St Suite 200	Chicago	IL	60611	312-670-6707	670-6787
Web: www.scgchicago.org					
Embassy 2134 Kalorama Rd NW	Washington	DC	20008	202-332-0333	332-3933
Web: www.serbiaembusa.org					
Seychelles Embassy 800 2nd Ave Suite 400C	New York	NY	10017	212-972-1785	972-1786
Singapore					
Consulate General 595 Market St Suite 2450	San Francisco	CA	94105	415-543-4775	543-4788
Web: www.mfa.gov.sg					
Embassy 3501 International Pl NW	Washington	DC	20008	202-537-3100	537-0876
Web: www.mfa.gov.sg					
Slovakia Embassy 3523 International Ct NW	Washington	DC	20008	202-237-1054	237-6438
Web: www.slovakembassy-us.org					
Slovenia					
Consulate General 120 E 56th St Suite 320	New York	NY	10022	212-370-3006	370-3581
Web: www.embassy.org					
Embassy 2410 California St NW	Washington	DC	20036	202-386-6601	386-6633
Web: washington.embassy.si					

Entry	City	State	ZIP	Phone	Fax
South Africa					
Consulate General 333 E 38th St 9th Fl	New York	NY	10016	212-213-4880	213-0102
Web: www.southafrica-newyork.net					
Consulate General 200 S Michigan Ave Suite 600	Chicago	IL	60604	312-939-7929	939-2588
Web: www.southafricachicago.com					
Embassy 3051 Massachusetts Ave NW	Washington	DC	20008	202-232-4400	265-1607
Web: www.saembassy.org					
South African Consulate-General 6300 Wilshire Blvd Suite 600	Los Angeles	CA	90048	323-651-0902	323-5969
Web: www.link2southafrica.com					
Spain					
Consulate General 150 E 58th St 30th Fl	New York	NY	10155	212-355-4080	644-3751
Consulate General 1405 Sutter St	San Francisco	CA	94109	415-922-2995	931-9706
Consulate General 2655 Le Jeune Rd Suite 203	Miami	FL	33134	305-446-5511	446-0585
Web: www.conspainmiami.org					
Consulate General 180 N Michigan Ave Suite 1500	Chicago	IL	60601	312-782-4588	782-1635
Web: www.consulate-spain-chicago.com					
Embassy 2375 Pennsylvania Ave NW	Washington	DC	20037	202-452-0100	833-5670
Web: www.maec.es/subwebs/embajadas/Washington/es/home/Paginas/Home.aspx					
Sri Lanka					
Consulate General 3250 Wilshire Blvd Suite 1405	Los Angeles	CA	90010	213-387-0210	387-0216
Web: www.srilankaconsulatela.com					
Embassy 2148 Wyoming Ave NW	Washington	DC	20008	202-483-4025	232-7181
Web: www.slembassyusa.org					
Sudan Embassy 2210 Massachusetts Ave NW	Washington	DC	20008	202-338-8565	667-2406
Web: www.sudanembassy.org					
Suriname Embassy 4301 Connecticut Ave NW Suite 460	Washington	DC	20008	202-244-7488	244-5878
Web: www.surinameembassy.org					
Sweden					
Consulate General 10940 Wilshire Blvd Suite 700	Los Angeles	CA	90024	310-445-4008	473-2229
Web: www.swedenabroad.se					
Consulate General 120 Montgomery St Suite 2175	San Francisco	CA	94104	415-788-2631	788-6841
Web: www.swedenabroad.com					
Consulate General 445 Park Ave Fl 21	New York	NY	10022	212-888-3000	888-3125
Web: www.swedenabroad.com					
Embassy 2900 K St NW	Washington	DC	20007	202-467-2600	467-2699
Web: www.swedenabroad.com					
Switzerland					
Consulate General 456 Montgomery St Suite 1500	San Francisco	CA	94104	415-788-2272	788-1402
Web: www.eda.admin.ch/washington_emb					
Consulate General 737 N Michigan Ave Suite 2301	Chicago	IL	60611	312-915-0061	915-0388
Web: www.eda.admin.ch/chicago					
Consulate General 11766 Wilshire Blvd Suite 1400	Los Angeles	CA	90025	310-575-1145	575-1982
Web: www.eda.admin.ch/losangeles					
Consulate General 1349 W Peachtree St Suite 1000 2 Mid-Town Plaza	Atlanta	GA	30309	404-870-2000	870-2011
Web: www.eda.admin.ch/washington_emb					
Embassy 2900 Cathedral Ave NW	Washington	DC	20008	202-745-7900	387-2564
Web: www.swissemb.org					
Tajikistan Embassy 1725 K St NW	Washington	DC	20006	202-223-6090	223-6091
Web: www.tjus.org					
Tanzania Embassy 1232 22nd St NW	Washington	DC	20037	202-939-6125	797-7408
Web: www.tanzaniaembassy-us.org					
Thailand					
Consulate General 611 N Larchmont Blvd 2nd Fl	Los Angeles	CA	90004	323-962-9574	962-2128
Web: www.thaiconsulatela.org					
Consulate General 351 E 52nd St	New York	NY	10022	212-754-1770	754-1907
Web: www.thaiconsulnewyork.com					
Embassy 1024 Wisconsin Ave NW Suite 401	Washington	DC	20007	202-944-3600	944-3611
Web: www.thaiembdc.org					
Togo Embassy 2208 Massachusetts Ave NW	Washington	DC	20008	202-234-4212	232-3190
Web: www.togoembassy.us					
Tonga Consulate General 360 Post St Suite 604	San Francisco	CA	94108	415-781-0365	781-3964
Web: www.tongaconsulate.com					
Trinidad & Tobago Embassy 1708 Massachusetts Ave NW	Washington	DC	20036	202-467-6490	785-3130
Web: www.ttembassy.com					
Turkey					
Consulate General 6300 Wilshire Blvd Suite 2010	Los Angeles	CA	90048	323-655-8832	655-8681
Web: www.turkishembassy.org					
Consulate General 360 N Michigan Ave Suite 1405	Chicago	IL	60601	312-263-0644	263-1449
Web: www.turkishembassy.org					
Consulate General 1990 Post Oak Blvd Suite 1300	Houston	TX	77056	713-622-5849	623-6639
TF: 888-566-7656 ■ *Web:* www.turkishembassy.org					
Consulate General 821 UN Plaza 5th Fl	New York	NY	10017	212-949-0160	983-1293
Web: www.turkishconsulateny.org					
Embassy 2525 Massachusetts Ave NW	Washington	DC	20008	202-612-6700	319-1639
Web: www.turkishembassy.org					
Turkmenistan					
Embassy 2207 Massachusetts Ave NW	Washington	DC	20008	202-588-1500	280-1003
Web: www.turkmenistanembassy.org					
Uganda Embassy 5911 16th St NW	Washington	DC	20011	202-726-7100	726-1727
Web: www.ugandaembassy.com					
Ukraine					
Consulate General 10 E Huron St	Chicago	IL	60611	312-642-4388	642-4385
Web: www.ukrchicago.com					
Embassy 3350 M St NW	Washington	DC	20007	202-333-0606	333-0817
TF: 800-779-8347 ■ *Web:* www.ukremb.com					
United Arab Emirates Embassy 3522 International Ct NW	Washington	DC	20008	202-243-2400	243-2432
Web: www.uae-embassy.org					
United Kingdom					
Consulate General 1 Sansome St Suite 850	San Francisco	CA	94104	415-617-1300	434-2018
Web: www.britainusa.com					
Consulate General 1001 Brickell Bay Dr Suite 2800	Miami	FL	33131	305-374-3500	374-8196
Web: www.britainusa.com/miami					
Consulate General 1 Memorial Dr Suite 1500	Cambridge	MA	02142	617-245-4500	621-0220
Web: www.britainusa.com					
Consulate General 400 N Michigan Ave Suite 1300	Chicago	IL	60611	312-970-3800	970-3854
Web: www.britainusa.com					
Consulate General 133 Peachtree St NE	Atlanta	GA	30303	404-954-7700	954-7702
Web: www.britainusa.com					
Consulate General 1000 Louisiana St Suite 1900	Houston	TX	77002	713-659-6270	659-7094
Web: www.britainusa.com					
Consulate General 11766 Wilshire Blvd Suite 1200	Los Angeles	CA	90025	310-481-0031	481-2960
Web: www.britainusa.com					
Consulate General 845 3rd Ave	New York	NY	10022	212-745-0200	754-3062
Web: www.britainusa.com					
Embassy 3100 Massachusetts Ave NW	Washington	DC	20008	202-588-6500	588-7870
Web: www.britainusa.com					
Uruguay					
Consulate General 420 Madison Ave 6th Fl	New York	NY	10017	212-753-8581	753-1603
Web: www.conuruyork.org					
Consulate General 429 Santa Monica Blvd Suite 400	Santa Monica	CA	90401	310-394-5777	394-5140
Web: www.conurula.org					
Embassy 1913 'I' St NW	Washington	DC	20006	202-331-1313	331-8142
Web: www.mrree.gub.uy/gxpsites/hgxpp001?7,7,442,O,S,0,MNU;E;309;1;MNU					
Uzbekistan					
Consulate General 801 2nd Ave 20th Fl	New York	NY	10017	212-754-7403	
Web: www.uzbekconsulny.org					
Embassy 1746 Massachusetts Ave NW	Washington	DC	20036	202-887-5300	293-6804
Web: www.uzbekistan.org					
Venezuela					
Consulate General 2401 Fountain View Dr	Houston	TX	77057	713-974-0028	974-1413
Web: www.consulvenhou.org					
Consulate General World Trade Ctr 2 Canal St Suite 2300	New Orleans	LA	70130	504-522-3284	522-7092
Web: www.embavenez-us.org/_neworleans					
Consulate General 7 E 51st St	New York	NY	10022	212-826-1660	644-7471
Web: www.consulado-ny.gov.ve					
Consulate General 545 Boylston St 3rd Fl	Boston	MA	02116	617-266-9368	266-2350
Embassy 1099 30th St NW	Washington	DC	20007	202-342-2214	342-6820
Web: www.embavenez-us.org					
Vietnam					
Consulate General 1700 California St Suite 580	San Francisco	CA	94109	415-922-1707	922-1848
Web: www.vietnamconsulate-sf.org					
Embassy 1233 20th St NW Suite 400	Washington	DC	20036	202-861-0737	861-0917
Web: www.vietnamembassy.us					
Yemen Embassy 2319 Wyoming Ave NW	Washington	DC	20008	202-965-4760	337-2017
Web: www.yemenembassy.org					
Zambia Embassy 2419 Massachusetts Ave NW	Washington	DC	20008	202-265-9717	332-0826
Web: www.zambiaembassy.org					
Zimbabwe Embassy 1608 New Hampshire Ave NW	Washington	DC	20009	202-332-7100	483-9326
Web: www.zimbabwe-embassy.us					

261 EMBROIDERY & OTHER DECORATIVE STITCHING

Entry	City	State	ZIP	Phone	Fax
Branded Emblem Co Inc 7920 Foster St	Overland Park	KS	66204	913-648-7920	648-7444
TF: 800-747-7920 ■ *Web:* www.brandedemblem.com					
Carolace Embroidery Co Inc 65 Railroad Ave Unit 3	Ridgefield	NJ	07657	201-945-2151	943-1990
Web: www.carolace.com					
CR Daniels Inc 3451 Ellicott Ctr Dr	Ellicott City	MD	21043	410-461-2100	461-2987
TF: 800-933-2638 ■ *Web:* www.crdaniels.com					
EmbroidMe Inc 2121 Vista Pkwy	West Palm Beach	FL	33411	561-640-7367	640-6062
TF: 877-877-0234 ■ *Web:* www.embroidme.com					
Fabri-Quilt Inc 901 E 14th Ave PO Box 12479	North Kansas City	MO	64116	816-421-2000	471-2853
TF: 800-279-0622 ■ *Web:* www.fabri-quilt.com					

				Phone	Fax
Herrschners Inc 2800 Hoover Rd *TF:* 800-713-1239 ■ *Web:* www.herrschners.com	Stevens Point	WI	54481	715-342-0741	341-2250
Jubilee Embroidery Co Inc 411 Hwy 601	Lugoff	SC	29078	803-438-2934	438-3733
Kasbar National Industries Inc 370 Reed Rd Suite 200 *Web:* www.kasbarnational.com	Broomall	PA	19008	610-544-7117	544-9799
Lion Bros Co Inc 10246 Reisterstown Rd *TF Cust Svc:* 800-365-6543 ■ *Web:* www.lionbrothers.com	Owings Mills	MD	21117	410-363-1000	363-0181
Luv N' Care Ltd 2805 St Charles Ave *TF:* 800-588-6227 ■ *Web:* www.luvncare.com	Monroe	LA	71201	318-388-4916	323-1899
Moritz Embroidery Works Inc 1455 Industrial Pk PO Box 187 *TF:* 800-533-4183 ■ *Web:* www.moritzembroidery.com	Mount Pocono	PA	18344	570-839-9600	839-9430
National Emblem Inc 17036 S Avalon Blvd *TF:* 800-877-6185 ■ *Web:* www.nationalemblem.com	Carson	CA	90746	310-515-5055	515-5966
Penn Emblem Co 10909 Dutton Rd *TF:* 800-793-7366 ■ *Web:* www.pennemblem.com	Philadelphia	PA	19154	215-632-7800	632-6166
Saint Louis Embroidery 1759 Scherer Pkwy *TF:* 800-423-0450	Saint Charles	MO	63303	636-724-2200	946-3296
Schweizer Emblem Co 1022 Busse Hwy *TF Cust Svc:* 800-942-5215 ■ *Web:* www.schweizer-emblem.com	Park Ridge	IL	60068	847-292-1022	292-1028
Superior Pleating & Stitching 3671 E Olympic Blvd	Los Angeles	CA	90023	323-261-3964	261-0122

262 EMPLOYMENT OFFICES - GOVERNMENT

				Phone	Fax
Employment & Training Administration 200 Constitution Ave NW Rm S2307 *Web:* www.doleta.gov	Washington	DC	20210	202-693-2700	693-2725
US Dept of Labor 200 Constitution Ave NW *Web:* www.dol.gov/vets	Washington	DC	20210	202-693-4700	693-4754
Alaska Employment Security Div PO Box 25509 *Web:* www.labor.state.ak.us/esd/home.htm	Juneau	AK	99802	907-465-2712	465-4537
Arizona Employment Administration PO Box 6123 *Web:* www.azdes.gov	Phoenix	AZ	85005	602-542-3957	542-2491
Arkansas Dept of Workforce Services 2 Capitol Mall *Web:* www.arkansas.gov	North Little Rock	AR	72201	501-682-2121	682-2273
California Employment Development Dept 800 Capitol Mall MIC 83 *Web:* www.edd.ca.gov	Sacramento	CA	95814	916-654-8210	657-5294
Colorado Labor & Employment Dept 633 17th St Suite 201 *TF:* 800-390-7936 ■ *Web:* www.coworkforce.com	Denver	CO	80203	303-318-8000	
Connecticut Labor Dept 200 Folly Brook Blvd *Web:* www.ctdol.state.ct.us	Wethersfield	CT	06109	860-263-6000	263-6699
Delaware Employment & Training Div 4425 N Market St *Web:* www.delawareworks.com	Wilmington	DE	19802	302-761-8085	
DEW's Columbia Campus 1550 Gadsden St PO Box 995 *Web:* www.sces.org	Columbia	SC	29202	803-737-2400	737-2642
Employment Services Dept 4049 S Capitol St SW *TF:* 877-319-7346 ■ *Web:* www.does.ci.washington.dc.us	Washington	DC	20032	202-724-7000	673-6994
Florida Workforce Florida Inc 1580 Waldo Palmer Ln Suite 1 *Web:* www.workforceflorida.com	Tallahassee	FL	32303	850-921-1119	921-1101
Georgia Employment Services Div 148 Andrew Young International Blvd NE *Web:* www.dol.state.ga.us	Atlanta	GA	30303	404-232-3515	
Hawaii Workforce Development Div 830 Punchbowl St Rm 209 *Web:* www.hawaii.gov	Honolulu	HI	96813	808-586-8877	586-8822
Idaho Labor Dept 317 W Main St *Web:* www.labor.idaho.gov/dnn/Default.aspx?alias=labor.idaho.gov/dnn/idl	Boise	ID	83735	208-332-3570	334-6300
Indiana Workforce Development Dept 10 N Senate Ave *TF:* 800-891-6499 ■ *Web:* www.in.gov	Indianapolis	IN	46204	317-232-7670	233-4793
Iowa Workforce Development 1000 E Grand Ave *TF:* 800-562-4692 ■ *Web:* www.iowaworkforce.org	Des Moines	IA	50319	515-281-5387	281-4698
Kansas Labor Dept 401 SW Topeka Blvd	Topeka	KS	66603	785-296-5000	296-1926
Kentucky Workforce Investment Dept 500 Mero St 20th Fl *Web:* www.workforce.ky.gov	Frankfort	KY	40601	502-564-4286	564-7967
Louisiana Labor Dept 1001 N 23rd St *TF:* 877-529-6757 ■ *Web:* www.laworks.net	Baton Rouge	LA	70802	225-342-3111	
Maine Employment Services Bureau 45 Commerce Dr *Web:* www.mainecareercenter.com	Augusta	ME	04330	207-623-7981	287-5933
Maryland Workforce Development Div 1100 N Eutaw St Rm 616 *Web:* www.dllr.state.md.us/employment	Baltimore	MD	21201	410-767-2400	767-2986
Massachusetts Workforce Development Dept 1 Ashburton Pl Rm 2112 *Web:* www.mass.gov	Boston	MA	02108	617-626-7100	727-1090
Michigan Career Education & Workforce Programs 201 N Washington Sq 3rd Fl *TF:* 888-253-6855 ■ *Web:* www.michigan.gov/mdcd	Lansing	MI	48913	517-241-4000	373-0314
Minnesota Public Safety Dept 444 Cedar St Town Sq Bldg *Web:* www.dps.state.mn.us	Saint Paul	MN	55101	651-201-7000	
Mississippi Employment Security Commission 1235 Echelon Pkwy PO Box 1699 *TF:* 888-844-3577 ■ *Web:* www.mdes.ms.gov	Jackson	MS	39215	601-321-6000	321-6004
Missouri Div of Employment Security 421 E Dunklin St PO Box 59 *Web:* www.labor.mo.gov	Jefferson City	MO	65104	573-751-7500	751-6552
Montana Workforce Services Div PO Box 1728 *Web:* wsd.dli.mt.gov	Helena	MT	59624	406-444-4100	444-3037
Nebraska Workforce Development - Dept of Labor 550 S 16th St PO Box 94600 *Web:* www.dol.nebraska.gov	Lincoln	NE	68508	402-471-9000	471-2318
Nevada Dept of Employment Training & Rehabilitation 500 E 3rd St Rm 200 *Web:* www.nvdetr.org	Carson City	NV	89713	775-684-3911	684-3908
New Hampshire Employment Security (NHES) 32 S Main St *TF:* 800-852-3400 ■ *Web:* www.nh.gov	Concord	NH	03301	603-224-3311	228-4145
New Jersey Workforce New Jersey PO Box 110 *Web:* www.wnjpin.net	Trenton	NJ	08625	609-292-2000	777-0483
New Mexico Dept of Workforce Solutions 301 W DeVargas *Web:* www.dws.state.nm.us	Santa Fe	NM	87501	505-827-7434	827-7346
New York Labor Dept WA Harriman Campus Bldg 12 *TF:* 888-469-7365 ■ *Web:* www.labor.state.ny.us	Albany	NY	12240	518-457-9000	457-6908
North Carolina Employment Security Commission PO Box 25903 *Web:* www.ncesc.com	Raleigh	NC	27611	919-733-4329	733-8745
North Dakota Job Service PO Box 5507 *TF:* 800-366-6888 ■ *Web:* www.jobsnd.com	Bismarck	ND	58506	701-328-2825	328-4000
Ohio Workforce Developement Office 4020 E 5th Ave *TF:* 800-342-4784 ■ *Web:* www.ohioworkforce.org	Columbus	OH	43216	614-752-3091	995-1298
Oklahoma Employment Security Commission 2401 N Lincoln Blvd Suite 504 *TF:* 888-900-9675 ■ *Web:* www.oesc.state.ok.us	Oklahoma City	OK	73105	405-557-7100	557-5355
Oregon Employment Dept 875 Union St NE *Web:* egov.oregon.gov/EMPLOY	Salem	OR	97311	503-451-2400	947-1472
Pennsylvania Workforce Investment Board 901 N 7th St Suite 103 *Web:* www.paworkforce.state.pa.us	Harrisburg	PA	17120	717-772-4966	783-4660
Rhode Island Labor & Training Dept 1511 Pontiac Ave *Web:* www.dlt.state.ri.us	Cranston	RI	02920	401-462-8000	462-8872
South Dakota Career Center Div 116 W Missouri Ave *Web:* www.sdjobs.org	Pierre	SD	57501	605-773-3372	773-6680
Tennessee Labor & Workforce Development Dept 220 French Landing Dr *Web:* www.state.tn.us	Nashville	TN	37243	615-741-6642	741-5078
Texas Workforce Commission 101 E 15th St *Web:* www.twc.state.tx.us	Austin	TX	78778	512-463-2222	936-3504
Workforce Services Dept 140 E 300 S *Web:* www.jobs.utah.gov	Salt Lake City	UT	84111	801-526-9675	526-9211
Vermont Labor Dept 5 Green Mountain Dr *Web:* www.labor.vermont.gov	Montpelier	VT	05601	802-828-4000	828-4022
Virginia Employment Commission 703 E Main St *Web:* www.vec.virginia.gov	Richmond	VA	23219	804-786-1485	225-3923
Washington Employment Security Dept 212 Maple Pk Ave SE *Web:* www.esd.wa.gov	Olympia	WA	98504	360-902-9500	902-9556
Wisconsin Workforce Development Dept 201 E Washington Ave *Web:* www.dwd.state.wi.us	Madison	WI	53702	608-267-9613	266-1784
Wyoming Dept of Employment 1510 E Pershing Blvd *Web:* www.doe.wyo.gov/Pages/default.aspx	Cheyenne	WY	82002	307-777-7672	777-5805

263 EMPLOYMENT SERVICES - ONLINE

				Phone	Fax
4Jobs.com 1060 1st Ave Suite 100 *TF:* 877-230-3885 ■ *Web:* www.4jobs.com	King of Prussia	PA	19406	610-878-2800	878-2801
agriCAREERS Inc 613 Main St *TF:* 888-224-5621 ■ *Web:* www.agricareersinc.com	Massena	IA	50853	712-779-3300	779-3366
Arbita 12 S 6th St Suite 730 *Web:* www.arbita.net	Minneapolis	MN	55402	612-278-0000	253-9392
Avjobs Inc PO Box 260830 **Fax Area Code:* 888 ■ *Web:* www.avjobs.com	Littleton	CO	80163	303-683-2322	624-8691*
BestJobsUSA.com 550 Heritage Dr Suite 200 *Web:* www.bestjobsusa.com	Jupiter	FL	33458	561-686-6800	686-8043
Beyond.com Inc 1060 1st Ave Suite 100 *Web:* www.beyond.com	King of Prussia	PA	19406	610-878-2800	
CareerBuilder.com 200 N LaSalle St Suite 1100 **Fax Area Code:* 877 ■ *TF:* 800-638-4212 ■ *Web:* www.careerbuilder.com	Chicago	IL	60601	773-527-3600	349-4467*
CareerExposure 3934 SW Corbett Ave *Web:* www.careerexposure.com	Portland	OR	97239	503-221-7779	221-7880
CareerMag.com 1060 First Ave Suite 100 *Web:* www.careermag.com	King of Prussia	PA	19406	610-878-2800	
CareerPark 101 N Pt Blvd *TF:* 800-396-3306 ■ *Web:* www.careerpark.com	Lancaster	PA	17601	717-581-1966	
CareerWomen.com 3934 SW Corbett Ave *Web:* www.careerwomen.com	Portland	OR	97239	503-221-7779	221-7780
Chronicle of Higher Education Career Network The 1255 23rd St NW 7th Fl *Web:* chronicle.com/jobs	Washington	DC	20037	202-466-1000	452-1033
CollegeGrad.com Inc 1051 E Hillsdale Blvd Suite 800 **Fax Area Code:* 262 ■ *TF:* 800-991-4262 ■ *Web:* www.collegegrad.com	Foster City	CA	94404	800-991-4262	375-6721*
ComputerJobs.com Inc 1995 N Pk Pl SE # 425 *TF:* 800-850-0045 ■ *Web:* www.computerjobs.com	Atlanta	GA	30339	770-850-0045	850-0369
Cool Works 511 Hwy 89 PO Box 272 *Web:* www.coolworks.com	Gardiner	MT	59030	406-848-2380	848-2320

Name / Address	City	State	Zip	Phone	Fax
Dice Inc 4101 NW Urbandale Dr. *TF:* 877-386-3323 ■ *Web:* www.dice.com	Urbandale	IA	50322	515-280-1144	280-1452
DiversitySearch 3934 SW Corbett Ave *Web:* www.diversitysearch.com	Portland	OR	97239	503-221-7779	221-7780
EmplawyerNet 2331 Westwood Blvd Suite 331 *TF:* 800-270-2688 ■ *Web:* www.emplawyernet.com	Los Angeles	CA	90025	800-270-2688	
Employer Central 297 Kingsbury Suite D PO Box 4470 **Fax Area Code:* 775 ■ *TF:* 800-442-3614 ■ *Web:* www.employercentral.com	Stateline	NV	89449	800-442-3614	546-6040*
EmploymentGuide.com 150 Granby St *TF:* 877-876-4039 ■ *Web:* www.employmentguide.com	Norfolk	VA	23510	877-876-4039	804-8095
Environmental Career Opportunities c/o Brubach Corp 700 Graves St **Fax Area Code:* 434 ■ *TF:* 800-315-9777 ■ *Web:* www.ecojobs.com	Charlottesville	VA	22902	800-315-9777	984-2331*
ExecUNet Inc 295 Westport Ave *TF:* 800-637-3126 ■ *Web:* www.execunet.com	Norwalk	CT	06851	203-750-1030	840-8320
Guru.com 5001 Baum Blvd Suite 760 *Web:* www.guru.com	Pittsburgh	PA	15213	412-687-1316	687-4466
HealthCareSource Inc 8 Winchester Pl Suite 201 *TF:* 800-869-5200 ■ *Web:* www.healthcaresource.com	Winchester	MA	01890	800-869-5200	829-6600
Ihispano.com 4265 N Knox Ave Suite 300 *TF:* 888-252-1220	Chicago	IL	60641	888-252-1220	
IMDiversity Inc 140 Carondelet St *Web:* www.imdiversity.com	New Orleans	LA	70130	504-598-3357	523-0271
International Foundation of Employee Benefit Plans (IFEBP) 18700 W Bluemound Rd *TF:* 888-334-3327 ■ *Web:* www.ifebp.org	Brookfield	WI	53045	262-786-6700	786-8670
JobBank USA Inc 1417 Sadler Rd PO Box 331 **Fax Area Code:* 404 ■ *Web:* www.jobbankusa.com	Fernandina Beach	FL	32034	678-318-1775	261-1357*
JobWeb 62 Highland Ave *TF:* 800-544-5272 ■ *Web:* www.jobweb.com	Bethlehem	PA	18017	610-868-1421	868-0208
MBA Careers 3934 SW Corbett Ave *Web:* www.mbacareers.com	Portland	OR	97239	503-221-7779	221-7780
Monster Jobs 5 Clock Tower Pl Suite 500 *TF:* 800-666-7837 ■ *Web:* www.monster.com	Maynard	MA	01754	978-461-8000	461-8100
MonsterTRAK 11845 W Olympic Blvd Suite 500 *TF:* 800-999-8725 ■ *Web:* www.monstertrak.monster.com	Los Angeles	CA	90064	310-474-3377	475-7912
National Diversity Newspaper Job Bank *c/o Morris Communications* PO Box 936 *TF:* 800-622-6358	Augusta	GA	30903	800-622-6358	828-3830
NationJob Inc 920 Morgan St Suite T *TF:* 800-292-7731 ■ *Web:* www.nationjob.com	Des Moines	IA	50309	515-280-3672	243-5384
Net-Temps Inc 55 Middlesex St Suite 220 *TF:* 800-307-0062 ■ *Web:* www.net-temps.com	North Chelmsford	MA	01863	978-251-7272	251-7250
Peterson's Nelnet LLC 2000 Lenox Dr 3rd Fl *TF:* 877-338-7772 ■ *Web:* www.essayedge.com	Lawrenceville	NJ	08648	609-896-8669	896-4565
ProcureStaff Ltd 560 Lexington Ave 15th Fl *TF:* 866-491-1795 ■ *Web:* www.procurestaff.com	New York	NY	10022	212-901-2828	704-2477
Project Connect EPCS On-Line Services WISC B150 Education Bldg 1000 Bascom Mall *Web:* www.careers.education.wisc.edu/projectconnect	Madison	WI	53706	608-262-1755	262-9074
Recruiters OnLine Network Inc (RON) 947 Essex Ln *TF:* 888-364-4667 ■ *Web:* www.recruitersonline.com	Medina	OH	44256	888-364-4667	237-8686
Vault Inc 93 Varick St *Web:* www.vault.com	New York	NY	10013	212-366-4212	366-6117

264 ENGINEERING & DESIGN

SEE ALSO Surveying, Mapping, Related Services p. 2680

Name / Address	City	State	Zip	Phone	Fax
A Epstein & Sons International Inc 600 W Fulton St *Web:* www.epsteinglobal.com	Chicago	IL	60661	312-454-9100	454-9100
ABM Engineering Services Co 5300 S Eastern Ave Suite 100 *TF Sales:* 866-678-0783 ■ *Web:* www.abm.com	Los Angeles	CA	90040	323-234-2001	724-9561
ADD Inc 311 Summer St *Web:* www.addinc.com	Boston	MA	02210	617-234-3100	661-7118
Advanced Engineering & Environmental Services Inc 2016 S Washington St *Web:* www.ae2s.com	Grand Forks	ND	58201	701-746-8087	
Advanced Technology & Research Corp 6650 Eli Whitney Dr **Fax Area Code:* 301 ■ *Web:* www.atrcorp.com	Columbia	MD	21046	443-766-7888	989-8000*
Advantis Technologies 1400 Bluegrass Lakes Pkwy *TF:* 888-452-7678 ■ *Web:* www.poolspacare.com	Alpharetta	GA	30004	770-521-5999	521-5959
AE Global Media Inc 2540 Beltway Blvd PO Box 668065 **Fax Area Code:* 704 ■ *TF:* 800-467-3709 ■ *Web:* www.audioethics.com	Charlotte	NC	28266	800-467-3709	394-7883*
AECOM Technology Corp 555 S Flower St 37th Fl *Web:* www.aecom.com	Los Angeles	CA	90071	213-593-8000	593-8730
AEP Pro Serv 347 Elizabeth Ave Suite 100 *TF:* 877-638-4552 ■ *Web:* www.aepnetworks.com	Somerset	NJ	08873	732-652-5200	764-8862
Affiliated Engineers Inc (AEI) 5802 Research Pk Blvd *Web:* www.aeieng.com	Madison	WI	53719	608-238-2616	238-2614
AGUIRRE Corp 10670 N Central Expwy 6th Fl *Web:* www.aguirreroden.com	Dallas	TX	75231	972-788-1508	788-1583
AI Signal Research Inc 3411 Triana Blvd SW *Web:* www.aisignal.com	Huntsville	AL	35805	256-551-0008	551-0099
AirPol Inc 199 Pomeroy Rd Suite 103 *Web:* www.airpol.com	Parsippany	NJ	07054	973-599-4418	428-6048
AKRF Inc 440 Pk Ave S *TF:* 800-899-2573 ■ *Web:* www.akrf.com	New York	NY	10022	212-696-0670	779-9721
Alan Plummer & Assoc Inc 1320 S University Dr *Web:* www.apaienv.com	Fort Worth	TX	76107	817-806-1700	870-2536
Albert Kahn Assoc Inc 7430 2nd Ave Albert Kahn Bldg *Web:* www.albertkahn.com	Detroit	MI	48202	313-202-7000	202-7001
Alion Science & Technology 1750 Tysons Blvd Suite 1300 *TF:* 877-771-6252 ■ *Web:* www.alionscience.com	McLean	VA	22102	703-918-4480	933-6774
Allen & Hoshall Inc 1661 International Dr Suite 100 *TF:* 888-819-5005 ■ *Web:* www.allenhoshall.com	Memphis	TN	38120	901-820-0820	683-1001
AM Kinney 150 E 4th St *TF:* 800-265-3682 ■ *Web:* www.amkinney.com	Cincinnati	OH	45202	513-421-2265	421-2264
Ambitech Engineering Corp 1333 Butterfield Rd Suite 200 *Web:* www.ambitech.com	Downers Grove	IL	60515	630-963-5800	963-8099
AMEC Earth & Environmental 221 18th St SE *Web:* www.amec.com/earthandenvironmental	Calgary	AB	T2E6J5	403-248-4331	248-2188
AMEC Inc 2020 Winston Pk Dr Suite 700 *Web:* www.amec.com	Oakview	ON	L6H6X7	905-829-5400	829-5401
American Consulting Engineers PLC 400 E Vine St Suite 300 *Web:* www.entran.us	Lexington	KY	40507	859-233-2100	254-9664
American Consulting Inc 7260 Shadeland Stn *Web:* www.structurepoint.com	Indianapolis	IN	46256	317-547-5580	543-0270
American Engineering Testing Inc 550 Cleveland Ave N *TF:* 800-972-6364 ■ *Web:* www.amengtest.com	Saint Paul	MN	55114	651-659-9001	659-1379
Ammann & Whitney Inc 96 Morton St *Web:* www.ammann-whitney.com	New York	NY	10014	212-462-8500	929-5356
Ams Mechanical Systems Inc 140 E Tower Dr *Web:* www.amsmechanicalsystems.com	Burr Ridge	IL	60527	630-887-7700	887-0770
AMSEC LLC 2829 Guardian Ln *Web:* www.amsec.com	Virginia Beach	VA	23452	757-463-6666	463-9110
Anvil Corp 1675 W Bakerview Rd *TF:* 877-412-6845 ■ *Web:* www.anvilcorp.com	Bellingham	WA	98226	360-671-1450	
Apex Environmental Inc 15850 Crabbs Branch Way Suite 200 *Web:* www.apexenv.com	Rockville	MD	20855	301-417-0200	975-0169
Applied Technology & Management Inc 5550 NW 111th Blvd **Fax Area Code:* 352 ■ *TF:* 800-275-6488 ■ *Web:* www.appliedtm.com	Gainesville	FL	32653	386-418-6400	375-0995*
APS Technology Inc 7 Laser Ln **Fax Area Code:* 203 ■ *Web:* www.aps-tech.com	Wallingford	CT	06492	860-613-4450	284-7428*
Arcadis 630 Plaza Dr Suite 200 *Web:* www.arcadis-us.com	Highlands Ranch	CO	80129	720-344-3500	344-3535
Ardaman & Assoc Inc 8008 S Orange Ave *TF:* 800-432-3143 ■ *Web:* www.ardaman.com	Orlando	FL	32809	407-855-3860	859-8121
Arkel International Inc PO Box 4621 *Web:* www.arkel.com	Baton Rouge	LA	70821	225-343-0525	336-1849
Arquitectonica International Corp 801 Brickell Ave Suite 1100 *Web:* www.arquitectonica.com	Miami	FL	33131	305-372-1812	372-1175
Arthur Dyson & Assoc 764 P St Suite B *Web:* www.arthurdyson.com	Fresno	CA	93721	559-486-3582	486-3582
ASCG Inc 300 W 31st Ave *Web:* www.whpacific.com	Anchorage	AK	99503	907-339-6500	339-5327
Asg Renaissance 22226 Garrison St *TF:* 800-238-0890 ■ *Web:* www.asgren.com	Dearborn	MI	48124	313-565-4700	565-4701
Astorino 227 Fort Pitt Blvd *TF:* 800-518-0464 ■ *Web:* www.ldastorino.com	Pittsburgh	PA	15222	412-765-1700	765-1711
Atlantic Testing Laboratories Ltd PO Box 29 *Web:* www.atlantictesting.com	Canton	NY	13617	315-386-4578	386-1012
Atrenta Inc 2077 Gateway Pl Suite 300 *Web:* www.atrenta.com	San Jose	CA	95110	408-453-3333	453-3322
Austin Co 6095 Parkland Blvd *Web:* www.theaustin.com	Cleveland	OH	44124	440-544-2600	544-2661
Ayres Assoc Inc 3433 Oakwood Hills Pkwy *Web:* www.ayresassociates.com	Eau Claire	WI	54701	715-834-3161	831-7500
B G Consultants Inc 4806 Vue Du Lac Pl *Web:* www.bgcons.com	Manhattan	KS	66503	785-537-7448	537-8793
Ballinger 833 Chestnut St Suite 1400 *Web:* www.ballinger-ae.com	Philadelphia	PA	19107	215-446-0900	446-0901
Bantu Inc 8133 Lessburg Pike Suite 250 **Fax Area Code:* 888 ■ *Web:* www.bantu.com	Vienna	VA	22182	703-766-4577	828-1726*
Bard Rao + Athanas Consulting Engineers Inc 311 Arsenal St The Arsenal on the Charles *Web:* www.brplusa.com	Watertown	MA	02472	617-254-0016	924-9339
Barge Waggoner Sumner & Cannon 211 Commerce St Suite 600 *Web:* www.bargewaggoner.com	Nashville	TN	37201	615-254-1500	255-6572
Barr Engineering Co 4700 W 77th St *TF:* 800-632-2277 ■ *Web:* www.barr.com	Minneapolis	MN	55435	952-832-2600	832-2601
Bartlett & West Engineers Inc 1200 SW Executive Dr *TF:* 888-200-6464 ■ *Web:* www.bartwest.com	Topeka	KS	66615	785-272-2252	272-5694
Barton Malow Design 26500 American Dr Suite 451 *Web:* www.bartonmalowdesign.com	Southfield	MI	48034	248-351-4500	436-5001
Baxter & Woodman Inc 8678 Ridgefield Rd *Web:* www.baxwood.com	Crystal Lake	IL	60012	815-459-1260	455-0450
BBG-BBGM 161 Sixth Ave 3rd Fl *Web:* www.bbg-bbgm.com	New York	NY	10013	212-888-7667	935-3868
Bechtel Corp 50 Beale St *Web:* www.bechtel.com	San Francisco	CA	94105	415-768-1234	768-9038
Bechtel North America 3000 Post Oak Blvd *Web:* www.bechtel.com	Houston	TX	77056	713-235-2000	960-9031
Belcan Engineering Group Inc 10200 Anderson Way *TF:* 800-423-5226 ■ *Web:* www.belcan.com	Cincinnati	OH	45242	513-891-0972	
Belt Collins 2153 N King St Suite 200 *Web:* www.beltcollins.com	Honolulu	HI	96819	808-521-5361	538-7819
Benesch 205 N Michigan Ave Suite 2400 *TF:* 877-222-9995 ■ *Web:* www.benesch.com	Chicago	IL	60601	312-565-0450	565-2497
Berger/ABAM Engineers Inc 33301 9th Ave S Suite 300 *Web:* www.abam.com	Federal Way	WA	98003	206-431-2300	431-2250

Company	City	State	ZIP	Phone	Fax
Bergmann Assoc Inc 28 E Main St 200 First Federal Plaza *TF:* 800-724-1168 ■ *Web:* www.bergmannpc.com	Rochester	NY	14614	585-232-5135	325-8493
Bermello Ajamil & Partners 2601 S Bayshore Dr *Web:* www.bamiami.com	Miami	FL	33133	305-859-2050	859-9638
Berryman & Henigar 11590 W Bernardo Ct Suite 100 *TF:* 800-964-4274	San Diego	CA	92127	858-451-6100	451-2846
Beyer Blinder Belle Architects & Planners LLC 41 E 11th St 2nd Fl *Web:* www.beyerblinderbelle.com	New York	NY	10003	212-777-7800	475-7424
Bionetics Corp 11833 Cannon Blvd Suite 100 *TF:* 800-868-0330 ■ *Web:* www.bionetics.com	Newport News	VA	23606	757-873-0900	873-6998
BKF Engineers 255 Shoreline Dr Suite 200 *Web:* www.bkf.com	Redwood City	CA	94065	650-482-6300	482-6399
BL Cos 355 Research Pkwy *TF:* 800-301-3077 ■ *Web:* www.blcompanies.com	Meriden	CT	06450	203-630-1406	630-2615
BLM Architects (BSA) 2520 Renaissance Blvd Suite 110 *Web:* www.blm-architects.com	King of Prussia	PA	19406	610-270-0599	270-0995
BMH Eagleton Inc 3900 Essex Ln Suite 300	Houston	TX	77027	713-871-8787	871-1914
Bolton & Menk Inc 1960 Premier Dr *Web:* www.bolton-menk.com	Mankato	MN	56001	507-625-4171	625-4177
Boswell Engineering 330 Phillips Ave *Web:* www.boswellengineering.com	South Hackensack	NJ	07606	201-641-0770	641-1831
Bowyer-Singleton & Assoc Inc 520 S Magnolia Ave *Web:* www.bsacorporate.com	Orlando	FL	32801	407-843-5120	649-8664
BP Barber & Assoc Inc 101 Research Dr *Web:* www.bpbarber.com	Columbia	SC	29203	803-254-4400	771-6676
Braun Intertec Corp 11001 Hampshire Ave S *TF:* 800-279-6100 ■ *Web:* www.braunintertec.com	Bloomington	MN	55438	952-995-2000	995-2020
Bresslergroup 2400 Market St Suite 1 *Web:* www.bresslergroup.com	Philadelphia	PA	19103	215-561-5100	561-5101
Bricmont Inc 500 Technology Dr Southpointe Industrial Pk *TF:* 888-274-2462 ■ *Web:* www.bricmont.com	Canonsburg	PA	15317	724-746-2300	746-9420
Brinjac Engineering Inc 114 N 2nd St # 1 *TF:* 877-274-6526 ■ *Web:* www.brinjac.com	Harrisburg	PA	17101	717-233-4502	233-0833
Brock Solutions Inc 86 Ardelt Ave *TF:* 877-702-7625 ■ *Web:* www.brocksolutions.com	Kitchener	ON	N2C2C9	519-571-1522	571-1721
Brown & Caldwell Consulting Engineers 201 N Civic Dr Suite 115 *Web:* www.brownandcaldwell.com	Walnut Creek	CA	94596	925-937-9010	937-9026
Brown & Gay Engineers Inc 11490 Westheimer Rd Suite 700 *Web:* www.browngay.com	Houston	TX	77077	281-558-8700	558-9701
BSA Life Structures 9365 Counselors Row *Web:* www.bsalifestructures.com	Indianapolis	IN	46240	317-819-7878	819-7288
BSK & Assoc 567 W Shaw Ave Suite B *Web:* www.bskinc.com	Fresno	CA	93704	559-497-2880	497-2864
Buchart Horn Inc/Basco Assoc 445 W Philadelphia St *TF:* 800-274-2224 ■ *Web:* www.bh-ba.com	York	PA	17401	717-852-1400	852-1401
Bucher Willis & Ratliff Corp 609 W N St *TF:* 800-942-9807 ■ *Web:* www.bwrcorp.com	Salina	KS	67401	785-827-3603	827-3029
Burgess & Niple Inc 5085 Reed Rd *TF:* 800-282-1761 ■ *Web:* www.burgessniple.com	Columbus	OH	43220	614-459-2050	451-1385
Burk-Kleinpeter Inc (BKI) 4176 Canal St *Web:* www.bkiusa.com	New Orleans	LA	70119	504-486-5901	483-6298
Burns & McDonnell 9400 Ward Pkwy *Web:* www.burnsmcd.com	Kansas City	MO	64114	816-333-9400	822-3412
Burns & Roe Enterprises Inc 800 Kinderkamack Rd *Web:* www.roe.com	Oradell	NJ	07649	201-265-2000	986-4459
Byers Engineering Co 6285 Barfield Rd 4th Fl *Web:* www.byers.com	Atlanta	GA	30328	404-843-1000	843-2116
C & S Cos (CSCOS) 499 Col Eileen Collins Blvd *TF:* 877-277-6583 ■ *Web:* www.cscos.com	Syracuse	NY	13212	315-455-2000	455-9667
Callison Architecture Inc 1420 5th Ave Suite 2400 *Web:* www.callison.com	Seattle	WA	98101	206-623-4646	623-4625
Camp Dresser & McKee Inc 50 Hampshire St 1 Cambridge Pl *TF:* 800-343-7004 ■ *Web:* www.cdm.com	Cambridge	MA	02139	617-452-6000	452-8000
Campbell Grinder Co 1226 Pontaluna Rd *Web:* www.campbellgrinder.com	Spring Lake	MI	49456	231-798-6464	798-6466
Cannon Design 2170 Whitehaven Rd *Web:* www.cannondesign.com	Grand Island	NY	14072	716-773-6800	773-5909
Carbide Products Inc 800 Clayton Ave *TF:* 877-863-2340 ■ *Web:* www.carbidepros.com	Georgetown	KY	40324	502-863-2390	863-8904
Carollo Engineers 3033 N 44th St Suite 101 *TF:* 800-523-5822 ■ *Web:* www.carollo.com	Phoenix	AZ	85018	602-263-9500	265-1422
Carroll Engineering Corp 949 Easton Rd Suite 100 *Web:* www.carrollengineering.com	Warrington	PA	18976	215-343-5700	343-0875

Company	City	State	ZIP	Phone	Fax
CAS Inc PO Box 11190 *TF:* 800-729-8686 ■ *Web:* www.cas-inc.com	Huntsville	AL	35814	256-971-6126	971-6105
CDI Engineering Solutions 1717 Arch St 35th Fl *TF:* 800-996-7566 ■ *Web:* www.cdicorp.com	Philadelphia	PA	19103	215-282-8050	636-1177
CDI Marine Co 9550 Regency Sq Blvd Suite 400 *Web:* www.cdi-gs.com	Jacksonville	FL	32225	904-805-0700	805-0701
CEI Engineering Assoc Inc 3317 SW 'I' St *TF:* 800-433-4173 ■ *Web:* www.ceieng.com	Bentonville	AR	72712	479-273-9472	273-0844
Centra Technology Inc 25 Burlington Mall Rd *Web:* www.centratechnology.com	Burlington	MA	01803	781-272-7887	272-7836
CH Guernsey & Co 5555 N Grand Blvd *TF:* 800-845-2061 ■ *Web:* www.chguernsey.com	Oklahoma City	OK	73112	405-416-8100	416-8111
Chastain-Skillman Inc 4705 Old Rd 37 *Web:* www.chastainskillman.com	Lakeland	FL	33813	863-646-1402	647-3806
Chemical & Industrial Engineering Inc 1930 Bishop Ln Suite 800 *Web:* www.cieng.com	Louisville	KY	40218	502-451-4977	451-9574
Chemstress Consultant Co 39 S Main St *Web:* www.chemstress.com	Akron	OH	44308	330-535-5591	535-1431
ChemTech Consultants Inc 1370 Washington Pke *Web:* www.chemtech88.com	Bridgeville	PA	15017	412-221-1360	221-5685
Chemtex International Inc 1979 Eastwood Rd *TF:* 877-243-6839 ■ *Web:* www.chemtex.com	Wilmington	NC	28403	910-509-4400	509-4567
Chevron Energy Solutions 345 California St 18th Fl *Web:* www.chevronenergy.com	San Francisco	CA	94104	415-733-4500	733-4950
Chiang Patel & Yerby 1820 Regal Row Suite 200 *Web:* www.cpyi.com	Dallas	TX	75235	214-638-0500	638-3723
Chl Systems 476 Meetinghouse Rd *Web:* www.chlsystems.com	Souderton	PA	18964	215-723-7284	723-9115
Civil & Environmental Consultants Inc 333 Baldwin Rd *TF:* 800-365-2324 ■ *Web:* www.cecinc.com	Pittsburgh	PA	15205	412-429-2324	429-2114
Civiltech Engineering Inc 450 E Devon Ave Suite 300 *Web:* www.civiltechinc.com	Itasca	IL	60143	630-773-3900	
Clough Harbour & Assoc (CHA) 3 Winners Cir PO Box 5269 *TF:* 800-836-0817 ■ *Web:* www.cloughharbour.com	Albany	NY	12205	518-453-4500	458-1735
Cochran Stephenson & Donkervoet Inc 323 W Camden St Suite 700 *Web:* www.csdarch.com	Baltimore	MD	21201	410-539-2080	752-5263
Coler & Colantonio Inc 101 Accord Pk Dr *Web:* www.col-col.com	Norwell	MA	02061	781-982-5400	982-5490
Columbia Group Inc The (TCG) 20 M St SE *Web:* www.columbiaresearch.com	Washington	DC	20003	202-546-1435	544-5645
Commonwealth Assoc Inc PO Box 1124 *Web:* www.cai-engr.com	Jackson	MI	49204	517-788-3848	788-3003
Compass Systems Inc 21471 Great Mills Rd *Web:* www.compass-sys-inc.com	Lexington Park	MD	20653	301-737-4640	863-9687
Comsearch 19700 Janelia Farm Blvd *Web:* www.comsearch.com	Ashburn	VA	20147	703-726-5500	726-5600
Concepts NREC 217 Billings Farm Rd *Web:* www.conceptsnrec.com	White River Junction	VT	05001	802-296-2321	296-2325
Conestoga-Rovers & Assoc 2055 Niagara Falls Blvd Suite 3 *Web:* www.craworld.com	Niagara Falls	NY	14304	716-297-6150	297-2265
Contech Control Services Inc PO Box 923 *Web:* www.contechnet.com	La Porte	TX	77572	281-471-8010	471-8065
Converse Consultants 222 E Huntington Dr Suite 211 *Web:* www.converseconsultants.com	Monrovia	CA	91016	626-930-1200	930-1212
Coon Engineering Inc (CEI) 2832 W Wilshire Blvd *Web:* www.coonengineering.com	Oklahoma City	OK	73116	405-842-0363	842-0364
Cooper Carry Inc 191 Peachtree St NE #2400 *Web:* www.coopercarry.com	Atlanta	GA	30303	404-237-2000	237-0276
Corestates Inc 4191 Pleasant Hill Rd *Web:* www.core-eng.com	Duluth	GA	30096	770-242-9550	
Corgan Assoc Inc 401 N Houston *Web:* www.corgan.com	Dallas	TX	75202	214-748-2000	653-8281
Corrpro Cos Inc 1055 W Smith Rd *TF:* 800-726-5082 ■ *Web:* www.corrpro.com	Medina	OH	44256	330-723-5082	722-7654
CPH Engineers 500 W Fulton St *TF:* 800-609-0688 ■ *Web:* www.cphengineers.com	Sanford	FL	32771	407-322-6841	330-0639
Crawford Murphy & Tilly Inc 2750 W Washington St *Web:* www.cmtengr.com	Springfield	IL	62702	217-787-8050	787-8054
Crb Engineers Inc 7410 NW Tiffany Springs Pkwy Suite 100 *TF:* 877-427-2872 ■ *Web:* www.crbusa.com	Kansas City	MO	64153	816-880-9800	880-9898
Crown Electrical Services & Automation Inc 5960 Southport Rd *Web:* www.crown-esa.com	Portage	IN	46368	219-762-0700	762-1636
CSA Group Inc 8790 Governor's Hill Dr Suite 111 *Web:* www.csagroup.com	Cincinnati	OH	45249	513-677-4440	677-4443
CT Consultants Inc 8150 Sterling Ct *Web:* www.ctconsultants.com	Mentor	OH	44060	440-951-9000	951-7487
CTA Architects Engineers 13 N 23rd St *Web:* www.ctagroup.com	Billings	MT	59101	406-248-7455	248-3779
Ctl Engineering Inc PO Box 44548 *Web:* www.ctleng.com	Columbus	OH	43204	614-276-8123	276-6377
CTL/Thompson Inc 1971 W 12th Ave *Web:* www.ctlt.com	Denver	CO	80204	303-825-0777	825-4252

	City	State	ZIP	Phone	Fax
D3 Technologies Inc 4838 Ronson Ct *TF:* 800-677-7868 ■ *Web:* www.d3tech.com	San Diego	CA	92111	858-571-1685	571-8563
Dataline LLC 7918 Jones Branch Dr Suite 650 *TF:* 800-666-9858 ■ *Web:* www.dataline.com	McLean	VA	23513	703-847-7412	847-7419
David Evans & Assoc Inc (DEA) 2100 SW River Pkwy *TF:* 800-721-1916 ■ *Web:* www.deainc.com	Portland	OR	97201	503-223-6663	223-2701
Davis & Floyd Inc 1319 Hwy 72 221 E *Web:* www.davisfloyd.com	Greenwood	SC	29649	864-229-5211	229-7844
Dayton T Brown Inc 1175 Church St *TF:* 800-232-6300 ■ *Web:* www.daytontbrown.com	Bohemia	NY	11716	631-589-6300	589-4046
Defense Group Inc 307 Annandale Rd Suite 110 *TF:* 877-233-5789 ■ *Web:* www.defensegroupinc.com	Falls Church	VA	22042	703-532-0802	532-0806
Degenkolb Engineers 225 Montgomery Suite 500 *Web:* www.degenkolb.com	San Francisco	CA	94104	415-392-6952	981-3157
Delex Systems Inc 1953 Gallows Rd Suite 700 *Web:* www.delex.com	Vienna	VA	22182	703-734-8300	893-5338
Delon Hampton & Assoc Chartered 900 7th St NW # 800 *Web:* www.delonhampton.com	Washington	DC	20001	202-898-1999	371-2073
DeStefano & Partners Ltd 330 N Wabash Ave Suite 3200 *Web:* www.destefanoandpartners.com	Suite 250	IL	60611	312-836-4321	836-4322
Dewberry & Davis 8401 Arlington Blvd *Web:* www.dewberry.com	Fairfax	VA	22031	703-849-0100	849-0100
Diversified Technology Consultants Inc 556 Washington Ave *Web:* www.teamdtc.com	North Haven	CT	06473	203-239-4200	234-7376
DLR Group Inc 400 Essex Ct *Web:* www.dlrgroup.com	Omaha	NE	68114	402-393-4100	393-8747
DLZ Corp 6121 Huntley Rd *TF:* 800-336-5352 ■ *Web:* www.dlzcorp.com	Columbus	OH	43229	614-888-0040	848-6712
Doerfer Engineering Corp PO Box 816 *TF:* 877-483-4700 ■ *Web:* www.doerfer.com	Waverly	IA	50677	319-277-3110	277-7023
DRS Technical Services Segment 8300 Boone Blvd Suite 555 *Web:* www.drs.com	Vienna	VA	22182	703-761-7616	761-6713
Durrant Group Inc 400 ice harbor Dr *Web:* www.durrant.com	Dubuque	IA	52001	563-583-9131	557-9078
Dvirka & Bartilucci Consulting Engineers 330 Crossways Pk Dr *TF:* 888-364-9890 ■ *Web:* www.dvirkaandbartilucci.com	Woodbury	NY	11797	516-364-9890	364-9045
Dyer Riddle Mills & Precourt Inc (DRMP) 941 Lk Baldwin Ln *TF:* 800-375-3767 ■ *Web:* www.drmp.com	Orlando	FL	32814	407-896-0594	896-4836
Dynamac Corp 1901 Research Blvd # 220 *Web:* www.dynamac.com	Rockville	MD	20850	301-417-9800	417-6132
E2 Consulting Engineers Inc 450 E 17th Ave *TF:* 888-835-9400 ■ *Web:* www.e2.com	Denver	CO	80203	303-232-9800	238-8972
EA Engineering Science & Technology Inc 11019 McCormick Rd *TF:* 800-777-9750 ■ *Web:* www.eaest.com	Hunt Valley	MD	21031	410-584-7000	771-1625
EADS Group 1126 8th Ave *TF:* 800-626-0904 ■ *Web:* www.eadsgroup.com	Altoona	PA	16602	814-944-5035	944-4862
ECS Corporate Services LLC 14026 Thunderbolt Pl Suite 300 **Fax Area Code:* 703 ■ *Web:* www.ecslimited.com	Chantilly	VA	20151	571-299-6000	834-5527*
EDO Technical Services Operations 254 E Ave K-4 *Web:* www.edotso.com	Lancaster	CA	93535	661-723-7368	948-7003
EI Assoc 8 Ridgedale Ave *Web:* www.eiassociates.com	Cedar Knolls	NJ	07927	973-775-7777	775-7770
Eichleay Engineers Inc of California 1390 Willow Pass Rd Suite 600 *Web:* www.eichleay.com	Concord	CA	94520	925-689-7000	689-7006
Elkus/Manfredi Architects 300 A St *Web:* www.elkus-manfredi.com	Boston	MA	02210	617-426-1300	426-7502
EMA Services Inc 1970 Oakcrest Ave Suite 100 *Web:* www.ema-inc.com	Saint Paul	MN	55113	651-639-5600	639-5730
EN Engineering 7135 James Ave *Web:* www.enengineering.com	Woodridge	IL	60517	630-353-4000	353-7777
Enercon Services Inc 5100 E Skelly Dr Suite 450 *TF:* 800-735-7693 ■ *Web:* www.enercon.com	Tulsa	OK	74135	918-665-7693	665-7232
Engineering & Environmental Consultants Inc 4625 E Fort Lowell Rd *Web:* www.eec-info.com	Tucson	AZ	85712	520-321-4625	321-0333
Engineering Planning & Management Inc 959 Concord St *Web:* www.epm-inc.com	Framingham	MA	01701	508-875-2121	879-3291
Ennead Architects 320 W 13 St *TF:* 800-939-7790 ■ *Web:* www.ennead.com	New York	NY	10014	212-807-7171	807-5917
ENSCO Inc 3110 Fairview Pk Dr Suite 300 *TF:* 800-367-2682 ■ *Web:* www.ensco.com	Falls Church	VA	22042	703-321-9000	321-4605
Envirocon Inc PO Box 16655 *Web:* www.envirocon.com	Missoula	MT	59808	406-523-1150	
Envisioneering Inc PO Box 7221 **Fax Area Code:* 703 ■ *Web:* www.envisioneeringinc.com	Alexandria	VA	22307	571-483-4100	317-1970*
ERM Group Inc 350 Eagle View Blvd *TF:* 800-662-1124 ■ *Web:* www.erm.com	Exton	PA	19341	610-524-3500	524-7335
Evans Mechwart Hambleton & Tilton Inc (EMHT) 5500 New Albany Rd *Web:* www.emht.com	Columbus	OH	43054	614-775-4500	775-4800
Ewing Cole 100 N 6th St *Web:* www.ewingcole.com	Philadelphia	PA	19106	215-923-2020	574-9163
Exodyne Inc 8433 N Black Canyon Hwy *TF:* 800-870-3676 ■ *Web:* www.exodyne.com	Phoenix	AZ	85021	602-995-3700	995-4091
Extrusion Technology Corp of America 7600 S Santa Fe Dr Bldg C	Houston	TX	77061	713-641-6010	641-6039
Facility Group Inc 2233 Lake Pk Dr Suite 100 *TF:* 800-525-2463 ■ *Web:* www.facilitygroup.com	Smyrna	GA	30080	770-437-2700	437-7554
Fanning/Howey Assoc Inc 1200 Irmscher Blvd *TF:* 888-499-2292 ■ *Web:* www.fhai.com	Celina	OH	45822	419-586-2292	586-3393
Farwest Corrosion Control Co 1480 W Artesia Blvd *TF:* 888-532-7937 ■ *Web:* www.farwestcorrosion.com	Gardena	CA	90248	310-532-9524	532-3934
Fata Hunter Inc 1040 Iowa Ave Suite 100 *TF:* 800-248-6837 ■ *Web:* www.fatahunter.com	Riverside	CA	92507	951-328-0200	328-9205
Fay Spofford & Thorndike LLC 5 Burlington Woods *TF:* 800-835-8666 ■ *Web:* www.fstinc.com	Burlington	MA	01803	781-221-1000	229-1115
Fentress Bradburn Architects Ltd 421 Broadway *Web:* www.fentressarchitects.com	Denver	CO	80203	303-722-5000	722-5080
Fishbeck Thompson Carr & Huber Inc 1515 Arboretum Dr SE *Web:* www.ftch.com	Grand Rapids	MI	49546	616-575-3824	464-3993
Flad & Assoc 644 Science Dr *Web:* www.flad.com	Madison	WI	53711	608-238-2661	238-6727
Fletcher-Thompson Inc 3 Corporate Dr Suite 500 *Web:* www.fletcherthompson.com	Shelton	CT	06484	203-225-6500	225-6701
Fluor Daniel Inc 3 Polaris Way *Web:* www.fluor.com	Aliso Viejo	CA	92698	949-349-2000	349-2585
Fluoresco Lighting & Sign Corp 5505 S Nogales Hwy PO Box 27042 *Web:* www.fluoresco.com	Tucson	AZ	85726	520-623-7953	884-0161
Ford Bacon & Davis 12021 Lakeland Pk Blvd *Web:* www.fbd.com	Baton Rouge	LA	70809	225-297-3201	297-3325
Fortress International Group Inc 7226 Lee Deforest Dr Suite 203 *PINK: FIGI* ■ *TF:* 888-329-4877 ■ *Web:* www.thefigi.com	Columbia	MD	21046	410-312-9988	312-9979
Foster Wheeler AG 53 Frontage Rd PO Box 9000 *NASDAQ: FWLT* ■ *TF:* 888-288-1464 ■ *Web:* www.fwc.com	Hampton	NJ	08827	908-730-4000	713-3245
Foster Wheeler Development Corp 12 Peach Tree Hill Rd	Livingston	NJ	07039	973-535-2300	535-2242
Foster Wheeler USA Corp Perryville Corporate Pk *Web:* www.fwc.com	Clinton	NJ	08809	908-730-4000	730-5315
Foth & Van Dyke & Assoc Inc 2737 S Ridge Rd *TF:* 800-236-8690 ■ *Web:* www.foth.com	Green Bay	WI	54304	920-497-2500	497-8516
Freese & Nichols Inc 4055 International Plaza Suite 200 *Web:* www.freese.com	Fort Worth	TX	76109	817-735-7300	735-7491
Fru-Con Engineering Inc 15933 Clayton Rd *Web:* www.frucon.com	Ballwin	MO	63011	636-391-6700	391-4513
FSB Texas 6850 Manhattan Blvd Suite 200	Fort Worth	TX	73120	817-727-8348	451-4925
Fugro Consultants LP 6100 Hillcroft Ave *Web:* www.fugroconsultants.com	Houston	TX	77081	713-369-5400	369-5518
Fuss & O'Neill Consulting Engineers Inc 146 Hartford Rd *TF:* 800-286-2469 ■ *Web:* www.fando.com	Manchester	CT	06040	860-646-2469	533-5143
Future Technologies Inc 3877 Fairfax Ridge Rd *Web:* www.ftechi.com	Fairfax	VA	22030	703-278-0199	385-0886
Galaxy Scientific Corp 3120 Fire Rd *Web:* www.galaxyscientific.com	Egg Harbor Township	NJ	08234	609-645-0900	645-3316
Gannett Fleming Inc 207 Senate Ave *TF:* 800-233-1055 ■ *Web:* www.gannettfleming.com	Camp Hill	PA	17106	717-763-7211	763-8150
Garver Engineers 4701 Northshore Dr *TF:* 800-264-3633 ■ *Web:* www.garverusa.com	North Little Rock	AR	72118	501-376-3633	372-8042
GDA Technologies Inc 1010 Rincon Cir *Web:* www.gdatech.com	San Jose	CA	95131	408-432-3090	432-3091
GDS Engineers Inc 9009 W Loop S Suite 800 *Web:* www.gdseng.com	Houston	TX	77096	713-667-9162	667-9241
GEI Consultants Inc 400 Unicorn Pk Dr *TF:* 800-678-1503 ■ *Web:* www.geiconsultants.com	Woburn	MA	01801	781-721-4000	721-4073
Gensler 2 Harrison St Suite 400 *Web:* www.gensler.com	San Francisco	CA	94105	415-433-3700	836-4599
Geo-Marine Inc 2201 Ave K Suite A2 *Web:* www.geo-marine.com	Plano	TX	75074	972-423-5480	422-2736
GeoEngineers Inc 8410 154th Ave NE *TF:* 800-533-2158 ■ *Web:* www.geoengineers.com	Redmond	WA	98052	425-861-6000	861-6050
Geomatrix Consultants Inc 2101 Webster St 12th Fl *TF:* 800-999-6879 ■ *Web:* www.geomatrix.com	Oakland	CA	94612	510-663-4100	663-4141
George Butler Assoc Inc 9801 Renner Blvd *TF:* 800-932-2468 ■ *Web:* www.gbutler.com	Lenexa	KS	66219	913-492-0400	577-8200
George G Sharp Inc 22 Cortlandt St # 10 *Web:* www.georgesharp.com	New York	NY	10007	212-732-2800	732-2809
GeoSyntec Consultants Inc 5901 Broken Sound Pkwy NW Suite 300 *TF:* 800-765-4436 ■ *Web:* www.geosyntec.com	Boca Raton	FL	33487	561-995-0900	995-0925
Ghafari Assoc Inc 17101 Michigan Ave **Fax:* Hum Res ■ *Web:* www.ghafari.com	Dearborn	MI	48126	313-441-3000	441-1545*
Gibbs & Cox Inc 2711 Jefferson Davis Hwy Suite 1000 *Web:* www.gibbscox.com	Arlington	VA	22202	703-416-3600	416-3679
Global Design Alliance Inc (GDA) 26 Grammercy Pk S 4B *Web:* www.globalda.com	New York	NY	10003	971-887-3860	
Global Marine Systems (Federal) Inc 1800 Eller Dr *Web:* www.globalmarinesystems.com	Fort Lauderdale	FL	33316	954-530-8088	766-8853
Golder Assoc Inc 3730 Chamblee Tucker Rd *Web:* www.golder.com	Atlanta	GA	30341	770-496-1893	934-9476
Gonzalez Design Group 29401 Stevenson Hwy *Web:* www.gonzalez-group.com	Madison Heights	MI	48071	248-548-6010	548-3160

	City	State	Zip	Phone	Fax
Gould Evans International 4041 Mill St *Web:* www.gouldevans.com	Kansas City	MO	64111	816-931-6655	931-9640
GPD Group 520 S Main St Suite 2531 *Web:* www.gpdco.com	Akron	OH	44311	330-572-2100	572-2101
GRAEF-USA Inc 1 Honey Creek Corporate Ctr 125 S 84th St Suite 401 *Web:* www.gasai.com	Milwaukee	WI	53214	414-259-1500	259-0037
Grant Geophysical Inc PO Box 219950 *TF:* 800-390-5530 ■ *Web:* www.grantgeo.com	Houston	TX	77218	281-398-9503	398-9996
Greeley & Hansen 100 S Wacker Dr Suite 1400 *TF:* 800-837-9779 ■ *Web:* www.greeley-hansen.com	Chicago	IL	60606	312-558-9000	558-1006
Greenberg Farrow 1420 W Peachtree St NW Suite 200 **Fax Area Code:* 770 ■ *Web:* www.greenbergfarrow.com	Atlanta	GA	30339	404-601-4000	303-2333*
Greenhorne & O'Mara Inc 6110 Frost Pl *TF:* 866-322-8905 ■ *Web:* www.g-and-o.com	Laurel	MD	20707	301-982-2800	220-2483
Greenman-Pedersen Inc 325 W Main St *TF:* 800-347-9221 ■ *Web:* www.gpinet.com	Babylon	NY	11702	631-587-5060	587-5029
Gresham Smith & Partners 511 Union St 1400 Nashville City Ctr *TF:* 800-867-3384 ■ *Web:* www.gspnet.com	Nashville	TN	37219	615-770-8100	770-8411
Gruzen Samton LLC 320 W 13th St 9th Fl *Web:* www.gruzensamton.com	New York	NY	10014	212-477-0900	477-1257
GRW Engineers Inc 801 Corporate Dr *TF:* 800-432-9537 ■ *Web:* www.grwinc.com	Lexington	KY	40503	859-223-3999	223-8917
Gstek Inc 1100 Madison Plaza Suite A *Web:* www.gstekinc.com	Chesapeake	VA	23320	757-548-1597	
Gulf Interstate Engineering Co 16010 Barkers Pt Ln Suite 600 *Web:* www.gie.com	Houston	TX	77079	713-850-3400	850-3579
H2M Group 575 Broad Hollow Rd *Web:* www.h2m.com	Melville	NY	11747	631-756-8000	694-4122
Haas Tcm Inc 1646 W Chester Pike **Fax Area Code:* 610 ■ *TF:* 800-220-4227 ■ *Web:* www.haastcm.com	West Chester	PA	19382	484-564-4510	436-9076*
HAKS Engineers PC 40 Wall St *Web:* www.haks.net	New York	NY	10038	212-747-1997	747-1947
Halcrow Yolles 207 Queens Quay W Suite 550 PO Box 132 *TF:* 800-572-1759 ■ *Web:* www.halcrow.com/halcrowyolles	Toronto	ON	M5J1A7	416-363-8123	363-0341
Haley & Aldrich Inc 465 Medford St Suite 2200 *Web:* www.haleyaldrich.com	Boston	MA	02129	617-886-7400	886-7600
Halff Assoc Inc 1201 N Bowser Rd *Web:* www.halff.com	Richardson	TX	75081	214-346-6200	739-0095
Hammel Green & Abrahamson Inc 701 Washington Ave N *TF:* 888-442-8255 ■ *Web:* www.hga.com	Minneapolis	MN	55401	612-758-4000	758-4199
Hanson Professional Services Inc 1525 S 6th St *TF:* 800-788-2450 ■ *Web:* www.hansonengineers.com	Springfield	IL	62703	217-788-2450	788-2503
Hardesty & Havover LLP 1501 Broadway Suite 310 *Web:* www.hardesty-hanover.com	New York	NY	10036	212-944-1150	391-0297
Harris & Assoc Inc 120 Mason Cir *Web:* www.harris-assoc.com	Concord	CA	94520	925-827-4900	
Harris Group Inc 300 Elliott Ave W *TF:* 800-488-7410 ■ *Web:* www.harrisgroup.com	Seattle	WA	98119	206-494-9400	494-9500
Hart Crowser Inc 1700 Westlake Ave N # 200 *TF:* 800-925-9530 ■ *Web:* www.hartcrowser.com	Seattle	WA	98109	206-324-9530	328-5581
Hatch Mott Macdonald Group 27 Bleeker St *Web:* www.hatchmott.com	Millburn	NJ	07041	973-379-3400	376-1072
Hazen & Sawyer PC 498 Seventh Ave 11th Fl *TF:* 800-858-9876 ■ *Web:* www.hazenandsawyer.com	New York	NY	10018	212-777-8400	614-9049
HC Nutting Co *Terracon Co* 611 Lunken Pk Dr *Web:* www.terracon.com	Cincinnati	OH	45226	513-321-5816	321-0294
HDR Engineering Inc 8404 Indian Hills Dr **Fax:* Hum Res ■ *TF:* 800-366-4411 ■ *Web:* www.hdrinc.com	Omaha	NE	68114	402-399-1000	548-5015*
Heery International Inc 999 Peachtree St NE Suite 300 *Web:* www.heery.com	Atlanta	GA	30309	404-881-9880	875-1283
Herbert Rowland & Grubic Inc 1820 Linglestown Rd *Web:* www.hrg-inc.com	Harrisburg	PA	17110	717-564-1121	564-1158
HF Lenz Co 1407 Scalp Ave *Web:* www.hflenz.com	Johnstown	PA	15904	814-269-9300	269-9301
Hill International Inc 303 Lippincott Ctr *Web:* www.hillintl.com	Marlton	NJ	08053	856-810-6200	810-0404
HKS Inc 1919 McKinney Ave *Web:* www.hksinc.com	Dallas	TX	75201	214-969-5599	969-3397
HLW International 115 5th Ave 5th Fl *Web:* www.hlw.com	New York	NY	10003	212-353-4600	353-4666
HMC Architiect 3546 Councours St *TF:* 800-350-9979 ■ *Web:* www.hmcarchitects.com	Ontario	CA	91764	909-989-9979	483-1400
HNTB Corp 715 Kirk Dr *Web:* www.hntb.com	Kansas City	MO	64105	816-472-1201	472-4060
Howard R Green Co 8710 Earhart Ln SW *TF:* 800-728-7805 ■ *Web:* www.hrgreen.com	Cedar Rapids	IA	52404	319-841-4000	841-4012
Howe-Baker Engineers Inc PO Box 956	Tyler	TX	75710	903-597-0311	595-7751
HPD Systems 23563 W Main St *TF:* 800-927-0319 ■ *Web:* www.hpdsystems.com	Plainfield	IL	60544	815-609-2000	609-0490
Hrl Laboratories LLC 3011 Malibu Canyon Rd *Web:* www.hrl.com	Malibu	CA	90265	310-317-5000	317-5483
Hubbell Roth & Clark Inc 555 Hulet Dr PO Box 824 *Web:* www.hrc-engr.com	Bloomfield Hills	MI	48303	248-454-6300	338-2592
Huitt-Zollars Inc 1717 McKinney Ave Suite 1400 *Web:* www.huitt-zollars.com	Dallas	TX	75202	214-871-3311	871-0757
Hunsaker & Assoc Irvine Inc 3 Hughes *Web:* www.hunsaker.com	Irvine	CA	92618	949-583-1010	583-0759
Hussey Gay Bell & DeYoung Inc 329 Commercial Dr Suite 200 *Web:* www.hgbd.com	Savannah	GA	31406	912-354-4626	354-6754
HW Lochner Inc 20 N Wacker Dr Suite 1200 *TF:* 800-327-7346 ■ *Web:* www.hwlochner.com	Chicago	IL	60606	312-372-7346	372-8208
ICF International Inc 9300 Lee Hwy *NASDAQ: ICFI* ■ *TF:* 800-532-4783 ■ *Web:* www.icfi.com	Fairfax	VA	22031	703-934-3603	934-3740
Icon Mechanical Construction & Engineering LLC 1616 Cleveland Blvd *TF:* 800-814-5670 ■ *Web:* www.iconmech.com	Granite City	IL	62040	618-452-0035	452-0037
IDEO 100 Forest Ave *Web:* www.ideo.com	Palo Alto	CA	94301	650-688-3400	289-3707
Imperial Electronic Assembly Inc 1000 Federal Rd *Web:* www.impea.com	Brookfield	CT	06804	203-740-8425	740-8450
Indus Technology Inc 2243 San Diego Ave *Web:* www.industechnology.com	San Diego	CA	92110	619-299-2555	299-2444
Innovation Genesis LLC The Old Corner Bookstore 3 School St *Web:* www.productgenesis.com	Cambridge	MA	02108	617-234-0070	337-9544
Integrity Applications Inc (IAI) 5160 Parkstone Dr Suite 230 *Web:* www.integrity-apps.com	Chantilly	VA	20151	703-378-8672	378-8978
Intelligent Automation Inc 15400 Calhoun Dr Suite 400 *Web:* www.i-a-i.com	Rockville	MD	20855	301-294-5200	294-5201
Interface Engineering Inc 708 SW 3rd Ave Suite 400 *Web:* www.interfaceengineering.com	Portland	OR	97204	503-382-2266	
International Electronic Machines Corp 60 4th Ave *Web:* www.iem.net	Albany	NY	12202	518-449-5504	449-5567
Intrinsix Corp 33 Lyman St *TF:* 800-783-0330 ■ *Web:* www.intrinsix.com	Westborough	MA	01581	508-836-4100	836-4222
Jacobs Engineering Group Inc 1111 S Arroyo Pkwy PO Box 7084 *NYSE: JEC* ■ **Fax:* Hum Res ■ *Web:* www.jacobs.com	Pasadena	CA	91105	626-578-3500	578-6914*
James Machine Works LLC 1521 Adams St *TF:* 800-259-6104 ■ *Web:* www.jmwinc.net	Monroe	LA	71201	318-322-6104	388-4245
Jeter Cook & Jepson Architects Inc 450 Church St *Web:* www.jcj.com	Hartford	CT	06103	860-247-9226	524-8067
John A Martin & Assoc Inc 950 S Grand Ave 4th Fl *Web:* www.johnmartin.com	Los Angeles	CA	90015	213-483-6490	483-3084
John M. Campbell & Co 1215 Crossroads Blvd *TF:* 800-821-5933 ■ *Web:* www.jmcampbell.com	Norman	OK	73072	405-321-1383	321-4533
Johnson Fain 1201 N Broadway *Web:* www.johnsonfain.com	Los Angeles	CA	90012	323-224-6000	224-6030
Johnson Mirmiran & Thompson (JMT) 72 Loveton Cir *TF:* 800-472-2310 ■ *Web:* www.jmt.com	Sparks	MD	21152	410-329-3100	472-2200
Jones Edmunds & Assoc Inc 730 NE Waldo Rd *Web:* www.jonesedmunds.com	Gainesville	FL	32641	352-377-5821	377-3166
Kadrmas Lee & Jackson Inc 677 27th Ave E PO Box 290 *Web:* www.kljeng.com	Dickinson	ND	58602	701-483-1284	483-2795
Kajima USA Inc 1251 Avenue of the Americas 9th Fl *Web:* www.kajimausa.com	New York	NY	10020	212-355-4571	355-4576
Kanawha Stone Co Inc 401 Jacobson Dr PO Box 503 *Web:* www.kanawhastone.com	Poca	WV	25159	304-755-8271	755-8274
Kaplan McLaughlin Diaz 222 Vallejo St *Web:* www.kmdarchitects.com	San Francisco	CA	94111	415-398-5191	394-7158
KBR Inc 4100 Clinton Dr *TF:* 800-231-8166 ■ *Web:* www.halliburton.com/kbr/index.jsp	Houston	TX	77020	713-753-3011	753-5353
KCI Technologies Inc 936 Ridgebrook Rd *TF:* 800-572-7496 ■ *Web:* www.kci.com/tech	Sparks	MD	21152	410-316-7800	316-7817
Keith & Schnars PA 6500 N Andrews Ave *Web:* www.keithandschnars.com	Fort Lauderdale	FL	33309	954-776-1616	771-7690
Kennedy/Jenks Consultants 303 2nd St # S300 *Web:* www.kennedyjenks.com	San Francisco	CA	94107	415-243-2150	896-0999
Kenvirons Inc 452 Versailles Rd *Web:* www.kenvirons.com	Frankfort	KY	40601	502-695-4357	695-4363
King Engineering Assoc Inc 4921 Memorial Hwy Suite 300 *TF:* 800-723-1403 ■ *Web:* www.kingengineering.com	Tampa	FL	33634	813-880-8881	
Kirkham Michael Inc 12700 W Dodge Rd PO Box 542030 *Web:* www.kirkham.com	Omaha	NE	68154	402-393-5630	255-3850
Kirksey 6909 Portwest Dr *Web:* www.kirksey.com	Houston	TX	77024	713-850-9600	850-7308
Kisinger Campo & Assoc Corp 201 N Franklin St # 400 *Web:* www.kcaeng.com	Tampa	FL	33602	813-871-5331	871-5135
KJWW Engineering Consultants PC 623 26th Ave *Web:* www.kjww.com	Rock Island	IL	61201	309-788-0673	786-5967
KKE Architects Inc 300 1st Ave N *TF:* 888-408-8569 ■ *Web:* www.kke.com	Minneapolis	MN	55401	612-339-4200	342-9267
Kleinfelder Inc 5015 Shoreham Pl *Web:* www.kleinfelder.com	San Diego	CA	92122	858-320-2000	320-2001
Klotz Assoc Inc 1160 Dairy Ashford St *Web:* www.klotz.com	Houston	TX	77079	281-589-7257	
Kohn Pedersen Fox Assoc PC 111 W 57th St *Web:* www.kpf.com	New York	NY	10019	212-977-6500	956-2526
Koltanbar Engineering Co PO Box 3456	Troy	MI	48007	248-362-2400	362-2316
KPFF Consulting Engineers Inc 1601 5th Ave Suite 1600 *Web:* www.kpff.com	Seattle	WA	98101	206-622-5822	622-8130
Kratos Defense & Security Solutions Inc 4820 Eastgate Mall Suite 200 *TF:* 866-606-5867 ■ *Web:* www.kratosdefense.com	San Diego	CA	92121	858-495-0508	812-7301

Company / Address	City	State	Zip	Phone	Fax
Krazan & Assoc Inc 215 W Dakota Ave — *Web:* www.krazan.com	Clovis	CA	93612	559-348-2200	348-2201
Kroeschell Inc 3222 N Kennicott Ave — *Web:* www.kroeschell.com	Arlington Heights	IL	60004	312-649-7980	649-3654
KSA Engineers Inc 140 E Tyler St Suite 600 PO Box 1552 — *Web:* www.ksaeng.com	Longview	TX	75601	903-236-7700	236-7779
Kta-Tator Inc 115 Technology Dr — *TF:* 800-245-6379 ■ *Web:* www.kta.com	Pittsburgh	PA	15275	412-788-1300	788-1306
Kuhlmann Design Group Inc (KDGI) 66 Progress Pkwy — *Web:* www.kdginc.com	Maryland Heights	MO	63043	314-434-8898	434-8280
Kuljian Corp 1880 JF Kennedy Blvd — *Web:* www.kuljian.com	Philadelphia	PA	19103	215-243-1900	243-1942
L Robert Kimball & Assoc Inc 615 W Highland Ave — *Web:* www.lrkimball.com	Ebensburg	PA	15931	814-472-7700	472-7712
Langan Engineering & Environmental Services Inc 619 River Dr Ctr 1 — *TF:* 800-352-6426 ■ *Web:* www.langan.com	Elmwood Park	NJ	07407	201-794-6900	794-7501
Langdon Wilson Architecture Planning Interiors 1055 Wilshire Blvd Suite 1500 — *Web:* www.langdonwilson.com	Los Angeles	CA	90017	213-250-1186	482-4654
Larson Design Group Inc 1000 Commerce Pk Dr Suite 201 PO Box 487 — *TF:* 877-323-6603 ■ *Web:* www.larsondesigngroup.com	Williamsport	PA	17701	570-323-6603	323-9902
Lauren Engineers & Constructors Inc PO Box 1761 — *Web:* www.laurenec.com	Abilene	TX	79604	325-670-9660	670-9663
Lawler Matusky & Skelly Engineers LLP 1 Blue Hill Plaza — *Web:* www.lmseng.com	Pearl River	NY	10965	845-735-8300	735-7466
LBA Group Inc 3400 Tupper Dr — *TF:* 800-522-4464 ■ *Web:* www.lbagroup.com	Greenville	NC	27834	252-757-0279	752-9155
Lee Burkhart Liu Inc 13335 Maxella Ave — *Web:* www.lblarch.com	Marina del Rey	CA	90292	310-829-2249	829-1736
Leighton Group Inc 17781 Cowan St — *Web:* www.leightongroup.com	Irvine	CA	92614	949-250-1421	250-1114
LeMessurier Consultants 675 Massachusetts Ave — *Web:* www.lemessurier.com	Cambridge	MA	02139	617-868-1200	661-7520
Leo A Daly 8600 Indian Hills Dr — *Web:* www.leoadaly.com	Omaha	NE	68114	402-391-8111	391-8111
Lhb Inc 21 W Superior St Suite 500 — *Web:* www.lhbcorp.com	Duluth	MN	55802	218-727-8446	
Lionakis Beaumont Design Group Inc 1919 19th St — *Web:* www.lbdg.com	Sacramento	CA	95814	916-558-1900	558-1919
LiRo Group 6 Aerial Way — *Web:* www.liro.com	Syosset	NY	11791	516-938-5476	938-5491
LJB Inc 3100 Research Blvd PO Box 20246 — *TF:* 866-552-3536 ■ *Web:* www.ljbinc.com	Dayton	OH	45420	937-259-5000	259-5100
LMN Architects 801 2nd Ave Suite 501 — *TF:* 800-966-3087 ■ *Web:* www.lmnarchitects.com	Seattle	WA	98104	206-682-3460	343-9388
Locating Inc 2575 Westside Pkwy Suite 100 — *Web:* www.locatinginc.com	Alpharetta	GA	30004	678-461-3900	461-3902
Lockwood Andrews & Newnam Inc 2925 Briar Pk Dr — *Web:* www.lan-inc.com	Houston	TX	77042	713-266-6900	266-2089
Lockwood Kessler & Bartlett Inc 1 Aerial Way — *Web:* www.lkbinc.com	Syosset	NY	11791	516-938-0600	931-6344
Lohan Caprile Goettsch Architects *Goettsch Partners* 224 S Michigan Ave 17th Fl — *Web:* www.gpchicago.com	Chicago	IL	60604	312-356-0600	356-0601
Loiederman Soltesz Assoc 1390 Piccard Dr Suite 100 — *Web:* www.lsassociates.net	Rockville	MD	20850	301-948-2750	948-6321
Looney Ricks Kiss Architects 175 Toyota Plaza Suite 600 — *Web:* www.lrk.com	Memphis	TN	38103	901-521-1440	525-2760
Louis Berger Group Inc 100 Halsted St — *TF:* 800-323-4098 ■ *Web:* www.louisberger.com	East Orange	NJ	07018	973-678-1960	672-4284
LPA Group Inc 700 Huger St — *Web:* www.lpagroup.com	Columbia	SC	29201	803-254-2211	779-8749
LPA Inc 5161 California Ave Suite 100 — *Web:* www.lpainc.com	Irvine	CA	92617	949-261-1001	260-1190
LS3P Assoc Ltd 205 1/2 King St — *Web:* www.ls3p.com	Charleston	SC	29401	843-577-4444	722-4789
Lumos & Assoc Inc 800 E College Pkwy — *TF:* 800-621-7155 ■ *Web:* www.lumosengineering.com	Carson City	NV	89706	775-883-7077	883-7114
M & W Zander US Operations Inc 549 W Randolph St	Chicago	IL	60661	312-577-3200	577-3525
M-E Engineers Inc 10055 W 43rd Ave — *Web:* www.me-engineers.com	Wheat Ridge	CO	80033	303-421-6655	421-0331
M/E Engineering PC 150 N Chestnut St — *Web:* www.meengineering.com	Rochester	NY	14604	585-288-5590	288-0233
Macaulay-Brown Inc 4021 Executive Dr — *Web:* www.macb.com	Dayton	OH	45430	937-426-3421	426-5364
MacKay & Somps (MSCE) 5142 Franklin Dr Suite B — *Web:* www.msce.com	Pleasanton	CA	94588	925-225-0690	225-0698
Magnusson Klemencic Assoc Inc 1301 5th Ave Suite 3200 — *Web:* www.mka.com	Seattle	WA	98101	206-292-1200	292-1201
Maguire Group Inc 33 Commercial St Suite 1 — *Web:* www.maguiregroup.com	Foxboro	MA	02035	508-543-1700	543-5157
Mahlum Architects Inc 71 Columbia St 4Fl — *Web:* www.mahlum.com	Seattle	WA	98104	206-441-4151	441-0478
Malcolm Pirnie Inc 104 Corporate Pk Dr — *TF:* 800-759-5020 ■ *Web:* www.pirnie.com	White Plains	NY	10602	914-694-2100	694-9286
Malouf Engineering International Inc 17950 Preston Rd Suite 720 — *Web:* www.maloufengineering.com	Dallas	TX	75252	972-783-2578	783-2583
Management Consulting Inc 1961 Diamond Springs Rd — *TF:* 877-624-8090 ■ *Web:* www.manconinc.com	Virginia Beach	VA	23455	757-460-0879	460-0317
Manufacturing & Engineering Excellence Inc 615 Dado St — *Web:* www.me2inc.com	San Jose	CA	95131	408-382-1900	382-1909
MAR Inc 1803 Research Blvd Suite 204 — **Fax Area Code:* 240 ■ *Web:* www.marinc.com	Rockville	MD	20850	301-231-0100	453-9871*
Marine Systems Corp 70 Fargo St Seaport Ctr — *Web:* www.mscorp.net	Boston	MA	02210	617-542-3345	542-2461
MARISA Industries Inc 1426 Pacific Dr — *Web:* www.marisaind.com	Auburn Hills	MI	48326	248-475-9600	475-9908
Mark Thomas & Co Inc 1960 Zanker Rd — *Web:* www.markthomas.com	San Jose	CA	95112	408-453-5373	453-5390
Marshall Miller & Assoc Rt 720 Bluefield Industrial Pk PO Box 848 — *Web:* www.mma1.com	Bluefield	VA	24605	276-322-5467	322-3102
Maser Consulting PA 331 Newman Springs Rd 1 River Centre Bldg 2 — *Web:* www.maserconsulting.com	Red Bank	NJ	07701	732-383-1950	383-1984
Matrix Design Group Inc 1601 Blake St Suite 200 — *Web:* www.matrixdesigngroup.com	Denver	CO	80202	303-572-0200	
MBH Architects 2470 Mariner Sq Loop — *TF:* 888-689-8880 ■ *Web:* www.mbharch.com	Alameda	CA	94501	510-865-8663	865-1611
Mbs Assoc Inc 10148 Commerce Pk Dr — *TF:* 888-469-9301 ■ *Web:* www.mbsassociates.com	Cincinnati	OH	45246	513-645-1600	680-4587
McCormick Taylor & Assoc Inc 2 Commerce Sq 10th Fl — *Web:* www.mccormicktaylor.com	Philadelphia	PA	19103	215-592-4200	592-0682
McCrone Inc 20 Ridgely Ave 2nd Fl — *Web:* www.mccrone-inc.com	Annapolis	MD	21401	410-267-8621	
McDonough Assoc Inc 130 E Randolph St Suite 1000 — *Web:* www.maiengr.com	Chicago	IL	60601	312-946-8600	946-7199
McDonough Bolyard Peck Inc (MBP) 3040 Williams Dr Williams Plaza 1 Suite 300 — *TF:* 800-898-9088 ■ *Web:* www.mbpce.com	Fairfax	VA	22031	703-641-9088	641-8965
MCG Architecture 1055 E Colorado Blvd Suite 400 — *Web:* www.mcgarchitecture.com	Pasadena	CA	91106	626-793-9119	796-9295
Mcgoodwin Williams & Yates Inc (MWY) 302 E Millsap Rd — *Web:* www.mwyusa.com	Fayetteville	AR	72703	479-443-3404	443-4340
McKim & Creed PA 243 N Front St — *Web:* www.mckimcreed.com	Wilmington	NC	28401	910-343-1048	251-8282
McLaren Performance Technologies Inc 32233 W Eight Mile Rd — *Web:* www.mclarenperformance.com	Livonia	MI	48152	248-477-6240	477-3349
McLaughlin Research Corp 132 Johnnycake Hill Rd — *TF:* 800-556-7154 ■ *Web:* www.mrcds.com	Middletown	RI	02842	401-849-4010	847-9716
McMahon Group 1445 McMahon Dr — *Web:* www.mcmgrp.com	Neenah	WI	54956	920-751-4200	751-4284
MCR LLC 2010 Corporate Ridge Suite 350 — *Web:* www.mcri.com	Mclean	VA	22102	703-506-4600	506-8601
Mda Information Systems Inc 6011 Executive Blvd — *TF:* 800-642-1687 ■ *Web:* www.mdafederal.com	Rockville	MD	20852	240-833-8200	833-8201
Mead & Hunt Inc 6501 Watts Rd — *Web:* www.meadhunt.com	Madison	WI	53719	608-273-6380	273-6391
Merrick & Co 2450 S Peoria St — *TF:* 800-544-1714 ■ *Web:* www.merrick.com	Aurora	CO	80014	303-751-0741	751-2581
Mesa Assoc Inc PO Box 196 — *Web:* www.mesainc.com	Madison	AL	35758	256-258-2100	258-2103
Michael Baker Corp 100 Airsite Dr Airsite Business Pk — *AMEX:* BKR ■ *TF:* 800-553-1153 ■ *Web:* www.mbakercorp.com	Moon Township	PA	15108	412-269-6300	375-3977
Michaud Cooley Erickson & Assoc Inc 1200 Metropolitan Ctr 333 S 7th St — *Web:* www.michaudcooley.com	Minneapolis	MN	55402	612-339-4941	339-8354
Middough Assoc Inc 1901 E 13th St — **Fax:* Hum Res ■ *Web:* www.middough.com	Cleveland	OH	44114	216-771-2060	367-6020*
Midrex Technologies 2725 Water Ridge Pkwy Suite 100 — *Web:* www.midrex.com	Charlotte	NC	28217	704-373-1600	373-1611
Miller Architects & Builders Inc 3335 W St Germain St # 101 — *TF:* 800-772-1758 ■ *Web:* www.millerab.com	Saint Cloud	MN	56301	320-251-4109	251-4693
Missman Inc 1011 27th Ave PO Box 6040 — *Web:* www.missman.com	Rock Island	IL	61204	309-788-7644	788-7691
Modern Technology Solutions Inc (MTSI) 5285 Shawnee Rd Suite 400 — *Web:* www.mtsi-va.com	Alexandria	VA	22312	703-564-3800	
Modjeski & Masters Inc PO Box 2345 — *Web:* www.modjeski.com	Harrisburg	PA	17105	717-790-9565	790-9564
Moffatt & Nichol Engineers 3780 Kilroy Airport Way # 750 — *Web:* www.moffattnichol.com	Long Beach	CA	90806	562-590-6500	590-6512
Monte R Lee & Co 100 NW 63rd St Suite 100 — *Web:* www.mrleng.com	Oklahoma City	OK	73116	405-842-2405	848-8018
Moody Nolan Inc 300 Spruce St Suite 300 — *TF:* 877-530-4984 ■ *Web:* www.moodynolan.com	Columbus	OH	43215	614-461-4664	280-8881
Moreland & Altobelli Assoc Inc 2211 Beaver Ruin Rd Suite 190 — *Web:* www.maai.net	Norcross	GA	30071	770-263-5945	263-0166

Company / Address	City	State	Zip	Phone	Fax
Morris Architects 1001 Fannin St Suite 300	Houston	TX	77002	713-622-1180	622-7021
Web: www.morrisarchitects.com					
Morrison-Maierle Inc 1 Engineering Pl	Helena	MT	59602	406-442-3050	442-8962
Web: www.m-m.net					
MS Consultants Inc 333 E Federal St	Youngstown	OH	44503	330-744-5321	744-5256
Web: www.msconsultants.com					
Mse Power Systems Inc 403 New Karner Rd	Albany	NY	12205	518-452-7718	452-7716
Web: www.msepower.com					
MSX International Inc 1950 Concept Dr	Warren	MI	48091	248-829-6300	
Web: www.msxi.com					
Mueser Rutledge Consulting Engineers (MRCE)					
14 Penn Plaza 225 W 34th St 2nd Fl	New York	NY	10122	917-339-9300	339-9400
Web: www.mrce.com					
Multax Systems Inc					
505 N Sepulveda Blvd Suite 7	Manhattan Beach	CA	90266	310-379-8398	379-1142
TF: 800-888-0199 ■ *Web:* www.multax.net					
MulvanneyG2 Architecture					
1110 112th Ave NE #500	Bellevue	WA	98004	425-463-2000	463-2002
Web: www.mulvannyg2.com					
Mustang Engineering LP 16001 Pk Ten Pl	Houston	TX	77084	713-215-8000	215-8506
Web: www.mustangeng.com					
Nadel Architects 1990 S Bundy Dr 4th Fl	Los Angeles	CA	90025	310-826-2100	826-0182
Web: www.nadelarc.com					
National Security Technologies LLC					
2621 Losee Rd	Las Vegas	NV	89030	702-295-1000	295-2448
Web: www.nstec.com					
NBBJ 223 Yale Ave N	Seattle	WA	98109	206-223-5555	621-2300
Web: www.nbbj.com					
Neel-Schaffer Inc					
125 S Congress St Suite 1100	Jackson	MS	39201	601-948-3178	948-3071
Web: www.neel-schaffer.com					
Neff Engineering Co 7114 Innovation Blvd	Fort Wayne	IN	46818	260-489-6007	489-6204
Web: www.neffengineering.com					
Nesbitt Engineering Inc (NEI) 227 N Upper St	Lexington	KY	40475	859-233-3111	259-2717
Web: www.nei-ky.com					
New Tech Engineering LP 1030 Regional Pk Dr	Houston	TX	77060	281-951-4330	951-8719
Web: www.newtechengineering.com					
Newcomb & Boyd					
303 Peachtree Ctr Ave NE Suite 525	Atlanta	GA	30303	404-730-8400	730-8401
Web: www.newcomb-boyd.com					
Niles Bolton Assoc Inc (NBA)					
3060 Peachtree Rd NW Suite 600	Atlanta	GA	30305	404-365-7600	365-7610
Web: www.nilesbolton.com					
Ninyo & Moore 5710 Ruffin Rd	San Diego	CA	92123	858-576-1000	576-9600
TF: 800-427-0401 ■ *Web:* www.ninyoandmoore.com					
Nolte Assoc Inc 2495 Natomas Pk Dr # 4	Sacramento	CA	95833	916-641-9100	641-9222
TF: 800-216-6583 ■ *Web:* www.nolte.com					
Northwestern Engineering Co PO Box 2624	Rapid City	SD	57709	605-394-3310	341-2558
Web: www.nwemanagement.com					
Nova Group Inc 185 Devlin Rd	Napa	CA	94558	707-257-3200	257-2774
Web: www.novagrp.com					
Novariant Inc 45700 Northport Loop E	Fremont	CA	94538	510-933-4800	933-4801
Web: www.novariant.com					
O'Brien & Gere Engineers Inc					
333 W Washington St	East Syracuse	NY	13202	315-437-6100	463-7554
Web: www.obg.com					
O'Neal Inc 10 Falcon Crest Dr	Greenville	SC	29607	864-298-2000	298-2200
Web: www.onealinc.com					
Odell Assoc Inc 800 W Hill St 3rd Fl	Charlotte	NC	28208	704-414-1000	414-1111
Web: www.odell.com					
Olsson Assoc 1111 Lincoln Mall	Lincoln	NE	68508	402-474-6311	474-5160
Web: www.oaconsulting.com					
Omni-Means Ltd 943 Reserve Dr Suite 100	Roseville	CA	95678	916-782-8688	782-8689
Web: www.omnimeans.com					
Operational Technologies Corp					
4100 NW Loop 410 Suite 230	San Antonio	TX	78229	210-731-0000	731-0008
TF: 800-677-8072 ■ *Web:* www.otcorp.com					
Optical Components Inc (OCI) 1175 E Edna Pl	Covina	CA	91724	626-967-5281	967-2513
Web: www.ocioptics.com					
Orbital Engineering Inc 1344 5th Ave	Pittsburgh	PA	15219	412-261-9100	261-2308
Web: www.orbitalengr.com					
Orchard Hiltz & McCliment Inc (OHM)					
34000 Plymouth Rd	Livonia	MI	48150	734-522-6711	522-6427
TF: 888-522-6711 ■ *Web:* www.ohm-advisors.com					
ORI Services Corp 4565 Ruffner St Suite 201	San Diego	CA	92111	858-576-4422	576-4475
Web: www.oriservices.com					
Ortloff Engineers Ltd					
415 W Wall Ave Suite 2000	Midland	TX	79701	432-685-0277	685-0258
Web: www.ortloff.com					
Otak Inc 17355 Boones Ferry Rd	Lake Oswego	OR	97035	503-635-3618	635-5395
Web: www.otak.com					
Overlook Systems Technologies Inc					
1950 Old Gallows Rd Suite 400	Vienna	VA	22182	703-893-1411	356-9029
Web: www.overlooksys.com					
Owen Group Inc 20 Morgan	Irvine	CA	92618	949-860-4800	860-4810
TF: 800-600-6936 ■ *Web:* www.owengroup.com					
Pacific Architects & Engineers Inc					
888 S Figueroa St Suite 1700	Los Angeles	CA	90017	213-481-2311	481-7189
Web: www.paegroup.com					
Pacific Blue Micro Inc (PBM)					
16800 Aston St Suite 175	Irvine	CA	92606	949-417-7000	
TF: 800-660-0720 ■ *Web:* www.pacblue.com					
Pacifica Services Inc					
106 S Mentor Ave Suite 200	Pasadena	CA	91106	626-405-0131	405-0059
Web: www.pacificaservices.com					
PageSoutherlandPage (PSPAEC)					
1100 Louisiana St Suite 1	Houston	TX	77002	713-871-8484	871-8440
Web: www.pspaec.com					
Pape-Dawson Engineers Inc 555 E Ramsey	San Antonio	TX	78216	210-375-9000	375-9010
Web: www.pape-dawson.com					
Paragon Engineering Services Inc					
2201 S Queen St	York	PA	17402	717-854-7374	854-5533
Web: www.peservices.org					

Company / Address	City	State	Zip	Phone	Fax
Parametrix Inc 1231 Fryar Ave	Sumner	WA	98390	253-863-5128	863-0946
Web: www.parametrix.com					
Parkhill Smith & Cooper Inc 4222 85th St	Lubbock	TX	79423	806-473-2200	473-3500
Web: www.team-psc.com					
Parsons 100 Summer St Suite 800	Boston	MA	02110	617-457-7900	457-7979
Web: www.parsons.com					
Parsons Brinckerhoff Inc 1 Penn Plaza 2nd Fl	New York	NY	10119	212-465-5000	465-5096
Web: www.pbworld.com					
Parsons Corp 100 W Walnut St	Pasadena	CA	91124	626-440-2000	440-2630
TF: 800-883-7300 ■ *Web:* www.parsons.com					
Parsons Harland Bartholomew & Assoc Inc					
400 S Woods Mill Rd # 33	Chesterfield	MO	63017	314-434-2900	576-2702
Web: www.parsons.com					
Parsons Infrastructure & Technology					
100 W Walnut St	Pasadena	CA	91124	626-440-4000	440-6200
TF: 800-883-7300 ■ *Web:* www.parsons.com					
Parsons Transportation Group					
1133 15th St NW Suite 800	Washington	DC	20005	202-775-3300	775-3422
Patrick Engineering Inc 4970 Varsity Dr	Lisle	IL	60532	800-799-7050	
TF: 800-799-7050 ■ *Web:* www.patrickengineering.com					
Patton Harris Rust & Assoc PC (PHRA)					
14532 Lee Rd	Chantilly	VA	20151	703-449-6700	449-6713
TF: 800-550-7472 ■ *Web:* www.phra.com					
Paul C Rizzo Assoc Inc 500 Penn Ctr Blvd	Pittsburgh	PA	15235	412-856-9700	
Web: www.rizzoassoc.com					
Paulus Sokolowski & Sartor LLC					
67 Mountain Blvd # B	Warren	NJ	07059	732-560-9700	
Web: www.psands.com					
Payette Assoc Inc 290 Congress St 5th Fl	Boston	MA	02210	617-895-1000	895-1002
Web: www.payette.com					
PB-KBB Inc 11757 Katy Fwy Suite 600	Houston	TX	77079	281-496-5590	589-5865
Web: www.pbworld.com					
PCA Engineering Inc					
57 Cannonball Rd PO Box 196	Pompton Lakes	NJ	07442	973-616-4501	616-4451
TF: 800-666-7221 ■ *Web:* www.cpbypca.com					
Pei Cobb Freed & Partners Architects LLP					
88 Pine St	New York	NY	10005	212-751-3122	872-5443
Web: www.pcfandp.com					
Pennoni Assoc Inc					
1 Drexel Plaza 3001 Market St 2nd Fl	Philadelphia	PA	19104	215-222-3000	222-0384
Web: www.pennoni.com					
Perkins & Will 330 N Wabash Ave Suite 3600	Chicago	IL	60611	312-755-0770	755-0775
TF: 800-837-9455 ■ *Web:* www.perkinswill.com					
Perkowitz + Ruth Architects					
111 W Ocean Blvd 21st Fl	Long Beach	CA	90802	562-628-8000	628-8001
Web: www.prarchitects.com					
Perteet Inc					
2707 Colby Ave Suite 900 PO Box 1186	Everett	WA	98201	425-252-7700	339-6018
TF: 800-615-9900 ■ *Web:* www.perteet.com					
Petrocon Engineering Inc PO Box 20397	Beaumont	TX	77720	409-840-2100	840-2200
TF: 800-256-5710 ■ *Web:* www.petrocon.com					
Phillips Swager Assoc					
401 SW Water St Suite 701	Peoria	IL	61602	309-282-8000	282-8001
Web: www.psa-ae.com					
Pierce Goodwin Alexander & Linville (PGAL)					
3131 Briarpark Suite 200	Houston	TX	77042	713-622-1444	968-9333
Web: www.pgal.com					
Pincock Allen & Holt A Div Of Runge Inc					
165 S Union Blvd Suite 950	Lakewood	CO	80228	303-986-6950	987-8907
Web: www.pincock.com					
Pittsburgh Design Services Inc PO Box 469	Carnegie	PA	15106	412-276-3000	276-1216
Poggemeyer Design Group Inc					
1168 N Main St	Bowling Green	OH	43402	419-352-7537	353-0187
Web: www.poggemeyer.com					
Power Engineering Corp PO Box 766	Wilkes-Barre	PA	18703	570-823-8822	823-8143
TF: 800-626-0903 ■ *Web:* www.powerengineeringcorp.com					
Power Engineers Inc					
3940 Glenbrook Dr PO Box 1066	Hailey	ID	83333	208-788-3456	788-2082
TF: 800-331-3902 ■ *Web:* www.powereng.com					
Ppi Technology Services LP					
800 Gessner Rd Suite 900	Houston	TX	77024	713-464-2200	699-1348*
**Fax Area Code:* 866 ■ *Web:* www.ppitech.net					
PPM Consultants Inc 2508 Ticheli Rd	Monroe	LA	71202	318-323-7270	323-6593
TF: 800-761-8675 ■ *Web:* www.ppmco.com					
Prein & Newhof Inc 3355 Evergreen Dr Ne	Grand Rapids	MI	49525	616-364-8491	364-6955
Web: www.preinnewhof.com					
Preston Partnership LLC					
1000 Abernathy Rd NE Suite 600	Atlanta	GA	30328	770-396-7248	396-2945
Web: www.theprestonpartnership.com					
Priority Designs Inc 501 Morrison Rd	Columbus	OH	43230	614-337-9979	337-9499
Web: www.prioritydesigns.com					
Pro-Inspect Inc 1710 Sens Rd	La Porte	TX	77571	281-470-7783	470-7785
TF: 800-762-8289 ■ *Web:* www.pro-inspect.com					
Product Development Technologies Inc					
1 Corporate Dr	Lake Zurich	IL	60047	847-821-3000	821-3020
Web: www.pdt.com					
Professional Engineering Consultants PA					
303 S Topeka St	Wichita	KS	67202	316-262-2691	262-3003
Web: www.pec1.com					
Professional Service Industries Inc (PSI)					
1901 S Meyers Rd Suite 400	Oakbrook Terrace	IL	60181	630-691-1490	691-1587
TF: 800-548-7901 ■ *Web:* www.psiusa.com					
Project Resources Inc					
3760 Convoy St Suite 230	San Diego	CA	92111	858-505-1000	505-1010
Web: www.priworld.com					
ProjectDesign Consultants					
701 B St Suite 800	San Diego	CA	92101	619-235-6471	234-0349
Web: www.projectdesign.com					
Psomas & Assoc					
11444 W Olympic Blvd Suite 750	West Los Angeles	CA	90064	310-954-3700	954-3777
Web: www.psomas.com					

	City	State	Zip	Phone	Fax
PTI Engineered Plastics Inc 50900 Corporate Dr *Web:* www.teampti.com	Macomb	MI	48044	586-263-5100	263-6680
Qk4 815 W Market St Suite 300 *TF:* 800-928-2222 ■ *Web:* www.qk4.com	Louisville	KY	40202	502-585-2222	581-0406
R T Patterson Co Inc 230 3rd Ave 2nd Fl *Web:* www.rtpatterson.net	Pittsburgh	PA	15222	412-227-6600	227-6672
RBA Group Inc 1 Evergreen Pl PO Box 1927 *Web:* www.rbagroup.com	Morristown	NJ	07962	973-898-0300	984-5421
RBC Inc 100 N Pitt St Suite 300 *Web:* www.rbcinc.com	Alexandria	VA	22314	703-549-6921	549-6926
RBF Consulting 14725 Alton Pkwy *TF:* 800-479-3808 ■ *Web:* www.rbf.com	Irvine	CA	92618	949-472-3505	472-8373
RCM Technologies Inc 2500 McClellan Ave Suite 350 *NASDAQ: RCMT* ■ *Web:* www.rcmt.com	Pennsauken	NJ	08109	856-356-4500	356-4600
Reimelt Corp 13330 Byrd Dr *Web:* www.reimelt.com	Odessa	FL	33556	813-920-7434	920-3864
Remington & Vernick Engineers Inc 232 Kings Hwy E *Web:* www.rve.com	Haddonfield	NJ	08033	856-795-9595	795-1882
Rentenbach Engineering Co 2400 Sutherland Ave *TF:* 800-621-4941 ■ *Web:* www.rentenbach.com	Knoxville	TN	37919	865-546-2440	546-3414
Research Management Consultants Inc 816 Camarillo Springs Rd Suite J *Web:* www.rmci.com	Camarillo	CA	93012	805-987-5538	987-2868
Respec Inc 3824 Jet Dr *TF:* 877-737-7321 ■ *Web:* www.respec.com	Rapid City	SD	57703	605-394-6400	394-6456
Rettew Assoc Inc 3020 Columbia Ave *TF:* 800-738-8395 ■ *Web:* www.rettew.com	Lancaster	PA	17603	717-394-3721	394-1063
Revak Cos The 12204 W Fairmont Pkwy PO Box 1645 *Web:* www.revak.com	La Porte	TX	77572	281-474-4458	474-5137
Reynolds Smith & Hills Inc 10748 Deerwood Pk Blvd *TF:* 800-741-2014 ■ *Web:* www.rsandh.com	Jacksonville	FL	32256	904-256-2500	256-2501
RK&K 81 W Mosher St *TF:* 800-787-3755 ■ *Web:* www.rkk.com	Baltimore	MD	21217	410-728-2900	728-0282
RM Towill Corp 2024 N King St Suite 200 *Web:* www.rmtowill.com	Honolulu	HI	96819	808-842-1133	842-1937
RMF Engineering Inc 5520 Research Pk Dr 3rd Fl *TF:* 800-938-5760 ■ *Web:* www.rmf.com	Baltimore	MD	21228	410-576-0505	385-0327
RMT Inc 744 Heartland Trail *TF:* 800-283-3443 ■ *Web:* www.rmtinc.com	Madison	WI	53717	608-831-4444	831-3334
RNL Design 1050 17th St # A200 *Web:* www.rnldesign.com	Denver	CO	80265	303-295-1717	292-0845
Roberts & Schaefer Co 222 S Riverside Plaza Suite 1800 *Web:* www.r-s.com	Chicago	IL	60606	312-236-7292	726-2872
Ross & Baruzzini 6 S Old Orchard Ave *Web:* www.rossbar.com	Webster Groves	MO	63119	314-918-8383	918-1766
Rosser International 524 W Peachtree St NW *Web:* www.rosser.com	Atlanta	GA	30308	404-876-3800	888-6863
Rothenbuhler Engineering 524 Rhodes Rd PO Box 708 *Web:* www.rothenbuhlereng.com	Sedro Woolley	WA	98284	360-856-0836	856-2183
RSP Architects 1220 Marshall St NE *Web:* www.rsparch.com	Minneapolis	MN	55413	612-677-7100	677-7499
RTKL Assoc Inc 901 S Bond St *TF:* 800-345-7855 ■ *Web:* www.rtkl.com	Baltimore	MD	21231	410-537-6000	276-2136
Ruekert & Mielke Inc W233 N2080 Ridgeview Pkwy *Web:* www.ruekert-mielke.com	Waukesha	WI	53188	262-542-5733	542-5631
S & B Engineers & Constructors Ltd 7825 Pk Pl Blvd *Web:* www.sbec.com	Houston	TX	77087	713-645-4141	643-8029
S E A Consultants Inc 215 1st St # 320 *Web:* www.seacon.com	Cambridge	MA	02142	617-497-7800	498-4630
S Systems Corp 5777 W Century Blvd Suite 520 *Web:* www.s-sc.com	Los Angeles	CA	90045	310-215-0248	642-3738
S/L/A/M Collaborative 80 Glastonbury Blvd *Web:* www.slamcoll.com	Glastonbury	CT	06033	860-657-8077	657-3141
SA Healy Co 1910 S Highland Ave Suite 300 *TF:* 888-724-3259 ■ *Web:* www.sahealy.com	Lombard	IL	60148	630-678-3110	678-3130
Sabre Industries Inc 1120 Welsh Rd Suite 210 *TF:* 888-722-7350 ■ *Web:* www.sabreindustriesinc.com	North Wales	PA	19454	267-263-1300	263-1301
SAI Consulting Engineers Inc 1400 Penn Ave Suite 101 *Web:* www.saiengr.com	Pittsburgh	PA	15222	412-392-8750	392-8785
Saipem America Inc 15950 Pk Row *Web:* www.saipemamerica.com	Houston	TX	77084	281-552-5600	552-5910
Sargent & Lundy LLC 55 E Monroe St *Web:* www.sargentlundy.com	Chicago	IL	60603	312-269-2000	269-3454
Sasaki Assoc Inc 64 Pleasant St *Web:* www.sasaki.com	Watertown	MA	02472	617-926-3300	924-2748
Savin Engineers PC 3 Campus Dr *Web:* www.savinengineers.com	Pleasantville	NY	10570	914-769-3200	747-6686
Scale Models Unlimited 400 S Front St Suite 300 *Web:* www.smu.com	Memphis	TN	38103	901-577-5155	577-5157
Schafer Corp 321 Billerica Rd **Fax: Hum Res* ■ *Web:* www.schafercorp.com	Chelmsford	MA	01824	978-256-2070	256-1404*
SchenkelShultz Architects 111 E Wayne St Suite 555 *Web:* www.schenkelshultz.com	Fort Wayne	IN	46802	260-424-9080	424-1222
Schnabel Engineering Inc 1054 Technology Pk Dr *Web:* www.schnabel-eng.com	Glen Allen	VA	23059	804-264-3222	264-3244
Schneider Corp 8901 Otis Ave *TF:* 800-898-0332 ■ *Web:* www.theschneidercorp.com	Indianapolis	IN	46216	317-826-7100	826-7200
Scientech Inc 200 S Woodruff Ave *TF:* 800-247-8818 ■ *Web:* www.scientech.com	Idaho Falls	ID	83401	208-529-1000	524-9282
SCS Engineers 3900 Kilroy Airport Way Suite 100 *TF:* 800-326-9544 ■ *Web:* www.scsengineers.com	Long Beach	CA	90806	562-426-9544	427-0805
SE Technologies LLC 98 Vanadium Rd Bldg D *TF:* 800-685-0354 ■ *Web:* www.se-env.com	Bridgeville	PA	15017	412-221-1100	257-6103
Sebesta Blomberg & Assoc Inc 2381 W Cleveland Service Dr *TF:* 877-706-6858 ■ *Web:* www.sebesta.com	Roseville	MN	55113	651-634-0775	634-7400
SEI Group Inc 303 Williams Ave SW Suite 135 *Web:* www.seigroupinc.com	Huntsville	AL	35801	256-533-0500	533-5516
SENTEL Corp 1101 King St Suite 550 *Web:* www.sentel.com	Alexandria	VA	22314	703-739-0084	739-6028
Shannon & Wilson Inc PO Box 300303 *TF Cust Svc:* 800-633-6800 ■ *Web:* www.shannonwilson.com	Seattle	WA	98103	206-632-8020	633-6777
Sheladia Assoc Inc 15825 Shady Grove Rd Suite 100 *Web:* www.sheladia.com	Rockville	MD	20850	301-590-3939	948-7174
Shepley Bulfinch 2 Seaport Ln *Web:* www.shepleybulfinch.com	Boston	MA	02210	617-423-1700	451-2420
Shive-Hattery Inc (SH) 316 2nd St SE Suite 500 PO Box 1599 *TF:* 800-798-0227 ■ *Web:* www.shive-hattery.com	Cedar Rapids	IA	52406	319-362-0313	362-2883
Short-Elliott-Hendrickson Inc 3535 Vadnais Ctr Dr *TF:* 800-325-2055 ■ *Web:* www.sehinc.com	Saint Paul	MN	55110	651-490-2000	490-2150
Simpson Gumpertz & Heger Inc 41 Seyon St Bldg 1 Suite 500 *Web:* www.sgh.com	Waltham	MA	02453	781-907-9000	907-9009
Sino Swearingen Aircraft Corp 1770 Skyplace Blvd *Web:* www.sj30jet.com	San Antonio	TX	78216	210-258-3959	258-8650
SJB Group Inc 5745 Essen Ln Suite 200 *Web:* www.sjbgroup.com	Baton Rouge	LA	70821	225-769-3400	769-3596
Skelly & Loy Inc 449 Eisenhower Blvd *TF:* 800-892-5653 ■ *Web:* www.skellyloy.com	Harrisburg	PA	17111	717-232-0593	232-1799
Skidmore Owings & Merrill 224 S Michigan Ave Suite 1000 *Web:* www.som.com	Chicago	IL	60604	312-554-9090	360-4545
Smallwood Reynolds Stewart Stewart & Assoc Inc (SRSSA) One Piedmont Ctr 3565 Piedmont Rd Bldg 1 Suite 303 *Web:* www.srssa.com	Atlanta	GA	30305	404-233-5453	264-0929
SmithGroup Inc 500 Griswold St Suite 1700 *Web:* www.smithgroup.com	Detroit	MI	48226	313-983-3600	983-3636
SMS Concast America Inc 100 Sandusky St *Web:* www.sms-concast.ch	Pittsburgh	PA	15212	412-237-8950	237-8951
SMS Demag Inc 100 Sandusky St	Pittsburgh	PA	15212	412-231-1200	231-3995
SNC Lavalin Group Inc 455 Rene-Levesque Blvd W *TSE: SNC* ■ *Web:* www.snc-lavalin.com	Montreal	QC	H2Z1Z3	514-393-1000	866-0795
Snyder & Assoc Inc PO Box 1159 *TF:* 888-964-2020 ■ *Web:* www.snyder-associates.com	Ankeny	IA	50021	515-964-2020	964-7938
Sofec Inc 14741 Yorktown Plaza *TF:* 800-462-6003 ■ *Web:* www.sofec.com	Houston	TX	77070	713-510-6600	510-6601
Soil Consultant Engineering (SCE) 9303 Ctr St *Web:* www.soilconsultants.net	Manassas	VA	20110	703-366-3000	366-3400
Solekai Systems Corp 3398 Carmel Mountain Rd *Web:* www.solekai.com	San Diego	CA	92121	858-436-2040	436-2041
Sonalysts Inc 215 Waterford PkwyNorth *TF:* 800-526-8091 ■ *Web:* www.sonalysts.com	Waterford	CT	06385	860-442-4355	447-8883
Southern Co Services Inc 42 Inverness Ctr Pkwy	Birmingham	AL	35242	205-992-6011	
SPACECO Inc 9575 W Higgins Rd Suite 700 *TF:* 888-772-2326 ■ *Web:* www.spacecoinc.com	Rosemont	IL	60018	847-696-4060	696-4065
SPEC Services Inc 17101 Bushard St *Web:* www.specservices.com	Fountain Valley	CA	92708	714-963-8077	963-0364
SPI/Mobile Pulley Works Inc 905 S Ann St *TF:* 866-334-6325 ■ *Web:* www.spimpw.com	Mobile	AL	36605	251-653-0606	653-0668
SRF Consulting Group Inc 1 Carlson Pkwy N Suite 150 *Web:* www.srfconsulting.com	Minneapolis	MN	55447	763-475-0010	475-2429
SRK Consulting Inc 7175 W Jefferson Ave Suite 3000 *Web:* www.na.srk.com	Lakewood	CO	80235	303-985-1333	985-9947
SSOE Inc 1001 Madison Ave *Web:* www.ssoe.com	Toledo	OH	43624	419-255-3830	255-6101
Stanley Consultants Inc 225 Iowa Ave *Web:* www.stanleygroup.com	Muscatine	IA	52761	563-264-6600	264-6658
Stantec Inc 10160-112 St *TSE: STN* ■ *Web:* www.stantec.com	Edmonton	AB	T5K2L6	780-917-7000	917-7330
Stellar Engineering Inc 5505 E 13-Mile Rd	Warren	MI	48092	586-978-8444	978-2315
Strand Assoc Inc 910 W Wingra Dr *Web:* www.strand.com	Madison	WI	53715	608-251-4843	251-8655
Stratasys Inc 7665 Commerce Way *NASDAQ: SSYS* ■ *TF:* 800-937-3010 ■ *Web:* www.stratasys.com	Eden Prairie	MN	55344	952-937-3000	937-0070
STV Group Inc 205 W Welsh Dr *Web:* www.stvinc.com	Douglassville	PA	19518	610-385-8200	385-8505
STV Inc 225 Pk Ave S 5th Fl *Web:* www.stvinc.com	New York	NY	10003	212-777-4400	777-8463
Sullivan International Group Inc 4750 Womble Rd *TF:* 888-744-1432 ■ *Web:* www.onesullivan.com	San Diego	CA	92106	619-260-1432	260-1421
Sunland Group Inc 1033 La Posada Dr Suite 370 *TF:* 866-732-8500 ■ *Web:* www.sunlandgrp.com	Austin	TX	78752	512-494-0208	494-0406

	City	State	Zip	Phone	Fax
Support Systems Assoc Inc (SSAI) 709 S Harbor City Blvd Suite 350 *TF:* 877-234-7724 ■ *Web:* www.ssai.org	Melbourne	FL	32901	321-724-5566	724-6673
Sur-Flo Plastics & Engineering Inc 24358 Groesbeck Hwy *Web:* www.sur-flo.com	Warren	MI	48089	586-773-0400	773-8946
Swanke Hayden Connell Architects (SHCA) 295 Lafayette St *Web:* www.shca.com	New York	NY	10012	212-226-9696	219-0059
Symmes Maini & McKee Assoc (SMMA) 1000 Massachusetts Ave *Web:* www.smma.com	Cambridge	MA	02138	617-547-5400	354-5758
Synchrony Inc 4655 Technology Dr *Web:* www.synchrony.com	Salem	VA	24153	540-989-1541	989-0467
Syska & Hennessy Group 11 W 42nd St *TF:* 800-328-1600 ■ *Web:* www.syska.com	New York	NY	10036	212-921-2300	556-3333
System Dynamics International Inc (SDI) 560 Discovery Dr NW *Web:* www.sdi-inc.com	Huntsville	AL	35806	256-895-9000	895-9443
Systems & Processes Engineering Corp (SPEC) 6800 Burleson Rd Suite 320 *Web:* www.spec.com	Austin	TX	78744	512-479-7732	494-0756
Systems Planning & Analysis Inc (SPA) 2001 N Beauregard St *Web:* www.spa.com	Alexandria	VA	22311	703-399-7550	399-7555
Systems Technologies Inc 185 Rt 36 *Web:* www.systek.com	West Long Branch	NJ	07764	732-571-6400	571-6401
T-solutions Inc 100 Bruton Ct Suite B *Web:* www.tsoln-inc.com	Chesapeake	VA	23322	757-410-9450	
Tait & Assoc Inc 701 Pk Ctr Dr *Web:* www.tait.com	Santa Ana	CA	92705	714-560-8200	560-8244
Tampa Bay Engineering Group Inc 380 Pk Pl Blvd Suite 300 *TF:* 800-861-8314 ■ *Web:* www.tbegroup.com	Clearwater	FL	33759	727-531-3505	539-1294
Taylor Wiseman & Taylor 124 Gaither Dr Suite 150 *Web:* www.taylorwiseman.com	Mount Laurel	NJ	08054	856-235-7200	722-9250
Teledyne Brown Engineering Inc 300 Sparkman Dr PO Box 070007 **Fax:* Hum Res ■ *TF:* 800-933-2091 ■ *Web:* www.tbe.com	Huntsville	AL	35807	256-726-1000	726-3570*
Terracon 18001 W 106th St *Web:* www.terracon.com	Olathe	KS	66061	913-599-6886	599-0574
Testwell Laboratories Inc 47 Hudson St *TF:* 800-444-9013 ■ *Web:* www.testwelllabs.com	Ossining	NY	10562	914-762-9000	762-9638
Tetra Tech EC Inc 1000 the American Rd *TF:* 800-580-3765 ■ *Web:* www.tteci.com	Morris Plains	NJ	07950	973-630-8000	630-8165
Tetra Tech Inc 3475 E Foothill Blvd *NASDAQ: TTEK* ■ *Web:* www.tetratech.com	Pasadena	CA	91107	626-351-4664	351-5291
Tetra Tech MPS 710 Avis Dr	Ann Arbor	MI	48108	734-665-6000	665-2570
Tetra Tech/KCM 1420 5th Ave Suite 600 *TF:* 800-443-5540	Seattle	WA	98101	206-883-9300	883-9301
Texas Energy Engineers Inc 808 Travis St Suite 200 *Web:* www.ccrd.com	Houston	TX	77002	713-237-8900	237-0123
Th Hill Assoc Inc 7676 Hillmont St Suite 360 *Web:* www.thhill.com	Houston	TX	77040	713-934-9215	
Thelen Assoc Inc 1398 Cox Ave *Web:* www.thelenassoc.com	Erlanger	KY	41018	859-746-9400	746-9408
Thompson Ventulett Stainback & Assoc Inc 1230 Peachtree St NE 2700 Promenade 2 *Web:* www.tvsa.com	Atlanta	GA	30309	404-888-6600	888-6700
Thornton-Tomasetti Group Inc (TTINC) 2000 L St NW Suite 840 *Web:* www.thorntontomasetti.com	Washington	DC	20036	202-580-6300	580-6301
Tighe & Bond Inc 53 Southampton Rd *Web:* www.tighebond.com	Westfield	MA	01085	413-562-1600	562-5317
Timmons Group Inc 1001 Boulders Pkwy Suite 300 *Web:* www.timmons.com	Richmond	VA	23225	804-794-3500	794-7639
Tj Cross Engineers Inc 200 New Stine Rd Suite 270 *Web:* www.tjcross.com	Bakersfield	CA	93309	661-831-8782	831-5019
TL Industries Inc 2541 Tracy Rd *Web:* www.tlindustries.com	Northwood	OH	43619	419-666-8144	666-6534
TLC Engineering for Architecture 255 S Orange Ave # 1600 *TF:* 800-835-9926 ■ *Web:* www.tlc-engineers.com	Orlando	FL	32801	407-841-9050	835-9926
TMAD Inc 320 N Halstead St Suite 200 *Web:* www.tmadengineers.com	Pasadena	CA	91107	626-351-8881	351-5319
TMP Architecture 1191 W Sq Lake Rd PO Box 289 *Web:* www.tmp-architecture.com	Bloomfield Hills	MI	48302	248-338-4561	338-0223
Toledo Engineering Co Inc 3400 Executive Pkwy PO Box 2927 *Web:* www.teco.com	Toledo	OH	43606	419-537-9711	537-1369
Tolz King Duvall Anderson & Assoc Inc 444 Cedar St Suite 1500 *TF:* 800-247-1714 ■ *Web:* www.tkda.com	Saint Paul	MN	55101	651-292-4400	292-0083
Trandes Corp 4601 Presidents Dr Suite 360 *TF:* 800-878-0201 ■ *Web:* www.trandes.com	Lanham	MD	20706	301-459-0200	459-1069
TransCore Holdings Inc 8158 Adams Dr Bldg 200 *TF:* 800-233-2172 ■ *Web:* www.transcore.com	Hummelstown	PA	17036	717-561-2400	561-5939
TranSystems Corp 2400 Pershing Rd Suite 400 *Web:* www.transystems.com	Kansas City	MO	64108	816-329-8700	329-8703
TRC Worldwide Engineering Inc (TRCWW) 217 Ward Cir *Web:* www.trcww.com	Brentwood	TN	37027	615-661-7979	661-0644
Tri Star Engineering Inc 3000 16th St *Web:* www.star3.com	Bedford	IN	47421	812-277-0208	277-0219
TriLeaf Inc 10845 Olive Blvd Suite 310 *Web:* www.trileaf.com	Saint Louis	MO	63141	314-997-6111	997-8066
Triodyne Inc 666 Dundee Rd Suite 103 *Web:* www.triodyne.com	Northbrook	IL	60062	847-677-4730	647-2047
Truevance Management Inc 7666 Blanding Blvd PO Box 440879 *TF:* 800-285-2028 ■ *Web:* www.truevance.com	Jacksonville	FL	32244	904-777-9052	777-9514
Tsoi/Kobus & Assoc Inc (TKA) 1 Brattle Sq PO Box 9114 *Web:* www.tka-architects.com	Cambridge	MA	02238	617-475-4000	475-4445
TY Lin International 2 Harrison St Suite 500 *Web:* www.tylin.com	San Francisco	CA	94111	415-291-3700	433-0807
Ulteig Engineers Inc 3350 38th Ave S PO Box 9615 *TF:* 888-557-9090 ■ *Web:* www.ulteig.com	Fargo	ND	58104	701-237-3211	237-3191
Unidyne Corp 3835 E Princess Anne Rd	Norfolk	VA	23502	757-855-8037	853-3046
Unified Industries Inc 6551 Loisdale Ct Suite 400 *Web:* www.uii.com	Springfield	VA	22150	703-922-9800	971-5892
United States Steel Corp 600 Grant St *TF:* 800-245-4450 ■ *Web:* www.uss.com	Pittsburgh	PA	15219	412-433-1121	
Universal Technical Resource Services Inc (UERS) 950 Kings Hwy N Suite 208 *Web:* www.utrs.com	Cherry Hill	NJ	08034	856-667-6770	667-7586
Universal Technology Corp (UTC) 1270 N Fairfield Rd *Web:* www.utcdayton.com	Dayton	OH	45432	937-426-2808	426-0839
UniversalPegasus International Inc 4848 Loop Central Dr *TF:* 800-966-1811 ■ *Web:* www.universalpegasus.com	Houston	TX	77081	713-425-6000	977-1047
Unwin Scheben Korynta Huetti Inc (USKH) 2515 A St *TF:* 888-706-8754 ■ *Web:* www.uskh.com	Anchorage	AK	99503	907-276-4245	258-4653
Urbahn Architects 49 W 37th St 6th Fl *Web:* www.urbahn.com	New York	NY	10018	212-239-0220	563-5621
Urban Engineers Inc 530 Walnut St 14th Fl *Web:* www.urbanengineers.com	Philadelphia	PA	19106	215-922-8080	922-8082
URS Corp 600 Montgomery St 25th Fl *NYSE: URS* ■ *TF:* 877-877-8970 ■ *Web:* www.urscorp.com	San Francisco	CA	94111	415-774-2700	398-1905
US Laboratories Inc 7895 Convoy Ct Suite 18 *TF:* 800-487-0355 ■ *Web:* www.uslaboratories.com	San Diego	CA	92111	858-715-5800	715-5810
Utility Engineering Park Central Bldg 1515 Arapahoe St Tower 1 Suite 800 *TF:* 800-403-5189 ■ *Web:* www.ue-corp.com	Denver	CO	80202	303-928-4400	928-4368
Van Dijk Westlake Reed Leskosky (WRL) 925 Euclid Ave Suite 1900 *Web:* www.wrldesign.com	Cleveland	OH	44115	216-522-1350	522-1357
Vanadium Group Corp 134 Three Degree Rd *TF:* 800-685-0354	Pittsburgh	PA	15237	412-367-6060	630-8430
Vanasse Hangen Brustlin Inc (VHB) 101 Walnut St PO Box 9151 *Web:* www.vhb.com	Watertown	MA	02472	617-924-1770	924-2286
Vanderweil Engineers 274 Summer St *TF:* 800-726-2840 ■ *Web:* www.vanderweil.com	Boston	MA	02210	617-423-7423	423-7401
Vanteon Corp 250 Cross Keys Office Pk 3rd Fl *TF:* 888-506-5677 ■ *Web:* www.vanteon.com	Fairport	NY	14450	585-419-9555	248-0537
Vaughn & Melton Inc PO Box 1425 *TF:* 800-388-6660 ■ *Web:* www.vaughnmelton.com	Middlesboro	KY	40965	606-248-6600	248-0372
Vectech Pharmaceutical Consultants Inc 26105 Orchard Lk Rd Suite 311 *TF:* 800-966-8832 ■ *Web:* www.vectech.com	Farmington Hills	MI	48334	248-478-5820	442-0060
Veenstra & Kimm Inc 3000 Westown Pkwy *TF:* 800-241-8000 ■ *Web:* www.v-k.net	West Des Moines	IA	50266	515-225-8000	225-7848
Versar Inc 6850 Versar Ctr *AMEX: VSR* ■ *TF Cust Svc:* 800-283-7727 ■ *Web:* www.versar.com	Springfield	VA	22151	703-750-3000	642-6825
Vigen Construction Inc PO Box 6109 *Web:* www.vigenconstruction.com	Grand Forks	ND	58206	218-773-1159	773-3454
Vitetta 4747 S Broad St *Web:* www.vitetta.com	Philadelphia	PA	19112	215-218-4747	218-4740
VOA Assoc Inc 224 S Michigan Ave Suite 1400 *Web:* www.voa.com	Chicago	IL	60604	312-554-1400	554-1412
Volkert & Assoc Inc 3809 Moffett Rd *TF:* 800-340-1070 ■ *Web:* www.volkert.com	Mobile	AL	36618	251-342-1070	342-7962
VSE Corp 2550 Huntington Ave *NASDAQ: VSEC* ■ *TF:* 800-455-4873 ■ *Web:* www.vsecorp.com	Alexandria	VA	22303	703-960-4600	329-4623
W & H Pacific 12100 NE 195th St #300 *Web:* www.whpacific.com	Bothell	WA	98011	425-951-4800	951-4808
Wade-Trim Group Inc 500 Griswold Ave Suite 2500 *TF:* 800-482-2864 ■ *Web:* www.wadetrim.com	Detroit	MI	48226	313-961-3650	961-0898
Waldemar S Nelson & Co Inc 1200 St Charles Ave *Web:* www.wsnelson.com	New Orleans	LA	70130	504-523-5281	523-4587
Walker Parking Consultants/Restoration Engineers Inc 2121 Hudson Ave *Web:* www.walkerparking.com	Kalamazoo	MI	49008	269-381-6080	343-5811
Wallace Roberts & Todd LLC 1700 Market St 28th Fl *TF:* 800-978-4450 ■ *Web:* www.wrtdesign.com	Philadelphia	PA	19103	215-732-5215	732-2551
Walter P Moore 1301 Mckinney St # 1100 *Web:* www.walterpmoore.com	Houston	TX	77010	713-630-7300	630-7396
Ware Malcomb 10 Edelman *Web:* www.waremalcomb.com	Irvine	CA	92618	949-660-9128	863-1581
Washington Corp PO Box 16630 *TF:* 800-832-7329 ■ *Web:* www.washcorp.com	Missoula	MT	59808	406-523-1300	523-1399
Watkins Hamilton Ross Architects Inc 1111 Louisiana St Suite 2600 *Web:* www.whrarchitects.com	Houston	TX	77002	713-665-5665	665-6213
WD Partners 1201 Dublin Rd *Web:* www.wdpartners.com	Columbus	OH	43215	614-221-0840	221-2484

	City	State	ZIP	Phone	Fax
Weidlinger Assoc 375 Hudson St 12th Fl *Web:* www.wai.com	New York	NY	10014	212-367-3000	367-3030
Wenck Assoc Inc PO Box 249 *Web:* www.wenck.com	Maple Plain	MN	55359	763-479-4200	479-4242
Wentz Group 555 Twin Dolphin Dr Suite 160 *Web:* www.wentzgroup.com	Redwood Shores	CA	94065	650-592-3950	593-5632
Westech International Inc 2500 La Blvd NE Suite 325 *Web:* www.westech-intl.com	Albuquerque	NM	87110	505-888-6666	837-9424
Westinghouse Electric Co PO Box 355 *Web:* www.westinghouse.com	Pittsburgh	PA	15230	412-374-4111	
Weston & Sampson Inc 5 Centennial Dr *TF:* 800-726-7766 ■ *Web:* www.westonandsampson.com	Peabody	MA	01960	978-532-1900	977-0100
Weston Solutions Inc 1400 Weston Way PO Box 2653 *TF:* 800-793-7866 ■ *Web:* www.westonsolutions.com	West Chester	PA	19380	610-701-3000	701-3186
Whitman Requardt & Assoc 801 S Caroline St *TF:* 800-787-7100 ■ *Web:* www.wrallp.com	Baltimore	MD	21231	410-235-3450	243-5716
Whitney Bailey Cox & Magnani LLC 849 Fairmount Ave Suite 100 *Web:* www.wbcm.com	Baltimore	MD	21286	410-512-4500	324-4100
Wight & Co 2500 N Frontage Rd *Web:* www.wightco.com	Darien	IL	60561	630-969-7000	969-7979
Wilbur Smith Assoc Inc 1301 Gervais St PO Box 92 *Web:* www.wilbursmith.com	Columbia	SC	29202	803-758-4500	251-2064
Willbros Downstream LLC 1900 N 161st E Ave *Web:* www.inservusa.com	Tulsa	OK	74116	918-234-4150	879-2730
Willbros Engineers Inc 2087 E 71st St *TF:* 800-434-8970 ■ *Web:* www.willbros.com	Tulsa	OK	74136	918-496-0400	491-9436
Willdan 2401 E Katella Ave Suite 300 *TF:* 800-424-9144 ■ *Web:* www.willdan.com	Anaheim	CA	92806	714-940-6300	940-4920
WilsonMiller Inc 3200 Bailey Ln Suite 200 *TF:* 800-649-4336 ■ *Web:* www.wilsonmiller.com	Naples	FL	34105	239-649-4040	643-5716
Wimberly Allison Tong & Goo 700 Bishop St Suite 1800 *Web:* www.watg.com	Honolulu	HI	96813	808-521-8888	521-3888
Wink Inc 8641 United Plaza Blvd Suite 204 *Web:* www.winkinc.com	Baton Rouge	LA	70809	225-932-6000	932-9035
Winzler & Kelly Consulting Engineers 2235 Mercury Way Suite 150 *Web:* www.w-and-k.com	Santa Rosa	CA	95407	707-523-1010	527-8679
Wiss Janney Elstner Assoc Inc 330 Pfingsten Rd *TF:* 800-345-3199 ■ *Web:* www.wje.com	Northbrook	IL	60062	847-272-7400	291-9599
Wolfberg Alvarez 1500 San Remo Ave Suite 300 *Web:* www.wolfbergalvarez.com	Coral Gables	FL	33146	305-666-5474	669-9875
Wood Patel & Assoc Inc 2051 W Northern Ave Suite 100 *Web:* www.woodpatel.com	Phoenix	AZ	85021	602-335-8500	335-8580
Woodard & Curran 41 Hutchins Dr *TF:* 800-426-4262 ■ *Web:* www.woodardcurran.com	Portland	ME	04102	207-774-2112	271-7952
Woolpert Inc 4454 IBA Central Blvd *Web:* www.woolpert.com	Dayton	OH	45430	937-461-5660	461-0743
Wright Water Engineers Inc 2490 W 26th Ave Suite 100a *Web:* www.wrightwater.com	Denver	CO	80211	303-480-1700	480-1020
Yoder 4899 Commerce Pkwy *TF:* 800-631-0520 ■ *Web:* www.krasnykaplan.com	Cleveland	OH	44128	216-292-4460	831-7948
Zephyr Environmental Corp 2600 Via Fortuna Suite 450 *TF:* 800-452-5558 ■ *Web:* www.zephyrenv.com	Austin	TX	78746	512-329-5544	329-8253

265 ENGINES & TURBINES

SEE ALSO Aircraft Engines & Engine Parts p. 1387; Automotive Parts & Supplies - Mfr p. 1497; Motors (Electric) & Generators p. 2263

	City	State	ZIP	Phone	Fax
Alturdyne Inc 660 Steele St *Web:* www.alturdyne.com	El Cajon	CA	92020	619-440-5531	442-0481
Arrow Engine Co 2301 E Independence St *TF:* 800-331-3662 ■ *Web:* www.arrowengines.com	Tulsa	OK	74110	918-583-5711	592-1481
Briggs & Stratton Corp 12301 W Wirth St *NYSE: BGG* ■ *TF:* 800-444-7774 ■ *Web:* www.briggsandstratton.com	Wauwatosa	WI	53222	414-259-5333	259-5338
Brunswick Corp 1 N Field Ct *NYSE: BC* ■ *Web:* www.brunswick.com	Lake Forest	IL	60045	847-735-4700	735-4765
Brunswick Corp Mercury Marine Div W 6250 Pioneer Rd *Web:* www.mercurymarine.com	Fond du Lac	WI	54935	920-929-5040	929-5893
Capstone Turbine Corp 21211 Nordhoff St *NASDAQ: CPST* ■ *Web:* www.capstoneturbine.com	Chatsworth	CA	91311	818-734-5300	734-5320
Caterpillar Inc 100 NE Adams St *NYSE: CAT* ■ **Fax:* PR ■ *Web:* www.cat.com	Peoria	IL	61629	309-675-1000	675-4332*
Caterpillar Remanufacturing Franklin 751 International Dr *TF Cust Svc:* 800-837-7697 ■ *Web:* www.franklinpower.com	Franklin	IN	46131	317-738-2117	738-4614
Chromium Corp 14911 Quorum Dr Suite 600 *Web:* www.chromcorp.com	Dallas	TX	75254	972-851-0460	851-0461
Clayton Industries 17477 Hurley St *TF:* 800-423-4585 ■ *Web:* www.claytonindustries.com	City of Industry	CA	91744	626-435-1200	435-0180
Concentric Inc 800 Hollywood Ave *Web:* www.concentricinc.com	Itasca	IL	60143	630-773-3355	773-1119
Cummins Inc 500 Jackson St PO Box 3005 *NYSE: CMI* ■ *TF:* 800-343-7357 ■ *Web:* www.cummins.com	Columbus	IN	47201	812-377-5000	377-3334
Delaware Mfg Industries Corp 3775 Commerce Ct *TF:* 800-248-3642 ■ *Web:* www.dmic.com	Wheatfield	NY	14120	716-743-4360	743-4370
Detroit Diesel Corp 13400 Outer Dr *Web:* www.detroitdiesel.com	Detroit	MI	48239	313-592-5000	592-7580
Dresser Inc Waukesha Engine Div 1101 W St Paul Ave *Web:* www.dresserwaukesha.com	Waukesha	WI	53188	262-547-3311	549-2795
Dresser-Rand Control Systems 1202 W Sam Houston Pkwy N *Web:* www.dresser-rand.com/products/controls	Houston	TX	77043	713-365-2630	
Dresser-Rand Steam Turbines 10205 Westheimer Rd *Web:* www.dresser-rand.com	Houston	TX	77042	713-354-6100	354-6110
Electro Steam Generator Corp 50 Indel Ave PO Box 438 *TF:* 866-617-0764 ■ *Web:* www.electrosteam.com	Rancocas	NJ	08073	609-288-9071	288-9078
EnPro Industries Inc 5605 Carnegie Blvd Suite 500 *NYSE: NPO* ■ *TF:* 866-663-6776 ■ *Web:* www.enproindustries.com	Charlotte	NC	28209	704-731-1500	731-1511
EnPro Industries Inc Fairbanks Morse Engine 701 White Ave **Fax:* Mktg ■ *TF:* 800-356-6955 ■ *Web:* www.fairbanksmorse.com	Beloit	WI	53511	608-364-4411	364-8302*
GE Aviation 1 Neumann Way *Web:* www.geaviation.com	Cincinnati	OH	45215	513-243-2000	
GE Energy 4200 Wildwood Pkwy **Fax Area Code:* 800 ■ *TF:* 800-368-1316 ■ *Web:* www.ge-energy.com	Atlanta	GA	30339	770-859-6000	368-1317*
Globe Turbocharger Specialties Inc 201 Edison Way PO Box 30009 *Web:* www.globeturbocharger.com	Reno	NV	89502	775-856-7337	856-7338
H & H Mfg Co Inc 2 Horne Dr	Folcroft	PA	19032	610-532-8100	461-4620
Hatch & Kirk Inc 5111 Leary Ave NW *TF:* 800-426-2818 ■ *Web:* www.hatchkirk.com	Seattle	WA	98107	206-783-2766	782-6482
HDM Hydraulics LLC 125 Fire Tower Dr *Web:* www.hdmco.com	Tonawanda	NY	14150	716-694-8004	694-4164
Hercules Engine Components Co 2770 S Erie St *TF:* 800-345-0662 ■ *Web:* www.herculesengine.com	Massillon	OH	44646	330-830-2498	830-4081
Industrial Parts Depot LLC 23231 Normandie Ave *Web:* www.ipdparts.com	Torrance	CA	90501	310-530-1900	
JASPER Engines & Transmissions 815 Wernsing Rd PO Box 650 *TF:* 800-827-7455 ■ *Web:* www.jasperengines.com	Jasper	IN	47547	812-482-1041	634-1820
John Deere Power Systems 3801 W Ridgeway Ave PO Box 5100 **Fax Area Code:* 319 ■ *TF:* 800-533-6446 ■ *Web:* www.deere.com	Waterloo	IA	50704	800-533-6446	292-5075*
KMS Ventures Inc 1301 W 25th St Suite 300	Austin	TX	78705	512-474-6312	474-6389
Kohler Engines 444 Highland Dr **Fax:* Sales ■ *TF:* 800-544-2444 ■ *Web:* www.kohlerengines.com	Kohler	WI	53044	920-457-4441	459-1570*
Marine Power Holding LLC 17506 Marine Power Industrial Pk *Web:* www.marinepowerusa.com	Ponchatoula	LA	70454	985-386-2081	386-4010
Northern Lights Inc 4420 14th Ave NW *TF:* 800-762-0165 ■ *Web:* www.northern-lights.com	Seattle	WA	98107	206-789-3880	782-5455
NREC Power Systems 5222 Hwy 311 *TF:* 800-851-6732 ■ *Web:* www.nrecps.com	Houma	LA	70360	985-872-5480	872-0611
Penske Corp Rt 10 Green Hills PO Box 563 **Fax:* Acctg ■ *TF:* 888-234-4201 ■ *Web:* www.penske.com	Reading	PA	19603	610-775-6000	775-5064*
Pratt & Whitney Canada Inc 1000 Marie-Victorin Blvd *TF:* 800-268-8000 ■ *Web:* www.pwc.ca	Longueuil	QC	J4G1A1	450-677-9411	647-3620
Rolls-Royce Energy System Inc 105 N Sandusky St *Web:* www.rolls-royce.com	Mount Vernon	OH	43050	740-393-8888	393-8336
Salem Preferred Partners LLC 236 Rowan St *Web:* www.spplc.com	Salem	VA	24153	540-389-3922	389-3926
Sierra International Inc 1 Sierra Pl *TF:* 877-663-8396 ■ *Web:* www.teleflexmarine.com	Litchfield	IL	62056	217-324-9400	324-4396
Solar Turbines Inc 2200 Pacific Hwy **Fax:* Sales ■ *Web:* www.mysolar.cat.com	San Diego	CA	92101	619-544-5000	544-2849*
Springfield ReManufacturing Corp 650 N Broadview Pl *TF:* 800-772-7733 ■ *Web:* www.srcreman.com	Springfield	MO	65802	417-862-3501	864-0625
SRC Holdings Corp 3140 E Division St	Springfield	MO	65802	417-862-4510	863-9778
Technetics Corp 1700 E International Speedway Blvd *Web:* www.techneticsfl.com	DeLand	FL	32724	386-736-7373	738-4533
Voith Siemens Hydro Power 760 E Berlin Rd *Web:* www.voith.com	York	PA	17408	717-792-7000	792-7263
Volvo Penta of the Americas Inc 1300 Volvo Penta Dr *Web:* www.volvopenta.com	Chesapeake	VA	23320	757-436-2800	436-5150
Walker Power Systems (WPS) 1301 E Jackson St **Fax:* Sales ■ *Web:* www.walkerpower.com	Phoenix	AZ	85034	602-257-8505	255-0569*
Wartsila North America Inc 16330 Air Ctr Blvd *TF:* 877-927-8745 ■ *Web:* www.wartsila.com	Houston	TX	77032	281-233-6200	233-6233
Westerbeke Corp 150 John Hancock Rd Miles Standish Industrial Pk *Web:* www.westerbeke.com	Taunton	MA	02780	508-823-7677	884-9688
Western Diesel Services Inc 1100 Research Blvd *TF:* 800-495-8620 ■ *Web:* www.ckpower.com	Saint Louis	MO	63132	314-868-8620	868-9314

266 ENVELOPES

	City	State	ZIP	Phone	Fax
ADM Corp 100 Lincoln Blvd *TF:* 800-327-0718 ■ *Web:* www.packinglist.com	Middlesex	NJ	08846	732-469-0900	469-0785
Alvah Bushnell Co 519 E Chelten Ave *TF:* 800-255-7434 ■ *Web:* www.bushnellco.com	Philadelphia	PA	19144	215-842-9520	843-7725

Phone | Fax

AmericanChurch Inc
525 McClurg Rd PO Box 3120 .... Youngstown OH 44513 330-758-4545 758-3361
TF: 800-446-3035 ■ *Web:* www.americanchurch.com

B & W Press Inc 401 E Main St. .... Georgetown MA 01833 978-352-6100 352-5955
Web: www.bwpress.com

Bowers Envelope Co 5331 N Tacoma Ave .... Indianapolis IN 46220 317-253-4321 254-2239
Web: www.bowersenvelope.com

Cenveo Inc 201 Broad St 1 Canterberry Green.......... Stamford CT 06901 203-595-3000 595-3070
NYSE: CVO ■ *Web:* www.cenveo.com

Colfax Envelope Corp 951 Commerce Ct. .... Buffalo Grove IL 60089 847-215-1122 215-1122

Colortree Inc of Virginia 8000 Villa Pk Dr .... Richmond VA 23228 804-358-4245 358-0488
TF: 800-222-2962 ■ *Web:* www.colortreeva.com

Curtis 1000 Inc
1725 Breckinridge Pkwy Suite 500.................... Duluth GA 30096 678-380-9095 594-0518*
**Fax Area Code:* 800 ■ **Fax:* Mktg ■ *TF:* 800-683-8162 ■ *Web:* www.curtis1000.com

Federal Envelope Co 608 Country Club Dr .... Bensenville IL 60106 630-595-2000 595-1212
Web: www.federalenvelope.com

Gaw-O'Hara Envelope Co 500 N Sacramento Blvd .... Chicago IL 60612 773-638-1200 638-1208

Heinrich Envelope Corp 925 Zane Ave N. .... Minneapolis MN 55422 763-544-3571 544-6287
TF: 800-346-7957 ■ *Web:* www.heinrichenvelope.com

Love Envelopes Inc 10733 E Ute St .... Tulsa OK 74116 918-836-3535 832-9978
TF: 800-532-9747 ■ *Web:* www.loveenvelopes.com

Mackay Envelope Corp 2100 Elm St SE .... Minneapolis MN 55414 612-331-9311 331-8229
TF: 800-622-5299 ■ *Web:* www.mackaymitchellenvelope.com

MeadWestvaco Corp Envelope Div
2001 Roosevelt Ave .... Springfield MA 01104 413-736-7211 787-9625
TF: 800-628-9265 ■ *Web:* www.meadwestvaco.com

Motion Envelope Inc 1455 Terre Colony Ct............. Dallas TX 75212 214-634-2131 634-2132
Web: www.motionenvelope.com

National Church Supply Co The PO Box 269.......... Chester WV 26034 304-387-5200 387-5266
TF: 800-627-9900 ■ *Web:* www.envelopeservice.com

Oles Envelope Corp 532 E 25th St.................... Baltimore MD 21218 410-243-1520 243-1541
TF: 800-822-6537 ■ *Web:* www.olesenvelope.com

Papercone Corp 3200 Fern Valley Rd.................. Louisville KY 40213 502-961-9493 961-9346
TF: 800-626-5308 ■ *Web:* www.papercone.com

Poly-Pak Industries Inc 125 Spagnoli Rd.............. Melville NY 11747 631-293-6767 454-6366
TF: 800-969-1995 ■ *Web:* www.poly-pak.com

Response Envelope Inc 1340 S Baker Ave .... Ontario CA 91761 909-923-5855 923-3639
TF: 800-890-5959 ■ *Web:* www.response-envelope.com

Royal Envelope Co 4114 S Peoria St .... Chicago IL 60609 773-376-1212 376-0011

Tension Envelope Corp 819 E 19th St.............. Kansas City MO 64108 816-471-3800 283-1498
TF: 800-388-5122 ■ *Web:* www.tension.com

Top Flight Inc 1300 Central Ave .... Chattanooga TN 37408 423-266-8171 266-6857
TF: 800-777-3740 ■ *Web:* www.topflightpaper.com

Western States Envelope & Label Co
4480 N 132nd St .... Butler WI 53007 262-781-5540 781-5791
TF: 800-558-0514 ■ *Web:* www.wsec.com

Worcester Envelope Co
22 Millbury St PO Box 406.......................... Auburn MA 01501 508-832-5394 832-3796*
**Fax:* Sales ■ *TF:* 800-343-1398 ■ *Web:* www.worcesterenvelope.com

267 EQUIPMENT RENTAL & LEASING

SEE ALSO Credit & Financing - Commercial p. 1773; Credit & Financing - Consumer p. 1775; Fleet Leasing & Management p. 1849

267-1 Computer Equipment Leasing

Phone | Fax

All Service Computer Rental
600 Sylvan Ave.......................... Englewood Cliffs NJ 07632 201-568-6555 568-4448
TF: 800-927-6555 ■ *Web:* www.ascr.com

Computer Sales International Inc (CSI)
9990 Old Olive St Rd .... Saint Louis MO 63141 314-997-7010 997-7844
TF: 800-955-0960 ■ *Web:* www.csileasing.com

Data Sales Co Inc 3450 W Burnsville Pkwy .... Burnsville MN 55337 952-890-8838 895-3369
TF: 800-328-2730 ■ *Web:* www.datasales.com

Econocom USA Inc 6750 Poplar Ave Suite 202 .... Memphis TN 38138 901-685-0021 685-0021

El Camino Resources International Inc
6233 Variel Ave............................ Woodland Hills CA 91367 818-226-6600 226-6600

Electro Rent Corp 6060 Sepulveda Blvd............. Van Nuys CA 91411 818-787-2100 786-4354
NASDAQ: ELRC ■ *TF Sales:* 800-688-1111 ■ *Web:* www.electrorent.com

First Equipment Co PO Box 2129..................... Addison TX 75001 972-380-2300 380-8350
TF: 888-780-8631 ■ *Web:* www.firstequipment.com

Forsythe MacArthur Assoc Inc 7770 Frontage Rd........ Skokie IL 60077 847-675-8000 675-2130
TF: 800-843-4488 ■ *Web:* www.forsythe.com

Hitachi Credit America Ltd
800 Connecticut Ave Suite 4n01...................... Norwalk CT 06854 203-956-3000
Web: www.hitachicreditamerica.com

LaSalle Systems Leasing Inc 6111 N River Rd........ Rosemont IL 60018 847-823-9600 823-1646
Web: www.elasalle.com

Leasing Technologies International Inc
221 Danbury Rd .... Wilton CT 06897 203-563-1100 563-1112
Web: www.ltileasing.com

Manufacturers' Lease Plans Inc
818 E Osborn Rd Suite 200 .... Phoenix AZ 85014 602-944-4411 944-4417
Web: www.leaseplans.com

Meridian Technology Leasing Services
Nine Pkwy N Suite 500.......................... Deerfield IL 60015 847-940-1200 319-2209
TF Cust Svc: 800-426-3090 ■ *Web:* www.meridianleasing.com

Newport Leasing Inc
4750 Von Karman Ave .... Newport Beach CA 92660 949-476-8476 476-9200
TF Cust Svc: 800-678-9426 ■ *Web:* www.newportleasing.com

Rent-A-PC Inc 265 Oser Ave...................... Hauppauge NY 11788 631-273-8888 273-8889
TF: 877-736-8272 ■ *Web:* www.smartsourcerentals.com

Stamford Computer Group Inc 74 W Pk Pl............ Stamford CT 06901 203-324-9495 324-3195

Summit Funding Group Inc
11500 Northlake Dr Suite 300 .... Cincinnati OH 45249 513-489-1222 489-1490
Web: www.summit-funding.com

Vicom Computer Services Inc
60 Carolyn Blvd .... Farmingdale NY 11735 631-694-3900 694-2640
Web: www.vicomnet.com

267-2 Home & Office Equipment Rental (General)

Phone | Fax

Bakercorp 3020 Old Ranch Pkwy Suite 220............ Seal Beach CA 90740 562-430-6262 430-4865
Web: www.bakercorp.com

Bay Cities Crane & Rigging Inc
457 Parr Blvd .... Richmond CA 94801 510-236-0101 234-2480
Web: www.braggnorcal.com

Bestway Inc 12400 Coit Rd Suite 950................... Dallas TX 75251 214-630-6655 630-8404
TF: 800-520-1107 ■ *Web:* www.bestwayrto.com

Bi-Rite Co Inc 6608 E Adamo Dr....................... Tampa FL 33619 813-623-5461 626-8195
Web: www.buddyrents.com

Brook Furniture Rental Inc
100 N Field Dr # 220 .... Lake Forest IL 60045 847-810-4000 283-0478
TF: 800-933-7368 ■ *Web:* www.bfr.com

Celtic Leasing Corp 4 Pk Plaza Suite 300 .... Irvine CA 92614 949-263-3880 263-1331
Web: www.celticleasing.com

Exhibitors Carpet Service Inc
4300 W Montrose Ave .... Chicago IL 60641 773-685-6100 283-3533
TF: 800-746-9784 ■ *Web:* www.chicagocarpet.com

GFC Leasing Co 2675 Research Pk Dr................. Madison WI 53711 608-274-7877 271-9703
TF: 800-333-5905

Grand Rental Station
1260 E Higgins Rd .... Elk Grove Village IL 60007 847-640-8860
Web: www.grandrental.com

Independent Rental Inc 2020 S Cushman St .... Fairbanks AK 99701 907-456-6595 456-2927
Web: www.independentrentalinc.com

Lease One Systems
7305 Manchester Rd Suite C-1.................... Saint Louis MO 63143 314-645-1300 645-2663
TF: 888-645-1300 ■ *Web:* www.lease-one.com

Leasing Experts Inc The
9710 E Indigo St Suite 203.......................... Miami FL 33157 305-235-1222 235-4177
TF: 800-700-0657 ■ *Web:* www.leasingexperts.com

Lmg Inc PO Box 770429.............................. Orlando FL 32877 407-850-0505 438-8422
TF: 888-226-3100 ■ *Web:* www.lmg.net

Marlin Business Services Inc
300 Fellowship Rd Suite 170 .... Mount Laurel NJ 08054 856-359-9111 479-1100*
NASDAQ: MRLN ■ **Fax Area Code:* 888 ■ *TF:* 888-479-9111 ■ *Web:* www.marlinleasing.com

Party Rental Ltd 275 N St.......................... Teterboro NJ 07608 201-727-4700 727-4701
Web: www.partyrentalltd.com

Projection Presentation Technology
5803 Rolling Rd Suite 207 .... Springfield VA 22152 703-912-1334 912-1350
Web: www.projection.com

Rent-A-Center Inc 5501 Headquarters Dr............... Plano TX 75024 972-801-1100 943-0113*
NASDAQ: RCII ■ **Fax:* Cust Svc ■ *TF:* 800-275-2696 ■ *Web:* www6.rentacenter.com

Royal Audio Video Supply Inc
235 N Cswy Blvd .... Metairie LA 70001 504-831-9779 831-9299
TF: 866-747-6483 ■ *Web:* www.royal-av.com

Rug Doctor LP 4701 Old Shepard Pl .... Plano TX 75093 972-673-1400 673-1401
TF: 800-234-6286 ■ *Web:* www.rugdoctor.com

Somerset Capital Group Ltd
612 Wheelers Farms Rd .... milford CT 06461 203-394-6182 394-6192
TF: 877-282-9922 ■ *Web:* www.somersetcapital.com

Swank Audio Visuals LLC
639 Gravois Bluffs Blvd .... Fenton MO 63026 314-534-1940 289-2182
TF: 877-792-6528 ■ *Web:* www.swankav.com

Taylor Rental 1547 Brandy Pkwy.................. Streamwood IL 60107 630-289-2550
Web: www.taylorrental.com

Television Rental Co Inc 5502 Broadway .... Woodside NY 11377 718-458-2211 672-7223
TF: 888-875-8872 ■ *Web:* www.tvrc.com

Tri-Rentals Inc 3103 E Broadway Suite 400 .... Phoenix AZ 85040 602-232-9900 232-6001
TF: 800-678-3854 ■ *Web:* www.trirentals.com

267-3 Industrial & Heavy Equipment Rental

Phone | Fax

Able Builders Equipment LLC 7475 NW 63rd St .... Miami FL 33166 305-592-5940 592-2793
TF: 800-831-4564 ■ *Web:* www.ablebuildersequipment.com

Aero Rental Inc 3808 E Golf Links Rd.................. Tucson AZ 85713 520-748-8776 745-3741
TF: 800-730-8776 ■ *Web:* www.aeroaz.com

Aggreko 4607 W Admiral Doyle Dr.................. New Iberia LA 70560 337-367-7884 367-0870
TF: 800-323-6086 ■ *Web:* www.aggreko.com

AH Harris & Son Inc 367 Alumni Rd................ Newington CT 06111 860-665-9494 665-9444
TF: 800-382-6555 ■ *Web:* www.ahharris.com

Ahern Rentals Inc 4241 Arville St .... Las Vegas NV 89103 702-362-0623 362-9316
TF: 800-589-6797 ■ *Web:* www.ahern.com

Allied Steel Construction Co Inc
2211 NW 1st Terr PO Box 1111 .... Oklahoma City OK 73101 405-232-7531 236-3705
TF: 800-522-4658 ■ *Web:* www.alliedsteelerectors.com

American Equipment Co 2106 Anderson Rd.......... Greenville SC 29611 864-295-7800 295-7956
Web: www.americanequipment.com

APi Supply Inc 624 Arthur St NE.................. Minneapolis MN 55413 612-379-8000 379-8038
Web: www.apisupplyinc.com

Atlas Lift Truck Rentals & Sales Inc
5050 N River Rd .... Schiller Park IL 60176 847-678-3450 678-1750
Web: www.atlaslift.com

Beco Equipment Co 5555 Dahlia St............. Commerce City CO 80022 303-288-2613
Web: www.becoequipment.com

Blanchard Machinery Inc
14301 NE 19th Ave.......................... North Miami FL 33181 305-949-2581 949-9813
TF: 800-330-4242 ■ *Web:* www.blanchardmachinery.com

Brockman Forklift Inc 15800 Tireman Ave .... Detroit MI 48228 313-584-4550 584-2423
TF: 800-228-1957

				Phone	Fax
Broussard Bros Inc 25817 Louisiana Hwy 333	Abbeville	LA	70510	337-893-5303	893-7148
TF: 800-299-5303 ■ *Web:* www.broussardbrothers.com					
Buck & Knobby Equipment Co 6220 Sterns Rd	Ottawa Lake	MI	49267	734-856-2811	856-2709
Web: www.buckandknobby.com					
Chesapeake Industrial Leasing Co Inc 9512 Harford Rd	Baltimore	MD	21234	410-661-5000	661-5053
TF: 800-782-1022 ■ *Web:* www.cilc.com					
Cloverdale Equipment Co 13133 Cloverdale St	Oak Park	MI	48237	248-399-6600	399-7730
TF: 800-822-7999 ■ *Web:* www.cloverdale-equip.com					
Cornell & Co Inc 224 Cornell Ln PO Box 807	Woodbury	NJ	08096	856-742-1900	742-8186
Web: www.cornellcraneandsteel.com					
D & D Equipment Rental Inc 10936 Shoemaker Ave	Santa Fe Springs	CA	90670	562-595-4555	595-1265
TF: 866-446-1100 ■ *Web:* www.ddrental.com					
Equipment Corp of America 1000 Stn St PO Box 306	Coraopolis	PA	15108	412-331-2000	264-1158
TF: 800-745-3872 ■ *Web:* www.ecanet.com					
Ervin Leasing Co 3893 Research Pk Dr	Ann Arbor	MI	48108	800-748-0015	968-2808
TF: 800-748-0015 ■ *Web:* www.ervinleasing.com					
Essex Crane Rental Corp 1110 Lake Cook Rd Suite 220	Buffalo Grove	IL	60089	847-215-6500	215-6535
Web: www.essexcrane.com					
Force Construction Co Inc 990 N National Rd	Columbus	IN	47201	812-372-8441	372-5424
Web: www.forceco.com					
G & C Equipment Corp 1875 W Redondo Beach Blvd Suite 102	Gardena	CA	90247	310-515-6715	515-5046
Web: www.gandccorp.com					
Gammaloy Holdings LP 2001 Kirby Dr Suite 715	Houston	TX	77019	713-522-9540	522-9559
H & E Equipment Services Inc 11100 Mead Rd Suite 200	Baton Rouge	LA	70816	225-298-5200	298-5377
NASDAQ: HEES ■ *TF:* 877-700-7368 ■ *Web:* www.he-equipment.com					
Hawthorne Machinery Co 16945 Camino San Bernardo	San Diego	CA	92127	858-674-7000	674-7160
TF: 800-437-4228 ■ *Web:* www.hawthornecat.com					
HB Rentals LC 5813 Hwy 90 E	Broussard	LA	70518	337-839-1641	839-1628
TF: 800-262-6790 ■ *Web:* www.hbrental.com					
Hertz equipment rental 5500 Commerce Blvd	Rohnert Park	CA	94928	707-586-4444	586-4421
Web: www.hertzequip.com					
Hertz Equipment Rental Corp 225 Brae Blvd	Park Ridge	NJ	07656	201-307-2000	307-2651
TF: 800-654-3131 ■ *Web:* www.hertzequip.com					
Horizon Fleet Services Inc 341 NW 122nd St	Oklahoma City	OK	73114	405-755-9703	755-6829
TF: 800-357-2444 ■ *Web:* www.horizonfleet.com					
Independent Rental Inc 2020 S Cushman St	Fairbanks	AK	99701	907-456-6595	456-2927
Web: www.independentrentalinc.com					
Klochko Equipment Rental Co Inc 2782 Corbin Ave	Melvindale	MI	48122	313-386-7220	386-2530
TF: 800-783-7368 ■ *Web:* www.klochko.com					
Leppo Inc PO Box 154	Tallmadge	OH	44278	330-630-6581	630-1599
TF: 800-453-7762 ■ *Web:* www.leppos.com					
Marco Crane & Rigging Co 221 S 35th Ave	Phoenix	AZ	85009	602-272-2671	352-0413
TF: 800-668-2671 ■ *Web:* www.marcocrane.com					
Maxim Crane Works 1225 Washington Pike	Bridgeville	PA	15017	412-504-0200	504-0126
TF: 866-629-4648 ■ *Web:* www.maximcrane.com					
Medico Industries Inc 1500 Hwy 315	Wilkes-Barre	PA	18711	570-825-7711	824-1169
TF: 800-633-0027 ■ *Web:* www.medicomfg.com					
Mitcham Industries Inc (MII) 8141 Hwy 75 S PO Box 1175	Huntsville	TX	77340	936-291-2277	295-1922*
NASDAQ: MIND ■ **Fax:* Sales ■ *Web:* www.mitchamindustries.com					
Modern Equipment Sales & Rental Co 24 Brookside Dr	Wilmington	DE	19804	302-658-5257	658-0135
TF: 800-227-2525 ■ *Web:* www.moderngroup.com					
Morris Kreitz & Sons Inc 220 N Pk Rd	Wyomissing	PA	19610	610-376-7187	375-8747
Web: www.morriskreitz.com					
Morrow Equipment Co LLC 3218 Pringle Rd SE	Salem	OR	97302	503-585-5721	363-1172
TF: 800-505-7766 ■ *Web:* www.morrowequipment.com					
Mustang Rental Services Inc 15907 E Fwy	Channelview	TX	77530	281-452-7368	457-0501
Web: www.mustangcat.com					
National Construction Rentals Inc 15319 Chatsworth St	Mission Hills	CA	91345	818-221-6000	221-6099
TF: 800-874-6285 ■ *Web:* www.rentnational.com					
National Equipment Services Inc 8770 W Brynmawr Ave Suite 400	Chicago	IL	60631	773-695-3999	714-0538
TF: 800-637-7368					
Neff Corp 3750 NW 87th Ave Suite 400	Miami	FL	33178	305-513-3350	513-4156
TF: 888-709-6333 ■ *Web:* www.neffrental.com					
Norcal Rental Group LLC 318 Stealth Ct	Livermore	CA	94551	925-961-0130	456-9760
TF: 800-649-6629 ■ *Web:* www.crescorent.com					
Quantum Analytics 363 Vintage Pk Dr	Foster City	CA	94404	650-312-0900	312-0313
TF: 800-992-4199 ■ *Web:* www.lqa.com					
Raymond Handling Concepts Corp 41400 Boyce Rd	Fremont	CA	94538	510-745-7500	745-7686
TF: 800-675-2500 ■ *Web:* www.raymondhandling.com					
RSC Equipment Rental Inc 6929 E Greenway Pkwy Suite 200	Scottsdale	AZ	85254	480-905-3300	905-3400
TF: 800-222-7777 ■ *Web:* www.rscrental.com					
Rush Enterprises Inc 555 IH 35 S Suite 500	New Braunfels	TX	78130	830-626-5200	626-5310
NASDAQ: RUSHA ■ *TF:* 800-973-7874 ■ *Web:* www.rushenterprises.com					
Safway Services Inc N 19 W 24200 Riverwood Dr	Waukesha	WI	53188	262-523-6500	523-9880
TF: 800-558-4772 ■ *Web:* www.safway.com					
Sims Crane & Equipment Co PO Box 11825	Tampa	FL	33680	813-626-8102	626-6255
TF: 888-846-8548 ■ *Web:* www.simscrane.com					
Skyworks LLC 100 Thielman Dr	Buffalo	NY	14206	716-822-5438	
TF: 866-983-1184 ■ *Web:* www.skyworksllc.com					
Stanley W Bowles Corp 2000 Virginia-Carolina Dr PO Box 4706	Martinsville	VA	24115	276-632-3446	632-7624
Web: www.bowlesproperties.com					
Star Rentals Inc 1919 4th Ave S	Seattle	WA	98134	206-622-7880	587-3280
TF: 800-825-7880 ■ *Web:* www.starrentals.com					
Stephenson Equipment Inc (SEI) 7201 Paxton St	Harrisburg	PA	17111	717-564-3434	564-7580
TF: 800-325-6455 ■ *Web:* www.stephensonequipment.com					
Sterling Crane 2440 76th Ave	Edmonton	AB	T6P1J5	780-440-4434	440-1954
Web: www.sterlingcrane.ca					
Sunbelt Rentals Inc 1337 Hundred Oaks Dr	Charlotte	NC	28217	704-348-2676	602-7538
TF Mktg: 866-786-2358 ■ *Web:* www.sunbeltrentals.com					
T & T Truck & Crane Service Inc 1375 N Olive St	Ventura	CA	93001	805-488-4475	648-5218
TF: 800-655-3348 ■ *Web:* www.truckandcrane.com					
Telogy Inc 3200 Whipple Rd	Union City	CA	94587	510-675-9500	675-1600
TF: 800-835-6494					
Tetra Corporate Services LLC 3165 Millrock Dr Suite 400	Salt Lake City	UT	84121	801-566-2600	365-6263
Web: www.tetracsi.com					
Thomas Instrument & Machine Co Inc 3440 First St	Brookshire	TX	77423	281-375-6300	375-5264
Web: www.thomasinstrument.com					
Timco Services Inc 1724 E Milton Rd	Lafayette	LA	70508	337-233-8664	856-8158
TF: 800-749-2054					
Traffic Control Service Inc 1881 Betmor Ln	Anaheim	CA	92805	714-937-0422	526-9501
TF: 800-222-8274 ■ *Web:* www.tcsi.biz					
United Crane Rentals Inc 111 N Michigan Ave	Kenilworth	NJ	07033	908-245-6260	245-1708
TF: 800-356-6260					
United Rentals Inc 5 Greenwich Office Pk	Greenwich	CT	06830	203-622-3131	622-6080
NYSE: URI ■ *TF:* 800-877-3687 ■ *Web:* www.ur.com					
Utility Equipment Leasing Corp N4 W22610 Bluemound Rd	Waukesha	WI	53186	262-547-1600	544-8546
TF: 800-558-0999 ■ *Web:* www.uelc.com					
Volvo Rents 1 Volvo Dr	Asheville	NC	28803	866-387-3687	650-2504*
**Fax Area Code:* 828 ■ *TF:* 866-387-3687 ■ *Web:* www.volvorentsconstructionequipment.com					
Waco Scaffolding & Equipment Co 4545 Spring Rd PO Box 318028	Cleveland	OH	44131	216-749-8900	741-8486
TF: 800-321-3150 ■ *Web:* www.wacoscaf.com					
Western Oilfields Supply Co 3404 State Rd	Bakersfield	CA	93308	661-399-9124	393-6897*
**Fax:* Acctg ■ *TF:* 800-350-7246 ■ *Web:* www.rainforrent.com					

267-4 Medical Equipment Rental

				Phone	Fax
American Shared Hospital Services 4 Embarcadero Ctr Suite 3700	San Francisco	CA	94111	415-788-5300	788-5660
AMEX: AMS ■ *TF:* 800-735-0641 ■ *Web:* www.ashs.com					
Dynasplint Systems Inc 770 Ritchie Hwy Suite W21	Severna Park	MD	21146	410-544-9530	380-3784*
**Fax Area Code:* 800 ■ *TF:* 800-638-6771 ■ *Web:* www.dynasplint.com					
First Lease Inc 185 Commerce Dr Unit 102	Fort Washington	PA	19034	215-283-9727	283-9870
TF: 800-544-7607 ■ *Web:* www.firstleaseonline.com					
Freedom Medical Inc 219 Welsh Pool Rd	Exton	PA	19341	610-903-0200	903-0180
TF: 800-784-8849 ■ *Web:* www.freedommedical.com					
King's Medical Co 1894 Georgetown Rd	Hudson	OH	44236	330-653-3968	656-0600
Web: www.kingsmedical.com					
Modern Medical Modalities Corp PO Box 957	Union	NJ	07083	908-687-8840	687-8842
Universal Hospital Services Inc 7700 France Ave S Suite 275	Edina	MN	55435	952-893-3200	893-0704
TF: 800-847-7368 ■ *Web:* www.uhs.com					

267-5 Transport Equipment Rental

				Phone	Fax
Andersons Inc Rail Group 480 W Dussel Dr PO Box 119	Maumee	OH	43537	419-893-5050	891-2749
TF: 866-234-0505 ■ *Web:* www.andersonsinc.com					
Chicago Freight Car Leasing Co 6250 N River Rd Suite 7000	Rosemont	IL	60018	847-318-8000	318-8045
Web: www.crdx.com					
Cronos Containers Inc 1 Front St Suite 925	San Francisco	CA	94111	415-677-8990	677-9396
TF: 800-821-7035 ■ *Web:* www.cronos.com					
Eurotainer Inc 5810 Wilson Rd Suite 200	Humble	TX	77396	832-300-5001	300-5050
Web: www.eurotainer.com					
EXSIF Worldwide Inc 2700 Westchester Ave Suite 400	Purchase	NY	10577	914-848-4200	848-4201
Web: www.exsifww.com					
Flexi-Van Leasing Inc 251 Monroe Ave	Kenilworth	NJ	07033	908-276-8000	276-7666
Web: www.flexi-van.com					
GATX Rail Canada 1801 Magill College Ave Suite 1475	Montreal	QC	H3A2N4	514-931-7343	931-5534
TF: 800-806-2489 ■ *Web:* www.cgtx.com					
GATX Rail Corp 222 W Adams St	Chicago	IL	60661	312-621-6200	621-6272*
**Fax:* Sales ■ *Web:* www.gatx.com/rail					
GE Rail Car Services 161 N Clark St 7th Fl	Chicago	IL	60601	312-853-5000	853-5605
TF: 888-272-5793 ■ *Web:* www.ge.com/capital/rail					
GLNX Corp 10077 Grogan's Mill Rd Suite 450	The Woodlands	TX	77380	281-363-0185	363-7060
Web: www.glnx.com					
Greenbrier Co 1 Centerpointe Dr Suite 200	Lake Oswego	OR	97035	503-684-7000	684-7553
NYSE: GBX ■ *TF:* 800-343-7188 ■ *Web:* www.gbrx.com					
Highway Technologies Inc 880 N Addison Rd	Villa Park	IL	60181	630-368-0920	932-7611
Web: www.hwy-tech.com					
Interpool Inc 211 College Rd E	Princeton	NJ	08540	609-452-8900	452-8211
TF: 800-388-7485 ■ *Web:* www.interpool.com					
Procor Ltd 2001 Speers Rd	Oakville	ON	L6J5E1	905-827-4111	827-0913
Web: www.procor.com					

	City	State	Zip	Phone	Fax
Railserve Inc 1691 Phoenix Blvd Suite 110 *TF:* 800-345-7245 ■ *Web:* www.railserveinc.com	Atlanta	GA	30349	770-996-6838	996-6830
TAL International Group Inc 100 Manhattanville Rd *NYSE:* TAL ■ *Web:* www.talinternational.com	Purchase	NY	10577	914-251-9000	697-2549
TTX Co 101 N Wacker Dr *TF:* 800-621-5854 ■ *Web:* www.ttx.com	Chicago	IL	60606	312-853-3223	984-3790
XTRA Corp 1801 Pk 270 Dr Suite 400 *TF:* 800-325-1453 ■ *Web:* www.xtralease.com	Saint Louis	MO	63146	314-579-9300	542-0783

268 ETHICS COMMISSIONS

	City	State	Zip	Phone	Fax
Federal Election Commission 999 E St NW *TF:* 800-424-9530 ■ *Web:* www.fec.gov	Washington	DC	20463	202-694-1100	
US Office of Government Ethics 1201 New York Ave NW Suite 500 *Web:* www.usoge.gov	Washington	DC	20005	202-482-9300	482-9237
Alabama Ethics Commission 100 N Union St Suite 104 *Web:* www.ethics.alabama.gov	Montgomery	AL	36104	334-242-2997	242-0248
Alaska Legislative Ethics Committee PO Box 101468 *Web:* www.ethics.legis.state.ak.us	Anchorage	AK	99510	907-269-0150	269-0152
Arakansas Ethics Commission 910 W 2nd St Suite 100 *TF:* 800-422-7773 ■ *Web:* www.arkansasethics.com	Little Rock	AR	72201	501-324-9600	324-9606
California Fair Political Practices Commission 428 J St Suite 620 *TF:* 866-275-3772 ■ *Web:* www.fppc.ca.gov	Sacramento	CA	95814	916-322-5660	322-0886
Connecticut Ethics Commission 18-20 Trinity St Suite 205 *Web:* www.ct.gov/ethics/site/default.asp	Hartford	CT	06106	860-263-2400	263-2402
Delaware Public Integrity Commission 410 Federal St Margaret O"Neill Bldg Suite 3 *Web:* www.depic.delaware.gov	Dover	DE	19901	302-739-2399	739-2398
District of Columbia Elections & Ethics Board 441 4th St NW Suite 250N *TF:* 866-328-6837 ■ *Web:* www.dcboee.org	Washington	DC	20001	202-727-2525	347-2648
Florida Ethics Commission 3600 Maclay Blvd S Suite 201 *Web:* www.ethics.state.fl.us	Tallahassee	FL	32312	850-488-7864	488-3077
Georgia Transparency & Campaign Finance Commission 200 Piedmont Ave SE Suite 1402 *TF:* 866-589-7327 ■ *Web:* www.ethics.state.ga.us	Atlanta	GA	30334	404-463-1980	463-1988
Indiana State Ethics Commission 402 W Washington St Rm W-198 *Web:* www.in.gov/ethics	Indianapolis	IN	46204	317-232-3850	232-0707
Iowa Ethics & Campaign Disclosure Board 510 E 12th St Suite 1-A *Web:* www.state.ia.us	Des Moines	IA	50319	515-281-4028	281-3701
Kansas Governmental Ethics Commission 109 W 9th St Suite 504 *Web:* www.accesskansas.org	Topeka	KS	66612	785-296-4219	296-2548
Kentucky Executive Branch Ethics Commission 700 Capitol Ave ;Rm 209 *Web:* www.ethics.ky.gov	Frankfort	KY	40601	502-564-7954	564-2686
Kentucky Legislative Ethics Commission 22 Mill Creek Pk *Web:* www.klec.ky.gov	Frankfort	KY	40601	502-573-2863	573-2929
Louisiana Ethics Board 617 N Third St LaSalle Bldg, Suite 10-36 *TF:* 800-842-6630 ■ *Web:* www.ethics.state.la.us	Baton Rouge	LA	70802	225-219-5600	381-7271
Maine Governmental Ethics & Election Practices Commission 45 Memorial Cir *Web:* www.state.me.us	Augusta	ME	04330	207-287-4179	287-6775
Maryland Ethics Commission 9 State Cir Suite 200 *TF:* 877-669-6085 ■ *Web:* ethics.gov.state.md.us	Annapolis	MD	21401	410-974-2068	974-2418
Massachusetts State Ethics Commission 1 Ashburton Pl Rm 619 *Web:* www.mass.gov/ethics	Boston	MA	02108	617-727-0060	723-5851
Minnesota Campaign Finance & Public Disclosure Board 658 Cedar St Suite 190 *TF:* 800-657-3889 ■ *Web:* www.cfboard.state.mn.us	Saint Paul	MN	55155	651-296-5148	296-1722
Mississippi Ethics Commission 146 E Amite St # 103 *Web:* www.ethics.state.ms.us	Jackson	MS	39201	601-359-1285	354-6253
Montana Commissioner of Political Practices 1205 8th Ave PO Box 202401 *Web:* www.politicalpractices.mt.gov	Helena	MT	59620	406-444-2942	444-1643
Nebraska Accountability & Disclosure Commission PO Box 95086 *Web:* www.nadc.nol.org	Lincoln	NE	68509	402-471-2522	471-6599
Nevada Commission on Ethics 704 W Nye Ln Suite 204 *Web:* www.ethics.nv.gov	Carson City	NV	89703	775-687-5469	687-1279
New Jersey Ethical Standards Commission 28 W State St Rm 1407 PO Box 082 *Web:* www.state.nj.us/lps/ethics	Trenton	NJ	08625	609-292-1892	633-9252
New Mexico Ethics Administration 325 Don Gaspar St Suite 300 *TF:* 800-477-3632 ■ *Web:* www.sos.state.nm.us/ethics.htm	Santa Fe	NM	87503	505-827-3600	827-4954
North Carolina Ethics Board 116 W Jones St *Web:* www.doa.state.nc.us/ethics	Raleigh	NC	27603	919-733-2780	733-2785
Ohio Ethics Commission 30 W Spring St L3 *Web:* www.ethics.ohio.gov	Columbus	OH	43215	614-466-7090	466-8368
Oklahoma Ethics Commission 2300 N Lincoln Blvd Rm B5 *Web:* www.ok.gov	Oklahoma City	OK	73105	405-521-3451	521-4905
Oregon Government Standards & Practices Commission 3218 Pringle Rd SE # 220 *Web:* www.gspc.state.or.us	Salem	OR	97302	503-378-5105	373-1456
Pennsylvania State Ethics Commission Rm 309 Finance Bldg PO Box 11470 *TF:* 800-932-0936 ■ *Web:* www.ethics.state.pa.us	Harrisburg	PA	17108	717-783-1610	787-0806
Rhode Island Ethics Commission 40 Fountain St	Providence	RI	02903	401-222-3790	222-3382
South Carolina Ethics Commission 5000 Thurmond Mall Suite 250 *Web:* www.state.sc.us	Columbia	SC	29201	803-253-4192	253-7539
Texas Ethics Commission 201 E 14th St 10th Fl *Web:* www.ethics.state.tx.us	Austin	TX	78701	512-463-5800	463-5777
Washington Public Disclosure Commission PO Box 40908 *Web:* www.pdc.wa.gov	Olympia	WA	98504	360-753-1111	753-1112
West Virginia Ethics Commission 210 Brooks St Suite 300 *Web:* www.wvethicscommission.org	Charleston	WV	25301	304-558-0664	558-2169
Wisconsin Ethics Board 212 E Washington Ave 3rd Fl *Web:* www.gab.wi.gov	Madison	WI	53703	608-266-8123	264-9319

269 EXECUTIVE RECRUITING FIRMS

	City	State	Zip	Phone	Fax
Aaron Consulting Inc 625 N Euclid Ave *Web:* www.aaronlaw.com	Saint Louis	MO	63108	314-367-2627	367-2919
Accretive Solutions Inc 311 S Wacker Dr Suite 5200 *Web:* www.accretivesolutions.com	Chicago	IL	60606	312-994-4600	994-4638
AT Kearney Executive Search 222 W Adams St *Web:* www.atkearney.com	Chicago	IL	60606	312-648-0111	223-6369
Barton Assoc Inc 701 Richmond Ave # 226 *Web:* www.bartona.com	Houston	TX	77006	713-961-9111	993-9399
Battalia Winston International 555 Madison Ave 19th Fl *Web:* www.battaliawinston.com	New York	NY	10022	212-308-8080	308-1309
Bishop Partners Ltd 28 W 44th St #1120 *Web:* www.bishoppartners.com	New York	NY	10036	212-986-3419	986-3350
Boardroom Consultants 530 5th Ave Suite 2100 *Web:* www.boardroomconsultants.com	New York	NY	10036	212-328-0440	328-0441
Boyden World Corp 50 Broadway *Web:* www.boyden.com	Hawthorne	NY	10532	914-747-0093	747-0108
Canny Bowen Inc 280 Pk Ave W Tower 30th Fl *Web:* www.cannybowen.com	New York	NY	10017	212-949-6611	949-5191
Chadick Ellig Inc 300 Pk Ave 25th Fl *Web:* www.chadickellig.com	New York	NY	10022	212-688-8671	308-4510
Chicago Legal Search Ltd 180 N LaSalle St Suite 3325 *Web:* www.chicagolegalsearch.com	Chicago	IL	60601	312-251-2580	251-0223
Choi & Burns LLC 156 W 56th St 18th Fl *Web:* www.choiburns.com	New York	NY	10019	212-755-7051	355-2610
Christian & Timbers 25825 Science Pk Dr Suite 100 *TF:* 800-380-9444 ■ *Web:* www.ctnet.com	Cleveland	OH	44122	216-464-8710	464-6160
Cole Warren & Long Inc 1500 John F Kennedy Blvd # 312 *TF:* 800-394-8517 ■ *Web:* www.cwl-inc.com	Philadelphia	PA	19102	215-563-0701	563-2907
Compass Group Ltd 401 S Old Woodward Ave Suite 310 *Web:* www.compassgroup.com	Birmingham	MI	48009	248-540-9110	647-8288
Cook Assoc Inc 212 W Kinzie St *Web:* www.cookassociates.com	Chicago	IL	60654	312-329-0900	329-1528
Dahl Morrow International 11260 Roger Bacon St Suite 204 *Web:* www.dahl-morrowintl.com	Reston	VA	20190	703-787-8117	787-8114
Daniel & Yeager (D&Y) 6767 Old Madison Pike Suite 690 **Fax Area Code:* 256 ■ *TF:* 800-955-1919 ■ *Web:* www.dystaffing.com	Huntsville	AL	35806	800-955-1919	551-1075*
DHR International 10 S Riverside Plaza Suite 2220 *TF:* 800-782-2210 ■ *Web:* www.dhrinternational.com	Chicago	IL	60606	312-782-1581	782-2096
Dieckmann & Assoc 500 N Michigan Ave # 300 *Web:* www.dieckmann-associates.com	Chicago	IL	60611	312-819-5900	819-5924
Diversified Search Cos 2005 Market St Suite 3300 *TF:* 800-423-3932 ■ *Web:* www.divsearch.com	Philadelphia	PA	19103	215-732-6666	568-8399
DP Parker & Assoc Inc 1 Hollis St Suite 103 *Web:* www.dpparker.com	Wellesley	MA	02482	781-237-1220	237-4702
Early Cochran & Olson LLC 1 E Wacker Dr Suite 2510 *Web:* www.ecollc.com	Chicago	IL	60601	312-595-4200	595-4209
Eastman & Beaudine Inc 7201 Bishop Rd Suite 220 *Web:* www.eastman-beaudine.com	Plano	TX	75024	972-312-1012	312-1020
Egon Zehnder International Inc 1 N Wacker Dr Suite 2300 *TF:* 800-800-5567 ■ *Web:* www.egonzehnder.com	Chicago	IL	60606	312-260-8800	782-2846
Exec Solutions 5655 Lindero Canyon Rd Suite 521	Westlake Village	CA	91362	818-575-8080	575-8099
Fergus Partnership Consulting Inc 14 Wall St # 3C *Web:* www.ferguslex.com	New York	NY	10005	212-767-1775	315-0351
Halbrecht Lieberman Assoc Inc 32 Surf Rd *Web:* www.hlassoc.com	Westport	CT	06880	203-222-4890	222-4895
HC Smith Ltd 20600 Chagrin Blvd Suite 101 *TF:* 800-442-7583 ■ *Web:* www.hcsmith.com	Shaker Heights	OH	44122	216-752-9966	752-9970
HealthCare Recruiters International 5220 Spring Valley Rd Suite 40 *Web:* www.hcrintl.com	Dallas	TX	75254	972-702-0444	702-0432
Heath/Norton Assoc 301 Crocus Ct Suite L-7	Dayton	NJ	08810	732-329-4663	

	City	State	ZIP	Phone	Fax
Heidrick & Struggles International Inc 233 S Wacker Dr Suite 7000 *NASDAQ: HSII* ■ *Web:* www.heidrick.com	Chicago	IL	60606	312-496-1000	496-1048
Herbert Mines Assoc Inc 375 Pk Ave *Web:* www.herbertmines.com	New York	NY	10152	212-355-0909	223-2186
Higdon Partners LLC *HigdonBraddockMatthews LLC* 230 Pk Ave Suite 951 *Web:* www.higdonbarrett.com	New York	NY	10169	212-986-4662	986-5002
Horton International LLC 433 S Main St	West Hartford	CT	06110	860-521-0101	521-0140
Howard Fischer Assoc International 1800 Kennedy Blvd Suite 700 *Web:* www.hfischer.com	Philadelphia	PA	19103	215-568-8363	568-4815
Howard-Sloan Search Inc 1140 Avenue of the Americas *TF:* 800-221-1326 ■ *Web:* www.howardsloan.com	New York	NY	10036	212-704-0444	869-7999
Hughes & Sloan Inc 1360 Peachtree St NE 1 Midtown Plaza Suite 1010 *Web:* www.hughesandsloan.com	Atlanta	GA	30309	404-873-3421	873-3861
Hunt Howe Partners LLC 1 Dag Hammarskjold Plaza 26th Fl *Web:* www.hunthowe.com	New York	NY	10017	212-758-2800	758-7710
IMC Group of Cos 120 White Plains Rd Suite 405 *Web:* www.the-imc.com	Tarrytown	NY	10591	914-468-7050	468-7051
Kenzer Corp 1 Penn Plaza *Web:* www.kenzer.com	New York	NY	10119	212-308-4300	308-1842
Klein Landau & Romm 1015 18th St NW Suite 508 *TF:* 866-807-1931 ■ *Web:* www.klrs.com	Washington	DC	20036	202-728-0100	728-0112
Korn/Ferry International 1900 Avenue of the Stars Suite 2600 *NYSE: KFY* ■ *Web:* www.kornferry.com	Los Angeles	CA	90067	310-552-1834	553-6452
Kovensky & Co 2121 K St NW # 850 **Fax Area Code:* 413 ■ *Web:* www.kovenskyandcompany.com	Washington	DC	20037	202-261-3555	832-1838*
Lawrence Glaser Assoc Inc 505 S Lenola Rd Suite 202 *Web:* www.lgasearch.com	Moorestown	NJ	08057	856-778-9500	778-4390
Major Lindsey & Africa 938 B St *TF:* 877-482-1010 ■ *Web:* www.mlaglobal.com	San Rafael	CA	94901	415-485-5111	485-5110
Management Recruiters International Worldwide Inc 1717 Arch St 36th Fl *TF:* 800-875-4000 ■ *Web:* www.mrinetwork.com	Philadelphia	PA	19103	215-636-1200	751-1759
Mestel & Co Inc 575 Madison Ave Suite 3000 *Web:* www.mestel.com	New York	NY	10022	646-356-0500	356-0545
Monster Worldwide Inc 622 3rd Ave 39th Fl *NASDAQ: MNST* ■ **Fax Area Code:* 646 ■ *TF:* 888-225-5867 ■ *Web:* www.about-monster.com	New York	NY	10017	212-351-7000	658-0541*
MSI International Inc 650 Pk Ave *TF:* 800-927-0919 ■ *Web:* www.msimsi.com	King of Prussia	PA	19406	610-265-2000	265-2213
National Search Assoc 2035 Corte del Nogal, Suite 100 Suite 100 *Web:* www.nsasearch.com	Carlsbad	CA	92011	760-431-1115	683-3044
Nordeman Grimm 65 E 55th St 33rd Fl *Web:* www.nordemangrimm.com	New York	NY	10022	212-935-1000	980-1443
Physicians Search 5581 E Stetson Ct *TF:* 800-748-6320	Anaheim	CA	92807	714-685-1047	685-1143
Pittleman & Assoc 336 E 43rd St *Web:* www.pittlemanassociates.com	New York	NY	10017	212-370-9600	370-9608
Rice Cohen International 301 Oxford Valley Rd Suite 1506A	Yardley	PA	19067	215-321-4100	
Rusher Loscavio & LoPresto 369 Pine St #221 *Web:* www.rll.com	San Francisco	CA	94104	415-765-6600	546-2201
Russell Reynolds Assoc Inc 200 Pk Ave 23rd Fl *TF:* 888-772-6200	New York	NY	10166	212-351-2000	370-0896
Skott/Edwards Consultants 7 Royal Dr *Web:* www.skottedwards.com	Cherry Quay	NJ	08723	732-920-1883	477-1541
Spectra International 3200 N Hayden Rd Suite 210 **Fax Area Code:* 800 ■ *TF:* 800-595-5617 ■ *Web:* www.spectra-az.com	Scottsdale	AZ	85251	480-481-0411	893-8483*
Spencer Reed Group Inc 6900 College Blvd Suite 1 *TF:* 800-477-5035 ■ *Web:* www.spencerreed.com	Overland Park	KS	66211	913-663-4400	663-4464
SpencerStuart 401 N Michigan Ave Suite 3400 *Web:* www.spencerstuart.com	Chicago	IL	60611	312-822-0080	822-0116
Stanton Chase International 400 E Pratt St # 420 *Web:* www.stantonchase.com	Baltimore	MD	21202	410-528-8400	528-8409
Swan Legal Search 1100 Glendon Ave 15th Fl *TF:* 888-860-1154 ■ *Web:* www.swanlegal.com	Los Angeles	CA	90024	310-201-2500	445-0621
Tyler & Co 400 Northridge Rd Suite 1250 *Web:* www.tylerandco.com	Atlanta	GA	30350	770-396-3939	396-6693
Whitney Partners 555 Fifth Ave 6th Fl *Web:* www.whitneygroup.com	New York	NY	10017	212-508-3500	508-3540
Witt/Kieffer Ford Hadelman & Lloyd 2015 Spring Rd Suite 510 *Web:* www.wittkieffer.com	Oak Brook	IL	60523	630-990-1370	990-1382
Wyatt & Jaffe 4999 France Ave S Suite 260 *Web:* www.wyattjaffe.com	Minneapolis	MN	55410	612-285-2858	285-2786

270 EXERCISE & FITNESS EQUIPMENT

SEE ALSO Sporting Goods p. 2664

	City	State	ZIP	Phone	Fax
All Pro Exercise Products Inc PO Box 8268 **Fax Area Code:* 908 ■ *TF:* 800-735-9287 ■ *Web:* www.allproweights.com	Longboat Key	FL	34228	941-387-9432	281-5793*
Body Masters Sports Industries Inc 700 E Texas Ave PO Box 259 *TF:* 800-325-8964	Rayne	LA	70578	337-334-9611	334-4827
Body-Solid Inc 1900 Des Plaines Ave *TF:* 800-833-1227 ■ *Web:* www.bodysolid.com	Forest Park	IL	60130	708-427-3500	427-3556
Cybex International Inc 10 Trotter Dr *AMEX: CYB* ■ *TF:* 888-462-9239 ■ *Web:* www.ecybex.com	Medway	MA	02053	508-533-4300	533-5500
Fitness Quest Inc 1400 Raff Rd SW *TF:* 800-321-9236 ■ *Web:* www.fitnessquest.com	Canton	OH	44750	330-478-0755	478-2159
Heart-Rate Inc 3190 Airport Loop Dr Bldg E *TF:* 800-237-2271 ■ *Web:* www.heartrateinc.com	Costa Mesa	CA	92626	714-850-9716	755-5749
Heartline Fitness Products Inc 19209 Orbit Dr *TF:* 800-262-3348 ■ *Web:* www.heartlinefitness.com	Gaithersburg	MD	20879	301-921-0661	330-5479
Hoggan Health Industries Inc 8020 S 1300 W *TF:* 800-678-7888 ■ *Web:* www.hogganhealth.com	West Jordan	UT	84088	801-572-6500	572-6514
Hoist Fitness Systems Inc 9990 Empire St Suite 130 *TF:* 800-548-5438 ■ *Web:* www.hoistfitness.com	San Diego	CA	92126	858-578-7676	578-9558
HYDRO-FIT Inc 160 Madison St *TF Cust Svc:* 800-346-7295 ■ *Web:* www.hydrofit.com	Eugene	OR	97402	541-484-4361	484-1443
ICON Health & Fitness Inc 1500 S 1000 W **Fax:* Cust Svc ■ *TF:* 800-999-3756 ■ *Web:* www.iconfitness.com	Logan	UT	84321	435-750-5000	750-3632*
IronMaster LLC 21828 87th Ave SE Suite E *TF:* 800-533-3339 ■ *Web:* www.ironmaster.com	Woodinville	WA	98072	425-408-9040	483-2868
Life Fitness 5100 N River Rd *TF:* 800-351-3737 ■ *Web:* www.lifefitness.com	Schiller Park	IL	60176	800-351-3737	216-8893
Nautilus Inc 16400 SE Nautilus Dr *NYSE: NLS* ■ *TF:* 800-628-8458 ■ *Web:* www.nautilusgroup.com	Vancouver	WA	98684	360-694-7722	694-7755
New York Barbells 160 Home St *TF:* 800-446-1833 ■ *Web:* www.newyorkbarbells.com	Elmira	NY	14904	607-733-8038	733-1010
Paramount Fitness Corp 6450 E Bandini Blvd *TF:* 800-721-2121 ■ *Web:* www.paramountfitness.com	Los Angeles	CA	90040	323-721-2121	724-2000
Precor Inc 20031 142nd Ave NE *TF:* 800-786-8404 ■ *Web:* www.precor.com	Woodinville	WA	98072	425-486-9292	486-3856
Pro Star Sports Inc 1133 Winchester Ave *TF:* 800-821-8482 ■ *Web:* www.prostarsports.com	Kansas City	MO	64126	816-241-9737	241-2459
Soloflex Inc 570 NE 53rd Ave *TF:* 800-547-8802 ■ *Web:* www.soloflex.com	Hillsboro	OR	97124	503-640-8891	648-0864
Spirit Mfg Inc 2601 Commerce Dr *TF:* 800-258-4555 ■ *Web:* www.spiritfitness.com	Jonesboro	AR	72402	870-935-1107	935-7611
Star Trac by Unisen Inc 14410 Myford Rd *TF:* 800-228-6635 ■ *Web:* www.startrac.com	Irvine	CA	92606	714-669-1660	838-6286
True Fitness Technology Inc 865 Hoff Rd *TF:* 800-426-6570 ■ *Web:* www.truefitness.com	O"Fallon	MO	63366	636-272-7100	272-7148
Vectra Fitness Inc 7901 S 190th St *Web:* www.vectrafitness.com	Kent	WA	98032	425-291-9550	291-9650
Woodway USA W229 N591 Foster Ct *TF:* 800-966-3929 ■ *Web:* www.woodway.com	Waukesha	WI	53186	262-548-6235	522-6235
York Barbell Co Inc 3300 Board Rd *TF Cust Svc:* 800-358-9675 ■ *Web:* www.yorkbarbell.com	York	PA	17402	717-767-6481	764-0044

271 EXPLOSIVES

	City	State	ZIP	Phone	Fax
Accurate Energetics Systems LLC 5891 Hwy 230 W *Web:* www.aesys.biz	McEwen	TN	37101	931-729-4207	729-4214
Action Mfg Co 100 E Erie Ave *Web:* www.action-mfg.com	Philadelphia	PA	19134	215-739-6400	423-7749
Alliant Powder Rt 114 PO Box 6 *TF:* 800-276-9337 ■ *Web:* www.alliantpowder.com	Radford	VA	24143	540-639-8503	639-8496
Austin Powder Co 25800 Science Pk Dr Suite 300 *TF:* 800-321-0752 ■ *Web:* www.austinpowder.com	Cleveland	OH	44122	216-464-2400	591-1568
Buckley Powder Co 42 Inverness Dr E *TF:* 800-333-2266 ■ *Web:* www.buckleypowder.com	Englewood	CO	80112	303-790-7007	790-7033
Can-Blast Inc 755 Wallace Rd Unit 3 *Web:* www.can-blast.com	North Bay	ON	P1B8K4	705-474-3431	476-7643
Cartridge Actuated Devices Inc 51 Dwight Pl *Web:* www.mcselph.com	Fairfield	NJ	07004	973-575-1312	575-6039
Dyno Nobel Inc 2795 E Cottonwood Pkwy # 500 # 500 *TF:* 800-473-2626 ■ *Web:* www.dynonobel.com	Salt Lake City	UT	84121	801-364-4800	328-6452
Ensign-Bickford Industries Inc 100 Grist Mill Rd *TF:* 800-828-9814 ■ *Web:* www.ensign-bickfordind.com	Simsbury	CT	06070	860-843-2000	843-1510
Hodgdon Powder Co Inc 6231 Robinson St *Web:* www.hodgdon.com	Shawnee Mission	KS	66202	913-362-9455	362-1307
Mil-Spec Industries Corp 10 Mineola Ave *Web:* www.milspecindustries.com	Roslyn Heights	NY	11577	516-625-5787	625-0988
Orica USA Inc 33101 E Quincy Ave *Web:* www.oricaminingservices.com	Watkins	CO	80137	303-268-5000	268-5250
Pyrotechnic Specialties Inc 1661 Juniper Creek Rd *Web:* www.pyrotechonline.com	Byron	GA	31008	478-956-5400	956-5108
Rozzi Inc 11605 N Lebanon Rd *Web:* www.rozzifireworks.com	Loveland	OH	45140	513-683-0620	683-2043
Schaefer Pyrotechnics Inc 376 Hartman Bridge Rd *TF:* 877-598-2264 ■ *Web:* www.schaeferfireworks.com	Ronks	PA	17572	717-687-0647	687-8982
Senex Explosives Inc 710 Millers Run Rd	Cuddy	PA	15031	412-221-3218	221-6032
Special Devices Inc 14370 White Sage Rd *TF:* 888-782-0082 ■ *Web:* www.specialdevices.com	Moorpark	CA	93021	805-553-1200	553-1201

	City	State	Zip	Phone	Fax
Stresau Laboratory Inc N8265 Medley Rd Web: www.stresau.com	Spooner	WI	54801	715-635-2777	635-7979
Technical Ordnance Inc 9200 Nike Rd Web: www.tekord.com	Saint Bonifacius	MN	55375	952-446-1526	446-1990
Teledyne Reynolds Inc 5005 McConnell Ave Web: www.teledynereynolds.com	Los Angeles	CA	90066	310-823-5491	822-8046
Zambelli Internationale Fireworks Mfg 20 S Mercer St 2nd Fl TF: 800-245-0397 ■ Web: www.zambellifireworks.com	New Castle	PA	16101	724-658-6611	658-8318

272 EYE BANKS

SEE ALSO Organ & Tissue Banks p. 2330; Transplant Centers - Blood Stem Cell p. 2726

Eye Banks Listed Here Are Members Of The Eye Bank Association Of America (Ebaa), An Accrediting Body For Eye Banks. The Ebaa Medical Standards For Member Eye Banks Are Endorsed By The American Academy Of Ophthalmology.

	City	State	Zip	Phone	Fax
Alabama Eye Bank 500 Robert Jemison Rd TF: 800-423-7811 ■ Web: www.alabamaeyebank.org	Birmingham	AL	35209	205-942-2120	942-2184
Alcon Laboratories Inc 6201 S Fwy TF: 800-862-5266 ■ Web: www.alcon.com	Fort Worth	TX	76134	817-293-0450	
Arkansas Lions Eye Bank & Laboratory 4301 W Markham St Slot 523-1 Web: www.uams.edu/jei/lions	Little Rock	AR	72205	501-686-8388	603-1463
Banque D'Yeux de Quebec 5415 Blvd l'Assomption	Montreal	QC	H1T2M4	514-252-3886	252-3821
Baton Rouge Regional Eye Bank 7777 Hennessy Blvd PMB 163 Web: www.eyebankbr.org	Baton Rouge	LA	70808	225-766-8996	765-4366
Center for Organ Recovery & Education (CORE) 204 Sigma Dr RIDC Pk TF: 800-366-6777 ■ Web: www.core.org	Pittsburgh	PA	15238	412-366-6777	963-3596
Central New York Eye & Tissue Bank 475 Irving Ave Suite 100 TF: 800-393-7487 ■ Web: www.cnyeyebank.org	Syracuse	NY	13210	315-476-0199	471-6060
Central Ohio Lions Eye Bank 262 Neil Ave Suite 140 TF: 800-301-4960 ■ Web: www.lionseyebank.net	Columbus	OH	43215	614-293-2057	545-2067
Cincinnati Eye Bank for Sight Restoration Inc 4015 Executive Pk Dr Suite 330 Web: www.cintieb.org	Cincinnati	OH	45241	513-861-3716	483-3984
Cleveland Eye Bank 11100 Euclid Ave Wearn Bldg Rm 615 TF: 800-251-9270	Cleveland	OH	44106	216-844-3937	983-0069
Connecticut Eye Bank & Visual Research Foundation Inc 389 John Downey Dr TF: 800-355-5520	New Britain	CT	06052	860-224-5550	224-5720
Donor Network of Arizona 201 W Coolidge St TF: 800-447-9477 ■ Web: www.dnaz.org	Phoenix	AZ	85013	602-222-2200	222-2202
East Tennessee Lions Eye Bank 1924 Alcoa Hwy	Knoxville	TN	37920	865-544-9625	523-4869
Eye Bank Assn of America (EBAA) 1015 18th St NW Suite 1010 Web: www.restoresight.org	Washington	DC	20036	202-775-4999	429-6036
Eye Bank for Sight Restoration Inc 120 Wall St 3rd Fl TF: 866-287-3937 ■ Web: www.eyedonation.org	New York	NY	10005	212-742-9000	269-3139
Eye Bank of British Columbia 2550 Willow St Eye Care Centre 3rd Fl Web: www.eyebankofbc.ca	Vancouver	BC	V5Z3N9	604-875-4567	875-5316
Eye Bank of Canada Ontario Div 1 Spadina Crescent Rm 114 TF: 877-363-8456 ■ Web: eyebank.med.utoronto.ca	Toronto	ON	M5S2J5	416-978-7355	978-1522
Great Plains Lions Eye Bank *Texas Tech University Health Sciences Ctr* 3601 4th St Suite BAB104-HSC Web: www.ttuhsc.edu/eye	Lubbock	TX	79430	806-743-2242	743-1431
Hawaii Lions Eye Bank & Makana Foundation 614 S St Suite 101 Web: www.eyebank.org	Honolulu	HI	96813	808-536-7416	528-5032
Heartland Lions Eye Bank 10100 N Ambassador Dr # 200 TF: 800-816-9264 ■ Web: www.mlerf.org	Kansas City	MO	64153	816-454-5454	454-5446
Heartland Lions Eye Bank 3506 S Culpepper Cir # D TF: 800-331-2636 ■ Web: www.mlerf.org	Springfield	MO	65804	417-882-1532	882-8206
Heartland Lions Eye Bank 4482 Woodson Rd Suite 7 TF: 800-331-2636 ■ Web: www.mlerf.org	Saint Louis	MO	63134	314-428-4373	428-3751
Idaho Lions Eye Bank 1055 N Curtis Rd TF: 800-546-6889 ■ Web: www.idaholions.org	Boise	ID	83706	208-367-2400	367-6843
International Cornea Project 9246 Lightwave Ave Suite 120 TF: 800-393-2265 ■ Web: www.sdeb.org	San Diego	CA	92123	858-694-0400	565-7368
International Sight Restoration Inc 3808 Gunn Hwy Suite B Web: www.internationalsight.com	Tampa	FL	33618	813-264-6003	264-6007
Iowa Lions Eye Bank 2346 Mormon Trek Blvd Suite 1500 TF: 866-435-7733 ■ Web: www.webeye.ophth.uiowa.edu	Iowa City	IA	52246	319-356-2871	384-9781
Laboratories at Bonfils 717 Yosemite St 2nd Fl TF: 800-321-6088 ■ Web: www.labsatbonfils.com	Denver	CO	80230	303-365-9000	343-6666
LifePoint Inc 4200 Faber Pl Dr TF: 800-462-0755 ■ Web: www.sceyebank.org	Charleston	SC	29405	843-763-7755	763-6393
LifePoint Inc 164 Lott Ct # B TF: 800-462-0755 ■ Web: www.sceyebank.org	West Columbia	SC	29169	803-796-2195	794-1831
LifeShare of the Carolinas 86 Victoria Rd Bldg B TF: 800-932-4483 ■ Web: www.lifesharecarolinas.org	Asheville	NC	28801	828-258-9703	258-3219
Lions Eye Bank Alberta Society 7007 14th St SW Web: www.act4sight.com	Calgary	AB	T2V1P9	403-943-3406	943-3244
Lions Eye Bank for Long Island *North Shore University Hospital* 350 Community Dr Web: www.lebli.org	Manhasset	NY	11030	516-465-8430	465-8434
Lions Eye Bank of Lexington 3290 Blazer Pkwy Suite 201 Web: www.mc.uky.edu	Lexington	KY	40509	859-323-6740	323-5927
Lions Eye Bank of Manitoba & Northwest Ontario Inc 691 Wolseley Ave Rm 105 TF: 800-552-6820	Winnipeg	MB	R3G1C3	204-788-8507	783-6823
Lions Eye Bank of Nebraska Inc *University of Nebraska Medical Ctr* UNMC 985541 TF: 800-225-7244 ■ Web: www.eyebanknebraska.org	Omaha	NE	68198	402-559-4039	559-7705
Lions Eye Bank of New Jersey 841 Mountain Ave. TF: 800-653-9379 ■ Web: www.lebnj.org	Springfield	NJ	07081	973-921-1222	921-1221
Lions Eye Bank of North Dakota 301 N 4th St TF: 800-372-3751	Bismarck	ND	58501	701-250-9390	250-0805
Lions Eye Bank of Northwest Pennsylvania Inc 5105 Richmond St	Erie	PA	16509	814-866-3545	864-1875
Lions Eye Bank of Oregon 1010 NW 22nd Ave Suite N144 TF: 800-843-7793 ■ Web: www.orlions.org	Portland	OR	97210	503-413-7523	413-6716
Lions Eye Bank of Puerto Rico PO Box 363311	San Juan	PR	00936	787-273-0597	273-0974
Lions Eye Bank of Saskatchewan Inc *Regina Pasqua Hospital* 4104 Dewdney Ave	Regina	SK	S4T1A5	306-655-8002	569-4122
Lions Eye Bank of Texas at Baylor College of Medicine *Dept of Opthalmology* 6565 Fannin St NC-205 Web: www.bcm.edu	Houston	TX	77030	713-798-5500	798-4645
Lions Eye Bank of West Central Ohio 1945 Southtown Blvd Suite E	Dayton	OH	45439	937-396-1000	396-1880
Lions Eye Bank of Wisconsin 2401 American Ln. TF: 877-233-2354 ■ Web: www.eyebankwis.com	Madison	WI	53704	608-233-2354	233-2895
Lions Medical Eye Bank & Research Center of Eastern Virginia Inc 600 Gresham Dr TF: 800-453-6059 ■ Web: www.lionseyebank.org	Norfolk	VA	23507	757-388-2748	388-3744
Lone Star Lions Eye Bank 102 E Wheeler St PO Box 347 TF: 800-977-3937 ■ Web: www.lsleb.org	Manor	TX	78653	512-457-0638	457-0658
Medical Eye Bank of Florida 2177 E Michigan St Suite 2 TF: 800-277-2020	Orlando	FL	32806	407-422-2020	425-7262
Medical Eye Bank of Maryland 815 Pk Ave TF: 800-756-4824 ■ Web: www.tbionline.org	Baltimore	MD	21201	410-752-2020	783-0183
Medical Eye Bank of West Virginia 3 Courtney Dr	Charleston	WV	25304	304-926-9200	926-6779
Mid-Continent Eye Bank 625 N Carriage Pkwy Suite 190 Web: www.wichitaeyebank.com	Wichita	KS	67208	316-260-8220	260-8225
Midwest Eye Banks 4889 Venture Dr TF: 800-247-7250 ■ Web: www.midwesteyebanks.org	Ann Arbor	MI	48108	734-780-2100	780-2143
Minnesota Lions Eye Bank 1000 Westgate Dr Suite 260 TF Cust Svc: 866-887-4448 ■ Web: www.mnlionseyebank.org	Saint paul	MN	55114	612-625-5159	626-1192
Mississippi Lions Eye Bank 431 Katherine Dr TF: 800-213-0403 ■ Web: www.mslionseyebank.org	Flowood	MS	39232	601-420-5739	420-5743
National Disease Research Interchange (NDRI) 1628 John F Kennedy Blvd 8 Penn Ctr 8th Fl TF: 800-222-6374 ■ Web: www.ndriresource.org	Philadelphia	PA	19103	215-557-7361	557-7154
New Brunswick Eye Bank *Saint Joseph""s Hospital* 130 Bayard Dr	Saint John	NB	E2L3L6	506-632-5541	632-5573
New England Eye & Tissue Transplant Bank 1 Gateway Pl Suite 309 TF: 800-462-2566	Newton	MA	02458	617-964-1809	965-1891
New Mexico Lions Eye Bank 2501 Yale Blvd SE Suite 100 TF: 888-616-3937	Albuquerque	NM	87106	505-266-3937	266-5560
North Carolina Eye Bank Inc 3900 Westpoint Blvd Suite F TF: 800-552-9956 ■ Web: www.nceyebank.org	Winston-Salem	NC	27103	336-765-0932	765-8803
Northeast Pennsylvania Lions Eye Bank Inc *Lehigh Valley Hospital* 17th & Chew Sts PO Box 7017 TF: 800-637-2393 ■ Web: www.paeyebank.org	Allentown	PA	18105	610-969-2155	969-4254
Northern California Transplant Bank 7700 Edgewater Dr Suite 526	Oakland	CA	94621	510-957-9595	957-9594
Northwest Lions Eye Bank 901 Boren Ave Suite 810 TF: 800-847-5786 ■ Web: www.nleb.org	Seattle	WA	98104	206-682-8500	682-8504
Northwest Louisiana Lions Eye Bank 721 Blvd St	Shreveport	LA	71104	318-222-7999	222-8779
Oklahoma Lions Eye Bank 3840 N Lincoln Blvd Web: www.lionnet-oklahoma.org	Oklahoma City	OK	73105	405-557-1393	557-0086
Old Dominion Eye Bank (ODEF) 9200 Arboretum Pkwy Suite 104 Web: www.odef.org	Richmond	VA	23236	804-560-7540	560-4752
Regional Tissue Bank QEII Health Sciences Centre 5788 University Ave Rm 431 McKenzie Bldg Ctr TF: 800-314-6515 ■ Web: www.cdha.nshealth.ca/tissuebank/tissueBank.html	Halifax	NS	B3H1V7	902-473-4171	473-2170
Rochester Eye & Human Parts Bank 524 White Spruce Blvd TF: 800-568-4321 ■ Web: www.rehpb.org	Rochester	NY	14623	585-272-7890	272-7897
Rocky Mountain Lions Eye Bank 1675 N Ursula Ave Rm El-2049 TF: 800-444-7479 ■ Web: www.corneas.org	Aurora	CO	80045	720-848-3937	848-3938

	City	State	Zip	Phone	Fax
San Antonio Eye Bank 8122 Datapoint Dr Suite 325 *Web:* www.tbionline.org	San Antonio	TX	78229	210-614-1209	614-1422
San Diego Eye Bank (SDEB) 9246 Lightwave Ave Suite 120 *TF:* 800-393-2265 ■ *Web:* www.sdeb.org	San Diego	CA	92123	858-694-0400	565-7368
Sight Society of Northeastern New York Inc *Lions Eye Bank at Albany* 6 Executive Pk Dr *TF:* 888-615-3937 ■ *Web:* www.lionseyebankalbany.org	Albany	NY	12203	518-489-7606	489-7607
South Dakota Lions Eye Bank 4501 W 61st St N *TF:* 800-245-7846 ■ *Web:* www.sdleb.org	Sioux Falls	SD	57107	605-373-1008	373-1261
Southeast Texas Lions Eye Bank Inc 700 University Blvd Suite 302 *TF:* 866-902-3937 ■ *Web:* www.utmb.edu/stleb	Galveston	TX	77550	409-747-5816	747-5817
Southern Eye Bank 2701 Kingman St Suite 200 *Web:* www.southerneyebank.com	Metairie	LA	70006	504-891-3937	891-2401
Tennessee District 12-0 Lions Eye Bank 979 E 3rd St Suite A250	Chattanooga	TN	37403	423-778-4000	778-4050
Tennessee Donor Services 1600 Hayes St *TF:* 888-234-4440 ■ *Web:* www.dcids.org	Nashville	TN	37203	615-234-5251	320-1655
Tissue Banks International 815 Pk Ave *TF:* 800-756-4824 ■ *Web:* www.tbionline.org	Baltimore	MD	21201	410-752-2020	783-6183
University of California San Francisco Tissue Bank 3924 Williams Rd Suite 201 *TF:* 800-553-5536	San Jose	CA	95117	408-345-3515	345-3520
University of Louisville Lions Eye Bank 301 E Muhammad Ali Blvd *Web:* www.ulleb.org	Louisville	KY	40202	502-852-5457	852-5471
Upstate New York Transplant Services Inc 110 Broadway *TF:* 800-227-4771 ■ *Web:* www.unyts.org	Buffalo	NY	14203	716-853-6667	853-6674
Utah Lions Eye Bank *John A Moran Eye Ctr* 65 Mario Capecchi Dr *Web:* www.utaheyebank.org	Salt Lake City	UT	84132	801-581-2039	585-5703
Vision Share 108 Acorn Hill Ln *TF:* 888-657-4448 ■ *Web:* www.visionshare.org	Apex	NC	27502	919-303-2584	303-2586
Western Texas Lions Eye Bank Alliance 2030 Pullman St Suite 4 *TF:* 866-226-7632 ■ *Web:* www.wtleb.org	San Angelo	TX	76902	325-653-8666	655-2847

273 FABRIC STORES

SEE ALSO Patterns - Sewing p. 2391

	City	State	Zip	Phone	Fax
Britex Fabrics LLC 146 Geary St *Web:* www.britexfabrics.com	San Francisco	CA	94108	415-392-2910	392-3906
Everfast Inc 203 Gale Ln *TF Cust Svc:* 800-213-6366 ■ *Web:* www.calicocorners.com	Kennett Square	PA	19348	610-444-9700	444-1221
Fabric Place Inc 136 Howard St *TF:* 800-556-3700	Framingham	MA	01702	508-872-4888	872-4888
Fishman's Fabrics Inc 1101 S Des Plaines St *Web:* www.fishmansfabrics.com	Chicago	IL	60607	312-922-7250	922-7402
Jo-Ann Fabrics & Crafts 5555 Darrow Rd *TF:* 888-739-4120 ■ *Web:* www.joann.com	Hudson	OH	44236	330-656-2600	463-6760
Jo-Ann Stores Inc (JAS) 5555 Darrow Rd *NYSE: JAS* ■ *TF:* 888-739-4120 ■ *Web:* www.joann.com	Hudson	OH	44236	330-656-2600	463-6760
Mary Maxim Inc 2001 Holland Ave PO Box 5019 *TF:* 800-962-9504 ■ *Web:* www.marymaxim.com	Port Huron	MI	48061	810-987-2000	987-5056
Vogue Fabrics 718 Main St *Web:* www.voguefabricsstore.com	Evanston	IL	60202	847-864-9600	475-8958

274 FACILITIES MANAGEMENT SERVICES

SEE ALSO Correctional & Detention Management (Privatized) p. 1764

	City	State	Zip	Phone	Fax
Akima Corp 1001 E Benson Blvd Suite 100 *Web:* www.akima.com	Anchorage	AK	99508	907-277-2058	277-2058
Alexander Co Inc The 145 E Badger Rd Suite 200 *Web:* www.alexandercompany.com	Madison	WI	53713	608-258-5580	258-5599
American Pool Enterprises Inc 11515 Cronridge Dr # Q *Web:* www.americanpool.com	Owings Mills	MD	21117	443-471-1190	471-1189
ARAMARK Conference Centers 372 Ridgefield Rd **Fax Area Code: 914* ■ *TF:* 800-422-6338 ■ *Web:* www.aramarkconferencecenters.com	Wilton	CT	06897	203-210-5226	631-8362*
ARAMARK Uniform & Career Apparel LLC 1101 Market St *TF:* 800-999-8989 ■ *Web:* www.aramark-uniform.com	Philadelphia	PA	19107	215-238-3000	238-3333
Arctic Slope World Services 2 N Cascade Ave Suite 510	Colorado Springs	CO	80903	719-473-8903	473-8907
CA One Services 40 Fountain Plaza *TF:* 800-828-7240	Buffalo	NY	14202	716-858-5000	858-5882
Creative Dining Services 1 Royal Pk Dr Suite 3 *Web:* www.creativedining.com	Zeeland	MI	49464	616-748-1700	748-1900
Delaware North Cos Gaming & Entertainment 40 Fountain Plaza *TF:* 800-828-7240 ■ *Web:* www.delawarenorth.com	Buffalo	NY	14202	716-858-5000	858-5926
Delaware North Cos Parks & Resorts 40 Fountain Plaza *TF:* 800-828-7240	Buffalo	NY	14202	716-858-5000	858-5882
Diversco Integrated Services Inc 105 Diversco Dr *TF:* 800-277-3420 ■ *Web:* www.diversco.com	Spartanburg	SC	29307	864-579-3420	579-9578
Elite Show Services Inc 2878 Camino Del Rio S Suite 260 *Web:* www.eliteservicesusa.com	San Diego	CA	92108	619-574-1589	574-1588
FLIK International Corp Conference Center Management 3 International Dr 2nd Fl *Web:* www.comptass-usa.com	Rye Brook	NY	10573	914-935-5300	935-5551
Johnson Controls Inc 7400 Birchmount Rd *TF:* 800-482-2778 ■ *Web:* www.bljc.com	Markham	ON	L3R4E6	905-475-7610	415-3299
Johnson Controls Inc 5757 N Green Bay Ave *NYSE: JCI* ■ *TF:* 800-972-8040 ■ *Web:* www.johnsoncontrols.com	Milwaukee	WI	53209	414-524-1200	524-3232
Kansas Turnpike Authority (KTA) 9401 E Kellogg PO Box 780007 *Web:* www.ksturnpike.com	Wichita	KS	67207	316-682-4537	651-0864
Kmm Telecommunications Inc 9 Law Dr Suite 12 *Web:* www.kmmtel.com	Fairfield	NJ	07004	973-482-9533	955-9009
L & M Technologies Inc 4209 Balloon Pk Rd NE *Web:* www.lmtechnologies.com	Albuquerque	NM	87109	505-343-0200	343-0300
Mainthia Technologies Inc 7055 Engle Rd Suite 502 *Web:* www.mainthia.com	Cleveland	OH	44130	440-816-0202	816-1121
Marenzana Group Inc 295 Main St S PO Box 845 *Web:* www.marenzana.com	Woodbury	CT	06798	203-263-3888	263-3815
Navis Corp 1000 Broadway Suite 150 *Web:* www.navis.com	Oakland	CA	94607	510-267-5000	267-5100
New York State Bridge Authority PO Box 1010 *Web:* www.nysba.state.ny.us	Highland	NY	12528	845-691-7245	691-3560
Olympia Entertainment Inc 2211 Woodward Ave *Web:* www.olympiaentertainment.com	Detroit	MI	48201	313-471-3200	471-3595
OMNIPLEX World Services Corp 14151 Pk Meadow Dr # 300 *TF:* 800-356-3406 ■ *Web:* www.omniplex.com	Chantilly	VA	20151	703-652-3100	652-3106
Philotechnics Ltd 201 Renovare Blvd *TF:* 888-723-9278 ■ *Web:* www.philotechnics.com	Oak Ridge	TN	37830	865-483-1551	
Phoenix Park 'n Swap 3801 E Washington St *TF:* 800-772-0852 ■ *Web:* www.americanparknswap.com	Buffalo	NY	85034	602-273-1250	273-7375
Serco Group Inc 2650 Pk Tower Dr Suite 800 **Fax Area Code: 703* ■ *Web:* www.serco.com	Vienna	VA	22180	571-226-5000	573-8215*
SKE Support Services Inc 14900 Landmark Blvd Suite 400 *Web:* www.firstvehicleservices.com/Newsletter/FSS.htm	Dallas	TX	75254	972-991-0800	233-2469
Sodexho Conferencing 9801 Washington Blvd Suite 1014 **Fax Area Code: 301* ■ *TF Hum Res:* 800-763-3946 ■ *Web:* www.sodexousa.com	Gaithersburg	MD	20878	800-763-3946	987-4068*
Terranear PMC LLC 5005 W Royal Ln Suite 216 *Web:* www.terranear.com	Irving	TX	75063	972-929-1095	
UNICCO Service Co 275 Grove St Suite 3-200 *TF:* 800-283-9222 ■ *Web:* www.ugl-unicco.com	Auburndale	MA	02466	617-527-5222	969-2210
United Space Alliance 1150 Gemini Ave *TF:* 800-329-4036 ■ *Web:* www.unitedspacealliance.com	Houston	TX	77058	281-212-6200	212-6636
VMS Inc 203 E Cary St Suite 200 *TF:* 888-547-4404 ■ *Web:* www.vmsom.com	Richmond	VA	23219	804-261-8000	264-1808
Xanterra Parks & Resorts 6312 S Fiddlers Green Cir Suite 600-N *Web:* www.xanterra.com	Greenwood Village	CO	80111	303-600-3400	600-3600

275 FACTORS

Factors Are Companies That Buy Accounts Receivable (Invoices) From Other Businesses At A Discount.

	City	State	Zip	Phone	Fax
Accord Financial Corp 77 Bloor St W *TSE: ACD* ■ *TF:* 800-967-0015 ■ *Web:* www.accordfinancial.com	Toronto	ON	M5S1M2	416-961-0007	961-9443
Accord Financial Corp 3500 de Maisonneuve Blvd W Suite 1510 *TF:* 800-231-2977 ■ *Web:* www.accordfinancial.com	Montreal	QC	H3Z3C1	514-932-8223	932-0076
Account Funding Inc 16055 Ventura Blvd Suite 924 *TF:* 800-666-3928 ■ *Web:* www.accountfunding.com	Encino	CA	91436	818-995-7272	995-3631
Accounts Receivable Funding Corp 317 Peoples St Suite 600 **Fax Area Code: 877* ■ *TF:* 800-992-1717 ■ *Web:* www.arfc.com	Corpus Christi	TX	78401	361-884-7196	884-1292*
Action Capital Corp 230 Peachtree St Suite 910 *TF:* 800-525-7767 ■ *Web:* www.actioncapital.com	Atlanta	GA	30343	404-524-3181	577-4880
Advantage Funding Corp 1000 Parkwood Cir Suite 300 *TF:* 800-241-2274 ■ *Web:* www.advantagefunding.com	Atlanta	GA	30339	770-955-2274	955-0643
AmeriFactors 215 Celebration Pl Suite 340 *TF:* 800-884-3863 ■ *Web:* www.amerifactors.com	Celebration	FL	34747	407-566-1150	566-1250
Applied Capital Inc 3700 Rio Grande Blvd NW Suite 4 *Web:* www.appliedcapital.net	Albuquerque	NM	87107	505-342-1840	342-2246
Asta Funding Inc 210 Sylvan Ave *NASDAQ: ASFI* ■ *TF:* 866-389-7627 ■ *Web:* www.astafunding.com	Englewood Cliffs	NJ	07632	201-567-5648	569-6198
Bibby Financial Services 101 N Westlake Blvd Suite 204 *TF:* 866-446-2888 ■ *Web:* www.bibbyusa.com	Westlake Village	CA	91362	805-446-6111	370-0235
Capital-Plus Inc 7620 Olentangy River Rd *Web:* www.capplus.com	Columbus	OH	43235	614-848-7620	841-3856
Crestmark Bank 5480 Corporate Dr Suite 350 *TF:* 888-999-6088 ■ *Web:* www.crestmark.com	Troy	MI	48098	248-641-5100	641-5101
Diversified Funding Services Inc PO Box 873 *TF:* 888-603-0055 ■ *Web:* www.divfunding.com	Jonesboro	GA	30237	770-603-0055	603-9823
DSA Factors 3126 N Lincoln Ave PO Box 577520 *Web:* www.dsafactors.com	Chicago	IL	60657	773-248-9000	248-9005

Company	City	State	Zip	Phone	Fax
Goodman Factors 3010 LBJ Fwy Suite 140	Dallas	TX	75234	972-241-3297	243-6285
TF: 877-446-6362 ■ *Web:* www.goodmanfactors.com					
Hamilton Group 100 Elwood Davis Rd.	North Syracuse	NY	13212	315-413-0086	413-0087
TF: 800-351-3066 ■ *Web:* www.hamiltongroup.net					
Interface Financial Group					
2182 Dupont Dr Suite 221	Irvine	CA	92612	949-477-0665	475-8688*
**Fax Area Code:* 866 ■ *TF:* 800-387-0860 ■ *Web:* www.interfacefinancial.com					
JD Factors 500 Silver Spur Rd Suite 306	Redondo Beach	CA	90275	310-544-5141	544-5142
TF: 866-585-2274 ■ *Web:* www.jdfactors.com					
LSQ Funding Group LC					
1403 W Colonial Dr Suite B	Orlando	FL	32804	407-206-0022	206-0025
TF: 800-474-7606 ■ *Web:* www.lsqgroup.com					
Magnolia Financial Inc 187 W Broad St	Spartanburg	SC	29306	864-573-9900	573-9912
Web: www.magfinancial.com					
Mazon Assoc Inc 600 W Airport Fwy	Irving	TX	75062	972-554-6967	554-0951
TF: 800-442-2740 ■ *Web:* www.mazon.com					
Merchant Factors Corp 1430 Broadway 18th Fl	New York	NY	10018	212-840-7575	869-1752
TF: 800-929-3293 ■ *Web:* www.merchantfactors.com					
Performance Funding 4105 N 20th St Suite 205	Phoenix	AZ	85016	602-912-0200	912-0480
Web: www.performancefunding.com					
Porter Capital Corp 2112 1st Ave N	Birmingham	AL	35203	205-322-5442	322-7719
TF: 800-737-7344 ■ *Web:* www.portercap.net					
Prestige Capital Corp					
2 Executive Dr400 Kelby St	Fort Lee	NJ	07024	201-944-4455	944-9477
Web: www.pcc-cash.com					
Quantum Corporate Funding Ltd					
1140 Avenue of the Americas 16th Fl	New York	NY	10036	212-768-1200	944-8216
TF: 800-352-2535 ■ *Web:* www.quantumfunding.com					
Riviera Finance 220 Ave I	Redondo Beach	CA	90277	800-872-7484	454-8122*
**Fax Area Code:* 651 ■ *TF:* 800-421-1327 ■ *Web:* www.rivierafinance.com					
Rosenthal & Rosenthal Inc 1370 Broadway	New York	NY	10018	212-356-1400	356-0910
TF: 800-999-4800 ■ *Web:* www.rosenthalinc.com					
RTS Financial Service 8601 Monrovia	Lenexa	KS	66215	913-492-6351	492-1998
TF: 800-860-7926 ■ *Web:* www.rtsfinancial.com					
Seven Oaks Capital					
5745 Essen Ln Suite 102	Baton Rouge	LA	70810	225-757-1919	757-1916
TF: 800-511-4588 ■ *Web:* www.sevenoakscapital.com					
TCE Capital Corp 505 Consumers Rd Suite 707	Toronto	ON	M2J4V8	416-497-7400	497-3139
TF: 800-465-0400 ■ *Web:* www.tcecapital.com					
Transport Clearing East Inc					
210 Woodlawn Grn Bldg 6	Charlotte	NC	28217	704-527-1820	527-1851
Web: www.tceast.com					
United Capital Funding Corp					
146 2nd St N Suite 200	Saint Petersburg	FL	33701	727-894-8232	898-4205
Web: www.ucfunding.com					

276 FARM MACHINERY & EQUIPMENT - MFR

SEE ALSO Lawn & Garden Equipment p. 2148

Company	City	State	Zip	Phone	Fax
ADM Alliance Nutrition Inc 1000 N 30th St	Quincy	IL	62301	217-222-7100	222-4069
TF: 800-292-3333 ■ *Web:* www.admani.com					
AGCO Corp (AGCO) 4205 River Green Pkwy	Duluth	GA	30096	770-813-9200	813-6140
NYSE: AG ■ *TF:* 877-525-4384 ■ *Web:* www.agcocorp.com					
Agile Mfg Inc 720 Industrial Pk Rd	Anderson	MO	64831	417-845-6065	845-6069
TF: 800-704-7356 ■ *Web:* www.agilemfg.net					
Alamo Group Inc 1627 E Walnut	Seguin	TX	78155	830-379-1480	372-9683
NYSE: ALG ■ *TF Cust Svc:* 800-356-6286 ■ *Web:* www.alamo-group.com					
All-American Coop PO Box 125	Stewartville	MN	55976	507-533-4222	280-0066
TF: 888-354-4058 ■ *Web:* www.allamericancoop.com					
Alliance Product Group 601 S Broad St	Kalida	OH	45853	419-532-3312	532-2468
TF: 800-322-6301 ■ *Web:* www.topairequip.com					
Allied Systems Co 21433 SW Oregon St	Sherwood	OR	97140	503-625-2560	625-7269
TF: 800-285-7000 ■ *Web:* www.alliedsystems.com					
Amadas Industries Inc 1100 Holland Rd	Suffolk	VA	23434	757-539-0231	934-3264
Web: www.amadas.com					
Amarillo Wind Machine Co 20513 Ave 256	Exeter	CA	93221	559-592-4256	592-4194
TF: 800-311-4498 ■ *Web:* www.amarillowind.com					
Amerequip Corp 1015 Calumet Ave	Kiel	WI	53042	920-894-7063	894-3799
Web: www.amerequip.com					
Arts-Way Mfg Co Inc 5556 Hwy 9 PO Box 288	Armstrong	IA	50514	712-864-3131	864-3154
NASDAQ: ARTW ■ *Web:* www.artsway-mfg.com					
Automatic Equipment Mfg Co					
1 Mill Rd Industrial Pk	Pender	NE	68047	402-385-3051	385-3360
TF: 800-228-9289 ■ *Web:* www.aemfg.com					
B & H Mfg Inc 141 County Rd 34 E	Jackson	MN	56143	507-847-2802	847-4655
TF: 800-240-3288 ■ *Web:* www.bhmfg.com					
Berg Equipment Co 2700 W Veterans Pkwy	Marshfield	WI	54449	715-384-2151	387-6777
TF: 800-494-1738 ■ *Web:* www.bergequipment.com					
Big Dutchman Inc 3900 John F Donnelly Dr	Holland	MI	49424	616-392-5981	392-6188
Web: www.bigdutchmanusa.com					
Bou-Matic 1919 Stoughton Rd	Madison	WI	53716	608-222-3484	222-9314
Web: www.bou-matic.com					
Bowie Industries Inc 1004 E Wise St	Bowie	TX	76230	940-872-1106	872-4792
TF: 800-433-0934 ■ *Web:* www.bowieindustries.com					
Brillion Iron Works Inc					
200 Pk Ave PO Box 127	Brillion	WI	54110	920-756-2121	756-3550
TF: 800-409-9749 ■ *Web:* www.brillionfarmeq.com					
Brock Grain Conditioning Group					
1750 W SR-28	Frankfort	IN	46041	765-654-8517	654-8510
TF: 800-541-7900 ■ *Web:* www.graindryers.com					
Brown Manufacturfing Corp 6001 E Hwy 27	Ozark	AL	36360	334-795-6603	795-3029
TF: 800-633-8909 ■ *Web:* www.brownmfgcorp.com					
Broyhill Co 1 N Market Sq	Dakota City	NE	68731	402-987-3412	987-3601
TF: 800-228-1003 ■ *Web:* www.broyhill.com					
Bucklin Tractor & Implement Co					
115 W Railroad PO Box 127	Bucklin	KS	67834	620-826-3271	826-3760
TF: 800-334-4823 ■ *Web:* www.btiequip.com					
Buhler Versatile Inc 1260 Clarence Ave	Winnipeg	MB	R3T1T2	204-661-8711	654-2503
TF: 888-524-1003 ■ *Web:* www.buhlerindustries.com					
Bush Hog LLC 2501 Griffin Ave	Selma	AL	36703	334-872-6261	874-2701
TF: 800-363-6096 ■ *Web:* www.bushhog.com					
Bushnell Illinois Tank Co 650 W Davis St	Bushnell	IL	61422	309-772-3106	772-2045
Web: www.schuldbushnell.com					
Cal-Coast Dairy Systems Inc 424 S Tegner Rd	Turlock	CA	95380	209-634-9026	634-3458
TF Cust Svc: 800-732-6826 ■ *Web:* www.calcoastinc.com					
Carter Day International Inc					
500 73rd Ave NE	Minneapolis	MN	55432	763-571-1000	571-3012
Web: www.carterday.com					
Case IH 621 State St	Racine	WI	53404	262-636-6011	
TF: 877-422-7344 ■ *Web:* www.caseih.com					
Chick Master Incubator Co					
945 Lafayette Rd PO Box 704	Medina	OH	44258	330-722-5591	723-0233
TF: 800-727-8726 ■ *Web:* www.chickmaster.com					
Conrad-American Inc PO Box 2000	Houghton	IA	52631	319-469-4111	469-4111
TF: 800-553-1791 ■ *Web:* www.conradamer.com					
Continental Eagle Corp					
201 Gin Shop Hill Rd	Prattville	AL	36067	334-365-8811	365-8811
TF: 866-266-3245 ■ *Web:* www.coneagle.com					
Covington Planter Co 410 Hodges Ave	Albany	GA	31701	229-888-2032	888-0448
Web: www.covingtonplanter.com					
CTB Inc 611 N Higbee St PO Box 2000	Milford	IN	46542	574-658-4191	658-3471
Web: www.ctbinc.com					
Custom Products of Litchfield Inc					
1715 S Sibley Ave	Litchfield	MN	55355	320-693-3221	693-7252
TF: 800-222-5463 ■ *Web:* www.800cabline.com					
Daco Inc 609 Airport Rd	North Aurora	IL	60542	630-897-8797	897-4076
Web: www.dacoinc.com					
Danuser Machine Co 500 E 3rd St	Fulton	MO	65251	573-642-2246	642-2240
Web: www.danuser.com					
David Mfg Co 1004 E Illinois St	Assumption	IL	62510	217-226-4421	226-4445
TF: 877-362-8033 ■ *Web:* www.dmc-davidmanufacturing.com					
Deereá&áCo 1 John Deere Pl	Moline	IL	61265	309-765-8000	765-8000
TF: 866-993-3373 ■ *Web:* www.deere.com					
Diamond Automations Inc					
23400 Haggerty Rd	Farmington Hills	MI	48335	248-476-7100	476-0849
Web: www.diamondsystem.com					
Dig Corp 1210 Activity Dr	Vista	CA	92081	760-727-0914	
TF: 800-322-9146 ■ *Web:* www.digcorp.com					
DuraTech Industries International Inc					
PO Box 1940	Jamestown	ND	58401	701-252-4601	252-0502
TF: 800-243-4601 ■ *Web:* www.duratechindustries.net					
Empire Plow Co Inc 3140 E 65th St	Cleveland	OH	44127	216-641-2290	441-4709
Web: www.mckayempire.com					
EVH Mfg LLC 4895 Red Bluff Rd	Loris	SC	29569	843-756-4051	756-4436
TF: 888-990-2555 ■ *Web:* www.evhmfg.com					
EZ Trail Inc Hwy 133 E PO Box 168	Arthur	IL	61911	217-543-3471	543-3473
TF Cust Svc: 800-677-2802 ■ *Web:* www.e-ztrail.com					
Finn Corp 9281 Le St Dr	Fairfield	OH	45014	513-874-2818	874-2914
TF: 800-543-7166 ■ *Web:* www.finncorp.com					
Flint Cliffs Mfg Co 1600 Bluff Rd	Burlington	IA	52601	319-752-2781	752-5538
Web: www.flintcliffsmanufacturing.com					
Forsbergs Inc					
1210 Pennington Ave PO Box 510	Thief River Falls	MN	56701	218-681-1927	681-2037
TF Cust Svc: 800-654-1927 ■ *Web:* www.forsbergs.com					
Gandy Co 528 Gandrud Rd	Owatonna	MN	55060	507-451-5430	451-2857
TF: 800-443-2476 ■ *Web:* www.gandy.net					
Gehl Co 1 Gehl Way	West Bend	WI	53095	262-334-9461	338-7517
Web: www.gehl.com					
GMP Metal Products Inc 3883 Delor St	Saint Louis	MO	63116	314-481-0300	481-1379
TF: 800-325-9808 ■ *Web:* www.gmpmetal.com					
GSI Group Inc 1004 E Illinois St PO Box 20	Assumption	IL	62510	217-226-5400	226-4445
Web: www.grainsystems.com					
Hagie Mfg Co 721 Central Ave W	Clarion	IA	50525	515-532-2861	532-3553
TF: 800-247-4885 ■ *Web:* www.hagie.com					
Hanson Silo Co 11587 County Rd 8 SE	Lake Lillian	MN	56253	320-664-4171	664-4140
TF: 800-450-4171 ■ *Web:* www.hansonsilo.com					
Hardi Inc 1500 W 76th St	Davenport	IA	52806	563-386-1730	386-1710
TF: 866-770-7063 ■ *Web:* www.hardi-us.com					
Hastings Equity Grain Bin Mfg Co					
1900 Summit Ave	Hastings	NE	68901	402-462-2189	462-2900
Web: www.hastingstanks.com					
HCC Inc 1501 1st Ave	Mendota	IL	61342	815-539-9371	539-3135
Web: www.hccincorporated.com					
HD Hudson Mfg Co					
500 N Michigan Ave Suite 2300	Chicago	IL	60611	312-644-2830	644-7989
TF: 800-523-9284 ■ *Web:* www.hdhudson.com					
Heartland Equipment Inc 2100 N Falls Blvd	Wynne	AR	72396	870-238-1234	238-8545
Web: www.tractorscraper.com					
Heik Holding Co Inc 2608 S Hume Ave	Marshfield	WI	54449	715-387-3414	384-5463
Web: www.hsmfgco.com					
Henderson Mfg Inc 1085 S 3rd St	Manchester	IA	52057	563-927-2828	927-2521
TF: 800-359-4970 ■ *Web:* www.henderson-mfg.com					
Herschel-Adams Inc 1301 N 14th St	Indianola	IA	50125	515-961-7481	524-7481*
**Fax Area Code:* 800 ■ *TF Cust Svc:* 800-247-2167 ■ *Web:* www.herschel-adams.com					
Hiniker Co 58766 240th St	Mankato	MN	56002	507-625-6621	625-5883*
**Fax:* Sales ■ *TF:* 800-433-5620 ■ *Web:* www.hiniker.com					
Honiron Corp 400 Canal St	Jeanerette	LA	70544	337-276-6314	276-3614
Web: www.honiron.com					
Howse Implement Co Inc					
2013 Hwy 184 E PO Box 86	Laurel	MS	39441	601-428-0841	425-4900
Web: www.howseimplement.com					
Hutchinson/Mayrath/TerraTrack Industries					
514 W Crawford St	Clay Center	KS	67432	785-632-3133	632-5964
TF: 800-523-6993					
Irridelco International Corp					
440 Sylvan Ave	Englewood Cliffs	NJ	07632	201-569-3030	569-9237
Web: www.irridelco.com					
J & M Mfg Co Inc					
284 Railroad St PO Box 547	Fort Recovery	OH	45846	419-375-2376	375-2708
Web: www.jm-inc.com					

Company	City	State	ZIP	Phone	Fax
Johnson Farm Machinery Co Inc 152 W Kentucky Ave *Web:* www.jfmco.com	Woodland	CA	95695	530-662-1788	666-5585
K & M Mfg Co 308 NW 2nd St PO Box 209 *Fax Area Code: 320 ■ TF: 800-328-1752 ■ Web:* www.kandmmanufacturing.com	Renville	MN	56284	800-328-1752	329-3709*
Kbh Corp The 395 Anderson Blvd *TF:* 800-843-5241 ■ *Web:* www.kbhequipment.com	Clarksdale	MS	38614	662-624-5471	
Kelley Mfg Co 80 Vernon Dr PO Box 1467 *TF:* 800-444-5449 ■ *Web:* www.kelleymfg.com	Tifton	GA	31793	229-382-9393	382-5259
Kelly Ryan Equipment Co 900 Kelly Ryan Dr *TF:* 800-640-6967 ■ *Web:* www.kryan.com	Blair	NE	68008	402-426-2151	426-2186
Kinze Mfg Inc 2172 M Ave	Williamsburg	IA	52361	319-668-1300	668-3069
Kirby Mfg Inc 484 S State Hwy 59 *Web:* www.kirbymfg.com	Merced	CA	95341	209-723-0778	723-3941
KMW Ltd PO Box 327 *TF:* 800-445-7388 ■ *Web:* www.kmwloaders.com	Sterling	KS	67579	620-278-3641	278-2388
Kubota Tractor Corp 3401 Del Amo Blvd *TF:* 800-582-6821 ■ *Web:* www.kubota.com	Torrance	CA	90503	310-370-3370	370-2370
Kuhn Knight Inc 1501 W 7th Ave PO BOX 0167 *Web:* www.kuhnknight.com	Brodhead	WI	53520	608-897-2131	897-2561
Kuhn Krause Inc 305 S Monroe *TF:* 800-957-2873 ■ *Web:* www.krauseco.com	Hutchinson	KS	67501	620-663-6161	662-5903
Lely USA Inc PO Box 437 *TF:* 888-245-4684 ■ *Web:* www.old.lely.com/en	Pella	IA	50219	641-621-7896	621-7881
Lewis/Mola Mfg LLC 183 Elle Dr *Web:* www.lewismola.com	Bennettsville	SC	29512	843-479-6231	479-7739
Lindsay Corp 2222 N 111th St *NYSE: LNN ■ TF:* 866-404-5049 ■ *Web:* www.lindsay.com	Omaha	NE	68164	402-829-6800	428-7289
Loftness Specialized Farm Equipment Inc 650 S Main St PO Box 337 *TF:* 800-828-7624 ■ *Web:* www.loftness.com	Hector	MN	55342	320-848-6266	848-6269
Lummus Carver Gump Corp 1 Lummus Dr *TF:* 800-458-6687 ■ *Web:* www.carver-inc.com	Savannah	GA	31407	912-748-5000	447-9250
Lund Precision Products 400 E Industrial Pk Rd *Web:* www.lundonline.com	Holly Springs	MS	38635	662-252-2340	252-3352
Mathews Co 500 Industrial Ave *TF:* 800-323-7045 ■ *Web:* www.mathewscompany.com	Crystal Lake	IL	60012	815-459-2210	459-5889
Mertz Mfg LLC 1701 N Waverly St *TF:* 800-654-6433 ■ *Web:* www.mertzok.com	Ponca City	OK	74601	580-762-5646	767-8411
Miller Saint Nazianz Inc 511 E Main St *TF:* 800-247-5557 ■ *Web:* www.millerstn.com	Saint Nazianz	WI	54232	920-773-2121	773-1200
Modern Group Ltd 1655 Louisiana St *TF Cust Svc:* 800-231-8198 ■ *Web:* www.modernusa.com	Beaumont	TX	77701	409-833-2665	833-1766
Montgomery Industries International Inc 2017 Thelma St *Web:* www.montgomeryindustries.com	Jacksonville	FL	32206	904-355-4055	355-0401
Moorfeed Corp 1336 W Wiley Ave *TF:* 888-545-7171 ■ *Web:* www.moorfeed.com	Bluffton	IN	46714	260-353-1042	824-0129
Moridge Mfg Inc 105 Old US Hwy 81 S *Web:* www.grasshoppermower.com	Moundridge	KS	67107	620-345-6301	345-2301
Orchard Machinery Corp 2700 Colusa Hwy *Web:* www.shakermaker.com	Yuba City	CA	95993	530-673-2822	673-0296
Orchard-Rite Ltd Inc PO Box 9308 *TF:* 800-676-4460 ■ *Web:* www.orchard-rite.com	Yakima	WA	98909	509-457-9196	457-9186
Orthman Mfg Inc 75765 Rd 435 PO Box 638 *TF:* 800-658-3270 ■ *Web:* www.orthman.com	Lexington	NE	68850	308-324-4654	324-5001
Osborne Industries Inc 120 N Industrial Ave *TF:* 800-255-0316 ■ *Web:* www.osborneindustries.com	Osborne	KS	67473	785-346-2192	346-2194
Oxbo International Corp 7275 Batavia Byron Rd *Web:* www.oxbocorp.com	Byron	NY	14422	585-548-2665	548-2599
P & H Mfg Co 604 S Lodge St *TF Sales:* 800-879-2123	Shelbyville	IL	62565	217-774-2123	774-5341
Peerless Mfg Co US Hwy 82 E *TF:* 800-225-4617 ■ *Web:* www.peerlessmfg.cc	Shellman	GA	39886	229-679-5353	679-5542
Performance Feeders Inc 251 Dunbar *Web:* www.performancefeeders.com	Oldsmar	FL	34677	813-855-2685	855-4296
Precision Tank & Equipment Co Inc 3503 Conover Rd *TF:* 800-258-4197 ■ *Web:* www.precisiontank.com	Virginia	IL	62691	217-452-7228	452-3956
Rainbow Mfg Co 101 Rainbow Dr *TF Cust Svc:* 800-841-0323 ■ *Web:* www.rainbowirrigation.com	Fitzgerald	GA	31750	229-423-4341	423-4645
Rayne Land Planes Inc 9107 Grand Prairie Hwy **Fax Area Code: 713 ■ Web:* www.rayneplane.com	Church Point	LA	70525	337-334-2101	634-2813*
Reinke Mfg Co Inc 5325 Reinke Rd *Web:* www.reinke.com	Deshler	NE	68340	402-365-7251	365-4370
Root-Lowell Mfg Co 1000 Foreman Rd PO Box 289 *TF:* 800-748-0098 ■ *Web:* www.rlflomaster.com	Lowell	MI	49331	616-897-9211	897-8223
Schuette Mfg & Steel Sales Inc 5028 Hwy 42 *Web:* www.knowlesmfgco.com	Manitowoc	WI	54220	920-758-2491	758-2599
Scranton Mfg Co Inc 101 State St PO Box 336 *TF:* 800-831-1858 ■ *Web:* www.scrantonmfg.com	Scranton	IA	51462	712-652-3396	652-3399
Shivvers Inc 614 W English St *TF:* 800-245-9093 ■ *Web:* www.shivvers.com	Corydon	IA	50060	641-872-1005	872-1593
Simonsen Industries Inc 500 Hwy 31 E *TF:* 800-831-4860 ■ *Web:* www.simonsen-industries.com	Quimby	IA	51049	712-445-2211	445-2626
Sioux Steel Co 196 1/2 E 6th St *TF:* 800-557-4689 ■ *Web:* www.siouxsteel.com	Sioux Falls	SD	57104	605-336-1750	965-4252
Spudnik Equipment Co 584 W 100 N Rd *Web:* www.spudnik.us	Blackfoot	ID	83221	208-785-0480	785-1497
Star Forge Inc 1801 S Ihm Blvd *Web:* www.starmfg.com	Freeport	IL	61032	815-235-7750	235-4813
Stock Equipment Co 16490 Chillicothe Rd *TF:* 800-268-3347 ■ *Web:* www.stockequipment.com	Chagrin Falls	OH	44023	440-543-6000	543-5944
Sudenga Industries Inc 2002 Kingbird Ave *TF:* 888-783-3642 ■ *Web:* www.sudenga.com	George	IA	51237	712-475-3301	475-3320
Sukup Mfg Co 1555 255th St PO Box 677 *Web:* www.sukup.com	Sheffield	IA	50475	641-892-4222	892-4629
T-I Irrigation Co 151 E Hwy 6 AB Rd PO Box 1047 **Fax Area Code: 800 ■ TF:* 800-330-4264 ■ *Web:* www.tlirr.com	Hastings	NE	68902	402-462-4128	330-4268*
Taylor Pittsburgh Mfg 7 Rocky Mt Rd *Web:* www.taylorpittsburgh.com	Athens	TN	37303	423-745-3110	744-9662
Toro Co Irrigation Div 5825 Jasmine St *TF:* 800-664-4740 ■ *Web:* www.toro.com	Riverside	CA	92502	800-654-1882	451-1390
Unverferth Mfg Co Inc 18107 US 224 W *TF:* 800-322-6301 ■ *Web:* www.unverferth.com	Kalida	OH	45853	419-532-3121	532-2468
Valmont Industries Inc 1 Valmont Plaza *NYSE: VMI ■ TF:* 800-825-6668 ■ *Web:* www.valmont.com	Omaha	NE	68154	402-963-1000	963-1100
Vermeer Corp 1210 Vermeer Rd E PO Box 200 *Web:* www2.vermeer.com	Pella	IA	50219	641-628-3141	621-7773
Wiese Industries Inc 1501 5th St PO Box 39 *TF:* 800-568-4391 ■ *Web:* www.wiesecorp.com	Perry	IA	50220	515-465-9854	465-9858
Woods Equipment Co 1000 W Cherokee St	Sioux Falls	SD	57104	605-336-3860	336-6750
Woods Equipment Co 2606 S Illinois Rt 2 PO Box 1000 **Fax: Sales ■ TF:* 800-319-6637 ■ *Web:* www.woodsonline.com	Oregon	IL	61061	815-732-2141	732-7580*
Wylie & Son Mfg Co 101 N Main St *TF Sales:* 800-722-4001 ■ *Web:* www.wyliesprayers.com	Petersburg	TX	79250	806-667-3566	667-3392
Yargus Mfg Inc PO Box 238 *Web:* www.yargus.com	Marshall	IL	62441	217-826-6352	
Yetter Mfg Inc 109 S McDonough St PO Box 358 *TF:* 800-447-5777 ■ *Web:* www.yetterco.com	Colchester	IL	62326	309-776-4111	776-3222

277 FARM MACHINERY & EQUIPMENT - WHOL

Company	City	State	ZIP	Phone	Fax
24 Century Equipment LLC PO Drawer L *TF:* 800-783-2621	Leoti	KS	67861	620-375-2621	375-4562
Abilene Machine Inc PO Box 129 *TF:* 800-255-0337 ■ *Web:* www.abilenemachine.com	Abilene	KS	67410	785-655-9455	655-3838
Ag-Land Implement Inc Hwy 63 N PO Box 31 *Web:* www.aglandimplement.com	New Hampton	IA	50659	641-394-4226	394-3936
Agri-Service 3204 Kimberly Rd E *TF:* 800-388-3599 ■ *Web:* www.agri-service.com	Twin Falls	ID	83301	208-734-7772	734-7775
Arends & Sons Inc 715 S Sangamon Ave *TF:* 800-637-6052 ■ *Web:* www.arends-sons.com	Gibson City	IL	60936	217-784-4241	784-8749
Arends Bros Inc Rt 54 N *Web:* www.arendsbros.com	Melvin	IL	60952	217-388-7717	388-2882
Baker Implement Co 421 E Main St *Web:* www.bakerimplement.com	Portageville	MO	63873	573-379-5455	379-5313
Barnett Implement Co Inc 4220 Old Hwy 99 S *TF:* 800-453-9274 ■ *Web:* www.barnettimplement.com	Mount Vernon	WA	98273	360-424-7995	424-0403
BE Implement Co 1645 FM 403 *TF:* 800-725-5435 ■ *Web:* www.beimplement.com	Brownfield	TX	79316	806-637-3594	637-8992
Belarus Tractor International Inc 7842 N Faulkner Rd **Fax: Sales ■ TF:* 800-356-2336 ■ *Web:* www.belarus.com	Milwaukee	WI	53224	414-355-2000	355-6903*
Bell Equipment Inc 118 W S St *TF:* 800-753-3373 ■ *Web:* www.jddealer.deere.com	Grangeville	ID	83530	208-983-1730	983-1903
Berchtold Equipment Co Inc 330 E 19th St *Web:* www.berchtold.com	Bakersfield	CA	93305	661-323-7817	325-4059
Blanchard Compact Equipment 1410 Ashville Hwy *TF:* 800-397-9075 ■ *Web:* www.blanchardmachinery.com	Spartanburg	SC	29303	864-582-1245	582-7121
Boston Tractor Co Inc PO Box 8	Dixie	GA	31629	229-263-4133	263-9178
Browning Equipment Inc 800 E Main St *Web:* www.browningequipment.com	Purcellville	VA	20132	540-338-7123	338-5835
Burks Tractor Co Inc 3140 Kimberly Rd *TF:* 800-247-7419 ■ *Web:* www.burkstractor.com	Twin Falls	ID	83301	208-733-5543	734-9852
Carco International Inc 2721 Midland Blvd *TF:* 800-824-3215	Fort Smith	AR	72904	479-441-3270	441-3273
Carrico Implement Co Inc 3160 US 24 Hwy *TF:* 877-542-4099 ■ *Web:* www.carricoimplement.com	Beloit	KS	67420	785-738-5744	738-2648
Coleman Equipment Inc 24000 W 43rd St *Web:* www.colemanequip.com	Bonner Springs	KS	66012	913-422-3040	422-3044
Deer Trail Implement Inc 1411 S Hwy 81 Bypass PO Box 1326 *TF:* 800-364-4020 ■ *Web:* www.deertrailinc.com	McPherson	KS	67460	620-241-3553	241-3572
Delta Implement Co Inc 3180 Hwy 82 E	Greenville	MS	38704	662-332-2683	332-2911
Delta Ridge Implement Inc 1150 US Hwy 425 *Web:* www.jddealer.deere.com/deltaridge	Rayville	LA	71269	318-728-6423	728-6426
EJ Smith Group PO Box 7247	Charlotte	NC	28241	704-583-0422	583-0429
Ernie Williams Ltd 2613 Hwy 18 E *Web:* www.erniewilliamsltd.com	Algona	IA	50511	515-295-3561	295-3419
Farm Equipment Co Inc 406 Hwy 165 N	Portland	AR	71663	870-737-2211	737-4298
Farm Implement & Supply Co Inc 1200 S Washington Hwy 183 *TF:* 888-589-6029 ■ *Web:* www.farmimp.com	Plainville	KS	67663	785-434-4824	434-7390
Farmer Boy Ag Systems Inc PO Box 435 *TF:* 800-845-3374 ■ *Web:* www.farmerboyag.com	Myerstown	PA	17067	717-866-7565	866-6233
Farmers Supply Sales Inc 1409 E Ave *TF:* 877-656-2291	Kalona	IA	52247	319-656-2291	656-3873
Ferriday Farm Equipment Co Inc 503 Lake Dr Hwy 568 *TF:* 800-256-4576	Ferriday	LA	71334	318-757-4576	757-4576
Finning International Inc 666 Burrard St Suite 1000 Pk Pl *TSX: FTT ■ TF:* 888-346-6464 ■ *Web:* www.finning.ca	Vancouver	AB	V6C2X8	604-691-6444	691-6440
Forks Equipment 5101 Gateway Dr *TF:* 888-456-0240 ■ *Web:* www.forksequipment.com	Grand Forks	ND	58203	701-746-4436	780-9550
French Implement Co Inc 497 S Hwy 105 *TF:* 800-325-8622 ■ *Web:* www.conmacmissouri.com	Charleston	MO	63834	573-649-3021	649-5389
Fruit Growers Supply Co Inc 14130 Riverside Dr *Web:* www.fruitgrowers.com	Sherman Oaks	CA	91423	818-986-6480	783-1941
Gardner Inc 3641 Interchange Rd *TF:* 800-848-8946 ■ *Web:* www.gardnerinc.com	Columbus	OH	43204	614-456-4000	456-4001

Company	City	State	Zip	Phone	Fax
Garton Tractor Inc 2400 N Golden State Blvd *TF:* 800-286-0490 ■ *Web:* www.garton-tractor.com	Turlock	CA	95380	209-632-3931	632-8006
Gebo Distributing Co Inc 3109 Olton Blvd PO Box 850	Plainview	TX	79073	806-293-4212	293-3992
Giles & Ransome Inc Ransome Engine Power Div 2975 Galloway Rd *TF:* 800-753-4228 ■ *Web:* www.ransome.com	Bensalem	PA	19020	215-639-4300	245-2831
Glade & Grove Supply Inc 1006 State Rd 80 PO Box 760 *Web:* www.gladeandgrove.com	Belle Glade	FL	33430	561-996-3095	996-2048
Golden Spike Equipment Co 1352 W Main St PO Box 70 *TF:* 800-821-4474 ■ *Web:* www.gspike.com	Tremonton	UT	84337	435-257-5346	257-5719
Greenline Equipment 6068 S Redwood Rd *TF:* 888-201-5500 ■ *Web:* www.greenlineequipment.com	Salt Lake City	UT	84123	801-966-4231	966-4313
Grossenburg Implement Inc 31341 US Hwy 18 *TF:* 800-658-3440 ■ *Web:* www.grossenburg.com	Winner	SD	57580	605-842-2040	842-3485
Hamilton Equipment Inc 567 S Reading Rd PO Box 478 *Web:* www.haminc.com	Ephrata	PA	17522	717-733-7951	733-1783
Harcourt Equipment 313 Hwy 169 & 175 E *TF:* 800-445-5646	Harcourt	IA	50544	515-354-5331	354-5328
Harry J Whelchel Co PO Box 5022	Chattanooga	TN	37406	423-698-4415	629-7395
HB Duvall Inc 901 E Patrick St PO Box 70 *TF:* 800-423-4032 ■ *Web:* www.hbduvall.com	Frederick	MD	21701	301-662-1125	695-0265
HC Clark Implement Co 4411 E Hwy 12 *TF:* 800-532-6747	Aberdeen	SD	57401	605-225-8170	225-4671
Heartland Farm & Lawn 1880 Missouri 13 *TF:* 877-532-6766 ■ *Web:* www.heartlandfarmandlawn.com	Higginsville	MO	64037	660-584-7434	584-7412
Heath's Inc 600 W Bridge St *TF:* 800-443-2847 ■ *Web:* www.heaths.com	Monticello	IL	61856	217-762-2534	762-8032
Hector Turf & Garden Inc 1301 NW 3rd St *TF:* 800-432-5512 ■ *Web:* www.hectorturf.com	Deerfield Beach	FL	33442	954-429-3200	360-7657
HH Halferty & Sons Inc PO Box 298	Smithville	MO	64089	816-532-0221	532-0242
Hillsboro Equipment Inc E18898 State Hwy 33 E PO Box 583 *TF:* 800-521-5133 ■ *Web:* www.hillsboroequipment.com	Hillsboro	WI	54634	608-489-2275	489-2717
Hollingsworth Inc 1775 SW 30th St *TF:* 800-541-1612 ■ *Web:* www.jddealer.deere.com	Ontario	OR	97914	541-889-7254	889-8364
HOLT Texas Ltd 3302 S WW White Rd *TF:* 800-275-4658 ■ *Web:* www.holtcat.com	San Antonio	TX	78222	210-648-1111	648-0079
Hoober Inc 3452 Old Philadelphia Pike PO Box 518 *TF:* 800-732-0017 ■ *Web:* www.hoober.com	Intercourse	PA	17534	717-768-8231	768-3005
Horizon Equipment 402 6th St *TF:* 800-458-4431	Manning	IA	51455	712-653-2574	
Hoxie Implement Co Inc 933 Oak Ave Hwy 23&24 *Web:* www.hoxieimplement.com	Hoxie	KS	67740	785-675-3201	675-3438
Hultgren Implements Inc 5698 State Hwy 175 *TF:* 800-827-1650	Ida Grove	IA	51445	712-364-3105	364-2197
Hurst Farm Supply Inc 105 Ave D *TF:* 800-535-8903 ■ *Web:* www.hurstfs.com	Abernathy	TX	79311	806-298-2541	298-2936
Implement Sales Co LLC 1574 Stone Ridge Dr *TF:* 800-955-9592 ■ *Web:* www.implementsalesga.com	Stone Mountain	GA	30083	770-908-9439	908-8123
Iowa Export-Import Trading Co 512 Tuttle St *TF:* 800-831-4145 ■ *Web:* www.iaexim.com	Des Moines	IA	50309	515-245-2464	283-3901
Jacobi Sales Inc 425 Main St NE *TF:* 800-489-3617 ■ *Web:* www.jacobisales.com	Palmyra	IN	47164	812-364-6141	364-6157
James River Equipment 11047 Leadbetter Rd *TF:* 800-969-6001 ■ *Web:* www.jrenet.com	Ashland	VA	23005	804-798-6001	752-7111
JD Equipment Inc 1660 US 42 NE *TF:* 800-659-5646 ■ *Web:* www.jdequipment.com	London	OH	43140	614-879-6620	879-5767
Jerry Pate Turf & Irrigation Inc 301 Schubert Dr *Web:* www.jerrypate.com	Pensacola	FL	32504	850-479-4653	484-8596
JJ Nichting Co Inc 1342 Pilot Grove Rd	Pilot Grove	IA	52648	319-469-4461	469-4703
John Day Co 6263 Abbott Dr *TF:* 800-767-2273 ■ *Web:* www.johnday.com	Omaha	NE	68110	402-455-8000	457-3812
JS Woodhouse Co Inc 1314 Union St *Web:* www.jswoodhouse.com	West Springfield	MA	01090	413-736-5462	732-3786
Kelly Sauder Rupiper Equipment LLC (KSR) 805 E Howard St PO Box 77 *Web:* www.ksrequipment.com	Pontiac	IL	61764	815-842-1149	842-1085
Landell-Thelen Inc 323 E Hwy 30 *TF:* 800-694-5674 ■ *Web:* www.landellthelen.com	Shelton	NE	68876	308-647-6811	647-9100
Lansdowne-Moody Co LP 8445 E Fwy *Web:* www.lansdowne-moody.com	Houston	TX	77029	713-672-8366	672-8173
Larchmont Engineering & Irrigation Co 11 Larchmont Ln *TF:* 877-862-2550 ■ *Web:* www.larchmont-eng.com	Lexington	MA	02420	781-862-2550	862-0173
Lawrence Tractor Co Inc 2530 E Main St *Web:* www.lawrencetractor.com	Visalia	CA	93292	559-734-7406	734-8325
Lefeld Implement Inc 5228 SR-118 *TF:* 888-678-2375 ■ *Web:* www.lefeldimp.com	Coldwater	OH	45828	419-678-2375	678-8705
Liechty Farm Equipment Inc 1701 S Defiance St *TF:* 800-272-5898 ■ *Web:* www.liechtyfarmequipment.com	Archbold	OH	43502	419-445-1565	445-1779
Linder Equipment Co 311 E Kern St *Web:* www.linderequipment.com	Tulare	CA	93274	559-685-5000	685-0452
Littau Harvester Inc 855 Rogue Ave *TF:* 866-262-2495 ■ *Web:* www.littauharvester.com	Stayton	OR	97383	503-769-5953	
Maine Potato Growers Inc 56 Parsons St *Web:* www.mpgco-op.com	Presque Isle	ME	04769	207-764-2471	764-8460
McCranie Implement Co US Hwy 341 Bypass *TF:* 800-245-9046	Hawkinsville	GA	31036	478-892-9046	783-0778
MDMA Equipment N6387 US Hwy 25	Durand	WI	54736	715-672-8444	
Mid-State Equipment Inc W 1115 Bristol Rd *TF:* 877-677-4020 ■ *Web:* www.midstateequipment.com	Columbus	WI	53925	920-623-4020	623-4500
Miller Machinery & Supply Co 127 NE 27th St *TF:* 800-273-3030	Miami	FL	33137	305-573-1300	576-9535
Monroe Tractor & Implement Co Inc 1001 Lehigh Stn Rd *Web:* www.monroetractor.com	Henrietta	NY	14467	585-334-3867	334-0001
NV Equipment 704 E 8th Ave *TF:* 800-848-5482	Yuma	CO	80759	970-848-5482	848-5143
Odessa Trading Co 9 W 1st Ave PO Box 277 *TF:* 800-726-2661 ■ *Web:* www.odessatrading.com	Odessa	WA	99159	509-982-2661	982-2540
Olsen Implement Inc 2025 US Hwy 14 W *TF:* 800-627-5469 ■ *Web:* www.olsenimplement.com	Huron	SD	57350	605-352-7100	352-7071
Peterson Tractor Co 955 Marina Blvd *TF:* 888-738-3776 ■ *Web:* www.petersontractor.com	San Leandro	CA	94577	510-357-6200	352-5952
Phillips Tractor 27225 Hwy 47	Gaston	OR	97119	503-662-3929	
Pioneer Equipment Co 2545 S Sarah St *Web:* www.pioneercvc.com	Fresno	CA	93706	559-486-7580	486-7587
Polk County Farmers Co-op 9055 Rickreall Rd *TF:* 800-842-2224 ■ *Web:* www.agwestsupply.com	Rickreall	OR	97371	503-363-2332	363-5662
Price Bros Equipment Co 619 S Washington St *Web:* www.pricebroseq.com	Wichita	KS	67211	316-265-9577	265-1062
R & W Supply Inc 2210 Hall Ave *TF:* 800-477-1191 ■ *Web:* www.rwsupply.com	Littlefield	TX	79339	806-385-4447	385-4449
RDO Equipment Co 700 7th St S *Web:* www.rdoequipment.com	Fargo	ND	58103	701-239-8730	271-6328
Revels Tractor Co Inc 2217 N Main St *TF:* 800-849-5469 ■ *Web:* www.revelstractor.com	Fuquay-Varina	NC	27526	919-552-5697	552-9321
RN Johnson Inc (RNJ) 269 Main St PO Box 448 *Web:* www.rnjohnsoninc.com	Walpole	NH	03608	603-756-3321	756-3452
Rockingham New Holland Inc 600 W Market St *TF:* 800-360-5313	Harrisonburg	VA	22802	540-434-6791	434-6780
Roeder Implement Inc 2550 Rockdale Rd *TF:* 800-557-1184 ■ *Web:* www.roederimplement.com	Dubuque	IA	52003	563-557-1184	583-1821
Rose Bros Inc 302 Main St	Lingle	WY	82223	307-837-2292	837-2922
Schilling Bros Inc 705 N Rt 49 PO Box 96 *TF:* 800-545-0568 ■ *Web:* www.schillingbros.com	Casey	IL	62420	217-932-5941	932-2616
Schilling Bros Inc 5400 US Hwy 45 *Web:* www.schillingbros.com	Mattoon	IL	61938	217-234-6478	235-3991
Schmidt Machine Co 7013 Ohio 199 *Web:* www.schmidtmachine.com	Upper Sandusky	OH	43351	419-294-3814	294-2607
Scott Truck & Tractor Co of Monroe Inc 1000 ML King Dr *Web:* www.scottcompanies.com	Monroe	LA	71203	318-387-4160	388-9297
Seedburo Equipment Co 1022 W Jackson Blvd *TF:* 800-284-5779 ■ *Web:* www.seedburo.com	Chicago	IL	60607	312-738-3700	738-3544
SEMA Equipment Inc 11555 Hwy 60 Blvd *TF:* 800-569-1377 ■ *Web:* www.semaequip.com	Wanamingo	MN	55983	507-824-2256	824-2668
Simpson Norton Corp 4144 S Bullard Ave *TF:* 877-859-8676 ■ *Web:* www.simpsonnorton.com	Goodyear	AZ	85338	623-932-5116	932-5299
Sioux Automation Center Inc 877 1st Ave NW *TF:* 866-722-1488 ■ *Web:* www.siouxautomation.com	Sioux Center	IA	51250	712-722-1488	722-1487
Sloan Implement Co Inc 120 N Business 51 *TF:* 800-745-4020 ■ *Web:* www.sloans.com	Assumption	IL	62510	217-226-4411	226-3351
Spartan Distributors Inc 487 W Division St *TF:* 800-822-2216	Sparta	MI	49345	616-887-7301	887-6288
Stoller International Inc 15521 E 1830 N Rd *Web:* www.stollerinternational.com	Pontiac	IL	61764	815-844-6197	842-3213
Straub International Inc 214 SW 40th Ave PO Box 1606 *TF:* 800-658-1706 ■ *Web:* www.straubint.com	Great Bend	KS	67530	620-792-5256	793-5167
Studer Super Service Inc PO Box 617 *Web:* www.studers.com	Monroe	WI	53566	608-328-8331	
Teeter Irrigation Inc 2295 S Old Hwy 83 *TF:* 800-834-7481 ■ *Web:* www.teeterirrigation.com	Garden City	KS	67846	620-276-8257	276-2652
Texas Timberjack Inc 6004 S First St *Web:* www.texastimberjack.com	Lufkin	TX	75901	936-634-3365	634-9636
Titan Machinery Inc 7955 179th Ave SE *Web:* www.titanmachinery.com	Wahpeton	ND	58075	701-642-8424	642-9514
Tom Hassenfritz Equipment Co 1300 W Washington St *TF:* 800-634-4885 ■ *Web:* www.the-co.com	Mount Pleasant	IA	52641	319-385-3114	385-3731
Torrence's Farm Implement Inc 190 E Hwy 86 PO Box C *Web:* www.torrencesfarmimplements.com	Heber	CA	92249	760-352-5355	352-8707
Tractor Supply Co 200 Powell Pl *NASDAQ: TSCO* ■ *TF:* 877-872-7721 ■ *Web:* www.tractorsupply.com	Brentwood	TN	37027	615-366-4600	366-4686
Turf Professionals Equipment Co 9108 Bond St *TF:* 800-299-3245	Overland Park	KS	66214	913-599-1449	599-0667
Unruh-Foster Inc 501 E Texcoco St *TF:* 800-279-7283 ■ *Web:* www.unruhfoster.com	Montezuma	KS	67867	620-846-2215	846-2371
Van-Wall Equipment Inc 22728 141st Dr PO Box 575 *TF:* 800-568-2381 ■ *Web:* www.vanwall.com	Perry	IA	50220	515-465-5681	
Wade Inc 1505 Hwy 82 W *Web:* www.wadeincorporated.com	Greenwood	MS	38930	662-453-6312	455-3287
Washington County Tractor Inc PO Box 1619 *TF:* 800-256-5655 ■ *Web:* www.wctractor.com	Brenham	TX	77834	979-836-4591	836-7446
West Central Co-op 406 1st St PO Box 68 *TF:* 800-522-1946 ■ *Web:* www.west-central.com	Ralston	IA	51459	712-667-3200	667-3215
Western Equipment Distributors Inc 20224 80th Ave S *TF:* 877-558-7710 ■ *Web:* www.western-equip.com	Kent	WA	98032	253-872-8858	872-6942
Western Implement Co Inc 2919 N Ave *Web:* www.westernimplement.com	Grand Junction	CO	81504	970-242-7960	242-5241
WG Leffelman & Sons Inc 340 N Metcalf Ave *TF:* 800-957-2513 ■ *Web:* www.wgleffelman.com	Amboy	IL	61310	815-857-2513	857-3105
White's Inc 4614 Navigation Blvd PO Box 2344 **Fax Area Code: 888* ■ *TF:* 800-231-9559 ■ *Web:* www.whitesinc.com	Houston	TX	77011	713-928-2632	944-8373*
Witmer's Inc 39821 SR 14 *TF:* 888-427-6025 ■ *Web:* www.witmersinc.com	Salem	OH	44460	330-427-2147	427-2611

Company	City	State	Zip	Phone	Fax
Wyandot Tractor & Implement Co PO Box 147 TF: 800-472-9554	Upper Sandusky	OH	43351	419-294-2349	294-5200
Wyatt-Quarles Seed Co 730 US Hwy 70 W TF: 800-662-7591 ■ Web: www.wqseeds.com	Garner	NC	27529	919-772-4243	772-4278

278 FARM PRODUCT RAW MATERIALS

Company	City	State	Zip	Phone	Fax
ADM Grain Co 4666 E Faries Pkwy	Decatur	IL	62526	217-424-5200	424-4650
ADM Rice Inc 4666 Faries Pkwy Web: www.adm.com	Decatur	IL	62526	217-424-5200	424-5580
ADM/Growmark River System Inc 4666 E Faries Pkwy *Fax: Hum Res ■ TF: 800-637-5843	Decatur	IL	62526	217-424-5900	424-4383*
Ag One Co-op Inc 141 W 500 N PO Box 2009	Anderson	IN	46018	765-643-6639	643-4396
Agri Co-op 310 Logan St TF: 800-658-4089 ■ Web: www.agrico-op.com	Holdrege	NE	68949	308-995-8626	995-5779
Ajinomoto Heartland LLC 8430 W Bryn Mawr Ave Suite 650 Web: www.lysine.com	Chicago	IL	60631	773-380-7000	380-7006
Allenberg Cotton Co 7255 Goodlett Farms Pkwy Web: www.allenberg.com	Cordova	TN	38016	901-383-5000	383-5010
Alliance Grain Co 1306 W 8th St TF: 800-222-2451 ■ Web: www.alliance-grain.com	Gibson City	IL	60936	217-784-4284	784-8949
Apache Farmers Co-op 201 W Floyd St Web: www.apachecoop.com	Apache	OK	73006	580-588-3351	588-9277
Aurora Co-op Elevator Co 605 12th St PO Box 209 TF: 800-642-6795 ■ Web: www.auroracoop.com	Aurora	NE	68818	402-694-2106	694-2060
Birdsong Peanuts 612 Madison Ave PO Box 1400	Suffolk	VA	23434	757-539-3456	539-7360
Bunge Ltd 50 Main St 6th Fl NYSE: BG ■ Web: www.bunge.com	White Plains	NY	10606	914-684-2800	684-3499
C & F Foods Inc 15620 E Valley Blvd Web: www.cnf-foods.com	City of Industry	CA	91744	626-723-1000	723-1212
Cargill Inc 15407 McGinty Rd W *Fax: Cust Svc ■ TF: 800-227-4455 ■ Web: www.cargill.com	Wayzata	MN	55391	952-742-7575	742-7209*
Cargill Ltd 240300 Graham Ave PO Box 5900 Web: www.cargill.com	Winnipeg	MB	R3C4C5	204-947-0141	947-6444
CBG Enterprises Inc PO Box 249 Web: www.cgb.com	Mandeville	LA	70470	985-867-3500	867-3500
Central Connecticut Co-op Farmers Assn 10 Apel Pl PO Box 8500 TF: 800-640-4523 ■ Web: www.cccfeeds.com	Manchester	CT	06040	860-649-4523	643-5305
Central Iowa Co-op 924 First St TF: 800-728-0017	Jewell	IA	50130	515-827-5431	827-5904
Ceres Solutions LLP 2112 Indianapolis Rd PO Box 432 TF: 800-878-0952 ■ Web: www.growerscoop.com	Crawfordsville	IN	47933	765-362-6700	362-7010
Chickasha Of Georgia LLC PO Box 1927 Web: www.chickashaofgeorgia.com	Tifton	GA	31793	229-388-8008	388-8866
Co-Alliance LLP 103 Lincoln St PO Box 560 TF: 800-525-0272 ■ Web: www.co-alliance.com	Danville	IN	46122	317-745-4491	718-1850
Co-op Elevator Co 7211 E Michigan Ave PO Box 619 TF Cust Svc: 800-968-0601 ■ Web: www.coopelev.com	Pigeon	MI	48755	989-453-4500	453-3942
Co-op Federee de Quebec *The Federated Coop* 9001 boul de l'Acadie Bureau 200 Web: www.lacoop.coop	Montreal	QC	H4N3H7	514-858-2222	384-7176
ConAgra Grain Cos 11 ConAgra Dr Suite 5024 Web: www.conagrafoods.com	Omaha	NE	68102	402-595-5637	943-5777
DeBruce Grain Inc 4100 N Mulberry Dr Suite 300 TF: 800-821-5210 ■ Web: www.debruce.com	Kansas City	MO	64116	816-421-8182	584-2350
Dunavant Enterprises Inc 3797 New Getwell Rd *Fax: Hum Res ■ Web: www.dunavant.com	Memphis	TN	38118	901-369-1500	369-1608*
Effingham Equity Inc 201 W Roadway Ave TF: 800-223-1337 ■ Web: www.effinghamequity.com	Effingham	IL	62401	217-342-4101	347-7601
Farmers Co-op 208 W Depot TF: 800-642-6439 ■ Web: www.farmersCooperativeerative.com	Dorchester	NE	68343	402-946-2211	946-2062
Farmers Co-op Co 2321 N Loop Dr Suite 220 Web: www.fccoop.com	Ames	IA	50010	515-817-2100	
Farmers Co-op Co 105 4th Ave	Dayton	IA	50530	515-547-2813	547-2282
Federated Co-operatives Ltd 401 22nd St E Web: www.fcl.ca	Saskatoon	SK	S7K0H2	306-244-3311	244-3403
Frick Services Inc 3154 Depot St TF: 800-552-1754	Wawaka	IN	46794	260-761-3311	761-3112
Frontier Co-op Co 211 S Lincoln St TF: 800-869-0379 ■ Web: www.frontiercooperative.com	Brainard	NE	68626	402-545-2811	545-2821
Heart of Iowa Co-op *Key Co-op* 13585 620 Ave TF: 800-662-4642 ■ Web: www.keycoop.com	Roland	IA	50236	515-388-4341	388-4589
Heartland Co-op 2829 Westown Pkwy Suite 350 TF: 800-513-3938 ■ Web: www.heartlandcoop.com	West Des Moines	IA	50266	515-225-1334	225-8511
Interstate Commodities Inc (ICI) 7 Madison St TF: 800-833-3636 ■ Web: www.icigrain.com	Troy	NY	12181	518-272-7212	272-7299
Italgrani Elevator Co 7900 Van Buren St	Saint Louis	MO	63111	314-638-1447	752-7621
James Richardson International (JRI) 1 Lombard Pl Suite 2700 Web: www.jri.ca	Winnipeg	MB	R3B0X8	204-934-5961	947-2647
John I Haas Inc 5185 MacArthur Blvd NW Suite 300 Web: www.johnihaas.com	Washington	DC	20016	202-777-4800	777-4895
Kelley Bean Co Inc 2407 Cir Dr Web: www.kelleybean.com	Scottsbluff	NE	69361	308-635-6438	635-7345
MaxYield Co-op 313 3rd Ave NE PO Box 49 TF: 800-383-0003 ■ Web: www.maxyieldcooperative.com	West Bend	IA	50597	515-887-7211	887-7291
Mont Eagle Mills Inc 804 W Main St	Oblong	IL	62449	618-592-4211	592-4214
NEW Co-op Inc 2626 1st Ave S TF: 800-362-2233 ■ Web: www.newcoop.com	Fort Dodge	IA	50501	515-955-2040	955-5565
New Image Global Inc 1672 Railroad St TF: 888-898-6879 ■ Web: www.royalblunts.com	Corona	CA	92880	951-371-8344	371-8345
NF Davis Drier & Elevator Inc 9421 N Dos Palos Ave	Firebaugh	CA	93622	559-659-3035	659-2275
Northwest Grain 315 Broadway Ave N PO Box 128 Web: www.northwestgrain.com	Saint Hilaire	MN	56754	218-964-5252	964-5818
Northwest Grain Growers Inc 850 N 4th Ave TF: 800-994-4290 ■ Web: www.nwgrgr.com	Walla Walla	WA	99362	509-525-6510	529-6050
Parrish & Heimbecker Ltd 201 Cottage Ave Suite 1400 TF: 800-665-8937 ■ Web: www.parrishandheimbecker.com	Winnipeg	MB	R3B3K6	204-956-2030	943-8233
Pendleton Grain Growers Inc 1000 SW Dorian St PO Box 1248 TF: 800-422-7611 ■ Web: www.pggcountry.com	Pendleton	OR	97801	541-276-7611	276-4839
Plains Cotton Co-op Assn 3301 E 50th St PO Box 2827 TF: 800-333-8011 ■ Web: www.pcca.com	Lubbock	TX	79408	806-763-8011	762-7400
PremierCo-op Inc 2104 W Pk Ct Web: www.grandprairiecoop.com	Champaign	IL	61821	217-355-1983	355-3478
Pro-Pet LLC 1400 McKinley Rd TF: 800-245-4125 ■ Web: www.joypetfood.com	Saint Marys	OH	45885	419-394-3374	394-8024
Rockingham Co-Operative 101 W Grace St Web: www.rockinghamcoop.com	Harrisonburg	VA	22801	540-434-3856	434-6890
Scoular Co 2027 Dodge St TF: 800-488-3500 ■ Web: www.scoular.com	Omaha	NE	68102	402-342-3500	342-5568
South Dakota Wheat Growers Assn 908 Lamont St SE TF: 888-429-4902 ■ Web: www.sdwg.com	Aberdeen	SD	57401	605-225-5500	225-0859
Southwestern Irrigated Cotton Growers Assn 3500 Doniphan Dr PO Box 1709	El Paso	TX	79949	915-581-5441	581-4138
Staplcotn Co-op Assn Inc 214 W Market St TF: 800-293-6231 ■ Web: www.staplcotn.com	Greenwood	MS	38930	662-453-6231	453-6274
Stratton Equity Co-op Co Inc 98 Colorado Ave PO Box 25 TF: 800-752-2068	Stratton	CO	80836	719-348-5347	348-5506
United Farmers Co-op 360 E Oak St TF: 800-742-7813 ■ Web: www.ufcoop.com	Shelby	NE	68662	402-527-5511	527-5515
Watertown Co-op Elevator Assn 811 Burlington Northern Dr TF: 888-882-3039 ■ Web: www.watertowncoop.com	Watertown	SD	57201	605-886-3039	886-0601
Watonwan Farm Service 233 W Ciro St TF: 800-657-3282 ■ Web: www.wfsag.com	Truman	MN	56088	507-776-2831	776-2871
Weil Bros Cotton Inc 4444 Pk Blvd Web: www.cotton.net	Montgomery	AL	36116	334-244-1800	271-4238
Western Iowa Co-op 3330 Moville St PO Box 106 TF: 800-488-3201 ■ Web: www.westerniowacoop.com	Hornick	IA	51026	712-874-3211	874-3230

279 FARM SUPPLIES

Company	City	State	Zip	Phone	Fax
Ag-Land FS Inc 1505 Valle Vista Blvd Web: www.aglandfs.com	Pekin	IL	61554	309-346-4145	
Agland Inc 260 Factory Rd PO Box 338 TF: 800-433-4688 ■ Web: www.aglandinc.com	Eaton	CO	80615	970-454-4000	454-2144
Agri Producers Inc 205 Main St Web: www.api.coop	Tampa	KS	67483	785-965-2221	965-2263
AgVantage FS Inc 1600 8th St SW TF: 800-346-0058 ■ Web: www.agvantagefs.com	Waverly	IA	50677	319-483-4900	483-4992
Allied Seed LLC 9311 Hwy 45 TF: 888-252-7573 ■ Web: www.alliedseed.com	Nampa	ID	83686	208-466-6700	466-9074
American Pride Co-Op 55 W Bromley Ln TF: 800-332-6478 ■ Web: www.americanpridecoop.com	Brighton	CO	80601	303-659-1230	659-7650
Battle Creek Farmers Co-op 400 W Front St PO Box 10 TF: 800-233-6679 ■ Web: www.bccoop.com	Battle Creek	NE	68715	402-675-2055	675-1645
BFG Supply Co LLC PO Box 479 Web: www.bfgsupply.com	Burton	OH	44021	440-834-1883	834-1885
BinghamCo-op Inc PO Box 887 Web: www.binghamcoop.com	Blackfoot	ID	83221	208-785-3440	785-3444
Bleyhl Farm Service Inc 940 E Wine Country Rd TF Cust Svc: 800-862-6806 ■ Web: www.bleyhl.com	Grandview	WA	98930	509-882-2248	882-4208
Bradley Caldwell Inc 200 Kiwanis Blvd *Fax: Cust Svc ■ TF Cust Svc: 800-257-9100 ■ Web: www.bradleycaldwell.com	Hazleton	PA	18202	570-455-7511	455-0385*
Cal/West Seeds 38001 County Rd 27 TF: 800-327-3337 ■ Web: www.calwestseeds.com	Woodland	CA	95695	530-666-3331	666-5317
Carroll Service Co 505 W Illinois Rt 64	Lanark	IL	61046	815-493-2181	493-6173
Caudill Seed & Warehouse Co Inc 1402 W Main St TF: 800-626-5357 ■ Web: www.caudillseed.com	Louisville	KY	40203	502-583-4402	583-4405
Central Valley Coop 900 30th Pl NW TF: 800-270-2339 ■ Web: centralvalleycoop.com	Owatonna	MN	55060	507-451-1230	451-7579
Central Wisconsin Co-op PO Box 14 TF: 800-472-3004 ■ Web: www.cwco-op.com	Stratford	WI	54484	715-687-4443	
Chem Nut Inc 800 Business Pk Dr Web: www.chemnut.com	Leesburg	GA	31706	229-883-7050	439-0842
CHS Inc 5500 Cenex Dr NASDAQ: CHSCP ■ TF: 800-232-3639 ■ Web: www.chsinc.com	Inver Grove Heights	MN	55077	651-355-6000	355-6432
Co-op Feed Dealers Inc 380 Broome Corporate Pkwy PO Box 670 TF Cust Svc: 800-333-0895 ■ Web: www.cfd.coop	Conklin	NY	13748	607-651-9078	651-9078
Countryside Co-op 514 E Main St TF: 800-236-7585 ■ Web: www.countrysidecoop.com	Durand	WI	54736	715-672-8947	672-5131
CropKing Inc 134 W Dr TF: 800-321-5656 ■ Web: www.cropking.com	Lodi	OH	44254	330-302-4203	302-4204
Customer One Co-op PO Box 215 Web: www.customeronecoop.com	Marathon	WI	54448	715-443-2241	443-3474

				Phone	Fax
Dragon Claw USA Inc 16033 Arrow Hwy	Irwindale	CA	91706	626-480-0068	480-0018
TF: 800-238-5296 ■ *Web:* www.dcamerica.net					
Edon Farmers Co-op Assn Inc					
205 S Michigan PO Box 308	Edon	OH	43518	419-272-2121	485-4509
TF: 800-878-4093 ■ *Web:* www.edonfarmerscoop.com					
Evergreen FS Inc 402 N Hershey Rd	Bloomington	IL	61704	309-663-2392	663-0494
TF: 877-963-2392 ■ *Web:* www.evergreen-fs.com					
Farm Country Co-op PO Box 1037	Pine Island	MN	55963	507-356-8313	356-8881
TF: 800-356-8313 ■ *Web:* www.farmcountrycoop.com					
Farm Service Co 4040 S Expy	Council Bluffs	IA	51502	712-323-7167	323-9667
TF: 800-705-7666 ■ *Web:* www.farmservicecompany.com					
Farm Service Co-op 2050 Chatburn Ave	Harlan	IA	51537	712-755-3185	755-7098
TF: 800-452-4372 ■ *Web:* www.fscoop.com					
Farmers Co-op Assn 105 Jackson St	Jackson	MN	56143	507-847-4160	847-2521
TF: 800-864-3847 ■ *Web:* www.fcajackson.com					
Farmers Co-op Supply & Shipping Assn					
570 Commerce St	West Salem	WI	54669	608-786-1100	786-1606
TF: 800-657-5189					
Farmers Feed & Grain Co Inc					
306 Birch St PO Box 291	Riceville	IA	50466	641-985-2147	985-4000
Web: www.ffgcoinc.com					
Farmway Inc 204 E Ct St PO Box 568	Beloit	KS	67420	785-738-2241	738-9659
Web: www.farmwaycoop.com					
Federation Co-op 108 N Water St	Black River Falls	WI	54615	715-284-5354	284-9672
TF: 800-944-1784 ■ *Web:* www.fedcoop.com					
Fifield Land Co 4307 Fifield Rd	Brawley	CA	92227	760-344-6391	344-6394
Web: www.kfseeds.com					
Florida Fertilizer Co Inc PO Box 1087	Wauchula	FL	33873	863-773-4159	
Web: www.floridafertilizer.com					
Frenchman Valley Farmers Co-op Exchange					
202 Broadway	Imperial	NE	69033	308-882-3200	882-3242
TF: 800-538-2667 ■ *Web:* www.fvcoop.com					
Gold Star FS Inc 101 N E St PO Box 79	Cambridge	IL	61238	309-937-3369	937-5465
TF: 800-443-8497 ■ *Web:* www.goldstarfs.com					
Gowan Co LLC PO Box 5569	Yuma	AZ	85366	928-783-8844	343-9255
TF: 800-883-1844 ■ *Web:* www.gowanco.com					
Grangetto's Farm & Garden Supply Co					
1105 W Mission Ave	Escondido	CA	92025	760-745-4671	745-5111
TF: 800-536-4671 ■ *Web:* www.grangettos.com					
GROWMARK Inc 1701 Towanda Ave	Bloomington	IL	61701	309-557-6000	829-8532
Web: www.growmark.com					
Hart Chemicals Inc 2424 4th St	Berkeley	CA	94710	510-549-3535	549-0890
Web: www.pcchem.com					
Hummert International Inc					
4500 Earth City Expy	Earth City	MO	63045	314-506-4500	506-4510
TF: 800-325-3055 ■ *Web:* www.hummert.com					
Hutchinson Co-Op PO Box 158	Hutchinson	MN	55350	320-587-4647	587-6964
TF: 800-795-1299 ■ *Web:* www.hutchcoop.com					
Intermountain Farmers Assn					
1147 W 2100 S	Salt Lake City	UT	84119	801-972-2122	972-2186
TF: 800-748-4432 ■ *Web:* www.ifa-coop.com					
International Commodities Export Corp (ICEC)					
10001 Woodloch Forest Dr Suite 400	The Woodlands	TX	77380	832-764-5000	764-5100
Web: www.icecglobal.com					
JS West & Cos 721 8th St	Modesto	CA	95354	209-577-3221	523-9828
TF: 800-675-9378 ■ *Web:* www.jswest.com					
Keller Grain & Feed Inc 7977 Main St	Greenville	OH	45331	937-448-2284	448-2102
Web: www.kellergrain.com					
Kreamer Feed Inc PO Box 38	Kreamer	PA	17833	570-374-8148	374-2007
TF: 800-767-4537 ■ *Web:* www.kreamerfeed.com					
Kugler Co 209 W 3rd St PO Box 1748	McCook	NE	69001	308-345-2280	345-7756
TF: 800-445-9116 ■ *Web:* www.kuglercompany.com					
La Salle Farmers Grain Co 317 4th St NE	Madelia	MN	56062	507-642-3276	642-3299
TF: 800-245-5857					
Legend Seeds Inc PO Box 241	De Smet	SD	57231	605-854-3346	854-3135
Web: www.legendseeds.net					
Loveland Industries Inc 14520 WCR # 64	Greeley	CO	80631	970-356-8920	356-8926
TF: 800-356-8920					
Luckey Farmers Inc					
1200 W Main St PO Box 217	Woodville	OH	43460	419-849-2711	849-2720
Web: www.luckeyfarmers.com					
Martrex Inc 14525 Hwy 7	Minnetonka	MN	55345	952-933-5000	933-1889
TF: 800-328-3627 ■ *Web:* www.martrexinc.com					
McFarlane Mfg Co Inc					
1259 Water St PO Box 100	Sauk City	WI	53583	608-643-3321	643-2309
TF: 800-627-8569 ■ *Web:* www.mcfarlanes.net					
Meherrin Agricultural & Chemical Co Inc					
413 Main St PO Box 200	Severn	NC	27877	252-585-1744	585-1718
TF: 800-775-0333					
MFA Inc 201 Ray Young Dr	Columbia	MO	65201	573-874-5111	876-5430
Web: www.mfaincorporated.com					
Midland Co-op 101 S Main St	Axtell	NE	68924	308-743-2424	743-2428
TF: 800-404-2420					
Miles Farm Supplies LLC 2760 Keller Rd	Owensboro	KY	42301	270-926-2420	683-7565
TF: 800-666-4537 ■ *Web:* www.milesnmore.com					
New Alliance FS Inc 110 NE St	Oskaloosa	IA	52577	319-728-2223	673-9735*
**Fax Area Code:* 641 ■ *TF:* 800-672-2589					
NEW Co-op Inc 2626 1st Ave S	Fort Dodge	IA	50501	515-955-2040	955-5565
TF: 800-362-2233 ■ *Web:* www.newcoop.com					
Northwest Wholesale Inc					
1567 N Wenatchee Ave	Wenatchee	WA	98801	509-662-2141	663-4540
TF: 800-874-6607 ■ *Web:* www.nwwinc.com					
Northwestern Supply Co Inc					
525 Progress Rd	Waite Park	MN	56387	320-251-0812	251-6210
TF: 800-397-6972					
Nu Way Co-op Inc PO Box Q	Trimont	MN	56176	507-639-2311	639-4006
TF: 800-445-4118 ■ *Web:* www.nuwaycoop.com					
Nyssa Co-op Supply 18 N 2nd St	Nyssa	OR	97913	541-372-2254	372-2453
Orange Belt Supply Co 25244 Rd 204	Lindsay	CA	93247	559-562-2574	562-6043
Web: www.orangebelt.net					
Orangeburg Pecan Co Inc PO Box 38	Orangeburg	SC	29116	803-534-4277	534-4279
TF: 800-845-6970 ■ *Web:* www.uspecans.com					
Orscheln Farm & Home LLC					
1800 Overcenter Dr PO Box 698	Moberly	MO	65270	800-498-5090	269-3500*
**Fax Area Code:* 660 ■ *TF:* 800-498-5090 ■ *Web:* www.orscheln.com					
Osborne Distributing Co 3908 Wilbarger St	Vernon	TX	76384	940-552-7711	553-4056
Panhandle Co-op Assn					
401 S Beltline Hwy W	Scottsbluff	NE	69361	308-632-5301	632-5375
TF Cust Svc: 800-732-4546 ■ *Web:* www.panhandlecoop.com					
Paris Farmers' Union PO Box D	South Paris	ME	04281	207-743-8976	743-8564
TF: 800-639-3603 ■ *Web:* www.parisfarmersunion.net					
Perham Co-op Creamery Assn 459 3rd Ave SE	Perham	MN	56573	218-346-6240	346-6241
Web: www.perhamcoop.com					
Pickseed West Disc Inc 33149 Hwy 99 E	Tangent	OR	97389	541-926-8886	926-2515
Web: www.pickseed.com					
Quality Liquid Feeds Inc PO Box 240	Dodgeville	WI	53533	608-935-2345	935-3198
TF: 800-236-2345 ■ *Web:* www.qlf.com					
Red River Specialties Inc PO Box 7241	Shreveport	LA	71137	318-425-5944	424-6562
TF: 800-256-3344 ■ *Web:* www.rrsi.com					
Reedsville Co-Operative Assn Inc					
PO Box 460	Reedsville	WI	54230	920-754-4321	754-4536
TF: 800-968-9484 ■ *Web:* www.countryvisionscoop.com					
Richardson Seeds Inc PO Box 60	Vega	TX	79092	806-267-2379	267-2820
Web: www.richardsonseeds.com					
Rolling Hills Farm Service Inc					
421 N 10th St	Winterset	IA	50273	515-462-2644	462-3410
TF: 800-352-3276					
S R C Corp PO Box 30676	Salt Lake City	UT	84130	801-268-4500	268-4596
Web: www.steveregan.com					
Seeds of Change Inc PO Box 15700	Santa Fe	NM	87592	505-438-8080	438-7052
TF: 888-762-7333 ■ *Web:* www.seedsofchange.com					
Siegers Seed Co 13031 Reflections Dr	Holland	MI	49424	616-786-4999	994-0333
TF: 800-962-4999 ■ *Web:* www.siegers.com					
Silver Edge Co-op 39999 Hilton Rd	Edgewood	IA	52042	563-928-6419	
TF: 800-632-5953 ■ *Web:* www.silveredgecoop.com					
South Central Co-op 40 W Pk Dr	Gibbon	MN	55335	507-834-6534	834-6140
TF: 800-690-6534					
Southern FS Inc 2002 E Main St PO Box 728	Marion	IL	62959	618-993-2833	997-2526
TF: 800-492-7684 ■ *Web:* www.home.southernfs.com					
Southern States Co-op Inc 6606 W Broad St	Richmond	VA	23230	804-281-1000	281-1141
TF: 800-826-2762 ■ *Web:* www.southernstates-coop.com					
Southern States Frederick Co-op Inc					
518 W S St	Frederick	MD	21701	301-663-6164	663-8173
Web: www.southernstates.com					
Stanislaus Farm Supply Co 624 E Service Rd	Modesto	CA	95358	209-538-7070	541-3191
TF: 800-323-0725 ■ *Web:* www.stanislausfarmsupply.com					
Tennessee Farmers Co-op					
180 Old Nashville Hwy	La Vergne	TN	37086	615-793-8011	793-8343
TF: 800-366-2667 ■ *Web:* www.ourcoop.com					
Transammonia Inc 320 Pk Ave	New York	NY	10022	212-223-3200	759-1410
Web: www.transammonia.com					
TriOak Foods Inc 103 W Railroad St PO Box 68	Oakville	IA	52646	319-766-2230	
Web: www.trioak.com					
United Suppliers Inc 30473 260th St	Eldora	IA	50627	641-858-2341	858-5493
TF: 800-782-5123 ■ *Web:* www.uniteds.com					
Universal Co-ops Inc (UCOOP)					
1300 Corporate Ctr Curve	Eagan	MN	55121	651-239-1000	239-1203
TF: 800-375-1121 ■ *Web:* www.ucoop.com					
Van Horn Inc PO Box 380	Cerro Gordo	IL	61818	217-677-2131	677-2134
TF: 800-252-1615 ■ *Web:* www.vanhorninc.com					
Wabash Valley Service Co Inc 909 N Ct St	Grayville	IL	62844	618-375-2311	375-5351
TF: 888-869-8127 ■ *Web:* www.home.wabashvalleyfs.com					
West Agro Inc 11100 N Congress Ave	Kansas City	MO	64153	816-891-1600	891-1606
Web: www.westagro.com					
Western Consolidated Coop					
520 Co Rd 9 PO Box 78	Holloway	MN	56249	320-394-2171	394-2180
Web: www.west-con.com					
Western Reserve Farm Co-op Inc					
14961 S State Ave PO Box 339	Middlefield	OH	44062	440-632-1192	632-1258
TF: 888-427-6672 ■ *Web:* www.wrfc.org					
Westland Co-op 2112 Indianapolis Rd	Crawfordsville	IN	47933	765-362-6700	362-7010
TF: 800-878-0952 ■ *Web:* www.westlandcoop.com					
Wheaton-Dumont Farmer Co-op 1115 Broadway	Wheaton	MN	56296	320-563-8152	563-4392
TF: 800-258-7444 ■ *Web:* www.wdcoop.com					
Wilbur-Ellis Co					
345 California St 27th Fl	San Francisco	CA	94104	415-772-4000	772-4011
Web: www.wilburellis.com/pages/Home.aspx					
Wilco Farmers 200 Industrial Way	Mount Angel	OR	97362	503-845-6122	845-9310
TF: 800-382-5339 ■ *Web:* www.wilco.coop					

280 FASHION DESIGN HOUSES

SEE ALSO Clothing & Accessories - Mfr p. 1607

				Phone	Fax
Anna Sui Corp 250 W 39th St 15th Fl	New York	NY	10018	212-768-1951	768-8825
Web: www.annasui.com					
Armani Exchange 568 Broadway	New York	NY	10012	212-431-6000	431-4669
TF: 800-717-2929 ■ *Web:* www.armaniexchange.com					
Badgley Mischka 550 7th Ave 22nd Fl	New York	NY	10018	212-921-1585	921-4171
Web: www.badgleymischka.com					
BCBG Max Azria 2761 Fruitland Ave	Vernon	CA	90058	323-589-2224	277-5454
TF: 888-636-2224 ■ *Web:* www.bcbg.com					
Betsey Johnson Inc 498 7th Ave 21st Fl	New York	NY	10018	212-244-0843	244-0855
Web: www.betseyjohnson.com					
Calvin Klein Inc 205 W 39th St 3rd Fl	New York	NY	10018	212-719-2600	730-4818
TF Cust Svc: 800-388-9122 ■ *Web:* www.pvh.com					
Carolina Herrera Ltd 501 7th Ave 17th Fl	New York	NY	10018	212-944-5757	944-7996
Web: www.carolinaherrera.com					
Christian Dior 712 5th Ave 37th Fl	New York	NY	10019	212-582-0500	582-0500
TF: 800-929-3467					

Company / Address	City	State	Zip	Phone	Fax
Cynthia Rowley 376 Bleecker St *Web:* www.cynthiarowley.com	New York	NY	10014	212-242-0847	242-4136
Diane Von Furstenberg 440 W 14th St *TF:* 888-472-2383 ■ *Web:* www.dvf.com	New York	NY	10014	212-753-1111	753-1180
Dolce & Gabbana 825 Madison Ave *Web:* www.dolcegabbana.it	New York	NY	10065	212-750-0055	750-5750
Donna Karan International Inc 550 7th Ave 15th Fl *TF:* 800-231-0884 ■ *Web:* www.donnakaran.com	New York	NY	10018	212-789-1500	789-1821
Ellen Tracy Inc 575 7th Ave 10th Fl *Web:* www.ellentracy.com	New York	NY	10018	212-944-6999	944-2446
Escada USA Inc 10 Mulholland Dr *Web:* www.escada.com	Hasbrouck Heights	NJ	07604	201-462-6000	462-6440
Evy Of California Inc 810A S Flower St *Web:* www.evy.com	Los Angeles	CA	90017	213-746-4647	746-9788
Halston 96 Spring St 13th Fl *Web:* www.halston.com	New York	NY	10012	212-282-1200	219-0936
Jessica McClintock Inc 1400 16th St *TF:* 800-333-5301 ■ *Web:* www.jessicamcclintock.com	San Francisco	CA	94103	415-553-8200	553-8329
Jhane Barnes Inc 119 W 40th St 20th Fl *TF:* 888-465-4263 ■ *Web:* www.jhanebarnes.com	New York	NY	10018	212-575-2448	575-2506
Jill Stuart Inc 550 7th Ave 24th Fl *Web:* www.jillstuart.com	New York	NY	10018	212-921-2600	921-2850
Kay Green Design Inc 859 Outer Rd *TF:* 800-226-5186 ■ *Web:* www.kaygreendesign.com	Orlando	FL	32814	407-246-7155	426-7873
Manolo Blahnik Manolo Blahnik Press Office 31 W 54th St	New York	NY	10019	212-582-1583	582-5778
Marc Bouwer 27 W 20th St Suite 1201 *Web:* www.marcbouwer.com	New York	NY	10011	212-242-7510	242-2687
Marc Jacobs International 72 Spring St 2nd Fl *Web:* www.marcjacobs.com	New York	NY	10012	212-343-0222	343-2960
Max Mara USA Inc 530 7th Ave 21st Fl	New York	NY	10018	212-536-6200	302-1134
Michael Kors 11 W 42nd St 21st Fl *Web:* www.michaelkors.com	New York	NY	10036	212-201-8100	
Nicole Miller 525 7th Ave 20th Fl *Web:* www.nicolemiller.com	New York	NY	10018	212-719-9200	391-4327
Norma Kamali 11 W 56th St *Web:* www.normakamalicollection.com	New York	NY	10019	212-957-9797	956-1060
Oscar De La Renta Ltd 550 7th Ave 8th Fl *Web:* www.oscardelarenta.com	New York	NY	10018	212-354-6777	768-9110
Prada 610 W 52nd St *Web:* www.prada.com	New York	NY	10019	212-307-9300	246-3653
Todd Oldham 120 Wooster St 3rd Fl *Web:* www.toddoldhamstudio.com	New York	NY	10012	212-226-4668	226-4873
Vera Wang 225 W 39th St 9th Fl **Fax:* PR ■ *TF:* 800-839-8372 ■ *Web:* www.verawang.com	New York	NY	10018	212-575-6400	354-2548*
Vivienne Tam 550 7th Ave 20th Fl *Web:* www.viviennetam.com	New York	NY	10018	212-840-6470	869-4043
Yves Saint Laurent 3 E 57th St *Web:* www.ysl.com	New York	NY	10022	212-980-2970	

281 FASTENERS & FASTENING SYSTEMS

SEE ALSO Hardware - Mfr p. 2003; Precision Machined Products p. 2443

Company / Address	City	State	Zip	Phone	Fax
Air Industries Corp 12570 Knott St *Web:* www.air-industries.com	Garden Grove	CA	92841	714-892-5571	892-7904
Allfast Fastening Systems Inc 15200 Don Julian Rd *Web:* www.allfastinc.com	City of Industry	CA	91745	626-968-9388	968-9393
Atlas Bolt & Screw Co 1628 Troy Rd *TF:* 800-321-6977 ■ *Web:* www.atlasfasteners.com	Ashland	OH	44805	419-289-6171	289-2564
Avibank Mfg Inc 11500 Sherman Way *Web:* www.avibank.com	North Hollywood	CA	91605	818-392-2100	255-2094
B & G Mfg Co Inc 3067 Unionville Pike **Fax:* Sales ■ *TF:* 800-366-3067 ■ *Web:* www.bgmfg.com	Hatfield	PA	19440	215-822-1925	822-1006*
Bristol Industries 630 E Lambert Rd **Fax:* Sales ■ *Web:* www.bristol-ind.com	Brea	CA	92821	714-990-4121	529-6726*
Captive Fastener Corp 19 Thornton Rd *Web:* www.captive-fastener.com	Oakland	NJ	07436	201-337-6800	337-1012
Chicago Rivet & Machine Co 901 Frontenac Rd *AMEX:* CVR ■ *Web:* www.chicagorivet.com	Naperville	IL	60563	630-357-8500	983-9314
Cold Heading Co 21777 Hoover Rd *Web:* www.coldheading.com	Warren	MI	48089	586-497-7000	497-7007
Decker Mfg Corp 703 N Clark St *Web:* www.deckernut.com	Albion	MI	49224	517-629-3955	629-3535
Detroit Heading LLC 6421 Lynch Rd *Web:* www.detroitheading.com	Detroit	MI	48234	313-267-2240	267-2061
DexTechnologies LLC 2110 Bishop Cir E	Dexter	MI	48130	734-426-5200	426-5870
Elgin Fastener Group 1414 S Benham Rd *Web:* www.elginfasteners.com	Versailles	IN	47042	812-689-8959	689-6635
Entegra Fastener Corp 321 E Foster Ave	Wood Dale	IL	60191	630-595-6250	595-6250
Etf Fastening Systems Inc 29019 Solon Rd *TF:* 800-248-2376 ■ *Web:* www.etf-fastening.com	Solon	OH	44139	440-248-8655	248-0423
Fastco Industries Inc PO Box 141427 *Web:* www.fastcoind.com	Grand Rapids	MI	49514	616-453-5428	453-2490
Ford Fasteners Inc 110 S Newman St *TF:* 800-272-3673 ■ *Web:* www.fordfasteners.com	Hackensack	NJ	07601	201-487-3151	487-1919
Gesipa Fasteners USA Inc 3150 Brunswick Pike Suite 310 *TF:* 800-257-9404 ■ *Web:* www.gesipausa.com	Lawrenceville	NJ	08648	609-883-8300	883-8301
Hohmann & Barnard Inc 30 Rasons Ct *TF:* 800-645-0616 ■ *Web:* www.h-b.com	Hauppauge	NY	11788	631-234-0600	234-0683
Huck Fasteners 24000 Western Ave *Web:* www.contmid.com	Park Forest	IL	60466	708-747-1200	747-9373
Indiana Automotive Fasteners Inc 1300 Anderson Blvd *Web:* www.iafi.com	Greenfield	IN	46140	317-467-0100	467-2782
ITW Brands 955 National Pkwy Suite 95500 *TF:* 800-982-7178 ■ *Web:* www.itwbrands.com	Schaumburg	IL	60173	847-944-2260	619-8344
ITW Buildex 1349 W Bryn Mawr *TF:* 800-284-5339 ■ *Web:* www.itwbuildex.com	Itasca	IL	60143	630-595-3500	595-3549
Lake Erie Screw Corp 13001 Athens Ave	Cleveland	OH	44107	216-521-1800	
Lawrence Screw Products Inc 7230 W Wilson Ave *Web:* www.lawscrew.com	Harwood Heights	IL	60706	708-867-5150	867-7052
Mid-States Bolt & Screw Co 4126 Somers Dr *TF:* 800-482-0867 ■ *Web:* www.midstatesbolt.com	Burton	MI	48529	810-744-0123	744-3798
Mid-States Screw Corp 1817 18th Ave *Web:* www.midstatesscrew.com	Rockford	IL	61104	815-397-2440	398-1047
Monogram Aerospace Fasteners 3423 S Garfield Ave *Web:* www.monogramaerospace.com	Los Angeles	CA	90040	323-722-4760	721-1851
Ms Aerospace Inc 13928 Balboa Blvd *Web:* www.msaerospace.com	Sylmar	CA	91342	818-833-9095	833-9525
National Rivet & Mfg Co 21 E Jefferson St *TF:* 888-324-5511 ■ *Web:* www.nationalrivet.com	Waupun	WI	53963	920-324-5511	324-3388
Ohio Nut & Bolt Co 33 1st Ave *TF:* 800-362-0291 ■ *Web:* www.on-b.com	Berea	OH	44017	440-243-0200	243-4006
Pan American Screw Inc 630 Reese Dr SW *TF Cust Svc:* 800-951-2222 ■ *Web:* www.panamericanscrew.com	Conover	NC	28613	828-466-0060	466-0070
PennEngineering & Mfg Corp 5190 Old Easton Rd *TF:* 800-237-4736 ■ *Web:* www.penn-eng.com	Danboro	PA	18916	215-766-8853	766-3680
Robertson Inc 97 Bronte St N *TF:* 800-268-5090 ■ *Web:* www.robertsonscrew.com	Milton	ON	L9T2N8	905-878-2866	878-2867
Scovill Fasteners Inc 1802 Scovill Dr **Fax:* Cust Svc ■ *TF Cust Svc:* 800-756-4734 ■ *Web:* www.scovill.com	Clarkesville	GA	30523	706-754-1000	754-4000*
Southern Fastening Systems Inc 635 Fairgrounds Rd *Web:* www.southernfastening.com	Muscle Shoals	AL	35661	256-381-3628	381-3631
SPS Technologies Inc 301 Highland Ave *Web:* www.spstech.com	Jenkintown	PA	19046	215-572-3000	572-3790
Stafast Products Inc 505 Lake Shore Blvd *TF:* 800-782-3278 ■ *Web:* www.stafast.com	Painesville	OH	44077	440-357-5546	357-7137
Textron Fastening Systems 840 W Long Lake Rd Suite 450 *Web:* www.textronfasteningsystems.com	Troy	MI	48098	248-879-8660	813-6372
Treadway Electric Co 3300 W 65th St *TF:* 800-666-8321 ■ *Web:* www.treadwayelectric.com	Little Rock	AR	72209	501-562-2111	562-3743
TriMas Corp 39400 Woodward Ave Suite 130 *Web:* www.trimascorp.com	Bloomfield Hills	MI	48304	248-631-5450	631-5455
Vertex Distribution 523 Pleasant St Bldg 10 *Web:* www.vertexdistribution.com	Attleboro	MA	02703	508-431-1120	431-1114

282 FENCES - MFR

SEE ALSO Recycled Plastics Products p. 2531

Company / Address	City	State	Zip	Phone	Fax
Acorn Wire & Iron Works Inc 2035 S Racine Ave *TF:* 800-552-2676 ■ *Web:* www.acornwire.com	Chicago	IL	60608	773-585-0600	585-2403
Dare Products Inc 157 Betterly Rd PO Box 157 *TF:* 800-922-3273 ■ *Web:* www.dareproducts.com	Battle Creek	MI	49016	269-965-2307	965-3261
Fi-Shock Inc 5360 N National Dr *TF:* 800-251-9288 ■ *Web:* www.fishock.com	Knoxville	TN	37914	865-524-7380	673-4770
Kalinich Fence Co Inc 12223 Prospect Rd *Web:* www.kalinichfenceco.com	Strongsville	OH	44149	440-238-6127	238-2178
Master Halco Inc 1321 Greenway Dr **Fax Area Code:* 800 ■ **Fax:* Cust Svc ■ *TF:* 800-883-8384 ■ *Web:* www.masterhalco.com	Irving	TX	75038	972-714-7300	542-8488*
Merchants Metals Inc 375 Northridge Road Suite 500 *TF:* 866-888-5611 ■ *Web:* www.merchantsmetals.com	Atlanta	GA	30350	678-731-8077	
Moultrie Mfg Co 1403 Georgia Hwy 133 S PO Box 2948 *TF:* 800-841-8674 ■ *Web:* www.moultriemanufacturing.com	Moultrie	GA	31776	229-985-1312	890-7245
Riverdale Mills Corp 130 Riverdale St PO Box 200 *TF:* 800-762-6374 ■ *Web:* www.riverdale.com	Northbridge	MA	01534	508-234-8715	234-9593
Tru-Link Fence Co 5440 Touhy Ave *TF:* 888-568-9300 ■ *Web:* www.tru-link.com	Skokie	IL	60077	847-568-9300	568-9600

283 FERTILIZERS & PESTICIDES

SEE ALSO Farm Supplies p. 1841

Company / Address	City	State	Zip	Phone	Fax
Abell Corp 2500 Sterlington Rd *TF:* 800-325-7204 ■ *Web:* www.abellfertilizer.net/html/Abell_New/index-Profile.html	Monroe	LA	71203	318-343-7565	343-8795
Agricultural Commodities Inc 2224 Oxford Rd *TF:* 800-359-8899	New Oxford	PA	17350	717-624-8249	624-3216
Agriliance 5500 Cenex Dr *TF:* 800-535-4635	Inver Grove Heights	MN	55077	651-451-5000	451-5404
Agrium Inc 13131 Lake Fraser Dr SE *NYSE:* AGU ■ **Fax:* PR ■ *TF:* 877-247-4861 ■ *Web:* www.agrium.com	Calgary	AB	T2J7E8	403-225-7000	225-7609*
Airgas Specialty Products 6340 Sugarloaf Pkwy Suite 300 *TF:* 800-226-4572 ■ *Web:* www.airgasspecialtyproducts.com	Duluth	GA	30097	770-717-2210	717-2222

Company	City	State	Zip	Phone	Fax
Alabama Farmers Co-op Inc PO Box 2227 *TF:* 800-737-6843 ■ *Web:* www.alafarm.com	Decatur	AL	35601	256-353-6843	350-1770
Alco Industries Inc 820 Adams Ave Suite 130 *Web:* www.alcoind.com	Norristown	PA	19403	610-666-0930	666-0752
Amvac Chemical Corp 4100 E Washington Blvd *TF:* 800-424-9300 ■ *Web:* www.amvac-chemical.com	Los Angeles	CA	90023	323-264-3910	268-1028
Andersons Inc Plant Nutrient Group 8086 E CR 900 S *TF:* 800-552-3769 ■ *Web:* www.andersonsinc.com/ag/pnd/index.html	Galveston	IN	46932	574-626-2522	626-3174
Apache Nitrogen Products Inc 1436 S Apache Powder Rd PO Box 700 *Web:* www.apachenitro.com	Benson	AZ	85602	520-720-2217	720-4158
Atlantic FEC Fertilizer & Chemical Co 18375 SW 260 St *TF:* 800-432-3413 ■ *Web:* www.atlanticfec.com	Homestead	FL	33031	305-247-8800	247-3328
Bay Zinc Co 301 W Charron Rd PO Box 167 *Web:* www.bayzinc.com	Moxee	WA	98936	509-248-4911	248-4916
Brandt Consolidated Inc 211 W Rt 125 PO Box 350 *Web:* www.brandtconsolidated.com	Pleasant Plains	IL	62677	217-626-1123	626-1927
California Ammonia Co (CALAMCO) 1776 W March Ln Suite 420 *TF:* 800-624-4200 ■ *Web:* www.calamco.com	Stockton	CA	95207	209-982-1000	983-0822
Cargill Inc North America 15407 McGinty Rd *TF:* 800-227-4455	Wayzata	MN	55391	952-742-7575	
Certis USA LLC 9145 Guilford Rd Suite 175 *TF:* 800-847-5620 ■ *Web:* www.certisusa.com	Columbia	MD	21046	301-604-7340	604-7015
CF Industries Inc 4 Pkwy N *Web:* www.cfindustries.com	Deerfield	IL	60015	847-405-2400	405-2711
CFC Farm & Home Ctr 15172 Brandy Rd PO Box 2002 *TF:* 800-284-2667 ■ *Web:* www.cfcfarmhome.net	Culpeper	VA	22701	540-825-2200	825-2200
Coastal Agrobusiness Inc 3702 Evans St PO Box 856 *TF:* 800-758-1828 ■ *Web:* www.coastalagro.com	Greenville	NC	27835	252-756-1126	756-3282
Coffeyville Resources LLC 10 E Cambridge Cir Dr *Web:* www.coffeyvillegroup.com	Kansas City	KS	66103	913-982-0500	981-0001
Degesch America Inc PO Box 116 *TF:* 800-330-2525 ■ *Web:* www.degeschamerica.com	Weyers Cave	VA	24486	540-234-9281	234-8225
Dow AgroSciences LLC 9330 Zionsville Rd **Fax Area Code:* 800 ■ *TF:* 800-258-1470 ■ *Web:* www.dowagro.com	Indianapolis	IN	46268	317-337-3000	905-7326*
Drexel Chemical Co 1700 Ch Ave PO Box 13327 *Web:* www.drexchem.com	Memphis	TN	38113	901-774-4370	774-4666
DuPont Agriculture & Nutrition 1007 Market St DuPont Bldg *TF:* 800-441-7515	Wilmington	DE	19898	302-774-1000	999-4399
DuPont Crop Protection PO Box 80705 *TF:* 888-638-7668 ■ *Web:* www2.dupont.com/Production_Agriculture/en_US/cpp_us.html	Wilmington	DE	19880	302-774-1000	999-4399
EDEN Bioscience Corp 11816 N Creek Pkwy N *TF:* 888-522-5976	Bothell	WA	98011	425-806-7300	806-7400
Enforcer Products Inc PO Box 1060 *TF:* 800-241-5656 ■ *Web:* www.enforcer.com	Cartersville	GA	30120	770-386-0801	386-1659
FMC Corp 1735 Market St *NYSE:* FMC ■ *Web:* www.fmc.com	Philadelphia	PA	19103	215-299-6000	299-5998
FMC Corp Agricultural Products Group 1735 Market St *Web:* www.fmccrop.com	Philadelphia	PA	19103	215-299-6000	299-5999
Frit Industries Inc 1792 Jodie Parker Rd *TF:* 800-633-7685 ■ *Web:* www.fritind.com	Ozark	AL	36360	334-774-2515	774-9306
Good Earth Inc 5960 Broadway *Web:* www.goodearth.org	Lancaster	NY	14086	716-684-8111	684-3722
Green Light Co 10511 Wetmore Rd *TF:* 800-777-5702 ■ *Web:* www.greenlightco.com	San Antonio	TX	78216	210-494-3481	494-5224
Helena Chemical Co 225 Schilling Blvd Suite 300 *Web:* www.helenachemical.com	Collierville	TN	38017	901-761-0050	821-5455
Hintzsche Fertilizer Inc 2 S 181 County Line Rd PO Box 367 *TF:* 800-446-3378 ■ *Web:* www.hintzsche.com	Maple Park	IL	60151	630-557-2406	557-2557
HJ Baker & Bros Inc 228 Saugatuck Ave *Web:* www.bakerbro.com	Westport	CT	06880	203-682-9200	227-8351
Ibe Trade Corp 950 3rd Ave FL 25 25th Fl *Web:* www.ibetrade.com	New York	NY	10022	212-593-3255	308-3642
Intrepid Potash Inc 700 17th St Suite 1700 *NYSE:* IPI ■ *Web:* www.intrepidpotash.com	Denver	CO	80202	303-296-3006	298-7502
JR Simplot Co 999 W Main St # 1300 *TF:* 800-635-5008 ■ *Web:* www.simplot.com	Boise	ID	83702	208-336-2110	389-7515
JR Simplot Co AgriBusiness Group 999 Main St PO Box 70013 *TF:* 800-635-9444 ■ *Web:* www.simplot.com/agricultural	Boise	ID	83707	208-672-2700	672-2760
Kellogg Supply Inc 350 W Sepulveda Blvd *TF Cust Svc:* 800-232-2322 ■ *Web:* www.kellogggarden.com	Carson	CA	90745	310-830-2200	835-6174
Kirby Agri Inc 500 Running Pump Rd PO Box 6277 *TF:* 800-745-7524 ■ *Web:* www.kirbyagri.com	Lancaster	PA	17607	717-299-2541	293-9306
Koch Nitrogen Co 4111 E 37th St N *Web:* www.kochind.com	Wichita	KS	67220	316-828-5500	828-4084
Landec Ag Inc 201 N Michigan *TF:* 800-241-7252 ■ *Web:* www.landecag.com	Oxford	IN	47971	765-385-1000	385-0598
Lebanon Seaboard Corp 1600 E Cumberland St *TF:* 800-233-0628 ■ *Web:* www.lebsea.com	Lebanon	PA	17042	717-273-1685	273-9466
Living Earth Technology Co 1901 California Crossing *Web:* www.livingearth.net	Dallas	TX	75220	972-506-8575	
MFA Inc 201 Ray Young Dr *Web:* www.mfaincorporated.com	Columbia	MO	65201	573-874-5111	876-5430
Miller Chemical & Fertilizer Corp 120 Radio Rd PO Box 333 *TF:* 800-233-2040 ■ *Web:* www.millerchemical.com	Hanover	PA	17331	717-632-8921	632-4581
Monsanto Co 800 N Lindbergh Blvd *NYSE:* MON ■ *Web:* www.monsanto.com	Saint Louis	MO	63167	314-694-1000	694-8506
Na-Churs/Alpine Solutions 421 Leader St *TF:* 800-622-4877 ■ *Web:* www.nachurs.com	Marion	OH	43302	740-382-5701	383-2615
Pace International LLC 1201 3rd Ave Suite 5450	Seattle	WA	98101	206-264-7599	436-5808
PBI/Gordon Corp 1217 W 12th St PO Box 014090 *TF:* 800-821-7925 ■ *Web:* www.pbigordon.com	Kansas City	MO	64101	816-421-4070	474-0462
Potash Corp 1101 Skokie Blvd *TF:* 800-645-2183 ■ *Web:* www.potashcorp.com	Northbrook	IL	60062	847-849-4200	849-4695
Potash Corp of Saskatchewan Inc 122 1st Ave S Suite 500 *NYSE:* POT ■ *TF:* 800-667-3930 ■ *Web:* www.potashcorp.com	Saskatoon	SK	S7K7G3	306-933-8500	652-2699
Pro-Serve Inc 400 E Brook Rd PO Box 161059 *TF:* 877-776-7375	Memphis	TN	38109	901-332-7052	346-7157
Rohm & Haas Co 100 Independence Mall W **Fax:* Hum Res ■ *Web:* www.rohmhaas.com	Philadelphia	PA	19106	215-592-3000	592-3377*
Safeguard Chemical Corp 411 Wales Ave *TF:* 800-536-3170 ■ *Web:* www.safeguardchemical.com	Bronx	NY	10454	718-585-3170	585-3657
Sara Lee Household & Body Care 707 Eagleview Blvd *TF:* 800-879-5494 ■ *Web:* www.saralee.com	Exton	PA	19341	610-321-1220	321-1440
SC Johnson & Son Inc 1525 Howe St *TF:* 800-494-4855 ■ *Web:* www.scjohnson.com	Racine	WI	53403	262-260-2154	260-2632
Scotts Miracle Gro Products Inc 14111 Scottslawn Rd *TF:* 888-270-3714 ■ *Web:* www.scotts.com/smg	Marysville	OH	43041	937-644-0011	644-7600
Scotts Miracle-Gro Co 14111 Scottslawn Rd *NYSE:* SMG ■ *TF Cust Svc:* 800-543-8873 ■ *Web:* www.scotts.com	Marysville	OH	43041	937-644-0011	644-7600
Share Corp 7821 N Faulkner Rd *TF:* 800-776-7192 ■ *Web:* www.sharecorp.com	Milwaukee	WI	53224	414-355-4000	355-0516
Southern States Chemical Co 1600 E President St *TF:* 888-337-8922 ■ *Web:* www.sschemical.com	Savannah	GA	31404	912-232-1101	232-1103
Spectrum Brands 601 Rayovac Dr **Fax Area Code:* 888 ■ *TF:* 800-341-0020 ■ *Web:* www.spectrumbrands.com	Madison	WI	53711	314-427-4886	677-4770*
Stoller USA 4001 W Sam Houston Pkwy N Suite 100 *TF:* 800-539-5283 ■ *Web:* www.stollerusa.com	Houston	TX	77043	713-461-1493	461-4467
Summit Chemical Co 235 S Kresson St *TF:* 800-227-8664 ■ *Web:* www.summitchemical.com	Baltimore	MD	21224	410-522-0661	522-0833
Sunniland Corp 1721 Hwy 1735 *TF:* 800-432-1130 ■ *Web:* www.sunniland.com	Sanford	FL	32773	407-322-2421	324-5784
Syngenta Corp 2200 Concord Pike PO Box 8353 *TF:* 800-759-4500 ■ *Web:* www2.syngenta.com	Wilmington	DE	19803	302-425-2000	425-2001
Syngenta Crop Protection Inc 410 Swing Rd PO Box 18300 **Fax:* Sales ■ *TF:* 800-334-9481 ■ *Web:* www2.syngenta.com	Greensboro	NC	27409	336-632-6000	632-7650*
Tender Corp 106 Burndy Rd *TF:* 800-258-4696 ■ *Web:* www.tendercorp.com	Littleton	NH	03561	603-444-5464	444-6735
Terra Nitrogen Co LP 600 4th St Terra Centre *Web:* www.terranitrogen.com	Sioux City	IA	51101	712-277-1340	277-7364
Trans-Resources Inc 200 W 57th St	New York	NY	10019	212-515-4100	515-4111
Valley Fertilizer & Chemical Co Inc 201 Valley Rd PO Box 816 *TF:* 800-571-3121 ■ *Web:* www.valleyfertilizer.com	Mount Jackson	VA	22842	540-477-3121	477-3123
Van Diest Supply Co 1434 220th St PO Box 610 *TF:* 800-779-2424 ■ *Web:* www.vdsc.com	Webster City	IA	50595	515-832-2366	832-2955
Woodstream Corp 69 N Locust St *TF:* 800-800-1819 ■ *Web:* www.woodstreamcorp.com	Lititz	PA	17543	717-626-2125	626-1912
Y-Tex Corp 1825 Big Horn Ave PO Box 1450 *TF:* 800-443-6401 ■ *Web:* www.y-tex.com	Cody	WY	82414	307-587-5515	527-6433

284 FESTIVALS - BOOK

Festival	City	State	Zip	Phone	Fax
Alabama Bound 2100 Pk Pl *Web:* www.alabamabound.org	Birmingham	AL	35203	205-226-3610	226-3743
Amelia Book Island Festival PO Box 824 *Web:* www.bookisland.org	Amelia Island	FL	32035	904-491-8176	
Arizona Book Festival 1242 N Central Ave *Web:* www.azbookfestival.org	Phoenix	AZ	85004	602-257-0335	257-0392
Baltimore Book Festival Baltimore Office of Promotion 7 E Redwood St Suite 500 *Web:* www.bop.org	Baltimore	MD	21202	410-752-8632	385-0361
Banff Mountain Book Festival The Banff Ctr PO Box 1020 Stn 38 *Web:* www.banffcentre.ca	Banff	AB	T1L1H5	403-762-6675	762-6277
Boston Globe Book Festival Public Affairs Dept PO Box 2378 *Web:* www.bostonglobe.com	Boston	MA	02107	617-929-2649	929-2606
Buckeye Book Fair 205 W Liberty St *Web:* www.buckeyebookfair.com	Wooster	OH	44691	330-262-3244	
Great Salt Lake Book Festival Utah Humanities Council 202 W 300 N *Web:* www.utahhumanities.org	Salt Lake City	UT	84103	801-359-9670	531-7869
Kentucky Book Fair PO Box 537 *Web:* www.kybookfair.com	Frankfort	KY	40602	502-564-8300	564-5773
Latino Book & Family Festival 2777 Jefferson St Suite 200 *Web:* www.latinofestivals.com	Carlsbad	CA	92008	760-434-4484	434-7476
Lee County Reading Festival 2050 Central Ave *Web:* www.lee-county.com	Fort Myers	FL	33901	239-479-4636	
Los Angeles Times Festival of Books Los Angeles Times 202 W 1st St *TF:* 800-528-4637 ■ *Web:* www.latimes.com/extras/festivalofbooks	Los Angeles	CA	90012	213-237-5000	237-2335

	City	State	Zip	Phone	Fax
Miami Book Fair International (MBFI) 401 NE Second Ave Suite 4102 *Web:* www.miamibookfair.com	Miami	FL	33132	305-237-3258	237-3978
Montana Festival of the Book University of Montana Ctr for the Book 311 Brantly Hall *Web:* www.bookfest-mt.org	Missoula	MT	59812	406-243-6022	243-4836
Much Ado About Books Jacksonville Public Library Foundation PO Box 40103 *Web:* www.muchadoaboutbooks.com	Jacksonville	FL	32203	904-630-1703	
National Book Festival Library of Congress 101 Independence Ave SE *TF:* 888-714-4696 ■ *Web:* www.loc.gov/bookfest	Washington	DC	20540	202-707-2777	707-9199
New York Center for Independent Publishing Small Press Ctr 20 W 44th St *Web:* www.nycip.org	New York	NY	10036	212-764-7021	840-2046
Northern Arizona Book Festival PO Box 1871 *Web:* www.nazbookfestival.org	Flagstaff	AZ	86002	928-380-8682	
NOVELLO Festival of Reading Public Library of Charlotte & Mecklenburg County 310 N Tryon St *Web:* www.plcmc.lib.nc.us/readers_club/features/feature.asp?id=52	Charlotte	NC	28202	704-416-0100	336-2002
Printers Row Book Fair Chicago Tribune 435 N Michigan Ave *Web:* www.chicagotribune.com	Chicago	IL	60611	312-527-8280	
South Carolina Book Festival PO Box 5287 *Web:* www.schumanities.org	Columbia	SC	29250	803-771-2477	771-2487
Southern Festival of Books Humanities Tennessee 306 Gay St Suite 306 *Web:* www.tn-humanities.org	Nashville	TN	37201	615-770-0006	321-4586
Southern Kentucky Book Fest Western Kentucky University Libraries & Museum Cravens Library Rm 106 *Web:* www.sokybookfest.org	Bowling Green	KY	42101	270-745-5016	745-6422
Texas Book Festival 610 Brazos St Suite 200 *Web:* www.texasbookfestival.org	Austin	TX	78701	512-477-4055	322-0722
Times Festival of Reading 490 1st Ave S 4th Fl St Petersburg Times Promotion Dept *TF:* 800-333-7505 ■ *Web:* www.festivalofreading.com	Saint Petersburg	FL	33701	727-445-4142	892-2992
Vancouver International Writers & Readers Festival 1398 Cartwright St *Web:* www.writersfest.bc.ca	Vancouver	BC	V6H3R8	604-681-6330	681-8400
Vegas Valley Book Festival Nevada Humanities Committee 4505 Maryland Pkwy *TF:* 800-382-5023 ■ *Web:* www.nevadahumanities.org	Las Vegas	NV	89154	702-895-1878	895-1877
Virginia Festival of the Book Virginia Foundation for the Humanities 145 Ednam Dr *Web:* www.vabook.org	Charlottesville	VA	22903	434-924-3296	296-4714

285 FESTIVALS - FILM

	City	State	Zip	Phone	Fax
AFI Fest American Film Institute 2021 N Western Ave *Web:* www.afifest.com	Los Angeles	CA	90027	323-856-7600	467-4578
Anchorage Film Festival 1410 Rudakof Cir *Web:* www.anchoragefilmfestival.com	Anchorage	AK	99508	907-338-3690	338-3857
Ann Arbor Film Festival 308 1/2 S State St #31 *Web:* www.aafilmfest.org	Ann Arbor	MI	48104	734-995-5356	995-5396
Arpa International Film Festival 2919 Maxwell St *Web:* www.affma.org	Los Angeles	CA	90027	323-663-1882	663-1882
Asian American International Film Festival 115 W 30th St Suite 708 *Web:* www.asiancinevision.org	New York	NY	10001	212-989-1422	727-3584
Atlanta Film Festival 535 Means St NW Suite C *Web:* www.atlantafilmfestival.com	Atlanta	GA	30318	404-352-4225	352-0173
Austin Film Festival 1145 W 5th St # 210 *TF:* 800-310-3378 ■ *Web:* www.austinfilmfestival.com	Austin	TX	78703	512-478-4795	478-6205
Beverly Hills Film Festival 9663 Santa Monica Blvd Suite 777 *Web:* www.beverlyhillsfilmfestival.com	Beverly Hills	CA	90210	310-779-1206	
Boston Film Festival 9B Hamilton Pl *Web:* www.bostonfilmfestival.org	Boston	MA	02108	617-523-8388	
Brooklyn International Film Festival 180 S 4th St Suite 2S *Web:* www.brooklynfilmfestival.org	Brooklyn	NY	11211	718-486-8181	599-5039
Chicago Indiefest Film Festival PO Box 148849 *Web:* www.indiefestchicago.com	Chicago	IL	60614	773-665-7600	665-7660
Chicago International Film Festival Cinema Chicago 30 E Adams St Suite 800 *Web:* www.chicagofilmfestival.com	Chicago	IL	60603	312-683-0121	683-0122
Cleveland International Film Festival 2510 Market Ave *Web:* www.clevelandfilm.org	Cleveland	OH	44133	216-623-3456	623-0103
DC Independent Film Festival 2950 Van Ness St NW *Web:* www.dciff.org	Washington	DC	20008	202-537-9493	686-8867
Denver International Film Festival 2601 Blake St *Web:* www.denverfilm.org	Denver	CO	80205	303-595-3456	595-0956
Film Fest New Haven PO Box 9644 *Web:* www.filmfest.org	New Haven	CT	06536	203-776-6789	776-4260
Fort Lauderdale International Film Festival 503 SE 6th St *Web:* www.fliff.com	Fort Lauderdale	FL	33301	954-760-9898	760-9099
Full Frame Documentary Film Festival 212 W Main St #104 *Web:* www.fullframefest.org	Durham	NC	27701	919-687-4100	687-4200
Green Mountain Film Festival 26 Main St *Web:* www.savoytheater.com	Montpelier	VT	05602	802-229-0598	229-2662
Heartland Film Festival 200 S Meridian St Suite 220 *Web:* www.heartlandfilmfestival.com	Indianapolis	IN	46225	317-464-9405	464-9409
High Falls Film Festival 45 E Ave Suite 400 *Web:* www.highfallsfilmfestival.com	Rochester	NY	14604	585-279-8330	232-4822
Hot Springs Documentary Film Festival 819 Central Ave *Web:* www.docufilminst.org	Hot Springs	AR	71901	501-321-4747	321-0211
Long Beach International Film Festival 2005 Palo Verde Suite 309 *Web:* www.longbeachfilmfestival.com	Long Beach	CA	90815	562-938-9687	938-9687
Los Angeles Film Festival 9911 W Pico Blvd, Film Independent *TF:* 866-345-6337 ■ *Web:* www.lafilmfest.com	Beverly Hills	CA	90211	310-432-1240	
Los Angeles International Short Film Festival 1610 Argyle Ave Suite 113 *Web:* www.lashortsfest.com	Hollywood	CA	90028	323-461-4400	
Malibu International Film Festival PO Box 4166 *Web:* www.malibufilmfestival.org	Venice	CA	90294	310-452-6688	
Maryland Film Festival 107 E Read St *Web:* www.mdfilmfest.com	Baltimore	MD	21202	410-752-8083	752-8273
Miami International Film Festival Miami Dade College 25 NE 2nd St Bldg 5 Rm 5501 *Web:* www.miamifilmfestival.com	Miami	FL	33132	305-237-3456	237-7344
Mill Valley Film Festival 38 Miller Ave Suite 6 *Web:* www.mvff.com	Mill Valley	CA	94941	415-383-5256	383-8606
Minneapolis/St Paul International Film Festival Minnesota Film Arts 309 Oak St SE *Web:* www.mnfilmarts.org	Minneapolis	MN	55414	612-331-7563	378-7750
Montreal World Film Festival 1432 Rue de Bleury *Web:* www.ffm-montreal.org	Montreal	QC	H3A2J1	514-848-3883	848-3886
Nashville Film Festival 161 Rains Ave *Web:* www.nashvillefilmfestival.org	Nashville	TN	37203	615-742-2500	742-1004
New Hampshire Film Expo 155 Fleet St *Web:* www.nhfilmexpo.com	Portsmouth	NH	03801	603-647-6439	
New Orleans Film Festival 843 Carondelet St Upper Suite 1 *Web:* www.neworleansfilmfest.com	New Orleans	LA	70130	504-309-6633	309-0923
New York Film Festival 70 Lincoln Ctr Plaza *Web:* www.filmlinc.com	New York	NY	10023	212-875-5638	875-5636
Newport International Film Festival PO Box 146 *Web:* www.newportfilmfestival.com	Newport	RI	02840	401-846-9100	846-6665
Olympia Film Festival 416 Washington St SE Suite 208 *Web:* www.olyfilm.org	Olympia	WA	98501	360-754-3675	943-9100
Outfest-Los Angeles Gay & Lesbian Film Festival 3470 Wilshire Blvd Suite 935 *Web:* www.outfest.org	Los Angeles	CA	90010	213-480-7088	480-7099
Philadelphia Film Festival 234 Market St 4th Fl **Fax Area Code:* 215 ■ *Web:* www.phillyfests.com	Philadelphia	PA	19106	267-765-9700	733-0668*
Phoenix Film Festival 2345 E Thomas Rd Suite 100 *Web:* www.phoenixfilmfestival.com	Phoenix	AZ	85016	602-955-6444	955-0966
Portland International Film Festival 1219 SW Pk Ave *Web:* www.nwfilm.org	Portland	OR	97205	503-221-1156	294-0874
Riverrun International Film Festival 870 W 4th St *Web:* www.riverrunfilm.com	Winston-Salem	NC	27101	336-724-1502	724-1112
Rochester International Film Festival PO Box 17746 *Web:* www.rochesterfilmfest.org	Rochester	NY	14617	585-234-7411	
Saint Louis International Film Festival 3547 Olive St *Web:* www.cinemastlouis.org	Saint Louis	MO	63103	314-289-4150	289-4159
San Diego Film Festival 10975 San Diego Mission Rd *Web:* www.sdff.org	San Diego	CA	92108	619-582-2368	286-8324
San Francisco International Asian American Film Festival 145 9th St Suite 350 *Web:* www.caamedia.org	San Francisco	CA	94103	415-863-0814	863-7428
San Francisco International Film Festival 39 Mesa St Suite 110 The Presidio *Web:* www.sfiff.org	San Francisco	CA	94129	415-561-5000	561-5099
San Jose Film Festival - CineQuest PO Box 720040 *Web:* www.cinequest.org	San Jose	CA	95172	408-995-5033	995-5713
Santa Barbara International Film Festival 1528 Chapala St Suite 203 *Web:* www.sbfilmfestival.org	Santa Barbara	CA	93101	805-963-0023	962-2524
Sarasota Film Festival 332 Cocoanut Ave *Web:* www.sarasotafilmfestival.com	Sarasota	FL	34236	941-364-9514	364-8411
Savannah Film Festival PO Box 3146 *Web:* www.scad.edu/filmfest	Savannah	GA	31402	912-525-5051	525-5052
Seattle International Film Festival 305 Harrison St *Web:* www.seattlefilm.com	Seattle	WA	98109	206-464-5830	264-7919

	City	State	Zip	Phone	Fax
Sidewalk Moving Picture Festival 2312 1st Ave N *Web:* www.sidewalkfest.com	Birmingham	AL	35203	205-324-0888	324-2488
Sonoma Valley Film Festival 103A E Napa St *Web:* www.sonomafilmfest.org	Sonoma	CA	95476	707-933-2600	933-2612
South by Southwest Film Festival 500 E Cesar Chavez St *Web:* www.sxsw.com	Austin	TX	78701	512-467-7979	451-0754
Sundance Film Festival 1895 Sidewinder Dr *Web:* www.sundance.org/festival	Park City	UT	84060	801-328-3456	575-5175
Tambay Film & Video Festival 16002 Saddle Creek Dr. *Web:* www.tambayfilmfest.com	Tampa	FL	33694	813-964-9781	
Telluride Film Festival 800 Jones St. *Web:* www.telluridefilmfestival.com	Berkeley	CA	94710	510-665-9494	665-9589
Telluride Indiefest PO Box 860 *Web:* www.tellurideindiefest.com	Telluride	CO	81435	970-708-1529	728-8128
Three Rivers Film Festival 477 Melwood Ave. *Web:* www.3rff.com	Pittsburgh	PA	15213	412-681-5449	681-5503
Toronto International Film Festival 2 Carlton St Suite 1600 *Web:* www.e.bell.ca	Toronto	ON	M5B1J3	416-967-7371	967-9477
Utah Short Film & Video Festival Utah Film & Video Ctr 20 SW Temple. *Web:* www.ufvc.org	Salt Lake City	UT	84101	801-534-1158	
Vermont International Film Festival 1 Main St Suite 307 *Web:* www.vtiff.org	Burlington	VT	05401	802-660-2600	860-9555
Worldfest Houston International Film Festival PO Box 56566 *TF:* 866-965-9955 ■ *Web:* www.worldfest.org	Houston	TX	77256	713-965-9955	965-9960

286 FIRE PROTECTION SYSTEMS

SEE ALSO Personal Protective Equipment & Clothing p. 2409; Safety Equipment - Mfr p. 2630; Security Products & Services p. 2649

	City	State	Zip	Phone	Fax
Autronics Corp 12701 Schabarum Ave *Web:* www.autronics.com	Irwindale	CA	91706	626-851-3100	960-8500
BRK Brands Inc 3901 Liberty St Rd. *TF:* 800-323-9005 ■ *Web:* www.firstalert.com	Aurora	IL	60504	630-851-7330	851-9015
Chemetron Fire Systems 4801 Southwick Dr 3rd Fl. *TF Cust Svc:* 800-878-5631 ■ *Web:* www.chemetron.com	Matteson	IL	60443	708-748-1503	748-2847
Fenwal Safety Systems 4200 Airport Dr NW. *Web:* www.fenwalsafety.com	Wilson	NC	27896	252-237-7004	246-7181
Fike Corp 704 SW 10th St *TF:* 877-342-3453 ■ *Web:* www.fike.com	Blue Springs	MO	64015	816-229-3405	228-9277
Fire & Life Safety America 3017 Vernon Rd PO Box 26747 *TF:* 800-252-5069 ■ *Web:* www.flsamerica.com	Richmond	VA	23228	804-222-1381	222-4393
Fire Systems West Inc 206 Frontage Rd N Suite C. *Web:* www.firesystemswest.com	Pacific	WA	98047	253-833-1248	735-0113
Firecom Inc 39-27 59th St. *TF:* 800-347-3266 ■ *Web:* www.firecominc.com	Woodside	NY	11377	718-899-6100	899-1932
First Alert Inc 3901 Liberty St Rd *TF:* 800-323-9005 ■ *Web:* www.firstalert.com	Aurora	IL	60504	630-851-7330	851-7538
Gamewell FCI 12 Clintonville Rd. *Web:* www.gamewell.com	Northford	CT	06472	203-484-7161	484-7118
General Monitors Inc 26776 Simpatica Cir *TF:* 866-686-0741 ■ *Web:* www.generalmonitors.com	Lake Forest	CA	92630	949-581-4464	581-1151
Harrington Signal Co 2519 4th Ave *TF:* 800-577-5758 ■ *Web:* www.harringtonsignal.com	Moline	IL	61265	309-762-0731	762-8215
Honeywell Fire Solutions 1 Fire-Lite Pl *TF:* 800-289-3473 ■ *Web:* www.firelite.com	Northford	CT	06472	203-484-7161	484-7118
Kidde Aerospace 4200 Airport Dr NW **Fax:* Hum Res ■ *Web:* www.kiddeaerospace.com	Wilson	NC	27896	252-237-7004	246-7184*
Meggitt Safety Systems Inc 1915 Voyager Ave. *Web:* www.meggitt.com	Simi Valley	CA	93063	805-584-4100	578-3400
Potter Electric Signal Co Inc 5757 Phantom Dr Suite 125 *TF:* 800-325-3936 ■ *Web:* www.pottersignal.com	Hazelwood	MO	63042	314-878-4321	595-6999
Siemens Bldg Technologies Inc Fire Safety Div 8 Fernwood Rd *TF:* 800-222-0108 ■ *Web:* www.sbt.siemens.com/fis	Florham Park	NJ	07932	973-593-2600	593-6670
Silent Knight 7550 Meridian Cir Suite 100 *TF:* 800-328-0103 ■ *Web:* www.silentknight.com	Maple Grove	MN	55369	763-493-6400	493-6475
SimplexGrinnell Ltd 50 Technology Dr. **Fax:* Hum Res ■ *TF:* 800-746-7539 ■ *Web:* www.simplexgrinnell.com	Westminster	MA	01441	978-731-2500	731-7867*
Smeal Fire Apparatus Co 610 W 4th St PO Box 8. *Web:* www.smeal.com	Snyder	NE	68664	402-568-2224	568-2346
Task Force Tips Inc 3701 Innovation Way *TF:* 800-348-2686 ■ *Web:* www.tft.com	Valparaiso	IN	46383	219-462-6161	464-7155
Viking Corp 210 N Industrial Pk Dr *TF:* 800-968-9501 ■ *Web:* www.vikingcorp.com	Hastings	MI	49058	269-945-9501	945-9599

287 FIREARMS & AMMUNITION (NON-MILITARY)

SEE ALSO Sporting Goods p. 2664; Weapons & Ordnance (Military) p. 2773

	City	State	Zip	Phone	Fax
Advanced Interactive Systems Inc (AIS) 665 Andover Pk W *TF:* 800-441-4487 ■ *Web:* www.ais-sim.com	Seattle	WA	98188	206-575-9797	575-8565
American Derringer Corp 127 N Lacy Dr *Web:* www.amderringer.com	Waco	TX	76705	254-799-9111	799-7935
Beeman Precision Airguns 5454 Argosy Dr *TF:* 800-227-2744 ■ *Web:* www.beeman.com	Huntington Beach	CA	92649	714-890-4800	890-4808
Beretta USA Corp 17601 Beretta Dr *TF:* 800-237-3882 ■ *Web:* www.berettausa.com	Accokeek	MD	20607	301-283-2191	283-0435
Colt's Mfg Co LLC PO Box 1868 *TF:* 800-962-2658 ■ *Web:* www.coltsmfg.com	Hartford	CT	06144	860-236-6311	244-1442
Connecticut Valley Arms (CVA) 1685 Boggs Rd Suite 300. *Web:* www.cva.com	Duluth	GA	30096	770-449-4687	242-8546
Crosman Corp 7629 Rt 5 & 20. *TF:* 800-724-7486 ■ *Web:* www.crosman.com	Bloomfield	NY	14469	585-657-6161	657-5405
Defense Technology/Federal Laboratories 1855 S Loop PO Box 248. *TF:* 877-248-3835 ■ *Web:* www.defense-technology.com	Caspar	WY	82601	307-235-2136	473-2713
Eldorado Cartridge Corp 12801 US Hwy 95 S. *Web:* www.pmcammo.com	Boulder City	NV	89005	702-294-0025	294-0121
Federal Cartridge Co 900 Ehlen Dr **Fax:* Hum Res ■ *TF:* 800-831-0850 ■ *Web:* www.federalpremium.com	Anoka	MN	55303	763-323-2300	323-2506*
Freedom Arms Inc 314 Wyoming 239 *TF:* 800-833-4432 ■ *Web:* www.freedomarms.com	Freedom	WY	83120	307-883-2468	883-2005
Galion LLC 515 N E St PO Box 447 *Web:* www.galionllc.com	Galion	OH	44833	419-468-5214	468-1661
Glock Inc 6000 Highlands Pkwy. *Web:* www.glock.com	Smyrna	GA	30082	770-432-1202	433-8719
Green Mountain Rifle Barrel Co 153 W Main St *Web:* www.gmriflebarrel.com	Conway	NH	03818	603-447-1095	447-1099
Gun Parts Corp 226 Williams Ln. **Fax Area Code:* 877 ■ *TF:* 866-686-7424 ■ *Web:* www.gunpartscorp.com	Kingston	NY	12401	845-679-4867	486-7278*
H & R 1871 60 Industrial Rowe. *TF:* 866-776-9292 ■ *Web:* www.hr1871.com	Gardner	MA	01440	978-632-9393	632-2300
Heckler & Koch Inc 5675 Transport Blvd. *Web:* www.hk-usa.com	Columbus	GA	31907	706-568-1906	568-9151
Heritage Mfg Inc 4600 NW 135th St *Web:* www.heritagemfg.com	Opa Locka	FL	33054	305-685-5966	687-6721
Hornady Mfg Co 3625 W Old Potash Hwy. *TF:* 800-338-3220 ■ *Web:* www.hornady.com	Grand Island	NE	68803	308-382-1390	382-5761
Knight Rifles 21852 Hwy J46 *Web:* www.knightrifles.com	Centerville	IA	52544	641-856-2626	856-2628
Lyman Products Corp 475 Smith St. *TF:* 800-225-9626 ■ *Web:* www.lymanproducts.com	Middletown	CT	06457	860-632-2020	632-1699
Marksman Products Inc 5482 Argosy Dr *TF:* 800-822-8005 ■ *Web:* www.marksman.com	Huntington Beach	CA	92649	714-898-7535	891-0782
Marlin Firearms Co PO Box 1871 *TF Cust Svc:* 800-544-8892 ■ *Web:* www.marlinfirearms.com	Madison	NC	27025	203-239-5621	234-7991
Meggitt Defense Systems Caswell (MDSC) 2540 2nd St NE	Minneapolis	MN	55418	612-379-2000	379-2367
OF Mossberg & Sons Inc 7 Grasso Ave. **Fax:* Mktg ■ *TF:* 800-363-3555 ■ *Web:* www.mossberg.com	North Haven	CT	06473	203-230-5300	230-5420*
Olin Corp Winchester Div 427 N Shamrock St. *TF:* 800-356-2666 ■ *Web:* www.winchester.com	East Alton	IL	62024	618-258-2000	258-3084
Remington Arms Co Inc 870 Remington Dr PO Box 700. *TF:* 800-243-9700 ■ *Web:* www.remington.com	Madison	NC	27025	336-548-8700	548-7801
Savage Arms Inc 100 Springdale Rd. *TF:* 800-370-0712 ■ *Web:* www.savagearms.com	Westfield	MA	01085	413-568-7001	562-7764
SIG SAUER Inc 18 Industrial Dr *TF:* 800-325-3693 ■ *Web:* www.sigsauer.com	Exeter	NH	03833	603-772-2302	772-9082
Smith & Wesson Corp 2100 Roosevelt Ave *TF Cust Svc:* 800-331-0852 ■ *Web:* www.smith-wesson.com	Springfield	MA	01104	413-781-8300	747-3317
Smith & Wesson Holding Corp 2100 Roosevelt Ave *NASDAQ: SWHC* ■ *TF:* 800-372-6454 ■ *Web:* www.smith-wesson.com	Springfield	MA	01104	413-781-8300	747-3317
Springfield Armory 420 W Main St. *TF:* 800-680-6866 ■ *Web:* www.springfield-armory.com	Geneseo	IL	61254	309-944-5631	944-3676
Taurus International Mfg Inc 16175 NW 49th Ave *Web:* www.taurususa.com	Miami	FL	33014	305-624-1115	624-1126
Thompson Center Arms Co Inc 400 N Main St PO Box 5002. *Web:* www.tcarms.com	Rochester	NH	03866	603-332-2333	332-5133
Weatherby Inc 1605 Commerce Way *Web:* www.weatherby.com	Paso Robles	CA	93446	805-227-2600	237-0427
Williams Gun Sight Co 7389 Lapeer Rd. *TF:* 800-530-9028 ■ *Web:* www.williamsgunsight.com	Davison	MI	48423	810-653-2131	658-2140

288 FISHING - COMMERCIAL

	City	State	Zip	Phone	Fax
American Seafoods Holdings LLC 2025 1st Ave Suite 900. *TF:* 800-275-2019 ■ *Web:* www.americanseafoods.com	Seattle	WA	98121	206-374-1515	374-1516
Arctic Storm Management Group LLC 2727 Alaskan Way Pier 69 *TF:* 800-929-0908 ■ *Web:* www.arcticstorm.com/index.html	Seattle	WA	98121	206-547-6557	547-3165
Blue North Fisheries Inc 2930 Westlake Ave N Suite 300 *TF:* 877-878-3263 ■ *Web:* www.bluenorthfisheries.com	Seattle	WA	98109	206-352-9252	352-9380
Bon Secour Fisheries Inc 17449 County Rd 49 S PO Box 60 *TF:* 800-633-6854 ■ *Web:* www.bonsecourfisheries.com	Bon Secour	AL	36511	251-949-7411	949-6478
Canadian Fishing Co Foot of Gore Ave *TF:* 888-526-2929 ■ *Web:* www.canfisco.com	Vancouver	BC	V6A2Y7	604-681-0211	681-3277
JH Miles & Co Inc 902 S Hampton Ave	Norfolk	VA	23510	757-622-9264	622-9261
Little Bay Lobster Co 158 Shattuck Way *TF:* 800-220-8484 ■ *Web:* www.littlebaylobster.com	Newington	NH	03801	603-431-3170	431-3496

				Phone	Fax
Lund's Fisheries Inc 997 Ocean Dr PO Box 830 *Web:* www.lundsfish.com	Cape May	NJ	08204	609-884-7600	884-0664
North Pacific Corp 5612 Lake Washington Blvd Suite 102 *Web:* www.npc-usa.com	Kirkland	WA	98033	425-822-1001	822-1004
Nova Fisheries 2532 Yale Ave E *TF:* 888-458-6682 ■ *Web:* www.novafish.com	Seattle	WA	98102	206-781-2000	781-9011
Ocean Beauty Seafoods Inc 1100 W Ewing St *TF:* 800-877-0185 ■ *Web:* www.oceanbeauty.com	Seattle	WA	98119	206-285-6800	285-9190
Point Judith Fishermen's Co 75 State St	Narragansett	RI	02882	401-782-1500	782-1599
Raffield Fisheries Inc 1624 Grouper Ave *Web:* www.raffieldfisheries.com	Port Saint Joe	FL	32456	850-229-8229	229-8782
Sahlman Seafoods Inc 1601 Sahlman Dr PO Box 5009 *Web:* www.sahlmanseafood.com	Tampa	FL	33605	813-248-5726	247-5787
Trident Seafood Corp 5303 Shilshole Ave NW *TF:* 800-426-5490 ■ *Web:* www.tridentseafoods.com	Seattle	WA	98107	206-783-3818	782-7195
Wanchese Fish Co 2000 Northgate Commerce Pkwy *Web:* www.wanchese.com	Suffolk	VA	23435	757-673-4500	673-4550

289 FIXTURES - OFFICE & STORE

SEE ALSO Commercial & Industrial Furniture p. 1894

				Phone	Fax
Able Steel Equipment Co Inc 50-02 23rd St *Web:* www.ablesteelequipment.com	Long Island City	NY	11101	718-361-9240	937-5742
Advanced Equipment Corp 2401 W Commonwealth Ave *Web:* www.advancedequipment.com	Fullerton	CA	92833	714-635-5350	525-6083
AGI Schutz Merchandising Co 376 Pine St Ext *TF:* 800-662-2150	Forest City	NC	28043	828-245-9871	248-4990
American Sanitary Partition Corp 300 Enterprise St PO Box 99 *Web:* www.am-sanitary-partition.com	Ocoee	FL	34761	407-656-0611	656-8189
Ampco Products Inc 11400 NW 36th Ave *Web:* www.ampco.com	Miami	FL	33167	305-821-5700	557-0764
Angola Wire Products Inc 803 Wohlert St *TF:* 800-800-7225 ■ *Web:* www.angolawire.com	Angola	IN	46703	260-665-9447	665-6182
Architectural Bronze Aluminum Corp 655 Deerfield Rd Suite 100 *TF:* 800-339-6581 ■ *Web:* www.architecturalbronze.com	Deerfield	IL	60015	847-266-7300	266-7301
Aspects Inc 9441 Opal Ave	Mentone	CA	92359	909-794-7722	794-6996
Bel-Mar Wire Products Inc 2343 N Damen Ave *Web:* www.belmarwire.net	Chicago	IL	60647	773-342-3800	342-0038
Benner-Nawman Inc 3450 Sabin Brown Rd *TF:* 800-992-3833 ■ *Web:* www.bnproducts.com	Wickenburg	AZ	85390	928-684-2813	684-7041
Bennett Mfg Co Inc 13315 Railroad St *TF:* 800-345-2142 ■ *Web:* www.bennettmfg.com	Alden	NY	14004	716-937-9161	937-3137
Best-Rite Mfg 2885 Lorraine Ave PO Box D *TF:* 800-749-2258 ■ *Web:* www.moorecoinc.com	Temple	TX	76501	800-749-2258	697-6258
Bob-Leon Plastics Inc 5151 Franklin Blvd *Web:* www.bob-leon.com	Sacramento	CA	95820	916-452-4063	452-3759
BodenAlexander 5335 NE 109th Ave *TF:* 800-733-1923 ■ *Web:* www.boden.com	Portland	OR	97220	503-252-4728	252-4932
Borroughs Corp 3002 N Burdick St *TF:* 800-748-0227 ■ *Web:* www.borroughs.com	Kalamazoo	MI	49004	269-342-0161	342-4161
Boston Retail Products 400 Riverside Ave *TF:* 800-225-1633 ■ *Web:* www.bostonretail.com	Medford	MA	02155	781-395-7417	391-5766
Cal-Partitions Inc 23814 President Ave *Web:* www.calpartitions.com	Harbor City	CA	90710	310-539-1911	539-5816
Cano Corp 225 Industrial Rd *TF:* 800-237-1358 ■ *Web:* www.canocorp.com	Fitchburg	MA	01420	978-342-0953	342-5082
Carolina Cabinet Co 3363 Highway 301 N *Web:* www.carolinacabinet.net	Wilson	NC	27893	252-291-5181	291-8039
Ceemco Inc 5313 Robert Ave *Web:* www.ceemco.com	Cincinnati	OH	45248	513-922-0088	922-0719
Churchill Cabinet Co 4616 W 19th St *TF Sales:* 800-379-9776 ■ *Web:* www.chicago-gaming.com	Cicero	IL	60804	708-780-0070	780-9762
ClosetMaid Corp 650 SW 27th Ave *TF Cust Svc:* 800-874-0008 ■ *Web:* www.closetmaid.com	Ocala	FL	34471	352-401-6000	867-8583
Consolidated Storage Cos 225 Main St **Fax Area Code:* 888 ■ *TF Cust Svc:* 800-323-0801 ■ *Web:* www.equipto.com	Tatamy	PA	18085	610-253-2775	859-2121*
Cres-Cor 5925 Heisley Rd *TF:* 877-273-7267 ■ *Web:* www.crescor.com	Mentor	OH	44060	440-350-1100	350-7267
Crown Metal Mfg Co 765 S SR 83 *Web:* www.crownmetal.com	Elmhurst	IL	60126	630-279-9800	279-9807
Custom Fold Doors Inc 110 W Ash Ave **Fax Area Code:* 818 ■ *TF:* 800-913-3573 ■ *Web:* www.customfold.net	Burbank	CA	91502	323-849-3225	846-0744*
Datum Filing Systems Inc 89 Church Rd *TF:* 800-828-8018 ■ *Web:* www.datumfiling.com	Emigsville	PA	17318	717-764-6350	764-6656
DeBourgh Mfg Co 27505 Otero Ave PO Box 981 *TF:* 800-328-8829 ■ *Web:* www.debourgh.com	La Junta	CO	81050	719-384-8161	384-8161
Design Workshops 486 Lesser St *Web:* www.design-workshops.com	Oakland	CA	94601	510-434-0727	434-0727
Dixie Store Fixtures & Sales Co Inc 2425 1st Ave N *TF:* 800-323-4943 ■ *Web:* www.dixiestorefixtures.com	Birmingham	AL	35203	205-322-2442	322-2445
Durham Mfg Co Inc 201 Main St PO Box 230 *TF:* 800-243-3774 ■ *Web:* www.durhammfg.com	Durham	CT	06422	860-349-3427	
Econoco Corp 300 Karin Ln **Fax Area Code:* 800 ■ *TF:* 800-645-7032 ■ *Web:* www.econoco.com	Hicksville	NY	11801	516-935-7700	505-8300*
Edsal Mfg Co Inc 4400 S Packers Ave *Web:* www.edsal.com	Chicago	IL	60609	773-254-0600	
Electrorack Inc 1443 S Sunkist St *TF:* 800-433-6745 ■ *Web:* www.electrorack.com	Anaheim	CA	92806	714-776-5420	776-9683
Environments Inc 13600 County Rd 62 *Web:* www.environmentsinc.com	Minnetonka	MN	55345	952-933-9981	933-6048
EQUIPTO 225 Main St **Fax Area Code:* 888 ■ *TF:* 800-323-0801 ■ *Web:* www.equipto.com	Tatamy	PA	18085	610-253-2775	859-2121*
Eugene Welding Co 2420 Wills St *TF:* 800-959-0857 ■ *Web:* www.ewco.net	Marysville	MI	48040	810-364-7421	364-4347
Ex-Cell Metal Products Inc 11240 Melrose St *TF:* 800-392-3557 ■ *Web:* www.ex-cell.com	Franklin Park	IL	60131	847-451-0451	451-0458
Eyelematic Mfg Co Inc 1 Seemar Rd *Web:* www.eyelematic.com	Watertown	CT	06795	860-274-6791	274-8464
Farmington Displays Inc 21 Hyde Rd *Web:* www.fdi-group.com	Farmington	CT	06032	860-677-2497	677-1418
Ferrante Mfg Co 6626 Gratiot Ave *Web:* www.ferrantemfg.com	Detroit	MI	48207	313-571-1111	571-1111
Fetzers' Inc 6223 W Double Eagle Cir *Web:* www.fetzersinc.com	Salt Lake City	UT	84118	801-484-6103	484-6122
Fixtures International Inc 501 Yale St PO Box 7774 *TF:* 800-444-1253 ■ *Web:* www.fixturesintl.com	Houston	TX	77007	713-869-3228	869-0970
Frazier Industrial Co 91 Fairview Ave *Web:* www.frazier.com	Long Valley	NJ	07853	908-876-3001	876-3615
General Partitions Mfg Corp 1702 Peninsula Dr PO Box 8370 *Web:* www.genpartitions.com	Erie	PA	16505	814-833-1154	838-3473
Giannelli Cabinets 19443 Londelius St	Northridge	CA	91324	818-882-9787	
Giffin Interior & Fixture Inc 500 Scotti Dr	Bridgeville	PA	15017	412-221-1166	221-3745
Goebel Fixture Co 528 Dale St *TF:* 800-727-4646 ■ *Web:* www.gf.com	Hutchinson	MN	55350	320-587-2112	587-2378
Hamilton Fixture 3550 Symmes Rd *TF:* 800-889-2165 ■ *Web:* www.hamiltonfixture.com	Hamilton	OH	45015	513-874-2016	870-8741
Hamilton Sorter Co Inc 3158 Production Dr **Fax Area Code:* 800 ■ *TF:* 800-503-9966 ■ *Web:* www.hamiltonsorter.com	Fairfield	OH	45014	513-870-4400	503-9968*
Handy Store Fixtures Inc 337 Sherman Ave *TF:* 800-631-4280 ■ *Web:* www.handysf.com	Newark	NJ	07114	973-242-1600	623-5058
Harbor Industries Inc 14130 172nd Ave *TF:* 800-968-6993 ■ *Web:* www.harbor-ind.com	Grand Haven	MI	49417	616-842-5330	842-1385
HMC Industries Inc 21020 63rd Ave N **Fax Area Code:* 206 ■ *Web:* www.hmcindinc.com	Lynnwood	WA	98036	425-778-3144	624-4434*
Holcomb & Hoke Mfg Co Inc 1545 Van Buren St *Web:* www.foldoor.com	Indianapolis	IN	46203	317-784-2448	781-9164
Hoosier Co 5421 W 86th St PO Box 681064 *TF:* 800-521-4184 ■ *Web:* www.hoosierco.com	Indianapolis	IN	46268	317-872-8125	872-7183
Hufcor Inc 2101 Kennedy Rd *TF:* 800-356-6968 ■ *Web:* www.hufcor.com	Janesville	WI	53545	608-756-1241	756-1246
Hurco Design & Mfg 200 W 33rd St *TF:* 877-859-6840 ■ *Web:* www.hurcoind.com	Ogden	UT	84401	801-394-9471	394-8218
IDX Baltimore Inc 1710 Midway Rd *TF:* 800-638-9667	Odenton	MD	21113	410-551-3600	551-9076
IDX Seattle 1301 N Levee Rd *Web:* www.idxcorporation.com	Puyallup	WA	98371	253-445-9000	445-8754
Imperial Counters Inc 725 Spiral Blvd *Web:* www.imperialcounters.com	Hastings	MN	55033	651-437-3903	438-3855
Inland Showcase & Fixture Co Inc 1473 N Thesta St	Fresno	CA	93703	559-237-4158	237-7238
InterMetro Industries Corp 651 N Washington St **Fax:* Hum Res ■ *TF Cust Svc:* 800-992-1776 ■ *Web:* www.metro.com	Wilkes-Barre	PA	18705	570-825-2741	824-7520*
International Visual Corp (IVC) 4765 Des Grandes Prairies *TF:* 866-643-0570 ■ *Web:* www.ivcweb.com	Montreal	QC	H1R1A5	514-643-0570	643-4867
Jaken Co Inc 6842 Walker St *Web:* www.jaken.com	La Palma	CA	90623	714-522-1700	522-1788
Jarke Corp - Div of Leggett & Platt 750 Pinecrest Dr *TF:* 800-722-5255 ■ *Web:* www.jarke.com	Prospect Heights	IL	60070	847-541-6500	325-1608
Jesco-Wipco Industries Inc 950 Anderson Rd PO Box 388 *TF:* 888-463-1246 ■ *Web:* www.jescoonline.com	Litchfield	MI	49252	517-542-2903	542-2501
JL Industries Inc 4450 W 78th St Cir *TF:* 800-554-6077 ■ *Web:* www.jlindustries.com	Bloomington	MN	55435	952-835-6850	835-2218
John Boos & Co 315 S 1st St PO Box 609 *Web:* www.johnboos.com	Effingham	IL	62401	217-347-7701	347-7705
JR Jones Fixture Co 3216 Winnetka Ave N	Minneapolis	MN	55427	763-544-4239	544-3106
Kardex Systems Inc 114 Westview Ave PO Box 171 **Fax:* Mktg ■ *TF:* 800-234-3654 ■ *Web:* www.kardex.com	Marietta	OH	45750	740-374-9300	374-9953*
Karges Furniture Co Inc 1501 W Maryland St *TF:* 800-252-7437 ■ *Web:* www.karges.com	Evansville	IN	47710	812-425-2291	425-4016
Kawneer Co Inc 555 Guthridge Ct *Web:* www.kawneer.com	Norcross	GA	30092	770-449-5555	734-1560
Kay Co Inc The 509 W Barner St	Frankfort	IN	46041	765-659-3388	659-2956
Kent Corp 4446 Pinson Valley Pkwy *TF:* 800-252-5368 ■ *Web:* www.kentcorp.com	Birmingham	AL	35215	205-853-3420	856-3622
Killion Industries Inc 1380 Poinsettia Ave *TF:* 800-421-5352 ■ *Web:* www.killionindustries.com	Vista	CA	92083	760-727-5102	727-5108
Knickerbocker Partition Corp 193 Hanse Ave PO Box 3035 *Web:* www.knickerbockerpartition.com	Freeport	NY	11520	516-546-0550	546-0549
Kwik-Wall Co 1010 E Edwards St *TF:* 800-280-5945 ■ *Web:* www.kwik-wall.com	Springfield	IL	62703	217-522-5553	522-1170
LA Darling Co 1401 Hwy 49B *TF:* 800-643-3499 ■ *Web:* www.ladarling.com	Paragould	AR	72450	870-239-9564	239-6427
Lista International Corp 106 Lowland St *TF Cust Svc:* 800-722-3020 ■ *Web:* www.listaintl.com	Holliston	MA	01746	508-429-1350	429-0711
Lodi Metal Tech 37555 Sycamore St	Newark	CA	94560	510-795-1602	794-6156*
Lozier Corp 6336 John J Pershing Dr **Fax:* Cust Svc ■ *TF:* 800-228-9882 ■ *Web:* www.lozier.com	Omaha	NE	68110	402-457-8000	457-8297*

Phone | Fax

Lyon Work Space Products 420 N Main St .... Montgomery IL 60538 630-892-8941 892-8966
TF: 800-433-8488 ■ *Web:* www.lyonworkspace.com
M.E.G. LLC 502 S Green St PO Box 240 .... Cambridge City IN 47327 765-478-3141 478-4439
TF Cust Svc: 800-645-3315 ■ *Web:* www.megfixtures.com
Madix Store Fixtures 500 Airport Rd .... Terrell TX 75160 214-515-5400 563-0792*
**Fax Area Code:* 972 ■ *TF Cust Svc:* 800-776-2349 ■ *Web:* www.madixinc.com
Metpar Corp 95 State St .... Westbury NY 11590 516-333-2600 333-2618
TF: 888-638-7271 ■ *Web:* www.metpar.com
MII Inc Lundia Div 600 Capitol Way .... Jacksonville IL 62650 217-243-8585 479-8191
TF: 800-726-9663 ■ *Web:* www.lundiausa.com
MII Inc Myers Div 2100 W 5th St Rd .... Lincoln IL 62656 217-735-1241 735-6645
Miller/Zell Inc 4715 Frederick Dr SW .... Atlanta GA 30336 404-691-7400 699-2189
Web: www.millerzell.com
Millrock Div Modular Brand Group LLC
405 W St .... West Bridgewater MA 02379 508-584-0084 687-7700*
**Fax Area Code:* 617 ■ *TF:* 800-645-7625 ■ *Web:* www.millrock.com
Modern Metals Industries Inc PO Box 888 .... El Segundo CA 90245 310-516-0611 516-0464
TF: 800-437-6633
Modern Woodcrafts LLC
72 NW Dr Farmington Industrial Pk .... Plainville CT 06062 860-677-7371 676-8381
Web: www.modernwoodcrafts.com
Modernfold Inc 215 W New Rd .... Greenfield IN 46140 317-468-6700 468-6760
TF: 800-869-9685 ■ *Web:* www.modernfold.com
Modular Systems Inc 169 Pk St .... Fruitport MI 49415 231-865-3167 865-6101
TF: 877-847-5989 ■ *Web:* www.mod-eez.com
Monarch Industries Inc 99 Main St .... Warren RI 02885 401-247-5200 247-5601*
**Fax:* Sales ■ *TF:* 800-669-9663 ■ *Web:* www.monarchinc.com
National Partitions & Interiors Inc
10300 Goldenfern Ln .... Knoxville TN 37931 800-999-7266 362-5688*
**Fax Area Code:* 305 ■ *TF:* 866-528-4616 ■ *Web:* www.n-p.com
Northway Industries Inc
434 Paxtonville Rd PO Box 277 .... Middleburg PA 17842 570-837-1564 837-1575
Web: www.northwayind.com
Northwestern Inc 15054 Oxnard St .... Van Nuys CA 91411 818-786-1581 786-5063
Oak & More Ltd 4949 SE 25th Ave .... Portland OR 97202 503-245-4522 245-4503
Osvold Co 2340 Lexington Ave N .... St.Paul MN 55113 651-415-9995 415-9996
Web: www.s225953489.onlinehome.us
Pacific Fixture Co Inc
12860 San Fernando Rd Unit B .... Sylmar CA 91342 818-362-2130 367-8968
TF: 800-272-2349 ■ *Web:* www.pacificfixture.com
Packard Industries Inc 1515 US 31 N .... Niles MI 49120 269-684-2550 684-2422
TF: 800-253-0866 ■ *Web:* www.packardindustries.com
Pan-Osten Co 6944 Louisville Rd .... Bowling Green KY 42101 270-783-3900 783-3911
TF: 800-472-6678
Panelfold Inc 10700 NW 36th Ave .... Miami FL 33167 305-688-3501 688-0185
Web: www.panelfold.com
Pentwater Wire Products Inc (PWP)
474 Carol St PO Box 947 .... Pentwater MI 49449 231-869-6911 869-4020
TF: 877-869-6911 ■ *Web:* www.pentwaterwire.com
Peterson Mfg Co 700 W 143rd .... Plainfield IL 60544 815-436-9201 436-2863
TF: 800-547-8995 ■ *Web:* www.peterson-mfg.com
Plasticrest Products Inc 4519 W Harrison St .... Chicago IL 60624 773-826-2163 826-4227
TF: 800-828-2163
Principle Fixture & Millwork
105 Prospect Way .... Osceola WI 54020 715-294-1400 294-1456
Racks Inc PO Box 530840 .... San Diego CA 92153 619-661-0987
TF: 877-920-7225 ■ *Web:* www.racksinc.com
Rapid Rack Industries Inc
14421 Bonelli St .... City of Industry CA 91746 626-333-7225 333-5265
TF: 800-736-7225 ■ *Web:* www.rapidrack.com
RC Smith Co 14200 Southcross Dr W .... Burnsville MN 55306 952-854-0711 854-8160
TF: 800-747-7648 ■ *Web:* www.rcsmith.com
Reeve Store Equipment Co
9131 Bermudez St PO Box 276 .... Pico Rivera CA 90660 562-949-2535 949-3862
TF: 800-927-3383 ■ *Web:* www.reeveco.com
Republic Storage Systems LLC
1038 Belden Ave NE .... Canton OH 44705 330-438-5800 454-7772
TF Sales: 800-477-1255 ■ *Web:* www.republicstorage.com
Ridg-U-Rak Inc 120 S Lake St PO Box 150 .... North East PA 16428 814-725-8751 725-5659
TF: 866-479-7225 ■ *Web:* www.ridgurak.com
Russ Bassett Co 8189 Byron Rd .... Whittier CA 90606 562-945-2445 698-8972
TF: 800-350-2445 ■ *Web:* www.russbassett.com
Salsbury Industries Inc 1010 E 62nd St .... Los Angeles CA 90001 323-846-6700 846-6800
TF: 800-624-5299 ■ *Web:* www.mailboxes.com
Sandusky Cabinets Inc
16125 Widmere Rd PO Box 517 .... Arvin CA 93203 661-854-5551 854-2003
TF Cust Svc: 800-336-0674 ■ *Web:* www.sanduskycabinets.com
Schulte Corp 12115 Ellington Ct .... Cincinnati OH 45249 513-489-9300 277-3701
TF: 800-669-3225 ■ *Web:* www.schultestorage.com
Semasys Inc 702 Ashland St .... Houston TX 77007 713-869-8331 869-5077
TF Cust Svc: 800-231-1425 ■ *Web:* www.semasys.com
Showbest Fixture Corp 4112 Sarellen Rd .... Richmond VA 23231 804-222-5535 222-7220
Web: www.showbest.com
Southern Imperial Inc 1400 Eddy Ave .... Rockford IL 61103 815-877-7041
TF Cust Svc: 800-747-4665 ■ *Web:* www.southernimperial.com
Southern Metal Industries Inc
8767 Alabama Hwy PO Box 219 .... Ringgold GA 30736 706-935-4486 935-6854
TF: 800-241-5246 ■ *Web:* www.southernmetal.com
SpaceGuard Products Inc 711 S Commerce Dr .... Seymour IN 47274 812-523-3044 428-5758*
**Fax Area Code:* 800 ■ *TF:* 800-841-0680 ■ *Web:* www.spaceguardproducts.com
Spacesaver Corp 1450 Janesville Ave .... Fort Atkinson WI 53538 920-563-6362 563-2702
TF: 800-492-3434 ■ *Web:* www.spacesaver.com
Sparks Custom Retail LLC
2828 Charter Rd .... Philadelphia PA 19154 215-602-8056 676-8020
TF: 800-925-7727 ■ *Web:* www.sparksretail.com
Sparks Marketing Group Inc
2828 Charter Rd .... Philadelphia PA 19154 215-676-6900
TF: 800-925-7727 ■ *Web:* www.sparksonline.com
Spectrum Industries Inc 925 1st Ave .... Chippewa Falls WI 54729 715-723-6750 335-0473*
**Fax Area Code:* 800 ■ *TF:* 800-235-1262 ■ *Web:* www.spectrumfurniture.com
SPG International 11230 Harland Dr .... Covington GA 30014 770-787-9830 577-2210*
**Fax Area Code:* 800 ■ *TF:* 877-503-4774 ■ *Web:* www.spgusa.com
Stanley Vidmar Storage Technologies
11 Grammes Rd .... Allentown PA 18103 610-797-6600 523-9934*
**Fax Area Code:* 800 ■ *TF:* 800-523-9462 ■ *Web:* www.stanleyvidmar.com
Stanly Fixtures Co Inc
11635 NC 138 Hwy PO Box 616 .... Norwood NC 28128 704-474-3184 474-3011
TF: 800-476-3184 ■ *Web:* www.stanlyfixtures.com
Stevens Industries Inc 704 W Main St .... Teutopolis IL 62467 217-857-6411 540-3101
Web: www.stevensind.com
Stevens Wire Products Inc
351 NW 'F' St PO Box 1146 .... Richmond IN 47375 765-966-5534 962-3586
Web: www.stevenswire.com
Store Kraft Mfg Co 500 Irving St .... Beatrice NE 68310 402-223-2348 223-1268
Web: www.storekraft.com
Storr Office Environments of Florida Inc
5112 W Linebaugh Ave .... Tampa FL 33624 813-418-3300 418-3301
Web: www.storr.com
Streater Inc 411 S 1st Ave .... Albert Lea MN 56007 507-373-0611 373-7630
TF: 800-527-4197 ■ *Web:* www.streater.com
Structural Concepts Corp 888 Porter Rd .... Muskegon MI 49441 231-798-8888 798-4960
TF: 800-433-9489 ■ *Web:* www.structuralconcepts.com
Stylmark Inc PO Box 32008 .... Minneapolis MN 55432 763-574-7474 574-1415
TF: 800-328-2495 ■ *Web:* www.stylmark.com
Sumner Group Inc 2121 Hampton Ave .... Saint Louis MO 63139 314-633-8000 633-8002
Web: www.sumner-group.com
Syndicate Systems 402 N Main St .... Middlebury IN 46540 574-825-9561 825-7194
Systems Mfg Corp 1037 Powers Rd .... Conklin NY 13748 607-775-1100 775-5080
TF Cust Svc: 800-762-7587 ■ *Web:* www.smcplus.com
Tarrant Interiors 5000 S Fwy .... Fort Worth TX 76115 817-922-5000 922-5015
Tesko Welding & Mfg Co 7350 W Montrose Ave .... Norridge IL 60706 708-452-0045 452-0112
TF: 800-621-4514
Timely Inc 10241 Norris Ave .... Pacoima CA 91331 818-896-3094 899-2677
TF: 800-247-6242 ■ *Web:* www.timelyframes.com
TJ Hale Co
W 139 N 9499 Hwy 145 PO Box 250 .... Menomonee Falls WI 53051 262-255-5555 255-5678
TF: 800-236-4253 ■ *Web:* www.tjhale.com
Transwall Office Systems Inc
1220 Wilson Dr PO Box 1930 .... West Chester PA 19380 800-441-9255 429-1411*
**Fax Area Code:* 610 ■ *TF:* 800-441-9255 ■ *Web:* www.transwall.com
Trendway Corp 13467 Quincy St PO Box 9016 .... Holland MI 49422 616-399-3900 399-2231
TF: 800-968-5344 ■ *Web:* www.trendway.com
Trion Industries Inc 297 Laird St .... Wilkes-Barre PA 18702 570-824-1000 824-0802
TF: 800-444-4665 ■ *Web:* www.triononline.com
Unarco Material Handling Inc
701 16th Ave E .... Springfield TN 37172 800-862-7261 382-2777*
**Fax Area Code:* 615 ■ *TF:* 800-862-7261 ■ *Web:* www.unarcorack.com
Viking Metal Cabinet Co Inc 5321 W 65th St .... Chicago IL 60638 708-594-1111 594-1028
TF: 800-776-7767 ■ *Web:* www.vikingmetal.com
Vira Mfg Inc 1 Buckingham Ave .... Perth Amboy NJ 08861 732-442-8472 442-8464
TF: 800-305-8472 ■ *Web:* www.viranet.com
W/M Display Group 1040-50 W 40th St .... Chicago IL 60609 773-254-3700 254-3188
TF: 800-443-2000 ■ *Web:* www.wmdisplay.com
Weis/Robart Partitions Inc 3737 S Venoy Rd .... Wayne MI 48184 734-467-8711 467-8710
Web: www.weisrobart.com
Westco Inc 4010 S Orchard St Suite 108 .... New York NY 10001 212-685-5050 213-1382
Western Pacific Storage Systems Inc
300 E Arrow Hwy .... San Dimas CA 91773 909-451-0303 451-0311
TF: 800-732-9777 ■ *Web:* www.wpss.com
WJ Egli Co Inc 205 E Columbia St .... Alliance OH 44601 330-823-3666 823-0011
Web: www.wjegli.com
Woodworkers of Denver Inc 1475 S Acoma St .... Denver CO 80223 303-777-7656 744-8550
Web: www.woodworkersofdenver.com

290 FLAGS, BANNERS, PENNANTS

Phone | Fax

Aaa Flag & Banner Mfg Co
8955 National Blvd .... Los Angeles CA 90034 800-266-4222 836-7253*
**Fax Area Code:* 310 ■ *TF:* 800-266-4222 ■ *Web:* www.aaaflag.com
Annin & Co 105 Eisenhower Pkwy .... Roseland NJ 07068 973-228-9400 228-4095
TF: 800-526-1390 ■ *Web:* www.annin.com
Collegiate Pacific Inc PO Box 300 .... Roanoke VA 24002 540-981-0281 981-0281
AMEX: BOO ■ *TF:* 800-336-5996 ■ *Web:* www.collegiatepacific.com
Eder Flag Mfg Co Inc 1000 W Rawson Ave .... Oak Creek WI 53154 414-764-3522 333-7329*
**Fax Area Code:* 800 ■ **Fax:* Orders ■ *TF:* 800-558-6044 ■ *Web:* www.ederflagnews.com
Metro Flag 47 Bassett Hwy .... Dover NJ 07801 973-366-1776 366-0956
TF: 800-666-3524
National Banner Co 11938 Harry Hines Blvd .... Dallas TX 75234 972-241-2131 241-6282
TF: 800-527-0860
Olympus Flag & Banner 9000 W Heather Ave .... Milwaukee WI 53224 414-355-2010 355-1931
TF: 800-558-9620 ■ *Web:* www.olympus-flag.com

291 FLASH MEMORY DEVICES

Phone | Fax

Advanced Micro Devices Inc (AMD)
1 AMD Pl PO Box 3453 .... Sunnyvale CA 94088 408-749-4000 749-4291
NYSE: AMD ■ *TF:* 800-538-8450 ■ *Web:* www.amd.com
Kingston Technology Co
17600 Newhope St .... Fountain Valley CA 92708 714-435-2600 435-2699
TF: 800-835-6575 ■ *Web:* www.kingston.com
Lexar Media Inc 47300 Bayside Pkwy .... Fremont CA 94538 510-413-1200 440-3499
Web: www.lexarmedia.com
Micron Technology Inc 8000 S Federal Way .... Boise ID 83707 208-368-4000 368-4617
NYSE: MU ■ *Web:* www.micron.com
PNY Technologies Inc 299 Webro Rd .... Parsippany NJ 07054 973-515-9700 560-5590*
**Fax:* Sales ■ *TF:* 800-769-7079 ■ *Web:* www3.pny.com
SanDisk Corp 601 McCarthy Blvd .... Milpitas CA 95035 408-801-1000 801-8657
NASDAQ: SNDK ■ *Web:* www.sandisk.com
Sharp Microelectronics of the Americas
5700 NW Pacific Rim Blvd .... Camas WA 98607 360-834-2500 834-8903
Web: www.sharpsma.com
Sony Electronics Inc 1 Sony Dr .... Park Ridge NJ 07656 201-930-1000 358-4058*
**Fax:* Hum Res ■ *TF Cust Svc:* 800-222-7669 ■ *Web:* www.sony.com

	City	State	ZIP	Phone	Fax
Spansion Inc 915 DeGuigne Dr *NYSE: CODE* ■ *TF:* 866-772-6746 ■ *Web:* www.spansion.com	Sunnyvale	CA	94085	408-962-2500	
STEC Inc 3001 Daimler St *TF:* 800-367-7330 ■ *Web:* www.stec-inc.com	Santa Ana	CA	92705	949-476-1180	476-1209

292 FLEET LEASING & MANAGEMENT

	City	State	ZIP	Phone	Fax
Allstate Leasing Inc 9428 Reisterstown Rd *TF:* 800-223-4885 ■ *Web:* www.allstateleasing.com	Owings Mills	MD	21117	410-363-6500	363-1784
Automotive Resources International 9000 Midlantic Dr *Web:* www.arifleet.com	Mount Laurel	NJ	08054	856-778-1500	778-6200
Avis Budget Group Inc 6 Sylvan Way *NYSE: CAR* ■ **Fax Area Code: 212* ■ *Web:* www.avisbudgetgroup.com	Parsippany	NJ	07054	973-496-4700	413-1924*
Donlen Corp 2315 Sanders Rd *TF:* 800-323-1483 ■ *Web:* www.donlen.com	Northbrook	IL	60062	847-714-1400	714-1500
Emkay Inc 805 W Thorndale Ave *TF:* 800-621-2001 ■ *Web:* www.emkay.com	Itasca	IL	60143	630-250-7400	250-7400
Enterprise Fleet Services 5105 Johnson Rd *TF:* 800-325-8007 ■ *Web:* www.enterprise.com	Coconut Creek	FL	33073	954-354-5400	
Executive Car Leasing Inc 7807 Santa Monica Blvd *TF:* 800-994-2277 ■ *Web:* www.executivecarleasing.com	Los Angeles	CA	90046	323-654-5000	848-9015
Frank Consolidated Enterprises Inc 666 Garland Pl	Des Plaines	IL	60016	847-699-7000	699-0681
GE Capital Fleet Services 3 Capital Dr **Fax:* Hum Res ■ *TF:* 800-469-0044 ■ *Web:* www.gefleet.com/fleet	Eden Prairie	MN	55344	952-828-1000	828-1040*
GE Equipment Services 260 Long Ridge Rd *Web:* www.geem.com	Stamford	CT	06927	203-357-4000	357-6489
Lease Plan USA 1165 Sanctuary Pkwy **Fax Area Code: 678* ■ *TF:* 800-457-8721 ■ *Web:* www.leaseplan.com	Alpharetta	GA	30004	770-933-9090	202-8700*
Leasing Assoc Inc PO Box 243 *TF:* 800-449-4807 ■ *Web:* www.theleasingcompany.com	Houston	TX	77001	713-522-9771	528-1259
Lily Transportation Corp 145 Rosemary St *Web:* www.lily.com	Needham	MA	02494	781-449-8811	449-7128
Motorlease Corp 1506 New Britain Ave *TF:* 800-243-0182 ■ *Web:* www.motorleasecorp.com	Farmington	CT	06032	860-677-9711	674-8677
Park Avenue Bmw Acura Motor Corp 250 W Passaic St *TF:* 877-568-8701 ■ *Web:* www.parkavemotors.com	Maywood	NJ	07607	201-843-7900	843-1052
PHH Arval 940 Ridgebrook Rd *TF:* 800-665-9744 ■ *Web:* www.phh.com	Sparks	MD	21152	410-771-1900	771-3362
RUAN Transportation Management Systems 666 Grand Ave Suite 3100 *TF:* 800-678-3210 ■ *Web:* www.ruan.com	Des Moines	IA	50309	515-245-2500	245-2684
Wheels Inc 666 Garland Pl **Fax:* Mail Rm ■ *Web:* www.wheels.com	Des Plaines	IL	60016	847-699-7000	699-4047*

FLOOR COVERINGS - MFR

SEE Carpets & Rugs p. 1557; Flooring - Resilient p. 1849; Tile - Ceramic (Wall & Floor) p. 2714

293 FLOOR COVERINGS STORES

	City	State	ZIP	Phone	Fax
Augusta Flooring Inc 202 Bobby Jones Expy *Web:* www.gcocarpet.com	Augusta	GA	30907	706-650-0400	650-2167
Award Hardwood Floors LLP 401 N 72nd Ave *TF:* 888-862-9273 ■ *Web:* www.awardfloors.com	Wausau	WI	54401	715-849-8080	849-8181
Budget Floor Store 3636 W Reno *Web:* www.budgetfloorstore.com	Oklahoma City	OK	73157	405-947-5575	942-5783
Carpet King Inc 1815 W River Rd *Web:* www.carpet-king.com	Minneapolis	MN	55411	612-287-1700	588-2401
Carpetile Plano Inc 8-10 W Main St	Plano	IL	60545	630-552-3400	552-3044
Century Tile Supply Co 747 E Roosevelt Rd *TF:* 888-345-3968 ■ *Web:* www.century-tile.com	Lombard	IL	60148	630-495-2300	495-8645
Chicago Granite & Marble Inc 415 Busse Rd *Web:* www.totalstonesolutions.com	Elk Grove Village	IL	60007	847-806-7000	806-7002
Clark-Dunbar Carpets 3232 Empire Dr *TF:* 800-256-1467	Alexandria	LA	71301	318-445-0262	473-9246
Coyle Carpet One Inc 250 W Beltline Hwy *TF:* 800-842-6953 ■ *Web:* www.coylecarpet.com	Madison	WI	53713	608-257-0291	258-7248
Everett Carpet Co 318 Ashman St	Midland	MI	48640	989-835-7191	835-7621
Finer Floor Covering Inc 1098 S 6th St *Web:* www.finerfloors.com	San Jose	CA	95112	408-297-0420	
Floor Coverings International 200 Technology Ct Suite 1200 *TF Sales:* 800-955-4324 ■ *Web:* www.floorcoveringsinternational.com	Smyrna	GA	30082	770-874-7600	874-7605
Floorcraft 15810 Bear Creek Pkwy *Web:* www.floorcraft.org	Redmond	WA	98052	425-885-4161	881-5617
Flooring Sales Group 1251 1st Ave S *Web:* www.greatfloors.com	Seattle	WA	98134	206-624-7800	622-8407
Furniture Outlets USA Inc 140 E Hinks Ln *TF:* 877-395-8998 ■ *Web:* www.furnitureoutletsusa.com	Sioux Falls	SD	57104	605-336-5000	336-5010
Harry L Murphy Inc 42 Bonaventura Dr *TF:* 800-439-6777	San Jose	CA	95134	408-955-1100	955-1111
J.e.k. Carpet Corp 3550 NW 77th Ct *Web:* www.dolphincarpet.com	Miami	FL	33122	305-591-4141	378-1700
Lumber Liquidators Inc 1455 VFW Pkwy *TF:* 877-645-5347 ■ *Web:* www.lumberliquidators.com	West Roxbury	MA	02132	617-327-1222	327-2039
Miller's Carpet One 15615 Hwy 99 *Web:* www.carpetone.com	Lynnwood	WA	98037	425-743-3213	742-4141
MMM Carpets Unlimited Inc 3100 Molinaro St *TF:* 800-355-4666 ■ *Web:* www.mmmcarpets.com	Santa Clara	CA	95054	408-988-4661	988-5181
Nationwide Floorcover & Window Coverings 111 E Kilbourn Ave Suite 2400 *TF:* 800-366-8088 ■ *Web:* www.floorsandwindows.com	Milwaukee	WI	53202	414-765-9900	765-1300
O'Krent Floor Covering Co 2075 N Loop 1604 E *TF:* 800-369-7387 ■ *Web:* www.okrentfloors.com	San Antonio	TX	78232	210-227-7387	227-7390
Pace Stone Inc 663 Washington St *TF:* 800-789-0236 ■ *Web:* www.pacestone.com	Eden	NC	27288	336-623-2158	623-3347
Redi-Carpet Inc 10225 Mula Rd Suite 120 *Web:* www.redicarpet.com	Stafford	TX	77477	832-310-2000	310-2001
Roysons Corp 40 Vanderhoof Ave *TF:* 888-769-7667 ■ *Web:* www.roysons.com	Rockaway	NJ	07866	973-625-7923	625-5917
Saint Paul Linoleum & Carpet Co 2956 Ctr Ct *Web:* www.stpaullinocpt.com	Eagan	MN	55121	651-686-7770	686-6660

294 FLOORING - RESILIENT

SEE ALSO Recycled Plastics Products p. 2531

	City	State	ZIP	Phone	Fax
American Biltrite Inc 57 River St *AMEX: ABL* ■ *Web:* www.ambilt.com	Wellesley Hills	MA	02481	781-237-6655	237-6880
American Floor Products Co Inc 7977 Cessna Ave *TF:* 800-342-0424 ■ *Web:* www.afco-usa.com	Gaithersburg	MD	20879	301-987-0490	987-0422
Amtico International Inc 6480 Roswell Rd *TF:* 800-268-4260 ■ *Web:* www.amtico.com	Atlanta	GA	30328	404-267-1900	267-1901
Armstrong World Industries Inc 2500 Columbia Ave **Fax:* Hum Res ■ *TF Cust Svc:* 800-233-3823 ■ *Web:* www.armstrong.com	Lancaster	PA	17603	717-397-0611	396-6133*
Columbia Forest Products Inc 222 SW Columbia St Suite 1575 *TF:* 800-547-4261 ■ *Web:* www.columbiaforestproducts.com	Portland	OR	97201	503-224-5300	224-5294
Congoleum Corp 3500 Quakerridge Rd PO Box 3127 *AMEX: CGM* ■ *TF:* 800-274-3266 ■ *Web:* www.congoleum.com	Mercerville	NJ	08619	609-584-3000	584-3305
Country Floors Inc 15 E 16th St *Web:* www.countryfloors.com	New York	NY	10003	212-627-8300	242-1604
Expanko Cork Co Inc 1129 W Lincoln Hwy *TF:* 800-345-6202 ■ *Web:* www.expanko.com	Coatesville	PA	19320	610-593-3000	380-0302
Florida Brick & Clay Co Inc (FBC) 1708 Turkey Creek Rd *Web:* www.floridabrickandclay.com	Plant City	FL	33567	813-754-1521	754-5469
Forbo Industries Inc PO Box 667 **Fax:* Cust Svc ■ *TF Cust Svc:* 800-842-7839 ■ *Web:* www.forbo-industries.com	Hazleton	PA	18201	570-459-0771	450-0258*
Formica Corp 10155 Reading Rd *TF:* 800-367-6422 ■ *Web:* www.formica.com	Cincinnati	OH	45241	513-786-3400	
Hambro Forest Products Inc 445 Elk Valley Rd PO Box 129 *Web:* www.cresdek.com	Crescent City	CA	95531	707-464-6131	464-9375
Mannington Commercial 345 Marine Dr PO Box 12281 *TF:* 800-241-2262 ■ *Web:* www.mannington.com	Calhoun	GA	30703	706-629-7301	629-2365
Mannington Mills Inc 75 Mannington Mills Rd *TF Cust Svc:* 800-356-6787 ■ *Web:* www.mannington.com	Salem	NJ	08079	856-935-3000	339-6099
Natco Products Corp 155 Brookside Ave	West Warwick	RI	02893	401-828-0300	823-7670
Pergo Inc 3128 Highwoods Blvd Suite 100 *TF:* 800-222-1827 ■ *Web:* www.pergo.com	Raleigh	NC	27604	919-773-6000	773-6004
Pionite Decorative Surfaces 1 Pionite Rd *TF:* 800-746-6483 ■ *Web:* www.pionite.com	Auburn	ME	04210	207-784-9111	784-0392
RCA Rubber Co 1833 E Market St *TF:* 800-321-2340 ■ *Web:* www.rcarubber.com	Akron	OH	44305	330-784-1291	794-6446
Regupol America 33 Keystone Dr **Fax Area Code: 717* ■ *TF:* 800-537-8737 ■ *Web:* www.regupol.com	Lebanon	PA	17042	800-537-8737	675-2199*
Roppe Corp 1602 N Union St *TF:* 800-537-9527 ■ *Web:* www.roppe.com	Fostoria	OH	44830	419-435-8546	435-1056
SRI Sports Inc 809 Kenner St *TF:* 800-723-8873 ■ *Web:* www.srisports.com	Dalton	GA	30721	706-272-4200	278-4898
Stonhard Inc 1 Pk Ave *TF Cust Svc:* 800-854-0310 ■ *Web:* www.stonhard.com	Maple Shade	NJ	08052	856-779-7500	321-7510
Superior Mfg Group 6655 W Ave 3rd *TF:* 800-621-2802 ■ *Web:* www.notrax.com	Chicago	IL	60638	708-458-4600	458-4723
Surface Shields Inc 10457 163rd Pl *TF:* 800-913-5667 ■ *Web:* www.surfaceshields.com	Orland Park	IL	60467	708-226-9810	226-9817
Tarkett Inc 1001 Yamaska St E *TF:* 800-363-9276 ■ *Web:* www.tarkettna.com	Farnham	QC	J2N1J7	450-293-3173	293-6644

295 FLORISTS

SEE ALSO Flowers-by-Wire Services p. 1851; Garden Centers p. 1901

	City	State	ZIP	Phone	Fax
1-800-Flowers.com Inc 1 Old Country Rd Suite 500 *NASDAQ: FLWS* ■ *TF:* 800-356-9377 ■ *Web:* www.ww2.1800flowers.com	Carle Place	NY	11514	516-237-6000	237-6124
Anthony's Florist & Gifts Inc 701 E Hallandale Beach Blvd *TF:* 800-989-8765	Hallandale	FL	33009	954-457-8520	457-8669
Arrow Florist & Park Avenue Greenhouses Inc 757 Pk Ave *TF:* 800-556-7097	Cranston	RI	02910	401-785-1900	785-4120
Bachman's Inc 6010 Lyndale Ave S *TF:* 888-222-4626 ■ *Web:* www.bachmans.com	Minneapolis	MN	55419	612-861-7311	861-7730
Boesen the Florist 3422 Beaver Ave *TF:* 800-274-4761 ■ *Web:* www.boesen.com	Des Moines	IA	50310	515-274-4761	274-6369

	City	State	Zip	Phone	Fax
Cactus Flower Florists 7077 E Bell Rd Suite 100 *Fax: Sales ■ TF: 800-922-2887 ■ Web: www.cactusflower.com	Scottsdale	AZ	85254	480-483-9200	483-9200*
Calyx & Corolla Inc 3975 20th St G Suite 6 Web: www.calyxandcorolla.com	Vero Beach	FL	32960	772-299-1377	299-1208
Carter's & La Rue's Flower Shop 2600 N MacArthur Blvd TF: 800-874-1462 ■ Web: www.cartersflowers.com	Oklahoma City	OK	73127	405-943-3314	948-1079
Connell's Map Lee Flowers & Gifts 2408 E Main St TF: 800-790-8980 ■ Web: www.cmlflowers.com	Bexley	OH	43209	614-237-8653	
Country Lane Flower Shop 729 S Michigan Ave TF: 800-764-7673 ■ Web: www.countrylaneflowers.com	Howell	MI	48843	517-546-1111	546-5168
DeLoache Flowers 2927 Millwood Ave TF: 800-922-2707 ■ Web: www.deloacheflowersonlie.com	Columbia	SC	29205	803-256-1681	256-5002
Don Wan Florist Ltd 5644 W 63rd St TF: 800-336-6926	Chicago	IL	60638	773-585-2225	585-9572
Dr Delphinium Designs & Events 5806 W Lovers Ln & Tollway TF: 800-783-8790 ■ Web: www.drdelphinium.com	Dallas	TX	75225	214-522-9911	525-1240
Eastern Floral & Gift Shop 818 Butterworth St SW TF: 800-494-2202 ■ Web: www.easternfloral.com	Grand Rapids	MI	49504	616-949-2200	949-9009
Felly's Flowers Inc PO Box 6620 TF: 800-993-7673 ■ Web: www.fellys.net	Madison	WI	53716	608-223-3285	
Field of Flowers Inc 5101 S University Dr TF: 800-963-7374 ■ Web: www.fieldofflowers.com	Davie	FL	33328	954-680-2406	680-2116
Florist 800 Network 973 Vale Terr Blvd Suite 102 *Fax Area Code: 800 ■ TF: 800-688-1299 ■ Web: www.800send.com	Vista	CA	92084	760-732-1260	947-8552*
Flower Patch Inc 4645 S Riverside Dr TF: 888-865-6858 ■ Web: www.flowerpatch.com	Murray	UT	84123	801-268-6566	266-6746
Flower Pot Florists 2314 N Broadway St TF: 800-824-7792 ■ Web: www.knoxvilleflowerpot.com	Knoxville	TN	37917	865-523-5121	524-8654
Flower World 1530 S Delaware St TF: 800-257-7880	Paulsboro	NJ	08066	856-224-4960	661-8049
FlowerClub PO Box 60910 TF: 800-800-7363 ■ Web: www.flowerclub.com	Los Angeles	CA	90060	405-440-6001	
Foster City Flowers & Gifts 1185 Chess Dr Suite G TF: 800-970-7673 ■ Web: www.fostercity-flowers.com	Foster City	CA	94404	650-573-6607	578-6756
FTD Inc 3113 Woodcreek Dr TF Cust Svc: 800-736-3383 ■ Web: www.ftd.com	Downers Grove	IL	60515	630-719-7800	724-6019
Greeters of Hawaii Ltd 3375 Koapaka St Suite B250 PO Box 29638 TF: 800-366-8559 ■ Web: www.greetersofhawaii.com	Honolulu	HI	96819	808-836-0161	833-7756
Grower Direct Fresh Cut Flowers Inc 4220 98th St Suite 118 Web: www.growerdirect.com	Edmonton	AB	T6E6A1	780-436-7774	436-3336
Higdon Florist 201 E 32nd St TF: 800-641-4726 ■ Web: www.higdonflorist.com	Joplin	MO	64804	417-624-7171	624-7244
Howard Bros Florists 8700 S Pennsylvania Ave TF: 800-648-0524 ■ Web: www.howardbrothersflorist.com	Oklahoma City	OK	73159	405-632-4747	632-1672
John Wolf Florist 6228 Waters Ave TF: 800-944-6435 ■ Web: www.ftdfloristsonline.com	Savannah	GA	31406	912-352-9843	353-8843
Johnston the Florist Inc 14179 Lincoln Way TF: 800-232-4795 ■ Web: www.johnstontheflorist.com	North Huntingdon	PA	15642	412-751-2821	751-2961
Joyce Florist 2729 S Hampton Rd TF: 800-527-1520 ■ Web: www.joyceflorist.com	Dallas	TX	75224	214-942-1776	331-6272
Ken's Flower Shop 140 W S Boundary St TF: 800-253-0100 ■ Web: www.kensflowers.com	Perrysburg	OH	43551	419-874-1333	874-3441
Kuhn Flowers Inc 3802 Beach Blvd TF: 800-458-5846 ■ Web: www.kuhnflowers.com	Jacksonville	FL	32207	904-398-8601	348-7379
Lehrer's Flowers Inc 3191 W 38th Ave TF: 800-537-1308 ■ Web: www.thinkflowers.com	Denver	CO	80211	303-455-1234	433-0028
Lester's Florist Inc 2100 Bull St TF: 800-841-1103 ■ Web: www.lestersflorist.com	Savannah	GA	31401	912-233-6066	233-3654
Lloyd's Florist 9216 Preston Hwy TF: 800-264-1825 ■ Web: www.lloydsflorist.net	Louisville	KY	40229	502-968-5428	964-5696
Locker's Florist 1640 S 83rd St TF: 877-276-7673 ■ Web: www.lockersflorist.com	West Allis	WI	53214	414-276-7673	
Martina's Flowers & Gifts 3830 Washington Rd TF: 800-927-1204 ■ Web: www.martinas.com	Martinez	GA	30907	706-863-7172	860-7590
Metropolitan Plant & Flower Exchange 2125 Fletcher Ave TF: 800-942-1050 ■ Web: www.metroplantexchange.com	Fort Lee	NJ	07024	201-944-1050	944-7970
Nanz & Kraft Florists Inc 141 Breckenridge Ln TF: 800-897-6551 ■ Web: www.nanzandkraft.com	Louisville	KY	40207	502-897-6551	897-2082
National Floral Supply Inc PO Box 190 Web: www.flowersonbase.com	Bryantown	MD	20617	301-932-7600	932-7906
Norton's Flowers & Gifts 2900 Washtenaw Ave TF: 800-682-8667 ■ Web: www.nortonsflowers.com	Ypsilanti	MI	48197	734-434-2700	434-1140
Phillip's Flower Shops Inc 524 N Cass Ave TF: 800-356-7257 ■ Web: www.800florals.com	Westmont	IL	60559	630-719-5200	719-2292
Phoenix Flower Shops 5733 E Thomas Rd Suite 4 TF: 888-311-0404 ■ Web: www.phoenixflowershops.com	Scottsdale	AZ	85251	480-289-4000	
Proflowers.com 4840 Eastgate Mall TF: 800-776-3569 ■ Web: www.proflowers.com	San Diego	CA	92121	858-729-2800	638-4725
Provide Commerce Inc 4840 Eastgate mall TF Cust Svc: 800-776-3569 ■ Web: www.prvd.com	San Diego	CA	92121	858-638-4900	909-4201
Russell Florist Inc 5001 Gravois Ave TF: 800-351-9003 ■ Web: www.russellflorist.com	Saint Louis	MO	63116	314-351-4676	351-6842
Schroeder's Flowerland Inc 1530 S Webster Ave TF: 800-236-4769 ■ Web: www.schroederflowers.com	Green Bay	WI	54301	920-436-6363	433-9685
Stephenson's Flower Shops 3015 Old Gettysburg Rd TF: 888-761-5990 ■ Web: www.ftdfloristsonline.com/stephensons	Camp Hill	PA	17011	717-761-5990	975-0481
Strange's Florist Inc 3313 Mechanicsville Pike TF: 800-421-4070 ■ Web: www.netfloral.com	Richmond	VA	23223	804-321-2200	329-5576
Thrifty Flowers Inc 24001 Telegraph Rd Web: www.thriftyflorist.net	Southfield	MI	48034	248-386-8900	386-4195
Veldkamp's Flowers 9501 W Colfax Ave TF: 800-247-3730 ■ Web: www.veldkamps.com	Lakewood	CO	80215	303-232-2673	234-5686
Villere's Florist 750 Martin Behrman Ave TF: 800-845-5373 ■ Web: www.villeresflowers.com	Metairie	LA	70005	504-833-3716	830-4513
Winston Bros Inc 131 Newbury St TF: 800-457-4901 ■ Web: www.winstonflowers.com	Boston	MA	02116	617-541-1100	541-1126

296 FLOWERS & NURSERY STOCK - WHOL

	City	State	Zip	Phone	Fax
Atwoods Distributing Inc 500 S Garland Rd Web: www.atwoods.com	Enid	OK	73703	580-233-3702	234-4332
Ball Horticultural Co 622 Town Rd TF: 800-879-2255 ■ Web: www.ballhort.com	West Chicago	IL	60185	630-231-3600	231-3605
Celebrity Inc 4520 Old Troup Hwy Suite C *Fax Area Code: 800 ■ TF: 800-527-8446	Tyler	TX	75707	903-561-3981	850-4329*
Central Garden & Pet Co 1340 Treat Blvd Suite 600 NASDAQ: CENT ■ Web: www.central.com	Walnut Creek	CA	94597	925-948-4000	287-0601
Claymore C Sieck Wholesale Florist 311 E Chase St TF: 800-624-7134 ■ Web: www.sieck.com	Baltimore	MD	21202	410-685-4660	685-1547
Cleveland Plant & Flower Co 12920 Corporate Dr TF: 800-688-8012 ■ Web: www.cpfco.com	Parma	OH	44130	216-898-3500	898-1075
Country Silk Inc 100 S Washington Ave Web: www.countrysilk.com	Dunellen	NJ	08812	732-752-5556	752-7550
Cut Flower Wholesale Inc 2122 Faulkner Rd TF: 888-997-8367 ■ Web: www.cutflower.com	Atlanta	GA	30324	404-320-1619	634-7922
Delaware Valley Wholesale Florist Inc (DVWF) 520 Mantua Blvd N TF: 800-676-1212 ■ Web: www.dvwf.com	Sewell	NJ	08080	856-468-7000	464-2772
Denver Wholesale Florists Co 4800 Dahlia St Web: www.dwfwholesale.com	Denver	CO	80216	303-399-0970	376-3123
Distinctive Designs International Inc 120 Sibley Dr TF: 800-243-4787 ■ Web: www.distinctivedesigns.com	Russellville	AL	35654	256-332-7390	332-7890
Esprit Miami 3043 NW 107th Ave TF: 800-327-2320 ■ Web: www.espritmiami.com	Miami	FL	33172	305-591-2244	591-2603
Florist Distributing Inc 2403 Bell Ave TF: 800-373-3741 ■ Web: www.fdionline.net	Des Moines	IA	50321	515-243-5228	282-9241
Greenleaf Wholesale Florists Inc 13239 Weld County Rd 4 TF: 800-659-8000 ■ Web: www.greenleafwholesale.com	Brighton	CO	80601	303-659-8000	659-4022
Holmberg Farms Inc 13430 Hobson Simmons Rd TF: 800-282-3562 ■ Web: www.holmbergfarms.com	Lithia	FL	33547	813-689-3601	
Karthauser & Sons Inc W 147 N 11100 Fond du Lac Ave TF: 800-338-8620 ■ Web: www.karthauser.net	Germantown	WI	53022	262-255-7815	255-6920
Kennicott Bros 452 N Ashland Ave Web: www.kennicott.com	Chicago	IL	60622	312-492-8200	492-8202
L & L Nursery Supply Co Inc 5350 G St TF: 800-624-2517 ■ Web: www.llnurserysupply.com	Chino	CA	91710	909-591-0461	591-3280
Manatee Cortez Floral Co 1320 33rd St W	Palmetto	FL	34221	941-721-0600	729-5151
Miramar Wholesale Nurseries Inc PO Box 22598 Web: www.miramarnurseries.com	San Diego	CA	92192	858-552-0658	
Norben Import Corp 99 S Newman St TF: 800-526-4652 ■ Web: www.norben.com	Hackensack	NJ	07601	201-487-0855	487-0787
Pennock Co 3601 Island Ave TF: 888-736-6625 ■ Web: www.pennock.com	Philadelphia	PA	19153	215-844-6600	492-7901
Pittsburgh Cut Flower Co 1901 Liberty Ave TF: 800-837-2837 ■ Web: www.pittsburghcutflower.com	Pittsburgh	PA	15222	412-355-7000	391-0649
Platz Flowers & Supply Inc 8501 Frontage Rd TF: 888-752-8048 ■ Web: www.platzwholesale.com	Morton Grove	IL	60053	847-966-3100	556-6471
Rexius Forest By-Products Inc 1275 Bailey Hill Rd TF: 800-473-9487 ■ Web: www.rexius.com	Eugene	OR	97402	541-342-1835	343-4802
Roman J Claprood Co 242 N Grant Ave TF: 800-966-7695	Columbus	OH	43215	614-221-5515	
Roy Houff Co The 6200 S Oak Pk Ave TF: 800-366-1769 ■ Web: www.royhouff.com	Chicago	IL	60638	773-586-8666	586-8790
Shemin Nurseries 1081 King St Web: www.sheminnurseries.com	Greenwich	CT	06831	203-531-6700	531-7393
Southern Importers Inc 3859 Battleground Ave Suite 300 TF Cust Svc: 800-334-9658	Greensboro	NC	27410	336-292-4521	852-6397
Spokane Flower Growers Inc 115 E Pacific Ave	Spokane	WA	99202	509-624-0121	747-8509
Tapscott's 1403 E 18th St TF: 800-626-1922 ■ Web: www.tapfloral.com	Owensboro	KY	42303	270-684-2308	683-3702
Teters Floral Products Inc 1425 S Lillian Ave TF: 800-999-5996 ■ Web: www.teters.com	Bolivar	MO	65613	417-326-7654	326-8061
Teufel Nursery Inc 100 SW Miller Rd TF: 800-483-8335 ■ Web: www.teufellandscape.com	Portland	OR	97225	503-646-1111	646-1112
Van Bloem Gardens 8079 Van Zyverden Rd PO Box 500 *Fax Area Code: 646 ■ TF: 800-332-2852 ■ Web: www.vanbloem.com	Meridian	MS	39302	601-679-1050	839-2605*
Van Well Nursery 2821 Grant Rd TF: 800-572-1553 ■ Web: www.vanwell.net	East Wenatchee	WA	98802	509-886-8189	886-0294

Company	City	State	ZIP	Phone	Fax
Van Zyverden Inc 8079 Van Zyverden Rd *TF:* 800-332-2852	Meridian	MS	39305	601-679-8274	679-8039
Western Organics Inc 420 E Southern Ave *TF:* 800-352-3245	Tempe	AZ	85202	602-269-5756	269-7621
Zelenka Nursery Inc 16127 Winans St *TF:* 800-253-3743 ■ *Web:* www.zelenkanursery.com	Grand Haven	MI	49417	616-842-1367	842-0304
Zieger & Sons Inc 6215 Ardleigh St *TF:* 800-752-2003 ■ *Web:* www.zieger.com	Philadelphia	PA	19138	215-438-7060	438-8729

297 FLOWERS-BY-WIRE SERVICES

Company	City	State	ZIP	Phone	Fax
Teleflora Inc 11444 Olympic Blvd *TF:* 800-321-2654 ■ *Web:* www.teleflora.com	Los Angeles	CA	90064	310-231-9199	966-3612

298 FOIL & LEAF - METAL

Company	City	State	ZIP	Phone	Fax
Api Foils Inc 329 New Brunswick Ave **Fax Area Code:* 785 ■ *Web:* www.apigroup.com	Rahway	NJ	07065	732-382-6800	842-9748*
Chemetal 39 O'Neil St *TF:* 800-807-7341 ■ *Web:* www.chmetal.com	EastHampton	MA	01027	413-529-0718	529-9898
Crown Roll Leaf Inc 91 Illinois Ave *TF:* 800-631-3831 ■ *Web:* www.crownrollleaf.com	Paterson	NJ	07503	973-742-4000	742-0219
Gould Electronics Inc 2929 W Chandler Blvd *Web:* www.gould.com	Chandler	AZ	85224	480-899-0343	963-2119
Oak-Mitsui Inc 80 1st St *Web:* www.oakmitsui.com	Hoosick Falls	NY	12090	518-686-4961	686-8080
October Co Inc 51 Ferry St *TF:* 800-628-9346	EastHampton	MA	01027	413-527-9380	527-0091

299 FOOD PRODUCTS - MFR

SEE ALSO Agricultural Products p. 1376; Bakeries p. 1505; Beverages - Mfr p. 1520; Ice - Manufactured p. 2103; Livestock & Poultry Feeds - Prepared p. 2182; Meat Packing Plants p. 2225; Pet Products p. 2411; Poultry Processing p. 2441; Salt p. 2631

Company	City	State	ZIP	Phone	Fax
Conchita Foods Inc 9115 NW 105th Way *Web:* www.conchita-foods.com	Miami	FL	33178	305-888-9703	888-1020
Flatout Inc 1422 Woodland Dr *TF:* 866-944-5445 ■ *Web:* www.flatoutbread.com	Saline	MI	48176	734-944-5445	944-5115
Rhee Bros Inc 7461 Coca Cola Dr *Web:* www.rheebros.com	Hanover	MD	21076	410-381-9000	381-4989
Sunny Dell Foods Inc 135 N 5th St *Web:* www.sunnydell.com	Oxford	PA	19363	610-932-5164	932-9479
Wixon Inc 1390 E Bolivar Ave *TF:* 800-841-5304 ■ *Web:* www.wixon.com	Milwaukee	WI	53235	414-769-3000	769-3024

299-1 Bakery Products - Fresh

Company	City	State	ZIP	Phone	Fax
Alessi Bakeries Inc 2909 W Cypress St *Web:* www.alessibakeries.com	Tampa	FL	33609	813-879-4544	872-9103
Alfred Nickles Bakery Inc 26 N Main St *TF:* 800-635-1110 ■ *Web:* www.nicklesbakery.com	Navarre	OH	44662	330-879-5635	879-5896
Alpha Baking Co Inc 4545 W Lyndale Ave *Web:* www.alphabaking.com	Chicago	IL	60639	773-489-5400	489-2711
Amoroso's Baking Co 845 S 55th St *TF:* 800-377-6557 ■ *Web:* www.amorosobaking.com	Philadelphia	PA	19143	215-471-4740	472-5299
Arnie's Inc 722 Leonard St NW *TF:* 800-343-4361	Grand Rapids	MI	49504	616-458-1107	458-3085
Bama Pie Ltd 2745 E 11th St *TF:* 800-756-2262	Tulsa	OK	74104	918-592-0778	732-2811
Barker Specialty Products LLC 703 Franklin St PO Box 478 *Web:* www.barkercompany.com	Keosauqua	IA	52565	319-293-3777	293-3776
Bays Corp PO Box 1455 *Web:* www.bays.com	Chicago	IL	60690	312-346-5757	226-3435
Better Baked Foods Inc 56 Smedley St *Web:* www.betterbaked.com	North East	PA	16428	814-725-8778	725-8785
Bimbo Bakeries USA 7301 S Fwy *Web:* www.bimbobakeriesusa.com	Fort Worth	TX	76134	817-293-6230	615-3091
Brown's Bakery Inc 505 Downs St	Defiance	OH	43512	419-784-3330	784-5346
Butter Krust Baking Co Inc 249 N 11th St *TF:* 800-332-8521 ■ *Web:* www.holsum.com	Sunbury	PA	17801	570-286-5845	286-0780
Byrnes & Kiefer Coompany 131 Kline Ave *TF:* 877-444-2240 ■ *Web:* www.bkcompany.com	Callery	PA	16024	724-538-5200	538-9292
Calise & Sons Bakery Inc 2 Quality Dr *TF:* 800-225-4737 ■ *Web:* www.calisebakery.com	Lincoln	RI	02865	401-334-3444	334-0938
Carolina Foods Inc 1807 S Tryon St *TF:* 800-234-0441	Charlotte	NC	28203	704-333-9812	940-0040
Cassones Bakery Inc 202 S Regent St	Port Chester	NY	10573	914-939-1568	939-3811
Chattanooga Bakery Inc 900 Manufacture Rd *TF:* 800-251-3404 ■ *Web:* www.moonpie.com	Chattanooga	TN	37401	423-267-3351	266-2169
Cloverhill Bakery Inc 2035 N Narragansett Ave *TF:* 800-745-9822 ■ *Web:* www.cloverhill.com	Chicago	IL	60639	773-745-9800	745-1647
Colchester Bakery 96 Lebanon Ave *Web:* www.colchesterbakery.com	Colchester	CT	06415	860-537-2415	
Country Oven Bakery Inc 2840 Pioneer Dr	Bowling Green	KY	42101	270-782-3200	782-7170
Dakota Brands International 2121 13th St NE *TF:* 800-844-5073 ■ *Web:* www.dakotabrands.com	Jamestown	ND	58401	701-252-5073	251-1047
De Wafelbakkers LLC PO Box 13570 *TF:* 800-924-3391 ■ *Web:* www.dewafelbakkers.com	North Little Rock	AR	72113	501-791-3320	791-0309
Delight Grecian Foods Inc 1201 Tonne Rd *TF:* 800-621-4387 ■ *Web:* www.greciandelight.com	Elk Grove Village	IL	60007	847-364-1010	635-7294
Dinkel's Bakery 3329 N Lincoln Ave *TF:* 800-822-8817 ■ *Web:* www.dinkels.com	Chicago	IL	60657	773-281-7300	281-6169
Dolly Madison Cakes 12 E Armour Blvd *TF:* 800-483-7253 ■ *Web:* www.dollymadison.com	Kansas City	MO	64111	816-502-4000	502-4126
Ellison Bakery 4108 W Ferguson Rd *Web:* www.ebakery.com	Fort Wayne	IN	46809	260-747-6136	747-1954
Fantini Baking Co Inc 375 Washington St *TF:* 800-223-9037 ■ *Web:* www.fantinibakery.com	Haverhill	MA	01832	978-373-1273	373-6250
FB Sale LLC 1688 N Wayneport Rd *Web:* www.fleischersbagels.com	Macedon	NY	14502	315-986-9999	
Federal Bakers USA 5015 Lee Hwy Suite 101	Arlington	VA	22207	703-469-1500	312-6051
Figi's Inc 3200 S Maple Ave *TF:* 800-422-3444	Marshfield	WI	54449	715-387-6311	384-1130
Flowers Foods Inc 1919 Flowers Cir *NYSE: FLO* ■ **Fax:* Mktg ■ *Web:* www.flowersfoods.com	Thomasville	GA	31757	229-226-9110	226-1318*
Franz Family Bakeries Gai's Div 2006 S Weller St *Web:* www.usbakery.com	Seattle	WA	98144	206-726-7535	726-7555
Franz Family Bakeries William's Div 2000 Nugget Way **Fax Area Code:* 503	Eugene	OR	97403	541-485-8211	546-7140*
Fresh Start Bakeries 145 S State College Blvd Suite 200 *Web:* www.freshstartbakeries.com	Brea	CA	92821	714-256-8900	256-8916
George Weston Bakeries Inc 55 Paradise Ln *TF:* 800-842-9595	Bay Shore	NY	11706	631-273-6000	
Granny's Kitchens LLC 178 Industrial Pk Dr *TF:* 800-311-9113 ■ *Web:* www.grannyskitchens.com	Frankfort	NY	13340	315-735-5000	735-3200
Greyston Bakery Inc 104 Alexander St *TF:* 800-289-2253 ■ *Web:* www.greystonbakery.com	Yonkers	NY	10701	914-375-1510	375-1514
H & S Bakery Inc 601 S Caroline St *TF:* 800-959-7655 ■ *Web:* www.hsbakery.com	Baltimore	MD	21231	410-276-7254	558-3096
Heinemann's Bakeries LLc PO Box 558265 *Web:* www.heinemanns.com	Chicago	IL	60655	616-885-9094	885-9031
Heiners Bakery Inc 1300 Adams Ave *TF:* 800-776-8411	Huntington	WV	25704	304-523-8411	525-9268
Herman Seekamp Inc 1120 W Fullerton Ave *Web:* www.clydesdonuts.com	Addison	IL	60101	630-628-6555	628-6838
Jtm Foods Inc 2126 E 33rd St *Web:* www.jtmfoods.net	Erie	PA	16510	814-899-0886	899-9862
Klosterman Baking Co Inc 4760 Paddock Rd *TF:* 877-301-1004 ■ *Web:* www.klostermanbakery.com	Cincinnati	OH	45229	513-242-1004	242-8257
Lawler Foods Ltd Inc PO Box 2558 *TF:* 800-541-8285 ■ *Web:* www.lawlers.com	Humble	TX	77347	281-446-0059	446-3806
Leidenheimer Baking Co 1501 Simon Bolivar Ave *TF:* 800-259-9099 ■ *Web:* www.leidenheimer.com	New Orleans	LA	70113	504-525-1575	525-1596
Lepage Bakeries Inc 1 Country Kitchen Plaza PO Box 1900 *Web:* www.lepagebakeries.com	Auburn	ME	04211	207-783-9161	783-3300
Lewis Bakeries Inc 500 N Fulton Ave *TF:* 800-365-2812	Evansville	IN	47710	812-425-4642	425-7609
Little Dutch Boy Bakery Inc 12349 S 970 E *TF:* 800-382-2594	Draper	UT	84020	801-571-3800	571-3802
Martin's Famous Pastry Shoppe Inc 1000 Potato Roll Ln *TF Cust Svc:* 800-548-1200 ■ *Web:* www.mfps.com	Chambersburg	PA	17201	717-263-9580	263-6687
Mary Ann's Baking Co 8371 Carbide Ct	Sacramento	CA	95828	916-681-7444	681-7470
Mary of Puddin Hill Inc 201 E I-30 *TF Orders:* 800-545-8889 ■ *Web:* www.puddinhill.com	Greenville	TX	75402	903-455-2651	455-4522
McKee Foods Corp PO Box 750 **Fax:* Hum Res ■ *TF Cust Svc:* 800-522-4499 ■ *Web:* www.mckeefoods.com	Collegedale	TN	37315	423-238-7111	238-7127*
Morabito Baking Co Inc 757 Kohn St *TF:* 800-525-7747 ■ *Web:* www.morabito.com	Norristown	PA	19401	610-275-5419	275-0358
Mrs Baird's Bakeries Inc 7301 S Fwy *TF:* 800-366-7921 ■ *Web:* www.mrsbairds.com	Fort Worth	TX	76134	817-293-6230	615-3091
Oak State Products Inc PO Box 549 *Web:* www.oakstate.com	Wenona	IL	61377	815-853-4348	853-4625
Old London Foods 1776 Eastchester Rd *TF:* 888-266-4445 ■ *Web:* www.oldlondonfoods.com	Bronx	NY	10461	718-409-1776	409-1776
Omni Baking Co 2621 Freddy Ln Bldg 7 *Web:* www.omnibaking.com	Vineland	NJ	08360	856-205-1485	
Orlando Baking Co Inc 7777 Grand Ave *TF:* 800-362-5504 ■ *Web:* www.orlandobaking.com	Cleveland	OH	44104	216-361-1872	391-3469
Ottenberg's Bakery Inc 655 Taylor St NE *TF:* 800-334-7264	Washington	DC	20017	202-529-5800	529-3121
Palagonia Bakery 508 Junius St	Brooklyn	NY	11212	718-272-5400	272-5427
Pan-O-Gold Baking Co 444 E St Germain St *TF:* 800-444-7005	Saint Cloud	MN	56304	320-251-9361	252-0249
Pechters Baking 840 Jersey St *TF:* 800-525-5779	Harrison	NJ	07029	973-483-3374	481-2319
Pepperidge Farm Inc 595 Westport Ave *TF PR:* 888-737-7374 ■ *Web:* www.pepperidgefarm.com	Norwalk	CT	06851	203-846-7000	846-7369
Piantedosi Baking Co Inc 240 Commercial St *TF:* 800-339-0080 ■ *Web:* www.piantedosi.com	Malden	MA	02148	781-321-3400	324-5647
Quality Bakery Products Inc 888 E Las Olas Blvd Suite 700 **Fax Area Code:* 305	Fort Lauderdale	FL	33301	954-779-3663	779-7678*
Quinzani's Bakery 380 Harrison Ave *TF:* 800-999-1062 ■ *Web:* www.quinzanisbakery.com	Boston	MA	02118	617-426-2114	451-8075

Phone | Fax

Ralcorp Frozen Bakery Products
3250 Lacey Rd Suite 600 Downers IL 60515 630-455-5200 455-5202
NYSE: RAH ■ *Web:* www.ralcorpfrozen.com

Richmond Baking Co 520 N 6th St Richmond IN 47374 765-962-8535 962-2253
Web: www.richmondbaking.com

Rockland Bakery Inc 94 Demarest Mill Rd W Nanuet NY 10954 845-623-5800 623-6921
Web: www.rocklandbakery.com

Roskam Baking Co PO Box 202 Grand Rapids MI 49501 616-574-5757 574-1117
TF: 877-684-2879

Schmidt Baking Co Inc 7801 Fitch Ln Baltimore MD 21236 410-668-8200 882-2051
TF: 800-456-2253 ■ *Web:* www.schmidtbaking.com

Schwebel Baking Co PO Box 6018 Youngstown OH 44501 330-783-2860 782-1774
TF: 800-860-2867 ■ *Web:* www.schwebels.com

Signature Breads Inc 100 Justin Dr Chelsea MA 02150 617-884-9800
TF: 888-602-6533 ■ *Web:* www.signaturebreads.com

Sokol & Co 5315 Dansher Rd Countryside IL 60525 708-482-8250 482-9750
TF Cust Svc: 800-328-7656 ■ *Web:* www.solofoods.com

Southern Bakeries LLC 2700 E 3rd St Hope AR 71802 870-777-9031 777-2406
TF: 800-643-1542 ■ *Web:* www.southernbakeries.com

Specialty Bakers Inc 450 S State Rd Marysville PA 17053 717-957-2131 957-0156
TF: 800-233-0778 ■ *Web:* www.sbiladyfingers.com

Svenhard's Swedish Bakery Inc 335 Adeline St Oakland CA 94607 510-834-5035 839-6797
TF: 800-333-7836 ■ *Web:* www.svenhards.com

Sweetheart Bakery 5150 Midland Rd Billings MT 59101 406-248-4800 248-1499

Table Talk Pies Inc 120 Washington St Worcester MA 01610 508-798-8811 798-0848
Web: www.tabletalkpie.com

Tasty Baking Co
Navy Yard Corporate Ctr 3 Crescent Dr
Suite 200 Philadelphia PA 19112 215-221-8500 223-3288
TF: 800-338-2789 ■ *Web:* www.tastykake.com

TJ Cinnamons 1155 Perimeter Ctr W Atlanta GA 30338 678-514-4100
TF: 800-487-2729

Turano Baking Co 6501 Roosevelt Rd Berwyn IL 60402 708-788-9220 788-3075
TF: 800-458-5662 ■ *Web:* www.turanobakery.com

Wenner Bread Products Inc 33 Rajon Rd Bayport NY 11705 631-563-6262 563-6546
TF: 800-869-6262 ■ *Web:* www.wenner-bread.com

Wolferman's Inc 14350 Santa Fe Trail Dr Lenexa KS 66215 913-888-4499 492-5195
TF Cust Svc: 800-919-1888 ■ *Web:* www.wolfermans.com

299-2 Bakery Products - Frozen

Phone | Fax

Athens Pastries & Frozen Foods Inc
13600 Snow Rd Cleveland OH 44142 216-676-8500 676-0609
TF: 800-837-5683 ■ *Web:* www.athens.com

Bako Products 1425 Del Paso Blvd Sacramento CA 95815 916-929-6868 922-9091
Web: www.bakoproducts.com

Bridgford Foods Corp 1308 N Patt St Anaheim CA 92801 714-526-5533 526-4360
NASDAQ: BRID ■ *TF:* 800-854-3255 ■ *Web:* www.bridgford.com

Brooks Food Group Inc 940 Orange St Bedford VA 24523 540-586-8284 586-1072
TF: 800-873-4934 ■ *Web:* www.brooksfoodgroup.com

Chef Solutions Inc 1000 Universal Dr North Haven CT 06473 203-234-0115 234-7620
TF: 800-877-1157 ■ *Web:* www.chefsolutions.com

Cookietree Bakeries 4122 S 500 W Salt Lake City UT 84123 801-268-2253 265-2727
TF: 800-998-0111 ■ *Web:* www.cookietree.com

Country Home Bakers Inc
3 Enterprise Dr Suite 404 Shelton CT 06484 203-225-2333 225-2333
TF Cust Svc: 800-243-0008

Country Oven Bakery Inc
2840 Pioneer Dr Bowling Green KY 42101 270-782-3200 782-7170

Dessert Innovations Inc 25-B Enterprise Blvd Atlanta GA 30336 404-691-5000 691-5001
TF: 800-359-7351 ■ *Web:* www.dessertinnovations.com

Eli's Cheesecake Co
6701 W Forest Preserve Dr Chicago IL 60634 773-736-3417 205-3801
TF: 800-999-8300 ■ *Web:* www.elicheesecake.com

Figi's Inc 3200 S Maple Ave Marshfield WI 54449 715-387-6311 384-1130
TF: 800-422-3444

Goodman Food Products 200 E Beach Ave Inglewood CA 90302 310-674-3180 673-7008

Guttenplans Frozen Dough 100 Hwy 36 Middletown NJ 07748 732-495-9480 495-2415
TF: 888-422-4357 ■ *Web:* www.guttenplan.com

James Skinner Baking Co 4657 G St Omaha NE 68117 402-734-1672 734-0516
TF: 800-358-7428 ■ *Web:* www.skinnerbaking.com

Main Street Gourmet Inc 170 Muffin Ln Cuyahoga Falls OH 44223 330-929-0000 920-8329
TF: 800-678-6246 ■ *Web:* www.mainstreetgourmet.com

Maplehurst Inc 50 Maplehurst Dr Brownsburg IN 46112 317-858-9000 858-9009
TF: 800-428-3200 ■ *Web:* www.maplehurstbakeries.com

New York Frozen Foods Inc
25900 Fargo Ave Bedford Heights OH 44146 216-292-5655 292-5978

Rhino Foods Inc 79 Industrial Pkwy Burlington VT 05401 802-862-0252 865-4145
TF: 800-639-3350 ■ *Web:* www.rhinofoods.com

Sara Lee Food & Beverage 3500 Lacey Rd Downers Grove IL 60515 630-598-7892 598-8221
TF: 866-727-2533 ■ *Web:* www.saraleefoods.com

Vie de France Yamazaki Inc
2070 Chain Bridge Rd Suite 500 Vienna VA 22182 703-442-9205 821-2695
TF: 800-446-4404 ■ *Web:* www.vdfy.com

299-3 Butter (Creamery)

Phone | Fax

AMPI 315 N Broadway New Ulm MN 56073 507-354-8295 359-8668
TF: 800-533-3580 ■ *Web:* www.ampi.com

Cabot Creamery 1 Home Farm Way Montpelier VT 05602 802-229-9361
TF: 888-792-2268 ■ *Web:* www.cabotcheese.com

California Dairies Inc 2000 N Plaza Dr Visalia CA 93291 559-625-2200 625-5433
TF: 800-821-5588 ■ *Web:* www.californiadairies.com

Challenge Dairy Products Inc
11875 Dublin Blvd Suite B230 Dublin CA 94568 925-828-6160 551-7591
TF: 800-733-2374 ■ *Web:* www.challengedairy.com

Farmers Co-op Creamery Inc
700 N Hwy 99 W McMinnville OR 97128 503-472-2157 472-3821

Grassland Dairy Products Co Inc
N 8790 Fairgrounds Ave PO Box 160 Greenwood WI 54437 715-267-6182 267-6044
TF: 800-428-8837 ■ *Web:* www.grassland.com

Land O'Lakes Inc 4001 Lexington Ave N Arden Hills MN 55126 651-481-2222 481-2488*
*Fax: Hum Res ■ *TF:* 800-328-9680 ■ *Web:* www.landolakesinc.com

O-AT-KA Milk Products Co-op Inc
700 Ellicott St Batavia NY 14020 585-343-0536 343-4473
TF: 800-828-8152 ■ *Web:* www.oatkamilk.com

Plainview Milk Products Co-Op
130 2nd St SW Plainview MN 55964 507-534-3872 534-3992
TF: 800-356-5606 ■ *Web:* www.plainviewmilk.com

Schreiber Foods Inc 425 Pine St Green Bay WI 54301 920-437-7601 455-2700
TF: 800-344-0333 ■ *Web:* www.schreiberfoods.com

Sommermaid Creamery Inc PO Box 350 Doylestown PA 18901 215-345-6160 345-4945
Web: www.sommermaid.com

299-4 Cereals (Breakfast)

Phone | Fax

Big G Cereals
1 General Mills Blvd PO Box 9452 Minneapolis MN 55426 800-248-7310 764-8330*
*Fax Area Code: 763 ■ *Fax: PR ■ *TF:* 800-248-7310 ■ *Web:* www.generalmills.com

Blue Planet Foods Inc PO Box 2178 Collegedale TN 37315 423-396-3145 396-3479
TF: 877-396-3145 ■ *Web:* www.blueplanetfoods.net

Bob's Red Mill Natural Foods Inc
3521 SE Pheasant Ct Milwaukie OR 97222 503-654-3215 653-1339
TF: 800-553-2258 ■ *Web:* www.bobsredmill.com

Breadshop Inc 16100 Foothill Blvd Irwindale CA 91706 800-334-3204 969-0939*
*Fax Area Code: 626 ■ *TF:* 800-334-3204

Gilster-Mary Lee Corp 1037 State St Chester IL 62233 618-826-2361 826-2973
TF: 800-851-5371

Healthy Times Inc 13200 Kirkham Way Bldg 104 Poway CA 92064 858-513-1550 513-1533

Homestead Mills 221 N River St PO Box 1115 Cook MN 55723 218-666-5233 666-5236
TF: 800-652-5233 ■ *Web:* www.homesteadmills.com

Honeyville Grain Inc
11600 Dayton Dr Rancho Cucamonga CA 91730 909-980-9500 980-6503
TF: 888-810-3212 ■ *Web:* www.honeyvillegrain.com

Hyde & Hyde Inc 300 El Sobrante Rd Corona CA 92879 951-817-2300 270-3526
Web: www.hydeandhyde.com

Kashi Co
4275 Executive Sq Suite 600 PO Box 8557 La Jolla CA 92037 858-274-8870 274-8894
Web: www.kashi.com

Kellogg Co 1 Kellogg Sq PO Box 3599 Battle Creek MI 49016 269-961-2000 961-2871
NYSE: K ■ *TF Cust Svc:* 800-962-1413 ■ *Web:* www2.kelloggs.com

Little Crow Foods 201 S Detroit St Warsaw IN 46580 574-267-7141 267-2370
TF: 800-288-2769 ■ *Web:* www.littlecrowfoods.com

Lundberg Family Farms
5370 Church St PO Box 369 Richvale CA 95974 530-882-4551 882-4500
Web: www.lundberg.com

Malt-O-Meal Inc 80 S 8th St Suite 2700 Minneapolis MN 55402 612-338-8551 359-5424
TF: 800-328-4452 ■ *Web:* www.malt-o-meal.com

Nature's Hand Inc 1800 E Cliff Rd Suite 7 Burnsville MN 55337 952-890-6033 890-6040

New England Natural Bakers
74 Fairview St E Greenfield MA 01301 413-772-2239 772-2936
Web: www.newenglandnaturalbakers.com

Organic Milling Co 505 W Allen Ave San Dimas CA 91773 909-599-0961 599-5180
TF: 800-638-8686

Quaker Foods North America 555 W Monroe St Chicago IL 60661 312-821-1000
TF: 800-555-6287 ■ *Web:* www.quakeroats.com

Ralston Foods PO Box 618 Saint Louis MO 63188 314-877-7000 877-7771
Web: www.ralstonfoods.com

Weetabix Co Inc 20 Cameron St Clinton MA 01510 978-368-0991 365-7268
TF: 800-343-0590

Wildtime Foods 1201 Pearl St Eugene OR 97441 541-747-1654 747-5067
TF: 800-356-4458 ■ *Web:* www.grizzliesbrand.com

299-5 Cheeses - Natural, Processed, Imitation

Phone | Fax

AMPI 315 N Broadway New Ulm MN 56073 507-354-8295 359-8668
TF: 800-533-3580 ■ *Web:* www.ampi.com

Barker Specialty Products LLC
703 Franklin St PO Box 478 Keosauqua IA 52565 319-293-3777 293-3776
Web: www.barkercompany.com

Bel/Kaukauna USA 1500 E N Ave Little Chute WI 54140 920-788-3524 788-9725
TF: 800-558-3500 ■ *Web:* www.kaukaunacheese.com

Berner Foods Inc 2034 E Factory Rd Dakota IL 61018 815-563-4222 563-4017
TF: 800-819-8199 ■ *Web:* www.bernerfoods.com

Biery Cheese Co 6544 Paris Ave Louisville OH 44641 330-875-3381 875-5896
TF: 800-243-3731 ■ *Web:* www.bierycheese.com

Boar's Head Provisions Co Inc
1819 Main St Suite 800 Sarasota FL 34236 941-955-0994 906-8213
Web: www.boarshead.com

Bongards' Creameries 13200 County Rd 51 Norwood MN 55368 952-466-5521 466-5556
Web: www.bongards.com

Brewster Dairy Inc
800 S Wabash Ave PO Box 98 Brewster OH 44613 330-767-3492 767-3386
TF: 800-874-8874 ■ *Web:* www.brewstercheese.com

Burnett Dairy Co-op 11631 SR- 70 Grantsburg WI 54840 715-689-2468 689-2135
Web: www.burnettdairy.com

Cabot Creamery 1 Home Farm Way Montpelier VT 05602 802-229-9361
TF: 888-792-2268 ■ *Web:* www.cabotcheese.com

Cacique Inc 14923 Procter Ave La Puente CA 91746 626-961-3399 961-4676*
*Fax: Sales ■ *TF:* 800-521-6987 ■ *Web:* www.caciqueusa.com

Calabro Cheese Corp
580 Coe Ave PO Box 120186 East Haven CT 06512 203-469-1311 469-6929
TF: 800-969-1311 ■ *Web:* www.calabrocheese.com

California Dairies Inc 2000 N Plaza Dr Visalia CA 93291 559-625-2200 625-5433
TF: 800-821-5588 ■ *Web:* www.californiadairies.com

Churny Co Inc 1 Kraft Ct Glenview IL 60025 847-646-5500 646-5590

Colonna Bros Inc 4102 Bergen Tpke North Bergen NJ 07047 201-864-1115 864-0144

ConAgra Foods Retail Products Co Deli Foods Group
215 W Field Rd Naperville IL 60563 630-857-1000 512-1124
TF: 800-325-7424

Dairiconcepts LP 3253 E Chestnut Expy Springfield MO 65802 417-829-3400 829-3401
TF: 877-596-4374 ■ *Web:* www.dairiconcepts.com

	City	State	Zip	Phone	Fax
Dairy Farmers of America Inc					
10220 N Ambassador Dr Northpointe Tower	Kansas City	MO	64153	816-801-6455	801-6592
TF: 888-332-6455 ■ *Web:* www.dfamilk.com					
Dairy Food USA Inc PO Box 7	Blue Mounds	WI	53517	608-437-5598	437-8850
TF Cust Svc: 800-236-3300 ■ *Web:* www.dairyfoodusa.com					
Ellsworth Co-op Creamery Inc					
232 N Wallace St	Ellsworth	WI	54011	715-273-4311	273-5318
Empire Cheese Inc 4520 County Rd 6	Cuba	NY	14727	585-968-1552	968-2660
F & A Dairy Products Inc PO Box 278	Dresser	WI	54009	715-755-3485	755-3480
Farmdale Creamery Inc					
1049 W Baseline St	San Bernardino	CA	92411	909-889-3002	888-2541
First District Assn 101 S Swift Ave	Litchfield	MN	55355	320-693-3236	693-6243
Web: www.firstdistrict.com					
Fleur de Lait BC USA 400 S Custer Ave	New Holland	PA	17557	717-355-8500	355-8546
TF: 800-322-2743					
Galaxy Nutritional Foods Inc					
2441 Viscount Row	Orlando	FL	32809	407-855-5500	855-7485
TF Cust Svc: 800-808-2325 ■ *Web:* www.galaxyfoods.com					
Golden Cheese Co of California					
1138 W Rincon St	Corona	CA	92880	951-493-4700	493-4749*
**Fax:* Hum Res ■ *TF Cust Svc:* 800-842-0264					
Gossner Foods Inc 1051 N 1000 W	Logan	UT	84321	435-752-9365	752-3147
TF: 800-944-0454 ■ *Web:* www.gossner.com					
Grande Cheese Co Dairy Rd	Brownsville	WI	53006	920-583-3122	269-1435*
**Fax:* Hum Res ■ *Web:* www.grandecig.com					
Great Lakes Cheese Co Inc					
17825 Great Lakes Pkwy	Hiram	OH	44234	440-834-2500	834-1002
TF: 800-677-7181 ■ *Web:* www.greatlakescheese.com					
Heluva Good 6551 Pratt Rd PO Box 410	Sodus	NY	14551	315-483-6971	483-9927
TF: 800-323-2188 ■ *Web:* www.heluvagood.com					
Hilmar Cheese Co Inc PO Box 910	Hilmar	CA	95324	209-667-6076	634-1408
TF: 888-300-4465 ■ *Web:* www.hilmarcheese.com					
Holmes Cheese Co 9444 SR-39	Millersburg	OH	44654	330-674-6451	674-6673
Jerome Cheese Co 547 W Nez Perce	Jerome	ID	83338	208-324-8806	324-8892
Klondike Cheese Co W7839 Hwy 81	Monroe	WI	53566	608-325-3021	325-3027
Web: www.klondikecheese.com					
Kraft Canada Inc 95 Moatfield Dr	Don Mills	ON	M3B3L6	416-441-5000	441-5328*
**Fax:* PR ■ *Web:* www.kraftcanada.com					
Kraft Foods Inc 3 Lakes Dr	Northfield	IL	60093	847-646-2000	646-6005
NYSE: KFT ■ *Web:* www.kraftfoodscompany.com					
Kraft Foods North America Inc 3 Lakes Dr	Northfield	IL	60093	847-646-2000	646-6005
Web: www.kraft.com					
Land O'Lakes Inc 4001 Lexington Ave N	Arden Hills	MN	55126	651-481-2222	481-2488*
**Fax:* Hum Res ■ *TF:* 800-328-9680 ■ *Web:* www.landolakesinc.com					
Le Sueur Cheese Co Inc 719 N Main St	Le Sueur	MN	56058	507-665-3353	665-2820
TF: 800-247-0871					
Leprino Foods Co 1830 W 38th Ave	Denver	CO	80211	303-480-2600	480-2682
TF: 800-537-7466 ■ *Web:* www.leprinofoods.com					
Los Altos Food Products Inc					
15130 Nelson Ave	City of Industry	CA	91744	626-330-6555	330-6755
Web: www.losaltosfoods.com					
Lucille Farms Inc 150 River Rd	Montville	NJ	07045	973-334-6030	402-6361
TF: 800-654-6844					
Mancuso Cheese Co 612 Mills Rd	Joliet	IL	60433	815-722-2475	722-1302
Marathon Cheese Corp PO Box 185	Marathon	WI	54448	715-443-2211	443-2211
Web: www.mchesse.com					
Miceli Dairy Products Co 2721 E 90th St	Cleveland	OH	44104	216-791-6222	231-2504
TF: 800-551-7196 ■ *Web:* www.miceli-dairy.com					
Minerva Cheese Factory Inc					
430 Radloff Ave PO Box 60	Minerva	OH	44657	330-868-4196	868-7947
Nelson Ricks Creamery Co					
1755 S Fremont Dr	Salt Lake City	UT	84104	801-364-3607	364-3600
Pace Dairy Foods Co 2700 Valleyhigh Dr NW	Rochester	MN	55901	507-288-6315	288-6856
TF: 800-533-1687					
Saputo Inc 6869 boul Metropolitain	Saint-Leonard	QC	H1P1X8	514-328-6662	328-3364
TSX: SAP ■ *Web:* www.saputo.com					
Sargento Foods Inc 1 Persnickety Pl	Plymouth	WI	53073	920-893-8484	893-8399
TF: 800-243-3737 ■ *Web:* www.sargento.com					
Sartori Food Corp 107 Pleasant View Rd	Plymouth	WI	53073	920-893-6061	892-2732
TF Cust Svc: 800-558-5888 ■ *Web:* www.sartoricheese.com					
Schreiber Foods Inc 425 Pine St	Green Bay	WI	54301	920-437-7601	455-2700
TF: 800-344-0333 ■ *Web:* www.schreiberfoods.com					
Sorrento Lactalis Inc 2376 S Pk Ave	Buffalo	NY	14220	716-823-6262	823-6454
TF: 800-828-7031 ■ *Web:* www.sorrentocheese.com					
Sun-Re Cheese Corp 178 Lenker Ave	Sunbury	PA	17801	570-286-1511	286-5123
Swiss Valley Farms Co 21100 Holden Dr	Davenport	IA	52806	563-391-3341	391-7479
TF: 800-747-6113 ■ *Web:* www.swissvalley.com					
Tillamook County Creamery Assn Inc					
4185 Hwy 101 N	Tillamook	OR	97141	503-842-4481	842-6039
Web: www.tillamook.com					
Trega Foods Ltd 2701 Freedom Rd	Appleton	WI	54140	920-788-2115	
Web: www.tregafoods.com					
Tropical Cheese Industries Inc					
450 Fayette St PO Box 1357	Perth Amboy	NJ	08861	732-442-4898	442-8227
TF: 888-874-4928 ■ *Web:* www.tropicalcheese.com					
Valley Queen Cheese Factory Inc					
200 E Railway Ave	Milbank	SD	57252	605-432-4563	432-9383
Web: www.vqcheese.com					
Wapsie Valley Creamery Inc					
300 10th St NE	Independence	IA	50644	319-334-7193	334-4914
Westby Co-op Creamery 401 S Main St	Westby	WI	54667	608-634-3181	634-3194
TF Cust Svc: 800-492-9282 ■ *Web:* www.westbycreamery.com					
Wisconsin Cheeseman Inc PO Box 1	Madison	WI	53782	608-837-5166	837-5493
TF Orders: 800-698-1721 ■ *Web:* www.wisconsincheeseman.com					
Zausner Foods Corp 400 S Custer Ave	New Holland	PA	17557	717-355-8505	355-8561
TF: 800-322-2743 ■ *Web:* www.alouettecheese.com					

299-6 Chewing Gum

	City	State	Zip	Phone	Fax
Concord Confections Ltd 345 Courtland Ave	Concord	ON	L4K5A6	905-660-8989	660-8979
TF: 800-267-0037 ■ *Web:* www.ic.gc.ca/eic/site/ic1.nsf/eng/home					
Ford Gum & Machine Co Inc 18 Newton Ave	Akron	NY	14001	716-542-4561	542-4610
TF: 800-225-5535 ■ *Web:* www.fordgum.com					
Lotte USA Inc 5243 Wayne Rd	Battle Creek	MI	49015	269-963-6664	963-6695
Topps Co Inc 1 Whitehall St	New York	NY	10004	212-376-0300	376-0573
TF: 800-489-9149 ■ *Web:* www.topps.com					
Wrigley Co The 410 N Michigan Ave	Chicago	IL	60611	312-644-2121	644-0353
NYSE: WWY ■ *TF:* 800-974-4539 ■ *Web:* www.wrigley.com					

299-7 Coffee - Roasted (Ground, Instant, Freeze-Dried)

	City	State	Zip	Phone	Fax
Allegro Coffee Co 12799 Claude Ct	Thornton	CO	80241	303-444-4844	920-5468
TF Cust Svc: 800-530-3993 ■ *Web:* www.allegro-coffee.com					
American Coffee Co Inc 800 Magazine St	New Orleans	LA	70130	504-581-7234	581-7518
TF Cust Svc: 800-554-7234 ■ *Web:* www.frenchmarketcoffee.com					
Andresen Ryan Coffee Co 2206 Winter St	Superior	WI	54880	715-392-4771	392-4776
TF: 800-293-2726					
Araban Coffee Co Inc 2 Keith Way	Hingham	MA	02043	781-740-4441	740-4005
TF: 800-225-2474					
Autocrat Coffee Inc 10 Blackstone Valley Pl	Lincoln	RI	02865	401-333-3300	333-3719
TF: 800-288-6272 ■ *Web:* www.autocrat.com					
Bargreen Coffee Co 2821 Rucker Ave	Everett	WA	98201	425-252-3161	259-4673
Web: www.bargreencoffee-store.stores.yahoo.net					
Boyd Coffee Co 19730 NE Sandy Blvd	Portland	OR	97230	503-666-4545	669-2223
TF Cust Svc: 800-545-4077 ■ *Web:* www.boyds.com					
Cadillac Coffee Co 1801 Michael St	Madison Heights	MI	48071	248-545-2266	584-4184
TF: 800-438-6900 ■ *Web:* www.cadillaccoffee.com					
Cafe Rico Inc PO Box 400	Caguas	PR	00726	787-745-7426	286-7426
Web: www.caferico.com					
Coffee Holding Co Inc					
3475 Victory Blvd	Staten Island	NY	11314	718-832-0800	832-0892
NASDAQ: JVA ■ *TF:* 800-458-2233 ■ *Web:* www.coffeeholding.com					
Community Coffee Co PO Box 791	Baton Rouge	LA	70821	225-291-3900	368-4510
TF: 800-688-0990 ■ *Web:* www.communitycoffee.com					
DeCoty Coffee Co Inc 1920 Austin St	San Angelo	TX	76903	325-655-5607	655-6837
TF: 800-588-8001 ■ *Web:* www.decotycoffee.com					
Excellent Coffee Co Inc 259 E Ave	Pawtucket	RI	02860	401-724-6393	724-0560
F Gavina & Sons Inc 2700 Fruitland Ave	Vernon	CA	90058	323-582-0671	581-1127
TF: 800-428-4627 ■ *Web:* www.gavina.com					
Farmer Bros Co 20333 S Normandie Ave	Torrance	CA	90502	310-787-5200	320-2436
NASDAQ: FARM ■ *TF:* 800-735-2878 ■ *Web:* www.farmerbrosco.com					
Folger Coffee Co The 1 Strawberry Ln	Orrville	OH	44667	800-937-9745	
TF: 800-937-9745 ■ *Web:* www.folgers.com					
Frontier Natural Products Co-op					
3021 78th St PO Box 299	Norway	IA	52318	319-227-7996	227-7966
TF: 800-669-3275 ■ *Web:* www.frontiercoop.com					
Great Atlantic & Pacific Tea Co Inc					
2 Paragon Dr	Montvale	NJ	07645	201-573-9700	571-8820
NYSE: GAP ■ *TF:* 866-443-7374 ■ *Web:* www.aptea.com					
Green Mountain Coffee Roasters Inc					
33 Coffee Ln	Waterbury	VT	05676	802-244-5621	244-6565*
NASDAQ: GMCR ■ **Fax:* Sales ■ *TF Cust Svc:* 888-879-4627 ■ *Web:* www.greenmountaincoffee.com					
Hawaiian Isles Kona Coffee Co					
2839 Mokumoa St	Honolulu	HI	96819	808-833-2244	833-6328
TF Orders: 800-749-9103 ■ *Web:* www.hawaiianisles.com					
Melitta Canada Inc 1 Greensboro Dr Suite 202	Rexdale	ON	M9W1C8	416-243-8979	243-1808
TF: 800-565-4882 ■ *Web:* www.melitta.ca					
Nestle USA Inc 800 N Brand Blvd	Glendale	CA	91203	818-549-6000	549-6952*
**Fax:* Sales ■ *Web:* www.nestle.com					
New England Coffee Co 100 Charles St	Malden	MA	02148	781-324-8094	388-2838
TF: 800-225-3537 ■ *Web:* www.newenglandcoffee.com					
Old Mansion Foods					
3811 Corporate Rd PO Box 1838	Petersburg	VA	23805	804-862-9889	861-8816
TF: 800-476-1877 ■ *Web:* www.oldmansionfoods.com					
Paul deLima Co Inc 7546 Morgan Rd	Liverpool	NY	13090	315-457-3725	457-3730
TF: 800-962-8864 ■ *Web:* www.delimacoffee.com					
Port City Java Inc					
101 Portwatch Way PO Box 785	Wilmington	NC	28412	910-796-6646	
Web: www.portcityjava.com					
Red Diamond Inc					
1701 Vanderbilt Rd PO Box 2168	Birmingham	AL	35201	205-254-3138	254-6062
TF: 800-292-4651 ■ *Web:* www.reddiamond.com					
Rowland Coffee Roasters Inc 5605 NW 82nd Ave	Miami	FL	33166	305-594-9039	594-7603
TF: 800-990-9039					
Royal Cup Inc 160 Cleage Dr	Birmingham	AL	35217	205-849-5836	271-6071
TF Cust Svc: 800-366-5836 ■ *Web:* www.royalcupcoffee.com					
S & D Coffee Inc 300 Concord Pkwy PO Box 1628	Concord	NC	28026	704-782-3121	721-5792
TF Cust Svc: 800-933-2210 ■ *Web:* www.sndcoffee.com					
SJ McCullagh Inc 245 Swan St	Buffalo	NY	14204	800-753-3473	856-3486
TF: 800-753-3473 ■ *Web:* www.mccullaghcoffee.com					
Stewarts Private Blend Food Inc					
4110 W Wrightwood Ave	Chicago	IL	60639	773-489-2500	489-2148
TF: 800-654-2862 ■ *Web:* www.stewarts.com					
Texas Coffee Co Inc					
3297 ML King Pkwy S PO Box 31	Beaumont	TX	77704	409-835-3434	835-4248
TF: 800-259-3400 ■ *Web:* www.texjoy.com					
Torke Coffee Roasting Co Inc					
3455 Paine Ave PO Box 694	Sheboygan	WI	53081	920-458-4114	458-0488
TF: 800-242-7671					
Van Roy Coffee Co The 4569 Spring Rd	Cleveland	OH	44131	216-749-7069	749-7039
TF: 877-826-7669 ■ *Web:* www.vanroycoffee.com					

	City	State	Zip	Phone	Fax
White Cloud Coffee Co 5125 N Sawyer Ave *TF:* 800-738-0989 ■ *Web:* www.whitecloudcoffee.com	Boise	ID	83714	208-322-1166	322-6226
White Coffee Corp 1835 38th St *TF:* 800-221-0140 ■ *Web:* www.whitecoffee.com	Long Island City	NY	11105	718-204-7900	956-8504

299-8 Confectionery Products

	City	State	Zip	Phone	Fax
Adams & Brooks Inc 1915 S Hoover St PO Box 7303 *TF Orders:* 800-999-9808 ■ *Web:* www.adams-brooks.com	Los Angeles	CA	90007	213-749-3226	746-7614
ADM Cocoa Div 4666 E Faries Pkwy *TF:* 800-558-9958	Decatur	IL	62526	217-424-5200	424-4296
Andes Candies Inc 1400 E Wisconsin St	Delavan	WI	53115	262-728-9121	728-6794
Anthony-Thomas Candy Co 1777 Arlingate Ct *TF:* 877-226-3921 ■ *Web:* www.anthony-thomas.com	Columbus	OH	43228	614-274-8405	274-0019
Asher's Chocolates 80 Wambold Rd *TF:* 800-223-4420 ■ *Web:* www.ashers.com	Souderton	PA	18964	215-721-3000	721-3265
Atkinson Candy Co 1608 W Frank Ave *TF:* 800-231-1203 ■ *Web:* www.atkinsoncandy.com	Lufkin	TX	75904	936-639-2333	639-2337
Barry Callebaut USA LLC 400 Industrial Pk Rd *TF:* 800-556-8845 ■ *Web:* www.barry-callebaut.com	Saint Albans	VT	05478	802-524-9711	524-5148
Best Sweet Inc 288 Mazeppa Rd **Fax:* Mktg ■ *TF:* 888-211-5530 ■ *Web:* www.bestsweet.com	Mooresville	NC	28115	704-664-4300	664-9640*
Blommer Chocolate Co 600 W Kinzie St *TF:* 800-621-1606 ■ *Web:* www.blommer.com	Chicago	IL	60654	312-226-7700	226-4141
Boyer Candy Inc 821 17th St *Web:* www.boyercandies.com	Altoona	PA	16602	814-944-9401	943-2354
Brown & Haley 1940 E 11th St *TF:* 800-426-8400 ■ *Web:* www.brown-haley.com	Tacoma	WA	98421	253-620-3000	272-6742
Cargill Inc North America 15407 McGinty Rd *TF:* 800-227-4455	Wayzata	MN	55391	952-742-7575	
Ce De Candy Inc 1091 Lousons Rd *TF:* 800-631-7968	Union	NJ	07083	908-964-0660	964-0911
Charms Co 7401 S Cicero Ave *TF:* 800-877-7655	Chicago	IL	60629	773-838-3400	838-3564
Cherrydale Farms Inc 1035 Mill Rd *TF:* 800-333-4525 ■ *Web:* www.cherrydale.com	Allentown	PA	18106	610-366-1606	391-9345
Chocolates a la Carte Inc 28455 Livingston Ave **Fax:* Sales ■ *TF Cust Svc:* 800-818-2462 ■ *Web:* www.chocolatesalacarte.com	Valencia	CA	91355	661-257-3700	257-4999*
ConAgra Foods Retail Products Co Grocery Foods Group 3353 Michelson Dr	Irvine	CA	92612	949-437-1018	437-3315
Decko Products Inc 2105 Superior St *TF:* 800-537-6143 ■ *Web:* www.decko.com	Sandusky	OH	44870	419-626-5757	626-3135
Eaton Farm Confectioners Inc 30 Burbank Rd *TF:* 800-343-9300 ■ *Web:* www.eatonfarmcandies.com	Sutton	MA	01590	508-865-5235	865-7087
Elmer Candy Corp PO Box 788 *TF:* 800-843-9537 ■ *Web:* www.elmercandy.com	Ponchatoula	LA	70454	985-386-6166	386-6166
Esther Price Candies Inc 1709 Wayne Ave *TF:* 800-782-0326 ■ *Web:* www.estherprice.com	Dayton	OH	45410	937-253-2121	253-3294
Farley's & Sathers Candy Co Inc 1 Sather Plaza *TF:* 800-533-0330 ■ *Web:* www.farleysandsathers.com	Round Lake	MN	56167	507-945-8181	945-8343
FB Washburn Candy Corp 137 Perkins Ave *Web:* www.fbwashburncandy.com	Brockton	MA	02302	508-588-0820	588-2205
Ferrara Bakery & Cafe Inc 195 Grand St 3rd Fl *TF:* 800-871-6068 ■ *Web:* www.ferraracafe.com	New York	NY	10013	212-226-6150	226-0667
Ferrara Pan Candy Co 7301 Harrison St *TF:* 800-323-1768 ■ *Web:* www.ferrarapan.com	Forest Park	IL	60130	708-366-0500	366-5921
Ferrero USA Inc 600 Cottontail Ln *TF:* 800-337-7376 ■ *Web:* www.ferrerousa.com	Somerset	NJ	08873	732-764-9300	764-9300
Fowler's Chocolate Co 100 River Rock Dr Suite 102 *TF:* 800-824-2263 ■ *Web:* www.fowlerschocolates.com	Buffalo	NY	14207	716-877-9983	877-9959
Frankford Candy & Chocolate Co Inc 9300 Ashton Rd *Web:* www.frankfordcandy.com	Philadelphia	PA	11914	215-735-5200	735-0721
Ganong Bros Ltd 1 Chocolate Dr *Web:* www.ganong.com	Saint Stephen	NB	E3L2X5	506-465-5600	465-5610
Gayle's Chocolates 417 S Washington Ave *Web:* www.gayleschocolates.com	Royal Oak	MI	48067	248-398-0001	399-5106
Gertrude Hawk Chocolates Inc 9 Keystone Pk *TF:* 800-822-2032 ■ *Web:* www.gertrudehawkchocolates.com	Dunmore	PA	18512	570-342-7556	342-0261
Ghirardelli Chocolate Co 1111 139th Ave *TF:* 800-877-9338 ■ *Web:* www.ghirardelli.com	San Leandro	CA	94578	510-483-6970	297-2649
Godiva Chocolatier Inc 355 Lexington Ave 16th Fl *TF:* 800-732-7333 ■ *Web:* www.godiva.com	New York	NY	10017	212-984-5900	984-5901
Goetze's Candy Co Inc 3900 E Monument St *TF Orders:* 800-295-8058 ■ *Web:* www.goetzecandy.com	Baltimore	MD	21205	410-342-2010	522-7681
Guittard Chocolate Co 10 Guittard Rd *TF:* 800-468-2462 ■ *Web:* www.guittard.com	Burlingame	CA	94010	650-697-4427	692-2761
Harry London Candies Inc 5353 Lauby Rd *TF Cust Svc:* 800-321-0444 ■ *Web:* www.londoncandies.com	North Canton	OH	44720	330-494-0833	499-6902
HB Reese Candy Co 925 Reese Ave *TF Cust Svc:* 800-468-1714	Hershey	PA	17033	717-534-4106	
Hershey Co 100 Crystal A Dr *NYSE:* HSY ■ *TF Cust Svc:* 800-362-8321 ■ *Web:* www.thehersheycompany.com	Hershey	PA	17033	717-534-4200	534-6760
Hillside Candy Co 35 Hillside Ave *TF:* 800-524-1304 ■ *Web:* www.hillsidecandy.com	Hillside	NJ	07205	973-926-2300	926-4440
James Candy Co 1519 Boardwalk *TF Orders:* 800-441-1404 ■ *Web:* www.seashoretaffy.com	Atlantic City	NJ	08401	609-344-1519	344-0246
Jelly Belly Candy Co 1 Jelly Belly Ln **Fax:* Cust Svc ■ *TF:* 800-323-9380 ■ *Web:* www.jellybelly.com	Fairfield	CA	94533	707-428-2800	428-0819*
Joyva Corp 53 Varick Ave *Web:* www.joyva.com	Brooklyn	NY	11237	718-497-0170	366-8504
Judson-Atkinson Candies 4266 Dividend St PO Box 200669 *Web:* www.judsonatkinsoncandies.com	San Antonio	TX	78220	210-359-8380	359-8392
Just Born Inc 1300 Stefko Blvd *TF:* 800-445-5787 ■ *Web:* www.justborn.com	Bethlehem	PA	18017	610-867-7568	867-7870
Katharine Beecher Candies 1250 Slate Hill Rd *TF:* 800-232-7082 ■ *Web:* www.padutchcandies.com	Camp Hill	PA	17011	717-761-5440	761-5702
Koeze Co PO Box 9470 **Fax Area Code:* 866 ■ *TF:* 800-555-9688 ■ *Web:* www.koeze.com	Grand Rapids	MI	49509	800-555-9688	817-0147*
Kopper's Chocolate 39 Clarkson St *TF:* 800-325-0026 ■ *Web:* www.kopperschocolate.com	New York	NY	10014	212-243-0220	
Lammes Candies Since 1885 Inc 200 B Parker Dr Suite 500 *TF Cust Svc:* 800-252-1885 ■ *Web:* www.lammes.com	Austin	TX	78728	512-310-1885	310-2280
Lincoln Snacks Co 5020 S 19th St	Lincoln	NE	68512	402-421-5500	421-5519
Lindt & Sprungli USA 1 Fine Chocolate Pl *TF:* 877-695-4638 ■ *Web:* www.lindtusa.com	Stratham	NH	03885	603-778-8100	778-3102
Lucks Co The 3003 S Pine St **Fax:* Orders ■ *TF:* 800-426-9778 ■ *Web:* www.lucks.com	Tacoma	WA	98409	253-383-4815	383-0071*
Madelaine Chocolate Novelties Inc 9603 Beach Ch Dr *TF:* 800-322-1505 ■ *Web:* www.madelainechocolate.com	Rockaway Beach	NY	11693	718-945-1500	318-4607
Malleys Chocolates 13400 Brookpark Rd *TF:* 800-835-5684 ■ *Web:* www.malleys.com	Cleveland	OH	44135	216-362-8700	362-7240
Mars Snack Food 800 High St *TF:* 800-432-1093 ■ *Web:* www.mars.com	Hackettstown	NJ	07840	908-852-1000	850-2734
Marshmallow Cone Co 5141 Fischer Pl *TF:* 800-641-8551 ■ *Web:* www.marshmallowcone.com	Cincinnati	OH	45217	513-641-2345	641-2557
Masterson Co Inc 4023 W National Ave *TF:* 800-558-0990 ■ *Web:* www.mastersoncompany.com	Milwaukee	WI	53215	414-647-1132	647-1170
Melster Candies Inc 500 E Madison St *TF:* 800-535-4401	Cambridge	WI	53523	608-423-3221	423-3195
Moonstruck Chocolate Co 6600 N Baltimore Ave *TF:* 800-557-6666 ■ *Web:* www.moonstruckchocolate.com	Portland	OR	97203	503-247-3448	247-3450
Morley Candy Makers Inc 23770 Hall Rd *TF:* 800-651-7263 ■ *Web:* www.sanderscandy.com	Clinton Township	MI	48036	586-468-4300	468-9407
Munson's Candy Kitchen Inc 174 Hop River Rd *TF:* 888-686-7667 ■ *Web:* www.munsonschocolates.com	Bolton	CT	06043	860-649-4332	649-7209
Nestle Canada Inc 25 Sheppard Ave W *TF:* 800-563-7853 ■ *Web:* www.nestle.ca	Toronto	ON	M2N6S8	416-512-9000	218-2654
Nestle USA Inc 800 N Brand Blvd **Fax:* Sales ■ *Web:* www.nestle.com	Glendale	CA	91203	818-549-6000	549-6952*
New England Confectionery Co (NECCO) 135 American Legion Hwy *TF:* 800-225-5508 ■ *Web:* www.necco.com	Revere	MA	02151	781-485-4500	485-4509
Palmer Candy Co 2600 Hwy 75 N PO Box 326 *TF:* 800-831-0828 ■ *Web:* www.palmercandy.com	Sioux City	IA	51102	712-258-5543	258-3224
Paradise Inc 1200 W MLK Blvd PO Drawer Y *TF:* 800-330-8952 ■ *Web:* www.paradisefruitco.com	Plant City	FL	33564	813-752-1155	754-3168
Pearson's Candy Co 2140 W 7th St *TF Cust Svc:* 800-328-6507 ■ *Web:* www.pearsoncandy.com	Saint Paul	MN	55116	651-698-0356	696-2222
Peerless Confection Co 1254 W Schubert Ave *Web:* www.peerlesscandy.com	Chicago	IL	60614	773-281-6100	281-5812
Pennsylvania Dutch Candies 1250 Slate Hill Rd *TF:* 800-233-7082 ■ *Web:* www.padutchcandies.com	Camp Hill	PA	17011	717-761-5440	761-5702
Pez Candy Inc 35 Prindle Hill Rd *TF:* 800-243-6087 ■ *Web:* www.pez.com	Orange	CT	06477	203-795-0531	799-1679
Plb Sports Inc Penn Ctr W Bldg 3 Suite 411 *TF:* 877-752-7778 ■ *Web:* www.plbsports.com	Pittsburgh	PA	15276	412-787-8800	787-8745
Primrose Candy Co 4111 W Parker Ave *Web:* www.primrosecandy.com	Chicago	IL	60639	773-276-9522	276-7411
Promotion In Motion PO Box 558 *TF:* 800-369-7391 ■ *Web:* www.promotioninmotion.com	Closter	NJ	07624	201-784-5800	784-1010
RM Palmer Co 77 S 2nd Ave *Web:* www.rmpalmer.com	West Reading	PA	19611	610-372-8971	378-5208
Russell Stover Candies Inc 4900 Oak St *TF:* 800-477-8683 ■ *Web:* www.russellstover.com	Kansas City	MO	64112	816-842-9240	
Santa Cruz Nutritionals 2200 Delaware Ave **Fax:* Sales ■ *Web:* www.santacruznutritionals.com	Santa Cruz	CA	95060	831-457-3200	460-0610*
Sconza Candy Co 1 Sconza Candy Ln *TF:* 888-726-6921 ■ *Web:* www.sconzacandy.com	Oakdale	CA	95361	209-845-3700	845-3737
See's Candies Inc 210 El Camino Real *TF Cust Svc:* 800-951-7337 ■ *Web:* www.sees.com	South San Francisco	CA	94080	650-761-2490	875-6825
Sherwood Brands Inc 9601 Blackwell Rd # 225 *Web:* www.sherwoodbrands.com	Rockville	MD	20850	301-309-6161	309-6162
Sorbee International Ltd 9990 Global Rd *TF:* 800-654-3997 ■ *Web:* www.sorbee.com	Philadelphia	PA	19115	215-677-5200	677-7736
Spangler Candy Co 400 N Portland St PO Box 71 *TF Sales:* 800-653-8638 ■ *Web:* www.spanglercandy.com	Bryan	OH	43506	419-636-4221	636-3695
Standard Candy Co Inc 715 Massman Dr *TF:* 800-226-4340 ■ *Web:* www.googoo.com	Nashville	TN	37210	615-889-6360	889-7775
Storck USA LP 325 N LaSalle St Suite 400 *TF:* 800-621-7772 ■ *Web:* www.storck.com	Chicago	IL	60610	312-467-5700	467-9722
Supreme Chocolatier LLC 1150 S Ave *Web:* www.supremechocolatier.com	Staten Island	NY	10314	718-761-9600	761-5279
Sweet Candy Co Inc 3780 W Directors Row *TF:* 800-669-8669 ■ *Web:* www.sweetcandy.com	Salt Lake City	UT	84104	801-886-1444	886-1404
T R Toppers Inc 320 Fairchild *TF:* 800-748-4635 ■ *Web:* www.trtoppers.com	Pueblo	CO	81001	719-948-4902	948-4908
Tootsie Roll Industries Inc 7401 S Cicero Ave *NYSE:* TR ■ *TF:* 800-877-7655 ■ *Web:* www.tootsie.com	Chicago	IL	60629	773-838-3400	838-3534
Vitasoy USA Inc 1 New England Way *TF:* 800-848-2769 ■ *Web:* www.nasoya.com	Ayer	MA	01432	978-772-6880	772-6881
Waymouth Farms Inc 5300 Boone Ave *TF:* 800-527-0094 ■ *Web:* www.goodsensesnacks.com	New Hope	MN	55428	763-533-5300	533-9890

				Phone	Fax
Wolfgang Candy Co 50 E 4th Ave	York	PA	17404	717-843-5536	845-2881
TF: 800-248-4273 ■ *Web:* www.wolfgangcandy.com					
World's Finest Chocolate Inc 4801 S Lawndale	Chicago	IL	60632	888-821-8452	256-2685*
**Fax Area Code:* 877 ■ *TF:* 888-821-8452 ■ *Web:* www.worldsfinestchocolate.com					
Y & S Candies 400 Running Pump Rd	Lancaster	PA	17603	717-299-1261	394-9109
Zachary Confections Inc 2130 W SR-28	Frankfort	IN	46041	765-659-4751	659-1491
TF Cust Svc: 800-445-4222 ■ *Web:* www.zacharyconfections.com					

299-9 Cookies & Crackers

				Phone	Fax
B Manischewitz Co LLC					
1 Manischewitz Plaza	Jersey City	NJ	07302	201-333-3700	333-1809
Web: www.manischewitz.com					
Bakery Express -Ms Desserts					
4711 Hollins Ferry Rd	halethrope	MD	21227	410-281-2000	944-5427
Web: www.ms					
Benzel's Pretzel Bakery Inc 5200 6th Ave	Altoona	PA	16602	814-942-5062	942-4133
TF: 800-344-4438 ■ *Web:* www.benzels.com					
Bremner Biscuit Co 4600 Joliet St	Denver	CO	80239	303-371-8180	371-8185
TF: 800-722-1871 ■ *Web:* www.bremnerbiscuitco.com					
Bremner Inc 800 Market St PO Box 618	Saint Louis	MO	63101	314-877-7000	877-7667
TF Cust Svc: 800-445-8338 ■ *Web:* www.bremnerbiscuit.com					
Christie Cookie Co 1205 3rd Ave N	Nashville	TN	37208	615-242-3817	242-5572
TF: 800-458-2447 ■ *Web:* www.christiecookies.com					
Deep Foods Inc 1090 Springfield Rd	Union	NJ	07083	908-810-7500	810-1518
Web: www.deepfoods.com					
Delyse Inc 505 Reactor Way	Reno	NV	89502	775-857-1811	857-4722
TF: 800-441-6887 ■ *Web:* www.delyse.com					
Ellison Bakery 4108 W Ferguson Rd	Fort Wayne	IN	46809	260-747-6136	747-1954
Web: www.ebakery.com					
Fehr Foods Inc 5425 N 1st St	Abilene	TX	79603	325-691-5425	691-5471
Web: www.fehrfoods.com					
Ferrara Bakery & Cafe Inc					
195 Grand St 3rd Fl	New York	NY	10013	212-226-6150	226-0667
TF: 800-871-6068 ■ *Web:* www.ferraracafe.com					
Interbake Foods LLC					
2821 Emerywood Pkwy Suite 210	Richmond	VA	23294	804-755-7107	
Web: www.interbakefoods.com					
J & J Snack Foods Corp 6000 Central Hwy	Pennsauken	NJ	08109	856-665-9533	665-6718
NASDAQ: JJSF ■ *TF:* 800-486-9533 ■ *Web:* www.jjsnack.com					
Joy Cone Co 3435 Lamor Rd	Hermitage	PA	16148	724-962-5747	962-7103
TF: 800-242-2663 ■ *Web:* www.joycone.com					
Joyce Food Products Inc 80 Ave K	Newark	NJ	07105	973-491-9696	589-6145*
Keebler Foods Co					
1 Kellogg Sq PO Box 3599	Battle Creek	MI	49016	269-961-2000	530-8773*
**Fax Area Code:* 630 ■ *Web:* www.keebler.com					
Keystone Pretzels 124 W Airport Rd	Lititz	PA	17543	717-560-1882	560-2241
TF: 888-572-4500 ■ *Web:* www.keystonepretzels.com					
Lance Inc PO Box 32368	Charlotte	NC	28232	704-557-8300	
NASDAQ: LNCE ■ *Web:* www.lance.com					
Little Dutch Boy Bakery Inc 12349 S 970 E	Draper	UT	84020	801-571-3800	571-3802
TF: 800-382-2594					
Norse Dairy Systems PO Box 1869	Columbus	OH	43216	614-294-4931	
TF: 800-338-7465 ■ *Web:* www.norse.com					
Pretzels Inc 123 Harvest Rd PO Box 503	Bluffton	IN	46714	260-824-4838	824-0895
TF: 800-456-4838 ■ *Web:* www.pretzels-inc.com					
Richmond Baking Co 520 N 6th St	Richmond	IN	47374	765-962-8535	962-2253
Web: www.richmondbaking.com					
Rudolph Foods Co Inc 6575 Bellefontaine Rd	Lima	OH	45804	419-648-3611	648-4087
TF: 800-241-7675 ■ *Web:* www.rudolphfoods.com					
Shur-Good Biscuit Co Inc					
2950 Robertson Ave 4th Fl	Cincinnati	OH	45209	513-458-6200	458-6212
Silver Lake Cookie Co Inc 141 Freeman Ave	Islip	NY	11751	631-581-4000	581-4510
TF: 800-645-9048 ■ *Web:* www.silverlakecookie.com					
Snyder's of Hanover 1250 York St PO Box 6917	Hanover	PA	17331	717-632-4477	632-7207
TF: 800-233-7125 ■ *Web:* www.snydersofhanover.com					
Stella D'oro Biscuit Co Inc 184 W 237th St	Bronx	NY	10463	718-549-3700	884-6494
Sweet Street Desserts PO Box 15127	Reading	PA	19612	610-921-8113	921-8195
TF Orders: 800-793-3897 ■ *Web:* www.sweetstreet.com					
T Marzetti Co Chatham Village Foods Div					
15 Kendrick Rd	Wareham	MA	02571	508-291-2304	291-0133
TF: 800-771-3888 ■ *Web:* www.marzetti.com					
Tom Sturgis Pretzels Inc 2267 Lancaster Pike	Reading	PA	19607	610-775-0335	796-1418*
**Fax:* PR ■ *TF:* 800-817-3834 ■ *Web:* www.tomsturgispretzels.com					
Venus Wafers Inc 70 Research Rd	Hingham	MA	02043	781-740-1002	749-7195
TF: 800-545-4538 ■ *Web:* www.venuswafers.com					
Vista Bakery Inc					
3000 Mt Pleasant St PO Box 888	Burlington	IA	52601	319-754-6551	752-0063
TF: 800-553-2343 ■ *Web:* www.vistabakery.com					
Wege Pretzel Co 116 N Blettner Ave	Hanover	PA	17331	800-233-1933	632-4190*
**Fax Area Code:* 717 ■ *TF:* 800-233-1933 ■ *Web:* www.wege.com					
Willmar Cookie & Nut Co Inc 1118 E Hwy 12	Willmar	MN	56201	320-235-0600	235-0659

299-10 Dairy Products - Dry, Condensed, Evaporated

				Phone	Fax
Abbott Laboratories Ross Products Div					
625 Cleveland Ave	Columbus	OH	43215	614-624-7677	624-7616*
**Fax:* PR ■ *TF PR:* 800-227-5767 ■ *Web:* www.rosslabs.com					
American Casein Co 109 Elbow Ln	Burlington	NJ	08016	609-387-3130	387-7204
TF: 800-699-6455 ■ *Web:* www.americancasein.com					
AMPI 315 N Broadway	New Ulm	MN	56073	507-354-8295	359-8668
TF: 800-533-3580 ■ *Web:* www.ampi.com					
California Dairies Inc 2000 N Plaza Dr	Visalia	CA	93291	559-625-2200	625-5433
TF: 800-821-5588 ■ *Web:* www.californiadairies.com					
Dairy Farmers of America Inc					
10220 N Ambassador Dr Northpointe Tower	Kansas City	MO	64153	816-801-6455	801-6592
TF: 888-332-6455 ■ *Web:* www.dfamilk.com					
Davisco International Inc 719 N Main St	Le Sueur	MN	56058	507-665-8811	665-3701
TF: 800-323-4503 ■ *Web:* www.daviscofoods.com					
Erie Foods International Inc					
401 7th Ave PO Box 648	Erie	IL	61250	309-659-2233	659-2822
TF: 800-447-1887 ■ *Web:* www.eriefoods.com					
Farmers Co-op Creamery Inc					
700 N Hwy 99 W	McMinnville	OR	97128	503-472-2157	472-3821
Foremost Farms USA E10889A Penny Ln	Baraboo	WI	53913	608-355-8700	355-6701
TF: 800-362-9196 ■ *Web:* www.foremostfarms.com					
Galloway Co Inc 601 S Commercial St	Neenah	WI	54956	920-722-7741	722-1927
Web: www.gallowaycompany.com					
Gehl's Guernsey Farms Inc					
N116 W15970 Main St	Germantown	WI	53022	262-251-8570	251-8744
TF: 800-521-2873 ■ *Web:* www.gehls.com					
Instantwhip Foods Inc 2200 Cardigan Ave	Columbus	OH	43215	614-488-2536	488-0307*
**Fax:* Sales ■ *TF Cust Svc:* 800-544-9447 ■ *Web:* www.instantwhip.com					
Jackson-Mitchell Inc PO Box 934	Turlock	CA	95381	209-667-2019	668-4753
TF: 800-343-1185 ■ *Web:* www.meyenberg.com					
Land O'Lakes Inc 4001 Lexington Ave N	Arden Hills	MN	55126	651-481-2222	481-2488*
**Fax:* Hum Res ■ *TF:* 800-328-9680 ■ *Web:* www.landolakesinc.com					
Maple Island Inc					
2497 7th Ave E Suite 105	North Saint Paul	MN	55109	651-773-1000	773-2155
TF: 800-369-1022 ■ *Web:* www.maple-island.com					
Mead Johnson Canada 333 Preston St Suite 600	Ottawa	ON	K1S5N4	613-567-3536	239-3996
Web: www.meadjohnson.ca					
Mead Johnson Nutritionals					
2701 Patriot Blvd 4th Fl	Glenview	IL	60026	847-832-2420	
Web: www.meadjohnson.com					
Milk Products LLC PO Box 150	Chilton	WI	53014	920-849-2348	849-9014
TF: 800-657-0793 ■ *Web:* www.milkproductsinc.com					
Milnot Co 100 S Fourth St Suite 1010	Saint Louis	MO	63102	314-436-7667	436-7679
TF Sales: 800-877-6455 ■ *Web:* www.milnot.com					
Morningstar Foods 2515 McKinney Ave Suite 1200	Dallas	TX	75201	214-303-3400	303-3499
Nestle USA Inc 800 N Brand Blvd	Glendale	CA	91203	818-549-6000	549-6952*
**Fax:* Sales ■ *Web:* www.nestle.com					
O-AT-KA Milk Products Co-op Inc					
700 Ellicott St	Batavia	NY	14020	585-343-0536	343-4473
TF: 800-828-8152 ■ *Web:* www.oatkamilk.com					
Ohio Processors Inc PO Box 594	London	OH	43140	740-852-9243	852-5445
Penn Maid Foods Inc 10975 Dutton Rd	Philadelphia	PA	19154	215-824-2800	824-2820
TF: 800-220-7063 ■ *Web:* www.pennmaid.com					
Rich Products Corp 1 Robert Rich Way	Buffalo	NY	14213	716-878-8000	
TF: 800-828-2021 ■ *Web:* www.richs.com					
Sinton Dairy Foods Co LLC					
3801 Sinton Rd	Colorado Springs	CO	80907	719-633-3821	633-4376
TF: 800-388-4970 ■ *Web:* www.sintondairy.com					
Valentine Enterprises Inc					
940 Collins Hill Rd	Lawrenceville	GA	30043	770-995-0661	995-0725
Web: www.veiusa.com					
Vern Dale Products Inc 8445 Lyndon St	Detroit	MI	48238	313-834-4190	834-6280
Web: www.verndaleproducts.com					

299-11 Diet & Health Foods

				Phone	Fax
Alle Processing Corp 56-20 59th St	Maspeth	NY	11378	718-894-2000	326-4642
Web: www.moncuisine.com					
AMS Health Sciences Inc 4000 N Lindsay	Oklahoma City	OK	73105	405-842-0131	843-4935
TF: 800-426-4267 ■ *Web:* www.amsonline.com					
Balance Bar Co					
800 W Chester Ave PO Box 1031	Rye Brook	NY	10573	800-678-4246	
TF: 800-678-4246					
BAZI Inc 1730 Blake St Suite 305	Denver	CO	80202	303-316-8577	316-8078
TF: 888-935-7808 ■ *Web:* www.drinkbazi.com					
Cascadian Farm Inc 719 Metcalf St	Sedro Woolley	WA	98284	360-855-0100	855-0444
TF: 800-624-4123 ■ *Web:* www.cascadianfarm.com					
ConAgra Foods Retail Products Co Grocery Foods Group					
3353 Michelson Dr	Irvine	CA	92612	949-437-1018	437-3315
Continental Culture Specialists Inc					
1358 E Colorado St	Glendale	CA	91205	818-240-7400	240-7400
Eden Foods Inc 701 Tecumseh Rd	Clinton	MI	49236	517-456-7424	456-6075
TF Cust Svc: 800-248-0320 ■ *Web:* www.edenfoods.com					
Golden Temple Inc 2545 Prairie Rd	Eugene	OR	97402	541-461-2160	461-2191
TF: 800-285-6457 ■ *Web:* www.goldentemple.com					
Great American Health Foods 4075 40th Ave SW	Fargo	ND	58104	701-356-2760	450-5047*
**Fax Area Code:* 800 ■ *TF:* 800-437-2733					
Grow Co Inc 55 Railroad Ave	Richfield	NJ	07657	201-941-8777	
Health Hut 1512 1st Ave NE	Cedar Rapids	IA	52402	319-362-7345	369-0440
Isagenix International LLC 2225 S Price Rd	Chandler	AZ	85286	480-889-5747	636-5386
TF: 877-877-8111 ■ *Web:* www.isagenix.com/us/en/home.dhtml					
Lehman Sugarfree Confections Inc					
4512 Farragut Rd	Brooklyn	NY	11203	718-469-3057	469-3060
TF: 800-438-3327					
Medifast Inc 11445 Cronhill Dr	Owings Mills	MD	21117	410-581-8042	581-8070
AMEX: MED ■ *TF:* 866-463-3432 ■ *Web:* www.medifast1.com					
Nutrition 21 Inc 4 Manhattanville Rd	Purchase	NY	10577	914-701-4500	696-0860
NASDAQ: NXXI ■ *TF:* 800-699-3533 ■ *Web:* www.nutrition21.com					
RC Fine Foods PO Box 236	Belle Mead	NJ	08502	908-359-5500	359-6957
TF: 800-526-3953 ■ *Web:* www.rcfinefoods.com					
Seasons' Enterprises Ltd					
1790 W Cortland Ct Suite B PO Box 965	Addison	IL	60101	630-628-0211	628-0385
TF: 800-789-0211 ■ *Web:* www.seasonssnacks.com					
Slim-Fast Foods Co 800 Sylvan Ave	Englewood Cliffs	NJ	07632	201-894-7760	871-8117
TF: 877-375-4632 ■ *Web:* www.slim-fast.com					
Tahitian Noni International 333 W Riverpark Dr	Provo	UT	84604	801-234-1000	234-1001
TF Cust Svc: 800-445-2969 ■ *Web:* www.tni.com/united_states					
TreeHouse Foods Inc					
2021 Spring Rd Suite 600	Oak Brook	IL	60523	708-483-1300	409-1062
NYSE: THS ■ *Web:* www.treehousefoods.com					
Vitaminerals Inc 1815 Flower St	Glendale	CA	91201	800-432-1856	240-2785*
**Fax Area Code:* 818 ■ *TF:* 800-432-1856 ■ *Web:* www.cryogel.tv					

Company	City	State	ZIP	Phone	Fax
Vitarich Foods Inc 4365 Arnold Ave *TF:* 800-817-9999 ■ *Web:* www.vitarichlabs.com	Naples	FL	34104	239-430-2266	430-4930
Worldwide Sport Nutrition 851 Broken Sound Pkwy NW Suite 133 **Fax Area Code:* 866 ■ *TF:* 800-854-5019 ■ *Web:* www.sportnutrition.com	Boca Raton	FL	33487	561-241-9400	857-6152*

299-12 Fats & Oils - Animal or Marine

Company	City	State	ZIP	Phone	Fax
Baker Commodities Inc 4020 Bandini Blvd *TF:* 800-427-0696	Los Angeles	CA	90023	323-268-2801	268-5166
Coast Packing Co 3275 E Vernon Ave *Web:* www.coastpacking.com	Los Angeles	CA	90058	323-277-7700	277-7712
Darling International Inc 251 O'Connor Ridge Blvd Suite 300 *AMEX:* DAR ■ *TF:* 800-800-4841 ■ *Web:* www.darlingii.com	Irving	TX	75038	972-717-0300	717-1588
GA Wintzer & Son Co 5 N Blackhoof St PO Box 406 *TF:* 800-331-1801	Wapakoneta	OH	45895	419-738-3771	
Griffin Industries 4221 Alexandria Pike *TF:* 800-743-7413 ■ *Web:* www.griffinind.com	Cold Spring	KY	41076	859-781-2010	572-2575
Griffin Industries Inc 4413 Tanner Church Rd *TF:* 800-536-3935	Ellenwood	GA	30294	404-363-1320	363-1335
Harbinger Group Inc 450 Pk Ave 27th Fl *NYSE:* HRG ■ **Fax Area Code:* 585 ■ *Web:* www.zapatacorp.com	New York	NY	10022	212-906-8555	242-8677*
Jacob Stern & Sons Inc 1464 E Valley Rd *TF:* 800-223-7054 ■ *Web:* www.jacobstern.com	Santa Barbara	CA	93108	805-565-1411	565-1415
Kaluzny Bros Inc 2324 Mound Rd	Joliet	IL	60436	815-744-1453	729-5078
National By-Products Inc 907 Walnut St Suite 400 *TF:* 888-773-5430	Des Moines	IA	50309	515-288-2166	288-1007
Omega Protein Corp 2105 City W Blvd Suite 500 **Fax Area Code:* 713 ■ *Web:* www.buyomegaprotein.com	Houston	TX	77042	877-866-3423	940-6166*
San Luis Tallow Co Inc PO Box 3835 *TF:* 800-281-8660	San Luis Obispo	CA	93403	805-543-8660	
Werner G Smith Inc 1730 Train Ave *TF:* 800-535-8343 ■ *Web:* www.wernergsmithinc.com	Cleveland	OH	44113	216-861-3676	861-3680

299-13 Fish & Seafood - Canned

Company	City	State	ZIP	Phone	Fax
Acme Smoked Fish Corp 30 Gem St *Web:* www.acmesmokedfish.com	Brooklyn	NY	11222	718-383-8585	
Alyeska Seafoods Inc PO Box 31359	Seattle	WA	98103	206-547-2100	547-1808
Annette Island Packing Co 100 Tait St *Web:* www.metlakatlaseafood.com	Metlakatla	AK	99926	907-886-4661	886-4660
Appert's Foodservice 900 S Hwy 10 *TF:* 800-225-3883 ■ *Web:* www.apperts.com	Saint Cloud	MN	56304	320-251-3200	259-0747
Beaver Street Fisheries Inc 1741 W Beaver St *TF:* 800-874-6426 ■ *Web:* www.beaverfish.com	Jacksonville	FL	32209	904-354-8533	
Bumble Bee Seafoods Inc 9655 Granite Ridge Dr # 100 *TF:* 800-800-8572 ■ *Web:* www.bumblebee.com	San Diego	CA	92123	858-715-4000	560-6045
Chicken of the Sea International Inc 9330 Scranton Rd Suite 500 PO Box 85568 *TF:* 800-456-1511 ■ *Web:* www.chickenofthesea.com	San Diego	CA	92186	858-558-9662	597-4574
High Liner Foods Inc PO Box 839 *Web:* www.highlinerfoods.com	Portsmouth	NH	03802	603-431-6865	430-9205
Icicle Seafoods Inc 4019 21st Ave W *Web:* www.icicleseafoods.com	Seattle	WA	98199	206-282-0988	282-7222
Inlet Fish Producers Inc 2000 Columbia St PO Box 114 *Web:* www.inletfish.com	Kenai	AK	99611	907-283-9275	283-4097
Los Angeles Smoking & Curing Co (LASCCO) PO Box 53236	Los Angeles	CA	90053	213-622-0724	624-2369
Nelson Crab Inc PO Box 520 *TF:* 800-262-0069 ■ *Web:* www.nelsoncrabonline.com	Tokeland	WA	98590	360-267-2911	267-2921
Noon Hour Food Products Inc 215 N Des Plaines *TF Cust Svc:* 800-621-6636	Chicago	IL	60661	312-382-1177	382-9420
Overwaitea Food Group 19855 92A Ave *TF:* 800-242-9229 ■ *Web:* www.owfg.com	Langley	BC	V1M3B6	604-888-1213	
Pacific Choice Seafoods Co 1 Commercial St	Eureka	CA	95501	707-442-2981	442-2985
Pacific Seafood Co PO Box 97 *TF:* 800-388-1101 ■ *Web:* www.pacseafood.com	Clackamas	OR	97015	503-657-1101	
Peter Pan Seafoods Inc 2200 6th Ave Suite 1000 *Web:* www.ppsf.com	Seattle	WA	98121	206-728-6000	441-9090
Petersburg Fisheries 411 N Nordic Dr *Web:* www.hookedonfish.com	Petersburg	AK	99833	907-772-4294	772-4472
Rich-SeaPak Corp PO Box 20670 *TF:* 800-654-9731 ■ *Web:* www.seapak.com	Saint Simons Island	GA	31522	912-638-5000	634-3104
RJ Peacock Canning Co PO Box 189	Lubec	ME	04652	207-733-5556	733-0936
Sea Safari Ltd 785 E Pantego St PO Box 369	Belhaven	NC	27810	252-943-3091	943-3083
Silver Lining Seafoods Co PO Box 6092 *Web:* www.silverliningseafoods.com	Ketchikan	AK	99901	907-225-9865	225-3891
Snow's/Doxsee Inc 994 Ocean Dr *TF:* 800-459-0396 ■ *Web:* www.snows.com	Cape May	NJ	08204	609-884-0440	898-2409
Vita Food Products Inc 2222 W Lake St *AMEX:* VSF ■ *TF:* 800-989-8482 ■ *Web:* www.vitafoodproducts.com	Chicago	IL	60612	312-738-4500	738-3215
Wards Cove Packing Co 88 E Hamlin St	Seattle	WA	98102	206-323-3200	323-9165
Westward Seafoods 2101 4th Ave Suite 1700 *Web:* www.westwardseafoods.com	Seattle	WA	98121	206-682-5949	682-1825

299-14 Fish & Seafood - Fresh or Frozen

Company	City	State	ZIP	Phone	Fax
America's Catch Inc PO Box 584 *TF:* 800-242-0041 ■ *Web:* www.catfish.com	Itta Bena	MS	38941	662-254-7207	254-9776
American Seafoods International 40 Herman Melville Blvd *TF:* 800-343-8046	New Bedford	MA	02740	508-997-0031	997-5820
Bama Sea Products 756 28th St S *TF:* 800-833-3474 ■ *Web:* www.bamasea.com	Saint Petersburg	FL	33712	727-327-3474	322-0580
Blount Seafood Corp 630 Currant Rd *TF:* 800-274-2526 ■ *Web:* www.blountseafood.com	Fall River	MA	02720	774-888-1300	888-1399
Bon Secour Fisheries Inc 17449 County Rd 49 S PO Box 60 *TF:* 800-633-6854 ■ *Web:* www.bonsecourfisheries.com	Bon Secour	AL	36511	251-949-7411	949-6478
Camanchaca Inc 7200 NW 19th St Suite 410 *TF:* 800-335-7553 ■ *Web:* www.camanchacainc.com	Miami	FL	33126	305-406-9560	
Chef John Folse & Co Inc 2517 S Philippe Ave *Web:* www.jfolse.com	Gonzales	LA	70737	225-644-6000	
Chesapeake Bay Packing Llc 800 Terminal Ave *Web:* www.chesapeakebaypacking.com	Newport News	VA	23607	757-244-8440	244-8500
Chesapeake Fish Co Inc 535 Harbor Ln *Web:* www.chesapeakefish.com	San Diego	CA	92101	619-238-0526	238-5592
ConFish Inc PO Box 271 *TF:* 800-228-3474 ■ *Web:* www.confish.com	Isola	MS	38754	662-962-3101	962-0114
Crocker & Winsor Seafoods Inc PO Box 51905 *TF:* 800-225-1597 ■ *Web:* www.crockerwinsor.com	Boston	MA	02205	617-269-3100	269-3376
Eastern Fisheries Inc 14 Hervey Tichon Ave *Web:* easternfisheries.com	New Bedford	MA	02740	508-993-5300	991-2226
Eastern Shore Seafood PO Box 38 *TF Sales:* 800-446-8550	Mappsville	VA	23407	757-824-5651	824-4135
Fishermen's Pride Processors 4510 S Alameda St *Web:* www.neptunefoods.com	Los Angeles	CA	90058	323-232-8300	232-8833
Freshwater Farm Products LLC 4554 State Hwy 12 E PO Box 850 *TF:* 800-748-9338 ■ *Web:* www.freshwatercatfish.com	Belzoni	MS	39038	662-247-4205	247-4442
Gorton's Inc 128 Rogers St *TF:* 800-225-0572 ■ *Web:* www.gortons.com	Gloucester	MA	01930	978-283-3000	281-8295
Graham & Rollins Inc 19 Rudd Ln	Hampton	VA	23669	757-723-3831	722-3762
Great Northern Products LTD 2700 PLAINFIELD PIKE *Web:* www.northernproducts.com	Cranston	RI	02921	401-490-4590	490-5595
Harris Soup Co The 17711 NE Riverside Pkwy *TF:* 800-307-7687 ■ *Web:* www.harrysfresh.com	Portland	OR	97230	503-257-7687	257-7363
Iceland Seafood Corp 190 Enterprise Dr	Newport News	VA	23603	757-820-4000	888-6250
Icelandic USA Inc 190 Enterprise Dr *Web:* www.icelandic.com	Newport News	VA	23603	757-820-4000	888-6250
Indian Ridge Shrimp Co 120 Dr Hugh St Martin Rd	Chauvin	LA	70344	985-594-3361	594-9641
King & Prince Seafood Corp 1 King & Prince Blvd *TF:* 800-841-0205 ■ *Web:* www.kpseafood.com	Brunswick	GA	31520	912-265-5155	264-4812
Kitchens Seafood 1001 E Baker St *TF:* 800-327-0132	Plant City	FL	33563	813-750-1888	750-1889
Metompkin Bay Oyster Co 101 N 11th St # 105 *Web:* www.metompkinseafood.com	Crisfield	MD	21817	410-968-0660	968-0670
Morey's Seafood International LLC 1218 Hwy 10 S *Web:* www.moreys.com	Motley	MN	56466	218-352-6345	352-6523
Netuno USA Inc 18501 Pines Blvd Suite 206 *Web:* www.netunousa.com	Pembroke Pines	FL	33029	305-513-0904	513-3904
Ocean Beauty Seafoods Inc 1100 W Ewing St *TF:* 800-877-0185 ■ *Web:* www.oceanbeauty.com	Seattle	WA	98119	206-285-6800	285-9190
Overwaitea Food Group 19855 92A Ave *TF:* 800-242-9229 ■ *Web:* www.owfg.com	Langley	BC	V1M3B6	604-888-1213	
Pacific Coast Seafood Co PO Box 70	Warrenton	OR	97146	503-861-2201	861-3302*
Pinnacle Foods Corp 121 Woodcrest Rd *TF:* 800-486-8816 ■ *Web:* www.pinnaclefoodscorp.com	Cherry Hill	NJ	08003	856-969-7100	
Riverside Foods Inc 2520 Wilson St	Two Rivers	WI	54241	920-793-4511	794-7332
Sea Harvest Packing Co PO Box 818 *TF:* 800-627-4300 ■ *Web:* www.seaharvest.com	Brunswick	GA	31521	912-264-3212	264-2749
Sea Watch International Ltd 8978 Glebe Pk Dr *TF:* 800-732-2526 ■ *Web:* www.seaclam.com	Easton	MD	21601	410-822-7500	822-1266
Seafood Producers Co-op 2875 Roeder Ave *Web:* www.spcsales.com	Bellingham	WA	98225	360-733-0120	733-0513
Simmons Farm Raised Catfish Inc 2628 Erickson Rd *Web:* www.simmonscatfish.com	Yazoo City	MS	39194	662-746-5687	746-8625
Smith Luther & Son Inc PO Box 67	Atlantic	NC	28511	252-225-3341	225-6391
Stoller Fisheries Inc 1301 18th St *TF:* 800-831-5174 ■ *Web:* www.stollerfisheries.com	Spirit Lake	IA	51360	712-336-1750	336-4681
Sugiyo USA Inc PO Box 468 *Web:* www.sugiyo.com	Anacortes	WA	98221	360-293-0180	293-6964
Tampa Bay Fisheries Inc 3060 Gallagher Rd *TF:* 800-234-2561 ■ *Web:* www.tampabayfisheries.com	Dover	FL	33527	813-752-8883	752-3168
Tampa Maid Foods Inc 1600 Kathleen Rd *TF:* 800-237-7637 ■ *Web:* www.tampamaid.com	Lakeland	FL	33805	863-687-4411	683-8713
Texas Pack Inc PO Box 1643	Port Isabel	TX	78578	956-943-5461	943-6630
Thomas Seafood of Carteret Inc 421 Merrimon Rd	Beaufort	NC	28516	252-728-2391	728-6792
Tichon Seafood Corp 7 Conway St	New Bedford	MA	02740	508-999-5607	990-8271
Trident Seafood Corp 5303 Shilshole Ave NW *TF:* 800-426-5490 ■ *Web:* www.tridentseafoods.com	Seattle	WA	98107	206-783-3818	782-7195
True World Foods International Inc 1515 Puyallup St *TF:* 800-935-6464 ■ *Web:* www.kanimi.com	Sumner	WA	98390	253-826-3700	826-2534

Company	City	State	Zip	Phone	Fax
UniSea Inc 15400 NE 90th St PO Box 97019 *TF:* 800-535-8509 ■ *Web:* www.unisea.com	Redmond	WA	98073	425-881-8181	861-5249
Viking Seafoods Inc 50 Crystal St *TF:* 800-225-3920 ■ *Web:* www.vikingseafoods.com	Malden	MA	02148	781-324-1050	397-0527
Wanchese Fish Co 2000 Northgate Commerce Pkwy *Web:* www.wanchese.com	Suffolk	VA	23435	757-673-4500	673-4550

299-15 Flavoring Extracts & Syrups

Company	City	State	Zip	Phone	Fax
Aroma Tech Inc 130 Industrial Pkwy *TF:* 800-542-7662 ■ *Web:* www.aromatec.com	Somerville	NJ	08876	908-707-0707	707-1704
Brady Enterprises Inc 167 Moore Rd *TF:* 800-225-5126 ■ *Web:* www.brady-ent.com	East Weymouth	MA	02189	781-337-5000	337-9338
Cleveland Syrup Corp 5000 Track Rd PO Box 91959	Cleveland	OH	44101	216-883-1845	883-6204
David Michael & Co Inc 10801 Decatur Rd *TF:* 800-523-3806 ■ *Web:* www.dmflavors.com	Philadelphia	PA	19154	215-632-3100	637-3920
DD Williamson & Co Inc 100 S Spring St *TF:* 800-227-2635 ■ *Web:* www.caramel.com	Louisville	KY	40206	502-895-2438	
Dr Pepper Snapple Group Inc 5301 Legacy Dr *TF:* 800-686-7398 ■ *Web:* www.drpeppersnapplegroup.com	Plano	TX	75024	972-673-7000	673-7980
Edlong Corp 225 Scott St *TF:* 888-698-2783 ■ *Web:* www.edlong.com	Elk Grove Village	IL	60007	847-439-9230	439-0053
Emerald Kalama Chemical LLC 1296 3rd St NW *Web:* www.emeraldmaterials.com	Kalama	WA	98625	360-673-2550	673-3564
Firmenich Inc PO Box 5880 *TF:* 800-257-9591 ■ *Web:* www.firmenich.com	Princeton	NJ	08543	609-452-1000	452-0564
Flavor Systems International Inc 10139 Commerce Pk Dr *TF:* 800-498-2783 ■ *Web:* www.flavorsystems.com	Cincinnati	OH	45246	513-870-4900	870-4909
Food Producers International 10505 Wayzata Blvd Suite 400 *TF:* 800-443-1336	Minnetonka	MN	55305	952-544-2763	
Frutarom Corp 9500 Railroad Ave **Fax:* Cust Svc ■ *TF:* 800-526-7147 ■ *Web:* www.frutarom.com	North Bergen	NJ	07047	201-861-9500	861-9267*
Givaudan Flavors Corp 1199 Edison Dr **Fax:* Cust Svc ■ *TF:* 800-892-1199 ■ *Web:* www.givaudan.com	Cincinnati	OH	45216	513-948-8000	948-2157*
I Rice & Co Inc 11500 Roosevelt Blvd Bldg D *TF:* 800-232-6022 ■ *Web:* www.iriceco.com	Philadelphia	PA	19116	215-673-7423	673-2616
Jel Sert Co The Rt 59 & Conde St PO Box 261 *TF:* 800-323-2592 ■ *Web:* www.jelsert.com	West Chicago	IL	60186	630-231-7590	231-3993
Kalsec Inc 3713 W Main St *TF:* 800-323-9320 ■ *Web:* www.kalsec.com	Kalamazoo	MI	49006	269-349-9711	382-3060
Kerry North America 3400 Millington Rd *TF:* 800-334-4788 ■ *Web:* www.kerrygroup.com	Beloit	WI	53511	608-363-1200	
Limpert Bros Inc 202 NW Blvd PO Box 1480 *TF:* 800-691-1353 ■ *Web:* www.limpertbrothers.com	Vineland	NJ	08362	856-691-1353	794-8968
Lyons Magnus Inc 3158 E Hamilton Ave *TF:* 800-344-7130 ■ *Web:* www.lyonsmagnus.com	Fresno	CA	93702	559-268-5966	233-8249
M & F Worldwide Corp 35 E 62nd St *NYSE: MFW* ■ *Web:* www.mandfworldwide.com	New York	NY	10021	212-572-8600	572-8400
Mastertaste 6133 N River Rd Suite 670 *Web:* www.mastertaste.com	Rosemont	IL	60018	847-823-9300	823-9301
Mother Murphy's Labs Inc 2826 S Elm St PO Box 16846 *TF:* 800-849-1277 ■ *Web:* www.mothermurphys.com	Greensboro	NC	27416	336-273-1737	273-2615
Nielsen-Massey Vanillas Inc 1550 S Shields Dr *TF:* 800-525-7873 ■ *Web:* www.nielsenmassey.com	Waukegan	IL	60085	847-578-1550	578-1570
Northwestern Flavors Inc 120 N Aurora St	West Chicago	IL	60185	630-231-6111	876-5042
Ottens Flavors 7800 Holstein Ave *TF:* 800-523-0767 ■ *Web:* www.ottensflavors.com	Philadelphia	PA	19153	215-365-7800	365-7801
Phillips Syrup Corp 28025 Ranney Pkwy *Web:* www.phillipssyrup.com	Westlake	OH	44145	440-835-8001	835-1148
Robertet Flavors Inc 10 Colonial Dr	Piscataway	NJ	08854	732-981-8300	981-1717
Sea Breeze Inc 441 Rt 202 *TF:* 800-732-2733 ■ *Web:* www.seabreezesyrups.com	Towaco	NJ	07082	973-334-7777	334-2617
Seco & Golden 100 Dairies of Florida Inc 1600 Essex Ave *Web:* www.golden100.com	DeLand	FL	32724	386-734-3906	738-1378
Sensient Technologies Corp 777 E Wisconsin Ave 11th Fl *NYSE: SXT* ■ *TF:* 800-558-9892 ■ *Web:* www.sensient-tech.com	Milwaukee	WI	53202	414-271-6755	347-4783
Sethness Products Co 3422 W Touhy Ave *TF:* 888-772-1880 ■ *Web:* www.sethness.com	Lincolnwood	IL	60712	847-329-2080	329-2090
Symrise Inc 300 N St *TF:* 800-422-1559 ■ *Web:* www.symrise.com	Teterboro	NJ	07608	201-288-3200	288-0843
T Hasegawa USA Inc 14017 183rd St *Web:* www.thasegawa.com	Cerritos	CA	90703	714-522-1900	522-6800
Virginia Dare Extract Co Inc 882 3rd Ave *TF:* 800-847-4500 ■ *Web:* www.virginiadare.com	Brooklyn	NY	11232	718-788-1776	768-3978
Western Syrup Co 13766 Milroy Pl *TF:* 800-229-6686 ■ *Web:* www.jogue.com	Santa Fe Springs	CA	90670	562-921-4485	921-5170
Wild Flavors Inc 1261 Pacific Ave **Fax:* Sales ■ *TF:* 888-945-3352 ■ *Web:* www.wildflavors.com	Erlanger	KY	41018	859-342-3600	342-3736*
Zink & Triest Co Inc 150 Domorah Dr *TF:* 800-537-5070	Montgomeryville	PA	18936	215-469-1950	469-1951

299-16 Flour Mixes & Doughs

Company	City	State	Zip	Phone	Fax
Abitec Corp Inc PO Box 569 *TF Sales:* 800-555-1255 ■ *Web:* www.abiteccorp.com	Columbus	OH	43216	614-429-6464	299-8279
Bake'n Joy Foods Inc 351 Willow St *TF:* 800-666-4937 ■ *Web:* www.bakenjoy.com	North Andover	MA	01845	978-683-1414	683-1713
Best Brands Corp 111 Cheshire Ln Suite 100 *TF:* 800-328-2068 ■ *Web:* www.bestbrandscorp.com	Minnetonka	MN	55305	952-404-7500	404-7501
Betty Crocker 1 General Mills Blvd PO Box 9452 **Fax:* PR ■ *TF:* 800-248-7310 ■ *Web:* www.bettycrocker.com	Minneapolis	MN	55426	763-764-7600	764-8330*
Caravan Products Co Inc 100 Adams Dr *TF:* 800-526-5261	Totowa	NJ	07512	973-256-8886	256-8395
Cereal Food Processors Inc 2001 Shawnee Mission Pkwy *TF:* 800-743-5687 ■ *Web:* www.cerealfood.com	Mission Woods	KS	66205	913-890-6300	890-6382
Continental Mills Inc PO Box 88176 *TF:* 800-457-7744 ■ *Web:* www.continentalmills.com	Seattle	WA	98138	253-872-8400	872-7954
CSM Bakery Products 1912 Montreal Rd *Web:* www.hcbrill.com	Tucker	GA	30084	770-938-3823	939-2934
Dawn Food Products Inc 3333 Sargent Rd *TF Cust Svc:* 800-292-1362 ■ *Web:* www.dawnfoods.com	Jackson	MI	49201	517-789-4400	789-4465
Gilster-Mary Lee Corp 1037 State St *TF:* 800-851-5371	Chester	IL	62233	618-826-2361	826-2973
Langlois Co 10810 San Sevaine Way *TF:* 800-962-5993	Mira Loma	CA	91752	951-360-3900	360-3465
Modern Products Inc PO Box 248	Thiensville	WI	53092	262-242-2400	242-2751
Pinnacle Foods Corp 121 Woodcrest Rd *TF:* 800-486-8816 ■ *Web:* www.pinnaclefoodscorp.com	Cherry Hill	NJ	08003	856-969-7100	
Puratos Corp 1941 Old Cuthbert Rd *TF:* 800-654-0036 ■ *Web:* www.puratos.com	Cherry Hill	NJ	08034	856-428-4300	428-2939
Rhodes International Inc PO Box 25487 *TF Cust Svc:* 800-876-7333 ■ *Web:* www.rhodesbread.com	Salt Lake City	UT	84125	801-972-0122	972-0286
Roman Meal Co 2101 S Tacoma Way *TF:* 800-426-3600 ■ *Web:* www.romanmeal.com	Tacoma	WA	98409	253-475-0964	475-1906
Southern Maid Donut Flour Co 3615 Cavalier Dr *TF:* 800-936-6887 ■ *Web:* www.southernmaiddonuts.com	Garland	TX	75042	972-272-6425	276-3549
Subco Foods Inc 4350 S Taylor Dr *TF:* 800-473-0757 ■ *Web:* www.subcofoods.com	Sheboygan	WI	53081	920-457-7761	457-3899
Watson Foods Co Inc 301 Heffernan Dr *TF:* 800-388-3481 ■ *Web:* www.watson-inc.com	West Haven	CT	06516	203-932-3000	932-8266

299-17 Food Emulsifiers

Company	City	State	Zip	Phone	Fax
ADM Specialty Food Ingredients Div 4666 E Faries Pkwy *TF:* 800-637-5843 ■ *Web:* www.admworld.com	Decatur	IL	62526	217-424-5200	424-4702
American Ingredients Co 3947 Broadway *TF:* 800-669-4092	Kansas City	MO	64111	816-561-9050	561-9909
American Lecithin Co Inc 115 Hurley Rd Unit 2B *TF:* 800-364-4416 ■ *Web:* www.americanlecithin.com	Oxford	CT	06478	203-262-7100	262-7101
Bunge Ltd 50 Main St 6th Fl *NYSE: BG* ■ *Web:* www.bunge.com	White Plains	NY	10606	914-684-2800	684-3499
Crest Foods Co Inc 905 Main St *Web:* www.crestfoods.com	Ashton	IL	61006	815-453-7411	453-7744
Frutarom Corp 9500 Railroad Ave **Fax:* Cust Svc ■ *TF:* 800-526-7147 ■ *Web:* www.frutarom.com	North Bergen	NJ	07047	201-861-9500	861-9267*

299-18 Fruits & Vegetables - Dried or Dehydrated

Company	City	State	Zip	Phone	Fax
Basic American Foods 2121 N California Blvd # 400 *TF:* 800-227-4050 ■ *Web:* www.baf.com	Walnut Creek	CA	94596	925-472-4000	472-4360
Bernard Food Industries Inc 1125 Hartrey Ave **Fax Area Code:* 800 ■ *TF:* 800-323-3663 ■ *Web:* www.bernardfoods.com	Evanston	IL	60204	847-869-5222	962-1546*
ConAgra Store Brands 21340 Hayes Ave	Lakeville	MN	55044	952-469-4971	469-5550
Concord Foods Inc 10 Minuteman Way *Web:* www.concordfoods.com	Brockton	MA	02301	508-580-1700	584-9425
Crystals International Inc 600 W ML King Jr Blvd *TF:* 800-237-7620	Plant City	FL	33563	813-754-2691	754-2691
Custom Culinary 2021 W Dr *TF Cust Svc:* 800-621-8827 ■ *Web:* www.customculinary.com	Oakbrook	IL	60532	630-928-4880	928-4899
Dean Distributors Inc 1350 Bayshore Hwy Suite 400 **Fax Area Code:* 800 ■ *TF:* 800-792-0816 ■ *Web:* www.deandistributors.com	Burlingame	CA	94010	650-340-1738	928-2090*
Del Monte Foods Co 1 Maritime Plaza *TF Cust Svc:* 800-543-3090 ■ *Web:* www.delmonte.com	San Francisco	CA	94111	415-247-3000	247-3565
Derco Holdings LLC 2670 W Shaw Ln *Web:* www.dercofoods.com	Fresno	CA	93711	559-435-2664	435-8520
Freskeeto Frozen Foods Inc 8019 Rt 209	Ellenville	NY	12428	845-647-5111	647-5611
Garry Packing Inc 11272 E Central Ave PO Box 249 *TF:* 800-248-2126 ■ *Web:* www.garrypacking.com	Del Rey	CA	93616	559-888-2126	888-2848
Givaudan INC PO Box 157 *TF:* 800-487-5003	Silverton	OR	97381	503-873-3600	873-7807
Graceland Fruit Inc 1123 Main St *TF:* 800-352-7181 ■ *Web:* www.gracelandfruit.com	Frankfort	MI	49635	231-352-7181	352-4711
Halben Food Mfg Co Inc 4553 Gustine Ave	Saint Louis	MO	63116	314-832-1906	832-4668
Idaho Fresh-Pak Inc 529 N 3500 E PO Box 130 *TF:* 800-635-6100 ■ *Web:* www.idahoan.com	Lewisville	ID	83431	208-754-4686	754-0094
Idaho Supreme Potatoes Inc 614 E 800 N PO Box 246	Firth	ID	83236	208-346-6841	346-4104
Idaho-Pacific Corp 4723 E 100 N PO Box 478 *TF Sales:* 800-238-5503 ■ *Web:* www.idahopacific.com	Ririe	ID	83443	208-538-6971	538-5082
Larsen Farms 2650 N 2375 E *TF Sales:* 800-767-6104 ■ *Web:* www.larsenfarms.com	Hamer	ID	83425	208-662-5501	662-5568
Meridian Foods 201 E Babb Rd	Eaton	IN	47338	765-396-3344	396-3430

Phone | Fax

MicroSoy Corp 300 Microsoy Dr. Jefferson IA 50129 515-386-2100 386-3287
Web: www.microsoyflakes.com

National Raisin Co PO Box 219 Fowler CA 93625 559-834-5981 834-1055
TF: 800-874-3726 ■ *Web:* www.nationalraisin.com

Nonpareil Corp 40 N 400 W Blackfoot ID 83221 208-785-5880 785-3656
TF: 800-522-2223 ■ *Web:* www.nonpareilpotato.com

Northwest Pea & Bean Co Inc
6109 E Desmet Ave. Spokane WA 99212 509-534-3821 534-4350

Oregon Freeze Dry Inc PO Box 1048 Albany OR 97321 541-926-6001 967-6527
TF: 800-547-4060 ■ *Web:* www.ofd.com

Oregon Potato Co PO Box 3110 Pasco WA 99302 509-545-4545
TF: 800-336-6311 ■ *Web:* www.oregonpotato.com

Sensient Dehydrated Flavors PO Box 1524 Turlock CA 95381 209-667-2777 634-6235

Small Planet Foods Inc 719 Metcalf St Sedro Woolley WA 98284 360-855-0100 855-0444
TF: 800-624-4123 ■ *Web:* www.smallplanetfoods.com

Stapleton-Spence Packing Co
1530 The Alameda Suite 320 San Jose CA 95126 408-297-8815 297-0611
TF: 800-297-8815 ■ *Web:* www.stapleton-spence.com

Sun-Maid Growers of California
13525 S Bethel Ave. Kingsburg CA 93631 559-896-8000 897-2362
TF Sales: 800-272-4746 ■ *Web:* www.sun-maid.com

Sunsweet Growers Inc 901 N Walton Ave Yuba City CA 95993 530-674-5010 751-5238
TF: 800-417-2253 ■ *Web:* www.sunsweet.com

Tree Top Inc 220 E 2nd Ave Selah WA 98942 509-697-7251 697-0421
TF: 800-237-0515 ■ *Web:* www.treetop.com

Tule River Co-op Dryer Inc
16548 Rd 168 PO Box 4477 Woodville CA 93258 559-784-3396 686-8061

Victor Packing Inc 11687 Rd 27 1/2 Madera CA 93637 559-673-5908 673-4225
Web: www.victorpacking.com

Z Foods Inc 9537 Rd 29 1/2 Madera CA 93637 559-673-6368 673-7508
Web: www.zfoods.com

299-19 Fruits & Vegetables - Pickled

Phone | Fax

B & G Foods Inc 4 Gatehall Dr Suite 110 Parsippany NJ 07054 973-401-6500 630-6553
NYSE: BGS ■ *Web:* www.bgfoods.com

Bay View Food Products Inc
2606 N Huron Rd Pinconning MI 48650 989-879-3555 879-2659
Web: www.bayviewfoods.com

Beaverton Foods Inc PO Box 687 Beaverton OR 97075 503-646-8138 644-9204
TF: 800-223-8076 ■ *Web:* www.beavertonfoods.com

Cain's Foods Inc 114 E Main St PO Box 347 Ayer MA 01432 978-772-0300 772-9254
TF: 800-225-0601 ■ *Web:* www.cainsfoods.com

Cajun Chef Products Inc PO Box 248 Saint Martinville LA 70582 337-394-7112 394-7115

Clorox Co 1221 Broadway Oakland CA 94612 510-271-7000 832-1463
NYSE: CLX ■ *TF Cust Svc:* 800-292-2808 ■ *Web:* www.thecloroxcompany.com

ConAgra Foods Retail Products Co Grocery Foods Group
3353 Michelson Dr. Irvine CA 92612 949-437-1018 437-3315

Conway Import Co Inc
11051 W Addison St. Franklin Park IL 60131 847-455-5600 455-5630
TF: 800-323-8801

Daltons Best Maid Products Inc
1400 S Riverside Dr Fort Worth TX 76104 817-335-5494 534-7117
TF: 800-447-3581 ■ *Web:* www.bestmaidproducts.com

Eastern Foods Inc 1000 Naturally Fresh Blvd. Atlanta GA 30349 404-765-9000 765-9016*
*Fax: Hum Res ■ *TF:* 800-765-1950 ■ *Web:* www.naturallyfresh.com

GLK Foods LLC 11 Clark St Shortsville WI 14548 585-289-4414
Web: www.greatlakeskraut.com

Gold Pure Food Products Inc 1 Brooklyn Rd Hempstead NY 11550 516-483-5600 483-5798
TF: 800-422-4681 ■ *Web:* www.goldshorseradish.com

Henri's Food Products Co Inc
8622 N 87th St Milwaukee WI 53224 414-365-5720 354-3958
TF Cust Svc: 800-338-8831

HV Food Products Co 1221 Broadway Oakland CA 94612 510-271-7000 832-1463
Web: www.hiddenvalley.com

JG Van Holten & Son Inc
703 W Madison St PO Box 66 Waterloo WI 53594 920-478-2144 478-2316
Web: www.vanholtenpickles.com

Kaplan & Zubrin Inc 146 Kaighns Ave Camden NJ 08103 856-964-1083 964-0510

Ken's Foods Inc 1 D'Angelo Dr Marlborough MA 01752 508-229-1100 229-1111
TF: 800-633-5800 ■ *Web:* www.kensfoods.com

Kikkoman Foods Inc
N 1365 6th Corners Rd PO Box 69 Walworth WI 53184 262-275-6181 275-9452
Web: www.kikkoman.com

Kruger Foods Inc 18362 E Hwy 4 Stockton CA 95215 209-941-8518 941-0345
Web: www.krugerfoods.com

KT's Kitchens Inc 1065 E Walnut St Carson CA 90746 310-764-0850 764-0855

Langlois Co 10810 San Sevaine Way Mira Loma CA 91752 951-360-3900 360-3465
TF: 800-962-5993

Lee Kum Kee Inc 14841 don Julian Rd City of Industry CA 91746 626-709-1888 709-1899
TF Orders: 800-654-5082 ■ *Web:* www.us.lkk.com

Litehouse Inc 1109 N Ella Ave. Sandpoint ID 83864 208-263-7569 263-7821
TF: 800-669-3169 ■ *Web:* www.litehousefoods.com

MA Gedney Co 2100 Stoughton Ave Chaska MN 55318 952-448-2612 448-1790
Web: www.gedneypickle.com

Maurice's Gourmet Barbeque PO Box 6847 West Columbia SC 29171 803-791-5887 791-8707
TF: 800-628-7423 ■ *Web:* www.mauricesbbq.com

McIlhenny Co Hwy 329 Avery Island LA 70513 337-365-8173 365-9613
TF Orders: 800-634-9599 ■ *Web:* www.tabasco.com

Meduri Farms Inc PO Box 636 Dallas OR 97338 503-623-0308
Web: www.medurifarms.com

Moody Dunbar Inc
2000 Waters Edge Dr Suite 21 Johnson City TN 37604 423-952-0100 952-0289
TF: 800-251-8202

Morehouse Foods Inc 760 Epperson Dr City of Industry CA 91748 626-854-1655 854-1656
Web: www.morehousefoods.com

Mount Olive Pickle Co PO Box 609 Mount Olive NC 28365 919-658-2535 658-6296
TF: 800-672-5041 ■ *Web:* www.mtolivepickles.com

Mullins Food Products Inc 2200 S 25th Ave Broadview IL 60155 708-344-3224 344-0153
Web: www.mullinsfood.com

Musco Olive Products Inc 17950 Via Nicolo Tracy CA 95377 209-836-4600 836-0518
TF Sales: 800-523-9828 ■ *Web:* www.olives.com

Newman's Own Inc 246 Post Rd E Westport CT 06880 203-222-0136 227-5630
Web: www.newmansown.com

NewStar Fresh Foods LLC 900 Work St. Salinas CA 93901 831-758-7800 758-7869
TF: 888-782-7220 ■ *Web:* www.newstarfresh.com

Old Dutch Mustard Co 98 Cutter Mill Rd Great Neck NY 11021 516-466-0522 466-0762

Olds Products Co 10700 88th Ave Pleasant Prairie WI 53158 262-947-3500 947-3517
TF: 800-233-8064

Pacific Choice Brands Inc 4667 E Date Ave Fresno CA 93725 559-237-5583 237-2078
Web: www.pacificchoicebrands.com

Piknik Products Co Inc 3806 Day St. Montgomery AL 36108 334-265-1567 265-9490
TF Cust Svc: 800-300-8557

Plochman Inc 1333 N Boudreau Rd. Manteno IL 60950 815-468-3434 468-8755
Web: www.plochman.com

Portion Pac Inc 7325 Snider Rd Mason OH 45040 513-398-0400 459-5300

Ralph Sechler & Son Inc
5686 State Rd 1 PO Box 152 Saint Joe IN 46785 260-337-5461 337-5771
TF: 800-332-5461 ■ *Web:* www.sl6dev.mailordercentral.com

Spring Glen Fresh Foods Inc
314 Spring Glen Dr PO Box 518 Ephrata PA 17522 717-733-2201 738-4335
TF: 800-641-2853 ■ *Web:* www.springglen.com

Swanson Pickle Co Inc
11561 Heights Ravenna Rd. Ravenna MI 49451 231-853-2289 853-6281

T Marzetti Co 1105 Schrock Rd Suite 300 Columbus OH 43229 614-846-2232 848-8330
Web: www.marzetti.com

Tasty-Toppings Inc PO Box 728 Columbus NE 68602 402-564-1347 563-1469
Web: www.dorothylynch.com

Van Law Food Products Inc PO Box 2388 Fullerton CA 92837 714-870-9091 870-5609

Victoria Packing Corp (VPC) 443 E 100th St Brooklyn NY 11236 718-927-3000 649-7069
Web: www.victoriapacking.com

Walden Farms 1209 W St Georges Ave Linden NJ 07036 908-925-9494 925-9537
TF: 800-229-1706 ■ *Web:* www.waldenfarms.com

William B Reily & Co Inc 640 Magazine St New Orleans LA 70130 504-524-6131 539-5427
TF: 800-535-1961

Yamasa Corp USA 3500 Fairview Industrial Dr SE Salem OR 97302 503-363-8550 363-8710
Web: www.yamasausa.com

299-20 Fruits, Vegetables, Juices - Canned or Preserved

Phone | Fax

All Juice Food & Beverage Corp
352 Jet St Hendersonville NC 28792 828-685-8821 685-8495
TF: 800-232-8717

Allen Canning Co 305 E Main St. Siloam Springs AR 72761 479-524-6431 524-3291
TF: 800-234-2553 ■ *Web:* www.allencanning.com

AM Braswell Jr Food Co Inc
226 N Zetterower Ave Statesboro GA 30458 912-764-6191 489-1572
TF: 800-673-9388 ■ *Web:* www.braswells.com

American Spoon Foods Inc 1668 Clarion Ave Petoskey MI 49770 231-347-9030 347-2512
TF: 800-222-5886 ■ *Web:* www.spoon.com

Apple & Eve Inc 2 Seaview Blvd Port Washington NY 11050 516-621-1122 625-9474
TF: 800-969-8018 ■ *Web:* www.appleandeve.com

Ardmore Farms Inc 1915 N Woodland Blvd DeLand FL 32720 386-734-4634 736-8894
TF: 800-365-8423 ■ *Web:* www.juice4u.com

Authentic Specialty Foods Inc
4340 Eucalyptus Ave. Chino CA 91710 909-631-2000 636-2100
TF: 888-236-2272

B & G Foods Inc 4 Gatehall Dr Suite 110 Parsippany NJ 07054 973-401-6500 630-6553
NYSE: BGS ■ *Web:* www.bgfoods.com

Baumer Foods Inc 2424 Edenborn Ave Suite 510 Metairie LA 70001 504-482-5761 483-2425
TF Sales: 800-222-0694 ■ *Web:* www.baumerfoods.com

Beckman & Gast Co Inc
282 W Kremer-Hoying Rd PO Box 307 Saint Henry OH 45883 419-678-4195
Web: www.beckmangast.com

Bonduelle Inc 8615 St Laurent Blvd Suite 200 Montreal QC H2P2M9 514-384-4281 384-7992
Web: www.bonduelle.ca

Brooklyn Bottling Co 643 S Rd Milton NY 12547 845-795-2171 795-2589

Bruce Foods Corp PO Drawer 1030 New Iberia LA 70561 337-365-8101 369-9026
TF: 800-299-9082 ■ *Web:* www.brucefoods.com

Burnette Foods Inc 701 US Hwy 31 Elk Rapids MI 49629 231-264-8116 264-9597
Web: www.burnettefoods.com

Bush Bros & Co 1016 E Weisgarber Rd Knoxville TN 37909 865-588-7685 584-8157
Web: www.bushbeans.com

California Fruit & Tomato Kitchen LLC
2906 Santa Fe St PO Box 827 Riverbank CA 95367 209-869-9300 869-9060

Campbell Soup Co 1 Campbell Pl Camden NJ 08103 856-342-4800 342-3878
NYSE: CPB ■ *TF:* 800-772-8467 ■ *Web:* www.campbellsoupcompany.com

Cargill Inc North America 15407 McGinty Rd Wayzata MN 55391 952-742-7575
TF: 800-227-4455

Carriage House Cos Inc The 196 Newton St. Fredonia NY 14063 716-673-1000 673-8443*
*Fax: Sales ■ *TF:* 800-828-8915 ■ *Web:* www.carriagehousecos.com

Cascadian Farm Inc 719 Metcalf St Sedro Woolley WA 98284 360-855-0100 855-0444
TF: 800-624-4123 ■ *Web:* www.cascadianfarm.com

Centennial Specialty Foods Corp
10700 E Geddes Ave Suite 170 Centennial CO 80112 303-292-4018 292-4364
Web: www.centennialspecialtyfoods.com

Cherry Growers Inc 6331 US Hwy 31 Grawn MI 49637 231-276-9241 276-7075
Web: www.cherrygrowers.net

Cincinnati Preserving Co Inc
3015 E Kemper Rd Sharonville OH 45241 513-771-2000 771-8381
TF Cust Svc: 800-222-9966 ■ *Web:* www.clearbrookfarms.com

Citrus Systems Inc 125 Jackson Ave N Hopkins MN 55343 952-935-0410
Web: www.citrussystems.com

Clement Pappas & Co Inc
1 colons Dr Suite 200 carneyspoint NJ 08069 856-455-1000 455-8746
TF: 800-257-7019 ■ *Web:* www.clementpappas.com

ConAgra Foods Retail Products Co Grocery Foods Group
3353 Michelson Dr. Irvine CA 92612 949-437-1018 437-3315

Company / Address	City	State	ZIP	Phone	Fax
ConAgra Hunt-Wesson Foodservice Co 3353 Michelson Dr. TF: 800-633-0112 ■ Web: www.conagrafoodservice.com	Irvine	CA	92612	949-437-1000	
Cornelius Seed Corn Co 14760 317th Ave. TF: 800-218-1862 ■ Web: www.corneliusseed.com	Bellevue	IA	52031	563-672-3463	672-3521
Country Pure Foods Inc 681 W Waterloo Rd. Web: www.countrypurefoods.com	Akron	OH	44314	330-753-2293	745-7838
Crookham Co Inc PO Box 520 Web: www.crookham.com	Caldwell	ID	83606	208-459-7451	454-2108
Daily Juice Products 1 Daily Way TF: 800-245-2929	Verona	PA	15147	412-828-9020	828-8876
Del Monte Foods Co 1 Maritime Plaza TF Cust Svc: 800-543-3090 ■ Web: www.delmonte.com	San Francisco	CA	94111	415-247-3000	247-3565
Del Monte Fresh Produce Co 241 Sevilla Ave. TF Cust Svc: 800-950-3683 ■ Web: www.freshdelmonte.com	Coral Gables	FL	33134	305-520-8400	520-8455
Diana Fruit Co Inc 651 Mathew St Web: www.dianafruit.com	Santa Clara	CA	95050	408-727-9631	727-9890
Dole Packaged Foods Co 1 Dole Dr	Westlake Village	CA	91362	818-874-4000	874-4893
Don Pepino Sales Co 123 Railroad Ave Web: www.donpepino.com	Williamstown	NJ	08094	856-629-7429	629-6340
ED Smith Foods Ltd 944 Hwy Suite 8 TF: 800-263-9246 ■ Web: www.edsmith.com	Winona	ON	L8E5S3	905-643-1211	643-3328
Escalon Premier Brands 1905 McHenry Ave TF: 800-343-9556 ■ Web: www.escalon.net	Escalon	CA	95320	209-838-7341	838-6785
Faribault Foods Inc 222 S 9th St Suite 3380 Web: www.faribaultfoods.com	Minneapolis	MN	55402	612-333-6461	342-2908
Fremont Co 802 N Front St	Fremont	OH	43420	419-334-8995	334-8120
Fruit Dynamics LLC 4206 Mercantile Ave. Web: www.incrediblefresh.com	Naples	FL	34104	239-280-3717	643-5447
Furmano Foods Inc 770 Cannery Rd PO Box 500 TF: 877-877-6032 ■ Web: www.furmanos.com	Northumberland	PA	17857	570-473-3516	473-7367
Giorgio Foods Inc PO Box 96 TF: 800-220-2139 ■ Web: www.giorgiofoods.com	Temple	PA	19560	610-926-2139	926-7012
Gray & Co 2331 23rd Ave. TF: 800-333-8876 ■ Web: www.cherryman.com	Forest Grove	OR	97116	503-357-3141	357-8837
Growers Co-op Grape Juice Co Inc 112 N Portage St PO Box 399 Web: www.concordgrapejuice.com	Westfield	NY	14787	716-326-3161	326-6566
Hanover Foods Corp 1550 York St PO Box 334 TF: 800-888-4646 ■ Web: www.hanoverfoods.com	Hanover	PA	17331	717-632-6000	632-6681
Hawaiian Sun Products Inc 259 Sand Island Access Rd Web: www.hawaiiansunproducts.com	Honolulu	HI	96819	808-845-3211	842-0532
Heinz North America 357 6th Ave Heinz 57 Ctr Web: www.heinz.com/our-food/products/north-america.aspx	Pittsburgh	PA	15222	412-237-5700	237-5377
Hirzel Canning Co & Farms 411 Lemoyne Rd. TF: 800-837-1631 ■ Web: www.hirzel.com	Toledo	OH	43619	419-693-0531	693-4859
HJ Heinz Co One PPG Pl NYSE: HNZ ■ TF: 800-255-5750 ■ Web: www.heinz.com	Pittsburgh	PA	15222	412-456-5700	456-6015
House Foods America Corp 7351 Orangewood Ave TF: 877-333-7077 ■ Web: www.house-foods.com	Garden Grove	CA	92841	714-901-4350	901-4235
Independent Food Processors 401 N 1st St	Yakima	WA	98901	509-457-6487	457-7983
Indian Summer Co-op 3958 W Chauvez Rd	Ludington	MI	49431	231-845-6248	843-9453*
Ingomar Packing Co 9950 S Ingomar Grade PO Box 1448 Web: www.ingomarpacking.com	Los Banos	CA	93635	209-826-9494	854-6292
International Juice Concentrates Inc 1532 W Esther St Web: www.intljuice.com	Long Beach	CA	90813	562-599-5831	599-5107
J. Lieb Foods Inc PO Box 389 Web: www.jliebfoods.com	Forest Grove	OR	97116	503-359-9279	
Jasper Wyman & Son 280 N Main St. TF: 800-341-1758 ■ Web: www.wymans.com	Milbridge	ME	04658	207-546-2311	546-2074
JM Smucker Co 1 Strawberry Ln. NYSE: SJM ■ TF: 888-550-9555 ■ Web: www.smucker.com	Orrville	OH	44667	330-682-3000	684-6410
JM Smucker Pennsylvania Inc 300 Keck Ave	New Bethlehem	PA	16242	814-275-1323	275-1340
Johanna Foods Inc 20 Johanna Farm Rd PO Box 272 TF: 800-727-6700 ■ Web: www.johannafoods.com	Flemington	NJ	08822	908-788-2409	788-2331
Juice Bowl Products Inc 2090 Bartow Rd.	Lakeland	FL	33802	863-665-5515	667-7137
Knouse Foods Co-op Inc 800 Peach Glen-Idaville Rd TF: 800-827-7537 ■ Web: www.knouse.com	Peach Glen	PA	17375	717-677-8181	677-7069
Lakeside Foods Inc 808 Hamilton St. Web: www.lakesidefoods.com	Manitowoc	WI	54220	920-684-3356	686-4033
Langers Juice Co Inc 16195 Stephens St Web: www.langers.com	City of Industry	CA	91745	626-336-1666	961-2021
Lawrence Foods Inc 2200 Lunt Ave. TF: 800-323-7848 ■ Web: www.lawrencefoods.com	Elk Grove Village	IL	60007	847-437-2400	437-2567
Leelanau Fruit Co 2900 SW Bayshore Dr. TF: 800-431-0718 ■ Web: www.leelanaufruit.com	Suttons Bay	MI	49682	231-271-3514	271-4367
LiDestri Foods Inc 815 Whitney Rd W TF: 800-397-5222	Fairport	NY	14450	585-377-7700	377-8150
Litehouse Chadalee Farms Inc 1400 Foreman Rd.	Lowell	MI	49331	616-897-5911	897-6720
Louis Maull Co The 219 N Market St Web: www.maull.com	Saint Louis	MO	63102	314-241-8410	
Lyons Magnus Inc 3158 E Hamilton Ave. TF: 800-344-7130 ■ Web: www.lyonsmagnus.com	Fresno	CA	93702	559-268-5966	233-8249
Maui Land & Pineapple Co Inc 120 Kane St PO Box 187 NYSE: MLP ■ Web: www.mauiland.com	Kahului	HI	96733	808-877-3351	871-0953
Mayer Bros Apple Products Inc 3300 Transit Rd. Web: www.mayerbrothers.com	West Seneca	NY	14224	716-668-1787	668-2437
Moody Dunbar Inc 2000 Waters Edge Dr Suite 21 TF: 800-251-8202	Johnson City	TN	37604	423-952-0100	952-0289
Morgan Foods Inc 90 W Morgan St TF: 888-430-1780 ■ Web: www.morganfoods.com	Austin	IN	47102	812-794-1170	794-1211
Mott's Inc 900 King St TF: 800-426-4891 ■ Web: www.motts.com	Rye Brook	NY	10573	914-612-4000	612-4100
Mrs Clark's Foods LLC 740 SE Dalby Dr TF: 800-736-5674 ■ Web: www.mrsclarks.com	Ankeny	IA	50021	515-964-8100	964-8397
Muir Glen Organic Tomato Products 719 Metcalf St TF: 800-832-6345 ■ Web: www.muirglen.com	Sedro Woolley	WA	98284	360-855-0100	
Mullins Food Products Inc 2200 S 25th Ave Web: www.mullinsfood.com	Broadview	IL	60155	708-344-3224	344-0153
Mushroom Co The 902 Woods Rd Web: www.themushroomcompany.com	Cambridge	MD	21613	410-221-8971	221-8952
National Fruit Product Co Inc 701 Fairmont Ave PO Box 2040 *Fax: Sales ■ TF: 800-551-5167 ■ Web: www.whitehousefoods.com	Winchester	VA	22604	540-662-3401	665-4670*
New Era Canning Co 4856 1st St	New Era	MI	49446	231-861-2151	861-4068
Ocean Spray Cranberries Inc 1 Ocean Spray Dr TF: 800-662-3263 ■ Web: www.oceanspray.com	Lakeville-Middleboro	MA	02349	508-946-1000	946-7704
Odwalla Inc 120 Stone Pine Rd TF: 800-639-2552 ■ Web: www.odwalla.com	Half Moon Bay	CA	94019	650-726-1888	560-9009
Pacific Coast Producers 631 N Cluff Ave. Web: www.pcoastp.com	Lodi	CA	95240	209-367-8800	367-1084
Pastorelli Food Products Inc 162 N Sangamon St TF: 800-767-2829 ■ Web: www.pastorelli.com	Chicago	IL	60607	312-666-2041	666-2415
President Global Corp 6965 Aragon Cir	Buena Park	CA	90620	714-994-2990	523-3142
Pro-Fac Co-op Inc 590 Willow Brook Office Pk PO Box 274 TF: 877-894-2869 ■ Web: www.profaccoop.com	Fairport	NY	14450	585-218-4210	218-4241
Ray Bros & Noble Canning Co Inc 3720 E 150 S PO Box 314 Web: www.noblecanning.com	Hobbs	IN	46047	765-675-7451	675-7400
Red Gold Inc 120 E Oak St. Web: www.redgold.com	Orestes	IN	46063	765-754-7527	754-3230
Rohtstein Corp 70 Olympia Ave TF: 800-225-1661	Woburn	MA	01888	781-935-8400	932-3917
Ryan Trading Corp 2500 Westchester Ave Suite 102 Web: www.ryantrading.com	Purchase	NY	10577	914-253-6767	253-6722
Seneca Foods Corp 3736 S Main St. NASDAQ: SENEA ■ Web: www.senecafoods.com	Marion	NY	14505	315-926-8100	926-8300
Simply Orange Juice Co 2659 Orange Ave TF: 800-871-2653 ■ Web: www.simplyorangejuice.com	Apopka	FL	32703	800-871-2653	
Southern Gardens Citrus 1820 Country Rd 833	Clewiston	FL	33440	863-983-3030	983-3060
Stanislaus Food Products Co 1202 D St TF: 800-327-7201 ■ Web: www.stanislausfoodproducts.com	Modesto	CA	95354	209-522-7201	521-4014
Stapleton-Spence Packing Co 1530 The Alameda Suite 320 TF: 800-297-8815 ■ Web: www.stapleton-spence.com	San Jose	CA	95126	408-297-8815	297-0611
Sun Orchard Inc 1198 W Fairmont Dr. TF: 800-505-8423 ■ Web: www.sunorchard.com	Tempe	AZ	85282	480-966-1770	921-1426
Talk O'Texas Brands Inc 1610 Roosevelt St TF: 800-749-6572 ■ Web: www.talkotexas.com	San Angelo	TX	76905	325-655-6077	655-7967
Texas Citrus Exchange 702 E Expy 83 Web: www.texascitrusexchange.com	Mission	TX	78572	956-585-8321	585-1655
Tip Top Canning Co 505 S 2nd St PO Box 126 TF: 800-352-2635	Tipp City	OH	45371	937-667-3713	667-3802
Tree Top Inc 220 E 2nd Ave TF: 800-237-0515 ■ Web: www.treetop.com	Selah	WA	98942	509-697-7251	697-0421
Truitt Bros Inc 1105 Front St NE *Fax: Sales ■ TF: 800-547-8712 ■ Web: www.truittbros.com	Salem	OR	97301	503-362-3674	588-2868*
TW Garner Food Co 4045 Indiana Ave PO Box 4239 Web: www.texaspete.com	Winston-Salem	NC	27115	336-661-1550	661-1901
Valley Processing Inc 108 E Blaine Ave PO Box 246	Sunnyside	WA	98944	509-837-8084	837-3481
Vegetable Juices Inc 7400 S Narragansett Ave. TF: 888-776-9752 ■ Web: www.vegetablejuices.com	Bedford Park	IL	60638	708-924-9500	924-9510
Vita-Pakt Citrus Products 707 N Barranca Ave Web: www.vita-pakt.com	Covina	CA	91723	626-332-1101	915-4107
Welch's Inc 3 Concord Farms 575 Virginia Rd Web: www.welchs.com	Concord	MA	01742	978-371-1000	
Whitlock Packaging Corp 1701 S Lee St TF: 800-833-9382 ■ Web: www.whitlockpkg.com	Fort Gibson	OK	74434	918-478-4300	478-7362
Zeigler Beverage Co 1513 N Broad St TF Sales: 800-854-6123 ■ Web: www.zeiglers.com	Lansdale	PA	19446	215-855-5161	855-4548

299-21 Fruits, Vegetables, Juices - Frozen

Company / Address	City	State	ZIP	Phone	Fax
American Fruit Processors 10725 Sutter Ave *Fax: Sales ■ Web: www.americanfruit.com	Pacoima	CA	91331	818-899-9574	899-6042*
Apio Inc PO Box 727 TF Sales: 800-454-1355 ■ Web: www.apioinc.com	Guadalupe	CA	93434	805-343-2835	
Ardmore Farms Inc 1915 N Woodland Blvd TF: 800-365-8423 ■ Web: www.juice4u.com	DeLand	FL	32720	386-734-4634	736-8894
Bernatello's PO Box 729 TF: 800-622-6935 ■ Web: www.bernatellos.com	Maple Lake	MN	55358	320-963-6191	963-6447
Birds Eye Foods Inc 90 Linden Oaks TF: 800-999-5044 ■ Web: www.birdseyefoods.com	Rochester	NY	14625	585-383-1850	385-2857
Bonduelle Inc 8615 St Laurent Blvd Suite 200 Web: www.bonduelle.ca	Montreal	QC	H2P2M9	514-384-4281	384-7992
Brooks Food Group Inc 940 Orange St TF: 800-873-4934 ■ Web: www.brooksfoodgroup.com	Bedford	VA	24523	540-586-8284	586-1072
Capitol City Produce 16550 Commercial Ave. TF: 800-349-1583 ■ Web: www.capitolcityproduce.com	Baton Rouge	LA	70816	225-272-8153	272-8152

Company	City	State	Zip	Phone	Fax
Cascadian Farm Inc 719 Metcalf St	Sedro Woolley	WA	98284	360-855-0100	855-0444
TF: 800-624-4123 ■ *Web:* www.cascadianfarm.com					
Cherry Growers Inc 6331 US Hwy 31	Grawn	MI	49637	231-276-9241	276-7075
Web: www.cherrygrowers.net					
Coloma Frozen Foods Inc 4145 Coloma Rd	Coloma	MI	49038	269-849-0500	849-0886
TF: 800-462-7608 ■ *Web:* www.colomafrozen.com					
ConAgra Foods Retail Products Co Frozen Foods Group 5 ConAgra Dr	Omaha	NE	68102	402-595-6000	
Web: www.conagrafoods.com					
Del Mar Food Products Corp 1720 Beach Rd	Watsonville	CA	95076	831-722-3516	722-7690
Dole Food Co Inc 1 Dole Dr	Westlake Village	CA	91362	818-879-6600	874-4893*
**Fax:* Hum Res ■ *TF:* 800-232-8888 ■ *Web:* www.dole.com					
Fresh Frozen Foods LLC 1814 Washington St PO Box 215	Jefferson	GA	30549	706-367-9851	367-4646
TF: 800-277-9851 ■ *Web:* www.freshfrozenfoods.com					
Frozsun Inc 701 W Kimberly Ave Suite 210	Placentia	CA	92870	714-630-2170	630-0920
Web: www.frozsun.com					
General Mills Green Giant 915 E Pleasant St	Belvidere	IL	61008	815-547-5311	547-5896*
**Fax:* Cust Svc ■ *Web:* www.greengiant.com					
Giorgio Foods Inc PO Box 96	Temple	PA	19560	610-926-2139	926-7012
TF: 800-220-2139 ■ *Web:* www.giorgiofoods.com					
GM Allen & Son Inc Rt 15 PO Box 454	Blue Hill	ME	04614	207-469-7060	469-2308
Graceland Fruit Inc 1123 Main St	Frankfort	MI	49635	231-352-7181	352-4711
TF: 800-352-7181 ■ *Web:* www.gracelandfruit.com					
HJ Heinz Co One PPG Pl	Pittsburgh	PA	15222	412-456-5700	456-6015
NYSE: HNZ ■ *TF:* 800-255-5750 ■ *Web:* www.heinz.com					
Holly Hill Fruit Products Co Inc 315 US Hwy 17-92 N	Davenport	FL	33837	863-422-1131	422-1136
Hpc Foods Ltd 288 Libby St	Honolulu	HI	96819	808-848-2431	841-4398
TF: 877-370-0919 ■ *Web:* hpcfoods.com					
Jewel Apple & Summer Prize Co PO Box 27	Yakima	WA	98907	509-248-7200	453-3835
JR Simplot Co 999 W Main St # 1300	Boise	ID	83702	208-336-2110	389-7515
TF: 800-635-5008 ■ *Web:* www.simplot.com					
JR Simplot Co Food Group 6360 S Federal Way	Boise	ID	83716	208-384-8000	384-8015
TF: 800-635-0408 ■ *Web:* www.simplot.com					
Lakeside Foods Inc 808 Hamilton St	Manitowoc	WI	54220	920-684-3356	686-4033
Web: www.lakesidefoods.com					
Lamb Weston Inc 8701 W Gage Blvd	Kennewick	WA	99336	509-735-4651	737-6621*
**Fax:* Sales ■ *Web:* www.lambweston.com					
Leelanau Fruit Co 2900 SW Bayshore Dr	Suttons Bay	MI	49682	231-271-3514	271-4367
TF: 800-431-0718 ■ *Web:* www.leelanaufruit.com					
Lewis Dreyfus Citrus Inc PO Box 770399	Winter Garden	FL	34777	407-656-1000	656-1229
TF: 800-549-4272 ■ *Web:* www.ldcitrusfl.com					
McCain Foods Ltd 181 Bay St Suite 3600	Toronto	ON	M5J2T3	416-955-1700	
TF: 866-622-2461 ■ *Web:* www.mccain.com					
McCain Foods USA Inc 2275 Cabot Dr	Lisle	IL	60532	630-955-0400	857-4560
TF: 800-938-7799 ■ *Web:* www.mccainusa.com					
Milne Fruit Products Inc 804 Bennett Ave	Prosser	WA	99350	509-786-2611	786-4915
Web: www.milnefruit.com					
Mr Dell Foods Inc 300 W Major St	Kearney	MO	64060	816-628-4644	628-4633
Web: www.mrdells.com					
Mrs Clark's Foods LLC 740 SE Dalby Dr	Ankeny	IA	50021	515-964-8100	964-8397
TF: 800-736-5674 ■ *Web:* www.mrsclarks.com					
National Frozen Foods Corp 1600 Fairview Ave E Suite 200	Seattle	WA	98102	206-322-8900	322-4458
Web: www.nffc.com					
NORPAC Foods Inc 930 W Washington St	Stayton	OR	97383	503-769-2101	769-1273
TF: 800-733-9311 ■ *Web:* www.norpac.com					
Ochoa Egg & Unlimited Foods Inc PO Box 747	Warden	WA	98857	509-349-2210	349-2375
Patterson Frozen Foods Inc PO Box 114	Patterson	CA	95363	209-892-2611	892-5209
TF: 800-821-1007 ■ *Web:* www.pattersonfrozenfoods.com					
Penobscot McCrum LLC 28 Pierce St	Belfast	ME	04915	207-338-4360	338-5742
TF: 800-435-4456 ■ *Web:* www.penobscotmccrum.com					
Peterson Farms Inc 3104 W Baseline Rd PO Box 115	Shelby	MI	49455	231-861-6333	861-6550
Web: www.petersonfarmsinc.com					
R.W. Knudsen & Sons Inc 1 Strawberry Ln PO Box 369	Orrville	OH	44667	888-569-6993	
TF: 888-569-6993 ■ *Web:* www.rwknudsenfamily.com					
Seabrook Bros & Sons Inc 85 Finley Rd	Seabrook	NJ	08302	856-455-8080	455-9282
Web: www.seabrookfarms.com					
Seneca Foods Corp 3736 S Main St	Marion	NY	14505	315-926-8100	926-8300
NASDAQ: SENEA ■ *Web:* www.senecafoods.com					
Sill Farms Market Inc 50241 Red Arrow Hwy	Lawrence	MI	49064	269-674-3755	674-3756
Smith Frozen Foods Inc 101 Depot St	Weston	OR	97886	541-566-3515	566-3772
Web: www.smithfrozenfoods.com					
Sun Orchard of Florida Inc 1200 S 30th St	Haines City	FL	33844	863-422-5062	422-5176
TF: 877-875-8423 ■ *Web:* www.sunorchard.com					
Sweet Ovations 1741 Tomlinson Rd	Philadelphia	PA	19116	215-676-3900	613-2115
TF: 800-280-9387 ■ *Web:* www.sweetovations.com					
Sysco Seattle Inc 22820 54th Ave S	Kent	WA	98032	206-622-2261	721-2787
Web: www.syscoseattle.com					
Townsend Farms Inc 23303 NE Sandy Blvd	Fairview	OR	97024	503-666-1780	618-8257
Tree Top Inc 220 E 2nd Ave	Selah	WA	98942	509-697-7251	697-0421
TF: 800-237-0515 ■ *Web:* www.treetop.com					
Twin City Foods Inc 10120 269th Pl NW	Stanwood	WA	98292	360-629-2111	515-2485*
**Fax Area Code:* 206 ■ *Web:* www.twincityfruts.com					
United Foods Inc 10 Pictsweet Dr	Bells	TN	38006	731-422-7600	561-8810*
**Fax Area Code:* 800 ■ *TF:* 800-367-7412 ■ *Web:* www.pictsweet.com					
Valley Foods Inc PO Box C	Lindsay	CA	93247	559-562-5169	562-5691
Ventura Coastal Corp 2325 Vista del Mar Dr	Ventura	CA	93002	805-653-7000	648-4915
Vita-Pakt Citrus Products 707 N Barranca Ave	Covina	CA	91723	626-332-1101	915-4107
Web: www.vita-pakt.com					
Wawona Frozen Foods Inc 100 W Alluvial Ave	Clovis	CA	93611	559-299-2901	299-1921
TF: 800-669-2966 ■ *Web:* www.wawona.com					

299-22 Gelatin

Company	City	State	Zip	Phone	Fax
ConAgra Hunt-Wesson Foodservice Co 3353 Michelson Dr	Irvine	CA	92612	949-437-1000	
TF: 800-633-0112 ■ *Web:* www.conagrafoodservice.com					
Gelita USA Inc PO Box 927	Sioux City	IA	51102	712-943-5516	943-3372
Web: www.gelita.com					
Langlois Co 10810 San Sevaine Way	Mira Loma	CA	91752	951-360-3900	360-3465
TF: 800-962-5993					
Milligan & Higgins 100 Maple Ave	Johnstown	NY	12095	518-762-4638	762-7039
Web: www.milligan1868.com					
Nitta Gelatin Inc 201 W Passaic St	Rochelle Park	NJ	07662	201-368-0071	368-0282
TF: 800-278-7680 ■ *Web:* www.nitta-gelatin.com					
PB Leiner 366 N Broadway Suite 307	Jericho	NY	11753	516-822-4040	822-4044
Web: www.pbgelatins.com					
Subco Foods Inc 4350 S Taylor Dr	Sheboygan	WI	53081	920-457-7761	457-3899
TF: 800-473-0757 ■ *Web:* www.subcofoods.com					
Swagger Foods Corp 900 Corporate Woods Pkwy	Vernon Hills	IL	60061	847-913-1200	913-1263
Web: www.swaggerfoods.com					

299-23 Grain Mill Products

Company	City	State	Zip	Phone	Fax
ACH Food Cos Inc 7171 Goodlet Farms Pkwy	Cordova	TN	38016	901-381-3000	381-2968
TF: 800-691-1106 ■ *Web:* www.achfood.com					
ADM Corn Processing Div 4666 E Faries Pkwy	Decatur	IL	62526	217-424-5200	424-5978
TF: 800-637-5843 ■ *Web:* www.adm.com					
ADM Milling Co 8000 W 110th St Suite 300	Overland Park	KS	66210	913-491-9400	491-0035
TF: 800-422-1688					
ADM Specialty Feed Ingredients Div 4666 E Faries Pkwy	Decatur	IL	62526	217-424-5200	424-5580
NYSE: adm ■ *Web:* www.adm.com					
Ag Processing Inc 12700 W Dodge Rd PO Box 2047	Omaha	NE	68103	402-496-7809	498-5548
TF: 800-247-1345 ■ *Web:* www.agp.com					
Allen Bros Milling Co PO Box 1437	Columbia	SC	29202	803-779-2460	252-0014
American Rice Inc 10700 N Fwy Suite 800	Houston	TX	77037	281-272-8800	272-9707
Web: www.amrice.com					
Bartlett & Co 4800 Main St Suite 600	Kansas City	MO	64112	816-753-6300	753-0063
TF: 800-888-6300 ■ *Web:* www.bartlettandco.com					
Bay State Milling Co 100 Congress St	Quincy	MA	02169	617-328-4400	479-8910
TF: 800-553-5687 ■ *Web:* www.bsm.com					
Beaumont Rice Mills Inc 1800 Pecos St	Beaumont	TX	77701	409-832-2521	832-6927
Birkett Mills 163 Main St	Penn Yan	NY	14527	315-536-3311	536-6740
Web: www.thebirkettmills.com					
Blendex Co Inc 11208 Electron Dr	Louisville	KY	40299	502-267-1003	267-1024
TF: 800-626-6354 ■ *Web:* www.blendex.com					
Cargill 616 S Jefferson St	Paris	IL	61944	217-465-5331	463-1644
Cargill Inc North America 15407 McGinty Rd	Wayzata	MN	55391	952-742-7575	
TF: 800-227-4455					
Cereal Food Processors Inc 2001 Shawnee Mission Pkwy	Mission Woods	KS	66205	913-890-6300	890-6382
TF: 800-743-5687 ■ *Web:* www.cerealfood.com					
Cereal Foods Inc 416 N Main St	McPherson	KS	67460	620-241-2410	241-7167
TF: 800-835-2067					
Chelsea Milling Co 201 W N St PO Box 460	Chelsea	MI	48118	734-475-1361	475-4630
Web: www.jiffymix.com					
Cormier Rice Milling Co Inc 501 W 3rd St PO Box 152	De Witt	AR	72042	870-946-3561	946-3029
Corn Products International Inc 5 Westbrook Corporate Ctr	Westchester	IL	60154	708-551-2600	551-2700
NYSE: CPO ■ *Web:* www.cornproducts.com					
Farmers Rice Co-op PO Box 15223	Sacramento	CA	95851	916-923-5100	920-3321
TF: 800-326-2799 ■ *Web:* www.farmersrice.com					
Farmers Rice Milling Co 3211 Hwy 397 S	Lake Charles	LA	70615	337-433-5205	433-1735
Web: www.frmco.com					
Florida Crystals Corp 1 N Clematis St Suite 200	West Palm Beach	FL	33401	561-655-6303	659-3206
Web: www.floridacrystals.com					
Foxtail Foods 6075 Poplar Ave Suite 800	Memphis	TN	38119	901-766-6400	537-7141
TF Cust Svc: 800-487-2253 ■ *Web:* www.foxtailfoods.com					
Gold Medal 1 General Mills Blvd	Minneapolis	MN	55426	763-764-7600	764-3232*
**Fax:* PR ■ *TF:* 800-248-7310 ■ *Web:* www.generalmills.com/Brands/Baking_Products/Gold_Medal.aspx					
Grain Processing Corp 1600 Oregon St	Muscatine	IA	52761	563-264-4211	264-4216
Web: www.grainprocessing.com					
Henry & Henry Inc 3765 Walden Ave	Lancaster	NY	14086	716-685-4000	685-0160
Hodgson Mill Inc 1100 Stevens Ave	Effingham	IL	62401	217-347-0105	347-0198
TF: 800-347-0105 ■ *Web:* www.hodgsonmill.com					
Hopkinsville Milling Co 2001 S Walnut St	Hopkinsville	KY	42240	270-886-1231	886-6407
House-Autry Mills Inc 7000 US Hwy 301 S	Four Oaks	NC	27524	919-963-6200	963-6458
TF: 800-849-0802 ■ *Web:* www.house-autry.com					
HR Wentzel Sons Inc 5521 Waggoners Gap Rd PO Box 125	Landisburg	PA	17040	717-789-3306	789-0128
Indian Harvest Specialtifoods Inc 1012 Paul Bunyan Dr SE	Bemidji	MN	56601	218-751-8500	751-8519
TF Orders: 800-346-7032 ■ *Web:* www.indianharvest.com					
JR Short Milling Co 1580 Grinnell Rd	Chicago	IL	60601	815-937-2633	937-8806
TF: 800-544-8734 ■ *Web:* www.shortmill.com					
King Milling Co 115 S Broadway St	Lowell	MI	49331	616-897-9264	897-4350
Web: www.kingmilling.com					
Knappen Milling Co 110 S Water St	Augusta	MI	49012	269-731-4141	731-5441
TF: 800-562-7736 ■ *Web:* www.knappen.com					
Lacey Milling Co 217 W 5th St	Hanford	CA	93230	559-584-6634	584-9165
Mallet & Co Inc 51 Arch St Ext	Carnegie	PA	15106	412-276-9000	276-9002
TF: 800-245-2757 ■ *Web:* www.malletoil.com					
Manildra Milling Corp 4210 Shawnee Mission Pkwy Suite 312A	Shawnee Mission	KS	66205	913-362-0777	362-0052
Mars Snack Food 800 High St	Hackettstown	NJ	07840	908-852-1000	850-2734
TF: 800-432-1093 ■ *Web:* www.mars.com					
McShares Inc PO Box 1460	Salina	KS	67402	785-825-2181	825-8908
TF: 800-234-7174 ■ *Web:* www.researchprod.com					
Mennel Milling Co 128 W Crocker St	Fostoria	OH	44830	419-435-8151	436-5150
TF: 800-688-8151 ■ *Web:* www.mennel.com					
MGP Ingredients Inc 100 Commercial St PO Box 130	Atchison	KS	66002	913-367-1480	367-0192

				Phone	Fax
NASDAQ: MGPI ■ *TF:* 800-255-0302 ■ *Web:* www.mgpingredients.com					
Midstate Mills Inc 324 E 'A' St	Newton	NC	28658	828-464-1611	465-5139
TF: 800-222-1032 ■ *Web:* www.midstatemills.com					
Minn-Dak Growers Ltd 4034 40th Ave N	Grand Forks	ND	58203	701-746-7453	780-9050
Web: www.minndak.com					
Minnesota Grain Pearling Co 1380 Corporate Ctr Curve Suite 101	Eagan	MN	55121	651-681-1460	681-7975
Morrison Milling Co 319 E Prairie St	Denton	TX	76201	940-387-6111	566-5992
TF: 800-866-5487					
North Dakota Mill & Elevator 1823 Mill Rd	Grand Forks	ND	58203	701-795-7000	795-7251
TF: 800-538-7721 ■ *Web:* www.ndmill.com					
Pacific Grain Products International Inc 351 Hanson Way PO Box 2060	Woodland	CA	95776	530-662-5056	662-6074
TF Cust Svc: 800-333-0110 ■ *Web:* www.pgpint.com/eshop.php					
Pacific International Rice Mills Inc PO Box 652	Woodland	CA	95776	530-666-1691	668-8515
TF: 800-747-4764					
Pan American Grain Co Inc Calle Claudia 9cnr	Guaynabo	PR	00968	787-273-6100	273-6872
Web: www.panamericangrain.com					
Producers Rice Mill Inc 518 E Harrison St	Stuttgart	AR	72160	870-673-4444	673-8131
Web: www.producersrice.com					
Riceland Foods Inc 2120 S Pk Ave	Stuttgart	AR	72160	870-673-5500	673-3366
TF Cust Svc: 800-264-1283 ■ *Web:* www.riceland.com					
RiceTec Inc 1925 FM 2917 PO Box 1305	Alvin	TX	77511	281-393-3502	393-3532
TF: 877-580-7423 ■ *Web:* www.ricetec.com					
Riviana Foods Inc PO Box 2636	Houston	TX	77252	713-529-3251	529-1661
Web: www.riviana.com					
Rock River Lumber & Grain Co 5502 Lyndon Rd PO Box 68	Prophetstown	IL	61277	815-537-5131	
TF: 800-605-4333 ■ *Web:* www.rockriverag.com					
Roman Meal Milling Co Inc 4014 15th Ave NW	Fargo	ND	58102	701-282-9656	282-9743
Roquette America Inc 1003 Commercial St	Keokuk	IA	52632	319-524-5757	526-2345
TF: 800-553-7030					
Shawnee Milling Co Inc 201 S Broadway PO Box 1567	Shawnee	OK	74802	405-273-7000	273-7333
TF: 800-654-2600 ■ *Web:* www.shawneemilling.com					
Siemer Milling Co 111 W Main St PO Box 670	Teutopolis	IL	62467	217-857-3131	857-3092
TF: 800-826-1065 ■ *Web:* www.siemermilling.com					
SunOpta Inc 2838 Bovaird Dr W	Brampton	ON	L7A0H2	905-455-2528	455-2529
NASDAQ: STKL ■ *Web:* www.sunopta.com					
Supreme Rice Mill Inc 4 S Ave D PO Box 490	Crowley	LA	70527	337-783-5222	783-3204
Thomas Monahan Co Inc 202 N Oak St	Arcola	IL	61910	217-268-4955	268-3113
TF: 800-637-7739 ■ *Web:* www.thomasmonahan.com					
Wilkins-Rogers Inc 27 Frederick Rd	Ellicott City	MD	21043	410-465-5800	750-0163
TF Cust Svc: 800-735-3585					

299-24 Honey

				Phone	Fax
Adee Honey Farm 517 Jay St	Bruce	SD	57220	605-627-5621	627-5622
Web: www.adeehoneyfarms.com					
Dutch Gold Honey Inc 2220 Dutch Gold Dr	Lancaster	PA	17601	717-393-1716	393-8687
Web: www.dutchgoldhoney.com					
Fisher Honey Co 1 Belle Ave Bldg 21	Lewistown	PA	17044	717-242-4373	242-3978
Web: www.fisherhoney.com					
Glorybee Foods Inc 120 N Seneca Rd	Eugene	OR	97402	541-689-0913	689-9692
TF: 800-456-7923 ■ *Web:* www.glorybee.com					
Golden Heritage Foods LLC 120 Santa Fe St	Hillsboro	KS	67063	620-947-3173	947-3640
TF: 800-947-3640 ■ *Web:* www.ghfllc.com					
Honey Acres 1557 Hwy 67 N	Ashippun	WI	53003	920-474-4411	474-4018
TF: 800-558-7745 ■ *Web:* www.honeyacres.com					
Honeytree Inc 8570 M 50	Onsted	MI	49265	517-467-2482	467-2056
TF: 800-968-1889					
Miller's Honey Co Inc 3000 S W Temple	Salt Lake City	UT	84115	801-486-8479	486-8494
Web: www.millerhoney.com					
Pure Sweet Honey Farm Inc 514 Commerce Pkwy	Verona	WI	53593	608-845-9601	
Silverbow Honey Co Inc 1120 E Wheeler Rd	Moses Lake	WA	98837	509-765-6616	765-6549
Web: www.silverbowhoney.com					
Sioux Honey Assn Co-op 301 Lewis Blvd	Sioux City	IA	51101	712-258-0638	258-1332
TF: 888-270-6956 ■ *Web:* www.suebee.com					
TW Burleson & Son Inc 301 Peters St	Waxahachie	TX	75165	972-937-4810	937-8711
Web: www.burlesons-honey.com					
Wixson Honey Inc 4937 Lakemont-Himrod Rd	Dundee	NY	14837	607-243-7301	243-7143

299-25 Ice Cream & Frozen Desserts

				Phone	Fax
Anderson Erickson Dairy Co 2420 E University Ave	Des Moines	IA	50317	515-265-2521	263-6301
TF: 800-234-7257 ■ *Web:* www.aedairy.com					
Baldwin Richardson Foods Co Inc 20201 S La Grange Rd Suite 200	Frankfort	IL	60423	815-464-9994	464-9995
TF Cust Svc: 800-762-6458 ■ *Web:* www.brfoods.com					
Barber Dairies Inc 36 Barber Ct	Birmingham	AL	35209	205-942-2351	943-0297
Web: www.barbersdairy.com					
Ben & Jerry's Homemade Inc 30 Community Dr	South Burlington	VT	05403	802-846-1500	846-1556
Web: www.benjerry.com					
Berkeley Farms Inc 25500 Clawiter Rd	Hayward	CA	94545	510-265-8600	265-8754*
**Fax:* Sales ■ *Web:* www.berkeleyfarms.com					
Blue Bell Creameries Inc 1101 S Blue Bell Rd	Brenham	TX	77833	979-836-7977	830-7398
Web: www.bluebell.com					
Broughton Foods Co 1701 Green St	Marietta	OH	45750	740-373-4121	373-2861
TF: 800-283-2479					
Cedar Crest Specialties Inc 7269 State Rd 60 # 4	Cedarburg	WI	53012	262-377-7252	377-5554
TF: 800-877-8341 ■ *Web:* www.cedarcresticecream.com					
Coleman Dairy Inc 6901 I-30	Little Rock	AR	72209	501-565-1551	568-1710
TF: 800-365-1551 ■ *Web:* www.colemandairy.com					
Country Fresh Inc 2555 Buchanan Ave SW	Grand Rapids	MI	49548	616-243-0173	243-5926
TF: 800-748-0480 ■ *Web:* www.enjoycountryfresh.com					
Creamland Dairies Inc 10 Indian School Rd NW	Albuquerque	NM	87105	505-247-0721	246-9696
TF: 800-334-3865 ■ *Web:* www.creamland.com					
Crossroad Farms Dairy 400 S Shortridge Rd	Indianapolis	IN	46219	317-229-7600	229-7676
TF: 800-334-7502					
Dairy Fresh Corp 915 Tuscaloosa St	Greensboro	AL	36744	334-624-3041	
Dreyer's Grand Ice Cream Holdings Inc 5929 College Ave	Oakland	CA	94618	510-317-1415	450-4621
TF: 800-888-3442 ■ *Web:* www.dreyersinc.com					
Driggs Farm of Indiana Inc 400 S Chamber Dr	Decatur	IN	46733	260-724-2136	724-2136
Edy's Grand Ice Cream 5929 College Ave	Oakland	CA	94618	510-652-8187	450-4621
TF: 800-888-3442					
Farr Better Foods 286 E 21st St	Ogden	UT	84401	801-393-8629	399-0516
Web: www.farrsicecream.com					
Galliker Dairy Co Inc 143 Donald Ln	Johnstown	PA	15907	814-266-8702	
TF: 800-477-6455 ■ *Web:* www.gallikers.com					
Gandy's Dairies Inc 201 University Blvd	Lubbock	TX	79415	800-338-6841	
TF: 800-338-6841 ■ *Web:* www.gandysdairy.com					
Heisler's Cloverleaf Dairy 743 Catawissa Rd	Tamaqua	PA	18252	570-668-3399	668-3041
Web: www.heislersdairy.com					
Hershey Creamery Co 301 S Cameron St	Harrisburg	PA	17101	717-238-8134	233-7195
TF: 888-240-1905 ■ *Web:* www.hersheyicecream.com					
Hiland Dairy Co 1133 E Kearney St PO Box 2270	Springfield	MO	65801	417-862-9311	837-1106
TF: 800-641-4022 ■ *Web:* www.hilanddairy.com					
Holland Dairies Inc 304 Main St	Holland	IN	47541	812-536-2310	536-4320
TF: 800-634-2509					
Ice Cream Specialties 8419 Hanley Industrial Dr	Saint Louis	MO	63144	314-962-2550	962-1990
TF: 800-662-7550					
J & J Snack Foods Corp 6000 Central Hwy	Pennsauken	NJ	08109	856-665-9533	665-6718
NASDAQ: JJSF ■ *TF:* 800-486-9533 ■ *Web:* www.jjsnack.com					
Jackson Ice Cream Co Inc 2600 E 4th Ave	Hutchinson	KS	67501	620-663-1244	663-1952
Klinke Bros Ice Cream Co 2450 Scaper Cove	Memphis	TN	38114	901-743-8250	743-8254
Land O'Sun Dairies LLC 2900 Bristol Hwy	Johnson City	TN	37601	423-283-5700	283-5716
TF Acctg: 800-683-0765					
Louis Trauth Dairy Inc 16 E 11th St	Newport	KY	41071	859-431-7553	431-0349
TF: 800-544-6455 ■ *Web:* www.trauthdairy.com					
Newport Creamery Inc 35 Stockanosset Rd	Cranston	RI	02920	401-946-4000	946-4392
Web: www.newportcreamery.com					
Perry's Ice Cream Co Inc 1 Ice Cream Plaza	Akron	NY	14001	716-542-5492	542-2544
TF: 800-873-7797 ■ *Web:* www.perrysicecream.com					
Philly's Famous Water Ice Inc 1102 N 28th St	Tampa	FL	33605	813-353-8645	
TF: 877-379-4757 ■ *Web:* www.phillyswirl.com					
Royal Ice Cream Co 6200 Euclid Ave	Cleveland	OH	44103	216-432-1144	432-0433
TF: 888-645-6606 ■ *Web:* www.pierres.com					
Schwan Food Co 115 W College Dr	Marshall	MN	56258	507-532-3274	
TF: 800-533-5290 ■ *Web:* www.theschwanfoodcompany.com					
Stonyfield Farm Inc 10 Burton Dr	Londonderry	NH	03053	603-437-4040	437-7594
TF: 800-776-2697 ■ *Web:* www.stonyfield.com					
Sugar Creek Foods Inc 301 N El Paso St	Russellville	AR	72810	479-968-1005	968-5651
TF: 800-445-2715 ■ *Web:* www.taghoneyhillfarm.com					
Tofutti Brands Inc 50 Jackson Dr	Cranford	NJ	07016	908-272-2400	272-9492
AMEX: TOF ■ *Web:* www.tofutti.com					
Turkey Hill Dairy Inc 2601 River Rd	Conestoga	PA	17516	717-872-5461	872-4130
TF: 800-688-7539 ■ *Web:* www.turkeyhill.com					
Umpqua Dairy Products Co 333 SE Sykes Ave PO Box 1306	Roseburg	OR	97470	541-672-2638	673-0256
TF: 888-672-6455 ■ *Web:* www.umpquadairy.com					
Upstate Farms Co-op 25 Anderson Rd	Buffalo	NY	14225	716-892-3156	892-3157
TF: 800-724-6455 ■ *Web:* www.upstatefarmscoop.com					
Wells Enterprises Inc 1 Blue Bunny Dr	Le Mars	IA	51031	712-546-4000	546-1782
TF: 800-942-3800 ■ *Web:* www.wellsdairy.com					
WH Braum Inc 3000 NE 63rd St	Oklahoma City	OK	73121	405-478-1656	475-2460
Web: www.braums.com					
Yarnell Ice Cream Co 205 S Spring St	Searcy	AR	72143	501-268-2414	279-0846
TF: 800-666-2414 ■ *Web:* www.yarnells.com					
YoCream International Inc 5858 NE 87th Ave	Portland	OR	97220	503-256-3754	256-3976
TF: 800-962-7326 ■ *Web:* www.yocream.com					

299-26 Meat Products - Prepared

				Phone	Fax
A to Z Kosher Meat Products Co Inc 123 Grand St	Brooklyn	NY	11211	718-384-7400	384-7403
Web: www.empirenational.com					
Aidells Sausage Co 1625 Alvarado St	San Leandro	CA	94577	510-614-5450	614-2287
TF: 877-243-3557 ■ *Web:* www.aidells.com					
Albertville Quality Foods Inc 130 Quality Dr PO Box 756	Albertville	AL	35950	256-840-9923	840-9906
TF: 866-226-5540 ■ *Web:* www.albertvillequalityfoods.com					
Alderfer Inc 382 Main St PO Box 2	Harleysville	PA	19438	215-256-8818	256-6120
TF Sales: 877-253-6328 ■ *Web:* www.alderfermeats.com					
American Foods Group Inc 544 Acme St	Green Bay	WI	54302	920-437-6330	436-6510
TF: 800-345-0293 ■ *Web:* www.americanfoodsgroup.com					
Ball Park Franks 3500 Lacey Rd	Downers Grove	IL	60515	630-598-7892	598-8221
TF Cust Svc: 866-727-2533 ■ *Web:* www.ballparkfranks.com					

Company / Address	City	State	ZIP	Phone	Fax
Ballard's Farm Sausage Inc 2131 Right Fork Wilson Creek Rd PO Box 699 — *TF:* 800-346-7675 ■ *Web:* www.ballardsfarm.com	Wayne	WV	25570	304-272-5147	272-5336
Bar-S Foods Co 3838 N Central Ave Suite 1900 — *Web:* www.bar-s.com	Phoenix	AZ	85012	602-264-7272	285-5252
Beef Products Inc 891 Two Rivers Dr — *Web:* www.beefproducts.com	Dakota Dunes	SD	57049	605-217-8000	217-8001
Berks Packing Co Inc 307-323 Bingaman St PO Box 5919 — *TF:* 800-882-3757 ■ *Web:* www.berksfoods.com	Reading	PA	19610	610-376-7291	378-1210
Best Provision Co Inc 144 Avon Ave — *TF:* 800-631-4466	Newark	NJ	07108	973-242-5000	648-0041
Blue Grass Quality Meats 2645 Commerce Dr — *TF:* 888-236-4455	Crescent Springs	KY	41017	859-331-7100	331-4273
Boar's Head Provisions Co Inc 1819 Main St Suite 800 — *Web:* www.boarshead.com	Sarasota	FL	34236	941-955-0994	906-8213
Bobak Sausage Co 5275 S Archer Ave — *Web:* www.bobak.com	Chicago	IL	60632	773-735-5334	735-8605
Boyle's Famous Corned Beef Co 1638 St Louis Ave — *TF:* 800-821-3626	Kansas City	MO	64101	816-221-6283	221-3888
Bridgford Foods Corp 1308 N Patt St — *NASDAQ: BRID* ■ *TF:* 800-854-3255 ■ *Web:* www.bridgford.com	Anaheim	CA	92801	714-526-5533	526-4360
Burger's Ozark Country Cured Hams Inc 32819 Missouri 87 — *TF:* 800-203-4424 ■ *Web:* www.smokehouse.com	California	MO	65018	573-796-3134	796-3137
Carando Inc 20 Carando Dr — *TF:* 800-628-9524 ■ *Web:* www.carando.com	Springfield	MA	01104	413-781-5620	737-7314
Cargill Inc North America 15407 McGinty Rd — *TF:* 800-227-4455	Wayzata	MN	55391	952-742-7575	
Cargill Value Added Meats 200 S Ember Ln — *TF:* 800-558-2000 ■ *Web:* www.cargill.com/about/organization/value_added_meats.htm	Milwaukee	WI	53233	414-645-6500	647-6009
Caribbean Products Ltd 3624 Falls Rd	Baltimore	MD	21211	410-235-7700	235-1513
Carl Buddig & Co 950 175th St — *TF:* 800-621-0868 ■ *Web:* www.buddig.com	Homewood	IL	60430	708-798-0900	798-3178
Carlton Food Products Inc 880 Hwy 46 E PO Box 311385 — *TF:* 800-628-9849	New Braunfels	TX	78131	830-625-7583	629-7814
Carmelita Chorizo 2901 W Floral Dr — *Web:* www.carmelitachorizo.com	Monterey Park	CA	91754	323-262-6751	262-3503
Carriage House Foods 1131 Dayton Ave — *TF:* 800-250-3860	Ames	IA	50010	515-232-2273	232-3003
Cattaneo Bros Inc 769 Caudill St — *TF:* 800-243-8537 ■ *Web:* www.cattaneobros.com	San Luis Obispo	CA	93401	805-543-7188	543-4698
Cher-Make Sausage Co 2915 Calumet Ave — *TF:* 800-242-7679 ■ *Web:* www.cher-make.com	Manitowoc	WI	54220	920-683-5980	682-2588
Chicago Meat Authority Inc (CMA) 1120 W 47th Pl — *TF:* 800-383-3811 ■ *Web:* www.chicagomeat.com	Chicago	IL	60609	773-254-3811	254-5851
Chicopee Provision Co Inc 19 Sitarz St — *TF:* 800-924-6328 ■ *Web:* www.bluesealkielbasa.com	Chicopee	MA	01014	413-594-4765	594-2584
Citterio USA Corp 2008 SR 940 — *TF:* 800-435-8888 ■ *Web:* www.citteriousa.com	Freeland	PA	18224	570-636-3171	636-3171
Clifty Farm Country Ham Co Inc 1500 Hwy 641 S PO Box 1146 — *TF:* 800-486-4267 ■ *Web:* www.cliftyfarm.com	Paris	TN	38242	731-642-9740	642-7129
Cloverdale Foods Co Inc 3015 34th St NW PO Box 667 — *TF:* 800-669-9511 ■ *Web:* www.cloverdalefoods.com	Mandan	ND	58554	701-663-9511	663-0690
Coleman Natural Foods 1667 Cole Blvd Bldg 19 Suite 300 — *TF:* 800-442-8666 ■ *Web:* www.colemannatural.com	Lakewood	CO	80401	303-468-2500	277-9263
Continental-Capri Inc 250 Jackson St	Englewood	NJ	07631	201-568-7100	568-7180
Cook's Ham Inc 200 S 2nd St — *Web:* www.cooksham.com	Lincoln	NE	68508	402-475-6700	
Counts Sausage Co Inc 220 Church St PO Box 390 — *TF:* 800-868-0041	Prosperity	SC	29127	803-364-2392	364-1570
Daniel Weaver Co 1415 Weavertown Rd PO Box 525 — *TF:* 800-932-8377 ■ *Web:* www.godshalls.com	Lebanon	PA	17046	717-274-6100	274-6103
Daniele International Inc 105 Davis Dr — *TF:* 800-451-2535 ■ *Web:* www.danielefoods.com	Pascoag	RI	02859	401-568-6228	
Dean Sausage Co Inc 3750 Pleasant Valley Rd PO Box 750 — *Web:* www.deansausage.com	Attalla	AL	35954	256-538-6082	538-2584
Dearborn Sausage Co Inc 2450 Wyoming Ave — *Web:* www.dearbornsausage.com	Dearborn	MI	48120	313-842-2375	842-2640
Dewied International Inc 5010 IH- 10 E — *TF:* 800-992-5600 ■ *Web:* www.dewied.com	San Antonio	TX	78219	210-661-6161	662-6112
Dietz & Watson Inc 5701 Tacony St — *TF:* 800-333-1974 ■ *Web:* www.dietzandwatson.com	Philadelphia	PA	19135	215-831-9000	831-1044
Dold Foods Inc 2929 N Ohio St	Wichita	KS	67204	316-838-9101	838-9053
Fabbri Sausage Mfg Co 166 N Aberdeen St — *Web:* www.fabbrisausage.com	Chicago	IL	60607	312-829-6363	
Family Brands International LLC 1001 Elm Hill Rd PO Box 429 — *TF:* 800-356-4455 ■ *Web:* www.fbico.com	Lenoir City	TN	37771	865-986-8005	986-7171
Fargo Packing & Sausage Co 307 E Main Ave	West Fargo	ND	58078	701-282-3211	282-0325
FB Purnell Sausage Co Inc 6931 Shelbyville Rd PO Box 366 — *TF:* 800-262-6584 ■ *Web:* www.itsgooo-od.com	Simpsonville	KY	40067	502-722-5626	722-5586
Fisher Meats Inc 85 Front St N	Issaquah	WA	98027	425-392-3131	392-0168
Frank Wardynski & Sons Inc 336 Peckham St — *Web:* www.wardynski.com	Buffalo	NY	14206	716-854-6083	854-4887
Fred Usinger Inc 1030 N Old World 3rd St — *TF:* 800-558-9998 ■ *Web:* www.usinger.com	Milwaukee	WI	53203	414-276-9100	291-5277
Freedom Sausage Inc 4155 E 1650th Rd	Earlville	IL	60518	815-792-8276	792-8283
Freirich Julian Food Products Inc 815 W Kerr St — *TF:* 800-554-4788 ■ *Web:* www.freirich.com	Salisbury	NC	28144	704-636-2621	636-4650
G & G Supermarket Inc 1211 W College Ave — *Web:* www.gandgmarket.com	Santa Rosa	CA	95401	707-546-6877	575-5921
Gallo Salami 2411 Baumann Ave — *TF:* 800-321-1097	San Lorenzo	CA	94580	510-276-1300	278-2177
Garcia Foods Inc PO Box 13280 — *Web:* www.garciafoods.com	San Antonio	TX	78213	210-349-6262	
Gold Star Sausage Co Inc 2800 Walnut St PO Box 4245 — *TF:* 800-258-7229	Denver	CO	80204	303-295-6400	294-0495
Golden State Foods 18301 Von Karman Ave Suite 1100 — *Web:* www.goldenstatefoods.com	Irvine	CA	92612	949-252-2000	252-2080
Great Lakes Packing Co 1535 W 43rd St	Chicago	IL	60609	773-927-6660	927-8587
Green Tree Packing Co 65 Central Ave — *TF:* 800-221-5754	Passaic	NJ	07055	973-473-1305	473-7975
Greenwood Packing Plant 1 Packer Ave — *Web:* www.carolinaprideonline.com	Greenwood	SC	29646	864-223-7125	229-5386
Grote & Weigel Inc 76 Granby St — *TF:* 800-973-6370 ■ *Web:* www.groteandweigel.com	Bloomfield	CT	06002	860-242-8528	242-4162
Habbersett Scrapple Inc 701 Ashland Ave Suite A-4 — *Web:* www.habbersettscrapple.com	Folcroft	PA	19032	610-532-9973	586-2396
Harper's Hams & Gifts 2955 US Hwy 51 N PO Box 122 — *TF:* 888-427-7377 ■ *Web:* www.hamtastic.com	Clinton	KY	42031	270-653-2081	653-2409
Hatfield Quality Meats Inc 2700 Clemens Rd — *TF:* 800-523-5291 ■ *Web:* www.hatfieldqualitymeats.com	Hatfield	PA	19440	215-368-2500	
Hazle Park Packing Co 260 Washington Ave Hazle Pk	Hazletownship	PA	18202	570-455-7571	455-6030
Henry's Hickory House Inc 249 Copeland St	Jacksonville	FL	32204	904-354-6839	354-6028
Hi Grade Meats Inc 2160 S W Temple St	Salt Lake City	UT	84115	801-487-5818	487-4343
Hormel Foods Corp 1 Hormel Pl — *NYSE: HRL* ■ **Fax:* Sales ■ *TF:* 800-523-4635 ■ *Web:* www.hormel.com	Austin	MN	55912	507-437-5248	437-5129*
Hormel Foods International Corp 1 Hormel Pl — *TF:* 800-523-4635 ■ *Web:* www.hormelfoods.com	Austin	MN	55912	507-437-5478	437-5113
Hummel Bros Inc 180 Sargent Dr — *TF:* 800-828-8978	New Haven	CT	06511	203-787-4113	498-1755
Indiana Packers Corp Hwy 421 S County Rd 100 N PO Box 318 — *TF:* 800-472-7201 ■ *Web:* www.inpac.com	Delphi	IN	46923	765-564-3680	564-3684
Ito Cariani Foods Div Itoham America Inc 3190 Corporate Pl	Hayward	CA	94545	510-887-0882	
John Hofmeister & Son Inc 2386 S Blue Island Ave — *Web:* www.hofhaus.com	Chicago	IL	60608	773-847-0700	847-6624
John Morrell & Co 805 E Kemper Rd — **Fax:* Cust Svc ■ *TF:* 800-445-2013 ■ *Web:* www.johnmorrell.com	Cincinnati	OH	45246	513-346-3540	346-7552*
Johnsonville Sausage LLC PO Box 906 — *Web:* www.johnsonville.com	Sheboygan Falls	WI	53085	920-467-2641	467-2818
Jones Dairy Farm 800 Jones Ave PO Box 808 — *TF:* 800-635-6637 ■ *Web:* www.jonesdairyfarm.com	Fort Atkinson	WI	53538	920-563-2431	563-6801
Karl Ehmer Inc 63-35 Fresh Pond Rd — *TF:* 800-487-5275 ■ *Web:* www.karlehmer.com	Ridgewood	NY	11385	718-456-8100	456-2270
Kayem Foods Inc 75 Arlington St — *TF:* 800-426-6100 ■ *Web:* www.kayem.com	Chelsea	MA	02150	617-889-1600	889-5931
Kent Quality Foods Inc 703 Leonard St NW — *TF:* 800-748-0141 ■ *Web:* www.kentqualityfoods.com	Grand Rapids	MI	49504	616-459-4595	459-8433
Kessler's Inc 1201 Hummel Ave — *TF:* 800-382-1328 ■ *Web:* www.kesslerfoods.com	Lemoyne	PA	17043	717-763-7162	763-4982
Keystone Foods LLC 300 Bar Harbor Dr Suite 600, 5 Tower Bridge — *Web:* www.keystonefoods.com	West Conshohocken	PA	19428	610-667-6700	667-1460
King's Command Foods Inc 7622 S 188th St — *Web:* www.kingscommand.com	Kent	WA	98032	425-251-6788	251-0523
Kiolbassa Provision Co 1325 S Brazos St — *Web:* www.kiolbassa.com	San Antonio	TX	78207	210-226-8127	226-7464
Klement Sausage Co Inc 207 E Lincoln Ave — *TF:* 800-553-6368 ■ *Web:* www.klements.com	Milwaukee	WI	53207	414-744-2330	744-2438
Koegel Meats Inc 3400 W Bristol Rd — *Web:* www.koegelmeats.com	Flint	MI	48507	810-238-3685	238-2467
Kowalski Sausage Co Inc 2270 Holbrook Ave — *TF:* 800-482-2400	Hamtramck	MI	48212	313-873-8200	873-4220
Kraft Foods Inc Oscar Mayer Foods Div 910 Mayer Ave	Madison	WI	53704	608-241-3311	242-6108
Kronos Products Inc 4501 W District Blvd — *Web:* www.kronosproducts.com	Chicago	IL	60632	773-847-2250	847-2492
Kunzler & Co Inc 652 Manor St — *TF Cust Svc:* 888-586-9537 ■ *Web:* www.kunzler.com	Lancaster	PA	17603	717-299-6301	390-2170
Land O'Frost Inc 16850 Chicago Ave — *TF:* 800-323-3308 ■ *Web:* www.landofrost.com	Lansing	IL	60438	708-474-7100	474-9329
Les Trois Petits Cochons Inc 4223 1st Ave 2nd Fl — *TF:* 800-537-7283 ■ *Web:* www.3pigs.com	Brooklyn	NY	11232	212-219-1230	941-9726
Levonian Bros Inc 27 River St PO Box 629 — *TF Cust Svc:* 800-538-6642	Troy	NY	12180	518-274-3610	274-0098
Louie's Finer Meats Inc PO Box 774 — *TF:* 800-270-4297 ■ *Web:* www.louiesfinermeats.com	Cumberland	WI	54829	715-822-4728	822-3150
Maid-Rite Steak Co Inc 105 Keystone Industrial Pk — *TF:* 800-233-4259	Dunmore	PA	18512	570-343-4748	969-2878
Makowski's Real Sausage Co 2710 S Poplar Ave	Chicago	IL	60608	312-842-5330	842-5414
Maple Leaf Consumer Foods 321 Cortland Ave E — *TF:* 800-567-3212 ■ *Web:* www.mapleleaf.ca	Kitchener	ON	N2G3X8	519-741-5000	749-7400
Maple Leaf Foods Inc 30 St Clair Ave W Suite 1500 — *TSE: MFI* ■ *Web:* www.mapleleaf.ca	Toronto	ON	M4V3A2	416-926-2000	926-2018
Marathon Enterprises Inc 9 Smith St — *TF:* 800-722-7388	Englewood	NJ	07631	201-935-3330	935-5693

Company	City	State	Zip	Phone	Fax
Martin Rosol Inc 45 Grove St *Web:* www.martinrosols.com	New Britain	CT	06053	860-223-2707	229-6690
Meadow Farms Sausage Co 6215 S Western Ave	Los Angeles	CA	90047	323-752-2300	752-5640
Milan Salami Co Inc 1155 67th St	Oakland	CA	94608	510-654-7055	654-7257
Miller Packing Co 1122 Industrial Way PO Box 1390 *TF:* 800-624-2328 ■ *Web:* www.millerhotdogs.com	Lodi	CA	95241	209-339-2310	334-0848
Mongolia Casing Corp 4706 Grand Ave *TF:* 800-221-4887	Maspeth	NY	11378	718-628-4500	628-5800
Mrs Ressler's Food Products Co 5501 Tabor Ave PO Box 5717 *Web:* www.ressler.com	Philadelphia	PA	19120	215-744-4700	744-4750
Murry's Inc 8300 Pennsylvania Ave *TF:* 800-638-0215 ■ *Web:* www.murrys.com	Upper Marlboro	MD	20772	301-420-6400	967-4816
Natural Casing Co 410 E Railroad St	Peshtigo	WI	54157	715-582-3736	582-3931
Neto Sausage Co Inc 3499 Alameda St PO Box 578 *TF:* 888-482-6386 ■ *Web:* www.netosausage.com	Santa Clara	CA	95052	408-296-0818	296-0538
Oberto Sausage Co 7060 S 238th St *TF:* 877-234-7902 ■ *Web:* www.oberto.com	Kent	WA	98032	253-437-6100	437-6153
Odom's Tennessee Pride Sausage Inc 1201 Neelys Bend Rd *TF:* 800-327-6269 ■ *Web:* www.tnpride.com	Madison	TN	37115	615-868-1360	860-4703
Old Wisconsin Sausage Co 5030 Claybird Rd *TF:* 800-558-7840	Sheboygan	WI	53083	920-458-4304	458-2716
OSI Industries LLC 1225 Corporate Blvd *Web:* www.osigroup.com	Aurora	IL	60504	630-851-6600	851-8223
Palama Meat Co Inc 2029 Lauwiliwili St	Kapolei	HI	96707	808-682-8305	834-8895
Palmyra Bologna Co Inc 230 N College St PO Box 111 *TF:* 800-282-6336 ■ *Web:* www.seltzerslebanonbologna.com	Palmyra	PA	17078	717-838-6336	838-5345
Park 100 Foods Inc 326 E Adams St *TF:* 800-854-6504 ■ *Web:* www.park100foods.com	Tipton	IN	46072	765-675-3480	675-3474
Peer Foods Group Inc 1200 W 35th St Suite 5E *TF:* 800-365-5644 ■ *Web:* www.peerfoods.com	Chicago	IL	60609	773-927-1440	927-9859
Phillips Bros Country Ham Inc 1523 S Fayetteville St *Web:* www.phillipsbrotherscountryhams.com	Asheboro	NC	27205	336-625-4321	625-4322
Pine Ridge Farms 1801 Maury St *Web:* www.pineridgefarmspork.com	Des Moines	IA	50317	515-266-4100	266-9889
Plumrose USA Inc 7 Lexington Ave *TF:* 800-526-4909 ■ *Web:* www.plumroseusa.com	East Brunswick	NJ	08816	732-257-6600	257-6644
Pocino Foods Co 14250 Lomitas Ave *Web:* www.pocinofoods.com	City of Industry	CA	91746	626-968-8000	968-0196
Premio Foods Inc 50 Utter Ave *TF:* 800-864-7622 ■ *Web:* www.premiofoods.com	Hawthorne	NJ	07506	973-427-1106	427-1140
Quaker Maid Meats Inc PO Box 350 *Web:* www.quakermaidmeats.com	shillington	PA	19607	610-376-1500	376-2678
Quality Sausage Co Ltd 1925 Lone Star Dr *Web:* www.qualitysausage.com	Dallas	TX	75212	214-634-3400	634-2296
Randolph Packing Co 275 Roma Jean Pkwy *TF:* 800-451-1607 ■ *Web:* www.randolphpacking.com	Streamwood	IL	60107	630-830-3100	830-1872
Reser's Fine Foods Inc 15570 SW Jenkins Rd PO Box 8 *TF:* 800-333-6431 ■ *Web:* www.resers.com	Beaverton	OR	97075	503-643-6431	
Saags Products Inc 1799 Factor Ave *TF:* 800-352-7224 ■ *Web:* www.saags.com	San Leandro	CA	94577	510-352-8000	352-4100
Sabrett Food Products Corp 9 Smith St *TF:* 800-722-7388 ■ *Web:* www.sabrett.com	Englewood	NJ	07631	201-935-3330	935-5693
Sadler's Smokehouse Ltd PO Box 1088 *TF:* 800-777-5581 ■ *Web:* www.sadlerssmokehouse.com	Henderson	TX	75653	903-657-5581	655-8404
Schaller & Weber Inc 22-35 46th St *TF Orders:* 800-847-4115 ■ *Web:* www.schallerweber.com	Astoria	NY	11105	718-721-5480	956-9157
Silver Star Meats Inc 1720 Middletown Rd PO Box 393 *TF:* 800-548-1321 ■ *Web:* www.silverstarmeats.com	McKees Rocks	PA	15136	412-771-5539	
Simeus Foods International Inc 812 S 5th Ave *TF:* 888-772-3663 ■ *Web:* www.simeusfoods.com	Mansfield	TX	76063	817-473-1562	473-2017
Smith Packing Co Inc 105-125 Washington St *Web:* www.smithpacking.com	Utica	NY	13503	315-732-5125	732-5129
Smithfield Foods Inc 200 Commerce St *NYSE: SFD* ■ *TF:* 800-276-6158 ■ *Web:* www.smithfieldfoods.com	Smithfield	VA	23430	757-365-3000	365-3017
Sparrer Sausage Co Inc 4320 W Ogden Ave *TF:* 800-666-3287 ■ *Web:* www.sparrers.com	Chicago	IL	60623	773-762-3334	521-9368
Specialty Foods Group Inc 21 Enterprise Pkwy 4th Fl *Web:* www.specialtyfoodsgroup.com	Hampton	VA	23666	757-952-1200	952-1201
Stampede Meat Inc 7351 S 78th Ave *TF:* 800-353-0933 ■ *Web:* www.stampedemeat.com	Bridgeview	IL	60455	773-376-4300	
Standard Casing Co Inc The 165 Chubb Ave *TF:* 800-847-4141 ■ *Web:* www.standardcasing.com/index.html	Lyndhurst	NJ	07071	201-434-6300	434-1508
Standard Meat Co LP 5105 Investment Dr *TF:* 866-859-6313 ■ *Web:* www.standardmeat.com	Dallas	TX	75236	214-561-0561	561-0560
Stevison Ham Co 125 Stevison Ham Rd	Portland	TN	37148	615-325-4161	
Stock Yards Packing Co Inc 340 N Oakley Blvd *TF:* 800-621-3687 ■ *Web:* www.stockyards.com	Chicago	IL	60612	312-733-6050	733-0738
Storer Meats Co Inc 3007 Clinton Ave *TF:* 800-355-7537	Cleveland	OH	44113	216-621-7538	361-0622
Sugar Creek Packing Co 2101 Kenskill Ave *TF:* 800-848-8205 ■ *Web:* www.sugarcreek.com	Wshngtn CT Hs	OH	43160	740-335-3586	335-7444
Suzanna's Kitchen Inc 4025 Buford Hwy *TF:* 800-241-2455 ■ *Web:* www.suzannaskitchen.com	Duluth	GA	30096	770-476-9900	476-8899
Sysco Kansas City Inc 1915 E Kansas City Rd *Web:* www.kc.sysco.com	Olathe	KS	66061	913-829-5555	780-8625
Taylor Provisions 63 Perrine Ave PO Box 5108	Trenton	NJ	08638	609-392-1113	392-1354
Tyson Prepared Foods Inc 5701 McNutt Rd **Fax:* Acctg ■ *TF:* 800-351-8184 ■ *Web:* www.tyson.com	Santa Teresa	NM	88008	575-589-0100	589-1903*
US Premium Beef LLC (USPB) 12200 N Ambassador Dr PO Box 20103 *TF:* 866-877-2525 ■ *Web:* www.uspremiumbeef.com	Kansas City	MO	64163	816-713-8800	713-8810
Vienna Sausage Mfg Co 2501 N Damen Ave *TF:* 800-621-8183 ■ *Web:* www.viennabeef.com	Chicago	IL	60647	773-278-7800	278-4759
Vincent Giordano Corp 2600 Washington Ave *Web:* www.vgiordano.com	Philadelphia	PA	19146	215-467-6629	467-6339
Vista International Packaging LLC 1126 88th Pl *TF:* 800-558-4058 ■ *Web:* www.vistapackaging.com	Kenosha	WI	53143	262-694-2276	694-4824
Vollwerth & Co 200 Hancock St PO Box 239 *TF:* 800-562-7620 ■ *Web:* www.vollwerth.com	Hancock	MI	49930	906-482-1550	482-0842
Webster City Custom Meats Inc 1611 E 2nd St *TF:* 888-786-3287 ■ *Web:* www.webstercitycustommeats.com	Webster City	IA	50595	515-832-1130	832-5515
Wimmer's Meat Products Inc 126 W Grant St PO Box 286 *TF Sales:* 800-358-0761 ■ *Web:* www.wimmersmeats.com	West Point	NE	68788	402-372-2437	372-5659
Wolfson Casing Corp 700 S Fulton Ave *TF:* 800-221-8042 ■ *Web:* www.wolfsoncasing.com	Mount Vernon	NY	10550	914-668-9000	668-5744
Zweigles Inc 651 Plymouth Ave N *Web:* www.zweigles.com	Rochester	NY	14608	585-546-1740	546-8721

299-27 Milk & Cream Products

Company	City	State	Zip	Phone	Fax
Agri-Mark Inc PO Box 5800 *Web:* www.agrimark.net	Lawrence	MA	01842	978-689-4442	794-8304
Alta Dena Dairy 17637 E Valley Blvd *TF Orders:* 800-535-1369 ■ *Web:* www.altadenadairy.com	City of Industry	CA	91744	214-721-1273	
AMPI 315 N Broadway *TF:* 800-533-3580 ■ *Web:* www.ampi.com	New Ulm	MN	56073	507-354-8295	359-8668
Anderson Dairy Inc 801 Searles Ave *Web:* www.andersondairy.com	Las Vegas	NV	89101	702-642-7507	642-3480
Anderson Erickson Dairy Co 2420 E University Ave *TF:* 800-234-7257 ■ *Web:* www.aedairy.com	Des Moines	IA	50317	515-265-2521	263-6301
Barber Dairies Inc 36 Barber Ct *Web:* www.barbersdairy.com	Birmingham	AL	35209	205-942-2351	943-0297
Bartlett Dairy Inc 150-03 150th St *Web:* www.bartlettny.com	Jamaica	NY	11433	718-658-2299	725-2527
Berkeley Farms Inc 25500 Clawiter Rd **Fax:* Sales ■ *Web:* www.berkeleyfarms.com	Hayward	CA	94545	510-265-8600	265-8754*
Broughton Foods Co 1701 Green St *TF:* 800-283-2479	Marietta	OH	45750	740-373-4121	373-2861
Brown Cow West Corp 3810 Delta Fair Blvd *TF:* 888-429-5459 ■ *Web:* www.browncowfarm.com	Antioch	CA	94509	925-757-9209	757-9160
California Dairies Inc 2000 N Plaza Dr *TF:* 800-821-5588 ■ *Web:* www.californiadairies.com	Visalia	CA	93291	559-625-2200	625-5433
Century Foods International 400 Century Ct PO Box 257 *Web:* www.centuryfoods.com	Sparta	WI	54656	608-269-1900	269-1910
Clover Farms Dairy 3300 Pottsville Pike *TF:* 800-323-0123 ■ *Web:* www.farmersdairy.com	Reading	PA	19605	610-921-9111	
Cloverland Green Spring Dairy Inc 2701 Loch Raven Rd *TF Orders:* 800-876-6455 ■ *Web:* www.cloverlanddairy.com	Baltimore	MD	21218	410-235-4477	889-3690
Coleman Dairy Inc 6901 I-30 *TF:* 800-365-1551 ■ *Web:* www.colemandairy.com	Little Rock	AR	72209	501-565-1551	568-1710
Country Fresh Inc 2555 Buchanan Ave SW *TF:* 800-748-0480 ■ *Web:* www.enjoycountryfresh.com	Grand Rapids	MI	49548	616-243-0173	243-5926
Crossroad Farms Dairy 400 S Shortridge Rd *TF:* 800-334-7502	Indianapolis	IN	46219	317-229-7600	229-7676
Dairy Fresh Corp 915 Tuscaloosa St	Greensboro	AL	36744	334-624-3041	
Dannon Co 100 Hillside Ave **Fax:* Hum Res ■ *Web:* www.dannon.com	White Plains	NY	10603	914-872-8400	872-1573*
Dean Foods Co 2711 N Haskell Ave Suite 3400 *NYSE: DF* ■ *TF:* 800-395-7004 ■ *Web:* www.deanfoods.com	Dallas	TX	75204	214-303-3400	303-3499
Eagle Family Foods Inc 1 Strawberry Ln **Fax Area Code:* 330 ■ *TF:* 888-656-3245 ■ *Web:* www.eaglebrand.com	Orrville	OH	44667	888-656-3245	684-6410*
Farmers Select LLC 7321 N Loop Rd	El Paso	TX	79915	915-772-2736	772-0907
Farmland Dairies LLC 520 Main Ave **Fax:* Sales ■ *Web:* www.farmlanddairies.com	Wallington	NJ	07057	973-777-2500	249-3838*
Flav-O-Rich 1105 N William St *TF:* 877-321-1158	Goldsboro	NC	27530	919-734-0728	735-6344
Galliker Dairy Co Inc 143 Donald Ln *TF:* 800-477-6455 ■ *Web:* www.gallikers.com	Johnstown	PA	15907	814-266-8702	
Garelick Farms Inc 124 Grove St Franklin Oaks Office Pk Suite 100 **Fax:* Sales ■ *TF:* 800-343-4982	Franklin	MA	02038	508-528-9000	553-5475*
Guida-Seibert Dairy Co 433 Pk St *TF:* 800-832-8929 ■ *Web:* www.supercow.com	New Britain	CT	06051	860-224-2404	225-0035
Gustafson's Dairy Inc 4169 County Rd 15-A *TF:* 800-342-1092 ■ *Web:* www.gustafsonsdairy.com	Green Cove Springs	FL	32043	904-284-3750	284-5570
Harrisburg Dairies Inc 2001 Herr St *TF:* 800-692-7429 ■ *Web:* www.harrisburgdairies.com	Harrisburg	PA	17105	717-233-8701	231-4584
Heritage Foods LLC 4002 Westminster Ave **Fax Area Code:* 800 ■ *TF Orders:* 800-321-5960	Santa Ana	CA	92703	714-775-5000	239-6027*
Hiland Dairy Co 1133 E Kearney St PO Box 2270 *TF:* 800-641-4022 ■ *Web:* www.hilanddairy.com	Springfield	MO	65801	417-862-9311	837-1106
Kemps LLC 1270 Energy Ln *TF:* 800-322-9566	Saint Paul	MN	55108	651-379-6500	379-6806
Kleinpeter Farms Dairy LLC 14444 Airline Hwy *Web:* www.kleinpeterdairy.com	Baton Rouge	LA	70817	225-753-2121	752-8964
Land O'Lakes Inc 4001 Lexington Ave N **Fax:* Hum Res ■ *TF:* 800-328-9680 ■ *Web:* www.landolakesinc.com	Arden Hills	MN	55126	651-481-2222	481-2488*

Company	City	State	ZIP	Phone	Fax
Land O'Lakes Inc Dairyman's Div 400 S 'M' St	Tulare	CA	93274	559-687-8287	685-6911*
Lehigh Valley Dairies Inc 880 Allentown Rd *TF:* 800-937-3233 ■ *Web:* www.lehighmilk.com	Lansdale	PA	19446	215-855-8205	855-9834
Lifeway Foods Inc 6431 W Oakton St *NASDAQ: LWAY* ■ *TF:* 877-281-3874 ■ *Web:* www.lifeway.net	Morton Grove	IL	60053	847-967-1010	967-6558
Maola Milk & Ice Cream Co 305 Ave C *TF:* 800-476-1021 ■ *Web:* www.maolamilk.com	New Bern	NC	28563	252-638-1131	638-2268
Maple Hill Farms Inc 12 Burr Rd PO Box 767 *TF:* 800-243-0067	Bloomfield	CT	06002	860-242-9689	243-2490
Marcus Dairy Inc 4 Eagle Rd *TF:* 800-243-2511 ■ *Web:* www.marcusdairy.com	Danbury	CT	06810	203-748-5611	791-2759
Mayfield Dairy Farms Inc PO Box 310 *TF:* 800-362-9546 ■ *Web:* www.mayfielddairy.com	Athens	TN	37371	423-745-2151	745-6385
McArthur Dairy Inc 500 Sawgrass Corporate Pkwy *TF:* 877-803-6565 ■ *Web:* www.mcarthurdairy.com	Sunrise	FL	33325	954-846-1234	846-0429
Meadow Brook Dairy 2365 Buffalo Rd *TF:* 800-352-4010 ■ *Web:* www.meadowbrookdairy.com	Erie	PA	16510	814-899-3191	464-9152
Michigan Milk Producers Assn 41310 Bridge St *Web:* www.mimilk.com	Novi	MI	48375	248-474-6672	474-0924
Milkco Inc 220 Deaverview Rd *TF:* 800-842-8021	Asheville	NC	28806	828-254-9560	252-9560
Oakhurst Dairy 364 Forest Ave *TF:* 800-482-0718 ■ *Web:* www.oakhurstdairy.com	Portland	ME	04101	207-772-7468	874-0714
Parmalat Canada Ltd 405 the W Mall 10th Fl *TF:* 800-563-1515 ■ *Web:* www.parmalat.ca	Toronto	ON	M9C5J1	416-626-1973	620-3123
Penn Maid Foods Inc 10975 Dutton Rd *TF:* 800-220-7063 ■ *Web:* www.pennmaid.com	Philadelphia	PA	19154	215-824-2800	824-2820
Prairie Farms Dairy Inc 1100 N Broadway St *TF:* 800-654-2547 ■ *Web:* www.prairiefarms.com	Carlinville	IL	62626	217-854-2547	854-6426
Pride of Main Street Dairy 214 Main St S	Sauk Centre	MN	56378	320-351-8300	351-8500
Producers Dairy Foods Inc 250 E Belmont Ave **Fax:* Orders ■ *TF Cust Svc:* 800-244-6024 ■ *Web:* www.producersdairy.com	Fresno	CA	93701	559-264-6583	457-4691*
Purity Dairies Inc 360 Murfreesboro Rd *TF:* 800-947-6455 ■ *Web:* www.puritydairies.com	Nashville	TN	37210	615-244-1900	242-8547
Readington Farms Inc 12 Mill Rd *TF General:* 800-426-1707 ■ *Web:* www.readington/wakefern.com	Whitehouse Station	NJ	08889	908-534-2121	534-5235
Royal Crest Dairy Inc 350 S Pearl St *Web:* www.royalcrestdairy.com	Denver	CO	80209	303-777-2227	744-9173
Rutter Dairy Inc 2100 N George St *Web:* www.rutters.com	York	PA	17404	717-848-9827	845-8751
Schneider Valley Farms Dairy 1860 E 3rd St *TF:* 800-332-8563	Williamsport	PA	17701	570-326-2021	326-2736
Schneider's Dairy Inc 726 Frank St	Pittsburgh	PA	15227	412-881-3525	881-7722
Shamrock Foods Co Inc 2540 N 29th Ave *TF:* 800-289-3663 ■ *Web:* www.shamrockfoods.com	Phoenix	AZ	85009	602-233-6400	477-6469
Smith Dairy 1381 Dairy Ln PO Box 87 *TF:* 800-776-7076 ■ *Web:* www.smithdairy.com	Orrville	OH	44667	330-683-8710	683-1079
Smith Dairy Wayne Div 1590 NW 11th St *TF:* 800-875-9296 ■ *Web:* www.smithsdairy.com	Richmond	IN	47375	765-935-7521	962-5269
Southeast Milk Inc 1950 SE Hwy 484 *TF:* 800-598-7866 ■ *Web:* www.southeastmilk.org	Belleview	FL	34420	352-245-2437	307-5528
Southern Belle Dairy Co Inc 607 Bourne Ave **Fax Area Code:* 800 ■ *TF:* 800-468-4798 ■ *Web:* www.southernbelledairy.com	Somerset	KY	42501	606-679-1131	441-8931*
Springfield Creamery Inc 29440 Airport Rd *Web:* www.nancysyogurt.com	Eugene	OR	97402	541-689-2911	689-2915
Steuben Foods Inc 155-04 Liberty Ave	Jamaica	NY	11433	718-291-3333	291-0560
Stonyfield Farm Inc 10 Burton Dr *TF:* 800-776-2697 ■ *Web:* www.stonyfield.com	Londonderry	NH	03053	603-437-4040	437-7594
Superior Dairy Inc 4719 Navarre Rd SW *TF:* 800-683-2479	Canton	OH	44706	330-477-4515	477-5908
T Marzetti Co Allen Milk Div 1709 Frank Rd	Columbus	OH	43223	614-279-8673	279-5674
TG Lee Foods Inc 315 N Bumby Ave	Orlando	FL	32803	407-894-4941	896-4757
UC Milk Co Inc 234 N Scott St *TF:* 800-462-2354 ■ *Web:* www.ucmilk.com	Madisonville	KY	42431	270-821-7221	821-7292
Umpqua Dairy Products Co 333 SE Sykes Ave PO Box 1306 *TF:* 888-672-6455 ■ *Web:* www.umpquadairy.com	Roseburg	OR	97470	541-672-2638	673-0256
United Dairy Farmers 3955 Montgomery Rd *TF:* 800-654-2809 ■ *Web:* www.udfinc.com	Cincinnati	OH	45212	513-396-8700	396-8736
United Dairy Inc 300 N 5th St *TF:* 800-252-1542 ■ *Web:* www.uniteddairy.com	Martins Ferry	OH	43935	740-633-1451	633-6759
Upstate Farms Co-op 25 Anderson Rd *TF:* 800-724-6455 ■ *Web:* www.upstatefarmscoop.com	Buffalo	NY	14225	716-892-3156	892-3157
Velda Farms LLC 402 S Kentucky Ave Suite 500 **Fax Area Code:* 888 ■ *TF Cust Svc:* 800-795-4649 ■ *Web:* www.veldafarms.com	Lakeland	FL	33801	863-686-4441	644-6113*
WestFarm Foods 635 Elliott Ave W *TF:* 800-333-6455	Seattle	WA	98119	206-284-7220	284-7220
WhiteWave Foods Co 12002 Airport Way *Web:* www.whitewave.com	Broomfield	CO	80021	303-635-4000	
Whittier Farms Inc 86 Douglas Rd *Web:* www.whittierfarms.com	West Sutton	MA	01590	508-865-0640	865-4128
Wilcox Farms Inc 40400 Harts Lake Valley Rd *TF:* 800-568-6456 ■ *Web:* www.wilcoxfarms.com	Roy	WA	98580	360-458-7774	458-6950

299-28 Nuts - Edible

Company	City	State	ZIP	Phone	Fax
Azar Nut Co 1800 Northwestern Dr *TF:* 800-351-8178	El Paso	TX	79912	915-877-4079	877-1198
Beer Nuts Inc 103 N Robinson St *TF:* 800-233-7688 ■ *Web:* www.beernuts.com	Bloomington	IL	61701	309-827-8580	827-0914
Dahlgren & Co Inc 1220 Sunflower St *TF:* 800-346-6050 ■ *Web:* www.sunflowerseed.com	Crookston	MN	56716	218-281-2985	281-2985
Diamond Foods Inc 1050 S Diamond St *NASDAQ: DMND* ■ *Web:* www.diamondfoods.com	Stockton	CA	95205	209-467-6000	461-7309
Hines Nut Co Inc 990 S St Paul St *TF:* 800-580-0580 ■ *Web:* www.hinesnut.com	Dallas	TX	75201	214-939-0253	761-0720
John B Sanfilippo & Son Inc 1703 N Randall Rd *NASDAQ: JBSS* ■ *TF:* 800-323-6887 ■ *Web:* www.jbssinc.com	Elgin	IL	60123	847-289-1800	289-1843
Kar Nut Products Co Inc 1200 E 14 Mile Rd *TF:* 800-527-6887 ■ *Web:* www.karsnuts.net/shop	Madison Heights	MI	48071	248-588-1903	588-1902
King Nut Co 31900 Solon Rd *TF:* 800-860-5464 ■ *Web:* www.kingnut.com	Solon	OH	44139	440-248-8484	248-0153
Koinonia Partners 1324 Georgia Hwy 49 S *TF:* 877-738-1741 ■ *Web:* www.koinoniapartners.org	Americus	GA	31719	229-924-0391	924-6504
Leavitt Corp 100 Santilli Hwy *Web:* www.teddie.com	Everett	MA	02149	617-389-2600	387-9085
Nutcracker Brands Inc PO Box 420 *TF:* 800-638-6887 ■ *Web:* www.nutcrackerbrands.com	Billerica	MA	01821	978-663-5400	667-8596
Pippin Snack Pecan Co PO Box 3330 *TF:* 800-748-8305	Albany	GA	31706	229-432-9316	438-0464
Priester Pecan Co Inc PO Box 381 *TF:* 800-277-3226 ■ *Web:* www.priesters.com	Fort Deposit	AL	36032	334-227-4301	227-4294
Ralcorp PO Box 8084 *TF:* 800-233-5979 ■ *Web:* www.ralcorp.com	Dothan	AL	36304	334-983-5643	983-4796
South Georgia Pecan Co 309 S Lee St *TF:* 800-627-6630 ■ *Web:* www.georgiapecan.com	Valdosta	GA	31601	229-244-1321	247-6361
Superior Nut Co Inc 225 Monsignor O'Brien Hwy *Web:* www.superiornut.com	Cambridge	MA	02141	617-876-3808	876-8225
Trophy Nut Co Inc 320 N 2nd St *TF:* 800-729-6887 ■ *Web:* www.trophynut.com	Tipp City	OH	45371	937-667-8478	667-4656
Willmar Cookie & Nut Co Inc 1118 E Hwy 12	Willmar	MN	56201	320-235-0600	235-0659
Wricley Nut Products Co 480 Pattison Ave *TF:* 800-523-1303	Philadelphia	PA	19148	215-467-1106	467-4127
Young Pecan Shelling Co PO Box 5779 *TF Sales:* 800-829-6864 ■ *Web:* www.youngpecan.com	Florence	SC	29502	843-664-2330	664-2344

299-29 Oil Mills - Cottonseed, Soybean, Other Vegetable Oils

Company	City	State	ZIP	Phone	Fax
Abitec Corp Inc PO Box 569 *TF Sales:* 800-555-1255 ■ *Web:* www.abiteccorp.com	Columbus	OH	43216	614-429-6464	299-8279
ADM North American Oilseed Processing Div 4666 E Faries Pkwy *TF:* 800-637-5843 ■ *Web:* www.adm.com	Decatur	IL	62526	217-424-5200	424-5978
ADM Quincy 1900 Gardner Expy	Quincy	IL	62301	217-224-1800	
Ag Processing Inc 12700 W Dodge Rd PO Box 2047 *TF:* 800-247-1345 ■ *Web:* www.agp.com	Omaha	NE	68103	402-496-7809	498-5548
American Lecithin Co Inc 115 Hurley Rd Unit 2B *TF:* 800-364-4416 ■ *Web:* www.americanlecithin.com	Oxford	CT	06478	203-262-7100	262-7101
Bunge Ltd 50 Main St 6th Fl *NYSE: BG* ■ *Web:* www.bunge.com	White Plains	NY	10606	914-684-2800	684-3499
Cargill Inc 15407 McGinty Rd W **Fax:* Cust Svc ■ *TF:* 800-227-4455 ■ *Web:* www.cargill.com	Wayzata	MN	55391	952-742-7575	742-7209*
Cargill Inc PO Box 9300 *TF:* 800-227-4455 ■ *Web:* www.cargill.com	Minneapolis	MN	55440	952-742-7575	
Cargill Inc North America 15407 McGinty Rd *TF:* 800-227-4455	Wayzata	MN	55391	952-742-7575	
ConAgra Foods Retail Products Co Grocery Foods Group 3353 Michelson Dr	Irvine	CA	92612	949-437-1018	437-3315
Delta Oil Mill PO Box 29 *Web:* www.deltaoilmill.com	Jonestown	MS	38639	662-358-4481	358-4629
Hartsville Oil Mill PO Box 1057	Darlington	SC	29540	843-393-1501	395-2690
Owensboro Grain Co 822 E 2nd St *TF:* 800-874-0305 ■ *Web:* www.owensborograin.com	Owensboro	KY	42303	270-926-2032	686-6509
Planters Cotton Oil Mill Inc 2901 Planters Dr *Web:* www.plantersoil.com	Pine Bluff	AR	71601	870-534-3631	534-1421
Producers Co-op Oil Mill 6 SE 4th St *Web:* www.producerscoop.net	Oklahoma City	OK	73129	405-232-7555	236-4887
Pyco Industries Inc PO Box 841 *Web:* www.pycoindustriesinc.com	Lubbock	TX	79041	806-747-3434	744-3221
Sessions Co Inc 801 N Main PO Box 311310 *Web:* www.peanutsouth.com	Enterprise	AL	36331	334-393-0200	393-0240
Valley Co-op Oil Mill PO Box 533609 *TF:* 800-775-3382	Harlingen	TX	78553	956-425-4545	425-4264
WA Cleary Products 1049 Rt 27 *TF:* 800-238-7813 ■ *Web:* www.waclearyproducts.com	Somerset	NJ	08873	732-247-8000	247-6977

299-30 Oils - Edible (Margarine, Shortening, Table Oils, etc)

Company	City	State	ZIP	Phone	Fax
Aarhuskarlshamn USA Inc 131 Marsh St *Web:* www.aak.com	Newark	NJ	07114	973-741-5049	344-6638
ACH Food Cos Inc 7171 Goodlet Farms Pkwy *TF:* 800-691-1106 ■ *Web:* www.achfood.com	Cordova	TN	38016	901-381-3000	381-2968
Bertolli USA Inc 920 Sylvan Ave *TF:* 800-908-9789 ■ *Web:* www.bertolli.com	Englewood Cliffs	NJ	07632	800-908-9789	
ConAgra Hunt-Wesson Foodservice Co 3353 Michelson Dr *TF:* 800-633-0112 ■ *Web:* www.conagrafoodservice.com	Irvine	CA	92612	949-437-1000	
Fuji Vegetable Oil Inc 1 Barker Ave *Web:* www.fujioilusa.com	White Plains	NY	10601	914-761-7900	
Golden Foods/Golden Brands LLC 2520 7th St Rd *TF:* 800-622-3055 ■ *Web:* www.gfgb.com	Louisville	KY	40208	502-636-3712	636-3904
Kagome Creative Foods LLC 710 N Pearl St *TF:* 800-643-0006 ■ *Web:* www.kagomeusa.com	Osceola	AR	72370	870-563-2601	563-2223
Mahoney Environmental 1819 Moen Ave *TF:* 800-892-9392 ■ *Web:* www.mahoneyenvironmental.com	Joliet	IL	60436	815-730-2080	730-2087
Par-Way Tryson Co 107 Bolte Ln *TF:* 800-844-4554 ■ *Web:* www.parwaytryson.com	Saint Clair	MO	63077	636-629-4545	629-1330

	Phone	Fax
Star Fine Foods 4652 E Date Ave . . . . . Fresno CA 93725 *TF:* 800-694-4872 ■ *Web:* www.starfinefoods.com	559-498-2900	498-2920
Unilever Bestfoods North America 800 Sylvan Ave. . . . . Englewood Cliffs NJ 07632 *Web:* www.bestfoods.com	201-894-4000	
Ventura Foods LLC 40 Pt Dr . . . . . Brea CA 92821 *TF:* 800-421-6257 ■ *Web:* www.venturafoods.com	714-257-3700	257-4009
Veronica Foods Co 1991 Dennison St . . . . . Oakland CA 94606 *TF:* 800-370-5554 ■ *Web:* www.evoliveoil.com	510-535-6833	532-2837

299-31 Pasta

	Phone	Fax
A Zerega's Sons Inc 20-01 Broadway . . . . . Fair Lawn NJ 07410 *Web:* www.zerega.com	201-797-1400	797-0148
American Italian Pasta Co (AIPC) 4100 N Mulberry Dr Suite 200 . . . . . Kansas City MO 64116 *Web:* www.aipc.com	816-584-5000	584-5100
Carla's Pasta Inc 50 Talbot Ln . . . . . South Windsor CT 06074 *Web:* www.carlaspasta.com	860-436-4042	436-4073
Dakota Growers Pasta Co Inc 1 Pasta Ave. . . . . Carrington ND 58421 *TF:* 800-543-5561 ■ *Web:* www.dakotagrowers.com	701-652-2855	652-3552
Everfresh Food Corp 501 Huron Blvd SE . . . . . Minneapolis MN 55414 *TF:* 800-428-9999	612-331-6393	331-1172
Foulds Inc 520 E Church St . . . . . Libertyville IL 60048	847-362-3062	362-6658
Gilster-Mary Lee Corp 1037 State St . . . . . Chester IL 62233 *TF:* 800-851-5371	618-826-2361	826-2973
Joyce Food Products Inc 80 Ave K . . . . . Newark NJ 07105	973-491-9696	589-6145*
Marzetti Frozen Pasta 803 8th St SW . . . . . Altoona IA 50009 *TF:* 800-247-4194 ■ *Web:* www.marzetti.com	515-967-4254	967-4147
Monterey Pasta Co 1528 Moffett St. . . . . Salinas CA 93905 *NASDAQ: PSTA* ■ *TF:* 800-588-7782 ■ *Web:* www.montereygourmetfoods.com	831-753-6262	753-6255
Nanka Seimen Co 3030 Leonis Blvd. . . . . Vernon CA 90058	323-585-9967	
New World Pasta Co 85 Shannon Rd . . . . . Harrisburg PA 17112 **Fax:* Sales ■ *TF Sales:* 800-227-2782 ■ *Web:* www.newworldpasta.com	717-526-2200	526-2469*
Nissin Foods USA Co Inc 2001 W Rosecrans Ave . . . . . Gardena CA 90249 **Fax:* Sales ■ *Web:* www.nissinfoods.com	310-327-8478	515-3751*
Noodles By Leonardo Inc 1702 Schwan Ave PO Box 860 . . . . . Devils Lake ND 58301	701-662-8300	662-2216
OB Macaroni Co PO Box 53 . . . . . Fort Worth TX 76101 *TF Orders:* 800-553-4336 ■ *Web:* www.obmacaroni.com	817-335-4629	335-4726
Peking Noodle Co Inc 1514 N San Fernando Rd . . . . . Los Angeles CA 90065 *TF:* 877-735-4648 ■ *Web:* www.pekingnoodle.com	323-223-2023	223-3211
Philadelphia Macaroni Co 760 S 11th St. . . . . Philadelphia PA 19147 *Web:* www.philamacaroni.com	215-923-3141	925-4298

299-32 Peanut Butter

	Phone	Fax
Algood Food Co 7401 Trade Port Dr . . . . . Louisville KY 40258 *Web:* www.algoodfood.com	502-637-3631	637-1502
Carriage House Cos Inc The 196 Newton St. . . . . Fredonia NY 14063 **Fax:* Sales ■ *TF:* 800-828-8915 ■ *Web:* www.carriagehousecos.com	716-673-1000	673-8443*
ConAgra Foods Retail Products Co Grocery Foods Group 3353 Michelson Dr. . . . . Irvine CA 92612	949-437-1018	437-3315
ConAgra Hunt-Wesson Foodservice Co 3353 Michelson Dr. . . . . Irvine CA 92612 *TF:* 800-633-0112 ■ *Web:* www.conagrafoodservice.com	949-437-1000	
Edwards-Freeman Inc 441 E Hector St . . . . . Conshohocken PA 19428 *TF:* 877-448-6887 ■ *Web:* www.edwardsfreeman.com	610-828-7441	832-0126
HB Reese Candy Co 925 Reese Ave . . . . . Hershey PA 17033 *TF Cust Svc:* 800-468-1714	717-534-4106	
Jimbo's Jumbos Inc 185 Peanut Dr PO Box 465 . . . . . Edenton NC 27932 *TF:* 800-334-4771 ■ *Web:* www.originalnuthouse.com	252-482-2193	482-7857
JM Smucker Co 1 Strawberry Ln. . . . . Orrville OH 44667 *NYSE: SJM* ■ *TF:* 888-550-9555 ■ *Web:* www.smucker.com	330-682-3000	684-6410
John B Sanfilippo & Son Inc 1703 N Randall Rd . . . . . Elgin IL 60123 *NASDAQ: JBSS* ■ *TF:* 800-323-6887 ■ *Web:* www.jbssinc.com	847-289-1800	289-1843
Leavitt Corp 100 Santilli Hwy . . . . . Everett MA 02149 *Web:* www.teddie.com	617-389-2600	387-9085
Producers Peanut Co Inc 337 Moore Ave. . . . . Suffolk VA 23434 *TF:* 800-847-5491 ■ *Web:* www.producerspeanut.com	757-539-7496	934-7730
Sessions Co Inc 801 N Main PO Box 311310 . . . . . Enterprise AL 36331 *Web:* www.peanutsouth.com	334-393-0200	393-0240

299-33 Salads - Prepared

	Phone	Fax
Chelten House Products Inc 607 Heron Dr . . . . . Bridgeport NJ 08014 *Web:* www.cheltenhouse.com	856-467-1600	467-4769
D'Arrigo Bros Co of California Inc PO Box 850 . . . . . Salinas CA 93902 *TF Cust Svc:* 800-995-5939 ■ *Web:* www.andyboy.com	831-455-4500	455-4445
Earth Island 9201 Owensmouth Ave . . . . . Chatsworth CA 91311	818-725-2820	725-2812
Herold's Salads Inc 17512 Miles Ave. . . . . Cleveland OH 44128 *TF:* 800-427-2523 ■ *Web:* www.heroldssalads.com	216-991-7500	991-9565
Home Made Brand Foods Inc 2 Opportunity Way . . . . . Newburyport MA 01950 *Web:* www.hmbf.com	978-462-3663	462-7117
Kayem Foods Inc 75 Arlington St . . . . . Chelsea MA 02150 *TF:* 800-426-6100 ■ *Web:* www.kayem.com	617-889-1600	889-5931
Ready Pac Produce Inc 4401 Foxdale Ave . . . . . Irwindale CA 91706 **Fax Area Code:* 626 ■ *TF:* 800-800-7822 ■ *Web:* www.readypac.com	800-800-7822	856-0088*
Reser's Fine Foods Inc 15570 SW Jenkins Rd PO Box 8. . . . . Beaverton OR 97075 *TF:* 800-333-6431 ■ *Web:* www.resers.com	503-643-6431	
Sandridge Food Corp (SFC) 133 Commerce Dr. . . . . Medina OH 44256 *TF:* 800-672-2523 ■ *Web:* www.sandridge.com	330-725-2348	722-3998
Suter Co Inc 258 May St . . . . . Sycamore IL 60178 *TF:* 800-435-6942 ■ *Web:* www.suterco.com	815-895-9186	895-4814
Sweet Earth Natural Foods 207 16th St. . . . . Pacific Grove CA 93950	831-375-8673	375-3441

299-34 Sandwiches - Prepared

	Phone	Fax
Bridgford Foods Corp 1308 N Patt St. . . . . Anaheim CA 92801 *NASDAQ: BRID* ■ *TF:* 800-854-3255 ■ *Web:* www.bridgford.com	714-526-5533	526-4360
Cloverdale Foods Co Inc 3015 34th St NW PO Box 667 . . . . . Mandan ND 58554 *TF:* 800-669-9511 ■ *Web:* www.cloverdalefoods.com	701-663-9511	663-0690
Hormel Foods Corp 1 Hormel Pl. . . . . Austin MN 55912 *NYSE: HRL* ■ **Fax:* Sales ■ *TF:* 800-523-4635 ■ *Web:* www.hormel.com	507-437-5248	437-5129*
Konop Cos 1725 Industrial Dr. . . . . Green Bay WI 54302 *TF:* 800-770-0477 ■ *Web:* www.konopcompanies.com	920-468-8517	468-1190
Landshire Inc 9200 W Main St . . . . . Belleville IL 62223 *TF:* 800-468-3354 ■ *Web:* www.landshire.com	618-398-8122	398-7627
Lloyd's Barbecue Co 1455 Mendota Hts Rd. . . . . Saint Paul MN 55120 *Web:* www.lloydsbbq.com	651-688-6000	688-8658
Southern Belle Sandwich Co 1969 N Lobdell Blvd. . . . . Baton Rouge LA 70806	225-927-4670	928-5661
Sunburst Foods Inc 1002 Sunburst Dr. . . . . Goldsboro NC 27534 *TF:* 800-849-3196 ■ *Web:* www.sunburstfoods.net	919-778-2151	778-9203
Sweet Earth Natural Foods 207 16th St. . . . . Pacific Grove CA 93950	831-375-8673	375-3441

299-35 Snack Foods

	Phone	Fax
American Pop Corn Co 1 Fun Pl PO Box 178 . . . . . Sioux City IA 51102 *Web:* www.jollytime.com	712-239-1232	239-1268
Azteca Foods Inc 5005 S Nagle Ave. . . . . Chicago IL 60638 *Web:* www.aztecafoods.com	708-563-6600	563-0331
Bachman Co 1 Pk Plaza . . . . . Wyomissing PA 19610 *TF:* 800-523-8253 ■ *Web:* www.bachmanco.com	610-320-7800	320-7897
Barrel O' Fun Snack Foods Co 800 4th St NW. . . . . Perham MN 56573 *TF:* 800-346-4910 ■ *Web:* www.barrelofunsnacks.com	218-346-7000	346-7003
Better Made Snack Foods Inc 10148 Gratiot Ave. . . . . Detroit MI 48213 *TF:* 800-332-2394 ■ *Web:* www.bmchips.com	313-925-4774	925-6028
Bickel's Snack Foods 1120 Zinns Quarry Rd. . . . . York PA 17404 **Fax:* Cust Svc ■ *TF:* 800-233-1933 ■ *Web:* www.bickelssnacks.com	717-843-0738	843-4569*
Cape Cod Potato Chip Co 100 Breed's Hill Rd . . . . . Hyannis MA 02601 *TF:* 888-881-2447 ■ *Web:* www.capecodchips.com	508-775-3358	775-2808
Chester Inc 555 Eastport Ctr Dr PO Box 2237. . . . . Valparaiso IN 46383 *TF:* 800-778-1131 ■ *Web:* www.chesters.com	219-464-9999	464-8488
CJ Vitner & Co 4202 W 45th St. . . . . Chicago IL 60632 *TF:* 800-397-7629	773-523-7900	523-9143
ConAgra Foods Retail Products Co Grocery Foods Group 3353 Michelson Dr. . . . . Irvine CA 92612	949-437-1018	437-3315
Evans Food Products Co 4118 S Halsted St . . . . . Chicago IL 60609 *TF:* 866-254-7400 ■ *Web:* www.evansfood.com	773-254-7400	254-7791
F & F Foods Inc 3501 W 48th Pl . . . . . Chicago IL 60632 *TF Cust Svc:* 800-621-0225 ■ *Web:* www.fffoods.com	773-927-3737	927-3906
Frito-Lay North America 7701 Legacy Dr . . . . . Plano TX 75024 *TF:* 866-374-8677 ■ *Web:* www.fritolay.com	972-334-7000	334-2019
Golden Flake Snack Foods Inc 1 Golden Flake Dr. . . . . Birmingham AL 35205 *TF:* 800-239-2447 ■ *Web:* www.goldenflake.com	205-323-6161	458-7121
Herr Foods Inc 20 Herr Dr PO Box 300 . . . . . Nottingham PA 19362 *TF:* 800-344-3777 ■ *Web:* www.herrs.com	610-932-9330	932-1190
Husman Snack Foods Co 1845 Airport Exchange Blvd Bldg B Suite 100 . . . . . Erlanger KY 41018 *TF:* 800-487-6267	859-282-7490	282-7491
Ideal Snacks Corp 89 Mill St . . . . . Liberty NY 12754 *Web:* www.idealsnacks.com	845-292-7000	292-7000
Keystone Food Products Inc 3767 Hecktown Rd . . . . . Easton PA 18045 *TF:* 800-523-9426	610-258-0888	250-0721
Lance Inc PO Box 32368 . . . . . Charlotte NC 28232 *NASDAQ: LNCE* ■ *Web:* www.lance.com	704-557-8300	
Martin's Potato Chips Inc 5847 Lincoln Hwy W PO Box 28. . . . . Thomasville PA 17364 *TF:* 800-272-4477 ■ *Web:* www.martinschips.com	717-792-3565	792-4906
Mike-Sell's Potato Chip Co 333 Leo St PO Box 115 . . . . . Dayton OH 45404 *TF:* 800-257-4742 ■ *Web:* www.mike-sells.com	937-228-9400	461-5707
Mission Foods 2110 Santa Fe Dr. . . . . Pueblo CO 81006 *TF:* 800-821-3187 ■ *Web:* www.missionfoods.com	719-543-4350	545-3681
Old Dutch Foods Inc 2375 Terminal Rd . . . . . Roseville MN 55113 *TF:* 800-989-2447 ■ *Web:* www.olddutchfoods.com	651-633-8810	633-8894
Ozuna Food Products Corp 510 Martin Ave . . . . . Santa Clara CA 95050	408-727-5481	727-2009
Snacks Unlimited 1 General Mills Blvd . . . . . Minneapolis MN 55426 **Fax:* PR ■ *TF:* 800-248-7310 ■ *Web:* www.generalmills.com	763-764-7600	764-3232*
Snyder of Berlin 1313 Stadium Dr . . . . . Berlin PA 15530 *TF:* 800-374-7949 ■ *Web:* www.birdseyefoods.com	814-267-4641	267-5648
Tim's Cascade Snacks 1150 Industry Dr N . . . . . Algona WA 98001 *TF:* 800-533-8467 ■ *Web:* www.timschips.com	253-833-0255	939-9411
Uncle Ray's Llc 14245 Birwood St . . . . . Detroit MI 48238 *TF:* 800-800-3286 ■ *Web:* www.unclerays.com	313-834-0800	931-6945
Utz Quality Foods Co 900 High St . . . . . Hanover PA 17331 *TF:* 800-367-7629 ■ *Web:* www.utzsnacks.com	717-637-6644	633-5102
Wachusett Potato Chip Co 759 Water St . . . . . Fitchburg MA 01420 *TF:* 800-551-5539	978-342-6038	345-4894
Wise Foods Inc 245 Townpark Dr Suite 450 . . . . . Kennesaw GA 30144 *TF:* 800-438-9473 ■ *Web:* www.wisesnacks.com	770-426-5821	426-0971
Wyandot Inc 135 Wyandot Ave . . . . . Marion OH 43302 **Fax:* Cust Svc ■ *TF:* 800-992-6368 ■ *Web:* www.wyandotsnacks.com	740-383-4031	382-0115*

299-36 Specialty Foods

Company	City	State	Zip	Phone	Fax
AFP Advanced Food Products LLC 402 S Custer Ave *Web:* www.afpllc.com	New Holland	PA	17557	717-355-8667	355-8848
Alphin Bros Inc 2302 US 301 S *TF:* 800-672-4502 ■ *Web:* www.alphinbrothers.com	Dunn	NC	28334	910-892-8751	892-2709
Ameriqual Group LLC 18200 Hwy 41 N *Web:* www.ameriqual.com	Evansville	IN	47725	812-867-1444	867-0278
Amy's Kitchen Inc 2227 Capricorn Way Suite 201 *Web:* www.amyskitchen.com	Santa Rosa	CA	95407	707-578-7188	578-7995
Appetizers & Inc 2555 N Elston Ave *TF:* 800-323-5472 ■ *Web:* www.appetizersandinc.com	Chicago	IL	60647	800-323-5472	
Arden International Kitchens Inc 21150 Hamburg Ave *TF:* 800-368-7337 ■ *Web:* www.ardenculinary.com	Lakeville	MN	55044	952-469-2000	985-5822
Armanino Foods of Distinction Inc 30588 San Antonio St *TF:* 800-255-5855 ■ *Web:* www.armaninofoods.com	Hayward	CA	94544	510-441-9300	441-0101
Ateeco Inc 600 E Ctr St PO Box 606 *TF:* 800-233-3170 ■ *Web:* www.pierogy.com	Shenandoah	PA	17976	570-462-2745	462-1392
Avanti Foods 109 Depot St *TF:* 800-243-3739 ■ *Web:* www.avantifoods.com	Walnut	IL	61376	815-379-2155	379-9357
Beech-Nut Nutrition Corp 100 Hero Dr *TF:* 800-233-2468 ■ *Web:* www.beechnut.com	Amsterdam	NY	12010	518-595-6600	
Bellisio Foods Inc 1201 Harman Pl Suite 302 **Fax Area Code:* 218 ■ *TF:* 800-368-7337 ■ *Web:* www.bellisiofoods.com	Minneapolis	MN	55403	612-371-8222	723-5577*
Border Foods Inc 4065 J St SE *TF:* 888-737-7751 ■ *Web:* www.borderfoodsinc.com	Deming	NM	88030	888-737-7751	737-7752
Bruce Foods Corp PO Drawer 1030 *TF:* 800-299-9082 ■ *Web:* www.brucefoods.com	New Iberia	LA	70561	337-365-8101	369-9026
Buddy's Kitchen Inc 12105 Nicollet Ave *Web:* www.buddyskitchen.com	Burnsville	MN	55337	952-894-2540	895-1664
Camino Real Foods Inc 2638 E Vernon Ave *TF:* 800-421-6201 ■ *Web:* www.caminorealkitchens.com	Vernon	CA	90058	323-585-6599	585-5420
Campbell Soup Co 1 Campbell Pl *NYSE: CPB* ■ *TF:* 800-772-8467 ■ *Web:* www.campbellsoupcompany.com	Camden	NJ	08103	856-342-4800	342-3878
Castleberry's Food Co 1621 15th St PO Box 1010 *TF:* 800-241-3520 ■ *Web:* www.castleberrys.com	Augusta	GA	30903	706-733-7765	736-5061
Champion Foods LLC 23900 Bell Rd *Web:* www.championfoods.com	New Boston	MI	48164	734-753-3663	753-5366
Chungs Gourmet Foods 3907 Dennis St *TF:* 800-824-8647 ■ *Web:* www.chungsfoods.com	Houston	TX	77004	713-741-2118	741-2330
ConAgra Foods Culinary Products 1805 N Santa Fe Ave *TF:* 800-388-5505 ■ *Web:* www.conagrafoods.com	Compton	CA	90221	310-223-1499	223-1698
ConAgra Foods Retail Products Co Frozen Foods Group 5 ConAgra Dr *Web:* www.conagrafoods.com	Omaha	NE	68102	402-595-6000	
ConAgra Foods Retail Products Co Grocery Foods Group 3353 Michelson Dr	Irvine	CA	92612	949-437-1018	437-3315
Continental Mills Inc PO Box 88176 *TF:* 800-457-7744 ■ *Web:* www.continentalmills.com	Seattle	WA	98138	253-872-8400	872-7954
Cromers Inc 1055 Berea Rd PO box 163 *TF:* 800-322-7688 ■ *Web:* www.cromers.com	Columbia	SC	29202	803-779-1147	779-4743
Cuisine Solutions Inc 2800 Eisenhower Ave Suite 450 *PINK: CUSI* ■ *TF:* 888-285-4679 ■ *Web:* www.cuisinesolutions.com	Alexandria	VA	22314	703-270-2900	750-1158
D & D Foods Inc 9425 N 48th St *TF:* 800-272-5234	Omaha	NE	68152	402-571-4113	571-8245
Del Monte Foods Co 1 Maritime Plaza *TF Cust Svc:* 800-543-3090 ■ *Web:* www.delmonte.com	San Francisco	CA	94111	415-247-3000	247-3565
Deli Express 16101 W 78th St *TF:* 866-787-8862 ■ *Web:* www.deliexpress.com	Eden Prairie	MN	55344	952-937-9440	937-0186
Don Miguel Mexican Foods Inc 1501 W Orangewood Ave *Web:* www.donmiguel.com	Orange	CA	92868	714-634-8441	978-3743
Durrset Amigos Ltd 600 Carswell *TF:* 800-580-3477 ■ *Web:* www.amigosfoods.com	San Antonio	TX	78226	210-798-5360	798-5365
Ebro Foods Inc 1330 W 43rd St *Web:* www.ebrofoods.com	Chicago	IL	60609	773-696-0150	696-0151
Eden Foods Inc 701 Tecumseh Rd *TF Cust Svc:* 800-248-0320 ■ *Web:* www.edenfoods.com	Clinton	MI	49236	517-456-7424	456-6075
El Encanto Inc 2001 4th St SW PO Box 293 *TF:* 800-888-7336 ■ *Web:* www.buenofoods.com	Albuquerque	NM	87103	505-243-2722	242-1680
Ener-G Foods Inc 5960 1st Ave S PO Box 84487 *TF:* 800-331-5222 ■ *Web:* www.ener-g.com	Seattle	WA	98124	206-767-3928	764-3398
Fairmont Foods of Minnesota 905 E 4th St *Web:* www.fairmontfoods.com	Fairmont	MN	56031	507-238-9001	238-9560
Fiesta Canning Co Inc 1480 E Bethany Home Suite 110 *TF:* 877-524-4537 ■ *Web:* www.fiestacan.com	Phoenix	AZ	85016	602-212-2424	274-7233
Fortitech Inc Riverside Technology Pk 2105 Technology Dr *TF:* 800-950-5156 ■ *Web:* www.fortitech.com	Schenectady	NY	12308	518-372-5155	372-5599
Frozen Specialties Inc 720 Barre Rd	Archbold	OH	43502	419-445-9015	445-9465
Gardenburger Inc 15615 Alton Pkwy Suite 350 *TF:* 800-636-0109 ■ *Web:* www.gardenburger.com	Irvine	CA	92618	949-255-2000	255-2010
Gerber Products Co 445 State St *TF:* 800-443-7237 ■ *Web:* www.gerber.com	Fremont	MI	49413	231-928-2000	928-2723
Goya Foods Inc 100 Seaview Dr *Web:* www.goya.com	Secaucus	NJ	07096	201-348-4900	348-6609
Grandma Brown's Beans Inc 5837 Scenic Ave	Mexico	NY	13114	315-963-7221	963-4072
Hain Celestial Group Inc 58 S Service Rd Suite 250 *NASDAQ: HAIN* ■ *TF:* 800-434-4246 ■ *Web:* www.hain-celestial.com	Melville	NY	01747	631-730-2200	730-2550
Hanover Foods Corp 1550 York St PO Box 334 *TF:* 800-888-4646 ■ *Web:* www.hanoverfoods.com	Hanover	PA	17331	717-632-6000	632-6681
HJ Heinz Co One PPG Pl *NYSE: HNZ* ■ *TF:* 800-255-5750 ■ *Web:* www.heinz.com	Pittsburgh	PA	15222	412-456-5700	456-6015
Home Market Foods Inc 140 Morgan Dr *TF:* 800-367-8325 ■ *Web:* www.homemarketfoods.com	Norwood	MA	02062	781-948-1500	702-6171
Home Run Inn Frozen Foods Corp 1300 International Pkwy *Web:* www.homeruninn.com	Woodridge	IL	60517	630-783-9696	783-0069
Homestead Pasta Co 315 S Maple Ave Bldg 106 *TF:* 800-334-3397 ■ *Web:* www.homesteadpasta.com	South San Francisco	CA	94080	650-615-0750	615-0764
Hormel Foods Corp 1 Hormel Pl *NYSE: HRL* ■ **Fax:* Sales ■ *TF:* 800-523-4635 ■ *Web:* www.hormel.com	Austin	MN	55912	507-437-5248	437-5129*
J & B Sausage Co Inc 100 Main St *Web:* www.jbfoods.com	Waelder	TX	78959	830-788-7511	788-7279
JM Smucker Co 1 Strawberry Ln *NYSE: SJM* ■ *TF:* 888-550-9555 ■ *Web:* www.smucker.com	Orrville	OH	44667	330-682-3000	684-6410
Joseph Seviroli Inc 601 Brook St *Web:* www.seviroli.com	Garden City	NY	11530	516-222-6220	222-0534
Juanita's Foods Inc 645 N Eubank St PO Box 847 *TF:* 800-303-2965 ■ *Web:* www.juanitasfoods.com	Wilmington	CA	90748	310-834-5339	835-6516
Kahiki Foods Inc 1100 Morrison Rd *TF:* 888-436-2500 ■ *Web:* www.kahiki.com	Gahanna	OH	43230	614-322-3180	751-0039
La Choy Foodservice 3353 Michelson Dr PO Box 57078 *TF:* 800-252-0672 ■ *Web:* www.lachoy.com	Irvine	CA	92612	949-255-4100	
La Reina Inc 316 N Ford Blvd *TF:* 800-367-7522 ■ *Web:* www.lareinainc.com	Los Angeles	CA	90022	323-268-2791	265-4295
La Tapatia Tortilleria Inc 104 E Belmont Ave *Web:* www.tortillas4u.com	Fresno	CA	93701	559-441-1030	441-1712
Lamb Weston Inc 8701 W Gage Blvd **Fax:* Sales ■ *Web:* www.lambweston.com	Kennewick	WA	99336	509-735-4651	737-6621*
Leon's Texas Cuisine Co 2100 Redbud Blvd *TF:* 800-527-1243 ■ *Web:* www.texascuisine.com	McKinney	TX	75069	972-529-5050	529-2244
Little Lady Foods Inc 2323 Pratt Blvd *TF:* 800-439-1440 ■ *Web:* www.littleladyfoods.com	Elk Grove Village	IL	60007	847-806-1440	806-0026
Logan International Ltd 100 Logan Dr *Web:* www.loganinternational.com	Boardman	OR	97818	541-481-2081	481-3081
Luigino's Inc 525 S Lake Ave PO Box 16630 *TF:* 800-521-1281 ■ *Web:* www.michelinas.com	Duluth	MN	55816	218-723-5555	723-8356
Mancini Foods PO Box 157 *TF:* 800-741-1778 ■ *Web:* www.mancinifoods.com	Zolfo Springs	FL	33890	863-735-2000	735-1172
Marzetti Frozen Pasta 803 8th St SW *TF:* 800-247-4194 ■ *Web:* www.marzetti.com	Altoona	IA	50009	515-967-4254	967-4147
McCain Foods Ltd 181 Bay St Suite 3600 *TF:* 866-622-2461 ■ *Web:* www.mccain.com	Toronto	ON	M5J2T3	416-955-1700	
McCain Foods USA Inc 2275 Cabot Dr *TF:* 800-938-7799 ■ *Web:* www.mccainusa.com	Lisle	IL	60532	630-955-0400	857-4560
Michael Angelo's Gourmet Foods Inc 200 Michael Angelo Way *TF:* 800-526-4918 ■ *Web:* www.michaelangelos.com	Austin	TX	78728	512-218-3500	218-3600
Morgan Foods Inc 90 W Morgan St *TF:* 888-430-1780 ■ *Web:* www.morganfoods.com	Austin	IN	47102	812-794-1170	794-1211
Mott's Inc 900 King St *TF:* 800-426-4891 ■ *Web:* www.motts.com	Rye Brook	NY	10573	914-612-4000	612-4100
Nardone Bros Baking Co Inc 420 New Commerce Blvd *TF:* 800-822-5320 ■ *Web:* www.nardonebros.com	Wilkes-Barre	PA	18706	570-823-0141	823-2581
Ole Mexican Foods Inc 6585 Crescent Dr *TF:* 800-878-6307 ■ *Web:* www.olemexicanfoods.com	Norcross	GA	30071	770-582-9200	582-9400
On-Cor Frozen Foods LLC 627 Landwehr Rd *Web:* www.on-cor.com	Northbrook	IL	60062	847-205-1040	205-1070
Overhill Farms Inc 2727 E Vernon Ave *AMEX: OFI* ■ *TF:* 800-859-6406 ■ *Web:* www.overhillfarms.com	Vernon	CA	90058	323-582-9977	582-6122
Panhandle Foods Inc 1980 Smith Township SR	Burgettstown	PA	15021	724-947-2216	947-4940
Papa John's International Inc PO Box 99900 *TF:* 877-547-7272 ■ *Web:* www.papajohns.com	Louisville	KY	40269	877-547-7272	
Pastorelli Food Products Inc 162 N Sangamon St *TF:* 800-767-2829 ■ *Web:* www.pastorelli.com	Chicago	IL	60607	312-666-2041	666-2415
Pinnacle Foods Corp 121 Woodcrest Rd *TF:* 800-486-8816 ■ *Web:* www.pinnaclefoodscorp.com	Cherry Hill	NJ	08003	856-969-7100	
Preferred Meal Systems Inc 5240 St Charles Rd *TF Cust Svc:* 800-886-6325	Berkeley	IL	60163	708-318-2500	493-2690
Proferas Inc 1136 Moosic St *TF:* 800-360-7763	Scranton	PA	18505	570-342-4181	342-4853
Progresso Quality Foods Co 500 W Elmer Rd *TF:* 800-200-9377 ■ *Web:* www.bettycrocker.com/products/prod_progresso.asp	Vineland	NJ	08360	856-691-1565	
Quaker Foods North America 555 W Monroe St *TF:* 800-555-6287 ■ *Web:* www.quakeroats.com	Chicago	IL	60661	312-821-1000	
Randall Food Products Inc 8050 Hosbrook Rd *Web:* www.randallbeans.com	Cincinnati	OH	45236	513-793-6525	793-6442
Request Foods Inc PO Box 2577 *TF Sales:* 800-748-0378 ■ *Web:* www.requestfoods.com	Holland	MI	49422	616-786-0900	820-6385
Reynaldo's Mexican Food Co Inc 3301 E Vernon Ave *TF:* 800-686-4911 ■ *Web:* www.rmfood.com	Vernon	CA	90058	562-803-3188	803-3196
Rich Products Corp 1 Robert Rich Way *TF:* 800-828-2021 ■ *Web:* www.richs.com	Buffalo	NY	14213	716-878-8000	
Rokeach Food Corp 80 Ave K	Newark	NJ	07105	973-589-4900	589-5298
Ruiz Foods Inc PO Box 37 *TF:* 800-477-6474 ■ *Web:* www.elmonterey.com	Dinuba	CA	93618	559-591-5510	591-1968

	City	State	ZIP	Phone	Fax
Schwan Food Co 115 W College Dr TF: 800-533-5290 ■ Web: www.theschwanfoodcompany.com	Marshall	MN	56258	507-532-3274	
Small Planet Foods Inc 719 Metcalf St TF: 800-624-4123 ■ Web: www.smallplanetfoods.com	Sedro Woolley	WA	98284	360-855-0100	855-0444
State Fair Foods 3900 Meacham Blvd TF: 800-641-6412	Haltom City	TX	76117	817-427-7700	427-7777
Suter Co Inc 258 May St TF: 800-435-6942 ■ Web: www.suterco.com	Sycamore	IL	60178	815-895-9186	895-4814
Tastefully Simple Inc 1920 Turning Leaf Ln SW PO Box 3006 TF: 866-448-6446 ■ Web: www.tastefullysimple.com	Alexandria	MN	56308	320-763-0695	763-2458
Unilever Food Solutions 2200 Cabot Dr *Fax: Cust Svc ■ TF: 800-786-6988 ■ Web: www.unileverusa.com	Lisle	IL	60532	630-955-5508	955-5231*
Vanee Foods Co Inc 5418 McDermott Dr TF Cust Svc: 800-654-6647 ■ Web: www.vaneefoods.com	Berkeley	IL	60163	708-449-7300	449-2558
Windsor Foods 3355 W Alabama St Suite 730 TF: 800-437-6936 ■ Web: www.windsorfoods.com	Houston	TX	77098	713-843-5200	960-9709
Winter Gardens Quality Foods Inc 304 Commerce St PO Box 339 TF: 800-242-7637 ■ Web: www.wintergardens.com	New Oxford	PA	17350	717-624-4911	624-7729
Wornick Co 4700 Creek Rd TF: 800-860-4555 ■ Web: www.wornick.com	Cincinnati	OH	45242	513-794-9800	794-0107

299-37 Spices, Seasonings, Herbs

	City	State	ZIP	Phone	Fax
Abco Laboratories Inc 2450 S Watney Way TF: 800-678-2226 ■ Web: www.abcolabs.com	Fairfield	CA	94533	707-432-2200	432-2240
Alberto-Culver Consumer Products Worldwide 2525 Armitage Ave TF: 800-333-0005 ■ Web: www.alberto.com	Melrose Park	IL	60160	708-450-3000	
All American Seasonings 10600 E 54th Ave Web: www.allamericanseasonings.com	Denver	CO	80239	303-623-2320	623-1920
Basic American Foods 2121 N California Blvd # 400 TF: 800-227-4050 ■ Web: www.baf.com	Walnut Creek	CA	94596	925-472-4000	472-4360
Benson's Gourmet Seasonings 850 W Foothill Blvd TF: 800-325-5619 ■ Web: www.bensonsgourmetseasonings.com	Azusa	CA	91702	626-969-4443	969-2912
Blendex Co Inc 11208 Electron Dr TF: 800-626-6354 ■ Web: www.blendex.com	Louisville	KY	40299	502-267-1003	267-1024
Frontier Natural Products Co-op 3021 78th St PO Box 299 TF: 800-669-3275 ■ Web: www.frontiercoop.com	Norway	IA	52318	319-227-7996	227-7966
Fuchs North America 9740 Reisterstown Rd TF: 800-365-3229 ■ Web: www.fuchsnorthamerica.com	Owings Mills	MD	21117	410-363-1700	363-6619
Griffith Laboratories Worldwide Inc 1 Griffith Ctr TF Cust Svc: 800-346-9494 ■ Web: www.griffithlaboratories.com	Alsip	IL	60803	708-371-0900	389-4055
Johnny's Fine Foods Inc 319 E 25th St TF Orders: 800-962-1462 ■ Web: www.johnnysfinefoods.com	Tacoma	WA	98421	253-383-4597	572-8742
Lisy Corp 3400 NW 67th St Web: www.lisycorp.com	Miami	FL	33147	305-836-5479	836-8752
Lucile's Famous Creole Seasonings 2124 14th St Web: www.luciles.com	Boulder	CO	80302	303-442-4743	939-9848
McCormick & Co Inc 18 Loveton Cir PO Box 6000 NYSE: MKC ■ TF: 800-632-5847 ■ Web: www.mccormickcorporation.com	Sparks	MD	21152	410-771-7301	527-8214
McCormick & Co Inc Food Service Div 226 Schilling Cir TF: 800-322-7742 ■ Web: www.mccormickforchefs.com	Hunt Valley	MD	21031	410-771-7500	771-1111
McCormick & Co Inc McCormick Flavor Div 226 Schilling Cir TF: 800-322-7742 ■ Web: www.mccormickforchefs.com	Hunt Valley	MD	21031	410-771-7500	771-1111
McCormick & Co Inc US Consumer Products Div 211 Schilling Cir TF: 800-292-5300 ■ Web: www.mccormick.com	Hunt Valley	MD	21031	410-527-6000	
McCormick Ingredients 10901 Gilroy Rd TF: 800-632-5847 ■ Web: www.mccormick.com	Hunt Valley	MD	21031	410-771-5025	527-6005
Newly Weds Foods Inc 2501 N Keeler Ave TF: 800-621-7521 ■ Web: www.newlywedsfoods.com	Chicago	IL	60639	773-489-7000	292-7612
Precision Foods Inc 11457 Olde Cabin Rd Suite 100 TF: 800-442-5242 ■ Web: www.precisionfoods.com	Saint Louis	MO	63141	314-567-7400	567-7421
Spice Hunter Inc 184 Suburban Rd PO Box 8110 *Fax: Cust Svc ■ TF: 800-444-3061 ■ Web: www.spicehunter.com	San Luis Obispo	CA	93403	805-544-4466	544-3824*
Spice World Inc 8101 Presidents Dr TF: 800-433-4979 ■ Web: www.spiceworldinc.com	Orlando	FL	32809	407-851-9432	857-7171
Tampico Spice Co Inc 5941 S Central Ave Web: www.tampicospice.com	Los Angeles	CA	90001	323-235-3154	232-8686
World Spice Inc 223 E Highland Pkwy TF: 800-234-1060 ■ Web: www.wsispice.com	Roselle	NJ	07203	908-245-0600	245-0696
Zatarain's Inc 82 1st St Web: www.zatarains.com	Gretna	LA	70053	504-367-2950	362-2004

299-38 Sugar & Sweeteners

	City	State	ZIP	Phone	Fax
Alma Plantation Ltd 4612 Alma Rd	Lakeland	LA	70752	225-627-6666	627-5138
Amalgamated Sugar Co LLC 1951 S Saturn Way # 100	Boise	ID	83709	208-383-6500	383-6684
American Crystal Sugar Co 101 3rd St N Web: www.crystalsugar.com	Moorhead	MN	56560	218-236-4400	236-4702
C & H Sugar Co Inc 830 Loring Ave TF: 800-888-0118 ■ Web: www.chsugar.com	Crockett	CA	94525	510-787-2121	787-1791
Cajun Sugar Co-op Inc 2711 Northside Rd	New Iberia	LA	70563	337-365-3401	365-7820
Cora-Texas Mfg Co Inc 32505 Texas Rd PO Box 280 Web: www.coratexas.com	White Castle	LA	70788	225-545-3679	545-8360
Cumberland Packing Corp 2 Cumberland St TF: 800-221-1763 ■ Web: www.sweetnlow.com	Brooklyn	NY	11205	718-858-4200	260-9017
Florida Crystals Corp 1 N Clematis St Suite 200 Web: www.floridacrystals.com	West Palm Beach	FL	33401	561-655-6303	659-3206
Hawaiian Commercial & Sugar Co 1 Hansen St Web: www.hcsugar.com	Puunene	HI	96784	808-877-0081	871-7663
Imperial Sugar Co 8016 Hwy 90 A NASDAQ: IPSU ■ TF: 800-727-8427 ■ Web: www.imperialsugar.com	Sugar Land	TX	77478	281-491-9181	490-9530
Lafourche Sugars Corp 141 Lake Leighton Quarters Rd	Thibodaux	LA	70301	985-447-3210	447-8728
Lantic Sugar Ltd 4026 Notre-Dame St NE Web: www.lantic.ca	Montreal	QC	H1W2K3	514-527-8686	527-8406
Louisiana Sugar Co-op Inc 6092 Resweber Hwy Web: www.lasuca.com	Saint Martinville	LA	70582	337-394-3255	394-5632
Lula Westfield LLC 451 Hwy 1005 PO Box 10	Paincourtville	LA	70391	985-369-6450	369-6139
MA Patout & Son Ltd 3512 J Patout Burns Rd Web: www.mapatout.com	Jeanerette	LA	70544	337-276-4592	276-4247
Merisant Worldwide Inc 33 N Dearborn St # 200 Web: www.merisant.com	Chicago	IL	60602	312-840-6000	840-5400
Michigan Sugar Co Inc 2600 S Euclid Ave Web: www.michigansugar.com	Bay City	MI	48706	989-686-0161	671-3695
Minn-Dak Farmers Co-op 7525 Red River Rd Web: www.mdfarmerscoop.com	Wahpeton	ND	58075	701-642-8411	642-6814
NutraSweet Co The 10 S Wacker Dr TF Cust Svc: 800-323-5321 ■ Web: www.nutrasweet.com	Chicago	IL	60606	312-873-5000	873-5050
Rio Grande Valley Sugar Growers PO Box 459 Web: www.rgvsugar.com	Santa Rosa	TX	78593	956-636-1411	636-1046
Saint Mary Sugar Co-op Inc 20056 Hwy 182 PO Box 269	Jeanerette	LA	70544	337-276-6761	276-4297
Southern Minnesota Beet Sugar Co-op 83550 CR 21 PO Box 500 Web: www.smbsc.com	Renville	MN	56284	320-329-8305	329-3252
Sterling Sugars Inc 611 Irish Bend Rd	Franklin	LA	70538	337-828-0620	828-1757
Sugar Cane Growers Co-op of Florida PO Box 666 Web: www.scgc.org	Belle Glade	FL	33430	561-996-5556	996-4747
US Sugar Corp 111 Ponce de Leon Ave Web: www.ussugar.com	Clewiston	FL	33440	863-983-8121	983-9827
Western Sugar Co-op 7555 E Hampden Ave Suite 600 TF: 800-523-7497 ■ Web: www.westernsugar.com	Denver	CO	80231	303-830-3939	830-3941

299-39 Syrup - Maple

	City	State	ZIP	Phone	Fax
Carriage House Cos Inc The 196 Newton St *Fax: Sales ■ TF: 800-828-8915 ■ Web: www.carriagehousecos.com	Fredonia	NY	14063	716-673-1000	673-8443*
Foxtail Foods 6075 Poplar Ave Suite 800 TF Cust Svc: 800-487-2253 ■ Web: www.foxtailfoods.com	Memphis	TN	38119	901-766-6400	537-7141
Golden Eagle Syrup Co Inc 205 1st Ave SE Web: www.goldeneaglesyrup.com	Fayette	AL	35555	205-932-5294	932-5296
H Fox & Co Inc 416 Thatford Ave Web: www.foxs-syrups.com	Brooklyn	NY	11212	718-385-4600	345-4283
Maple Grove Farms of Vermont Inc 1052 Portland St TF: 800-525-2540 ■ Web: www.maplegrove.com	Saint Johnsbury	VT	05819	802-748-5141	748-9647
Maple Hollow/Waterloo USA W 1887 Robinson Dr	Merrill	WI	54452	715-536-7251	536-1295
Pinnacle Foods Corp 121 Woodcrest Rd TF: 800-486-8816 ■ Web: www.pinnaclefoodscorp.com	Cherry Hill	NJ	08003	856-969-7100	
Richards Maple Products Inc 545 Water St TF: 800-352-4052 ■ Web: www.richardsmapleproducts.com	Chardon	OH	44024	440-286-4160	286-7203
Sea Breeze Inc 441 Rt 202 TF: 800-732-2733 ■ Web: www.seabreezesyrups.com	Towaco	NJ	07082	973-334-7777	334-2617
Spring Tree Maple Products 28 Vernon St Suite 412	Brattleboro	VT	05301	802-254-8784	254-8648

299-40 Tea

	City	State	ZIP	Phone	Fax
4C Foods Corp 580 Fountain Ave Web: www.4c.com	Brooklyn	NY	11208	718-272-4242	272-2899
Celestial Seasonings Inc 4600 Sleepytime Dr *Fax: Cust Svc ■ TF: 800-525-0347 ■ Web: www.celestialseasonings.com	Boulder	CO	80301	303-530-5300	581-1520*
Eastern Tea Corp 1 Engelhard Dr TF: 800-221-0865 ■ Web: www.easterntea.com	Monroe Township	NJ	08831	609-860-1100	860-1105
Fee Bros Inc 453 Portland Ave TF: 800-961-3337 ■ Web: www.feebrothers.com	Rochester	NY	14605	585-544-9530	
Lipton Co 800 Sylvan Ave Web: www.lipton.com	Englewood Cliffs	NJ	07632	201-894-7760	871-8117
Oregon Chai Inc 20925 Watertown Rd TF: 888-874-2424 ■ Web: www.oregonchai.com	Waukesha	WI	53186	262-317-3900	317-3993
R C Biglow Inc 201 Black Rock Tpke TF: 888-244-3569 ■ Web: www.bigelowtea.com	Fairfield	CT	06825	203-334-1212	334-5114
Redco Foods Inc 1 Hansen Island TF: 800-556-6674 ■ Web: www.redrosetea.com	Little Falls	NY	13365	315-823-1300	823-2069
S & D Coffee Inc 300 Concord Pkwy PO Box 1628 TF Cust Svc: 800-933-2210 ■ Web: www.sndcoffee.com	Concord	NC	28026	704-782-3121	721-5792
Stash Tea Co 16655 SW 72nd Ave Suite 200 *Fax: Orders ■ TF: 800-547-1514 ■ Web: www.stashtea.com	Tigard	OR	97224	503-684-4482	624-4424*

299-41 Vinegar & Cider

				Phone	Fax
Assouline & Ting Inc 2050 Richmond St *TF:* 800-521-4491	Philadelphia	PA	19125	215-627-3000	627-3517
Bertolli USA Inc 920 Sylvan Ave *TF:* 800-908-9789 ■ *Web:* www.bertolli.com	Englewood Cliffs	NJ	07632	800-908-9789	
Boyajian Inc 144 Will Dr *TF:* 800-965-0665 ■ *Web:* www.boyajianinc.com	Canton	MA	02021	781-828-9966	828-9922
Consumers Vinegar & Spice Co Inc 4723 S Washtenaw Ave	Chicago	IL	60632	773-376-4100	376-6224
Creole Fermentation Industries Inc 7331 Den Frederick Rd	Abbeville	LA	70510	337-898-9377	898-9376
Gold Pure Food Products Inc 1 Brooklyn Rd *TF:* 800-422-4681 ■ *Web:* www.goldshorseradish.com	Hempstead	NY	11550	516-483-5600	483-5798
Heintz & Weber Co Inc 150 Reading Ave *Web:* www.webersmustard.com	Buffalo	NY	14220	716-852-7171	852-7173
Knouse Foods Co-op Inc 800 Peach Glen-Idaville Rd *TF:* 800-827-7537 ■ *Web:* www.knouse.com	Peach Glen	PA	17375	717-677-8181	677-7069
MA Gedney Co 2100 Stoughton Ave *Web:* www.gedneypickle.com	Chaska	MN	55318	952-448-2612	448-1790
Mizkan Americas Inc 1661 Feehanville Dr Suite 300 *TF:* 800-323-4358 ■ *Web:* www.mizkan.com	Mount Prospect	IL	60056	847-590-0059	590-0405
National Fruit Product Co Inc 701 Fairmont Ave PO Box 2040 **Fax:* Sales ■ *TF:* 800-551-5167 ■ *Web:* www.whitehousefoods.com	Winchester	VA	22604	540-662-3401	665-4670*
Pastorelli Food Products Inc 162 N Sangamon St *TF:* 800-767-2829 ■ *Web:* www.pastorelli.com	Chicago	IL	60607	312-666-2041	666-2415
Rex Wine Vinegar Co 828-30 Raymond Blvd	Newark	NJ	07105	973-589-6911	589-5788
Silver Palate 300 Knickerbocker Rd PO Box 512 *TF:* 800-872-5283 ■ *Web:* www.shop.silverpalate.com	Cresskill	NJ	07626	201-568-0110	568-8844

299-42 Yeast

				Phone	Fax
Bakon Yeast Inc PO Box 651	Rhinelander	WI	54501	715-362-6533	362-6530
Brolite Products Inc 1900 S Pk Ave *TF:* 888-276-5483 ■ *Web:* www.bakewithbrolite.com	Streamwood	IL	60107	630-830-0340	830-0356
DSM Food Specialties Inc 45 Waterview Blvd **Fax Area Code:* 610 ■ *TF:* 800-662-4478 ■ *Web:* www.dsm.com	Parsippany	NJ	07054	800-662-4478	650-8599*
Lesaffre Yeast Corp 7475 W Main St *TF Cust Svc:* 800-558-7279 ■ *Web:* www.lesaffreyeastcorp.com	Milwaukee	WI	53214	877-677-7000	
Minn-Dak Yeast Co Inc 18175 Red River Rd W *TF:* 800-348-0991	Wahpeton	ND	58075	701-642-3300	642-1908
Sensient Flavors Inc 5600 W Raymond St **Fax:* Sales ■ *TF:* 800-445-0073 ■ *Web:* www.sensient-tech.com	Indianapolis	IN	46241	317-243-3521	240-1524*

300 FOOD PRODUCTS - WHOL

SEE ALSO Beverages - Whol p. 1522

				Phone	Fax
Saladino's Inc 3325 W Figarden Dr PO Box 12266 *Web:* www.saladinos.com	Fresno	CA	93777	559-271-3700	271-3701

300-1 Baked Goods - Whol

				Phone	Fax
Fresh Start Bakeries 145 S State College Blvd Suite 200 *Web:* www.freshstartbakeries.com	Brea	CA	92821	714-256-8900	256-8916
Horizon Food Group 7066 Las Positas Rd Suite G *TF:* 800-229-2552 ■ *Web:* www.horizonfoodgroup.com	Livermore	CA	94551	925-373-7700	373-8271
Interstate Bakeries Corp *Hostess Brands Inc* 12 E Armour Blvd **Fax Area Code:* 816 ■ *TF:* 800-483-7253 ■ *Web:* www.hostessbrands.com	Kansas City	MO	64111	800-483-7253	502-4126*
Tri-State Baking Co 6800 S Washington St	Amarillo	TX	79120	806-373-6696	345-7893
Turano Baking Co 6501 Roosevelt Rd *TF:* 800-458-5662 ■ *Web:* www.turanobakery.com	Berwyn	IL	60402	708-788-9220	788-3075
Wheat Montana Farms Inc 10778 US Hwy 287 *Web:* www.wheatmontana.com	Three Forks	MT	59752	406-285-3614	285-3749

300-2 Coffee & Tea - Whol

				Phone	Fax
Barrie House Coffee Co Inc 945 Nepperhan Ave *Web:* www.barriehouse.com	Yonkers	NY	10703	914-423-8400	423-8499
Becharas Bros Coffee Co Inc 14501 Hamilton Ave *TF:* 800-944-9675	Highland Park	MI	48203	313-869-4700	869-7940
Capricorn Coffees Inc 353 10th St *TF:* 800-541-0758 ■ *Web:* www.capricorncoffees.com	San Francisco	CA	94103	415-621-8500	621-9875
Coffee Bean International 9120 NE Alderwood Rd *TF:* 800-877-0474 ■ *Web:* www.coffeebeanintl.com	Portland	OR	97220	503-227-4490	225-9604
Coffee Masters Inc 7606 Industrial Ct *TF:* 800-334-6485 ■ *Web:* www.coffeemasters.com	Spring Grove	IL	60081	815-675-0088	675-3166
Paramount Coffee Co 130 N Larch Ave *TF:* 800-968-1222 ■ *Web:* www.paramountcoffee.com	Lansing	MI	48912	517-372-5500	372-2870
Red Diamond Inc 1701 Vanderbilt Rd PO Box 2168 *TF:* 800-292-4651 ■ *Web:* www.reddiamond.com	Birmingham	AL	35201	205-254-3138	254-6062
Royal Cup Inc 160 Cleage Dr *TF Cust Svc:* 800-366-5836 ■ *Web:* www.royalcupcoffee.com	Birmingham	AL	35217	205-849-5836	271-6071

300-3 Confectionery & Snack Foods - Whol

				Phone	Fax
AMCON Distributing Co 7405 Irvington Rd *AMEX:* DIT ■ *TF:* 800-369-6200 ■ *Web:* www.amcon.com	Omaha	NE	68122	402-331-3727	331-4834
Annabelle Candy Co Inc 27211 Industrial Blvd *Web:* www.annabelle-candy.com	Hayward	CA	94545	510-783-2900	785-7675
Anpesil Distribution Services 333 Swedesboro Ave *Web:* www.anpesil.com	Gibbstown	NJ	08027	856-687-0000	687-0017
AW Marshall Co PO Box 16127 *TF:* 800-273-4713	Salt Lake City	UT	84116	801-328-4713	328-9600
Brown & Haley 1940 E 11th St *TF:* 800-426-8400 ■ *Web:* www.brown-haley.com	Tacoma	WA	98421	253-620-3000	272-6742
Burklund Distributors Inc 2500 N Main St Suite 3 *TF:* 800-322-2876 ■ *Web:* www.burklund.com	East Peoria	IL	61611	309-694-1900	694-6788
Candy Direct 745 Design Ct Suite 602 *TF:* 888-922-6390 ■ *Web:* www.candydirect.com	Chula Vista	CA	91911	619-216-0116	374-2930
Continental Concession Supplies Inc 250 Fulton Ave *TF:* 800-516-0090 ■ *Web:* www.ccsicandy.com	New Hyde Park	NY	11040	516-739-8777	739-8750
Diamond Bakery Co 756 Moowaa St *Web:* www.diamondbakery.com	Honolulu	HI	96817	808-847-3551	847-7482
Eby-Brown Co 280 W Shuman Blvd Suite 280 *TF:* 800-553-8249 ■ *Web:* www.eby-brown.com	Naperville	IL	60563	630-778-2800	778-2831
Edward A. Berg & Sons PO Box 1187 *Web:* www.eaberg.com	Maywood	NJ	07607	201-845-8200	845-8201
Foreign Candy Co Inc 1 Foreign Candy Dr *TF:* 800-767-4575 ■ *Web:* www.foreigncandy.com	Hull	IA	51239	712-439-1496	439-1434
Frito-Lay North America 7701 Legacy Dr *TF:* 866-374-8677 ■ *Web:* www.fritolay.com	Plano	TX	75024	972-334-7000	334-2019
Hammons Products Co 105 Hammons Dr PO Box 140 *TF:* 888-429-6887 ■ *Web:* www.hammonsproducts.com	Stockton	MO	65785	417-276-5181	276-5187
Harold Levinson Assoc (HLA) 21 Banfi Plaza *TF:* 800-325-2512 ■ *Web:* www.hlacigars.com	Farmingdale	NY	11735	631-962-2400	962-9000
Hines Nut Co Inc 990 S St Paul St *TF:* 800-580-0580 ■ *Web:* www.hinesnut.com	Dallas	TX	75201	214-939-0253	761-0720
Keilson-Dayton Co 107 Commerce Pk Dr *TF:* 800-759-3174	Dayton	OH	45404	937-236-1070	236-2124
Kennedy Wholesale Inc 16014 Adelante St *TF:* 877-292-2639 ■ *Web:* www.kennedywholesale.com	Irwindale	CA	91706	818-241-9977	241-3046
McDonald Candy Co 2350 W Broadway St *TF:* 877-722-5503	Eugene	OR	97402	541-345-8421	345-7146
New Britain Candy Co 24 Maple St *TF:* 800-382-0515 ■ *Web:* www.newbritaincandy.com	Wethersfield	CT	06129	860-257-7058	257-7495
Old Dutch Foods Inc 2375 Terminal Rd *TF:* 800-989-2447 ■ *Web:* www.olddutchfoods.com	Roseville	MN	55113	651-633-8810	633-8894
Perugina Brands of America 800 N Brand Blvd 8th Fl *TF:* 800-544-1672 ■ *Web:* www.nestleusa.com	Glendale	CA	91203	818-551-3530	549-6952
Showtime Concession Supply Inc 200 SE 19th St *TF:* 800-882-6496 ■ *Web:* www.showtimeconcession.com	Moore	OK	73160	405-895-9902	895-9904
Sultana Distribution Services Inc 600 Food Ctr Dr *TF:* 877-617-5500 ■ *Web:* www.sultanadist.com	Bronx	NY	10474	718-617-5500	617-5225
Superior Nut & Candy Co Inc 1111 W 40th St *Web:* www.superiornutandcandy.com	Chicago	IL	60609	773-254-7900	254-9171
Superior Nut Co Inc 225 Monsignor O'Brien Hwy *Web:* www.superiornut.com	Cambridge	MA	02141	617-876-3808	876-8225
Taste of Nature Inc 2828 Donald Douglas Loop N Suite A *Web:* www.candyasap.com	Santa Monica	CA	90405	310-396-4433	396-4432
Torn & Glasser Inc 1622 E Olympic Blvd PO Box 21823 *Web:* www.tornandglasser.com	Los Angeles	CA	90021	213-627-6496	688-0941
Trophy Nut Co Inc 320 N 2nd St *TF:* 800-729-6887 ■ *Web:* www.trophynut.com	Tipp City	OH	45371	937-667-8478	667-4656
Tzetzo Bros Inc 1100 Military Rd *TF:* 800-248-2881	Buffalo	NY	14217	716-877-0800	877-0385

300-4 Dairy Products - Whol

				Phone	Fax
Ambriola Co Inc 2 Burma Rd *TF:* 800-962-8224 ■ *Web:* www.ambriola.com	Jersey City	NJ	07305	201-434-6289	434-5505
AMPI 315 N Broadway *TF:* 800-533-3580 ■ *Web:* www.ampi.com	New Ulm	MN	56073	507-354-8295	359-8668
Broughton Foods Co 1701 Green St *TF:* 800-283-2479	Marietta	OH	45750	740-373-4121	373-2861
Clofine Dairy Products Inc 1407 New Rd *TF:* 800-441-1001 ■ *Web:* www.clofinedairy.com	Linwood	NJ	08221	609-653-1000	653-0127
Clover-Stornetta Farms Inc PO Box 750369 *TF:* 800-237-3315 ■ *Web:* www.clover-stornetta.com	Petaluma	CA	94975	707-778-8448	778-0509
Country Classic Dairies Inc PO Box 968 *TF:* 800-321-4563 ■ *Web:* www.darigold-mt.com	Bozeman	MT	59771	406-586-5426	586-5110
Country Fresh Inc 2555 Buchanan Ave SW *TF:* 800-748-0480 ■ *Web:* www.enjoycountryfresh.com	Grand Rapids	MI	49548	616-243-0173	243-5926
Cream-O-Land Dairy Inc 529 Cedar Ln PO Box 146 *TF:* 800-220-6455 ■ *Web:* www.creamoland.com	Florence	NJ	08518	609-499-3601	499-3896

	City	State	Zip	Phone	Fax
Dairylea Co-op Inc					
5001 Brittonfield Pkwy	East Syracuse	NY	13057	315-433-0100	433-2345
TF: 800-654-8838 ■ *Web:* www.dairylea.com					
Erie Foods International Inc					
401 7th Ave PO Box 648	Erie	IL	61250	309-659-2233	659-2822
TF: 800-447-1887 ■ *Web:* www.eriefoods.com					
Fonterra USA 100 Corporate Ctr Dr Suite 101	Camp Hill	PA	17011	717-920-4000	920-4089
TF: 800-358-9096 ■ *Web:* www.fonterra.com					
Graf Creamery Co PO Box 49	Zachow	WI	54182	715-758-2137	758-8020
Hautly Cheese Co Inc 251 Axminister Dr	Saint Louis	MO	63026	636-533-4400	533-4401
TF: 800-729-9339 ■ *Web:* www.hautly.com					
Hillcrest Foodsß 2695 E 40th St	Cleveland	OH	44115	216-361-4625	361-0764
TF: 800-952-4344 ■ *Web:* www.hillcrestfoods.com					
Lowville Producers Dairy Co-op					
7396 Utica Blvd	Lowville	NY	13367	315-376-3921	376-3442
Web: www.gotgoodcheese.com					
Luberski Inc 310 N Harbor Blvd Suite 205	Fullerton	CA	92832	714-680-3447	680-3380
TF: 800-326-3220 ■ *Web:* www.hiddenvilla.com					
Maryland & Virginia Milk Producers Co-op Assn Inc					
1985 Isaac Newton Sq W	Reston	VA	20190	703-742-6800	742-7459
TF: 800-552-1976 ■ *Web:* www.mdvamilk.com					
Masters Gallery Foods Inc					
328 County Hwy PP PO Box 170	Plymouth	WI	53073	920-893-9145	
TF: 800-236-8431 ■ *Web:* www.mastersgalleryfoods.com					
Matanuska Maid Dairy					
814 W Northern Lights Blvd	Anchorage	AK	99503	907-561-5223	563-7492
TF: 800-478-5223					
Plains Dairy Products 300 N Taylor St	Amarillo	TX	79107	806-374-0385	374-0396
TF: 800-365-5608 ■ *Web:* www.plainsdairy.com					
Prairie Farms Dairy Inc					
1100 N Broadway St	Carlinville	IL	62626	217-854-2547	854-6426
TF: 800-654-2547 ■ *Web:* www.prairiefarms.com					
Purity Dairies Inc 360 Murfreesboro Rd	Nashville	TN	37210	615-244-1900	242-8547
TF: 800-947-6455 ■ *Web:* www.puritydairies.com					
Queensboro Farm Products Inc					
156-02 Liberty Ave	Jamaica	NY	11433	718-658-5000	658-0408
TF General: 800-696-8970					
Reilly Dairy & Food Co PO Box 130197	Tampa	FL	33681	813-839-8458	839-0394
Web: www.reillydairy.com					
Roberts Dairy Co 2901 Cuming St	Omaha	NE	68131	402-344-4321	346-0277
TF: 800-779-4321 ■ *Web:* www.robertsdairy.com					
Rockview Dairies Inc 7011 Stewart & Gray Rd	Downey	CA	90241	562-927-5511	928-9866
TF: 800-423-2479 ■ *Web:* www.rockviewfarms.com					
Schenkel's Dairy 1019 Flax Mill Rd	Huntington	IN	46750	260-356-4225	359-5045
TF General: 800-552-2791					
Schneider's Dairy Inc 726 Frank St	Pittsburgh	PA	15227	412-881-3525	881-7722
Select Milk Producers Inc 320 W Hermosa Dr	Artesia	NM	88210	575-746-6698	746-1752*
**Fax Area Code:* 505 ■ *Web:* www.selectmilk.com					
Simco Sales Service of Pennsylvania Inc					
101 Commerce Dr	Moorestown	NJ	08057	856-813-2300	
TF: 800-220-2300 ■ *Web:* www.jackjillicecream.com					
Sunshine Dairy Foods Inc 801 NE 21st Ave	Portland	OR	97232	503-234-7526	233-9441
TF: 800-544-0554 ■ *Web:* www.sunshinedairyfoods.com					
Sure Winner Foods Inc 2 Lehner Rd	Saco	ME	04072	207-282-1258	286-1410
TF: 800-640-6447 ■ *Web:* www.swfoods.com					
Umpqua Dairy Products Co					
333 SE Sykes Ave PO Box 1306	Roseburg	OR	97470	541-672-2638	673-0256
TF: 888-672-6455 ■ *Web:* www.umpquadairy.com					
United Dairymen of Arizona Inc PO Box 26877	Tempe	AZ	85285	480-966-7211	829-7491
Vince Deconna Distributing Inc PO Box 39	Orange Lake	FL	32681	352-591-1530	591-4418
TF: 800-824-8254 ■ *Web:* www.deconna.com					

300-5 Fish & Seafood - Whol

	City	State	Zip	Phone	Fax
American Seafood Co 3657 Old Getwell Rd	Memphis	TN	38118	901-542-5100	542-5150
TF: 800-747-9771 ■ *Web:* www.cassidyfoods.com					
Arrowac Fisheries Inc					
4039 21st Ave W					
Suite 200, Fisherman's Commerce Bldg	Seattle	WA	98199	206-282-5655	282-9329
Web: www.arrowac-merco.com					
Beaver Street Fisheries Inc					
1741 W Beaver St	Jacksonville	FL	32209	904-354-8533	
TF: 800-874-6426 ■ *Web:* www.beaverfish.com					
Blount Seafood Corp 630 Currant Rd	Fall River	MA	02720	774-888-1300	888-1399
TF: 800-274-2526 ■ *Web:* www.blountseafood.com					
Bon Secour Fisheries Inc					
17449 County Rd 49 S PO Box 60	Bon Secour	AL	36511	251-949-7411	949-6478
TF: 800-633-6854 ■ *Web:* www.bonsecourfisheries.com					
California Shellfish Co PO Box 2028	San Francisco	CA	94126	415-923-7400	923-1677
ConAgra Foods Foodservice Co 1 ConAgra Dr	Omaha	NE	68102	402-595-4000	
Web: www.conagrafoodservice.com					
Del Mar Seafoods Inc 331 Ford St	Watsonville	CA	95076	831-763-3000	763-2444
Web: www.delmarseafoods.com					
Eiwa International Inc 500 E 7th St	Los Angeles	CA	90014	213-680-0497	680-0317
Web: www.intmarine.com					
Empress International Ltd					
5 Dakota Dr Suite 303	Lake Success	NY	11042	516-740-4100	621-8318
TF Sales: 800-645-6244					
Fishery Products International					
18 Electronics Ave	Danvers	MA	01923	978-777-2660	777-6849
TF: 800-374-4770 ■ *Web:* www.fisheryproducts.com					
Golden-Tech International Inc					
2461 152nd Ave Ne	Redmond	WA	98052	425-869-1461	867-1368
TF: 800-311-8090 ■ *Web:* www.gtiinc.com					
Inland Seafood Corp 1651 Montreal Cir	Atlanta	GA	30084	404-350-5850	350-5871
TF: 800-883-3474 ■ *Web:* www.choicemall.com					
Interamerican Trading & Products Corp					
PO Box 402427	Miami Beach	FL	33140	305-885-9666	885-0402
TF: 800-999-7123					
Intersea Fisheries Ltd					
777 Terr Ave Heights Plaza	Hasbrouck Heights	NJ	07604	201-692-9000	692-9460
Web: www.intersea-fish.com					
Ipswich Shellfish Co Inc 8 Hayward St	Ipswich	MA	01938	978-356-4371	356-9235
TF: 800-477-9424 ■ *Web:* www.ipswichshellfish.com					
Isf Trading Inc PO Box 772	Portland	ME	04104	207-879-1575	761-5877
Web: www.seaurchinmaine.com					
John Keeler & Co Inc 3000 NW 109th Ave	Miami	FL	33172	305-836-6858	836-6859
TF: 888-663-2722 ■ *Web:* www.onecrab.com					
LD Amory & Co Inc 101 S King St	Hampton	VA	23669	757-722-1915	723-1184
TF: 800-338-3755					
Maine Lobster Direct 48 Union Wharf	Portland	ME	04101	207-772-9056	772-0169
TF: 800-556-2783 ■ *Web:* www.mainelobsterdirect.com					
Mazzetta Co 1990 St Johns Ave	Highland Park	IL	60035	847-433-1150	433-8973
Web: www.mazzetta.com					
Metropolitan Poultry & Seafood Co					
1920 Stanford Ct	Landover	MD	20785	301-772-0060	772-1013
TF: 800-522-0060 ■ *Web:* www.metropoultry.com					
Morey's Seafood International LLC					
1218 Hwy 10 S	Motley	MN	56466	218-352-6345	352-6523
Web: www.moreys.com					
Morley Sales Co Inc 809 W Madison St	Chicago	IL	60607	312-829-1125	829-3680
TF: 800-828-0424					
Oceanpro Industries Ltd					
1900 Fenwick St Ne	Washington	DC	20002	202-529-3003	
Web: www.profish.com					
Ore-Cal Corp 634 S Crocker St	Los Angeles	CA	90021	213-680-9540	228-6557
TF: 800-827-7474 ■ *Web:* www.ore-cal.com					
Pacific Giant Inc 4625 District Blvd	Vernon	CA	90058	323-587-5000	587-5050
Web: www.pacificgiant.com					
Peninsula Seafood of San Bruno Inc					
135 El Camino Real	San Bruno	CA	94066	650-875-3933	875-3936
Web: www.wehaveseafood.com/retail.html					
Premier Pacific Seafoods Inc					
111 W Harrison St	Seattle	WA	98119	206-286-8584	286-8810
Quirch Foods Co 7600 NW 82nd Pl	Miami	FL	33166	305-691-3535	593-0272
TF: 800-458-5252 ■ *Web:* www.quirchfoods.com					
Red Chamber Co 1912 E Vernon Ave	Vernon	CA	90058	323-234-9000	231-8888
Web: www.redchamber.com					
Sager's Seafood Plus Inc					
4802 Bridal Wreath Dr	Richmond	TX	77406	281-342-8833	342-8891
TF: 800-929-3474 ■ *Web:* www.sagersseafoodplus.com					
SeaSpecialties Inc 1111 NW 159th Dr	Miami	FL	33169	305-625-5112	625-5528
TF: 800-654-6682 ■ *Web:* www.seaspecialties.com					
Seawise Inc 4 Greenleaf Woods Dr Suite 201	Portsmouth	NH	03801	603-433-6677	433-2703
Web: www.seawiseinc.com					
Slade Gorton Co Inc 225 Southampton St	Boston	MA	02118	617-442-5800	442-9090
TF: 800-225-1573 ■ *Web:* www.sladegorton.com					
Southeast Alaska Smoked Salmon Co Inc					
550 S Franklin St	Juneau	AK	99801	907-463-4617	463-4644
TF: 800-582-5122 ■ *Web:* www.takustore.com					
Southern Foods Inc					
3500 Old Battleground Rd	Greensboro	NC	27410	336-545-3800	545-3822
TF: 800-441-3663 ■ *Web:* www.southernfoods.com					
Stavis Seafoods Inc 212 Northern Ave Suite 305	Boston	MA	02210	617-482-6349	482-1340
TF: 800-390-5103 ■ *Web:* www.stavis.com					
Sunnyvale Seafood Corp 1651 Pomona Ave	San Jose	CA	95110	408-289-9198	280-9100
Web: www.sunnyvaleseafood.com					
Town Dock The PO Box 608	Narragansett	RI	02882	401-789-2200	
Web: www.towndockinc.com					
Tri Marine Fish Co 220 Cannery St	San Pedro	CA	90731	310-547-1144	547-1166
Web: www.trimarinegroup.com					
Tropic Fish & Vegetable Center Inc					
1020 Auahi St	Honolulu	HI	96814	808-591-2936	591-2934
Web: www.tropicfishhawaii,.com					
Troyer Foods Inc 17141 State Rd 4	Goshen	IN	46528	574-533-0302	533-3851
TF: 800-876-9377 ■ *Web:* www.troyers.com					
Val's Distributing Co					
6124 E 30th St N PO Box 581583	Tulsa	OK	74115	918-835-9987	835-3808
TF: 800-274-9987 ■ *Web:* www.valsdist.com					

300-6 Frozen Foods (Packaged) - Whol

	City	State	Zip	Phone	Fax
Advantage Sales & Marketing					
18100 Von Karman Ave Suite 1000	Irvine	CA	92612	949-797-2900	797-9112
Web: www.asmnet.com					
Baja Foods LLC 636 W Root St	Chicago	IL	60609	773-376-9030	376-9245
Web: www.bajafoodsllc.com					
Cedar Farms 2100 Hornig Rd	Philadelphia	PA	19116	215-934-7100	934-5851
TF: 800-220-2217 ■ *Web:* www.cedarfarms.com					
ConAgra Foods Foodservice Co 1 ConAgra Dr	Omaha	NE	68102	402-595-4000	
Web: www.conagrafoodservice.com					
Dot Foods Inc 1 Dot Way PO Box 192	Mount Sterling	IL	62353	217-773-4411	773-3321
TF: 800-366-3687 ■ *Web:* www.dotfoods.com					
Happy & Healthy Products Inc					
1600 S Dixie Hwy Suite 200	Boca Raton	FL	33432	561-367-0739	368-5267
TF: 800-378-4854 ■ *Web:* www.fruitfull.com					
Mrs Smith's Bakeries LLC 2855 Rolling Pin Ln	Suwanee	GA	30024	678-482-3000	482-3451
Web: www.mrssmiths.schwansfoodservice.com					
Paris Foods Corp 1632 Carman St	Camden	NJ	08105	856-964-0915	964-9719
Web: www.parisfoods.com					
Quality Frozen Foods Inc 1663 62nd St	Brooklyn	NY	11204	718-256-9100	234-3755
Web: www.qualityfrozenfoods.com					
Sun Belt Food Co Inc					
951 Broken Sound Pkwy	Boca Raton	FL	33487	561-995-9100	997-5664
Web: www.sunbeltfoods.com					
Trudeau Distributing Co					
25 Cliff Rd W Suite 115	Burnsville	MN	55337	952-882-8295	882-8397
Web: www.trudeaudistributing.com					

Company / Address	City	State	ZIP	Phone	Fax
Wilcox Frozen Foods Inc 2200 Oakdale Ave TF: 800-827-7858	San Francisco	CA	94124	415-282-4116	282-3044

300-7 Fruits & Vegetables - Fresh - Whol

Company / Address	City	State	ZIP	Phone	Fax
Adams Bros Produce Co 302 Fenley Ave W PO Box 2682 TF: 800-292-6532	Birmingham	AL	35202	205-323-7161	251-4867
Albert's Organics Inc 3268 E Vernon Ave TF: 800-899-4595 ■ Web: www.albertsorganics.com	Vernon	CA	90058	323-587-6367	587-6567
Alpine Fresh Inc 9300 NW 58th St Suite 201 Web: www.alpinefresh.com	Miami	FL	33178	305-594-9117	594-8506
Amerifresh 16100 N 71st St Suite 520 TF: 800-568-3235 ■ Web: www.amerifresh.com	Scottsdale	AZ	85254	480-927-4000	927-4909
Anthony Marano Co Inc 3000 S Ashland Ave Web: www.anthonymarano.com	Chicago	IL	60608	773-321-7500	321-7800
Banacol Marketing Corp 2655 Le Jeune Rd Suite 1015 TF: 877-324-7619 ■ Web: www.banacol.com	Coral Gables	FL	33134	305-441-9036	446-4291
Belair Produce Co Inc 7226 Pkwy Dr TF: 888-782-8008 ■ Web: www.belairproduce.com	Hanover	MD	21076	410-782-8000	782-8009
Bernard Zell Anshe Emet Day School 3751 N Broadway St Web: www.bzaeds.org	Chicago	IL	60613	773-281-1858	281-4709
Bix Produce Co 1415 L'Orient St TF: 800-642-9514 ■ Web: www.bixproduce.com	Saint Paul	MN	55117	651-487-8000	489-1310
Bland Farms Inc 1126 Raymond Bland Rd TF: 800-440-9543 ■ Web: www.blandfarms.com	Glennville	GA	30427	912-654-1426	654-3532
Bouten Construction Co 627 N Napa St PO Box 3507 Web: www.boutenconstruction.com	Spokane	WA	99220	509-535-3531	535-6047
Brothers Produce Inc 3173 Produce Row Web: www.brothersproduce.com	Houston	TX	77023	713-924-4196	921-3060
Calavo Growers Inc 1141-A Cummings Rd NASDAQ: CVGW ■ TF: 800-422-5286 ■ Web: www.calavo.com	Santa Paula	CA	93060	805-525-1245	921-3287
Caro Foods Inc 2324 Bayou Blue Rd TF: 800-395-2276 ■ Web: www.performancefoodservice.com/Caro	Houma	LA	70364	985-872-1483	876-0825
Castellini Co 2 Plum St PO Box 721610 TF Cust Svc: 800-843-2676 ■ Web: castellinico.com	Newport	KY	41066	859-442-4600	442-4666
Cleveland Growers Marketing Co 12200 Corporate Dr	Cleveland	OH	44130	216-898-3900	898-3901
CM Holtzinger Fruit Co 1312 N 6th Ave PO Box 169 Web: www.holtzingerfruit.com	Yakima	WA	98902	509-457-5115	248-1514
Community Suffolk Inc 304 2nd St TF: 800-225-4470	Everett	MA	02149	617-389-5200	389-6680
Consumers Produce Co 1 21st St TF: 800-245-0698 ■ Web: www.consumersproduce.com	Pittsburgh	PA	15222	412-281-0722	281-6541
Costa Fruit & Produce 18 Bunker Hill Industrial Pk PO Box 290754 TF: 800-343-0836 ■ Web: www.freshideas.com	Boston	MA	02129	617-241-8007	241-8007
Country Fresh Mushroom Co PO Box 489 Web: www.countryfreshmushrooms.com	Avondale	PA	19311	610-268-3033	268-0479
Crosset Co Inc 10295 Toebben Dr TF: 800-347-4902	Independence	KY	41051	859-283-5830	817-7634
D'Arrigo Bros Co of New York Inc 315 NYC Terminal Market TF: 800-223-8080	Bronx	NY	10474	718-991-5900	960-0544
Del Monte Fresh Produce Co 241 Sevilla Ave TF Cust Svc: 800-950-3683 ■ Web: www.freshdelmonte.com	Coral Gables	FL	33134	305-520-8400	520-8455
DiMare Bros/New England Farms Packing Co 84 New England Produce Ctr Web: www.dimareinc.com	Chelsea	MA	02150	617-889-3800	889-2067
DiMare Fresh Inc 1049 Ave H E TF: 800-322-2184 ■ Web: www.dimarefresh.com	Arlington	TX	76011	817-385-3000	385-3015
Dole Food Co Hawaii 802 Mapunapuna St TF: 800-697-9100 ■ Web: www.dolefruithawaii.com	Honolulu	HI	96819	808-861-8015	861-8020
East Coast Fruit Co Inc 3335 Edgewood Ave N TF: 800-541-4602	Jacksonville	FL	32254	904-355-7591	355-7591
Egan Bernard & Co 1900 Old Dixie Hwy *Fax Area Code: 772 ■ TF: 800-327-6676 ■ Web: www.dneworld.com	Fort Pierce	FL	34946	800-327-6676	465-1181*
Federal Fruit & Produce Co 1890 E 58th Ave TF: 800-621-7166 ■ Web: www.fedfruit.com	Denver	CO	80216	303-292-1303	292-1303
FreshPoint Inc 1390 Enclave Pkwy Web: www.freshpoint.com	Houston	TX	77077	281-899-4242	899-4231
Freshway Foods 601 Stolle Ave Web: www.freshwayfoods.com	Sidney	OH	45365	937-498-4664	498-1529
Frieda's Inc 4465 Corporate Ctr Dr *Fax: Sales ■ TF: 800-421-9477 ■ Web: www.friedas.com	Los Alamitos	CA	90720	714-826-6100	816-0273*
General Produce Co 1330 N 'B' St TF: 800-366-4985 ■ Web: www.generalproduce.com	Sacramento	CA	95814	916-441-6431	441-2483
Giumarra Bros Fruit Co Inc 1601 E Olympic Blvd Bldg 400 Suite 408 Web: www.giumarra.com	Los Angeles	CA	90021	213-627-2900	628-4878
Global Tropical Fresh Fruit Corp 91 Brooklyn Terminal Market TF: 800-734-5622 ■ Web: www.globaltropical.com	Brooklyn	NY	11236	718-763-4603	531-7467
Gold Harbor Commodities Inc 9750 3rd Ave NE	Seattle	WA	98115	206-527-6138	
Graves Menu Maker Foods Inc 913 Big Horn Dr TF: 800-557-6623 ■ Web: www.menumakerfoods.com	Jefferson City	MO	65109	573-893-3000	893-2172
H Smith Packing Corp 99 Fort Fairfield Rd Web: www.smithsfarm.com	Presque Isle	ME	04769	207-764-4540	764-2816
HC Schmeiding Produce Co 2330 N Thompson St PO Box 369 TF: 800-643-3607	Springdale	AR	72764	479-751-4517	751-6831
Hearn Kirkwood 7251 Standard Dr TF: 888-866-2905 ■ Web: www.hearnkirkwood.com	Hanover	MD	21076	410-712-6000	712-0020
Heeren Bros Inc 1060 Hall St SW TF: 800-253-4620 ■ Web: www.heerenbros.com	Grand Rapids	MI	49503	616-452-2101	243-7070
Hollar & Greene Produce Co Inc 230 Cabbage Rd PO Box 3500 TF: 800-222-1077 ■ Web: www.hollarandgreene.com	Boone	NC	28607	828-264-2177	264-4413
Indianapolis Fruit Co Inc 4501 Massachusetts Ave TF: 800-377-2425 ■ Web: www.indyfruit.com	Indianapolis	IN	46218	317-546-2425	543-0521
Kegel's Produce Inc 2851 Old Tree Dr TF: 800-535-3435 ■ Web: www.kegels.com	Lancaster	PA	17603	717-392-6612	392-6482
L & M Cos Inc 2925 Huntleigh Dr Suite 204 Web: www.lmcompanies.com	Raleigh	NC	27604	919-981-8000	954-9984
Melissa's/World Variety Produce Inc 5325 S Soto St TF: 800-468-7111 ■ Web: www.melissas.com	Vernon	CA	90058	323-588-0151	588-1768
Mission Produce Inc 2500 E Vineyard Ave # 300 Web: www.missionpro.com	Oxnard	CA	93036	805-981-3650	981-3660
Moore Food Distributors Co 9910 Page Ave TF: 800-467-7878 ■ Web: www.moorefooddist.com	Saint Louis	MO	63132	314-426-1300	426-6690
Mountain View Fruit Sales Inc 4275 Ave 416 Web: www.mountainviewfruit.com	Reedley	CA	93654	559-637-9933	637-9733
Muir Enterprises Inc 3575 W 900 S PO Box 26775 *Fax: Sales ■ TF: 877-268-2002 ■ Web: www.coppercanyonfarms.com	Salt Lake City	UT	84104	801-363-7695	322-1640*
Natural Selection Foods 1721 San Juan Hwy TF: 888-624-1004 ■ Web: www.nsfoods.com	San Juan Bautista	CA	95045	831-623-7880	623-4988
North Bay Produce Inc PO Box 988 *Fax Area Code: 231 ■ TF: 800-678-1941 ■ Web: www.northbayproduce.com	Traverse City	MI	49685	800-678-1941	946-1902*
Oneonta Trading Corp 1 Oneonta Way TF: 800-688-2191 ■ Web: www.oneonta.com	Wenatchee	WA	98801	509-663-2631	663-6333
Organic Valley Family of Farms 1 Organic Way *Fax Area Code: 608 ■ TF: 888-444-6455 ■ Web: www.organicvalley.coop	LaFarge	WI	54639	888-444-6455	625-3025*
Pacific Coast Fruit Co 201 NE 2nd Ave Suite 100 TF: 800-445-8082 ■ Web: www.pcfruit.com	Portland	OR	97232	503-234-6411	234-0072
Pandol Bros Inc 401 Rd 192 Web: www.pandol.com	Delano	CA	93215	661-725-3755	725-4741
Paramount Export Co 175 Filbert St Suite 201 TF: 800-869-0150 ■ Web: www.paramountexport.net	Oakland	CA	94607	510-839-0150	839-1002
Peak of the Market 1200 King Edward St TF: 888-289-7325 ■ Web: www.peakmarket.com	Winnipeg	MB	R3H0R5	204-633-7325	694-7325
Peirone Produce Co 524 Spokane Falls Blvd TF: 800-552-5837 ■ Web: www.peirone.com	Spokane	WA	99202	509-838-3515	838-3916
Procacci Bros Sales Corp 3333 S Front St Web: www.procaccibrothers.com	Philadelphia	PA	19148	215-463-8000	467-1144
Produce Source Partners 8411 Sanford Dr TF: 800-344-4728 ■ Web: www.producesourcepartners.com	Richmond	VA	23228	804-262-8300	
Progressive Produce Co 5790 Peachtree St TF: 800-900-0757 ■ Web: www.progressiveproduce.com	Los Angeles	CA	90040	323-890-8100	890-8113
ProPacificfresh 70 pepsi way PO Box 1069 Web: www.propacificfresh.com	Durham	CA	95938	530-893-0596	893-5973
Sambazon Inc 1160 Calle Cordillera TF: 877-726-2296 ■ Web: www.sambazon.com	San Clemente	CA	92673	949-498-8618	498-8619
Sandridge Food Corp (SFC) 133 Commerce Dr TF: 800-672-2523 ■ Web: www.sandridge.com	Medina	OH	44256	330-725-2348	722-3998
Simonian Fruit Co 511 N 7th St PO Box 340 Web: www.simonianfruit.com	Fowler	CA	93625	559-834-5921	834-2363
Snokist Growers Co-op 10 W Mead Ave PO Box 1587 TF: 800-258-0470 ■ Web: www.snokist.com	Yakima	WA	98907	509-453-5631	453-9359
Strobe Celery & Vegetable Co 2404 S Wolcott Ave *Fax Area Code: 312 ■ Web: www.strube.com	Chicago	IL	60608	773-446-4000	226-7644*
Sunkist Growers Inc 14130 Riverside Dr *Fax: PR ■ TF: 800-383-7141 ■ Web: www.sunkist.com	Sherman Oaks	CA	91423	818-986-4800	379-7511*
Sunnyridge Farm Inc 1900 5th St N W PO Box 3036 Web: www.sunnyridge.com	Winter Haven	FL	33881	863-294-8856	595-4095
Superior Foods Inc 275 Westgate Dr TF: 888-373-7871 ■ Web: www.superiorfoods.com	Watsonville	CA	95076	831-728-3691	722-0926
Sysco Food Services of San Francisco Inc 5900 Stewart Ave NYSE: SYY ■ TF: 800-877-7012 ■ Web: www.syscosf.com	Fremont	CA	94538	510-226-3000	226-3085
Taylor Farms Inc 911 Blanco Cir # B Web: www.taylorfarms.com	Salinas	CA	93901	831-754-0471	754-0473
Tonly Vitrano Co Maryland Wholesale Produce Market Bldg B	Jessup	MD	20794	410-799-7444	799-2464
W. R. Vernon Produce Co PO Box 4054 TF: 800-222-6406 ■ Web: www.vernonproduce.com	Winston Salem	NC	27115	336-725-9741	761-1841

300-8 Groceries - General Line

Company / Address	City	State	ZIP	Phone	Fax
Abbott Sysco Food Service 2400 Harrison Rd *Fax: Sales ■ TF: 800-686-3663 ■ Web: www.abbottfoods.com	Columbus	OH	43204	614-272-0658	272-8409*
Advantage Sales & Marketing 18100 Von Karman Ave Suite 1000 Web: www.asmnet.com	Irvine	CA	92612	949-797-2900	797-9112
Affiliated Foods Inc 1401 W Farmers Ave TF: 800-234-3661 ■ Web: www.afiama.com	Amarillo	TX	79118	806-372-3851	374-1721
Affiliated Foods Midwest 1301 W Omaha Ave Web: www.afmidwest.com	Norfolk	NE	68701	402-371-0555	371-1884
AJC International 5188 Roswell Rd NW TF: 800-252-3663 ■ Web: www.ajcfood.com	Atlanta	GA	30342	404-252-6750	252-9340
Albert Guarnieri Co 1133 E Market St TF: 800-686-2639 ■ Web: www.albertguarnieri.com	Warren	OH	44483	330-394-5636	394-4982
AMCON Distributing Co 7405 Irvington Rd AMEX: DIT ■ TF: 800-369-6200 ■ Web: www.amcon.com	Omaha	NE	68122	402-331-3727	331-4834
American Seaway Foods Inc 5300 Richmond Rd *Fax Area Code: 412	Bedford Heights	OH	44146	216-292-7000	968-1618*
Amster-Kirtz Co 2830 Cleveland Ave NW TF: 800-257-9338	Canton	OH	44709	330-493-1800	493-8207
Anderson-DuBose Co 6575 Davis Industrial Pkwy TF: 800-248-1080	Solon	OH	44139	440-248-8800	248-6208
Associated Food Stores Inc 1850 W 2100 S TF Cust Svc: 888-574-9000 ■ Web: www.afstores.com	Salt Lake City	UT	84119	801-973-4400	978-8551

Company	City	State	Zip	Phone	Fax
Associated Grocers Inc 8600 Anselmo Ln	Baton Rouge	LA	70810	225-769-2020	763-6194
TF: 800-637-2021 ■ *Web:* www.agbr.com					
Associated Grocers of Florida Inc 1141 SW 12th Ave	Pompano Beach	FL	33069	954-876-3000	876-3039
Web: www.agfla.com					
Associated Grocers of New England Inc 11 Co-op Way	Pembroke	NH	03275	603-223-6710	223-5672
TF: 800-242-2248 ■ *Web:* www.agne.com					
Associated Grocers of the South 3600 Vanderbilt Rd	Birmingham	AL	35217	205-841-6781	808-4920
TF: 800-695-6051 ■ *Web:* www.agsouth.com					
Associated Wholesale Grocers Inc 5000 Kansas Ave	Kansas City	KS	66106	913-288-1000	288-1587
Web: www.awginc.com					
Associated Wholesalers Inc PO Box 67	Robesonia	PA	19551	610-693-3161	693-3171*
**Fax:* Orders ■ *TF:* 800-927-7771 ■ *Web:* www.awiweb.com					
Atalanta Corp 1 Atalanta Plaza	Elizabeth	NJ	07206	908-351-8000	351-1693
Web: www.atalanta1.com					
Avico Distributing Inc 729 Broad St	Utica	NY	13501	315-724-8243	724-7697
TF: 800-734-8243 ■ *Web:* www.avicospice.com					
Bozzuto's Inc 275 School House Rd	Cheshire	CT	06410	203-272-3511	250-2880*
**Fax:* Sales ■ *Web:* www.bozzutos.com					
Brenham Wholesale Grocery Co 602 W 1st St	Brenham	TX	77833	979-836-7925	830-0346
TF: 800-324-3232 ■ *Web:* www.bwgroc.com					
C & S Wholesale Grocers Inc 889 Putney Rd	Brattleboro	VT	05301	802-257-4371	257-6613
Web: www.cswg.com					
Camp Olympia 723 Olympia Dr	Trinity	TX	75862	936-594-2541	594-8143
TF: 800-735-6190 ■ *Web:* www.campolympia.com					
Cash-Wa Distributing Co 401 W 4th St	Kearney	NE	68845	308-237-3151	234-6018
TF: 800-652-0010 ■ *Web:* www.cashwa.com					
CB Ragland Co 2720 Eugenia Ave	Nashville	TN	37211	615-254-2841	254-2130*
**Fax:* Hum Res ■ *TF:* 800-234-4455 ■ *Web:* www.cbragland.com					
CD Hartnett Co 302 N Main St	Weatherford	TX	76086	817-594-3813	594-9714
TF: 877-594-3813 ■ *Web:* www.cd-hartnett.com					
Central Grocers Co-op Inc 11100 Belmont Ave	Franklin Park	IL	60131	847-451-0660	288-8710
Web: www.central-grocers.com					
Certified Grocers Midwest Inc 1 Certified Dr	Hodgkins	IL	60525	708-579-2100	579-9786
Web: www.certisaver.com					
Coastal Pacific Food Distributors Inc (CPFD) 1015 Performance Dr	Stockton	CA	95206	209-983-2454	983-8009*
**Fax:* Cust Svc ■ *TF:* 800-500-2611 ■ *Web:* www.cpfd.com					
ConAgra Grocery Products Co 3353 Michelson Dr	Irvine	CA	92612	949-437-1000	437-3305
Web: www.conagrafoods.com					
Core-Mark International Inc 395 Oyster Pt Blvd Suite 415	South San Francisco	CA	94080	650-589-9445	952-4284
TF: 800-622-1713 ■ *Web:* www.coremark.com					
Dearborn Wholesale Grocers Inc 2801 S Western Ave	Chicago	IL	60608	773-254-4300	254-4300
TF: 800-999-3663 ■ *Web:* www.dearbornwholesale.com					
Di Giorgio Corp 380 Middlesex Ave	Carteret	NJ	07008	732-541-5555	541-3602
Web: www.whiterose.com					
Di Giorgio Corp White Rose Food Div 380 Middlesex Ave	Carteret	NJ	07008	732-541-5555	541-3730
Web: www.whiterose.com					
DiCarlo Distributors Inc 1630 N Ocean Ave	Holtsville	NY	11742	631-758-6000	758-6096
TF: 800-342-2756 ■ *Web:* www.dicarlofood.com					
Dismex Food Inc 12255 SW 133rd Ct	Miami	FL	33186	305-238-6146	238-4032
Web: www.dismexfood.com					
Dpi-epicurean Fine Foods 246 S Robson St	Mesa	AZ	85210	480-969-9333	461-3645
Web: www.epicurean-foods.com					
Dutch Valley Bulk Food Distributors Inc 7615 Lancaster Ave	Myerstown	PA	17067	717-933-4191	933-5466
TF: 800-733-4191 ■ *Web:* www.dutchvalleyfoods.com					
E. G. Ayers Distributing Inc 5819 S Broadway St	Eureka	CA	95503	707-445-2077	445-5719
Web: www.ayersdistributing.com					
Empire Food Brokers of Ohio Inc 11243 Cornell Pk Dr	Cincinnati	OH	45242	513-793-6241	
Web: www.empirefoods.com					
Europa Market Co Inc The 8100 Water St	Saint Louis	MO	63111	314-631-7288	
Web: www.europa-market.com					
Farner-Bocken Co 1751 US Hwy 30 E PO Box 368	Carroll	IA	51401	712-792-3503	792-3503
TF: 800-274-8692 ■ *Web:* www.mrc.farner-bocken.com/fbpublic					
Feesers Inc 5561 Grayson Rd	Harrisburg	PA	17111	717-564-4636	558-7450
TF: 800-326-2828 ■ *Web:* www.feesers.com					
Food Services of America Inc 4025 Delridge Way SW Suite 400	Seattle	WA	98106	206-933-5000	933-5283
TF: 800-372-3663 ■ *Web:* www.fsafood.com					
Glazier Foods Co 11303 Antoine Dr	Houston	TX	77066	832-375-6303	375-6114
TF: 800-989-6411 ■ *Web:* www.glazierfoods.com					
Gordon Food Service 333 50th St SW	Grand Rapids	MI	49548	616-530-7000	717-7600
TF: 800-968-7500 ■ *Web:* www.gfs.com					
Grocers Supply International Inc 3131 E Holcombe Blvd PO Box 14200	Houston	TX	77021	713-747-5000	749-9362*
**Fax:* Acctg ■ *TF:* 800-352-8003 ■ *Web:* www.grocerssupply.com					
Grocery Supply Co 1301 Main St	Sulphur Springs	TX	75482	903-885-7621	439-3249
TF: 800-231-1938 ■ *Web:* www.grocerysupply.com					
Hannaford Bros Co 145 Pleasant Hill Rd	Scarborough	ME	04074	207-883-2911	
TF: 800-341-6393 ■ *Web:* www.hannaford.com					
HT Hackney Inc 1200 Burris Rd	Newton	NC	28658	828-464-1010	466-3464
TF: 800-876-4641 ■ *Web:* www.hthackney.com					
Imperial Trading Co Inc 701 Edwards Ave PO Box 23508	Elmwood	LA	70123	504-733-1400	736-4156
TF Cust Svc: 800-743-1761 ■ *Web:* www.imperialtrading.com					
Institution Food House Inc 543 12th St Dr NW	Hickory	NC	28603	828-323-4500	725-4500
TF: 800-800-0434 ■ *Web:* www.institutionfoodhouse.com					
JM Swank Co 395 Herky St	North Liberty	IA	52317	319-626-3683	626-3662
TF: 800-593-6375 ■ *Web:* www.jmswank.com/index2.html					
Johnson O'hare Co Inc 1 Progress Rd	Billerica	MA	01821	978-663-9000	262-2200
Web: www.johare.com					
Jordano's Inc 550 S Patterson Ave	Santa Barbara	CA	93111	805-964-0611	964-3821
TF: 800-325-2278 ■ *Web:* www.jordanos.com					
JT Davenport & Sons Inc 1144 Broadway Rd	Sanford	NC	27332	919-774-9444	774-9444
TF Cust Svc: 800-868-7550 ■ *Web:* www.mail01.jtdavenport.com/jtdweb.nsf					
Just Bagels Mfg Inc 527 Casanova St	Bronx	NY	10474	718-328-9700	328-9997
Web: www.justbagels.com					
Key Food Stores Co-op Inc 1200 S Ave	Staten Island	NY	10314	718-370-4200	370-4232*
**Fax:* Mktg ■ *Web:* www.keyfoods.com					
Koa Trading Co PO Box 1031	Lihue	HI	96766	808-245-6961	245-8036
TF: 877-794-6341 ■ *Web:* www.koatradingcoinc.com					
Kraft Foods International Inc 3 Lakes Dr	Northfield	IL	60093	847-646-2000	335-9395*
**Fax Area Code:* 914 ■ *TF:* 800-323-0768 ■ *Web:* www.kraftfoodscompany.com					
Labatt Food Service 4500 Industry Pk Dr	San Antonio	TX	78218	210-661-4216	661-0973
TF: 800-324-8732 ■ *Web:* www.labattfood.com					
Laurel Grocery Co Inc 129 Barbourville Rd	London	KY	40744	606-878-6601	864-5693
TF: 800-467-6601 ■ *Web:* www.laurelgrocery.com					
Long Wholesale Distributors Inc 5173 Pioneer Dr PO Box 70	Meridian	MS	39301	601-482-3144	482-3109
TF: 800-748-3847 ■ *Web:* www.longdistribution.com					
Luke Soules Acosta 1920 Westridge Dr	Irving	TX	75038	972-518-1442	751-0983
TF: 800-486-0928					
Maines Paper & Food Service Co 101 Broome Corporate Pkwy	Conklin	NY	13748	607-779-1200	723-3245*
**Fax:* Cust Svc ■ *TF:* 800-366-3669 ■ *Web:* www.maines.net					
Maya Overseas Foods Inc 48-85 Maspeth Ave	Maspeth	NY	11378	718-894-5145	894-5178
Web: www.mayafoods.com					
MBM Corp PO Box 800	Rocky Mount	NC	27801	252-985-7200	985-7241*
McLane Co Inc 4747 McLane Pkwy	Temple	TX	76504	254-771-7500	771-7244
TF: 800-299-1401 ■ *Web:* www.mclaneco.com					
McLane Foodservice Inc 2085 Midway Rd	Carrollton	TX	75006	972-364-2000	364-2088
TF: 888-792-9300 ■ *Web:* www.mclaneco.com					
Mendez & Co PO Box 363348	San Juan	PR	00936	787-793-8888	783-9498
Merchants Co 1100 Edwards St	Hattiesburg	MS	39401	601-583-4351	582-5333
TF: 800-844-3663 ■ *Web:* www.themerchantscompany.com					
Merchants Distributors Inc 5001 Alex Lee Blvd	Hickory	NC	28601	828-323-4100	323-4527
TF: 800-800-2634 ■ *Web:* www.merchantsdistributors.com					
Metro Inc 11011 Maurice-Duplessis Blvd	Montreal	QC	H1C1V6	514-643-1055	643-1215
TF: 800-361-4681 ■ *Web:* www.metro.ca					
Millbrook Distribution Services 88 Huntoon Memorial Hwy	Leicester	MA	01524	508-892-8171	892-4827
TF: 800-225-7398 ■ *Web:* www.millbrookds.com					
Nash Finch Co 7600 France Ave S	Minneapolis	MN	55440	952-832-0534	844-1237
NASDAQ: NAFC ■ *Web:* www.nashfinch.com					
Norman's Inc 86 Division St S	Battle Creek	MI	49017	269-968-6136	968-6988
TF: 800-695-5696 ■ *Web:* www.normanfoods.com					
Olean Wholesale Grocery Co-op Inc 1587 County Rd 27	Olean	NY	14760	716-372-2020	372-2039
TF: 866-774-9751 ■ *Web:* www.oleanwholesale.com					
Oppenheimer Cos Inc 877 W Main St Suite 700	Boise	ID	83702	208-343-4883	343-4490
TF: 800-727-9939 ■ *Web:* www.oppcos.com					
Paris Gourmet of New York Inc 145 Grand St	Carlstadt	NJ	07072	201-939-5656	939-5613
Web: www.parisgourmet.com					
Penn Traffic Co 1200 State Fair Blvd	Syracuse	NY	13209	315-453-7284	461-2387*
**Fax:* Acctg ■ *TF:* 800-275-9005 ■ *Web:* www.penntraffic.com					
Performance Food Group Co 12500 W Creek Pkwy	Richmond	VA	23238	804-484-7700	484-7701
Web: www.pfgc.com					
Performance Foodservice 12500 W Creek Pkwy	Richmond	VA	23238	804-484-7700	
Web: performancefoodservice.com					
Perishable Distributors of Iowa Ltd 2741 SE PDI Pl	Ankeny	IA	50021	515-965-6300	965-1105
Web: www.contactpdi.com					
Piggly Wiggly Alabama Distributing Co Inc 2400 JT Wooten Dr	Bessemer	AL	35020	205-481-2300	481-2383
Web: www.pwadc.com					
Piggly Wiggly Carolina Co Inc PO Box 118047	Charleston	SC	29423	843-554-9880	745-2730
TF: 800-243-9880 ■ *Web:* www.thepig.net					
Pocahontas Foods USA Inc PO Box 9729	Richmond	VA	23228	804-262-8614	261-4394
Purity Wholesale Grocers Inc 5400 Broken Sound Blvd NW Suite 100	Boca Raton	FL	33487	561-994-9360	994-9629
TF: 800-323-6838 ■ *Web:* www.pwg-inc.com					
Robin's Food Distribution Inc PO Box 617637	Chicago	IL	60661	312-243-8800	243-9495
Web: www.robinsfoods.com					
Roundy's Inc 875 E Wisconsin Ave	Milwaukee	WI	53202	414-231-5000	231-7939
Web: www.roundys.com					
S Abraham & Sons Inc PO Box 1768	Grand Rapids	MI	49501	616-453-6358	453-9309
TF: 877-477-5455 ■ *Web:* www.sasinc.com					
Schiff's Restaurant Service Inc 3410 N Main Ave	Scranton	PA	18508	570-343-1294	969-6255
Web: www.myschiffs.com					
Shaheen Bros Inc PO Box 897	Amesbury	MA	01913	978-688-1844	388-6617
Web: www.shaheenbros.com					
Shamrock Foods Co Inc 2540 N 29th Ave	Phoenix	AZ	85009	602-233-6400	477-6469
TF: 800-289-3663 ■ *Web:* www.shamrockfoods.com					
Southco Distributing Co 2201 S John St	Goldsboro	NC	27530	919-735-8012	735-0097
TF: 800-969-3172 ■ *Web:* www.southcodistributing.com					
Spartan Stores Inc 850 76th St SW PO Box 8700	Grand Rapids	MI	49518	616-878-2000	
NASDAQ: SPTN ■ *TF:* 800-343-4422 ■ *Web:* www.spartanstores.com					

Company / Address	City	State	Zip	Phone	Fax
Specialty Brands Of America Inc					
1400 Old Country Rd	Westbury	NY	11590	516-997-6969	997-0778
TF: 877-652-2797 ■ *Web:* www.sbamerica.com					
Super Store Industries					
16888 McKinley Ave PO Box 549	Lathrop	CA	95330	209-858-2010	858-5674
SUPERVALU Inc 7075 Flying Cloud Dr	Eden Prairie	MN	55344	952-828-4000	828-8998
NYSE: SVU ■ *TF Cust Svc:* 888-256-2800 ■ *Web:* www.supervalu.com					
SUPERVALU International 495 E 19th St	Tacoma	WA	98421	253-593-3198	593-7828
TF: 877-787-8254 ■ *Web:* www.supervaluinternational.com					
SYGMA Network Inc 2000 Westbelt Dr	Columbus	OH	43228	614-771-3801	771-3830
TF: 800-347-7344 ■ *Web:* www.sygmanetwork.com					
SYSCO Corp 1390 Enclave Pkwy	Houston	TX	77077	281-584-1390	584-2721*
NYSE: SYY ■ **Fax:* PR ■ *Web:* www.sysco.com					
Sysco Denver Inc 5000 Beeler St	Denver	CO	80238	303-585-2000	
TF: 800-366-6696 ■ *Web:* www.syscodenver.com					
Sysco Food Services Of Idaho Inc					
5710 Pan Am Ave	Boise	ID	83716	208-345-9500	387-2598
TF: 800-747-9726 ■ *Web:* www.syscoidaho.com					
Sysco Food Services of Metro New York LLC					
20 Theodore Conrad Dr	Jersey City	NJ	07305	201-433-2000	433-1338
Web: www.syscometrony.com					
Sysco Foodservice 21 Four Seasons Dr	Etobicoke	ON	M9B6J8	416-234-2668	234-2650
Web: www.sysco.ca					
Sysco Hampton Roads Inc					
7000 Harbour View Blvd	Suffolk	VA	23435	757-673-4000	673-4148
TF: 800-234-2451 ■ *Web:* www.syscohamptonroads.com					
Thomas & Howard Wholesale Grocers Inc					
209 Flintlake Rd PO Box 23659	Columbia	SC	29223	803-788-5520	699-9097
TF: 800-251-1383 ■ *Web:* www.tohoco.com					
Thoms Proestler Co 8001 TPC Rd	Rock Island	IL	61204	309-787-1234	787-1254
TF: 800-747-1234 ■ *Web:* www.performancefoodservice.com					
Topco Assoc LLC 7711 Gross Pt Rd	Skokie	IL	60077	847-676-3030	676-4949
TF: 888-423-0139 ■ *Web:* www.topco.com					
Tripifoods Inc 1427 William St	Buffalo	NY	14206	716-853-7400	852-7400
TF: 800-851-7400 ■ *Web:* www.tripifoods.com					
Unified Grocers Inc 5200 Sheila St	Commerce	CA	90040	323-264-5200	265-4006
TF: 800-724-7762 ■ *Web:* www.unifiedgrocers.com					
UniPro Foodservice Inc					
2500 Cumberland Pkwy Suite 600	Atlanta	GA	30339	770-952-0871	952-0872
TF: 800-366-7723 ■ *Web:* www.uniprofoodservice.com					
United Natural Foods Inc (UNFI)					
313 Iron Horse Way	Providence	RI	02908	401-528-8634	
NASDAQ: UNFI ■ *Web:* www.unfi.com					
Vend Mart Inc 1950 Williams St	San Leandro	CA	94577	510-297-5132	352-8363
Web: www.vendmart.com					
Vistar/VSA Corp 12650 E Arapahoe Rd Bldg D	Centennial	CO	80112	303-662-7234	662-7570
TF: 800-880-9900 ■ *Web:* www.vistar.com					
W L Halsey Grocery Co Inc PO Box 6485	Huntsville	AL	35824	256-772-9691	461-8386
TF: 800-621-0240 ■ *Web:* www.halseyfoodservice.com					
Wakefern Food Corp 600 York St	Elizabeth	NJ	07207	908-527-3300	527-3397
TF: 800-746-7748 ■ *Web:* www.shoprite.com					
Western Family Foods Inc 6700 SW Sandburg St	Tigard	OR	97223	503-639-6300	684-3469
Web: www.westernfamily.com					
Winkler Inc 535 E Medcalf St	Dale	IN	47523	812-937-4421	937-2044
TF: 800-621-3843 ■ *Web:* www.winklerinc.com					
Wood-Fruitticher Grocery Co Inc					
2900 Alton Rd	Birmingham	AL	35210	205-836-9663	836-9681
TF: 800-489-4500 ■ *Web:* www.woodfruitticher.com					

300-9 Meats & Meat Products - Whol

Company / Address	City	State	Zip	Phone	Fax
Agar Supply Co Inc 225 John Hancock Rd	Taunton	MA	02780	508-821-2060	880-5113*
**Fax Area Code:* 617 ■ **Fax:* Sales ■ *TF:* 800-669-6040 ■ *Web:* www.agarsupply.com					
Amigos Meat Distributors-East LP					
611 Crosstimber	Houston	TX	77022	713-928-3111	694-0610
Web: www.amigosfoods.biz					
Aurora Packing Co Inc 125 S Grant St	North Aurora	IL	60542	630-897-0551	897-0647
Auth Bros Inc 1905 Clarkson Way	Landover	MD	20785	301-322-8400	322-3185
TF: 800-424-2610					
Bruss Co 3548 N Kostner Ave	Chicago	IL	60641	773-282-2900	282-6966
TF: 800-621-3882					
Calumet Diversified Meats Inc					
10000 80th Ave	Pleasant Prairie	WI	53158	262-947-7200	947-7209
TF: 800-752-7427 ■ *Web:* www.porkchops.com					
Cambridge Packing Co Inc 41 Food Mart Rd	Boston	MA	02118	617-269-6700	269-9390
TF: 800-722-6726 ■ *Web:* www.cambridgepacking.com					
Colorado Boxed Beef Co PO Box 899	Winter Haven	FL	33882	863-967-0636	965-2222
TF: 800-955-0636 ■ *Web:* www.coloradoboxedbeef.com					
ConAgra Foods Foodservice Co 1 ConAgra Dr	Omaha	NE	68102	402-595-4000	
Web: www.conagrafoodservice.com					
Cusack Wholesale Meat Inc					
301 SW 12th St	Oklahoma City	OK	73109	405-232-2114	232-2127
TF: 800-241-6328 ■ *Web:* www.cusackmeats.com					
Cypress Food Distributors Inc					
3111 N University Dr Suite 612	Coral Springs	FL	33065	954-344-2900	344-3607
Web: www.cypressfood.com					
Dairyland Corp 1300 Viele Ave	Bronx	NY	10474	718-842-8700	378-2234
Web: www.dairylandonline.com					
Day-Lee Foods Inc 13055 Molette St	Santa Fe Springs	CA	90670	562-802-6800	926-0646
Web: www.day-lee.com					
Deen Wholesale Meats 813 E Northside Dr	Fort Worth	TX	76102	817-335-2257	338-9256
TF: 800-333-3953 ■ *Web:* www.deenmeat.com					
Ditta Meat Co PO Box 5623	Pasadena	TX	77508	281-487-2010	
Web: www.dittameat.com					
Durham Meat Co 2026 Martin Ave	Santa Clara	CA	95050	800-444-5687	748-1267*
**Fax Area Code:* 408 ■ *TF:* 800-233-8742					
Empire Packing Co LP PO Box 13408	Memphis	TN	38113	901-948-4788	948-4713
Web: www.ledbetterfoods.com					
Freedman Food Service of San Antonio					
4241 Director Dr	San Antonio	TX	78219	210-337-1011	333-9410
TF: 800-552-3234 ■ *Web:* www.freedmanfoods.com					
Green Tree Packing Co 65 Central Ave	Passaic	NJ	07055	973-473-1305	473-7975
TF: 800-221-5754					
Heartland Meat Co Inc 3461 Main St	Chula Vista	CA	91911	619-407-3668	407-3678
TF: 888-407-3668 ■ *Web:* www.heartlandmeat.com					
Holten Meat Inc 1682 Sauget Business Blvd	Sauget	IL	62206	618-337-8400	337-3292
TF: 800-851-4684 ■ *Web:* www.holtenmeat.com					
Jensen Meat Co Inc 2525 Birch St	Vista	CA	92081	760-727-6700	727-8598
Web: www.jensenmeat.com					
Keystone Foods LLC					
300 Bar Harbor Dr					
Suite 600, 5 Tower Bridge	West Conshohocken	PA	19428	610-667-6700	667-1460
Web: www.keystonefoods.com					
Manda Fine Meats 2445 Sorrel Ave	Baton Rouge	LA	70802	225-344-7636	344-7647
TF: 800-343-2642 ■ *Web:* www.mandafinemeats.com					
Maryland Quality Meats Inc					
701 W Hamburg St	Baltimore	MD	21230	410-539-7055	685-6720
TF: 800-368-2579 ■ *Web:* www.mqm.biz					
Merchants Export Inc					
200 Dr Maritn Luther King Blvd	West Palm Beach	FL	33404	561-844-7000	844-0071
Web: www.merchantexport.com					
Michael's Finer Meats & Seafoods					
3775 Zane Trace Dr	Columbus	OH	43228	614-527-4900	527-4520
TF: 800-282-0518 ■ *Web:* www.michaelsmeats.com					
Midamar Corp PO Box 218	Cedar Rapids	IA	52406	319-362-3711	362-4111
TF: 800-362-3711 ■ *Web:* www.midamar.com					
Northwestern Meat Inc 2100 NW 23rd St	Miami	FL	33142	305-633-8112	633-6907
Web: www.numeat.com					
Orrell's Food Service 9827 S NC Hwy 150	Linwood	NC	27299	336-752-2114	752-2060
Web: www.orrellsfoodservice.com					
Paper Pak Industries (PPI) 1941 N White Ave	La Verne	CA	91750	909-392-1750	392-1760
TF: 888-293-6529 ■ *Web:* www.paperpakindustries.com					
Porky Products Corp 400 Port Carteret Dr	Carteret	NJ	07008	732-541-0200	969-6043
TF: 800-952-0265 ■ *Web:* www.porkyproducts.com					
Pucci Foods 25447 Industrial Blvd	Hayward	CA	94545	510-300-6800	300-6805
Web: www.puccifoods.com					
Quality Meats & Seafoods 700 Ctr St	West Fargo	ND	58078	701-282-0202	282-0583
TF: 800-959-4250 ■ *Web:* www.qualitymeats.com					
Quirch Foods Co 7600 NW 82nd Pl	Miami	FL	33166	305-691-3535	593-0272
TF: 800-458-5252 ■ *Web:* www.quirchfoods.com					
Sampco Inc 651 W Washington Blvd Suite 300	Chicago	IL	60661	312-346-1506	346-8302
TF: 800-767-0689					
Scavuzzo's Inc 2840 Gwinnot St	Kansas City	MO	64120	816-231-1517	231-1590
TF: 800-800-4707 ■ *Web:* www.Scavuzzo"s.com					
Schisa Bros Inc PO Box 3350	Syracuse	NY	13220	315-463-0213	463-0248
TF: 800-676-3287					
Sherwood Food Distributors					
18615 Sherwood Ave	Detroit	MI	48234	313-659-7300	366-8825
Southern Foods Inc					
3500 Old Battleground Rd	Greensboro	NC	27410	336-545-3800	545-3822
TF: 800-441-3663 ■ *Web:* www.southernfoods.com					
Tapia Bros Co 6067 District Blvd	Maywood	CA	90270	323-560-7415	560-8924
Web: www.tapiabrothers.com					
Thumann Inc 670 Dell Rd	Carlstadt	NJ	07072	201-935-3636	935-2226
Web: www.thumanns.com					
Tri-City Meats Inc 1346 N Hickory Ave	Meridian	ID	83642	208-884-2600	884-2601
TF: 800-955-6423 ■ *Web:* www.tricitymeats.com					
Trim-Rite Food Corp					
801 Commerce Pkwy	Carpentersville	IL	60110	847-649-3400	649-3420
TF: 800-626-9442 ■ *Web:* www.trim-rite.com					
Troyer Foods Inc 17141 State Rd 4	Goshen	IN	46528	574-533-0302	533-3851
TF: 800-876-9377 ■ *Web:* www.troyers.com					
U W Provision Co Inc PO Box 620038	Middleton	WI	53562	608-836-7421	836-6328
TF: 800-832-0517 ■ *Web:* www.uwprovision.com					
Williams Sausage Co Inc					
5132 Old Troy Hickman Rd	Union City	TN	38261	731-885-5841	885-5884
TF: 800-844-4242 ■ *Web:* www.williams-sausage.com					

300-10 Poultry, Eggs, Poultry Products - Whol

Company / Address	City	State	Zip	Phone	Fax
Acme Farms Inc PO Box 3065	Seattle	WA	98114	206-323-4300	323-3900
TF: 800-542-8309					
Agar Supply Co Inc 225 John Hancock Rd	Taunton	MA	02780	508-821-2060	880-5113*
**Fax Area Code:* 617 ■ **Fax:* Sales ■ *TF:* 800-669-6040 ■ *Web:* www.agarsupply.com					
Butts Foods Inc 432 N Royal St PO Box 2466	Jackson	TN	38301	731-423-3456	423-4566
TF: 800-962-8570 ■ *Web:* www.buttsfoods.com					
Chino Valley Ranchers 5611 Peck Rd	Arcadia	CA	91006	626-652-0890	652-0893
TF: 800-354-4503 ■ *Web:* www.chinovalleyranchers.com					
Consolidated Poultry & Egg Co PO Box 11958	Memphis	TN	38111	901-322-6466	324-7283
Crystal Farms Refrigerated Distribution Co					
6465 Wayzata Blvd Suite 200	Minneapolis	MN	55426	952-544-8101	544-8069
TF: 877-279-7825 ■ *Web:* www.crystalfarms.com					
Dutt & Wagner of Virginia Inc					
1142 W Main St	Abingdon	VA	24210	276-628-2116	628-4619
TF: 800-688-2116					
Harker's Distribution Inc 801 6th St SW	Le Mars	IA	51031	712-546-8171	546-3109*
**Fax:* Sales ■ *TF:* 800-798-9800 ■ *Web:* www.harkers.com					
Hemmelgarn & Sons Inc 3763 Philothea Rd	Coldwater	OH	45828	419-678-2351	678-4922
House of Raeford Farms Inc 520 E Central Ave	Raeford	NC	28376	910-875-5161	875-8300
TF: 800-888-7539 ■ *Web:* www.houseofraeford.com					
Lincoln Poultry & Egg Co 800 Cattail Rd	Lincoln	NE	68521	402-477-3757	477-1800
TF: 800-477-4433 ■ *Web:* www.lincolnpoultry.com					
Metropolitan Poultry & Seafood Co					
1920 Stanford Ct	Landover	MD	20785	301-772-0060	772-1013
TF: 800-522-0060 ■ *Web:* www.metropoultry.com					
Norbest Inc 6875 S 900 E	Midvale	UT	84047	801-566-5656	255-2309
TF: 800-453-5327					

Company	City	State	ZIP	Phone	Fax
Nulaid Foods Inc 200 W 5th St *TF:* 800-788-8871 ■ *Web:* www.nulaid.com	Ripon	CA	95366	209-599-2121	599-5220
Petaluma Poultry Inc PO Box 7368 *TF:* 800-556-6789 ■ *Web:* www.petalumapoultry.com	Petaluma	CA	94955	707-763-1904	763-3924
Quirch Foods Co 7600 NW 82nd Pl *TF:* 800-458-5252 ■ *Web:* www.quirchfoods.com	Miami	FL	33166	305-691-3535	593-0272
RW Sauder Inc 570 Furnace Hills Pike *Web:* www.sauderegs.com	Lititz	PA	17543	717-626-2074	626-0493
Troyer Foods Inc 17141 State Rd 4 *TF:* 800-876-9377 ■ *Web:* www.troyers.com	Goshen	IN	46528	574-533-0302	533-3851
Will Poultry Co Inc PO Box 1146 *Web:* www.willpoultry.com	Buffalo	NY	14240	716-853-2000	853-2011
Zacky Farms 13200 Crossroads Pkwy N Suite 250 *TF:* 800-888-0235 ■ *Web:* www.zacky.com	City of Industry	CA	91746	562-641-2020	641-2040

300-11 Specialty Foods - Whol

Company	City	State	ZIP	Phone	Fax
Alamo Distributors Inc PO Box 11946 *Web:* www.ablesales.com	San Juan	PR	00922	787-620-4141	620-4101
Camerican International Inc 45 Eisenhower Dr	Paramus	NJ	07652	201-587-0101	587-2043*
Charles C. Parks Co 500 Belvedere Dr *TF:* 800-873-2406 ■ *Web:* www.charlescparks.com	Gallatin	TN	37066	615-452-2406	451-4212
ConAgra Foods Foodservice Co 1 ConAgra Dr *Web:* www.conagrafoodservice.com	Omaha	NE	68102	402-595-4000	
Condal Distributors 531 Dupont St *Web:* www.condalfoods.com	Bronx	NY	10474	718-589-1100	589-9200
Connell Rice & Sugar Co Inc 200 Connell Dr *Web:* www.connellco.com/CRISU.htm	Berkeley Heights	NJ	07922	908-673-3700	673-3800
Conway Import Co Inc 11051 W Addison St *TF:* 800-323-8801	Franklin Park	IL	60131	847-455-5600	455-5630
Crs Onesource 2803 Tamarack Rd PO Box 1984 *TF:* 800-264-0710 ■ *Web:* www.crsonesource.com	Owensboro	KY	42302	270-684-1469	685-5696
Diaz Wholesale & Mfg Co Inc 5501 Fulton Industrial Blvd *TF:* 800-394-4639 ■ *Web:* www.diazfoods.com	Atlanta	GA	30336	404-344-5421	344-3003
Ellis Coffee Co 2835 Bridge St *TF:* 800-822-3984 ■ *Web:* www.elliscoffee.com	Philadelphia	PA	19137	215-537-9500	535-5311
Essex Grain Products 9 Lee Blvd *TF:* 800-441-1017 ■ *Web:* www.essexgrain.com	Frazer	PA	19355	610-647-3800	647-4990
Garden Spot Distributors Inc 191 Commerce Dr *Fax Area Code: 877 ■ *Web:* www.gardenspotdist.com	New Holland	PA	17557	717-354-4936	829-5100*
Ginsburg Bakery Inc 300 N Tennessee Ave *Web:* www.ginsburgbakery.com	Atlantic City	NJ	08401	609-345-2265	345-2268
Gregory's Foods Inc 1301 Trapp Rd *Fax Area Code: 651 ■ *TF:* 800-231-4734 ■ *Web:* www.gregorysfoods.com	Eagan	MN	55121	800-231-4734	454-2254*
Hain Celestial Group Inc 58 S Service Rd Suite 250 *NASDAQ: HAIN* ■ *TF:* 800-434-4246 ■ *Web:* www.hain-celestial.com	Melville	NY	01747	631-730-2200	730-2550
Harlan Bakeries-Avon LLC 7597 E US Hwy 36 *Web:* www.harlanbakeries.com	Avon	IN	46123	317-272-3600	272-1110
I & K Distributors Inc 1600 Gressel Dr *TF:* 800-472-9920 ■ *Web:* www.ikdist.com	Delphos	OH	45833	419-695-5015	695-7585
Indiana Sugars Inc 911 Virginia St *TF:* 800-333-9666 ■ *Web:* www.sugars.com	Gary	IN	46402	219-886-9151	886-5124
Industrial Commodities Inc PO Box 4380 *Web:* www.industrialcommodities.com	Glen Allen	VA	23058	804-935-1700	935-1760
J Sosnick & Sons Inc 258 Littlefield Ave *TF:* 800-443-6737 ■ *Web:* www.sosnick.com	South San Francisco	CA	94080	650-952-2226	952-2439
JFC International Inc 540 Forbes Blvd *TF:* 800-633-1004 ■ *Web:* www.jfc.com	South San Francisco	CA	94080	650-873-8400	952-3272
Joffrey's Coffee & Tea Co 3803 Corporex Pk Dr *TF:* 800-458-5282 ■ *Web:* www.joffreys.com	Tampa	FL	33619	813-250-0404	250-0303
John E Koerner & Co Inc PO Box 10218 *TF:* 800-333-1913 ■ *Web:* www.koerner-co.com	New Orleans	LA	70181	504-734-1100	734-0630
King Milling Co 115 S Broadway St *Web:* www.kingmilling.com	Lowell	MI	49331	616-897-9264	897-4350
Lecoq Cuisine Corp 35 Union Ave *Web:* www.lecoqcuisine.com	Bridgeport	CT	06607	203-334-1010	334-1800
Liberty Richter Inc 300 Broadacres Dr *Web:* www.libertyrichter.com	Bloomfield	NJ	07003	973-338-0300	338-0382
Lomar Distributing 2500 Dixon St *TF:* 800-369-3663	Des Moines	IA	50316	515-244-3105	244-0515
Losurdo Foods Inc 20 Owens Rd *TF:* 888-567-8736 ■ *Web:* www.losurdofoods.com	Hackensack	NJ	07601	201-343-6680	343-8078
Love & Quiches Desserts 178 Hanse Ave *TF:* 800-525-5251 ■ *Web:* www.loveandquiches.com	Freeport	NY	11520	516-623-8800	623-8817
Mitsui Foods Inc 35 Maple St *TF:* 800-777-2322 ■ *Web:* www.mitsui-foods.com	Norwood	NJ	07648	201-750-0500	750-0150
Morris J Golombeck Inc 960 Franklin Ave *Web:* www.golombeckspice.com	Brooklyn	NY	11225	718-284-3505	693-1941
Mutual Trading Co Ltd 431 Crocker St *Web:* www.lamtc.com	Los Angeles	CA	90013	213-626-9458	626-5130
Nantze Springs Inc 156 W Carroll St PO Box 1273 *TF:* 800-239-7873 ■ *Web:* www.nantzesprings.com	Dothan	AL	36301	334-794-4218	
Neiman Bros Co Inc 3322 W Newport Ave *Web:* www.neimanbrothers.com	Chicago	IL	60618	773-463-3000	463-3181
O S F Flavors Inc 40 Baker Hollow Rd *TF:* 800-466-6015 ■ *Web:* www.osfflavors.com	Windsor	CT	06095	860-298-8350	298-8363
Otis McAllister Inc 160 Pine St Suite 350 *Web:* www.otismac.com	San Francisco	CA	94111	415-421-6010	421-6016
Otto Brehm Inc PO Box 249 *TF:* 800-272-6886 ■ *Web:* www.ottobrehm.com	Yonkers	NY	10710	914-968-6100	968-8926
Pacific Spice Co Inc 6430 E Slauson Ave *TF:* 800-281-0614 ■ *Web:* www.pacspice.com	Los Angeles	CA	90040	323-726-9190	726-9442
Pbm Holdings Inc 204 N Main St *Web:* www.pbmproducts.com	Gordonsville	VA	22942	540-832-3282	832-3522
Pharmline Inc PO Box 291 *Web:* www.pharmlineinc.com	Florida	NY	10921	845-651-4443	651-6900
Pocono Produce Co Inc Rte 191 & Chipperfield Dr *TF:* 800-366-4550 ■ *Web:* www.poconoproduce.com	Stroudsburg	PA	18360	570-421-4990	424-5271
Producers Rice Mill Inc 518 E Harrison St *Web:* www.producersrice.com	Stuttgart	AR	72160	870-673-4444	673-8131
Rain Creek Baking Co The 2401 W Almond Ave *TF:* 800-530-0505 ■ *Web:* www.raincreekbaking.com	Madera	CA	93637	559-674-4445	674-4466
ReNew Life Formulas Inc 2076 Sunnydale Blvd *Fax Area Code: 866 ■ *TF:* 800-830-1800 ■ *Web:* www.renewlife.com	Clearwater	FL	33765	727-450-1061	594-5468*
Riceland Foods Inc 2120 S Pk Ave *TF Cust Svc:* 800-264-1283 ■ *Web:* www.riceland.com	Stuttgart	AR	72160	870-673-5500	673-3366
Ron-Son Foods Inc PO Box 38 *Web:* www.ronsonfoods.com	Swedesboro	NJ	08085	856-241-7333	241-7338
Roxy Trading Inc 389 Humane Way *Web:* www.roxytrading.com	Pomona	CA	91768	626-610-1388	610-1339
Royal Pacific Tea Co Inc The PO Box 6277 *Web:* www.royalpacificintl.com	Scottsdale	AZ	85261	480-951-8251	951-0092
Schreiber Foods International Inc PO Box 299 *TF:* 800-631-7070 ■ *Web:* www.ambrosia-foods.com	Ramsey	NJ	07446	201-327-3535	327-2812
Setton Pistachio of Terra Bella Inc 9370 Rd 234 PO Box 11089 *Web:* www.settonfarms.com	Terra Bella	CA	93270	559-535-6050	535-6089
Shonfeld's USA Inc 3100 S Susan St *TF:* 877-447-8933 ■ *Web:* www.shonfelds.com	Santa Ana	CA	92704	714-429-1922	429-7971
Silver Springs Bottled Water Co Inc PO Box 926 *TF:* 800-556-0334 ■ *Web:* www.ssbwc.com	Silver Springs	FL	34489	352-368-6806	368-2374
Sk Food International Inc 4666 Amber Valley Pkwy *Web:* www.skfood.com	Fargo	ND	58104	701-356-4106	356-4102
Specialty Baking Co 1365 N 10th St *Web:* www.specialtybaking.com	San Jose	CA	95112	408-298-6914	298-6950
Sturm Foods Inc PO Box 287 *TF:* 800-347-8876 ■ *Web:* www.sturmfoods.com	Manawa	WI	54949	920-596-2511	596-3040
Sugar Foods Corp 950 3rd Ave 21st Fl *TF:* 800-732-8963 ■ *Web:* www.sugarfoods.com	New York	NY	10022	212-753-6900	753-6988
Sunsweet Growers Inc 901 N Walton Ave *TF:* 800-417-2253 ■ *Web:* www.sunsweet.com	Yuba City	CA	95993	530-674-5010	751-5238
Syrian Bakery & Grocery Inc 5400 W 35th St *Web:* www.ziyad.com	Cicero	IL	60804	708-222-8330	222-1442
SYSCO Food Services of Cleveland Inc 4747 Grayton Rd *TF:* 800-584-4580 ■ *Web:* www.syscocleveland.com	Cleveland	OH	44135	216-201-3100	201-3511
Sysco Indianapolis LLC 4000 W 62nd St *TF:* 800-347-3920 ■ *Web:* www.syscoindy.com	Indianapolis	IN	46268	317-291-2020	216-9346
SYSCO Philadelphia LLC 600 Packer Ave PO Box 6499 *Web:* www.syscophilly.com/ordereze/1000/Page.aspx	Philadelphia	PA	19145	215-463-8200	463-1618
T. J. Harkins Co 279 Beaudin Blvd *Fax Area Code: 603 ■ *TF:* 800-527-5552 ■ *Web:* www.tjharkins.com	Bolingbrook	IL	60440	630-427-3400	783-1806*
United Sugars Corp 7401 Metro Blvd Suite 350 *Web:* www.unitedsugars.com	Edina	MN	55439	952-896-0131	
Westway Trading Corp 365 Canal St Suite 2900 *Web:* www.westwaytrading.com	New Orleans	LA	70130	504-525-9741	522-1638
Wildflower Bread Co 7755 E Gray Rd Suite 101 *Web:* www.wildflowerbread.com	Scottsdale	AZ	85260	480-951-9453	951-9464
William George Co Inc 1002 Mize Ave PO Box 1387 *Web:* www.wmgeorgeco.com	Lufkin	TX	75904	936-634-7738	634-7872
Woodland Foods Inc 3751 Sunset Ave *Web:* www.woodlandfoods.com	Waukegan	IL	60087	847-625-8600	625-5050
Yamamoto of Orient Inc 122 Voyager St *Web:* www.yamamotoyama.com	Pomona	CA	91768	909-594-7356	595-5849

301 FOOD PRODUCTS MACHINERY

SEE ALSO Food Service Equipment & Supplies p. 1876

Company	City	State	ZIP	Phone	Fax
Abec Inc 3998 Schelden Cir *TF:* 800-736-3677 ■ *Web:* www.abec.com	Bethlehem	PA	18017	610-861-4666	861-2636
Acme Pizza & Bakery Equipment Inc 7039 E Slauson Ave *TF:* 800-428-2263 ■ *Web:* www.acmepbe.com	Commerce	CA	90040	323-722-7900	726-4700
Adamatic Corp 607 Industrial Way W *TF:* 800-526-2807 ■ *Web:* www.adamatic.com	Eatontown	NJ	07724	732-544-8400	544-0735
Alto-Shaam Inc W 164 N 9221 Water St PO Box 450 *TF:* 800-329-8744 ■ *Web:* www.alto-shaam.com	Menomonee Falls	WI	53052	262-251-3800	251-7067
American Permanent Ware Inc 729 3rd Ave *TF:* 800-527-2100 ■ *Web:* www.apwwyott.com	Dallas	TX	75226	214-421-7366	565-0976
Anderson International Corp 6200 Harvard Ave *TF:* 800-336-4730 ■ *Web:* www.andersonintl.net	Cleveland	OH	44105	216-641-1112	641-0709
Anetsberger Bros Inc 1052 Briarwood Ln *TF:* 800-837-2638 ■ *Web:* www.anetsberger.com	Northbrook	IL	60062	847-272-0770	272-1095
APV Canada Inc 3280 Langstaff Rd *TF:* 800-263-3958	Concord	ON	L4K4Z8	905-760-1852	760-1865
Atlas Metal Industries 1135 NW 159th Dr *TF Cust Svc:* 800-762-7565 ■ *Web:* www.atlasfoodserv.com	Miami	FL	33169	305-625-2451	623-0475

Phone | Fax

Atlas Pacific Engineering Co 1 Atlas Ave . . . . Pueblo CO 81001 719-948-3040 948-3058
TF: 800-227-0682 ■ *Web:* www.atlaspacific.com
Baader-Johnson 2955 Fairfax Trafficway. . . . . Kansas City KS 66115 913-621-3366 621-1729
TF: 800-288-3434 ■ *Web:* www.baader-johnson.com
Baker Perkins Inc 3223 Kraft Ave SE . . . . Grand Rapids MI 49512 616-784-3111 784-0973
Web: www.bakerperkinsgroup.com
Belshaw Bros Inc 1750 22nd Ave S . . . . Seattle WA 98144 206-322-5474 322-5425
TF: 800-578-2547 ■ *Web:* www.belshaw.com
Bepex International LLC 333 Taft St NE . . . . Minneapolis MN 55413 612-331-4370 627-1444
Web: www.bepex.com
Bettcher Industries Inc PO Box 336 . . . . Vermilion OH 44089 440-965-4422 967-6166
TF: 800-321-8763 ■ *Web:* www.bettcher.com
BIRO Mfg Co 1114 W Main St . . . . Marblehead OH 43440 419-798-4451 798-9106
Web: www.birosaw.com
Blakeslee Inc 1228 capital Drve . . . . Addison IL 60101 708-656-0660 532-5020*
**Fax Area Code:* 630 ■ *TF Cust Svc:* 888-656-0660 ■ *Web:* www.blakesleeinc.com
Brewmatic Co
20333 S Normandie Ave PO Box 2959 . . . . Torrance CA 90509 310-787-5444 787-5412
TF: 800-421-6860 ■ *Web:* www.brewmatic.com
C Cretors & Co 3243 N California Ave. . . . . Chicago IL 60618 773-588-1690 588-7141
TF: 800-228-1885 ■ *Web:* www.cretors.com
Carlisle Cos Inc
13925 Ballantyne Corporate Pl Suite 400. . . . . Charlotte NC 28277 704-501-1100 501-1190
NYSE: CSL ■ *Web:* www.carlisle.com
Carpigiani USA 3760 Industrial Dr. . . . . Winston-Salem NC 27115 336-661-9883 661-9883
TF: 800-648-4889 ■ *Web:* www.carpigiani.com
Carrier Commercial Refrigeration Inc
9300 Harris Corners Pkwy Suite 200 . . . . Charlotte NC 28269 704-494-2600 494-2558
Web: www.ccr.carrier.com
Casa Herrerra Inc 2655 N Pine St . . . . Pomona CA 91767 909-392-3930 392-0231
TF: 800-624-3916 ■ *Web:* www.casaherrera.com
CE Rogers Co 1895 Frontage Rd . . . . Mora MN 55051 320-679-2172 679-2180
TF: 800-279-8081 ■ *Web:* www.cerogers.com
Chester-Jensen Co Inc PO Box 908 . . . . Chester PA 19016 610-876-6276 876-0485
TF: 800-685-3750 ■ *Web:* www.chester-jensen.com
Cleveland Range Co 1333 E 179th St . . . . Cleveland OH 44110 216-481-4900 481-3782
TF: 800-338-2204 ■ *Web:* www.clevelandrange.com
Colborne Corp 28495 N Ballard Dr . . . . Lake Forest IL 60045 847-371-0101 371-0101
TF: 800-279-1879 ■ *Web:* www.colbornefoodbotics.com
CPM Wolverine Proctor LLC 251 Gibraltar Rd . . . . Horsham PA 19044 215-443-5200 443-5206
Web: www.cpm.net
Crown Iron Works Co The PO Box 1364 . . . . Minneapolis MN 55440 651-639-8900 639-8051
TF: 888-703-7500 ■ *Web:* www.crowniron.com
Delfield Co 980 S Isabella Rd. . . . . Mount Pleasant MI 48858 989-773-7981 773-3210
TF: 800-733-8821 ■ *Web:* www.delfield.com
Duke Mfg Co 2305 N Broadway . . . . Saint Louis MO 63102 314-231-1130 231-5074
TF: 800-735-3853 ■ *Web:* www.dukemfg.com
Dunkley International Inc 1910 Lake St. . . . . Kalamazoo MI 49001 269-343-5583 343-5614
TF: 800-666-1264 ■ *Web:* www.dunkleyintl.com
Dupps Co 548 N Cherry St . . . . Germantown OH 45327 937-855-6555 855-6554
Web: www.dupps.com
Edlund Co Inc 159 Industrial Pkwy . . . . Burlington VT 05401 802-862-9661 862-4822
TF: 800-772-2126 ■ *Web:* www.edlundco.com
Evergreen Packaging Equipment
2400 6th St SW . . . . Cedar Rapids IA 52406 319-399-3200 399-3543
Web: www.evergreenpackaging.com
Fedco Systems Co Super Grain Div
500 Vandenmark Rd PO Box 769 . . . . Sidney OH 45365 937-492-4158 492-3688
TF: 800-999-3327 ■ *Web:* www.fedcosystems.com
Feldmeier Equipment Inc
6800 Townline Rd PO Box 474. . . . . Syracuse NY 13211 315-454-8608 454-3701
Web: www.feldmeier.com
Fish Oven & Equipment Corp 120 W Kemp Ave. . . . . . . Wauconda IL 60084 847-526-8686 526-7447
TF: 877-526-8720 ■ *Web:* www.fishoven.com
Fitzpatrick Co 832 Industrial Dr . . . . Elmhurst IL 60126 630-530-3333 530-0832
Web: www.fitzmill.com
Food Warming Equipment Co Inc
7900 S Rt 31. . . . . Crystal Lake IL 60014 815-459-7500 459-7989
TF Sales: 800-222-4393 ■ *Web:* www.fwe.com
Frymaster LLC 8700 Line Ave . . . . Shreveport LA 71106 318-865-1711 868-5987
TF Cust Svc: 800-221-4583 ■ *Web:* www.frymaster.com
Fulton Iron & Mfg LLC 3844 Walsh St. . . . . Saint Louis MO 63116 314-752-2400 353-2987
Web: www.fultoniron.net
Garland Commercial Industries 185 S St . . . . Freeland PA 18224 570-636-1000 624-0218*
**Fax Area Code:* 800 ■ *TF:* 800-424-2411 ■ *Web:* www.garland-group.com
Gem Equipment of Oregon Inc PO Box 359. . . . . Woodburn OR 97071 503-982-9902 981-6316
Web: www.gemequipment.com
Globe Food Equipment Co 2153 Dryden Rd . . . . Dayton OH 45439 937-299-5493 299-8623
TF: 800-347-5423 ■ *Web:* www.globeslicers.com
Great Western Mfg Co Inc
2017 S 4th St PO Box 149 . . . . Leavenworth KS 66048 913-682-2291 682-1431
TF: 800-682-3121 ■ *Web:* www.gwmfg.com
Grindmaster Crathco Systems Inc
4003 Collins Ln . . . . Louisville KY 40245 502-425-4776 425-4664
TF: 800-695-4500 ■ *Web:* www.grindmaster.com
GS Blodgett Corp 44 Lakeside Ave . . . . Burlington VT 05401 802-658-6600 864-0183
TF: 800-331-5842 ■ *Web:* www.blodgett.com
Hayes & Stolz Industrial Mfg Co
3521 Hemphill St PO Box 11217 . . . . Fort Worth TX 76110 817-926-3391 926-4133
TF: 800-725-7272 ■ *Web:* www.hayes-stolz.com
Heat & Control Inc 21121 Cabot Blvd . . . . Hayward CA 94545 510-259-0500 259-0600
TF: 800-227-5980 ■ *Web:* www.heatandcontrol.com
Henny Penny Corp 1219 US 35 W PO Box 60 . . . . Eaton OH 45320 937-456-8400 417-8402*
**Fax Area Code:* 800 ■ *TF:* 800-417-8417 ■ *Web:* www.hennypenny.com
Hobart Corp 701 S Ridge Ave. . . . . Troy OH 45374 937-332-3000 332-2852
TF Cust Svc: 800-333-7447 ■ *Web:* www.hobartcorp.com
Hollymatic Corp 600 E Plainfield Rd. . . . . Countryside IL 60525 708-579-3700 579-1057
Web: www.hollymatic.com
Horix Mfg Co 1384 Island Ave . . . . McKees Rocks PA 15136 412-771-1111 331-8599
Web: www.horixmfg.com

Phone | Fax

Idaho Steel Products Co
255 E Anderson St . . . . Idaho Falls ID 83401 208-522-1275 522-6041
Web: www.idahosteel.com
Insinger Machine Co 6245 State Rd . . . . Philadelphia PA 19135 215-624-4800 624-6966
ITW Food Equipment Group 701 S Ridge Ave. . . . . Troy OH 45374 937-332-3000 332-2852
TF Cust Svc: 800-333-7447
Jarvis Products Corp 33 Anderson Rd. . . . . Middletown CT 06457 860-347-7271 347-6978
Web: www.jarvisproducts.com
Key Technology Inc 150 Avery St. . . . . Walla Walla WA 99362 509-529-2161 527-1331
NASDAQ: KTEC ■ *Web:* www.keyww.com
Kuhl Corp 39 Kuhl Rd PO Box 26 . . . . Flemington NJ 08822 908-782-5696 782-2751
Web: www.kuhlcorp.com
Kwik Lok Corp 2712 S 16th Ave PO Box 9548 . . . . Yakima WA 98909 509-248-4770 457-6531
TF: 800-688-5945 ■ *Web:* www.kwiklok.com
Lawrence Equipment Inc 2034 Peck Rd. . . . . El Monte CA 91733 626-442-2894 350-5181
TF: 800-423-4500 ■ *Web:* www.lawrenceequipment.com
Lewis M Carter Mfg Co Hwy 84 W . . . . Donalsonville GA 39845 229-524-2197 524-2531
Web: www.lmcarter.com
LK Industries 1357 W Beaver St . . . . Jacksonville FL 32209 904-354-8882 353-1984
TF: 800-531-4975 ■ *Web:* www.loadking.com
Lucks Co The 3003 S Pine St . . . . Tacoma WA 98409 253-383-4815 383-0071*
**Fax:* Orders ■ *TF:* 800-426-9778 ■ *Web:* www.lucks.com
Luker Inc 514 National Ave. . . . . Augusta GA 30901 706-724-0244 724-1050
TF: 800-982-9534 ■ *Web:* www.lukerinc.com
Luthi Machinery Co Inc 1 Magnuson Ave. . . . . Pueblo CO 81003 719-948-1110 948-3058
TF: 800-227-0682 ■ *Web:* www.luthi.com
M-E-C Co 1400 W Main St . . . . Neodesha KS 66757 620-325-2673 325-2678
Web: www.m-e-c.com
Manitowoc Beverage Equipment
2100 Future Dr . . . . Sellersburg IN 47172 812-246-7000 246-9922
TF: 800-367-4233 ■ *Web:* www.manitowocbeverage.com
Manitowoc Co Inc 2400 S 44th St . . . . Manitowoc WI 54220 920-684-4410 652-9778
NYSE: MTW ■ *Web:* www.manitowoc.com
Market Forge Industries Inc 35 Garvey St. . . . . Everett MA 02149 617-387-4100 227-2659*
**Fax Area Code:* 800 ■ *TF:* 866-698-3188 ■ *Web:* www.mfii.com
Marlen International Inc
9202 Barton St . . . . Overland Park KS 66214 800-862-7536 888-6440*
**Fax Area Code:* 913 ■ *TF:* 800-862-7536 ■ *Web:* www.marlen.com
Merco-Savory Inc 1111 N Hadley Rd . . . . Fort Wayne IN 46804 260-459-8200 436-0735
TF Cust Svc: 888-417-5462 ■ *Web:* www.mercoproducts.com
Meyer Machine Co Inc
3528 Fredericksburg Rd PO Box 5460 . . . . San Antonio TX 78201 210-736-1811 736-9452
Web: www.meyer-industries.com
Microfluidics International Corp
30 Ossipee Rd PO Box 9101. . . . . Newton MA 02464 617-969-5452 965-1213
TF: 800-370-5452 ■ *Web:* www.microfluidicscorp.com
Middleby Corp 1400 Toastmaster Dr . . . . Elgin IL 60120 847-741-3300 741-0015
NASDAQ: MIDD ■ *Web:* www.middleby.com
Myers Engineering Inc 8376 Salt Lake Ave . . . . Bell CA 90201 323-560-4723 771-7789
Web: www.myersmixer.com
Nitta Casings Inc
141 Southside Ave PO Box 858 . . . . Somerville NJ 08876 908-218-4400 725-2835
TF Cust Svc: 800-526-3970 ■ *Web:* www.nittacasings.com
Oliver Products Co 445 6th St NW. . . . . Grand Rapids MI 49504 616-456-7711 456-5820
TF: 800-253-3893 ■ *Web:* www.oliverproducts.com
Peerless Machinery Corp
500 S Vandenmark Rd PO Box 769 . . . . Sidney OH 45365 937-492-4158 492-3688
TF: 800-999-3327 ■ *Web:* www.thepeerlessgroup.us
Peters Machinery Inc 500 S Vandemark Rd . . . . Sidney OH 45365 937-492-4158 492-3688
TF: 800-999-3327 ■ *Web:* www.petersmachinery.com
Philadelphia Gear Corp 1221 E Main St . . . . Palmyra PA 17078 717-838-1341 832-1740
TF: 800-956-4937 ■ *Web:* www.philamixers.com
Piper Products Inc 300 S 84th Ave . . . . Wausau WI 54401 715-842-2724 842-3125
TF: 800-544-3057 ■ *Web:* www.piperonline.net
Pitco Frialator Inc PO Box 501 . . . . Concord NH 03302 603-225-6684 225-8472
TF: 800-258-3708 ■ *Web:* www.blodgett.com/pitco_hm.shtml
Planet Products Corp 4200 Malsbary Rd . . . . Cincinnati OH 45242 513-984-5544 984-5580
Web: www.planet-products.com
Prince Castle Inc 355 E Kehoe Blvd. . . . . Carol Stream IL 60188 630-462-8800 462-1460
TF: 800-722-7853 ■ *Web:* www.princecastle.com
Resina West Inc 27455 Bostik Ct . . . . Temecula CA 92590 951-296-6585 296-5018
Web: www.resina.com
RMF Steel Products Co 4417 E 119th St. . . . . Grandview MO 64030 816-765-4101 765-0067
Web: www.rmfsteel.com
Ross Industries Inc 5321 Midland Rd . . . . Midland VA 22728 540-439-3271 439-2740
TF: 800-336-6010 ■ *Web:* www.rossindinc.com
S Howes Co Inc 25 Howard St. . . . . Silver Creek NY 14136 716-934-2611 934-2081
TF: 888-255-2611 ■ *Web:* www.showes.com
SaniServ Inc 451 E County Line Rd. . . . . Mooresville IN 46158 317-831-7030 831-7036
TF: 800-733-8073 ■ *Web:* www.saniserv.com
Schebler Co 5665 Senno Rd PO Box 1008 . . . . Bettendorf IA 52722 563-359-0110 359-8430
Web: www.schebler.com
Schlueter Co 112 E Centerway St . . . . Janesville WI 53545 608-755-5455 755-5440
TF: 800-359-1700
Server Products Inc
3601 Pleasant Hill Rd PO Box 98 . . . . Richfield WI 53076 262-628-5600 628-5110
TF: 800-558-8722 ■ *Web:* www.server-products.com
Sonic Corp 1 Research Dr. . . . . Stratford CT 06615 203-375-0063 378-4079
Web: www.sonicmixing.com
Southbend Co Inc 1100 Old Honeycutt Rd . . . . Fuquay-Varina NC 27526 919-552-9161 552-9798
TF: 800-348-2558 ■ *Web:* www.southbendnc.com
Stoelting LLC 502 Hwy 67 . . . . Kiel WI 53042 920-894-2293 894-7029
TF: 800-558-5807 ■ *Web:* www.stoelting.com
Stolle Machinery Co LLC 6949 S Potomac St. . . . . Centennial CO 80112 303-708-9044 708-9045
TF: 800-228-4593 ■ *Web:* www.stollemachinery.com
Stork Gamco Inc
1024 Airport Pkwy PO Box 1258 . . . . Gainesville GA 30503 770-532-7041 536-0585
Stork Townsend Inc
2425 Hubbell Ave PO Box 1433. . . . . Des Moines IA 50317 515-265-8181 263-3333
TF: 800-247-8609 ■ *Web:* www.townsendeng.com
Taylor 750 N Blackhawk Blvd . . . . Rockton IL 61072 815-624-8333 624-8000
TF: 800-624-8333 ■ *Web:* www.taylor-company.com

	City	State	ZIP	Phone	Fax
Tomlinson Industries					
13700 Broadway Ave	Garfield Heights	OH	44125	216-587-3400	526-9634*
*Fax Area Code: 800 ■ TF: 800-945-4589 ■ Web: www.tomlinsonind.com					
Town Food Service Equipment Co 72 Beadel St	Brooklyn	NY	11222	718-388-5650	388-5860
TF: 800-221-5032 ■ Web: www.townfood.com					
Ultrafryer Systems Inc 302 Spencer Ln	San Antonio	TX	78201	210-731-5000	731-5099
TF: 888-331-5013 ■ Web: www.ultrafryer.com					
Union Standard Equipment Co 801 E 141st St	Bronx	NY	10454	718-585-0200	993-2650
TF: 800-237-8873 ■ Web: www.unionmachinery.com					
United Bakery Equipment Co Inc					
15815 W 110th St	Lenexa	KS	66219	913-541-8700	541-0781
Web: www.ubeusa.com					
Univex Corp 3 Old Rockingham Rd	Salem	NH	03079	603-893-6191	893-1249
TF: 800-258-6358 ■ Web: www.univexcorp.com					
Urschel Laboratories Inc					
2503 Calumet Ave PO Box 2200	Valparaiso	IN	46384	219-464-4811	462-3879
Web: www.urschel.com					
Van Doren Sales Inc 10 NE Cascade Ave	East Wenatchee	WA	98802	509-886-1837	886-2837
Web: www.vandorensales.com					
Vendome Copper & Brass Works Inc					
729 Franklin St	Louisville	KY	40202	502-587-1930	589-0639
Web: www.vendomecopper.com					
Viking Range Corp 111 Front St	Greenwood	MS	38930	662-455-1200	455-3127
Web: www.vikingrange.com					
Volckening Inc 6700 3rd Ave	Brooklyn	NY	11220	718-836-4000	748-2811
TF: 800-221-0876 ■ Web: www.volckening.com					
Walker Stainless Equipment Co LLC					
625 State St	New Lisbon	WI	53950	608-562-3151	562-3142
TF: 800-356-5734 ■ Web: www.walkerstainless.com					
Weiler & Co Inc 1116 E Main St	Whitewater	WI	53190	262-473-5254	473-5867
TF Sales: 800-558-9507 ■ Web: www.weilerinc.com					
Wells Bloomfield Industries 10 Sunnen Dr	St. Louis	MO	63143	888-356-5362	264-6666*
*Fax Area Code: 800 ■ TF: 888-356-5362 ■ Web: www.wellsbloomfield.com					
Wenger Mfg Inc 714 Main St	Sabetha	KS	66534	785-284-2133	284-3771
Web: www.wenger.com					
Wilbur Curtis Co Inc 6913 Acco St	Montebello	CA	90640	323-837-2300	837-2406
TF: 800-421-6150 ■ Web: www.wilburcurtis.com					
Winston Industries LLC 2345 Carton Dr	Louisville	KY	40299	502-495-5400	495-5458
TF: 800-234-5286 ■ Web: www.winstonind.com					
Witte Co Inc 507 Rt 31 S PO Box 47	Washington	NJ	07882	908-689-6500	537-6806
TF: 866-265-4071 ■ Web: www.witte.com					
Wolf Range Co 2006 Northwestern Pkwy	Louisville	KY	40203	310-637-3737	

302 FOOD SERVICE

SEE ALSO Restaurant Companies p. 2555

	City	State	ZIP	Phone	Fax
Advance Food Co Inc 301 W Broadway	Enid	OK	73701	580-237-4400	213-4707
Web: www.advf.com					
Aircraft Service International Group					
201 S Orange Ave Suite 1100	Orlando	FL	32801	407-648-7373	206-5391
TF: 800-557-2744 ■ Web: www.asig.com					
All Seasons Services Inc					
5 Campanelli Cir 2nd Fl	Canton	MA	02021	781-828-2345	828-0427
TF: 888-558-2557 ■ Web: www.allseasonsservices.com					
American Food & Vending Corp					
124 Metropolitan Pk Dr	Syracuse	NY	13088	315-457-9950	457-0186
TF: 800-466-9261 ■ Web: www.americanfoodandvending.com					
ARAMARK Food & Support Services					
1101 Market St	Philadelphia	PA	19107	215-238-3000	238-3333
TF: 800-999-8989 ■ Web: www.aramark.com					
Atlas Food Systems & Services Inc					
205 Woods Lake Rd	Greenville	SC	29607	864-232-1885	232-1671
TF: 800-476-1123 ■ Web: www.atlasfoods.com					
Blue Line Foodservice Distribution					
24120 Haggerty Rd	Farmington Hills	MI	48335	248-478-6200	442-4570
TF: 800-892-8272 ■ Web: www.bluelinedist.com					
Bon Appetit Management Co					
100 Hamilton Ave Suite 300	Palo Alto	CA	94301	650-798-8000	798-8090
Web: www.bamco.com					
Bran-Zan Holdings Inc					
1548 Barclay Blvd	Buffalo Grove	IL	60089	847-342-0000	297-3970
TF: 866-266-9670 ■ Web: www.branzan.com					
Canteen Vending Services					
compass group 2400 Yorkmont Rd	Charlotte	NC	28217	704-329-4000	424-5086
TF: 800-357-0012 ■ Web: www.canteen-usa.com					
Cara Operations Ltd 199 Four Valley Dr	Vaughan	ON	L4K0B8	905-760-2244	405-6777
TF: 800-860-4082 ■ Web: www.cara.com					
Centerplate 2187 Atlantic St	Stamford	CT	06902	800-698-6992	
TF: 800-698-6992 ■ Web: www.centerplate.com					
Chefs' Warehouse Holdings LLC					
100 E Ridge Rd	Ridgefield	CT	06871	718-842-8700	
Web: www.chefswarehouse.com					
CL Swanson Corp 4501 Femrite Dr	Madison	WI	53716	608-221-7640	221-7648
Web: www.swansons.net					
COI Foodservice 2629 Eugenia Ave	Nashville	TN	37211	615-231-4300	231-4334
TF: 877-503-5212 ■ Web: www.coifood.com					
Compass Group North American Div (CGNAD)					
2400 Yorkmont Rd	Charlotte	NC	28217	704-329-4000	424-5086*
*Fax: Hum Res ■ TF: 800-357-0012 ■ Web: www.compass-usa.com					
Culinaire International					
2100 Ross Ave Suite 3100	Dallas	TX	75201	214-754-1880	754-1881
TF: 866-324-9093 ■ Web: www.culinaireintl.com					
Edsung Foodservice Equipment Co					
PO Box 17100	Honolulu	HI	96817	808-845-3931	842-4702
Excelsior Grand 2380 Hylan Blvd	Staten Island	NY	10306	718-987-4800	987-4803
Web: www.excelsiorgrand.com					
Filterfresh Coffee Service Inc					
378 University Ave	Westwood	MA	02090	781-461-8734	461-8732
TF: 800-461-8734 ■ Web: www.filterfresh.com					

	City	State	ZIP	Phone	Fax
Five Star Food Service Inc 1019 14th St	Columbus	GA	31901	706-327-0303	324-1038
TF: 800-327-0043 ■ Web: www.fivestar-food.com					
Flying Food Group 212 N Sangamon St Suite 1-A	Chicago	IL	60607	312-243-2122	243-5088
Web: www.flyingfood.com					
Food Bank For New York City					
39 Broadway 10th Fl	New York	NY	10006	212-566-7855	566-1463
Web: www.foodbanknyc.org					
Food Fast Corp 4703 DC Dr Suite 100	Tyler	TX	75701	903-534-0028	534-3767
Web: www.foodfastcorp.com					
Forever/NPC Resorts LLC					
7501 McCormick Blvd	Scottsdale	AZ	85258	480-998-8888	998-8887
TF: 800-455-3509 ■ Web: www.foreverlivings.com					
Ga Food Service Inc 12200 32nd Ct N	Saint Petersburg	FL	33716	727-573-2211	572-8209
TF: 800-852-2211 ■ Web: www.sunmeadow.com					
Garb-ko Inc 3925 Fortune Blvd	Saginaw	MI	48603	989-799-6937	799-9206
Web: www.garbko.com					
Gate Gourmet 11710 Plaza America Dr Suite 800	Reston	VA	20190	703-964-2300	964-2399*
*Fax: Sales ■ Web: www.gategourmet.com					
Gc Partners Inc 3816 Forrestgate Dr	Winston Salem	NC	27103	336-767-1600	744-2610
Web: www.gcpartners.com					
General Mills Inc 1 General Mills Blvd	Minneapolis	MN	55426	800-248-7310	764-8330*
*Fax Area Code: 763 ■ *Fax: PR ■ TF: 800-248-7310 ■ Web: www.generalmills.com					
Guckenheimer Enterprises Inc					
3 Lagoon Dr Suite 325	Redwood Shores	CA	94065	650-592-3800	592-0406
TF: 800-466-5303 ■ Web: www.guckenheimer.com					
Guest Services Inc 3055 SR 699	Fairfax	VA	22031	703-849-9300	641-4690
TF: 800-345-7534 ■ Web: www.guestservices.com					
HMSHost Corp 6905 Rockledge Dr # 1	Bethesda	MD	20817	240-694-4100	694-4626
Web: www.hmshost.com					
Host America Corporate Dining					
1 Leonardo Dr	North Haven	CT	06473	203-239-4678	234-1503
Web: www.hostamericacorp.com					
Hot Stuff Foods LLC 2930 W Maple St	Sioux Falls	SD	57107	605-330-7531	336-0141
Web: www.hotstuffoods.com					
Hq Sustainable Maritime Industries Inc					
Melbourne Towers, 1511 Third Ave Suite 788	Seattle	WA	98101	206-621-9888	621-0318
PINK: HQSM ■ Web: www.hqfish.com					
Institution Food House Inc 543 12th St Dr NW	Hickory	NC	28603	828-323-4500	725-4500
TF: 800-800-0434 ■ Web: www.institutionfoodhouse.com					
Institutional Distributors Inc					
PO Box 520	East Bernstadt	KY	40729	606-843-2100	843-2108
TF: 800-442-7885					
Institutional Wholesale Co					
535 Dry Valley Rd	Cookeville	TN	38503	931-537-4000	537-4017*
*Fax: Cust Svc ■ TF: 800-239-9588					
Island Oasis 141 Norfolk St PO Box 769	Walpole	MA	02081	508-660-1176	
TF: 800-777-4752 ■ Web: www.islandoasis.com					
Lackmann Culinary Services					
303 Crossways Pk Dr	Woodbury	NY	11797	516-364-2300	364-9788
Web: www.lackmann.com					
Lee Bros Foodservice Inc 640 N 9th St	San Jose	CA	95112	408-275-0700	275-0416
Web: www.leebros.com					
Love & Quiches Desserts 178 Hanse Ave	Freeport	NY	11520	516-623-8800	623-8817
TF: 800-525-5251 ■ Web: www.loveandquiches.com					
Martin's Inc 6821 Dogwood Rd	Baltimore	MD	21244	410-265-1300	265-1328
Maximum Quality Foods Inc 3351 Tremley Pt Rd	Linden	NJ	07036	908-474-0003	474-1320
Web: www.maximumqualityfoods.com					
Morrison Management Specialists Inc					
5801 Peachtree Dunwoody Rd	Atlanta	GA	30342	404-845-3330	845-3333
TF: 800-622-1035 ■ Web: www.iammorrison.com					
Nantze Springs Inc					
156 W Carroll St PO Box 1273	Dothan	AL	36301	334-794-4218	
TF: 800-239-7873 ■ Web: www.nantzesprings.com					
Open Kitchen Inc 1161 W 21st St	Chicago	IL	60608	312-666-5335	666-9242
TF: 800-339-5334 ■ Web: www.openkitchens.com					
Port City Java Inc					
101 Portwatch Way PO Box 785	Wilmington	NC	28412	910-796-6646	
Web: www.portcityjava.com					
Rodrigo's Online Store 1320 N Manzanita St	Orange	CA	92867	714-633-7844	
Web: www.rodrigos-shop.com					
Romeo & Sons Inc 100 Romeo Ln	Uniontown	PA	15401	724-438-5561	438-1149
Web: www.romeofoods.com					
Sanese Services Inc 6465 Busch Blvd	Columbus	OH	43229	614-436-1234	436-1592
TF: 800-589-3410 ■ Web: www.sanese.com					
SeamlessWeb Professional Solutions LLC					
232 Madison Ave Suite 1409	New York	NY	10016	212-944-7755	
Web: www.seamlessweb.com					
Signature Services Corp					
2705 Hawes Ave PO Box 35885	Dallas	TX	75235	214-353-2661	353-4843
TF: 800-929-5519 ■ Web: www.signatureservices.com					
Sodexo Inc 9801 Washingtonian Blvd	Gaithersburg	MD	20878	301-987-4000	987-4438
TF: 800-763-3946 ■ Web: www.sodexousa.com					
Spartan Foods Of America Inc PO Box 1003	Fairforest	SC	29336	864-595-6262	576-5972
Web: www.mamamarys.com					
Sportservice Corp 40 Fountain Plaza	Buffalo	NY	14202	716-858-5000	858-5424
TF: 800-828-7240 ■ Web: www.dncinc.com					
Stepherson's 2155 Covington Pike	Memphis	TN	38128	901-382-5701	683-2477
Web: www.superlofoods.com					
Summit Food Service Distributors Inc					
580 Industrial Rd	London	ON	N5V1V1	519-453-3410	453-5148
TF: 800-265-9267 ■ Web: www.summitfoods.com					
SYSCO Food Services of Cleveland Inc					
4747 Grayton Rd	Cleveland	OH	44135	216-201-3100	201-3511
TF: 800-584-4580 ■ Web: www.syscocleveland.com					
Sysco Jacksonville Inc					
1501 Lewis Industrial Dr PO Box 37045	Jacksonville	FL	32254	904-786-2600	695-8135
TF: 800-786-2611 ■ Web: www.sysco-jax.com					
SYSCO Philadelphia LLC					
600 Packer Ave PO Box 6499	Philadelphia	PA	19145	215-463-8200	463-1618
Web: www.syscophilly.com/ordereze/1000/Page.aspx					
Sysco Portland Inc 26250 SW Pkwy Ctr Dr	Wilsonville	OR	97070	503-682-8700	682-6699
Web: www.syscoportland.com					

	City	State	Zip	Phone	Fax
Taher Inc 5570 Smetana Dr *Web:* www.taher.com	Minnetonka	MN	55343	952-945-0505	945-0444
Trujillo & Sons Inc 1100 NW 23rd St *Web:* www.trujilloandsons.com	Miami	FL	33127	305-633-6482	638-5013
Universal Sodexho 5749 Susitna Dr *TF:* 800-535-1946	Harahan	LA	70123	504-733-5761	733-2017
V/Gladieux Enterprises Inc 3400 Executive Pkwy	Toledo	OH	43606	419-473-3009	473-2335
Valley Inc 4400 Mangum Dr *TF:* 800-748-9985 ■ *Web:* www.valleyservicesi.com	Flowood	MS	39232	601-664-3100	664-3399
Value Creation Partners Inc 445 Hutchinson Ave Suite 800 *Web:* www.vcponline.com	Columbus	OH	43235	614-785-6401	785-6402
Williams Food Service 227 S 30th St *Web:* www.williamsfood.com	Louisville	KY	40212	502-778-1641	213-5675
Yancey's Food Service Co 5820 Piper Dr *Web:* www.yanceys.com	Loveland	CO	80538	970-613-4333	613-4334
Zaugs Inc 4100 W Wisconsin Ave *Web:* www.zaugs.com	Appleton	WI	54913	920-734-9881	734-4322

303 FOOD SERVICE EQUIPMENT & SUPPLIES

SEE ALSO Food Products Machinery p. 1873

	City	State	Zip	Phone	Fax
Adams-Burch Inc 1901 Stanford Ct *TF Cust Svc:* 800-347-8093 ■ *Web:* www.adams-burch.com	Landover	MD	20785	301-341-1600	341-5114
Advance Tabco 200 Heartland Blvd *TF:* 800-645-3166 ■ *Web:* www.advancetabco.com	Edgewood	NY	11717	631-242-4800	242-6900
Anderson-DuBose Co 6575 Davis Industrial Pkwy *TF:* 800-248-1080	Solon	OH	44139	440-248-8800	248-6208
Atlanta Fixture & Sales Co 3185 NE Expy *TF:* 800-282-1977 ■ *Web:* www.atlantafixture.com	Atlanta	GA	30341	770-455-8844	986-9202
Bargreen Ellingson Inc 2925 70th Ave E *TF:* 866-722-2665 ■ *Web:* www.bargreen.com	Fife	WA	98424	253-722-2600	896-3620
Boelter Cos Inc N22W23685 Ridgeview Pkwy W *TF:* 800-263-5837 ■ *Web:* www.boelter.com	Milwaukee	WI	53188	262-523-6200	523-6003
Bolton & Hay Inc 2701 Delaware Ave *TF:* 800-362-1861 ■ *Web:* www.boltonhay.com	Des Moines	IA	50317	515-265-2554	265-6090
Browne & Co 100 Esna Pk Dr *TF:* 877-327-6963 ■ *Web:* www.browneco.com	Markham	ON	L3R2S1	905-475-6104	475-5843
Browne-Halco Inc 2840 Morris Ave *TF:* 888-289-1005 ■ *Web:* www.halco.com	Union	NJ	07083	908-964-9200	964-6677
Buffalo Hotel Supply Co Inc 375 Commerce Dr PO Box 646 *TF:* 800-333-1678 ■ *Web:* www.ebhsonline.com	Amherst	NY	14228	716-691-8080	691-3255
Cambro Mfg Co 5801 Skylab Rd **Fax:* Cust Svc ■ *TF:* 800-833-3003 ■ *Web:* www.cambro.com	Huntington Beach	CA	92647	714-848-1555	842-3430*
Carlisle FoodService Products Inc 4711 E Hefner Rd *TF:* 800-654-8210 ■ *Web:* www.carlislefsp.com	Oklahoma City	OK	73131	405-475-5600	475-5607
Chudnow Mfg Co Inc 3055 New St PO Box 10 *Web:* www.chudnowmfg.com	Oceanside	NY	11572	516-593-4222	593-4156
Curtis Restaurant Supply & Equipment Co 6577 E 40th St *TF:* 800-766-2878 ■ *Web:* www.curtisequipment.com	Tulsa	OK	74145	918-622-7390	665-0990
Eagle Group Inc 100 Industrial Blvd *TF:* 800-441-8440 ■ *Web:* www.eaglegrp.com	Clayton	DE	19938	302-653-3000	653-2065
Edsung Foodservice Equipment Co PO Box 17100	Honolulu	HI	96817	808-845-3931	842-4702
Edward Don & Co 2500 S Harlem Ave *TF Cust Svc:* 800-777-4366 ■ *Web:* www.don.com	North Riverside	IL	60546	708-883-8000	883-8676
Genpak Carthage 505 E Cotton St **Fax Area Code:* 800 ■ *TF:* 800-340-4005 ■ *Web:* www.genpak.com	Carthage	TX	75633	903-693-7151	932-5222*
Gordon Food Service 333 50th St SW *TF:* 800-968-7500 ■ *Web:* www.gfs.com	Grand Rapids	MI	49548	616-530-7000	717-7600
HB Hunter Co 1512 Brown Ave PO Box 1599	Norfolk	VA	23504	757-664-5200	664-2372
Hotel & Restaurant Supply Inc 5020 Arundel Rd PO Box 6 *TF:* 800-782-6651 ■ *Web:* www.hnrsupply.com	Meridian	MS	39302	601-482-7127	482-7170
Intedge Mfg 1875 Chumley Rd *TF:* 866-969-9605 ■ *Web:* www.intedge.com	Woodruff	SC	29388	864-969-9601	969-9604
InterMetro Industries Corp 651 N Washington St **Fax:* Hum Res ■ *TF Cust Svc:* 800-992-1776 ■ *Web:* www.metro.com	Wilkes-Barre	PA	18705	570-825-2741	824-7520*
Kittredge Equipment Co Inc 100 Bowles Rd *TF:* 800-423-7082 ■ *Web:* www.kittredgeequipment.com	Agawam	MA	01001	413-304-4100	
Lakeside Mfg Inc 4900 W Electric Ave *TF:* 800-558-8565 ■ *Web:* www.elakeside.com	West Milwaukee	WI	53219	414-902-6400	902-6446
Lancaster Colony Commercial Products Inc 3902 Indianola Ave *TF:* 800-292-7260 ■ *Web:* www.lccpinc.com	Columbus	OH	43214	614-263-2850	263-2857
Maines Equipment & Supply Co 650 Conklin Rd *TF:* 800-306-3669 ■ *Web:* www.maines.net	Conklin	NY	13748	607-772-0055	772-0550
Maines Paper & Food Service Co 101 Broome Corporate Pkwy **Fax:* Cust Svc ■ *TF:* 800-366-3669 ■ *Web:* www.maines.net	Conklin	NY	13748	607-779-1200	723-3245*
Manitowoc Foodservice 2227 Welbilt Blvd *Web:* www.enodis.com	New Port Richey	FL	34655	727-375-7010	
McLane Foodservice Inc 2085 Midway Rd *TF:* 888-792-9300 ■ *Web:* www.mclaneco.com	Carrollton	TX	75006	972-364-2000	364-2088
N Wasserstrom & Sons Inc 2300 Lockbourne Rd *TF:* 800-444-4697 ■ *Web:* www.wasserstrom.com	Columbus	OH	43207	614-228-5550	737-8501
PBI Market Equipment Inc 2667 Gundry Ave *TF:* 800-421-3753 ■ *Web:* www.pbimarketing.com	Signal Hill	CA	90755	562-595-4785	426-2262
Perkins Equipment Div 7 Perimeter Rd *TF:* 800-258-3040 ■ *Web:* www.perkins1.com	Manchester	NH	03103	603-669-3400	641-6140
PrimeSource FoodService Equipment Inc 1409 S Lamar St Suite 1007 *TF:* 800-737-8567 ■ *Web:* www.primesourcefse.com	Dallas	TX	75215	214-273-4900	273-4999
RAPIDS Wholesale Equipment Co 6201 S Gateway Dr *TF:* 800-472-7431 ■ *Web:* www.rapidswholesale.com	Marion	IA	52302	319-447-1670	447-1680
Regal Ware Inc 1675 Reigle Dr *Web:* www.regalware.com	Kewaskum	WI	53040	262-626-2121	626-8565
Reinhart Food Service 7735 Westside Industrial Dr *TF:* 888-781-5464 ■ *Web:* www.rfsdelivers.com	Jacksonville	FL	32219	904-781-9888	786-7035
Restaurant & Stores Equipment Co 230 W 700 S *TF:* 800-877-0087 ■ *Web:* www.refcosls.com	Salt Lake City	UT	84101	801-364-1981	355-2029
Restaurant Technologies Inc 2250 Pilot Knob Rd Suite 100 *TF:* 888-796-4997 ■ *Web:* www.rti-inc.com	Mendota Heights	MN	55120	651-796-1600	379-4082
Ricos Products Co Inc 830 S Presa St *Web:* www.ricos.com	San Antonio	TX	78210	210-222-1415	226-6453
Service Ideas Inc 2354 Ventura Dr *TF:* 800-328-4493 ■ *Web:* www.serviceideas.com	Woodbury	MN	55125	651-730-8800	730-8880
Smith & Greene Co 19015 66th Ave S *TF:* 800-232-8050 ■ *Web:* www.smithandgreene.com	Kent	WA	98032	425-656-8000	656-8075
Southern Foods Inc 3500 Old Battleground Rd *TF:* 800-441-3663 ■ *Web:* www.southernfoods.com	Greensboro	NC	27410	336-545-3800	545-3822
Standex International Corp Food Service Equipment Group 908 Hwy 15 N *TF:* 800-647-1284 ■ *Web:* www.standex.com	New Albany	MS	38652	662-534-9061	534-8180
Sunlow Master Marketing 1071 Howell Mill Rd NW *TF:* 800-678-6569	Atlanta	GA	30318	404-872-8135	872-0471
Superior Products Catalog Co 510 W County Rd D *TF Sales:* 800-328-9800 ■ *Web:* www.superprod.com	Saint Paul	MN	55112	651-636-1110	636-3671
SYSCO Corp 1390 Enclave Pkwy *NYSE:* SYY ■ **Fax:* PR ■ *Web:* www.sysco.com	Houston	TX	77077	281-584-1390	584-2721*
TriMark USA Inc 505 Collins St *TF:* 800-755-5580 ■ *Web:* www.trimarkusa.com	South Attleboro	MA	02703	508-399-2400	761-3600
Unified Foodservice Purchasing Co-op LLC 950 Breckenridge Ln *TF:* 800-444-4144 ■ *Web:* www.ufpc.com	Louisville	KY	40207	502-896-5900	893-4150
United Restaurant Equipment Co Inc 297 Central St *Web:* www.unitedrestaurant.com	Lowell	MA	01852	978-453-7223	453-2765
Vollrath Co LLC The 1236 N 18th St PO Box 611 *TF:* 800-624-2051 ■ *Web:* www.vollrathco.com	Sheboygan	WI	53081	920-457-4851	459-6570
Wasserstrom Co 477 S Front St *TF:* 800-999-9277 ■ *Web:* www.wasserstrom.com	Columbus	OH	43215	614-228-6525	228-8776
Western Pioneer Sales Co 406 E Colorado St **Fax Area Code:* 323	Glendale	CA	91205	818-244-1466	245-7285*

304 FOOTWEAR

	City	State	Zip	Phone	Fax
Acor Orthopaedic Inc 18530 S Miles Pkwy *TF:* 800-237-2267 ■ *Web:* www.acor.com	Cleveland	OH	44128	216-662-4500	662-4547
Acton Enterprises Inc 253 America Pl *Web:* www.actonenterprises.com	Jeffersonville	IN	47130	812-288-7659	288-7747
Acushnet Co 333 Bridge St **Fax:* Hum Res ■ *TF:* 800-225-8500 ■ *Web:* www.acushnet.com	Fairhaven	MA	02719	508-979-2000	979-3900*
Adidas America 5055 N Greeley Ave *TF:* 888-234-3270 ■ *Web:* www.adidas.com	Portland	OR	97217	971-234-2300	234-2450
Aerosoles Inc 201 Meadow Rd *TF:* 800-798-9478 ■ *Web:* www.aerosoles.com	Edison	NJ	08817	732-985-6900	985-1332
Aldo Shoes 2300 Emile Belanger *TF:* 888-818-2536 ■ *Web:* www.aldoshoes.com	Saint-Laurent	QC	H4R3J4	514-747-2536	747-7993
Allen-Edmonds Shoe Corp 201 E Seven Hills Rd *TF Cust Svc:* 800-235-2348 ■ *Web:* www.allenedmonds.com	Port Washington	WI	53074	262-235-6512	235-6265
Asics America Corp 29 Parker # 100 *TF:* 800-333-8404 ■ *Web:* www.asicsamerica.com	Irvine	CA	92618	949-453-8888	453-0292
ATP Mfg LLC 761 Great Rd *TF:* 800-315-5246 ■ *Web:* www.atp-usa.com	North Smithfield	RI	02896	401-765-8600	766-5327
BA Mason 1251 1st Ave **Fax Area Code:* 800 ■ *TF:* 800-893-8508	Chippewa Falls	WI	54774	715-723-1871	446-2329*
Badorf Shoe Co Inc 1633 Rothsville Rd PO Box 367 *TF:* 800-325-1545 ■ *Web:* www.badorfshoe.com	Lititz	PA	17543	717-626-8521	627-4952
Bakers Footwear Group Inc 2815 Scott Ave *OTC:* BKRS ■ *TF:* 866-454-2062 ■ *Web:* www.bakersshoes.com	Saint Louis	MO	63103	314-621-0699	621-1018
Barbour Welting Co Div Barbour Corp 1001 N Montello St *TF:* 800-955-9649 ■ *Web:* www.barbourcorp.com	Brockton	MA	02301	508-583-8200	583-4113
Bates Shoe Co 9341 Courtland Dr NE *Web:* www.wolverineworldwide.com	Rockford	MI	49351	616-866-5500	866-5658
Belleville Shoe Mfg Co 100 Premier Dr *Web:* www.bellevilleshoe.com	Belleville	IL	62220	618-233-5600	257-1112
Benchmark Brands Inc 5250 Triangle Pkwy Suite 200 *Web:* www.benchmarkbrands.com	Norcross	GA	30092	770-242-1254	242-1962
Brooks Sports Inc 19910 N Creek Pkwy Suite 200 *TF:* 800-227-6657 ■ *Web:* www.brooksrunning.com	Bothell	WA	98011	425-488-3131	489-1975
Brown Shoe Co Inc 8300 Maryland Ave *NYSE:* BWS ■ *TF Cust Svc:* 800-766-6465 ■ *Web:* www.brownshoe.com	Saint Louis	MO	63105	314-854-4000	854-4274
Capezio/Ballet Makers Inc 1 Campus Rd *TF Acctg:* 800-595-9002 ■ *Web:* www.capeziodance.com	Totowa	NJ	07512	973-595-9000	595-9120
Cardinal Shoe Corp 468 Canal St	Lawrence	MA	01840	978-686-9706	686-9707
Cels Enterprises Inc 3485 S La Cienega Blvd *Web:* www.chineselaundry.com	Los Angeles	CA	90016	310-838-2103	838-8732

	City	State	Zip	Phone	Fax
Charles David of California 5731 Buckingham Pkwy *Web:* www.charlesdavid.com	Culver City	CA	90230	310-348-5050	348-5041
Cherokee Inc 6835 Valjean Ave *NASDAQ: CHKE* ■ *Web:* www.thecherokeegroup.com	Van Nuys	CA	91406	818-908-9868	908-9191
Chinese Laundry Shoes 3485 S La Cienega Blvd *TF:* 855-852-8637 ■ *Web:* www.chineselaundry.com	Los Angeles	CA	90016	310-838-2103	838-8732
Clark Cos NA 156 Oak St *TF Cust Svc:* 800-425-2757 ■ *Web:* www.clarksusa.com	Newton Upper Falls	MA	02464	617-964-1222	243-4213
Cole-Haan 1 Cole Haan Dr *TF:* 800-488-2000 ■ *Web:* www.colehaan.com	Yarmouth	ME	04096	207-846-2500	846-1491
Connors Footwear 20 Whitcher St *Web:* www.whitemt.com	Lisbon	NH	03585	603-838-6694	838-2278
Consolidated Shoe Co Inc 22290 Timberlake Rd **Fax:* Sales ■ *TF:* 800-368-7463 ■ *Web:* www.nicoleshoes.com	Lynchburg	VA	24502	434-239-0391	582-5631*
Converse Inc 1 High St **Fax:* Mktg ■ *TF Cust Svc:* 800-428-2667 ■ *Web:* www.converse.com	North Andover	MA	01845	978-983-3300	983-3521*
Cowtown Boot Co 11401 Gateway Blvd W *TF:* 800-580-2698	El Paso	TX	79936	915-593-2565	593-9441
Crocs Inc 6328 Monarch Pk Pl *NASDAQ: CROX* ■ *TF:* 866-306-3179 ■ *Web:* www.crocs.com	Niwot	CO	80503	303-848-7000	468-4266
D Myers & Sons Inc 4311 Erdman Ave *TF:* 800-367-7463	Baltimore	MD	21213	410-522-7500	522-7575
Dan Post Boot Co 1751 Alpine Dr *TF:* 800-340-2668 ■ *Web:* www.danpostboots.com	Clarksville	TN	37040	931-645-4466	645-6557
Danner Shoe Mfg Co 17634 NE Airport *TF Cust Svc:* 800-345-0430 ■ *Web:* www.danner.com	Portland	OR	97230	503-251-1100	251-1119
Deckers Outdoor Corp 495-A S Fairview Ave *NASDAQ: DECK* ■ *TF:* 800-858-5342 ■ *Web:* www.deckers.com	Goleta	CA	93117	805-967-7611	967-9722
Director's Showcase International (DSI) 505 Sroufe St PO Box 229 *TF:* 800-893-8171 ■ *Web:* www.dshowcase.com	Ligonier	IN	46767	260-894-7158	894-3628
Drew Shoe Corp 252 Quarry Rd *TF:* 800-837-3739 ■ *Web:* www.drewshoe.com	Lancaster	OH	43130	740-653-4271	654-4979
East Lion Corp 18525 Railroad St *TF:* 877-939-1818 ■ *Web:* www.eastlioncorp.com	City of Industry	CA	91748	626-912-1818	935-5858
Eastland Shoe Mfg Corp 4 Meeting House Rd *Web:* www.eastlandshoe.com	Freeport	ME	04032	207-865-6314	865-9261
Easy Spirit Shoes 1129 Westchester Ave **Fax Area Code:* 914 ■ *Web:* www.easyspirit.com	White Plains	NY	10604	512-501-8292	640-1612*
ES Originals Inc 450 W 33rd St 9th Fl *TF:* 800-677-6577 ■ *Web:* www.esoriginals.com	New York	NY	10001	212-736-8124	736-8366
Famous Footwear 7010 Mineral Pt Rd *TF Cust Svc:* 800-888-7198 ■ *Web:* www.famousfootwear.com	Madison	WI	53717	608-829-3668	827-3353
Fancy Feet Inc 26650 Harding St *TF:* 800-858-8460	Oak Park	MI	48237	248-398-8460	398-5650
Fendi NA Inc 720 5th Ave 5th Fl *TF:* 800-336-3469 ■ *Web:* www.fendi.com	New York	NY	10019	212-920-8100	767-0545
Finish Line Inc The 3308 N Mitthoeffer Rd *NASDAQ: FINL* ■ *TF:* 800-370-6061 ■ *Web:* www.finishline.com	Indianapolis	IN	46235	317-899-1022	899-0237
Florsheim Inc 333 W Estabrook Blvd **Fax Area Code:* 414 ■ *TF:* 866-454-0449 ■ *Web:* www.florsheim.com	Glendale	WI	53212	866-454-0449	908-1601*
Foot Locker Inc 112 W 34th St *NYSE: FL* ■ *TF:* 800-991-6682 ■ *Web:* www.footlocker-inc.com	New York	NY	10120	212-720-3700	720-4460
Foot Solutions Inc 2359 Windy Hill Rd Suite 400 *TF:* 866-338-2597 ■ *Web:* www.footsolutions.com	Marietta	GA	30067	770-955-0099	953-6270
Foot-So-Port Shoe Corp 405 E Forest St PO Box 247 *TF:* 800-679-7463 ■ *Web:* www.footsoport.com	Oconomowoc	WI	53066	262-567-4416	567-5323
Footaction INC 112 W 34th St *TF:* 800-991-6686 ■ *Web:* www.footaction.com	New York	NY	10120	715-261-9588	
Footstar Inc 933 MacArthur Blvd *TF:* 800-777-1330 ■ *Web:* www.footstar.com	Mahwah	NJ	07430	201-934-2000	934-0398
Gateway Shoe Co 910 Kehro Mill Rd Suite 112 *TF:* 800-539-6063 ■ *Web:* www.gatewayshoes.com	Ballwin	MO	63011	636-256-7050	527-3797
Genesco Inc 1415 Murfreesboro Rd *NYSE: GCO* ■ *Web:* www.genesco.com	Nashville	TN	37217	615-367-7000	
Georgia Boot Inc 235 Noah Dr *TF:* 800-251-3388 ■ *Web:* www.georgiaboot.com	Franklin	TN	37068	615-794-1556	790-4229
GH Bass & Co Inc 1001 Frontier Rd Suite 100 *TF Cust Svc:* 800-950-2277 ■ *Web:* www.pvh.com	Bridgewater	NJ	08807	908-685-0050	
HH Brown Shoe Co Inc 124 W Putnam Ave *TF:* 888-444-2769 ■ *Web:* www.hhbrown.com	Greenwich	CT	06830	203-661-2424	661-1818
Hush Puppies Co 9341 Courtland Dr NE **Fax:* Acctg ■ *TF:* 800-626-8696 ■ *Web:* www.hushpuppies.com	Rockford	MI	49351	616-866-5500	866-5625*
Ilani Shoes Ltd 1350 Broadway	New York	NY	10018	212-947-5830	947-2319
IMA International Marketing Inc 10821 Lakeview Ave *TF:* 800-321-1098 ■ *Web:* www.imalimited.com	Lenexa	KS	66219	913-599-5995	599-2288
Impo International Inc 3510 Black Rd *TF:* 800-367-4676	Santa Maria	CA	93455	805-922-7753	925-0450
Inter-Pacific Corp 2257 Colby Ave	Los Angeles	CA	90064	310-473-7591	479-8701
Island Import & Export Co 7570 Hwy 65 NE *Web:* www.i-i-e.com	Fridley	MN	55432	763-783-7338	783-1106
Jimlar Corp 160 Great Neck Rd *Web:* www.jimlar.com	Great Neck	NY	11021	516-829-1717	829-2970
John Reyer Shoe Store Reyers City Ctr 40 S Water Ave *TF Cust Svc:* 800-245-1550 ■ *Web:* www.reyers.com	Sharon	PA	16146	724-981-2200	983-8269
Johnston & Murphy Inc 1415 Murfreesboro Rd *TF:* 800-424-2854 ■ *Web:* www.johnstonmurphy.com	Nashville	TN	37217	615-367-8101	367-7139
Justin Boot Co Inc 610 W Daggett St **Fax:* Cust Svc ■ *TF Cust Svc:* 866-240-8853 ■ *Web:* www.justinboots.com	Fort Worth	TX	76104	817-332-4385	348-2809*
K-Swiss Inc 31248 Oak Crest Dr *NASDAQ: KSWS* ■ *TF:* 800-938-8000 ■ *Web:* www.kswiss.com	Westlake Village	CA	91361	818-706-5100	706-5390
Kaepa USA Inc 9050 Autobahn Dr Suite 500 *TF:* 800-880-9200 ■ *Web:* www.kaepa.com	Dallas	TX	75237	972-296-7300	296-7319
Keds Corp 191 Spring St *TF:* 800-428-6575 ■ *Web:* www.keds.com	Lexington	MA	02421	617-824-6000	824-6868
Kenneth Cole Productions Inc 603 W 50th St *NYSE: KCP* ■ **Fax Area Code:* 201 ■ **Fax:* Cust Svc ■ *TF:* 800-536-2653 ■ *Web:* www.kennethcole.com	New York	NY	10019	212-265-1500	583-3811*
LA Gear Inc 844 Moraga Dr *TF Cust Svc:* 800-252-4327 ■ *Web:* www.lagear.com	Los Angeles	CA	90049	310-889-3410	889-3500
La Sportiva North America Inc 3850 Frontier Ave Suite 100 *Web:* www.sportiva.com	Boulder	CO	80301	303-443-8710	442-7541
LaCrosse Footwear Inc 17634 NE Airport *NASDAQ: BOOT* ■ *TF Cust Svc:* 800-323-2668 ■ *Web:* www.lacrosse-outdoors.com	Portland	OR	97230	503-766-1010	766-1015
Lady Foot Locker (LFL) 112 W 34th St *TF:* 800-991-6686 ■ *Web:* www.ladyfootlocker.com	New York	NY	10120	715-261-9588	
Lake Catherine Footwear 190 Elmwood Dr *TF Cust Svc:* 800-826-8676 ■ *Web:* www.munroshoe.com	Hot Springs	AR	71901	501-262-6000	262-6165
Lamey-Wellehan Inc 940 Turner St *TF:* 800-370-6906 ■ *Web:* www.lwshoes.com	Auburn	ME	04210	207-784-6595	784-9650
Lehigh Safety Shoe Co 39 E Canal St *TF:* 800-444-4086 ■ *Web:* www.lehighsafetyshoes.com	Nelsonville	OH	45764	800-444-4086	
Lucchese Boot Co 40 Walter Jones Blvd **Fax Area Code:* 888 ■ **Fax:* Cust Svc ■ *TF:* 800-637-6888 ■ *Web:* www.lucchese.com	El Paso	TX	79906	915-778-8585	238-0468*
Lugz Inc 155 6th Ave 9th Fl *TF:* 800-648-8602 ■ *Web:* www.lugz.com	New York	NY	10013	212-691-4700	691-5350
Lyn-Flex West Inc 405 Red Oak Rd PO Box 570 *Web:* www.lynflex.com	Owensville	MO	65066	573-437-4125	437-2350
Marty's Shoe Outlet Inc 121 Carver Ave *TF Cust Svc:* 800-262-7897 ■ *Web:* www.martyshoes.com	Westwood	NJ	07675	201-497-6636	497-6639
Meramec Group Inc 338 Ramsey St *Web:* www.meramec.com	Sullivan	MO	63080	573-468-3101	860-3101
Mercury International 19 Alice Agnew Dr PO Box 222	North Attleboro	MA	02761	508-699-9000	699-9099
Merrell Footwear 9341 Courtland Dr NE *TF Cust Svc:* 888-637-7001 ■ *Web:* www.merrell.com/US/en	Rockford	MI	49351	616-866-5500	866-5625
Mizuno USA 4925 Avalon Ridge Pkwy *TF:* 800-333-7888 ■ *Web:* www.mizunousa.com	Norcross	GA	30071	770-441-5553	448-3234
Montello Heel Mfg Inc 13 Emerson Ave *TF:* 800-245-4335	Brockton	MA	02305	508-586-0603	559-9270
Munro & Co Inc 3770 Malvern Rd 71901 PO Box 6048 *TF:* 800-826-8676 ■ *Web:* www.munroshoe.com	Hot Springs	AR	71902	501-262-6000	262-6084
New Balance Athletic Shoe Inc 20 Guest St Brighton Landing *TF:* 800-343-4648 ■ *Web:* www.newbalance.com	Boston	MA	02135	617-783-4000	783-7050
Nike Inc 1 Bowerman Dr *NYSE: NKE* ■ *TF Cust Svc:* 800-344-6453 ■ *Web:* www.nike.com	Beaverton	OR	97005	503-671-6453	646-6926
Nina Footwear Co Inc 730 5th Ave 8th Fl *TF:* 800-233-6462 ■ *Web:* www.ninashoes.com	New York	NY	10019	212-399-2323	246-6837
Nine West Group Inc 1129 Westchester Ave Nine W Plaza *TF:* 800-999-1877 ■ *Web:* www.ninewest.com	White Plains	NY	10604	914-640-6400	640-1676
Nocona Boot Co 610 W Daggett St **Fax:* Cust Svc ■ *TF:* 866-240-8854 ■ *Web:* www.nocona.com	Fort Worth	TX	76104	817-332-4385	390-2566*
Novus Inc 655 Calle Cubitas *TF:* 888-530-4546 ■ *Web:* www.novushoes.com	Guaynabo	PR	00969	787-272-4546	272-4500
Nunn-Bush Shoe Co Inc 333 W Estabrook Blvd	Milwaukee	WI	53201	414-908-1600	908-1605
ONGUARD Industries 1850 Clark Rd *TF:* 800-365-2282 ■ *Web:* www.onguardindustries.com	Havre de Grace	MD	21078	410-272-2000	272-3346
Otomix Inc 3691 Lenawee Ave *TF:* 800-701-7867 ■ *Web:* www.otomix.com	Los Angeles	CA	90016	310-815-4700	815-4720
Payless ShoeSource Inc 3231 SE Sixth Ave *NYSE: PSS* ■ *TF:* 800-426-1141 ■ *Web:* www.collectivebrands.com	Topeka	KS	66607	785-233-5171	295-6049
Pentland USA Inc 3333 New Hyde Pk Rd Suite 200 *Web:* www.pentland.com	New Hyde Park	NY	11042	516-365-1333	365-2333
Phoenix Footwear Group Inc 5937 Darwin Court Suite 109 *AMEX: PXG* ■ *TF:* 800-341-1550 ■ *Web:* www.phoenixfootwear.com	Carlsbad	CA	92008	760-602-9688	602-0152
Propet USA Inc 25612 74th Ave S *TF:* 800-877-6738 ■ *Web:* www.propetusa.com	Kent	WA	98032	253-854-7600	854-7607
Puma North America Inc 10 Lyberty Way *TF:* 800-662-7862 ■ *Web:* www.puma.com	Westford	MA	01886	978-698-1000	698-1150
PW Minor & Son Inc 3 Tread Easy Ave PO Box 678 *TF:* 800-524-1084 ■ *Web:* www.pwminor.com	Batavia	NY	14020	585-343-1500	343-1514
Quabaug Corp 18 School St *TF:* 800-325-5022 ■ *Web:* www.vibram.com	North Brookfield	MA	01535	508-867-7731	867-4600
Rack Room Shoes 8310 Technology Dr *Web:* www.rackroomshoes.com	Charlotte	NC	28262	704-547-9200	547-8159
Red Wing Shoe Co Inc 314 Main St *TF Cust Svc:* 800-733-9464 ■ *Web:* www.redwingshoes.com	Red Wing	MN	55066	651-388-8211	388-7415
Reebok International Ltd 1895 JW Foster Blvd **Fax:* Cust Svc ■ *TF:* 800-843-4444 ■ *Web:* www.reebok.com	Canton	MA	02021	781-401-5000	401-4516*
RG Barry Corp 13405 Yarmouth Dr NW *AMEX: DFZ* ■ *TF:* 800-848-7560 ■ *Web:* www.rgbarry.com	Pickerington	OH	43147	614-864-6400	866-9787
Riddell Inc 669 Sugar Ln *TF:* 800-275-5338 ■ *Web:* www.riddell.com	Elyria	OH	44035	440-366-8225	336-6292
Rockport Co Inc 1895 JW Foster Blvd **Fax:* Cust Svc ■ *TF:* 800-828-0545 ■ *Web:* www.rockport.com	Canton	MA	02021	781-401-5000	401-5230*
Rocky Shoes & Boots Inc 39 E Canal St *NASDAQ: RCKY* ■ *TF:* 800-421-5151 ■ *Web:* www.rockyboots.com	Nelsonville	OH	45764	740-753-1951	753-4024
Romika USA LLC 3405 Del Webb Ave NE *Web:* www.romikausa.com	Salem	OR	97301	503-393-0963	588-3013
Ryka Inc 101 Enterprise Suite 100 *TF:* 888-834-7952 ■ *Web:* www.ryka.com	Aliso Viejo	CA	92653	888-834-7952	
Salomon North America 5055 N Greeley Ave *TF:* 877-272-5666 ■ *Web:* www.salomonsports.com	Portland	OR	97217	971-234-2300	234-2450
SAS Shoemakers 1717 SAS Dr *TF:* 877-782-7463 ■ *Web:* www.sasshoes.com	San Antonio	TX	78224	210-924-6561	921-7896
Saucony Inc 191 Spring St *TF:* 800-282-6575 ■ *Web:* www.saucony.com	Lexington	MA	02420	617-824-6000	
Saxon Shoes Inc 11800 W Broad St Suite 2750 *TF:* 800-686-5616 ■ *Web:* www.saxonshoes.com	Richmond	VA	23233	804-285-3473	285-8526

	City	State	Zip	Phone	Fax
Schwartz & Benjamin Inc 20 W 57th St 4th Fl	New York	NY	10019	212-541-9092	974-0609
Sebago Inc 9341 Courtland Dr	Rockford	MI	49351	616-866-5500	866-5625
TF: 800-253-2184 ■ *Web:* www.sebago.com					
SG Footwear Inc 20 E Broadway	Hackensack	NJ	07601	201-342-1200	342-4405
Web: www.sgfootwear.com					
Sherman Shoes 116 N Old Woodward Ave	Birmingham	MI	48009	248-646-8431	646-5018
Shiekh LLC 4083 E Airport Dr	Ontario	CA	91761	909-230-6620	732-2955*
**Fax Area Code:* 510 ■ *TF:* 888-574-4354 ■ *Web:* www.shiekhshoes.com					
Shoe Carnival Inc 7500 E Columbia St	Evansville	IN	47715	812-867-6471	867-3625
NASDAQ: SCVL ■ *TF Cust Svc:* 800-430-7463 ■ *Web:* www.shoecarnival.com					
Shoe Show of Rocky Mountain Inc 2201 Trinity Church Rd	Concord	NC	28027	704-782-4143	782-3411
TF Cust Svc: 888-557-4637 ■ *Web:* www.shoeshow.com					
Shoes.com Inc 6755 Hollywood Blvd 4th Fl	Los Angeles	CA	90028	888-233-6743	566-7933*
**Fax Area Code:* 310 ■ *TF:* 888-233-6743 ■ *Web:* www.shoes.com					
Shtofman Co 1905 W Gentry Pkwy	Tyler	TX	75702	903-592-0861	592-8380
Skechers USA Inc 228 Manhattan Beach Blvd Suite 200	Manhattan Beach	CA	90266	310-318-3100	318-5019
NYSE: SKX ■ *TF Cust Svc:* 800-243-0443 ■ *Web:* www.skechers.com					
South Cone Inc 9660 Chesapeake Dr	San Diego	CA	92123	858-514-3600	514-3620
TF: 800-423-6855 ■ *Web:* www.reef.com					
Spalding 150 Brookdale Dr	Springfield	MA	01104	413-735-1400	735-1570
TF Cust Svc: 800-772-5346 ■ *Web:* www.spalding.com					
Sperry Top-Sider 4200 S A St	Richmond	IN	47374	800-617-2239	
TF: 800-617-2239 ■ *Web:* www.sperrytopsider.com					
Stanbee Co Inc 70 Broad St	Carlstadt	NJ	07072	201-933-9666	933-7985
Web: www.stanbee.com					
Steven Madden Ltd 52-16 Barnett Ave	Long Island City	NY	11104	718-446-1800	446-5599
NASDAQ: SHOO ■ *TF:* 800-747-6233 ■ *Web:* www.stevemadden.com					
Stride Rite Corp 191 Spring St	Lexington	MA	02420	617-824-6000	428-2767*
**Fax Area Code:* 800 ■ *TF Cust Svc:* 800-666-5689 ■ *Web:* www.striderite.com					
Super Shoe Stores Inc 601 Dual Hwy	Hagerstown	MD	21740	301-739-2130	
Web: www.supershoes.com					
Teva Sport Sandals 515 N Beaver St	Flagstaff	AZ	86001	928-779-5938	779-6004
TF Orders: 800-367-8382 ■ *Web:* www.teva.com					
Timberland Co The 200 Domain Dr	Stratham	NH	03885	603-772-9500	926-9239
NYSE: TBL ■ *TF:* 800-258-0855 ■ *Web:* www.timberland.com					
Tony Lama Boot Co Inc 1137 Tony Lama St	El Paso	TX	79915	915-778-8311	771-6107
TF: 800-866-9526 ■ *Web:* www.tonylama.com					
Topline Corp 13150 SE 32nd St	Bellevue	WA	98005	425-643-3003	643-3846
Web: www.toplinecorp.com					
Trimfoot Co LLC 115 Trimfoot Terr	Farmington	MO	63640	573-756-6616	756-8482
TF: 800-325-6116 ■ *Web:* www.trimfootco.com					
TT Group Inc 702 Carnation Dr	Aurora	MO	65605	417-678-2181	678-6901
TF: 800-445-0886 ■ *Web:* www.tt-group.com					
Unisa America Inc 10814 NW 33rd St Suite 100	Miami	FL	33172	305-591-9397	594-2154
Web: www.unisashoes.com					
Vans Inc 15700 Shoemaker Ave	Santa Fe Springs	CA	90670	562-565-8267	565-8407
TF: 800-826-7800 ■ *Web:* www.vans.com					
Weinbrenner Shoe Co Inc 108 S Polk St	Merrill	WI	54452	715-536-5521	536-1172
TF Cust Svc: 800-826-0002 ■ *Web:* www.weinbrennerusa.com					
Wellco Enterprises Inc 614 Mabry Hood Rd Suite 100	Waynesville	NC	28786	828-456-3545	456-3547
TF: 800-840-3155 ■ *Web:* www.wellco.com					
West Coast Shoe Co 52828 NW Shoe Factory Ln PO Box 607	Scappoose	OR	97056	503-543-7114	543-7110
TF: 800-326-2711 ■ *Web:* www.westcoastshoe.com					
Weyco Group Inc 333 W Estabrook Blvd	Glendale	WI	53212	414-908-1880	908-1603
NASDAQ: WEYS ■ *Web:* www.weycogroup.com					
Willits Footwear Worldwide Inc 208 N River Rd	Halifax	PA	17032	717-896-3411	896-3470
TF: 800-544-3633 ■ *Web:* www.willitshoe.com					
Wolff Shoe Co 1705 Larkin williams Rd	Fenton	MO	63026	636-343-7770	326-4922
Wolverine World Wide Inc 9341 Courtland Dr	Rockford	MI	49351	616-866-5500	862-6230*
NYSE: WWW ■ **Fax Area Code:* 800 ■ *TF:* 800-365-5505 ■ *Web:* www.wolverineworldwide.com					
Wolverine Worldwide Inc 9341 Courtland Dr	Rockford	MI	49351	616-866-5500	325-8164*
NYSE: WWW ■ **Fax Area Code:* 800 ■ *TF:* 800-253-2184 ■ *Web:* www.wolverineworldwide.com					

305 FORESTRY SERVICES

SEE ALSO Timber Tracts p. 2714

	City	State	Zip	Phone	Fax
American Forest Management Inc PO Box 1919	Sumter	SC	29151	803-773-5461	773-4248
Web: www.americanforestmanagement.com					
Cascade Timber Consulting Inc 3210 Hwy 20	Sweet Home	OR	97386	541-367-2111	367-2117
Columbia River Log Scaling & Grading Bureau 260 Oakway Ctr	Eugene	OR	97401	541-342-6007	485-3086
Web: www.crls.com					
Environmental Consultants Inc 295 Buck Rd # 203	SouthHampton	PA	18966	215-322-4040	322-9404
Web: www.eci-consulting.com					
Fountains Forestry Inc 175 Barnstead Rd	Pittsfield	NH	03263	603-435-8234	435-7274
Web: www.fountainforestry.com					
Georgia Timberlands Inc 3250 Waterville Rd	Macon	GA	31206	478-788-4660	781-0246
Web: gatimberlands.com					
Hal Hays Construction Inc 1835 Chicago Ave Suite C	Riverside	CA	92507	951-788-0703	
TF: 888-425-4297 ■ *Web:* www.halhays.com					
International Air Response Inc 22000 S Old Price Rd	Chandler	AZ	85248	520-796-5188	796-1064
Web: www.internationalairresponse.com					
Lake County Forest Preserve District 2000 N Milwaukee Ave	Libertyville	IL	60048	847-367-6640	367-6649
Web: www.lcfpd.org					
Lower Dixie Timber Co 500 S Industrial PO Box 248	Thomasville	AL	36784	334-636-1500	636-1861
TF: 800-824-9525					
Resource Management Service LLC 31 Inverness Ctr Pkwy Suite 360	Birmingham	AL	35242	205-991-9516	991-2807
TF: 800-995-9516 ■ *Web:* www.resourcemgt.com					
Sealaska Corp 1 Sealaska Plaza Suite 400	Juneau	AK	99801	907-586-1512	586-2304
Web: www.sealaska.com					

306 FOUNDATIONS - COMMUNITY

SEE ALSO Charitable & Humanitarian Organizations p. 1412

	City	State	Zip	Phone	Fax
Adelphoi Village Inc 1119 Village Way	Latrobe	PA	15650	724-520-1111	520-1878
Web: www.adelphoivillage.org					
Arizona Community Foundation 2201 E Camelback Rd Suite 202	Phoenix	AZ	85016	602-381-1400	381-1575
TF: 800-222-8221 ■ *Web:* www.azfoundation.org					
Boston Foundation 75 Arlington St 10th Fl	Boston	MA	02116	617-338-1700	338-1604
Web: www.tbf.org					
California Community Foundation 445 S Figueroa St Suite 3400	Los Angeles	CA	90071	213-413-4130	383-2046
Web: www.calfund.org					
California Endowment 21650 Oxnard St Suite 1200	Woodland Hills	CA	91367	818-703-3311	703-4193
TF: 800-449-4149 ■ *Web:* www.calendow.org					
California Wellness Foundation (CWF) 6320 Canoga Ave Suite 1700	Woodland Hills	CA	91367	818-702-1900	702-1999
Web: www.calwellness.org					
Chicago Community Trust & Affiliates 111 E Wacker Dr Suite 1400	Chicago	IL	60601	312-616-8000	616-7955
Web: www.cct.org					
Cleveland Foundation 1422 Euclid Ave Suite 1300	Cleveland	OH	44115	216-861-3810	861-1729
TF: 800-869-3810 ■ *Web:* www.clevelandfoundation.org					
Colorado Trust 1600 Sherman St	Denver	CO	80203	303-837-1200	839-9034
TF: 888-847-9140 ■ *Web:* www.coloradotrust.org					
Columbus Foundation 1234 E Broad St	Columbus	OH	43205	614-251-4000	251-4009
Web: www.columbusfoundation.org					
Communities Foundation of Texas Inc 5500 Caruth Haven Ln	Dallas	TX	75225	214-750-4222	750-4210
Web: www.cftexas.org					
Community Foundation for Greater Atlanta Inc 50 Hurt Plaza Suite 449	Atlanta	GA	30303	404-688-5525	688-3060
Web: www.cfgreateratlanta.org					
Community Foundation for Greater New Haven 70 Audubon St	New Haven	CT	06510	203-777-2386	787-6584
Web: www.cfgnh.org					
Community Foundation for the National Capital Region 1201 15th St NW Suite 420	Washington	DC	20005	202-955-5890	955-8084
Web: www.cfncr.org					
Community Foundation of Greater Memphis 1900 Union Ave	Memphis	TN	38104	901-728-4600	722-0010
Web: www.cfgm.org					
Community Foundation Serving Richmond & Central Virginia 7325 Beaufont Springs Dr Suite 210	Richmond	VA	23225	804-330-7400	330-5992
Web: www.tcfrichmond.org					
Community Foundation Silicon Valley 60 S Market St Suite 1000	San Jose	CA	95113	408-278-2200	278-0280
Web: www.cfsv.org					
Dayton Foundation 40 N Main St # 500	Dayton	OH	45423	937-222-0410	222-0636
TF: 877-222-0410 ■ *Web:* www.daytonfoundation.org					
El Pomar Foundation 10 Lake Cir	Colorado Springs	CO	80906	719-633-7733	577-5702
TF: 800-554-7711 ■ *Web:* www.elpomar.org					
Foundation for the Carolinas 217 S Tryon St	Charlotte	NC	28202	704-973-4500	973-4599
TF: 800-973-7244 ■ *Web:* www.fftc.org					
Greater Cincinnati Foundation 200 W 4th St	Cincinnati	OH	45202	513-241-2880	852-6886
Web: www.greatercincinnatifdn.org					
Greater Kansas City Community Foundation & Affiliated Trusts (GKCCF) 1055 Broadway Suite 130	Kansas City	MO	64105	816-842-0944	842-8079
Web: www.gkccf.org					
Greater Milwaukee Foundation 101 W Pleasant St Suite 210	Milwaukee	WI	53212	414-272-5805	272-6235
Web: www.greatermilwaukeefoundation.org					
Hartford Foundation for Public Giving 10 Columbus Blvd	Hartford	CT	06106	860-548-1888	524-8346
Web: www.hfpg.org					
Hawaii Community Foundation 1164 Bishop St Suite 800	Honolulu	HI	96813	808-537-6333	521-6286
TF: 888-731-3863 ■ *Web:* www.hawaiicommunityfoundation.org					
Houston Endowment Inc 600 Travis St Suite 6400	Houston	TX	77002	713-238-8100	238-8101
Web: www.houstonendowment.org					
Marin Community Foundation 5 Hamilton Landing Suite 200	Novato	CA	94949	415-464-2500	464-2555
TF: 800-270-0295 ■ *Web:* www.marincf.org					
Minneapolis Foundation 80 8th St 800 IDS Ctr	Minneapolis	MN	55402	612-672-3878	672-3846
TF: 866-305-0543 ■ *Web:* www.minneapolisfoundation.org					
National Heritage Foundation 6201 Leesburg Pike Suite 405	Falls Church	VA	22044	703-536-8708	820-5100
Web: www.nhf.org					
New York Community Trust 909 3rd Ave 22nd Fl	New York	NY	10022	212-686-0010	532-8528
Web: www.nycommunitytrust.org					
Northwest Area Foundation 60 Plato Blvd E Suite 400	Saint Paul	MN	55107	651-224-9635	225-7701
TF: 888-904-9821 ■ *Web:* www.nwaf.org					
Oklahoma City Community Foundation 1300 N Broadway Dr	Oklahoma City	OK	73103	405-235-5603	235-5612
Web: www.occf.org					
Omaha Community Foundation (OCF) 302 S 36th St Suite 100	Omaha	NE	68131	402-342-3458	342-3582
TF: 800-794-3458 ■ *Web:* www.omahafoundation.org					

Phone Fax

Oregon Community Foundation The
1221 SW Yamhill St Suite 100 . . . . Portland OR 97205 503-227-6846 274-7771
Web: www.oregoncf.org
Peninsula Community Foundation
1700 S El Camino Real Suite 300. . . . . San Mateo CA 94402 650-358-9369 358-9817
Web: www.pcf.org
Pittsburgh Foundation 1 PPG Pl 30th Fl. . . . . Pittsburgh PA 15222 412-391-5122 391-7259
Web: www.pittsburghfoundation.org
Rhode Island Foundation 1 Union Stn . . . . Providence RI 02903 401-274-4564 331-8085
Web: www.rifoundation.org
Saint Paul Foundation
55 E 5th St Suite 600 . . . . Saint Paul MN 55101 651-224-5463 224-8123
TF: 800-875-6167 ■ *Web:* www.saintpaulfoundation.org
San Diego Foundation
1420 Kettner Blvd Suite 500. . . . . San Diego CA 92101 619-235-2300 239-1710
Web: www.sdfoundation.org
San Francisco Foundation
225 Bush St Suite 500 . . . . San Francisco CA 94104 415-733-8500 477-2783
Web: www.sff.org
Seattle Foundation 1200 5th Ave Suite 1300 . . . . Seattle WA 98101 206-622-2294 622-7673
Web: www.seattlefoundation.org

307 FOUNDATIONS - CORPORATE

SEE ALSO Charitable & Humanitarian Organizations p. 1412

Phone Fax

Abbott Laboratories Fund
100 Abbott Pk Rd Dept 379 Bldg 6D. . . . . Abbott Park IL 60064 847-935-0853 935-5051
Web: www.abbott.com/citizenship/fund/fund.shtml
Aetna Foundation Inc 151 Farmington Ave. . . . . Hartford CT 06156 860-273-6382 273-4764
Web: www.aetna.com
Alabama Power Foundation Inc
600 N 18th St . . . . Birmingham AL 35291 205-257-2508 257-1860
Web: www.southerncompany.com
Alcoa Foundation 201 Isabella St. . . . . Pittsburgh PA 15212 412-553-2348 553-4498
Web: www.alcoa.com/foundation
Allstate Foundation
2775 Sanders Rd Suite F4 . . . . Northbrook IL 60062 847-402-5502 326-7517
Web: www.allstate.com
Archer Daniels Midland Foundation
4666 E Faries Pkwy . . . . Decatur IL 62526 217-424-5200 424-5581
TF: 800-637-5843
Bank of America Charitable Foundation
100 N Tryon St . . . . Charlotte NC 28255 800-218-9946 622-3469*
**Fax Area Code:* 415 ■ *TF:* 888-488-9802 ■ *Web:* www.bankofamerica.com/foundation
Baxter International Foundation
1 Baxter Pkwy . . . . Deerfield IL 60015 847-948-4605 948-4559
Web: www.baxter.com
Bristol-Myers Squibb Foundation Inc
345 Pk Ave . . . . New York NY 10154 212-546-4000 546-9574
Web: www.bms.com/sr/philanthropy
Burroughs Wellcome Fund
21 TW Alexander Dr
PO Box 13901 . . . . Research Triangle Park NC 27709 919-991-5100 941-5160
Web: www.bwfund.org
Cargill Foundation
15407 McGinty Rd W MS PA-50 . . . . Wayzata MN 55391 952-742-2546 742-7224
TF: 800-227-4455 ■ *Web:* www.cargill.com
Caterpillar Foundation 100 NE Adams St. . . . . Peoria IL 61629 309-675-4464 675-4332
Web: www.cat.com/foundation
CIGNA Foundation 1601 Chestnut St . . . . Philadelphia PA 19192 215-761-1000 761-5715
Web: www.cigna.com/general/about/community/contributions.html
Cisco Systems Foundation 170 W Tasman Dr . . . . San Jose CA 95134 408-527-3040
TF: 800-553-6387 ■ *Web:* www.cisco.com
Citigroup Foundation 153 East 53rd St. . . . . New York NY 10022 212-559-9124 793-5906
Web: www.citigroup.com/citigroup/citizen
Coca-Cola Foundation Inc PO Box 1734 . . . . Atlanta GA 30301 404-676-2568 676-8804
TF: 800-438-2653 ■
Web: www2.coca-cola.com/citizenship/foundation_coke.html
DaimlerChrysler Corp Fund
1000 Chrysler Dr . . . . Auburn Hills MI 48326 248-576-5741 576-4742
TF: 800-247-9753 ■ *Web:* www.fund.daimlerchrysler.com
Dow Chemical Co Foundation 2030 Dow Ctr. . . . . Midland MI 48674 989-636-1000 636-4460
TF: 800-331-6451 ■ *Web:* www.dow.com/about/corp/social/social.htm
Eli Lilly & Co Foundation
Lilly Corporate Ctr . . . . Indianapolis IN 46285 317-276-2000 277-6719
TF: 800-545-5979 ■ *Web:* www.lilly.com
Emerson Charitable Trust
8000 W Florissant Ave . . . . Saint Louis MO 63136 314-553-3621
ExxonMobil Foundation Inc
5959 Las Colinas Blvd . . . . Irving TX 75039 972-444-1000 444-1405
Fidelity Foundation 82 Devonshire St Suite S-2 . . . . Boston MA 02109 617-563-6806 476-9130
Web: www.fidelityfoundation.org
Freddie Mac Foundation 8250 Jones Branch Dr . . . . McLean VA 22102 703-918-8888 918-8895
TF: 800-373-3343 ■ *Web:* www.freddiemacfoundation.org
GE Foundation 3135 Easton Tpke . . . . Fairfield CT 06828 203-373-3216 373-3029
Web: www.ge.com
General Mills Foundation
1 General Mills Blvd. . . . . Minneapolis MN 55426 763-764-2211 764-4114
Web: www.generalmills.com
General Motors Foundation Inc
3044 W Grand Blvd 11-134 GM Bldg. . . . . Detroit MI 48202 313-665-0824
Web: www.gm.com
Georgia Power Foundation Inc
241 Ralph McGill Blvd NE Bin 10131. . . . . Atlanta GA 30308 404-506-6784 506-1485
Web: www.southerncompany.com
GlaxoSmithKline Foundation
5 Moore Dr. . . . . Research Triangle Park NC 27709 919-483-2140 315-3015
TF: 888-825-5249 ■ *Web:* www.gsk.com
Hallmark Corp Foundation 2501 McGee St . . . . Kansas City MO 64108 816-274-8516 274-8547

Phone Fax

Hasbro Children's Foundation The
10 Rockefeller Plaza 16th Fl . . . . New York NY 10020 212-713-7654
Web: www.hasbro.com
HCA Foundation 1 Pk Plaza. . . . . Nashville TN 37203 615-344-2343 344-5722
Web: www.hcacaring.org
Hess Foundation Inc
1185 Avenue of the Americas . . . . New York NY 10036 212-997-8500 536-8390
HJ Heinz Co Foundation
600 Grant St 60th Fl . . . . Pittsburgh PA 15219 412-456-5773 442-3227
Web: www.heinz.com
Honeywell International Foundation
101 Columbia Rd . . . . Morristown NJ 07962 973-455-2000 455-4807
Humana Foundation Inc
500 W Main St Humana Bldg . . . . Louisville KY 40202 502-580-3613 580-1256
Web: www.humanafoundation.org
IBM International Foundation 1 New Orchard Rd . . . . Armonk NY 10504 914-499-5242 499-7684
Web: www.ibm.com
Kimberly-Clark Foundation 351 Phelps Dr. . . . . Irving TX 75038 972-281-1477 281-1490
Web: www.kimberly-clark.com
Koch Foundation Inc
4421 NW 39th Ave Suite 1 . . . . Gainesville FL 32606 352-373-7491
Web: www.kochenterprises.com
Levi Strauss Foundation
1155 Battery St. . . . . San Francisco CA 94111 415-501-6000 501-6575
Web: www.levistrauss.com/about/foundations/levi-strauss-foundation
Lutheran Community Foundation
625 4th Ave S Suite 200. . . . . Minneapolis MN 55415 612-340-4110 340-4109
TF: 800-365-4172 ■ *Web:* www.thelcf.org
Mead Corp Foundation Courthouse Plaza NE . . . . Dayton OH 45463 937-495-6323 495-4103
TF: 800-345-6323
Merck Co Foundation
1 Merck Dr PO Box 100 . . . . Whitehouse Station NJ 08889 908-423-2042
MetLife Foundation
2701 Queens Plaza N 1 MetLife Plaza. . . . . Long Island City NY 11101 212-578-6272 578-0617
Web: www.metlife.org
Motorola Foundation 1303 E Algonquin Rd . . . . Schaumburg IL 60196 847-576-5000 538-4055
Web: www.motorola.com/MotorolaFoundation
New York Life Foundation
51 Madison Ave Suite 1600 . . . . New York NY 10010 212-576-7341
Web: www.newyorklife.com
New York Times Co Foundation Inc
229 W 43rd St . . . . New York NY 10036 212-556-1091 556-4450
Web: www.nytco.com/company/foundation
PepsiCo Foundation Inc 700 Anderson Hill Rd. . . . . Purchase NY 10577 914-253-2000 253-3553
Pfizer Foundation Inc 235 E 42nd St. . . . . New York NY 10017 212-733-2323 573-2883
TF: 800-733-4717 ■ *Web:* www.pfizer.com
Playboy Foundation 680 N Lake Shore Dr. . . . . Chicago IL 60611 312-751-8000 751-2818
Web: www.playboyenterprises.com/foundation
Principal Financial Group Foundation Inc
711 High St . . . . Des Moines IA 50392 515-247-7227 246-5475
TF: 800-986-3343 ■ *Web:* www.principal.com/about/giving
Procter & Gamble Fund PO Box 599. . . . . Cincinnati OH 45201 513-983-1100
Revlon Foundation Inc 237 Pk Ave . . . . New York NY 10017 212-527-6974
TF Cust Svc: 800-473-8566 ■ *Web:* www.revlon.com
Sara Lee Foundation 3 First National Plaza. . . . . Chicago IL 60602 312-558-8448 419-3192
TF: 800-727-2533 ■ *Web:* www.saraleefoundation.org
SBC Foundation 130 E Travis St Suite 350 . . . . San Antonio TX 78205 800-591-9663 351-2599*
**Fax Area Code:* 210 ■ *TF:* 800-591-9663 ■ *Web:* www.sbc.com/foundation
Scripps Howard Foundation
312 Walnut St PO Box 5380. . . . . Cincinnati OH 45201 513-977-3035 977-3800
TF: 800-888-3000 ■ *Web:* www.scripps.com/foundation
Siemens Foundation 170 Wood Ave S. . . . . Iselin NJ 08830 732-603-5886 603-5890
TF: 877-822-5233 ■ *Web:* www.siemens-foundation.org
State Farm Cos Foundation
1 State Farm Plaza Suite B-4 . . . . Bloomington IL 61710 309-766-2161 994-5272
TF Cust Svc: 866-604-5480 ■ *Web:* www.easymatch.com/statefarm
Target Foundation
1000 Nicollete Mall TPS 3080 . . . . Minneapolis MN 55403 612-696-6098 696-5088
TF: 800-440-0680 ■ *Web:* www.targetcorp.com
Tenet Healthcare Foundation
13737 Noel Rd Suite 100 . . . . Dallas TX 75240 469-893-6502
Web: www.tenethealth.com
Union Pacific Foundation
1400 Douglas St MS 1560. . . . . Omaha NE 68179 402-544-5600
Web: www.up.com/found
UPS Foundation 55 Glenlake Pkwy NE . . . . Atlanta GA 30328 404-828-6451 828-7435
Web: www.community.ups.com/philanthropy/main.html
Verizon Foundation 1255 Corporate Dr . . . . Irving TX 75038 800-360-7955 840-6988*
**Fax Area Code:* 212 ■ *TF:* 800-360-7955 ■ *Web:* www.foundation.verizon.com
Wachovia Foundation 301 S College St . . . . Charlotte NC 28288 704-374-4085 374-2484
Web: www.wachovia.com/wachoviafoundation
Wal-Mart Foundation 702 SW 8th St. . . . . Bentonville AR 72716 800-530-9925 273-6850*
**Fax Area Code:* 479 ■ *TF:* 800-530-9925 ■ *Web:* www.walmartfoundation.org
Whirlpool Foundation 2000 N M-63 . . . . Benton Harbor MI 49022 269-923-5584 925-0154
TF: 800-446-2574 ■ *Web:* www.whirlpoolcorp.com
Xerox Foundation 45 Glover Ave PO Box 4504 . . . . Norwalk CT 06856 203-968-3000
TF: 800-334-6200

308 FOUNDATIONS - PRIVATE

SEE ALSO Charitable & Humanitarian Organizations p. 1412

Phone Fax

Adolph Coors Foundation
4100 E Mississippi Ave Suite 1850 . . . . Denver CO 80246 303-388-1636 388-1684
Web: www.acoorsfdn.org
Ahmanson Foundation 9215 Wilshire Blvd . . . . Beverly Hills CA 90210 310-278-0770
Web: www.theahmansonfoundation.org
Alfred P Sloan Foundation
630 5th Ave Suite 2550 . . . . New York NY 10111 212-649-1649 757-5117
Web: www.sloan.org

Foundation	City	State	ZIP	Phone	Fax
Amon G Carter Foundation 201 Main St # 1945 *Web:* www.agcf.org	Fort Worth	TX	76102	817-332-2783	332-2787
Andrew W Mellon Foundation 140 E 62nd St *Web:* www.mellon.org	New York	NY	10021	212-838-8400	888-4172
Annenberg Foundation 150 N Radnor-Chester Rd Suite 200 *Web:* www.annenbergfoundation.org	Radnor	PA	19087	610-341-9066	964-8688
Annie E Casey Foundation 701 St Paul St *TF:* 800-222-1099 ■ *Web:* www.aecf.org	Baltimore	MD	21202	410-547-6600	547-6624
Archibald Bush Foundation 332 Minnesota St Suite E-900 *Web:* www.bushfoundation.org	Saint Paul	MN	55101	651-227-0891	297-6485
Arthur S DeMoss Foundation 777 S Flagler Dr Suite 1600-W	West Palm Beach	FL	33401	561-804-9000	804-9025
Arthur Vining Davis Foundations 225 Water St Suite 1510 *Web:* www.avdfdn.org	Jacksonville	FL	32202	904-359-0670	359-0675
Ave Maria Foundation 1 Ave Maria Dr PO Box 373 *Web:* www.avemariafoundation.org	Ann Arbor	MI	48106	734-930-3150	930-4453
Barr Foundation 136 NE Olive Way *Web:* www.oandp.com	Boca Raton	FL	33432	561-394-6514	391-7601
Benton Foundation 1625 K St NW 11th Fl *Web:* www.benton.org	Washington	DC	20006	202-638-5770	638-5771
Bill & Melinda Gates Foundation PO Box 23350 *TF:* 888-452-6352 ■ *Web:* www.gatesfoundation.org	Seattle	WA	98102	206-709-3100	709-3180
Brown Foundation Inc 2217 Welch St *Web:* www.brownfoundation.org	Houston	TX	77019	713-523-6867	523-2917
Carnegie Corp of New York 437 Madison Ave 26th Fl *Web:* www.carnegie.org	New York	NY	10022	212-371-3200	754-4073
Center Township Trustee of Marion Co Indiana 863 Massachusetts Ave *Web:* www.centergov.org	Indianapolis	IN	46204	317-633-3610	289-4324
Champlin Foundations The 300 Centerville Rd *Web:* www.fdncenter.org/grantmaker/champlin	Warwick	RI	02886	401-736-0370	736-7248
Charles & Helen Schwab Foundation 1650 S Amphlett Blvd Suite 300 *Web:* www.schwabfoundation.org	San Mateo	CA	94402	650-655-2412	655-2411
Charles Hayden Foundation 140 Broadway 51st Fl *Web:* www.fdncenter.org	New York	NY	10005	212-785-3677	785-3689
Charles Stewart Mott Foundation 503 S Saginaw St Suite 1200 *Web:* www.mott.org	Flint	MI	48502	810-238-5651	766-1753
Chatlos Foundation 710 Miami Springs Dr # 200 *Web:* www.chatlos.org	Longwood	FL	32779	407-862-5077	862-0708
Colonial Williamsburg Foundation PO Box 1776 **Fax:* Hum Res ■ *TF:* 800-447-8679 ■ *Web:* www.history.org	Williamsburg	VA	23187	757-229-1000	220-7259*
Commonwealth Fund 1 E 75th St *Web:* www.cmwf.org	New York	NY	10021	212-606-3800	606-3500
Conrad N Hilton Foundation 100 W Liberty St Suite 840 *Web:* www.hiltonfoundation.org	Reno	NV	89501	775-323-4221	323-4150
Corporation for Public Broadcasting (CPB) 401 9th St NW *TF:* 800-272-2190 ■ *Web:* www.cpb.org	Washington	DC	20004	202-879-9600	879-9700
Dave Thomas Foundation for Adoption 525 Metro Pl Suite 220 *TF:* 800-275-3832 ■ *Web:* www.davethomasfoundation.org	Dublin	OH	43017	614-764-8454	766-3871
David & Lucile Packard Foundation 300 2nd St *Web:* www.packard.org	Los Altos	CA	94022	650-948-7658	948-5793
Donald W Reynolds Foundation 1701 Village Ctr Cir *Web:* www.dwreynolds.org	Las Vegas	NV	89134	702-804-6000	804-6099
Doris Duke Charitable Foundation (DDCF) 650 5th Ave 19th Fl *Web:* www.ddcf.org	New York	NY	10019	212-974-7000	974-7590
Duke Endowment 100 N Tryon St Suite 3500 *Web:* www.dukeendowment.org	Charlotte	NC	28202	704-376-0291	376-9336
Edna McConnell Clark Foundation 415 Madison Ave 10th Fl *Web:* www.emcf.org	New York	NY	10017	212-551-9100	421-9325
Educational Foundation of America 35 Church Ln *Web:* www.efaw.org	Westport	CT	06880	203-226-6498	227-0424
Ellison Medical Foundation 4710 Bethesda Ave Suite 204 *Web:* www.ellisonfoundation.org	Bethesda	MD	20814	301-657-1830	657-1828
Evelyn & Walter Haas Jr Fund 1 Market St Suite 400 Landmark Bldg *Web:* www.haasjr.org	San Francisco	CA	94105	415-856-1400	856-1500
Ewing Marion Kauffman Foundation (EMKF) 4801 Rockhill Rd *TF:* 800-489-4900 ■ *Web:* www.kauffman.org	Kansas City	MO	64110	816-932-1000	932-1100
First Nonprofit Insurance Co 111 N Canal St Suite 801 *TF:* 800-526-4352 ■ *Web:* www.firstnonprofit.com	Chicago	IL	60606	312-930-9500	930-0375
Ford Family Foundation 1600 NW Stewart Pkwy *Web:* www.tfff.org	Roseburg	OR	97470	541-957-5574	957-5720
Ford Foundation 320 E 43rd St *Web:* www.fordfound.org	New York	NY	10017	212-573-5000	351-3677
Gates Family Foundation 3575 Cherry Creek N Dr Suite 100 *Web:* www.gatesfamilyfoundation.org	Denver	CO	80209	303-722-1881	316-3038
George S & Dolores Dore Eccles Foundation 79 S Main St 12th Fl *Web:* www.gsecclesfoundation.org	Salt Lake City	UT	84111	801-246-5355	350-3510
Geraldine R Dodge Foundation 14 Maple Ave *Web:* www.grdodge.org	Morristown	NJ	07962	973-540-8442	540-1211
Goizueta Foundation 4401 Northside Pkwy Suite 520 *Web:* www.goizuetafoundation.org	Atlanta	GA	30327	404-239-0390	239-0018
Hall Family Foundation 2501 McGee St PO Box 419580 MD 323 *Web:* www.hallfamilyfoundation.org	Kansas City	MO	64141	816-274-8516	274-8547
Hearst Foundation The 300 W 57th St 26th Fl *Web:* hearstfdn.org	New York	NY	10019	212-586-5404	586-1917
Henry J Kaiser Family Foundation 2400 Sand Hill Rd *Web:* www.kff.org	Menlo Park	CA	94025	650-854-9400	854-4800
Henry Luce Foundation Inc 111 W 50th St Suite 4601 *Web:* www.hluce.org	New York	NY	10020	212-489-7700	581-9541
Herbert H & Grace A Dow Foundation 1018 W Main St *TF:* 800-362-4849 ■ *Web:* www.hhdowfoundation.org	Midland	MI	48640	989-631-3699	631-0675
Horace W Goldsmith Foundation 375 Pk Ave Rm 1602	New York	NY	10152	212-319-8700	319-2881
Hudson-Webber Foundation 333 W Fort St Suite 1310 *Web:* www.hudson-webber.org	Detroit	MI	48226	313-963-7777	963-2818
J Bulow Campbell Foundation 50 Hurt Plaza Suite 850 *Web:* www.jbcf.org	Atlanta	GA	30303	404-658-9066	659-4802
J Paul Getty Trust 1200 Getty Ctr Dr Suite 403 *Web:* www.getty.edu	Los Angeles	CA	90049	310-440-7340	440-7722
JA & Kathryn Albertson Foundation PO Box 70002 *Web:* www.jkaf.org	Boise	ID	83707	208-424-2600	424-2626
James Irvine Foundation 1 Market Plaza *Web:* www.irvine.org	San Francisco	CA	94105	415-777-2244	777-0869
JE & LE Mabee Foundation Inc 401 S Boston Ave 30th Fl *Web:* www.mabeefoundation.com	Tulsa	OK	74103	918-584-4286	585-5540
John D & Catherine T MacArthur Foundation 140 S Dearborn St *Web:* www.macfound.org	Chicago	IL	60603	312-726-8000	920-6258
John S & James L Knight Foundation 200 S Biscayne Blvd Suite 3300 *TF:* 800-711-2004 ■ *Web:* www.knightfdn.org	Miami	FL	33131	305-908-2600	908-2698
John Simon Guggenheim Memorial Foundation 90 Pk Ave 33rd Fl *Web:* www.gf.org	New York	NY	10016	212-687-4470	697-3248
John Templeton Foundation 300 Conshohocken State Rd Suite 500 *Web:* www.templeton.org	West Conshohocken	PA	19428	610-941-2828	825-1730
Joyce Foundation 70 W Madison St Suite 2750 *Web:* www.joycefdn.org	Chicago	IL	60602	312-782-2464	782-4160
Kate B Reynolds Charitable Trust 128 Reynolda Village *TF:* 800-485-9080 ■ *Web:* www.kbr.org	Winston-Salem	NC	27106	336-397-5500	723-7765
Kiwanis International Foundation 3636 Woodview Trace *TF:* 800-549-2647 ■ *Web:* www.kif.kiwanis.org	Indianapolis	IN	46268	317-217-6254	471-8323
Koret Foundation 33 New Montgomery St Suite 1090 *Web:* www.koretfoundation.org	San Francisco	CA	94105	415-882-7740	882-7775
Liberty Fund Inc 8335 Allison Pointe Trial Suite 300 *TF:* 800-955-8335 ■ *Web:* www.libertyfund.org	Indianapolis	IN	46250	317-842-0880	579-6060
Lilly Endowment Inc 2801 N Meridian St *Web:* www.lillyendowment.org	Indianapolis	IN	46208	317-924-5471	926-4431
Lois Pope LIFE Foundation 6274 Linton Blvd Suite 103 *Web:* www.life-edu.org	Delray Beach	FL	33484	561-865-0955	865-0938
Lumina Foundation for Education 30 S Meridian St Suite 700 *TF:* 800-834-5756 ■ *Web:* www.luminafoundation.org	Indianapolis	IN	46204	317-951-5342	951-5063
Lynde & Harry Bradley Foundation Inc 1241 N Franklin Pl *Web:* www.bradleyfdn.org	Milwaukee	WI	53202	414-291-9915	291-9991
Lyndhurst Foundation 517 E 5th St *Web:* www.lyndhurstfoundation.org	Chattanooga	TN	37403	423-756-0767	756-0770
Magic Johnson Foundation Inc 9100 Wilshire Blvd Suite 700-E *TF:* 888-624-4205 ■ *Web:* www.magicjohnson.org	Beverly Hills	CA	90212	310-246-4400	246-1106
McCune Foundation 6 PPG Pl Suite 750 *Web:* www.mccune.org	Pittsburgh	PA	15222	412-644-8779	644-8059
McKnight Foundation 710 2nd St S Suite 400 *Web:* www.mcknight.org	Minneapolis	MN	55401	612-333-4220	332-3833
Meadows Foundation Inc 3003 Swiss Ave *TF:* 800-826-9431 ■ *Web:* www.mfi.org	Dallas	TX	75204	214-826-9431	827-7042
Meyer Memorial Trust 425 NW 10th Ave Suite 400 *Web:* www.mmt.org	Portland	OR	97209	503-228-5512	228-5840
Michael J Fox Foundation for Parkinson's Research Grand Central Stn PO Box 4777 *TF:* 800-708-7644 ■ *Web:* www.michaeljfox.org	New York	NY	10163	800-708-7644	
Milken Family Foundation 1250 4th St *Web:* www.mff.org	Santa Monica	CA	90401	310-570-4800	570-4801
MJ Murdock Charitable Trust 703 Broadway St Suite 710 *Web:* www.murdock-trust.org	Vancouver	WA	98660	360-694-8415	694-1819
Moody Foundation 2302 Post Office St Suite 704 *TF:* 866-742-1133 ■ *Web:* www.moodyf.org	Galveston	TX	77550	409-763-5333	763-5564

Name / Address	City	State	ZIP	Phone	Fax
Morris & Gwendolyn Cafritz Foundation 1825 K St NW 14th Fl	Washington	DC	20006	202-223-3100	296-7567
Web: www.cafritzfoundation.org					
National Foundation for Cancer Research (NFCR) 4600 E W Hwy Suite 525	Bethesda	MD	20814	301-654-1250	654-5824
TF: 800-321-2873 ■ *Web:* www.nfcr.org					
Nellie Mae Education Foundation 1250 Hancock St Suite 205N	Quincy	MA	02169	781-348-4200	348-4299
TF: 877-635-5436 ■ *Web:* www.nmefdn.org					
Oceanside Produce Inc 5780 Mission Ave	Oceanside	CA	92057	760-758-2942	758-3813
Web: www.vineripe.com					
Open Society Institute 400 W 59th St	New York	NY	10019	212-548-0600	548-4679
Web: www.soros.org					
Packard Humanities Institute 300 2nd St	Los Altos	CA	94022	650-948-0150	948-4135
Web: www.packhum.org					
Paul G Allen Family Foundation 505 5th Ave S Suite 900	Seattle	WA	98104	206-342-2000	342-3000
Web: www.pgafamilyfoundation.org					
Peter Kiewit Foundation 8805 Indian Hills Dr Suite 225	Omaha	NE	68114	402-344-7890	344-8099
Pew Charitable Trusts 2005 Market St 1 Commerce Sq Suite 1700	Philadelphia	PA	19103	215-575-9050	575-4939
TF: 800-634-4850 ■ *Web:* www.pewtrusts.org					
Public Welfare Foundation 1200 U St NW	Washington	DC	20009	202-965-1800	265-8852
TF: 800-275-7934 ■ *Web:* www.publicwelfare.org					
Research Corp 4703 E Camp Lowell Dr Suite 201	Tucson	AZ	85712	520-571-1111	571-1119
Web: www.rescorp.org					
Retirement Research Foundation 8765 W Higgins Rd Suite 430	Chicago	IL	60631	773-714-8080	714-8089
Web: www.rrf.org					
Richard King Mellon Foundation 500 Grant St Suite 4106	Pittsburgh	PA	15219	412-392-2800	392-2837
Web: www.fdncenter.org/grantmaker/rkmellon					
Robert A Welch Foundation 5555 San Felipe St Suite 1900	Houston	TX	77056	713-961-9884	961-5168
Web: www.welch1.org					
Robert R McCormick Tribune Foundation 205 N Michigan Ave Suite 4300	Chicago	IL	60611	312-445-5000	445-5001
Web: www.mccormickfoundation.org					
Robert W Woodruff Foundation Inc 50 Hurt Plaza Suite 1200	Atlanta	GA	30303	404-522-6755	522-7026
Web: www.woodruff.org					
Robert Wood Johnson Foundation PO Box 2316	Princeton	NJ	08543	609-452-8701	627-6701
Web: www.rwjf.org					
Rockefeller Bros Fund 475 Riverside Dr Suite 900	New York	NY	10115	212-812-4200	812-4299
Web: www.rbf.org					
Rockefeller Foundation 420 5th Ave	New York	NY	10018	212-869-8500	764-3468*
**Fax:* Mail Rm ■ *TF:* 800-645-1133 ■ *Web:* www.rockefellerfoundation.org					
Rosie's For All Kids Foundation Inc PO Box 1001	New York	NY	10108	212-703-7388	703-7381
Web: www.forallkids.org					
Roy J Carver Charitable Trust 202 Iowa Ave	Muscatine	IA	52761	563-263-4010	263-1547
Web: www.carvertrust.org					
Skillman Foundation The 100 Falon Centre Dr Suite 100	Detroit	MI	48207	313-393-1185	393-1187
Web: www.skillman.org					
Smith Richardson Foundation Inc 60 Jesup Rd	Westport	CT	06880	203-222-6222	222-6282
Web: www.srf.org					
Spencer Foundation 625 N Michigan Ave Suite 1600	Chicago	IL	60611	312-337-7000	337-0282
Web: www.spencer.org					
Starr Foundation 399 Pk Ave 17th Fl	New York	NY	10022	212-909-3600	750-3536
Web: www.starrfoundation.org					
Stowers Institute For Medical Research 1000 E 50th St	Kansas City	MO	64110	816-926-4000	926-2000
Web: www.stowers-institute.org					
Sunshine Lady Foundation Inc 4900 Randall Pkwy Suite H	Wilmington	NC	28403	910-397-7742	397-0023
TF: 866-255-7742 ■ *Web:* www.sunshineladyfdn.org					
Surdna Foundation Inc 330 Madison Ave 30th Fl	New York	NY	10017	212-557-0010	557-0003
Web: www.surdna.org					
Terra Foundation for American Art 980 N Michigan Ave Suite 1315	Chicago	IL	60611	312-664-3939	664-2052
Web: www.terraamericanart.org					
Thomas Jefferson Foundation PO Box 316	Charlottesville	VA	22902	434-984-9808	977-7757
Web: www.monticello.org					
Turner Foundation Inc 133 Luckie St 2nd Fl	Atlanta	GA	30303	404-681-9900	681-0172
Web: www.turnerfoundation.org					
Van Andel Institute 333 Bostwick Ave NE	Grand Rapids	MI	49503	616-234-5000	234-5001
Web: www.vai.org					
Vira I Heinz Endowment 625 Liberty Ave 30 Dominion Tower	Pittsburgh	PA	15222	412-281-5777	281-5788
Web: www.heinz.org					
Wallace Foundation The 5 Penn Plaza 7th Fl	New York	NY	10001	212-251-9700	679-6990
Web: www.wallacefoundation.org/Pages/default.aspx					
Walter & Elise Haas Fund 1 Lombard St Suite 305	San Francisco	CA	94111	415-398-4474	
Web: www.haassr.org					
Walton Family Foundation Inc (WFF) PO Box 2030	Bentonville	AR	72712	479-464-1570	464-1580
Web: www.waltonfamilyfoundation.org					
Wayne & Gladys Valley Foundation 1939 Harrison St Suite 510	Oakland	CA	94612	510-466-6060	466-6067
Weingart Foundation 1055 W 7th St Suite 3050	Los Angeles	CA	90017	213-688-7799	688-1515
Web: www.weingartfnd.org					
Whitehall Foundation Inc 125 Worth Ave	Palm Beach	FL	33480	561-655-4474	659-4978
Web: www.whitehall.org					
William & Flora Hewlett Foundation 2121 Sand Hill Rd	Menlo Park	CA	94025	650-234-4500	234-4501
Web: www.hewlett.org					
William K Warren Foundation 6585 S Yale Ave Suite 900	Tulsa	OK	74136	918-492-8100	481-7935
William Penn Foundation 100 N 18th St 2 Logan Sq 11th Fl	Philadelphia	PA	19103	215-988-1830	988-1823
Web: www.wpennfdn.org					
WK Kellogg Foundation 1 Michigan Ave E	Battle Creek	MI	49017	269-968-1611	968-0413
Web: www.wkkf.org					
WM Keck Foundation 550 S Hope St Suite 2500	Los Angeles	CA	90071	213-680-3833	
Web: www.wmkeck.org					

309 FOUNDRIES - INVESTMENT

Name / Address	City	State	ZIP	Phone	Fax
Aero Metals Inc 1201 E Lincoln Way	La Porte	IN	46350	219-326-1976	326-1972
Web: www.aerometals.com					
Bescast Inc 4600 E 355th St	Willoughby	OH	44094	440-946-5300	946-8437
Web: www.bescast.com					
Bimac Corp 3034 Dryden Rd	Dayton	OH	45439	937-299-7333	299-7367
Web: www.bimac.com					
Consolidated Casting Corp 1501 S I-45	Hutchins	TX	75141	972-225-7305	225-2970
Web: www.consolicast.com					
Dolphin Inc 740 S 59th Ave	Phoenix	AZ	85043	602-272-6747	233-9570
Web: www.dolphincasting.com					
Engineered Precision Casting Co Inc 952 Palmer Ave	Middletown	NJ	07748	732-671-2424	671-8615
Web: www.epcast.com					
FS Precision Tech Co LLC 3025 E Victoria St	Rancho Dominguez	CA	90221	310-638-0595	631-2884
Web: www.fs-precision.com					
Hitchiner Mfg Co Inc 117 Old Wilton Rd PO Box 2001	Milford	NH	03055	603-673-1100	673-7960
Web: www.hitchiner.com					
Northern Precision Casting Co 300 Interchange N PO Box 580	Lake Geneva	WI	53147	262-248-4461	248-1796
TF: 800-934-4903 ■ *Web:* www.northernprecision.com					
PCC Structurals Inc 4600 SE Harney Dr	Portland	OR	97206	503-777-3881	652-3593
Web: www.pccstructurals.com					
Pennsylvania Precision Cast Parts Inc 521 N 3rd Ave PO Box 1429	Lebanon	PA	17042	717-273-3338	273-2662
Web: www.ppcpinc.com					
Post Precision Castings Inc 21 Walnut St	Strausstown	PA	19559	610-488-1011	488-6928
Web: www.postprecision.com					
Precision Castparts Corp 4650 SW Macadam Ave Suite 440	Portland	OR	97239	503-417-4800	417-4817
NYSE: PCP ■ *Web:* www.precast.com					
Precision Metalsmiths Inc 1081 E 200th St	Cleveland	OH	44117	216-481-8900	481-1101
Web: www.precisionmetalsmiths.com					
Remet Corp 210 Commons Rd	Utica	NY	13502	315-797-8700	797-4477
TF: 800-445-2424 ■ *Web:* www.remet.com					
Stainless Foundry & Engineering Inc 5110 N 35th St	Milwaukee	WI	53209	414-462-7400	462-7303
Web: www.stainlessfoundry.com					
Waltek Inc 14310 Sunfish Lake Blvd NW	Ramsey	MN	55303	763-427-3181	427-3216
TF: 800-937-9496 ■ *Web:* www.waltekinc.com					
Wyman-Gordon Co 10825 Telge Rd PO Box 40456	Houston	TX	01536	281-856-9900	839-7500*
**Fax Area Code:* 508 ■ *TF:* 800-343-6070 ■ *Web:* www.wyman-gordon.com					

310 FOUNDRIES - IRON & STEEL

SEE ALSO Foundries - Nonferrous (Castings) p. 1883

Name / Address	City	State	ZIP	Phone	Fax
Aarrowcast Inc 2900 E Richmond St	Shawano	WI	54166	715-526-3600	526-9758
Web: www.aarrowcast.com					
Allegheny Technologies Inc 1000 Six PPG Pl	Pittsburgh	PA	15222	412-394-2800	394-3034*
NYSE: ATI ■ **Fax:* Hum Res ■ *TF Sales:* 800-258-3586 ■ *Web:* www.alleghenytechnologies.com					
Alloy Engineering & Casting Co 1700 W Washington St	Champaign	IL	61821	866-352-8001	897-2525*
**Fax Area Code:* 260 ■ *TF:* 866-352-8001 ■ *Web:* www.aecco.com					
American Cast Iron Pipe Co (ACIPCO) 1501 31st Ave N	Birmingham	AL	35207	205-325-7701	307-2747
TF: 800-442-2347 ■ *Web:* www.acipco.com					
AMSTED Industries Inc 180 N Stetson St Suite 1800	Chicago	IL	60601	312-645-1700	819-8504*
**Fax:* Hum Res ■ *Web:* www.amsted.com					
ASF-Keystone Inc 1700 Walnut St	Granite City	IL	62040	618-225-6593	225-6595
Atlantic States Cast Iron Pipe Co 183 Sitgreaves St	Phillipsburg	NJ	08865	908-454-1161	454-1026
TF: 800-859-1161 ■ *Web:* www.atlanticstates.com					
Atlas Foundry Co Inc 601 N Henderson Ave	Marion	IN	46952	765-662-2525	662-2902
Web: www.atlasfdry.com					
Badger Foundry Co 1058 E Mark St	Winona	MN	55987	507-452-5760	452-6469
Web: www.badgerfoundry.com					
Baker Mfg Co 133 Enterprise St	Evansville	WI	53536	608-882-5100	882-6776
Web: www.bakermfg.com					
Bay Cast Inc 2611 Ctr Ave	Bay City	MI	48708	989-892-0511	892-0599
Web: www.baycastinc.com					
Benton Foundry Inc 5297 SR 487	Benton	PA	17814	570-925-6711	925-6929
Web: www.bentonfoundry.com					
Blackhawk Foundry & Machine Co 323 S Clark St	Davenport	IA	52802	563-323-3621	323-2105
Bremen Castings Inc 500 N Baltimore St	Bremen	IN	46506	574-546-2411	546-5016
TF: 800-837-2411 ■ *Web:* www.bremencastings.com					
Buck Co Inc 897 Lancaster Pike	Quarryville	PA	17566	717-284-4114	284-3737
Web: www.buckcompany.com					

Company	City	State	ZIP	Phone	Fax
Burnham Foundry LLC 2345 Licking Rd *Web:* www.burnhamfoundry.com	Zanesville	OH	43701	740-452-9371	450-8081
Campbell Foundry Co 800 Bergen St *TF:* 800-843-4766 ■ *Web:* www.campbellfoundry.com	Harrison	NJ	07029	973-483-5480	483-1843
Canada Alloy Casting Co 529 Manitou Dr *Web:* www.cac.ca	Kitchener	ON	N2C1S2	519-895-1161	895-1169
Cast-Fab Technologies Inc 3040 Forrer St *Web:* www.cast-fab.com	Cincinnati	OH	45209	513-758-1000	758-1002
Castalloy Inc 1701 Industrial Ln PO Box 827 *TF:* 800-211-0900 ■ *Web:* www.castalloycorp.com	Waukesha	WI	53189	262-547-0070	547-2215
Casting Service 300 Philadelphia St *Web:* www.castingservice.com	La Porte	IN	46350	219-362-1000	362-0119
Citation Corp 2700 Corporate Dr Suite 100 *Web:* www.citation.net	Birmingham	AL	35242	205-871-5731	870-8211
Clow Water Systems Co 2266 S 6th St *Web:* www.clowwatersystems.com	Coshocton	OH	43812	740-622-6651	622-8551
Columbia Steel Casting Co Inc 10425 N Bloss Ave *TF:* 800-547-9471 ■ *Web:* www.columbiasteel.com	Portland	OR	97203	503-286-0685	286-1743
Columbus Castings 2211 Parsons Ave *Web:* www.columbussteel.com	Columbus	OH	43207	614-444-2121	445-2125
Complex Steel & Wire Corp 36254 Annapolis St *TF:* 800-521-0666 ■ *Web:* www.complexsteel.com	Wayne	MI	48184	734-326-1600	326-7421
Dalton Corp PO Box 230 *Web:* www.daltonfoundries.com	Warsaw	IN	46581	574-267-8111	371-5299
Delta Centrifugal Corp PO Box 1043 *TF Sales:* 800-433-3100 ■ *Web:* www.deltacentrifugal.com	Temple	TX	76503	254-773-9055	773-9055
Didion & Sons Foundry Co 4894 N Service Rd	Saint Peters	MO	63376	314-928-1130	447-8640
Dixie Southern Industrial Inc 1060 N Commonwealth Ave *Web:* www.dsisteel.com	Polk City	FL	33868	863-984-1900	984-1825
Donsco Inc 124 N Front St *Web:* www.donsco.com	Wrightsville	PA	17368	717-252-1561	252-4530
Dotson Co Inc 200 W Rock St *Web:* www.dotson.com	Mankato	MN	56001	507-345-5018	345-1270
Douglas Steel Fabricating Corp 1312 S Waverly Rd *Web:* www.douglassteel.com	Lansing	MI	48917	517-322-2050	322-0050
Duraloy Technologies Inc 120 Bridge St **Fax:* Sales ■ *TF:* 800-823-5101 ■ *Web:* www.duraloy.com	Scottdale	PA	15683	724-887-5100	887-5224*
Eagle Foundry Co Inc PO Box 250 *Web:* www.eaglefoundryco.com	Eagle Creek	OR	97022	503-637-3048	637-3091
East Jordan Iron Works Inc 301 Spring St *TF:* 800-874-4100 ■ *Web:* www.ejiw.com	East Jordan	MI	49727	231-536-2261	536-4458
Elyria Foundry Co 120 Filbert St *Web:* www.elyriafoundry.com	Elyria	OH	44036	440-322-4657	323-1101
Eureka Foundry Co 1601 Reggie White Blvd *Web:* www.eurekafoundryco.com	Chattanooga	TN	37402	423-267-3328	756-2607
Farrar Corp 142 W Burns St *Web:* www.farrarusa.com	Norwich	KS	67118	620-478-2212	478-2200
Frazier & Frazier Industries Inc 817 Ranch Rd 1951 *Web:* www.ffcastings.com	Coolidge	TX	76635	254-786-2293	786-2284
Frog Switch & Mfg Co 600 E High St *TF:* 800-233-7194 ■ *Web:* www.frogswitch.com	Carlisle	PA	17013	717-243-2454	243-7768
Gartland Foundry Co Inc 330 Grant St *TF:* 800-237-0226 ■ *Web:* www.gartlandfoundry.com	Terre Haute	IN	47802	812-232-0226	232-7569
Goldens' Foundry & Machine Co (GFMCO) 600 12th St PO Box 96 *TF:* 800-328-8379 ■ *Web:* www.gfmco.com	Columbus	GA	31902	706-323-0471	596-2850
Great Lakes Castings LLC 800 N Washington Ave *Web:* www.greatlakescastings.com	Ludington	MI	49431	231-843-2501	845-1534
Grede Foundries Inc 9898 W Bluemound Rd **Fax:* Sales ■ *Web:* www.grede.com	Milwaukee	WI	53226	414-257-3600	256-9399*
Gregg Industries Inc 10460 Hickson St *Web:* www.greggind.com	El Monte	CA	91731	626-575-7664	401-0971
Harrison Steel Castings Co Inc 900 S Mound St *Web:* www.hscast.com	Attica	IN	47918	765-762-2481	762-2487
Hensley Industries Inc 2108 Joe Field Rd PO Box 29779 **Fax:* Cust Svc ■ *TF:* 888-406-6262 ■ *Web:* www.hensleyind.com	Dallas	TX	75229	972-241-2321	241-0915*
Hitachi Metals America Ltd 2 Manhattanville Rd Suite 301 *TF:* 877-787-3120 ■ *Web:* www.hitachimetals.com	Purchase	NY	10577	914-694-9200	694-9279
Howco Metals Management 9611 Telge Rd *TF:* 800-392-7720 ■ *Web:* www.howcogroup.com	Houston	TX	77095	281-649-8800	649-8900
Huron Casting Inc 7050 Hartley St PO Box 679 *Web:* www.huroncasting.com	Pigeon	MI	48755	989-453-3933	453-3319
Intat Precision Inc 2148 N State Rd 3 PO Box 488 *Web:* www.intat.com	Rushville	IN	46173	765-932-5323	932-3032
Interstate Castings Co 3823 Massachusetts Ave *Web:* www.interstatecastings.com	Indianapolis	IN	46218	317-546-2427	546-4004
Jencast 1004 W 14th *TF:* 800-796-6630 ■ *Web:* www.jencast.com	Coffeyville	KS	67337	620-251-7802	251-3622
Johnson Brass & Machine Foundry Inc 270 N Mill St PO Box 219 *Web:* www.johnsoncentrifugal.com	Saukville	WI	53080	262-377-9440	284-7066
Johnstown Specialty Castings Inc 545 Central Ave	Johnstown	PA	15902	814-535-9000	536-0868*
Lufkin Industries Inc 601 S Raguet St *NASDAQ: LUFK* ■ *Web:* www.lufkin.com	Lufkin	TX	75902	936-634-2211	637-5474
Mabry Iron Castings Ltd 6531 Industrial Rd PO Box 21777 *Web:* www.mabrycastings.com	Beaumont	TX	77705	409-842-2223	842-2894
Maddox Foundry & Machine Works Inc 13370 SW 170th St *TF:* 800-347-0789 ■ *Web:* www.maddoxfoundry.com	Archer	FL	32618	352-495-2121	495-3962
Maynard Steel Casting Co 2856 S 27th St *Web:* www.maynardsteel.com	Milwaukee	WI	53215	414-645-0440	645-7378
McWane Cast Iron Pipe Co 1201 Vanderbilt Rd	Birmingham	AL	35234	205-322-3521	324-7250*
McWane Inc 2900 Hwy 280 Suite 300 *Web:* www.mcwane.com	Birmingham	AL	35223	205-414-3100	414-3170
Milwaukee Malleable & Grey Iron Works PO Box 2039	Milwaukee	WI	53201	414-645-0200	645-2892
Minnotte Corp Minnotte Sq *TF:* 800-809-7068 ■ *Web:* www.minnotte.com	Pittsburgh	PA	15220	412-922-1633	922-5051
Motor Castings Co 1323 S 65th St *Web:* www.motorcastings.com	Milwaukee	WI	53214	414-476-1434	476-2845
Neenah Foundry Co 2121 Brooks Ave *TF:* 800-558-5075 ■ *Web:* www.nfco.com	Neenah	WI	54956	920-725-7000	729-3661
Northern Iron & Machine 867 Forest St *Web:* www.northernim.com	Saint Paul	MN	55106	651-778-3300	778-1321
Omaha Steel Castings Co 4601 Farnam St	Omaha	NE	68106	402-558-6000	558-0327
Osco Industries Inc PO Box 1388 *Web:* www.oscoind.com	Portsmouth	OH	45662	740-354-3183	353-1504
Pacific States Cast Iron Pipe Co 1401 E 2000 S *Web:* www.pscipco.com	Provo	UT	84603	801-373-6910	377-0338
Pacific Steel Casting Co Inc 1333 2nd St *Web:* www.pacificsteel.com	Berkeley	CA	94710	510-525-9200	524-4673
Paxton-Mitchell Co 2614 Martha St *Web:* www.paxton-mitchell.com	Omaha	NE	68105	402-345-6767	345-6772
Prospect Foundry Inc 1225 Winter St NE *Web:* www.prospectfoundry.com	Minneapolis	MN	55413	612-331-9282	331-4122
Quaker City Castings Inc 310 E Euclid Ave *Web:* www.qccast.com	Salem	OH	44460	330-332-1566	332-1159
Quality Castings Co 1200 N Main St *Web:* www.qcfoundry.com	Orrville	OH	44667	330-682-6010	683-3153
Richmond Foundry 126 Collins Rd *Web:* www.matrixmetalsllc.com	Richmond	TX	77469	281-342-5511	342-0542
Robinson Foundry Inc 505 Robinson Ct *Web:* www.robinsonfoundry.com	Alexander City	AL	35010	256-329-8481	329-0503
Rodney Hunt Co 46 Mill St *TF:* 800-448-8860 ■ *Web:* www.rodneyhunt.com	Orange	MA	01364	978-544-2511	544-7204
Samuel Steel Pickling Co 1400 Enterprise Pkwy *Web:* www.samuelsteel.com	Twinsburg	OH	44087	330-963-3777	963-0770
Sawbrook Steel Castings Co 425 Shepherd Ave *Web:* www.sawbrooksteel.com	Cincinnati	OH	45215	513-554-1700	554-0092
Sentinel Bldg Systems Inc 237 S 4th St PO Box 348 *Web:* www.sentinelbuildings.com	Albion	NE	68620	402-395-5076	395-6369
Sharon Coating LLC 277 Sharpsville Ave *TF:* 800-430-8586 ■ *Web:* www.sharoncoating.com	Sharon	PA	16146	724-981-3545	981-3009
Sioux City Foundry Co 801 Division St *TF:* 800-831-0874 ■ *Web:* www.siouxcityfoundry.com	Sioux City	IA	51102	712-252-4181	252-4197
Sivyer Steel Corp 225 S 33rd St *TF:* 800-474-8937 ■ *Web:* www.sivyersteel.com	Bettendorf	IA	52722	563-355-1811	355-3946
Smith Foundry Co 1855 E 28th St *Web:* www.smithfoundry.com	Minneapolis	MN	55407	612-729-9395	725-2519
Spokane Steel Foundry Co 3808 N Sullivan Rd Bldg 1 *TF:* 800-541-3601	Spokane	WA	99216	509-924-0440	924-9448
Standard Alloys & Mfg PO Box 969 *TF:* 800-231-8240 ■ *Web:* www.standardalloys.com	Port Arthur	TX	77640	409-983-3201	983-7837
Steel Service Corp 2260 Flowood Dr PO Box 321425 *TF:* 800-844-9222 ■ *Web:* www.steelservicecorp.com	Jackson	MS	39232	601-939-9222	939-9359
T & B Foundry Co 2469 E 71st St	Cleveland	OH	44104	216-391-4200	391-4206
Talladega Castings & Machine Co Inc 228 N Ct St *TF:* 800-766-6708 ■ *Web:* www.tmsco.com	Talladega	AL	35160	256-362-5550	362-1321
Talladega Machinery & Supply Co Inc 301 N Johnson Ave PO Box 736 *TF Cust Svc:* 800-289-8672 ■ *Web:* www.tmsco.com	Talladega	AL	35161	256-362-4124	761-2565
Taylor & Fenn Co 22 Deerfield Rd *Web:* www.taylorfenn.com	Windsor	CT	06095	860-249-7531	525-2961
ThyssenKrupp Budd Co 3155 W Big Beaver Rd PO Box 2601 *Web:* www.buddcompany.com	Troy	MI	48007	248-643-3500	643-3593
Thyssenkrupp Waupaca Inc 1955 Brunner Dr PO Box 249 *Web:* www.waupacafoundry.com	Waupaca	WI	54981	715-258-6611	258-9268
Tyler Pipe Co 11910 CR 492 **Fax Area Code:* 800 ■ *TF:* 800-527-8478 ■ *Web:* www.tylerpipe.com	Tyler	TX	75706	903-882-5511	248-9537*
Unicast Co 241 N Washington St *Web:* www.unicastco.com	Boyertown	PA	19512	610-367-0155	367-2787
Union Electric Steel Corp 726 Bell Ave *Web:* www.uniones.com	Carnegie	PA	15106	412-429-7655	276-1711
Universal Stainless Inc 14002 E 33rd Pl	Aurora	CO	80011	303-375-1511	375-1626
Urick Foundry Co 1501 Cherry St *Web:* www.urick.net	Erie	PA	16502	814-454-2461	454-1397
US Pipe & Foundry Co 3300 1st Ave N PO Box 10406 *TF:* 866-347-7473 ■ *Web:* www.uspipe.com	Birmingham	AL	35202	205-254-7000	254-7149
Walker Machine & Foundry Corp PO Box 4587 *Web:* www.walkerfoundry.com	Roanoke	VA	24015	540-344-6265	342-2278
Waukesha Foundry Co Inc 1300 Lincoln Ave **Fax:* Sales ■ *TF:* 800-727-0741 ■ *Web:* www.waukeshafoundry.com	Waukesha	WI	53186	262-542-0741	549-8440*
Wells Mfg Co 2100 W Lake Shore Dr *TF:* 800-227-6455 ■ *Web:* www.wellsmanufacturing.com	Woodstock	IL	60098	815-338-3900	338-3950
Wheeling-Nisshin Inc 400 Penn St *Web:* www.wheeling-nisshin.com	Follansbee	WV	26037	304-527-2800	527-0985
Willman Industries Inc 338 S Main St *Web:* www.willmanind.com	Cedar Grove	WI	53013	920-668-8526	668-8998
Winsert Inc 2645 Industrial Pkwy S PO Box 0198 *Web:* www.winsert.com	Marinette	WI	54143	715-732-1703	732-2824

	City	State	Zip	Phone	Fax
Wollaston Alloys Inc 205 Wood Rd *Web:* www.wollastonalloys.com	Braintree	MA	02184	781-848-3333	848-3993
Zurn Cast Metals Operation 1302 Raspberry St *TF:* 877-875-1404 ■ *Web:* www.zurn.com	Erie	PA	16502	814-455-0921	456-2754

311 FOUNDRIES - NONFERROUS (CASTINGS)

SEE ALSO Foundries - Iron & Steel p. 1881

	City	State	Zip	Phone	Fax
Ace Precision Castings LLC 610 S 12th Ave PO Box 657 *Web:* www.aceprecisioncastings.com	Marshalltown	IA	50158	641-753-5566	753-0150
Advance Die Casting Co 3760 N Holton St *Web:* www.advancediecasting.com	Milwaukee	WI	53212	414-964-0284	963-6088
Ahresty Wilmington Corp 2627 S S St *Web:* www.ahresty.com	Wilmington	OH	45177	937-382-6112	382-5871
Akron Foundry Co 2728 Wingate Ave *Web:* www.akronfoundry.com	Akron	OH	44314	330-745-3101	745-7999
Alloy Die Casting Co 6550 Caballero Blvd	Buena Park	CA	90620	714-521-9800	521-5510*
Arrow Acme Inc PO Box 218	Webster City	IA	50595	515-832-3120	832-3145
Arrow Pattern & Foundry Co 9725 Industrial Dr	Bridgeview	IL	60455	708-598-0300	598-0310
Aurora Metals Divison LLC 1995 Greenfield Ave *Web:* www.aurorametals.com	Montgomery	IL	60538	630-844-4900	844-6839
Bardane Mfg PO Box 70 *Web:* www.bardane.com	Jermyn	PA	18433	570-876-4844	876-1938
Basic Aluminum Castings Co 1325 E 168th St *Web:* www.basicaluminum.com	Cleveland	OH	44110	216-481-5606	481-7031
Blaser Die Casting Co 5700 3rd Ave S PO Box 80286 *Web:* www.blaser-die.com	Seattle	WA	98108	206-767-7800	767-7055
Brillcast Inc 3400 Wentworth Dr SW *Web:* www.brillcast.com	Grand Rapids	MI	49519	616-534-4977	534-0880
Buck Co Inc 897 Lancaster Pike *Web:* www.buckcompany.com	Quarryville	PA	17566	717-284-4114	284-3737
Bunting Bearings Corp 1001 Holland Pk Blvd *TF:* 888-228-9899 ■ *Web:* www.buntingbearings.com	Holland	OH	43528	419-866-7000	866-0653
C & H Die Casting Inc PO Box 1170 *TF:* 800-433-3148 ■ *Web:* www.chdiecasting.com	Temple	TX	76503	254-938-2541	938-7117
Cast Technologies Inc 1100 SW Washington St	Peoria	IL	61602	309-676-2157	676-2167
Cast-Rite Corp 515 E Airline Way *Web:* www.cast-rite.com	Gardena	CA	90248	310-532-2080	532-0605
Chicago White Metal Casting Inc 649 N Rt 83 *Web:* www.cwmdiecast.com	Bensenville	IL	60106	630-595-4424	595-4474
Consolidated Metco Inc 13940 N Rivergate Blvd **Fax:* Sales ■ *TF Sales:* 800-547-9473 ■ *Web:* www.conmet.com	Portland	OR	97203	503-286-5741	240-5488*
Consolidated Precision Products 8333 Wilcox Ave *Web:* www.cfi-pac.com	Cudahy	CA	90201	323-773-2363	562-3174
Deco Products Co 506 Sanford St *TF:* 800-327-9751 ■ *Web:* www.decoprod.com	Decorah	IA	52101	563-382-4264	382-9845
Del Mar Die Casting Co 12901 S Western Ave *TF:* 800-624-7468 ■ *Web:* www.delmarindustries.com	Gardena	CA	90249	323-321-0600	321-0600
Denison Industries 22 Fielder Dr *Web:* www.denisonindustries.com	Denison	TX	75020	903-786-4444	786-6570
Dynacast Inc 14045 Ballantyne Corporate Pl *TF:* 800-811-7839 ■ *Web:* www.dynacast.com	Charlotte	NC	28277	704-927-2790	927-2791
Eck Industries Inc 1602 N 8th St PO Box 967 *Web:* www.eckindustries.com	Manitowoc	WI	54221	920-682-4618	682-9298
Electric Materials Co 50 S Washington St *TF:* 800-356-2211 ■ *Web:* www.elecmat.com	North East	PA	16428	814-725-9621	725-3620
Empire Die Casting Co Inc 635 Highland Rd E *Web:* www.empiredie.com	Macedonia	OH	44056	330-467-0750	908-3052
Falcon Foundry Co 96 6th St *TF:* 800-253-8624 ■ *Web:* www.falconfoundry.com	Lowellville	OH	44436	330-536-6221	536-6221
Fall River Group 670 S Main St	Fall River	WI	53932	920-484-3311	484-2233
Fansteel/Wellman Dynamics Corp 1746 Commerce Rd *Web:* www.fansteel.com/wellman	Creston	IA	50801	641-782-8521	782-7672
Foundry Systems International 5159 S Prospect St	Ravenna	OH	44266	330-296-9053	296-1921
General Die Casters Inc 2150 Highland Rd *TF:* 800-332-2278 ■ *Web:* www.generaldie.com	Twinsburg	OH	44087	330-657-2300	657-2192
Gibbs Die Casting Corp 369 Community Dr *Web:* www.gibbsdc.com	Henderson	KY	42420	270-827-1801	827-7840
Globalfoundries Inc 840 N McCarthy Blvd *Web:* www.globalfoundries.com	Milpitas	CA	95035	408-462-3900	
H-J Enterprises Inc 3010 High Ridge Blvd *Web:* www.h-jenterprises.com	High Ridge	MO	63049	636-677-3421	376-1915
Halex Co 23901 Aurora Rd *TF:* 800-749-3261 ■ *Web:* www.halexco.com	Bedford Heights	OH	44146	440-439-1616	439-1792
Harmony Castings LLC 251 Perry Hwy *Web:* www.harmonycastings.com	Harmony	PA	16037	724-452-5811	452-0118
Heick Die Casting Corp 6550 W Diversey Ave	Chicago	IL	60707	773-637-1100	637-1101
Hoffmann Die Cast Corp 229 Kerth St *Web:* www.hoffmanndc.com	Saint Joseph	MI	49085	269-983-1102	983-2928
Howmet Castings 1 Misco Dr *Web:* www.alcoa.com	Whitehall	MI	49461	231-894-5686	894-7607
ICG Castings Inc 101 Poplar St	Dowagiac	MI	49047	269-783-3100	783-3104
Imperial Die Casting Co 2249 Old Liberty Rd *Web:* www.rcmindustries.com	Liberty	SC	29657	864-859-0202	855-1597
Johnson Brass & Machine Foundry Inc 270 N Mill St PO Box 219 *Web:* www.johnsoncentrifugal.com	Saukville	WI	53080	262-377-9440	284-7066
Kitchen-Quip Inc 405 E Marion St *Web:* www.kqcasting.com	Waterloo	IN	46793	260-837-8311	837-7919
Lansco Die Casting Inc 711 S Stimson Ave	City of Industry	CA	91745	626-961-3449	369-7129
Lee Brass Co 1800 Golden Springs Dr *TF Cust Svc:* 800-876-1811 ■ *Web:* www.leebrass.com	Anniston	AL	36207	256-831-2501	831-8380
Littlestown Foundry Inc 150 Charles St PO Box 69 *TF:* 800-471-0844 ■ *Web:* www.littlestownfoundry.com	Littlestown	PA	17340	717-359-4141	359-5010
Madison Precision Products Inc 94 E 400 N *Web:* www.madisonprecision.com	Madison	IN	47250	812-273-4702	273-2451
Madison-Kipp Corp 201 Waubesa St **Fax:* Mktg ■ *Web:* www.madison-kipp.com	Madison	WI	53704	608-244-3511	242-5284*
Magnolia Metal Corp 10675 Bedford Ave # 200 *TF:* 800-228-4043 ■ *Web:* www.magnoliabronze.com	Omaha	NE	68134	402-455-8760	455-8762
Martin Brass Foundry Inc 2341 Jefferson St **Fax Area Code:* 310	Torrance	CA	90501	323-775-3803	320-4971*
Matthews International Corp 2 Northshore Ctr Suite 200 *NASDAQ:* MATW ■ *TF:* 800-223-4964	Pittsburgh	PA	15212	412-442-8200	442-8291
New Products Corp 448 N Shore Dr *Web:* www.npc.com	Benton Harbor	MI	49022	269-925-2161	934-6180
NGK Metals Corp 917 Hwy 11 S **Fax Area Code:* 877 ■ *TF:* 800-523-8268 ■ *Web:* www.ngkmetals.com	Sweetwater	TN	37874	423-337-5500	645-2328*
Ohio Aluminum Industries Inc 4840 Warner Rd *Web:* www.ohioaluminum.com/index.html	Garfield Heights	OH	44125	216-641-8865	641-8847
Ohio Decorative Products Inc 220 S Elizabeth St *Web:* www.ohiodec.com	Spencerville	OH	45887	419-647-4191	647-4202
Pace Industries Inc PO Box 1198	Harrison	AR	72601	870-741-8255	741-4998
Pacific Die Casting Corp 6155 S Eastern Ave *Web:* www.pacdiecast.com	Commerce	CA	90040	323-725-1332	728-1115
Park-Ohio Holdings Corp (PKOH) 6065 Parkland Blvd *NASDAQ:* PKOH ■ *Web:* www.pkoh.com	Cleveland	OH	44124	440-947-2000	947-2099
PHB Inc 7900 W Ridge Rd *Web:* www.phbcorp.com	Fairview	PA	16415	814-474-5511	474-2063
Piad Precision Casting Corp 112 Industrial Pk Rd *TF:* 800-441-9858 ■ *Web:* www.piad.com	Greensburg	PA	15601	724-838-5500	838-5520
Premier Die Casting Co 1177 Rahway Ave *TF:* 800-394-3006 ■ *Web:* www.diecasting.com	Avenel	NJ	07001	732-634-3000	634-0590
Premier Tool & Die Cast Corp 9886 N Tudor Rd *TF:* 800-417-8717 ■ *Web:* www.premierdiecast.com	Berrien Springs	MI	49103	269-471-7715	471-3855
Progress Casting Group Inc 2600 Niagara Ln N *TF:* 800-866-3025	Plymouth	MN	55447	763-557-1000	557-0320
Quad City Die Casting Co 3800 River Dr	Moline	IL	61265	309-762-7346	762-3134
Reliable Castings Corp 3530 Spring Grove Ave *Web:* www.reliablecastings.com	Cincinnati	OH	45223	513-541-2627	541-5696
Ridco Casting Co 6 Beverage Hill Ave *Web:* www.ridco.com	Pawtucket	RI	02860	401-724-0400	724-6320
Robinson Foundry Inc 505 Robinson Ct *Web:* www.robinsonfoundry.com	Alexander City	AL	35010	256-329-8481	329-0503
Ross Aluminum Foundries 815 N Oak Ave *Web:* www.rossal.com	Sidney	OH	45365	937-492-4134	498-1883
Saint Clair Die Casting LLC 225 St Clair Industrial Pk Dr *Web:* www.stclairdiecasting.com	Saint Clair	MO	63077	636-629-2550	629-0594
Selmet Inc 33992 SE 7 Mile Ln PO Box 689 *Web:* www.selmetinc.com	Albany	OR	97322	541-926-7731	928-9346
Southern Centrifugal Inc 4180 S Creek Rd *TF:* 800-722-7277 ■ *Web:* www.metaltek.com	Chattanooga	TN	37406	423-622-4131	622-2227
Stroh Die Casting Co Inc 11123 W Burleigh St *TF Cust Svc:* 800-843-2871	Milwaukee	WI	53222	414-771-7100	771-1329
Talladega Castings & Machine Co Inc 228 N Ct St *TF:* 800-766-6708 ■ *Web:* www.tmsco.com	Talladega	AL	35160	256-362-5550	362-1321
Tampa Brass & Aluminum 8511 Florida Mining Blvd *Web:* www.tampabrass.com	Tampa	FL	33634	813-885-6064	882-3271
Techni-Cast Corp 11220 Garfield Ave **Fax:* Sales ■ *TF:* 800-923-4585 ■ *Web:* www.techni-cast.com	South Gate	CA	90280	562-923-4585	861-4259*
Texas Die Casting Inc 600 S Loop 485 *Web:* www.texasdiecasting.com	Gladewater	TX	75647	903-845-2224	845-6155
ThyssenKrupp Stahl Co 11 E Pacific PO Box 6 *TF:* 888-395-1042 ■ *Web:* www.stahlspecialty.com	Kingsville	MO	64061	816-597-3322	597-3485
Top Die Casting Co 13910 Dearborn Ave *Web:* www.topdie.com	South Beloit	IL	61080	815-389-2599	389-3057
Travis Pattern & Foundry Inc 1413 E Hawthorne Rd *Web:* www.pduinc.com	Spokane	WA	99218	509-466-3545	467-6465
Twin City Die Castings Co 1070 33rd Ave SE *Web:* www.tcdcinc.com	Minneapolis	MN	55414	651-645-3611	644-5280
United Titanium Inc 3450 Old Airport Rd *TF:* 800-321-4938 ■ *Web:* www.unitedtitanium.com	Wooster	OH	44691	330-264-2111	263-1336
Walker Die Casting Inc 1125 Higgs Rd PO Box 1189 *Web:* www.walkerdiecasting.com	Lewisburg	TN	37091	931-359-6206	359-8030
Ward Aluminum Casting Co 642 Growth Ave *TF:* 866-427-8700 ■ *Web:* www.wardcorp.com	Fort Wayne	IN	46808	260-426-8700	420-1919
Watry Industries Inc 3312 Lakeshore Dr *Web:* www.watry.com	Sheboygan	WI	53081	920-457-4886	457-5241
Wisconsin Aluminum Foundry Co Inc 838 S 16th St *Web:* www.wafco.com	Manitowoc	WI	54220	920-682-8286	682-7285
Wollaston Alloys Inc 205 Wood Rd *Web:* www.wollastonalloys.com	Braintree	MA	02184	781-848-3333	848-3993
Wolverine Bronze Co 28178 Hayes Rd **Fax:* Sales ■ *Web:* www.wolverinebronze.com	Roseville	MI	48066	586-776-8180	776-4510*

	City	State	ZIP	Phone	Fax
Yoder Die Casting Corp 727 Kiser St	Dayton	OH	45404	937-222-6734	222-6805
Yoder Industries Inc 2520 Needmore Rd	Dayton	OH	45414	937-278-5769	278-6321
Web: www.yoderindustries.com					

312 FRAMES & MOULDINGS

	City	State	ZIP	Phone	Fax
Alexander Moulding Mill Co Hwy 281 S	Hamilton	TX	76531	254-386-3187	386-3675
Alexandria Moulding 20352 Powerdam Rd	Alexandria	ON	K0C1A0	613-525-2784	525-4677
TF: 866-377-2539 ■ *Web:* www.alexmo.com					
Best Moulding Corp 100 Alameda Rd NW	Albuquerque	NM	87114	505-898-6770	898-1301
Web: www.bestmoulding.com					
Groovfold Inc 1050 W State St	Newcomerstown	OH	43832	740-498-8363	498-8782
TF: 800-367-1133 ■ *Web:* www.groovfold.com					
Homeshield Colonial Craft 2270 Woodale Dr	Mounds View	MN	55112	763-231-4000	783-7218
TF: 800-727-5187 ■ *Web:* www.home-shield.com					
Kendall-Hartcraft 1480 Independence Ave PO Box 270465	Hartford	WI	53027	262-673-3440	673-3052
TF: 800-558-7834 ■ *Web:* www.kendallhartcraft.com					
Kendall-Hartcraft Inc 5838 Research Pk Blvd NW	Huntsville	AL	35806	256-859-5533	545-0398*
**Fax Area Code:* 888 ■ *TF:* 800-421-7435 ■ *Web:* www.kendallhartcraft.com					
Larson-Juhl 3900 Steve Reynolds Blvd	Norcross	GA	30093	770-279-5200	279-5297*
**Fax:* Hum Res ■ *TF:* 800-438-5031 ■ *Web:* www.larsonjuhl.com					
Lasercraft Inc 800 A St	San Rafael	CA	94901	415-472-8388	472-8389
Web: www.elsal.com					
Monarch Industries Inc 99 Main St	Warren	RI	02885	401-247-5200	247-5601*
**Fax:* Sales ■ *TF:* 800-669-9663 ■ *Web:* www.monarchinc.com					
North American Enclosures Inc 65 Jetson Ln	Central Islip	NY	11722	631-234-9500	234-9504
TF: 800-645-9209 ■ *Web:* www.naeframes.com					
PB & H Moulding Corp 124 Pickard Dr E	Syracuse	NY	13211	315-455-5602	455-8748
TF: 800-746-9724 ■ *Web:* www.pbhmoulding.com					
Peterson Picture Frame Co Inc 2720 W Belmont Ave	Chicago	IL	60618	773-463-8888	463-4603
Web: www.peterson-picture.com					
Royal Mouldings Ltd 135 Bearcreek Rd PO Box 610	Marion	VA	24354	276-783-8161	782-3285
TF: 800-368-3117 ■ *Web:* www.royalbuildingproducts.com					
Sunset Moulding Co Inc 2231 Paseo Ave	Live Oak	CA	95953	530-695-1801	695-2560
Web: www.sunsetmoulding.com					
Uniek Inc 805 Uniek Dr	Waunakee	WI	53597	608-849-9999	849-9799*
**Fax:* Mktg ■ *TF:* 800-248-6435 ■ *Web:* www.uniekinc.com					
Woodgrain Distribution 80 Shelby St	Montevallo	AL	35115	205-665-2546	665-3432
TF: 800-756-0199 ■ *Web:* www.woodgraindistribution.com					

FRAMES & MOULDINGS - METAL

SEE Doors & Windows - Metal p. 1786

313 FRANCHISES

SEE ALSO Auto Supply Stores p. 1489; Automotive Services p. 1500; Bakeries p. 1505; Beauty Salons p. 1517; Business Service Centers p. 1550; Candles p. 1553; Car Rental Agencies p. 1554; Children's Learning Centers p. 1604; Cleaning Services p. 1606; Remodeling, Refinishing, Resurfacing Contractors p. 1729; Convenience Stores p. 1748; Health Food Stores p. 2009; Home Inspection Services p. 2025; Hotels & Hotel Companies p. 2081; Ice Cream & Dairy Stores p. 2103; Laundry & Drycleaning Services p. 2144; Optical Goods Stores p. 2328; Pest Control Services p. 2410; Printing Companies - Commercial Printers p. 2451; Real Estate Agents & Brokers p. 2518; Restaurant Companies p. 2555; Staffing Services p. 2673; Travel Agency Networks p. 2731; Weight Loss Centers & Services p. 2774

Please See The Category On Hotel & Resort Operation & Management For Listings Of Hotel Franchises.

	City	State	ZIP	Phone	Fax
1-800-DryClean LLC 3948 Ranchero Dr	Ann Arbor	MI	48108	866-822-6115	822-6888*
**Fax Area Code:* 734 ■ *TF:* 800-379-2532 ■ *Web:* www.1-800-dryclean.com					
1-800-Got-Junk 1523 W 3rd Ave 3rd Fl	Vancouver	BC	V6J1J8	800-468-5865	751-0634*
**Fax Area Code:* 801 ■ *TF:* 800-468-5865 ■ *Web:* www.1800gotjunk.com					
1-800-Water Damage 1167 Mercer St	Seattle	WA	98109	206-381-3041	381-3052
TF: 800-940-9745 ■ *Web:* www.1800waterdamage.com					
A & W Restaurants Inc 1441 Gardiner Ln	Louisville	KY	40213	502-874-8300	874-3183
Web: www.awrestaurants.com					
ABC Seamless 3001 Fiechtner Dr	Fargo	ND	58103	701-293-5952	293-3107
TF: 800-732-6577 ■ *Web:* www.abcseamless.com					
Abrakadoodle Inc 1800 Robert Fulton Dr	Reston	VA	22191	703-860-6570	860-6574
Web: www.abrakadoodle.com					
ActionCOACH 5781 S Fort Apache Rd	Las Vegas	NV	89148	702-795-3188	795-3183
TF: 888-483-2828 ■ *Web:* www.actioncoach.com					
Affiliated Car Rental 96 Freneau Ave Suite 2	Matawan	NJ	07747	732-583-8500	290-8305
TF: 800-367-5159					
AIM Mail Centers 15550-D Rockfield Blvd	Irvine	CA	92618	949-837-4151	837-4537
TF: 800-669-4246 ■ *Web:* www.aimmailcenters.com					
Aire Serv Heating & Air Conditioning Inc 1020 N University Parks Dr	Waco	TX	76707	800-583-2662	745-5098*
**Fax Area Code:* 254 ■ *TF:* 800-583-2662 ■ *Web:* www.aireserv.com					
Aire-Master of America Inc 1821 N State Hwy Cc	Nixa	MO	65714	417-725-2691	725-5737
TF: 800-525-0957 ■ *Web:* www.airemaster.com					
All Tune & Lube Brakes & More Inc 8334 Veteran's Hwy	Millersville	MD	21108	410-987-1011	987-9080
TF: 800-935-8863 ■ *Web:* www.alltuneandlube.com					
American Leak Detection 888 Research Dr Suite 100	Palm Springs	CA	92262	760-320-9991	320-1288
TF: 800-755-6697 ■ *Web:* www.americanleakdetection.com					
AmeriSpec Inc 889 Ridge Lake Blvd	Memphis	TN	38120	901-820-8500	820-8520
TF: 800-426-2270 ■ *Web:* www.amerispec.com					
Anago Cleaning Systems 1100 Pk Central Blvd S Suite 1200	Pompano Beach	FL	33064	954-752-3111	752-1200
TF: 800-213-5857 ■ *Web:* www.anagousa.com					
Arby's Restaurant Group Inc 1155 Perimeter Ctr W	Atlanta	GA	30338	678-514-4100	
TF: 800-487-2729 ■ *Web:* www.arbys.com					
Archadeck 2924 Emerywood Pkwy # 101	Richmond	VA	23294	804-353-6999	353-2364
TF: 800-722-4668 ■ *Web:* www.archadeck.com					
Avalar Network Inc 6430 Medical Ctr St # 100	Las Vegas	NV	89148	702-895-8988	895-8998
TF: 877-895-8988 ■ *Web:* www.avalar.biz					
Bad Ass Coffee Co of Hawaii Inc 155 W Malvern Ave	Salt Lake City	UT	84115	801-463-1966	463-2606
TF: 888-422-3277 ■ *Web:* www.badasscoffee.com					
Barnie's Coffee & Tea Co Inc 2126 Landstreet Rd Suite 300	Orlando	FL	32809	407-854-6600	854-6601
TF: 800-854-1416 ■ *Web:* www.barniescoffee.com					
Baskin-Robbins Inc 130 Royall St	Canton	MA	02021	781-737-3000	
TF: 800-859-5339 ■ *Web:* www.baskinrobbins.com					
Beef O'Bradys Inc 5510 W LaSalle St Suite 200	Tampa	FL	33607	813-226-2333	226-0030
TF: 800-728-8878 ■ *Web:* www.beefobradys.com					
Bellacino's Corp 10096 Shaver Rd	Portage	MI	49024	269-329-0782	329-0930
TF: 877-379-0700 ■ *Web:* www.bellacinos.com					
Ben & Jerry's Homemade Inc 30 Community Dr	South Burlington	VT	05403	802-846-1500	846-1556
Web: www.benjerry.com					
Ben Franklin Stores Promotions Unlimited Corp 7601	Racine	WI	53408	262-681-7000	
TF: 800-992-9307 ■ *Web:* www.benfranklinstores.com					
Benjamin Franklin Plumbing Plaza Five Pt 50 Central Ave Suite 920	Sarasota	FL	34236	941-366-9692	951-0942
TF: 800-695-3579 ■ *Web:* www.benjaminfranklinplumbing.com					
Bevinco Bar Systems Ltd 510-505 Consumers Rd	Toronto	ON	M2J4V8	416-490-6266	490-6899
TF: 888-238-4626 ■ *Web:* www.bevinco.com					
Big Apple Bagels 500 Lake Cook Rd Suite 475	Deerfield	IL	60015	847-948-7520	405-8140
TF: 800-251-6101 ■ *Web:* www.babcorp.com					
Big Boy Restaurants International LLC 4199 Marcy St	Warren	MI	48091	586-759-6000	755-8531*
**Fax:* Cust Svc ■ *TF:* 800-837-3003 ■ *Web:* www.bigboy.com					
Big O Tires Inc 823 Donald Ross Rd	Florida	CA	33408	561-383-3000	
TF: 800-926-8473 ■ *Web:* www.bigotires.com					
Bojangles' Restaurants Inc 9432 Southern Pine Blvd	Charlotte	NC	28273	704-527-2675	523-6676
TF: 800-366-9921 ■ *Web:* www.bojangles.com					
Bonus Bldg Care Inc 14331 Proton Rd	Dallas	TX	75244	972-789-9400	789-9399
TF: 800-931-1102 ■ *Web:* www.bonusbuildingcare.com					
Boston Pizza International Inc 5500 Parkwood Way	Richmond	BC	V6V2M4	604-270-1108	270-4168
Web: www.bostonpizza.com					
Boston Pizza Restaurants LP 1501 LBJ Fwy Suite 450	Dallas	TX	75234	972-484-9022	484-7630
TF: 866-277-8721 ■ *Web:* www.bostons.com					
BrickKicker Inc 849 N Ellsworth St	Naperville	IL	60563	630-420-9900	420-2270
TF: 800-821-1820 ■ *Web:* www.brickkicker.com					
Bruegger's Enterprises 159 Bank St	Burlington	VT	05401	802-660-4020	652-9293
Web: www.brueggers.com					
Bruster's Ice Cream Inc 1525 Riverside Dr	Bridgewater	PA	15009	724-774-4155	774-6384
Web: www.brusters.com					
BuildingStars Inc 11489 Page Service Dr	Saint Louis	MO	63146	314-991-3356	991-3198
Web: www.buildingstars.com					
Camille's Sidewalk Cafe 8801 S Yale Suite 400	Tulsa	OK	74137	918-488-9727	497-1916
Web: www.camillescafe.com					
Candy Bouquet International Inc 510 Mclean St	Little Rock	AR	72202	501-375-9990	375-9998
TF: 877-226-3901 ■ *Web:* www.candybouquet.com					
Captain D's LLC 1717 Elm Hill Pike Suite A-1	Nashville	TN	37210	615-391-5461	231-2309
TF: 800-314-4819 ■ *Web:* www.captainds.com					
Car-X Assoc Corp 1375 E Woodfield Rd Suite 500	Schaumburg	IL	60173	847-273-8920	619-3310
TF: 800-359-2359 ■ *Web:* www.carx.com					
CardSmart Retail Corp 430 Pine St	Central Falls	RI	02863	877-227-3762	726-2384*
**Fax Area Code:* 401 ■ *TF:* 877-227-3762 ■ *Web:* www.cardsmart.com					
Carlson Wagonlit Travel Inc 701 Carlson Pkwy	Minnetonka	MN	55305	763-212-5000	212-5458
TF: 800-335-8747 ■ *Web:* www.carlsonwagonlit.com					
Cartex Ltd 42816 Mound Rd	Sterling Heights	MI	48314	586-739-4330	739-4331
TF: 800-421-7328 ■ *Web:* www.fabrion.net					
Cartridge World 6460 Hollis St	Emeryville	CA	94608	510-594-9900	594-9991
TF: 888-997-3345 ■ *Web:* www.cartridgeworld.com					

Company / Address	City	State	ZIP	Phone	Fax
Carvel Franchising					
200 Glenridge Pt Pkwy Suite 200	Atlanta	GA	30342	404-255-3250	255-4978
TF: 800-227-8353 ■ *Web:* www.carvel.com					
Century 21 Real Estate Corp 1 Campus Dr	Parsippany	NJ	07054	973-428-9700	496-7564
TF: 877-221-2765 ■ *Web:* www.century21.com					
CertaPro Painters Ltd					
150 Green Tree Rd Suite 1003	Oaks	PA	19456	610-983-9411	650-9997
TF: 800-462-3782 ■ *Web:* www.certapro.com					
Certified Restoration DryCleaning Network LLC					
2060 Coolidge Hwy	Berkley	MI	48072	800-963-2736	246-7868*
**Fax Area Code:* 248 ■ *TF:* 800-963-2736 ■ *Web:* www.restorationdrycleaning.com					
Charley's Grilled Subs					
2500 Farmers Dr Suite 140	Columbus	OH	43235	614-923-4700	923-4701
TF: 800-437-8325 ■ *Web:* www.charleys.com					
Checkers Drive-In Restaurants Inc					
4300 W Cypress St Suite 600	Tampa	FL	33607	813-283-7000	283-7001
TF: 800-800-8072 ■ *Web:* www.checkers.com					
Cheeburger Cheeburger Restaurants Inc					
11595 Kelly Rd Suite 316	Fort Myers	FL	33908	239-437-1611	437-1512
TF: 800-487-6211 ■ *Web:* www.cheeburger.com					
Chem-Dry 1530 N 1000 W	Logan	UT	84321	435-755-0099	755-0021
TF: 800-243-6379 ■ *Web:* www.chemdry.com					
Chester's International LLC					
3500 Colonnade Pkwy Suite 325	Birmingham	AL	32543	205-949-4690	298-0332
Web: www.chestersinternational.com					
Christmas Decor Inc 206 23rd St	Lubbock	TX	79404	800-687-9551	722-9627*
**Fax Area Code:* 806 ■ *TF:* 800-687-9551 ■ *Web:* www.christmasdecor.net					
CiCi Enterprises LP 1080 W Bethel Rd	Coppell	TX	75019	972-745-4200	745-4204
Web: www.cicispizza.com					
Cinnabon Inc 200 Glenridge Pt Pkwy Suite 200	Atlanta	GA	30342	404-255-3250	255-4978
Web: www.cinnabon.com					
Cleaning Authority					
6994 Columbia Gateway Dr Suite 100	Columbia	MD	21046	410-740-1900	685-6243*
**Fax Area Code:* 866 ■ *TF:* 800-783-6243 ■ *Web:* www.thecleaningauthority.com					
Closet Factory 12800 S Broadway	Los Angeles	CA	90061	310-516-7000	516-8065
TF: 800-318-8800 ■ *Web:* www.closetfactory.com					
Club Z! Inc 15310 Amberly Dr Suite 185	Tampa	FL	33647	813-931-5516	932-2485
TF: 800-434-2582 ■ *Web:* www.clubztutoring.com					
Coffee Beanery LTD The 3429 Pierson Pl	Flushing	MI	48433	810-733-1020	733-1536
TF: 800-728-2326 ■ *Web:* www.coffeebeanery.com					
Coffee News USA 120 Linden St	Bangor	ME	04401	207-941-0860	941-1050
Web: www.coffeenewsusa.com					
Cold Stone Creamery Inc					
9311 E Via De Ventura	Scottsdale	AZ	85258	480-362-4800	362-4812
TF Cust Svc: 866-464-9467 ■ *Web:* www.coldstonecreamery.com					
Color Me Mine Enterprises Inc					
5140 Lankershim Blvd	North Hollywood	CA	91601	818-505-2108	509-9772
TF: 888-265-6764 ■ *Web:* www.colormemine.com					
Color-Glo International 7111 Ohms Ln	Minneapolis	MN	55439	952-835-1338	835-1395
TF: 800-328-6347 ■ *Web:* www.colorglo.com					
Comet Cleaners 406 W Division St	Arlington	TX	76011	817-461-3555	861-4779
Web: www.cometcleaners.com					
ComForcare Senior Services Inc					
2510 Telegraph Rd Suite 100	Bloomfield Hills	MI	48302	248-745-9700	745-9763
TF: 800-886-4044 ■ *Web:* www.comforcare.com					
Comfort Keepers Franchising Inc					
6640 Poe Ave Suite 200	Dayton	OH	45414	937-264-1933	264-3103
TF: 800-387-2415 ■ *Web:* www.comfortkeepers.com					
Computer Explorers 12715 Telge Rd	Cypress	TX	77429	281-256-4100	373-4450
TF: 800-531-5053 ■ *Web:* www.computerexplorers.com					
Computer Renaissance					
500 S Florida Ave Suite 400	Lakeland	FL	33801	863-669-1155	665-6324*
**Fax Area Code:* 800 ■ *Web:* www.compren.com					
Computer Troubleshooters USA					
755 Commerce Dr Suite 412	Decatur	GA	30030	404-477-1300	234-6162*
**Fax Area Code:* 770 ■ *TF:* 877-704-1702 ■ *Web:* www.comptroub.com					
Contours Express Inc 156 Imperial Way	Nicholasville	KY	40356	859-885-6441	241-2234
TF: 877-227-2282 ■ *Web:* www.contoursexpress.com					
Cookies By Design Inc 1865 Summit Ave Suite 605	Plano	TX	75074	972-398-9536	398-9542
TF: 800-945-2665 ■ *Web:* www.cookiesbydesign.com					
Coverall Cleaning Concepts					
5201 Congress Ave Suite 275	Boca Raton	FL	33487	561-922-2500	922-2423
TF: 800-537-3371 ■ *Web:* www.coverall.com					
Craters & Freighters 331 Corporate Cir Suite J	Golden	CO	80401	800-736-3335	399-9964*
**Fax Area Code:* 303 ■ *TF:* 800-736-3335 ■ *Web:* www.cratersandfreighters.com					
Creative Colors International Inc					
19015 S Jodi Rd Suite E	Mokena	IL	60448	708-478-1437	478-1636
TF: 800-933-2656 ■ *Web:* www.creativecolorsintl.com					
Crest Foods Inc 101 W Renner Rd Suite 240	Richardson	TX	75802	214-495-9533	853-5347
Web: www.nestlecafe.com					
Crestcom International Ltd					
6900 E Belleview Ave Suite 300	Greenwood Village	CO	80111	303-267-8200	267-8207
TF: 888-273-7826 ■ *Web:* www.crestcom.com					
Critter Control Inc					
9435 E Cherry Bend Rd	Traverse City	MI	49684	231-947-2400	947-9440
TF: 800-451-6544 ■ *Web:* www.crittercontrol.com					
Crown Trophy 9 Skyline Dr	Hawthorne	NY	10532	800-583-8228	347-0211*
**Fax Area Code:* 914 ■ *TF:* 800-583-8228 ■ *Web:* www.crowntrophy.com					
Cruise Holidays International Inc					
3033 Campus Dr Suite 320	Plymouth	MN	55401	800-866-7245	212-5266*
**Fax Area Code:* 763 ■ *TF:* 800-866-7245 ■ *Web:* www.cruiseholidays.com					
CruiseOne Inc					
1415 NW 62nd St Suite 205	Fort Lauderdale	FL	33309	954-958-3700	958-3703
TF: 800-832-3592 ■ *Web:* www.cruiseone.com					
Culver Franchising System Inc					
1240 Water St	Prairie du Sac	WI	53578	608-643-7980	643-7982
Web: www.culvers.com					
Curves International Inc 100 Ritchie Rd	Waco	TX	76712	254-399-9285	399-9731
TF: 800-848-1096 ■ *Web:* www.curves.com					
Cuts Fitness For Men 1120 Raritan Rd	Clark	NJ	07066	732-381-9300	574-1130
D'Angelo Sandwich Shops 600 Providence Hwy	Dedham	MA	02026	781-461-1200	461-1896
TF: 800-727-2446 ■ *Web:* www.dangelos.com					
Dairy Queen 7505 Metro Blvd	Minneapolis	MN	55439	952-830-0200	830-0480
TF: 800-679-6556 ■ *Web:* www.dairyqueen.com					
Decor & You Inc 900 Main St S Bldg 2	Southbury	CT	06488	203-264-3500	264-5095
TF: 800-477-3326 ■ *Web:* www.decorandyou.com					
Decorating Den Systems Inc 8659 Commerce Dr	Easton	MD	21601	410-822-9001	
TF: 800-332-3367 ■ *Web:* www.decoratingden.com					
Denny's Inc 203 E Main St	Spartanburg	SC	29319	864-597-8000	597-8780*
**Fax:* Mktg ■ *Web:* www.dennys.com					
Dingo Inc 250 Lehow Ave Suite B	Englewood	CO	80110	303-471-4935	283-2819*
**Fax Area Code:* 720 ■ *TF:* 877-500-2275 ■ *Web:* www.barkbusters.com					
DirectBuy Inc 101 W 84th Dr Suite C	Merrillville	IN	46410	219-755-6211	755-6208
TF: 800-827-6400 ■ *Web:* www.directbuy.com					
Domino's Pizza Inc					
30 Frank Lloyd Wright Dr	Ann Arbor	MI	48106	734-930-3030	930-3580*
NYSE: DPZ ■ **Fax:* Mail Rm ■ *TF:* 888-366-4667 ■ *Web:* www.express.dominos.com					
Dr Vinyl & Assoc Ltd					
201 NW Victoria Dr	Lee"s Summit	MO	64086	816-525-6060	525-6333
TF: 800-531-6600 ■ *Web:* www.drvinyl.com					
DreamMaker Bath & Kitchen by Worldwide					
1020 N University Parks Dr	Waco	TX	76707	254-745-2477	745-2588
TF: 800-583-9099 ■ *Web:* www.dreammaker-remodel.com					
Dunkin' Donuts 130 Royall St	Canton	MA	02021	781-737-3000	737-4000
TF Cust Svc: 800-859-5339 ■ *Web:* www.dunkindonuts.com					
Duraclean International Inc					
220 W Campus Dr # A	Arlington Heights	IL	60004	847-704-7100	704-7101
TF: 800-251-7070 ■ *Web:* www.duraclean.com					
East of Chicago Pizza Co 512 E Tiffin St	Willard	OH	44890	419-935-3033	935-3278
Web: www.eastofchicago.com					
Edible Arrangements LLC 95 Barnes Rd	Wallingford	CT	06492	203-907-0066	230-0792
TF Cust Svc: 800-236-7101 ■ *Web:* www.ediblearrangements.com					
EmbroidMe Inc 2121 Vista Pkwy	West Palm Beach	FL	33411	561-640-7367	640-6062
TF: 877-877-0234 ■ *Web:* www.embroidme.com					
Emerging Vision Inc 520 Eighth Ave 23rd Fl	New York	NY	10018	646-737-1500	
Web: www.emergingvision.com					
ERA Franchise Systems Inc 1 Campus Dr	Parsippany	NJ	07054	973-407-5807	407-7354
TF: 800-869-1260 ■ *Web:* www.era.com					
Express Employment Professionals					
8516 NW Expy	Oklahoma City	OK	73162	405-840-5000	717-5665
TF: 800-222-4057 ■ *Web:* www.expresspros.com					
Express Oil Change 1880 S Pk Dr	Hoover	AL	35244	205-945-1771	940-6025
TF: 888-945-1771 ■ *Web:* www.expressoil.com					
Express Tax Franchise Corp					
3030 Hartley Rd Suite 320	Jacksonville	FL	32257	904-262-0031	262-2864
TF: 888-417-4461 ■ *Web:* www.expresstaxservice.com					
Extreme Pita 2187 Dunwin Dr	Mississauga	ON	L5L1X2	905-820-7887	820-8448
TF: 888-729-7482 ■ *Web:* www.extremepita.com					
Famous Dave's of America Inc					
12701 Whitewater Dr Suite 200	Minnetonka	MN	55343	952-294-1300	294-0242
NASDAQ: DAVE ■ *TF:* 800-210-4040 ■ *Web:* www.famousdaves.com					
Fantastic Sams Inc 50 Dunham Rd 3rd Fl	Beverly	MA	01915	978-232-5600	232-5601
Web: www.fantasticsams.com					
Fast-Fix Jewelry & Watch Repairs					
1300 NW 17th Ave Suite 170	Delray Beach	FL	33445	561-330-6060	330-6062
TF: 800-359-0407 ■ *Web:* www.fastfix.com					
FasTracKids International Ltd					
6900 E Belleview Ave Suite 100	Greenwood Village	CO	80111	303-224-0200	224-0222
TF: 888-576-6888 ■ *Web:* www.fastrackids.com					
Figaro's Italian Pizza Inc					
1500 Liberty St SE Suite 160	Salem	OR	97302	503-371-9318	363-5364
TF: 888-344-2767 ■ *Web:* www.figaros.com					
Firehouse Restaurant Group Inc					
3400 Kori Rd # 8	Jacksonville	FL	32257	904-886-8300	886-2111
TF: 800-388-3473 ■ *Web:* www.firehousesubs.com					
Fish Window Cleaning Services Inc					
200 Enchanted Pkwy	Saint Louis	MO	63021	636-530-7334	530-7856
TF: 877-707-3474 ■ *Web:* www.fishwindowcleaning.com					
Floor Coverings International					
200 Technology Ct Suite 1200	Smyrna	GA	30082	770-874-7600	874-7605
TF Sales: 800-955-4324 ■ *Web:* www.floorcoveringsinternational.com					
Flowerama of America Inc 3165 W Airline Hwy	Waterloo	IA	50703	319-291-6004	291-8676
TF: 800-728-6004 ■ *Web:* www.flowerama.com					
Foot Solutions Inc					
2359 Windy Hill Rd Suite 400	Marietta	GA	30067	770-955-0099	953-6270
TF: 866-338-2597 ■ *Web:* www.footsolutions.com					
Fox's Pizza Den Inc					
4425 Willaim Penn Hwy	Murrysville	PA	15668	724-733-7888	325-5479
TF: 800-899-3697 ■ *Web:* www.foxspizza.com					
Framing & Art Centre 1800 Appleby Line Rd	Burlington	ON	L7L6A1	800-563-7263	565-5755
TF: 800-563-7263 ■ *Web:* www.framingartcentre.com					
Friendly Computers					
3440 W Cheyenne Suite 100	North Las Vegas	NV	89032	702-458-2780	869-2780
TF: 800-656-3115 ■ *Web:* www.friendlycomputers.com					
Furniture Medic 3839 S Forest Hill Irene Rd	Memphis	TN	38125	901-597-8600	597-8630
TF: 800-877-9933 ■ *Web:* www.furnituremedic.com					
Glass Doctor 1020 N University Parks Dr	Waco	TX	76707	254-745-2400	745-2590
Web: www.glassdoctor.com					
GNC Corp 300 6th Ave	Pittsburgh	PA	15222	412-288-4600	338-8905*
**Fax:* Cust Svc ■ *TF Cust Svc:* 888-462-2548 ■ *Web:* www.gnc.com					
Goddard Systems Inc 1016 W Ninth Ave	King of Prussia	PA	19406	610-265-8510	265-8867
TF: 800-463-3273 ■ *Web:* www.goddardschool.com					
Gold's Gym International Inc					
125 E John Carpenter Fwy Suite 1300	Irving	TX	75062	214-574-4653	
TF: 800-457-5375 ■ *Web:* www.goldsgym.com					
Golden Chick 11488 Luna Rd Suite 100B	Dallas	TX	75234	972-831-0911	831-0401
Web: www.goldenchick.com					
Golden Corral Corp 5151 Glenwood Ave	Raleigh	NC	27612	919-781-9310	881-4485
TF: 800-284-5673 ■ *Web:* www.goldencorral.net					
Golden Krust Carribean Bakery & Grill					
3958 Pk Ave	Bronx	NY	10457	718-655-7878	583-1883
Web: www.goldenkrustbakery.com					
Grease Monkey International Inc					
7100 E Belleview Ave Suite 305	Greenwood Village	CO	80111	303-308-1660	308-5908
TF: 800-822-7706 ■ *Web:* www.greasemonkeyintl.com					
Great American Cookie Co Inc					
4685 Frederick Dr SW	Atlanta	GA	30336	404-696-1700	699-0887
TF: 800-332-4856 ■ *Web:* www.greatamericancookies.com					
Great Clips Inc					
7700 France Ave S Suite 425	Minneapolis	MN	55435	952-893-9088	844-3444
TF: 800-999-5959 ■ *Web:* www.greatclips.com					
Great Harvest Bread Co 28 S Montana St	Dillon	MT	59725	406-683-6842	683-5537
TF: 800-442-0424 ■ *Web:* www.greatharvest.com					
Great Steak & Potato Co					
9311 E Via de Ventura	Scottsdale	AZ	85258	480-362-4800	362-4812
TF: 866-452-4252 ■ *Web:* www.thegreatsteak.com					

Company	City	State	ZIP	Phone	Fax
Griswold Special Care Inc 717 Bethlehem Pike Suite 300 *TF:* 888-777-7630 ■ *Web:* www.griswoldspecialcare.com	Erdenheim	PA	19038	215-402-0200	402-0202
Growth Coach The 10700 Montgomery Rd Suite 300 **Fax Area Code:* 513 ■ *TF:* 888-292-7992 ■ *Web:* www.thegrowthcoach.com	Cincinnati	OH	45242	888-292-7992	563-2691*
Gymboree Corp 500 Howard St *NASDAQ: GYMB* ■ *TF:* 877-449-6932 ■ *Web:* www.gymboree.com	San Francisco	CA	94105	415-278-7000	278-7100
Gymboree Corp Play & Music Program 500 Howard St *TF:* 800-520-7529 ■ *Web:* www.gymboree.com	San Francisco	CA	94105	415-278-7000	278-7100
Handyman Matters Inc 12567 W Cedar Dr Suite 250 *TF:* 866-808-8401 ■ *Web:* www.handymanmatters.com	Lakewood	CO	80228	303-984-0177	984-0133
Happy & Healthy Products Inc 1600 S Dixie Hwy Suite 200 *TF:* 800-378-4854 ■ *Web:* www.fruitfull.com	Boca Raton	FL	33432	561-367-0739	368-5267
Hayes Handpiece Franchises Inc 5375 Avenida Encinas Suite C *TF:* 800-228-0521 ■ *Web:* www.hayeshandpiece.com	Carlsbad	CA	92008	760-602-0521	602-0505
Hobbytown USA 1233 Libra Dr *TF Cust Svc:* 800-869-0424 ■ *Web:* www.hobbytown.com	Lincoln	NE	68512	402-434-5385	
Hollywood Tans 1120 Rt 73 # 400 *Web:* www.hollywoodtans.com	Mount Laurel	NJ	08054	856-914-9090	914-9099
Homes & Land Magazine Affiliates LLC 1830 E Pk Ave *TF:* 800-726-6683 ■ *Web:* www.homesandland.com	Tallahassee	FL	32301	850-574-2111	575-9567
HomeTeam Inspection Service Inc 575 Chamber Dr *TF:* 800-598-5297 ■ *Web:* www.hometeaminspection.com	Milford	OH	45150	513-831-1300	831-6010
HomeVestors of America Inc 6500 Greenville Ave Suite 400 *TF:* 800-442-8937 ■ *Web:* www.homevestors.com	Dallas	TX	75206	972-761-0046	761-9022
Honeybaked Ham Co 5445 Triangle Pkwy Suite 400 *TF:* 800-367-2426 ■ *Web:* www.honeybakedonline.com	Norcross	GA	30092	678-966-3100	966-3134
Hot Stuff Foods LLC 2930 W Maple St *Web:* www.hotstufffoods.com	Sioux Falls	SD	57107	605-330-7531	336-0141
Houlihan's Restaurant Group Inc 8700 State Line Rd Suite 100 *Web:* www.houlihans.com	Leawood	KS	66206	913-901-2500	901-2651
House Doctors 575 Chamber Dr *TF:* 800-319-3359 ■ *Web:* www.housedoctors.com	Milford	OH	45150	513-831-0100	831-6010
HouseMaster 421 W Union Ave *TF:* 800-526-3939 ■ *Web:* www.housemaster.com	Bound Brook	NJ	08805	732-469-6565	469-7405
Hungry Howie's Pizza & Subs Inc 30300 Stephenson Hwy Suite 200 *TF:* 800-624-8122 ■ *Web:* www.hungryhowies.com	Madison Heights	MI	48071	248-414-3300	414-3301
Ident-A-Kid Services of America 2810 Scherer Dr Suite 100 *TF:* 800-890-1000 ■ *Web:* www.identakid.com	Saint Petersburg	FL	33716	727-577-4646	576-8258
IHOP Corp 450 N Brand Blvd *TF:* 800-241-4467 ■ *Web:* www.ihop.com	Glendale	CA	91203	818-240-6055	637-4730
Instant Imprints 5897 Oberlin Dr # 200 *TF:* 800-542-3437 ■ *Web:* www.instantimprints.com	San Diego	CA	92121	858-642-4848	453-6513
Interface Financial Group 2182 Dupont Dr Suite 221 **Fax Area Code:* 866 ■ *TF:* 800-387-0860 ■ *Web:* www.interfacefinancial.com	Irvine	CA	92612	949-477-0665	475-8688*
Interim HealthCare Inc 1601 Sawgrass Corporate Pkwy *TF:* 800-338-7786 ■ *Web:* www.interimhealthcare.com	Sunrise	FL	33323	954-858-6000	858-2820
iSold It 260 S Lake Ave129 N Hill Ave	Pasadena	CA	91101	626-584-0440	584-6540
It's A Grind Inc 6272 E Pacific Coast Hwy Suite E *TF:* 866-424-5282 ■ *Web:* www.itsagrind.com	Long Beach	CA	90803	562-594-5600	594-4100
Jackson Hewitt Inc 3 Sylvan Way Suite 301 *NYSE: JTX* ■ *TF:* 800-234-1040 ■ *Web:* www.jacksonhewitt.com	Parsippany	NJ	07054	800-234-1040	
Jazzercise Inc 2460 Impala Dr *TF Cust Svc:* 800-348-4748 ■ *Web:* www.jazzercise.com	Carlsbad	CA	92010	760-476-1750	602-7180
Jenny Craig International Inc 5770 Fleet St *TF:* 800-443-2331 ■ *Web:* www.jennycraig.com	Carlsbad	CA	92008	760-696-4000	696-4506
Jet's America Inc 37501 Mound Rd *TF:* 888-446-5870 ■ *Web:* www.jetspizza.com	Sterling Heights	MI	48130	586-268-5870	268-6762
Juice It Up! Franchise Corp 17915 Sky Pk Cir Suite J *Web:* www.juiceitup.com	Irvine	CA	92614	949-475-0146	475-0137
Karmelkorn Shoppes Inc 7505 Metro Blvd *Web:* www.karmelkorn.com	Minneapolis	MN	55439	952-830-0200	830-0270
Keller Williams Realty Inc 807 Las Cimas Pkwy Suite 200 *Web:* www.kw.com	Austin	TX	78746	512-327-3070	328-1433
KFC Corp 1441 Gardiner Ln *TF:* 800-544-5774 ■ *Web:* www.kfc.com	Louisville	KY	40213	502-874-8300	874-2759
Kid to Kid 170 S 1000E *TF:* 888-543-2543 ■ *Web:* www.kidtokid.com	Salt Lake City	UT	84102	801-359-0071	359-3207
Kinderdance International Inc 1333 Gateway Dr Suite 1033 *TF:* 800-554-2334 ■ *Web:* www.kinderdance.com	Melbourne	FL	32901	321-984-4448	984-4490
Kitchen Tune-Up Inc 813 Cir Dr *TF:* 800-333-6385 ■ *Web:* www.kitchentuneup.com	Aberdeen	SD	57401	605-225-4049	225-1371
L & W Investigations Inc 23332 Mill Creek Dr Suite 130 *Web:* www.lwfranchise.com	Laguna Hills	CA	92653	949-305-7383	305-8928
LA Weight Loss Centers 747 Dresher Rd Suite 100 *TF:* 877-524-3571 ■ *Web:* www.laweightloss.com	Horsham	PA	19044	215-346-4300	
Lady of America Franchise Corp 500 E Broward Blvd Suite 1650 *TF:* 800-833-5239 ■ *Web:* www.ladyofamerica.com	Fort Lauderdale	FL	33394	954-527-5373	527-5436
Lawn Doctor Inc 142 SR 34 *TF:* 800-631-5660 ■ *Web:* www.lawndoctor.com	Holmdel	NJ	07733	732-946-0029	946-9089
Learning Express Inc 29 Buena Vista St *TF:* 800-924-2296 ■ *Web:* www.learningexpress.com	Devens	MA	01434	978-889-1000	889-1010
Liberty Tax Service Inc 1716 Corporate Landing Pkwy *TF Cust Svc:* 800-790-3863 ■ *Web:* www.libertytax.com	Virginia Beach	VA	23454	757-493-8855	493-0169
Lil' Angels LLC 4041 Hatcher Cir *TF:* 800-358-9101 ■ *Web:* www.angelsus.com	Memphis	TN	38118	901-682-4470	682-2018
Little Caesars Inc 2211 Woodward Ave **Fax:* Cust Svc ■ *TF:* 800-722-3727 ■ *Web:* www.littlecaesars.com	Detroit	MI	48201	313-983-6000	983-6166*
Little Gym International Inc 7001 N Scottsdale Rd # 1050 *TF:* 888-228-2878 ■ *Web:* www.thelittlegym.com	Scottsdale	AZ	85253	480-948-2878	948-2765
Living Assistance Services Inc 28 W Eagle Rd Suite 204 *TF:* 800-365-4189 ■ *Web:* www.livingassistance.com	Havertown	PA	19083	610-924-0630	924-9690
Long John Silver's Restaurants Inc 1441 Gardiner Ln *Web:* www.ljsilvers.com	Louisville	KY	40213	502-874-8300	874-8306
Mad Science Group 8360 Bougainville St Suite 201 *TF:* 800-586-5231 ■ *Web:* www.madscience.org	Montreal	QC	H4P2G1	514-344-4181	344-6695
MaggieMoo's International LLC 10025 Governor Warfield Pkwy Suite 301 **Fax Area Code:* 410 ■ *TF:* 800-949-8114 ■ *Web:* www.maggiemoos.com	Columbia	MD	21044	800-949-8114	740-1500*
Magnetsigns Adv Inc 4225 38th St *TF:* 800-219-8977 ■ *Web:* www.magnetsigns.com	Camrose	AB	T4V3Z3	780-672-8720	672-8716
Maid Brigade USA/Minimaid Canada 4 Concourse Pkwy Suite 200 *TF:* 800-722-6243 ■ *Web:* www.maidbrigade.com	Atlanta	GA	30328	770-551-9630	391-9092
MaidPro Corp 180 Canal St *TF:* 888-624-3776 ■ *Web:* www.maidpro.com	Boston	MA	02114	617-742-8787	720-0700
Mail Boxes Etc 6060 Cornerstone Ct W *TF:* 800-789-4623 ■ *Web:* www.mbe.com	San Diego	CA	92121	858-455-8800	546-7493
Manhattan Bagel Co Inc 100 Horizon Ctr Blvd *TF:* 800-308-2457 ■ *Web:* www.manhattanbagel.com	Hamilton	NJ	08691	609-631-7000	631-7068
MARS International Inc 2001 E Division St Suite 101 **Fax Area Code:* 800	Arlington	TX	76011	817-226-6277	230-2859*
Martinizing Dry Cleaning 422 Wards Corner Rd *TF:* 800-827-0207 ■ *Web:* www.martinizing.com	Loveland	OH	45140	513-351-6211	731-0818
Mathnasium LLC 5120 W Goldleaf Cir Suite 300 **Fax Area Code:* 310 ■ *TF:* 877-531-6284 ■ *Web:* www.mathnasium.com	Los Angeles	CA	90056	877-531-6284	943-2111*
Maui Wowi Inc 5445 DTC Pkwy Suite 1050 *Web:* www.mauiwowi.com	Greenwood Village	CO	80111	303-781-7800	781-2438
McDonald's Corp 1 McDonald's Plaza *NYSE: MCD* ■ *TF:* 800-234-6227 ■ *Web:* www.mcdonalds.com	Oak Brook	IL	60523	630-623-3000	623-5500
Medicap Pharmacies Inc 4350 Westown Pkwy Suite 400 *TF Cust Svc:* 800-445-2244 ■ *Web:* www.medicaprx.com	West Des Moines	IA	50266	515-224-8400	224-8415
Merle Norman Cosmetics Inc 9130 Bellanca Ave *TF:* 800-421-2060 ■ *Web:* www.merlenorman.com	Los Angeles	CA	90045	310-641-3000	641-7144
Merlin Corp 1 N River Ln Suite 206 *TF:* 800-637-5467 ■ *Web:* www.merlins.com	Geneva	IL	60134	630-208-9900	208-8601
Midas International Corp 1300 Arlington Heights Rd *TF:* 800-621-0144 ■ *Web:* www.midas.com	Itasca	IL	60143	630-438-3000	438-3700
Minuteman Press International Inc 61 Executive Blvd *TF:* 800-645-3006 ■ *Web:* www.minutemanpress.com	Farmingdale	NY	11735	631-249-1370	249-5618
Molly Maid Inc 3948 Ranchero Dr *TF:* 800-665-5962 ■ *Web:* www.mollymaid.com	Ann Arbor	MI	48108	734-822-6800	822-6888
Money Mailer LLC 12131 Western Ave *TF:* 800-234-2771 ■ *Web:* www.moneymailer.com	Garden Grove	CA	92841	714-889-3800	889-4618
Mr Appliance Corp 1010 N University Parks Dr **Fax Area Code:* 254 ■ *TF:* 800-290-1422 ■ *Web:* www.mrappliance.com	Waco	TX	76707	800-290-1422	745-5073*
Mr Electric Corp 1010 N University Parks Dr **Fax Area Code:* 254 ■ *TF:* 800-253-9151 ■ *Web:* www.mrelectric.com	Waco	TX	76707	800-253-9151	745-5068*
Mr Handyman International LLC 3948 Ranchero Dr **Fax Area Code:* 734 ■ *TF Cust Svc:* 800-289-4600 ■ *Web:* www.mrhandyman.com	Ann Arbor	MI	48108	800-289-4600	822-6888*
Mr Hero Restaurants 7010 Engle Rd Suite 100 *TF:* 888-860-5082 ■ *Web:* www.mrhero.com	Middleburg Heights	OH	44130	440-625-3080	625-3081
Mr Sub 4576 Yonge St Suite 600 *TF:* 800-668-7827 ■ *Web:* www.mrsub.ca	Toronto	ON	M2N6P1	416-225-5545	225-5536
Mrs Fields Original Cookies Inc 2855 E Cottonwood Pkwy Suite 400 *TF:* 800-348-6311 ■ *Web:* www.mrsfields.com	Salt Lake City	UT	84121	801-736-5600	736-5970
My Favorite Muffin 500 Lake Cook Rd Suite 475 *TF:* 800-251-6101 ■ *Web:* www.babcorp.com	Deerfield	IL	60015	847-948-7520	405-8140
My Gym Enterprises Inc 15300 Ventura Blvd Suite 414 **Fax Area Code:* 818 ■ *TF:* 800-426-4573 ■ *Web:* www.my-gym.com	Sherman Oaks	CA	91403	800-469-4967	907-0735*
N-Hance 1530 N 1000 W *TF:* 866-642-6231 ■ *Web:* www.nhancefranchise.com	Logan	UT	84321	435-755-0099	755-0021
Nathan's Famous Inc One Jericho Plaza 2nd Fl *NASDAQ: NATH* ■ *TF:* 800-628-4267 ■ *Web:* www.nathansfamous.com	Jericho	NY	11753	516-338-8500	338-7220

Company / Address	City	State	ZIP	Phone	Fax
National Property Inspections Inc (NPI) 9375 Burt St Suite 201	Omaha	NE	68114	402-333-9807	933-2508*
*Fax Area Code: 800 ■ TF: 800-333-9807 ■ Web: www.npiweb.com					
Nationwide Floorcover & Window Coverings 111 E Kilbourn Ave Suite 2400	Milwaukee	WI	53202	414-765-9900	765-1300
TF: 800-366-8088 ■ Web: www.floorsandwindows.com					
Navis Pack & Ship Centers 5675 DTC Blvd Suite 280	Greenwood Village	CO	80111	303-741-6626	741-6653
TF: 800-525-6309 ■ Web: www.gonavis.com					
NOVUS Auto Glass Eagle Creek Commerce Ctr 12800 Hwy 13 S Suite 500	Minneapolis	MN	55378	952-944-8000	944-2542
TF: 800-328-1137 ■ Web: www.novusglass.com					
Nutrilawn Inc 202-2077 Dundas St E Suite 202	Mississauga	ON	L4X1M2	416-620-7100	620-7771
Web: www.nutri-lawn.com					
OctoClean Franchising Systems 3357 Chicago Ave	Riverside	CA	92507	951-683-5859	779-0270
Web: www.octoclean.com					
One Hour Air Conditioning & Heating 2 N Tamiami Trail Suite 806	Sarasota	FL	34236	941-552-5100	951-0942
TF: 800-746-0458 ■ Web: www.onehourheatandair.com					
OpenWorks 4742 N 24th St Suite 300	Phoenix	AZ	85016	602-224-0440	468-3788
TF: 800-777-6736 ■ Web: www.openworksweb.com					
Orange Julius of America 7505 Metro Blvd PO Box 39286	Minneapolis	MN	55439	952-830-0200	830-0480*
*Fax: Mktg ■ TF: 800-679-6556 ■ Web: www.dairyqueen.com					
Outdoor Connection Inc 424 Neosho	Burlington	KS	66839	620-364-5500	364-5563
Web: www.outdoor-connection.com					
Oxford Learning Centers Inc 97B S Livingston Ave	Livingston	NJ	07039	973-597-4300	
TF: 888-559-2212 ■ Web: www.oxfordlearning.com					
Padgett Business Services 160 Hawthorne Pk	Athens	GA	30606	706-548-1040	543-8537
TF: 800-723-4388 ■ Web: www.smallbizpros.com					
Pak Mail Centers of America Inc 7173 S Havana St Suite 600	Englewood	CO	80112	303-957-1000	790-9445
TF Cust Svc: 800-778-6665 ■ Web: www.pakmail.com					
Palm Beach Tan Inc 13800 Senlac Dr Suite 200	Farmers Branch	TX	75234	972-406-2400	406-2515
Web: www.palmbeachtan.com					
Papa John's International Inc 2002 Papa John's Blvd	Louisville	KY	40299	502-261-7272	261-4331*
NASDAQ: PZZA ■ *Fax: Cust Svc ■ TF: 877-547-7272 ■ Web: www.papajohns.com					
Papa Murphy's International Inc 8000 NE Pkwy Dr Suite 350	Vancouver	WA	98662	360-260-7272	260-0500
Web: www.papamurphys.com					
Party America 980 Atlantic Ave Suite 103	Alameda	CA	94501	510-747-1800	747-1810
Web: www.partyamerica.com					
Party City Corp 25 Green Pond Rd Suite 1	Rockaway	NJ	07866	925-965-7112	
TF: 800-727-8924 ■ Web: www.partycity.com					
Paul Davis Restoration Inc 1 Independent Dr Suite 2300	Jacksonville	FL	32202	904-737-2779	737-4204
TF: 800-722-1818 ■ Web: www.pdrestoration.com					
Pearle Vision Inc 4000 Luxottica Pl	Mason	OH	45040	877-486-6486	486-3596*
*Fax Area Code: 330 ■ TF: 800-282-3931 ■ Web: www.pearlevision.com					
Perkins Restaurant & Bakery 6075 Poplar Ave Suite 800	Memphis	TN	38119	901-766-6400	766-6482
TF: 800-877-7375 ■ Web: www.perkinsrestaurants.com					
Perma-Glaze Inc 1638 Research Loop Rd Suite 160	Tucson	AZ	85710	520-722-9718	296-4393
TF: 800-332-7397 ■ Web: www.permaglaze.com					
Pet Supplies "Plus" Inc 22710 Haggerty Rd Suite 100	Farmington Hills	MI	48335	248-374-1900	374-7900
TF: 866-477-7747 ■ Web: www.petsuppliesplus.com					
Petland Inc 250 Riverside St	Chillicothe	OH	45601	740-775-2464	775-2574
TF: 800-221-5935 ■ Web: www.petland.com					
Physicians Weight Loss Centers of America Inc 395 Springside Dr	Akron	OH	44333	330-666-7952	666-2197
TF: 800-205-7887 ■ Web: www.pwlc.com					
Pinch A Penny Inc 14480 62nd St N	Clearwater	FL	33760	727-531-8913	536-8066
TF: 800-509-5571 ■ Web: www.pinchapenny.com					
PIP Printing & Document Services Inc 26722 Plaza Dr Suite 200	Mission Viejo	CA	92691	949-282-3800	282-3899
Web: www.pip.com					
Pizza Inn Inc 3551 Plano Pkwy	The Colony	TX	75056	469-384-5000	384-5054
NASDAQ: PZZI ■ TF: 800-880-9955 ■ Web: www.pizzainn.com					
Pizza Pizza Ltd 580 Jarvis St	Toronto	ON	M4Y2H9	416-967-1010	967-0891
TF: 800-265-9762 ■ Web: www.pizzapizza.ca					
Pizza Ranch Inc 204 19th St SE	Orange City	IA	51041	800-321-3401	439-1125*
*Fax Area Code: 712 ■ TF: 800-321-3401 ■ Web: www.pizzaranch.com					
Plato's Closet 4200 Dahlberg Dr Suite 100	Minneapolis	MN	55422	763-520-8500	520-8410
Web: www.platoscloset.com					
Play It Again Sports 4200 Dahlberg Dr Suite 100	Minneapolis	MN	55422	763-520-8500	520-8470
TF: 800-433-2540 ■ Web: www.playitagainsports.com					
Postal Connections of America 1081 Camino del Rio S Suite 109	San Diego	CA	92108	619-294-7550	294-4550
TF: 800-767-8257 ■ Web: www.postalconnections.com					
PostalAnnex+ Inc 7580 Metropolitan Dr Suite 200	San Diego	CA	92108	619-563-4800	563-9850
TF: 800-456-1525 ■ Web: www.postalannex.com					
PostNet International Franchise Corp 1819 Wazee St	Denver	CO	80202	303-771-7100	771-7133
TF: 800-841-7171 ■ Web: www.postnet.com					
Powerhouse Gym International 355 S Old Woodward Suite 150	Birmingham	MI	48009	248-476-2888	530-9816*
*Fax Area Code: 249 ■ Web: www.powerhousegym.com					
Precision Auto Care Inc 748 Miller Dr SE	Leesburg	VA	20175	703-777-9095	771-7108
TF: 800-438-8863 ■ Web: www.precisiontune.com					
PremierGarage Systems LLC 21405 N 15th Ln	Phoenix	AZ	85027	480-483-3030	483-7895
TF: 866-483-4272 ■ Web: www.premiergarage.com					
Pressed4Time Inc 8 Clock Tower Pl Suite 110	Maynard	MA	01754	978-823-8300	823-8301
TF: 800-423-8711 ■ Web: www.pressed4time.com					
Primrose School Franchising Co 3660 Cedarcrest Rd	Acworth	GA	30101	770-529-4100	529-1551
TF: 800-745-0677 ■ Web: www.primroseschools.com					
Priority Management Systems Inc 11160 Silversmith Pl	Richmond	BC	V7A5E4	604-214-7772	214-7773
Web: www.prioritymanagement.com					
Pro Image Franchise LC 233 N 1250 W Suite 200	Centerville	UT	84014	801-296-9999	296-1319
TF: 888-477-6326 ■ Web: www.proimage.net					
ProForma 8800 E Pleasant Valley Rd	Independence	OH	44131	216-520-8400	520-8444
TF: 800-825-1525 ■ Web: www.proforma.com					
Property Damage Appraisers Inc PO Box 9230	Fort Worth	TX	76147	817-731-5555	866-4732*
*Fax Area Code: 800 ■ TF Cust Svc: 800-749-7324 ■ Web: www.pdacorporation.com					
Qdoba Restaurant Corp 4865 Ward Rd Suite 500	Wheat Ridge	CO	80033	720-898-2300	898-2396
Web: www.qdoba.com					
RadioShack 320 Trinity Campus Cir	Fort Worth	TX	76102	817-415-3011	415-3240
TF: 800-843-7422 ■ Web: www.radioshack.com					
Rainbow International 1010 N University Pk Dr	Waco	TX	76707	254-745-2444	745-2592
TF: 800-583-9100 ■ Web: www.rainbowintl.com					
Re-Bath LLC 1055 S Country Club Dr	Mesa	AZ	85210	480-844-1575	833-7199
TF: 800-426-4573 ■ Web: www.re-bath.com					
RE/MAX International Inc 5075 S Syracuse St	Denver	CO	80237	303-770-5531	796-3599
TF Cust Svc: 800-525-7452 ■ Web: www.remax.com					
Real Living Inc 77 E Nationwide Blvd	Columbus	OH	43215	614-459-7400	457-6807
TF: 800-848-7400 ■ Web: www.realliving.com					
Realty Executives International Inc 2398 E Camelback Rd Suite 900	Phoenix	AZ	85016	602-957-0747	224-5542
TF: 800-252-3366 ■ Web: www.realtyexecutives.com					
Red Robin Gourmet Burgers Inc 6312 S Fiddlers Green Cir Suite 200-N	Greenwood Village	CO	80111	303-846-6000	846-6013
NASDAQ: RRGB ■ Web: www.redrobin.com					
Regis Corp Supercuts Div 7201 Metro Blvd	Minneapolis	MN	55439	952-947-7777	947-7801
TF: 888-888-7778 ■ Web: www.supercuts.com					
Relax The Back Corp 6 Ctr Pt Dr Suite 350	La Palma	CA	90623	800-222-5728	523-2419*
*Fax Area Code: 714 ■ TF: 800-222-5728 ■ Web: www.relaxtheback.com					
Rescuecom Corp 2560 Burnet Ave	Syracuse	NY	13206	800-737-2837	433-5228*
*Fax Area Code: 315 ■ TF: 800-737-2837 ■ Web: www.rescuecom.com					
Results Travel 701 Carlson Pkwy	Minnetonka	MN	55305	763-212-5000	212-2302
TF: 800-523-2200 ■ Web: www.resultstravel.com					
Right at Home Inc 11949 Q St Suite 118	Omaha	NE	68137	402-697-7537	697-0289
TF: 877-697-7537 ■ Web: www.rightathome.net					
Rita's Water Ice Franchise Co LLC 1210 Northbrook Dr	Trevose	PA	19053	215-876-9300	
TF: 800-677-7482 ■ Web: www.ritasice.com					
Rooter-Man 268 Rangeway Rd	North Billerica	MA	01862	978-667-1144	663-0061
TF: 800-700-8062 ■ Web: www.rooterman.com					
RSVP Publications 6730 W Linebaugh Ave Suite 201	Tampa	FL	33625	813-960-7787	725-0621*
*Fax Area Code: 877 ■ TF: 800-360-7787 ■ Web: www.rsvppublications.com					
Ruby Tuesday Inc 150 W Church Ave	Maryville	TN	37801	865-379-5700	380-7639*
NYSE: RT ■ *Fax: Mktg ■ TF: 800-325-0755 ■ Web: www.rubytuesday.com					
Saladworks LLC Eight Tower Bridge 161 Washington St Suite 300	Conshohocken	PA	19428	610-825-3080	825-3280
Web: www.saladworks.com					
Sandler Sales Institute 10411 Stevenson Rd	Stevenson	MD	21153	410-653-1993	358-7858
TF: 800-638-5686 ■ Web: www.sandler.com					
Screenmobile 72-050A Corporate Way	Thousand Palms	CA	92276	760-343-3500	343-7543
Web: www.screenmobile.com					
Sea Tow Services International Inc 1560 Youngs Ave PO Box 1178	Southold	NY	11971	631-765-3660	765-5208
TF: 800-473-2869 ■ Web: www.seatow.com					
Second Cup Ltd 6303 Airport Rd	Mississauga	ON	L4V1R8	877-212-1818	
TF: 877-212-1818 ■ Web: www.secondcup.com					
Shefield Group 2265 W Railway St	Abbotsford	BC	V2S2E3	604-859-1014	859-1711
Web: www.shefield.com					
Signs by Tomorrow USA Inc 8681 Robert Fulton Dr	Columbia	MD	21046	410-312-3600	312-3520
TF: 800-765-7446 ■ Web: www.signsbytomorrow.com					
Sir Speedy Inc 26722 Plaza Dr	Mission Viejo	CA	92691	949-348-5000	348-5010
TF: 800-854-8297 ■ Web: www.sirspeedy.com					
Snap-on Inc 2801 80th St	Kenosha	WI	53143	262-656-5200	656-5577
NYSE: SNA ■ TF: 877-762-7664 ■ Web: www.snapon.com					
Sonny's Franchise Co 2605 Maitland Ctr Pkwy Suite C	Maitland	FL	32751	407-660-8888	660-9050
Web: www.sonnysbbq.com					
Spherion Corp 2050 Spectrum Blvd	Fort Lauderdale	FL	33309	954-308-7600	351-8117
NYSE: SFN ■ TF: 866-435-7456 ■ Web: www.sfngroup.com					
Sport Clips Inc 110 Briarwood Dr	Georgetown	TX	78628	512-869-1201	869-0366
TF: 800-872-4247 ■ Web: www.sportclips.com					
Spring-Green Lawn Care Corp 11909 Spaulding School Dr	Plainfield	IL	60544	815-436-8777	436-9056
TF: 800-435-4051 ■ Web: www.spring-green.com					

Phone Fax

Stained Glass Overlay Inc 1827 N Case St..............Orange CA 92865 714-974-6124 974-6529
TF: 800-944-4746 ■ *Web:* www.stainedglassoverlay.com

Stork News of America Inc
1305 Hope Mills Rd Suite A...................... Fayetteville NC 28304 910-426-1357 426-2473
TF: 800-633-6395 ■ *Web:* www.storknews.com

Stretch-N-Grow International Inc
PO Box 7599 ....Seminole FL 33775 727-596-7614
TF: 800-348-0166 ■ *Web:* www.stretch-n-grow.com

StrollerFit Inc
100 E-Business Way Suite 290..................... Cincinnati OH 45241 513-489-2920 489-2964
TF: 866-222-9348 ■ *Web:* www.strollerfit.com

Successories Inc 1040 Holland Dr................. Boca Raton FL 33487 630-820-7200 998-7716*
**Fax Area Code:* 561 ■ *TF:* 800-621-1423 ■ *Web:* www.successories.com

Super Wash Inc 707 W Lincolnway PO Box 188......... Morrison IL 61270 815-772-2111 772-7160
Web: www.superwash.com

SuperCoups 350 Revolutionary Dr................. East Taunton MA 02718 508-977-2000 977-0644
TF: 800-626-2620 ■ *Web:* www.supercoups.com

SuperShuttle International Inc
14500 N Northsight Blvd Suite 329 .... Scottsdale AZ 85260 480-609-3000 607-9317
Web: www.supershuttle.com

TCBY Enterprises Inc
2855 E Cottonwood Pkwy Suite 400.............. Salt Lake City UT 84121 801-736-5600 736-5970
TF: 888-900-8229 ■ *Web:* www.tcby.com

Terminix International Co LP
860 Ridge Lake Blvd..............................Memphis TN 38120 901-766-1333 766-1491*
**Fax:* Mktg ■ *TF:* 800-654-7848 ■ *Web:* www.terminix.com

Treats International Franchise Corp
1550-A Laperriere Ave Suite 201 ....Ottawa ON K1Z7T2 613-563-4073 563-1982
TF: 800-461-4003 ■ *Web:* www.treats.com

Tropical Smoothie Cafe 12598 US Hwy 98 W............ Destin FL 32550 850-269-9850 269-9845
Web: www.tropicalsmoothie.com

Truly Nolen of America Inc
3636 E Speedway Blvd ....Tucson AZ 85716 520-327-3447 322-4011
TF: 800-528-3442 ■ *Web:* www.trulynolen.com

Tuffy Assoc Corp 7150 Granite Cir..................... Toledo OH 43617 419-865-6900 865-7343
TF: 800-228-8339 ■ *Web:* www.tuffy.com

United Financial Services Group
325 Chestnut St # 3000 .... Philadelphia PA 19106 215-238-0300 238-9056
TF: 800-826-0787 ■ *Web:* www.unitedfsg.com

United Shipping Solutions
6985 Union Pk Ctr Suite 565 ....Midvale UT 84047 801-352-0012 352-0339
TF: 866-744-7486 ■ *Web:* www.usshipit.com

UPS Store The 6060 Cornerstone Ct W............ San Diego CA 92121 858-455-8800 546-7492
TF: 800-789-4623 ■ *Web:* www.theupsstore.com

V2K Window Fashions Inc
1127 Auraria Pkwy Suite 204........................Denver CO 80204 800-200-0835 202-5201*
**Fax Area Code:* 303 ■ *TF:* 800-200-0835 ■ *Web:* www.v2k.com

Valpak Direct Marketing Systems Inc
8605 Largo Lakes Dr ....Largo FL 33773 727-393-1270 393-8060
TF: 800-237-6266 ■ *Web:* www.valpak.com

We the People USA Inc
1436 Lancaster Ave Suite 300 .... Berwyn PA 19312 866-429-2790 296-2038*
**Fax Area Code:* 610 ■ *TF:* 866-429-2790 ■ *Web:* www.wethepeopleusa.com

Weed Man 1645 Finfar Ct........................ Mississauga ON L5J4K1 905-823-8550 823-4594
Web: www.weedmancanada.com

Western Sizzlin Corp
416 S Jefferson St # 600 .... Roanoke VA 24011 540-345-3195 345-0831
TF: 800-247-8325 ■ *Web:* www.western-sizzlin.com

Wetzel's Pretzels LLC
35 Hugus Alley Suite 300..........................Pasadena CA 91103 626-432-6900 432-6904
Web: www.wetzels.com

Wild Birds Unlimited Inc
11711 N College Ave Suite 146 ....Carmel IN 46032 317-571-7100 571-7110
TF: 800-326-4928 ■ *Web:* www.wbu.com

WineStyles Inc 5100 W Copans Rd Suite 310 .... Margate FL 33063 954-984-0070 984-0074
TF: 866-424-9463 ■ *Web:* www.winestylesstore.com

Wing Zone Franchise Corp
900 Cir 75 Pkwy Suite 930..........................Atlanta GA 30339 404-875-5045 875-6631
TF: 877-946-4966 ■ *Web:* www.wingzone.com

Wingstop Restaurants Inc
1101 E Arapaho Rd Suite 150..................... Richardson TX 75081 972-686-6500 686-6502
Web: www.wingstop.com

Wireless Toyz Ltd
23399 Commerce Dr Suite B-1................ Farmington Hills MI 48335 248-426-8200 671-0346
TF: 866-237-2624 ■ *Web:* www.wirelesstoyz.com

Wireless Zone 34 Industrial Pk Pl.................. Middletown CT 06457 860-632-9494 632-9343
TF: 800-411-2355 ■ *Web:* www.wirelesszone.com

Women's Health Boutique Franchise System Inc
12715 Telge Rd..................................Cypress TX 77429 888-708-9982 373-4450*
**Fax Area Code:* 281 ■ *TF:* 888-708-9982 ■ *Web:* www.w-h-b.com

Woodcraft Supply LLC
1177 Rosemar Rd PO Box 1686....................Parkersburg WV 26105 800-535-4482 428-8271*
**Fax Area Code:* 304 ■ *TF:* 800-535-4482 ■ *Web:* www.woodcraft.com

World Inspection Network International Inc
6500 6th Ave NW ....Seattle WA 98117 206-728-8100
TF: 800-967-8127 ■ *Web:* www.wini.com

Worldwide Express 2828 Routh St Suite 400............ Dallas TX 75201 214-720-2400 720-2446
TF: 800-758-7447 ■ *Web:* www.wwex.com

WSI Internet 5580 Explorer Dr Suite 600............ Mississauga ON L4W4Y1 905-678-7588 678-7242
TF: 888-678-7588 ■ *Web:* www.wsicorporate.com

Yogen Fruz 210 Shields Ct........................ Markham ON L3R8V2 905-479-8762 479-5235
Web: www.yogenfruz.com

Young Rembrandts 23 N Union St .... Elgin IL 60123 847-742-6966 742-7197
Web: www.youngrembrandts.com

Ziebart International Corp 1290 E Maple Rd............. Troy MI 48083 248-588-4100 588-2513*
**Fax:* Orders ■ *TF:* 800-877-1312 ■ *Web:* www.ziebart.com

314 FREIGHT FORWARDERS

SEE ALSO Logistics Services (Transportation & Warehousing) p. 2183

Phone Fax

Airways Freight Corp
3849 W Wedington Dr .... Fayetteville AR 72704 479-442-6301 442-6522
TF: 800-643-3525 ■ *Web:* www.airwaysfreight.com

Alba Wheels Up International Inc
525 Washington Blvd Suite 2402..................Jersey City NJ 07310 201-435-7050 435-5650
Web: www.albawheelsup.com

ALG Admiral Inc 745 Dillon Dr ....Wood Dale IL 60191 630-766-3900 350-7616
TF: 800-323-0289 ■ *Web:* www.admiralusa.com

Alliance International Forwarders Inc
7155 Old Katy Rd Suite 100 S ....Houston TX 77024 713-428-3100 428-3101
Web: www.aifi.com

Allstates WorldCargo Inc
1 Pelican Dr Suite 1 .... Bayville NJ 08721 732-831-6868 831-6869
TF: 800-575-5575 ■ *Web:* www.allstatesair.com

American Fast Freight Inc 450 Shattuck Ave S ....Renton WA 98057 253-680-2582 624-8334*
**Fax Area Code:* 206 ■ *TF:* 800-642-6664 ■ *Web:* www.americanfast.com

AmeriQuest Transportation Services Inc
457 Haddonfield Rd Suite 220 ....Cherry Hill NJ 08002 856-773-0600 773-0609
TF: 800-608-0809 ■ *Web:* www.ameriquestcorp.com

Argents Express Group 7025 Metroplex Dr............ Romulus MI 48174 734-326-9499 326-1172
TF: 800-229-2231 ■ *Web:* www.argents.com

Arrow Freight Management Inc PO Box 371974........ El Paso TX 79937 915-778-3999 778-4282
TF: 888-598-9891 ■ *Web:* www.arrowelp.com

Astar USA 1200 Brickell Ave 16th Flr.................... Miami FL 33131 305-982-0500 416-9564
Web: www.astaraircargo.us

Atlantic & Pacific Freightways Inc
PO Box 17007 ....Portland OR 97217 360-699-2057 567-0987
TF: 800-628-6419 ■ *Web:* www.apfreightservices.com

Barthco International Inc
5101 S Broad St.............................. Philadelphia PA 19112 215-238-8600 592-1254
TF: 888-227-8426 ■ *Web:* www.barthco.com

Big Daddy Drayage Inc 575 Ave P.................... Newark NJ 07105 973-522-1717
Web: www.bigdaddydrayage.com

Casas International Brokerage Inc
9355 Airway Rd Suite 4 .... San Diego CA 92154 619-661-6162 661-6800
Web: www.casasinternational.com

Central Global Express 29000 Smith Rd.............. Romulus MI 48174 734-955-2555 729-8120
TF: 800-982-3924 ■ *Web:* www.gocge.com

Concordia International Forwarding Inc
70 E Sunrise Hwy Suite 605.................... Valley Stream NY 11581 516-561-1100 561-1323
Web: www.concordiafreight.com

Continental Traffic Service Inc (CTSI)
5100 Poplar Ave Clark Tower Bldg Suite 1750..........Memphis TN 38137 901-766-1500 766-1520
Web: www.continental-traffic.com

Corporate Traffic Inc
2002 Southside Blvd ....Jacksonville FL 32216 904-727-0051 727-6804
Web: www.corporate-traffic.com

Dynamic Ocean Services International Inc
1201 Hahlo St....................................Houston TX 77020 713-672-0515 672-0786
Web: www.dynamicosi.com

Evans Delivery Co Inc PO Box 268 .... Pottsville PA 17901 570-385-9048 385-9058
TF: 800-666-7885 ■ *Web:* www.evansdelivery.com

FESCO Agencies NA Inc 1000 2nd Ave Suite 1310 .... Seattle WA 98104 206-583-0860 583-0889
TF: 800-275-3372 ■ *Web:* www.fesco-na.com

Fetch Logistics Inc
25 Northpointe Pkwy Suite 200 .... Amherst NY 14228 716-689-4556 689-9676
TF: 800-964-4940 ■ *Web:* www.fetchlogistics.com

Freight Logistics Inc PO Box 1712..................Medford OR 97501 541-734-5617
TF: 800-866-7882 ■ *Web:* www.shipfli.com

Frontier Logistics LP 1806 S 16th St.................La Porte TX 77571 800-610-6808 307-2399*
**Fax Area Code:* 281 ■ *TF:* 800-610-6808 ■ *Web:* www.frontierlogistics.com

Fts International Express Inc
400 Country Club Dr .... Bensenville IL 60106 630-694-0644 694-0778
Web: www.fts.com

Gold Coast Freightways Inc 12250 NW 28th Ave......... Miami FL 33167 305-687-3560 685-8056
TF: 800-531-4775 ■ *Web:* www.gcfreight.com

Graulich International Inc 6411 NW 35th Ave........... Miami FL 33147 305-836-1700 836-1763
TF: 800-836-2709 ■ *Web:* www.graulichinternational.com

Guaranteed Air Freight & Forwarding Inc
4555 McDonnell Blvd........................... Saint Louis MO 63134 314-427-7709 427-5392
TF: 800-445-0738 ■ *Web:* www.gaffinc.com

Ha Logistics Inc 5175 Johnson Dr..................Pleasanton CA 94588 925-251-9300 251-9333
TF: 800-449-5778 ■ *Web:* www.halogistics.com

Harbor Freight Transport Corp 301 Craneway St........ Newark NJ 07114 973-589-6700 589-6677
Web: www.harborfrt.com

Hassett Air Express 877 S Rt 83 .... Elmhurst IL 60126 630-530-6524 530-6539
TF: 800-323-9422 ■ *Web:* www.hassettair.com

Hawaiian Express Service Inc
3623 Munster Ave PO Box 57136.................... Hayward CA 94545 510-783-6100 782-5794
Web: www.hawaiianexpressinc.com

I. C. S. Customs Service Inc
1099 Morse Ave ....Elk Grove Village IL 60007 630-350-9998 718-9987*
**Fax Area Code:* 847 ■ *Web:* www.icscustoms.com

Knitney Lines Inc PO Box 350 .... Scranton PA 18501 570-457-5060 457-6725
TF: 866-564-8639 ■ *Web:* www.knitneylines.com

L E Coppersmith Inc 525 S Douglas St .... El Segundo CA 90245 310-607-8000 607-8001
TF: 888-827-4388 ■ *Web:* www.coppersmith.com

LeanLogistics Inc 1351 S Waverly Rd .... Holland MI 49423 616-738-6400 738-6462
TF: 866-584-7280 ■ *Web:* www.leanlogistics.com

				Phone	Fax
Leman USA Inc 1860 Renaissance Blvd.	Sturtevant	WI	53177	262-884-4700	884-4690
Web: www.lemanusa.com					
Logfret Inc 101 Pk Ave Suite 1	Hoboken	NJ	07030	201-656-7728	656-7876
Web: www.logfret.com					
Logistics Plus Inc 1406 Peach St.	Erie	PA	16501	814-461-7600	761-7625
TF: 866-564-7587 ■ *Web:* www.logisticsplus.net					
Lynden Inc 18000 International Blvd Suite 800	Seattle	WA	98188	206-241-8778	243-8415
TF: 888-596-3361 ■ *Web:* www.lynden.com					
Masterpiece International Ltd					
39 Broadway 14th Fl.	New York	NY	10006	212-825-4800	825-7010
Web: www.masterpieceintl.com					
MG Maher & Co Inc 1 Canal Pl Suite 1600	New Orleans	LA	70130	504-581-3320	529-2611
Web: www.mgmaher.com					
Mhf Inc 613 E Butler Rd	Butler	PA	16002	724-431-0365	431-0462
Web: www.mhf.com					
Mike's Loading Service Inc (MLS)					
1802 S Expy 281	Edinburg	TX	78542	956-292-2700	292-2755
TF: 800-645-3562 ■ *Web:* www.mikesloadingservice.com					
Morrison Express Corp USA					
2000 S Hughes Way	El Segundo	CA	90245	310-322-8999	322-6688
Web: www.morrisonexpress.com					
Nippon Express USA Inc					
590 Madison Ave Suite 2401	New York	NY	10022	212-758-6100	758-2595
Web: www.nipponexpressusa.com					
Norvanco International Inc					
3514 142nd Ave E Suite 400	Sumner	WA	98390	253-987-4031	987-4015
Web: www.norvanco.com					
OTS Astracon LLC 3115 Beam Rd PO Box 19413	Charlotte	NC	28217	704-424-5522	424-5622
Web: www.otsusa.net					
Pacific Alaska Freightways Inc 2812 70th Ave E	Fife	WA	98424	253-926-3292	926-3161
TF: 800-426-9940 ■ *Web:* www.pafak.com					
Phoenix International Freight Services Ltd					
712 N Central Ave.	Wood Dale	IL	60191	630-766-9444	766-6395
TF: 800-959-9590 ■ *Web:* www.phoenixintl.com					
Pioneer Transfer LLC					
2034 S St Aubin St PO Box 2567	Sioux City	IA	51106	712-274-2332	274-2946
TF: 800-325-4650 ■ *Web:* www.pioneertransfer.com					
Poten & Partners Inc 805 3rd Ave 19th Fl.	New York	NY	10022	212-230-2000	355-0295
Web: www.poten.com					
Pulau Electronics Corp 12633 Challenger Pkwy.	Orlando	FL	32826	407-380-9191	380-9786
Web: www.pulau.com					
Quality Customs Broker Inc					
4464 S Whitnall Ave	St. Francis	WI	53235	414-482-9447	482-9448
TF: 888-813-4647 ■ *Web:* www.qualitybrokers.com					
Quality Transportation 319 5th Ave 4th Fl.	New York	NY	10016	212-308-6333	308-6595
Web: www.qualityca.com					
Ram International Inc					
4664 World Pkwy Cir	Saint Louis	MO	63134	314-427-3000	427-5068
TF: 800-884-4726 ■ *Web:* www.ram-intl.com					
Raymond Express International (REI)					
320 Harbor Way	South San Francisco	CA	94080	650-871-8560	952-3288
Web: www.reiexpress.com					
Rmx Global Logistics 35715 US Hwy 40 Bldg B	Evergreen	CO	80439	888-824-7365	674-3803*
**Fax Area Code:* 303 ■ *TF:* 888-824-7365 ■ *Web:* www.rmxglobal.com					
Rock-It Cargo USA Inc					
5438 W 104th St PO Box 90519	Los Angeles	CA	90045	310-410-0935	410-0628
TF: 800-973-1727 ■ *Web:* www.rockitcargo.com					
Romar Transportation Systems Inc					
3500 S Kedzie Ave	Chicago	IL	60632	773-376-8800	650-1644
TF: 800-621-5416 ■ *Web:* www.romartrans.com					
Scott Logistics Corp PO Box 391	Rome	GA	30162	706-234-1184	234-9258
Web: www.scottlogistics.com					
Sea Shipping Line Inc 520 3rd St Suite 207	Oakland	CA	94607	510-639-7447	663-0104
TF: 800-624-7447 ■ *Web:* www.seashipping.com					
Senderex Cargo Inc					
10425 S La Cienega Blvd	Los Angeles	CA	90045	310-342-2900	642-0427
TF: 800-421-5846 ■ *Web:* www.senderex.com					
Sho-Air International					
5401 Argosy Ave.	Huntington Beach	CA	92649	949-476-9111	476-9991
TF: 800-227-9111 ■ *Web:* www.shoair.com					
Sky Logistics & Distribution 4001 32nd St N	Fargo	ND	58102	701-298-0349	298-8009
TF: 800-882-9745 ■ *Web:* www.skylogistics.com					
Tech Transport Inc PO Box 431	Milford	NH	03055	603-673-0898	
Web: www.techtransport.com					
Terminal Corp The					
1657 S Highland Ave Suite A	Baltimore	MD	21224	800-560-7207	246-0519*
**Fax Area Code:* 410 ■ *Web:* www.termcorp.com					
Total Quality Logistics Inc (TQL) PO Box 799	Milford	OH	45150	513-831-2600	965-7630
TF: 800-580-3101 ■ *Web:* www.tql.com					
Towne Air Freight 24805 US 20 W	South Bend	IN	46628	574-233-3183	
TF: 800-468-6963 ■ *Web:* www.towneair.com					
TRANSInternational System Inc					
130 E Wilson Bridge Rd Suite 150					
PO Box 109	Worthington	OH	43085	614-891-4942	891-4929
Web: www.trnj.com					
Transportation Management Assoc Inc					
PO Box 907	Mocksville	NC	27028	336-751-1097	
TF: 800-745-8292 ■ *Web:* www.tmaco.com					
Transvantage Solutions Inc PO Box 1259	Somerville	NJ	08876	908-526-8700	526-6943
TF: 800-526-3972 ■ *Web:* www.transvantage.com					
TranzAct Technologies Inc					
360 W Butterfield Rd 4th Fl.	Elmhurst	IL	60126	630-833-0890	833-8538
Web: www.tranzact.com					
Tricor America Inc					
717 Airport Blvd	South San Francisco	CA	94080	650-877-3650	583-3197
TF: 800-669-7631 ■ *Web:* www.tricor.com					
U-Freight America Inc					
320 Corey Way PO Box 1890	South San Francisco	CA	94080	650-583-6527	583-8122
Web: www.ufreight.com					
Velocity Express					
1 Morningside Dr N Bldg B Suite 300	Westport	CT	06880	888-839-7669	489-6974*
**Fax Area Code:* 201 ■ *TF:* 800-899-7296 ■ *Web:* www.velocityexp.com					
WR Zanes & Co of Louisiana Inc					
223 Tchoupitoulas St	New Orleans	LA	70130	504-524-1301	524-1309
Web: www.wrzanes.com					

315 FREIGHT TRANSPORT - DEEP SEA (DOMESTIC PORTS)

				Phone	Fax
Alaska Marine Lines Inc					
5615 W Marginal Way SW	Seattle	WA	98106	206-763-4244	764-5782
TF Cust Svc: 800-950-4265 ■ *Web:* www.shipaml.com					
Coastal Transportation Inc 4025 13th Ave W.	Seattle	WA	98119	206-282-9979	283-9121
TF: 800-544-2580 ■ *Web:* www.coastaltransportation.com					
Crowley Maritime Corp 555 12th St Suite 2130	Oakland	CA	94607	510-251-7500	251-7510
TF: 800-276-9539 ■ *Web:* www.crowley.com					
Econocaribe Consolidators Inc 2401 NW 69th St.	Miami	FL	33147	305-693-5133	696-9350
TF: 866-326-6648 ■ *Web:* www.econocaribe.com					
Express Marine Inc PO Box 329	Pennsauken	NJ	08110	856-541-4600	541-0338
Web: www.expressmarine.com					
Freightquote.com Inc 16025 W 113th St	Lenexa	KS	66219	913-642-4700	642-6773
TF: 800-323-5441 ■ *Web:* www.freightquote.com					
Hapag-Lloyd America Inc 401 E Jackson St	Tampa	FL	33631	813-276-4600	276-4873
TF: 800-276-4600 ■ *Web:* www.hapag-lloyd.com/en					
Horizon Lines Inc 4064 Colony Rd Suite 200	Charlotte	NC	28211	704-973-7000	973-7075
NYSE: HRZ ■ *TF Cust Svc:* 877-678-7447 ■ *Web:* www.horizonlines.com					
Inchcape Shipping Services Inc					
11 N Water St # 9290	Mobile	AL	36602	251-461-2700	461-5067
Web: www.iss-shipping.com					
International Shipholding Corp					
11 N Water Suite 18290	Mobile	AL	36602	251-243-9100	529-5745*
NYSE: ISH ■ **Fax Area Code:* 504 ■ *TF:* 800-826-3513 ■ *Web:* www.intship.com					
Keystone Shipping Co					
1 Bala Plaza E Suite 600	Bala Cynwyd	PA	19004	610-617-6800	617-6899
Web: www.keyship.com					
Marine Transport Corp					
9487 Regency Sq Blvd	Jacksonville	FL	32225	904-727-2200	727-2501
Web: www.crowley.com/petroleum-chemical-transportation					
Maritrans Inc 2 Harbor Pl 302 Knights Run Ave	Tampa	FL	33602	813-209-0600	221-2769
NYSE: TUG					
Matson Navigation Co 555 12th St	Oakland	CA	94607	510-628-4000	628-7380
TF Cust Svc: 800-462-8766 ■ *Web:* www.matson.com					
Mormac Marine Group Inc					
1 Landmark Sq Suite 710	Stamford	CT	06901	203-977-8900	977-8933
Northland Services Inc					
6700 W Marginal Way S W	Seattle	WA	98106	206-763-3000	767-5579
TF: 800-426-3113 ■ *Web:* www.northlandservicesinc.com					
Overseas Shipholding Group Inc 666 3rd Ave	New York	NY	10017	212-953-4100	578-1832
NYSE: OSG ■ *TF:* 800-223-1722 ■ *Web:* www.osg.com					
Penn-Attransco Corp					
10 E Baltimore St Suite 1102	Baltimore	MD	21202	410-347-7000	347-7001
SC Loveland Co Inc PO Box 368	Pennsville	NJ	08070	856-935-8100	935-7417
TF: 800-523-2687					
Sea Star Line LLC					
100 Bell Tel Way Suite 300	Jacksonville	FL	32216	904-855-1260	724-3011
TF: 877-775-7447 ■ *Web:* www.seastarline.com					
Seaboard Marine 8001 NW 79th Ave	Miami	FL	33166	305-863-4444	863-4400
TF: 800-753-0681 ■ *Web:* www.seaboardmarine.com					
TECO Ocean Shipping 1300 E 8th Ave Suite S-300	Tampa	FL	33605	813-209-4200	242-4849
TF: 800-835-4161 ■ *Web:* www.tecooceanshipping.com					
TECO Transport 702 N Franklin St.	Tampa	FL	33602	813-228-1111	273-0248
TF: 800-835-4161 ■ *Web:* www.tecotransport.com					
Totem Ocean Trailer Express Inc					
32001 32nd Ave S Suite 200	Federal Way	WA	98001	253-449-8100	449-8225
TF: 800-426-0074 ■ *Web:* www.totemocean.com					
Trailer Bridge Inc					
10405 New Berlin Rd E	Jacksonville	FL	32226	904-751-7100	751-7444
NASDAQ: TRBR ■ *TF:* 800-554-1589 ■ *Web:* www.trailerbridge.com					
US Shipping Corp 399 Thornall St 8th Fl.	Edison	NJ	08837	732-635-1500	635-1918
NYSE: USS ■ *TF:* 866-942-6592 ■ *Web:* www.usshipllc.com					
Western Pioneer Inc 4601 Shilshole Ave NW	Seattle	WA	98107	206-789-1930	781-2486
TF: 800-426-6783 ■ *Web:* www.westernpioneer.com					
Young Bros Ltd PO Box 3288	Honolulu	HI	96801	808-543-9311	543-9458
TF: 800-572-2743 ■ *Web:* www.htbyb.com					

316 FREIGHT TRANSPORT - DEEP SEA (FOREIGN PORTS)

				Phone	Fax
American Overseas Marine Corp					
100 Newport Ave Ext.	Quincy	MA	02171	617-786-8300	472-4925
Antillean Marine Shipping Corp					
3038 NW N River Dr	Miami	FL	33142	305-633-6361	894-3880
Web: www.antillean.com					
APL Ltd 16220 N Scottsdale Rd Suite 300	Scottsdale	AZ	85254	602-586-4800	
TF: 800-999-7733 ■ *Web:* www.apl.com					
Atlantic Container Line (ACL) 50 Cardinal Dr	Westfield	NJ	07090	908-518-5300	452-5492*
**Fax Area Code:* 732 ■ *TF:* 800-225-1235 ■ *Web:* www.aclcargo.com					
Csl International Inc 152 Conant St	Beverly	MA	01915	978-922-1300	922-1772
Web: www.cslint.com					

				Phone	Fax
Fednav Ltd 1000 Rue de la GauchetiFre O Bureau 3500	Montreal	QC	H3B4W5	514-878-6500	878-6642
TF: 800-678-4842 ■ *Web:* www.fednav.com					
Gdb International Inc 1 Home News Row	New Brunswick	NJ	08901	732-246-3001	246-3004
Web: www.gdbinternational.com					
Genco Shipping & Trading Ltd 299 Pk Ave 20th Fl	New York	NY	10171	646-443-8550	443-8551
NYSE: GNK ■ *Web:* www.gencoshipping.com					
General Maritime Corp 299 Pk Ave 2nd Fl	New York	NY	10171	212-763-5600	763-5603
NYSE: GMR ■ *Web:* www.generalmaritimecorp.com					
Hamburg Sud North America Inc 465 S St	Morristown	NJ	07960	973-775-5300	775-5310
TF: 800-901-7447 ■ *Web:* www.hamburgsud.com					
Hapag-Lloyd America Inc 401 E Jackson St	Tampa	FL	33631	813-276-4600	276-4873
TF: 800-276-4600 ■ *Web:* www.hapag-lloyd.com/en					
Hoegh Autoliners Inc 500 N Broadway Jericho Atrium Bldg Suite 233	Jericho	NY	11753	516-935-1600	935-2604
Web: www.hoegh.com/autoliners					
Inchcape Shipping Services Inc 11 N Water St # 9290	Mobile	AL	36602	251-461-2700	461-5067
Web: www.iss-shipping.com					
Interlog USA Inc 2818A Anthony Ln S	Minneapolis	MN	55418	612-789-3456	789-2118
TF: 800-603-6030 ■ *Web:* www.interlogusa.com					
International Shipholding Corp 11 N Water Suite 18290	Mobile	AL	36602	251-243-9100	529-5745*
NYSE: ISH ■ **Fax Area Code:* 504 ■ *TF:* 800-826-3513 ■ *Web:* www.intship.com					
K Line America Inc 8730 Stony Pt Pkwy Suite 400	Richmond	VA	23235	804-560-3600	560-3463
TF: 800-609-3221 ■ *Web:* www.k-line.com					
Liberty Maritime Corp 1979 Marcus Ave Suite 200	Lake Success	NY	11042	516-488-8800	488-8806
Web: www.libertymar.com					
Maersk Inc 2 Giralda Farms PO Box 880	Madison	NJ	07940	973-514-5000	514-5410
TF Cust Svc: 800-321-8807 ■ *Web:* www.maersksealand.com					
Marine Transport Corp 9487 Regency Sq Blvd	Jacksonville	FL	32225	904-727-2200	727-2501
Web: www.crowley.com/petroleum-chemical-transportation					
Maywood International Sales Inc PO Box 9292	Santa Fe	NM	87504	505-984-8484	982-9780
Web: www.maywoodinternational.com					
OMI Corp 1 Stn Pl Metro Ctr	Stamford	CT	06902	203-602-6700	602-6701*
NYSE: OMM ■ **Fax:* Hum Res ■ *TF:* 800-344-9711					
Orient Overseas Container Line Inc 17777 Ctr Ct Dr N Suite 500	Cerritos	CA	90703	562-499-2600	499-4401
TF: 800-822-6625 ■ *Web:* www.oocl.com					
Overseas Shipholding Group Inc 666 3rd Ave	New York	NY	10017	212-953-4100	578-1832
NYSE: OSG ■ *TF:* 800-223-1722 ■ *Web:* www.osg.com					
Pasha Group Inc 5725 Paradise Dr Suite 1000	Corte Madera	CA	94925	415-927-6400	924-5672
Web: www.pashagroup.com					
Red River Shipping Corp 6110 Executive Blvd Suite 620	Rockville	MD	20852	301-230-0854	770-6131
Seaboard Marine 8001 NW 79th Ave	Miami	FL	33166	305-863-4444	863-4400
TF: 800-753-0681 ■ *Web:* www.seaboardmarine.com					
Stolt-Nielsen Transportation Group 800 Connecticut Ave 4th Fl E	Norwalk	CT	06854	203-838-7100	299-0067
NASDAQ: SNSA ■ *Web:* www.stoltnielsen.com					
Sunmar Shipping Inc 500 108th Ave NE Suite 1710	Bellevue	WA	98004	425-577-1870	577-1880
TF: 800-443-4127					
TECO Ocean Shipping 1300 E 8th Ave Suite S-300	Tampa	FL	33605	813-209-4200	242-4849
TF: 800-835-4161 ■ *Web:* www.tecooceanshipping.com					
Tidewater Inc 601 Poydras St Suite 1900	New Orleans	LA	70130	504-568-1010	566-4580
NYSE: TDW ■ *TF:* 800-678-8433 ■ *Web:* www.tdw.com					
Tropical Shipping 5 E 11th St	Riviera Beach	FL	33404	561-881-3900	840-2840
TF: 800-367-6200 ■ *Web:* www.tropical.com					
Wallenius Wilhelmsen Lines Americas 188 Broadway PO Box 1232	Woodcliff Lake	NJ	07677	201-505-5100	307-9030
Web: www.2wglobal.com					
Wallenius Wilhelmsen Logistics PO Box 1232	Woodcliff Lake	NJ	07677	201-307-1300	307-0069*
**Fax:* Cust Svc ■ *Web:* www.2wglobal.com					
Westwood Shipping Lines 840 S 333rd St PO Box 9777	Federal Way	WA	98063	253-924-4399	924-5956
TF: 800-200-9751 ■ *Web:* www.weyerhaeuser.com					

317 FREIGHT TRANSPORT - INLAND WATERWAYS

				Phone	Fax
American Commercial Barge Lines Inc 1701 E Market St	Jeffersonville	IN	47130	812-288-0100	288-1664
TF: 800-457-6377 ■ *Web:* www2.aclines.com					
American Commercial Lines Inc 1701 E Market St	Jeffersonville	IN	47130	812-288-0100	288-0413
TF: 800-457-6377 ■ *Web:* www.aclines.com					
American River Transportation Co 4666 E Faries Pkwy	Decatur	IL	62526	217-424-5200	451-4270
TF: 800-637-5824					
American Steamship Co 500 Essjay Rd Centerpointe Corporate Pk	Williamsville	NY	14221	716-635-0222	635-0220
Web: www.americansteamship.com					
Amherst madison inc 2 Port Amherst Dr	Charleston	WV	25306	304-926-1100	926-1136
Web: www.amherstmadison.com					
Andrie Inc 561 E Western Ave PO Box 1548	Muskegon	MI	49442	231-728-2226	726-6747
Web: www.andrie.com					
Boston Towing & Transportation Co LP 36 New St	East Boston	MA	02128	617-567-9100	567-2583
TF: 800-836-8847					
Bouchard Transportation Co Inc 58 S Service Rd Suite 150	Melville	NY	11747	631-390-4900	390-4905
Web: www.bouchardtransport.com					
Canal Barge Co Inc 835 Union St	New Orleans	LA	70112	504-581-2424	584-1505
Web: www.canalbarge.com					
Cargill Cargo Carriers 15407 McGinty Rd	Wayzata	MN	55391	952-742-7575	742-6289
Web: www.cargill.com					
Celtic Marine Corp 3888 S Sherwood Forest Blvd Celtic Ctr Bldg 1	Baton Rouge	LA	70816	225-752-2490	752-2582
Web: www.celticmarine.com					
Crounse Corp 400 Marine Way	Paducah	KY	42003	270-444-9611	444-9615
Web: www.crounse.com					
Crowley Maritime Corp 555 12th St Suite 2130	Oakland	CA	94607	510-251-7500	251-7510
TF: 800-276-9539 ■ *Web:* www.crowley.com					
Fednav Ltd 1000 Rue de la GauchetiFre O Bureau 3500	Montreal	QC	H3B4W5	514-878-6500	878-6642
TF: 800-678-4842 ■ *Web:* www.fednav.com					
Hannah Marine Corp 13155 Grant Rd	Lemont	IL	60439	630-257-5457	257-9049
TF: 800-257-5458 ■ *Web:* www.hannahmarine.com					
Ingram Barge Co 4400 Harding Rd 1 Belle Meade Pl	Nashville	TN	37205	615-298-8200	298-8379
TF: 800-876-2047 ■ *Web:* www.ingrambarge.com					
K-Sea Transportation Partners LP 3245 Richmond Terr	Staten Island	NY	10303	718-720-7207	390-0627
NYSE: KSP ■ *Web:* www.k-sea.com					
Kirby Corp 55 Waugh Dr Suite 1000	Houston	TX	77007	713-435-1000	435-1011
NYSE: KEX ■ *TF:* 800-324-2441 ■ *Web:* www.kirbycorp.com					
L & M Botruc Rental Inc 18692 W Main St	Galliano	LA	70354	985-475-5733	475-5669
TF: 800-256-1186 ■ *Web:* www.botruc.com					
M-G Transport Service Inc 7000 Midland Blvd	Amelia	OH	45102	513-943-7300	947-4026
Web: www.mgtransport.com					
Marquette Transportation Co LLC 150 Ballard Cir	Paducah	KY	42001	270-443-9404	441-7544
TF: 800-456-9404 ■ *Web:* www.marquettetrans.com					
Midwest Energy Resources Co W Winter St & Ajax Rd	Superior	WI	54880	715-392-9807	392-9137
Web: www.midwestenergy.com					
Seafreight Agencies Inc 2800 NW 105th Ave	Miami	FL	33172	305-592-6060	471-9555
Web: www.seafreightagencies.com					
Shaver Transportation Co Inc 4900 NW Front Ave	Portland	OR	97210	503-228-8850	274-7098
TF: 888-228-8850					
TECO Transport 702 N Franklin St	Tampa	FL	33602	813-228-1111	273-0248
TF: 800-835-4161 ■ *Web:* www.tecotransport.com					
Tidewater Barge Lines Inc 6305 NW Old Lower River Rd	Vancouver	WA	98660	360-693-1491	694-8981
TF: 800-562-4345 ■ *Web:* www.tidewater.com					
Transerve Marine Inc 500 E Indian River Rd	Norfolk	VA	23523	757-545-7301	545-5692
Warrior & Gulf Navigation Co 50 Viaduct Rd PO Box 11397	Chickasaw	AL	36671	251-452-6000	452-6014
TF: 800-452-6100 ■ *Web:* www.tstarinc.com					

318 FRUIT GROWERS

SEE ALSO Crop Preparation Services p. 1380; Wines - Mfr p. 1521

318-1 Berry Growers

				Phone	Fax
AD Makepeace Co Inc 158 Tihonet Rd	Wareham	MA	02571	508-295-1000	291-7453
Web: www.admakepeace.com					
Atlantic Blueberry Co 7201 Weymouth Rd	Hammonton	NJ	08037	609-561-8600	561-5033
Web: www.atlanticblueberry.com					
Brady Farms Inc 14786 Winans St	West Olive	MI	49460	616-842-3916	842-8357
California Giant Inc 75 Sakata Ln	Watsonville	CA	95076	831-728-1773	728-0613
Web: www.calgiant.com					
Cherryfield Foods Inc PO Box 128	Cherryfield	ME	04622	207-546-7573	546-2713
Cutler Cranberry Co N11569 County Rd H	Camp Douglas	WI	54618	608-427-3268	
Driscoll Strawberry Assoc Inc 345 Westridge Dr	Watsonville	CA	95077	831-763-5100	761-1090
TF: 800-871-3333 ■ *Web:* www.driscolls.com					
Fujii Farms 2511 S Troutdale Rd	Troutdale	OR	97060	503-665-6659	661-2799
Habelman Bros Co Inc PO Box 150	Tomah	WI	54660	608-372-2444	372-2566
Jasper Wyman & Son 280 N Main St	Milbridge	ME	04658	207-546-2311	546-2074
TF: 800-341-1758 ■ *Web:* www.wymans.com					
Merrill Blueberry Farms Inc PO Box 149	Ellsworth	ME	04605	207-667-9750	667-4052
TF: 800-711-6551 ■ *Web:* www.merrillwildblueberries.com					
Michigan Blueberry Growers Assn 4726 County Rd 215	Grand Junction	MI	49056	269-434-6791	434-6997
TF: 866-269-1511 ■ *Web:* www.blueberries.com					
Naturipe Berry Growers PO Box 4280	Salinas	CA	93912	831-722-2430	728-9398
Web: www.naturipeberrygrowers.com					
Northland Cranberries Inc 2321 W Grand Ave PO Box 8020	Wisconsin Rapids	WI	54495	715-424-4444	422-6800
Reenders Blueberries Farms 14079 168th Ave	Grand Haven	MI	49417	616-842-5238	842-0890

	City	State	ZIP	Phone	Fax
Reiter Affiliated Cos 1767 San Juan Rd	Aromas	CA	95004	831-726-3256	726-3219
Sandy Farms 34500 SE Hwy 211 *Web:* www.sandyfarms.com	Boring	OR	97009	503-668-4525	668-8813
Sunrise Growers 701 W Kimberly St Suite 210 *Web:* www.sunrisegrowers.com	Placentia	CA	92870	714-630-2050	630-0215

318-2 Citrus Growers

	City	State	ZIP	Phone	Fax
A Duda & Sons Inc 1200 Duda Trail *Web:* www.duda.com	Oviedo	FL	32765	407-365-2111	365-2147
Alico Inc PO Box 338 *NASDAQ: ALCO* ■ *Web:* www.alicoinc.com	La Belle	FL	33975	863-675-2966	675-6928
Ben Hill Griffin Inc 700 S SR 17 PO Box 127	Frostproof	FL	33843	863-635-2251	635-7333
Blood's Hammock Groves 4600 Linton Blvd **Fax:* Orders ■ *TF:* 800-255-5188 ■ *Web:* www.bloodsgroves.com	Delray Beach	FL	33445	561-498-3938	498-0285*
Blue Banner Co Inc 2601 3rd St PO Box 226 *TF:* 800-426-2422	Riverside	CA	92502	951-686-2422	686-6440
Callery-Judge Grove 4001 Seminole-Pratt Whitney Rd *TF:* 800-967-2643 ■ *Web:* www.cjgrove.com	Loxahatchee	FL	33470	561-793-1676	790-5466
Consolidated Citrus LP 4210 Metro Pkwy Suite 250	Fort Myers	FL	33916	239-275-4060	275-4973
Corona College Heights Orange & Lemon Assn 8000 Lincoln Ave *Web:* www.cchcitrus.com	Riverside	CA	92504	951-688-1811	689-5115
Edinburg Citrus Assn 401 W Chapin Rd	Edinburg	TX	78539	956-383-2743	383-2435
Egan Bernard & Co 1900 Old Dixie Hwy **Fax Area Code: 772* ■ *TF:* 800-327-6676 ■ *Web:* www.dneworld.com	Fort Pierce	FL	34946	800-327-6676	465-1181*
G & S Packing Co Inc 16600 S Hwy C 25 *Web:* www.gspacking.com	Weirsdale	FL	32195	352-821-2251	821-5000
Gracewood Fruit Co 1626 90th Ave	Vero Beach	FL	32966	772-567-1151	567-2719
Graves Bros Co 2770 Indian River Blvd Suite 201 *Web:* www.gravesbrotherscompany.com	Vero Beach	FL	32960	772-562-3886	562-3565
Heller Bros Packing Corp 288 9th St *TF:* 800-823-2124 ■ *Web:* www.hellerbros.com	Winter Garden	FL	34787	407-656-2124	656-1751
Highland Exchange Service Co-op 5916 SR 540 E PO Box K *TF:* 800-237-3989	Waverly	FL	33877	863-439-3661	439-5383
Lake Wales Citrus Growers Assn 111 N 1st St PO Box 1739	Dundee	FL	33838	863-439-5710	439-1535
Leroy E Smith's Sons Inc 4776 Old Dixie Hwy	Vero Beach	FL	32967	772-567-3421	567-8428*
Limoneira Co 1141 Cummings Rd *TF:* 800-350-5541 ■ *Web:* www.limoneira.com	Santa Paula	CA	93060	805-525-5541	525-8211
Nelson & Co Inc 110 E Broadway PO Box 620789	Oviedo	FL	32762	407-365-6631	366-0145
Paramount Citrus Assn 1901 S Lexington St *Web:* www.paramountcitrus.com	Delano	CA	93215	661-720-2400	720-2403
Saticoy Lemon Assn 7560 E Bristol Rd *Web:* www.saticoylemon.com	Ventura	CA	93003	805-654-6500	654-6587
Seald-Sweet Growers Inc 1991 74th Ave *TF Sales:* 800-336-2926 ■ *Web:* www.sealdsweet.com	Vero Beach	FL	32966	772-569-2244	562-9038
Silver Springs Citrus Inc 25411 N Mare Ave *TF:* 800-940-2277 ■ *Web:* www.silverspringscitrus.com	Howey in the Hills	FL	34737	352-324-2101	324-3422
Southern Gardens Citrus 1820 Country Rd 833	Clewiston	FL	33440	863-983-3030	983-3060
Sunkist Growers Inc 14130 Riverside Dr **Fax:* PR ■ *TF:* 800-383-7141 ■ *Web:* www.sunkist.com	Sherman Oaks	CA	91423	818-986-4800	379-7511*
Villa Park Orchards Assn 960 3rd St PO Box 307	Fillmore	CA	93016	805-524-0411	524-5912

318-3 Deciduous Tree Fruit Growers

	City	State	ZIP	Phone	Fax
All State Apple Exchange PO Box 246	Milton	NY	12547	845-795-2121	795-2618
Auvil Fruit Co 21902 SR 97 *Web:* www.auvilfruit.com	Orondo	WA	98843	509-784-1711	784-1712
Barbee Orchards 131 Bella Terra Rd	Zillah	WA	98953	509-865-4591	865-3220
Bertuccio Farms 2410 Airline Hwy *Web:* www.bertuccios.com	Hollister	CA	95023	831-636-0821	637-9393
Big Six Farms 5575 Zenith Mill Rd	Fort Valley	GA	31030	478-825-7504	825-1194
Blue Bird Inc 10135 Mill Rd *TF:* 800-548-1700	Peshastin	WA	98847	509-548-1700	548-0288
Blue Mountain Growers Inc 231 E Broadway PO Box 156	Milton-Freewater	OR	97862	541-938-4401	938-5304
Blue Star Growers Inc 100 SE Blue Star Way	Cashmere	WA	98815	509-782-2922	782-3646
Borton & Sons Inc 2550 Borton Rd *Web:* www.bortonfruit.com	Yakima	WA	98903	509-966-3905	966-3994
Broetje Orchards 1111 Fishhook Pk Rd	Prescott	WA	99348	509-749-2217	749-2354
Capital Agricultural Property Services Inc 801 Warrenville Rd Suite 150 *TF:* 800-243-2060 ■ *Web:* www.capitalag.com	Lisle	IL	60532	630-434-9150	434-9343
Chappell Farms Inc 166 Boiling Springs Rd *Web:* www.chappellfarms.com	Barnwell	SC	29812	803-584-2565	584-3676
Chelan Fruit Co 5 Howser Rd	Chelan	WA	98816	509-682-2591	682-2656
Cherry Central Co-op Inc 1771 N US Hwy 31 S PO Box 988 *TF:* 800-678-1860 ■ *Web:* www.cherrycentral.com	Traverse City	MI	49685	231-946-1860	941-4167
Cowiche Growers Inc 251 Cowiche City Rd *Web:* www.cowichegrowers.com	Cowiche	WA	98923	509-678-4168	678-4160
Danna & Danna Inc 625 Cooper St	Yuba City	CA	95992	530-673-5131	673-5131
Evans Fruit Farm 200 Cowiche City Rd *TF:* 800-255-7513	Cowiche	WA	98923	509-678-4127	
EW Brandt & Sons Inc PO Box B *Web:* www.ewbrandt.com	Parker	WA	98939	509-877-3193	877-2737
Fagundes Agribusiness 8700 Fargo Ave *Web:* www.oldworldcheese.com	Hanford	CA	93230	559-582-4080	582-0683
Fowler Packing Co Inc 8570 S Cedar Ave	Fresno	CA	93725	559-834-5911	834-5272
Gerawan Farming 15749 E Ventura St	Sanger	CA	93657	559-787-8780	787-8798
Gerbbers Farms 908 Hwy 97 *TF:* 800-967-3634	Brewster	WA	98812	509-689-3424	689-2997
Henggeler Packing Co Inc 6730 Elmore Rd PO Box 313	Fruitland	ID	83619	208-452-4212	452-5416
Highland Fruit Growers Inc 8304 Wide Hollow Rd	Yakima	WA	98908	509-966-3990	966-3992
Ito Packing Co Inc PO Box 707 *Web:* www.itopack.com	Reedley	CA	93654	559-638-2531	638-2282
Marchese Family Properties 270 E Main St	Los Gatos	CA	95030	408-395-8375	395-9675
McDougal & Sons 3887 Pioneer Way	Monitor	WA	98801	509-662-2136	665-4078
Mount Konocti Growers Inc 2550 Big Valley Rd PO Box 365	Kelseyville	CA	95451	707-279-4213	279-2251
National Fruit Product Co Inc 701 Fairmont Ave PO Box 2040 **Fax:* Sales ■ *TF:* 800-551-5167 ■ *Web:* www.whitehousefoods.com	Winchester	VA	22604	540-662-3401	665-4670*
Naumes Inc 2 Barnett Rd PO Box 996 *Web:* www.naumes.com	Medford	OR	97501	541-772-6268	772-2135
Orchard View Farms Inc 4055 Skyline Rd *Web:* www.orchardviewfarms.com	The Dalles	OR	97058	541-298-4496	298-1808
Oregon Cherry Growers Inc 1520 Woodrow NE *TF:* 800-367-2536 ■ *Web:* www.orcherry.com	Salem	OR	97301	503-364-8421	585-7710
P-R Farms Inc 2917 E Shepherd Ave *Web:* www.prfarms.com	Clovis	CA	93619	559-299-0201	299-7292
Premiere Partners 2004 fox Dr	Champaign	IL	61820	217-352-6000	352-9048
Rice Fruit Co 2760 Carlisle Rd PO Box 66 *TF:* 800-627-3359 ■ *Web:* www.ricefruit.com	Gardners	PA	17324	717-677-8131	677-9842
Southern Orchard Supply Co 50 Ln Rd PO Box 1087 *TF:* 800-277-3224 ■ *Web:* www.lanepacking.com	Fort Valley	GA	31030	478-825-3592	825-7995
Stadelman Fruit Inc 111 Meade St	Zillah	WA	98953	509-829-5145	829-5164
Stemilt Growers Inc PO Box 2779 *Web:* www.stemilt.com	Wenatchee	WA	98807	509-663-1451	665-4376
Sun Valley Packing Co 7381 Ave 432 PO Box 351	Reedley	CA	93654	559-591-1515	591-1616
Sun World International Inc 16350 Driver Rd *Web:* www.sun-world.com	Bakersfield	CA	93308	661-392-5000	392-4678
Symms Fruit Ranch Inc 14068 Sunny Slope Rd	Caldwell	ID	83607	208-459-4821	459-6932
Taylor Orchards 1665 E Fall Line Fwy *Web:* www.taylororchards.com	Reynolds	GA	31076	478-847-4186	847-4464
Thiara Bros Orchards 1205 Kibby Rd	Merced	CA	95340	209-383-6126	383-1012
Titan Farms 5 RW Du Bose Rd *TF:* 888-848-2672 ■ *Web:* www.titanfarms.com	Ridge Spring	SC	29129	803-685-5381	685-5885
Twin Hill Ranch 1689 Pleasant Hill Rd *Web:* www.twinhillranch.com	Sebastopol	CA	95472	707-823-2815	823-6268
Valley View Packing Co Inc PO Box 5699 *Web:* www.valleyviewpacking.com	San Jose	CA	95150	408-289-8300	289-8897

318-4 Fruit Growers (Misc)

	City	State	ZIP	Phone	Fax
Brooks Tropicals Inc 18400 SW 256th St PO Box 900160 **Fax:* Sales ■ *TF:* 800-327-4833 ■ *Web:* www.brookstropicals.com	Homestead	FL	33090	305-247-3544	246-5827*
Calavo Growers Inc 1141-A Cummings Rd *NASDAQ: CVGW* ■ *TF:* 800-422-5286 ■ *Web:* www.calavo.com	Santa Paula	CA	93060	805-525-1245	921-3287
Chiquita Brands International Inc 250 E 5th St *NYSE: CQB* ■ *Web:* www.chiquitabrands.com	Cincinnati	OH	45202	513-784-8000	784-8030
Del Monte Fresh Produce Co 241 Sevilla Ave *TF Cust Svc:* 800-950-3683 ■ *Web:* www.freshdelmonte.com	Coral Gables	FL	33134	305-520-8400	520-8455
Dole Food Co Inc 1 Dole Dr **Fax:* Hum Res ■ *TF:* 800-232-8888 ■ *Web:* www.dole.com	Westlake Village	CA	91362	818-879-6600	874-4893*
Elmore & Stahl Inc 4012 E Goodwin Rd	Mission	TX	78574	956-205-7300	585-5825
Growers Express LLC 1219 Abbott St PO Box 948 **Fax:* Sales ■ *Web:* www.growersexpress.com	Salinas	CA	93901	831-757-9700	422-4246*
Gw Palmer & Co Inc 1080 W Rex Rd *Web:* www.gwpalmer.net	Memphis	TN	38119	901-761-7900	682-4141
Healds Valley Farms Inc 6715 W Monte Cristo Rd *Web:* www.healdsvalley.com	Edinburg	TX	78539	956-380-0102	380-1063
Jewel Date Co 84675 60th Ave *Web:* www.jeweldate.com	Thermal	CA	92274	760-399-4474	399-4476
Martori Farms 7332 E Butherus Dr *TF:* 800-627-8674 ■ *Web:* www.martorifarms.com	Scottsdale	AZ	85260	480-998-1444	483-6723
Maui Land & Pineapple Co Inc 120 Kane St PO Box 187 *NYSE: MLP* ■ *Web:* www.mauiland.com	Kahului	HI	96733	808-877-3351	871-0953
Mission Produce Inc 2500 E Vineyard Ave # 300 *Web:* www.missionpro.com	Oxnard	CA	93036	805-981-3650	981-3660
Mount Dora Farms 16398 Jacinto Fort Blvd *Web:* www.mountdorafarms.com	Houston	TX	77015	713-821-7400	821-7342
Valley Fig Growers 2028 S 3rd St *Web:* www.valleyfig.com	Fresno	CA	93702	559-237-3893	237-3898
Van Drunen Farms 300 W 6th St *Web:* www.vandrunenfarms.com	Momence	IL	60954	815-472-3100	472-3850
West Pak Avocado Inc 42322 Avenida Alvarado *TF:* 800-266-4414 ■ *Web:* www.westpak.com	Temecula	CA	92590	951-296-5757	296-5745

318-5 Grape Vineyards

				Phone	Fax
Baker Farming Co 45499 W Panoche Rd	Firebaugh	CA	93622	559-659-3942	659-7114
Del Rey Packing 5287 S Del Rey Ave	Del Rey	CA	93616	559-888-2031	888-2715
Giumarra Vineyards Corp 11220 Edison Hwy	Edison	CA	93220	661-395-7000	366-7134
John Kautz Farms 5490 Bear Creek Rd	Lodi	CA	95240	209-334-4786	339-1689
Lion Raisins 9500 S De Wols Ave PO Box 1350 *Web:* www.lionraisins.com	Selma	CA	93662	559-834-6677	834-6622
National Grape Co-op Assn Inc 2 S Portage St *Web:* www.nationalgrape.com	Westfield	NY	14787	716-326-5200	326-5494
National Raisin Co PO Box 219 *TF:* 800-874-3726 ■ *Web:* www.nationalraisin.com	Fowler	CA	93625	559-834-5981	834-1055
Pacific Agri Lands Inc 5206 Hammett Rd	Modesto	CA	95358	209-545-1623	
Pandol & Sons 401 Rd 192 *Web:* www.pandol.com	Delano	CA	93215	661-725-3755	725-4741
Paragon Vineyard Co Inc 4915 Orcutt Rd *Web:* www.baileyana.com	San Luis Obispo	CA	93401	805-544-9080	781-3635
Scheid Vineyards Inc 305 Hilltown Rd *PINK: SVIN* ■ *TF:* 888-772-4343 ■ *Web:* www.scheidvineyards.com	Salinas	CA	93908	831-455-9990	455-9998
Spring Mountain Vineyards 2805 Spring Mountain Rd *TF:* 877-769-4637 ■ *Web:* www.springmtn.com	Saint Helena	CA	94574	707-967-4188	963-2753
Ste Michelle Wine Estates 14111 NE 145th St *TF:* 800-267-6793 ■ *Web:* www.ste-michelle.com	Woodinville	WA	98072	425-488-1133	415-3657
Sun Valley Packing Co 7381 Ave 432 PO Box 351	Reedley	CA	93654	559-591-1515	591-1616
Sun World International Inc 16350 Driver Rd *Web:* www.sun-world.com	Bakersfield	CA	93308	661-392-5000	392-4678
Symms Fruit Ranch Inc 14068 Sunny Slope Rd	Caldwell	ID	83607	208-459-4821	459-6932
Trinchero Family Estates 100 St Helena Hwy S PO Box 248 **Fax:* Mktg ■ *Web:* www.tfewines.com	Saint Helena	CA	94574	707-963-3104	963-2381*
Vino Farms Inc 1377 E Lodi Ave	Lodi	CA	95240	209-334-6975	369-8765
Windsor Vineyards 205 Concourse Blvd *TF:* 800-289-9463 ■ *Web:* www.windsorvineyards.com	Santa Rosa	CA	95403	707-836-5000	

319 FUEL DEALERS

				Phone	Fax
AC & T Co Inc 11535 Hopewell Rd *TF:* 800-458-3835 ■ *Web:* www.acandt.com	Hagerstown	MD	21740	301-582-2700	582-2719
Acree Oil Co 402 W Currahee St PO Box 699 *Web:* www.acreeoil.com	Toccoa	GA	30577	706-886-2838	886-4461
Alvin Hollis & Co 1 Hollis St *TF:* 800-649-5090 ■ *Web:* www.alvinhollis.com	South Weymouth	MA	02190	781-335-2100	335-6134
AmeriGas Inc 460 N Gulph Rd *Web:* www.amerigas.com	King of Prussia	PA	19406	610-337-7000	768-7647
AmeriGas Partners LP 460 N Gulph Rd *NYSE: APU* ■ *TF:* 800-427-4968 ■ *Web:* www.amerigas.com	King of Prussia	PA	19406	610-337-7000	992-3259
Apollo Oil LLC 1175 Early Dr *TF:* 800-473-5823 ■ *Web:* www.apollooil.com	Winchester	KY	40391	859-744-5444	745-5823
Automotive Service Inc 910 Mountain Home Rd PO Box 2157 *TF:* 800-383-3421	Reading	PA	19608	610-678-3421	678-3515
Besche Oil Co Inc 3045 Old Washington Rd *Web:* www.bescheoil.com	Waldorf	MD	20601	301-645-7061	645-8727
Blossman Gas Inc 809 Washington Ave *TF:* 800-234-1110 ■ *Web:* www.blossmangas.com	Ocean Springs	MS	39564	228-875-2261	875-9307
Bowden Oil Co Inc PO Box 145 *TF:* 800-280-0393 ■ *Web:* www.bowdenoil.com	Sylacauga	AL	35150	256-245-5611	249-2975
Carroll Independent Fuel Co 2700 Loch Raven Rd *TF:* 800-834-8590 ■ *Web:* www.carrollfuel.com	Baltimore	MD	21218	410-235-1066	235-3842
Consumer Oil & Supply Co 100 Railroad St	Braymer	MO	64624	660-645-2215	645-2426
District Petroleum Products Inc 1814 River Rd Suite 100	Huron	OH	44839	419-433-8373	433-9646
E Osterman Inc 1 Memorial Sq PO Box 150 *TF:* 800-407-3930 ■ *Web:* www.ostermangas.com	Whitinsville	MA	01588	508-234-9902	234-0645
Empire State Fuel Co 1640 McDonald Ave *Web:* www.empirefuel.com	Brooklyn	NY	11230	718-627-5100	627-5100
Energy Transfer Equity LP 3738 Oak Lawn Ave *NYSE: ETE* ■ *Web:* www.energytransfer.com	Dallas	TX	75219	214-981-0700	981-0703
Energy Transfer Partners LP 3738 Oak Lawn Ave *NYSE: ETP* ■ *Web:* www.energytransfer.com	Dallas	TX	75219	214-981-0700	981-0703
Farm & Home Oil Co 3115 State Rd PO Box 389 *TF:* 800-473-1562 ■ *Web:* www.fhoil.com	Telford	PA	18969	215-257-0131	257-2088
Farmers Union Oil Co of Southern Valley 204 S Front St *TF:* 800-382-9046 ■ *Web:* www.fuosv.com	Fairmount	ND	58030	701-474-5440	474-5445
FC Haab Co Inc 2314 Market St *TF:* 800-486-5663 ■ *Web:* www.fchaab.com	Philadelphia	PA	19103	215-563-0800	563-9448
Ferrellgas Partners LP 1 Liberty Plaza *NYSE: FGP* ■ *TF:* 800-816-3048 ■ *Web:* www.ferrellgas.com	Liberty	MO	64068	816-792-1600	792-7985
First Corporate Sedans Inc 60 E 42nd St Suite 2424 *TF:* 800-473-8876 ■ *Web:* www.fcsny.com	New York	NY	10165	212-972-2282	286-9130
Fred M Schildwachter & Sons Inc 1400 Ferris Pl *TF:* 800-642-3646 ■ *Web:* www.schildwachteroil.com	Bronx	NY	10461	718-828-2500	828-3661
Gas Inc 77 Jefferson Pkwy *Web:* www.gasincorporated.com	Newnan	GA	30263	770-502-8800	502-8833
Glassmere Fuel Service Inc 1967 Saxonburg Blvd *TF:* 800-235-9054 ■ *Web:* www.glassmerefuel.com	Tarentum	PA	15084	724-265-4646	265-3588
Griffith Energy Services Inc 2510 Schuster Dr **Fax:* Cust Svc ■ *TF:* 800-633-4328 ■ *Web:* www.griffithoil.com	Cheverly	MD	20781	301-322-5100	772-8183*
Herring Gas Co Inc 33 Main St E *TF:* 800-543-9049	Meadville	MS	39653	601-384-5833	384-2205
Hometown Inc 1518 E N Ave	Milwaukee	WI	53202	414-276-9311	276-6061
Huntley Oil & Gas Co Inc 137 Hwy 74 PO Box 369	Wadesboro	NC	28170	704-694-2144	694-2145
Jenkins Gas & Oil Co Inc 221 Main St *Web:* www.jenkinsgas.com	Pollocksville	NC	28573	252-224-4551	224-1443
JS West & Cos 721 8th St *TF:* 800-675-9378 ■ *Web:* www.jswest.com	Modesto	CA	95354	209-577-3221	523-9828
Kingston Oil Supply Corp 15 N Broadway PO Box 760	Port Ewen	NY	12466	845-331-0770	331-3760
Kolkhorst Petroleum Co 1685 E Washington PO Box 410 *TF:* 800-548-6671 ■ *Web:* www.kolkhorst.com	Navasota	TX	77868	936-825-6868	870-3355
Landmark Industries Ltd 11111 Wilcrest Green Dr Suite 100 PO Box 42374 *Web:* www.landmarkindustries.com	Houston	TX	77042	713-789-0310	789-2907
Lansing Ice & Fuel Co 911 Ctr St	Lansing	MI	48906	517-372-3850	485-9482
Lawes Coal Co Inc 499 Sycamore Ave	Shrewsbury	NJ	07702	732-741-6300	741-8527
Lewis & Raulerson Inc 1759 State St PO Box 289 *Web:* www.lewisandraulerson.com	Waycross	GA	31501	912-283-5951	283-8281
Lincoln Land Oil Co 2026 Republic St *TF:* 800-238-4912 ■ *Web:* www.lincolnlandoil.com	Springfield	IL	62702	217-523-5050	523-5001
Local Oil Co Inc 2015 7th Ave N	Anoka	MN	55303	763-421-4923	421-0304
Martin LP Gas Inc PO Box 191 *TF:* 800-256-6644 ■ *Web:* www.martinlpgas.com	Kilgore	TX	75663	903-983-6200	983-6271
Meenan Oil Co Inc 520 Broadhollow Rd Suite 200-W	Melville	NY	11747	516-495-1100	495-1101
Metro Energy Group 1011 Hudson Ave *TF:* 800-866-4680 ■ *Web:* www.metroenergynj.com	Ridgefield	NJ	07657	201-941-3470	941-6854
Midwest Bottle Gas Co 3600 State Trunk Hwy 157 *TF:* 800-522-1055	La Crosse	WI	54602	608-781-1010	781-3094
Mirabito Fuel Group 49 Ct St PO Box 5306 *TF:* 800-934-9480 ■ *Web:* www.mirabitofuel.com	Binghamton	NY	13902	607-352-2800	584-5130
Mitchell Supreme Fuel Co 532 Freeman St *TF:* 800-832-7090 ■ *Web:* www.mitchellsupreme.com	Orange	NJ	07050	973-678-1800	672-0148
Mutual Liquid Gas & Equipment Co Inc 17117 S Broadway St **Fax Area Code:* 310 ■ *Web:* www.mutualpropane.com	Gardena	CA	90248	323-321-3771	515-2633*
New London Energy 410 Bank St *TF:* 800-944-8803	New London	CT	06320	860-271-2020	271-2050
Oliver Oil Co Inc PO Box 248 *TF:* 800-634-8729	Chambersburg	PA	17201	717-264-5165	264-1733
Peoples Community Oil Co-op 427 Main St	Darlington	WI	53530	608-776-4437	776-3156
Petroleum Marketers Inc 3000 Ogden Rd *Web:* www.petroleummarketers.com	Roanoke	VA	24014	540-772-4900	772-6900
Planters Oil Inc 217 S Main St	Fitzgerald	GA	31750	229-423-2096	423-4836
Polsinello Fuels Inc 41 Riverside Ave *TF:* 800-334-5823 ■ *Web:* www.polsinello.com	Rensselaer	NY	12144	518-463-0084	463-4086
Prairie Pride Co-op 1100 E Main St *TF:* 888-532-9686 ■ *Web:* www.prairieridecoop.com	Marshall	MN	56258	507-532-9686	532-4394
Pro-Gas Sales & Service Co 1535 S Walker Rd	Muskegon	MI	49442	231-773-3261	773-3463
Range Co-op Inc 102 S Hoover Rd *TF General:* 800-862-8628	Virginia	MN	55792	218-741-7393	741-7396
Richard Oil & Fuel Holding Co Inc 2330 Hwy 70 PO Box 686 *TF:* 800-375-8389 ■ *Web:* www.richardoil.com	Donaldsonville	LA	70346	225-473-8389	473-8458
Robison Oil Corp 500 Executive Blvd *Web:* www.robisonoil.com	Elmsford	NY	10523	914-345-5700	345-5792
Rose Fuel & Materials Inc 918 Oliver Plow Ct *Web:* www.rosebrick.com	South Bend	IN	46601	574-234-2133	232-2695
Sharp Energy Inc 648 Ocean Hwy *Web:* www.sharpenergy.com	Pocomoke City	MD	21851	410-957-0422	957-0716
Shipley Energy 550 E King St *TF:* 800-839-1849 ■ *Web:* www.shipleyenergy.com	York	PA	17405	717-848-4100	854-5496
SJ Fuel Co Inc 601 Union St *Web:* www.sjfuelco.com	Brooklyn	NY	11215	718-855-6060	625-5696
Southeast Fuels Inc 604 Green Valley Rd Suite 207 *Web:* www.southeastfuels.com	Greensboro	NC	27408	336-854-1106	547-8720
Spencer Oil Co Inc 16410 Common Rd *TF:* 800-445-7562	Roseville	MI	48066	586-775-5022	775-3111
Star Gas Partners LP 2187 Atlantic St *NYSE: SGU* ■ *TF:* 800-966-9827 ■ *Web:* www.Star-Gas.com	Stamford	CT	06902	203-328-7310	328-7422
Streicher Mobile Fueling Inc 200 W Cypress Creek Rd Suite 400 *NASDAQ: FUEL* ■ *TF:* 800-383-5734 ■ *Web:* www.mobilefueling.com	Fort Lauderdale	FL	33309	954-308-4200	308-4222
Suburban Gas Inc 2800 Dartmouth Ave	Bessemer	AL	35020	205-424-4464	424-0667
Suburban Propane LP 1 Suburban Pl 240 Rt 10 W PO Box 206 *NYSE: SPH* ■ *TF:* 800-776-7263 ■ *Web:* www.suburbanpropane.com	Whippany	NJ	07981	973-887-5300	
Surner Heating Co Inc 60 Shumway St *Web:* www.surnerheat.com	Amherst	MA	01002	413-253-5999	253-9063
Susser Holdings LLC 4433 Baldwin Blvd *TF:* 800-569-3585 ■ *Web:* www.susser.com	Corpus Christi	TX	78408	361-693-3600	884-2494
SW Rawls Inc 100 Bowers Rd *Web:* www.swrawls.com	Franklin	VA	23851	757-562-3115	562-1227

Company	City	State	Zip	Phone	Fax
Western Natural Gas Co 2960 Strickland St *Web:* www.westernnaturalgas.com	Jacksonville	FL	32254	904-387-3511	387-6034
WH Riley & Son Inc 35 Chestnut St *Web:* www.whriley.com	North Attleboro	MA	02761	508-695-9391	699-7712
William R Peterson Oil Co 276 Main St Suite 1 PO Box 31 *TF:* 800-622-6971	Portland	CT	06480	860-342-3560	342-2543
Wilson of Wallingford Inc 221 Rogers Ln PO box 185 *Web:* www.wilsonoilandpropane.com	Wallingford	PA	19086	610-566-7600	566-7608
Woodruff Energy 73 Water St PO Box 777 *TF:* 800-557-1121 ■ *Web:* www.woodruffenergy.com	Bridgeton	NJ	08302	856-455-1111	455-4085
Worley & Obetz Inc 85 White Oak Rd PO Box 429 *TF:* 800-697-6891 ■ *Web:* www.worleyobetz.com	Manheim	PA	17545	717-665-6891	665-2867

320 FUND-RAISING SERVICES

Company	City	State	Zip	Phone	Fax
Adams Hussey & Assoc 1600 Wilson Blvd Suite 300 *Web:* www.ahadirect.com	Arlington	VA	22209	703-248-0025	248-0029
Advantage Fund Raising Consulting Inc 208 Passaic Ave *TF:* 888-540-2372 ■ *Web:* www.advantageconsulting.com	Fairfield	NJ	07004	973-575-9196	575-5614
Alford Group Inc 1603 Orrington Ave 2nd Fl. *TF:* 800-291-8913 ■ *Web:* www.alford.com	Evanston	IL	60201	847-425-9800	425-4114
Barton Cotton Inc 3030 Waterview Ave *TF:* 800-638-4652 ■ *Web:* www.bartoncotton.com	Baltimore	MD	21230	410-247-4800	247-3681
Bentz Whaley Flessner 7251 Ohms Ln *TF:* 800-921-0111 ■ *Web:* www.bwf.com	Minneapolis	MN	55439	952-921-0111	921-0109
Brakeley Briscoe Inc 51 Locust Ave Suite 204 *TF:* 800-486-5171 ■ *Web:* www.brakeleybriscoe.com	New Canaan	CT	06804	203-972-0282	972-0263
Cargill Assoc Inc 4701 Altamesa Blvd *TF:* 800-433-2233 ■ *Web:* www.cargillassociates.com	Fort Worth	TX	76133	817-292-9374	292-6205
Carlton & Co 101 Federal St Suite 1900 **Fax Area Code:* 252 ■ *TF General:* 800-622-0194	Boston	MA	02110	617-342-7257	738-8962*
Changing Our World Inc 220 E 42nd St 5th Fl. **Fax Area Code:* 202 ■ *Web:* www.changingourworld.com	New York	NY	10017	212-499-0866	499-9075*
Community Counselling Service 461 5th Ave 3rd Fl *TF:* 800-223-6733 ■ *Web:* www.ccsfundraising.com	New York	NY	10017	212-695-1175	967-6451
Cramer & Assoc *Hodge Cramer & Assoc* 555 Metro Pl N Suite 500 *TF:* 800-926-4483 ■ *Web:* www.cramerfundraising.com	Dublin	OH	43017	614-766-4483	568-7685
Cull Martin & Assoc Inc 320 N Jensen Rd *Web:* www.cullmartin.com	Vestal	NY	13850	607-722-3884	722-4264
Dragul Group 312 Walnut St Suite 1600	Cincinnati	OH	45202	513-762-7828	721-4628
Economic Opportunity Board Of Clark County 330 W Washington Ave Suite 7 *Web:* www.eobccnv.org	Las Vegas	NV	89127	702-647-3307	647-3125
Fam Funds 384 N Grand St PO Box 310 *TF:* 800-721-5391 ■ *Web:* www.famfunds.com	Cobleskill	NY	12043	518-234-4393	234-4473
Gift Planning Assoc 223 Clipper St *Web:* www.giftplanner1.com	San Francisco	CA	94114	415-970-2380	
Gonser Gerber Tinker Stuhr LLP 400 E Diehl Rd Suite 380 *TF:* 800-446-4487 ■ *Web:* www.ggts.com	Naperville	IL	60563	630-505-1433	505-7710
Grenzebach Glier & Assoc Inc 401 N Michigan Ave Suite 2800 *Web:* www.grenzebachglier.com	Chicago	IL	60611	312-372-4040	372-7911
Institutional Advancement Programs Inc 65 Main St Suite 208	Tuckahoe	NY	10707	914-779-4092	961-3114
Jackson & Assoc Inc 30294 Inverness Ln *TF:* 800-824-8447 ■ *Web:* www.jacksonandassoc.com	Evergreen	CO	80439	303-670-1100	670-1127
John B Cummings Co Inc 3333 Lee Pkwy Suite 600 *Web:* www.cummingsco.com	Dallas	TX	75219	214-526-1772	665-9590
John Brown Ltd Inc 46 Grove St PO Box 296 *Web:* www.johnbrownlimited.com	Peterborough	NH	03458	603-924-3834	924-7998
KMA Direct Communications 7160 Dallas Pkwy Suite 400 *TF:* 800-562-4161 ■ *Web:* www.kma.com	Plano	TX	75024	972-244-1900	244-1901
Lipman Hearne Inc 200 S Michigan Ave Suite 1600 *Web:* www.lipmanhearne.com	Chicago	IL	60604	312-356-8000	356-4005
LW Robbins Assoc 201 Summer St. *TF:* 800-229-5972 ■ *Web:* www.lwra.com	Holliston	MA	01746	508-893-0210	893-0212
MacIntyre Assoc Inc 106 W State St *TF:* 888-575-0903 ■ *Web:* www.macintyreassociates.com	Kennett Square	PA	19348	610-925-5925	
Netzel Grigsby Assoc Inc 9696 Culver Blvd Suite 105 *Web:* www.netzelgrigsby.com	Culver City	CA	90232	310-836-7624	836-9357
PEP Direct Inc 19 Stoney Brook Dr *TF:* 877-782-3782 ■ *Web:* www.pep-direct.com	Wilton	NH	03086	603-654-6141	654-2159
Phillips & Assoc PO Box 241040 *Web:* www.phillipsontheweb.com	Los Angeles	CA	90024	310-247-0963	247-0966
Ruotolo Assoc Inc (RA) 29 Broadway Suite 210 *TF:* 800-786-8656 ■ *Web:* www.ruotoloassociates.com	Cresskill	NJ	07626	201-568-3898	568-8783
Sanky Perlowin Assoc Inc *Sanky Communications Inc* 589 8th Ave 10th Fl *Web:* www.sankyinc.com	New York	NY	10018	212-868-4300	868-4310
Skystone Ryan *Skystone Partners LLC* 635 W 7th St Suite 107 *TF:* 800-883-0801 ■ *Web:* www.skystoneryan.com	Cincinnati	OH	45203	513-241-6778	241-0551
Stanford Group 211 W 56th St Suite 3-M	New York	NY	10019	212-333-5514	581-4202
Ter Molen Watkins & Brandt LLC 500 N Dearborn St Suite 726 *Web:* www.twbfundraising.com	Chicago	IL	60610	312-222-0560	222-0565
Van Groesbeck & Co 2211 Dickens Rd Suite 300 *Web:* www.vangroesbeckco.com	Richmond	VA	23230	804-285-3175	285-2059
Whitney Jones Inc 119 Brookstown Ave Suite 302 *Web:* www.whitneyjonesinc.com	Winston-Salem	NC	27101	336-722-2371	

321 FURNACES & OVENS - INDUSTRIAL PROCESS

Company	City	State	Zip	Phone	Fax
AFC Holcroft LLC 49630 Pontiac Trail *Web:* www.afc-holcroft.com	Wixom	MI	48393	248-624-8191	624-3710
AGF Burner Inc 1955 Swarthmore Ave Unit 2 *Web:* www.agfburner.com	Lakewood	NJ	08701	732-730-8090	730-8060
AJAX Electric Co 60 Tomlinson Rd. *Web:* www.ajaxelectric.com	Huntingdon Valley	PA	19006	215-947-8500	947-6757
Ajax Tocco Magnethermic Corp 1745 Overland Ave NE *TF:* 800-321-0153 ■ *Web:* www.ajaxtocco.com	Warren	OH	44483	330-372-8511	372-8644
Alabama Specialty Products Inc 152 Metal Samples Rd PO Box 8 *Web:* www.alspi.com	Munford	AL	36268	256-358-5200	358-4515
Alpha 1 Induction Service Center Inc 1525 Old Alum Creek Dr. *TF:* 800-991-2599 ■ *Web:* www.alpha1induction.com	Columbus	OH	43209	614-253-8900	253-8981
AVS Inc 60 Fitchburg Rd *TF:* 800-272-0710 ■ *Web:* www.avsinc.com	Ayer	MA	01432	978-772-0710	772-6462
Belco Industries Inc 115 E Main St *Web:* www.belcoind.com	Belding	MI	48809	616-794-0410	794-3424
Bloom Engineering Co Inc 5460 Curry Rd *TF:* 800-451-5491 ■ *Web:* www.bloomeng.com	Pittsburgh	PA	15236	412-653-3500	653-2253
BriskHeat Corp 1055 Gibbard Ave. *TF:* 800-848-7673 ■ *Web:* www.bhthermal.com	Columbus	OH	43201	614-294-3376	294-3807
Callidus Technologies Inc 7130 S Lewis St Suite 335 *Web:* www.callidus.com	Tulsa	OK	74136	918-496-7599	496-7587
Cambridge Engineering Inc PO Box 1010 *TF:* 800-899-1989 ■ *Web:* www.cambridge-eng.com	Chesterfield	MO	63006	636-532-2233	530-6133
CCI Thermal Technologies Inc 5918 Roper Rd *TF Cust Svc:* 800-661-8529 ■ *Web:* www.ccithermal.com	Edmonton	AB	T6B3E1	780-466-3178	468-5904
CI Hayes 33 Fwy Dr. *Web:* www.cihayes.com	Cranston	RI	02920	401-467-5200	467-2108
Cincinnati Industrial Machinery An Armor Metal Group Co 4600 N Mason-Montgomery Rd **Fax:* Sales ■ *TF:* 800-677-0076 ■ *Web:* www.armormetal.com	Mason	OH	45040	513-923-5600	923-5694*
CMI EFCO Inc 435 W Wilson St *Web:* www.cmigroupe.com	Salem	OH	44460	330-332-4661	332-4661
Consarc Corp 100 Indel Ave **Fax:* Sales ■ *Web:* www.consarc.com	Rancocas	NJ	08073	609-267-8000	267-1366*
Consutech Systems LLC PO Box 15119 *Web:* www.consutech.com	Richmond	VA	23227	804-746-4120	730-9056
Delta Mfg/Acra 8717 W 84th St *Web:* www.acraelectric.com	Tulsa	OK	74131	918-224-6755	224-6866
Despatch Industries Inc 8860 207th St W *Web:* www.despatch.com	Lakeville	MN	55044	952-469-5424	469-4513
Detroit Radiant Product Co 21400 Hoover Rd *TF:* 800-222-1100 ■ *Web:* www.reverberray.com	Warren	MI	48089	586-756-0950	756-2626
Detroit Stoker Co 1510 E 1st St *TF:* 800-786-5374 ■ *Web:* www.detroitstoker.com	Monroe	MI	48161	734-241-9500	241-0216
Eclipse Inc 1665 Elmwood Rd **Fax:* Cust Svc ■ *TF:* 800-676-3254 ■ *Web:* www.eclipsenet.com	Rockford	IL	61103	815-877-3031	877-3336*
Eisenmann Corp 150 E Dartmoor Dr *Web:* www.eisenmann.com	Crystal Lake	IL	60014	815-455-4100	455-1018
Electric Heating Equipment Co 1240 Oronoque Rd *TF:* 800-958-9998	Milford	CT	06460	203-882-0199	882-8937
Fast Heat Inc 776 Oaklawn Ave *TF:* 800-982-4328 ■ *Web:* www.fastheat.com	Elmhurst	IL	60126	630-833-5400	833-2040
Fostoria Industries Inc 1200 N Main St PO Box 986 *TF:* 800-495-4525 ■ *Web:* www.fostoriaindustries.com	Fostoria	OH	44830	419-435-9201	435-0842
Gas-Fired Products Inc 305 Doggett St. *TF:* 800-830-3983 ■ *Web:* www.gasfiredproducts.com	Charlotte	NC	28203	704-372-3485	332-5843
GC Broach Co 7667 E 46th Pl *Web:* www.broach.com	Tulsa	OK	74145	918-664-7420	627-4083
Glenn Electric Heater Corp 2111 E 30th St *Web:* www.glennelectricheater.com	Erie	PA	16510	814-898-4000	898-1719
Glenro Inc 39 McBride Ave. *TF:* 800-922-0106 ■ *Web:* www.glenro.com	Paterson	NJ	07501	973-279-5900	279-9103
Glo-Quartz Electric Heater Co Inc 7084 Maple St *TF Sales:* 800-321-3574 ■ *Web:* www.gloquartz.com	Mentor	OH	44060	440-255-9701	255-7852
Global Finishing Solutions LLC 1625 W Crosby Rd Suite 124 *TF:* 800-848-8738 ■ *Web:* globalfinishing.com	Carrollton	TX	75006	800-848-8738	633-1108
Harper International Corp 100 W Drullard Ave. *Web:* www.harperintl.com	Lancaster	NY	14086	716-684-7400	684-7405

Company	City	State	ZIP	Phone	Fax
Hauck Mfg Co PO Box 90 Web: www.hauckburner.com	Lebanon	PA	17042	717-272-3051	273-9882
Heatrex Inc 21371 Blooming Valley Rd TF: 800-394-6589 ■ Web: www.heatrex.com	Meadville	PA	16335	814-724-1800	333-6580
Henry F Teichmann Inc 3009 Washington Rd Web: www.hft.com	McMurray	PA	15317	724-941-9550	941-3479
Hotwatt Inc 128 Maple St *Fax: Sales ■ Web: www.hotwatt.com	Danvers	MA	01923	978-777-0070	774-2409*
Huppert Industries Inc 16808 S Lathrop Ave Web: www.huppert.com	Harvey	IL	60426	708-339-2020	339-2225
Inductoheat Inc 32251 N Avis Dr TF: 800-642-8903 ■ Web: www.inductoheat.com	Madison Heights	MI	48071	248-585-9393	589-1062
Inductotherm Corp 10 Indel Ave TF: 800-257-9527 ■ Web: www.inductotherm.com	Rancocas	NJ	08073	609-267-9000	267-3537
Inductotherm Industries Inc 10 Indel Ave PO Box 157 TF: 800-257-9527 ■ Web: www.inductothermgroup.com	Rancocas	NJ	08073	609-267-9000	267-7894
Industrial Combustion Inc 351 21st St Web: www.ind-comb.com	Monroe	WI	53566	608-325-3141	325-4379
Industrial Engineering & Equipment Co 425 Hanley Industrial Ct Web: www.indeeco.com	Saint Louis	MO	63144	314-644-4300	644-5332
Industrial Heater Corp 30 Knotter Dr TF: 800-822-4426 ■ Web: www.industrialheater.com	Cheshire	CT	06410	203-250-0500	250-0599
Industronics Service Co 489 Sullivan Ave PO Box 649 TF: 800-878-1551 ■ Web: www.industronics.com	South Windsor	CT	06074	860-289-1551	289-3526
International Thermal Systems LLC (ITS) 4697 W Greenfield Ave TF: 877-683-6797 ■ Web: www.itsllcusa.com	Milwaukee	WI	53214	414-672-7700	672-8800
IntriCon Corp 1260 Red Fox Rd AMEX: IIN ■ TF: 800-523-6500 ■ Web: www.IntriCon.com	Arden Hills	MN	55112	651-636-9770	636-9503
Ipsen Inc PO Box 6266 TF: 800-727-7625 ■ Web: www.ipsenusa.com	Rockford	IL	61125	815-332-4941	332-4995
John Zink Co LLC 11920 E Apache St TF: 800-421-9242 ■ Web: www.johnzink.com	Tulsa	OK	74116	918-234-1800	234-2700
Johnson Gas Appliance Co 520 E Ave NW TF: 800-553-5422 ■ Web: www.mendotahearth.com	Cedar Rapids	IA	52405	319-365-5267	365-6282
JT Thorpe & Son Inc 1060 Hensley St TF: 800-577-1755 ■ Web: www.jtthorpe.com	Richmond	CA	94801	510-233-2500	233-2901
Koch Chemical Technology Group LLC 4111 E 37th St N PO Box 2256 Web: www.kochind.com/IndustryAreas/process.aspx	Wichita	KS	67220	316-828-5500	828-4704
Lanly Co The 26201 Tungsten Rd Web: www.lanly.com	Cleveland	OH	44132	216-731-1115	731-7900
Larose RF Systems Inc 150 Dover Rd Web: www.radiofrequency.com	Millis	MA	02054	508-376-0850	376-9944
Lepel Corp 200-G Executive Dr TF: 800-548-8520	Edgewood	NY	11717	631-586-3300	586-3232
Novatec Inc 222 Thomas Ave TF: 800-237-8379 ■ Web: www.novatec.com	Baltimore	MD	21225	410-789-4811	789-4638
Nutec Bickley USA 480 State Rd # B Web: www.nutecbickley.com	Bensalem	PA	19020	215-638-4500	
Paragon Industries Inc 2011 S Town E Blvd TF: 800-876-4328 ■ Web: www.paragonweb.com	Mesquite	TX	75149	972-288-7557	222-0646
Phoenix Solutions Co 3324 Winpark Dr Web: www.phoenixsolutionsco.com	Crystal	MN	55427	763-544-2721	546-5617
Pillar Induction Co 21905 Gateway Rd TF: 800-558-7733 ■ Web: www.pillar.com	Brookfield	WI	53045	262-317-5300	317-5353
Procedyne Corp 11 Industrial Dr Web: www.procedyne.com	New Brunswick	NJ	08901	732-249-8347	249-7220
Process Combustion Corp 5460 Curry Rd Web: www.pcc-sterling.com	Pittsburgh	PA	15236	412-655-0955	650-5569
Pyronics Inc 17700 Miles Rd Web: www.pyronics.com	Cleveland	OH	44128	216-662-8800	663-8954
Radiant Technology Corp 1335 S Acacia Ave	Fullerton	CA	92831	714-991-0200	991-0600
Radio Frequency Co Inc 150 Dover Rd PO Box 158 Web: www.radiofrequency.com	Millis	MA	02054	508-376-9555	376-9944
Radyne Corp 211 W Boden St TF: 800-236-8360 ■ Web: www.radyne.com	Milwaukee	WI	53207	414-481-8360	481-8303
Rapid Engineering Inc 1100 7-Mile Rd NW TF: 800-536-3461 ■ Web: www.rapidengineering.com	Comstock Park	MI	49321	616-784-0500	784-1910
Ray Burner/RD Miners Co 401 Parr Blvd TF: 800-729-2876 ■ Web: www.rayburner.com	Richmond	CA	94801	510-236-4972	236-4083
Red-Ray Mfg Co Inc 10-22 County Line Rd Web: www.red-ray.com	Branchburg	NJ	08876	908-722-0040	722-2535
SECO/Warwick Corp 180 Mercer St TF: 800-458-6071 ■ Web: www.secowarwick.com	Meadville	PA	16335	814-724-1400	724-1407
SPX Corp Lindberg Div 3827 Riverside Rd TF: 800-873-4468 ■ Web: www.heat-treat.com	PO Box 131	MI	49084	269-849-2700	849-3021
ST Johnson Co 925 Stanford Ave Web: www.stjohnson.com	Oakland	CA	94608	510-652-6000	652-4302
Steelman Industries Inc 2800 Hwy 135 N PO Box 1461 TF: 800-287-6633 ■ Web: www.steelman.com	Kilgore	TX	75662	903-984-3061	984-1384
StrikoDynarad 501 E Roosevelt Ave Web: www.strikodynarad.com	Zeeland	MI	49464	616-772-3705	772-5271
Surface Combustion Inc 1700 Indian Wood Cir TF: 800-537-8980 ■ Web: www.surfacecombustion.com	Maumee	OH	43537	419-891-7150	891-7151
Swindell Dressler International Co 5100 Casteel Dr Web: www.swindelldressler.com	Coraopolis	PA	15108	412-788-7100	
T-M Vacuum Products Inc 630 S Warrington Ave Web: www.tmvacuum.com	Cinnaminson	NJ	08077	856-829-2000	829-0990
Tempco Electric Heater Corp 607 N Central Ave TF: 888-268-6396 ■ Web: www.tempco.com	Wood Dale	IL	60191	630-350-2252	350-0232
Tenova Core 100 Corporate Ctr Dr TF: 800-355-4826 ■ Web: www.corefurnace.com	Coraopolis	PA	15108	412-262-2240	262-2055
Thermal Circuits Inc 1 Technology Way TF: 800-808-4328 ■ Web: www.thermalcircuits.com	Salem	MA	01970	978-745-1162	741-3420
Thermal Engineering Corp 2741 The Blvd TF: 800-331-0097 ■ Web: www.tecinfrared.com	Columbia	SC	29209	803-783-0750	783-0756
Thermal Equipment Corp 1301 W 228th St Web: www.thermalequipment.com	Torrance	CA	90501	310-328-6600	320-2692
Thermcraft Inc PO Box 12037 Web: www.thermcraftinc.com	Winston Salem	NC	27117	336-784-4800	784-0634
Trent Inc 201 Leverington Ave TF: 800-544-8736 ■ Web: www.trentheat.com	Philadelphia	PA	19127	215-482-5000	482-9389
Truheat Inc 700 Grand St TF: 800-879-6199 ■ Web: www.truheat.com	Allegan	MI	49010	269-673-2145	673-7219
Watlow Electric Mfg Co 12001 Lackland Rd TF: 800-492-8569 ■ Web: www.watlow.com	Saint Louis	MO	63146	314-878-4600	878-6814
Webster Engineering & Mfg Co LLC 619 Industrial Rd Web: www.webster-engineering.com	Winfield	KS	67156	620-221-7464	221-9447
Wisconsin Oven Corp 2675 Main St Web: www.wisoven.com	East Troy	WI	53120	262-642-3938	363-4018

322 FURNITURE - MFR

SEE ALSO Baby Products p. 1504; Cabinets - Wood p. 1551; Fixtures - Office & Store p. 1847; Mattresses & Adjustable Beds p. 2223; Recycled Plastics Products p. 2531

Company	City	State	ZIP	Phone	Fax
Unisource Solutions Inc 8350 Rex Rd Web: www.unisourceit.com	Pico Rivera	CA	90660	562-949-1111	949-7110

322-1 Commercial & Industrial Furniture

Company	City	State	ZIP	Phone	Fax
Abco Office Furniture 4121 Rushton St TF: 800-336-0070 ■ Web: www.abcofurniture.com	Florence	AL	35630	256-767-4100	760-1247
Adelphia Steel Equipment Co 7372 State Rd TF: 800-865-8211 ■ Web: www.adelphiafurniture.com	Philadelphia	PA	19136	215-333-6300	331-6090
Allied Plastics Co Inc 2001 Walnut St TF Cust Svc: 800-999-0386 ■ Web: www.alliedplasticsco.com	Jacksonville	FL	32206	904-359-0386	353-4746
Allsteel Inc 2210 2nd Ave TF Cust Svc: 888-255-7833 ■ Web: www.allsteeloffice.com	Muscatine	IA	52761	563-272-4800	272-4887
American of Martinsville 128 E Church St Web: www.americanofmartinsville.com	Martinsville	VA	24112	276-632-2061	638-8810
Anthro Corp 10450 SW Manhasset Dr *Fax Area Code: 800 ■ TF: 800-325-3841 ■ Web: www.anthro.com	Tualatin	OR	97062	503-691-2556	325-0045*
Artistic Frame Corp 985 3rd Ave Web: www.artisticframe.com	New York	NY	10022	212-289-2100	289-2101
Bernhardt Furniture Co Inc 1839 Morganton Blvd SW TF: 800-523-8824 ■ Web: www.bernhardt.com	Lenoir	NC	28645	828-758-9811	759-6634
Bestar Inc 4220 Villeneuve St CNQ: BES ■ TF: 888-823-7827 ■ Web: www.bestar.ca	Lac-Megantic	QC	G6B2C3	819-583-1017	583-5370
Bevco Precision Mfg Co 21320 Doral Rd TF: 800-864-2991 ■ Web: www.bevco.com	Waukesha	WI	53186	262-798-9200	798-9201
BGD Cos Inc 5323 Lakeland Ave N TF: 800-699-3537 ■ Web: www.bgdmidwest.com	Minneapolis	MN	55429	612-338-6804	338-4942
Biofit Engineered Products 15500 Biofit Way TF: 800-597-0246 ■ Web: www.biofit.com	Bowling Greene	OH	43402	419-823-1089	823-1342
BK Barrit Corp 4011 G St *Fax Area Code: 215 ■ TF: 888-256-2020 ■ Web: www.bkbarrit.com	Philadelphia	PA	19124	267-345-1200	739-1709*
Boling Furniture Co 311 NE Church Rd PO Box 1059 TF: 888-779-6546	Mount Olive	NC	28365	919-635-2400	635-4845
Borroughs Corp 3002 N Burdick St TF: 800-748-0227 ■ Web: www.borroughs.com	Kalamazoo	MI	49004	269-342-0161	342-4161
Bright Chair Co 51 Railroad Ave PO Box 269 TF: 888-524-5997 ■ Web: www.brightchair.com	Middletown	NY	10940	845-343-2196	343-4958
CabotWrenn 405 Rink Dam Rd PO Box 1767 Web: www.cabotwrenn.com	Hickory	NC	28603	828-495-4607	495-1294
Carolina Business Furniture LLC 535 Archdale Blvd TF: 800-763-0212 ■ Web: www.carolinabusinessfurniture.com	Archdale	NC	27263	336-431-9400	431-9511
Carson's Inc 4299 Cheyenne Dr PO Box 14186 Web: www.carsonsofhp.com	Archdale	NC	27263	336-431-1101	431-0677
Chairmasters Inc 200 E 146th St Web: www.chairmasters.com	Bronx	NY	10451	718-292-0600	292-0613

				Phone	Fax
Cramer Inc 1222 Quebec St	North Kansas City	MO	64116	816-471-4433	471-7188
TF: 800-366-6700 ■ *Web:* www.cramerinc.com					
CTB Corp 26327 Fallbrook Ave	Wyoming	MN	55092	651-462-3550	462-8806
Web: www.ctbcorp.com					
Danver 1 Grand St	Wallingford	CT	06492	203-269-2300	265-6190
TF: 888-441-0537 ■ *Web:* www.danver.com					
Dar-Ran Furniture Industries					
2402 Shore St	High Point	NC	27263	336-861-2400	861-6485
TF: 800-334-7891 ■ *Web:* www.darran.com					
Dauphin North America 300 Myrtle Ave	Boonton	NJ	07005	973-263-1100	220-3844*
**Fax Area Code:* 800 ■ *TF Cust Svc:* 800-631-1186 ■ *Web:* www.dauphin.com					
Davis Furniture Industries Inc					
2401 S College Dr	High Point	NC	27261	336-889-2009	889-0031
TF: 877-463-2847 ■ *Web:* www.davis-furniture.com					
Delco Office Systems Div Delco Assoc Inc					
55 Old Field Pt Rd	Greenwich	CT	06830	203-661-5101	661-5101
TF: 800-243-8528					
Design Options 5455 W Waters Ave # 214	Tampa	FL	33634	813-885-4950	885-2994
TF: 877-800-3560 ■ *Web:* www.designoptions.com					
Easi File Mfg Corp 6 Wrigley St	Irvine	CA	92618	949-855-4121	380-0561*
**Fax:* Sales ■ *TF:* 800-800-5563 ■ *Web:* www.easifileusa.com					
Emeco Industries Inc 805 W Elm Ave PO Box 179	Hanover	PA	17331	717-637-5951	637-5951
TF: 800-366-5951 ■ *Web:* www.emeco.net					
Engineered Data Products Inc 1250 W 124th Ave	Denver	CO	80234	303-465-2800	465-4936
TF: 800-432-1337 ■ *Web:* www.edp-usa.com					
Ergotron Inc 1181 Trapp Rd	Eagan	MN	55121	651-681-7600	681-7710
TF Sales: 800-888-8458 ■ *Web:* www.ergotron.com					
Executive Office Concepts Inc					
1705 S Anderson Ave	Compton	CA	90220	310-537-1657	603-9100
TF: 800-421-5927 ■ *Web:* www.eoccorp.com					
Fillip Metal Cabinet Co 4500 W 47th St	Chicago	IL	60632	773-826-7373	826-6420
TF: 800-535-0733 ■ *Web:* www.fillipmetal.com					
First Office 1204 E 6th St PO Box 100	Huntingburg	IN	47542	812-683-4848	683-7155*
**Fax:* Cust Svc ■ *TF:* 800-521-5381 ■ *Web:* www.firstoffice.com					
Flex-Y-Plan Industries Inc 6960 W Ridge Rd	Fairview	PA	16415	814-474-1565	474-2129
TF Cust Svc: 800-458-0552 ■ *Web:* www.fyp.com					
Flexible-Montisa 323 Acorn St	Plainwell	MI	49080	269-685-6831	685-9195
TF Cust Svc: 800-875-6836 ■ *Web:* www.flexiblemontisa.com					
Flexsteel Industries Inc 3400 Jackson St	Dubuque	IA	52001	563-556-7730	556-8345*
NASDAQ: FLXS ■ **Fax:* Cust Svc ■ *Web:* www.flexsteel.com					
Foldcraft Co 615 Centennial Dr	Kenyon	MN	55946	507-789-5111	544-0480*
**Fax Area Code:* 800 ■ *TF:* 800-759-6653 ■ *Web:* www.plymold.com					
Furniture Values International LLC					
2929 NW Grand Ave 601 N 75 Th Ave	Phoenix	AZ	85043	602-233-0224	269-6810
TF Cust Svc: 888-484-5874					
Geiger International Inc					
6095 Fulton Industrial Blvd SW	Atlanta	GA	30336	404-344-1100	836-7519
TF: 800-456-6452 ■ *Web:* www.geigerintl.com					
GF Office Furniture Ltd 525 Steam Plant Rd	Gallatin	TN	37066	615-452-9120	230-1533
TF Cust Svc: 800-321-4005					
Global Industries Inc 17 W Stow Rd	Marlton	NJ	08053	856-596-3390	596-5684
TF: 800-220-1900 ■ *Web:* www.globaltotaloffice.com					
Groupe Lacasse LLC 99 St-Pierre St	Sainte-Pie	QC	J0H1W0	450-772-2495	248-1865*
**Fax Area Code:* 888 ■ **Fax:* Cust Svc ■ *TF:* 888-522-2773 ■ *Web:* www.groupelacasse.com					
Gunlocke Co LLC 1 Gunlocke Dr	Wayland	NY	14572	585-728-5111	728-8334*
**Fax:* Hum Res ■ *TF Cust Svc:* 800-828-6300 ■ *Web:* www.gunlocke.com					
H Wilson Co 2245 Delany Rd	Waukegan	IL	60087	708-339-5111	327-1698*
**Fax Area Code:* 800 ■ *TF:* 800-323-4656 ■ *Web:* www.hwilson.com					
Hausmann Industries Inc 130 Union St	Northvale	NJ	07647	201-767-0255	767-1369
TF: 888-428-7626 ■ *Web:* www.hausmann.com					
Haworth Inc 1 Haworth Ctr	Holland	MI	49423	616-393-3000	393-1570
TF: 800-765-4100 ■ *Web:* www.haworth.com					
Herman Miller Inc 855 E Main Ave	Zeeland	MI	49464	616-654-3000	654-5385
NASDAQ: MLHR ■ *TF:* 888-443-4357 ■ *Web:* www.hermanmiller.com					
High Point Furniture Industries Inc					
1104 Bedford St PO Box 2063	High Point	NC	27261	336-431-7101	434-1964
TF: 800-447-3462 ■ *Web:* www.hpfi.com					
Hirsh Industries Inc 11229 Aurora Ave	Urbandale	IA	50322	515-299-3200	299-3374
TF: 800-383-7414 ■ *Web:* www.hirshindustries.com					
HON Co 200 Oak St	Muscatine	IA	52761	563-272-7100	264-7206
TF: 800-553-8230 ■ *Web:* www.hon.com					
Huot Mfg Co 550 Wheeler St N	Saint Paul	MN	55104	651-646-1869	646-0457
TF: 800-832-3838 ■ *Web:* www.huot.com					
IAC Industries 895 Beacon St	Brea	CA	92821	714-990-8997	990-0557
TF: 800-229-1422 ■ *Web:* www.iacindustries.com					
Indiana Furniture 1224 Mill St	Jasper	IN	47546	812-482-5727	482-9035
TF: 800-422-5727 ■ *Web:* www.indianafurniture.com					
Institutional & Office Services Inc					
4 Cara Ct	Randolph	NJ	07869	973-895-9002	895-9003
TF: 800-223-1210					
Interior Crafts Inc 2513 W Cullerton Ave	Chicago	IL	60608	773-376-8160	376-9578
Intrex LLC 40 Pk St	Brooklyn	NY	11206	718-455-5042	919-5202
TF: 877-946-8739 ■ *Web:* www.intrexfurniture.com					
Invincible Office Furniture Co					
842 S 26th St PO Box 1117	Manitowoc	WI	54220	920-682-4601	683-2970
TF: 800-558-4417 ■ *Web:* www.invinciblefurniture.com					
Inwood Office Invironments					
1108 E 15th St PO Box 646	Jasper	IN	47546	812-482-6121	482-9732
TF: 800-786-6121 ■ *Web:* www.inwood.net					
izzydesign 17237 Van Wagoner Rd	Spring Lake	MI	49456	616-847-7000	847-7000
Web: www.izzyplus.com					
Jasper Desk Co 415 E 6th St	Jasper	IN	47546	812-482-4132	482-9552
TF Cust Svc: 800-365-7994 ■ *Web:* www.jasperdesk.com					
Jasper Seating Co Inc					
Jasper Group 225 Clay St	Jasper	IN	47546	812-482-3204	482-1548
TF: 800-622-5661 ■ *Web:* www.jaspergroup.us.com					
Jebco Inc 405 Mayfield Rd	Warrenton	GA	30828	706-465-3378	465-2481
Web: www.jebcomfg.com					
Jofco International 402 E 13th St	Jasper	IN	47546	812-482-5154	634-2392
TF: 800-235-6326 ■ *Web:* www.jofco.com					
JSJ Corp 700 Robbins Rd	Grand Haven	MI	49417	616-842-6350	847-3112
Web: www.jsjcorp.com					
Khoury Inc 1129 Webster Ave PO Box 1746	Waco	TX	76703	254-754-5481	754-1606
TF: 800-725-6765 ■ *Web:* www.khouryinc.com					
KI 1330 Bellevue St	Green Bay	WI	54302	920-468-8100	468-0280
TF: 800-424-2432 ■ *Web:* www.ki-inc.com					
Kimball Hospitality 1180 E 16th St	Jasper	IN	47549	812-482-1600	634-4324
TF: 800-634-9510 ■ *Web:* www.kimballhospitality.com					
Kimball Office Furniture Co 1600 Royal St	Jasper	IN	47549	812-482-1600	482-8300
TF: 800-482-1818 ■ *Web:* www.kimballoffice.com					
Knoll Inc 1235 Water St	East Greenville	PA	18041	215-679-7991	679-1755
NYSE: KNL ■ *TF Cust Svc:* 800-343-5665 ■ *Web:* www.knoll.com					
Lakeside Mfg Inc 4900 W Electric Ave	West Milwaukee	WI	53219	414-902-6400	902-6446
TF: 800-558-8565 ■ *Web:* www.elakeside.com					
LB Furniture Industries LLC 99 S 3rd St	Hudson	NY	12534	518-828-1501	828-3219
TF: 800-403-0833 ■ *Web:* www.lbempire.com					
Liberty Furniture Industries					
6195 Purdue Dr SW	Atlanta	GA	30336	404-629-1003	629-0717
Web: www.mylibertyfurniture.com					
Luxor Div EBSCO Industries Inc					
2245 Delany Rd	Waukegan	IL	60087	847-244-1800	327-1698*
**Fax Area Code:* 800 ■ *TF:* 800-323-4656 ■ *Web:* www.luxorfurn.com					
Magna Design Inc 26246 Twelve Trees Ln NW	Poulsbo	WA	98370	360-394-1300	394-1321
TF: 800-426-1202 ■ *Web:* www.magnadesign.com					
Martin Furniture 2345 britannia Blvd	San Diego	CA	92154	619-671-5100	671-5199
TF Cust Svc: 800-268-5669 ■ *Web:* www.martinfurniture.com					
Marvel Group Inc 3843 W 43rd St	Chicago	IL	60632	773-523-4804	237-0358*
**Fax Area Code:* 800 ■ **Fax:* Cust Svc ■ *TF Cust Svc:* 800-621-8846 ■ *Web:* www.marvelgroup.com					
Maxon Furniture Inc 660 SW 39th St Suite 150	Renton	WA	98057	253-872-0396	872-7572
TF Cust Svc: 800-289-1274 ■ *Web:* www.maxonfurniture.com					
Mayline Group 619 N Commerce St PO Box 728	Sheboygan	WI	53082	920-457-5537	457-7388
TF: 800-822-8037 ■ *Web:* www.mayline.com					
McDowell-Craig Office Furniture					
13146 Firestone Blvd	Norwalk	CA	90650	562-921-4441	921-9638
TF: 877-921-2100 ■ *Web:* www.mcdowellcraig.com					
Metro 7220 Edgewater Dr	Oakland	CA	94621	510-567-5200	562-2915
Web: www.metrofurniture.com					
Midwest Commercial Interiors					
987 S W Temple	Salt Lake City	UT	84101	801-359-7681	355-2713
TF: 800-351-4553 ■ *Web:* www.midwestcommercialinteriors.com					
MLP Seating Corp 2125 Lively Blvd	Elk Grove Village	IL	60007	847-956-1700	956-1776
TF: 800-723-3030 ■ *Web:* www.mlpseating.com					
MTS Seating Inc 7100 Industrial Dr	Temperance	MI	48182	734-847-3875	329-0687*
**Fax Area Code:* 800 ■ *Web:* www.mtsseating.com					
National Business Services 1601 Magoffin Ave	El Paso	TX	79901	915-544-1271	544-0325
TF Sales: 800-777-7807 ■ *Web:* www.nbsinc.com					
National Office Furniture 1205 Kimball Blvd	Jasper	IN	47549	812-482-1717	482-8800
TF: 800-482-1717 ■ *Web:* www.nationalofficefurniture.com					
NER Data Products Inc 307 S Delsea Dr	Glassboro	NJ	08028	856-881-5524	637-2217*
**Fax Area Code:* 800 ■ *TF:* 800-257-5235 ■ *Web:* www.nerdata.com					
Neutral Posture Inc 3904 N Texas Ave	Bryan	TX	77803	979-778-0502	778-0408
TF: 800-446-3746 ■ *Web:* www.igoergo.com					
Nomanco Inc 501 Nmc Dr	Zebulon	NC	27597	919-269-6500	269-7936
TF: 800-345-7279 ■ *Web:* www.nomaco.com					
Nova Solutions Inc 421 Industrial Ave	Effingham	IL	62401	217-342-7070	940-6682*
**Fax Area Code:* 800 ■ *TF:* 800-730-6682 ■ *Web:* www.novadesk.com					
Office Chairs Inc 14815 Radburn Ave	Santa Fe Springs	CA	90670	562-802-0464	926-5561
TF: 866-624-4968					
Omni International Inc					
435 12th St SW PO Box 1409	Vernon	AL	35592	205-695-9173	695-6465
TF: 800-844-6664 ■ *Web:* www.omniinternational.com					
Open Plan Systems Inc					
14140 N Washington Hwy PO Box 1810	Ashland	VA	23005	804-228-5600	228-5656
TF: 800-849-7239 ■ *Web:* www.openplan.com					
Orna Metal Inc 1200 Stafford St PO Box 608	Washington	MO	63090	636-239-7867	239-0789
Paoli Inc 201 E Martin St	Orleans	IN	47452	812-723-2791	865-1516
TF: 800-457-7415 ■ *Web:* www.paoli.com					
Penco Products Inc 99 Brower Ave	Oaks	PA	19456	610-666-0500	666-7561
TF: 800-562-1000 ■ *Web:* www.pencoproducts.com					
Reconditioned Systems Inc (RSI)					
2636 S Wilson St Suite 105	Tempe	AZ	85282	480-968-1772	894-1907
TF: 800-280-5000 ■ *Web:* www.resy.net					
Robertson Furniture Co Inc 890 Elberton St	Toccoa	GA	30577	706-886-1494	886-8998
TF: 800-241-0713 ■ *Web:* www.robertson-furniture.com					
Rush Industries Inc 118 N Wrenn St	High Point	NC	27260	336-886-7700	886-2227
Web: www.rushfurniture.com					
Safco Products Co 9300 W Research Ctr Rd	New Hope	MN	55428	763-536-6700	536-6784
TF Cust Svc: 800-328-3020 ■ *Web:* www.safcoproducts.com					
Sedgewick Industries 667 W Ward Ave	High Point	NC	27260	336-885-9300	885-9174
TF: 888-882-8565 ■ *Web:* www.sedgewick.com					
Shafer Commercial Seating Inc 4101 E 48th Ave	Denver	CO	80216	303-322-7792	393-1836
Web: www.shafer.com					
Shure Mfg Corp 1901 W Main St	Washington	MO	63090	636-390-7100	390-7171
TF: 800-227-4873 ■ *Web:* www.shureusa.com					
Signore Inc 55-57 Jefferson St	Ellicottville	NY	14731	716-699-2361	699-8025
TF: 800-828-2808 ■ *Web:* www.signore.com					
Sligh Furniture Co 217 E 24th St Suite 102	Holland	MI	49423	616-392-7101	392-9495
TF: 866-277-0258 ■ *Web:* www.sligh.com					
Southwood Furniture Corp 2860 Nathan St	Hickory	NC	28602	828-465-1776	465-0858
TF: 800-345-1777 ■ *Web:* www.southwoodfurn.com					
Spectrum Industries Inc 925 1st Ave	Chippewa Falls	WI	54729	715-723-6750	335-0473*
**Fax Area Code:* 800 ■ *TF:* 800-235-1262 ■ *Web:* www.spectrumfurniture.com					
Statton Furniture Mfg Co Inc 504 E 1st St	Hagerstown	MD	21740	301-739-0360	739-8421
Web: www.statton.com					
Steelcase Inc 801 44th St SE PO Box 1967	Grand Rapids	MI	49501	616-247-2710	247-2256*
NYSE: SCS ■ **Fax:* Mail Rm ■ *TF:* 888-783-3522 ■ *Web:* www.steelcase.com					
Stevens Industries Inc 704 W Main St	Teutopolis	IL	62467	217-857-6411	540-3101
Web: www.stevensind.com					
Studios Q Furniture 3060 Main Ave SE	Hickory	NC	28602	828-322-1794	322-8462
TF: 800-356-5732 ■ *Web:* www.studioqfurniture.com					
Stylex Inc 740 Coopertown Rd	Delanco	NJ	08075	856-461-5600	461-5574
TF: 800-257-5742 ■ *Web:* www.stylexseating.com					

			Phone	Fax
TAB Products Co 605 4th St....Mayville TF: 888-822-9777 ■ Web: www.tab.com	WI	53050	920-387-3131	387-1805
Taylor Cos 1 Taylor Pkwy....Bedford TF: 888-758-2956 ■ Web: www.thetaylorcompanies.com	OH	44146	440-232-0700	439-6720
Techline USA LLC 500 S Division St....Waunakee TF: 800-356-8400 ■ Web: www.techlineusa.com	WI	53597	608-849-4181	850-2379
Teknion Corp 1150 Flint Rd....Toronto Web: www.teknion.com	ON	M3J2J5	416-661-3370	661-4586
Tennsco Corp 201 Tennsco Dr PO Box 1888....Dickson *Fax Area Code: 800 ■ TF Cust Svc: 866-446-8686 ■ Web: www.tennsco.com	TN	37056	615-446-8000	722-0134*
Trendway Corp 13467 Quincy St PO Box 9016....Holland TF: 800-968-5344 ■ Web: www.trendway.com	MI	49422	616-399-3900	399-2231
Tuohy Furniture Corp 42 St Albans Pl....Chatfield TF Cust Svc: 800-533-1696 ■ Web: www.tuohyfurniture.com	MN	55923	507-867-4280	867-3374
Turnbull Enterprises Inc 3100 Viona Ave....Baltimore Web: www.turnbullenterprises.com	MD	21230	410-789-1700	789-1706
Ulrich Planfiling Equipment Corp 2120 4th Ave PO Box 135....Lakewood TF: 800-346-2875 ■ Web: www.ulrichcorp.com	NY	14750	716-763-1815	763-1818
United Chair Co 147 St-Pierre St....Sainte-Pie *Fax Area Code: 888 ■ TF: 888-522-2773 ■ Web: www.unitedchair.com	QC	J0H1W0	450-772-2495	248-1865*
Van San Corp 16735 E Johnson Dr....City of Industry TF: 800-423-1829 ■ Web: www.vansan.com	CA	91745	626-961-7211	369-9510
Viking Acoustical Corp 21480 Heath Ave....Lakeville TF: 800-328-8385 ■ Web: www.vikingusa.com	MN	55044	952-469-3405	469-4503
Vitro Seating Products Inc 201 Madison St....Saint Louis TF Cust Svc: 800-325-7093 ■ Web: www.vitroseating.com	MO	63102	314-241-2265	241-8723
Watson Furniture Group Inc 26246 Twelve Trees Ln NW....Poulsbo TF: 800-426-1202 ■ Web: www.watsonfurniture.com	WA	98370	360-394-1300	
West Coast Industries Inc 10 Jackson St....San Francisco TF: 800-243-3150 ■ Web: www.westcoastindustries.com	CA	94111	415-621-6656	552-5368
Whitehall Furniture 201 E Martin St....Orleans *Fax Area Code: 800 ■ TF: 800-467-3585 ■ Web: www.wfi.com	IN	47452	812-865-3898	888-5817*
Woodland Products Co Inc 1480 E Grand Ave....Pomona	CA	91766	909-622-3456	622-2042
Workdeck Furniture 4990 W Greenbrooke SE....Kentwood Web: www.workdeckfurniture.com	MI	49512	616-698-2664	698-2665
Workplace Systems Inc 562 Mammoth Rd....Londonderry TF: 800-258-9700 ■ Web: www.workplacesystemsinc.com	NH	03053	603-622-3727	622-0174
Workspaces Inc 14311 SE 77th Ct....Newcastle TF: 800-466-4123 ■ Web: www.workspaces.com	WA	98059	425-226-4398	226-9468
Wright Line LLC 160 Gold Star Blvd....Worcester TF: 800-225-7348 ■ Web: www.wrightline.com	MA	01606	508-852-4300	853-8904

322-2 Household Furniture

			Phone	Fax
Aaron Rents Inc Woodhaven Furniture Industries Div 309 E Paces Ferry Rd NE....Atlanta Web: www.aaronrents.com	GA	30305	866-352-4927	
Acacia Home & Garden Inc 101 McLin Creek Rd N PO Box 426....Conover Web: www.acaciahomeandgarden.com	NC	28613	828-465-1700	465-4205
Advantage Furniture Hwy 145 S PO Box 369....Nettleton Web: www.advantagefurniture.com	MS	38858	662-895-3800	963-0574
Alan White Co 1122 E Antigo St....Stamps Web: www.alanwhiteco.com	AR	71860	870-533-4471	533-8858
Albany Industries Inc 504 N Glenfield Rd....New Albany Web: www.albanyindustries.com	MS	38652	662-534-9800	534-9805
American Drew 4620 Grandover Pkwy....Greensboro TF: 800-933-0243 ■ Web: www.americandrew.com	NC	27417	336-294-5233	315-4391
Ameriwood Industries Inc 410 E S 1st St....Wright City TF: 800-454-0283 ■ Web: www.ameriwood.com	MO	63390	636-745-3351	745-1007
Ashley Furniture Industries Inc 1 Ashley Way....Arcadia TF: 800-477-2222 ■ Web: www.ashleyfurniture.com	WI	54612	608-323-3377	323-6008
Baby's Dream Furniture Inc 411 Industrial Blvd PO Box 579....Buena Vista TF: 800-835-2742 ■ Web: www.babysdream.com	GA	31803	229-649-4404	649-2007
Baker Furniture 1661 Monroe Ave NW....Grand Rapids *Fax: Acctg ■ TF: 800-592-2537 ■ Web: www.kohlerinteriors.com	MI	49505	616-361-7321	361-7067*
Bassett Furniture Industries Inc 3525 Fairystone Pk Hwy....Bassett NASDAQ: BSET ■ Web: www.bassettfurniture.com	VA	24055	276-629-6000	629-6346
Bauhaus USA Inc 1 Bauhaus Dr....Saltillo Web: www.bauhaususa.com	MS	38866	662-869-2664	869-5910
Bellini 495 Central Ave....Scarsdale Web: www.bellini.com	NY	10583	914-472-7336	
Berg Furniture Inc 120 E Gloucester Pike....Barrington Web: www.bergfurniture.com	NJ	08007	856-310-0511	310-0512
Berkline BenchCraft LLC 1 Berkline Dr....Morristown Web: www.berkline.com	TN	37814	423-585-1500	585-1760
Best Home Furnishings Inc 1 Best Dr....Ferdinand Web: www.besthf.com	IN	47532	812-367-1761	367-2345
Bielecky Bros Inc 979 Third Ave....New York Web: www.bieleckybrothers.com	NY	10022	212-753-2355	751-9369
Bradington-Young 920 E 1st St....Cherryville Web: www.bradington-young.com	NC	28021	704-435-5881	435-4276
Brooks Furniture Mfg Inc 110 Maples Ln....Tazewell TF: 800-427-6657	TN	37879	423-626-1111	626-8346
Broyhill Furniture Industries Inc 1 Broyhill Pk....Lenoir *Fax: Sales ■ TF Cust Svc: 800-327-6944 ■ Web: www.broyhillfurn.com	NC	28633	828-758-3111	758-3538*
Brueton Industries Inc 146 Hanse Ave....Freeport TF Cust Svc: 800-221-6783 ■ Web: www.brueton.com	NY	11520	516-379-3400	543-4520
Bush Industries Inc 1 Mason Dr....Jamestown TF: 800-228-2874 ■ Web: www.bushfurniture.com	NY	14701	716-665-2000	665-2074
Bushline Inc 707 Industrial Pk Dr....New Tazewell TF: 800-627-1682 ■ Web: www.bushline.com	TN	37825	423-626-5246	626-7237
Canadel Furniture Inc 700 Canadel Ave....Louiseville Web: www.canadel.com	QC	J5V2L6	819-228-8471	228-8389
Capris Furniture Industries Inc 1401 NW 27th Ave....Ocala *Fax Area Code: 800 ■ Web: www.caprisfurniture.com	FL	34475	352-629-8889	226-0765*
Carson's Inc 4299 Cheyenne Dr PO Box 14186....Archdale Web: www.carsonsofhp.com	NC	27263	336-431-1101	431-0677
Century Furniture LLC 401 11th St NW....Hickory Web: www.centuryfurniture.com	NC	28601	828-328-1851	328-2176
Charles Inc 600 N 10th St....Council Bluffs TF: 800-831-5878 ■ Web: www.charlesfurniture.com	IA	51503	712-328-2603	328-8270
Charles Schneider Furniture 518 N 10th St....Council Bluffs TF: 800-831-5878 ■ Web: charlesfurniture.com/cschneider	IA	51503	712-328-1587	328-8270
Chromcraft Revington Inc 1330 Win Hentschel Blvd....West Lafayette AMEX: CRC ■ Web: www.chromcraft-revington.com	IN	47906	765-807-2640	807-2660
Classic Leather Inc 203 Simpson St....Conover Web: www.classic-leather.com	NC	28613	828-328-2046	324-6212
Clayton Marcus Co Inc 166 Teague Town Rd....Hickory Web: www.claytonmarcus.com	NC	28601	828-495-2200	495-2260
Cochrane Furniture Co 190 Cochrane Rd....Lincolnton *Fax Area Code: 800 ■ Web: www.cochrane-furniture.com	NC	28092	704-732-1151	752-6109*
Conleasco Inc 13150 1st St PO Box 367....Becker TF: 800-261-4188 ■ Web: www.beckerfurnitureworld.com	MN	55308	763-262-9000	262-9114
Conover Chair Co Inc 210 4th St SW....Conover	NC	28613	828-464-0251	464-0251
Councill Cos LLC 267 Councill Access Rd....Denton Web: www.councill.com	NC	27239	336-859-2155	859-5284
Craftmaster Furniture Corp 221 Craftmaster Rd....Hiddenite Web: www.cmfurniture.com	NC	28636	828-632-9786	632-0301
Crawford Furniture Mfg Corp 1021 Allen St Ext....Jamestown TF: 800-325-7368 ■ Web: www.crawfordfurniture.com	NY	14701	716-661-9100	483-2634
Cresent Mfg Co 350 Maple St....Gallatin Web: www.cresent.com	TN	37066	615-452-1671	451-0332
DeFehr Furniture Ltd 125 Furniture Pk....Winnipeg TF: 877-333-3471 ■ Web: www.defehr.com	MB	R2G1B9	204-988-5630	663-4458
DMI Furniture Inc 9780 Ormsby Stn Rd Suite 2000....Louisville *Fax Area Code: 800 ■ TF: 888-372-1927 ■ Web: www.dmifurniture.com	KY	40223	502-426-4351	755-2878*
Dorel Industries Inc 1255 Greene Ave Suite 300....Montreal PINK: DIIBF ■ Web: www.dorel.com	QC	H3Z2A4	514-934-3034	934-9379
Drexel Heritage Furnishings Inc 1925 Eastchester Dr....High Point TF: 866-450-3434 ■ Web: www.drexelheritage.com	NC	27265	336-888-4800	888-4815
Durham Furniture Inc 450 Lambton St W....Durham Web: www.durhamfurniture.com	ON	N0G1R0	519-369-2345	369-6515
Dutailier Group Inc 299 Rue Chaput....Sainte-Pie TF: 800-363-9817 ■ Web: www.dutailier.com	QC	J0H1W0	450-772-2403	772-5055
Eagle Industries LLC 601 Double Springs Rd....Bowling Green TF Cust Svc: 888-809-4700 ■ Web: www.eagle-ind.com	KY	42102	270-843-3363	843-3609
El Ran Furniture Ltd 2751 Transcanada Hwy....Pointe-Claire TF: 800-361-6546 ■ Web: www.elran.com	QC	H9R1B4	514-630-5656	630-9150
Elegant Bebe 1430 W Pine Lake....Montgomery *Fax Area Code: 713 ■ TF: 888-886-8307 ■ Web: www.elegantbebe.com	TX	77316	281-584-0190	416-7923*
Elliott's Designs Inc 2473 E Rancho Del Amo Pl....Rancho Dominguez TF: 800-435-5468 ■ Web: www.elliottsdesigns.com	CA	90220	310-631-4931	631-4531
Ello Furniture Mfg Co 1350 Preston St....Rockford Web: www.ellofurniture.com	IL	61102	815-964-8601	964-9985
Entourage LA 100 Wilshire Blvd Suite 800....Santa Monica Web: www.entouragela.com	CA	90401	310-656-0499	656-0269
Ethan Allen Interiors Inc Ethan Allen Dr....Danbury NYSE: ETH ■ Web: www.ethanallen.com	CT	06811	203-743-8000	743-8298
Evenflo Co Inc 1801 Commerce Dr....Piqua *Fax: Hum Res ■ TF: 800-233-5921 ■ Web: www.evenflo.com	OH	45356	937-415-3300	415-3112*
Fairfield Chair Co 1331 Harper Ave SW....Lenoir Web: www.fairfieldchair.com	NC	28645	828-758-5571	758-0211
Ficks Reed Co 6245 Creek Rd....Cincinnati Web: www.ficksreed.com	OH	45242	513-985-0606	985-9293
Finnleo Sauna 575 Cokato St E....Cokato *Fax Area Code: 320 ■ TF: 800-346-6536 ■ Web: www.finnleo.com	MN	55321	800-346-6536	286-2224*
Flexsteel Industries Inc 3400 Jackson St....Dubuque NASDAQ: FLXS ■ *Fax: Cust Svc ■ Web: www.flexsteel.com	IA	52001	563-556-7730	556-8345*
Founders Furniture Rt 460 E....Appomattox *Fax: Cust Svc ■ TF: 800-548-7704 ■ Web: www.foundersfurniture.com	VA	24522	434-352-7181	352-8726*
Fraenkel Co Inc PO Box 15385....Baton Rouge TF: 800-847-2580 ■ Web: www.fraenkel.com	LA	70895	225-275-4242	272-7319
Franklin Corp 600 Franklin Dr....Houston Web: www.franklincorp.com	MS	38851	662-456-4286	456-3156
Furniture Brands International Inc 1 N Brentwood Blvd 15th Fl....Saint Louis NYSE: FBN ■ TF: 866-873-3667 ■ Web: www.furniturebrands.com	MO	63105	314-863-1100	863-5306
Furniture Values International LLC 2929 NW Grand Ave 601 N 75 Th Ave....Phoenix TF Cust Svc: 888-484-5874	AZ	85043	602-233-0224	269-6810
Hammary Furniture Co 2464 Norwood St SW....Lenoir *Fax Area Code: 800 ■ TF: 800-362-3387 ■ Web: www.hammary.com	NC	28645	828-728-3231	443-2920*
Hancock & Moore Inc 166 Hancock & Moore Ln....Hickory Web: www.hancockandmoore.com	NC	28601	828-495-8235	495-3021
Harden Furniture Inc 8550 Mill Pond Way....McConnellsville Web: www.hardenfurniture.com	NY	13401	315-245-1000	245-2884
Hekman 860 E Main Ave....Zeeland TF: 800-253-9249 ■ Web: www.hekman.com	MI	49464	616-748-2660	748-2645
Henkel Harris Co Inc 2983 S Pleasant Valley Rd PO Box 2170....Winchester Web: www.henkelharris.com	VA	22601	540-667-4900	667-8261

Company / Address	City	State	Zip	Phone	Fax
Henredon Furniture Industries Inc 400 Henredon Rd	Morganton	NC	28655	828-437-5261	437-5264
TF: 800-444-3682 ■ *Web:* www.henredon.com					
Hickory Chair Co 37 9th St Pl SE	Hickory	NC	28602	828-328-1801	328-8954
TF: 800-349-4579 ■ *Web:* www.hickorychair.com					
Hickory White Co 856 7th Ave SE	Hickory	NC	28602	828-322-8624	322-3942
Web: www.hickorywhite.com					
Hooker Furniture Corp 440 E Commonwealth Blvd	Martinsville	VA	24112	276-632-0459	388-2289*
NASDAQ: HOFT ■ **Fax Area Code:* 800 ■ **Fax:* Cust Svc ■ *TF Cust Svc:* 888-462-6877 ■ *Web:* www.hookerfurniture.com					
Hughes Furniture Industries Inc 952 S Stout Rd	Randleman	NC	27317	336-498-8700	498-8750
Web: www.hughesfurniture.com					
Interactive Health Inc 3030 Walnut Ave	Long Beach	CA	90807	562-426-8700	426-9690
TF: 800-742-5493 ■ *Web:* www.interhealth.com					
Interior Crafts Inc 2513 W Cullerton Ave	Chicago	IL	60608	773-376-8160	376-9578
J-Art Iron Co 9435 Jefferson Blvd	Culver City	CA	90232	310-202-1126	202-1642
Web: www.jartiron.com					
Jackson Furniture Industries Inc 1910 King Edward Ave	Cleveland	TN	37311	423-476-8544	961-7343
Web: www.catnapper.com					
Jensen Industries Inc 1946 E 46th St	Los Angeles	CA	90058	323-235-6800	235-6878
TF: 800-325-8351					
Johnston Tombigbee Furniture Mfg Co 1402 Waterworks Rd PO Box 2128	Columbus	MS	39704	662-328-1685	327-1814
TF: 800-654-3876 ■ *Web:* www.jtbfurniture.com					
Kessler Industries 8600 Gateway Blvd E	El Paso	TX	79907	915-591-8161	598-7353
Web: www.kesslerind.com					
KidsChairs Inc 1364 London Bridge Rd Suite 101	Virginia Beach	VA	23453	757-301-7464	301-7551
Web: www.kidschairs.com					
Kimball Home Furniture 1600 Royal St	Jasper	IN	47549	812-482-1600	482-8012*
**Fax:* Cust Svc ■ *TF:* 800-482-1616 ■ *Web:* www.kimball.com					
Kincaid Furniture Co Inc 240 Pleasant Hill Rd	Hudson	NC	28638	828-728-3261	728-0223
TF: 800-438-8207 ■ *Web:* www.kincaidfurniture.com					
Kindel Furniture Co 100 Garden St SE	Grand Rapids	MI	49507	616-243-3676	243-6248
Web: www.kindelfurniture.com					
King Hickory Furniture Co 1820 Main Ave SE	Hickory	NC	28601	828-322-6025	328-2159
Web: www.kinghickory.com					
Klaussner Furniture Industries Inc 405 Lewallen Rd	Asheboro	NC	27205	336-625-6174	626-0905
TF Cust Svc: 800-828-9534 ■ *Web:* www.klaussner.com					
La-Z-Boy Inc 1284 N Telegraph Rd	Monroe	MI	48162	734-242-1444	457-2005*
NYSE: LZB ■ **Fax:* Sales ■ *TF:* 800-375-6890 ■ *Web:* www.la-z-boy.com					
Lamont Ltd 1530 Bluff Rd	Burlington	IA	52601	319-753-5131	753-0946
TF: 800-553-5621 ■ *Web:* www.lamontlimited.com					
Lane Furniture Industries Inc Hwy 145 S PO Box 1627	Tupelo	MS	38802	662-566-7211	566-3474
TF: 800-467-9555 ■ *Web:* www.lanefurniture.com					
Lea Industries Inc 4620 Grandover Pkwy	Greensboro	NC	27417	336-294-5233	315-4391
TF: 888-299-5619 ■ *Web:* www.leaindustries.com					
Leathercraft 102 Section House Rd	Hickory	NC	28601	800-627-1561	627-1562
TF: 800-627-1561 ■ *Web:* www.leathercraft-furniture.com					
Lexington Home Brands 1300 National Hwy	Thomasville	NC	27360	336-474-5300	474-5506
TF: 800-539-4636 ■ *Web:* www.lexington.com					
Little Tikes Co The 2180 Barlow Rd	Hudson	OH	44236	330-650-3000	
TF Cust Svc: 800-321-0183 ■ *Web:* www.littletikes.com					
Mantua Mfg Co 7900 Northfield Rd	Walton Hills	OH	44146	800-333-8333	929-8014
TF Orders: 800-333-8333 ■ *Web:* www.bedframes.com					
Marge Carson Inc 9056 Garvey Ave	Rosemead	CA	91770	626-571-1111	571-0924
Web: www.margecarson.com					
McGuire Furniture Co 1201 Bryant St	San Francisco	CA	94103	415-626-1414	864-8593
TF: 800-662-4847 ■ *Web:* www.mcguirefurniture.com					
Michael Thomas Furniture Inc 100 E Newberry St	Liberty	NC	27298	336-622-3075	622-4112
Web: www.michaelthomasfurniture.com					
Million Dollar Baby 841 Washington Blvd	Montebello	CA	90640	323-728-8988	722-8866
Web: www.milliondollarbaby.com					
Mitchell Gold & Bob Williams Co (MGBW) 135 One Comfortable Pl	Taylorsville	NC	28681	828-632-9200	632-2693
TF: 800-789-5401 ■ *Web:* www.mgbwhome.com					
New England Woodcraft Inc PO Box 165	Forest Dale	VT	05745	802-247-8211	247-8042
Web: www.newoodcraft.com					
Nichols & Stone 1 Stickley Dr PO Box 480	Manlius	NY	13104	315-682-1554	
Web: www.nichols-stone.com					
Norwalk Furniture Corp 100 Furniture Pkwy	Norwalk	OH	44857	419-744-3200	668-6223
TF Orders: 800-837-2565 ■ *Web:* www.norwalkfurniture.com					
Orleans Furniture Inc 1481 N Main St	Columbia	MS	39429	601-736-9002	731-2823
Web: www.orleansfurniture.com					
Pearson Co 1420 Progress Ave	High Point	NC	27260	336-882-8135	885-5508
Web: www.pearsoncompany.com					
Pennsylvania House Co 166 Teague Town Rd	Hickory	NC	28601	828-495-2200	456-2788*
**Fax Area Code:* 800 ■ *TF:* 800-782-9663 ■ *Web:* www.pennsylvaniahouse.com					
Perdue Woodworks Inc 2415 Creek Dr	Rapid City	SD	57703	605-341-2101	341-1565
Web: www.perduesinc.com					
Progressive Furniture Inc 502 Middle St PO Box 308	Archbold	OH	43502	419-446-4500	446-4550
Web: www.progressivefurniture.com					
Pulaski Furniture Corp 1 Pulaski Sq	Pulaski	VA	24301	540-980-7330	994-5468
Web: www.pulaskifurniture.com					
Realistic Furniture Industries 405 Lewallen Rd	Asheboro	NC	27205	336-625-6174	626-0905
TF: 800-828-9534 ■ *Web:* www.klaussnerfurnitures.com					
Richardson Bros Co 904 Monroe St	Sheboygan Falls	WI	53085	920-467-4631	467-2222*
**Fax:* Cust Svc ■ *TF:* 800-242-7676 ■ *Web:* www.richardsonindustries.com					
Riverside Furniture Corp 1400 S 6th St	Fort Smith	AR	72902	479-785-8100	785-8149
Web: www.riverside-furniture.com					
Robern Inc 701 N Wilson Ave	Bristol	PA	19007	215-826-9800	826-9633
TF: 800-877-2376 ■ *Web:* www.robern.com					
Rochelle Furniture PO Box 649	Ludington	MI	49431	800-223-6047	843-9276*
**Fax Area Code:* 231 ■ *TF:* 800-223-6047 ■ *Web:* www.rochellefurniture.com					
Room & Board Inc 4600 Olson Memorial Hwy	Minneapolis	MN	55422	763-287-7135	520-0811
Web: www.roomandboard.com					
Roomstore Inc 12501 Patterson Ave	Richmond	VA	23238	804-784-7600	784-7653
OTC: ROOM ■ *Web:* www.roomstore.com					
Rowe Fine Furniture Inc 8300 Greensboro Dr Suite 425	McLean	VA	22102	703-847-8670	847-8686
TF: 800-334-7693 ■ *Web:* www.rowefurniture.com					
RT Mfg 232 S 1250 W	Lindon	UT	84042	801-609-8168	796-2688
TF: 855-228-8388 ■ *Web:* www.rumbletuff.com					
Rush Industries Inc 118 N Wrenn St	High Point	NC	27260	336-886-7700	886-2227
Web: www.rushfurniture.com					
Sam Moore Furniture Industries 1556 Dawn Dr	Bedford	VA	24523	540-586-8253	586-8497
Web: www.sammoore.com					
Sandberg Furniture Mfg Co Inc PO Box 58291	Los Angeles	CA	90058	323-582-0711	589-5507
Web: www.sandbergfurniture.com					
Sauder Woodworking Co 502 Middle St PO Box 156	Archbold	OH	43502	419-446-2711	446-3692
TF Cust Svc: 800-523-3987 ■ *Web:* www.sauder.com					
Schnadig Corp 1111 E Touhy Ave Suite 500	Des Plaines	IL	60018	847-803-6000	803-6050
TF: 800-468-8730 ■ *Web:* www.schnadig.com					
Shermag Inc 2171 King St W	Sherbrooke	QC	J1J2G1	819-566-1515	566-8985
TF Sales: 800-363-2635 ■ *Web:* www.shermag.com					
Sherrill Furniture Co 2405 Highland Ave NE	Hickory	NC	28601	828-322-2640	324-8207
Web: www.sherrillfurniture.com					
Sico North America Inc 7525 Cahill Rd	Minneapolis	MN	55439	952-941-1700	941-6737
TF: 800-328-6138 ■ *Web:* www.sicoinc.com					
Sligh Furniture Co 217 E 24th St Suite 102	Holland	MI	49423	616-392-7101	392-9495
TF: 866-277-0258 ■ *Web:* www.sligh.com					
Southern Motion Inc PO Box 1064	Pontotoc	MS	38863	662-488-4007	488-4008
Web: www.southernmotion.com					
Southwood Furniture Corp 2860 Nathan St	Hickory	NC	28602	828-465-1776	465-0858
TF: 800-345-1777 ■ *Web:* www.southwoodfurn.com					
Standard Furniture Mfg Co Inc 801 Hwy 31 S	Bay Minette	AL	36507	251-937-6741	520-7667*
**Fax Area Code:* 800 ■ **Fax:* Cust Svc ■ *TF:* 800-827-7866 ■ *Web:* www.standard-furniture.com					
Stanley Furniture Co Inc 1641 Fairystone Pk Hwy	Stanleytown	VA	24168	276-627-2000	629-4334
NASDAQ: STLY ■ *Web:* www.stanleyfurniture.com					
Statton Furniture Mfg Co Inc 504 E 1st St	Hagerstown	MD	21740	301-739-0360	739-8421
Web: www.statton.com					
Storkcraft Baby 7433 Nelson Rd	Richmond	BC	V6W1G3	604-274-5121	274-9727
TF: 877-274-0277 ■ *Web:* www.storkcraftdirect.com					
Style Line Furniture Inc 116 Godfrey Rd	Verona	MS	38879	662-566-1113	566-7657
Suncast Corp 701 N Kirk Rd	Batavia	IL	60510	630-879-2050	879-6112
TF: 800-444-3310 ■ *Web:* suncast.com					
Swaim Inc 1801 S College Dr	High Point	NC	27260	336-885-6131	885-6227
Web: www.swaim-inc.com					
Techline USA LLC 500 S Division St	Waunakee	WI	53597	608-849-4181	850-2379
TF: 800-356-8400 ■ *Web:* www.techlineusa.com					
Thomasville Furniture Industries Inc 401 E Main St PO Box 339	Thomasville	NC	27361	336-472-4000	472-4085
Web: www.thomasville.com					
Vanguard Furniture Co Inc 109 Simpson St	Conover	NC	28613	828-328-5601	
TF: 800-968-1702 ■ *Web:* www.vanguardfurniture.com					
Vaughan Furniture Co Inc PO Box 1489	Galax	VA	24333	276-236-6111	238-3238
Web: www.vaughanfurniture.com					
Vermont Tubbs 1 Tubbs Ave	Brandon	VT	05733	802-247-3414	247-6395
TF: 800-327-7026 ■ *Web:* www.vermonttubbs.com					
Walter E Smithe Furniture Inc 1251 W Thorndale Ave	Itasca	IL	60143	630-285-8000	285-8022
TF: 800-948-4263 ■ *Web:* www.smithe.com					
Webb Furniture Enterprises Inc PO Box 1277	Galax	VA	24333	276-236-2984	236-2899
Whitecraft Inc 1025 S Federal Hwy	Dania	FL	33004	954-927-0237	
Web: www.whitecraftinc.net					
Whittier Wood Products 3787 W 1st Ave PO Box 2827	Eugene	OR	97402	541-687-0213	687-2060
TF: 800-653-3336 ■ *Web:* www.whittierwood.com					
Winners Only Inc 1365 Pk Ctr Dr	Vista	CA	92081	760-599-0300	597-0899
Web: www.winnersonly.com					
Woodland Furniture LLC 4475 S 15th W	Idaho Falls	ID	83402	208-523-9006	523-9194
Web: www.woodlandfurniture.com					
Zenith Products Corp 400 Lukens Dr	New Castle	DE	19720	800-892-3986	326-8400*
**Fax Area Code:* 302 ■ **Fax:* Cust Svc ■ *TF:* 800-892-3986 ■ *Web:* www.zenith-interiors.com					

322-3 Institutional & Other Public Buildings Furniture

Company / Address	City	State	Zip	Phone	Fax
A. C. Furniture Co Inc PO Box 200	Axton	VA	24054	276-650-3356	650-3747
Web: www.acfurniture.com					
Achieva Inc 197 Funder Dr PO Box 729	Mocksville	NC	27028	336-751-3501	751-5623
TF: 800-788-7213 ■ *Web:* www.achievaweb.com					
Adden Furniture Inc 710 Chelmsford St	Lowell	MA	01851	978-454-7848	453-1449
TF: 800-625-3876 ■ *Web:* www.addenfurniture.com					
American Desk 1302 Industrial Blvd	Temple	TX	76504	254-899-3621	773-7370
TF: 800-433-3142 ■ *Web:* www.amdesk.com					
American of Martinsville 128 E Church St	Martinsville	VA	24112	276-632-2061	638-8810
Web: www.americanofmartinsville.com					
American Seating Co 401 American Seating Ctr NW	Grand Rapids	MI	49504	616-732-6600	732-6401
TF Cust Svc: 800-748-0268 ■ *Web:* www.americanseating.com					
Artco-Bell Corp 1302 Industrial Blvd	Temple	TX	76504	254-899-3621	773-7370
TF: 800-433-3142 ■ *Web:* www.artcobell.com					
Bay Concepts Inc (BCI) 1036-47th Ave PO Box 7229	Oakland	CA	94601	510-534-4511	534-4515
TF: 888-534-4511 ■ *Web:* www.bayconcepts.com					
Bretford Mfg Inc 11000 Seymour Ave	Franklin Park	IL	60131	847-678-2545	343-1779*
**Fax Area Code:* 800 ■ *TF:* 800-521-9614 ■ *Web:* www.bretford.com					
Brice Mfg Co Inc 10262 Norris Ave	Pacoima	CA	91331	818-896-2938	897-3748
Web: www.timco.aero					
Brodart Co 500 Arch St	Williamsport	PA	17701	570-326-2461	326-6769
TF: 800-233-8467 ■ *Web:* www.brodart.com					

Company	City	State	Zip	Phone	Fax
Buckstaff Co 1127 S Main St TF: 800-755-5890 ■ Web: www.buckstaff.com	Oshkosh	WI	54902	920-235-5890	235-2018
Columbia Mfg Inc 1 Cycle St Web: www.columbiamfginc.com	Westfield	MA	01085	413-562-3664	568-5345
Conleasco Inc 13150 1st St PO Box 367 TF: 800-261-4188 ■ Web: www.beckerfurnitureworld.com	Becker	MN	55308	763-262-9000	262-9114
Enochs Medical Furniture Inc 3950 Priority Way S Dr # 116 TF: 800-428-2305 ■ Web: www.enochsmed.com	Indianapolis	IN	46240	317-580-2940	580-2944
ErgoGenesis LLC 1 BodyBilt Pl TF: 800-364-5299 ■ Web: www.ergogenesis.com	Navasota	TX	77868	936-825-1700	825-1725
Fetzers' Inc 6223 W Double Eagle Cir Web: www.fetzersinc.com	Salt Lake City	UT	84118	801-484-6103	484-6122
Fleetwood Group Inc 11832 James St TF: 800-257-6390 ■ Web: www.fleetwoodgroup.com	Holland	MI	49424	616-396-1142	396-8022
Fordham Equipment Co 3308 Edson Ave TF: 800-249-5922	Bronx	NY	10469	718-379-7300	379-7312
Furniture by Thurston 12250 Charles Dr Web: www.furniturebythurston.com	Grass Valley	CA	95945	530-272-4331	272-4962
Gaylord Bros 7282 William Barry Blvd TF: 800-634-6304 ■ Web: www.gaylord.com	Syracuse	NY	13212	315-457-5070	457-8387
Gunlocke Co LLC 1 Gunlocke Dr *Fax: Hum Res ■ TF Cust Svc: 800-828-6300 ■ Web: www.gunlocke.com	Wayland	NY	14572	585-728-5111	728-8334*
Hard Mfg Co Inc 230 Grider St TF: 800-873-4273 ■ Web: www.hardmfg.com	Buffalo	NY	14215	716-893-1800	896-2579
Herman Miller for Health Care 855 E Main Ave PO Box 302 TF: 888-443-4357 ■ Web: www.hermanmiller.com/healthcare	Zeeland	MI	49464	616-654-3000	
Hill-Rom Services Inc 1069 SR 46 E *Fax: Hum Res ■ Web: www.hill-rom.com	Batesville	IN	47006	812-934-7777	931-3592*
Hussey Seating Co 38 Dyer St Ext *Fax: Sales ■ TF: 800-341-0401 ■ Web: www.husseyseating.com	North Berwick	ME	03906	207-676-2271	676-0257*
Imperial Woodworks Inc 7201 Mars Dr PO Box 7835 *Fax Area Code: 254 ■ TF: 800-234-6624 ■ Web: www.pews.com	Waco	TX	76714	800-234-6624	741-0736*
Interkal Inc 5981 E Cork St Web: www.interkal.com	Kalamazoo	MI	49048	269-349-1521	349-6530
Inwood Office Invironments 1108 E 15th St PO Box 646 TF: 800-786-6121 ■ Web: www.inwood.net	Jasper	IN	47546	812-482-6121	482-9732
Irwin Seating Co Inc 3251 Fruit Ridge NW PO Box 2429 *Fax: Sales ■ TF: 800-759-7328 ■ Web: www.irwinseating.com	Grand Rapids	MI	49544	616-574-7400	574-7411*
Kimball Hospitality 1180 E 16th St TF: 800-634-9510 ■ Web: www.kimballhospitality.com	Jasper	IN	47549	812-482-1600	634-4324
KLN Steel Products Co 2 Winnco Dr TF: 800-624-9101 ■ Web: www.kln.com	San Antonio	TX	78218	210-227-4747	227-4047
LB Furniture Industries LLC 99 S 3rd St TF: 800-403-0833 ■ Web: www.lbempire.com	Hudson	NY	12534	518-828-1501	828-3219
List Industries Inc 401 Jim Moran Blvd TF: 800-776-1342 ■ Web: www.listindustries.com	Deerfield Beach	FL	33442	954-429-9155	428-3843
Luxor Div EBSCO Industries Inc 2245 Delany Rd *Fax Area Code: 800 ■ TF: 800-323-4656 ■ Web: www.luxorfurn.com	Waukegan	IL	60087	847-244-1800	327-1698*
Mastercraft Specialties Inc 800 Maple St TF: 866-521-1816 ■ Web: www.mastercraftspecialties.com	York	PA	17356	717-244-8508	244-9483
Meadows Office Furniture Co 71 W 23rd St Web: www.meadowsoffice.com	New York	NY	10010	212-741-0333	741-0303
Meco Corp 1500 Industrial Rd TF: 800-251-7558 ■ Web: www.meco.net	Greeneville	TN	37745	423-639-1171	639-1055
Midwest Folding Products Inc 1414 S Western Ave TF: 800-621-4716 ■ Web: www.midwestfolding.com	Chicago	IL	60608	312-666-3366	666-2606
Mitchell Furniture Systems Inc 1700 W St Paul Ave TF: 800-290-5960 ■ Web: www.mitchell-tables.com	Milwaukee	WI	53201	414-342-3111	342-4239
Mity-Lite Inc 1301 W 400 N NASDAQ: MITY ■ TF: 800-909-8034 ■ Web: www.mitylite.com	Orem	UT	84057	801-224-0589	224-6191
MLP Seating Corp 2125 Lively Blvd TF: 800-723-3030 ■ Web: www.mlpseating.com	Elk Grove Village	IL	60007	847-956-1700	956-1776
Monroe Table Co 316 N Walnut St TF: 800-247-2488	Colfax	IA	50054	515-674-3511	674-3513
Nemschoff Chairs Inc 909 N 8th St TF Cust Svc: 800-203-8916 ■ Web: www.nemschoff.com	Sheboygan	WI	53081	920-457-7726	459-1234
New Holland Church Furniture 313 Prospect St PO Box 217 TF: 800-648-9663 ■ Web: www.newhollandwood.com	New Holland	PA	17557	717-354-4521	354-2481
Omni International Inc 435 12th St SW PO Box 1409 TF: 800-844-6664 ■ Web: www.omniinternational.com	Vernon	AL	35592	205-695-9173	695-6465
Parisi Royal Inc 305 Pheasant Run Web: www.parisi-royal.com	Newtown	PA	18940	215-968-6677	968-3580
Royal Seating Ltd 1110 Industrial Blvd TF Cust Svc: 800-460-4916 ■ Web: www.royalseating.com	Cameron	TX	76520	254-605-5500	605-5517
Scholarcraft Inc PO Box 170748 TF Cust Svc: 888-765-5200 ■ Web: www.scholarcraft.com	Birmingham	AL	35217	205-841-1922	841-1992
Shelby Williams Industries Inc 150 Shelby Williams Dr TF: 800-732-8464 ■ Web: www.shelbywilliams.com	Morristown	TN	37813	423-586-7000	586-2260
Sico North America Inc 7525 Cahill Rd TF: 800-328-6138 ■ Web: www.sicoinc.com	Minneapolis	MN	55439	952-941-1700	941-6737
Spectrum Industries Inc 925 1st Ave *Fax Area Code: 800 ■ TF: 800-235-1262 ■ Web: www.spectrumfurniture.com	Chippewa Falls	WI	54729	715-723-6750	335-0473*
Sturdisteel Co 131 Ava Dr TF: 800-433-3116 ■ Web: www.sturdisteel.com	Hewitt	TX	76643	254-666-5155	666-4472
Sunrise Medical Continuing Care Group 5001 Joerns Dr TF: 800-972-7581	Stevens Point	WI	54481	715-341-3600	341-3962
Tesco Industries LP 1035 E Hacienda *Fax Area Code: 979 ■ TF: 800-699-5824 ■ Web: www.tesco-ind.com	Bellville	TX	77418	800-699-5824	865-9074*
Texwood Furniture Corp 1203 Industrial Blvd TF: 888-878-0000 ■ Web: www.texwood.com	Cameron	TX	76520	254-605-5500	605-5552
TMI Systems Design Corp 50 S 3rd Ave W TF: 800-456-6716 ■ Web: www.tmisystems.com	Dickinson	ND	58601	701-456-6716	456-6700
Trinity Furniture Mfg 2885 Lorraine Ave TF: 800-256-7397 ■ Web: www.pews.com	Temple	TX	76501	254-778-4727	773-0500
United Metal Fabricators Inc 1316 Eisenhower Blvd TF Sales: 800-638-5322 ■ Web: www.umf-exam.com	Johnstown	PA	15904	814-266-8726	266-1870
Valley City Mfg Co Ltd 64 Hatt St TF: 800-828-7628 ■ Web: www.valleycity.com	Dundas	ON	L9H2G3	905-628-2255	628-4470
Virco Mfg Corp 2027 Harpers Way AMEX: VIR ■ *Fax Area Code: 800 ■ TF Cust Svc: 800-448-4726 ■ Web: www.virco.com	Torrance	CA	90501	310-533-0474	258-7367*
Wieland 13737 Main St PO Box 1000 TF: 800-777-5055 ■ Web: www.wielandhealthcare.com	Grabill	IN	46741	260-627-3686	627-6496
Winco Inc 5516 SW 1st Ln TF: 800-237-3377 ■ Web: www.wincomfg.com	Ocala	FL	34474	352-854-2929	854-9544
Worden Co Inc 199 E 17th St TF: 800-748-0561 ■ Web: www.wordencompany.com	Holland	MI	49423	616-392-1848	392-2542

322-4 Outdoor Furniture

Company	City	State	Zip	Phone	Fax
Belson Outdoors Inc 111 N River Rd TF: 800-323-5664 ■ Web: www.belson.com	North Aurora	IL	60542	630-897-8489	897-0573
Bemis Mfg Co 300 Mill St TF: 800-558-7651 ■ Web: www.bemismfg.com	Sheboygan Falls	WI	53085	920-467-4621	467-8573
Brown Jordan Co 9860 Gidley St TF: 800-743-4252 ■ Web: www.brownjordan.com	El Monte	CA	91731	626-443-8971	575-0126
Brown Jordan International Inc 1801 N Andrews Ave Web: www.brownjordan.com	Pompano Beach	FL	33069	954-960-1117	960-1849
CFI Mfg Inc 2150 Whitfield Ave Web: www.cartergrandle.com	Sarasota	FL	34243	941-751-1000	755-0977
Cox Industries Inc 860 Cannon Bridge Rd PO Box 1124 TF: 800-476-4401 ■ Web: www.coxwood.com	Orangeburg	SC	29116	803-534-7467	534-1410
DuMor Inc 15 Industrial Cir TF: 800-598-4018 ■ Web: www.dumor.com	Mifflintown	PA	17059	717-436-2106	436-9839
Gardenside Ltd 999 Andersen Dr Suite 140 TF: 888-999-8325 ■ Web: www.gardenside.com	San Rafael	CA	94901	415-455-4500	455-4505
Hatteras Hammocks Inc 305 Industrial Blvd TF: 800-643-3522 ■ Web: www.hatterashammocks.com	Greenville	NC	27834	252-758-0641	758-0375
Hill Co 8615 Germantown Ave Web: www.hill-company.com	Philadelphia	PA	19118	215-247-7600	247-7603
Homecrest Industries Inc 1250 Homecrest Ave SE TF: 888-346-4852 ■ Web: www.homecrest.com	Wadena	MN	56482	218-631-1000	631-2609
J Robert Scott Inc 500 N Oak St TF: 877-207-5130 ■ Web: www.jrobertscott.com	Inglewood	CA	90302	310-680-4300	672-3710
Kay Park Recreation Corp 1301 Pine St *Fax: Cust Svc ■ TF Cust Svc: 800-553-2476 ■ Web: www.kaypark.com	Janesville	IA	50647	319-987-2313	987-2900*
Kessler Industries 8600 Gateway Blvd E Web: www.kesslerind.com	El Paso	TX	79907	915-591-8161	598-7353
Kingsley-Bate Ltd 7200 Gateway Ct Web: www.kingsleybate.com	Manassas	VA	20109	703-361-7000	361-7001
Lloyd/Flanders Industries Inc 3010 10th St TF: 800-526-9894 ■ Web: www.lloydflanders.com	Menominee	MI	49858	906-863-4491	863-6700
Mallin Casual Furniture 1 Minson Way TF: 800-251-6537 ■ Web: www.mallinfurniture.com	Montebello	CA	90640	323-513-1041	513-1047
Minson Corp 1 Minson Way TF: 800-251-6537 ■ Web: www.minson.com	Montebello	CA	90640	323-513-1041	513-1047
Moultrie Mfg Co 1403 Georgia Hwy 133 S PO Box 2948 TF: 800-841-8674 ■ Web: www.moultriemanufacturing.com	Moultrie	GA	31776	229-985-1312	890-7245
OW Lee Co Inc 1822 E Francis St TF: 800-776-9533 ■ Web: www.owlee.com	Ontario	CA	91761	909-947-3771	947-6614
Plantation Patterns Furniture Co 4241 12th Ave E Suite 600 *Fax Area Code: 952 ■ TF: 888-446-4766 ■ Web: www.plantationpatterns.com	Shakopee	MN	55379	888-446-4766	746-9579*
RIO Brands 10981 Decatur Rd Web: www.all-luminum.com	Philadelphia	PA	19154	215-632-2800	824-1172
RJ Thomas Mfg Co Inc PO Box 946 TF: 800-725-5115 ■ Web: www.pilotrock.com	Cherokee	IA	51012	712-225-5115	225-5796
Telescope Casual Furniture Inc 82 Church St Web: www.telescopecasual.com	Granville	NY	12832	518-642-1100	642-2536
Tropitone Furniture Co Inc 5 Marconi *Fax Area Code: 800 ■ *Fax: Cust Svc ■ TF Cust Svc: 800-654-7000 ■ Web: www.tropitone.com	Irvine	CA	92618	949-951-2010	972-5714*
Twin Oaks Hammocks 138 Twin Oaks Rd TF: 800-688-8946 ■ Web: www.twinoakstore.com	Louisa	VA	23093	540-894-5125	894-4112
Wabash Valley Mfg Inc 505 E Main St TF: 800-253-8619 ■ Web: www.wabashvalley.com	Silver Lake	IN	46982	260-352-2102	352-2160
Walpole Woodworkers Inc 767 E St PO Box 151 TF Cust Svc: 800-343-6948 ■ Web: www.walpolewoodworkers.com	Walpole	MA	02081	508-668-2800	668-7301
Winston Furniture 540 Dolphin Rd Web: www.winstonfurniture.com	Haleyville	AL	35565	205-486-9211	486-9349

323 FURNITURE - WHOL

Company	City	State	Zip	Phone	Fax
A Pomerantz & Co 9987 Bustleton Ave TF: 800-344-9135 ■ Web: www.pomerantz.com	Philadelphia	PA	19115	215-408-2100	408-2110
Adirondack Direct 3040 48th Ave TF: 800-221-2444 ■ Web: www.adirondackdirect.com	Long Island City	NY	11101	718-204-4500	204-4537
AFD Contract Furniture Inc 810 7th Ave # 2 Web: www.afd-inc.com	New York	NY	10019	212-721-7100	721-7175
Amini Innovation Corp 8725 Rex Rd Web: www.amini.com	Pico Rivera	CA	90660	562-222-2500	222-2525
Angel Line 88 Industrial Pk Rd Web: www.angelline.com	Pennsville	NJ	08070	856-678-6300	678-6328

				Phone	Fax
ATD-American Co 135 Greenwood Ave	Wyncote	PA	19095	215-576-1380	523-2300*
**Fax Area Code: 800* ■ *TF:* 866-283-9327 ■ *Web:* www.atd.com					
Bank & Office Interiors 5601-6th Ave S	Seattle	WA	94145	206-768-8000	768-0236
TF: 800-762-8002 ■ *Web:* www.bankandoffice.com					
Barclay Dean Interiors 11100 NE 8th St Suite 900	Bellevue	WA	98004	425-451-8940	454-1705
Web: www.barclaydean.com					
BCinteriors 1930 Central Ave	Boulder	CO	80301	303-443-3666	443-0406
Web: www.bcinteriors.com					
BKM Enterprises Inc 300 E River Dr	East Hartford	CT	06108	860-528-9981	528-1843
TF: 800-786-4350 ■ *Web:* www.bkm.com					
Brown & Saenger 1409 N C Ave	Sioux Falls	SD	57104	605-336-1960	332-0963
TF: 800-952-3509 ■ *Web:* www.brown-saenger.com					
Business Furniture Corp 6102 Victory Way	Indianapolis	IN	46278	317-216-1600	216-1602
TF: 800-774-5544 ■ *Web:* www.bfcindy.com					
Business Furniture Inc 10 Lanidex Ctr W	Parsippany	NJ	07054	973-503-0730	503-1565
Web: www.bfionline.com					
California Office Furniture 1724 10th St	Sacramento	CA	95811	916-442-6959	442-3480
TF: 877-442-6959 ■ *Web:* www.caloffice.com					
Carithers Wallace Courtenay Co 4343 NE Expy	Atlanta	GA	30340	770-493-8200	491-6374
TF: 800-292-8220 ■ *Web:* www.c-w-c.com					
Carroll Seating Co Inc 2105 Lunt Ave	Elk Grove Village	IL	60007	847-434-0909	434-0910
TF: 800-972-3779 ■ *Web:* www.carrollseating.com					
Champion Industries Inc 2450-90 First Ave PO Box 2968	Huntington	WV	25728	304-528-2700	528-2765
NASDAQ: CHMP ■ *TF:* 800-624-3431 ■ *Web:* www.champion-industries.com					
COECO Office Systems Co 2521 N Church St PO Box 2088	Rocky Mount	NC	27804	252-977-1121	985-1566
TF: 800-682-6844 ■ *Web:* www.coeco.com					
Commercial Furniture Interiors Inc 1135 Spruce Dr	Mountainside	NJ	07092	908-518-1670	654-8436
Web: www.cfioffice.com					
Contract Furnishers Of Hawaii Inc 1600 Kapiolani Blvd	Honolulu	HI	96814	808-599-2411	599-2617
Web: www.op-hawaii.com					
Corporate Environments 1636 NE Expwy	Atlanta	GA	30329	404-492-8775	679-8950
Web: www.corporateenvironments.com					
CSN Stores LLC 177 Huntington Ave Suite 6000	Boston	MA	02115	617-880-8593	880-8594
TF: 800-593-5251 ■ *Web:* www.csnstores.com					
Dancker Sellew & Douglas 236 W 30th St # 4	New York	NY	10001	212-267-2200	619-6799
TF: 800-326-2537 ■ *Web:* www.dancker.com					
Douron Inc 30 New Plant Ct	Owings Mills	MD	21117	410-363-2600	363-1659
TF: 888-833-8350 ■ *Web:* www.douron.com					
Empire Office Inc 105 Madison Ave # 15	New York	NY	10016	212-607-5500	607-5650
TF: 877-533-6747 ■ *Web:* www.empireoffice.com					
Enriching Spaces 1360 Kemper Meadow Dr	Cincinnati	OH	45240	513-851-0933	742-6415
Web: www.enrichingspaces.com					
Evergreen Enterprises Inc 5915 Midlothian Trnpk	Richmond	VA	23225	804-231-1800	231-2888
TF: 800-774-3837 ■ *Web:* www.myevergreen.com					
Facilitech Inc 1111 Valley View Ln	Irving	TX	75061	817-858-2000	858-2108
TF: 800-568-9281 ■ *Web:* www.businessinteriors.com					
Forrer Business Interiors Inc 555 W Estabrook Blvd	Glendale	WI	53212	414-906-3200	906-3299
Web: www.forrersbi.com					
Furniture Consultants Inc 641 Avenue of the Americas 2nd Fl	New York	NY	10011	212-229-4500	807-0036
Web: www.e-fci.com					
General Office Environment Inc 18 Railroad Ave	Rochelle Park	NJ	07662	201-845-0010	845-0034
Web: www.goeinc.com					
General Office Products Co 4521 Hwy 7	Minneapolis	MN	55416	952-925-7500	925-7531
Web: www.gopco.com					
GI Seaman & Co 4201 International Pkwy	Carrollton	TX	75007	214-764-6400	764-6420
Web: www.glseamancompany.com					
Glover Equipment Sales Group LLC 221 Cockeysville Rd PO Box 405	Hunt Valley	MD	21030	410-771-8000	771-8010
TF: 800-966-9016 ■ *Web:* www.gloverequipment.com					
GuildMaster Inc 1938 E Phelps St	Springfield	MO	65802	417-879-3326	879-3330
PINK: GLDU ■ *TF:* 877-669-3326 ■ *Web:* www.guildmaster.com					
Haldeman-Homme Inc 430 Industrial Blvd NE	Minneapolis	MN	55413	612-331-4880	378-2236
TF: 800-795-0696 ■ *Web:* www.haldemanhomme.com					
Hart Furniture Co Inc 12 Harold Hart Rd	Siler City	NC	27344	919-742-4141	663-2925
Web: www.hartfurnitureco.com					
Henricksen & Co 1101 W River Pkwy Suite 100	Minneapolis	MN	55415	612-455-2200	877-3300
Web: www.henricksen.com					
Hudson Seating & Mobility 151 Rockwell Rd	Newington	CT	06111	860-666-7500	666-7501
TF: 800-321-4442 ■ *Web:* www.hudsonhhc.com					
Intereum 845 Berkshire Ln N	Plymouth	MN	55441	763-417-3300	417-3309
Web: www.intereum.com					
Interiors Inc 1325 N Dutton Ave	Santa Rosa	CA	95401	707-544-4770	544-0722
J L Business Interiors Inc 515 Schoenhaar Dr PO Box 303	West Bend	WI	53090	262-338-2221	338-2269
TF: 866-338-5524 ■ *Web:* www.jlbusinessinteriors.com					
Jules Seltzer Assoc 8833 Beverly Blvd	Los Angeles	CA	90048	310-274-7243	274-7243
Web: www.julesseltzer.com					
KBM Workspace 320 S 1st St	San Jose	CA	95113	408-351-7100	938-0699
Web: www.kbmworkspace.com					
Kentwood Office Furniture Inc 3063 Breton Rd SE	Grand Rapids	MI	49512	616-957-2320	957-2361
TF: 800-878-5572 ■ *Web:* www.kentwoodoffice.com					
Kimbrell Furniture Distributors PO Box 11117	Charlotte	NC	28220	704-523-3424	522-1137
Web: www.kimbrells.com					
Lake County Office Equipment Inc 1428 Glen Flora Ave PO Box 8758	Waukegan	IL	60079	847-662-5393	662-8761
Web: www.getofficeplus.com					
Lee Co Inc 27 S 12th St PO Box 567	Terre Haute	IN	47808	812-235-8155	235-3587

				Phone	Fax
Lenoir Empire Furniture 1625 Cherokee Rd	Johnson City	TN	37604	423-929-7283	929-7040
Loth Inc 3574 E Kemper Rd	Cincinnati	OH	45241	513-554-4900	554-8700
Web: www.lothexperts.com					
Marnoy Interests Ltd 6807 Portwest Dr	Houston	TX	77024	713-803-0000	803-0001
Web: www.ophouston.com					
MG West 2 Shaw Alley 3rd Fl PO Box 7231	San Francisco	CA	94105	415-284-4800	284-0150
Web: www.mgwest.com					
MISSCO Contract Sales 2510 Lakeland Terr Suite 100	Jackson	MS	39216	601-987-8600	987-3038
TF: 800-647-5333 ■ *Web:* www.missco.com					
Najarian Furniture Co Inc 17560 Rowland St	City of Industry	CA	91748	626-839-8700	839-8707
TF: 888-781-3088 ■ *Web:* www.najarianfurniture.com					
National Business Furniture Inc 735 N Water St Suite 440	Milwaukee	WI	53202	414-276-8511	276-8371
TF Sales: 800-558-1010 ■ *Web:* www.nationalbusinessfurniture.com					
Nickerson Corp PO Box 5751	Bay Shore	NY	11706	631-666-0200	666-2667
Web: www.nickersoncorp.com					
North Country Business Products Inc PO Box 910	Bemidji	MN	56619	218-751-4140	755-6039
TF: 866-819-7403 ■ *Web:* www.ncbpinc.com					
Nova International Inc 3401 K St NW Suite 201	Washington	DC	20007	202-338-4009	338-4138
TF: 800-257-6682 ■ *Web:* www.novainternational.com					
OEC Bsuiness Interiors 900 N Church Rd	Elmhurst	IL	60126	630-589-5500	589-5637
Web: www.oecbusinessinteriors.com					
Office Concepts 965 W Chicago Ave	Chicago	IL	60622	312-942-1100	942-9840
Web: www.officeconcepts.com					
Office Environments Inc 11407 Granite St	Charlotte	NC	28273	704-714-7200	714-7400
Web: www.office-environments.com					
Office Star Products 1901 S Archibald PO Box 3520	Ontario	CA	91761	909-930-2000	930-5419
TF: 800-950-7262 ■ *Web:* www.officestar.net					
Ohio Desk Co 1122 Prospect Ave E	Cleveland	OH	44115	216-623-0600	623-0611
TF: 800-326-0601 ■ *Web:* www.ohiodesk.com					
OneWorkplace 475 Brannan St Suite 210	San Francisco	CA	94107	415-357-2200	357-2201
Web: www.oneworkplace.com					
Pacific Design Ctr 8687 Melrose Ave	West Hollywood	CA	90069	310-657-0800	652-8576
Web: www.pacificdesigncenter.com					
Peabody Office Furniture Corp 234 Congress St	Boston	MA	02110	617-542-1902	542-1609
Web: www.peabodyoffice.com					
Pear Commercial Interiors Inc 1515 Arapahoe St Suite 100	Denver	CO	80202	303-824-2000	824-2001
Web: www.pearcom.com					
Pigott Inc 3815 Ingersoll Ave	Des Moines	IA	50312	515-279-8879	279-7338
Web: www.pigottnet.com					
Pivot Interiors 2740 Zanker Rd Suite 100	San Jose	CA	95134	408-432-5600	432-5601
Web: www.pivotinteriors.com					
R & M Office Furniture Inc 9615 Oates Dr	Sacramento	CA	95827	916-362-1756	362-1086
TF: 800-660-1756 ■ *Web:* www.randmoffice.com					
Red Willow Office Interiors 558 E Castle Pines Pkwy	Castle Rock	CO	80108	303-373-9950	371-3710
Web: www.redwillowoffice.com					
RH Kyle Furniture Co 1352 Hansford St	Charleston	WV	25301	304-346-0671	346-0674
TF: 800-624-9170 ■ *Web:* www.kylefurniture.com					
Sarreid Ltd 3905 Airport Dr NW	Wilson	NC	27896	252-291-1414	237-1592
Web: www.sarreid.com					
Southern Office Furniture Distributors Inc 719 N Regional Rd	Greensboro	NC	27409	336-668-4192	668-2076
TF: 800-933-6369					
Sterling Collection Inc The 1730 1st St	San Fernando	CA	91340	818-837-4680	361-2250
Web: www.sterling-collection.com					
Tangram Interiors Inc 9200 Sorensen Ave	Santa Fe Springs	CA	90670	562-365-5000	365-5399
TF: 800-700-1377 ■ *Web:* www.tangraminteriors.com					
Trade Products Corp 12124 Popes Head Rd	Fairfax	VA	22030	703-502-9000	502-9399
TF: 888-352-3580 ■ *Web:* www.tradeproductscorp.com					
Waldner's Business Environment 125 Rt 110	Farmingdale	NY	11735	631-694-1522	694-3503
Web: www.waldners.com					
Wasserstrom Co 477 S Front St	Columbus	OH	43215	614-228-6525	228-8776
TF: 800-999-9277 ■ *Web:* www.wasserstrom.com					
WB Wood 100 5th Ave 12th Fl	New York	NY	10011	212-206-9500	206-9222
Web: www.wbwood.com					
Western Office Interiors 500 Citadel Dr Suite 250	Los Angeles	CA	90040	323-271-1800	271-1801
Web: www.westernoffice.com					
Winners Only Inc 1365 Pk Ctr Dr	Vista	CA	92081	760-599-0300	597-0899
Web: www.winnersonly.com					
Workplace Solutions 30800 Telegraph Rd Suite 2985	Bingham Farms	MI	48025	248-430-2500	430-2346
TF: 800-429-9172 ■ *Web:* www.wp-int.com					
Workscapes Inc 1173 N Orange Ave	Orlando	FL	32804	407-599-6770	599-6780
Web: www.workscapes.com					
World Imports Ltd Inc 11000 Roosevelt Blvd	Philadelphia	PA	19116	215-676-9900	676-5224
TF: 800-486-4710 ■ *Web:* www.worldimportsltd.com					

324 FURNITURE STORES

SEE ALSO Department Stores p. 1783

				Phone	Fax
A D Wynne Co Inc 710 Baronne St	New Orleans	LA	70113	504-522-9558	522-7070
Web: www.adwynne.com					
Aaron Investments Inc 100 Robin Rd Ext	Acworth	GA	30102	678-255-1000	255-1019
Web: www.woodstockoutlet.com					
American Furniture Warehouse Co 8501 Grant St	Thornton	CO	80229	303-289-3300	288-1726
TF: 888-615-9415 ■ *Web:* www.afwonline.com					

	City	State	Zip	Phone	Fax
American Home Furnishings 3535 Menaul Blvd NE	Albuquerque	NM	87107	505-883-2211	883-2119
TF: 800-876-4454 ■ *Web:* www.americanhome.com					
Arizona Leather Co Inc 4235 Schaefer Ave	Chino	CA	91710	909-364-2571	
TF: 888-669-5328 ■ *Web:* www.arizonaleather.com					
Art Van Furniture Co 6500 E14-Mile Rd	Warren	MI	48092	586-939-0800	979-9064*
**Fax:* Mktg ■ *TF:* 877-511-8364 ■ *Web:* www.artvan.com					
Atlantic Corporate Interiors Inc (ACCINC) 4600 Powder Mill Rd Suite 300	Beltsville	MD	20705	301-931-3600	931-3601
Web: www.aciinc.com					
Badcock's Economy Furniture Store Inc 3931 RCA Blvd Suite 3122	Palm Beach Gardens	FL	33410	561-694-8588	694-8113
Web: www.badcock.com					
Barn Furniture Mart Inc 6206 N Sepulveda Blvd	Van Nuys	CA	91411	818-780-4070	780-4749
TF: 888-302-2276 ■ *Web:* www.barnfurniture.com					
Bedroom Store Inc 2440 Adie Rd	Saint Louis	MO	63043	314-569-3669	814-0077
Web: www.thebedroomstore.com					
Big Sandy Furniture Co Inc 8375 Gallia Pike	Franklin Furnace	OH	45629	740-574-2113	574-1078
Web: www.bigsandysuperstore.com					
Big Sur Waterbeds Inc 13333 E 37th Ave	Denver	CO	80239	303-371-8560	371-9420
Boss Chair Inc 5353 Jillson St	Commerce	CA	90040	323-262-1919	262-2300
Web: www.bosschair.com					
Cabot House Inc 10 Industrial Way	Amesbury	MA	01913	978-834-9280	388-0792
Web: www.cabothouse.com					
Carls Furniture 6650 N Federal Hwy	Boca Raton	FL	33487	561-226-1111	226-1497
Web: www.carls.com					
Carol House Furniture Co 2332 Millpark Dr	Maryland Heights	MO	63043	314-427-4200	427-8176
Web: www.carolhouse.com					
City Furniture Inc 6701 N Hiatus Rd	Tamarac	FL	33321	954-597-2200	718-3328
TF: 866-208-2489 ■ *Web:* www.city-furniture.com					
Coulter's Furniture 1324 Windsor Ave	Windsor	ON	N8X3L9	519-253-7422	253-3744
TF: 888-238-4778 ■ *Web:* www.coulters.com					
CS Wo & Sons Ltd 702 S Beretenia St	Honolulu	HI	96813	808-545-5966	543-5366
Web: www.cswo.com					
Darvin Furniture 15400 S La Grange Rd	Orland Park	IL	60462	708-460-4100	460-9132
TF: 800-232-7846 ■ *Web:* www.darvin.com					
Dearden's Furniture Co 700 S Main St	Los Angeles	CA	90014	213-627-9600	627-9600
Web: www.deardens.com					
Desks Inc Business Furniture 445 Bryant St Unit #8	Denver	CO	80204	303-777-7778	698-7139
Web: www.dibf.net					
Domain Home 51 Morgan Dr	Norwood	MA	02062	781-769-9130	769-3580
TF: 877-436-6246 ■ *Web:* www.domain-home.com					
Dufresne Furniture Ltd 230 Panet Rd	Winnipeg	MB	R2J0S3	204-989-9907	237-4923*
**Fax:* Claims ■ *TF:* 800-737-3233 ■ *Web:* www.dufresne.ca					
Ed Marling Stores Inc 2950 Mcclure Rd	Topeka	KS	66614	785-273-6970	271-2910
Web: www.marlings.com					
El Dorado Furniture Corp 4200 NW 167th St	Miami	FL	33054	305-624-2400	
TF: 800-236-6256 ■ *Web:* www.eldoradofurniture.com					
Empresas Berrios Inc PO Box 674	Cidra	PR	00739	787-653-9393	
Ethan Allen Interiors Inc Ethan Allen Dr	Danbury	CT	06811	203-743-8000	743-8298
NYSE: ETH ■ *Web:* www.ethanallen.com					
Finger Furniture Co Inc 1601 Gillingham Ln	Sugar Land	TX	77478	713-221-4441	221-4601
Web: www.fingerfurniture.com					
Franklin Interiors Inc 2740 Smallman St Suite 600	Pittsburgh	PA	15222	412-261-2525	255-4089
TF: 800-371-5001 ■ *Web:* www.franklininteriors.com					
Freed's Fine Furnishings Inc 3645 Sturgis Rd	Rapid City	SD	57702	605-343-2538	343-3662
Web: www.sdfreeds.com					
Furnitureland South Inc 5635 Riverdale Dr PO Box 1550	Jamestown	NC	27282	336-841-4328	822-3031*
**Fax:* Cust Svc ■ *Web:* www.furniturelandsouth.com					
Gabberts Inc 3501 Galleria	Minneapolis	MN	55435	952-927-1500	927-1555
Web: www.gabberts.com					
Gorman's Gallery Inc 29145 Telegraph Rd	Southfield	MI	48034	248-353-9880	353-6855
Web: www.gormans.com					
Grand Furniture Discount Store 836 E Little Creek Rd	Norfolk	VA	23518	757-588-1331	583-9075
Web: www.grandfurniture.com					
Grand Home Furnishings 4235 Electric Rd SW Suite 100	Roanoke	VA	24018	540-776-7000	776-5528
Web: www.grandhomefurnishings.com					
Hansen's Furniture Co 916 W Division St	Mount Vernon	WA	98273	360-424-7188	
Hart Furniture Co Inc 12 Harold Hart Rd	Siler City	NC	27344	919-742-4141	663-2925
Web: www.hartfurnitureco.com					
Haverty Furniture Cos Inc 780 Johnson Ferry Rd NE Suite 800	Atlanta	GA	30342	404-443-2900	443-4180
NYSE: HVT ■ *TF:* 800-241-4599 ■ *Web:* www.havertys.com					
Haynes Furniture Co Inc 5324 Virginia Beach Blvd	Virginia Beach	VA	23462	757-497-9681	552-1545
Web: www.haynesfurniture.com					
Home Furniture Co of Lafayette Inc 909 W Pont Des Mouton Rd	Lafayette	LA	70507	337-291-7900	234-8577
TF: 800-641-8578 ■ *Web:* www.homefurn.com					
Hurwitz-Mintz Furniture Co 1751 Airline Dr	Metairie	LA	70001	504-378-1000	523-7273
TF: 800-597-9555 ■ *Web:* www.hurwitzmintz.com					
IKEA 420 Alan Wood Rd	Conshohocken	PA	19428	610-834-0180	834-0872
TF: 800-434-4532 ■ *Web:* www.ikea.com					
International Contract Furnishings Inc (ICF) 19 Ohio Ave	Norwich	CT	06360	860-886-1700	784-8209*
**Fax Area Code:* 888 ■ *TF:* 800-237-1625 ■ *Web:* www.icfsource.com					
Jerome's Furniture Warehouse 16960 Mesamint St	San Diego	CA	92127	858-753-1500	753-0826
TF: 888-537-6637 ■ *Web:* www.jeromes.com					
Johnny Janosik Inc 11151 Trussum Pond Rd	Laurel	DE	19956	302-875-5955	
Web: www.johnnyjanosik.com					
K-Town Furniture Co Inc 136 Oak Ave	Kannapolis	NC	28081	704-932-3111	938-2990
Kane Furniture Corp 5700 70th Ave N	Pinellas Park	FL	33781	727-545-9555	541-6960
Web: www.kanesfurniture.com					
Knoxville Wholesale Furniture Co Inc 10461 Parkside Dr	Knoxville	TN	37922	865-671-5300	671-5301
Web: www.knoxvillewholesalefurniture.com					
Lack's Stores Inc 200 S Ben Jordan PO Box 2088	Victoria	TX	77901	361-578-3571	576-9814
TF: 800-242-1123 ■ *Web:* www.lacks.com					
Lack's Valley Stores Ltd 1300 San Patricia St	Pharr	TX	78577	956-702-3361	782-5740
Web: www.lacksvalley.com					
Levin Furniture Co 301 Fritzhenry Rd	Smithton	PA	15479	724-872-2050	872-2060
Web: www.levinfurniture.com					
Low's Furniture 906 Main St	Fortuna	CA	95540	707-725-3331	725-1268
Web: www.lows.com					
Macy's 111 N State St	Chicago	IL	60602	312-781-1000	
Web: www.macys.com					
Market Square 305 W High St	High Point	NC	27260	336-821-1500	821-1575
Web: www.mmpihighpoint.com					
Mathis Bros Furniture Inc 6611 S 101 St E Ave	Tulsa	OK	74133	918-461-7785	
TF Cust Svc: 800-329-3434 ■ *Web:* www.mathisbrothers.com					
Mazer's Discount Home Centers Inc 816 Green Springs Hwy	Birmingham	AL	35209	205-942-2744	986-0229
Web: www.mazers.com					
McGregor Co 111 W Main St	Marshalltown	IA	50158	641-753-6627	753-0175
Web: www.mcgregorsfurniture.com					
Miskelly Furniture 101 Airport Rd	Jackson	MS	39208	601-939-6288	933-5975
Web: www.miskellys.com					
Nebraska Furniture Mart Inc 700 S 72nd St	Omaha	NE	68114	402-397-6100	392-3386
TF: 800-336-9136 ■ *Web:* www.nfm.com					
Office Furniture Partnership Inc The 67 E Pk Pl	Morristown	NJ	07960	973-267-6966	
TF: 800-758-6409 ■ *Web:* www.officefurniturepartnership.com					
Olinde's Furniture 9536 Airline Hwy	Baton Rouge	LA	70815	225-926-3380	924-2063
Web: www.olindes.com					
Olum's of Binghamton Inc 3701 Vestal Pkwy E	Vestal	NY	13850	607-729-5775	729-6166
TF Cust Svc: 800-964-5690 ■ *Web:* www.olums.com					
Parker Furniture 10375 SW Beaverton-Hillsdale Hwy	Beaverton	OR	97005	503-644-0155	644-0170
TF: 800-877-9491 ■ *Web:* www.parker-furniture.com					
Peerless Mattress & Furniture Co G-3437 Miller Rd	Flint	MI	48507	810-230-7440	230-0143
TF: 800-253-0937					
Philip Linder & Assoc Inc 12821 Knott St Suite B	Garden Grove	CA	92841	714-657-7599	657-7163
TF: 888-412-1743 ■ *Web:* www.lindersfurniture.com					
Pier 1 Kids 100 Pier 1 Pl	Fort Worth	TX	76102	817-252-8000	252-8995
TF: 800-433-4035 ■ *Web:* www.pier1.com					
Porters of Racine 301 6th St	Racine	WI	53403	262-633-6363	633-5011
TF: 800-558-3245 ■ *Web:* www.portersofracine.com					
Raymour & Flanigan Furniture PO Box 220	Liverpool	NY	13088	315-453-2500	453-2551*
**Fax:* Mktg ■ *Web:* www.raymourflanigan.com					
RH Kuhn Co 2250 Roswell Dr	Pittsburgh	PA	15227	412-444-2300	444-2330
TF: 888-696-7378					
Robb & Stucky Furniture Inc 14550 Plantation Rd	Fort Myers	FL	33912	239-437-7997	437-5940
Web: www.robbstucky.com					
Rooms to Go Inc 11540 US Hwy 92 E	Seffner	FL	33584	813-623-5400	620-1717
TF Cust Svc: 800-766-6786 ■ *Web:* www.roomstogo.com					
Roomstores of Phoenix LLC The 3011 E Broadway Rd	Phoenix	AZ	85040	602-268-1111	305-7561
Web: www.arizonaroomstore.com					
Rothman Furniture Stores Inc 2101 E Terra Ln	O'Fallon	MO	63366	314-291-1199	978-7057*
**Fax Area Code:* 636 ■ *Web:* www.rothmanfurniture.com					
Rotmans Furniture & Carpet 725 Southbridge St	Worcester	MA	01610	508-755-5276	752-4258
TF: 800-768-6267 ■ *Web:* www.rotmans.com					
Routzahn's 1931 N Market St	Frederick	MD	21701	301-662-2141	662-7215
Web: www.routzahns.com					
Royal Discount Furniture Co Inc 122 S Main St	Memphis	TN	38103	901-527-6407	527-8166
Web: www.royalfurniture.com					
Royals Inc 324 SW 16th St	Belle Glade	FL	33430	561-996-6581	996-1369
Sam Levitz Furniture 3430 E 36th St	Tucson	AZ	85713	520-624-7443	628-4175
Web: www.samlevitz.com					
San Francisco Design Ctr 2 Henry Adams St Suite 450	San Francisco	CA	94103	415-490-5800	490-5885
Web: www.sfdesigncenter.com					
Scan International Inc 1800-I Rockville Pike	Rockville	MD	20852	301-984-2960	984-0755
TF: 800-386-0989					
Schewel Furniture Co Inc 1031 Main St	Lynchburg	VA	24504	434-522-0200	522-0207
Schmidt-Goodman Office Products 1920 N Broadway	Rochester	MN	55906	507-282-3870	282-7355*
**Fax Area Code:* 517 ■ *TF:* 800-247-0663 ■ *Web:* www.schmidtgoodman.com					
Schottenstein Stores Corp 1800 Moler Rd	Columbus	OH	43207	614-221-9200	449-0403
TF: 800-743-4577					
Scott Rice Office Works 14720 W 105th St	Lenexa	KS	66215	913-888-7600	227-7793
Web: www.scottrice.com					
Seattle Office Furniture LLC 3035 1st Ave	Seattle	WA	98121	206-728-5710	728-5716
Web: www.seattleofficefurniture.com					
Sedlak Interiors Inc 34300 Solon Rd	Solon	OH	44139	440-248-2424	349-8724
TF: 800-260-2949 ■ *Web:* www.sedlakinteriors.com					
Selden's Home Furnishings & Interior Design 1802 62nd Ave E	Tacoma	WA	98424	253-922-5700	922-2924
TF: 800-870-7880					
Shops at Carolina Furniture of Williamsburg 5425 Richmond Rd	Williamsburg	VA	23188	757-565-3000	565-4476
TF: 800-582-8916 ■ *Web:* www.carolina-furniture.com					
Sit 'n Sleep 14300 S Main St	Gardena	CA	90248	310-842-6850	842-6844
Web: www.sitnsleep.com					

	City	State	ZIP	Phone	Fax
Sleepy's Inc 1000 S Oister Bay Rd	Hickszille	NY	11801	516-861-8800	861-8887
TF: 800-753-3797 ■ *Web:* www.sleepys.com					
Smith's Furniture 8055 National Tpke	Louisville	KY	40214	502-368-9917	368-5369
Web: www.smithsfurniture.net					
Smulekoff's Fine Home Furnishings PO Box 74090	Cedar Rapids	IA	52407	319-362-2181	362-2180
TF: 888-384-6995 ■ *Web:* www.smulekoffs.com					
Star Furniture Co Inc 16666 Barker Springs Rd	Houston	TX	77084	281-492-6661	579-5900
TF: 800-364-6661 ■ *Web:* www.starfurniture.com					
Steinhafels W 231 N 1013 County Hwy F	Waukesha	WI	53186	262-436-4600	436-4601
TF Cust Svc: 866-351-4600 ■ *Web:* www.steinhafels.com					
Sterling Furniture Co 2051 S 1100 E	Salt Lake City	UT	84106	801-467-1579	
Stevens Furniture Co 1258 Hickory Blvd SW	Lenoir	NC	28645	828-728-5511	728-5518
Stevens Office Interiors 1449 Erie Blvd E	Syracuse	NY	13210	315-479-5595	428-1688
TF: 800-724-0099 ■ *Web:* www.stevensinteriors.com					
Storehouse Inc 4200 Perimeter Pk S	Atlanta	GA	30341	770-457-1176	
Web: www.storehouse.com					
Town & Country Furniture 6545 Airline Hwy	Baton Rouge	LA	70805	225-355-6666	355-7459
TF: 800-375-6660 ■ *Web:* www.tcfurniture.com					
United Factory Furniture Corp 301 S Martin L King Blvd	Las Vegas	NV	89106	702-384-9300	384-7672
Web: www.walkerfurniture.com					
USA Baby 793 Springer Dr	Lombard	IL	60148	630-652-0600	652-9080
TF: 800-323-4108 ■ *Web:* www.usababy.com					
Value City Furniture 1800 Moler Rd	Columbus	OH	43207	614-221-9200	449-4880*
**Fax:* Cust Svc ■ *TF:* 800-743-4577 ■ *Web:* www.vcf.com					
Walker's Furniture Inc 2611 N Woodruff Rd	Spokane	WA	99206	509-535-1995	534-0013
TF: 866-667-6655 ■ *Web:* www.walkersfurniture.com					
Warehouse Home Furnishings Distributors Inc 1851 Telfair St PO Box 1140	Dublin	GA	31021	478-275-3150	275-6276
TF: 800-456-0424 ■ *Web:* www.farmersfurniture.com					
Wayside Furniture Inc 1367 Canton Rd	Akron	OH	44312	330-733-6221	733-6420
TF: 877-499-3968 ■ *Web:* www.wayside-furniture.com					
Weekends Only Inc 349 Marshall Ave 3rd Fl	Saint Louis	MO	63119	314-447-1500	447-1591
Web: www.weekendsonly.com					
Wenger Furniture Appliance & Electronics 4552 Whittier Blvd	Los Angeles	CA	90022	323-261-1136	261-0968
Web: www.wengerfurniture.com					
Western Contract 11455 Folsom Blvd	Rancho Cordova	CA	95742	916-638-3338	638-2698
Web: www.westerncontract.com					
Wieser & Cawley Inc 1301 Colegate Dr	Marietta	OH	45750	740-373-1676	373-9336
TF: 800-339-0094 ■ *Web:* www.wiesercawleyfurnitures.com					
Wolf Furniture Inc 1620 N Tuckahoe St	Bellwood	PA	16617	814-742-4380	742-4389
Web: www.wolffurniture.com					
Wood You Distributors Inc 3333 N Canal St PO Box 12469	Jacksonville	FL	32209	904-354-0300	354-6983
Web: www.woodyou.com					
Workplace Resource LLC 4400 NE Loop 410 Suite 130	San Antonio	TX	78218	210-226-5141	
TF: 800-580-3000 ■ *Web:* www.hmwrasa.com					
WS Badcock Corp 200 NW Phosphate Blvd	Mulberry	FL	33860	863-425-4921	425-7513
TF: 800-223-2625 ■ *Web:* www.badcock.com					

325 GAMES & GAMING

SEE ALSO Casino Companies p. 1557; Casinos p. 1558; Lotteries, Games, Sweepstakes p. 2189; Toys, Games, Hobbies p. 2723

	City	State	ZIP	Phone	Fax
Ac Coin & Slot 201 W Decatur Ave	Pleasantville	NJ	08232	609-641-7811	383-2758
TF: 800-284-7568 ■ *Web:* www.ac-coin.com					
Alaska Bingo Supply 3707 Woodland Dr Suite 3	Anchorage	AK	99517	907-243-7003	248-0895
TF: 800-478-7003 ■ *Web:* www.alaskabingosupply.com					
American Gaming & Electronics 9500 W 55th St	McCook	IL	60525	708-290-2100	290-2200
TF: 800-336-6630 ■ *Web:* www.age-gaming.com					
American Wagering Inc 675 Grier Dr	Las Vegas	NV	89119	702-735-0101	735-0142
Web: www.americanwagering.com					
Amtote International Inc 11200 Pepper Rd	Hunt Valley	MD	21031	410-771-8700	785-5299*
**Fax:* Acctg ■ *TF:* 800-345-1566 ■ *Web:* www.amtote.com					
Arachnid Inc 6212 Material Ave	Loves Park	IL	61111	815-654-0212	654-0447
TF: 800-435-8319 ■ *Web:* www.bullshooter.com					
Aristocrat Technologies 7230 Amigo St	Las Vegas	NV	89119	702-270-1000	270-1469
TF: 800-748-4156 ■ *Web:* www.aristocrat.com.au					
Bally Gaming & Systems 6601 S Bermuda Rd	Las Vegas	NV	89119	702-896-7700	896-7823*
**Fax:* Sales ■ *TF:* 877-462-2559 ■ *Web:* www.ballygaming.com					
Bmi Gaming Inc 3500 NW Boca Raton Blvd Suite 721	Boca Raton	FL	33431	561-391-7200	391-8040
Web: www.bmigaming.com					
Douglas Press Inc 2810 Madison St	Bellwood	IL	60104	708-547-8400	547-0296
TF: 800-323-0705 ■ *Web:* www.douglaspress.com					
eLottery Inc 46 Southfield Ave 3 Stamford Landing Suite 370	Stamford	CT	06902	203-388-1808	388-1808
Web: www.elottery.com					
Florida Gaming Corp 3500 NW 37th Ave	Miami	FL	33142	305-633-6400	633-4386
Web: www.fla-gaming.com					
FortuNet Inc 2950 S Highland Dr Suite C	Las Vegas	NV	89109	702-796-9090	796-9069
Web: www.fortunet.com					
GameTech International Inc 8850 Double Diamond Pkwy	Reno	NV	89521	775-850-6000	850-6199
NASDAQ: GMTC ■ *TF:* 800-487-8510 ■ *Web:* www.gametech-inc.com					
Gaming Partners International Corp 1700 Industrial Rd	Las Vegas	NV	89102	702-384-2425	384-1965
NASDAQ: GPIC ■ *TF:* 800-728-5766 ■ *Web:* www.gpigaming.com					
GTECH Corp GTECH Ctr 10 Memorial Blvd	Providence	RI	02903	401-392-1000	392-1234
Web: www.gtech.com					
Hands-On Mobile 580 California St Suite 600	San Francisco	CA	94104	415-848-0400	399-1666
Web: www.mforma.com					
IGT Inc 9295 Prototype Dr	Reno	NV	89521	775-448-7777	
Web: www.igt.com					
Interactive Systems Worldwide Inc (ISWI) 2 Andrews Dr Fl 2	West Paterson	NJ	07424	973-256-8181	256-8211
NASDAQ: ISWI ■ *Web:* www.sportxction.com					
International Game Technology (IGT) 9295 Prototype Dr	Reno	NV	89521	775-448-7777	448-1600*
NYSE: IGT ■ **Fax:* Hum Res ■ *TF:* 800-688-7890 ■ *Web:* www.igt.com					
Jacobs Entertainment Inc 17301 W Colfax Ave Suite 250	Golden	CO	80401	303-215-5200	
Konami Gaming Inc 585 Trade Ctr Dr	Las Vegas	NV	89119	702-616-1400	367-0001
TF: 866-544-7568 ■ *Web:* www.konamigaming.com					
Littlefield Corp 2501 N Lamar Blvd	Austin	TX	78705	512-476-5141	476-5680
Web: www.littlefield.com					
Mondial International Corp 101 Secor Ln PO Box 889	Pelham Manor	NY	10803	914-738-7411	738-7521
Web: www.mondialgroup.com					
Monolith Productions Inc 10516 NE 37th Cir	Kirkland	WA	98033	425-739-1500	827-3901
Web: www.lith.com					
Multimedia Games Inc 206 Wild Basin Rd Bldg B, Fourth Fl	Austin	TX	78746	512-334-7500	334-7695
NASDAQ: MGAM ■ *Web:* www.multimediagames.com					
Newport Diversified Inc 19200 Von Karman Ave Suite 1000	Irvine	CA	92612	949-851-1355	851-6304
Web: www.nd-inc.com					
Nickels & Dimes Inc 4534 Old Denton Rd	Carrollton	TX	75010	972-939-4220	492-7505
Web: www.tilt.com					
PokerTek Inc 1150 Crews Rd Suite F	Matthews	NC	28105	888-484-5178	
NASDAQ: PTEK ■ *TF:* 888-484-5178 ■ *Web:* www.pokertek.com					
Scientific Games Corp 750 Lexington Ave 25th Fl	New York	NY	10022	212-754-2233	754-2372
NASDAQ: SGMS ■ *TF:* 800-367-9345 ■ *Web:* www.scientificgames.com					
SED Gaming Inc 2055 Boggs Rd	Duluth	GA	30096	678-473-1260	473-1175
TF Cust Ser: 877-208-9955 ■ *Web:* www.vision-gaming.com					
Shuffle Master Inc 1106 Palms Airport Dr	Las Vegas	NV	89119	702-897-7150	897-2284
NASDAQ: SHFL ■ *Web:* www.shufflemaster.com					
Skee-Ball Amusement Games 121 Liberty Ln	Chalfont	PA	18914	215-997-8900	997-8982
Web: www.skeeball.com					
Smart Industries Corp 1626 Delaware Ave	Des Moines	IA	50317	515-265-9900	265-3148
TF: 800-553-2442 ■ *Web:* www.smartind.com					
United Coin Machine Co 600 Pilot Rd Suite E	Las Vegas	NV	89119	702-270-7500	270-7501
Web: www.unitedcoin.com					
United Tote Co 700 Central Ave	Louisville	KY	40208	502-636-4400	
TF: 800-283-3729 ■ *Web:* www.unitedtote.com					
Valley-Dynamo 7224 Burns Rd	Richland Hills	TX	76118	972-595-5365	595-5380
TF: 800-248-2837 ■ *Web:* www.valley-dynamo.com					
VendingData Corp 6830 Spencer St	Las Vegas	NV	89119	702-733-7195	733-7197
Video King Gaming Systems 2717 N 118 Cir Suite 210	Omaha	NE	68164	402-951-2970	951-2990
TF: 800-635-9912 ■ *Web:* www.bingoking.com					
VirtGame Corp 6969 Corte Santa Fe Suite A	San Diego	CA	92121	858-373-5001	373-5007
Western Regional Off-Track Betting Corp 700 Ellicott St	Batavia	NY	14020	585-343-1423	343-6873
TF: 800-724-2000 ■ *Web:* www.westernotb.com					
WMS Gaming Inc 800 S Northpoint Blvd	Waukegan	IL	60085	847-785-3000	785-3058
NYSE: WMS ■ *TF:* 800-522-4700 ■ *Web:* www.wms.com					

326 GARDEN CENTERS

SEE ALSO Horticultural Products Growers p. 2026; Seed Companies p. 2650

	City	State	ZIP	Phone	Fax
Armstrong Garden Centers Inc (AGC) 2200 E Rt 66 Suite 200	Glendora	CA	91740	626-914-1091	335-0257
TF: 800-229-1707 ■ *Web:* www.armstronggarden.com					
Behnke Nurseries Co 11300 Baltimore Ave	Beltsville	MD	20705	301-937-1100	937-8034
Web: www.behnkes.com					
Breck's US Reservation Centre PO Box 65	Guilford	IN	47022	812-537-3149	537-9653
Web: www.brecks.com					
Bwi Cos Inc 1355 N Kings Hwy PO Box 990	Nash	TX	75569	903-838-8561	831-4799
Web: www.bwicompanies.com					
Cal Herbold Nursery 9403 E Ave	Hesperia	CA	92340	760-244-6125	
Calloway's Nursery Inc 4200 Airport Fwy Suite 200	Fort Worth	TX	76117	817-222-1122	302-0031
Web: www.calloways.com					
Capital Nursery Co 4700 Freeport Blvd	Sacramento	CA	95822	916-455-2601	455-2141
Web: www.capitalnursery.com					
Champlain Valley Equipment Inc PO Box 522	Middlebury	VT	05753	802-388-4967	
Web: www.champlainvalleyequipment.com					
DA Hoerr & Sons Inc 8020 N Shadetree Dr	Peoria	IL	61615	309-691-4561	691-1834
Web: www.hoerrnursery.com					
Earl May Seed & Nursery 208 N Elm St	Shenandoah	IA	51603	712-246-1020	246-2210
TF: 800-843-9608 ■ *Web:* www.earlmay.com					
Farmers Market Garden Center Inc 4110 N Elston Ave	Chicago	IL	60618	773-539-1200	539-1482
Web: www.gardenchicago.com					
Flowerwood Garden Ctr 7645 US Hwy 14	Crystal Lake	IL	60012	815-459-6200	459-3711
TF: 800-852-3114 ■ *Web:* www.flowerwoodinc.com					
Fruit Basket Flowerland 765 28th St SW	Wyoming	MI	49509	616-532-7404	531-7858
Web: www.myflowerland.com					
Gardener's Supply Co 128 Intervale Rd	Burlington	VT	05401	802-660-3500	660-3501
TF: 800-863-1700 ■ *Web:* www.gardeners.com					
Green Thumb International Inc 21812 Sherman Way	Canoga Park	CA	91303	818-340-6400	340-8598
Web: www.supergarden.com					
Greenbrier Farms Inc 225 Sign Pine Rd	Chesapeake	VA	23322	757-421-2141	421-2159
TF: 800-821-2141 ■ *Web:* www.greenbrierfarms.info					

Company	City	State	ZIP	Phone	Fax
Home & Garden Showplace 8600 W Bryn Mawr *TF:* 888-474-9752 ■ *Web:* www.gardenplace.com	Chicago	IL	60631	773-695-5000	695-7049
Home Depot Inc 2455 Paces Ferry Rd NW *NYSE:* HD ■ *TF Cust Svc:* 800-553-3199 ■ *Web:* www.homedepot.com	Atlanta	GA	30339	770-433-8211	384-2356
Johnson's Garden Centers 2707 W 13th St *TF:* 888-542-8463 ■ *Web:* www.johnsonsgarden.com	Wichita	KS	67203	316-942-1443	942-1494
Johnson's Nursery Inc W180 N 6275 Marcy Rd *Web:* www.johnsonsnursery.com	Menomonee Falls	WI	53051	262-252-4988	252-4495
JW Jung Seed Co 335 S High St **Fax Area Code:* 800 ■ *TF:* 800-297-3123 ■ *Web:* www.jungseed.com	Randolph	WI	53956	920-326-3121	692-5864*
L. J. Thalmann Co 3132 Lake Ave *Web:* www.chaletnursery.com	Wilmette	IL	60091	847-256-0561	256-4978
Langeveld Bulb Co Inc 725 Vassar Ave *TF:* 800-526-0467	Lakewood	NJ	08701	732-367-2000	942-3801
Lowe's Cos Inc 1000 Lowe's Blvd *NYSE:* LOW ■ **Fax Area Code:* 336 ■ *TF:* 800-445-6937 ■ *Web:* www.lowes.com	Mooresville	NC	28117	704-758-1000	658-4766*
M & R Nurseries Inc 1601 W Beauregard Ave	San Angelo	TX	76901	325-653-3341	653-3342
Mahoney's Garden Ctr 242 Cambridge St *Web:* www.mahoneysgarden.com	Winchester	MA	01890	781-729-5900	721-1277
McKay Nursery Co Inc 750 S Monroe St PO Box 185 *TF:* 800-236-4242 ■ *Web:* www.mckaynursery.com	Waterloo	WI	53594	920-478-2121	478-3615
Merrygro Farms Inc 34135 Cardinal Ln *TF:* 888-637-7947	Eustis	FL	32736	352-589-0868	589-8138
Michigan Bulb Co PO Box 4180 *Web:* www.michiganbulb.com	Lawrenceburg	IN	47025	513-354-1498	354-1499
Milaeger's Inc 4838 Douglas Ave *TF:* 800-669-1229 ■ *Web:* www.milaegers.com	Racine	WI	53402	262-639-2040	681-6192
North Haven Gardens Inc 7700 Northaven Rd *TF:* 800-347-2342 ■ *Web:* www.nhg.com	Dallas	TX	75230	214-363-6715	987-1511
Oakland Nursery Inc 1156 Oakland Pk Ave *Web:* www.oaklandnursery.com	Columbus	OH	43224	614-268-3511	
Panhandle Co-op Assn 401 S Beltline Hwy W *TF Cust Svc:* 800-732-4546 ■ *Web:* www.panhandlecoop.com	Scottsbluff	NE	69361	308-632-5301	632-5375
Pike Nurseries Holding LLC 4020 Steve Reynolds Blvd *Web:* www.pikenursery.com	Norcross	GA	30093	770-921-1022	638-6940
Plant Delights Nursery Inc 9241 Sauls Rd *Web:* www.plantdel.com	Raleigh	NC	27603	919-772-4794	662-0370
Plants of the Southwest 3095 Agua Fria St *TF:* 800-788-7333 ■ *Web:* www.plantsofthesouthwest.com	Santa Fe	NM	87507	505-438-8888	438-8800
Pleasant View Gardens Inc 7316 Pleasant St **Fax Area Code:* 603 ■ *TF:* 800-343-4784 ■ *Web:* www.pvg.com	Loudon	NH	03307	800-343-4784	435-6849*
Pursley Inc 9115 58th Dr E Suite A	Bradenton	FL	34202	941-753-7851	751-5176
Rain or Shine LandscapeUSA 13126 NE Airport Way **Fax Area Code:* 503 ■ *TF:* 800-248-1981 ■ *Web:* www.landscapeusa.com	Portland	OR	97230	800-966-1033	255-9201*
Ritchie Tractor Cy LLC 1746 W Lmar Alexander Pkwy *TF:* 888-319-0282 ■ *Web:* www.ritchietractor.com	Maryville	TN	37801	865-981-3199	981-1740
Round Butte Seed Growers Inc PO Box 117 *TF:* 866-385-7001 ■ *Web:* www.rbseed.com	Culver	OR	97734	541-546-5222	546-2237
San Gabriel Nursery & Florist 632 S San Gabriel Blvd *Web:* www.sgnurserynews.com/site	San Gabriel	CA	91776	626-286-3782	286-0047
Shanti Bithi Nursery Inc 3047 High Ridge Rd *Web:* www.webcom.com	Stamford	CT	06903	203-329-0768	329-8872
Siebenthaler Co 3001 Catalpa Dr *Web:* www.siebenthaler.com	Dayton	OH	45405	937-274-1154	274-9448
Sloat Garden Center Inc 420 Coloma St *Web:* www.sloatgardens.com	Sausalito	CA	94965	415-332-0657	332-1009
Stein Garden & Gift Centers Inc 5400 S 27th St *Web:* www.steingg.com	Milwaukee	WI	53221	414-761-5400	761-5420
Summerwinds Nursery 17826 N Tatum Blvd *Web:* www.summerwindsnursery.com	Phoenix	AZ	85032	602-867-1822	
Target Stores 1000 Nicollet Mall *TF:* 800-440-0680 ■ *Web:* www.target.com	Minneapolis	MN	55403	612-304-6073	307-8870
TLC Florist & Greenhouse Inc 105 W Memorial Rd *TF:* 800-366-4852 ■ *Web:* www.tlcgarden.com	Oklahoma City	OK	73114	405-751-0630	751-1300
Treelands Inc 1000 Huntington Tpke	Bridgeport	CT	06610	203-372-3511	371-6023
Twombly Nursery 163 Barn Hill Rd *Web:* www.twomblynursery.com	Monroe	CT	06468	203-261-2133	261-9230
Van Bourgondien & Sons Inc 245 Rt 109 *TF:* 800-622-9997 ■ *Web:* www.dutchbulbs.com	Babylon	NY	11702	631-669-3500	669-1228
Village Nurseries 1589 N Main St *TF:* 800-542-0209 ■ *Web:* www.villagenurseries.com	Orange	CA	92867	714-279-3100	279-3199
Wal-Mart Stores Inc 702 SW 8th St *NYSE:* WMT ■ **Fax:* PR ■ *TF Cust Svc:* 800-925-6278 ■ *Web:* www.walmartstores.com	Bentonville	AR	72716	479-273-4000	273-4053*
Waterloo Gardens Inc 200 N Whitford Rd *Web:* www.waterloogardens.com	Exton	PA	19341	610-363-0800	363-6416
Weingartz Supply Co 46061 Van Dyke Ave *TF:* 855-669-7278 ■ *Web:* www.weingartz.com	Utica	MI	48317	586-731-7240	731-9319
White Flower Farm Inc 30 Irene St *TF Cust Svc:* 800-411-6159 ■ *Web:* www.whiteflowerfarm.com	Torrington	CT	06790	860-496-9624	496-1418
Zamzows Inc 1201 N Franklin Blvd *Web:* www.zamzows.com	Nampa	ID	83687	208-465-3630	465-3468

327 GAS STATIONS

SEE ALSO Convenience Stores p. 1748

Company	City	State	ZIP	Phone	Fax
Alpena Oil Co Inc 235 Water St *TF:* 800-968-1098 ■ *Web:* www.alpenaoil.net	Alpena	MI	49707	989-356-1098	356-9486
AMBEST Inc 5115 Maryland Way *TF:* 800-910-7220 ■ *Web:* www.am-best.com	Brentwood	TN	37027	615-371-5187	371-5186
Arfa Enterprises Inc 4350 Haddonfield Rd Suite 200 *Web:* www.arfaoil.com	Pennsauken	NJ	08109	856-486-0550	486-0058
Bi-Mor Stations Inc 1890 S Pacific Hwy PO Box 1220 *Web:* www.bimorstations.com	Medford	OR	97501	541-772-2053	779-2602
Blossman Oil Co Inc PO Box 89 *Web:* www.blossmanoil.com	Covington	LA	70434	985-898-2663	
BP Plc 28100 Torch Pkwy *NYSE:* BP ■ **Fax Area Code:* 281 ■ *TF:* 866-427-6947 ■ *Web:* www.bp.com	Warrenville	IL	60555	630-420-5111	298-0738*
Busler Enterprises Inc 2601 St Joseph Ave *TF:* 800-457-3232	Evansville	IN	47720	812-424-7511	429-0669
Chevron Corp 6001 Bollinger Canyon Rd *NYSE:* CVX ■ **Fax Area Code:* 866 ■ *TF Cust Svc:* 800-243-8766 ■ *Web:* www.chevron.com	San Ramon	CA	94583	925-842-1000	420-0335*
Colonial Group Inc 101 N Lathrop Ave	Savannah	GA	31415	912-236-1331	235-2938
Commercial Energy of Montana Inc 118 E Main St PO Box 548 *Web:* www.commercialenergy.net	Cut Bank	MT	59427	406-873-3300	873-2598
Commercial Truck Terminal Inc 35647 Hwy 27	Haines City	FL	33844	863-422-1148	422-1148
Cone Oil Co Inc 6185 Cockrill Bend Cir	Nashville	TN	37209	615-350-6141	350-6137
Crystal Flash Petroleum Corp 5221 Ivy Tech Dr *TF:* 800-886-3835 ■ *Web:* www.crystal-flash.com	Indianapolis	IN	46268	317-879-2849	879-2855
Dakota Plains Co-op 151 9th Ave NW *TF:* 800-288-7922 ■ *Web:* www.dakotaplains.coop	Valley City	ND	58072	701-845-0812	845-2680
Detroiter Travel Ctr 21055 W Rd *Web:* www.detroiter.net	Woodhaven	MI	48183	734-675-4982	692-4015
Dixie Oil Co Inc 1284 US Hwy 82	Tifton	GA	31794	229-382-2700	387-6905
Dunlap Oil Co Inc 759 S Haskell Ave	Willcox	AZ	85643	520-384-2240	384-5159
Edward H Wolf & Sons Inc 414 Kettle Moraine Dr S PO Box 348 *TF:* 800-236-9653 ■ *Web:* www.ehwolf.com	Slinger	WI	53086	262-644-5030	644-5424
Englefield Oil Co 1935 James Pkwy *TF:* 800-282-1675 ■ *Web:* www.englefieldoil.com	Heath	OH	43056	740-928-8215	928-3844
Erickson Oil Products Inc 1231 Industrial St *TF:* 800-521-0104 ■ *Web:* www.freedomvalu.com	Hudson	WI	54016	715-386-8241	386-2022
Exxon Mobil Corp 5959 Las Colinas Blvd *NYSE:* XOM ■ *TF:* 800-252-1800 ■ *Web:* www.exxonmobil.com	Irving	TX	75039	972-444-1000	444-1348
Fabian Oil Inc 20 Oak St PO Box 99 *Web:* www.fabianoil.com	Oakland	ME	04963	207-465-2000	
FL Roberts & Co Inc 93 W Broad St *TF:* 800-628-4004 ■ *Web:* www.flroberts.com	Springfield	MA	01105	413-781-7444	781-4328
Fleming Oil Co Inc 1 Putney Rd *TF:* 800-287-6095 ■ *Web:* www.flemoil.com	Brattleboro	VT	05301	802-254-6095	254-3725
Flying J Inc 1104 Country Hill Dr *TF Sales:* 877-218-9290 ■ *Web:* www.flyingj.com	Ogden	UT	84403	801-624-1000	395-8005
Forward Corp 219 N Front St *TF:* 800-664-4501 ■ *Web:* www.forwardcorp.com	Standish	MI	48658	989-846-4501	846-4412
Freedom Oil Co 814 W Chestnut St *TF:* 800-397-6147 ■ *Web:* www.freedomoil.com	Bloomington	IL	61701	309-828-7750	829-3813
Gas 'n' Shop Inc 701 Marina Bay Pl *Web:* www.gasnshop.com	Lincoln	NE	68528	402-475-1101	475-0976
GasAmerica Services Inc 2700 W Main St *TF:* 866-427-9900 ■ *Web:* www.gasamerica.com	Greenfield	IN	46140	317-468-2515	468-2525
Gate Petroleum Co 9540 San Jose Blvd PO Box 23627 *Web:* www.gatepetro.com	Jacksonville	FL	32241	904-737-7220	732-7660
Gawfco Enterprises Inc 587 Ygnacio Valley Rd *Web:* www.gawfco.com	Walnut Creek	CA	94596	925-979-0560	
Getty Realty Corp 125 Jericho Tpke Suite 103 *NYSE:* GTY ■ *TF:* 866-399-4335 ■ *Web:* www.gettyrealty.com	Jericho	NY	11753	516-478-5400	478-5490
Graham Enterprise Inc 446 Morris Ave	Mundelein	IL	60060	847-837-0777	837-0778
Harper Oil Co 2319 W Jefferson	Springfield	IL	62702	217-698-4088	698-7088
Hawkeye Oil Co Inc PO Box 1506	Cedar Rapids	IA	52406	319-364-7146	364-7148
Hunt & Sons Inc 5750 S Watt Ave *TF:* 800-734-2999 ■ *Web:* www.huntnsons.com	Sacramento	CA	95829	916-383-4868	383-1005
Imperial Oil Resources Ltd 237 4th Ave SW PO Box 2480 Stn M *TF:* 800-567-3776 ■ *Web:* www.imperialoil.ca	Calgary	AB	T2P3M9	403-237-3737	237-2072
Iowa 80 Group Inc PO Box 639 *TF:* 800-336-9889 ■ *Web:* www.iowa80group.com	Walcott	IA	52773	563-284-6965	284-6475
J & H Oil Co 2696 Chicago Dr SW *TF:* 800-442-9110 ■ *Web:* www.jhoil.com	Wyoming	MI	49519	616-534-2181	534-1663
Jubitz Corp 33 NE Middlefield Rd *TF:* 800-399-5480 ■ *Web:* www.jubitz.com	Portland	OR	97211	503-283-1111	240-5834
Kent Oil Inc PO Box 908001 *TF:* 800-375-5368 ■ *Web:* www.thekentcompanies.com	Midland	TX	79708	432-520-4000	697-8911
Lassus Bros Oil Inc 1800 Magnavox Way *TF:* 800-686-2836	Fort Wayne	IN	46804	260-436-1415	436-0340
MAPCO Express Inc 7102 Commerce Way *TF:* 877-888-0002 ■ *Web:* www.mapcoexpress.com	Brentwood	TN	37027	615-771-6701	771-8098
MM Fowler Inc 4220 Neal Rd *TF:* 800-313-6635	Durham	NC	27705	919-309-2925	309-9924
Monroe Oil Co 519 E Franklin St PO Box 1109 *TF:* 800-452-2717 ■ *Web:* www.monroeoilinc.com	Monroe	NC	28111	704-289-5438	
NELLA Oil Co 2360 Lindbergh St *TF:* 800-995-0401 ■ *Web:* www.nellaoil.com	Auburn	CA	95602	530-885-0401	885-5851
Ney Oil Co Inc 145 S Water St PO Box 155 *TF:* 800-962-9839 ■ *Web:* www.neyoil.com	Ney	OH	43549	419-658-2324	658-2723
O'Connell Oil Assoc Inc 275 Elm St *TF:* 800-464-4894 ■ *Web:* www.baygo.com	Pittsfield	MA	01201	413-499-4800	499-6072
Olds-olympic Inc PO Box 180 *Web:* www.olds-olympic.com	Lynnwood	WA	98046	425-778-4004	771-4346
Pilot Travel Centers LLC PO Box 10146 **Fax:* Cust Svc ■ *TF:* 800-562-6210 ■ *Web:* www.pilotcorp.com	Knoxville	TN	37939	865-588-7487	450-2800*
Platolene 500 Inc PO Box 3088	Terre Haute	IN	47803	812-877-1556	877-2510
Premium Oil Co 2005 S 300 W	Salt Lake City	UT	84115	801-487-4721	
Quality Oil Co LLC 1540 Silas Creek Pkwy *Web:* www.qualityoilnc.com	Winston-Salem	NC	27127	336-722-3441	721-9520

	City	State	Zip	Phone	Fax
RaceTrac Petroleum Inc 3225 Cumberland Blvd Suite 100	Atlanta	GA	30339	770-431-7600	563-8129
TF: 888-636-5589 ■ *Web:* www.racetrac.com					
Rip Griffin Truck Travel Center Inc 4710 4th St	Lubbock	TX	79416	806-795-8785	795-6574
TF: 800-333-9330 ■ *Web:* www.ripgriffin.com					
Sampson-Bladen Oil Co Inc 932 US Hwy 421 N PO Box 469	Clinton	NC	28329	910-592-4177	592-0504
TF: 800-849-4177 ■ *Web:* www.sboil.com					
Sapp Bros Truck Stops Inc 9915 S 148th St	Omaha	NE	68138	402-895-7038	895-1957
Web: www.sappbrostruckstops.com					
Schmitt Sales Inc 2101 St Rita's Ln	Buffalo	NY	14221	716-639-1500	639-1511
TF: 800-873-8080 ■ *Web:* www.schmittsales.com					
Schmuckal Oil Co 1516 Barlow St	Traverse City	MI	49686	231-946-2800	941-7435
Web: www.schmuckaloil.com					
Scott-Gross Co Inc 664 Magnolia Ave	Lexington	KY	40505	859-252-7667	737-5452
TF: 800-967-6874 ■ *Web:* www.scottgross.com					
Service Oil Inc 1718 E Main Ave	West Fargo	ND	58078	701-277-1050	277-1723
TF: 800-726-0133 ■ *Web:* www.stamart.com					
Shirtcliff Oil Co PO Box 6003	Myrtle Creek	OR	97457	541-863-5268	863-5144
TF: 800-422-0536 ■ *Web:* www.shirtcliffoil.com					
Speedway SuperAmerica LLC 500 Speedway Dr	Enon	OH	45323	937-864-3000	
TF Cust Svc: 800-643-1948 ■ *Web:* www.speedway.com					
Spencer Cos Inc 120 Woodson St NW	Huntsville	AL	35801	256-533-1150	535-2910
TF: 800-633-2910 ■ *Web:* www.spencercos.com					
Swifty Oil Co Inc PO Box 1002	Seymour	IN	47274	812-522-1640	522-8554
TF: 800-742-8497					
Thornton Oil Corp 10101 Linn Stn Rd Suite 200	Louisville	KY	40223	502-425-8022	327-9026
TF: 800-928-8022 ■ *Web:* www.thorntonsinc.com					
TOWN PUMP INC 600 S Main St	Butte	MT	59702	406-497-6700	497-6704
TF: 800-823-4931 ■ *Web:* www.townpump.com					
TravelCenters of America 24601 Ctr Ridge Rd Suite 200	Westlake	OH	44145	440-808-9100	808-3209*
*Fax: Mktg ■ *TF:* 800-872-7024 ■ *Web:* www.tatravelcenters.com					
Tri Star Marketing Inc 2211 W Bradley Ave	Champaign	IL	61821	217-367-8386	367-3920
Web: www.superpantry.com					
Triple A Oil 12342 Inwood Rd	Dallas	TX	75244	972-503-3333	503-0007
TF Cust Svc: 800-657-9595					
True North Energy LLC 5565 Airport Hwy	Toledo	OH	43615	419-868-6800	868-1458
Web: www.truenorth.org					
Tucson Truck Terminal Inc 5451 E Benson Hwy	Tucson	AZ	85706	520-574-0050	574-9606
Urbieta Enterprises Inc 9701 NW 89th Ave	Medley	FL	33178	305-884-0008	883-1927
Web: www.urbietaoil.com					
Vermont Gas Systems Inc 85 Swift St	South Burlington	VT	05403	802-863-4511	863-8872
TF: 800-639-8081 ■ *Web:* www.vermontgas.com					
W & H Co-op Oil Co 407 13th St N	Humboldt	IA	50548	515-332-2782	332-1559
TF: 800-392-3816					
Wallace Enterprises Inc 5370 Oakdale Rd	Smyrna	GA	30082	404-799-9400	799-0322
Wallis Oil Co 106 E Washington St	Cuba	MO	65453	573-885-2277	885-4760
TF: 800-467-6652 ■ *Web:* www.wallisco.com					
Wesco Inc 1460 Whitehall Rd	Muskegon	MI	49445	231-719-4300	719-4301
TF: 800-968-0200 ■ *Web:* www.gowesco.com					

328 GAS TRANSMISSION - NATURAL GAS

Companies That Transmit Or Store Natural Gas But Do Not Distribute It.

	City	State	Zip	Phone	Fax
Aka Energy Group LLC 65 Mercado St Suite 250	Durango	CO	81301	970-375-6405	375-2216
Web: www.akaenergy.com					
ANR Pipeline Co 717 Texas St	Houston	TX	77002	403-920-7473	
NYSE: TCP ■ *TF:* 800-827-5267 ■ *Web:* www.anrpl.com					
Atlas Pipeline Partners LP 1550 Coraopolis Heights Rd	Moon Township	PA	15108	918-574-3500	896-8518*
NYSE: APL ■ *Fax Area Code: 330 ■ *TF:* 877-950-7473 ■ *Web:* www.atlaspipeline.com					
Boardwalk Pipeline Partners LP 3800 Frederica St	Owensboro	KY	42301	270-926-8686	688-5872
NYSE: BWP ■ *TF:* 877-686-3620					
British Gas Services Inc 5444 Westheimer Rd Suite 1775	Houston	TX	77056	713-622-7100	622-7244
Cheniere Energy Inc 700 Milam St Suite 800	Houston	TX	77002	713-375-5000	375-6000
AMEX: LNG ■ *TF:* 888-948-2036 ■ *Web:* www.cheniere.com					
CMS Gas Transmission & Storage Co 1 Energy Plaza	Jackson	MI	49201	517-788-0550	
Web: www.cmsenergy.com					
Colorado Interstate Gas Co PO Box 1087	Colorado Springs	CO	80944	719-473-2300	473-2300
Web: www.cigco.com					
Columbia Gas Transmission Corp 1700 MacCorkle Ave SE	Charleston	WV	25314	304-357-2000	357-2000
TF: 800-832-3242 ■ *Web:* www.columbiagastrans.com/tco.html					
Columbia Gulf Transmission Co 2603 Augusta Dr Suite 300	Houston	TX	77057	713-267-4100	267-4100
TF: 888-880-4853 ■ *Web:* www.columbiagastrans.com/cgt.html					
ConocoPhillips Alaska Inc PO Box 100360	Anchorage	AK	99510	907-276-1215	263-4731
TF: 800-622-5501 ■ *Web:* www.alaska.conocophillips.com					
Copano Energy LLC 2727 Allen Pkwy Suite 1200	Houston	TX	77019	713-621-9547	
NASDAQ: CPNO ■ *TF:* 800-621-9556 ■ *Web:* www.copanoenergy.com					
Crossroads Pipeline Co 12801 Fair Lakes Pkwy	Fairfax	VA	22033	703-227-3200	227-3378
TF: 888-499-3450					
Crosstex Energy LP 2501 Cedar Springs Rd Suite 600	Dallas	TX	75201	214-953-9500	953-9501
NASDAQ: XTEX ■ *TF:* 866-427-8732 ■ *Web:* www.crosstexenergy.com					
DCP Midstream Partners LP 370 17th St Suite 2775	Denver	CO	80202	303-633-2900	605-2225
NYSE: DPM					
Duke Energy Algonquin Gas 1284 Soldiers Field Rd	Brighton	MA	02135	617-254-4050	
Duke Energy Trading & Marketing 5400 Westheimer Ct	Houston	TX	77056	713-260-1800	627-4145
TF: 800-873-3853 ■ *Web:* www.duke-energy.com					
El Paso Corp 1001 Louisiana St	Houston	TX	77002	713-420-2600	420-4417
NYSE: EP ■ *TF:* 800-351-0004 ■ *Web:* www.elpaso.com					
El Paso Natural Gas Co PO Box 1087	Colorado Springs	CO	80944	719-473-2300	473-2300*
*Fax: Mktg ■ *Web:* www.elpaso.com					
Enogex Inc 515 Central Pk Dr Suite 600	Oklahoma City	OK	73105	405-525-7788	557-7904
TF: 800-736-8492 ■ *Web:* www.oge.com/enogex					
Enterprise Products Partners LP 1100 Louisiana St 10th Fl	Houston	TX	77002	713-381-6500	880-6668
NYSE: EPD ■ *Web:* www.epplp.com					
Equitrans LP 625 Liberty Ave	Pittsburgh	PA	15222	724-627-5176	852-7310
TF: 800-654-6335 ■ *Web:* www.equitrans.eqt.com					
Gulf South Pipeline Co LP 20 E Greenway Plaza Suite 900	Houston	TX	77046	713-544-6000	
TF: 866-820-6000 ■ *Web:* www.gulfsouthpl.com					
Hiland Partners LP 205 W Maple Ave Suite 1100	Enid	OK	73701	580-242-6040	616-2080
Web: www.hilandpartners.com					
IGS Energy Inc 5020 Bradenton Ave	Dublin	OH	43017	614-923-1000	923-1010
Web: www.igsenergy.com					
Iroquois Gas Transmission System LP 1 Corporate Dr Suite 600	Shelton	CT	06484	203-925-7200	929-9501
Web: www.iroquois.com					
Kern River Gas Transmission Co 2755 E Cottonwood Pkwy Suite 300	Salt Lake City	UT	84158	801-937-6000	
TF: 800-420-7500					
Kinder Morgan Energy Partners LP 500 Dallas St Suite 1000	Houston	TX	77002	713-369-9000	369-9411*
NYSE: KMP ■ *Fax: Hum Res ■ *TF:* 888-844-5657 ■ *Web:* www.kindermorgan.com					
Kinder Morgan Management LLC 500 Dallas St 1 Allen Ctr Suite 1000	Houston	TX	77002	713-369-9000	369-9100
NYSE: KMR ■ *TF:* 800-324-2900 ■ *Web:* www.kindermorgan.com					
Kinder Morgan Texas Pipeline LLC 500 Dallas St Suite 1000	Houston	TX	77002	713-369-9000	369-9100
TF: 800-324-2900 ■ *Web:* www.kindermorgan.com					
Mississippi River Transmission Inc 1600 S Brentwood Blvd Suite 590	Saint Louis	MO	63144	314-991-9900	991-2317
TF Cust Svc: 800-325-4005					
NGL Supply LLC 6120 S Yale Ave Suite 805	Tulsa	OK	74136	918-481-1119	492-0990
Web: www.nglsupplyinc.com					
Northern Natural Gas Co 1111 S 103rd St	Omaha	NE	68124	402-398-7200	398-7214
Paiute Pipeline Co 5241 W Spring Mountain Rd	Las Vegas	NV	89146	702-876-7178	873-3820
Web: www.paiutepipeline.com					
Penn Octane Corp 77-530 Enfield Ln Bldg D	Palm Desert	CA	92211	760-772-9080	772-8588
NASDAQ: POCC					
PG & E Gas Transmission-Northwest 1400 SW 5th Ave Suite 900	Portland	OR	97201	503-833-4000	833-4906
Questar Gas Management Co PO Box 45360	Salt Lake City	UT	84145	801-324-5111	
TF: 800-323-5517 ■ *Web:* www.questargas.com					
Questar Pipeline Co PO Box 45360	Salt Lake City	UT	84145	801-324-2400	324-2684*
*Fax: Cust Svc ■ *Web:* www.questarpipeline.com					
Regency Energy Partners LP 1700 Pacific Suite 2900	Dallas	TX	75201	214-750-1771	750-1749
NASDAQ: RGNC ■ *Web:* www.regencyenergy.com					
SemGroup LP 6120 S Yale Ave Suite 700	Tulsa	OK	74136	918-388-8100	388-8290
Web: www.semgroupcorp.com					
Seminole Energy Services LLC 1323 E 71st St Suite 300	Tulsa	OK	74136	918-492-2840	492-3075
Web: www.seminoleenergy.com					
Spark Energy Gas LP 2105 Citywest Blvd	Houston	TX	77042	713-977-5645	374-8007*
*Fax Area Code: 877 ■ *TF:* 800-332-7143 ■ *Web:* www.sparkenergy.com					
Tennessee Gas Pipeline Co (TGP) PO Box 2511	Houston	TX	77252	713-420-4600	
TF: 800-231-2800 ■ *Web:* www.tennesseeadvantage.com					
Trailblazer Pipeline Co PO Box 27	Heartwell	NE	68945	308-563-3221	563-2270
TransCanada Pipelines Ltd 450 1st St SW	Calgary	AB	T2P5H1	403-920-2000	920-2200
NYSE: TRP ■ *TF:* 800-661-3805 ■ *Web:* www.transcanada.com					
Transwestern Pipeline Co 5444 Westheimer Rd	Houston	TX	77056	713-989-7000	646-2551
Web: www.tw.enron.com					
Tri-Gas & Oil Co Inc 3941 Federalsburg Hwy PO Box 465	Federalsburg	MD	21632	410-754-8184	754-9158
TF: 800-638-7802 ■ *Web:* www.trigas-oil.com					
TXU Lone Star Pipeline 301 S Harwood St	Dallas	TX	75201	214-875-4887	875-5134
Web: www.txu.com/us/ourbus/pipeline					
Veresen Inc 222 3rd Ave SW Suite 440	Calgary	AB	T2P0B4	403-296-0140	213-3648
Web: www.fortchicago.com					
WBI Holdings Inc PO Box 5601	Bismarck	ND	58506	701-530-1500	530-1599
TF: 800-238-8350 ■ *Web:* www.wbip.com					
Williams Gas Pipeline Gulfstream 1905 Intermodal Cir Suite 310	Palmetto	FL	34221	800-440-8475	
TF: 888-427-4352 ■ *Web:* www.williams.com/gas_pipeline					
Williams Gas Pipelines West PO Box 58900	Salt Lake City	UT	84158	801-583-8800	584-6483
Williams Partners LP 1 Williams Ctr	Tulsa	OK	74172	918-573-2000	573-8805
NYSE: WPZ ■ *TF:* 800-945-5426 ■ *Web:* www.williamslp.com					
Williston Basin Interstate Pipeline Co 1250 W Century Ave	Bismarck	ND	58503	701-530-1600	530-1699
TF: 800-238-8350 ■ *Web:* www.wbip.com					

329 GASKETS, PACKING, SEALING DEVICES

SEE ALSO Automotive Parts & Supplies - Mfr p. 1497

	City	State	Zip	Phone	Fax
Accratronics Seals Corp 2211 Kenmere Ave	Burbank	CA	91504	818-843-1500	841-2117
Web: www.accratronics.com					
Accro Gasket Inc 17365 Daimler St	Irvine	CA	92614	949-261-5846	261-5840
Web: www.accrogasket.com					
Akron Gasket & Packing Enterprises Inc 1244 Home Ave	Akron	OH	44310	330-633-3742	888-2088*
*Fax Area Code: 800 ■ *TF:* 800-289-7318 ■ *Web:* www.akrongasket.com					

Company	City	State	ZIP	Phone	Fax
American Casting & Mfg Corp 51 Commercial St *TF:* 800-342-0333 ■ *Web:* www.americancasting.com	Plainview	NY	11803	516-349-7010	349-8389
American Gasket & Rubber Co 119 E Commerce Dr	Schaumburg	IL	60173	847-882-8333	882-9333
American Packing & Gasket Co (APG) 6039 Armour Dr PO Box 213 *TF:* 800-888-5223 ■ *Web:* www.apandg.com	Houston	TX	77020	713-675-5271	675-2730
Amesbury Group Inc 57 Hunt Rd **Fax Area Code:* 800 ■ *Web:* www.amesbury.com	Amesbury	MA	01913	978-388-0581	289-6699*
APM Hexseal Corp 44 Honeck St *Web:* www.apmhexseal.com	Englewood	NJ	07631	201-569-5700	569-4106
Apple Rubber Products Inc 310 Erie St *TF Cust Svc:* 800-828-7745 ■ *Web:* www.applerubber.com	Lancaster	NY	14086	716-684-6560	684-8302
Artus Corp 201 S Dean St *Web:* www.artuscorp.com	Englewood	NJ	07631	201-568-1000	568-8865
Atlantic Gasket Corp 3908 Frankford Ave *TF:* 800-229-8881 ■ *Web:* www.atlanticgasket.com	Philadelphia	PA	19124	215-533-6400	533-4130
Auburn Mfg Co 29 Stack St *TF:* 800-427-5387 ■ *Web:* www.auburn-mfg.com	Middletown	CT	06457	860-346-6677	346-1334
Avica Inc 1785 Voyager Ave *Web:* www.avicausa.com	Simi Valley	CA	93063	805-584-4150	584-4155
AW Chesterton Co 500 Unicorn Pk Dr *Web:* www.chesterton.com	Woburn	MA	01801	781-438-7000	481-2500
Bal Seal Engineering Co Inc 19650 Pauling *TF:* 800-366-1006 ■ *Web:* www.balseal.com	Foothill Ranch	CA	92610	949-460-2100	460-2300
Bar's Products 10386 N Holly Rd *TF:* 800-521-7475 ■ *Web:* www.barsproducts.com	Holly	MI	48442	248-634-8278	634-1505
Basic Rubber & Plastics Co 8700 Boulder Ct *Web:* www.basicrubber.com	Walled Lake	MI	48390	248-360-7400	360-7101
Bentley Mfg Co Inc 520 Pk Industrial Dr *TF:* 800-424-2425 ■ *Web:* www.gasketsonline.com	La Habra	CA	90723	562-501-2955	697-5319
Burly Seal Products Co 1865 W D Ave *TF:* 800-877-7325 ■ *Web:* www.sealsandpackings.com	Tooele	UT	84074	800-877-7325	877-6979
California Gasket & Rubber Corp 533 W Collins Ave **Fax Area Code:* 714 ■ *TF:* 800-635-7084 ■ *Web:* www.calgasket.com	Orange	CA	92867	310-323-4250	639-0586*
Calpico Inc 1387 San Mateo Ave **Fax Area Code:* 800 ■ *TF:* 800-998-9115 ■ *Web:* www.calpicoinc.com	South San Francisco	CA	94080	650-588-2241	872-7325*
CE Conover & Co Inc 4106 Blanche Rd *TF:* 800-266-6837	Bensalem	PA	19020	215-639-6666	639-1799
CGR Products Inc 4655 US Hwy 29 N *TF:* 877-313-6785 ■ *Web:* www.cgrproducts.com	Greensboro	NC	27405	336-621-4568	375-5324
Chambers Gasket & Mfg Co 4701 W Rice St *Web:* www.chambersgasket.com	Chicago	IL	60651	773-626-8800	626-1430
Chicago Gasket Co 1285 W N Ave *TF:* 800-833-5666 ■ *Web:* www.chicagogasket.com	Chicago	IL	60622	773-486-3060	486-3784
Chicago-Wilcox Mfg Co 16928 State St *TF:* 800-323-5282 ■ *Web:* www.chicagowilcox.com	South Holland	IL	60473	708-339-5000	339-9876
Cincinnati Gasket Packing & Mfg Inc 40 Illinois Ave *Web:* www.cincinnatigasket.com	Cincinnati	OH	45215	513-761-3458	761-2994
Cooper Mfg Co 410 S 1st Ave	Marshalltown	IA	50158	641-752-6736	752-7476
Corpus Christi Gasket & Fastener Inc PO Box 4074 *TF:* 800-460-6366 ■ *Web:* www.ccgasket.com	Corpus Christi	TX	78469	361-884-6366	884-0695
DAR Industrial Products Inc 128 Front St *Web:* www.darindustrial.com	West Conshohocken	PA	19428	610-825-4900	825-4901
Delta Rubber Co 39 Wauregan Rd PO Box 300 *Web:* www.nnbr.com	Danielson	CT	06239	860-779-0300	774-0402
Eagle Burgmann Industries LP 10035 Brookriver Dr *TF Cust Svc:* 800-303-7735 ■ *Web:* www.eagleburgmann.com	Houston	TX	77040	713-939-9515	939-9091
EnPro Industries Inc 5605 Carnegie Blvd Suite 500 *NYSE:* NPO ■ *TF:* 866-663-6776 ■ *Web:* www.enproindustries.com	Charlotte	NC	28209	704-731-1500	731-1511
Excelsior Inc 720 Chestnut St *TF:* 800-435-4671 ■ *Web:* www.excelsiorinc.com	Rockford	IL	61105	815-987-2900	962-5466
Fast Group Houston Inc 8103 Rankin Rd *Web:* www.fast-houston.com	Humble	TX	77396	281-446-6662	446-7034
Flexitallic LP 6915 Hwy 225 *Web:* www.flexitallic.com	Deer Park	TX	77536	281-604-2400	604-2415
Flow Dry Technology Ltd 379 Albert Rd *TF:* 800-533-0077 ■ *Web:* www.stanhope.com	Brookville	OH	45309	937-833-2161	833-3208
Flowserve Corp 5215 N O'Connor Blvd Suite 2300 *NYSE:* FLS ■ *Web:* www.flowserve.com	Irving	TX	75039	972-443-6500	443-6800
Forest City Technologies Inc 299 Clay St *Web:* www.forestcitytech.com	Wellington	OH	44090	440-647-2115	647-2644
Freudenberg-NOK General Partnership 47690 E Anchor Ct *TF:* 800-533-5656 ■ *Web:* www.freudenberg-nok.com	Plymouth	MI	48170	734-451-0020	451-0125
Garlock Sealing Technologies 1666 Division St **Fax:* Cust Svc ■ *TF:* 800-448-6688 ■ *Web:* www.garlock.net	Palmyra	NY	14522	315-597-4811	597-3290*
Gasket Engineering Co Inc 4500 E 75th Terr PO Box 320288 *Web:* www.gasketeng.com	Kansas City	MO	64132	816-363-8333	363-3558
Gasket Mfg Co 18001 Main St *TF:* 800-442-7538 ■ *Web:* www.gasketmfg.com	Gardena	CA	90248	310-217-5600	217-5608
Gaskets Inc 301 State Rd 16 *TF:* 800-558-1833 ■ *Web:* www.gasketsinc.com	Rio	WI	53960	920-992-3137	992-3124
Greene Tweed & Co 2075 Detwiler Rd *Web:* www.gtweed.com	Kulpsville	PA	19443	215-256-9521	256-0189
Gunite Supply & Equipment Co - West 1726 S Magnolia Ave *TF:* 888-393-8635 ■ *Web:* www.gunitesupply.com	Monrovia	CA	91016	626-358-0143	359-7985
Hahn Elastomer Corp 14601 Keel St *Web:* www.hahnelastomer.com	Plymouth	MI	48170	734-455-3300	455-3300
Higbee Inc 6741 Thompson Rd *TF:* 800-255-4800 ■ *Web:* www.higbee-inc.com	Syracuse	NY	13211	315-432-8021	432-0227
Holm Industries Inc 745 S Gardner St	Scottsburg	IN	47170	812-752-2526	752-3563
Hoosier Gasket Corp 3333 Massachusetts Ave *TF:* 800-442-7705 ■ *Web:* www.hoosiergasket.com	Indianapolis	IN	46218	317-545-2000	545-5500
Ilene Industries Inc 301 Stanley Blvd *TF:* 800-251-1602 ■ *Web:* www.ileneindustries.com	Shelbyville	TN	37160	931-684-8731	684-8735
Indian Springs Mfg Co Inc 2095 W Genesse Rd PO Box 469 *Web:* www.indiansprings.com	Baldwinsville	NY	13027	315-635-6101	635-7473
Industrial Custom Products Inc 2801 37th Ave NE *TF:* 800-654-0886 ■ *Web:* www.industrialcustom.com	Minneapolis	MN	55421	612-781-2255	781-1144
Industrial Gasket & Shim Co Inc (IGS) 200 Country Club Rd *TF:* 800-229-1447 ■ *Web:* www.igscorp.com	Meadow Lands	PA	15347	724-222-5800	222-5898
Industrial Gasket Inc (IG) 720 S Sara Rd *TF:* 800-654-8433 ■ *Web:* www.igok.com	Mustang	OK	73137	405-376-9393	376-3933
Intek Plastic Inc 1000 Spiral Blvd *TF:* 800-451-4544 ■ *Web:* www.intekplastics.com	Hastings	MN	55033	651-437-7700	437-3805
Interface Solutions Inc 216 Wohlsen Way *TF:* 800-942-7538 ■ *Web:* www.sealinfo.com	Lancaster	PA	17603	717-207-6000	207-6080
International Seal Co Inc 2041 E Wilshire Ave	Santa Ana	CA	92705	714-834-0602	834-0590
ITT Conoflow 5154 Hwy 78 PO Box 768 **Fax:* Cust Svc ■ *Web:* www.ittconoflow.com	Saint George	SC	29477	843-563-9281	563-2131*
Jade Engineered Plastic Inc 121 Broadcommon Rd *TF:* 800-557-9155 ■ *Web:* www.jadeplastics.com	Bristol	RI	02809	401-253-4440	253-1605
JM Clipper Corp 403 Industrial Dr PO Drawer 632340 *TF:* 800-233-3900	Nacogdoches	TX	75964	936-560-5419	560-8998
John Crane Canada Inc 423 Green Rd N *Web:* www.johncrane.com	Stoney Creek	ON	L8E2R4	905-662-6191	662-1564
John Crane Inc 6400 W Oakton St *TF:* 800-732-5464 ■ *Web:* www.johncrane.com	Morton Grove	IL	60053	847-967-2400	967-2400
Kaydon Ring & Seal Inc 1600 Wicomico St PO Box 626 *Web:* www.kaydonringandseal.com	Baltimore	MD	21230	410-547-7700	576-9059
Lamons Gasket Co 7300 Airport Blvd *TF:* 800-231-6906 ■ *Web:* www.lamonsgasket.com	Houston	TX	77061	713-222-0284	547-9502
Manufactured Rubber Products Co 4501 Tacony St	Philadelphia	PA	19124	215-533-3600	533-3912
Marsh Industries Inc 49680 Leona Dr *Web:* www.marshindustries.com	Chesterfield	MI	48051	586-949-9300	949-1290
Melrath Gasket Inc 1500 John F Kennedy Blvd # 200 *TF:* 800-635-7284 ■ *Web:* www.melrath.com	Philadelphia	PA	19102	215-223-6000	229-6235
Mesa Rubber Co - West 1726 S Magnolia Ave *TF:* 888-393-8635 ■ *Web:* www.mesarubber.com	Monrovia	CA	91016	626-359-9361	359-7985
MG Industries Inc 1427 W 16th St	Long Beach	CA	90813	562-436-9095	436-6844
Mr Gasket Inc 10601 Memphis Ave Bldg 12-A *Web:* www.mrgasket.com	Cleveland	OH	44144	216-688-8300	688-8305
Netherland Rubber Co 2931 Exon Ave *TF:* 800-582-1877 ■ *Web:* www.netherlandrubber.com	Cincinnati	OH	45241	513-733-0883	733-1096
Newco Automotive Inc 101 Ellen Dr	Orion Township	MI	48359	248-333-2320	239-3900
Novagard Solutions Inc 5109 Hamilton Ave *TF:* 800-380-0138 ■ *Web:* www.novagard.com	Cleveland	OH	44114	216-881-8111	881-6977
Ohio Gasket & Shim Co Inc 976 Evans Ave *TF:* 800-321-2438 ■ *Web:* www.ogsindustries.com	Akron	OH	44305	330-630-2030	630-2075
Omega Shielding Products Inc 1384 Pompton Ave *TF:* 800-828-5784 ■ *Web:* www.omegashielding.com	Cedar Grove	NJ	07009	973-890-7455	890-9714
Pacific States Felt & Mfg Co Inc 23850 Clawiter Rd *TF:* 800-566-8866 ■ *Web:* www.pacificstatesfelt.com	Hayward	CA	94545	510-783-0277	783-4725
Parco Inc 1801 S Archibald Ave *Web:* www.parcoinc.com	Ontario	CA	91761	909-947-2200	923-0288
Parker EPS Redmond Plastics Ops 3967 Buffalo St *Web:* www.acadiapolymers.com	Marion	NY	14505	315-926-4211	926-4498
Parker Hannifin Corp TechSeal Div 3025 W Croft Cir *Web:* www.parker.com	Spartanburg	SC	29302	864-573-7332	583-4299
Pemko Mfg Co Inc 4226 Transport St *TF:* 800-283-9988 ■ *Web:* www.pemko.com	Ventura	CA	93003	805-642-2600	642-4109
Performance Polymer Technologies Co 8801 Washington Blvd Suite 109 *Web:* www.pptech.com	Roseville	CA	95678	916-677-1414	677-1474
PerkinElmer Fluid Sciences Inc Centurion Products 15 Pioneer Ave *Web:* www.perkinelmer.com	Warwick	RI	02888	401-781-4700	781-0930
PPC Mechanical Seals 2769 Mission Dr *TF:* 800-731-7325 ■ *Web:* www.ppcmechanicalseals.com	Baton Rouge	LA	70805	225-356-4333	355-2126
Precision Gasket Co 5625 W 78th St *Web:* www.precisiongasket.com	Minneapolis	MN	55439	952-942-6711	942-6712
Presray Corp 159 Charles Coleman Blvd *Web:* www.presray.com	Pawling	NY	12564	845-855-1220	855-1137
Press-Seal Gasket Corp 2424 W State Blvd *TF:* 800-348-7325 ■ *Web:* www.press-seal.com	Fort Wayne	IN	46808	260-436-0521	436-1908
Presscut Industries Inc 1730 Briercroft Ct *TF:* 800-442-4924 ■ *Web:* www.presscut.com	Carrollton	TX	75006	972-389-0615	245-2488
Pureflex Inc 4617 E Paris Ave SE *Web:* www.pureflex.com	Kentwood	MI	49512	616-554-1100	554-3633
Rhopac Fabricators Inc 450 Enterprise Pkwy *Web:* www.rhopac.com	Lake Zurich	IL	60047	847-540-7400	540-6690
Rotor Clip Co Inc 187 Davidson Ave *TF Cust Svc:* 800-631-5857 ■ *Web:* www.rotorclip.com	Somerset	NJ	08873	732-469-7333	469-7898
Rubbercraft Corp of California 15627 S Broadway *TF:* 800-782-2379 ■ *Web:* www.rubbercraft.com	Gardena	CA	90248	310-328-5402	618-1832

Phone | Fax

Santa Fe Rubber Products Inc
12306 E Washington Blvd .... Whittier CA 90606 562-693-2776 693-4936
Web: www.santaferubber.com
Schlegel Systems Inc 1555 Jefferson Rd .... Rochester NY 14623 585-427-7200 427-9913*
**Fax:* Cust Svc ■ *TF:* 800-828-6237 ■ *Web:* www.schlegel.com
Seal Methods Inc
11915 Shoemaker Ave .... Santa Fe Springs CA 90670 562-944-0291 946-9439
TF: 800-423-4777 ■ *Web:* www.sealmethodsinc.com
Sealing Devices Inc 4400 Walden Ave .... Lancaster NY 14086 716-684-7600 684-0760
TF Cust Svc: 800-727-3257 ■ *Web:* www.sealingdevices.com
Sealing Equipment Products Co Inc
123 Airpark Industrial Rd .... Alabaster AL 35007 205-403-7500 403-7592
TF Cust Svc: 800-633-4770 ■ *Web:* www.sepcousa.com
Serra Mfg Corp
3039 E Las Hermanas St .... Rancho Dominguez CA 90221 310-537-4560 537-1153*
**Fax:* Cust Svc ■ *Web:* www.serramfg.com
Southern Rubber Co Inc 2209 Patterson St .... Greensboro NC 27407 336-299-2456 294-4970
Specification Rubber Products Inc
1568 1st St N .... Alabaster AL 35007 205-663-2521 663-1875
TF: 800-633-3415 ■ *Web:* www.specrubber.com
Standco Industries Inc 2701 Clinton Dr .... Houston TX 77020 713-224-6311 229-9312
TF: 800-231-6018 ■ *Web:* www.standco.net
Stanley Harrison Corp 3020 Empire Ave .... Burbank CA 91504 818-842-2131 842-6042
Stein Seal Co Inc 1500 Industrial Blvd .... Kulpsville PA 19443 215-256-0201 256-4818
Web: www.steinseal.com
Sur-Seal Gasket & Packing Inc
6156 Wesselman Rd .... Cincinnati OH 45248 513-574-8500 574-2220
TF: 800-345-8966 ■ *Web:* www.sur-seal.com
T & E Industries Inc 215 Watchung Ave .... Orange NJ 07050 973-672-5454 672-0180
TF Sales: 800-245-7080 ■ *Web:* www.teindustries.com
Trelleborg Sealing Solutions
5503 Distribution Dr .... Fort Wayne IN 46825 260-749-2709
Web: www.trelleborg.com
Trostel Ltd 901 Maxwell St .... Lake Geneva WI 53147 262-248-4481 248-6406
Web: www.trostel.com
United Gasket Corp 1633 55th Ave .... Cicero IL 60804 708-656-3700 656-6292
Web: www.unitedgasket.com
UTEX Industries Inc 10810 Katy Fwy # 100 .... Houston TX 77043 713-467-1000 467-3609
TF: 800-359-9230 ■ *Web:* www.utexind.com
Vellumoid Inc 54 Rockdale St .... Worcester MA 01606 508-853-2500 852-0741
TF: 800-609-5558 ■ *Web:* www.vellumoid.com
William H Harvey 4334 S 67th St .... Omaha NE 68117 402-331-1175 331-9532*
**Fax Area Code:* 800 ■ *TF:* 800-321-9532 ■ *Web:* www.wmharvey.com
Zero International Inc 415 Concord Ave .... Bronx NY 10455 718-585-3230 292-2243
TF: 800-635-5335 ■ *Web:* www.zerointernational.com

330 GIFT SHOPS

SEE ALSO Card Shops p. 1555; Duty-Free Shops p. 1791; Home Furnishings Stores p. 2023

Phone | Fax

Afromart Gift Enterprises 20 La Rue St .... Riverside CA 92508 951-686-0078
TF: 877-215-0284 ■ *Web:* www.afromart.net
Arribas Bros Inc 1500 Live Oak Ln .... Lake Buena vista FL 32830 407-828-4840 828-8019
TF: 888-828-4840 ■ *Web:* www.arribasbrothers.com
Barbeques Galore 10 Orchard Rd Suite 200 .... Lake Forest CA 92630 949-597-2400 597-2434
TF: 800-752-3085 ■ *Web:* www.bbqgalore.com
Brookstone Inc 1 Innovation Way .... Merrimack NH 03054 603-880-9500 577-8003
TF Cust Svc: 800-846-3000 ■ *Web:* www.brookstone.com
Chicago Symphony Orchestra Ass
220 S Michigan Ave .... Chicago IL 60604 312-294-3000 294-3329
Web: www.cso.org
Christmas Tree Shops 261 White's Path .... South Yarmouth MA 02664 508-394-1206 394-7153
Web: www.christmastreeshops.com
CM Paula Co 6049 Hi-Tek Ct .... Mason OH 45040 513-336-3100 336-3119
TF: 800-543-4464 ■ *Web:* www.cmpaula.com
Decorative Concepts Inc 401 Milford Pkwy .... Milford OH 45150 513-248-1144 248-3553
Disney Consumer Products
500 S Buena Vista St .... Burbank CA 91521 818-560-1000 560-1930*
**Fax:* Cust Svc ■ *TF PR:* 800-723-4763
EBSCO Industries Inc Military Service Co Div
PO Box 1943 .... Birmingham AL 35201 205-991-6600
Web: www.ebscoind.com
Evelyn Hill Inc 1 Liberty Is Frnt 1 .... New York NY 10004 212-363-3180 480-2460
Web: www.thestatueofliberty.com
Friendly Gift Shop Inc 4 Branmar Plaza .... Wilmington DE 19810 302-475-6560 475-4605
GiftCertificates.com 11510 Blondo St .... Omaha NE 68164 800-522-8207 445-0075*
**Fax Area Code:* 402 ■ *TF:* 800-773-7368 ■ *Web:* www.giftcertificates.com
GoCollect Inc 65 Broadway 7th Fl .... New York NY 10006 212-430-6520
Web: www.gocollect.com
Hazelwood Enterprises Inc 402 N 32nd St .... Phoenix AZ 85008 602-275-7709 275-4658
TF: 800-680-4667 ■ *Web:* www.hazelwoods.com
Historical Research Center International Inc
2019 Corporate Dr .... Boynton Beach FL 33426 561-732-5263 740-0497
TF: 800-940-7991 ■ *Web:* www.names.com
Hummel Gift Shop 1656 E Garfield Rd .... New Springfield OH 44443 330-549-3728 549-0879
TF: 800-354-5438 ■ *Web:* www.hummelgiftshop.com
Illuminations 1736 Corporate Cir .... Petaluma CA 94954 707-769-2700 769-8700
TF: 800-226-3537 ■ *Web:* www.illuminations.com
Kirlins Inc 532 Maine St .... Quincy IL 62305 217-224-8953 224-9400
Web: www.kirlins.com
Limited Edition 2170 Sunrise Hwy .... Merrick NY 11566 516-623-4400 867-3701
TF: 800-645-2864
Mole Hollow Candles Ltd
3 Deerfield Ave .... Shelburne Falls MA 01370 413-625-6337 625-9669
TF Cust Svc: 800-445-6653 ■ *Web:* www.molehollowcandles.com
Napa Valley Candle Factory & Gift Shop
3037 California Blvd .... Napa CA 94558 707-255-0902 255-0902
Web: www.napanet.net/~candlman
New Seasons Market 7300 SW Beaverton Hwy .... Portland OR 97225 503-292-6838 292-2349
Web: www.newseasonsmarket.com
Only in San Francisco
Pier 39 Space B-11 .... San Francisco CA 94133 415-397-0143 956-8124
Web: www.onlyinsanfrancisco.net
Oregon Connection 1125 S 1st St .... Coos Bay OR 97420 541-267-7804 267-6497
TF: 800-255-5318 ■ *Web:* www.oregonconnection.com
Pacific Trade International Inc
5515 Security Ln Suite 1100 .... Rockville MD 20852 301-816-4200 816-4220
Paradies Shops
5950 Fulton Industrial Blvd SW .... Atlanta GA 30336 404-344-7905 349-3226
Web: www.theparadiesshops.com
Razorback Gift Shops Inc
579 W Vanburen St .... Eureka Springs AR 72632 479-253-8294 253-9232
San Francisco Music Box Co 6411 Burleson Rd .... Austin TN 78744 800-227-2190 369-6192*
**Fax Area Code:* 512 ■ *TF:* 800-227-2190 ■ *Web:* www.sfmusicbox.com
Sanrio Inc 570 Eccles Ave .... South San Francisco CA 94080 650-952-2880 872-2730
TF: 800-325-8316 ■ *Web:* www.sanrio.com
Silver Towne LP
120 E Union City Pike PO Box 424 .... Winchester IN 47394 765-584-7481 584-1246
TF: 800-788-7481 ■ *Web:* www.silvertowne.com
Soap Plant 4633 Hollywood Blvd .... Los Angeles CA 90027 323-663-0122 663-0243
Web: www.soapplant.com
Tuesday Morning Corp 6250 LBJ Fwy .... Dallas TX 75240 972-387-3562 991-5403
NASDAQ: TUES ■ *TF:* 800-457-0099 ■ *Web:* www.tuesdaymorning.com
Wall Drug Store Inc PO Box 401 .... Wall SD 57790 605-279-2175 279-2699
Web: www.walldrug.com
WeddingChannel.com 700 S Flower Suite 600 .... Los Angeles CA 90017 877-335-5252 599-4180*
**Fax Area Code:* 213 ■ *TF:* 877-335-5252 ■ *Web:* www.weddings.weddingchannel.com
Wendell August Forge Inc 620 Madison Ave .... Grove City PA 16127 724-458-8360 458-5952
TF: 800-923-4438 ■ *Web:* www.wendellaugust.com
Yankee Candle Co Inc PO Box 110 .... South Deerfield MA 01373 413-665-8306 665-4815
NYSE: YCC ■ *TF:* 877-803-6890 ■ *Web:* www.yankeecandle.com

331 GIFTS & NOVELTIES - WHOL

Phone | Fax

ABC Distributing Inc 2800 Lakeside Dr .... Bannockburn IL 60015 847-615-7366 735-9720
Web: www.abcdistributing.com
Accoutrements PO Box 30811 .... Seattle WA 98113 425-349-3838 349-5188
TF: 800-886-2221 ■ *Web:* www.accoutrements.com
Admiral Exchange Co Inc 1443 Union St .... San Diego CA 92101 619-239-2165 239-1843
Web: www.admiralexchange.com
Aerial Photography Services Inc (APS)
2511 S Tryon St .... Charlotte NC 28203 704-333-5144 333-4911
Web: www.aps-1.com
Angel Sales Inc 4147 N Ravenswood Ave .... Chicago IL 60613 773-883-8858 883-8889
Web: www.angelsales.com
Blair Cedar & Novelty Works Inc
680 W US Hwy 54 .... Camdenton MO 65020 573-346-2235 346-5534
TF: 800-325-3943 ■ *Web:* www.blaircedar.com
Boyds Collection Ltd 350 S St .... McSherrystown PA 17344 717-633-9898 633-5511
TF: 800-377-3050 ■ *Web:* www.boydsstuff.com
Bright Ideas in Broad Ripple Inc
7425 Westfield Blvd .... Indianapolis IN 46240 317-257-4111 257-4174
Web: www.bright-ideas.org
Drysdales Inc 3220 S Memorial Dr .... Tulsa OK 74145 918-664-6481 664-1431
TF: 800-444-6481 ■ *Web:* www.drysdales.com
Enesco Group Inc 225 Windsor Dr .... Itasca IL 60143 630-875-5300 875-5350
TF Cust Svc: 800-436-3726 ■ *Web:* www.enesco.com
Fridgedoor.com 65 School St .... Quincy MA 02169 617-770-7913 801-8026
TF: 800-955-3741 ■ *Web:* www.fridgedoor.com
Hayes Specialties Corp 1761 E Genesee .... Saginaw MI 48601 989-755-6541 755-2341
TF: 800-248-3603 ■ *Web:* www.ehayes.com
Hollywood Ribbon Industries Inc
3400 E Medford St PO Box 63187 .... Los Angeles CA 90063 323-266-0670 266-6709
TF: 800-457-7652 ■ *Web:* www.hollywoodribbon.com
Hornung's Golf Products Inc
815 Morris St .... Fond du Lac WI 54935 920-922-2640 922-4986
TF: 800-323-3569 ■ *Web:* www.hornungs.com
Kurt S Adler Inc 7 W 34th St .... New York NY 10001 212-924-0900 807-0575
TF: 866-919-9757 ■ *Web:* www.kurtadler.com
Morrow Enterprises 350 130th Ave .... Vero Beach FL 32968 772-257-3300 770-9175
Web: morrowent.com
Northwestern Products Inc
721 Industrial Pk Rd .... Ashland WI 54806 715-685-9500 685-9545
TF: 800-328-7317 ■ *Web:* www.nwproductsinc.com
Sanrio Inc 570 Eccles Ave .... South San Francisco CA 94080 650-952-2880 872-2730
TF: 800-325-8316 ■ *Web:* www.sanrio.com
Service Systems Assoc Inc 4699 Marion St .... Denver CO 80216 303-322-3031 815-1698
Web: www.kmssa.com
Specialty Co 6250 W Howard St .... Niles IL 60714 800-621-5165 367-3557*
**Fax Area Code:* 877 ■ *TF:* 800-621-5165 ■ *Web:* www.shopelks.com
Star Sales Co Inc 1803 N Central St .... Knoxville TN 37917 865-524-0771 524-4889
TF: 800-347-9494 ■ *Web:* www.starsalescompany.com
Trends International LLC 5188 W 74th St .... Indianapolis IN 46268 317-388-1212 388-1414
Web: www.trendsinternational.com
Unique Industries Inc
4750 League Island Blvd .... Philadelphia PA 19112 215-336-4300 888-1490*
**Fax Area Code:* 800 ■ *TF:* 800-888-0559 ■ *Web:* www.favors.com
Us Balloon Mfg Co Inc 140 58th St .... Brooklyn NY 11220 718-492-9700 832-9872*
**Fax Area Code:* 800 ■ *TF:* 800-285-4000 ■ *Web:* www.usballoon.com
Variety Distributors Inc 609 7th St .... Harlan IA 51537 712-755-2184 755-5041
TF: 800-274-1095 ■ *Web:* www.varietydistributors.com
WinCraft Inc 1124 W 5th St PO Box 888 .... Winona MN 55987 507-454-5510 453-0690
TF: 800-533-8006 ■ *Web:* www.wincraft.com
Zims Inc 4370 S 300 W .... Salt Lake City UT 84107 801-268-2505 268-9859
TF Orders: 800-453-6420

332 GLASS - FLAT, PLATE, TEMPERED

	City	State	Zip	Phone	Fax
AGC Flat Galss North America Inc					
11175 Cicero Dr Suite 400	Alpharetta	GA	30022	404-446-4200	446-4221
TF: 800-251-0441 ■ *Web:* www.na.agc-flatglass.com					
Anthony International 12391 Montera Ave	Sylmar	CA	91342	818-365-9451	361-9611
TF: 800-772-0900 ■ *Web:* www.anthonydoors.com					
Apogee Enterprises Inc					
4400 W 78th St Suite 520	Minneapolis	MN	55435	952-835-1874	835-3196
NASDAQ: APOG ■ *TF:* 877-752-3432 ■ *Web:* www.apog.com					
Basco Shower Enclosures 7201 Snider Rd	Mason	OH	45040	513-573-1900	573-1919
TF: 800-543-1938 ■ *Web:* www.bascoshowerdoor.com					
Binswanger Glass					
965 Ridge Lake Blvd Suite 300	Memphis	TN	38120	901-767-7111	683-9351
TF: 800-238-6057 ■ *Web:* www.binswangerglass.com					
Bullseye Glass Co 3722 SE 21st Ave	Portland	OR	97202	503-232-8887	238-9963
TF: 888-220-3002 ■ *Web:* www.bullseyeglass.com					
Cameron Glass Inc 3550 W Tacoma St	Broken Arrow	OK	74012	918-254-6000	252-4665
TF: 800-331-3666 ■ *Web:* www.camglass.com					
Cardinal Glass Co 1087 Research Pkwy	Rockford	IL	61109	815-394-1400	397-1750
TF Cust Svc: 800-728-3468					
Corning Display Technologies					
1 Riverfront Plaza	Corning	NY	14831	607-974-5439	974-7097
Web: www.corning.com/displaytechnologies					
D & W Inc 941 Oak St	Elkhart	IN	46514	574-264-9674	264-9859
TF: 800-255-0829 ■ *Web:* www.dwincorp.com					
Gemtron Corp 615 Hwy 68	Sweetwater	TN	37874	423-337-3522	337-7979
Web: www.gemtron.com					
Gentex Corp 600 N Centennial St	Zeeland	MI	49464	616-772-1800	772-7348
NASDAQ: GNTX ■ *TF:* 800-444-4689 ■ *Web:* www.gentex.com					
Glaz-Tech Industries Inc 2207 E Elvira Rd	Tucson	AZ	85756	520-629-0268	629-8811
TF: 800-755-8062 ■ *Web:* www.glaztech.com					
Globe Amerada Glass Co					
2001 Greenleaf Ave	Elk Grove Village	IL	60007	847-364-2900	364-3625
TF: 800-323-8776					
Gray Glass Co 217-44 98th Ave	Queens Village	NY	11429	718-217-2943	217-0280
TF: 800-523-3320 ■ *Web:* www.grayglass.net					
Guardian Industries Corp 2300 Harmon Rd	Auburn Hills	MI	48326	248-340-1800	340-9988
TF: 800-327-5888 ■ *Web:* www.guardian.com					
Hartung Agalite Glass Co 17830 W Valley Hwy	Tukwila	WA	98188	425-656-2626	656-2601
TF: 800-552-2227 ■ *Web:* www.hartung-glass.com					
Hehr International Inc 3333 Casitas Ave	Los Angeles	CA	90039	323-663-1261	666-9458
Web: www.hehrintl.com					
Kokomo Opalescent Glass Co 1310 S Market St	Kokomo	IN	46902	765-457-8136	459-5177
Web: www.kog.com					
Magna Donnelly 49 W 3rd St	Holland	MI	49423	616-786-7000	786-6233
Web: www.magnadon.com					
Maran-Wurzell Glass & Mirror Co					
1683 Mt Vernon Ave	Pomona	CA	91768	909-623-1665	623-1695
Naturalite 750 Airport Rd	Terrell	TX	75160	972-551-6400	551-6420
TF: 800-527-4018 ■ *Web:* www.naturalite.com					
Northwestern Industries Inc					
2500 W Jameson St	Seattle	WA	98199	206-285-3140	285-3603
TF: 800-426-2771 ■ *Web:* www.nwiglass.com					
ODL Inc 215 E Roosevelt Ave	Zeeland	MI	49464	616-772-9111	772-9110*
**Fax:* Cust Svc ■ *TF:* 800-288-1800 ■ *Web:* www.odl.com					
Oregon Glass Co 10450 SW Ridder Rd	Wilsonville	OR	97070	503-682-3846	682-0252
TF: 800-547-0217 ■ *Web:* www.oregonglass.com					
Paul Wissmach Glass Co Inc					
420 Stephen St PO Box 228	Paden City	WV	26159	304-337-2253	337-8800
Web: www.wissmachglass.com					
Pilkington Holdings Inc					
811 Madison Ave PO Box 0799	Toledo	OH	43697	419-247-3731	247-3821
Web: www.pilkington.com					
PPG Industries Inc 1 PPG Pl	Pittsburgh	PA	15272	412-434-3131	434-2011*
NYSE: PPG ■ **Fax:* Hum Res ■ *Web:* www.ppg.com					
Rainbow Art Glass Inc 1761 Rt 34 S	Wall	NJ	07727	732-681-6003	681-4984
TF: 800-526-2356 ■ *Web:* www.rainbowartglass.com					
Rambusch Decorating Co					
160 Cornelison Ave	Jersey City	NJ	07304	201-333-2525	433-3355
Web: www.rambusch.com					
Saint-Gobain Corp 750 E Swedesford Rd	Valley Forge	PA	19482	610-341-7000	341-7797
TF: 800-274-8530 ■ *Web:* www.saint-gobain.com/us					
Schott North America Inc 555 Taxter Rd	Elmsford	NY	10523	914-831-2200	831-2201
Web: www.us.schott.com					
Spectrum Glass Co PO Box 646	Woodinville	WA	98072	425-483-6699	483-9007
TF: 800-426-3120 ■ *Web:* www.spectrumglass.com					
Stanley Home Decor 480 Myrtle St	New Britain	CT	06053	860-225-5111	827-3895
TF: 800-782-6539					
Thermoseal Glass Corp 400 Water St	Gloucester	NJ	08130	856-456-3109	456-0989
TF: 800-456-7788 ■ *Web:* www.thermoseal.com					
Torstenson Glass Co 3233 N Sheffield Ave	Chicago	IL	60657	773-525-0435	525-0009
Web: www.tglass.com					
Tru-Vue Glass & Artboard Co 9400 W 55th St	McCook	IL	60525	708-485-5080	485-5980
TF Cust Svc: 800-621-8339 ■ *Web:* www.tru-vue.com					
Viracon Inc 800 Pk Dr	Owatonna	MN	55060	507-451-9555	444-3555
TF: 800-533-2080 ■ *Web:* www.viracon.com					
Virginia Mirror Co Inc 300 Moss St S	Martinsville	VA	24112	276-632-9816	632-2488
TF: 800-826-4776					
VVP America Inc 965 Ridge Lake Blvd Suite 300	Memphis	TN	38120	901-767-7111	683-9351
TF: 800-238-6057 ■ *Web:* www.vvpamerica.com					
Wasco Products Inc 22 Pioneer Ave PO Box 351	Sanford	ME	04073	207-324-8060	490-1218
TF: 800-388-0293 ■ *Web:* www.wascoproducts.com					

333 GLASS FIBERS

	City	State	Zip	Phone	Fax
Corning Inc 1 Riverfront Plaza	Corning	NY	14831	607-974-9000	974-8688*
NYSE: GLW ■ **Fax:* Hum Res ■ *Web:* www.corning.com					
Evanite Fiber Corp PO Box E	Corvallis	OR	97339	541-753-1211	753-1211
TF Cust Svc: 800-441-5567					
FGX International Holdings Ltd					
500 George Washington Hwy	Smithfield	RI	02917	401-231-3800	232-7235
TF: 800-283-3090 ■ *Web:* www.fgxi.com					
Fiberoptics Technology Inc 1 Quassett Rd	Pomfret	CT	06258	860-928-0443	928-7664
TF Cust Svc: 800-433-5248 ■ *Web:* www.fiberoptix.com					
Incom Inc PO Box G	Southbridge	MA	01550	508-765-9151	765-0041
Web: www.incomusa.com					

334 GLASS JARS & BOTTLES

	City	State	Zip	Phone	Fax
Arkansas Glass Container Corp					
516 W Johnson Ave	Jonesboro	AR	72401	870-932-4564	268-6217
Web: www.agcc.com					
Glenshaw Glass Co Inc					
1101 William Flynn Hwy	Glenshaw	PA	15116	412-486-9100	486-9252
TF: 800-326-2467					
Gujarat Glass International Inc					
401 Rt 73 N Bldg 10 Suite 202					
Lake Ctr Executive Pk	Marlton	NJ	08053	856-293-6400	293-6401
Web: www.theglassgroup.com					
Jarden Corp 555 Theodore Fremd Ave Suite B-302	Rye	NY	10580	914-967-9400	
NYSE: JAH ■ *Web:* www.jardencorp.com					
Leone Industries Co 443 SE Ave	Bridgeton	NJ	08302	856-455-2000	455-3491
Web: www.leoneglass.com					
New High Glass Inc 12713 SW 125th Ave	Miami	FL	33186	305-232-0840	251-4622
TF: 800-452-7787 ■ *Web:* www.newhighglass.net					
Owens-Illinois Inc One Michael Owens Way	Perrysburg	OH	43551	567-336-5000	247-1132*
NYSE: OI ■ **Fax Area Code:* 419 ■ *Web:* www.o-i.com					
Saint-Gobain Containers Inc					
1509 S Macedonia Ave	Muncie	IN	47302	765-741-7000	741-7012
TF: 800-428-8642 ■ *Web:* www.sgcontainers.com					

335 GLASS PRODUCTS - INDUSTRIAL (CUSTOM)

	City	State	Zip	Phone	Fax
Abrisa USPG PO Box 3258	Ventura	CA	93006	805-525-4902	525-8604
TF: 800-350-5000 ■ *Web:* www.abrisa.com					
Bassett Mirror Co Inc PO Box 627	Bassett	VA	24055	276-629-3341	629-3709
Web: www.bassettmirror.com					
Elan Technology 11829 E Oglethorpe Hwy # E	Midway	GA	31320	912-880-3526	880-3000
Web: www.elantechnology.com					
Flex-O-Lite Inc					
50 Crestwood Executive Ctr Suite 522	Saint Louis	MO	63126	800-325-9525	541-3193
TF: 800-325-9525 ■ *Web:* www.flexolite.com					
Fredericks Co The					
2400 Philmont Ave PO Box 67	Huntingdon Valley	PA	19006	215-947-2500	947-7464
Web: www.frederickscom.com					
Garner Glass Co 177 S Indian Hill Blvd	Claremont	CA	91711	909-624-5071	625-0173
Headwest Inc 15650 S Avalon Blvd	Compton	CA	90220	310-532-5420	532-5920
Web: www.headwestinc.com					
Henderson Glass Inc 715 S Blvd E	Rochester Hills	MI	48307	248-829-4700	829-4799
TF: 800-694-0672 ■ *Web:* www.hendersonglass.com					
Lang-Mekra North America LLC					
101 Tillessen Blvd	Ridgeway	SC	29130	803-337-5264	337-5265
Web: www.lang-mekra.com					
Lenoir Mirror Co Inc 401 Kincaid St	Lenoir	NC	28645	828-728-3271	728-5010
TF: 800-438-8204 ■ *Web:* www.lenoirmirror.com					
Naugatuck Glass Co PO Box 71	Naugatuck	CT	06770	203-729-5227	729-8781*
**Fax:* Sales ■ *TF:* 800-533-3513					
North American Specialty Glass					
2175 Kumry Rd PO Box 70	Trumbauersville	PA	18970	215-536-0333	536-6872
TF: 888-785-5962 ■ *Web:* www.naspecialtyglass.com					
Precision Electronic Glass Inc					
1013 Hendee Rd	Vineland	NJ	08360	856-691-2234	691-3090
TF: 800-982-4734 ■ *Web:* www.pegglass.com					
Richland Glass Co Inc 1640 SW Blvd	Vineland	NJ	08360	800-959-0312	691-4525*
**Fax Area Code:* 856 ■ *TF:* 800-959-0312 ■ *Web:* www.richlandglass.com					
Swift Glass Co Inc 131 W 22nd St	Elmira Heights	NY	14903	607-733-7166	732-5829
TF: 800-537-9438 ■ *Web:* www.swiftglass.com					

336 GLASSWARE - LABORATORY & SCIENTIFIC

	City	State	Zip	Phone	Fax
Ace Glass Inc 1430 NW Blvd PO Box 688	Vineland	NJ	08360	856-692-3333	543-6752*
**Fax Area Code:* 800 ■ *TF:* 800-223-4524 ■ *Web:* www.aceglass.com					
Bellco Glass Inc 340 Edrudo Rd	Vineland	NJ	08360	856-691-1075	691-3247
TF: 800-257-7043 ■ *Web:* www.bellcoglass.com					
Bioscreen Testing Services Inc					
3904 Del AMO Blvd Suite 801	Torrance	CA	90503	310-214-0043	370-3642
Web: www.bioscreen.com					
Corning Inc 1 Riverfront Plaza	Corning	NY	14831	607-974-9000	974-8688*
NYSE: GLW ■ **Fax:* Hum Res ■ *Web:* www.corning.com					
Eden Labs 1601 W 5th St Suite 240	Columbus	OH	43212	614-374-2455	469-0148*
**Fax Area Code:* 801 ■ *Web:* www.edenlabs.org					
Gujarat Glass International Coded Products					
5176 Harding Hwy	Mays Landing	NJ	08330	856-728-9300	293-6401
Quadrex Corp PO Box 3881	Woodbridge	CT	06525	203-393-3112	393-0391
TF Sales: 800-275-7033 ■ *Web:* www.quadrexcorp.com					
Schott North America Inc 555 Taxter Rd	Elmsford	NY	10523	914-831-2200	831-2201
Web: www.us.schott.com					
Wale Apparatus Co Inc 400 Front St	Hellertown	PA	18055	610-838-7047	838-7440
TF: 800-444-9253 ■ *Web:* www.waleapparatus.com					

337 GLASSWARE & POTTERY - HOUSEHOLD

SEE ALSO Table & Kitchen Supplies - China & Earthenware p. 2680

Company	City	State	Zip	Phone	Fax
Anchor Hocking Co 519 Pierce Ave *Web:* www.anchorhocking.com	Lancaster	OH	43130	740-681-6478	681-6040
Berney-Karp Inc 3350 E 26th St *TF:* 800-237-6395 ■ *Web:* www.ceramic-source.com	Los Angeles	CA	90023	323-260-7122	260-7245
Blenko Glass Co Inc Fairground Rd PO Box 67 *TF:* 877-425-3656 ■ *Web:* www.blenko.com	Milton	WV	25541	304-743-9081	743-0547
Carolina Mirror Co 600 Elkin Hwy *TF:* 800-334-7245 ■ *Web:* www.carolinamirror.com	North Wilkesboro	NC	28659	336-838-2151	838-9734
Ceramo Co Inc 681 Kasten Dr *TF:* 800-325-8303 ■ *Web:* www.ceramousa.com	Jackson	MO	63755	573-243-3138	243-3130
Crystal Clear Industries 2 Bergen Tpke *TF Orders:* 800-841-4014	Ridgefield Park	NJ	07660	201-440-4200	440-1758
Culver Industries Inc 1000 Industrial Blvd Hopewell Industrial Pk *TF:* 800-862-0070	Aliquippa	PA	15001	724-857-5770	857-5770
Enesco Corp 225 Windsor Dr *TF:* 800-436-3726 ■ *Web:* www.enesco.com	Itasca	IL	60143	630-875-5300	875-5350
Fenton Art Glass Co 700 Elizabeth St *TF Cust Svc:* 800-933-6766 ■ *Web:* www.fentonartglass.com	Williamstown	WV	26187	304-375-6122	375-6459
Friedman Bros Decorative Arts Inc 9015 NW 105th Way *TF:* 800-327-1065 ■ *Web:* www.homeportfolio.com	Medley	FL	33178	305-887-3170	885-5331
Gainey Ceramics Inc 1200 Arrow Hwy *TF Cust Svc:* 800-451-8155 ■ *Web:* www.gaineyceramics.com	La Verne	CA	91750	909-593-3533	596-9337
Gardner Glass Products Inc 600 Elkin Hwy *TF:* 800-334-7267 ■ *Web:* www.gardnerglass.com	North Wilkesboro	NC	28659	336-651-9300	667-0185
Haeger Industries Inc 7 Maiden Ln *TF Cust Svc:* 800-288-2529 ■ *Web:* www.haegerpotteries.com	Dundee	IL	60118	847-426-3441	426-0017
Haeger Potteries of Macomb 411 W Calhoun St *Web:* www.haegerpotteries.com	Macomb	IL	61455	309-833-2171	833-3860
Haggerty Enterprises Inc 321 W Lake St *TF:* 800-336-5282 ■ *Web:* www.lavalamp.com	Elmhurst	IL	60126	630-315-3300	315-3392
Indiana Glass Co Div Lancaster Colony Corp 717 W E St *Web:* www.indianaglass.com	Dunkirk	IN	47336	765-768-6789	768-1272
LE Smith Glass Co 1900 Liberty St *TF:* 800-537-6484 ■ *Web:* www.lesmithglass.com	Mount Pleasant	PA	15666	724-547-3544	547-2077
Libbey Inc 300 Madison Ave PO Box 10060 *NYSE: LBY* ■ *TF:* 888-794-8469 ■ *Web:* www.libbey.com	Toledo	OH	43699	419-325-2100	325-2369
Marshall Pottery 4901 Elysian Fields Rd *TF:* 888-768-8721 ■ *Web:* www.marshallpottery.com	Marshall	TX	75670	903-927-5400	938-8222
Mikasa Inc 100 Plaza Dr *TF Cust Svc:* 800-833-4681 ■ *Web:* www.mikasa.com	Secaucus	NJ	07094	201-867-9210	867-0580
Pfaltzgraff Co 140 E Market St **Fax:* Cust Svc ■ *TF:* 800-999-2811 ■ *Web:* www.pfaltzgraff.com	York	PA	17401	717-848-5500	771-1433*
Rauch Industries Inc 2408 Forbes Rd	Gastonia	NC	28056	704-867-5333	864-2081
Steuben Glass 1 Steuben Way *TF:* 800-424-4240 ■ *Web:* www.steuben.com	Corning	NY	14830	607-974-8584	974-8850
Swarovski North America Ltd 1 Kenney Dr **Fax Area Code:* 800 ■ *TF:* 800-289-4900 ■ *Web:* www.swarovski.com	Cranston	RI	02920	401-463-6400	870-5660*
Waterford Wedgwood USA Inc 1330 Campus Pkwy *Web:* www.wwusa.com	Wall	NJ	07719	732-938-5800	938-6915
World Kitchen Inc 11911 Freedom Dr Suite 600 *TF Cust Svc:* 800-999-3436 ■ *Web:* www.worldkitchen.com	Reston	VA	20190	703-456-4700	456-2020

338 GLOBAL DISTRIBUTION SYSTEMS (GDSS)

A Global Distribution System (Gds) Is A Computer Reservations System That Includes Reservations Databases Of Air Travel Suppliers In Many Countries. Gdss Typically Are Owned Jointly By Airlines Operating In Different Countries.

Company	City	State	Zip	Phone	Fax
Amadeus North America Inc 9250 NW 36 St *TF:* 888-262-3387 ■ *Web:* www.amadeus.com	Miami	FL	33178	305-499-6000	499-6889
American Sales Co Inc 4201 Walden Ave *Web:* www.americansalescompany.net	Lancaster	NY	14086	716-686-7000	685-6142
Century Distributors Inc 15710 Crabbs Branch Way *Web:* www.centurydist.com	Rockville	MD	20855	301-212-9100	212-9681
Pegasus Solutions Inc 8350 N Central Expy Suite 1900 *TF:* 800-528-2422 ■ *Web:* www.pegs.com	Dallas	TX	75206	214-234-4000	234-4040
Sabre Inc 3150 Sabre Dr *Web:* www.sabre-holdings.com	Southlake	TX	76092	682-605-1000	
Travelport 7 Sylvan Way *Web:* www.travelport.com	Parsippany	NJ	07054	973-428-9700	

339 GOURMET SPECIALTY SHOPS

Company	City	State	Zip	Phone	Fax
Dean & DeLuca Inc 4115 E Harry **Fax Area Code:* 800 ■ *TF:* 800-221-7714 ■ *Web:* www.deandeluca.com	Wichita	KS	67218	316-821-3200	781-4050*
Graber Olive House Inc 315 E 4th St *TF:* 800-996-5483 ■ *Web:* www.graberolives.com	Ontario	CA	91764	909-983-1761	984-2180
Harry & David Holdings Inc 2500 S Pacific Hwy **Fax Area Code:* 877 ■ *TF Cust Svc:* 800-345-5655 ■ *Web:* www.harryanddavid.com	Medford	OR	97501	541-776-2121	233-2300*
Hickory Farms Inc 1505 Holland Rd *TF:* 800-288-7327 ■ *Web:* www.hickoryfarms.com	Maumee	OH	43537	419-893-7611	893-0164
Honeybaked Ham Co 5445 Triangle Pkwy Suite 400 *TF:* 800-367-2426 ■ *Web:* www.honeybakedonline.com	Norcross	GA	30092	678-966-3100	966-3134
Jerky Hut International PO Box 308 *TF:* 800-223-5759 ■ *Web:* www.jerkyhut.com	Hubbard	OR	97032	503-981-7191	981-7692
Logan Farms Honey Glazed Hams 10560 Westheimer Rd *TF:* 800-833-4267 ■ *Web:* www.loganfarmsinc.com	Houston	TX	77042	713-781-3773	977-0532
M&M Meat Shops 640 Trillium Dr PO Box 2488 *Web:* www.mmmeatshops.com	Kitchener	ON	N2H6M3	519-895-1075	895-0762
Omaha Steaks International Inc 10909 John Galt Blvd **Fax:* Hum Res ■ *TF:* 800-960-8400 ■ *Web:* www.omahasteaks.com	Omaha	NE	68137	402-597-8370	597-8125*
Stew Leonard's 100 Westport Ave **Fax:* Hum Res ■ *TF:* 800-729-7839 ■ *Web:* www.stew-leonards.com	Norwalk	CT	06851	203-750-6106	750-6178*
Your Northwest 31461 NE Bell Rd *TF:* 888-252-0699 ■ *Web:* www.yournw.com	Sherwood	OR	97140	503-554-9060	537-9693
Zabar's & Co Inc 2245 Broadway *TF:* 800-697-6301 ■ *Web:* www.zabars.com	New York	NY	10024	212-787-2000	580-4477

340 GOVERNMENT - CITY

Company	City	State	Zip	Phone	Fax
Abilene City Hall 555 Walnut St *Web:* www.abilenetx.com	Abilene	TX	79601	325-676-6200	676-6229
Akron City Hall 166 S High St Rm 202 *Web:* www.ci.akron.oh.us	Akron	OH	44308	330-375-2133	375-2468
Albany City Hall 24 Eagle St *Web:* www.albanyny.org	Albany	NY	12207	518-434-5100	434-5013
Albuquerque City Hall PO Box 1293 *Web:* www.cabq.gov	Albuquerque	NM	87103	505-768-3000	768-3019
Alexandria City Hall 301 King St *Web:* www.alexandriava.gov	Alexandria	VA	22314	703-838-4000	838-6433
Allentown City Hall 435 Hamilton St *Web:* www.allentownpa.gov	Allentown	PA	18101	610-437-7539	437-7554
Amarillo City Hall 509 E 7th Ave *Web:* www.ci.amarillo.tx.us	Amarillo	TX	79101	806-378-3000	378-9394
Anaheim City Hall 200 S Anaheim Blvd *Web:* www.anaheim.net	Anaheim	CA	92805	714-765-5162	765-5164
Anchorage City Hall 632 6th Ave 2nd Fl Suite 250 PO Box 196650 *Web:* www.muni.org	Anchorage	AK	99519	907-343-4431	343-4499
Ann Arbor City Hall 100 N 5th Ave *Web:* www.a2gov.org	Ann Arbor	MI	48107	734-994-2700	332-5966
Annapolis City Hall 160 Duke of Gloucester St *Web:* www.ci.annapolis.md.us	Annapolis	MD	21401	410-263-7997	216-9284
Arlington (TX) City Hall 101 W Abram St *Web:* www.ci.arlington.tx.us	Arlington	TX	76010	817-275-3271	459-6120
Asheville City Hall 70 Ct Plaza PO Box 7148 *Web:* www.ashevillenc.gov	Asheville	NC	28802	828-259-5600	259-5499
Atlanta City Hall 55 Trinity Ave SW Suite 2500 *Web:* www.atlantaga.gov	Atlanta	GA	30303	404-330-6004	658-6893
Atlantic City City Hall 1301 Bacharach Blvd *Web:* www.cityofatlanticcity.org	Atlantic City	NJ	08401	609-347-5300	347-6408
Augusta (GA) Municipal Hall 530 Greene St *Web:* www.augustaga.gov	Augusta	GA	30911	706-821-1820	821-1838
Augusta (ME) City Hall 16 Cony St *Web:* www.ci.augusta.me.us	Augusta	ME	04330	207-626-2310	626-2304
Aurora City Hall 15151 E Alameda Pkwy *Web:* www.auroragov.org	Aurora	CO	80012	303-739-7015	739-7594
Austin City Hall PO Box 1088 *Web:* www.cityofaustin.org	Austin	TX	78767	512-974-2000	974-2337
Bakersfield City Hall 1600 Truxtun Ave # 300 *Web:* www.bakersfieldcity.us	Bakersfield	CA	93301	661-326-3751	324-1850
Bangor City Hall 73 Harlow St *Web:* www.bangormaine.gov	Bangor	ME	04401	207-992-4200	945-4449
Bar Harbor Town Hall 93 Cottage St *Web:* www.barharbormaine.gov	Bar Harbor	ME	04609	207-288-4098	288-4461
Baton Rouge City Hall 222 St Louis St # 301 *Web:* www.brgov.com	Baton Rouge	LA	70802	225-389-3100	389-5203
Billings City Hall 210 N 27th St *Web:* www.ci.billings.mt.us	Billings	MT	59101	406-657-8210	657-8390
Biloxi City Hall PO Box 429 *Web:* www.biloxi.ms.us	Biloxi	MS	39533	228-435-6254	435-6129
Birmingham City Hall 710 N 20th St *Web:* www.informationbirmingham.com	Birmingham	AL	35203	205-254-2000	254-2115
Bismarck City Hall 500 E Front St *Web:* www.bismarck.org	Bismarck	ND	58501	701-355-1300	222-6470
Bloomington City Hall 401 N Morton St *Web:* www.bloomington.in.gov	Bloomington	IN	47404	812-339-2261	349-3570
Boise City Hall 150 N Capitol Blvd *Web:* www.cityofboise.org	Boise	ID	83702	208-384-4422	384-4420
Boston City Hall 1 City Hall Plaza *Web:* www.cityofboston.gov	Boston	MA	02201	617-635-4601	248-1937
Boulder City Hall PO Box 791 *Web:* www.ci.boulder.co.us	Boulder	CO	80306	303-441-3388	441-4478
Branson City Hall 110 W Maddux St Suite 205 *Web:* www.cityofbranson.org	Branson	MO	65616	417-334-3345	335-4354
Bridgeport City Hall 999 Broad St *Web:* www.ci.bridgeport.ct.us	Bridgeport	CT	06604	203-576-7201	576-3913
Brownsville City Hall 1001 E Elizabeth St *Web:* www.cob.us	Brownsville	TX	78520	956-548-6000	546-4021
Buffalo City Hall 65 Niagara Sq *Web:* www.ci.buffalo.ny.us	Buffalo	NY	14202	716-851-4200	851-4360

Name / Address	City	State	ZIP	Phone	Fax
Burlington City Hall 149 Church St	Burlington	VT	05401	802-865-7000	865-7014
Web: www.ci.burlington.vt.us					
Calgary City Hall 800 Macleod Trail SE PO Box 2100	Calgary	AB	T2P2M5	403-268-2489	538-6111
Web: www.calgary.ca/portal/server.pt					
Carson City City Hall 201 N Carson St	Carson City	NV	89701	775-887-2100	882-8408
Web: www.carson-city.nv.us					
Casper City Hall 200 N David St	Casper	WY	82601	307-235-8400	235-7575
Web: www.cityofcasperwy.com					
Cedar Rapids City Hall 3851 River Ridge Dr NE	Cedar Rapids	IA	52402	319-286-5060	286-5130
Web: www.cedar-rapids.org					
Champaign City Hall 102 N Neil St	Champaign	IL	61820	217-403-8700	403-8980
Web: www.ci.champaign.il.us					
Charleston (SC) City Hall 50 Broad St	Charleston	SC	29401	843-577-6970	720-3959
Web: www.charlestoncity.info					
Charleston (WV) City Hall 200 Civic Ctr Dr	Charleston	WV	25301	304-348-8000	348-8157
Web: www.cityofcharleston.org					
Charlotte City Hall Charlotte-Mecklenburg Government Ctr 600 E 4th St	Charlotte	NC	28202	704-336-2241	336-6644
Web: www.ci.charlotte.nc.us					
Chattanooga City Hall 101 E 11th St Suite 100	Chattanooga	TN	37402	423-757-5152	757-0005
Web: www.chattanooga.gov					
Chesapeake City Hall 306 Cedar Rd	Chesapeake	VA	23322	757-382-2489	421-3176
Web: www.cityofchesapeake.net					
Cheyenne City Hall 2101 O'Neil Ave	Cheyenne	WY	82001	307-637-6200	637-6454
Web: www.cheyennecity.org					
Chicago City Hall 121 N La Salle St	Chicago	IL	60602	312-744-4000	744-8045
Web: egov.cityofchicago.org					
Chula Vista City Hall 276 4th Ave	Chula Vista	CA	91910	619-691-5044	476-5379
Web: www.ci.chula-vista.ca.us					
Cincinnati City Hall 801 Plum St	Cincinnati	OH	45202	513-352-3000	352-5020
Web: www.cincinnati-oh.gov					
Cleveland City Hall 601 Lakeside Ave	Cleveland	OH	44114	216-664-2000	664-3837
Web: www.cleveland-oh.gov					
Colorado Springs City Hall 107 N Nevada Ave Suite 205	Colorado Springs	CO	80903	719-385-5900	385-5488
Web: www.springsgov.com					
Columbia (MO) City Hall 701 E Broadway 5th Fl	Columbia	MO	65201	573-874-7214	442-8828
Web: www.ci.columbia.mo.us					
Columbus Consolidated Government Center 100 10th St	Columbus	GA	31901	706-653-4000	653-4970
Web: www.columbusga.org					
Concord City Hall 41 Green St	Concord	NH	03301	603-225-8500	225-8592
Web: www.ci.concord.nh.us					
Corpus Christi City Hall 1201 Leopard St PO Box 9277	Corpus Christi	TX	78469	361-880-3000	880-3113
Web: www.cctexas.com					
Dallas City Hall 1500 Marilla St	Dallas	TX	75201	214-670-3011	670-3946
Web: www.dallascityhall.com					
Dayton City Hall 101 W 3rd St	Dayton	OH	45402	937-333-3333	333-4297
Web: www.ci.dayton.oh.us					
Daytona Beach City Hall 301 S Ridgewood Ave Rm 210 PO Box 2451	Daytona Beach	FL	32114	386-671-8100	671-8115
Web: www.ci.daytona-beach.fl.us					
Denver City Hall 201 W Colfax Ave 1st Fl	Denver	CO	80202	720-865-8400	865-8580
Web: www.denvergov.org					
Des Moines City Hall 400 Robert D Ray Dr	Des Moines	IA	50309	515-283-4500	237-1645
Web: www.dmgov.org					
Detroit City Hall 2 Woodward Ave Suite 200	Detroit	MI	48226	313-224-3270	224-1466
Web: www.ci.detroit.mi.us					
Dover City Hall 15 ELoockerman St	Dover	DE	19901	302-736-7008	736-7177
Web: www.cityofdover.com					
Dubuque City Hall 50 W 13th St	Dubuque	IA	52001	563-589-4100	589-0890
Web: www.cityofdubuque.org					
Duluth City Hall 411 W 1st St	Duluth	MN	55802	218-730-5500	730-5923
Web: www.duluthmn.gov					
Durham City Hall 101 City Hall Plaza	Durham	NC	27701	919-560-1200	560-4835
Web: www.durhamnc.gov					
Edmonton City Hall 1 Sir Winston Churchill Sq 3rd Fl	Edmonton	AB	T5J2R7	780-442-5311	496-8210
Web: www.edmonton.ca					
El Paso City Hall 2 Civic Ctr Plaza	El Paso	TX	79901	915-541-4000	541-4501
Web: www.elpasotexas.gov					
Erie City Hall 626 State St	Erie	PA	16501	814-870-1234	870-1296
Web: www.ci.erie.pa.us					
Eugene City Hall 777 Pearl St Rm 105	Eugene	OR	97401	541-682-5010	682-5414
Web: www.eugene-or.gov					
Evansville City Hall 1 NW ML King Jr Blvd	Evansville	IN	47708	812-436-4992	436-4999
Web: www.evansvillegov.net					
Fairbanks City Hall 800 Cushman St	Fairbanks	AK	99701	907-459-6771	459-6710*
**Fax:* City Clerk ■ *Web:* www.ci.fairbanks.ak.us					
Fargo City Hall 200 N 3rd St	Fargo	ND	58102	701-241-1310	476-4136
Web: www.cityoffargo.com					
Flagstaff City Hall 211 W Aspen Ave	Flagstaff	AZ	86001	928-774-5281	779-7696
Web: www.flagstaff.az.gov					
Flint City Hall 1101 S Saginaw St Rm 101	Flint	MI	48502	810-766-7346	766-7218
Web: www.cityofflint.com					
Fort Collins City Hall 300 Laporte Ave	Fort Collins	CO	80521	970-221-6505	224-6107
Web: www.fcgov.com					
Fort Lauderdale City Hall 100 N Andrews Ave	Fort Lauderdale	FL	33301	954-828-5000	828-5017
Web: www.fortlauderdale.gov					
Fort Smith City Hall 623 Garrison Ave Rm 303	Fort Smith	AR	72901	479-784-2208	784-2256
Web: www.fsark.com					
Fort Wayne City Hall 1 Main St	Fort Wayne	IN	46802	260-427-1221	427-1371
Web: www.cityoffortwayne.org					
Fort Worth City Hall 1000 Throckmorton St	Fort Worth	TX	76102	817-392-8900	392-6187
Web: www.fortworthgov.org					
Frankfort City Hall PO Box 697	Frankfort	KY	40602	502-875-8523	223-7193
Web: frankfort.ky.gov					
Fremont City Hall PO Box 5006	Fremont	CA	94537	510-284-4000	284-4001
Web: www.fremont.gov					
Fresno City Hall 2600 Fresno St Rm 2064	Fresno	CA	93721	559-621-7770	621-7776
Web: www.fresno.gov					
Garden Grove City Hall 11222 Acacia Pkwy	Garden Grove	CA	92840	714-741-5000	741-5044
Web: www.ci.garden-grove.ca.us					
Garland City Hall 200 N 5th St	Garland	TX	75040	972-205-2000	205-2504
Web: www.ci.garland.tx.us					
Gettysburg Borough Hall 59 E High St	Gettysburg	PA	17325	717-334-1160	334-7258
Web: www.gettysburg-pa.gov					
Glendale (AZ) City Hall 5850 W Glendale Ave	Glendale	AZ	85301	623-930-2000	915-2690
Web: www.glendaleaz.com					
Glendale (CA) City Hall 613 E Broadway Rm 110	Glendale	CA	91206	818-548-2090	241-5386
Web: www.ci.glendale.ca.us					
Grand Forks City Hall 255 N 4th St	Grand Forks	ND	58203	701-746-2626	787-3740
Web: www.grandforksgov.com					
Grand Rapids City Hall 300 Monroe Ave NW	Grand Rapids	MI	49503	616-456-3010	456-4607
Web: www.ci.grand-rapids.mi.us					
Great Falls City Hall 2 Pk Dr S	Great Falls	MT	59403	406-771-1180	727-0005
Web: www.ci.great-falls.mt.us					
Green Bay City Hall 100 N Jefferson St Rm 106	Green Bay	WI	54301	920-448-3010	448-3016
Web: www.ci.green-bay.wi.us					
Greensboro City Hall 300 W Washington St PO Box 3136	Greensboro	NC	27401	336-373-2489	373-2117
Web: www.greensboro-nc.gov					
Greenville City Hall 206 S Main St	Greenville	SC	29601	864-232-2273	467-5725
TF: 800-849-4339 ■ *Web:* www.greatergreenville.com					
Gulfport City Hall 2309 15th St	Gulfport	MS	39501	228-868-5700	868-5800
Web: www.ci.gulfport.ms.us					
Halifax City Hall 1841 Argyle St PO Box 1749	Halifax	NS	B3J3A5	902-490-4210	490-4012
Web: www.halifax.ca/community/HalifaxCityHall					
Harrisburg City Hall 10 N 2nd St	Harrisburg	PA	17101	717-255-3060	255-3081
Web: www.harrisburgpa.gov					
Hartford City Hall 550 Main St	Hartford	CT	06103	860-522-4888	
Web: www.hartford.gov					
Hattiesburg City Hall 200 Forest St PO Box 1898	Hattiesburg	MS	39401	601-545-4500	545-4529
Web: www.hattiesburgms.com					
Helena City Hall 316 N Pk Ave	Helena	MT	59623	406-447-8410	447-8434
Web: www.ci.helena.mt.us					
Hialeah City Hall 501 Palm Ave Suite 310	Hialeah	FL	33010	305-883-5820	883-5814
Web: www.ci.hialeah.fl.us					
Hilton Head Island Town Hall 1 Town Center Ct	Hilton Head Island	SC	29928	843-341-4600	842-7728
Web: www.hiltonheadislandsc.gov					
Honolulu City Hall 530 S King St	Honolulu	HI	96813	808-523-4385	527-6888
Web: www.co.honolulu.hi.us					
Hot Springs City Hall PO Box 700	Hot Springs	AR	71902	501-321-6800	321-6809
Web: www.ci.hot-springs.ar.us					
Houston City Hall 901 Bagby St	Houston	TX	77002	713-247-1000	247-2355
Web: www.houstontx.gov					
Huntington Beach City Hall 18381 Gothard St	Huntington Beach	CA	92648	714-536-5511	374-1557
Web: www.ci.huntington-beach.ca.us					
Huntsville City Hall PO Box 308	Huntsville	AL	35804	256-427-5240	427-5257
Web: www.hsvcity.com					
Independence City Hall 111 E Maple Ave	Independence	MO	64050	816-325-7000	325-7012
Web: www.ci.independence.mo.us					
Indianapolis City Hall 200 E Washington St Suite 2501	Indianapolis	IN	46204	317-327-3601	327-3980
Web: www.indygov.org					
Irving City Hall 825 W Irving Blvd	Irving	TX	75060	972-721-2600	721-2420
Web: www.ci.irving.tx.us					
Jackson (MS) City Hall 219 S President St	Jackson	MS	39201	601-960-1084	960-2193
Web: www.city.jackson.ms.us					
Jackson (WY) Town Hall 150 E Pearl Ave	Jackson	WY	83001	307-733-3932	739-0919
Web: www.ci.jackson.wy.us					
Jacksonville City Hall 117 W Duval St Suite 400	Jacksonville	FL	32202	904-630-1776	630-2391
Web: www.coj.net					
Jefferson City City Hall 320 E McCarty St	Jefferson City	MO	65101	573-634-6304	634-6329
Web: www.jeffcitymo.org					
Jersey City City Hall 280 Grove St	Jersey City	NJ	07302	201-547-5000	547-5461
Web: www.cityofjerseycity.com					
Johnson City City Hall 601 E Main St	Johnson City	TN	37601	423-434-6000	434-6295
Web: www.johnsoncitytn.com					
Juneau City Hall 155 S Seward St	Juneau	AK	99801	907-586-5278	586-2536
Web: www.juneau.org					
Kansas City (KS) City Hall 701 N 7th St	Kansas City	KS	66101	913-573-5000	573-5210
Web: www.wycokck.org					
Kansas City (MO) City Hall 414 E 12th St 25th Fl	Kansas City	MO	64106	816-513-3360	513-3353
Web: www.kcmo.org					
Key West City Hall 525 Angela St	Key West	FL	33040	305-809-3834	809-3833
Web: www.keywestcity.com					
Knoxville City Hall 400 W Main St	Knoxville	TN	37902	865-215-2000	215-2085
Web: www.ci.knoxville.tn.us					
Lafayette City Hall 705 W University Ave	Lafayette	LA	70506	337-291-8200	291-8399
Web: www.lafayettegov.org					
Lansing City Hall 124 W Michigan Ave 9th Fl	Lansing	MI	48933	517-483-4131	377-0068
Web: www.cityoflansingmi.com					
Las Cruces City Hall 200 N Church St	Las Cruces	NM	88001	575-541-2000	541-2117
Web: www.las-cruces.org					

				Phone	Fax
Las Vegas City Hall 400 Stewart Ave 1st Fl ... Las Vegas *Web:* www.lasvegasnevada.gov	NV	89101		702-229-6011	386-9108
Lincoln City Hall 555 S 10th St ... Lincoln *Web:* www.lincoln.ne.gov	NE	68508		402-441-7515	441-6533
Little Rock City Hall 500 W Markham St ... Little Rock *Web:* www.littlerock.org	AR	72201		501-371-4500	371-4498
Long Beach City Hall 333 W Ocean Blvd ... Long Beach *Web:* www.longbeach.gov	CA	90802		562-570-6101	570-6789
Los Angeles City Hall 200 N Spring St Rm 360 ... Los Angeles *Web:* www.lacity.org	CA	90012		213-978-1022	978-1027
Louisville City Hall 601 W Jefferson St ... Louisville *Web:* www.louisvilleky.gov	KY	40202		502-574-1100	574-4420
Lubbock City Hall 1625 13th St ... Lubbock *Web:* www.ci.lubbock.tx.us	TX	79401		806-775-3000	775-3002
Macon City Hall 700 Poplar St ... Macon *Web:* www.macon.ga.us	GA	31201		478-751-7170	751-7931
Madison City Hall 210 Martin Luther King Jr Blvd Rm 403 ... Madison *Web:* www.cityofmadison.com	WI	53703		608-266-4611	267-8671
Manchester City Hall 1 City Hall Plaza ... Manchester *Web:* www.manchesternh.gov	NH	03101		603-624-6455	624-6481
Memphis City Hall 125 N Main St ... Memphis *Web:* www.cityofmemphis.org	TN	38103		901-576-6500	576-6200
Mesa City Hall PO Box 1466 ... Mesa *Web:* www.cityofmesa.org	AZ	85211		480-644-2011	644-2821
Miami City Hall 3500 Pan American Dr ... Miami *Web:* www.ci.miami.fl.us	FL	33133		305-250-5400	250-5410
Milwaukee City Hall 200 E Wells St ... Milwaukee *Web:* www.city.milwaukee.gov	WI	53202		414-286-2200	286-3191
Minneapolis City Hall 350 S 5th St ... Minneapolis *Web:* www.ci.minneapolis.mn.us	MN	55415		612-673-3000	673-3812
Mobile City Hall 205 Government St ... Mobile *Web:* www.cityofmobile.org	AL	36602		251-208-7411	208-7576
Modesto City Hall PO Box 642 ... Modesto *Web:* www.modestogov.com	CA	95353		209-577-5200	571-5152
Monterey City Hall 580 Pacific St ... Monterey *Web:* www.monterey.org	CA	93940		831-646-3935	646-3702
Montgomery City Hall 103 N Perry St ... Montgomery *Web:* www.montgomeryal.gov	AL	36104		334-241-4400	241-2266
Montpelier City Hall 39 Main St ... Montpelier *Web:* montpelier-vt.org	VT	05602		802-223-9502	223-9519
Montreal City Hall 275 Notre-Dame St E ... Montreal *Web:* www.ville.montreal.qc.ca	QC	H2Y1C6		514-872-3101	872-4059
Morgantown City Hall 389 Spruce St ... Morgantown *Web:* www.morgantown.com	WV	26505		304-284-7439	284-7525
Myrtle Beach City Hall 937 Broadway St ... Myrtle Beach *Web:* www.cityofmyrtlebeach.com	SC	29577		843-918-1000	918-1028
Naples City Hall 735 8th St S ... Naples *Web:* www.naplesgov.com	FL	34102		239-213-1015	213-1025
Nashville & Davidson County Metropolitan City Hall 100 Metropolitan Courthouse ... Nashville *Web:* www.nashville.gov	TN	37201		615-862-6000	862-6040
New Haven City Hall 165 Church St ... New Haven *Web:* www.cityofnewhaven.com	CT	06510		203-946-8200	946-7683
New Orleans City Hall 421 Loyola Ave ... New Orleans *Web:* www.cityofno.com	LA	70112		504-658-4000	658-4938
New York City Hall Broadway & Murray Sts ... New York *Web:* www.nyc.gov	NY	10007		212-788-2656	
Newark City Hall 920 Broad St ... Newark *Web:* www.ci.newark.nj.us	NJ	07102		973-733-8004	733-5352
Newport City Hall 43 Broadway ... Newport *Web:* www.cityofnewport.com	RI	02840		401-846-9600	845-2510
Newport News City Hall 2400 Washington Ave ... Newport News *Web:* www.ci.newport-news.va.us	VA	23607		757-926-8000	926-3503
Norfolk City Hall 810 Union St ... Norfolk *Web:* www.norfolk.gov	VA	23510		757-664-4000	664-4226
Oakland City Hall 1 Frank H Ogawa Plaza ... Oakland *Web:* www.oaklandnet.com	CA	94612		510-444-2489	
Ocean City City Hall 301 Baltimore Ave ... Ocean City *TF:* 800-626-2326 ■ *Web:* www.town.ocean-city.md.us	MD	21842		410-289-8931	289-7385
Ogden City Hall 2549 Washington Blvd ... Ogden *Web:* www.ogdencity.com	UT	84401		801-629-8150	629-8154
Oklahoma City City Hall 200 N Walker Ave ... Oklahoma City *Web:* www.okc.gov	OK	73102		405-297-2578	297-3124
Olympia City Hall PO Box 1967 ... Olympia *Web:* www.ci.olympia.wa.us	WA	98507		360-753-8447	709-2791
Omaha City Hall 1819 Farnam St Suite LC1 ... Omaha *Web:* www.ci.omaha.ne.us	NE	68183		402-444-5550	444-5263
Orlando City Hall 400 S Orange Ave ... Orlando *Web:* www.cityoforlando.net	FL	32801		407-246-2221	246-2842
Ottawa City Hall 110 Laurier Ave W ... Ottawa *TF:* 866-261-9799 ■ *Web:* www.ottawa.ca/city_hall/index_en.html	ON	K1P1J1		613-580-2400	580-2495
Oxnard City Hall 305 W 3rd St ... Oxnard *Web:* www.ci.oxnard.ca.us	CA	93030		805-385-7803	385-7806
Palm Springs City Hall 3200 E Tahquitz Canyon Way ... Palm Springs *Web:* www.ci.palm-springs.ca.us	CA	92262		760-323-8299	322-8332
Paterson City Hall 155 Market St ... Paterson *Web:* www.patcity.com	NJ	07505		973-321-1500	321-1311
Pensacola City Hall 180 Governmental Ctr ... Pensacola *Web:* www.ci.pensacola.fl.us	FL	32521		850-435-1626	436-5208
Peoria City Hall 419 Fulton St Suite 401 ... Peoria *Web:* www.ci.peoria.il.us	IL	61602		309-494-8565	494-8574
Philadelphia City Hall 1234 Market St 17th Fl ... Philadelphia *Web:* www.phila.gov	PA	19107		215-686-9749	686-9801
Phoenix City Hall 200 W Washington St 11th Fl ... Phoenix *Web:* www.phoenix.gov	AZ	85003		602-262-7111	495-5583
Pierre City Hall 222 E Dakota Ave ... Pierre *Web:* www.ci.pierre.sd.us	SD	57501		605-773-7407	773-7406
Pittsburgh City Hall 414 Grant St City-County Bldg ... Pittsburgh *Web:* www.city.pittsburgh.pa.us	PA	15219		412-255-2100	255-2821
Plano City Hall 1520 Ave K ... Plano *Web:* www.plano.gov	TX	75074		972-941-7000	423-9587
Pocatello City Hall 911 N 7th Ave ... Pocatello *Web:* www.pocatello.us	ID	83201		208-234-6163	234-6297
Portland (ME) City Hall 389 Congress St ... Portland *Web:* www.portlandmaine.gov	ME	04101		207-874-8610	874-8612
Portland (OR) City Hall 1221 SW 4th Ave ... Portland *Web:* www.portlandonline.com	OR	97204		503-823-4000	823-3588
Providence City Hall 25 Dorrance St ... Providence *Web:* www.providenceri.com	RI	02903		401-421-7740	421-6492
Provo City Hall 351 W Ctr St ... Provo *Web:* www.provo.org	UT	84601		801-852-6100	852-6107
Quebec City Hall 2 Rue des Jardins Suite 115 ... Quebec *Web:* www.ville.quebec.qc.ca	QC	G1R4S9		418-641-6434	641-6318
Rapid City City Hall 300 6th St ... Rapid City *Web:* www.rcgov.org	SD	57701		605-394-4110	394-6793
Rehoboth Beach City Hall 229 Rehoboth Ave ... Rehoboth Beach *Web:* www.cityofrehoboth.com	DE	19971		302-227-6181	227-4643
Reno City Hall PO Box 1900 ... Reno *Web:* www.cityofreno.com	NV	89505		775-334-2030	334-2432
Richmond City Hall 900 E Broad St Rm 201 ... Richmond *Web:* www.richmondgov.com	VA	23219		804-646-7000	646-7978
Riverside City Hall 3900 Main St ... Riverside *Web:* www.riversideca.gov	CA	92522		951-826-5312	826-5470
Roanoke City Hall 215 Church Ave SW ... Roanoke *Web:* www.roanokegov.com	VA	24011		540-853-2000	853-1145
Rochester (MN) City Hall 201 4th St SE ... Rochester *Web:* www.ci.rochester.mn.us	MN	55904		507-285-8082	287-7979
Rochester (NY) City Hall 30 Church St ... Rochester *Web:* www.ci.rochester.ny.us	NY	14614		585-428-7045	428-6059
Rockford City Hall 425 E State St ... Rockford *Web:* www.ci.rockford.il.us	IL	61104		815-987-5590	967-6952
Sacramento City Hall 915 'I' St ... Sacramento *Web:* www.cityofsacramento.org	CA	95814		916-808-7200	808-7672
Saint Augustine City Hall PO Box 210 ... Saint Augustine *Web:* www.staugustinegovernment.com	FL	32085		904-825-1007	825-1008
Saint Louis City Hall 1200 Market St ... Saint Louis *Web:* stlouis.missouri.org	MO	63103		314-622-3201	622-4061
Saint Paul City Hall 15 W Kellogg Blvd 390 City Hall ... Saint Paul *Web:* www.stpaul.gov	MN	55101		651-266-8500	266-8513
Saint Petersburg City Hall 175 5th St N ... Saint Petersburg *Web:* www.stpete.org	FL	33701		727-893-7111	892-5102
Salem City Hall 555 Liberty St SE Rm 220 ... Salem *Web:* www.cityofsalem.net	OR	97301		503-588-6255	588-6354
Salt Lake City City Hall 451 S State St ... Salt Lake City *Web:* www.slcgov.com	UT	84111		801-535-7704	535-6331
San Antonio City Hall PO Box 839966 ... San Antonio *Web:* www.sanantonio.gov	TX	78283		210-207-7040	207-7027
San Bernardino City Hall 300 N 'D' St ... San Bernardino *Web:* www.ci.san-bernardino.ca.us	CA	92418		909-384-5211	384-5158
San Diego City Hall 202 C St ... San Diego *Web:* www.sandiego.gov	CA	92101		619-533-4000	533-4045
San Jose City Hall 200 Santa Clara St ... San Jose *Web:* www.sanjoseca.gov	CA	95113		408-535-3500	292-6731
Santa Ana City Hall 20 Civic Ctr Plaza ... Santa Ana *Web:* www.ci.santa-ana.ca.us	CA	92701		714-647-6900	647-6954
Santa Fe City Hall 200 Lincoln Ave ... Santa Fe *Web:* www.santafenm.gov	NM	87501		505-955-6520	955-6910
Savannah City Hall PO Box 1027 ... Savannah *Web:* www.ci.savannah.ga.us	GA	31402		912-651-6441	651-4260
Scottsdale City Hall 7447 E Indian School Rd ... Scottsdale *Web:* www.scottsdaleaz.gov	AZ	85251		480-312-3111	312-2888
Scranton City Hall 340 N Washington Ave ... Scranton *Web:* www.scrantonpa.gov	PA	18503		570-348-4100	348-4207
Seattle City Hall 600 4th Ave 2nd Fl ... Seattle *Web:* www.seattle.gov	WA	98104		206-684-8888	684-8587
Shreveport City Hall PO Box 31109 ... Shreveport *Web:* www.ci.shreveport.la.us	LA	71130		318-673-2489	673-5099
Sioux Falls City Hall 224 W 9th St ... Sioux Falls *Web:* www.siouxfalls.org	SD	57104		605-367-8000	367-7801
South Bend City Hall 227 W Jefferson Blvd 455 County-City Bldg ... South Bend *Web:* www.ci.south-bend.in.us	IN	46601		574-235-9221	235-9173
Spokane City Hall 808 W Spokane Falls Blvd ... Spokane *Web:* www.spokanecity.org	WA	99201		509-625-6350	625-6217
Springfield (IL) City Hall 800 E Monroe St Rm 300 ... Springfield *Web:* www.springfield.il.us	IL	62701		217-789-2200	789-2109
Springfield (MA) City Hall 36 Ct St ... Springfield *Web:* www.springfieldcityhall.com	MA	01103		413-787-6000	
Springfield (MO) City Hall 840 Boonville Ave ... Springfield *Web:* www.springfieldmo.gov/home	MO	65802		417-864-1000	864-1649
Stamford City Hall 888 Washington Blvd 10th Fl ... Stamford *Web:* www.cityofstamford.org	CT	06901		203-977-4150	977-5845
Stockton City Hall 425 N El Dorado St ... Stockton *Web:* www.stocktongov.com	CA	95202		209-937-8212	937-7149
Syracuse City Hall 233 E Washington St ... Syracuse *Web:* www.syracuse.ny.us	NY	13202		315-448-8216	448-8489
Tacoma City Hall 747 Market St ... Tacoma *Web:* www.cityoftacoma.org	WA	98402		253-591-5000	591-5300

				Phone	Fax
Tallahassee City Hall 300 S Adams St	Tallahassee	FL	32301	850-891-0010	891-8542
Web: www.talgov.com					
Tampa City Hall 306 E Jackson St	Tampa	FL	33602	813-274-8251	274-7050
Web: www.tampagov.net					
Tempe City Hall 31 E 5th St	Tempe	AZ	85281	480-350-8221	350-8930
Web: www.tempe.gov					
Toledo City Hall 1 Government Ctr	Toledo	OH	43604	419-245-1001	245-1370
Web: www.ci.toledo.oh.us					
Topeka City Hall 215 SE 7th St	Topeka	KS	66603	785-368-3754	368-3966
Web: www.topeka.org					
Toronto City Hall 100 Queen St W	Toronto	ON	M5H2N2	416-392-8016	392-2980
Web: www.toronto.ca					
Trenton City Hall 319 E State St	Trenton	NJ	08608	609-989-3185	989-3190
Web: www.trentonnj.org					
Tucson City Hall 255 W Alameda St	Tucson	AZ	85701	520-791-4204	791-5198
Web: www.ci.tucson.az.us					
Tulsa City Hall 200 Civic Ctr	Tulsa	OK	74103	918-596-2100	596-9010
Web: www.cityoftulsa.org					
Tupelo City Hall 71 E Troy St	Tupelo	MS	38804	662-841-6513	840-2075
Web: www.tupeloms.gov					
Tuscaloosa City Hall 2201 University Blvd	Tuscaloosa	AL	35401	205-349-2010	349-0147
Web: www.ci.tuscaloosa.al.us					
Vancouver (BC) City Hall					
453 W 12th Ave PO Box 7747	Vancouver	BC	V5Y1V4	604-873-7000	873-7051
Web: vancouver.ca					
Vancouver (WA) City Hall PO Box 1995	Vancouver	WA	98668	360-487-8000	696-8049
Web: www.cityofvancouver.us					
Virginia Beach City Hall					
2401 Courthouse Dr					
Municipal Ctr Bldg 1	Virginia Beach	VA	23456	757-385-8151	
Web: www.vbgov.com					
Washington (DC) City Hall					
1350 Pennsylvania Ave NW	Washington	DC	20004	202-727-1000	727-0505
Web: www.dc.gov					
West Palm Beach City Hall 200 2nd St	West Palm Beach	FL	33401	561-822-1200	822-1424
Web: www.cityofwpb.com					
Wheeling City Council Chambers					
1500 Chapline St	Wheeling	WV	26003	304-234-3694	234-6419
Web: www.wheelingchamber.com					
Wichita City Hall 455 N Main St 1st Fl	Wichita	KS	67202	316-268-4331	268-4567
Web: www.wichita.gov					
Williamsburg City Hall 401 Lafayette St	Williamsburg	VA	23185	757-220-6100	220-6107
Web: www.williamsburgva.gov					
Wilmington City Hall 800 N French St	Wilmington	DE	19801	302-576-2489	571-4607
Web: www.ci.wilmington.de.us					
Winnipeg City Hall 510 Main St Main Fl	Winnipeg	MB	R3B1B9	204-986-6432	947-3452
Web: www.winnipeg.ca/interhom					
Winston-Salem City Hall					
101 N Main St Po Box 2511	Winston-Salem	NC	27101	336-727-8000	748-3060
Web: www.cityofws.org					
Yonkers City Hall 40 S Broadway	Yonkers	NY	10701	914-377-6000	377-6029
Web: www.cityofyonkers.com					
Youngstown City Hall 26 S Phelps St 6th Fl	Youngstown	OH	44503	330-742-8709	742-8707
Web: www.cityofyoungstownoh.org					

341 GOVERNMENT - COUNTY

				Phone	Fax
Abbeville County 102 Ct Sq	Abbeville	SC	29620	864-366-5312	366-4595
Web: www.sccounties.org					
Accomack County 23296 Courthouse Ave #203	Accomac	VA	23301	757-787-5700	787-2468
Web: www.co.accomack.va.us					
Ada County 200 W Front St Suite 3255	Boise	ID	83702	208-287-7000	287-7009
Web: www.adaweb.net					
Adair County 424 Public Sq	Columbia	KY	42728	270-384-2801	384-4805
Web: www.columbia-adaircounty.com					
Adair County 400 Public Sq	Greenfield	IA	50849	641-743-2546	743-2565
Adair County					
106 W Washington St County Courthouse	Kirksville	MO	63501	660-665-3350	785-3233
Adair County PO Box 169	Stilwell	OK	74960	918-696-7198	696-2603
Adams County 450 S 4th Ave	Brighton	CO	80601	303-659-2120	654-6011
Web: www.co.adams.co.us					
Adams County PO Box 484	Corning	IA	50841	641-322-4711	322-4523
Web: www.co.adams.ia.us					
Adams County 201 Industrial Ave PO Box 48	Council	ID	83612	208-253-6125	253-6127
Web: www.co.adams.id.us					
Adams County 313 W Jefferson St	Decatur	IN	46733	260-724-5300	724-5313
Web: www.co.adams.in.us					
Adams County PO Box 2067	Hastings	NE	68902	402-461-7104	461-7185
Web: www.adamscounty.org					
Adams County PO Box 1006	Natchez	MS	39121	601-446-6684	445-7913
Adams County 507 Vermont St	Quincy	IL	62301	217-277-2150	277-2155
Web: www.co.adams.il.us					
Adams County 210 W Broadway	Ritzville	WA	99169	509-659-3257	659-0118
Web: www.co.adams.wa.us					
Adams County					
110 W Main St Rm 25 County Courthouse	West Union	OH	45693	937-544-2011	544-8911
Web: www.adamscountytravel.org					
Addison County 7 Mahady Ct	Middlebury	VT	05753	802-388-7741	388-4621
Web: www.addisoncountychamber.com					
Aiken County 828 Richland Ave W	Aiken	SC	29801	803-642-2012	642-2124
TF: 866-876-7074 ■ *Web:* www.aikencounty.net					
Alachua County 12 SE 1st St	Gainesville	FL	32601	352-374-5210	338-7303
Web: www.alachuacounty.us					
Alamance County 124 W Elm St	Graham	NC	27253	336-228-1312	570-6788
Web: www.alamance-nc.com					
Alameda County 1221 Oak St Suite 555	Oakland	CA	94612	510-272-6984	272-3784
Web: www.acgov.org					
Alamosa County 8900 Independence Way	Alamosa	CO	81101	719-589-4848	589-1900
Web: www.ccionline.org					
Albany County 112 State St Rm 200	Albany	NY	12207	518-447-7040	447-5589
Web: www.albanycounty.com					
Albemarle County 401 McIntire Rd	Charlottesville	VA	22902	434-296-5841	296-5800
Web: www.albemarle.org					
Alcorn County 305 S Fulton Dr	Corinth	MS	38834	662-286-5521	286-7773
Web: www.alcorncounty.org					
Aleutians East Borough 100 Mossberry Ln	Sand Point	AK	99661	907-383-2699	383-3496
TF: 888-383-2699 ■ *Web:* www.aleutianseast.org					
Alexander County 2000 Washington Ave	Cairo	IL	62914	618-734-7000	734-7002
Alexander County 621 Liledoun Rd	Taylorsville	NC	28681	828-632-9332	632-0059
Web: www.co.alexander.nc.us					
Alexandria (Independent City)					
301 King St Suite 2300	Alexandria	VA	22314	703-838-4500	838-6433
Web: www.ci.alexandria.va.us					
Alfalfa County 300 S Grand Ave	Cherokee	OK	73728	580-596-3158	
Alger County 100 Ct St	Munising	MI	49862	906-387-2076	387-2156
Allamakee County 110 Allamakee St	Waukon	IA	52172	563-568-3318	568-6353
Web: www.allamakeecounty.com					
Allegany County 7 Ct St County Courthouse	Belmont	NY	14813	585-268-9270	268-9659
Web: www.alleganyco.com					
Allen County					
715 S Calhoun St County Courthouse Rm 201	Fort Wayne	IN	46802	260-449-7245	449-7929
Web: www.co.allen.in.us					
Allen County 1 N Washington St	Iola	KS	66749	620-365-1407	365-1441
Web: www.allencounty.org					
Allen County 301 N Main St	Lima	OH	45801	419-228-3700	222-8427
Web: www.allencountyohio.com					
Allen County 201 W Main St Rm 6	Scottsville	KY	42164	270-237-3706	237-9206
Web: www.allencountykentucky.com					
Allen Parish 602 Ct St	Oberlin	LA	70655	337-639-4396	639-4326
Web: www.allenparish.com					
Allendale County 526 Memorial Ave	Allendale	SC	29810	803-584-3438	584-7042
Web: www.allendalecounty.com					
Alpena County 720 W Chisholm St	Alpena	MI	49707	989-356-0930	354-9648
Web: www.alpenacounty.org					
Alpine County 99 Waters St	Markleeville	CA	96120	530-694-2281	694-2491
Web: www.alpinecountyca.com					
Amador County 810 Ct St	Jackson	CA	95642	209-223-6470	257-0619
Web: www.co.amador.ca.us					
Amelia County PO Box A	Amelia Court House	VA	23002	804-561-3039	561-6039
Web: www.ameliacova.us					
Amherst County 153 Washington St	Amherst	VA	24521	434-946-9400	946-9370
Web: www.countyofamherst.com					
Amite County PO Box 680	Liberty	MS	39645	601-657-8022	657-8288
Web: www.amitecounty.ms					
Anaconda-Deer Lodge County 800 Main St	Anaconda	MT	59711	406-563-4060	563-4001
Web: www.anacondamt.org					
Anchorage Municipality 632 W 6th Ave # 250	Anchorage	AK	99501	907-343-4311	343-4313
Web: www.muni.org					
Anderson County 101 S Main St	Anderson	SC	29624	864-260-4000	260-4106
Web: www.andersoncountysc.org					
Anderson County 100 N Main St Rm 111	Clinton	TN	37716	865-457-5400	259-0116
Web: www.andersoncountychamber.org					
Anderson County 100 E 4th Ave	Garnett	KS	66032	785-448-6841	448-5621
Anderson County 151 S Main St	Lawrenceburg	KY	40342	502-839-3041	839-3043
Anderson County 500 N Church St	Palestine	TX	75801	903-723-7432	723-4625
Web: www.co.anderson.tx.us					
Andrew County PO Box 206	Savannah	MO	64485	816-324-3624	324-6154
Andrews County 215 NW 1st St Annex Bldg	Andrews	TX	79714	432-524-1426	
Web: www.co.andrews.tx.us					
Androscoggin County 2 Turner St Unit 2	Auburn	ME	04210	207-784-8390	782-5367
Web: www.androscoggincounty.com					
Anne Arundel County 44 Calvert St	Annapolis	MD	21401	410-222-7000	
Web: www.co.anne-arundel.md.us					
Anoka County 325 E Main St	Anoka	MN	55303	763-422-7350	422-6919
Web: www.co.anoka.mn.us					
Anson County					
114 N Green St Courthouse Rm 30	Wadesboro	NC	28170	704-694-2796	694-7015
Web: www.co.anson.nc.us					
Antelope County 501 Main St	Neligh	NE	68756	402-887-4410	887-4719
Web: www.co.antelope.ne.us					
Antrim County 203 E Cayuga St	Bellaire	MI	49615	231-533-6353	533-6935
Web: www.antrimcounty.org					
Apache County 395 S 1st W	Saint Johns	AZ	85936	928-337-4364	337-2771
Web: www.co.apache.az.us					
Appling County 69 Tippins St	Baxley	GA	31513	912-367-8100	367-8161
Web: www.baxley.org					
Appomattox County 297 Ct St	Appomattox	VA	24522	434-352-5275	352-2781
Web: www.appomattox.com					
Aransas County 301 N Live Oak St	Rockport	TX	78382	361-790-0122	790-0119
Web: www.aransascounty.org					
Arenac County PO Box 747	Standish	MI	48658	989-846-4626	
Web: www.arenaccountygov.com					
Arkansas County PO Box 719	Stuttgart	AR	72160	870-673-7311	
Arlington County					
2100 Clarendon Blvd Suite 300	Arlington	VA	22201	703-228-3130	228-7430
Web: www.co.arlington.va.us					
Armstrong County PO Box 309	Claude	TX	79019	806-226-2081	226-5301
Web: www.co.armstrong.tx.us					
Armstrong County					
450 E Market St Courthouse Complex	Kittanning	PA	16201	724-543-2500	548-3285
Web: www.armstrongcounty.com					
Arthur County PO Box 126	Arthur	NE	69121	308-764-2203	764-2216
Ascension Parish 208 E Railroad St	Gonzales	LA	70737	225-621-5709	621-5704
Web: www.ascensionparish.net					
Ashe County Chamber of Commerce					
1 N Jefferson Ave Suite C	West Jefferson	NC	28694	336-846-9550	846-8671
TF: 888-343-2743 ■ *Web:* www.ashechamber.com					
Ashland County 142 W 2nd St	Ashland	OH	44805	419-289-0000	282-4240
Web: www.ashlandcounty.org					
Ashland County 201 W Main St Rm 202	Ashland	WI	54806	715-682-7000	682-7032
Web: www.co.ashland.wi.us					
Ashley County 205 E Jefferson St PO Box 5	Hamburg	AR	71646	870-853-2020	853-2082

Entry	City	State	ZIP	Phone	Fax
Asotin County 135 2nd St	Asotin	WA	99402	509-243-2081	243-4978
Web: www.co.asotin.wa.us					
Assumption Parish 4809 Louisiana 1	Napoleonville	LA	70390	985-369-6653	369-2032
Web: www.assumptionla.com					
Atascosa County 1 Courthouse Cir Dr Suite 102	Jourdanton	TX	78026	830-767-2511	769-1021
Web: www.co.atascosa.tx.us					
Atchison County 423 N 5th St	Atchison	KS	66002	913-367-1653	367-0227
Web: www.atchisoncountyks.org					
Atchison County PO Box 280	Rock Port	MO	64482	660-744-2707	744-5705
Athens County Board of Developmental Disabilities 801 W Union St	Athens	OH	45701	740-594-3539	
Web: www.athenscountygovernment.com					
Athens-Clarke County PO Box 1868	Athens	GA	30603	706-613-3031	613-3033
Web: www.athensclarkecounty.com					
Atkinson County PO Box 518	Pearson	GA	31642	912-422-3391	422-3429
Atlantic County 5901 E Main St	Mays Landing	NJ	08330	609-641-7867	625-4738
Web: www.aclink.org					
Atoka County 200 E Ct St	Atoka	OK	74525	580-889-2643	889-2608
Web: www.atokacity.org					
Attala County 230 W Washington St	Kosciusko	MS	39090	662-289-2921	289-7662
Audrain County 101 N Jefferson St Rm 101	Mexico	MO	65265	573-473-5820	581-2380
Web: www.audraincounty.org					
Audubon County 318 Leroy St No 6	Audubon	IA	50025	712-563-4275	563-4276
Web: www.auduboncounty.org					
Auglaize County 209 S Blackhoof St Suite 201	Wapakoneta	OH	45895	419-739-6710	738-7953
Web: www.auglaizecounty.org					
Augusta County 18 Government Ctr Ln	Verona	VA	24482	540-245-5600	245-5621
Web: www.co.augusta.va.us					
Augusta-Richmond County 530 Greene St	Augusta	GA	30911	706-821-2400	821-2819
Web: www.augustaga.gov					
Aurora County PO Box 366	Plankinton	SD	57368	605-942-7165	942-7170
Austin County 1 E Main St	Bellville	TX	77418	979-865-5911	865-8786
Web: www.austincounty.com					
Avery County PO Box 115	Newland	NC	28657	828-733-2900	733-8410
Web: www.averycounty.com					
Avoyelles Parish 312 N Main St Courthouse Bldg Suite D	Marksville	LA	71351	318-253-9208	253-4614
Baca County 741 Main St	Springfield	CO	81073	719-523-4372	523-4881
Web: www.springfieldcolorado.com					
Bacon County PO Box 356	Alma	GA	31510	912-632-5214	632-2757
Bailey County 300 S 1st St	Muleshoe	TX	79347	806-272-3044	272-3538
Web: www.co.bailey.tx.us					
Baker County 1995 3rd St Suite 150	Baker City	OR	97814	541-523-8207	523-8240
Web: www.bakercounty.org					
Baker County 339 E Macclenny Ave	Macclenny	FL	32063	904-259-8113	259-4176
Web: www.bakercountyfl.org					
Baker County PO Box 10	Newton	GA	39870	229-734-3004	734-7770
Baldwin County 322 Courthouse Sq	Bay Minette	AL	36507	251-937-9561	580-2500
Web: www.co.baldwin.al.us					
Baldwin County 121 N Wilkinson St Suite 314	Milledgeville	GA	31061	478-445-4791	445-6320
Web: www.baldwincountyga.com					
Ballard County 132 N 4th St	Wickliffe	KY	42087	270-335-5168	335-3081
Web: www.ballardconet.com					
Baltimore County 401 Bosley Ave	Towson	MD	21204	410-887-2697	887-3062
Web: www.co.ba.md.us					
Bamberg County PO Box 150	Bamberg	SC	29003	803-245-3025	245-3088
Web: www.bambergsc.com					
Banks County 144 Yonah Homer Rd PO Box 337	Homer	GA	30547	706-677-6240	677-6294
Web: www.bankscountyga.org					
Banner County 206 State St	Harrisburg	NE	69345	308-436-5265	436-4180
Web: www.co.banner.ne.us					
Bannock County PO Box 4016	Pocatello	ID	83205	208-236-7211	236-7363
Web: www.co.bannock.id.us					
Baraga County 16 N 3rd St	L'Anse	MI	49946	906-524-6183	524-6186
Barber County Development Inc 215 S Iliff Hwy 281 PO Box 4	Medicine Lodge	KS	67104	620-886-3988	886-5425
Web: www.barbercounty.net					
Barbour County PO Box 398	Clayton	AL	36016	334-775-3203	775-1102
Barbour County 8 N Main St	Philippi	WV	26416	304-457-2232	457-5983
Barnes County 230 4th St NW Rm 202	Valley City	ND	58072	701-845-8500	845-8548
Web: www.co.barnes.nd.us					
Barnstable County 3195 Main St	Barnstable	MA	02630	508-362-2511	362-4136
Web: www.tsic.com					
Barnwell County 141 Main St	Barnwell	SC	29812	803-541-1020	541-1025
Web: www.barnwellcountysc.com					
Barren County 117 N Public Sq Suite 1A	Glasgow	KY	42141	270-651-3783	651-1083
Web: www.barrencounty.com					
Barron County 330 E LaSalle Ave Rm 210	Barron	WI	54812	715-537-6200	537-6277
Web: www.co.barron.wi.us					
Barrow County 233 E Broad St	Winder	GA	30680	770-307-3005	307-3141
Web: www.barrowga.org					
Barry County 700 Main St Suite 2	Cassville	MO	65625	417-847-2561	847-5311
Barry County 220 W State St	Hastings	MI	49058	269-948-4810	945-0209
Web: www.barrycounty.org					
Bartholomew County 234 Washington St	Columbus	IN	47201	812-379-1600	379-1675
Web: www.bartholomewco.com					
Barton County 1400 Main St Suite 202	Great Bend	KS	67530	620-793-1835	793-1990
Web: www.bartoncounty.org					
Barton County 1004 Gulf St	Lamar	MO	64759	417-682-3529	682-4100
Web: www.bartoncounty.com					
Bartow County 135 W Cherokee Ave Suite 251	Cartersville	GA	30120	770-387-5030	387-5023
Web: www.bartowga.org					
Bastrop County 804 Pecan St	Bastrop	TX	78602	512-581-4000	332-7269
Web: www.bastropcounty.com					
Bates County 1 N Delaware St	Butler	MO	64730	660-679-3371	679-9922
Web: www.batescounty.net					
Bath County PO Box 609	Owingsville	KY	40360	606-674-2613	674-9526
Bath County 65 Courthouse Hill	Warm Springs	VA	24484	540-839-7221	839-7222
Web: www.bathcountyva.org					
Baxter County 1 E 7th St Rm 103	Mountain Home	AR	72653	870-425-3475	424-5105
Web: www.baxtercounty.org					
Bay County 515 Ctr Ave Suite 101	Bay City	MI	48708	989-895-4280	895-4284
Web: www.co.bay.mi.us					
Bay County 300 E 4th St	Panama City	FL	32401	850-763-9061	747-5188
Web: www.co.bay.fl.us					
Bayfield County PO Box 878	Washburn	WI	54891	715-373-6100	373-6153
Web: www.bayfieldcounty.org					
Baylor County PO Box 689	Seymour	TX	76380	940-889-3322	
Beadle County PO Box 1358	Huron	SD	57350	605-353-7165	353-0118
Web: www.beadlecounty.org					
Bear Lake County 7 E Ctr St PO Box 190	Paris	ID	83261	208-945-2212	945-2780
Web: www.bearlakecounty.info					
Beaufort County 102 Ribaut Rd	Beaufort	SC	29902	843-470-5218	470-5248
Web: www.co.beaufort.sc.us					
Beaufort County 121 W 3rd St	Washington	NC	27889	252-946-0079	946-7722
Web: www.co.beaufort.nc.us					
Beauregard Parish 201 W 1st St	DeRidder	LA	70634	337-463-8595	462-3916
Beaver County PO Box 338	Beaver	OK	73932	580-625-3151	625-3430
Web: www.okcounties.org					
Beaver County 810 3rd St Courthouse	Beaver	PA	15009	724-728-3934	728-0725
Web: www.co.beaver.pa.us					
Beaver County 105 E Ctr St PO Box 789	Beaver	UT	84713	435-438-6490	438-6466
Web: www.beaver.state.ut.us					
Beaverhead County 2 S Pacific St	Dillon	MT	59725	406-683-5245	683-3769
Web: www.beaverhead.com					
Becker County 915 Lake Ave	Detroit Lakes	MN	56501	218-846-7301	846-7257*
**Fax:* Acctg ■ *Web:* www.co.becker.mn.us					
Beckham County PO Box 67	Sayre	OK	73662	580-928-2457	928-2467
Bedford (Independent City) 215 E Main St	Bedford	VA	24523	540-587-6001	586-7134
Web: www.ci.bedford.va.us					
Bedford County 211 S Juliana St	Bedford	PA	15522	814-623-4807	623-0991
Web: www.bedford.sapdc.org					
Bedford County 122 E Main St Suite 202	Bedford	VA	24523	540-586-7601	586-0406
Web: www.co.bedford.va.us					
Bedford County 104 Public Sq N	Shelbyville	TN	37160	931-684-1921	685-9590
Web: www.shelbyvilletn.com					
Bee County 105 W Corpus Christi St Rm 103	Beeville	TX	78102	361-362-3245	362-3247
Web: www.co.bee.tx.us					
Belknap County 34 County Dr	Laconia	NH	03246	603-527-5400	527-5409
Web: www.belknapcounty.org					
Bell County 101 E Central Ave PO Box 480	Belton	TX	76513	254-939-3521	933-5179
TF: 800-460-2355 ■ *Web:* www.bellcountytx.com					
Bell County PO Box 157	Pineville	KY	40977	606-337-6143	337-5415
Belmont County 101 W Main St Courthouse	Saint Clairsville	OH	43950	740-695-2121	695-5305
Beltrami County 619 Beltrami Ave NW Courthouse	Bemidji	MN	56601	218-333-4120	333-4209
Web: www.co.beltrami.mn.us					
Ben Hill County 402A E Pine St	Fitzgerald	GA	31750	229-426-5112	426-5106
Web: www.benhillcounty.com					
Benewah County 701 College Ave	Saint Maries	ID	83861	208-245-3212	245-3046
Bennett County PO Box 281	Martin	SD	57551	605-685-6969	685-1075
Bennington County 207 S St	Bennington	VT	05201	802-447-2700	447-2703
Web: www.bennington.com					
Benson County PO Box 213	Minnewaukan	ND	58351	701-473-5345	473-5571
Bent County 725 Bent Ave	Las Animas	CO	81054	719-456-1600	456-0375
Web: www.bentcounty.org					
Benton County PO Box 218	Ashland	MS	38603	662-224-6300	224-6303
Benton County 215 E Central St Suite 217	Bentonville	AR	72712	479-271-1013	271-1019
Web: www.co.benton.ar.us					
Benton County 1 E Ct Sq Rm 102	Camden	TN	38320	731-584-6011	584-4640
Benton County 408 SW Monroe Ave Suite 111	Corvallis	OR	97339	541-766-6800	766-6893
Web: www.co.benton.or.us					
Benton County 615 Hwy 23 PO Box 189	Foley	MN	56329	320-968-5205	968-5353
Web: www.co.benton.mn.us					
Benton County 706 E 5th St Suite 37	Fowler	IN	47944	765-884-0930	884-0322
Web: www.bentoncounty.org					
Benton County 7122 W Okanogan Pl Bldg A	Kennewick	WA	99336	509-735-3591	736-3066
Web: www.co.benton.wa.us					
Benton County PO Box 719	Vinton	IA	52349	319-472-2766	
Web: www.cobentoniaus.com					
Benton County PO Box 1238	Warsaw	MO	65355	660-438-7326	438-3275
Benzie County 448 Ct Pl	Beulah	MI	49617	231-882-9671	882-5941
Web: www.benzieco.net					
Bergen County 1 Bergen County Plaza Rm 580	Hackensack	NJ	07601	201-336-7300	336-7304
Web: www.co.bergen.nj.us					
Berkeley County PO Box 219	Moncks Corner	SC	29461	843-719-4403	719-4511
Web: www.co.berkeley.sc.us					
Berkeley County Council 400 W Stephen St Suite 201	Martinsburg	WV	25401	304-264-1923	267-1794
Web: www.berkeleycountycomm.org					
Berks County *Law Library* 633 Court St 4th Fl	Reading	PA	19601	610-478-3370	478-6375
Web: www.co.berks.pa.us					
Berkshire County 76 E St	Pittsfield	MA	01201	413-499-1940	499-7990
Bernalillo County 1 Civic Plaza NW 10th Fl	Albuquerque	NM	87102	505-768-4240	768-4329
Web: www.bernco.gov					
Berrien County 201 N Davis St	Nashville	GA	31639	229-686-5421	686-2785
Berrien County 701 Main St	Saint Joseph	MI	49085	269-983-7111	982-8642
Web: www.berriencounty.org					
Bertie County 106 Dundee St PO Box 530	Windsor	NC	27983	252-794-5300	794-5327
Web: www.co.bertie.nc.us					
Bexar County 100 Dolorosa St	San Antonio	TX	78205	210-335-2011	335-2252
Web: www.bexar.org					
Bibb County 35 Ct Sq E # 101	Centreville	AL	35042	205-926-3103	926-3132
Web: www.bibbcountyalabama.com					
Bibb County 601 Mulberry St	Macon	GA	31201	478-621-6400	621-6329
Web: www.co.bibb.ga.us					

				Phone	Fax
Bienville Parish 100 Courthouse Dr Rm 100	Arcadia	LA	71001	318-263-2123	263-7426
Web: www.bienvilleparish.org					
Big Horn County 420 W C St	Basin	WY	82410	307-568-2357	568-9375
Web: www.bighorncountywy.gov					
Big Horn County 121 W 3rd St	Hardin	MT	59034	406-665-9735	665-9738
Big Stone County 20 SE 2nd St	Ortonville	MN	56278	320-839-2537	839-2537
Web: www.bigstonecounty.org					
Billings County PO Box 138	Medora	ND	58645	701-623-4491	623-4896
Bingham County 501 N Maple St Suite 205	Blackfoot	ID	83221	208-782-3163	785-4131
Web: www.co.bingham.id.us					
Black Hawk County 316 E 5th St	Waterloo	IA	50703	319-833-3012	833-3170
Web: www.co.black-hawk.ia.us					
Blackford County 110 W Washington St	Hartford City	IN	47348	765-348-1620	348-7222*
*Fax: Acctg ■ *Web:* www.supertiles.com					
Bladen County 166 E Broad St Rm 105	Elizabethtown	NC	28337	910-862-6700	862-6767
Web: www.bladeninfo.org					
Blaine County 145 Lincoln Ave	Brewster	NE	68821	308-547-2222	547-2228
Web: www.blainecounty.ne.gov					
Blaine County 420 Ohio St	Chinook	MT	59523	406-357-3250	357-2199
Web: co.blaine.mt.gov					
Blaine County 206 1st Ave S Suite 200	Hailey	ID	83333	208-788-5505	788-5501
Web: www.co.blaine.id.us					
Blaine County 212 N Weigle	Watonga	OK	73772	580-623-5890	
Web: www.watonga.com					
Blair County 423 Allegheny St Suite 142	Hollidaysburg	PA	16648	814-693-3030	693-3033
Blanco County 101 E Pecan Dr Po Box 65	Johnson City	TX	78636	830-868-7357	868-7788
Web: www.co.blanco.tx.us					
Bland County 612 Main St # 104	Bland	VA	24315	276-688-4562	688-2438
Web: www.bland.org					
Bleckley County 306 SE 2nd St	Cochran	GA	31014	478-934-3200	934-0822
Web: www.bleckley.org					
Bledsoe County 104 N Frazier St	Pikeville	TN	37367	423-447-6855	447-7265
Blount County 341 Ct St	Maryville	TN	37804	865-273-5700	273-5705
Web: www.blounttn.org					
Blount County 220 2nd Ave E Rm 106	Oneonta	AL	35121	205-625-4160	625-5961
Web: www.co.blount.al.us					
Blue Earth County 204 S 5th St	Mankato	MN	56001	507-304-4000	389-8437
Web: www.co.blue-earth.mn.us					
Boise County 420 Main St PO Box 1300	Idaho City	ID	83631	208-392-4431	392-4473
Web: www.co.boise.id.us					
Bolivar County 200 S Ct St	Cleveland	MS	38732	662-846-5877	846-5880
Web: www.co.bolivar.ms.us					
Bollinger County PO Box 110	Marble Hill	MO	63764	573-238-1900	238-4511
Bon Homme County 300 W 18th Ave	Tyndall	SD	57066	605-589-4215	589-4245
Bond County 203 W College Ave	Greenville	IL	62246	618-664-0449	664-9414
Bonner County 215 S 1st Ave	Sandpoint	ID	83864	208-265-1432	265-1447
Web: www.co.bonner.id.us					
Bonneville County 900 Environmental Way	Idaho Falls	ID	83402	208-529-1354	529-1379
Web: www.co.bonneville.id.us					
Boone County 222 S 4th St	Albion	NE	68620	402-395-2055	
Web: www.co.boone.ne.us					
Boone County 601 N Main St Suite 201	Belvidere	IL	61008	815-547-4770	547-3579
Web: www.boonecountyil.org					
Boone County 201 State St	Boone	IA	50036	515-433-0500	432-8102
Web: www.co.boone.ia.us					
Boone County 2950 E Washington St	Burlington	KY	41005	859-334-3642	334-2193
Web: www.boonecountyky.org					
Boone County 801 E Walnut St	Columbia	MO	65201	573-886-4295	886-4300
Web: www.co.boone.mo.us					
Boone County 100 N Main St Suite 201	Harrison	AR	72601	870-741-8428	741-9724
Boone County 212 Courthouse Sq	Lebanon	IN	46052	765-482-3510	485-0150
Boone County 200 State St	Madison	WV	25130	304-369-3925	369-7329
Web: www.boonecountywv.org					
Borden County PO Box 156	Gail	TX	79738	806-756-4391	756-4405
Web: www.co.borden.tx.us					
Bosque County PO Box 617	Meridian	TX	76665	254-435-2201	435-2152
Web: users.htcomp.net/bosque					
Bossier Parish 204 Burt Blvd 2nd Fl	Benton	LA	71006	318-965-2336	965-2713
Web: www.mybossier.com					
Botetourt County 1 W Main St 1st Fl	Fincastle	VA	24090	540-473-8220	
Web: www.co.botetourt.va.us					
Bottineau County 314 W 5th St	Bottineau	ND	58318	701-228-3983	228-2336
Web: www.bottineau.com					
Boulder County 1750 33rd St Suite 201	Boulder	CO	80301	303-413-7770	413-7775
Web: www.co.boulder.co.us					
Boundary County					
6452 Kootenai Trail Rd # 22	Bonners Ferry	ID	83805	208-267-5504	267-7814
Web: www.boundarycountyid.org					
Bourbon County 210 S National Ave	Fort Scott	KS	66701	620-223-3800	223-5832
Web: www.bourboncountyks.org					
Bourbon County 301 Main St Suite 106	Paris	KY	40361	859-987-2142	987-5660
Web: www.parisky.com					
Bowie County 710 James Bowie Dr	New Boston	TX	75570	903-628-2571	628-6729
Web: www.co.bowie.tx.us					
Bowman County 104 1st St NW # 3	Bowman	ND	58623	701-523-3450	523-5443
Web: www.bowmannd.com					
Box Butte County 1790 CR 69 PO Box 170	Alliance	NE	69301	308-762-1246	762-2867
Web: www.co.box-butte.ne.us					
Box Elder County 01 S Main St	Brigham City	UT	84302	435-734-3300	723-7562
Web: www.boxeldercounty.org					
Boyd County PO Box 26	Butte	NE	68722	402-775-2391	775-2146
Boyd County 2800 Louisa St # 106	Catlettsburg	KY	41129	606-739-5116	739-6357
Boyle County 321 W Main St Rm 123	Danville	KY	40422	859-238-1110	238-1114
Web: www.danville-ky.com					
Bracken County PO Box 147	Brooksville	KY	41004	606-735-2952	735-2867
Bradford County 945 N Temple Ave PO Drawer B	Starke	FL	32091	904-964-6280	964-4454
Web: www.bradford-co-fla.org					
Bradford County 301 Main St Courthouse	Towanda	PA	18848	570-265-1727	265-1729
Web: www.bradfordcountypa.org					
Bradley County 155 N Ocoee St	Cleveland	TN	37311	423-728-7226	478-8845
Web: www.bradleyco.net					
Bradley County 101 E Cedar St	Warren	AR	71671	870-226-3853	226-8401
Branch County 31 Division St	Coldwater	MI	49036	517-279-4301	278-4130
Web: www.co.branch.mi.us					
Brantley County PO Box 398	Nahunta	GA	31553	912-462-6285	462-5538
Web: www.brantleycounty.org					
Braxton County 300 Main St PO Box 486	Sutton	WV	26601	304-765-2833	765-2093
Web: www.braxtonwv.org					
Brazoria County 111 E Locust St Suite 200	Angleton	TX	77515	979-849-5711	864-1358
Web: www.brazoria-county.com					
Brazos County 300 E 26th St Suite 120	Bryan	TX	77803	979-361-4135	361-4125
Web: www.co.brazos.tx.us					
Breathitt County 1137 Main St	Jackson	KY	41339	606-666-3810	666-3807
Web: www.breathittcounty.com					
Breckinridge County PO Box 538	Hardinsburg	KY	40143	270-756-2246	756-1569
Web: www.breckinridgecounty.net					
Bremer County 415 E Bremer Ave	Waverly	IA	50677	319-352-0130	352-0602
Web: www.co.bremer.ia.us					
Brevard County 400 S St Suite 1-A	Titusville	FL	32780	321-264-6750	264-6751
Web: www.brevardcounty.us					
Brewster County 201 W Ave E	Alpine	TX	79830	432-837-3366	837-6217
Web: www.co.brewster.tx.us					
Briscoe County PO Box 555	Silverton	TX	79257	806-823-2134	823-2359
Web: www.co.briscoe.tx.us					
Bristol (Independent City)					
497 Cumberland St Rm 210	Bristol	VA	24201	276-645-7321	821-6097
Web: www.bristolva.org					
Bristol Bay Borough PO Box 189	Naknek	AK	99633	907-246-4224	246-6633
Web: www.theborough.com					
Bristol County 9 Ct St	Taunton	MA	02780	508-824-9681	821-3101
Web: www.countyofbristol.net					
Bristol County 10 Ct St	Bristol	RI	02809	401-253-7000	253-3080
Web: www.bristolri.us					
Broadwater County 515 Broadway	Townsend	MT	59644	406-266-3443	266-3674
Bronx County 851 Grand Concourse Suite 301	Bronx	NY	10451	718-590-3500	590-3537
Web: www.nyc.gov					
Brooke County 632 Main St	Wellsburg	WV	26070	304-737-3661	737-4023
Brookings County 314 6th Ave	Brookings	SD	57006	605-692-6284	696-8211
Web: www.brookingscountysd.gov					
Brooks County PO Box 427	Falfurrias	TX	78355	361-325-5604	325-4944
Brooks County 610 S Highland Rd	Quitman	GA	31643	229-263-5561	263-9345
Web: www.brooks-county.org					
Broome County 44 Hawley St	Binghamton	NY	13901	607-778-2451	778-2243
Web: www.gobroomecounty.com					
Broomfield City & County 1 DesCombes Dr	Broomfield	CO	80020	303-469-3301	438-6296
Web: www.ci.broomfield.co.us					
Broward County					
115 S Andrews Ave Rm 421	Fort Lauderdale	FL	33301	954-357-7000	357-7295
Web: www.co.broward.fl.us					
Brown County 25 Market St Suite 1	Aberdeen	SD	57401	605-626-7105	626-4010
Web: www.brown.sd.us					
Brown County 148 W 4th St	Ainsworth	NE	69210	402-387-2705	387-0918
Web: www.co.brown.ne.us					
Brown County 800 Mt Orab Pike Suite 101	Georgetown	OH	45121	937-378-3956	378-6324
Web: www.county.brown.oh.us					
Brown County 305 E Walnut Suite 120	Green Bay	WI	54301	920-448-4016	448-4498
Web: www.co.brown.wi.us					
Brown County 601 Oregon St	Hiawatha	KS	66434	785-742-2581	742-7705
Web: www.brown.kansasgov.com					
Brown County 200 Ct St Rm 4	Mount Sterling	IL	62353	217-773-3421	773-2233
Brown County PO Box 85	Nashville	IN	47448	812-988-5510	988-5562
Web: www.browncounty.org					
Brown County 14 S State St PO Box 248	New Ulm	MN	56073	507-233-6600	359-1430
Web: www.co.brown.mn.us					
Brule County 300 S Courtland St Suite 111	Chamberlain	SD	57325	605-734-4580	734-4582
Web: www.bruleco.tripod.com					
Brunswick County 45 Courthouse Dr	Bolivia	NC	28422	910-253-2000	253-2022
Web: www.brunsco.net					
Brunswick County 216 N Main St	Lawrenceville	VA	23868	434-848-2215	848-4307
Web: www.tourbrunswick.org					
Bryan County PO Box 1789	Durant	OK	74702	580-924-2202	924-2289
Bryan County 51 N Courthouse St	Pembroke	GA	31321	912-653-3819	653-4691
Web: www.bryancountyga.org					
Buchanan County PO Box 950	Grundy	VA	24614	276-935-6500	935-4479
Buchanan County 210 5th Ave NE	Independence	IA	50644	319-334-2196	334-7455
Web: www.buchanancounty.com					
Buchanan County 411 Jules St	Saint Joseph	MO	64501	816-271-1411	271-1535
Web: www.co.buchanan.mo.us					
Buckingham County					
13360 W James Anderson Hwy	Buckingham	VA	23921	434-969-4242	969-1638
Bucks County 55 E Ct St	Doylestown	PA	18901	215-348-6000	348-6571
Web: www.buckscounty.org					
Buena Vista County 215 E 5th St	Storm Lake	IA	50588	712-749-2546	749-2700
Web: www.co.buena-vista.ia.us					
Buffalo County 407 S 2nd St	Alma	WI	54610	608-685-6209	685-6213
Web: www.buffalocounty.com					
Buffalo County PO Box 1270	Kearney	NE	68848	308-236-1226	233-3649
Web: www.buffalogov.org					
Bullitt County 300 S Buckman St	Shepherdsville	KY	40165	502-543-2513	543-9121
Web: www.bullittcounty.org					
Bulloch County 115 N Main St	Statesboro	GA	30458	912-764-6245	764-8634
Web: www.bullochcounty.net					
Bullock County 212 Prairie St N	Union Springs	AL	36089	334-738-2720	738-5068
Web: www.unionspringsalabama.com					
Buncombe County 205 College St Suite 300	Asheville	NC	28801	828-250-4100	250-6077
Web: www.buncombecounty.org					
Bureau County 700 S Main St	Princeton	IL	61356	815-875-2014	879-4803
Web: www.bureaucounty-il.com					
Burke County 103 Main St NE	Bowbells	ND	58721	701-377-2718	377-2020
Web: www.burkecountynd.com					
Burke County PO Box 219	Morganton	NC	28680	828-439-4340	438-2782
Web: www.co.burke.nc.us					
Burke County PO Box 89	Waynesboro	GA	30830	706-554-2324	554-0350
Web: www.burkecounty-ga.gov					

	City	State	Zip	Phone	Fax
Burleigh County PO Box 1055	Bismarck	ND	58502	701-222-6761	221-3756
Web: www.co.burleigh.nd.us					
Burleson County 100 W Buck St Suite 203	Caldwell	TX	77836	979-567-2329	567-2376
Web: www.co.burleson.tx.us					
Burlington County 49 Rancocas Rd	Mount Holly	NJ	08060	609-265-5122	265-0696
Web: www.co.burlington.nj.us					
Burnet County 220 S Pierce St	Burnet	TX	78611	512-756-5420	756-5410
Web: www.burnetcountytexas.org					
Burnett County 7410 County Rd K	Siren	WI	54872	715-349-2181	
Web: www.burnettcounty.com/gov					
Burt County 111 N 13th St PO Box 8787	Tekamah	NE	68061	402-374-2955	374-2956
Web: www.burtcounty.ne.gov					
Butler County 428 6th St	Allison	IA	50602	319-267-2487	267-2488
Web: www.butlercoiowa.org					
Butler County 290 S Main St PO Box 1208	Butler	PA	16003	724-284-5233	284-5244
Web: www.co.butler.pa.us					
Butler County 451 N 5th St	David City	NE	68632	402-367-7430	367-3329
Web: www.co.butler.ne.us					
Butler County 205 W Central Ave	El Dorado	KS	67042	316-322-4300	322-4387
TF: 800-822-6104 ■ *Web:* www.bucoks.com					
Butler County PO Box 756	Greenville	AL	36037	334-382-3612	382-3506
Butler County 315 High St	Hamilton	OH	45011	513-887-3278	887-3966
Web: www.butlercountyohio.org					
Butler County PO Box 449	Morgantown	KY	42261	270-526-5676	526-2658
Butler County 100 N Main St Courthouse Rm 202	Poplar Bluff	MO	63901	573-686-8050	686-8066
Butte County 248 W Grand Ave PO Box 737	Arco	ID	83213	208-527-3021	527-3295
Butte County PO Box 250	Belle Fourche	SD	57717	605-892-2516	892-2836
Butte County 25 County Ctr Dr	Oroville	CA	95965	530-538-7691	538-7975
Web: www.buttecounty.net					
Butte-Silver Bow County 155 W Granite St	Butte	MT	59703	406-497-6200	497-6328
Web: www.co.silverbow.mt.us					
Butts County 625 W 3rd St # 4	Jackson	GA	30233	770-775-8200	775-8211
Web: www.buttscounty.org					
Cabarrus County 65 Church St S	Concord	NC	28025	704-920-2100	920-2820
Web: www.cabarruscounty.us					
Cabell County 750 5th Ave Suite 108	Huntington	WV	25701	304-526-8625	526-8632
Web: www.cabellcounty.org					
Cache County 179 N Main St Suite 102	Logan	UT	84321	435-716-7150	752-3597
Web: www.cachecounty.org					
Caddo County 201 W Oklahoma Ave	Anadarko	OK	73005	405-247-6609	
Web: www.rootsweb.ancestry.com/~okcaddo/ccpage.htm					
Caddo Parish 505 Travis St 8th Fl	Shreveport	LA	71101	318-226-6900	429-7630
Web: www.caddo.org					
Calaveras County 891 Mountain Ranch Rd	San Andreas	CA	95249	209-754-6370	754-6733
Web: www.co.calaveras.ca.us					
Calcasieu Parish 1000 Ryan St # 5	Lake Charles	LA	70601	337-437-3550	437-3350
Web: www.cppj.net					
Caldwell County PO Box 67	Kingston	MO	64650	816-586-2571	586-3600
Caldwell County PO Box 2200	Lenoir	NC	28645	828-757-1300	757-1295
Web: www.co.caldwell.nc.us					
Caldwell County 110 S Main St	Lockhart	TX	78644	512-398-1824	398-1816
Web: www.co.caldwell.tx.us					
Caldwell County 100 E Market St Rm 23	Princeton	KY	42445	270-365-6754	365-7447
Caldwell Parish PO Box 1737	Columbia	LA	71418	318-649-2681	649-5930
Caledonia County 1126 Main St	Saint Johnsbury	VT	05819	802-748-6600	748-6603
Calhoun County 1702 Noble St Suite 103	Anniston	AL	36201	256-241-2800	231-1744
Web: www.calhounchamber.com					
Calhoun County 20859 Central Ave E Rm 130	Blountstown	FL	32424	850-674-4545	674-5553
Web: www.calhounco.org					
Calhoun County PO Box 230	Grantsville	WV	26147	304-354-6725	354-6725
Calhoun County PO Box 1175	Hampton	AR	71744	870-798-2517	798-2428
Calhoun County 102 County Rd PO Box 187	Hardin	IL	62047	618-576-2351	576-2895
Calhoun County 315 W Green St	Marshall	MI	49068	269-781-0730	781-0721
Web: www.calhouncountymi.org					
Calhoun County PO Box 226	Morgan	GA	39866	229-849-4835	849-2100
Calhoun County PO Box 8	Pittsboro	MS	38951	662-412-3117	412-3128
Calhoun County 211 S Ann St	Port Lavaca	TX	77979	361-553-4411	553-4420
Web: www.tisd.net					
Calhoun County 416 4th St Suite 5	Rockwell City	IA	50579	712-297-8122	297-5082
Web: www.calhouncountyiowa.com					
Calhoun County 102 Courthouse Dr Suite 108 Courthouse Annex	Saint Matthews	SC	29135	803-874-2435	874-1242
Callahan County 100 W 4th St	Baird	TX	79504	325-854-1155	854-1227
Web: www.co.callahan.tx.us					
Callaway County 10 E 5th St	Fulton	MO	65251	573-642-0730	642-7181
Web: www.callaway.county.missouri.org					
Calloway County 101 S 5th St 2nd Fl	Murray	KY	42071	270-753-3923	759-9611
Calumet County 206 Ct St	Chilton	WI	53014	920-849-2361	849-1469
Web: www.co.calumet.wi.us					
Calvert County 175 Main St	Prince Frederick	MD	20678	410-535-1600	535-9572
Web: www.co.cal.md.us					
Camas County PO Box 430	Fairfield	ID	83327	208-764-2242	764-2349
Cambria County 200 S Ctr St	Ebensburg	PA	15931	814-472-1540	472-0761
Web: www.co.cambria.pa.us					
Camden County 117 N NC 343 PO Box 190	Camden	NC	27921	252-338-1919	333-1603
Web: camdencountync.besavvy2.egovlink.com					
Camden County 520 Market St Rm 102	Camden	NJ	08102	856-225-5300	225-5316
Web: www.co.camden.nj.us					
Camden County 826 N Business Rt 5	Camdenton	MO	65020	573-346-4440	346-5181
Web: www.camdenmo.org					
Camden County PO Box 99	Woodbine	GA	31569	912-576-5649	576-5647
Web: www.co.camden.ga.us					
Cameron County 964 E Harrison St	Brownsville	TX	78520	956-544-0815	544-0813
Web: www.co.cameron.tx.us					
Cameron County 20 E 5th St	Emporium	PA	15834	814-486-2315	486-3176
Web: www.cameroncountypa.com					
Cameron Parish PO Box 549	Cameron	LA	70631	337-775-5316	775-7172
Web: www.cameronparish.net					
Camp County 126 Church St	Pittsburg	TX	75686	903-856-2731	856-2309
Web: www.co.camp.tx.us					
Campbell County PO Box 3010	Gillette	WY	82717	307-682-7285	687-6455
Web: ccg.co.campbell.wy.us					
Campbell County 570 Main St # A21	Jacksboro	TN	37757	423-562-4985	566-3852
Web: www.co.campbell.tn.us					
Campbell County PO Box 146	Mound City	SD	57646	605-955-3536	955-5303
Campbell County 1098 Monmouth St # 204	Newport	KY	41071	859-292-3845	292-0615
Web: www.campbellcountyky.org					
Campbell County 732 Village Hwy	Rustburg	VA	24588	434-332-9517	332-9518
Web: www.co.campbell.va.us					
Canadian County 201 N Choctaw St	El Reno	OK	73036	405-262-1070	422-2411
Web: www.canadiancounty.org					
Candler County 705 N Lewis St	Metter	GA	30439	912-685-2835	685-4823
Cannon County 1 County Courthouse Public Sq	Woodbury	TN	37190	615-563-4278	563-1289
Web: www.cannoncounty.info					
Canyon County 1115 Albany St	Caldwell	ID	83605	208-454-7574	454-7525
Web: www.canyoncounty.org					
Cape Girardeau County 1 Barton Sq	Jackson	MO	63755	573-243-3547	204-2418
Web: www.showme.net					
Cape May County 7 N Main St PO Box 5000	Cape May Court House	NJ	08210	609-465-1010	465-8625
Web: www.capemaycountygov.net					
Carbon County 2 Hazard Sq PO Box 129	Jim Thorpe	PA	18229	570-325-3611	325-3622
Web: www.carboncounty.com					
Carbon County 120 E Main St	Price	UT	84501	435-636-3200	636-3210
Web: www.co.carbon.ut.us					
Carbon County PO Box 1017	Rawlins	WY	82301	307-328-2668	328-2669
TF: 800-228-3547 ■ *Web:* www.wyomingcarboncounty.com					
Carbon County 17 W 11th St	Red Lodge	MT	59068	406-446-1220	446-2640
Web: www.co.carbon.mt.us					
Caribou County PO Box 775	Soda Springs	ID	83276	208-547-4324	547-4759
Carlisle County PO Box 176	Bardwell	KY	42023	270-628-3233	628-0191
Carlton County PO Box 130	Carlton	MN	55718	218-384-9166	384-9182
Web: www.co.carlton.mn.us					
Caroline County 117 Ennis St	Bowling Green	VA	22427	804-633-5380	633-4970
Web: www.co.caroline.va.us					
Caroline County 109 Market St	Denton	MD	21629	410-479-0660	479-4060
Web: www.carolinemd.org					
Carroll County 210 W Church St	Berryville	AR	72616	870-423-2022	423-7400
TF: 888-423-2087					
Carroll County 114 E 6th St	Carroll	IA	51401	712-792-4923	792-9423
Web: www.co.carroll.ia.us					
Carroll County 423 College St Rm 408 PO Box 338	Carrollton	GA	30112	770-830-5800	830-5992
Web: www.carrollcountyga.com					
Carroll County 440 Main St Courthouse	Carrollton	KY	41008	502-732-7005	732-7007
Web: www.carrollcountyky.com					
Carroll County 8 S Main St Suite 6	Carrollton	MO	64633	660-542-0615	542-0621
Carroll County PO Box 60	Carrollton	MS	38917	662-237-9274	237-9642
Carroll County 119 S Lisbon St Suite 201	Carrollton	OH	44615	330-627-4869	627-6656
Web: www.carrollcountyohio.net					
Carroll County 101 W Main St	Delphi	IN	46923	765-564-4485	564-1835
Web: www.carrollnet.org					
Carroll County 605 Pine St # A230	Hillsville	VA	24343	276-730-3070	730-3071
Web: www.chillsnet.org					
Carroll County 625 High St Suite 103	Huntingdon	TN	38344	731-986-1936	986-1935
Web: www.carrollcounty-tn-chamber.com					
Carroll County 8216 Black Oak Rd PO Box 152	Mount Carroll	IL	61053	815-244-0221	244-3709
TF: 800-485-0145 ■ *Web:* www.gocarrollcounty.com					
Carroll County PO Box 152	Ossipee	NH	03864	603-539-2428	539-4287
Carroll County 225 N Ctr St Rm 300	Westminster	MD	21157	410-386-2400	386-2485
Web: www.ccgov.carr.org					
Carson City (Independent City) 201 N Carson St	Carson City	NV	89701	775-887-2100	887-2286
Web: www.carson-city.nv.us					
Carson County PO Box 487	Panhandle	TX	79068	806-537-3873	537-3623
Web: www.co.carson.tx.us					
Carter County 101 1st St SW	Ardmore	OK	73401	580-223-8162	
TF: 800-231-8668 ■ *Web:* www.brightok.net/cartercounty					
Carter County 214 Park St PO Box 315	Ekalaka	MT	59324	406-775-8749	775-8750
Web: www.cartercountymt.info					
Carter County 801 E Elk Ave Courthouse Bldg	Elizabethton	TN	37643	423-542-1814	547-1502
Web: www.tourelizabethton.com					
Carter County 300 W Main St Rm 232	Grayson	KY	41143	606-474-5188	474-6883
Web: www.cartercountyclerksoffice.com					
Carter County 105 Main St PO Box 445	Van Buren	MO	63965	573-323-4527	323-4527
Carteret County Courthouse Sq	Beaufort	NC	28516	252-728-8450	728-2092
Web: www.co.carteret.nc.us					
Carver County 606 E 4th St	Chaska	MN	55318	952-361-1500	361-1491
Web: www.co.carver.mn.us					
Cascade County 325 2nd Ave N # 100	Great Falls	MT	59401	406-454-6800	454-6703
Web: www.co.cascade.mt.us					
Casey County PO Box 306	Liberty	KY	42539	606-787-6154	787-6154
Cass County 5 W 7th St	Atlantic	IA	50022	712-243-4570	243-6660
Web: www.casscountyiowa.org					
Cass County PO Box 132	Cassopolis	MI	49031	269-445-3701	445-5018
Web: casscountymi.org					
Cass County 211 9th St S	Fargo	ND	58103	701-241-5601	241-5728
Web: www.casscountynd.gov					
Cass County 2502 W Mechanic St	Harrisonville	MO	64701	816-380-8100	380-8101
Web: www.casscounty.com					
Cass County PO Box 449	Linden	TX	75563	903-756-5071	756-8057
Web: www.co.cass.tx.us					
Cass County 200 Ct Pk	Logansport	IN	46947	574-753-7740	722-1556
Cass County 346 Main St	Plattsmouth	NE	68048	402-296-9300	296-9332
Web: www.cassne.org					
Cass County 100 E Springfield St	Virginia	IL	62691	217-452-7217	452-7219
Cassia County 1459 Overland Ave	Burley	ID	83318	208-878-7302	878-9109
Web: www.cassiacounty.org					
Castro County 100 E Bedford St	Dimmitt	TX	79027	806-647-3338	647-5438
Web: www.co.castro.tx.us					

Entry	City	State	ZIP	Phone	Fax
Caswell County 139 Church St	Yanceyville	NC	27379	336-694-4171	694-7338
Web: www.caswellcountync.gov					
Catahoula Parish PO Box 654	Harrisonburg	LA	71340	318-744-5497	744-5488
Catawba County PO Box 389	Newton	NC	28658	828-465-8201	465-8392
Web: www.co.catawba.nc.us					
Catoosa County 875 Lafayette St	Ringgold	GA	30736	706-935-4231	
Web: www.catoosa.com					
Catron County 100 Main St	Reserve	NM	87830	505-533-6423	533-6433
Web: www.mylocalgov.com/catroncountynm					
Cattaraugus County 303 Ct St	Little Valley	NY	14755	716-938-9111	938-6009
Web: www.co.cattaraugus.ny.us					
Cavalier County 901 3rd St Suite 15	Langdon	ND	58249	701-256-2229	256-2566
Web: www.ccjda.org					
Cayuga County 160 Genesee St	Auburn	NY	13021	315-253-1271	253-1673
Web: www.co.cayuga.ny.us					
Cecil County 129 E Main St Rm 108	Elkton	MD	21921	410-996-5375	392-6032
Web: www.ccgov.org					
Cedar County 101 S Broadway	Hartington	NE	68739	402-254-7411	254-7410
Web: www.co.cedar.ne.us					
Cedar County 113 S St PO Box 126	Stockton	MO	65785	417-276-6700	276-2207
Cedar County 400 Cedar St	Tipton	IA	52772	563-886-2101	886-3594
Web: www.cedarcounty.org					
Centre County 420 Holmes St Willowbank Office Bldg	Bellefonte	PA	16823	814-355-6700	355-6980
Web: www.co.centre.pa.us					
Cerro Gordo County 220 N Washington Ave	Mason City	IA	50401	641-421-3022	421-3072
Web: www.co.cerro-gordo.ia.us					
Chaffee County 104 Crestone Ave	Salida	CO	81201	719-539-4004	539-8588
Web: www.chaffeecounty.org					
Chambers County 404 Washington Ave	Anahuac	TX	77514	409-267-8309	267-8315
Web: www.co.chambers.tx.us					
Chambers County 2 Lafayette St S Suite B Courthouse	Lafayette	AL	36862	334-864-4348	
Web: www.chamberscounty.com					
Champaign County 1776 E Washington St	Urbana	IL	61802	217-384-3776	384-3896
Web: www.co.champaign.il.us					
Champaign County 1512 S US Hwy 68 Suite A100	Urbana	OH	43078	937-484-1611	484-1609
Web: www.co.champaign.oh.us					
Chariton County 306 S Cherry St	Keytesville	MO	65261	660-288-3273	288-3403
Charles County 200 Baltimore St	La Plata	MD	20646	301-645-0600	645-0560
Web: www.charlescounty.org					
Charles Mix County PO Box 490	Lake Andes	SD	57356	605-487-7131	487-7221
Charleston County 4045 Bridge View	Charleston	SC	29405	843-958-4030	958-4035
Web: www.charlestoncounty.org					
Charlevoix County 203 Antrim St	Charlevoix	MI	49720	231-547-7200	547-7217
Web: www.charlevoixcounty.org					
Charlotte County 250 LeGrande Ave Suite A PO Box 608	Charlotte Court House	VA	23923	434-542-5147	542-5248
Web: www.co.charlotte.va.us					
Charlotte County 18500 Murdoch Cir	Port Charlotte	FL	33948	941-743-1300	743-1530
Web: www.charlottecountyfl.com					
Charlottesville (Independent City) 605 E Main St	Charlottesville	VA	22902	434-970-3101	970-3890
Web: www.charlottesville.org					
Charlton County 100 S 3rd St	Folkston	GA	31537	912-496-2549	496-1156
Chase County 300 Pearl St	Cottonwood Falls	KS	66845	620-273-6423	273-6617
Web: www.chasecountyks.org					
Chase County PO Box 1299	Imperial	NE	69033	308-882-5266	882-7552
Web: www.co.chase.ne.us					
Chatham County 12 E St PO Box 369	Pittsboro	NC	27312	919-542-3240	542-1402
Web: www.co.chatham.nc.us					
Chatham County 124 Bull St	Savannah	GA	31401	912-652-7869	652-7874
Web: www.chathamcounty.org					
Chattooga County PO Box 211	Summerville	GA	30747	706-857-0701	857-0742
Web: www.chattoogacountyga.com					
Chautauqua County 3 N Erie St Gerace Office Bldg	Mayville	NY	14757	716-753-4211	753-4756
Web: www.chautco.com					
Chautauqua County 215 N Chautauqua St	Sedan	KS	67361	620-725-5800	725-5801
Cheatham County 100 Public Sq Suite 105	Ashland City	TN	37015	615-792-4316	792-2001
Web: www.cheathamcounty.net					
Cheboygan County 870 S Main St	Cheboygan	MI	49721	231-627-8808	627-8453
Web: www.cheboygancounty.net					
Chelan County 350 Orondo Ave	Wenatchee	WA	98801	509-667-6380	667-6611
Web: www.co.chelan.wa.us					
Chemung County 210 Lake St PO Box 588	Elmira	NY	14902	607-737-2920	737-2897
Web: www.chemungcounty.com					
Chenango County 5 Court St	Norwich	NY	13815	607-337-1700	337-1455
Web: www.co.chenango.ny.us					
Cherokee County 90 N St Suite 310	Canton	GA	30114	678-493-6511	493-6013
Web: www.cherokeega.com					
Cherokee County 260 Cedar Bluff Rd Suite 103	Centre	AL	35960	256-927-3668	927-3669
Web: www.cherokee-chamber.org					
Cherokee County 520 W Main St PO Box F	Cherokee	IA	51012	712-225-6744	225-6749
Web: www.cherokeeia.com					
Cherokee County PO Box 14	Columbus	KS	66725	620-429-2042	429-1042
Web: www.cherokeecountyks.com					
Cherokee County 210 N Limestone St	Gaffney	SC	29340	864-487-2562	487-2594
Web: www.cherokeecounty-sc.org					
Cherokee County 75 Peachtree St	Murphy	NC	28906	828-837-5527	837-9684
Web: www.cherokeecounty-nc.org					
Cherokee County PO Box 420	Rusk	TX	75785	903-683-2350	683-5931
Web: www.co.cherokee.tx.us					
Cherokee County 213 W Delaware St Rm 200	Tahlequah	OK	74464	918-456-3171	458-6508
Cherry County PO Box 120	Valentine	NE	69201	402-376-2771	376-3095
Web: www.co.cherry.ne.us					
Chesapeake (Independent City) 306 Cedar Rd	Chesapeake	VA	23322	757-382-6151	382-6678
Web: www.chesapeake.va.us					
Cheshire County 12 Ct St	Keene	NH	03431	603-352-6902	
Web: www.co.cheshire.nh.us					
Chester County 140 Main St # A1	Chester	SC	29706	803-385-2605	581-7975
Web: www.chesterchamber.com					
Chester County 313 W Market St Suite 6202 PO Box 2748	West Chester	PA	19380	610-344-6100	344-5995
TF: 800-692-1100 ■ *Web:* dsf.chesco.org					
Chesterfield County 200 W Main St # K	Chesterfield	SC	29709	843-623-2574	623-6944
Web: www.chesterfield.k12.sc.us					
Chesterfield County PO Box 70	Chesterfield	VA	23832	804-748-1201	751-4993
Web: www.co.chesterfield.va.us					
Cheyenne County PO Box 567	Cheyenne Wells	CO	80810	719-767-5685	767-8730
Web: www.co.cheyenne.co.us					
Cheyenne County 212 E Washington	Saint Francis	KS	67756	785-332-8800	332-8825
Web: www.cheyennecounty.org					
Cheyenne County 1000 10th Ave PO Box 217	Sidney	NE	69162	308-254-2141	254-5049*
**Fax:* Hum Res ■ *Web:* www.co.cheyenne.ne.us					
Chickasaw County 797 S Jackson St	Houston	MS	38851	662-456-2513	456-5295
Chickasaw County 8 E Prospect St	New Hampton	IA	50659	641-394-2100	394-5541
Web: www.chickasawcoia.org					
Chicot County 108 Main St County Courthouse	Lake Village	AR	71653	870-265-8000	265-8018
Childress County Court house PO Box 4	Childress	TX	79201	940-937-6143	937-3479
Chilton County PO Box 1948	Clanton	AL	35046	205-755-1551	280-7204
Web: www.chiltoncounty.org					
Chippewa County 711 N Bridge St	Chippewa Falls	WI	54729	715-726-7980	726-7987
Web: www.co.chippewa.wi.us					
Chippewa County 629 N 11th St	Montevideo	MN	56265	320-269-7447	269-7412*
**Fax:* Acctg ■ *Web:* www.co.chippewa.mn.us					
Chippewa County 319 Ct St	Sault Sainte Marie	MI	49783	906-635-6300	635-6851
Web: www.users.lighthouse.net					
Chisago County 313 N Main St Suite 174	Center City	MN	55012	651-213-8879	213-0359
Web: www.co.chisago.mn.us					
Chittenden County 175 Main St	Burlington	VT	05401	802-863-3467	
Web: www.ccrpcvt.org					
Choctaw County PO Box 250	Ackerman	MS	39735	662-285-6329	285-3444
Choctaw County 117 S Mulberry St Suite 9	Butler	AL	36904	205-459-2417	459-4248
Choctaw County 300 E Duke St	Hugo	OK	74743	580-326-3778	326-6787
Chouteau County 1308 Franklin St	Fort Benton	MT	59442	406-622-5151	622-3012
Web: www.co.chouteau.mt.us					
Chowan County 113 E King St	Edenton	NC	27932	252-482-8431	482-0126
Web: www.chowancounty-nc.gov					
Christian County 511 S Main St	Hopkinsville	KY	42240	270-887-4105	885-5925
Web: www.christiancounty.org					
Christian County 100 W Church St Rm 206	Ozark	MO	65721	417-581-6360	581-8331
Web: www.christiancountymo.gov					
Christian County 101 S Main St PO Box 647	Taylorville	IL	62568	217-824-4969	824-5105
Churchill County 155 N Taylor St Suite 153	Fallon	NV	89406	775-423-5136	423-0717
Web: www.churchillcounty.org					
Cibola County 515 W High Ave	Grants	NM	87020	505-287-9431	285-2562
Web: www.grants.org					
Cimarron County Courthouse Sq PO Box 788	Boise City	OK	73933	580-544-2221	544-2251
Citrus County 110 N Apopka Ave	Inverness	FL	34450	352-341-6400	341-6491
Web: www.clerk.citrus.fl.us					
City of Buena Vista 2039 Sycamore Ave	Buena Vista	VA	24416	540-261-6121	
Web: www.bvcity.org					
Clackamas County 2051 Kaen Rd	Oregon City	OR	97045	503-655-8551	650-5688
Web: www.co.clackamas.or.us					
Claiborne County 410 Market St	Port Gibson	MS	39150	601-437-5841	437-4543
Claiborne County 1740 Main St	Tazewell	TN	37879	423-626-3284	626-3604
Web: claibornecounty.com					
Claiborne Parish 512 E Main St PO Box 330	Homer	LA	71040	318-927-9601	927-2345
Web: www.claiborneone.org					
Clallam County 223 E 4th St Suite 2	Port Angeles	WA	98362	360-452-7831	417-2493
Web: www.clallam.net					
Clare County 225 W Main St	Harrison	MI	48625	989-539-7131	539-6616
Web: www.clarecountyinternet.com					
Clarendon County 3 W Key St	Manning	SC	29102	803-435-8424	435-8258
Web: www.clarendoncounty.com					
Clarion County 421 Main St Courthouse	Clarion	PA	16214	814-226-4000	227-2501
Web: www.co.clarion.pa.us					
Clark County 401 Clay St	Arkadelphia	AR	71923	870-246-4491	246-6505
Web: www.clarkcountyarkansas.com					
Clark County 913 Highland St	Ashland	KS	67831	620-635-2813	635-2051
Web: www.clarkcountyks.com					
Clark County 200 N Commercial St	Clark	SD	57225	605-532-5921	532-5931
Clark County 320 W Main St PO Box 205	Dubois	ID	83423	208-374-5402	374-5609
Clark County 501 E Court Ave	Jeffersonville	IN	47130	812-285-6275	285-6366
Web: www.co.clark.in.us					
Clark County 111 E Ct St	Kahoka	MO	63445	660-727-3283	727-1051
Clark County 500 S Grand Central Pkwy	Las Vegas	NV	89155	702-455-4011	
Web: www.co.clark.nv.us					
Clark County 501 Archer Ave County Courthouse	Marshall	IL	62441	217-826-8311	826-2519
Web: www.clarkcountyil.org					
Clark County 517 Ct St	Neillsville	WI	54456	715-743-5148	743-5154
Web: www.co.clark.wi.us					
Clark County 101 N Limestone St	Springfield	OH	45502	937-328-2458	328-2436
Web: www.co.clark.oh.us					
Clark County PO Box 5000	Vancouver	WA	98666	360-397-2000	397-6099
Web: www.co.clark.wa.us					
Clark County 34 S Main St Rm 103	Winchester	KY	40391	859-745-0200	737-5678
Clarke County 101 N Church Ct Suite B	Berryville	VA	22611	540-955-5100	955-4002
Web: www.co.clarke.va.us					
Clarke County PO Box 548	Grove Hill	AL	36451	251-275-3507	275-8517
Clarke County 100 S Main St Courthouse	Osceola	IA	50213	641-342-6096	342-2463
Web: www.clarkecountyia.org					
Clarke County PO Box 689	Quitman	MS	39355	601-776-2126	776-2756
Clatsop County 820 Exchange St 2nd Fl	Astoria	OR	97103	503-325-8511	325-9307
Web: www.co.clatsop.or.us					
Clay County PO Box 187	Ashland	AL	36251	256-354-7888	354-3208
Clay County 609 E National Ave Rm 213	Brazil	IN	47834	812-448-9024	446-9602
Web: www.claycountyin.org					
Clay County 424 Brown St PO Box 387	Celina	TN	38551	931-243-2161	
Web: www.dalehollowlake.org					

	Phone	Fax
Clay County PO Box 190 ... Clay WV 25043	304-587-4259	587-7329
Clay County 712 5th St ... Clay Center KS 67432 *Web:* www.claycountyks.org	785-632-2552	632-5856
Clay County 111 W Fairfield St PO Box 67 ... Clay Center NE 68933 *Web:* www.claycounty.ne.gov	402-762-3463	762-3506
Clay County 155 Wilson St ... Fort Gaines GA 39851 *Web:* www.claycountyga.org	229-768-3238	768-3672
Clay County 825 N Orange Ave ... Green Cove Springs FL 32043 *Web:* www.claycountygov.com	904-269-6302	
Clay County 261 Courthouse Dr # 1 ... Hayesville NC 28904 *Web:* www.main.nc.us	828-389-8334	389-3329
Clay County PO Box 548 ... Henrietta TX 76365 *Web:* www.co.clay.tx.us	940-538-4631	538-5597
Clay County 1 Courthouse Sq ... Liberty MO 64068 *Web:* www.claycogov.com	816-792-7733	792-7777
Clay County PO Box 160 ... Louisville IL 62858	618-665-3626	665-3607
Clay County 316 Main St Suite 108 ... Manchester KY 40962	606-598-3663	598-4047
Clay County 807 11th St N ... Moorhead MN 56560 *Web:* www.co.clay.mn.us	218-299-5002	299-5195
Clay County PO Box 306 ... Piggott AR 72454	870-598-2813	598-2813
Clay County 215 W 4th St ... Spencer IA 51301 *Web:* www.co.clay.ia.us	712-262-4335	262-6042
Clay County 211 W Main St Suite 200 ... Vermillion SD 57069 *Web:* www.claycountysd.org	605-677-7120	677-7104
Clay County PO Box 815 ... West Point MS 39773 *Web:* www.claycountyms.com	662-494-3124	492-4059
Clayton County 111 High St NE ... Elkader IA 52043 *Web:* www.claytoncountyiowa.net	563-245-2204	245-1175
Clayton County 112 Smith St ... Jonesboro GA 30236 *Web:* www.co.clayton.ga.us	770-477-3211	477-3217
Clear Creek County PO Box 2000 ... Georgetown CO 80444 *Web:* www.co.clear-creek.co.us	303-679-2312	679-2440
Clearfield County 230 E Market St ... Clearfield PA 16830 *Web:* www.clearfieldco.org	814-765-2641	765-2640
Clearwater County 213 Main Ave N ... Bagley MN 56621 **Fax: Acctg ■ Web:* www.co.clearwater.mn.us	218-694-6520	694-6244*
Clearwater County 150 Michigan Ave ... Orofino ID 83544 *Web:* www.clearwatercounty.org	208-476-3615	476-3127
Cleburne County 301 W Main St ... Heber Springs AR 72543	501-362-4620	362-4622
Cleburne County 120 Vickery St Rm 202 ... Heflin AL 36264	256-463-2651	463-2257
Clermont County 101 E Main St Rm 322 ... Batavia OH 45103 *Web:* www.clermontcountyohio.gov	513-732-7300	732-7826
Cleveland County 201 S Jones Ave ... Norman OK 73071 *Web:* www.ccok.us	405-366-0230	366-0234
Cleveland County PO Box 368 ... Rison AR 71665	870-325-6521	325-6144
Cleveland County 311 E Marion St ... Shelby NC 28150 *Web:* www.clevelandcounty.com	704-484-4800	484-4930
Clinch County PO Box 433 ... Homerville GA 31634	912-487-5854	487-3083
Clinton County 810 Franklin St ... Carlyle IL 62231 *Web:* www.clintonco.org	618-594-2464	594-0195
Clinton County 612 N 2nd St ... Clinton IA 52732 *Web:* www.clintoncountyiowa.com	563-243-6210	243-5869
Clinton County 265 Courthouse Sq ... Frankfort IN 46041	765-659-6335	
Clinton County 232 E Main St 3rd Fl ... Lock Haven PA 17745 *Web:* www.clintoncountypa.com	570-893-4000	893-4041
Clinton County PO Box 245 ... Plattsburg MO 64477	816-539-3713	539-3072
Clinton County 137 Margaret St Suite 208 ... Plattsburgh NY 12901 *Web:* www.co.clinton.ny.us	518-565-4600	565-4616
Clinton County 100 E State St # 2600 ... Saint Johns MI 48879 *Web:* www.clinton-county.org	989-224-5140	224-5102
Clinton County 46 S S St ... Wilmington OH 45177 *Web:* www.co.clinton.oh.us	937-382-2103	383-2884
County Courthouse 100 S Cross St ... Albany KY 42602 *Web:* www.clintoncounty.ky.gov	606-387-5234	387-7651
Cloud County 811 Washington St ... Concordia KS 66901 *Web:* www.cloudcountyks.org	785-243-8110	243-8123
Coahoma County PO Box 98 ... Clarksdale MS 38614	662-624-3000	624-3040
Coal County 4 N Main St ... Coalgate OK 74538	580-927-3122	927-4003
Cobb County 100 Cherokee St Suite 300 ... Marietta GA 30090 *Web:* www.cobbcounty.org	770-528-1000	528-2606
Cochise County 1415 W Melody Ln Bldg G ... Bisbee AZ 85603 *Web:* cochise.az.gov	520-432-9200	432-5016
Cochran County County Courthouse Rm 102 ... Morton TX 79346	806-266-5450	266-9027
Cocke County 360 E Main St Rm 146 Courthouse Annex ... Newport TN 37821 *Web:* www.cockecounty.com	423-623-8791	623-8792
Coconino County 219 E Cherry Ave ... Flagstaff AZ 86001 *TF:* 800-559-9289 ■ *Web:* www.coconino.az.gov	928-774-5011	779-6785
Codington County 14 Ist Ave SE ... Watertown SD 57201 *Web:* www.codington.org	605-882-6288	882-5384
Coffee County 101 S Peterson Ave ... Douglas GA 31533 *Web:* www.coffeecountygov.com	912-384-4799	384-0291
Coffee County 2 County Complex ... New Brockton AL 36323 *Web:* www.coffeecounty.us	334-894-5556	
Coffee County 1329 McArthur Dr ... Manchester TN 37355 *Web:* www.coffeecountytn.org	931-723-5106	723-8248
Coffey County 110 S 6th St ... Burlington KS 66839 *Web:* www.coffeycountyks.org	620-364-2191	364-8975
Coke County PO Box 150 ... Robert Lee TX 76945	325-453-2631	453-2650
Colbert County 201 N Main St ... Tuscumbia AL 35674 *Web:* www.colbertcounty.org	256-386-8500	386-8510
Cole County 301 E High St # 100 ... Jefferson City MO 65101 *Web:* www.colecounty.org	573-634-9100	634-8031
Coleman County PO Box 591 ... Coleman TX 76834 *Web:* www.co.coleman.tx.us	325-625-2889	
Coles County 651 Jackson Ave Rm 122 ... Charleston IL 61920 *Web:* www.co.coles.il.us	217-348-0501	348-7337
Colfax County 230 N 3rd St PO Box 159 ... Raton NM 87740	505-445-5551	445-4031
Colfax County 411 E 11th St ... Schuyler NE 68661 *Web:* www.colfaxcounty.ne.gov	402-352-8504	352-8515
Colleton County 31 Klein St ... Walterboro SC 29488 *Web:* www.colletoncounty.org	843-549-1725	549-7215
Collier County 3301 Tamiami Trail E ... Naples FL 34112 *Web:* www.colliergov.net	239-252-8383	252-4010
Collin County 200 S McDonald St Suite 120 ... McKinney TX 75069 *Web:* www.co.collin.tx.us	972-548-4134	547-5731
Collingsworth County County Courthouse 800 W Ave PO Box 10 ... Wellington TX 79095 *Web:* www.co.collingsworth.tx.us.com	806-447-2408	447-2409
Colonial Heights (Independent City) 201 James Ave PO Box 3401 ... Colonial Heights VA 23834 *Web:* www.colonial-heights.com	804-520-9265	520-9207
Colorado County 318 Springs St Suite 103 ... Columbus TX 78934 *Web:* www.co.colorado.tx.us	979-732-2155	732-8852
Colquitt County PO Box 517 ... Moultrie GA 31776	229-890-1805	
Columbia County 35 W Main St ... Bloomsburg PA 17815 *Web:* www.columbiapa.org	570-389-5600	784-0257
Columbia County 341 E Main St ... Dayton WA 99328 *Web:* www.columbiaco.com	509-382-4542	382-2490
Columbia County PO Box 498 ... Evans GA 30809 *Web:* www.columbiacountyga.gov	706-868-3379	868-3348
Columbia County 560 Warren St ... Hudson NY 12534 *Web:* www.govt.co.columbia.ny.us	518-828-3339	
Columbia County 135 NE Hernando Ave # 203 ... Lake City FL 32055 *Web:* www.columbiacountyfla.com	386-755-4100	758-1337
Columbia County 1 Ct Sq Suite 1 ... Magnolia AR 71753	870-235-3774	235-3773
Columbia County PO Box 177 ... Portage WI 53901 *Web:* www.co.columbia.wi.us	608-742-9654	742-9602
Columbia County 230 Strand St ... Saint Helens OR 97051 *Web:* www.co.columbia.or.us	503-397-3796	397-7266
Columbiana County 105 S Market St ... Lisbon OH 44432 *Web:* www.columbianacounty.org	330-424-7777	
Columbus County PO Box 1587 ... Whiteville NC 28472 *Web:* www.columbusco.org	910-641-3000	641-3027
Columbus-Muscogee County PO Box 1340 ... Columbus GA 31902 *Web:* www.columbusga.com	706-653-4013	653-4016
Colusa County 546 Jay St ... Colusa CA 95932 *Web:* www.colusacountyclerk.com	530-458-0500	458-0512
Comal County 199 Main Plaza ... New Braunfels TX 78130 *TF:* 877-724-9475 ■ *Web:* www.co.comal.tx.us	830-221-1100	608-2026
Comanche County 201 S New York PO Box 268 ... Coldwater KS 67029 *Web:* www.comanchecounty.com	620-582-2361	582-2426
Comanche County County Courthouse 101 W Central Ave ... Comanche TX 76442	325-356-2655	356-5764
Comanche County 315 SW 5th St Suite 304 ... Lawton OK 73501 *Web:* www.comanchecounty.us	580-355-5214	
Concho County PO Box 98 ... Paint Rock TX 76866 *Web:* www.co.concho.tx.us	325-732-4322	732-2040
Concordia Parish PO Box 790 ... Vidalia LA 71373	318-336-4204	336-8777
Conecuh County 409 Bellville St ... Evergreen AL 36401	251-578-2066	578-7013
Conejos County PO Box 157 ... Conejos CO 81129	719-376-5565	376-5661
Contra Costa County 651 Pine St 3rd Fl ... Martinez CA 94553 *Web:* www.co.contra-costa.ca.us	925-335-1080	335-1098
Converse County 107 N 5th St Suite 114 ... Douglas WY 82633 *Web:* www.conversecounty.org	307-358-2244	358-5998
Conway County 117 S Moose St ... Morrilton AR 72110	501-354-9621	354-9610
Cook County 118 N Clark St Rm 820 ... Chicago IL 60602 *Web:* www.co.cook.il.us	312-603-4660	603-4479
Cook County 411 W 2nd St ... Grand Marais MN 55604 *Web:* www.co.cook.mn.us	218-387-3000	387-3007
Cooke County 216 W Pecan St ... Gainesville TX 76240 *Web:* www.co.cooke.tx.us	940-668-5420	668-5522
Cooper County 200 Main St ... Boonville MO 65233	660-882-2114	882-5645
Coos County 250 N Baxter St ... Coquille OR 97423 *Web:* www.co.coos.or.us	541-396-3121	396-4861
Coos County 55 School St Suite 301 ... Lancaster NH 03584	603-788-4900	
Coosa County PO Box 10 ... Rockford AL 35136	256-377-2420	377-2524
Copiah County 122 S Lowe St PO Box 507 ... Hazlehurst MS 39083 *Web:* www.copiahcounty.org	601-894-3021	894-4081
Corson County PO Box 175 ... McIntosh SD 57641	605-273-4201	273-4597
Cortland County 46 Greenbush St Suite 101 ... Cortland NY 13045 *Web:* www.cortland-co.org	607-753-5021	753-5378
Coryell County 620 E Main St PO Box 237 ... Gatesville TX 76528 *Web:* www.co.coryell.tx.us	254-865-5911	865-8631
Coshocton County 401 1/2 Main St ... Coshocton OH 43812 *Web:* www.co.coshocton.oh.us	740-622-1753	622-4917
Costilla County 401 S Church Pl ... San Luis CO 81152 *Web:* www.costilla-county.com	719-672-3681	672-4493
Cottle County PO Box 717 ... Paducah TX 79248 *Web:* www.co.cottle.tx.us	806-492-3823	492-2625
Cotton County 301 N Broadway ... Walters OK 73572	580-875-3026	875-3756
Cottonwood County 900 3rd Ave ... Windom MN 56101 *Web:* www.co.cottonwood.mn.us	507-831-1905	831-4553
County of Greene 93 E High St ... Waynesburg PA 15370 *TF:* 888-852-5399 ■ *Web:* www.co.greene.pa.us	724-852-5210	852-5327
Covington (Independent City) 333 W Locust St ... Covington VA 24426 *Web:* www.covington.va.us	540-965-6300	965-6303
Covington County 1 N Ct Sq County Courthouse ... Andalusia AL 36420 *Web:* flagshipgis.com	334-428-2540	428-2575
Covington County PO Box 1679 ... Collins MS 39428	601-765-4242	765-5016
Coweta County 22 E Broad St ... Newnan GA 30263 *Web:* www.coweta.ga.us	770-254-2601	254-2606
Cowley County 311 E 9th Ave ... Winfield KS 67156 *Web:* www.cowleycounty.org	620-221-5400	221-5498
Cowlitz County 312 SW 1st Ave ... Kelso WA 98626 *Web:* www.co.cowlitz.wa.us	360-577-3016	577-2323
Craig County PO Box 308 ... New Castle VA 24127 *Web:* www.craigcountyva.gov	540-864-5010	864-5590
Craig County PO Box 397 ... Vinita OK 74301	918-256-2507	256-3617
Craighead County 511 S Main St # 202 ... Jonesboro AR 72401 *Web:* www.craigheadcounty.org	870-933-4520	933-4514

Name / Address	City	State	ZIP	Phone	Fax
Crane County 201 W 6th St	Crane	TX	79731	432-558-3581	558-1185
Web: www.co.crane.tx.us					
Craven County 406 Craven St	New Bern	NC	28560	252-636-6600	637-0526
Web: www.co.craven.nc.us					
Crawford County 112 E Mansfield St	Bucyrus	OH	44820	419-562-5876	562-3491
Web: www.crawford-co.org					
Crawford County 1202 Broadway Suite 7	Denison	IA	51442	712-263-2648	263-3131
Web: www.crawfordcounty.org					
Crawford County PO Box 375	English	IN	47118	812-338-2565	338-2507
Crawford County 111 E Forest Ave	Girard	KS	66743	620-724-6115	724-6007
Web: www.crawfordcountykansas.org					
Crawford County 200 W Michigan Ave	Grayling	MI	49738	989-344-3206	344-3223
Web: www.crawfordco.org					
Crawford County 1011 Hwy 341 N PO Box 1059	Roberta	GA	31078	478-836-3782	836-5818
Crawford County 903 Diamond Pk	Meadville	PA	16335	814-333-7400	337-0457
Web: www.co.crawford.pa.us					
Crawford County 220 N Beaumont Rd	Prairie du Chien	WI	53821	608-326-0200	326-0213
Web: www.wisconline.com					
Crawford County 100 Douglas St	Robinson	IL	62454	618-546-1212	546-0140
Web: www.crawfordcountycentral.com					
Crawford County 302 Main St PO Box AS	Steelville	MO	65565	573-775-2376	775-3066
Web: crawfordcountymo.net					
Crawford County 300 Main St County Courthouse Rm 7	Van Buren	AR	72956	479-474-1312	471-3236
Creek County 317 E Lee St Rm 100	Sapulpa	OK	74066	918-224-4084	
Web: www.okcountyrecords.com					
Crenshaw County 29 S Glenwood Ave	Luverne	AL	36049	334-335-6568	335-3616
Crisp County 210 S 7th St	Cordele	GA	31015	229-276-2672	276-2675
Web: www.crispcounty.com					
Crittenden County 100 Ct St County Courthouse	Marion	AR	72364	870-739-4434	739-3072
Crittenden County 107 S Main St	Marion	KY	42064	270-965-4200	965-4572
Crockett County 1 S Bellis St Suite 3	Alamo	TN	38001	731-696-5460	696-4101
Crockett County PO Box C	Ozona	TX	76943	325-392-2022	392-3742
Web: www.co.crockett.tx.us					
Crook County 300 NE 3rd St Rm 23	Prineville	OR	97754	541-447-6553	416-2145
Web: www.co.crook.or.us					
Crook County 309 Cleveland St PO Box 37	Sundance	WY	82729	307-283-1323	283-3038
Web: www.crookcounty.wy.gov					
Crosby County 201 W Aspen St Suite 102	Crosbyton	TX	79322	806-675-2334	
Web: www.co.crosby.tx.us					
Cross County 705 E Union St Rm 8	Wynne	AR	72396	870-238-5735	238-5739
Crow Wing County 326 Laurel St	Brainerd	MN	56401	218-824-1067	824-1054
TF: 888-829-6680 ■ *Web:* www.co.crow-wing.mn.us					
Crowley County 631 Main St Suite 102	Ordway	CO	81063	719-267-4643	267-4608
Web: www.crowleycounty.net					
Culberson County PO Box 158	Van Horn	TX	79855	432-283-2058	283-9234
Web: www.co.culberson.tx.us					
Cullman County 500 2nd Ave SW Rm 202	Cullman	AL	35055	256-739-3530	739-3525
Web: www.co.cullman.al.us					
Culpeper County 151 N Main St # 201	Culpeper	VA	22701	540-727-3427	727-3460
Web: www.culpepercounty.gov					
Cumberland County 27 Fayette St	Bridgeton	NJ	08302	856-451-8000	455-1410
Web: www.co.cumberland.nj.us					
Cumberland County 212 N Main St	Burkesville	KY	42717	270-864-3726	864-5884
Cumberland County 1 Courthouse Sq	Carlisle	PA	17013	717-240-6150	240-6448
Web: www.ccpa.net					
Cumberland County 2 N Main St Suite 206	Crossville	TN	38555	931-484-6442	484-6440
Web: www.crossville-chamber.com					
Cumberland County 1 Courthouse Cir PO Box 77	Cumberland	VA	23040	804-492-4280	492-3342
Web: www.cumberlandcounty.virginia.gov					
Cumberland County PO Box 1829	Fayetteville	NC	28302	910-678-7700	678-7717
Web: www.co.cumberland.nc.us					
Cumberland County 142 Federal St Rm 102	Portland	ME	04101	207-871-8380	871-8292
Web: www.cumberlandcounty.org					
Cumberland County 140 Courthouse Sq PO Box 146	Toledo	IL	62468	217-849-2631	849-2968
Cuming County 200 S Lincoln St PO Box 290	West Point	NE	68788	402-372-6002	372-6013
Web: www.co.cuming.ne.us					
Currituck County 153 Courthouse Rd Suite 204 PO Box 39	Currituck	NC	27929	252-232-2075	232-3551
Web: www.co.currituck.nc.us					
Curry County 700 N Main St Suite 7	Clovis	NM	88101	575-763-6016	
Web: www.mylocalgov.com/currycountynm					
Curry County 29821 Ellensburg Ave PO Box 746	Gold Beach	OR	97444	541-247-3296	247-6440
Web: www.co.curry.or.us					
Cusseta-Chattahoochee County PO Box 299	Cusseta	GA	31805	706-989-3602	989-2005
Web: chattahoocheecounty.georgia.gov					
Custer County PO Box 300	Arapaho	OK	73620	580-323-1221	331-1131
Web: custer.okcounties.org					
Custer County 431 S 10th St	Broken Bow	NE	68822	308-872-5701	872-2811
Web: www.co.custer.ne.us					
Custer County 801 E Main Ave	Challis	ID	83226	208-879-2360	879-5246
Web: www.co.custer.id.us					
Custer County 420 Mt Rushmore Rd # 1	Custer	SD	57730	605-673-8100	
Web: www.custercountysd.com					
Custer County 1010 Main St	Miles City	MT	59301	406-874-3343	874-3452
Web: www.co.chouteau.mt.us					
Custer County 205 S 6th St	Westcliffe	CO	81252	719-783-2441	783-2885
Web: www.custercountygov.com					
Cuyahoga County 1219 Ontario St	Cleveland	OH	44113	216-443-7010	443-5091
Web: www.cuyahogacounty.us					
Dade County 300 W Water St	Greenfield	MO	65661	417-637-2724	637-1006
Dade County 75 Case Ave	Trenton	GA	30752	706-657-4778	657-8284
Web: www.dadega.com					
Daggett County 95 N & 100 W PO Box 219	Manila	UT	84046	435-784-3154	784-3335
Web: www.dsdf.org					
Dakota County 1601 Broadway	Dakota City	NE	68731	402-987-2126	494-9228
Web: www.dakotacountyne.org					
Dakota County 1560 Hwy 55	Hastings	MN	55033	651-438-8100	438-4405
Web: www.co.dakota.mn.us					
Dale County 202 Hwy 123 S Suite C	Ozark	AL	36360	334-774-6025	774-1841
Dallam County 414 Denver Ave # 201	Dalhart	TX	79022	806-244-4751	244-3751
Web: www.dallam.org					
Dallas County 801 Ct St	Adel	IA	50003	515-993-5814	993-4752
Web: www.co.dallas.ia.us					
Dallas County 102 S Cedar St	Buffalo	MO	65622	417-345-2632	345-5321
Dallas County 411 Elm St	Dallas	TX	75202	214-653-7361	653-7057
Web: www.dallascounty.org					
Dallas County 206 W 3rd St	Fordyce	AR	71742	870-352-2307	352-7179
Dallas County PO Box 987	Selma	AL	36702	334-874-2560	874-2587
Dane County 210 ML King Jr Blvd Rm 106	Madison	WI	53703	608-266-4121	
Web: www.co.dane.wi.us					
Daniels County 213 Main St Suite 2	Scobey	MT	59263	406-487-5561	487-5583
Danville (Independent City) 401 Patton St	Danville	VA	24544	434-799-5168	799-6502
Web: www.ci.danville.va.us					
Dare County 954 Marshall Collins Dr	Manteo	NC	27954	252-475-5800	473-1817
Web: www.co.dare.nc.us					
Darke County 520 S Broadway St	Greenville	OH	45331	937-547-7370	547-7367
Web: www.co.darke.oh.us					
Darlington County 1 Public Sq # B4	Darlington	SC	29532	843-398-4330	393-6871
Web: www.darcosc.com					
Dauphin County 2 S 2nd St 3rd Fl	Harrisburg	PA	17101	717-780-6636	780-6468
TF: 800-328-0058 ■ *Web:* www.dauphincounty.org					
Davidson County 913 Greensboro St PO Box 1067	Lexington	NC	27293	336-242-2000	248-8440
Web: www.co.davidson.nc.us					
Davidson County 205 Metro Courthouse	Nashville	TN	37201	615-862-6770	862-6774
Web: www.nashville.gov					
Davie County 123 S Main St	Mocksville	NC	27028	336-751-5513	751-7408
Web: www.co.davie.nc.us					
Daviess County 102 N Main St	Gallatin	MO	64640	660-663-2641	663-3376
Daviess County 212 St Ann St # 104	Owensboro	KY	42303	270-685-8434	686-7111
Web: www.daviessky.org					
Daviess County 200 E Walnut St	Washington	IN	47501	812-254-8664	254-8698
Web: www.daviesscounty.org					
Davis County 100 Courthouse Sq	Bloomfield	IA	52537	641-664-2011	664-2041
Web: www.daviscounty.org					
Davis County 28 E State St PO Box 618	Farmington	UT	84025	801-451-3324	451-3421
Web: www.co.davis.ut.us					
Davison County 200 E 4th Ave	Mitchell	SD	57301	605-995-8608	995-8618
Web: www.davisoncounty.org					
Dawes County 451 Main St	Chadron	NE	69337	308-432-0100	432-5179
Web: www.co.dawes.ne.us					
Dawson County 78 Howard Ave E # 100	Dawsonville	GA	30534	706-344-3501	344-3504
Web: www.dawsoncounty.org					
Dawson County 207 W Bell St	Glendive	MT	59330	406-377-3058	377-1717
Web: www.dawsoncountymontana.org					
Dawson County PO Box 1268	Lamesa	TX	79331	806-872-3778	872-2473
Web: www.co.dawson.tx.us					
Dawson County PO Box 370	Lexington	NE	68850	308-324-2127	324-6106
Web: www.dawsoncountyne.net					
Day County 711 W 1st St	Webster	SD	57274	605-345-3771	345-3818
De Baca County 548 E Ave C	Fort Sumner	NM	88119	505-355-2601	355-2441
Deaf Smith County 235 E 3rd St Rm 203	Hereford	TX	79045	806-363-7077	363-7023
Dearborn County 215 W High St	Lawrenceburg	IN	47025	812-537-8877	532-2021
Web: www.dearborncounty.org					
Decatur County PO Box 726	Bainbridge	GA	39818	229-248-3030	246-2062
Decatur County 22 W Main St	Decaturville	TN	38329	731-852-2131	852-2130
Web: www.decaturcountytn.org					
Decatur County 150 Courthouse Sq Suite 244	Greensburg	IN	47240	812-663-8223	662-6627
Web: www.decaturcounty.in.gov					
Decatur County 207 N Main St	Leon	IA	50144	641-446-4382	446-7159
Decatur County PO Box 28	Oberlin	KS	67749	785-475-8102	475-8130
Web: www.oberlinkansas.org					
Defiance County 500 Ct St Suite A	Defiance	OH	43512	419-782-4761	782-8449
Web: www.defiance-county.com					
DeKalb County PO Box 248	Maysville	MO	64469	816-449-5402	449-2440
DeKalb County 556 N McDonough St Administrative Tower Rm G10	Decatur	GA	30030	404-371-2000	371-2002
Web: www.co.dekalb.ga.us					
DeKalb County 111 Grand Ave SW Suite 200	Fort Payne	AL	35967	256-845-8500	845-8502
Web: www.dekalbcountyal.us					
DeKalb County 1 Public Sq Rm 205	Smithville	TN	37166	615-597-5177	597-1404
Web: www.smithvilletn.com					
DeKalb County 110 E Sycamore St	Sycamore	IL	60178	815-895-7149	895-7148
Web: www.dekalbcounty.org					
Del Norte County 981 H St Suite 200	Crescent City	CA	95531	707-464-7204	464-1165
Web: www.co.del-norte.ca.us					
Delaware County 101 N Sandusky St	Delaware	OH	43015	740-833-2100	833-2099
Web: www.co.delaware.oh.us					
Delaware County PO Box 426	Delhi	NY	13753	607-746-2123	746-6924
Web: www.co.delaware.ny.us					
Delaware County PO Box 309	Jay	OK	74346	918-253-4520	253-8352
Web: www.delawareclerk.org					
Delaware County 301 E Main St	Manchester	IA	52057	563-927-4942	927-3074
Web: www.delawarecountyia.com					
Delaware County 201 W Front St Government Ctr Bldg	Media	PA	19063	610-891-4000	891-0647
Web: www.co.delaware.pa.us					
Delaware County 100 W Main St	Muncie	IN	47305	765-747-7730	747-7899
Web: www.co.delaware.in.us					
Delta County 90 Texas Hwy 24 S	Cooper	TX	75432	903-395-4118	395-4455
Delta County 501 Palmer St Suite 211	Delta	CO	81416	970-874-2150	874-2161
Web: www.deltacounty.com					
Delta County 310 Ludington St	Escanaba	MI	49829	906-789-5105	789-5196
Web: www.deltami.org					
Denali Borough PO Box 480	Healy	AK	99743	907-683-1330	683-1340
Web: www.denaliborough.govoffice.com					
Dent County 400 N Main St	Salem	MO	65560	573-729-4144	729-6106
Web: www.salemmissouri.com/government.html					
Denton County 1450 E McKinney	Denton	TX	76209	940-349-2012	349-2019
Web: www.co.denton.tx.us					

Entry	City	State	Zip	Phone	Fax
Denver City & County 201 W Colfax Ave 1st Fl	Denver	CO	80202	720-865-8400	
Web: www.denvergov.org					
Des Moines County PO Box 158	Burlington	IA	52601	319-753-8272	753-8253
Web: www.co.des-moines.ia.us					
Deschutes County 1300 NW Wall St Suite 200	Bend	OR	97701	541-388-6570	385-3202
Web: www.co.deschutes.or.us					
Desha County PO Box 188	Arkansas City	AR	71630	870-877-2426	877-2531
DeSoto County 201 E Oak St	Arcadia	FL	34266	863-993-4800	993-4809
Web: www.co.desoto.fl.us					
DeSoto County 365 Losher St	Hernando	MS	38632	662-429-1460	429-4116
Web: www.desotoms.com					
DeSoto Parish PO Box 1206	Mansfield	LA	71052	318-872-3110	872-4202
Deuel County 718 3rd St	Chappell	NE	69129	308-874-3308	874-3472
Web: www.co.deuel.ne.us					
Deuel County 408 4th St W	Clear Lake	SD	57226	605-874-2120	874-2916
Web: www.deuelcountysd.com					
Dewey County Broadway & Ruble PO Box 368	Taloga	OK	73667	580-328-5521	
Dewey County PO Box 277	Timber Lake	SD	57656	605-865-3672	865-3691
DeWitt County 201 W Washington St PO Box 439	Clinton	IL	61727	217-935-2119	935-4596
Web: www.dewittcountyill.com					
DeWitt County 307 N Gonzales St	Cuero	TX	77954	361-275-3724	275-8994
Web: www.co.dewitt.tx.us					
Dickens County PO Box 120	Dickens	TX	79229	806-623-5531	623-5319
Dickenson County 293 Main St	Clintwood	VA	24228	276-926-1616	926-6465
Web: www.dickensonctyva.com					
Dickey County PO Box 215	Ellendale	ND	58436	701-349-3249	349-4639
Dickinson County PO Box 248	Abilene	KS	67410	785-263-3774	263-2045
Web: www.dkcoks.com					
Dickinson County 705 S Stephenson Ave	Iron Mountain	MI	49801	906-774-0988	774-4660
Web: www.dickinsoncountymi.org					
Dickinson County 1802 Hill Ave	Spirit Lake	IA	51360	712-336-3356	336-2677
Web: www.co.dickinson.ia.us					
Dickson County PO Box 267	Charlotte	TN	37036	615-789-7003	789-6075
Web: www.dicksoncounty.net					
Dillon County 109 S 3rd Ave	Dillon	SC	29536	843-774-1400	774-1443
Web: www.dilloncounty.org					
Dimmit County 103 N 5th St	Carrizo Springs	TX	78834	830-876-2323	876-5036
Web: www.dimmitcountytx.com					
Dinwiddie County 14016 Boydton Plank Rd	Dinwiddie	VA	23841	804-469-4500	469-4503
Web: www.dinwiddieva.us					
Divide County PO Box 68	Crosby	ND	58730	701-965-6831	965-6943
Dixie County 214 NE 351 Hwy # M	Cross City	FL	32628	352-498-1200	498-1201
Web: www.dixiecounty.org					
Dixon County 302 W 3rd St	Ponca	NE	68770	402-755-2881	755-2632
Web: www.co.dixon.ne.us					
Doddridge County 118 E Ct St Rm 102	West Union	WV	26456	304-873-2631	873-1840
Dodge County 5016 Courthouse Cir Suite 102	Eastman	GA	31023	478-374-4361	374-8121
Dodge County 435 N Pk Ave Rm 102	Fremont	NE	68025	402-727-2767	727-2764
Web: www.dodgecounty.ne.gov					
Dodge County 127 E Oak St	Juneau	WI	53039	920-386-3602	386-3928
Web: www.co.dodge.wi.us					
Dodge County 22 6th St E	Mantorville	MN	55955	507-635-6239	635-6265
Web: www.co.dodge.mn.us					
Dolores County 409 N Main St	Dove Creek	CO	81324	970-677-2383	677-2815
Web: www.dolorescounty.org					
Dona Ana County 845 N Motel Blvd	Las Cruces	NM	88007	575-647-7200	647-7302
Web: www.co.dona-ana.nm.us					
Doniphan County PO Box 278	Troy	KS	66087	785-985-3513	985-3723
Web: www.dpcountyks.com					
Donley County 300 S Sully St	Clarendon	TX	79226	806-874-3436	874-3351
Web: www.donleytx.com					
Dooly County 117 S 3rd St	Vienna	GA	31092	229-268-4228	268-4230
Web: www.doolychamber.com					
Door County 421 Nebraska St	Sturgeon Bay	WI	54235	920-746-2200	746-2330
Web: www.co.door.wi.gov					
Dorchester County 501 Ct Ln	Cambridge	MD	21613	410-228-1700	228-9641
Web: www.commissioners.net					
Dorchester County 101 Ridge St	Saint George	SC	29477	843-563-0121	563-0178
Web: www.dorchestercounty.net					
Dougherty County 222 Pine Ave	Albany	GA	31701	229-431-2121	438-3967
Web: www.dougherty.ga.us					
Douglas County 305 8th Ave W	Alexandria	MN	56308	320-762-3877	762-2389
Web: www.co.douglas.mn.us					
Douglas County 706 Braddock St	Armour	SD	57313	605-724-2585	724-2508
Douglas County 283 SE 2nd Ave	Ava	MO	65608	417-683-4714	683-1017
Douglas County 100 3rd St	Castle Rock	CO	80104	303-660-7401	688-1293
Web: www.douglas.co.us					
Douglas County 8700 Hospital Dr	Douglasville	GA	30134	770-949-2000	
Web: www.celebratedouglascounty.com					
Douglas County					
1100 Massachusetts St 1st level	Lawrence	KS	66044	785-832-5167	
Web: www.douglas-county.com					
Douglas County PO Box 218	Minden	NV	89423	775-782-9020	782-9016
Web: cltr.co.douglas.nv.us					
Douglas County 1819 Farnam St	Omaha	NE	68183	402-444-6762	444-6456
Web: www.douglascounty-ne.gov					
Douglas County 1036 SE Douglas St	Roseburg	OR	97470	541-440-4323	440-4408
Web: www.co.douglas.or.us					
Douglas County 1313 Belknap St	Superior	WI	54880	715-395-1341	395-1421
Web: www.douglascountywi.org					
Douglas County 401 S Ctr St PO Box 467	Tuscola	IL	61953	217-253-2411	253-2233
Web: www.clerk&recorder@netcare-il.com					
Douglas County 213 Rainer St	Waterville	WA	98858	509-745-8537	745-9045
Web: www.douglascountywa.net					
Drew County 210 S Main St	Monticello	AR	71655	870-460-6250	460-6255
Dubois County 1 Courthouse Sq	Jasper	IN	47546	812-481-7035	481-7044
Web: www.duboiscounty.org					
Dubuque County 720 Central Ave	Dubuque	IA	52001	563-589-4418	
Web: www.dubuquecounty.org					
Duchesne County 734 N Ctr St	Duchesne	UT	84021	435-738-1101	738-5522
Web: www.duchesnegov.net					
Dukes County PO Box 190	Edgartown	MA	02539	508-696-3840	696-3841
Web: www.dukescounty.org					
Dundy County PO Box 506	Benkelman	NE	69021	308-423-2058	
Web: www.co.dundy.ne.us					
Dunklin County Courthouse Sq PO Box 188	Kennett	MO	63857	573-888-1374	888-2832
Dunn County PO Box 105	Manning	ND	58642	701-573-4448	573-4323
Dunn County 800 Wilson Ave	Menomonie	WI	54751	715-232-1677	232-2534
Web: dunncountywi.govoffice2.com					
DuPage County 421 N County Farm Rd	Wheaton	IL	60187	630-407-5500	407-5501
Web: www.dupageco.org					
Duplin County 112 Duplin St # 101	Kenansville	NC	28349	910-296-1686	296-2310
Web: www.duplincounty.org					
Durham County 200 E Main St	Durham	NC	27701	919-560-0000	560-0020
Web: www.co.durham.nc.us					
Dutchess County 22 Market St	Poughkeepsie	NY	12601	845-486-2120	
Web: www.co.dutchess.ny.us					
Duval County 117 W Duval St	Jacksonville	FL	32202	904-630-1178	630-2906
Web: www.coj.net					
Duval County PO Box 248	San Diego	TX	78384	361-279-6274	
Dyer County 115 Market St PO Box 1360	Dyersburg	TN	38025	731-286-7814	288-7719
Eagle County PO Box 850	Eagle	CO	81631	970-328-8612	328-8716
Web: www.eaglecounty.us					
Early County PO Box 849	Blakely	GA	39823	229-723-3033	723-4411
Web: gsccca.org					
East Baton Rouge Parish 1755 Florida St	Baton Rouge	LA	70802	225-389-3129	389-3118
Web: www.brgov.com					
East Carroll Parish 400 1st St	Lake Providence	LA	71254	318-559-2399	559-0037
Web: www.eastcarroll.net					
East Feliciana Parish 12305 St Helena St	Clinton	LA	70722	225-683-5145	683-3556
Web: www.felicianatourism.org					
Eastland County 100 W Main PO Box 110	Eastland	TX	76448	254-629-1583	629-8125
Web: www.eastlandcountytexas.com					
Eaton County 1045 Independence Blvd	Charlotte	MI	48813	517-543-7500	541-0666
Web: www.co.eaton.mi.us					
Eau Claire County 721 Oxford Ave	Eau Claire	WI	54703	715-839-4801	839-4854
Echols County 110 General Beloach St	Statenville	GA	31648	229-559-6538	559-6158
Web: www.echolscountygeorgia.com					
Ector County 300 N Grant Ave Rm 111	Odessa	TX	79761	432-498-4130	498-4177
Web: www.co.ector.tx.us					
Eddy County 101 W Greene St Suite 110	Carlsbad	NM	88220	505-887-9511	234-1835*
**Fax Area Code:* 575 ■ *Web:* www.co.eddy.nm.us					
Eddy County 524 Central Ave	New Rockford	ND	58356	701-947-2434	947-2067
Edgar County 115 W Ct St Rm J County Courthouse	Paris	IL	61944	217-466-7433	466-7430
Web: www.edgarcounty-il.gov					
Edgecombe County 201 St Andrew St PO Box 10	Tarboro	NC	27886	252-641-7833	641-0456
Web: www.edgecombecountync.gov					
Edgefield County					
129 Courthouse Sq Suite 205	Edgefield	SC	29824	803-637-4080	637-4007
Web: www.edgefieldcounty.sc.gov					
Edmonson County PO Box 830	Brownsville	KY	42210	270-597-2624	597-9714
Web: edmonsoncountyclerk.com					
Edmunds County PO Box 384	Ipswich	SD	57451	605-426-6671	426-6323
Edwards County 50 E Main St	Albion	IL	62806	618-445-2115	445-4941
Edwards County 108 E 6th St PO Box 161	Kinsley	KS	67547	620-659-2711	659-3304
Web: www.edwardscounty.org					
Edwards County PO Box 184	Rocksprings	TX	78880	830-683-2235	683-5376
Effingham County 101 N 4th St PO Box 628	Effingham	IL	62401	217-342-6535	342-3577
Web: www.co.effingham.il.us					
Effingham County 601 N Laurel St	Springfield	GA	31329	912-754-2153	754-4157
Web: www.effinghamcounty.org					
El Dorado County 360 Fair Ln Bldg B	Placerville	CA	95667	530-621-5490	621-2147
Web: www.co.el-dorado.ca.us					
El Paso County 200 S Cascade Ave	Colorado Springs	CO	80903	719-520-6200	520-6212
Web: www.elpasoco.com					
El Paso County 500 E San Antonio Ave	El Paso	TX	79901	915-546-2000	546-2012
Web: www.co.el-paso.tx.us					
Elbert County 12 S Oliver St	Elberton	GA	30635	706-283-2005	213-7286
Web: www.elbertga.com					
Elbert County 215 Comanche St PO Box 7	Kiowa	CO	80117	303-621-2341	621-2343
Web: www.elbertcounty-co.gov					
Elk County 127 N Pine	Howard	KS	67349	620-374-2490	374-2771
Web: www.elk.kansasgov.com					
Elk County 250 Main St	Ridgway	PA	15853	814-776-1161	776-5379
Web: www.co.elk.pa.us					
Elkhart County 117 N 2nd St	Goshen	IN	46526	574-535-6743	
Web: www.elkhartcountygov.org					
Elko County 569 Ct St	Elko	NV	89801	775-738-5398	753-8535
Web: www.elkocountynv.net					
Elliott County PO Box 788	Sandy Hook	KY	41171	606-738-5238	738-6962
Ellis County PO Box 197	Arnett	OK	73832	580-885-7301	885-7258
Ellis County 1204 Fort St	Hays	KS	67601	785-628-9410	628-9413
Web: www.ellisco.org					
Ellis County 1201 N Hwy 77 Suite B	Waxahachie	TX	75165	972-825-5071	923-5010
Web: www.co.ellis.tx.us					
Ellsworth County 210 N Kansas St	Ellsworth	KS	67439	785-472-4161	472-3818
Web: www.ellsworthcounty.org					
Elmore County 150 S 4th E St Suite 5	Mountain Home	ID	83647	208-587-2129	587-2134
Web: www.elmorecounty.org					
Elmore County PO Box 310	Wetumpka	AL	36092	334-567-1124	567-5957
Web: www.elmoreco.org					
Emanuel County 101 N Main St	Swainsboro	GA	30401	478-237-3881	237-2593
Emery County 75 E Main PO Box 907	Castle Dale	UT	84513	435-381-5106	381-5183
Web: www.emerycounty.com					
Emmet County 609 1st Ave N	Estherville	IA	51334	712-362-4261	362-7454
Web: www.emmetcountyia.com					
Emmet County 200 Division St	Petoskey	MI	49770	231-348-1744	348-0602
Web: www.co.emmet.mi.us					
Emmons County PO Box 129	Linton	ND	58552	701-254-4807	254-4012
Emporia (Independent City) 201 S Main St	Emporia	VA	23847	434-634-3332	634-0003
Web: www.ci.emporia.va.us					
Erath County 112 W College St	Stephenville	TX	76401	254-965-1482	965-5732
Web: www.co.erath.tx.us					
Erie County 92 Franklin St	Buffalo	NY	14202	716-858-8785	858-6550
Web: www.erie.gov					

				Phone	Fax
Erie County 140 W 6th St Rm 116	Erie	PA	16501	814-451-6303	451-6350
Web: www.eriecountygov.org					
Erie County 323 Columbus Ave	Sandusky	OH	44870	419-627-7705	624-6873
Web: www.erie-county-ohio.net					
Escambia County 314 Belleville Ave	Brewton	AL	36426	251-867-0305	867-0365
Web: www.co.escambia.al.us					
Escambia County PO Box 1591	Pensacola	FL	32591	850-595-4900	595-4908
Web: www.co.escambia.fl.us					
Esmeralda County PO Box 547	Goldfield	NV	89013	775-485-6367	485-6376
Web: www.governet.net					
Essex County 7559 Court St PO Box 247	Elizabethtown	NY	12932	518-873-3600	873-3548
Web: www.co.essex.ny.us					
Essex County PO Box 75	Guildhall	VT	05905	802-676-3910	676-3463
Essex County 465 Dr Martin Luther King Jr Blvd Rm 558	Newark	NJ	07102	973-621-4921	621-5695
Web: www.essex-countynj.org					
Essex County 36 Federal St County Administration Bldg 1st Fl	Salem	MA	01970	978-741-0200	
Essex County 305 Prince St	Tappahannock	VA	22560	804-443-3541	445-1216
Web: www.essex-virginia.org					
Estill County PO Box 59	Irvine	KY	40336	606-723-5156	723-5108
Web: www.estill.net					
Etowah County 800 Forrest Ave	Gadsden	AL	35901	256-549-5300	549-5400
Web: www.etowahcounty.org					
Eureka County 10 S Main St	Eureka	NV	89316	775-237-5262	237-6015
Web: www.co.eureka.nv.us					
Evangeline Parish 200 Court St PO Drawer 347	Ville Platte	LA	70586	337-363-5671	363-5780
Web: www.laclerksofcourt.org					
Evans County 3 Freeman St	Claxton	GA	30417	912-739-1141	739-0111
Web: www.claxtonevanschamber.com					
Fairbanks North Star Borough 809 Pioneer Rd	Fairbanks	AK	99701	907-459-1000	459-1224
Web: www.co.fairbanks.ak.us					
Fairfax (Independent City) 10455 Armstrong St	Fairfax	VA	22030	703-385-7936	385-7811
Web: www.co.fairfax.va.us					
Fairfax County 12000 Government Ctr Pkwy	Fairfax	VA	22035	703-324-2531	324-3956
Web: www.co.fairfax.va.us					
Fairfield County 210 E Main St	Lancaster	OH	43130	740-687-7090	687-6048
Web: www.co.fairfield.oh.us					
Fairfield County 101 S Congress St PO Box 299	Winnsboro	SC	29180	803-712-6526	712-1506
Web: www.fairfieldsc.com					
Fairfield County 1061 Main St	Bridgeport	CT	06604	203-579-6527	382-8406
Fall River County 906 N River St	Hot Springs	SD	57747	605-745-5131	745-6835
Web: www.sdjudicial.com					
Fallon County 10 W Fallon St	Baker	MT	59313	406-778-7114	778-2815
Web: www.falloncounty.net					
Falls Church (Independent City) 300 Pk Ave	Falls Church	VA	22046	703-248-5001	248-5146
Web: www.ci.falls-church.va.us					
Falls County PO Box 458	Marlin	TX	76661	254-883-1408	883-1406
Fannin County 400 W Main St Suite 100	Blue Ridge	GA	30513	706-632-2203	632-2507
Web: www.fannincountyga.org					
Fannin County 101 Sam Rayburn Dr County Courthouse Suite 102	Bonham	TX	75418	903-583-7486	640-4241
Web: www.co.fannin.tx.us					
Faribault County 415 N Main St	Blue Earth	MN	56013	507-526-6277	526-3054
Web: www.co.faribault.mn.us					
Faulk County PO Box 309	Faulkton	SD	57438	605-598-6224	598-6680
Faulkner County 801 Locust St	Conway	AR	72034	501-450-4909	450-4938
Web: www.faulknercounty.org					
Fauquier County 10 Hotel St Suite 204	Warrenton	VA	20186	540-422-8001	422-8022
Web: www.fauquiercounty.gov					
Fayette County 401 N Central Ave # 6	Connersville	IN	47331	765-825-1813	827-4902
Web: www.co.fayette.in.us					
Fayette County 103 1st Ave NW Courthouse Annex Suite 2	Fayette	AL	35555	205-932-4510	932-2902
Fayette County 140 Stonewall Ave W	Fayetteville	GA	30214	770-460-5730	460-9412
Web: www.fayettecountyga.gov					
Fayette County 100 Ct St	Fayetteville	WV	25840	304-574-4348	574-4314
Web: www.fayettecounty.com					
Fayette County 246 W Colorado St	La Grange	TX	78945	979-968-3251	968-8531
Web: www.co.fayette.tx.us					
Fayette County 1 Ct Sq # 101	Somerville	TN	38068	901-465-5213	465-5293
Web: www.fayettecountychamber.com					
Fayette County 61 E Main St	Uniontown	PA	15401	724-430-1201	430-1265
Web: www.fayettepa.org					
Fayette County 221 S 7th St # 106	Vandalia	IL	62471	618-283-5000	283-5004
Fayette County 133 S Main St Suite 401	Washington Court House	OH	43160	740-335-0720	333-3530
Web: www.fayette-co-oh.com					
Fayette County 114 N Vine St	West Union	IA	52175	563-422-5694	422-3137
Fentress County 101 S Main St	Jamestown	TN	38556	931-879-8014	879-8438
Web: www.jamestowntn.org					
Fergus County 712 W Main St	Lewistown	MT	59457	406-535-5026	535-6076
Web: www.co.fergus.mt.us					
Ferry County 290 E Tessie Ave	Republic	WA	99166	509-775-5229	775-5230
Web: www.ferry-county.com					
Fillmore County 900 G St	Geneva	NE	68361	402-759-4931	759-4307
Web: www.fillmorecounty.org					
Fillmore County 101 Fillmore St	Preston	MN	55965	507-765-3356	765-4571
Web: www.co.fillmore.mn.us					
Finney County 311 N 9th St PO Box M	Garden City	KS	67846	620-272-3542	272-3599
Web: www.finneycounty.org					
Fisher County PO Box 368	Roby	TX	79543	325-776-2401	776-3274
Web: www.co.fisher.tx.us					
Flagler County 1769 E Moody Blvd Bldg 2	Bunnell	FL	32110	386-313-4000	
Web: www.flaglercounty.org					
Flathead County 800 S Main St	Kalispell	MT	59901	406-758-5503	758-5861
Web: www.co.flathead.mt.us					
Fleming County 201 Ct Sq	Flemingsburg	KY	41041	606-845-7571	845-1312
Web: www.flemingcountyky.org					
Florence County 180 N Irby	Florence	SC	29501	843-665-3031	665-3097
Web: www.florenceco.org					
Florence County 501 Lake Ave	Florence	WI	54121	715-528-3201	528-4762
Web: www.florencewisconsin.com					
Floyd County 101 S Main St	Charles City	IA	50616	641-228-7777	228-7772
Web: www.floydcoia.org					
Floyd County 120 W Oxford St	Floyd	VA	24091	540-745-9300	745-9305
Web: www.fin.org					
Floyd County 100 Main St Courthouse Rm 101	Floydada	TX	79235	806-983-4900	983-4909
Floyd County PO Box 1056	New Albany	IN	47151	812-948-5415	948-4711
Web: www.warrickcounty.gov					
Floyd County 149 S Central Ave # 1	Prestonsburg	KY	41653	606-886-3816	886-8089
Web: www.floydcountykentucky.com					
Floyd County 12 E 4th Ave Suite 209	Rome	GA	30162	706-291-5110	291-5248
Web: www.floydcountyga.org					
Fluvanna County 132 Main St	Palmyra	VA	22963	434-591-1910	591-1911
Web: www.co.fluvanna.va.us					
Foard County PO Box 539	Crowell	TX	79227	940-684-1365	684-1918
Fond du Lac County PO Box 1557	Fond du Lac	WI	54936	920-929-3000	929-3293
Web: www.fdlco.wi.gov					
Ford County 100 Gunsmoke St 4th fl	Dodge City	KS	67801	620-227-4500	227-4699
Web: www.fordcounty.net					
Ford County 200 W State St Rm 101	Paxton	IL	60957	217-379-2721	379-3258
Web: www.fordiroq.prairienet.org					
Forest County 200 E Madison St	Crandon	WI	54520	715-478-2422	478-5175
Web: www.forestcountywi.com					
Forest County 526 Elm St Suite 3	Tionesta	PA	16353	814-755-3537	755-8837
Web: www.co.forest.pa.us					
Forrest County 700 N Main St	Hattiesburg	MS	39401	601-582-3213	545-6065
Web: www.co.forrest.ms.us					
Forsyth County 100 Courthouse Sq Suite 010	Cumming	GA	30040	770-781-2120	886-2858
Web: www.co.forsyth.ga.us					
Forsyth County 200 N Main St	Winston-Salem	NC	27101	336-761-2250	761-2018
Web: www.co.forsyth.nc.us					
Fort Bend County 301 Jackson St Suite 101	Richmond	TX	77469	281-342-3411	341-8669
Web: www.co.fort-bend.tx.us					
Foster County PO Box 257	Carrington	ND	58421	701-652-1001	652-2173
Web: www.fostercounty.com					
Fountain County PO Box 183	Covington	IN	47932	765-793-2192	793-5002
Web: www.co.fountain.in.us					
Franklin (Independent City) 120 Pretlow St	Franklin	VA	23851	757-562-8559	562-8561
Franklin County 33 Market St Suite 203	Apalachicola	FL	32320	850-653-8861	653-2261
Web: www.franklincountyflorida.com					
Franklin County PO Box 607	Benton	IL	62812	618-438-3221	435-3405
Franklin County 459 Main St	Brookville	IN	47012	765-647-5111	647-3224
Franklin County 9592 Lavonia Rd	Carnesville	GA	30521	706-384-2514	
Web: www.franklin-county.com					
Franklin County 14 N Main St	Chambersburg	PA	17201	717-261-3810	267-3438
Web: www.co.franklin.pa.us					
Franklin County 369 S High St 3rd Fl	Columbus	OH	43215	614-462-3650	462-4325
Web: www.co.franklin.oh.us					
Franklin County 140 Main St	Farmington	ME	04938	207-778-6614	778-5899
Web: www.franklincountymaine.com					
Franklin County 315 W Main St	Frankfort	KY	40602	502-875-8702	875-8718
Franklin County 405 15th Ave	Franklin	NE	68939	308-425-6202	425-6093
Franklin County 425 Main St Suite 20 PO Box 1573	Greenfield	MA	01302	413-774-3167	
Web: www.frcog.org					
Franklin County 12 1st Ave NW PO Box 28	Hampton	IA	50441	641-456-5626	456-5628
Franklin County 113 Market St	Louisburg	NC	27549	919-496-5994	496-2683
Web: www.co.franklin.nc.us					
Franklin County 355 W Main St PO Box 70	Malone	NY	12953	518-481-1681	483-9143
Web: www.adirondacklakes.org					
Franklin County PO Box 297	Meadville	MS	39653	601-384-2330	384-5864
Web: www.franklincountyms.com					
Franklin County PO Box 68	Mount Vernon	TX	75457	903-537-4252	
Web: www.co.franklin.tx.us					
Franklin County 315 S Main St	Ottawa	KS	66067	785-229-3410	229-3419
Web: www.co.franklin.ks.us					
Franklin County 211 W Commercial St	Ozark	AR	72949	479-667-3607	667-4247
Franklin County 1016 N 4th Ave	Pasco	WA	99301	509-545-3535	545-3573
Web: www.co.franklin.wa.us					
Franklin County 39 W Oneida St	Preston	ID	83263	208-852-1090	852-1094
Franklin County 1255 Franklin St	Rocky Mount	VA	24151	540-483-3030	483-3035
Web: www.franklincountyva.org					
Franklin County 405 N Jackson Ave	Russellville	AL	35653	256-332-8851	332-8855
Web: www.franklincountychamber.org					
Franklin County PO Box 808	Saint Albans	VT	05478	802-524-3863	524-7996
Franklin County 300 E Main St Rm 201	Union	MO	63084	636-583-6355	583-7320
Web: www.franklinmo.org					
Franklin County 1 S Jefferson St	Winchester	TN	37398	931-967-2905	962-1473
Web: www.franklincotn.us					
Franklin Parish 6550 Main St	Winnsboro	LA	71295	318-435-5133	435-5134
Frederick County 107 N Kent St	Winchester	VA	22601	540-665-5600	667-0370
Web: www.co.frederick.va.us					
Fredericksburg (Independent City) 715 Princess Ann St	Fredericksburg	VA	22401	540-372-1010	372-1201
Web: www.fredericksburgchamber.org					
Freeborn County 411 S Broadway	Albert Lea	MN	56007	507-377-5116	377-5109
Web: www.co.freeborn.mn.us					
Freestone County PO Box 1010	Fairfield	TX	75840	903-389-2635	389-6533
Fremont County 136 Justice Ctr Rd Rm 103	Canon City	CO	81212	719-269-0100	269-0134
Web: www.fremontco.com					
Fremont County 450 N 2nd St Rm 220	Lander	WY	82520	307-332-2405	332-1132
Web: www.fremontcounty.org					
Fremont County 151 W 1st N St	Saint Anthony	ID	83445	208-624-7332	624-7335
Web: www.co.fremont.id.us					

	City	State	ZIP	Phone	Fax
Fremont County PO Box 549	Sidney	IA	51652	712-374-2232	374-3330
Web: www.co.fremont.ia.us					
Fresno County 1100 Van Ness Ave	Fresno	CA	93721	559-488-1710	488-1830
Web: www.co.fresno.ca.us					
Frio County 500 E San Antonio St Rm 6	Pearsall	TX	78061	830-334-2214	334-0021
Web: www.co.frio.tx.us					
Frontier County PO Box 40	Stockville	NE	69042	308-367-8641	367-8730
Web: www.co.frontier.ne.us					
Fulton County 141 Pryor St SW Suite 10061	Atlanta	GA	30303	404-730-8320	893-6511
Web: www.co.fulton.ga.us					
Fulton County PO Box 126	Hickman	KY	42050	270-236-2727	236-2522
Fulton County 2 N Main St	Gloversville	NY	12095	518-725-0641	725-0643
Web: www.fultoncountyny.org					
Fulton County 100 N Main St	Lewistown	IL	61542	309-547-3041	547-3326
Web: www.outfitters.com					
Fulton County 116 W Market St Suite 203	McConnellsburg	PA	17233	717-485-3691	485-9411
Web: www.fulton.sapdc.org					
Fulton County 815 Main St	Rochester	IN	46975	574-223-4824	223-8304
Web: www.co.fulton.in.us					
Fulton County PO Box 219	Salem	AR	72576	870-895-3310	895-3383
Fulton County 152 S Fulton St Suite 270	Wauseon	OH	43567	419-337-9255	337-9285
Web: www.fultoncountyoh.com					
Furnas County PO Box 387	Beaver City	NE	68926	308-268-4145	268-3205
Gadsden County 10 E Jefferson St	Quincy	FL	32351	850-875-8601	875-8612
Web: www.gadsdengov.net					
Gage County 612 Grant St # 3	Beatrice	NE	68310	402-223-1300	223-1371
Web: www.co.gage.ne.us					
Gaines County 101 S Main St Rm 107	Seminole	TX	79360	432-758-4003	758-1442
Web: www.gainescountyonline.us					
Galax (Independent City) 111 E Grayson St	Galax	VA	24333	276-236-5773	236-2889
Web: www.ingalax.net					
Gallatin County 311 W Main St Rm 203	Bozeman	MT	59715	406-582-3050	582-3068
Web: www.co.gallatin.mt.us					
Gallatin County PO Box 550	Shawneetown	IL	62984	618-269-3025	269-3343
Gallatin County 102 W High St	Warsaw	KY	41095	859-567-5411	567-5444
Web: www.gallatincountyky.com					
Gallia County 18 Locust St	Gallipolis	OH	45631	740-446-4374	446-4804
Web: www.galliacounty.org					
Galveston County 600 59th St 2nd Fl Suite 2001 PO Box 17253	Galveston	TX	77550	409-766-2200	770-5133
Web: www.co.galveston.tx.us					
Garden County 611 Main St	Oshkosh	NE	69154	308-772-3924	772-0124
Web: www.co.garden.ne.us					
Garfield County 250 S 8th PO Box 218	Burwell	NE	68823	308-346-4161	
Web: www.garfieldcounty.ne.gov					
Garfield County 114 W Broadway	Enid	OK	73701	580-237-0225	249-5951
Garfield County 109 8th St Suite 200	Glenwood Springs	CO	81601	970-945-2377	947-1078
Web: www.garfield-county.com					
Garfield County 352 Leavitt St	Jordan	MT	59337	406-557-6254	557-2567
Web: www.garfieldcounty.com					
Garfield County 55 S Main St	Panguitch	UT	84759	435-676-1100	676-8239
TF: 800-636-8826					
Garfield County 789 Main St PO Box 915	Pomeroy	WA	99347	509-843-3731	843-1224
Web: www.co.garfield.wa.us					
Garland County 501 Ouachita Ave	Hot Springs	AR	71901	501-622-3610	624-0665
Web: www.garlandcounty.org					
Garrard County 15 Public Sq County Courthouse	Lancaster	KY	40444	859-792-3071	792-6751
Garrett County 203 S 4th St Rm 207	Oakland	MD	21550	301-334-8970	334-5000
Web: www.garrettcounty.org					
Garvin County 201 W Grant St	Pauls Valley	OK	73075	405-238-2772	238-6283
Garza County PO Box 366	Post	TX	79356	806-495-4430	495-4431
Web: www.garzacounty.net					
Gasconade County 119 E 1st St Rm 2	Hermann	MO	65041	573-486-5427	486-8893
Web: www.gscnd.com					
Gaston County PO Box 1578	Gastonia	NC	28053	704-866-3100	866-3147
Web: www.co.gaston.nc.us					
Gates County 200 Ct St	Gatesville	NC	27938	252-357-1240	357-0073
Web: www.albemarle-nc.com					
Geary County 200 E 8th PO Box 927	Junction City	KS	66441	785-238-3912	238-5419
Web: ks-geary.manatron.com					
Geauga County 470 Ctr St Bldg 4	Chardon	OH	44024	440-285-2222	286-9177
Web: www.co.geauga.oh.us					
Gem County 415 E Main St	Emmett	ID	83617	208-365-4561	365-7795
Web: www.co.gem.id.us					
Genesee County 15 Main St # 1	Batavia	NY	14020	585-344-2550	344-8582
Web: www.co.genesee.ny.us					
Genesee County 900 S Saginaw St Rm 202	Flint	MI	48502	810-257-3282	257-3464
Web: www.co.genesee.mi.us					
Geneva County PO Box 86	Geneva	AL	36340	334-684-5620	684-5605
Gentry County 200 W Clay St	Albany	MO	64402	660-726-3618	726-4102
Georgetown County 715 Prince St	Georgetown	SC	29440	843-545-3063	545-3292
Web: www.georgetowncountysc.org					
Gibson County PO Box 630	Princeton	IN	47670	812-386-8401	385-5025
Gibson County 1 Ct Sq Suite 100	Trenton	TN	38382	731-855-7642	855-7643
Web: www.gibsoncountytn.com					
Gila County 1400 E Ash St	Globe	AZ	85501	928-425-3231	425-0319
TF: 800-304-4452 ■ *Web:* co.gila.az.us/index.html					
Gilchrist County PO Box 37	Trenton	FL	32693	352-463-3170	463-3166
Web: www.co.gilchrist.fl.us					
Giles County 501 Wenonah Ave	Pearisburg	VA	24134	540-921-1722	921-3825
Web: www.gilescounty.org					
Giles County 222 W Madison St	Pulaski	TN	38478	931-363-1509	424-4795
Web: www.gilescounty-tn.us					
Gillespie County 101 W Main St Unit 13	Fredericksburg	TX	78624	830-997-6515	997-9958
Web: www.gillespiecounty.org					
Gilmer County 368 Craig Str PO Box 505	Ellijay	GA	30540	706-635-7400	635-7410
Web: www.gilmerchamber.com					
Gilmer County 10 Howard St	Glenville	WV	26351	304-462-7641	462-8855
Gilpin County 203 Eureka St	Central City	CO	80427	303-582-5321	582-3086
Web: www.co.gilpin.co.us					
Glacier County 512 E Main St	Cut Bank	MT	59427	406-873-5063	873-2125
Web: www.glaciercountymt.org					
Glades County 500 Ave K PO Box 1018	Moore Haven	FL	33471	863-946-6000	946-2860
Web: www.myglades.com					
Gladwin County 401 W Cedar Ave	Gladwin	MI	48624	989-426-7351	426-6917
Web: www.gladwinco.com					
Glascock County PO Box 231	Gibson	GA	30810	706-598-2084	598-2577
Glasscock County 117 E Currie St	Garden City	TX	79739	432-354-2612	
Web: www.co.glasscock.tx.us					
Glenn County 526 W Sycamore St Suitr B1	Willows	CA	95988	530-934-6400	934-6419
Web: www.countyofglenn.net					
Gloucester County 6467 Main St	Gloucester	VA	23061	804-693-4042	693-6004
Web: www.co.gloucester.va.us					
Gloucester County 1 N Broad St Rm 101	Woodbury	NJ	08096	856-853-3237	853-3327
Web: www.co.gloucester.nj.us					
Glynn County 701 G St	Brunswick	GA	31520	912-554-7400	554-7596
Web: www.glynncounty.org					
Gogebic County 200 N Moore St	Bessemer	MI	49911	906-663-4518	663-4660
Web: www.gogebic.org					
Golden Valley County 150 1st Ave SE PO Box 9	Beach	ND	58621	701-872-3713	
Web: www.beachnd.com					
Golden Valley County 107 Kemp St PO Box 10	Ryegate	MT	59074	406-568-2231	568-2428
Web: www.co.golden-valley.mt.us					
Goliad County 127 N Courthouse Sq PO Box 50	Goliad	TX	77963	361-645-3294	645-3858
Web: www.co.goliad.tx.us					
Gonzales County 1709 Sarah Dewitt Dr	Gonzales	TX	78629	830-672-2801	672-2636
Goochland County 1800 Sandy Hook Rd	Goochland	VA	23063	804-556-5800	556-4617
Web: www.co.goochland.va.us					
Goodhue County 454 W 6th St	Red Wing	MN	55066	651-267-4800	267-4986
Web: www.co.goodhue.mn.us					
Gooding County 624 Main St	Gooding	ID	83330	208-934-4841	934-5085
Web: www.goodingidaho.net					
Gordon County 201 N Wall St	Calhoun	GA	30701	706-629-3795	629-9516
Web: www.gordoncounty.org					
Goshen County 2125 E 'A' St PO Box 160	Torrington	WY	82240	307-532-4051	532-7375
Web: www.goshencounty.org					
Gosper County 507 Smith Ave PO Box 136	Elwood	NE	68937	308-785-2611	785-2300
Web: www.co.gosper.ne.us					
Gove County 520 Washington St Suite 105 PO Box 128	Gove	KS	67736	785-938-2300	938-4486
Grady County 250 N Broad St	Cairo	GA	39828	229-377-1512	377-1039
Web: www.gradycountyga.gov					
Grady County 326 Choctaw St	Chickasha	OK	73018	405-224-7388	222-4506
Web: www.gradycountyok.com					
Grafton County 3855 Dartmouth College Hwy PO Box 1	North Haverhill	NH	03774	603-787-6941	787-2345
Web: www.graftoncountynh.us					
Graham County 410 N Pomeroy St	Hill City	KS	67642	785-421-3453	421-6374
Graham County 12 N Main St	Robbinsville	NC	28771	828-479-7973	479-6417
Web: www.main.nc.us					
Graham County 921 W Thatcher Blvd	Safford	AZ	85546	928-428-3250	428-5951
Web: www.graham.az.gov					
Grainger County 8095 Rutledge Pike # 100	Rutledge	TN	37861	865-828-3513	828-4284
Web: www.graingertn.com					
Grand County 308 W Byers Ave	Hot Sulphur Springs	CO	80451	970-725-3347	725-0100
Web: www.co.grand.co.us					
Grand County 125 E Ctr St	Moab	UT	84532	435-259-1321	259-2959
Web: www.grandcountyutah.net					
Grand Forks County 124 S 4th St	Grand Forks	ND	58201	701-787-2715	787-2716
Web: www.grandforkscountygov.com					
Grand Isle County 9 Hyde Rd PO Box 49	Grand Isle	VT	05458	802-372-8830	372-8815
Grand Traverse County 400 Boardman Ave	Traverse City	MI	49684	231-922-4760	922-4658
Web: www.grandtraverse.org					
Granite County 220 N Sansome St PO Box 925	Philipsburg	MT	59858	406-859-3771	859-3817
Web: www.co.granite.mt.us					
Grant County 201 S Humbolt St Suite 290	Canyon City	OR	97820	541-575-1675	575-2248
Web: www.grantcounty.cc					
Grant County 106 2nd Ave	Carson	ND	58529	701-622-3615	622-3717
Web: grantcountynd.com					
Grant County 10 2nd Ave NE	Elbow Lake	MN	56531	218-685-4825	685-5349
Web: www.co.grant.mn.us					
Grant County 457 1st Ave NW	Ephrata	WA	98823	509-754-2011	754-6098
Web: www.co.grant.wa.us					
Grant County 105 E Harrison St PO Box 139	Hyannis	NE	69350	308-458-2488	458-2780
Grant County 111 S Jefferson St	Lancaster	WI	53813	608-723-2675	723-4048
Web: www.grantcounty.org					
Grant County 101 E 4th St	Marion	IN	46952	765-668-8121	668-6541
Web: www.grantcounty.net					
Grant County 112 E Guthrie St PO Box 167	Medford	OK	73759	580-395-2274	395-2086
Grant County 210 E 5th Ave	Milbank	SD	57252	605-432-6711	432-9004*
Grant County 5 Highland Ave	Petersburg	WV	26847	304-257-4422	257-9645
Web: www.grantcounty-wv.com					
Grant County 101 W Ctr St Rm 106	Sheridan	AR	72150	870-942-2631	942-3564
Web: grantcountyar.com					
Grant County 1400 Hwy 180	Silver City	NM	88061	575-574-0000	574-0073
Web: www.grantcountynm.com					
Grant County 108 S Glenn St	Ulysses	KS	67880	620-356-1335	356-3081
Web: www.grantcoks.org					
Grant County 107 N Main St	Williamstown	KY	41097	859-824-3321	824-3367
Web: grantcounty.ky.gov					
Grant Parish PO Box 263	Colfax	LA	71417	318-627-3246	627-3201
Web: www.gpsb.org					
Granville County PO Box 906	Oxford	NC	27565	919-693-4761	690-1766
Web: www.granvillecounty.org					
Gratiot County County Courthouse, 214 E Center St PO Box 437	Ithaca	MI	48847	989-875-5215	875-5284
Web: www.co.gratiot.mi.us					
Graves County 101 E S St	Mayfield	KY	42066	270-247-3626	247-1274
Web: gravescounty.ky.gov					
Gray County PO Box 487	Cimarron	KS	67835	620-855-3618	855-3107
Web: www.grayco.org					

Name / Address	City	State	ZIP	Phone	Fax
Gray County PO Box 1902	Pampa	TX	79066	806-669-8004	669-8054
Web: www.co.gray.tx.us					
Grays Harbor County					
102 W Broadway St Rm 203	Montesano	WA	98563	360-249-3842	249-6381
Web: www.co.grays-harbor.wa.us					
Grayson County 129 Davis St PO Box 130	Independence	VA	24348	276-773-2231	773-3338
Web: www.ls.net					
Grayson County 10 Public Sq	Leitchfield	KY	42754	270-259-3201	259-9264
Web: www.graysoncountychamber.com					
Grayson County 100 W Houston St	Sherman	TX	75090	903-813-4207	868-9691
Web: www.co.grayson.tx.us					
Greeley County PO Box 287	Greeley	NE	68842	308-428-3625	428-3022
Greeley County PO Box 277	Tribune	KS	67879	620-376-4256	376-2294
Web: www.greeleycountygovernment.org					
Green County 203 W Ct St	Greensburg	KY	42743	270-932-5386	932-6241
Green County 2841 6th St	Monroe	WI	53566	608-328-9430	328-2835
Web: www.greencounty.org					
Green Lake County 492 Hill St	Green Lake	WI	54941	920-294-4005	294-4009
Web: www.co.green-lake.wi.us					
Greenbrier County 200 W Washington St	Lewisburg	WV	24901	304-647-6602	647-6694
TF: 800-833-2068 ■ *Web:* www.greenbrierwv.com					
Greene County PO Box 229	Bloomfield	IN	47424	812-384-8532	384-8458
Web: www.in-map.net					
Greene County 519 N Main St	Carrollton	IL	62016	217-942-5443	942-9323
Web: www.greene-county.com					
Greene County 411 Main St	Catskill	NY	12414	518-719-3270	719-3793
Web: www.greenegovernment.com					
Greene County PO Box 307	Eutaw	AL	35462	205-372-3598	372-1510
Web: www.greenecountyalabama.com					
Greene County 204 N Cutler St	Greeneville	TN	37745	423-798-1708	798-1822
Web: www.greenecountytngovt.com					
Greene County					
113 N Main St 3rd Fl Suite 306	Greensboro	GA	30642	706-453-7716	453-9555
Web: www.greenecountyga.gov					
Greene County 114 N Chestnut St	Jefferson	IA	50129	515-386-2516	386-2321
Web: www.jeffersoniowa.com					
Greene County PO Box 610	Leakesville	MS	39451	601-394-2377	394-4445
Greene County PO Box 62	Paragould	AR	72451	870-239-6311	239-3550
Greene County 301 N Greene St	Snow Hill	NC	28580	252-747-3505	747-2700
Web: www.co.greene.nc.us					
Greene County 940 N Boonville Ave	Springfield	MO	65802	417-868-4055	868-4170
Web: www.greenecountymo.org					
Greene County 22 Ct St	Stanardsville	VA	22973	434-985-5208	985-6723
Web: www.gcva.us					
Greene County 35 Green St	Xenia	OH	45385	937-562-5006	562-5331
Web: www.co.greene.oh.us					
Greenlee County 223 5th St	Clifton	AZ	85533	928-865-2072	865-4417
Web: www.co.greenlee.az.us					
Greensville County 337 S Main St	Emporia	VA	23847	434-348-4215	348-4020
Web: www.greensvillecountyva.gov					
Greenup County 301 Main St	Greenup	KY	41144	606-473-7394	473-5354
Greenville County 305 E N St	Greenville	SC	29601	864-467-8551	467-8540
Web: www.greenvillecounty.org					
Greenwood County 311 N Main St	Eureka	KS	67045	620-583-8121	583-8124
Greenwood County					
600 Monument St PO Box P-103	Greenwood	SC	29646	864-942-8500	942-8566
Web: www.co.greenwood.sc.us					
Greer County PO Box 207	Mangum	OK	73554	580-782-3664	782-3803
Web: www.greercounty-ok.com					
Gregg County 101 E Methvin PO Box 3049	Longview	TX	75601	903-236-8430	237-2574
Web: www.co.gregg.tx.us					
Gregory County PO Box 430	Burke	SD	57523	605-775-2665	775-2965
Grenada County PO Box 1517	Grenada	MS	38902	662-226-1941	227-2865
Web: www.grenadacircuitclerk.webs.com					
Griggs County 808 Rollin Ave SW	Cooperstown	ND	58425	701-797-2772	797-3587
Web: www.cooperstownnd.com					
Grundy County PO Box 177	Altamont	TN	37301	931-692-3718	692-3721
Grundy County 706 G Ave	Grundy Center	IA	50638	319-824-5229	824-3447
Web: www.grundycounty.org					
Grundy County PO Box 675	Morris	IL	60450	815-941-3222	942-2222
Web: www.grundyco.org					
Grundy County 700 Main St	Trenton	MO	64683	660-359-6305	359-6786
Guadalupe County 420 Parker Ave Suite 1	Santa Rosa	NM	88435	505-472-3791	472-4791
Guadalupe County PO Box 990	Seguin	TX	78156	830-303-4188	401-0300
Web: www.co.guadalupe.tx.us					
Guernsey County 627 Wheeling Ave Suite 300	Cambridge	OH	43725	740-432-9200	432-9359
Web: www.guernseycounty.org					
Guilford County PO Box 3427	Greensboro	NC	27402	336-641-3383	641-6833
Web: www.co.guilford.nc.us					
Gulf County					
1000 Cecil Costin Sr Blvd Rm 148	Port Saint Joe	FL	32456	850-229-6112	229-6174
Web: www.gulfcounty-fl.gov					
Gunnison County 221 N Wisconsin St Suite C	Gunnison	CO	81230	970-641-1516	641-7956
Web: www.co.gunnison.co.us					
Guthrie County 200 N 5th St	Guthrie Center	IA	50115	641-747-3415	747-2420
Gwinnett County					
75 Langley Dr					
Gwinnett Justice & Administration Ctr	Lawrenceville	GA	30045	770-822-7000	822-7097
Web: www.co.gwinnett.ga.us					
Haakon County PO Box 698	Philip	SD	57567	605-859-2800	
Habersham County 555 Monroe St Unit 20	Clarkesville	GA	30523	706-754-6270	754-1014
Web: www.co.habersham.ga.us					
Haines Borough 103 3rd Ave S PO Box 1209	Haines	AK	99827	907-766-2231	766-2716
Web: www.hainesborough.us					
Hale County 1001 Main St PO Box 396	Greensboro	AL	36744	334-624-4257	624-1715
Hale County 500 Broadway St Suite 140	Plainview	TX	79072	806-291-5261	291-9810
Web: www.texasonline.net					
Halifax County 33 S Granville St	Halifax	NC	27839	252-583-1131	583-9921
Web: www.halifaxnc.com					
Halifax County 13 N Main St	Halifax	VA	24558	434-476-3300	476-3384
Web: www.halifax.com					
Hall County 225 Green St SE	Gainesville	GA	30501	770-531-7025	531-7070
Web: www.hallcounty.org					
Hall County 121 S Pine St	Grand Island	NE	68801	308-385-5080	385-5184
Web: www.hcgi.org					
County Courthouse 512 Main St	Memphis	TX	79245	806-259-2627	
Hamblen County 511 W 2nd N St	Morristown	TN	37814	423-586-1993	318-2508
Web: www.hamblencountygovernment.us					
Hamilton County 1111 13th St Suite 1	Aurora	NE	68818	402-694-3443	694-2397
Web: www.co.hamilton.ne.us					
Hamilton County 625 Georgia Ave Rm 201	Chattanooga	TN	37402	423-209-6500	209-6501
Web: www.hamiltontn.gov					
Hamilton County 138 E Ct St Rm 603	Cincinnati	OH	45202	513-946-4400	946-4444
Web: www.hamilton-co.org					
Hamilton County					
County Courthouse 102 N Rice Suite 107	Hamilton	TX	76531	254-386-3518	386-8727
Web: www.hamiltoncountytx.org					
Hamilton County 207 NE 1st St Rm 106	Jasper	FL	32052	386-792-1288	792-3524
Web: www.hamiltoncountyflorida.com					
Hamilton County 102 County View Dr	Lake Pleasant	NY	12108	518-548-7111	548-9740
Web: www.hamiltoncounty.com					
Hamilton County					
100 S Jackson St County Courthouse	McLeansboro	IL	62859	618-643-2721	
Hamilton County					
1 Hamilton County Sq Suite 106	Noblesville	IN	46060	317-776-9629	776-9664
Web: www.co.hamilton.in.us					
Hamilton County PO Box 1167	Syracuse	KS	67878	620-384-5629	384-5853
Web: www.hamiltoncountyks.com					
Hamilton County 2300 Superior St	Webster City	IA	50595	515-832-9510	832-9514
Web: www.hamiltoncounty.org					
Hamlin County PO Box 256	Hayti	SD	57243	605-783-3751	783-2157
Hampden County 50 State St	Springfield	MA	01102	413-748-8600	
Hampshire County 99 Main St Rm 205	NorthHampton	MA	01060	413-584-0557	584-1465
Hampshire County 66 N High St	Romney	WV	26757	304-822-5112	822-4039
Web: www.co.hampshire.wv.us					
Hampton (Independent City) 22 Lincoln St	Hampton	VA	23669	757-727-8311	
Web: www.hampton.va.us					
Hampton County					
201 Jackson Ave W					
B T Deloach Administrative Bldg	Hampton	SC	29924	803-914-2103	914-2107
Web: www.hamptoncountysc.org					
Hancock County 3068 Longfellow Dr	Bay Saint Louis	MS	39520	228-467-5404	467-3159
Web: www.hancockcountyms.org					
Hancock County PO Box 39	Carthage	IL	62321	217-357-3911	
Hancock County 50 State St Suite 7	Ellsworth	ME	04605	207-667-9542	667-1412
Web: www.co.hancock.me.us					
Hancock County 300 S Main St	Findlay	OH	45840	419-424-7037	424-7801
Web: www.co.hancock.oh.us					
Hancock County PO Box 70	Garner	IA	50438	641-923-2532	923-3521
Web: www.hancockcountyia.org					
Hancock County 9 E Main St Rm 201	Greenfield	IN	46140	317-462-1109	
Web: www.hancockcoingov.org					
Hancock County PO Box 146	Hawesville	KY	42348	270-927-6117	927-8639
Web: www.hancockcounty-ky.com					
Hancock County PO Box 367	New Cumberland	WV	26047	304-564-3311	564-5941
Hancock County 418 Harrison St Suite 96	Sneedville	TN	37869	423-733-2519	733-4509
Hancock County 601 Broad St	Sparta	GA	31087	706-444-5746	444-6221
Hand County 415 W 1st Ave	Miller	SD	57362	605-853-3337	853-3779
Hanover County 7497 County Complex Rd	Hanover	VA	23069	804-365-6000	365-6234
Web: www.co.hanover.va.us					
Hansford County 15 NW Court	Spearman	TX	79081	806-659-4110	659-4168
Web: www.co.hansford.tx.us					
Hanson County PO Box 127	Alexandria	SD	57311	605-239-4446	239-9446
Haralson County 155 Van Wert St	Buchanan	GA	30113	770-646-2002	646-2035
Web: www.haralsoncountyga.org					
Hardee County 412 W Orange St Rm A-203	Wauchula	FL	33873	863-773-6952	773-0958
Web: www.hardeecounty.net					
Hardeman County 100 N Main St	Bolivar	TN	38008	731-658-3541	658-3482
Web: www.hardemancotn.org					
Hardeman County PO Box 30	Quanah	TX	79252	940-663-2901	
Hardin County					
1215 Edgington Ave County Courthouse	Eldora	IA	50627	641-939-8109	939-8245
Web: www.hardincountyonline.com					
Hardin County 1 N Main St	Elizabethtown	IL	62931	618-287-2251	287-2661
Web: www.hardincountyil.org					
Hardin County 14 Public Sq	Elizabethtown	KY	42701	270-765-2171	765-6193
Web: www.hccoky.org					
Hardin County 1 Courthouse Sq Suite 100	Kenton	OH	43326	419-674-2205	674-2272
Web: www.co.hardin.oh.us					
Hardin County 300 Monroe St Suite B-110	Kountze	TX	77625	409-246-5185	
Hardin County 65 Ct St # 1	Savannah	TN	38372	731-925-3921	926-4313
Web: www.tourhardincounty.org					
Harding County 410 Ramsland St PO Box 534	Buffalo	SD	57720	605-375-3351	375-3432
Harding County 35 Pine St PO Box 1002	Mosquero	NM	87733	505-673-2301	673-2922
Web: www.hardingcounty.org					
Hardy County 204 Washington St Rm 111	Moorefield	WV	26836	304-530-0250	530-0251
Web: www.hardycountywv.com					
Harlan County PO Box 698	Alma	NE	68920	308-928-2173	928-2079
Harlan County PO Box 670	Harlan	KY	40831	606-573-3636	573-0064
Harmon County 114 W Hollis St	Hollis	OK	73550	580-688-3658	688-9784
Harnett County PO Box 759	Lillington	NC	27546	910-893-7555	814-2662
Web: www.harnett.org					
Harney County 450 N Buena Vista Suite 14	Burns	OR	97720	541-573-6641	573-8370
Web: www.co.harney.or.us					
Harper County 201 N Jennings Ave	Anthony	KS	67003	620-842-5555	842-3455
Web: www.harpercounty.org					
Harper County PO Box 369	Buffalo	OK	73834	580-735-2130	735-6034
Harris County PO Box 528	Hamilton	GA	31811	706-628-4944	628-7039
Web: www.harriscountychamber.org					
Harris County 201 Caroline St 4th Fl	Houston	TX	77002	713-755-5000	
Web: www.co.harris.tx.us					
Harrison County PO Box 525	Bethany	MO	64424	660-425-6424	425-3772
Harrison County 100 W Market St	Cadiz	OH	43907	740-942-8861	942-8860
Web: www.harrisoncountyohio.org					

				Phone	Fax
Harrison County					
301 W Main St County Courthouse	Clarksburg	WV	26301	304-624-8500	624-8673
Web: www.harrisoncountywv.com					
Harrison County 300 N Capitol Ave Rm 203	Corydon	IN	47112	812-738-4289	738-3126
Web: harrisoncounty.in.gov					
Harrison County 313 Oddville Ave	Cynthiana	KY	41031	859-234-7130	234-8049
Harrison County 1801 23rd Ave	Gulfport	MS	39501	228-865-4036	868-1480
Web: www.co.harrison.ms.us					
Harrison County 111 N 2nd Ave	Logan	IA	51546	712-644-3123	644-2643
Web: www.harrisoncountyia.org					
Harrison County PO Box 1365	Marshall	TX	75671	903-935-8403	
Web: www.co.harrison.tx.us					
Harrisonburg (Independent City)					
345 S Main St	Harrisonburg	VA	22801	540-432-7701	432-7778
Web: www.ci.harrisonburg.va.us					
Hart County 800 Chandler St	Hartwell	GA	30643	706-376-2024	376-9477
Web: www.hartcountyga.org					
Hart County 200 Main St	Munfordville	KY	42765	270-524-2751	524-0458
Web: www.hartcounty.com					
Hartley County PO Box Q	Channing	TX	79018	806-235-3582	235-2316
Web: www.co.hartley.tx.us					
Harvey County 800 N Main PO Box 687	Newton	KS	67114	316-284-6840	284-6856
Web: www.harveycounty.com					
Haskell County PO Box 725	Haskell	TX	79521	940-864-2451	864-6164
Web: www.co.haskell.tx.us					
Haskell County 202 E Main St	Stigler	OK	74462	918-967-2884	967-2885
Haskell County PO Box 518	Sublette	KS	67877	620-675-2263	675-2681
Web: www.haskellcounty.org					
Hawaii County 333 Kilauea Ave # 2	Hilo	HI	96720	808-961-8255	961-8912
Web: www.hawaii-county.com					
Hawkins County 110 E Main St	Rogersville	TN	37857	423-272-7002	272-5801
Web: www.hawkinscounty.org					
Hayes County 505 Troth St PO Box 370	Hayes Center	NE	69032	308-286-3413	286-3208
Web: www.hayescounty.ne.gov					
Hays County 110 E Martin Luther King St	San Marcos	TX	78666	512-393-7738	393-7735
Web: www.co.hays.tx.us					
Haywood County 1 N Washington St	Brownsville	TN	38012	731-772-1432	772-3864
Haywood County 215 N Main St	Waynesville	NC	28786	828-452-6625	452-6715
Web: www.gov.co.haywood.nc.us					
Heard County PO Box 40	Franklin	GA	30217	706-675-3821	675-2493
Hemphill County PO Box 867	Canadian	TX	79014	806-323-6212	
Hempstead County PO Box 1420	Hope	AR	71802	870-777-2241	777-7829
Henderson County					
100 E Tyler Courthouse Suite 107 PO Box 632	Athens	TX	75751	903-675-6140	675-6105
Web: www.co.henderson.tx.us					
Henderson County 20 N Main St	Henderson	KY	42420	270-826-3906	826-9677
Web: www.hendersonky.com					
Henderson County					
1 Historic Courthouse Sq	Hendersonville	NC	28792	828-697-4808	692-9855
Web: www.hendersoncountync.org					
Henderson County 17 Monroe Ave Suite 2	Lexington	TN	38351	731-968-2856	968-6644
Henderson County PO Box 308	Oquawka	IL	61469	309-867-2911	867-2033
Web: www.outfitters.com					
Hendricks County 1 Courthouse Sq	Danville	IN	46122	317-745-9231	745-9306
Web: www.co.hendricks.in.us					
Hendry County PO Box 1760	La Belle	FL	33975	863-675-5217	675-5238
Web: www.hendryfla.net					
Hennepin County 300 S 6th St	Minneapolis	MN	55487	612-348-3081	348-8701
Web: www.co.hennepin.mn.us					
Henrico County PO Box 27032	Richmond	VA	23273	804-501-4202	501-5214
Web: www.co.henrico.va.us					
Henry County 101 Ct Sq Suite J	Abbeville	AL	36310	334-585-2753	585-5006
Henry County 307 W Ctr St	Cambridge	IL	61238	309-937-3575	
Web: www.co.henry.il.us					
Henry County 100 W Franklin St	Clinton	MO	64735	660-885-7204	890-2693
Henry County PO Box 7	Collinsville	VA	24078	276-634-4601	634-4781
Web: www.henrycountyva.gov/Collinsville-District.html					
Henry County 140 Henry Pkwy	McDonough	GA	30253	770-954-2400	954-2418
Web: www.co.henry.ga.us					
Henry County PO Box 176	Mount Pleasant	IA	52641	319-385-2632	385-4144
Web: www.co.henry.ia.us					
Henry County 1853 Oakwood Ave	Napoleon	OH	43545	419-592-4876	
Web: www.henrycountyohio.com					
Henry County PO Box B	New Castle	IN	47362	765-529-6401	521-7046
Henry County 27 S Property Rd	New Castle	KY	40050	502-845-5705	845-5708
Web: www.henryweb.com					
Henry County					
101 W Washington St Suite 100 PO Box 24	Paris	TN	38242	731-642-2412	644-0947
Web: www.henryco.com					
Herkimer County 109 Mary St Suite 1111	Herkimer	NY	13350	315-867-1129	867-1349
Web: www.herkimercounty.org					
Hernando County 16110 Aviation Loop Dr	Brooksville	FL	34604	352-754-4000	754-4477
Web: www.co.hernando.fl.us					
Hertford County 701 N King St	Winton	NC	27986	252-358-7845	358-0793
Web: www.co.hertford.nc.us					
Hettinger County 336 Pacific Ave	Mott	ND	58646	701-824-2645	824-2717
Web: www.hettingercounty.org					
Hickman County 114 N Central Ave # 202	Centerville	TN	37033	931-729-2621	729-9951
Web: www.hickmanco.com					
Hickman County					
110 E Clay St County Courthouse	Clinton	KY	42031	270-653-2131	653-4248
Hickory County PO Box 3	Hermitage	MO	65668	417-745-6450	745-6057
Hidalgo County PO Box 58	Edinburg	TX	78540	956-318-2100	318-2105
Web: www.co.hidalgo.tx.us					
Highland County					
119 Governor Foraker Pl # 211	Hillsboro	OH	45133	937-393-1911	393-5850
Web: www.highland-co.com					
Highland County 165 W Main St	Monterey	VA	24465	540-468-2447	468-3447
Web: www.highlandcova.org					
Highlands County 430 S Commerce Ave	Sebring	FL	33870	863-402-6500	402-6507
Web: www.hcbcc.net					
Hill County 315 4th St	Havre	MT	59501	406-265-5481	265-3693
Web: www.co.hill.mt.us					
Hill County PO Box 398	Hillsboro	TX	76645	254-582-4030	582-4003
Web: www.co.hill.tx.us					
Hillsborough County 329 Mast Rd	Golfstown	NH	03045	603-627-5600	627-5603
Web: www.hillsboroughcountynh.org					
Hillsborough County 800 E Twigg St	Tampa	FL	33602	813-276-8100	276-2437
Web: www.hillsboroughcounty.org					
Hillsdale County 29 N Howell St	Hillsdale	MI	49242	517-437-3391	437-3392
Web: www.co.hillsdale.mi.us					
Hinds County 316 S President St	Jackson	MS	39205	601-968-6501	968-6794
Web: www.co.hinds.ms.us					
Hinsdale County 311 N Henson St	Lake City	CO	81235	970-944-2225	944-2630
Web: www.hinsdalecountycolorado.us					
Hitchcock County 229 E D St	Trenton	NE	69044	308-334-5646	334-5398
Web: www.co.hitchcock.ne.us					
Hocking County 1 E Main St	Logan	OH	43138	740-385-5195	385-1105
Web: www.co.hocking.oh.us					
Hockley County 802 Houston St Suite 213	Levelland	TX	79336	806-894-4404	
Web: www.co.hockley.tx.us					
Hodgeman County PO Box 247	Jetmore	KS	67854	620-357-6421	357-6161
Hoke County 227 N Main St	Raeford	NC	28376	910-875-8751	875-9222
TF: 800-597-8751 ■ *Web:* www.hoke-raeford.com					
Holmes County PO Box 397	Bonifay	FL	32425	850-547-1100	547-6630
Web: www.holmescountyonline.com					
Holmes County PO Box 239	Lexington	MS	39095	662-834-2508	834-3020
Holmes County 2 Ct St	Millersburg	OH	44654	330-674-0286	674-0566
Web: www.holmescounty.com/gov					
Holt County 204 N 4th St PO Box 329	O'Neill	NE	68763	402-336-1762	336-1762
Web: www.co.holt.ne.us					
Holt County PO Box 437	Oregon	MO	64473	660-446-3303	446-3353
Honolulu City & County 530 S King St Rm 100	Honolulu	HI	96813	808-768-3810	768-3835
Web: www.co.honolulu.hi.us					
Hood County 100 E Pearl St # 5	Granbury	TX	76048	817-579-3222	579-3227
Web: www.co.hood.tx.us					
Hood River County 601 State St	Hood River	OR	97031	541-386-3970	386-9392
Web: www.co.hood-river.or.us					
Hooker County PO Box 184	Mullen	NE	69152	308-546-2244	546-2490
Web: www.co.hooker.ne.us					
Hopewell (Independent City)					
300 N Main St Rm 217	Hopewell	VA	23860	804-541-2243	541-2248
Web: www.hopewellva.gov					
Hopkins County 24 Union St	Madisonville	KY	42431	270-821-7361	825-5009
Web: www.hopkinscounty.net					
Hopkins County PO Box 288	Sulphur Springs	TX	75483	903-438-4074	438-4110
Web: www.hopkinscountytx.org					
Horry County 1301 2nd Ave	Conway	SC	29526	843-915-5080	915-6081
Web: www.horrycounty.org					
Hot Spring County 210 Locust St	Malvern	AR	72104	501-332-2291	332-2221
Hot Springs County 415 Arapahoe St	Thermopolis	WY	82443	307-864-3515	864-3333
Web: www.hscounty.com					
Houghton County 401 E Houghton Ave	Houghton	MI	49931	906-482-1150	483-0364
Web: www.houghtoncounty.net					
Houston County 304 S Marshall St	Caledonia	MN	55921	507-725-5806	725-5550
Web: www.geocities.com					
Houston County PO Box 370	Crockett	TX	75835	936-544-3256	544-1954
Web: www.co.houston.tx.us					
Houston County 462 N Oates St PO Box 6406	Dothan	AL	36303	334-677-4740	794-6633
Web: www.houstoncounty.org					
Houston County PO Box 388	Erin	TN	37061	931-289-4165	289-2603
Houston County 200 Carl Vinson Pkwy	Warner Robins	GA	31088	478-542-2115	923-5697
Web: www.houstoncountyga.com					
Howard County 300 Main St	Big Spring	TX	79720	432-264-2213	264-2215
Web: www.co.howard.tx.us					
Howard County 137 N Elm St County Courthouse	Cresco	IA	52136	563-547-2661	547-3605
Web: www.crescoia.com/howardcounty/index.html					
Howard County 3430 Courthouse Dr	Ellicott City	MD	21043	410-313-2011	313-3051
Web: www.co.ho.md.us					
Howard County 1 Courthouse Sq	Fayette	MO	65248	660-248-2284	248-1075
Howard County 104 N Buckeye St # 114	Kokomo	IN	46901	765-456-2204	456-2267
Web: www.co.howard.in.us					
Howard County 421 N Main St Rm 10	Nashville	AR	71852	870-845-7502	845-7505
Howard County PO Box 25	Saint Paul	NE	68873	308-754-4343	754-4125
Web: www.howardcounty.ne.gov					
Howell County 1 Courthouse	West Plains	MO	65775	417-256-2591	256-2512
Web: www.howellcounty.net					
Hubbard County					
301 Ct Ave County Courthouse	Park Rapids	MN	56470	218-732-2300	732-3645*
**Fax:* Acctg ■ *Web:* www.co.hubbard.mn.us					
Hudson County 257 Cornelison Ave 4th Fl	Jersey City	NJ	07302	201-369-3470	369-3478
Web: www.hudsoncountyclerk.org					
Hudspeth County PO Box 58	Sierra Blanca	TX	79851	915-369-2301	369-0055
Huerfano County 401 Main St Suite 201	Walsenburg	CO	81089	719-738-2370	738-3996
Web: www.huerfanococc.com					
Hughes County 200 N Broadway St Suite 7	Holdenville	OK	74848	405-379-2746	379-6739
Hughes County 104 E Capitol Ave PO Box 1238	Pierre	SD	57501	605-773-3713	
Web: www.hughescounty.org					
Humboldt County 203 Main St	Dakota City	IA	50529	515-332-1571	332-1738
Web: www.ci.humboldt.ia.us					
Humboldt County 421 I St	Eureka	CA	95501	707-445-7256	
Web: www.co.humboldt.ca.us					
Humboldt County 50 W 5th St	Winnemucca	NV	89445	775-623-6300	623-6302
Web: www.hcnv.us					
Humphreys County 102 Castleman St PO Box 547	Belzoni	MS	39038	662-247-1740	247-0101
Humphreys County Courthouse Annex Rm 1	Waverly	TN	37185	931-296-7795	296-5011
Hunt County PO Box 1316	Greenville	TX	75403	903-408-4130	408-4287
Web: www.huntcounty.net					
Hunterdon County 71 Main St	Flemington	NJ	08822	908-788-1221	782-4068
Web: www.co.hunterdon.nj.us					
Huntingdon County					
223 Penn St County Courthouse	Huntingdon	PA	16652	814-643-3091	643-8152
Web: www.huntingdoncounty.net					

				Phone	Fax
Huntington County 201 N Jefferson St County Courthouse Rm 103	Huntington	IN	46750	260-358-4822	358-4823
Web: www.huntington.in.us					
Huron County 250 E Huron Ave Rm 305	Bad Axe	MI	48413	989-269-8242	269-6152
Web: www.huroncounty.com					
Huron County County Courthouse 2 E Main St 2nd Fl	Norwalk	OH	44857	419-668-5113	663-4048
Web: www.hccommissioners.com					
Hutchinson County 140 Euclid St Rm 36	Olivet	SD	57052	605-387-4215	387-4208
Hutchinson County PO Box 1186	Stinnett	TX	79083	806-878-4002	
Web: www.co.hutchinson.tx.us					
Hyde County PO Box 306	Highmore	SD	57345	605-852-2512	852-2767
Hyde County 30 Oyster Creek Rd	Swanquarter	NC	27885	252-926-4178	926-3701
Web: www.hydecounty.org					
Iberia Parish 300 Iberia St Suite 400	New Iberia	LA	70560	337-365-8246	369-4470
Web: www.iberiaparishgovernment.com					
Iberville Parish 58050 Meriam St	Plaquemine	LA	70764	225-687-5160	687-5260
Web: www.ibervilleparish.com					
Ida County 401 Moorehead St	Ida Grove	IA	51445	712-364-2626	364-3929
Idaho County 320 W Main St Rm 5	Grangeville	ID	83530	208-983-2751	983-1458
Web: www.idahocounty.org					
Imperial County 940 W Main St Rm 202	El Centro	CA	92243	760-482-4427	482-4271
Web: www.co.imperial.ca.us					
Independence County 192 E Main St	Batesville	AR	72501	870-793-8828	793-8831
Indian River County 2145 14th Ave	Vero Beach	FL	32960	772-567-8000	978-1822
Web: www.indian-river.fl.us					
Indiana County 825 Philadelphia St Courthouse	Indiana	PA	15701	724-465-3805	465-3953
Web: www.indianacounty.org					
Ingham County 315 S Jefferson St Fl 1 PO Box 179	Mason	MI	48854	517-676-7201	676-7254
Web: www.ingham.org					
Inyo County PO Drawer N	Independence	CA	93526	760-878-0292	878-2241
Web: www.countyofinyo.org					
Ionia County 100 W Main St	Ionia	MI	48846	616-527-5322	527-8201
Web: www.ioniacounty.org					
Iosco County 422 W Lake St	Tawas City	MI	48763	989-362-4212	984-1002
Web: www.iosco.m33access.com					
Iowa County 222 N Iowa St Suite 102	Dodgeville	WI	53533	608-935-5445	935-3024
Web: www.iowacounty.org					
Iowa County PO Box 266	Marengo	IA	52301	319-642-3914	
Web: www.co.iowa.ia.us					
Iredell County 200 S Ctr St PO Box 788	Statesville	NC	28687	704-878-3000	878-5355
Web: www.co.iredell.nc.us					
Irion County PO Box 736	Mertzon	TX	76941	325-835-2421	835-2008
Web: www.co.irion.tx.us					
Iron County 2 S 6th St	Crystal Falls	MI	49920	906-875-3221	875-6775
Web: www.iron.org					
Iron County 300 Taconite St	Hurley	WI	54534	715-561-3375	561-2928
Web: www.ironcountywi.com					
Iron County 25 S Main St	Ironton	MO	63650	573-546-2912	546-6499
Web: www.ironcounty.org					
Iron County 68 S 100 E	Parowan	UT	84761	435-477-3375	477-8847
Web: www.ironcounty.net					
Iroquois County 1001 E Grant St	Watseka	IL	60970	815-432-6960	432-3894
Web: www.fordiroq.prairienet.org					
Irwin County 207 S Irwin Ave Suite 2	Ocilla	GA	31774	229-468-9441	468-9672
Web: www.irwincounty.net					
Isabella County 200 N Main St	Mount Pleasant	MI	48858	989-772-0911	773-7431
Web: www.isabellacounty.org					
Isanti County 555 18th Ave SW	Cambridge	MN	55008	763-689-3859	689-8226
Web: www.co.isanti.mn.us					
Island County 1 NE 7th St # 214	Coupeville	WA	98239	360-679-7354	679-7381
Web: www.islandcounty.net					
Isle of Wight County 17090 Monument Cir # 123	Isle of Wight	VA	23397	757-365-6204	357-9171
Web: www.co.isle-of-wight.va.us					
Issaquena County PO Box 27	Mayersville	MS	39113	662-873-2761	873-2061
Itasca County 123 NE 4th St	Grand Rapids	MN	55744	218-327-2847	327-2848
Web: www.co.itasca.mn.us					
Itawamba County PO Box 776	Fulton	MS	38843	662-862-3421	862-3421
Web: www.itawamba.com					
Izard County PO Box 95	Melbourne	AR	72556	870-368-4316	368-4748
Jack County 100 Main St	Jacksboro	TX	76458	940-567-2111	567-6641
Jackson County 101 N Main St # 203	Altus	OK	73521	580-482-4070	482-4472
Web: www.intplsrv.net					
Jackson County 307 Main St	Black River Falls	WI	54615	715-284-0208	284-0270
Web: www.co.jackson.wi.us					
Jackson County PO Box 318	Brownstown	IN	47220	812-358-6116	358-6187
Jackson County 115 W Main St Rm 101	Edna	TX	77957	361-782-3563	
Web: www.co.jackson.tx.us					
Jackson County PO Box 617	Gainesboro	TN	38562	931-268-9888	268-9060
Web: www.jacksonco.com					
Jackson County 400 New York Ave 2nd Fl	Holton	KS	66436	785-364-2891	364-4204
Web: www.jackson.kansasgov.com					
Jackson County 312 S Jackson St 1st Fl	Jackson	MI	49201	517-788-4265	788-4601
Web: www.co.jackson.mi.us					
Jackson County 405 4th St # 5	Jackson	MN	56143	507-847-2763	847-4718
Web: www.co.jackson.mn.us					
Jackson County 275 Portsmouth St	Jackson	OH	45640	740-286-3301	286-4061
Jackson County 67 Athens St	Jefferson	GA	30549	706-367-6312	367-9083
Web: www.jacksoncountygov.com					
Jackson County PO Box 128	Kadoka	SD	57543	605-837-2121	837-2120
Jackson County 415 E 12th St	Kansas City	MO	64106	816-881-3000	881-3133
Web: www.co.jackson.mo.us					
Jackson County 201 W Platt St	Maquoketa	IA	52060	563-652-3144	652-6975
Web: www.jacksoncountyiowa.com					
Jackson County 4445 Lafayette St	Marianna	FL	32446	850-482-9552	482-7849
Web: www.jacksoncounty-fl.com					
Jackson County PO Box 339	McKee	KY	40447	606-287-7800	287-4505
Web: www.eastky.net/jacksonco					
Jackson County 10 S Oakdale Ave Rm 214 Courthouse	Medford	OR	97501	541-774-6035	774-6455
Web: www.co.jackson.or.us					

				Phone	Fax
Jackson County 1001 Walnut St County Courthouse	Murphysboro	IL	62966	618-687-7360	687-7359
Web: www.co.jackson.il.us					
Jackson County 208 Main St County Courthouse	Newport	AR	72112	870-523-7420	523-7404
Jackson County PO Box 998	Pascagoula	MS	39568	228-769-3089	769-3348
Web: www.co.jackson.ms.us					
Jackson County PO Box 800	Ripley	WV	25271	304-373-2250	372-1107
Jackson County 102 E Laurel St Suite 47 Courthouse	Scottsboro	AL	35768	256-574-9280	574-9321
Jackson County 401 Grindstaff Cove Rd	Sylva	NC	28779	828-586-4055	586-7528
Web: www.jacksonnc.org					
Jackson County 404 4th St	Walden	CO	80480	970-723-4660	723-4706
Jackson Parish 500 E Ct St # 103	Jonesboro	LA	71251	318-259-2424	395-0386
Web: www.jacksonparishpolicejury.org					
James City County PO Box 8784	Williamsburg	VA	23187	757-253-6728	253-6833
Web: www.james-city.va.us					
Jasper County PO Box 1047	Bay Springs	MS	39422	601-764-3368	764-3999
Jasper County 302 S Main St Rm 102	Carthage	MO	64836	417-358-0416	358-0415
Web: www.jaspercounty.org					
Jasper County P121 N Austin St Rm 103	Jasper	TX	75951	409-384-2632	384-7198
Web: www.co.jasper.tx.us					
Jasper County 126 W Greene St Suite 18	Monticello	GA	31064	706-468-4900	468-4942
Jasper County 101 1st St N	Newton	IA	50208	641-792-7016	792-1053
Web: www.co.jasper.ia.us					
Jasper County 204 W Washington St Suite 2	Newton	IL	62448	618-783-3124	783-4137
Jasper County 115 W Washington St # 204	Rensselaer	IN	47978	219-866-4926	866-9450
Web: www.jaspercountyin.com					
Jasper County PO Box 248	Ridgeland	SC	29936	843-726-7710	726-7782
Web: www.jaspersc.org					
Jay County 120 N Ct St 2nd Fl	Portland	IN	47371	260-726-6920	726-6922
Web: www.co.jay.in.us					
Jeff Davis County 100 Woodward Ave	Fort Davis	TX	79734	432-426-3251	426-3760
Web: www.co.jeff-davis.tx.us					
Jefferson County 114 Pearl St	Beaumont	TX	77701	409-835-8475	839-2394
Web: www.co.jefferson.tx.us					
Jefferson County 716 Richard Arrington Jr Blvd N Suite 210	Birmingham	AL	35203	205-325-5555	325-4860
Web: www.jeffcointouch.com					
Jefferson County PO Box H	Boulder	MT	59632	406-225-4020	225-4149
Web: www.co.jefferson.mt.us					
Jefferson County 155 Main St Jefferson Pl	Brookville	PA	15825	814-849-1653	849-4084
Web: www.jeffersoncountypa.com					
Jefferson County PO Box 208	Charles Town	WV	25414	304-728-3215	728-1957
Web: www.jeffersoncountywv.org					
Jefferson County 214 W Main St	Dandridge	TN	37725	865-397-2935	397-3839
Web: www.jefferson-tn-chamber.org					
Jefferson County 411 4th St	Fairbury	NE	68352	402-729-2323	729-2016
Web: www.co.jefferson.ne.us					
Jefferson County 51 E Briggs Ave	Fairfield	IA	52556	641-472-2840	
Web: www.jeffersoniowa.com					
Jefferson County PO Box 145	Fayette	MS	39069	601-786-3021	786-6009
Jefferson County 100 Jefferson County Pkwy	Golden	CO	80419	303-271-8106	271-8197
Web: www.jeffco.us					
Jefferson County 729 Maple St	Hillsboro	MO	63050	636-797-5478	797-5360
Web: www.jeffcomo.org					
Jefferson County 320 S Main St Rm 109	Jefferson	WI	53549	920-674-7140	674-7368
Web: www.co.jefferson.wi.us					
Jefferson County 217 E Broad St	Louisville	GA	30434	478-625-3332	625-4007
Web: www.jeffersoncounty.org					
Jefferson County 300 E Main St Courthouse Rm 203	Madison	IN	47250	812-265-8922	265-8950
Web: www.madisonindiana.org					
Jefferson County 66 SE 'D' St Suite C	Madras	OR	97741	541-475-4451	325-5018
Jefferson County 1456 S Jefferson Hwy	Monticello	FL	32344	850-342-0218	342-0222
Web: www.co.jefferson.fl.us					
Jefferson County 100 S 10th St County Courthouse	Mount Vernon	IL	62864	618-244-8000	244-8111
Jefferson County 300 Jefferson St PO Box 321	Oskaloosa	KS	66066	785-863-2272	863-3135
Web: www.jfcountyks.com					
Jefferson County PO Box 6317	Pine Bluff	AR	71611	870-541-5322	541-5324
Web: www.jeffersoncountyark.com					
Jefferson County 1820 Jefferson St	Port Townsend	WA	98368	360-385-9100	385-9382
Web: www.co.jefferson.wa.us					
Jefferson County 210 Courthouse Way Suite 100	Rigby	ID	83442	208-745-7756	745-9397
Web: www.co.jefferson.id.us					
Jefferson County 301 Market St Courthouse	Steubenville	OH	43952	740-283-8500	283-8599
Web: www.jeffersoncountyoh.com					
Jefferson County 175 Arsenal St	Watertown	NY	13601	315-785-3081	785-5145
Web: www.co.jefferson.ny.us					
Jefferson County 220 N Main St Rm 103	Waurika	OK	73573	580-228-2029	228-3608
Jefferson Davis County PO Box 1137	Prentiss	MS	39474	601-792-4204	792-2894
Jefferson Davis Parish 300 State St # 106	Jennings	LA	70546	337-824-8340	
Web: www.jeffdavis.org					
Jefferson Parish 200 Derbigny St # 3100	Gretna	LA	70053	504-364-2600	
Web: www.jeffparish.net					
Jenkins County 611 Winthrop Ave	Millen	GA	30442	478-982-2563	982-4750
Web: www.jenkinscountyga.com					
Jennings County 25 N Pike St	Vernon	IN	47282	812-352-3070	352-3076
Web: www.jenningsco.org					
Jerauld County PO Box 435	Wessington Springs	SD	57382	605-539-1202	539-1203
Jerome County 300 N Lincoln Ave Rm 301	Jerome	ID	83338	208-644-2704	644-2709
Web: www.co.jerome.id.us					
Jersey County 200 N Lafayette St Suite 1	Jerseyville	IL	62052	618-498-5571	498-7721
Web: www.jerseycounty.org					
Jessamine County 101 N Main St	Nicholasville	KY	40356	859-885-4161	885-5837
Web: www.jessamineco.com					
Jewell County 307 N Commercial St	Mankato	KS	66956	785-378-4020	378-4075
Jim Hogg County PO Box 878	Hebbronville	TX	78361	361-527-4031	527-5843
Jim Wells County PO Box 1459	Alice	TX	78333	361-668-5702	
Web: www.co.jim-wells.tx.us					

	City	State	Zip	Phone	Fax
Jo Daviess County 330 N Bench St	Galena	IL	61036	815-777-0161	777-3688
Web: www.jodaviess.org					
Johnson County 76 N Main St	Buffalo	WY	82834	307-684-7272	684-2708
Web: www.johnsoncountywyoming.org					
Johnson County 215 Main St	Clarksville	AR	72830	479-754-2175	
Web: local.arkansas.gov					
Johnson County 204 S Buffalo Ave	Cleburne	TX	76033	817-556-6323	556-6327
Web: www.johnsoncountytx.org					
Johnson County 5 E Jefferson St PO Box 368	Franklin	IN	46131	317-736-3708	736-3749
Web: www.co.johnson.in.us					
Johnson County 913 S Dubuque St Suite 201	Iowa City	IA	52240	319-356-6000	356-6036
Web: www.jacksoncountyiowa.com					
Johnson County 222 W Main St	Mountain City	TN	37683	423-727-9633	727-7047
Web: www.johnsoncountytn.org					
Johnson County 111 S Cherry St Suite 1200	Olathe	KS	66061	913-715-0775	715-0800
Web: www.jocoks.com					
Johnson County 230 Ct St	Paintsville	KY	41240	606-789-2557	789-2559
Johnson County 351 Broadway	Tecumseh	NE	68450	402-335-6300	335-6311
Web: www.co.johnson.ne.us					
Johnson County PO Box 96	Vienna	IL	62995	618-658-3611	658-2908
Johnson County					
300 N Holden St County Courthouse	Warrensburg	MO	64093	660-747-6161	747-9332
Web: www.jaspercounty.org					
Johnson County PO Box 321	Wrightsville	GA	31096	478-864-3484	864-1343
Johnston County PO Box 297	Smithfield	NC	27577	919-934-3191	934-5857
Johnston County 403 W Main St	Tishomingo	OK	73460	580-371-3058	371-2174
Jones County PO Box 19	Anamosa	IA	52205	319-462-4341	462-5827
Web: www.co.jones.ia.us					
Jones County PO Box 552	Anson	TX	79501	325-823-3762	823-4223
Web: www.co.jones.tx.us					
Jones County PO Box 1359	Gray	GA	31032	478-986-6405	986-9682
Web: www.jonescounty.org					
Jones County 415 N 5th Ave	Laurel	MS	39440	601-428-0527	428-3610
Web: www.edajones.com					
Jones County PO Box 448	Murdo	SD	57559	605-669-2361	669-2641
Jones County 101 Market St	Trenton	NC	28585	252-448-7351	448-1607
Web: www.co.jones.nc.us					
Josephine County 500 NW 6th St	Grants Pass	OR	97526	541-474-5240	474-5246
Web: www.co.josephine.or.us					
Juab County 160 N Main St	Nephi	UT	84648	435-623-3410	623-5936
Web: www.co.juab.ut.us					
Judith Basin County 11 3rd St NW PO Box 307	Stanford	MT	59479	406-566-2277	566-2211
Web: co.judith-basin.mt.us					
Juneau City & Borough 155 S Seward St	Juneau	AK	99801	907-586-5278	586-5385
Web: www.juneau.org					
Juneau County 220 E State St	Mauston	WI	53948	608-847-9300	847-9402
Web: www.juneaucounty.com					
Juniata County 498 Jefferson St	Mifflintown	PA	17059	717-436-7715	436-7734
Web: www.co.juniata.pa.us					
Kalamazoo County 201 W Kalamazoo Ave	Kalamazoo	MI	49007	269-383-8840	384-8143
Web: www.kalcounty.com					
Kalkaska County PO Box 10	Kalkaska	MI	49646	231-258-3300	258-3337
Web: www.kalkaskami.com					
Kanabec County 18 N Vine St	Mora	MN	55051	320-679-6466	679-6431
Web: www.kanabeccounty.org					
Kanawha County 409 Virginia St E	Charleston	WV	25301	304-357-0130	357-0585
Web: www.kanawha.us					
Kandiyohi County PO Box 936	Willmar	MN	56201	320-231-6202	231-6263
Web: www.co.kandiyohi.mn.us					
Kane County 719 Batavia Ave Bldg A	Geneva	IL	60134	630-232-5930	232-9188
Web: www.countyofkane.org					
Kane County 78 S 100 E	Kanab	UT	84741	435-644-5033	644-2052
TF: 800-733-5263 ■ *Web:* www.kaneutah.com					
Kankakee County 189 E Ct St	Kankakee	IL	60901	815-937-2990	939-8831
Web: www.co.kankakee.il.us					
Karnes County					
101 N Panna Maria Ave Suite 9	Karnes City	TX	78118	830-780-3938	780-4576
Web: www.co.karnes.tx.us					
Kauai County 4386 Rice St Suite 101	Lihue	HI	96766	808-241-4800	241-6207
Web: www.kauai.gov					
Kaufman County 100 W Mulberry St	Kaufman	TX	75142	972-932-4331	932-8018
Web: www.kaufmancounty.net					
Kay County 201 S Main St	Newkirk	OK	74647	580-362-2537	362-3300
Web: www.courthouse.kay.ok.us					
Kearney County 424 N Colorado Ave	Minden	NE	68959	308-832-2723	832-2729
Web: www.kearneycounty.ne.gov					
Kearny County PO Box 86	Lakin	KS	67860	620-355-6422	355-7382
Web: www.kearnycountykansas.com					
Keith County 511 N Spruce St Suite 102	Ogallala	NE	69153	308-284-4726	284-6277
Web: www.co.keith.ne.us					
Kemper County PO Box 188	De Kalb	MS	39328	601-743-2460	743-2789
Kenai Peninsula Borough 144 N Binkley St	Soldotna	AK	99669	907-262-4441	262-8615
Web: www.borough.kenai.ak.us					
Kendall County 201 E San Antonio St	Boerne	TX	78006	830-249-9343	249-1763
Web: www.co.kendall.tx.us					
Kendall County 111 W Fox St	Yorkville	IL	60560	630-553-4104	553-4119
Web: www.co.kendall.il.us					
Kenedy County PO Box 227	Sarita	TX	78385	361-294-5220	294-5218
Kennebec County 125 State St	Augusta	ME	04330	207-622-0971	623-4083
Web: www.kennebeccounty.org					
Kenosha County 1010 56th St	Kenosha	WI	53140	262-653-2552	653-2564
Web: www.co.kenosha.wi.us					
Kent County 400 High St	Chestertown	MD	21620	410-778-7435	778-7482
Web: www.kentcounty.com					
Kent County 555 S Bay Rd	Dover	DE	19901	302-744-2305	736-2279
Web: www.co.kent.de.us					
Kent County 300 Monroe Ave NW	Grand Rapids	MI	49503	616-632-7640	632-7645
Web: www.accesskent.com					
Kent County PO Box 9	Jayton	TX	79528	806-237-3881	237-2632
Web: www.co.kent.tx.us					
Kenton County 303 Ct St	Covington	KY	41011	859-392-1600	392-1639
Web: www.kentoncounty.org					

	City	State	Zip	Phone	Fax
Keokuk County 101 S Main St	Sigourney	IA	52591	641-622-2210	622-2171
Web: www.keokukcountyia.com					
Kern County 1115 Truxtun Ave 5th Fl	Bakersfield	CA	93301	661-868-3198	868-3190
Web: www.co.kern.ca.us					
Kerr County 700 Main St Rm 122	Kerrville	TX	78028	830-792-2255	792-2274
Web: www.kerrcounty.org					
Kershaw County 1121 Broad St Rm 202	Camden	SC	29020	803-425-1500	425-6044
Web: www.kershawcountysc.org					
Ketchikan Gateway Borough					
1900 1st Ave Suite 115	Ketchikan	AK	99901	907-228-6604	247-8439
Web: www.borough.ketchikan.ak.us					
Kewaunee County 613 Dodge St	Kewaunee	WI	54216	920-388-7144	388-3199
Web: www.kewauneeco.org					
Keweenaw County 5095 4th St	Eagle River	MI	49950	906-337-2229	337-2795
Web: www.keweenaw.org					
Keya Paha County PO Box 349	Springview	NE	68778	402-497-3791	497-3799
Web: www.co.keya-paha.ne.us					
Kidder County					
120 E Broadway Kidder County Courthouse	Steele	ND	58482	701-475-2632	475-2202
Kimball County 114 E 3rd St	Kimball	NE	69145	308-235-2241	235-3654
Web: www.co.kimball.ne.us					
Kimble County 501 Main St Courthouse	Junction	TX	76849	325-446-3353	446-2986
Web: www.co.kimble.tx.us					
King & Queen County					
242 Allens Cir Suite L					
PO Box 177	King & Queen Court House	VA	23085	804-785-5975	785-5999
Web: www.kingandqueenco.net					
King County PO Box 135	Guthrie	TX	79236	806-596-4412	596-4664
King County 701 5th Ave Suite 3210	Seattle	WA	98104	206-296-4040	296-0194
TF: 800-325-6165 ■ *Web:* www.metrokc.gov					
King George County 9483 Kings Hwy Suite 3	King George	VA	22485	540-775-3322	775-5466
Web: www.king-george.va.us					
King William County PO Box 215	King William	VA	23086	804-769-4927	769-4964
Web: www.co.king-william.va.us					
Kingfisher County 101 S Main St Rm 3	Kingfisher	OK	73750	405-375-3887	375-6033
Kingman County 130 N Spruce St	Kingman	KS	67068	620-532-2521	532-2037
Kings County 360 Adams St Rm 189	Brooklyn	NY	11201	347-404-9772	
Web: www.nycourts.gov/courts/2jd/kingsclerk/index.shtml					
Kings County 680 Campus Dr	Hanford	CA	93230	559-582-3211	582-6639
Web: www.co.kings.ca.us					
Kingsbury County PO Box 176	De Smet	SD	57231	605-854-3811	854-9080
Kinney County PO Box 9	Brackettville	TX	78832	830-563-2521	563-2644
Web: www.co.kinney.tx.us					
Kiowa County 1305 Goff	Eads	CO	81036	719-438-5421	438-5327
Web: www.kiowacountycolo.com					
Kiowa County 211 E Florida Ave	Greensburg	KS	67054	620-723-3366	723-3234
Kiowa County PO Box 73	Hobart	OK	73651	580-726-5286	726-6033
Kit Carson County 251 16th St # 103	Burlington	CO	80807	719-346-8638	346-7242
Web: www.kitcarsoncounty.org					
Kitsap County 614 Division St MS 4	Port Orchard	WA	98366	360-337-7146	337-4632
Web: www.kitsapgov.com					
Kittitas County 205 W 5th Ave Suite 108	Ellensburg	WA	98926	509-962-7508	962-7679
Web: www.co.kittitas.wa.us					
Kittson County 410 5th St SE # 214	Hallock	MN	56728	218-843-2655	843-2656
Web: www.visitnwminnesota.com					
Klamath County 305 Main St	Klamath Falls	OR	97601	541-883-5134	883-5165
TF: 800-377-6094 ■ *Web:* www.klamathcounty.org					
Kleberg County PO Box 1327	Kingsville	TX	78364	361-595-8548	593-1355
Web: www.co.kleberg.tx.us					
Klickitat County					
205 S Columbus Ave Rm 204 MS CH3	Goldendale	WA	98620	509-773-5744	773-4559
Web: www.klickitatcounty.org					
Knott County PO Box 446	Hindman	KY	41822	606-785-5651	785-0996
Knox County 401 Ct Sq # 6	Barbourville	KY	40906	606-546-8915	546-6196
Knox County PO Box 196 Courthouse 1st Fl	Benjamin	TX	79505	940-459-2441	459-2005
Web: www.knoxcountytexas.com					
Knox County 206 Main St	Center	NE	68724	402-288-5604	288-5605
Web: www.co.knox.ne.us					
Knox County 107 N 4th St	Edina	MO	63537	660-397-2184	397-3331
Knox County 200 S Cherry St	Galesburg	IL	61401	309-343-3121	345-0098
Web: www.knoxcountyil.com					
Knox County 400 W Main St # 603	Knoxville	TN	37902	865-215-2534	215-2038
Web: www.knoxcounty.org					
Knox County 117 E High St Suite 161	Mount Vernon	OH	43050	740-393-6703	393-6705
Web: www.knoxcountyohio.org					
Knox County 62 Union St	Rockland	ME	04841	207-594-0420	594-0443
Web: www.knoxcounty.midcoast.com					
Knox County 101 N 7th St	Vincennes	IN	47591	812-885-2521	895-4929
Kodiak Island Borough 710 Mill Bay Rd	Kodiak	AK	99615	907-486-9311	486-9391
Web: www.kib.co.kodiak.ak.us					
Koochiching County 715 4th St	International Falls	MN	56649	218-283-1152	283-1151
Web: www.co.koochiching.mn.us					
Kootenai County 451 N Government Way	Coeur d'Alene	ID	83814	208-446-1000	446-1188
Web: www.co.kootenai.id.us					
Kosciusko County 121 N Lake St	Warsaw	IN	46580	574-372-2331	372-2338
Web: www.kcgov.com					
Kossuth County 114 W State St	Algona	IA	50511	515-295-2718	295-3071
Web: www.co.kossuth.ia.us					
La Crosse County 400 N 4th St Rm 1210	La Crosse	WI	54601	608-785-9581	785-9741
Web: www.co.la-crosse.wi.us					
La Paz County 1108 S Joshua Ave	Parker	AZ	85344	928-669-6115	669-9709
Web: www.co.la-paz.az.us					
La Plata County 1060 E 2nd Ave Suite 134	Durango	CO	81301	970-382-6280	382-6285
Web: www.co.laplata.co.us					
La Porte County 813 Lincolnway	La Porte	IN	46350	216-326-6808	326-5615
Web: www.alco.org					
La Salle County 100 N Stewart	Cotulla	TX	78014	830-879-3033	879-2933
Web: www.lasallecountytx.org					
Labette County 501 Merchant St	Oswego	KS	67356	620-795-2138	795-2928
Web: www.labettecounty.com					
Lac qui Parle County (LQP) 600 6th St	Madison	MN	56256	320-598-7444	598-3125
Web: www.lqpco.com					

Name / Address	City	State	Zip	Phone	Fax
Lackawanna County 436 Spruce St	Scranton	PA	18503	570-963-6723	963-6387
Web: www.lackawannacounty.org					
Laclede County 200 N Adams Ave	Lebanon	MO	65536	417-532-5471	588-9288
Web: www.lacledecountymissouri.org					
Lafayette Consolidated Government 705 W University Ave PO Box 4017-C	Lafayette	LA	70506	337-291-8200	291-6392
Web: www.lafayettegov.org					
Lafayette County 626 Main St PO Box 40	Darlington	WI	53530	608-776-4850	776-8893
Web: www.co.lafayette.wi.gov					
Lafayette County 1 Courthouse Sq	Lewisville	AR	71845	870-921-4858	921-4505
Lafayette County 1001 Main St	Lexington	MO	64067	660-259-4315	259-6109
Web: www.lafayettecountymo.com					
Lafayette County 300 N Lamar Blvd # 100	Oxford	MS	38655	662-234-7563	234-5038
Web: www.oxfordms.com					
Lafourche Parish 402 Green St	Thibodaux	LA	70301	985-446-8427	446-8459
Web: www.lapage.com					
LaGrange County 105 N Detroit St	LaGrange	IN	46761	260-499-6368	463-2187
Web: www.lagrangecounty.com					
Lake & Peninsula Borough PO Box 495	King Salmon	AK	99613	907-246-3421	246-6602
Lake County 800 10th St Suite 200	Baldwin	MI	49304	231-745-2725	745-8632
Web: www.lakecountymichigan.com					
Lake County 2293 N Main St	Crown Point	IN	46307	219-755-3440	755-3447
Web: www.lakecountyin.org					
Lake County 255 N Forbes St	Lakeport	CA	95453	707-263-2371	263-2207
Web: www.co.lake.ca.us					
Lake County 513 Ctr St	Lakeview	OR	97630	541-947-6006	947-6015
Web: www.lakecountyor.org					
Lake County PO Box 917	Leadville	CO	80461	719-486-1410	486-3972
Lake County 200 E Ctr St	Madison	SD	57042	605-256-5644	256-5080
Lake County 25 N Pk Pl	Painesville	OH	44077	440-350-2500	
Web: www.lakecountyohio.org					
Lake County 106 4th Ave E	Polson	MT	59860	406-883-7208	883-7283
Web: www.lakecounty-mt.org					
Lake County 550 W Main St	Tavares	FL	32778	352-742-4102	742-4110
Web: www.lakecountyclerk.org					
Lake County 116 S Ct St	Tiptonville	TN	38079	731-253-7582	253-6815
Lake County 601 3rd Ave	Two Harbors	MN	55616	218-834-8300	834-8360
Web: www.co.lake.mn.us					
Lake County 18 N County St	Waukegan	IL	60085	847-377-2000	
Web: www.co.lake.il.us					
Lake of the Woods County 206 8th Ave SE	Baudette	MN	56623	218-634-2836	634-2509
Web: www.co.lake-of-the-woods.mn.us					
Lamar County 229 Roberta Dr	Barnesville	GA	30204	770-358-5146	358-5149
Web: www.barnesville.org					
Lamar County 119 N Main St Rm 109	Paris	TX	75460	903-737-2420	782-1000
Web: www.dryelf.com					
Lamar County 403 Main St PO Box 247	Purvis	MS	39475	601-794-3406	794-1049
Web: www.lamarcounty.com					
Lamar County PO Box 338	Vernon	AL	35592	205-695-7333	695-8522
Lamb County 100 6th St Rm 103	Littlefield	TX	79339	806-385-4222	385-6485
Lamoille County PO Box 490	Hyde Park	VT	05655	802-888-2207	
Web: www.lamoilleeconomy.org					
LaMoure County PO Box 128	La Moure	ND	58458	701-883-5301	883-4240
Web: www.lamoco.drtel.net					
Lampasas County 409 Pecan St PO Box 347	Lampasas	TX	76550	512-556-8271	556-8270
Web: www.co.lampasas.tx.us					
Lancaster County 50 N Duke St	Lancaster	PA	17602	717-299-8000	293-7208
Web: www.co.lancaster.pa.us					
Lancaster County PO Box 1809	Lancaster	SC	29721	803-285-1581	416-9388
Web: www.lancastercountysc.net					
Lancaster County PO Box 99	Lancaster	VA	22503	804-462-5611	462-9978
Web: www.lancova.com					
Lancaster County 555 S 10th St Rm 108	Lincoln	NE	68508	402-441-7481	441-8728
Web: www.lancaster.ne.gov					
Lander County 315 S Humboldt St	Battle Mountain	NV	89820	775-635-5738	635-5761
Web: www.landercounty.org					
Lane County PO Box 788	Dighton	KS	67839	620-397-5356	397-5419
Lane County 125 E 8th Ave	Eugene	OR	97401	541-682-4203	682-4616
Web: www.co.lane.or.us					
Langlade County 800 Clermont St	Antigo	WI	54409	715-627-6200	627-6303
Web: www.co.langlade.wi.us					
Lanier County 56 W Main St # 9	Lakeland	GA	31635	229-482-2088	482-8187
Lapeer County 255 Clay St	Lapeer	MI	48446	810-667-0356	667-0362
Web: www.county.lapeer.org					
Laramie County 309 W 20th St	Cheyenne	WY	82001	307-633-4264	633-4240
Web: www.webgate.co.laramie.wy.us					
Larimer County 1 Old Town Sq	Fort Collins	CO	80524	970-498-7860	498-7906
Web: www.larimer.org					
LaRue County 209 W High St	Hodgenville	KY	42748	270-358-3544	358-4528
Web: www.laruecounty.org					
Las Animas County PO Box 115	Trinidad	CO	81082	719-846-3314	845-2573
LaSalle County 707 E Etna Rd	Ottawa	IL	61350	815-434-8205	434-8319
Web: www.lasallecounty.org					
LaSalle Parish PO Box 1288	Jena	LA	71342	318-992-2101	992-2103
Lassen County 220 S Lassen St Suite 5	Susanville	CA	96130	530-251-8217	257-3480
Web: www.co.lassen.ca.us					
Latah County 522 S Adams St PO Box 8068	Moscow	ID	83843	208-882-8580	883-7203
Web: www.latah.id.us					
Latimer County 109 N Central St	Wilburton	OK	74578	918-465-2021	465-3736
Lauderdale County 200 S Ct St # 303	Florence	AL	35630	256-760-5750	760-5703
Web: www.lauderdalecountyonline.com					
Lauderdale County 410 Constitution Ave 11th Fl	Meridian	MS	39301	601-482-9746	482-9744
Web: www.lauderdalecounty.org					
Lauderdale County 100 Ct Sq	Ripley	TN	38063	731-635-2561	635-9682
Laurel County 101 S Main St Rm 203	London	KY	40741	606-864-5158	864-7369
Laurens County 117 E Jackson St	Dublin	GA	31040	478-272-4755	272-3895
Web: www.co.laurens.ga.us					
Laurens County 100 Hillcrest Sq # B	Laurens	SC	29360	864-984-3538	984-3726
Web: www.laurenscountysc.org					
Lavaca County 412 N Texana	Hallettsville	TX	77964	361-798-3612	798-1610
Web: www.co.lavaca.tx.us					
Lawrence County 916 15th St Rm 31	Bedford	IN	47421	812-275-7543	277-2024
Web: www.bedfordonline.com					
Lawrence County 90 Sherman St	Deadwood	SD	57732	605-578-1941	578-1065*
**Fax:* Acctg ■ *Web:* www.lawrence.sd.us					
Lawrence County 111 S 4th St # 11	Ironton	OH	45638	740-533-4355	533-4383
Web: www.lawrencecountyohio.org					
Lawrence County 240 W Gaines St	Lawrenceburg	TN	38464	931-762-7700	766-2291
Web: www.co.lawrence.tn.us					
Lawrence County 1100 State St County Courthouse	Lawrenceville	IL	62439	618-943-2346	943-5205
Web: www.lawrencecountyillinois.com					
Lawrence County 122 S Main Cross St	Louisa	KY	41230	606-638-4102	638-0618
Web: www.lawrencekentucky.com					
Lawrence County PO Box 821	Monticello	MS	39654	601-587-7162	587-0750
Lawrence County PO Box 307	Moulton	AL	35650	256-974-0663	974-2403
Web: www.naiap.com					
Lawrence County 1 Courthouse Sq Suite 101	Mount Vernon	MO	65712	417-466-2638	466-4348
Lawrence County County Courthouse 430 Court St	New Castle	PA	16101	724-658-2541	652-9646
TF: 855-564-6116 ■ *Web:* www.co.lawrence.pa.us					
Lawrence County PO Box 526	Walnut Ridge	AR	72476	870-886-1111	886-1122
Le Sueur County 88 S Pk Ave	Le Center	MN	56057	507-357-2251	357-6433
Web: www.co.le-sueur.mn.us					
Lea County 100 N Main St Suite 11	Lovington	NM	88260	575-396-8619	396-3293
Web: www.leacounty.net					
Leake County PO Box 72	Carthage	MS	39051	601-267-7371	267-6137
Web: www.leakems.com					
Leavenworth County 300 Walnut St Suite 106	Leavenworth	KS	66048	913-684-0421	684-0406
Web: www.leavenworthcounty.org					
Lebanon County 400 S 8th St Rms 102 Municipal Bldg	Lebanon	PA	17042	717-228-4419	228-4467
Web: www.lebcounty.org					
Lee County PO Box 551	Beattyville	KY	41311	606-464-4115	464-4102
Lee County PO Box 387	Bishopville	SC	29010	803-484-5341	484-1632
Lee County 112 E 2nd St PO Box 329	Dixon	IL	61021	815-288-3309	288-6492
Web: www.countyoflee.org					
Lee County 933 Ave H	Fort Madison	IA	52627	319-372-6557	372-8200
Web: www.leecounty.org					
Lee County PO Box 398	Fort Myers	FL	33902	239-533-2259	485-2143
Web: www.lee-county.com					
Lee County PO Box 419	Giddings	TX	78942	979-542-3684	542-2623
Web: www.co.lee.tx.us					
Lee County PO Box 417	Pennington Gap	VA	24277	276-337-9277	346-7712
Web: www.leecountyvachamber.org					
Lee County 104 Leslie Hwy PO Box 889	Leesburg	GA	31763	229-759-6000	759-6050
Web: www.lee.ga.us					
Lee County 15 E Chestnut St	Marianna	AR	72360	870-295-7715	295-7783
Lee County PO Box 666	Opelika	AL	36803	334-745-9767	742-9478
Lee County PO Box 4209	Sanford	NC	27331	919-708-4400	775-3483
Web: www.leecountync.com					
Lee County 200 W Jefferson St	Tupelo	MS	38804	662-841-9100	680-6091
Web: www.leecoms.com					
Leelanau County 8527 E Government Ctr Dr Suite 103	Suttons Bay	MI	49682	231-256-9824	256-8295
Web: www.leelanaucounty.com					
LeFlore County PO Box 218	Poteau	OK	74953	918-647-5738	647-8930
Leflore County 306 W Market St	Greenwood	MS	38930	662-453-1435	455-1278
Lehigh County 455 W Hamilton St Rm 132	Allentown	PA	18101	610-782-3148	770-3840
Web: www.lehighcounty.org					
Lemhi County 206 Courthouse Dr	Salmon	ID	83467	208-756-2815	756-8424
Web: www.lemhicountyidaho.org					
Lenawee County 425 N Main St 3rd Fl Judicial Bldg	Adrian	MI	49221	517-264-4599	264-4790
Web: www.lenawee.mi.us					
Lenoir County 130 S Queen St PO Box 3289	Kinston	NC	28502	252-559-6450	559-6454
Web: www.co.lenoir.nc.us					
Leon County PO Box 98	Centerville	TX	75833	903-536-2352	
Web: www.co.leon.tx.us					
Leon County 301 S Monroe St 5th Fl	Tallahassee	FL	32301	850-606-5302	606-5303
Web: www.co.leon.fl.us					
Leslie County 22010 Main St	Hyden	KY	41749	606-672-3200	672-7373
Web: www.lesliecounty.net					
Letcher County 156 Main St Suite 102	Whitesburg	KY	41858	606-633-2432	632-9282
Web: www.letchercounty.ky.gov					
Levy County 355 S Court St PO Box 310	Bronson	FL	32621	352-486-5218	486-5167
Web: www.levycounty.org					
Lewis & Clark County 316 N Pk Ave	Helena	MT	59623	406-447-8200	447-8370
Web: www.co.lewis-clark.mt.us					
Lewis County 360 NW N St	Chehalis	WA	98532	360-748-9121	748-1639
Web: www.fortress.wa.gov					
Lewis County 110 N Pk St Rm 108	Hohenwald	TN	38462	931-796-3378	796-6010
Web: www.lewisedc.org					
Lewis County 7660 N State St	Lowville	NY	13367	315-376-5333	376-3768
Web: www.lewiscountyny.org					
Lewis County 100 Lafayette St	Monticello	MO	63457	573-767-5205	767-8245
Lewis County 510 Oak St Rm 1	Nezperce	ID	83543	208-937-2251	937-9233
Web: www.lewiscountyid.org					
Lewis County 112 Second St # 201	Vanceburg	KY	41179	606-796-2722	796-0822
Lewis County 499 US Hwy 33 E Suite 102	Weston	WV	26452	304-269-7328	269-8202
TF: 800-296-7329 ■ *Web:* www.stonewallcountry.com					
Lexington (Independent City) 300 E Washington St	Lexington	VA	24450	540-462-3700	463-5310
Web: www.ci.lexington.va.us					
Lexington County 205 E Main St County Courthouse	Lexington	SC	29072	803-785-8212	785-8314
Web: www.co.lexington.sc.us					
Lexington-Fayette County 162 E Main St	Lexington	KY	40507	859-253-3344	231-9619
Web: www.lfucg.com					
Liberty County 10818 NW State Rd 20	Bristol	FL	32321	850-643-5404	643-2866
Web: www.libertycountyflorida.com					

	City	State	ZIP	Phone	Fax
Liberty County 316 N Park Ave Rm 304	Helena	MT	59623	406-447-8304	447-8370
Web: www.co.lewis-clark.mt.us					
Liberty County 112 N Main St	Hinesville	GA	31310	912-876-2164	369-0204
Web: www.libertycounty.org					
Liberty County 1923 Sam Houston St	Liberty	TX	77575	936-336-4600	336-4640
Web: www.co.liberty.tx.us					
Licking County 20 S 2nd St	Newark	OH	43055	740-670-5110	670-5119
Web: www.lcounty.com					
Limestone County 310 W Washington St	Athens	AL	35611	256-233-6400	233-6403
Web: www.limestonecounty.al.gov					
Limestone County PO Box 350	Groesbeck	TX	76642	254-729-5504	729-2951
Web: www.co.limestone.tx.us					
Lincoln County PO Box 555 County Courthouse	Brookhaven	MS	39602	601-835-3479	835-3423
Lincoln County 104 N Main St	Canton	SD	57013	605-764-2581	764-0134*
*Fax: Acctg ■ *Web:* www.lincolncountysd.org					
Lincoln County 300 Central Ave	Carrizozo	NM	88301	505-648-2394	648-2381*
*Fax Area Code: 575 ■ *TF:* 800-687-2705 ■ *Web:* www.lincolncountynm.net					
Lincoln County 811 Manuel St Suite 5	Chandler	OK	74834	405-258-1264	258-0439
Lincoln County 450 Logan St	Davenport	WA	99122	509-725-1401	725-1150
Web: www.co.lincoln.wa.us					
Lincoln County 112 Main St S	Fayetteville	TN	37334	931-433-2454	433-9304
Web: www.vallnet.com					
Lincoln County PO Box 497	Hamlin	WV	25523	304-824-7990	824-2444
Web: www.co.lincoln.wv.us					
Lincoln County 103 3rd Ave	Hugo	CO	80821	719-743-2444	743-2524
Web: www.lincolncountyco.us					
Lincoln County 319 N Rebecca St	Ivanhoe	MN	56142	507-694-1529	694-1198*
*Fax: Acctg ■ *Web:* www.co.lincoln.mn.us					
Lincoln County PO Box 670	Kemmerer	WY	83101	307-877-9056	877-3101
Web: www.lcwy.org					
Lincoln County 512 California Ave	Libby	MT	59923	406-293-7781	293-8577
Web: www.lincolncountymt.us					
Lincoln County 216 E Lincoln Ave	Lincoln	KS	67455	785-524-4757	524-5008
Web: www.lincolncoks.com					
Lincoln County 210 Humphrey St	Lincolnton	GA	30817	706-359-4444	359-4729
Web: www.lincolncountyga.com					
Lincoln County 115 W Main St	Lincolnton	NC	28092	704-736-8471	736-8718
Web: www.co.lincoln.nc.us					
Lincoln County 1110 E Main St	Merrill	WI	54452	715-536-0312	536-6528
Web: www.co.lincoln.wi.us					
Lincoln County 225 W Olive St Rm 201	Newport	OR	97365	541-265-4131	265-4950
Web: www.co.lincoln.or.us					
Lincoln County 301 N Jeffers St	North Platte	NE	69101	308-534-4350	535-3527
Web: www.co.lincoln.ne.us					
Lincoln County PO Box 90	Pioche	NV	89043	775-962-5390	962-5180
Web: www.co.lincoln.nv.us					
Lincoln County 111 W 'B' St Suite C	Shoshone	ID	83352	208-886-7641	886-2798
Lincoln County 102 E Main St County Courthouse	Stanford	KY	40484	606-365-4570	365-4572
Web: www.lincolnky.com					
Lincoln County 300 S Drew St	Star City	AR	71667	870-628-5114	628-5794
Lincoln County 201 Main St	Troy	MO	63379	636-528-6300	528-5528
Web: www.lcmo.us					
Lincoln County PO Box 249	Wiscasset	ME	04578	207-882-6311	882-4320
Web: www.lincolncountymain.me					
Lincoln Parish 100 W Texas Ave	Ruston	LA	71270	318-251-5150	251-5149
Web: www.lincolnparish.org					
Linn County 300 4th Ave SW	Albany	OR	97321	541-967-3831	926-5109
Web: www.co.linn.or.us					
Linn County 123 5th St SE	Cedar Rapids	IA	52401	319-892-5005	892-5009
Web: www.linncounty.org					
Linn County 108 N High St	Linneus	MO	64653	660-895-5417	895-5527
Linn County PO Box 350	Mound City	KS	66056	913-795-2660	795-2004
Web: www.linncountyks.com					
Lipscomb County 1 Courthouse Sq PO Box 70	Lipscomb	TX	79056	806-862-3091	862-3004
Web: www.co.lipscomb.tx.us					
Litchfield County 15 W St	Litchfield	CT	06759	860-567-0885	567-4779
Web: www.litchfieldcty.com					
Little River County 351 N 2nd St	Ashdown	AR	71822	870-898-7208	898-2860
Live Oak County PO Box 280	George West	TX	78022	361-449-2733	
Web: www.co.live-oak.tx.us					
Livingston County 6 Ct St Rm 201	Geneseo	NY	14454	585-243-7010	
Web: www.co.livingston.state.ny.us					
Livingston County 200 E Grand River Ave	Howell	MI	48843	517-546-0500	546-4354
Web: www.co.livingston.mi.us					
Livingston County 112 W Madison St	Pontiac	IL	61764	815-844-2006	842-1844
Web: www.livingstoncounty-il.org					
Livingston County 335 Ct St	Smithland	KY	42081	270-928-2162	928-2162
Web: www.livingstonco.ky.gov					
Livingston Parish 29261 S Frost Rd	Livingston	LA	70754	225-686-2266	686-7079
Web: www.lapage.com					
Llano County PO Box 40	Llano	TX	78643	325-247-4455	247-2406
Web: www.co.llano.tx.us					
Logan County 117 E Columbus St	Bellefontaine	OH	43311	937-599-7283	599-7268
Web: www.co.logan.oh.us					
Logan County 366 N Broadway Ave	Booneville	AR	72927	479-675-2951	675-2952
Logan County 301 E Harrison Ave Suite 102	Guthrie	OK	73044	405-282-0266	282-0267
Logan County 601 Broadway St PO Box 278	Lincoln	IL	62656	217-732-4148	732-6064
Web: www.co.logan.il.us					
Logan County 421 Main St	Logan	WV	25601	304-792-8600	792-8621
Web: www.logancountychamberofcommerce.com					
Logan County 301 Broadway St	Napoleon	ND	58561	701-754-2751	754-2270
Web: www.napoleonnd.com					
Logan County 710 W 2nd St	Oakley	KS	67748	785-672-4244	672-3341
Logan County 116 S Main St PO Box 358	Russellville	KY	42276	270-726-2206	726-2237
Web: www.loganchamber.com					
Logan County 317 Main St PO Box 8	Stapleton	NE	69163	308-636-2311	
Logan County 315 Main St	Sterling	CO	80751	970-522-0888	522-4018
Web: www.logancountyco.gov					
Long County 49 E McDonald St	Ludowici	GA	31316	912-545-2143	545-2150
Lonoke County 301 N Ctr St	Lonoke	AR	72086	501-676-2368	676-3038
Lorain County 225 Ct St	Elyria	OH	44035	440-329-5536	329-5404
Web: www.loraincounty.us					
Los Alamos County 2300 Trinity Dr Rm 230	Los Alamos	NM	87544	505-662-8080	662-8079
Web: www.lac-nm.us					
Los Angeles County 500 W Temple St	Los Angeles	CA	90012	213-974-1311	680-1122
Web: www.lacounty.info					
Loudon County 101 Mulberry St Suite 200	Loudon	TN	37774	865-458-2726	458-9891
Web: www.loudoncounty.org					
Loudoun County 1 Harrison St SE PO Box 7000	Leesburg	VA	20177	703-777-0200	777-0325
Web: www.loudoun.gov					
Louisa County 1 Woolfolk Ave	Louisa	VA	23093	540-967-0401	967-3411
Web: www.louisacounty.com					
Louisa County 117 S Main St	Wapello	IA	52653	319-523-4541	523-4542
Web: www.louisacountyiowa.org					
Louisville-Jefferson County 527 W Jefferson St	Louisville	KY	40202	502-574-5700	574-5784
Web: www.louisvilleky.gov					
Loup County 408 4th St PO Box 187	Taylor	NE	68879	308-942-3135	942-3103
Web: www.co.loup.ne.us					
Love County 405 W Main St Suite 203	Marietta	OK	73448	580-276-3059	
Loving County 100 Bell St PO Box 194	Mentone	TX	79754	432-377-2441	377-2701
Web: www.co.loving.tx.us					
Lowndes County 505 2nd Ave N	Columbus	MS	39701	662-329-5888	329-5881
Lowndes County PO Box 65	Hayneville	AL	36040	334-548-2331	548-5101
Lowndes County 325 W Savannah Ave	Valdosta	GA	31601	229-671-2400	245-5222
Web: www.lowndescounty.com					
Lubbock County 904 Broadway St Rm 207	Lubbock	TX	79401	806-775-1043	
Web: www.co.lubbock.tx.us					
Lucas County 916 Braden St	Chariton	IA	50049	641-774-4421	774-8669
Lucas County 1 Government Ctr Suite 800	Toledo	OH	43604	419-213-4500	213-4532
Web: www.co.lucas.oh.us					
Luce County 407 W Harrie St	Newberry	MI	49868	906-293-5521	293-0050
Lumpkin County 99 Courthouse Hill Suite A	Dahlonega	GA	30533	706-864-3742	864-4760
Web: www.lumpkincounty.gov					
Lunenburg County 11435 Courthouse Rd	Lunenburg	VA	23952	434-696-2230	696-3931
Web: www.lunenburgva.org					
Luzerne County 200 N River St	Wilkes-Barre	PA	18711	570-825-1500	825-9343
Web: www.luzernecounty.org					
Lycoming County 48 W 3rd St	Williamsport	PA	17701	570-327-2256	327-2505
Web: www.lyco.org					
Lyman County PO Box 38	Kennebec	SD	57544	605-869-2247	869-2203*
Lynchburg (Independent City) 900 Church St	Lynchburg	VA	24504	434-847-1443	847-1536
Web: www.lynchburgva.gov					
Lynn County PO Box 937	Tahoka	TX	79373	806-561-4750	561-4988
Web: www.co.lynn.tx.us					
Lyon County PO Box 310	Eddyville	KY	42038	270-388-2331	388-0634
Web: www.lyoncounty.ky.gov					
Lyon County 430 Commercial St	Emporia	KS	66801	620-341-3243	341-3415
Web: www.lyoncounty.org					
Lyon County 607 W Main St	Marshall	MN	56258	507-537-6728	537-6091*
*Fax: Acctg ■ *Web:* www.lyonco.org					
Lyon County 206 S 2nd Ave	Rock Rapids	IA	51246	712-472-8530	
Web: www.lyoncountyiowa.com					
Lyon County 27 S Main St	Yerington	NV	89447	775-463-6501	463-5305
Web: www.lyon-county.org					
Mackinac County 100 S Marley St	Saint Ignace	MI	49781	906-643-7300	643-7302
Web: www.mackinaccounty.net					
Macomb County 40 N Main St 1st Fl	Mount Clemens	MI	48043	586-469-5120	
Web: www.macombcountymi.gov					
Macon County 141 S Main St Rm 104	Decatur	IL	62523	217-424-1305	423-0922
Macon County 5 W Main St	Franklin	NC	28734	828-349-2025	349-2400
Web: www.maconnc.org					
Macon County 201 County Courthouse	Lafayette	TN	37083	615-666-2363	666-5323
Web: www.maconcountytn.com					
Macon County 102 Vine St PO Box 135	Macon	MO	63552	660-385-5627	385-3972
Web: www.maconcounty.org					
Macon County 121 S Sumter St	Oglethorpe	GA	31068	478-472-7021	472-5643
Web: www.maconcountyga.org					
Macon County 101 E Northside St Courthouse	Tuskegee	AL	36083	334-727-5120	724-2621
Macoupin County PO Box 107	Carlinville	IL	62626	217-854-3214	854-7347
Web: www.macoupincountyonline.net					
Madera County 200 W 4th St	Madera	CA	93637	559-675-7703	673-3302
Web: www.madera-county.com					
Madison County 16 E 9th St	Anderson	IN	46016	765-641-9419	648-1375
Web: www.madisoncty.com					
Madison County 146 W Ctr St	Canton	MS	39046	601-859-1177	859-5875
Web: www.madison-co.com					
Madison County 91 Albany Ave	Danielsville	GA	30633	706-795-5664	795-2997
Web: www.madisonco.us					
Madison County 157 N Main St Suite 109	Edwardsville	IL	62025	618-692-6290	692-8903
Web: www.co.madison.il.us					
Madison County 1 Courthouse Sq	Fredericktown	MO	63645	573-783-2176	783-5351
Madison County 100 Northside Sq	Huntsville	AL	35801	256-532-3492	532-6994
Web: www.co.madison.al.us					
Madison County 201 Main St	Huntsville	AR	72740	479-738-2747	738-2735
Madison County 100 E Main St Suite 105	Jackson	TN	38301	731-423-6022	424-4903
Web: www.co.madison.tn.us					
Madison County PO Box 618	London	OH	43140	740-852-2972	845-1660
Web: www.co.madison.oh.us					
Madison County PO Box 237	Madison	FL	32341	850-973-1500	973-2059
Web: www.madisonfl.org					
Madison County 1313 N Main St # 2	Madison	NE	68748	402-454-3311	454-6682
Web: www.co.madison.ne.us					
Madison County PO Box 373	Madison	VA	22727	540-948-4455	948-3759
Web: www.madison-va.com					
Madison County 101 W Main St Rm 102	Madisonville	TX	77864	936-348-2638	348-5858
Web: www.co.madison.tx.us					
Madison County PO Box 579	Marshall	NC	28753	828-649-2531	649-2829
Web: www.main.nc.us					
Madison County PO Box 389	Rexburg	ID	83440	208-356-3662	356-8396
Web: www.co.madison.id.us					
Madison County 101 W Main St	Richmond	KY	40475	859-624-4703	623-3071

Entry	City	State	ZIP	Phone	Fax
Madison County 100 Wallace St PO Box 185	Virginia City	MT	59755	406-843-4230	843-5207
Web: madison.mt.gov					
Madison County 138 N Court St Bldg 4 PO Box 668	Wampsville	NY	13163	315-366-2261	366-2615
Web: www.madisoncounty.org					
Madison County 112 N 1st St	Winterset	IA	50273	515-462-4451	462-9825
Web: www.madisoncounty.com					
Madison Parish PO Box 1710	Tallulah	LA	71282	318-574-0655	574-3961
Magoffin County PO Box 430	Salyersville	KY	41465	606-349-2313	349-2109
Mahaska County 106 S 1st St Mahaska Courthouse 2nd Fl	Oskaloosa	IA	52577	641-673-7786	672-1256
Web: www.mahaskacounty.org					
Mahnomen County PO Box 379	Mahnomen	MN	56557	218-935-5669	935-5946*
Mahoning County 120 Market St	Youngstown	OH	44503	330-740-2104	740-2105
Web: www.mahoningcountyoh.gov					
Major County 500 E Broadway	Fairview	OK	73737	580-227-4732	227-2736
Malheur County 251 B St W	Vale	OR	97918	541-473-5151	473-5523
Web: www.malheurco.org					
Manassas (Independent City) 9027 Ctr St	Manassas	VA	20110	703-257-8200	335-0042
Web: www.manassascity.org					
Manassas Park (Independent City) 1 Pk Ctr Ct	Manassas Park	VA	20111	703-335-8800	335-0053
Web: www.cityofmanassaspark.us					
Manatee County 1112 Manatee Ave W	Bradenton	FL	34205	941-748-4501	
Web: www.mymanatee.org					
Manistee County 415 3rd St	Manistee	MI	49660	231-398-5000	723-1795
Web: www.manisteecounty.net					
Manitowoc County PO Box 2000	Manitowoc	WI	54221	920-683-4030	683-2733
Web: www.co.manitowoc.wi.us					
Marathon County 500 Forest St	Wausau	WI	54403	715-261-1500	261-1515
Web: www.co.marathon.wi.us					
Marengo County PO Box 480715	Linden	AL	36748	334-295-2200	295-2254
Maricopa County 301 W Jefferson St 10th Fl	Phoenix	AZ	85003	602-506-3415	506-6402
Web: www.maricopa.gov					
Maries County 211 4th St	Vienna	MO	65582	573-422-3388	422-3269
Marin County 3501 Civic Ctr Dr	San Rafael	CA	94903	415-499-6450	
Web: www.marin.org					
Marinette County 1926 Hall Ave	Marinette	WI	54143	715-732-7406	732-7532
Web: www.marinettecounty.com					
Marion County PO Box 481	Buena Vista	GA	31803	229-649-2603	649-3702
Marion County 250 Broad St Suite 2	Columbia	MS	39429	601-736-2691	444-0206
Marion County 217 Adams St	Fairmont	WV	26554	304-367-5440	367-5448
Web: www.marioncountywv.com					
Marion County 132 Military St S # 204	Hamilton	AL	35570	205-921-7451	952-9851
Web: www.sonet.net					
Marion County 200 E Washington St City County Bldg Rm W122	Indianapolis	IN	46204	317-327-4740	327-3893
Web: www.indygov.org/county					
Marion County 24 Courthouse Sq Rm 101 PO Box 789	Jasper	TN	37347	423-942-2515	942-0815
Marion County PO Box 763	Jefferson	TX	75657	903-665-3971	665-8732
Web: www.co.marion.tx.us					
Marion County 214 E Main St PO Box 497	Knoxville	IA	50138	641-828-2257	828-7580
Web: www.redrockarea.com					
Marion County 120 W Main St Suite 3	Lebanon	KY	40033	270-692-2651	692-9811
Web: www.lebanonky.org					
Marion County 200 S 3rd St Suite 104	Marion	KS	66861	620-382-2185	382-3420
TF: 800-305-8851 ■ *Web:* www.marioncoks.net					
Marion County 100 N Main St	Marion	OH	43302	740-223-4270	223-4279
Web: www.co.marion.oh.us					
Marion County PO Box 183	Marion	SC	29571	843-423-3904	423-8306
Web: www.co.marion.sc.us					
Marion County 601 SE 25th Ave	Ocala	FL	34471	352-620-3307	620-3392
Web: www.marioncountyfl.org					
Marion County 100 S Main St	Palmyra	MO	63461	573-769-2549	769-4312
Marion County PO Box 637	Salem	IL	62881	618-548-3400	548-2226
Marion County PO Box 14500	Salem	OR	97309	503-588-5225	373-4408
Web: www.co.marion.or.us					
Marion County PO Box 545	Yellville	AR	72687	870-449-6231	449-4979
Mariposa County 5100 Bullion St PO Box 784	Mariposa	CA	95338	209-966-3222	966-5147
Web: www.mariposacounty.org					
Marlboro County PO Box 419	Bennettsville	SC	29512	843-479-5600	479-5639
Web: www.marlborocounty.sc.gov					
Marquette County 234 W Baraga Ave	Marquette	MI	49855	906-225-8151	225-8155
Web: www.co.marquette.mi.us					
Marquette County PO Box 186	Montello	WI	53949	608-297-9136	297-7609
Web: www.co.marquette.wi.us					
Marshall County 1101 Main St	Benton	KY	42025	270-527-4740	527-4738
Web: www.marshallcounty.net					
Marshall County PO Box 130	Britton	SD	57430	605-448-5213	448-5213
Marshall County 424 Blount Ave	Guntersville	AL	35976	256-571-7701	571-7703
Web: www.marshallco.org					
Marshall County PO Box 219	Holly Springs	MS	38635	662-252-4431	551-3302
Marshall County PO Box 328	Lacon	IL	61540	309-246-6325	246-3667
Web: www.co.marshall.il.us					
Marshall County 1 County Courthouse Rm 106	Madill	OK	73446	580-795-3165	795-3165
Marshall County 1 E Main St 3rd Fl	Marshalltown	IA	50158	641-754-6355	754-6349
Web: www.co.marshall.ia.us					
Marshall County 1201 Broadway	Marysville	KS	66508	785-562-5361	562-5262
Web: www.marshall.kansasgov.com					
Marshall County PO Box 459	Moundsville	WV	26041	304-845-1220	845-5891
Web: www.marshallcountywv.org					
Marshall County 211 W Madison St	Plymouth	IN	46563	574-936-8922	936-8893
Web: www.co.marshall.in.us					
Marshall County 208 E Colvin Ave	Warren	MN	56762	218-745-4851	745-5089
Web: www.visitnwminnesota.com					
Martin County 201 Lake Ave Suite 201	Fairmont	MN	56031	507-238-3211	238-3259*
*Fax: Acctg ■ *Web:* www.co.martin.mn.us					
Martin County PO Box 460	Inez	KY	41224	606-298-2810	298-0143
Martin County PO Box 120	Shoals	IN	47581	812-247-3651	247-2791
Martin County 301 N St Peter St	Stanton	TX	79782	432-756-3412	607-2212
Martin County PO Box 9016	Stuart	FL	34995	772-288-5576	288-5548
Web: www.martin.fl.us					
Martin County 305 E Main St PO Box 308	Williamston	NC	27892	252-792-2515	
Web: www.martincountyncgov.com					
Martinsville (Independent City) PO Box 1112	Martinsville	VA	24114	276-656-5180	403-5280
Web: www.ci.martinsville.va.us					
Mason County 125 N Plum PO Box 77	Havana	IL	62644	309-543-6661	543-2085
Web: www.masoncountyil.org					
Mason County 304 E Ludington Ave	Ludington	MI	49431	231-843-8202	843-1972
Web: www.masoncounty.net					
Mason County PO Box 702	Mason	TX	76856	325-347-5253	347-6868
Web: www.co.mason.tx.us					
Mason County 221 Stanley Reed Court St	Maysville	KY	41056	606-564-6706	564-7315
Web: www.masoncountykentucky.com					
Mason County 200 6th St	Point Pleasant	WV	25550	304-675-1110	675-4982
Mason County PO Box 340	Shelton	WA	98584	360-427-9670	
Web: www.co.mason.wa.us					
Massac County PO Box 429	Metropolis	IL	62960	618-524-5213	524-8514
Matagorda County 1700 7th St Rm 202	Bay City	TX	77414	979-244-7680	244-7688
Web: www.co.matagorda.tx.us					
Matanuska-Susitna Borough 350 E Dahlia Ave	Palmer	AK	99645	907-745-4801	745-9845
Web: www.co.mat-su.ak.us					
Mathews County PO Box 463	Mathews	VA	23109	804-725-2550	725-7456
Web: www.co.mathews.va.us					
Maui County 200 S High St	Wailuku	HI	96793	808-270-7748	270-7171
Web: www.co.maui.hi.us					
Maury County 10 Public Sq	Columbia	TN	38401	931-381-3690	381-1016
Web: www.mauryalliance.com					
Maverick County PO Box 4050	Eagle Pass	TX	78853	830-773-2829	752-4479
Mayes County 1 Ct Pl Suite 120	Pryor	OK	74361	918-825-2426	825-3803
Web: okcountyrecruits.com					
McClain County 121 N 2nd St Suite 303	Purcell	OK	73080	405-527-3360	
McCone County 1004 C Ave	Circle	MT	59215	406-485-3505	485-2689
Web: www.circle-montana.com					
McCook County PO Box 504	Salem	SD	57058	605-425-2781	425-3144
McCormick County 133 S Mine St Rm 102	McCormick	SC	29835	864-465-2195	
Web: www.mccormickcountysc.org					
McCracken County PO Box 609	Paducah	KY	42002	270-444-4700	444-4704
Web: www.co.mccracken.ky.us					
McCreary County PO Box 699	Whitley City	KY	42653	606-376-2411	376-3898
Web: www.mccrearycounty.com					
McCulloch County 199 County Courthouse Rm 103	Brady	TX	76825	325-597-0733	597-0606
McCurtain County 108 N Central St	Idabel	OK	74745	580-286-2370	286-1040
McDonald County 602 Main St	Pineville	MO	64856	417-223-4717	223-7519
McDonough County 1 Courthouse Sq	Macomb	IL	61455	309-833-2474	836-3368
Web: www.outfitters.com/illinois/mcdonough					
McDowell County 60 E Ct St	Marion	NC	28752	828-652-7121	659-3484
Web: www.mcdowellgov.com					
McDowell County 90 Wyoming St Suite 109	Welch	WV	24801	304-436-8544	436-8576
McDuffie County PO Box 158	Thomson	GA	30824	706-595-2134	595-9150
Web: www.dca.state.ga.us					
McHenry County PO Box 117	Towner	ND	58788	701-537-5729	537-5969
McHenry County 2200 N Seminary Ave	Woodstock	IL	60098	815-334-4000	334-8727
Web: www.co.mchenry.il.us					
McIntosh County PO Box 179	Ashley	ND	58413	701-288-3450	288-3671
McIntosh County PO Box 584	Darien	GA	31305	912-437-6671	437-6416
Web: mcintoshcounty.georgia.gov/03/home/0,2230,8871558,00.html					
McIntosh County PO Box 110	Eufaula	OK	74432	918-689-2741	689-3385
McKean County PO Box 1507	Smethport	PA	16749	814-887-5571	887-2242
Web: www.mckeancountypa.org					
McKenzie County PO Box 524	Watford City	ND	58854	701-444-3452	444-3916
Web: www.4eyes.net					
McKinley County 207 W Hill Ave	Gallup	NM	87301	505-863-6866	863-1419
Web: www.co.mckinley.nm.us					
McLean County 115 E Washington St Rm 102	Bloomington	IL	61701	309-888-5190	888-5932
Web: www.co.mclean.il.us					
McLean County PO Box 57	Calhoun	KY	42327	270-273-3082	273-5084
McLean County 712 5th Ave	Washburn	ND	58577	701-462-8541	462-8212
Web: www.visitmcleancounty.com					
McLennan County 215 N 5th St # 223B	Waco	TX	76701	254-757-5078	757-5146
Web: www.co.mclennan.tx.us					
McLeod County 830 11th St	Glencoe	MN	55336	320-864-5551	
Web: www.co.mcleod.mn.us					
McMinn County 5 S Hill St Suite A	Athens	TN	37303	423-745-4440	744-1657
Web: www.mcminnco.org					
McMullen County PO Box 235	Tilden	TX	78072	361-274-3215	274-3858
McNairy County County Courthouse Rm 102	Selmer	TN	38375	731-645-3511	
Web: www.mcnairycountytn.com					
McPherson County PO Box 248	Leola	SD	57456	605-439-3361	439-3394
McPherson County 117 N Maple Courthouse PO Box 425	McPherson	KS	67460	620-241-3656	241-1168
Web: www.mcphersoncountyks.us					
Meade County PO Box 614	Brandenburg	KY	40108	270-422-2152	422-2158
Web: countyclerk.meadecounty.ky.gov					
Meade County PO Box 278	Meade	KS	67864	620-873-8700	873-8713
Web: www.meadeco.org					
Meade County 1425 Sherman St PO Box 939	Sturgis	SD	57785	605-347-4411	347-3526
Web: www.meadecounty.org					
Meagher County 15 W Main St	White Sulphur Springs	MT	59645	406-547-3612	547-3388
Mecklenburg County 393 Washington St PO Box 307	Boydton	VA	23917	434-738-6191	738-6861
Web: www.mecklenburgva.com					
Mecklenburg County 600 E 4th St 11th Fl Charlotte-Mecklenburg Government Ctr	Charlotte	NC	28202	704-336-2472	336-5887
Web: www.co.mecklenburg.nc.us					
Mecosta County 400 Elm St	Big Rapids	MI	49307	231-796-2505	592-0121
Web: www.co.mecosta.mi.us					
Medina County 1100 16th St Rm 109	Hondo	TX	78861	830-741-6001	741-6015

				Phone	Fax
Meeker County 325 N Sibley Ave	Litchfield	MN	55355	320-693-5200	
Web: www.co.meeker.mn.us					
Meigs County 17214 State Hwy 58 N PO Box 218	Decatur	TN	37322	423-334-5747	
Meigs County 100 E 2nd St PO Box 151	Pomeroy	OH	45769	740-992-2895	992-2270
Web: www.meigscountyohio.com					
Mellette County PO Box 257	White River	SD	57579	605-259-3230	259-3030
Menard County PO Box 1038	Menard	TX	76859	325-396-4682	396-2047
Menard County PO Box 465	Petersburg	IL	62675	217-632-2415	632-4301
Web: www.menardil.com					
Mendocino County 501 Low Gap Rd Rm 1020	Ukiah	CA	95482	707-463-4376	463-4257
Web: www.co.mendocino.ca.us					
Menifee County PO Box 123	Frenchburg	KY	40322	606-768-3512	768-6738
Menominee County PO Box 279	Keshena	WI	54135	715-799-3311	799-1322
Web: www.wisconline.com/counties/menominee					
Menominee County 839 10th Ave	Menominee	MI	49858	906-863-9968	863-8839
Web: www.menomineecounty.com					
Merced County 2222 M St	Merced	CA	95340	209-385-7637	385-7375
Web: www.co.merced.ca.us					
Mercer County PO Box 66	Aledo	IL	61231	309-582-7021	582-7022
Web: www.mercercountyil.org					
Mercer County 220 W Livingston St Rm A201	Celina	OH	45822	419-586-3178	586-1699
Web: www.mercercountyohio.org					
Mercer County 235 S Main St	Harrodsburg	KY	40330	859-734-6310	734-6309
Web: www.merceronline.com					
Mercer County 109 Courthouse	Mercer	PA	16137	724-662-7548	
Web: www.mcc.co.mercer.pa.us					
Mercer County 802 Main St County Courthouse	Princeton	MO	64673	660-748-3425	748-3180
Mercer County 1501 Main St	Princeton	WV	24740	304-487-8311	487-9842
Web: www.mccvb.com					
Mercer County PO Box 39	Stanton	ND	58571	701-745-3262	745-3710
Web: www.mercercountynd.com					
Mercer County PO Box 8068	Trenton	NJ	08650	609-989-6470	989-1111
Web: www.nj.gov/counties/mercer					
Meriwether County PO Box 428	Greenville	GA	30222	706-672-1314	672-1886
Merrick County PO Box 27	Central City	NE	68826	308-946-2881	946-2332
Web: www.merrickcounty.ne.gov					
Merrimack County 4 Ct St Suite 2	Concord	NH	03301	603-228-0331	224-2665
Web: www.ci.concord.nh.us					
Mesa County PO Box 20000	Grand Junction	CO	81502	970-244-1800	256-1588
Web: www.mesacounty.us					
Metcalfe County 100 E Stockton # 1	Edmonton	KY	42129	270-432-4821	432-5176
Miami County 201 S Pearl St Suite 102	Paola	KS	66071	913-294-3976	294-9544
Web: www.miamicountyks.org					
Miami County PO Box 184	Peru	IN	46970	765-472-3901	472-1778
Miami County 201 W Main St	Troy	OH	45373	937-440-5900	
Web: www.co.miami.oh.us					
Miami-Dade County 111 NW 1st St Suite 220	Miami	FL	33128	305-375-5924	375-5569
Web: www.miamidade.gov					
Middlesex County PO Box 871	New Brunswick	NJ	08901	732-745-3082	
Web: co.middlesex.nj.us					
Middlesex County Rtes 17 & 33 Courthouse PO Box 158	Saluda	VA	23149	804-758-5317	758-8637
Web: www.co.middlesex.va.us					
Middlesex County 1 Ct St	Middletown	CT	06457	860-343-6400	343-6423
Midland County 220 W Ellsworth St	Midland	MI	48640	989-832-6739	832-6680
Web: www.co.midland.mi.us					
Midland County 500 N Loraine St 4th Fl PO Box 1350	Midland	TX	79702	432-688-4401	688-4926
Web: www.co.midland.tx.us					
Mifflin County 20 N Wayne St	Lewistown	PA	17044	717-248-6733	248-3695
Web: www.co.mifflin.pa.us					
Milam County 107 W Main St	Cameron	TX	76520	254-697-7049	697-7055
Web: www.milamcounty.net					
Millard County 765 S Hwy 99 Suite 6	Fillmore	UT	84631	435-743-6223	743-6923
Web: www.millardcounty.com					
Mille Lacs County 635 2nd St SE	Milaca	MN	56353	320-983-8313	983-8384
Web: www.co.mille-lacs.mn.us					
Miller County 400 Laurel St Rm 105	Texarkana	AR	71854	870-774-1501	773-4090
Web: www.millercountyar.org					
Miller County 2001 Missouri 52	Tuscumbia	MO	65082	573-369-1900	369-2910
Mills County 418 Sharp St County Courthouse	Glenwood	IA	51534	712-527-4880	527-4936
Web: www.millscoia.us					
Mills County PO Box 646	Goldthwaite	TX	76844	325-648-2711	648-3251
Web: www.co.mills.tx.us					
Milwaukee County 901 N 9th St	Milwaukee	WI	53233	414-278-4067	278-4075
Web: www.co.milwaukee.wi.us					
Miner County 401 N Main St	Howard	SD	57349	605-772-4612	772-4412
Web: www.howardsd.com					
Mineral County 1201 N Main St PO Box 70	Creede	CO	81130	719-658-2575	658-2764
Web: www.mineralcountycolorado.com					
Mineral County PO Box 1450	Hawthorne	NV	89415	775-945-2446	945-0706
Mineral County 150 Armstrong St	Keyser	WV	26726	304-788-3924	788-4109
Web: www.mineralcountywv.com					
Mineral County 300 River St PO Box 396	Superior	MT	59872	406-822-3520	822-3579
Web: www.co.mineral.mt.us					
Mingo County 75 E 2nd Ave	Williamson	WV	25661	304-235-0381	235-0365
Minidoka County 715 G St PO Box 368	Rupert	ID	83350	208-436-7111	436-0737
Web: www.minidoka.id.us					
Minnehaha County 415 N Dakota Ave	Sioux Falls	SD	57104	605-367-4206	367-8314
Web: www.minnehahacounty.org					
Missaukee County 111 S Canal PO Box 800	Lake City	MI	49651	231-839-4967	839-3684
Web: www.missaukee.org					
Mississippi County 200 W Walnut St Rm 103	Blytheville	AR	72315	870-762-2411	838-7784
Web: mcagov.missconet.com					
Mississippi County 200 N Main St	Charleston	MO	63834	573-683-2146	683-6071
Web: www.misscomo.net					
Missoula County 200 W Broadway St	Missoula	MT	59802	406-523-4780	258-4899
Web: www.co.missoula.mt.us					
Mitchell County 26 Crimson Laurel Cir # 5	Bakersville	NC	28705	828-688-2434	688-4443
Web: www.mitchellcounty.org					
Mitchell County PO Box 190	Beloit	KS	67420	785-738-3652	738-5524
Web: www.mcks.org					
Mitchell County 26 N Ct St PO Box 187	Camilla	GA	31730	229-336-2000	336-2003
Web: www.mitchellcountyga.net					
Mitchell County 349 Oak St Rm 103	Colorado City	TX	79512	325-728-3481	728-5322
Mitchell County 508 State St	Osage	IA	50461	641-732-3726	732-3728
Mobile County 205 Government St	Mobile	AL	36644	251-574-5077	
Web: www.mobilecounty.org					
Modoc County 204 S Ct St Rm 204	Alturas	CA	96101	530-233-6200	233-2434
Web: www.modoccounty.us					
Moffat County 221 W Victory Way	Craig	CO	81625	970-824-9104	824-4975
Web: www.co.moffat.co.us					
Mohave County PO Box 7000	Kingman	AZ	86402	928-753-0729	753-5103
Web: www.co.mohave.az.us					
Moniteau County 200 E Main St	California	MO	65018	573-796-4661	796-3082
Monmouth County 1 E Main St	Freehold	NJ	07728	732-431-7324	409-7566
Web: www.co.monmouth.nj.us					
Mono County PO Box 237	Bridgeport	CA	93517	760-932-5530	932-5531
Web: www.monocounty.ca.gov					
Monona County 610 Iowa Ave	Onawa	IA	51040	712-423-2491	423-2744
Monongalia County 243 High St Rm 123	Morgantown	WV	26505	304-291-7230	291-7233
Web: www.co.monongalia.wv.us					
Monroe County PO Box 578	Aberdeen	MS	39730	662-369-8143	369-7928
Web: www.gomonroe.org					
Monroe County 10 Benton Ave E	Albia	IA	52531	641-932-5212	932-3245
Monroe County 301 N College Ave Rm 201	Bloomington	IN	47404	812-349-2600	349-2610
Web: www.co.monroe.in.us					
Monroe County 123 Madison St	Clarendon	AR	72029	870-747-3632	747-5961
Monroe County 38 W Main St PO Box 189	Forsyth	GA	31029	478-994-7000	994-7294
Web: www.monroecountygeorgia.com					
Monroe County 1100 SimontonSt	Key West	FL	33040	305-294-4641	
Web: monroecofl.virtualtownhall.net					
Monroe County 103 College St Suite 1	Madisonville	TN	37354	423-442-2220	442-9542
Web: www.monroegovernment.org					
Monroe County 106 E 1st St	Monroe	MI	48161	734-240-7020	240-7045
Web: www.co.monroe.mi.us					
Monroe County PO Box 8	Monroeville	AL	36461	251-743-4107	575-7934
Web: www.monroecountyal.com					
Monroe County 300 N Main St Rm 204	Paris	MO	65275	660-327-5106	327-1019
Web: www.monroecounty.gov					
Monroe County 39 W Main St Rm 101	Rochester	NY	14614	585-428-5151	753-1650
Web: www.monroecounty.gov					
Monroe County 202 S K St Rm 1	Sparta	WI	54656	608-269-8705	269-8747
Web: www.co.monroe.wi.us					
Monroe County 610 Monroe St	Stroudsburg	PA	18360	570-517-3009	517-3866
Web: www.co.monroe.pa.us					
Monroe County 200 N Main St Suite D	Tompkinsville	KY	42167	270-487-5471	487-5976
Monroe County 216 Main St PO Box 350	Union	WV	24983	304-772-3096	772-4191
Web: www.monroecountywv.net					
Monroe County 100 S Main St	Waterloo	IL	62298	618-939-8681	939-8639
Monroe County 101 N Main St Rm 12	Woodsfield	OH	43793	740-472-5181	472-2526
Web: www.monroecountyohio.net					
Montague County PO Box 77	Montague	TX	76251	940-894-2461	894-3110
Web: www.co.montague.tx.us					
Montcalm County PO Box 368	Stanton	MI	48888	989-831-7339	831-7474
Monterey County 168 W Alisal St	Salinas	CA	93901	831-755-5115	757-5792
Web: www.co.monterey.ca.us					
Montezuma County 601 N Mildred Rd	Cortez	CO	81321	970-565-8317	565-3420
Web: www.co.montezuma.co.us					
Montgomery County 755 Roanoke St Suite 2E	Christiansburg	VA	24073	540-382-6954	382-6943
Web: www.montva.com					
Montgomery County PO Box 687	Clarksville	TN	37041	931-648-5711	553-5160
Web: www.montgomerycountytn.org					
Montgomery County PO Box 959	Conroe	TX	77305	936-539-7885	760-6990
Web: www.co.montgomery.tx.us					
Montgomery County PO Box 768	Crawfordsville	IN	47933	765-364-6430	364-6355
Web: www.mcedonline.com					
Montgomery County 41 N Perry St	Dayton	OH	45422	937-496-7591	496-7627
Web: www.co.montgomery.oh.us					
Montgomery County PO Box 1500	Fonda	NY	12068	518-853-3834	853-8220
Web: www.co.montgomery.ny.us					
Montgomery County 1 Courthouse Sq PO Box 595	Hillsboro	IL	62049	217-532-9530	532-9581
Web: www.montgomeryco.com					
Montgomery County PO Box 446	Independence	KS	67301	620-330-1200	330-1202
Web: www.mgcountyks.org					
Montgomery County PO Box 1667	Montgomery	AL	36102	334-832-1210	832-2533
Web: www.mc-ala.org					
Montgomery County 211 E 3rd St	Montgomery City	MO	63361	573-564-3357	564-8088
Web: www.montgomerycountymo.org					
Montgomery County PO Box 717	Mount Ida	AR	71957	870-867-3114	867-4354
Montgomery County PO Box 414	Mount Sterling	KY	40353	859-498-8700	498-8729
Montgomery County 310 W Broad St	Mount Vernon	GA	30445	912-583-2363	583-2026
Montgomery County PO Box 311	Norristown	PA	19404	610-278-3346	278-5188
Web: www.montcopa.org					
Montgomery County PO Box 469	Red Oak	IA	51566	712-623-4986	623-4987
Montgomery County 101 Monroe St	Rockville	MD	20850	240-777-2500	777-2517
Web: www.montgomerycountymd.gov					
Montgomery County PO Box 527	Troy	NC	27371	910-576-4211	576-5020
Web: www.montgomery-county.com					
Montgomery County PO Box 71	Winona	MS	38967	662-283-2333	283-2233
Montmorency County PO Box 789	Atlanta	MI	49709	989-785-8013	785-8014
Montour County 29 Mill St	Danville	PA	17821	570-271-3010	271-3089
Web: www.montourco.org					
Montrose County 161 S Townsend	Montrose	CO	81401	970-249-3362	249-7761
Web: www.co.montrose.co.us					
Moody County 101 E Pipestone Ave	Flandreau	SD	57028	605-997-3181	997-3861
Moore County PO Box 905	Carthage	NC	28327	910-947-6363	947-1874
Web: www.co.moore.nc.us					
Moore County 715 S Dumas Ave Rm 105	Dumas	TX	79029	806-935-6164	935-9004
Web: www.co.moore.tx.us					
Moore County 196 Main St PO Box 206	Lynchburg	TN	37352	931-759-7346	759-6394
Web: www.lynchburgtn.com					

Entry	City	State	Zip	Phone	Fax
Mora County 518 Mile Marker 29 PO Box 360	Mora	NM	87732	505-387-2448	387-9023
Morehouse Parish 100 E Madison Ave.	Bastrop	LA	71221	318-281-3343	281-3775
Morgan County 77 Fairfax St Suite 1A	Berkeley Springs	WV	25411	304-258-8547	258-8545
Web: www.morgancountywv.gov.com					
Morgan County PO Box 668	Decatur	AL	35602	256-351-4730	351-4738
Web: www.co.morgan.al.us					
Morgan County PO Box 1399	Fort Morgan	CO	80701	970-542-3521	542-3520
Web: www.co.morgan.co.us					
Morgan County PO Box 1387	Jacksonville	IL	62651	217-243-8581	243-8368
Web: www.morgancounty-il.com					
Morgan County 355 Hancock St	Madison	GA	30650	706-342-0725	343-6450
Web: www.morganga.org					
Morgan County PO Box 1556	Martinsville	IN	46151	765-342-1025	342-1111
Morgan County 19 E Main St	McConnelsville	OH	43756	740-962-4752	962-4522
Web: www.morgancounty.org					
Morgan County PO Box 886	Morgan	UT	84050	801-845-4011	829-6176
Web: www.morgan-county.net					
Morgan County 100 E Newton St.	Versailles	MO	65084	573-378-5436	378-5991
Morgan County 415 Kingston St.	Wartburg	TN	37887	423-346-3480	346-4161
Web: www.morgancountytn.org					
Morgan County PO Box 26	West Liberty	KY	41472	606-743-3949	743-2111
Morrill County 606 L St.	Bridgeport	NE	69336	308-262-0860	262-1469
Web: www.co.morrill.ne.us					
Morris County 501 W Main St.	Council Grove	KS	66846	620-767-5518	767-6861
Morris County 500 Broadnax St.	Daingerfield	TX	75638	903-645-3911	645-5729
Web: www.co.morris.tx.us					
Morris County PO Box 315	Morristown	NJ	07963	973-285-6120	285-5231
Web: www.co.morris.nj.us					
Morrison County 213 SE 1st Ave	Little Falls	MN	56345	320-632-0293	632-0294
Web: www.co.morrison.mn.us					
Morrow County 100 Court St PO Box 788	Heppner	OR	97836	541-676-9061	676-9876
Web: morrowcountyoregon.com					
Morrow County 48 E High St.	Mount Gilead	OH	43338	419-947-4085	947-1860
Web: www.co.morrow.oh.us					
Morton County PO Box 1116	Elkhart	KS	67950	620-697-2157	697-2159
Web: www.mtcoks.com					
Morton County 210 2nd Ave NW	Mandan	ND	58554	701-667-3300	667-3453
Web: www.co.morton.nd.us					
Motley County PO Box 660	Matador	TX	79244	806-347-2621	347-2220
Web: www.co.motley.tx.us					
Moultrie County					
County Courthouse 10 S Main St Suite 6	Sullivan	IL	61951	217-728-4389	728-8178
Mountrail County PO Box 69	Stanley	ND	58784	701-628-2915	628-3975
Mower County 201 1st St NE.	Austin	MN	55912	507-437-9535	437-9471
Web: www.co.mower.mn.us					
Muhlenberg County PO Box 525	Greenville	KY	42345	270-338-1441	338-1774
Multnomah County 1221 SW 4th Ave.	Portland	OR	97204	503-823-4000	988-5773
Web: www.co.multnomah.or.us					
Murray County PO Box 1129	Chatsworth	GA	30705	706-695-2413	695-8721
Murray County 2500 28th St	Slayton	MN	56172	507-836-6148	836-8904
Web: www.murray-countymn.com					
Murray County PO Box 240	Sulphur	OK	73086	580-622-3777	622-6209
Muscatine County 401 E 3rd St	Muscatine	IA	52761	563-263-5821	263-7248
Web: www.co.muscatine.ia.us					
Muskegon County 141 Terr St # 209	Muskegon	MI	49442	231-724-6221	724-6262
Web: www.co.muskegon.mi.us					
Muskingum County 401 Main St	Zanesville	OH	43701	740-455-7104	
Web: www.muskingumcounty.org					
Muskogee County PO Box 1008	Muskogee	OK	74402	918-682-7781	682-8803
Web: www.okcountyrecord.com					
Musselshell County 506 Main St.	Roundup	MT	59072	406-323-1104	323-3303
Nacogdoches County 101 W Main St Rm 205	Nacogdoches	TX	75961	936-560-7733	559-5926
Web: www.co.nacogdoche					
Nance County 209 Esther St PO Box 338	Fullerton	NE	68638	308-536-2331	536-2742
Web: www.co.nance.ne.us					
Nantucket County 16 Broad St.	Nantucket	MA	02554	508-228-7216	325-5313
Napa County 1195 3rd St Rm 310	Napa	CA	94559	707-253-4421	253-4176
Web: www.co.napa.ca.us					
Nash County 120 W Washington St Suite 3072	Nashville	NC	27856	252-459-9800	459-9817
Web: www.co.nash.nc.us					
Nassau County PO Box 456	Fernandina Beach	FL	32035	904-548-4600	321-5723
Web: www.nassauclerk.org					
Nassau County 240 Old Country Rd	Mineola	NY	11501	516-571-2664	742-4099
Web: www.nassaucountyny.gov					
Natchitoches Parish 200 Church St # 210	Natchitoches	LA	71457	318-352-2714	357-2208
Web: www.nppj.org					
Natrona County 200 N Ctr St.	Casper	WY	82601	307-235-9200	
Web: www.natronacounty-wy.gov					
Navajo County PO Box 668	Holbrook	AZ	86025	928-524-4188	524-4261
Web: www.co.navajo.az.us					
Navarro County PO Box 423	Corsicana	TX	75151	903-654-3036	654-3097
Web: www.co.navarro.tx.us					
Nelson County 113 E Steven Foster St.	Bardstown	KY	40004	502-348-1820	348-1822
Nelson County 210 B Ave W Suite 203	Lakota	ND	58344	701-247-2462	247-2412
Nelson County 84 Courthouse Sq PO Box 336	Lovingston	VA	22949	434-263-7000	263-7004
Web: nelsoncounty.com					
Nemaha County 1824 N St	Auburn	NE	68305	402-274-4213	274-4389
Web: www.nemahacounty.ne.gov					
Nemaha County PO Box 186	Seneca	KS	66538	785-336-3570	336-3373
Web: www.nemaha.kansasgov.com					
Neosho County PO Box 138	Erie	KS	66733	620-244-3811	244-3810
Neshoba County 401 Beacon St Suite 107	Philadelphia	MS	39350	601-656-3581	656-5915
Web: www.neshoba.org					
Ness County 105 S Pennsylvania	Ness City	KS	67560	785-798-4864	798-3680
Web: www.nesscountyks.com					
Nevada County 950 Maidu Ave	Nevada City	CA	95959	530-265-1218	
Web: www.co.nevada.ca.us					
Nevada County PO Box 621	Prescott	AR	71857	870-887-2710	887-5795
New Castle County					
87 Reads Way New Castle Corporate Commons	New Castle	DE	19720	302-395-5101	395-5268
Web: www.co.new-castle.de.us					
New Kent County					
12001 Courthouse Cir PO Box 98	New Kent	VA	23124	804-966-9520	966-9528
Web: www.co.new-kent.va.us					
New London County 70 Huntington St	New London	CT	06320	860-443-5363	442-7703
New York County 60 Centre St	New York	NY	10007	646-386-5955	374-5790*
**Fax Area Code: 212* ■ *Web:* www.nyc.gov					
Newaygo County 1087 Newell St	White Cloud	MI	49349	231-689-7200	689-7205
Web: www.countyofnewaygo.com					
Newberry County 1226 College St PO Drawer 10	Newberry	SC	29108	803-321-2110	321-2111
Web: www.newberrycounty.net					
Newport County 45 Washington Sq	Newport	RI	02840	401-841-8330	846-1673
Web: www.courts.ri.gov					
Newport News (Independent City)					
2400 Washington Ave.	Newport News	VA	23607	757-926-8411	926-3503
Web: www.newport-news.va.us					
Newton County 1124 Clark St	Covington	GA	30014	678-625-1202	
Web: www.co.newton.ga.us					
Newton County PO Box 447	Decatur	MS	39327	601-635-2368	635-3210
Newton County PO Box 410	Jasper	AR	72641	870-446-5125	446-5755
Web: www.newtonclark@arkansaclarks.com					
Newton County PO Box 49	Kentland	IN	47951	219-474-6081	474-5749
TF: 888-663-9866					
Newton County 101 S Wood St.	Neosho	MO	64850	417-451-8220	451-7434
Newton County 115 Court St PO Box 484	Newton	TX	75966	409-379-5341	379-9049
Web: www.co.newton.tx.us					
Nez Perce County 1230 Main St PO Box 896	Lewiston	ID	83501	208-799-3020	799-3070
Web: www.co.nezperce.id.us					
Niagara County PO Box 461	Lockport	NY	14095	716-439-7022	439-7066
Web: www.niagaracounty.com					
Nicholas County PO Box 227	Carlisle	KY	40311	859-289-3730	289-3705
Web: www.carlisle-nicholascounty.org					
Nicholas County 700 Main St Suite 2	Summersville	WV	26651	304-872-7848	872-9602
Web: www.nicholascountywv.gov					
Nicollet County 501 S Minnesota Ave.	Saint Peter	MN	56082	507-931-6800	931-9220
Web: www.co.nicollet.mn.us					
Niobrara County PO Box 420	Lusk	WY	82225	307-334-2211	334-3013
Web: www.county-clerk.net/countyclerk.asp?state=Wyoming&county=Niobrara					
Noble County 101 N Orange St	Albion	IN	46701	260-636-2736	636-4000
Web: www.nobleco.org					
Noble County 210 Ct House	Caldwell	OH	43724	740-732-2969	732-5702
Web: www.noblecountyohio.com					
Noble County 300 Courthouse Dr Rm 11	Perry	OK	73077	580-336-2141	336-2481
Web: www.okcountyrecords.com					
Nobles County 1530 Airport Rd	Worthington	MN	56187	507-372-8263	372-4994
Web: www.co.nobles.mn.us					
Nodaway County 403 N Market PO Box 218	Maryville	MO	64468	660-582-2251	582-5282
Nolan County 100 E 3rd St Suite 108	Sweetwater	TX	79556	325-235-2462	236-9416
Web: www.co.nolan.tx.us					
Norfolk (Independent City)					
810 Union St Rm 1101	Norfolk	VA	23510	757-664-4242	664-4239
Web: www.norfolk.gov					
Norfolk County 614 High St	Dedham	MA	02026	781-461-6105	326-6480
Web: www.norfolkcounty.org					
Norman County 16 3rd Ave E PO Box 146	Ada	MN	56510	218-784-5473	784-4531
Web: www.co.norman.mn.us					
North Slope Borough PO Box 69	Barrow	AK	99723	907-852-2611	852-0229
Web: www.co.north-slope.ak.us					
Northampton County 669 Washington St.	Easton	PA	18042	610-559-6700	559-6702
Web: www.northamptoncounty.org					
Northampton County PO Box 36	Eastville	VA	23347	757-678-0465	678-5410
Web: www.co.northampton.va.us					
Northampton County PO Box 808	Jackson	NC	27845	252-534-2501	534-1166
Web: www.northamptonnc.com					
Northumberland County PO Box 217	Heathsville	VA	22473	804-580-3700	580-2261
Web: www.co.northumberland.va.us					
Northumberland County 201 Market St Rt 7	Sunbury	PA	17801	570-988-4151	988-4497
TF: 800-692-7208 ■ *Web:* www.northumberlandco.org					
Northwest Arctic Borough PO Box 1110	Kotzebue	AK	99752	907-442-2500	442-2930
Web: www.nwabor.org					
Norton (Independent City)					
618 Virginia Ave PO Box 618	Norton	VA	24273	276-679-1160	679-3510
Web: www.nortonva.org					
Norton County PO Box 70	Norton	KS	67654	785-877-5720	877-5722
Nottoway County 325 W Court House Rd.	Nottoway	VA	23955	434-645-9043	645-2201
Nowata County 229 N Maple St	Nowata	OK	74048	918-273-0175	273-1936
Noxubee County PO Box 147	Macon	MS	39341	662-726-4243	726-2272
Web: www.noxubeecounty.org					
Nuckolls County PO Box 366	Nelson	NE	68961	402-225-4361	225-4301
Web: www.nuckollscounty.ne.gov					
Nueces County 901 Leopard St Suite 201	Corpus Christi	TX	78401	361-888-0580	888-0329
Web: www.co.nueces.tx.us					
Nye County PO Box 1031	Tonopah	NV	89049	775-482-8127	482-8133
Web: www.co.nye.nv.us					
O'Brien County PO Box 340	Primghar	IA	51245	712-957-3045	957-3046
Web: www.obriencounty.com					
Oakland County 1200 N Telegraph Rd.	Pontiac	MI	48341	248-858-0582	452-9221
Web: www.co.oakland.mi.us					
Obion County 2 Bill Burnett Cir	Union City	TN	38261	731-885-3831	885-0287
Web: www.obioncountytennessee.com					
Ocean County 118 Washington St.	Toms River	NJ	08753	732-929-2018	349-4336
Web: www.co.ocean.nj.us					
Oceana County 100 State St Suite 1	Hart	MI	49420	231-873-4328	873-1391
Web: www.oceana.mi.us					
Ochiltree County 511 S Main St.	Perryton	TX	79070	806-435-8039	435-2081
Web: www.co.ochiltree.tx.us					
Oconee County 415 S Pine St PO Box 678	Walhalla	SC	29691	864-638-4280	638-4280
Web: www.oconeesc.com					
Oconee County PO Box 145	Watkinsville	GA	30677	706-769-5120	769-0705
Web: www.oconeecounty.net					
Oconto County 301 Washington St	Oconto	WI	54153	920-834-6800	834-6867
Web: www.co.oconto.wi.us					
Ogemaw County 806 W Houghton Ave	West Branch	MI	48661	989-345-0215	345-7223

Name / Address	City	State	ZIP	Phone	Fax
Ogle County PO Box 357	Oregon	IL	61061	815-732-3201	732-6273
Web: www.oglecounty.org					
Oglethorpe County 341 W Main St	Lexington	GA	30648	706-743-5270	743-8371
Ohio County 301 S Main Suite 201	Hartford	KY	42347	270-298-4423	298-4426
Ohio County 413 Main St PO Box 185	Rising Sun	IN	47040	812-438-2610	438-1215
Ohio County 1500 Chapline St Rm 205	Wheeling	WV	26003	304-234-3656	234-3829
Web: www.ohiocounty.wv.gov/countygovernmentagencies/Pages/countyclerk.aspx					
Okaloosa County 101 E James Lee Blvd	Crestview	FL	32536	850-689-5000	689-5818
Web: www.co.okaloosa.fl.us					
Okanogan County 149 N 3rd Ave PO Box 72	Okanogan	WA	98840	509-422-7275	422-7277
Web: www.okanogancounty.org					
Okeechobee County 304 NW 2nd St	Okeechobee	FL	34972	863-763-6441	763-9529
Web: www.co.okeechobee.fl.us					
Okfuskee County PO Box 26	Okemah	OK	74859	918-623-0939	623-0635
Oklahoma County 320 Robert S Kerr Ave	Oklahoma City	OK	73102	405-270-0082	
Web: www.oklahomacounty.org					
Okmulgee County PO Box 904	Okmulgee	OK	74447	918-756-0788	758-1261
Oktibbeha County 101 E Main St	Starkville	MS	39759	662-323-5834	338-1064
Web: www.gtpdd.com/counties/oktibbeha					
Oldham County 100 W Jefferson St	LaGrange	KY	40031	502-222-9311	222-3208
Web: www.oldhamcounty.net					
Oldham County PO Box 360	Vega	TX	79092	806-267-2667	267-2671
Web: www.co.oldham.tx.us					
Oliver County PO Box 125	Center	ND	58530	701-794-8777	794-3476
Oneida County 10 Court St	Malad City	ID	83252	208-766-4116	766-2448
Web: www.co.oneida.id.us					
Oneida County 1 S Oneida Ave PO Box 400	Rhinelander	WI	54501	715-369-6144	369-6230
Web: www.co.oneida.wi.gov					
Oneida County 800 Pk Ave	Utica	NY	13501	315-798-5776	798-6440
Web: www.oneidacounty.org					
Onondaga County 401 Montgomery St	Syracuse	NY	13202	315-435-2226	435-3455
Web: www.ongov.net					
Onslow County 4024 Richland Hwy	Jacksonville	NC	28540	910-347-4717	455-7878
Web: www.co.onslowcountync.gov					
Ontario County 20 Ontario St	Canandaigua	NY	14424	585-396-4200	393-2951
Web: www.co.ontario.ny.us					
Ontonagon County 725 Greenland Rd	Ontonagon	MI	49953	906-884-4255	884-2916
Orange County 5 Ct St	Chelsea	VT	05038	802-685-4610	685-3246
Orange County 255 Main St	Goshen	NY	10924	845-291-2700	291-2724
Web: www.co.orange.ny.us					
Orange County 106 E Margaret Ln	Hillsborough	NC	27278	919-732-8181	644-3043
Web: www.co.orange.nc.us					
Orange County 801 W Division	Orange	TX	77631	409-882-7055	882-7012
Web: www.co.orange.tx.us					
Orange County 112 W Main St Suite 202 PO Box 111	Orange	VA	22960	540-672-3313	672-1679*
**Fax Area Code: 276* ■ *Web:* www.orangecova.com					
Orange County 201 S Rosalind Ave 5th Fl	Orlando	FL	32802	407-836-7350	836-5879
Web: www.orangecountyfl.net					
Orange County 1 Court St	Paoli	IN	47454	812-723-2649	723-0239
Web: www.co.orange.in.us					
Orange County 12 Civic Ctr Plaza	Santa Ana	CA	92702	714-834-2500	834-2675
Web: www.oc.ca.gov					
Orangeburg County 1406 Amelia St	Orangeburg	SC	29118	803-533-6263	534-3848
Web: www.orangeburgcounty.org					
Oregon County PO Box 324	Alton	MO	65606	417-778-7475	778-7488
Orleans County 3 S Main St	Albion	NY	14411	585-589-5334	589-0181
Web: www.orleansny.com					
Orleans County 247 Main St	Newport	VT	05855	802-334-3344	334-3385
Orleans Parish 1300 Perdido St Rm 9-E-06	New Orleans	LA	70112	504-658-4000	658-8647
Web: www.neworleans.com					
Osage County 106 E Main St	Linn	MO	65051	573-897-2139	897-4741
Web: www.osagecountymo.com					
Osage County PO Box 226	Lyndon	KS	66451	785-828-4812	828-4749
Web: www.osage.kansasgov.com					
Osage County PO Box 87	Pawhuska	OK	74056	918-287-3136	287-4979
Osborne County PO Box 160	Osborne	KS	67473	785-346-2431	346-5252
Web: www.osbornecounty.org					
Osceola County 1 Courthouse Sq	Kissimmee	FL	34741	407-343-3500	343-3699
Web: www.osceola.org					
Osceola County 301 W Upton Ave	Reed City	MI	49677	231-832-3261	832-6149
Web: www.osceola-county.org					
Osceola County 300 7th St	Sibley	IA	51249	712-754-2241	754-3743
Web: www.osceolacountyia.com					
Oscoda County PO Box 399	Mio	MI	48647	989-826-1109	826-1136
Oswego County 46 E Bridge St	Oswego	NY	13126	315-349-8235	349-8237
Web: www.co.oswego.ny.us					
Otero County 1000 New York Ave Suite 109	Alamogordo	NM	88310	505-437-7427	443-2904
Web: www.co.otero.nm.us					
Otero County PO Box 511	La Junta	CO	81050	719-383-3020	383-3026
Web: www.hotelgov.org					
Otoe County 1021 Central Ave Rm 103	Nebraska City	NE	68410	402-873-9500	873-9506
Web: www.co.otoe.ne.us					
Otsego County 197 Main St	Cooperstown	NY	13326	607-547-4202	547-4260
Web: www.otsegocounty.com					
Otsego County 225 W Main St	Gaylord	MI	49735	989-732-6484	732-1562
Web: www.otsegocountymi.gov					
Ottawa County 414 Washington St	Grand Haven	MI	49417	616-846-8312	846-8138
Web: www.co.ottawa.mi.us					
Ottawa County 102 E Central Ave Suite 203	Miami	OK	74354	918-542-3332	542-8260
Ottawa County 307 N Concord St Suite 130	Minneapolis	KS	67467	785-392-2279	392-2011
Web: www.ottawacounty.org					
Ottawa County 315 Madison St	Port Clinton	OH	43452	419-734-6710	734-6898
Web: www.co.ottawa.oh.us					
Otter Tail County 520 Fir Ave W	Fergus Falls	MN	56537	218-998-8000	998-8438
Web: www.co.ottertail.mn.us					
Ouachita County PO Box 644	Camden	AR	71711	870-837-2210	837-2218
Ouachita Parish PO Box 1862	Monroe	LA	71210	318-327-1444	327-1462
Web: www.opclerkofcourt.com					
Ouray County PO Box C	Ouray	CO	81427	970-325-4961	325-0452
Web: www.co.ouray.co.us					
Outagamie County 410 S Walnut St	Appleton	WI	54911	920-832-5077	832-2200
Web: www.co.outagamie.wi.us					
Overton County 317 E University St Rm 22	Livingston	TN	38570	931-823-2631	823-2696
Web: www.overtoncountytn.com					
Owen County 100 N Thomas St	Owenton	KY	40359	502-484-3405	484-1004
Web: www.owenton.net					
Owen County 60 S Main St County Courthouse	Spencer	IN	47460	812-829-5000	829-5004
Web: www.owencounty.org					
Owsley County PO Box 500	Booneville	KY	41314	606-593-5735	593-5737
Web: www.owsleycountykentucky.org					
Owyhee County PO Box 128	Murphy	ID	83650	208-495-2421	495-1173
Web: www.owyheecounty.net					
Oxford County 26 Western Ave PO Box 179	South Paris	ME	04281	207-743-6359	743-1545
Web: www.oxfordcounty.org					
Ozark County PO Box 416	Gainesville	MO	65655	417-679-3516	679-3209
Ozaukee County PO Box 994	Port Washington	WI	53074	262-284-8110	284-8100
Web: www.co.ozaukee.wi.us					
Pacific County PO Box 67	South Bend	WA	98586	360-875-9300	875-9321
Web: www.co.pacific.wa.us					
Page County PO Box 263	Clarinda	IA	51632	712-542-3214	542-5460
Page County 117 S Ct St	Luray	VA	22835	540-743-4142	743-4533
Web: www.co.page.va.us					
Palm Beach County 301 N Olive Ave	West Palm Beach	FL	33401	561-355-2001	355-3990
Web: www.co.palm-beach.fl.us					
Palo Alto County 1010 Broadway Suite 200	Emmetsburg	IA	50536	712-852-3603	852-2274
Palo Pinto County PO Box 219	Palo Pinto	TX	76484	940-659-1277	
Web: www.co.palo-pinto.tx.us					
Pamlico County PO Box 776	Bayboro	NC	28515	252-745-3133	745-5514
Web: www.co.pamlico.nc.us					
Panola County 151 Public Sq	Batesville	MS	38606	662-563-6205	563-6277
Panola County 110 Sycamore St Rm 201	Carthage	TX	75633	903-693-0302	693-2726
Web: www.carthagetexas.com					
Park County 1002 Sheridan Ave	Cody	WY	82414	307-527-8510	527-8515
TF: 800-786-2844 ■ *Web:* www.parkcounty.us					
Park County PO Box 220	Fairplay	CO	80440	719-836-4227	836-4348
Web: www.co.park.co.us					
Park County 414 E Callender St	Livingston	MT	59047	406-222-4110	
Web: www.parkcounty.org					
Parke County 116 W High St Rm 204	Rockville	IN	47872	765-569-5132	569-4222
Web: www.parkecounty-in.gov					
Parker County PO Box 819	Weatherford	TX	76086	817-594-7461	594-9540
Web: www.co.parker.tx.us					
Parmer County PO Box 356	Farwell	TX	79325	806-481-3691	
Web: www.co.parmer.tx.us					
Pasco County 7530 Little Rd	New Port Richey	FL	34654	727-847-2411	847-8969
Web: www.pascocountyfl.net					
Pasquotank County PO Box 39	Elizabeth City	NC	27907	252-335-0865	335-0866
Web: www.co.pasquotank.nc.us					
Passaic County 401 Grand St	Paterson	NJ	07505	973-225-3632	754-1920
Web: www.passaiccountynj.org					
Patrick County PO Box 148	Stuart	VA	24171	276-694-7213	694-6943
Web: www.co.patrick.va.us					
Paulding County 240 Constitution Blvd	Dallas	GA	30132	770-443-7550	443-7537
Web: www.paulding.gov					
Paulding County 115 N Williams St Rm 104	Paulding	OH	45879	419-399-8210	399-8248
Pawnee County 715 Broadway	Larned	KS	67550	620-285-3721	285-2559
Web: www.pawneecountykansas.com					
Pawnee County 500 Harrison St Rm 203	Pawnee	OK	74058	918-762-3741	762-3714
Web: www.cityofpawnee.com					
Pawnee County 625 6th St PO Box 431	Pawnee City	NE	68420	402-852-2963	852-2963
Web: www.co.pawnee.ne.us					
Payette County 1130 3rd Ave N Rm 104	Payette	ID	83661	208-642-6000	642-6011
Web: www.payettecounty.org					
Payne County 315 W 6th St Suite 202	Stillwater	OK	74074	405-747-8310	747-8304
Web: www.paynecounty.org					
Peach County 205 W Church St	Fort Valley	GA	31030	478-825-2535	825-2678
Web: www.peachcounty.net					
Pearl River County 200 S Main St PO Box 431	Poplarville	MS	39470	601-403-2300	795-3093
Web: www.pearlrivercounty.net					
Pecos County 103 W Callaghan St	Fort Stockton	TX	79735	432-336-7555	336-7557
Web: www.co.pecos.tx.us					
Pembina County 301 Dakota St W Suite 6	Cavalier	ND	58220	701-265-4275	265-4876
Web: www.pembinacountynd.gov					
Pemiscot County 610 Ward Ave	Caruthersville	MO	63830	573-333-4203	333-0440
Pend Oreille County 229 S Garden Ave	Newport	WA	99156	509-447-2435	447-2734
Web: www.pendoreilleco.org					
Pender County PO Box 5	Burgaw	NC	28425	910-259-1200	259-1402
Web: www.pender-county.com					
Pendleton County 233 Main St	Falmouth	KY	41040	859-654-4321	654-5047
Web: www.pendletoncountyky.org					
Pendleton County PO Box 1167	Franklin	WV	26807	304-358-2505	358-2473
Pennington County 315 St Joseph St	Rapid City	SD	57701	605-394-2171	394-6833
Web: www.co.pennington.sd.us					
Pennington County 115 South Main	Warren	MN	56762	218-745-6733	683-7026
Web: www.visitnwminnesota.com/Pennington.htm					
Penobscot County 97 Hammond St	Bangor	ME	04401	207-942-8535	945-6027
Peoria County 324 Main St Rm 101	Peoria	IL	61602	309-672-6059	672-6054
Web: www.co.peoria.il.us					
Pepin County 740 7th Ave W	Durand	WI	54736	715-672-8857	672-8677
Web: www.co.pepin.wi.us					
Perkins County PO Box 426	Bison	SD	57620	605-244-5626	244-7110
Perkins County PO Box 156	Grant	NE	69140	308-352-4643	352-2455
Web: www.co.perkins.ne.us					
Perquimans County PO Box 45	Hertford	NC	27944	252-426-8484	426-4034
Web: www.co.perquimans.nc.us					
Perry County 2219 Payne St	Tell City	IN	47586	812-547-3741	547-9782
Web: www.perrycountyin.org					
Perry County PO Box 150	Hazard	KY	41702	606-436-4614	439-0557
Perry County PO Box 16	Linden	TN	37096	931-589-2216	589-2215
Web: www.perrycountytennessee.com/government/perry-county-government					
Perry County PO Box 505	Marion	AL	36756	334-683-6106	683-2207
Perry County PO Box 198	New Augusta	MS	39462	601-964-8398	964-8746

	City	State	Zip	Phone	Fax
Perry County 25 W Main St PO Box 37	New Bloomfield	PA	17068	717-582-2131	582-5162
Web: www.perryco.org					
Perry County 121 W Brown St PO Box 248	New Lexington	OH	43764	740-342-2045	342-5505
Web: www.perrycountyohiocofc.com					
Perry County 310 W Main St Suite 105	Perryville	AR	72126	501-889-5126	889-5759
Perry County 3764 State Rts 13-127 Rm 204 PO Box 438	Pinckneyville	IL	62274	618-357-5116	357-3365
Web: www.perrycountyil.org					
Pershing County 398 Main St PO Box 820	Lovelock	NV	89419	775-273-2208	273-3015
Web: www.pershingcounty.net					
Person County 304 S Morgan St Rm 212	Roxboro	NC	27573	336-597-1720	599-1609
Web: www.personcounty.net					
Petersburg (Independent City) 135 N Union St # 202	Petersburg	VA	23803	804-733-2301	732-9212
Web: www.petersburg-va.org					
Petroleum County 302 E Main PO Box 226	Winnett	MT	59087	406-429-5311	429-6328
Web: www.petroleumcountymt.com					
Pettis County 415 S Ohio St	Sedalia	MO	65301	660-826-5395	829-0717
Phelps County PO Box 404	Holdrege	NE	68949	308-995-4469	995-4368
Web: www.phelpsgov.org					
Phelps County 200 N Main St	Rolla	MO	65401	573-458-6000	458-6119
Web: www.phelpscounty.org					
Philadelphia County City Hall Broad & Market Sts	Philadelphia	PA	19107	215-686-1776	567-7380
Web: www.phila.gov					
Phillips County 620 Cherry St Suite 202 County Courthouse	Helena	AR	72342	870-338-5505	338-5509
Phillips County 221 W Interocean Dr	Holyoke	CO	80734	970-854-3131	854-4745
Web: www.phillipscountyco.org					
Phillips County 314 S 2nd Ave W PO Box 360	Malta	MT	59538	406-654-2423	654-2429
Phillips County 301 State St	Phillipsburg	KS	67661	785-543-6825	543-6827
Piatt County PO Box 558	Monticello	IL	61856	217-762-9487	762-7563
Web: www.piattcounty.org					
Pickaway County 139 W Franklin St	Circleville	OH	43113	740-474-6093	474-8988
Web: www.pickaway.org					
Pickens County PO Box 460	Carrollton	AL	35447	205-367-2020	367-2025
Pickens County PO Box 130	Jasper	GA	30143	706-253-8766	
Web: www.georgiamarble-mountain.org					
Pickens County PO Box 215	Pickens	SC	29671	864-898-5866	898-5863
Web: www.co.pickens.sc.us					
Pickett County 1 Courthouse Sq Suite 201	Byrdstown	TN	38549	931-864-3879	864-7195
TF: 888-406-4704 ■ *Web:* www.dalehollow.com/government.htm					
Pierce County PO Box 679	Blackshear	GA	31516	912-449-2022	449-2024
Pierce County 414 W Main St PO Box 119	Ellsworth	WI	54011	715-273-6851	273-6853
Web: www.co.pierce.wi.us					
Pierce County 111 W Ct St Rm 1	Pierce	NE	68767	402-329-4225	329-6439
Web: www.co.pierce.ne.us					
Pierce County 240 SE 2nd St PO Box 258	Rugby	ND	58368	701-776-6161	776-5707
Pierce County 930 Tacoma Ave S Rm 110	Tacoma	WA	98402	253-798-7455	798-3428
Web: www.co.pierce.wa.us					
Pike County 115 W Main St	Bowling Green	MO	63334	573-324-2412	324-5154
Web: www.pikecountytourism.com					
Pike County PO Box 309	Magnolia	MS	39652	601-783-3362	
Web: www.co.pike.ms.us					
Pike County 506 Broad St	Milford	PA	18337	570-296-7613	296-6055
Web: www.pikepa.org					
Pike County PO Box 219	Murfreesboro	AR	71958	870-285-2231	285-3281
Pike County PO Box 125	Petersburg	IN	47567	812-354-6025	354-6369
Pike County PO Box 631	Pikeville	KY	41502	606-432-6240	432-6222
Web: www.kentucky.gov					
Pike County 100 E Washington St Courthouse	Pittsfield	IL	62363	217-285-6812	285-5820
Web: www.pikeil.org					
Pike County PO Box 1147	Troy	AL	36081	334-566-6374	566-0142
Pike County 100 E 2nd St	Waverly	OH	45690	740-947-2715	947-1729
Web: www.piketravel.com					
Pike County PO Box 377	Zebulon	GA	30295	770-567-3406	567-2006
Web: www.co.pike.ga.us					
Pima County 130 W Congress St 10th Fl	Tucson	AZ	85701	520-740-8661	740-8171
Web: www.pima.gov					
Pinal County 31 N Pinal St	Florence	AZ	85232	520-866-6000	866-6512
Web: www.co.pinal.az.us					
Pine County 315 Main St S Suite 9	Pine City	MN	55063	320-629-5634	629-5762
Web: www.pinecounty.org					
Pinellas County 315 Court St Rm 601	Clearwater	FL	33756	727-464-3485	464-4384
Web: www.pinellascounty.org					
Pipestone County 416 S Hiawatha Ave	Pipestone	MN	56164	507-825-6740	825-6741*
**Fax:* Acctg ■ *Web:* www.mncounties.org					
Piscataquis County 159 E Main St	Dover-Foxcroft	ME	04426	207-564-2161	564-3022
Web: www.pcedc.org					
Pitkin County 530 E Main St Suite 101	Aspen	CO	81611	970-920-5180	920-5196
Web: www.county.aspenpitkin.com					
Pitt County 1717 W 5th St	Greenville	NC	27834	252-902-2950	830-6311
Web: www.pittcountync.gov					
Pittsburg County 115 E Carl Albert Pkwy Suite 1A	McAlester	OK	74501	918-423-6865	423-7304
Pittsylvania County 21 N Main St PO Box 426	Chatham	VA	24531	434-432-7700	
Web: www.pittgov.org					
Piute County 550 N Main St	Junction	UT	84740	435-577-2840	577-2433
Web: www.millardcounty.com					
Placer County 2954 Richardson Dr	Auburn	CA	95603	530-886-5600	886-5687
Web: www.placer.ca.gov					
Plaquemines Parish 301 Main St	Belle Chasse	LA	70037	504-392-4969	297-5195
Web: www.plaqueminesparish.com					
Platte County 2610 14th St	Columbus	NE	68601	402-563-4904	564-4164
Web: www.plattecounty.net					
Platte County 415 3rd St	Platte City	MO	64079	816-858-2232	858-3363
Web: www.co.platte.mo.us					
Platte County PO Box 728	Wheatland	WY	82201	307-322-3555	322-2245
Pleasants County 301 Ct Ln Rm 101	Saint Marys	WV	26170	304-684-7542	684-7569
Plumas County 520 Main St Rm 104	Quincy	CA	95971	530-283-6305	283-6415
Web: www.countyofplumas.com					
Plymouth County 215 4th Ave SE	Le Mars	IA	51031	712-546-6100	546-5784*
**Fax:* Acctg ■ *Web:* www.co.plymouth.ia.us					
Plymouth County 52 Obery St # 5	Plymouth	MA	02360	508-747-6911	830-0676
Web: www.seeplymouth.com					
Pocahontas County 900C 10th Ave	Marlinton	WV	24954	304-799-4549	799-6947
Web: www.pocahontascountywv.com					
Pocahontas County 99 Ct Sq County Courthouse	Pocahontas	IA	50574	712-335-4208	335-5045
Poinsett County County Courthouse 401 Market St	Harrisburg	AR	72432	870-578-5333	578-4401
Web: www.poinsettcounty.us					
Pointe Coupee Parish 201 E Main St	New Roads	LA	70760	225-638-9596	638-9590
Polk County 100 Polk County Plaza Suite 110	Balsam Lake	WI	54810	715-485-9226	485-9104
Web: www.co.polk.wi.us					
Polk County 330 W Church St	Bartow	FL	33830	863-534-6000	534-7655
Web: www.polk-county.net					
Polk County 6239 Hwy 411	Benton	TN	37307	423-338-4524	338-8611
Web: www.ocoeetn.org					
Polk County 102 E Broadway Suite 14	Bolivar	MO	65613	417-326-4912	
Polk County PO Box 948	Cedartown	GA	30125	770-749-2114	749-2148
Web: www.polkcountygeorgia.us					
Polk County 40 Courthouse Sq PO Box 308	Columbus	NC	28722	828-894-3301	894-2263
Web: www.co.polk.nc.us					
Polk County 816 Marion Ave Suite 210	Crookston	MN	56716	218-281-2332	281-2204
Web: www.co.polk.mn.us					
Polk County 850 Main St	Dallas	OR	97338	503-623-9217	623-0717
Web: www.co.polk.or.us					
Polk County 111 Court Ave	Des Moines	IA	50309	515-286-3000	323-5225
Web: www.polkcountyiowa.gov					
Polk County PO Box 2119	Livingston	TX	77351	936-327-6804	327-6874
Web: www.co.polk.tx.us					
Polk County 507 Church Ave	Mena	AR	71953	479-394-8123	394-8115
Polk County PO Box 276	Osceola	NE	68651	402-747-5431	747-2656
Web: www.polkcounty.ne.gov					
Pondera County 20 4th Ave SW	Conrad	MT	59425	406-271-4000	271-4070
Web: www.ponderacountymontana.org					
Pontotoc County 100 W 13th St	Ada	OK	74820	580-332-1425	
Pontotoc County PO Box 209	Pontotoc	MS	38863	662-489-3900	489-3940
Pope County 130 E Minnesota Ave	Glenwood	MN	56334	320-634-5705	634-3087*
**Fax:* Acctg ■ *Web:* www.mncounties.org					
Pope County PO Box 216	Golconda	IL	62938	618-683-4466	683-4466
Pope County 102 W Main St County Courthouse Suite 6	Russellville	AR	72801	479-968-6064	967-2291
Poquoson (Independent City) 500 City Hall Ave	Poquoson	VA	23662	757-868-3000	868-3101
Web: www.ci.poquoson.va.us					
Portage County 449 S Meridian St 7th Fl	Ravenna	OH	44266	330-297-3600	297-3610
TF: 800-772-3799 ■ *Web:* www.co.portage.oh.us					
Portage County 1516 Church St	Stevens Point	WI	54481	715-346-1351	346-1486
Web: www.co.portage.wi.us/countyclerk					
Porter County 155 Indiana Ave	Valparaiso	IN	46383	219-465-3445	465-3592
Web: www.co.porter.in.us					
Portsmouth (Independent City) PO Box 820	Portsmouth	VA	23705	757-393-8746	393-5378
Web: www.portsmouth.va.gov					
Posey County 126 E 3rd St Rm 220	Mount Vernon	IN	47620	812-838-1300	838-1344
Web: www.poseycounty.org					
Pottawatomie County 325 N Broadway	Shawnee	OK	74801	405-273-8222	275-6898
Pottawatomie County PO Box 187	Westmoreland	KS	66549	785-457-3314	457-3507
Web: www.pottcounty.org					
Pottawattamie County PO Box 476	Council Bluffs	IA	51502	712-328-5604	
Web: www.pottcounty.com					
Potter County 900 S Polk St Rm 418 PO Box 9638	Amarillo	TX	79105	806-379-2275	379-2296
Web: www.co.potter.tx.us					
Potter County 1 E 2nd St Rm 22	Coudersport	PA	16915	814-274-8290	274-8284
Web: www.pottercountypa.net					
Potter County 201 S Exene St PO Box 67	Gettysburg	SD	57442	605-765-9472	765-9670
Powder River County PO Box 270	Broadus	MT	59317	406-436-2657	436-2151
Powell County 409 Missouri Ave	Deer Lodge	MT	59722	406-846-3680	846-2784
Web: www.powellcountymontana.com					
Powell County PO Box 548	Stanton	KY	40380	606-663-6444	663-6406
Power County 543 Bannock Ave	American Falls	ID	83211	208-226-7611	226-7612
Web: www.co.power.id.us					
Poweshiek County PO Box 218	Montezuma	IA	50171	641-623-5644	623-5320
Powhatan County PO Box 37	Powhatan	VA	23139	804-598-5660	598-5608
Web: www.powhatanva.com					
Prairie County PO Box 1011	Des Arc	AR	72040	870-256-4434	
Prairie County 217 W Park St PO Box 125	Terry	MT	59349	406-635-5575	635-5576
Pratt County PO Box 885	Pratt	KS	67124	620-672-4115	672-9541
Web: www.prattcounty.org					
Preble County 101 E Main St	Eaton	OH	45320	937-456-8143	456-8114
Web: www.prebco.org					
Prentiss County PO Box 477	Booneville	MS	38829	662-728-8151	728-2007
Presidio County PO Box 789	Marfa	TX	79843	432-729-4812	729-4313
Presque Isle County PO Box 110	Rogers City	MI	49779	989-734-3288	734-7635
Preston County 101 W Main St Rm 201	Kingwood	WV	26537	304-329-0070	329-0198
Price County 126 Cherry St	Phillips	WI	54555	715-339-3325	339-3089
Web: www.co.price.wi.us					
Prince Edward County 111 S St 2nd Fl PO Box 304	Farmville	VA	23901	434-392-5145	392-3913
Web: www.co.prince-edward.va.us					
Prince George County 6602 Courts Dr PO Box 68	Prince George	VA	23875	804-722-8669	732-1967
Web: www.princegeorgeva.org					
Prince George's County 14741 Governor Oden Bowie Dr	Upper Marlboro	MD	20772	301-952-3600	952-4862
Web: www.goprincegeorgescounty.com					
Prince William County 1 County Complex Ct	Prince William	VA	22192	703-792-6600	792-7484
Web: www.pwcgov.org					
Providence County 1 Dorrance Plaza	Providence	RI	02903	401-458-5400	

	City	State	ZIP	Phone	Fax
Prowers County 301 S Main St Suite 215	Lamar	CO	81052	719-336-8030	336-2255
Web: www.prowerscounty.net					
Pueblo County 215 W 10th St	Pueblo	CO	81003	719-583-6000	583-4894
Web: www.co.pueblo.co.us					
Pulaski County 105 Lumpkin St	Hawkinsville	GA	31036	478-783-4154	783-9209
Pulaski County 401 W Markham St Suite 100	Little Rock	AR	72201	501-340-8500	340-8340
Web: www.co.pulaski.ar.us					
Pulaski County PO Box 118	Mound City	IL	62963	618-748-9360	748-9305
Pulaski County 143 3rd St NW Suite 1	Pulaski	VA	24301	540-980-7705	980-7717
Web: www.pulaskicounty.org					
Pulaski County 100 N Main St Suite 208 PO Box 724	Somerset	KY	42501	606-679-2042	678-0073
Web: www.pcgovt.com					
Pulaski County 301 Historic 66 E Suite 101	Waynesville	MO	65583	573-774-4701	774-5601
Web: www.visitpulaskicounty.org					
Pulaski County 112 E Main St Rm 230	Winamac	IN	46996	574-946-3313	946-4953
Pushmataha County 304 SW 'B' St	Antlers	OK	74523	580-298-2512	298-5299
Putnam County 40 Gleneida Ave Rm 100	Carmel	NY	10512	845-225-3641	228-0231
Web: www.putnamcountyny.com					
Putnam County 121 S Dixie Ave	Cookeville	TN	38501	931-526-7106	372-8201
Web: www.putnamcountytn.gov					
Putnam County 108 S Madison Ave Suite 300	Eatonton	GA	31024	706-485-5826	485-5578
Web: www.putnamcountyga.us					
Putnam County Courthouse Rm 21 & 23	Greencastle	IN	46135	765-653-2648	
Web: www.putnamcountyin.org					
Putnam County PO Box 236	Hennepin	IL	61327	815-925-7129	925-7549
Putnam County 245 E Main St Suite 101	Ottawa	OH	45875	419-523-3656	523-9213
Web: www.putnamcountyohio.com					
Putnam County PO Box 758	Palatka	FL	32178	386-329-0361	329-0888
Web: www.co.putnam.fl.us					
Putnam County Rm 204 County Courthouse	Unionville	MO	63565	660-947-2674	947-4214
Putnam County 3389 Winfield Rd	Winfield	WV	25213	304-586-0202	586-0280
Web: www.putnamcounty.org					
Quay County 300 S 3rd St	Tucumcari	NM	88401	505-461-2112	461-6208
Queen Anne's County 107 N Liberty St	Centreville	MD	21617	410-758-4098	758-1170
Web: www.qac.org					
Queens County 120-55 Queens Blvd	Kew Gardens	NY	11424	718-286-3000	286-2876
Quitman County PO Box 307	Georgetown	GA	39854	229-334-2578	334-3991
Quitman County 230 Chestnut St County Courthouse	Marks	MS	38646	662-326-2661	326-8004
Rabun County 25 Courthouse Sq Suite 201	Clayton	GA	30525	706-782-5271	782-7588
Web: www.gamountains.com					
Racine County 730 Wisconsin Ave	Racine	WI	53403	262-636-3121	636-3491
Web: www.racineco.com					
Radford (Independent City) 619 2nd St	Radford	VA	24141	540-731-3603	731-3699
Web: www.radford.va.us					
Raleigh County 215 Main St	Beckley	WV	25801	304-255-9126	255-9355
Ralls County 311 S Main St	New London	MO	63459	573-985-7111	985-6100
Ramsey County 524 4th Ave Rm 4	Devils Lake	ND	58301	701-662-7006	662-7063
Web: www.co.ramsey.nd.us					
Ramsey County 15 W Kellogg Blvd Rm 250	Saint Paul	MN	55102	651-266-8000	266-8039
TF: 866-520-7225 ■ *Web:* www.co.ramsey.mn.us					
Randall County PO Box 660	Canyon	TX	79015	806-468-5505	468-5509
Web: www.randallcounty.org					
Randolph County 725 McDowell Rd 2nd Fl	Asheboro	NC	27205	336-318-6300	318-6853
Web: www.co.randolph.nc.us					
Randolph County 1 Taylor St	Chester	IL	62233	618-826-2510	826-3750
Randolph County PO Box 221	Cuthbert	GA	39840	229-732-6440	732-5364
Randolph County PO Box 368	Elkins	WV	26241	304-636-0543	636-0544
Randolph County 110 S Main St	Huntsville	MO	65259	660-277-4717	277-3246
Web: www.randolphcountymo.com					
Randolph County PO Box 328	Wedowee	AL	36278	256-357-4551	357-9012
Randolph County 100 S Main St PO Box 230	Winchester	IN	47394	765-584-7207	584-2958
Web: www.randolphcounty.us					
Rankin County 211 E Government St Suite A	Brandon	MS	39042	601-825-1475	825-9600
Web: www.rankincounty.org					
Ransom County PO Box 626	Lisbon	ND	58054	701-683-5823	683-5826
Rapides Parish PO Box 952	Alexandria	LA	71309	318-473-8153	473-4667
Rappahannock County 290 Gay St PO Box 519	Washington	VA	22747	540-675-5330	675-5331
Web: www.rappahannockcountyva.gov					
Ravalli County 215 S 4th St Suite C	Hamilton	MT	59840	406-375-6212	375-6326
Web: www.co.ravalli.mt.us					
Rawlins County 607 Main St	Atwood	KS	67730	785-626-3351	626-9019
Web: www.rawlinscounty.info					
Ray County 100 W Main St County Courthouse	Richmond	MO	64085	816-776-4502	776-4512
Reagan County PO Box 100	Big Lake	TX	76932	325-884-2442	884-1503
Real County PO Box 750	Leakey	TX	78873	830-232-5202	232-6888
Web: www.co.real.tx.us					
Red Lake County PO Box 367	Red Lake Falls	MN	56750	218-253-2598	253-4894
Web: www.prairieagcomm.com					
Red River County 200 N Walnut St	Clarksville	TX	75426	903-427-2401	427-5510
Web: www.co.red-river.tx.us					
Red River Parish PO Box 485	Coushatta	LA	71019	318-932-6741	932-3126
Red Willow County 502 Norris Ave	McCook	NE	69001	308-345-1552	345-4460
Web: www.co.red-willow.ne.us					
Redwood County 3rd & Jefferson Courthouse Sq PO Box 130	Redwood Falls	MN	56283	507-637-4013	637-4072*
**Fax:* Acctg ■ *Web:* www.mncounties2.org/redwood					
Reeves County 100 E 4th St	Pecos	TX	79772	432-445-5467	445-3997
Refugio County 808 Commerce St PO Box 704	Refugio	TX	78377	361-526-2233	526-1325
Web: www.co.refugio.tx.us					
Reno County 206 W 1st St	Hutchinson	KS	67501	620-694-2934	694-2534
Web: www.rngov.org					
Rensselaer County 1600 7th Ave	Troy	NY	12180	518-270-2900	270-2961
Web: www.rensco.com					
Renville County 205 Main St E	Mohall	ND	58761	701-756-6398	756-6398
Renville County 500 E DePue Ave 3rd Fl	Olivia	MN	56277	320-523-3680	523-3689
Web: www.co.renville.mn.us					
Republic County 1815 M St	Belleville	KS	66935	785-527-7231	527-2668
Web: www.nckcn.com					
Reynolds County PO Box 10	Centerville	MO	63633	573-648-2494	648-2296
Rhea County 1475 Market St 1st Fl	Dayton	TN	37321	423-775-7818	
Web: www.rheacountytn.gov					
Rice County 320 NW 3rd St	Faribault	MN	55021	507-332-6101	332-5999
Web: www.co.rice.mn.us					
Rice County 101 W Commercial St	Lyons	KS	67554	620-257-2232	257-3039
Web: www.ricecounty.us					
Rich County 20 S Main St	Randolph	UT	84064	435-793-2415	793-2410
Web: www.utahreach.org					
Richardson County 1700 Stone St	Falls City	NE	68355	402-245-2911	245-2946
Web: www.co.richardson.ne.us					
Richland County 2020 Hampton St	Columbia	SC	29204	803-576-2050	576-2137
Web: www.richlandonline.com					
Richland County 50 Pk Ave E	Mansfield	OH	44902	419-774-5549	774-5547
Web: www.richlandcountyohio.org					
Richland County 103 W Main St	Olney	IL	62450	618-392-3111	393-4005
Richland County 181 W Seminary St PO Box 310	Richland Center	WI	53581	608-647-2197	647-6134
Web: www.co.richland.wi.us					
Richland County 201 W Main St	Sidney	MT	59270	406-433-1708	482-3731
Web: www.richland.org					
Richland County 418 2nd Ave N	Wahpeton	ND	58075	701-671-1524	671-1512
Web: www.mylocalgov.com					
Richland Parish 708 Julia St	Rayville	LA	71269	318-728-2061	728-7004
Richmond (Independent City) 900 E Broad St Rm 201	Richmond	VA	23219	804-780-7970	646-7987
Web: www.ci.richmond.va.us					
Richmond County 125 S Hancock St	Rockingham	NC	28379	910-997-8211	997-8208
Web: www.co.richmond.nc.us					
Richmond County 130 Stuyvesant Pl	Staten Island	NY	10301	718-390-5393	390-5269
Web: www.nyc.gov					
Richmond County 101 Court Cir	Warsaw	VA	22572	804-333-3781	333-5396
Web: www.co.richmond.va.us					
Riley County 110 Courthouse Plaza	Manhattan	KS	66502	785-537-6300	537-6394
Web: www.co.riley.ks.us					
Ringgold County 109 W Madison St	Mount Ayr	IA	50854	641-464-3234	464-2478
Rio Blanco County 555 Main St PO Box 1067	Meeker	CO	81641	970-878-9460	878-3587
Web: www.co.rio-blanco.co.us					
Rio Grande County 965 6th St PO Box 160	Del Norte	CO	81132	719-657-3334	657-2621
Web: www.riograndecounty.org					
Ripley County County Courthouse 100 Courthouse Sq	Doniphan	MO	63935	573-996-3215	996-9774
Ripley County 115 N Main St	Versailles	IN	47042	812-689-6115	689-6000
Web: www.ripleycounty.com					
Ritchie County 115 E Main St Rm 201	Harrisville	WV	26362	304-643-2164	643-2906
Riverside County 4080 Lemon St 4th Fl	Riverside	CA	92501	951-955-1100	955-1105
Web: www.co.riverside.ca.us					
Roane County 200 E Race St	Kingston	TN	37763	865-376-5556	717-4121
Web: www.roanealliance.org					
Roane County 200 Main St	Spencer	WV	25276	304-927-2860	927-2489
Roanoke (Independent City) 210 Reserve Ave SW	Roanoke	VA	24016	540-853-2000	853-1138
Web: www.roanokeva.gov					
Roanoke County 5204 Bernard Dr	Roanoke	VA	24018	540-772-2004	561-2884
Web: www.co.roanoke.va.us					
Roberts County PO Box 477	Miami	TX	79059	806-868-2341	868-3381
Web: www.co.roberts.tx.us					
Roberts County 411 2nd Ave E	Sisseton	SD	57262	605-698-7336	698-4277*
Robertson County PO Box 1029	Franklin	TX	77856	979-828-4130	828-1260
Web: www.co.robertson.tx.us					
Robertson County 26 Court St	Mount Olivet	KY	41064	606-724-5212	724-5022
Web: www.robertsoncounty.ky.gov					
Robertson County 511 S Brown St	Springfield	TN	37172	615-384-5895	384-2218
Web: www.robertsoncountytn.org					
Robeson County 701 N Elm St	Lumberton	NC	28358	910-671-3000	671-3010
Web: www.co.robeson.nc.us					
Rock County 400 State St PO Box 367	Bassett	NE	68714	402-684-3933	684-2741
Web: www.co.rock.ne.us					
Rock County 51 S Main St	Janesville	WI	53545	608-757-5660	757-5662
Web: www.co.rock.wi.us					
Rock County 204 E Brown St	Luverne	MN	56156	507-283-5020	283-5017
Web: www.co.rock.mn.us					
Rock Island County 1504 3rd Ave	Rock Island	IL	61201	309-786-4451	
Web: www.co.rock-island.il.us					
Rockbridge County 150 S Main St	Lexington	VA	24450	540-463-4361	463-5981
Web: www.co.rockbridge.va.us					
Rockcastle County 205 E Main St PO Box 6	Mount Vernon	KY	40456	606-256-2831	256-4302
Web: www.rockcastlecountyky.com					
Rockdale County 922 Court St	Conyers	GA	30012	770-278-7900	278-7921
Web: rockdaleclerk.com					
Rockingham County 10 Rt 125	Brentwood	NH	03833	603-679-9350	
Web: www.co.rockingham.nh.us					
Rockingham County Ct Sq	Harrisonburg	VA	22801	540-564-3000	564-3127
Web: www.co.rockingham.va.us					
Rockingham County 371 US Hwy 65 PO Box 101	Wentworth	NC	27375	336-342-8101	342-8105
Web: www.co.rockingham.nc.us					
Rockland County 11 New Hempstead Rd	New City	NY	10956	845-638-5100	638-5675
Web: www.co.rockland.ny.us					
Rockwall County 1101 Ridge Rd Suite 101	Rockwall	TX	75087	972-882-0220	882-0229
Web: www.rockwallcountytexas.com					
Roger Mills County PO Box 708	Cheyenne	OK	73628	580-497-3365	497-3199
Rogers County 219 S Missouri St	Claremore	OK	74017	918-341-2518	341-4529
Web: www.rogerscounty.org					
Rolette County PO Box 276	Rolla	ND	58367	701-477-3816	477-8594
Web: www.rolettecounty.com					
Rooks County 115 N Walnut St	Stockton	KS	67669	785-425-6391	425-6015
Web: www.rookscounty.net					
Roosevelt County 109 W 1st St 4th Fl of the Roosevelt County Courthouse	Portales	NM	88130	575-356-4990	356-8307
Web: www.rooseveltcounty.com					
Roosevelt County 400 2nd Ave S	Wolf Point	MT	59201	406-653-6250	653-6289

Entry	City	State	ZIP	Phone	Fax
Roscommon County 500 Lake St	Roscommon	MI	48653	989-275-5923	275-8640
Web: www.roscommoncounty.net					
Roseau County 606 5th Ave SW Rm 20	Roseau	MN	56751	218-463-2541	463-1889
Web: www.visitnwminnesota.com/Roseau.htm					
Rosebud County 1200 Main St	Forsyth	MT	59327	406-346-2251	356-7551
Ross County 2 N Paint St Suite B	Chillicothe	OH	45601	740-702-3010	702-3018
Web: www.co.ross.oh.us					
Routt County 136 6th St PO Box 775227	Steamboat Springs	CO	80477	970-870-5405	871-8140
Web: www.co.routt.co.us					
Rowan County 627 E Main St 2nd Fl	Morehead	KY	40351	606-784-5212	784-2923
Rowan County 130 W Innes St	Salisbury	NC	28144	704-636-0361	638-3092
Web: www.co.rowan.nc.us					
Runnels County PO Box 189	Ballinger	TX	76821	325-365-2720	365-3408
Web: www.co.runnels.tx.us					
Rush County 715 Elm PO Box 220	La Crosse	KS	67548	785-222-2731	222-3559
Web: www.rushcounty.org					
Rush County 101 E 2nd St County Courthouse	Rushville	IN	46173	765-932-2077	938-1163*
**Fax: Acctg ■ Web:* www.rushcounty.in.gov					
Rusk County 115 N Main St Suite 206	Henderson	TX	75652	903-657-0330	
Web: www.co.rusk.tx.us					
Rusk County 311 Miner Ave E	Ladysmith	WI	54848	715-532-2100	532-2237
Web: www.ruskcounty.org					
Russell County 410 Monument Sq PO Box 397	Jamestown	KY	42629	270-343-2112	343-2134
Web: www.russellcounty.ky.gov					
Russell County 137 Highland Dr	Lebanon	VA	24266	276-889-8000	889-8011
Web: www.russellcountyva.org					
Russell County 501 14th St	Phenix City	AL	36867	334-298-0516	297-6250
Russell County 401 N Main St PO Box 113	Russell	KS	67665	785-483-4641	483-5725
Web: ks-russellco.manatron.com					
Rutherford County 319 N Maple St Suite 121	Murfreesboro	TN	37130	615-898-7800	898-7830
Rutherford County 289 N Main St	Rutherfordton	NC	28139	828-287-6060	287-6262
Web: www.rutherfordgov.org					
Rutland County 83 Ctr St Suite 3	Rutland	VT	05701	802-775-4394	775-2291
Web: www.rutlandvermont.com					
Sabine County PO Box 580	Hemphill	TX	75948	409-787-3786	787-2044
Web: www.sabinecountytexas.com					
Sabine Parish 400 S Capitol St	Many	LA	71449	318-256-6223	256-9037
Web: www.sabineparishclerk.com					
Sac County PO Box 368	Sac City	IA	50583	712-662-7791	662-7978
Web: www.saccounty.org					
Sacramento County 700 H St Rm 7650	Sacramento	CA	95814	916-874-5833	874-5885
Web: www.saccounty.net					
Sagadahoc County 752 High St	Bath	ME	04530	207-443-8200	443-8213
Web: www.sagcounty.com					
Saginaw County 111 S Michigan Ave	Saginaw	MI	48602	989-790-5251	790-5254
Web: www.saginawcounty.com					
Saguache County 501 4th St PO Box 176	Saguache	CO	81149	719-655-2512	655-2730
Web: www.saguachecounty.net					
Saint Charles County 397 Turner Blvd	Saint Peters	MO	63376	636-949-7550	949-7552
Web: election.sccmo.org					
Saint Charles Parish 15045 River Rd	Hahnville	LA	70057	985-783-5000	783-2067
Web: www.st-charles.la.us					
Saint Clair County 165 5th Ave Suite 100	Ashville	AL	35953	205-594-2100	594-2110
Web: www.stclairco.com					
Saint Clair County 10 Public Sq	Belleville	IL	62220	618-277-6600	277-8783
Web: www.co.st-clair.il.us					
Saint Clair County PO Box 525	Osceola	MO	64776	417-646-2315	646-8080
Web: stclaircountymissouri.com					
Saint Clair County 201 McMorran Blvd	Port Huron	MI	48060	810-985-2200	985-4796
Web: www.stclaircounty.org					
Saint Croix County 1101 Carmichael Rd	Hudson	WI	54016	715-386-4600	381-4400
Web: www.co.saint-croix.wi.us					
Saint Francis County PO Box 1653	Forrest City	AR	72336	870-261-1725	630-1210
Saint Francois County 1 N Washington St Rm 206	Farmington	MO	63640	573-756-5411	431-6967
Saint Helena Parish PO Box 308	Greensburg	LA	70441	225-222-4514	222-3443
TF: 866-345-6185					
Saint James Parish 5800 Hwy 44 PO Box 106	Convent	LA	70723	225-562-2270	562-2279
Web: www.stjamesla.com					
Saint John the Baptist Parish 1801 W Airline Hwy	LaPlace	LA	70068	985-652-9569	652-4131
Web: www.sjbparish.com					
Saint Johns County 4010 Lewis Speedway	Saint Augustine	FL	32084	904-819-3600	819-3661
Web: www.co.st-johns.fl.us					
Saint Joseph County 125 W Main St PO Box 189	Centreville	MI	49032	269-467-5602	467-5628
Web: www.stjosephcountymi.org					
Saint Joseph County 101 S Main St	South Bend	IN	46601	574-235-9635	235-9838
Web: www.stjosephcountyindiana.com					
Saint Landry Parish 118 S Court St PO Box 750	Opelousas	LA	70571	337-942-5606	948-7265
Web: www.stlandry.org					
Saint Lawrence County 48 Court St Bldg 2	Canton	NY	13617	315-379-2237	379-2302
Web: www.co.st-lawrence.ny.us					
Saint Louis County 41 S Central Ave	Clayton	MO	63105	314-615-5000	615-7890
Web: www.stlouisco.com					
Saint Louis County 100 N 5th Ave W Rm 214	Duluth	MN	55802	218-726-2380	725-5060*
**Fax: Acctg ■ Web:* www.co.st-louis.mn.us					
Saint Lucie County PO Box 700	Fort Pierce	FL	34954	772-462-6900	
Web: www.stlucieco.gov					
Saint Martin Parish 301 Port St PO Box 9	Saint Martinville	LA	70582	337-394-2200	394-2203
Web: stmartinparish-la.org					
Saint Mary Parish 500 Main St PO Box 1231	Franklin	LA	70538	337-828-4100	828-2509
Web: www.parish.st-mary.la.us					
Saint Mary's County 41770 Baldridge St PO Box 653	Leonardtown	MD	20650	301-475-4200	475-4935
Web: www.co.saint-marys.md.us					
Saint Tammany Parish 701 N Columbia St	Covington	LA	70433	985-809-8700	
Web: www.stpgov.org					
Sainte Genevieve County 55 S 3rd St	Sainte Genevieve	MO	63670	573-883-5589	883-5312
Salem (Independent City) 114 N Broad St PO Box 869	Salem	VA	24153	540-375-3000	
Web: www.ci.salem.va.us					
Salem County PO Box 18	Salem	NJ	08079	856-935-7510	935-8882
Web: www.salemco.org					
Saline County 215 N Main St Suite 9	Benton	AR	72015	501-303-5630	776-2412
Web: www.salinecounty.org					
Saline County 10 E Poplar St	Harrisburg	IL	62946	618-253-8197	252-3073
Saline County 19 E Arrow St County Courthouse	Marshall	MO	65340	660-886-3331	886-2603
Saline County PO Box 5040	Salina	KS	67402	785-309-5820	309-5826
Web: www.co.saline.ks.us					
Saline County 215 S Ct St	Wilber	NE	68465	402-821-2374	821-3381
Web: www.co.saline.ne.us					
Salt Lake County 2001 S State St Suite S2200	Salt Lake City	UT	84190	801-468-3000	468-3440
Web: www.co.slc.ut.us					
Saluda County 100 E Church St Suite 6	Saluda	SC	29138	864-445-3303	445-3772
Web: www.saludacounty.sc.gov					
Sampson County 435 Rowan Rd	Clinton	NC	28328	910-592-6308	592-1945
Web: www.sampsonnc.com					
San Augustine County 223 N Harrison	San Augustine	TX	75972	936-275-2452	275-2263
Web: www.co.san-augustine.tx.us					
San Benito County 440 5th St Rm 206	Hollister	CA	95023	831-636-4029	636-2939
Web: www.san-benito.ca.us					
San Bernardino County 222 W Hospitality Ln	San Bernardino	CA	92415	909-387-8306	376-8940
Web: www.co.san-bernardino.ca.us					
San Diego County 1600 Pacific Hwy	San Diego	CA	92101	858-694-3900	557-4155*
**Fax Area Code: 619 ■ Web:* www.co.san-diego.ca.us					
San Francisco City & County 1 Dr Carlton B Goodlett Pl City Hall Rm 168	San Francisco	CA	94102	415-554-4950	554-4951
Web: www.sfgov2.org					
San Jacinto County 1 State Hwy 150 Rm 2	Coldspring	TX	77331	936-653-2324	653-8312
Web: www.co.san-jacinto.tx.us					
San Joaquin County 222 E Weber Ave 2nd Fl RM 202 PO Box 990	Stockton	CA	95201	209-468-2400	468-0371
Web: www.sjgov.org					
San Juan County 100 S Oliver Dr	Aztec	NM	87410	505-334-9471	334-3635
Web: www.co.san-juan.nm.us					
San Juan County 350 Court St Rm 7	Friday Harbor	WA	98250	360-378-2163	378-3967
Web: www.co.san-juan.wa.us					
San Juan County PO Box 338	Monticello	UT	84535	435-587-3223	587-2425
Web: www.sanjuancounty.org					
San Juan County PO Box 466	Silverton	CO	81433	970-387-5671	387-5671
San Luis Obispo County 1055 Monterey St Rm D-120	San Luis Obispo	CA	93408	805-781-5080	781-1111
Web: www.slocounty.org					
San Mateo County 555 County Ctr	Redwood City	CA	94063	650-363-4500	363-1903
Web: www.co.sanmateo.ca.us					
San Miguel County 500 W National St Suite 200	Las Vegas	NM	87701	505-425-9333	425-7019
Web: www.smcounty.net					
San Miguel County PO Box 548	Telluride	CO	81435	970-728-3954	728-4808
Web: www.sanmiguelcounty.org					
San Saba County 500 E Wallace St County Courthouse	San Saba	TX	76877	325-372-3614	372-6484
Web: www.co.san-saba.tx.us					
Sanborn County PO Box 56	Woonsocket	SD	57385	605-796-4515	796-4502
Sanders County 111 Main St PO Box 519	Thompson Falls	MT	59873	406-827-6942	827-4388
Web: www.sanderscounty.mt.gov					
Sandoval County 1500 Idalia Road Bldg D	Bernalillo	NM	87004	505-867-7500	771-7600
Web: www.sandovalcounty.com					
Sandusky County 622 Croghan St	Fremont	OH	43420	419-334-6100	334-6104
Web: www.sandusky-county.org					
Sangamon County 200 S 9th St Rm 201	Springfield	IL	62701	217-753-6700	535-3233
Web: www.co.sangamon.il.us					
Sanilac County 60 W Sanilac Ave Rm 203	Sandusky	MI	48471	810-648-3212	648-5466
Web: www.sanilaccounty.net					
Sanpete County 160 N Main St	Manti	UT	84642	435-835-2131	835-2135
Web: www.utahreach.org					
Santa Barbara County PO Box 159	Santa Barbara	CA	93102	805-568-2550	568-3247
Web: www.countyofsb.org					
Santa Clara County 70 W Hedding St 11th Fl E Wing	San Jose	CA	95110	408-299-5105	293-5649
Web: www.claraweb.co.santa-clara.ca.us					
Santa Cruz County 2150 N Congress Dr	Nogales	AZ	85621	520-761-7800	761-7700
Web: www.co.santa-cruz.az.us					
Santa Cruz County 701 Ocean St Rm 230	Santa Cruz	CA	95060	831-454-2800	
Web: www.co.santa-cruz.ca.us					
Santa Fe County 102 Grant Ave	Santa Fe	NM	87504	505-986-6200	995-2740
TF: 800-894-7028 ■ *Web:* www.co.santa-fe.nm.us					
Santa Rosa County 6495 Caroline St Suite F	Milton	FL	32570	850-983-1900	983-1829
Web: data2.santarosa.fl.gov					
Sarasota County PO Box 3079	Sarasota	FL	34230	941-861-7400	
Web: www.co.sarasota.fl.us					
Saratoga County 40 McMaster St	Ballston Spa	NY	12020	518-885-5381	884-4726
Web: www.co.saratoga.ny.us					
Sargent County PO Box 176	Forman	ND	58032	701-724-6241	724-6244
Web: www.mylocalgov.com					
Sarpy County 1210 Golden Gate Dr Suite 1118	Papillion	NE	68046	402-593-2105	593-4360
Web: www.co.sarpy.ne.us					
Sauk County 505 S Broadway St	Baraboo	WI	53913	608-355-3286	355-3522
Web: www.co.sauk.wi.us					
Saunders County PO Box 61	Wahoo	NE	68066	402-443-8101	443-5010
Web: www.co.saunders.ne.us					
Sawyer County 10610 Main St Suite 10 PO Box 836	Hayward	WI	54843	715-634-4866	634-3666
TF: 877-699-4110 ■ *Web:* www.sawyercountygov.org					

	City	State	Zip	Phone	Fax
Schenectady County 620 State St	Schenectady	NY	12305	518-388-4222	388-4224
Web: www.schenectadycounty.com					
Schleicher County PO Drawer 580	Eldorado	TX	76936	325-853-2833	853-2768
Web: www.co.schleicher.tx.us					
Schley County PO Box 352	Ellaville	GA	31806	229-937-2609	937-5880
Schoharie County 284 Main St PO Box 429	Schoharie	NY	12157	518-295-8347	295-8482
Web: www.schohariecounty-ny.gov					
Schoolcraft County 300 Walnut St Rm 164	Manistique	MI	49854	906-341-3618	341-5680
Schuyler County PO Box 187	Lancaster	MO	63548	660-457-3842	457-3016
Schuyler County PO Box 200	Rushville	IL	62681	217-322-4734	322-6164
Schuyler County 105 9th St	Watkins Glen	NY	14891	607-535-8133	535-8130
Web: www.schuylercounty.us					
Schuylkill County 401 N 2nd St	Pottsville	PA	17901	570-622-5570	628-1210
Web: www.co.schuylkill.pa.us					
Scioto County 602 7th St Rm 205	Portsmouth	OH	45662	740-355-8218	354-2057
Web: www.sciotocountyohio.com					
Scotland County PO Box 489	Laurinburg	NC	28353	910-277-2406	277-2411
Web: www.scotlandcounty.org					
Scotland County County Courthouse 117 S Market St	Memphis	MO	63555	660-465-7027	465-7785
Scott County 131 S Winchester St PO Box 188	Benton	MO	63736	573-545-3549	545-3540
Web: www.scottcountymo.com					
Scott County 416 W 4th St	Davenport	IA	52801	563-326-8647	326-8298
Web: www.scottcountyiowa.com					
Scott County 100 E Main St	Forest	MS	39074	601-469-1922	469-5180
Scott County 336 Water St	Gate City	VA	24251	276-386-6521	386-9198
Web: www.scottcountyva.com					
Scott County 101 E Main St	Georgetown	KY	40324	502-863-7850	863-7852
Web: www.scottky.com					
Scott County 282 Court St	Huntsville	TN	37756	423-663-2588	663-3969
Web: www.scottcounty.com					
Scott County 303 Ct St	Scott City	KS	67871	620-872-2420	872-7145
Web: www.scott.kansasgov.com					
Scott County 1 E McClain Ave Suite 120	Scottsburg	IN	47170	812-752-4769	752-5459
Web: www.greatscottindiana.org					
Scott County 200 4th Ave W	Shakopee	MN	55379	952-445-7750	496-8257
Web: www.co.scott.mn.us					
Scott County 190 W 1st St PO Box 10	Waldron	AR	72958	479-637-2642	637-0124
Scott County 35 E Market St	Winchester	IL	62694	217-742-3178	742-5853
Scotts Bluff County 1825 10th St	Gering	NE	69341	308-436-6600	436-3178
Web: www.scottsbluffcounty.org					
Screven County PO Box 159	Sylvania	GA	30467	912-564-7535	564-2562
Scurry County 1806 25th St Suite 300	Snyder	TX	79549	325-573-5332	573-7396
Web: www.co.scurry.tx.us					
Searcy County PO Box 998	Marshall	AR	72650	870-448-3807	448-5005
Sebastian County 35 S 6th St Rm 102	Fort Smith	AR	72901	479-782-5065	784-1567
Web: www.sebastiancountyonline.com					
Sedgwick County PO Box 50	Julesburg	CO	80737	970-474-3346	474-0954
Sedgwick County 525 N Main St Rm 211	Wichita	KS	67203	316-660-9222	383-7961
Web: www.sedgwickcounty.org					
Seminole County 200 S Knox Ave	Donalsonville	GA	39845	229-524-2878	524-8984
Seminole County 1101 E 1st St	Sanford	FL	32771	407-665-7945	665-7939*
**Fax:* Hum Res ■ *Web:* www.seminolecountyfl.gov					
Seminole County PO Box 1180	Wewoka	OK	74884	405-257-2501	257-6422
Seneca County 111 Madison St	Tiffin	OH	44883	419-447-4550	447-0556
Web: www.senecacounty.com					
Seneca County 1 DiPronio Dr	Waterloo	NY	13165	315-539-1770	539-3789
Web: www.co.seneca.ny.us					
Sequatchie County 22 Cherry St PO BOX 595	Dunlap	TN	37327	423-949-2522	949-6316
Web: www.sequatchie.com					
Sequoyah County 120 E Chickasaw Ave	Sallisaw	OK	74955	918-775-4516	775-1218
Sevier County County Courthouse 115 N 3rd St Rm 102	De Queen	AR	71832	870-642-2852	642-3896
Web: www.seviercounty-ar.com					
Sevier County 125 Ct Ave Suite 202 E	Sevierville	TN	37862	865-453-5502	453-6830
Web: www.seviercountytn.org					
Seward County 415 N Washington Ave Suite 109	Liberal	KS	67901	620-626-3200	626-3211
Web: www.seward.kansasgov.com					
Seward County PO Box 190	Seward	NE	68434	402-643-2883	643-9243
Web: www.connectseward.org					
Shackelford County PO Box 247	Albany	TX	76430	325-762-2232	762-2830
Web: www.co.shackelford.tx.us					
Shannon County 111 N Main St	Eminence	MO	65466	573-226-3414	226-5321
Shannon County 906 N River St	Hot Springs	SD	57747	605-745-5131	745-5688
Sharkey County PO Box 218	Rolling Fork	MS	39159	662-873-2755	873-6045
Sharp County PO Box 307	Ash Flat	AR	72513	870-994-7361	994-7712
Web: www.sharpcounty.org					
Shasta County 1643 Market St	Redding	CA	96099	530-225-5378	225-5454
Web: www.co.shasta.ca.us					
Shawano County 311 N Main St	Shawano	WI	54166	715-526-9150	524-5157
Web: www.co.shawano.wi.us					
Shawnee County 200 SE 7th St	Topeka	KS	66603	785-233-8200	291-4912
Web: www.co.shawnee.ks.us					
Sheboygan County 615 N 6th St	Sheboygan	WI	53081	920-459-3003	459-0304
Web: www.co.sheboygan.wi.us					
Shelby County PO Box 1987	Center	TX	75935	936-598-6361	598-3701
Web: www.co.shelby.tx.us					
Shelby County PO Box 1810	Columbiana	AL	35051	205-669-3760	669-3786
Web: www.shelbycountyalabama.com					
Shelby County 612 Court St Rm 301 PO Box 431	Harlan	IA	51537	712-755-5543	755-2667
TF: 800-735-3942 ■ *Web:* www.shco.org					
Shelby County 160 N Main St Suite 450	Memphis	TN	38103	901-545-4301	545-4283
Web: www.co.shelby.tn.us					
Shelby County PO Box 230	Shelbyville	IL	62565	217-774-4421	774-5291
Shelby County 25 W Polk St	Shelbyville	IN	46176	317-392-6330	392-6393
Web: www.co.shelby.in.us					
Shelby County 419 Washington St	Shelbyville	KY	40065	502-633-1220	633-7623
Web: www.shelbyvilleky.com					
Shelby County 100 E Main St	Shelbyville	MO	63469	573-633-2181	633-1004
Shelby County 129 E Ct St Suite 100	Sidney	OH	45365	937-498-7226	498-1293
Web: www.co.shelby.oh.us					
Shenandoah County 600 N Main St Suite 102	Woodstock	VA	22664	540-459-6165	459-6168
Web: www.co.shenandoah.va.us					
Sherburne County 13880 Hwy 10	Elk River	MN	55330	763-241-2800	241-2816
Web: www.co.sherburne.mn.us					
Sheridan County PO Box 899	Hoxie	KS	67740	785-675-3361	675-3487
Sheridan County PO Box 409	McClusky	ND	58463	701-363-2207	363-2953
Web: www.mylocalgov.com					
Sheridan County 100 W Laurel Ave	Plentywood	MT	59254	406-765-1660	765-2609
Web: www.co.sheridan.mt.us					
Sheridan County 301 E 2nd St PO Box 39	Rushville	NE	69360	308-327-5650	327-5624
Sheridan County 224 S Main St Suite B-2	Sheridan	WY	82801	307-674-2500	
Web: www.sheridancounty.com					
Sherman County 813 Broadway Rm 102	Goodland	KS	67735	785-899-4800	899-4844
Web: www.sherman.kansasgov.com					
Sherman County PO Box 456	Loup City	NE	68853	308-745-1513	745-1820
Web: www.co.sherman.ne.us					
Sherman County 500 Court St PO Box 365	Moro	OR	97039	541-565-3606	565-3771
Web: www.sherman-county.com					
Sherman County PO Box 270	Stratford	TX	79084	806-366-2371	366-5670
Web: www.co.sherman.tx.us					
Shiawassee County 208 N Shiawassee St	Corunna	MI	48817	989-743-2242	743-2241
Web: www.co.shiawassee.mi.us					
Shoshone County 700 Bank St	Wallace	ID	83873	208-752-3331	752-4304
Web: www.shoshonecounty.org					
Sibley County 400 Ct St	Gaylord	MN	55334	507-237-4051	237-4062
Web: www.co.sibley.mn.us					
Sierra County 100 Courthouse Sq Suite 11 PO Box D	Downieville	CA	95936	530-289-3295	289-2830
Web: www.sierracounty.ws					
Simpson County 103 W Cedar St	Franklin	KY	42134	270-586-8161	586-6464
Web: www.simpsoncountyclerk.ky.gov					
Simpson County PO Box 367	Mendenhall	MS	39114	601-847-2626	847-7004
Sioux County PO Box L	Fort Yates	ND	58538	701-854-3481	854-3854*
Sioux County PO Box 158	Harrison	NE	69346	308-668-2401	668-2443
Web: www.co.sioux.ne.us					
Sioux County 210 Central Ave SE	Orange City	IA	51041	712-737-2286	737-8908
Web: www.siouxcounty.org					
Siskiyou County 201 4th St	Yreka	CA	96097	530-842-8005	842-8013
Web: www.co.siskiyou.ca.us					
Sitka City & Borough 100 Lincoln St	Sitka	AK	99835	907-747-3294	747-7403
Web: www.cityofsitka.com					
Skagit County 205 W Kincaid St Rm 103	Mount Vernon	WA	98273	360-336-9440	
Web: www.skagitcounty.net					
Skamania County 240 Vancouver Ave PO Box 790	Stevenson	WA	98648	509-427-3770	427-3777
Web: www.skamaniacounty.org					
Slope County PO Box JJ	Amidon	ND	58620	701-879-6275	879-6278
Smith County 122 Turner High Cir	Carthage	TN	37030	615-735-9833	735-8252
Web: www.smithcountychamber.org					
Smith County PO Box 517	Raleigh	MS	39153	601-782-4751	782-4007
Smith County 218 S Grant St	Smith Center	KS	66967	785-282-5110	282-5114
Smith County PO Box 1018	Tyler	TX	75710	903-535-0630	535-0684
Web: www.smith-county.com					
Smyth County 109 W Main St Rm 144	Marion	VA	24354	276-782-4044	782-4045
Web: www.smythcounty.org					
Snohomish County 3000 Rockefeller Ave MS 605	Everett	WA	98201	425-388-3466	388-3806
Web: www.co.snohomish.wa.us					
Snyder County 9 W Market St	Middleburg	PA	17842	570-837-4207	837-4282
Web: www.snydercounty.org					
Socorro County 200 Church St PO Box I	Socorro	NM	87801	505-835-0589	835-4629
Web: www.socorro-nm.com					
Solano County 675 Texas St Suite 1900	Fairfield	CA	94533	707-784-7485	784-6311
Web: www.co.solano.ca.us					
Somerset County 11916 Somerset Ave Rm 111	Princess Anne	MD	21853	410-651-0320	651-0366
Web: www.visitsomerset.com					
Somerset County 41 Court St	Skowhegan	ME	04976	207-474-9861	474-7405
Web: www.somersetcounty-me.org					
Somerset County 300 N Ctr Ave	Somerset	PA	15501	814-445-1400	445-1447
Web: www.co.somerset.pa.us					
Somerset County 20 Grove St	Somerville	NJ	08876	908-231-7006	253-8853
Web: www.co.somerset.nj.us					
Somervell County PO Box 1098	Glen Rose	TX	76043	254-897-4427	897-3233
Web: www.glenrose.org					
Sonoma County 575 Administration Dr Suite 104A	Santa Rosa	CA	95403	707-565-2431	565-3778
Web: www.sonoma-county.org					
Southampton County 22350 Main St	Courtland	VA	23837	757-653-2200	653-2547
Web: www.southamptoncounty.org					
Spalding County PO Box 1087	Griffin	GA	30224	770-467-4200	
Web: www.spaldingcounty.com					
Spartanburg County 180 Magnolia St	Spartanburg	SC	29306	864-596-2591	596-2239
Web: www.spartanburgcounty.org					
Spencer County 200 Main St PO Box 12	Rockport	IN	47635	812-649-6028	649-6030
Web: spencercounty.in.gov					
Spencer County 2 W Main St	Taylorsville	KY	40071	502-477-3215	477-3216
Web: www.spencercountyky.gov					
Spokane County 1116 W Broadway Ave	Spokane	WA	99260	509-477-2265	477-2274
Web: www.spokanecounty.org					
Spotsylvania County 1905 Courthouse Rd PO Box 99	Spotsylvania	VA	22553	540-507-7010	507-7019
Web: www.spotsylvania.va.us					
Stafford County 209 N Broadway St	Saint John	KS	67576	620-549-3295	549-3298
Web: www.staffordcounty.org					
Stafford County 1300 Court House Rd	Stafford	VA	22554	540-658-8750	
Web: www.co.stafford.va.us					
Stanislaus County 1021 I St Suite 101	Modesto	CA	95354	209-525-5250	525-5804
Web: www.stancounty.com					
Stanley County PO Box 595	Fort Pierre	SD	57532	605-223-7780	223-7791
Stanly County 201 S 2nd St PO Box 668	Albemarle	NC	28001	704-986-7000	983-7001
Web: www.co.stanly.nc.us					
Stanton County PO Box 190	Johnson	KS	67855	620-492-2140	492-2688
Stanton County PO Box 347	Stanton	NE	68779	402-439-2222	439-2200
Web: www.co.stanton.ne.us					

Name / Address	City	State	Zip	Phone	Fax
Stark County 225 4th St NE	Canton	OH	44702	330-451-7432	451-7190
Web: www.co.stark.oh.us					
Stark County PO Box 130	Dickinson	ND	58602	701-456-7630	456-7634*
Stark County 130 W Main St PO Box 97	Toulon	IL	61483	309-286-5911	286-4039
Web: starkco.illinois.gov					
Starke County					
53 E Washington St County Courthouse	Knox	IN	46534	574-772-9128	772-9169
Starr County Industrial Foundation					
601 E Main St Rm 201	Rio Grande City	TX	78582	956-487-2709	
Web: www.starrcounty.org					
Staunton (Independent City)					
113 E Beverley St	Staunton	VA	24401	540-332-3874	332-3970
Web: www.staunton.va.us					
Stearns County 705 Courthouse Sq Rm 121	Saint Cloud	MN	56303	320-656-3601	656-6393
Web: www.co.stearns.mn.us					
Steele County PO Box 296	Finley	ND	58230	701-524-2152	524-1325
Steele County 111 E Main St	Owatonna	MN	55060	507-444-7700	444-7491
Web: www.co.steele.mn.us					
Stephens County 200 W Walker St	Breckenridge	TX	76424	254-559-3700	559-9645
Web: www.co.stephens.tx.us					
Stephens County 101 S 11th St	Duncan	OK	73533	580-255-4193	255-1771
Stephens County PO Box 386	Toccoa	GA	30577	706-886-9491	886-2185
Web: www.stephenscounty-ga.gov					
Stephenson County 50 W Douglas St # 500	Freeport	IL	61032	815-235-8289	235-8378
Web: www.co.stephenson.il.us					
Sterling County PO Box 55	Sterling City	TX	76951	325-378-5191	378-2266
Web: www.co.sterling.tx.us					
Steuben County 206 E Gale St	Angola	IN	46703	260-668-1000	668-3702
Web: www.co.steuben.in.us					
Steuben County 3 E Pulteny Sq	Bath	NY	14810	607-664-2563	664-2158
Web: www.steubencony.org					
Stevens County 215 S Oak St	Colville	WA	99114	509-684-3751	684-8310
Web: www.co.stevens.wa.us					
Stevens County 200 E 6th St	Hugoton	KS	67951	620-544-2541	544-4094
Web: www.stevenscoks.org					
Stevens County 400 Colorado Ave PO Box 530	Morris	MN	56267	320-589-7289	589-7288
Web: www.co.stevens.mn.us					
Stewart County 225 Donelson Pkwy PO Box 67	Dover	TN	37058	931-232-7616	232-4934
Web: www.stewartcountygovernment.com					
Stewart County PO Box 157	Lumpkin	GA	31815	229-838-6769	838-9856
Web: www.stewartcountyga.gov					
Stillwater County 400 3rd Ave N PO Box 149	Columbus	MT	59019	406-322-8000	322-8007
Web: www.stillwater.mt.gov					
Stoddard County 316 S Prairie St	Bloomfield	MO	63825	573-568-3339	568-2194
Stokes County 1012 Main St PO Box 250	Danbury	NC	27016	336-593-4400	593-4401
Web: www.co.stokes.nc.us					
Stone County 108 E 4th St	Galena	MO	65656	417-357-6127	357-6861
Web: www.stoneco-mo.us					
Stone County 107 W Main St Suite C	Mountain View	AR	72560	870-269-3351	269-3176
Stone County 323 E Cavers Ave PO Drawer 7	Wiggins	MS	39577	601-928-5266	928-6464
Web: www.stonecountygov.com					
Stonewall County PO Box P	Aspermont	TX	79502	940-989-2272	989-2715
Web: www.stonewallcountytexas.us					
Storey County 26 S B St	Virginia City	NV	89440	775-847-0968	847-0949
Web: storeycounty.org					
Story County 1315 S B Ave	Nevada	IA	50201	515-382-7410	
Web: www.storycounty.com					
Strafford County 259 County Farm Rd	Dover	NH	03820	603-742-1458	743-4407
Web: www.co.strafford.nh.us					
Stutsman County 511 2nd Ave SE	Jamestown	ND	58401	701-252-9035	251-6325
Web: www.co.stutsman.nd.us					
Sublette County PO Box 250	Pinedale	WY	82941	307-367-4372	367-6396
Web: www.visitsublettecounty.com					
Suffolk (Independent City) 441 Market St	Suffolk	VA	23434	757-514-4000	
Web: www.suffolkva.us					
Suffolk County 3 Pemberton Sq Government Ctr	Boston	MA	02108	617-725-8787	
Suffolk County 310 Ctr Dr	Riverhead	NY	11901	631-852-2000	852-2004
Web: www.co.suffolk.ny.us					
Sullivan County 3258 Hwy 126	Blountville	TN	37617	423-323-6428	279-2725
Web: www.sullivancounty.org					
Sullivan County 245 Muncy St PO Box 157	Laporte	PA	18626	570-946-5201	946-4421
Web: www.sullivancounty-pa.us					
Sullivan County 109 N Main St	Milan	MO	63556	660-265-3786	265-3724
Sullivan County 100 N St	Monticello	NY	12701	845-794-3000	794-6928
Web: www.co.sullivan.ny.us					
Sullivan County 14 Main St	Newport	NH	03773	603-863-2560	863-9314
Web: www.sullivancountynh.gov					
Sullivan County 100 Ct House Sq # 304	Sullivan	IN	47882	812-268-4657	268-7027
Web: www.sctb.net					
Sully County PO Box 188	Onida	SD	57564	605-258-2535	258-2270
Summers County PO Box 97	Hinton	WV	25951	304-466-7104	466-7146
Web: www.summerscvb.com					
Summit County 175 S Main St	Akron	OH	44308	330-643-2500	643-2507
Web: www.co.summit.oh.us					
Summit County PO Box 1538	Breckenridge	CO	80424	970-453-2561	453-3540
Web: www.co.summit.co.us					
Summit County 60 N Main St	Coalville	UT	84017	435-336-3203	336-3030
Web: www.co.summit.ut.us					
Sumner County 101 Public Sq PO Box 549	Gallatin	TN	37066	615-452-4367	451-6027
Web: www.sumnertn.org					
Sumner County 501 N Washington Ave	Wellington	KS	67152	620-326-3395	326-2116
Web: co.sumner.ks.us					
Sumter County 500 W Lamar St PO Box 295	Americus	GA	31709	229-928-4500	928-4503
Web: sumtercountyga.us					
Sumter County 209 N Florida St	Bushnell	FL	33513	352-793-0200	793-0207
Web: www.bocc.co.sumter.fl.us					
Sumter County PO Box 936	Livingston	AL	35470	205-652-2291	
Sumter County 141 N Main St	Sumter	SC	29150	803-436-2227	436-2223
Web: www.sumtercountysc.org					
Sunflower County PO Box 988	Indianola	MS	38751	662-887-4703	887-7054
Surry County 202 Kapp St	Dobson	NC	27017	336-386-3700	386-9879
Web: www.co.surry.nc.us					
Surry County PO Box 65	Surry	VA	23883	757-294-5271	294-5204
Web: www.surrycounty.govoffice2.com					
Susquehanna County 75 Public Ave	Montrose	PA	18801	570-278-4600	278-9268
Web: www.susquehanna.pa.us					
Sussex County 2 The Cr PO Box 589	Georgetown	DE	19947	302-855-7743	855-7749
Web: www.sussexcountyde.gov					
Sussex County 4 Pk Pl	Newton	NJ	07860	973-579-0900	383-7493
Web: www.sussex.nj.us					
Sussex County 20233 Thornton Sq PO Box 1397	Sussex	VA	23884	434-246-1000	246-6013
Web: sussexcounty.govoffice.com					
Sutter County 433 2nd St	Yuba City	CA	95991	530-822-7134	822-7214
Web: www.co.sutter.ca.us					
Sutton County 300 E Oak St Suite 3	Sonora	TX	76950	325-387-3815	387-6028
Web: www.co.sutton.tx.us					
Suwannee County 200 S Ohio Ave	Live Oak	FL	32064	386-364-3498	362-0548
Web: www.suwanneechamber.com					
Swain County PO Box 1397	Bryson City	NC	28713	828-488-2288	488-9360
Web: www.swaincounty.org					
Sweet Grass County					
200 W 1st Ave PO Box 888	Big Timber	MT	59011	406-932-5152	932-3026
Web: www.co.sweetgrass.mt.us					
Sweetwater County PO Box 730	Green River	WY	82935	307-872-6400	872-6337
Web: www.co.sweet.wy.us					
Swift County PO Box 110	Benson	MN	56215	320-843-2744	843-4124
Web: www.swiftcounty.com					
Swisher County					
County Courthouse 119 S Maxwell St	Tulia	TX	79088	806-995-3294	995-4121
Web: www.co.swisher.tx.us					
Switzerland County					
212 W Main St County Courthouse	Vevay	IN	47043	812-427-3302	427-3179
Talbot County					
11 N Washington St County Courthouse	Easton	MD	21601	410-770-8010	770-8007
Web: www.co.talbot.md.us					
Talbot County PO Box 325	Talbotton	GA	31827	706-665-3239	665-8637
Taliaferro County PO Box 182	Crawfordville	GA	30631	706-456-2123	456-2749
Talladega County 1 Ct Sq	Talladega	AL	35160	256-362-1357	761-2147
Web: www.talladegacounty.com					
Tallahatchie County PO Box 350	Charleston	MS	38921	662-647-5551	647-8490
Tallapoosa County 125 N Broadnax St Rm 131	Dadeville	AL	36853	256-825-4268	825-1009
Tama County 104 W State St PO Box 61	Toledo	IA	52342	641-484-3980	484-5127
Web: www.tamacounty.org					
Taney County 132 David St PO Box 156	Forsyth	MO	65653	417-546-7200	546-2519
Web: www.co.taney.mo.us					
Tangipahoa Parish 206 E Mulberry St	Amite	LA	70422	985-748-3211	748-7576
Web: www.tangipahoa.org					
Taos County 105 Albright St Suite A	Taos	NM	87571	575-737-6300	737-6314
Web: www.taoscounty.org					
Tarrant County 100 W Weatherford St	Fort Worth	TX	76196	817-884-1195	884-3295
Web: www.tarrantcounty.com					
Tate County PO Box 309	Senatobia	MS	38668	662-562-5661	560-6205
Tattnall County PO Box 25	Reidsville	GA	30453	912-557-4335	557-6088
Web: www.tattnall.com					
Taylor County 300 Oak St	Abilene	TX	79602	325-674-1202	674-1279
Web: www.taylorcountytexas.org					
Taylor County					
405 Jefferson St County Courthouse	Bedford	IA	50833	712-523-2095	523-2936
Taylor County 109 Ivy St PO Box 278	Butler	GA	31006	478-862-3336	862-2871
Web: www.taylorga.us/page39.php					
Taylor County 203 N Ct St Suite 5	Campbellsville	KY	42718	270-465-6677	789-1144
Taylor County 214 W Main St	Grafton	WV	26354	304-265-1401	265-3016
Taylor County 224 S 2nd St	Medford	WI	54451	715-748-1460	748-1415
Web: www.co.taylor.wi.us					
Taylor County PO Box 620	Perry	FL	32348	850-838-3506	838-3549
Web: www.taco.perryfl.com					
Tazewell County 11 S 4th St Fl 2 Suite 203	Pekin	IL	61554	309-477-2264	477-2244
Web: www.tazewell.com					
Tazewell County PO Box 968	Tazewell	VA	24651	276-988-1222	988-7501
Tehama County 633 Washington St Rm 11	Red Bluff	CA	96080	530-527-3350	527-1745
Web: www.co.tehama.ca.us					
Telfair County 713 Telfair Ave	McRae	GA	31055	229-868-5688	868-7950
Teller County PO Box 959	Cripple Creek	CO	80813	719-689-2988	686-7900
Web: www.co.teller.co.us					
Tensas Parish PO Box 78	Saint Joseph	LA	71366	318-766-3921	766-3926
Terrebonne Parish PO Box 1569	Houma	LA	70361	985-868-5660	868-5143
Web: terrebonneclerk.org					
Terrell County PO Box 525	Dawson	GA	39842	229-995-4476	995-4320
Terrell County 105 E Hackberry	Sanderson	TX	79848	432-345-2391	345-2740
Web: www.co.terrell.tx.us					
Terry County 500 W Main St Rm 105	Brownfield	TX	79316	806-637-8551	637-4874
Web: www.co.terry.tx.us					
Teton County 1 S Main St PO Box 610	Choteau	MT	59422	406-466-2151	466-2138
Web: www.tetoncomt.org					
Teton County 89 N Main St Suite 1	Driggs	ID	83422	208-354-2905	354-8776
Teton County PO Box 1727	Jackson	WY	83001	307-733-4430	739-8681
Web: www.tetonwyo.org					
Texas County PO Box 197	Guymon	OK	73942	580-338-3141	338-4311
Web: www.txcountyok.com					
Texas County 210 N Grand Ave	Houston	MO	65483	417-967-2112	967-3837
Thayer County 225 N 4th St Rm 201 PO Box 208	Hebron	NE	68370	402-768-6126	768-2129
Web: www.thayercounty.ne.gov					
Thomas County 300 N Ct Ave	Colby	KS	67701	785-460-4500	460-4503
Web: www.thomascountyks.com					
Thomas County PO Box 226	Thedford	NE	69166	308-645-2261	645-2623
Thomas County					
110 N Crawford St PO Box 920	Thomasville	GA	31799	229-225-4100	226-3430
Web: www.thomascountyboc.org					
Throckmorton County PO Box 309	Throckmorton	TX	76483	940-849-2501	849-3220
Web: www.co.throckmorton.tx.us					
Thurston County 2000 Lakeridge Dr SW Bldg 2	Olympia	WA	98502	360-786-5430	753-4033
Web: www.co.thurston.wa.us					
Thurston County PO Box G	Pender	NE	68047	402-385-2343	385-3544

Entry	City	State	Zip	Phone	Fax
Tift County 225 N Tift Ave PO Box 354	Tifton	GA	31794	229-386-7856	386-7813
Web: www.tiftcounty.org					
Tillamook County 201 Laurel Ave	Tillamook	OR	97141	503-842-3403	842-1384
Web: www.co.tillamook.or.us					
Tillman County 201 N Main St	Frederick	OK	73542	580-335-3421	335-3795
Tioga County 16 Court St PO Box 307	Owego	NY	13827	607-687-8660	687-8686
Web: www.tiogacountyny.com					
Tippah County 101 E Spring St	Ripley	MS	38663	662-837-7374	837-7148
Web: www.tippahcounty.ripley.ms					
Tippecanoe County 20 N 3rd St	Lafayette	IN	47901	765-423-9215	423-9196
Web: www.county.tippecanoe.in.us					
Tipton County PO Box 528	Covington	TN	38019	901-476-0207	476-0227
Web: www.tiptonco.com					
Tipton County 101 E Jefferson St	Tipton	IN	46072	765-675-2794	675-3194*
**Fax:* Acctg ■ *Web:* www.tiptoncounty.org					
Tishomingo County 1008 Battleground Dr	Iuka	MS	38852	662-423-7010	423-7005
Web: www.tunicacounty.com					
Titus County 100 W 1st Suite 204	Mount Pleasant	TX	75455	903-577-6796	572-5078
Web: www.co.titus.tx.us					
Todd County 221 1st Ave S Suite 200	Long Prairie	MN	56347	320-732-4469	732-4001*
**Fax:* Acctg ■ *Web:* www.co.todd.mn.us					
Todd County 200 E 3rd St	Winner	SD	57580	605-842-3727	842-1116
Tolland County 69 Brooklyn St	Rockville	CT	06066	860-896-4920	
Tom Green County 124 W Beauregard Ave	San Angelo	TX	76903	325-659-6553	659-3251
Web: www.co.tom-green.tx.us/county/index.html					
Tompkins County 320 N Tioga St	Ithaca	NY	14850	607-274-5431	274-5445
Web: www.co.tompkins.ny.us					
Tooele County 47 S Main St	Tooele	UT	84074	435-843-3140	882-7317
Web: www.co.tooele.ut.us					
Toole County 226 1st St S	Shelby	MT	59474	406-424-8310	424-8301
Toombs County 100 Courthouse Sq	Lyons	GA	30436	912-526-3311	526-1004
Torrance County 205 9th St PO BOX 48	Estancia	NM	87016	505-246-4725	384-5294
Web: www.torrancecountynm.org					
Towner County PO Box 517	Cando	ND	58324	701-968-4340	968-4344
Web: www.mylocalgov.com					
Towns County 48 River St Suite B	Hiawassee	GA	30546	706-896-2276	896-4628
Web: www.mountaintopga.com					
Transylvania County 28 E Main St	Brevard	NC	28712	828-884-3100	884-3119
Web: www.transylvaniacounty.org					
Traverse County PO Box 428	Wheaton	MN	56296	320-563-4242	563-4424*
Travis County PO Box 1748	Austin	TX	78767	512-854-9343	854-9542
Web: www.co.travis.tx.us					
Treasure County PO Box 392	Hysham	MT	59038	406-342-5547	342-5445
Trego County 216 N Main St	WaKeeney	KS	67672	785-743-5773	743-5594
Trempealeau County 36245 Main St	Whitehall	WI	54773	715-538-2311	538-4210
Web: www.tremplocounty.com					
Treutlen County					
302 Martin Luther King JR Dr	Soperton	GA	30457	912-529-3664	529-6062
Trigg County PO Box 1310	Cadiz	KY	42211	270-522-6661	522-6662
Trimble County 4874 Hwy 421 N PO Box 312	Bedford	KY	40006	502-255-0062	255-0063
Web: www.trimblecounty.com					
Trinity County PO Box 456	Groveton	TX	75845	936-642-1208	642-3004
Web: www.co.trinity.tx.us					
Trinity County 101 Court St PO Box 1215	Weaverville	CA	96093	530-623-1220	623-8398
Web: www.trinitycounty.org					
Tripp County Historical Society 200 E 3rd St	Winner	SD	57580	605-842-2266	842-2267
Troup County PO Box 866	LaGrange	GA	30241	706-883-1740	883-1724
Web: www.troupcountyga.org					
Trousdale County 200 E Main St Rm 2	Hartsville	TN	37074	615-374-2906	374-1100
Trumbull County					
160 High St NW 5th Fl Administration Bldg	Warren	OH	44481	330-675-2451	675-2462
Web: www.co.trumbull.oh.us					
Tucker County 215 1st St Suite 201	Parsons	WV	26287	304-478-2414	478-2217
Web: www.tuckercounty.wv.gov					
Tulare County 2800 W Burrel Ave	Visalia	CA	93291	559-636-5000	733-6898
Web: www.co.tulare.ca.us					
Tulsa County 500 S Denver Ave Suite 120	Tulsa	OK	74103	918-596-5801	596-5819
Web: www.tulsacounty.org					
Tunica County 1058 S Court St	Tunica	MS	38676	662-363-1465	
Web: tunicacounty.com					
Tuolumne County 2 S Green St	Sonora	CA	95370	209-533-5511	533-5510
Web: www.co.tuolumne.ca.us					
Turner County PO Box 191	Ashburn	GA	31714	229-567-2011	567-0450
TF: 800-471-9696 ■ *Web:* turnercounty.georgia.gov					
Turner County 400 S Main St	Parker	SD	57053	605-297-3115	297-2115
Tuscaloosa County 714 Greensboro Ave	Tuscaloosa	AL	35401	205-349-3870	
Web: www.tuscco.com					
Tuscarawas County					
125 E High Ave Rm 230	New Philadelphia	OH	44663	330-365-3243	343-4682
Web: www.co.tuscarawas.oh.us					
Twiggs County 425 N Railroad St	Jeffersonville	GA	31044	478-945-3629	945-3988
Web: www.twiggscounty.us					
Twin Falls County					
427 Shoshone St N PO Box 126	Twin Falls	ID	83301	208-736-4004	736-4155
Web: www.twinfallscounty.org					
Tyler County PO Box 66	Middlebourne	WV	26149	304-758-2102	758-2126
Tyler County 100 Bluff St Rm 110	Woodville	TX	75979	409-283-2281	283-6305
Web: www.co.tyler.tx.us					
Tyrrell County 108 S Water St PO Box 449	Columbia	NC	27925	252-796-1371	796-1188*
**Fax:* Acctg ■ *Web:* www.visittyrrellcounty.com					
Uinta County 225 9th St PO Box 810	Evanston	WY	82931	307-783-0306	783-0376
Web: www.uintacounty.com					
Uintah County 147 E Main St	Vernal	UT	84078	435-781-0770	781-6701
TF: 800-966-4680 ■ *Web:* www.co.uintah.ut.us					
Ulster County 240 Fair St	Kingston	NY	12401	845-340-3288	340-3299
Web: www.co.ulster.ny.us					
Umatilla County 216 SE 4th St	Pendleton	OR	97801	541-278-6236	278-6345
Web: www.co.umatilla.or.us					
Unicoi County 100 Main St PO Box 713	Erwin	TN	37650	423-743-3000	743-0942
Web: www.unicoicounty.org					
Unified Government of Wyandotte County/Kansas City					
701 N 7th St Suite 323	Kansas City	KS	66101	913-573-5260	573-5005
Web: www.wycokck.org					
Union County 114 Courthouse St PO Box 1	Blairsville	GA	30512	706-439-6000	439-6004
Web: www.unioncounty.gov					
Union County 1103 S 1st St	Clayton	NM	88415	575-374-9253	374-9442*
**Fax Area Code:* 505 ■ *TF:* 800-390-7858 ■ *Web:* www.claytonnewmexico.org					
Union County 300 N Pine St Suite 6	Creston	IA	50801	641-782-7315	782-8241
Web: www.unioncountyiowa.org					
Union County					
101 N Washington Rm 102 County Courthouse	El Dorado	AR	71730	870-864-1910	864-1927
Union County 2 Broad St Rm 115	Elizabeth	NJ	07207	908-527-4999	558-2589
Web: www.unioncountynj.org					
Union County 209 E Main St Suite 230	Elk Point	SD	57025	605-356-2132	356-3687
Union County 309 W Market St PO Box H	Jonesboro	IL	62952	618-833-5711	833-8712
Union County 1106 K Ave	La Grande	OR	97850	541-963-1001	963-1079
Web: www.union-county.org					
Union County 55 W Main St Rm 103	Lake Butler	FL	32054	386-496-3331	496-1718
Union County 103 S 2nd St	Lewisburg	PA	17837	570-524-8600	524-8635
Web: www.unionco.org					
Union County 26 W Union St	Liberty	IN	47353	765-458-6121	458-5263
Union County 233 W 6th St	Marysville	OH	43040	937-645-3006	645-3162
Web: www.co.union.oh.us/GD/Templates/Pages/UC/UCPageDefault.aspx?page=1					
Union County 901 Main St Suite 119	Maynardville	TN	37807	865-992-8043	992-4992
Web: www.unioncountytn.org					
Union County 500 N Main St Rm 925	Monroe	NC	28112	704-283-3810	282-0121
Web: www.co.union.nc.us					
Union County PO Box 119	Morganfield	KY	42437	270-389-1334	389-9135
Union County PO Box 847	New Albany	MS	38652	662-534-1900	534-1907
Web: www.ucda-newalbany.com					
Union County PO Box 703	Union	SC	29379	864-429-1630	429-1715
Web: www.countyofunion.com					
Union Parish 100 E Bayou St Suite 105	Farmerville	LA	71241	318-368-3055	368-3861
Upshur County 40 W Main St Rm 101	Buckhannon	WV	26201	304-472-1068	472-1029
Web: www.buchamber.com					
Upshur County PO Box 730	Gilmer	TX	75644	903-843-4015	843-4504
Web: www.countyofupshur.com					
Upson County 106 E Lee St Suite 110	Thomaston	GA	30286	706-647-7012	647-7030
Upton County 205 E 10th St	Rankin	TX	79778	432-693-2861	693-2129
Utah County 100 E Center St Suite 2200	Provo	UT	84606	801-851-8000	
Web: www.co.utah.ut.us					
Uvalde County PO Box 284	Uvalde	TX	78802	830-278-6614	278-8692
Web: www.uvaldecounty.com					
Val Verde County PO Box 1267	Del Rio	TX	78841	830-774-7564	774-7608
Valencia County 444 Luna Ave	Los Lunas	NM	87031	505-866-2073	866-2023
Web: www.co.valencia.nm.us					
Valley County 219 N Main St	Cascade	ID	83611	208-382-4297	382-7107
Web: www.co.valley.id.us					
Valley County 501 Ct Sq PO Box 2	Glasgow	MT	59230	406-228-6220	228-9027
Valley County 125 S 15th St	Ord	NE	68862	308-728-3700	728-7725
Web: www.co.valley.ne.us					
Van Buren County 451 Main St Suite 2	Clinton	AR	72031	501-745-4140	745-7400
Van Buren County PO Box 475	Keosauqua	IA	52565	319-293-3129	293-6404
Web: www.800-tourvbc.com					
Van Buren County 212 E Paw Paw St Suite 101	Paw Paw	MI	49079	269-657-8218	657-8298
Web: www.vbco.org					
Van Buren County PO Box 827	Spencer	TN	38585	931-946-2121	946-7572
Van Wert County 114 E Main St	Van Wert	OH	45891	419-238-6159	238-4528
Web: www.vanwertcounty.org					
Van Zandt County 121 E Dallas St Rm 202	Canton	TX	75103	903-567-6503	567-6722
Web: www.vanzandtcounty.org					
Vance County 122 Young St Suite E	Henderson	NC	27536	252-738-2040	
Web: www.vancecounty.org					
Vanderburgh County 1 NW ML King Jr Blvd	Evansville	IN	47708	812-435-5241	435-5963
Web: www.vanderburghgov.org					
Venango County Courthouse Annex 1174 Elk St	Franklin	PA	16323	814-432-9510	432-3149
Web: www.co.venango.pa.us					
Ventura County 800 S Victoria Ave	Ventura	CA	93009	805-654-2267	662-6543
Web: www.countyofventura.org					
Vermilion County					
6 N Vermilion St Fl 1 Courthouse Annex	Danville	IL	61832	217-554-1900	554-1914
Web: www.co.vermilion.il.us					
Vermilion Parish					
County Courthouse 100 N State St Suite 101	Abbeville	LA	70510	337-898-1992	898-9803
Web: www.vermilionparishclerkofcourt.com					
Vermillion County PO Box 10	Newport	IN	47966	765-492-3500	492-5001
Vernon County 100 W Cherry St	Nevada	MO	64772	417-448-2500	667-6035
Web: www.vernoncountymo.org					
Vernon County Courthouse Annex Rm 108	Viroqua	WI	54665	608-637-5380	637-5556
Web: www.wisconline.com/counties/vernon					
Vernon Parish 215 N 4th St	Leesville	LA	71446	337-238-1384	238-9902
Victoria County 115 N Bridge St # 103	Victoria	TX	77901	361-575-1478	575-6276
Web: www.victoriacountytx.org					
Vigo County PO Box 8449	Terre Haute	IN	47808	812-462-3211	232-2921
Web: www.vigocountyin.com					
Vilas County 330 Ct St	Eagle River	WI	54521	715-479-3600	479-3605
Web: www.co.vilas.wi.us					
Vinton County					
100 E Main St County Courthouse	McArthur	OH	45651	740-596-4571	596-4571
Web: www.vintoncounty.com					
Virginia Beach (Independent City)					
2401 Courthouse Dr					
Municipal Ctr Bldg 1	Virginia Beach	VA	23456	757-427-4242	427-5626
Web: www.vbgov.com					
Volusia County 123 W Indiana Ave	DeLand	FL	32720	386-736-5920	822-5707
Web: volusia.org					
Wabash County PO Box 277	Mount Carmel	IL	62863	618-262-4561	
Wabash County 69 W Hill St	Wabash	IN	46992	260-563-0661	569-1352
Web: www.wabashcountycvb.com					
Wabasha County 625 Jefferson Ave	Wabasha	MN	55981	651-565-2648	565-2774*
**Fax:* Acctg ■ *Web:* www.co.wabasha.mn.us					
Wabaunsee County 215 Kansas Ave PO Box 278	Alma	KS	66401	785-765-2414	765-3704
Web: www.wabaunsee.kansasgov.com					
Wadena County 415 S Jefferson St	Wadena	MN	56482	218-631-7634	631-7635
Web: www.co.wadena.mn.us					

Name / Address	City	State	ZIP	Phone	Fax
Wagoner County PO Box 156	Wagoner	OK	74477	918-485-6171	485-7709
Wahkiakum County 64 Main St	Cathlamet	WA	98612	360-795-3558	795-8813
Web: www.co.wahkiakum.wa.us					
Wake County 336 Fayetteville St	Raleigh	NC	27601	919-856-6160	856-6168
Web: www.wakegov.com					
Wakulla County 3056 Crawfordville Hwy	Crawfordville	FL	32327	850-926-0905	926-0938
Web: www.clerk.wakulla.fl.us					
Waldo County PO Box D	Belfast	ME	04915	207-338-1710	338-6360
Web: www.waldocountyme.gov					
Walker County PO Box 1207	Huntsville	TX	77342	936-436-4933	436-4930
Web: www.co.walker.tx.us					
Walker County 1801 3rd Ave S PO Box 1447	Jasper	AL	35502	205-384-7230	384-7003
Web: www.walkercounty.com					
Walker County PO Box 445	La Fayette	GA	30728	706-638-1437	638-1453
Web: www.co.walker.ga.us					
Walla Walla County 315 W Main St	Walla Walla	WA	99362	509-527-3200	527-3235
Web: www.co.walla-walla.wa.us					
Wallace County PO Box 70	Sharon Springs	KS	67758	785-852-4282	852-4783
Waller County 836 Austin St	Hempstead	TX	77445	979-826-3357	826-8317
Web: www.wallercounty.org					
Wallowa County 101 S River St Rm 100	Enterprise	OR	97828	541-426-4543	426-5901
Web: www.co.wallowa.or.us					
Walsh County 600 Cooper Ave	Grafton	ND	58237	701-352-2851	352-3340
Web: www.mylocalgov.com					
Walthall County 200 Ball Ave	Tylertown	MS	39667	601-876-4947	876-6026
Web: www.walthallcountychamber.org					
Walton County PO Box 1260	De Funiak Springs	FL	32435	850-892-8115	892-7551
Web: www.co.walton.fl.us					
Walton County 303 S Hammond Dr Suite 330	Monroe	GA	30655	770-267-1301	267-1400
Web: www.waltoncountyga.org					
Walworth County 100 W Walworth St PO Box 1001	Elkhorn	WI	53121	262-741-4241	741-4287
Web: www.co.walworth.wi.us					
Walworth County PO Box 199	Selby	SD	57472	605-649-7878	649-7867*
Wapello County 101 W 4th St	Ottumwa	IA	52501	641-683-0060	683-0064
Web: www.wapellocounty.org					
Ward County PO Box 5005	Minot	ND	58702	701-857-6600	857-6623
Web: www.co.ward.nd.us					
Ward County					
County Courthouse 400 S Allen St Suite 101	Monahans	TX	79756	432-943-3294	943-6054
Web: www.co.ward.tx.us					
Ware County 800 Church St	Waycross	GA	31501	912-287-4300	287-4301
Web: www.warecounty.com					
Warren County 413 2nd St	Belvidere	NJ	07823	908-475-6211	475-6208
Web: www.co.warren.nj.us					
Warren County					
429 E 10th St Suite 100 Courthouse	Bowling Green	KY	42102	270-842-9416	843-5319
Web: www.warrencounty.state.ky.us					
Warren County					
220 N Commerce Ave Suite 100	Front Royal	VA	22630	540-636-4600	636-6066
Web: www.warrencountyva.net					
Warren County 115 N Howard St	Indianola	IA	50125	515-961-1033	961-1071
Web: www.co.warren.ia.us					
Warren County 1340 State Rt 9	Lake George	NY	12845	518-761-6429	761-6551
Web: www.co.warren.ny.us					
Warren County 550 Justice Dr	Lebanon	OH	45036	513-695-1242	695-2990
Web: www.co.warren.oh.us					
Warren County 201 E. Locust St Suite 16	McMinnville	TN	37110	931-473-6652	473-6655
Web: www.warrentn.com					
Warren County 100 W Broadway	Monmouth	IL	61462	309-734-8592	734-7406
Web: www.outfitters.com/illinois/warren					
Warren County 1009 Cherry St	Vicksburg	MS	39183	601-636-4415	630-8016
Web: www.co.warren.ms.us					
Warren County 204 4th Ave	Warren	PA	16365	814-728-3400	728-3479
Web: www.warren-county.net					
Warren County 521 Main St PO Box 46	Warrenton	GA	30828	706-465-2171	465-1300
Web: www.warrencountyga.com					
Warren County 104 W Main St	Warrenton	MO	63383	636-456-3331	456-1801
Warren County 109 S Main St	Warrenton	NC	27589	252-257-3261	257-5529
Web: www.warrencountync.org					
Warren County 125 N Monroe St Suite 11	Williamsport	IN	47993	765-762-3510	762-7251
Web: www.warrenco.net					
Warrick County 107 W Locust St Suite 301	Boonville	IN	47601	812-897-6120	897-6189
Web: www.warrickcounty.gov					
Wasatch County 25 N Main St	Heber City	UT	84032	435-654-3211	654-9924
Web: www.co.wasatch.ut.us					
Wasco County 511 Washington St	The Dalles	OR	97058	541-506-2500	298-3607
Web: www.co.wasco.or.us					
Waseca County 307 N State St	Waseca	MN	56093	507-835-0610	835-0633*
**Fax: Acctg ■ Web:* www.co.waseca.mn.us					
Washakie County PO Box 260	Worland	WY	82401	307-347-3131	347-9366
Web: www.washakiecounty.net					
Washburn County PO Box 639	Shell Lake	WI	54871	715-468-4600	468-4725
Web: www.co.washburn.wi.us					
Washington County 205 Academy Dr	Abingdon	VA	24210	276-525-1300	525-1309
Web: www.washcova.com					
Washington County 150 Ash Ave	Akron	CO	80720	970-345-2701	345-2702
Washington County					
400 S Johnstone Ave Rm 100	Bartlesville	OK	74003	918-337-2840	337-2894
Web: www.co.washington.ok.us					
Washington County PO Box 466	Blair	NE	68008	402-426-6822	426-6825
Washington County 100 E Main St Suite 102	Brenham	TX	77833	979-277-6200	277-6278
Web: www.co.washington.tx.us					
Washington County PO Box 146	Chatom	AL	36518	251-847-2208	847-3677
Washington County PO Box 647	Chipley	FL	32428	850-638-6285	638-6297
Web: www.washingtonfl.com					
Washington County					
280 N College Ave Suite 300	Fayetteville	AR	72701	479-444-1711	444-1894
Web: www.co.washington.ar.us					
Washington County 383 Broadway Bldg A	Fort Edward	NY	12828	518-746-2170	746-2177
Web: www.co.washington.ny.us					
Washington County PO Box 309	Greenville	MS	38702	662-378-8355	
Web: www.thedelta.org					
Washington County 100 W Washington St	Hagerstown	MD	21740	240-313-2200	313-2201
Web: www.washco-md.net					
Washington County 155 N 1st Ave Rm 340	Hillsboro	OR	97124	503-846-8747	846-8636
Web: www.co.washington.or.us					
Washington County 100 E Main St	Jonesborough	TN	37659	423-753-1621	753-4716
Web: www.washingtoncountytn.com					
Washington County PO Box 297	Machias	ME	04654	207-255-3127	255-3313
Web: www.washingtoncountymaine.com					
Washington County 205 Putnam St	Marietta	OH	45750	740-373-6623	373-2085
Web: www.co.washington.oh.us					
Washington County 65 State St	Montpelier	VT	05602	802-828-2091	
Washington County					
101 E St Louis St County Courthouse	Nashville	IL	62263	618-327-8314	327-3582
Washington County 116 Adams St	Plymouth	NC	27962	252-793-5823	793-1183
Web: www.washingtoncountygov.com					
Washington County 102 N Missouri St	Potosi	MO	63664	573-438-4901	438-4038
Washington County 197 E Tabernacle St	Saint George	UT	84770	435-634-5700	634-5753
Web: www.washco.state.ut.us					
Washington County 99 Public Sq Suite 102	Salem	IN	47167	812-883-5748	883-8108
Web: www.washingtoncountyindiana.com					
Washington County 119 Jones St	Sandersville	GA	31082	478-552-2325	552-7424
Web: www.washingtoncounty-ga.com					
Washington County PO Box 446	Springfield	KY	40069	859-336-5425	336-5408
Washington County 14949 62nd St N	Stillwater	MN	55082	651-430-6001	430-6017
Web: www.co.washington.mn.us					
Washington County 4800 Tower Hill Rd	Wakefield	RI	02879	401-782-4121	782-4190
Washington County PO Box 391	Washington	IA	52353	319-653-7741	653-7787
Web: co.washington.ia.us					
Washington County 214 C St	Washington	KS	66968	785-325-2974	325-2303
Washington County 1 S Main St Suite 1005	Washington	PA	15301	724-228-6787	
Web: www.co.washington.pa.us					
Washington County PO Box 670	Weiser	ID	83672	208-414-2092	414-3925
Web: www.co.washington.id.us					
Washington County					
432 E Washington St Suite 2027 PO Box 1986	West Bend	WI	53095	262-335-4400	306-2208
Web: www.co.washington.wi.us					
Washington Parish 909 Pearl St	Franklinton	LA	70438	985-839-7825	839-7828
Washita County PO Box 380	Cordell	OK	73632	580-832-2284	832-3526
Washoe County 75 Court St Rm 131 PO Box 30083	Reno	NV	89501	775-328-3260	328-3582
Web: www.co.washoe.nv.us					
Washtenaw County PO Box 8645	Ann Arbor	MI	48107	734-222-6850	222-6715
Web: www.ewashtenaw.org					
Watauga County 842 W King St Courthouse	Boone	NC	28607	828-265-8000	264-3230
Web: www.wataugacounty.org					
Watonwan County 710 7th Ave S PO Box 518	Saint James	MN	56081	507-375-1236	375-5010
Web: www.co.watonwan.mn.us					
Waukesha County 515 W Moreland Blvd Rm 120	Waukesha	WI	53188	262-548-7010	548-7722
Web: www.waukeshacounty.gov					
Waupaca County 811 Harding St	Waupaca	WI	54981	715-258-6200	258-6212
Web: www.co.waupaca.wi.us					
Waushara County 209 S St Marie St	Wautoma	WI	54982	920-787-0441	787-0481
Web: www.1waushara.com					
Wayne County PO Box 424	Corydon	IA	50060	641-872-2264	872-2431
Web: www.waynecountyiowa.com					
Wayne County					
Coleman A Young Municipal Ctr					
2 Woodward Ave 2nd Fl	Detroit	MI	48226	313-224-6262	224-5364
Web: www.co.wayne.mi.us					
Wayne County PO Box 187	Fairfield	IL	62837	618-842-5182	842-6427
Wayne County 224 E Walnut St # 466	Goldsboro	NC	27530	919-731-1435	731-1446
Web: www.waynegov.com					
Wayne County 109 Walnut St	Greenville	MO	63957	573-224-3011	224-5609
Wayne County 925 Ct St	Honesdale	PA	18431	570-253-5970	253-5432
Web: www.co.wayne.pa.us					
Wayne County 341 E Walnut St	Jesup	GA	31546	912-427-5900	427-5906
Web: www.co.wayne.ga.us					
Wayne County 18 S Main St PO Box 189	Loa	UT	84747	435-836-2765	836-2479
Web: www.waynecnty.com					
Wayne County 26 Church St	Lyons	NY	14489	315-946-5400	946-5407
Web: www.co.wayne.ny.us					
Wayne County 55 N Main St Suite 106	Monticello	KY	42633	606-348-5721	
Web: www.waynecounty.ky.gov					
Wayne County 401 E Main St	Richmond	IN	47374	765-973-9237	973-9321
Web: www.co.wayne.in.us					
Wayne County PO Box 248	Wayne	NE	68787	402-375-2288	375-4137
Web: www.county.waynene.org					
Wayne County PO Box 248	Wayne	WV	25570	304-272-6369	272-5318
Wayne County					
609 Azalea Dr County Courthouse	Waynesboro	MS	39367	601-735-6242	735-6224
Wayne County PO Box 848	Waynesboro	TN	38485	931-722-3653	722-5994
Web: www.waynecountytn.org					
Wayne County 428 W Liberty St	Wooster	OH	44691	330-287-5400	287-5407
Web: www.wayneohio.org					
Waynesboro (Independent City)					
503 W Main St	Waynesboro	VA	22980	540-942-6600	942-6671
Web: www.waynesboro.va.us					
Weakley County					
116 W Main St Rm 104 PO Box 587	Dresden	TN	38225	731-364-2285	364-5236
Web: www.weakleycountytn.gov					
Webb County 1110 Washington St	Laredo	TX	78040	956-523-4143	523-5012
Web: www.webbcounty.com					
Weber County 2380 Washington Blvd Suite 350	Ogden	UT	84401	801-399-8454	399-8314
Web: www.co.weber.ut.us					
Webster County 25 Us Hwy 41A S	Dixon	KY	42409	270-639-5042	639-7009
Web: www.webstercountyky.com					
Webster County 701 Central Ave	Fort Dodge	IA	50501	515-574-3719	574-3714
Web: www.webstercountyia.org					
Webster County					
101 S Crittenden St					
County Courthouse Rm 12	Marshfield	MO	65706	417-468-2223	468-5307
Webster County PO Box 29	Preston	GA	31824	229-828-5775	828-2105

Entry	City	State	ZIP	Phone	Fax
Webster County 621 N Cedar St # 2	Red Cloud	NE	68970	402-746-2716	746-2710
Web: www.co.webster.ne.us					
Webster County 515 Carroll St	Walthall	MS	39771	662-258-4131	258-6657
Web: www.webstercountyms.com					
Webster County 139 Baker St Rm G1	Webster Springs	WV	26288	304-847-2145	847-5198
Web: www.websterwv.com					
Webster Parish PO Box 370	Minden	LA	71058	318-371-0366	371-0226
Web: www.wppj.org					
Weld County PO Box 758	Greeley	CO	80632	970-336-7204	352-0242
Web: www.co.weld.co.us					
Wells County 102 W Market St Rm 205	Bluffton	IN	46714	260-824-6470	824-6475
Web: www.wellscounty.org					
Wells County PO Box 155	Fessenden	ND	58438	701-547-3122	547-3840
Web: www.mylocalgov.com					
West Baton Rouge Parish PO Box 757	Port Allen	LA	70767	225-383-4755	387-0218
Web: www.wbrcouncil.org					
West Carroll Parish PO Box 1078	Oak Grove	LA	71263	318-428-3281	428-9896
West Feliciana Parish PO Box 1921	Saint Francisville	LA	70775	225-635-3864	635-3705
Web: www.westfelicianaparish.org					
Westchester County 110 Dr Martin Luther King Jr Blvd 3rd Fl	White Plains	NY	10601	914-995-3080	995-4030
Web: www.westchesterclerk.com					
Westmoreland County 2 N Main St Courthouse Sq Suite 101	Greensburg	PA	15601	724-830-3100	830-3029
Web: www.co.westmoreland.pa.us					
Westmoreland County PO Box 1000	Montross	VA	22520	804-493-0130	493-0134
Web: www.westmoreland-county.org					
Weston County 1 W Main St	Newcastle	WY	82701	307-746-4775	746-9505
Wetzel County PO Box 156	New Martinsville	WV	26155	304-455-8224	455-5256
Wexford County 437 E Division St	Cadillac	MI	49601	231-779-9453	779-9745
Web: www.wexfordcounty.org					
Wharton County PO Box 69	Wharton	TX	77488	979-532-2381	532-8426
Web: www.co.wharton.tx.us					
Whatcom County 311 Grand Ave Rm 301	Bellingham	WA	98225	360-676-6777	676-6693
Web: www.co.whatcom.wa.us					
Wheatland County 201 A Ave NW	Harlowton	MT	59036	406-632-4893	632-4880
Wheeler County PO Box 181	Alamo	GA	30411	912-568-7135	568-1909
Wheeler County PO Box 127	Bartlett	NE	68622	308-654-3235	654-3470
Wheeler County 701 Adams St PO Box 447	Fossil	OR	97830	541-763-2911	763-2026
Web: www.wheelercounty-oregon.com					
Wheeler County PO Box 465	Wheeler	TX	79096	806-826-5544	826-3282
Web: www.co.wheeler.tx.us					
White County 301 E Main St PO Box 339	Carmi	IL	62821	618-382-7211	382-2322
Web: www.whitecounty-il.gov					
White County 59 S Main St Suite A	Cleveland	GA	30528	706-865-2235	865-1324
Web: www.whitecounty.net					
White County 110 N Main St	Monticello	IN	47960	574-583-7032	583-1532
White County 300 N Spruce St	Searcy	AR	72143	501-279-6200	279-6233
Web: www.whitecountyar.org					
White County County Courthouse Rm 205	Sparta	TN	38583	931-836-3203	836-3204
Web: www.sparta-chamber.net					
White Pine County 801 Clark St Suite 4	Ely	NV	89301	775-289-2341	289-2544
Web: www.whitepinecounty.net					
Whiteside County 200 E Knox St	Morrison	IL	61270	815-772-5100	772-7673
Web: www.whiteside.org					
Whitfield County PO Box 248	Dalton	GA	30722	706-876-2559	275-7540
Web: www.whitfieldcountyga.com					
Whitley County 101 W Van Buren St	Columbia City	IN	46725	260-248-3102	248-3137
Whitley County PO Box 8	Williamsburg	KY	40769	606-549-6002	549-2790
Whitman County 404 N Main St	Colfax	WA	99111	509-397-4622	397-6355
Web: www.co.whitman.wa.us					
Wibaux County 200 S Wibaux St	Wibaux	MT	59353	406-796-2481	796-2625
Wichita County PO Box 968	Leoti	KS	67861	620-375-2731	375-4350
Wichita County 900 7th St # 250	Wichita Falls	TX	76301	940-766-8144	716-8554
Web: www.co.wichita.tx.us					
Wicomico County 125 N Division St	Salisbury	MD	21803	410-548-4801	548-4803
Web: www.wicomicocounty.org					
Wilbarger County 1700 Wilbarger St County Courthouse Rm 15	Vernon	TX	76384	940-552-5486	553-1202
Web: www.co.wilbarger.tx.us					
Wilcox County 103 N Broad St	Abbeville	GA	31001	229-467-2737	467-2000
Wilkes County 23 E Ct St Rm 222	Washington	GA	30673	706-678-2511	678-3033
Web: www.washingtonwilkes.org					
Wilkes County 110 N St	Wilkesboro	NC	28697	336-651-7345	651-7546
Web: www.wilkescounty.net					
Wilkin County PO Box 219	Breckenridge	MN	56520	218-643-7172	643-7167
Web: www.co.wilkin.mn.us					
Wilkinson County 100 Bacon St	Irwinton	GA	31042	478-946-2236	946-3767
Wilkinson County PO Box 516	Woodville	MS	39669	601-888-4381	888-6776
Will County 302 N Chicago St	Joliet	IL	60432	815-740-4615	740-4699
Web: www.willcountyillinois.com					
Willacy County 576 W Main St 1st Fl	Raymondville	TX	78580	956-689-2710	689-9849
Web: www.willacy.tx.us					
Williams County 1 Courthouse Sq	Bryan	OH	43506	419-636-2059	636-0643
Web: www.co.williams.oh.us					
Williams County PO Box 2047	Williston	ND	58802	701-577-4540	577-4535
Web: www.williamsnd.com					
Williamsburg (Independent City) 401 Lafayette St	Williamsburg	VA	23185	757-220-6100	220-6107
Web: www.williamsburgva.gov					
Williamsburg County 147 W Main St	Kingstree	SC	29556	843-355-9321	355-2106
Web: www.williamsburgsc.com					
Williamson County 1320 W Main St PO Box 624	Franklin	TN	37065	615-790-5712	790-5610
Web: www.williamson-tn.org					
Williamson County 405 ML King St	Georgetown	TX	78626	512-930-4300	943-1616
Williamson County 200 W Jefferson St	Marion	IL	62959	618-997-1301	993-2071
Web: www.williamsoncounty.com					
Wilson County PO Box 27	Floresville	TX	78114	830-393-7308	393-7334
Wilson County 615 Madison St Rm 104	Fredonia	KS	66736	620-378-2186	378-3841
Web: ks-wilson.manatron.com					
Wilson County 228 E Main St Rm 101	Lebanon	TN	37087	615-444-0314	443-2615
Web: www.wilsoncountytn.com					
Wilson County PO Box 1728	Wilson	NC	27894	252-399-2810	237-4341
Web: www.wilson-co.com					
Winchester (Independent City) 5 N Kent St	Winchester	VA	22601	540-667-5770	545-8711
Web: www.ci.winchester.va.us					
Windham County PO Box 207	Newfane	VT	05345	802-365-7979	365-4360
Windham County PO Box 191	Putnam	CT	06260	860-928-7749	928-7076
Windsor County PO Box 458	Woodstock	VT	05091	802-457-2121	457-3446
Winkler County 100 E Winkler St	Kermit	TX	79745	432-586-3401	
Web: www.co.wichita.tx.us					
Winn Parish PO Box 951	Winnfield	LA	71483	318-628-5824	628-7336
Winnebago County PO Box 2808	Oshkosh	WI	54903	920-236-4800	303-3025
Web: www.co.winnebago.wi.us					
Winnebago County 404 Elm St	Rockford	IL	61101	815-987-3050	969-0259
Web: www.co.winnebago.il.us					
Winneshiek County 201 W Main St	Decorah	IA	52101	563-382-2469	382-0603
Winona County 177 Main St	Winona	MN	55987	507-457-6350	454-9365
Web: www.co.winona.mn.us					
Winston County PO Box 309	Double Springs	AL	35553	205-489-5533	489-5140
Winston County PO Box 69	Louisville	MS	39339	662-773-3631	773-8814
Web: www.winstoncounty.com					
Wirt County PO Box 53	Elizabeth	WV	26143	304-275-4271	275-3418
Wise County 200 N Trinity St	Decatur	TX	76234	940-627-3351	627-2138
Web: www.co.wise.tx.us					
Wise County 206 E Main St Suite 223 PO Box 570	Wise	VA	24293	276-328-2321	328-9780
Web: www.wisecounty.org					
Wolfe County PO Box 400	Campton	KY	41301	606-668-3515	668-3492
Wood County 1 Courthouse Sq PO Box 829	Bowling Green	OH	43402	419-354-9280	354-9241
Web: www.co.wood.oh.us					
Wood County 1 Court Sq PO Box 1474	Parkersburg	WV	26102	304-424-1850	424-1864
Web: www.woodcountywv.com					
Wood County PO Box 1796	Quitman	TX	75783	903-763-2711	763-2902
Web: www.co.wood.tx.us					
Wood County PO Box 8095	Wisconsin Rapids	WI	54495	715-421-8460	421-8808
Web: www.co.wood.wi.us					
Woodbury County 620 Douglas St	Sioux City	IA	51101	712-279-6611	279-6021
Web: www.woodbury-ia.com					
Woodford County 103 S Main St County Courthouse	Versailles	KY	40383	859-873-3421	873-0196
Web: www.woodfordchamber-ky.com					
Woodruff County Woodruff County Courthouse 500 N 3rd St	Augusta	AR	72006	870-347-2871	347-2608
Woods County 407 Government St	Alva	OK	73717	580-327-2126	327-1219
Woodson County 105 W Rutledge St Rm 103	Yates Center	KS	66783	620-625-8605	625-8670
Web: www.woodsoncounty.net					
Woodward County 1600 Main St Suite 9	Woodward	OK	73801	580-256-8097	254-6840
Worcester County 1 W Market St Rm 1103	Snow Hill	MD	21863	410-632-1194	632-3131
Web: www.co.worcester.md.us					
Worcester County 110 Front St	Worcester	MA	01608	508-798-7717	798-7746
Worth County PO Box 450	Grant City	MO	64456	660-564-2219	564-2432
Worth County 1000 Central Ave	Northwood	IA	50459	641-324-2840	324-2360
Web: www.worthcounty.org					
Worth County 201 N Main St Rm 30	Sylvester	GA	31791	229-776-8200	776-8232
Web: www.worthcounty.com					
Wright County 10 2nd St NW Rm 201	Buffalo	MN	55313	763-682-7539	682-7300
Web: www.co.wright.mn.us					
Wright County 115 N Main St	Clarion	IA	50525	515-532-2771	532-2669
Web: www.wrightcounty.org					
Wright County 125 Court Sq PO Box 98	Hartville	MO	65667	417-741-6661	741-6142
Web: www.wcida.com					
Wyandot County 109 S Sandusky Ave County Courthouse	Upper Sandusky	OH	43351	419-294-1432	294-6414
Web: www.co.wyandot.oh.us					
Wyoming County PO Box 309	Pineville	WV	24874	304-732-8000	732-9659
Wyoming County 1 Courthouse Sq	Tunkhannock	PA	18657	570-836-3200	
Web: www.wyocopa.org					
Wyoming County 143 N Main St Suite 104	Warsaw	NY	14569	585-786-8810	786-3703
Web: www.wyomingco.net					
Wythe County 340 S 6th St	Wytheville	VA	24382	276-223-6020	223-6030
Web: www.wytheco.org					
Yadkin County 217 E Willow St	Yadkinville	NC	27055	336-679-4200	679-6005
Web: www.yadkincounty.gov					
Yakima County 128 N 2nd St Rm 323	Yakima	WA	98901	509-574-1430	574-1473
Web: www.co.yakima.wa.us					
Yakutat City & Borough PO Box 160	Yakutat	AK	99689	907-784-3323	784-3281
Web: www.yakutat.net					
Yalobusha County PO Box 664	Water Valley	MS	38965	662-473-5024	473-3622
Yamhill County 414 NE Evans St	McMinnville	OR	97128	503-434-7518	434-7520
Web: www.co.yamhill.or.us					
Yancey County 110 Town Sq Rm 11	Burnsville	NC	28714	828-682-3971	682-4301
Web: www.main.nc.us					
Yankton County 410 Walnut St Suite 205	Yankton	SD	57078	605-668-3080	668-5411
Web: www.co.yankton.sd.us					
Yates County 417 Liberty St	Penn Yan	NY	14527	315-536-5120	536-5545
Web: www.yatescounty.org					
Yavapai County 1015 Fair St Rm 310	Prescott	AZ	86305	928-771-3200	771-3257
Web: www.co.yavapai.az.us					
Yazoo County 211 E Broadway	Yazoo City	MS	39194	662-746-2661	746-3893
Web: www.yazoo.org					
Yell County PO Box 219	Danville	AR	72833	479-495-4850	
Yellow Medicine County 415 9th Ave	Granite Falls	MN	56241	320-564-3325	564-4435
Web: www.yellowmedicine.govoffice.com					
Yellowstone County 217 N 27th St Rm 401	Billings	MT	59101	406-256-2785	256-2736
Web: www.co.yellowstone.mt.us					
Yoakum County PO Box 309	Plains	TX	79355	806-456-2721	456-2258
Web: www.co.yoakum.tx.us					
Yolo County 625 Court St Suite 202	Woodland	CA	95695	530-666-8150	668-4029
Web: www.yolocounty.org					
York County 45 Kennebunk Rd PO Box 399	Alfred	ME	04002	207-324-1571	324-9494
Web: www.yorkcountyme.gov					
York County 510 N Lincoln Ave	York	NE	68467	402-362-7759	362-7558
Web: www.yorkcounty.ne.gov					

Phone Fax

York County 45 N George St .... York PA 17401 717-771-9612 771-9096
Web: www.york-county.org

York County 2 S Congress St PO Box 649 .... York SC 29745 803-684-8507 684-8575
Web: www.yorkcountygov.com

York County 300 Ballard St PO Box 316 .... Yorktown VA 23690 757-890-3450 890-3459
Web: www.co.york.va.us

Young County 516 4th St Rm 104 .... Graham TX 76450 940-549-8432 521-0305

Yuba County 915 8th St Suite 115 .... Marysville CA 95901 530-749-7575 749-7312
Web: www.co.yuba.ca.us

Yuma County 310 Ash St Suite F .... Wray CO 80758 970-332-5809 332-5919
Web: www.yumacounty.net

Yuma County 198 S Main St .... Yuma AZ 85364 928-373-1010 373-1120
Web: www.co.yuma.az.us

Zapata County 200 E 7th St # 138 .... Zapata TX 78076 956-765-9915 765-9933
Web: www.zapatausa.com

Zavala County
200 E Uvalde St County Courthouse .... Crystal City TX 78839 830-374-2331 374-5955
Web: www.co.zavala.tx.us

342 GOVERNMENT - STATE

SEE ALSO Correctional Facilities - State p. 1764; Employment Offices - Government p. 1822; Ethics Commissions p. 1834; Governors - State p. 1999; Legislation Hotlines p. 2150; Lotteries, Games, Sweepstakes p. 2189; Parks-State p. 2346; Sports Commissions & Regulatory Agencies - State p. 2667; Student Assistance Programs p. 2678; Veterans Nursing Homes - State p. 2760

342-1 Alabama

Phone Fax

State Government Information
3 S Jackson St Suite 200 .... Montgomery AL 36104 334-242-8000
TF: 866-353-3468 ■ *Web:* www.alabama.gov

Administrative Office of Alabama Courts
300 Dexter Ave .... Montgomery AL 36104 334-242-0300 242-2099
Web: www.judicial.state.al.us

Agriculture & Industries Dept
1445 Federal Dr PO Box 3336 .... Montgomery AL 36109 334-240-7171 240-7190
Web: www.agi.state.al.us

Archives & History Dept
624 Washington Ave .... Montgomery AL 30130 334-242-4435 240-3433
Web: www.archives.state.al.us

Arts Council 201 Monroe St Suite 110 .... Montgomery AL 36130 334-242-4076 240-3269
Web: www.arts.alabama.gov

Attorney General
State House 11 S Union St .... Montgomery AL 36130 334-242-7300 242-7458
Web: www.ago.state.al.us

Banking Dept 401 Adams Ave Suite 680 .... Montgomery AL 36130 334-242-3452 242-3500
Web: www.bank.state.al.us

Bill Status-Senate
State House 11 S Union St Rm 716 .... Montgomery AL 36130 334-242-7826 242-8819
TF: 800-499-3051 ■ *Web:* www.alisdb.legislature.state.al.us

Child Support Enforcement Div
50 Ripley St .... Montgomery AL 36130 334-242-9300 242-0606

Children"s Affairs Dept
135 S Union St Suite 215 PO Box 302755 .... Montgomery AL 36130 334-353-2700 353-2701
Web: www.dca.state.al.us

Commission on Higher Education
100 N Union St PO Box 302000 .... Montgomery AL 36130 334-242-1998 242-0268
Web: www.ache.state.al.us/StudentAsst/Programs.htm

Conservation & Natural Resources Dept
64 N Union St PO Box 301450 .... Montgomery AL 36130 334-242-3486 242-1880
TF: 800-262-3151 ■ *Web:* www.outdooralabama.com

Consumer Affairs Office 11 S Union St .... Montgomery AL 36130 334-242-7334 242-2433
Web: www.ago.state.al.us/consumer.cfm

Corrections Dept 301 S Ripley St .... Montgomery AL 36104 334-353-3883 353-3891
Web: www.doc.state.al.us

Crime Victims Compensation Commission
5845 Carmichael Rd .... Montgomery AL 36117 334-290-4420 290-4455
TF: 800-541-9388 ■ *Web:* acvcc.alabama.gov

Department of Industrial Relations
649 Monroe St .... Montgomery AL 36131 334-242-8005 242-3960
Web: dir.alabama.gov

Department of Transportation
1409 Coliseum Blvd .... Montgomery AL 36130 334-242-6207 353-6530
Web: www.dot.state.al.us

Economic & Community Affairs Dept
PO Box 5690 .... Montgomery AL 36103 334-242-5100 242-5099
Web: www.adeca.state.al.us

Education Dept
50 N Ripley St PO Box 302101 .... Montgomery AL 36104 334-242-9700 242-9708
Web: www.alsde.edu

Emergency Management Agency
5898 County Rd 41 PO Drawer 2160 .... Clanton AL 35046 205-280-2200 280-2410
TF: 800-843-0699 ■ *Web:* www.ema.alabama.gov

Environmental Management Dept
1400 Coliseum Blvd .... Montgomery AL 36110 334-271-7700 271-7950
Web: www.adem.state.al.us

Ethics Commission 100 N Union St Suite 104 .... Montgomery AL 36104 334-242-2997 242-0248
Web: www.ethics.alabama.gov

Finance Dept 600 Dexter Ave Suite N-105 .... Montgomery AL 36130 334-242-7160 353-3300
Web: www.finance.state.al.us

Forensic Sciences Dept PO Box 3510 .... Montgomery AL 36131 334-844-4648 877-7531
Web: www.adfs.state.al.us

Highway Patrol Div PO Box 1511 .... Montgomery AL 36102 334-242-4393 242-4385
Web: www.dps.state.al.us/public/highwaypatrol

Historical Commission 468 S Perry St .... Montgomery AL 36104 334-242-3184 240-3477
Web: www.preserveala.org

Homeland Security Dept PO Box 304115 .... Montgomery AL 36130 334-353-3050 223-1120
TF: 800-361-4454 ■ *Web:* www.dhs.alabama.gov

Housing Finance Authority PO Box 242967 .... Montgomery AL 36124 334-244-9200 244-9214
Web: www.ahfa.com

Human Resources Dept
Gordon Persons Bldg
50 N Ripley St Suite 2104 .... Montgomery AL 36130 334-242-1310 353-1115
Web: www.dhr.state.al.us

Information Services Div
64 N Union St Suite 200 .... Montgomery AL 36130 334-242-3800 242-7002
Web: www.isd.state.al.us

Insurance Dept 201 Monroe St Suite 1700 .... Montgomery AL 36104 334-269-3550 241-4192
Web: www.aldoi.org

Labor Dept RSA Union 6th Fl PO Box 303500 .... Montgomery AL 36130 334-242-3460 240-3417
Web: www.alalabor.state.al.us

Legislature 11 S Union St .... Montgomery AL 36130 334-242-7800 242-8819
Web: www.legislature.state.al.us

Lieutenant Governor
11 S Union St Suite 725 .... Montgomery AL 36130 334-242-7900 242-4661
Web: www.ltgov.state.al.us

Mental Health & Mental Retardation Dept
100 N Union St PO Box 301410 .... Montgomery AL 36130 334-242-3454 242-0725
TF: 800-367-0955 ■ *Web:* www.mh.state.al.us

Motor Vehicle Div 50 N Ripley St 12th Fl .... Montgomery AL 36104 334-242-9000 242-8038
Web: www.ador.state.al.us

National Guard PO Box 3711 .... Montgomery AL 36109 334-271-7200 271-7426
Web: www.alguard.state.al.us

Pardons & Paroles Board
301 S Ripley St PO Box 302405 .... Montgomery AL 36130 334-353-7771 242-1809
Web: www.pardons.state.al.us

Prepaid Affordable College Tuition (PACT) Program
100 N Union St Suite 660 .... Montgomery AL 36130 334-242-7514 242-7041
TF: 800-252-7228 ■ *Web:* www.treasury.state.al.us

Public Health Dept 201 Monroe St .... Montgomery AL 36104 334-206-5300 206-5534
TF: 800-252-1818 ■ *Web:* www.adph.org

Public Safety Dept PO Box 1511 .... Montgomery AL 36102 334-242-4371 353-8477
Web: www.dps.state.al.us

Public Service Commission
100 N Union St RSA Union PO Box 304260 .... Montgomery AL 36130 334-242-5218 242-0509
TF: 800-392-8050 ■ *Web:* www.psc.state.al.us

Rehabilitation Services Dept
602 S Lawrence St .... Montgomery AL 36104 334-293-7500 293-7383
TF: 800-441-7607 ■ *Web:* www.rehab.state.al.us

Revenue Dept 50 N Ripley St Rm 4112 .... Montgomery AL 36104 334-242-1170 242-0550
Web: www.ador.state.al.us

Robert Bentley Governor
State Capitol 600 Dexter Ave Suite N-104 .... Montgomery AL 36130 334-242-7100 353-0004
Web: www.governor.alabama.gov

Secretary of State PO Box 5616 .... Montgomery AL 36103 334-242-7200 242-4993
Web: www.sos.state.al.us

Securities Commission
770 Washington Ave Suite 570 .... Montgomery AL 36130 334-242-2984 242-0240
TF: 800-222-1253 ■ *Web:* www.asc.state.al.us

Senior Services Dept
770 Washington Ave Suite 470 .... Montgomery AL 36130 334-242-5743 242-5594
TF: 877-425-2243 ■ *Web:* www.adss.state.al.us

State Parks Div 64 N Union St .... Montgomery AL 36130 334-242-3334 353-8629
TF: 800-252-7275 ■ *Web:* www.alapark.com

State Port Authority PO Box 1588 .... Mobile AL 36633 251-441-7200 441-7216
Web: www.asdd.com

Tourism & Travel Bureau
401 Adams Ave Suite 126 .... Montgomery AL 36104 334-242-4169 242-4554
TF: 800-252-2262 ■ *Web:* www.touralabama.org

Treasury Dept 600 Dexter Ave Suite S-106 .... Montgomery AL 36130 334-242-7500 242-7592
Web: www.treasury.state.al.us

Veterans Affairs Dept
770 Washington Ave # 530 .... Montgomery AL 36104 334-242-5077 242-5102
Web: www.va.state.al.us

Vital Records PO Box 5625 .... Montgomery AL 36103 334-206-5418 262-9563
Web: ph.state.al.us/chs/Index.htm

Weights & Measures Div PO Box 3336 .... Montgomery AL 36109 334-240-7133 240-7175

Wildlife & Freshwater Fisheries Div
64 N Union St .... Montgomery AL 36104 334-242-3465 242-3032
Web: www.dcnr.state.al.us/about/awff

Workers" Compensation Div 649 Monroe St .... Montgomery AL 36131 334-353-0990 353-8262
Web: dir.alabama.gov/wc

Higher Education Commission
100 N Union St PO Box 302000 .... Montgomery AL 36130 334-242-1998 242-0268
Web: www.ache.state.al.us

342-2 Alaska

Phone Fax

State Government Information
333 Willoughby Ave PO Box 110230 .... Juneau AK 99811 907-465-2111
Web: doa.alaska.gov

Aging Commission 150 Third St PO Box 116093 .... Juneau AK 99801 907-465-3250 465-1396
Web: www.alaskaaging.org

Arts Council 411 W 4th Ave Suite 1E .... Anchorage AK 99501 907-269-6610 269-6601
Web: www.eed.state.ak.us

Attorney General PO Box 110300 .... Juneau AK 99811 907-465-3600 465-2075
Web: www.law.state.ak.us

	City	State	Zip	Phone	Fax
Banking Securities & Corporations Div 150 W 3rd St # 217 *Web:* www.dced.state.ak.us	Juneau	AK	99801	907-465-2521	465-2549
Behavioral Health Div PO Box 110620 *Web:* www.hss.state.ak.us/dbh	Juneau	AK	99811	907-465-3370	465-2668
Child Support Enforcement Div 550 W 7th Ave Suite 310 *Web:* www.csed.state.ak.us	Anchorage	AK	99501	907-269-6900	269-6650
Children's Services Office PO Box 110630 *Web:* www.hss.state.ak.us/ocs	Juneau	AK	99811	907-465-3191	465-3397
Commerce Community & Economic Development Dept 333 Willoughby Ave PO Box 11080 *Web:* www.commerce.state.ak.us	Juneau	AK	99811	907-465-2500	465-5442
Commission on Postsecondary Education PO Box 110510 *TF:* 800-441-2962 ■ *Web:* www.alaskaadvantage.state.ak.us	Juneau	AK	99811	907-465-2962	465-5316
Corrections Dept PO Box 112000 *Web:* www.correct.state.ak.us	Juneau	AK	99811	907-465-3342	465-3253
Court System 303 K St *Web:* www.state.ak.us/courts	Anchorage	AK	99501	907-264-0547	264-0585
Education & Early Development Dept 801 W 10th St Suite 200 *Web:* www.eed.state.ak.us	Juneau	AK	99801	907-465-2800	465-4156
Employment Security Div PO Box 25509 *Web:* www.labor.state.ak.us/esd/home.htm	Juneau	AK	99802	907-465-2712	465-4537
Enterprise Technology Services Div PO Box 110206 *Web:* www.state.ak.us	Juneau	AK	99811	907-465-2220	465-3450
Environmental Conservation Dept 410 Willoughby Ave Suite 303 *Web:* www.state.ak.us	Juneau	AK	99801	907-465-5066	465-5070
Fish & Game Dept 1255 W 8th St PO Box 25526 *Web:* www.adfg.state.ak.us	Juneau	AK	99802	907-465-4100	465-2332
Health & Social Services Dept PO Box 110601 *Web:* www.hss.state.ak.us	Juneau	AK	99811	907-465-3030	465-3068
History & Archeology Office 550 W 7th Ave Suite 1310 *Web:* dnr.alaska.gov/parks/oha	Anchorage	AK	99501	907-269-8721	269-8908
Homeland Security & Emergency Services Div PO Box 5750 *Web:* www.ak-prepared.com	Fort Richardson	AK	99505	907-428-7000	428-7009
Housing Finance Corp PO Box 101020 *Web:* www.ahfc.state.ak.us	Anchorage	AK	99510	907-338-6100	338-7940
Insurance Div PO Box 110805 *Web:* www.commerce.state.ak.us/insurance	Juneau	AK	99811	907-465-2515	465-3422
Labor & Workforce Development Dept 111 W 8th St PO Box 21149 *Web:* www.labor.state.ak.us	Juneau	AK	99802	907-465-2700	465-2784
Legislative Ethics Committee PO Box 101468 *Web:* www.ethics.legis.state.ak.us	Anchorage	AK	99510	907-269-0150	269-0152
Lieutenant Governor 240 Main St # 301 *Web:* www.gov.state.ak.us	Juneau	AK	99801	907-465-3520	465-5400
Measurement Standards Div 12050 Industry Way Bldg O Suite 6 *Web:* www.dot.state.ak.us	Anchorage	AK	99515	907-345-7750	345-6835
Military & Veterans Affairs Dept PO Box 5800 *Web:* www.ak-prepared.com/dmva	Fort Richardson	AK	99505	907-428-6003	428-6019
Motor Vehicles Div 3300 B Fairbanks St *Web:* www.state.ak.us	Anchorage	AK	99503	907-269-5559	269-6084
Natural Resources Dept 500 W 7th Ave Suite 1400 *Web:* www.dnr.state.ak.us	Anchorage	AK	99501	907-269-8431	269-8918
Occupational Licensing Div 333 Willoughby Ave # 9 *Web:* www.dced.state.ak.us	Juneau	AK	99801	907-465-2534	465-2974
Parks & Outdoor Recreation Div 550 W 7th Ave Suite 1380 *Web:* www.dnr.state.ak.us/parks	Anchorage	AK	99501	907-269-8700	269-8907
Parole Board PO Box 112000 *Web:* www.correct.state.ak.us/corrections/Parole	Juneau	AK	99811	907-465-3384	465-3110
Permanent Fund Dividend Div 333 Willoughby Ave 11th Fl *Web:* www.pfd.state.ak.us	Juneau	AK	99811	907-465-2326	465-3470
Personnel Div 333 Willoughby Ave PO Box 110201 *Web:* www.dop.state.ak.us	Juneau	AK	99811	907-465-4430	465-2576
Postsecondary Education Commission 3030 Vintage Blvd *TF Cust Svc:* 800-441-3293 ■ *Web:* www.alaskaadvantage.state.ak.us	Juneau	AK	99801	907-465-6740	465-5316
Public Assistance Div PO Box 110640 *Web:* www.hss.state.ak.us/dpa	Juneau	AK	99811	907-465-3347	465-5154
Real Estate Commission 550 W 7th Ave Suite 1500 *Web:* www.commerce.state.ak.us/occ/prec.htm	Anchorage	AK	99501	907-269-8197	269-8196
Regulatory Commission 550 W 8th Ave Suite 300 *Web:* www.state.ak.us	Anchorage	AK	99501	907-276-6222	276-0160
Revenue Dept PO Box 110400 *Web:* www.revenue.state.ak.us	Juneau	AK	99811	907-465-2300	465-2389
State Legislature State Capitol *Web:* www.legis.state.ak.us	Juneau	AK	99801	907-465-4648	465-2864
State Libraries Archives & Museums Div 333 Willoughby Ave PO Box 110571 *Web:* www.eed.state.ak.us/lam	Juneau	AK	99811	907-465-2910	465-2151
State Medical Examiner 5455 Dr Martin Luther King Jr Ave *Web:* www.hss.state.ak.us/dph/sme	Anchorage	AK	99507	907-334-2200	334-2216
State Troopers Div 5700 E Tudor Rd *Web:* www.dps.state.ak.us	Anchorage	AK	99507	907-269-5641	337-2059
Supreme Court 303 K St	Anchorage	AK	99501	907-264-0612	264-0878
Tourism Development Office PO Box 11800 *Web:* www.commerce.state.ak.us/oed/toubus/home.cfm	Juneau	AK	99811	907-465-2500	
Transportation & Public Facilities Dept 3132 Ch Dr *Web:* www.dot.state.ak.us	Juneau	AK	99801	907-465-3900	586-8365
Violent Crimes Compensation Board 333 Willoughby Ave State Office Bldg Fl 10 *Web:* doa.alaska.gov	Juneau	AK	99801	907-465-3040	465-2379
Vital Statistics Bureau 5441 Commercial Blvd *Web:* www.hss.state.ak.us/dph/bvs	Juneau	AK	99801	907-465-3391	465-3618
Vocational Rehabilitation Div 801 W 10th St Suite 200 *TF:* 800-478-2815 ■ *Web:* www.labor.state.ak.us	Juneau	AK	99801	907-465-2814	465-2856
Workers' Compensation Div 1111 W 8th St Rm 305 PO Box 115512 *Web:* www.labor.state.ak.us/wc	Juneau	AK	99801	907-465-2790	465-2797

342-3 Arizona

	City	State	Zip	Phone	Fax
State Government Information 100 N 15th Ave Suite 440 *Web:* az.gov	Phoenix	AZ	85007	602-542-4900	
Administrative Office of the Cts 1501 W Washington St *Web:* www.azcourts.gov	Phoenix	AZ	85007	602-542-9301	542-9484
Aging & Adult Administration 1789 W Jefferson St MS 001A *Web:* www.de.state.az.us	Phoenix	AZ	85007	602-542-6572	542-6575
Agriculture Dept 1688 W Adams St *Web:* www.azda.gov	Phoenix	AZ	85007	602-542-4373	542-5420
Arts Commission 417 W Roosevelt St *Web:* www.azarts.gov	Phoenix	AZ	85003	602-255-5882	256-0282
Attorney General 1275 W Washington St *TF:* 888-377-6108 ■ *Web:* www.azag.gov	Phoenix	AZ	85007	602-542-5025	542-4085
Boxing Commission 1110 W Washington St Suite 260	Phoenix	AZ	85007	602-364-1721	364-1703
Child Support Enforcement Div PO Box 40458 **Fax:* Cust Svc ■ *Web:* www.de.state.az.us/dcse	Phoenix	AZ	85067	602-274-7646	274-8250*
Children Youth & Families Div 1789 W Jefferson St *TF:* 877-543-7633 ■ *Web:* www.de.state.az.us	Phoenix	AZ	85007	602-542-2277	542-3330
Commerce Dept 1700 W Washington St Suite 600 *Web:* www.azcommerce.com	Phoenix	AZ	85007	602-771-1100	771-1200
Consumer Protection & Antitrust Unit 1275 W Washington St *Web:* www.azag.gov	Phoenix	AZ	85007	602-542-5763	542-4579
Corp Commission 1200 W Washington St *Web:* www.cc.state.az.us	Phoenix	AZ	85007	602-542-2237	542-4111
Corrections Dept 1601 W Jefferson St *Web:* www.adc.state.az.us	Phoenix	AZ	85007	602-542-5497	542-2859
Criminal Justice Commission 1110 W Washington St Suite 230 *Web:* acjc.state.az.us	Phoenix	AZ	85007	602-364-1146	364-1175
Economic Security Dept 1717 W Jefferson St *Web:* www.de.state.az.us	Phoenix	AZ	85007	602-542-4791	542-5339
Education Dept 1535 W Jefferson St *Web:* www.ade.state.az.us	Phoenix	AZ	85007	602-542-4361	542-5440
Emergency & Military Affairs Dept 5636 E McDowell Rd *Web:* www.azdema.gov	Phoenix	AZ	85008	602-267-2700	267-2954
Employment Administration PO Box 6123 *Web:* www.azdes.gov	Phoenix	AZ	85005	602-542-3957	542-2491
Environmental Quality Dept 1110 W Washington St *TF:* 800-234-5677 ■ *Web:* www.azdeq.gov	Phoenix	AZ	85007	602-207-2300	207-2218
Executive Clemency Board 1645 W Jefferson St Rm 101 *Web:* www.azboec.gov	Phoenix	AZ	85007	602-542-5656	542-5680
Financial Institutions 2910 N 44th St Suite 310 *Web:* www.azbanking.com	Phoenix	AZ	85018	602-771-2800	381-1225
Game & Fish Dept 5000 W Carefree Hwy *Web:* www.azgfd.com	Phoenix	AZ	85086	602-942-3000	789-3924
Government Information Technology Agency 100 N 15th Ave Suite 440 *Web:* www.azgita.gov	Phoenix	AZ	85007	602-364-4482	364-4799
Governor 1700 W Washington St Executive Tower 9th Fl *Web:* www.governor.state.az.us	Phoenix	AZ	85007	602-542-4331	542-7601
Health Services Dept 150 N 18th Ave *Web:* www.azdhs.gov	Phoenix	AZ	85007	602-364-3150	542-1062
Highway Patrol Div PO Box 6638 *Web:* www.dps.state.az.us	Phoenix	AZ	85005	602-223-2000	223-2916
Historic Preservation Office 1300 W Washington St *TF:* 800-285-3703 ■ *Web:* www.azstateparks.com	Phoenix	AZ	85007	602-542-4174	542-4180
Housing Dept 1700 W Washington St Suite 210 *Web:* www.housingaz.com	Phoenix	AZ	85007	602-771-1000	771-1002
Industrial Commission 800 W Washington St *Web:* www.ica.state.az.us	Phoenix	AZ	85007	602-542-4411	542-3373
Insurance Dept 2910 N 44th St 2nd Fl *Web:* www.id.state.az.us	Phoenix	AZ	85018	602-912-8400	912-8452
Land Dept 1616 W Adams St *Web:* www.land.state.az.us	Phoenix	AZ	85007	602-542-4602	542-5223
Legislature Capitol Complex 1700 W Washington St *TF:* 800-352-8404 ■ *Web:* www.azleg.state.az.us	Phoenix	AZ	85007	602-926-3559	542-3429
Lottery 4740 E University Dr *Web:* www.arizonalottery.com	Phoenix	AZ	85034	480-921-4400	921-5512
Medical Board 9545 Doubletree Ranch Rd *Web:* www.azmdboard.org	Scottsdale	AZ	85258	480-551-2700	551-2704
Motor Vehicle Div 1801 W Jefferson St *Web:* www.dot.state.az.us/mvd	Phoenix	AZ	85007	602-712-8152	712-6539

	City	State	Zip	Phone	Fax
Nursing Board 4747 N 7th St Suite 200 *Web:* www.azbn.gov	Phoenix	AZ	85014	602-771-7800	771-7888
Postsecondary Education Commission 2020 N Central Ave Suite 550 *Web:* www.azhighered.org	Phoenix	AZ	85004	602-258-2435	258-2483
Racing Dept 1110 W Washington St Suite 260 *Web:* www.azracing.gov	Phoenix	AZ	85007	602-364-1700	364-1703
Real Estate Dept 2910 N 44th St Suite 100 *Web:* www.re.state.az.us	Phoenix	AZ	85018	602-771-7799	468-0562
Rehabilitation Services Administration 1789 W Jefferson St 2nd Fl NW *TF:* 800-563-1221 ■ *Web:* www.azdes.gov	Phoenix	AZ	85007	602-542-3332	542-3778
Revenue Dept 1600 W Monroe St *Web:* www.azdor.gov	Phoenix	AZ	85007	602-716-6090	542-4772
Secretary of State 1700 W Washington St W Wing 7th Fl *Web:* www.azsos.gov	Phoenix	AZ	85007	602-542-4285	542-1575
Securities Div 1300 W Washington St 3rd Fl *Web:* www.ccsd.cc.state.az.us	Phoenix	AZ	85007	602-542-4242	594-7470
State Boards Office 1400 W Washington St Suite 230	Phoenix	AZ	85007	602-542-3095	542-3093
State Compensation Fund 3030 N 3rd St *Web:* www.scfaz.com	Phoenix	AZ	85012	602-631-2000	631-2213
State Parks 1300 W Washington St *Web:* www.azstateparks.com	Phoenix	AZ	85007	602-542-4174	542-4188
Supreme Court 1501 W Washington St *Web:* www.supreme.state.az.us	Phoenix	AZ	85007	602-542-9300	542-9480
Tourism Office 1110 W Washington St Suite 155 *TF:* 888-520-3434 ■ *Web:* www.arizonaguide.com	Phoenix	AZ	85007	602-364-3700	364-3701
Transportation Dept 206 S 17th Ave *Web:* www.dot.state.az.us	Phoenix	AZ	85007	602-712-7227	712-6941
Treasurer 1700 W Washington St W Wing 1st Fl *Web:* www.aztreasury.state.az.us	Phoenix	AZ	85007	602-542-1463	542-7176
Veterans'' Service Dept 3839 N 3rd St Suite 200 *Web:* www.azdvs.gov	Phoenix	AZ	85012	602-255-3373	255-1038
Vital Records Office 1818 W Adams St *Web:* www.azdhs.gov	Phoenix	AZ	85007	602-364-1300	364-1257
Weights & Measures Dept 4425 W Olive Ave Suite 134 **Fax Area Code:* 623 ■ *TF:* 800-277-6675 ■ *Web:* www.azdwm.gov	Glendale	AZ	85302	602-771-4920	939-8586*

342-4 Arkansas

	City	State	Zip	Phone	Fax
State Government Information 425 W Capitol Suite 1620 *Web:* portal.arkansas.gov	Little Rock	AR	72201	501-682-3000	
Administrative Office of the Cts 625 Marshall St *Web:* www.courts.state.ar.us	Little Rock	AR	72201	501-682-9400	682-9410
Aging & Adult Services Div PO Box 1437 *Web:* www.arkansas.gov/dhhs/aging	Little Rock	AR	72203	501-682-2441	682-8155
Arts Council 323 Ctr St Suite 1400 *Web:* www.arkansasarts.com	Little Rock	AR	72201	501-324-9766	324-9207
Attorney General 323 Ctr St Suite 200 *TF Consumer Info:* 800-482-8982 ■ *Web:* www.ag.state.ar.us	Little Rock	AR	72201	501-682-2007	682-8084
Bank Dept 400 Hardin Rd Suite 100 *Web:* www.state.ar.us	Little Rock	AR	72211	501-324-9019	324-9028
Bill Status-House State Capitol Rm 350 *Web:* www.arkleg.state.ar.us	Little Rock	AR	72201	501-682-7771	
Bill Status-Senate State Capitol Rm 320 *Web:* www.arkleg.state.ar.us	Little Rock	AR	72201	501-682-5951	
Bureau of Standards 4608 W 61st St *Web:* plantboard.arkansas.gov/Standards	Little Rock	AR	72209	501-570-1159	562-7605
Child Support Enforcement Office PO Box 8133 *Web:* www.state.ar.us	Little Rock	AR	72203	501-682-6169	682-6002
Children & Family Services Div Slot 5560 PO Box 1437 *Web:* www.arkansas.gov/dhhs/chilnfam	Little Rock	AR	72203	501-682-8772	682-6968
Consumer Protection Div 323 Ctr St Tower Bldg Suite 200 *TF:* 800-482-8982 ■ *Web:* www.ag.state.ar.us/consumer/home.htm	Little Rock	AR	72201	501-682-6150	682-8118
Contractors Licensing Board 4100 Richards Rd *Web:* www.state.ar.us	North Little Rock	AR	72117	501-372-4661	372-2247
Correction Dept PO Box 8707 *Web:* www.state.ar.us	Pine Bluff	AR	71611	870-267-6200	267-6258
Cosmetology Board 101 E Capitol Ave Suite 108 *Web:* www.accessarkansas.org	Little Rock	AR	72201	501-682-2168	682-5640
Crime Victims Reparations Board 323 Ctr St Suite 200 *TF:* 800-448-3014 ■	Little Rock	AR	72201	501-682-1020	682-5313
Development Finance Authority 423 Main St Suite 500 *Web:* www.accessarkansas.org/adfa	Little Rock	AR	72201	501-682-5900	682-5859
Economic Development Dept 1 Capitol Mall Suite 4C-300 *TF:* 800-275-2672 ■ *Web:* www.1800arkansas.com	Little Rock	AR	72201	501-682-1121	682-7394
Education Dept 4 Capitol Mall *Web:* www.arkedu.state.ar.us	Little Rock	AR	72201	501-682-4475	682-1079
Environmental Quality Dept 5301 Northshore Dr *Web:* www.adeq.state.ar.us	Little Rock	AR	72118	501-682-0744	682-0798
Ethics Commission 910 W 2nd St Suite 100 *TF:* 800-422-7773 ■ *Web:* www.arkansasethics.com	Little Rock	AR	72201	501-324-9600	324-9606
Finance & Administration Dept 1509 W 7th St *Web:* www.state.ar.us	Little Rock	AR	72201	501-682-2242	682-1029
Financial Aid Office 114 E Capitol St *TF:* 800-547-8839 ■ *Web:* www.arkansashighered.com/financial.html	Little Rock	AR	72201	501-371-2013	371-2001
Game & Fish Commission 2 Natural Resource Dr *TF:* 800-364-4263 ■ *Web:* www.agfc.state.ar.us	Little Rock	AR	72205	501-223-6300	223-6444
General Assembly State Capitol Bldg *Web:* www.arkleg.state.ar.us	Little Rock	AR	72201	501-682-6107	682-2917
Governor State Capitol Bldg *Web:* www.arkansas.gov	Little Rock	AR	72201	501-682-2345	682-1382
Health & Human Services Dept 4815 W Markham St *Web:* www.healthyarkansas.com	Little Rock	AR	72205	501-661-2000	671-1450
Heritage Dept 323 Ctr St Suite 1500 *Web:* www.arkansasheritage.com	Little Rock	AR	72201	501-324-9150	324-9154
Highway & Transportation Dept 10324 Interstate 30 *TF:* 800-245-1672 ■ *Web:* www.arkansashighways.com	Little Rock	AR	72209	501-569-2000	569-2400
Human Services Dept PO Box 1437 *Web:* www.arkansas.gov/dhhs	Little Rock	AR	72203	501-682-1001	682-6571
Information Systems Dept PO Box 3155 *Web:* www.dis.state.ar.us	Little Rock	AR	72203	501-682-3038	682-4310
Insurance Dept 1200 W 3rd St *TF:* 800-282-9134 ■ *Web:* www.state.ar.us/insurance	Little Rock	AR	72201	501-371-2600	371-2618
Labor Dept 10421 W Markham St *Web:* www.arkansas.gov/labor	Little Rock	AR	72205	501-682-4500	682-4506
Lieutenant Governor State Capitol Bldg Suite 270 *Web:* www.ltgovernor.arkansas.gov	Little Rock	AR	72201	501-682-2144	682-2894
Motor Vehicle Office 1900 W 7th St Rm 2030 *Web:* www.state.ar.us/dfa/motorvehicle	Little Rock	AR	72203	501-682-4630	682-1116
Natural Resources Commission 101 E Capitol Suite 350 *Web:* www.aswcc.arkansas.gov	Little Rock	AR	72201	501-682-1611	682-3991
Parks & Tourism Dept 1 Capitol Mall *TF:* 800-628-8725 ■ *Web:* www.arkansas.com	Little Rock	AR	72201	501-682-7777	682-1364
Public Accountancy Board 101 E Capitol Ave Suite 450 *Web:* www.state.ar.us/asbpa	Little Rock	AR	72201	501-682-1520	682-5538
Public Service Commission PO Box 400 *Web:* www.state.ar.us/psc	Little Rock	AR	72203	501-682-2051	682-5731
Racing Commission 1515 W 7th St Rm 505 *Web:* www.state.ar.us/dfa/racing	Little Rock	AR	72203	501-682-1467	682-5273
Real Estate Commission 612 S Summit St *Web:* www.arec.arkansa.gov	Little Rock	AR	72201	501-683-8010	683-8020
Rehabilitation Services 1616 Brookwood Dr *TF:* 800-330-0632 ■ *Web:* www.arsinfo.org	Little Rock	AR	72202	501-296-1600	296-1655
Revenue Div PO Box 1272 *Web:* www.dfa.arkansas.gov	Little Rock	AR	72203	501-682-7025	682-7900
Secretary of State State Capitol Bldg Rm 256 *Web:* www.sos.arkansas.gov	Little Rock	AR	72201	501-682-1010	682-3510
Securities Dept 201 E Markham St Rm 300 *TF:* 800-981-4429 ■ *Web:* www.accessarkansas.org/arsec	Little Rock	AR	72201	501-324-9260	324-9268
State Medical Board 2100 Riverfront Dr *Web:* www.armedicalboard.org	Little Rock	AR	72202	501-296-1802	296-1805
State Police 1 State Police Plaza Dr *Web:* www.asp.state.ar.us	Little Rock	AR	72209	501-618-8000	618-8222
Supreme Court 625 Marshall St 1320 Justice Bldg *Web:* courts.arkansas.gov/cotc	Little Rock	AR	72201	501-682-6849	682-6877
Treasurer 220 State Capitol Rm 220 *Web:* www.artreasury.gov	Little Rock	AR	72201	501-682-5888	682-3842
Veterans Affairs Dept 2200 Fort Roots Dr Bldg 65 Rm 119 *Web:* www.veterans.arkansas.gov	North Little Rock	AR	72114	501-370-3820	370-3829
Vital Records Div 4815 W Markham St Slot 44 *TF:* 800-637-9314 ■ *Web:* www.healthyarkansas.com	Little Rock	AR	72205	501-661-2174	663-2832
Worker's Compensation Commission PO Box 950 *TF:* 800-622-4472 ■ *Web:* www.awcc.state.ar.us	Little Rock	AR	72203	501-682-3930	682-2777
Workforce Services Dept 2 Capitol Mall *Web:* www.arkansas.gov	North Little Rock	AR	72201	501-682-2121	682-2273
Higher Education Dept 114 E Capitol Ave *Web:* www.arkansashighered.com	Little Rock	AR	72201	501-371-2000	371-2001

342-5 California

	City	State	Zip	Phone	Fax
State Government Information 630 Sequoia Pacific Blvd *TF:* 800-807-6755 ■ *Web:* www.ca.gov	Sacramento	CA	95811	916-657-9900	
Administrative Office of the Cts 455 Golden Gate Ave 3rd Fl *Web:* www.courtinfo.ca.gov	San Francisco	CA	94102	415-865-4200	865-4205
Aging Dept 1300 National Dr Suite 200 *Web:* www.aging.ca.gov	Sacramento	CA	95834	916-419-7500	928-2268
Arts Council 1300 'I' St Suite 930 *TF:* 800-201-6201 ■ *Web:* www.cac.ca.gov	Sacramento	CA	95814	916-322-6555	322-6575
Athletic Commission 1430 Howe Ave *Web:* www.dca.ca.gov	Sacramento	CA	95825	916-263-2195	263-2197
Attorney General PO Box 944255 *Web:* www.caag.state.ca.us	Sacramento	CA	95244	916-445-9555	324-5341
Bill Status-Assembly State Capitol Rm 3196 *Web:* www.leginfo.ca.gov/bilinfo.html	Sacramento	CA	95814	916-445-2323	

	City	State	ZIP	Phone	Fax
Bill Status-Senate State Capitol Rm 3044	Sacramento	CA	95814	916-445-4251	445-4450
Web: www.leginfo.ca.gov/bilinfo.html					
Child Support Services Dept PO Box 269112	Sacramento	CA	95826	916-464-5000	464-5211
TF: 866-249-0773 ■ *Web:* www.childsup.ca.gov					
Community Services & Development Dept					
PO Box 1947	Sacramento	CA	95814	916-341-4200	341-4203
Web: www.csd.ca.gov					
Conservation Dept 801 K St MS 24-01	Sacramento	CA	95814	916-322-1080	445-0732
Web: www.consrv.ca.gov					
Consumer Affairs Dept 400 R St	Sacramento	CA	95814	916-445-1254	445-3755
Web: www.dca.ca.gov					
Corporations Dept 1515 K St Suite 200	Sacramento	CA	95814	916-445-7205	322-3205
Web: www.corp.ca.gov					
Corrections Dept PO Box 942883	Sacramento	CA	94283	916-445-7682	322-2877
Web: www.corr.ca.gov					
Economic Development Dept					
801 K St Suite 1700	Sacramento	CA	95814	916-322-1394	322-2865
Web: www.commerce.ca.gov					
Education Dept 1430 N St Suite 5602	Sacramento	CA	95812	916-319-0800	319-0100
Web: www.cde.ca.gov					
Emergency Services Office 3650 Schriever Ave	Mather	CA	95655	916-845-8510	845-8910
Web: www.oes.ca.gov					
Employment Development Dept					
800 Capitol Mall MIC 83	Sacramento	CA	95814	916-654-8210	657-5294
Web: www.edd.ca.gov					
Energy Commission 1516 9th St	Sacramento	CA	95814	916-654-4287	654-4420
Web: www.energy.ca.gov					
Environmental Protection Agency					
555 Capitol Mall	Sacramento	CA	95814	916-445-3846	445-6401
Web: www.calepa.ca.gov					
Fair Political Practices Commission					
428 J St Suite 620	Sacramento	CA	95814	916-322-5660	322-0886
TF: 866-275-3772 ■ *Web:* www.fppc.ca.gov					
Finance Dept State Capitol Rm 1145	Sacramento	CA	95814	916-445-3878	324-7311
Web: www.dof.ca.gov					
Financial Institutions Dept					
111 Pine St Suite 1100	San Francisco	CA	94111	415-263-8500	989-5310
TF Consumer Info: 800-622-0620 ■ *Web:* www.dfi.ca.gov					
Fish & Game Dept 1416 9th St 12th Fl	Sacramento	CA	95814	916-445-0411	653-7387
TF: 888-334-2258 ■ *Web:* www.dfg.ca.gov					
Food & Agriculture Dept 1220 N St	Sacramento	CA	95814	916-654-0433	654-0403
Web: www.cdfa.ca.gov					
Governor State Capitol 1st Fl	Sacramento	CA	95814	916-445-2841	445-4633
Web: www.governor.ca.gov					
Health Care Services Dept PO Box 942732	Sacramento	CA	94234	800-735-2929	
TF: 800-735-2929 ■ *Web:* www.dhcs.ca.gov					
Highway Patrol PO Box 942898	Sacramento	CA	94298	916-843-3000	657-8639
Web: www.chp.ca.gov					
Historic Preservation Office					
PO Box 942896	Sacramento	CA	94296	916-653-6624	653-9824
Web: www.ohp.parks.ca.gov					
Horse Racing Board 1010 Hurley Way Rm 300	Sacramento	CA	95825	916-263-6000	263-6042
Web: www.chrb.ca.gov					
Housing & Community Development Dept					
1800 3rd St Suite 450	Sacramento	CA	95814	916-445-4782	323-9242
Web: www.hcd.ca.gov					
Housing Finance Agency					
1121 L St Fl 7 Conference Rm	Sacramento	CA	95814	916-322-3991	322-1994
Web: www.calhfa.ca.gov					
Industrial Relations Dept					
455 Golden Gate Ave	San Francisco	CA	94102	415-703-5050	703-5058
Web: www.dir.ca.gov					
Insurance Dept 300 Capitol Mall Suite 1700	Sacramento	CA	95814	916-492-3500	445-5280
Web: www.insurance.ca.gov					
Lieutenant Governor State Capitol Rm 1114	Sacramento	CA	95814	916-445-8994	323-4998
Web: www.ltg.ca.gov					
Medical Board 2005 Evergreen St # 1200	Sacramento	CA	95815	916-263-2382	263-2944
Web: www.medbd.ca.gov					
Mental Health Dept 1600 9th St Rm 151	Sacramento	CA	95814	916-654-3890	654-3198
TF: 800-896-2512 ■ *Web:* www.dmh.ca.gov					
Military Dept 9800 Goethe Rd PO Box 269101	Sacramento	CA	95826	916-854-3000	854-3671
TF: 800-321-2752 ■ *Web:* www.calafornianationalguard.com					
Motor Vehicles Dept PO Box 942869	Sacramento	CA	95818	916-657-6437	657-5716
Web: www.dmv.ca.gov					
Office of Vital Records PO Box 997410	Sacramento	CA	95899	916-445-2684	858-5553*
**Fax Area Code:* 800 ■ *Web:* www.cdph.ca.gov/certlic/birthdeathmar/Pages/ContactUs.aspx					
Parks & Recreation Dept PO Box 942896	Sacramento	CA	94296	916-653-6995	657-3903
TF: 800-777-0369 ■ *Web:* www.parks.ca.gov					
Postsecondary Education Commission					
1303 J St Suite 500	Sacramento	CA	95814	916-445-7933	327-4417
Web: www.cpec.ca.gov					
Prison Terms Board 1515 K St Suite 600	Sacramento	CA	95814	916-445-4072	445-5242
Web: www.cdcr.ca.gov					
Public Utilities Commission					
505 Van Ness Ave	San Francisco	CA	94102	415-703-2782	703-1758
TF: 800-848-5580 ■ *Web:* www.cpuc.ca.gov					
Real Estate Dept					
2201 Broadway PO Box 187000	Sacramento	CA	95818	916-227-0782	227-0777
Web: www.dre.ca.gov					
Rehabilitation Dept 721 Capitol Mall	Sacramento	CA	95814	916-324-1313	
Web: www.rehab.cahwnet.gov					
Secretary of State 1500 11th St	Sacramento	CA	95814	916-653-6814	653-4620
Web: www.ss.ca.gov					
Social Services Dept 744 P St	Sacramento	CA	95814	916-445-6951	445-7311
Web: www.dss.cahwnet.gov					
State Legislature State Capitol	Sacramento	CA	95814	916-324-4676	445-1830
Web: www.leginfo.ca.gov					
State Lottery Commission 600 N 10th St	Sacramento	CA	95814	916-323-7095	323-7087
Web: www.calottery.com					
Student Aid Commission PO Box 419027	Rancho Cordova	CA	95741	916-526-8999	526-8002
TF: 888-224-7268 ■ *Web:* www.csac.ca.gov					
Supreme Court					
333 W Santa Clara St Suite 1060	San Jose	CA	95113	408-277-1004	
Web: www.courts.ca.gov					
Teacher Credentialing Commission					
1900 Capitol Ave	Sacramento	CA	95814	916-445-7254	
TF: 888-921-2682 ■ *Web:* www.ctc.ca.gov					
Transportation Dept 1120 N St	Sacramento	CA	95814	916-654-5266	654-6608
Web: www.dot.ca.gov					
Travel & Tourism Commission PO Box 1499	Sacramento	CA	95812	916-444-4429	322-3402
Web: www.visitcalifornia.com					
Treasurer PO Box 942809	Sacramento	CA	94209	916-653-2995	653-3125
Web: www.treasurer.ca.gov					
Veterans Affairs Dept 1227 'O' St	Sacramento	CA	95814	916-653-2158	653-2456
TF: 800-221-8998 ■ *Web:* www.cdva.ca.gov					
Victim Compensation Program PO Box 3036	Sacramento	CA	95812	916-324-0400	
TF: 800-777-9229 ■ *Web:* www.boc.ca.gov					
Workers' Compensation Div					
PO Box 420603	San Francisco	CA	94142	415-703-4600	703-4664
Web: www.dir.ca.gov/dwc					

342-6 Colorado

	City	State	ZIP	Phone	Fax
State Government Information 1525 Sherman St	Denver	CO	80203	303-866-5000	
Web: www.colorado.gov					
Aging & Adult Services Div					
1575 Sherman St 10th Fl	Denver	CO	80203	303-866-2800	866-2696
Agriculture Dept 700 Kipling St Suite 4000	Lakewood	CO	80215	303-239-4100	239-4125
Web: www.colorado.gov/ag					
Arts Council 1560 Broadway Suite 1600	Denver	CO	80202	303-866-2723	866-4266
TF: 800-291-2787 ■ *Web:* www.coloarts.state.co.us					
Attorney General 1525 Sherman St 5th Fl	Denver	CO	80203	303-866-3617	866-5691
Web: www.ago.state.co.us					
Banking Div 1560 Broadway St Suite 975	Denver	CO	80202	303-894-7575	894-7570
Web: www.dora.state.co.us					
Bill Status 200 E Colfax Ave	Denver	CO	80203	303-866-3055	866-4543
Web: www.leg.state.co.us					
Child Support Enforcement Div					
1575 Sherman St 5th Fl	Denver	CO	80203	303-866-4300	866-4360
Web: www.childsupport.state.co.us					
Children Youth & Families Office					
1575 Sherman St	Denver	CO	80203	303-866-5700	866-2214
Web: www.cdhs.state.co.us					
CollegeInvest 1560 Broadway Suite 1700	Denver	CO	80202	303-295-1981	296-4811
TF: 800-448-2424 ■ *Web:* www.collegeinvest.org					
Consumer Protection Div 1525 Sherman St 5th Fl	Denver	CO	80203	303-866-5189	866-5691
Web: www.cdphe.state.co.us/cp					
Corrections Dept 2862 S Cir Dr	Colorado Springs	CO	80906	719-226-4701	226-4755
Web: www.doc.state.co.us					
Economic Development Commission					
1625 Broadway Suite 1700	Denver	CO	80202	303-892-3840	892-3848
Web: www.state.co.us/oed/edc					
Education Dept 201 E Colfax Ave	Denver	CO	80203	303-866-6600	830-0793
Web: www.cde.state.co.us					
Educator Licensing Unit 201 E Colfax Ave	Denver	CO	80203	303-866-6628	866-6866
Web: www.cde.state.co.us					
Emergency Management Office					
9195 E Mineral Ave Suite 200	Centennial	CO	80112	720-852-6600	852-6750
Web: www.dola.state.co.us					
General Assembly					
Colorado State Capitol					
200 E Colfax Ave Rm 048	Denver	CO	80203	303-866-3521	866-3855
Web: www.leg.state.co.us					
Governor 136 State Capitol Bldg	Denver	CO	80203	303-866-2471	866-2003
Web: www.colorado.gov/governor					
Higher Education Commission					
1380 Lawrence St Suite 1200	Denver	CO	80203	303-866-2723	866-4266
Web: www.state.co.us					
Historical Society 1300 Broadway	Denver	CO	80203	303-866-3682	866-5739
Web: www.coloradohistory.org					
Housing & Finance Authority 1981 Blake St	Denver	CO	80202	303-297-2432	297-2615
TF: 800-877-2432 ■ *Web:* www.colohfa.org					
Human Services Dept 1575 Sherman St	Denver	CO	80203	303-866-5700	866-4214
Web: www.cdhs.state.co.us					
Insurance Div 1560 Broadway Suite 850	Denver	CO	80202	303-894-7499	894-7455
Web: www.dora.state.co.us					
Labor & Employment Dept 633 17th St Suite 201	Denver	CO	80203	303-318-8000	
TF: 800-390-7936 ■ *Web:* www.coworkforce.com					
Lieutenant Governor 130 State Capitol Bldg	Denver	CO	80203	303-866-2087	866-5469
Lottery 212 W 3rd St Suite 210	Pueblo	CO	81003	719-546-2400	546-5208
TF: 800-999-2959 ■ *Web:* www.coloradolottery.com					
Measurements Standards Section					
3125 Wyandot St	Denver	CO	80211	303-477-4220	477-4248
Web: www.ag.state.co.us					
Medical Examiners Board					
1560 Broadway Suite 1300	Denver	CO	80202	303-894-7690	894-7692
Web: www.dora.state.co.us					
Motor Vehicle Div 1881 Pierce St	Lakewood	CO	80214	303-205-5600	205-5975
Web: www.mv.state.co.us/mv.html					
Natural Resources Dept 1313 Sherman St Rm 718	Denver	CO	80203	303-866-3311	866-2115
TF: 800-536-5308 ■ *Web:* www.dnr.state.co.us					
Office of Information Technology					
601 E 18th Ave Suite 250	Denver	CO	80203	303-764-7700	764-7725
Web: www.colorado.gov/cs/Satellite/OIT-Main/CBON/1249667231891					
Parks & Outdoor Recreation Div					
1313 Sherman St Rm 618	Denver	CO	80203	303-866-3437	866-3206
TF Campground Resv: 800-678-2267 ■ *Web:* www.parks.state.co.us					
Parole Board 1600 W 24th St Bldg 54	Pueblo	CO	81003	719-583-5800	583-5805
Web: www.ccjrc.org/resources.shtml					
Public Health & Environment Dept					
4300 Cherry Creek Dr S	Denver	CO	80246	303-692-2000	782-0095
TF: 800-886-7689 ■ *Web:* www.cdphe.state.co.us					

	City	State	ZIP	Phone	Fax
Public Utilities Commission 1580 Logan St 2nd Fl *Web:* www.dora.state.co.us/puc	Denver	CO	80203	303-894-2000	894-2065
Real Estate Commission 1900 Grant St Suite 600 *Web:* www.dora.state.co.us/real-estate	Denver	CO	80203	303-894-2166	894-2683
Regulatory Agencies Dept 1560 Broadway Suite 1550 *TF:* 800-886-7675 ■ *Web:* www.dora.state.co.us	Denver	CO	80202	303-894-7855	894-7885
Revenue Dept 1375 Sherman St Rm 404 *Web:* www.revenue.state.co.us	Denver	CO	80261	303-866-3091	866-2400
Secretary of State 1700 Broadway 2nd Fl *Web:* www.sos.state.co.us	Denver	CO	80290	303-894-2200	894-4860
Securities Div 1560 Broadway Suite 900 *Web:* www.dora.state.co.us/securities	Denver	CO	80202	303-894-2320	
State Court Administrator 1301 Pennsylvania St Suite 300 *TF:* 800-888-0001 ■ *Web:* www.courts.state.co.us	Denver	CO	80203	303-837-3668	837-2340
State Patrol 700 Kipling St *Web:* www.csp.state.co.us	Lakewood	CO	80215	303-239-4500	239-4485
Supreme Court 2 E 14th Ave 4th Fl *Web:* www.courts.state.co.us/supct/supctindex.htm	Denver	CO	80203	303-837-3790	
Tourism Office 1625 Broadway Suite 1700 *TF:* 800-265-6723 ■ *Web:* www.colorado.com	Denver	CO	80202	303-892-3885	892-3848
Transportation Dept 4201 E Arkansas Ave *Web:* www.dot.state.co.us	Denver	CO	80222	303-757-9228	757-9153
Treasurer 200 E Colfax Ave # 140 *Web:* www.treasurer.state.co.us	Denver	CO	80203	303-866-2441	866-2123
Victims Programs Office 700 Kipling St Suite 1000 *TF:* 888-282-1080 ■ *Web:* dcj.state.co.us/ovp	Denver	CO	80215	303-239-5719	239-4491
Vital Records Section 4300 Cherry Creek Dr S *Web:* www.cdphe.state.co.us/hs/certs.asp	Denver	CO	80246	303-692-2200	691-9307
Vocational Rehabilitation Div 2211 W Evans Ave Bldg B *Web:* www.cdhs.state.co.us	Denver	CO	80223	303-866-4150	866-3419
Wildlife Div 6060 Broadway *Web:* www.wildlife.state.co.us	Denver	CO	80216	303-297-1192	294-0874
Workers Compensation Div 633 17th St Suite 400 *TF:* 888-390-7936 ■ *Web:* www.coworkforce.com/dwc	Denver	CO	80202	303-318-8700	318-8710

342-7 Connecticut

	City	State	ZIP	Phone	Fax
State Government Information 101 E River Dr *Web:* www.ct.gov	East Hartford	CT	06108	860-622-2200	
Accountancy Board 30 Trinity St	Hartford	CT	06106	860-509-6179	509-6247
Administrative Services Dept 165 Capitol Ave 4th Fl *Web:* www.das.state.ct.us	Hartford	CT	06106	860-713-5000	713-7459
Aging Commission 210 Capitol Ave Suite 508 *Web:* www.cga.ct.gov	Hartford	CT	06106	860-240-5200	240-5204
Agriculture Dept 165 Capitol Ave *TF:* 800-861-9931 ■ *Web:* www.ct.gov/doag	Hartford	CT	06106	860-713-2500	713-2515
Attorney General 55 Elm St *Web:* www.cslib.org/attygenl	Hartford	CT	06106	860-808-5318	808-5387
Banking Dept 260 Constitution Plaza *TF:* 800-831-7225 ■ *Web:* www.state.ct.us	Hartford	CT	06103	860-240-8299	240-8178
Bill Status Legislative Office Bldg	Hartford	CT	06106	860-240-0555	
Chief Medical Examiner 11 Shuttle Rd *TF:* 800-846-8820 ■ *Web:* www.state.ct.us	Farmington	CT	06032	860-679-3980	679-1257
Child Support Assistance 55 Elm St	Hartford	CT	06106	860-808-5150	808-5383
Commission on Culture & Tourism 1 Constitution Plaza *Web:* www.cultureandtourism.org	Hartford	CT	06103	860-256-2800	256-2811
Consumer Protection Dept 165 Capitol Ave *TF:* 800-842-2649 ■ *Web:* www.ct.gov/dcp	Hartford	CT	06106	860-713-6020	713-7239
Correction Dept 24 Wolcott Hill Rd *Web:* www.ct.gov/doc	Wethersfield	CT	06109	860-692-7780	692-7783
Dept of Consumer Protection 165 Capitol Ave *TF:* 800-842-2649 ■ *Web:* www.ct.gov	Hartford	CT	06106	860-713-6100	713-7239
Dept of Consumer Protection 165 Capitol Ave *TF:* 800-842-2649 ■ *Web:* www.ct.gov	Hartford	CT	06106	860-713-6100	713-7239
Economic & Community Development Dept 505 Hudson St *Web:* www.ct.gov	Hartford	CT	06106	860-270-8000	270-8188
Education Dept 165 Capitol Ave *Web:* www.state.ct.us	Hartford	CT	06106	860-713-6548	713-7005
Environmental Protection Dept 79 Elm St *Web:* www.dep.state.ct.us	Hartford	CT	06106	860-424-3000	424-4051
Ethics Commission 18-20 Trinity St Suite 205 *Web:* www.ct.gov/ethics/site/default.asp	Hartford	CT	06106	860-263-2400	263-2402
General Assembly 300 Capitol Ave Rm 5100 *Web:* www.cga.ct.gov	Hartford	CT	06106	860-240-0100	240-0122
Governor 210 Capitol Ave *Web:* www.ct.gov	Hartford	CT	06106	860-566-4840	524-7395
Higher Education Dept 61 Woodland St *Web:* www.ctdhe.org/SFA	Hartford	CT	06105	860-947-1800	947-1310
Higher Education Dept 61 Woodland St *TF:* 800-842-0229 ■ *Web:* www.ctdhe.org	Hartford	CT	06105	860-947-1800	947-1310
Homeland Security Div 25 Sigourney St 6th Fl *Web:* www.ct.gov/hls	Hartford	CT	06106	860-256-0800	256-0815
Housing Finance Authority 999 W St *Web:* www.chfa.org	Rocky Hill	CT	06067	860-721-9501	571-4367
Information Technology Dept 101 E River Dr *Web:* www.ct.gov	East Hartford	CT	06108	860-622-2400	610-0672
Insurance Dept 153 Market St # 7 *Web:* www.ct.gov	Hartford	CT	06103	860-297-3800	566-7410
Judicial Branch 231 Capitol Ave *Web:* www.jud.state.ct.us	Hartford	CT	06106	860-757-2100	757-2130
Labor Dept 200 Folly Brook Blvd *Web:* www.ctdol.state.ct.us	Wethersfield	CT	06109	860-263-6000	263-6699
Lieutenant Governor 210 Capitol Ave Rm 304 *Web:* www.ct.gov	Hartford	CT	06106	860-524-7384	524-7304
Motor Vehicles Dept 60 State St *Web:* www.ct.gov	Wethersfield	CT	06161	860-263-5700	524-4898
Parole Board 55 W Main St Suite 520 *Web:* www.ct.gov	Waterbury	CT	06702	203-805-6605	805-6652
Public Health Dept 410 Capitol Ave *Web:* www.dph.state.ct.us	Hartford	CT	06134	860-509-8000	509-7111
Public Utility Control Dept 10 Franklin Sq *TF:* 800-382-4586 ■ *Web:* www.state.ct.us	New Britain	CT	06051	860-827-2622	827-2613
Regulatory Services Bureau 410 Capitol Ave PO Box 340308	Hartford	CT	06134	860-509-8045	509-7539
Rehabilitation Services Bureau 25 Sigourney St 11th Fl *TF:* 800-537-2549 ■ *Web:* www.brs.state.ct.us	Hartford	CT	06106	860-424-4844	424-4850
Revenue Services Dept 25 Sigourney St *Web:* www.ct.gov/drs	Hartford	CT	06106	860-297-5650	297-5714
Secretary of State 210 Capitol Ave Rm 104 *Web:* www.sots.state.ct.us	Hartford	CT	06106	860-509-6200	509-6209
Securities & Business Investments Div 260 Constitution Plaza *Web:* www.state.ct.us	Hartford	CT	06103	860-240-8230	240-8295
State of Connecticut Dept of Education Certificati PO Box 150471 *Web:* www.state.ct.us	Hartford	CT	06115	860-713-6969	713-7017
State Parks Div 79 Elm St *TF:* 866-287-2757 ■ *Web:* www.dep.state.ct.us	Hartford	CT	06106	860-424-3200	424-4070
State Police Div 1111 Country Club Rd *Web:* www.state.ct.us	Middletown	CT	06457	860-685-8000	685-8354
Supreme Court 231 Capitol Ave *Web:* www.jud.state.ct.us/external/supapp	Hartford	CT	06106	860-757-2200	757-2217
Tourism Div 505 Hudson St *TF:* 888-288-4748 ■ *Web:* www.ctbound.org	Hartford	CT	06106	860-270-8080	270-8077
Transportation Dept 2800 Berlin Tpke *Web:* www.ct.gov	Newington	CT	06111	860-594-2000	594-3008
Treasurer 55 Elm St *Web:* www.state.ct.us	Hartford	CT	06106	860-702-3000	702-3043
Veterans Affairs Dept 287 W St *TF:* 800-447-0961 ■ *Web:* www.ct.gov/ctva	Rocky Hill	CT	06067	860-721-5891	721-5904
Victim Services Office 31 Cookes St *TF:* 800-822-8428 ■ *Web:* www.jud.state.ct.us	Plainville	CT	06062	860-747-3994	747-6428
Vital Records Unit PO Box 340308 *Web:* www.dph.state.ct.us	Hartford	CT	06134	860-509-7897	509-7964
Workers' Compensation Commission 21 Oak St 4th Fl *TF:* 800-223-9675 ■ *Web:* www.wcc.state.ct.us	Hartford	CT	06106	860-493-1500	247-1361

342-8 Delaware

	City	State	ZIP	Phone	Fax
State Government Information 401 Federal St *TF:* 800-464-4357 ■ *Web:* www.delaware.gov	Dover	DE	19901	302-739-4000	
Administrative Office of the Cts 500 N King St 11th Fl *Web:* www.courts.delaware.gov	Wilmington	DE	19801	302-255-0090	255-2217
Aging & Adults with Physical Disabilites Services Div 1901 N DuPont Hwy *Web:* www.dhss.delaware.gov	New Castle	DE	19720	302-255-9390	577-4445
Agriculture Dept 2320 S DuPont Hwy *TF:* 800-286-8685 ■ *Web:* www.state.de.us/deptagri	Dover	DE	19901	302-739-4811	697-6287
Arts Div 820 N French St 4th Fl *Web:* www.artsdel.org	Wilmington	DE	19801	302-577-8278	577-6561
Attorney General 820 N French St *Web:* www.state.de.us/attgen	Wilmington	DE	19801	302-577-8400	577-6630
Bank Commissioner 555 E Loockerman St Suite 210	Dover	DE	19901	302-739-4235	739-3609
Chief Medical Examiner 200 S Adam St *Web:* www.dhss.delaware.gov	Wilmington	DE	19801	302-577-3420	577-3416
Child Support Enforcement Div 1901 N Du Pont Highway, Main Bldg *Web:* www.dhss.delaware.gov/dhss/dcse	New Castle	DE	19720	302-577-7171	577-4873
Consumer Protection Unit 820 N French St 5th Fl *Web:* www.state.de.us/attgen	Wilmington	DE	19801	302-577-8600	577-6499
Correction Dept 245 McKee Rd **Fax:* Mail Rm ■ *Web:* www.state.de.us/correct	Dover	DE	19904	302-739-5601	739-8223*
Dover Division of Motor Vehicles 303 Transportation Cir PO Box 698 *Web:* www.dmv.de.gov	Dover	DE	19903	302-744-2500	739-3152
Economic Development Office 99 Kings Hwy *Web:* www.state.de.us/dedo	Dover	DE	19901	302-739-4271	739-5749
Education Dept 401 Federal St Suite 2 *Web:* www.doe.state.de.us	Dover	DE	19901	302-739-4601	739-4654
Emergency Management Agency 165 Brick Store Landing Rd *TF:* 877-729-3362 ■ *Web:* www.state.de.us/dema	Smyrna	DE	19977	302-659-3362	659-6855
Finance Dept 820 N French St 8th Fl *Web:* www.state.de.us/finance	Wilmington	DE	19801	302-577-8979	577-8982
Fish & Wildlife Div 89 Kings Hwy *Web:* www.dnrec.state.de.us/fw	Dover	DE	19901	302-739-9910	739-6157
General Assembly Legislative Hall PO Box 1401 *Web:* www.legis.delaware.gov	Dover	DE	19903	302-744-4162	739-6890
Governor 150 William Penn St 2nd Fl *Web:* www.state.de.us/governor	Dover	DE	19901	302-577-3210	739-2775
Harness Racing Commission 2320 S Dupont Hwy *Web:* www.state.de.us/deptagri/harness	Dover	DE	19901	302-698-4599	697-6287

Name / Address	City	State	Zip	Phone	Fax
Health & Social Services Dept 1901 N DuPont Hwy *Web:* www.dhss.delaware.gov/dhss	New Castle	DE	19720	302-355-9040	255-4429
Historical & Cultural Affairs Div 21 The Green	Dover	DE	19901	302-739-5313	739-6711
Housing Authority 18 The Green *Web:* www.state.de.us	Dover	DE	19901	302-739-4263	739-6122
Labor Dept 4425 N Market St *Web:* www.delawareworks.com	Wilmington	DE	19802	302-761-8000	761-6621
Lieutenant Governor 150 William Penn St 3rd Fl *Web:* www.state.de.us/ltgov	Dover	DE	19901	302-744-4333	739-6965
Natural Resources & Environmental Control Dept 89 Kings Hwy *Web:* www.dnrec.state.de.us	Dover	DE	19901	302-739-9902	739-6242
Parks & Recreation Div 89 Kings Hwy *TF Campground Resv:* 877-987-2757 ■ *Web:* www.destateparks.com	Dover	DE	19901	302-739-9200	739-3817
Parole Board 820 N French St 5th Fl *Web:* www.state.de.us/parole	Wilmington	DE	19801	302-577-5233	577-3501
Professional Regulation Div 861 Silver Lake Blvd Suite 203 *Web:* www.professionallicensing.state.de.us	Dover	DE	19904	302-739-4500	739-2711
Professional Standards Board 401 Federal St Suite 2 *Web:* www.doe.k12.de.us/csa/profstds/default.shtml	Dover	DE	19901	302-735-4000	739-4654
Public Integrity Commission 410 Federal St Margaret O'Neill Bldg Suite 3 *Web:* www.depic.delaware.gov	Dover	DE	19901	302-739-2399	739-2398
Revenue Div 820 N French St 1st Fl *Web:* www.state.de.us/revenue	Wilmington	DE	19801	302-577-8200	577-8202
Secretary of State 401 Federal St Suite 3 *Web:* www.state.de.us/sos/sos.shtml	Dover	DE	19901	302-739-4111	739-3811
Securities Div 820 N French St 5th Fl *Web:* www.state.de.us/securities	Wilmington	DE	19801	302-577-8424	577-6987
Services for Children Youth & Their Families Dept 1825 Faulkland Rd *Web:* www.state.de.us	Wilmington	DE	19805	302-633-2500	995-8290
State Police Div PO Box 430 *Web:* www.state.de.us/dsp	Dover	DE	19903	302-739-5911	739-5966
Supreme Court 820 N French St *Web:* www.courts.delaware.gov	Wilmington	DE	19899	302-577-8425	577-3702
Technology & Information Dept 801 Silver Lake Blvd *Web:* www.state.de.us/dti	Dover	DE	19904	302-739-9500	739-6251
Thoroughbred Racing Commission 2320 S DuPont Hwy **Fax Area Code:* 512 ■ *Web:* www.state.de.us/deptagri/thoroughbred	Dover	DE	19901	302-698-4599	463-1376*
Tourism Office 99 Kings Hwy *TF:* 866-284-7483 ■ *Web:* www.visitdelaware.net	Dover	DE	19901	302-739-4271	739-5749
Treasurer 540 S DuPont Hwy Suite 4 *Web:* www.state.de.us/treasure	Dover	DE	19903	302-744-1000	739-5635
Unemployment Insurance Div 4425 N Market St *Web:* www.delawareworks.com/Unemployment/welcome.shtml	Wilmington	DE	19802	302-761-8351	761-6637
Veterans Affairs Commission 802 Silverlake Blvd Suite 100 *Web:* www.state.de.us/veteran	Dover	DE	19904	302-739-2792	739-2794
Violent Crimes Compensation Board 240 N James St Suite 203 *Web:* regulations.delaware.gov	Newport	DE	19804	302-995-8383	995-8387
Vital Statistics Office PO Box 637 *TF:* 800-464-4357 ■ *Web:* www.dhss.delaware.gov	Dover	DE	19903	302-739-4721	736-1862
Vocational Rehabilitation Div 4425 N Market St *Web:* www.delawareworks.com/divisions/dvr/welcome.htm	Wilmington	DE	19809	302-761-8300	761-6633
Weights & Measures Office 2320 S DuPont Hwy *TF:* 800-282-8685 ■ *Web:* www.state.de.us/deptagri/weightsm	Dover	DE	19901	302-739-4811	697-6287
Higher Education Commission 820 N French St 5th Fl *TF:* 800-292-7935 ■ *Web:* www.doe.state.de.us	Wilmington	DE	19801	302-577-3240	577-6765

342-9 District of Columbia

Name / Address	City	State	Zip	Phone	Fax
Government Information 920 Varnum St NE *Web:* dc.gov	Washington	DC	20017	202-727-1000	
Aging Office 441 4th St NW Suite 900 S *Web:* www.dcoa.dc.gov	Washington	DC	20001	202-724-5622	724-4979
Banking Bureau PO Box 96378	Washington	DC	20090	202-727-8000	535-1197
Bill Status 1350 Pennsylvania Ave NW Suite 10 *Web:* www.dccouncil.washington.dc.us/lims/default.asp	Washington	DC	20004	202-724-8050	
Commission on the Arts & Humanities 1371 Harvard St NW *Web:* www.dcarts.dc.gov/dcarts	Washington	DC	20009	202-724-5613	727-4135
Consumer & Regulatory Affairs Dept 941 N Capitol St NE *Web:* dc.gov/DC	Washington	DC	20002	202-442-4400	442-9445
Convention & Tourism Corp 901 7th St NW 4th Fl *TF:* 800-422-8644 ■ *Web:* www.washington.org	Washington	DC	20001	202-789-7000	789-7037
Crime Victims Compensation Program 515 5th St NW Rm 109 Court Bldg A *Web:* www.dccourts.gov	Washington	DC	20001	202-879-4216	879-4230
Dept of Insurance Securities & Banking 810 1st St NE Suite 701 *Web:* www.disr.washingtondc.gov	Washington	DC	20002	202-727-8000	
Economic Development 1350 Pennsylvania Ave NW Suite 317 *Web:* www.dcbiz.dc.gov	Washington	DC	20004	202-727-6365	727-6703
Elections & Ethics Board 441 4th St NW Suite 250N *TF:* 866-328-6837 ■ *Web:* www.dcboee.org	Washington	DC	20001	202-727-2525	347-2648
Employment Services Dept 4049 S Capitol St SW *TF:* 877-319-7346 ■ *Web:* www.does.ci.washington.dc.us	Washington	DC	20032	202-724-7000	673-6994
Historic Preservation Office 801 N Capitol St NE	Washington	DC	20002	202-442-8800	
Homeland Security & Emergency Management Agency 2720 Martin Luther King Jr Ave SE 8th Fl *Web:* dcema.dc.gov/dcema	Washington	DC	20032	202-727-6161	
Housing Finance Agency 815 Florida Ave NW *Web:* www.dchfa.org	Washington	DC	20001	202-777-1600	
Human Services Dept 64 New York Ave NE 6th Fl *Web:* www.dhs.dc.gov	Washington	DC	20002	202-671-4200	
Lottery & Charitable Games Control Board 2101 ML King Jr Ave SE *Web:* www.dclottery.com	Washington	DC	20020	202-645-8000	645-8077
Occupational & Professional Licensing Administration 941 N Capitol St NE *Web:* dc.gov/DC	Washington	DC	20002	202-442-4320	442-4528
Paternity & Child Support Enforcement Office 441 4th St NW Suite 550N *Web:* dc.gov/DC	Washington	DC	20001	202-442-9900	
Public Service Commission 1333 'H' St NW 2nd Fl W *Web:* www.dcpsc.org	Washington	DC	20005	202-626-5100	393-1389
Rehabilitation Services Administration 810 1st St NE *Web:* dc.gov/DC	Washington	DC	20002	202-442-8663	442-8742
Securities Bureau 810 1st St NE Suite 701 *Web:* app.dc.gov	Washington	DC	20002	202-727-8000	535-1196
Tuition Assistance Grant Program 810 First St NE *TF:* 877-485-6751 ■ *Web:* www.osse.dc.gov	Washington	DC	20001	202-727-2824	727-2834
Vital Records Branch 825 N Capitol St NE 1st Fl *Web:* www.dchealth.dc.gov	Washington	DC	20002	202-671-5000	
Weights & Measures Office 1110 U St SE	Washington	DC	20020	202-698-2130	

342-10 Florida

Name / Address	City	State	Zip	Phone	Fax
State Government Information 404 S Monroe St Suite 409 *TF:* 800-342-1827 ■ *Web:* www.myflorida.com	Tallahassee	FL	32399	850-488-1234	
Agriculture & Consumer Services Dept State Capitol PL-10 *Web:* www.doacs.state.fl.us	Tallahassee	FL	32399	850-488-3022	488-7585
Attorney General State Capitol PL-01 *TF:* 866-966-7226 ■ *Web:* myfloridalegal.com	Tallahassee	FL	32399	850-487-1963	487-2564
Bill Status 111 W Madison St Rm 704 *TF:* 800-342-1827 ■ *Web:* www.leg.state.fl.us	Tallahassee	FL	32399	850-488-4371	922-1534
Business & Professional Regulation Dept 1940 N Monroe St *Web:* www.myflorida.com/dbpr	Tallahassee	FL	32399	850-487-1395	488-1830
Chief Financial Officer 200 E Gaines St *Web:* www.fldfs.com	Tallahassee	FL	32399	850-413-2850	
Child Support Enforcement Program PO Box 8030 *TF:* 800-622-5437 ■ *Web:* www.myflorida.com/dor/childsupport	Tallahassee	FL	32314	800-622-5437	
Citrus Dept 605 E Main St **Fax Area Code:* 877 ■ *Web:* www.floridajuice.com	Bartow	FL	33830	863-537-3999	352-2487*
Colleges & Universities Div 325 W Gaines St *Web:* www.fldcu.org	Tallahassee	FL	32399	850-254-0466	245-9685
Consumer Services Div 2005 Apalachee Pkwy *TF:* 800-435-7352 ■ *Web:* www.800helpfla.com	Tallahassee	FL	32399	850-922-2966	487-4177
Corrections Dept 2601 Blair Stone Rd **Fax:* Hum Res ■ *Web:* www.dc.state.fl.us	Tallahassee	FL	32399	850-488-5021	488-4534*
Cultural Affairs Div 1001 DeSoto Pk Dr *Web:* www.florida-arts.org	Tallahassee	FL	32301	850-254-6470	245-6497
Education Dept 325 W Gaines St *Web:* www.fldoe.org	Tallahassee	FL	32399	850-245-0505	245-9667
Elder Affairs Dept 4040 Esplanade Way *Web:* www.elderaffairs.state.fl.us	Tallahassee	FL	32399	850-414-2000	414-2004
Emergency Management Div 2555 Shumard Oak Blvd *Web:* www.floridadisaster.org	Tallahassee	FL	32399	850-413-9900	488-7841
Environmental Protection Dept 3900 Commonwealth Blvd MS 10 *Web:* www.dep.state.fl.us	Tallahassee	FL	32399	850-245-2118	245-2128
Ethics Commission 3600 Maclay Blvd S Suite 201 *Web:* www.ethics.state.fl.us	Tallahassee	FL	32312	850-488-7864	488-3077
Financial Regulation Office 200 E Gaines St *Web:* www.fldfs.com	Tallahassee	FL	32399	850-410-9111	410-9448
Financial Services Dept 200 E Gaines St *TF:* 800-342-2762 ■ *Web:* www.fldfs.com	Tallahassee	FL	32399	850-413-3100	488-2349
Fish & Wildlife Conservation Commission 620 S Meridian St *Web:* www.floridaconservation.org	Tallahassee	FL	32399	850-488-4676	488-6988
Florida Prepaid College Board PO Box 6448 **Fax:* Cust Svc ■ *TF:* 800-552-4723 ■ *Web:* www.myfloridaprepaid.com	Tallahassee	FL	32314	850-488-8514	309-1766*
Governor State Capitol *Web:* www.myflorida.com	Tallahassee	FL	32399	850-488-4441	487-0801
Health Dept 4052 Bald Cypress Way Bin A00 *Web:* www.doh.state.fl.us	Tallahassee	FL	32399	850-245-4443	487-3729
Highway Safety & Motor Vehicles Dept 2900 Apalachee Pkwy *Web:* www.hsmv.state.fl.us	Tallahassee	FL	32399	850-922-9000	922-6274

				Phone	Fax
Historical Resources Div					
500 S Bronough St Suite 305	Tallahassee	FL	32399	850-245-6300	245-6435
Web: dhr.dos.state.fl.us					
Housing Finance Corp					
227 N Bronough St Suite 5000	Tallahassee	FL	32301	850-488-4197	488-9809
Web: www.floridahousing.org					
Insurance Regulation Office					
200 E Gaines St	Tallahassee	FL	32399	850-413-3132	
TF: 800-342-2762 ■ *Web:* www.fldfs.com					
Law Enforcement Dept PO Box 1489	Tallahassee	FL	32302	850-410-7000	410-7440
Web: www.fdle.state.fl.us					
Legislature 111 W Madison St	Tallahassee	FL	32399	850-488-4371	922-0183
Web: www.leg.state.fl.us					
Lieutenant Governor State Capitol PL-05	Tallahassee	FL	32399	850-488-4711	921-6114
Lottery Dept 250 Marriott Dr	Tallahassee	FL	32301	850-487-7777	487-7796*
**Fax:* Hum Res ■ *Web:* www.flalottery.com					
Medical Quality Assurance Div					
4052 Bald Cypress Way	Tallahassee	FL	32399	850-488-0595	487-9622
Web: www.doh.state.fl.us					
Military Affairs Dept					
St Francis Barracks 82 Marine St	Saint Augustine	FL	32084	904-823-0364	823-0125
Web: www.dma.state.fl.us					
Parole Commission 4070 Esplanade Way	Tallahassee	FL	32399	850-488-3417	414-1915
Web: https://fpc.state.fl.us					
Public Service Commission					
2540 Shumard Oak Blvd	Tallahassee	FL	32399	850-413-6042	487-1716
Web: www.floridapsc.com					
Recreation & Parks Div					
3900 Commonwealth Blvd MS 500	Tallahassee	FL	32399	850-245-2157	245-3041
TF Campground Resv: 800-326-3521 ■ *Web:* www.dep.state.fl.us					
Revenue Dept 501 S Calhoun St Suite 104	Tallahassee	FL	32399	850-488-5050	488-0024
Web: www.myflorida.com/dor					
Secretary of State 500 S Bronough St	Tallahassee	FL	32399	850-245-6500	245-6125
Web: www.dos.state.fl.us					
State Boxing Commission 1940 N Monroe St	Tallahassee	FL	32399	850-488-8500	922-2249
Web: www.state.fl.us					
State Cts Administrator Office					
500 S Duval St	Tallahassee	FL	32399	850-922-5081	488-0156
Web: www.flcourts.org					
State Technology Office					
4030 Esplanade Way	Tallahassee	FL	32399	850-410-4777	922-5162
Web: www.sto.myflorida.com					
Student Financial Assistance Office					
1940 N Monroe St Suite 70	Tallahassee	FL	32303	850-410-5200	488-3612
TF: 888-827-2004 ■ *Web:* www.floridastudentfinancialaid.org					
Supreme Court 500 S Duval St	Tallahassee	FL	32399	850-488-0125	
Web: www.flcourts.org					
Tourism Commission					
661 E Jefferson St Suite 300	Tallahassee	FL	32301	850-488-5607	224-2938
TF: 888-735-2872 ■ *Web:* www.visitflorida.com					
Transportation Dept 605 Suwannee St	Tallahassee	FL	32399	850-414-5200	414-5201
Web: www.dot.state.fl.us					
Veterans' Affairs Dept					
11351 Ulmerton Rd Rm 311-K	Largo	FL	33778	727-518-3202	518-3216
Web: www.floridavets.org					
Victim Services & Criminal Justice Programs					
State Capitol PL-01	Tallahassee	FL	32399	850-414-3300	487-1595
TF: 866-966-7226 ■ *Web:* myfloridalegal.com/victims					
Vital Records Bureau PO Box 210	Jacksonville	FL	32231	904-359-6900	359-6993
Web: www.doh.state.fl.us					
Vocational Rehabilitation Services Div					
2002 Old St Augustine Rd Bldg A	Tallahassee	FL	32301	850-245-3399	
TF: 800-451-4327 ■ *Web:* www.rehabworks.org					
Workers' Compensation Div					
200 E Gaines St	Tallahassee	FL	32399	850-413-1601	
Web: www.fldfs.com					
Workforce Florida Inc					
1580 Waldo Palmer Ln Suite 1	Tallahassee	FL	32303	850-921-1119	921-1101
Web: www.workforceflorida.com					

342-11 Georgia

				Phone	Fax
State Government Information					
100 Peachtree St NW Suite 2300	Atlanta	GA	30303	404-656-2000	
TF: 800-436-7442 ■ *Web:* www.georgia.gov/00/home/0,2061,4802,00.html					
Administrative Office of the Cts					
244 Washington St SW Suite 300	Atlanta	GA	30334	404-656-5171	651-6449
Web: www.georgiacourts.org					
Aging Services Div					
2 Peachtree St NW Suite 9-385	Atlanta	GA	30303	404-657-5255	657-5285
Web: www.aging.dhr.georgia.gov					
Agriculture Dept 19 ML King Jr Dr SW	Atlanta	GA	30334	404-656-3600	656-9380
Web: www.agr.state.ga.us					
Arts Council 260 14th St NW Suite 401	Atlanta	GA	30318	404-685-2787	685-2788
Web: www.gaarts.org					
Attorney General 40 Capitol Sq SW	Atlanta	GA	30334	404-656-3300	657-8733
Web: www.state.ga.us/ago					
Banking & Finance Dept					
2990 Brandywine Rd Suite 200	Atlanta	GA	30341	770-986-1633	986-1654
Web: www.ganet.org					
Bill Status-House State Capitol Rm 309	Atlanta	GA	30334	404-656-5015	
Web: www.legis.state.ga.us					
Bill Status-Senate State Capitol Rm 353	Atlanta	GA	30334	404-656-5040	656-5043
Web: www.legis.state.ga.us					
Child Support Enforcement Office					
2 Peachtree St NW	Atlanta	GA	30303	404-657-0634	
Web: www.ocse.dhr.georgia.gov					
Community Affairs Dept 60 Executive Pk S NE	Atlanta	GA	30329	404-656-4940	679-0589
Web: www.dca.state.ga.us					
Corrections Dept 2 ML King Jr Dr SE Suite 866	Atlanta	GA	30334	404-656-9770	651-8335
Web: www.dcor.state.ga.us					
Defense Dept PO Box 17965	Atlanta	GA	30316	404-624-6001	624-6005
Web: www.dod.state.ga.us					
Economic Development Dept					
75 5th St NW # 1200	Atlanta	GA	30308	404-962-4000	463-7299
Web: www.georgia.org					
Education Dept					
205 Jesse Hill Jr Dr SE Suite 2066E	Atlanta	GA	30334	404-656-2800	651-8737
Web: www.gadoe.org					
Emergency Management Agency					
935 E Confederate Ave SE	Atlanta	GA	30316	404-635-7000	635-7205
Web: www.gema.state.ga.us					
Employment Services Div					
148 Andrew Young International Blvd NE	Atlanta	GA	30303	404-232-3515	
Web: www.dol.state.ga.us					
Environmental Protection Div					
2 ML King Jr Dr SE Suite 1152E	Atlanta	GA	30334	404-657-5947	651-5778
TF: 888-373-5947 ■ *Web:* www.dnr.state.ga.us/dnr/environ					
Family & Children Services Div					
2 Peachtree St NW Suite 19-400	Atlanta	GA	30303	404-651-9361	657-5105
Web: dfcs.dhr.georgia.gov					
General Assembly State Capitol	Atlanta	GA	30334	404-656-5020	651-8086
Web: www.legis.state.ga.us					
Governor 203 State Capitol SW	Atlanta	GA	30334	404-656-1776	657-7332
Web: www.gov.state.ga.us					
Governor's Office of Consumer Protection					
2 ML King Jr Dr Suite 356	Atlanta	GA	30334	404-656-6800	651-9018
TF: 800-869-1123 ■ *Web:* consumer.georgia.gov					
Historic Preservation Div					
254 Washington St SW	Atlanta	GA	30334	404-656-2840	651-8739
Web: www.gashpo.org					
Housing Finance Div 60 Executive Pk S NE	Atlanta	GA	30329	404-679-0607	679-4837
Web: www.dca.state.ga.us					
Human Resources Dept					
2 Peachtree St NW Suite 29-250	Atlanta	GA	30303	404-656-5680	651-8669
Web: www.dhr.georgia.gov					
Information Technology Office					
2 Peachtree St NW Suite 4-400	Atlanta	GA	30303	404-656-5540	
Web: www.oit.dhr.georgia.gov/portal/site/DHS-OIT					
Insurance Commissioner					
2 ML King Jr Dr SE 7th Fl	Atlanta	GA	30334	404-656-2056	656-4030
Web: www.gainsurance.org					
Labor Dept					
148 Andrew Young International Blvd NE	Atlanta	GA	30303	404-232-7300	657-9996
Web: www.dol.state.ga.us					
Lieutenant Governor 240 State Capitol	Atlanta	GA	30334	404-656-5030	656-6739
Web: ltgov.georgia.gov					
Medical Examiners Composite State Board					
2 Peachtree St NW 36th Fl	Atlanta	GA	30303	404-656-3913	656-9723
Web: medicalboard.georgia.gov					
Mental Health Developmental Disabilities & Addicti					
2 Peachtree St NW Suite 22-224	Atlanta	GA	30303	404-657-2252	657-1137
Web: www.mhddad.dhr.georgia.gov					
Motor Vehicle Safety Dept 2206 E View Pkwy	Conyers	GA	33013	678-413-8650	
Web: www.dmvs.ga.gov					
Natural Resources Dept					
2 ML King Jr Dr SE Suite 1252E	Atlanta	GA	30334	404-656-3500	656-0770
Web: www.gadnr.org					
Pardons & Paroles Board					
2 ML King Jr Dr SE E Tower Suite 458	Atlanta	GA	30334	404-656-5651	651-8502
Web: www.pap.state.ga.us					
Parks Recreation & Historic Sites Div					
2 ML King Jr Dr SE Suite 1352E	Atlanta	GA	30334	404-656-2770	651-5871
TF: 800-862-7275 ■ *Web:* www.gastateparks.org					
Ports Authority PO Box 2406	Savannah	GA	31402	912-964-3811	964-3921
TF: 800-342-8012 ■ *Web:* www.gaports.com					
Professional Licensing Boards Div					
237 Coliseum Dr	Macon	GA	31217	478-207-1300	207-1363
Web: www.sos.state.ga.us					
Public Health Div					
2 Peachtree St NW Suite 15-470	Atlanta	GA	30303	404-657-2700	657-2715
Web: www.health.state.ga.us					
Public Service Commission					
244 Washington St SW Suite 126	Atlanta	GA	30334	404-656-4501	656-2341
Web: www.psc.state.ga.us					
Rehabilitation Services Div					
148 Andrew Young International Blvd NE					
Suite 510 Sussex Pl	Atlanta	GA	30303	404-232-3910	
Web: www.vocrehabga.org					
Revenue Dept 1800 Century Ctr Blvd NE	Atlanta	GA	30345	404-417-4477	417-2101
Web: www.etax.dor.ga.gov					
Secretary of State State Capitol Rm 214	Atlanta	GA	30334	404-656-2881	656-0513
Web: www.sos.state.ga.us					
Securities & Business Regulation Div					
2 Martin Luther King Jr Dr W Tower Suite 802	Atlanta	GA	30334	404-656-3920	657-8410
Web: sos.georgia.gov/securities/securitiesdiv.htm					
State Patrol PO Box 1456	Atlanta	GA	30371	404-624-7000	624-7498
Web: www.dps.georgia.gov					
Student Finance Commission					
2082 E Exchange Pl Suite 200	Tucker	GA	30084	770-724-9000	724-9089
TF: 800-505-4732 ■ *Web:* www.gsfc.org					
Supreme Court					
244 Washington St SW					
Rm 572 State Office Annex Bldg	Atlanta	GA	30334	404-656-3470	656-2253
Web: www.gasupreme.us					
Tourism Div					
285 Peachtree Ctr Ave NE Suite 1000	Atlanta	GA	30303	404-656-2000	651-9063
TF: 800-847-4842 ■ *Web:* www.georgiaonmymind.org					
Transparency & Campaign Finance Commission					
200 Piedmont Ave SE Suite 1402	Atlanta	GA	30334	404-463-1980	463-1988
TF: 866-589-7327 ■ *Web:* www.ethics.state.ga.us					
Transportation Dept 2 Capitol Sq	Atlanta	GA	30334	404-656-5267	656-3507
Web: www.dot.state.ga.us					

	City	State	ZIP	Phone	Fax
Treasury & Fiscal Services Office 200 Piedmont Ave Suite 1202W *Web:* www.otfs.georgia.gov	Atlanta	GA	30334	404-656-2168	656-9048
University System Board of Regents 270 Washington St SW *Web:* www.usg.edu	Atlanta	GA	30334	404-656-2250	651-9301
Veterans Service Dept Floyd Veterans Memorial Bldg Suite 970E *Web:* sdvs.georgia.gov	Atlanta	GA	30334	404-656-2300	656-7006
Vital Records Office 2600 Skyland Dr NE *Web:* www.health.state.ga.us	Atlanta	GA	30319	404-679-4701	524-4278
Wildlife Resources Div 2070 US Hwy 278 SE **Fax Area Code: 706* ■ *Web:* www.georgiawildlife.dnr.state.ga.us	Social Circle	GA	30025	770-918-6400	557-3030*
Workers' Compensation Board 270 Peachtree St NW *Web:* www.sbwc.georgia.gov	Atlanta	GA	30303	404-656-2048	651-9467

342-12 Hawaii

	City	State	ZIP	Phone	Fax
State Government Information 201 Merchant St Suite 1805 *Web:* portal.ehawaii.gov	Honolulu	HI	96813	808-695-4620	695-4618
Administrative Office of the Cts 417 S King St Rm 206 *Web:* www.courts.state.hi.us	Honolulu	HI	96812	808-539-4900	539-4855
Aging Office 250 S Hotel St Rm 406 *Web:* www.hawaii.gov	Honolulu	HI	96813	808-586-0100	586-0185
Agriculture Dept 1428 S King St *Web:* www.hawaii.gov	Honolulu	HI	96814	808-973-9600	973-9613
Attorney General 425 Queen St *Web:* www.state.hi.us/ag	Honolulu	HI	96813	808-586-1500	586-1239
Bill Status 415 S Beretania St Rm 401 *Web:* www.capitol.hawaii.gov	Honolulu	HI	96813	808-587-0478	587-0793
Budget & Finance Dept PO Box 150 *Web:* www.state.hi.us	Honolulu	HI	96810	808-586-1518	586-1976
Business Economic Development & Tourism Dept PO Box 2359 *Web:* www.hawaii.gov	Honolulu	HI	96804	808-586-2355	586-2377
Child Support Enforcement Agency 601 Kamokila Blvd Suite 251 *TF:* 888-317-9081 ■ *Web:* www.hawaii.gov	Kapolei	HI	96707	808-692-7000	692-7060
Civil Defense Div 3949 Diamond Head Rd *Web:* www.scd.state.hi.us	Honolulu	HI	96816	808-733-4300	733-4287
Commerce & Consumer Affairs Dept PO Box 541 *Web:* www.state.hi.us/dcca	Honolulu	HI	96809	808-586-2830	586-2877
Consumer Protection Office 235 S Beretania St Rm 801 *Web:* www.hawaii.gov	Honolulu	HI	96813	808-586-2630	586-2640
Corrections Div 919 Ala Moana Blvd 4th Fl	Honolulu	HI	96814	808-587-1340	587-1282
Crime Victims Compensation Commission 1136 Union Mall Rm 600 *Web:* www.hawaii.gov	Honolulu	HI	96813	808-587-1143	587-1146
Education Dept 1390 Miller St *Web:* www.doe.k12.hi.us	Honolulu	HI	96813	808-586-3230	586-3234
Financial Institutions Div PO Box 2054 *Web:* www.hawaii.gov	Honolulu	HI	96805	808-586-2820	586-2818
Forestry & Wildlife Div 1151 Punchbowl St Rm 325 *Web:* www.dofaw.net	Honolulu	HI	96813	808-587-0166	587-0160
Governor 415 S Beretania St State Capitol *Web:* www.gov.state.hi.us	Honolulu	HI	96813	808-586-0034	586-0006
Health Dept 1250 Punchbowl St *Web:* www.state.hi.us	Honolulu	HI	96813	808-586-4400	586-4444
Historic Preservation Div 601 Kamokila Blvd Rm 555 *Web:* www.hawaii.gov/dlnr/hpd/hpgreeting.htm	Kapolei	HI	96707	808-692-8015	692-8020
Housing & Community Development Corp 677 Queen St Suite 300 *Web:* www.hcdch.state.hi.us	Honolulu	HI	96813	808-587-0597	587-0588
Human Resources Development Dept 235 S Beretania St Rm 1400 *Web:* www.state.hi.us	Honolulu	HI	96813	808-587-1100	587-1106
Human Services Dept PO Box 339 *Web:* www.state.hi.us	Honolulu	HI	96809	808-586-4997	586-4890
Information & Communication Services Div 1151 Punchbowl St Rm B-10 *Web:* www.hawaii.gov	Honolulu	HI	96813	808-586-1920	586-1922
Insurance Div PO Box 3614 *Web:* www.hawaii.gov	Honolulu	HI	96811	808-586-2790	586-2806
Labor & Industrial Relations Dept 830 Punchbowl St *Web:* www.dlir.state.hi.us	Honolulu	HI	96813	808-586-8842	586-9099
Land & Natural Resources Dept 1151 Punchbowl St *Web:* www.hawaii.gov/dlnr	Honolulu	HI	96813	808-587-0400	587-0390
Legislature 415 S Beretania St *Web:* www.capitol.hawaii.gov	Honolulu	HI	96813	808-587-0666	587-0681
Lieutenant Governor 415 S Beretania St 5th Fl *Web:* www.hawaii.gov/ltgov	Honolulu	HI	96813	808-586-0255	586-0231
Measurement Standards Branch 1851 Auiki St *Web:* www.hawaiiag.org	Honolulu	HI	96819	808-832-0690	832-0683
Motor Vehicle Safety Office 601 Kamokila Blvd Rm 511	Kapolei	HI	96707	808-692-7650	692-7665
Paroling Authority 1177 Alakea St 1st Fl	Honolulu	HI	96813	808-587-1293	587-1314
Postsecondary Education Commission 2444 Dole St Bachman Hall Rm 209	Honolulu	HI	96822	808-956-8213	956-5156
Professional & Vocational Licensing Div PO Box 3469 *Web:* www.hawaii.gov	Honolulu	HI	96801	808-586-3000	586-3031
Public Utilities Commission 465 S King St Rm 103 *Web:* www.state.hi.us	Honolulu	HI	96813	808-586-2020	586-2066
Securities Compliance Div 335 Merchant St Rm 203 *Web:* www.hawaii.gov	Honolulu	HI	96813	808-586-2744	586-2733
Sheriffs Div 1111 Alakea St 2nd Fl	Honolulu	HI	96813	808-538-5665	538-5661
Social Services Div 810 Richards St Suite 400 *Web:* www.state.hi.us/dhs	Honolulu	HI	96813	808-586-5701	586-5700
State Foundation for Culture & the Arts 250 S Hotel St 2nd Fl *Web:* www.state.hi.us	Honolulu	HI	96813	808-586-0300	586-0308
State Parks Div PO Box 621 *Web:* www.state.hi.us	Honolulu	HI	96809	808-587-0300	587-0311
Supreme Court 417 S King St *Web:* www.courts.state.hi.us	Honolulu	HI	96813	808-539-4919	539-4928
Taxation Dept PO Box 259 *TF:* 800-222-3229 ■ *Web:* www.state.hi.us	Honolulu	HI	96809	808-587-1510	587-1506
Teacher Standards Board 650 Iwilei Rd Suite 201 *Web:* www.htsb.org	Honolulu	HI	96817	808-586-2600	586-2606
Tourism Authority 1801 Kalakaua Ave *Web:* www.hawaii.gov	Honolulu	HI	96815	808-973-2255	973-2253
Transportation Dept 869 Punchbowl St *Web:* www.hawaii.gov	Honolulu	HI	96813	808-587-2160	587-2313
Veterans Services Office 459 Patterson Rd E Wing Suite 1-A103 *Web:* www.dod.state.hi.us	Honolulu	HI	96819	808-433-0420	433-0385
Vital Records Section PO Box 3378 *Web:* www.state.hi.us	Honolulu	HI	96801	808-586-4533	586-4606
Vocational Rehabilitation Div 601 Kamokila Blvd Rm 514	Kapolei	HI	96707	808-692-7715	692-7727
Workforce Development Div 830 Punchbowl St Rm 209 *Web:* www.hawaii.gov	Honolulu	HI	96813	808-586-8877	586-8822

342-13 Idaho

	City	State	ZIP	Phone	Fax
State Government Information 999 Main St Suite 910 *TF:* 877-443-3468 ■ *Web:* www.idaho.gov	Boise	ID	83702	208-334-2411	332-0106
Accountancy Board 3101 W Main St # 210 *Web:* www.isba.idaho.gov	Boise	ID	83702	208-334-2490	334-2615
Administrative Director of the Courts PO Box 83720 *Web:* www.isc.idaho.gov	Boise	ID	83720	208-334-2246	947-7590
Aging Commission 3380 W Americana Ter # 120 *Web:* www.idahoaging.com	Boise	ID	83706	208-334-3833	334-3033
Agriculture Dept 2270 Old Penitentiary Rd *Web:* www.agri.state.id.us	Boise	ID	83712	208-332-8500	334-2170
Arts Commission 2410 Old Penitentiary Rd *TF:* 800-278-3863 ■ *Web:* www.arts.idaho.gov	Boise	ID	83712	208-334-2119	334-2488
Attorney General PO Box 83720 *TF:* 800-432-3545 ■ *Web:* www.state.id.us	Boise	ID	83720	208-334-2400	334-2530
Bill Status PO Box 83720 *Web:* www3.state.id.us/legislat/legtrack.html	Boise	ID	83720	208-334-2475	334-2125
Board of Medicine 1755 Westgate Dr Suite 140 *TF:* 800-333-0073 ■ *Web:* www.bom.state.id.us	Boise	ID	83704	208-327-7000	327-7005
Child Support Services Bureau PO Box 83720 *Web:* www.healthandwelfare.idaho.gov	Boise	ID	83720	208-334-2479	334-0666
Consumer Protection Unit PO Box 83720 *Web:* www.state.id.us	Boise	ID	83720	208-334-2424	334-4151
Correction Board 1299 N Orchard St Suite 110 *Web:* www.corr.state.id.us	Boise	ID	83706	208-658-2000	327-7404
Crime Victims Compensation Program PO Box 83720 *TF:* 800-950-2110 ■ *Web:* www.iic.idaho.gov	Boise	ID	83720	208-334-6000	334-2321
Economic Development Div 700 W State St PO Box 83720 *TF:* 800-842-5858 ■ *Web:* commerce.idaho.gov	Boise	ID	83720	208-334-2470	334-2631
Education Dept 650 W State St PO Box 83720 *Web:* www.sde.state.id.us	Boise	ID	83720	208-332-6800	334-2228
Family & Community Services Div 450 W State St *Web:* www.healthandwelfare.idaho.gov	Boise	ID	83702	208-334-5700	332-7330
Finance Dept PO Box 83720 *Web:* www.finance.state.id.us	Boise	ID	83720	208-332-8000	332-8096
Fish & Game Dept 600 S Walnut St *Web:* www.fishandgame.idaho.gov	Boise	ID	83712	208-334-3700	334-2114
Governor 700 W Jefferson St # 228 *Web:* www.gov.idaho.gov	Boise	ID	83720	208-334-2100	334-3454
Health & Welfare Dept 450 W State St 10th Fl PO Box 83720 **Fax: PR* ■ *Web:* www.healthandwelfare.idaho.gov	Boise	ID	83720	208-334-5500	334-5926*
Historical Society 2205 Old Penitentiary Rd *TF:* 877-653-4367 ■ *Web:* history.idaho.gov	Boise	ID	83712	208-334-2682	334-2774
Homeland Security Bureau 4040 W Guard St Bldg 600 *TF:* 800-344-0984 ■ *Web:* www.bhs.idaho.gov	Boise	ID	83705	208-422-3040	422-3044
Housing & Finance Assn 565 W Myrtle Ave *TF:* 800-526-7145 ■ *Web:* www.ihfa.org	Boise	ID	83702	208-331-4882	331-4804
Information Technology & Communication Services Di 650 W State St Rm 100 *Web:* www.adm.idaho.gov	Boise	ID	83702	208-332-1841	334-5315
Insurance Dept 700 W State St 3rd Fl PO Box 83720 *Web:* www.doi.state.id.us	Boise	ID	83720	208-334-4250	334-4398
Lands Dept PO Box 83720 *Web:* www.idl.idaho.gov/index.htm	Boise	ID	83720	208-334-0200	334-2339

	City	State	Zip	Phone	Fax
Legislature PO Box 83720 *Web:* www.legislature.idaho.gov	Boise	ID	83720	208-334-2475	334-2125
Lieutenant Governor 700 W Jefferson St *Web:* www.lgo.idaho.gov	Boise	ID	83720	208-334-2200	334-3259
Lottery 1199 Shoreline Ln Suite 100 *TF:* 800-432-5688	Boise	ID	83702	208-334-2600	334-2610
Motor Vehicles Div 3311 W State St PO Box 7129 *Web:* www.apps.itd.idaho.gov	Boise	ID	83707	208-334-8000	334-8739
National Board For Professional Teaching Standards PO Box 83720 *Web:* www.sde.idaho.gov	Boise	ID	83720	208-332-6882	334-4664
Occupational Licenses Bureau 700 West State St. *Web:* www.ibol.idaho.gov	Boise	ID	83702	208-334-3233	334-3945
Pardon & Parole Commission PO Box 83720 *Web:* www.state.id.us	Boise	ID	83720	208-334-2520	334-3501
Parks & Recreation Dept 5657 Warm Springs Ave. *Web:* www.idahoparks.org	Boise	ID	83716	208-334-4199	334-3741
Public Utilities Commission PO Box 83720. *TF:* 800-432-0369 ■ *Web:* www.puc.state.id.us	Boise	ID	83720	208-334-0300	334-3762
Racing Commission PO Box 700 *Web:* www.isp.state.id.us/race	Meridian	ID	83680	208-884-7080	884-7098
Real Estate Commission 633 N 4th St *Web:* www.idahorealestatecommission.com	Boise	ID	83720	208-334-3285	334-2050
Secretary of State 700 W Jefferson St Rm 203 *Web:* www.idsos.state.id.us	Boise	ID	83720	208-334-2300	334-2282
State Police Div PO Box 700 *Web:* www.isp.state.id.us	Meridian	ID	83680	208-884-7000	884-7290
Supreme Court PO Box 83720. *Web:* www.isc.idaho.gov	Boise	ID	83720	208-334-2210	334-2616
Tax Commission 800 E Pk Blvd. *TF:* 800-972-7660 ■ *Web:* www.tax.idaho.gov	Boise	ID	83712	208-334-7660	334-7844
Tourism Development Div 700 W State St PO Box 83720 *TF:* 800-842-5858 ■ *Web:* www.visitid.org	Boise	ID	83720	208-334-2470	334-2631
Transportation Dept PO Box 7129 *Web:* www.itd.idaho.gov	Boise	ID	83707	208-334-8000	334-3858
Treasurer 700 W Jefferson St Suite 126 PO Box 83720 *Web:* sto.idaho.gov	Boise	ID	83720	208-334-3200	332-2959
Veterans Services Div 351 Collins Rd. *Web:* www.veterans.idaho.gov	Boise	ID	83702	208-577-2310	334-2627
Vital Records & Health Statistics Bureau PO Box 83720 *Web:* www.healthandwelfare.idaho.gov	Boise	ID	83720	208-334-5988	
Vocational Rehabilitation Div 650 W State St Rm 150. *Web:* www.vr.idaho.gov	Boise	ID	83720	208-334-3390	334-5305
Weights & Measures Bureau 2216 Kellogg Ln *Web:* www.agri.state.id.us	Boise	ID	83712	208-332-8690	334-2378

342-14 Illinois

	City	State	Zip	Phone	Fax
State Government Information 401 S 2nd St. *Web:* www.illinois.gov	Springfield	IL	62701	217-782-2000	
Administrative Office of the Illinois Courts 3101 Old Jacksonville Rd *Web:* www.state.il.us/court	Springfield	IL	62704	217-558-4490	785-3903
Aging Dept 421 E Capitol Ave Suite 100 *Web:* www.state.il.us/aging	Springfield	IL	62701	217-785-3356	785-4477
Agriculture Dept PO Box 19281 *Web:* www.agr.state.il.us	Springfield	IL	62794	217-782-2172	785-4505
Attorney General 500 S 2nd St. *Web:* www.illinoisattorneygeneral.gov	Springfield	IL	62706	217-782-1090	782-7046
Banks & Real Estate Div 500 E Monroe St 3rd Fl *Web:* www.idfpr.com	Springfield	IL	62701	217-782-3000	558-4297
Bill Status 705 Stratton Bldg *Web:* www.ilga.gov/legislation	Springfield	IL	62706	217-782-3944	524-6059
Child Support Enforcement Div 509 S 6th St **Fax Area Code:* 217 ■ *TF:* 800-447-4278 ■ *Web:* www.ilchildsupport.com	Springfield	IL	62701	800-447-4278	524-4608*
Children & Family Services Dept 406 E Monroe St. *Web:* www.state.il.us/dcfs	Springfield	IL	62701	217-785-2509	524-0014
Commerce & Economic Opportunity Dept 620 E Adams St *Web:* www.commerce.state.il.us	Springfield	IL	62701	217-782-7500	524-0864
Commerce Commission 527 E Capitol Ave *Web:* www.state.il.us/icc	Springfield	IL	62701	217-782-7295	524-0673
Community College Board 401 E Capitol Ave. *Web:* www.iccb.state.il.us	Springfield	IL	62701	217-785-0123	524-4981
Consumer Protection Div 100 W Randolph St 12th Fl. *Web:* www.illinoisattorneygeneral.gov	Chicago	IL	60601	312-814-3000	814-2549
Corrections Dept 1301 Concordia Ct *Web:* www.idoc.state.il.us	Springfield	IL	62702	217-522-2666	522-0355
Crime Victims Services Div 100 W Randolf Rd 13th Fl. *TF:* 800-228-3368 ■ *Web:* www.illinoisattorneygeneral.gov	Chicago	IL	60601	312-814-2581	814-7105
Driver Services Office 2701 S Dirksen Pkwy *Web:* www.cyberdriveillinois.com/departments/drivers	Springfield	IL	62723	217-785-6212	
Emergency Management Agency 2200 S Dirksen Pkwy *Web:* www.state.il.us/iema	Springfield	IL	62703	217-782-7860	782-2589
Environmental Protection Agency 1021 N Grand Ave E *Web:* www.epa.state.il.us	Springfield	IL	62794	217-782-2829	782-9039
General Assembly 705 Stratton Bldg *Web:* www.ilga.gov	Springfield	IL	62706	217-782-2000	
Governor State Capitol Bldg Rm 207 *Web:* www.illinois.gov/gov	Springfield	IL	62706	217-782-6830	524-4049
Healthcare & Family Services Dept 201 S Grand Ave E 3rd Fl *Web:* www.hfs.illinois.gov	Springfield	IL	62763	217-782-1200	524-7979
Historic Preservation Agency 1 Old State Capitol Plaza *Web:* www.state.il.us	Springfield	IL	62701	217-785-7930	785-7937
Housing Development Authority 401 N Michigan Ave Suite 900 *Web:* www.ihda.org	Chicago	IL	60611	312-836-5200	832-2136
Human Services Dept 100 S Grand Ave E 3rd Fl *TF:* 800-843-6154 ■ *Web:* www.dhs.state.il.us	Springfield	IL	62762	217-557-1601	557-1651
Insurance Div 320 W Washington St 4th Fl. *Web:* www.ins.state.il.us	Springfield	IL	62767	217-782-4515	782-5020
Labor Dept 160 N LaSalle St Suite C-1300 *Web:* www.state.il.us/agency/idol	Chicago	IL	60601	312-793-2800	793-5257
Lottery 101 W Jefferson St *TF:* 800-252-1775 ■ *Web:* www.illinoislottery.com	Springfield	IL	62702	217-524-5155	558-2468
Mental Health Div 100 W Randolf St Suite 3-400 *TF:* 800-252-2923 ■ *Web:* www.commerce.state.il.us	Chicago	IL	60601	312-814-2811	814-6732
Military Affairs Dept 1301 N MacArthur Blvd *Web:* www.il.ngb.army.mil	Springfield	IL	62702	217-761-3569	761-3527
Natural Resources Dept 1 Natural Resources Way *Web:* dnr.state.il.us	Springfield	IL	62702	217-782-6302	782-0179
Professional Regulation Div 320 W Washington St 3rd Fl. *Web:* www.ildpr.com	Springfield	IL	62786	217-785-0800	782-7645
Public Health Dept 535 W Jefferson St *Web:* www.idph.state.il.us	Springfield	IL	62761	217-782-4977	782-3987
Racing Board 100 W Randolph St Suite 11-100 *Web:* www.state.il.us/agency/irb	Chicago	IL	60601	312-814-2600	814-5062
Revenue Dept 101 W Jefferson St. *TF:* 800-732-8866 ■ *Web:* www.revenue.state.il.us	Springfield	IL	62702	217-782-3336	782-4217
Secretary of State 213 State Capitol *TF:* 800-252-8980 ■ *Web:* www.cyberdriveillinois.com	Springfield	IL	62756	217-782-2201	785-0358
Securities Dept 300 W Jefferson St Suite 300-A *Web:* www.cyberdriveillinois.com	Springfield	IL	62702	217-782-2256	782-8876
State Board of Education 100 N 1st St. *Web:* www.isbe.state.il.us	Springfield	IL	62777	217-782-4321	524-4928
State Police 801 S Seventh St PO Box 19461 *Web:* www.isp.state.il.us	Springfield	IL	62794	217-782-7263	785-2821
Student Assistance Commission 1755 Lake Cook Rd **Fax:* Cust Svc ■ *TF:* 800-899-4722 ■ *Web:* www.collegeillinois.org	Deerfield	IL	60015	847-948-8500	831-8549*
Supreme Court 200 E Capitol Ave *Web:* www.state.il.us/court	Springfield	IL	62701	217-782-2035	782-3520
Tourism Bureau 100 W Randolph St Suite 3-400 *TF:* 800-226-6632 ■ *Web:* www.enjoyillinois.com	Chicago	IL	60601	312-814-4732	814-6175
Treasurer State Capitol Bldg Rm 219 *Web:* www.treasurer.il.gov	Springfield	IL	62706	217-782-2211	785-2777
Veterans Affairs Dept 833 S Spring St *TF:* 800-437-9824 ■ *Web:* www.state.il.us/agency/dva	Springfield	IL	62794	217-782-6641	524-0344
Vital Records Div 605 W Jefferson St. *Web:* www.idph.state.il.us/vitalrecords	Springfield	IL	62702	217-782-6553	785-3209
Wildlife Resources Div 1 Natural Resources Way *Web:* www.dnr.state.il.us	Springfield	IL	62702	217-782-6384	
Workers' Compensation Commission 100 W Randolph St 8th Fl. *TF:* 866-352-3033 ■ *Web:* www.iwcc.il.gov	Chicago	IL	60601	312-814-6611	814-6523
Higher Education Board 431 E Adams St 2nd Fl *Web:* www.ibhe.org	Springfield	IL	62701	217-782-2551	782-8548

342-15 Indiana

	City	State	Zip	Phone	Fax
State Government Information 402 W Washington St Rm W160A *TF:* 800-457-8283 ■ *Web:* www.in.gov	Indianapolis	IN	46204	317-233-0800	
Agriculture Dept 101 W Ohio St Suite 1200 *Web:* www.in.gov/isda	Indianapolis	IN	46204	317-232-8770	232-1362
Arts Commission 150 W Market St Suite 618 *Web:* www.in.gov/arts	Indianapolis	IN	46204	317-232-1268	232-5595
Attorney General 302 W Washington St 5th Fl *Web:* www.in.gov/attorneygeneral	Indianapolis	IN	46204	317-232-6201	232-7979
Bill Status State House 200 W Washington St Suite 301 *Web:* www.in.gov/apps/lsa/session/billwatch	Indianapolis	IN	46204	317-232-9856	
Child Support Bureau 402 W Washington St Rm W360 *Web:* www.in.gov/dcs/support	Indianapolis	IN	46204	317-232-4877	233-4925
Community Development Div 1 N Capitol Ave Suite 600. *TF:* 800-824-2476 ■ *Web:* www.iedc.in.gov	Indianapolis	IN	46204	317-232-8911	233-3597
Consumer Protection Div 402 W Washington St 5th Fl *TF:* 800-382-5516 ■ *Web:* www.in.gov	Indianapolis	IN	46204	317-232-6330	233-4393

				Phone	Fax
Correction Dept 302 W Washington St Rm E334 *Web:* www.in.gov/indcorrection	Indianapolis	IN	46204	317-232-5715	232-6798
Disability Aging & Rehabilitative Services Div 402 W Washington St Rm W451 *TF:* 800-545-7763 ■ *Web:* www.in.gov	Indianapolis	IN	46207	317-232-1147	232-1240
Economic Development Corp 1 N Capitol Ave Suite 700 *Web:* www.iedc.in.gov	Indianapolis	IN	46204	317-232-8800	232-4146
Education Dept State House 200 W Washington St Rm 229 *Web:* www.doe.state.in.us	Indianapolis	IN	46204	317-232-6610	232-9121
Environmental Management Dept 100 N Senate Ave Rm 1301 *TF:* 800-451-6027 ■ *Web:* www.in.gov/idem	Indianapolis	IN	46204	317-232-8611	233-6647
Family & Social Services Administration 402 W Washington St Rm W461 *TF:* 800-545-7763 ■ *Web:* www.in.gov/fssa	Indianapolis	IN	46207	317-233-4454	233-4693
Finance Authority 1 N Capitol Ave Suite 900 *Web:* www.in.gov	Indianapolis	IN	46204	317-233-4332	232-6786
Financial Institutions Dept 402 W Washington St *Web:* www.in.gov	Indianapolis	IN	46204	317-232-3955	232-7655
Fish & Wildlife Div 402 W Washington St Rm W273 *Web:* www.in.gov/dnr/fishwild	Indianapolis	IN	46204	317-232-4080	232-8150
General Assembly State House 200 W Washington St *TF:* 800-382-9842 ■ *Web:* www.in.gov/legislative	Indianapolis	IN	46204	317-232-9600	232-2554
Governor State House 200 W Washington St Rm 206 *Web:* www.in.gov	Indianapolis	IN	46204	317-232-4567	232-3443
Health Dept 2 N Meridian St *Web:* www.in.gov	Indianapolis	IN	46204	317-233-1325	233-7394
Higher Education Commission 101 W Ohio St Suite 550 *Web:* www.in.gov	Indianapolis	IN	46204	317-464-4400	464-4410
Historical Bureau 140 N Senate Ave Rm 130 *Web:* www.in.gov/history	Indianapolis	IN	46204	317-232-2537	232-3728
Homeland Security Dept 302 W Washington St Rm E208 *Web:* www.in.gov/dhs	Indianapolis	IN	46204	317-232-3980	232-3895
Horse Racing Commission 150 W Market St Suite 530 *Web:* www.in.gov	Indianapolis	IN	46204	317-233-3119	233-4470
Housing Finance Authority 30 S Meridian St Suite 1000 *Web:* www.in.gov	Indianapolis	IN	46204	317-232-7777	232-7778
Insurance Dept 311 W Washington St Suite 300 *TF Cust Svc:* 800-622-4461 ■ *Web:* www.in.gov	Indianapolis	IN	46204	317-232-2385	232-5251
Labor Dept 402 W Washington St Rm W195 *Web:* www.in.gov/labor	Indianapolis	IN	46204	317-232-2655	233-3790
Lieutenant Governor State House 200 W Washington St Rm 333 *Web:* www.in.gov/lgov	Indianapolis	IN	46204	317-232-4545	232-4788
Lottery 201 S Capitol Ave Suite 1100 *TF:* 800-955-6886 ■ *Web:* www.in.gov	Indianapolis	IN	46225	317-264-4800	264-4933
Motor Vehicles Bureau 100 N Senate Ave Rm N440 *Web:* www.in.gov	Indianapolis	IN	46204	317-233-6000	233-3135
Natural Resources Dept 402 W Washington St *Web:* www.in.gov/dnr	Indianapolis	IN	46204	317-232-4200	233-6811
Parole Services Div 302 W Washington St *Web:* www.in.gov/idoc/reentry/2513.htm	Indianapolis	IN	46204	317-233-6984	232-5728
Port Commission 150 W Market St Suite 100 *TF:* 800-232-7678 ■ *Web:* www.portsofindiana.com	Indianapolis	IN	46204	317-232-9200	232-0137
Professional Licensing Agency 302 W Washington St Rm E034 *Web:* www.in.gov/pla	Indianapolis	IN	46204	317-232-2980	232-2312
Professional Standards Div 101 W Ohio St Suite 300 *Web:* www.doe.state.in.us	Indianapolis	IN	46204	317-232-9010	232-9023
Revenue Dept 100 N Senate Ave Rm N128 *Web:* www.in.gov/dor	Indianapolis	IN	46204	317-232-2240	232-2103
Secretary of State 200 W Washington St Rm 201 *Web:* www.in.gov	Indianapolis	IN	46204	317-232-6531	233-3283
Securities Div 302 W Washington St Rm E111 *Web:* www.in.gov	Indianapolis	IN	46204	317-232-6681	233-3675
State Court Administration Div 30 S Meridian St #500 *Web:* www.in.gov	Indianapolis	IN	46204	317-232-2542	233-6586
State Ethics Commission 402 W Washington St Rm W-198 *Web:* www.in.gov/ethics	Indianapolis	IN	46204	317-232-3850	232-0707
State Parks & Reservoirs Div 402 W Washington Rm W-298 *TF:* 800-622-4931 ■ *Web:* www.in.gov/dnr/parks	Indianapolis	IN	46204	317-232-4124	232-4132
State Police 100 N Senate Ave 3rd Fl *Web:* www.in.gov/isp	Indianapolis	IN	46204	317-232-8248	232-0652
Students Assistance Commission 150 W Market St Suite 500 *TF:* 888-528-4719 ■ *Web:* www.in.gov	Indianapolis	IN	46204	317-232-2350	232-3260
Supreme Court State House 200 W Washington St Rm 315 *Web:* www.in.gov/judiciary/supreme	Indianapolis	IN	46204	317-232-2540	232-8372
Technology Office 100 N Senate Ave Suite N-551 *Web:* www.in.gov	Indianapolis	IN	46204	317-232-3172	232-0748
Tourism Development Office 1 N Capitol Ave Suite 100 *TF:* 888-365-6946 ■ *Web:* www.in.gov	Indianapolis	IN	46204	317-232-8860	233-6887
Transportation Dept 100 N Senate Ave Rm N755 *Web:* www.in.gov	Indianapolis	IN	46204	317-232-5533	232-0238
Treasurer State House 200 W Washington St Rm 242 *Web:* www.in.gov/tos	Indianapolis	IN	46204	317-232-6386	233-1780
Utility Regulatory Commission 302 W Washington St Rm E306 *Web:* www.in.gov/iurc	Indianapolis	IN	46204	317-232-2701	232-6758
Veterans' Affairs Dept 302 W Washington St Rm E120 *Web:* www.in.gov	Indianapolis	IN	46204	317-232-3910	232-7721
Victims Services Div 1 N Capitol Ave Suite 1000 *TF:* 800-353-1484 ■ *Web:* www.in.gov	Indianapolis	IN	46204	317-232-1233	233-3912
Vital Records Office 6 W Washington St *Web:* www.in.gov/isdh/bdcertifs/bdcert.html	Indianapolis	IN	46204	317-233-2700	233-7210
Weights & Measures Div 2525 Shadeland Ave Unit D3 *Web:* www.in.gov/isdh/regsvcs/wtmsr/welcome.html	Indianapolis	IN	46219	317-356-7078	351-2877
Worker's Compensation Board 402 W Washington St Rm W196 *Web:* www.in.gov/workcomp	Indianapolis	IN	46204	317-232-3808	233-5493
Workforce Development Dept 10 N Senate Ave *TF:* 800-891-6499 ■ *Web:* www.in.gov	Indianapolis	IN	46204	317-232-7670	233-4793

342-16 Iowa

				Phone	Fax
State Government Information 1305 E Walnut St *Web:* www.iowa.gov	Des Moines	IA	50319	515-281-5011	
Adult Children & Family Services Div 1305 E Walnut St 5th Fl *TF:* 800-972-2017 ■ *Web:* www.dhs.state.ia.us/ACFS/ACFS.asp	Des Moines	IA	50319	515-281-5521	281-4597
Agriculture & Land Stewardship Dept 502 E 9th St *Web:* www.agriculture.state.ia.us	Des Moines	IA	50319	515-281-5321	281-6236
Arts Council 600 E Locust *Web:* www.iowaartscouncil.org	Des Moines	IA	50319	515-242-6194	242-6498
Attorney General 1305 E Walnut St 2nd Fl *Web:* www.state.ia.us/government/ag	Des Moines	IA	50319	515-281-8373	281-4209
Banking Div 200 E Grand Ave Suite 300 *Web:* www.state.ia.us	Des Moines	IA	50309	515-281-4014	281-4862
Child Support Recovery Unit 1901 Bell Ave *TF:* 888-229-9223 ■ *Web:* https://childsupport.dhs.state.ia.us	Des Moines	IA	50309	515-242-5530	
Commerce Dept 1918 SE Hulsizer Rd *Web:* www.state.ia.us	Ankeny	IA	50021	515-281-7400	281-5329
Community Development Div 200 E Grand Ave *Web:* www.state.ia.us/government/ided/crd	Des Moines	IA	50309	515-242-4780	242-4809
Conservation & Recreation Div 502 E 9th St *Web:* www.iowadnr.com	Des Moines	IA	50319	515-281-5529	281-6794
Consumer Protection Div 1305 E Walnut St 2nd Fl *Web:* www.iowaattorneygeneral.org	Des Moines	IA	50319	515-281-5926	281-6771
Corrections Dept 420 Watson Powell Jr Way *Web:* www.doc.state.ia.us	Des Moines	IA	50309	515-242-5702	281-7345
Crime Victim Assistance Div 321 E 12th St Rm 018 Lucas State Office Bldg *TF:* 800-373-5044 ■	Des Moines	IA	50319	515-281-5044	281-8199
Economic Development Dept 200 E Grand Ave *Web:* www.state.ia.us/government/ided	Des Moines	IA	50309	515-242-4700	242-4722
Education Dept 400 E 14th St *Web:* www.state.ia.us/educate	Des Moines	IA	50319	515-281-3436	242-4722
Educational Examiners Board 400 E 14th St Grimes State Office Bldg *TF:* 800-778-7856 ■ *Web:* www.state.ia.us/boee	Des Moines	IA	50319	515-281-5849	281-7669
Elder Affairs Dept 200 10th St 3rd Fl *TF:* 800-532-3213 ■ *Web:* www.state.ia.us/elderaffairs	Des Moines	IA	50309	515-242-3333	242-3300
Emergency Management Div 1305 E Walnut St Level A *Web:* www.iowahomelandsecurity.org	Des Moines	IA	50319	515-281-3231	281-7539
Environmental Services Div 502 E 9th St *Web:* www.iowadnr.com/epc	Des Moines	IA	50319	515-281-5918	281-8895
Ethics & Campaign Disclosure Board 510 E 12th St Suite 1-A *Web:* www.state.ia.us	Des Moines	IA	50319	515-281-4028	281-3701
General Assembly State Capitol 1007 E Grand Ave *Web:* www.legis.iowa.gov	Des Moines	IA	50319	515-281-5129	
Governor State Capitol Bldg *Web:* www.governor.state.ia.us	Des Moines	IA	50319	515-281-5211	281-6611
Human Services Dept 1305 E Walnut St *TF:* 800-972-2017 ■ *Web:* www.dhs.state.ia.us	Des Moines	IA	50319	515-281-2817	281-4457
Information Technology Dept 1305 E Walnut St Level B *Web:* www.state.ia.us	Des Moines	IA	50319	515-281-5503	281-6137
Insurance Div 330 Maple St *Web:* www.iid.state.ia.us	Des Moines	IA	50319	515-281-5705	281-3059
Lieutenant Governor State Capitol Bldg	Des Moines	IA	50319	515-281-5211	281-6611

	City	State	Zip	Phone	Fax
Lottery 2323 Grand Ave	Des Moines	IA	50312	515-281-7900	281-7882*
*Fax: Hum Res ■ Web: www.ialottery.com					
Medical Examiners Board 1007 E Grand Ave	Des Moines	IA	50319	515-281-5171	242-5908
Web: www.docboard.org					
Motor Vehicle Div PO Box 9204	Des Moines	IA	50306	515-244-9124	237-3152
TF: 800-532-1121 ■ Web: www.dot.state.ia.us					
Natural Resources Dept 502 E 9th St	Des Moines	IA	50319	515-281-5918	281-6794
Web: www.iowadnr.com					
Parks & Preserves Bureau 502 E 9th St	Des Moines	IA	50319	515-281-5918	281-6794
Parole Board 510 E 12th St Suite 3	Des Moines	IA	50319	515-725-5747	242-5762
Web: www.bop.state.ia.us					
Professional Licensing & Regulation Div					
200 E Grand Ave Suite 390	Des Moines	IA	50309	515-243-4723	281-4862
Web: www.state.ia.us/government/com/prof					
Public Health Dept 321 E 12th St	Des Moines	IA	50319	515-281-5787	281-4958
Web: www.idph.state.ia.us					
Regents Board 11260 Aurora Ave	Urbandale	IA	50322	515-281-3934	281-6420
Web: www.state.ia.us/regents					
Revenue & Finance Dept					
1305 E Walnut St 4th Fl	Des Moines	IA	50319	515-281-3204	242-6040
Web: www.state.ia.us/tax					
Secretary of State 321 E 12th St 1st Fl	Des Moines	IA	50319	515-281-5204	242-5953
Web: www.sos.state.ia.us					
Securities Bureau 321 E 12th St	Des Moines	IA	50319	515-281-4441	281-3059
Web: www.iid.state.ia.us					
State Court Administration 1111 E Ct Ave	Des Moines	IA	50319	515-281-5241	242-0014
Web: www.judicial.state.ia.us					
State Historical Society 600 E Locust St	Des Moines	IA	50319	515-281-5111	242-6498
Web: www.iowahistory.org					
State Patrol Div 502 E 9th St	Des Moines	IA	50319	515-281-5824	242-6305
Web: www.state.ia.us/government/dps/isp					
Supreme Court					
1111 E Court Ave					
Iowa Judicial Branch Bldg	Des Moines	IA	50319	515-281-5911	242-6164
Web: www.iowacourts.gov/Supreme_Court					
Tourism Office 200 E Grand Ave	Des Moines	IA	50309	515-242-4705	242-4718
TF: 888-472-6035 ■ Web: www.traveliowa.com					
Transportation Dept 800 Lincoln Way	Ames	IA	50010	515-239-1101	239-1639
Web: www.dot.state.ia.us					
Treasurer 1007 E Grand Ave Capitol Bldg	Des Moines	IA	50319	515-281-5368	281-7562
Web: www.treasurer.state.ia.us					
Utilities Board 1375 E Court Ave Rm 69	Des Moines	IA	50319	515-725-7300	725-7399
TF: 877-565-4450 ■ Web: www.state.ia.us/government/com/util					
Veterans Affairs Dept					
7105 NW 70th Ave Camp Dodge Bldg A6A	Johnston	IA	50131	515-242-5331	242-5659
TF: 800-838-4692 ■ Web: www.state.ia.us/icva					
Vital Records Bureau					
321 E 12th St					
Lucas State Office Bldg 1st Fl	Des Moines	IA	50319	515-281-4944	281-0479
Web: www.idph.state.ia.us/eh/health_statistics.asp#vital					
Vocational Rehabilitation Services Div					
510 E 12th St	Des Moines	IA	50319	515-281-4311	281-7645
Web: www.dvrs.state.ia.us					
Weights & Measures Bureau 2230 S Ankeny Blvd	Ankeny	IA	50021	515-725-1492	725-1459
Workforce Development 1000 E Grand Ave	Des Moines	IA	50319	515-281-5387	281-4698
TF: 800-562-4692 ■ Web: www.iowaworkforce.org					

342-17 Kansas

	City	State	Zip	Phone	Fax
State Government Information					
534 S Kansas Ave Suite 1210	Topeka	KS	66603	785-296-0111	296-5563
TF: 800-452-6727 ■ Web: www.kansas.gov					
Accountancy Board 900 SW Jackson St Suite 556	Topeka	KS	66612	785-296-2162	291-3501
Web: www.ksboa.org					
Aging Dept 503 S Kansas Ave	Topeka	KS	66603	785-296-4986	296-0256
Web: www.agingkansas.org					
Agriculture Dept 109 SW 9th St	Topeka	KS	66612	785-296-3556	296-8389
Web: www.accesskansas.org/kda					
Arts Commission 700 SW Jackson St Suite 1004	Topeka	KS	66603	785-296-3335	296-4989
Web: www.arts.state.ks.us					
Attorney General 120 SW 10th Ave 2nd Fl	Topeka	KS	66612	785-296-2215	296-6296
Web: www.ksag.org					
Banking Commissioner					
700 SW Jackson St Suite 300	Topeka	KS	66603	785-296-2266	296-0168
Web: www.osbckansas.org					
Bill Status					
300 SW 10th Ave State Capitol Bldg Rm 343N	Topeka	KS	66612	785-296-3296	296-6650
Web: www.kslegislature.org					
Certification & Teacher Education Div					
120 SE 10th Ave	Topeka	KS	66612	785-296-8010	296-4318
Web: www.ksbe.state.ks.us/cert/cert.html					
Commerce Dept 1000 SW Jackson St Suite 100	Topeka	KS	66612	785-296-3481	296-5055
Web: kdoch.state.ks.us					
Conservation Commission					
109 SW 9th St Suite 500	Topeka	KS	66612	785-296-3600	296-6172
Web: www.accesskansas.org/kscc					
Consumer Protection Div 120 SW 10th Ave Rm 430	Topeka	KS	66612	785-296-3751	291-3699
TF: 800-432-2310 ■ Web: www.accesskansas.org					
Corp Commission 1500 SW Arrowhead Rd	Topeka	KS	66604	785-271-3220	271-3354
Web: www.kcc.state.ks.us					
Corrections Dept 900 SW Jackson St Suite 400	Topeka	KS	66612	785-296-3317	296-0014
Web: docnet.dc.state.ks.us					
Cosmetology Board 714 SW Jackson St Suite 100	Topeka	KS	66603	785-296-3155	296-3002
Web: www.accesskansas.org/kboc					
Crime Victims Compensation Board					
120 SW 10th Ave 2nd Fl	Topeka	KS	66612	785-296-2359	296-0652
Web: www.accesskansas.org/ksag/Divisions/Cvcb/main.htm					
Education Dept 120 SE 10th Ave	Topeka	KS	66612	785-296-3201	296-7933
Web: www.ksbe.state.ks.us					
Emergency Management Div 2800 SW Topeka Blvd	Topeka	KS	66611	785-274-1409	274-1426
Web: www.accesskansas.org					
Governmental Ethics Commission					
109 W 9th St Suite 504	Topeka	KS	66612	785-296-4219	296-2548
Web: www.accesskansas.org					
Governor State Capitol Bldg 2nd Fl	Topeka	KS	66612	785-296-3232	296-7973
Web: www.ksgovernor.org					
Healing Arts Board					
800 SW Jackson Lower Level-Suite A	Topeka	KS	66612	785-296-7413	296-0852
TF: 888-886-7205 ■ Web: www.ksbha.org					
Health & Environment Dept 1000 SW Jackson St	Topeka	KS	66612	785-296-1500	296-6231
Web: www.kdhe.state.ks.us					
Highway Patrol 122 SW 7th St	Topeka	KS	66603	785-296-6800	296-5956
Web: www.kansashighwaypatrol.org					
Historical Society 6425 SW 6th Ave	Topeka	KS	66615	785-272-8681	272-8682
Web: www.kshs.org					
Housing Resources Corp					
611 S Kansas Ave Suite 300	Topeka	KS	66603	785-296-5865	296-8985
Web: www.kshousingcorp.org					
Information Systems & Communications Div					
900 SW Jackson Rm 751S	Topeka	KS	66612	785-296-3343	296-1168
Web: www.da.state.ks.us					
Insurance Dept 420 SW 9th St	Topeka	KS	66612	785-296-3071	296-2283
TF: 800-432-2484 ■ Web: www.ksinsurance.org					
Judicial Administrator					
301 W 10th St Kansas Judicial Ctr	Topeka	KS	66612	785-296-2256	296-7076
Web: www.kscourts.org					
Kansas Inc 632 SW Van Buren St Suite 100	Topeka	KS	66603	785-296-1460	296-1463
Web: www.kansasinc.org					
Labor Dept 401 SW Topeka Blvd	Topeka	KS	66603	785-296-5000	296-1926
Legislature 300 SW 10th Ave State Capitol Bldg	Topeka	KS	66612	785-296-2391	296-1153
Web: www.kslegislature.org					
Lieutenant Governor					
300 SW 10th Ave State Capitol Bldg Rm 222	Topeka	KS	66612	785-296-2213	296-5669
Web: www.ksgovernor.org/lt_gov.html					
Lottery 128 N Kansas Ave	Topeka	KS	66603	785-296-5700	296-5712
TF: 800-544-9467					
Motor Vehicles Div 915 SW Harrison St Rm 162	Topeka	KS	66626	785-296-3601	291-3755
Web: www.ksrevenue.org/dmv.htm					
Parole Board 900 SW Jackson St 4th Fl	Topeka	KS	66612	785-296-3469	296-7949
Real Estate Commission					
120 SE 6th Ave Suite 200	Topeka	KS	66603	785-296-3411	296-1771
Web: www.accesskansas.org/krec					
Regents Board 1000 SW Jackson St Suite 520	Topeka	KS	66612	785-296-3421	296-0983
Web: www.kansasregents.org					
Rehabilitation Services Div					
3640 SW Topeka Blvd Suite 150	Topeka	KS	66611	785-267-5301	267-0263
Revenue Dept 915 SW Harrison St	Topeka	KS	66612	785-296-3041	368-8392
Web: www.ksrevenue.org					
Secretary of State 120 SW 10th Ave 1st Fl	Topeka	KS	66612	785-296-4564	296-4570
Web: www.kssos.org					
Securities Commission 618 S Kansas Ave 2nd Fl	Topeka	KS	66603	785-296-3307	296-6872
Web: www.securities.state.ks.us					
Social & Rehabilitation Services Dept					
915 SW Harrison St 6th Fl	Topeka	KS	66612	785-296-3959	296-2173
Web: www.srskansas.org					
Supreme Court 301 SW 10th Ave Rm 374	Topeka	KS	66612	785-296-3229	296-1028
Web: www.kscourts.org/supct					
Technical Professions Board					
900 SW Jackson St Suite 507	Topeka	KS	66612	785-296-3053	
Web: www.accesskansas.org/ksbtp					
Transportation Dept 700 SW Harrison St	Topeka	KS	66603	785-296-3566	296-1095
Web: www.ink.org/public/kdot					
Travel & Tourism Development Div					
1000 SW Jackson St Suite 100	Topeka	KS	66612	785-296-5403	296-6988
TF: 800-252-6727 ■ Web: www.travelks.org					
Treasurer 900 SW Jackson St Suite 201	Topeka	KS	66612	785-296-3171	296-7950
Web: www.treasurer.state.ks.us					
Veterans Affairs Commission					
700 SW Jackson St Suite 701	Topeka	KS	66603	785-296-3976	296-1462
Web: www.kcva.org					
Vital Statistics Div					
1000 SW Jackson St Suite 120	Topeka	KS	66612	785-296-1400	296-8075
Web: www.kdhe.state.ks.us/vital					
Weights & Measures Div PO Box 19282	Topeka	KS	66619	785-862-2415	862-2460
Web: www.accesskansas.org					
Wildlife & Parks Dept					
1020 S Kansas Ave Suite 200	Topeka	KS	66612	785-296-2281	296-6953
Web: www.kdwp.state.ks.us					
Workers' Compensation Div					
800 SW Jackson St Suite 600	Topeka	KS	66612	785-296-4000	296-0839
TF: 800-332-0353 ■ Web: www.hr.state.ks.us					

342-18 Kentucky

	City	State	Zip	Phone	Fax
State Government Information					
229 W Main St Suite 400	Frankfort	KY	40601	502-875-3733	875-3722
TF: 877-855-3573 ■ Web: kentucky.gov					
Accountancy Board 332 W Broadway Suite 310	Louisville	KY	40202	502-595-3037	595-4500
Web: www.cpa.ky.gov					
Administrative Office of the Cts					
100 Millcreek Pk	Frankfort	KY	40601	502-573-2350	695-1759
TF: 800-928-2350 ■ Web: www.kycourts.net					
Aging Services Office					
275 E Main St 3rd Fl W	Frankfort	KY	40621	502-564-6930	564-4595
Web: chs.state.ky.us/aging					
Agriculture Dept					
Capitol Annex 702 Capitol Ave Suite 188	Frankfort	KY	40601	502-564-5126	564-5016
Web: www.kyagr.com					
Arts Council 500 Mero St 21st Fl	Frankfort	KY	40601	502-564-3757	564-2839
TF: 888-833-2787 ■ Web: www.kyarts.org					

Name / Address	City	State	ZIP	Phone	Fax
Athletic Commission 500 Mero St # 5 *Web:* www.ppr.ky.gov	Frankfort	KY	40601	502-564-7760	564-3969
Attorney General State Capitol Bldg 700 Capitol Ave Suite 120 *Web:* www.e-archives.ky.gov	Frankfort	KY	40601	502-696-5614	564-2894
Bill Status State Capitol Bldg 700 Capitol Ave Rm 300 *Web:* www.lrc.state.ky.us/legislat/legislat.htm	Frankfort	KY	40601	502-564-8100	564-6543
Child Support Div 730 Schenkel Ln *TF:* 800-248-1163 ■ *Web:* www.chfs.ky.gov	Frankfort	KY	40601	502-564-2285	564-5988
Consumer Protection Div 1024 Capital Ctr Dr Suite 200 *TF:* 888-432-9257 ■ *Web:* www.ag.ky.gov	Frankfort	KY	40601	502-696-5389	573-8317
Corrections Dept 275 E Main St Rm G-41 PO Box 2400 *Web:* www.corrections.ky.gov	Frankfort	KY	40602	502-564-4726	564-5037
Crime Victims Compensation Board 130 Brighton Pk Blvd *TF:* 800-469-2120 ■ *Web:* www.cvcb.ppr.ky.gov	Frankfort	KY	40601	502-573-2290	573-4817
Economic Development Cabinet 500 Mero St 24th Fl *Web:* www.thinkkentucky.com	Frankfort	KY	40601	502-564-7670	564-3256
Education Dept 500 Mero St *Web:* www.education.ky.gov/KDE	Frankfort	KY	40601	502-564-4770	564-5680
Education Professional Standards Board 100 Airport Dr 3rd Fl *TF:* 888-598-7667 ■ *Web:* www.kyepsb.net	Frankfort	KY	40601	502-564-4606	564-7080
Emergency Management Div 100 Minuteman Pkwy *Web:* www.kyem.ky.gov	Frankfort	KY	40601	502-607-1680	607-1614
Environmental Protection Dept 200 Fair Oaks Ln *Web:* www.dep.ky.gov	Frankfort	KY	40601	502-564-2150	564-4245
Executive Branch Ethics Commission 700 Capitol Ave ;Rm 209 *Web:* www.ethics.ky.gov	Frankfort	KY	40601	502-564-7954	564-2686
Finance & Administration Cabinet Capitol Annex 702 Capitol Ave Rm 383 *Web:* www.state.ky.us/agencies/finance	Frankfort	KY	40601	502-564-4240	564-6785
Financial Institutions Dept 1025 Capital Ctr Dr Suite 200 *TF:* 800-223-2579 ■ *Web:* www.dfi.state.ky.us	Frankfort	KY	40601	502-573-3390	573-8787
Fish & Wildlife Resources Dept 1 Game Farm Rd *TF:* 800-858-1549 ■ *Web:* www.kdfwr.state.ky.us	Frankfort	KY	40601	502-564-3400	564-6508
General Assembly State Capitol Bldg 700 Capitol Ave *TF:* 800-372-7181 ■ *Web:* www.lrc.state.ky.us	Frankfort	KY	40601	502-564-8100	564-6543
Governor State Capitol Bldg 700 Capitol Ave Rm 100 *Web:* www.governor.ky.gov	Frankfort	KY	40601	502-564-2611	564-2517
Governor's Office for Technology 101 Cold Harbor Dr *Web:* www.got.state.ky.us	Frankfort	KY	40601	502-564-7680	564-6856
Hairdressers & Cosmetologists Board 111 St James Ct Suite A	Frankfort	KY	40601	502-564-4262	564-0481
Health & Family Services Cabinet 275 E Main St 4th Fl W *Web:* www.chfs.ky.gov	Frankfort	KY	40621	502-564-7130	564-3866
Health Services Cabinet 275 E Main St 5th Fl W *Web:* www.chfs.ky.gov	Frankfort	KY	40621	502-564-7042	564-7091
Higher Education Assistance Authority PO Box 798 *TF:* 800-928-8926	Frankfort	KY	40602	502-696-7200	696-7345
Historical Society 100 W Broadway *TF:* 877-444-7867 ■ *Web:* www.kyhistory.org	Frankfort	KY	40601	502-564-1792	564-4701
Horse Racing Authority 4063 Iron Works Pkwy Bldg B *Web:* www.krc.ppr.ky.gov	Lexington	KY	40602	859-246-2040	246-2039
Housing Corp 1231 Louisville Rd *TF:* 800-633-8896 ■ *Web:* www.kyhousing.org	Frankfort	KY	40601	502-564-7630	564-5708
Insurance Dept 215 W Main St *TF:* 800-595-6053 ■ *Web:* doi.ppr.ky.gov/kentucky	Frankfort	KY	40602	502-564-3630	564-6090
Labor Cabinet 1047 US Hwy 127 S Suite 4 *Web:* www.labor.ky.gov	Frankfort	KY	40601	502-564-3070	564-5387
Legislative Ethics Commission 22 Mill Creek Pk *Web:* www.klec.ky.gov	Frankfort	KY	40601	502-573-2863	573-2929
Lieutenant Governor State Capitol Bldg 700 Capitol Ave Suite 142 *Web:* www.ltgovernor.ky.gov	Frankfort	KY	40601	502-564-2611	564-2849
Lottery Corp 1011 W Main St *TF:* 800-937-8946 ■ *Web:* www.kylottery.com	Louisville	KY	40202	502-560-1500	560-1532
Medical Licensure Board 310 Whittington Pkwy Suite 1B *Web:* www.kbml.org	Louisville	KY	40222	502-429-7150	429-7158
Natural Resources Dept 2 Hudson Hollow *Web:* www.naturalresources.ky.gov	Frankfort	KY	40601	502-564-6940	564-5848
Parks Dept 500 Mero St Suite 1100 *TF:* 800-255-7275 ■ *Web:* www.parksky.gov	Frankfort	KY	40601	502-564-2172	564-6100
Parole Board PO Box 2400 *Web:* www.justice.ky.gov/parolebd	Frankfort	KY	40602	502-564-3620	564-8995
Postsecondary Education Council 1024 Capital Ctr Dr Suite 320 *Web:* www.cpe.ky.gov	Frankfort	KY	40601	502-573-1555	573-1535
Public Service Commission PO Box 615 *TF:* 800-772-4636 ■ *Web:* www.psc.state.ky.us	Frankfort	KY	40602	502-564-3940	564-3460
Real Estate Commission 10200 Linn Stn Rd Suite 201 *TF:* 888-373-3300 ■ *Web:* www.krec.net	Louisville	KY	40223	502-429-7250	429-7246
Revenue Cabinet 200 Fair Oaks Ln *Web:* www.revenue.state.ky.us	Frankfort	KY	40620	502-564-4581	564-3685
Secretary of State The Capitol Bldg 700 Capital Ave Suite 152 *Web:* www.sos.ky.gov	Frankfort	KY	40601	502-564-3490	564-5687
State Police Dept 919 Versailles Rd *Web:* www.kentuckystatepolice.org	Frankfort	KY	40601	502-695-6300	573-1479
Supreme Court 700 Capitol Ave Rm 235 *Web:* apps.courts.ky.gov	Frankfort	KY	40601	502-564-5444	564-2665
Travel Dept 500 Mero St Suite 2200 *TF:* 800-225-8747 ■ *Web:* www.kentuckytourism.com	Frankfort	KY	40601	502-564-4930	564-5695
Treasury 1050 US Hwy 127 S Suite 100 *Web:* www.kytreasury.com	Frankfort	KY	40601	502-564-4722	564-6545
Vehicle Regulation Div 200 Mero St 3rd Fl *Web:* www.kytc.state.ky.us	Frankfort	KY	40622	502-564-7000	564-6403
Veterans Affairs Dept 111 Louisville Rd # B *Web:* www.kdva.net	Frankfort	KY	40601	502-564-9203	564-9240
Vital Statistics Div 275 E Main St Suite 1EA *Web:* www.chfs.ky.gov	Frankfort	KY	40621	502-564-4212	227-0032
Vocational Rehabilitation Dept 209 St Clair St Rm 200 *TF:* 800-372-7172	Frankfort	KY	40601	502-564-4440	564-6745
Workers Claims Dept 657 Chamberlin Ave *TF:* 800-554-8601 ■ *Web:* dwc.state.ky.us	Frankfort	KY	40601	502-564-5550	564-5732
Workforce Investment Dept 500 Mero St 20th Fl *Web:* www.workforce.ky.gov	Frankfort	KY	40601	502-564-4286	564-7967

342-19 Louisiana

Name / Address	City	State	ZIP	Phone	Fax
State Government Information 1201 N 3rd St Suite G-150 PO Box 44124 *TF:* 800-354-9548 ■ *Web:* www.louisiana.gov	Baton Rouge	LA	70802	225-342-7000	
Agriculture & Forestry Dept 5825 Florida Blvd *Web:* www.ldaf.state.la.us	Baton Rouge	LA	70806	225-922-1234	922-1253
Arts Div PO Box 44247 *Web:* www.crt.state.la.us/arts	Baton Rouge	LA	70804	225-342-8180	342-8173
Attorney General PO Box 94005 *Web:* www.ag.state.la.us	Baton Rouge	LA	70804	225-326-6705	326-6793
Bill Status State Capitol 900 N 3rd St 13th Fl *TF:* 800-256-3793 ■ *Web:* www.legis.state.la.us	Baton Rouge	LA	70804	225-342-2456	
Board of Regents PO Box 3677 *Web:* www.regents.state.la.us	Baton Rouge	LA	70821	225-342-4253	342-6926
Certified Public Accountants Board 601 Poydras St Suite 1770 *Web:* www.cpaboard.state.la.us	New Orleans	LA	70130	504-566-1244	566-1252
Child Support Enforcement Services PO Box 260222 *Web:* www.dss.state.la.us	Baton Rouge	LA	70826	225-342-4780	
Community Services Office 333 Laurel St *Web:* www.dss.state.la.us	Baton Rouge	LA	70801	225-342-2297	342-2268
Consumer Protection Office PO Box 94095 *Web:* www.ag.state.la.us/Consumers.aspx	Baton Rouge	LA	70804	225-342-7900	342-9637
Contractors Licensing Board 2525 Quail Dr *Web:* www.lslbc.state.la.us	Baton Rouge	LA	70808	225-765-2301	765-2431
Crime Victims Reparations Board 1885 Wooddale Blvd Rm 1230 *Web:* www.lcle.state.la.us	Baton Rouge	LA	70806	225-342-1689	
Culture Recreation & Tourism Dept PO Box 94361 *Web:* www.crt.state.la.us	Baton Rouge	LA	70804	225-342-8115	342-3207
Economic Development Dept PO Box 94185 *TF:* 800-450-8115 ■ *Web:* www.lded.state.la.us	Baton Rouge	LA	70804	225-342-3000	342-9095
Education Dept PO Box 94064 **Fax Area Code:* 225 ■ *TF:* 877-453-2721 ■ *Web:* www.doe.state.la.us	Baton Rouge	LA	70804	877-453-2721	342-0193*
Elderly Affairs Office 525 Florida St 4th Fl *Web:* goea.louisiana.gov	Baton Rouge	LA	70802	225-342-7100	342-7133
Environmental Quality Dept 602 N Fifth St *TF:* 866-896-5337 ■ *Web:* www.deq.state.la.us	Baton Rouge	LA	70802	225-219-5337	
Ethics Board 617 N Third St LaSalle Bldg, Suite 10-36 *TF:* 800-842-6630 ■ *Web:* www.ethics.state.la.us	Baton Rouge	LA	70802	225-219-5600	381-7271
Financial Institutions Office PO Box 94095 *Web:* www.ofi.state.la.us	Baton Rouge	LA	70804	225-925-4660	925-4548
Governor PO Box 94004 *TF:* 866-366-1121 ■ *Web:* www.gov.state.la.us	Baton Rouge	LA	70804	225-342-7015	342-7099
Health & Hospitals Dept PO Box 629 *Web:* www.dhh.state.la.us	Baton Rouge	LA	70821	225-342-9500	342-5568
Historic Preservation Div 1051 N 3rd St # 402 *Web:* www.crt.state.la.us	Baton Rouge	LA	70802	225-342-8160	342-8173
Homeland Security & Emergency Preparedness Office 7667 Independence Blvd *Web:* www.loep.state.la.us	Baton Rouge	LA	70806	225-925-7500	925-7501
Housing Finance Agency 2415 Quail Dr *TF:* 888-454-2001 ■ *Web:* www.lhfa.state.la.us	Baton Rouge	LA	70808	225-763-8700	763-8710
Information Services Office 1201 N 3rd St *Web:* www.doa.state.la.us	Baton Rouge	LA	70802	225-342-0900	342-0902
Insurance Dept PO Box 94214 *TF:* 800-259-5300 ■ *Web:* www.ldi.state.la.us	Baton Rouge	LA	70804	225-342-5900	342-8622

Agency / Address	City	State	ZIP	Phone	Fax
Judicial Administrators Office 400 Royal St Suite 1190 *Web:* www.lasc.org	New Orleans	LA	70130	504-310-2550	
Labor Dept 1001 N 23rd St. *TF:* 877-529-6757 ■ *Web:* www.laworks.net	Baton Rouge	LA	70802	225-342-3111	
Legislature PO Box 94062 *TF:* 800-256-3793 ■ *Web:* www.legis.state.la.us	Baton Rouge	LA	70804	225-342-2456	
Lieutenant Governor 1051 N Third St *Web:* www.crt.state.la.us	Baton Rouge	LA	70802	225-342-7009	342-1949
Lottery Corp 555 Laurel St. *Web:* www.louisianalottery.com	Baton Rouge	LA	70801	225-297-2000	297-2005
Medical Examiners Board 1515 Poydras St *Web:* www.lsbme.org	New Orleans	LA	70112	504-568-6820	
Motor Vehicles Office PO Box 64886 *TF:* 877-368-5463 ■ *Web:* www.omv.dps.state.la.us	Baton Rouge	LA	70896	225-925-6335	925-1838
Natural Resources Dept PO Box 94396 *Web:* www.dnr.state.la.us	Baton Rouge	LA	70804	225-342-4500	342-5861
Office of Student Financial Assistance 602 N 5th St PO Box 91202 *TF:* 800-259-5626 ■ *Web:* www.osfa.la.gov	Baton Rouge	LA	70802	225-922-1011	208-1496
Public Safety & Corrections Dept 504 Mayflower St PO Box 94304 *Web:* www.doc.louisiana.gov	Baton Rouge	LA	70804	225-342-6741	342-3095
Public Service Commission PO Box 91154 *TF:* 800-256-2397 ■ *Web:* www.lpsc.org	Baton Rouge	LA	70821	225-342-4404	342-2831
Racing Commission 320 N Carrollton Ave Suite 2-B *Web:* www.horseracing.la.gov	New Orleans	LA	70119	504-483-4000	483-4898
Real Estate Commission PO Box 14785 *TF:* 800-821-4529 ■ *Web:* www.lrec.state.la.us	Baton Rouge	LA	70898	225-765-0191	765-0637
Rehabilitation Services 627 N 4th St *TF:* 800-737-2958	Baton Rouge	LA	70802	225-219-2225	
Revenue Dept 617 N 3rd St PO Box 201 *Web:* www.rev.state.la.us	Baton Rouge	LA	70801	225-219-2700	
Secretary of State PO Box 94125 *Web:* www.sec.state.la.us	Baton Rouge	LA	70804	225-922-1000	922-0002
Securities Commission 8660 United Plaza Blvd 2nd Fl	Baton Rouge	LA	70809	225-925-4660	925-4548
Social Services Dept 627 N Fourth St *Web:* www.dss.state.la.us	Baton Rouge	LA	70802	225-342-0286	342-8636
State Parks Office PO Box 44426 *TF:* 888-677-1400 ■ *Web:* www.lastateparks.com	Baton Rouge	LA	70804	225-342-8111	342-8107
State Police PO Box 66614 *Web:* www.lsp.org	Baton Rouge	LA	70896	225-925-6006	
Supreme Court 400 Royal St *Web:* www.lasc.org	New Orleans	LA	70112	504-310-2300	
Teacher Standards Assessment & Certification Div 1201 N 3rd St PO Box 94064 **Fax Area Code: 225* ■ *TF:* 877-453-2721 ■ *Web:* www.doe.state.la.us	Baton Rouge	LA	70802	877-453-2721	342-0193*
Tourism Office PO Box 94291 *Web:* www.louisianatravel.com	Baton Rouge	LA	70804	225-342-8100	342-8390
Treasurer 900 N 3rd St Fl 3 PO Box 44154 *Web:* www.treasury.state.la.us/default.aspx	Baton Rouge	LA	70802	225-342-0010	342-0046
Veterans Affairs Dept 1885 Wooddale Blvd *Web:* www.ldva.org	Baton Rouge	LA	70806	225-922-0500	922-0511
Weights & Measures Div PO Box 3098	Baton Rouge	LA	70821	225-925-3780	923-4877
Wildlife & Fisheries Dept PO Box 98000 *TF:* 800-442-2511 ■ *Web:* www.wlf.louisiana.gov	Baton Rouge	LA	70898	225-765-2800	765-2892
Workers' Compensation Office PO Box 94040 *Web:* www.laworks.net/WorkersComp/OWC_WorkerMenu.asp	Baton Rouge	LA	70804	225-342-7555	342-5665

342-20 Maine

Agency / Address	City	State	ZIP	Phone	Fax
State Government Information 26 Edison Dr *TF:* 888-577-6690 ■ *Web:* www.maine.gov	Augusta	ME	04330	207-624-9494	
Administrative Office of the Cts PO Box 4820 *Web:* www.courts.state.me.us	Portland	ME	04112	207-822-0792	
Agriculture Dept 28 State House Stn *Web:* www.state.me.us	Augusta	ME	04333	207-287-3871	287-7548
Arts Commission 193 State St. *Web:* www.mainearts.com	Augusta	ME	04330	207-287-2724	287-2725
Attorney General 6 State House Stn *Web:* www.state.me.us	Augusta	ME	04333	207-626-8800	
Chief Medical Examiner 37 State House Stn *Web:* www.state.me.us	Augusta	ME	04333	207-624-7180	624-7178
Child & Family Services Office 221 State St *Web:* www.maine.gov/dhhs/bcfs	Augusta	ME	04333	207-287-5060	287-5031
Conservation Dept 22 State House Stn *Web:* www.state.me.us/doc	Augusta	ME	04333	207-287-2211	287-2400
Consumer Protection Unit 6 State House Stn *TF:* 800-436-2131 ■ *Web:* www.state.me.us	Augusta	ME	04333	207-626-8849	
Corrections Dept 25 Tyson Dr 3rd Fl 111 State House Stn *Web:* www.state.me.us	Augusta	ME	04333	207-287-2711	287-4370
Economic & Community Development Dept 59 State House Stn *TF:* 800-541-5872 ■ *Web:* www.econdevmaine.com	Augusta	ME	04333	207-624-9800	
Education Dept 23 State House Stn *Web:* www.maine.gov/education	Augusta	ME	04333	207-624-6600	624-6700
Elder Services Office 11 State House Stn 442 Civic Ctr Dr. *Web:* www.maine.gov/dhhs/beas	Augusta	ME	04333	207-287-9200	287-9229
Emergency Management Agency 72 State House Stn *TF:* 800-452-8735 ■ *Web:* www.state.me.us	Augusta	ME	04333	207-624-4432	287-3189
Employment Services Bureau 45 Commerce Dr *Web:* www.mainecareercenter.com	Augusta	ME	04330	207-623-7981	287-5933
Environmental Protection Dept 17 State House Stn *TF:* 800-452-1942 ■ *Web:* www.state.me.us	Augusta	ME	04333	207-287-7688	287-7814
Finance Authority of Maine 5 Community Dr PO Box 949 *TF:* 800-228-3734 ■ *Web:* www.famemaine.com	Augusta	ME	04332	207-623-3263	623-0095
Financial Institutions Bureau 36 State House Stn *Web:* www.state.me.us	Augusta	ME	04333	207-624-8570	624-8590
Governmental Ethics & Election Practices Commission 45 Memorial Cir *Web:* www.state.me.us	Augusta	ME	04330	207-287-4179	287-6775
Governor 1 State House Stn *TF:* 888-577-6690 ■ *Web:* www.maine.gov/governor	Augusta	ME	04333	207-287-3531	287-1034
Health Bureau 11 State House Stn *Web:* www.mainepublichealth.gov	Augusta	ME	04333	207-287-8016	287-9058
Historic Preservation Commission 65 State House Stn *Web:* www.state.me.us	Augusta	ME	04333	207-287-2132	287-2335
Housing Authority 353 Water St *Web:* www.mainehousing.org	Augusta	ME	04330	207-626-4600	626-4678
Human Services Dept 11 State House Stn *Web:* www.state.me.us	Augusta	ME	04333	207-287-3707	287-3005
Information Services Bureau 145 State House Stn *Web:* www.state.me.us	Augusta	ME	04333	207-624-8800	287-4563
Inland Fisheries & Wildlife Dept 41 State House Stn *Web:* www.state.me.us	Augusta	ME	04333	207-287-8000	287-6395
Insurance Bureau 34 State House Stn *TF:* 800-300-5000 ■ *Web:* www.maine.gov/pfr/insurance	Augusta	ME	04333	207-624-8475	624-8599
Labor Dept PO Box 259 *Web:* www.state.me.us/labor	Augusta	ME	04332	207-623-7900	
Legislature 115 State House Stn *Web:* janus.state.me.us/legis	Augusta	ME	04333	207-287-1615	287-1621
Licensing & Registration Office 35 State House Stn *Web:* www.state.me.us	Augusta	ME	04333	207-624-8500	624-8637
Licensure in Medicine Board 161 Capitol St *Web:* www.docboard.org	Augusta	ME	04330	207-287-3601	287-6590
Motor Vehicles Bureau 29 State House Stn *Web:* www.maine.gov/sos/bmv	Augusta	ME	04333	207-624-9000	624-9013
Parks & Land Bureau 22 State House Stn *TF Campground Resv:* 800-332-1501 ■ *Web:* www.state.me.us	Augusta	ME	04333	207-287-3821	287-6170
Parole Board 111 State House Stn	Augusta	ME	04333	207-287-4381	287-4370
Public Utilities Commission 18 State House Stn *Web:* www.state.me.us	Augusta	ME	04333	207-287-3831	287-1039
Quality Assurance & Regulations Div 28 State House Stn *Web:* www.state.me.us	Augusta	ME	04333	207-287-2161	287-5576
Rehabilitation Services Bureau 150 State House Stn **Fax Area Code: 207* ■ *TF:* 800-760-1573 ■ *Web:* www.maine.gov/rehab	Augusta	ME	04333	800-698-4440	287-5292*
Revenue Services 24 State House Stn *Web:* www.state.me.us	Augusta	ME	04333	207-287-2076	287-3618
Secretary of State 148 State House Stn *Web:* www.maine.gov/sos	Augusta	ME	04333	207-626-8400	287-8598
Securities Div 121 State House Stn *Web:* www.maine.gov	Augusta	ME	04333	207-624-8551	624-8590
State Police 45 Commerce Dr *Web:* www.maine.gov/dps/msp	Augusta	ME	04333	207-624-7200	624-7088
Support Enforcement & Recovery Div 11 State House Stn *Web:* www.state.me.us	Augusta	ME	04333	207-624-4100	287-5096
Supreme Court PO Box 368 *Web:* www.courts.state.me.us/mainecourts/supreme	Portland	ME	04112	207-822-4146	
Teacher Certification & Placement Office 23 State House Stn *Web:* www.state.me.us	Augusta	ME	04333	207-624-6603	624-6851
Tourism Office 59 State House Stn *TF:* 888-624-6345 ■ *Web:* www.visitmaine.com	Augusta	ME	04333	207-287-5711	287-8070
Transportation Dept 16 State House Stn *Web:* www.maine.gov/mdot	Augusta	ME	04333	207-624-3000	624-3001
Treasurer 39 State House Stn *Web:* www.state.me.us	Augusta	ME	04333	207-624-7477	287-2367
University of Maine System Board of Trustees 16 Central St. *Web:* www.maine.edu	Bangor	ME	04401	207-973-3211	973-3296
Veterans' Services Bureau 117 State House Stn *Web:* www.state.me.us	Augusta	ME	04333	207-626-4271	626-4509
Victims' Compensation Program 6 State House Sta *Web:* www.maine.gov	Augusta	ME	04333	207-624-7882	624-7730
Vital Records Office 11 State House Stn *Web:* www.maine.gov/dhhs	Augusta	ME	04333	207-287-3181	287-1093
Workers' Compensation Board 27 State House Stn *Web:* www.state.me.us	Augusta	ME	04333	207-287-3751	287-7198

342-21 Maryland

Agency / Address	City	State	ZIP	Phone	Fax
State Government Information State House *TF:* 800-811-8336 ■ *Web:* www.maryland.gov	Annapolis	MD	21401	410-974-3901	
Administrative Office of the Cts 580 Taylor Ave *Web:* www.courts.state.md.us	Annapolis	MD	21401	410-260-1400	974-2169
Aging Dept 301 W Preston St Rm 1007 *Web:* www.mdoa.state.md.us	Baltimore	MD	21201	410-767-1100	333-7943

	City	State	Zip	Phone	Fax
Agriculture Dept 50 Harry S Truman Pkwy *Web:* www.mda.state.md.us	Annapolis	MD	21401	410-841-5700	841-5914
Assessments & Taxation Dept 301 W Preston St 8th Fl *Web:* www.dat.state.md.us	Baltimore	MD	21201	410-767-1184	333-5873
Attorney General 200 St Paul Pl 16th Fl. *Web:* www.oag.state.md.us	Baltimore	MD	21202	410-576-6300	576-7040
Business & Economic Development Dept 217 E Redwood St *Web:* www.choosemaryland.org	Baltimore	MD	21202	410-767-6300	333-6911
Chief Medical Examiner 111 Penn St	Baltimore	MD	21201	410-333-3250	333-3063
Court of Appeals 361 Rowe Blvd 4th Fl *TF:* 800-926-2583 ■ *Web:* www.courts.state.md.us/coappeals	Annapolis	MD	21401	410-260-1500	
Criminal Injuries Compensation Board 6776 Reisterstown Rd Suite 206 *TF:* 888-679-9347 ■ *Web:* www.dpscs.state.md.us	Baltimore	MD	21215	410-585-3010	764-3815
Dept of Legislative Services 90 State Cir *TF:* 800-492-7122 ■ *Web:* www.mlis.state.md.us	Annapolis	MD	21401	410-946-5400	946-5405
Education Dept 200 W Baltimore St *TF:* 888-246-0016 ■ *Web:* www.marylandpublicschools.org	Baltimore	MD	21201	410-767-0100	333-2226
Emergency Management Agency 5401 Rue St Lo Dr *TF:* 877-636-2872 ■ *Web:* www.memaportal.mema.state.md.us	Reisterstown	MD	21136	410-517-3600	517-3610
Environment Dept 1800 Washington Blvd *TF:* 800-633-6101 ■ *Web:* www.mde.state.md.us	Baltimore	MD	21230	410-537-3000	537-3888
Ethics Commission 9 State Cir Suite 200 *TF:* 877-669-6085 ■ *Web:* ethics.gov.state.md.us	Annapolis	MD	21401	410-974-2068	974-2418
Financial Regulation Div 500 N Calvert St Rm 402 *TF:* 888-784-0136 ■ *Web:* www.dllr.state.md.us	Baltimore	MD	21202	410-230-6097	333-0475
Fisheries Service 580 Taylor Ave *Web:* www.dnr.state.md.us/fisheries	Annapolis	MD	21401	410-260-8281	260-8279
General Assembly 90 State Cir *Web:* www.mlis.state.md.us	Annapolis	MD	21401	410-841-3000	841-3850
Governor State House 100 State Cir *Web:* www.gov.state.md.us	Annapolis	MD	21401	410-974-3901	974-3275
Health & Mental Hygiene Dept 201 W Preston St 5th Fl *Web:* www.dhmh.state.md.us	Baltimore	MD	21201	410-767-6500	767-6489
Higher Education Commision 839 Bestgate Rd Suite 400 *TF:* 800-974-0203 ■ *Web:* www.mhec.state.md.us	Annapolis	MD	21401	410-260-4500	260-3200
Historical & Cultural Programs Div 100 Community Pl 3rd Fl *Web:* www.marylandhistoricaltrust.net	Crownsville	MD	21032	410-514-7600	514-7678
Housing & Community Development Dept 100 Community Pl *TF:* 800-756-0119 ■ *Web:* www.dhcd.state.md.us	Crownsville	MD	21032	410-514-7206	987-4070
Information Technology Office 45 Calvert St *Web:* www.dbm.state.md.us	Annapolis	MD	21401	410-260-7259	
Insurance Administration 525 St Paul Pl *TF:* 800-492-6116 ■ *Web:* www.mdinsurance.state.md.us	Baltimore	MD	21202	410-468-2000	468-2020
Labor & Industry Div 1100 N Eutaw St Rm 606 *Web:* www.dllr.state.md.us	Baltimore	MD	21201	410-767-2241	767-2986
Lieutenant Governor 100 State Cir. *TF:* 800-811-8336 ■ *Web:* www.gov.state.md.us	Annapolis	MD	21401	410-974-2804	974-5882
Motor Vehicle Administration 6601 Ritchie Hwy NE *Web:* www.mva.state.md.us	Glen Burnie	MD	21062	410-768-7274	768-7506
Natural Resources Dept 580 Taylor Ave *TF:* 877-620-8367 ■ *Web:* www.dnr.state.md.us	Annapolis	MD	21401	410-260-8021	260-8024
Occupational & Professional Licensing Div 500 N Calvert St 3rd Fl *Web:* www.dllr.state.md.us/license/occprof	Baltimore	MD	21202	410-230-6231	333-6314
Parole & Probation Div 6776 Reisterstown Rd Suite 305 *TF:* 877-227-8031 ■ *Web:* www2.dpscs.state.md.us	Baltimore	MD	21215	410-585-3500	764-4091
Physician Quality Assurance Board 4201 Patterson Ave *Web:* www.bpqa.state.md.us	Baltimore	MD	21215	410-764-4777	358-2252
Public Safety & Correctional Services Dept 300 E Joppa Rd Suite 1000 *TF:* 877-379-8636 ■ *Web:* www.dpscs.state.md.us	Towson	MD	21286	410-339-5000	339-4240
Public Service Commission 6 St Paul St 16th Fl *TF:* 800-492-0474 ■ *Web:* www.psc.state.md.us	Baltimore	MD	21202	410-767-8000	333-6495
Racing Commission 500 N Calvert St Rm 201 *Web:* www.dllr.state.md.us	Baltimore	MD	21202	410-230-6330	333-8308
Rehabilitation Services Div 2301 Argonne Dr *TF:* 888-554-0334 ■ *Web:* www.dors.state.md.us	Baltimore	MD	21218	410-554-9385	554-9412
Secretary of State 16 Francis St Jeffery Bldg 1st Fl *Web:* www.sos.state.md.us	Annapolis	MD	21401	410-974-5521	974-5190
Securities Div 200 St Paul Pl 20th Fl *Web:* www.oag.state.md.us/Securities	Baltimore	MD	21202	410-576-6360	576-6532
Social Services Administration 311 W Saratoga St *Web:* www.dhr.state.md.us	Baltimore	MD	21201	410-767-7216	333-0127
State Arts Council 175 W Ostend St Suite E *Web:* www.msac.org	Baltimore	MD	21230	410-767-6555	333-1062
State Athletic Commission 500 N Calvert St Rm 304 *Web:* www.dllr.state.md.us/license/occprof/athlet.html	Baltimore	MD	21202	410-230-6223	333-6314
State Forest & Park Service 580 Taylor Ave Rm E-3 *TF Campground Resv:* 800-830-3970 ■ *Web:* www.dnr.state.md.us	Annapolis	MD	21401	410-260-8186	260-8191
State Lottery 1800 Washington Blvd Suite 330 *Web:* www.mdlottery.com	Baltimore	MD	21230	410-230-8790	230-8728
State Police 1201 Reisterstown Rd *Web:* www.mdsp.maryland.gov	Pikesville	MD	21208	410-486-3101	653-4269
Teacher Certification & Accreditation Div 200 W Baltimore St *TF:* 866-772-8922 ■ *Web:* www.certification.msde.state.md.us	Baltimore	MD	21201	410-767-0412	
Tourism Development Office 217 E Redwood St 9th Fl *TF:* 800-543-1036 ■ *Web:* www.mdisfun.org	Baltimore	MD	21202	410-767-3400	333-6643
Treasurer 80 Calvert St Rm 109 *TF:* 800-974-0468 ■ *Web:* www.treasurer.state.md.us	Annapolis	MD	21401	410-260-7533	974-3530
Veterans Affairs Dept 31 Hopkins Plaza Rm 1231 *TF:* 800-446-4926 ■ *Web:* www.mdva.state.md.us	Baltimore	MD	21201	410-230-4444	230-4445
Vital Records Div 6550 Reisterstown Rd *TF:* 800-832-3277 ■ *Web:* www.mdpublichealth.org	Baltimore	MD	21215	410-764-3038	358-0738
Weights & Measures Section 50 Harry S Truman Pkwy Rm 410 *Web:* www.mda.state.md.us	Annapolis	MD	21401	410-841-5790	841-2765
Workers' Compensation Commission 10 E Baltimore St *Web:* www.wcc.state.md.us	Baltimore	MD	21202	410-864-5100	564-5101
Workforce Development Div 1100 N Eutaw St Rm 616 *Web:* www.dllr.state.md.us/employment	Baltimore	MD	21201	410-767-2400	767-2986

342-22 Massachusetts

	City	State	Zip	Phone	Fax
Agricultural Resources Dept 251 Cswy St Suite 500 *Web:* www.mass.gov	Boston	MA	02114	617-626-1700	626-1850
Attorney General 1 Ashburton Pl Suite 2010 *Web:* www.ago.state.ma.us	Boston	MA	02108	617-727-2200	727-6016
Banks Div 1000 Washington St Fl 10 *TF:* 800-495-2265 ■ *Web:* www.mass.gov	Boston	MA	02118	617-956-1501	956-1599
Bill Status 1 Ashburton Pl Rm 1611 *TF:* 800-392-6090 ■ *Web:* www.mass.gov/legis/ltsform.htm	Boston	MA	02108	617-727-7030	742-4528
Business Development Office 10 Pk Plaza Rm 3720 *Web:* www.state.ma.us	Boston	MA	02116	617-973-8600	973-8797
Child Support Enforcement Div 51 Sleeper St 3rd Fl *TF:* 800-332-2733 ■ *Web:* www.cse.state.ma.us	Boston	MA	02205	617-626-4170	626-3894
Correction Dept 50 Maple St *Web:* www.mass.gov	Milford	MA	01757	508-422-3300	422-3386
Cultural Council 10 St James Ave 3rd Fl *Web:* www.massculturalcouncil.org	Boston	MA	02116	617-727-3668	727-0044
Education Dept 350 Main St *Web:* www.doe.mass.edu	Malden	MA	02148	781-388-3300	388-3392
Elder Affairs Office 1 Ashburton Pl 5th Fl *TF:* 800-243-4636 ■ *Web:* www.state.ma.us/elder	Boston	MA	02108	617-727-7750	727-9368
Emergency Management Agency 400 Worcester Rd *Web:* www.mass.gov	Framingham	MA	01702	508-820-2000	820-2030
Environmental Protection Dept 1 Winter St 2nd Fl *Web:* www.mass.gov/eops	Boston	MA	02108	617-292-5856	574-6880
Executive Office of Transportation 10 Pk Plaza Rm 3170 *Web:* www.eot.state.ma.us	Boston	MA	02116	617-973-7000	973-8031
Fish & Game Dept 251 Cswy St Suite 400 *Web:* www.mass.gov/dfwele	Boston	MA	02214	617-626-1500	626-1505
General Court State House *Web:* www.mass.gov/legis	Boston	MA	02133	617-722-2000	267-8658
Governor State House Executive Office Rm 360 *Web:* www.mass.gov	Boston	MA	02133	617-725-4000	727-9725
Historical Commission 220 William T Morrissey Blvd *Web:* www.sec.state.ma.us	Boston	MA	02125	617-727-8470	727-5128
Housing & Community Development Dept 100 Cambridge St *Web:* www.mass.gov/dhcd	Boston	MA	02114	617-573-1100	573-1285
Housing Finance Agency 1 Beacon St *Web:* www.masshousing.com	Boston	MA	02108	617-854-1000	854-1029
Information Technology Div 1 Ashburton Pl Rm 804 *Web:* www.mass.gov	Boston	MA	02108	617-727-2040	727-2779
Insurance Div 1 S Stn 5th Fl *Web:* www.mass.gov/doi	Boston	MA	02110	617-521-7794	521-7770
Lieutenant Governor State House Rm 280 *TF:* 888-870-7770 ■ *Web:* www.mass.gov/gov	Boston	MA	02133	617-727-4005	727-9725
Medical Examiner 720 Albany St *Web:* www.mass.gov	Boston	MA	02118	617-267-6767	266-6763
Mental Health Dept 25 Staniford St *Web:* www.mass.gov/dmh	Boston	MA	02214	617-626-8000	
Parole Board 12 Mercer Rd *TF:* 888-298-6272 ■ *Web:* www.mass.gov/parole	Natick	MA	01760	508-650-4500	650-4599
Professional Licensure Div 239 Cswy St 5th Fl *Web:* www.mass.gov/dpl	Boston	MA	02114	617-727-3074	727-2197
Public Health Dept 250 Washington St *Web:* www.mass.gov/dph	Boston	MA	02108	617-624-6000	624-5206
Public Protection & Advocacy Bureau 100 Cambridge St	Boston	MA	02114	617-727-2200	727-5762
Public Utilities Dept 1 S Stn *Web:* www.mass.gov/dte	Boston	MA	02202	617-305-3500	345-9101
Registry of Motor Vehicles PO Box 55891 *Web:* www.mass.gov/rmv/regs/reg7.htm	Boston	MA	02205	617-351-4500	351-9519
Rehabilitation Commission 27 Wormwood St Suite 600 *Web:* www.state.ma.us	Boston	MA	02210	617-204-3600	727-1539

	City	State	Zip	Phone	Fax
Revenue Dept 51 Sleeper St *Web:* www.dor.state.ma.us	Boston	MA	02205	617-626-2201	626-2299
Secretary of the Commonwealth State House Rm 337 *Web:* www.sec.state.ma.us	Boston	MA	02133	617-727-9180	742-4722
Securities Div 1 Ashburton Pl 17th Fl *Web:* www.sec.state.ma.us/sct	Boston	MA	02108	617-727-3548	248-0177
Social Services Dept 24 Farnsworth St *Web:* www.mass.gov	Boston	MA	02210	617-748-2000	261-7435
Standards Div 1 Ashburton Pl Rm 1115 *Web:* www.mass.gov	Boston	MA	02108	617-727-3480	727-5705
State Boxing Commission 1 Ashburton Pl Rm 1301 *Web:* www.mass.gov/mbc	Boston	MA	02108	617-727-3200	727-5732
State Ethics Commission 1 Ashburton Pl Rm 619 *Web:* www.mass.gov/ethics	Boston	MA	02108	617-727-0060	723-5851
State Lottery Commission 60 Columbian St *Web:* www.masslottery.com	Braintree	MA	02184	781-849-5555	849-5546
State Parks & Recreation Div 251 Cswy St Suite 600 *Web:* www.mass.gov/dcr/forparks.htm	Boston	MA	02214	617-626-4986	626-4999
State Police Dept 470 Worcester Rd *Web:* www.state.ma.us/msp	Framingham	MA	01702	508-820-2300	820-2211
State Racing Commission 1 Ashburton Pl Rm 1313 *Web:* www.state.ma.us	Boston	MA	02108	617-727-2581	227-6062
Supreme Judicial Ct 1 Pemberton Sq Suite 2500 *Web:* www.mass.gov/courts	Boston	MA	02108	617-557-1000	723-3577
Transitional Assistance Dept 600 Washington St *Web:* www.mass.gov/dta	Boston	MA	02111	617-348-8400	348-8575
Travel & Tourism Office 10 Pk Plaza Suite 4510 *TF:* 800-227-6277 ■ *Web:* www.mass-vacation.com	Boston	MA	02116	617-973-8500	973-8525
Treasurer State House Rm 227 *Web:* www.mass.gov/?pageID=trehomepage&L=1&L0=Home&sid=Ctre	Boston	MA	02133	617-367-6900	248-0372
Veterans'' Services Dept 600 Washington St Suite 1100 *Web:* www.state.ma.us/veterans	Boston	MA	02111	617-727-3578	727-5903
Victim Compensation & Assistance Div 1 Ashburton Pl *Web:* www.ago.state.ma.us	Boston	MA	02108	617-727-2200	367-3906
Vital Records & Statistics Registry 150 Mt Vernon St 1st Fl *Web:* www.mass.gov	Dorchester	MA	02125	617-740-2600	423-2038
Workforce Development Dept 1 Ashburton Pl Rm 2112 *Web:* www.mass.gov	Boston	MA	02108	617-626-7100	727-1090
Higher Education Board 1 Ashburton Pl Rm 1401 *Web:* www.mass.edu	Boston	MA	02108	617-994-6950	727-6397

342-23 Michigan

	City	State	Zip	Phone	Fax
State Government Information PO Box 30013 *Web:* www.michigan.gov	Lansing	MI	48909	517-373-1837	
Aging Services Office 7109 W Saginaw PO Box 30676 *Web:* www.miseniors.net	Lansing	MI	48909	517-373-8230	373-4092
Agriculture Dept PO Box 30017 *TF:* 800-292-3939 ■ *Web:* www.michigan.gov/mda	Lansing	MI	48909	517-373-1104	335-7071
Arts & Cultural Affairs Council 702 W Kalamazoo St PO Box 30705 *Web:* www.michigan.gov	Lansing	MI	48909	517-241-4011	241-3979
Attorney General 525 W Ottawa St *TF:* 877-765-8388 ■ *Web:* www.michigan.gov	Lansing	MI	48933	517-373-1110	373-3042
Bill Status PO Box 30036 *Web:* www.legislature.mi.gov	Lansing	MI	48909	517-373-0630	
Career Education & Workforce Programs 201 N Washington Sq 3rd Fl *TF:* 888-253-6855 ■ *Web:* www.michigan.gov/mdcd	Lansing	MI	48913	517-241-4000	373-0314
Child Support Office 235 S Grand Ave Suite 1215 *TF:* 866-661-0005 ■ *Web:* www.michigan.gov/dhs	Lansing	MI	48933	866-661-0005	
Civil Rights Dept 110 W Michigan Ave Suite 800 Capitol Tower Bldg *Web:* www.michigan.gov/mdcr	Lansing	MI	48933	517-335-3165	241-0546
Civil Service Dept Capitol Commons Ctr 400 S Pine St *TF:* 800-788-1766 ■ *Web:* www.michigan.gov	Lansing	MI	48913	517-373-3030	373-7690
Community Health Dept Capitol View Bldg 201 Townsend St *TF:* 800-649-3777 ■ *Web:* www.michigan.gov/mdch	Lansing	MI	48913	517-373-3740	
Consumer Protection Div PO Box 30213 *Web:* www.michigan.gov/ag	Lansing	MI	48909	517-373-1140	241-3771
Corrections Dept 206 E Michigan Ave Grandview Plaza PO Box 30003 *Web:* www.michigan.gov/corrections	Lansing	MI	48909	517-335-1426	373-6883
Crime Victims Services Commission 320 S Walnut St 5th Fl *Web:* www.mivictims.org	Lansing	MI	48913	517-373-7373	
Driver & Vehicle Bureau 7064 Crowner Dr *Web:* www.michigan.gov/sos	Lansing	MI	48918	517-322-1460	322-5458
Drug Control Policy Office 320 S Walnut St Lewis Cass Bldg 5th Fl *Web:* www.michigan.gov/mdch	Lansing	MI	48913	517-373-4700	241-2199
Economic Development Corp 300 N Washington Sq *TF:* 888-522-0103 ■ *Web:* www.michiganadvantage.org	Lansing	MI	48913	517-373-9808	241-3683
Education Dept 608 W Allegan St PO Box 30008 *Web:* www.michigan.gov	Lansing	MI	48909	517-373-3324	
Education Trust PO Box 30198 *TF:* 800-638-4543 ■ *Web:* www.michigan.gov/treasury	Lansing	MI	48909	517-335-4767	373-6967
eLibrary Information 702 W Kalamazoo St PO Box 30007 *Web:* www.michigan.gov/hal	Lansing	MI	48909	517-373-4331	373-5700
Emergency Management & Homeland Security Div PO Box 30636	Lansing	MI	48909	517-336-6198	333-4987
Environmental Quality Dept 3423 N Logan St *Web:* www.michigan.gov	Lansing	MI	48906	517-373-7917	
Financial & Insurance Regulation PO Box 30220 *TF:* 877-999-6442 ■	Lansing	MI	48909	517-373-0220	335-4978
Gaming Control Board 1500 Abbott Rd Suite 400 *Web:* www.michigan.gov/mgcb	East Lansing	MI	48823	517-241-0040	241-0510
Governor PO Box 30013 *Web:* www.michigan.gov/gov	Lansing	MI	48909	517-373-3400	335-6863
Human Services Dept 235 S Grand Ave PO Box 30037 *Web:* www.michigan.gov/dhs	Lansing	MI	48909	517-373-2035	335-6101
Information Technology Dept George W Romney Bldg 8th Fl 111 S Capitol Ave *Web:* www.michigan.gov/dit	Lansing	MI	48913	517-335-4000	373-8213
Labor & Economic Growth Dept 611 W Ottawa St *Web:* www.michigan.gov	Lansing	MI	48933	517-373-1820	373-2129
Legislature State Capitol PO Box 30014 *Web:* www.legislature.mi.gov	Lansing	MI	48909	517-373-6339	373-0171
Lieutenant Governor PO Box 30013 *Web:* www.michigan.gov/ltgov	Lansing	MI	48909	517-373-6800	241-3956
Management & Budget Dept PO Box 30026 *Web:* www.michigan.gov/dmb	Lansing	MI	48909	517-373-1004	373-7268
Military & Veterans Affairs Dept 3411 N ML King Blvd *Web:* www.michigan.gov/dmva	Lansing	MI	48906	517-481-8000	
Natural Resources Dept PO Box 30028 *Web:* www.michigan.gov/dnr	Lansing	MI	48909	517-241-3230	
Parks & Recreation Bureau PO Box 30257 *TF Campground Resv:* 800-447-2757 ■ *Web:* www.michigan.gov/dnr	Lansing	MI	48909	517-373-9900	373-4625
Public Service Commission PO Box 30221 *Web:* www.michigan.gov/mpsc	Lansing	MI	48909	517-241-6180	241-6181
Racing Commissioners Office 525 W Allegan St PO Box 30773 *Web:* www.michigan.gov	Lansing	MI	48909	517-335-1420	241-3018
Rehabilitation Services 201 N Washington Sq 4th Fl *Web:* www.michigan.gov	Lansing	MI	48933	517-373-3390	335-7277
Secretary of State 430 W Allegan St 4th Fl *Web:* www.michigan.gov	Lansing	MI	48918	517-373-2510	241-3442
State Court Administrator 925 W Ottawa St *Web:* www.courts.michigan.gov/scao	Lansing	MI	48913	517-373-0130	373-7517
State Historic Preservation Office 702 W Kalamazoo St PO Box 30740 *Web:* www.michigan.gov	Lansing	MI	48909	517-373-1630	335-0348
State Housing Development Authority PO Box 30044 *Web:* www.michigan.gov/mshda	Lansing	MI	48909	517-373-8370	335-4797
State Lottery 101 E Hillsdale St PO Box 30023 *Web:* www.michigan.gov/lottery	Lansing	MI	48909	517-335-5600	335-5644
State Police Dept 714 S Harrison Rd *Web:* www.michigan.gov/msp	East Lansing	MI	48823	517-332-2521	336-6255
Student Financial Services Bureau Austin Bldg 430 W Allegan *TF:* 800-642-5626 ■ *Web:* www.michigan.gov/mistudentaid	Lansing	MI	48922	517-373-4897	
Supreme Court PO Box 30052 *Web:* www.courts.michigan.gov/supremecourt	Lansing	MI	48909	517-373-0120	
Transportation Dept PO Box 30050 *Web:* www.michigan.gov/mdot	Lansing	MI	48909	517-373-2090	373-0167
Travel Michigan 300 N Washington Sq *TF:* 888-784-7328 ■ *Web:* www.michigan.org	Lansing	MI	48913	517-373-0670	373-0059
Treasurer 430 W Allegan St *Web:* www.michigan.gov/treasury	Lansing	MI	48922	517-373-3200	373-4968
Unemployment Insurance Agency Cadillac Pl 3024 W Grand Blvd *Web:* www.michigan.gov/uia	Detroit	MI	48202	313-456-2400	456-2424
Vital Records Div 201 Townsend St Capitol View Bldg 3rd Fl *Web:* www.michigan.gov/mdch	Lansing	MI	48913	517-335-8656	321-5884
Wildlife Div PO Box 30444 *Web:* www.michigan.gov/dnr	Lansing	MI	48909	517-373-1263	373-6705
Workers Compensation Agency PO Box 30016 *Web:* www.michigan.gov/wca	Lansing	MI	48909	517-322-1106	322-6689

342-24 Minnesota

	City	State	Zip	Phone	Fax
State Government Information 100 Rev Dr Mlk Jr Blvd *Web:* www.state.mn.us	Saint Paul	MN	55155	651-296-6013	
Aging Board 540 Cedar St *TF:* 800-657-3889 ■ *Web:* www.mnaging.org	Saint Paul	MN	55155	651-431-2500	431-7415
Arts Board 400 Sibley St Suite 200 *TF:* 800-866-2787 ■ *Web:* www.arts.state.mn.us	Saint Paul	MN	55101	651-215-1600	215-1602
Attorney General 1400 Bremer Tower 445 Minnesota St *TF:* 800-657-3787 ■ *Web:* www.ag.state.mn.us	Saint Paul	MN	55101	651-296-3353	297-4193
Bill Status-House 75 ML King Jr Blvd Rm 211 *Web:* www.leg.state.mn.us/leg/legis.asp	Saint Paul	MN	55155	651-296-6646	

				Phone	Fax
Bill Status-Senate 75 ML King Jr Blvd Rm 231 *Web:* www.leg.state.mn.us/leg/legis.asp	Saint Paul	MN	55155	651-296-2887	
Campaign Finance & Public Disclosure Board 658 Cedar St Suite 190 *TF:* 800-657-3889 ■ *Web:* www.cfboard.state.mn.us	Saint Paul	MN	55155	651-296-5148	296-1722
Child Support Enforcement Div 444 Lafayette Rd *Web:* www.dhs.state.mn.us	Saint Paul	MN	55155	651-431-2000	431-7517
Children Families & Learning Dept 1500 Hwy 36 W *Web:* education.state.mn.us	Roseville	MN	55113	651-582-8200	582-8202
Children's Services Administration PO Box 64943 *Web:* www.dhs.state.mn.us	Saint Paul	MN	55164	651-431-4660	431-7522
Commerce Dept 85 7th Pl E Suite 500 *Web:* www.commerce.state.mn.us	Saint Paul	MN	55101	651-296-4026	297-1959
Consumer Protection Office 445 Minnesota St Suite 1400 *TF:* 800-657-3787 ■ *Web:* www.ag.state.mn.us	Saint Paul	MN	55101	651-296-3353	
Corrections Dept 1450 Energy Pk Dr Suite 200 *Web:* www.corr.state.mn.us	Saint Paul	MN	55108	651-361-7200	642-0223
Crime Victims Reparations Board 445 Minnesota St Suite 2300 *TF:* 888-622-8799	Saint Paul	MN	55101	651-201-7300	296-5787
Driver & Vehicle Services Div 445 Minnesota St Suite 190 Town Sq Bldg. *Web:* https://dps.mn.gov/divisions/dvs	Saint Paul	MN	55101	651-297-3298	296-3141
Employment & Economic Development Dept 332 Minnesota St Suite E200 *TF:* 800-657-3858 ■ *Web:* www.deed.state.mn.us	Saint Paul	MN	55101	651-259-7114	
Enterprise Technology Office 658 Cedar St.	Saint Paul	MN	55155	651-296-8888	
Finance Dept 658 Cedar St Suite 400 *TF:* 800-627-3529 ■ *Web:* www.finance.state.mn.us	Saint Paul	MN	55155	651-201-8000	296-8685
Fish & Wildlife Div 500 Lafayette Rd *Web:* www.dnr.state.mn.us	Saint Paul	MN	55155	651-259-5180	297-7272
Governor 130 State Capitol 75 Rev Dr Martin Luther King Jr Blvd *TF:* 800-657-3717 ■ *Web:* www.governor.state.mn.us	Saint Paul	MN	55155	651-296-3391	296-2089
Health Dept PO Box 64975 *TF:* 888-345-0823 ■ *Web:* www.health.state.mn.us	Saint Paul	MN	55164	651-201-5000	
Historical Society 345 Kellogg Blvd W *TF:* 800-657-3773 ■ *Web:* www.mnhs.org	Saint Paul	MN	55102	651-259-3000	
Homeland Security & Emergency Management Div 444 Cedar St Suite 223 *Web:* www.dps.state.mn.us	Saint Paul	MN	55101	651-201-7400	296-0459
Housing Finance Authority 400 Sibley St Suite 300 *TF:* 800-657-3769 ■ *Web:* www.mhfa.state.mn.us	Saint Paul	MN	55101	651-296-7608	296-8139
Human Services Dept 444 Lafayette Rd *Web:* www.dhs.state.mn.us	Saint Paul	MN	55155	651-431-2000	296-6244
Labor & Industry Dept 443 Lafayette Rd N. *TF:* 800-342-5354 ■ *Web:* www.doli.state.mn.us	Saint Paul	MN	55155	651-284-5005	284-5727
Legislature 75 Constitution Ave State Capitol *TF:* 800-657-3550 ■ *Web:* www.leg.state.mn.us	Saint Paul	MN	55155	651-296-2146	
Licensing Div 85 7th Pl E Suite 600 *TF:* 800-657-3978	Saint Paul	MN	55101	651-296-6319	284-4107
Medical Practice Board 2829 University Ave SE Suite 500 *TF:* 800-657-3709 ■ *Web:* www.bmp.state.mn.us	Minneapolis	MN	55414	612-617-2130	617-2166
Natural Resources Dept 500 Lafayette Rd. *TF:* 888-646-6367 ■ *Web:* www.dnr.state.mn.us	Saint Paul	MN	55155	651-296-6157	296-3618
Office of Higher Education 1450 Energy Pk Dr Suite 350 *TF:* 800-657-3866 ■ *Web:* www.ohe.state.mn.us	Saint Paul	MN	55108	651-642-0567	642-0675
Office of State Registrar 85 E 7th Pl 3rd Fl PO Box 64882 *Web:* www.health.state.mn.us/divs/chs/osr	Saint Paul	MN	55164	651-201-5970	
Pardon Board 1450 Energy Pk Dr Suite 200	Saint Paul	MN	55108	651-642-0284	643-2575
Parks & Recreation Div 500 Lafayette Rd	Saint Paul	MN	55155	651-259-5591	
Public Safety Dept 444 Cedar St Town Sq Bldg *Web:* www.dps.state.mn.us	Saint Paul	MN	55101	651-201-7000	
Public Utilities Commission 121 7th Pl E Suite 350 *TF:* 800-657-3782 ■ *Web:* www.puc.state.mn.us	Saint Paul	MN	55101	651-296-7124	297-7073
Revenue Dept 600 N Roberts St *Web:* www.taxes.state.mn.us	Saint Paul	MN	55101	651-296-3403	297-5309
Secretary of State 60 Empire Dr Suite 100 *Web:* www.sos.state.mn.us	Saint Paul	MN	55103	651-296-2803	215-0682
Securities Div 85 7th Pl E	Saint Paul	MN	55101	651-296-4973	
State Court Administrator 25 Rev Dr Martin Luther King Jr Blvd Rm 135 *Web:* www.mncourts.gov	Saint Paul	MN	55155	651-296-2474	297-5636
State Lottery 2645 Long Lake Rd *Web:* www.mnlottery.com	Roseville	MN	55113	651-297-7456	
State Patrol Div 444 Cedar St Suite 130 *Web:* www.dps.state.mn.us	Saint Paul	MN	55101	651-201-7100	
Supreme Court 25 Rev Dr Martin Luther King Jr Blvd *Web:* www.courts.state.mn.us	Saint Paul	MN	55155	651-297-7650	
Teacher Licensing Office 1500 Hwy 36 W	Roseville	MN	55113	651-582-8691	582-8809
Tourism Office 121 7th Pl E Suite 100 *TF:* 888-868-7476 ■ *Web:* www.exploreminnesota.com	Saint Paul	MN	55101	651-296-5029	
Transportation Dept 395 John Ireland Blvd *TF:* 800-657-3774 ■ *Web:* www.dot.state.mn.us	Saint Paul	MN	55155	651-296-3000	
Veterans Affairs Dept 20 W 12th St Fl 2 Rm 206-C *Web:* www.mdva.state.mn.us	Saint Paul	MN	55155	651-296-2562	296-3954

				Phone	Fax
Weights & Measures Div 14305 Southcross Dr Suite 150 **Fax Area Code:* 952	Burnsville	MN	55306	651-215-5821	435-4040*
Workers" Compensation Div 443 Lafayette Rd *TF:* 800-342-5354 ■ *Web:* www.doli.state.mn.us/workcomp.html	Saint Paul	MN	55155	651-284-5005	296-9634

342-25 Mississippi

				Phone	Fax
State Government Information 301 N Lamar Suite 508 *TF:* 866-671-3468 ■ *Web:* www.mississippi.gov	Jackson	MS	39201	601-359-3468	576-3468
Administrative Office of the Courts 450 High St PO Box 117 *Web:* www.mssc.state.ms.us/aoc/aoc.html	Jackson	MS	39205	601-576-4630	576-4630
Aging & Adult Services Div 421 W Pascagoula St *Web:* www.mdhs.state.ms.us	Jackson	MS	39203	601-359-4929	359-4370
Archives & History Dept 200 N St PO Box 571 *Web:* www.mdah.state.ms.us	Jackson	MS	39201	601-576-6850	576-6975
Arts Commission 501 N W St Suite 1101-A *Web:* www.arts.state.ms.us	Jackson	MS	39201	601-359-6030	359-6008
Attorney General PO Box 220 *Web:* www.ago.state.ms.us	Jackson	MS	39205	601-359-3680	359-3796
Banking & Consumer Finance Dept PO Box 23729 *TF:* 800-844-2499 ■ *Web:* www.dbcf.state.ms.us	Jackson	MS	39225	601-359-1031	359-3557
Bill Status PO Box 1018 *Web:* billstatus.ls.state.ms.us	Jackson	MS	39215	601-359-3719	
Child Support Enforcement Div PO Box 352 *TF:* 800-948-4010 ■ *Web:* www.mdhs.state.ms.us/cse.html	Jackson	MS	39205	601-359-4861	359-4415
Consumer Protection Div PO Box 22947 *TF:* 800-281-4418 ■ *Web:* www.ago.state.ms.us/index.php/sections/consumer	Jackson	MS	39225	601-359-4230	359-4231
Contractors Board 215 Woodline Dr Suite B *TF:* 800-880-6161 ■ *Web:* www.msboc.state.ms.us	Jackson	MS	39232	601-354-6161	354-6715
Corrections Dept 723 N President St *Web:* www.mdoc.state.ms.us	Jackson	MS	39202	601-359-5600	359-5624
Crime Victim Compensation Program PO Box 220 *TF:* 800-829-6766 ■	Jackson	MS	39205	601-359-6766	576-4445
Development Authority 501 N W St # 601 *Web:* www.mississippi.org	Jackson	MS	39201	601-359-3449	359-2832
Education Dept PO Box 771 *Web:* www.mde.k12.ms.us	Jackson	MS	39205	601-359-3513	359-2566
Emergency Management Agency PO Box 4501 *TF:* 800-222-6362 ■ *Web:* www.msema.org	Jackson	MS	39296	601-933-6875	933-6800
Employment Security Commission 1235 Echelon Pkwy PO Box 1699 *TF:* 888-844-3577 ■ *Web:* www.mdes.ms.gov	Jackson	MS	39215	601-321-6000	321-6004
Enviromental Quality Dept PO Box 20305 *Web:* www.deq.state.ms.us	Jackson	MS	39289	601-961-5611	354-6356
Ethics Commission 146 E Amite St # 103 *Web:* www.ethics.state.ms.us	Jackson	MS	39201	601-359-1285	354-6253
Family & Children Services Div 750 N State St. *Web:* www.mdhs.state.ms.us/fcs.html	Jackson	MS	39202	601-359-4500	359-4363
Finance & Administration Dept 1301 Wolfolk Bldg # B *Web:* www.dfa.state.ms.us	Jackson	MS	39201	601-359-3402	359-2405
Governor PO Box 139 *TF:* 877-405-0733 ■ *Web:* www.governorbarbour.com	Jackson	MS	39205	601-359-3150	359-3741
Health Dept PO Box 1700 *Web:* www.msdh.state.ms.us	Jackson	MS	39215	601-576-7400	576-7948
Higher Learning Institutions Board of Trustees 3825 Ridgewood Rd Suite 915 *TF:* 800-327-2980 ■ *Web:* www.ihl.state.ms.us	Jackson	MS	39211	601-432-6198	432-6972
Highway Safety Patrol PO Box 958	Jackson	MS	39205	601-987-1212	987-1498
Historic Preservation Div PO Box 571 *Web:* www.mdah.state.ms.us/hpres	Jackson	MS	39205	601-576-6940	576-6955
Home Corp 735 Riverside Dr *Web:* www.mshomecorp.com	Jackson	MS	39202	601-718-4642	718-4643
Human Services Dept 750 N State St. *Web:* www.mdhs.state.ms.us	Jackson	MS	39205	601-359-4500	359-4510
Information Technology Services Dept 301 N Lamar St Suite 508 *Web:* www.its.state.ms.us	Jackson	MS	39201	601-359-1395	354-6016
Insurance Dept 501 N W St # 1001 *Web:* www.doi.state.ms.us	Jackson	MS	39201	601-359-3569	359-2474
Legislature New Capitol PO Box 1018 *Web:* www.ls.state.ms.us	Jackson	MS	39215	601-359-3770	359-3935
Lieutenant Governor 400 High St # 316 *Web:* www.ls.state.ms.us	Jackson	MS	39201	601-359-3200	359-4054
Medical Licensure Board 1867 Crane Ridge Dr Suite 200-B *Web:* www.msbml.state.ms.us	Jackson	MS	39216	601-987-3079	987-4159
Motor Vehicle Commission PO Box 16873 *Web:* www.mmvc.state.ms.us	Jackson	MS	39236	601-987-3995	987-3997
Parks & Recreation Div PO Box 451 *TF:* 800-467-2757 ■ *Web:* www.mdwfp.com/parks.asp	Jackson	MS	39205	601-432-2266	432-2236
Parole Board 660 N St Suite 100 A *Web:* www.mpb.state.ms.us	Jackson	MS	39202	601-576-3520	576-3528
Public Accountancy Board 5 Old River Pl Suite 104 *Web:* www.msbpa.state.ms.us	Jackson	MS	39202	601-354-7320	354-7290
Public Health Statistics Bureau 571 Stadium Dr PO Box 1700 *Web:* www.msdh.state.ms.us/phs	Jackson	MS	39215	601-576-7960	576-7505
Public Service Commission PO Box 1174 *Web:* www.psc.state.ms.us	Jackson	MS	39215	601-961-5434	961-5469
Real Estate Commission 2506 Lakeland Dr Suite 300 *Web:* www.mrec.state.ms.us	Flowood	MS	39232	601-932-6770	932-2990

				Phone	Fax
Rehabilitation Services Dept 3895 Beasley Rd *TF:* 800-443-1000 ■ *Web:* www.mdrs.state.ms.us	Jackson	MS	39213	601-853-5100	853-5205
Securities Div PO Box 136 *Web:* www.sos.ms.gov	Jackson	MS	39205	601-359-1048	359-1499
State Medical Examiner 1700 E Woodrow Wilson Ave *Web:* www.dps.state.ms.us	Jackson	MS	39216	601-987-1600	987-1445
Student Financial Aid Office 3825 Ridgewood Rd *TF:* 800-327-2980 ■ *Web:* www.ihl.state.ms.us/financialaid	Jackson	MS	39211	601-432-6997	432-6527
Supreme Court PO Box 117 *Web:* www.mssc.state.ms.us	Jackson	MS	39205	601-359-3694	359-2407
Tax Commission PO Box 22828 *Web:* www.mstc.state.ms.us	Jackson	MS	39225	601-923-7000	923-7404
Teacher Licensure Office PO Box 771 *Web:* www.mde.k12.ms.us	Jackson	MS	39205	601-359-3483	359-2778
Tourism Development Div PO Box 849 *TF:* 866-733-6477 ■ *Web:* www.visitmississippi.org	Jackson	MS	39205	601-359-3297	359-5757
Treasury Dept 501 N W St Suite 1101 *TF:* 800-987-4450 ■ *Web:* www.collegesavingsmississippi.com	Jackson	MS	39201	601-359-5255	359-5234
Treasury Dept PO Box 138 *Web:* www.treasury.state.ms.us	Jackson	MS	39205	601-359-3600	359-2001
Veterans Affairs Board 3466 Hwy 80 E *Web:* www.vab.state.ms.us	Pearl	MS	39208	601-576-4850	576-4868
Weights & Measures Div PO Box 1609	Jackson	MS	39215	601-359-1149	359-1175
Wildlife Fisheries & Parks Dept 1505 Eastover Dr *Web:* www.mdwfp.com	Jackson	MS	39211	601-432-2400	432-2024
Worker's Compensation Commission PO Box 5300 *Web:* www.mwcc.state.ms.us	Jackson	MS	39296	601-987-4200	987-4233

342-26 Missouri

				Phone	Fax
State Government Information 301 W High St *Web:* dor.mo.gov	Jefferson City	MO	65101	573-751-2000	
Agriculture Dept PO Box 630 *Web:* www.mda.state.mo.us	Jefferson City	MO	65102	573-751-4211	751-1784
Arts Council 815 Olive St Suite 16 *Web:* www.missouriartscouncil.org	Saint Louis	MO	63101	314-340-6845	340-7215
Attorney General PO Box 899 *Web:* www.moago.org	Jefferson City	MO	65102	573-751-3321	751-0774
Bill Status 117A State Capitol *Web:* www.house.state.mo.us	Jefferson City	MO	65101	573-751-4633	751-0130
Child Support Enforcement Div 221 W High St PO Box 1527 *TF:* 800-859-7999 ■ *Web:* www.dss.missouri.gov/cse	Jefferson City	MO	65102	573-751-4301	751-8450
Conservation Dept 2901 W Truman Blvd *Web:* www.mdc.mo.gov	Jefferson City	MO	65109	573-751-4115	751-4467
Consumer Protection Div PO Box 899 *Web:* www.moago.org/divisions/consumerprotection.htm	Jefferson City	MO	65102	573-751-6887	751-7948
Corrections Dept PO Box 236 *Web:* www.corrections.state.mo.us	Jefferson City	MO	65102	573-526-6500	751-4099
Crime Victims' Compensation Unit PO Box 3001 *Web:* www.dolir.state.mo.us	Jefferson City	MO	65102	573-526-6006	526-4940
Economic Development Dept PO Box 1157 *Web:* www.ded.state.mo.us	Jefferson City	MO	65102	573-751-3946	751-7258
Educator Certification Section PO Box 480 *Web:* dese.mo.gov/divteachqual/teachcert/certstaff.html	Jefferson City	MO	65102	573-751-0051	
Elementary & Secondary Education Dept PO Box 480 *Web:* www.dese.state.mo.us	Jefferson City	MO	65102	573-751-4212	751-8613
Emergency Management Agency PO Box 116 *Web:* www.sema.state.mo.us	Jefferson City	MO	65102	573-526-9101	634-7966
Employment Security Div 421 E Dunklin St PO Box 59 *Web:* www.labor.mo.gov	Jefferson City	MO	65104	573-751-7500	751-6552
Family Services Div PO Box 2320 *Web:* www.dss.missouri.gov/dfs	Jefferson City	MO	65102	573-751-3221	751-3203
Finance Div PO Box 716 *TF:* 888-246-7225 ■ *Web:* www.finance.mo.gov	Jefferson City	MO	65102	573-751-3242	751-9192
General Assembly State Capitol **Fax:* PR ■ *Web:* www.moga.mo.gov	Jefferson City	MO	65101	573-751-4633	751-8640*
Governor PO Box 720 *Web:* www.gov.state.mo.us	Jefferson City	MO	65102	573-751-3222	751-1495
Healing Arts Board PO Box 4 *Web:* www.ded.state.mo.us	Jefferson City	MO	65102	573-751-0098	751-3166
Health & Senior Services Dept PO Box 570 *Web:* www.dhss.state.mo.us	Jefferson City	MO	65102	573-751-6400	751-6010
Higher Education Dept 3515 Amazonas Dr *TF:* 800-473-6757 ■ *Web:* www.dhe.mo.gov	Jefferson City	MO	65109	573-751-2361	751-6635
Historical Preservation Office 1101 Riverside Dr *Web:* www.dnr.mo.gov	Jefferson City	MO	65101	573-751-7858	522-6262
Homeland Security Office PO Box 809 *Web:* www.homelandsecurity.state.mo.us	Jefferson City	MO	65102	573-522-3007	751-7819
Housing Development Commission 3435 Broadway *Web:* www.mhdc.com	Kansas City	MO	64111	816-759-6600	759-6828
Insurance Dept 301 W High St Suite 530 *Web:* www.insurance.state.mo.us	Jefferson City	MO	65101	573-751-4126	751-1165
Labor & Industrial Relations Dept PO Box 504 *Web:* www.dolir.state.mo.us	Jefferson City	MO	65102	573-751-4091	526-4135
Lieutenant Governor State Capitol Bldg Rm 224 *Web:* ltgov.mo.gov	Jefferson City	MO	65101	573-751-4727	751-9422
Lottery 1823 Southridge Dr PO Box 1603 *Web:* www.molottery.com	Jefferson City	MO	65109	573-751-4050	751-5188
Motor Vehicles & Drivers Licensing Div 301 W High St Rm 360 *Web:* dor.mo.gov/drivers	Jefferson City	MO	65101	573-751-4450	526-4774
Natural Resources Dept PO Box 176 *TF Cust Svc:* 800-361-4827 ■ *Web:* www.dnr.mo.gov	Jefferson City	MO	65102	573-751-3443	751-7627
Probation & Parole Board 1511 Christy Dr *Web:* www.corrections.state.mo.us/division/prob/prob.htm	Jefferson City	MO	65101	573-751-8488	751-8501
Professional Registration Div PO Box 1335 *Web:* www.ded.state.mo.us	Jefferson City	MO	65102	573-751-0293	751-4176
Public Service Commission PO Box 360 *Web:* www.psc.state.mo.us	Jefferson City	MO	65102	573-751-3234	751-1847
Real Estate Commission PO Box 1339 *Web:* www.ded.state.mo.us	Jefferson City	MO	65102	573-751-2628	751-2777
Revenue Dept PO Box 311 *Web:* www.dor.state.mo.us	Jefferson City	MO	65105	573-751-4450	751-7150
Secretary of State PO Box 778 *Web:* www.sos.mo.gov	Jefferson City	MO	65102	573-751-4936	526-4903
Securities Div 600 W Main St 2nd Fl *Web:* www.sos.state.mo.us/securities	Jefferson City	MO	65101	573-751-4136	526-3124
Social Services Dept PO Box 1527 *Web:* www.dss.state.mo.us	Jefferson City	MO	65102	573-751-4815	751-3203
State Courts Administrator PO Box 104480 *Web:* www.osca.state.mo.us	Jefferson City	MO	65110	573-751-3585	522-6152
State Highway Patrol PO Box 568 *Web:* www.mshp.state.mo.us	Jefferson City	MO	65102	573-751-3313	751-9419
State Parks Div PO Box 176 *TF:* 800-334-6946 ■ *Web:* www.mostateparks.com	Jefferson City	MO	65102	573-751-2479	751-8656
Student Assistance Resource Services (MOSTARS) 205 Jefferson St PO Box 1469 *TF:* 800-473-6757 ■ *Web:* www.dhe.mo.gov	Jefferson City	MO	65109	573-751-2361	751-6635
Supreme Court PO Box 150 *Web:* www.osca.state.mo.us/sup/index.nsf	Jefferson City	MO	65102	573-751-4144	751-7514
Tourism Div PO Box 1055 *TF:* 800-877-1234 ■ *Web:* www.missouritourism.org	Jefferson City	MO	65102	573-526-5900	751-5160
Transportation Dept PO Box 270 *TF:* 888-275-6636 ■ *Web:* www.modot.state.mo.us	Jefferson City	MO	65102	573-751-2551	751-6555
Treasurer PO Box 210 *Web:* www.sto.state.mo.us	Jefferson City	MO	65102	573-751-2411	751-9443
Veterans Commission 205 Jefferson St Fl 12 Jefferson Bldg PO Drawer 147 *TF:* 866-838-4636 ■ *Web:* mvc.dps.mo.gov	Jefferson City	MO	65102	573-751-3779	751-6836
Vital Records Bureau PO Box 570 *Web:* www.dhss.state.mo.us	Jefferson City	MO	65102	573-751-6387	526-3846
Vocational & Adult Education Div 3024 Dupont Cir PO Box 480 *TF:* 877-222-8963 ■ *Web:* dese.mo.gov/divcareered	Jefferson City	MO	65109	573-751-3251	751-1441
Weights & Measures Div PO Box 630 *Web:* www.mda.state.mo.us/Consumer/j.htm	Jefferson City	MO	65102	573-751-4278	751-0281
Workers'' Compensation Div PO Box 58 *Web:* www.dolir.state.mo.us/wc	Jefferson City	MO	65102	573-751-4231	751-2012

342-27 Montana

				Phone	Fax
State Government Information PO Box 200113 *Web:* www.mt.gov	Helena	MT	59620	406-444-2511	444-2701
Arts Council PO Box 202201 *TF:* 800-282-3092 ■ *Web:* www.art.mt.gov	Helena	MT	59620	406-444-6430	444-6548
Attorney General 215 N Sanders St *Web:* www.doj.mt.gov	Helena	MT	59601	406-444-2026	444-3549
Banking & Financial Institutions Div PO Box 200546 *TF:* 800-914-8423 ■ *Web:* www.banking.mt.gov	Helena	MT	59620	406-841-2920	841-2930
Business & Occupational Licensing Bureau PO Box 200513 *Web:* www.state.mt.us	Helena	MT	59620	406-841-2300	841-2305
Child & Family Services Div 1400 Broadway PO Box 8005 *Web:* www.dphhs.mt.gov	Helena	MT	59604	406-444-5900	841-2487
Child Support Enforcement Div PO Box 202943 *Web:* www.dphhs.state.mt.us	Helena	MT	59620	406-444-9767	444-9626
Commerce Dept PO Box 200501 *Web:* www.commerce.state.mt.us	Helena	MT	59620	406-841-2700	841-2701
Commissioner of Political Practices 1205 8th Ave PO Box 202401 *Web:* www.politicalpractices.mt.gov	Helena	MT	59620	406-444-2942	444-1643
Community Development Div 1424 9th Ave *Web:* www.commerce.state.mt.us	Helena	MT	59620	406-444-3814	444-1872
Consumer Protection Office 2225 11th Ave PO Box 200501 *TF:* 800-481-6896 ■ *Web:* www.doj.mt.gov	Helena	MT	59620	406-444-4500	444-9680
Corrections Dept PO Box 201301 *Web:* www.cor.state.mt.us	Helena	MT	59620	406-444-3930	444-4920
Court Administration 215 N Sanders St Rm 315 *Web:* www.montanacourts.org	Helena	MT	59620	406-444-2621	444-0834
Disability Services Div 111 N Sanders St *Web:* www.dphhs.mt.gov	Helena	MT	59604	406-444-2590	444-3632
Disaster & Emergency Services Div PO Box 4789 *Web:* www.dma.mt.gov/des	Fort Harrison	MT	59636	406-841-3911	841-3965

				Phone	Fax
Environmental Quality Dept PO Box 200901 *Web:* www.deq.state.mt.us	Helena	MT	59620	406-444-2544	444-4386
Fish Wildlife & Parks Dept 1420 E 6th Ave *Web:* www.fwp.state.mt.us	Helena	MT	59620	406-444-2535	444-4952
Forensic Science Div 2679 Palmer St *Web:* www.doj.mt.gov	Missoula	MT	59808	406-728-4970	549-1067
Governor PO Box 200801 *Web:* www.governor.mt.gov	Helena	MT	59620	406-444-3111	444-5529
Healthcare Licensing Bureau 301 S Pk Ave Rm 430 *Web:* www.discoveringmontana.com	Helena	MT	59620	406-841-2303	841-2305
Higher Education Board of Regents 2500 Broadway St PO Box 203201 *TF:* 877-501-1722 ■ *Web:* www.mus.edu	Helena	MT	59620	406-444-6570	444-1469
Highway Patrol Div 2550 Prospect Ave *Web:* www.doj.state.mt.us	Helena	MT	59620	406-444-7000	444-4169
Historical Society 225 N Roberts St *TF:* 800-243-9900 ■ *Web:* www.his.state.mt.us	Helena	MT	59601	406-444-2694	444-2696
Horse Racing Board 1424 9th Ave *Web:* www.mt.gov	Helena	MT	59601	406-444-4287	444-4305
Housing Div PO Box 200528 *Web:* www.housing.mt.gov	Helena	MT	59620	406-841-2840	841-2841
Information Technology Services Div 125 N Roberts St *TF:* 800-628-4917 ■ *Web:* www.itsd.mt.gov	Helena	MT	59601	406-444-2700	444-2701
Insurance Div 840 Flelena Ave *Web:* www.discoveringmontana.com/sao/insurance	Helena	MT	59601	406-444-2040	444-3497
Labor & Industry Dept PO Box 1728 *Web:* www.dli.mt.gov	Helena	MT	59624	406-444-2840	444-1394
Legislative Services PO Box 201706 *Web:* www.leg.state.mt.us	Helena	MT	59620	406-444-4800	444-3036
Lieutenant Governor 1301 E 6th Ave *Web:* www.governor.mt.gov	Helena	MT	59601	406-444-5551	444-4648
Motor Vehicle Div PO Box 201430 *Web:* www.doj.mt.gov	Helena	MT	59620	406-444-1772	444-1631
Natural Resources & Conservation Dept 1625 11th Ave *Web:* www.dnrc.mt.gov	Helena	MT	59620	406-444-2074	444-2684
Parks Div PO Box 200701 *Web:* www.fwp.state.mt.us	Helena	MT	59620	406-444-3750	444-4952
Promotion Div (Travel Montana) PO Box 200533 *TF:* 800-847-4868 ■ *Web:* www.visitmt.com	Helena	MT	59620	406-841-2870	841-2871
Public Education Board 46 N Last Chance Gulch PO Box 200601 *Web:* www.bpe.state.mt.us	Helena	MT	59620	406-444-6576	444-0847
Public Health & Human Services Dept PO Box 4210 *Web:* www.dphhs.mt.gov	Helena	MT	59604	406-444-5622	444-1970
Public Instruction Office PO Box 202501 *TF:* 888-231-9393 ■ *Web:* www.opi.state.mt.us	Helena	MT	59620	406-444-3680	444-2893
Public Service Commission PO Box 202601 *Web:* www.psc.state.mt.us	Helena	MT	59620	406-444-6199	444-7618
Revenue Dept PO Box 5805 *Web:* www.discoveringmontana.com	Helena	MT	59604	406-444-6900	444-3696
Secretary of State PO BOx 202801 *Web:* www.sos.state.mt.us	Helena	MT	59620	406-444-2034	444-3976
Securities Dept 840 Helena Ave *Web:* www.sao.mt.gov	Helena	MT	59601	406-444-2040	444-5558
Senior & Long Term Care Div 111 N Sanders St Rm 210 *Web:* www.dphhs.state.mt.us	Helena	MT	59604	406-444-4077	444-7743
State Auditor Office 840 Helena Ave *Web:* www.sao.mt.gov	Helena	MT	59601	406-444-2040	444-3497
State Legislature State Capitol *Web:* www.leg.state.mt.us	Helena	MT	59620	406-444-4800	444-3036
Supreme Court 215 N Sanders St Rm 323 *Web:* www.lawlibrary.state.mt.us	Helena	MT	59620	406-444-3858	444-5705
Transportation Dept 2701 Prospect Ave PO Box 201001 *Web:* www.mdt.mt.gov	Helena	MT	59620	406-444-6200	444-7643
Veterans' Affairs Board PO Box 5715 *Web:* www.dma.mt.gov	Helena	MT	59604	406-324-3740	324-3145
Victim Services Office PO Box 201410 *Web:* www.doj.state.mt.us	Helena	MT	59620	406-444-3653	444-9680
Vital Records Bureau PO Box 4210 *TF:* 888-877-1946 ■ *Web:* www.dphhs.mt.gov	Helena	MT	59604	406-444-4228	444-1803
Weights & Measures Program PO Box 200516 *Web:* www.bsd.dli.mt.gov/bc/ms_index.asp	Helena	MT	59620	406-443-8065	443-8163
Worker's Compensation Ct PO Box 537 *Web:* www.wcc.dli.mt.gov	Helena	MT	59624	406-444-7794	444-7798

342-28 Nebraska

				Phone	Fax
State Government Information 521 S 14th St Suite 300 *Web:* www.nebraska.gov	Lincoln	NE	68508	402-471-2311	
Accountability & Disclosure Commission PO Box 95086 *Web:* www.nadc.nol.org	Lincoln	NE	68509	402-471-2522	471-6599
Aging Div PO Box 95026 *Web:* www.hhs.state.ne.us/ags/agsindex.htm	Lincoln	NE	68509	402-471-2307	471-4619
Agriculture Dept 301 Centennial Mall S *Web:* www.agr.state.ne.us	Lincoln	NE	68509	402-471-2341	471-2759
Arts Council 1004 Farnam St *TF:* 800-341-4067 ■ *Web:* www.nebraskaartscouncil.org	Omaha	NE	68131	402-595-2122	595-2334
Attorney General 1445 K St # 2115 *Web:* www.ago.state.ne.us	Lincoln	NE	68508	402-471-2682	471-3297
Banking & Finance Dept 1230 'O' St Suite 400 PO Box 95006 *Web:* www.ndbf.org	Lincoln	NE	68509	402-471-2171	471-3062
Child Support Enforcement Div PO Box 94728 *TF:* 877-631-9973 ■ *Web:* www.hhs.state.ne.us	Lincoln	NE	68509	402-471-8715	471-7311
Children's Services Div PO Box 95026 *Web:* www.hhs.state.ne.us/chs/chsindex.htm	Lincoln	NE	68509	402-471-9331	471-9034
Consumer Protection Div 2115 State Capitol Bldg *TF:* 800-727-6432 ■ *Web:* www.ago.state.ne.us	Lincoln	NE	68509	402-471-2682	471-0006
Coordinating Commission for Postsecondary Educatio 140 N 8th St Suite 300 PO Box 95005 *Web:* www.ccpe.state.ne.us	Lincoln	NE	68509	402-471-2847	471-2886
Correctional Services Dept PO Box 94661 *Web:* www.corrections.state.ne.us	Lincoln	NE	68509	402-471-2654	479-5119
Crime Victim Reparations Programs PO Box 94946	Lincoln	NE	68509	402-471-2828	471-2837
Economic Development Dept 301 Centennial Mall S PO Box 94666 *TF:* 800-426-6505 ■ *Web:* www.neded.org	Lincoln	NE	68509	402-471-3747	471-3778
Education Dept PO Box 94987 *Web:* www.education.ne.gov	Lincoln	NE	68509	402-471-2295	471-0117
Emergency Management Agency 1300 Military Rd *TF:* 877-297-2368 ■ *Web:* www.nema.ne.gov	Lincoln	NE	68508	402-471-7421	471-7433
Environmental Quality Dept 1200 N St Suite 400 *TF:* 877-253-2603 ■ *Web:* www.deq.state.ne.us	Lincoln	NE	68508	402-471-2186	471-2909
Game & Parks Commission PO Box 30370 *Web:* www.ngpc.state.ne.us	Lincoln	NE	68503	402-471-0641	471-5528
Governor PO Box 94848 *Web:* gov.nol.org	Lincoln	NE	68509	402-471-2244	471-6031
Health & Human Services Dept 301 Centennial Mall S *TF:* 800-430-3244 ■ *Web:* www.hhs.state.ne.us	Lincoln	NE	68508	402-471-3121	471-9449
Health Regulations & Licensure Div PO Box 95026 *Web:* www.hhs.state.ne.us	Lincoln	NE	68509	402-471-2133	471-9449
Historical Society 1500 R St *TF:* 800-833-6747 ■ *Web:* www.nebraskahistory.org	Lincoln	NE	68501	402-471-3270	471-3100
Insurance Dept 941 O St Suite 400 *TF:* 877-564-7323 ■ *Web:* www.doi.ne.gov	Lincoln	NE	68508	402-471-2201	471-4610
Investment Finance Authority 1230 'O' St Suite 200 *TF:* 800-204-6432 ■ *Web:* www.nifa.org	Lincoln	NE	68508	402-434-3900	434-3921
Lieutenant Governor 1445 K St # 2315 *Web:* www.ltgov.ne.gov	Lincoln	NE	68508	402-471-2256	471-6031
Motor Vehicles Dept PO Box 94789 *Web:* www.dmv.state.ne.us	Lincoln	NE	68509	402-471-3900	471-9594
Natural Resources Dept 301 Centennial Mall S 4th Fl *Web:* www.dnr.state.ne.us	Lincoln	NE	68509	402-471-2363	471-2900
Parks Div 2200 N 33rd St *Web:* www.ngpc.state.ne.us	Lincoln	NE	68503	402-471-0641	471-5528
Parole Board PO Box 94754 *Web:* www.parole.state.ne.us	Lincoln	NE	68509	402-471-2156	471-2453
Power Review Board 301 Centennial Mall S *Web:* www.nprb.state.ne.us	Lincoln	NE	68508	402-471-2301	471-3715
Public Accountancy Board 140 N 8th St # 290 *Web:* www.nbpa.ne.gov	Lincoln	NE	68508	402-471-3595	471-4484
Public Service Commission 1200 N St Suite 300 *TF:* 800-526-0017 ■ *Web:* www.psc.state.ne.us	Lincoln	NE	68508	402-471-3101	471-0254
Real Estate Commission 1200 N St Suite 402 PO Box 94667 *Web:* www.nrec.state.ne.us	Lincoln	NE	68509	402-471-2004	471-4492
Revenue Dept 301 Centennial Mall S 2nd Fl PO Box 94818 *TF:* 800-742-7474 ■ *Web:* www.revenue.state.ne.us	Lincoln	NE	68509	402-471-5729	471-5608
Secretary of State 1445 K St # 2300 *Web:* www.sos.state.ne.us	Lincoln	NE	68508	402-471-2554	471-3237
Securities Bureau 1230 'O' St Suite 400 PO Box 95006 *Web:* www.ndbf.org	Lincoln	NE	68509	402-471-3445	471-3062
State Court Administrator State Capitol Bldg Rm 1213	Lincoln	NE	68509	402-471-3730	471-2197
State Patrol PO Box 94907 *Web:* www.nsp.state.ne.us	Lincoln	NE	68509	402-471-4545	479-4002
State Racing Commission 301 Centennial Mall S 6th Fl PO Box 95014 *Web:* www.horseracing.state.ne.us	Lincoln	NE	68509	402-471-4155	471-2339
Supreme Court State Capitol Bldg *Web:* court.nol.org	Lincoln	NE	68509	402-471-3731	471-3480
Teacher Certification Office PO Box 94987 *Web:* www.nde.state.ne.us/tcert/tcert.html	Lincoln	NE	68509	402-471-2496	471-9735
Travel & Tourism Div PO Box 98907 *TF:* 877-632-7275 ■ *Web:* www.visitnebraska.org	Lincoln	NE	68509	402-471-3796	471-3026
Treasurer PO Box 94788 *Web:* www.treasurer.state.ne.us	Lincoln	NE	68509	402-471-2455	471-4390
Unicameral Legislature PO Box 94604 *Web:* www.nebraskalegislature.gov	Lincoln	NE	68509	402-471-2271	471-2126
Veterans' Affairs Dept 301 Centennial Mall S # 4 *Web:* www.vets.state.ne.us	Lincoln	NE	68508	402-471-2458	471-2491

	City	State	ZIP	Phone	Fax
Vital Statistics Div 1033 "O" St Suite 130 PO Box 95065 *Web:* www.hhs.state.ne.us/vitalrecords	Lincoln	NE	68509	402-471-2871	
Vocational Rehabilitation Services Div PO Box 94987 *TF:* 877-637-3422 ■ *Web:* www.vocrehab.state.ne.us	Lincoln	NE	68509	402-471-3644	471-0788
Weights & Measures Div 301 Centennial Mall S *Web:* www.agr.state.ne.us	Lincoln	NE	68508	402-471-4292	471-2759
Workers' Compensation Court PO Box 98908 *TF:* 800-599-5155 ■ *Web:* www.wcc.ne.gov	Lincoln	NE	68509	402-471-6468	471-2700
Workforce Development - Dept of Labor 550 S 16th St PO Box 94600 *Web:* www.dol.nebraska.gov	Lincoln	NE	68508	402-471-9000	471-2318

342-29 Nevada

	City	State	ZIP	Phone	Fax
State Government Information 101 N Carson St *Web:* nv.gov	Carson City	NV	89701	775-687-5000	
Accountancy Board 1325 Airmotive Way Suite 220 *Web:* www.nvaccountancy.com	Reno	NV	89502	775-786-0231	786-0234
Administrative Office of the Courts 201 S Carson St Suite 250 *Web:* nevadajudiciary.us/index.php/administrativeofficesofthecourt	Carson City	NV	89701	775-684-1700	684-1723
Aging Services Div 1860 E Sahara Ave *Web:* www.aging.state.nv.us	Las Vegas	NV	89104	702-486-3545	486-3572
Arts Council 716 N Carson St Suite A *Web:* www.dmla.clan.lib.nv.us	Carson City	NV	89701	775-687-6680	687-6688
Attorney General 100 N Carson St *Web:* www.ag.state.nv.us	Carson City	NV	89701	775-684-1100	684-1108
Bill Status 401 S Carson St *TF:* 800-992-6761 ■ *Web:* www.leg.state.nv.us	Carson City	NV	89701	775-684-3360	
Business & Industry Dept 555 E Washington Ave Suite 4900 *Web:* www.dbi.state.nv.us	Las Vegas	NV	89101	702-486-2750	486-2758
Child & Family Services Div 4126 Technology Way 3rd Fl *Web:* www.dcfs.state.nv.us	Carson City	NV	89706	775-684-4400	684-4455
Child Support Enforcement Office 1470 College Pkwy *TF:* 800-992-0900 ■ *Web:* dwss.nv.gov	Carson City	NV	89706	775-684-0500	684-0646
Commission on Ethics 704 W Nye Ln Suite 204 *Web:* www.ethics.nv.gov	Carson City	NV	89703	775-687-5469	687-1279
Conservation & Natural Resources Dept 901 S Stewart St Suite 5001 *Web:* www.dcnr.nv.gov	Carson City	NV	89701	775-684-2700	684-2715
Consumer Affairs Div 1850 E Sahara Ave Suite 101 *Web:* www.fyiconsumer.org	Las Vegas	NV	89104	702-486-7355	486-7371
Corrections Dept PO Box 7011 *Web:* www.doc.nv.gov	Carson City	NV	89702	775-887-3285	687-6715
Cultural Affairs Dept 716 N Carson St Suite B *Web:* www.dmla.clan.lib.nv.us	Carson City	NV	89701	775-687-8393	684-5446
Economic Development Commission 808 W Nye Ln *TF:* 800-336-1600 ■ *Web:* www.diversifynevada.com	Carson City	NV	89703	775-687-9900	687-9924
Education Dept 700 E 5th St *Web:* www.nde.state.nv.us	Carson City	NV	89701	775-687-9200	687-9101
Emergency Management Div 2478 Fairview Dr *Web:* www.dem.state.nv.us	Carson City	NV	89701	775-687-0300	687-0322
Employment Training & Rehabilitation Dept 500 E 3rd St Rm 200 *Web:* www.nvdetr.org	Carson City	NV	89713	775-684-3911	684-3908
Environmental Protection Div 901 S Stewart St Suite 4001 *Web:* www.ndep.nv.gov	Carson City	NV	89701	775-687-4670	687-5856
Financial Institutions Div 2785 E Desert Inn Rd Suite 180 *Web:* www.fid.state.nv.us	Las Vegas	NV	89121	775-486-4120	486-4563
Gaming Commission 1919 College Pkwy PO Box 8003 *Web:* gaming.nv.gov/ngc_main.htm	Carson City	NV	89706	775-684-7750	687-5817
Governor 101 N Carson St *Web:* gov.state.nv.us	Carson City	NV	89701	775-684-5670	684-5683
Health Div 4150 Technology Way Suite 300 *Web:* health2k.state.nv.us	Carson City	NV	89706	775-684-4200	684-4211
Highway Patrol Div 555 Wright Way *Web:* www.ps.state.nv.us	Carson City	NV	89711	775-687-5300	684-4879
Historic Preservation Office 100 N Stewart St *Web:* www.dmla.clan.lib.nv.us	Carson City	NV	89701	775-684-3440	684-3442
Housing Div 1535 Old Hot Springs Rd Suite 50 *Web:* www.nvhousing.state.nv.us	Carson City	NV	89706	775-687-2040	687-4040
Human Resources Dept 4126 Technology Way Rm 100 *Web:* hr.state.nv.us	Carson City	NV	89706	775-684-4000	684-4010
Information Technology Dept 400 W King St Suite 300 *Web:* www.doit.nv.gov	Carson City	NV	89703	775-684-5800	684-5846
Insurance Div 1818 E College Pkwy Suite 103 *Web:* doi.state.nv.us	Carson City	NV	89706	775-687-0700	687-0787
Legislature 401 S Carson St *Web:* www.leg.state.nv.us	Carson City	NV	89701	775-684-6800	687-5962
Lieutenant Governor 101 N Carson St Suite 2 *Web:* www.ltgov.nv.gov	Carson City	NV	89701	775-684-7111	684-7110
Medical Examiners Board 1105 Terminal Way Suite 301 *Web:* www.medboard.nv.gov	Reno	NV	89502	775-688-2559	688-2321
Motor Vehicles Dept 555 Wright Way *TF:* 877-368-7828 ■ *Web:* www.dmvnv.com	Carson City	NV	89711	775-684-4368	684-4770
Parole & Probation Div 1445 Old Hot Springs Rd Suite 104 *Web:* www.dps.nv.gov	Carson City	NV	89706	775-687-5040	684-2699
Postsecondary Education Commission 3663 E Sunset Rd # 202 *Web:* www.cpe.state.nv.us	Las Vegas	NV	89120	702-486-7330	486-7340
Public Safety Dept 555 Wright Way	Carson City	NV	89711	775-684-4556	684-4809
Public Utilities Commission 1150 E William St *Web:* puc.nv.gov	Carson City	NV	89701	775-684-6101	684-6110
Real Estate Div 2501 E Sahara Ave Suite 102 *Web:* www.red.state.nv.us	Las Vegas	NV	89104	702-486-4033	486-4275
Rehabilitation Div 1370 S Curry St *Web:* www.nv.gov	Carson City	NV	89703	775-684-4040	684-4184
Secretary of State 101 N Carson St Suite 3 *TF:* 800-450-8594 ■ *Web:* sos.state.nv.us	Carson City	NV	89701	775-684-5708	684-5725
Securities Div 555 E Washington Ave Suite 5200 *TF:* 800-758-6440 ■ *Web:* www.sos.state.nv.us	Las Vegas	NV	89101	702-486-2440	486-2452
State Athletic Commission 555 E Washington Ave Suite 3300 *Web:* www.boxing.nv.gov	Las Vegas	NV	89101	702-486-2575	486-2577
State Parks Div 901 S Stewart St 5th Fl *Web:* www.parks.nv.gov	Carson City	NV	89701	775-684-2770	684-2777
Supreme Court 201 S Carson St Suite 250 *Web:* www.nevadajudiciary.us	Carson City	NV	89701	775-684-1600	
System of Higher Education 2601 Enterprise Rd *Web:* www.nevada.edu	Reno	NV	89512	775-784-4901	784-1127
Taxation Dept 1550 E College Pkwy Suite 115 *Web:* tax.state.nv.us	Carson City	NV	89706	775-684-2000	684-2020
Teacher Licensure Office 700 E 5th St *Web:* www.doe.nv.gov	Carson City	NV	89701	775-687-9115	687-9101
Tourism Commission 401 N Carson St *TF:* 800-237-0774 ■ *Web:* www.travelnevada.com	Carson City	NV	89701	775-687-4322	687-6159
Transportation Dept 1263 S Stewart St *Web:* www.nevadadot.com	Carson City	NV	89712	775-888-7000	888-7115
Treasurer 101 N Carson St Suite 4 *Web:* https://nevadatreasurer.gov/index.htm	Carson City	NV	89701	775-684-5600	684-5781
Veterans Services Office 5460 Reno Corporate Dr *Web:* www.veterans.nv.gov	Reno	NV	89511	775-688-1653	688-1656
Vital Statistics Office 4150 Technology Way Suite 104 *Web:* health2k.state.nv.us/vital	Carson City	NV	89706	775-684-4242	684-4156
Weights & Measures Bureau 2150 Frazier Ave *Web:* www.agri.state.nv.us	Sparks	NV	89431	775-688-1166	688-2533
Welfare Div 1470 College Pkwy *TF:* 800-992-0900 ■ *Web:* welfare.state.nv.us	Carson City	NV	89706	775-684-0500	684-0646

342-30 New Hampshire

	City	State	ZIP	Phone	Fax
State Government Information 64 S St *Web:* www.nh.gov	Concord	NH	03301	603-271-1110	
Accountancy Board 78 Regional Dr Bldg 2 *Web:* www.nh.gov	Concord	NH	03301	603-271-3286	271-8702
Administrative Office of the Courts 2 Charles Doe Dr *Web:* www.courts.state.nh.us/aoc	Concord	NH	03301	603-271-2521	513-5454
Agriculture Markets & Food Dept PO Box 2042 *Web:* agriculture.nh.gov	Concord	NH	03302	603-271-3551	271-1109
Arts Council 2 1/2 Beacon St 2nd Fl *Web:* www.nh.gov/nharts	Concord	NH	03301	603-271-2789	271-3584
Attorney General 33 Capitol St *Web:* www.nh.gov	Concord	NH	03301	603-271-3658	271-2110
Banking Dept 53 Regional Dr Suite 200 *TF:* 800-437-5991 ■ *Web:* www.nh.gov	Concord	NH	03301	603-271-3561	271-1090
Board of Medicine 2 Industrial Pk Dr Suite 8 *Web:* www.nh.gov	Concord	NH	03301	603-271-1203	271-6702
Bureau of Elderly & Adult Services 129 Pleasant St *Web:* www.dhhs.nh.gov	Concord	NH	03301	603-271-4680	271-4643
Chief Medical Examiner 246 Pleasant St Suite 218	Concord	NH	03301	603-271-1235	271-6308
Child Support Services 129 Pleasant St *Web:* www.dhhs.state.nh.us/DHHS/DCSS	Concord	NH	03301	603-271-8140	271-4787
Children Youth & Families Div 129 Pleasant St 4th Fl *Web:* www.dhhs.state.nh.us	Concord	NH	03301	603-271-4451	271-4729
Consumer Protection Bureau 33 Capitol St *Web:* www.doj.nh.gov	Concord	NH	03301	603-271-3641	271-2110

				Phone	Fax
Corrections Dept PO Box 1806 *Web:* www.state.nh.us/nhdoc	Concord	NH	03302	603-271-5600	271-5643
Education Dept 101 Pleasant St *Web:* www.ed.state.nh.us	Concord	NH	03301	603-271-3494	271-1953
Emergency Management Office 33 Hazen Dr *Web:* www.nhoem.state.nh.us	Concord	NH	03305	603-271-2231	225-7341
Employment Security 32 S Main St *TF:* 800-852-3400 ■ *Web:* www.nh.gov	Concord	NH	03301	603-224-3311	228-4145
Environmental Services Dept 29 Hazen Dr PO Box 95 *TF:* 800-735-2964 ■ *Web:* des.nh.gov	Concord	NH	03301	603-271-3503	271-2867
Fish & Game Dept 11 Hazen Dr *Web:* www.wildlife.state.nh.us	Concord	NH	03301	603-271-3511	271-1438
General Court 107 N Main St Rm 302 *Web:* gencourt.state.nh.us	Concord	NH	03301	603-271-2111	271-2105
Governor State House 107 N Main St Rm 208 *Web:* www.nh.gov	Concord	NH	03301	603-271-2121	271-7680
Health & Human Services Dept 6 Hazen Dr *Web:* www.dhhs.state.nh.us	Concord	NH	03301	603-271-4685	271-4912
Historical Resources Div 19 Pillsbury St *Web:* www.nh.gov/nhdhr	Concord	NH	03301	603-271-3483	271-3433
Housing Finance Authority PO Box 5087 *TF:* 800-439-7247 ■ *Web:* www.nhhfa.org	Manchester	NH	03108	603-472-8623	472-8501
Insurance Dept 21 S Fruit St Suite 14 *Web:* www.nh.gov	Concord	NH	03301	603-271-2261	271-1406
Joint Board of Licensure & Certification 57 Regional Dr *Web:* www.state.nh.us/jtboard	Concord	NH	03301	603-271-2219	271-6990
Labor Dept 95 Pleasant St *Web:* www.labor.state.nh.us	Concord	NH	03301	603-271-3171	271-6852
Lottery Commission 14 Integra Dr *TF:* 800-852-3324 ■ *Web:* www.nhlottery.org	Concord	NH	03301	603-271-3391	271-1160
Motor Vehicles Div 23 Hazen Dr *Web:* www.nh.gov/dmv	Concord	NH	03305	603-271-2251	271-1061
Parks & Recreation Div 172 Pembroke Rd *Web:* www.nhparks.state.nh.us	Concord	NH	03301	603-271-3556	271-3553
Parole Board PO Box 14 *Web:* www.nh.gov/nhdoc/divisions/parole/index.html	Concord	NH	03302	603-271-2569	271-6179
Postsecondary Education Commission 3 Barrell Ct Suite 300 *TF:* 800-735-2964 ■ *Web:* www.nh.gov	Concord	NH	03301	603-271-2555	271-2696
Public Utilities Commission 21 S Fruit St Suite 10 *TF Consumer Assistance:* 800-852-3793 ■ *Web:* www.puc.state.nh.us	Concord	NH	03301	603-271-2431	271-3878
Real Estate Commission 25 Capitol St Rm 434 *Web:* www.nh.gov/nhrec	Concord	NH	03301	603-271-2701	271-1039
Resources & Economic Development Dept PO Box 1856 *Web:* www.dred.state.nh.us	Concord	NH	03302	603-271-2412	271-2629
Revenue Administration Dept 45 Chenell Dr *Web:* www.nh.gov/revenue	Concord	NH	03301	603-271-2191	271-1756
Secretary of State 107 N Main St State House Rm 204 *Web:* www.sos.nh.gov	Concord	NH	03301	603-271-3242	271-6316
Securities Regulation Bureau State House Rm 204 *Web:* www.sos.nh.gov/securities	Concord	NH	03301	603-271-1463	271-7933
State Police Div 10 Hazen Dr *Web:* www.nh.gov/safety/nhsp	Concord	NH	03305	603-271-2575	271-2527
Supreme Court 1 Charles Doe Dr *Web:* www.courts.state.nh.us	Concord	NH	03301	603-271-2646	513-4575
Teacher Credentialing Bureau 101 Pleasant St *Web:* www.education.nh.gov	Concord	NH	03301	603-271-2408	271-1953
Transportation Dept PO Box 483 *Web:* www.nh.gov/dot	Concord	NH	03301	603-271-3734	271-3914
Travel & Tourism Development Office PO Box 1856 *TF:* 800-262-6660 ■ *Web:* www.visitnh.gov	Concord	NH	03302	603-271-2665	271-6870
Treasury Dept 25 Capitol St Rm 121 *Web:* www.nh.gov/treasury	Concord	NH	03301	603-271-2621	271-3922
Veterans Council 275 Chestnut St Rm 517 *Web:* www.nh.gov	Manchester	NH	03101	603-624-9230	624-9236
Victims' Assistance Commission 33 Capitol St *TF:* 800-300-4500 ■ *Web:* www.nh.gov	Concord	NH	03301	603-271-1284	223-6291
Vital Records Bureau 71 S Fruit St *TF:* 800-735-2964 ■ *Web:* www.sos.nh.gov/vitalrecords	Concord	NH	03301	603-271-4650	271-3447
Vocational Rehabilitation Office 21 S Fruit St Suite 20 *TF:* 800-299-1647 ■ *Web:* www.education.nh.gov	Concord	NH	03301	603-271-3471	271-7095
Weights & Measures Bureau PO Box 2042 *Web:* agriculture.nh.gov/about/weights_measures.htm	Concord	NH	03302	603-271-3709	271-1109
Worker's Compensation Div 95 Pleasant St *TF:* 800-272-4353 ■ *Web:* www.labor.state.nh.us	Concord	NH	03301	603-271-3176	271-6149

342-31 New Jersey

				Phone	Fax
State Government Information PO Box 212 *Web:* www.newjersey.gov	Trenton	NJ	08625	609-292-2121	633-8888
Administrative Office of the Cts 25 Market St PO Box 037 *Web:* www.judiciary.state.nj.us	Trenton	NJ	08625	609-984-0275	984-6968
Aging & Community Services Div PO Box 807 *Web:* www.newjersey.gov	Trenton	NJ	08625	609-943-3437	588-3317
Agriculture Dept PO Box 330 *Web:* www.state.nj.us/agriculture	Trenton	NJ	08625	609-292-3976	292-3978
Arts Council 225 W State St PO Box 306 *Web:* www.njartscouncil.org	Trenton	NJ	08625	609-292-6130	989-1440
Attorney General 25 Market St PO Box 080 *Web:* www.state.nj.us	Trenton	NJ	08625	609-292-4925	292-3508
Banking & Insurance Dept 20 W State St PO Box 325 *TF:* 800-446-7467 ■ *Web:* www.state.nj.us/dobi	Trenton	NJ	08625	609-292-7272	984-5273
Bill Status State House Annex PO Box 068 *TF:* 800-792-8630 ■ *Web:* www.njleg.state.nj.us	Trenton	NJ	08625	609-292-4840	777-2440
Child Support Office PO Box 716 *TF:* 800-621-5437 ■ *Web:* www.njchildsupport.org	Trenton	NJ	08625	609-588-2385	588-2354
Commerce Economic Growth & Tourism Commission 20 W State St PO Box 820 *Web:* www.state.nj.us/commerce	Trenton	NJ	08625	609-777-0885	777-4097
Community Affairs Dept 101 S Broad St PO Box 204 *Web:* www.nj.gov/dca	Trenton	NJ	08625	609-777-3474	292-3292
Consumer Affairs Div 124 Halsey St *Web:* www.state.nj.us	Newark	NJ	07102	973-504-6200	648-3538
Corrections Dept PO Box 863 *Web:* www.state.nj.us	Trenton	NJ	08625	609-292-4036	292-9083
Economic Development Authority PO Box 990 **Fax:* PR ■ *Web:* www.njeda.com	Trenton	NJ	08625	609-292-1800	292-5722*
Education Dept PO Box 500 *Web:* www.state.nj.us/education	Trenton	NJ	08625	609-292-4450	777-4099
Emergency Management Office PO Box 7068 *Web:* www.njsp.org/feedback.html	West Trenton	NJ	08628	609-882-2000	538-0345
Environmental Protection Dept 401 E State St PO Box 402 *Web:* www.state.nj.us/dep	Trenton	NJ	08625	609-292-2885	292-1921
Ethical Standards Commission 28 W State St Rm 1407 PO Box 082 *Web:* www.state.nj.us/lps/ethics	Trenton	NJ	08625	609-292-1892	633-9252
Fish Game & Wildlife Div PO Box 400 *Web:* www.state.nj.us/dep/fgw	Trenton	NJ	08625	609-292-9410	984-1414
Governor 125 W State St PO Box 001 *Web:* www.state.nj.us/governor	Trenton	NJ	08625	609-292-6000	292-3454
Health & Senior Services Dept PO Box 360 *Web:* www.state.nj.us/health	Trenton	NJ	08625	609-292-7837	984-5474
Higher Education Student Assistance Authority 4 Quakerbridge Plaza PO Box 540 *TF:* 800-792-8670 ■ *Web:* www.hesaa.org	Trenton	NJ	08625	609-588-7944	588-7389
Historical Commission 225 W State St PO Box 305 *Web:* www.state.nj.us	Trenton	NJ	08625	609-292-6062	633-8168
Housing & Mortgage Finance Agency 637 S Clinton Ave PO Box 18550 *Web:* www.state.nj.us/dca/hmfa	Trenton	NJ	08650	609-278-7400	278-1754
Human Services Dept 240 W State St PO Box 700 *Web:* www.state.nj.us/humanservices	Trenton	NJ	08625	609-292-3717	292-3824
Information Technology Office PO Box 212 *Web:* www.nj.gov/it/oit	Trenton	NJ	08625	609-777-3861	633-8888
Labor & Workforce Development Dept PO Box 110 *Web:* www.state.nj.us/labor	Trenton	NJ	08625	609-292-2323	633-9271
Lottery PO Box 041 *Web:* www.state.nj.us	Trenton	NJ	08625	609-599-5800	599-5935
Mental Health Services Div PO Box 272 *TF:* 800-382-9717 ■ *Web:* www.state.nj.us/humanservices/dmhs	Trenton	NJ	08625	609-777-0700	777-0662
Military & Veterans' Affairs Dept 101 Eggert Crossing Rd *TF:* 800-624-0508 ■ *Web:* www.state.nj.us	Lawrenceville	NJ	08648	609-530-4600	530-7100
Motor Vehicle Commission 225 E State St PO Box 160 *TF:* 888-486-3339 ■ *Web:* www.state.nj.us/mvc	Trenton	NJ	08666	609-292-6500	777-4171
Parks & Forestry Div PO Box 404 *Web:* www.state.nj.us/dep/parksandforests	Trenton	NJ	08625	609-292-2733	984-0503
Parole Board PO Box 862 *Web:* www.state.nj.us/parole	Trenton	NJ	08625	609-292-4257	943-4769
Personnel Dept 44 S Clinton Ave PO Box 317 *Web:* www.nj.gov	Trenton	NJ	08625	609-292-4145	984-1064
Public Utilities Board 2 Gateway Ctr *Web:* www.state.nj.us/bpu	Newark	NJ	07102	973-648-2013	648-4195
Racing Commission 140 E Front St *Web:* www.njpublicsafety.org	Trenton	NJ	08625	609-292-0613	599-1785
Real Estate Commission 20 W State St PO Box 328 *Web:* www.state.nj.us/dobi/remnu.shtml	Trenton	NJ	08625	609-292-8300	292-0944
Secretary of State 125 W State St PO Box 300 *Web:* www.state.nj.us	Trenton	NJ	08625	609-984-1900	292-7665
Securities Bureau PO Box 47029 *Web:* www.state.nj.us/lps/ca/bos.htm	Newark	NJ	07101	973-504-3610	504-3639
State Athletic Control Board 140 E Front St *Web:* www.state.nj.us/lps/sacb	Trenton	NJ	08625	609-292-0317	292-3756
State Legislature State House Annex PO Box 068 *Web:* www.njleg.state.nj.us	Trenton	NJ	08625	609-292-4840	777-2440
State Medical Examiner 325 Norfolk St *Web:* www.state.nj.us/lps/dcj/sme.htm	Newark	NJ	07103	973-648-4500	648-4469
State Police PO Box 7068 *Web:* www.state.nj.us/lps/njsp	West Trenton	NJ	08628	609-882-2000	882-6920
Supreme Court PO Box 970 *Web:* www.judiciary.state.nj.us/supreme/index.htm	Trenton	NJ	08625	609-292-4837	396-9056
Transportation Dept 1035 PkwyAve PO Box 600 *Web:* www.state.nj.us/transportation	Trenton	NJ	08625	609-530-2000	530-3294

				Phone	Fax
Travel & Tourism Div PO Box 820	Trenton	NJ	08625	609-777-0885	633-7418
TF: 800-847-4865 ■ Web: www.state.nj.us/travel					
Treasurer PO Box 002	Trenton	NJ	08625	609-292-5031	984-3888
Web: www.state.nj.us/treasury					
Victims of Crime Compensation Board 50 Park Pl	Newark	NJ	07102	973-648-2107	648-3937
TF: 877-658-2221 ■ Web: www.nj.gov/oag/njvictims					
Vital Statistics Bureau 120 E Front St	Trenton	NJ	08608	609-292-4087	392-4292
Web: www.state.nj.us					
Vocational Rehabilitation Services Div PO Box 398	Trenton	NJ	08625	609-292-7318	
Web: www.state.nj.us/labor/dvrs/vrsindex.html					
Weights & Measures Office 1261 US Hwy 1 # 9	Avenel	NJ	07001	732-815-4840	382-5298
Web: www.state.nj.us					
Workers' Compensation Div PO Box 381	Trenton	NJ	08625	609-292-2414	984-2515
Web: www.state.nj.us/labor/wc/wcindex.html					
Workforce New Jersey PO Box 110	Trenton	NJ	08625	609-292-2000	777-0483
Web: www.wnjpin.net					
Higher Education Commission 20 W State St PO Box 542	Trenton	NJ	08625	609-292-4310	292-7225
Web: www.state.nj.us					

342-32 New Mexico

				Phone	Fax
State Government Information 490 Old Santa Fe Trail	Santa Fe	NM	87501	505-476-2200	
Web: www.newmexico.gov					
Accountancy Board 5200 Oakland Ave NE # C	Albuquerque	NM	87113	505-841-9108	476-6511
Web: www.rld.state.nm.us					
Administrative Office of the Cts 237 Don Gaspar St Rm 25	Santa Fe	NM	87501	505-827-4800	827-4824
Web: www.nmcourts.com					
Adult Parole Board 45 Penitentiary Rd	Santa Fe	NM	87508	505-827-8825	827-8933
Aging Agency 2550 Cerrillos Rd	Santa Fe	NM	87505	505-476-4799	476-4836
Web: www.nmaging.state.nm.us					
Agriculture Dept 3190 S Espina PO Box 30005	Las Cruces	NM	88003	575-646-3007	646-8120
Web: nmdaweb.nmsu.edu					
Arts Div 407 Galisteo St Suite 270	Santa Fe	NM	87501	505-827-6490	827-6043
Web: www.nmarts.org					
Attorney General PO Drawer 1508	Santa Fe	NM	87504	505-827-6000	827-5826
Web: www.nmag.gov					
Child Support Enforcement Div PO Box 25110	Santa Fe	NM	87504	505-476-7207	476-7045
Web: www.state.nm.us					
Children Youth & Families Dept PO Drawer 5160	Santa Fe	NM	87502	505-827-7610	827-9978
TF: 800-610-7610 ■ Web: www.cyfd.org					
Consumer Protection Div PO Drawer 1508	Santa Fe	NM	87504	505-827-6060	827-6685
Web: www.ago.state.nm.us					
Corrections Dept PO Box 27116	Santa Fe	NM	87502	505-827-8709	827-8220
Web: www.state.nm.us/corrections					
Crime Victims Reparation Commission 8100 Mountain Rd NE Suite 106	Albuquerque	NM	87110	505-841-9432	841-9437
TF: 800-306-6262 ■ Web: www.state.nm.us/cvrc					
Dept of Workforce Solutions 401 Broadway NE PO Box 1928	Albuquerque	NM	87103	505-841-8409	841-8491
Web: www.dws.state.nm.us					
Economic Development Dept PO Box 20003	Santa Fe	NM	87504	505-827-0300	827-0328
TF: 800-374-3061 ■ Web: www.edd.state.nm.us					
Education Dept 300 Don Gaspar St	Santa Fe	NM	87501	505-827-5800	827-6696
Web: www.sde.state.nm.us					
Energy Minerals & Natural Resources Dept PO Box 6429	Santa Fe	NM	87505	505-476-3200	476-3220
Web: www.emnrd.state.nm.us					
Environment Dept 1190 St Francis Dr Suite 4050	Santa Fe	NM	87502	505-827-2855	827-2836
TF: 800-219-6157 ■ Web: www.nmenv.state.nm.us					
Ethics Administration 325 Don Gaspar St Suite 300	Santa Fe	NM	87503	505-827-3600	827-4954
TF: 800-477-3632 ■ Web: www.sos.state.nm.us/ethics.htm					
Finance & Administration Dept 407 Galisteo St Rm 180	Santa Fe	NM	87501	505-827-4985	827-4984
Web: www.state.nm.us					
Financial Aid & Student Services Unit 1068 Cerrillos Rd	Santa Fe	NM	87505	505-476-6500	476-6511
TF: 800-279-9777 ■ Web: www.hed.state.nm.us					
Financial Institutions Div 2550 Cerrillos Rd	Santa Fe	NM	87505	505-476-4885	476-4670
Web: www.rld.state.nm.us					
Game & Fish Dept 1 Wildlife Way	Santa Fe	NM	87507	505-476-8000	476-8116
Web: www.wildlife.state.nm.us					
Governor State Capitol Bldg 490 Santa Fe Trail Rm 400	Santa Fe	NM	87501	505-827-3000	476-2226
Web: www.governor.state.nm.us					
Health Dept 1190 S St Francis Dr Suite N-4100	Santa Fe	NM	87505	505-827-2613	827-2530
Web: www.health.state.nm.us					
Highway & Transportation Dept PO Box 1149	Santa Fe	NM	87504	505-827-5100	827-3214
TF: 877-887-7094 ■ Web: www.nmshtd.state.nm.us					
Historic Preservation Div 228 E Palace Ave Rm 320	Santa Fe	NM	87501	505-827-6320	827-6338
Web: www.nmoca.com					
Human Services Dept PO Box 2348	Santa Fe	NM	87504	505-827-7750	827-6286
Web: www.state.nm.us/hsd					
Information Technology Management Office 715 Alta Vista	Santa Fe	NM	87505	505-827-2051	
Web: www.cio.state.nm.us					
Legislative Council Services 490 Old Santa Fe Trail Rm 411	Santa Fe	NM	87501	505-986-4600	986-4680
Web: www.legis.state.nm.us					
Lieutenant Governor State Capitol Bldg Rm 417	Santa Fe	NM	87501	505-476-2250	476-2257
TF: 800-432-4406					
Lottery 4511 Osuna Rd NE PO Box 93190	Albuquerque	NM	87199	505-342-7600	342-7511
Web: www.nmlottery.com					
Medical Board 2055 S Pacheco Bldg 400	Santa Fe	NM	87505	505-476-7220	476-7237
Web: www.nmmb.state.nm.us					
Medical Investigator UNM Health Science Ctr MSC11 6030	Albuquerque	NM	87131	505-272-6053	272-0727
Web: www.omi.unm.edu					
Mortgage Finance Authority 344 4th St SW	Albuquerque	NM	87102	505-843-6880	243-3289
TF: 800-444-6880 ■ Web: www.nmmfa.org					
Motor Vehicles Div PO Box 1028	Santa Fe	NM	87504	505-827-2296	827-2267
TF: 888-683-4636 ■ Web: www.state.nm.us					
Professional (Educator) Licensure Unit 300 Don Gaspar St	Santa Fe	NM	87501	505-827-6581	827-4148
Web: www.ped.state.nm.us					
Public Regulation Commission PO Box 1269	Santa Fe	NM	87504	505-827-4500	827-4747
Web: www.nmprc.state.nm.us					
Public Safety Dept PO Box 1628	Santa Fe	NM	87504	505-827-9000	827-3434
Web: www.dps.nm.org					
Racing Commission 300 San Mateo NE Suite 110	Albuquerque	NM	87108	505-841-6400	841-6413
Web: www.nmrc.state.nm.us					
Regulation & Licensing Dept 2550 Cerrillos Rd	Santa Fe	NM	87505	505-476-4500	476-4511
Web: www.rld.state.nm.us					
Secretary of State 325 Don Gaspar Ave Suite 300	Santa Fe	NM	87503	505-827-3600	827-8081
TF: 800-477-3632 ■ Web: www.sos.state.nm.us					
Securities Div 2550 Cerrillos Rd	Santa Fe	NM	87505	505-476-4580	984-0617
Web: www.rld.state.nm.us/Securities					
Standards & Consumers Services Div MSC 3170 PO Box 30005	Las Cruces	NM	88003	575-646-1616	646-2361
TF: 800-371-7099 ■					
State Legislature State Capitol Rm 100	Santa Fe	NM	87501	505-986-4751	986-4680
Web: legis.state.nm.us					
State Parks Div PO Box 1147	Santa Fe	NM	87504	505-476-3355	476-3361
TF: 888-667-2757 ■ Web: www.emnrd.state.nm.us/nmparks					
State Police Div 4491 Cerrillos Rd PO Box 1628	Santa Fe	NM	87507	505-827-9300	827-3394
Web: www.nmsp.dps.state.nm.us					
Supreme Court 237 Don Gaspar Ave	Santa Fe	NM	87501	505-827-4860	827-4837
Web: nmsupremecourt.nmcourts.gov					
Taxation & Revenue Dept PO Box 630	Santa Fe	NM	87504	505-827-0700	827-0331
Web: www.state.nm.us/tax					
Tourism Dept 491 Old Santa Fe Trail	Santa Fe	NM	87503	505-827-7400	827-7402
TF: 800-545-2070 ■ Web: www.newmexico.org					
Treasurer PO Box 608	Santa Fe	NM	87504	505-995-1120	995-1195
Web: www.stonm.org					
Veterans' Service Commission PO Box 2324	Santa Fe	NM	87504	505-827-6300	827-6372
TF: 866-433-8387 ■ Web: www.state.nm.us					
Vital Records & Health Statistics Bureau 1105 S St Francis Dr	Santa Fe	NM	87505	505-827-0121	984-1048
Web: www.dohewbs2.health.state.nm.us					
Vocational Rehabilitation Div 435 St Michaels Dr Bldg D	Santa Fe	NM	87505	505-954-8500	954-8562
TF: 800-224-7005 ■ Web: www.dvrgetsjobs.com					
Workers'' Compensation Administration PO Box 27198	Albuquerque	NM	87125	505-841-6000	841-6009
TF: 800-255-7965 ■ Web: www.state.nm.us/wca					
Workforce Solutions Dept 301 W DeVargas	Santa Fe	NM	87501	505-827-7434	827-7346
Web: www.dws.state.nm.us					
Higher Education Dept 1068 Cerrillos Rd	Santa Fe	NM	87505	505-476-1100	476-6511
TF: 800-279-9777 ■ Web: www.hed.state.nm.us					

342-33 New York

				Phone	Fax
State Government Information NYS State Capitol Bldg	Albany	NY	12224	518-474-8390	
Web: www.ny.gov					
Aging Office 2 Empire State Plaza	Albany	NY	12223	518-474-7158	
Web: www.aging.state.ny.us					
Arts Council 175 Varick St 3rd Fl	New York	NY	10014	212-627-4455	620-5911
Web: www.nysca.org					
Athletic Commission 123 William St 20th Fl	New York	NY	10038	212-417-5700	417-4987
TF: 866-269-3769 ■ Web: www.dos.state.ny.us					
Attorney General State Capitol	Albany	NY	12224	518-474-7330	474-5481
Web: www.oag.state.ny.us					
Banking Dept 1 State St	New York	NY	10004	212-709-5470	709-3582*
*Fax: Hum Res ■ TF: 877-226-5697 ■ Web: www.banking.state.ny.us					
Bill Status 55 Elk St	Albany	NY	12210	518-455-7545	455-7681
TF: 800-342-9860 ■ Web: www.assembly.state.ny.us					
Child Support Enforcement Div 40 N Pearl St	Albany	NY	12243	518-474-9081	
Web: www.newyorkchildsupport.com					
Children & Family Services Office 52 Washington St	Rensselaer	NY	12144	518-473-7793	486-7550
Web: www.ocfs.state.ny.us					
Consumer Protection Board 5 Empire State Plaza Suite 2101	Albany	NY	12223	518-474-3514	474-2474
TF: 800-697-1220 ■ Web: www.consumer.state.ny.us					

				Phone	Fax
Correctional Services Dept 1220 Washington Ave Bldg 2 *Web:* www.docs.state.ny.us	Albany	NY	12226	518-457-8126	457-7070
Court of Appeals 20 Eagle St *Web:* www.nycourts.gov	Albany	NY	12207	518-455-7700	
Crime Victims Board 845 Central Ave *Web:* www.cvb.state.ny.us	Albany	NY	12206	518-457-8727	457-8658
Education Dept 89 Washington Ave **Fax:* Hum Res ■ *Web:* www.nysed.gov	Albany	NY	12234	518-474-3852	474-5631*
Emergency Management Office 1220 Washington Ave Bldg 22 Suite 101 *Web:* www.nysemo.state.ny.us	Albany	NY	12226	518-457-8900	457-8924
Empire State Development 30 S Pearl St *TF:* 800-782-8369 ■ *Web:* www.empire.state.ny.us	Albany	NY	12245	518-292-5100	292-5812
Environmental Conservation Dept 625 Broadway 14th Fl *Web:* www.dec.state.ny.us	Albany	NY	12233	518-402-8540	402-9016
Fish Wildlife & Marine Resources Div 50 Wolf Rd # 560C *Web:* www.dec.state.ny.us	Albany	NY	12205	518-402-8924	402-8925
Governor State Capitol Executive Chamber *Web:* www.state.ny.us	Albany	NY	12224	518-474-8390	474-1513
Health Dept Empire State Plaza Corning II Tower *Web:* www.health.state.ny.us	Albany	NY	12237	518-473-8600	473-7071
Higher Education Services Corp 99 Washington Ave *TF:* 888-697-4372 ■ *Web:* www.hesc.com	Albany	NY	12255	518-473-1574	473-3749
Historic Preservation Div PO Box 189 *TF:* 800-456-2267 ■ *Web:* www.nysparks.com	Waterford	NY	12188	518-237-8643	
Housing Finance Agency 641 Lexington Ave *Web:* www.nyhomes.org	New York	NY	10022	212-688-4000	872-0789
Insurance Dept 1 Commerce Plaza *Web:* www.ins.state.ny.us	Albany	NY	12257	518-474-6600	473-6814
Investor Protection & Securities Bureau 120 Broadway 23rd Fl *Web:* www.oag.state.ny.us	New York	NY	10271	212-416-8200	416-8816
Labor Dept WA Harriman Campus Bldg 12 *TF:* 888-469-7365 ■ *Web:* www.labor.state.ny.us	Albany	NY	12240	518-457-9000	457-6908
Lieutenant Governor NYS State Capitol Bldg *Web:* www.governor.ny.gov	Albany	NY	12224	518-474-8390	
Lower Manhattan Development Corp 1 Liberty Plaza 20th Fl *Web:* www.renewnyc.com	New York	NY	10006	212-962-2300	962-2431
Mental Health Office 44 Holland Ave *TF:* 800-597-8481 ■ *Web:* www.omh.state.ny.us	Albany	NY	12229	518-474-4403	474-2149
Military & Naval Affairs Div 330 Old Niskayuna Rd *Web:* www.dmna.state.ny.us	Latham	NY	12110	518-786-4500	786-4785
Motor Vehicles Dept 6 Empire State Plaza *Web:* www.nydmv.state.ny.us	Albany	NY	12228	518-473-5595	474-9578
Office of Court Administration 25 Beaver St Rm 852 *TF:* 800-268-7869 ■ *Web:* www.courts.state.ny.us/admin	New York	NY	10004	212-428-2100	428-2188
Office of the Professions 89 Washington Ave 2nd Fl *Web:* www.op.nysed.gov	Albany	NY	12234	518-474-3817	474-1449
Parks Recreation & Historic Preservation Office 1 Empire State Plaza *TF Campground Resv:* 800-456-2267 ■ *Web:* www.nysparks.com	Albany	NY	12238	518-474-0456	486-2924
Parole Div 97 Central Ave *Web:* www.parole.state.ny.us	Albany	NY	12206	518-473-9400	473-6037
Power Authority 30 S Pearl St 10th Fl *Web:* www.nypa.gov	Albany	NY	12207	518-433-6700	433-6780
Public Service Commission 3 Empire State Plaza *Web:* www.dps.state.ny.us	Albany	NY	12223	518-474-7080	473-2838
Racing & Wagering Board 1 Broadway Ctr Suite 600 *Web:* www.racing.state.ny.us	Schenectady	NY	12305	518-395-5400	
Secretary of State 41 State St *Web:* www.dos.state.ny.us	Albany	NY	12231	518-474-0050	474-4765
State Comptroller 110 State St 15th Fl *Web:* www.osc.state.ny.us	Albany	NY	12236	518-474-4404	473-3004
State Legislature Legislative Office Bldg *Web:* public.leginfo.state.ny.us	Albany	NY	12247	518-455-2800	456-3332
State Police Div 1220 Washington Ave Bldg 22 *Web:* www.troopers.state.ny.us	Albany	NY	12226	518-457-6811	457-3207
Taxation & Finance Dept WA Harriman Campus Bldg 8 *TF:* 800-225-5829 ■ *Web:* www.tax.state.ny.us	Albany	NY	12227	518-457-2244	457-2486
Technology Office PO Box 2062 *Web:* www.oft.state.ny.us	Albany	NY	12220	518-473-9450	402-2976
Temporary & Disability Assistance Office 40 N Pearl St 16th Fl *TF:* 800-342-3009 ■ *Web:* www.otda.ny.gov	Albany	NY	12243	518-473-1090	474-7870
Tourism Div PO Box 2603 *TF:* 800-225-5697 ■ *Web:* www.iloveny.com	Albany	NY	12220	518-474-4116	486-6416
Transportation Dept 50 Wolf Rd *Web:* www.dot.state.ny.us	Albany	NY	12232	518-457-4422	457-5583
Veterans' Affairs Div 5 Empire State Plaza FL 28 *TF:* 888-838-7697 ■ *Web:* veterans.ny.gov	Albany	NY	12223	518-474-6784	473-0379
Vital Records Office PO Box 2602 *Web:* www.health.state.ny.us	Albany	NY	12220	518-474-3077	474-9168
Vocational & Educational Services for Individuals 1 Commerce Plaza Rm 1606 *Web:* www.vesid.nysed.gov	Albany	NY	12234	518-474-2714	474-8802
Workers' Compensation Board 20 Pk St *Web:* www.wcb.state.ny.us	Albany	NY	12207	518-474-6674	473-1415
Education Dept 89 Washington Ave 5N EB *Web:* www.highered.nysed.gov	Albany	NY	12234	518-474-3901	

342-34 North Carolina

				Phone	Fax
State Government Information 301 N Wilmington St Raleigh *Web:* www.ri.gov	Raleigh	NC	27601	919-733-1110	
Administrative Office of the Cts PO Box 2448 *Web:* www.nccourts.org	Raleigh	NC	27602	919-733-7107	715-5779
Aging & Adult Service Div 693 Palmer Dr *Web:* www.dhhs.state.nc.us	Raleigh	NC	27603	919-733-3983	733-0443
Agriculture Dept 2 W Edenton St 1001 MSC *Web:* www.agr.state.nc.us	Raleigh	NC	27699	919-733-7125	733-1141
Arts Council MSC 4632 Dept of Cultural Resources *Web:* www.ncarts.org	Raleigh	NC	27699	919-807-6500	807-6532
Attorney General 114 W Edenton St *Web:* www.ncdoj.com	Raleigh	NC	27603	919-716-6400	716-6750
Banking Commission 316 W Edenton St *Web:* www.nccob.org	Raleigh	NC	27603	919-733-3016	733-6918
Bill Status 16 W Jones St Rm 2226 *Web:* www.ncleg.net	Raleigh	NC	27601	919-733-7778	
Chief Medical Examiner CB 7580 *TF:* 800-672-7024 ■ *Web:* www.ocme.med.unc.edu	Chapel Hill	NC	27599	919-966-2253	962-6263
Child Support Enforcement Section PO Box 20800 *Web:* www.dhhs.state.nc.us	Raleigh	NC	29619	919-255-3800	
Commerce Dept 301 N Wilmington St *Web:* www.nccommerce.com	Raleigh	NC	27699	919-733-4151	733-9299
Consumer Protection Section 114 W Edenton St *Web:* www.ncdoj.com	Raleigh	NC	27603	919-716-6000	716-6050
Correction Dept 214 W Jones St 4201 MSC *Web:* www.doc.state.nc.us	Raleigh	NC	27699	919-716-3700	716-3794
Cultural Resources Dept 109 E Jones St *Web:* www.ncdcr.gov	Raleigh	NC	27601	919-807-7385	733-1620
Emergency Management Div 116 W Jones St *Web:* www.ncem.org	Raleigh	NC	27611	919-715-8000	733-5406
Employment Security Commission PO Box 25903 *Web:* www.ncesc.com	Raleigh	NC	27611	919-733-4329	733-8745
Environment & Natural Resources Dept 512 N Salisbury St *Web:* www.enr.state.nc.us	Raleigh	NC	27604	919-733-4984	715-3060
Ethics Board 116 W Jones St *Web:* www.doa.state.nc.us/ethics	Raleigh	NC	27603	919-733-2780	733-2785
General Assembly 16 W Jones St *Web:* www.ncleg.net	Raleigh	NC	27601	919-733-7928	715-2880
Governor 166 W Jones St 20301 MSC *Web:* www.governor.state.nc.us	Raleigh	NC	27699	919-733-5811	733-2120
Health & Human Services Dept 2001 MSC *Web:* www.dhhs.state.nc.us	Raleigh	NC	27699	919-733-4534	715-4645
Housing Finance Agency 3508 Bush St *Web:* www.nchfa.com	Raleigh	NC	27609	919-877-5700	877-5701
Information Technology Services Office 3700 Wake Forest Rd *Web:* www.its.state.nc.us	Raleigh	NC	27609	919-981-5555	981-2548
Insurance Dept 1201 MSC *Web:* www.ncdoi.com	Raleigh	NC	27699	919-733-7349	733-0085
Labor Dept 4 W Edenton St *Web:* www.dol.state.nc.us	Raleigh	NC	27601	919-733-7166	733-6197
Lieutenant Governor 310 N Blount St 20401 MSC *Web:* www.ltgov.state.nc.us	Raleigh	NC	27699	919-733-7350	733-6595
Marine Fisheries Div PO Box 769 *TF:* 800-682-2632 ■ *Web:* www.ncfisheries.net	Morehead City	NC	28557	252-726-7021	
Mental Health Developmental Disabilities & Substan 3009 MSC *Web:* www.dhhs.state.nc.us	Raleigh	NC	27699	919-715-3197	733-4962
Motor Vehicles Div 1100 New Bern Ave *Web:* www.ncdot.org	Raleigh	NC	27697	919-861-3015	733-0126
Parks & Recreation Div 1615 MSC *Web:* www.ils.unc.edu	Raleigh	NC	27699	919-733-4181	715-3085
Parole Commission 4222 MSC *Web:* www.doc.state.nc.us/parole	Raleigh	NC	27699	919-716-3010	716-3987
Public Instruction Dept 301 N Wilmington St *Web:* www.ncpublicschools.org	Raleigh	NC	27601	919-807-3300	807-3445
Real Estate Commission 1313 Navajo Dr *Web:* www.ncrec.state.nc.us	Raleigh	NC	27609	919-875-3700	877-4221
Revenue Dept 501 N Wilmington St *Web:* www.dor.state.nc.us	Raleigh	NC	27604	919-733-7211	733-0023
Secretary of State PO Box 29622 *Web:* www.secstate.state.nc.us	Raleigh	NC	27699	919-807-2005	807-2010
Securities Div PO Box 29622 *Web:* www.secretary.state.nc.us	Raleigh	NC	27626	919-733-3924	821-0818
Social Services Div 2401 MSC *Web:* www.dhhs.state.nc.us	Raleigh	NC	27699	919-733-3055	733-9386
Standards Div 2 W Edenton St 1050 MSC *Web:* www.agr.state.nc.us	Raleigh	NC	27699	919-733-3313	715-0524
State Highway Patrol 512 N Salisbury St *Web:* www.nccrimecontrol.org	Raleigh	NC	27603	919-733-7952	733-1189
State Personnel Office 116 W Jones St *Web:* www.osp.state.nc.us	Raleigh	NC	27603	919-807-4800	733-0653
State Ports Authority 2202 Burnett Blvd PO Box 9002 *TF:* 800-334-0682 ■ *Web:* www.ncports.com	Wilmington	NC	28402	910-763-1621	343-6225
State Treasurer 325 N Salisbury St *Web:* www.nctreasurer.com	Raleigh	NC	27603	919-508-5176	508-5167
Supreme Court 2 E Morgan St PO Box 2170 *Web:* www.nccourts.org	Raleigh	NC	27602	919-831-5700	733-0105

				Phone	Fax
Tourism Div 301 N Wilmington St TF: 800-847-4862 ■ Web: www.visitnc.com	Raleigh	NC	27601	919-733-4171	733-8582
Transportation Dept 1 S Wilmington St Web: www.ncdot.org	Raleigh	NC	27611	919-733-2520	733-9150
Utilities Commission 4325 Mail Service Ctr TF: 866-380-9816 ■ Web: www.ncuc.commerce.state.nc.us	Raleigh	NC	27699	919-733-7328	733-7300
Veterans Affairs Div 1315 Mail Service Ctr Web: www.doa.nc.gov	Raleigh	NC	27699	919-733-3851	733-2834
Victims Compensation Services Div 4703 MSC Web: www.nccrimecontrol.org	Raleigh	NC	27699	919-733-7974	715-4209
Vital Records Unit 225 N McDowell St Web: www.vitalrecords.dhhs.state.nc.us	Raleigh	NC	27603	919-733-3526	829-1359
Vocational Rehabilitation Services Div 2801 MSC Web: dvr.dhhs.state.nc.us	Raleigh	NC	27699	919-855-3500	733-7968
Community College System 200 W Jones St Web: www.ncccs.cc.nc.us	Raleigh	NC	27603	919-807-7100	807-7164

342-35 North Dakota

				Phone	Fax
State Government Information 600 E Blvd Ave Dept 130 Web: www.nd.gov	Bismarck	ND	58505	701-328-2471	328-3230
Accountancy Board 2701 S Columbia Rd TF: 800-532-5904 ■ Web: www.state.nd.us	Grand Forks	ND	58201	701-775-7100	775-7430
Aging Services Div 1237 W Divide Ave Suite 6 Web: www.nd.gov	Bismarck	ND	58501	701-328-4601	328-8744
Agriculture Dept 600 E Blvd Ave Dept 602 TF: 800-242-7535 ■ Web: www.agdepartment.com	Bismarck	ND	58505	701-328-2231	328-4567
Attorney General 600 E Blvd Ave Dept 125 Web: www.ag.state.nd.us	Bismarck	ND	58505	701-328-2210	328-2226
Child Support Enforcement Div 1600 E Century Ave Suite 7 TF: 800-231-4255 ■ Web: www.nd.gov/dhs/services/childsupport	Bismarck	ND	58501	701-328-3582	328-6575
Children & Family Services Div 600 E Blvd Ave Web: www.nd.gov	Bismarck	ND	58505	701-328-2316	328-3538
Consumer Protection Div 4205 State St Web: www.ag.state.nd.us	Bismarck	ND	58503	701-328-3404	328-5568
Corrections & Rehabilitation Dept 3100 Railroad Ave Web: www.state.nd.us	Bismarck	ND	58501	701-328-6390	328-6651
Court Administrator Office 600 E Blvd Ave Dept 180 Web: www.ndcourts.com	Bismarck	ND	58505	701-328-4216	328-2092
Crime Victims Compensation Program PO Box 5521	Bismarck	ND	58506	701-328-6195	328-6186
Drivers License & Traffic Safety Div 608 E Blvd Ave Web: www.dot.nd.gov/public/divdist/dlts.htm	Bismarck	ND	58505	701-328-2600	328-2435
Economic Development & Finance Div 1600 E Century Ave Suite 200-B TF: 866-432-5682 ■ Web: www.growingnd.com	Bismarck	ND	58503	701-328-5300	328-5320
Education Standards & Practices Board 2718 Gateway Ave Dept 303 Web: www.state.nd.us	Bismarck	ND	58503	701-328-9641	328-9647
Emergency Management Div PO Box 5511 Web: www.nd.gov/des	Bismarck	ND	58506	701-328-8100	328-8181
Financial Institutions Dept 2000 Schafer St Suite G TF: 800-366-6888 ■ Web: www.nd.gov/dfi	Bismarck	ND	58501	701-328-9933	328-0290
Game & Fish Dept 100 N Bismarck Expy Web: www.gf.nd.gov	Bismarck	ND	58501	701-328-6300	328-6352
Governor 600 E Blvd Ave Dept 101 Web: www.governor.state.nd.us	Bismarck	ND	58505	701-328-2200	328-2205
Health Dept 600 E Blvd Ave Dept 301 Web: www.health.state.nd.us	Bismarck	ND	58505	701-328-2372	328-4727
Highway Patrol 600 E Blvd Ave Dept 504 Web: www.state.nd.us	Bismarck	ND	58505	701-328-2455	328-1717
Historical Society 612 E Blvd Ave Web: www.state.nd.us	Bismarck	ND	58505	701-328-2666	328-3710
Housing Finance Agency PO Box 1535 TF: 800-292-8621 ■ Web: www.ndhfa.org	Bismarck	ND	58502	701-328-8080	328-8090
Human Services Dept 600 E Blvd Ave Dept 325 TF: 800-472-2622 ■ Web: www.state.nd.us	Bismarck	ND	58505	701-328-2310	328-2359
Indian Affairs Commission 600 E Blvd Ave Rm 117 Web: www.health.state.nd.us/ndiac	Bismarck	ND	58505	701-328-2428	328-1537
Information Technology Dept 600 E Blvd Ave Dept 112 Web: www.nd.gov/itd	Bismarck	ND	58505	701-328-3190	328-3000
Insurance Dept 600 E Blvd Ave Dept 401 TF: 800-247-0560 ■ Web: www.state.nd.us	Bismarck	ND	58505	701-328-2440	328-4880
Job Service PO Box 5507 TF: 800-366-6888 ■ Web: www.jobsnd.com	Bismarck	ND	58506	701-328-2825	328-4000
Labor Dept 600 E Blvd Ave Dept 406 Web: www.nd.gov/labor	Bismarck	ND	58505	701-328-2660	328-2031
Legislative Assembly State Capitol 600 E Blvd Ave Web: www.legis.nd.gov	Bismarck	ND	58505	701-328-2916	328-3615
Lieutenant Governor 600 E Blvd Ave Web: governor.nd.gov	Bismarck	ND	58505	701-328-2200	328-2205
Medical Examiners Board 418 E Broadway Suite 12 Web: www.ndbomex.com	Bismarck	ND	58501	701-328-6500	328-6505
Parks & Recreation Dept 1600 E Century Ave Suite 3 TF: 800-807-4723 ■ Web: www.parkrec.nd.gov	Bismarck	ND	58503	701-328-5357	328-5363
Parole & Probation Div 3100 E Railroad Ave Web: www.nd.gov/docr	Bismarck	ND	58501	701-328-6190	328-6651
Public Instruction Dept 600 E Blvd Ave Dept 201 Web: www.dpi.state.nd.us	Bismarck	ND	58505	701-328-2260	328-2461
Public Service Commission 600 E Blvd Ave Dept 408 Web: www.psc.state.nd.us	Bismarck	ND	58505	701-328-2400	328-2410
Racing Commission 500 N 9th St Web: www.ndracingcommission.com	Bismarck	ND	58501	701-328-4290	328-4300
Real Estate Commission 200 E Main Ave Suite 204 Web: www.realestatend.org	Bismarck	ND	58501	701-328-9749	328-9750
Secretary of State 600 E Blvd Ave Dept 108 TF: 800-352-0867 ■ Web: www.nd.gov/sos	Bismarck	ND	58505	701-328-2900	328-2992
Securities Dept 600 E Blvd Ave Dept 414 Web: www.ndsecurities.com	Bismarck	ND	58505	701-328-2910	328-2946
Student Financial Assistance Program 600 E Blvd Ave 10th Fl Dept 215 Web: www.ndus.nodak.edu	Bismarck	ND	58505	701-328-2960	328-2961
Supreme Court 600 E Blvd Ave Dept 180 Web: www.ndcourts.com	Bismarck	ND	58505	701-328-2221	328-4480
Tax Dept 600 E Blvd Ave Web: www.nd.gov	Bismarck	ND	58505	701-328-2770	328-3700
Testing & Safety Div 600 E Blvd Ave Dept 408 Web: www.psc.state.nd.us	Bismarck	ND	58505	701-328-2400	328-2410
Tourism Div 1600 Century Ave Suite 200S TF: 800-435-5663 ■ Web: www.ndtourism.com	Bismarck	ND	58502	701-328-2525	328-4878
Transportation Dept 608 E Blvd Ave Web: www.state.nd.us/dot	Bismarck	ND	58505	701-328-2500	328-1420
Treasurer 600 E Blvd Ave Web: www.nd.gov/ndtreas	Bismarck	ND	58505	701-328-2643	328-3002
University System 600 E Blvd Ave Dept 215 Web: www.ndus.edu	Bismarck	ND	58505	701-328-2960	328-2961
Veterans Affairs Dept 4201 38th St S # 104 TF: 866-634-8387 ■ Web: www.nd.gov	Fargo	ND	58104	701-239-7165	239-7166
Vital Records Div 600 E Blvd Ave Dept 301 Web: www.vitalnd.com	Bismarck	ND	58505	701-328-2360	328-1850
Vocational Rehabilitation Div 1237 W Divide Ave Suite 1B TF: 800-755-2745	Bismarck	ND	58501	701-328-8950	328-8969
Workers Compensation 1600 E Century Ave Suite 1000 TF: 800-777-5033 ■ Web: www.workforcesafety.com	Bismarck	ND	58503	701-328-3800	328-3820

342-36 Ohio

				Phone	Fax
State Government Information 1320A Arthur E Adams Dr Web: www.ohio.gov	Columbia	OH	43221	614-466-2000	
Adjutant General Dept 2825 W Dublin-Granville Rd Web: www.ohionationalguard.com	Columbus	OH	43235	614-336-7000	336-7410
Administrative Director of the Supreme Court 65 S Front St Web: www.supremecourt.ohio.gov/AD/hollon.asp	Columbus	OH	43215	614-387-9000	387-9509
Adoption Services Section 50 W Town St Suite 400 TF: 866-635-3748 ■ Web: jfs.ohio.gov/oapl	Columbus	OH	43215	614-466-9274	728-6726
Aging Dept 50 W Broad St 9th Fl Web: www.goldenbuckeye.com	Columbus	OH	43215	614-466-5500	466-5741
Agriculture Dept 8995 E Main St TF: 800-282-1955 ■ Web: www.agri.ohio.gov	Reynoldsburg	OH	43068	614-728-6201	728-6310
Arts Council 30 E Broad St # 33 Web: www.oac.state.oh.us	Columbus	OH	43215	614-466-2613	466-4494
Attorney General 30 E Broad St 17th Fl Web: www.ag.state.oh.us	Columbus	OH	43215	614-466-4320	466-5087
Child Support Office 30 E Broad St 32nd Fl TF: 800-686-1556 ■ Web: www.jfs.ohio.gov/OCS	Columbus	OH	43215	614-752-6561	752-9760
Commerce Dept 77 S High St 23rd Fl Web: www.com.state.oh.us	Columbus	OH	43215	614-466-3636	644-8292
Consumer Protection Section 30 E Broad St 14th Fl TF: 800-282-0515 ■ Web: www.ohioattorneygeneral.gov	Columbus	OH	43215	614-466-8831	728-7583
Crime Victim Services 150 E Gay St 25th Fl TF: 800-582-2877 ■ Web: www.ag.state.oh.us	Columbus	OH	43215	614-466-5610	752-2732
Development Dept 77 S High St TF: 800-848-1300 ■ Web: www.odod.state.oh.us	Columbus	OH	43215	614-466-2480	644-5167
Education Dept 25 S Front St TF: 877-644-6338 ■ Web: www.ode.state.oh.us	Columbus	OH	43215	614-466-3641	466-0599
Emergency Management Agency 2855 W Dublin-Granville Rd Web: www.ema.ohio.gov	Columbus	OH	43235	614-889-7150	889-7183
Environmental Protection Agency 122 S Front St PO Box 1049 Web: www.epa.state.oh.us	Columbus	OH	43216	614-644-3020	644-3184
Ethics Commission 30 W Spring St L3 Web: www.ethics.ohio.gov	Columbus	OH	43215	614-466-7090	466-8368
Financial Institutions Div 77 S High St 21st Fl TF: 866-278-0003 ■ Web: com.ohio.gov/fiin	Columbus	OH	43266	614-728-8400	728-0380

	City	State	Zip	Phone	Fax
General Assembly State House *Web:* www.legislature.state.oh.us	Columbus	OH	43215	614-466-8842	
Governor 77 S High St 30th Fl *Web:* www.governor.ohio.gov	Columbus	OH	43215	614-466-3555	466-9354
Governor's Office on Veterans Affairs 77 S High St 7th Fl *Web:* www.veteransaffairs.ohio.gov	Columbus	OH	43215	614-644-0898	
Health Dept 246 N High St *Web:* www.odh.ohio.gov	Columbus	OH	43215	614-466-3543	644-0085
Highway Patrol 1970 W Broad St PO Box 182074 *TF:* 877-772-8765 ■ *Web:* statepatrol.ohio.gov	Columbus	OH	43223	614-466-2660	644-9749
Historical Society 1982 Velma Ave *Web:* www.ohiohistory.org	Columbus	OH	43211	614-297-2300	297-2411
Housing Finance Agency 57 E Main St *Web:* www.ohiohome.org	Columbus	OH	43215	614-466-7970	644-5393
Information Technology Office 30 E Broad St Suite 4040	Columbus	OH	43215	614-466-6930	644-8151
Insurance Dept 2100 Stella Ct *TF:* 800-686-1526 ■ *Web:* www.ohioinsurance.gov	Columbus	OH	43215	614-644-2658	644-3743
Job & Family Services Dept 30 E Broad St 32nd Fl *Web:* www.jfs.ohio.gov	Columbus	OH	43215	614-466-6282	466-2815
Legislative Information Office 77 S High St *TF:* 800-282-0253 ■ *Web:* www.legislature.state.oh.us	Columbus	OH	43215	614-466-8842	644-1721
Lieutenant Governor 77 S High St 30th Fl *Web:* governor.ohio.gov	Columbus	OH	43215	614-466-3396	
Mental Health Dept 30 E Broad St 8th Fl *TF:* 888-636-4889 ■ *Web:* www.mh.state.oh.us	Columbus	OH	43215	614-466-2596	752-9453
Motor Vehicles Bureau 1970 W Broad St PO Box 16520 *Web:* www.bmv.ohio.gov	Columbus	OH	43216	614-752-7500	752-7972
Natural Resources Dept 2045 Morse Rd *Web:* www.ohiodnr.com	Columbus	OH	43229	614-265-6565	261-9601
Parks & Recreation Div 2045 Morse Rd Bldg C-3 *TF:* 800-282-7275 ■ *Web:* www.ohiodnr.com	Columbus	OH	43229	614-265-6561	261-8407
Parole Board 1050 Fwy Dr N *Web:* www.drc.state.oh.us	Columbus	OH	43229	614-752-1200	752-1251
Public Utilities Commission 180 E Broad St *Web:* www.puco.ohio.gov	Columbus	OH	43215	614-466-3016	644-9546
Racing Commission 77 S High St 18th Fl *Web:* www.racing.ohio.gov	Columbus	OH	43215	614-466-2757	466-1900
Regents Board 30 E Broad St 36th Fl *TF:* 800-233-6734 ■ *Web:* www.ohiohighered.org	Columbus	OH	43215	614-466-6000	466-5866
Rehabilitation & Correction Dept 770 W Broad St *Web:* www.drc.state.oh.us	Columbus	OH	43222	614-752-1159	752-1086
Rehabilitation Services Commission 400 E Campus View Blvd *TF:* 800-282-4536 ■ *Web:* rsc.ohio.gov	Columbus	OH	43235	614-438-1200	438-1257
Secretary of State 180 E Broad St 16th Fl *Web:* www.sos.state.oh.us	Columbus	OH	43215	614-466-2655	644-0649
Securities Div 77 S High St 22nd Fl *Web:* www.securities.state.oh.us	Columbus	OH	43215	614-644-7381	466-3316
State Grants & Scholarships Office 30 E Broad St 36th Fl PO Box 182452 *TF:* 888-833-1133 ■ *Web:* regents.ohio.gov/sgs	Columbus	OH	43218	614-466-7420	752-5903
Supreme Court 65 S Front St *Web:* www.sconet.state.oh.us	Columbus	OH	43215	614-387-9530	387-9539
Taxation Dept 30 E Broad St 22nd Fl PO Box 530 *TF:* 888-405-4089 ■ *Web:* tax.ohio.gov	Columbus	OH	43215	614-466-2166	466-6401
Transportation Dept 1980 W Broad St *Web:* www.dot.state.oh.us	Columbus	OH	43223	614-466-7170	644-8662
Travel & Tourism Div PO Box 1001 *TF:* 800-282-5393 ■ *Web:* www.discoverohio.com	Columbus	OH	43216	614-466-8844	466-6744
Treasurer 30 E Broad St 9th Fl *Web:* www.treasurer.state.oh.us	Columbus	OH	43215	614-466-2160	644-7313
Tuition Trust Authority 580 S High St Suite 208 *TF Cust Svc:* 800-233-6734 ■ *Web:* www.collegeadvantage.com	Columbus	OH	43215	614-752-9400	466-4486
Vital Statistics Unit 246 N High St PO Box 15098 *Web:* www.odh.ohio.gov	Columbus	OH	43215	614-466-2531	
Weights & Measures Div 8995 E Main St *Web:* www.ohioagriculture.gov/weights	Reynoldsburg	OH	43068	614-728-6290	728-6424
Wildlife Div 2045 Morse Rd Bldg G *TF:* 800-945-3543 ■ *Web:* www.ohiodnr.com/wildlife	Columbus	OH	43229	614-265-6300	262-1143
Workers' Compensation Bureau 30 W Spring St **Fax Area Code:* 877 ■ *TF:* 800-644-6292 ■ *Web:* www.ohiobwc.com	Columbus	OH	43215	614-644-6292	526-6446*
Workforce Developement Office 4020 E 5th Ave *TF:* 800-342-4784 ■ *Web:* www.ohioworkforce.org	Columbus	OH	43216	614-752-3091	995-1298
Youth Services Dept 51 N High St *Web:* www.dys.ohio.gov	Columbus	OH	43215	614-466-4314	728-9859

342-37 Oklahoma

	City	State	Zip	Phone	Fax
State Government Information 2101 N Lincoln Blvd *Web:* www.ok.gov	Oklahoma City	OK	73105	405-521-2011	
Administrative Office of the Courts 1915 N Stiles Ave Suite 305	Oklahoma City	OK	73105	405-521-2450	521-6815
Aging Services Div 312 NE 28th St *Web:* www.okdhs.org/aging	Oklahoma City	OK	73105	405-521-2327	521-2086
Agriculture Food & Forestry Dept 2800 N Lincoln Blvd *Web:* www.oda.state.ok.us	Oklahoma City	OK	73105	405-521-3864	521-4912
Arts Council 2101 N Lincoln Blvd # 640 *Web:* www.arts.state.ok.us	Oklahoma City	OK	73152	405-521-2931	521-6418
Attorney General 313 NE 21st St *Web:* www.oag.state.ok.us	Oklahoma City	OK	73105	405-521-3921	521-6246
Banking Dept 4545 N Lincoln Blvd Suite 164 *Web:* www.osbd.state.ok.us	Oklahoma City	OK	73105	405-521-2782	522-2993
Chief Medical Examiner 901 N Stonewall Ave *Web:* www.state.ok.us	Oklahoma City	OK	73117	405-239-7141	239-2430
Child Support Enforcement Div PO Box 53552 *Web:* www.okdhs.org/childsupport	Oklahoma City	OK	73152	405-522-5871	522-2753
Children & Family Services Div PO Box 25352 *Web:* www.okdhs.org/dcfs	Oklahoma City	OK	73125	405-521-3777	521-4373
Commerce Dept 900 N Stiles Ave *TF:* 800-879-6552 ■ *Web:* www.okcommerce.gov	Oklahoma City	OK	73104	405-815-6552	815-5199
Conservation Commission 2800 N Lincoln Blvd Suite 160 *Web:* www.okcc.state.ok.us	Oklahoma City	OK	73105	405-521-2384	521-6686
Consumer Protection Div 313 NE 21st St *Web:* www.oag.state.ok.us	Oklahoma City	OK	73105	405-521-4274	528-1867
Corporation Commission 2101 N Lincoln PO Box 52000 *Web:* www.occ.state.ok.us	Oklahoma City	OK	73152	405-521-2211	522-1623
Corrections Dept 3400 N Martin Luther King Ave *Web:* www.doc.state.ok.us	Oklahoma City	OK	73111	405-425-2500	425-2886
Development Finance Authority 5900 N Classen Ct	Oklahoma City	OK	73118	405-842-1145	848-3314
Education Dept 2500 N Lincoln Blvd *Web:* www.sde.state.ok.us	Oklahoma City	OK	73105	405-521-3301	521-6205
Emergency Management Dept 4600 N Martin Luther King Ave *Web:* www.ok.gov	Oklahoma City	OK	73111	405-521-2481	521-4053
Employment Security Commission 2401 N Lincoln Blvd Suite 504 *TF:* 888-900-9675 ■ *Web:* www.oesc.state.ok.us	Oklahoma City	OK	73105	405-557-7100	557-5355
Environmental Quality Department 707 N Robinson Ave PO Box 1677 *TF:* 800-869-1400 ■ *Web:* www.deq.state.ok.us	Oklahoma City	OK	73101	405-702-1000	702-7101
Ethics Commission 2300 N Lincoln Blvd Rm B5 *Web:* www.ok.gov	Oklahoma City	OK	73105	405-521-3451	521-4905
Health Dept 1000 NE 10th St *Web:* www.health.state.ok.us	Oklahoma City	OK	73117	405-271-4200	271-3431
Highway Patrol PO Box 11415 *Web:* www.dps.state.ok.us	Oklahoma City	OK	73136	405-425-2006	419-2029
Historical Society 800 Nahzi Zuhzi Dr *Web:* www.ok-history.mus.ok.us	Oklahoma City	OK	73105	405-521-2491	521-2492
Housing Finance Agency 1140 NW 63rd St Suite 200 *TF:* 800-256-1489 ■ *Web:* www.ohfa.org	Oklahoma City	OK	73116	405-848-1144	840-1109
Human Services Dept 2400 N Lincoln Blvd *Web:* www.okdhs.org	Oklahoma City	OK	73105	405-521-3646	521-6458
Indian Affairs Commission 2500 N Lincoln Blvd Suite 282 *Web:* www.oiac.state.ok.us	Oklahoma City	OK	73105	405-521-3828	522-4447
Insurance Department 3625 NW 56th Suite 100 *TF:* 800-522-0071 ■ *Web:* www.ok.gov/oid	Oklahoma City	OK	73152	405-521-2828	521-6635
Labor Dept 4001 N Lincoln Blvd *Web:* www.okdol.state.ok.us	Oklahoma City	OK	73105	405-528-1500	528-5751
Legislation Service Bureau 2300 N Lincoln Blvd Rm B30 *Web:* www.lsb.state.ok.us	Oklahoma City	OK	73105	405-521-4081	521-5507
Legislature 2300 N Lincoln Blvd *Web:* www.lsb.state.ok.us	Oklahoma City	OK	73105	405-524-0126	521-5507
Lieutenant Governor 2300 N Lincoln Blvd Suite 211 *Web:* www.ltgov.state.ok.us	Oklahoma City	OK	73105	405-521-2161	525-2702
Mental Health & Substance Abuse Services Dept 1200 NE 13th St PO Box 53277 *Web:* www.odmhsas.org	Oklahoma City	OK	73152	405-522-3908	522-3650
Motor Vehicle Commission 4334 NW Expy Suite 183 *Web:* www.youroklahoma.com/omvc	Oklahoma City	OK	73116	405-607-8227	607-8909
National Guard 3501 Military Cir *Web:* www.ok.ngb.army.mil	Oklahoma City	OK	73111	405-228-5000	228-5524

Name / Address	City	State	Zip	Phone	Fax
Pardon & Parole Board 120 N Robinson Ave Suite 900W *Web:* www.ppb.state.ok.us	Oklahoma City	OK	73102	405-602-5863	602-6437
Parks Div PO Box 52002 *TF:* 800-654-8240 ■ *Web:* www.touroklahoma.com	Oklahoma City	OK	73152	405-230-8300	521-2428
Personnel Management Office 2101 N Lincoln Blvd Suite G-80 *Web:* www.opm.state.ok.us	Oklahoma City	OK	73105	405-521-2177	524-6942
Real Estate Commission 2401 NW 23rd St Suite 18 *Web:* www.orec.state.ok.us	Oklahoma City	OK	73107	405-521-3387	521-2189
Rehabilitative Services Dept 5501 N Portland Ave *TF:* 800-845-8476 ■ *Web:* www.okrehab.org	Oklahoma City	OK	73112	405-951-3400	951-3529
Secretary of State 2300 N Lincoln Blvd Rm 101 *Web:* www.sos.state.ok.us	Oklahoma City	OK	73105	405-521-3912	521-3771
Securities Dept 120 N Robinson St Suite 860 *Web:* www.securities.state.ok.us	Oklahoma City	OK	73102	405-280-7700	280-7742
State Regents for Higher Education 655 Research Pkwy Suite 200 *Web:* www.okhighered.org	Oklahoma City	OK	73104	405-225-9100	225-9235
Supreme Court 2100 N Lincoln Blvd Suite 4 *Web:* www.oscn.net	Oklahoma City	OK	73105	405-521-2163	528-1607
Tax Commission 2501 N Lincoln Blvd *Web:* www.oktax.state.ok.us	Oklahoma City	OK	73194	405-521-3160	521-3826
Tourism & Recreation Dept 15 N Robinson St Suite 100 *TF:* 800-652-6552 ■ *Web:* tourism.state.ok.us	Oklahoma City	OK	73105	405-521-2406	521-3992
Treasurer 2300 N Lincoln Rd Rm 217 *Web:* www.treasurer.state.ok.us	Oklahoma City	OK	73105	405-521-3191	521-4994
Veterans Affairs Dept 2311 N Central Ave *Web:* www.odva.state.ok.us	Oklahoma City	OK	73105	405-521-3684	521-6533
Victim Services Unit 313 NE 21st St *Web:* www.oag.ok.gov/oagweb.nsf/vservices.html	Oklahoma City	OK	73105	405-521-3921	521-6246
Vital Records Div 1000 NE 10th St Rm 111 *Web:* www.health.state.ok.us/program/vital	Oklahoma City	OK	73117	405-271-4040	
Weights & Measures 2800 N Lincoln Blvd *Web:* www.ok.gov/~okag/index.htm	Oklahoma City	OK	73105	405-521-3864	522-4584
Wildlife Conservation Dept PO Box 53465 *TF:* 800-522-8039 ■ *Web:* www.wildlifedepartment.com	Oklahoma City	OK	73152	405-521-4660	521-6505

342-38 Oregon

Name / Address	City	State	Zip	Phone	Fax
Arts Commission 775 Summer St NE Suite 200 *Web:* www.oregonartscommission.org	Salem	OR	97301	503-986-0082	986-0260
Attorney General 1162 Ct St NE Justice Bldg *Web:* www.doj.state.or.us	Salem	OR	97301	503-378-4400	378-4017
Child Support Div 494 State St Suite 300 *Web:* dcs.state.or.us	Salem	OR	97301	503-986-6166	986-6158
Children Adults & Families Div 500 Summer St NE *Web:* egov.oregon.gov/DHS/children	Salem	OR	97310	503-945-5600	373-7032
Community Colleges & Workforce Development Dept 255 Capitol St NE *Web:* www.workforce.state.or.us	Salem	OR	97310	503-378-8648	378-8434
Corrections Dept 2575 Ctr St NE *Web:* www.oregon.gov/DOC	Salem	OR	97301	503-945-9090	373-1173
Crime Victims Service Div 1162 Ct St NE *TF:* 877-877-9392 ■ *Web:* www.doj.state.or.us/CrimeV/welcome1.htm	Salem	OR	97301	503-378-4400	378-5738
Department of Human Services 500 Summer St NE *Web:* www.oregon.gov/DHS	Salem	OR	97310	503-945-5944	378-2897
Dept of Consumer & Business Services 350 Winter St NE PO Box 14480 *Web:* egov.oregon.gov/DCBS	Salem	OR	97309	503-378-4100	378-6444
Dept of Transportation 355 Capitol St NE Suite 135 Rm 222 *TF:* 888-275-6368 ■ *Web:* www.oregon.gov/ODOT	Salem	OR	97301	503-986-4000	986-3432
Driver & Motor Vehicle Services Div 1905 Lana Ave NE *Web:* www.oregon.gov/ODOT/DMV	Salem	OR	97314	503-945-5000	945-5254
Education Dept 255 Capitol St NE *Web:* www.ode.state.or.us	Salem	OR	97310	503-378-3600	373-5156
Emergency Management 3225 State St # 115 *Web:* www.egov.oregon.gov	Salem	OR	97301	503-378-2911	373-7933
Energy Dept 625 Marion St NE *Web:* www.egov.oregon.gov	Salem	OR	97301	503-378-4040	373-7806
Environmental Quality Dept 811 SW 6th Ave *Web:* www.deq.state.or.us	Portland	OR	97204	503-229-5696	229-6124
Finance & Corporate Securities Div PO Box 14480 *Web:* www.cbs.state.or.us/external/dfcs	Salem	OR	97309	503-378-4140	947-7862
Financial Fraud/Consumer Protection Section 1162 Ct St NE *TF:* 877-877-9392 ■ *Web:* www.doj.state.or.us/finfraud	Salem	OR	97301	503-378-4400	373-7067
Fish & Wildlife Dept 3406 Cherry Ave NE *TF:* 800-720-6339 ■ *Web:* www.dfw.state.or.us	Salem	OR	97303	503-947-6000	947-6042
Forestry Dept 2600 State St Suite 110 *Web:* www.egov.oregon.gov	Salem	OR	97310	503-945-7200	945-7212
Government Standards & Practices Commission 3218 Pringle Rd SE # 220 *Web:* www.gspc.state.or.us	Salem	OR	97302	503-378-5105	373-1456
Governor 900 Ct St NE *Web:* www.governor.state.or.us	Salem	OR	97301	503-378-3111	378-6827
Heritage Conservation Div 725 Summer St NE Suite C *Web:* egov.oregon.gov/OPRD/HCD	Salem	OR	97301	503-986-0671	986-0793
Housing & Community Services Dept 725 Summer St NE Suite B PO Box 14508 *Web:* www.egov.oregon.gov	Salem	OR	97309	503-986-2000	986-2020
Information Resources Management Div 1225 Ferry St SE *Web:* www.irmd.das.state.or.us	Salem	OR	97301	503-378-2135	373-5200
Insurance Div 350 Winter St NE Rm 440 *Web:* www.cbs.state.or.us	Salem	OR	97301	503-947-7980	378-4351
Labor & Industries Bureau 800 NE Oregon St Suite 1045 *Web:* www.boli.state.or.us	Portland	OR	97232	503-731-4200	731-4103
Land Conservation & Development Dept 635 Capitol St NE Suite 150 *Web:* www.lcd.state.or.us	Salem	OR	97302	503-373-0050	378-5518
Legislative Assembly 900 Ct St NE *Web:* www.leg.state.or.us	Salem	OR	97310	503-986-1180	373-1527
Lottery 500 Airport Rd SE *Web:* www.oregonlottery.org	Salem	OR	97301	503-540-1000	540-1001
Measurement Standards Div 635 Capitol St NE *Web:* egov.oregon.gov/ODA/MSD	Salem	OR	97301	503-986-4670	986-4784
Military Dept 1776 Militia Way SE PO Box 14350 *Web:* www.egov.oregon.gov	Salem	OR	97309	503-584-3980	584-3987
Oregon Business Development Department 775 Summer St NE Suite 200 *TF:* 866-467-3466 ■ *Web:* www.oregon.gov/OBDD/index.shtml	Salem	OR	97301	503-986-0123	581-5115
Parks & Recreation Dept 725 Summer St NE Suite C *TF:* 800-551-6949 ■ *Web:* www.oregon.gov/OPRD	Salem	OR	97301	503-986-0707	986-0794
Parole & Post-Prison Supervision Board 2575 Ctr St NE Suite 100 *Web:* www.paroleboard.state.or.us	Salem	OR	97301	503-945-0900	373-7558
Public Health Div 800 NE Oregon St Suite 465-B *Web:* public.health.oregon.gov/PHD	Portland	OR	97232	503-731-4000	731-4031
Public Utility Commission 550 Capitol St NE Suite 215 PO Box 2148 *Web:* www.oregon.gov/PUC	Salem	OR	97308	503-378-6611	378-5505
Publication & Distribution Services 900 Ct St NE Rm 49 *Web:* www.leg.state.or.us	Salem	OR	97310	503-986-1180	373-1527
Racing Commission 800 NE Oregon St Suite 310 *Web:* racing.oregon.gov	Portland	OR	97232	971-673-0207	673-0213
Revenue Dept 955 Ctr St NE *Web:* www.egov.oregon.gov	Salem	OR	97301	503-378-4988	945-8738
Secretary of State 900 Ct St NE Rm 136 *Web:* www.sos.state.or.us	Salem	OR	97301	503-986-1500	986-1616
Seniors & People with Disabilities Div 500 Summer St NE 2nd Fl *TF:* 800-282-2096 ■ *Web:* www.egov.oregon.gov	Salem	OR	97310	503-945-5811	378-7823
State Court Administrator Office 1163 State St *Web:* www.ojd.state.or.us	Salem	OR	97301	503-986-5500	986-5503
State Police Dept 225 Capitol St NE 4th Fl *Web:* www.oregon.gov	Salem	OR	97310	503-378-3720	378-8282
Student Assistance Commission 1500 Valley River Dr Suite 100 *TF:* 800-452-8807 ■ *Web:* www.osac.state.or.us	Eugene	OR	97401	541-687-7400	687-7419
Supreme Court 1163 State St *Web:* www.ojd.state.or.us	Salem	OR	97301	503-986-5550	986-5560
Tourism Commission 670 Hawthorne Ave SE Suite 240 *TF:* 800-547-7842 ■ *Web:* www.traveloregon.com	Salem	OR	97301	503-378-8850	
Treasurer 350 Winter St NE Suite 100 *Web:* www.ost.state.or.us	Salem	OR	97301	503-378-4000	373-7051
Veterans' Affairs Dept 700 Summer St NE *Web:* www.odva.state.or.us	Salem	OR	97301	503-373-2000	373-2362
Vital Records Unit PO Box 14050 *Web:* www.dhs.state.or.us	Portland	OR	97293	503-731-4095	234-8417
Vocational Rehabilitation Services Office 500 Summer St NE E-87 *TF:* 877-277-0513 ■ *Web:* egov.oregon.gov/DHS/vr	Salem	OR	97301	503-945-5880	947-5010
Workers'' Compensation Board 2601 SE 25th St Suite 150 *Web:* www.cbs.state.or.us/wcb	Salem	OR	97302	503-378-3308	373-1684

342-39 Pennsylvania

Agency / Address	City	State	Zip	Phone	Fax
State Government Information 209 Finance Bldg *Web:* www.state.pa.us	Harrisburg	PA	17120	717-787-2121	787-4523
Administrative Office of the Cts 1515 Market St Suite 1414 *Web:* www.courts.state.pa.us	Philadelphia	PA	19102	215-560-6300	560-6315
Aging Dept 555 Walnut St 5th Fl *Web:* www.aging.state.pa.us	Harrisburg	PA	17101	717-783-1550	783-6842
Agriculture Dept 2301 N Cameron St *Web:* www.agriculture.state.pa.us	Harrisburg	PA	17110	717-772-2853	705-8402
Attorney General Strawberry Sq 16th Fl *Web:* www.attorneygeneral.gov	Harrisburg	PA	17120	717-787-3391	787-8242
Banking Dept 333 Market St 16th Fl *Web:* www.banking.state.pa.us	Harrisburg	PA	17101	717-214-8343	787-8773
Bill Status Main Capitol Bldg Rm 648 *Web:* www.legis.state.pa.us	Harrisburg	PA	17120	717-787-2342	
Child Support Enforcement Bureau PO Box 8018 *Web:* www.dpw.state.pa.us	Harrisburg	PA	17105	717-787-2600	787-9706
Community & Economic Development Dept 400 N St 4th Fl *Web:* www.newpa.com	Harrisburg	PA	17120	717-787-3003	787-6866
Conservation & Natural Resources Dept 400 Market St # 7 *Web:* www.dcnr.state.pa.us	Harrisburg	PA	17120	717-787-2869	705-2832
Consumer Advocate 555 Walnut St 5th Fl *Web:* www.oca.state.pa.us	Harrisburg	PA	17101	717-783-5048	783-7152
Corrections Dept PO Box 598 *Web:* www.cor.state.pa.us	Camp Hill	PA	17001	717-975-4859	787-0132
Driver & Vehicle Services Bureau 1101 S Front St *Web:* www.dmv.state.pa.us	Harrisburg	PA	17104	717-787-2977	705-1046
Education Dept 333 Market St *Web:* www.pde.state.pa.us	Harrisburg	PA	17126	717-783-6788	783-4517
Emergency Management Agency 2605 I- Dr *Web:* www.pema.state.pa.us	Harrisburg	PA	17110	717-651-2001	651-2021
Environmental Protection Dept PO Box 2063 *Web:* www.dep.state.pa.us	Harrisburg	PA	17105	717-783-2300	783-8926
Fish & Boat Commission 1601 Elmerton Ave *Web:* www.fish.state.pa.us	Harrisburg	PA	17110	717-705-7800	705-7802
Game Commission 2001 Elmerton Ave *Web:* www.pgc.state.pa.us	Harrisburg	PA	17110	717-787-4250	772-2411
General Assembly Capitol Bldg *Web:* www.legis.state.pa.us	Harrisburg	PA	17120	717-787-5920	772-2344
General Services Dept 515 N Office Bldg PO Box 1365 *Web:* www.dgs.state.pa.us	Harrisburg	PA	17125	717-785-5996	772-2026
Governor 225 Main Capitol Bldg *Web:* www.governor.state.pa.us	Harrisburg	PA	17120	717-787-2500	772-8284
Health Dept Health & Welfare Bldg PO Box 90 *Web:* www.dsf.health.state.pa.us	Harrisburg	PA	17108	717-787-6436	772-6959
Higher Education Assistance Agency 1200 N 7th St *TF:* 800-692-7392 ■ *Web:* www.pheaa.org	Harrisburg	PA	17102	717-720-2860	720-3644
Historical & Museum Commission 300 N St *Web:* www.phmc.state.pa.us	Harrisburg	PA	17120	717-787-3362	783-9924
Homeland Security Office 2605 I- Dr *Web:* www.homelandsecurity.state.pa.us	Harrisburg	PA	17110	717-772-8052	
Housing Finance Agency 211 N Front St *Web:* www.phfa.org	Harrisburg	PA	17101	717-780-3800	780-3905
Information Technology Office 209 Finance Bldg *Web:* www.oit.state.pa.us	Harrisburg	PA	17120	717-787-5440	787-4523
Insurance Dept 1326 Strawberry Sq *Web:* www.ins.state.pa.us	Harrisburg	PA	17120	717-787-7000	783-3898
Labor & Industry Dept 1700 Labor & Industry Bldg *Web:* www.dli.state.pa.us	Harrisburg	PA	17120	717-787-5279	787-8826
Lieutenant Governor Capitol Bldg Suite 200 *Web:* www.governor.state.pa.us	Harrisburg	PA	17120	717-787-3300	783-0150
Mental Health & Substance Abuse Office PO Box 2675 *Web:* www.dpw.state.pa.us/Family	Harrisburg	PA	17105	717-787-6443	
Military & Veterans Affairs Dept Fort Indiantown Gap Bldg S-0-47 *Web:* www.dmva.state.pa.us	Annville	PA	17003	717-861-8500	861-8314
Probation & Parole Board 1101 S Front St Suite 5100 *Web:* www.pbpp.state.pa.us	Harrisburg	PA	17104	717-787-5100	705-1774
Professional & Occupational Affairs Bureau PO Box 2649 *Web:* www.dos.state.pa.us/bpoa	Harrisburg	PA	17105	717-783-7192	783-0510
Public Utility Commission 400 N St Keystone Bldg PO Box 3265 *TF:* 800-692-7380 ■ *Web:* www.puc.state.pa.us	Harrisburg	PA	17120	717-783-1740	787-6641
Public Welfare Dept PO Box 2675 *Web:* www.dpw.state.pa.us	Harrisburg	PA	17105	717-787-2600	772-2062
Revenue Dept Strawberry Sq 11th Fl *Web:* www.revenue.state.pa.us	Harrisburg	PA	17128	717-783-3680	787-3990
Secretary of the Commonweath North Office Bldg	Harrisburg	PA	17120	717-787-6458	787-1734
Securities Commission 1010 N 7th St 2nd Fl *Web:* www.psc.state.pa.us	Harrisburg	PA	17102	717-787-8061	783-5122
State Ethics Commission Rm 309 Finance Bldg PO Box 11470 *TF:* 800-932-0936 ■ *Web:* www.ethics.state.pa.us	Harrisburg	PA	17108	717-783-1610	787-0806
State Parks Bureau PO Box 8551 *TF:* 888-727-2757 ■ *Web:* www.dcnr.state.pa.us	Harrisburg	PA	17105	717-787-6640	787-8817
State Police 1800 Elmerton Ave *Web:* www.psp.state.pa.us	Harrisburg	PA	17110	717-783-5599	
Supreme Court City Hall Suite 468 *Web:* www.courts.state.pa.us	Philadelphia	PA	19107	215-560-6370	
Tourism Office 404 N St 4th Fl *TF:* 800-847-4872 ■ *Web:* www.visitpa.com	Harrisburg	PA	17120	717-720-1301	787-0687
Transportation Dept 400 N St *TF:* 800-932-4600 ■ *Web:* www.dot.state.pa.us	Harrisburg	PA	17120	717-787-2838	787-1739
Treasury Dept 129 Finance Bldg *Web:* www.treasury.state.pa.us	Harrisburg	PA	17120	717-787-2465	783-9760
Tuition Account Plan (TAP 529) 2005 Market St PO Box 42529 *TF:* 866-244-9877 ■	Philadelphia	PA	19103	866-244-9877	
Victims Compensation Assistance Program PO Box 1167 *Web:* www.pccd.state.pa.us	Harrisburg	PA	17101	717-783-5153	787-4306
Vital Records Div PO Box 1528 *Web:* www.health.state.pa.us	New Castle	PA	16103	724-656-3100	652-8951
Vocational Rehabilitation Office 909 Green St *TF:* 800-442-6351	Harrisburg	PA	17120	717-787-5244	783-5221
Workers Compensation Bureau 1171 S Cameron St Rm 324	Harrisburg	PA	17104	717-783-5421	772-0342
Workforce Investment Board 901 N 7th St Suite 103 *Web:* www.paworkforce.state.pa.us	Harrisburg	PA	17120	717-772-4966	783-4660
State System of Higher Education 2986 N 2nd St *TF:* 800-457-7743 ■ *Web:* www.passhe.edu	Harrisburg	PA	17110	717-720-4000	720-4011

342-40 Rhode Island

Agency / Address	City	State	Zip	Phone	Fax
State Government Information 40 Fountain St *Web:* www.ri.gov	Providence	RI	02903	401-222-2000	
Adjutant General''s Office 645 New London Ave	Cranston	RI	02920	401-275-4100	275-4338
Agriculture & Resource Marketing Div 235 Promenade St *Web:* www.dem.ri.gov	Providence	RI	02908	401-222-2781	222-6047
Arts Council 1 Capitol Hill 3rd Fl *Web:* www.arts.ri.gov	Providence	RI	02908	401-222-3880	222-3018
Attorney General 150 S Main St *Web:* www.riag.state.ri.us	Providence	RI	02903	401-274-4400	222-1331
Bill Status State House Rm 1 *Web:* www.rilin.state.ri.us	Providence	RI	02903	401-222-3580	
Board of Governors for Higher Education 80 Washington St Shepard Bldg *Web:* www.ribghe.org	Providence	RI	02903	401-456-6000	456-6028
Child Support Services 77 Dorrance St	Providence	RI	02903	401-222-2847	222-2887
Children Youth & Families Dept 101 Friendship St *Web:* www.dcyf.state.ri.us	Providence	RI	02903	401-528-3575	528-3590
Consumer Protection Unit 150 S Main St *Web:* www.riag.ri.gov	Providence	RI	02903	401-274-4400	222-5110
Corrections Dept 40 Howard Ave *Web:* www.doc.state.ri.us	Cranston	RI	02920	401-462-1000	462-2630
Court Administrators Office 250 Benefit St *Web:* www.courts.state.ri.us	Providence	RI	02903	401-222-3263	222-5131
Crime Victim Compensation Program 40 Fountain St 1st Fl *Web:* www.treasury.state.ri.us/vcfund.htm	Providence	RI	02903	401-222-8590	222-4577
Economic Development Corp 1 W Exchange St *Web:* www.riedc.com	Providence	RI	02903	401-222-2601	222-2102
Elderly Affairs Dept 35 Howard Ave *Web:* www.dea.state.ri.us	Cranston	RI	02920	401-462-4000	462-0586
Elementary & Secondary Education Dept 255 Westminster St *Web:* www.ride.ri.gov	Providence	RI	02903	401-222-4600	222-6178
Emergency Management Agency 645 New London Ave *Web:* www.riema.ri.gov	Cranston	RI	02920	401-946-9996	944-1891
Environmental Management Dept 235 Promenade St Suite 450 *Web:* www.state.ri.us/dem	Providence	RI	02908	401-222-6800	222-6802
Ethics Commission 40 Fountain St	Providence	RI	02903	401-222-3790	222-3382
General Assembly State House *Web:* www.rilin.state.ri.us	Providence	RI	02903	401-222-2466	222-6142
Governor State House *Web:* www.governor.state.ri.us	Providence	RI	02903	401-222-2080	273-5729
Health Dept 3 Capitol Hill *Web:* www.health.ri.gov	Providence	RI	02908	401-222-2231	222-6548
Higher Education Assistance Authority 560 Jefferson Blvd *TF:* 800-922-9855 ■ *Web:* www.riheaa.org	Warwick	RI	02886	401-736-1100	732-3541
Historical Preservation & Heritage Commission 150 Benefit St *Web:* www.preservation.ri.gov	Providence	RI	02903	401-222-2678	222-2968
Housing & Mortgage Finance Corp 44 Washington St *Web:* www.rihousing.com	Providence	RI	02903	401-751-5566	
Human Services Dept 600 New London Ave *Web:* www.dhs.state.ri.us	Cranston	RI	02920	401-462-5300	462-1876
Labor & Training Dept 1511 Pontiac Ave *Web:* www.dlt.state.ri.us	Cranston	RI	02920	401-462-8000	462-8872

Phone | Fax

Library & Information Services Office
1 Capitol Hill ... Providence RI 02908 401-222-4444 222-2083
Web: www.olis.state.ri.us
Lieutenant Governor 82 Smith St ... Providence RI 02903 401-222-2371 222-2012
Web: www.ltgov.state.ri.us
Lottery 1425 Pontiac Ave ... Cranston RI 02920 401-463-6500 463-5008
Web: www.rilot.com
Medical Examiner 48 Orms St ... Providence RI 02904 401-222-5500 222-5517
Parks & Recreation Div 2321 Hartford Ave ... Johnston RI 02919 401-222-2632 934-0610
Web: www.riparks.com
Professional Regulation Div
1511 Pontiac Ave Howard Ctr Bldg 70 ... Cranston RI 02920 401-462-8580
Web: www.dlt.ri.gov/profregs
Public Utilities Commission
89 Jefferson Blvd ... Warwick RI 02888 401-941-4500 941-1694
Web: www.ripuc.org
Rehabilitation Services Office
40 Fountain St ... Providence RI 02903 401-421-7005 222-3574
Web: www.ors.state.ri.us
Secretary of State
82 Smith St Rm 217 State House ... Providence RI 02903 401-222-2357 222-1356
Web: sos.ri.gov
State Police 311 Danielson Pike ... North Scituate RI 02857 401-444-1000 444-1105
Web: www.risp.state.ri.us
Supreme Court 250 Benefit St ... Providence RI 02903 401-222-3272 222-3599
Web: www.courts.state.ri.us
Tourism Div 315 Iron Horse Way Suite 101 ... Providence RI 02908 800-250-7384 273-8270*
**Fax Area Code:* 401 ■ *TF:* 800-556-2484 ■ *Web:* www.visitrhodeisland.com
Transportation Dept 2 Capitol Hill ... Providence RI 02903 401-222-2481 222-2086
Web: www.dot.state.ri.us
Treasurer State House Rm 102 ... Providence RI 02903 401-222-2397 222-6140
Web: www.treasury.state.ri.us
Veterans'' Affairs Div 600 New London Ave ... Cranston RI 02910 401-462-0350
Web: www.dhs.state.ri.us/dhs/dvetaff.htm
Vital Records Div 3 Capitol Hill Rm 101 ... Providence RI 02908 401-222-2811 222-4393
Web: www.health.state.ri.us/chic/vital
Weights & Measures Office
1511 Pontiac Ave Bldg 70 ... Cranston RI 02920 401-457-8555
Worker's Compensation Div
1511 Pontiac Ave Bldg 69 2nd Fl ... Cranston RI 02920 401-460-8100 462-8105
Web: www.dlt.ri.gov/wc

342-41 South Carolina

Phone | Fax

State Government Information
1301 Gervais St Suite 710 ... Columbia SC 29201 803-771-0131 771-0131
TF: 866-340-7105 ■ *Web:* www.sc.gov
Adoption Services Div PO Box 1520 ... Columbia SC 29202 803-898-7561 898-7641
Web: www.state.sc.us/dss/adoption
Agriculture Dept 1200 Senate St PO Box 11280 ... Columbia SC 29211 803-734-2190 734-2192
Web: www.scda.state.sc.us
Arts Commission 1800 Gervais St ... Columbia SC 29201 803-734-8696 734-8526
Web: www.state.sc.us
Attorney General 1000 Assembly St ... Columbia SC 29201 803-734-3970 734-3971
Web: www.scattorneygeneral.org
Business Carolina Inc 1441 Main St Suite 900 ... Columbia SC 29201 803-461-3801 461-3826
Web: businesscarolina.net
Child Support Enforcement Office
3150 Harden St Ext ... Columbia SC 29203 803-898-9210 898-9126
TF: 800-768-5858 ■ *Web:* www.state.sc.us
Commerce Dept 1201 Main St Suite 1600 ... Columbia SC 29201 803-737-0400 737-0418
TF: 800-868-7232 ■ *Web:* www.sccommerce.com
Consumer Affairs Dept PO Box 5757 ... Columbia SC 29250 803-734-4200 734-4286
TF: 800-922-1594 ■ *Web:* www.scconsumer.gov
Corrections Dept 4444 Broad River Rd ... Columbia SC 29210 803-896-8500 896-3972
Web: www.doc.sc.gov
Court Administration 1015 Sumter St 2nd Fl ... Columbia SC 29201 803-734-1800 734-1821
Web: www.judicial.state.sc.us
Disabilities & Special Needs Dept
3440 Harden St Ext PO Box 4706 ... Columbia SC 29240 803-898-9600 898-9653
TF: 888-376-4636 ■ *Web:* www.state.sc.us
Education Dept 1429 Senate St ... Columbia SC 29201 803-734-8500 734-8527
Web: www.myscschools.com
Education Lottery 1333 Main St 4th Fl ... Columbia SC 29201 803-737-2002 737-2005
Web: www.sceducationlottery.com
Emergency Management Div
1100 Fish Hatchery Rd ... West Columbia SC 29172 803-737-8500 737-8570
Web: www.scemd.org
Employment Security Commission
1550 Gadsden St PO Box 995 ... Columbia SC 29202 803-737-2400 737-2642
Web: www.sces.org
Ethics Commission
5000 Thurmond Mall Suite 250 ... Columbia SC 29201 803-253-4192 253-7539
Web: www.state.sc.us
Financial Institutions Board
1015 Sumter St # 309 ... Columbia SC 29201 803-734-2001 734-2013
Web: www.state.sc.us
Governor PO Box 12267 ... Columbia SC 29211 803-734-2100 734-5167
Web: www.scgovernor.com
Health & Environmental Control Dept
2600 Bull St ... Columbia SC 29201 803-898-3432 898-3323
Web: www.scdhec.gov
Health & Human Services Dept 1801 Main St ... Columbia SC 29201 803-898-2500 898-4515
Web: www.dhhs.state.sc.us
Higher Education Tuition Grants Commission
101 Business Pk Blvd Suite 2100 ... Columbia SC 29203 803-896-1120 896-1126
Web: www.sctuitiongrants.com
Highway Patrol 5400 Broad River Rd ... Columbia SC 29210 803-896-7920 896-7922
Web: www.schp.org
Historic Preservation Office
8301 Parklane Rd ... Columbia SC 29223 803-896-6100 896-6167
Web: www.state.sc.us/scdah/histrcpl.htm
Insurance Dept 300 Arbor Lake Suite 1200 ... Columbia SC 29223 803-737-6160 737-6229
Web: www.doi.state.sc.us
Labor Licensing & Regulation Dept
110 Centerview Dr # 116 ... Columbia SC 29210 803-896-4300 896-4393
Web: www.llr.state.sc.us
Law Enforcement Div
4400 Broad River Rd PO Box 21398 ... Columbia SC 29210 803-896-7001 896-7041
Web: www.sled.sc.gov
Legislature State House PO Box 142 ... Columbia SC 29202 803-212-6200 212-6299
Web: www.scstatehouse.gov
Lieutenant Governor PO Box 142 ... Columbia SC 29202 803-734-2080 734-2082
Web: www.state.sc.us/ltgov
Medical Examiners Board
110 Centerview Dr # 202 ... Columbia SC 29210 803-896-4500 896-4515
Web: www.llr.state.sc.us
Mental Health Dept 2414 Bull St PO Box 485 ... Columbia SC 29202 803-898-8581 898-8316
Web: www.state.sc.us
Motor Vehicles Div PO Box 1498 ... Blythewood SC 29016 803-896-5000
TF: 800-422-1368 ■ *Web:* www.scdps.org
Natural Resources Dept PO Box 167 ... Columbia SC 29202 803-734-4007 734-4300
Web: www.dnr.state.sc.us
Parks Recreation & Tourism Dept
1205 Pendleton St ... Columbia SC 29201 803-734-1650 734-0133
Web: www.southcarolinaparks.com
Probation Parole & Pardon Services Dept
2221 Devine st Suite 600 PO Box 50666 ... Columbia SC 29250 803-734-9220 734-9440
Web: www.dppps.sc.gov
Professional & Occupational Licensing Boards
110 Centerview Dr ... Columbia SC 29210 803-896-4300 896-4310
Web: www.llr.state.sc.us/pol.asp
Public Service Commission PO Drawer 11649 ... Columbia SC 29211 803-896-5133 896-5246
Web: www.psc.state.sc.us
Revenue Dept 301 Gervais St PO Box 125 ... Columbia SC 29214 803-898-5000 898-5822
Web: www.sctax.org
Secretary of State
1205 Pendleton St Suite 525 ... Columbia SC 29201 803-734-2170 734-1661
Web: www.scsos.com
Securities Div PO Box 11549 ... Columbia SC 29211 803-734-9916 734-0032
TF: 877-232-5378 ■ *Web:* www.scsecurities.com
Senior Services Bureau 1801 Main St ... Columbia SC 29202 803-549-0820 898-4515
Web: www.dhhs.state.sc.us/InsideDHHS/Bureaus
Social Services Dept PO Box 1520 ... Columbia SC 29202 803-898-7601 898-7277
Web: www.state.sc.us/dss
State Housing Finance & Development Authority
300 Outlet Pointe Blvd Suite C ... Columbia SC 29210 803-896-9001 896-9012
Web: www.sha.state.sc.us
State Ports Authority 176 Concord St ... Charleston SC 29401 843-723-8651 577-8626
TF: 800-845-7106 ■ *Web:* www.scspa.com
Supreme Court
1231 Gervais St Supreme Court Bldg ... Columbia SC 29201 803-734-1080 734-1499
Web: www.judicial.state.sc.us/supreme
Transportation Dept 955 Park St PO Box 191 ... Columbia SC 29202 803-737-1302 737-2038
Web: www.scdot.org
Treasurer PO Box 11778 ... Columbia SC 29211 803-734-2101 734-2690
Web: www.state.sc.us/treas
Veterans Affairs Div
1205 Pendleton St Rm 447 ... Columbia SC 29201 803-734-0200 734-0197
Web: www.govoepp.state.sc.us/vetaff.htm
Victim Assistance Div
1205 Pendleton St Rm 401 ... Columbia SC 29201 803-734-1900 734-1708
Web: www.govoepp.state.sc.us
Vital Records Div 2600 Bull St ... Columbia SC 29201 803-898-3630 898-3761
Web: www.scdhec.gov/vr
Vocational Rehabilitation Dept
1410 Boston Ave PO Box 15 ... West Columbia SC 29171 803-896-6500 896-6529
TF: 800-832-7526 ■ *Web:* www.scvrd.net
Wildlife & Freshwater Fisheries Div
PO Box 167 ... Columbia SC 29202 803-734-3889 734-6020
Web: www.dnr.state.sc.us/wild
Workers' Compensation Commission
1333 Main St # 500 ... Columbia SC 29201 803-737-5700 737-5764
Web: www.wcc.state.sc.us
Commission on Higher Education
1333 Main St Suite 200 ... Columbia SC 29201 803-737-2260 737-2297
Web: www.che400.state.sc.us

342-42 South Dakota

Phone | Fax

State Government Information
500 E Capitol Ave ... Pierre SD 57501 605-773-3011
Web: www.sd.gov
Adult Services & Aging Office
700 Governors Dr ... Pierre SD 57501 605-773-3656 773-6834
Web: www.state.sd.us
Agriculture Dept 523 E Capitol Ave ... Pierre SD 57501 605-773-3375 773-5926
Web: www.state.sd.us
Arts Council 800 Governors Dr ... Pierre SD 57501 605-773-3131 773-6962
Web: www.artscouncil.sd.gov
Attorney General 1302 E Hwy 14 ... Pierre SD 57501 605-773-3215 773-4106
Web: www.state.sd.us
Banking Div 217 1/2 W Missouri Ave ... Pierre SD 57501 605-773-3421 773-5367
Web: www.state.sd.us/drr2/reg/bank
Bill Status 500 E Capitol ... Pierre SD 57501 605-773-3251
Web: www.legis.state.sd.us
Career Center Div 116 W Missouri Ave ... Pierre SD 57501 605-773-3372 773-6680
Web: www.sdjobs.org
Child Protection Services 700 Governors Dr ... Pierre SD 57501 605-773-3227 773-6834
Web: www.state.sd.us/social/CPS
Child Support Div 700 Governors Dr ... Pierre SD 57501 605-773-3641 773-7295
TF: 800-286-9145 ■ *Web:* www.state.sd.us/social/DCS

				Phone	Fax
Consumer Protection Div 500 E Capitol Ave. Web: www.state.sd.us	Pierre	SD	57501	605-773-4400	773-7163
Corrections Dept 500 E Capital Ave Web: www.state.sd.us/corrections/corrections.html	Pierre	SD	57501	605-773-3478	773-3194
Crime Victims' Compensation Program 700 Governors Dr TF: 800-696-9476 ■ Web: www.state.sd.us	Pierre	SD	57501	605-773-6317	773-6834
Economic Development Office 711 E Wells Ave TF: 800-872-6190 ■ Web: www.sdgreatprofits.com	Pierre	SD	57501	605-773-3301	773-3256
Education Dept 700 Governors Dr Web: www.doe.sd.gov	Pierre	SD	57501	605-773-3134	773-6139
Emergency Management Office 118 W Capitol Ave Web: www.oem.sd.gov	Pierre	SD	57501	605-773-3231	773-5380
Environment & Natural Resources Dept 523 E Capitol Ave Web: www.state.sd.us	Pierre	SD	57501	605-773-3151	773-6035
Finance & Management Bureau 500 E Capitol Ave Rm A-216 Web: www.state.sd.us/bfm	Pierre	SD	57501	605-773-3411	773-4711
Gaming Commission 221 W Capitol Ave Suite 101 Web: www.state.sd.us	Pierre	SD	57501	605-773-6050	773-6053
Governor 500 E Capitol Ave Web: www.state.sd.us	Pierre	SD	57501	605-773-3212	773-5844
Health Dept 600 E Capitol Ave. Web: www.state.sd.us	Pierre	SD	57501	605-773-3361	773-5683
Highway Patrol Div 118 W Capitol Ave Web: www.hp.state.sd.us	Pierre	SD	57501	605-773-3105	773-6046
Historical Society 900 Governors Dr Web: www.sdhistory.org	Pierre	SD	57501	605-773-3458	773-6041
Housing Development Authority PO Box 1237 Web: www.sdhda.org	Pierre	SD	57501	605-773-3181	773-5154
Information & Telecommunications Bureau 700 Governors Dr Web: www.state.sd.us	Pierre	SD	57501	605-773-5110	773-6040
Insurance Div 445 E Capitol Ave Web: www.state.sd.us/drr2/reg/insurance	Pierre	SD	57501	605-773-3563	773-5369
Labor Dept 700 Governors Dr. Web: www.state.sd.us/dol	Pierre	SD	57501	605-773-3101	773-4211
Legislature Capitol Bldg 500 E Capitol Ave 3rd Fl Web: legis.state.sd.us	Pierre	SD	57501	605-773-3251	773-4576
Lieutenant Governor 500 E Capitol Ave. Web: www.state.sd.us/Lt.Gov	Pierre	SD	57501	605-773-3661	773-4711
Military & Veterans Affairs Dept 2823 W Main St Web: www.state.sd.us	Rapid City	SD	57702	605-737-6200	737-6677
Motor Vehicle Div 445 E Capital Ave Web: www.state.sd.us/drr2/motorvehicle	Pierre	SD	57501	605-773-3541	773-5129
Pardons & Parole Board PO Box 5911 Web: www.state.sd.us	Sioux Falls	SD	57117	605-367-5040	367-5025
Parks & Recreation Div 523 E Capitol Ave TF Campground Resv: 800-710-2267 ■ Web: www.sdgfp.info	Pierre	SD	57501	605-773-3391	773-6245
Personnel Bureau 500 E Capitol Ave Web: www.state.sd.us/jobs	Pierre	SD	57501	605-773-3148	773-4356
Public Utilities Commission 500 E Capitol Ave Web: www.state.sd.us	Pierre	SD	57501	605-773-3201	773-3809
Real Estate Commission 221 W Capitol Ave Suite 101 Web: www.state.sd.us	Pierre	SD	57501	605-773-3600	773-4356
Regents Board 306 E Capitol Ave Suite 200 Web: www.sdbor.edu	Pierre	SD	57501	605-773-3455	733-5320
Rehabilitation Services Div 500 E Capitol Ave TF: 800-265-9684 ■ Web: www.state.sd.us	Pierre	SD	57501	605-773-3195	773-5483
Revenue 445 E Capitol Ave. Web: www.state.sd.us/drr	Pierre	SD	57501	605-773-3311	773-5129
Secretary of State 500 E Capitol Ave Suite 204 Web: www.sdsos.gov	Pierre	SD	57501	605-773-3537	773-6580
Securities Div 445 E Capitol Ave. Web: www.state.sd.us	Pierre	SD	57501	605-773-4823	773-5953
Social Services Dept 700 Governors Dr Web: www.state.sd.us/social	Pierre	SD	57501	605-773-3165	773-4855
State Court Administrator 500 E Capitol Ave Web: www.sdjudicial.com	Pierre	SD	57501	605-773-8459	773-8437
Supreme Court 500 E Capitol Ave Web: www.sdjudicial.com	Pierre	SD	57501	605-773-3511	773-6128
Tourism Office 711 E Wells Ave. TF: 800-952-3625 ■ Web: www.travelsd.com	Pierre	SD	57501	605-773-3301	773-3256
Treasurer 500 E Capitol Ave Suite 212 Web: www.sdtreasurer.com	Pierre	SD	57501	605-773-3378	773-3115
Tribal Government Relations Office 711 E Wells Ave Web: www.sdtribalrelations.com	Pierre	SD	57501	605-773-3415	773-6592
Vital Records 600 E Capitol Ave TF: 800-738-2301 ■ Web: www.state.sd.us	Pierre	SD	57501	605-773-4961	773-5683
Weights & Measures Office 118 W Capitol Ave Web: www.state.sd.us/dps/wm	Pierre	SD	57501	605-773-3697	773-6631

342-43 Tennessee

				Phone	Fax
State Government Information 400 Deaderick St 15th Fl Web: www.tennessee.gov	Nashville	TN	37243	615-741-3011	
Administrative Office of the Cts 511 Union St Suite 600 Web: www.tsc.state.tn.us	Nashville	TN	37219	615-741-2687	741-6285
Aging & Disability Commission 500 Deaderick St 8th Fl Web: www.state.tn.us/comaging	Nashville	TN	37243	615-741-2056	741-3309
Agriculture Dept 440 Hogan Rd PO Box 40627 Web: www.state.tn.us/agriculture	Nashville	TN	37204	615-837-5100	837-5333
Arts Commission 401 Charlotte Ave Web: www.arts.state.tn.us	Nashville	TN	37243	615-741-1701	741-8559
Attorney General PO Box 20207 Web: www.attorneygeneral.state.tn.us	Nashville	TN	37202	615-741-3491	741-2009
Bill Status 320 6th Ave N 1st Fl Web: www.legislature.state.tn.us	Nashville	TN	37243	615-741-3511	
Boxing & Racing Board 500 James Robertson Pkwy 2nd Fl	Nashville	TN	37243	615-741-2384	741-5995
Child Support Services Div 400 Deaderick St 12th Fl TF: 800-838-6911 ■ Web: www.state.tn.us/humanserv/child_support.htm	Nashville	TN	37248	615-313-4880	532-2791
Children's Services Dept 436 6th Ave N 7th Fl Web: www.state.tn.us	Nashville	TN	37243	615-741-9699	532-8079
Commerce & Insurance Dept 500 James Robertson Pkwy 5th Fl Web: www.state.tn.us/commerce	Nashville	TN	37423	615-741-6007	532-6934
Consumer Affairs Div 500 James Robertson Pkwy 5th Fl Web: www.state.tn.us	Nashville	TN	37243	615-741-4737	532-4994
Correction Dept 320 6th Ave N 4th Fl Web: www.state.tn.us	Nashville	TN	37243	615-741-1000	741-4605
Div of Claims Administration 502 Deaderick St Web: treasury.tn.gov	Nashville	TN	37243	615-741-2734	532-4979
Economic & Community Development Dept 312 8th Ave N 11th Fl TF: 877-768-6374 ■ Web: www.tn.gov/ecd	Nashville	TN	37243	615-741-1888	741-7306
Education Dept 710 James Robertson Pkwy 6th Fl Web: www.state.tn.us	Nashville	TN	37243	615-741-2731	532-4791
Emergency Management Agency 3041 Sidco Dr Web: www.tnema.org	Nashville	TN	37204	615-741-0001	242-9635
Environment & Conservation Dept 401 Church St L & C Annex 1st Fl Web: www.state.tn.us/environment	Nashville	TN	37243	615-532-0109	532-0120
Finance & Administration Dept 312 Rosa L Parks Ave Web: www.state.tn.us/finance	Nashville	TN	37243	615-741-0320	741-9872
Financial Institutions Dept 414 Union St Suite 1000 Web: www.tn.gov	Nashville	TN	37219	615-741-2236	
General Assembly 320 6th Ave N Web: www.legislature.state.tn.us	Nashville	TN	37243	615-741-3511	532-6973
Governor State Capitol 1st Fl Web: www.tennessee.gov	Nashville	TN	37243	615-741-2001	532-9711
Health Dept 425 5th Ave N 3rd Fl Web: www.state.tn.us	Nashville	TN	37247	615-741-3111	741-2491
Highway Patrol 1150 Foster Ave Web: www.state.tn.us	Nashville	TN	37249	615-251-5175	532-1051
Historical Commission 2941 Lebanon Rd Web: www.state.tn.us	Nashville	TN	37214	615-532-1550	532-1549
Homeland Security Office 312 Rosa L Parks Ave Web: www.tennessee.gov	Nashville	TN	37243	615-532-7825	253-5379
Housing Development Agency 404 James Robertson Pkwy Suite 1114 Web: www.state.tn.us/thda	Nashville	TN	37243	615-741-2400	741-9634
Human Services Dept 400 Deaderick St. Web: www.state.tn.us	Nashville	TN	37248	615-313-4700	741-4165
Information Resources Office 312 Rosa L Parks Ave Web: www.state.tn.us	Nashville	TN	37243	615-741-3700	532-0471
Insurance Div 500 James Robertson Pkwy Web: www.tn.gov	Nashville	TN	37243	615-741-2176	532-2788
Labor & Workforce Development Dept 220 French Landing Dr Web: www.state.tn.us	Nashville	TN	37243	615-741-6642	741-5078
Lottery 200 Athens Way Suite 200 *Fax: Hum Res ■ Web: www.tnlottery.com	Nashville	TN	37228	615-324-6500	324-8013*
Mental Health & Developmental Disabilities Dept 425 5th Ave N 3rd Fl TF: 800-669-1851 ■ Web: www.state.tn.us	Nashville	TN	37243	615-532-6500	532-6514
Military Dept 3041 Sidco Dr Web: www.tnmilitary.org	Nashville	TN	37204	615-313-0633	313-3129
Personnel Dept 505 Deaderick St Web: www.state.tn.us	Nashville	TN	37243	615-741-2958	532-0728
Probation & Parole Board 404 James Robertson Pkwy Suite 1300 Web: www.tennessee.gov/bopp	Nashville	TN	37243	615-741-1673	532-8581
Real Estate Commission 500 James Robertson Pkwy Suite 180 TF: 800-342-4031 ■ Web: www.state.tn.us/commerce/boards/trec	Nashville	TN	37243	615-741-2273	741-0313
Regulatory Authority 460 James Robertson Pkwy Web: www.state.tn.us/tra	Nashville	TN	37243	615-741-2904	741-5015
Regulatory Boards Div 500 James Robertson Pkwy Web: www.state.tn.us/commerce/boards	Nashville	TN	37243	615-741-3449	741-6470
Rehabilitation Services Div 400 Deaderick St 11th Fl Web: www.state.tn.us/humanserv/rehabilitation.htm	Nashville	TN	37248	615-313-4700	741-4165
Revenue Dept 500 Deaderick St Web: www.state.tn.us/revenue	Nashville	TN	37242	615-741-2461	741-0682
Secretary of State State Capitol 1st Fl Web: www.state.tn.us/sos	Nashville	TN	37243	615-741-2819	532-9547
Securities Div 500 James Robertson Pkwy Suite 680 Web: www.state.tn.us/commerce/securities	Nashville	TN	37243	615-741-2947	532-8375
State Parks Div 401 Church St 7th Fl TF: 888-867-2757 ■ Web: www.state.tn.us/environment/parks	Nashville	TN	37243	615-532-0001	532-0732

Phone | Fax

Student Assistance Corp
404 James Robertson Pkwy Suite 1510 . . . . . Nashville TN 37243 615-741-1346 741-6101
TF: 800-257-6526 ■ *Web:* www.state.tn.us/tsac

Supreme Court
511 Union St Nashville City Ctr Suite 600 . . . . . Nashville TN 37219 615-741-2687
TF: 800-448-7970 ■ *Web:* www.tsc.state.tn.us

Title & Registration Div
44 Vantage Way Suite 160 . . . . . Nashville TN 37243 615-741-3101 401-6782
Web: www.state.tn.us/safety/titleandregistration

Tourist Development Dept
312 8th Ave N 25th Fl. . . . . . Nashville TN 37243 615-741-2159 741-7225
Web: www.state.tn.us/tourdev

Transportation Dept
505 Deaderick St Suite 700 . . . . . Nashville TN 37243 615-741-2848 741-2508
Web: www.tdot.state.tn.us

Treasurer
Tennessee State Capitol
1st Fl 600 Charlotte Ave. . . . . . Nashville TN 37243 615-741-2956
Web: www.treasury.state.tn.us

Treasury Dept 600 Charlotte Ave. . . . . . Nashville TN 37243 615-741-2956 532-1591
Web: www.treasury.state.tn.us

Veterans Affairs Dept 215 8th Ave N. . . . . . Nashville TN 37243 615-741-2931 741-4785
Web: www.state.tn.us/veteran

Vital Records Div 421 5th Ave N 1st Fl. . . . . . Nashville TN 37247 615-741-1763 741-9860
Web: www.state.tn.us/health/vr

Wildlife Resources Agency PO Box 40747 . . . . . Nashville TN 37204 615-781-6500 741-4606
Web: www.state.tn.us/twra

Workers Compensation Div
710 James Robertson Pkwy 2nd Fl. . . . . . Nashville TN 37243 615-741-2395 532-1468
Web: www.state.tn.us/labor-wfd/wcomp.html

Higher Education Commission
404 James Robertson Pkwy Suite 1900 . . . . . Nashville TN 37243 615-741-3605 741-6230
Web: www.state.tn.us

342-44 Texas

Phone | Fax

State Government Information PO Box 13564 . . . . . Austin TX 78711 512-463-4630
TF: 877-452-9060 ■ *Web:* www.texas.gov/en/Pages/default.aspx

Aging & Disability Services Dept
701 W 51st St PO Box 149030. . . . . . Austin TX 78714 512-438-3011 438-4220
TF: 800-458-9858

Agriculture Dept PO Box 12847. . . . . . Austin TX 78711 512-463-7476 463-1104
TF Cust Svc: 800-835-5832 ■ *Web:* www.agr.state.tx.us

Arts Commission PO Box 13406. . . . . . Austin TX 78711 512-463-5535 475-2699
TF: 800-252-9415 ■ *Web:* www.arts.state.tx.us

Assistive & Rehabilitation Services Dept
4800 N Lamar Blvd 3rd Fl. . . . . . Austin TX 78756 512-377-0500 407-3251
TF: 800-252-5204 ■ *Web:* www.dars.state.tx.us

Attorney General PO Box 12548. . . . . . Austin TX 78711 512-463-2191 463-2063
Web: www.oag.state.tx.us

Banking Dept 2601 N Lamar Blvd . . . . . Austin TX 78705 512-475-1300 475-1313
TF: 877-276-5554 ■ *Web:* www.banking.state.tx.us

Bill Status
State Capitol 1100 Congress Ave Rm 2N-3 . . . . . Austin TX 78711 512-463-2182 475-4626
TF: 877-824-7038 ■ *Web:* www.capitol.state.tx.us

Child Support Div 300 W 15th St . . . . . Austin TX 78701 512-460-6000 834-9712
TF: 800-252-8014 ■ *Web:* www.oag.state.tx.us

Comptroller of Public Accounts 111 E 17th St. . . . . . Austin TX 78774 512-463-4600 475-0352
TF: 800-531-5441 ■ *Web:* www.cpa.state.tx.us

Consumer Protection Div PO Box 12548 . . . . . Austin TX 78711 512-463-2185 473-8301
TF: 800-621-0508 ■ *Web:* www.oag.state.tx.us/consumer/consumer.shtml

Crime Victims Services Div PO Box 12198 . . . . . Austin TX 78711 512-936-1200 320-8270
TF: 800-983-9933 ■ *Web:* www.oag.state.tx.us

Criminal Justice Dept PO Box 13084 . . . . . Austin TX 78711 512-475-3250 305-9398
Web: www.tdcj.state.tx.us

Economic Development
1700 N Congress Ave PO Box 12728. . . . . . Austin TX 78711 512-936-0100 936-0440
Web: www.tded.state.tx.us

Education Agency 1701 N Congress Ave. . . . . . Austin TX 78701 512-463-9734 463-9838
Web: www.tea.state.tx.us

Emergency Management Div PO Box 4087. . . . . . Austin TX 78773 512-424-2138 424-2444
Web: www.demwmd.net

Environmental Quality Commission
12115 Pk Thirty 5 Cir. . . . . . Austin TX 78753 512-239-1000 239-5533
Web: www.tceq.state.tx.us

Ethics Commission 201 E 14th St 10th Fl . . . . . Austin TX 78701 512-463-5800 463-5777
Web: www.ethics.state.tx.us

Family & Protective Services Dept
701 W 51st St PO Box 149030. . . . . . Austin TX 78752 512-438-4800 438-3525
Web: www.dfps.state.tx.us

General Land Office
1700 N Congress Ave Suite 935. . . . . . Austin TX 78701 512-463-5001 475-1558
TF: 800-998-4456 ■ *Web:* www.glo.texas.gov

Governor PO Box 12428. . . . . . Austin TX 78711 512-463-2000 463-1849
TF: 800-843-5789 ■ *Web:* www.governor.state.tx.us

Higher Education Coordinating Board
1200 E Anderson Ln. . . . . . Austin TX 78752 512-427-6101 427-6169
Web: www.thecb.state.tx.us

Historical Commission 108 W 16th St. . . . . . Austin TX 78701 512-463-6100 463-8222
Web: www.thc.state.tx.us

Housing & Community Affairs Dept
507 Sabine St PO Box 13941. . . . . . Austin TX 78711 512-475-3800 472-8526
Web: www.tdhca.state.tx.us

Information Resources Dept
300 W 15th St Suite 1300. . . . . . Austin TX 78701 512-475-4700 475-4759
Web: www.dir.state.tx.us

Insurance Dept 333 Guadalupe St PO Box 149104. . . . . . Austin TX 78714 512-463-6169 475-2005
TF: 800-252-3439 ■ *Web:* www.tdi.state.tx.us

Phone | Fax

Legislature State Capitol . . . . . Austin TX 78711 512-463-0124 463-0694
Web: www.capitol.state.tx.us

Licensing & Regulation Dept PO Box 12157. . . . . . Austin TX 78711 512-463-6599 475-2874
Web: www.license.state.tx.us

Lieutenant Governor PO Box 12068 . . . . . Austin TX 78711 512-463-0001 463-0677
Web: www.ltgov.state.tx.us

Lottery Commission PO Box 16630. . . . . . Austin TX 78761 512-344-5000 344-5240*
**Fax:* Hum Res ■ *TF:* 800-375-6886 ■ *Web:* www.txlottery.org

Medical Board PO Box 2018. . . . . . Austin TX 78768 512-305-7010 305-7008
TF Cust Svc: 800-248-4062 ■ *Web:* www.tmb.state.tx.us

Motor Vehicle Div 125 E 11th St . . . . . Austin TX 78701 512-416-4800 416-4890
Web: www.dot.state.tx.us/mvd

Office of Court Administration
205 W 14th St Suite 600. . . . . . Austin TX 78711 512-463-1625 463-1648
Web: www.courts.state.tx.us

Pardons & Parole Board PO Box 13401 . . . . . Austin TX 78701 512-936-6351 463-8120
Web: www.tdcj.state.tx.us/bpp

Parks & Wildlife Dept 4200 Smith School Rd. . . . . . Austin TX 78744 512-389-4800 389-4814
TF: 800-792-1112 ■ *Web:* www.tpwd.state.tx.us

Public Safety Dept 5805 N Lamar Blvd . . . . . Austin TX 78752 512-424-2000 424-5708
Web: www.txdps.state.tx.us

Public Utility Commission PO Box 13326 . . . . . Austin TX 78711 512-936-7000 936-7003
TF: 888-782-8477 ■ *Web:* www.puc.state.tx.us

Racing Commission 8505 Cross Pk Dr Suite 110 . . . . . Austin TX 78754 512-833-6699 833-6907
Web: www.txrc.state.tx.us

Railroad Commission PO Box 12967. . . . . . Austin TX 78711 512-463-7131 463-7161
TF: 877-228-5740 ■ *Web:* www.rrc.state.tx.us

Real Estate Commission PO Box 12188. . . . . . Austin TX 78711 512-465-3900 465-3910
Web: www.trec.state.tx.us

Secretary of State PO Box 12887 . . . . . Austin TX 78711 512-463-5770 475-2761
Web: www.sos.state.tx.us

State Health Services Dept 1100 W 49th St . . . . . Austin TX 78756 512-458-7111 458-7750
Web: www.tdh.texas.gov

State Securities Board 208 E 10th St Fl 5. . . . . . Austin TX 78701 512-305-8300 305-8310
Web: www.ssb.state.tx.us

Supreme Court
201 W 14th St Rm 104 PO Box 12248 . . . . . Austin TX 78711 512-463-1312 463-1365
Web: www.supreme.courts.state.tx.us

Transportation Dept 125 E 11th St. . . . . . Austin TX 78701 512-463-8585 463-9896
Web: www.dot.state.tx.us

Veterans Commission PO Box 12277 . . . . . Austin TX 78711 512-463-5538 475-2395
TF: 800-252-8387 ■ *Web:* www.tvc.state.tx.us

Vital Statistics Bureau PO Box 12040 . . . . . Austin TX 78711 888-963-7111 458-7111*
**Fax Area Code:* 512 ■ *TF:* 888-963-7111 ■ *Web:* www.tdh.state.tx.us/bvs

Workers Compensation Commission
7551 Metro Ctr Dr . . . . . Austin TX 78744 512-804-4000 804-4001
TF Cust Svc: 800-252-7031 ■ *Web:* www.twcc.state.tx.us

Workforce Commission 101 E 15th St. . . . . . Austin TX 78778 512-463-2222 936-3504
Web: www.twc.state.tx.us

Youth Commission 4900 N Lamar Blvd PO Box 4260 . . . . . Austin TX 78765 512-424-6130 424-6236
Web: www.tyc.state.tx.us

342-45 Utah

Phone | Fax

State Government Information
136 E S Temple Suite 1150. . . . . . Salt Lake City UT 84111 801-538-3000 860-7680*
**Fax Area Code:* 877 ■ *Web:* www.utah.gov

Administrative Office of the Courts
450 S State St N31 . . . . . Salt Lake City UT 84114 801-578-3800 578-3843
Web: www.utcourts.gov

Aging & Adult Services Div
120 N 200 W Rm 325. . . . . . Salt Lake City UT 84103 801-538-3910 538-4395
Web: www.hsdaas.utah.gov

Agriculture & Food Dept
350 N Redwood Rd. . . . . . Salt Lake City UT 84116 801-538-7100 538-7126
Web: www.ag.utah.gov

Arts Council 617 E S Temple. . . . . . Salt Lake City UT 84102 801-236-7555 236-7556
Web: artsandmuseums.utah.gov

Attorney General PO Box 142320. . . . . . Salt Lake City UT 84114 801-538-9600 538-1121
Web: www.attorneygeneral.utah.gov

Child & Family Services Div
195 N 1950 W Rm 225. . . . . . Salt Lake City UT 84116 801-538-4100 538-3993
TF: 855-323-3237 ■ *Web:* www.hsdcfs.utah.gov

Child Support Div 515 E 100 S 8th Fl. . . . . . Salt Lake City UT 84114 801-536-8300 536-8315
Web: attorneygeneral.utah.gov/childsupport.html

Commerce Dept 160 E Broadway # 4 . . . . . Salt Lake City UT 84111 801-530-6701 530-6446
Web: www.commerce.utah.gov

Community & Economic Development Dept
324 S State St Suite 500. . . . . . Salt Lake City UT 84111 801-538-8700 538-8888
Web: dced.utah.gov

Consumer Protection Div
160 E Broadway . . . . . Salt Lake City UT 84111 801-530-6601 530-6001
Web: www.commerce.utah.gov

Corrections Dept 14717 S Minuteman Dr. . . . . . Draper UT 84020 801-265-5500 265-5726
Web: www.corrections.utah.gov

Crime Victim Reparations Office
350 E 500 S Suite 200 . . . . . Salt Lake City UT 84111 801-238-2360 533-4127
Web: www.crimevictim.utah.gov

Education Office 250 E 500 S. . . . . . Salt Lake City UT 84111 801-538-7500 538-7521
Web: www.usoe.k12.ut.us

Emergency Services & Homeland Security Div
1110 State Office Bldg . . . . . Salt Lake City UT 84114 801-538-3400 538-3770
Web: des.utah.gov

Environmental Quality Dept
195 N 1950 W . . . . . Salt Lake City UT 84116 801-536-4400 536-0061
TF: 800-458-0145 ■ *Web:* www.deq.utah.gov

Financial Institutions Dept
PO Box 146800 . . . . . Salt Lake City UT 84111 801-538-8830 538-8894
Web: www.dfi.utah.gov

				Phone	Fax
Governor					
350 N State St Suite 200					
PO Box 142220	Salt Lake City	UT	84114	801-538-1000	538-1528
TF: 800-705-2464 ■ *Web:* www.utah.gov/governor					
Health Dept 288 Garside St	Salt Lake City	UT	84116	801-538-6111	538-6306
Web: www.health.utah.gov					
Higher Education Assistance Authority					
PO Box 145112	Salt Lake City	UT	84114	801-321-7294	366-8430
TF: 877-336-7378 ■ *Web:* www.uheaa.org					
Higher Education System 60 S 400 W	Salt Lake City	UT	84101	801-321-7101	321-7199
Web: www.utahsbr.edu					
Highway Patrol 4501 S 2700 W	Salt Lake City	UT	84119	801-965-4518	965-4716
Web: www.highwaypatrol.utah.gov					
Housing Corp 2479 Lake Pk Blvd	West Valley City	UT	84120	801-902-8200	
Web: www.utahhousingcorp.org					
Human Resource Management Dept					
2120 State Office Bldg	Salt Lake City	UT	84114	801-538-3025	538-3403
Web: www.dhrm.utah.gov					
Human Services Dept 195 N 1950 W	Salt Lake City	UT	84116	801-538-4171	538-4016
Web: www.dhs.utah.gov					
Information Technology Services					
6000 State Office Bldg	Salt Lake City	UT	84114	801-538-3833	538-3622
Web: www.its.state.ut.us					
Insurance Dept 3110 State Office Bldg	Salt Lake City	UT	84114	801-538-3800	538-3829
Web: www.insurance.utah.gov					
Labor Commission PO Box 146600	Salt Lake City	UT	84114	801-530-6800	530-6390
TF: 800-530-5090 ■ *Web:* www.laborcommission.utah.gov					
Legislature					
State Capitol Complex W Bldg	Salt Lake City	UT	84114	801-538-1029	538-1908
Web: www.le.utah.gov					
Lieutenant Governor PO Box 142325	Salt Lake City	UT	84114	800-705-2464	538-1133*
**Fax Area Code:* 801 ■ *TF:* 800-705-2464 ■ *Web:* www.utah.gov/ltgovernor					
Medical Examiner's Office					
48 Medical Dr	Salt Lake City	UT	84113	801-584-8410	584-8435
Web: health.utah.gov/ome					
Motor Vehicle Div PO Box 30412	Salt Lake City	UT	84130	801-297-7780	297-3570
TF: 800-368-8824 ■ *Web:* dmv.utah.gov					
Natural Resources Dept					
1594 W N Temple Suite 3710	Salt Lake City	UT	84116	801-538-7200	538-7315
Web: www.nr.utah.gov					
Occupational & Professional Licensing Div					
PO Box 146741	Salt Lake City	UT	84111	801-530-6628	530-6511
TF: 866-275-3675 ■ *Web:* www.dopl.utah.gov					
Pardons & Parole Board					
448 East Winchester St Suite 300	Murray	UT	84107	801-261-6464	261-6481
Web: bop.utah.gov					
Parks & Recreation Div					
1594 W N Temple # 116	Salt Lake City	UT	84116	801-538-7220	538-7378
TF: 800-322-3770 ■ *Web:* www.stateparks.utah.gov					
Public Service Commission					
160 E 300 S PO Box 45585	Salt Lake City	UT	84114	801-530-6716	530-6796
Web: www.psc.state.ut.us					
Real Estate Div PO Box 146711	Salt Lake City	UT	84114	801-530-6747	526-4387
Web: realestate.utah.gov					
Rehabilitation Office 250 E 500 S	Salt Lake City	UT	84111	801-538-7530	538-7522
TF: 800-473-7530 ■ *Web:* www.usor.utah.gov					
Securities Div 160 E Broadway # 2	Salt Lake City	UT	84111	801-530-6600	530-6980
Web: www.securities.state.ut.us					
Sports Commission					
201 S Main St Suite 2002	Salt Lake City	UT	84111	801-328-2372	328-2389
Web: www.utahsportscommission.com					
State Treasurer					
315 State Capitol Bldg # E	Salt Lake City	UT	84114	801-538-1042	538-1465
Web: www.treasurer.utah.gov					
Supreme Court 450 S State St	Salt Lake City	UT	84114	801-238-7967	238-7980
Web: www.utcourts.gov/courts/sup					
Tax Commission 210 N 1950 W	Salt Lake City	UT	84134	801-297-2200	297-3891
Web: www.tax.utah.gov					
Transportation Dept					
4501 Constitution Blvd	Salt Lake City	UT	84119	801-965-4000	965-4338
Web: www.udot.utah.gov					
Travel Development Div 300 N State St	Salt Lake City	UT	84114	801-538-1900	538-1399
TF: 800-200-1160 ■ *Web:* www.travel.utah.gov					
Veterans' Affairs Office					
550 Foothills Blvd Suite 206	Salt Lake City	UT	84108	801-326-2372	326-2369
Web: www.ut.ngb.army.mil					
Vital Records & Statistics Office					
288 Garside St	Salt Lake City	UT	84116	801-538-6105	538-9467
Web: www.health.utah.gov					
Wildlife Resources Div					
1594 W N Temple Suite 2110	Salt Lake City	UT	84116	801-538-4700	538-4709
Web: www.wildlife.utah.gov					
Workers" Compensation Fund PO Box 57929	Murray	UT	84157	801-288-8000	288-8938
Workforce Services Dept 140 E 300 S	Salt Lake City	UT	84111	801-526-9675	526-9211
Web: www.jobs.utah.gov					

342-46 Vermont

				Phone	Fax
State Government Information					
535 Stone Cutters Way Fl 3 Suite 2	Montpelier	VT	05602	802-828-1110	
Web: www.vermont.gov					
Aging & Disabilities Dept 103 S Main St	Waterbury	VT	05671	802-241-2401	241-2325
Web: www.dail.vermont.gov					
Agriculture Food & Markets Dept					
116 State St	Montpelier	VT	05620	802-828-2430	828-2361
Web: www.vermontagriculture.com					
Arts Council 136 State St	Montpelier	VT	05633	802-828-3291	828-3363
Web: www.vermontartscouncil.org					
Attorney General 109 State St	Montpelier	VT	05609	802-828-3171	828-2154
Web: www.state.vt.us					
Banking Div 89 Main St	Montpelier	VT	05620	802-828-3307	828-1477
Web: www.bishca.state.vt.us					
Bill Status 115 State St State House	Montpelier	VT	05633	802-828-2231	828-2424
Web: www.leg.state.vt.us					
Board of Medical Practice					
101 Cherry St 3rd Fl PO Box 70	Burlington	VT	05402	802-657-4220	657-4227
Web: healthvermont.gov					
Chief Medical Examiner 111 Colchester Ave	Burlington	VT	05401	802-863-7320	863-7265
Child Support Office 103 S Main St	Waterbury	VT	05671	802-241-2319	244-1483
TF: 800-786-3214 ■ *Web:* www.ocs.state.vt.us					
Children & Families Dept					
103 S Main St 2nd Fl 5 N	Waterbury	VT	05671	802-241-2100	241-2407
TF: 800-786-3214 ■ *Web:* dcf.vermont.gov					
Consumer Assistance Program					
146 University Pl	Burlington	VT	05405	802-656-3183	656-1423
TF: 800-649-2424 ■ *Web:* www.atg.state.vt.us					
Corrections Dept 103 S Main St	Waterbury	VT	05671	802-241-2442	241-2565
Web: www.doc.state.vt.us					
Court Administrator 111 State St	Montpelier	VT	05609	802-828-3278	828-3457
Web: www.vermontjudiciary.org					
Crime Victim Services Ctr 58 S Main St	Waterbury	VT	05676	802-241-1250	241-4337
Web: www.ccvs.state.vt.us					
Dept for Children & Families 103 S Main St	Waterbury	VT	05671	802-241-2853	241-2830
Web: www.dpath.state.vt.us					
Economic Development Dept PO Box 20	Montpelier	VT	05601	802-828-3080	828-3258
Web: www.thinkvermont.com					
Education Dept 120 State St	Montpelier	VT	05620	802-828-3135	828-3140
Web: www.state.vt.us					
Educator Licensing Div 120 State St	Montpelier	VT	05620	802-828-2445	828-5107
Web: education.vermont.gov					
Emergency Management Office 103 S Main St	Waterbury	VT	05671	802-244-8721	241-5556
TF: 800-347-0488 ■ *Web:* www.dps.state.vt.us					
Environmental Conservation Dept					
103 S Main St	Waterbury	VT	05671	802-241-3800	244-5141
Web: www.anr.state.vt.us/dec/dec.htm					
Fish & Wildlife Dept 103 S Main St Bldg 10S	Waterbury	VT	05671	802-241-3700	241-3295
Web: www.anr.state.vt.us					
General Assembly 115 State St	Montpelier	VT	05633	802-828-2228	828-2424
Web: www.leg.state.vt.us					
Governor 109 State St 5th Fl	Montpelier	VT	05609	802-828-3333	828-3339
Web: www.vermont.gov					
Health Dept 108 Cherry St	Burlington	VT	05402	802-863-7200	865-7754
Web: www.healthvermont.gov					
Historic Preservation Div					
National Life Bldg 6th Fl	Montpelier	VT	05620	802-828-3213	828-3206
TF: 800-341-2211 ■ *Web:* www.historicvermont.org					
Housing & Community Affairs Dept					
1 National Life Dr 6th Fl	Montpelier	VT	05620	802-828-3211	828-3258
TF: 800-253-0191 ■ *Web:* www.dhca.state.vt.us					
Insurance Div 89 Main St	Montpelier	VT	05620	802-828-3301	
Web: www.bishca.state.vt.us					
Labor & Industry Dept					
5 Green Mountain Dr PO Box 488	Montpelier	VT	05601	802-828-2288	828-2195
Web: www.state.vt.us/labind					
Labor Dept 5 Green Mountain Dr	Montpelier	VT	05601	802-828-4000	828-4022
Web: www.labor.vermont.gov					
Licensing & Professional Regulation Office					
National Life Bldg N 2nd Fl	Montpelier	VT	05620	802-828-2367	828-2368
Web: www.vtprofessionals.org					
Lieutenant Governor State House	Montpelier	VT	05633	802-828-2226	828-3198
Web: www.ltgov.vermont.gov					
Lottery Commission 1311 US Rt 302 Suite 100	Barre	VT	05641	802-479-5686	479-4294
TF: 800-322-8800 ■ *Web:* www.vtlottery.com					
Motor Vehicles Dept 120 State St	Montpelier	VT	05603	802-828-2000	828-2098
Web: www.aot.state.vt.us/dmv/dmvhp.htm					
Natural Resources Agency 103 S Main St	Waterbury	VT	05671	802-241-3600	244-1102
Web: www.anr.state.vt.us					
Parks Div 103 S Main St Bldg 10S	Waterbury	VT	05671	802-241-3655	244-1481
TF Campground Resv: 888-409-7579 ■ *Web:* www.vtstateparks.com					
Public Service Board 112 State St 4th Fl	Montpelier	VT	05620	802-828-2358	828-3351
Web: www.state.vt.us/psb					
Real Estate Commission					
81 River St Drawer 9	Montpelier	VT	05609	802-828-3228	828-2368
Secretary of State 26 Terr St Drawer 9	Montpelier	VT	05609	802-828-2363	828-2496
Web: www.sec.state.vt.us					
Securities Div 89 Main St	Montpelier	VT	05620	802-828-3420	828-2896
Web: www.bishca.state.vt.us					
State Police 103 S Main St	Waterbury	VT	05671	802-244-7345	241-5551
Web: www.dps.state.vt.us/vtsp					
Supreme Court 111 State St	Montpelier	VT	05609	802-828-3278	828-3457
Web: www.vermontjudiciary.org					
Taxes Dept 133 State St	Montpelier	VT	05609	802-828-2505	828-2701
Web: www.state.vt.us/tax					
Tourism & Marketing Dept					
6 Baldwin St drawer 22	Montpelier	VT	05633	802-828-3237	828-3233
TF: 800-837-6668 ■ *Web:* www.vermontvacation.com					
Transportation Agency 1 National Life Dr	Montpelier	VT	05633	802-828-2657	828-2024
Web: www.aot.state.vt.us					
Treasurer 109 State St 4th Fl	Montpelier	VT	05609	802-828-2301	828-2772
Web: www.vermonttreasurer.gov					
Veterans Affairs Office 118 State St	Montpelier	VT	05620	802-828-3379	828-5932
Web: www.va.state.vt.us					
Vital Records Section PO Box 70	Burlington	VT	05402	802-863-7275	651-1787
Web: www.healthvermont.gov					
Vocational Rehabilitation Div					
103 S Main St	Waterbury	VT	05671	802-241-2186	241-3359
TF: 866-879-6757 ■ *Web:* www.vocrehab.vermont.gov					
Workers' Compensation Div					
5 Green Mountain Dr	Montpelier	VT	05601	802-828-2286	828-2195
Web: www.labor.vermont.gov					

342-47 Virginia

				Phone	Fax
State Government Information 1111 E Main St Suite 901 *TF:* 877-482-3468 ■ *Web:* portal.virginia.gov	Richmond	VA	23219	804-786-0000	
Aging Dept 1610 Forest Ave # 100 *Web:* www.vda.virginia.gov	Richmond	VA	23229	804-662-9333	662-9354
Agriculture & Consumer Services Dept 1100 Bank St Suite 210 *Web:* www.vdacs.virginia.gov	Richmond	VA	23219	804-786-3501	371-2945
Arts Commission 223 Governor St 2nd Fl *Web:* www.arts.state.va.us	Richmond	VA	23219	804-225-3132	225-4327
Attorney General 900 E Main St *Web:* www.oag.state.va.us	Richmond	VA	23219	804-786-2071	786-1991
Chief Medical Examiner 400 E Jackson St *Web:* www.vdh.virginia.gov/medexam	Richmond	VA	23219	804-786-3174	371-8595
Child Support Enforcement Div 730 E Broad St *TF:* 800-468-8894 ■ *Web:* www.dss.state.va.us	Richmond	VA	23219	804-692-1501	692-2553
Commerce & Trade Office 202 N 9th St Suite 723 *Web:* www.commerce.virginia.gov	Richmond	VA	23219	804-786-7831	371-0250
Conservation & Recreation Dept 203 Governor St Suite 302 *Web:* www.dcr.state.va.us	Richmond	VA	23219	804-786-6124	786-6141
Consumer Affairs Office PO Box 1163 *Web:* www.vdacs.virginia.gov/consumers	Richmond	VA	23218	804-786-2042	225-2666
Corrections Dept 6900 Atmore Dr *Web:* www.vadoc.state.va.us	Richmond	VA	23225	804-674-3000	674-3509
Criminal Injuries Compensation Fund 11513 Allecingie Pkwy *TF:* 800-522-4007 ■ *Web:* www.vwc.state.va.us	Richmond	VA	23235	804-378-3434	378-4390
Economic Development Partnership 901 E Byrd St *Web:* www.yesvirginia.org	Richmond	VA	23219	804-371-8100	371-8112
Education Dept PO Box 2120 *Web:* www.pen.k12.va.us	Richmond	VA	23218	804-225-2020	371-2099
Emergency Management Dept 10501 Trade Ct *Web:* www.vdem.state.va.us	Richmond	VA	23236	804-897-6500	897-6506
Employment Commission 703 E Main St *Web:* www.vec.virginia.gov	Richmond	VA	23219	804-786-1485	225-3923
Environmental Quality Dept 629 E Main St *Web:* www.deq.state.va.us	Richmond	VA	23240	804-698-4000	698-4500
Financial Institutions Bureau 1300 E Main St Suite 800 PO Box 640 *Web:* www.scc.virginia.gov	Richmond	VA	23218	804-371-9657	371-9416
Game & Inland Fisheries Dept 4010 W Broad St *Web:* www.dgif.state.va.us	Richmond	VA	23230	804-367-1000	367-0405
General Assembly General Assembly Bldg 1000 Bank St	Richmond	VA	23219	804-698-1788	
Governor 1111 E Broad St PO Box 1475 *TF:* 800-828-1120 ■ *Web:* www.governor.virginia.gov	Richmond	VA	23219	804-786-2211	371-6351
Health Dept 109 Governor St # 13 *Web:* www.vdh.virginia.gov	Richmond	VA	23219	804-864-7001	864-7022
Health Professions Dept 9960 Mayland Dr Suite 300 *TF:* 800-533-1560 ■ *Web:* www.dhp.virginia.gov	Henrico	VA	23233	804-367-4400	527-4475
Historic Resources Dept 2801 Kensington Ave *Web:* www.dhr.state.va.us	Richmond	VA	23221	804-367-2323	367-2391
Housing Development Authority 601 S Belvidere St *TF:* 800-968-7837 ■ *Web:* www.vhda.com	Richmond	VA	23220	804-782-1986	783-6704
Human Resource Management Dept 101 N 14th St 12th Fl *Web:* www.dhrm.virginia.gov	Richmond	VA	23219	804-225-2131	371-7401
Information Technologies Agency 411 E Franklin St Suite 500 *Web:* www.vita.virginia.gov	Richmond	VA	23219	804-225-8482	
Insurance Bureau PO Box 1157 *Web:* www.scc.virginia.gov/division/boi	Richmond	VA	23218	804-371-9741	371-9873
Labor & Industry Dept 13 S 13th St *Web:* www.doli.state.va.us	Richmond	VA	23219	804-371-2327	371-6524
Lieutenant Governor 900 E Main St 1st Fl W *Web:* www.ltgov.virginia.gov	Richmond	VA	23219	804-786-2078	786-7514
Lottery 900 E Main St *Web:* www.valottery.com	Richmond	VA	23219	804-692-7777	692-7775
Mental Health Mental Retardation & Substance Abuse Services Dept 1220 Bank St *Web:* www.dmhmrsas.virginia.gov	Richmond	VA	23219	804-786-3921	371-6638
Parole Board 6900 Atmore Dr	Richmond	VA	23225	804-674-3081	674-3284
Port Authority 600 World Trade Ctr *Web:* www.vaports.com	Norfold	VA	23510	757-683-8000	683-8500
Professional & Occupational Regulation Dept 9960 Mayland Dr # 400 *Web:* www.state.va.us	Richmond	VA	23233	804-367-8500	367-9537
Racing Commission 10700 Horsemen's Rd *Web:* www.vrc.virginia.gov	New Kent	VA	23124	804-966-7400	966-7418
Rehabilitative Services Dept 8004 Franklin Farms Dr *TF:* 800-552-5019 ■ *Web:* www.vadrs.org	Richmond	VA	23229	804-662-7000	662-9532
Secretary of the Commonwealth 830 E Main St 14th Fl *Web:* www.soc.state.va.us	Richmond	VA	23219	804-786-2441	371-0017
Securities Div PO Box 1197 *Web:* www.scc.virginia.gov/division/srf	Richmond	VA	23218	804-371-9051	371-9911
Social Services Dept 801 E Main St *Web:* www.dss.state.va.us	Richmond	VA	23219	804-726-7000	
State Corp Commission 1300 E Main St PO Box 1197 *Web:* www.scc.virginia.gov	Richmond	VA	23218	804-371-9967	371-9836
State Council of Higher Education 101 N 14th St 9th Fl *Web:* www.schev.edu	Richmond	VA	23219	804-225-2600	225-2604
State Court Administrator 100 N 9th St *Web:* www.courts.state.va.us	Richmond	VA	23219	804-786-6455	786-4542
State Parks Div 203 Governor St Suite 213 *TF Resv:* 800-933-7275 ■ *Web:* www.dcr.virginia.gov/parks	Richmond	VA	23219	804-786-1712	786-9294
State Police 7700 Midlothian Tpke *Web:* www.vsp.state.va.us	Richmond	VA	23235	804-674-2000	674-2936
Supreme Court 100 N 9th St *Web:* www.courts.state.va.us/scv	Richmond	VA	23219	804-786-2251	786-6249
Taxation Dept 3610 W Broad St # 101 *Web:* www.tax.virginia.gov	Richmond	VA	23230	804-367-8031	786-3536
Tourism Corp 901 E Byrd St *TF:* 800-847-4882 ■ *Web:* www.vatc.org	Richmond	VA	23219	804-786-2051	786-1919
Treasury Dept 101 N 14th St # 4th *Web:* www.trs.virginia.gov	Richmond	VA	23219	804-225-2142	225-3187
Vital Records Div PO Box 1000 *Web:* www.vdh.virginia.gov/vitalrec	Richmond	VA	23218	804-662-6200	644-2550
Workers Compensation Commission 1000 DMV Dr *Web:* www.vwc.state.va.us	Richmond	VA	23220	804-367-8600	367-9740
Community College System 101 N 14th St 15th Fl *Web:* www.vccs.edu	Richmond	VA	23219	804-819-4901	819-4766

342-48 Washington

				Phone	Fax
State Government Information PO Box 40234 *Web:* access.wa.gov	Olympia	WA	98504	360-753-5000	
Administrative Office of the Courts 1112 Quince St SE PO Box 41174 *Web:* www.courts.wa.gov	Olympia	WA	98504	360-753-3365	586-8869
Aging & Disability Services Administration PO Box 45600 *Web:* www.aasa.dshs.wa.gov	Olympia	WA	98504	360-725-2300	407-0369
Agriculture Dept PO Box 42560 *Web:* www.agr.wa.gov	Olympia	WA	98504	360-902-1800	902-2092
Arts Commission 711 Capitol Way S Suite 600 *Web:* www.arts.wa.gov	Olympia	WA	98504	360-753-3860	586-5351
Attorney General PO Box 40100 *Web:* www.atg.wa.gov	Olympia	WA	98504	360-753-6200	664-0228
Bill Status PO Box 40600 *TF:* 800-562-6000 ■ *Web:* www.leg.wa.gov	Olympia	WA	98504	360-786-7573	
Child Support Div PO Box 45860 *TF:* 800-457-6202 ■ *Web:* www.dshs.wa.gov	Olympia	WA	98504	360-664-5440	586-3274
Children's Administration PO Box 45710 *Web:* www.dshs.wa.gov	Olympia	WA	98504	360-902-7920	902-7903
Community Trade & Economic Development Dept PO Box 42525 *Web:* www.cted.wa.gov	Olympia	WA	98504	360-725-4000	586-8440
Consumer Protection Div 1125 Washington St SE PO Box 40100 *Web:* www.atg.wa.gov/page.aspx?id=1792	Olympia	WA	98504	360-753-6200	
Corrections Dept PO Box 41100 *Web:* www.doc.wa.gov	Olympia	WA	98504	360-753-1573	664-4056
Crime Victim Compensation Program PO Box 44520 *TF:* 800-762-3716 ■	Olympia	WA	98504	360-902-5355	902-5333
Ecology Dept PO Box 47600 *Web:* www.ecy.wa.gov	Olympia	WA	98504	360-407-6000	407-6989
Emergency Management Div Camp Murray Bldg 20 TA-20 *Web:* www.emd.wa.gov	Tacoma	WA	98430	253-512-7000	512-7200
Employment Security Dept 212 Maple Pk Ave SE *Web:* www.esd.wa.gov	Olympia	WA	98504	360-902-9500	902-9556
Financial Institutions Dept PO Box 41200 *TF:* 877-746-4334 ■ *Web:* www.dfi.wa.gov/cs	Olympia	WA	98504	360-902-8703	
Fish & Wildlife Dept 600 Capitol Way N *Web:* www.wdfw.wa.gov	Olympia	WA	98501	360-902-2200	902-2156
Governor 302 14th St SW PO Box 40002 *Web:* www.governor.wa.gov	Olympia	WA	98504	360-902-4111	753-4110
Health Dept PO Box 47890 *TF:* 800-525-0127 ■ *Web:* www.doh.wa.gov	Olympia	WA	98504	360-236-4501	586-7424
Historical Society 1911 Pacific Ave *TF:* 888-238-4378 ■ *Web:* www.wshs.org	Tacoma	WA	98402	253-272-3500	272-9518
Horse Racing Commission 6326 Martin Way Suite 209 *Web:* www.whrc.wa.gov	Olympia	WA	98516	360-459-6462	459-6461
Housing Finance Commission 1000 2nd Ave Suite 2700 *TF:* 800-767-4663 ■ *Web:* www.wshfc.org	Seattle	WA	98104	206-464-7139	587-5113
Indeterminate Sentence Review Board PO Box 40907 *Web:* www.srb.wa.gov	Olympia	WA	98504	360-493-9266	493-9287
Information Services Dept PO Box 42445 *Web:* www.dis.wa.gov	Olympia	WA	98504	360-902-3470	664-0733
Insurance Commissioner PO Box 40255 *Web:* www.insurance.wa.gov	Olympia	WA	98504	360-725-7000	586-3535
Labor & Industries Dept PO Box 44000 *Web:* www.lni.wa.gov	Olympia	WA	98504	360-902-5800	902-4202
Legislature State Capitol *Web:* www.leg.wa.gov	Olympia	WA	98504	360-786-7550	786-7520
Licensing Dept PO Box 9020 *Web:* www.dol.wa.gov	Olympia	WA	98504	360-902-3600	902-4042
Lieutenant Governor 416 Sid Snyder Ave SW *Web:* www.ltgov.wa.gov	Olympia	WA	98501	360-786-7700	786-7749
Mental Health Div PO Box 45320 *TF:* 888-713-6010 ■ *Web:* www1.dshs.wa.gov/mentalhealth	Olympia	WA	98504	360-902-8070	902-0809

	City	State	Zip	Phone	Fax
Natural Resources Dept PO Box 47001	Olympia	WA	98504	360-902-1000	902-1775
Web: www.wa.gov/dnr					
Office of Superindent Public Instruction Dept					
600 Washington St SE PO Box 47200	Olympia	WA	98504	360-753-6000	753-6712
Web: www.k12.wa.us					
Personnel Dept PO Box 47500	Olympia	WA	98504	360-664-1960	586-4694
Web: hr.dop.wa.gov					
Professional Educator Standards Board					
PO Box 47236	Olympia	WA	98504	360-725-6275	586-4548
Web: www.pesb.wa.gov					
Public Disclosure Commission PO Box 40908	Olympia	WA	98504	360-753-1111	753-1112
Web: www.pdc.wa.gov					
Revenue Dept PO Box 47478	Olympia	WA	98504	360-753-5574	705-6655
TF: 800-647-7706 ■ *Web:* dor.wa.gov					
Secretary of State PO Box 40220	Olympia	WA	98504	360-902-4151	586-5629
Web: www.secstate.wa.gov					
Securities Div PO Box 9033	Olympia	WA	98507	360-902-8760	902-0524
Web: www.dfi.wa.gov/sd					
Social & Health Services Dept PO Box 45010	Olympia	WA	98504	360-902-8400	902-7848
Web: www.wa.gov/dshs					
State Lottery PO Box 43000	Olympia	WA	98504	360-664-4720	664-2630
TF: 800-732-5101 ■ *Web:* www.walottery.com					
State Parks & Recreation Commission					
1111 Israel Rd SW	Olympia	WA	98504	360-902-8500	
TF Campground Resv: 888-226-7688 ■ *Web:* www.parks.wa.gov					
State Patrol PO Box 42600	Olympia	WA	98504	360-753-6540	704-2297*
**Fax:* Hum Res ■ *Web:* www.wsp.wa.gov					
Supreme Court PO Box 40929	Olympia	WA	98504	360-357-2077	
Web: www.courts.wa.gov					
Tourism Div PO Box 42525	Olympia	WA	98504	360-725-4172	753-4470
Web: www.experiencewashington.com					
Transportation Dept PO Box 47300	Olympia	WA	98504	360-705-7000	705-6800
Web: www.wsdot.wa.gov					
Treasurer					
416 Sid Snyder Ave SW Rm 230 PO Box 40200	Olympia	WA	98504	360-902-9000	902-9044
Web: www.tre.wa.gov					
Utilities & Transportation Commission					
1300 S Evergreen Park Dr SW PO Box 47250	Olympia	WA	98504	360-664-1234	664-1150
TF: 888-333-9882 ■ *Web:* www.wutc.wa.gov					
Vehicle Services Div PO Box 9020	Olympia	WA	98507	360-902-3820	586-6703
Web: www.dol.wa.gov					
Veterans Affairs Dept PO Box 41150	Olympia	WA	98504	360-753-5586	725-2197
TF: 800-562-2308 ■ *Web:* www.dva.wa.gov					
Vital Records Div PO Box 9709	Olympia	WA	98507	360-236-4300	352-2586
Web: www.doh.wa.gov/EHSPHL/CHS/cert.htm					
Vocational Rehabilitation Div PO Box 45340	Olympia	WA	98504	360-438-8000	438-8007
TF: 800-637-5627 ■ *Web:* www.dshs.wa.gov					
Higher Education Coordinating Board					
917 Lakeridge Way PO Box 43430	Olympia	WA	98504	360-753-7800	753-7808
Web: www.hecb.wa.gov					

342-49 West Virginia

	City	State	Zip	Phone	Fax
State Government Information 100 Dee Dr	Charleston	WV	25311	304-558-3456	
Web: www.wv.gov					
Accountancy Board 106 Capitol St Suite 100	Charleston	WV	25301	304-558-3557	558-1325
Web: www.wvboacc.org					
Administrative Office of the Courts					
1900 Kanawha Blvd E Bldg 1 Rm E-100	Charleston	WV	25305	304-558-0145	558-1212
Web: www.state.wv.us					
Agriculture Dept					
1900 Kanawha Blvd E Bldg 1 Rm E-28	Charleston	WV	25305	304-558-2201	558-2203
Web: www.wvagriculture.org					
Arts Commission					
1900 Kanawha Blvd E Cultural Ctr	Charleston	WV	25305	304-558-0220	558-2779
Web: www.wvculture.org/arts					
Attorney General					
1900 Kanawha Blvd E Bldg 1 Rm 26-E	Charleston	WV	25305	304-558-2021	558-0140
Web: www.wvago.gov					
Banking Div					
1900 Kanawha Blvd E Bldg 3 Rm 311	Charleston	WV	25305	304-558-2294	558-0442
Web: www.wvdob.org					
Bill Status State Capitol Rm MB27	Charleston	WV	25305	304-347-4831	347-4901
TF: 877-565-3447 ■ *Web:* www.legis.state.wv.us					
Board of Medicine 101 Dee Dr Suite 103	Charleston	WV	25311	304-558-2921	558-2084
Web: www.wvdhhr.org					
Bureau for Public Health					
350 Capitol St Rm 702	Charleston	WV	25301	304-558-2971	558-1035
Web: www.wvdhhr.org/bph					
Chief Medical Examiner 619 Virginia St W	Charleston	WV	25302	304-558-5319	558-7886
Web: www.wvdhhr.org/ocme					
Child Support Enforcement Bureau					
231 Capitol St # 2	Charleston	WV	25301	304-558-3780	558-4092
TF: 800-249-3778 ■ *Web:* www.wvdhhr.org					
Children & Families Bureau					
350 Capitol St Rm R-730	Charleston	WV	25301	304-558-0628	558-4194
TF: 800-642-8589 ■ *Web:* www.wvdhhr.org/bcf					
Commerce Bureau 80 MacCorkle Ave SW	South Charleston	WV	25303	304-558-2200	558-2956
TF: 800-225-5982 ■ *Web:* www.boc.state.wv.us					
Community Development Div					
1900 Kanawha Blvd E Bldg 6 Rm 553	Charleston	WV	25305	304-558-4010	558-3248
TF: 800-982-3386 ■ *Web:* www.wvdo.org					
Consumer Protection Div					
812 Quarrier St 1st Fl	Charleston	WV	25301	304-558-8986	558-0184
TF: 800-368-8808 ■ *Web:* www.state.wv.us					
Corrections Div					
112 California Ave Bldg 4 Rm 300	Charleston	WV	25305	304-558-2036	558-5367
Web: www.wvdoc.com					
Crime Victims Compensation Fund					
1900 Kanawha Blvd E Rm W-334	Charleston	WV	25305	304-347-4850	347-4915
TF: 877-562-6878 ■ *Web:* www.legis.state.wv.us					
Dept of Revenue					
State Capitol Bldg 1 Rm W-300	Charleston	WV	25305	304-558-1017	558-2324
Web: www.revenue.wv.gov					
Development Office					
1900 Kanawah Blvd E Bldg 6 Rm 525B	Charleston	WV	25305	304-558-2234	558-1189
TF: 800-982-3386 ■ *Web:* www.wvdo.org					
Div of Natural Resources					
324 Fourth Ave Bldg 74	South Charleston	WV	25303	304-558-2754	558-2768
Web: www.wvdnr.gov					
Education Dept					
1900 Kanawha Blvd E Bldg 6 Rm 358	Charleston	WV	25305	304-558-2681	558-0048
Web: www.wvde.state.wv.us					
Emergency Services Office					
1900 Kanawha Blvd E Bldg 1 Rm EB-80	Charleston	WV	25305	304-558-5380	344-4538
Web: www.wvdhsem.gov					
Environmental Protection Dept 601 57th St	Charleston	WV	25304	304-926-0440	926-0446
Web: www.dep.state.wv.us					
Ethics Commission 210 Brooks St Suite 300	Charleston	WV	25301	304-558-0664	558-2169
Web: www.wvethicscommission.org					
Governor					
State Capitol Bldg 1900 Kanawha Blvd E	Charleston	WV	25305	304-558-2000	342-7025
Web: www.wvgov.org					
Historic Preservation Unit					
1900 Kanawha Blvd E	Charleston	WV	25305	304-558-0220	558-2779
Web: www.wvculture.org/shpo					
Housing Development Fund					
814 Virginia St E	Charleston	WV	25301	304-345-6475	340-9943
TF: 800-933-9843 ■ *Web:* www.wvhdf.com					
Insurance Commission PO Box 50540	Charleston	WV	25305	304-558-3354	558-0412
TF: 888-879-9842 ■ *Web:* www.wvinsurance.gov					
Labor Div					
1900 Kanawha Blvd E Bldg 6 Rm 749-B	Charleston	WV	25305	304-558-7890	558-3797
TF: 877-558-5134 ■ *Web:* www.state.wv.us/labor					
Lottery PO Box 2067	Charleston	WV	25327	304-558-0500	558-0129
TF: 800-982-4946 ■ *Web:* www.wvlottery.com					
Motor Vehicles Div					
1800 Kanawha Blvd E Bldg 3	Charleston	WV	25317	304-558-3900	558-1987
Web: www.wvdot.com					
Office of Technology 321-323 Capitol St	Charleston	WV	25305	304-558-5472	
Web: www.state.wv.us/ot					
Parks & Recreation					
1900 Kanawha Blvd E # 3	Charleston	WV	25305	304-558-2764	558-0077
TF: 800-225-5982 ■ *Web:* www.wvstateparks.com					
Probation & Parole Board					
1409 greenbrier Suite 220	Charleston	WV	25311	304-558-6366	558-5678
Public Service Commission					
208 Brooke St PO Box 812	Charleston	WV	25301	304-340-0300	340-0325
TF: 800-344-5113 ■ *Web:* www.psc.state.wv.us					
Racing Commission 106 Dee Dr	Charleston	WV	25311	304-558-2150	558-6319
Web: www.wvf.state.wv.us					
Real Estate Commission					
300 Capitol St Suite 400	Charleston	WV	25301	304-558-3555	558-6442
Web: www.wvrec.org					
Rehabilitation Services Div					
State Capitol PO Box 50890	Charleston	WV	25305	304-766-4600	766-4905
TF: 800-642-8207 ■ *Web:* www.wvdrs.org					
Secretary of State					
1900 Kanawha Blvd E Bldg 1 Suite 157K	Charleston	WV	25305	304-558-6000	558-0900
TF: 866-767-8683 ■ *Web:* www.wvsos.com					
Securities Div					
1900 Kanawha Blvd E Bldg 1 Rm W-100	Charleston	WV	25305	304-558-2257	558-4211
TF: 877-982-9148 ■ *Web:* www.wvsao.gov					
Senior Services Bureau					
1900 Kanawha Blvd E Bldg 10	Charleston	WV	25305	304-558-3317	558-0004
TF: 877-987-3646 ■ *Web:* www.state.wv.us/seniorservices					
State Legislature State Capitol Rm 212	Charleston	WV	25305	304-347-4836	347-4919
Web: www.legis.state.wv.us					
State Police 725 Jefferson Rd	South Charleston	WV	25309	304-746-2100	746-2230
Web: www.wvstatepolice.com					
Supreme Court of Appeals					
1900 Kanawha Blvd E Bldg 1 Rm E-317	Charleston	WV	25305	304-558-2601	558-3815
Web: www.state.wv.us/wvsca					
Teacher Certification Office					
1900 Kanawha Blvd E	Charleston	WV	25305	304-558-7010	558-7843
TF: 800-982-2378 ■ *Web:* wvde.state.wv.us/certification					
Tourism Div 90 MacCorkle Ave SW	Charleston	WV	25303	304-558-2200	558-2956
TF: 800-225-5982 ■ *Web:* www.wvtourism.com					
Transportation Dept					
1900 Kanawha Blvd E Bldg 5 Rm A-109	Charleston	WV	25305	304-558-0444	558-1004
Web: www.wvdot.com					
Treasurer					
1900 Kanawha Blvd E Bldg 1 Suite E-145	Charleston	WV	25305	304-558-5000	558-4097
TF: 800-422-7498 ■ *Web:* www.wvtreasury.com					
Veterans Affairs Div					
1321 Plaza E Suite 101	Charleston	WV	25301	304-558-3540	558-8197
TF: 888-838-2332 ■ *Web:* www.state.wv.us/va					
Vital Statistics 350 Capitol St Rm 165	Charleston	WV	25301	304-558-2931	558-1051
Web: www.wvdhhr.org/bph/oehp/hsc/vr/birtcert.htm					
Weights & Measures Div					
570 W MacCorkle Ave	Saint Albans	WV	25177	304-722-0602	722-0605
Higher Education Policy Commission					
1018 Kanawha Blvd E Suite 700	Charleston	WV	25301	304-558-2101	558-5719
TF: 888-825-5707 ■ *Web:* www.wvhepcnew.wvnet.edu					

342-50 Wisconsin

	City	State	Zip	Phone	Fax
State Government Information					
1 E Main Suite 200 PO Box 2037	Madison	WI	53701	608-266-2211	
Web: www.wisconsin.gov					

	City	State	Zip	Phone	Fax
Aging & Long Term Care Resources Bureau PO Box 7851 *Web:* www.dhfs.state.wi.us/aging	Madison	WI	53707	608-266-2536	267-3203
Agriculture Trade & Consumer Protection Dept PO Box 8911 *Web:* www.datcp.state.wi.us	Madison	WI	53708	608-224-5012	224-5045
Arts Board 101 E Wilson St 1st Fl *Web:* www.arts.state.wi.us	Madison	WI	53702	608-266-0190	267-0380
Attorney General PO Box 7857 *Web:* www.doj.state.wi.us	Madison	WI	53707	608-266-1221	267-2779
Bill Status 1 E Main St *TF:* 800-362-9472 ■ *Web:* www.legis.state.wi.us	Madison	WI	53708	608-266-9960	
Board of Regents 1220 Linden Dr 1860 Van Hise Hall *Web:* www.wisconsin.edu/bor	Madison	WI	53706	608-262-2324	262-5739
Child Support Bureau 201 E Washington Ave *Web:* www.dwd.state.wi.us	Madison	WI	53703	608-266-9909	267-2824
Children & Family Services Div PO Box 8916 *Web:* www.dhfs.state.wi.us/aboutDHFS/DCFS/dcfs.htm	Madison	WI	53708	608-267-3905	266-6836
Commerce Dept 201 W Washington Ave *Web:* www.commerce.state.wi.us	Madison	WI	53707	608-266-1018	266-3447
Consumer Protection Office PO Box 7857 *Web:* www.doj.state.wi.us/columns	Madison	WI	53707	608-266-3861	267-2779
Corrections Dept PO Box 7925 *Web:* www.wi-doc.com	Madison	WI	53707	608-240-5000	240-3300
Crime Victims Services Office PO Box 7951 *TF:* 800-446-6564 ■ *Web:* www.doj.state.wi.us	Madison	WI	53707	608-264-9497	264-6368
Director of State Courts 16E Capitol Bldg PO Box 1688 *Web:* www.wicourts.gov	Madison	WI	53701	608-266-6828	267-0980
Economic Development Div PO Box 7970	Madison	WI	53707	608-266-9467	264-6451
Emergency Management Div PO Box 7865 *Web:* www.emergencymanagement.wi.gov	Madison	WI	53707	608-242-3232	242-3247
Ethics Board 212 E Washington Ave 3rd Fl *Web:* www.gab.wi.gov	Madison	WI	53703	608-266-8123	264-9319
Fisheries Management PO Box 7921 *Web:* www.dnr.state.wi.us/fish	Madison	WI	53707	608-267-7498	266-2244
Governor PO Box 7863 *Web:* walker.wi.gov	Madison	WI	53707	608-266-1212	267-8983
Health & Family Services Dept PO Box 7850 *Web:* www.dhfs.state.wi.us	Madison	WI	53707	608-266-1865	266-7882
Health Professions Bureau Dept of Regulation & Licensing PO Box 8935 *Web:* drl.wi.gov	Madison	WI	53708	608-266-2112	261-7083
Historical Society 816 State St *Web:* www.wisconsinhistory.org	Madison	WI	53706	608-264-6400	
Housing & Economic Development Authority 201 W Washington Ave # 700 *TF:* 800-334-6873 ■ *Web:* www.wheda.com	Madison	WI	53703	608-266-7884	267-1099
Insurance Commission PO Box 7873 *TF:* 800-236-8517 ■ *Web:* www.oci.wi.gov	Madison	WI	53707	608-266-3585	266-9935
Legislature State Capitol *Web:* www.legis.state.wi.us	Madison	WI	53702	608-266-2211	266-7038
Lieutenant Governor 19 E State Capitol *Web:* www.ltgov.state.wi.us	Madison	WI	53702	608-266-3516	267-3571
Lottery PO Box 8941 *Web:* www.wilottery.com	Madison	WI	53708	608-261-4916	264-6644
Motor Vehicles Div 4802 Sheboygan Ave *Web:* www.dot.wisconsin.gov/drivers	Madison	WI	53707	608-266-2233	261-0136
Natural Resources Dept 101 S Webster St PO Box 7921 *Web:* www.dnr.state.wi.us	Madison	WI	53707	608-266-2621	261-4380
Parks & Recreation Bureau 101 S Webster St # Pr6 *Web:* www.dnr.wi.gov	Madison	WI	53703	608-266-2181	267-7474
Parole Commission PO Box 7960 *Web:* www.wisconsin.gov	Madison	WI	53707	608-240-7280	240-7299
Public Instruction Dept PO Box 7841 *Web:* www.dpi.state.wi.us	Madison	WI	53707	608-266-1771	267-1052
Public Service Commission PO Box 610 N Whitney Way PO Box 7854 *Web:* psc.wi.gov	Madison	WI	53707	608-266-5481	266-3957
Regulation & Licensing Dept PO Box 8935 *Web:* www.drl.wi.gov	Madison	WI	53708	608-266-2112	267-0644
Revenue Dept 2135 Rimrock Rd PO Box 8933 *Web:* www.dor.state.wi.us	Madison	WI	53708	608-266-6466	266-5718
Secretary of State 30 W Mifflin Fl 10 *Web:* www.sos.state.wi.us	Madison	WI	53703	608-266-8888	266-3159
Securities Div PO Box 1768 *Web:* www.wdfi.org/fi/securities	Madison	WI	53701	608-266-1064	264-7979
State Patrol Div PO Box 7912 *Web:* www.dot.wisconsin.gov/statepatrol	Madison	WI	53707	608-266-3212	267-4495
Supreme Court PO Box 1688 *Web:* www.courts.state.wi.us/supreme	Madison	WI	53701	608-266-1880	267-0640
Teacher Education & Licensing Bureau 125 S Webster St *Web:* www.dpi.state.wi.us	Madison	WI	53703	608-266-1879	264-9558
Tourism Dept 201 W Washington Ave 2nd Fl *TF:* 800-432-8747 ■ *Web:* www.travelwisconsin.com	Madison	WI	53703	608-266-2161	266-3403
Treasurer PO Box 7871 *Web:* www.ost.state.wi.us	Madison	WI	53707	608-266-1714	266-2647
Veterans Affairs Dept 30 W Mifflin St # 306 *TF:* 800-947-8387 ■ *Web:* www.dva.state.wi.us	Madison	WI	53703	608-266-1311	267-0403
Vital Records Office PO Box 309 *Web:* www.dhfs.state.wi.us/vitalrecords	Madison	WI	53701	608-266-1373	255-2035
Vocational Rehabilitation Div PO Box 7852 *TF:* 800-442-3477 ■ *Web:* www.dwd.state.wi.us/dvr	Madison	WI	53707	608-261-0050	266-1133
Worker's Compensation Div PO Box 7901 *Web:* www.dwd.state.wi.us/wc	Madison	WI	53707	608-266-1340	267-0394
Workforce Development Dept 201 E Washington Ave *Web:* www.dwd.state.wi.us	Madison	WI	53702	608-267-9613	266-1784

342-51 Wyoming

	City	State	Zip	Phone	Fax
State Government Information 123 Capitol Bldg *Web:* wyoming.gov	Cheyenne	WY	82002	307-777-7841	777-6869
Aging Div 6101 Yellowstone Rd N Rm 259B *TF:* 800-442-2766 ■ *Web:* wdhfs.state.wy.us/aging	Cheyenne	WY	82002	307-777-7986	777-5340
Agriculture Dept 2219 Carey Ave *Web:* wyagric.state.wy.us	Cheyenne	WY	82002	307-777-7321	777-6593
Arts Council 2320 Capitol Ave *Web:* wyoarts.state.wy.us	Cheyenne	WY	82002	307-777-7742	777-5499
Attorney General 123 Capitol 200 W 24th St *Web:* www.attorneygeneral.state.wy.us	Cheyenne	WY	82002	307-777-7841	777-6869
Banking Div 122 W 25th St Herschler Bldg 3rd Fl E *Web:* www.audit.state.wy.us	Cheyenne	WY	82202	307-777-7797	777-3555
Board of Medicine 320 W 25th St # 200 *Web:* www.wyomedboard.state.wy.us	Cheyenne	WY	82001	307-778-7053	778-2069
Business Council 214 W 15th St *Web:* www.wyomingbusiness.org	Cheyenne	WY	82002	307-777-2800	777-2838
Certified Public Accountants Board 2020 Carey Ave Suite 702 *Web:* www.cpaboard.state.wy.us	Cheyenne	WY	82002	307-777-7551	777-3796
Child Support Enforcement 122 West 25th St Herschler Bldg 1301 First Fl E *Web:* dfsweb.state.wy.us/child-support-enforcement	Cheyenne	WY	82002	307-777-6948	777-5588
Community Development Authority PO Box 634 *Web:* www.wyomingcda.com	Casper	WY	82602	307-265-0603	266-5414
Consumer Protection Unit 122 W 25th St *Web:* www.attorneygeneral.state.wy.us	Cheyenne	WY	82001	307-777-7874	777-7956
Corrections Dept 700 W 21st St *Web:* www.doc.state.wy.us	Cheyenne	WY	82002	307-777-7208	777-7479
Dept of Employment 1510 E Pershing Blvd *Web:* www.doe.wyo.gov/Pages/default.aspx	Cheyenne	WY	82002	307-777-7672	777-5805
Education Dept 2300 Capitol Ave 2nd Fl *Web:* www.edu.wyoming.gov	Cheyenne	WY	82002	307-777-7675	777-6234
Environmental Quality Dept 122 W 25th St Herschler Bldg *Web:* deq.state.wy.us	Cheyenne	WY	82002	307-777-7937	777-7682
Family Services Dept 2300 Capitol Ave 3rd Fl *Web:* www.dfsweb.state.wy.us	Cheyenne	WY	82002	307-777-7561	777-7747
Game & Fish Dept 5400 Bishop Blvd *Web:* www.gf.state.wy.us	Cheyenne	WY	82006	307-777-4600	777-4610
Governor State Capitol 200 W 24th St Rm 124 *Web:* www.wyoming.gov	Cheyenne	WY	82202	307-777-7434	632-3909
Health Dept 2300 Capitol Ave Suite 401 *Web:* www.wdhfs.state.wy.us	Cheyenne	WY	82002	307-777-7656	777-7439
Highway Patrol 5300 Bishop Blvd *Web:* www.whp.state.wy.us	Cheyenne	WY	82009	307-777-4301	777-4288
Historic Preservation Office 2301 Central Ave 3rd Fl *Web:* www.wyoshpo.state.wy.us	Cheyenne	WY	82002	307-777-7697	777-6421
Homeland Security Office 122 W 25th St Herschler Bldg 1st Fl *Web:* www.wyohomelandsecurity.state.wy.us	Cheyenne	WY	82002	307-777-4900	635-6017
Information Technology Div 2001 Capitol Ave *Web:* www.ai.state.wy.us	Cheyenne	WY	82002	307-777-5003	
Insurance Dept 106 E 6th Ave *Web:* www.insurance.state.wy.us	Cheyenne	WY	82002	307-777-7401	777-2446
Legislative Service Office State Capitol Bldg Rm 213 *TF:* 800-342-9570 ■ *Web:* www.legisweb.state.wy.us	Cheyenne	WY	82002	307-777-7881	777-5466
Legislature 213 State Capitol *Web:* legisweb.state.wy.us	Cheyenne	WY	82002	307-777-7881	777-5466
Motor Vehicles Services Div 5300 Bishop Blvd *Web:* www.dot.state.wy.us	Cheyenne	WY	82009	307-777-4714	777-4772
Probation & Parole Div 700 W 21st St Suite 200	Cheyenne	WY	82002	307-777-7208	777-5386
Professional Teaching Standards Board 1920 Thomes Ave Suite 400 *Web:* www.ptsb.state.wy.us	Cheyenne	WY	82002	307-777-7291	777-8718
Public Service Commission 2515 Warren Ave Suite 300 *Web:* www.psc.state.wy.us	Cheyenne	WY	82002	307-777-7427	777-5700
Real Estate Commission 2020 Carey Ave Suite 702 *Web:* realestate.state.wy.us	Cheyenne	WY	82002	307-777-7141	777-3796
Revenue Dept Herschler Bldg 2nd Fl W *Web:* revenue.state.wy.us	Cheyenne	WY	82002	307-777-7961	777-7722
Secretary of State 200 W 24th St *Web:* www.soswy.state.wy.us	Cheyenne	WY	82002	307-777-7378	777-6217
Securities Div 200 W 24th St *Web:* soswy.state.wy.us	Cheyenne	WY	82002	307-777-7370	777-7640
State Parks & Historical Sites Div 122 W 25th St 1st Fl E *TF Campground Resv:* 877-996-7275 ■ *Web:* www.wyoparks.state.wy.us	Cheyenne	WY	82002	307-777-5598	777-6472
Supreme Court 2301 Capitol Ave *Web:* courts.state.wy.us	Cheyenne	WY	82002	307-777-7316	777-6129
Technical Services Div 2219 Carey Ave *Web:* wyagric.state.wy.us	Cheyenne	WY	82202	307-777-7324	777-6593
Tourism Div 1520 Etchepare Cir *TF:* 800-225-5996 ■ *Web:* www.wyomingtourism.org	Cheyenne	WY	82007	307-777-7777	777-2877
Transportation Dept 5300 Bishop Blvd *Web:* www.dot.state.wy.us	Cheyenne	WY	82009	307-777-4375	777-4163
Treasurer 200 W 24th St *Web:* www.treasurer.state.wy.us	Cheyenne	WY	82002	307-777-7408	777-5411

	City	State	Zip	Phone	Fax
Veterans' Affairs Commission					
851 Werner Ct Suite 120	Casper	WY	82601	307-265-7372	265-7392
TF: 800-833-5987					
Victims Services Div 200 W 24th St # 110	Cheyenne	WY	82001	307-777-7200	777-6683
TF: 888-996-8816 ■ *Web:* www.vssi.state.wy.us					
Vital Records Services Hathaway Bldg	Cheyenne	WY	82002	307-777-7591	
Web: www.wdhfs.state.wy.us					
Vocational Rehabilitation Div					
122 W 25th St Suite 1100	Cheyenne	WY	82002	307-777-7389	777-5939
Web: www.wyomingworkforce.org					
Workers'' Safety & Compensation Div					
1510 E Pershing Blvd	Cheyenne	WY	82002	307-777-7159	777-6552
Web: wydoe.state.wy.us/wscd					
Workforce Services Dept					
122 W 25th St 2nd Fl E	Cheyenne	WY	82002	307-777-8650	777-7106
Web: www.wyomingworkforce.org					
Community College Commission					
2020 Carey Ave 8th Fl	Cheyenne	WY	82002	307-777-7763	777-6567
Web: www.commission.wcc.edu					

343 GOVERNMENT - US - EXECUTIVE BRANCH

SEE ALSO Cemeteries - National p. 1561; Coast Guard Installations p. 1615; Correctional Facilities - Federal p. 1764; Military Bases p. 2246; Parks - National - US p. 2340

	City	State	Zip	Phone	Fax
Office of the President					
1600 Pennsylvania Ave NW	Washington	DC	20500	202-456-1414	456-2461
Web: www.whitehouse.gov					
Office of the Vice President					
1650 Pennsylvania Ave NW	Washington	DC	20501	202-456-0373	
Web: www.whitehouse.gov/vicepresident					
Council of Economic Advisers					
1800 G St NW 8th Fl	Washington	DC	20502	202-395-5084	395-6958
Web: www.whitehouse.gov					
Council on Environmental Quality					
730 Jackson Pl NW	Washington	DC	20503	202-395-5750	456-6546
Web: www.whitehouse.gov/ceq					
Domestic Policy Council					
1600 Pennsylvania Ave NW	Washington	DC	20500	202-456-5594	456-5557
Web: www.whitehouse.gov/dpc					
National Economic Council					
1600 Pennsylvania Ave NW	Washington	DC	20500	202-456-2800	456-2223
Web: www.whitehouse.gov/nec					
National Security Council (NSC)					
1600 Pennsylvania Ave NW	Washington	DC	20500	202-456-9491	456-9270
Web: www.whitehouse.gov/nsc					
Office of Faith-Based & Neighborhood Partnerships					
1600 Pennsylvania Ave NW	Washington	DC	20500	202-456-6708	456-7019
Web: www.whitehouse.gov/administration/eop/ofbnp					
Office of Management & Budget (OMB)					
725 17th St NW	Washington	DC	20503	202-395-3080	395-3888
Web: www.whitehouse.gov/omb					
Office of National AIDS Policy					
736 Jackson Pl NW	Washington	DC	20503	202-456-7320	456-7315
Web: www.whitehouse.gov/onap/aids.html					
Office of National Drug Control Policy					
PO Box 6000	Rockville	MD	20849	800-666-3332	519-5212*
**Fax Area Code:* 301 ■ *TF:* 800-666-3332 ■ *Web:* www.whitehousedrugpolicy.gov					
Office of Science & Technology Policy					
725 17th St NW Rm 5228	Washington	DC	20502	202-456-7116	456-6021
Web: www.ostp.gov					
Office of the First Lady					
1600 Pennsylvania Ave NW 200 E Wing	Washington	DC	20500	202-456-7064	456-6771
Web: www.whitehouse.gov/firstlady					
Office of the US Trade Representative					
600 17th St NW	Washington	DC	20508	202-395-7360	
Web: www.ustr.gov					
President's Foreign Intelligence Advisory Board (PIAB)					
White House 1600 Pennsylvania Ave	Washington	DC	20500	202-456-1414	456-2461
Web: www.whitehouse.gov/administration/eop/piab					
USA Freedom Corps					
1600 Pennsylvania Ave NW	Washington	DC	20500	877-872-2677	
TF: 877-872-2677 ■ *Web:* www.usafreedomcorps.gov					
White House Office					
1600 Pennsylvania Ave NW	Washington	DC	20500	202-456-1414	
Web: www.whitehouse.gov					
White House Press Secretary					
1600 Pennsylvania Ave NW	Washington	DC	20500	202-456-2673	456-0126

343-1 US Department of Agriculture

	City	State	Zip	Phone	Fax
Dept of Agriculture (USDA)					
1400 Independence Ave SW	Washington	DC	20250	202-720-3631	720-2166
Web: www.usda.gov					
Agricultural Marketing Service					
1400 Independence Ave SW	Washington	DC	20250	202-720-5115	720-8477
Web: www.ams.usda.gov					
Agricultural Research Service					
US Dept of Agriculture					
1400 Independence Ave SW	Washington	DC	20250	202-720-3656	720-5427
Web: www.ars.usda.gov					
Animal & Plant Health Inspection Service (APHIS)					
National Veterinary Services Laboratories					
2300 Dayton Ave	Ames	IA	50010	515-663-7200	663-7402
Web: www.aphis.usda.gov					
Center for Nutrition Policy & Promotion (CNPP)					
3101 Pk Ctr Dr 10th Fl	Alexandria	VA	22302	703-305-7600	305-3300
TF: 888-779-7264 ■ *Web:* www.cnpp.usda.gov					
Co-op State Research Education & Extension Service					
US Dept of Agriculture					
1400 Independence Ave SW MS 2201	Washington	DC	20250	202-720-7441	720-8987
Web: www.csrees.usda.gov					
Commodity Credit Corp					
1400 Independence Ave SW	Washington	DC	20250	202-720-3111	720-9105
Web: www.fsa.usda.gov/ccc					
Economic Research Service (ERS)					
US Dept of Agriculture 1800 M St NW	Washington	DC	20036	202-694-5050	694-5757
Web: www.ers.usda.gov					
Farm Service Agency					
1400 Independence Ave SW MS 0506	Washington	DC	20250	202-720-3865	
Web: www.fsa.usda.gov					
Food & Nutrition Service 3101 Pk Ctr Dr	Alexandria	VA	22302	703-305-2062	305-2908
Web: www.fns.usda.gov					
Food Stamp Program 3101 Pk Ctr Dr	Alexandria	VA	22302	703-305-2022	305-2454
TF: 800-221-5689 ■ *Web:* www.fns.usda.gov					
Food & Nutrition Service Regional Offices					
Mid-Atlantic Region 300 Corporate Blvd	Robbinsville	NJ	08691	609-259-5025	259-5185
Web: www.fns.usda.gov/fns					
Midwest Region 77 W Jackson Blvd 20th Fl	Chicago	IL	60604	312-353-6664	
Mountain Plains Region 1244 Speer Blvd Rm 903	Denver	CO	80204	303-844-0300	844-6203
Northeast Region					
10 Cswy St Rm 501 Federal Bldg	Boston	MA	02222	617-565-6370	565-6473
Web: www.fns.usda.gov					
Southeast Region 61 Forsyth St SW Suite 8T36	Atlanta	GA	30303	404-562-1801	562-1807
Southwest Region USDA 1100 Commerce St Rm 522	Dallas	TX	75242	214-290-9800	767-0271
Western Region 90 7th St Suite 10-100	San Francisco	CA	94103	415-705-1310	705-1353
Food Safety & Inspection Service					
1400 Independence Ave SW Rm 331E	Washington	DC	20250	202-720-7025	205-0158
Web: www.fsis.usda.gov					
Foreign Agricultural Service					
1400 Independence Ave SW	Washington	DC	20250	202-720-3935	690-2159
Web: www.fas.usda.gov					
Forest Service (USFS)					
1400 Independence Ave SW	Washington	DC	20050	202-205-8333	
TF: 800-832-1355 ■ *Web:* www.fs.fed.us					
Forest Service Regional Offices					
Region 1 (Northern Region) PO Box 7669	Missoula	MT	59807	406-329-3511	329-3347
Web: www.fs.fed.us					
Region 10 (Alaska Region) PO Box 21628	Juneau	AK	99802	907-586-8806	586-7876
Web: www.fs.fed.us					
Region 2 (Rocky Mountain Region) 740 Simms St	Golden	CO	80401	303-275-5350	275-5366
Web: www.fs.fed.us					
Region 3 (Southwestern Region)					
333 Broadway Blvd SE	Albuquerque	NM	87102	505-842-3292	
Web: www.fs.fed.us					
Region 4 (Intermountain Region) 324 25th St	Ogden	UT	84401	801-625-5306	625-5127
Web: www.fs.fed.us/r4					
Region 5 (Pacific Southwest Region)					
1323 Club Dr	Vallejo	CA	94592	707-562-8737	562-9130
Web: www.fs.fed.us/r5					
Region 6 (Pacific Northwest Region)					
333 SW 1st Ave PO Box 3623	Portland	OR	97208	503-808-2468	808-2469
Web: www.fs.fed.us/r6					
Region 8 (Southern Region)					
1720 Peachtree St Suite 760S	Atlanta	GA	30309	404-347-4177	347-4821
TF: 877-372-7248 ■ *Web:* www.fs.fed.us					
Region 9 (Eastern Region)					
626 E Wisconsin Ave	Milwaukee	WI	53202	414-297-3600	297-3808
Web: www.fs.fed.us					
Grain Inspection Packers & Stockyards Administration					
1400 Independence Ave SW MS-3601	Washington	DC	20250	202-720-0219	205-9237
TF: 800-998-3447 ■ *Web:* www.gipsa.usda.gov					
National Agricultural Library					
Abraham Lincoln Bldg 10301 Baltimore Ave	Beltsville	MD	20705	301-504-5755	504-6110
Web: www.nal.usda.gov					
National Agricultural Statistics Service (NASS)					
1400 Independence Ave SW	Washington	DC	20250	202-720-2707	720-9013
TF: 800-727-9540 ■ *Web:* www.nass.usda.gov					
Natural Resources Conservation Service					
1400 Independence Ave SW Rm 5105A	Washington	DC	20250	202-720-7246	720-7690
Web: www.nrcs.usda.gov					
Risk Management Agency					
1400 Independence Ave SW MS 0801	Washington	DC	20250	202-690-2803	690-2818
Web: www.rma.usda.gov					
Rural Business-Co-op Service					
1400 Independence Ave SW	Washington	DC	20250	202-690-4730	690-4737
Web: www.rurdev.usda.gov					
Rural Development					
1400 Independence Ave SW	Washington	DC	20250	202-720-4581	720-2080
Web: www.rurdev.usda.gov					
Rural Housing Service					
1400 Independence Ave SW Rm 5014	Washington	DC	20250	202-690-1533	690-0500
Web: www.rurdev.usda.gov/rhs					
Rural Utilities Service					
1400 Independence Ave SW Rm 5135S	Washington	DC	20250	202-720-9540	720-1725
Web: www.rurdev.usda.gov/rus					
Secretary of Agriculture					
1400 Independence Ave SW Rm 200A	Washington	DC	20250	202-720-3631	720-2166
Web: www.usda.gov					

				Phone	Fax
USDA Graduate School 600 Maryland Ave SW	Washington	DC	20024	202-314-3300	329-4723*
*Fax Area Code: 866 ■ TF: 888-744-4723 ■ Web: grad.usda.gov					
World Agricultural Outlook Board					
1400 Independence Ave SW	Washington	DC	20250	202-720-6030	720-4043
Web: www.usda.gov/oce/commodity					

343-2 US Department of Commerce

				Phone	Fax
Dept of Commerce					
1401 Constitution Ave NW Hoover Bldg	Washington	DC	20230	202-482-4883	482-5168
Web: www.commerce.gov					
Bureau of Economic Analysis (BEA)					
1441 L St NW	Washington	DC	20005	202-606-9900	606-5311
Web: www.bea.gov					
Bureau of Industry & Security					
1401 Constitution Ave NW Hoover Bldg	Washington	DC	20230	202-482-2000	
Web: www.bis.doc.gov					
Economic Development Administration					
1401 Constitution Ave NW	Washington	DC	20230	202-482-4687	482-5671
Web: www.eda.gov					
Economic Development Administration Regional Offices					
Atlanta 401 W Peachtree St NW Suite 1820	Atlanta	GA	30308	404-730-3002	730-3025
Web: www.eda.gov					
Austin 504 Lavaca St Suite 1100	Austin	TX	78701	512-381-8144	381-8177
Web: www.eda.gov					
Chicago 111 N Canal St Suite 855	Chicago	IL	60606	312-353-7706	353-8575
Denver 410 17th St # 250	Denver	CO	80202	303-844-4715	844-3968
Philadelphia					
Curtis Ctr 601 Walnut St Suite 140-S	Philadelphia	PA	19106	215-597-4603	597-1063
Seattle Federal Bldg 915 2nd Ave Rm 1890	Seattle	WA	98174	206-220-7660	220-7669
Web: www.eda.gov/AboutEDA/Regions.xml					
Economics & Statistics Administration					
1401 Constitution Ave NW	Washington	DC	20230	202-482-5710	482-3417
Web: www.esa.doc.gov					
International Trade Administration					
1401 Constitution Ave NW	Washington	DC	20230	202-482-3809	482-5819
Web: www.ita.doc.gov					
Minority Business Development Agency (MBDA)					
1401 Constitution Ave NW	Washington	DC	20230	202-482-5061	501-4698
Web: www.mbda.gov					
Minority Business Development Agency Regional Offices					
Atlanta Region					
401 W Peachtree St NW Suite 1715	Atlanta	GA	30308	404-730-3300	730-3313
Web: www.mbda.gov					
Chicago Region 55 E Monroe St Suite 2810	Chicago	IL	60603	312-353-0182	353-0191
TF: 888-324-1551 ■ Web: www.mbda.gov					
Dallas Region 1100 Commerce St Rm 726	Dallas	TX	75242	214-767-8001	767-0613
Web: www.mbda.gov					
New York Region 26 Federal Plaza Suite 3720	New York	NY	10278	212-264-3262	264-0725
Web: www.mbda.gov					
San Francisco Region					
221 Main St Suite 1280	San Francisco	CA	94105	415-744-3001	744-3061
Web: www.mbda.gov					
National Environmental Satellite Data & Information Service					
1335 East-West Hwy SSMC1 8th Fl	Silver Spring	MD	20910	301-713-3578	713-1249
Web: www.nesdis.noaa.gov					
National Climatic Data Ctr					
151 Patton Ave Rm 120	Asheville	NC	28801	828-271-4800	271-4876
Web: www.ncdc.noaa.gov					
National Coastal Data Development Ctr					
Bldg 1100 Suite 101	Stennis Space Center	MS	39529	228-688-2936	688-2010
TF: 866-732-2382 ■ Web: www.ncddc.noaa.gov					
National Geophysical Data Ctr					
E/GC 325 Broadway	Boulder	CO	80305	303-497-6826	497-6513
Web: www.ngdc.noaa.gov					
National Oceanographic Data Ctr					
1315 East-West Hwy 4th Fl	Silver Spring	MD	20910	301-713-3277	713-3302
Web: www.nodc.noaa.gov					
National Institute of Standards & Technology (NIST)					
100 Bureau Dr Sp 1070	Gaithersburg	MD	20899	301-975-6478	926-1630
TF: 800-877-8339 ■ Web: www.nist.gov/index.html					
National Marine Fisheries Service Regional Offices					
Alaska Region PO Box 21668	Juneau	AK	99802	907-586-7221	586-7249
Web: www.fakr.noaa.gov					
NortheastRegion 1 Blackburn Dr	Gloucester	MA	01930	978-281-9300	281-9333
Web: www.nero.noaa.gov					
Northwest Region 7600 Sand Pt Way NE	Seattle	WA	98115	206-526-6150	526-6426
Web: www.nwr.noaa.gov					
Pacific Islands Region					
1601 Kapiolani Blvd Rm 1110	Honolulu	HI	96814	808-944-2200	973-2906
TF: 888-674-7411 ■ Web: www.fpir.noaa.gov					
Southeast Region 263 13th Ave S	Saint Petersburg	FL	33701	727-824-5301	824-5320
Web: www.sero.nmfs.noaa.gov					
Southwest Region					
501 W Ocean Blvd Suite 4200	Long Beach	CA	90802	562-980-4000	980-4018
Web: www.swr.nmfs.noaa.gov					
National Ocean Service					
1305 East-West Hwy	Silver Spring	MD	20910	301-713-3074	713-4269
Web: www.nos.noaa.gov					
National Oceanic & Atmospheric Administration (NOAA)					
1401 Constitution Ave NW	Washington	DC	20910	202-482-6090	482-3154
Web: www.noaa.gov					
National Sea Grant Program					
1315 East-West Hwy SSMC-3 11th Fl	Silver Spring	MD	20910	301-734-1077	713-0799
Web: www.nsgo.seagrant.org					
National Technical Information Service (NTIS)					
5285 Port Royal Rd	Springfield	VA	22161	703-605-6000	605-6900
TF Orders: 800-553-6847 ■ Web: www.ntis.gov					
National Telecommunications & Information Administration (NTIA)					
1401 Constitution Ave NW Hoover Bldg	Washington	DC	20230	202-482-7002	
Web: www.ntia.doc.gov					
National Weather Service (NWS)					
1325 East-West Hwy	Silver Spring	MD	20910	301-713-0689	713-0662
Web: www.weather.gov					
National Hurricane Ctr 11691 SW 17th St	Miami	FL	33165	305-229-4470	553-1901
Web: www.nhc.noaa.gov					
National Weather Service Regional Offices					
Alaska Region 222 W 7th Ave # 23 Rm 517	Anchorage	AK	99513	907-271-5088	271-3711
Web: www.arh.noaa.gov					
Central Region 7220 NW 101st Terr	Kansas City	MO	64153	816-891-7734	891-8362
Web: www.crh.noaa.gov					
Eastern Region 630 Johnson Ave	Bohemia	NY	11716	631-244-0101	244-0167
Web: www.erh.noaa.gov					
Pacific Region 737 Bishop St Suite 2200	Honolulu	HI	96813	808-532-6416	532-5569
Web: www.prh.noaa.gov/pr					
Southern Region 819 Taylor St Rm 10A05C	Fort Worth	TX	76102	817-978-1000	978-4740
Web: www.srh.noaa.gov					
Western Region 125 S State St	Salt Lake City	UT	84103	801-524-5122	524-5270
Web: www.wrh.noaa.gov					
North American Industry Classification System (NAICS)					
US Census Bureau 4600 Silver Hill Rd	Washington	DC	20233	301-763-4636	
TF: 800-923-8282 ■ Web: www.census.gov/eos/www/naics					
Secretary of Commerce					
1401 Constitution Ave NW HCHB Rm 5858	Washington	DC	20230	202-482-2112	482-2741
Web: www.commerce.gov					
US Census Bureau 4600 Silver Hill Rd	Washington	DC	20233	301-763-2135	763-3761
Web: www.census.gov					
US Census Bureau Regional Offices					
Atlanta 101 Marietta St NW Suite 3200	Atlanta	GA	30303	404-730-3832	730-3835
TF: 800-424-6974 ■ Web: www.census.gov					
Boston 4 Copley Pl Suite 301	Boston	MA	02117	617-424-4501	424-0547
TF: 800-562-5721 ■ Web: www.census.gov					
Charlotte 901 Ctr Pk Dr Suite 106	Charlotte	NC	28217	704-424-6400	424-6944
TF: 800-331-7360 ■ Web: www.census.gov					
Chicago 1111 W 22nd St Suite 400	Oak Brook	IL	60523	630-288-9200	288-9288
TF: 800-865-6384 ■ Web: www.census.gov					
Dallas 8585 N Stemmons Fwy Suite 800-S	Dallas	TX	75247	214-253-4400	655-5362
TF: 800-835-9752 ■ Web: www.census.gov					
Denver 6900 W Jefferson Ave Suite 100	Denver	CO	80235	303-264-0202	969-6777
TF: 800-852-6159 ■ Web: www.census.gov					
Detroit 1395 Brewery Pk Blvd Suite 100	Detroit	MI	48207	313-259-1158	259-5045
TF: 800-432-1495 ■ Web: www.census.gov					
Kansas City 1211 N 8th St	Kansas City	KS	66101	913-551-6728	551-6789
TF: 800-728-4748 ■ Web: www.census.gov					
Los Angeles 15350 Sherman Way Suite 300	Van Nuys	CA	91406	818-267-1700	904-6429
TF: 800-992-3530 ■ Web: www.census.gov/rolax/www					
New York 395 Hudson St Suite 800	New York	NY	10014	212-584-3400	478-4800
TF: 800-991-2520 ■ Web: www.census.gov/ronyc/www					
Philadelphia 833 Chestnut St Suite 504	Philadelphia	PA	19107	215-717-1800	717-0755
TF: 800-262-4236 ■ Web: www.census.gov					
Seattle 601 Union St Suite 3800	Seattle	WA	98101	206-381-6200	381-6310
TF: 800-233-3308 ■ Web: www.census.gov					
US Patent & Trademark Office PO Box 1450	Alexandria	VA	22313	571-272-1000	273-8300
TF: 800-786-9199 ■ Web: www.uspto.gov					

343-3 US Department of Defense

				Phone	Fax
Dept of Defense (DOD) The Pentagon	Washington	DC	20301	703-545-6700	
Web: www.defenselink.mil					
American Forces Information Service (AFIS)					
601 N Fairfax St	Alexandria	VA	22314	703-428-1200	428-0903
Web: www.defenselink.mil					
Defense Advanced Research Projects Agency (DARPA)					
3701 N Fairfax Dr	Arlington	VA	22203	703-526-6630	528-3655
Web: www.darpa.mil					
Defense Commissary Agency 1300 E Ave	Fort Lee	VA	23801	804-734-8253	
TF: 800-699-5063 ■ Web: www.commissaries.com					
Defense Contract Audit Agency					
8725 John J Kingman Rd Suite 2135	Fort Belvoir	VA	22060	703-767-3265	767-3267
Web: www.dcaa.mil					
Defense Contract Management Agency					
6350 Walker Ln Suite 300	Alexandria	VA	22310	703-428-1833	
TF: 888-576-3262 ■ Web: www.dcma.mil					
Defense Finance & Accounting Service					
1851 Bell St Rm 920	Arlington	VA	22240	703-607-2616	607-1384
Web: www.dod.mil					
Defense Hotline for Fraud Waste & Abuse					
The Pentagon	Washington	DC	20301	703-604-8799	604-8567
TF: 800-424-9098 ■ Web: www.dodig.mil/hotline/fwacompl.htm					
Defense Information Systems Agency					
PO Box 4502	Arlington	VA	22204	703-607-6900	607-4081
Web: www.disa.mil					
Defense Intelligence Agency					
7400 Defense Pentagon	Washington	DC	20301	703-695-0071	
Web: www.dia.mil					
Defense Logistics Agency					
8725 John J Kingman Rd Rm 2545	Fort Belvoir	VA	22060	703-767-6200	767-6287

	City	State	Zip	Phone	Fax
Defense Office of Economic Adjustment					
400 Army-Navy Dr Suite 200	Arlington	VA	22202	703-604-6020	604-5843
Web: www.oea.gov					
Defense Prisoner of War/Missing Personnel Office					
2900 Defense Pentagon	Washington	DC	20301	703-699-1102	602-1890
Web: www.dtic.mil					
Defense Security Cooperation Agency					
201 12th St S Suite 203	Arlington	VA	22202	703-604-6604	602-5403
Web: www.dsca.osd.mil					
Defense Security Service					
Office of Communication 1340 Braddock Pl	Alexandria	VA	22314	703-325-9471	325-6545
Web: www.dss.mil					
Defense Technical Information Ctr (DTIC)					
8725 John J Kingman Rd Suite 0944	Fort Belvoir	VA	22060	703-767-9100	767-9183
TF: 800-225-3842 ■ *Web:* www.dtic.mil					
Defense Threat Reduction Agency					
8725 John T Kingman Rd MS 6201	Fort Belvoir	VA	22060	703-767-5870	767-4450
TF: 800-701-5096 ■ *Web:* www.dtra.mil					
Joint Chiefs of Staff					
Chairman					
9999 Joint Chiefs of Staff Pentagon	Washington	DC	20318	703-697-9121	697-6002
Web: www.dtic.mil					
Missile Defense Agency					
7100 Defense Pentagon	Washington	DC	20301	703-693-0891	693-1526
Web: www.mda.mil					
National Defense University					
Fort McNair 300 5th Ave SW	Washington	DC	20319	202-685-4700	
Web: www.ndu.edu					
National Security Agency 9800 Savage Rd	Fort Meade	MD	20755	301-688-6524	688-6198
Web: www.nsa.gov					
Secretary of Defense					
1000 Defense Pentagon	Washington	DC	20301	703-692-7100	571-8951
Web: www.defenselink.mil					
Uniformed Services University of the Health Sciences					
4301 Jones Bridge Rd	Bethesda	MD	20814	301-295-1956	295-1960
TF: 800-772-1743 ■ *Web:* www.usuhs.mil					

343-4 US Department of Defense - Department of the Air Force

	City	State	Zip	Phone	Fax
Dept of the Air Force					
1670 Air Force Pentagon	Washington	DC	20330	703-695-9664	693-9601
Web: www.af.mil					
North American Aerospace Defense Command					
250 Vandenberg St Suite B-016	Peterson AFB	CO	80914	719-554-6889	554-3165
Web: www.norad.mil					
Air Combat Command 205 Dodd Blvd	Langley AFB	VA	23665	757-764-3204	764-3589
Web: www.acc.af.mil					
Air Education & Training Command					
100 H St Suite 4	Randolph AFB	TX	78150	210-652-6307	652-2027
Web: www.aetc.randolph.af.mil					
Air Force Chief of Staff					
1670 Air Force Pentagon	Washington	DC	20330	703-697-9225	693-9297
Web: www.af.mil/library/afchain.asp					
Air Force Materiel Command					
4375 Chidlaw Rd	Wright-Patterson AFB	OH	45433	937-257-6033	
Web: www.afmc.af.mil					
Air Force Reserve Command					
155 Richard Ray Blvd	Robins AFB	GA	31098	478-327-1009	327-0082
Web: www.afrc.af.mil					
Air Force Space Command					
150 Vandenberg St	Peterson AFB	CO	80914	719-554-3731	554-6013
Web: www.afspc.af.mil					
Air Force Special Operations Command					
229 Cody Ave Suite 103	Hurlburt Field	FL	32544	850-884-5515	884-7249
Web: www.afsoc.af.mil					
Air Mobility Command 503 Ward Dr Suite 214	Scott AFB	IL	62225	618-229-7843	
Web: www.amc.af.mil					
Air National Guard					
1411 Jefferson Davis Hwy	Arlington	VA	22202	703-607-2388	607-3678
Web: www.ang.af.mil					

343-5 US Department of Defense - Department of the Army

	City	State	Zip	Phone	Fax
Dept of the Army 1500 Army Pentagon	Washington	DC	20310	703-697-4200	
Web: www.army.mil					
Army Board for Correction of Military Records					
1901 S Bell St 2nd Fl	Arlington	VA	22202	703-607-1600	602-0935
Web: arba.army.pentagon.mil/abcmr-overview.cfm					
Army Discharge Review Board					
1901 S Bell St 2nd Fl	Arlington	VA	22202	703-607-1600	
Web: arba.army.pentagon.mil/adrb-overview.cfm					
Chief of Staff of the US Army					
200 Army Pentagon	Washington	DC	20310	703-697-0900	614-5268
Web: www.army.mil/leaders/csa					
Judge Advocate General's Corps					
1777 N Kent St	Rosslyn	VA	22209	703-697-5151	588-0155
TF: 800-208-7178 ■ *Web:* www.jagcnet.army.mil					
US Army Center of Military History					
103 3rd Ave SW Fort McNair Bldg 35	Washington	DC	20319	202-685-2194	685-2081
Web: www.history.army.mil					
US Army Legal Services Agency					
901 N Stuart St Suite 700	Arlington	VA	22203	703-588-6357	696-8403
Web: www.jagcnet.army.mil					
Army National Guard					
Army National Guard Readiness Ctr					
111 S George Mason Dr	Arlington	VA	22204	703-607-7000	607-7088
Web: www.arng.army.mil					
US Army Corps of Engineers 441 G St NW	Washington	DC	20314	202-761-0010	761-1803
Web: www.usace.army.mil					
US Army Corps of Engineers Regional Offices					
Great Lakes & Ohio River Div 550 Main St	Cincinnati	OH	45202	513-684-3010	684-3755
Web: www.lrd.usace.army.mil					
Mississippi Valley Div 1400 Walnut St	Vicksburg	MS	39180	601-634-7783	
Web: www.mvd.usace.army.mil					
North Atlantic Div					
302 General Lee Ave Fort Hamilton	Brooklyn	NY	11252	718-765-7018	765-7170
Web: www.nad.usace.army.mil					
Northwestern Div PO Box 2870	Portland	OR	97208	503-808-3700	808-3706
Web: www.nwd.usace.army.mil					
Pacific Ocean Div Fort Shafter Bldg 525	Honolulu	HI	96858	808-438-8319	438-2656
Web: www.pod.usace.army.mil					
South Atlantic Div 60 Forsyth St SW Rm 9M15	Atlanta	GA	30303	404-562-5011	
Web: www.sad.usace.army.mil					
South Pacific Div 1455 Market St	San Francisco	CA	94103	415-503-6514	
Web: www.spd.usace.army.mil					
Southwestern Div 1100 Commerce St	Dallas	TX	75242	469-487-7007	
Web: www.swd.usace.army.mil					
US Army Criminal Investigation Command					
Public Affairs Office 6010 6th St	Fort Belvoir	VA	22060	703-806-0372	
Web: www.cid.army.mil					
US Army Forces Command					
1777 Hardee Ave SW	Fort McPherson	GA	30330	404-464-7276	464-5628
Web: www.forscom.army.mil					
US Army Intelligence & Security Command					
8825 Beulah St	Fort Belvoir	VA	22060	703-706-2002	
Web: www.inscom.army.mil					
US Army Materiel Command 9301 Chapek Rd	Fort Belvoir	VA	22060	703-806-8010	806-8031
Web: www.amc.army.mil					
US Army Military District of Washington					
103 3rd Ave SW Bldg 39 Fort McNair	Washington	DC	20319	202-685-2812	685-3481
Web: www.mdw.army.mil					
US Army Reserve Command					
1401 Deshler St SW	Fort McPherson	GA	30330	404-464-8500	
Web: www.armyreserve.army.mil/ARWEB					
US Army Space & Missile Defense Command					
PO Box 1500	Huntsville	AL	35807	256-955-6338	955-6344
Web: www.smdc.army.mil					
US Army Special Operations Command (USASOC)					
2929 Desert Storm Dr	Fort Bragg	NC	28310	910-432-6005	432-1046
Web: www.soc.mil					
US Army War College 122 Forbes Ave	Carlisle	PA	17013	717-245-3131	245-4224
TF: 800-453-0992 ■ *Web:* www.carlisle.army.mil					
Walter Reed Army Medical Ctr					
6900 Georgia Ave NW	Washington	DC	20307	202-782-3501	782-2478
Web: www.wramc.amedd.army.mil					

343-6 US Department of Defense - Department of the Navy

	City	State	Zip	Phone	Fax
Dept of the Navy 1000 Navy Pentagon	Washington	DC	20350	703-695-8400	
Web: www.navy.mil					
Chief of Naval Operations					
2000 Navy Pentagon	Washington	DC	20350	703-695-5664	693-9408
Web: www.navy.mil					
Judge Advocate General's Corps					
1322 Patterson Ave Suite 3000	Washington Navy Yard	DC	20374	202-685-5275	
Web: www.jag.navy.mil					
Medicine & Surgery Bureau 2300 E St NW	Washington	DC	20372	202-762-3211	
Web: www.med.navy.mil					
Office of Naval Intelligence					
4251 Suitland Rd	Washington	DC	20395	301-669-3400	669-3099
Web: www.navy.mil/swf/index.asp					
Office of Naval Research					
1 Liberty Ctr 875 N Randolph St Suite 1425	Arlington	VA	22203	703-696-5031	696-5940
Web: www.onr.navy.mil					
Military Sealift Command					
914 Charles Morris Ct SE					
Washington Navy Yard	Washington	DC	20398	202-685-5055	685-5067
TF: 888-732-5438 ■ *Web:* www.msc.navy.mil					
Naval Air Systems Command					
47123 Buse Rd Bldg 2272 Suite 075	Patuxent River	MD	20670	301-757-1487	757-1525
Web: www.navair.navy.mil					
Naval Education & Training Command					
250 Dallas St	Pensacola	FL	32508	850-452-4858	452-4900
Web: www.cnet.navy.mil					
Naval Facilities Engineering Command					
1322 Patterson Ave SE					
Washington Navy Yard	Washington	DC	20374	202-685-1423	685-1484
Web: www.navfac.navy.mil					
Naval Network Warfare Command					
2465 Guadalcanal Rd	Norfolk	VA	23521	757-417-6706	
Web: www.netwarcom.navy.mil					
Naval Sea Systems Command					
1333 Isaac Hull Ave SE					
Washington Navy Yard	Washington	DC	20376	202-781-3889	
Web: www.navsea.navy.mil					
Naval Special Warfare Command					
2000 Trident Way	Coronado	CA	92155	619-522-2824	522-2831
Web: www.navsoc.navy.mil					
Navy Personnel Command 5720 Integrity Dr	Millington	TN	38055	901-874-3165	874-3165
Web: www.npc.navy.mil					

Phone | Fax

Space & Naval Warfare Systems Command
4301 Pacific Hwy . . . San Diego CA 92110 619-524-7000 524-7010
Web: www.spawar.navy.mil
US Naval Observatory
3450 Massachusetts Ave NW . . . Washington DC 20392 202-762-1438 762-1489*
**Fax:* PR ■ *Web:* www.usno.navy.mil

343-7 US Department of Defense - US Marine Corps

Phone | Fax

US Marine Corps
USMC Headquarters
3000 Marine Corps Pentagon . . . Washington DC 20350 703-614-2500 697-7246
Web: www.marines.mil/Pages/Default.aspx
Commandant The Pentagon . . . Washington DC 20350 703-614-2500 697-7246
Web: www.usmc.mil
Public Affairs Div The Pentagon . . . Washington DC 20350 703-614-8010 697-5362
Web: www.usmc.mil
Marine Corps Recruiting Command
3280 Russell Rd . . . Quantico VA 22134 703-784-9400 784-9863
Web: www.marines.com
Marine Corps Systems Command 2200 Lester St . . . Quantico VA 22134 703-432-1800 432-3535
Web: www.marcorsyscom.usmc.mil

343-8 US Department of Education

Phone | Fax

Dept of Education 400 Maryland Ave SW . . . Washington DC 20202 202-401-2000 401-0689
TF: 800-872-5327 ■ *Web:* www.ed.gov
Inspector General's Fraud & Abuse Hotline
400 Maryland Ave Sw . . . Washington DC 20202 800-647-8733 245-7047*
**Fax Area Code:* 202 ■ *TF:* 800-647-8733 ■ *Web:* www.ed.gov/about/offices/list/oig/hotline.html
Institute of Education Sciences
555 New Jersey Ave NW Rm 600 . . . Washington DC 20208 202-219-1385 219-1402
Web: www.ed.gov/about/offices/list/ies
Office of Elementary & Secondary Education
400 Maryland Ave SW . . . Washington DC 20202 202-401-0113 205-0303
Web: www.ed.gov/about/offices/list/oese
Office of English Language Acquisition
400 Maryland Ave . . . Washington DC 20202 202-401-4300 205-1229
Web: www2.ed.gov/about/offices/list/oela/index.html
Office of Innovation & Improvement
400 Maryland Ave SW . . . Washington DC 20202 202-205-4500 401-4123
Web: www.ed.gov
Office of Postsecondary Education
1990 K St NW . . . Washington DC 20006 202-502-7750 502-7677
Web: www.ed.gov/about/offices/list/ope
Office of Safe & Drug-Free Schools
400 Maryland Ave SW Rm 3E300 . . . Washington DC 20202 202-260-3954 260-7767
Web: www.ed.gov/about/offices/list/osdfs
Office of Special Education & Rehabilitation Services
400 Maryland Ave . . . Washington DC 20202 202-245-7468
Web: www2.ed.gov/about/offices/list/osers/index.html
Office of Vocational & Adult Education
550 12th St SW . . . Washington DC 20202 202-245-7700 245-7837
TF: 800-872-5327 ■ *Web:* www.ed.gov/about/offices/list/ovae
Dept of Education Regional Offices
Region 1
5 Post Office Sq 9th Fl Rm 24 POCH Bldg . . . Boston MA 02110 617-289-0100 289-0151
Web: www2.ed.gov/about/contacts/gen/regions.html
Region 10
915 2nd Ave Rm 3362 Jackson Federal Bldg . . . Seattle WA 98174 206-607-1655 607-1661
Web: www2.ed.gov
Region 2 Financial Sq 32 Old Slip 25th Fl . . . New York NY 10005 646-428-3905 428-3904
Region 3 100 Penn Sq E Suite 505 . . . Philadelphia PA 19107 215-656-6010 656-6020
Region 4
Federal Ctr 61 Forsyth St SW Suite 19T40 . . . Atlanta GA 30303 404-974-9450 974-9459
Web: www.ed.gov
Region 5 500 W Madison St Suite 1427 . . . Chicago IL 60661 312-730-1700 730-1704
Web: www.ed.gov
Region 7 8930 Ward Pkwy Suite 2002 . . . Kansas City MO 64114 816-268-0405 823-1400
Region 8
Federal Bldg 1244 Speer Blvd Suite 615 . . . Denver CO 80204 303-844-3544 844-2524
Web: www.ed.gov
Region 9 50 Beale St Rm 9100 . . . San Francisco CA 94105 415-486-5700
US Dept of Education
Region 6 1999 Bryan St Suite 1510 . . . Dallas TX 75201 214-661-9500 661-9594
Web: www.ed.gov
National Center for Education Statistics
1990 K St NW . . . Washington DC 20006 202-502-7300 502-7466
Web: nces.ed.gov
National Institute for Literacy (NIFL)
1775 'I' St NW Suite 730 . . . Washington DC 20006 202-233-2025 233-2050
TF: 800-228-8813 ■ *Web:* www.lincs.ed.gov
Office of Federal Student Aid
Union Ctr Plaza 830 1st St NE . . . Washington DC 20202 202-377-3000 275-5000
TF: 800-433-3243 ■ *Web:* www.ed.gov/about/offices/list/fsa
Secretary of Education
400 Maryland Ave SW . . . Washington DC 20202 202-401-3000 260-7867
TF: 800-872-5327 ■ *Web:* www.ed.gov/news/staff/bios/spellings.html

Phone | Fax

National Library of Education
400 Maryland Ave SW . . . Washington DC 20202 202-205-5015 260-7364
TF: 800-424-1616 ■
Web: www.ies.ed.gov/ncee/projects/nat_ed_library.asp

343-9 US Department of Energy

Phone | Fax

Dept of Energy (DOE)
1000 Independence Ave SW . . . Washington DC 20585 202-586-5575 586-5823
Web: www.energy.gov
Office of Civilian Radioactive Waste Management
1000 Independence Ave SW . . . Washington DC 20585 202-586-6842 586-6638
TF: 800-225-6972 ■ *Web:* www.ocrwm.doe.gov
Office of Electricity Delivery & Energy Reliability
1000 Independence Ave SW . . . Washington DC 20585 202-586-1411 586-1472
Web: www.electricity.doe.gov
Office of Energy Efficiency & Renewable Energy
1000 Independence Ave SW . . . Washington DC 20585 202-586-5570 586-9260
TF: 877-337-3463 ■ *Web:* www.eere.energy.gov
Office of Environmental Management
1000 Independence Ave SW . . . Washington DC 20585 202-586-7709 586-7757
Web: www.em.doe.gov
Office of Fossil Energy
1000 Independence Ave SW . . . Washington DC 20585 202-586-6660 586-7847
Web: www.fe.doe.gov
Office of Legacy Management
Office of Stakeholder Relations LM-5 . . . Washington DC 20585 202-586-7550 586-1540
Web: www.lm.doe.gov
Office of Nuclear Energy
1000 Independence Ave SW . . . Washington DC 20585 202-586-6630 586-0544
Web: www.ne.doe.gov
Office of Science
1000 Independence Ave SW . . . Washington DC 20585 202-586-5430 586-4120
Web: www.sc.doe.gov
Energy Information Administration
1000 Independence Ave SW . . . Washington DC 20585 202-586-8800 586-0727
Web: www.eia.doe.gov
Federal Energy Regulatory Commission
888 1st St NE . . . Washington DC 20426 202-502-8004 208-2106
TF: 866-208-3372 ■ *Web:* www.ferc.gov
Federal Energy Regulatory Commission Regional Offices
Atlanta 3700 Crestwood Pkwy NW 9th Fl . . . Atlanta GA 30096 678-245-3075 245-3010
Web: www.ferc.gov/contact-us/tel-num/regional/atlanta.asp
Chicago
Federal Bldg 230 S Dearborn St Rm 3130 . . . Chicago IL 60604 312-596-4438 596-4460
Web: www.ferc.gov/contact-us/tel-num/regional.asp
New York 19 W 34th St Suite 400 . . . New York NY 10001 212-273-5911 631-8124
Web: www.ferc.gov/contact-us/tel-num/regional/newyork.asp
Portland 805 SW Broadway Suite 550 . . . Portland OR 97205 503-552-2700 552-2799
Web: www.ferc.gov/contact-us/tel-num/regional.asp
San Francisco 901 Market St Suite 350 . . . San Francisco CA 94103 415-369-3300 369-3322
Web: www.ferc.gov
National Nuclear Security Administration (NNSA)
1000 Independence Ave SW . . . Washington DC 20585 202-586-5000 586-4892
TF: 800-342-5363 ■ *Web:* www.nnsa.doe.gov
Power Marketing Administrations
Bonneville Power Administration
905 NE 11th Ave . . . Portland OR 97232 503-230-3000
Web: www.bpa.gov
Southeastern Power Administration
1166 Athens Tech Rd . . . Elberton GA 30635 706-213-3800 213-3884
Web: www.sepa.doe.gov
Southwestern Power Administration 1 W 3rd St . . . Tulsa OK 74103 918-595-6600 595-6656
Web: www.swpa.gov
Western Area Power Administration
PO Box 281213 . . . Lakewood CO 80228 720-962-7000 962-7200
Web: www.wapa.gov
Secretary of Energy
1000 Independence Ave SW . . . Washington DC 20585 202-586-6210 586-4403
Web: www.energy.gov/organization

343-10 US Department of Health & Human Services

Phone | Fax

Dept of Health & Human Services (HHS)
330 Independence Ave SW . . . Washington DC 20201 202-619-0257
TF: 877-696-6775 ■ *Web:* www.dhhs.gov
Dept of Health & Human Services Regional Offices
Region 1 JFK Federal Bldg Suite 2100 . . . Boston MA 02203 617-565-1500 565-1491
Web: www.hhs.gov/region1
Region 10 2201 6th Ave Rm 1036 . . . Seattle WA 98121 206-615-2010 615-2087
Web: www.hhs.gov/region10
Region 2 26 Federal Plaza . . . New York NY 10278 212-264-4600 264-3620
Web: www.hhs.gov/region2
Region 3 150 S Independence Mall W . . . Philadelphia PA 19106 215-861-4633 861-4625
Web: www.hhs.gov/region3
Region 4 Federal Ctr 61 Forsyth St SW . . . Atlanta GA 30303 404-562-7888 562-7899
Web: www.hhs.gov/region4
Region 5 233 N Michigan Ave Suite 1300 . . . Chicago IL 60601 312-353-5160 353-4144
Web: www.hhs.gov/region5
Region 6 1301 Young St Suite 1124 . . . Dallas TX 75202 214-767-3301 767-3617
Web: www.hhs.gov/region6

Phone | Fax

Region 7 601 E 12th St . . . . . . Kansas City MO 64106 816-426-2821 426-2178
Web: www.hhs.gov/region7
Region 8 Federal Bldg 1961 Stout St. . . . . . . Denver CO 80294 303-844-3372 844-4545
Web: www.hhs.gov/region8
Region 9 50 United Nations Plaza Rm 431 . . . . . . San Francisco CA 94102 415-437-8500 437-8505
Web: www.hhs.gov/region9

Administration for Children & Families (ACF)
901 D St SW. . . . . . . Washington DC 20447 202-401-9215 401-5450
Web: www.acf.dhhs.gov

Administration for Children & Families Regional Offices
Atlanta 61 Forsyth St SW Suite 4M60 . . . . . . Atlanta GA 30303 404-562-2900 562-2981
Web: www.acf.hhs.gov/programs/region4
Boston JFK Federal Bldg Rm 2000 . . . . . . Boston MA 02203 617-565-1020 565-2493
Web: www.acf.hhs.gov/programs/region1
Chicago 233 N Michigan Ave Suite 400 . . . . . . Chicago IL 60601 312-353-4237 353-2204
Web: www.acf.hhs.gov/programs/region5
Dallas 1301 Young St Suite 914 . . . . . . Dallas TX 75202 214-767-9648 767-3743
Web: www.acf.hhs.gov/programs/region6
New York 26 Federal Plaza Rm 4114. . . . . . New York NY 10278 212-264-2890 264-4881
Web: www.acf.hhs.gov/programs/region2
Philadelphia
150 S Independence Mall W Suite 864 . . . . . . Philadelphia PA 19106 215-861-4000 861-4070
Web: www.acf.hhs.gov/programs/region3
San Francisco
50 United Nations Plaza Rm 450 . . . . . . San Francisco CA 94102 415-437-8400 437-8444
Web: www.acf.hhs.gov/programs/region9

Administration on Aging (AoA)
1 Massachusetts Ave NW . . . . . . Washington DC 20201 202-619-0724 357-3555
Web: www.aoa.gov

Administration on Aging Regional Offices
Region I JFK Federal Bldg Rm 2075 . . . . . . Boston MA 02203 617-565-1158 565-4511
Web: www.aoa.gov
Region IV
Atlanta Federal Ctr 61 Forsyth St SW
Suite 5M69 . . . . . . Atlanta GA 30303 404-562-7600 562-7598
Web: www.aoa.gov/about/contact/contact.asp
Region IX
50 United Nations Plaza Rm 455 . . . . . . San Francisco CA 94102 415-437-8780 437-8782
Web: www.aoa.gov/about/contact/contact.asp
Region V 233 N Michigan Ave Suite 790. . . . . . Chicago IL 60601 312-353-3141 886-8533
Web: www.aoa.gov
Region VI 1301 Young St Suite 736 . . . . . . Dallas TX 75201 214-767-2971 767-2951
Web: www.aoa.gov/about/contact/contact.asp
Region VII 601 E 12th St Suite 1731. . . . . . Kansas City MO 64106 312-353-3141 886-8533
Web: www.aoa.gov/about/contact/contact.asp
Region VIII 999 18th St S Terr Suite 496. . . . . . Denver CO 80202 303-844-2951 844-2943
Web: www.aoa.gov
Region X
Blanchard Plaza 2201 6th Ave MS RX-33 . . . . . . Seattle WA 98121 206-615-2298 615-2305
Web: www.aoa.gov/about/contact/contact.asp
Regions II & III 26 Federal Plaza Rm 38-102. . . . . . New York NY 10278 212-264-2977 264-0114
Web: www.aoa.gov/about/contact/contact.asp

Agency for Healthcare Research & Quality
540 Gaither Rd . . . . . . Rockville MD 20850 301-427-1200 427-1201
TF: 800-358-9295 ■ *Web:* www.ahrq.gov

Agency for Toxic Substances & Disease Registry
1600 Clifton Rd NE Bldg 37 MS E-29. . . . . . Atlanta GA 30333 404-498-0110 498-0093
TF: 888-422-8737 ■ *Web:* www.atsdr.cdc.gov

AIDSinfo PO Box 6303 . . . . . . Rockville MD 20849 301-519-0459 519-6616
TF: 800-448-0440 ■ *Web:* www.aidsinfo.nih.gov

Centers for Disease Control & Prevention (CDC)
1600 Clifton Rd NE. . . . . . Atlanta GA 30333 404-639-7000 639-7111
Web: www.cdc.gov
National Center for Chronic Disease Prevention & Health Promotion
2900 Woodcock Blvd. . . . . . Atlanta GA 30341 404-639-8000 639-8600
Web: www.cdc.gov/nccdphp
National Center for Emerging & Zoonotic Infectious Diseases
1600 Clifton Rd . . . . . . Atlanta GA 30333 404-639-3311
TF: 800-232-4636 ■ *Web:* www.cdc.gov/nczved
National Center for Environmental Health
4770 Buford Hwy Bldg 101 . . . . . . Chamblee GA 30341 404-639-3311 488-0083*
**Fax Area Code:* 770 ■ *TF:* 800-232-4636 ■ *Web:* www.cdc.gov
National Center for Health Marketing
1600 Clifton Rd NE . . . . . . Atlanta GA 30333 404-498-1515
TF: 800-311-3435 ■ *Web:* www.cdc.gov/healthmarketing
National Center for Health Statistics
6525 Belcrest Rd . . . . . . Hyattsville MD 20782 301-458-4000
Web: www.cdc.gov
National Center for HIV/AIDS Viral Hepatitis STD & TB Prevention
1600 Clifton Rd . . . . . . Atlanta GA 30333 800-232-4636
Web: www.cdc.gov/nchstp/od/nchstp.html
National Center for Immunization & Respiratory Diseases
1600 Clifton Rd NE MS E-05. . . . . . Atlanta GA 30333 800-232-4636
TF: 800-232-4636 ■ *Web:* www.cdc.gov/vaccines
National Center for Injury Prevention & Control
2858 Woodcock Blvd. . . . . . Atlanta GA 30333 770-488-4696 488-4422
Web: www.cdc.gov/ncipc
National Center for Preparedness Detection & Control of Infectious Diseases
1600 Clifton Rd NE MS C-14 . . . . . . Atlanta GA 30333 404-639-3534 639-2945
TF: 800-311-3435 ■ *Web:* www.cdc.gov/ncpdcid
National Center for Public Health Informatics
1600 Clifton Rd NE MS E-78. . . . . . Atlanta GA 30333 404-498-2475 498-6570
Web: www.cdc.gov/ncphi
National Center on Birth Defects & Developmental Disabilities
12 Executive Pk Dr W NE. . . . . . Atlanta GA 30329 770-498-3800 498-3070
Web: www.cdc.gov/ncbddd
National Institute for Occupational Safety & Health
200 Independence Ave SW . . . . . . Washington DC 20201 404-639-3286
TF: 800-356-4674 ■ *Web:* www.cdc.gov/niosh
National Office of Public Health Genomics
4770 Buford Hwy MS K-89 . . . . . . Atlanta GA 30341 770-488-8510 488-8355
Web: www.cdc.gov/genomics
Travelers" Health 1600 Clifton Rd NE . . . . . . Atlanta GA 30333 800-232-4636 232-3299*
**Fax Area Code:* 888 ■ *TF:* 800-232-4636 ■ *Web:* wwwnc.cdc.gov/travel

Centers for Medicare & Medicaid Services (CMS)
7500 Security Blvd . . . . . . Baltimore MD 21244 410-786-1800 786-1810
Web: www.cms.hhs.gov
Medicare Hotline 7500 Security Blvd. . . . . . . Baltimore MD 21244 800-633-4227
TF: 800-633-4227 ■ *Web:* www.medicare.gov

Centers for Medicare & Medicaid Services Regional Offices
Region I JFK Federal Bldg Rm 2325 . . . . . . Boston MA 02203 617-565-1188 565-1339
Web: www.cms.hhs.gov/RegionalOffices
Region II 26 Federal Plaza 38th Fl. . . . . . . New York NY 10278 212-616-2205 264-6189
Web: www.cms.hhs.gov/RegionalOffices
Region III
150 S Independence Mall W Suite 216 . . . . . . Philadelphia PA 19106 215-861-4140 861-4240
Web: www.cms.hhs.gov/RegionalOffices
Region IV 61 Forsyth St SW Suite 4T20 . . . . . . Atlanta GA 30303 404-562-7500 562-7162
Web: www.cms.hhs.gov/RegionalOffices
Region IX 90 7th St # 5-300 . . . . . . San Francisco CA 94105 415-744-3501 744-3517
Web: www.cms.hhs.gov
Region V 233 N Michigan Ave Suite 600. . . . . . Chicago IL 60601 312-886-6432 353-0252
Web: www.cms.hhs.gov/RegionalOffices
Region VI 1301 Young St Suite 714 . . . . . . Dallas TX 75202 214-767-6423 767-6400
Web: www.cms.hhs.gov/RegionalOffices
Region VII
Federal Bldg 601 E 12th St Rm 235. . . . . . Kansas City MO 64106 816-426-5925 426-3548
Web: www.cms.hhs.gov/RegionalOffices
Region VIII 1600 Broadway Suite 700 . . . . . . Denver CO 80202 303-844-2111 844-6374
Web: www.cms.hhs.gov/RegionalOffices
Region X 2201 6th Ave MS 40 . . . . . . Seattle WA 98121 206-615-2306 615-2027
Web: www.cms.hhs.gov/RegionalOffices

Child Welfare Information Gateway
1250 Maryland Ave SW 8th Fl . . . . . . Washington DC 20024 703-385-7565 385-3206
TF: 800-394-3366 ■ *Web:* www.childwelfare.gov

Food & Drug Administration (FDA)
5600 Fishers Ln . . . . . . Rockville MD 20857 301-827-2410 443-3100
TF: 888-463-6332 ■ *Web:* www.fda.gov
Center for Biologics Evaluation & Research
1401 Rockville Pike Suite 200N MS HFM-4 . . . . . . Rockville MD 20852 301-827-0372
Web: www.fda.gov/cber
Center for Devices & Radiological Health
9200 Corporate Blvd Suite 100G. . . . . . Rockville MD 20850 800-638-2041 443-8818*
**Fax Area Code:* 301 ■ *TF:* 800-638-2041 ■ *Web:* www.fda.gov/cdrh
Center for Drug Evaluation & Research
Hillandale Bldg 4th Fl . . . . . . Silver Spring MD 20993 301-796-3400
TF: 888-463-6332 ■
Web: www.fda.gov/AboutFDA/CentersOffices/CDER/default.htm
Center for Food Safety & Applied Nutrition
5100 Paint Branch Pkwy . . . . . . College Park MD 20740 301-436-1600 436-2668
TF: 888-723-3366 ■ *Web:* www.cfsan.fda.gov
Center for Veterinary Medicine
7519 Standish Pl Metro Pk N 4 . . . . . . Rockville MD 20855 240-276-9000
Web: www.fda.gov/cvm
National Center for Toxicological Research
3900 N Ctr Rd . . . . . . Jefferson AR 72079 870-543-7000 543-7576
TF: 800-638-3321 ■ *Web:* www.fda.gov/nctr

Food & Drug Administration Regional Offices
Central Region
900 US Custom House 200 Chestnut St . . . . . . Philadelphia PA 19106 215-597-4390
Northeast Region 158-15 Liberty Ave . . . . . . Jamaica NY 11433 718-662-5416 662-5434
Pacific Region
Federal Bldg 1301 Clay St Suite 1180N. . . . . . Oakland CA 94612 510-637-3960 637-3976
Web: www.hhs.gov
Southeast Region 60 8th St NE . . . . . . Atlanta GA 30309 404-253-1171 253-1207
Southwest Region
4040 N Central Expwy Suite 900 . . . . . . Dallas TX 75204 214-253-4904 253-4965

Health Resources & Services Administration (HRSA)
5600 Fishers Ln . . . . . . Rockville MD 20857 301-443-2216 443-2605
TF: 888-275-4772 ■ *Web:* www.hrsa.gov

Indian Health Service (IHS)
801 Thompson Ave Suite 400. . . . . . Rockville MD 20852 301-443-1083 443-4794
Web: www.ihs.gov

National Child Care Information & Technical Assistance Ctr (NCCIC)
9300 Lee Hwy. . . . . . Fairfax VA 22031 800-616-2242 716-2242
TF: 800-616-2242 ■ *Web:* www.nccic.acf.hhs.gov

National Clearinghouse for Alcohol & Drug Information
11426 Rockville Pk PO Box 2345. . . . . . Rockville MD 20847 800-729-6686
TF: 800-729-6686 ■ *Web:* www.ncadi.samhsa.gov

National Hansen's Disease Program (NHDP)
1770 Physicians Pk Dr . . . . . . Baton Rouge LA 70816 225-756-3700
TF: 800-642-2477

National Health Information Ctr (NHIC)
PO Box 1133 . . . . . . Washington DC 20013 301-565-4167 984-4256
TF: 800-336-4797 ■ *Web:* www.health.gov/nhic

Phone Fax

National Institutes of Biomedical Imaging & Bioengineering (NIBIB)
National Institute of Biomedical Imaging & Bioengineering
6707 Democracy Blvd .... Bethesda MD 20892 301-496-8859 480-0679
Web: www.nibib.nih.gov

National Institutes of Health (NIH)
9000 Rockville Pike .... Bethesda MD 20892 301-496-4000
Web: www.nih.gov
Center for Scientific Review
6701 Rockledge Dr MSC 7768 .... Bethesda MD 20892 301-435-1115
Web: cms.csr.nih.gov
Clinical Ctr 10 Ctr Dr Bldg 10 .... Bethesda MD 20892 301-496-2563 402-2984
Web: www.cc.nih.gov
John E Fogarty International Ctr
31 Ctr Dr MSC 2220 .... Bethesda MD 20892 301-496-2075 594-1211
Web: www.fic.nih.gov
National Cancer Institute
Public Inquiries Office 6116 Executive Blvd
Rm 3036A .... Bethesda MD 20892 301-435-3848 402-2594
TF: 800-422-6237 ■ *Web:* www.cancer.gov
National Cancer Institute - Cancer Information Service
6116 Executive Blvd Suite 300 .... Bethesda MD 20892 800-422-6237
TF: 800-422-6237 ■ *Web:* www.cancer.gov
National Center for Complementary & Alternative Medicine
31 Ctr Dr Bldg 31 .... Bethesda MD 20892 301-594-7103
TF: 888-644-6226 ■ *Web:* www.nccam.nih.gov
National Center on Minority Health & Health Disparities
6707 Democracy Blvd Suite 800 MSC 5465 .... Bethesda MD 20892 301-402-1366 480-4049
Web: ncmhd.nih.gov
National Eye Institute 2020 Vision Pl .... Bethesda MD 20892 301-496-5248 402-1065
Web: www.nei.nih.gov
National Heart Lung & Blood Institute
31 Ctr Dr Bldg 31 Rm 5A52 MSC 2486 .... Bethesda MD 20892 301-496-5166 402-0818
Web: www.nhlbi.nih.gov
National Human Genome Research Institute
31 Ctr Dr Bldg 31 Rm 4B09 .... Bethesda MD 20892 301-402-0911 402-2218
Web: www.genome.gov
National Institute of Allergy & Infectious Diseases
6610 Rockledge Dr MSC 6612 .... Bethesda MD 20892 301-496-5717 402-3573
TF: 866-284-4107 ■ *Web:* www.niaid.nih.gov
National Institute of Arthritis & Musculoskeletal & Skin Diseases
31 Ctr Dr MSC 2350 Bldg 31 Rm 4C02 .... Bethesda MD 20892 301-496-8190 480-2814
Web: www.niams.nih.gov
National Institute of Child Health & Human Development
31 Ctr Dr Bldg 31 Rm 2A32 .... Bethesda MD 20892 301-496-5133 496-7101
TF: 800-370-2943 ■ *Web:* www.nichd.nih.gov
National Institute of Dental & Craniofacial Research
31 Ctr Dr .... Bethesda MD 20892 301-496-3571 402-2185
Web: www.nidcr.nih.gov
National Institute of Diabetes & Digestive & Kidney Diseases
31 Center Dr MSC 2560 .... Bethesda MD 20892 301-496-3583 496-7422
Web: www.niddk.nih.gov
National Institute of Environmental Health Sciences
PO Box 12233 .... Research Triangle Park NC 27709 919-541-3201 541-2260
Web: www.niehs.nih.gov
National Institute of General Medical Sciences
45 Ctr Dr MSC 6200 .... Bethesda MD 20892 301-496-7301
Web: www.nigms.nih.gov
National Institute of Mental Health
6001 Executive Blvd Rm 8184 MSC 9663 .... Bethesda MD 20892 301-443-4513 443-4279
TF: 866-615-6464 ■ *Web:* www.nimh.nih.gov
National Institute of Neurological Disorders & Stroke
PO Box 5801 .... Bethesda MD 20824 301-496-5751
TF: 800-352-9424 ■ *Web:* www.ninds.nih.gov
National Institute of Nursing Research
31 Ctr Dr Bldg 31 Rm 5B05 .... Bethesda MD 20892 301-496-8230 594-3405
Web: www.nih.gov/ninr
National Institute on Aging
31 Ctr Dr Bldg 31 Rm 5C27 MSC 2292 .... Bethesda MD 20892 301-496-1752 496-1072
Web: www.nia.nih.gov
National Institute on Alcohol Abuse & Alcoholism
5635 Fishers Ln MSC 9304 .... Bethesda MD 20892 301-443-3885 443-7043
Web: www.niaaa.nih.gov
National Institute on Deafness & Other Communication Disorders
31 Ctr Dr Bldg 31 Rm 3C35 .... Bethesda MD 20892 301-496-7243 402-0018
TF: 800-241-1044 ■ *Web:* www.nidcd.nih.gov
National Institute on Drug Abuse
6001 Executive Blvd Rm 4123 .... Bethesda MD 20892 301-443-6480 443-8908
Web: www.nida.nih.gov
National Library of Medicine
8600 Rockville Pike Bldg 38 .... Bethesda MD 20894 301-594-5983 402-1384
TF: 888-346-3656 ■ *Web:* www.nlm.nih.gov
Office of Communications & Public Liason
1 Ctr Dr Bldg 1 Rm 344 .... Bethesda MD 20892 301-496-4461 496-0017
Web: www.nih.gov
Office of Dietary Supplements
6100 Executive Blvd Suite 3B01 .... Bethesda MD 20892 301-435-2920 480-1845
Web: www.ods.od.nih.gov
Office of Rare Diseases
6100 Executive Blvd Suite 3B01 .... Bethesda MD 20892 301-402-4336 480-9655
Web: www.rarediseases.info.nih.gov

Phone Fax

National Library of Medicine
Lister Hill National Center for Biomedical Communications
8600 Rockville Pike Bldg 38A 7th Fl .... Bethesda MD 20894 301-496-4441 480-3035
Web: www.lhncbc.nlm.nih.gov
National Center for Biotechnology Information
8600 Rockville Pike Bldg 38A .... Bethesda MD 20894 301-496-2475 480-9241
Web: www.ncbi.nlm.nih.gov

National Mental Health Information Ctr
PO Box 42557 .... Washington DC 20015 240-747-5484 747-5470
TF: 800-789-2647 ■ *Web:* www.samhsa.gov

National Women's Health Information Ctr
8270 Willow Oaks Corporate Dr .... Fairfax VA 22031 800-994-9662
TF: 800-994-9662 ■ *Web:* www.womenshealth.gov

NIH Osteoporosis & Related Bone Diseases - National Resource Ctr
2 AMS Cir .... Bethesda MD 20892 202-223-0344 293-2356
TF: 800-624-2663 ■ *Web:* www.niams.nih.gov/bone

Office of Public Health & Science
200 Independence Ave SW Rm 716G .... Washington DC 20201 202-690-7694 690-6960
Web: www.hhs.gov/ophs

Office of Public Health & Science Regional Offices
Region I JFK Federal Bldg Rm 2100 .... Boston MA 02203 617-565-1505 565-1491
Web: www.hhs.gov/ophs/rha
Region II 26 Federal Plaza Suite 3835 .... New York NY 10278 212-264-2560
Web: www.hhs.gov/ophs/rha
Region III
150 S Independence Mall W Suite 436 .... Philadelphia PA 19106 215-861-4639
Web: www.hhs.gov/ophs/rha
Region IV 61 Forsyth St SW Suite 5B95 .... Atlanta GA 30303 404-562-7888 562-7899
Web: www.hhs.gov/ophs/rha
Region IX
50 United Nations Plaza Suite 327 .... San Francisco CA 94102 415-437-8096 437-8004
Web: www.hhs.gov/ophs/rha
Region V 233 N Michigan Ave Suite 1300 .... Chicago IL 60601 312-353-1385 353-0718
Web: www.hhs.gov/ophs/rha
Region VI 1301 Young St Suite 1124 .... Dallas TX 75202 214-767-3879 767-3617
Web: www.hhs.gov/ophs/rha
Region VII Federal Bldg 601 E 12th St .... Kansas City MO 64106 816-426-3291 426-2178
Region VIII Federal Bldg 1961 Stout St .... Denver CO 80294 303-844-5101
Web: directory.psc.gov/os/691.html
Region X 2201 6th Ave MS RX-20 .... Seattle WA 98121 206-615-2469 615-2481
Web: www.hhs.gov/ophs/rha

President's Council on Physical Fitness Sports & Nutrition
1101 Wootton Pkwy .... Rockville MD 20852 240-276-9567 276-9860
Web: www.fitness.gov

Secretary of Health & Human Services
200 Independence Ave SW Rm 615-F .... Washington DC 20201 202-690-7000 690-7755
Web: www.hhs.gov/about

Substance Abuse & Mental Health Services Administration
1 Choke Cherry Rd .... Rockville MD 20857 240-276-2000 276-2010
TF: 877-726-4727 ■ *Web:* www.samhsa.gov
Center for Mental Health Services
1 Choke Cherry Ln .... Rockville MD 20857 877-726-4727 221-4292*
**Fax Area Code: 240* ■ *Web:* www.samhsa.gov
Center for Substance Abuse Prevention
1 Choke Cherry Rd .... Rockville MD 20850 240-276-2420 276-2760
TF: 800-729-6686 ■ *Web:* www.prevention.samhsa.gov
Center for Substance Abuse Treatment
1 Choke Cherry Rd PO Box 2345 .... Rockville MD 20857 240-276-2130 221-4292
TF: 877-726-4727 ■ *Web:* www.samhsa.gov

US Surgeon General 5600 Fishers Ln Rm 18-67 .... Rockville MD 20857 301-443-4000 443-5890
Web: www.surgeongeneral.gov

343-11 US Department of Homeland Security

Phone Fax

Dept of Homeland Security (DHS)
245 Murray Dr SW Bldg 410 .... Washington DC 20528 202-282-8000 282-8401
Web: www.dhs.gov
Ready Campaign 500 C St SW .... Washington DC 20472 202-282-8000 282-8401
Web: www.ready.gov

Federal Emergency Management Agency (FEMA)
500 C St SW .... Washington DC 20472 800-621-3362
TF: 800-621-3362 ■ *Web:* www.fema.gov
FEMA for Kids 500 C St SW .... Washington DC 20472 202-646-4600
Web: www.fema.gov/kids
National Flood Insurance Program
500 C St SW .... Washington DC 20472 888-379-9531 646-2818*
**Fax Area Code: 202* ■ *TF:* 888-379-9531 ■ *Web:* www.floodsmart.gov
US Fire Administration 16825 S Seton Ave .... Emmitsburg MD 21727 301-447-1000 447-1346
Web: www.usfa.dhs.gov

Federal Emergency Management Agency Regional Offices
Region 1 99 High St 6th Fl .... Boston MA 02110 877-336-2734
TF: 877-336-2734 ■ *Web:* www.fema.gov/about/regions
Region 10
Federal Regional Ctr 130 228th St SW .... Bothell WA 98021 425-487-4600 487-4622
TF: 800-772-1252 ■ *Web:* www.fema.gov
Region 2 26 Federal Plaza Suite 1311 .... New York NY 10278 212-680-3600 680-3681
Web: www.fema.gov/about/regions
Region 3
1 Independence Mall
615 Chestnut St 6th Fl .... Philadelphia PA 19106 215-931-5600 931-5621
TF: 800-621-3362 ■ *Web:* www.fema.gov

	City	State	ZIP	Phone	Fax
Region 4 3003 Chamblee-Tucker Rd	Atlanta	GA	30341	770-220-5200	220-5230
Web: www.fema.gov					
Region 5 536 S Clark St 6th Fl	Chicago	IL	60605	312-408-5500	408-5234
TF: 877-336-2564 ■ *Web:* www.fema.gov					
Region 6 800 N Loop 288	Denton	TX	76209	940-898-5399	898-5325
TF: 800-426-5460 ■ *Web:* www.fema.gov					
Region 7 9221 Ward Pkwy Suite 300	Kansas City	MO	64114	816-283-7061	283-7582
Web: www.fema.gov/about/regions					
Region 8					
Denver Federal Ctr Bldg 710 PO Box 25267	Denver	CO	80225	303-235-4900	235-4976
Web: www.fema.gov					
Region 9 1111 Broadway Suite 1200	Oakland	CA	94607	510-627-7100	627-7112
Web: www.fema.gov/about/regions					
Federal Law Enforcement Training Ctr					
1131 Chapel Crossing Rd	Glynco	GA	31524	912-267-2100	
Web: www.fletc.gov					
Secretary of Homeland Security					
Naval Security Stn	Washington	DC	20528	202-282-8000	282-8401
Web: www.dhs.gov/dhspublic					
Transportation Security Administration (TSA)					
601 S 12th St	Arlington	VA	22202	202-282-8000	227-1300
TF: 866-289-9673 ■ *Web:* www.tsa.gov					
Federal Air Marshal Service 601 S 12th St	Arlington	VA	22202	703-487-3400	487-3405
Web: www.tsa.gov					
US Citizenship & Immigration Services (USCIS)					
20 Massachusetts Ave NW	Washington	DC	20529	202-272-1000	272-1134
TF: 800-375-5283 ■ *Web:* www.uscis.gov					
US Citizenship & Immigration Services Regional Offices					
Central Region 7701 N Stemmons Fwy	Dallas	TX	75247	214-905-5430	905-5435
Eastern Region 70 Kimball Ave	South Burlington	VT	05403	802-660-5000	660-5114
Western Region					
24000 Avila Rd PO Box 30080	Laguna Niguel	CA	92607	949-360-2995	360-3081
TF: 800-375-5283 ■ *Web:* www.uscis.gov					
US Coast Guard (USCG) 2100 2nd St SW	Washington	DC	20593	202-372-4620	372-4986
Web: www.uscg.mil					
Boating Safety Office					
2100 2nd St SW Rm 3100	Washington	DC	20593	202-372-1051	372-1933
Web: www.uscgboating.org					
Law Enforcement Office 2100 2nd St SW	Washington	DC	20593	202-372-2183	
Web: www.uscg.mil/hq/g-o/g-opl					
National Maritime Ctr 100 Forbes Dr	Martinsburg	WV	25404	304-433-3400	
TF: 888-427-5662 ■ *Web:* www.uscg.mil					
National Pollution Funds Ctr					
4200 Wilson Blvd Suite 1000	Arlington	VA	20598	202-493-6700	493-6900
Web: www.uscg.mil/hq/npfc					
Navigation Ctr 7323 Telegraph Rd	Alexandria	VA	22315	703-313-5900	313-5920
Web: www.navcen.uscg.gov					
Search & Rescue Office					
2100 2nd St SW Rm 3106	Washington	DC	20593	202-372-2076	
Web: www.uscg.mil/hq/g-o/g-opr/g-opr.htm					
US Computer Emergency Readiness Team					
245 Murray Ln SW Bldg 410	Washington	DC	20598	703-235-5110	
TF: 888-282-0870 ■ *Web:* www.us-cert.gov					
US Customs & Border Protection					
1300 Pennsylvania Ave NW	Washington	DC	20229	703-526-4200	
TF: 877-227-5511 ■ *Web:* www.customs.ustreas.gov					
US Immigration & Customs Enforcement (ICE)					
425 'I' St NW	Washington	DC	20536	202-514-1900	
TF: 866-347-2423 ■ *Web:* www.ice.gov					
US Secret Service 245 Murray Dr Bldg 410	Washington	DC	20223	202-406-5830	
Web: www.secretservice.gov					
US Coast Guard Academy 15 Mohegan Ave	New London	CT	06320	860-444-8500	701-6700
TF: 800-883-8724 ■ *Web:* www.cga.edu					

343-12 US Department of Housing & Urban Development

	City	State	ZIP	Phone	Fax
Dept of Housing & Urban Development (HUD)					
451 7th St SW	Washington	DC	20410	202-708-0685	619-8153
TF: 800-569-4287 ■ *Web:* www.hud.gov					
Public Affairs Office 451 7th St SW MC W	Washington	DC	20410	202-708-0980	619-8153
Dept of Housing & Urban Development Regional Offices					
Boston 10 Cswy St Federal Bldg	Boston	MA	02222	617-994-8200	565-6558
Web: portal.hud.gov/portal/page/portal/HUD					
Great Plains Region 400 State Ave	Kansas City	KS	66101	913-551-5642	551-5469
Web: portal.hud.gov					
Mid-Atlantic Region 100 Penn Sq E	Philadelphia	PA	19107	215-656-0500	656-3445
TF: 800-225-5342					
New York/New Jersey Region					
26 Federal Plaza Suite 3541	New York	NY	10278	212-264-8000	264-3068
TF: 800-496-4294 ■ *Web:* portal.hud.gov					
Pacific/Hawaii Region					
600 Harrison St 3rd Fl	San Francisco	CA	94107	415-489-6572	436-8412
TF: 800-347-3739 ■ *Web:* portal.hud.gov					
Region 5 - Chicago					
Federal Bldg 77 W Jackson Blvd	Chicago	IL	60604	312-353-6236	353-5417
Web: portal.hud.gov					
Rocky Mountain Region 1670 Broadway 25th Fl	Denver	CO	80202	303-672-5440	672-5004
Seattle Federal Bldg 909 1st Ave Suite 200	Seattle	WA	98104	509-368-3200	
Web: www.hud.gov/localoffices.cfm					
Southeast/Caribbean Region					
Five Points Plaza Bldg 40 Marietta St	Atlanta	GA	30303	404-331-5001	730-2392
Southwest Region					
801 N Cherry St Unit 45 Suite 2500	Fort Worth	TX	76102	817-978-5965	978-5569
Government National Mortgage Assn					
451 7th St SW Suite B-133	Washington	DC	20410	202-708-1535	708-0490
Web: www.ginniemae.gov					
HUD Office of Community Planning & Development					
451 7th St SW MC-D	Washington	DC	20410	202-708-2690	708-3336
Web: www.hud.gov/offices/cpd					
Affordable Housing Programs Office					
451 7th St SW MS-DGH	Washington	DC	20410	202-708-2684	708-1744
Web: www.hud.gov/offices/cpd/affordablehousing/programs					
Block Grant Assistance Office					
451 7th St SW MS-DGB	Washington	DC	20410	202-708-3587	
Web: www.hud.gov/offices/cpd/communitydevelopment					
HIV/AIDS Housing Office					
451 7th St SW Rm 7212	Washington	DC	20410	202-708-1934	708-9313
Web: www.hud.gov/offices/cpd/aidshousing					
Special Needs Assistance Programs Office					
451 7th St SW MS-DESP	Washington	DC	20410	202-708-4300	708-0053
Web: www.hud.gov/offices/cpd/homeless					
HUD Office of Fair Housing & Equal Opportunity					
451 7th St SW MC E	Washington	DC	20410	202-708-4252	708-4483
TF: 800-669-9777 ■ *Web:* www.hud.gov/offices/fheo					
Housing Discrimination Hotline					
451 7th St SW	Washington	DC	20410	202-708-1112	
TF: 800-669-9777 ■					
Web: portal.hud.gov/hudportal/HUD?src=/program_offices/fair_housing_equal_opp					
HUD Office of Healthy Homes & Lead Hazard Control					
451 7th St SW MC-L	Washington	DC	20410	202-708-0310	755-1000
Web: www.hud.gov/offices/lead					
HUD Office of Housing - Federal Housing Administration (FHA)					
451 7th St SW Suite 9100	Washington	DC	20410	202-708-1112	
TF: 800-767-7468 ■ *Web:* www.hud.gov/offices/hsg/fhahistory.cfm					
HUD Office of Policy Development & Research					
451 7th St SW MC R	Washington	DC	20410	202-708-1600	619-8000
Web: www.huduser.org					
HUD Office of Public & Indian Housing					
451 7th St SW Rm 4100	Washington	DC	20410	202-708-0950	619-8478
TF: 800-955-2232 ■ *Web:* www.hud.gov/offices/pih					
Real Estate Assessment Ctr					
550 12th St SW Suite 100	Washington	DC	20410	888-245-4860	
TF: 888-245-4860 ■ *Web:* www.hud.gov/offices/reac					
Secretary of Housing & Urban Development					
451 7th St SW	Washington	DC	20410	202-708-0417	619-8365
Web: www.hud.gov/about					

343-13 US Department of the Interior

	City	State	ZIP	Phone	Fax
Dept of the Interior (DOI) 1849 C St NW	Washington	DC	20240	202-208-3100	
Web: www.doi.gov					
Nationalatlas.gov					
US Geological Survey 508 National Ctr					
12201 Sunrise Valley Dr	Reston	VA	20192	703-648-5953	
TF: 888-275-8747 ■ *Web:* www.nationalatlas.gov					
Bureau of Indian Affairs (BIA)					
1849 C St NW MS 4141	Washington	DC	20240	202-208-7163	208-5320
Web: www.doi.gov/bureau-indian-affairs.html					
Bureau of Indian Affairs Regional Offices					
Alaska Region 709 W 9th St 3rd Fl PO Box 25520	Juneau	AK	99802	907-586-7177	586-7252
TF: 800-645-8397					
Eastern Oklahoma Region PO Box 8002	Muskogee	OK	74402	918-781-4600	781-4604
Eastern Region 545 Marriott Dr Suite 700	Nashville	TN	37214	615-564-6700	564-6701
TF: 888-258-6118					
Great Plains Region 115 4th Ave SE	Aberdeen	SD	57401	605-226-7343	226-7446
Web: www.bia.gov					
Midwest Region					
Federal Bldg 1 Federal Dr Rm 550	Minneapolis	MN	55111	612-713-4400	713-4401
Navajo Region PO Box 1060	Gallup	NM	87305	505-863-8314	863-8324
Northwest Region					
Federal Complex 911 NE 11th Ave	Portland	OR	97232	503-231-6702	231-2201
Pacific Region					
Federal Bldg					
2800 Cottage Way Suite W-2820	Sacramento	CA	95825	916-978-6000	978-6099
Rocky Mountain Region					
Federal Courthouse 316 N 26th St	Billings	MT	59101	406-247-7943	247-7976
Southern Plains Region PO Box 368	Anadarko	OK	73005	405-247-6673	247-5611
Southwest Region					
1001 Indian School Rd NW	Albuquerque	NM	87104	505-563-3103	563-3101
Western Region					
400 N 5th St 12th Fl 12 Arizona Ctr	Phoenix	AZ	85001	602-379-6600	379-4413
Bureau of Land Management (BLM) 1849 C St NW	Washington	DC	20240	202-208-3801	208-5242
Web: www.blm.gov					
National Wild Horse & Burro Program					
PO Box 3270	Sparks	NV	89432	775-475-2222	
TF: 866-468-7826 ■ *Web:* www.blm.gov					
Bureau of Land Management Regional Offices					
Alaska State Office 222 W 7th Ave Suite 13	Anchorage	AK	99513	907-271-5960	271-3684
Web: www.blm.gov					
Arizona State Office					
1 N Central Ave Suite 800	Phoenix	AZ	85004	602-417-9200	417-9556
Web: www.blm.gov					

	City	State	Zip	Phone	Fax
California State Office					
2800 Cottage Way Suite W-1834	Sacramento	CA	95825	916-978-4400	978-4416
Web: www.blm.gov					
Colorado State Office 2850 Youngfield St	Lakewood	CO	80215	303-239-3600	239-3933
Web: www.co.blm.gov					
Eastern States Office 7450 Boston Blvd	Springfield	VA	22153	703-440-1600	
Web: www.es.blm.gov					
Idaho State Office 1387 S Vinnell Way	Boise	ID	83709	208-373-4000	373-3899
Web: www.id.blm.gov					
Montana State Office 5001 Southgate Dr	Billings	MT	59101	406-896-5000	
Web: www.mt.blm.gov					
Nevada State Office 1340 Financial Blvd	Reno	NV	89502	775-861-6400	861-6606
Web: www.nv.blm.gov					
Oregon/Washington State Office					
333 SW 1st Ave	Portland	OR	97204	503-808-6001	808-6422
Web: www.blm.gov					
Utah State Office PO Box 45155	Salt Lake City	UT	84145	801-539-4001	539-4013
Web: www.ut.blm.gov					
Wyoming State Office					
5353 Yellowstone Rd PO Box 1828	Cheyenne	WY	82003	307-775-6256	775-6129
Web: www.wy.blm.gov					
Bureau of Reclamation 1849 C St NW	Washington	DC	20240	202-513-0501	513-0314
Web: www.usbr.gov					
Bureau of Reclamation Regional Offices					
Great Plains Region PO Box 36900	Billings	MT	59107	406-247-7600	247-7604
Web: www.usbr.gov					
Lower Colorado Region PO Box 61470	Boulder City	NV	89006	702-293-8411	293-8333
Web: www.usbr.gov					
Mid-Pacific Region					
Federal Bldg 2800 Cottage Way	Sacramento	CA	95825	916-978-5000	978-5005
Web: www.usbr.gov					
Pacific Northwest Region					
1150 N Curtis Rd Suite 100	Boise	ID	83706	208-378-5012	378-5019
Web: www.usbr.gov					
Upper Colorado Region					
125 S State St Rm 6107	Salt Lake City	UT	84138	801-524-3600	524-5499
Web: www.usbr.gov/uc					
Minerals Management Service 1849 C St NW	Washington	DC	20240	202-208-3500	208-7242
Web: www.mms.gov					
National Interagency Fire Ctr					
3833 S Development Ave	Boise	ID	83705	208-387-5512	387-5797
Web: www.nifc.gov					
Conservation & Outdoor Recreation Programs					
1849 C St NW Org Code 2220	Washington	DC	20240	202-354-6900	371-5179
Web: www.nps.gov/ncrc					
National Register of Historic Places					
1201 Eye St NW 8th Fl	Washington	DC	20005	202-354-2213	
Web: www.cr.nps.gov					
National Park Service Regional Offices Southeast Region					
100 Alabama St SW 1924 Bldg	Atlanta	GA	30303	404-507-5817	562-3201
Web: www.nps.gov/legacy/regions.html					
Office of Surface Mining Reclamation & Enforcement					
1951 Constitution Ave NW					
S Interior Bldg Rm 233	Washington	DC	20240	202-208-4006	
Web: www.osmre.gov					
Office of Surface Mining Reclamation & Enforcement Regional Offices					
Appalachian Region 3 Parkway Ctr	Pittsburgh	PA	15220	412-937-2828	
Web: www.arcc.osmre.gov					
Mid-Continent Region 501 Belle St Rm 216	Alton	IL	62002	618-463-6460	463-6470
Web: www.mcrcc.osmre.gov/MCR					
Western Region 1999 Broadway Suite 3320	Denver	CO	80202	303-293-5000	293-5006
Web: www.wrcc.osmre.gov					
Secretary of the Interior					
1849 C St NW Rm 6156	Washington	DC	20240	202-208-7351	208-5048
Web: www.doi.gov/welcome.html					
US Board on Geographic Names					
US Geological Survey 12201 Sunrise Valley Dr					
MS 523	Reston	VA	20192	703-605-4575	
Web: www.geonames.usgs.gov					
US Fish & Wildlife Service (USFWS)					
1849 C St NW	Washington	DC	20240	202-208-4717	208-6965
TF: 800-344-9453 ■ *Web:* www.fws.gov					
US Fish & Wildlife Service Regional Offices					
Alaska Region 1011 E Tudor Rd	Anchorage	AK	99503	907-786-3309	786-3495
Web: www.alaska.fws.gov					
California & Nevada Region					
2800 Cottage Way	Sacramento	CA	95825	916-414-6464	414-6486
Web: www.fws.gov					
Great Lakes/Big Rivers Region					
5600 American Blvd W Suite 900	Bloomington	MN	55437	612-713-5360	713-5280
TF: 800-877-8339 ■ *Web:* www.fws.gov/midwest					
Mountain-Prairie Region 134 Union Blvd	Lakewood	CO	80228	303-236-7905	236-8295
Web: www.fws.gov/mountain-prairie					
NortheastRegion 300 Westgate Ctr Dr	Hadley	MA	01035	413-253-8200	253-8308
Web: www.fws.gov					
Pacific Region					
Eastside Federal Complex 911 NE 11th Ave	Portland	OR	97232	503-231-6838	231-6161
Web: www.fws.gov/pacific					
Southeast Region 1875 Century Blvd Suite 400	Atlanta	GA	30345	404-679-4000	679-4006
Web: www.fws.gov/southeast					
Southwest Region					
500 Gold Ave SW PO Box 1306	Albuquerque	NM	87102	505-248-6911	248-6910
Web: www.fws.gov/southwest					
US Geological Survey (USGS)					
12201 Sunrise Valley Dr	Reston	VA	20192	703-648-4000	648-4454
TF: 888-275-8747 ■ *Web:* www.usgs.gov					

	City	State	Zip	Phone	Fax
Ask USGS 12201 Sunrise Valley Dr	Reston	VA	20192	703-648-5953	
TF: 888-275-8747 ■ *Web:* www.ask.usgs.gov					
National Park Service Regional Offices					
Alaska Region 240 W 5th Ave Suite 114	Anchorage	AK	99501	907-644-3510	644-3816
National Park Service Regional Offices Pacific West Region					
1111 Jackson St Suite 700	Oakland	CA	94607	510-817-1304	817-1485
National Park Service Regional Offices Intermountain Region					
12795 W Alameda Pkwy	Denver	CO	80225	303-969-2500	
National Park Service (NPS)					
1849 C St NW Rm 1013	Washington	DC	20240	202-208-6843	219-0910
Web: www.nps.gov					
National Park Service Regional Offices National Capital Region					
1100 Ohio Dr SW	Washington	DC	20242	202-619-7000	619-7220
Web: www.nps.gov/ncro					
National Park Service Regional Offices Midwest Region					
601 Riverfront Dr	Omaha	NE	68102	402-661-1524	661-1984
National Park Service Regional Offices NortheastRegion					
200 Chestnut St # 3	Philadelphia	PA	19106	215-597-7013	597-0815
Web: www.nps.gov					

343-14 US Department of Justice

	City	State	Zip	Phone	Fax
Department of Justice Antitrust Div Regional Offices					
Chicago Field Office					
209 S LaSalle St Suite 600	Chicago	IL	60604	312-353-5559	353-1046
Web: www.justice.gov					
Cleveland Field Office					
55 Erieview Plaza Suite 700	Cleveland	OH	44114	216-522-4070	522-8332
Web: www.justice.gov					
Dept of Justice (DOJ)					
950 Pennsylvania Ave NW	Washington	DC	20530	202-514-2007	514-5331
Web: www.justice.gov					
Antitrust Div 950 Pennsylvania Ave NW	Washington	DC	20530	202-514-2401	616-2645
Web: www.usdoj.gov/atr					
Civil Div 950 Pennsylvania Ave NW	Washington	DC	20530	202-514-3301	514-8071
Web: www.usdoj.gov/civil					
Civil Rights Div 950 Pennsylvania Ave NW	Washington	DC	20530	202-514-4609	307-2572
Web: www.usdoj.gov/crt					
Community Relations Service 600 E St NW	Washington	DC	20530	202-305-2935	305-3009
Web: www.usdoj.gov/crs					
Criminal Div 601 D St NW	Washington	DC	20530	202-514-7200	514-9412
Web: www.usdoj.gov/criminal					
Environment & Natural Resources Div					
950 Pennsylvania Ave NW	Washington	DC	20530	202-514-2701	514-0557
Web: www.usdoj.gov/enrd					
National Security Division					
950 Pennsylvania Ave NW	Washington	DC	20530	202-514-1057	353-9836
Web: www.usdoj.gov/nsd					
Office of Information & Privacy					
1425 New York Ave NW Suite 11050	Washington	DC	20530	202-514-3642	514-1009
Web: www.usdoj.gov/oip/oip.html					
Public Affairs Office					
950 Pennsylvania Ave NW	Washington	DC	20530	202-616-2777	
Web: www.usdoj.gov/opa					
Tax Div 950 Pennsylvania Ave NW 4th Fl	Washington	DC	20530	202-514-2901	514-5479
Web: www.usdoj.gov/tax					
Dept of Justice Antitrust Div Regional Office					
Dallas Field Office 1601 Elm St Suite 4950	Dallas	TX	75201	214-880-9401	880-9423
Web: www.justice.gov					
Dept of Justice Antitrust Div Regional Offices					
Atlanta Field Office					
Federal Bldg 75 Spring St SW Suite 1176	Atlanta	GA	30303	404-331-7100	331-7110
New York Field Office					
26 Federal Plaza Rm 3630	New York	NY	10278	212-264-0383	264-0678
Web: www.justice.gov/atr					
Philadelphia Field Office					
7th & Walnut St Suite 650	Philadelphia	PA	19106	215-597-7405	597-8838
Web: www.justice.gov					
San Francisco Field Office					
450 Golden Gate Ave Rm 10-0101	San Francisco	CA	94102	415-436-6660	436-6687
Federal Bureau of Prisons 320 1st St NW	Washington	DC	20534	202-307-3250	514-6620
Web: www.bop.gov					
Bureau of Alcohol Tobacco Firearms & Explosives (ATF)					
650 Massachusetts Ave NW	Washington	DC	20226	202-927-7777	927-7862
Web: www.atf.gov					
Bureau of Alcohol Tobacco Firearms & Explosives Regional Offices					
Atlanta Field Div 2600 Century Pkwy NE	Atlanta	GA	30345	404-417-2600	417-2601
Web: www.atf.gov					
Baltimore Field Div 31 Hopkins Plaza 5th Fl	Baltimore	MD	21201	410-779-1700	779-1701
Web: www.atf.gov/field/baltimore					
Boston Field Div 10 Cswy St Suite 791	Boston	MA	02222	617-557-1200	577-1201
Web: www.atf.gov/field/boston					
Charlotte Field Div					
6701 Carmel Rd Suite 200	Charlotte	NC	28226	704-716-1800	716-1801
Web: www.atf.gov/field/charlotte					
Chicago Field Div					
525 W Van Buren St Suite 600	Chicago	IL	60607	312-846-7200	846-7201
Web: www.atf.gov/field/chicago					
Columbus Field Div 37 W Broad St Suite 200	Columbus	OH	43215	614-827-8400	827-8401
Web: www.atf.gov					

Entry	City	State	ZIP	Phone	Fax
Dallas Field Div 1114 Commerce St Rm 303	Dallas	TX	75242	469-227-4300	227-4330
Web: www.atf.gov					
Denver Field Div					
Byron Rogers Federal Bldg					
1961 Stout St Rm 674	Denver	CO	80294	303-844-7450	844-7535
Web: www.atf.gov					
Detroit Field Div					
1155 Brewery Park Blvd Suite 300	Detroit	MI	48207	313-202-3400	202-3445
Web: www.atf.gov/field/detroit					
Houston Field Div 333 W Loop N # 111	Houston	TX	77032	281-372-2900	372-2919
Web: www.atf.gov					
Kansas City Field Div					
2600 Grand Ave Suite 200	Kansas City	MO	64108	816-559-0700	559-0701
Web: www.atf.gov/field/kansascity					
Los Angeles Field Div					
350 S Figueroa St Suite 800	Los Angeles	CA	90071	213-534-2450	534-2415
Web: www.atf.gov/field/losangeles					
Louisville Field Div					
600 Martin Luther King Pl #322	Louisville	KY	40202	502-753-3400	753-3401
Web: www.atf.gov					
Miami Field Div 11410 NW 20 St Suite 201	Miami	FL	33172	305-597-4800	597-4801
Web: www.atf.gov/field/miami					
Nashville Field Div					
5300 Maryland Way Suite 200	Brentwood	TN	37027	615-565-1400	565-1401
Web: www.atf.gov/field/nashville					
New Orleans Field Div					
1 Galleria Blvd Suite 1700	Metairie	LA	70001	985-246-7000	246-7039
Web: www.atf.gov/field/neworleans					
New York Field Div 241 37th St 3rd Fl	Brooklyn	NY	11232	718-650-4000	650-4001
Web: www.atf.gov					
Philadelphia Field Div 601 Walnut St	Philadelphia	PA	19106	215-446-7800	446-7811
Web: www.atf.gov					
Phoenix Field Div					
201 E Washington St Suite 940	Phoenix	AZ	85004	602-776-5400	776-5429
Web: www.atf.gov					
Saint Paul Field Div					
30 E 7th St Suite 1900	Saint Paul	MN	55101	651-726-0200	726-0201
Web: www.atf.gov/field/stpaul					
San Francisco Field Div					
5601 Arnold Rd Suite 400	Dublin	CA	94568	925-479-7500	829-7612
Web: www.atf.gov					
Seattle Field Div 915 2nd Ave Rm 790	Seattle	WA	98174	206-389-5800	389-5829
Web: www.atf.gov/field/seattle					
Tampa Field Div 400 N Tampa St Suite 2100	Tampa	FL	33602	813-202-7300	202-7301
Web: www.atf.gov/field/tampa					
Washington (DC) Field Div					
1401 H St NW Suite 900	Washington	DC	20226	202-648-8010	648-8001
Web: www.atf.gov/field/washington					
Community Oriented Policing Services (COPS)					
1100 Vermont Ave NW 10th Fl	Washington	DC	20530	202-616-2888	
TF: 800-421-6770 ■ *Web:* www.cops.usdoj.gov					
Drug Enforcement Administration (DEA)					
700 Army-Navy Dr	Arlington	VA	22202	202-307-8000	
Web: www.dea.gov					
DEA Training Academy PO Box 1475	Quantico	VA	22134	703-632-5000	
Web: www.usdoj.gov					
El Paso Intelligence Ctr 11339 Simms St	El Paso	TX	79908	915-760-2000	
Web: www.dea.gov					
Drug Enforcement Administration Regional Offices					
Atlanta Div Federal Bldg 75 Spring St SW	Atlanta	GA	30303	404-893-7000	893-7110
Web: www.dea.gov					
Boston Div 15 New Sudbury St Rm E400	Boston	MA	02203	617-557-2100	557-2135
Web: www.dea.gov					
Chicago Div Federal Bldg 230 S Dearborn St	Chicago	IL	60604	312-353-7875	886-8439
Web: www.dea.gov					
Dallas Div 10160 Technology Blvd E	Dallas	TX	75220	214-366-6900	366-6914
Web: www.dea.gov/pubs/states/dallas.html					
Denver Div 115 Inverness Dr E	Englewood	CO	80112	303-705-7300	705-7414
Web: www.dea.gov/pubs/states/denver.html					
Detroit Div 431 Howard St	Detroit	MI	48226	313-234-4000	234-4141
Web: www.dea.gov/pubs/states/detroit.html					
El Paso Div 660 S Mesa Hills Suite 2000	El Paso	TX	79912	915-832-6000	832-6001
Web: www.dea.gov					
Houston Div 1433 W Loop S Suite 600	Houston	TX	77027	713-693-3000	
Web: www.dea.gov/pubs/states/houston.html					
Los Angeles Div					
Federal Bldg 255 E Temple St 20th Fl	Los Angeles	CA	90012	213-621-6700	
Web: www.dea.gov					
Miami Div 8400 NW 53rd St	Miami	FL	33166	305-994-4870	994-4500
Web: www.dea.gov/pubs/states/miami.html					
New Orleans Div 3838 N Cswy Blvd Suite 1800	Metairie	LA	70002	504-840-1100	
Web: www.dea.gov					
New York Div 99 10th Ave	New York	NY	10011	212-337-3900	337-2799
Web: www.usdoj.gov					
Philadelphia Div					
Federal Bldg 600 Arch St Rm 10224	Philadelphia	PA	19106	215-861-3474	861-1979
Web: www.dea.gov					
Phoenix Div 3010 N 2nd St Suite 301	Phoenix	AZ	85012	602-664-5600	664-5616
Web: www.dea.gov					
Saint Louis Div 317 S 16th St	Saint Louis	MO	63103	314-538-4600	538-4798
Web: www.dea.gov					

Entry	City	State	ZIP	Phone	Fax
San Diego Div 4560 Viewridge Ave	San Diego	CA	92123	858-616-4100	616-4084
Web: www.dea.gov					
San Francisco Div 450 Golden Gate Ave	San Francisco	CA	94102	415-436-7900	436-7810
Web: www.dea.gov/pubs/states/sanfran.html					
Seattle Div 400 2nd Ave W	Seattle	WA	98119	206-553-5443	553-1576
Web: www.dea.gov/pubs/states/seattle.html					
Washington DC Div 800 K St NW Suite 500	Washington	DC	20001	202-305-8500	305-5760
Web: www.dea.gov/pubs/states/wdo.html					
Executive Office for Immigration Review					
5107 Leesburg Pike	Falls Church	VA	22041	703-305-0289	605-0365
Web: www.usdoj.gov/eoir					
Executive Office for US Trustees					
20 Massachusetts Ave NW Suite 8000	Washington	DC	20530	202-307-1391	307-0672
Web: www.justice.gov/usd					
Federal Bureau of Investigation (FBI)					
935 Pennsylvania Ave NW	Washington	DC	20535	202-324-3000	
Web: www.fbi.gov					
Criminal Justice Information Services					
1000 Custer Hollow Rd	Clarksburg	WV	26306	304-625-2700	625-4498
Web: www.fbi.gov/hq/cjisd/cjis.htm					
FBI Academy 1 Hoover Rd	Quantico	VA	22135	703-632-1000	
Web: www.fbi.gov					
FBI Laboratory FBI Academy	Quantico	VA	22135	703-632-1000	
Web: www.fbi.gov/about-us/lab					
Management & Specialty Training Ctr					
791Chambers Rd	Aurora	CO	80011	303-340-7800	
Web: www.bop.gov/about/train					
National Institute of Corrections					
320 1st St NW	Washington	DC	20534	202-307-3106	
TF: 800-995-6423 ■ *Web:* www.nicic.org					
National Institute of Corrections Information Cent					
1860 Industrial Cir Suite A	Longmont	CO	80501	303-682-0213	682-0558
TF: 800-877-1461 ■ *Web:* www.nicic.org					
Federal Bureau of Prisons Regional Offices					
Mid-Atlantic Region					
302 Sentinel Dr Suite 200	Annapolis Junction	MD	20701	301-317-3100	
Web: www.bop.gov					
North Central Region					
400 State Ave Suite 800	Kansas City	KS	66101	913-621-3939	
Web: www.bop.gov/about/ro/ncr					
Northeast Region					
2nd & Chestnut St 7th Fl	Philadelphia	PA	19106	215-521-7301	
Web: www.bop.gov					
South Central Region 4211 Cedar Springs Rd	Dallas	TX	75219	214-224-3389	
Web: www.bop.gov					
Southeast Region					
3800 Camp Creek Pk SW Bldg 2000	Atlanta	GA	30331	678-686-1200	
Web: www.bop.gov					
Western Region 7950 Dublin Blvd 3rd Fl	Dublin	CA	94568	925-803-4700	
Web: www.bop.gov					
Foreign Claims Settlement Commission of the US					
600 E St NW	Washington	DC	20579	202-616-6975	616-6993
Web: www.usdoj.gov/fcsc					
National Criminal Justice Reference Service					
PO Box 6000	Rockville	MD	20849	301-519-5500	519-5212
TF: 800-851-3420 ■ *Web:* www.ncjrs.org					
National Drug Intelligence Ctr					
319 Washington St 5th Fl	Johnstown	PA	15901	814-532-4601	532-4690
Web: www.usdoj.gov					
Office of Justice Programs (OJP)					
810 7th St NW	Washington	DC	20531	202-307-0703	
Web: www.ojp.usdoj.gov					
Bureau of Justice Assistance					
810 7th St NW	Washington	DC	20531	202-616-6500	305-1367
Web: www.ojp.usdoj.gov/BJA					
Bureau of Justice Statistics					
810 7th St NW	Washington	DC	20531	202-307-0765	307-5846
TF: 800-851-3420 ■ *Web:* www.ojp.usdoj.gov/bjs					
Community Capacity Development Office					
810 7th St NW	Washington	DC	20531	202-616-1152	616-1159
Web: www.ojp.usdoj.gov/ccdo					
National Institute of Justice					
810 7th St NW	Washington	DC	20531	202-307-2942	307-6394
Web: www.ojp.usdoj.gov/nij					
Office for Victims of Crime					
810 7th St NW 8th Fl	Washington	DC	20531	202-307-5983	514-6383
Web: www.ojp.usdoj.gov/ovc					
Office of Juvenile Justice & Delinquency Prevention					
810 7th St NW	Washington	DC	20531	202-307-5911	307-2093
Web: ojjdp.ncjrs.org					
Office of Special Counsel for Immigration-Related Unfair Employment Practices					
950 Pennsylvania Ave NW	Washington	DC	20038	202-616-5594	616-5509
TF: 800-255-7688 ■ *Web:* www.usdoj.gov/crt/osc					
Office of the Pardon Attorney					
1425 New York Ave NW Suite 1100	Washington	DC	20530	202-616-6070	616-6069
Web: www.usdoj.gov/pardon					
Office of Tribal Justice					
950 Pennsylvania Ave NW Rm 2200C	Washington	DC	20530	202-514-8812	514-9078
Web: www.usdoj.gov/otj					
Office on Violence Against Women					
145 N St Suite 10W 121	Washington	DC	20530	202-307-6026	307-2277
Web: www.ovw.usdoj.gov					
US Marshals Service					
1735 Jefferson Davis Hwy	Arlington	VA	22202	202-307-9100	307-8729
TF: 800-336-0102 ■ *Web:* www.usmarshals.gov					

Phone | Fax

US National Central Bureau of INTERPOL (INTERPOL)
600 E St NW Suite 600 .... Washington DC 20530 202-616-9000 616-8400
Web: www.justice.gov

US Parole Commission
5550 Friendship Blvd Rm 420 .... Chevy Chase MD 20815 301-492-5990 492-5543
TF: 888-585-9103 ■ *Web:* www.usdoj.gov/uspc

343-15 US Department of Labor

Phone | Fax

Dept of Labor (DOL) 200 Constitution Ave NW .... Washington DC 20210 202-693-4650 693-4674
TF: 866-487-2365 ■ *Web:* www.dol.gov
GovBenefits.gov 200 Constitution Ave NW .... Washington DC 20210 800-333-4636
TF: 866-487-2365 ■ *Web:* www.govbenefits.gov
Job Corps
200 Constitution Ave NW Suite N4463 .... Washington DC 20210 202-693-3000 693-2767
Web: jobcorps.dol.gov
Office of Administrative Law Judges
800 K St NW Suite 400 N .... Washington DC 20001 202-693-7300 693-7365
Web: www.oalj.dol.gov
Public Affairs Office
200 Constitution Ave NW Rm S2514 .... Washington DC 20210 202-693-4676 693-5057
TF: 866-487-2365 ■ *Web:* www.dol.gov

Dept of Labor Regional Offices
Region 1 - Boston JFK Federal Bldg Rm 525A .... Boston MA 02203 617-565-2072 565-2076
Web: www.dol.gov
Region 10 - Seattle 1111 3rd Ave Suite 920 .... Seattle WA 98101 206-553-0574 553-2086
Region 2 - New York 201 Varick St Rm 983 .... New York NY 10014 646-264-3650
Web: www.dol.gov
Region 3 - Philadelphia
170 S Independence Mall W Suite 635E .... Philadelphia PA 19106 215-861-5083
Web: www.dol.gov
Region 4 - Atlanta
Federal Ctr 400 W Bay St Rm 943 .... jacksonville FL 32202 904-357-4776
Region 5 - Chicago
Federal Bldg 230 S Dearborn St .... Chicago IL 60604 312-596-5400 596-5401
Web: www.doleta.gov
Region 6 - Dallas
Federal Bldg 525 S Griffin St Rm 407 .... Dallas TX 75202 972-850-2409 850-2401
Web: www.dol.gov/owcp/contacts/dallas/arf.htm
Region 8 - Denver 1999 Broadway Suite 1620 .... Denver CO 80202 303-844-1286 844-1283
Web: www.dol.gov

Employment & Training Administration
200 Constitution Ave NW Rm S2307 .... Washington DC 20210 202-693-2700 693-2725
Web: www.doleta.gov

US Dept of Labor 200 Constitution Ave NW .... Washington DC 20210 202-693-4700 693-4754
Web: www.dol.gov/vets

Bureau of International Labor Affairs
200 Constitution Ave NW .... Washington DC 20210 202-693-4770 693-4780
Web: www.dol.gov/ilab

Bureau of Labor Statistics
2 Massachusetts Ave NE .... Washington DC 20212 202-691-5200 691-7890
Web: www.bls.gov
Consumer Price Index
2 Massachusetts Ave NE Suite 3130 .... Washington DC 20212 202-691-7000 691-6325
Web: www.bls.gov/cpi

Bureau of Labor Statistics Regional Offices
Mid-Atlantic Information Office
170 S Independence Mall W Suite 610 E .... Philadelphia PA 19106 215-597-3282 861-5720
Web: www.bls.gov/ro3
Midwest Information Office
230 S Dearborn St # 1086 .... Chicago IL 60604 312-353-1880 353-1886
Web: www.bls.gov
Mountain-Plains Information Office
2300 Main St Suite 1190 .... Kansas City MO 64108 816-285-7000 285-7009
Web: www.bls.gov/ro7
New England Information Office
JFK Federal Bldg Rm E-310 .... Boston MA 02203 617-565-2327 565-4182
Web: www.bls.gov/ro1
New York-New Jersey Information Office
201 Varick St Rm 808 .... New York NY 10014 212-264-3600 337-2532
Web: www.bls.gov/ro2
Southeast Information Office 61 Forsyth St .... Atlanta GA 30303 404-893-4222 893-4221
Web: www.bls.gov
Southwest Information Office
Federal Bldg 525 Griffin St Rm 221 .... Dallas TX 75202 972-850-4800 767-8881*
**Fax Area Code:* 214 ■ *Web:* www.bls.gov/ro6
Western Information Office
PO Box 193766 .... San Francisco CA 94119 415-625-2270 625-2351
Web: www.bls.gov

Employee Benefits Security Administration
200 Constitution Ave NW Rm S2524 .... Washington DC 20210 202-693-8300 219-5526
Web: www.dol.gov/ebsa

Phone | Fax

Employment & Training Administration Regional Offices
Region I - Boston JFK Federal Bldg Rm E-350 .... Boston MA 02203 617-788-0170 788-0101
Web: www.doleta.gov/regions/reg01bos
Region II - Philadelphia
The Curtis Crt 170 S Independence Mall West
Suite 825E .... Philadelphia PA 19106 215-861-5200 861-5260
Web: www.doleta.gov
Region III - Atlanta
Federal Ctr 61 Forsyth St SW Rm 6M12 .... Atlanta GA 30303 404-302-5300 302-5382
Web: www.doleta.gov/regions/reg03
Region IV - Dallas
Federal Bldg 525 Griffin St Rm 317 .... Dallas TX 75202 972-850-4600 850-4605
Web: www.doleta.gov/regions/reg04
Region V - Chicago
Federal Bldg 230 S Dearborn St 6th Fl .... Chicago IL 60604 312-596-5400 596-5401
Web: www.doleta.gov/regions/reg05
Region VI - San Francisco
90 7th St Suite 17-300 .... San Francisco CA 94103 415-625-7900 625-7903
Web: www.doleta.gov/regions/reg06

Employment Standards Administration
200 Constitution Ave NW Rm S2321 .... Washington DC 20210 202-693-0200 693-0218
TF: 866-487-2365 ■ *Web:* www.dol.gov/esa
Office of Labor-Management Standards
200 Constitution Ave NW Rm N5605 .... Washington DC 20210 202-693-0122
Web: www.dol.gov/esa/olms_org.htm
Office of Workers' Compensation Programs
200 Constitution Ave Rm S3524 .... Washington DC 20210 202-693-0031 693-1378
Web: www.dol.gov/esa/owcp_org.htm
Wage & Hour Div 200 Constitution Ave NW .... Washington DC 20210 202-693-0051 693-1406
Web: www.dol.gov/esa/whd

Labor Racketeering & Fraud Investigations Office
200 Constitution Ave NW Rm S5014 .... Washington DC 20210 202-693-5229
Web: www.oig.dol.gov/olrfi.htm

Mine Safety & Health Administration (MSHA)
1100 Wilson Blvd .... Arlington VA 22209 202-693-9400 693-9401
TF: 800-746-1553 ■ *Web:* www.msha.gov
Coal Mine Safety & Health Office
1100 Wilson Blvd .... Arlington VA 22209 202-693-9500 693-9501
Web: www.msha.gov/programs/coal.htm
Metal & Non-Metal Mine Safety & Health Office
1100 Wilson Blvd .... Arlington VA 22209 202-693-9600 693-9601
Web: www.msha.gov/programs/metal.htm
National Mine Health & Safety Academy
1301 Airport Rd .... Beaver WV 25813 304-256-3100 256-3324
Web: www.msha.gov

Occupational Safety & Health Administration (OSHA)
200 Constitution Ave NW .... Washington DC 20210 202-693-1999 693-1659
TF: 800-321-6735 ■ *Web:* www.osha.gov

Occupational Safety & Health Administration Regional Offices
Region 1 JFK Federal Bldg Rm E-340 .... Boston MA 02203 617-565-9860 565-9827
TF: 800-321-6742 ■ *Web:* www.osha.gov/oshdir/r01.html
Region 10 1111 3rd Ave Suite 715 .... Seattle WA 98101 206-553-5930 553-6499
TF: 800-321-6742 ■ *Web:* www.osha.gov/oshdir/r10.html
Region 2 201 Varick St Suite 670 .... New York NY 10014 212-337-2378 337-2371
TF: 800-321-6742 ■ *Web:* www.osha.gov/oshdir/r02.html
Region 3
Curtis Ctr 170 S Independence Mall W
Suite 740W .... Philadelphia PA 19106 215-861-4900 861-4904
TF: 800-321-6742 ■ *Web:* www.osha.gov
Region 4 61 Forsyth St SW Rm 6T50 .... Atlanta GA 30303 404-562-2300 562-2295
Web: www.osha.gov/oshdir/r04.html
Region 5
Federal Bldg 230 S Dearborn St Rm 3244 .... Chicago IL 60604 312-353-2220 353-7774
Web: www.osha.gov/oshdir/r05.html
Region 6 Federal Bldg 525 Griffin St Suite 602 .... Dallas TX 75202 972-850-4145 850-4149
Web: www.osha.gov/oshdir/r06.html
Region 7 2300 Main St Suite 1010 .... Kansas City MO 64108 816-283-8745 283-0547
Web: www.osha.gov/oshdir/r07.html
Region 8 1999 Broadway Suite 1690 .... Denver CO 80202 720-264-6550 264-6585
Web: www.osha.gov/oshdir/r08.html
Region 9 90 7th St Suite 18100 .... San Francisco CA 94103 415-625-2547 625-2534
Web: www.osha.gov/oshdir/r09.html

Office of Disability Employment Policy
200 Constitution Ave NW Suite S1303 .... Washington DC 20210 202-693-7880 693-7888
TF: 866-633-7365 ■ *Web:* www.dol.gov/odep

Secretary of Labor
200 Constitution Ave NW Rm S2018 .... Washington DC 20210 202-693-6000 693-6111
TF: 866-487-2365 ■ *Web:* www.dol.gov

Women's Bureau
200 Constitution Ave NW Rm S3002 .... Washington DC 20210 202-693-6710 693-6746
TF: 800-827-5335 ■ *Web:* www.dol.gov/wb

Women's Bureau Regional Offices
Region 1 JFK Federal Bldg Rm 525-A .... Boston MA 02203 617-565-1988 565-1986
Web: www.dol.gov/wb
Region 10 1111 3rd Ave Rm 925 .... Seattle WA 98101 206-553-1534 553-5085
TF: 800-827-5335 ■ *Web:* www.dol.gov
Region 2 201 Varick St Rm 602 .... New York NY 10014 212-337-2389 337-2394
TF: 800-827-5335 ■ *Web:* www.dol.gov/wb
Region 3
170 S Independence Mall W Suite 631E .... Philadelphia PA 19106 215-861-4860 861-4867
TF: 800-827-5335 ■ *Web:* www.dol.gov/wb
Region 4
Federal Ctr 61 Forsyth St SW Suite 7T95 .... Atlanta GA 30303 404-562-2336 562-2413
TF: 800-827-5335 ■ *Web:* www.dol.gov
Region 5
Federal Bldg 230 S Dearborn St Rm 1022 .... Chicago IL 60604 312-353-6985 353-6986
TF: 800-827-5335 ■ *Web:* www.dol.gov
Region 6 Federal Bldg 525 Griffin St Suite 735 .... Dallas TX 75202 972-850-4700 850-4704
TF: 800-827-5335 ■ *Web:* www.dol.gov/wb
Region 7 2300 Main St Suite 1050 .... Kansas City MO 64108 816-285-7233 285-7237
TF: 800-827-5335 ■ *Web:* www.dol.gov

	City	State	ZIP	Phone	Fax
Region 8 1999 Broadway Suite 1620 PO Box 46550	Denver	CO	80201	303-844-1286	844-1283
TF: 800-827-5335 ■ *Web:* www.dol.gov/wb					
Region 9 90 7th St Suite 2650	San Francisco	CA	94103	415-625-2638	625-2641
TF: 800-827-5335 ■ *Web:* www.dol.gov					

343-16 US Department of State

	City	State	ZIP	Phone	Fax
Dept of State 2201 C St NW	Washington	DC	20520	202-647-4000	647-3344
Web: www.state.gov					
Bureau of Consular Affairs					
2201 C St NW SA-29	Washington	DC	20520	202-501-4444	647-9622
TF: 888-407-4747 ■ *Web:* travel.state.gov					
Office of Children's Issues					
2201 C St NW 4th Fl MS SA-29	Washington	DC	20520	202-736-9130	736-9133
TF: 888-407-4747 ■ *Web:* www.travel.state.gov/family					
Overseas Citizens Services					
2201 C St NW 4th Fl SA-29	Washington	DC	20520	202-647-5225	
TF: 888-407-4747 ■ *Web:* travel.state.gov					
Passport Services					
1111 19th St NW 1st Fl Sidewalk Level	Washington	DC	20036	877-487-2778	
TF: 877-487-2778 ■ *Web:* travel.state.gov/passport					
Visa Services 2401 E St NW SA-1	Washington	DC	20522	202-663-1225	663-3899
Web: www.travel.state.gov/visa					
Bureau of Diplomatic Security					
DS Public Affairs 2201 C St NW	Washington	DC	20522	571-345-2502	
Web: www.state.gov					
Foreign Service Institute					
4000 Arlington Blvd Rt 50	Arlington	VA	22204	703-302-6703	302-7461
Web: www.state.gov/m/fsi					
International Boundary & Water Commission - US & Mexico					
4171 N Mesa Suite C-100	El Paso	TX	79902	915-832-4790	832-4190
TF: 800-262-8857 ■ *Web:* www.ibwc.state.gov					
International Boundary Commission - US & Canada					
2000 L St NW Suite 615	Washington	DC	20036	202-736-9102	632-2008
Web: www.internationalboundarycommission.org					
Passport Services Regional Offices					
Boston Agency					
10 Cswy St Rm 247 Tip O'Neill Federal Bldg	Boston	MA	02222	877-487-2778	
TF: 877-487-2778 ■ *Web:* www.travel.state.gov					
Chicago Agency					
Kluczynski Federal Bldg					
230 S Dearborn St Suite 1803	Chicago	IL	60604	877-487-2778	
TF: 877-487-2778 ■ *Web:* www.travel.state.gov					
Colorado Agency 3151 S Vaughn Way Suite 600	Aurora	CO	80014	877-487-2778	
TF: 877-487-2778					
Connecticut Agency 50 Washington St	Norwalk	CT	06854	877-487-2778	299-3434*
**Fax Area Code:* 203 ■ *TF:* 877-487-2778 ■ *Web:* www.travel.state.gov					
Honolulu Agency					
300 Ala Moana Bld Suite 1-330	Honolulu	HI	96850	877-487-2778	
TF: 877-487-2778 ■ *Web:* www.travel.state.gov					
Houston Agency					
Federal Bldg 1919 Smith St Suite 1100	Houston	TX	77002	713-209-3483	209-3470
Web: www.state.gov/m/ds/rls/rpt/18892.htm					
Los Angeles Agency					
11000 Wilshire Blvd Suite 1000	Los Angeles	CA	90024	877-487-2778	
TF: 877-487-2778 ■ *Web:* www.travel.state.gov					
Miami Agency					
Claude Pepper Federal Bldg					
51 SW 1st Ave 3rd Fl	Miami	FL	33130	877-487-2778	
TF: 877-487-2778 ■ *Web:* www.travel.state.gov					
New Orleans Agency					
365 Canal St Suite 1300	New Orleans	LA	70130	877-487-2778	
TF: 877-487-2778 ■					
Web: travel.state.gov/passport/npic/agencies/agencies_911.html					
New York Agency 376 Hudson St 10th Fl	New York	NY	10014	877-487-2778	
TF: 877-487-2778 ■ *Web:* www.travel.state.gov					
Philadelphia Agency					
US Custom House 200 Chesnut St Rm 103	Philadelphia	PA	19106	877-487-2778	
TF: 877-487-2778 ■ *Web:* www.travel.state.gov					
San Francisco Agency					
95 Hawthorne St 5th Fl	San Francisco	CA	94105	877-487-2778	538-2715*
**Fax Area Code:* 415 ■ *TF:* 877-487-2778 ■ *Web:* www.travel.state.gov					
Seattle Agency 915 2nd Ave Suite 3410	Seattle	WA	98174	206-220-7721	220-7723
Web: www.state.gov/m/ds/rls/rpt/18892.htm					
Washington (DC) Agency					
1111 19th St NW Rm 300	Washington	DC	20036	877-487-2778	
TF: 877-487-2778 ■ *Web:* www.travel.state.gov					
Secretary of State 2201 C St NW 7th Fl	Washington	DC	20520	202-647-9572	647-2283
Web: www.state.gov/secretary					
Bureau of Intelligence & Research					
2201 C St NW Rm 6531	Washington	DC	20520	202-647-9177	736-4688
Web: www.state.gov/s/inr					
Office of the Chief of Protocol					
2201 C St NW Rm 1238	Washington	DC	20520	202-647-2648	647-3980
Web: www.state.gov/s/cpr					
Office of the Coordinator for Counterterrorism					
2201 C St NW Rm 2509	Washington	DC	20520	202-647-9892	647-9256
Web: www.state.gov/s/ct					
Under Secretary for Arms Control & International Security					
Bureau of International Security & Nonproliferatio					
2201 C St NW Rm 7531	Washington	DC	20520	202-647-9610	647-4920
Web: www.state.gov					
Bureau of Political-Military Affairs					
2201 C St NW Rm 6212	Washington	DC	20520	202-647-9022	
Web: www.state.gov/t/pm					
Bureau of Verification Compliance & Implementation					
2201 C St NW Rm 5950	Washington	DC	20520	202-647-5315	647-1321
Web: www.state.gov					
Under Secretary for Democracy & Global Affairs					
Bureau of Democracy Human Rights & Labor					
2201 C St NW Rm 7802	Washington	DC	20520	202-647-2590	647-3209
Web: www.state.gov					
Bureau of Oceans & International Environmental & S					
2201 C St NW Rm 7831	Washington	DC	20520	202-647-1554	647-0217
Web: www.state.gov					
Bureau of Population Refugees & Migration					
2201C St NW	Washington	DC	20520	202-647-7360	647-8162
Web: www.state.gov					
Under Secretary for Economic Energy & Agricultural Affairs					
Bureau of Economic Energy & Business Affairs					
2201 C St NW	Washington	DC	20520	202-647-7971	647-5713
Web: www.state.gov					
Under Secretary for Political Affairs					
Bureau of African Affairs					
2201 C St NW Rm 6234A	Washington	DC	20520	202-647-2530	647-6301
Web: www.state.gov/p/af					
Bureau of East Asian & Pacific Affairs					
2201 C St NW Rm 6205	Washington	DC	20520	202-647-9596	647-7350
Web: www.state.gov/p/eap					
Bureau of European & Eurasian Affairs					
2201 C St NW Rm 4515	Washington	DC	20520	202-647-9761	647-5116
Web: www.state.gov/p/eur					
Bureau of International Narcotics & Law Enforcement Affairs					
2201 C St NW Rm 7333	Washington	DC	20520	202-647-8464	736-4885
Web: www.state.gov/p/inl					
Bureau of International Organization Affairs					
2201 C St NW	Washington	DC	20520	202-647-9600	736-4116
Web: www.state.gov/p/io					
Bureau of Near Eastern Affairs					
2201 C St NW Rm 6242	Washington	DC	20520	202-647-7209	736-4462
Web: www.state.gov/p/nea					
Bureau of South & Central Asian Affairs					
2201 C St NW Rm 6254	Washington	DC	20520	202-736-4325	736-4333
Web: www.state.gov/p/sca					
Bureau of Western Hemisphere Affairs					
2201 C St NW Rm 6262	Washington	DC	20520	202-647-5780	647-0834
Under Secretary for Public Diplomacy & Public Affairs					
Bureau of Educational & Cultural Affairs					
301 4th St SW Suite 800	Washington	DC	20547	202-203-5118	203-5115
Web: www.exchanges.state.gov					
Bureau of International Information Programs					
301 4th St SW	Washington	DC	20547	202-736-4405	
Web: www.state.gov					
Bureau of Public Affairs					
2201 C St NW Rm 2206	Washington	DC	20520	202-647-8411	647-3344
Web: www.state.gov					

343-17 US Department of Transportation

	City	State	ZIP	Phone	Fax
Dept of Transportation (DOT)					
1200 New Jersey Ave SE	Washington	DC	20590	202-366-4000	
Web: www.dot.gov					
Federal Aviation Administration (FAA)					
800 Independence Ave SW	Washington	DC	20591	866-835-5322	
TF: 866-835-5322 ■ *Web:* www.faa.gov					
Accident Investigation Office					
800 Independence Ave SW Rm 840	Washington	DC	20591	202-267-9612	267-5265
Web: www.faa.gov/about/office_org/headquarters_offices/avs					
Air Traffic Organization					
800 Independence Ave SW Rm 1002	Washington	DC	20591	202-267-3666	267-5456
Web: www.faa.gov/about/office_org/headquarters_offices/ato					
Aircraft Certification Service					
800 Independence Ave SW Suite 800 E	Washington	DC	20591	202-267-8235	267-5364
Web: www.faa.gov/about/office_org/headquarters_offices/avs/offices/air					
Commercial Space Transportation Office					
800 Independence Ave SW Rm 331	Washington	DC	20591	202-267-7793	267-5450
Web: ast.faa.gov					
FAA Academy					
Mike Monroney Aeronautical Ctr					
6500 S MacArthur Blvd	Oklahoma City	OK	73169	405-954-6900	954-3018
Web: www.academy.faa.gov					
Flight Standards Service					
800 Independence Ave SW Rm 821	Washington	DC	20591	202-267-8237	267-5230
Web: www.faa.gov/about/office_org/headquarters_offices/avs					
Great Lakes Region 2300 E Devon Ave	Des Plaines	IL	60018	847-294-7272	294-7036
Web: www.faa.gov					

Phone | Fax

International Aviation Office
800 Independence Ave SW .... Washington DC 20591 202-385-8900 267-7198
Web: www.intl.faa.gov
Mike Monroney Aeronautical Ctr
6500 S MacArthur Blvd .... Oklahoma City OK 73125 405-954-3011
Web: www.faa.gov/about/office_org
Safety Hotline 800 Independence Ave SW .... Washington DC 20591 800-255-1111
TF: 866-835-5322 ■ *Web:* www.faa.gov
William J Hughes Technical Ctr
Atlantic City International Airport .... Atlantic City NJ 08405 609-485-4000
Web: www.faa.gov/about/office_org/tc

Federal Aviation Administration Northwest Mountain Region
1601 Lind Ave SW .... Renton WA 98057 425-227-2001 227-1006
TF: 800-220-5715 ■ *Web:* www.faa.gov

Federal Aviation Administration Regional Offices (FAA)
Alaskan Region 222 W 7th Ave .... Anchorage AK 99513 907-271-5296
Web: www.alaska.faa.gov
Central Region Federal Bldg 901 Locust St .... Kansas City MO 64106 816-329-3050 329-3055
Web: www.faa.gov/cen
Eastern Region
1 Aviation Plaza 159-30 Rockaway Blvd .... Jamaica NY 11434 718-553-3001
Web: www.aea.faa.gov
New England Region
12 New England Executive Pk .... Burlington MA 01803 781-238-7020 238-7608
Web: www.faa.gov/airports/new_england
Western Pacific Region 15000 Aviation Blvd .... Lawndale CA 90261 310-725-7800 725-6811
Web: www.faa.gov/airports/western_pacific

Federal Aviation Administration Southern Region
1701 Columbia Ave .... College Park GA 30337 404-305-5000 305-5010
Web: www.faa.gov

Federal Highway Administration (FHWA)
400 7th St SW .... Washington DC 20590 202-366-0660
Web: www.fhwa.dot.gov
National Highway Institute
4600 Fairfax Dr # 800 .... Arlington VA 22203 703-235-0500 235-0593
TF: 877-558-6873 ■ *Web:* www.nhi.fhwa.dot.gov

Federal Motor Carrier Safety Administration (FMCSA)
1200 New Jersey Ave SE .... Washington DC 20590 800-832-5660
TF: 800-832-5660 ■ *Web:* www.fmcsa.dot.gov

Federal Railroad Administration
1200 New Jersey Ave Se .... Washington DC 20590 202-493-6000
Web: www.fra.dot.gov

Federal Railroad Administration Regional Offices
Region 1 55 Broadway Suite 1077 .... Cambridge MA 02142 617-494-2302 494-2967
Region 2
Baldwin Tower Suite 660 1510 Chester Pike .... Crum Lynne PA 19022 610-521-8200 521-8225
Region 3 61 Forsyth St SW Suite 16T20 .... Atlanta GA 30303 404-562-3800 562-3830
TF: 800-724-5993
Region 4 200 W Adams St .... Chicago IL 60606 312-353-6203 886-9634
TF: 800-724-5040 ■ *Web:* www.fra.dot.gov
Region 5
4100 International Plaza Suite 450 .... Fort Worth TX 76109 817-862-2200 862-2204
Region 6 901 Locust St Suite 464 .... Kansas City MO 64106 816-329-3840 329-3867
TF: 800-724-5996
Region 7 801 'I' St Suite 466 .... Sacramento CA 95814 916-498-6540 498-6546
Web: www.fra.dot.gov
Region 8 703 Broadway St # 650 .... Vancouver WA 98660 360-696-7536 696-7548
TF: 800-724-5998 ■ *Web:* www.fra.dot.gov

Federal Transit Administration
1200 New Jersey Ave SE .... Washington DC 20590 202-366-4043 366-9854
Web: www.fta.dot.gov

Federal Transit Administration Regional Offices
Region 1 55 Broadway Suite 920 .... Cambridge MA 02142 617-494-2055 494-2865
Web: www.fta.dot.gov
Region 10 Federal Bldg 915 2nd Ave Suite 3142 .... Seattle WA 98174 206-220-7954 220-7959
Web: www.fta.dot.gov
Region 2 1 Bowling Green Suite 429 .... New York NY 10004 212-668-2170 668-2136
Web: www.fta.dot.gov
Region 3 1760 Market St Suite 500 .... Philadelphia PA 19103 215-656-7100 656-7260
Web: www.fta.dot.gov
Region 4 230 Peachtree St NW Suite 800 .... Atlanta GA 30303 404-865-5600 865-5605
Web: www.fta.dot.gov
Region 5 200 W Adams St Suite 320 .... Chicago IL 60606 312-353-2789 886-0351
Web: www.fta.dot.gov
Region 6 819 Taylor St Rm 8A36 .... Fort Worth TX 76102 817-978-0550 978-0575
Web: www.fta.dot.gov
Region 7 901 Locust St Suite 404 .... Kansas City MO 64106 816-329-3920 329-3921
Web: www.fta.dot.gov
Region 8 12300 W Dakota Ave Suite 310 .... Lakewood CO 80228 720-963-3300 963-3333
Web: www.fta.dot.gov
Region 9 201 Mission St Suite 1650 .... San Francisco CA 94105 415-744-3133 744-2726
Web: www.fta.dot.gov

Maritime Administration (MARAD)
1200 New Jersey Ave SE .... Washington DC 20590 202-366-5807 366-3791
TF Hotline: 800-996-2723 ■ *Web:* www.marad.dot.gov
Div of Gulf Operations
500 Poydras St Suite 1223 .... New Orleans LA 70130 504-589-2000 589-6559
Web: www.marad.dot.gov
National Maritime Resource & Education Ctr
1200 New Jersey Ave SE .... Washington DC 20590 202-366-1931 366-6988
Web: www.marad.dot.gov/NMREC
US Merchant Marine Academy
300 Steamboat Rd .... Kings Point NY 11024 516-773-5387 773-5509
Web: www.usmma.edu

Phone | Fax

Maritime Administration Regional Offices
Great Lakes Region
1701 E Woodfield Rd Suite 203 .... Schaumburg IL 60173 847-995-0122 995-0133
Web: www.marad.dot.gov
North Atlantic Region 1 Bowling Green Rm 418 .... New York NY 10004 212-668-3330 668-3382
Web: www.marad.dot.gov/Offices/MRG-2100.html
South Atlantic Region 7737 Hampton Blvd .... Norfolk VA 23505 757-441-6393 440-0812
Web: www.marad.dot.gov
Western Region
201 Mission St Suite 2200 .... San Francisco CA 94105 415-744-3125 744-2576
Web: www.marad.dot.gov/Offices/MRG-4100.html

National Highway Traffic Safety Administration (NHTSA)
1200 New Jersey Ave SE .... Washington DC 20590 202-366-9550 366-6916
TF: 888-327-4236 ■ *Web:* www.nhtsa.dot.gov
Defects Investigation Office
1200 New Jersey Ave SE .... Washington DC 20590 202-366-9550 366-1767
TF: 888-327-4236 ■ *Web:* www-odi.nhtsa.dot.gov
National Center for Statistics & Analysis
1200 New Jersey Ave SE .... Washington DC 20590 202-366-1503 366-7078
TF: 800-934-8517 ■ *Web:* www.nhtsa.gov
Vehicle Research & Test Ctr
10820 SR 347 PO Box B37 .... East Liberty OH 43319 937-666-4511 666-3590
TF: 800-262-8309 ■ *Web:* www.nhtsa.gov

National Highway Traffic Safety Administration Regional Offices
NHTSA Region 1 Volpe Ctr Kendall Sq MS 903 .... Cambridge MA 02142 617-494-3427 494-3646
Web: www.nhtsa.dot.gov
NHTSA Region 10 915 2nd Ave Suite 3140 .... Seattle WA 98174 206-220-7640 220-7651
Web: www.nhtsa.dot.gov/nhtsa/whatis/regions/Region10
NHTSA Region 2
222 Mamaroneck Ave Suite 204 .... White Plains NY 10605 914-682-6162 682-6239
Web: www.nhtsa.dot.gov
NHTSA Region 3 10 S Howard St Suite 6700 .... Baltimore MD 21201 410-962-0900 962-2770
Web: www.nhtsa.dot.gov
NHTSA Region 4
Federal Ctr 61 Forsyth St SW Suite 17T30 .... Atlanta GA 30303 404-562-3739 562-3763
Web: www.nhtsa.dot.gov/nhtsa/whatis/regions/Region06
NHTSA Region 5
19900 Governors Dr Suite 201 .... Olympia Fields IL 60461 708-503-8822 503-8991
TF: 888-327-4235 ■ *Web:* www.nhtsa.dot.gov
NHTSA Region 6
Federal Bldg 819 Taylor St Rm 8A38 .... Fort Worth TX 76102 817-978-3653 978-8339
Web: www.nhtsa.dot.gov/nhtsa/whatis/regions/Region06
NHTSA Region 7 901 Locust St Rm 466 .... Kansas City MO 64106 816-329-3900 329-3910
Web: www.nhtsa.dot.gov
NHTSA Region 8 12300 W Dakota Ave Suite 140 .... Lakewood CO 80228 720-963-3100 963-3124
Web: www.nhtsa.dot.gov
NHTSA Region 9
201 Mission St Suite 2230 .... San Francisco CA 94105 415-744-3089 744-2532
Web: www.nhtsa.dot.gov

Pipeline & Hazardous Materials Safety Administration (PHMSA)
1200 New Jersey Ave SE E Bldg 2nd Fl .... Washington DC 20590 202-366-4433 366-3666
Web: www.phmsa.dot.gov
Office of Hazardous Materials Safety
1200 New Jersey Ave SE .... Washington DC 20590 202-366-0656 366-5713
TF: 800-467-4922 ■ *Web:* www.hazmat.dot.gov
Office of Pipeline Safety
1200 New Jersey Ave SE E Bldg 2nd Fl .... Washington DC 20590 202-366-4595 366-4566
Web: ops.dot.gov

Pipeline & Hazardous Materials Safety Administration Regional Offices
Central Region (Pipeline)
901 Locust St Rm 462 .... Kansas City MO 64106 816-329-3800 329-3831
Web: www.phmsa.dot.gov/about/region.html
Eastern Region (Pipeline)
409 3rd St SW Suite 300 .... Washington DC 20024 202-260-8500 260-8530
Web: www.phmsa.dot.gov/about/region.html
Southern Region 233 Peachtree St NE Suite 602 .... Atlanta GA 30303 404-832-1140 832-1168
Web: www.phmsa.dot.gov/about/region.html
Southwest Region 8701 Gessner Rd Suite 1110 .... Houston TX 77074 713-272-2820 272-2821
Web: www.phmsa.dot.gov/about/region.html
Western Region (Pipeline)
12300 W Dakota Ave Suite 110 .... Lakewood CO 80228 720-963-3160 963-3161
Web: www.phmsa.dot.gov/about/region.html

Research & Innovative Technology Administration (RITA)
1200 New Jersey Ave SE .... Washington DC 20590 202-366-7582 366-3759
TF: 800-853-1351 ■ *Web:* www.rita.dot.gov
Bureau of Transportation Statistics
1200 New Jersey Ave SE .... Washington DC 20590 202-366-1270 366-3640
TF: 800-853-1351 ■ *Web:* www.bts.gov
Office of Research Development & Technology
1200 New Jersey Ave SE .... Washington DC 20590 202-366-3492
TF: 800-853-1351 ■ *Web:* www.rita.dot.gov/agencies_and_offices/research
Transportation Safety Institute
6500 S MacArthur Blvd PO Box 25082 .... Oklahoma City OK 73125 405-954-3153 954-3521
TF: 800-954-3521 ■ *Web:* www.tsi.dot.gov
Volpe National Transportation Systems Ctr
55 Broadway .... Cambridge MA 02142 617-494-2000
Web: www.volpe.dot.gov

Saint Lawrence Seaway Development Corp
1200 New Jersey Ave SE Suite W-32-300 .... Washington DC 20590 202-366-0091 366-7147
TF: 800-785-2779 ■ *Web:* www.seaway.dot.gov

Secretary of Transportation
1200 New Jersey Ave SE Suite W-96-300 .... Washington DC 20590 202-366-1111 366-7202
Web: www.dot.gov/ost

	City	State	Zip	Phone	Fax
Surface Transportation Board 395 E St SW	Washington	DC	20423	202-245-0245	245-0461
Web: www.stb.dot.gov					

343-18 US Department of the Treasury

	City	State	Zip	Phone	Fax
Dept of the Treasury					
1500 Pennsylvania Ave NW	Washington	DC	20220	202-622-2000	622-6415
Web: www.ustreas.gov					
Treasurer of the US					
1500 Pennsylvania Ave NW	Washington	DC	20220	202-622-0100	622-6464
Web: www.treas.gov/offices/treasurer					
Alcohol & Tobacco Tax & Trade Bureau					
1310 G St NW Suite 300	Washington	DC	20220	202-453-2000	927-5611
TF: 877-882-3277 ■ Web: www.ttb.gov					
National Revenue Ctr					
550 Main St Suite 8002	Cincinnati	OH	45202	513-684-3334	684-2159
TF: 877-882-3277 ■ Web: www.ttb.gov/nrc					
Bureau of Engraving & Printing					
14th & C Sts SW	Washington	DC	20228	202-874-8888	874-3177
TF: 877-874-4114 ■ Web: www.moneyfactory.gov					
Bureau of the Public Debt 799 9th St NW	Washington	DC	20239	202-504-3500	504-3630
Web: www.publicdebt.treas.gov					
TreasuryDirect PO Box 7015	Parkersburg	WV	26106	304-480-7711	
TF: 800-722-2678 ■ Web: www.savingsbonds.gov					
Comptroller of the Currency 250 E St SW	Washington	DC	20219	202-874-5000	874-4950
TF Cust Svc: 800-613-6743 ■ Web: www.occ.treas.gov					
Financial Crimes Enforcement Network					
2070 Chain Bridge Rd PO Box 39	Vienna	VA	22182	703-905-3591	905-3690
Web: www.fincen.gov					
Financial Management Service					
401 14th St SW	Washington	DC	20227	202-874-6950	
Web: www.fms.treas.gov					
Internal Revenue Service (IRS)					
1111 Constitution Ave NW	Washington	DC	20224	202-622-9511	622-5156
TF: 800-829-1040 ■ Web: www.irs.gov					
Appeals Office 1099 14th St NW	Washington	DC	20005	202-435-5600	994-1804
Web: www.irs.gov					
Large & Mid-Size Business Div					
1111 Constitution Ave NW	Washington	DC	20224	202-283-8710	283-8508
Web: www.irs.gov/businesses					
Small Business/Self-Employed Div					
1111 Constitution Ave NW	Washington	DC	20442	202-622-0600	622-5046
Web: www.irs.gov/businesses					
Tax Exempt & Government Entities Div					
1111 Constitution Ave NW	Washington	DC	20224	202-283-2500	283-9973
Web: www.irs.gov/charities					
Taxpayer Advocate Service					
1111 Constitution Ave NW Rm 3031	Washington	DC	20224	202-622-6100	622-7854
TF: 877-777-4778 ■ Web: www.irs.gov/advocate					
Wage & Investment Div 401 W Peachtree St NW	Atlanta	GA	30308	404-338-7060	338-7054
Office of Thrift Supervision 1700 G St NW	Washington	DC	20552	202-906-6000	898-0230
Web: www.ots.treas.gov					
Secretary of the Treasury					
1500 Pennsylvania Ave NW Rm 3330	Washington	DC	20220	202-622-1100	622-0073
Web: www.treas.gov/organization/officials.html					
US Mint 801 9th St NW	Washington	DC	20220	202-354-7200	
TF Cust Svc: 800-872-6468 ■ Web: www.usmint.gov					
Denver 320 W Colfax Ave	Denver	CO	80204	303-405-4600	405-4604
Philadelphia 151 N Independence Mall E	Philadelphia	PA	19106	215-408-0367	408-2700
San Francisco 155 Hermann St	San Francisco	CA	94102	415-575-8000	575-7765
TF: 800-872-6468 ■ Web: www.usmint.gov					
West Point (NY) PO Box 37	West Point	NY	10996	845-446-6200	446-6258

343-19 US Department of Veterans Affairs

	City	State	Zip	Phone	Fax
Dept of Veterans Affairs (VA)					
810 Vermont Ave NW	Washington	DC	20420	202-461-7600	
TF Cust Svc: 800-827-1000 ■ Web: www.va.gov					
Public & Intergovernmental Affairs Office					
810 Vermont Ave NW	Washington	DC	20420	202-273-5750	273-7635
Web: www1.va.gov/opa					
National Center for Post-Traumatic Stress Disorder					
215 N Main St	White River Junction	VT	05009	802-296-5132	296-5135
Web: www.ptsd.va.gov					
National Cemetery Administration					
810 Vermont Ave NW	Washington	DC	20420	202-273-5146	273-6709
Web: www.cem.va.gov					
Secretary of Veterans Affairs					
810 Vermont Ave NW	Washington	DC	20420	202-273-4809	273-4877
Web: www1.va.gov/opa/bios					
Board of Veterans' Appeals					
811 Vermont Ave NW	Washington	DC	20420	202-565-5001	565-5587
Web: www.va.gov/opa/bios/secretary.asp					
Center for Minority Veterans					
810 Vermont Ave NW Rm 436	Washington	DC	20420	202-273-6708	273-7092
Web: www1.va.gov/centerforminorityveterans					
Center for Veterans Enterprise					
1722 I St NW Rm UM2	Washington	DC	20006	202-303-3260	254-0238
TF: 866-584-2344 ■ Web: www.vetbiz.gov					
Center for Women Veterans					
810 Vermont Ave NW Rm 438	Washington	DC	20420	202-273-6193	273-7092
Web: www1.va.gov/womenvet					
Veterans Benefits Administration					
810 Vermont Ave NW	Washington	DC	20420	202-273-6763	275-3591
TF: 800-827-1000 ■ Web: www.vba.va.gov					
Veterans Canteen Service					
1 Jefferson Barracks Rd Bldg 25	Saint Louis	MO	63125	314-652-4100	845-1201
Web: www.va.gov					
Veterans Health Administration					
810 Vermont Ave NW	Washington	DC	20420	202-273-5400	
Web: www2.va.gov					
Gulf War Veterans Information					
50 Irving St NW	Washington	DC	20422	202-745-8000	
Office of Research & Development					
810 Vermont Ave NW MC 12	Washington	DC	20420	202-254-0185	254-0460
Web: www.research.va.gov					

343-20 US Independent Agencies Government Corporations & Quasi-Official Agencies

Included Also Among These Listings Are Selected Federal Boards, Committees, And Commissions.

	City	State	Zip	Phone	Fax
Federal Election Commission 999 E St NW	Washington	DC	20463	202-694-1100	
TF: 800-424-9530 ■ Web: www.fec.gov					
US Office of Government Ethics					
1201 New York Ave NW Suite 500	Washington	DC	20005	202-482-9300	482-9237
Web: www.usoge.gov					
Advisory Council on Historic Preservation					
1100 Pennsylvania Ave NW Rm 803	Washington	DC	20004	202-606-8503	606-8647
Web: www.achp.gov					
African Development Foundation					
1400 'I' St NW 10th Fl	Washington	DC	20005	202-673-3916	673-3810
Web: www.adf.gov					
American Battle Monuments Commission					
Courthouse Plaza II Suite 500					
2300 Clarendon Blvd	Arlington	VA	22201	703-696-6900	696-6666
Web: www.abmc.gov					
Architectural & Transportation Barriers Compliance Board					
1331 F St NW Suite 1000	Washington	DC	20004	202-272-0080	272-0081
TF: 800-872-2253 ■ Web: www.access-board.gov					
Broadcasting Board of Governors					
330 Independence Ave SW	Washington	DC	20237	202-203-4545	203-4585
Web: www.bbg.gov					
International Broadcasting Bureau					
330 Independence Ave SW	Washington	DC	20237	202-203-4515	
Web: www.ibb.gov					
Office of Cuba Broadcasting					
4201 NW 77th Ave PO Box 521868	Miami	FL	33152	305-437-7000	437-7004
Web: www.martinoticias.com					
Voice of America 330 Independence Ave SW	Washington	DC	20237	202-203-4959	203-4960
Web: www.voanews.com					
Central Intelligence Agency (CIA)					
Office of Public Affairs	Washington	DC	20505	703-482-0623	482-1739
Web: www.cia.gov					
Commission of Fine Arts					
401 F St NW Suite 312	Washington	DC	20001	202-504-2200	504-2195
Web: www.cfa.gov					
Commission on Presidential Scholars					
Dept of Education					
400 Maryland Ave SW Rm 5E115	Washington	DC	20202	202-401-0961	260-7464
Web: www.ed.gov/programs/psp/commission.html					
Commission on Security & Cooperation in Europe					
234 Ford House Office Bldg 3rd & D Sts SW	Washington	DC	20515	202-225-1901	226-4199
Web: www.csce.gov					
Committee for Purchase from People Who Are Blind or Severely Disabled					
1421 Jefferson Davis Hwy					
Jefferson Plaza 2 Suite 10800	Arlington	VA	22202	703-603-7740	603-0655
Web: www.abilityone.gov					
Committee on Foreign Investments in the US					
Dept of the Treasury Office of Intl Investment					
1500 Pennsylvania Ave NW Rm 5221	Washington	DC	20220	202-622-9066	
Web: www.treas.gov					
Commodity Futures Trading Commission					
3 Lafayette Ctr 1155 21 St NW	Washington	DC	20581	202-418-5000	418-5521
TF: 866-366-2382 ■ Web: www.cftc.gov					
Commodity Futures Trading Commission Regional Offices					
Central Region 525 W Monroe St	Chicago	IL	60661	312-596-0700	596-0713
Web: www.cftc.gov					
Eastern Region 140 Broadway 19th Fl	New York	NY	10005	646-746-9700	746-9938
Web: www.cftc.gov					
Southwestern Region					
2 Emanuel Cleaver II Blvd Suite 300	Kansas City	MO	64112	816-960-7700	960-7750
Web: www.cftc.gov					
Consumer Product Safety Commission (CPSC)					
4340 E W Hwy # 502	Bethesda	MD	20814	301-504-7923	504-0051
TF: 800-638-0127 ■ Web: www.cpsc.gov					
Coordinating Council on Juvenile Justice & Delinquency Prevention					
810 7th St NW	Washington	DC	20531	202-307-5911	307-2093
Web: www.juvenilecouncil.gov					
Corp for National & Community Service					
AmeriCorps USA 1201 New York Ave NW	Washington	DC	20525	202-606-5000	
TF: 800-833-3722 ■ Web: www.americorps.gov					
Learn & Serve America					
1201 New York Ave NW	Washington	DC	20525	202-606-5000	
TF: 800-942-2677 ■ Web: www.learnandserve.org					

	City	State	Zip	Phone	Fax
Senior Corps 1201 New York Ave NW	Washington	DC	20525	202-606-5000	
TF: 800-833-3722 ■ *Web:* www.seniorcorps.gov					
Court Services & Offender Supervision Agency for the District of Columbia					
633 Indiana Ave NW	Washington	DC	20004	202-220-5300	220-5350
Web: www.csosa.gov					
Defense Nuclear Facilities Safety Board					
625 Indiana Ave NW Suite 700	Washington	DC	20004	202-694-7000	
TF: 800-788-4016 ■ *Web:* www.dnfsb.gov					
Denali Commission 510 L St Suite 410	Anchorage	AK	99501	907-271-1414	271-1415
TF: 888-480-4321 ■ *Web:* www.denali.gov					
Environmental Protection Agency (EPA)					
1200 Pennsylvania Ave NW	Washington	DC	20460	202-564-4700	501-1450
TF: 888-372-8255 ■ *Web:* www.epa.gov					
US National Response Team					
1200 Pennsylvania Ave NW	Washington	DC	20593	202-267-2675	267-1322
TF: 800-424-9346 ■ *Web:* www.nrt.org					
Environmental Protection Agency Regional Offices					
Region 1 1 Congress St Suite 1100	Boston	MA	02114	617-918-1111	918-0101
TF: 888-372-7341 ■ *Web:* www.epa.gov					
Region 10 1200 6th Ave Suite 900	Seattle	WA	98101	206-553-1200	553-0059
TF: 800-424-4372 ■ *Web:* www.epa.gov					
Region 2 290 Broadway	New York	NY	10007	212-637-3000	
Web: www.epa.gov					
Region 3 1650 Arch St	Philadelphia	PA	19103	215-814-5000	
TF: 800-438-2474 ■ *Web:* www.epa.gov					
Region 4 Federal Ctr 61 Forsyth St SW	Atlanta	GA	30303	404-562-9900	562-8174
TF: 800-241-1754 ■ *Web:* www.epa.gov					
Region 5 77 W Jackson Blvd	Chicago	IL	60604	312-353-2000	
Web: www.epa.gov					
Region 6 1445 Ross Ave Suite 1200	Dallas	TX	75202	214-665-2200	665-2182
TF: 800-887-6063 ■ *Web:* www.epa.gov					
Region 7 901 N 5th St	Kansas City	KS	66101	913-551-7003	
Web: www.epa.gov					
Region 8 1595 Wynkoop St	Denver	CO	80202	303-312-6312	
TF: 800-227-8917 ■ *Web:* www.epa.gov					
Region 9 75 Hawthorne St	San Francisco	CA	94105	415-947-8000	947-3598
TF: 866-372-9378 ■ *Web:* www.epa.gov					
Equal Employment Opportunity Commission (EEOC)					
1801 L St NW	Washington	DC	20507	202-663-4191	
TF: 800-669-4000 ■ *Web:* www.eeoc.gov					
Equal Employment Opportunity Commission Regional Offices					
Atlanta District 100 Alabama St SW Suite 4R30	Atlanta	GA	30303	404-562-6800	562-6909
TF: 800-669-4000 ■ *Web:* www.eeoc.gov					
Birmingham District					
1130 22nd St S Suite 2000	Birmingham	AL	35205	205-212-2100	212-2105
TF: 800-669-4000 ■ *Web:* www.eeoc.gov					
Charlotte District 129 W Trade St Suite 400	Charlotte	NC	28202	704-344-6682	344-6734
TF: 800-669-4000 ■ *Web:* www.eeoc.gov					
Chicago District 500 W Madison St Suite 2800	Chicago	IL	60661	312-353-2713	353-4041
Web: www.eeoc.gov					
Dallas District 207 S Houston St 3rd Fl	Dallas	TX	75202	214-253-2700	253-2720
TF: 800-669-4000 ■ *Web:* www.eeoc.gov					
Houston District					
Federal Bldg 1919 Smith St 6th Fl	Houston	TX	77002	713-209-3377	209-3381
TF: 800-669-4000 ■ *Web:* www.eeoc.gov/houston					
Indianapolis District					
101 W Ohio St Suite 1900	Indianapolis	IN	46204	317-226-7212	226-7953
Web: www.eeoc.gov					
Los Angeles District					
255 E Temple St 4th Fl	Los Angeles	CA	90012	213-894-1096	894-1118
TF: 800-669-4000 ■ *Web:* www.eeoc.gov					
Memphis District 1407 Union Ave Suite 621	Memphis	TN	38104	901-544-0115	544-0111
TF: 800-669-4000 ■ *Web:* www.eeoc.gov					
Miami District 2 S Biscayne Blvd Suite 2700	Miami	FL	33131	305-808-1740	808-1834
Web: www.eeoc.gov					
New York District 33 Whitehall St 5th Fl	New York	NY	10004	212-336-3620	336-3790
TF: 866-408-8075 ■ *Web:* www.eeoc.gov					
Philadelphia District					
21 S 5th St Suite 400	Philadelphia	PA	19106	215-440-2600	440-2606
TF: 866-408-8075 ■ *Web:* www.eeoc.gov					
Phoenix District 3300 N Central Ave Suite 690	Phoenix	AZ	85012	602-640-5000	640-5071
Web: www.eeoc.gov					
Saint Louis District					
1222 Spruce St Suite 8.100	Saint Louis	MO	63103	314-539-7800	539-7894
TF: 800-669-4000 ■ *Web:* www.eeoc.gov					
San Francisco District					
350 The Embarcadero Suite 500	San Francisco	CA	94105	415-625-5600	625-5609
Web: www.eeoc.gov					
Export-Import Bank of the US					
811 Vermont Ave NW	Washington	DC	20571	202-565-3946	
TF: 800-565-3946 ■ *Web:* www.exim.gov					
Farm Credit Administration					
1501 Farm Credit Dr	McLean	VA	22102	703-883-4000	734-5784
Web: www.fca.gov					

	City	State	Zip	Phone	Fax
Farm Credit Administration Regional Offices					
Bloomington (MN) Field Office					
2051 Killebrew Dr Suite 610	Bloomington	MN	55425	952-854-7151	854-4736
TF: 877-322-2566 ■ *Web:* www.fca.gov					
Dallas Field Office					
511 E Carpenter Fwy Suite 650	Irving	TX	75062	972-869-0550	869-9531
Denver Field Office					
3131 S Vaughn Way Suite 250	Aurora	CO	80014	303-696-9737	696-7114
Web: www.fca.gov					
McLean Field Office 1501 Farm Credit Dr	McLean	VA	22102	703-883-4497	883-2704
TF: 877-625-3261 ■ *Web:* www.fca.gov					
Sacramento Field Office					
2180 Harvard St Suite 300	Sacramento	CA	95815	916-648-1118	649-0512
Web: www.fca.gov					
Federal Accounting Standards Advisory Board					
441 G St NW Suite 6814	Washington	DC	20548	202-512-7350	512-7366
Web: www.fasab.gov					
Federal Communications Commission (FCC)					
445 12th St SW	Washington	DC	20554	888-225-5322	418-0232*
**Fax Area Code:* 202 ■ *TF:* 888-225-5322 ■ *Web:* www.fcc.gov					
Federal Deposit Insurance Corp					
550 17th St NW	Washington	DC	20429	202-898-7192	
TF: 877-275-3342 ■ *Web:* www.fdic.gov					
Federal Deposit Insurance Corp Regional Offices					
Atlanta Area Office 10 10th St NW # 800	Atlanta	GA	30309	678-916-2200	
TF: 800-765-3342 ■ *Web:* www.fdic.gov					
Boston Area Office					
15 Braintree Hill Office Pk Suite 300	Braintree	MA	02184	781-794-5500	794-5533
TF: 866-728-9953 ■ *Web:* www.fdic.gov					
Chicago Area Office					
300 S Riverside Plaza # 1700	Chicago	IL	60606	312-382-6000	282-7507
TF: 800-944-5343 ■ *Web:* www.fdic.gov					
Dallas Area Office 1601 Bryan St	Dallas	TX	75201	214-754-0098	
TF: 800-568-9161 ■ *Web:* www.fdic.gov					
Kansas City Area Office					
2345 Grand Blvd Suite 1200	Kansas City	MO	64108	816-234-8000	234-8004
TF: 800-209-7459 ■ *Web:* www.fdic.gov					
Memphis Area Office					
5100 Poplar Ave Suite 1900	Memphis	TN	38137	901-685-1603	821-5308
TF: 800-210-6354 ■ *Web:* www.fdic.gov					
New York Area Office 20 Exchange Pl 4th Fl	New York	NY	10005	917-320-2500	320-2903
TF: 800-334-9594					
San Francisco Area Office					
25 Jessie St at Ecker Sq Suite 2300	San Francisco	CA	94105	415-546-0160	
TF: 800-756-3558 ■ *Web:* www.fdic.gov					
Federal Financing Bank					
Dept of the Treasury					
1500 Pennsylvania Ave NW	Washington	DC	20220	202-622-2470	622-0707
Web: www.treas.gov					
Federal Housing Finance Board					
1625 'I' St NW	Washington	DC	20006	202-408-2500	408-1435
Web: www.fhfb.gov					
Federal Labor Relations Authority					
1400 K St NW	Washington	DC	20424	202-357-6029	482-6724
Web: www.flra.gov					
Federal Labor Relations Authority Regional Offices					
Atlanta Region 225 Peachtree St NE	Atlanta	GA	30303	404-331-5300	331-5280
Web: www.flra.gov					
Boston Region					
Federal Bldg 10 Cswy St Suite 472	Boston	MA	02222	617-565-5100	565-6262
Web: www.flra.gov					
Chicago Region 55 W Monroe St Suite 1150	Chicago	IL	60603	312-886-3465	886-5977
Web: www.flra.gov					
Dallas Region					
525 S Griffin St Suite 926 LB-107	Dallas	TX	75202	214-767-6266	767-0156
Web: www.flra.gov					
Denver Region 1391 Speer Blvd # 300	Denver	CO	80204	303-844-5224	844-2774
San Francisco Region					
901 Market St Suite 220	San Francisco	CA	94103	415-356-5000	356-5017
Web: www.cftc.gov					
Washington (DC) Region 1400 K St NW 2nd Fl	Washington	DC	20424	202-357-6029	482-6724
Web: www.flra.gov					
Federal Laboratory Consortium for Technology Transfer					
950 Kings Hwy N # 208	Cherry Hill	NJ	08034	856-667-7727	667-8009
Web: www.federallabs.org					
Federal Maritime Commission					
800 N Capitol St NW	Washington	DC	20573	202-523-5725	523-0014
Web: www.fmc.gov					
Federal Maritime Commission Regional Offices					
Los Angeles Area 839 S Beacon St Rm 1018	San Pedro	CA	90733	310-514-4905	514-3931
New Orleans Area 1515 Poydras St Rm 1723	New Orleans	LA	70112	504-589-6662	589-6663
Web: www.fmc.gov					
New York Area					
JFK International Airport Bldg 75 Rm 205B	Jamaica	NY	11430	718-553-2228	553-2229
Web: www.fca.gov					
South Florida Area PO Box 813609	Hollywood	FL	33081	954-963-5362	963-5630
Web: www.fmc.gov					
Federal Mediation & Conciliation Service					
2100 K St NW	Washington	DC	20427	202-606-8100	606-4251
Web: www.fmcs.gov					
Federal Mediation & Conciliation Service Regional Offices					
Eastern Region					
6161 Oak Tree Blvd Suite 120	Independence	OH	44131	216-520-4800	520-4819
Web: www.fmcs.gov/internet					
Western Region 1300 Godward St Suite 3950	Minneapolis	MN	55413	612-331-6670	331-5272
Web: www.fmcs.gov					
Federal Mine Safety & Health Review Commission					
601 New Jersey Ave NW	Washington	DC	20001	202-434-9900	434-9944
Web: www.fmshrc.gov					
Federal Reserve System					
20th St & Constitution Ave NW	Washington	DC	20551	202-452-3000	452-3819
Web: www.federalreserve.gov					
Federal Retirement Thrift Investment Board					
1250 H St NW	Washington	DC	20005	202-942-1600	942-1675
Web: www.frtib.gov					

	City	State	Zip	Phone	Fax
Federal Trade Commission (FTC)					
600 Pennsylvania Ave NW	Washington	DC	20580	202-326-2222	326-2396
TF: 877-382-4357 ■ *Web:* www.ftc.gov					
National Do Not Call Registry					
600 Pennsylvania Ave NW	Washington	DC	20580	888-382-1222	
TF: 888-382-1222 ■ *Web:* www.ftc.gov					
Federal Trade Commission Regional Offices					
East Central Region					
1111 Superior Ave Suite 200	Cleveland	OH	44114	216-263-3455	263-3426
TF: 877-382-4357 ■ *Web:* www.ftc.gov					
Midwest Region 55 W Monroe St Suite 1825	Chicago	IL	60603	312-960-5634	960-5600
Web: www.ftc.gov/ro/midwest.htm					
NortheastRegion 1 Bowling Green Suite 318	New York	NY	10004	212-607-2829	607-2822
Web: www.ftc.gov					
Northwest Region 915 2nd Ave Suite 2896	Seattle	WA	98174	206-220-6350	220-6366
Web: www.ftc.gov/ro/northwest.htm					
Southeast Region 60 Forsyth St SW	Atlanta	GA	30303	404-656-1390	656-1379
TF: 877-282-4357 ■ *Web:* www.ftc.gov					
Southwest Region 1999 Bryan St Suite 2150	Dallas	TX	75201	214-979-9350	953-3079
Web: www.ftc.gov/ro/southwest.htm					
Western Region					
18077 Wilshire Blvd Suite 700	Los Angeles	CA	90024	310-824-4343	824-4380
TF: 877-382-4357 ■ *Web:* www.ftc.gov					
General Services Administration (GSA)					
1275 F St NE	Washington	DC	20417	202-501-0800	
Web: www.gsa.gov					
FCIC National Contact Ctr PO Box 100	Pueblo	CO	81009	888-878-3256	948-9724*
**Fax Area Code:* 719 ■ *TF:* 888-878-3256 ■ *Web:* www.pueblo.gsa.gov					
Regulatory Information Service Ctr					
1800 F St NW Rm 3039	Washington	DC	20405	202-482-7340	482-7360
Web: www.gsa.gov					
General Services Administration Regional Offices					
Region 1 - New England					
10 Cswy St Rm 1010					
Thomas P O'Neill Federal Bldg	Boston	MA	02222	617-565-5860	
TF: 866-734-1727 ■ *Web:* www.gsa.gov					
Region 10 - Northwest/Arctic 400 15th St SW	Auburn	WA	98001	253-931-7000	
Web: www.gsa.gov					
Region 11 - National Capital Region					
301 7th St SW	Washington	DC	20407	202-708-9100	708-9966
Web: www.gsa.gov					
Region 2 - Northeast & Caribbean					
26 Federal Plaza	New York	NY	10278	212-264-2600	
Web: www.gsa.gov					
Region 3 - Mid-Atlantic					
Strawbridge Bldg 20 N 8th St	Philadelphia	PA	19107	215-446-5100	
TF: 800-333-4636 ■ *Web:* www.gsa.gov					
Region 4 - Southeast Sunbelt					
77 Forsyth St Suite 600	Atlanta	GA	30303	404-331-3200	331-0931
Web: www.gsa.gov					
Region 5 - Great Lakes 230 S Dearborn St	Chicago	IL	60604	312-886-8900	886-8901
Web: www.gsa.gov					
Region 6 - Heartland 1500 E Bannister Rd	Kansas City	MO	64131	816-926-7201	926-7513
Web: www.gsa.gov					
Region 7 - Greater Southwest					
819 Taylor St	Fort Worth	TX	76102	817-978-2321	978-4867
Web: www.gsa.gov					
Region 8 - Rocky Mountain					
Denver Federal Ctr Bldg 41	Denver	CO	80225	303-236-7329	
TF: 888-999-4777 ■ *Web:* www.gsa.gov					
Region 9 - Pacific Rim					
450 Golden Gate Ave	San Francisco	CA	94102	415-522-3001	522-3005
Web: www.gsa.gov					
Harry S Truman Scholarship Foundation					
712 Jackson Pl NW	Washington	DC	20006	202-395-4831	395-6995
Web: www.truman.gov					
Indian Arts & Crafts Board					
Dept of the Interior 1849 C St NW					
MS 2528-MIB	Washington	DC	20240	202-208-3773	208-5196
TF: 888-278-3253 ■ *Web:* www.iacb.doi.gov					
Inter-American Foundation (IAF)					
901 N Stuart St 10th Fl	Arlington	VA	22203	703-306-4301	306-4365
Web: www.iaf.gov					
Interagency Council on Homelessness					
409 3rd St SW Suite 310	Washington	DC	20024	202-708-4663	708-1216
Web: www.ich.gov					
Japan-US Friendship Commission					
1201 15th St NW Suite 330	Washington	DC	20005	202-653-9800	653-9802
Web: www.jusfc.gov					
Joint Board for the Enrollment of Actuaries					
Internal Revenue Service SE:OPR					
1111 Constitution Ave NW	Washington	DC	20224	202-622-8229	622-8300
Web: www.irs.gov					
Legal Services Corp 3333 K St NW 3rd Fl	Washington	DC	20007	202-295-1500	337-6797
Web: www.lsc.gov					
Marine Mammal Commission 4340 E W Hwy Rm 700	Bethesda	MD	20814	301-504-0087	504-0099
Web: www.mmc.gov					
Merit Systems Protection Board (MSPB)					
1615 M St NW	Washington	DC	20419	202-653-7200	653-7130
TF: 800-209-8960 ■ *Web:* www.mspb.gov					
Merit Systems Protection Board Regional Offices					
Atlanta Region 401 W Peachtree St NW 10th Fl	Atlanta	GA	30308	404-730-2755	730-2767
TF: 800-209-8960 ■ *Web:* www.mspb.gov					
Central Region 230 S Dearborn St 31st Fl	Chicago	IL	60604	312-353-2923	886-4231
Web: www.mspb.gov					
Dallas Field Office 1100 Commerce St Rm 620	Dallas	TX	75242	214-767-0555	767-0102
Web: www.mspb.gov					
Denver Field Office 12567 W Cedar Dr # 100	Lakewood	CO	80228	303-969-5101	969-5109
New York Field Office					
26 Federal Plaza Rm 3137-A	New York	NY	10278	212-264-9372	264-1417
Web: www.mspb.gov					
Northeastern Region					
1601 Market St Suite 1700	Philadelphia	PA	19103	215-597-9960	597-3456
Washington (DC) Region					
1800 Diagonal Rd Suite 205	Alexandria	VA	22314	703-756-6250	756-7112
Web: www.mspb.gov					
Western Region					
201 Mission St Suite 2310	San Francisco	CA	94105	415-904-6772	904-0580
Web: www.mspb.gov					
Migratory Bird Conservation Commission					
4401 N Fairfax Dr MS ARLSQ-622	Arlington	VA	22203	703-358-1716	358-2223
Web: www.fws.gov					
Millenium Challenge Corp 875 15th St NW	Washington	DC	20005	202-521-3600	
Web: www.mcc.gov					
Morris K Udall Foundation 110 S Church # 3350	Tucson	AZ	85709	520-670-5529	670-5530
Web: www.udall.gov					
National Aeronautics & Space Administration (NASA)					
300 E St SW	Washington	DC	20546	202-358-0001	358-3469
Web: www.nasa.gov					
National Archives & Records Administration (NARA)					
8601 Adelphi Rd	College Park	MD	20740	866-272-6272	837-0483*
**Fax Area Code:* 301 ■ *TF:* 866-272-6272 ■ *Web:* www.archives.gov					
Archival Research Catalog					
8601 Adelphi Rd	College Park	MD	20740	866-272-6272	
TF: 866-272-6272 ■ *Web:* www.archives.gov/research/arc					
Office of Presidential Libraries					
8601 Adelphi Rd Rm 2200	College Park	MD	20740	301-837-3250	837-3199
Web: www.archives.gov					
Office of the Federal Register					
800 N Capitol St NW Suite 700-K	Washington	DC	20002	202-741-6000	741-6012
Web: www.archives.gov/federal-register					
National Archives & Records Administration Regional Offices					
Central Plains Region 400 W Pershing Rd	Kansas City	MO	64131	816-268-8000	
Web: www.archives.gov					
Great Lakes Region 7358 S Pulaski Rd	Chicago	IL	60629	773-948-9001	948-9050
Web: www.archives.gov/great-lakes					
Mid Atlantic Region 900 Market St	Philadelphia	PA	19107	215-606-0100	606-0116
Web: www.archives.gov/midatlantic					
Northeast Region 380 Trapelo Rd	Waltham	MA	02452	781-663-0130	663-0154
TF: 866-406-2379 ■ *Web:* www.archives.gov					
Pacific Alaska Region 6125 Sand Pt Way NE	Seattle	WA	98115	206-336-5115	336-5112
TF: 866-325-7208 ■ *Web:* www.archives.gov					
Pacific Region 1000 Commodore Dr	San Bruno	CA	94066	650-238-3500	238-3507
Web: www.archives.gov/pacific					
Rocky Mountain Region PO Box 25307	Denver	CO	80225	303-407-5700	407-5761
Web: www.archives.gov/rocky-mountain					
Southeast Region 5780 Jonesboro Rd	Morrow	GA	30260	770-968-2100	968-2547
Web: www.archives.gov/southeast					
Southwest Region					
501 W Felix St Bldg 1 PO Box 6216	Fort Worth	TX	76115	817-334-5515	334-5621
Web: www.archives.gov/southwest					
National Capital Planning Commission					
401 9th St NW N Lobby Suite 500	Washington	DC	20004	202-482-7200	482-7272
Web: www.ncpc.gov					
National Council on Disability (NCD)					
1331 F St NW Suite 850	Washington	DC	20004	202-272-2004	272-2022
Web: www.ncd.gov					
National Credit Union Administration					
1775 Duke St	Alexandria	VA	22314	703-518-6300	518-6319
TF Fraud Hotline: 800-827-9650 ■ *Web:* www.ncua.gov					
National Credit Union Administration Regional Offices					
Region 1 9 Washington Sq Washington Ave Ext	Albany	NY	12205	518-862-7400	862-7420
Web: www.ncua.gov					
Region 2 1775 Duke St Suite 4206	Alexandria	VA	22314	703-519-4600	519-4620
Web: www.ncua.gov					
Region 3 7000 Central Pkwy Suite 1600	Atlanta	GA	30328	678-443-3000	443-3020
Web: www.ncua.gov					
Region 4 4807 Spicewood Springs Rd Suite 5200	Austin	TX	78759	512-342-5600	342-5620
Web: www.ncua.gov					
Region 5 1230 W Washington St Suite 301	Tempe	AZ	85281	602-302-6000	302-6024
Web: www.ncua.gov					
National Endowment for the Arts (NEA)					
1100 Pennsylvania Ave NW	Washington	DC	20506	202-682-5400	
Web: www.arts.gov					
National Endowment for the Humanities (NEH)					
1100 Pennsylvania Ave NW	Washington	DC	20506	202-606-8400	
TF: 800-634-1121 ■ *Web:* www.neh.gov					
National Indian Gaming Commission					
1441 L St NW Suite 9100	Washington	DC	20005	202-632-7003	632-7066
Web: www.nigc.gov					
National Labor Relations Board (NLRB)					
1099 14th St NW	Washington	DC	20570	202-273-1991	
TF: 866-667-6572 ■ *Web:* www.nlrb.gov					
National Labor Relations Board Regional Offices					
Region 1 10 Cswy St # 601	Boston	MA	02222	617-565-6700	565-6725
TF: 866-667-6572 ■ *Web:* www.nlrb.gov					
Region 10 233 Peachtree St NE Suite 1000	Atlanta	GA	30303	404-331-2896	331-2858
Web: www.nlrb.gov					

Phone Fax

Region 11
4035 University Pkwy Suite 200 ... Winston-Salem NC 27106 336-631-5201 631-5210
TF: 866-667-6572 ■ *Web:* www.nlrb.gov
Region 12 201 E Kennedy Blvd Suite 530 ... Tampa FL 33602 813-228-2641 228-2874
Web: www.nlrb.gov
Region 13 200 W Adams St ... Chicago IL 60606 312-353-7570 886-1341
Web: www.nlrb.gov
Region 14 1222 Spruce St Rm 8.302 ... Saint Louis MO 63103 314-539-7770 539-7794
TF: 866-667-6572 ■ *Web:* www.nlrb.gov
Region 15 1515 Poydras St Rm 610 ... New Orleans LA 70112 504-589-6361 589-4069
Web: www.nlrb.gov
Region 16
Federal Bldg 819 Taylor St Rm 8A24 ... Fort Worth TX 76102 817-978-2921 978-2928
TF: 866-667-6572 ■ *Web:* www.nlrb.gov
Region 17 8600 Farley St Suite 100 ... Overland Park KS 66212 913-967-3000 967-3010
Web: www.nlrb.gov
Region 18 330 2nd Ave S Suite 790 ... Minneapolis MN 55401 612-348-1757 348-1785
TF: 866-667-6572 ■ *Web:* www.nlrb.gov
Region 19 915 2nd Ave # 2948 ... Seattle WA 98174 206-220-6300 220-6305
Web: www.nlrb.gov
Region 2 26 Federal Plaza Rm 3614 ... New York NY 10278 212-264-0300 264-2450
Web: www.nlrb.gov
Region 20 901 Market St Suite 400 ... San Francisco CA 94103 415-356-5130 356-5156
TF: 866-667-6572 ■ *Web:* www.nlrb.gov
Region 21 888 S Figueroa St 9th Fl ... Los Angeles CA 90017 213-894-5200 894-2778
Web: www.nlrb.gov
Region 22 20 Washington Pl 5th Fl ... Newark NJ 07102 973-645-2100 645-3852
Web: www.nlrb.gov
Region 24 525 FD Roosevelt Ave Suite 1002 ... San Juan PR 00918 787-766-5347 766-5478
Web: www.nlrb.gov
Region 25 575 N Pennsylvania St # 238 ... Indianapolis IN 46204 317-226-7381 226-5103
TF: 866-667-6572 ■ *Web:* www.nlrb.gov
Region 26 80 Monroe Ave Suite 350 ... Memphis TN 38103 901-544-0018 544-0008
Web: www.nlrb.gov
Region 27 600 17th St 7th Fl N Tower ... Denver CO 80202 303-844-3551 844-6249
Web: www.nlrb.gov
Region 28 2600 N Central Ave Suite 1800 ... Phoenix AZ 85004 602-640-2160 640-2178
Web: www.nlrb.gov
Region 29 1 Metrotech Ctr N # A ... Brooklyn NY 11201 718-330-7713 330-7579
Web: www.nlrb.gov
Region 3
Niagara Ctr Bldg 130 S Elmwood Ave Suite 630 ... Buffalo NY 14202 716-551-4931 551-4972
TF: 866-667-6572 ■ *Web:* www.nlrb.gov
Region 30 310 W Wisconsin Ave Suite 700 ... Milwaukee WI 53203 414-297-3861 297-3880
Web: www.nlrb.gov
Region 31 11150 W Olympic Blvd Suite 700 ... Los Angeles CA 90064 310-235-7352 235-7420
TF: 866-667-6572 ■ *Web:* www.nlrb.gov
Region 32 1301 Clay St Rm 300N ... Oakland CA 94612 510-637-3300 637-3315
Web: www.nlrb.gov
Region 34 450 Main St ... Hartford CT 06103 860-240-3522 240-3564
Web: www.nlrb.gov/category/regions
Region 4 615 Chestnut St 7th Fl ... Philadelphia PA 19106 215-597-7601 597-7658
Web: www.nlrb.gov
Region 5 103 S Gay St 8th Fl ... Baltimore MD 21202 410-962-2822 962-2198
Web: www.nlrb.gov
Region 6 112 Washington Pl ... Pittsburgh PA 15219 412-395-4400 395-5986
Web: www.nlrb.gov
Region 7 477 Michigan Ave Rm 300 ... Detroit MI 48226 313-226-3200 226-2090
Web: www.nlrb.gov
Region 8 1240 E 9th St Rm 1695 ... Cleveland OH 44199 216-522-3715 522-2418
TF: 866-667-6572 ■ *Web:* www.nlrb.gov
Region 9 550 Main St Rm 3003 ... Cincinnati OH 45202 513-684-3686 684-3946
TF: 866-667-6572 ■ *Web:* www.nlrb.gov

National Mediation Board
1301 K St NW Suite 250E ... Washington DC 20005 202-692-5050
Web: www.nmb.gov

National Railroad Passenger Corp
60 Massachusetts Ave NE ... Washington DC 20002 202-906-3741 906-3285
TF: 800-872-7245 ■ *Web:* www.amtrak.com

National Science Foundation (NSF)
4201 Wilson Blvd ... Arlington VA 22230 703-292-5111 292-9232
TF: 800-877-8339 ■ *Web:* www.nsf.gov

National Transportation Safety Board (NTSB)
490 L'Enfant Plaza SW ... Washington DC 20594 202-314-6000 314-6293
Web: www.ntsb.gov

Nuclear Regulatory Commission Regional Offices
Region 1 475 Allendale Rd ... King of Prussia PA 19426 610-337-5000
TF: 800-432-1156
Region 2 61 Forsyth St SW Suite 23T85 ... Atlanta GA 30303 404-562-4400 562-4900
TF: 800-577-8510 ■ *Web:* www.nrc.gov
Region 3 2443 Warrenville Rd Suite 210 ... Lisle IL 60532 630-829-9500 515-1078
TF: 800-522-3025 ■ *Web:* www.nrc.gov
Region 4
Texas Health Resources Tower
611 Ryan Plaza Suite 400 ... Arlington TX 76011 817-860-8100 860-8210
TF: 800-952-9677

Nuclear Waste Technical Review Board (NWTRB)
2300 Clarendon Blvd Suite 1300 ... Arlington VA 22201 703-235-4473 235-4495
Web: www.nwtrb.gov

Occupational Safety & Health Review Commission
1120 20th St NW 9th Fl ... Washington DC 20036 202-606-5400 606-5050
Web: www.oshrc.gov

Occupational Safety & Health Review Commission Regional Offices
Atlanta Region 100 Alabama St SW Rm 2R90 ... Atlanta GA 30303 404-562-1640 562-1650
Web: www.oshrc.gov

Office of Compliance
110 2nd St SE Rm LA 200 ... Washington DC 20540 202-724-9250 426-1913
Web: www.compliance.gov

Office of Personnel Management (OPM)
1900 E St NW ... Washington DC 20415 202-606-1800
Web: www.opm.gov

Office of Special Counsel
1730 M St NW Suite 218 ... Washington DC 20036 202-254-3600 653-5151
TF: 800-872-9855 ■ *Web:* www.osc.gov

Office of Special Counsel Regional Offices
Dallas Field Office
525 Griffin St Rm 824 PO Box 103 ... Dallas TX 75202 214-747-1519 767-2764
TF: 800-872-9855 ■ *Web:* www.osc.gov
San Francisco Bay Area Field Office
Federal Bldg 1301 Clay St Suite 1220-N ... Oakland CA 94612 510-637-3460 637-3474
TF: 800-872-9855 ■ *Web:* www.osc.gov

Office of the National Counterintelligence Executive (NCIX)
CS5 Rm 300 ... Washington DC 20511 703-682-4500 682-4510
Web: www.ncix.gov

Overseas Private Investment Corp (OPIC)
1100 New York Ave NW ... Washington DC 20527 202-336-8400 408-9859
Web: www.opic.gov

Peace Corps 1111 20th St NW ... Washington DC 20526 202-692-2100 692-2101
TF: 800-424-8580 ■ *Web:* www.peacecorps.gov

Peace Corps Regional Offices
Atlanta Regional Office
100 Alabama St Bldg 1924 Suite 2R70 ... Atlanta GA 30303 404-562-3456 562-3455
TF: 800-424-8508 ■ *Web:* www.peacecorps.gov
Boston 10 Cswy St Suite 559, Federal Bldg ... Boston MA 02222 617-565-5555 565-5539
TF: 800-424-8580 ■ *Web:* www.peacecorps.gov
Chicago Regional Office
55 W Monroe St Suite 450 ... Chicago IL 60603 312-353-4990 353-4192
TF: 800-424-8580 ■ *Web:* www.peacecorps.gov
Dallas Regional Office
110 Commerce St Suite 427 ... Dallas TX 75242 214-253-5400 253-5401
TF: 800-424-8580 ■ *Web:* www.peacecorps.gov
Denver Regional Office
1999 Broadway Suite 2205 ... Denver CO 80202 303-844-7020 844-7010
TF: 800-424-8580 ■ *Web:* www.peacecorps.gov
Los Angeles Regional Office
2361 Rosecrans Ave Suite 155 ... El Segundo CA 90245 310-356-1100 356-1125
TF: 800-424-8580 ■ *Web:* www.peacecorps.gov
Mid-Atlantic Regional Office
1525 Wilson Blvd Suite 100 ... Arlington VA 22209 202-692-1040 692-1041
TF: 800-424-8580 ■ *Web:* www.peacecorps.gov
Minneapolis Regional Office
330 2nd Ave S Suite 420 ... Minneapolis MN 55401 612-348-1480 348-1474
TF: 800-424-8580 ■ *Web:* www.peacecorps.gov
New York Regional Office
201 Varick St Suite 1025 ... New York NY 10014 212-352-5440 352-5441
TF: 800-424-8580 ■ *Web:* www.peacecorps.gov
Northwest Regional Office
1601 5th Ave Suite 605 ... Seattle WA 98101 206-553-5490 553-2343
TF: 800-424-8580 ■ *Web:* www.peacecorps.gov
San Francisco Regional Office
1301 Clay St Suite 620-N ... Oakland CA 94610 510-452-8444 452-8441
TF: 800-424-8580 ■ *Web:* www.peacecorps.gov

Pension Benefit Guaranty Corp
1200 K St NW ... Washington DC 20005 202-326-4000 326-4047
TF Cust Svc: 800-400-7242 ■ *Web:* www.pbgc.gov

Postal Regulatory Commission
901 New York Ave NW Suite 200 ... Washington DC 20268 202-789-6800 789-6891
Web: www.prc.gov

Presidio Trust
34 Graham St PO Box 29052 ... San Francisco CA 94129 415-561-5300 561-5315
Web: www.presidio.gov

Railroad Retirement Board 844 N Rush St ... Chicago IL 60611 312-751-4500
TF: 800-808-0772 ■ *Web:* www.rrb.gov

Securities & Exchange Commission (SEC)
100 F St NE ... Washington DC 20549 202-942-8088 772-9295
TF: 800-732-0330 ■ *Web:* www.sec.gov
Office of Investor Education & Advocacy
100 F St NE ... Washington DC 20549 202-942-8088 772-9295
Web: www.sec.gov/investor.shtml

Securities & Exchange Commission Regional Offices
Atlanta Regional Office
3475 Lenox Rd NE Suite 1000 ... Atlanta GA 30326 404-842-7600
Web: www.sec.gov
Boston Regional Office 33 Arch St 23rd Fl ... Boston MA 02110 617-573-8900
Web: www.sec.gov/contact/addresses.htm
Chicago Regional Office
175 W Jackson Blvd Suite 900 ... Chicago IL 60604 312-353-7390 353-7398
Web: www.sec.gov
Denver Regional Office
1801 California St Suite 1500 ... Denver CO 80202 303-844-1000 844-1010
Web: www.sec.gov
Fort Worth Regional Office
801 Cherry St Unit 18 ... Fort Worth TX 76102 817-978-3821
Los Angeles Regional Office
5670 Wilshire Blvd 11th Fl ... Los Angeles CA 90036 323-965-3998 965-3815
Web: www.sec.gov

	City	State	Zip	Phone	Fax
Miami Regional Office					
801 Brickell Ave Suite 1800	Miami	FL	33131	305-982-6300	
Web: www.sec.gov					
New York Regional Office					
3 World Financial Ctr Suite 400	New York	NY	10281	212-336-1100	
Web: www.sec.gov					
Philadelphia Regional Office					
Mellon Independence Ctr 701 Market St	Philadelphia	PA	19106	215-597-3100	
Salt Lake Regional Office					
15 W S Temple St Suite 1800	Salt Lake City	UT	84101	801-524-5796	
San Francisco Regional Office					
44 Montgomery St Suite 2600	San Francisco	CA	94104	415-705-2500	
Selective Service System 1515 Wilson Blvd	Arlington	VA	22209	703-605-4000	
Web: www.sss.gov					
Selective Service System Regional Offices					
Region 1					
2500 Green Bay Rd Bldg 3400 Suite 276	North Chicago	IL	60064	847-688-4540	688-3433
Region 2 PO Box 94638	Palatine	IL	60094	847-688-6888	
TF: 888-655-1825 ■ *Web:* www.sss.gov					
Region 3 3401 Quebec St	Denver	CO	80207	720-941-1670	941-1685
Web: www.sss.gov					
Small Business Administration (SBA)					
409 3rd St SW	Washington	DC	20416	202-205-6600	205-6802
TF: 800-827-5722 ■ *Web:* www.sba.gov					
National Women's Business Council					
409 3rd St SW Suite 210	Washington	DC	20024	202-205-3850	205-6825
Web: www.nwbc.gov					
Small Business Administration Regional Offices					
Region 1 10 Cswy St Suite 812	Boston	MA	02222	617-565-8415	565-8420
Web: www.sba.gov/region1					
Region 10 2401 4th Ave Suite 400	Seattle	WA	98121	206-553-5231	553-4155
Web: www.sba.gov/content/regional-local-media-contacts-0#reg10					
Region 2 26 Federal Plaza Suite 3108	New York	NY	10278	212-264-1450	264-0038
Web: www.sba.gov/region2					
Region 3 900 Market St 5th Fl	Philadelphia	PA	19107	215-580-2807	580-2800
Web: www.sba.gov/region3					
Region 4 233 Peachtree St NE Suite 1800	Atlanta	GA	30303	404-331-4999	331-2354
Web: www.sba.gov/region4					
Region 5 500 W Madison St Suite 1150	Chicago	IL	60661	312-353-7327	353-3426
Web: www.sba.gov/content/regional-local-media-contacts-0#reg5					
Region 6 4300 Amon Carter Blvd Suite 108	Fort Worth	TX	76155	817-684-5581	684-5588
Web: www.sba.gov					
Region 7 100 Walnut Suite 530	Kansas City	MO	64106	816-426-4840	426-4848
Web: www.sba.gov					
Region 8 721 19th St Suite 426	Denver	CO	80202	303-844-2607	292-3582*
**Fax Area Code:* 202 ■ *Web:* www.sba.gov/content/regional-local-media-contacts-0#reg8					
Region 9 330 N Brand Blvd Suite 1270	Glendale	CA	91203	818-552-3434	552-3440
Web: www.sba.gov					
Social Security Administration (SSA)					
6401 Security Blvd	Baltimore	MD	21235	410-965-5738	966-1463
TF: 800-772-1213 ■ *Web:* www.ssa.gov					
Social Security Administration Regional Offices					
Region 1 JFK Federal Bldg Rm 1900	Boston	MA	02203	617-565-2870	565-2143
Web: www.ssa.gov/boston					
Region 10 701 5th Ave Suite 2900	Seattle	WA	98104	206-615-2100	615-2193
TF: 800-772-1213 ■ *Web:* www.ssa.gov					
Region 2 26 Federal Plaza Rm 40-102	New York	NY	10278	212-264-3915	264-6847
TF: 800-772-1213 ■ *Web:* www.ssa.gov/ny					
Region 3					
300 Spring Garden St PO Box 8788	Philadelphia	PA	19101	215-597-5157	597-2827
TF: 800-772-1213 ■ *Web:* www.ssa.gov					
Region 4 61 Forsyth St SW Suite 23T30	Atlanta	GA	30303	404-562-5600	562-5608
Web: www.ssa.gov/atlanta					
Region 5 600 W Madison St PO Box 8280	Chicago	IL	60680	312-575-4000	575-4016
TF: 800-772-1213 ■ *Web:* www.ssa.gov					
Region 6 1301 Young St	Dallas	TX	75202	214-767-4212	767-8986
TF: 800-772-1213 ■ *Web:* www.ssa.gov/dallas					
Region 7					
Federal Bldg 601 E 12th St Rm 436	Kansas City	MO	64106	816-936-5700	936-5972
Web: www.ssa.gov/kc					
Region 8 1244 Speer Blvd Suite 600	Denver	CO	80204	888-397-9803	844-6092*
**Fax Area Code:* 303 ■ *TF:* 888-397-9803 ■ *Web:* www.ssa.gov/denver					
Region 9 PO Box 4201	Richmond	CA	94804	510-970-8430	970-8218
TF: 800-772-1213 ■ *Web:* www.ssa.gov					
Social Security Advisory Board					
400 Virginia Ave SW Suite 625	Washington	DC	20024	202-475-7700	475-7715
Web: www.ssab.gov					
State Justice Institute (SJI)					
1650 King St Suite 600	Alexandria	VA	22314	703-684-6100	684-7618
Web: www.statejustice.org					
Susquehanna River Basin Commission					
1721 N Front St	Harrisburg	PA	17102	717-238-0423	238-2436
Web: www.srbc.net					
Tennessee Valley Authority (TVA)					
400 W Summit Hill Dr	Knoxville	TN	37902	865-632-2101	
Web: www.tva.gov					
US Agency for International Development (USAID)					
1300 Pennsylvania Ave NW	Washington	DC	20523	202-712-0000	216-3524
Web: www.usaid.gov					
US Arctic Research Commission					
4350 N Fairfax Dr Suite 510	Arlington	VA	22203	703-525-0111	525-0114
Web: www.arctic.gov					
US Chemical Safety & Hazard Investigation Board					
2175 K St NW Suite 400	Washington	DC	20037	202-261-7600	261-7650
Web: www.chemsafety.gov					
US Commission on Civil Rights					
624 9th St NW	Washington	DC	20425	202-376-7700	376-7672
Web: www.usccr.gov					
US Commission on Civil Rights Regional Offices					
Central Regional Office					
400 State Ave Suite 908	Kansas City	KS	66101	913-551-1400	551-1413
Web: www.usccr.gov					
Eastern Regional Office					
624 9th St NW Suite 700	Washington	DC	20425	202-376-7700	376-7672
Web: www.usccr.gov					
Midwestern Regional Office					
55 W Monroe St Suite 410	Chicago	IL	60603	312-353-8311	353-8324
TF: 800-552-6843 ■ *Web:* www.usccr.gov					
Rocky Mountain Regional Office 1700 Broadway	Denver	CO	80290	303-866-1040	866-1050
Web: www.usccr.gov					
Southern Regional Office					
61 Forsyth St SW Suite 18T40	Atlanta	GA	30303	404-562-7000	562-7005
Western Regional Office					
300 N Los Angeles St Suite 2010	Los Angeles	CA	90012	213-894-3437	894-0508
Web: www.usccr.gov					
US Commission on International Religious Freedom (USCIRF)					
800 N Capitol St NW Suite 790	Washington	DC	20002	202-523-3240	523-5020
Web: www.uscirf.gov					
US Election Assistance Commission					
1201 New York Ave NW # 300	Washington	DC	20005	202-566-3100	566-3127
TF: 866-747-1471 ■ *Web:* www.eac.gov					
US General Services Administration					
1275 First St NE	Washington	DC	20417	202-208-7642	
Web: www.gsa.gov/portal/category/100000					
US General Services Administration					
1800 F St NW	Washington	DC	20405	800-488-3111	
TF: 800-333-4636 ■ *Web:* www.usa.gov					
US Institute of Peace					
2301 Constitution Ave NW	Washington	DC	20037	202-457-1700	429-6063
Web: www.usip.org					
US International Trade Commission					
500 E St SW	Washington	DC	20436	202-205-2000	205-2316
Web: www.usitc.gov					
US Postal Service (USPS)					
475 L'Enfant Plaza W SW	Washington	DC	20260	202-268-2000	
TF Cust Svc: 800-275-8777 ■ *Web:* www.usps.com					
US Trade & Development Agency					
1000 Wilson Blvd Suite 1600	Arlington	VA	22209	703-875-4357	875-4009
Web: www.ustda.gov					
Vietnam Education Foundation (VEF)					
2111 Wilson Blvd Suite 700	Arlington	VA	22201	703-351-5053	351-1423
Web: www.vef.gov					
White House Commission on Remembrance					
1750 New York Ave NW	Washington	DC	20006	202-783-4665	783-1168
Web: www.remember.gov					

344 GOVERNMENT - US - JUDICIAL BRANCH

	City	State	Zip	Phone	Fax
Alien Terrorist Removal Court					
US Courthouse 333 Constitution Ave NW	Washington	DC	20001	202-354-3050	354-3067
Federal Judicial Ctr					
Thurgood Marshall Federal Judiciary Bldg					
1 Columbus Cir NE	Washington	DC	20002	202-502-4000	502-4099
Web: www.fjc.gov					
Judicial Conference of the US					
Thurgood Marshall Federal Judiciary Bldg					
1 Columbus Cir NE Rm 7-425 S	Washington	DC	20544	202-502-2400	502-1144
Web: www.uscourts.gov/judconf.html					
Judicial Panel on Multidistrict Litigation					
Thurgood Marshall Federal Judiciary Bldg					
1 Columbus Cir NE Rm G-255 N Lobby	Washington	DC	20544	202-502-2800	502-2888
Web: www.jpml.uscourts.gov					
Supreme Court of the US					
US Supreme Court Bldg 1 First St NE	Washington	DC	20543	202-479-3211	
Web: www.supremecourt.gov					
US Court of Appeals for the Armed Forces					
450 E St NW	Washington	DC	20442	202-761-1448	761-4672
Web: www.armfor.uscourts.gov					
US Court of Appeals for Veterans Claims					
625 Indiana Ave NW Suite 900	Washington	DC	20004	202-501-5970	501-5848
Web: www.uscourts.cavc.gov					
US Court of Federal Claims					
717 Madison Pl NW	Washington	DC	20005	202-357-6400	
Web: www.uscfc.uscourts.gov					
US Court of International Trade					
1 Federal Plaza	New York	NY	10278	212-264-2800	264-1085
Web: www.cit.uscourts.gov					
US Sentencing Commission					
Thurgood Marshall Federal Judiciary Bldg					
1 Columbus Cir NE S Lobby	Washington	DC	20002	202-502-4500	
Web: www.ussc.gov					
US Tax Court 400 2nd St NW	Washington	DC	20217	202-521-0700	
Web: www.ustaxcourt.gov					

344-1 US Appeals Courts

	City	State	Zip	Phone	Fax
Federal Circuit 717 Madison Pl NW	Washington	DC	20439	202-633-6550	633-9623
Web: www.fedcir.gov					

US Court of Appeals

	City	State	Zip	Phone	Fax
Circuit 1 1 Courthouse Way # 2500	Boston	MA	02210	617-748-9057	
Web: www.ca1.uscourts.gov					
Circuit 10 1823 Stout St	Denver	CO	80202	303-844-3157	
Web: www.ca10.uscourts.gov					
Circuit 11 56 Forsyth St NW 1st Fl	Atlanta	GA	30303	404-335-6100	
Web: www.ca11.uscourts.gov					
Circuit 2 US Courthouse 40 Foley Sq	New York	NY	10007	212-857-8500	
Web: www.ca2.uscourts.gov					
Circuit 3 US Courthouse 601 Market St	Philadelphia	PA	19106	215-597-2995	
Web: www.ca3.uscourts.gov					
Circuit 4 US Courthouse Annex 1100 E Main St	Richmond	VA	23219	804-916-2700	
Web: www.ca4.uscourts.gov					
Circuit 5 600 Camp St	New Orleans	LA	70130	504-310-7700	
Web: www.ca5.uscourts.gov					
Circuit 6 100 E 5th St # 532	Cincinnati	OH	45202	513-564-7000	564-7090
Web: www.ca6.uscourts.gov					
Circuit 7 219 S Dearborn St # 2722	Chicago	IL	60604	312-435-5850	
Web: www.ca7.uscourts.gov					
Circuit 8 111 S 10th St # 22.300	Saint Louis	MO	63102	314-244-2400	244-2780
Web: www.ca8.uscourts.gov					
Circuit 9 95 7th St PO Box 193939	San Francisco	CA	94103	415-556-9890	
Web: www.ca9.uscourts.gov					
District of Columbia Circuit					
33 Constitution Ave NW Rm 5523	Washington	DC	20001	202-216-7000	
Web: www.cadc.uscourts.gov					

344-2 US Bankruptcy Courts

US Bankruptcy Court

	City	State	Zip	Phone	Fax
Alabama Middle 1 Church St	Montgomery	AL	36104	334-954-3800	954-3819
Web: www.almb.uscourts.gov					
Alabama Northern 1800 5th Ave N Rm 120	Birmingham	AL	35203	205-714-4000	714-3913
Web: www.alnb.uscourts.gov					
Alabama Southern 201 St Louis St	Mobile	AL	36602	251-441-5391	441-6286
Web: www.alsb.uscourts.gov					
Alaska 605 W 4th Ave Suite 138	Anchorage	AK	99501	907-271-2655	271-2645
TF: 800-859-8059 ■ *Web:* www.akb.uscourts.gov					
Arizona 230 N 1st Ave Suite 101	Phoenix	AZ	85003	602-682-4000	
Web: www.azb.uscourts.gov					
Arkansas 300 W 2nd St	Little Rock	AR	72201	501-918-5500	918-5520
Web: www.arb.uscourts.gov					
California Central 255 E Temple St	Los Angeles	CA	90012	213-894-3118	
Web: www.cacb.uscourts.gov					
California Eastern 501 'I' St Suite 3-200	Sacramento	CA	95814	916-930-4400	
Web: www.caeb.uscourts.gov					
California Northern 235 Pine St # 19	San Francisco	CA	94120	415-268-2300	
Web: www.canb.uscourts.gov					
California Southern 325 W F St	San Diego	CA	92101	619-557-5620	
Web: www.casb.uscourts.gov					
Central District of Illinois					
600 E Monroe St 2nd Fl Rm 226	Springfield	IL	62701	217-492-4551	
Web: www.ilcb.uscourts.gov					
Colorado US Custom House 721 19th St	Denver	CO	80202	720-904-7300	
Web: www.cob.uscourts.gov					
Connecticut 450 Main St 7th Fl	Hartford	CT	06103	860-240-3675	240-3595
Web: www.ctb.uscourts.gov					
Delaware 824 N Market St 3rd Fl	Wilmington	DE	19801	302-252-2900	
Web: www.deb.uscourts.gov					
District of Columbia					
333 Constitution Ave NW	Washington	DC	20001	202-565-2500	
Web: www.dcb.uscourts.gov					
Florida Middle 801 N Florida Ave Suite 727	Tampa	FL	33602	813-301-5162	
Web: www.flmb.uscourts.gov					
Florida Northern 110 E Pk Ave Suite 100	Tallahassee	FL	32301	850-521-5001	
Web: www.flnb.uscourts.gov					
Florida Southern 51 SW 1st Ave	Miami	FL	33130	305-714-1800	
Web: www.flsb.uscourts.gov					
Georgia Middle 433 Cherry St PO Box 1957	Macon	GA	31202	478-752-3506	
Web: www.gamb.uscourts.gov					
Georgia Northern 75 Spring St SW	Atlanta	GA	30303	404-215-1000	
Web: www.ganb.uscourts.gov					
Georgia Southern 125 Bull St	Savannah	GA	31401	912-650-4100	
Web: www.gasb.uscourts.gov					
Hawaii 1132 Bishop St	Honolulu	HI	96813	808-522-8100	522-8120
Web: www.hib.uscourts.gov					
Idaho 550 W Fort St	Boise	ID	83724	208-334-1074	
Web: www.id.uscourts.gov					
Illinois Northern 219 S Dearborn St Rm 713	Chicago	IL	60604	312-435-5694	408-7750
Web: www.ilnb.uscourts.gov					
Illinois Southern 750 Missouri Ave	East Saint Louis	IL	62201	618-482-9400	
Web: www.ilsb.uscourts.gov					
Indiana Northern 401 S Michigan St	South Bend	IN	46601	574-968-2100	
Web: www.innb.uscourts.gov					
Indiana Southern 46 E Ohio St	Indianapolis	IN	46204	317-229-3800	229-3801
Web: www.insb.uscourts.gov					
Iowa Northern 425 2nd St SE # 800	Cedar Rapids	IA	52401	319-286-2200	286-2280
Web: www.ianb.uscourts.gov					
Iowa Southern 110 E Ct Ave PO Box 9264	Des Moines	IA	50306	515-284-6230	284-6303
TF: 888-219-5534 ■ *Web:* www.iasb.uscourts.gov					
Kansas 401 N Market St Rm 167	Wichita	KS	67202	316-269-6486	269-6181
Web: www.ksb.uscourts.gov					
Kentucky Eastern 100 E Vine St Suite 200	Lexington	KY	40507	859-233-2608	
Web: www.kyeb.uscourts.gov					
Kentucky Western 601 W Broadway Suite 450	Louisville	KY	40202	502-627-5700	
Web: www.kywb.uscourts.gov					
Louisiana Eastern					
500 Poydras St Suite B-601	New Orleans	LA	70130	504-589-7878	
Web: www.laeb.uscourts.gov					
Louisiana Middle 707 Florida St Suite 119	Baton Rouge	LA	70801	225-389-0211	
Web: www.lamb.uscourts.gov					
Louisiana Western 300 Fannin St Suite 2201	Shreveport	LA	71101	318-676-4267	
Web: www.lawb.uscourts.gov					
Maine 537 Congress St 2nd Fl	Portland	ME	04101	207-780-3482	780-3679
Web: www.meb.uscourts.gov					
Maryland 101 W Lombard St Suite 8308	Baltimore	MD	21201	410-962-2688	
Web: www.mdb.uscourts.gov					
Massachusetts 10 Cswy St Rm 1101 Federal Bldg	Boston	MA	02222	617-565-8950	565-6650
Web: www.mab.uscourts.gov/mab					
Michigan Eastern 211 W Fort St Suite 2100	Detroit	MI	48226	313-234-0065	
Web: www.mieb.uscourts.gov					
Michigan Western 1 Division Ave N Rm 200	Grand Rapids	MI	49503	616-456-2693	
Web: www.miwb.uscourts.gov					
Minnesota 300 S 4th St 7W US Courthouse	Minneapolis	MN	55415	612-664-5260	
TF: 800-959-9002 ■ *Web:* www.mnb.uscourts.gov					
Mississippi Northern 703 Hwy 145 N	Aberdeen	MS	39730	662-369-2596	
Web: www.msnb.uscourts.gov					
Mississippi Southern PO Box 2448	Jackson	MS	39225	601-965-5301	
Web: www.mssb.uscourts.gov					
Missouri Eastern 111 S 10th St 4th Fl	Saint Louis	MO	63102	314-244-4500	244-4990
TF: 866-803-9517 ■ *Web:* www.moeb.uscourts.gov					
Missouri Western 400 E 9th St Rm1510	Kansas City	MO	64106	816-512-1800	
Web: www.mow.uscourts.gov					
Montana 400 NW Main St	Butte	MT	59701	406-782-3354	
Web: www.mtb.uscourts.gov					
Nebraska 111 S 18th Plaza Suite 1125	Omaha	NE	68102	402-661-7444	
Web: www.neb.uscourts.gov					
Nevada 300 Las Vegas Blvd S	Las Vegas	NV	89101	702-388-6257	
Web: www.nvb.uscourts.gov					
New Hampshire 1000 Elm St 10th Fl	Manchester	NH	03101	603-222-2600	222-2697
Web: www.nhb.uscourts.gov					
New Jersey PO Box 1352	Newark	NJ	07102	973-645-4764	
Web: www.njb.uscourts.gov					
New Mexico PO Box 546	Albuquerque	NM	87103	505-348-2500	348-2473
TF: 866-291-6805 ■ *Web:* www.nmcourt.fed.us					
New York Eastern 271 Cadman Plaza E	Brooklyn	NY	11201	347-394-1700	
Web: www.nyeb.uscourts.gov					
New York Northern 445 Broadway Suite 330	Albany	NY	12207	518-257-1661	257-1643
Web: www.nynb.uscourts.gov					
New York Southern					
US Custom House 1 Bowling Green	New York	NY	10004	212-668-2870	668-2878
Web: www.nysb.uscourts.gov					
New York Western 100 State St Rm 1220	Rochester	NY	14614	585-613-4200	
Web: www.nywb.uscourts.gov					
North Carolina Eastern 1760-A Parkwood Blvd	Wilson	NC	27893	252-237-0248	243-4870
Web: www.nceb.uscourts.gov					
North Carolina Middle					
101 S Edgeworth St 1st Fl PO Box 26100	Greensboro	NC	27420	336-358-4000	
Web: www.ncmb.uscourts.gov					
North Carolina Western					
401 W Trade St PO Box 34189	Charlotte	NC	28234	704-350-7500	344-6403
TF: 800-884-9868 ■ *Web:* www.ncwb.uscourts.gov					
North Dakota 655 1st Ave N Suite 210	Fargo	ND	58102	701-297-7100	297-7166
Web: www.ndb.uscourts.gov					
Ohio Northern 201 Superior Ave	Cleveland	OH	44114	216-615-4300	
Web: www.ohnb.uscourts.gov					
Ohio Southern 120 W 3rd St	Dayton	OH	45402	937-225-2516	225-7574
Web: www.ohsb.uscourts.gov					
Oklahoma Eastern 111 W 4th St PO Box 1347	Okmulgee	OK	74447	918-758-0126	756-9248
Web: www.okeb.uscourts.gov					
Oklahoma Northern 224 S Boulder Ave Rm 105	Tulsa	OK	74103	918-699-4000	699-4045
Web: www.oknb.uscourts.gov					
Oklahoma Western 215 Dean A McGee Ave	Oklahoma City	OK	73102	405-609-5700	609-5752
Web: www.okwb.uscourts.gov					
Oregon 1001 SW 5th Ave Rm 700	Portland	OR	97204	503-326-1500	
Web: www.orb.uscourts.gov					
Pennsylvania Eastern					
900 Market St Suite 400	Philadelphia	PA	19107	215-408-2800	
Web: www.paeb.uscourts.gov					
Pennsylvania Middle 197 S Main St	Wilkes-Barre	PA	18701	570-831-2500	829-0249
TF: 877-298-2053 ■ *Web:* www.pamb.uscourts.gov					
Pennsylvania Western					
5414 US Steel Tower 600 Grant St	Pittsburgh	PA	15219	412-644-2700	644-6512
Web: www.pawb.uscourts.gov					
Puerto Rico 300 Calle Del Recinto Sur	San Juan	PR	00901	787-977-6000	977-6008
Web: www.prb.uscourts.gov					
Rhode Island					
The Federal Ctr					
380 Westminster Mall 6th Fl	Providence	RI	02903	401-626-3100	626-3150
Web: www.rib.uscourts.gov					
South Carolina 1100 Laurel St	Columbia	SC	29201	803-765-5436	
Web: www.scb.uscourts.gov					

	City	State	Zip	Phone	Fax
South Dakota 400 S Phillips Ave Rm 104 *Web:* www.sdb.uscourts.gov	Sioux Falls	SD	57104	605-357-2430	357-2401
Tennessee Eastern 800 Market St Suite 330 *Web:* www.tneb.uscourts.gov	Knoxville	TN	37902	865-545-4279	
Tennessee Middle 701 Broadway Rm 170 *Web:* www.tnmb.uscourts.gov	Nashville	TN	37203	615-736-5584	736-2305
Tennessee Western 200 Jefferson Ave Suite 413 *Web:* www.tnwb.uscourts.gov	Memphis	TN	38103	901-328-3500	
Texas Eastern 110 N College Ave 9th Fl *Web:* www.txeb.uscourts.gov	Tyler	TX	75702	903-590-3200	
Texas Northern 1100 Commerce St Rm 1254 *TF:* 800-442-6850 ■ *Web:* www.txnb.uscourts.gov	Dallas	TX	75242	214-753-2000	753-2038
Texas Southern PO Box 61010 *Web:* www.txs.uscourts.gov	Houston	TX	77208	713-250-5500	
Texas Western 615 E Houston St Rm 597 PO Box 1439 *Web:* www.txwb.uscourts.gov	San Antonio	TX	78205	210-472-6720	472-5196
US Virgin Islands US Courthouse 5500 Veterans Dr Rm 310 *Web:* www.vid.uscourts.gov	Saint Thomas	VI	00802	340-774-8310	776-5615
Utah 350 S Main St Rm 301 *Web:* www.utb.uscourts.gov	Salt Lake City	UT	84101	801-524-6687	524-4409
Vermont 67 Merchants Row PO Box 6648 *Web:* www.vtb.uscourts.gov	Rutland	VT	05702	802-776-2000	776-2020
Virginia Eastern 1100 E Main St Rm 301 *Web:* www.vaeb.uscourts.gov	Richmond	VA	23219	804-916-2400	
Virginia Western 210 Church Ave SW Rm 200 *Web:* www.vawb.uscourts.gov	Roanoke	VA	24011	540-857-2391	857-2873
Washington Eastern 904 W Riverside Ave Suite 304 *TF:* 800-519-2549 ■ *Web:* www.waeb.uscourts.gov	Spokane	WA	99201	509-353-2404	
Washington Western 700 Stewart St 6th Fl *Web:* www.wawb.uscourts.gov	Seattle	WA	98101	206-370-5200	
West Virginia Northern 1125 Chapline St 3rd Fl PO Box 70 *Web:* www.wvnb.uscourts.gov	Wheeling	WV	26003	304-233-1655	233-0185
West Virginia Southern 300 Virginia St E Rm 3200 *Web:* www.wvsb.uscourts.gov	Charleston	WV	25301	304-347-3003	
Wisconsin Eastern US Courthouse 517 E Wisconsin Ave Rm 126 *TF:* 877-781-7277 ■ *Web:* www.wieb.uscourts.gov	Milwaukee	WI	53202	414-297-3291	
Wisconsin Western 120 N Henry St Rm 340 PO Box 548 *Web:* www.wiwb.uscourts.gov	Madison	WI	53701	608-264-5178	
Wyoming 2120 Capitol Ave Suite 6004 *Web:* www.wyb.uscourts.gov	Cheyenne	WY	82001	307-433-2200	433-2214

344-3 US District Courts

	City	State	Zip	Phone	Fax
US District Court Alabama Northern 1729 5th Ave N *Web:* www.alnd.uscourts.gov	Birmingham	AL	35203	205-278-1700	
US District Court Arizona 401 W Washington St Suite 130 *Web:* www.azd.uscourts.gov	Phoenix	AZ	85003	602-322-7200	322-7209
US District Court Arkansas Western 30 S 6th St # 10308 *Web:* www.arwd.uscourts.gov	Fort Smith	AR	72901	479-783-6833	783-6308
US District Court California Central 312 N Spring St *Web:* www.cacd.uscourts.gov	Los Angeles	CA	90012	213-894-1565	
US District Court California Eastern 501 I St *Web:* www.caed.uscourts.gov	Sacramento	CA	95814	916-930-4000	
US District Court California Northern 450 Golden Gate Ave 16th Fl Rm 161111 *Web:* www.cand.uscourts.gov	San Francisco	CA	94102	415-522-2000	
US District Court California Southern 880 Front St Rm 4290 *Web:* www.casd.uscourts.gov	San Diego	CA	92101	619-557-6348	702-9900
US District Court Colorado 901 19th St 2nd Fl *Web:* www.co.uscourts.gov	Denver	CO	80294	303-844-3433	335-2040
US District Court Connecticut 141 Church St *Web:* www.ctd.uscourts.gov	New Haven	CT	06510	203-773-2140	773-2334
US District Court Delaware 844 N King St # 18 *Web:* www.ded.uscourts.gov	Wilmington	DE	19801	302-573-6170	
US District Court District of Columbia 333 Constitution Ave NW # 6822 *Web:* www.dcd.uscourts.gov	Washington	DC	20001	202-354-3000	
US District Court Florida Middle 401 W Central Blvd Suite 1200 *Web:* www.flmd.uscourts.gov	Orlando	FL	32801	407-835-4200	
US District Court Florida Northern 111 N Adams St 3rd Fl *Web:* www.flnd.uscourts.gov	Tallahassee	FL	32301	850-521-3501	521-3656
US District Court Florida Southern 301 N Miami Ave *Web:* www.flsd.uscourts.gov	Miami	FL	33128	305-523-5100	
US District Court for the District of Alaska 222 W 7th Ave Suite 4 *TF:* 866-243-3814 ■ *Web:* www.akd.uscourts.gov	Anchorage	AK	99513	907-677-6100	
US District Court Georgia Middle 475 Mulberry St PO Box 128 *Web:* www.gamd.uscourts.gov	Macon	GA	31202	478-752-3497	752-3496
US District Court Georgia Northern 75 Spring St SW Rm 2211 *Web:* www.gand.uscourts.gov	Atlanta	GA	30303	404-215-1600	
US District Court Georgia Southern PO Box 8286 *Web:* www.gasd.uscourts.gov	Savannah	GA	31412	912-650-4020	
US District Court Guam 520 W Soledad Ave 4th Fl *Web:* www.gud.uscourts.gov	Hagatna	GU	96910	671-473-9100	
US District Court Hawaii 300 Ala Moana Blvd Rm C-338 *Web:* www.hid.uscourts.gov	Honolulu	HI	96850	808-541-1300	
US District Court Idaho 550 W Fort St *Web:* www.id.uscourts.gov	Boise	ID	83724	208-334-1361	
US District Court Illinois Central 600 E Monroe St *Web:* www.ilcd.uscourts.gov	Springfield	IL	62701	217-492-4020	492-4028
US District Court Illinois Northern 219 S Dearborn St 20th Fl *Web:* www.ilnd.uscourts.gov	Chicago	IL	60604	312-435-5670	
US District Court Illinois Southern PO Box 249 *Web:* www.ilsd.uscourts.gov	East Saint Louis	IL	62202	618-482-9371	482-9383
US District Court Indiana Northern 204 S Main St *Web:* www.innd.uscourts.gov	South Bend	IN	46601	574-246-8000	
US District Court Indiana Southern 46 E Ohio St *Web:* www.insd.uscourts.gov	Indianapolis	IN	46204	317-229-3700	229-3959
US District Court Iowa Northern 101 1st St SE *Web:* www.iand.uscourts.gov	Cedar Rapids	IA	52401	319-286-2300	286-2301
US District Court Iowa Southern PO Box 9344 *Web:* www.iasd.uscourts.gov	Des Moines	IA	50306	515-284-6421	284-6418
US District Court Kansas 500 State Ave *Web:* www.ksd.uscourts.gov	Kansas City	KS	66101	913-551-6719	551-6942
US District Court Kentucky Eastern 101 Barr St *Web:* www.kyed.uscourts.gov	Lexington	KY	40507	859-233-2503	
US District Court Kentucky Western 601 W Broadway Rm 106 *Web:* www.kywd.uscourts.gov	Louisville	KY	40202	502-625-3500	625-3880
US District Court Louisiana Eastern 500 Poydras St Rm C-151 *Web:* www.laed.uscourts.gov	New Orleans	LA	70130	504-589-7650	589-7697
US District Court Louisiana Middle 777 Florida St Suite 139 *Web:* www.lamd.uscourts.gov	Baton Rouge	LA	70801	225-389-3500	389-3501
US District Court Louisiana Western 300 Fannin St Suite 1167 *Web:* www.lawd.uscourts.gov	Shreveport	LA	71101	318-676-4273	676-3962
US District Court Maine 156 Federal St *Web:* www.med.uscourts.gov	Portland	ME	04101	207-780-3356	
US District Court Maryland 101 W Lombard St *Web:* www.mdd.uscourts.gov	Baltimore	MD	21201	410-962-2600	
US District Court Massachusetts 1 Courthouse Way Suite 2300 *Web:* www.mad.uscourts.gov	Boston	MA	02210	617-748-9152	
US District Court Michigan Eastern 231 W Lafayette Blvd *Web:* www.mied.uscourts.gov	Detroit	MI	48226	313-234-5005	
US District Court Michigan Western 110 Michigan St NW Rm 399 *Web:* www.miwd.uscourts.gov	Grand Rapids	MI	49503	616-456-2381	456-2058
US District Court Minnesota 300 S 4th St Suite 202 *Web:* www.mnd.uscourts.gov	Minneapolis	MN	55415	612-664-5000	664-5033
US District Court Mississippi Northern 911 Jackson Ave E Rm 369 *Web:* www.msnd.uscourts.gov	Oxford	MS	38655	662-234-1971	236-5210
US District Court Mississippi Southern PO Box 23552 *Web:* www.mssd.uscourts.gov	Jackson	MS	39225	601-965-4439	
US District Court Missouri Eastern 111 S 10th St Suite 3.300 *Web:* www.moed.uscourts.gov	Saint Louis	MO	63102	314-244-7900	244-7909
US District Court Missouri Western 400 E 9th St *Web:* www.mow.uscourts.gov	Kansas City	MO	64106	816-512-5000	
US District Court Montana PO Box 8537 *Web:* www.mtd.uscourts.gov	Missoula	MT	59807	406-542-7260	542-7272
US District Court Nebraska 111 S 18th Plaza Suite 1152 *TF:* 866-220-4381 ■ *Web:* www.ned.uscourts.gov	Omaha	NE	68102	402-661-7350	661-7387
US District Court Nevada 333 Las Vegas Blvd S 1st Fl *Web:* www.nvd.uscourts.gov	Las Vegas	NV	89101	702-464-5400	
US District Court New Hampshire 55 Pleasant St Rm 110 *Web:* www.nhd.uscourts.gov	Concord	NH	03301	603-225-1423	
US District Court New Jersey 50 Walnut St Rm 4015 *Web:* www.pacer.njd.uscourts.gov	Newark	NJ	07102	973-645-3730	
US District Court New Mexico 333 Lomas Blvd NW *Web:* www.nmcourt.fed.us	Albuquerque	NM	87102	505-348-2000	348-2028

	City	State	Zip	Phone	Fax
US District Court New York Eastern 225 Cadman Plaza E *Web:* www.nyed.uscourts.gov	Brooklyn	NY	11201	718-613-2600	
US District Court New York Northern 100 S Clinton St PO Box 7367 *Web:* www.nynd.uscourts.gov	Syracuse	NY	13261	315-234-8500	
US District Court New York Southern 500 Pearl St *Web:* www.nysd.uscourts.gov	New York	NY	10007	212-805-0136	
US District Court New York Western 68 Ct St *Web:* www.nywd.uscourts.gov	Buffalo	NY	14202	716-551-4211	551-4850
US District Court North Carolina Eastern PO Box 25670 *Web:* www.nced.uscourts.gov	Raleigh	NC	27611	919-645-1700	645-1750
US District Court North Carolina Middle 324 W Market St 4th Fl *Web:* www.ncmd.uscourts.gov	Greensboro	NC	27401	336-332-6000	332-6060
US District Court North Carolina Western 401 W Trade St *TF:* 866-851-1605 ■ *Web:* www.ncwd.uscourts.gov	Charlotte	NC	28202	704-350-7400	350-7421
US District Court North Dakota PO Box 1193 *Web:* www.ndd.uscourts.gov	Bismarck	ND	58502	701-530-2300	530-2312
US District Court Ohio Northern 801 W Superior Ave *Web:* www.ohnd.uscourts.gov	Cleveland	OH	44113	216-357-7000	357-7040
US District Court Ohio Southern 85 Marconi Blvd *Web:* www.ohsd.uscourts.gov	Columbus	OH	43215	614-719-3000	719-3005
US District Court Oklahoma Eastern PO Box 607 *Web:* www.oked.uscourts.gov	Muskogee	OK	74402	918-684-7920	684-7902
US District Court Oklahoma Northern 333 W 4th St *TF:* 866-213-1957 ■ *Web:* www.oknd.uscourts.gov	Tulsa	OK	74103	918-699-4700	
US District Court Oklahoma Western 200 NW 4th St Rm 1210 *Web:* www.okwd.uscourts.gov	Oklahoma City	OK	73102	405-609-5000	609-5099
US District Court Oregon 1000 SW 3rd Ave Suite 740 *Web:* www.ord.uscourts.gov	Portland	OR	97204	503-326-8008	
US District Court Pennsylvania Eastern 601 Market St *Web:* www.paed.uscourts.gov	Philadelphia	PA	19106	215-597-7704	597-6390
US District Court Pennsylvania Middle 235 N Washington Ave PO Box 1148 *Web:* www.pamd.uscourts.gov	Scranton	PA	18501	570-207-5600	207-5650
US District Court Pennsylvania Western 700 Grant St *Web:* www.pawd.uscourts.gov	Pittsburgh	PA	15219	412-208-7500	
US District Court Puerto Rico 150 Carlos Chardon Ave Rm 150 Federal Bldg *Web:* www.prd.uscourts.gov	San Juan	PR	00918	787-772-3000	766-5693
US District Court Rhode Island 2 Exchange Ter # 234 *Web:* www.rid.uscourts.gov	Providence	RI	02903	401-752-7200	752-7247
US District Court South Carolina 1845 Assembly St # 1 *Web:* www.scd.uscourts.gov	Columbia	SC	29201	803-765-5816	765-5960
US District Court South Dakota 400 S Phillips Ave Rm 128 *Web:* www.sdd.uscourts.gov	Sioux Falls	SD	57104	605-330-6600	330-6601
US District Court Tennessee Eastern 800 Market St Suite 130 *Web:* www.tned.uscourts.gov	Knoxville	TN	37902	865-545-4228	545-4247
US District Court Tennessee Middle 801 Broadway Rm 800 *Web:* www.tnmd.uscourts.gov	Nashville	TN	37203	615-736-5498	736-7488
US District Court Tennessee Western 167 N Main St Rm 242 *Web:* www.tnwd.uscourts.gov	Memphis	TN	38103	901-495-1200	495-1250
US District Court Texas Eastern 211 W Ferguson St *Web:* www.txed.uscourts.gov	Tyler	TX	75702	903-590-1000	
US District Court Texas Northern 1100 Commerce St Rm 1452 *Web:* www.txnd.uscourts.gov	Dallas	TX	75242	214-753-2200	753-2266
US District Court Texas Southern PO Box 61010 *Web:* www.txs.uscourts.gov	Houston	TX	77208	713-250-5500	
US District Court Texas Western 655 E Durango Blvd Rm G65 *TF:* 800-659-2497 ■ *Web:* www.txwd.uscourts.gov	San Antonio	TX	78206	210-472-6550	472-6513
US District Court US Virgin Islands 3013 Estate Golden Rock *Web:* www.vid.uscourts.gov	Saint Croix	VI	00820	340-773-1130	773-1563
US District Court Utah 350 S Main St Rm 150 *Web:* www.utd.uscourts.gov	Salt Lake City	UT	84101	801-524-6100	526-1175
US District Court Vermont 11 Elmwood Ave Rm 506 PO Box 945 *TF:* 800-837-8718 ■ *Web:* www.vtd.uscourts.gov	Burlington	VT	05402	802-951-6301	
US District Court Virginia Eastern 401 Courthouse Sq 2nd Fl *Web:* www.vaed.uscourts.gov	Alexandria	VA	22314	703-299-2100	
US District Court Virginia Western 210 Franklin Rd Rm 540 PO Box 1234 *Web:* www.vawd.uscourts.gov	Roanoke	VA	24011	540-857-5100	857-5110
US District Court Washington Eastern 920 W Riverside Ave Suite 840 *Web:* www.waed.uscourts.gov	Spokane	WA	99201	509-458-3400	458-3420
US District Court Washington Western 700 Stewart St *Web:* www.wawd.uscourts.gov	Seattle	WA	98101	206-370-8400	
US District Court West Virginia Northern 300 3rd St PO Box 1518 *Web:* www.wvnd.uscourts.gov	Elkins	WV	26241	304-636-1445	636-5746
US District Court West Virginia Southern 300 Virginia St E Suite 2400 *Web:* www.wvsd.uscourts.gov	Charleston	WV	25301	304-347-3000	
US District Court Wisconsin Eastern 517 E Wisconsin Ave *Web:* www.wied.uscourts.gov	Milwaukee	WI	53202	414-297-3372	
US District Court Wisconsin Western 120 N Henry St Rm 320 PO Box 432 *Web:* www.wiwd.uscourts.gov	Madison	WI	53701	608-264-5156	264-5925
US District Court Wyoming 2120 Capitol Ave 2nd Fl *Web:* www.wyd.uscourts.gov	Cheyenne	WY	82001	307-433-2120	433-2152

344-4 US Supreme Court

	City	State	Zip	Phone	Fax
Roberts John G Jr US Supreme Court Bldg 1 1st St NE *Web:* www.supremecourt.gov	Washington	DC	20543	202-479-3000	
Alito Samuel A Jr US Supreme Court Bldg 1 1st St NE *Web:* www.supremecourt.gov	Washington	DC	20543	202-479-3000	
Breyer Stephen G US Supreme Court Bldg 1 1st St NE *Web:* www.supremecourt.gov	Washington	DC	20543	202-479-3000	
Ginsburg Ruth Bader US Supreme Court Bldg 1 1st St NE *Web:* www.supremecourt.gov	Washington	DC	20543	202-479-3000	
Kennedy Anthony M US Supreme Court Bldg 1 1st St NE *Web:* www.supremecourt.gov	Washington	DC	20543	202-479-3000	
Scalia Antonin US Supreme Court Bldg 1 1st St NE *Web:* www.supremecourt.gov	Washington	DC	20543	202-479-3000	
Stevens John Paul US Supreme Court Bldg 1 1st St NE *Web:* www.supremecourt.gov	Washington	DC	20543	202-479-3000	
Thomas Clarence US Supreme Court Bldg 1 1st St NE *Web:* www.supremecourt.gov	Washington	DC	20543	202-479-3000	

345 GOVERNMENT - US - LEGISLATIVE BRANCH

SEE ALSO Legislation Hotlines p. 2150

	City	State	Zip	Phone	Fax
Congressional Budget Office Ford House Office Bldg 4th Fl *Web:* www.cbo.gov	Washington	DC	20515	202-226-2602	
Government Accountability Office (GAO) 441 G St NW *Web:* www.gao.gov	Washington	DC	20548	202-512-4800	
Atlanta Office 2635 Century Pkwy Suite 700 *Web:* www.gao.gov	Atlanta	GA	30345	404-679-1900	679-1819
Boston Office 10 Cswy St Rm 575 *Web:* www.gao.gov	Boston	MA	02222	617-788-0500	788-0505
Dallas Office 1999 Bryan St Suite 2200 *Web:* www.gao.gov	Dallas	TX	75201	214-777-5600	777-5758
Dayton Office 2196 D St Area B Bldg 39 *Web:* www.gao.gov	Wright-Patterson AFB	OH	45433	937-258-7900	258-7118
Denver Office 1244 Speer Blvd Suite 800 *Web:* www.gao.gov	Denver	CO	80204	303-572-7306	572-7433
Huntsville Office 6767 Old Madison Pike Bldg 5 Suite 520 *Web:* www.gao.gov	Huntsville	AL	35806	256-922-7500	971-9240
Los Angeles Office 350 S Figueroa St Suite 1010 *Web:* www.gao.gov	Los Angeles	CA	90071	213-830-1000	830-1180
Norfolk Office 5029 Corporate Woods Dr Suite 300 *Web:* www.gao.gov	Virginia Beach	VA	23462	757-552-8100	552-8197
San Francisco Office 301 Howard St Suite 1200 *Web:* www.gao.gov	San Francisco	CA	94105	415-904-2000	904-2111
Seattle Office 701 5th Ave Suite 2700 *Web:* www.gao.gov	Seattle	WA	98104	206-287-4800	287-4872
Library of Congress					
American Folklife Ctr 101 Independence Ave SE *Web:* www.loc.gov/folklife	Washington	DC	20540	202-707-5510	707-2076
Congressional Research Service 101 Independence Ave SE *Web:* www.loc.gov/crsinfo	Washington	DC	20540	202-707-5700	707-6745
Law Library of Congress 101 Independence Ave SE *Web:* www.loc.gov/rr/law	Washington	DC	20540	202-707-5079	707-1820
National Library Service for the Blind & Physically Handicapped 1291 Taylor St NW *TF:* 888-657-7323 ■ *Web:* www.loc.gov/nls	Washington	DC	20011	202-707-5100	707-0712

				Phone	Fax
THOMAS: Legislative Information on the Internet					
101 Independence Ave SE	Washington	DC	20540	202-707-5000	707-5844
Web: www.thomas.loc.gov					
US Copyright Office					
101 Independence Ave SE	Washington	DC	20559	202-707-3000	
Web: www.copyright.gov					
US Government Accountability Office (US GAO)					
Chicago Office 200 W Adams St Suite 700	Chicago	IL	60606	312-220-7600	220-7726
Web: www.gao.gov					
US Government Printing Office Bookstore (GPO)					
732 N Capitol St NW	Washington	DC	20401	202-512-1800	512-2104
TF: 866-512-1800 ■ *Web:* bookstore.gpo.gov					
US Government Printing Office Federal Register Online (GPO)					
800 N Capitol St NW	Washington	DC	20001	202-741-6000	741-6012
Web: www.gpoaccess.gov/fr					
US House of Representatives					
100 Cannon House Office Bldg	Washington	DC	20515	202-225-3121	225-1904
Web: www.house.gov					
US Senate 455 Dirksen Senate Office Bldg	Washington	DC	20510	202-224-3121	
Web: www.senate.gov					

345-1 US Congressional Committees

				Phone	Fax
United States Senate Special Committee on Aging					
G31 Dirksen Senate Office Bldg	Washington	DC	20510	202-224-5364	224-9926
Web: aging.senate.gov					
US Congress					
Joint Committee on Printing					
305 Russell Senate Office Bldg	Washington	DC	20510	202-224-3205	224-1912
Web: www.house.gov/jcp					
Joint Economic Committee					
G-01 Dirksen Bldg	Washington	DC	20510	202-224-5171	224-0240
Web: www.jec.senate.gov					
The Joint Committee on Taxation					
1625 Longworth House Office Bldg	Washington	DC	20515	202-225-3621	225-0832
Web: www.jct.gov					
US House of Representatives					
Agriculture Committee 1301 Longworth Bldg	Washington	DC	20515	202-225-2171	225-0917
Web: www.agriculture.house.gov					
Armed Services Committee					
2120 Rayburn House Office Bldg	Washington	DC	20515	202-225-4151	225-0858
Web: www.armedservices.house.gov					
Budget Committee					
Cannon House Office Bldg Suite B-71	Washington	DC	20515	202-226-7270	226-7174
Web: www.budget.house.gov					
Committee on Education & Labor					
2181 Rayburn Bldg	Washington	DC	20515	202-225-4527	
Web: www.edlabor.house.gov					
Committee on Natural Resources					
1324 Longworth Bldg	Washington	DC	20515	202-225-6065	225-1031
Web: resourcescommittee.house.gov					
Energy & Commerce Committee					
2125 Rayburn Bldg	Washington	DC	20515	202-225-2927	225-2525
Web: www.energycommerce.house.gov					
Government Reform Committee					
2157 Rayburn Bldg	Washington	DC	20515	202-225-5074	225-3974
Web: www.reform.house.gov					
Homeland Security Committee					
117 Ford House Office Bldg	Washington	DC	20515	202-226-8417	226-3399
Web: www.hsc.house.gov					
House Administration Committee					
1309 Longworth Bldg	Washington	DC	20515	202-225-2061	226-2774
Web: www.house.gov/cha					
House Committee on Foreign Affairs					
2170 Rayburn Bldg	Washington	DC	20515	202-225-5021	225-2035
Web: www.internationalrelations.house.gov					
Judiciary Committee 2138 Rayburn Bldg	Washington	DC	20515	202-225-3951	225-7680
Web: www.judiciary.house.gov					
Permanent Select Committee on Intelligence					
H-405 Capitol Bldg	Washington	DC	20515	202-225-4121	226-5068
TF: 877-858-9040 ■ *Web:* www.intelligence.house.gov					
Rules Committee H-312 Capitol Bldg	Washington	DC	20515	202-225-9191	225-1061
Web: www.rules.house.gov					
Science Committee 2320 Rayburn Bldg	Washington	DC	20515	202-225-6371	225-0113
Web: www.house.gov/science					
Select Committee on Ethics 220 Hart Bldg	Washington	DC	20510	202-224-2981	224-7416
Web: ethics.senate.gov					
Small Business Committee					
2361 Rayburn Bldg	Washington	DC	20515	202-225-5821	225-3587
Web: www.smallbusiness.house.gov					
Transportation & Infrastructure Committee					
2165 Rayburn Bldg	Washington	DC	20515	202-225-9446	225-6782
Web: www.house.gov/transportation					
Veterans Affairs Committee					
335 Cannon Bldg	Washington	DC	20515	202-225-3527	
Web: www.house.gov/va					
Ways & Means Committee					
1102 Longworth Bldg	Washington	DC	20515	202-225-3625	225-2610
Web: www.waysandmeans.house.gov					
Agriculture Nutrition & Forestry Committee					
SR-328A Russell Bldg	Washington	DC	20510	202-224-2035	228-2125
Web: agriculture.senate.gov					
Budget Committee					
624 Drksen Senate Bldg # 624D	Washington	DC	20510	202-224-0642	224-4835
Web: www.senate.gov					
Commerce Science & Transportation Committee					
508 Dirksen Bldg	Washington	DC	20510	202-224-5115	
Web: www.commerce.senate.gov					
Committee on Small Business & Entrepreneurship					
428A Russell Senate Office Bldg	Washington	DC	20510	202-224-5175	224-5619
Web: sbc.senate.gov					
Energy & Natural Resources Committee					
304 Dirksen Senate Bldg	Washington	DC	20510	202-224-4971	224-6163
Web: energy.senate.gov					
Environment & Public Works Committee					
410 Dirksen Senate Office Bldg	Washington	DC	20510	202-224-8832	224-1273
Web: epw.senate.gov					
Finance Committee					
219 Dirksen Senate Office Bldg	Washington	DC	20510	202-224-4515	228-0554
Web: finance.senate.gov					
Foreign Relations Committee					
446 Dirksen Senate Office Bldg	Washington	DC	20510	202-224-4651	228-3612
Web: foreign.senate.gov					
Health Education Labor & Pensions Committee					
428 Dirksen Bldg	Washington	DC	20510	202-224-5375	228-4000
Web: www.help.senate.gov					
Homeland Security & Governmental Affairs Committee					
340 Dirksen Bldg	Washington	DC	20510	202-224-4751	224-9603
Web: www.senate.gov/~gov_affairs					
Judiciary Committee SD-224 Dirksen Bldg	Washington	DC	20510	202-224-5225	224-9102
Web: www.judiciary.senate.gov					
Rules & Administration Committee					
305 Russell Bldg	Washington	DC	20510	202-224-6352	224-2401*
**Fax:* Admin ■ *Web:* rules.senate.gov					
Veterans Affairs Committee					
412 Russell Bldg	Washington	DC	20510	202-224-9126	224-9575
Web: veterans.senate.gov					
US Senate					
Standards of Official Conduct Committee					
HT-2 Capitol Bldg	Washington	DC	20515	202-225-7103	225-7392
Web: www.house.gov/ethics					
US Senate Committee on Indian Affairs					
838 Hart Bldg	Washington	DC	20510	202-224-2251	228-2589
Web: indian.senate.gov					
US Senate Select Committee on Intelligence					
211 Hart Senate Office Bldg	Washington	DC	20510	202-224-1700	224-1772
Web: intelligence.senate.gov					

345-2 US Senators, Representatives, Delegates

The circled letter S denotes that a listing is for a senator.

Alabama

				Phone	Fax
Jo Bonner (Rep R-AL)					
2236 Rayburn House Office Bldg	Washington	DC	20515	202-225-4931	225-0562
TF: 800-288-8721 ■ *Web:* bonner.house.gov					
Martha Roby (Rep R-AL)					
414 Cannon House Office Building	Washington	DC	20515	202-225-2901	225-8913
Web: roby.house.gov					
Mo Brooks (Rep R-AL)					
1641 Longworth House Office Building	Washington	DC	20515	202-225-4801	225-4392
Web: brooks.house.gov					
Ⓢ**Richard C Shelby (Sen R-AL)**					
304 Russell Senate Office Bldg	Washington	DC	20510	202-224-5744	224-3416
Web: shelby.senate.gov					
Robert Aderholt (Rep R-AL)					
2264 Rayburn House Office Bldg	Washington	DC	20515	202-225-4876	225-5587
Web: aderholt.house.gov					
Rogers Mike D (Rep R-AL) 2246 Rayburn Bldg	Washington	DC	20515	202-225-4921	225-2082
Web: bachus.house.gov					
Ⓢ**Sessions Jeff (Sen R-AL)** 335 Russell Bldg	Washington	DC	20510	202-224-4124	224-3149
Web: www.sessions.senate.gov					
Spencer Bachus (Rep R-AL)					
2246 Rayburn House Bldg	Washington	DC	20515	202-225-4921	225-2082
Web: bachus.house.gov					
Terri A Sewell (Rep D-AL)					
1133 Longworth House Office Building	Washington	DC	20515	202-225-2665	226-9567
Web: www.sewell.house.gov					

Alaska

				Phone	Fax
Don Young (Rep R-AK)					
2314 Rayburn House Office Bldg	Washington	DC	20515	202-225-5765	225-0425
Web: donyoung.house.gov					
Ⓢ**Murkowski Lisa (Sen R-AK)** 709 Hart Bldg	Washington	DC	20510	202-224-6665	224-5301
Web: www.murkowski.senate.gov					
Ⓢ**Stevens Ted (Sen D-AK)**					
111 Russell Senate Office Bldg	Washington	DC	20510	202-224-3004	224-2354
Web: begich.senate.gov					

American Samoa

				Phone	Fax

Name / Address	City	State	ZIP	Phone	Fax
Faleomavaega Eni FH (Del D-AS) 2422 Rayburn Bldg	Washington	DC	20515	202-225-8577	225-8757
Web: www.house.gov/faleomavaega					

Arizona

Name / Address	City	State	ZIP	Phone	Fax
Ben Quayle (Rep R-AZ) 1419 Longworth House Office Bldg	Washington	DC	20515	202-225-3361	225-3462
Web: quayle.house.gov					
David Schweikert (Rep R-AZ) 1205 Longworth House Office Bldg	Washington	DC	20515	202-225-2190	225-0096
Web: schweikert.house.gov					
Ed Pastor (Rep D-AZ) 2465 Rayburn House Office Building	Washington	DC	20515	202-225-4065	225-1655
Web: www.pastor.house.gov					
Flake Jeff (Rep R-AZ) 240 Cannon Bldg	Washington	DC	20515	202-225-2635	226-4386
Web: flake.house.gov					
Franks Trent (Rep R-AZ) 1237 Longworth Bldg	Washington	DC	20525	202-225-4576	225-6328
Web: www.house.gov/franks					
Gabrielle Giffords (Rep D-AZ) 1030 Longworth House Office Bldg	Washington	DC	20515	202-225-2542	225-0378
Web: giffords.house.gov					
Grijalva Raul M (Rep D-AZ) 1440 Longworth Bldg	Washington	DC	20515	202-225-2435	225-1541
Web: www.house.gov/grijalva					
Ⓢ**John McCain (Sen R-AZ)** 241 Russell Senate Office Bldg	Washington	DC	20510	202-224-2235	228-2862
Web: mccain.senate.gov/public					
Ⓢ**Jon Kyl (Sen R-AZ)** 730 Hart Bldg	Washington	DC	20510	202-224-4521	224-2207
Web: kyl.senate.gov					
Paul Gosar (Rep R-AZ) 418 Cannon Bldg	Washington	DC	20515	202-225-2315	226-9739
TF: 866-537-2800 ■ *Web:* www.gosar.house.gov					

Arkansas

Name / Address	City	State	ZIP	Phone	Fax
Ⓢ**John Boozman (Sen R-AR)** 320 Hart Senate Office Bldg	Washington	DC	20515	202-224-4843	228-1371
Web: boozman.senate.gov/public					
Ⓢ**Mark Pryor (Sen D-AR)** 255 Dirksen Senate Office Bldg	Washington	DC	20510	202-224-2353	228-0908
Web: pryor.senate.gov					
Rick Crawford (Rep R-AR) 1408 Longworth House Office Building	Washington	DC	20515	202-225-4076	225-5602
Web: www.crawford.house.gov					
Ross Mike (Rep D-AR) 314 Cannon Bldg	Washington	DC	20515	202-225-3772	225-1314
Web: www.house.gov/ross					
Snyder Vic (Rep R-AR) 1232 Longworth House Office Building	Washington	DC	20515	202-225-2506	225-5903
Web: griffin.house.gov					

California

Name / Address	City	State	ZIP	Phone	Fax
Adam B Schiff (Rep D-CA) 2411 Rayburn House Office Bldg	Washington	DC	20515	202-225-4176	225-5828
Web: schiff.house.gov					
Anna G Eshoo (Rep D-CA) 205 Cannon Bldg	Washington	DC	20515	202-225-8104	225-8890
Web: eshoo.house.gov					
Baca Joe (Rep D-CA) 1527 Longworth Bldg	Washington	DC	20515	202-225-6161	225-8671
Web: www.house.gov/baca					
Ⓢ**Barbara Boxer (Sen D-CA)** 112 Hart Bldg	Washington	DC	20510	202-224-3553	224-0454
Web: boxer.senate.gov					
Bilbray Brian (Rep R-CA) 227 Cannon Bldg	Washington	DC	20515	202-225-0508	225-2558
Web: www.house.gov/bilbray					
Bono Mary (Rep R-CA) 104 Cannon Bldg	Washington	DC	20515	202-225-5330	225-2961
Web: bono.house.gov					
Brad Sherman (Rep D-CA) 2242 Rayburn House Office Building	Washington	DC	20515	202-225-5911	225-5879
Web: www.bradsherman.house.gov					
Buck McKeon (Rep R-CA) 2184 Rayburn House Office Building	Washington	DC	20515	202-225-1956	226-0683
Web: mckeon.house.gov					
Cardoza Dennis (Rep D-CA) 435 Cannon Bldg	Washington	DC	20515	202-225-6131	225-0819
Web: www.house.gov/cardoza					
Costa Jim (Rep D-CA) 1314 Longworth House Office Bldg	Washington	DC	20515	202-225-3341	225-9308
Web: www.house.gov/costa					
Daniel E Lungren (Rep R-CA) 2313 Rayburn House Office Building	Washington	DC	20515	202-225-5716	226-1298
Web: lungren.house.gov					
David Dreier (Rep R-CA) 233 Cannon Bldg	Washington	DC	20515	202-225-2305	225-7018
Web: dreier.house.gov/index.shtml					
Davis Susan A (Rep D-CA) 1526 Longworth Bldg	Washington	DC	20515	202-225-2040	225-2948
Web: www.house.gov/susandavis					
Devin Nunes (Rep R-CA) Longworth House Office Bldg Suite 1013	Washington	DC	20515	202-225-2523	225-3404
Web: www.nunes.house.gov					
Doolittle John T (Rep D-CA) 205 Cannon Building	Washington	DC	20515	202-225-8104	
Web: eshoo.house.gov					
Ed Royce (Rep R-CA) 2185 Rayburn Bldg	Washington	DC	20515	202-225-4111	226-0335
Web: www.royce.house.gov					
Ⓢ**Feinstein Dianne (Sen D-CA)** 331 Hart Bldg	Washington	DC	20510	202-224-3841	228-3954
Web: www.feinstein.senate.gov					
Filner Bob (Rep D-CA) 2428 Rayburn Bldg	Washington	DC	20515	202-225-8045	225-9073
Web: filner.house.gov					
Gallegly Elton (Rep R-CA) 2309 Rayburn Bldg	Washington	DC	20515	202-225-5811	225-1100
Web: www.house.gov/gallegly					
Gary G Miller (Rep R-CA) 2349 Rayburn House office Bldg	Washington	DC	20515	202-225-3201	226-6962
Web: www.garymiller.house.gov					
George Miller (Rep D-CA) 2205 Rayburn Bldg	Washington	DC	20515	202-225-2095	225-5609
Web: georgemiller.house.gov					
Grace Flores Napolitano (Rep D-CA) 1610 Longworth Bldg	Washington	DC	20515	202-225-5256	225-0027
Web: napolitano.house.gov					
Herger Wally (Rep R-CA) 2268 Rayburn Bldg	Washington	DC	20515	202-225-3076	226-0852
Web: www.house.gov/herger					
Howard L Berman (Rep D-CA) 2221 Rayburn House Office Bldg	Washington	DC	20515	202-225-4695	225-3196
Web: www.house.gov/berman					
Hunter Duncan (Rep R-CA) 2265 Rayburn Bldg	Washington	DC	20515	202-225-5672	225-0235
Web: www.hunter.house.gov					
Issa Darrell E (Rep R-CA) 2347 Rayburn House Office Building	Washington	DC	20515	202-225-3906	225-3303
Web: www.issa.house.gov					
Jackie Speier (Rep D-CA) 211 Cannon House Office Bldg	Washington	DC	20515	202-225-3531	226-4183
Web: speier.house.gov					
Jeff Denham (Rep R-CA) 1605 Longworth House Office Building	Washington	DC	20515	202-225-4540	225-3402
Web: denham.house.gov					
Jerry Lewis (Rep R-CA) 2112 Rayburn House Office Bldg	Washington	DC	20515	202-225-5861	225-6498
Web: www.jerrylewis.house.gov					
Jerry McNerney (Rep D-CA) 1210 Longworth House Office Bldg	Washington	DC	20515	202-225-1947	225-4060
Web: mcnerney.house.gov					
John Campbell (Rep R-CA) 1507 Longworth House Office Building	Washington	DC	20515	202-225-5611	225-9177
Web: campbell.house.gov					
Judy Chu (Rep D-CA) 1520 Longworth House Office Building	Washington	DC	20515	202-225-5464	225-5467
Web: chu.house.gov					
Ken Calvert (Rep R-CA) 2269 Rayburn Bldg	Washington	DC	20515	202-225-1986	225-2004
Web: calvert.house.gov					
Lee Barbara (Rep D-CA) 2444 Rayburn Bldg	Washington	DC	20515	202-225-2661	225-9817
Web: www.house.gov/lee					
Lofgren Zoe (Rep D-CA) 102 Cannon Bldg	Washington	DC	20515	202-225-3072	225-3336
Web: lofgren.house.gov					
Lois Capps (Rep D-CA) 2231 Rayburn House Office Bldg	Washington	DC	20515	202-225-3601	225-5632
Web: www.capps.house.gov					
Loretta Sanchez (Rep D-CA) 1114 Longworth House Office Building	Washington	DC	20515	202-225-2965	225-5859
Web: www.lorettasanchez.house.gov					
Lynn C Woolsey (Rep D-CA) 2263 Rayburn Bldg	Washington	DC	20515	202-225-5161	225-5163
Web: woolsey.house.gov					
McCarthy Kevin (Rep R-CA) 1523 Longworth Bldg	Washington	DC	20515	202-225-2915	225-2908
Web: www.kevinmccarthy.house.gov					
Michael M Honda (Rep D-CA) 1713 Longworth House Office Building	Washington	DC	20515	202-225-2631	225-2699
Web: www.honda.house.gov					
Pelosi Nancy (Rep D-CA) 235 Cannon Bldg	Washington	DC	20515	202-225-4965	225-4188
Web: www.house.gov/pelosi					
Roybal-Allard Lucille (Rep D-CA) 2330 Rayburn Bldg	Washington	DC	20515	202-225-1766	226-0350
Web: roybal-allard.house.gov					
Sam Farr (Rep D-CA) 1126 Longworth House Office Building	Washington	DC	20515	202-225-2861	225-6791
Web: www.farr.house.gov					
Sanchez Linda T (Rep D-CA) 1222 Longworth Bldg	Washington	DC	20515	202-225-6676	226-1012
Web: www.house.gov/lindasanchez					
Stark Pete (Rep D-CA) 239 Cannon Bldg	Washington	DC	20515	202-225-5065	226-3805
Web: www.stark.house.gov					
Tauscher Ellen (Rep D-CA) 228 Cannon House Office Building	Washington	DC	20515	202-225-1880	225-5914
Web: garamendi.house.gov					
Waters Maxine (Rep D-CA) 2344 Rayburn Bldg	Washington	DC	20515	202-225-2201	225-7854
Web: waters.house.gov					
Watson Diane E (Rep D-CA) 408 Cannon House Office Building	Washington	DC	20515	202-225-7084	225-2422
Web: karenbass.house.gov					
Waxman Henry A (Rep D-CA) 2204 Rayburn Bldg	Washington	DC	20515	202-225-3976	225-4099
Web: waxman.house.gov					
Xavier Becerra (Rep D-CA) 1119 Longworth Bldg	Washington	DC	20515	202-225-6235	225-2202
Web: becerra.house.gov					

Colorado

Name / Address	City	State	ZIP	Phone	Fax
Ⓢ**Allard Wayne (Sen D-CO)** 458 Russell Senate Office Building	Washington	DC	20510	202-224-5852	228-5036
Web: bennet.senate.gov					
DeGette Diana (Rep D-CO) 2421 Rayburn Bldg	Washington	DC	20515	202-225-4431	225-5657
Web: degette.house.gov					
Doug Lamborn (Rep R-CO) 437 Cannon House Office Building	Washington	DC	20515	202-225-4422	226-2638
Web: lamborn.house.gov					
Ed Perlmutter (Rep D-CO) 1221 Longworth House Office Bldg	Washington	DC	20515	202-225-2645	225-5278
Web: perlmutter.house.gov					
Ⓢ**Mark Udall (Sen D-CO)** Hart Office Bldg Suite SH-328	Washington	DC	20515	202-224-5941	224-6471
Web: markudall.senate.gov					
Mike Coffman (Rep R-CO) 1222 Longworth House Office Building	Washington	DC	20515	202-225-7882	226-4623
Web: coffman.house.gov					
Scott Tipton (Rep R-CO) 218 Cannon House Office Building	Washington	DC	20515	202-225-4761	226-9669
Web: www.tipton.house.gov					

Connecticut

Name / Address	City	State	ZIP	Phone	Fax
Chris Murphy (Rep D-CT) 412 Cannon House Office Building	Washington	DC	20515	202-225-4476	225-5933
Web: chrismurphy.house.gov					
James A Himes (Rep D-CT) 119 Cannon House Office Bldg	Washington	DC	20515	202-225-5541	225-9629
Web: www.himes.house.gov					
Joe Courtney (Rep D-CT) 215 Cannon House Office Bldg	Washington	DC	20515	202-225-2076	225-4977
Web: courtney.house.gov					
Ⓢ**Joseph Lieberman I (Sen D-CT)** 706 Hart Office Bldg	Washington	DC	20510	202-224-4041	224-9750
Web: lieberman.senate.gov					
Larson John B (Rep D-CT) 1005 Longworth Bldg	Washington	DC	20515	202-225-2265	225-1031
Web: www.house.gov/larson					
Rosa L DeLauro (Rep D-CT) 2262 Rayburn House Office Building	Washington	DC	20515	202-225-3661	225-4890
Web: www.delauro.house.gov					

Delaware

				Phone	Fax
John C Carney Jr (Rep D-DE) 1429 Longworth House Office Building Web: johncarney.house.gov	Washington	DC	20515	202-225-4165	225-2291
Ⓢ**Thomas Carper (Sen D-DE)** 513 Hart Bldg. Web: carper.senate.gov	Washington	DC	20510	202-224-2441	228-2190

District of Columbia

				Phone	Fax
Brown-Waite Ginny (Rep R-DC) 414 Cannon Bldg Web: www.house.gov	Washington	DC	20515	202-225-1002	226-6559
Eleanor Holmes Norton (Del D-DC) 2136 Rayburn House Office Building Web: www.norton.house.gov	Washington	DC	20515	202-225-8050	225-3002

Florida

				Phone	Fax
Allen West (Rep R-FL) 1708 Longworth House Office Building Web: west.house.gov	Washington	DC	20515	202-225-3026	225-8398
Ander Crenshaw (Rep R-FL) 440 Cannon House Office Bldg. Web: crenshaw.house.gov	Washington	DC	20515	202-225-2501	225-2504
Ⓢ**Bill Nelson (Sen D-FL)** 716 Senate Hart Office Bldg Web: billnelson.senate.gov	Washington	DC	20510	202-224-5274	228-2183
Bill Posey (Rep R-FL) 120 Cannon House Office Building. Web: posey.house.gov	Washington	DC	20515	202-225-3671	225-3516
Boyd Allen (Rep D-FL) 1229 Longworth House Office Building Web: southerland.house.gov	Washington	DC	20515	202-225-5235	225-5615
Brown Corrine (Rep D-FL) 2336 Rayburn Bldg Web: www.house.gov	Washington	DC	20515	202-225-0123	225-2256
Connie Mack IV (Rep R-FL) 115 Cannon Bldg Web: mack.house.gov	Washington	DC	20515	202-225-2536	226-0439
Daniel Webster (Rep D-FL) 1039 LHouse Office Building Web: webster.house.gov	Washington	DC	20515	202-225-2176	225-0999
Diaz-Balart Mario (Rep R-FL) 328 Cannon Bldg. Web: mariodiazbalart.house.gov	Washington	DC	20515	202-225-2778	226-0346
Frederica Wilson (Rep D-FL) 208 Cannon House Office Building. Web: wilson.house.gov	Washington	DC	20515	202-225-4506	226-0777
Gus Michael Bilirakis (Rep R-FL) 407 Cannon House Office Building. Web: www.bilirakis.house.gov	Washington	DC	20515	202-225-5755	225-4085
Jeff Miller (Rep R-FL) 2416 Rayburn House Office Bldg Web: jeffmiller.house.gov	Washington	DC	20515	202-225-4136	225-3414
John L Mica (Rep R-FL) 2187 Rayburn House Office Bldg Web: www.mica.house.gov	Washington	DC	20515	202-225-4035	226-0821
Kathy Castor (Rep D-FL) 137 Cannon House Office Bldg. Web: castor.house.gov	Washington	DC	20515	202-225-3376	225-5652
Ⓢ**Martinez Mel R (Sen R-FL)** 317 Hart Senate Office Bldg Web: rubio.senate.gov/public	Washington	DC	20510	202-224-3041	
Putnam Adam (Rep R-FL) 404 Cannon House Office Building. TF: 866-534-3530 ■ Web: dennisross.house.gov	Washington	DC	20515	202-225-1252	226-0585
Ros-Lehtinen Ileana (Rep R-FL) 2160 Rayburn Bldg. Web: ros-lehtinen.house.gov	Washington	DC	20515	202-225-3931	225-5620
Sandy Adams (Rep R-FL) 216 Cannon House Office Building. Web: www.adams.house.gov	Washington	DC	20515	202-225-2706	226-6299
Ted Deutch (Rep D-FL) 1024 Longworth House Office Bldg Web: wexler.house.gov	Washington	DC	20515	202-225-3001	225-5974
Tom Rooney (Rep R-FL) 1529 Longworth House Office Building Web: rooney.house.gov	Washington	DC	20515	202-225-5792	225-3132
Vern Buchanan (Rep R-FL) 221 Cannon House Office Building. Web: buchanan.house.gov	Washington	DC	20515	202-225-5015	226-0828
Wasserman Schultz Debbie (Rep D-FL) 118 Cannon Bldg Web: wassermanschultz.house.gov	Washington	DC	20515	202-225-7931	226-2052
Young CW Bill (Rep R-FL) 2407 Rayburn Bldg Web: www.house.gov/young	Washington	DC	20515	202-225-5961	225-9764

Georgia

				Phone	Fax
Barrow John (Rep D-GA) 2202 Rayburn House Office Building Web: barrow.house.gov	Washington	DC	20515	202-225-2823	225-3377
Ⓢ**Chambliss Saxby (Sen R-GA)** 416 Russell Bldg Web: www.chambliss.senate.gov	Washington	DC	20510	202-224-3521	224-0103
David Scott (Rep D-GA) 225 Cannon House Office Bldg. Web: davidscott.house.gov	Washington	DC	20515	202-225-2939	225-4628
Gingrey Phil (Rep R-GA) 119 Cannon Bldg Web: gingrey.house.gov	Washington	DC	20515	202-225-2931	225-2944
Henry C Johnson (Rep D-GA) 1427 Longworth House Office Building Web: hankjohnson.house.gov	Washington	DC	20515	202-225-1605	226-0691
Ⓢ**Isakson Johnny (Sen R-GA)** 120 Russell Bldg. Web: www.isakson.senate.gov	Washington	DC	20510	202-224-3643	228-0724
Jack Kingston (Rep R-GA) 2372 Rayburn House Office Building Web: www.kingston.house.gov	Washington	DC	20515	202-225-5831	226-2269
John Lewis (Rep D-GA) 343 Cannon House Office Bldg. Web: johnlewis.house.gov	Washington	DC	20515	202-225-3801	225-0351
Marshall James C (Rep R-GA) 516 Cannon House Office Building. Web: austinscott.house.gov	Washington	DC	20515	202-225-6531	225-3013
Rob Woodall (Rep R-GA) 1725 Longworth House Office Building Web: woodall.house.gov	Washington	DC	20515	202-225-4272	225-4696
Sanford D Bishop Jr (Rep D-GA) 2429 Rayburn House Office Building Web: www.bishop.house.gov	Washington	DC	20515	202-225-3631	225-2203
Tom Graves (Rep R-GA) 1113 Longworth House Office Bldg Web: www.tomgraves.house.gov	Washington	DC	20515	202-225-5211	225-8272
Tom Price (Rep R-GA) 403 Cannon House Office Bldg. Web: tomprice.house.gov	Washington	DC	20515	202-225-4501	225-4656
Westmoreland Lynn (Rep R-GA) 1213 Longworth Bldg. Web: westmoreland.house.gov	Washington	DC	20515	202-225-5901	225-2515

Guam

				Phone	Fax
Bordallo Madeleine Z (Del D-GU) 427 Cannon Bldg Web: www.house.gov/bordallo	Washington	DC	20515	202-225-1188	226-0341

Hawaii

				Phone	Fax
Ⓢ**Akaka Daniel K (Sen D-HI)** 141 Hart Bldg Web: www.akaka.senate.gov	Washington	DC	20510	202-224-6361	224-2126
Ⓢ**Byrd Robert C (Sen D-HI)** 722 Hart Bldg Web: inouye.senate.gov/Home/Home_1.cfm	Washington	DC	20510	202-224-3934	224-6747
Colleen Hanabusa (Rep D-HI) 238 Cannon House Office Building. Web: www.hanabusa.house.gov	Washington	DC	20515	202-225-2726	225-0688
Ⓢ**Inouye Daniel K (Sen D-HI)** 722 Hart Bldg. Web: www.inouye.senate.gov	Washington	DC	20510	202-224-3934	224-6747
Mazie K Hirono (Rep D-HI) 1410 Longworth House Office Building Web: hirono.house.gov	Washington	DC	20515	202-225-4906	225-4987

Idaho

				Phone	Fax
Ⓢ**Mike Crapo (Sen R-ID)** 239 Dirksen Senate Bldg Web: crapo.senate.gov	Washington	DC	20510	202-224-6142	228-1375
Mike Simpson (Rep R-ID) 2312 Rayburn House Office Bldg Web: www.simpson.house.gov	Washington	DC	20515	202-225-5531	225-8216
Raul Labrador (Rep R-ID) 1523 Longworth House Office Building Web: labrador.house.gov	Washington	DC	20515	202-225-6611	225-3029

Illinois

				Phone	Fax
Aaron Schock (Rep R-IL) 328 Cannon House Office Bldg. Web: www.schock.house.gov	Washington	DC	20515	202-225-6201	225-9249
Adam Kinzinger (Rep R-IL) 1218 Longworth House Office Building Web: kinzinger.house.gov	Washington	DC	20515	202-225-3635	225-3521
Bean Melissa L (Rep D-IL) 432 Cannon House Office Building. Web: walsh.house.gov	Washington	DC	20515	202-225-3711	225-7830
Bobby L Rush (Rep D-IL) 2268 Rayburn House Office Bldg Web: www.rush.house.gov	Washington	DC	20515	202-225-4372	226-0333
Bobby Schilling (Rep R-IL) 507 Cannon House Office Building. Web: schilling.house.gov	Washington	DC	20515	202-225-5905	225-5396
Daniel Lipinski (Rep D-IL) 1717 Longworth House Office Building TF: 866-822-5701 ■ Web: www.lipinski.house.gov	Washington	DC	20515	202-225-5701	225-1012
Davis Danny (Rep D-IL) 2159 Rayburn Bldg. Web: www.davis.house.gov	Washington	DC	20515	202-225-5006	225-5641
Donald Manzullo (Rep R-IL) 2228 Rayburn Bldg Web: manzullo.house.gov	Washington	DC	20515	202-225-5676	225-5284
Jackson Jesse Jr (Rep D-IL) 2419 Rayburn Bldg. Web: www.house.gov/jackson	Washington	DC	20515	202-225-0773	225-0899
James T Walsh (Rep R-IL) 432 Cannon House Office Building. Web: walsh.house.gov	Washington	DC	20515	202-225-3711	225-7830
Janice D Schakowsky (Rep D-IL) 2367 Rayburn House Office Building Web: www.schakowsky.house.gov	Washington	DC	20515	202-225-2111	226-6890
Jerry F Costello (Rep D-IL) 2408 Rayburn House Office Building Web: www.costello.house.gov	Washington	DC	20515	202-225-5661	225-0285

	City	State	Zip	Phone	Fax
John Shimkus (Rep R-IL) 2452 Rayburn House Office Bldg *Web:* www.shimkus.house.gov	Washington	DC	20515	202-225-5271	225-5880
Johnson Timothy V (Rep R-IL) 1207 Longworth Bldg *Web:* timjohnson.house.gov	Washington	DC	20515	202-225-2371	226-0791
Judy Biggert (Rep R-IL) 2113 Rayburn House Office Bldg *Web:* judybiggert.house.gov	Washington	DC	20515	202-225-3515	225-9420
Kirk Mark Steven (Rep D-IL) 212 Cannon House Office Building *Web:* dold.house.gov	Washington	DC	20515	202-225-4835	225-0837
Luis V Gutierrez (Rep D-IL) 2266 Rayburn Bldg *Web:* www.gutierrez.house.gov	Washington	DC	20515	202-225-8203	225-7810
Ⓢ**mark kirk (Sen R-IL)** 524 hart bldg *Web:* www.kirk.senate.gov	Washington	DC	20510	202-224-2854	228-4611
Michael Quigley (Rep D-IL) 1124 Longworth House Office Bldg *Web:* www.quigley.house.gov	Washington	DC	20515	202-225-4061	225-5603
Randy Hultgren (Rep R-IL) 427 Cannon House Office Building *Web:* hultgren.house.gov	Washington	DC	20515	202-225-2976	225-0697
Ⓢ**Richard J Durbin (Sen D-IL)** 711 Hart Senate Bldg *Web:* durbin.senate.gov	Washington	DC	20510	202-224-2152	228-0400
Roskam Peter J (Rep R-IL) 507 Cannon Bldg *Web:* roskam.house.gov/default.aspx	Washington	DC	20515	202-225-4561	225-1166

Indiana

	City	State	Zip	Phone	Fax
Andre Carson (Rep D-IN) 425 Cannon House Office Building *Web:* carson.house.gov	Washington	DC	20515	202-225-4011	225-5633
Dan Burton (Rep R-IN) 2308 Rayburn House Office Bldg *Web:* www.burton.house.gov	Washington	DC	20515	202-225-2276	225-0016
Joe Donnelly (Rep D-IN) 1530 Longworth House Office Building *Web:* donnelly.house.gov	Washington	DC	20515	202-225-3915	225-6798
Larry Bucshon (Rep R-IN) 1123 Longworth House Office Building *Web:* bucshon.house.gov	Washington	DC	20515	202-225-4636	225-3284
Ⓢ**Lugar Richard G (Sen R-IN)** 306 Hart Bldg *Web:* www.lugar.senate.gov	Washington	DC	20510	202-224-4814	228-0360
Mike Pence (Rep R-IN) 100 Cannon House Office Building *Web:* mikepence.house.gov	Washington	DC	20515	202-225-3021	225-3382
Todd Rokita (Rep R-IN) 236 Cannon House Office Building *Web:* rokita.house.gov	Washington	DC	20515	202-225-5037	226-0544
Todd Young (Rep R-IN) 1721 Longworth House Office Bldg *Web:* toddyoung.house.gov	Washington	DC	20515	202-225-5315	226-6866
Visclosky Peter J (Rep D-IN) 2256 Rayburn Bldg *Web:* visclosky.house.gov	Washington	DC	20515	202-225-2461	225-2493

Iowa

	City	State	Zip	Phone	Fax
Boswell Leonard L (Rep D-IA) 1427 Longworth Bldg *Web:* boswell.house.gov	Washington	DC	20515	202-225-3806	225-5608
Bruce Braley (Rep D-IA) 1727 Longworth House Office Building *Web:* braley.house.gov	Washington	DC	20515	202-225-2911	225-6666
Ⓢ**Charles E Grassley (Sen R-IA)** 135 Hart Senate Office Bldg *Web:* grassley.senate.gov	Washington	DC	20510	202-224-3744	224-6020
David Loebsack (Rep D-IA) 1527 Longworth House Office Bldg *Web:* loebsack.house.gov	Washington	DC	20515	202-225-6576	226-0757
Steve King (Rep R-IA) 1131 Longworth Office Bldg *Web:* www.steveking.house.gov	Washington	DC	20515	202-225-4426	225-3193
Ⓢ**Tom Harkin (Sen D-IA)** 731 Hart Senate Office Bldg *Web:* harkin.senate.gov	Washington	DC	20510	202-224-3254	224-9369
Tom Latham (Rep R-IA) 2217 Rayburn House Office Building *TF:* 866-428-5642 ■ *Web:* www.tomlatham.house.gov	Washington	DC	20515	202-225-5476	225-3301

Kansas

	City	State	Zip	Phone	Fax
Ⓢ**Brownback Sam (Sen R-KS)** Russell Senate Office Building *Web:* moran.senate.gov	Washington	DC	20510	202-224-6521	228-6966
Ⓢ**Jerry Moran (Sen R-KS)** Russell Senate Office Bldg Rm 354 *Web:* moran.senate.gov	Washington	DC	20515	202-224-6521	228-6966
Kevin Yoder (Rep R-KS) 214 Cannon House Office Building *Web:* yoder.house.gov	Washington	DC	20515	202-225-2865	225-2807
Lynn Jenkins (Rep R-KS) 1122 Longworth House Office Building *Web:* lynnjenkins.house.gov	Washington	DC	20515	202-225-6601	225-7986
Michael Richard Pompeo (Rep R-KS) 107 Cannon House Office Building *Web:* www.pompeo.house.gov	Washington	DC	20515	202-225-6216	225-3489
Ⓢ**Roberts Pat (Sen R-KS)** 109 Hart Bldg *Web:* www.roberts.senate.gov	Washington	DC	20510	202-224-4774	224-3514

Kentucky

	City	State	Zip	Phone	Fax
Ben Chandler (Rep D-KY) 1504 Longworth Bldg *Web:* chandler.house.gov	Washington	DC	20515	202-225-4706	225-2122
Ed Whitfield (Rep R-KY) 2368 Rayburn House Office Building *TF:* 800-328-5629 ■ *Web:* www.whitfield.house.gov	Washington	DC	20515	202-225-3115	225-3547
Geoff Davis (Rep R-KY) 1119 Longworth House Office Bldg *Web:* geoffdavis.house.gov	Washington	DC	20515	202-225-3465	225-0003
John Yarmuth (Rep D-KY) 435 Cannon House Office Bldg *Web:* yarmuth.house.gov	Washington	DC	20515	202-225-5401	225-5776
Lewis Ron (Rep R-KY) 308 Cannon House Office Building *Web:* www.house.gov/ronlewis	Washington	DC	20515	202-225-3501	226-2019
Ⓢ**McConnell Mitch (Sen R-KY)** 361A Russell Bldg *Web:* www.mcconnell.senate.gov/public	Washington	DC	20510	202-224-2541	224-2499
Rogers Harold (Rep R-KY) 2406 Rayburn Bldg *Web:* halrogers.house.gov	Washington	DC	20515	202-225-4601	225-0940

Louisiana

	City	State	Zip	Phone	Fax
Alexander Rodney M (Rep R-LA) 316 Cannon Bldg *Web:* alexander.house.gov	Washington	DC	20515	202-225-8490	225-5639
Cedric L Richmond (Rep D-LA) 415 Cannon House Office Building *Web:* www.richmond.house.gov	Washington	DC	20515	202-225-6636	225-1988
Charles W Boustany Jr (Rep R-LA) 1431 Longworth House Office Bldg *Web:* boustany.house.gov	Washington	DC	20515	202-225-2031	225-5724
Ⓢ**David Vitter (Sen R-LA)** 516 Hart Bldg *Web:* vitter.senate.gov/public	Washington	DC	20510	202-224-4623	228-5061
Jeff Landry (Rep R-LA) 206 Cannon Bldg *Web:* landry.house.gov	Washington	DC	20515	202-225-4031	226-3944
John C. Fleming (Rep R-LA) 416 Cannon House Office Building *Web:* fleming.house.gov	Washington	DC	20515	202-225-2777	225-8039
Ⓢ**Mary Landrieu (Sen D-LA)** 431 Dirksen Senate Office Bldg *Web:* landrieu.senate.gov	Washington	DC	20510	202-224-5824	224-9735
Scalise Steve (Rep R-LA) 429 Cannon House Office Building *Web:* www.scalise.house.gov	Washington	DC	20515	202-225-3015	225-0739

Maine

	City	State	Zip	Phone	Fax
Chellie Pingree (Rep D-ME) 1318 Longworth House Office Building *Web:* pingree.house.gov	Washington	DC	20515	202-225-6116	225-5590
Ⓢ**Collins Susan (Sen R-ME)** 413 Dirksen Bldg *Web:* collins.senate.gov	Washington	DC	20510	202-224-2523	224-2693
Mike Michaud (Rep D-ME) 1724 Longworth House Office Bldg *Web:* michaud.house.gov	Washington	DC	20515	202-225-6306	225-2943
Ⓢ**Olympia J Snowe (Sen R-ME)** 154 Russell Senate Office Bldg *TF:* 800-432-1599 ■ *Web:* snowe.senate.gov	Washington	DC	20510	202-224-5344	224-1946

Maryland

	City	State	Zip	Phone	Fax
Andy Harris (Rep R-MD) 506 Cannon House Office Bldg *Web:* harris.house.gov	Washington	DC	20515	202-225-5311	225-0254
Ⓢ**Barbara A Mikulski (Sen D-MD)** 503 Hart Senate Office Bldg *Web:* mikulski.senate.gov	Washington	DC	20510	202-224-4654	224-8858
Ⓢ**Benjamin L Cardin (Sen D-MD)** 509 Hart Senate Office Bldg *Web:* cardin.senate.gov	Washington	DC	20510	202-224-4524	224-1651
Christopher Van Hollen Jr (Rep D-MD) 1707 Longworth House Office Building *Web:* www.vanhollen.house.gov	Washington	DC	20515	202-225-5341	225-0375
Cummings Elijah (Rep D-MD) 2235 Rayburn Bldg *Web:* cummings.house.gov	Washington	DC	20515	202-225-4741	225-3178
Donna Edwards (Rep D-MD) 318 Cannon House Office Bldg *Web:* donnaedwards.house.gov	Washington	DC	20515	202-225-8699	225-8714
John P Sarbanes (Rep D-MD) 2444 Rayburn House Office Building *Web:* sarbanes.house.gov	Washington	DC	20515	202-225-4016	225-9219
Roscoe G Bartlett (Rep R-MD) 2412 Rayburn House Office Bldg *Web:* www.bartlett.house.gov	Washington	DC	20515	202-225-2721	225-2193
Ruppersberger Dutch (Rep D-MD) 2453 Rayburn House Office Building *Web:* www.dutch.house.gov	Washington	DC	20515	202-225-3061	225-3094

Massachusetts

	City	State	Zip	Phone	Fax
Capuano Michael E (Rep D-MA) 1530 Longworth Bldg *Web:* www.house.gov/capuano	Washington	DC	20515	202-225-5111	225-9322
Edward J Markey (Rep D-MA) 2108 Rayburn House office Bldg *Web:* www.markey.house.gov	Washington	DC	20515	202-225-2836	226-0092
Frank Barney (Rep D-MA) 2252 Rayburn Bldg *Web:* www.house.gov/frank	Washington	DC	20515	202-225-5931	225-0182
Ⓢ**John F Kerry (Sen D-MA)** 218 Russell Bldg 2nd Fl *Web:* kerry.senate.gov	Washington	DC	20510	202-224-2742	224-8525
Ⓢ**Kennedy Edward M (Sen R-MA)** 359 Dirksen Senate Office Bldg *Web:* scottbrown.senate.gov	Washington	DC	20510	202-224-4543	228-2646
Lynch Stephen F (Rep D-MA) 221 Cannon Bldg	Washington	DC	20515	202-225-8273	225-3984

				Phone	Fax
Web: lynch.house.gov					
McGovern James P (Rep D-MA) 438 Cannon Bldg *Web:* mcgovern.house.gov	Washington	DC	20515	202-225-6101	225-5759
Neal Richard E (Rep D-MA) 2208 Rayburn Bldg *Web:* www.house.gov/neal	Washington	DC	20515	202-225-5601	225-8112
Olver John W (Rep D-MA) 1111 Longworth Bldg *Web:* olver.house.gov	Washington	DC	20515	202-225-5335	226-1224
Tierney John F (Rep D-MA) 2238 Rayburn Bldg *Web:* tierney.house.gov	Washington	DC	20515	202-225-8020	225-5915
William R Keating (Rep D-MA) 2454 Rayburn Bldg *Web:* www.keating.house.gov	Washington	DC	20515	202-225-3111	225-5658

Michigan

				Phone	Fax
Bill Huizenga (Rep R-MI) 1217 Longworth House Office Building *Web:* huizenga.house.gov	Washington	DC	20515	202-225-4401	226-0779
Camp Dave (Rep R-MI) 341 Cannon House Office Bldg *TF:* 800-342-2455 ■ *Web:* camp.house.gov	Washington	DC	20515	202-225-3561	225-9679
Candice S Miller (Rep R-MI) 1034 Longworth House Office Building *Web:* candicemiller.house.gov	Washington	DC	20515	202-225-2106	226-1169
Ⓢ**Carl Levin (Sen D-MI)** 269 Russell Office Bldg *Web:* levin.senate.gov	Washington	DC	20510	202-224-6221	224-1388
Conyers John Jr (Rep D-MI) 2426 Rayburn Bldg *Web:* conyers.house.gov	Washington	DC	20515	202-225-5126	225-0072
Dan Benishek (Rep R-MI) 514 Cannon House Office Building *Web:* www.benishek.house.gov	Washington	DC	20515	202-225-4735	225-4744
Ⓢ**Debbie Stabenow (Sen D-MI)** 133 Hart Bldg *Web:* stabenow.senate.gov	Washington	DC	20510	202-224-4822	228-0325
Dingell John D (Rep D-MI) 2328 Rayburn Bldg *Web:* www.house.gov	Washington	DC	20515	202-225-4071	226-0371
Fred Upton (Rep R-MI) 2183 Rayburn House Office Bldg *Web:* www.upton.house.gov	Washington	DC	20515	202-225-3761	225-4986
Gary Peters (Rep D-MI) 1609 Longworth House Office Building *Web:* peters.house.gov	Washington	DC	20515	202-225-5802	226-2356
Hansen Clarke (Rep D-MI) 1319 Longworth House Office Building *Web:* www.hansenclarke.house.gov	Washington	DC	20515	202-225-2261	225-5730
Justin Amash (Rep R-MI) 114 Cannon House Office Building *Web:* www.amash.house.gov	Washington	DC	20515	202-225-3831	225-5144
Kildee Dale E (Rep D-MI) 2107 Rayburn Bldg *Web:* www.house.gov/kildee	Washington	DC	20515	202-225-3611	225-6393
Levin Sander M (Rep D-MI) 1236 Longworth Bldg *Web:* levin.house.gov	Washington	DC	20515	202-225-4961	226-1033
Mike Rogers (Rep R-MI) 133 Cannon House Office Bldg *TF:* 877-333-6453 ■ *Web:* www.mikerogers.house.gov	Washington	DC	20515	202-225-4872	225-5820
Thaddeus G McCotter (Rep R-MI) 2243 Rayburn House Office Bldg *Web:* mccotter.house.gov	Washington	DC	20515	202-225-8171	225-2667
Tim Walberg (Rep R-MI) 418 Cannon House Office Building *Web:* walberg.house.gov	Washington	DC	20515	202-225-6276	225-6281

Minnesota

				Phone	Fax
Betty McCollum (Rep D-MN) 1714 Longworth House Office Building *Web:* www.mccollum.house.gov	Washington	DC	20515	202-225-6631	225-1968
Chip Cravaack (Rep D-MN) 508 Cannon House Office Building *Web:* cravaack.house.gov	Washington	DC	20515	202-225-6211	225-0699
Ⓢ**Coleman Norm (Sen D-MN)** 320 Hart Senate Office Bldg *TF:* 800-642-6041 ■ *Web:* franken.senate.gov	Washington	DC	20510	202-224-5641	
John P Kline (Rep R-MN) 2439 Rayburn House Office Bldg *Web:* www.kline.house.gov	Washington	DC	20515	202-225-2271	225-2595
Keith Ellison (Rep D-MN) 1027 Longworth Bldg *Web:* ellison.house.gov	Washington	DC	20515	202-225-4755	225-4886
Ⓢ**Klobuchar Amy (Sen D-MN)** 302 Hart Bldg *Web:* www.klobuchar.senate.gov	Washington	DC	20510	202-224-3244	228-2186
Michele Bachmann (Rep R-MN) 103 Cannon House Office Building *Web:* bachmann.house.gov	Washington	DC	20515	202-225-2331	225-6475
Peterson Collin C (Rep D-MN) 2211 Rayburn Bldg *Web:* www.collinpeterson.house.gov	Washington	DC	20515	202-225-2165	225-1593
Ramstad Jim (Rep R-MN) 127 Cannon House Office Building *Web:* paulsen.house.gov	Washington	DC	20515	202-225-2871	225-6351
Tim Walz (Rep D-MN) 1722 Longworth House Office Building *Web:* walz.house.gov	Washington	DC	20515	202-225-2472	225-3433

Mississippi

				Phone	Fax
Alan Nunnelee (Rep R-MS) 1432 Longworth House Office Building *Web:* nunnelee.house.gov	Washington	DC	20515	202-225-4306	225-3549
Ⓢ**Cochran Thad (Sen R-MS)** 113 Dirksen Bldg *Web:* www.cochran.senate.gov	Washington	DC	20510	202-224-5054	224-9450
Pickering Chip (Rep R-MS) 307 Cannon House Office Building *Web:* harper.house.gov	Washington	DC	20515	202-225-5031	225-5797
Ⓢ**Roger Wicker (Sen R-MS)** 487 Russell Bldg *Web:* wicker.senate.gov	Washington	DC	20510	202-224-6253	228-0378

				Phone	Fax
Taylor Gene (Rep R-MS) 331 Cannon House Office Building *Web:* palazzo.house.gov	Washington	DC	20515	202-225-5772	225-7074
Thompson Bennie G (Rep D-MS) 2432 Rayburn Bldg *Web:* www.benniethompson.house.gov	Washington	DC	20515	202-225-5876	225-5898

Missouri

				Phone	Fax
Akin Todd (Rep R-MO) 117 Cannon Bldg *Web:* www.house.gov/akin	Washington	DC	20515	202-225-2561	225-2563
Blaine Luetkemeyer (Rep R-MO) 1740 Longworth House Office Building *Web:* luetkemeyer.house.gov	Washington	DC	20515	202-225-2956	225-5712
Ⓢ**Bond Kit (Sen R-MO)** 260 Russell Senate Office Bldg *Web:* blunt.senate.gov	Washington	DC	20510	202-224-5721	224-8149
Ⓢ**Claire McCaskill (Sen D-MO)** Hart Senate Office Bldg Suite 506 *Web:* mccaskill.senate.gov	Washington	DC	20510	202-224-6154	228-6326
Cleaver Emanuel (Rep D-MO) 1641 Longworth Bldg *Web:* www.house.gov/cleaver	Washington	DC	20515	202-225-4535	225-4403
Emerson Jo Ann (Rep R-MO) 2440 Rayburn Bldg *Web:* www.house.gov/emerson	Washington	DC	20515	202-225-4404	226-0326
Graves Sam (Rep R-MO) 1415 Longworth Bldg *Web:* graves.house.gov	Washington	DC	20515	202-225-7041	225-8221
Ⓢ**Roy Blunt (Sen R-MO)** 260 Russell Senate Office Bldg *Web:* blunt.senate.gov	Washington	DC	20510	202-224-5721	224-8149
Russ Carnahan (Rep D-MO) 1710 Longworth House Office Bldg *Web:* www.carnahan.house.gov	Washington	DC	20515	202-225-2671	225-7452
Skelton Ike (Rep R-MO) 1023 Longworth House Office Building *Web:* hartzler.house.gov	Washington	DC	20515	202-225-2876	225-0148
William Lacy Clay (Rep D-MO) 2418 Rayburn House Office Bldg *Web:* lacyclay.house.gov	Washington	DC	20515	202-225-2406	226-3717

Montana

				Phone	Fax
Ⓢ**Baucus Max (Sen D-MT)** 511 Hart Bldg *Web:* www.baucus.senate.gov	Washington	DC	20510	202-224-2651	224-4700
Ⓢ**Jon Tester (Sen D-MT)** 724 Hart Senate Office Bldg *Web:* tester.senate.gov	Washington	DC	20510	202-224-2644	224-8594
Rehberg Dennis R (Rep R-MT) 516 Cannon Bldg *TF:* 888-232-2626 ■ *Web:* rehberg.house.gov	Washington	DC	20515	202-225-3211	225-5687

Nebraska

				Phone	Fax
Adrian M Smith (Rep R-NE) 503 Cannon Bldg *Web:* adriansmith.house.gov	Washington	DC	20515	202-225-6435	225-0207
Jeff Fortenberry (Rep R-NE) 1514 Longworth House Office *Web:* fortenberry.house.gov	Washington	DC	20515	202-225-4806	225-5686
Ⓢ**Nelson Ben (Sen D-NE)** 720 Hart Bldg *Web:* www.bennelson.senate.gov	Washington	DC	20510	202-224-6551	228-0012

Nevada

				Phone	Fax
Berkley Shelley (Rep D-NV) 405 Cannon Bldg *TF:* 877-409-2488 ■ *Web:* www.berkley.house.gov	Washington	DC	20515	202-225-5965	225-3119
Harman Jane (Rep D-NV) 2400 Rayburn Bldg *Web:* www.house.gov/harman	Washington	DC	20515	202-225-8220	226-7290
Ⓢ**Harry Reid (Sen D-NV)** 522 Hart Senate Office Bldg *Web:* reid.senate.gov	Washington	DC	20510	202-224-3542	224-7327
Porter Jon (Rep R-NV) 132 Cannon House Office Building *Web:* heck.house.gov	Washington	DC	20515	202-225-3252	225-2185

New Hampshire

				Phone	Fax
Charles F Bass (Rep R-NH) 2350 Rayburn House Office Building *Web:* bass.house.gov	Washington	DC	20515	202-225-5206	225-2946
Frank Guinta (Rep R-NH) 1223 Longworth House Office Building *Web:* guinta.house.gov	Washington	DC	20515	202-225-5456	225-5822

				Phone	Fax
ⓢGregg Judd (Sen R-NH) 144 Russell Senate Office Bldg *Web:* ayotte.senate.gov	Washington	DC	20510	202-224-3324	224-4952
ⓢSununu John E (Sen D-NH) 520 Hart SOB *Web:* shaheen.senate.gov	Washington	DC	20510	202-224-2841	228-3194

New Jersey

				Phone	Fax
Albio Sires (Rep D-NJ) 2342 Rayburn House Office Bldg *Web:* www.sires.house.gov	Washington	DC	20515	202-225-7919	226-0792
Andrews Robert E (Rep D-NJ) 2265 Rayburn House Office Building *Web:* www.house.gov/andrews	Washington	DC	20515	202-225-6501	225-6583
Bill Pascrell (Rep D-NJ) 2370 Rayburn House Office Bldg *Web:* www.pascrell.house.gov	Washington	DC	20515	202-225-5751	225-5782
Christopher H Smith (Rep R-NJ) 2373 Rayburn House Office Bldg *Web:* www.chrissmith.house.gov	Washington	DC	20515	202-225-3765	225-7768
Ferguson Mike (Rep R-NJ) 426 Cannon House Office Building *Web:* lance.house.gov	Washington	DC	20515	202-225-5361	225-9460
Jon Runyan (Rep R-NJ) 1239 Longworth House Office Building *Web:* www.runyan.house.gov	Washington	DC	20515	202-225-4765	225-0778
ⓢLautenberg Frank R (Sen D-NJ) 324 Hart Bldg *Web:* www.lautenberg.senate.gov	Washington	DC	20510	202-224-3224	228-4054
LoBiondo Frank A (Rep R-NJ) 2427 Rayburn Bldg *Web:* www.house.gov/lobiondo	Washington	DC	20510	202-225-6572	225-3318
Pallone Frank Jr (Rep D-NJ) 237 Cannon Bldg *Web:* www.house.gov/pallone	Washington	DC	20515	202-225-4671	225-9665
Payne Donald M (Rep D-NJ) 2209 Rayburn Bldg *Web:* payne.house.gov	Washington	DC	20515	202-225-3436	225-4160
ⓢRobert Menendez (Sen D-NJ) 528 Senate Hart Office Bldg *Web:* menendez.senate.gov	Washington	DC	20510	202-224-4744	228-2197
Rodney Frelinghuysen (Rep R-NJ) 2369 Rayburn House Office Bldg *Web:* frelinghuysen.house.gov	Washington	DC	20515	202-225-5034	225-3186
Rothman Steven R (Rep D-NJ) 2303 Rayburn Bldg *Web:* www.house.gov/rothman	Washington	DC	20515	202-225-5061	225-5851
Rush Holt (Rep D-NJ) 1214 Longworth House Office Building *Web:* holt.house.gov	Washington	DC	20515	202-225-5801	225-6025
Scott Garrett (Rep R-NJ) 2244 Rayburn House Office Bldg *Web:* www.garrett.house.gov	Washington	DC	20515	202-225-4465	225-9048

New Mexico

				Phone	Fax
Ben R Lujan (Rep D-NM) 330 Cannon House Office Building *Web:* lujan.house.gov	Washington	DC	20515	202-225-6190	226-1528
ⓢJeff Bingaman (Sen D-NM) 703 Hart Senate Office Bldg *TF:* 800-443-8658 ■ *Web:* bingaman.senate.gov	Washington	DC	20510	202-224-5521	224-2852
Martin Heinrich (Rep D-NM) 336 Cannon House Office Building *Web:* heinrich.house.gov	Washington	DC	20515	202-225-6316	225-4975
Steve Pearce (Rep R-NM) 2432 Rayburn House Office Bldg *TF:* 855-473-2723 ■ *Web:* pearce.house.gov	Washington	DC	20515	202-225-2365	225-9599

New York

				Phone	Fax
Ackerman Gary L (Rep D-NY) 2243 Rayburn Bldg *Web:* ackerman.house.gov	Washington	DC	20515	202-225-2601	225-1589
Bill Owens (Rep D-NY) 431 Cannon House Office Bldg *Web:* owens.house.gov	Washington	DC	20515	202-225-4611	226-0621
Carolyn B Maloney (Rep D-NY) 2332 Rayburn House Office Bldg *Web:* www.maloney.house.gov	Washington	DC	20515	202-225-7944	225-4709
Carolyn McCarthy (Rep D-NY) 2346 Rayburn House Office Bldg *Web:* carolynmccarthy.house.gov	Washington	DC	20515	202-225-5516	225-5758
ⓢCharles E Schumer (Sen D-NY) 322 Hart Senate Office Bldg *Web:* schumer.senate.gov	Washington	DC	20510	202-224-6542	228-3027
Eliot L Engel (Rep D-NY) 2161 Rayburn House Office Building *Web:* www.engel.house.gov	Washington	DC	20515	202-225-2464	225-5513
gibson (Rep R-NY) 502Cannon Bldg *Web:* gibson.house.gov	Washington	DC	20515	202-225-5614	225-1168
ⓢGillibrand (Sen D-NY) 476 Russell Bldg *Web:* cillibrang.senate.gov	Washington	DC	20510	202-224-4451	228-0282
Higgins Brian M (Rep D-NY) 431 Cannon Bldg *Web:* www.house.gov/higgins	Washington	DC	20515	202-225-3306	226-0347
Israel Steve (Rep D-NY) 2457 Rayburn House Office Building *Web:* israel.house.gov	Washington	DC	20515	202-225-3335	225-4669
Jerrold Nadler (Rep D-NY) 2334 Rayburn House Office Bldg *Web:* www.nadler.house.gov	Washington	DC	20515	202-225-5635	225-6923
Jose E Serrano (Rep D-NY) 2227 Rayburn House Office Building *Web:* serrano.house.gov	Washington	DC	20515	202-225-4361	225-6001
Joseph Crowley (Rep D-NY) 2404 Rayburn House Office Bldg *Web:* crowley.house.gov	Washington	DC	20515	202-225-3965	225-1909
Louise M Slaughter (Rep D-NY) 2469 Rayburn House Office Building *Web:* www.slaughter.house.gov	Washington	DC	20515	202-225-3615	225-7822
Maurice D Hinchey (Rep D-NY) 2431 Rayburn House Office Building *Web:* www.hinchey.house.gov	Washington	DC	20515	202-225-6335	226-0774
McNulty Michael R (Rep D-NY) 422 Cannon House Office Building *Web:* tonko.house.gov	Washington	DC	20515	202-225-5076	225-5077
Meeks Gregory W (Rep D-NY) 2342 Rayburn Bldg *Web:* www.house.gov/meeks	Washington	DC	20515	202-225-3461	226-4169
Michael Gerard Grimm (Rep R-NY) 512 Cannon House Office Building *Web:* www.grimm.house.gov	Washington	DC	20515	202-225-3371	226-1272
Nan Hayworth (Rep R-NY) 1440 Longworth House Office Building *Web:* hayworth.house.gov	Washington	DC	20515	202-225-5441	225-3289
Nita M Lowey (Rep D-NY) 2365 Rayburn House Office Building *Web:* www.lowey.house.gov/index.html	Washington	DC	20515	202-225-6506	225-0546
Peter T King (Rep R-NY) 339 Cannon House Office Bldg *Web:* peteking.house.gov	Washington	DC	20515	202-225-7896	226-2279
Rangel Charles B (Rep D-NY) 2354 Rayburn Bldg *Web:* www.house.gov	Washington	DC	20515	202-225-4365	225-0816
Reynolds Thomas M (Rep D-NY) 1711 Longworth House Office Building *Web:* hochul.house.gov	Washington	DC	20515	202-225-5265	225-5910
Richard Hanna (Rep D-NY) 319 Cannon House Office Building *Web:* hanna.house.gov	Washington	DC	20515	202-225-3665	225-1891
Timothy Bishop (Rep D-NY) 306 Cannon House Office Building *Web:* timbishop.house.gov	Washington	DC	20515	202-225-3826	225-3143
Tom Reed (Rep R-NY) 1037 Longworth House Office Building *Web:* reed.house.gov	Washington	DC	20515	202-225-3161	226-6599
Towns Edolphus (Rep D-NY) 2232 Rayburn Bldg *Web:* www.house.gov/towns	Washington	DC	20515	202-225-5936	225-1018
Velazquez Nydia M (Rep D-NY) 2466 Rayburn Bldg *Web:* velazquez.house.gov/index.shtml	Washington	DC	20515	202-225-2361	226-0327
Weiner Anthony D (Rep D-NY) 2332 Rayburn House Office Building *Web:* maloney.house.gov	Washington	DC	20515	202-225-7944	225-4709
Yvette D Clarke (Rep D-NY) 1029 Longworth House Office Building *Web:* clarke.house.gov	Washington	DC	20515	202-225-6231	226-0112

North Carolina

				Phone	Fax
Butterfield GK Jr (Rep D-NC) 413 Cannon Bldg *Web:* butterfield.house.gov	Washington	DC	20515	202-225-3101	225-3354
ⓢDole Elizabeth H (Sen R-NC) 555 Dirksen Bldg *Web:* burr.senate.gov	Washington	DC	20510	202-224-6342	228-1100
Etheridge Bob (Rep R-NC) 1533 Longworth House Office Building *Web:* ellmers.house.gov	Washington	DC	20515	202-225-4531	225-5662
Heath Shuler (Rep D-NC) 229 Cannon House Office Bldg *Web:* shuler.house.gov	Washington	DC	20515	202-225-6401	226-6422
Howard Coble (Rep R-NC) 2188 Rayburn House Office Bldg *Web:* coble.house.gov	Washington	DC	20515	202-225-3065	225-8611
Jones Walter B (Rep D-NC) 2333 Rayburn Bldg *Web:* www.jones.house.gov	Washington	DC	20515	202-225-3415	225-3286
Larry Kissell (Rep D-NC) 1632 Longworth House Office Building *Web:* kissell.house.gov	Washington	DC	20515	202-225-3715	225-4036
McHenry Patrick (Rep R-NC) 224 Cannon House Office Bldg *Web:* mchenry.house.gov	Washington	DC	20515	202-225-2576	225-0316
Melvin L Watt (Rep D-NC) 2304 Rayburn Bldg *Web:* www.watt.house.gov	Washington	DC	20515	202-225-1510	225-1512
Mike McIntyre (Rep D-NC) 2133 Rayburn House Office *Web:* mcintyre.house.gov	Washington	DC	20515	202-225-2731	225-5773
Miller Brad (Rep D-NC) 1722 Longworth Bldg *Web:* www.house.gov/bradmiller	Washington	DC	20515	202-225-3032	225-0181
Price David (Rep D-NC) 2162 Rayburn Bldg *Web:* www.price.house.gov	Washington	DC	20515	202-225-1784	225-2014
Sue Myrick (Rep R-NC) 230 Cannon House Office Bldg *Web:* myrick.house.gov	Washington	DC	20515	202-225-1976	225-3389
Virginia Foxx (Rep R-NC) 1230 Longworth House Office Bldg *Web:* foxx.house.gov	Washington	DC	20515	202-225-2071	225-2995

North Dakota

				Phone	Fax
ⓢDorgan Byron L (Sen R-ND) 120 Russell Senate Office Bldg *Web:* hoeven.senate.gov/public	Washington	DC	20510	202-224-2551	224-7999
ⓢKent Conrad (Sen D-ND) 530 Hart Senate Office Bldg *Web:* conrad.senate.gov	Washington	DC	20510	202-224-2043	224-7776
Rick Berg (Rep R-ND) 323 Cannon House Office Building *Web:* berg.house.gov	Washington	DC	20515	202-225-2611	226-0893

Ohio

				Phone	Fax
Betty Sutton (Rep D-OH) 1519 Longworth House Office Bldg *Web:* sutton.house.gov	Washington	DC	20515	202-225-3401	225-2266
Bob Gibbs (Rep R-OH) 329 Cannon House Office Building *Web:* gibbs.house.gov	Washington	DC	20515	202-225-6265	225-3394
Chabot Steve (Rep R-OH) 129 Cannon Bldg *Web:* www.house.gov/chabot	Washington	DC	20515	202-225-2216	225-3012
Dennis J Kucinich (Rep D-OH) 2445 Rayburn House Office Building *Web:* kucinich.house.gov	Washington	DC	20515	202-225-5871	225-5745
James D Jordan (Rep R-OH) 1524 Longworth House Office Bldg *Web:* jordan.house.gov	Washington	DC	20515	202-225-2676	226-0577
Jim Renacci (Rep R-OH) 130 Cannon House Office Bldg *Web:* renacci.house.gov	Washington	DC	20515	202-225-3876	225-3059
John A Boehner (Rep R-OH)					

				Phone	Fax
1011 Longworth Bldg *Web:* johnboehner.house.gov	Washington	DC	20515	202-225-6205	225-0704
Marcia Fudge (Rep D-OH) 1019 Longworth House Office Bldg *Web:* www.fudge.house.gov	Washington	DC	20515	202-225-7032	225-1339
Pryce Deborah (Rep R-OH) 1007 Longworth House Office Building *Web:* stivers.house.gov	Washington	DC	20515	202-225-2015	225-3529
Schmidt Jean (Rep R-OH) 418 Cannon House Office Building *Web:* www.house.gov/schmidt	Washington	DC	20515	202-225-3164	225-1992
Ⓢ**Sherrod Brown (Sen D-OH)** 455 Russell Bldg *TF:* 888-896-6446 ■ *Web:* brown.senate.gov	Washington	DC	20510	202-224-2315	228-6321
Steve Austria (Rep R-OH) 439 Cannon House Bldg *Web:* austria.house.gov	Washington	DC	20515	202-225-4324	225-1984
Steve C LaTourette (Rep R-OH) 2371 Rayburn House Office Bldg *Web:* www.latourette.house.gov	Washington	DC	20515	202-225-5731	225-3307
Tiberi Patrick J (Rep R-OH) 113 Cannon Bldg *Web:* www.house.gov/tiberi	Washington	DC	20515	202-225-5355	226-4523
Timothy J Ryan (Rep D-OH) 1421 Longworth House Office Bldg *TF:* 800-856-4152 ■ *Web:* timryan.house.gov	Washington	DC	20515	202-225-5261	225-3719
Turner Michael (Rep R-OH) 1740 Longworth Bldg *Web:* turner.house.gov	Washington	DC	20515	202-225-6465	225-6754

Oklahoma

				Phone	Fax
Boren Dan (Rep D-OK) 216 Cannon Bldg *Web:* www.house.gov/boren	Washington	DC	20515	202-225-2701	225-3038
Cole Tom (Rep R-OK) 236 Cannon Bldg *Web:* www.cole.house.gov	Washington	DC	20515	202-225-6165	225-3512
Ⓢ**James M Inhofe (Sen R-OK)** 205 Russell Senate Office Bldg *Web:* inhofe.senate.gov	Washington	DC	20510	202-224-4721	228-0380
John Sullivan (Rep R-OK) 434 Cannon House Office Building *Web:* sullivan.house.gov	Washington	DC	20515	202-225-2211	225-9187
Lucas Frank D (Rep R-OK) 2311 Rayburn Bldg *Web:* www.house.gov/lucas	Washington	DC	20515	202-225-5565	225-8698

Oregon

				Phone	Fax
Earl Blumenauer (Rep D-OR) 1502 Longworth House Office Bldg *Web:* blumenauer.house.gov	Washington	DC	20515	202-225-4811	225-8941
Greg Walden (Rep R-OR) 2182 Rayburn House Office Bldg *Web:* www.walden.house.gov	Washington	DC	20515	202-225-6730	225-5774
Kurt Schrader (Rep D-OR) 314 Cannon House Office Building *Web:* schrader.house.gov	Washington	DC	20515	202-225-5711	225-5699
Peter A DeFazio (Rep D-OR) 2134 Rayburn Office Bldg *Web:* www.defazio.house.gov	Washington	DC	20515	202-225-6416	225-0032
Ⓢ**Smith Gordon (Sen D-OR)** 313 Hart Senate Office Bldg *Web:* merkley.senate.gov	Washington	DC	20510	202-224-3753	228-3997
Wu David (Rep D-OR) 2338 Rayburn Bldg *Web:* www.house.gov/wu	Washington	DC	20515	202-225-0855	225-9497
Ⓢ**Wyden Ron (Sen D-OR)** 223 Dirksen Bldg *Web:* www.wyden.senate.gov	Washington	DC	20510	202-224-5244	228-2717

Pennsylvania

				Phone	Fax
Allyson Y Schwartz (Rep D-PA) 1227 Longworth Office Bldg *Web:* schwartz.house.gov	Washington	DC	20515	202-225-6111	226-0611
Brady Robert A (Rep D-PA) 206 Cannon Bldg *Web:* www.house.gov/robertbrady	Washington	DC	20515	202-225-4731	225-0088
Charles W Dent (Rep R-PA) 1009 Longworth House Office Bldg *Web:* dent.house.gov	Washington	DC	20515	202-225-6411	226-0778
Doyle Mike (Rep D-PA) 401 Cannon Bldg *Web:* doyle.house.gov	Washington	DC	20515	202-225-2135	225-3084
Fattah Chaka (Rep D-PA) 2301 Rayburn Bldg *Web:* fattah.house.gov	Washington	DC	20515	202-225-4001	225-5392
Jason Altmire (Rep D-PA) 332 Cannon House Office Building *Web:* altmire.house.gov	Washington	DC	20515	202-225-2565	226-2274
Jim Gerlach (Rep R-PA) 2442 Rayburn House Office Bldg *Web:* gerlach.house.gov	Washington	DC	20515	202-225-4315	225-8440
Lou Barletta (Rep R-PA) 510 Cannon House Office Bldg *TF:* 855-241-5144 ■ *Web:* barletta.house.gov	Washington	DC	20515	202-225-6511	225-0764
Mark S Critz (Rep D-PA) 1022 Longworth House Office Building *Web:* www.critz.house.gov	Washington	DC	20515	202-225-2065	225-5709
Michael Fitzpatrick (Rep R-PA) 1224 Longworth House Office Building *Web:* fitzpatrick.house.gov	Washington	DC	20515	202-225-4276	225-9511
Mike Kelly (Rep R-PA) 515 Cannon House Office Building *Web:* www.kelly.house.gov	Washington	DC	20515	202-225-5406	225-3103
Patrick Meehan (Rep R-PA) 513 Cannon House Office Building *Web:* meehan.house.gov	Washington	DC	20515	202-225-2011	226-0280
Peterson John (Rep R-PA) 124 Cannon House Office Building *Web:* thompson.house.gov	Washington	DC	20515	202-225-5121	225-5796
Pitts Joseph R (Rep R-PA) 420 Cannon Bldg *Web:* www.house.gov/pitts	Washington	DC	20515	202-225-2411	225-2013
Platts Todd Russell (Rep R-PA) 1032 Longworth Bldg *Web:* www.house.gov/platts	Washington	DC	20515	202-225-5836	226-1000
Ⓢ**Robert P Casey Jr (Sen D-PA)** 393 Russell Senate Office Bldg *TF:* 866-802-2833 ■ *Web:* casey.senate.gov	Washington	DC	20510	202-224-6324	228-0604
Shuster Bill (Rep R-PA) 204 Cannon Bldg *Web:* www.house.gov/shuster	Washington	DC	20515	202-225-2431	225-2486
Specter Arlen (Rep R-PA) 1009 Longworth House Office Building *Web:* dent.house.gov	Washington	DC	20515	202-225-6411	226-0778
Tim Holden (Rep D-PA) 2417 Rayburn House Office Building *Web:* www.holden.house.gov	Washington	DC	20515	202-225-5546	226-0996
Timothy F Murphy (Rep R-PA) 322 Cannon Office Bldg *Web:* murphy.house.gov	Washington	DC	20515	202-225-2301	225-1844
Tom Marino (Rep R-PA) 410 Cannon House Office Bldg *Web:* marino.house.gov	Washington	DC	20515	202-225-3731	225-9594

Puerto Rico

				Phone	Fax
Fortuno Luis G (Rep D-PR) 1218 Longworth House Office Building *Web:* pierluisi.house.gov	Washington	DC	20515	202-225-2615	225-2154

Rhode Island

				Phone	Fax
David Cicilline (Rep D-RI) 128 Cannon House Office Building *Web:* cicilline.house.gov	Washington	DC	20515	202-225-4911	225-3290
Ⓢ**Jack Reed (Sen D-RI)** 728 Hart Senate Office Bldg *Web:* reed.senate.gov	Washington	DC	20510	202-224-4642	224-4680
James R Langevin (Rep D-RI) 109 Cannon House Office Bldg *Web:* www.langevin.house.gov	Washington	DC	20515	202-225-2735	225-5976
Ⓢ**Sheldon Whitehouse (Sen D-RI)** Hart Senate Office Bldg Rm 717 *Web:* whitehouse.senate.gov	Washington	DC	20510	202-224-2921	228-6362
Stearns Cliff (Rep R-RI) 2370 Rayburn Bldg *Web:* www.house.gov/stearns	Washington	DC	20515	202-225-5744	225-3973

South Carolina

				Phone	Fax
Barrett J Gresham (Rep R-SC) 116 Cannon House Office Building *Web:* jeffduncan.house.gov	Washington	DC	20515	202-225-5301	225-3216
Clyburn James E (Rep D-SC) 2135 Rayburn Bldg *Web:* clyburn.house.gov	Washington	DC	20515	202-225-3315	225-2313
Ⓢ**Inglis Bob (Sen R-SC)** 167 Russell *Web:* demint.senate.gov	Washington	DC	20510	202-224-6121	228-5143
Joe Wilson (Rep R-SC) 2229 Rayburn House Office Bldg *Web:* joewilson.house.gov	Washington	DC	20515	202-225-2452	225-2455
Ⓢ**Lindsey Graham (Sen R-SC)** 290 Russell Senate Office Bldg *Web:* lgraham.senate.gov	Washington	DC	20510	202-224-5972	224-3808
Tim Scott (Rep R-SC) 1117 Longworth House Office Building *TF:* 888-868-0737 ■ *Web:* www.timscott.house.gov	Washington	DC	20515	202-225-3176	225-3407

South Dakota

				Phone	Fax
Herseth Stephanie (Rep R-SD) 226 Cannon House Office Building *Web:* noem.house.gov	Washington	DC	20515	202-225-2801	225-5823
Ⓢ**John Thune (Sen R-SD)** United States Senate SD-511 *TF:* 866-850-3855 ■ *Web:* thune.senate.gov/public	Washington	DC	20510	202-224-2321	228-5429
Ⓢ**Tim Johnson (Sen D-SD)** 136 Hart Senate Office Bldg *Web:* johnson.senate.gov	Washington	DC	20510	202-224-5842	228-5765

Tennessee

				Phone	Fax
Blackburn Marsha W (Rep R-TN) 509 Cannon Bldg *Web:* www.house.gov/blackburn	Washington	DC	20515	202-225-2811	225-3004
Ⓢ**Bob Corker (Sen R-TN)** Dirksen Senate Office Bldg Suite 185 *Web:* corker.senate.gov	Washington	DC	20510	202-224-3344	228-0566
Charles J Fleischmann (Rep R-TN) 511 Cannon House Office Building *Web:* www.fleischmann.house.gov	Washington	DC	20515	202-225-3271	225-3494
Davis Lincoln (Rep R-TN) 410 Cannon Bldg *Web:* www.house.gov	Washington	DC	20515	202-225-6831	226-5172
Diane Black (Rep R-TN) 1531 Longworth House Office Building *Web:* black.house.gov	Washington	DC	20515	202-225-4231	225-6887
Duncan John J Jr (Rep R-TN) 2207 Rayburn Bldg *Web:* duncan.house.gov	Washington	DC	20515	202-225-5435	225-6440
Jim Cooper (Rep D-TN) 1536 Longworth Bldg *Web:* www.cooper.house.gov	Washington	DC	20515	202-225-4311	226-1035
Ⓢ**Lamar Alexander (Sen R-TN)**					

Phone Fax

455 Dirksen Senate Office Bldg .... Washington DC 20510 202-224-4944 228-3398
Web: alexander.senate.gov

Steve Cohen (Rep D-TN)
1005 Longworth House Office Bldg .... Washington DC 20515 202-225-3265 225-5663
Web: cohen.house.gov

Tanner John S (Rep R-TN)
1118 Longworth House Office Building .... Washington DC 20515 202-225-4714 225-1765
Web: fincher.house.gov

Texas

Phone Fax

Bill Flores (Rep R-TX)
1505 Longworth House Office Building .... Washington DC 20515 202-225-6105 225-0350
Web: flores.house.gov

Brady Kevin (Rep R-TX) 301 Cannon Bldg. .... Washington DC 20515 202-225-4901 225-5524
Web: www.house.gov/brady

Carter John R (Rep R-TX) 408 Cannon Bldg .... Washington DC 20515 202-225-3864 225-5886
Web: carter.house.gov

Charles A Gonzalez (Rep D-TX)
1436 Longworth Bldg .... Washington DC 20515 202-225-3236 225-1915
Web: gonzalez.house.gov

Cuellar Henry (Rep D-TX) 336 Cannon Bldg .... Washington DC 20515 202-225-1640 225-1641
Web: cuellar.house.gov

Doggett Lloyd (Rep D-TX) 201 Cannon Bldg. .... Washington DC 20515 202-225-4865 225-3073
Web: doggett.house.gov

Eddie Bernice Johnson (Rep D-TX)
2468 Rayburn Office Bldg .... Washington DC 20515 202-225-8885 226-1477
Web: www.ebjohnson.house.gov

Green Al (Rep D-TX) 425 Cannon Bldg. .... Washington DC 20515 202-225-7508 225-2947
Web: www.house.gov/algreen

Green Gene (Rep D-TX) 2335 Rayburn Bldg. .... Washington DC 20515 202-225-1688 225-9903
Web: www.house.gov/green

Hall Ralph M (Rep R-TX) 2405 Rayburn Bldg .... Washington DC 20515 202-225-6673 225-3332
Web: ralphhall.house.gov

Henry Cuellar (Rep D-TX)
2463 Rayburn House Office Bldg .... Washington DC 20515 202-225-1640 225-1641
TF: 877-780-0028 ■ *Web:* cuellar.house.gov

Hensarling Jeb (Rep R-TX) 132 Cannon Bldg. .... Washington DC 20515 202-225-3484 226-4888
Web: www.house.gov/hensarling

Joe Barton (Rep R-TX) 2109 Rayburn Bldg .... Washington DC 20515 202-225-2002 225-3052
Web: joebarton.house.gov

ⓈJohn Cornyn (Sen R-TX)
517 Hart Senate Office Bldg .... Washington DC 20510 202-224-2934 228-2856
Web: cornyn.senate.gov/public

John Culberson (Rep R-TX)
2352 Rayburn House Office Bldg .... Washington DC 20515 202-225-2571 225-4381
Web: www.culberson.house.gov

ⓈKay Bailey Hutchison (Sen R-TX)
284 Russell Senate Office Bldg .... Washington DC 20510 202-224-5922 224-0776
Web: hutchison.senate.gov

Kay Granger (Rep R-TX)
320 Cannon House Office Building .... Washington DC 20515 202-225-5071 225-5683
Web: kaygranger.house.gov

Kenny Marchant (Rep R-TX)
1110 Longworth House Office Building .... Washington DC 20515 202-225-6605 225-0074
Web: www.marchant.house.gov

Lamar Smith (Rep R-TX)
2409 Rayburn House Office Bldg .... Washington DC 20515 202-225-4236 225-8628
Web: lamarsmith.house.gov

Louie Gohmert (Rep R-TX)
2440 Rayburn House Office Building .... Washington DC 20515 202-225-3035 226-1230
TF: 866-535-6302 ■ *Web:* gohmert.house.gov

MacThornberry (Rep R-TX)
2209 Rayburn House Office Bldg .... Washington DC 20515 202-225-3706 225-3486
Web: www.thornberry.house.gov

McCaul Michael (Rep R-TX) 131 Cannon Bldg .... Washington DC 20515 202-225-2401 225-5955
Web: mccaul.house.gov

Michael C Burgess (Rep R-TX)
2241 Rayburn House Office Bldg .... Washington DC 20515 202-225-7772 225-2919
Web: burgess.house.gov

Mike Conaway (Rep R-TX)
1527 Longworth House Office Bldg .... Washington DC 20515 202-225-3605 225-1783
TF: 866-882-3811 ■ *Web:* conaway.house.gov

Paul Ron (Rep R-TX) 203 Cannon Bldg .... Washington DC 20515 202-225-2831
Web: paul.house.gov

Pete Olson (Rep R-TX)
312 Cannon House Office Building .... Washington DC 20515 202-225-5951 225-5241
Web: olson.house.gov

Pete Sessions (Rep R-TX)
2233 Rayburn House Office Bldg .... Washington DC 20515 202-225-2231 225-5878
Web: sessions.house.gov

Poe Ted (Rep R-TX) 1605 Longworth Bldg .... Washington DC 20515 202-225-6565 225-5547
TF: 866-425-6565 ■ *Web:* poe.house.gov

Randolph Blake Farenthold (Rep R-TX)
2110 Rayburn House Office Building .... Washington DC 20515 202-225-7742 226-1134
Web: www.farenthold.house.gov

Randy Neugebauer (Rep R-TX)
1424 Longworth House Office Building .... Washington DC 20515 202-225-4005 225-9615
Web: www.randy.house.gov

Ruben Hinojosa (Rep D-TX)
2262 Rayburn House Office Bldg .... Washington DC 20515 202-225-2531 225-5688
Web: hinojosa.house.gov

Sam Johnson (Rep R-TX) 1211 Longworth Bldg .... Washington DC 20515 202-225-4201 225-1485
Web: www.samjohnson.house.gov

Sheila Jackson Lee (Rep D-TX)
2160 Rayburn Bldg .... Washington DC 20515 202-225-3816 225-3317
Web: www.jacksonlee.house.gov

Phone Fax

Silvestre Reyes (Rep D-TX)
2210 Rayburn House Office Bldg .... Washington DC 20515 202-225-4831 225-2016
Web: reyes.house.gov

Utah

Phone Fax

Bishop Rob (Rep R-UT) 124 Cannon Bldg .... Washington DC 20515 202-225-0453 225-5857
Web: www.house.gov/robbishop

ⓈHatch Orrin G (Sen R-UT) 104 Hart Bldg .... Washington DC 20510 202-224-5251 224-6331
Web: www.hatch.senate.gov

Jason E Chaffetz (Rep R-UT)
1032 Longworth House Office Building .... Washington DC 20515 202-225-7751 225-5629
Web: www.chaffetz.house.gov

Jim Matheson (Rep D-UT)
2434 Rayburn House Office Building .... Washington DC 20515 202-225-3011 225-5638
Web: matheson.house.gov

Vermont

Phone Fax

ⓈPatrick J Leahy (Sen D-VT)
437 Russell Senate Bldg .... Washington DC 20510 202-224-4242 224-3479
Web: leahy.senate.gov

Peter Welch (Rep D-VT)
1404 Longworth House Office Bldg .... Washington DC 20515 202-225-4115 225-6790
TF: 888-605-7270 ■ *Web:* welch.house.gov

ⓈSanders Bernard (Sen D-VT) 332 Dirksen Bldg. .... Washington DC 20510 202-224-5141 228-0776
Web: www.sanders.senate.gov

Virgin Islands

Phone Fax

Christensen Donna (Del D-VI)
1510 Longworth Bldg .... Washington DC 20515 202-225-1790 225-5517
Web: donnachristensen.house.gov

Virginia

Phone Fax

Eric Cantor (Rep R-VA)
303 Canon House Office Building .... Washington DC 20515 202-225-2815 225-0011
Web: cantor.house.gov

Forbes J Randy (Rep R-VA) 307 Cannon Bldg .... Washington DC 20515 202-225-6365 226-1170
Web: forbes.house.gov

Frank R Wolf (Rep R-VA) 241 Cannon Bldg. .... Washington DC 20515 202-225-5136 225-0437
Web: www.wolf.house.gov

ⓈGerry Connolly (Sen D-VA)
424 Cannon House Office Building .... Washington DC 20515 202-225-1492 225-3071
Web: cornyn.senate.gov

Goodlatte Robert W (Rep R-VA)
2240 Rayburn Bldg .... Washington DC 20515 202-225-5431 225-9681
Web: goodlatte.house.gov

Howard Morgan Griffith (Rep R-VA)
1108 Longworth House Office Building .... Washington DC 20515 202-225-3861 225-0776
Web: www.morgangriffith.house.gov

James Moran (Rep D-VA) 2239 Rayburn Bldg .... Washington DC 20515 202-225-4376 225-0017
Web: moran.house.gov

ⓈJim Webb (Sen D-VA)
248 Russell Senate Office Bldg .... Washington DC 20510 202-224-4024 228-6363
Web: webb.senate.gov

ⓈMark R. Warner (Sen D-VA)
459A Russell Senate Office Bldg .... Washington DC 20510 202-224-2023 224-6295
TF: 877-676-2759 ■ *Web:* warner.senate.gov

Rahall Nick (Rep D-VA) 2307 Rayburn Bldg .... Washington DC 20515 202-225-3452 225-9061
Web: www.rahall.house.gov

Rob Wittman (Rep R-VA)
1317 Longworth House Office Bldg .... Washington DC 20515 202-225-4261 225-4382
Web: www.wittman.house.gov

Robert Hurt (Rep R-VA)
1516 Longworth House Office Building .... Washington DC 20515 202-225-4711 225-5681
Web: www.hurt.house.gov

Scott Rigell (Rep R-VA)
327 Cannon House Office Building .... Washington DC 20515 202-225-4215 225-4218
Web: rigell.house.gov

Scott Robert C (Rep D-VA)
1201 Longworth Bldg .... Washington DC 20515 202-225-8351 225-8354
Web: www.bobbyscott.house.gov

Washington

Phone Fax

Baird Brian (Rep R-WA)
1130 Longworth House Office Building .... Washington DC 20515 202-225-3536 225-3478
Web: herrerabeutler.house.gov

ⓈCantwell Maria (Sen D-WA) 511 Dirksen Bldg .... Washington DC 20510 202-224-3441 228-0514
Web: www.cantwell.senate.gov

Cathy McMorris (Rep R-WA)
2421 Rayburn House Office Bldg .... Washington DC 20515 202-225-2006 225-3392
Web: www.mcmorris.house.gov

Dave Reichert (Rep R-WA) 1730 Longworth Bldg. .... Washington DC 20515 202-225-7761 225-4282
Web: www.reichert.house.gov

Dicks Norman D (Rep D-WA) 2467 Rayburn Bldg .... Washington DC 20515 202-225-5916 226-1176
Web: www.house.gov/dicks

Doc Hastings (Rep R-WA)
1203 Longworth House Office Bldg .... Washington DC 20515 202-225-5816 225-3251
Web: hastings.house.gov

Inslee Jay (Rep D-WA) 403 Cannon Bldg. .... Washington DC 20515 202-225-6311 226-1606
TF: 800-422-5521 ■ *Web:* www.house.gov/inslee

Jim McDermott (Rep D-WA)
1035 Longworth House Office Building .... Washington DC 20515 202-225-3106 225-6197
Web: www.mcdermott.house.gov

Larsen Rick (Rep D-WA) 107 Cannon Bldg .... Washington DC 20515 202-225-2605 225-4420
Web: www.house.gov/larsen

ⓈPatty Murray (Sen D-WA)
448 Russell Senate Office Bldg .... Washington DC 20510 202-224-2621 224-0238
TF: 866-481-9186 ■ *Web:* murray.senate.gov/public

Smith Adam (Rep R-WA) 2402 Rayburn Bldg. .... Washington DC 20515 202-225-8901 225-5893
Web: www.house.gov/adamsmith

West Virginia

Phone Fax

ⓈJay Rockefeller (Sen D-WV) 531 Hart Bldg .... Washington DC 20510 202-224-6472 224-7665
Web: rockefeller.senate.gov

Mollohan Alan B (Rep R-WV)

Listing	City	State	Zip	Phone	Fax
313 Cannon House Office Building *Web:* mckinley.house.gov	Washington	DC	20515	202-225-4172	225-7564
Shelley Moore Capito (Rep R-WV) 2443 Rayburn House Office Building *Web:* capito.house.gov	Washington	DC	20515	202-225-2711	225-7856

Wisconsin

Listing	City	State	Zip	*Phone*	*Fax*
Gwen Moore (Rep D-WI) 2245 Rayburn House Office Building *Web:* www.gwenmoore.house.gov	Washington	DC	20515	202-225-4572	225-8135
ⓢ**Herbert H Kohl (Sen D-WI)** 330 Hart Bldg *Web:* www.kohl.senate.gov	Washington	DC	20510	202-224-5653	224-9787
Kind Ron (Rep D-WI) 1406 Longworth Bldg *Web:* www.house.gov/kind	Washington	DC	20515	202-225-5506	225-5739
Paul Ryan (Rep R-WI) 1233 Longworth House Office Bldg *Web:* www.paulryan.house.gov	Washington	DC	20515	202-225-3031	225-3393
Reid Ribble (Rep R-WI) 1513 Longworth House Office Building *Web:* ribble.house.gov	Washington	DC	20515	202-225-5665	225-5729
Sean Duffy (Rep R-WI) 1208 Longworth House Office Building *TF:* 855-585-4251 ■ *Web:* duffy.house.gov	Washington	DC	20515	202-225-3365	225-3240
Spratt John M Jr (Rep R-WI) 1233 Longworth House Office Bldg *Web:* paulryan.house.gov	Washington	DC	20515	202-225-3031	225-3393
Tammy Baldwin (Rep D-WI) 2446 Rayburn House Office Building *Web:* tammybaldwin.house.gov	Washington	DC	20515	202-225-2906	225-6942
Thomas E Petri (Rep R-WI) 2462 Rayburn House Office Building *Web:* www.petri.house.gov	Washington	DC	20515	202-225-2476	225-2356

Wyoming

Listing	City	State	Zip	*Phone*	*Fax*
Cubin Barbara (Rep R-WY) 113 Cannon House Office Building *Web:* lummis.house.gov	Washington	DC	20515	202-225-3311	225-3057
ⓢ**John Barrasso (Sen R-WY)** 307 Dirksen Senate Office Bldg *TF:* 866-235-9553 ■ *Web:* barrasso.senate.gov/public	Washington	DC	20510	202-224-6441	224-1724
ⓢ**Mike Enzi (Sen R-WY)** 379A Senate Russell Office Bldg *TF:* 888-250-1879 ■ *Web:* enzi.senate.gov	Washington	DC	20510	202-224-3424	228-0359

346 GOVERNORS - STATE

Listings For Governors Are Organized By State Names.

Listing	City	State	Zip	*Phone*	*Fax*
Sean Parnell (R) (Governor) PO Box 110001 *Web:* www.gov.state.ak.us	Juneau	AK	99811	907-465-3500	465-3532
Togiola TA Tulafono(D) (Governor) American Samoa Government *Web:* www.americansamoa.gov	Pago Pago	AS	96799	684-633-4116	633-2269
Michael Beebe (D) (Governor) State Capitol Bldg Suite 250 *Web:* www.accessarkansas.org/governor	Little Rock	AR	72201	501-682-2345	682-1382
Edmund G Brown (R) (Governor) c/o State Capitol Suite 1173 *Web:* www.governor.ca.gov	Sacramento	CA	95814	916-445-2841	558-3160
Ritter Bill (D) (Governor) 136 State Capitol Bldg *Web:* www.colorado.gov/governor	Denver	CO	80203	303-866-2471	866-2003
Jodi M Rell (R) (Governor) 210 Capitol Ave *TF:* 800-406-1527 ■ *Web:* www.ct.gov	Hartford	CT	06106	860-566-4840	524-7395
Crist Charlie (R) (Governor) State Capitol *Web:* www.flgov.com	Tallahassee	FL	32399	850-488-4441	487-0801
Nathan Deal (R) (Governor) 203 State Capitol *Web:* www.gov.georgia.gov	Atlanta	GA	30334	404-656-1776	657-7332
Clement L Otter (R) (Governor) State Capitol Bldg PO Box 83720 *Web:* www.gov.idaho.gov	Boise	ID	83720	208-334-2100	334-3454
Pat Quinn (D) (Governor) Office of the Governor 207 State House *Web:* www.illinois.gov/gov	Springfield	IL	62706	217-782-0244	782-1853
Terry Branstad (D) (Governor) 1007 E Grand Ave *Web:* www.governor.iowa.gov	Des Moines	IA	50319	515-281-5211	281-6611
Sam Brownback (D) (Governor) 300 SW 10th Ave Suite 241S *TF:* 877-579-6757 ■ *Web:* www.governor.ks.gov	Topeka	KS	66612	785-296-3232	296-7973
Jindal Bobby (R) (Governor) PO Box 94004 *Web:* www.gov.state.la.us	Baton Rouge	LA	70804	225-342-7015	342-7099
Paul R LePage (D) (Governor) 1 State House Stn *Web:* www.maine.gov/governor/lepage	Augusta	ME	04333	207-287-3531	287-1034
O'Malley Martin (D) (Governor) State House 100 State Cir *TF:* 800-811-8336 ■ *Web:* www.gov.state.md.us	Annapolis	MD	21401	410-974-3901	974-3275
Deval Patrick (D) (Governor) Rm 280 *TF:* 888-870-7770 ■ *Web:* www.mass.gov	Boston	MA	02133	617-725-4005	727-9725
Rick Snyder (D) (Governor) PO Box 30013 *Web:* www.michigan.gov/snyder	Lansing	MI	48909	517-373-3400	335-6863
Mark Dayton (R) (Governor) 130 State Capitol 75 Rev Dr Martin Luther King Jr Blvd *TF:* 800-657-3717 ■ *Web:* www.mn.gov/governor	Saint Paul	MN	55155	651-201-3400	797-1850
Haley Reeves Barbour (R) (Governor) PO Box 139 *TF:* 877-405-0733 ■ *Web:* www.governorbarbour.com	Jackson	MS	39205	601-359-3150	359-3741
Jay Nixon (R) (Governor) PO Box 720 *Web:* www.governor.mo.gov	Jefferson City	MO	65102	573-751-3222	751-1495
Brian Schweitzer (D) (Governor) PO Box 200801 *Web:* www.governor.mt.gov	Helena	MT	59620	406-444-3111	444-5529
Dave Heineman (R) (Governor) PO Box 94848 *Web:* www.governor.nebraska.gov	Lincoln	NE	68509	402-471-2244	471-6031
Brian Sandoval (R) (Governor) 101 N Carson St *Web:* www.nv.gov	Carson City	NV	89701	775-684-5670	684-5683
John Lynch (D) (Governor) State House 107 N Main St *TF:* 800-852-3456 ■ *Web:* www.governor.nh.gov	Concord	NH	03301	603-271-2121	271-7640
Chris Christie (D) (Governor) PO Box 001 *Web:* www.state.nj.us/governor	Trenton	NJ	08625	609-292-6000	292-3454
Susana Martinez (Governor) State Capitol Bldg 490 Old Santa Fe Trail Rm 400 *Web:* www.governor.state.nm.us	Santa Fe	NM	87501	505-476-2200	476-2226
Andrew M. Cuomo (Governor) NYS State Capitol Bldg *Web:* www.state.ny.us/governor	Albany	NY	12224	518-474-8390	474-1513
Benigno Fitial (Governor) Office of the Governor CB 10007 Capitol Hill *Web:* www.gov.mp	Saipan	MP	96950	670-664-2200	664-2211
John Kitzhaber (D) (Governor) 900 Ct St NE *Web:* www.governor.oregon.gov	Salem	OR	97301	503-378-4582	378-6827
Tom Corbett (D) (Governor) 225 Main Capitol Bldg *Web:* www.governor.state.pa.us	Harrisburg	PA	17120	717-787-2500	772-8284
Luis G Hon (PPD) (Governor) 2ndo Piso, Puerta de Tierra *TF:* 866-266-6678 ■ *Web:* www.fortaleza.gobierno.pr	San Juan	PR	00901	787-723-6333	729-7738
Governor Lincoln D (R) (Governor) 222 State House *Web:* www.governor.state.ri.us	Providence	RI	02903	401-222-2080	273-5729
Nimrata Nikki Randhawa Haley 800 Richland St *Web:* www.nikkihaley.com	Columbia	SC	29201	803-734-2100	734-5167
Dennis Daugaard (R) (Governor) 500 E Capitol Ave *Web:* www.sd.gov	Pierre	SD	57501	605-773-3212	773-5844
Bill Haslam (D) (Governor) State Capitol 1st Fl *Web:* www.tennesseeanytime.org/governor	Nashville	TN	37243	615-741-2001	532-9711
Rick Perry (R) (Governor) PO Box 12428 *TF:* 800-843-5789 ■ *Web:* www.governor.state.tx.us	Austin	TX	78711	512-463-2000	463-1849
John P de Jongh Jr (D) (Governor) 21-22 Kongens Gade *Web:* www.governordejongh.com	Saint Thomas	VI	00802	340-774-0001	774-1361
Earl Ray Tomblin (Governor) State Capitol Bldg 1900 Kanawha Blvd E *Web:* www.wvgov.org	Charleston	WV	25305	304-558-2000	342-7025
Doyle Jim (D) (Governor) State Capitol PO Box 7863 *Web:* www.wisgov.state.wi.us	Madison	WI	53707	608-266-1212	267-8983
Freudenthal David D (D) (Governor) State Capitol 200 W 24th St Rm 124 *Web:* www.wyoming.gov/governor	Cheyenne	WY	82002	307-777-7434	632-3909

347 GRAPHIC DESIGN

SEE ALSO Typesetting & Related Services p. 2742

Listing	City	State	Zip	*Phone*	*Fax*
3 Strikes Inc 1905 Elizabeth Ave *TF:* 888-725-8483 ■ *Web:* www.3strikes.com	Rahway	NJ	07065	732-382-3820	382-4082
Addis Group Inc 2515 9th St *Web:* www.addiscreson.com	Berkeley	CA	94710	510-704-7500	704-7501
B&B Image Group 1712 Marshall St NE *TF:* 888-788-9461 ■ *Web:* www.bbimagegroup.com	Minneapolis	MN	55413	612-788-9461	788-3253
Bendsen Signs & Graphics Inc 2901 N Woodford St *Web:* www.bendsensigns.com	Decatur	IL	62526	217-877-2345	877-2347
BrandEquity International 2330 Washington St *TF:* 800-969-3150 ■ *Web:* www.brandequity.com	Newton	MA	02462	617-969-3150	969-1944
Champion Awards Inc 3649 Winplace Rd *TF:* 800-242-6781 ■ *Web:* www.champion-awards.com	Memphis	TN	38118	901-365-4830	365-2796
CMI Inc 1716 W Grand Ave *Web:* www.cmiart.com	Chicago	IL	60622	312-666-4000	666-4001
Corporate Visions Inc 2000 M St NW 8th Fl *Web:* www.corpvisions.com	Washington	DC	20036	202-833-4333	833-4332
Creative Assoc 1 Snoopy Pl	Santa Rosa	CA	95403	707-546-7121	526-7361
Curran & Connors Inc 333 Marcus Blvd *Web:* www.curran-connors.com	Hauppauge	NY	11788	631-435-0400	435-0422
Deskey Assoc Inc 120 E 8th St *TF:* 877-433-7539 ■ *Web:* www.deskey.com	Cincinnati	OH	45202	513-721-6800	639-7575
Flavia Co The 111 El Paseo *Web:* flaviastore.artehouse.com/perl/home.pl	Santa Barbara	CA	93101	805-884-9626	884-0172

Company	City	State	ZIP	Phone	Fax
Girvin Inc 121 Stewart St Suite 212	Seattle	WA	98101	206-623-7808	674-7909
Web: www.girvin.com					
Great Lakes Graphics Inc 5555 W Howard St	Skokie	IL	60077	847-679-6710	
Imprimis Group Inc 4835 Lyndon B Johnson Fwy	Dallas	TX	75244	972-419-1700	419-1799
Web: www.imprimis.com					
Kane Graphical Corp 2255 W Logan Blvd	Chicago	IL	60647	773-384-1200	384-1207
TF: 800-992-2921 ■ *Web:* www.kanegraphical.com					
Mentus 6755 Mira Mesa Blvd Suite 123-137	San Diego	CA	92121	858-455-5500	455-6872
Web: www.mentus.com					
Metro Creative Graphics Inc 519 8th Ave	New York	NY	10018	212-947-5100	714-9139
TF: 800-223-1600 ■ *Web:* www.metrocreativegraphics.com					
NESCO Inc Service Group					
6140 Parkland Blvd	Mayfield Heights	OH	44124	440-461-6000	449-3111
P & R Group 222 W Hubbard St	Chicago	IL	60610	312-329-9600	822-9592
Web: www.pandrgroup.com					
Primary Color Systems Corp 265 Briggs Ave	Costa Mesa	CA	92626	949-660-7080	975-1557
Web: www.primarycolor.com					
Prism Studios Inc 2505 Kennedy St NE	Minneapolis	MN	55413	612-331-1000	331-4106
TF: 800-659-2001					
Signature Graphics Inc 1000 Signature Dr	Porter	IN	46304	219-926-4994	926-7231
TF: 800-356-3235 ■ *Web:* www.signaturegraph.com					
Smith Design Assoc					
205 Thomas St PO Box 8278	Glen Ridge	NJ	07028	973-429-2177	429-7119
Web: www.smithdesign.com					
Spire Inc 65 Bay St	Dorchester	MA	02125	617-426-3323	426-4114
TF: 800-653-3323 ■ *Web:* www.spire.net					
Subia Corp 6612 Gulton Ct NE	Albuquerque	NM	87109	505-345-2636	344-9177
TF: 800-275-2636 ■ *Web:* www.subia.com					
Unimac Graphics 350 Michele Pl	Carlstadt	NJ	07072	201-372-9650	372-9896
Web: www.unimacgraphics.com					
Vista Color Lab Inc 2048 Fulton Rd	Cleveland	OH	44113	216-651-2830	651-5004
TF: 800-890-0062 ■ *Web:* www.vistacolorimaging.com					
WBK Marketing & Design LLC					
537 E Pete Rose Way Suite 100	Cincinnati	OH	45202	513-784-0066	784-0986
Wesco Graphics Inc 410 E Grantline Rd Suite B	Tracy	CA	95376	209-832-1000	832-7800

348 GROCERY STORES

SEE ALSO Bakeries p. 1505; Convenience Stores p. 1748; Gourmet Specialty Shops p. 1907; Health Food Stores p. 2009; Ice Cream & Dairy Stores p. 2103; Wholesale Clubs p. 2775

Company	City	State	ZIP	Phone	Fax
A.g. Ferrari Foods 14234 Catalina St	San Leandro	CA	94577	510-346-2100	351-2672
TF: 877-878-2783 ■ *Web:* www.agferrari.com					
Acme Markets Inc 75 Valley Stream Pkwy	Malvern	PA	19355	610-889-4000	644-6814
TF: 800-767-2312 ■ *Web:* www.acmemarkets.com					
Alaska Commercial Co					
550 W 64th Ave Suite 200	Anchorage	AK	99518	907-273-4600	273-4800
TF: 800-478-4484 ■ *Web:* www.alaskacommercial.com					
ALDI Inc 1200 N Kirk Rd	Batavia	IL	60510	630-879-8100	879-9901
TF: 800-388-2534 ■ *Web:* www.aldi.us					
Allen's of Hastings Inc 1115 W 2nd St	Hastings	NE	68901	402-463-5633	463-5730
Web: www.allensuperstore.com					
Alliance Foods Inc 605 W Chicago Rd	Coldwater	MI	49036	517-278-2396	278-7936
TF: 800-388-4158 ■ *Web:* www.alliance-foods.com					
American Consumers Inc 55 Hannah Way	Rossville	GA	30741	706-861-3347	861-3364
TF: 800-742-3347					
Andronico's Market 1109 Washington Ave	Albany	CA	94706	510-559-2800	524-3601
Web: www.andronicos.com					
Atkinsons' Market Inc 451 4th St E	Ketchum	ID	83340	208-726-5668	726-3603
Web: www.atkinsons.com					
Autry Greer & Sons Inc 2850 W Main St	Prichard	AL	36612	251-457-8655	456-3744
TF: 800-477-9490 ■ *Web:* www.greers.com					
Ava Ruha Corp 225 E 17th St	Costa Mesa	CA	92627	949-631-4741	548-4232
Web: www.mothersmarket.com					
B & B Corporate Holdings Inc 927 US Hwy 301 S	Tampa	FL	33619	813-621-6411	622-8163*
B. Green & Co 1300 S Monroe St	Baltimore	MD	21230	410-539-6134	
Web: www.bgreenco.com					
Balls Food Stores Inc 5300 Speaker Rd	Kansas City	KS	66106	913-321-4223	551-8500
Web: www.henhouse.com					
Bashas Inc 22402 S Bashas Rd	Chandler	AZ	85248	480-895-9350	895-5292*
**Fax:* PR ■ *TF:* 800-755-7292 ■ *Web:* www.bashas.com					
Berkot Super Foods 20005 Wolf Rd	Mokena	IL	60448	708-479-7411	
Web: www.berkotfoods.com					
BI-LO LLC PO Box 99	Mauldin	SC	29662	800-862-9293	
TF: 800-862-9293 ■ *Web:* www.bi-lo.com					
Big Save Inc 4416 Waielo Rd PO Box 68	Eleele	HI	96705	808-335-3145	335-5049
Big Saver Foods Inc 4260 Charter St	Vernon	CA	90058	323-582-7222	582-2331
Web: www.bigsaverfoods.com					
Big Y Foods Inc 2145 Roosevelt Ave	Springfield	MA	01102	413-784-0600	732-8475
TF Cust Svc: 800-828-2688 ■ *Web:* www.bigy.com					
BiLo/Riverside Markets PO Box 607	Du Bois	PA	15801	814-375-3663	375-2974
TF: 800-922-1026 ■ *Web:* www.bilofoods.com					
Bordner PJ Co Inc 2100 Wales Rd NE	Massillon	OH	44646	330-832-7522	832-9691
Breadbox Food Stores Inc 10904 McBride Ln	Knoxville	TN	37932	865-777-2162	777-2167
Web: www.breadbox.biz					
Bristol Farms 915 E 230th St	Carson	CA	90745	310-233-4700	233-4701
Web: www.bristolfarms.com					
Brookshire Bros Ltd 1201 Ellen Trout Dr	Lufkin	TX	75904	936-634-8155	633-4611
TF: 800-364-6690 ■ *Web:* www.brookshirebrothers.com					
Brookshire Grocery Co 1600 W SW Loop 323	Tyler	TX	75701	903-534-3000	
Web: www.brookshires.com					
Bruno's Supermarkets 800 Lakeshore Pkwy	Birmingham	AL	35211	205-940-9400	912-4217*
**Fax:* Hum Res ■ *TF:* 877-247-4440 ■ *Web:* www.brunos.com					
Buehler Food Markets Inc					
1401 Old Mansfield Rd	Wooster	OH	44691	330-264-4355	
Web: www.buehlers.com					
Butera Finer Foods Inc 1 Clock Tower Plaza	Elgin	IL	60120	847-741-1010	741-9674
Web: www.buteramarket.com					
C & K Markets Inc 615 5th St	Brookings	OR	97415	541-469-3113	469-6717
TF: 800-932-7297 ■ *Web:* www.ckmarket.com					
Calhoun Enterprises 4155 Lomac St Suite G	Montgomery	AL	36106	334-272-4400	272-7799
TF: 800-294-1995 ■ *Web:* www.calhounenterprises.com					
Camellia Foods					
1300 Diamond Springs Rd Suite 500	Virginia Beach	VA	23445	757-855-3371	853-7405
Capitol Distributing Inc					
3500 E Commercial Ct	Meridian	ID	83642	208-888-5112	888-5989
Web: www.capitoldist.com					
Capri IGA Foodliner 224 E Harris Ave	Greenville	IL	62246	618-664-0022	664-4629
Cefco Convenience Stores Inc 2002 Scott Blvd	Temple	TX	76504	254-791-0009	791-0018
Web: www.cefcostores.com					
Certi-Saver Supermarket 1 Certified Dr	Hodgkins	IL	60525	708-579-2100	354-7502
Web: www.certisaver.com					
Chief Super Market Inc					
1340 W High St Suite E	Defiance	OH	43512	419-782-0950	782-6047
City Market 555 Sandhill Ln	Grand Junction	CO	81505	970-241-0750	255-0941
Web: www.citymarket.com					
Clark Gas & Oil PO Box 31	Stuart	VA	24171	276-694-3722	694-4684
Web: www.clarkgasandoil.com					
Clemens Markets Inc					
1555 Bustard Rd PO Box 1555	Kulpsville	PA	19443	215-361-9000	361-9000*
Clines Corners 1 Yacht Club Dr	Clines Corners	NM	87070	505-472-5488	472-5487
Web: www.clinescorners.com					
Coborn's Inc 1445 E Hwy 23	Saint Cloud	MN	56302	320-252-4222	252-0014
TF: 888-269-6201 ■ *Web:* www.cobornsinc.com					
Consun Food Industries Inc 123 N Gateway Blvd	Elyria	OH	44035	440-322-6301	322-8196
Covington Foods Inc 419 4th St PO Box 206	Covington	IN	47932	765-793-2470	793-0209
Crest Discount Foods Inc					
249 N Douglas Blvd	Midwest City	OK	73130	405-733-2330	733-5126
Web: www.crestfoodsok.com					
Cub Foods Stores 421 S 3rd St	Stillwater	MN	55082	651-439-7200	439-7200
Web: www.cub.com					
Cubby's Inc 9230 Mormon Bridge Rd	Omaha	NE	68152	402-453-2468	453-4513
Web: www.cubbys.com					
Dahl's Food Marts 4343 Merle Hay Rd	Des Moines	IA	50310	515-276-4845	278-0012
Delsea Shop Rite 215 N Delsea Dr	Vineland	NJ	08360	856-691-9395	691-6167
Web: www.shoprite.com					
DeMoulas Super Markets Inc 875 E St	Tewksbury	MA	01876	978-851-8000	640-8390
Dierbergs Markets Inc					
16690 Swingley Ridge Rd	Chesterfield	MO	63017	636-532-8884	812-1603
Web: www.dierbergs.com					
Dominick's Finer Foods Inc 711 Jorie Blvd	Oak Brook	IL	60523	630-891-5000	891-5180*
**Fax:* PR ■ *TF:* 877-723-3929 ■ *Web:* www.dominicks.com					
Dorignac's Food Center Inc					
710 Veterans Memorial Blvd	Metairie	LA	70005	504-837-4650	832-8944
Web: dorignacs.com					
Dorothy Lane Market Inc 2710 Far Hills Ave	Dayton	OH	45419	937-299-3561	299-3568
Web: www.dorothylane.com					
Double 8 Foods Inc 2201 E 46th St	Indianapolis	IN	46205	317-253-3417	257-0209
Web: www.double8foods.com					
Draeger's Super Markets Inc 222 E 4th Ave	San Mateo	CA	94401	650-685-3715	244-6548
Web: www.draegers.com					
Easy Way Food Stores Inc					
4545 S Mendenhall Rd	Memphis	TN	38141	901-527-6256	462-3965
Web: www.easywayproduce.com					
Econo Foods 1600 Stephenson PO Box 1107	Iron Mountain	MI	49801	906-774-1911	774-1915
TF: 877-295-4558 ■ *Web:* www.econotnc.com					
Essential Baking Co The 5601 1st Ave S	Seattle	WA	98108	206-545-3804	876-3768
Web: www.essentialbaking.com					
Fareway Stores Inc 2300 E 8th St PO Box 70	Boone	IA	50036	515-432-2623	433-4416
Farmer Jack 18718 Borman Ave	Detroit	MI	48228	313-270-1226	
TF: 877-327-5225 ■ *Web:* www.farmerjack.com					
Fastop Inc PO Box 806	Jasper	IN	47547	812-634-1074	482-6676
Web: www.ackoil.com					
Federated Group Inc					
3025 W Salt Creek Ln	Arlington Heights	IL	60005	847-577-1200	632-8302
TF: 800-234-0011 ■ *Web:* www.fedgroup.com					
Felpausch Food Centers 127 S Michigan Ave	Hastings	MI	49058	269-945-3485	945-3485
TF: 800-648-6433					
Fiesta Mart Inc 5235 Katy Fwy	Houston	TX	77007	713-869-6197	
TF: 800-123-4567 ■ *Web:* www.fiestamart.com					
First Coast Energy LLP					
7014 A C Skinner Pkwy Suite 290	Jacksonville	FL	32256	904-596-3200	596-8550
Web: www.dailysstores.com					
Food City 1005 N Arizona Ave	Chandler	AZ	85244	480-857-2198	
TF: 800-755-7292 ■ *Web:* www.myfoodcity.com					
Food Country USA 566 E Main St	Abingdon	VA	24210	276-628-3332	628-4613
Web: foodcountryusainc.com					
Food Emporium Inc The 42 W 39th St 18th Fl	New York	NY	10018	212-915-2202	226-5911*
**Fax Area Code:* 914 ■ *TF:* 866-443-7374 ■ *Web:* www.thefoodemporium.com					
Food Giant Supermarkets 120 Industrial Dr	Sikeston	MO	63801	573-471-3500	472-3135
TF: 800-388-3745					
Foodarama Supermarkets Inc					
922 Hwy 33 Bldg 6 Suite 1	Freehold	NJ	07728	732-462-4700	294-2322
Foodland Super Market Ltd 3536 Harding Ave	Honolulu	HI	96816	808-732-0791	737-4583
Web: www.foodland.com					
Foodmaster Supermarkets Inc					
100 Everett Ave Unit 12	Chelsea	MA	02150	617-660-1300	660-1399
Web: www.foodmastersupermarketinc.com					
Four B Corp 5300 Speaker Rd	Kansas City	KS	66106	913-321-4223	551-8500
Web: www.henhous.com					
Fred Meyer Inc 3800 SE 22nd PO Box 42121	Portland	OR	97202	503-232-8844	797-5395*
**Fax:* Cust Svc ■ *TF:* 800-858-9202 ■ *Web:* www.fredmeyer.com					
Fresh Brands Inc 2215 Union Ave PO Box 419	Sheboygan	WI	53081	920-457-4433	208-5000
TF: 800-530-7286 ■ *Web:* www.fresh-brands.com					
Fresh Encounter Inc 317 W Main Cross St	Findlay	OH	45840	419-422-8090	424-3932
Web: www.freshencounter.com					

				Phone	Fax
FreshDirect Inc 23-30 Borden Ave	Long Island City	NY	11101	718-928-1000	928-1050
TF: 866-511-1240 ■ Web: www.freshdirect.com					
Fry's Food Stores of Arizona Inc 500 S 99th Ave	Tolleson	AZ	85353	623-936-2100	907-4966
TF: 800-828-5235 ■ Web: www.frysfood.com					
Gelson's Markets 2020 S Central Ave	Compton	CA	90220	310-638-2842	631-0950
Web: www.gelsons.com					
Gerland's Corp 3131 Pawnee St	Houston	TX	77054	713-746-3600	746-3621
Web: www.gerlands.com					
Giant Eagle Inc 101 Kappa Dr	Pittsburgh	PA	15238	412-963-6200	967-3700
TF Cust Svc: 800-553-2324 ■ Web: www.gianteagle.com					
Giant Food Inc 8301 Professional Pl Suite 115	Landover	MD	20785	301-341-4100	618-4998*
*Fax: Cust Svc ■ TF: 888-469-4426 ■ Web: www.giantfood.com					
Giant Food Stores Inc 1149 Harrisburg Pike	Carlisle	PA	17013	717-249-4000	960-1356*
*Fax: Mail Rm ■ TF: 800-380-3814 ■ Web: www.giantfoodstores.com					
Golub Corp 461 Nott St	Schenectady	NY	12308	518-355-5000	379-3515
TF: 800-666-7667 ■ Web: www.pricechopper.com					
Goodsons' Supermarkets Inc Rt 52 Premier Mountain PO Box 858	Welch	WV	24801	304-436-8482	436-6888
Grade A Markets Inc 563 Newfield Ave	Stamford	CT	06905	203-356-1662	961-8135
Great Atlantic & Pacific Tea Co Inc 2 Paragon Dr	Montvale	NJ	07645	201-573-9700	571-8820
NYSE: GAP ■ TF: 866-443-7374 ■ Web: www.aptea.com					
Great Atlantic & Pacific Tea Co Inc The (A&p) 2 Paragon Dr	Montvale	NJ	07645	201-571-4806	571-4821
Web: www.aptea.com					
Groupon Inc 600 W Chicago Ave Suite 620	Chicago	IL	60654	312-676-5773	676-2728
Web: www.groupon.com					
Gs Foods Inc 5925 S Alcoa Ave	Vernon	CA	90058	323-581-6161	589-2106
Web: www.gsfoods.com					
Haggen Inc 2211 Rimland Dr	Bellingham	WA	98226	360-733-8720	
Web: www.haggen.com					
Hancock County Co-op Oil Assn 245 State St	Garner	IA	50438	641-923-2635	
TF: 800-924-2667 ■ Web: www.hancockcountycoop.com					
Hannaford Bros Co 145 Pleasant Hill Rd	Scarborough	ME	04074	207-883-2911	
TF: 800-341-6393 ■ Web: www.hannaford.com					
Harmons Grocery 3540 S 4000 W	West Valley City	UT	84120	801-969-8261	964-1299
Web: www.harmonsgrocery.com					
Harps Food Stores Inc 918 S Gutensohn Rd	Springdale	AR	72762	479-751-7601	751-3625
TF: 877-772-8193 ■ Web: www.harpsfood.com					
Harris Teeter Inc 701 Crestdale Rd PO Box 10100	Matthews	NC	28105	704-844-3100	
TF Cust Svc: 800-432-6111 ■ Web: www.harristeeter.com					
Hastings Co-op Creamery Co 1701 Vermillion St PO Box 217	Hastings	MN	55033	651-437-9414	437-3547
Web: www.hastingscreamery.com					
HE Butt Grocery Co (HEB) PO Box 839999	San Antonio	TX	78283	210-938-8357	938-8169
TF: 800-432-3113 ■ Web: www.heb.com					
Heinen's Inc 4540 Richmond Rd	Warrensville Heights	OH	44128	216-475-2300	514-4788
Web: www.heinens.com					
Hi Nabor Supermarket Inc 7201 Winbourne Ave	Baton Rouge	LA	70805	225-357-1448	357-7109
Hollywood Super Market Inc 2670 W Maple Rd PO Box 1286	Troy	MI	48084	248-643-6770	643-0309
Web: www.hollywoodmarkets.net					
Hornbacher's 2510 N Broadway	Fargo	ND	58102	701-293-5444	293-8770
Web: www.hornbachers.com					
Houchens Industries Inc 700 Church St	Bowling Green	KY	42102	270-843-3252	
TF: 800-843-3252					
Hy-Vee Inc 5820 Westown Pkwy	West Des Moines	IA	50266	515-267-2800	267-2817*
*Fax: Mail Rm ■ Web: www.hy-vee.com					
IGA Inc 8725 W Higgins Rd Suite 725	Chicago	IL	60631	773-693-4520	693-1271
TF: 800-321-5442 ■ Web: www.iga.com					
Ingles Markets Inc 2913 US Hwy 70 W	Black Mountain	NC	28711	828-669-2941	669-3536
NASDAQ: IMKTA ■ TF: 800-635-5066 ■ Web: www.ingles-markets.com					
Inserra ShopRite PO Box 7812	Edison	NJ	08818	201-529-5900	529-1189
TF: 800-746-7748 ■ Web: www.shoprite.com					
Ira Higdon Grocery Co Inc 150 IGA WAY PO Box 488	Cairo	GA	39828	229-377-1272	377-8756
Web: www.irahigdongc.com					
Jack Young's Supermarket Inc 3513 W Walnut Ave PO Box 3167	Visalia	CA	93278	559-625-9252	627-1945*
JC Pace Ltd 420 Throckmorton St Suite 710	Fort Worth	TX	76102	817-332-1219	332-3296
Jerry Lee's Grocery Inc 1411 Hwy 90	Gautier	MS	39553	228-497-3281	497-1026
Jerry's Foods 5101 Vernon Ave S	Edina	MN	55436	952-929-2685	
Web: www.jerrysfoods.com					
K-VA-T Food Stores Inc PO Box 1158	Abingdon	VA	24212	276-623-5100	623-5441
TF: 800-826-8451 ■ Web: www.foodcity.com					
Kash N' Karry Food Stores Inc 3801 Sugar Palm Dr	Tampa	FL	33619	813-620-1139	626-9550*
*Fax: Mail Rm ■ Web: www.sweetbaysupermarket.com					
Kennies Market Inc 217 W Middle St	Gettysburg	PA	17325	717-334-0402	334-2848
Web: www.kenniesmarket.com					
Kessler's Inc 621 6th Ave SE	Aberdeen	SD	57401	605-225-1692	225-0954
King Kullen Grocery Co Inc 185 Central Ave	Bethpage	NY	11714	516-733-7100	827-6325
Web: www.kingkullen.com					
Kirby Foods Inc 4102-B Fieldstone Rd PO Box 6268	Champaign	IL	61826	217-352-2600	352-9394
Web: www.kirbyfoods.com					
Klass Ingredients Inc 3885 N Buffalo St	Orchard Park	NY	14127	716-662-6665	662-0285
Web: www.klassingredients.com					
Kroger Co 1014 Vine St	Cincinnati	OH	45202	513-762-4000	
NYSE: KR ■ TF: 800-576-4377 ■ Web: www.kroger.com					
Kuukpik Corp PO Box 89187	Nuiqsut	AK	99789	907-480-6220	
TF: 866-480-6220 ■ Web: www.kuukpik.com					
L & L Food Centers 4924 S ML King Jr Blvd	Lansing	MI	48910	517-887-1877	393-2477
Leevers Supermarkets Inc 2195 N Hwy 83 Unit AA	Franktown	CO	80116	303-814-8646	814-8645
Web: www.leevers.com					
Loblaw Cos Ltd 1áPresident'sáChoiceáCir	Brampton	ON	L6Y5S5	905-459-2500	
TF: 877-525-4762 ■ Web: www.loblaw.com					

				Phone	Fax
Lowe's 1804 Hall Ave PO Box 1430	Littlefield	TX	79339	806-385-3366	385-8629
Web: www.lowesmarket.com					
Lowes Food Stores Inc 1381 Old Mill Cir Suite 200	Winston-Salem	NC	27103	336-659-0180	768-4702
TF: 800-669-5693 ■ Web: www.lowesfoods.com					
Mal Enterprises Inc 1219 Broadway St	Sweetwater	TX	79556	915-236-6351	236-6336
Market Day Corp 555 W Pierce Rd Suite 200	Itasca	IL	60143	630-285-1470	285-3340
TF: 877-632-7753 ■ Web: www.marketday.com					
Market Grocery Co 16 Forest Pkwy Bldg K	Forest Park	GA	30297	404-361-8620	361-3773
Web: www.marketgrocery.com					
Markets LLC The PO Box 9797	Bellingham	WA	98227	360-714-9797	
Web: www.themarketsllc.com					
Mars Supermarkets Inc 9627 Philadelphia Rd	Rosedale	MD	21237	410-590-0500	
TF: 888-284-7773 ■ Web: www.marsfood.com					
Marsh Supermarkets Inc 333 S Franklin Rd	Indianapolis	IN	46219	317-594-2100	594-2707*
*Fax: Hum Res ■ Web: www.marsh.net					
Martin & Bayley Inc 1311 A W Main	Carmi	IL	62821	618-382-2334	382-8956
TF: 800-876-2511 ■ Web: www.martinandbayley.com					
Martin's Marketplace 130 Tichenal Way	Cashmere	WA	98815	509-782-3801	782-2212
Mass Marketing Inc 401 Isom Rd Bldg 100	San Antonio	TX	78216	210-344-1960	341-6326
TF: 800-279-1149					
Meijer Inc 2929 Walker Ave NW	Grand Rapids	MI	49544	616-453-6711	453-6067
TF: 800-543-3704 ■ Web: www.meijer.com					
Meijer Stores Inc 2929 Walker Ave NW	Grand Rapids	MI	49544	616-453-6711	791-5131
TF: 800-543-3704 ■ Web: www.meijer.com					
Merchants Grocery Co 800 Maddox Dr PO Box 1268	Culpeper	VA	22701	540-825-0786	825-9016
TF: 877-897-9893 ■ Web: www.merchants-grocery.com					
Metro Inc 5559 Dundas St W	Etobicoke	ON	M9B1B9	416-239-7171	234-6583*
*Fax: Hum Res ■ TF: 800-268-2564 ■ Web: www.metro.ca					
Metro Inc 11011 boul Maurice Duplessis	Montreal	QC	H1C1V6	514-643-1000	
Web: www.metro.ca					
Mi Pueblo San Jose Inc 1745 Story Rd PO Box 3288	San Jose	CA	95122	408-259-3421	928-1172
TF: 888-997-7717 ■ Web: www.mipueblofoods.com					
Minyard Food Stores Inc 777 Freeport Pkwy	Coppell	TX	75019	972-393-8700	393-8550
Web: www.minyards.com					
Mohar Inc 550 Gravenstein Hwy N	Sebastopol	CA	95472	707-823-1418	823-1473
Web: www.fiestamkt.com					
Musser's Inc 35 Friendly Dr	Quarryville	PA	17566	717-284-4147	284-4145
Web: www.mussersmarket.com					
Nature's Best 6 Pointe Dr Suite 300	Brea	CA	92822	714-255-4600	255-4691*
*Fax Area Code: 741 ■ TF: 800-800-7799 ■ Web: www.naturesbest.net					
Netgrocer.com 14 Post Rd	Oakland	NJ	07436	201-337-3900	405-0578
TF: 888-638-4762 ■ Web: www.netgrocer.com					
Niemann Foods Inc 1501 N 12th St	Quincy	IL	62306	217-221-5600	221-5920
TF: 800-477-0156 ■ Web: www.discountfoods.com					
No Frills Supermarkets Inc 11163 Mills Alley Rd	Omaha	NE	68154	402-399-9244	399-0264
Norman Bros Produce Inc 7621 SW 87th Ave	Miami	FL	33173	305-274-9363	596-4541
Web: www.normanbrothers.com					
Norrenberns Foods Inc 205 E Harnett St	Mascoutah	IL	62258	618-566-7010	566-2366
Northgate Gonzalez Inc 1201 N Magnolia Ave	Anaheim	CA	92801	714-778-3784	778-3295
Web: www.northgatemarkets.com					
Novelty Inc 351 W Muskegon Dr	Greenfield	IN	46140	317-462-3121	462-8569
TF: 800-334-4354 ■ Web: www.noveltyinc.com					
Nugget Markets 157 Main St	Woodland	CA	95695	530-662-5479	668-1246
Web: www.nuggetmarket.com					
Overwaitea Food Group 19855 92A Ave	Langley	BC	V1M3B6	604-888-1213	
TF: 800-242-9229 ■ Web: www.owfg.com					
P & C Foods 1200 State Fair Blvd	Syracuse	NY	13209	315-457-9460	461-2353*
*Fax: Mail Rm ■ TF Cust Svc: 800-724-0205 ■ Web: www.pandcfoods.com					
Pathmark Stores Inc 2 Paragon Dr	Montvale	NJ	07008	732-499-3000	499-3072*
*Fax: PR ■ TF: 866-443-7374 ■ Web: www.pathmark.com					
Peapod LLC 9933 Woods Dr	Skokie	IL	60077	847-583-9400	583-9494
TF: 800-573-2763 ■ Web: www.peapod.com					
Penn Traffic Co 1200 State Fair Blvd	Syracuse	NY	13209	315-453-7284	461-2387*
*Fax: Acctg ■ TF: 800-275-9005 ■ Web: www.penntraffic.com					
Perlmart Inc 954 Rt 166	Toms River	NJ	08753	732-341-0700	240-9291
Pete's County Market 2612 S Broadway St	Alexandria	MN	56308	320-762-1158	762-0486
Web: www.petescountymarket.com					
Petrey W L Wholesale Co Inc 10345 Petrey Hwy	Luverne	AL	36049	334-230-5674	335-2422
Web: www.petrey.com					
Pick N Save 6950 W State St	Wauwatosa	WI	53213	414-475-7181	
Web: www.picknsave.com					
Piggly Wiggly Carolina Co Inc PO Box 118047	Charleston	SC	29423	843-554-9880	745-2730
TF: 800-243-9880 ■ Web: www.thepig.net					
Price Chopper Food Stores 5300 Speaker Rd	Kansas City	KS	66106	913-321-4223	551-8500
Web: www.mypricechopper.com					
Publix Super Markets Inc 3300 Publix Corporate Pkwy	Lakeland	FL	33811	863-688-1188	284-3331*
*Fax: Hum Res ■ TF PR: 800-342-1227 ■ Web: www.publix.com					
Pueblo International LLC 1300 NW 22nd St	Pompano Beach	FL	33069	954-977-2500	968-2648*
*Fax: Hum Res ■ Web: www.puebloxtra.com					
Quality Food Centers Inc 10116 NE 8th St	Bellevue	WA	98004	425-455-3761	462-2162
TF: 800-201-6261 ■ Web: www.qfc.com					
Quillin's Inc 700 N 3rd St Suite 105	La Crosse	WI	54601	608-785-1424	785-7175
Web: www.quillinsfoods.com					
Raley's 500 W Capitol Ave PO Box 15618	Sacramento	CA	95852	916-373-3333	373-0881*
*Fax: Cust Svc ■ TF: 800-925-9989 ■ Web: www.raleys.com					
Ralphs Grocery Co 1100 W Artesia Blvd	Compton	CA	90220	310-884-9000	884-2600
TF Cust Svc: 888-437-3496 ■ Web: www.ralphs.com					
Redner's Markets Inc 3 Quarry Rd	Reading	PA	19605	610-926-3700	926-6327
Web: www.rednersmarkets.com					
Remke Markets Inc 1299 Cox Ave	Erlanger	KY	41018	859-594-3400	594-3488
Web: www.remkes.com					
Reopco Inc 4930 E State St PO Box 4745	Rockford	IL	61110	815-387-1700	387-7884
Web: www.roadrangerusa.com					

Company / Address	City	State	ZIP	Phone	Fax
Resource Plus 9636 Heckscher Dr *Web:* www.resourcep.com	Jacksonville	FL	32226	888-678-8966	
RF Owens Co Inc 1062 Broadway *Web:* www.trucchis.com	Raynham	MA	02767	508-824-7515	824-7576
Rice Epicurean Markets Inc 5333 Gulfton St. *Web:* www.riceepicurean.com	Houston	TX	77081	713-662-7700	662-7757
Riesbeck Food Markets Inc 48661 National Rd *Web:* www.riesbeckfoods.com	Saint Clairsville	OH	43950	740-695-7050	695-7555
Roche Bros Supermarkets Inc 70 Hastings St *Web:* www.rochebros.com	Wellesley Hills	MA	02481	781-235-9400	235-3153
Rosauers Super Markets Inc 1815 W Garland Ave. *Web:* www.rosauers.com	Spokane	WA	99205	509-326-8900	328-2483
Roth's Family Markets 4895 Indian School Rd NE *TF:* 800-722-7684 ■ *Web:* www.roths.com	Salem	OR	97305	503-393-7684	393-4456
Safeway Inc 5918 Stoneridge Mall Rd. *NYSE: SWY* ■ *Web:* www.safeway.com	Pleasanton	CA	94588	925-467-3000	467-3323
Save Mart Supermarkets Inc PO Box 4278 **Fax:* Mktg ■ *Web:* www.savemart.com	Modesto	CA	95352	209-577-1600	577-3845*
Save-A-Lot Ltd 100 Corporate Office Dr *Web:* www.save-a-lot.com	Earth City	MO	63045	314-592-9100	592-9619
Schnuck Markets Inc 11420 Lackland Rd *TF:* 800-264-4400 ■ *Web:* www.schnucks.com	Saint Louis	MO	63146	314-994-9900	994-4337
Scolari's Food & Drug Co 255 S McCarran Blvd. *Web:* www.scolaristores.com	Sparks	NV	89431	775-331-7700	331-0675
Sedano's Supermarkets 3100 W 76th St. *Web:* www.sedanos.com	Hialeah	FL	33018	305-824-1034	556-6981
Shop 'n Save 10461 Manchester Rd **Fax:* Hum Res ■ *TF:* 800-368-7052 ■ *Web:* www.shopnsave.com	Kirkwood	MO	63122	314-984-0900	984-1390*
Shop-Rite Supermarkets Inc 55 Hannah Way PO Box 2328 *TF:* 800-742-3347	Fort Oglethorpe	GA	30742	706-861-3347	861-3364
Shoppers Food & Pharmacy 4600 Forbes Blvd *TF:* 800-775-9888 ■ *Web:* www.shoppersfood.com	Lanham	MD	20706	301-306-8600	
ShopRite Supermarkets Inc 600 York St *TF:* 800-746-7748 ■ *Web:* www.shoprite.com	Elizabeth	NJ	07207	908-527-3300	
SKH Management Co Inc 813 Lititz Pike PO Box 1500 *Web:* www.skh.com	Lititz	PA	17543	717-626-4771	626-0499
Smart & Final Inc 600 Citadel Dr *TF:* 800-894-0511 ■ *Web:* www.smartandfinal.com	Commerce	CA	90040	323-869-7500	869-7865
Sobeys Inc 115 King St *TF Cust Svc:* 888-944-0442 ■ *Web:* www.sobeys.ca	Stellarton	NS	B0K1S0	902-752-8371	752-2960
Spivey Enterprises Inc 6148 Brookshire Blvd *Web:* www.quikshoppe.com	Charlotte	NC	28216	704-399-4802	393-1940
Star Markets Ltd 1620 N School St *Web:* www.star-markets.com	Honolulu	HI	96817	808-832-8400	832-8420
Starco Impex Inc 2710 S 11th St **Fax Area Code:* 888 ■ *TF:* 866-740-9601 ■ *Web:* www.starcoimpex.com	Beaumont	TX	77701	866-740-9601	842-5650*
Stop & Shop Supermarket Co 1385 Hancock St. *Fax Area Code:* 617 ■ **Fax:* Hum Res ■ *Web:* www.stopandshop.com	Quincy	MA	02169	781-380-8000	770-8190*
Sunset Food Mart Inc 1812 Green Bay Rd. *Web:* www.sunsetfoods.com	Highland Park	IL	60035	847-432-5500	432-9335
Super A Foods Inc 7200 Dominion Cir *Web:* www.superafoods.com	Commerce	CA	90040	323-869-0600	869-0611
Super Center Concepts Inc 15510 Carmenita Rd *Web:* www.superiorgrocers.com	Santa Fe Springs	CA	90670	562-345-9000	345-9052
Super Fresh Food Markets Inc 2 Paragon Dr *TF:* 866-443-7374 ■ *Web:* www.superfreshfood.com/pages_aboutUs_CU.asp	Montvale	NJ	07645	866-443-7374	
Super H Mart Inc 2550 Pleasant Hill Rd *TF:* 877-427-7386 ■ *Web:* www.hmart.com	Duluth	GA	30096	678-543-4000	
SUPERVALU Inc 7075 Flying Cloud Dr *NYSE: SVU* ■ *TF Cust Svc:* 888-256-2800 ■ *Web:* www.supervalu.com	Eden Prairie	MN	55344	952-828-4000	828-8998
Sure Save Supermarkets Ltd 16-586 Old Volcano Rd *Web:* www.suresave.com	Keaau	HI	96749	808-966-9009	966-6200
Tamura Superette Inc 86-032 Farrington Hwy	Waianae	HI	96792	808-696-3321	696-8127
Thriftway Stores Inc 6433 SE Lake Rd *Web:* www.thriftwaystores.com	Portland	OR	97222	503-833-1288	944-3030
Thruway Food Market & Shopping Ctr 78 Oak St *Web:* www.shopthruway.com	Walden	NY	12586	845-778-3535	778-3659
Times Super Market Ltd 3375 Koapaka St Suite D108 *Web:* www.timessupermarkets.com	Honolulu	HI	96819	808-831-0811	831-0830
Tom's Food Markets 1311 S Division St *Web:* www.toms-foodmarkets.com	Traverse City	MI	49684	231-946-6431	
Tops Markets Inc PO Box 1027 *TF:* 800-522-2522 ■ *Web:* www.topsmarkets.com	Buffalo	NY	14240	716-635-5000	
Town & Country Markets Inc 20148 10th Ave NE *Web:* shared.central-market.com	Poulsbo	WA	98370	360-779-1881	
Trader Joe's Co 800 S Shamrock Ave *Web:* www.traderjoes.com	Monrovia	CA	91016	626-599-3700	
Treasure Island Foods Inc 3460 N Broadway Ave.	Chicago	IL	60657	773-327-4265	327-6337
Ukrop's Super Markets Inc 2001 Maywill St Suite 100 **Fax:* Hum Res ■ *TF:* 800-868-2270 ■ *Web:* www.ukropshomestylefoods.com	Richmond	VA	23230	804-340-3000	340-5198*
United Supermarkets Ltd 7830 Orlando Ave. *Web:* www.unitedtexas.com	Lubbock	TX	79423	806-791-0220	791-7491
Uwajimaya Inc 600 5th Ave S *TF:* 800-889-1928 ■ *Web:* www.uwajimaya.com	Seattle	WA	98104	206-624-6248	405-2996
Valu Discount Inc 315 Whittington Pkwy *Web:* www.valumarket.com	Louisville	KY	40222	502-327-8840	426-3731
Village Super Market Inc 733 Mountain Ave. *NASDAQ: VLGEA* ■ *TF:* 800-746-7748 ■ *Web:* www.shoprite.com	Springfield	NJ	07081	973-467-2200	467-6582
Waldbaums 2 Paragon Dr **Fax Area Code:* 201 ■ *TF:* 866-443-7374 ■ *Web:* www.waldbaums.com	Montvale	NJ	07645	866-443-7374	571-8748*
Wally's Supermarket 155 E 12TH St *Web:* www.wallyssupermarkets.com	Grafton	ND	58237	701-352-0770	352-1861
Walter Lagestee Inc 16145 S State St *Web:* www.waltsfoods.com	South Holland	IL	60473	708-333-5500	333-8713
Wedge Community Co-Op Inc 2105 Lyndale Ave S *Web:* www.wedge.coop	Minneapolis	MN	55405	612-871-3993	871-0734
Wegmans Food Markets Inc 1500 Brooks Ave PO Box 30844 **Fax:* Mail Rm ■ *TF:* 800-934-6267 ■ *Web:* www.wegmans.com	Rochester	NY	14603	585-328-2550	464-4626*
Weis Markets Inc 1000 S 2nd St PO Box 471 *NYSE: WMK* ■ *TF:* 866-999-9347 ■ *Web:* www.weismarkets.com	Sunbury	PA	17801	570-286-4571	286-3286
Western Bagel Baking Corp 7814 Sepulveda Blvd *Web:* www.westernbagel.com	Van Nuys	CA	91405	818-786-5847	787-3221
Western Beef Inc 47-05 Metropolitan Ave *Web:* www.westernbeef.com	Ridgewood	NY	11385	718-417-3770	628-2356
Western Supermarkets Inc 2614 19th St S *Web:* www.westernsupermarkets.com	Birmingham	AL	35209	205-879-3471	879-3476
Wilson Mills 5612 Wilson Mills Rd *TF:* 800-991-5444 ■ *Web:* www.catalano.com	Highland Heights	OH	44143	440-442-8800	461-6759
WinCo Foods Inc 650 N Armstrong Pl *TF:* 800-635-5167 ■ *Web:* www.wincofoods.com	Boise	ID	83705	208-377-0110	377-0474
Winegars Super Markets Inc 574 W 3400 S *Web:* www.winegars.com	Bountiful	UT	84010	801-298-5407	298-5463
Winn-Dixie Stores Inc 5050 Edgewood Ct. *Web:* www.winndixie.com	Jacksonville	FL	32254	904-783-5000	783-5294
Yokes Foods Inc 3426 S University Rd Suite 200 *Web:* www.yokesfoods.com	Spokane	WA	99206	509-921-2292	921-6801
Zallie Supermarkets 1230 Blackwood-Clementon Rd *Web:* www.shopripe.com	Clementon	NJ	08021	856-627-6501	627-8650

349 GYM & PLAYGROUND EQUIPMENT

Company / Address	City	State	ZIP	Phone	Fax
American Athletic Inc (AAI) 200 American Ave *TF:* 800-247-3978 ■ *Web:* www.americanathletic.com	Jefferson	IA	50129	515-386-3125	386-4566
American Playground Corp 6406 Production Dr *TF:* 800-541-1602	Anderson	IN	46013	765-642-0288	649-7162
BCI Burke Co Inc 660 Van Dyne Rd *TF:* 800-356-2070 ■ *Web:* www.bciburke.com	Fond du Lac	WI	54937	920-921-9220	921-9566
Columbia Cascade Co 1300 SW 6th Ave # 310 *TF:* 800-547-1940 ■ *Web:* www.timberform.com	Portland	OR	97201	503-223-1157	223-4530
Florida Playground & Steel Co 4701 S 50th St *TF:* 800-444-2655 ■ *Web:* www.fla-playground.com	Tampa	FL	33619	813-247-2812	247-1068
Game-Time Inc 150 Playcore Dr SE *TF:* 800-235-2440 ■ *Web:* www.gametime.com	Fort Payne	AL	35967	256-845-5610	997-5408
Grounds For Play Inc 1401 E Dallas St *TF:* 800-552-7529 ■ *Web:* www.groundsforplay.com	Mansfield	TX	76063	817-477-5482	477-1140
Jaypro Sports Inc 976 Hartford Tpke *TF Cust Svc:* 800-243-0533 ■ *Web:* www.jaypro.com	Waterford	CT	06385	860-447-3001	444-1779
Landscape Structures Inc 601 7th St S *TF:* 800-328-0035 ■ *Web:* www.playlsi.com	Delano	MN	55328	763-972-3391	972-3185
Miracle Recreation Equipment Co 878 Hwy 60 *TF:* 800-523-4202 ■ *Web:* www.miracle-recreation.com	Monett	MO	65708	417-235-6917	235-3551
PlayCore Inc 430 Chestnut St Suite 300 **Fax Area Code:* 877 ■ *TF:* 888-404-5737 ■ *Web:* www.playcore.com	Chattanooga	TN	37402	423-756-0015	762-7565*
Playworld Systems Inc 1000 Buffalo Rd *TF:* 800-233-8404 ■ *Web:* www.playworldsystems.com	Lewisburg	PA	17837	570-522-9800	522-3030
PW Athletic Mfg Co 140 N Gilbert Rd *TF:* 800-687-5768 ■ *Web:* www.pwathletic.com	Mesa	AZ	85203	928-778-4232	962-5290
School-Tech Inc 745 State Cir PO Box 1941 **Fax Area Code:* 800 ■ *TF:* 800-521-2832 ■ *Web:* www.school-tech.com	Ann Arbor	MI	48106	734-761-5072	654-4321*
SportsPlay Equipment Inc 5642 Natural Bridge Ave. *TF:* 800-727-8180 ■ *Web:* www.sportsplayinc.com	Saint Louis	MO	63120	314-389-4140	389-9034

350 GYPSUM PRODUCTS

Company / Address	City	State	ZIP	Phone	Fax
American Gypsum Co 3811 Turtle Creek Blvd Suite 1200 *TF:* 866-439-5800 ■ *Web:* www.americangypsum.com	Dallas	TX	75219	214-530-5500	
BPB Gypsum Inc 27442 Portola Pkwy Suite 100 *TF:* 800-426-3669	Foothill Ranch	CA	92610	949-282-5300	282-5334
Canadian Gypsum Co Inc 350 Burnhamthorpe Rd W 5th Fl *TF:* 800-565-6607 ■ *Web:* www.cgcinc.com	Mississauga	ON	L5B3J1	905-803-5600	803-5688
CertainTeed Gypsum 2424 Lakeshore Rd W *TF:* 800-731-3323 ■ *Web:* www.certainteed.com	Mississauga	ON	L5J1K4	905-823-9881	823-4860
Eagle Materials Inc 3811 Turtle Creek Blvd Suite 1100 *NYSE: EXP* ■ *TF:* 800-759-7625 ■ *Web:* www.eaglematerials.com	Dallas	TX	75219	214-432-2000	432-2100
G-P Gypsum Corp 133 Peachtree St NE **Fax:* Sales ■ *Web:* www.gp.com	Atlanta	GA	30303	404-652-4000	586-8140*
Hamilton Materials Inc 345 W Meats Ave. *TF:* 800-331-5569 ■ *Web:* www.hamiltonmaterials.com	Orange	CA	92865	714-637-2770	627-9033
Lafarge North America Inc 12950 Worldgate Dr Suite 600 *Web:* www.lafargenorthamerica.com	Herndon	VA	20170	703-480-3600	480-3899
National Gypsum Co 2001 Rexford Rd **Fax Area Code:* 800 ■ *TF:* 800-628-4662 ■ *Web:* www.national-gypsum.com	Charlotte	NC	28211	704-365-7300	329-6421*
PABCO Gypsum 37851 Cherry St. *TF:* 800-829-1577 ■ *Web:* www.pabcogypsum.paccoast.com	Newark	CA	94560	510-792-1577	797-8820
USG Corp 550 W Adams St *NYSE: USG* ■ *TF:* 800-621-9622 ■ *Web:* www.usg.com	Chicago	IL	60661	312-436-4000	672-4093

351 HAIRPIECES, WIGS, TOUPEES

Company / Address	City	State	Zip	Phone	Fax
Afro World Hair Goods Inc 7276 Natural Bridge Rd	Saint Louis	MO	63121	314-389-5194	389-8508
TF: 800-228-9424 ■ *Web:* www.afroworld.com					
Alkinco 129 W 29th St	New York	NY	10001	212-719-3070	764-7804
TF: 800-424-7118 ■ *Web:* www.alkincohair.com					
Amekor Industries 500 Brook Rd Suite 100	Conshohocken	PA	19428	610-825-6747	834-8427
TF: 800-345-6332 ■ *Web:* www.amekor.com					
Charles Alfieri Collection 4390 N Federal Hwy Suite 203	Fort Lauderdale	FL	33308	954-928-1755	928-1858
TF: 800-321-2413 ■ *Web:* www.charles-alfieri.com					
Eva Gabor International Ltd 5900 Equitable Rd	Kansas City	MO	64120	816-231-3700	231-8030
TF: 800-236-0326					
Freeda Wigs 779 E Newyork Ave	Brooklyn	NY	11203	718-771-2000	756-1503
Web: www.freeda.com					
Headcovers Unlimited 5 S Commerce Suite 39	Ardmore	OK	73401	580-226-5871	632-2728*
**Fax Area Code:* 832 ■ *Web:* www.headcovers.com					
Headstart Hair For Men Inc 3395 Cypress Gardens Rd	Winter Haven	FL	33884	863-324-5559	324-5673
TF: 800-645-6525 ■ *Web:* www.headstarthairformen.com					
Henry Margu Inc 540 Commerce Dr	Yeadon	PA	19050	610-622-0515	259-6541
TF: 800-345-8284					
HPH Corp 1529 SE 47th Terr	Cape Coral	FL	33904	239-540-0085	540-0892
TF: 800-654-9884 ■ *Web:* www.discounthairpiece.com					
Jacquelyn Wigs 15 W 37th St 4th Fl	New York	NY	10018	212-302-2266	302-0991
TF: 800-272-2424 ■ *Web:* www.jacquelynwigs.com					
Jean Paree Weegs Inc 4041 S 700 E Suite 2	Salt Lake City	UT	84107	801-328-9756	747-2509
TF Orders: 800-422-9447 ■ *Web:* www.jeanparee.com					
Jon Renau Collection 2510 Island View Way	Vista	CA	92081	760-598-0067	598-1205
TF: 800-462-9447 ■ *Web:* www.jonrenau.com					
Look of Love International 7095 B Rt 27 S	Edison	NJ	08817	908-687-9502	687-9509
TF: 800-526-7627 ■ *Web:* www.lookoflove.com					
Louis Ferre Inc 302 5th Ave 10th Fl	New York	NY	10001	212-239-1600	239-1601
TF: 800-695-1061 ■ *Web:* www.louisferre.com					
National Fiber Technology LLC 300 Canal St	Lawrence	MA	01840	978-686-2964	
TF Cust Svc: 800-842-2751 ■ *Web:* www.nftech.com					
Peggy Knight Solutions Inc 1750 Bridgeway	Sausalito	CA	94965	415-289-1777	331-8839
TF: 800-997-7753 ■ *Web:* www.peggyknight.com					
Rene Of Paris 15551 Cabrito Rd	Van Nuys	CA	91406	818-908-3100	988-2496
TF: 800-353-7363 ■ *Web:* www.reneofparis.com					
TressAllure/General Wig 5800 NW 163rd St	Miami Lakes	FL	33014	305-823-0600	823-0626
TF: 800-777-9447 ■ *Web:* www.tressallure.com					
Wig America Co 27317 industrial Blvd	Hayward	CA	94545	510-887-9579	887-9574
TF: 800-338-7600 ■ *Web:* www.wigamerica.com					
World of Wigs 2305 E 17th St	Santa Ana	CA	92705	714-547-4461	547-6063
TF: 800-794-5572 ■ *Web:* www.worldofwigs.com					
Yaffa Wigs 4118 13th Ave	Brooklyn	NY	11219	718-436-4280	436-1601
TF: 800-233-0660 ■ *Web:* www.yaffawigs.com					
YK International Co 3246 W Montrose Ave	Chicago	IL	60618	773-583-5270	583-5272
TF: 800-621-0086					

352 HANDBAGS, TOTES, BACKPACKS

SEE ALSO Leather Goods - Personal p. 2149; Luggage, Bags, Cases p. 2189; Sporting Goods p. 2664; Tarps, Tents, Covers p. 2682

Company / Address	City	State	Zip	Phone	Fax
Accurate Flannel Bag Co 468 Totowa Ave	Paterson	NJ	07522	973-720-1800	689-6774
TF General: 800-234-9200 ■ *Web:* www.accuratebags.com					
Allegro Mfg Inc 7250 Oxford Way	Commerce	CA	90040	323-724-0101	722-7341
TF: 800-833-5562 ■ *Web:* www.allegromfg.com					
Dow Cover Co Inc 373 Lexington Ave	New Haven	CT	06513	203-469-5394	469-5394
TF: 800-735-8877 ■ *Web:* www.dowcover.com					
Fabriko Inc 318 E Confederate Blvd	Appomattox	VA	24522	434-352-7145	243-9862*
**Fax Area Code:* 866 ■ *TF:* 800-558-0242 ■ *Web:* www.fabriko.com					
Innovo Group Inc 2633 Kingston Pike Suite 100	Knoxville	TN	37919	865-546-1110	546-9277
NASDAQ: INNO ■ *TF:* 800-627-2621 ■ *Web:* www.innovogroup.com					
Judith Leiber LLC 600 Madison Ave 17th Fl	New York	NY	10022	212-736-4244	736-4331
Web: www.judithleiber.com					
Kate Spade 48 W 25th St 7th Fl	New York	NY	10010	212-739-6550	
Web: www.katespade.com					
LBU Inc 217 Brook Ave	Passaic	NJ	07055	973-773-4800	773-6005
TF: 800-678-4528 ■ *Web:* www.lbuinc.com					
LeSportsac Inc 350 5th Ave # 402	New York	NY	10118	212-736-6262	643-8009
TF: 800-486-2247 ■ *Web:* www.lesportsac.com					
Ohio Bag Corp 6044 Rossmoor Lakes Ct	Boynton Beach	FL	33437	561-736-3131	735-0150
Web: www.ohiobag.com					
SeamCraft Inc 932 W Dakin St	Chicago	IL	60613	773-281-5150	975-9200
TF: 800-322-2441 ■ *Web:* www.seamcraft.com					
Service Mfg Corp 5414 W Roosevelt Rd	Chicago	IL	60644	773-287-5500	287-5585
TF: 800-338-7082 ■ *Web:* www.servicemfg.com					
Vera Bradley Designs 2208 Production Rd	Fort Wayne	IN	46808	260-482-4673	484-2278
TF: 800-975-8372 ■ *Web:* www.verabradley.com					

353 HARDWARE - MFR

Company / Address	City	State	Zip	Phone	Fax
Adams Rite Mfg Co 260 W Santa Fe St	Pomona	CA	91767	909-632-2300	632-2370
TF: 800-872-3267 ■ *Web:* www.adamsrite.com					
AdelWiggins Group 5000 Triggs St	Los Angeles	CA	90022	323-269-9181	269-3759
Web: www.adelwiggins.com					
Aehi Inc 14586 Central Ave	Chino	CA	91710	909-606-6998	606-6885
Web: www.aehiinc.com					
Agm Container Controls Inc PO Box 40020	Tucson	AZ	85717	520-881-2130	881-4983
TF: 800-995-5590 ■ *Web:* www.agmcontainer.com					
AL Hansen Mfg Co 701 Pershing Rd	Waukegan	IL	60085	847-244-8900	244-7222
Web: www.alhansen.com					
AmerTac 1 Rt 17 S	Saddle River	NJ	07458	201-934-3224	934-3224
Web: www.amertac.com					
Anderson Electrical Products Inc 1615 Moores St PO Box 455	Leeds	AL	35094	573-682-5521	682-8714
TF: 800-423-0730 ■ *Web:* www.hubbell.com					
Arrow Lock Co 100 Arrow Dr	New Haven	CT	06511	800-839-3157	421-6615
TF: 800-221-6529 ■ *Web:* www.arrowlock.com					
ASSA Inc 110 Sargent Dr	New Haven	CT	06511	203-624-5225	892-3256*
**Fax Area Code:* 800 ■ *TF:* 800-235-7482 ■ *Web:* www.assalock.com					
Atco Products Inc 189-V Frelinghuysen Ave	Newark	NJ	07114	973-242-5757	242-0131
Web: www.atcoproducts.com					
Attwood Corp 1016 N Monroe St	Lowell	MI	49331	616-897-9241	897-8358
Web: www.attwoodmarine.com					
Automotive Racing Products Inc 1863 Eastman Ave	Ventura	CA	93003	805-339-2200	650-0742
TF: 800-826-3045 ■ *Web:* www.arp-bolts.com					
Baden Steelbar & Bolt Corp 852 Big Sewickly Crk Rd R	Sewickley	PA	15143	724-266-3003	266-1619
Web: www.badensteel.com					
Baldwin Hardware Corp 841 E Wyomissing Blvd	Reading	PA	19611	610-777-7811	796-4600
TF: 800-437-7448 ■ *Web:* www.baldwinhardware.com					
Band-It-IDEX Inc 4799 Dahlia St	Denver	CO	80216	303-320-4555	333-6549
TF: 800-525-0758 ■ *Web:* www.band-it-idex.com					
Baron Mfg Co 1200 W Capitol Dr	Addison	IL	60101	630-628-9110	628-9141
TF: 800-368-8585 ■ *Web:* www.baronsnaps.com					
Basic Industries International Inc 302 S Milliken Ave Suite F	Ontario	CA	91761	909-390-6782	605-7647
Belwith International Ltd 3100 Broadway Ave	Grandville	MI	49418	800-235-9484	858-2119
TF: 800-235-9484 ■ *Web:* www.belwith.com					
Bete Fog Nozzle Inc 50 Greenfield St	Greenfield	MA	01301	413-772-0846	772-6729
TF: 800-235-0049 ■ *Web:* www.bete.com					
Blum Inc 7733 Old Plank Rd	Stanley	NC	28164	704-827-1345	827-0799
TF: 800-438-6788 ■ *Web:* www.blum.com					
Bomar Inc PO Box 1200	Charlestown	NH	03603	603-826-5791	826-4125
Web: www.pompanette.com/bomar					
Bommer Industries Inc PO Box 187	Landrum	SC	29356	864-457-3301	457-2487
TF: 800-334-1654 ■ *Web:* www.bommer.com					
Bourdon Forge Co Inc 99 Tuttle Rd	Middletown	CT	06457	860-632-2740	632-7247
Web: www.bourdonforge.com					
Brainerd Mfg Co Inc 140 Business Pk Dr	Winston-Salem	NC	27107	336-769-4077	771-6077*
**Fax:* Cust Svc ■ *TF:* 800-652-7277 ■ *Web:* www.libertyhardware.com					
Bronze Craft Corp 37 Will St	Nashua	NH	03060	603-883-7747	883-0222
TF: 800-488-7747 ■ *Web:* www.bronzecraft.com					
Chamberlain Group 845 Larch Ave	Elmhurst	IL	60126	630-279-3600	530-6091
TF: 800-282-6225 ■ *Web:* www.chamberlaingroup.com					
Charles Leonard Inc 145 Kennedy Dr	Hauppauge	NY	11788	631-273-6700	273-6777
TF: 800-999-7202 ■ *Web:* www.charlesleonard.com					
Charles Leonard Western Inc 235 W 140th St	Los Angeles	CA	90061	310-715-7464	715-7474
Chicago Hardware & Fixture Co 9100 Parklane Ave	Franklin Park	IL	60131	847-455-6609	455-0012
Web: www.chicagohardware.com					
Colonial Bronze Co 511 Winsted Rd	Torrington	CT	06790	860-489-9233	482-8760
TF: 800-355-7894 ■ *Web:* www.colonialbronze.com					
Component Hardware Group Inc 1890 Swarthmore Ave	Lakewood	NJ	08701	732-363-4700	364-8110
TF: 800-526-3694 ■ *Web:* www.componenthardware.com					
CompX International Inc 5430 LBJ Fwy Suite 1700	Dallas	TX	75240	972-448-1400	448-1408
AMEX: CIX ■ *Web:* www.compx.com					
Corbin Russwin Inc 225 Episcopal Rd	Berlin	CT	06037	203-225-7411	828-7266*
**Fax Area Code:* 860 ■ *TF:* 800-438-1951 ■ *Web:* www.corbin-russwin.com					
Craft Inc 1929 County St PO Box 3049	South Attleboro	MA	02703	508-761-7917	399-7240
TF: 800-827-2388 ■ *Web:* www.craft-inc.com					
Dayton Superior Corp 1125 Byers Rd	Miamisburg	OH	45342	937-866-0711	
TF: 800-745-3700 ■ *Web:* www.daytonsuperior.com					
DE-STA-CO 1025 Doris Rd	Auburn Hills	MI	48326	248-836-6700	836-6741*
**Fax:* Sales ■ *TF:* 888-337-8226 ■ *Web:* www.destaco.com					
Detmar Corp 2001 W Alexandrine Ave PO Box 08098	Detroit	MI	48208	313-831-1155	831-0624
Web: www.detmarcorp.com					
Dixie Industries 3510 N Orchard Knob Ave	Chattanooga	TN	37406	423-698-3323	622-3058
TF: 800-933-4943					
DORMA Group North America Dorma Dr	Reamstown	PA	17567	717-336-3881	336-2106
TF: 800-523-8483 ■ *Web:* www.dorma-usa.com					
East Teak Trading Group Inc 1106 Drake Rd	Donalds	SC	29638	360-793-3754	793-7835
TF: 800-338-5636 ■ *Web:* www.eastteak.com					
Eastern Co The 112 Bridge St PO Box 460	Naugatuck	CT	06770	203-729-2255	723-8653
AMEX: EML ■ *Web:* www.easterncompany.com					
Eberhard Mfg Co PO Box 368012	Cleveland	OH	44149	440-238-9720	572-2732
Web: www.eberhard.com					
Edward W Daniel Co Inc 11700 Harvard Ave	Cleveland	OH	44105	216-295-2750	295-2758
TF Cust Svc: 800-338-2658 ■ *Web:* www.ewdaniel.com					
Emtek Products Inc 15250 Stafford St	City of Industry	CA	91744	626-961-0413	336-2812
TF: 800-356-2741 ■ *Web:* www.emtek.com					
Engineered Products Co (EPCO) 601 Kelso St PO Box 108	Flint	MI	48506	810-767-2050	767-5084
TF: 888-414-3726 ■ *Web:* www.epcohardware.com					
ER Wagner Mfg Co Inc 4611 N 32nd St	Milwaukee	WI	53209	414-871-5080	449-8228
TF: 800-558-5596 ■ *Web:* www.erwagner.com					
ESPE Mfg Co Inc 9220 Ivanhoe St	Schiller Park	IL	60176	847-678-8950	678-0253
TF Cust Svc: 800-367-3773 ■ *Web:* www.espemfg.com					

Phone Fax

FKI Industries Faultless Caster Div
3438 Briley Pk Blvd N. Nashville TN 37207 615-687-6300 322-9329*
*Fax Area Code: 800 ■ TF Cust Svc: 800-322-7359 ■ Web: www.faultlesscaster.com

Folger Adam Security Inc 4634 S Presa St. San Antonio TX 78223 210-533-1231 533-2211
TF: 800-966-6739 ■ Web: www.southernfolger.com

Fortune Brands Home & Hardware Inc
520 Lake Cook Rd Deerfield IL 60015 847-484-4400
Web: www.fortunebrands.com

Fried Bros Inc 467 N 7th St. Philadelphia PA 19123 215-627-3205 592-1255
TF: 800-523-2924 ■ Web: www.fbisecurity.com

Fulton Corp 303 8th Ave Fulton IL 61252 815-589-3211 589-4433
TF: 800-252-0002 ■ Web: www.fultoncorp.com

G G Schmitt & Sons Inc 2821 Old Tree Dr Lancaster PA 17603 717-394-3701 291-9739
TF: 888-252-5446 ■ Web: www.ggschmitt.com

Genie Co 22790 County Rd 268 Alliance OH 44601 330-821-5360 821-1927
TF: 800-654-3643 ■ Web: www.geniecompany.com

HA Guden Co Inc 99 Raynor Ave Ronkonkoma NY 11779 631-737-2900 737-2933
TF: 800-344-6437 ■ Web: www.guden.com

Hager Co 139 Victor St. Saint Louis MO 63104 314-772-4400 782-0149*
*Fax Area Code: 800 ■ *Fax: Sales ■ TF: 800-325-9995 ■ Web: www.hagerco.com

Hamilton Caster & Mfg Co 1637 Dixie Hwy Hamilton OH 45011 513-863-3300 863-5508
Web: www.hamiltoncaster.com

Hartwell Corp 900 Richfield Rd. Placentia CA 92870 714-993-4200 579-4419
Web: www.hartwellcorp.com

Hindley Mfg Co Inc 9 Havens St. Cumberland RI 02864 401-722-2550 722-3083
TF: 800-323-9031 ■ Web: www.hindley.com

Hudson Lock Inc 81 Apsley St Hudson MA 01749 978-562-3481 562-9859
TF: 800-434-8960 ■ Web: www.hudsonlock.com

Hydraflow Inc 1881 W Malvern Ave. Fullerton CA 92833 714-773-2600 773-6351
Web: www.hydraflowusa.com

Ideal Clamp 3200 Parker Dr. Saint Augustine FL 32084 904-829-1000 825-1121
TF: 800-221-0100

Ingersoll-Rand Co Von Duprin Exit Device Div
2720 Tobey Dr Indianapolis IN 46219 317-613-8944 999-0328*
*Fax Area Code: 800 ■ TF Cust Svc: 800-999-0408 ■
Web: www.w3.securitytechnologies.com/irst/Pages/default.aspx

Jacknob Corp 290 Oser Ave PO Box 18032 Hauppauge NY 11788 631-546-6560 231-0330
TF: 866-452-3672 ■ Web: www.jacknob.com

Jacob Holtz Co
10 Industrial Hwy, MS-6
Airport Business Complex B. Lester PA 19029 215-423-2800 634-7454
TF: 800-445-4337 ■ Web: www.jacobholtz.com

James L Howard & Co Inc 10 Britton Dr Bloomfield CT 06002 860-242-3581 242-9966

Jarvis Caster Co 881 Lower Brownsville Rd Jackson TN 38301 731-554-2138 881-5701*
*Fax Area Code: 800 ■ TF: 800-995-9876 ■ Web: www.jarviscaster.com

Jonathan Engineered Solutions
410 Exchange St Suite 200. Irvine CA 92602 714-665-4400 368-7002
Web: www.jonathanengr.com

Kaba Ilco Corp 400 Jeffreys Rd Rocky Mount NC 27804 252-446-3321 446-4702
TF: 800-334-1381 ■ Web: www.kaba-ilco.com

Kason Industries Inc 57 Amlajack Blvd Shenandoah GA 30265 770-304-3000 251-4854
TF: 800-935-3550 ■ Web: www.kasonind.com

Keystone Electronics Corp 31-07 20th Rd. Astoria NY 11105 718-956-8900 956-9040
TF: 800-221-5510 ■ Web: www.keyelco.com

Knape & Vogt Mfg Co
2700 Oak Industrial Dr NE Grand Rapids MI 49505 616-459-3311 459-3290
TF: 800-253-1561 ■ Web: www.knapeandvogt.com

La Gard Inc 749 W Short St Lexington KY 40508 859-253-4744 255-2655
TF: 877-524-2732 ■ Web: www.lagard.com

Larson Hardware Mfg Co PO Box E. Sterling IL 61081 815-625-0503 625-8786
Web: www.larsonhardware.com

Lawrence Hardware Inc 4713 Hammermill Rd Tucker GA 30084 800-435-9568 892-7026
TF: 800-435-9568 ■ Web: www.lawrencehardware.com

LE Johnson Products Inc 2100 Sterling Ave. Elkhart IN 46516 574-293-5664 294-4697
TF: 800-837-5664 ■ Web: www.johnsonhardware.com

Liberty Hardware Mfg Corp
140 Business Pk Dr Winston-Salem NC 27107 336-769-4077 769-7306
TF: 800-542-3789 ■ Web: www.libertyhardware.com

Master Lock Co LLC
137 W Forest Hill Ave PO Box 927. Oak Creek WI 53154 414-571-5625 308-9245*
*Fax Area Code: 800 ■ TF: 800-464-2088 ■ Web: www.masterlock.com

McKinney Products Co 225 Episcopal Rd. Berlin CT 06037 570-346-7551 541-1073*
*Fax Area Code: 800 ■ TF: 800-346-7707 ■ Web: www.mckinneyhinge.com

Medeco Security Locks Inc 3625 Alleghany Dr. Salem VA 24153 540-380-5000 421-6615*
*Fax Area Code: 800 ■ TF: 800-839-3157 ■ Web: www.medeco.com

Murray Corp 260 Schilling Cir. Hunt Valley MD 21031 410-771-0380 771-5576
Web: www.murraycorp.com

Nagel Chase Inc 2377 Delaney Rd Gurnee IL 60031 847-336-4494 336-6542

National Mfg Co 1 1st Ave Sterling IL 61081 815-625-1320 625-1333
TF Cust Svc: 800-346-9445 ■ Web: www.natman.com

Newell Rubbermaid Inc Tools & Hardware Group
8935 NorthPointe Executive Dr. Huntersville NC 28078 704-987-4555
TF: 800-464-7946 ■ Web: www.newellrubbermaid.com

Nik-O-Lok Co 3130 N Mitthoeffer Rd Indianapolis IN 46235 317-899-6955 899-6977
TF: 800-428-4348 ■ Web: www.nikolok.com

Norton Industries Inc 20670 Corsair Blvd. Hayward CA 94545 510-786-3638 786-3082

Nucor Corp Fastener Div PO Box 6100. Saint Joe IN 46785 260-337-1600 337-1717
TF: 800-955-6826 ■ Web: www.nucor-fastener.com

Paneloc Corp PO Drawer 547 Farmington CT 06034 860-677-6711 677-8606
Web: www.paneloc.com

Parker International Products
243 Stafford St Worcester MA 01603 508-791-7131 753-7928
TF: 800-225-9011 ■ Web: www.parkerinternationalproducts.com

Payson Casters Inc 2323 N Delaney Rd. Gurnee IL 60031 847-336-6200 336-6542
TF: 800-323-4552 ■ Web: www.paysoncasters.com

PE Guerin Inc 23 Jane St. New York NY 10014 212-243-5270 727-2290
Web: www.peguerin.com

Perko Inc 16490 NW 13th Ave. Miami FL 33169 305-621-7525 620-9978
Web: www.perko.com

PL Porter Co 3000 Winona Ave Burbank CA 91504 818-526-2600 842-6117

Polar Hardware Mfg Co 1813 W Montrose Ave. Chicago IL 60613 773-935-8600 935-8749
Web: www.polarmfg.com

Phone Fax

Precision Brand Products Inc
2250 Curtiss St. Downers Grove IL 60515 630-969-7200 969-0310*
*Fax: Sales ■ TF: 800-535-3727 ■ Web: www.precisionbrand.com

PrimeSource Bldg Products Inc
2115 E Beltline Rd Carrollton TX 75006 972-416-1976 416-8331
TF: 800-745-3341 ■ Web: www.primesourcebp.com

Qual-Craft Industries PO Box 559. Stoughton MA 02072 781-344-1000 344-0056
TF: 800-231-5647 ■ Web: www.qualcraft.com

Railway Specialties Corp PO Box 29 Bristol PA 19007 215-788-9242 788-9244
Web: www.railwayspecialties.com

Renosol Corp 1512 Woodland Dr Saline MI 48176 734-429-5418 429-5351
Web: www.renosol.com

Renovator's Supply Inc
Renovators Old ML. Millers Falls MA 01349 413-423-3300 423-3800
TF: 800-659-2211 ■ Web: www.rensup.com

Riback Supply Co
2412 Business Loop 70 E PO Box 937 Columbia MO 65205 573-875-3131 449-8738
Web: www.riback.com

Rockford Process Control Inc 2020 7th St Rockford IL 61104 815-966-2000 966-2026
TF: 800-228-3779 ■ Web: www.rockfordprocess.com

Rocky Mountain Hardware Inc
1020 Airport Way PO Box 4108 Hailey ID 83333 208-788-2013 788-2577
TF: 888-788-2013 ■ Web: www.rockymountainhardware.com

Root Bros Mfg & Supply Co
10317-25 S Michigan Ave Chicago IL 60628 773-264-5000 264-6365
Web: www.rootbrothers.com

RWM Casters Co PO Box 668 Gastonia NC 28053 704-866-8533 868-4205
TF: 800-634-7704 ■ Web: www.rwmcasters.com

S Parker Hardware Mfg Corp PO Box 9882 Englewood NJ 07631 201-569-1600 569-1082
TF: 800-772-7537 ■ Web: www.sparker.com

Sargent & Greenleaf Inc
One Security Dr Nicholasville KY 40356 859-885-9411 885-3063
TF: 800-826-7652 ■ Web: www.sargentandgreenleaf.com

Sargent Mfg Co 100 Sargent Dr New Haven CT 06511 203-562-2151 498-5677*
*Fax: Sales ■ Web: www.sargentlock.com

Savant Mfg Inc 2930 Hwy 383 PO Box 520 Kinder LA 70648 337-738-5896 738-3215
TF: 800-326-6880 ■ Web: www.savantmfg.com

Schlage Lock Co 11819 N Pennsylvania St Carmel IN 40632 317-810-3700
TF: 800-847-1864 ■ Web: www.schlagelock.com

Securitron Magnalock Corp 550 Vista Blvd. Sparks NV 89434 775-355-5625 355-5636
TF Sales: 800-624-5625 ■ Web: www.securitron.com

Selby Furniture Hardware Co 321 Rider Ave Bronx NY 10451 718-993-3700 993-3143
TF: 800-224-0058 ■ Web: www.selbyhardware.com

Shelburne Corp 6221 Shelburne Rd Shelburne VT 05482 802-985-3321

Simpson Strong-Tie Co Inc
5956 W Las Positas Blvd Pleasanton CA 94588 925-560-9000 847-1597
TF: 800-925-5099 ■ Web: www.strongtie.com

Solus Industrial Innovations LLC
30152 Aventura. Rancho Santa Margarita CA 92688 949-589-3900 858-0300
TF Cust Svc: 800-825-8364 ■ Web: www.solusii.com

Southco Inc
210 N Brinton Lake Rd PO Box 0116 Concordville PA 19331 610-459-4000 459-4012
Web: www.southco.com

Trimark Corp PO Box 350 New Hampton IA 50659 641-394-3188
TF: 800-447-0343 ■ Web: www.trimarkcorp.com

Trimco/Builders Brass Works
3528 Emery St Los Angeles CA 90023 323-262-4191 264-7214
TF: 800-637-8746 ■ Web: www.trimcobbw.com

Truth Hardware Inc 700 W Bridge St Owatonna MN 55060 507-451-5620 451-5655*
*Fax: Cust Svc ■ TF Cust Svc: 800-866-7884 ■ Web: www.truth.com

Ultra Hardware Products LLC
1777 Hylton Rd. Pennsauken NJ 08110 856-663-5050 858-7210*
*Fax Area Code: 800 ■ TF: 800-426-6379 ■ Web: www.ultrahardware.com

Unicorp 291 Cleveland St Orange NJ 07050 973-674-1700 674-3803
TF: 800-526-1389 ■ Web: www.unicorpinc.com

Universal Tool Co Inc 33 Rose Pl. Springfield MA 01104 413-732-7738 733-6996

Voss Industries Inc 2168 W 25th St. Cleveland OH 44113 216-771-7655 771-2887
Web: www.vossind.com

Weber-Knapp Co 441 Chandler St PO Box 518. Jamestown NY 14701 716-484-9135 484-9142
Web: www.weberknapp.com

Weiser Lock A Masco Co 19701 Da Vinci. Lake Forest CA 92610 800-677-5625 713-7080
TF: 800-677-5625 ■ Web: www.weiserlock.com

Yale Norton Inc 3000 Hwy 74 E Monroe NC 28112 877-974-2255 233-1608*
*Fax Area Code: 704 ■ TF: 877-974-2255 ■ Web: www.nortondoorcontrols.com

Yale Residential Security Products Inc
100 Yale Ave. Lenoir City GA 37771 678-728-7400 989-8630*
*Fax Area Code: 865 ■ *Fax: Cust Svc ■ TF Cust Svc: 800-542-7562 ■ Web: www.yaleresidential.com

Yale Security Group 1902 Airport Rd. Monroe NC 28110 704-283-2101 338-0965*
*Fax Area Code: 800 ■ TF: 800-438-1951 ■ Web: www.yaleresidential.com/en/yale/yale-USA

Yardley Products Corp 10 W College Ave Yardley PA 19067 215-493-2700 493-6796
TF: 800-457-0154 ■ Web: www.yardleyproducts.com

354 HARDWARE - WHOL

Phone Fax

AB Wholesale Co 710 S College Ave Bluefield VA 24605 276-322-4686 326-1060
TF: 888-864-8642 ■ Web: www.magicmartstores.com

Ace Bolt & Screw Co of The Rio Grande Valley Inc
200 Brooklyn Ave San Antonio TX 78215 210-226-0244
TF: 800-292-5890 ■ Web: www.acebolt.com

Action Bolt & Tool Co PO Box 10864 Riviera Beach FL 33419 561-845-8800 845-0255
Web: www.actionboltandtool.com

Adtec Digital 408 Russell St Nashville TN 37206 615-256-6619 330-0691*
*Fax: Sales ■ Web: www.adtecinc.com

Aero-Space Southwest Inc 21450 N 3rd Ave Phoenix AZ 85027 623-582-2779 582-2019*
*Fax Area Code: 602 ■ TF: 800-289-2779 ■ Web: www.aerospacesw.com

All-Pro Fasteners Inc 1916 Peyco Dr N. Arlington TX 76001 817-467-5700 467-5365
TF: 800-361-6627 ■ Web: www.all-profasteners.com

Allied International 13207 Bradley Ave. Sylmar CA 91342 818-364-2333 362-9066
TF: 800-533-8333 ■ Web: www.alliedtools.com

	City	State	Zip	Phone	Fax
Amarillo Hardware Co 622 S Grant St PO Box 1891	Amarillo	TX	79101	806-376-4722	374-5520
TF: 800-949-4722					
Associated Steel Corp 18200 Miles Rd.	Cleveland	OH	44128	216-475-8000	475-6067
TF: 800-441-9303 ■ *Web:* www.associatedsteel.com					
B & T Wholesale Distributors Inc 846 Lind Ave SW	Renton	WA	98055	425-235-3592	235-3599
Baer Supply Co 909 Forest Edge Dr	Vernon Hills	IL	60061	847-913-2237	913-2230
TF: 800-944-2237 ■ *Web:* www.baersupply.com					
Bargain Supply Co 844 E Jefferson St	Louisville	KY	40206	502-562-5000	562-5051
TF: 800-322-5226 ■ *Web:* www.bargainsupply.com					
Barnett Inc 801 W Bay St.	Jacksonville	FL	32204	904-384-6530	388-2723*
**Fax:* Mktg ■ *TF:* 800-288-2000 ■ *Web:* www.e-barnett.com					
Bashlin Industries Inc PO Box 867	Grove City	PA	16127	724-458-8340	458-8342
Web: www.bashlin.com					
Blish-Mize Co 223 S 5th St	Atchison	KS	66002	913-367-1250	367-0667
TF: 800-995-0525 ■ *Web:* www.blishmize.com					
Bostwick-Braun Co PO Box 912	Toledo	OH	43697	419-259-3600	259-3959
TF: 800-777-9640					
Builders Hardware & Supply Co Inc 1516 15th Ave W PO Box C-79005	Seattle	WA	98119	206-281-3700	281-3747
TF: 800-828-1437 ■ *Web:* www.builders-hardware.com					
California Hardware Co 3601 E Jurupa St.	Ontario	CA	91761	909-390-6100	390-8799
TF: 800-995-9223					
Cascade Wholesale Hardware Inc PO Box 1659	Hillsboro	OR	97123	503-614-2600	629-5793
TF: 800-877-9987 ■ *Web:* www.cascade.com					
Clark Security Products Inc 4775 Viewridge Ave	San Diego	CA	92123	619-718-9750	495-0775*
**Fax Area Code:* 858 ■ *TF:* 800-854-2088 ■ *Web:* www.clarksecurity.com					
Desoto Sales Inc 20945 Osborne St	Canoga Park	CA	91304	818-998-0853	998-7542
TF: 800-826-9779 ■ *Web:* www.desotosales.com					
Dillon Poe Supply Corp 215 Pelham Davis Cir.	Greenville	SC	29615	864-213-9000	213-9700
TF: 800-849-4300 ■ *Web:* www.dillonsupply.com					
Dixie Construction Products Inc 970 Huff Rd NW	Atlanta	GA	30318	404-351-1100	350-2359
TF: 800-992-1180 ■ *Web:* www.dixieconstruction.com					
Do it Best Corp 6502 Nelson Ave	Fort Wayne	IN	46803	260-748-5300	493-1245
Web: www.doitbest.com					
Earnest Machine Products Co 12502 Plaza Dr	Parma	OH	44130	216-362-1100	362-9970
TF: 800-327-6378 ■ *Web:* www.earnestmachine.com					
EB Bradley Co 5080 S Alameda St.	Los Angeles	CA	90058	323-585-9201	585-5414
TF: 800-533-3030 ■ *Web:* www.ebbradley.com					
Emhart Teknologies Inc 50 Shelton Technology Ctr PO Box 859	Shelton	CT	06484	203-924-9341	925-3109
Web: www.emhart.com					
Fastec Industrial Corp 23348 County Rd 6.	Elkhart	IN	46514	574-262-2505	262-8634*
**Fax:* Sales ■ *TF:* 800-837-2505 ■ *Web:* www.fastecindustrial.com					
Fastenal Co PO Box 978	Winona	MN	55987	507-454-5374	453-8049
NASDAQ: FAST ■ *TF:* 877-327-8362 ■ *Web:* www.fastenal.com					
Faucet Queens Inc 650 Forest Edge Dr	Vernon Hills	IL	60061	847-478-2800	821-0277
Web: www.store.helpinghandtools.net					
General Fasteners Co 37584 Amrhein Rd Suite 150	Livonia	MI	48150	734-452-2400	591-6387
TF: 800-945-2658 ■ *Web:* www.genfast.com					
Handy Hardware Wholesale Inc 8300 Tewantin Dr	Houston	TX	77061	713-644-1495	644-3167
TF: 800-364-3835 ■ *Web:* www.handyhardware.com					
Hans Johnsen Co 8901 Chancellor Row	Dallas	TX	75247	214-879-1550	879-1520
TF Sales: 800-879-1515 ■ *Web:* www.hjc.com					
Harbor Freight Tools 3491 Mission Oaks Blvd.	Camarillo	CA	93011	805-445-4791	
Web: www.harborfreight.com					
Hardware Distribution Warehouses Inc (HDW) 6900 Woolworth Rd	Shreveport	LA	71129	318-686-8527	686-8550
TF Cust Svc: 800-256-8527 ■ *Web:* www.hdwinc.com					
Hardware Suppliers Of America PO Box 2208	Winterville	NC	28590	252-355-9400	
Web: www.hardwaresuppliers.com					
Heads & Threads International LLC 200 Kennedy Dr	Sayreville	NJ	08872	732-727-5800	727-5888
TF: 800-929-1950					
Hillman Group Inc 10590 Hamilton Ave	Cincinnati	OH	45231	513-851-4900	851-4997
TF: 800-800-4900 ■ *Web:* www.hillmangroup.com					
Hodell-natco Industries Inc 7825 Hub Pkwy	Cleveland	OH	44125	216-447-0165	447-5078
TF: 800-321-4862 ■ *Web:* www.hodell-natco.com					
Home Depot Supply 10641 Scripps Summit Ct	San Diego	CA	92131	858-831-2000	352-5354*
**Fax Area Code:* 800 ■ **Fax:* Sales ■ *TF:* 800-233-6166 ■ *Web:* www.hdsupply.com					
Horizon Distribution Inc PO Box 1021	Yakima	WA	98907	509-453-3181	457-5769
Web: www.horizondistribution.com					
House-Hasson Hardware Inc 3125 Water Plant Rd	Knoxville	TN	37914	865-525-0471	525-6178
TF: 800-333-0520 ■ *Web:* www.househasson.com					
Interline Brands Inc 801 W Bay St.	Jacksonville	FL	32204	904-421-1400	288-2828*
NYSE: IBI ■ **Fax Area Code:* 800 ■ *TF:* 800-288-2000 ■ *Web:* www.interlinebrands.com					
Jensen Distribution Services 314 W Riverside Ave.	Spokane	WA	99201	509-624-1321	838-2432
TF: 800-234-1321 ■ *Web:* www.jensenonline.com					
JSJ Corp 700 Robbins Rd	Grand Haven	MI	49417	616-842-6350	847-3112
Web: www.jsjcorp.com					
JSJ Corp Dake Div 724 Robbins Rd	Grand Haven	MI	49417	616-842-7110	842-0859
TF: 800-846-3253 ■ *Web:* www.dakecorp.com					
Kentec Inc 3250 Centerville Hwy.	Snellville	GA	30039	770-985-1907	985-6989
TF: 800-241-0148 ■ *Web:* www.kentec.com					
Leight Sales Co Inc 1051 E Artesia Blvd	Carson	CA	90746	310-223-1000	604-4702
Web: www.leightsales.com					
Long-Lewis Hardware 430 9th St N	Birmingham	AL	35203	205-322-2561	322-2504
TF: 800-322-0492 ■ *Web:* www.long-lewis.com					
Max Tool Inc 119b Citation Ct.	Birmingham	AL	35209	205-942-2466	942-7144
TF: 800-783-6298 ■ *Web:* www.maxtoolinc.com					
Mclendon Hardware Inc 440 Rainier Ave S.	Renton	WA	98057	425-235-3555	235-3569
Web: www.mclendons.com					
Monroe Hardware Co 101 N Sutherland Ave	Monroe	NC	28110	704-289-3121	289-2838
TF: 800-222-1974 ■ *Web:* www.monroehardware.com					
Omaha Wholesale Hardware Co PO Box 3628	Omaha	NE	68103	402-444-1673	444-1664
TF: 800-238-4566 ■ *Web:* www.omahawh.com					
Onity Inc 2232 Northmont Pkwy	Duluth	GA	30096	770-248-7535	
Web: www.onity.com					
Orgill Inc 3742 Tyndale Dr	Memphis	TN	38125	901-754-8850	752-8989
TF: 800-347-2860 ■ *Web:* www.orgill.com					
Parts Assoc Inc 12420 Plaza Dr	Parma	OH	44130	216-433-7700	433-9051
TF: 800-321-1128 ■ *Web:* www.pai-net.com					
Porteous Fastener Co 1300 Morse Ave	Elk Grove Village	IL	60007	847-228-6313	228-6761
TF: 800-935-2002 ■ *Web:* www.porteousfastener.com					
Ram Tool & Supply Co PO Box 320979	Birmingham	AL	35232	205-591-2527	599-7053
TF: 800-292-6027 ■ *Web:* www.ram-tool.com					
Regitar USA Inc 2575 Container Dr.	Montgomery	AL	36109	334-244-1885	244-1901
TF: 877-734-4827 ■ *Web:* www.regitar.com					
Reid Tool Supply Co Inc 2265 Black Creek Rd	Muskegon	MI	49444	231-777-3951	438-1145*
**Fax Area Code:* 800 ■ **Fax:* Sales ■ *TF Sales:* 800-253-0421 ■ *Web:* www.reidsupply.com					
Repairclinic.com Inc 48600 Michigan Ave	Canton	MI	48188	734-495-3079	495-3150
TF: 800-269-2609 ■ *Web:* www.repairclinic.com					
Ryobi Technologies Inc 1428 Pearman Dairy Rd	Anderson	SC	29625	864-226-6511	261-9435
TF: 800-525-2579 ■ *Web:* www.ryobitools.com					
Serv-a-lite Products Inc 3451 Morton Dr.	East Moline	IL	61244	309-752-1255	752-1266
TF: 800-447-6760 ■ *Web:* www.servalite.com					
Specialty Bolt & Screw Inc 235 Bowles Rd	Agawam	MA	01001	413-789-6700	789-9340
TF: 800-322-7878 ■ *Web:* www.specialtybolt.com					
Standard Supply & Distributing Co 1431 Regal Row	Dallas	TX	75247	214-630-7800	630-1894
Web: www.standardsupplyhvac.com					
Star Stainless Screw Co 30 W End Rd	Totowa	NJ	07511	973-256-2300	256-6519
TF: 800-631-3540					
Supply Technologies LLC 6065 Parkland Blvd	Cleveland	OH	44124	440-947-2100	947-2299
Web: www.ilsonline.com					
Techni-Tool Inc 1547 N Trooper Rd PO Box 1117	Worcester	PA	19490	610-941-2400	828-5623
TF Cust Svc: 800-832-4866 ■ *Web:* www.techni-tool.com					
Thruway Fasteners Inc 2910 Niagara Falls Blvd	North Tonawanda	NY	14120	716-694-1434	694-3865*
**Fax:* Sales ■ *TF:* 800-201-1619 ■ *Web:* www.thruwayfasteners.com					
Tomarco Contractor Specialties Inc 14848 Northam St	La Mirada	CA	90638	714-523-1771	523-1284
Web: www.tomarco.com					
Triangle Fastener Corp 1925 Preble Ave.	Pittsburgh	PA	15233	412-321-5000	321-7838
TF: 800-486-7832 ■ *Web:* www.trianglefastener.com					
United Hardware Distributing Co PO Box 410	Minneapolis	MN	55440	763-559-1800	559-5031
TF: 800-835-6560					
Wallace Hardware Co Inc 5050 S Davy Crockett Pky PO Box 6004	Morristown	TN	37815	423-586-5650	581-0766
TF: 800-776-0976 ■ *Web:* www.wallacehardware.com					
WBH Industries PO Box 98	Arlington	TX	76004	817-649-5700	649-5701
WCL Co PO Box 3588	City of Industry	CA	91744	626-968-5523	369-9805
TF: 800-331-3816 ■ *Web:* www.wclco.com					
Western Tool Supply PO Box 13430	Salem	OR	97309	503-588-8222	588-8225
Web: www.westerntool.com					
Wright & Wilhelmy Co Inc 11005 E St	Omaha	NE	68137	402-593-0600	593-0610
Web: www.counterfeitcop.com					
Wurth Service Supply Inc 4935 W 86th St	Indianapolis	IN	46268	317-704-1000	704-8469*
**Fax:* Cust Svc ■ *TF:* 800-428-4686 ■ *Web:* www.servicesupply.com					
WW Grainger Inc 100 Grainger Pkwy	Lake Forest	IL	60045	847-535-1000	
NYSE: GWW ■ *TF:* 888-361-8649 ■ *Web:* www.grainger.com					

355 HEALTH CARE PROVIDERS - ANCILLARY

SEE ALSO Home Health Services p. 2023; Hospices p. 2028; Vision Correction Centers p. 2762

	City	State	Zip	Phone	Fax
Amedisys Inc 5959 S Sherwood Forest Blvd Suite 300	Baton Rouge	LA	70816	225-292-2031	292-8163
NASDAQ: AMED ■ *TF:* 800-467-2662 ■ *Web:* www.amedisys.com					
American Family Care 2147 Riverchase Office Rd	Birmingham	AL	35244	205-403-8902	
TF: 800-258-7535 ■ *Web:* www.americanfamilycare.com					
American Red Cross In Greater New York (inc) 520 W 49th St.	New York	NY	10019	212-787-1000	
TF: 877-733-2767 ■ *Web:* www.nyredcross.org					
AmeriHealth Mercy Health Plan 8040 Carlson Rd Suite 500	Harrisburg	PA	17112	717-651-3540	937-8776*
**Fax Area Code:* 215 ■ *TF:* 888-991-7200 ■ *Web:* www.amerihealthmercyhp.com					
AmSurg Corp 20 Burton Hills Blvd 5th Fl	Nashville	TN	37215	615-665-1283	665-0755
NASDAQ: AMSG ■ *TF:* 800-945-2301 ■ *Web:* www.amsurg.com					
Apex Fitness Group 100 Camino Ruiz	Camarillo	CA	93012	805-449-1330	449-1370
TF: 800-656-2739 ■ *Web:* www.my.apexfitness.com					
Aptium Oncology 8201 Beverly Blvd.	Los Angeles	CA	90048	323-966-3400	966-3597
Web: www.aptiumoncology.com					
Arizona Physicians Ipa Inc 3141 N 3rd Ave	Phoenix	AZ	85013	602-651-6127	277-5475
Web: www.myapipa.com					
Baycare Health Network Inc 16255 Bay Vista Dr.	Clearwater	FL	33760	877-692-2922	
TF: 877-692-2922 ■ *Web:* www.baycare.org					
BriteSmile Inc 460 N Wiget Ln	Walnut Creek	CA	94598	925-941-6260	941-6266
TF: 800-274-8376 ■ *Web:* www.britesmile.com					
CareSource 230 N Main St	Dayton	OH	45402	937-224-3300	
TF: 800-488-0134 ■ *Web:* www.caresource.com					
Central Washington Comprehensive Mental Health PO Box 959	Yakima	WA	98907	509-575-4084	
Web: www.cwcmh.org					

Name / Address	City	State	Zip	Phone	Fax
Children's Bureau of Southern California					
1910 Magnolia Ave	Los Angeles	CA	90004	213-342-0100	342-0200
Web: www.all4kids.org					
Country Villa Service Corp					
5120 W Goldleaf Cir Suite 400	Los Angeles	CA	90056	310-574-3733	574-1322
TF: 866-227-3778 ■ *Web:* www.countryvillahealth.com					
DaVita Inc 1551 Wewatta St	Denver	CO	80202	303-405-2100	
NYSE: DVA ■ *TF:* 800-310-4872 ■ *Web:* www.davita.com					
Denver Rescue Mission					
3501 E 46th Ave PO Box 5206	Denver	CO	80216	303-297-1815	295-1566
Web: www.denverrescuemission.org					
Dynacq Healthcare Inc 10304 I-10 E Suite 369	Houston	TX	77029	713-378-2000	378-3166
NASDAQ: DYII ■ *Web:* www.dynacq.com					
Executive Health Group					
10 Rockefeller Plaza 4th Fl	New York	NY	10020	212-332-3030	332-1170*
**Fax:* Hum Res ■ *TF:* 800-362-8671					
Fresenius Medical Care North America					
920 Winter St	Waltham	MA	02451	781-699-9000	
NYSE: FMS ■ *TF:* 800-662-1237 ■ *Web:* www.fmcna.com					
Gambro Healthcare Inc 5200 Virginia Way	Brentwood	TN	37027	615-320-4200	320-4528
TF: 800-467-4736					
Hanger Orthopedic Group Inc					
10910 Domain Dr Suite 300	Austin	TX	78758	301-986-0701	986-0702
NYSE: HGR ■ *TF:* 877-442-6437 ■ *Web:* www.hanger.com					
Health Fitness Corp					
1650 W 82nd St Suite 1100	Minneapolis	MN	55431	952-831-6830	831-7264
TF: 800-639-7913 ■ *Web:* www.hfit.com					
HealthDrive Corp 25 Needham St	Newton	MA	02461	617-964-6681	964-0989
TF: 888-964-6681 ■ *Web:* www.healthdrive.com					
HealthSouth Corp					
3660 Grandview Pkwy Suite 200	Birmingham	AL	35243	205-967-7116	969-4740*
NYSE: HLS ■ **Fax:* Hum Res ■ *TF:* 800-765-4772					
Healthways Inc					
701 Cool Springs Blvd Suite 300	Franklin	TN	37067	800-327-3822	665-7697*
NASDAQ: HWAY ■ **Fax Area Code:* 615 ■ *TF:* 800-327-3822 ■ *Web:* www.americanhealthways.com					
Hooper Holmes Inc 170 Mt Airy Rd	Basking Ridge	NJ	07920	908-766-5000	766-5824
AMEX: HH ■ *TF:* 800-782-7373 ■ *Web:* www.hooperholmes.com					
Hudson River Healthcare Inc 1037 Main St	Peekskill	NY	10566	914-734-8800	734-8745
Web: www.hrhcare.org					
Med Tech 135 NW 100 Ave	Plantation	FL	33324	954-434-4341	434-0526
TF: 800-377-5869					
MedCath Inc 10720 Sikes Pl Suite 300	Charlotte	NC	28277	704-708-6600	708-5035
NASDAQ: MDTH ■ *Web:* www.medcath.com					
Midwest Medical Services 14217 W 95th St	Lenexa	KS	06215	913-956-4065	
TF: 866-931-6798 ■ *Web:* www.midwestmedservices.com					
Miracle-Ear Inc 5000 Cheshire Ln N Suite 1	Plymouth	MN	55446	763-268-4000	268-4365
TF: 800-234-7714 ■ *Web:* www.miracle-ear.com					
NovaCare Inc 680 American Ave	King of Prussia	PA	19406	610-992-7200	992-7264*
**Fax:* Hum Res ■ *TF:* 800-331-8840 ■ *Web:* www.novacare.com					
Open Door Family Medical Center Inc					
165 Main St	Ossining	NY	10562	914-941-1263	
Web: www.opendoormedical.org					
Orion HealthCorp Inc					
1805 Old Alabama Rd Suite 350	Roswell	GA	30076	678-832-1800	832-1888
PINK: ORNH ■ *Web:* www.orionhealthcorp.com					
PainCare Holdings Inc					
1030 N Orange Ave Suite 105	Orlando	FL	32801	407-367-0944	367-0950
PINK: PRXZ					
Radiation Therapy Services Inc					
2270 Colonial Blvd	Fort Myers	FL	33907	239-931-7275	931-7380
TF: 888-376-9729 ■ *Web:* www.rtsx.com					
SCAN Health Plan					
3800 Kilroy Airport Way Suite 100	Long Beach	CA	90806	562-989-5100	989-5200
TF: 800-247-5091 ■ *Web:* www.scanhealthplan.com					
Shapco Inc 1666 20th St Suite 100	Santa Monica	CA	90404	310-264-1666	264-1675
Sonus Corp 5000 Cheshire Ln N	Plymouth	MN	55446	800-432-7464	268-4353*
**Fax Area Code:* 763 ■ *TF:* 800-432-7464 ■ *Web:* www.sonus.com					
Spectrum Dental Inc 8554 Hayden Pl	Culver City	CA	90232	310-845-3160	845-1538
TF: 800-291-2828 ■ *Web:* www.specdent.com					
SunDance Rehabilitation Agency Inc					
18831 Von Karman Suite 400	Irvine	CA	92612	949-255-7100	468-4458*
**Fax Area Code:* 505 ■ *TF:* 800-729-6600 ■ *Web:* www.sundancerehab.com					
Symbion Inc 40 Burton Hills Blvd Suite 500	Nashville	TN	37215	615-234-5900	234-5998
Web: www.symbion.com					
Theo & Alfred M Landon Center on Aging					
3901 Rainbow Blvd	Kansas City	KS	66160	913-588-1203	588-1201
Web: www2.kumc.edu/coa					
Trailblazer Health Enterprises LLC					
8330 LBJ Fwy Executive Ctr III PO Box 650422	Dallas	TX	75265	469-372-2000	
Web: www.trailblazerhealth.com					
Trucks For You Inc 3250 N 32nd St	Muskogee	OK	74401	918-687-7708	687-9963
TF: 800-256-4805 ■ *Web:* www.trucksforyou.com					
United Surgical Partners International Inc (USPI)					
15305 Dallas Pkwy Suite 1600	Addison	TX	75001	972-713-3500	713-3550
Web: www.unitedsurgical.com					
Unity Physician Group Pc 1155 W 3rd St	Bloomington	IN	47404	812-323-3529	257-9182*
**Fax Area Code:* 866 ■ *Web:* www.unitypg.com					
US Physical Therapy					
1300 W Sam Houston Pkwy S Suite 300	Houston	TX	77042	713-297-7000	297-7090
NASDAQ: USPH ■ *TF:* 800-580-6285 ■ *Web:* www.corporate.usph.com					

356 HEALTH CARE SYSTEMS

SEE ALSO General Hospitals - US p. 2041

Health Care Systems Are One Or More Hospitals Owned, Leased, Sponsored, Or Managed By A Central Organization. Single-Hospital Systems Are Not Included Here; However, Some Large Hospital Networks Or Alliances May Be Listed.

Name / Address	City	State	Zip	Phone	Fax
Addus HealthCare Inc 2401 S Plum Grove Rd	Palatine	IL	60067	847-303-5300	303-5376
NASDAQ: ADUS ■ *Web:* www.addus.com					
Adventist Health 2100 Douglas Blvd	Roseville	CA	95661	916-781-2000	774-3390
TF: 800-847-9840 ■ *Web:* www.adventisthealth.org					
Adventist Health System					
111 N Orlando Ave	Winter Park	FL	32789	407-647-4400	975-1469
TF: 800-327-9290 ■ *Web:* www.adventisthealthsystem.com					
Advocate Health Care 2025 Windsor Dr	Oak Brook	IL	60523	630-572-9393	572-9139
TF: 800-323-8622 ■ *Web:* www.advocatehealth.com					
Albert Einstein Healthcare Network					
5501 Old York Rd	Philadelphia	PA	19141	215-456-7010	456-6199
TF: 800-346-7834 ■ *Web:* www.einstein.edu					
Alexian Bros Health System					
3040 Salt Creek Ln	Arlington Heights	IL	60005	847-230-3764	483-7040
Web: www.alexianhealthsystem.org					
Allina Health System 710 E 24th St	Minneapolis	MN	55404	612-813-3600	775-9733
Web: www.allina.com					
American Caresource Holdings Inc					
5429 LBJ Fwy Suite 850	Dallas	TX	75240	972-308-6830	980-2560
NASDAQ: ANCI ■ *TF:* 800-370-5994 ■ *Web:* www.americancaresource.com					
American Kidney Stone Management Ltd (AKSM)					
797 Thomas Ln	Columbus	OH	43214	614-447-0281	447-9374
TF: 800-637-5188 ■ *Web:* www.aksm.com					
American Renal Assoc Inc 66 Cherry Hill Dr	Beverly	MA	01915	978-922-3080	
TF: 877-997-3625 ■ *Web:* www.americanrenal.com					
Amerihealth Hmo 919 Market St Suite 1200	Wilmington	DE	19801	302-777-6400	
Web: www.amerihealth.com					
Amery Regional Medical Ctr 265 Griffin St E	Amery	WI	54001	715-268-8000	268-0311
TF: 800-424-5273 ■ *Web:* www.amerymedicalcenter.org					
Ancilla Systems Inc 1419 S Lake Pk Ave	Hobart	IN	46342	219-947-8500	947-4037
Web: www.ancilla.org					
ApolloMD Inc 5665 New Northside Dr Suite 320	Atlanta	GA	30328	770-874-5400	874-5433
Web: www.apollomd.com					
Appalachian Regional Healthcare Service					
1220 S Broadway	Lexington	KY	40504	859-226-2440	226-2586
Web: www.arh.org					
Ardent Health Services					
1 Burton Hills Blvd Suite 250	Nashville	TN	37215	615-296-3000	296-6005
Web: www.ardenthealth.com					
Ascension Health 4600 Edmundson Rd	Saint Louis	MO	63134	314-733-8000	733-8000
Aurora Health Care Inc					
750 W Virginia St PO Box 341880	Milwaukee	WI	53234	414-647-3000	647-3494
Web: www.aurorahealthcare.com					
Avera Health 3900 W Avera Dr	Sioux Falls	SD	57108	605-322-4700	322-4799
Web: www1.avera.org					
Banner Health 1441 N 12th St	Phoenix	AZ	85006	602-495-4000	495-4689
Web: www.bannerhealth.com					
Baptist Health Medical Ctr (BHMC)					
9601 IH- 630 Exit 7	Little Rock	AR	72205	501-202-2000	202-1159
Web: www.baptist-health.com					
Baptist Health South Florida Inc					
6855 Red Rd Suite 600	Coral Gables	FL	33143	786-662-7111	662-7334
TF: 800-327-2491 ■ *Web:* www.baptisthealth.net					
Baptist Health System 3201 4th Ave S	Birmingham	AL	35222	205-715-5000	715-5251*
**Fax:* Hum Res ■ *Web:* www.bhsala.com					
Baptist Healthcare System 4007 Kresge Way	Louisville	KY	40207	502-896-5000	896-5020
Baptist Hospital 2000 Church St	Nashville	TN	37236	615-284-5555	284-1592
Web: www.baptist-hosp.org					
Baptist Memorial Health Care Corp					
350 N Humphreys Blvd	Memphis	TN	38120	901-227-2727	226-5661*
**Fax:* Admissions ■ *TF:* 800-422-7847 ■ *Web:* www.bmhcc.org					
Baylor Health Care System 3500 Gaston Ave	Dallas	TX	75246	214-820-0111	820-2594
Web: www.baylorhealth.com					
Baystate Health Systems Inc					
280 Chestnut St	Springfield	MA	01199	413-784-0000	794-3325*
**Fax:* Hum Res ■ *Web:* www.baystatehealth.com					
Benedictine Health System					
503 E 3rd St Suite 400	Duluth	MN	55805	218-786-2370	786-2373
TF: 800-833-7208 ■ *Web:* www.bhshealth.org					
BJC HealthCare					
4444 Forest Pk Ave Suite 500	Saint Louis	MO	63108	314-286-2000	286-2060
Web: www.bjc.org					
Bon Secours Health System Inc					
1505 Marriottsville Rd	Marriottsville	MD	21104	410-442-5511	442-1082
Web: www.bshsi.com					
California Family Health Council Inc (CFHC)					
3600 Wilshire Blvd Suite 600	Los Angeles	CA	90010	213-386-5614	368-4410
Web: www.cfhc.org					
CAMC Health System Inc 501 Morris St	Charleston	WV	25301	304-388-5432	
Web: www.camc.org					
CareGroup Inc 375 Longwood Ave	Boston	MA	02215	617-975-5000	
Web: www.caregroup.org					
Carolinas HealthCare System					
1000 Blythe Blvd PO Box 32861	Charlotte	NC	28232	704-355-2000	355-4084*
**Fax:* Mktg ■ *Web:* www.carolinas.org					
Catholic Health East					
4211 W Boy Scout Blvd Suite 160	Tampa	FL	33607	813-874-0758	874-0710
Web: www.che.org					
Catholic Health Initiatives					
1999 Broadway Suite 2600	Denver	CO	80202	303-298-9100	298-9690
Catholic Healthcare Partners					
615 Elsinore Pl	Cincinnati	OH	45202	513-639-2800	639-2700*
**Fax:* Hum Res ■ *TF:* 800-367-9212 ■ *Web:* www.health-partners.org					
Catholic Healthcare West					
185 Berry St Suite 300	San Francisco	CA	94107	415-438-5500	438-5724
Web: www.chwhealth.org					
Centra Health Inc 1920 Atherholt Rd	Lynchburg	VA	24501	434-947-4700	947-4892
TF: 800-777-4325 ■ *Web:* www.centrahealth.com					
Chase Brexton Health Services Inc					
1001 Cathedral St	Baltimore	MD	21201	410-837-2050	
Web: www.chasebrexton.org					
Chesapeake Medical Systems Inc					
118 Cedar St	Cambridge	MD	21613	410-228-0221	228-4561
Web: www.chesapeakemed.com					

	City	State	ZIP	Phone	Fax
Childhaven 316 Broadway *Web:* www.childhaven.org	Seattle	WA	98122	206-464-3923	621-8374
Christiana Care Health System 501 W 14th St. *Web:* www.christianacare.org	Wilmington	DE	19801	302-428-2203	428-2564
CHRISTUS Health 6363 N Hwy 161 Suite 450 *Web:* www.christushealth.org	Irving	TX	75038	214-492-8500	492-8540
CHRISTUS Schumpert Health System 1 St Mary Pl *TF:* 888-336-8115 ■ *Web:* www.christusschumpert.org	Shreveport	LA	71101	318-681-4500	681-4232
CHRISTUS Spohn Health System 1702 Santa Fe St *TF:* 800-247-6574 ■ *Web:* www.christusspohn.org	Corpus Christi	TX	78404	361-881-3000	885-0566
Clarent Hospital Corp 12337 Jones Rd Suite 218 *Web:* www.clarenthospital.com	Houston	TX	77070	281-970-5104	774-5120
Community Health Systems Inc 4000 Meridian Blvd *NYSE:* CYH ■ *TF:* 888-373-9600 ■ *Web:* www.chs.net	Franklin	TN	37067	615-465-7000	370-3548
Community Services Group (CSG) 320 Highland Dr PO Box 597 *TF:* 877-907-7970 ■ *Web:* www.csgonline.org	Mountville	PA	17554	717-285-7121	285-2658
Covenant Health System 3615 19th St *Web:* www.covenanthealth.org	Lubbock	TX	79410	806-725-1011	725-1055
Covenant Health Systems Inc 10 Pelham Rd. *Web:* www.covenanths.com	Lexington	MA	02421	781-861-3535	862-5477
Crozer-Keystone Health System (CKHS) 190 W Sproul Rd *TF:* 800-254-3258 ■ *Web:* www.crozerkeystone.org	Springfield	PA	19064	610-328-8700	328-8725
DCH Health System 809 University Blvd E *Web:* www.dchsystem.com	Tuscaloosa	AL	35401	205-759-7111	750-5541
Detroit Medical Ctr (DMC) 4707 St Antoine *Web:* www.dmc.org	Detroit	MI	48201	313-745-6035	966-2040
Eastern Maine Healthcare Systems (EMHS) 43 Whiting Hill Rd *Web:* www.emh.org	Brewer	ME	04412	207-973-7050	973-7139
Edinburg Center Inc The 1040 Waltham St. *Web:* www.edinburgcenter.org	Lexington	MA	02421	781-862-3600	863-5903
Encore Healthcare LLC 7150 Columbia Gateway Dr Suite J *Web:* www.encore-healthcare.com	Columbia	MD	21046	443-539-2350	539-2351
Essent Healthcare Inc 3100 W End Ave Suite 900 *Web:* www.essenthealthcare.com	Nashville	TN	37203	615-312-5100	312-5101
Fairview Health Services 2450 Riverside Ave *TF:* 800-824-1953 ■ *Web:* www.fairview.org	Minneapolis	MN	55454	612-672-6000	672-7186
Franciscan Missionaries of Our Lady Health System (FMOLHS) 4200 Essen Ln *Web:* www.fmolhs.org	Baton Rouge	LA	70809	225-923-2701	926-4846
Franciscan Services Corp 6832 Convent Blvd *Web:* www.fscsylvania.org	Sylvania	OH	43560	419-882-8373	882-7360
Franciscan Sisters of Christian Charity HealthCare Ministry Inc 1415 S Rapids Rd. *Web:* www.fhcm.org	Manitowoc	WI	54220	920-684-7071	684-6417
Geisinger Health System 100 N Academy Ave *TF:* 800-275-6401 ■ *Web:* www.geisinger.org	Danville	PA	17822	570-271-6211	
General Health System (GHS) 3600 Florida Blvd. *Web:* www.brgeneral.org	Baton Rouge	LA	70806	225-387-7000	237-1623
Great Plains Health Alliance Inc 625 3rd St. *TF:* 800-432-2779 ■ *Web:* www.gpha.com	Phillipsburg	KS	67661	785-543-2111	
Greenville Hospital System (GHS) 701 Grove Rd *TF:* 877-447-4636 ■ *Web:* www.ghs.org	Greenville	SC	29605	864-455-8976	455-6218
Guthrie Healthcare System 1 Guthrie Sq *TF:* 888-448-8474 ■ *Web:* www.guthrie.org	Sayre	PA	18840	570-882-4312	882-5152
Hartford Health Care Corp 80 Seymour St *Web:* www.harthosp.com	Hartford	CT	06102	860-545-5000	
Harvard Vanguard Medical Assoc Inc 275 Grove St Suite 300. *Web:* www.harvardvanguard.org	Newton	MA	02466	617-559-8444	
HCA Holdings Inc 1 Pk Plaza. *NYSE:* HCA ■ *TF:* 800-828-2561 ■ *Web:* www.hcahealthcare.com	Nashville	TN	37203	615-344-9551	344-2830
HCA Midwest Health System 903 E 104th St Suite 500 *TF:* 800-386-9355 ■ *Web:* www.hcamidwest.com	Kansas City	MO	64131	816-508-4000	508-4036
Health Management Assoc Inc 5811 Pelican Bay Blvd Suite 500 *NYSE:* HMA ■ *Web:* www.hma.com	Naples	FL	34108	239-598-3131	597-5794
Health Net Of Arizona Inc 1230 W Washington St *TF:* 888-527-8688 ■ *Web:* www.healthnet.com	Tempe	AZ	85281	602-794-1400	
Healtheast 559 Capitol Blvd *Web:* www.healtheast.org	Saint Paul	MN	55103	651-232-2000	232-2315
Henry Ford Health System 1 Ford Pl *Fax Area Code: 313 ■ *TF:* 800-436-7936 ■ *Web:* www.henryford.com	Detroit	MI	48202	800-436-7936	874-6380*
Hospital Sisters Health System 4938 Laverna Rd. *Web:* www.hshs.org	Springfield	IL	62707	217-523-4747	523-0542
I-Trax Inc 4 Helman Dr Suite 130 *Web:* www.i-trax.com	Chadds Ford	PA	19317	610-459-2405	459-4705
IASIS Healthcare Corp 117 Seaboard Ln Bldg E *TF:* 877-898-6080 ■ *Web:* www.iasishealthcare.com	Franklin	TN	37067	615-844-2747	846-3006
Infirmary Health System Inc (IHS) 5 Mobile Infirmary Cir PO Box 2226. *Web:* www.mobileinfirmary.org	Mobile	AL	36607	251-435-2400	435-2060
Inova Health System 8110 Gatehouse Rd *Web:* www.inova.com	Falls Church	VA	22042	703-289-2069	289-2070
Integrated Healthcare Holdings Inc 1301 N Tustin Ave. *OTC:* IHCH ■ *Web:* www.ihhioc.com	Santa Ana	CA	92705	714-953-3652	953-3384

	City	State	ZIP	Phone	Fax
INTEGRIS Health Inc 3300 NW Expy *Web:* www.integrisok.com	Oklahoma City	OK	73112	405-951-2277	951-2733
Intermountain Health Care Inc (IHC) 36 S State St 22nd Fl *Fax: Hum Res ■ *TF Hum Res:* 800-843-7820 ■ *Web:* www.intermountainhealthcare.org	Salt Lake City	UT	84111	801-442-2000	442-3388*
Iowa Health System 1200 Pleasant St *Web:* www.ihs.org	Des Moines	IA	50309	515-241-6161	241-5994
Island Peer Review Organization Inc (IPRO) 1979 Marcus Ave *Web:* www.ipro.org	Lake Success	NY	11042	516-326-7767	328-2310
Jefferson Health System 259 N Radnor-Chester Rd Suite 290. *Web:* www.jeffersonhealth.org	Radnor	PA	19087	610-225-6200	225-6260
Johns Hopkins Health System (JHH) 600 N Wolfe St *Web:* www.hopkinsmedicine.org	Baltimore	MD	21287	410-955-5000	
Kindred Healthcare Inc 680 S 4th Ave *NYSE:* KND ■ *TF:* 800-545-0749 ■ *Web:* www.kindredhealthcare.com	Louisville	KY	40202	502-596-7300	596-4052
Legacy Health System 1720 NW Lovejoy St *Web:* www.legacyhealth.org	Portland	OR	97206	503-415-5600	415-5777
LifePoint Hospitals Inc 103 Powell Ct Suite 200 *NASDAQ:* LPNT ■ *Web:* www.lifepointhospitals.com	Brentwood	TN	37027	615-372-8500	
Lifespring Inc 460 Spring St *TF:* 800-456-2117 ■ *Web:* www.lifespr.com	Jeffersonville	IN	47130	812-280-2080	
Loris Community Hospital 3655 Mitchell St PO Box 690001 *Web:* www.lorishealth.org	Loris	SC	29569	843-716-7000	716-7195
Los Angeles County Dept of Health Services (LACDHS) 313 N Figueroa St Rm 708 *TF:* 800-711-5366 ■ *Web:* www.dhs.co.la.ca.us	Los Angeles	CA	90012	213-240-8101	481-0503
Marian Health System Inc PO Box 4753	Tulsa	OK	74159	918-742-9988	744-2716
Mayo Foundation 200 SW 1st St *Web:* www.mayoclinic.org	Rochester	MN	55905	507-284-2511	284-0161
MedCath Inc 10720 Sikes Pl Suite 300 *NASDAQ:* MDTH ■ *Web:* www.medcath.com	Charlotte	NC	28277	704-708-6600	708-5035
MedStar Health 5565 Sterrett Pl 5th Fl *TF:* 877-772-6505 ■ *Web:* www.medstarhealth.org	Columbia	MD	21044	410-772-6500	715-3754
Memorial Health Services Inc 7677 Ctr Ave. *Web:* www.memorialcare.org	Huntington Beach	CA	92647	562-933-1800	981-1336
Memorial Health Systems 875 Sterthaus Ave. *Web:* www.memorial-health.com	Ormond Beach	FL	32174	386-676-6000	
Memorial Hermann Healthcare System 7600 Beechnut St *Fax: Cust Svc ■ *Web:* www.memorialhermann.org	Houston	TX	77074	713-776-5500	776-5144*
Mercy Health System 1 W Elm St *Web:* www.mercyhealth.org	Conshohocken	PA	19428	610-567-6100	567-6444
Meridian Healthcare Group Inc 3500 Fincl Plaza Suite 200 *Web:* www.meridianhg.com	Tallahassee	FL	32312	850-325-7777	325-7778
Methodist Health Care System 6565 Fannin St. *Fax: Admitting ■ *Web:* www.methodisthealth.com	Houston	TX	77030	713-790-3311	793-1362*
Methodist Healthcare Inc 1265 Union Ave *Web:* www.methodisthealth.org	Memphis	TN	38104	901-516-7000	516-2394
Methodist Healthcare Ministries of South Texas Inc 4507 Medical Dr *TF:* 800-959-6673 ■ *Web:* www.mhm.org	San Antonio	TX	78229	210-692-0234	614-7563
Methodist Hospitals of Dallas 1441 N Beckley Ave *TF:* 800-725-9664 ■ *Web:* www.methodisthealthsystem.org	Dallas	TX	75203	214-947-8181	947-6501
MultiCare Health System 315 ML King Jr Way PO Box 5299 *Web:* www.multicare.org	Tacoma	WA	98415	253-403-1251	403-1180
New Center Community Mental Health Services 2051 W Grand Blvd *Web:* www.newcentercmhs.org	Detroit	MI	48208	313-961-3200	
New York City Health & Hospitals Corp 125 Worth St. *Fax: PR ■ *Web:* www.nyc.gov/html/hhc/html/home/home.shtml	New York	NY	10013	212-788-3339	788-3348*
New York-Presbyterian Healthcare System 622 W 168th St. *TF:* 877-697-9355 ■ *Web:* www.nyp.org/system	New York	NY	10032	212-305-2500	
North Broward Hospital District 303 SE 17th St *Web:* www.browardhealth.org	Fort Lauderdale	FL	33316	954-355-5100	355-4966
North Mississippi Health Services 830 S Gloster St *Web:* www.nmhs.net	Tupelo	MS	38801	662-377-3000	377-3990
Northwestern Counseling Support & Services Inc 107 Fisher Pond Rd *TF:* 800-834-7793 ■ *Web:* www.ncssinc.org	Saint Albans	VT	05478	802-524-6554	527-7801
Norton Healthcare 415 E Broadway PO Box 35070 *Web:* www.nortonhealthcare.com	Louisville	KY	40232	502-629-8025	629-8059
Novant Health Inc 3333 Silas Creek Pkwy *Web:* www.novanthealth.org	Winston-Salem	NC	27103	336-718-5000	297-1481
Oakwood Healthcare Inc 18101 Oakwood Blvd PO Box 2500 *TF:* 800-543-9355 ■ *Web:* www.oakwood.org	Dearborn	MI	48124	313-593-7000	436-2038
OhioHealth Corporate Offices 1087 Dennison Ave 3rd Fl *Web:* www.ohiohealth.com	Columbus	OH	43201	614-544-4485	544-5244
Optimus Health Care Inc 982 E Main St *Web:* www.optimushealthcare.org	Bridgeport	CT	06608	203-696-3260	339-7677
OSF Healthcare System 800 NE Glen Oak Ave *Web:* www.osfhealthcare.org	Peoria	IL	61603	309-655-2850	655-6869
Palomar Pomerado Health 15615 Pomerado Rd *TF:* 800-628-2880 ■ *Web:* www.pph.org	Poway	CA	92064	858-613-4000	675-5467

	City	State	Zip	Phone	Fax
Partners HealthCare System Inc 800 Boylston St Suite 1150 *Web:* www.partners.org	Boston	MA	02199	617-278-1000	278-1049
Planned Parenthood of Indiana Inc 200 S Meridian St PO Box 397 *Web:* www.ppin.org	Indianapolis	IN	46206	317-637-4343	637-4344
Portland Clinic The 800 SW 13th Ave *Web:* www.theportlandclinic.com	Portland	OR	97205	503-221-0161	
Premier Inc 12255 El Camino Real *TF:* 877-777-1552 ■ *Web:* www.premierinc.com	San Diego	CA	92130	858-481-2727	481-8919
Provena Health 19065 Hickory Creek Dr Suite 310 *Web:* www.provena.org	Mokena	IL	60448	708-478-7900	
Providence Health & Services 9 E 9th Ave *Web:* www2.providence.org	Spokane	WA	99202	509-474-7337	474-4882
Riverside Health System 701 Town Ctr Dr Suite 1000	Newport News	VA	23606	757-534-7000	534-7087
Riverside-San Bernardino County Indian Health Inc (RSBCIH) 11555 1/2 Potrero Rd *Web:* www.rsbcihi.org	Banning	CA	92220	951-849-4761	849-5631
Rush System for Health 1653 W Congress Pkwy Kidston Bldg Suite 305 *Web:* www.rush.edu	Chicago	IL	60612	312-942-5000	942-5831
Saint David's HealthCare 98 San Jacinto Blvd Suite 1800 **Fax:* Mktg ■ *Web:* www.stdavids.com	Austin	TX	78701	512-708-9700	482-4126*
Saint Francis Care 114 Woodland St *Web:* www.stfranciscare.org	Hartford	CT	06105	860-714-4000	714-7809
Saint Joseph Health System 500 S Main St *Web:* www.stjhs.org	Orange	CA	92868	714-347-7500	347-7501
Saint Mary's Good Samaritan Inc 605 N 12th St *TF:* 800-310-0484 ■ *Web:* www.smgsi.com	Mount Vernon	IL	62864	618-242-4600	241-3810
Saint Michael's Medical Ctr 1160 Raymond Blvd *Web:* www.cathedralhealth.org	Newark	NJ	07102	973-690-3500	
Saint Vincent Catholic Medical Centers 170 W 12th St **Fax Area Code:* 718 ■ *Web:* www.svcmc.org	New York	NY	10011	212-604-7000	558-2425*
Schumacher Group 200 Corporate Blvd Suite 201 PO Box 82368 *TF:* 800-893-9698 ■ *Web:* www.schumachergroup.com	Lafayette	LA	70508	337-354-1332	371-4477
Scottsdale Healthcare 7301 E 2nd St #106 *Web:* www.smhsi.com	Scottsdale	AZ	85251	480-481-4327	994-1597
Scranton Counseling Center Inc 326 Adams Ave *Web:* www.scrantonscc.org	Scranton	PA	18503	570-348-6100	
Scripps Health 4275 Campus Pt Ct *TF:* 800-727-4777 ■ *Web:* www.scripps.org	San Diego	CA	92121	858-678-6111	678-6767
Sea Mar Community Health Ctr 1040 S Henderson St *Web:* www.seamar.org	Seattle	WA	98108	206-763-5277	788-3204
Senior Whole Health LLC (SWH) 58 Charles St 2nd Fl *Web:* www.seniorwholehealth.com	Cambridge	MA	02141	617-494-5353	494-5599
Sentara Healthcare 6015 Poplar Hall Dr **Fax:* Mktg ■ *Web:* www.sentara.com	Norfolk	VA	23502	757-455-7000	455-7964*
Sharp Healthcare 8695 Spectrum Ctr Blvd *Web:* www.sharp.com	San Diego	CA	92123	858-499-4000	499-5237
Shriners Hospitals for Children 2900 N Rocky Pt Dr **Fax:* Hum Res ■ *TF:* 800-237-5055 ■ *Web:* www.shrinershospitalsforchildren.org	Tampa	FL	33607	813-281-0300	281-8113*
Sisters of Charity of Leavenworth Health System 9801 Renner Blvd Suite 100 *Web:* www.sclhsc.org	Lenexa	KS	66219	913-895-2800	895-2900
Sisters of Charity of Saint Augustine Health System 2475 E 22nd St *Web:* www.sistersofcharityhealth.org	Cleveland	OH	44115	216-696-5560	696-2204
Sisters of Mary of the Presentation Health System 1202 Page Dr SW PO Box 10007 *Web:* www.smphs.org	Fargo	ND	58106	701-237-9290	235-0906
Sisters of Mercy Health System 14528 S Outer Forty Suite 100 *Web:* www.mercy.net	Chesterfield	MO	63017	314-579-6100	628-3723
Sisters of Saint Francis Health Services Inc 1515 Dragoon Trail PO Box 1290 *Web:* www.franciscanalliance.org	Mishawaka	IN	46546	574-256-3935	256-0267
Sisters of the Holy Family of Nazareth Sacred Heart Province 310 N River Rd	Des Plaines	IL	60016	847-298-6760	803-1941
Solaris Health System Inc 80 James St *Web:* www.solarishs.org	Edison	NJ	08820	732-744-5888	205-1497
Southern Illinois Healthcare 1239 E Main St *TF:* 866-744-2468 ■ *Web:* www.sih.net	Carbondale	IL	62902	618-457-5200	549-7522
Spartanburg Regional Healthcare System 101 E Wood St **Fax:* Mail Rm ■ *Web:* www.spartanburgregional.com	Spartanburg	SC	29303	864-560-6000	560-6001*
St Elizabeth's Medical Ctr 736 Cambridge St *Web:* www.caritaschristi.org	Brighton	MA	02135	617-789-3000	
Summit Medical Group 1 Diamond Hill Rd *Web:* www.summitmedicalgroup.com	Berkeley Heights	NJ	07922	908-273-4300	790-6593
Suncoast Center Inc PO Box 10970 *Web:* www.suncoastcenter.com	Saint Petersbu	FL	33733	727-327-7656	323-8978
SunLink Health Systems Inc 900 Cir 75 Pkwy Suite 1120 *AMEX:* SSY ■ *Web:* www.sunlinkhealth.com	Atlanta	GA	30339	770-933-7000	933-7010
Sutter Health 2200 River Plaza *TF:* 800-606-7070 ■ *Web:* www.sutterhealth.org	Sacramento	CA	95833	916-733-8800	286-6611
Tenet Healthcare Corp 1445 Ross Ave *NYSE:* THC ■ *TF:* 800-743-6333 ■ *Web:* www.tenethealth.com	Dallas	TX	75240	469-893-2000	893-8600
Terros Inc 3003 N Central Ave Suite 200 *TF:* 800-631-1314 ■ *Web:* www.terros.org	Phoenix	AZ	85012	602-222-9444	
Texas Health Resources 611 Ryan Plaza Dr Suite 900 *Web:* www.texashealth.org	Arlington	TX	76011	817-462-7900	462-6230
TheraCare 116 W 32nd St 8th Fl *Web:* www.theracare.com	New York	NY	10001	212-564-2350	564-5896
Trinity Health 27870 Cabot Dr *Web:* www.trinity-health.org	Novi	MI	48377	248-489-6000	489-6775
Trinity Health System 380 Summit Ave *Web:* www.trinityhealth.com	Steubenville	OH	43952	740-283-7000	283-7425
Truman Medical Ctr 2301 Holmes St *Web:* www.trumed.org	Kansas City	MO	64108	816-404-1000	404-2573
United Health Centers of The San Joaquin Valley 650 Zediker Ave PO Box 790 *Web:* www.unitedhealthcenters.org	Parlier	CA	93648	559-646-3561	646-3642
United Health Services Hospitals 10-42 Mitchell Ave *Web:* www.uhs.net	Binghamton	NY	13903	607-762-2200	762-3874
United Medical Corp 603 Main St	Windermere	FL	34786	407-876-2200	876-5959
Universal Health Services Inc 367 S Gulph Rd *NYSE:* UHS ■ *TF:* 800-347-7750 ■ *Web:* www.uhsinc.com	King of Prussia	PA	19406	610-768-3300	768-3336
University Health Network 190 Elizabeth St **Fax:* PR ■ *Web:* www.uhn.ca	Toronto	ON	M5G2C4	416-340-3388	340-4896*
University of California Health System 1111 Franklin St **Fax:* Hum Res ■ *Web:* www.universityofcalifornia.edu	Oakland	CA	94607	510-987-0700	987-0894*
University of Maryland Medical System 22 S Greene St *TF:* 800-492-5538 ■ *Web:* www.umm.edu	Baltimore	MD	21201	410-328-8667	328-2412
University of Pittsburgh Medical Center Health System 200 Lothrop St **Fax:* Hum Res ■ *TF:* 800-533-8762 ■ *Web:* www.upmc.edu	Pittsburgh	PA	15213	412-647-2345	647-4522*
University of Texas System Office of Health Affairs 601 Colorado St *Web:* www.utsystem.edu/hea	Austin	TX	78701	512-499-4224	499-4313
US Public Health Service Indian Health Service 801 Thompson Ave Suite 400 **Fax:* PR ■ *Web:* www.ihs.gov	Rockville	MD	20852	301-443-1083	443-0507*
Valeo Behavioral Health Care Inc 5401 SW 7th St *Web:* www.valeotopeka.org	Topeka	KS	66606	785-233-1730	
Vanguard Health Systems Inc 20 Burton Hills Blvd Suite 100 *Web:* www.vanguardhealth.com	Nashville	TN	37215	615-665-6000	665-6099
Vantage Health Plan Inc 130 Desiard St Suite 300 *Web:* www.vhpla.com	Monroe	LA	71201	318-361-0900	
Venice Family Clinic 604 Rose Ave *Web:* www.venicefamilyclinic.org	Venice	CA	90291	310-392-8630	392-6642
Verde Valley Medical Ctr (VVMC) 269 S Candy Ln *Web:* www.verdevalleymedicalcenter.com	Cottonwood	AZ	86326	928-634-2251	
Veterans Health Administration 810 Vermont Ave NW *Web:* www2.va.gov	Washington	DC	20420	202-273-5400	
Via Christi Health System 3720 E Bayley St *Web:* www.via-christi.org	Wichita	KS	67218	316-858-4939	858-4186
Vibra Healthcare 4550 Lena Dr *Web:* www.vibrahealthcare.com	Mechanicsburg	PA	17055	717-591-5700	591-5710
Virginia Commonwealth University Medical Ctr (VCU) 1250 E Marshall St *Web:* www.vcuhealth.org	Richmond	VA	23298	804-828-9000	828-6727
Virtua Health 94 Brick Rd Suite 200 *Web:* www.virtua.org	Marlton	NJ	08053	856-355-0004	355-0012
VistaCare Inc 4800 N Scottsdale Rd Suite 5000 *TF:* 888-608-4665 ■ *Web:* www.vistacare.com	Scottsdale	AZ	85251	480-648-4545	648-4547
Washington County Mental Health Services Inc (WCMHS) PO Box 647 *Web:* www.wcmhs.org	Montpelier	VT	05601	802-229-0591	223-8623
WellMed Medical Management Inc 8637 Fredericksburg Rd Suite 360 *TF:* 888-781-9355 ■ *Web:* www.wellmedmedicalgroup.com	San Antonio	TX	78240	216-615-9355	
West Oakland Health Council Inc (WOHC) 700 Adeline St *Web:* www.wohc.org	Oakland	CA	94607	510-835-9610	272-0209
West Penn Allegheny Health System 4800 Friendship Ave *TF:* 877-284-2000 ■ *Web:* www.wpahs.org	Pittsburgh	PA	15224	412-359-8782	359-6516
West Tennessee Healthcare 620 Skyline Dr *Web:* www.wth.net	Jackson	TN	38301	731-541-5000	541-6802
Wheaton Franciscan Healthcare 26 W 171 Roosevelt Rd PO Box 667 *Web:* www.wfhealthcare.org	Wheaton	IL	60187	630-909-6900	909-8001
William Beaumont Hospital 3601 W 13-Mile Rd **Fax:* Admitting ■ *Web:* www.beaumonthospitals.com	Royal Oak	MI	48073	248-551-5000	898-0400*
Yakima Neighborhood Health Services (YNHS) 12 S 8 th St PO Box 2605 *Web:* www.ynhs.org	Yakima	WA	98907	509-454-4143	454-3651

357 HEALTH & FITNESS CENTERS

SEE ALSO Spas - Health & Fitness p. 2659; Weight Loss Centers & Services p. 2774

	City	State	Zip	Phone	Fax
24 Hour Fitness Worldwide Inc 12647 Alcosta Blvd 5th fl *TF:* 888-256-5485 ■ *Web:* www.24hourfitness.com	San Ramon	CA	94583	925-543-3100	543-3200
Bally Total Fitness Holding Corp 8700 W Bryn Mawr Ave *Web:* www.ballyfitness.com	Chicago	CA	60631	773-380-3000	693-2982

Phone | Fax

Brick Bodies Fitness Services Inc
201 Old Padonia Rd . . . Cockeysville MD 21030 410-252-8058 560-3299
TF: 877-348-3861 ■ *Web:* www.brickbodies.com
Butterfly Life
2404 San Ramon Valley Blvd Suite 200 . . . San Ramon CA 94583 800-288-8373 743-8820*
**Fax Area Code:* 925 ■ *TF:* 800-288-8373 ■ *Web:* www.butterflylife.com
Capital City Club Inc 7 Harris St . . . Atlanta GA 30303 404-523-8221 659-3498
Web: www.capitalcityclub.org
Chelsea Piers Sports & Entertainment Complex
23rd St & Hudson River . . . New York NY 10011 212-336-6666 336-6130
Web: www.chelseapiers.com
Club One Inc 555 Market St 13th fl . . . San Francisco CA 94105 415-477-3000 477-3001
Web: www.clubone.com
Clubsport of San Ramon
350 Bollinger Canyon Ln . . . San Ramon CA 94582 925-735-8500 735-7916
Web: www.clubsportsr.com
Contours Express Inc 156 Imperial Way . . . Nicholasville KY 40356 859-885-6441 241-2234
TF: 877-227-2282 ■ *Web:* www.contoursexpress.com
Court Sport 1 150 Clearbrook Rd. . . . Elmsford NY 10523 914-592-3005 347-7432
Web: www.court-sports.com
Courthouse Athletic Club
495 State St 6th Fl PO Box 3125 . . . Salem OR 97301 503-364-1731 371-0773
Web: www.fitfx.com
Crunch Fitness International
22 W 19th St # 4. . . . New York NY 10011 212-993-0300 993-0343
TF: 888-227-8624 ■ *Web:* www.crunch.com
Curves International Inc 100 Ritchie Rd. . . . Waco TX 76712 254-399-9285 399-9731
TF: 800-848-1096 ■ *Web:* www.curves.com
Denver Athletic Club 1325 Glenarm Pl . . . Denver CO 80204 303-534-1211 534-1125
Web: www.denverathleticclub.cc
Detroit Athletic Club 241 Madison St. . . . Detroit MI 48226 313-963-9200 963-8891
Web: www.thedac.com
East Bank Club 500 N Kingsbury St . . . Chicago IL 60654 312-527-5800 644-3868
Web: www.eastbankclub.com
Equinox Fitness Holdings Inc 895 Broadway. . . . New York NY 10003 212-677-0180 777-9510
TF: 866-332-6549 ■ *Web:* www.equinox.com
Fitcorp 111 Huntington Ave . . . Boston MA 02199 617-375-5600 262-2058
Web: www.fitcorp.com
Fitness Co The 2137 Hwy 35 N Suite 15. . . . Holmdel NJ 07733 732-203-1220 203-1660
Fitness Ctr 2508 Galen Dr . . . Champaign IL 61821 217-356-1616 356-7920
Web: www.fitcen.com
FitWorks
26391 Curtiss Wright Pkwy Suite 104 . . . Richmond Heights OH 44143 216-289-3100 289-3714
TF: 877-333-5348 ■ *Web:* www.fitworks.com
Gold's Gym International Inc
125 E John Carpenter Fwy Suite 1300 . . . Irving TX 75062 214-574-4653
TF: 800-457-5375 ■ *Web:* www.goldsgym.com
GoodLife Fitness
355 Wellington St PO Box 23091. . . . London ON N6A3N7 519-433-0601 661-0416
Web: www.goodlifefitness.com
Greenwood Athletic Club
5801 S Quebec St. . . . Greenwood Village CO 80111 303-770-2582 850-9219
Web: www.greenwoodathleticclub.com
Greenwood Athletic Club
1330 Bypass 72 NE Piedmont Plaza. . . . Greenwood SC 29649 864-229-7500 229-5479
Web: www.gwdac.com
Health Fitness Corp
1650 W 82nd St Suite 1100 . . . Minneapolis MN 55431 952-831-6830 831-7264
TF: 800-639-7913 ■ *Web:* www.hfit.com
Healthtrax Fitness & Wellness
2345 Main St . . . Glastonbury CT 06033 860-633-5572 652-7066
TF: 800-998-0880 ■ *Web:* www.healthtrax.com
In-Shape Sports Club
1016 E Bianchi Rd Suite A-1 . . . Stockton CA 95210 209-472-2231 474-7586
Web: www.inshapeclubs.com
Kinderdance International Inc
1333 Gateway Dr Suite 1033 . . . Melbourne FL 32901 321-984-4448 984-4490
TF: 800-554-2334 ■ *Web:* www.kinderdance.com
LA Fitness International 2880 Michelle Dr. . . . Irvine CA 92606 714-505-8958
Web: www.lafitness.com
Lady of America Franchise Corp
500 E Broward Blvd Suite 1650 . . . Fort Lauderdale FL 33394 954-527-5373 527-5436
TF: 800-833-5239 ■ *Web:* www.ladyofamerica.com
Lake Shore Athletic Club Inc
2401 NW 94th St . . . Vancouver WA 98665 360-574-1991 574-9233
Web: www.lsac.com
Las Vegas Athletic Club
2655 S Maryland Pkwy Suite 201. . . . Las Vegas NV 89109 702-734-8944 733-7771
Web: www.lvac.com
Lexington Health Care Ctr 178 Lowell St . . . Lexington MA 02420 781-862-7400 862-7855
Web: www.healthbridgemanagement.com/lexington
Little Gym International Inc
7001 N Scottsdale Rd # 1050. . . . Scottsdale AZ 85253 480-948-2878 948-2765
TF: 888-228-2878 ■ *Web:* www.thelittlegym.com
Lucille Roberts Health Clubs Inc
4 E 80th St . . . New York NY 10021 212-734-0616 734-4151
Web: www.lucilleroberts.com
Milwaukee Athletic Club 758 N Broadway. . . . Milwaukee WI 53202 414-273-5080 273-4118
Web: www.macwi.org
Multnomah Athletic Club 1849 SW Salmon St. . . . Portland OR 97205 503-223-6251 525-8998
Web: www.themac.com
My Gym Enterprises Inc
15300 Ventura Blvd Suite 414 . . . Sherman Oaks CA 91403 800-469-4967 907-0735*
**Fax Area Code:* 818 ■ *TF:* 800-426-4573 ■ *Web:* www.my-gym.com
New York Sports Club 888 7th Ave 25th Fl . . . New York NY 10106 212-246-6700 246-8422
TF: 800-301-1231 ■ *Web:* www.mysportsclubs.com
Omni Fitness Club 40 E Norton St . . . Muskegon MI 49444 231-739-3391 733-0156
Web: www.omnifitnessclub.com
Philadelphia Sports Clubs 888 7th Ave . . . New York NY 10106 212-246-6700 246-8422
TF: 800-301-1231 ■ *Web:* www.mysportsclubs.com
Powerhouse Gym International
355 S Old Woodward Suite 150. . . . Birmingham MI 48009 248-476-2888 530-9816*
**Fax Area Code:* 249 ■ *Web:* www.powerhousegym.com
Premier & Curzons Fitness Clubs
5100 Dixie Rd. . . . Mississauga ON L4W1C9 905-602-9911 602-9922
Web: www.premierfitness.ca
Rivers Club Inc 301 Grant St. . . . Pittsburgh PA 15219 412-391-5227 391-5016
Web: www.clubcorp.com
Riviera Fitness Centers 3908 Veterans Blvd. . . . Metairie LA 70002 504-454-5855 454-7717
Web: www.rivierafitnesscenters.com
San Francisco Bay Club The
150 Greenwich St . . . San Francisco CA 94111 415-433-2000 433-7161
Web: www.sfbayclub.com
Seattle Athletic Club 2020 Western Ave . . . Seattle WA 98121 206-443-1111 443-2632
Web: www.sacdt.com
Spectrum Clubs Inc 15759 San Pedro Ave. . . . San Antonio TX 78232 210-490-1980
Web: www.spectrumclubs.com
Sports Club Co The 11151 Missouri Ave . . . Los Angeles CA 90025 310-479-5200 479-8350
PINK: SCYL ■ *Web:* www.thesportsclubla.com
StrollerFit Inc
100 E-Business Way Suite 290. . . . Cincinnati OH 45241 513-489-2920 489-2964
TF: 866-222-9348 ■ *Web:* www.strollerfit.com
Town Sports International Inc 888 7th Ave . . . New York NY 10106 212-246-6700 246-8422
TF: 800-301-1231 ■ *Web:* www.mysportsclubs.com
Washington Sports Clubs 888 7th Ave . . . New York NY 10106 212-246-6700 246-8422
TF: 800-301-1231 ■ *Web:* www.mysportsclubs.com
Washington Tennis Services Inc
3200 Tower Oaks Blvd . . . Rockville MD 20852 301-622-7800 622-3373
Web: www.wtsinternational.com
Wellbridge Co
8400 E Crescent Pkwy Suite 200 . . . Greenwood Village CO 80111 303-866-0800 860-0440
TF: 888-458-0489 ■ *Web:* www.wellbridge.com
Western Athletic Clubs 1 Lombard St. . . . San Francisco CA 94111 415-781-1874 394-5570
Web: www.clubwest.com
YMCA Birmingham 5414 Hwy 280 . . . Birmingham AL 35242 205-981-0144
Web: www.sportsfirst.com

358 HEALTH FOOD STORES

Phone | Fax

Christopher Enterprises 155 W 250 N . . . Spanish Fork UT 84660 801-794-6800 794-6801
TF Cust Svc: 800-453-1406 ■ *Web:* www.drchristophers.com
Ginsberg's Foods Inc 29 Ginsberg Ln PO Box 17 . . . Hudson NY 12534 518-828-4004 828-8728
TF: 800-999-6006 ■ *Web:* www.ginsbergs.com
GNC Corp 300 6th Ave. . . . Pittsburgh PA 15222 412-288-4600 338-8905*
**Fax:* Cust Svc ■ *TF Cust Svc:* 888-462-2548 ■ *Web:* www.gnc.com
Juice It Up! Franchise Corp
17915 Sky Pk Cir Suite J . . . Irvine CA 92614 949-475-0146 475-0137
Web: www.juiceitup.com
Netrition Inc 20 Petra Ln. . . . Albany NY 12205 518-464-0765 456-9673
TF: 888-817-2411 ■ *Web:* www.netrition.com
Pilgrims Fine Foods Inc PO Box 14686 . . . Spokane WA 99214 509-924-7781 924-1441
Ream's Food Stores
160 E Claybourne Ave. . . . Salt Lake City UT 84115 801-485-8451 485-0845
Web: www.reamsfoods.com
Ripple Creek USA LLC PO Box 1165 . . . Southport CT 06890 203-331-0363 382-0044
Smoothie King Franchises Inc 121 Pk Pl . . . Covington LA 70433 985-635-6973 635-6987
TF: 800-577-4200 ■ *Web:* www.smoothieking.com
Sysco Food Services Of Los Angeles Inc
20701 E Currier Rd. . . . Walnut CA 91789 909-595-9595 598-6383
TF: 800-800-1199
Vincit Group The
412 Georgia Ave Suite 300. . . . Chattanooga TN 37403 423-265-7090 265-9070
Web: www.vincitgroup.com
Whole Foods Market Inc 550 Bowie St. . . . Austin TX 78703 512-477-4455 482-7000
NASDAQ: WFM ■ *TF:* 888-746-7936 ■ *Web:* www.wholefoodsmarket.com

359 HEALTH & MEDICAL INFORMATION - ONLINE

Phone | Fax

AIDS Education Global Information System
32234 Paseo Adelanto Suite B . . . San Juan Capistrano CA 92675 949-248-5843 248-2839
Web: www.aegis.com
Alternative Medicine.com
Natural Solutions Magazine
2995 Wilderness Pl Suite 205 . . . Boulder CO 80301 303-440-7402 440-7446
TF: 800-333-4325 ■ *Web:* www.naturalsolutionsmag.com
At Health Inc
14241 NE Woodinville-Duvall Rd Suite 104. . . . Woodinville WA 98072 360-668-3808 668-2216
TF: 888-284-3258 ■ *Web:* www.athealth.com
BabyCenter LLC 163 Freelon St. . . . San Francisco CA 94107 415-537-0900 537-0909
TF: 866-241-2229 ■ *Web:* www.babycenter.com
Body The 250 W 57th St. . . . New York NY 10107 212-541-8500 541-4911
Web: www.thebody.com
Cancerfacts.com 1725 Westlake Ave N Suite 300 . . . Seattle WA 98109 206-270-0225 270-0229
TF Cust Svc: 877-422-3228 ■ *Web:* www.cancerfacts.com
drgreene.com 9000 Crow Canyon Rd Suite S220. . . . Danville CA 94506 925-964-1793 964-1794
Web: www.drgreene.com
eDiets.com Inc 1000 Corporate Dr. . . . Fort Lauderdale FL 33334 954-360-9022 360-9095
NASDAQ: DIET ■ *TF:* 800-265-6170 ■ *Web:* www.ediets.com
eMedicine.com Inc 8420 W Dodge Rd Suite 402 . . . Omaha NE 68114 402-341-3222 341-3336
TF: 866-363-3362 ■ *Web:* www.emedicine.com
eMedicineHealth.com 8420 W Dodge Rd Suite 402. . . . Omaha NE 68114 402-341-3222 341-3336
TF: 866-363-3362 ■ *Web:* www.emedicinehealth.com
HealthBoards.com 6601 Ctr Dr W Suite 500 . . . Los Angeles CA 90045 310-348-8120 348-8127
Web: www.healthboards.com
HealthCentral.com Inc
1655 N Ft Myer Dr Suite 400 . . . Arlington VA 22209 703-302-1040 248-0830
Web: www.healthcentral.com

Phone Fax

Medicine Online Inc
18800 Delaware St Suite 650 . . . . . Huntington Beach CA 92648 714-848-0444 242-1484
Web: www.medicineonline.com

MedlinePlus
National Library of Medicine
8600 Rockville Pike . . . . . Bethesda MD 20894 301-594-5983 402-1384
TF: 888-346-3656 ■ *Web:* www.nlm.nih.gov/medlineplus

Medscape 669 River Dr Ctr 2 . . . . . Elmwood Park NJ 07407 201-703-3400 703-3401
TF: 800-809-0703 ■ *Web:* www.medscape.com

Pain.com
Dannemiller Memorial Educational Foundation
5711 NW Pkwy Suite 100 . . . . . San Antonio TX 78249 210-641-8311 641-8329
TF: 800-328-2308 ■ *Web:* www.pain.com

PubMed
US National Library of Medicine
8600 Rockville Pike . . . . . Bethesda MD 20894 301-594-5983 402-1384
TF: 888-346-3656 ■ *Web:* www.ncbi.nlm.nih.gov

Quackwatch Inc PO Box 1747 . . . . . Allentown PA 18105 610-437-1795
Web: www.quackwatch.org

Scientific Technologies Corp
4400 E Broadway Blvd Suite 705 . . . . . Tucson AZ 85711 520-202-3333 202-3340
Web: www.stchome.com

WebMD 111 8th Ave . . . . . New York NY 10011 212-624-3700
Web: www.webmd.com

HEATING EQUIPMENT - ELECTRIC

SEE Air Conditioning & Heating Equipment - Residential p. 1384

360 HEATING EQUIPMENT - GAS, OIL, COAL

SEE ALSO Air Conditioning & Heating Equipment - Commercial/Industrial p. 1382; Air Conditioning & Heating Equipment - Residential p. 1384; Boiler Shops p. 1532; Furnaces & Ovens - Industrial Process p. 1893

Phone Fax

Aerco International Inc 159 Paris Ave . . . . . Northvale NJ 07647 201-768-2400 784-8073
TF: 800-526-0288 ■ *Web:* www.aerco.com

Airtherm Mfg Inc
10805 Sunset Office Dr Suite L110 . . . . . Saint Louis MO 63127 314-835-9911 835-9692
Web: www.airthermhvac.com

Appalachian Stove & Fabricators Inc
329 Emma Rd . . . . . Asheville NC 28806 828-253-0164 254-7803
Web: www.appalachianstove.com

Aquatherm Industries Inc
1940 Rutgers University Blvd . . . . . Lakewood NJ 08701 732-905-0440 905-9899
TF: 800-535-6307 ■ *Web:* www.warmwater.com

Barnes & Jones Corp 91 Pacella Pk Dr . . . . . Randolph MA 02368 781-963-8000 963-3322
Web: www.barnesandjones.com

Besicorp Ltd 1151 Flatbush Rd . . . . . Kingston NY 12401 845-336-7700 336-7172
Web: www.besicorp.com

BFS Industries LLC 200 Industrial Dr . . . . . Butner NC 27509 919-575-6711 575-4275
Web: www.bfs-ind.com

Bosch Water Heating 340 Mad River Pk . . . . . Waitsfield VT 05673 802-496-4436 496-6924
Web: www.boschhotwater.com

Burner Systems International Inc (BSI)
3600 Cummings Rd . . . . . Chattanooga TN 37419 423-822-3600 825-3710
TF: 800-251-6318 ■ *Web:* www.burnersystems.com

Burnham Corp 2920 Old Tree Dr PO Box 3020 . . . . . Lancaster PA 17603 717-397-4701 293-5827
TF: 888-432-8887 ■ *Web:* www.burnham.com

Casso-Solar Corp 230 US Rt 202 PO Box 163 . . . . . Pomona NY 10970 845-354-2500 362-1856
TF: 800-988-4455 ■ *Web:* www.cassosolar.com

Charles A Hones Inc
607 Albany Ave PO Box 518 . . . . . North Amityville NY 11701 631-842-8886 842-9300
Web: www.charlesahones.com

Cryoquip Inc 25720 Jefferson Ave . . . . . Murrieta CA 92562 951-677-2060 677-2066
Web: www.cryoquip.com

DESA International 2701 Industrial Dr . . . . . Bowling Green KY 42101 270-781-9600 781-9600
TF Cust Svc: 800-432-5212 ■ *Web:* www.desaint.com

Dunkirk Boilers 85 Middle Rd . . . . . Dunkirk NY 14048 716-366-5500 366-1209*
**Fax:* Cust Svc ■ *Web:* www.dunkirk.com

Ebner Furnaces Inc 224 Quadral Dr . . . . . Wadsworth OH 44281 330-335-1600 335-1605
Web: www.ebnerfurnaces.com

EFM Sales Co 302 S 4th St . . . . . Emmaus PA 18049 610-965-9041 967-6593
TF: 800-935-0933 ■ *Web:* www.efmheating.com

Electro-Flex Heat Inc 5 Northwood Rd . . . . . Bloomfield CT 06002 860-242-6287 242-7298
TF: 800-585-4213 ■ *Web:* www.electroflexheat.com

Embassy Industries Inc 300 Smith St . . . . . Farmingdale NY 11735 631-694-1800 694-1832
Web: www.embassyind.com

Empire Comfort Systems Inc
918 Freeburg Ave . . . . . Belleville IL 62222 618-233-7420 233-7097
TF: 800-851-3153 ■ *Web:* www.empirecomfort.com

Enercor Inc 6354 Pershing Ave . . . . . University City MO 63130 314-381-1907 275-2416*
**Fax Area Code:* 208

Erie Power Technologies Inc
5300 Knowledge Pkwy Suite 200 . . . . . Erie PA 16510 814-897-7000 897-1090
TF: 800-323-3743 ■ *Web:* www.eriepower.com

Freeman Gas Inc
1186 Asheville Hwy PO Box 4366 . . . . . Spartanburg SC 29303 864-582-5475 582-0937
TF: 800-277-5730 ■ *Web:* www.freemangas.com

Fulton Cos 972 Centerville Rd PO Box 257 . . . . . Pulaski NY 13142 315-298-5121 298-6390
Web: www.fulton.com

Hago Mfg Co Inc 1120 Globe Ave . . . . . Mountainside NJ 07092 908-232-8687 232-7246
Web: www.hagonozzles.com

Hamworthy Peabody Combustion Inc
70 Shelton Technology Ctr . . . . . Shelton CT 06484 203-922-1199 922-8866
TF: 877-732-2639 ■ *Web:* www.peabodyengineering.com

Hayward Pool Products Inc 620 Division St . . . . . Elizabeth NJ 07207 908-351-5400 351-4700
Web: www.haywardnet.com

Phone Fax

Hearth & Home Technologies Inc
7571 215th St W . . . . . Lakeville MN 55044 952-985-6000 985-6001
TF: 800-669-4328 ■ *Web:* www.hearthtech.com

Heat Controller Inc 1900 Wellworth Ave . . . . . Jackson MI 49203 517-787-2100 787-9341
Web: www.heatcontroller.com

Heatilator Inc 1915 W Saunders St . . . . . Mount Pleasant IA 52641 319-385-9211 986-4430
TF: 800-669-4328 ■ *Web:* www.heatilator.com

John Zink Co LLC 11920 E Apache St . . . . . Tulsa OK 74116 918-234-1800 234-2700
TF: 800-421-9242 ■ *Web:* www.johnzink.com

Johnston Boiler Co 300 Pine St . . . . . Ferrysburg MI 49409 616-842-5050 842-1854*
**Fax:* Cust Svc ■ *TF:* 800-748-0295 ■ *Web:* www.johnstonboiler.com

LB White Co Inc W 6636 LB White Rd . . . . . Onalaska WI 54650 608-783-5691 783-6115
TF: 800-345-7200 ■ *Web:* www.lbwhite.com

Lennox Hearth Products 1110 W Taft Ave . . . . . Orange CA 92865 714-921-6100 655-2008*
**Fax Area Code:* 866 ■ *TF:* 800-854-0257 ■ *Web:* www.lennoxhearthproducts.com

M. P. N. Inc 3675 Amber St . . . . . Philadelphia PA 19134 215-289-9480 289-9490
TF: 800-783-4030 ■ *Web:* www.activeradiator.com

Meeder Equipment Co 12323 6th St . . . . . Rancho Cucamonga CA 91739 909-463-0600 463-0102
TF: 800-423-3711 ■ *Web:* www.meeder.com

Messer Machine & Mfg Inc
1751 1st Ave PO Box 105 . . . . . Windom MN 56101 507-831-1904 831-1908

New Buck Corp 8000 Hwy 226 S PO Box 69 . . . . . Spruce Pine NC 28777 828-765-6144 765-0462
Web: www.buckstove.com

New Yorker Boiler Co Inc
21 E Lincoln Ave Suite 100 . . . . . Hatfield PA 19440 215-855-8055 855-8229
TF: 800-535-4679 ■ *Web:* www.newyorkerboiler.com

North American Mfg Co Ltd 4455 E 71st St . . . . . Cleveland OH 44105 216-271-6000 641-7852
TF: 800-626-3477 ■ *Web:* www.namfg.com

Parker Boiler Co 5930 Bandini Blvd . . . . . Los Angeles CA 90040 323-727-9800 722-2848
Web: www.parkerboiler.com

Power Flame Inc 2001 S 21st St PO Box 974 . . . . . Parsons KS 67357 620-421-0480 421-0948
Web: www.powerflame.com

Powrmatic Inc
2906 Baltimore Blvd PO Box 439 . . . . . Finksburg MD 21048 410-833-9100 833-7971
TF: 800-966-9100 ■ *Web:* www.powrmatic.com

ProVision Technologies Inc
69 Railroad Ave Suite A-7 . . . . . Hilo HI 96720 808-969-3281 934-7462
Web: www.provisiontechnologies.com

Rasmussen Iron Works Inc
12028 E Philadelphia St . . . . . Whittier CA 90601 562-696-8718 698-3510
Web: www.rasmussen.biz

Raypak Inc 2151 Eastman Ave . . . . . Oxnard CA 93030 805-278-5300 278-5468
TF: 800-947-2975 ■ *Web:* www.raypak.com

Reimers Electra Steam Inc
4407 Martinsburg Pike PO Box 37 . . . . . Clear Brook VA 22624 540-662-3811 726-4215*
**Fax Area Code:* 800 ■ *TF:* 800-872-7562 ■ *Web:* www.reimersinc.com

Rite Engineering & Mfg Corp
5832 Garfield . . . . . City of Commerce CA 90040 562-862-2135 861-9821
Web: www.riteboiler.com

Roberts-Gordon Inc 1250 William St PO Box 44 . . . . . Buffalo NY 14240 716-852-4400 852-0854
TF: 800-828-7450 ■ *Web:* www.rg-inc.com

RW Beckett Corp PO Box 1289 . . . . . Elyria OH 44036 440-327-1060 327-1064
TF: 800-645-2876 ■ *Web:* www.beckettcorp.com

Schwank Inc 2 Schwank Way at Hwy 56N . . . . . Waynesboro GA 30830 706-554-6191 554-9390
TF: 877-446-3727 ■ *Web:* www.schwankgroup.com/en/home.asp

Smith Cast Iron Boilers 260 N Elm St . . . . . Westfield MA 01085 413-562-9631 562-3799
Web: www.smithboiler.com

Spectrolab Inc 12500 Gladstone Ave . . . . . Sylmar CA 91342 818-365-4611 898-7534
TF: 800-936-4888 ■ *Web:* www.spectrolab.com

Taco Inc 1160 Cranston St . . . . . Cranston RI 02920 401-942-8000 942-2360*
**Fax:* Cust Svc ■ *TF:* 800-822-6007 ■ *Web:* www.taco-hvac.com

Temco Fireplace Products Inc
410 Admiral Blvd . . . . . Mississauga ON L5T2N6 905-670-7777 565-4690

Templeton Coal Co 701 Wabash Ave . . . . . Terre Haute IN 47807 812-232-7037 232-3752

Thermal Solutions Products LLC PO Box 3244 . . . . . Lancaster PA 17605 717-239-7642 501-5212*
**Fax Area Code:* 877 ■ *Web:* www.thermalsolutions.com

US Stove Co Inc
400 Pedar Ave PO Box 151 . . . . . South Pittsburg TN 37380 423-837-2100 837-2109
TF: 800-750-2723 ■ *Web:* www.usstove.com

Utica Boilers Inc PO Box 4729 . . . . . Utica NY 13504 315-797-1310 797-3762
TF: 800-325-5479 ■ *Web:* www.uticaboilers.com

Vermont Castings Inc PO Box 501 . . . . . Bethel VT 05032 802-234-2300 234-2340
TF Prod Info: 800-227-8683 ■ *Web:* www.vermontcastings.com

Water Furnace International Inc
9000 Conservation Way . . . . . Fort Wayne IN 46809 260-478-5667 479-3284*
**Fax:* Hum Res ■ *TF:* 800-222-5667 ■ *Web:* www.waterfurnace.com

Wayne Combustion Systems 801 Glasgow Ave . . . . . Fort Wayne IN 46814 260-425-9200 345-0341*
**Fax Area Code:* 800 ■ *TF:* 800-443-4625 ■ *Web:* www.waynecombustion.com

Weil-McLain Co 500 Blaine St . . . . . Michigan City IN 46360 219-879-6561 879-4025
Web: www.weil-mclain.com

Williams Comfort Products 250 W Laurel St . . . . . Colton CA 92324 909-825-0993 824-8009
Web: www.williamscomfortprod.com

Zeeco Inc 22151 E 91st St S . . . . . Broken Arrow OK 74014 918-258-8551 251-5519
Web: www.zeeco.com

361 HEAVY EQUIPMENT DISTRIBUTORS

SEE ALSO Farm Machinery & Equipment - Whol p. 1839; Industrial Equipment & Supplies (Misc) - Whol p. 2104

Phone Fax

Admar Supply Co Inc 1950 Brighton Henriett . . . . . Rochester NY 14623 585-272-9390 272-9165
Web: www.admarsupply.com

Advanced Specialty Products
428 Clough St . . . . . Bowling Green OH 43402 419-354-2844 352-9663
Web: www.aspohio.com

Alban Tractor Co 8531 Pulaski Hwy . . . . . Baltimore MD 21237 410-686-7777 780-3481*
**Fax:* Hum Res ■ *TF:* 800-492-6994 ■ *Web:* www.albancat.com

Company	City	State	ZIP	Phone	Fax
Anderson Equipment Co 1000 Washington Pike *Fax: Sales ■ TF: 800-414-4554 ■ Web: www.andersonequip.com	Bridgeville	PA	15017	412-343-2300	504-4251*
Anderson Machinery Co Inc 6535 Leopard St TF: 800-308-6043 ■ Web: www.andersonmachinerytexas.com	Corpus Christi	TX	78409	361-289-6043	289-6047
Aring Equipment Co Inc 13001 W Silver Spring Dr Web: www.aringequipment.com	Butler	WI	53007	262-781-3770	779-2737
Arnold Machinery Co 2975 W 2100 S TF Cust Svc: 800-821-0548 ■ Web: www.arnoldmachinery.com	Salt Lake City	UT	84119	801-972-4000	975-9749
Bacon-Universal Co Inc 918 Ahua St TF: 800-352-3508 ■ Web: www.baconuniversal.com	Honolulu	HI	96819	808-839-7202	834-8110
Balzer Pacific Equipment Co 2136 SE 8th Ave TF: 800-442-0966 ■ Web: www.balzerpacific.com	Portland	OR	97214	503-232-5141	232-9556
Bane Machinery Inc PO Box 541355 TF: 800-594-2263 ■ Web: www.banemachinery.com	Dallas	TX	75354	214-352-2468	352-2460
Brandeis Machinery & Supply Co 1801 Watterson Trail TF: 800-274-7253 ■ Web: www.brandeismachinery.com	Louisville	KY	40299	502-493-4380	499-3180
Carlson Tractor & Equipment Co 15125 S Robert Trial TF: 800-642-4441 ■ Web: www.carlsontractorinc.com	Rosemount	MN	55068	651-423-2222	423-4551
Chadwick-BaRoss Inc 160 Warren Ave TF: 800-477-4963 ■ Web: www.chadwick-baross.com	Westbrook	ME	04092	207-854-8411	854-8237
Cleveland Bros Equipment Co Inc 5300 Paxton St TF: 800-482-2378 ■ Web: www.clevelandbrothers.com	Harrisburg	PA	17111	717-564-2121	564-6931
Cogar Mine Supply Inc PO Box 532 Web: www.cogarminesupply.com	Beckley	WV	25802	304-252-4435	252-4514
Conmaco/Rector LP 1602 Engineers Rd Web: www.conmaco.com	Belle Chasse	LA	70037	504-394-7330	393-8715
Cooke Sales & Service Co Inc 1422 Washington St	Chillicothe	MO	64601	660-646-1166	646-0381
Croushorn Equipment Co Inc 101 Cs-1064 TF: 800-861-5070	Harlan	KY	40831	606-573-2454	573-2482
Dean Machinery Co 5701 E 87th St Web: www.deancat.com	Kansas City	MO	64132	816-753-5300	753-5300
Diamond Equipment Inc 1060 E Diamond Ave TF: 800-258-4428 ■ Web: www.diamondequipment.com	Evansville	IN	47711	812-425-4428	421-1036
Empire Southwest Co 1725 S Country Club Dr TF: 800-367-4731 ■ Web: www.empire-cat.com	Mesa	AZ	85210	480-633-4000	633-4000
Erb Equipment Co Inc 200 Erb Industrial Dr Web: www.erbequipment.com	Fenton	MO	63026	636-349-0200	349-4426
Fabco Equipment Inc 11200 W Silver Spring Rd Web: www.fabco.com	Milwaukee	WI	53225	414-461-9100	461-8899
Feenaughty Machinery Co 4800 NE Columbia Blvd TF: 800-875-2566 ■ Web: www.feenaughty.com	Portland	OR	97218	503-282-2566	282-2566
Foley Equipment Co 1550 S W St *Fax: Sales ■ Web: www.foleyeq.com	Wichita	KS	67213	316-943-4211	943-0896*
Franks Supply Co Inc 3311 Stanford Dr Ne TF: 800-432-5254 ■ Web: www.franks-supply.com	Albuquerque	NM	87107	505-884-0000	884-1787
Garden State Engine & Equipment Co 3509 US Hwy 22 TF: 800-479-3857 ■ Web: www.gsee-crane.com	Somerville	NJ	08876	908-534-5444	534-5623
General Equipment & Supplies Inc 4300 Main Ave TF: 800-437-2924 ■ Web: www.genequip.com	Fargo	ND	58103	701-282-2662	281-9067
Global Equipment Marketing Inc PO Box 810483 TF: 866-750-8662 ■ Web: www.globalmagnetics.com	Boca Raton	FL	33481	561-750-8662	750-9507
Golden Equipment Co PO Box 6038 TF: 800-880-8580 ■ Web: www.goldenequipment.com	Albuquerque	NM	87197	505-345-7811	345-0401
Heavy Machines Inc 3926 E Rains Rd TF: 800-238-5591 ■ Web: www.heavymachinesinc.com	Memphis	TN	38118	901-260-2200	260-2276
HO Penn Machinery Co Inc 122 Noxon Rd *Fax: Mktg ■ Web: www.hopenn.com	Poughkeepsie	NY	12603	845-452-1200	452-3698*
Hoffman Equipment Inc 300 S Randolphville Rd TF: 800-446-3362 ■ Web: www.hoffmanequip.com	Piscataway	NJ	08854	732-752-3600	968-8371
Improved Construction Methods 1040 N Redmond Rd TF: 800-877-4571 ■ Web: www.improvedconstructionmethods.com	Jacksonville	AR	72076	501-982-7715	982-9794
James W Bell Co Inc 1720 I Ave NE Web: www.jwbell.com	Cedar Rapids	IA	52402	319-362-1151	362-4876
JC Smith Inc 345 Peat St Web: www.jcsmithinc.com	Syracuse	NY	13210	315-428-9903	428-9841
JCB Inc 2000 Bamford Blvd TF: 800-522-7522 ■ Web: www.jcbna.com	Pooler	GA	31322	912-447-2000	447-2299
John Fabick Tractor Co 1 Fabick Dr TF Cust Svc: 800-845-9188 ■ Web: www.fabickcat.com	Fenton	MO	63026	636-343-5900	343-4910
Kdr Supply Inc PO Box 10130 Web: www.kdrsupply.com	Liberty	TX	77575	936-336-6267	336-1034
Komatsu Equipment Co 2350 W 1500 S *Fax Area Code: 866 ■ Web: www.komatsu.com	Salt Lake City	UT	84104	801-972-3660	246-4487*
M R L Equipment Co Inc PO Box 31154 TF: 877-788-2907 ■ Web: www.markritelines.com	Billings	MT	59107	406-869-9900	
MacAllister Machinery Co Inc 7515 E 30th St TF: 800-227-3228 ■ Web: www.macallister.com	Indianapolis	IN	46219	317-545-2151	860-3310
Mankato Implement Inc 1150 S Victory Dr TF: 800-624-8983 ■ Web: www.mankatoimplement.com	Mankato	MN	56001	507-387-8201	388-3565
Milton CAT 554 Maple St Web: www.miltoncat.com	Hopkinton	NH	03229	603-746-4611	746-8686
Mississippi Valley Equipment Co Inc 1198 Pershall Rd TF: 800-325-8001 ■ Web: www.mve-stl.com	Saint Louis	MO	63137	314-869-8600	869-6862
Monroe Tractor & Implement Co Inc 1001 Lehigh Stn Rd Web: www.monroetractor.com	Henrietta	NY	14467	585-334-3867	334-0001
Moodie Implement Co Hwy 87 W TF: 800-823-3373 ■ Web: www.moodieimplement.com	Lewistown	MT	59457	406-538-5433	538-2604
Mustang Tractor & Equipment Co 12800 NW Fwy TF: 800-256-1001 ■ Web: www.mustangcat.com	Houston	TX	77040	713-460-2000	460-8473
Nortrax Equipment Co 310 Industrial Pk Dr TF: 800-472-6685 ■ Web: www.nortrax.com	Ashland	WI	54806	715-682-5522	682-8476
Ohio Machinery Co 3993 E Royalton Rd TF: 800-837-6200 ■ Web: www.ohiomachinery.com	Broadview Heights	OH	44147	440-526-6200	526-9513
Oldenburg Group Inc 1717 W Civic Dr Web: www.oldenburggroup.com	Milwaukee	WI	53209	414-977-1717	977-1700
Patten Industries Inc 635 W Lake St TF: 877-688-2228 ■ Web: www.pattencat.com	Elmhurst	IL	60126	630-279-4400	279-7892
Pioneer Machinery Co 55 Madison Ave Suite 400 *Fax Area Code: 866 ■ Web: www.pioneermachinery.us	Morristown	NJ	07960	973-285-3211	892-8724*
Power Motive Corp 5000 Vasquez Blvd TF: 800-627-0087 ■ Web: www.powermotivecorp.com	Denver	CO	80216	303-355-5900	388-9328
Production Specialty Services LLC PO Box 3176 Web: www.productionss.com	Midland	TX	79702	432-620-0059	620-0056
RDO Equipment Co 700 7th St S Web: www.rdoequipment.com	Fargo	ND	58103	701-239-8730	271-6328
Ring Power Corp 500 World Commerce Pkwy Web: www.ringpower.com	Saint Augustine	FL	32092	904-737-7730	281-9110
Rish Equipment Co PO Box 330 Web: www.rish.com	Bluefield	WV	24701	304-327-5124	327-8821
Road Machinery Co 716 S 7th St Web: www.roadmachinery.com	Phoenix	AZ	85034	602-252-7121	253-9690
Roland Machinery Co 816 N Dirksen Pkwy TF: 800-252-2926 ■ Web: www.rolandmachinery.com	Springfield	IL	62702	217-789-7711	744-7314
Rudd Equipment Co 4344 Poplar Level Rd TF: 800-283-7833 ■ Web: www.ruddequipment.com	Louisville	KY	40213	502-456-4050	459-8695
Scott Machinery Co 4055 S 500 W TF: 800-734-7441	Salt Lake City	UT	84123	801-262-7441	261-1857
Sellers Tractor Co Inc 400 N Chicago St Web: www.sellersequipment.com	Salina	KS	67401	785-823-6378	823-8083
Sequoia Equipment Co Inc PO Box 2747 Web: www.sequoiaequipment.com	Fresno	CA	93745	559-441-1122	441-0454
Southeastern Equipment Co Inc 10874 E Pike Rd TF: 800-798-5438 ■ Web: www.southeasternequip.com	Cambridge	OH	43725	740-432-6303	432-3303
Spreitzer Inc 3145 16th Ave SW TF: 800-823-0399	Cedar Rapids	IA	52404	319-365-9155	365-2525
Stan Houston Equipment Co 501 S Marion Rd TF: 800-952-3033 ■ Web: www.stanhouston.com	Sioux Falls	SD	57106	605-336-3727	336-7860
Stone & Stemle Inc 2951 N 600w Web: www.stoneandstemle.net	Jasper	IN	47546	812-634-1717	634-1740
Stowers Machinery Corp 6301 Old Rutledge Pike NE Web: www.stowerscat.com	Knoxville	TN	37924	865-546-1414	595-1030
Toromont Industries Ltd 3131 Hwy 7 W PO Box 5511 TSE: TIH ■ Web: www.investor.toromont.com	Concord	ON	L4K1B7	416-667-5511	667-5555
Tyler Equipment Corp 251 Shaker Rd PO Box 544 TF: 800-292-6351 ■ Web: www.tylerequipment.com	East Longmeadow	MA	01028	413-525-6351	525-5909
Valin Corp 555 E California Ave Web: www.valin.com	Sunnyvale	CA	94086	408-730-9850	730-1363
Victor L Phillips Co 4100 Gardner Ave TF: 800-878-9290 ■ Web: www.vlpco.com	Kansas City	MO	64120	816-241-9290	241-1738
Wajax Corp 3280 Wharton Way TSE: WJX ■ Web: www.wajax.com	Mississauga	ON	L4X2C5	905-212-3300	624-6020
West Side Tractor Sales Co 1400 W Ogden Ave Web: www.westsidetractorsales.com	Naperville	IL	60563	630-355-7150	355-7173
Western Power & Equipment 6407-B NE 117th Ave TF: 800-333-2346	Vancouver	WA	98662	360-253-2346	253-4830
Western States Equipment Co 500 E Overland Rd PO Box 38 TF: 800-852-2287 ■ Web: www.westernstatescat.com	Meridian	ID	83642	208-888-2287	884-2314
White's Farm Supply Inc 4154 Rt 31 Web: www.whitesfarmsupply.com	Canastota	NY	13032	315-697-2214	697-8024
Winchester Equipment Co 121 Indian Hollow Rd *Fax Area Code: 540 ■ Web: www.winchesterequipment.com	Winchester	VA	22603	800-323-3581	665-3058*
Wyoming Machinery Co 5300 Old W Yellowstone Hwy Web: www.wyomingcat.com	Casper	WY	82604	307-472-1000	261-4491

362 HELICOPTER TRANSPORT SERVICES

SEE ALSO Air Charter Services p. 1381; Ambulance Services p. 1394

Company	City	State	ZIP	Phone	Fax
Air Logistics Inc 4605 Industrial Dr NYSE: BRS ■ TF: 800-365-6771 ■ Web: www.bristowgroup.com	New Iberia	LA	70560	337-365-6771	364-8222
Air Logistics of Alaska 1915 Donald Ave	Fairbanks	AK	99701	907-452-1197	452-4539
Aircoastal Helicopters Inc 2615 Lantana Rd Suite J Web: www.aircoastal.com	Lantana	FL	33462	561-642-6840	642-5393
Biscayne Helicopters Inc 13955 SW 127th St Bldg 121 Web: www.biscaynehelicopters.com	Miami	FL	33186	305-252-3883	252-8154
Carson Helicopters 952 Blooming Glen Rd TF: 800-523-2335 ■ Web: www.carsonhelicopters.com	Perkasie	PA	18944	215-249-3535	249-1352
CHC Helicopter Corp 4740 Agar Dr NYSE: FLI ■ TF: 866-233-4227 ■ Web: www.chc.ca	Richmond	BC	V7B1A3	604-276-7500	

				Phone	Fax
Coastal Helicopters Inc 8995 Yandukin Dr	Juneau	AK	99801	907-789-5600	789-7076
TF: 800-789-5610 ■ *Web:* www.coastalhelicopters.com					
Columbia Helicopters Inc 14452 Arndt Rd NE	Aurora	OR	97002	503-678-1222	678-1222
Web: www.colheli.com					
Corporate Helicopters of San Diego 3753 John J Montgomery Dr Suite 2	San Diego	CA	92123	858-505-5650	874-3038
TF: 800-345-6737 ■ *Web:* www.corporatehelicopters.com					
Cougar Helicopters Inc Saint John's International Airport 40 Craig Dobbins' Way	Saint John's	NL	A1A4Y3	709-758-4800	758-4850
Web: www.cougar.ca					
Crescent Helicopters 1620 SW 75th Ave Nh Perry Airport	Pembroke Pines	FL	33023	954-987-1900	987-1912
Web: www.crescentair.com					
Era Helicopters Inc 4700 Old International Airport Rd	Anchorage	AK	99502	907-248-4422	266-8300
TF: 800-843-1947 ■ *Web:* www.flyera.com					
Evergreen Helicopters of Alaska Inc 1936 Merrill Field Dr	Anchorage	AK	99501	907-257-1500	279-6816
TF: 800-958-2454 ■ *Web:* www.evergreenaviation.com					
Gateway Helicopters Ltd PO Box 21028	North Bay	ON	P1B9N8	705-268-3334	474-1813
TF: 888-474-4214					
Helicopter Transport Services Inc (HTS) 701 Wilson Pt Rd PO Box E	Baltimore	MD	21220	410-391-7722	686-4507
Web: www.htshelicopters.com					
Helinet Aviation Services LLC 16644 Roscoe Blvd Hangar 2	Van Nuys	CA	91406	818-902-0229	902-9278
TF: 800-221-8389 ■ *Web:* www.helinet.com					
Highland Helicopters Ltd 4240 Agar Dr	Richmond	BC	V7B1A3	604-273-6161	273-6088
Web: www.highland.ca					
Houston Helicopters Inc 3506 Lockheed St	Pearland	TX	77581	281-485-1777	485-3701
Island Express Helicopter Service 1175 Queens Hwy S	Long Beach	CA	90802	310-510-2525	510-9671
TF Cust Svc: 800-228-2566 ■ *Web:* www.islandexpress.com					
Midwest Helicopter Airways Inc 525 Executive Dr	Willowbrook	IL	60527	630-325-7860	325-3313
TF: 800-323-7609 ■ *Web:* www.midwesthelicopter.com					
PHI Inc 2001 SE Evangeline Thwy	Lafayette	LA	70508	337-235-2452	235-3424
NASDAQ: PHII ■ *TF:* 800-235-2452 ■ *Web:* www.phihelico.com					
San Joaquin Helicopters 1407 S Lexington	Delano	CA	93215	661-725-1898	725-5401
Web: www.sjhelicopters.com					
Skydance Helicopters 2207 Bellanca St Suite B	Minden	NV	89423	775-782-4040	782-0140
TF: 800-882-1651 ■ *Web:* www.skydanceheli.com					
Tex-Air Helicopters Inc 8919 Paul B Koonce St	Houston	TX	77061	713-649-6344	649-0572
Victoria International Airport 1962 Canso Rd	North Saanich	BC	V8L5V5	250-656-3987	655-6839
TF: 866-844-4354 ■ *Web:* www.vih.com					
VIH Logging Ltd 1962 Canso Rd	North Saanich	BC	V8L5V5	250-656-1220	655-6839
Web: www.vih.com					
Westcor Aviation Inc 7305 E Greenway Rd	Scottsdale	AZ	85260	480-991-6558	991-7827
Wiggins Airways Inc 1 Garside Way	Manchester	NH	03103	603-629-9191	665-9644
Web: www.wiggins-air.com					
Yellowhead Helicopters Ltd 3010 Selwyn Rd PO Box 190	Valemount	BC	V0E2Z0	250-566-4401	566-4333
TF: 888-566-4401 ■ *Web:* www.yhl.ca					

363 HOLDING COMPANIES

SEE ALSO Conglomerates p. 1701

A Holding Company Is A Company That Owns Enough Voting Stock In Another Firm To Control Management And Operations By Influencing Or Electing Its Board Of Directors.

363-1 Airlines Holding Companies

				Phone	Fax
Alaska Air Group Inc 19300 International Blvd	Seattle	WA	98188	206-392-5040	392-5860
NYSE: ALK ■ *TF:* 800-451-0384 ■ *Web:* www.alaskaair.com					
AMR Corp 4333 Amon Carter Blvd	Fort Worth	TX	76155	817-963-1234	967-4162
NYSE: AMR ■ *Web:* www.aa.com					
ExpressJet Holdings Inc 990 Toffie Terrac	Atlanta	GA	30354	404-856-1000	
Web: www.expressjet.com					
Frontier Airlines Inc 7001 Tower Rd	Denver	CO	80249	720-374-4200	374-4622
TF: 800-432-1359 ■ *Web:* www.frontierairlines.com					
JetBlue Airways Corp 118-29 Queens Blvd	Forest Hills	NY	11375	718-286-7900	709-3621
NASDAQ: JBLU ■ *TF:* 800-538-2583 ■ *Web:* www.jetblue.com					
Republic Airways Holdings Inc 8909 Purdue Rd Suite 300	Indianapolis	IN	46268	317-484-6000	484-6040
NASDAQ: RJET ■ *TF:* 800-432-1359 ■ *Web:* www.republicairways.com					
SkyWest Inc 444 S River Rd	Saint George	UT	84790	435-634-3000	634-3105
NASDAQ: SKYW ■ *Web:* www.skywest.com					
UAL Corp 1200 E Algonquin Rd	Elk Grove Township	IL	60007	847-700-4000	700-2214
NASDAQ: UAUA ■ *TF:* 800-241-6522 ■ *Web:* www.united.com					
US Airways Group Inc 111 W Rio Salado Pkwy	Tempe	AZ	85281	480-693-5050	
NYSE: LCC ■ *TF:* 800-428-4322 ■ *Web:* www.usairways.com					

363-2 Bank Holding Companies

				Phone	Fax
1st Constitution Bancorp 2650 Rt 130 & Dey Rd	Cranbury	NJ	08512	609-655-4500	655-5653
NASDAQ: FCCY ■ *Web:* www.1stconstitution.com					
1st Source Corp 100 N Michigan St	South Bend	IN	46601	574-235-2254	235-2936*
NASDAQ: SRCE ■ **Fax:* Hum Res ■ *TF Cust Svc:* 800-513-2360 ■ *Web:* www.1stsource.com					
Abington Community Bancorp Inc 180 Old York Rd	Jenkintown	PA	19046	215-886-8280	887-4100
NASDAQ: ABBC ■ *TF:* 800-523-4175 ■ *Web:* www.abingtonbank.com					
Access National Corp 1800 Robert Fulton Dr Suite 310	Reston	VA	20191	703-871-2100	766-3386
NASDAQ: ANCX ■ *TF:* 800-931-0370 ■ *Web:* www.accessnationalbank.com					
Aliant National Corp PO Box 1237	Alexander City	AL	35011	256-329-7400	
TF: 866-888-8330 ■ *Web:* www.aliantbank.com					
Allegheny Valley Bank 5137 Butler St	Pittsburgh	PA	15201	412-781-1464	781-6474
OTC: AVLY ■ *Web:* www.avbpgh.com					
Alliance Financial Corp 120 Madison St 18th Fl	Syracuse	NY	13202	315-475-2100	475-4421
NASDAQ: ALNC ■ *TF:* 800-310-6275 ■ *Web:* www.alliancebankna.com					
Alpine Bank of Colorado 2200 Grand Ave PO Box 10000	Glenwood Springs	CO	81602	970-945-2424	947-1242
TF: 888-425-7463 ■ *Web:* www.alpinebank.com					
Amarillo National Bancorp Inc 410 S Taylor St	Amarillo	TX	79101	806-378-8000	378-8066*
**Fax:* Hum Res ■ *TF:* 800-262-3733					
AMB Financial Corp 8230 Hohman Ave	Munster	IN	46321	219-836-5870	836-5883
Web: www.ambfinancial.com					
Amboy Bancorp 3590 US Hwy 9 S	Old Bridge	NJ	08857	732-591-8700	591-0726
TF: 800-942-6269 ■ *Web:* www.amboybank.com					
Amegy Bancorp Inc 4400 Post Oak Pkwy	Houston	TX	77027	713-235-8800	571-5060*
**Fax:* Hum Res ■ *TF:* 800-324-6705					
Ameriana Bancorp 2118 Bundy Ave PO Box H	New Castle	IN	47362	765-529-2230	529-2232
NASDAQ: ASBI ■ *TF:* 866-844-7584 ■ *Web:* www.ameriana.com					
American Bank Inc 4029 W Tilghman St	Allentown	PA	18104	610-366-1800	289-3326
NASDAQ: AMBK ■ *TF:* 888-366-6622 ■ *Web:* www.pcbanker.com					
American National bank 628 Main St	Danville	VA	24541	434-792-5111	792-1582
NASDAQ: AMNB ■ *TF:* 800-240-8190 ■ *Web:* www.amnb.com					
American River Bankshares 3100 Zinfandel Dr Suite 450	Rancho Cordova	CA	95670	800-544-0545	851-1025*
NASDAQ: AMRB ■ **Fax Area Code:* 916 ■ *TF:* 800-544-0545 ■ *Web:* www.amrb.com					
American State Bank 1401 Ave Q	Lubbock	TX	79408	806-767-7000	747-5921
TF: 800-531-1401 ■ *Web:* www.asbonline.com					
American State Bank Holding Co 223 Main St	Williston	ND	58801	701-774-4100	774-4175
TF: 800-486-8173 ■ *Web:* www.asbt.com					
AmericanWest Bancorporation 41 W Riverside Ave Suite 400	Spokane	WA	99201	509-927-3028	465-9681
PINK: AWBC ■ *TF:* 800-772-5479 ■ *Web:* www.awbank.net					
Ameris Bancorp 24 2nd Ave SE	Moultrie	GA	31768	229-890-1111	890-2235
NASDAQ: ABCB ■ *TF:* 800-845-5219 ■ *Web:* www.amerisbank.com					
AmeriServe Financial Inc 216 Franklin St PO Box 520	Johnstown	PA	15907	814-533-5300	533-5427
NASDAQ: ASRV ■ *TF Cust Svc:* 800-837-2265 ■ *Web:* www.ameriservfinancial.com					
Ames National Corp 405 5th St PO Box 846	Ames	IA	50010	515-232-6251	663-3033
NASDAQ: ATLO ■ *Web:* www.amesnational.com					
Anchor BanCorp Wisconsin Inc 25 W Main St	Madison	WI	53707	608-252-8700	252-1889*
NASDAQ: ABCW ■ **Fax:* Hum Res ■ *TF:* 800-252-6246 ■ *Web:* www.anchorbank.com					
Andrew R Mancini Assoc Inc 129 Odell Ave	Endicott	NY	13760	607-754-7070	786-0410
Andrus Transportation Services LLC 3185 E Deseret Dr N PO Box 880	Saint George	UT	84790	435-673-1566	
TF: 800-888-5838 ■ *Web:* www.andrustrans.com					
Annapolis Bancorp Inc 1000 Bestgate Rd	Annapolis	MD	21401	410-224-4455	224-3132
NASDAQ: ANNB ■ *TF:* 800-582-2651 ■ *Web:* www.bankannapolis.com					
Arrow Financial Corp 250 Glen St	Glens Falls	NY	12801	518-745-1000	761-6741
NASDAQ: AROW ■ *Web:* www.arrowfinancial.com					
Associated Banc-Corp 1200 Hansen Rd	Green Bay	WI	54304	920-491-7000	491-7180*
NASDAQ: ASBC ■ **Fax:* Hum Res ■ *TF PR:* 800-236-2722 ■ *Web:* www.associatedbank.com					
Astoria Financial Corp 1 Astoria Federal Plaza	Lake Success	NY	11042	516-327-3000	
NYSE: AF					
Atlantic Coast Federal Corp (ACFC) 505 Haines Ave	Waycross	GA	31501	912-283-4711	284-2284
NASDAQ: ACFC ■ *TF:* 800-342-2824					
Auburn Enlarged City School District 78 Thornton Ave	Auburn	NY	13021	315-255-8800	255-5910
Web: www.auburn.cnyric.org					
Auburn National Bancorporation Inc PO Box 3110	Auburn	AL	36831	334-821-9200	887-2796
NASDAQ: AUBN ■ *TF:* 888-988-2162 ■ *Web:* www.auburnbank.com					
Bancorp Rhode Island One Turks Head Pl	Providence	RI	02903	401-456-5000	456-5154
NASDAQ: BARI ■ *TF:* 800-554-8969 ■ *Web:* www.bankri.com					
BancorpSouth Inc 2910 W Jackson St	Tupelo	MS	38801	662-680-2000	678-7299
NYSE: BXS ■ *TF:* 888-797-7711 ■ *Web:* www.bancorpsouthonline.com					
BancTrust Financial Group Inc 100 St Joseph St PO Box 3067	Mobile	AL	36652	251-431-7800	431-7851
NASDAQ: BTFG ■ *TF:* 800-689-7929 ■ *Web:* www.banctrustfinancialgroupinc.com					
BancWest Corp PO Box 3200	Honolulu	HI	96847	808-525-7000	525-5758
TF: 888-844-4444 ■ *Web:* www.bancwestcorp.com					
Bank Independent 710 S Montgomery Ave	Sheffield	AL	35660	256-386-5000	386-0710
TF: 877-865-5050 ■ *Web:* www.bibank.com					
Bank Mutual Corp 4949 W Brown Deer Rd	Milwaukee	WI	53223	414-354-1500	354-5450
NASDAQ: BKMU ■ *TF:* 888-358-5070 ■ *Web:* www.bankmutual.com					
Bank of America Corp 100 N Tryon St Suite 200 Corporate Ctr	Charlotte	NC	28255	704-386-5681	386-6699
NYSE: BAC ■ *TF:* 800-432-1000 ■ *Web:* www.bankofamerica.com					
Bank of Commerce Holdings 1901 Churn Creek Rd	Redding	CA	96002	530-722-3939	224-3337
NASDAQ: BOCH ■ *Web:* www.reddingbankofcommerce.com					
Bank of Granite Corp PO Box 128	Granite Falls	NC	28630	828-496-2000	496-2077
NASDAQ: GRAN ■ *Web:* www.bankofgranite.com					
Bank of Hawaii Corp 130 Merchant St 20th Fl	Honolulu	HI	96813	888-643-3888	
NYSE: BOH ■ *TF:* 888-643-3888 ■ *Web:* www.boh.com					
Bank of New York Mellon Corp The 1 Wall St	New York	NY	10286	212-495-1784	635-1799*
NYSE: BK ■ **Fax:* PR ■ *Web:* www.bnymellon.com					
Bank of South Carolina Corp 256 Meeting St	Charleston	SC	29401	843-724-1500	723-1513
NASDAQ: BKSC ■ *TF:* 800-523-4175 ■ *Web:* www.banksc.com					

Phone Fax

Bank of the Ozarks Inc
12615 Chenal Pkwy Suite 3100 .... Little Rock AR 72211 501-978-2265 978-2224
NASDAQ: OZRK ■ *TF:* 800-628-3552 ■ *Web:* www.bankozarks.com

BankAtlantic Bancorp Inc
2100 W Cypress Creek Rd .... Fort Lauderdale FL 33309 954-940-5000 940-5320
NYSE: BBX ■ *TF:* 800-741-1700 ■ *Web:* www.bankatlanticbancorp.com

BankFinancial Corp 15 W 60 N Frontage Rd .... Burr Ridge IL 60527 630-242-7321 614-3090*
NASDAQ: BFIN ■ **Fax Area Code:* 708 ■ *TF:* 800-894-6900 ■ *Web:* www.bankfinancial.com

Banner Bank PO Box 907 .... Walla Walla WA 99362 509-527-3636 526-8717*
NASDAQ: BANR ■ **Fax:* Hum Res ■ *TF:* 800-272-9933 ■ *Web:* www.bannerbank.com

Bar Harbor Bankshares
82 Main St PO Box 400 .... Bar Harbor ME 04609 207-288-3314 288-2626
AMEX: BHB ■ *TF:* 888-853-7100 ■ *Web:* www.bhbt.com

Barnes Transportation Services Inc
2309 Whitley Rd .... Wilson NC 27895 800-898-5897 281-2787*
**Fax Area Code:* 252 ■ *Web:* www.barnestransport.com

BB & T Corp 200 W 2nd St .... Winston-Salem NC 27101 336-733-2000
NYSE: BBT ■ *TF:* 800-682-6902 ■ *Web:* www.bbandt.com

BCB Bancorp Inc 104-110 Ave C .... Bayonne NJ 07002 201-823-0700 339-0403
NASDAQ: BCBP ■ *Web:* www.bcbbancorp.com

BCSB Bankcorp Inc 4111 E Joppa Rd Suite 300 .... Baltimore MD 21236 410-256-5000 529-1672
NASDAQ: BCSB

Beck-ford Construction LP 6750 Mayard Rd .... Houston TX 77041 713-896-7774 937-1942
Web: www.beck-ford.com

Benny Whitehead Inc 3265 S Eufaula Ave .... Eufaula AL 36027 334-687-8055 687-1345
TF: 800-633-7617 ■ *Web:* www.bwitruck.com

Berkshire Bancorp Inc 160 Broadway .... New York NY 10038 212-791-5362 791-5367
NASDAQ: BERK ■ *TF:* 800-773-5601 ■ *Web:* www.berkshirebank.com

Berkshire Hills Bancorp Inc 24 N St .... Pittsfield MA 01201 413-443-5601 443-3587
NASDAQ: BHLB ■ *TF:* 800-773-5601 ■ *Web:* www.berkshirebank.com

Beverly Hills Bancorp Inc
14523 SW Millikan Way Suite 200 .... Beaverton OR 97005 503-223-5600 223-8799
PINK: BHBC

Big Spring School District 45 Mt Rock Rd .... Newville PA 17241 717-776-2000
Web: www.bigspringsd.org

Blue River Bancshares Inc
29 E Washington St .... Shelbyville IN 46176 317-398-9721 392-6208
OTC: BRBI ■ *TF:* 800-298-3132 ■ *Web:* www.blueriverbancshares.com

BNC Bancorp 1226 Eastchester Dr .... High Point NC 27265 336-476-9200 889-8451
NASDAQ: BNCN ■ *Web:* www.bankofnc.com

BNCCORP Inc 322 E Main Ave .... Bismarck ND 58501 701-250-3040 222-3653
NASDAQ: BNCC ■ *Web:* www.bnccorp.com

BofI Holding Inc
Bank of Internet USA
12777 High Bluff Dr Suite 100 .... San Diego CA 92130 858-755-6381 350-0443
NASDAQ: BOFI ■ *TF:* 877-541-2634 ■ *Web:* www.bankofinternet.com

BOK Financial Corp PO Box 2300 .... Tulsa OK 74192 918-588-6000 588-6853
NASDAQ: BOKF

Boston Private Financial Holdings Inc
10 Post Office Sq .... Boston MA 02109 617-912-3799 912-4511
NASDAQ: BPFH ■ *Web:* www.bostonprivate.com

Brannen Banks Of Florida Inc PO Box 1929 .... Inverness FL 34451 352-726-1221 726-1156
Web: www.brannenbanks.com

Bridge Capital Holdings
55 Almaden Blvd Suite 200 .... San Jose CA 95113 408-423-8500 423-8520
NASDAQ: BBNK ■ *TF:* 800-937-5449 ■ *Web:* www.bridgebank.com

Britton & Koontz Capital Corp
500 Main St PO Box 1407 .... Natchez MS 39120 601-445-5576 445-2488
NASDAQ: BKBK ■ *TF:* 866-425-2265 ■ *Web:* www.bkbank.com

Broadway Financial Corp
4800 Wilshire Blvd .... Los Angeles CA 90010 323-634-1700 634-1728
NASDAQ: BYFC ■ *TF:* 888-988-2265 ■ *Web:* www.broadwayfederalbank.com

Brookline Bank 160 Washington St .... Brookline MA 02445 617-730-3520 730-3569
NASDAQ: BRKL ■ *TF Cust Svc:* 877-668-2265 ■ *Web:* www.brooklinebank.com

Brooklyn Federal Bancorp Inc 81 Ct St .... Brooklyn NY 11201 718-855-8500 858-5174
NASDAQ: BFSB ■ *Web:* www.brooklynbank.com

Brunswick Bank & trust
439 Livingston Ave .... New Brunswick NJ 08901 732-247-5800 247-5990
OTC: BRBW ■ *Web:* www.brunswickbank.com

Bryn Mawr Bank Corp 801 Lancaster Ave .... Bryn Mawr PA 19010 610-525-1700 526-2450*
NASDAQ: BMTC ■ **Fax:* Cust Svc ■ *TF:* 888-732-2080 ■ *Web:* www.bmtc.com

C & F Financial Corp
802 Main St PO Box 391 .... West Point VA 23181 804-843-4584 843-3017
NASDAQ: CFFI ■ *TF:* 800-583-3863 ■ *Web:* www.cffc.com

Cadence Financial Corp
5980 Horton St Suite 550 .... Emeryville CA 94608 510-899-8800 225-0371
AMEX: NBY ■ *TF:* 888-622-7341 ■ *Web:* www.novabaypharma.com

California First National Bancorp
18201 Von Karman Ave Suite 700 .... Irvine CA 92612 949-255-0500 255-0501
NASDAQ: CFNB ■ *TF:* 800-496-4640 ■ *Web:* www.calfirstbancorp.com

Camden National Corp 2 Elm St .... Camden ME 04843 207-236-8821 236-6256
AMEX: CAC ■ *TF:* 800-860-8821 ■ *Web:* www.camdennational.com

Capital City Bank Group Inc PO Box 900 .... Tallahassee FL 32302 850-402-7500 878-9133
NASDAQ: CCBG ■ *TF:* 888-671-0400 ■ *Web:* www.ccbg.com

Capitol Bancorp Ltd 200 N Washington Sq .... Lansing MI 48933 517-487-6555 374-2576
PINK: CBC ■ *Web:* www.capitolbancorp.com

Capitol City Bancshares Inc 562 Lee St .... Atlanta GA 30310 404-752-6067
TF: 866-758-6395 ■ *Web:* www.capitolcitybank-atl.com

Capitol Federal Financial 700 Kansas Ave .... Topeka KS 66603 785-235-1341 231-6216
NASDAQ: CFFN ■ *TF:* 888-822-7333 ■ *Web:* www.capfed.com

Cardinal Financial Corp
8270 Greensboro Dr Suite 500 .... McLean VA 22102 703-584-3400 584-3518*
NASDAQ: CFNL ■ **Fax:* Hum Res ■ *TF:* 800-473-3247 ■ *Web:* www.cardinalbank.com

Carolina Bank Holdings Inc
101 N Spring St .... Greensboro NC 27401 336-288-1898 387-4359
NASDAQ: CLBH ■ *TF:* 800-523-4175 ■ *Web:* www.carolinabank.com

Carrollton Bancorp
7151 Columbia Gateway Dr Suite A .... Baltimore MD 21046 410-312-5400
NASDAQ: CRRB ■ *TF:* 800-222-6566 ■ *Web:* www.carrolltonbank.com

Carver Bancorp Inc 75 W 125th St .... New York NY 10027 718-230-2900 426-6159*
NASDAQ: CARV ■ **Fax Area Code:* 212 ■ *TF:* 866-476-6587 ■ *Web:* www.carverbank.com

Cascade Bancorp 1100 NW Wall St .... Bend OR 97701 541-385-6205 382-8780
NASDAQ: CACB ■ *TF Cust Svc:* 877-617-3400 ■ *Web:* www.botc.com

Cascade Financial Corp 2828 Colby Ave .... Everett WA 98201 425-339-5500 259-8688*
NASDAQ: CASB ■ **Fax:* Hum Res ■ *TF:* 800-326-8787 ■ *Web:* www.cascadebank.com

Cathay General Bancorp Inc
777 N Broadway .... Los Angeles CA 90012 213-625-4700 625-1368
NASDAQ: CATY ■ *TF:* 800-922-8429 ■ *Web:* www.cathaybank.com

Center Bancorp Inc 2455 Morris Ave .... Union NJ 07083 908-688-9500 810-7304
NASDAQ: CNBC ■ *TF:* 800-862-3683 ■ *Web:* www.centerbancorp.com

Center Financial Corp
3435 Wilshire Blvd Suite 700 .... Los Angeles CA 90010 213-251-2222 251-2204
NASDAQ: CLFC ■ *TF:* 888-699-7788 ■ *Web:* www.investor.centerbank.com

Central Bancorp Inc 399 Highland Ave .... Somerville MA 02145 617-628-4000 629-4236
NASDAQ: CEBK ■ *Web:* www.centralbk.com

Central Bank 101 W Commercial St .... Lebanon MO 65536 417-532-2151 532-2001
Web: www.central-bank.net

Central Federal Corp PO Box 345 .... Wellsville OH 43968 330-532-1517 532-3875
NASDAQ: CFBK ■ *TF:* 888-273-8255

Central Pacific Financial Corp PO Box 3590 .... Honolulu HI 96811 808-544-0500 544-0500
NYSE: CPF ■ *TF:* 800-342-8422 ■ *Web:* www.centralpacificbank.com

Central Valley Community Bancorp
7100 N Financial Dr Suite 101 .... Fresno CA 93720 559-298-1775 298-1483
NASDAQ: CVCY ■ *TF:* 866-294-9588 ■ *Web:* www.cvcb.com

Central Virginia Bankshares Inc
2036 New Dorset Rd PO Box 39 .... Powhatan VA 23139 804-403-2000 598-7768
NASDAQ: CVBK ■ *TF:* 888-282-4030 ■ *Web:* www.centralvabank.com

Century Bancorp Inc 400 Mystic Ave .... Medford MA 02155 781-393-4160 393-4077
NASDAQ: CNBKA ■ *TF:* 800-442-1859 ■ *Web:* www.centurybank.com

CFS Bancorp Inc 707 Ridge Rd .... Munster IN 46321 219-836-5500 836-2950
NASDAQ: CITZ ■ *TF:* 888-226-5237 ■ *Web:* www.cfsbancorp.com

Chemical Financial Corp
333 E Main St PO Box 569 .... Midland MI 48640 989-839-5350 839-5255
NASDAQ: CHFC ■ *TF:* 800-867-9757 ■ *Web:* www.chemicalbankmi.com

Citizens & Northern Corp 90-92 Main St .... Wellsboro PA 16901 570-724-3411 724-6395
NASDAQ: CZNC

Citizens Banking Corp 328 S Saginaw St .... Flint MI 48502 810-766-7500 768-4724
NASDAQ: CBCF ■ *TF Cust Svc:* 800-676-6276 ■ *Web:* www.citizensonline.com

Citizens Financial Group Inc 1 Citizens Dr .... Riverside RI 02915 401-456-7000 455-5921
TF: 800-922-9999 ■ *Web:* www.citizensbank.com

Citizens Holding Co
521 Main St PO Box 209 .... Philadelphia MS 39350 601-656-4692 656-4264
NASDAQ: CIZ ■ *Web:* www.investor.citizensholdingcompany.com

Citizens Republic Bancorp
1 Citizens Banking Ctr 328 S Saginaw St .... Flint MI 48502 810-257-2506
NASDAQ: CRBC ■ *TF:* 800-676-6276 ■ *Web:* www.citizensbanking.com

Citizens South Banking Corp
519 S New Hope Rd PO Box 2249 .... Gastonia NC 28054 704-868-5200 868-2192*
NASDAQ: CSBC ■ **Fax:* Hum Res ■ *TF:* 800-218-8619 ■ *Web:* www.citizenssouth.com

City Holding Co 25 Gatewater Rd .... Charleston WV 25313 304-769-1100 769-1111
NASDAQ: CHCO ■ *TF:* 800-922-9236 ■ *Web:* www.cityholding.com

CKF Bancorp Inc PO Box 400 .... Danville KY 40423 859-236-4181 236-4363
Web: www.centralkyssb.com

Clifton Savings Bancorp Inc
1433 Van Houten Ave PO Box 2149 .... Clifton NJ 07015 973-473-2200 473-0451
NASDAQ: CSBK ■ *TF:* 888-562-6727 ■ *Web:* www.cliftonsavings.com

CNB Financial Corp 1 S 2nd St PO Box 42 .... Clearfield PA 16830 814-765-9621 765-8294
NASDAQ: CCNE ■ *TF:* 800-492-3221 ■ *Web:* www.bankcnb.com

CoBiz Inc 821 17th St .... Denver CO 80202 303-293-2265 244-9700
NASDAQ: COBZ ■ *TF:* 800-574-4714

Colonial Bankshares Inc 85 W Broad St .... Bridgeton NJ 08302 856-451-5800 451-5110
NASDAQ: COBK ■ *Web:* www.colonialbankfsb.com

Colony Bankcorp Inc
115 S Grant St PO Box 989 .... Fitzgerald GA 31750 229-426-6049 426-6039
NASDAQ: CBAN ■ *TF:* 800-873-6404 ■ *Web:* www.colonybank.com

Columbia Bank 1301 A St Suite 800 .... Tacoma WA 98402 253-305-1900 304-0050
NASDAQ: COLB ■ *TF:* 800-305-1905 ■ *Web:* www.columbiabank.com

CommerceFirst Bancorp Inc
1804 W St Suite 200 .... Annapolis MD 21401 410-280-6695 280-8565
NASDAQ: CMFB ■ *Web:* www.commerce1st.com

Commercial Bankshares Inc 1550 SW 57th Ave .... Miami FL 33144 305-267-1200 266-2939
TF: 800-752-7999

Commercial National Financial Corp
900 Ligonier St .... Latrobe PA 15650 724-539-3501 539-0816*
NASDAQ: CNAF ■ **Fax:* Hum Res ■ *TF:* 800-803-2265 ■ *Web:* www.cnbthebankonline.com

Commonwealth Bankshares Inc 403 Boush St .... Norfolk VA 23510 757-446-6900 446-6929
NASDAQ: CWBS ■ *TF:* 888-446-9862 ■ *Web:* www.bankofthecommonwealth.com

Community Bank & Trust
604 N 8th St PO Box 1409 .... Sheboygan WI 53082 920-459-4444 459-4450
TF: 888-582-4440 ■ *Web:* www.communitybankandtrust.com

Community Bank Shares of Indiana Inc
101 W Spring St .... New Albany IN 47150 812-944-2224 949-6870
NASDAQ: CBIN ■ *TF:* 866-944-2004 ■ *Web:* www.yourcommunitybank.com

Community Bank System Inc
5790 Widewaters Pkwy .... DeWitt NY 13214 315-445-2282 445-2282*
NYSE: CBU ■ **Fax:* Acctg ■ *TF:* 800-724-2262 ■ *Web:* www.communitybankna.com

Community Bankshares Inc
5570 DTC Blvd .... Greenwood Village CO 80111 720-529-3336
Web: www.cobnks.com

Community Financial Corp 38 N Central Ave .... Staunton VA 24401 540-886-0796 885-0643
NASDAQ: CFFC ■ *Web:* www.cbnk.com

Community First Bank Na PO Box 39 .... Forest OH 45843 419-273-2595 273-2598
Web: www.com1stbank.com

Community Investors Bancorp Inc
119 S Sandusky Ave .... Bucyrus OH 44820 419-562-7055 562-5516
TF: 800-222-4955 ■ *Web:* www.ffcb.com

Community Shores Bank Corp
1030 W Norton Ave .... Muskegon MI 49441 231-780-1800 780-3006
NASDAQ: CSHB ■ *TF:* 888-853-6633 ■ *Web:* www.communityshores.com

Community State Bank Bancshare PO Box 378 .... Shelbina MO 63468 573-588-4101 588-4408
TF: 877-568-4121 ■ *Web:* www.commbankonline.com

Community Trust Bancorp Inc
346 N Mayo Trail .... Pikeville KY 41501 606-432-1414 433-4637*
NASDAQ: CTBI ■ **Fax:* Hum Res ■ *TF:* 800-422-1090 ■ *Web:* www.ctbi.com

Community West Bancshares 445 Pine Ave .... Goleta CA 93117 805-692-5821 692-8902
NASDAQ: CWBC ■ *Web:* www.communitywest.com

				Phone	Fax
Compass Bancshares Inc 15 S 20th St	Birmingham	AL	35233	205-933-3305	297-3702
TF: 800-239-2265 ■ *Web:* www.bbvacompass.com					
Connecticut Bank & Trust Co 58 State House Sq	Hartford	CT	06103	860-246-5200	
NASDAQ: CTBC ■ *Web:* www.thecbt.com					
Country Club Bank 2310 S 4th St	Leavenworth	KS	66048	913-682-2300	
Web: www.countryclubbank.com					
Cowlitz Bancorporation 927 Commerce Ave	Longview	WA	98632	360-423-9800	578-0918*
NASDAQ: CWLZ ■ **Fax:* Hum Res ■ *TF:* 800-340-8865 ■ *Web:* www.cowlitzbancorp.com					
Crazy Woman Creek Bancorp Inc PO Box 1020	Buffalo	WY	82834	307-684-5591	684-7854
TF: 800-348-8971 ■ *Web:* www.buffalofed.com					
Crescent Financial Corp 1005 High House Rd	Cary	NC	27512	919-460-7770	460-2512
NASDAQ: CRFN ■ *Web:* www.crescentstatebank.com					
Crofutt & Smith Moving & Storage 1 Lenel Rd PO Box 8001	Landing	NJ	07850	973-347-7200	347-8143
TF: 800-524-1793 ■ *Web:* www.crofuttsmith.com					
Cullen/Frost Bankers Inc 100 W Houston St	San Antonio	TX	78205	210-220-4011	220-4087*
NYSE: CFR ■ **Fax:* Mail Rm ■ *TF:* 800-562-6732 ■ *Web:* www.frostbank.com					
CVB Financial Corp 701 N Haven Ave PO Box 51000	Ontario	CA	91764	909-980-4030	481-2130*
NASDAQ: CVBF ■ **Fax:* Hum Res ■ *TF:* 888-222-5432 ■ *Web:* www.cbbank.com					
Dearborn Bancorp Inc 22290 Michigan Ave	Dearborn	MI	48124	313-274-1000	274-5050
NASDAQ: DEAR ■ *TF:* 866-278-4848 ■ *Web:* www.fidbank.com					
Dickinson Financial Corp 1111 Main St # 302	Kansas City	MO	64105	816-472-5244	412-0024
Dime Community Bancshares Inc 209 Havemeyer St	Brooklyn	NY	11211	718-782-6200	486-7535*
NASDAQ: DCOM ■ **Fax:* Hum Res ■ *TF:* 800-321-3463 ■ *Web:* www.dime.com					
Doral Financial Corp 1441 F D Roosevelt Ave	San Juan	PR	00920	787-749-4949	749-4191
NYSE: DRL ■ *TF:* 866-296-3743 ■ *Web:* www.snl.com					
Eagle Bancorp Inc 7815 Woodmont Ave	Bethesda	MD	20814	240-497-2044	986-8529*
NASDAQ: EGBN ■ **Fax Area Code:* 301 ■ *TF:* 800-364-8313 ■ *Web:* www.eaglebankcorp.com					
East West Bancorp Inc 1881 W Main St	Alhambra	CA	91801	626-308-2012	308-2034
NASDAQ: EWBC ■ *TF:* 888-895-5650 ■ *Web:* www.eastwestbank.com					
Eastern Bank Corp 265 Franklin St	Boston	MA	02110	617-897-1008	
TF Cust Svc: 800-327-8376 ■ *Web:* www.easternbank.com					
Eastern Virginia Bankshares Inc 330 Hospital Rd	Tappahannock	VA	22560	804-443-8400	445-1047
NASDAQ: EVBS ■ *TF:* 888-464-2265 ■ *Web:* www.snl.com					
ECB Bancorp Inc 35050 US Hwy 264 PO Box 337	Engelhard	NC	27824	252-925-9411	925-8491
NASDAQ: ECBE ■ *TF:* 800-849-2265 ■ *Web:* www.myecb.com					
Enterprise Bancorp Inc 222 Merrimack St	Lowell	MA	01852	978-459-9000	656-5813
NASDAQ: EBTC ■ *Web:* www.enterprisebanking.com					
Enterprise Financial Services Corp 150 N Meramec Ave	Clayton	MO	63105	314-725-5500	721-6793
NASDAQ: EFSC ■ *TF:* 800-396-8141 ■ *Web:* www.enterprisebank.com					
ESB Financial Corp 600 Lawrence Ave	Ellwood City	PA	16117	724-758-5584	758-0576
NASDAQ: ESBF ■ *TF:* 800-533-4193 ■ *Web:* www.esbbank.com					
Evans Bancorp Inc 1 Grimsby Dr	Hamburg	NY	14075	716-926-2000	926-2005*
AMEX: EVBN ■ **Fax:* Hum Res ■ *TF:* 866-310-0763 ■ *Web:* www.evansbank.com					
Farmer State Bank of Sublette 303 S Pennsylvania Ave PO Box 20	Sublette	IL	61367	815-849-5242	849-5494
TF: 866-269-1722 ■ *Web:* www.sublettebank.com					
Farmers Capital Bank Corp PO Box 309	Frankfort	KY	40602	502-227-1668	227-1692
NASDAQ: FFKT ■ *Web:* www.farmerscapital.com					
Fauquier Bankshares Inc 10 Courthouse Sq	Warrenton	VA	20186	540-347-2700	349-2093
NASDAQ: FBSS ■ *TF:* 800-638-3798 ■ *Web:* www.fauquierbank.com					
FFD Financial Corp 321 N Wooster Ave	Dover	OH	44622	330-364-7777	364-7779
NASDAQ: FFDF ■ *TF:* 800-558-3424 ■ *Web:* www.onlinefirstfed.com/index.html					
FFW Corp 1205 N Cass St	Wabash	IN	46992	260-563-3185	563-4841
TF: 800-377-4984 ■ *Web:* www.crossroadsbanking.com					
Fidelity Bancorp Inc 1009 Perry Hwy	Pittsburgh	PA	15237	412-367-3300	364-6504
NASDAQ: FSBI ■ *TF:* 800-242-2500 ■ *Web:* www.fidelitybancorp-pa.com					
Fidelity Federal Bancorp 18 NW 4th St	Evansville	IN	47708	812-424-0921	469-2150
Web: www.unitedfidelity.com					
Fidelity Southern Corp 3490 Piedmont Rd Suite 1550	Atlanta	GA	30305	404-639-6500	814-8060
NASDAQ: LION ■ *TF:* 888-248-5466 ■ *Web:* www.fidelitysouthern.com					
Financial Institutions Inc 220 Liberty St	Warsaw	NY	14569	585-786-1100	786-5254
NASDAQ: FISI ■ *TF:* 866-344-2677 ■ *Web:* www.snl.com					
First American Bank Corp 1650 Louis Ave	Elk Grove Village	IL	60009	847-952-3700	364-7467
Web: www.firstambank.com					
First BanCorp 1519 Ponce de Leon Ave Sp 23	Santurce	PR	00908	787-729-8200	729-8139
NYSE: FBP ■ *TF:* 888-448-2511 ■ *Web:* www.firstbankpr.com					
First Bancorp 341 N Main St	Troy	NC	27371	910-576-6171	576-1070
NASDAQ: FBNC ■ *TF:* 800-548-9377 ■ *Web:* www.secure.firstbancorp.com					
First Bancorp of Indiana Inc 5001 Davis Lant Dr	Evansville	IN	47715	812-423-3196	421-4107
OTC: FBEI					
First Bancshares Inc 142 E 1st St	Mountain Grove	MO	65711	417-926-5151	926-4362
NASDAQ: FBSI					
First Banctrust Corp 101 S Central Ave	Paris	IL	61944	217-465-6381	465-0234
PINK: FIRT ■ *TF:* 800-228-6381 ■ *Web:* www.firstbanktrust.com					
First Banks Inc 135 N Meramec Ave	Clayton	MO	63105	314-854-4600	854-5454
TF: 800-760-2265 ■ *Web:* www.firstbanks.com					
First Busey Corp PO Box 17125	Urbana	IL	61803	217-365-4516	365-4592
NASDAQ: BUSE ■ *TF:* 800-672-8739 ■ *Web:* www.busey.com					
First Capital Inc 220 Federal Dr NW	Corydon	IN	47112	812-738-2198	738-2202
NASDAQ: FCAP ■ *TF:* 800-390-1465 ■ *Web:* www.firstherrison.com					
First Citizens Bancorporation Inc PO Box 29	Columbia	SC	29202	803-771-8700	931-8519
TF: 888-612-4444 ■ *Web:* www.firstcitizensonline.com					
First Citizens BancShares Inc 4300 Six Forks Rd	Raleigh	NC	27609	919-716-7000	716-7074
NASDAQ: FCNCA ■ *Web:* www.firstcitizens.com					
First Citizens Bank 1801 Century Pk E Suite 800	Los Angeles	CA	90067	310-552-1776	552-1772
NASDAQ: FRGB ■ *TF:* 888-323-4732 ■ *Web:* www.firstcitizens.com					
First Citizens National Bank Charitable Foundation PO Box 1708	Mason City	IA	50402	641-423-1600	423-4600
Web: www.firstcitizensnb.com					
First Commonwealth Financial Corp 601 Philadelphia St	Indiana	PA	15701	724-349-7220	349-7220*
NYSE: FCF ■ **Fax:* Hum Res ■ *TF:* 800-711-2265 ■ *Web:* www.fcfbank.com					
First Community Corp (FCC) 5455 Sunset Blvd	Lexington	SC	29072	803-951-0555	951-1722*
NASDAQ: FCCO ■ **Fax:* Cust Svc ■ *TF:* 888-951-2265 ■ *Web:* www.firstcommunitysc.com					
First Defiance Financial Corp 601 Clinton St	Defiance	OH	43512	419-782-5015	784-3467*
NASDAQ: FDEF ■ **Fax:* Hum Res ■ *TF:* 800-472-6292 ■ *Web:* www.fdef.com					
First Federal 420 2nd Ave SW	Cullman	AL	35055	256-734-4863	737-8900*
**Fax Area Code:* 203 ■ *Web:* www.firstfederalcullman.com					
First Federal Bancshares of Arkansas Inc 1401 Hwy 62-65 N	Harrison	AR	72601	870-741-7641	365-8355
NASDAQ: FFBH ■ *TF:* 866-242-3324 ■ *Web:* www.ffbh.com					
First Federal Capital Corp 605 State St	La Crosse	WI	54601	608-784-8000	784-6807*
**Fax:* Cust Svc ■ *TF:* 800-657-4636 ■ *Web:* www.firstfed.com					
First Financial Bancorp 300 High St	Hamilton	OH	45011	513-867-4700	867-4700
NASDAQ: FFBC ■ *TF:* 800-543-2265					
First Financial Bankshares Inc PO Box 701	Abilene	TX	79604	325-627-7155	627-7393
NASDAQ: FFIN ■ *Web:* www.ffin.com					
First Financial Corp 1 First Financial Plaza	Terre Haute	IN	47807	812-238-6000	232-5336
NASDAQ: THFF ■ *TF:* 800-511-0045 ■ *Web:* www.first-online.com					
First Financial Holdings Inc 2440 Mall Dr PO Box 118068	Charleston	SC	29423	843-529-5933	529-5933*
NASDAQ: FFCH ■ **Fax:* Mktg ■ *Web:* www.ir.firstfinancialholdings.com					
First FSB of Frankfort 216 W Main St PO Box 535	Frankfort	KY	40602	502-223-1638	223-7136
NASDAQ: KFFB ■ *TF:* 888-818-3372 ■ *Web:* www.ffsbfrankfort.com					
First Horizon National Corp 165 Madison	Memphis	TN	38103	901-523-4444	
NYSE: FHN ■ *TF:* 800-489-4040 ■ *Web:* www.fhnc.com					
First Independence Corp 112 E Myrtle St	Independence	KS	67301	620-331-1660	331-1600
TF: 800-455-0744					
First Interstate Bancsystem Inc 401 N 31st St	Billings	MT	59101	406-255-5300	255-5213*
**Fax:* Hum Res ■ *TF:* 800-342-0633 ■ *Web:* www.firstinterstatebank.com					
First M & F Corp 134 W Washington St	Kosciusko	MS	39090	662-289-5121	856-5524
NASDAQ: FMFC					
First Mariner Bancorp 1501 S Clinton St	Baltimore	MD	21224	410-342-2600	563-1594
NASDAQ: FMAR ■ *TF:* 888-561-2265 ■ *Web:* www.firstmarina.com					
First Merchants Corp 200 E Jackson St	Muncie	IN	47305	765-747-1500	741-7283*
NASDAQ: FRME ■ **Fax:* Mktg ■ *TF:* 800-205-3464 ■ *Web:* www.firstmerchants.com					
First Midwest Bancorp Inc 1 Pierce Pl Suite 1500	Itasca	IL	60143	630-875-7200	875-7396*
NASDAQ: FMBI ■ **Fax:* Mktg ■ *TF:* 800-322-3623					
First Mutual Bancshares Inc 400 108th Ave NE PO Box 1647	Bellevue	WA	98004	425-455-7300	455-7330
TF: 800-735-7303 ■ *Web:* www.firstmutual.com					
First National Bank of Tennessee 214 E Main St	Livingston	TN	38570	931-823-1261	
Web: www.fnbotn.com					
First National Lincoln Corp 223 Main St PO Box 940	Damariscotta	ME	04543	207-563-3195	563-3356
NASDAQ: FNLC ■ *TF:* 800-564-3195 ■ *Web:* www.thefirstbancorp.com					
First National of Nebraska Inc 1 First National Ctr	Omaha	NE	68197	402-341-0500	342-4332
TF: 800-688-7070 ■ *Web:* www.firstnational.com					
First Niagara Financial Group Inc 726 Exchange St Suite 618	Buffalo	NY	14210	716-625-7583	
NASDAQ: FNFG ■ *TF:* 800-421-0004 ■ *Web:* www.fnfg.com					
First Niles Financial Inc 55 N Main St	Niles	OH	44446	330-652-2539	652-0911
NASDAQ: FNFI					
First of Long Island Corp 10 Glen Head Rd	Glen Head	NY	11545	516-671-4900	656-3971*
NASDAQ: FLIC ■ **Fax:* Hum Res ■ *Web:* www.fngli.com					
First Security Group Inc 531 Broad St	Chattanooga	TN	37402	423-266-2000	267-3383
NASDAQ: FSGI ■ *Web:* www.fsgbank.com					
First South Bancorp Inc 1311 Carolina Ave	Washington	NC	27889	252-946-4178	946-3873
NASDAQ: FSBK ■ *TF:* 800-946-4178 ■ *Web:* www.firstsouthnc.com					
First Southern Bancshares Inc 102 S Ct St	Florence	AL	35630	256-764-7131	718-4260
TF: 800-625-7131					
First State Bancorp Inc 19230 SR- 136	Winchester	OH	45697	937-695-0331	695-0355
TF: 800-987-2566 ■ *Web:* www.fsbadamscounty.com					
First United Corp 19 S 2nd St	Oakland	MD	21550	301-334-9471	334-5784*
NASDAQ: FUNC ■ **Fax:* Hum Res ■ *TF:* 888-692-2654 ■ *Web:* www.mybankfirstunited.com					
First West Virginia Bancorp Inc 590 national Rd	Wheeling	WV	26003	304-277-1100	218-2458*
AMEX: FWV ■ **Fax:* Administration					
Firstbank Corp 311 Woodworth Ave	Alma	MI	48801	989-463-3131	463-6438
NASDAQ: FBMI ■ *Web:* www.firstbankmi.com					
FirstFed Bancorp Inc 1630 4th Ave N PO Box 340	Bessemer	AL	35020	205-428-8472	428-8652
TF: 800-436-5112 ■ *Web:* www.firstfedbessemer.com					
FirstMerit Corp III Cascade Plaza 7th Fl	Akron	OH	44308	330-996-6300	384-7321
NASDAQ: FMER ■ *TF:* 888-554-4362 ■ *Web:* www.firstmerit.com					
Flagstar Bancorp Inc 5151 Corporate Dr	Troy	MI	48098	248-312-2000	312-6842*
NYSE: FBC ■ **Fax:* Hum Res ■ *TF:* 800-945-7700 ■ *Web:* www.flagstar.com					
Flushing Financial Corp 1979 Marcus Ave Suite E-140	Lake Success	NY	11042	718-961-5400	
NASDAQ: FFIC ■ *TF:* 800-581-2889 ■ *Web:* www.flushingbank.com					
FMB Equibanc Inc 201 N Main St PO Box 2789	Statesboro	GA	30458	912-489-2600	764-2149
Web: www.fmbnk.com					
FNB Corp 101 Sunset Ave	Asheboro	NC	27203	336-626-8300	626-8374
NASDAQ: FNBN ■ *TF:* 800-873-1172 ■ *Web:* www.fnbnc.com					
FNB Corp 1 FNB Blvd	Hermitage	PA	16148	724-981-6000	983-3512
NYSE: FNB ■ *TF:* 888-981-6000 ■ *Web:* www.fnbcorporation.com					
Fulton Financial Corp 1 Penn Sq	Lancaster	PA	17602	717-291-2411	295-2561*
NASDAQ: FULT ■ **Fax:* Mktg ■ *TF:* 800-752-9580 ■ *Web:* www.fult.com					
German American Bancorp 711 Main St	Jasper	IN	47546	812-482-1314	482-0758
NASDAQ: GABC ■ *TF:* 800-482-1314 ■ *Web:* www.germanamerican.com					
Glacier Bancorp Inc PO Box 27	Kalispell	MT	59903	406-756-4200	
NASDAQ: GBCI ■ *TF:* 800-735-4371 ■ *Web:* www.glacierbank.com					
Gouverneur Bancorp Inc 400 Centre St	Newton	MA	02458	617-219-1440	219-1441
AMEX: GOV ■ *Web:* www.govreit.com					

				Phone	Fax
Great American Bancorp Inc 1311 S Neil St PO Box 1010 *Web:* www.greatamericanbancorp.com	Champaign	IL	61820	217-356-2265	356-2502
Great Southern Bancorp Inc 1451 E Battlefield *NASDAQ: GSBC* ■ *TF Cust Svc:* 800-749-7113 ■ *Web:* www.greatsouthernbank.com	Springfield	MO	65804	417-887-4400	895-4595
Greater Atlantic Financial Corp 10700 Parkridge Blvd *PINK: GAFC*	Reston	VA	20191	703-391-1300	391-1506
Greene County Bancorp Inc 302 Main St *NASDAQ: GCBC* ■ *TF:* 888-439-4272 ■ *Web:* www.thebankofgreenecounty.com	Catskill	NY	12414	518-943-2600	943-3756
Guaranty Bancshares Inc 100 W Arkansas St PO Box 1158 *TF:* 888-572-9881 ■ *Web:* www.gnty.com	Mount Pleasant	TX	75455	903-572-9881	572-5860
Guaranty Federal Bancshares Inc 1341 W Battlefield St *NASDAQ: GFED* ■ *Web:* www.gfed.com	Springfield	MO	65807	417-520-4333	
Habersham Bancorp 282 Historic Hwy 441 N *NASDAQ: HABC* ■ *TF:* 800-822-0316 ■ *Web:* www.habcorp.com	Cornelia	GA	30531	706-778-1000	778-6886
Hamm & Phillips Services Co 1312 E Willow Rd PO Box 3907 *TF:* 800-366-6024 ■ *Web:* www.hammphillips.com	Enid	OK	73701	580-242-1876	242-7339
Hancock Holding Co One Hancock Plaza 2510 14th St *NASDAQ: HBHC* ■ *TF:* 800-522-6542 ■ *Web:* www.hancockbank.com	Gulfport	MS	39502	228-868-4000	868-4627
Hanmi Bank 3660 Wilshire Blvd Suite PH-A *NASDAQ: HAFC* ■ *TF:* 877-808-4266 ■ *Web:* www.hanmi.com	Los Angeles	CA	90010	213-382-2200	384-8608
Harleysville Savings Financial Corp 271 Main St *NASDAQ: HARL* ■ *TF:* 888-256-8828 ■ *Web:* www.harleysvillesavings.com	Harleysville	PA	19438	215-256-8828	513-9393
Harris Bankcorp Inc 111 W Monroe St *Web:* www4.harrisbank.com	Chicago	IL	60603	312-461-7447	461-5788
Hawthorn Bancshares Inc 300 SW Longview Blvd *NASDAQ: HWBK* ■ *TF:* 800-761-8362 ■ *Web:* www.exchangebancshares.com	Lee's Summit	MO	64081	816-347-8100	
Heartland Financial USA Inc 1398 Central Ave *NASDAQ: HTLF* ■ **Fax Area Code:* 319 ■ *TF:* 888-739-2100 ■ *Web:* www.htlf.com	Dubuque	IA	52001	563-589-2100	589-2011*
Heritage Bank 101 N Main St *OTC: CCFH* ■ *TF:* 866-971-0106 ■ *Web:* www.heritagebank.com	Jonesboro	GA	30236	770-478-8881	478-8929
Heritage Commerce Corp 150 Almaden Blvd *NASDAQ: HTBK* ■ *Web:* www.heritagecommercecorp.com	San Jose	CA	95113	408-947-6900	947-6910
Heritage Financial Corp 201 5th Ave SW *NASDAQ: HFWA* ■ *TF:* 800-455-6126 ■ *Web:* www.hf-wa.com	Olympia	WA	98501	360-943-1500	352-0864
HF Financial Corp 225 S Main Ave *NASDAQ: HFFC* ■ *TF:* 800-244-2149 ■ *Web:* www.homefederal.com	Sioux Falls	SD	57104	605-333-7556	333-7621
HFB Financial Corp 1602 Cumberland Ave **Fax:* Hum Res ■ *TF:* 800-354-0182 ■ *Web:* www.homefederalbank.com	Middlesboro	KY	40965	606-248-1095	242-1010*
High Country Bancorp Inc 7360 W Hwy 50 *TF:* 800-201-0557 ■ *Web:* www.highcountry.net	Salida	CO	81201	719-539-2516	530-8880
HMN Financial Inc 1016 Civic Ctr Dr NW *NASDAQ: HMNF* ■ *TF:* 888-644-4142 ■ *Web:* www.justcallhome.com	Rochester	MN	55901	507-535-1200	346-1111
Home City Financial Corp 2454 N Limestone St PO Box 1288 *HCFL: OTC* ■ *TF:* 866-421-2331 ■ *Web:* www.homecityfederal.com	Springfield	OH	45503	937-390-0470	390-0876
Home Loan Financial Corp 413 Main St *Web:* www.homeloansavingsbank.com	Coshocton	OH	43812	740-622-0444	623-6000
Home Street Bank Inc 601 Union St Suite 2000 **Fax:* Mail Rm ■ *TF:* 800-654-1075 ■ *Web:* www.homestreet.com	Seattle	WA	98101	206-623-3050	389-6351*
Homestead Bancorp Inc 195 N 6th St *Web:* www.homesteadbank.com	Ponchatoula	LA	70454	985-386-3379	386-2400
Honat Bancorp Inc 733 Main St PO Box 350 *OTC: HONT* ■ *TF:* 800-462-9515 ■ *Web:* www.hnbbank.com	Honesdale	PA	18431	570-253-3355	253-5263
HopFed Bancorp Inc 2700 Fort Campbell Blvd *NASDAQ: HFBC* ■ *Web:* www.bankwithheritage.com	Hopkinsville	KY	42240	270-885-1171	889-0313
HSBC North America Holdings Inc 2700 Sanders Rd *TF:* 800-975-4722 ■ *Web:* www.hsbc.com	Prospect Heights	IL	60070	847-564-5000	205-7452
Hudson City Bancorp Inc West 80 Century Rd *NASDAQ: HCBK* ■ *TF:* 800-967-2200 ■ *Web:* www.hcsbonline.com	Paramus	NJ	07652	201-967-1900	967-0559
Hudson Valley Holding Corp 21 Scarsdale Rd *Web:* www.hudsonvalleybank.com	Yonkers	NY	10707	914-961-6100	961-7378
Huntington Bancshares Inc 7 Easton Oval *NASDAQ: HBAN* ■ **Fax Area Code:* 614 ■ *TF:* 800-480-2265 ■ *Web:* www.huntington.com	Columbus	OH	43219	616-355-8828	331-5862*
IBERIABANK Corp 200 W Congress St *NASDAQ: IBKC* ■ *TF:* 800-968-0801 ■ *Web:* www.iberiabank.com	Lafayette	LA	70501	337-521-4003	364-1171
IBT Bancorp Inc 309 Main St *AMEX: IRW*	Irwin	PA	15642	724-863-3100	863-3069
Independent Bank Corp 230 W Main St PO Box 491 *NASDAQ: IBCP* ■ *TF:* 800-662-0102 ■ *Web:* www.independentbank.com	Ionia	MI	48846	616-527-9450	527-4004
International Bancshares Corp 1200 San Bernardo Ave *NASDAQ: IBOC* ■ *Web:* www.ibc.com	Laredo	TX	78040	956-722-7611	726-6659
Intervest Bancshares Corp 1 Rockefeller Plaza Suite 400 *NASDAQ: IBCA* ■ *TF:* 877-226-5462 ■ *Web:* www.intervestnatbank.com	New York	NY	10020	212-218-8383	218-8390
INTRUST Financial Corp 1544 S Webb Rd *TF:* 800-895-2265 ■ *Web:* www.intrustbank.com	Wichita	KS	67207	316-383-1111	383-1828
ITLA Capital Corp 888 Prospect St Suite 110 *NASDAQ: ITLA* ■ *TF:* 888-551-4852 ■ *Web:* www.itlacapital.com	La Jolla	CA	92037	858-551-0511	551-1212
Jacksonville Bancorp Inc 100 N Laura St *NASDAQ: JAXB* ■ *TF:* 888-699-5292 ■ *Web:* www.jaxbank.com	Jacksonville	FL	32202	904-421-3040	421-3050
Jacksonville Bancorp Inc 1211 W Morton Ave *NASDAQ: JXSB* ■ *Web:* www.jacksonvillesavings.com	Jacksonville	IL	62650	217-245-4111	245-2010
Jeffersonville Bancorp 4866 SR 52 PO Box 398 *NASDAQ: JFBC* ■ *TF:* 888-216-2265 ■ *Web:* www.jeffbank.com	Jeffersonville	NY	12748	845-482-4000	482-3544
Johnson Financial Group Inc 555 Main St Suite 400 *Web:* www.johnsonbank.com	Racine	WI	53403	262-619-2790	619-2795

				Phone	Fax
Joy State Bank 101 W Main St *Web:* www.joystatebank.com	Joy	IL	61260	309-584-4146	584-4148
Kaiser Federal Bank 1359 N Grand Ave PO Box 6107 *NASDAQ: KFED* ■ *TF:* 800-524-2274 ■ *Web:* www.kaiserfederal.biz	Covina	CA	91724	626-339-9663	646-2032
Kearny Financial Corp 120 Passaic Ave *NASDAQ: KRNY*	Fairfield	NJ	07004	973-244-4500	439-3985
Keweenaw Financial Corp 235 Quincy St *TF:* 866-482-0404 ■ *Web:* www.snb-t.com	Hancock	MI	49930	906-482-0404	482-4403
KeyCorp 127 Public Sq *NYSE: KEY* ■ *TF:* 800-539-6070 ■ *Web:* www.key.com	Cleveland	OH	44114	216-689-6300	689-0519
Lake Sunapee Bank 9 Main St PO Box 29 *NASDAQ: NHTB* ■ *TF:* 800-281-5772 ■ *Web:* www.lakesunbank.com	Newport	NH	03773	603-863-5772	863-5025
Lakeland Bancorp Inc 250 Oak Ridge Rd *NASDAQ: LBAI* ■ *TF:* 866-224-1379 ■ *Web:* www.lakelandbank.com	Oak Ridge	NJ	07438	973-697-2000	697-8385
Lakeland Financial Corp 202 E Ctr St *NASDAQ: LKFN* ■ **Fax:* Hum Res ■ *TF:* 800-827-4522 ■ *Web:* www.lakecitybank.com	Warsaw	IN	46580	574-267-6144	267-9180*
Landmark Bancorp Inc 701 Poyntz Ave *NASDAQ: LARK* ■ *TF:* 800-322-6344 ■ *Web:* www.landmarkbancorpinc.com	Manhattan	KS	66502	785-565-2000	537-0619
Lexington B & L Financial Corp 205 S 13th St PO Box 190 *Web:* www.bl-bank.com	Lexington	MO	64067	660-259-2247	259-2384
Linkous Construction Co Inc 1715 Aaron Brenner Dr Suite 207 *Web:* www.linkousconstruction.com	Memphis	TN	38120	901-754-0700	754-0302
LNB Bancorp Inc 457 Broadway *NASDAQ: LNBB* ■ *TF:* 800-860-1007 ■ *Web:* www.4lnb.com	Lorain	OH	44052	440-989-3348	244-9507
Logansport Financial Corp 723 E Broadway PO Box 569 *TF:* 800-541-9154 ■ *Web:* www.logansportsavings.com	Logansport	IN	46947	574-722-3855	722-3857
LSB Financial Corp 101 Main St *NASDAQ: LSBI* ■ *TF:* 800-704-3084 ■ *Web:* www.lsbank.com	Lafayette	IN	47902	765-742-1064	742-1507
M & T Bank Corp 1 M & T Plaza 13th Fl *NYSE: MTB* ■ **Fax:* Hum Res ■ *TF:* 800-724-2440 ■ *Web:* www.mtb.com	Buffalo	NY	14203	716-842-4691	842-4691*
Macatawa Bank Corp 10753 Macatawa Dr *NASDAQ: MCBC* ■ *TF:* 877-820-2265 ■ *Web:* www.macatawabank.com	Holland	MI	49422	616-820-1444	494-7644
MainSource Financial Group Inc 201 N Broadway PO Box 87 *NASDAQ: MSFG* ■ *TF:* 800-530-9223 ■ *Web:* www.mainsourcebank.com	Greensburg	IN	47240	812-663-0157	663-4812
Malaga Financial Corp 2514 Via Tejon *OTC: MLGF* ■ *Web:* www.malagabank.com	Palos Verdes Estates	CA	90274	310-375-9000	373-3615
Marquette Financial Corp 9533 W 143rd St # 1 *TF:* 888-254-9500 ■ *Web:* www.emarquettebank.com	Orland Park	IL	60462	888-254-9500	
Marshall & Ilsley Corp 770 N Water St *NYSE: MI* ■ **Fax:* Hum Res ■ *TF:* 800-342-2265 ■ *Web:* www.mibank.com	Milwaukee	WI	53202	414-765-7801	298-2929*
MASSBANK Corp 123 Haven St *NASDAQ: MASB* ■ *TF:* 800-447-1052 ■ *Web:* www.massbank.com	Reading	MA	01867	781-662-0100	942-8194
MB Financial Inc 6111 N River Rd *NASDAQ: MBFI* ■ **Fax Area Code:* 773 ■ *TF:* 888-422-6562 ■ *Web:* www.mbfinancial.com	Rosemont	IL	60018	888-422-6562	278-4523*
MBT Financial Corp 102 E Front St *NASDAQ: MBTF* ■ *TF:* 800-321-0032 ■ *Web:* www.mbandt.com	Monroe	MI	48161	734-241-3431	384-8230
Mercantil Commercebank Holding Corp 220 Alhambra Cir **Fax:* Cust Svc ■ *Web:* www.commercebankfl.com	Coral Gables	FL	33134	305-460-8701	460-4010*
Mercantile Bancorp Inc 200 N 33rd St PO Box 3455 *AMEX: MBR* ■ *TF:* 800-405-6372 ■ *Web:* www.mercbanx.com	Quincy	IL	62305	217-223-7300	223-8938
Mercantile Bank Corp 310 Leonard St NW *NASDAQ: MBWM* ■ *TF:* 888-345-6296 ■ *Web:* www.mercbank.com	Grand Rapids	MI	49504	616-406-3000	454-5807
Merchants Bancshares Inc PO Box 1009 *NASDAQ: MBVT* ■ **Fax:* Cust Svc ■ *TF:* 800-322-5222 ■ *Web:* www.mbvt.com	Burlington	VT	05402	802-658-3400	865-1943*
Mesa Systems Inc 681 Railroad Blvd *Web:* www.mesasystemsgrandjunction.com	Grand Junction	CO	81505	888-229-1409	
Meta Financial Group Inc 121 E 5th St PO Box 1307 *NASDAQ: CASH* ■ *TF:* 800-792-6815 ■ *Web:* www.bankmeta.com	Storm Lake	IA	50588	712-732-4117	732-8122
MetroCorp Bancshares Inc 9600 Bellaire Blvd Suite 252 *NASDAQ: MCBI* ■ **Fax:* Hum Res ■ *TF:* 888-414-3556	Houston	TX	77036	713-776-3876	414-3507*
Metropolitan Bank Group 1110 W 35th St *Web:* www.metrobankgroup.com	Chicago	IL	60609	773-843-7800	890-3548
Mid Country Financial Corp PO Box 4164 *Web:* www.midcountryfinancial.com	Macon	GA	31208	478-746-8222	746-8005
Mid Penn Bancorp Inc 349 Union St *NASDAQ: MBP* ■ *TF:* 866-642-7736 ■ *Web:* www.midpennbank.com	Millersburg	PA	17061	717-692-2133	692-4861
MidSouth Bancorp Inc 102 Versailles Blvd *AMEX: MSL* ■ *TF:* 800-213-2265 ■ *Web:* www.midsouthbank.com	Lafayette	LA	70501	337-237-8343	267-4316
MidWestOne Financial Group Inc 102 S Clinton St PO Box 1700 *NASDAQ: MOFG* ■ *TF:* 800-303-6740 ■ *Web:* www.midwestonefinancial.com	Iowa City	IA	52240	319-356-5800	356-5849
Millennium Bankshares Corp 1601 Washington Plaza *NASDAQ: MBVA* ■ *TF:* 800-937-5449 ■ *Web:* www.millenniumbankshares.com	Reston	VA	20190	703-464-0100	464-0064
Miner-Dederick Construction LLP 1532 Peden PO Box 130067 *Web:* www.minerdederick.com	Houston	TX	77219	713-529-3001	529-6321
MutualFirst Financial Inc 110 E Charles St *NASDAQ: MFSF* ■ *TF:* 800-382-8031 ■ *Web:* www.mfsbank.com	Muncie	IN	47305	765-747-2800	
Nara Bancorp Inc 3731 Wilshire Blvd Suite 1000 *NASDAQ: NARA* ■ *TF:* 888-811-6272 ■ *Web:* www.narabank.com	Los Angeles	CA	90010	213-639-1700	235-3033
NASB Financial Inc 12498 S 71st Hwy *NASDAQ: NASB* ■ *TF:* 800-677-6272 ■ *Web:* www.nasb.com	Grandview	MO	64030	816-765-2200	316-4504
National Bankshares Inc 101 Hubbard St *NASDAQ: NKSH* ■ *TF:* 800-552-4123 ■ *Web:* www.nationalbankshares.com	Blacksburg	VA	24060	540-951-6300	951-6324
National Penn Bancshares Inc PO Box 547 *NASDAQ: NPBC* ■ *TF:* 800-822-3321 ■ *Web:* www.nationalpenn.com	Boyertown	PA	19512	610-705-9101	369-6118
NBT Bancorp Inc 52 S Broad St *NASDAQ: NBTB* ■ *TF:* 800-628-2265 ■ *Web:* www.nbtbancorp.com	Norwich	NY	13815	607-337-2265	336-7538

Company / Address	City	State	ZIP	Phone	Fax
New York Community Bancorp Inc 615 Merrick Ave *NYSE: NYB* ■ *TF:* 888-550-9888 ■ *Web:* www.mynycb.com	Westbury	NY	11590	516-683-4100	683-8360
Nexity Financial Corp 3500 Blue Lake Dr Suite 330 PO Box 43600 *PINK: NXTY* ■ *TF:* 877-738-6391 ■ *Web:* www.nexitybank.com	Birmingham	AL	35243	205-298-6391	298-6395
Nittany Financial Corp 116 E College Ave. *Web:* www.nittanybank.com	State College	PA	16801	814-234-7320	238-2167
North Central Bancshares Inc 825 Central Ave *NASDAQ: FFFD* ■ *TF:* 800-272-3445 ■ *Web:* www.firstfederaliowa.com	Fort Dodge	IA	50501	515-576-7531	576-7962
North State Bank Inc 6204 Falls of Neuse Rd *TF:* 877-357-2265 ■ *Web:* www.northstatebank.com	Raleigh	NC	27609	919-787-9696	719-4481
North Valley Bancorp 300 Pk Marina Cir. *NASDAQ: NOVB* ■ *TF:* 866-869-6673 ■ *Web:* www.novb.com	Redding	CA	96001	530-226-2900	221-4877
Northeast Bancorp 500 Canal St *AMEX: NBN* ■ *TF:* 800-284-5989 ■ *Web:* www.northeastbank.com	Lewiston	ME	04240	207-786-3245	782-7230
Northeast Indiana Bancorp Inc 648 N Jefferson St *TF:* 800-550-3372	Huntington	IN	46750	260-356-3311	358-0036
Northern States Financial Corp 1601 N Lewis Ave. *NASDAQ: NSFC* ■ *TF:* 800-339-4432 ■ *Web:* www.norstatesbank.com	Waukegan	IL	60085	847-244-6000	244-7485
Northern Trust Corp 50 S LaSalle St *NASDAQ: NTRS* ■ *Web:* www.northerntrust.com	Chicago	IL	60603	312-630-6000	444-7843
Northwest Bancorp Inc PO Box 128 *NASDAQ: NWSB* ■ *TF:* 800-859-1000 ■ *Web:* www.northwestsavingsbank.com	Warren	PA	16365	814-728-7263	
Norwood Financial Corp 717 Main St. *NASDAQ: NWFL* ■ *TF:* 800-598-5002 ■ *Web:* www.waynedank.com	Honesdale	PA	18431	570-253-1455	253-3725
Oak Park School District (OPSD) 13900 Granzon *Web:* www.oakparkschools.org	Oak Park	MI	48237	248-336-7700	336-7738
Ocean Bankshares Inc 780 NW 42nd Ave. *TF:* 877-310-2265 ■ *Web:* www.oceanbank.com	Miami	FL	33126	305-442-2660	446-2494
OceanFirst Financial Corp 975 Hooper Ave. *NASDAQ: OCFC* ■ *TF:* 888-623-2633 ■ *Web:* www.oceanfirstonline.com	Toms River	NJ	08753	732-240-4500	349-5070
Ocwen Financial Corp 1661 Worthington Rd Suite 100 PO Box 24737 *NYSE: OCN* ■ **Fax:* Hum Res ■ *TF:* 800-746-2936 ■ *Web:* www.ocwen.com	West Palm Beach	FL	33409	561-681-8000	682-8150*
Ohio Savings Financial Corp 1801 E 9th St Suite 200 *TF:* 800-860-2025	Cleveland	OH	44114	216-622-4100	588-4472
Ohio Valley Banc Corp 420 3rd Ave. *NASDAQ: OVBC* ■ *TF:* 800-468-6682 ■ *Web:* www.ovbc.com	Gallipolis	OH	45631	740-446-2631	446-4643
Old National Bancorp One Main St *NYSE: ONB* ■ *TF:* 800-731-2265 ■ *Web:* www.oldnational.com	Evansville	IN	47708	812-464-1294	464-1567
Old Point Financial Corp 1 W Mellen St PO Box 3392 *NASDAQ: OPOF* ■ *TF:* 800-952-0051 ■ *Web:* www.oldpoint.com	Hampton	VA	23663	757-722-7451	728-1279
Old Second Bancorp Inc 37 S River St *NASDAQ: OSBC* ■ **Fax:* Mktg ■ *TF:* 888-892-6565 ■ *Web:* www.o2bancorp.com	Aurora	IL	60506	630-892-0202	892-9630*
Oneida Financial Corp 182 Main St *NASDAQ: ONFC* ■ *TF:* 800-211-0564 ■ *Web:* www.oneidabank.com	Oneida	NY	13421	315-363-2000	366-3709
Oriental Financial Group Inc 997 San Roberto St 9th Fl. *NYSE: OFG*	San Juan	PR	00926	787-474-1993	474-1998
Owen Community Bank 279 E Morgan St PO Box 187 *OTC: HWEN* ■ *TF:* 800-690-2095 ■ *Web:* www.hfbancorp.com/holding	Spencer	IN	47460	812-829-2095	829-3069
Pacific & Western Credit Corp 140 Fullarton St Suite 2002 *TF:* 866-979-1919 ■ *Web:* www.pwbank.com	London	ON	N6A5P2	519-645-1919	645-2060
Pacific Capital Bancorp 20 E Carrillo St PO Box 60839 *NASDAQ: PCBC* ■ *TF:* 800-272-7200 ■ *Web:* www.pcbancorp.com	Goleta	CA	93117	805-564-6405	882-3856
Pacific Mercantile Bancorp 949 S Coast Dr 3rd Fl. *NASDAQ: PMBC* ■ *TF:* 877-450-2265 ■ *Web:* www.pmbank.com	Costa Mesa	CA	92626	714-438-2500	438-1059
Pacific Premier Bancorp Inc 1600 Sunflower Ave *NASDAQ: PPBI* ■ *TF:* 888-388-5433 ■ *Web:* www.ppbi.com	Costa Mesa	CA	92626	714-431-4000	433-3000
Park Bancorp Inc 5400 S Pulaski Rd *NASDAQ: PFED* ■ *TF:* 888-727-5333 ■ *Web:* www.parkfed.com	Chicago	IL	60632	773-582-8616	434-6043
Park Bank 7540 W Capitol Dr *Web:* www.parkbankonline.com	Milwaukee	WI	53216	414-466-8000	466-7773
Park National Corp 50 N 3rd St PO Box 3500 *AMEX: PRK* ■ *TF:* 800-762-2616 ■ *Web:* www.parknationalcorp.com	Newark	OH	43058	740-349-8451	349-3787
Parkvale Bank 4220 William Penn Hwy *NASDAQ: PVSA* ■ *Web:* www.parkvale.com	Monroeville	PA	15146	412-373-4804	374-9634
Pathfinder Bancorp Inc 214 W 1st St *NASDAQ: PBHC* ■ *TF:* 800-811-5620 ■ *Web:* www.pathfinderbank.com	Oswego	NY	13126	315-343-0057	342-9403
Patriot National Bancorp Inc 900 Bedford St *NASDAQ: PNBK* ■ *TF:* 800-762-7620 ■ *Web:* www.pnbk.com	Stamford	CT	06901	203-324-7500	324-8804
Peapack-Gladstone Bank 500 Hills Dr Suite 300 PO Box 700 *NASDAQ: PGC* ■ *TF:* 800-742-7595 ■ *Web:* www.pgbank.com	Bedminster	NJ	07921	908-234-0700	781-2046
People's Mutual Holdings 850 Main St *TF:* 800-392-3009 ■ *Web:* www.peoples.com	Bridgeport	CT	06604	203-338-7171	338-3600
Peoples Bancorp 212 W 7th St. *NASDAQ: PFDC* ■ *TF:* 800-374-6123 ■ *Web:* www.peoplesbancorp.com	Auburn	IN	46706	260-925-2500	925-8303
Peoples Bancorp Inc 138 Putnam St. *NASDAQ: PEBO* ■ **Fax:* Mail Rm ■ *TF:* 800-374-6123 ■ *Web:* www.peoplesbancorp.com	Marietta	OH	45750	740-373-3155	374-2020*
Peoples Bancorp of North Carolina Inc 518 W 'C' St *NASDAQ: PEBK* ■ *TF:* 800-948-7195 ■ *Web:* www.peoplesbanknc.com	Newton	NC	28658	828-464-5620	466-5043
Peoples-Sidney Financial Corp 101 E Ct St PO Box 727 *TF:* 800-235-8041	Sidney	OH	45365	937-492-6129	498-4554
Perry Bancshares Inc PO Box 797 *Web:* www.ebankperry.net	Perry	OK	73077	580-336-5531	336-3297
Pinnacle Bancshares Inc 1811 2nd Ave. *Web:* www.pinnaclebancshares.com	Jasper	AL	35501	205-221-4111	221-8860
PlainsCapital Corp 2323 Victory Ave Suite 1400 *TF:* 800-538-9990 ■ *Web:* www.plainscapital.com	Dallas	TX	75219	214-252-4100	252-4147
PNC Financial Services Group Inc 249 5th Ave 1 PNC Plaza *NYSE: PNC* ■ **Fax:* Hum Res ■ *TF:* 877-762-2000 ■ *Web:* www.pnc.com	Pittsburgh	PA	15222	412-762-2000	762-3257*
Popular Inc 209 Ponce de Leon Ave *NASDAQ: BPOP* ■ *TF:* 888-724-3650 ■ *Web:* www.popular.com	San Juan	PR	00918	787-765-9800	753-9434
Premier Community Bankshares Inc 4095 Valley Pike *TF:* 800-526-2265	Winchester	VA	22602	540-869-6600	869-4994
Premier Financial Bancorp Inc 2883 5th Ave. *NASDAQ: PFBI* ■ **Fax Area Code:* 502 ■ *TF:* 866-269-0298	Huntington	WV	25702	304-525-1600	863-7503*
Princeton National Bancorp Inc 606 S Main St. *NASDAQ: PNBC* ■ *Web:* www.citizens1st.com	Princeton	IL	61356	815-875-4444	872-0247
PrivateBancorp Inc 120 S LaSalle St. *NASDAQ: PVTB* ■ *TF:* 800-662-7748 ■ *Web:* www.privatebk.com	Chicago	IL	60603	312-683-7100	683-7111
Prosperity Bancshares Inc 1301 N Mechanic *NASDAQ: PRSP* ■ *TF:* 800-383-8000 ■ *Web:* www.prosperitybanktx.com	El Campo	TX	77437	979-578-8181	543-1906
Provident Community Bancshares Inc 2700 Celanese Rd. *NASDAQ: PCBS* ■ *TF:* 888-427-9002 ■ *Web:* www.provcombank.com	Rock Hill	SC	29732	803-325-9400	
Provident Financial Holdings Inc 3756 Central Ave *NASDAQ: PROV* ■ *TF:* 800-442-5201	Riverside	CA	92506	951-686-6060	782-6132
Provident Financial Services Inc 830 Bergen Ave. *NYSE: PFS* ■ *TF:* 800-742-2943 ■ *Web:* www.providentnj.com	Jersey City	NJ	07306	201-333-1000	
Provident New York Bancorp 400 Rella Blvd PO Box 600. *NASDAQ: PBNY* ■ **Fax:* Hum Res	Montebello	NY	10901	845-918-5707	369-8066*
Pulaski Financial Corp 12300 Olive Blvd *NASDAQ: PULB* ■ *TF:* 888-649-3320 ■ *Web:* www.pulaskibankstl.com	Saint Louis	MO	63141	314-878-2210	878-7130
PVF Capital Corp 30000 Aurora Rd *NASDAQ: PVFC* ■ *TF:* 800-676-2572 ■ *Web:* www.parkviewfederal.com	Solon	OH	44139	440-248-7171	914-3658
QCR Holdings Inc 3551 7th St Suite 204. *NASDAQ: QCRH* ■ *TF:* 866-676-0551 ■ *Web:* www.qcbt.com	Moline	IL	61265	309-736-3580	736-3581
Rabobank America 245 Pk Ave *Web:* www.rabobankamerica.com	New York	NY	10167	212-916-7800	916-7993
RBC Centura Banks Inc PO Box 1220 *TF:* 877-722-2265 ■ *Web:* www.rbcbankusa.com	Rocky Mount	NC	27802	252-454-4400	
Reece-Campbell Inc 320 S Wayne Ave *Web:* reececampbell.com	Cincinnati	OH	45215	513-542-4600	542-4753
Regions Financial Corp 1900 5th Ave N *NYSE: RF* ■ *TF:* 800-734-4667 ■ *Web:* www.regions.com	Birmingham	AL	35203	205-326-7100	326-7571
Renasant Corp 209 Troy St PO Box 709 *NASDAQ: RNST* ■ **Fax:* Hum Res ■ *TF Cust Svc:* 800-680-1601 ■ *Web:* www.renasantbank.com	Tupelo	MS	38802	662-680-1001	680-1448*
Republic Bancorp Inc 601 W Market St. *NASDAQ: RBCAA* ■ *TF:* 888-540-5363 ■ *Web:* www.republicbank.com	Louisville	KY	40202	502-584-3600	561-7188
Republic First Bancorp Inc 50 S 16th St Suite 2400 *NASDAQ: FRBK* ■ *TF:* 877-438-4338 ■ *Web:* www.myrepublicbank.com	Philadelphia	PA	19102	215-735-4422	735-5373
River Valley Bancorp 430 Clifty Dr *NASDAQ: RIVR* ■ **Fax:* Hum Res ■ *TF:* 800-994-4849 ■ *Web:* www.rvfbank.com	Madison	IN	47250	812-273-4949	265-6730*
River Wood Bank PO Box 458 *TF:* 800-749-9606	Bemidji	MN	56619	218-751-5120	751-5814
Riverbank The PO Box 188 *TF:* 888-294-2183 ■ *Web:* www.theriverbank.com	Osceola	WI	54020	715-294-2183	
Riverview Bancorp Inc 900 Washington St Suite 900 *NASDAQ: RVSB* ■ *Web:* www.riverviewbank.com	Vancouver	WA	98660	360-693-6650	693-6275
Rome Bancorp Inc 66 W St *NASDAQ: ROME* ■ *TF:* 800-220-6956 ■ *Web:* www.virtualbank.com	Pittsfield	MA	01201	413-445-8365	445-8355
S & T Bancorp Inc 800 Philadelphia St. *NASDAQ: STBA* ■ **Fax:* Cust Svc ■ *TF:* 800-325-2265 ■ *Web:* www.stbank.com	Indiana	PA	15701	724-465-1466	465-6874*
Salisbury Bancorp Inc 5 Bissell St PO Box 1868 *AMEX: SAL* ■ *TF:* 800-222-9801 ■ *Web:* www.salisburybank.com	Lakeville	CT	06039	860-435-9801	435-0631
Sandy Spring Bancorp Inc 17801 Georgia Ave *NASDAQ: SASR* ■ *TF:* 800-399-5919 ■ *Web:* www.sandyspringbank.com	Olney	MD	20832	301-774-6400	483-6701
Savannah Bancorp Inc 25 Bull St PO Box 188 *NASDAQ: SAVB* ■ *Web:* www.savb.com	Savannah	GA	31401	912-629-6486	651-4141
SCBT Financial Corp 950 John C Calhoun Dr *NASDAQ: SCBT* ■ *TF:* 800-277-2175 ■ *Web:* www.scbandt.com	Orangeburg	SC	29115	803-534-2175	531-8744
Seacoast Banking Corp of Florida 815 Colorado Ave PO Box 9012 *NASDAQ: SBCF* ■ *TF:* 800-706-9991 ■ *Web:* www.seacoastbanking.net	Stuart	FL	34994	772-287-4000	288-6012
Shore Bancshares Inc 18 E Dover St. *NASDAQ: SHBI* ■ *Web:* www.shbi.net	Easton	MD	21601	410-822-1400	820-4238
Shore Financial Corp 25020 Shore Pkwy *NASDAQ: SHBK* ■ *TF:* 800-852-8176	Onley	VA	23418	757-787-1335	789-3745
Sierra Bancorp 86 N Main St *NASDAQ: BSRR* ■ *TF Cust Svc:* 888-307-3772	Porterville	CA	93257	559-782-4900	782-4994
Simmons First National Corp 501 Main St. *NASDAQ: SFNC* ■ **Fax:* Hum Res ■ *TF:* 866-246-2400 ■ *Web:* www.simmonsfirst.com	Pine Bluff	AR	71601	870-541-1000	541-1138*
South Street Financial Corp 155 W S St *NASDAQ: SSFC*	Albemarle	NC	28001	704-982-9184	983-1308
Southern Banc Co Inc 221 S 6th St *Web:* www.sobanco.com	Gadsden	AL	35901	256-543-3860	543-3864
Southern Connecticut Bancorp Inc 215 Church St *AMEX: SSE* ■ *Web:* www.scbancorponline.com	New Haven	CT	06510	203-782-1100	782-1100
Southern Missouri Bancorp Inc 531 Vine St. *NASDAQ: SMBC* ■ *Web:* www.bankwithsouthern.com	Poplar Bluff	MO	63901	573-778-1800	686-2920
SouthFirst Bancshares Inc 126 N Norton Ave PO Box 167 *PINK: SZBI* ■ *TF:* 800-239-1492 ■ *Web:* www.southfirst.com	Sylacauga	AL	35150	256-245-4365	245-6341
Southside Bancshares Inc 1201 S Beckham Ave *NASDAQ: SBSI* ■ *TF:* 800-962-4284 ■ *Web:* www.southside.com	Tyler	TX	75701	903-531-7111	592-3692

				Phone	Fax
Southwest Bancorp Inc 608 S Main St PO Box 1988	Stillwater	OK	74076	405-377-4762	742-1928*
NASDAQ: OKSB ■ *Fax: Hum Res ■ TF: 888-762-4762 ■ Web: www.banksnb.com					
Southwest Georgia Financial Corp 201 1st St SE	Moultrie	GA	31768	229-985-1120	980-2211*
AMEX: SGB ■ *Fax: Hum Res ■ TF: 888-683-2265 ■ Web: www.sgfc.com					
State Bancorp Inc 699 Hillside Ave	New Hyde Park	NY	11040	516-437-1000	465-2222
NASDAQ: STBC ■ TF: 800-554-8969 ■ Web: www.statebankofli.com					
Sterling Bancorp 650 5th Ave	New York	NY	10019	212-757-3300	490-8852
NYSE: STL ■ TF: 800-523-4175 ■ Web: www.sterlingnationalbank.com					
Sterling Bancshares Inc 919 Milam St Suite 115	Houston	TX	77002	713-466-8300	
NASDAQ: SBIB ■ TF: 888-777-8735 ■ Web: www.banksterling.com					
Sterling Financial Corp 111 N Wall St	Spokane	WA	99201	509-624-4114	358-6161*
NASDAQ: STSA ■ *Fax: Hum Res ■ TF: 800-772-7791 ■ Web: www.sterlingsavingsbank.com					
Suburban Illinois Bank Corp PO Box 419	Elmhurst	IL	60126	630-279-1300	279-2509
TF: 877-279-1300 ■ Web: www.sbtbanknow.com					
Suffolk Bancorp 4 W 2nd St PO Box 9000	Riverhead	NY	11901	631-208-2200	727-3210
NASDAQ: SUBK ■ Web: www.scnb.com					
Sun Bancorp Inc (SNBC) 226 Landis Ave	Vineland	NJ	08360	856-691-7700	691-6763
NASDAQ: SNBC ■ TF: 800-691-7701 ■ Web: www.sunnbnj.com					
Sunflower Holdings Inc PO Box 800	Salina	KS	67402	785-827-5564	826-2293
TF: 888-827-5564 ■ Web: www.sunflowerbank.com					
SunTrust Banks Inc 303 Peachtree St NE	Atlanta	GA	30308	404-588-7711	335-2686
NYSE: STI ■ TF: 800-688-7878 ■ Web: www.suntrust.com					
Superior Bancorp 17 N 20th St	Birmingham	AL	35203	205-327-1400	324-8060
PINK: SUPR ■ Web: www.superiorbank.com					
Susquehanna Bancshares Inc 26 N Cedar St PO Box 1000	Lititz	PA	17543	717-626-4721	626-1874*
NASDAQ: SUSQ ■ *Fax: Edit ■ TF: 800-311-3182 ■ Web: www.susquehanna.net					
Sussex Bank 200 Munsonhurst Rd	Franklin	NJ	07416	973-827-2914	827-2926
NASDAQ: SBBX ■ TF: 800-511-9900 ■ Web: www.sussexbank.com					
SVB Financial Group 3005 Tasman Dr	Santa Clara	CA	95054	408-654-7400	496-2405
NASDAQ: SIVB ■ TF: 800-760-9644 ■ Web: www.svb.com					
SY Bancorp Inc 1040 E Main St	Louisville	KY	40206	502-582-2571	625-2431
NASDAQ: SYBT ■ TF: 800-625-9066 ■ Web: www.syb.com					
Synovus Financial Corp 1111 Bay Ave, Suite 500 PO Box 120	Columbus	GA	31902	706-649-2311	641-6555
NYSE: SNV ■ Web: www.synovus.com					
Tandem Transport Corp 1111 US Hwy 20 W Suite A	Michigan City	IN	46360	219-874-6271	873-7051
TF: 800-348-8532 ■ Web: www.tand.com					
Taylor Capital Group Inc 9550 W Higgins Rd 5th Fl	Rosemont	IL	60018	847-653-7978	653-7978
NASDAQ: TAYC ■ TF: 800-727-2265					
TCF Financial Corp 801 Marquette Ave	Minneapolis	MN	55402	612-661-6500	661-8277*
NYSE: TCB ■ *Fax: Hum Res ■ TF: 800-533-1723 ■ Web: www.tcfbank.com					
TD Banknorth Inc 2 Portland Sq PO Box 9540	Portland	ME	04112	800-462-3666	
TF: 800-462-3666 ■ Web: www.tdbanknorth.com					
Teche Holding Co 1120 Jefferson Terr	New Iberia	LA	70560	337-560-7151	365-7130
AMEX: TSH ■ TF: 800-256-1500 ■ Web: www.teche.com					
Texas Regional Bancshares Inc 3900 N 10th St 11th Fl PO Box 5910	McAllen	TX	78502	956-631-5400	631-5450
Web: www.trbsinc.com					
TF Financial Corp 3 Penns Trail	Newtown	PA	18940	215-579-4000	579-4748
NASDAQ: THRD ■ TF: 888-918-4473 ■ Web: www.thirdfedbank.com					
TIB Financial Corp 559 9th St N	Naples	FL	34102	239-263-3344	263-4543
NASDAQ: TIBB ■ TF: 800-233-6330 ■ Web: www.tibbank.com					
Timberland Bancorp Inc 624 Simpson Ave	Hoquiam	WA	98550	360-533-4747	533-4743
NASDAQ: TSBK ■ TF: 800-562-8761 ■ Web: www.timberlandbank.com					
Titonka Bancshares Inc PO Box 309	Titonka	IA	50480	515-928-2142	928-2042
TF: 866-985-3247 ■ Web: www.tsbbank.com					
Tonganoxie Bankshares Inc PO Box 219	Tonganoxie	KS	66086	913-845-0050	845-5100
TF: 888-845-2220 ■ Web: www.firststateks.com					
Tower Financial Corp 116 E Berry St	Fort Wayne	IN	46802	260-427-7000	427-7180
NASDAQ: TOFC ■ TF: 877-427-7220 ■ Web: www.towerbank.net					
TriCo Bancshares 63 Constitution Dr	Chico	CA	95973	530-898-0300	898-0310
NASDAQ: TCBK ■ TF: 800-922-8742 ■ Web: www.tcbk.com					
Trustco Bank Corp NY PO Box 1082	Schenectady	NY	12301	518-377-3311	381-3839
NASDAQ: TRST ■ TF: 800-670-3110 ■ Web: www.trustcobank.com					
Trustmark Corp 248 E Capitol St PO Box 291	Jackson	MS	39201	601-208-5111	944-5491*
NASDAQ: TRMK ■ *Fax: Cust Svc ■ TF Cust Svc: 800-243-2524 ■ Web: www.trustmark.com					
UMB Financial Corp 1010 Grand Blvd	Kansas City	MO	64106	816-860-7000	860-4952
NASDAQ: UMBF ■ TF: 800-821-2171 ■ Web: www.umb.com					
Umpqua Holdings Corp 1 SW Columbia St Suite 1200	Portland	OR	97258	503-727-4100	544-3250*
NASDAQ: UMPQ ■ *Fax Area Code: 971 ■ TF: 866-486-7782 ■ Web: www.umpquabank.com					
Union Bankshares Corp 211 N Main St	Bowling Green	VA	22427	804-633-5031	633-1310
NASDAQ: UBSH ■ TF: 800-990-4828 ■ Web: www.snl.com					
Union Bankshares Inc 20 Lower Main St	Morrisville	VT	05661	802-888-6600	888-4921
AMEX: UNB ■ TF: 866-862-1891 ■ Web: www.unionbankvt.com					
UnionBanCal Corp 400 California St 1st Fl	San Francisco	CA	94104	415-705-7000	765-3507*
*Fax: PR ■ Web: www.unionbank.com					
United Bancorp Inc 201 S 4th St	Martins Ferry	OH	43935	740-633-0445	633-1448
NASDAQ: UBCP ■ TF: 888-275-5566 ■ Web: www.unitedbancorp.com					
United Bancshares Inc 100 S High St PO Box 67	Columbus Grove	OH	45830	419-659-2141	659-2069
NASDAQ: UBOH ■ TF: 800-837-8111 ■ Web: www.theubank.com					
United Bankshares Inc 514 Market St	Parkersburg	WV	26101	304-424-8800	424-8833
NASDAQ: UBSI ■ TF: 800-345-4862 ■ Web: www.unitedbank-wv.com					
United Community Banks Inc PO Box 398	Blairsville	GA	30514	706-781-2265	745-8960
NASDAQ: UCBI ■ TF: 866-270-7200 ■ Web: www.ucbi.com					
United Community Financial Corp PO Box 1111	Youngstown	OH	44501	330-742-0500	742-0532
NASDAQ: UCFC ■ Web: www.ucfconline.com					
United Security Bancshares Inc PO Box 249	Thomasville	AL	36784	334-636-5424	636-9606
NASDAQ: USBI ■ TF: 866-546-8273 ■ Web: www.firstusbank.com					
United Tennessee Bankshares Inc 170 W Broadway	Newport	TN	37821	423-623-6088	625-0301
United Western Bancorp Inc 700 17th St Suite 2100	Denver	CO	80202	303-595-9898	390-0952
TF: 800-594-2079 ■ Web: www.uwbancorp.com					
Unity Bancorp Inc 64 Old Hwy 22	Clinton	NJ	08809	908-730-7630	730-9430
NASDAQ: UNTY ■ TF: 800-618-2265 ■ Web: www.unitybank.com					
University Bancorp Inc 2015 Washtenaw Ave	Ann Arbor	MI	48104	734-741-5858	741-5859
NASDAQ: UNIB ■ TF: 888-944-5004 ■ Web: www.university-bank.com					
Univest Corp of Pennsylvania 14 N Main St PO Box 64197	Souderton	PA	18964	215-721-2400	721-2433
NASDAQ: UVSP ■ TF: 877-723-5571 ■ Web: www.univest.net					
US Bancorp 800 Nicollet Mall	Minneapolis	MN	55402	651-466-3000	
NYSE: USB ■ TF Cust Svc: 800-872-2657 ■ Web: www.usbank.com					
Valley National Bancorp 1455 Valley Rd	Wayne	NJ	07470	973-305-8800	686-3491
NYSE: VLY ■ TF: 800-522-4100 ■ Web: www.valleynationalbank.com					
Veteran's Truck Line Inc 800 Black Hawk Dr	Burlington	WI	53105	262-539-3400	539-2720
TF: 800-456-9476 ■ Web: www.vetstruck.com					
Virginia Commerce Bancorp Inc (VCB) 5350 Lee Hwy	Arlington	VA	22207	703-534-0700	534-7216
NASDAQ: VCBI ■ TF: 877-822-5015 ■ Web: www.vcbonline.com					
VIST Financial Corp 1240 Broadcasting Rd PO Box 6219	Wyomissing	PA	19610	610-921-2210	372-5705
NASDAQ: FLPB ■ TF: 888-238-3330 ■ Web: www.vistfc.com					
Wachovia Bank 1 Front St 21st fl	San Francisco	CA	94111	800-798-2815	975-6558*
*Fax Area Code: 415 ■ TF: 800-798-2815 ■ Web: www.wachovia.com					
Washington Banking Co 450 SW Bayshore Dr	Oak Harbor	WA	98277	360-679-3121	675-7282
NASDAQ: WBCO ■ TF: 800-290-6508 ■ Web: www.wibank.com					
Washington Federal Inc 425 Pike St	Seattle	WA	98101	206-624-7930	467-0524
NASDAQ: WFSL ■ TF: 800-324-9375 ■ Web: www.washingtonfederal.com					
Washington Trust Bancorp Inc 23 Broad St	Westerly	RI	02891	401-348-1200	348-1470
NASDAQ: WASH ■ TF: 800-475-2265 ■ Web: www.washtrust.com					
Wayne Savings Bancshares Inc 151 N Market St	Wooster	OH	44691	330-264-5767	264-5908
NASDAQ: WAYN ■ TF: 800-414-1103 ■ Web: www.waynesavings.com					
Webster City Federal Bancorp 820 Des Moines St	Webster City	IA	50595	515-832-3071	832-3085
TF: 866-263-0293					
Webster Financial Corp PO Box 10305	Waterbury	CT	06726	800-325-2424	
NYSE: WBS ■ TF: 800-995-9995 ■ Web: www.websteronline.com					
Wells Fargo & Co 420 Montgomery St 12th Fl	San Francisco	CA	94104	800-869-3557	677-9075*
NYSE: WFC ■ *Fax Area Code: 415 ■ *Fax: Hum Res ■ TF: 800-333-0343 ■ Web: www.wellsfargo.com					
West Bancorp Inc 1601 22nd St	West Des Moines	IA	50266	515-222-2300	222-2345
NASDAQ: WTBA ■ TF: 800-810-2301 ■ Web: www.westbankiowa.com					
West Coast Bancorp 5335 Meadows Rd Suite 201	Lake Oswego	OR	97035	503-603-8052	684-0781
NASDAQ: WCBOD ■ TF: 800-895-3345 ■ Web: www.wcb.com					
Westfield Financial Inc 141 Elm St	Westfield	MA	01085	413-568-1911	562-7939
AMEX: WFD ■ TF: 800-995-5734 ■ Web: www.westfieldbank.com					
Westwood Holdings Group Inc 200 Crescent Ct Suite 1200	Dallas	TX	75201	214-756-6900	756-6979
NYSE: WHG ■ Web: www.westwoodgroup.com					
Winona National Holding Co PO Box 499	Winona	MN	55987	507-454-4320	
TF: 800-546-4392 ■ Web: www.winonanationalbank.com					
Wintrust Financial Corp 727 N Bank Ln	Lake Forest	IL	60045	847-615-4096	615-4091
NASDAQ: WTFC ■ Web: www.wintrust.com					
WSFS Financial Corp 500 Delaware Ave	Wilmington	DE	19801	302-792-6000	571-6842
NASDAQ: WSFS ■ TF: 888-973-7226 ■ Web: www.wsfsbank.com					
WTB Financial Corp PO Box 2127	Spokane	WA	99210	509-353-3939	
Web: www.watrust.com					
WVS Financial Corp 9001 Perry Hwy	Pittsburgh	PA	15237	412-364-1911	364-4120
NASDAQ: WVFC ■ Web: www.wvsbank.com					
Zions Bancorp 1 S Main St Suite 1380	Salt Lake City	UT	84111	801-974-8800	594-8402*
NASDAQ: ZION ■ *Fax: Mktg ■ TF: 800-789-2265 ■ Web: www.zionsbank.com					

363-3 Holding Companies (General)

				Phone	Fax
4Kids Entertainment Inc 53 W 23rd St 11th FL	New York	NY	10010	212-758-7666	980-0933
NYSE: KDE ■ Web: www.4kidsentertainment.com					
A-Mark Financial Corp 429 Santa Monica Blvd # 230	Santa Monica	CA	90401	310-319-0200	319-0279
Web: www.amark.com					
Acuity Brands Inc 1170 Peachtree St NE Suite 2400	Atlanta	GA	30309	404-853-1400	853-1411
NYSE: AYI ■ Web: www.acuitybrands.com					
Advanced Disposal Services Inc 7915 Bymadows Way Suite 300	Jacksonville	FL	32256	904-737-7900	
Web: www.advanceddisposal.com					
Affiliated Managers Group Inc (AMG) 600 Hale St	Prides Crossing	MA	01965	617-747-3300	747-3380
NYSE: AMG ■ Web: www.amg.com					
Alex Lee Inc 120 4th St SW	Hickory	NC	28602	828-323-4424	323-4435
Web: www.alexlee.com					
Alliance Holdings Gp LP 1717 S Boulder Ave Suite 400	Tulsa	OK	74119	918-295-1415	295-7361
NASDAQ: AHGP ■ Web: www.ahgp.com					
AllianceBernstein LP 1345 Avenue of the Americas	New York	NY	10105	212-969-1000	969-2229
TF: 800-221-5672 ■ Web: www.alliancebernstein.com					
Allied Systems Holdings Inc 2302 ParkLake Dr Bldg 15 Suite 600	Atlanta	GA	30345	404-370-4206	373-4285
Web: www.alliedholdings.com					
Alpine Group Inc 1 Meadowlands Plaza Suite 801	East Rutherford	NJ	07073	201-549-4400	549-4428
Alutiiq LLC 3909 Arctic Blvd Suite 400	Anchorage	AK	99503	907-222-9500	222-9501
Web: www.alutiiq.com					
American Standard Cos Inc 1 Centennial Ave PO Box 6820	Piscataway	NJ	08854	732-980-6000	980-3335
NYSE: ASD ■ TF: 800-442-1902 ■ Web: www.americanstandard-us.com					
AMETEK Inc 1100 Cassatt Rd PO Box 1764	Berwyn	PA	19312	610-647-2121	323-9337*
NYSE: AME ■ *Fax Area Code: 215 ■ TF: 800-473-1286 ■ Web: www.ametek.com					
Arden Group Inc 2020 S Central Ave	Compton	CA	90220	310-638-2842	604-4896*
NASDAQ: ARDNA ■ *Fax: Hum Res ■ Web: www.ardengroupinc.com					

Company / Address	City	State	Zip	Phone	Fax
Atlas Copco North America Inc 34 Maple Ave *Web:* www.atlascopco.com	Pine Brook	NJ	07058	973-439-3400	439-9188
Atlas World Group Inc 1212 St George Rd. *TF:* 800-252-8885 ■ *Web:* www.atlasworldgroup.com	Evansville	IN	47711	812-424-2222	421-7125
Augusta National Inc 2604 Washington Rd.	Augusta	GA	30904	706-667-6000	736-2321
Austin Industries Inc 3535 Travis St Suite 300 **Fax:* Acctg ■ *Web:* www.austin-ind.com	Dallas	TX	75204	214-443-5500	443-5581*
Bayer 6 W Belt Rd	Wayne	NJ	07470	973-694-4100	487-2005
Bell Canada Enterprises Inc 1000 de la Gauchetiere St W Suite 3700 *NYSE: BCE* ■ *TF:* 888-932-6666 ■ *Web:* www.bce.ca	Montreal	QC	H3B5H4	514-870-4385	870-3970
Bertelsmann Inc 1540 Broadway 24th Fl *Web:* www.bertelsmann.com	New York	NY	10036	212-782-1000	782-1010
BET Holdings II Inc 1235 W St NE **Fax:* PR ■ *TF:* 800-626-9911 ■ *Web:* www.bet.com	Washington	DC	20018	202-608-2000	608-2589*
Biglari Holdings Inc 175 E Houston St Suite 1300 *NYSE: BH* ■ *Web:* www.biglariholdings.com	San Antonio	TX	78205	210-344-3400	344-3411
Block Communications Inc 405 Madison Ave Suite 2100 *Web:* www.blockcommunications.com	Toledo	OH	43604	419-724-6212	724-6167
Blount International Inc 4909 SE International Way *NYSE: BLT* ■ **Fax:* Hum Res ■ *Web:* www.blount.com	Portland	OR	97222	503-653-8881	653-4402*
BNS Holding Inc 49 Stanton Ave *PINK: BNSSA* ■ *Web:* www.bnsholding.com	Riverside	RI	02915	401-848-6300	886-7407
Boca Resorts 501 E Camino Real *TF:* 888-543-1277 ■ *Web:* www.bocaresort.com	Boca Raton	FL	33432	561-447-3000	447-3183
Boler Co 500 Pk Blvd Suite 1000	Itasca	IL	60143	630-773-9111	773-9121
Boral Industries Inc 200 Mansell Ct E Suite 310	Roswell	GA	30076	770-645-4500	645-2888
Brose North America Inc 3933 Automation Ave *Web:* www.brose.com	Auburn Hills	MI	48326	248-339-4000	339-4099
Burlington Northern Santa Fe Corp (BNSF) 2650 Lou Menk Dr **Fax Area Code:* 817 ■ *TF:* 800-795-2673 ■ *Web:* www.bnsf.com	Fort Worth	TX	76131	800-795-2673	352-7925*
California Sports Inc 555 N Nash St	El Segundo	CA	90245	310-426-6000	426-6115
Cameron Holdings Corp 1200 Prospect St *Web:* www.cameron-holdings.com	La Jolla	CA	92037	858-551-1335	551-1343
Cardinal Health Inc 7000 Cardinal Pl *NYSE: CAH* ■ *TF:* 800-234-8701 ■ *Web:* www.cardinal.com	Dublin	OH	43017	614-757-5000	757-6000
Carnival Corp 3655 NW 87th Ave *NYSE: CCL* ■ *TF:* 800-438-6744 ■ *Web:* www.phx.corporate-ir.net	Miami	FL	33178	305-599-2600	406-4700
Cavs/Gund Arena Co 1 Ctr Ct. *TF General:* 800-332-2287 ■ *Web:* www.qarena.com	Cleveland	OH	44115	216-420-2000	420-2101
CBRL Group Inc PO Box 787 *NASDAQ: CBRL* ■ *TF:* 800-333-9566	Lebanon	TN	37088	615-444-5533	443-9818
Celadon Group Inc 9503 E 33rd St. *NASDAQ: CLDN* ■ *TF:* 800-235-2366 ■ *Web:* www.celadontrucking.com	Indianapolis	IN	46235	317-972-7000	890-8099
CenturyTel Inc 100 Centurylink Dr PO Box 4065 *NYSE: CTL* ■ *TF:* 877-290-5458 ■ *Web:* www.centurytel.com	Monroe	LA	71211	318-388-9000	388-9562
CF Industries Holdings Inc 4 Pkwy N Suite 400 *NYSE: CF* ■ *Web:* www.cfindustries.com	Deerfield	IL	60015	847-405-2400	405-2711
Cgf Industries Inc 2420 N Woodlawn Bldg 500 *Web:* www.cgfind.com	Wichita	KS	67220	316-691-4500	691-4545
Charles Schwab Corp 211 Main St *NASDAQ: SCHW* ■ *TF:* 800-435-4000 ■ *Web:* www.schwab.com	San Francisco	CA	94105	415-636-7000	636-9820
CIC Group Inc 530 Maryville Centre Dr Suite 100 *Web:* www.cicgroup.com	Saint Louis	MO	63141	314-682-2900	
Citigroup Inc 399 Pk Ave. *NYSE: C* ■ **Fax:* Hum Res ■ *Web:* www.citigroup.com	New York	NY	10043	212-559-1000	559-5138*
Clark Enterprises Inc 7500 Old Georgetown Rd 15th Fl *Web:* www.clarkenterprisesinc.com	Bethesda	MD	20814	301-657-7100	657-7263
Clayton Holdings LLC 2 Corporate Dr Suite 800 *TF:* 888-449-4055 ■ *Web:* www.clayton.com	Shelton	CT	06484	203-926-5600	926-5750
Comcast Corp One Comcast Ctr *NASDAQ: CMCSK* ■ *TF:* 800-266-2278 ■ *Web:* www.comcast.com	Philadelphia	PA	19103	215-665-1700	981-7790
ConAgra Foods Inc 1 ConAgra Dr *NYSE: CAG* ■ **Fax:* Hum Res ■ *TF:* 877-266-2472 ■ *Web:* www.conagrafoods.com	Omaha	NE	68102	402-595-4000	595-4707*
Conning Corp 1 Financial Plaza *TF:* 888-266-6464 ■ *Web:* www.conning.com	Hartford	CT	06103	860-527-1131	520-1240
CONSOL Energy Inc 1000 Consol Energy Dr. *NYSE: CNX* ■ *TF:* 800-544-8024 ■ *Web:* www.consolenergy.com	Canonsburg	PA	15317	724-485-4000	
Consolidated Communications Holdings Inc 121 S 17th St *NASDAQ: CNSL*	Mattoon	IL	61938	217-235-3311	235-3311
Consulier Engineering Inc 2391 Old Dixie Hwy *PINK: CSLR* ■ *Web:* www.consulier.com	Riviera Beach	FL	33404	561-842-2492	845-3237
Cookson America Inc 1 Cookson Pl *Web:* www.cooksongroup.co.uk	Providence	RI	02903	401-521-1000	521-5273
Core-Mark Holding Co Inc 395 Oyster Pt Blvd Suite 415 *NASDAQ: CORE* ■ *TF:* 800-622-1713 ■ *Web:* www.core-mark.com	South San Francisco	CA	94080	650-589-9445	589-4010
Cui Global Inc 20050 SW 112th Ave *OTC: CUGI* ■ **Fax Area Code:* 727 ■ *Web:* www.cuiglobal.com	Tualatin	OR	97062	503-612-2300	797-7770*
Dash Multi-Corp Inc 2500 Adie Rd *TF:* 800-899-9665 ■ *Web:* www.dashmulticorp.com	Maryland Heights	MO	63043	314-432-3200	432-3200
Dectron International Inc 4300 Poirier Blvd *TF:* 888-332-8766 ■ *Web:* www.dectron.com	Montreal	QC	H4R2C5	514-334-9609	334-9184
Delhaize America Inc 2110 Executive Dr PO Box 1330 *NYSE: DEG* ■ **Fax:* Hum Res ■ *Web:* www.delhaizegroup.com	Salisbury	NC	28145	704-633-8250	637-2581*
Deluxe Corp 3680 N Victoria St *NYSE: DLX* ■ *TF:* 800-328-7205 ■ *Web:* www.deluxe.com	Shoreview	MN	55126	651-483-7111	
DME Holdings LLC 2441 Bellevue Ave *TF:* 877-720-0082 ■ *Web:* www.dmecorporate.com	Daytona Beach	FL	32114	386-257-2500	271-3001
DNP America LLC 335 Madison Ave 3rd Fl *Web:* www.dnpamerica.com	New York	NY	10017	212-503-1060	
Duchossois Industries Inc 845 Larch Ave *TF:* 800-282-6225	Elmhurst	IL	60126	630-279-3600	530-6091
Dundee Bancorp Inc 1 Adelaide St E 28th Fl *TSX: DBCA* ■ *Web:* www.dundeecorp.com	Toronto	ON	M5C2V9	416-863-6990	363-4536
Dwyer Group Inc The 1020 N University Parks Dr *Web:* www.dwyergroup.com	Waco	TX	76707	254-745-2400	745-2590
E & A Industries Inc 101 W Ohio St Suite 1350 *Web:* www.eaindustries.com	Indianapolis	IN	46204	317-684-3150	681-5068
Edelman Financial Group The 5800 JPMorgan Chase Tower 600 Travis Suite 5800 *NASDAQ: EF* ■ *TF:* 800-538-0020 ■ *Web:* www.edelmanfinancial.com	Houston	TX	77002	713-224-3100	993-4677
Edward J DeBartolo Corp 7620 Marcus St *TF:* 888-965-3532	Youngstown	OH	44512	330-965-2000	965-2077
Elecsys Corp 846 N Mart-Way Ct *NASDAQ: ESYS* ■ *Web:* www.elecsyscorp.com	Olathe	KS	66219	913-647-0158	647-0132
Elvis Presley Enterprises Inc 3734 Elvis Presley Blvd *TF:* 800-238-2000 ■ *Web:* www.elvis.com	Memphis	TN	38186	901-332-3322	344-3116
Emergency Medical Services LP 6200 S Syracuse Way Suite 200 *NYSE: EMS* ■ *Web:* www.emsc.net	Greenwood Village	CO	80111	303-495-1200	495-1466
Eni Corp 485 Madison Ave *Web:* www.eni.it/home/home_en.html	New York	NY	10022	646-264-2250	
ESCO Technologies Inc 9900A Clayton Rd *NYSE: ESE* ■ *TF:* 888-622-3726 ■ *Web:* www.escotechnologies.com	Saint Louis	MO	63124	314-213-7200	213-7250
Esmark Steel Group 2500 Euclid Ave. *TF:* 800-323-0340 ■ *Web:* www.esmark.com	Chicago Heights	IL	60411	708-756-0400	756-0099
EVCI Career Colleges Holding Corp 1 Van Der Donck St 2nd Fl *NASDAQ: EVCI* ■ *Web:* www.evcinc.com	Yonkers	NY	10701	914-623-0700	964-8222
FedEx Corp 3610 Hacks Cross Rd *NYSE: FDX* ■ *TF:* 800-463-3339 ■ *Web:* www.fedex.com	Memphis	TN	38125	901-369-3600	434-9836
Fortune Diversified Industries Inc 6402 Corporate Dr *AMEX: FFI* ■ *Web:* www.fdvi.net	Indianapolis	IN	46278	317-532-1374	532-1376
Fresh Del Monte Produce Co 241 Sevilla Ave PO Box 149222 *NYSE: FDP* ■ *TF Cust Svc:* 800-950-3683 ■ *Web:* www.freshdelmonte.com	Coral Gables	FL	33134	305-520-8400	567-0320
Furmanite Corp 2435 N Central Expy Suite 700 *NYSE: XNR* ■ *Web:* www.furmanite.com	Richardson	TX	75080	972-699-4000	699-4025
Genmar Holdings Inc 80 S 8th St Suite 2900	Minneapolis	MN	55402	612-337-1944	337-1975
George Weston Ltd 22 St Clair Ave E *TSE: WN* ■ *TF:* 800-564-6253 ■ *Web:* www.weston.ca	Toronto	ON	M4T2S7	416-922-2500	922-4395
Global Entertainment Corp 1600 N Desert Dr Suite 301 *OTC: GNTP* ■ *Web:* www.globalentertainment2000.com	Tempe	AZ	85281	480-994-0772	994-0759
Golden Enterprises Inc 1 Golden Flake Dr *NASDAQ: GLDC* ■ *TF:* 800-239-2447	Birmingham	AL	35205	205-458-7316	458-7335
Goodman Global Inc 2550 N Loop W Suite 400 *TF:* 888-593-9988 ■ *Web:* www.goodmanglobal.com	Houston	TX	77092	713-861-2500	861-3207
Grand Vehicle Works Holdings Corp (GVW) 600 Central Ave Suite 214 *Web:* www.gvwholdings.com	Highland Park	IL	60035	847-681-8417	681-8515
GSC Enterprises Inc 130 N Hillcrest Dr *Web:* www.grocerysupply.com	Sulphur Springs	TX	75482	903-885-0829	885-6928
H&A Holdings Group Inc 300 N LaSalle St Suite 4925 *Web:* haholdings.com	Chicago	IL	60654	949-885-1152	
Hartz Group 667 Madison Ave 24th Fl *Web:* www.hartz.com	New York	NY	10065	212-308-3336	644-5987
Hickory Tech Corp 221 E Hickory St PO Box 3248 *NASDAQ: HTCO* ■ *TF:* 866-442-5679 ■ *Web:* www.hickorytech.com	Mankato	MN	56002	507-387-1151	625-9191
Hines Corp 1218 Pontaluna Rd Suite B *Web:* www.hinescorp.com	Spring Lake	MI	49456	231-799-6240	799-6298
Hitch Enterprises Inc 309 Northridge Cir PO Box 1308 *TF:* 800-634-8678 ■ *Web:* www.hitchok.com	Guymon	OK	73942	580-338-8575	338-0132
Holberg Industries Inc 545 Steamboat Rd	Greenwich	CT	06830	203-661-2500	661-5756
Home Capital Group Inc 145 King St W Suite 2300 *TSE: HCG* ■ *TF:* 800-990-7881 ■ *Web:* www.homecapital.com	Toronto	ON	M5H1J8	416-360-4663	363-7611
Hunt Consolidated Inc 1900 N Akard St Suite 1500 *TF:* 800-435-7794 ■ *Web:* www.huntoil.com	Dallas	TX	75201	214-978-8000	978-8888
Icahn Enterprises LP 767 5th Ave 47th Fl *NYSE: IEP* ■ *TF:* 800-255-2737 ■ *Web:* www.ielp.com	New York	NY	10153	212-702-4300	750-5841
iGATE Corp 2000 Cliff Mine Rd *NASDAQ: IGTE* ■ *TF:* 877-924-4283 ■ *Web:* www.igatecorp.com	Pittsburgh	PA	15275	412-490-9620	494-9272
Inergy Holdings LLC 2 Brush Creek Blvd Suite 200 *NASDAQ: NRGP* ■ **Fax Area Code:* 816 ■ *TF:* 877-446-3749 ■ *Web:* www.inergylp.com	Kansas City	MO	64112	877-446-3749	842-1904*
International Textile Group 804 Green Valley Rd Suite 300 **Fax:* Hum Res ■ *TF:* 800-763-0123 ■ *Web:* www.itg-global.com	Greensboro	NC	27408	336-379-6220	379-3310*
Investors Management Corp 5151 Glenwood Ave *TF:* 800-284-5673	Raleigh	NC	27612	919-781-9310	881-4686
INX Inc 350 Hills St Suite 106 *AMEX: ISR* ■ *TF:* 877-447-6729 ■ *Web:* www.isoray.com	Richland	WA	99354	509-375-1202	375-3473
ITOCHU International Inc 335 Madison Ave *Web:* www.itochu.com	New York	NY	10017	212-818-8000	818-8282
Japan Railways Group 1 Rockefeller Plaza Suite 1410 *Web:* www.japanrail.com	New York	NY	10020	212-332-8686	332-8690
Jmk International 4800 Bryant Irvin Ct *Web:* www.jmkint.com	Fort Worth	TX	76107	817-737-3703	735-1669

Company	City	State	Zip	Phone	Fax
Joy Global Inc 100 E Wisconsin Ave Suite 2780 PO Box 554 *NASDAQ: JOYG* ■ *Web:* www.joyglobal.com	Milwaukee	WI	53202	414-319-8500	319-8520
Juut Holdings Inc 201 Main St SE Suite 324 *Web:* www.juut.com	Minneapolis	MN	55414	612-676-2250	676-2251
K W Muth Co Inc PO Box 418 *TF:* 800-844-6616 ■ *Web:* www.muthco.com	Sheboygan	WI	53082	920-451-2000	451-2015
Kawasaki Heavy Industries USA Inc 60 E 42nd St Suite 2501 *Web:* www.khi.co.jp	New York	NY	10165	212-759-4950	759-6421
Kyocera International Inc 8611 Balboa Ave *Web:* www.global.kyocera.com	San Diego	CA	92123	858-576-2600	569-9412
Landmark Communications Inc 150 W Brambleton Ave *TF:* 800-446-2004	Norfolk	VA	23510	757-446-2010	446-2489
Lanoga Corp 17946 NE 65th St *Web:* www.lanoga.com	Redmond	WA	98052	425-883-4125	882-2959
Levitt Corp 2100 W Cypress Creek Rd	Fort Lauderdale	FL	33300	954-940-4950	940-4960
Liberty Diversified International Inc 5600 Hwy 169 N *TF:* 800-799-5346 ■ *Web:* www.libertydiversified.com	New Hope	MN	55428	763-536-6600	536-6685
Liberty Media Holding Corp 12300 Liberty Blvd *Web:* www.libertymedia.com	Englewood	CO	80112	720-875-5400	875-7469
Lincoln Electric Holdings Inc 22801 St Clair Ave *NASDAQ: LECO* ■ *TF:* 800-833-9353 ■ *Web:* www.lincolnelectric.com	Cleveland	OH	44117	216-481-8100	486-1751
Major Automotive Cos Inc 43-40 Northern Blvd *Web:* www.majorworld.com	Long Island City	NY	11101	718-937-3700	
Manifold Capital Corp 140 Broadway 47th Fl *PINK: MANF* ■ *Web:* www.aca.com	New York	NY	10005	212-375-2000	375-2100
Marsh & McLennan Cos Inc 1166 Avenue of the Americas *NYSE: MMC* ■ *TF:* 866-374-2662 ■ *Web:* www.mmc.com	New York	NY	10036	212-345-5000	345-4808
Maxco Inc 1005 Charlevoix Dr Suite 100 *Web:* www.maxc.com	Grand Ledge	MI	48837	517-627-1734	627-4951
McKesson Corp 1 Post St *NYSE: MCK* ■ *TF:* 800-482-3784 ■ *Web:* www.mckesson.com	San Francisco	CA	94104	415-983-8300	983-8453
MDC Holdings Inc 4350 S Monaco St Suite 500 *NYSE: MDC* ■ *Web:* www.richmondamerican.com	Denver	CO	80237	303-773-1100	771-3461
Merriman Holdings Inc 600 California St 9th Fl *NASDAQ: MERR* ■ *TF Sales:* 888-595-0999 ■ *Web:* www.merrimanco.com	San Francisco	CA	94108	415-248-5600	274-5651
Mitchel Group 1841 Ludlow Ave *Web:* www.tennscrewmach.com	Indianapolis	IN	46201	317-684-2600	532-9177
Mondial International Corp 101 Secor Ln PO Box 889 *Web:* www.mondialgroup.com	Pelham Manor	NY	10803	914-738-7411	738-7521
Morgan Keegan Inc 50 N Front St 17th Fl *TF:* 800-366-7426	Memphis	TN	38103	901-524-4100	579-4406
Natixis North America LLC 9 W 57th St 35th Fl *Web:* www.cm.natixis.com	New York	NY	10019	212-891-6100	891-6288
Navistar International Corp 4201 Winfield Rd *NYSE: NAV* ■ *TF:* 800-448-7825 ■ *Web:* www.navistar.com	Warrenville	IL	60555	630-753-5000	753-3982
NBC Universal Inc 30 Rockefeller Plaza *Web:* www.nbcuni.com	New York	NY	10112	212-664-4444	664-4085
Nes Holdings Inc 3724 National Dr Suite 109	Raleigh	NC	27612	919-510-5500	510-5059
NewMarket Corp 330 S 4th St *NYSE: NEU* ■ *TF:* 800-625-5191 ■ *Web:* www.newmarket.com	Richmond	VA	23219	804-788-5000	788-5688
NextWave Wireless Inc 10350 Science Ctr Dr Suite 210 *PINK: WAVE* ■ *TF:* 800-461-9330 ■ *Web:* www.nextwave.com	San Diego	CA	92121	858-480-3100	480-3105
Nordenia International 14591 State Hwy 177 *Web:* www.nordenia.com	Jackson	MO	63755	573-335-4900	335-6172
North Pittsburgh Systems Inc 4008 Gibsonia Rd *NASDAQ: NPSI* ■ *TF:* 800-541-9225	Gibsonia	PA	15044	724-443-9600	443-9431
NOWNESS LLC 19 E 57th St *Web:* www.nowness.com	New York	NY	10022	212-931-2000	931-2111
Nustar GP Holdings LLC 2330 N Loop 1604 W *NYSE: NSH* ■ *TF:* 800-866-9060 ■ *Web:* www.nustargpholdings.com	San Antonio	TX	78248	210-918-2000	345-2646
Oki Developments Inc 1416 112th Ave Ne *TF:* 877-465-3654 ■ *Web:* www.okigolf.com	Bellevue	WA	98004	425-454-2800	646-6999
Omnicom Group Inc 437 Madison Ave *NYSE: OMC* ■ **Fax:* Hum Res ■ *TF:* 800-332-3336 ■ *Web:* www.omnicomgroup.com	New York	NY	10022	212-415-3600	415-3530*
Orca Bay Sports & Entertainment 800 Griffiths Way *Web:* www.canucks.com	Vancouver	BC	V6B6G1	604-899-7400	899-7401
Otc Global Holdings LP 5718 Westheimer Rd Suite 1300 *Web:* www.otcgh.com	Houston	TX	77057	713-358-5450	
Otter Tail Corp 4334 18th Ave SW PO Box 9156 *NASDAQ: OTTR* ■ *TF:* 866-410-8780 ■ *Web:* www.ottertail.com	Fargo	ND	58106	701-232-6414	232-4108
Owl Cos 2465 Campus Dr *Web:* www.owlcompanies.com	Irvine	CA	92612	949-797-2000	660-4936
Pacer International Inc 2300 Clayton Rd Suite 1200 *NASDAQ: PACR* ■ *TF:* 877-917-2237 ■ *Web:* www.pacer.com	Concord	CA	94520	925-887-1400	887-1503
Pearson Inc 1330 Avenue of the Americas 7th Fl *Web:* www.pearson.com	New York	NY	10019	212-641-2400	641-2500
Peter Kiewit Sons' Inc 3555 Farnam St **Fax:* Hum Res ■ *Web:* www.kiewit.com	Omaha	NE	68131	402-342-2052	271-2939*
Phazar Corp 101 SE 25th Ave *NASDAQ: ANTP* ■ *TF:* 800-553-1507 ■ *Web:* www.antennaproducts.com	Mineral Wells	TX	76067	940-325-3301	325-0716
PHC Inc 200 Lake St Suite 102 *Web:* www.phc-inc.com	Peabody	MA	01960	978-536-2777	536-2677
Phillips Service Industries Inc 11878 Hubbard *Web:* www.psi-online.com	Livonia	MI	48150	734-853-5000	853-5032
Platinum Group of Cos Inc 9121 Oakdale Ave Sute 201 *Web:* www.platinumgroup.org	Chatsworth	CA	91311	818-721-3800	721-3811
Pro-Dex Inc 151 E Columbine Ave *NASDAQ: PDEX* ■ *TF:* 800-562-6204 ■ *Web:* www.pdex.com	Santa Ana	CA	92707	714-546-4045	513-7617
Pulte Homes Inc 100 Bloomfield Hills Pkwy Suite 300 *NYSE: PHM* ■ *TF:* 800-777-8583 ■ *Web:* www.pulte.com	Bloomfield Hills	MI	48304	248-647-2750	433-4598
RAB Holdings Inc 444 Madison Ave Suite 601	New York	NY	10022	212-688-4500	888-5025
Ralcorp Holdings Inc 800 Market St PO Box 618 *NYSE: RAH* ■ *Web:* www.ralcorp.com	Saint Louis	MO	63188	314-877-7000	877-7900
Red Apple Group Inc 823 11th Ave	New York	NY	10019	212-956-5803	247-4509
Relco LLC PO Box 1689 *Web:* www.relco.net	Willmar	MN	56201	320-231-2210	231-2282
Resource America Inc 1845 Walnut St 10th Fl *NASDAQ: REXI*	Philadelphia	PA	19103	215-546-5005	546-5388
Reunion Industries Inc 11 Stanwix St Suite 1400 *AMEX: RUN* ■ *Web:* www.reunionindustries.com	Pittsburgh	PA	15222	412-281-2111	281-4747
Revlon Inc 237 Pk Ave *NYSE: REV* ■ *TF:* 800-473-8566 ■ *Web:* www.revlon.com	New York	NY	10017	212-527-4000	527-4995
Reyes Holdings LLC 9500 Bryn Mawr Ave # 700 *Web:* www.reyesholdings.com	Rosemont	IL	60018	847-227-6500	671-4725
Rockwood Holdings Inc 100 Overlook Ctr *NYSE: ROC* ■ *Web:* www.rockwoodspecialties.com	Princeton	NJ	08540	609-514-0300	514-8720
Rosbottom Interests LLC 2640 Youree Dr *Web:* www.rosbottom.com	Shreveport	LA	71104	318-219-1212	
Rosen's Diversified Inc 1120 Lake Ave PO Box 933 *Web:* www.rosensdiversifiedinc.com	Fairmont	MN	56031	507-238-6001	
S & P Co 100 Shoreline Hwy Bldg B Suite 395	Mill Valley	CA	94941	415-332-0550	332-0567
Sabre Holdings Corp 3150 Sabre Dr *NYSE: TSG* ■ *Web:* www.sabre-holdings.com	Southlake	TX	76092	682-605-1000	
Sandvik Inc 1702 Nevins Rd *TF:* 800-726-3845 ■ *Web:* www.sandvik.com	Fair Lawn	NJ	07410	201-794-5000	794-5165
Sara Lee Corp 3500 Lacey Rd *NYSE: SLE* ■ *TF:* 800-621-5235 ■ *Web:* www.saralee.com	Downers Grove	IL	60515	630-598-6000	598-8482
Schott North America Inc 555 Taxter Rd *Web:* www.us.schott.com	Elmsford	NY	10523	914-831-2200	831-2201
Schuff International Inc 420 S 19th Ave *TF:* 800-528-0513 ■ *Web:* www.schuff.com	Phoenix	AZ	85009	602-252-7787	452-4468
Sears Holdings Corp 3333 Beverly Rd *NASDAQ: SHLD* ■ *Web:* www.searsholdings.com	Hoffman Estates	IL	60179	847-286-2500	286-7829
SGS North America Inc 201 State Rt 17 N *TF:* 800-747-9047 ■ *Web:* www.us.sgs.com	Rutherford	NJ	07070	201-508-3000	508-3193
Shamrock Cos Inc The 24090 Detroit Rd *Web:* www.shamrockcompanies.net	Westlake	OH	44145	440-899-9510	250-2180
Shenandoah Telecommunications Co 500 Shentel Way *NASDAQ: SHEN* ■ *TF:* 800-743-6835 ■ *Web:* www.shentel.com	Edinburg	VA	22824	540-984-5224	984-3438
Siebert Financial Corp 885 3rd Ave *NASDAQ: SIEB* ■ *TF:* 877-327-8379 ■ *Web:* www.siebertnet.com	New York	NY	10022	212-644-2400	486-2784
Simpson Investment Co 917 E 11th St	Tacoma	WA	98421	253-779-6400	280-9000
Speedus Corp 1 Dag Hammarskjold Blvd *PINK: SPDE* ■ **Fax Area Code:* 212 ■ *TF:* 888-773-3669 ■ *Web:* www.speedus.com	Freehold	NJ	07728	888-773-3669	937-5230*
Sumitomo Canada Ltd 150 King St W Suite 2304	Toronto	ON	M5H1J9	416-860-3800	365-3141
Sumitomo Corp of America 600 3rd Ave 42nd Fl *Web:* www.sumitomocorp.com	New York	NY	10016	212-207-0700	207-0456
Suntory International Corp 7 Times Sq 21st Fl *Web:* www.suntory.com	New York	NY	10036	212-891-6600	891-6601
Superior Group Inc 100 Front St Suite 525, 1 Tower Bridge Bldg *Web:* www.superior-group.com	West Conshohocken	PA	19428	610-397-2040	397-2720
T Rowe Price Group Inc 100 E Pratt St *NASDAQ: TROW* ■ **Fax:* Hum Res ■ *TF:* 800-638-7890 ■ *Web:* www.corporate.troweprice.com	Baltimore	MD	21202	410-345-2000	345-2394*
Taylor Corp 1725 Roe Crest Dr *TF:* 800-545-6620	North Mankato	MN	56003	507-625-2828	
TD Ameritrade Holding Corp 4211 S 102nd St PO Box 3288 *NASDAQ: AMTD* ■ *TF:* 800-237-8692 ■ *Web:* www.amtd.com	Omaha	NE	68127	800-237-8692	
Teijin Holdings USA 600 Lexington Ave 27th Fl *Web:* www.teijin.co.jp/english	New York	NY	10022	212-308-8744	308-8902
Telephone & Data Systems Inc 30 N La Salle St Suite 4000 *AMEX: TDS* ■ *TF:* 877-337-1575 ■ *Web:* www.teldta.com	Chicago	IL	60602	312-630-1900	630-9299
Terremark Worldwide Inc 1 Biscayne Tower 2 S Biscayne Blvd Suite 2800 *AMEX: TWW* ■ *TF:* 800-983-7060 ■ *Web:* www.terremark.com	Coconut Grove	FL	33131	305-856-3200	856-8190
Toyota Motor North America Inc 9 W 57th St Suite 4900 *TF:* 800-331-4331 ■ *Web:* www.toyota.com	New York	NY	10019	212-223-0303	759-7670
TransDigm Group Inc 1301 E 9th St Suite 3000 *NYSE: TDG* ■ *Web:* www.transdigm.com	Cleveland	OH	44114	216-706-2690	
Transtar Inc 1200 Penn Ave Suite 300 **Fax:* Hum Res ■ *Web:* www.tstarinc.com	Pittsburgh	PA	15222	412-829-3390	829-6694*
Tredegar Corp 1100 Boulders Pkwy Suite 200 *NYSE: TG* ■ *TF:* 800-411-7441 ■ *Web:* www.tredegar.com	Richmond	VA	23225	804-330-1000	330-1177
Trian Partners 280 Pk Ave 41st Fl **Fax:* Mail Rm ■ *TF:* 800-787-4272	New York	NY	10017	212-451-3000	451-3000*
Trump Organization 725 5th Ave 26th Fl *Web:* www.trump.com	New York	NY	10022	212-832-2000	935-0141

				Phone	Fax
Tsi Holding Co 999 Executive Pkwy Dr ... Saint Louis *Web:* www.tsiholding.com	MO	63141		314-628-6000	628-6099
Turner Corp 375 Hudson St ... New York *Web:* www.turnerconstruction.com	NY	75202		212-229-6000	
Um Holding Co 56 N Haddon Ave PO Box 200 ... Haddonfield *Web:* www.umholdings.com	NJ	08033		856-354-2200	
Unilever Canada Ltd 160 Bloor St E Suite 1500 ... Toronto *Web:* www.unilever.ca	ON	M4W3R2		416-964-1857	964-8831
Union Pacific Corp 1400 Douglas St ... Omaha *NYSE: UNP* ■ *TF:* 888-870-8777 ■ *Web:* www.up.com	NE	68179		402-544-5000	
US Merchants Financial Group Inc 1118 S La Cienega Blvd ... Los Angeles	CA	90035		310-855-1946	855-9649
Vector Group Ltd 100 SE 2nd St 32nd Fl ... Miami *NYSE: VGR* ■ *Web:* www.vectorgroupltd.com	FL	33131		305-579-8000	579-8001
Warnaco Group Inc 501 7th Ave ... New York *NYSE: WRC* ■ *Web:* www.warnaco.com	NY	10018		212-287-8000	287-8297
Warren Equities Inc 27 Warren Way ... Providence *Web:* www.warreneq.com	RI	02905		401-781-9900	461-7160
Waste Industries USA Inc 3301 Benson Dr Suite 601 ... Raleigh *TF:* 800-647-9946 ■ *Web:* www.waste-ind.com	NC	27609		919-325-3000	325-4040
WebMD Health Holdings Inc 111 8th Ave 7th Fl ... New York *NASDAQ: WBMD* ■ *Web:* www.webmd.com	NY	10011		212-624-3700	624-3800
Welch Allyn Inc 4341 State St Rd ... Skaneateles Falls **Fax:* Cust Svc ■ *TF Cust Svc:* 800-535-6663 ■ *Web:* www.welchallyn.com	NY	13153		315-685-4100	685-3361*
WESCO International Inc 225 W Stn Sq Dr Suite 700 ... Pittsburgh *NYSE: WCC* ■ *Web:* www.wesco.com	PA	15219		412-454-2200	454-2505
Williams Cos Inc 1 Williams Ctr ... Tulsa *NYSE: WMB* ■ *TF:* 800-945-5426 ■ *Web:* www.williams.com	OK	74102		918-573-2000	573-6714
Wood Resources LLC 1 Sound Shore Dr Suite 304 ... Greenwich *Web:* www.atlasholdingsllc.com	CT	06830		203-622-9138	622-0151
YRC Worldwide Inc 10990 Roe Ave ... Overland Park *NASDAQ: YRCW* ■ *TF:* 800-846-4300 ■ *Web:* www.yrc.com	KS	66211		913-696-6100	344-4717

363-4 Insurance Holding Companies

			Phone	Fax
21st Century Holding Co PO Box 407193 ... Fort Lauderdale *NASDAQ: TCHC* ■ *TF General:* 800-333-3477	FL	33340	954-581-9993	584-0724
AEGON USA Inc 4333 Edgewood Rd NE ... Cedar Rapids *Web:* www.aegonins.com	IA	52499	319-398-8511	
Affirmative Insurance Holdings Inc 4450 Sojourn Dr Suite 500 ... Addison *NASDAQ: AFFM* ■ **Fax Area Code:* 972 ■ *TF:* 800-877-0226 ■ *Web:* www.affirmativeholdings.com	TX	75001	630-560-7205	991-0882*
AFLAC Inc 1932 Wynnton Rd ... Columbus *NYSE: AFL* ■ **Fax:* Mktg ■ *TF:* 800-992-3522 ■ *Web:* www.aflac.com	GA	31999	706-323-3431	660-7103*
AIG SunAmerica Inc 21650 Oxnard St ... Woodland Hills *TF:* 800-445-7862 ■ *Web:* www.sunamerica.com	CA	91367	800-445-7862	
Alfa Insurance Corp PO Box 11000 ... Montgomery *NASDAQ: ALFA* ■ **Fax:* Hum Res ■ *TF:* 888-964-2532	AL	36191	334-288-3900	613-4732*
Allstate Corp 2775 Sanders Rd Allstate Plaza ... Northbrook *NYSE: ALL* ■ **Fax:* Hum Res ■ *TF:* 800-255-7828 ■ *Web:* www.allstate.com	IL	60062	847-402-5000	836-3998*
AMBAC Financial Group Inc 1 State St Plaza 15th Fl ... New York *NYSE: ABK* ■ *TF:* 800-221-1854 ■ *Web:* www.ambac.com	NY	10004	212-668-0340	509-9190
American Equity Investment Life Holding Co 6000 Westown Pkwy Suite 440 PO Box 71216 ... West Des Moines *NYSE: AEL* ■ *TF:* 888-221-1234 ■ *Web:* www.american-equity.com	IA	50266	515-221-0002	221-9947
American Family Insurance Group 6000 American Pkwy ... Madison **Fax:* Mail Rm ■ *TF:* 800-374-0008 ■ *Web:* www.amfam.com	WI	53783	608-249-2111	243-4924*
American Fidelity Group 2000 N Classen Blvd ... Oklahoma City **Fax:* Hum Res ■ *TF:* 800-654-8489 ■ *Web:* www.afadvantage.com	OK	73106	405-523-2000	523-5645*
American Financial Group Inc 1 E 4th St ... Cincinnati *NYSE: AFG* ■ *Web:* www.afginc.com	OH	45202	513-579-2121	579-2580
American International Group Inc (AIG) 180 Maiden Ln ... New York *NYSE: AIG* ■ *TF:* 877-638-4244 ■ *Web:* www.aig.com	NY	10038	212-770-6580	770-6293
American Medical Security (AMS) 3100 AMS Blvd PO Box 19032 ... Green Bay *TF:* 800-232-5432 ■ *Web:* www.eams.com	WI	54307	920-661-1111	
American Re Corp 555 College Rd E ... Princeton **Fax:* Mail Rm ■ *TF:* 800-255-5676 ■ *Web:* www.amre.com	NJ	08543	609-243-4200	243-4257*
American Skandia Prudential Financial Co 1 Corporate Dr ... Shelton **Fax Area Code:* 800 ■ *TF:* 888-778-2888 ■ *Web:* www.annuities.prudential.com	CT	06484	203-926-1888	207-7806*
American United Mutual Insurance Holding Co (AUMIHC) 1 American Sq PO Box 368 ... Indianapolis *Web:* www.oneamerica.com	IN	46206	317-285-1111	
Americo Life Inc 1055 Broadway ... Kansas City **Fax Area Code:* 800 ■ *TF Cust Svc:* 800-982-8144 ■ *Web:* www.americo.com	MO	64105	816-391-2000	395-9238*
Ameritas Holding Co 5900 O St ... Lincoln *TF:* 800-311-7871 ■ *Web:* www.ameritas.com	NE	68510	402-467-1122	467-7790
Anthem Insurance Cos Inc 120 Monument Cir Suite 200 ... Indianapolis **Fax:* Hum Res ■ *TF:* 800-331-1476 ■ *Web:* www.anthem.com	IN	46204	317-488-6000	488-6028*
Aon Corp 200 E Randolph St ... Chicago *NYSE: AOC* ■ *TF:* 877-384-4276 ■ *Web:* www.aon.com	IL	60601	312-381-1000	
Assicurazioni Generali US Branch 7 World Trade Ctr 250 Greenwich St 33rd Fl ... New York *Web:* www.generaliusa.com	NY	10006	212-602-7600	587-9537
Assurant Group 11222 Quail Roost Dr ... Miami *TF:* 800-852-2244 ■ *Web:* www.assurant.com	FL	33157	305-253-2244	252-6947
Assurant Inc 1 Chase Manhattan Plaza 41st Fl ... New York *NYSE: AIZ* ■ **Fax:* Hum Res ■ *TF:* 800-859-5676 ■ *Web:* www.assurant.com	NY	10005	212-859-7000	859-7058*
Assurity Security Group Inc 1526 K St ... Lincoln	NE	68508	402-476-6500	
Atlantic American Corp 4370 Peachtree Rd NE ... Atlanta *NASDAQ: AAME* ■ **Fax:* Mail Rm ■ *TF:* 800-241-1439 ■ *Web:* www.atlam.com	GA	30319	404-266-5500	266-5629*
Benfield Inc 500 N Akard St Suite 3700 ... Dallas *Web:* www.benfieldgroup.com	TX	75201	214-756-7000	756-7001
Bexil Corp 11 Hanover Sq ... New York *PINK: BXLC* ■ *Web:* www.bexil.com	NY	10005	212-785-0400	363-1101
Capitol Transamerica Corp 1600 Aspen Commons ... Middleton **Fax:* Hum Res ■ *TF:* 800-475-4450 ■ *Web:* www.capitolindemnity.com	WI	53562	608-829-4200	829-7409*
Chubb Corp 15 Mountain View Rd ... Warren *NYSE: CB* ■ **Fax:* Mail Rm ■ *Web:* www.chubb.com	NJ	07059	908-903-2000	903-2027*
CIGNA Corp 1601 Chestnut St ... Philadelphia *NYSE: CI* ■ *Web:* www.cigna.com	PA	19192	215-761-1000	761-5597
Cincinnati Financial Corp 6200 S Gilmore Rd ... Fairfield *NASDAQ: CINF*	OH	45014	513-870-2000	870-2911
Citizens Financial Corp 12910 Shelbyville Rd Suite 300 ... Louisville *NASDAQ: CNFL* ■ *TF:* 800-843-7752 ■ *Web:* www.citizensfinancialcorp.com	KY	40243	502-244-2420	244-2439
Citizens Inc 400 E Anderson Ln ... Austin *NYSE: CIA* ■ *TF:* 800-880-5044 ■ *Web:* www.citizensinc.com	TX	78752	512-837-7100	836-9785
CNA Financial Corp 333 S Wabash Ave ... Chicago *NYSE: CNA* ■ *TF:* 800-262-2000 ■ *Web:* www.cna.com	IL	60604	312-822-5000	
Commerce Group Inc 9503 E 33rd St One Celadon Dr ... Indianapolis *NYSE: CGI* ■ *TF:* 800-221-1605 ■ *Web:* www.celadontrucking.com	IN	46235	317-972-7000	890-9414
Conseco Inc 11825 N Pennsylvania St ... Carmel *NYSE: CNO* ■ **Fax:* Hum Res ■ *TF:* 800-541-2254 ■ *Web:* www.conseco.com	IN	46032	317-817-6100	817-6721*
Cumberland Technologies Inc 4311 W Waters Ave Suite 401 ... Tampa *TF:* 800-723-0171 ■ *Web:* www.cumberlandtech.com	FL	33614	813-885-2112	880-0901
CUNA Mutual Group 5910 Mineral Pt Dr ... Madison *TF:* 800-937-2644 ■ *Web:* www.cunamutual.com	WI	53705	608-238-5851	231-7875
Delphi Financial Group Inc 1105 N Market St Suite 1230 ... Wilmington *NYSE: DFG* ■ *Web:* www.delphifin.com	DE	19801	302-478-5142	
Deutsche Bank Americas Holding Corp 60 Wall St ... New York *Web:* www.db.com	NY	10005	212-250-2500	
Donegal Group Inc 1195 River Rd ... Marietta *NASDAQ: DGICB* ■ **Fax:* Hum Res ■ *TF:* 800-877-0600 ■ *Web:* www.donegalgroup.com	PA	17547	717-426-1931	426-7030*
E-L Financial Corp Ltd 165 University Ave 10th Fl ... Toronto *TSE: ELF*	ON	M5H3B8	416-947-2578	362-2592
EMC Insurance Group Inc 717 Mulberry St ... Des Moines *NASDAQ: EMCI* ■ *TF:* 800-447-2295 ■ *Web:* www.emcins.com	IA	50309	515-280-2511	
Everest Re Group Ltd 477 Martinsville Rd PO Box 830 ... Liberty Corner *NYSE: RE* ■ *TF:* 800-269-6660 ■ *Web:* www.everestre.com	NJ	07938	908-604-3000	604-3322
Fairfax Financial Holdings Ltd 95 Wellington St W Suite 800 ... Toronto *Web:* www.fairfax.ca	ON	M5J2N7	416-367-4941	367-4946
Farmers Insurance Group 4680 Wilshire Blvd ... Los Angeles *Web:* www.farmersinsurance.com	CA	90010	323-932-3200	936-8479
FBL Financial Group Inc 5400 University Ave ... West Des Moines *NYSE: FFG* ■ *Web:* www.fblfinancial.com	IA	50266	515-225-5400	226-6053
Federated Insurance Cos 121 E Pk Sq PO Box 328 ... Owatonna *TF:* 800-533-0472 ■ *Web:* www.federatedinsurance.com	MN	55060	507-455-5200	444-6778
Fidelity National Financial Inc 601 Riverside Ave ... Jacksonville *NYSE: FNF* ■ **Fax Area Code:* 805 ■ *TF:* 888-934-3354 ■ *Web:* www.fnf.com	FL	32204	904-854-8100	696-7823*
First Investors Corp 110 Fieldcrest Ave RARITAN Plaza I ... Edison *TF:* 800-432-4026 ■ *Web:* www.firstinvestors.com	NJ	08837	732-855-2500	855-2579
FPIC Insurance Group Inc 1000 Riverside Ave Suite 800 ... Jacksonville *NASDAQ: FPIC* ■ *TF:* 800-221-2101 ■ *Web:* www.fpic.com	FL	32204	904-354-2482	475-1159
GEICO 1 GEICO Plaza ... Washington *TF:* 800-824-5404 ■ *Web:* www.geico.com	DC	20076	301-986-2500	986-3757
General Re Corp 695 E Main St Financial Ctr ... Stamford *TF:* 800-431-9994 ■ *Web:* www.genre.com	CT	06901	203-328-5000	328-6423
GMAC Insurance Holdings Inc 13736 Riverport Dr Suite 700 ... Maryland Heights *TF:* 877-468-3466 ■ *Web:* www.gmacinsurance.com	MO	63043	314-493-8000	493-8113
Goran Capital Inc 2 Eva Rd Suite 200 ... Etobicoke	ON	M9C2A8	416-622-0660	622-8809
Great American Financial Resources Inc (GAFRI) 250 E 5th St ... Cincinnati *TF:* 888-497-8556 ■ *Web:* www.gafri.com	OH	45202	513-333-5300	
Great-West Lifeco Inc 100 Osborne St N ... Winnepeg *Web:* www.greatwestlifeco.com	MB	R3C3A5	204-946-8366	946-4139
Hallmark Financial Services Inc 777 Main St Suite 1000 ... Fort Worth *NASDAQ: HALL* ■ *Web:* www.hallmarkgrp.com	TX	76102	817-348-1600	348-1815
Hanover Insurance Group Inc 440 Lincoln St ... Worcester *NYSE: THG* ■ *TF:* 800-533-7881 ■ *Web:* www.hanover.com	MA	01653	508-855-1000	853-6332
Harleysville Group Inc 355 Maple Ave ... Harleysville *NASDAQ: HGIC* ■ **Fax:* Mktg ■ *TF:* 800-523-6344 ■ *Web:* www.harleysvillegroup.com	PA	19438	215-256-5000	256-5678*
Hartford Financial Services Group Inc 690 Asylum Ave ... Hartford *NYSE: HIG* ■ **Fax:* PR ■ *Web:* www.thehartford.com	CT	06115	860-547-5000	547-3799*
HCC Insurance Holdings Inc 13403 NW Fwy ... Houston *NYSE: HCC* ■ *Web:* www.hcc.com	TX	77040	713-462-1000	462-4210
HealthMarkets Inc 9151 Grapevine Hwy ... North Richland Hills *TF:* 800-527-5504 ■ *Web:* www.healthmarketsinc.com	TX	76180	817-255-5200	255-8164
HM Insurance Group 120 5th Ave ... Pittsburgh *TF:* 800-328-5433 ■ *Web:* www.hminsurancegroup.com	PA	15222	412-544-2000	544-1334

	City	State	Zip	Phone	Fax
Horace Mann Educators Corp 1 Horace Mann Plaza	Springfield	IL	62715	217-789-2500	788-5161
NYSE: HMN ■ *TF:* 800-999-1030 ■ *Web:* www.horacemann.com					
Industrial Alliance Insurance & Financial Services Inc 1080 Grande Allee W	Quebec	QC	G1K7M3	418-684-5026	688-8599
TSE: IAG-A ■ *TF:* 800-463-5261 ■ *Web:* www.inalco.com					
ING North America Insurance Corp 5780 Powers Ferry Rd NW	Atlanta	GA	30327	770-980-5100	980-3301
Web: www.ing.us					
Investors Title Co 121 N Columbia St	Chapel Hill	NC	27514	919-968-2200	690-6105*
NASDAQ: ITIC ■ **Fax Area Code:* 800 ■ *TF:* 800-326-4842					
John Hancock Financial Services Inc 601 Congress St	Boston	MA	02210	617-663-3000	663-4790*
**Fax:* PR ■ *Web:* www.johnhancock.com					
Kansas City Life Insurance Co 3520 Broadway	Kansas City	MO	64111	816-753-7000	753-4902
NASDAQ: KCLI ■ *TF:* 800-821-6164 ■ *Web:* www.kclife.com					
Kingsway America Inc (KAI) 150 NW Pt Blvd	Elk Grove Village	IL	60007	847-700-9100	700-9170
TF: 800-232-0631 ■ *Web:* www.univcas.com					
Legal & General America Inc 1701 Research Blvd	Rockville	MD	20850	301-279-4800	294-6960*
**Fax:* Cust Svc ■ *TF:* 800-638-8428 ■ *Web:* www.lgamerica.com					
Liberty Mutual Holding Co Inc 175 Berkeley St	Boston	MA	02116	617-357-9500	350-7648
Web: www.libertymutual.com					
Lifetime Healthcare Cos The 165 Ct St	Rochester	NY	14647	585-454-1700	238-4224
TF: 800-847-1200 ■ *Web:* www.lifethc.com					
Lincoln National Corp (LNC) 150 N Radnor-Chester Rd	Radnor	PA	19087	484-583-1400	448-3962*
NYSE: LNC ■ **Fax Area Code:* 215 ■ **Fax:* PR ■ *TF:* 877-275-5462 ■ *Web:* www.lfg.com					
Lykes Bros Inc PO Box 2879	Tampa	FL	33601	813-223-3911	221-1857*
**Fax:* Hum Res ■ *TF:* 800-243-0494					
Manulife Financial Corp 200 Bloor St E	Toronto	ON	M4W1E5	416-852-7792	926-5410
NYSE: MFC ■ *TF:* 800-795-9767 ■ *Web:* www.manulife.com					
Markel Corp 4521 Highwoods Pkwy	Glen Allen	VA	23060	804-747-0136	965-1600
NYSE: MKL ■ *TF:* 800-446-6671					
MBIA Inc 113 King St	Armonk	NY	10504	914-273-4545	765-3299*
NYSE: MBI ■ **Fax:* Hum Res ■ *Web:* www.mbia.com					
Meadowbrook Insurance Group Inc 26255 American Dr	Southfield	MI	48034	248-358-1100	358-1614
NYSE: MIG ■ *TF:* 800-482-2726 ■ *Web:* www.meadowbrookinsgrp.com					
MEEMIC Holdings Inc 1685 N Opdyke Rd PO Box 217019	Auburn Hills	MI	48321	248-373-5700	377-8518
TF: 888-463-3642 ■ *Web:* www.meemic.com					
Merchants Group Inc 250 Main St	Buffalo	NY	14202	716-849-3333	849-3388*
**Fax:* Hum Res ■ *TF:* 800-462-1077 ■ *Web:* www.merchantsgroup.com					
Mid Atlantic Medical Services Inc (MAMSI) 4 Taft Ct	Rockville	MD	20850	301-762-8205	360-8647
TF: 800-331-2102 ■ *Web:* www.mamsiunitedhealthcare.com					
Midland Co 7000 Midland Blvd	Amelia	OH	45102	513-943-7100	
NASDAQ: MLAN ■ *TF:* 800-759-9008 ■ *Web:* www.midlandcompany.com					
Mutual of Omaha Co Mutual of Omaha Plaza	Omaha	NE	68175	402-342-7600	351-2775
TF: 800-775-6000 ■ *Web:* www.mutualofomaha.com					
Nationwide Investment Services Corp 5100 Rings Rd	Dublin	OH	43017	614-249-7111	854-5036
NYSE: NFS ■ *TF:* 877-669-6877 ■ *Web:* www.nationwidefinancial.com					
Navigators Group Inc 1 Penn Plaza 55th Fl	New York	NY	10119	212-244-2333	244-4077
NASDAQ: NAVG ■ *TF:* 800-496-2901 ■ *Web:* www.navigators-insurance.com					
NGL Insurance Group 2 E Gilman St	Madison	WI	53703	800-548-2962	257-3940*
**Fax Area Code:* 608 ■ *TF:* 800-548-2962 ■ *Web:* www.nglic.com					
Ohio National Financial Services Inc 1 Financial Way Suite 100	Cincinnati	OH	45242	513-794-6100	794-4504*
**Fax:* Hum Res ■ *TF:* 800-366-6654 ■ *Web:* www.ohionational.com					
Old Republic International Corp 307 N Michigan Ave	Chicago	IL	60601	312-346-8100	726-0309
NYSE: ORI ■ *TF:* 800-621-0365 ■ *Web:* www.oldrepublic.com					
Pacific Mutual Holding Co 700 Newport Ctr Dr	Newport Beach	CA	92660	949-219-3011	219-5378
TF: 800-347-7787 ■ *Web:* www.pacificlife.com					
Patriot Risk Management Inc 401 E Las Olas Blvd Suite 1540	Fort Lauderdale	FL	33301	954-670-2937	779-3556
NYSE: PMG ■ *Web:* www.prmigroup.com					
Penn Treaty American Corp 3440 Lehigh St	Allentown	PA	18103	610-965-2222	967-4616
NYSE: PTA ■ *TF:* 800-222-3469 ■ *Web:* www.penntreaty.com					
Penn-America Group Inc 420 S York Rd	Hatboro	PA	19040	215-443-3600	443-3604*
**Fax:* Claims ■ *Web:* www.penn-america.com					
Phoenix Cos Inc The 1 American Row PO Box 5056	Hartford	CT	06102	860-403-5000	
NYSE: PNX ■ *TF:* 800-628-1936 ■ *Web:* www.phoenixwm.phl.com					
PICO Holdings Inc 875 Prospect St Suite 301	La Jolla	CA	92037	858-456-6022	456-6480
NASDAQ: PICO ■ *TF:* 888-389-3222 ■ *Web:* www.picoholdings.com					
PMA Capital Corp 380 Sentry Pkwy	Blue Bell	PA	19422	610-397-5298	397-5422
Web: www.pmacompanies.com					
PMI Group Inc 3003 Oak Rd	Walnut Creek	CA	94597	800-288-1970	
NYSE: PMI ■ *TF:* 800-288-1970 ■ *Web:* www.pmigroup.com					
Power Financial Corp 751 Victoria Sq	Montreal	QC	H2Y2J3	514-286-7400	286-7424
TF: 800-890-7440 ■ *Web:* www.powerfinancial.com					
Presidential Life Corp 69 Lydecker St	Nyack	NY	10960	845-358-2300	353-0273
NASDAQ: PLFE ■ *TF:* 800-926-7599 ■ *Web:* www.presidentiallife.com					
Principal Financial Group Inc 711 High St	Des Moines	IA	50392	515-247-5111	247-5874
NYSE: PFG ■ *TF:* 800-986-3343 ■ *Web:* www.principal.com					
ProAssurance Corp 100 Brookwood Pl Suite 300	Birmingham	AL	35209	205-877-4400	802-4799*
NYSE: PRA ■ **Fax:* Cust Svc ■ *TF:* 800-282-6242 ■ *Web:* www.proassurance.com					
Progressive Corp 6300 Wilson Mills Rd	Mayfield Village	OH	44143	440-461-5000	446-7436
NYSE: PGR ■ *TF Cust Svc:* 800-776-4737 ■ *Web:* www.progressive.com					
Protective Life Corp 2801 Hwy 280 S	Birmingham	AL	35203	205-268-1000	268-3196*
NYSE: PL ■ **Fax:* Hum Res ■ *TF:* 800-333-3418 ■ *Web:* www.protective.com					
Reinsurance Group of America Inc 1370 Timberlake Manor Pkwy	Chesterfield	MO	63017	636-736-7000	736-7100
NYSE: RGA ■ *TF:* 888-736-5445 ■ *Web:* www.rgare.com					
RLI Corp 9025 N Lindbergh Dr	Peoria	IL	61615	309-692-1000	692-1068
NYSE: RLI ■ *TF Cust Svc:* 800-331-4929 ■ *Web:* www.rlicorp.com					
SAFECO Corp 1001 4th Ave	Seattle	WA	98154	206-545-5000	545-5995
TF: 800-562-1018 ■ *Web:* www.safeco.com					
Scottish Re Inc 14120 Ballantyne Corporate Pl Suite 300	Charlotte	NC	28277	704-542-9192	542-5744
Web: www.scottishre.com					
Securian Financial Group Inc 400 Robert St N	Saint Paul	MN	55101	651-665-3500	665-4488
Web: www.securian.com					
Security Benefit Group of Cos 1 Security Benefit Pl	Topeka	KS	66636	785-438-3000	368-1772*
**Fax:* Cust Svc ■ *TF:* 800-888-2461 ■ *Web:* www.securitybenefit.com					
Selective Insurance Group Inc 40 Wantage Ave	Branchville	NJ	07890	973-948-3000	948-0292
NASDAQ: SIGI ■ *TF:* 800-777-9656 ■ *Web:* www.selectiveinsurance.com					
Sentry Insurance Group 1800 N Pt Dr	Stevens Point	WI	54481	715-346-6000	346-6770
TF: 800-373-6879 ■ *Web:* www.sentry.com					
Southwestern Life Holdings Inc 8710 Freeport Pkwy Suite 150	Irving	TX	75063	800-792-4368	333-7833*
**Fax Area Code:* 803 ■ *TF:* 800-792-4368					
StanCorp Financial Group Inc 1100 SW 6th Ave	Portland	OR	97204	971-321-6127	
NYSE: SFG ■ *TF:* 800-642-9888 ■ *Web:* www.investor.stancorpfinancial.com					
State Auto Financial Corp 518 E Broad St	Columbus	OH	43215	614-464-5000	464-5374
NASDAQ: STFC ■ *TF:* 800-444-9950 ■ *Web:* www.stfc.com					
Summit Holding Southeast Inc PO Box 600	Gainesville	GA	30503	678-450-5825	
TF: 800-971-2667 ■ *Web:* www.summitholdings.com					
Sun Life Financial Inc 150 King St W	Toronto	ON	M5H1J9	416-979-9966	888-2990*
NYSE: SLF ■ **Fax Area Code:* 518 ■ *TF:* 877-786-5438 ■ *Web:* www.sunlife.com					
Swiss Re Life & Health America Inc 175 King St	Armonk	NY	10504	914-828-8000	828-7000
TF: 877-794-7773 ■ *Web:* www.swissre.com					
Torchmark Corp 3700 S Stonebridge Dr	McKinney	TX	75070	972-569-4000	569-3282
NYSE: TMK ■ *Web:* www.torchmarkcorp.com					
Transatlantic Holdings Inc 80 Pine St	New York	NY	10005	212-365-2200	365-2362*
NYSE: TRH ■ **Fax:* Claims ■ *Web:* www.transre.com					
Travelers Cos Inc 385 Washington St	Saint Paul	MN	55102	651-310-7911	310-8204*
NYSE: TRV ■ **Fax:* Hum Res ■ *TF:* 800-328-2189 ■ *Web:* www.travelers.com					
ULLICO Inc 1625 Eye St NW	Washington	DC	20006	202-682-0900	
TF: 800-431-5425 ■ *Web:* www.ullico.com					
UNIFI Mutual Holding Co 5900 O St	Lincoln	NE	68510	402-467-1122	467-7939
TF: 800-311-7871 ■ *Web:* www.unificompanies.com					
United Fire Group 118 2nd Ave SE PO Box 73909	Cedar Rapids	IA	52407	319-399-5700	399-5499
TF: 800-332-7977 ■ *Web:* www.unitedfiregroup.com					
United Trust Group Inc (UTGI) 5250 S 6th St	Springfield	IL	62705	217-241-6410	241-6578
TF: 800-323-0050 ■ *Web:* www.utgins.com					
UnitedHealthcare Co 9900 Bren Rd E	Minnetonka	MN	55343	952-936-1300	936-7430
Web: www.uhc.com					
Unitrin Inc 1 E Wacker Dr	Chicago	IL	60601	312-661-4600	661-4690
NYSE: UTR ■ *Web:* www.unitrin.com					
Universal American Financial Corp (UAFC) 6 International Dr Suite 190	Rye Brook	NY	10573	914-934-5200	934-0700
NASDAQ: UHCO ■ *TF:* 866-249-8668 ■ *Web:* www.universalamerican.com					
UnumProvident Corp 1 Fountain Sq	Chattanooga	TN	37402	423-294-1011	294-3962
NYSE: UNM ■ *TF:* 800-887-2180 ■ *Web:* www.unum.com					
Utica Mutual Insurance Co PO Box 530	Utica	NY	13503	315-734-2000	734-2680
TF: 800-274-1914 ■ *Web:* www.uticanational.com					
Western & Southern Financial Group 400 Broadway	Cincinnati	OH	45202	513-629-1800	629-1212
TF: 800-333-5222 ■ *Web:* www.westernsouthern.com					
White Mountains Insurance Group Ltd 80 S Main St	Hanover	NH	03755	603-640-2200	643-4592
NYSE: WTM ■ *TF:* 866-295-3762 ■ *Web:* www.whitemountains.com					
White Mountains Re America 1 Liberty Plaza	New York	NY	10006	212-312-2500	385-2279
Web: www.folksamerica.com					
WR Berkley Corp 475 Steamboat Rd	Greenwich	CT	06830	203-629-3000	629-3073
NYSE: BER ■ *Web:* www.wrbc.com					

363-5 Utilities Holding Companies

	City	State	Zip	Phone	Fax
AGL Resources Inc 10 Peachtree Pl PO Box 4569	Atlanta	GA	30309	404-584-4000	584-3945*
NYSE: AGL ■ **Fax:* Hum Res ■ *TF Cust Svc:* 800-427-5463 ■ *Web:* www.aglresources.com					
ALLETE Inc 30 W Superior St	Duluth	MN	55802	218-279-5000	723-3944
NYSE: ALE ■ *TF:* 800-228-4966 ■ *Web:* www.allete.com					
Ameren Corp 1901 Chouteau Ave	Saint Louis	MO	63103	314-621-3222	621-2888
NYSE: AEE ■ *TF:* 800-552-7583					
American Electric Power Co Inc 1 Riverside Plaza	Columbus	OH	43215	614-716-1000	716-1823
NYSE: AEP ■ *TF Cust Svc:* 800-277-2177 ■ *Web:* www.aep.com					
American States Water Co 630 E Foothill Blvd	San Dimas	CA	91773	909-394-3600	394-9708
NYSE: AWR ■ *TF:* 800-999-4033 ■ *Web:* www.aswater.com					
American Water Works Co Inc 1025 Laurel Oak Rd	Voorhees	NJ	08043	856-346-8200	346-8360
Web: www.amwater.com					
Artesian Resources Corp 664 Churchmans Rd	Newark	DE	19702	302-453-6900	453-6957
NASDAQ: ARTNA ■ *TF:* 800-332-5114 ■ *Web:* www.artesianwater.com					
Atmos Energy Corp 5430 LBJ Fwy Suite 1800	Dallas	TX	75240	972-934-9227	855-3040
NYSE: ATO ■ *TF:* 888-954-4321 ■ *Web:* www.atmosenergy.com					
BayCorp Holdings Ltd 1 New Hampshire Ave Suite 207	Portsmouth	NH	03801	603-294-4850	457-6013
Black Hills Corp 625 9th St	Rapid City	SD	57701	605-721-1700	721-2596*
NYSE: BKH ■ **Fax:* Hum Res ■ *TF:* 800-843-8849 ■ *Web:* www.blackhillscorp.com					
CenterPoint Energy Inc 1111 Louisiana St	Houston	TX	77002	713-207-1111	207-0050*
NYSE: CNP ■ **Fax:* Hum Res ■ *TF Cust Svc:* 866-735-4268 ■ *Web:* www.centerpointenergy.com					
CH Energy Group Inc 284 S Ave	Poughkeepsie	NY	12601	845-452-2000	486-5415
NYSE: CHG ■ *TF:* 800-527-2714 ■ *Web:* www.chenergygroup.com					

	City	State	Zip	Phone	Fax
Cleco Corp 2030 Donahue Ferry Rd *NYSE: CNL* ■ **Fax:* Cust Svc ■ *TF Cust Svc:* 800-622-6537 ■ *Web:* www.cleco.com	Pineville	LA	71360	318-484-7400	641-8196*
CMS Energy Corp 1 Energy Plaza *NYSE: CMS* ■ *TF:* 800-477-5050 ■ *Web:* www.cmsenergy.com	Jackson	MI	49201	517-788-0550	
Connecticut Water Service Inc 93 W Main St *NASDAQ: CTWS* ■ **Fax:* Cust Svc ■ *TF:* 800-286-5700 ■ *Web:* www.ctwater.com	Clinton	CT	06413	860-669-8636	664-8081*
Consolidated Edison Inc 4 Irving Pl *NYSE: ED* ■ **Fax:* Hum Res ■ *TF:* 800-752-6633 ■ *Web:* www.conedison.com	New York	NY	10003	212-460-4600	260-8647*
Dominion Resources Inc 120 Tredegar St *NYSE: D* ■ *TF:* 800-552-4034 ■ *Web:* www.dom.com	Richmond	VA	23219	804-819-2000	819-2233
DPL Inc 1065 Woodman Dr *NYSE: DPL* ■ *TF:* 800-322-9244 ■ *Web:* www.dplinc.com	Dayton	OH	45432	937-224-6000	259-7147
DTE Energy Co One Energy Plaza *NYSE: DTE* ■ *TF:* 800-477-4747 ■ *Web:* www.dteenergy.com	Detroit	MI	48226	313-235-4000	235-6743
Duke Energy Corp 526 S Church St *NYSE: DUK* ■ **Fax:* Hum Res ■ *Web:* www.duke-energy.com	Charlotte	NC	28202	704-594-6200	382-3781*
Duquesne Light Holdings Inc 411 7th Ave *NYSE: DQE* ■ *TF:* 888-393-7000 ■ *Web:* www.duquesnelight.com	Pittsburgh	PA	15219	412-393-7000	393-7000
Dynegy Inc 1000 Louisiana St Suite 5800 *NYSE: DYN* ■ *TF:* 800-633-4704 ■ *Web:* www.dynegy.com	Houston	TX	77002	713-507-6400	
Edison International 2244 Walnut Grove Ave *NYSE: EIX* ■ *TF Cust Svc:* 800-655-4555 ■ *Web:* www.edison.com	Rosemead	CA	91770	626-302-1212	
Emera Inc 1894 Barrington St *TSE: EMA* ■ *TF:* 888-450-0507 ■ *Web:* www.emera.com	Halifax	NS	B3J2W5	902-450-0507	428-6112
Enbridge Energy Management LLC 1100 Louisiana St Suite 3300 *NYSE: EEQ* ■ *TF:* 866-337-4636 ■ *Web:* www.enbridgemanagement.com	Houston	TX	77002	713-821-2000	821-2232
Energen Corp 605 Richard Arrington Blvd N *NYSE: EGN* ■ *TF:* 800-292-4005 ■ *Web:* www.energen.com	Birmingham	AL	35203	205-326-2700	326-2590
Entergy Corp 639 Loyola Ave *NYSE: ETR* ■ *TF:* 800-368-3749 ■ *Web:* www.entergy.com	New Orleans	LA	70113	504-576-4000	576-4428
Exelon Corp 10 S Dearborn St 37th Fl *NYSE: EXC* ■ *TF:* 800-334-7661 ■ *Web:* www.exeloncorp.com	Chicago	IL	60690	312-394-7398	394-3110
FirstEnergy Corp 76 S Main St *NYSE: FE* ■ **Fax Area Code:* 330 ■ *TF:* 800-646-0400 ■ *Web:* www.firstenergycorp.com	Akron	OH	44308	800-646-0400	384-3866*
Fortis Inc 139 Water St Suite 201 *TSE: FTS* ■ *Web:* www.fortisinc.com	Saint John's	NL	A1B3T2	709-737-2800	737-5307
FPL Group Inc *NextEra Energy Inc* 700 Universe Blvd *NYSE: FPL* ■ *Web:* www.nexteraenergy.com	Juno Beach	FL	33408	561-694-4000	694-4620
Great Plains Energy Inc 1200 Main St PO Box 418679 *NYSE: GXP* ■ *Web:* www.greatplainsenergy.com	Kansas City	MO	64106	816-556-2200	556-2884
Holly Energy Partners LP 100 Crescent Ct Suite 1600 *NYSE: HEP* ■ *TF:* 800-453-5658 ■ *Web:* www.hollyenergy.com	Dallas	TX	75201	214-871-3555	871-3829
IDACORP Inc 1221 W Idaho St *NYSE: IDA* ■ *Web:* www.idacorpinc.com	Boise	ID	83702	208-388-2200	388-6914
Integrys Energy Group Inc 130 E Randolph Dr *NYSE: TEG* ■ *TF:* 800-699-1269 ■ *Web:* www.integrysgroup.com	Chicago	IL	60601	312-228-5400	
ITC Holdings Corp 39500 Orchard Hill Pl Suite 200 *NYSE: ITC* ■ *Web:* www.itctransco.com	Novi	MI	48375	248-374-7100	374-7136
Kaiser Midwest Inc 808 Hwy 34 W *Web:* www.cdcstihl.net	Marble Hill	MO	63764	573-238-2675	238-3088
Laclede Group Inc 720 Olive St Rm 1517 *NYSE: LG* ■ *TF:* 800-887-4173 ■ *Web:* www.thelacledegroup.com	Saint Louis	MO	63101	314-342-0500	
LG & E Energy Corp 220 W Main St *TF:* 800-331-7370 ■ *Web:* www.lgeenergy.com	Louisville	KY	40202	502-627-2000	627-3690
MidAmerican Energy Holdings Co 666 Grand Ave PO Box 657 *Web:* www.midamerican.com	Des Moines	IA	50303	515-242-4300	281-2981
National Fuel Gas Co 6363 Main St *NYSE: NFG* ■ *TF Cust Svc:* 800-365-3234 ■ *Web:* www.nationalfuelgas.com	Williamsville	NY	14221	716-857-7000	857-7206
National Grid 25 Research Dr *TF:* 888-424-2113 ■ *Web:* www.nationalgridus.com	Westborough	MA	01582	508-389-2000	389-2028
New Jersey Resources Corp 1415 Wyckoff Rd *NYSE: NJR* ■ **Fax:* Hum Res ■ *Web:* www.njresources.com	Wall	NJ	07719	732-938-1000	938-2134*
NSTAR 800 Boylston St *NYSE: NST* ■ **Fax Area Code:* 781 ■ *TF:* 800-592-2000 ■ *Web:* www.nstaronline.com	Boston	MA	02199	617-424-2000	441-8886*
OGE Energy Corp 321 N Harvey St *NYSE: OGE* ■ *TF:* 800-272-9741 ■ *Web:* www.oge.com	Oklahoma City	OK	73102	405-553-3000	553-3326
PG & E Corp 1 Market Plaza Suite 2400 *NYSE: PCG* ■ **Fax:* Hum Res ■ *TF:* 800-743-5000 ■ *Web:* www.pgecorp.com	San Francisco	CA	94105	415-267-7000	817-8245*
Pinnacle West Capital Corp 400 N 5th St *NYSE: PNW* ■ **Fax:* Investor Rel ■ *TF:* 800-457-2983 ■ *Web:* www.pinnaclewest.com	Phoenix	AZ	85004	602-250-1000	250-2741*
PNM Resources Inc Alvarado Sq *NYSE: PNM* ■ *TF:* 800-687-7854 ■ *Web:* www.pnmresources.com	Albuquerque	NM	87158	505-241-2700	241-4311
PPL Corp 2 N 9th St *NYSE: PPL* ■ *TF:* 800-342-5775 ■ *Web:* www.pplweb.com	Allentown	PA	18101	610-774-5151	774-6043
Progress Energy Inc 410 S Wilmington St PO Box 2041 *NYSE: PGN* ■ *TF:* 800-452-2777 ■ *Web:* www.progress-energy.com	Raleigh	NC	27601	919-546-6111	546-2920
Public Service Enterprise Group Inc 80 Pk Plaza *NYSE: PEG* ■ *TF Cust Svc:* 800-436-7734 ■ *Web:* www.pseg.com	Newark	NJ	07102	973-430-7000	623-5389
Puget Energy Inc 10885 NE 4th St *Web:* www.pugetenergy.com/pages/terms.html	Bellevue	WA	98004	425-454-6363	
Questar Corp 180 E 100 S PO Box 45360 *NYSE: STR* ■ *TF:* 800-323-5517 ■ *Web:* www.questarcorp.com	Salt Lake City	UT	84145	801-324-5000	324-3880
RGC Resources Inc 519 Kimball Ave PO Box 13007 *NASDAQ: RGCO* ■ **Fax:* Hum Res ■ *Web:* www.rgcresources.com	Roanoke	VA	24016	540-777-4427	777-3957*
SCANA Corp 220 Operation Way *NYSE: SCG* ■ *TF:* 800-251-7234 ■ *Web:* www.scana.com	Cayce	SC	29033	803-217-9000	933-8224
SEMCO Energy Inc 1411 3rd St Suite A *TF:* 888-427-1427 ■ *Web:* www.semcoenergy.com	Port Huron	MI	48060	888-427-1427	
Sempra Energy Corp 101 Ash St *NYSE: SRE* ■ *TF:* 800-411-7343 ■ *Web:* www.sempra.com	San Diego	CA	92101	619-696-2000	696-9202
SJW Corp 110 W Taylor St *NYSE: SJW* ■ *Web:* www.sjwater.com	San Jose	CA	95110	408-279-7900	279-7917
South Jersey Industries Inc (SJI) Rt 54 1 S Jersey Plaza *NYSE: SJI* ■ *TF Cust Svc:* 888-766-9900 ■ *Web:* www.sjindustries.com	Folsom	NJ	08037	609-561-9000	561-8225
Southern Co 30 Ivan Allen Jr Blvd NW *NYSE: SO* ■ *Web:* www.southernco.com	Atlanta	GA	30308	404-506-5000	506-0455
Sprint Nextel Corp 2001 Edmund Halley Dr PO Box 4600 *NYSE: S* ■ **Fax Area Code:* 800 ■ *Web:* www.sprint.com	Reston	VA	20195	703-433-4000	327-5182*
Tokyo Gas Co Ltd 1540 Broadway Suite 3920 *Web:* www.tokyo-gas.co.jp/index_e.html	New York	NY	10036	646-865-0577	865-0592
UGI Corp 460 N Gulph Rd *NYSE: UGI* ■ **Fax:* Hum Res ■ *Web:* www.ugicorp.com	King of Prussia	PA	19406	610-337-1000	992-3215*
UIL Holdings Corp 157 Church St *NYSE: UIL* ■ *TF:* 800-722-5584 ■ *Web:* www.uil.com	New Haven	CT	06510	203-499-2000	499-3664
UniSource Energy Corp 1 S Church Ave Suite 100 *NYSE: UNS* ■ *TF:* 866-537-8709 ■ *Web:* www.uns.com	Tucson	AZ	85702	520-571-4000	884-3601
United Water Resources Inc 200 Old Hook Rd **Fax:* Hum Res ■ *Web:* www.unitedwater.com	Harrington Park	NJ	07640	201-767-9300	767-7142*
Unitil Corp 6 Liberty Ln W *AMEX: UTL* ■ *TF:* 800-852-3339 ■ *Web:* www.unitil.com	Hampton	NH	03842	603-772-0775	773-6605
Vectren Corp 411 NW Riverside Dr PO Box 209 *NYSE: VVC* ■ *TF:* 800-227-1376 ■ *Web:* www.vectren.com	Evansville	IN	47708	812-491-4000	491-4706
Westar Energy Inc 818 S Kansas Ave *NYSE: WR* ■ *TF:* 800-383-1183 ■ *Web:* www.westarenergy.com	Topeka	KS	66612	785-575-6300	575-6596
WGL Holdings Inc 101 Constitution Ave NW *NYSE: WGL* ■ *TF:* 800-752-7520 ■ *Web:* www.wglholdings.com	Washington	DC	20080	703-750-2000	750-4858
Wisconsin Energy Corp 231 W Michigan St *NYSE: WEC* ■ **Fax:* Mktg ■ *TF:* 800-558-3303 ■ *Web:* www.wisconsinenergy.com	Milwaukee	WI	53203	414-221-2345	221-4906*

364 HOME FURNISHINGS - WHOL

	City	State	Zip	Phone	Fax
AA Importing Co Inc 7700 Hall St *TF Cust Svc:* 800-325-0602 ■ *Web:* www.aaimporting.com	Saint Louis	MO	63147	314-383-8800	383-2608
Acme Linen Co Inc 5136 E Triggs St *TF:* 800-255-2263 ■ *Web:* www.acmelinen.com	City of Commerce	CA	90022	323-266-4000	267-5771
Adleta Co 1645 Diplomat Dr Suite 200 *TF:* 800-423-5382 ■ *Web:* www.adleta.com	Carrollton	TX	75006	972-620-5600	620-5666
Advanced M & D Sales Inc 2335 N Clark Ave *Web:* www.advancedmanddsales.com	Portland	OR	97227	503-284-7601	460-0612
Allure Home Creation Co Inc 85 Fulton St	Boonton	NJ	07005	973-402-8888	334-2383
American Accessories International Inc 550 W Main St Suite 825	Knoxville	TN	37902	865-525-9100	525-0889
B & F System Inc 3920 S Walton Walker *Web:* www.bnfusa.com	Dallas	TX	75236	214-333-2111	333-1511
Bishop Distributing Co 5200 36th St SE *TF Cust Svc:* 800-748-0363 ■ *Web:* www.bishopdistributing.com	Grand Rapids	MI	49512	616-942-9734	942-6073
Boston Warehouse Trading Corp 59 Davis Ave *TF:* 888-923-2982 ■ *Web:* www.bwtc.com	Norwood	CA	02062	781-769-8550	769-9468
BR Funsten & Co 5200 Watt Ct Suite B *TF:* 800-999-9260 ■ *Web:* www.brfunsten.com	Fairfield	CA	94543	707-864-5143	863-3879
Cambridge Silversmith Ltd 116 Lehigh Dr *TF:* 800-890-3366 ■ *Web:* www.cambridgesilversmiths.com	Fairfield	NJ	07004	973-227-4400	227-5600
CCA Global Partners 4301 Earth City Expy *TF:* 800-466-6984 ■ *Web:* www.ccaglobalpartners.com	St. Louis	MO	63045	314-506-0000	291-6674
CDC Distributors 10511 Medallion Dr	Cincinnati	OH	45241	513-771-3100	771-2920
Decorative Crafts Inc 50 Chestnut St *TF:* 800-431-4455 ■ *Web:* www.decorativecrafts.com	Greenwich	CT	06830	203-531-1500	531-1590
Derr Flooring Co Inc 525 Davisville Rd PO Box 912 *TF:* 800-523-3457 ■ *Web:* www.derrflooring.com	Willow Grove	PA	19090	215-657-6300	657-9830
Dimock Gould & Co 190 22nd St *TF:* 800-274-4013	Moline	IL	61265	309-797-0650	764-9922
Fabricut Inc 9303 E 46th St *TF:* 800-999-8200 ■ *Web:* www.fabricut.com	Tulsa	OK	74145	918-622-7700	627-1916
General Floor Industries Inc 190 Benigno Blvd *Web:* www.generalfloor.com	Bellmawr	NJ	08031	856-931-0012	931-0731
Harold Import Co Inc 747 Vassar Ave *TF:* 800-526-2163 ■ *Web:* www.haroldimport.com	Lakewood	NJ	08701	732-367-2800	364-3253
Hoboken Floors 5600 Bucknell Dr Sw *TF:* 877-356-2687	Atlanta	GA	30336	404-629-1425	349-9975
Home Essentials & Beyond Inc 3001 Woodbridge Ave *Web:* www.homeessentials.com	Edison	NJ	08837	732-590-3600	590-3665
Jacobs Trading Co 8090 Excelsior Blvd *Web:* www.jacobstrading.com	hopkins	MN	55341	763-843-2000	843-2101
James G Hardy & Co 24919 148th Rd *TF:* 800-847-4076 ■ *Web:* www.hardylinen.com	Rosedale	NY	11422	212-689-6680	686-1827
Jay Franco & Sons Inc 295 5th Ave 3rd Fl *Web:* www.jfranco.com	New York	NY	10016	212-679-3022	685-4864
JJ Haines & Co Inc 6950 Aviation Blvd *TF:* 800-922-9248 ■ *Web:* www.jjhaines.com	Glen Burnie	MD	21061	410-760-4040	760-4045
Kiefer Specialty Flooring Inc 2910 Falling Waters Blvd *TF:* 800-322-5448 ■ *Web:* www.kieferfloors.com	Lindenhurst	IL	60046	847-245-8450	245-8589
KovalWilliamson 11208 47th Ave W *TF:* 800-972-4782 ■ *Web:* www.kwawest.com	Mukilteo	WA	98275	425-347-4249	347-2368
Larson Distributing Co Inc 5925 Broadway *TF:* 800-736-3750 ■ *Web:* www.larsondistributing.com	Denver	CO	80216	303-296-7253	296-8583
Longust Distributing Inc 2432 W Birchwood Ave *TF:* 800-352-0521 ■ *Web:* www.longust.com	Mesa	AZ	85202	480-820-6244	345-0324
Lonseal Inc 928 E 238th St *TF:* 800-832-7111 ■ *Web:* www.lonseal.com	Carson	CA	90745	310-830-7111	830-9986
Louis Bornstein & Co 321 Washington St *TF Sales:* 800-842-1111	Somerville	MA	02143	617-776-3555	623-1913
M Block & Sons Inc 5020 W 73rd St *TF:* 800-621-8845 ■ *Web:* www.mblock.com	Bedford Park	IL	60638	708-728-8400	728-0022

				Phone	Fax
Momeni Inc 36 E 31st St 2nd Fl	New York	NY	10016	212-532-9577	779-9568
TF: 800-536-6778 ■ *Web:* www.momeni.com					
Mottahedeh & Co 41 Madison Ave	New York	NY	10010	212-685-3050	213-3978
TF: 800-242-3050 ■ *Web:* www.mottahedeh.com					
Naturwood Home Furnishings Inc 2711 Mercantile Dr	Rancho Cordova	CA	95742	916-638-2424	638-7571
Web: www.naturwood.com					
OneCoast Network LLC 230 Spring St Suite 1800	Atlanta	GA	30303	610-524-6400	524-6429
TF: 866-592-5514 ■ *Web:* www.onecoast.com/index.asp					
Onthank Co Inc PO Box 1462	Des Moines	IA	50306	515-265-9801	
TF: 800-747-1811 ■ *Web:* www.onthank.com					
Palo Duro Hardwoods Inc 12655 E 42nd Ave Suite 60	Denver	CO	80239	303-375-0280	375-9747
TF: 800-783-3309 ■ *Web:* www.palodurocollection.com					
Peking Handicraft Inc 1388 San Mateo Ave	South San Francisco	CA	94080	650-871-3788	871-3781
TF: 800-872-6888 ■ *Web:* www.pkhc.com					
Retro Inc 295 5th Ave Suite 1102	New York	NY	10016	212-213-8838	213-8999
Web: www.aussino.com					
Revere Mills Inc 2860 S River Rd Suite 250	Des Plaines	IL	60018	847-759-6800	759-6840
TF: 800-367-8258					
Sewing Source Inc The PO Box 639	Spring Hope	NC	27882	252-478-3900	
TF: 800-849-6945 ■ *Web:* www.thesewingsourceinc.com					
Shaheen Carpet Mills Inc 3742 US Hwy 41 NW PO Box 167	Resaca	GA	30735	706-629-9544	625-5341
Web: www.shaheencarpet.com					
Sobel Westex Inc 2670 Western Ave	Las Vegas	NV	89109	702-735-4973	735-4957
TF: 800-282-3041 ■ *Web:* www.sobelwestex.com					
Southern Tile Distributors Inc PO Box 12209	Norfolk	VA	23541	757-855-8041	
TF: 800-333-8970 ■ *Web:* www.southerntile.com					
Stark Carpet Corp D & D Bldg 979 3rd Ave 11th Fl	New York	NY	10022	212-752-9000	758-4342
TF: 800-223-1224 ■ *Web:* www.starkcarpetcorp.com					
T & A Supply Co Inc 6821 S 216th St Bldg A PO Box 927	Kent	WA	98032	253-872-3682	282-3796*
**Fax Area Code:* 206 ■ *TF:* 800-562-2857 ■ *Web:* www.tasupply.com					
Thompson Olde Inc 3250 Camino Del Sol	Oxnard	CA	93030	805-983-0388	983-1849
TF: 800-827-1565 ■ *Web:* www.oldethompson.com					
Three Hands Corp 13259 Ralston Ave	Sylmar	CA	91342	818-833-1200	833-1212
TF: 800-443-5443 ■ *Web:* www.threehands.com					
Tin Box Co of America Inc The PO Box 9068	Farmingdale	NY	11735	631-845-1600	845-1610
TF: 800-888-8467 ■ *Web:* www.tinboxco.com					
Trade Am International Inc 6045 Atlantic Bolevard	Norcross	GA	30071	770-263-6144	333-9448*
**Fax Area Code:* 800 ■ *Web:* www.tradeam.com					
Wanke Cascade Co 6330 N Cutter Cir	Portland	OR	97217	503-289-8609	285-5640
TF: 800-365-5053 ■ *Web:* www.wanke.com					
WMF/USA 85 Price Pkwy Fl 14	Farmingdale	NY	11735	631-293-3990	293-3561
TF: 800-999-6347 ■ *Web:* www.corporate.wmfamericas.com					
Zak Designs Inc 1604 S Garfield Rd	Airway Heights	WA	99001	509-244-0555	244-0704
TF: 800-331-1089 ■ *Web:* www.zak.com					

365 HOME FURNISHINGS STORES

SEE ALSO Department Stores p. 1783; Furniture Stores p. 1899

				Phone	Fax
Altmeyer Home Stores Inc 6515 Rt 22	Delmont	PA	15626	724-468-3434	468-3233
TF: 800-394-6628 ■ *Web:* www.altmeyers.com					
Anna's Linens Inc 3550 Hyland Ave	Costa Mesa	CA	92626	714-850-0504	850-9170
Web: www.annaslinens.com					
Bazaar Home Fashions 7958 Ohio River Rd	Wheelersburg	OH	45694	740-574-0777	574-0779
TF: 877-764-0305 ■ *Web:* www.bazaarhomefashions.com					
Bed Bath & Beyond Inc 650 Liberty Ave	Union	NJ	07083	908-688-0888	688-6483
NASDAQ: BBBY ■ *TF:* 800-462-3966 ■ *Web:* www.bedbathandbeyond.com					
Besco Electric Supply Co 711 S 14th St	Leesburg	FL	34748	352-787-4542	365-0554
TF: 800-541-6618 ■ *Web:* www.bescoelectric.com					
Bridge Kitchenware Inc 711 3rd Ave	New York	NY	10017	212-688-4220	758-5387
TF: 800-274-3435 ■ *Web:* www.bridgekitchenware.com					
Bromberg & Co Inc 123 N 20th St	Birmingham	AL	35203	205-252-0221	458-0458
TF: 800-633-4616 ■ *Web:* www.brombergs.com					
Calvert Retail LP 100 W Rockland Rd Suite A PO Box 302	Montchanin	DE	19710	302-622-8811	622-8602
Web: www.calvertretail.com					
Chef's Catalog 5070 Centennial Blvd	Colorado Springs	CO	80919	972-969-3100	967-2433*
**Fax Area Code:* 800 ■ *TF Cust Svc:* 800-884-2433 ■ *Web:* www.chefscatalog.com					
Container Store The 500 Freeport Pkwy	Coppell	TX	75019	972-538-6000	
TF: 800-733-3532 ■ *Web:* www.containerstore.com					
Cooking.com 2850 Ocean Pk Blvd Suite 310	Santa Monica	CA	90405	310-450-3270	450-0615
TF: 800-663-8810 ■ *Web:* www.cooking.com					
Cost Plus Inc 200 4th St	Oakland	CA	94607	510-893-7300	893-3681
NASDAQ: CPWM ■ *TF:* 800-777-4665 ■ *Web:* www.worldmarket.com					
Design Within Reach Inc 225 Bush St 20th Fl	San Francisco	CA	94104	415-676-6500	676-6794
NASDAQ: DWRI ■ *TF:* 800-944-2233 ■ *Web:* www.dwr.com					
DirectBuy Inc 101 W 84th Dr Suite C	Merrillville	IN	46410	219-755-6211	755-6208
TF: 800-827-6400 ■ *Web:* www.directbuy.com					
Edward Joy Electric 905 Canal St	Syracuse	NY	13217	315-474-3361	479-8604
Web: www.edwardjoyelectric.com					
Euromarket Designs Inc 1250 Techny Rd	Northbrook	IL	60062	847-272-2888	272-5276
Web: www.crateandbarrel.com					
Flowerama of America Inc 3165 W Airline Hwy	Waterloo	IA	50703	319-291-6004	291-8676
TF: 800-728-6004 ■ *Web:* www.flowerama.com					
Foreside Co 33 Hutcherson Dr	Gorham	ME	04038	207-854-4000	854-3300
TF Cust Svc: 800-359-8380 ■ *Web:* www.foreside.com					
FurnitureFind.com Inc 311 W Jefferson Blvd	South Bend	IN	46601	574-299-2700	299-2645
TF: 800-362-7632 ■ *Web:* www.furniturefind.com					
Garden Ridge Corp 19411 Atrium Pl Suite 170	Houston	TX	77084	832-391-7201	
Web: www.gardenridge.com					
Geary's Stores Inc 351 N Beverly Dr	Beverly Hills	CA	90210	310-273-4741	859-8950
TF: 800-793-6670 ■ *Web:* www.gearys.com					
Gracious Home 1220 3rd Ave	New York	NY	10021	212-517-6300	249-1534
TF: 800-338-7809 ■ *Web:* www.gracioushome.com					
Granite City Electric Supply Co 19 Quincy Ave	Quincy	MA	02169	617-472-6500	472-8661
TF: 800-850-9400 ■ *Web:* www.granitecityelectric.com					
Gump's 135 Post St	San Francisco	CA	94108	415-982-1616	984-9374
TF: 800-766-7628 ■ *Web:* www.gumps.com					
Habitat Housewares 3801 Old Seward Hwy Suite 7	Anchorage	AK	99503	907-561-1856	563-5863
Web: www.habitathousewares.com					
Hammacher Schlemmer & Co 9307 N Milwaukee Ave	Niles	IL	60714	847-581-8600	581-8616
TF: 800-233-4800 ■ *Web:* www.hammacher.com					
Happi Stores Inc 6645 Poplar Ave Suite 105	Germantown	TN	38138	901-758-0034	758-8018
Home Accents Mart 2300 McFarland Blvd	Northport	AL	35476	205-339-6550	339-6553
HomeGoods Inc 770 Cochituate Rd	Framingham	MA	01701	508-390-3000	
Web: www.homegoods.com					
HomePortfolio Inc 288 Walnut St Suite 300	Newton	MA	02460	617-965-0565	965-4082
TF: 800-246-8136 ■ *Web:* www.homeportfolio.com					
International Cutlery Ltd 155 E 55th St Suite 6D	New York	NY	10022	212-924-7300	865-0806*
**Fax Area Code:* 646 ■ *TF:* 866-487-6164 ■ *Web:* www.internationalcutlery.com					
Jackalope Pottery 2820 Cerrillos Rd	Santa Fe	NM	87507	505-471-8539	471-6710
TF: 800-753-7757 ■ *Web:* www.jackalope.com					
Kirkland's Inc 431 Smith Ln	Jackson	TN	38301	615-872-4995	
NASDAQ: KIRK ■ *TF:* 877-208-6668 ■ *Web:* www.kirklands.com					
Kitchen Collection Inc 71 E Water St	Chillicothe	OH	45601	740-773-9150	774-0590
TF: 800-292-9150 ■ *Web:* www.kitchencollection.com					
Kitchen Fantasy 27576 Ynez Rd Suite H9	Temecula	CA	92591	951-693-4264	693-4265
Web: www.kitchenfantasy.com					
Linens 'n Things Inc 6 Brighton Rd	Clifton	NJ	07015	973-778-1300	778-0822
TF: 866-568-7378 ■ *Web:* www.lnt.com					
Linon Home Décor Products Inc 22 Jericho Tpke	Mineola	NY	11501	516-699-1000	699-1001
Web: www.linon.com					
Luxury Linens Corp 1830 Rt 130 N	Burlington	NJ	08016	609-387-7800	239-8242
Mattress Firm Inc 5815 Gulf Fwy	Houston	TX	77023	713-923-1090	923-1096
Web: www.mattressfirm.com					
Michael C Fina Inc 545 5th Ave	New York	NY	10017	212-557-2500	557-3862
TF: 800-289-3462 ■ *Web:* www.michaelcfina.com					
Mikasa Inc 100 Plaza Dr	Secaucus	NJ	07094	201-867-9210	867-0580
TF Cust Svc: 800-833-4681 ■ *Web:* www.mikasa.com					
Nevada Contract Carpet 6840 W Patrick Ln	Las Vegas	NV	89118	702-362-3033	362-5455
Web: www.nccfloors.com					
Pier 1 Imports Inc 100 Pier 1 Pl	Fort Worth	TX	76102	817-878-8000	
NYSE: PIR ■ *TF:* 800-245-4595 ■ *Web:* www.pier1.com					
Pierce's Flooring PO Box 80667	Billings	MT	59108	406-652-4666	652-1884
Web: www.pierceflooring.com					
Replacements Ltd PO Box 26029	Greensboro	NC	27420	336-697-3000	697-3100
TF: 800-737-5223 ■ *Web:* www.replacements.com					
Restoration Hardware Inc 2900 N MacArthur Dr Suite 100	Tracy	CA	95376	800-910-9836	
TF: 800-910-9836 ■ *Web:* www.restorationhardware.com					
Seattle Lighting Fixture Co 222 2nd Ave Ext S	Seattle	WA	98104	206-622-1962	447-1660
TF Cust Svc: 800-689-1000 ■ *Web:* www.seattlelighting.com					
Shreve Crump & Low Co Inc 440 Boylston St	Boston	MA	02116	617-267-9100	247-6450
TF: 800-225-7088 ■ *Web:* www.shrevecrumpandlow.com					
Southern Wholesale Flooring Co Inc 955B Cobb Pl Blvd PO Box 440069	Kennesaw	GA	30160	770-514-7110	514-7310
TF: 800-282-7590 ■ *Web:* www.swfloor.com					
Sultan & Sons 6601 lions Rd Suite E8	coconut creek	FL	33069	954-782-6600	590-3898
TF: 800-299-6601 ■ *Web:* www.sultanandsons.com					
Sur La Table 5701 6th Ave S Suite 486	Seattle	WA	98108	206-682-7175	
TF: 800-243-0852 ■ *Web:* www.surlatable.com					
TJX Cos Inc 770 Cochituate Rd	Framingham	MA	01701	508-390-1000	390-2091
NYSE: TJX ■ *TF:* 800-926-6299 ■ *Web:* www.tjx.com					
Villeroy & Boch Tableware Ltd 5 Vaughn Dr Suite 303	Princeton	NJ	08540	609-734-7800	734-7840
TF: 800-845-5376 ■ *Web:* www.villeroy-boch.com					
Waterford Wedgwood USA Inc 1330 Campus Pkwy	Wall	NJ	07719	732-938-5800	938-6915
Web: www.wwusa.com					
Williams-Sonoma Inc 3250 Van Ness Ave	San Francisco	CA	94109	415-421-7900	616-8359
NYSE: WSM ■ *TF:* 800-541-1262 ■ *Web:* www.williams-sonomainc.com					
Williamsburg Pottery PO Box 123	Lightfoot	VA	23090	757-564-3326	564-7514
TF: 800-768-8379 ■ *Web:* www.williamsburgpottery.com					
Winsome Trading Inc 16111 Woodinville Redmo	Woodinville	WA	98072	425-483-8888	483-4141
Web: www.winsomewood.com					
Z Gallerie Inc 1855 W 139th St	Gardena	CA	90249	310-630-1200	527-2792
TF: 800-358-8288 ■ *Web:* www.zgallerie.com					
Zabar's & Co Inc 2245 Broadway	New York	NY	10024	212-787-2000	580-4477
TF: 800-697-6301 ■ *Web:* www.zabars.com					

366 HOME HEALTH SERVICES

SEE ALSO Hospices p. 2028

				Phone	Fax
Access Plans Inc 900 36th Ave NW, Suite 105	Norman	OK	73072	405-579-8525	734-9253*
OTC: APNC ■ **Fax Area Code:* 770 ■ *TF:* 800-699-9472 ■ *Web:* www.alliancehealthcard.com					
AdCare Health Systems Inc 5057 Troy Rd	Springfield	OH	45502	937-964-8974	864-8961
AMEX: ADK ■ *Web:* www.adcarehealth.com					
Alacare Home Health & Hospice 2400 John Hawkins Pkwy	Birmingham	AL	35244	205-981-8000	981-8743
TF: 800-852-4724 ■ *Web:* www.alacare.com					

Phone | Fax

Allied Healthcare International Inc
245 Pk AVe 39th Fl ... New York NY 10167 212-750-0064 750-7221
NASDAQ: AHCI ■ *Web:* www.alliedhealthcare.com
Almost Family Inc
9510 Ormsby Stn Rd Suite 300 ... Louisville KY 40223 502-891-1000 891-8067
NASDAQ: AFAM ■ *TF:* 800-845-6987 ■ *Web:* www.almostfamily.com
Altamed Health Services Corp
500 Citadel Dr Suite 490 ... Los Angeles CA 90040 323-725-8751 889-7399
TF: 877-462-2582 ■ *Web:* www.altamed.org
Amedisys Inc
5959 S Sherwood Forest Blvd Suite 300 ... Baton Rouge LA 70816 225-292-2031 292-8163
NASDAQ: AMED ■ *TF:* 800-467-2662 ■ *Web:* www.amedisys.com
American HomePatient Inc
5200 Maryland Way Suite 400 ... Brentwood TN 37027 615-221-8884 373-1947
TF: 800-890-7271 ■ *Web:* www.ahom.com
Androscoggin Home Health Services Inc
PO Box 819 ... Lewiston ME 04243 207-777-7740 777-7748
TF: 800-482-7412 ■ *Web:* www.ahch.org
Anthelio Healthcare Solutions Inc
5400 LBJ Fwy Suite 200 ... Dallas TX 75240 214-257-7000 257-7042
Web: www.antheliohealth.com
Apria Healthcare Group Inc
26220 Enterprise Ct ... Lake Forest CA 92630 949-639-2000
NYSE: AHG ■ *TF:* 800-277-4288 ■ *Web:* www.apria.com
Aroostook Home Health Services
658 Main St Suite 2 ... Caribou ME 04736 207-492-8290 492-8245
TF: 877-688-9977
Ashtabula Regional Home Health Services
PO Box 1428 ... Ashtabula OH 44005 440-992-4663 992-0687
TF: 800-722-3330 ■ *Web:* www.acmchealth.org
Bayada Nurses Home Care Specialists
290 Chester Ave ... Moorestown NJ 08057 856-231-1000 231-1955
Web: www.bayada.com
Brandywine Nursing & Rehabilitation Center Inc
505 Greenbank Rd ... Wilmington DE 19808 302-998-0101 998-2922
Web: www.brandywinenursing.org
Cambridge Home Health Care Inc
4085 Embassy Pkwy ... Akron OH 44333 800-772-2929 668-1060*
**Fax Area Code:* 330 ■ *TF:* 800-772-2929 ■ *Web:* www.cambridgehomehealth.com
Care Partners 68 Sweeten Creek Rd ... Asheville NC 28803 828-252-2255 252-9355
TF: 800-627-1533 ■ *Web:* www.carepartners.org
CareSouth Homecare Professionals
1 10th St # 500 ... Augusta GA 30901 706-855-5533 854-7398
TF: 800-241-3363 ■ *Web:* www.caresouth.com
Carter Healthcare 3105 S Meridian Ave ... Oklahoma City OK 73119 405-947-7700 947-7300
TF: 888-951-1112 ■ *Web:* www.carterhealthcare.com
Christian Homes Inc 200 N Postville Dr ... Lincoln IL 62656 217-732-9651 732-8686
Web: www.christianhomes.org
ComForcare Senior Services Inc
2510 Telegraph Rd Suite 100 ... Bloomfield Hills MI 48302 248-745-9700 745-9763
TF: 800-886-4044 ■ *Web:* www.comforcare.com
Comfort Keepers Franchising Inc
6640 Poe Ave Suite 200 ... Dayton OH 45414 937-264-1933 264-3103
TF: 800-387-2415 ■ *Web:* www.comfortkeepers.com
Confident Care Corp 3 University Plaza Dr ... Hackensack NJ 07601 201-498-9400 498-1556
TF: 866-839-2273 ■ *Web:* www.confidentcarecorp.com
Continucare Corp
7200 Corporate Ctr Dr Suite 600 ... Miami FL 33126 305-500-2000 500-2080
AMEX: CNU ■ *TF:* 888-350-7515 ■ *Web:* www.continucare.com
Coram Healthcare Corp 1675 Broadway Suite 900 ... Denver CO 80202 303-292-4973 298-0043
TF: 800-267-2642 ■ *Web:* www.coramhc.com
Delaware Hospice Inc 3515 Silverside Rd ... Wilmington DE 19810 302-478-5707 479-2586
TF: 800-838-9800 ■ *Web:* www.delawarehospice.org
Episcopal Health Services Inc
700 Hicksville Rd ... Bethpage NY 11714 516-349-6100 349-6149
Web: www.ehs.org
General Healthcare Resources Inc
2250 Hickory Rd Suite 240 ... Plymouth Meeting PA 19462 610-834-1122 834-7525
TF: 800-879-4471 ■ *Web:* www.ghresources.com
Gentiva Health Services Inc
3350 Riverwood Pkwy Suite 1400 ... Atlanta GA 30339 770-951-6450
NASDAQ: GTIV ■ *Web:* www.gentiva.com
Griswold Special Care Inc
717 Bethlehem Pike Suite 300 ... Erdenheim PA 19038 215-402-0200 402-0202
TF: 888-777-7630 ■ *Web:* www.griswoldspecialcare.com
Gurwin Jewish Nursing & Rehabilitation Ctr
68 Hauppauge Rd ... Commack NY 11725 631-715-2600 715-2940
Web: www.gurwin.org
Help At Home Inc 1 N State St Suite 800 ... Chicago IL 60602 312-762-0900 704-0022
TF: 800-404-3191 ■ *Web:* www.helpathome.com
Home Bound Healthcare Inc 1615 Vollmer Rd ... Flossmoor IL 60422 708-798-0800
TF: 800-444-7028 ■ *Web:* www.homeboundhealth.com
Home Health Corp of America Inc
Healthcare Investment Corp of America
620 Freedom Business Ctr Suite 105 ... King of Prussia PA 19406 484-690-1200 751-9100
Web: www.healthinvcorp.com
Home Helpers Inc
10700 Montgomery Rd Suite 300 ... Cincinnati OH 45242 800-216-4196 563-2691*
**Fax Area Code:* 513 ■ *TF:* 800-216-4196 ■ *Web:* www.homehelpers.cc
Home Instead Inc 13330 California St Suite 200 ... Omaha NE 68154 402-498-4466 498-5757
TF: 888-484-5759 ■ *Web:* www.homeinstead.com
Home IV Care & Nutritional Service
PO Box 700 ... Stuarts Draft VA 24477 540-932-3000 932-3028
TF: 800-552-6576 ■ *Web:* www.homeivcare.com
Interim HealthCare Inc
1601 Sawgrass Corporate Pkwy ... Sunrise FL 33323 954-858-6000 858-2820
TF: 800-338-7786 ■ *Web:* www.interimhealthcare.com
Kelly Home Care Services Inc
999 W Big Beaver Rd ... Troy MI 48084 248-362-4444 244-4922*
**Fax:* Hum Res ■ *TF:* 800-937-5355 ■ *Web:* www.kellyassistedliving.com
Legum Home Health Care PO Box 700 ... Stuarts Draft VA 24477 540-932-3000 932-3028
LHC Group LLC 420 W Pinhook Rd Suite A ... Lafayette LA 70503 337-233-1307 235-8037
NASDAQ: LHCG ■ *TF:* 800-489-1307 ■ *Web:* www.lhcgroup.com

Phone | Fax

Lifetime Care 3111 Winton Rd S ... Rochester NY 14623 585-214-1000 214-1136
Web: www.lifetimecare.org
Lincare Holdings Inc 19387 US 19 N ... Clearwater FL 33764 727-530-7700 532-9692
NASDAQ: LNCR ■ *TF:* 800-284-2006 ■ *Web:* www.lincare.com
Living Assistance Services Inc
28 W Eagle Rd Suite 204 ... Havertown PA 19083 610-924-0630 924-9690
TF: 800-365-4189 ■ *Web:* www.livingassistance.com
Long Hill Co The 580 Long Hill Ave ... Shelton CT 06484 203-944-8283
Web: www.longhillcompany.com
Maxim Healthcare Services
7227 Lee Deforest Dr ... Columbia MD 21046 410-910-1500 910-1615
TF: 866-401-5586 ■ *Web:* www.maxhealth.com
Medical Center at Princeton Home Care
208 Bunn Dr ... Princeton NJ 08540 609-497-4900 497-4933
TF: 800-584-4153 ■ *Web:* www.princetonhcs.org
Medical Services of America Inc (MSA)
171 Monroe Ln ... Lexington SC 29072 803-957-0500 342-6190*
**Fax Area Code:* 888 ■ *TF:* 800-845-5850 ■ *Web:* www.msa-corp.com
Minnesota Visiting Nurse Agency
3433 Broadway St Ne ... Minneapolis MN 55413 612-617-4600 617-4782
Web: www.mvna.org
National Home Health Care Corp
700 White Plains Rd Suite 275 ... Scarsdale NY 10583 914-722-9000 722-9239
Web: www.nhhc.net
New York Health Care Inc 1850 McDonald Ave ... Brooklyn NY 11223 718-375-6700 375-1555
Web: www.nyhc.com
North Los Angel County Regional Ctr
15400 Sherman Way Suite 170 ... Van Nuys CA 91406 818-778-1900 756-6140
Web: www.nlacrc.org
Ohel Children's Home & Family Services Inc
4510 16th Ave ... Brooklyn NY 11204 718-851-6300
TF: 800-603-6435 ■ *Web:* www.ohelfamily.org
Pediatric Services of America Inc
310 Technology Pkwy ... Norcross GA 30092 770-441-1580 417-3252*
NASDAQ: PSAI ■ **Fax:* Hum Res ■ *TF:* 800-897-6373 ■ *Web:* www.psahealthcare.com
Personal-Touch Home Care Inc
186-18 Hillside Ave ... Jamaica NY 11432 718-468-2500 264-5834*
**Fax:* Hum Res ■ *TF:* 800-937-4747 ■ *Web:* www.pthomecare.com
Prs Inc 1761 Old Meadow Rd Suite 100 ... McLean VA 22102 703-536-9000 448-3723
Web: www.prsinc.org
Right at Home Inc 11949 Q St Suite 118 ... Omaha NE 68137 402-697-7537 697-0289
TF: 877-697-7537 ■ *Web:* www.rightathome.net
Selfhelp Community Services Inc
520 8th Ave 5th Fl ... New York NY 10018 212-971-7600 967-4784
Web: www.selfhelp.net
Sta-Home Health Agency Inc
406 Briarwood Dr Bldg 200 ... Jackson MS 39206 601-956-5100 956-3003
TF: 800-782-4663 ■ *Web:* www.sta-home.com
Star Multi Care Services Inc
115 Broad Hollow Rd Suite 275 ... Melville NY 11747 631-423-6689 427-5466
TF: 877-920-0600 ■ *Web:* www.starmulticare.com
Tender Loving Care Health Care Services (TLC)
1983 Marcus Ave Suite 200 ... Lake Success NY 11042 516-358-1000 358-2465
Ultra Care Home Medical 1815 Gardner Rd ... Broadview IL 60155 800-244-7404 450-1638*
**Fax Area Code:* 708 ■ *TF:* 800-222-9444 ■ *Web:* www.ultracarehm.com
Visiting Nurse Assn of Morris County (inc)
38 Elm St ... Morristown NJ 07960 973-539-1216
TF: 800-938-4748 ■ *Web:* www.vnannj.org
Visiting Nurse Assn Of Se Michigan
25900 Greenfield Rd ... Oak Park MI 48237 248-967-1440
TF: 800-882-5720 ■ *Web:* www.vna.org
VITAS Healthcare Corp
100 S Biscayne Blvd Suite 1500 ... Miami FL 33131 305-374-4143 350-6784*
**Fax:* Acctg ■ *TF:* 866-418-4827 ■ *Web:* www.vitas.com
We Care Health Services Inc
151 Bloor St W Suite 602 ... Toronto ON M5S1S3 416-922-7601 922-6280
TF: 888-429-3227 ■ *Web:* www.wecare.ca
Williamsville Suburban LLC
193 S Union Rd PO Bos 9039 ... Williamsville NY 14221 716-632-6152
Web: www.legacyhealthcarellc.com
Hospice Atlanta-Visiting Nurse Health System
1244 Pk Vista Dr ... Atlanta GA 30319 404-869-3000 869-3098
TF: 800-287-7849 ■ *Web:* www.vnhs.org

367 HOME IMPROVEMENT CENTERS

SEE ALSO Construction Materials p. 1732

Phone | Fax

Acadiana Shell & Limestone Inc PO Box 280 ... Abbeville LA 70511 337-893-1111
Web: www.acadianashell.com
Ace Hardware Corp 2200 Kensington Ct ... Oak Brook IL 60523 630-990-6600 990-6572*
**Fax:* Mktg ■ *Web:* www.acehardware.com
Ace Miner's Hardware Inc
1056 W Grand Ave ... Grover Beach CA 93433 805-489-0158 489-2971
Web: www.minershardware.com
Alaska Industrial Hardware Inc
2192 Viking Dr ... Anchorage AK 99501 907-276-7201 258-3054
TF: 800-478-7201 ■ *Web:* www.aihalaska.com
All American Home Ctr 7201 Firestone Blvd ... Downey CA 90241 562-927-8666 928-0633
Web: www.aahc.com
Arlington Coal & Lumber Co Inc 41 Pk Ave ... Arlington MA 02476 781-643-8100 643-7414
TF: 800-649-8101 ■ *Web:* www.arlcoal.com
Atlanta Hardwood Corp 5596 Riverview Rd SE ... Mableton GA 30126 404-792-2290
TF: 800-476-5393 ■ *Web:* www.hardwoodweb.com
Beronio Lumber Co 2525 Marin St ... San Francisco CA 94124 415-824-4300 824-3706
Web: www.beronio.com
Big B Lumberteria 6600 Brentwood Blvd ... Brentwood CA 94513 925-634-2442 634-9839
Web: www.bigblumber.com
Big L Corp PO Box 134 ... Sheridan MI 48884 989-291-3232 291-5751
Web: www.big-l-lumber.com

				Phone	Fax
Bloedorn Lumber Co Inc PO Box 1077 *Web:* www.bloedornlumber.com	Torrington	WY	82240	307-532-2151	532-3760
BMC West Corp PO Box 70006 *Web:* www.bmcwest.com	Boise	ID	83707	208-331-4300	331-4366
Brunsell Bros Ltd 4611 W Beltline Hwy *Web:* www.brunsell.com	Madison	WI	53711	608-275-7171	275-7179
Busy Beaver Bldg Centers Inc 3130 William Pitt Way Uparc Bldg A-6 *Web:* www.busybeaver.com	Pittsburgh	PA	15238	412-828-2323	828-2395
Cape Cod Lumber Co Inc PO Box 2013 *TF:* 800-698-8225 ■ *Web:* www.cclco.com	Abington	MA	02351	781-878-0715	871-6726
Carter Cos 601 Tallmadge Rd *TF:* 877-586-2374 ■ *Web:* www.carterlumber.com	Kent	OH	44240	330-673-6100	678-6134
Carter Lumber Co Inc 601 Tallmadge Rd *TF:* 877-586-2374 ■ *Web:* www.carterlumber.com	Kent	OH	44240	330-673-6100	678-6134
Carter-Jones Lumber Co 601 Tallmadge Rd *TF:* 877-586-2374 ■ *Web:* www.carterlumber.com/main.asp?id=25	Kent	OH	44240	330-673-6100	678-6134
Century Everglades LLC 6991 SW 8th St *Web:* www.evergladesdesign.com	Miami	FL	33144	305-261-1155	261-2772
Chinook Lumber Inc 17606 SR- 9 SE *Web:* www.chinooklumber.com	Snohomish	WA	98296	360-668-8800	863-6498
Choo Choo Build-it Mart 325 Commerce Loop *Web:* www.choochoobuilditmart.com	Vidalia	GA	30474	912-537-8964	537-4839
City Mill Co Ltd 660 N Nimitz Hwy *Web:* www.citymill.com	Honolulu	HI	96817	808-533-3811	524-8092
Contractor's Warehouse 3222 Winona Way Suite 201 **Fax:* Hum Res ■ *TF:* 800-789-8060 ■ *Web:* www.contractorswarehouse.com	North Highlands	CA	95660	916-331-5934	331-4658*
Cox Lumber Co 3300 Fairfield Ave S *Web:* www.coxlumber.com	Saint Petersburg	FL	33712	727-327-4503	327-5393
Dixieline Lumber Co Inc 3250 Sports Arena Blvd *Web:* www.dixieline.com	San Diego	CA	92110	619-224-4120	225-8192
Doug Ashy Bldg Materials Inc 4950 Johnston St *Web:* www.dougashybuilding.com	Lafayette	LA	70503	337-984-2110	989-9569
EBS Bldg Supplies 261 State St *TF:* 800-244-7134 ■ *Web:* www.ebsbuild.com	Ellsworth	ME	04605	207-667-7134	667-6043
Elementis Specialties Inc 329 Wyckoffs Mill Rd *Web:* www.elementis-specialties.com	Hightstown	NJ	08520	609-443-2000	443-2422
Ganahl Lumber Co 1220 E Ball Rd *Web:* www.ganahl.com	Anaheim	CA	92805	714-772-5444	772-0639
Grossman's Inc 90 Hawes Way *Web:* www.bargain-outlets.com	Stoughton	MA	02072	781-297-3300	297-0180
Hacienda Home Centers Inc PO Box 30148 *Web:* www.hacienda.doitbest.com	Albuquerque	NM	87190	505-884-8811	884-8959
Hamshaw Lumber Inc PO Box 725 *Web:* www.hamshawlumber.com	Keene	NH	03431	603-352-6506	352-8455
Hayward Lumber Co 429 Front St *Web:* www.haywardlumber.com	Salinas	CA	93901	831-755-8800	755-8821
Herrman Lumber Co 1917 S State Hwy N *TF:* 888-238-9778 ■ *Web:* www.herrmanlumber.com	Springfield	MO	65802	417-862-3737	862-8934
Home Depot Inc 2455 Paces Ferry Rd NW *NYSE:* HD ■ *TF Cust Svc:* 800-553-3199 ■ *Web:* www.homedepot.com	Atlanta	GA	30339	770-433-8211	384-2356
Jackson Lumber & Millwork Co Inc PO Box 449 *Web:* www.jacksonlumber.com	Lawrence	MA	01842	978-686-4141	689-1066
Jaeger Lumber & Supply Co Inc PO Box 126 *Web:* www.jaegerlumber.com	Union	NJ	07083	908-686-0070	686-0196
Jones Cassity Inc 302 Pine Tree Rd *Web:* www.cassityjones.com	Longview	TX	75604	903-759-0736	759-1406
Junior's Bldg Materials Inc 7574 Battlefield Pkwy *Web:* www.juniorsbuildingmaterials.com	Ringgold	GA	30736	706-937-3400	937-4100
Kuhns Bros Log Homes Inc 390 Swartz Rd *TF:* 800-326-9614 ■ *Web:* www.kuhnsbros.com	Lewisburg	PA	17837	570-568-1412	568-1187
Lampert Yards Inc 1850 Como Ave *Web:* www.lampertyards.com	Saint Paul	MN	55108	651-695-3600	695-3601
Len-Co Lumber Corp 1445 Seneca St *Web:* www.lencobuffalo.com	Buffalo	NY	14210	716-822-0243	822-1821
Lester Bldg Supply 14 Liberty St *Web:* www.lestergroup.com	Martinsville	VA	24112	276-638-8834	632-2117
Lowe's Cos Inc 1000 Lowe's Blvd *NYSE:* LOW ■ **Fax Area Code:* 336 ■ *TF:* 800-445-6937 ■ *Web:* www.lowes.com	Mooresville	NC	28117	704-758-1000	658-4766*
Lowe's Home Centers Inc PO Box 1111 *TF:* 800-445-6937 ■ *Web:* www.lowes.com	North Wilkesboro	NC	28656	800-445-6937	
MarJam Supply Co Inc 20 Rewe St *TF:* 800-462-7526 ■ *Web:* www.marjam.com	Brooklyn	NY	11211	718-388-6465	989-0029
Marson & Marson Lumber Inc PO Box 218 *Web:* www.marsonandmarson.com	Leavenworth	WA	98826	509-548-5829	548-6372
Martin Door Mfg Inc 2828 S 900 W *TF:* 800-388-9310 ■ *Web:* www.martindoor.com	Salt Lake City	UT	84119	801-973-9310	688-8182
McCoy's Bldg Supply 1200 N IH 35 *Web:* www.mccoys.com	San Marcos	TX	78666	512-353-5400	395-6608
Menard Inc 5101 Menard Dr *Web:* www.menards.com	Eau Claire	WI	54703	715-876-5911	876-2868
Montalbano Lumber Co Inc 1309 Houston Ave *Web:* www.montalbanolumber.com	Houston	TX	77007	713-228-9011	228-8222
National Lumber 71 Maple St *TF:* 800-370-9663 ■ *Web:* www.national-lumber.com	Mansfield	MA	02048	508-339-8020	339-4518
Nickerson Lumber Co 15 Main St	Orleans	MA	02653	508-255-0200	255-0599
Norcross Co The PO Box 637 *Web:* www.prestonfeather.com	Petoskey	MI	49770	231-347-2501	347-1154
Northern Tool & Equipment Co 2800 Southcross Dr W *TF Cust Svc:* 800-222-5381 ■ *Web:* www.northerntool.com	Burnsville	MN	55306	952-894-9510	894-1020
Olshan Lumber Co PO Box 1274 *Web:* www.olshanlumber.com	Houston	TX	77251	713-225-5551	220-9400
Orchard Supply Hardware 6450 Via del Oro *Web:* www.osh.com	San Jose	CA	95119	408-281-3500	365-2702
Paramount Builders Inc 501 Central Dr *TF:* 888-340-9002 ■ *Web:* www.paramountbuilders.com	Virginia Beach	VA	23454	757-340-9000	431-8200
Plainfield Lumber Co 3669 Plainfield Ave Ne *Web:* www.plc.doitbest.com	Grand Rapids	MI	49525	616-363-9021	363-9593
Pro-Build 3020 Willamette Dr NE *TF:* 800-842-8256 ■ *Web:* www.lumbermens-building.com	Lacey	WA	98516	360-456-1880	456-1884
Ray Mart Inc PO Box 5548 **Fax:* Mktg ■ *Web:* www.trisupplyhometeam.com	Beaumont	TX	77726	409-835-4744	924-7253*
Reisterstown Lumber Co The PO Box 337 *Web:* www.reisterstownlumber.com	Reisterstown	MD	21136	410-833-1300	833-6803
RONA Inc 220 Ch du Tremblay *TF:* 877-599-5900 ■ *Web:* www.rona.ca	Boucherville	QC	J4B8H7	514-599-5100	599-5137
S & W Lumber Co Inc 720 Camden Ave *Web:* www.economylumber.com	Campbell	CA	95008	408-378-5231	378-0258
Seigle's 1331 Davis Rd *Web:* www.seigles.com	Elgin	IL	60123	847-742-2000	697-6521
Sliters PO Box 130 *Web:* www.sliters.com	Somers	MT	59932	406-857-3306	857-3369
Spenard Builders Supply Inc 840 K St Suite 200 *TF:* 800-478-3141 ■ *Web:* www.sbsalaska.com	Anchorage	AK	99501	907-261-9105	261-9142
Standale Lumber & Supply Co 4100 Lake Michigan Dr NW *TF:* 800-968-8201 ■ *Web:* www.standalelumber.com	Grand Rapids	MI	49504	616-530-8200	534-4404
Star Lumber & Supply Co Inc 325 S W St *Web:* www.starlumber.com	Wichita	KS	67213	316-942-2221	941-0136
Stenerson Bros Lumber Co PO Box 500 *Web:* www.stenersonlumber.com	Moorhead	MN	56561	218-233-2754	233-2819
Sutherland Lumber Co 4000 Main St *TF:* 800-821-2252 ■ *Web:* www.sutherlands.com	Kansas City	MO	64111	816-756-3000	360-2195
True Value Co 8600 W Bryn Mawr Ave *Web:* www.truevaluecompany.com	Chicago	IL	60631	773-695-5000	695-6516
Viola Bros Inc 180 Washington Ave *Web:* www.violabros.com	Nutley	NJ	07110	973-667-7000	667-2048
WE Aubuchon Co Inc 95 Aubuchon Dr *TF:* 800-431-2712 ■ *Web:* www.aubuchonhardware.com	Westminster	MA	01473	978-874-0521	874-2096
Wheelwright Lumber Co 3127 Midland Dr *Web:* www.wheelwrightlumber.com	Ogden	UT	84401	801-627-0850	627-9933

368 HOME INSPECTION SERVICES

				Phone	Fax
AmeriSpec Inc 889 Ridge Lake Blvd *TF:* 800-426-2270 ■ *Web:* www.amerispec.com	Memphis	TN	38120	901-820-8500	820-8520
BrickKicker Inc 849 N Ellsworth St *TF:* 800-821-1820 ■ *Web:* www.brickkicker.com	Naperville	IL	60563	630-420-9900	420-2270
HomeTeam Inspection Service Inc 575 Chamber Dr *TF:* 800-598-5297 ■ *Web:* www.hometeaminspection.com	Milford	OH	45150	513-831-1300	831-6010
HouseMaster 421 W Union Ave *TF:* 800-526-3939 ■ *Web:* www.housemaster.com	Bound Brook	NJ	08805	732-469-6565	469-7405
National Property Inspections Inc (NPI) 9375 Burt St Suite 201 **Fax Area Code:* 800 ■ *TF:* 800-333-9807 ■ *Web:* www.npiweb.com	Omaha	NE	68114	402-333-9807	933-2508*
World Inspection Network International Inc 6500 6th Ave NW *TF:* 800-967-8127 ■ *Web:* www.wini.com	Seattle	WA	98117	206-728-8100	

369 HOME SALES & OTHER DIRECT SELLING

				Phone	Fax
4Life Research 9850 S 300 W *TF Sales:* 888-454-3374 ■ *Web:* www.4-life.com	Sandy	UT	84070	801-256-3102	562-3611
Amway Corp 7575 Fulton St E *TF:* 800-253-6500 ■ *Web:* www.amway.com	Ada	MI	49355	616-787-6000	682-4000
Avon Products Inc 1345 Avenue of the Americas *NYSE:* AVP ■ *TF Cust Svc:* 800-367-2866 ■ *Web:* www.avon.com	New York	NY	10105	212-282-5000	282-6825
Color Me Beautiful 7000 Infantry Ridge Rd Suite 200 *TF:* 800-533-5503 ■ *Web:* www.colormebeautiful.com	Manassas	VA	20109	703-471-6400	471-0127
Colorado Prime Foods 500 Bi-County Blvd Suite 400 **Fax Area Code:* 800 ■ **Fax:* Cust Svc ■ *TF:* 800-365-2404 ■ *Web:* www.coloradoprimefoods.com	Farmingdale	NY	11735	631-694-1111	288-5938*
Conklin Co Inc 551 Valley Pk Dr *TF:* 800-888-8838 ■ *Web:* www.conklin.com	Shakopee	MN	55379	952-445-6010	496-4281
Cutco Cutlery Corp 1116 E State St *TF:* 800-828-0448 ■ *Web:* www.cutco.com	Olean	NY	14760	716-373-6148	790-7184
Dial-A-Mattress Operating Corp 31-10 48th Ave *TF:* 800-999-1000 ■ *Web:* www.mattress.com	Long Island City	NY	11101	718-472-1200	472-1024
Discovery Toys Inc 7364 Marathon Dr Suite A *TF Cust Svc:* 800-341-8697 ■ *Web:* www.discoverytoysinc.com	Livermore	CA	94550	925-606-2600	606-2600
Gibraltar Trade Center Inc 15525 Racho Blvd *Web:* www.gibraltartrade.com	Taylor	MI	48180	734-287-2000	287-8330
Golden Neo-Life Diamite International 3500 Gateway Blvd *TF:* 800-432-5848 ■ *Web:* www.gnld.com	Fremont	CA	94538	510-651-0405	440-2818
Goldshield Elite 1501 Northpoint Pkwy Suite 100 **Fax Area Code:* 800 ■ *TF:* 866-218-8142 ■ *Web:* www.goldshieldelite.com	West Palm Beach	FL	33407	561-615-4701	423-3135*
JR Watkins Inc 150 Liberty St PO Box 5570 *TF:* 800-243-9423 ■ *Web:* www.watkinsonline.com	Winona	MN	55987	507-457-3300	452-6723
Mannatech Inc 600 S Royal Ln Suite 200 *NASDAQ:* MTEX ■ *TF:* 800-281-4469 ■ *Web:* www.us.mannatech.com	Coppell	TX	75019	972-471-7400	471-8135
Mary Kay Inc PO Box 799045 **Fax:* Cust Svc ■ *TF Cust Svc:* 800-627-9529 ■ *Web:* www.marykay.com	Dallas	TX	75379	972-687-6300	687-1623*
Melaleuca Inc 3910 S Yellowstone Hwy **Fax Area Code:* 888 ■ *TF Sales:* 800-282-3000 ■ *Web:* www.melaleuca.com	Idaho Falls	ID	83402	208-522-0700	528-2090*

Company	City	State	ZIP	Phone	Fax
Midwest Marketing Inc 239 Hwy 61 PO Box 125 *TF:* 800-662-7538 ■ *Web:* www.mwmktg.com	Bloomsdale	MO	63627	573-483-2577	483-9747
Noevir USA Inc 1095 Main St *TF:* 800-872-8817 ■ *Web:* www.noevirusa.com	Irvine	CA	92614	949-660-1111	553-3224
North American Membership Group Inc (NAMG) 12301 Whitewater Dr *TF:* 800-634-8598 ■ *Web:* www.namginc.com	Minnetonka	MN	55343	952-936-9333	988-7499
Nu Skin Enterprises Inc 75 W Ctr St *NYSE: NUS* ■ *Web:* www.nuskinenterprises.com	Provo	UT	84601	801-345-1000	345-5999
Nutrilite Products Inc 5600 Beach Blvd PO Box 5940 *Web:* www.nutrilite.com	Buena Park	CA	90621	714-562-6200	736-7610
Pampered Chef Ltd 1 Pampered Chef Ln *TF:* 888-687-2433 ■ *Web:* www.pamperedchef.com	Addison	IL	60101	630-261-8900	261-8992
Partylite Gifts Inc 59 Armstrong Rd **Fax Area Code:* 508 ■ *TF:* 888-999-5706 ■ *Web:* www.partylite.com	Plymouth	MA	02360	888-999-5706	732-5818*
Periodical Publishers Service Bureau 1 N Superior St *TF:* 800-654-9204 ■ *Web:* www.ppsb.com	Sandusky	OH	44870	419-626-0623	621-4383
Pola USA Inc 251 E Victoria St *TF:* 800-222-6564 ■ *Web:* www.pola.com	Carson	CA	90746	310-527-9696	515-1195
Princess House Inc 470 Miles Standish Blvd *TF Sales:* 800-622-0039 ■ *Web:* www.princesshouse.com	Taunton	MA	02780	508-823-0711	823-5182
Reliv International Inc 136 Chesterfield Industrial Blvd *NASDAQ: RELV* ■ *TF:* 800-735-4887 ■ *Web:* www.reliv.com	Chesterfield	MO	63005	636-537-9715	537-9753
Rena Ware International Inc 15885 NE 28th St *Web:* www.renaware.com	Bellevue	WA	98008	425-881-6171	882-7500
Rexair Inc 50 W Big Beaver Rd Suite 350 *Web:* www.rainbowsystem.com	Troy	MI	48084	248-643-7222	643-7676
Saladmaster Inc 230 Westway Pl Suite 101 *TF:* 800-765-5795 ■ *Web:* www.saladmaster.com	Arlington	TX	76018	817-633-3555	633-5544
Shaklee Corp 4747 Willow Rd *TF:* 800-742-5533 ■ *Web:* www.shaklee.com	Pleasanton	CA	94588	925-924-2000	924-2862
Sk Food Group Inc 4600 37th Ave SW *TF:* 800-722-6290 ■ *Web:* www.skfoodgroup.com	Seattle	WA	98126	206-935-8100	
Smartpak Equine LLC 40 Grissom Rd Suite 500 *TF:* 888-752-5171 ■ *Web:* www.smartpakequine.com	Plymouth	MA	02360	774-773-1114	
Specialty Merchandise Corp 996 Flower Glen St *TF Orders:* 800-877-7621 ■ *Web:* www.smcorp.com	Simi Valley	CA	93065	805-578-5500	584-8267
Stanley Home Products 1 Fuller Way *TF Cust Svc:* 800-628-9032 ■ *Web:* www.shponline.com	Great Bend	KS	67530	620-792-1711	792-1906
Success Motivation International Inc 4567 Lakeshore Dr *TF Sales:* 888-391-0050 ■ *Web:* www.success-motivation.com	Waco	TX	76710	254-776-9966	776-1230
Sunrider International 1625 Abalone Ave **Fax:* Hum Res ■ *TF Orders:* 888-278-6743 ■ *Web:* www.sunrider.com	Torrance	CA	90501	310-781-3808	222-6329*
UndercoverWear Inc 30 Commerce Way Suite 2 *TF:* 800-733-0007 ■ *Web:* www.undercoverwear.com	Tewksbury	MA	01876	978-851-8580	640-2882
University Subscription Service 1213 Butterfield Rd *TF:* 800-876-1213 ■ *Web:* www.ussmag.com	Downers Grove	IL	60515	630-960-3233	960-3246
Vector Marketing Co 322 Houghton Ave **Fax Area Code:* 585 ■ *TF:* 800-828-0448	Olean	NY	14760	716-373-6148	790-7173*
Vorwerk USA Co LP 1964 Corporate Sq *TF:* 800-562-6726 ■ *Web:* www.vorwerkusa.com	Longwood	FL	32750	407-830-9988	830-9958
World Book Inc 233 N Michigan Ave 20th Fl *TF:* 800-255-1750 ■ *Web:* www.worldbook.com	Chicago	IL	60601	312-729-5800	729-5600
Yves Rocher Inc PO Box 1701 *TF:* 888-909-0771 ■ *Web:* www.yvesrocherusa.com	Champlain	NY	12919	800-321-3434	321-4909

370 HOME WARRANTY SERVICES

Company	City	State	ZIP	Phone	Fax
American Home Shield 889 Ridge Lake Blvd PO Box 851 *TF:* 800-247-1644 ■ *Web:* www.ahscustomer.com	Memphis	TN	38120	901-537-8000	537-8005
Blue Ribbon Home Warranty Inc 95 S Wadsworth Blvd *TF:* 800-571-0475 ■ *Web:* www.brhw.com	Lakewood	CO	80226	303-986-3900	986-3152
Cross Country Group LLC 1 Cabot Rd # 4 *Web:* www.ccgroup.com	Medford	MA	02155	781-396-3700	391-7504
Cross Country Home Services 1625 NW 136th Ave Suite 200 *TF Cust Svc:* 800-327-9787 ■ *Web:* www.cchs.com	Fort Lauderdale	FL	33323	954-845-9100	845-2260
First American Home Buyers Protection Corp 7833 Haskell Ave PO Box 10180 **Fax Area Code:* 800 ■ *TF:* 800-444-9030 ■ *Web:* www.homewarranty.firstam.com	Van Nuys	CA	91410	818-781-5050	772-1151*
HMS National Inc 1625 NW 136th Ave Suite 200 *TF:* 800-432-1033 ■ *Web:* www.hmsnational.com	Fort Lauderdale	FL	33323	954-845-9100	845-2263
Home Buyers Warranty Corp 2675 S Abilene St *Web:* www.2-10.com	Aurora	CO	80014	303-368-4805	368-0529
Home Security of America Inc 310 N Midvale Blvd **Fax Area Code:* 877 ■ *TF:* 800-367-1448 ■ *Web:* www.onlinehsa.com	Madison	WI	53705	608-231-0010	638-1741*
Warrantech Corp Inc 2200 Hwy 121 *TF:* 800-544-9510 ■ *Web:* www.warrantech.com	Bedford	TX	76021	817-283-7267	
Warrantech International Inc 2200 Hwy 121 **Fax:* Hum Res ■ *TF:* 800-544-9510 ■ *Web:* www.warrantech.com	Beford	TX	76021	817-283-7267	785-6151*

371 HORSE BREEDERS

SEE ALSO Livestock Improvement Services p. 1380

Company	City	State	ZIP	Phone	Fax
Airdrie Stud Inc 2641 Old Frankfort Pike PO Box 487 *Web:* www.airdriestud.com	Midway	KY	40347	859-873-7270	873-6140
Ashford Stud 5095 Frankfort Rd PO Box 823 *Web:* www.coolmore.com/america	Versailles	KY	40383	859-873-7088	879-5756
Calumet Farm 3301 Versailles Rd *Web:* www.calumetfarm.com	Lexington	KY	40510	859-231-8272	254-4258
Claiborne Farm 703 Winchester Rd *Web:* www.clairbornefarm.com	Paris	KY	40361	859-233-4252	987-0008
Country Life Farm 319 Old Joppa Rd *Web:* www.countrylifefarm.com	Bel Air	MD	21014	410-879-1952	879-6207
Creston Farms 9010 Creston Rd *Web:* www.crestonfarms.com	Paso Robles	CA	93446	805-239-0711	239-4473
Darby Dan Farm 3225 Old Frankfort Pike *Web:* www.darbydan.com	Lexington	KY	40510	859-254-0424	281-6612
Gainesway Farm 3750 Paris Pike *Web:* www.gainesway.com	Lexington	KY	40511	859-293-2676	299-9371
Glencrest Farm 1576 Moores Mill Rd PO Box 4468 *TF:* 800-903-0136 ■ *Web:* www.glencrest.com	Midway	KY	40347	859-233-7032	233-9404
Grant's Farm 10501 Gravois Rd *Web:* www.grantsfarm.com	Saint Louis	MO	63123	314-843-1700	525-0822
Lane's End Farm 1500 Midway Rd PO Box 626 *Web:* www.lanesend.com	Versailles	KY	40383	859-873-7300	873-3746
Margaux Farm LLC 596 Moores Mill Rd PO Box 4220 *Web:* www.margauxfarm.com	Midway	KY	40347	859-846-4433	846-4486
Mill Ridge Farm 2800 Bowman Mill Rd *Web:* www.millridge.com	Lexington	KY	40513	859-231-0606	255-6010
Millford Farm 377 Weisenberger Mill Rd PO Box 4351 *Web:* www.millford.com	Midway	KY	40347	859-846-4705	846-4226
Northview Stallion Station 55 Northern Dancer Dr *Web:* www.northviewstallions.com	Chesapeake City	MD	21915	410-885-2855	
Old Frankfort Stud 3800 Old Frankfort Pike *Web:* www.oldfrankfortstud.com	Lexington	KY	40510	859-233-1717	233-1719
Pin Oak Stud 830 Grassy Spring Rd PO Box 68 *Web:* www.pinoakstud.com	Versailles	KY	40383	859-873-1420	873-2391
Stone Farm 200 Stoney Pt Rd *Web:* www.stonefarm.com	Paris	KY	40361	859-987-3737	987-1474
Sugar Maple Farm 5 Sugar Ln *Web:* www.sugarmaple-farm.com	Poughquag	NY	12570	845-724-3500	724-5889
Three Chimneys Farm PO Box 114 *Web:* www.threechimneys.com	Midway	KY	40347	859-873-7053	873-5723
Vinery Kentucky LLC 4241 Spurr Rd *Web:* www.vinerykentucky.com	Lexington	KY	40511	859-455-9388	455-9588
Wafare Farm 3808 Old Frankfort Pike *Web:* www.5000tableaux.info	Midway	KY	40347	859-846-5202	846-5645
Walmac International Stud Farm LLC 3395 Paris Pike *Web:* www.walmac.com	Lexington	KY	40511	859-299-0473	299-1259
Wimbledon Farm 1725 Walnut Hill Rd *Web:* www.wimbledonfarm.com	Lexington	KY	40515	859-272-0636	271-1435
Windfield Farms Ltd 2300 Simcoe St N PO Box 67	Oshawa	ON	L1H7K8	905-725-1195	579-7552
Windfields Farm 2525 DeLong Rd	Lexington	KY	40515	859-273-3050	273-3035
WinStar Farm LLC 3301 Pisgah Rd *Web:* www.winstarfarm.com	Versailles	KY	40383	859-873-1717	873-1612

372 HORTICULTURAL PRODUCTS GROWERS

SEE ALSO Garden Centers p. 1901; Seed Companies p. 2650

Company	City	State	ZIP	Phone	Fax
Ades & Gish Nurseries 2222 N Twin Oaks Valley Rd *Web:* www.agnurseries.com	San Marcos	CA	92069	760-410-0400	410-0433
Aldershot of New Mexico Inc 4884 S Main St *TF:* 888-768-6867	Mesilla Park	NM	88047	505-523-8621	523-8688
Alex R Masson Inc 12819 198th St *TF:* 800-444-6210 ■ *Web:* www.armasson.com	Linwood	KS	66052	913-301-3281	301-3288
Altman Specialty Plants Inc 3742 Bluebird Canyon Rd *TF:* 800-348-4881 ■ *Web:* www.livingtreasures.com	Vista	CA	92084	760-744-8191	744-8835
Aris Horticulture Inc 115 3rd St SE PO Box 230 **Fax Area Code:* 330 ■ *TF:* 800-321-9573 ■ *Web:* www.arishort.com	Barberton	OH	44203	800-232-9557	745-3098*
B & H Flowers Inc 3516 Foothill Rd *TF:* 800-682-5666 ■ *Web:* www.bandhflowers.com	Carpinteria	CA	93013	805-684-4550	684-1677
Battlefield Farms Inc 23190 Clarks Mountain Rd *TF:* 800-722-0744 ■ *Web:* www.battlefieldfarms.com	Rapidan	VA	22733	540-854-6485	854-6486
Bay City Flower Co Inc 2265 Cabrillo Hwy 5 PO Box 186 *TF Sales:* 800-399-5858	Half Moon Bay	CA	94019	650-726-5535	720-2004
Bell Nursery Inc 3838 Bell Rd *Web:* www.bellnursery.com	Burtonsville	MD	20866	301-421-1500	421-4269
Bettinger Farms Inc 11602 County Rd 28	Swanton	OH	43558	419-829-2771	829-2147
Blue Ridge Growers Inc 21409 Germanna Hwy *TF:* 800-368-2030 ■ *Web:* www.blueridgegrowers.com	Stevensburg	VA	22741	540-399-1636	399-9068
Burgett Floral Inc 868 Fuller NE *TF:* 800-404-2999 ■ *Web:* www.burgettflorist.com	Grand Rapids	MI	49503	616-456-1999	
California Pajarosa 133 Hughes Rd PO Box 684 *TF:* 800-565-6374 ■ *Web:* www.pajarosa.com	Watsonville	CA	95077	831-722-6374	722-1316
CD Ford & Sons Inc 16243 Ford Rd *TF:* 800-383-4661 ■ *Web:* www.cdford.com	Geneseo	IL	61254	309-944-4661	944-3703

Company	City	State	Zip	Phone	Fax
Color Spot Nurseries Inc 2575 Olive Hill Rd *Fax Area Code: 800 ■ TF: 800-554-4065 ■ Web: www.colorspot.com	Fallbrook	CA	92028	760-695-1430	250-5135*
Colorama Wholesale Nursery 1025 N Todd Ave	Azusa	CA	91720	626-969-3585	969-0481
Costa Nursery Farms Inc 22290 SW 162nd Ave *Fax Area Code: 786 ■ TF: 800-327-7074 ■ Web: www.costafarms.com	Goulds	FL	33170	305-247-3248	247-0591*
Cuthbert Greenhouses Inc 4900 Hendron Rd TF: 800-321-1939	Groveport	OH	43125	614-836-3866	836-3767
Dallas Johnson Greenhouse Inc 2802 Twin City Dr TF: 800-445-4794 ■ Web: www.djgreenhouses.com	Council Bluffs	IA	51501	712-366-0407	366-4510
Dan Schantz Farm & Greenhouses LLC 8025 Spinnerstown Rd TF: 800-451-3064 ■ Web: www.danschantz.com	Zionsville	PA	18092	610-967-2181	965-4506
DeLeon's Bromeliads Co 13745 SW 216th St TF: 800-448-8649 ■ Web: www.deleons4color.com	Goulds	FL	33170	305-238-6028	235-2354
Delray Plants Inc 955 Old SR 8 TF: 800-854-5393	Venus	FL	33960	863-465-1557	465-4365
Dramm & Echter Inc 1150 Quail Gardens Dr TF: 800-854-7021 ■ Web: www.drammechter.com	Encinitas	CA	92024	760-436-0188	436-2974
El Modeno Gardens Inc 11911 Jeffrey Rd TF: 800-776-8111	Irvine	CA	92602	949-559-1234	559-6760
Ever-Bloom Inc 4701 Foothill Rd TF: 800-388-8112 ■ Web: www.ever-bloom.com	Carpinteria	CA	93013	805-684-5566	684-7288
Farmers West 5300 Foothill Rd TF: 800-549-0085 ■ Web: www.farmerswest.com	Carpinteria	CA	93013	805-684-5531	684-1528
Garden State Growers 99 Locust Grove Rd TF: 800-288-8484 ■ Web: www.gardenstategrowers.com	Pittstown	NJ	08867	908-730-8888	730-6676
Green Circle Growers Inc 15650 SR-511 TF: 800-533-4266	Oberlin	OH	44074	440-775-1411	774-1465
Green Valley Floral Co 24999 Potter Rd TF: 800-228-1255 ■ Web: www.greenvalleyfloral.com	Salinas	CA	93908	831-424-7691	424-4473
Greenleaf Nursery Co 28406 Hwy 82 TF: 800-331-2982 ■ Web: www.glnsy.com	Park Hill	OK	74451	918-457-5172	457-5550
Harts Nursery of Jefferson Inc 4049 Jefferson-Scio Rd TF: 800-356-9335 ■ Web: www.hartsnursery.com	Jefferson	OR	97352	541-327-3366	327-1603
Hermann Engelmann Greenhouses Inc 2009 Marden Rd TF: 800-722-6435 ■ Web: www.exoticangel.com	Apopka	FL	32703	407-886-3434	886-0094
Imperial Nurseries Inc 90 Salmon Brook St TF: 800-343-3132 ■ Web: www.imperialnurseries.com	Granby	CT	06035	860-653-4541	653-2919
Ingleside Plantation Nurseries 5870 Leedstown Rd Web: www.inglesidenurseries.com	Oak Grove	VA	22443	804-224-7111	224-2032
Johannes Flowers Inc 4990 Foothill Rd TF: 800-365-9476 ■ Web: www.johannesflowers.com	Carpinteria	CA	93013	805-684-5686	566-2199
Johnsen Nurseries Inc 2897 Freedom Blvd TF: 800-322-6529 ■ Web: www.ameri-cal.com	Watsonville	CA	95076	831-728-4205	724-9281
Kerry's Bromeliad Nursery Inc 21840 SW 258th St TF: 800-331-9127 ■ Web: www.kerrys.com	Homestead	FL	33031	305-247-7096	247-3392
Knox Nursery Inc 940 Avalon Rd TF: 800-441-5669 ■ Web: www.knoxnursery.com	Winter Garden	FL	34787	407-293-3721	290-1702
Kocher Flower Growers 950 Brittany Rd TF: 800-821-4421	Encinitas	CA	92024	760-436-1458	607-9105
Kurt Weiss Greenhouses Inc 95 Main St TF: 800-858-8555 ■ Web: www.kurtweiss.com	Center Moriches	NY	11934	631-878-2500	878-2553
Layser's Flowers Inc 523 W Washington Ave Web: www.laysersflowers.com	Myerstown	PA	17067	717-866-5746	866-6099
Matsui Nursery Inc 1645 Old Stage Rd TF: 800-793-6433 ■ Web: www.matsuinursery.net	Salinas	CA	93908	831-422-6433	422-2387
McLellan Botanicals 688 Brannan St TF: 800-467-2443 ■ Web: www.orchidexperts.com	San Francisco	CA	94107	415-546-4049	543-6836
Metrolina Greenhouses Inc 16400 Huntersville-Concord Rd TF: 800-222-2905 ■ Web: www.metrolinagreenhouses.com	Huntersville	NC	28078	704-875-1371	875-6741
Mid American Growers Inc 14240 Greenhouse Ave TF: 800-892-6888	Granville	IL	61326	815-339-6831	339-2747
Monrovia Nursery Growers 18331 E Foothill Blvd TF: 800-999-9321 ■ Web: www.monrovia.com	Azusa	CA	91702	626-334-9321	334-3126
Mountain States Plants Corp 1421 W Gentile St TF: 800-326-4490 ■ Web: www.msplants.com	Layton	UT	84041	801-544-8878	544-1175
Nurserymen's Exchange 2651 N Cabrillo Hwy TF: 800-227-5229 ■ Web: www.bloomrite.com	Half Moon Bay	CA	94019	650-726-6361	712-4280
Ocean Breeze International (OBI) 3910 N Via Real TF: 888-715-8888 ■ Web: www.oceanbreezeintl.com	Carpinteria	CA	93013	805-684-1747	684-0235
OF Nelson & Sons Nursery Inc 3207 Clarona Rd Web: www.nelsonsfloridaroses.com	Apopka	FL	32703	407-886-3111	886-1489
Oglevee Ltd 152 Oglevee Ln TF: 800-437-4733	Connellsville	PA	15425	724-628-8360	628-7270
Panzer Nursery Inc 17980 SW Baseline Rd TF: 888-212-5327 ■ Web: www.panzernursery.com	Beaverton	OR	97006	503-645-1185	629-9023
Parks Bros Farm Inc 6733 Parks Rd TF: 800-334-5770 ■ Web: www.parksbrothers.com	Van Buren	AR	72956	479-474-1125	471-7051
Paul Ecke Ranch Inc 441 Saxony Rd TF: 800-468-3253 ■ Web: www.ecke.com	Encinitas	CA	92024	760-753-1134	944-4000
Petitti Garden Centers 24964 Broadway Ave Web: www.petittigardencenter.com	Oakwood Village	OH	44146	440-439-6511	439-7736
Post Gardens Inc 21189 Huron River Dr	Rockwood	MI	48173	734-379-9688	379-3008
Rockwell Farms Inc 6055 Hwy 152 E TF: 800-635-6576 ■ Web: www.rockwellfarms.com	Rockwell	NC	28138	704-279-5589	279-8573
Sedan Floral Inc 406 S School St PO Box 339 Web: www.sedanfloral.com	Sedan	KS	67361	620-725-3111	725-5257
Silver Terrace Nurseries Inc 501 N St TF: 800-323-5977 ■ Web: www.citywreaths.com	Pescadero	CA	94060	650-879-2110	879-2164
Smith Gardens Inc 1265 Marine Dr TF: 800-755-6256 ■ Web: www.northwestgrown.com	Bellingham	WA	98225	360-733-4671	647-1468
South Florida Growers 16885 SW 256th St TF: 866-948-3722	Homestead	FL	33031	305-248-3722	248-9886
Speedling Inc 4300 Old 41 Hwy S PO Box 7238 TF: 800-881-4769 ■ Web: www.speedling.com	Sun City	FL	33586	813-645-3221	645-0086
Sun Valley Floral Farms Inc 3160 Upper Bay Rd TF: 800-747-0396 ■ Web: www.sunvalleyfloral.com	Arcata	CA	95521	707-826-8700	826-8708
Sunshine Foliage World 2060 Steve Roberts Special TF: 800-872-0607 ■ Web: www.interiorscape.com	Zolfo Springs	FL	33890	863-735-0501	735-1810
Van Wingerden International Inc 1856 Jeffress Rd TF: 800-226-3597	Fletcher	NC	28732	828-891-4116	891-8581
Westerlay Orchids 3504 Via Real TF: 800-959-7673 ■ Web: www.westerlayorchids.com	Carpinteria	CA	93013	805-684-5411	684-5414
Westland Floral Co 1400 Cravens Ln Web: www.westlandfloral.com	Carpinteria	CA	93013	805-684-4011	684-0685
White's Nursery & Greenhouses Inc 3133 Old Mill Rd TF: 800-966-9969 ■ Web: www.whitesnursery.com	Chesapeake	VA	23323	757-487-1300	487-7845
Woodburn Nursery & Azaleas 13009 McKee School Rd NE TF Sales: 888-634-2232 ■ Web: www.woodburnnursery.com	Woodburn	OR	97071	503-634-2231	634-2238
Worthington Farms Inc 3661 Ballards Crossroads Rd Web: www.worthingtonfarms.com	Greenville	NC	27834	252-756-3827	756-9442
Young's Plant Farm Inc 863 Airport Rd TF: 800-304-8609	Auburn	AL	36830	334-821-3500	821-3526

373 HOSE & BELTING - RUBBER OR PLASTICS

SEE ALSO Automotive Parts & Supplies - Mfr p. 1497

Company	City	State	Zip	Phone	Fax
Abc Industrie PO Box 77 TF: 800-426-0921 ■ Web: www.abc-industries.net	Warsaw	IN	46581	574-267-5166	267-2045
American Hose & Industrial Rubber Inc 2545 N Broad St TF: 800-533-1134 ■ Web: www.americanhoseandrubber.com	Philadelphia	PA	19132	215-223-7710	223-7713
Ammeraal Beltech USA 7501 N St Louis Ave TF Cust Svc: 800-323-4170 ■ Web: www.ammeraal-beltechusa.com	Skokie	IL	60076	847-673-6720	673-6373
Apache Hose & Belting Co Inc 4805 Bowling St SW PO Box 1719 TF Sales: 800-553-5455 ■ Web: www.apachehb.com	Cedar Rapids	IA	52406	319-365-0471	365-2522
Atco Rubber Products Inc 7101 Atco Dr TF: 800-877-3828 ■ Web: www.atcoflex.com	Fort Worth	TX	76118	817-595-2894	595-4634
Atcoflex Inc 14261 172nd Ave PO Box 118	Grand Haven	MI	49417	616-842-4661	842-4623
Belting Industries Co Inc 20 Boright Ave TF: 800-843-2358 ■ Web: www.beltingindustries.com	Kenilworth	NJ	07033	908-272-8591	272-3825
Carlisle Power Transmission Products Inc 430 Southpointe Dr TF: 866-773-2926 ■ Web: www.cptbelts.com	Miamisburg	OH	45342	937-847-1500	847-1550
Chemprene Inc 483 Fishkill Ave PO Box 471 TF: 800-431-9981 ■ Web: www.chemprene.com	Beacon	NY	12508	845-831-2800	831-4639
Coilhose Pneumatics Inc 19 Kimberly Rd TF: 800-526-2100 ■ Web: www.coilhose.com	East Brunswick	NJ	08816	732-390-8480	390-9693
Colorite Plastics Co 101 Railroad Ave TF: 800-800-4673 ■ Web: www.coloriteplastics.com	Ridgefield	NJ	07657	201-941-2900	941-0308
Cooper Tire & Rubber Co 701 Lima Ave NYSE: CTB ■ TF: 800-854-6288 ■ Web: www.coopertire.com	Findlay	OH	45840	419-423-1321	424-4108
Copper State Rubber of Arizona Inc 750 S 59th Ave	Phoenix	AZ	85043	602-269-5927	269-8106
Cosmoflex Inc 4142 Industrial Dr PO Box 994	Hannibal	MO	63401	573-221-0242	221-9290
Couse & Bolten Co 90 S St TF: 800-360-1324	Newark	NJ	07114	973-344-6330	344-6335
Dormont Mfg Co 6015 Enterprise Dr *Fax Area Code: 724 ■ TF: 800-367-6668 ■ Web: www.dormont.com	Export	PA	15632	800-367-6668	327-9611*
Dynacraft Co 650 Milwaukee Ave N	Algona	WA	98001	253-333-3000	333-3041
Eaton Corp 1111 Superior Ave Eaton Ctr NYSE: ETN ■ Web: www.eaton.com	Cleveland	OH	44114	216-523-5000	523-4787
Fenner Drives 311 W Stiegel St TF Sales: 800-243-3374 ■ Web: www.fennerdrives.com	Manheim	PA	17545	717-665-2421	664-8214
Fenner Dunlop Conveyor Belting Americas 10125 S Tryon St TF Cust Svc: 800-922-1735 ■ Web: www.fennerdunlop.com	Charlotte	NC	28273	704-943-5669	334-7126
Flexaust Co 1510 Armstrong Rd *Fax Area Code: 800 ■ TF: 800-343-0428 ■ Web: www.flexaust.com	Warsaw	IN	46580	574-267-7909	382-8464*
Flexfab LLC 1699 W M-43 Hwy TF: 800-331-0003 ■ Web: www.flexfab.com	Hastings	MI	49058	269-945-2433	945-4802
Flexon Industries Corp 1 Flexon Plaza TF: 800-327-4673 ■ Web: www.flexonhose.com	Newark	NJ	07114	973-824-5530	824-1208
Freelin-Wade Co 1730 NE Miller St TF: 888-373-9233 ■ Web: www.freelin-wade.com	McMinnville	OR	97128	503-434-5561	472-1989
Gates Corp 1551 Wewatta St Web: www.gates.com	Denver	CO	80202	303-744-1911	744-4000
Habasit ABT Inc 150 Industrial Pk Rd TF: 800-522-2358 ■ Web: www.habasitabt.com	Middletown	CT	06457	860-632-2211	632-1710
Habasit Belting Inc 1400 Clinton St TF: 800-325-1585 ■ Web: www.habasitusa.com	Buffalo	NY	14206	716-824-8484	821-1316
HBD/Thermoid Inc 1301 W Sandusky Ave TF: 800-543-8070 ■ Web: www.hbdthermoid.com	Bellefontaine	OH	43311	937-593-5010	593-4354
Hi-Tech Duravent Inc 400 E Main St TF: 800-451-5985 ■ Web: www.hitechduravent.com	Georgetown	MA	01833	978-352-2077	352-2487
Hutchinson FTS Inc 1835 Technology Dr Web: www.hutchinsonworldwide.com	Troy	MI	48083	248-589-7710	589-7710
Jason Industrial Inc 340 Kaplan Dr Web: www.jasonindustrial.com	Fairfield	NJ	07004	973-227-4904	227-1651
JGB Enterprises Inc 115 Metropolitan Dr *Fax Area Code: 888 ■ Web: www.jgbhose.com	Liverpool	NY	13088	315-451-2770	451-6743*

Company	City	State	ZIP	Phone	Fax
Key Fire Hose Corp (KFH) PO Box 7107 *TF:* 800-447-5666 ■ *Web:* www.keyfire.com	Dothan	AL	36302	334-671-5532	671-5616
Legg Co Inc 325 E 10th St *TF Sales:* 800-835-1003 ■ *Web:* www.leggbelting.com	Halstead	KS	67056	316-835-2256	835-3218
Lockwood Products Inc 5615 Willow Ln. *TF:* 800-423-1625 ■ *Web:* www.loc-line.com	Lake Oswego	OR	97035	503-635-8113	635-2844
Mark IV Industries LLC PO Box 810 *Web:* www.mark-iv.com	Amherst	NY	14226	716-689-4972	689-6098
MBL USA Corp 1040 N Ridge Ave	Lombard	IL	60148	630-620-1050	620-7538
Mercer Rubber Co 350 Rabro Dr *Web:* www.mercer-rubber.com	Hauppauge	NY	11788	631-582-1524	348-0279
Mulhern Belting Inc 148 Bauer Dr. *TF:* 800-253-6300 ■ *Web:* www.mulhernbelting.com	Oakland	NJ	07436	201-337-5700	337-6540
NewAge Industries Inc 145 James Way *TF:* 800-506-3924 ■ *Web:* www.newageindustries.com	SouthHampton	PA	18966	215-526-2300	526-2190
Parker Fluid Connectors Group 6035 Parkland Blvd *TF:* 800-272-7537 ■ *Web:* www.parker.com/fcg	Cleveland	OH	44124	216-896-3000	896-4000
Performance Polymer Technologies Co 8801 Washington Blvd Suite 109 *Web:* www.pptech.com	Roseville	CA	95678	916-677-1414	677-1474
Ro-Lab American Rubber Co Inc 8830 W Linne Rd. *TF:* 888-276-2993 ■ *Web:* www.rolabamerican.com	Tracy	CA	95304	209-836-0965	836-0465
Salem-Republic Rubber Co 475 W California Ave *TF:* 800-686-4199 ■ *Web:* www.salem-republic.com	Sebring	OH	44672	330-938-9801	938-9809
Snap-Tite Inc 8325 Hessinger Dr *Web:* www.snap-tite.com	Erie	PA	16509	814-838-5700	833-0145
Sparks Belting Co 3800 Stahl Dr SE. *TF:* 800-451-4537 ■ *Web:* www.sparksbelting.com	Grand Rapids	MI	49546	616-949-2750	949-8518
Standco Industries Inc 2701 Clinton Dr *TF:* 800-231-6018 ■ *Web:* www.standco.net	Houston	TX	77020	713-224-6311	229-9312
Tigerflex Corp 801 Estes Ave.	Elk Grove Village	IL	60007	847-640-8366	640-8372
Titeflex Corp 603 Hendee St *TF:* 800-765-2525 ■ *Web:* www.titeflex.com	Springfield	MA	01139	413-739-5631	788-7593
Unaflex LLC 3901 NE 12th Ave. *TF:* 800-327-1286 ■ *Web:* www.unaflex.com	Pompano Beach	FL	33064	954-943-5002	946-3583
Voss Belting & Specialty Co 6965 N Hamlin Ave. *TF:* 800-323-3935 ■ *Web:* www.vossbelting.com	Lincolnwood	IL	60712	847-673-8900	673-1408

374 HOSPICES

SEE ALSO Specialty Hospitals p. 2075

ALABAMA

Hospice	City	State	ZIP	Phone	Fax
Hospice of Cullman County 1912 Al Hwy 157 *Web:* www.hospiceofcullmancounty.org	Cullman	AL	35058	256-739-5185	737-0985
Hospice of EAMC 665 Opelika Rd. *TF:* 888-822-5515 ■ *Web:* www.hospiceadvantage.com	Auburn	AL	36830	989-893-2904	895-3977
Hospice of Marshall County 408 Martling Rd *TF:* 888-334-9336 ■ *Web:* www.hospicemc.org	Albertville	AL	35951	256-891-7724	891-7754
Hospice of the Valley 240 Johnston St SE *TF:* 877-260-3657 ■ *Web:* www.hospiceofthevalley.net	Decatur	AL	35601	256-350-5585	350-5567
Hospice of West Alabama 3851 Loop Rd. *TF:* 877-362-7522 ■ *Web:* www.hospiceofwestalabama.com	Tuscaloosa	AL	35404	205-523-0101	523-0102
McAuley Hospice PO Box 1090	Daphne	AL	36526	251-626-2694	621-4424

ALASKA

Hospice	City	State	ZIP	Phone	Fax
Hospice of Anchorage 2612 E Northern Lights Blvd. *Web:* www.hospiceofanchorage.org	Anchorage	AK	99508	907-561-5322	561-0334

ARIZONA

Hospice	City	State	ZIP	Phone	Fax
Banner Home Care & Hospice 1325 N Fiesta Blvd Suite 1 *TF:* 800-293-6989	Gilbert	AZ	85233	480-497-5535	497-8250
Carondelet Hospice Services 630 N Alvernon Suite 361.	Tucson	AZ	85711	520-205-7700	205-7598
Hospice Family Care 1550 S Alma School Rd Suite 102 *Web:* www.hfc-az.com	Mesa	AZ	85210	480-461-3144	844-9711
Hospice Family Care 6300 E El Dorado Plaza Suite A-100. *TF:* 800-839-3288	Tucson	AZ	85715	520-790-9299	790-9211
Hospice of Arizona 19820 N 7th Ave Suite 130 *TF:* 800-890-9046 ■ *Web:* www.americanhospice.com	Phoenix	AZ	85027	602-678-1313	242-2178
Hospice of the Valley 777 W Southern Ave Suite 301	Mesa	AZ	85210	480-730-5980	730-6078
Hospice of the Valley 1510 E Flower St *Web:* www.hov.org	Phoenix	AZ	85014	602-530-6900	530-6901
Odyssey HealthCare Hospice 202 E Earll Dr Suite 160 *TF:* 800-478-1682 ■ *Web:* www.odsyhealth.com	Phoenix	AZ	85012	602-279-0677	279-1085
VistaCare of Arizona 202 E Earll Dr Suite 160. *TF:* 800-851-3522 ■ *Web:* www.vistacare.com	Phoenix	AZ	85012	602-648-6911	648-6912

ARKANSAS

Hospice	City	State	ZIP	Phone	Fax
Arkansas Hospice 14 Parkstone Cir *TF:* 877-257-3400 ■ *Web:* www.arkansashospice.org	North Little Rock	AR	72116	501-748-3333	748-3334
Hospice Home Care 1501 N University Ave Suite 340 *TF:* 800-479-2503	Little Rock	AR	72207	501-666-9697	666-4616
Hospice of the Ozarks 701 Burnett Dr *Web:* www.baxterregional.org	Mountain Home	AR	72653	870-424-1771	

CALIFORNIA

Hospice	City	State	ZIP	Phone	Fax
AseraCare Hospice - Orange 750 The City Dr Suite 120 *TF:* 877-508-0644 ■ *Web:* www.aserahospiceorange.com	Orange	CA	92868	714-980-0900	980-0910
Citrus Valley Hospice 820 N Phillips Ave *TF:* 877-422-7301 ■ *Web:* www.cvhp.org/facilities/cvh/cvh_q&a.htm	West Covina	CA	91791	626-859-2263	974-0332
Community Hospice Inc 4368 Spyres Way *TF:* 866-645-4567 ■ *Web:* www.hospiceheart.org	Modesto	CA	95356	209-578-6300	578-6391
Desert Hospital Hospice of the Desert Communities 555 E Tachevah Dr *TF:* 800-962-3765	Palm Springs	CA	92262	760-323-6642	327-8086
Elizabeth Hospice 150 W Crest St *TF:* 800-797-2050 ■ *Web:* www.elizabethhospice.org	Escondido	CA	92025	760-737-2050	796-3788
Hinds Hospice 1416 W Twain Ave *TF:* 800-400-4677 ■ *Web:* www.hindshospice.com	Fresno	CA	93711	559-222-0793	222-4782
Hoffmann Hospice of the Valley 5300 California Ave Suite 1 *TF:* 888-833-7900	Bakersfield	CA	93309	661-833-3900	716-1700
Hospice & Palliative Care of Contra Costa 3470 Buskirk Ave	Pleasant Hill	CA	94523	925-887-5678	609-1841
Hospice by the Bay 1902 Van Ness Ave 2nd Fl *Web:* www.hospicebythebay.citysearch.com	San Francisco	CA	94109	415-626-5900	626-7800
Hospice By the Bay 17 E Sir Francis Drake Blvd *Web:* www.hospicebythebay.org	Larkspur	CA	94939	415-927-2273	925-1004
Hospice Caring Project of Santa Cruz County 940 Disc Dr *Web:* www.hospicesantacruz.org	Scotts Valley	CA	95066	831-430-3000	430-9272
Hospice of Presbyterian 15050 Imperial Hwy.	La Mirada	CA	90638	562-944-1629	944-6169
Hospice of Redlands Community Hospital 350 Terracina Blvd	Redlands	CA	92373	909-335-5643	335-5648
Hospice of San Joaquin 3888 Pacific Ave. *Web:* www.hospicesj.org	Stockton	CA	95204	209-957-3888	957-3986
Hospice of the Valley 4850 Union Ave *Web:* www.hov.org	San Jose	CA	95124	408-947-1233	288-4172
Kaiser Hayward Hospice Program 30116 Eigenbrodt Way	Union City	CA	94587	510-675-5777	675-5778
Kaiser Permanente Hospital Hospice Dept 280 W MacArthur Blvd	Oakland	CA	94611	510-752-6390	752-7734
Kaiser Permanente Los Angeles Hospice 3699 Wilshire Blvd 3rd Fl.	Los Angeles	CA	90010	323-783-7416	667-7455
Kaiser Walnut Creek Hospice 200 Muir Rd.	Martinez	CA	94553	925-229-7800	229-7805
Livingston Memorial Visiting Nurse Assn Hospice 1996 Eastman Ave Suite 101 *TF:* 800-540-0543 ■ *Web:* www.lmvna.org	Ventura	CA	93003	805-642-1608	642-0830
Mission Hospice Inc of San Mateo County 1670 S Amphlett Blvd #300 *Web:* www.missionhospice.org	San Mateo	CA	94402	650-554-1000	554-1001
San Diego Hospice 4311 3rd Ave. *TF:* 800-696-9474 ■ *Web:* www.sdhospice.com	San Diego	CA	92103	619-688-1600	688-9665
Sutter Hospice/Sacramento 7300 Folsom Blvd # 100 *Web:* www.sutterhealth.org	Sacramento	CA	95826	916-454-6525	454-6526
Sutter VNA & Hospice 1625 Van Ness Ave Suite 4-A. *TF:* 800-557-9777 ■ *Web:* www.suttervnaandhospice.org	San Francisco	CA	94109	415-600-7500	600-7530
Torrance Memorial Home Health & Hospice 3330 Lomita Blvd Bldg 1 S. *Web:* www.torrancememorial.org	Torrance	CA	90505	310-784-3739	784-3717
Visiting Nurse & Hospice Care 222 E Canon Perdido St *Web:* www.sbvna.org/html/hospice_services.html	Santa Barbara	CA	93101	805-965-5555	568-5178
VITAS Healthcare Corp of California 990 W 190th St Suite 120. *TF:* 800-966-7757 ■ *Web:* www.vitas.com	Torrance	CA	90502	310-324-2273	225-5959
VITAS Healthcare Corp of California 16830 Ventura Blvd Suite 315 *TF:* 800-757-4242 ■ *Web:* www.vitas.com	Encino	CA	91436	818-385-0273	971-3580
VITAS Healthcare Corp of California 220 Commerce Suite 100. *TF:* 800-486-6157 ■ *Web:* www.vitas.com	Irvine	CA	92602	714-921-2273	734-2780
VITAS Healthcare Corp of California 9655 Granite Ridge Dr Suite 300 *TF:* 800-966-8705 ■ *Web:* www.vitas.com	San Diego	CA	92123	858-499-8901	503-4785
VITAS Healthcare Corp of San Gabriel Cities 1343 N Grand Ave. *TF:* 800-966-8709 ■ *Web:* www.vitas.com	Covina	CA	91724	626-918-2273	960-8587
VNA & Hospice of Northern California 1900 Powell St Suite 300 *TF:* 888-600-7744 ■ *Web:* www.suttervnaandhospice.org	Emeryville	CA	94608	510-450-8596	450-8532
VNA & Hospice of Southern California 150 W 1st St Suite 270. *TF:* 888-357-3574	Claremont	CA	91711	909-624-3574	624-1559
VNA Home Health Systems (VNAHHS) 2500 Red Hill Ave Suite 105. *Web:* www.vnahhs.com	Santa Ana	CA	92705	949-263-4700	263-4809
VNA of the Inland Counties 6235 River Crest Dr Suite L *Web:* www.vna-ic.org	Riverside	CA	92507	951-413-1200	656-0045

COLORADO

Name / Address	City	State	ZIP	Phone	Fax
Centura Home Care & Hospice 1391 Speer Blvd Suite 600 — *Web:* www.centurahealthathome.org	Denver	CO	80204	303-561-5000	561-5050
Denver Hospice The 501 S Cherry St Suite 700 — *Web:* www.thedenverhospice.org	Denver	CO	80246	303-321-2828	321-7171
Hospice & Palliative Care of Northern Colorado 2726 W 11th St Rd — *TF:* 800-564-5563 ■ *Web:* www.hpcnc.org	Greeley	CO	80634	970-352-8487	475-0037
Hospice & Palliative Care of Western Colorado 2754 Compass Dr Suite 377 — *TF:* 866-310-8900 ■ *Web:* www.hospicewco.com	Grand Junction	CO	81506	970-241-2212	257-2400
Hospice of Boulder County 2594 Trailridge Dr E — *Web:* www.hospicecareonline.org	Lafayette	CO	80026	303-449-7740	449-6961
Pikes Peak Hospice 825 E Pikes Peak Ave Suite 600 — *Web:* www.pikespeakhospice.org	Colorado Springs	CO	80903	719-633-3400	633-3800
Sangre de Cristo Hospice 1207 Pueblo Blvd Way	Pueblo	CO	81005	719-542-0032	542-1413

CONNECTICUT

Name / Address	City	State	ZIP	Phone	Fax
Abbott Terrace Health Ctr 44 Abbott Terr	Waterbury	CT	06702	203-755-4870	755-9016
Connecticut Hospice 100 Double Beach Rd — *Fax: Hum Res ■ *Web:* www.hospice.com	Branford	CT	06405	203-315-7500	315-7561*
Hospice of Southeastern Connecticut Inc 227 Dunham St — *TF:* 877-654-4035 ■ *Web:* www.hospicesect.org	Norwich	CT	06360	860-848-5699	848-6898
Regional Hospice of Western Connecticut 405 Main St — *Web:* www.danbury.org/hospice	Danbury	CT	06810	203-702-7400	792-1402
Visiting Nurse & Health Services of Connecticut Inc 8 Keynote Dr — *Web:* www.vnhsc.org	Vernon	CT	06066	860-872-9163	872-3030
Visiting Nurse & Hospice Care of Southwestern Connecticut 1029 E Main St — *Web:* www.vnhcsw.org	Stamford	CT	06902	203-276-3000	276-3001
VNA Health Care Hospice 103 Woodland St — *Web:* www.vnastl.com	Hartford	CT	06105	860-525-7001	278-0581

DELAWARE

Name / Address	City	State	ZIP	Phone	Fax
Compassionate Care Hospice of Delaware 5610 Kirkwood Hwy — *TF:* 800-219-0092 ■ *Web:* www.cchnet.net	Wilmington	DE	19808	302-683-1000	683-1006

DISTRICT OF COLUMBIA

Name / Address	City	State	ZIP	Phone	Fax
Hospice Care of the District of Columbia 50 F St NW Suite 3300 — *TF:* 800-869-2136 ■ *Web:* www.capitalhospice.org	Washington	DC	20001	202-244-8300	244-1413

FLORIDA

Name / Address	City	State	ZIP	Phone	Fax
Avow Hospice 1095 Whippoorwill Ln — *Web:* www.hospiceofnaples.org	Naples	FL	34105	239-261-4404	262-2429
Bigbend Hospice 1723 Mahan Ctr Blvd — *TF:* 800-772-5862 ■ *Web:* www.bigbendhospice.org	Tallahassee	FL	32308	850-878-5310	309-1638
Catholic Hospice Inc 14875 NW 77th Ave Suite 100 — *Web:* www.catholichospice.org	Miami Lakes	FL	33014	305-822-2380	824-0665
Community Hospice of Northeast Florida 655 W 8th St — *Web:* www.communityhospice.com	Jacksonville	FL	32209	904-244-1651	244-1656
Comprehensive Home Health & Hospice Care 7270 NW 12th St PH 6	Miami	FL	33126	305-591-1606	591-1618
Covenant Hospice 5041 N 12th Ave — *TF:* 800-541-3072 ■ *Web:* www.covenanthospice.org	Pensacola	FL	32504	850-433-2155	433-7212
Good Shepherd Hospice of Mid-Florida Inc 105 Arneson Ave — *TF:* 800-753-1880 ■ *Web:* www.goodshepherdhospice.org	Auburndale	FL	33823	863-297-1880	965-5601
Gulfside Regional Hospice Inc 6224 Lafayette St — *TF:* 800-561-4883 ■ *Web:* www.gulfsideregionalhospice.org	New Port Richey	FL	34652	727-845-5707	845-7254
Hernando Pasco Hospice 12107 Majestic Blvd — *TF:* 800-486-8784 ■ *Web:* www.hphospice.org	Hudson	FL	34667	727-863-7971	868-9261
Hope Hospice 9470 HealthPark Cir — *TF:* 800-835-1673 ■ *Web:* www.hopehospice.org	Fort Myers	FL	33908	239-482-4673	482-7298
Hospice & VNA of the Florida Keys 1319 William St — *Web:* www.hospicevna.com	Key West	FL	33040	305-294-8812	292-9466
Hospice by the Sea 1531 W Palmetto Pk Rd — *Fax: Admissions ■ *TF:* 800-633-2577 ■ *Web:* www.hospicebytheseafl.org	Boca Raton	FL	33486	561-395-5031	393-7137*
Hospice of Citrus County 4005 N Lecanto Hwy — *TF:* 866-642-0962 ■ *Web:* www.hospiceofcitruscounty.org	Beverly Hills	FL	34465	352-527-2020	527-0386
Hospice of Lake & Sumter Inc 12300 Ln Pk Rd — *TF:* 888-728-6234 ■ *Web:* www.hospicels.com	Tavares	FL	32778	352-343-1341	343-6115
Hospice of Marion County 3231 SW 34th Ave — *Web:* www.hospiceofmarion.com	Ocala	FL	34474	352-873-7400	873-7435
Hospice of North Central Florida Inc 4200 NW 90th Blvd — *TF:* 800-727-1889 ■ *Web:* www.hospice-cares.com	Gainesville	FL	32606	352-378-2121	379-6290
Hospice of Northeast Florida 4266 Sunbeam Rd — *TF:* 800-658-8898 ■ *Web:* www.communityhospice.com	Jacksonville	FL	32257	904-268-5200	268-9795
Hospice of Palm Beach County 5300 E Ave — *TF:* 800-287-4722 ■ *Web:* www.hpbc.com	West Palm Beach	FL	33407	561-848-5200	863-2044
Hospice of Saint Francis 1250 Grumman Pl # B — *TF:* 866-269-4240 ■ *Web:* www.nbbd.com	Titusville	FL	32780	321-269-4240	269-5428
Hospice of the Comforter 480 W Central Pkwy — *Fax: Admissions ■ *TF:* 800-767-9952 ■ *Web:* www.hospiceofthecomforter.org	Altamonte Springs	FL	32714	407-682-0808	682-5787*
Hospice of the Florida Suncoast 5771 Roosevelt Blvd — *Web:* www.thehospice.com	Clearwater	FL	33760	727-586-4432	523-2145
Hospice of the Treasure Coast 5090 Dunn Rd — *TF:* 800-299-4677 ■ *Web:* www.tchospice.org	Fort Pierce	FL	34981	772-462-8900	
Hospice of Volusia/Flagler 3800 Woodbriar Trail — *TF:* 800-272-2717 ■ *Web:* www.hfch.org	Port Orange	FL	32129	386-322-4701	322-4702
HospiceCare of Southeast Florida Inc 309 SE 18th St — *TF:* 800-372-1757 ■ *Web:* www.hospicecareflorida.org	Fort Lauderdale	FL	33316	954-467-7423	524-6067
Lifepath Hospice 3010 W Azeele St — *TF:* 800-209-2200 ■ *Web:* www.lifepath-hospice.org	Tampa	FL	33609	813-877-2200	872-7037
Tidewell Hospice 5955 Rand Blvd — *TF:* 800-959-4291 ■ *Web:* www.tidewell.org	Sarasota	FL	34238	941-923-5822	925-0969
Treasure Coast Hospice 1201 SE Indian St — *TF:* 800-299-4677 ■ *Web:* www.tchospice.org	Stuart	FL	34997	772-403-4500	403-4518
Visiting Nurse Assn of the Treasure Coast 1110 35th Ln — *TF:* 800-749-5760 ■ *Web:* www.vnatc.com	Vero Beach	FL	32960	772-567-5551	569-4174
VITAS Healthcare Corp of Central Florida 5151 Adanson St Suite 200 — *Web:* www.vitas.com	Orlando	FL	32804	407-875-0028	691-4517
VITAS Healthcare Corp of Florida 18001 Old Cutler Rd Suite 454 — *TF:* 800-950-9200 ■ *Web:* www.vitas.com	Palmetto Bay	FL	33157	786-573-1379	573-7870
VITAS Innovative Hospice Care 100 S Biscayne Blvd Suite 1500 — *Fax: Hum Res ■ *TF:* 866-418-4827 ■ *Web:* www.vitas.com	Miami	FL	33131	305-374-4143	350-6797*

GEORGIA

Name / Address	City	State	ZIP	Phone	Fax
Columbus Hospice 7020 Moon Rd — *Web:* www.columbushospice.com	Columbus	GA	31909	706-569-7992	569-8560
Heyman HospiceCare 420 E Second Ave — *TF:* 800-324-1078 ■ *Web:* www.floydmed.org	Rome	GA	30161	706-509-3200	509-3201
Hospice Atlanta-Visiting Nurse Health System 1244 Pk Vista Dr — *TF:* 800-287-7849 ■ *Web:* www.vnhs.org	Atlanta	GA	30319	404-869-3000	869-3098
Hospice of Central Georgia 6261 peak Rd — *TF:* 800-211-1084	Macon	GA	31210	478-633-5660	633-6247
Hospice of NE Georgia Medical Ctr 2150 Limestone Pkwy Suite 222 — *Web:* www.nghs.com	Gainesville	GA	30501	770-533-8888	219-8887
Hospice of Southwest Georgia 818 Gordon Ave — *TF:* 800-290-6567	Thomasville	GA	31792	229-227-5520	227-5526
Hospice Savannah Inc PO Box 13190 — *TF:* 888-355-4911 ■ *Web:* www.hospicesavannah.org	Savannah	GA	31416	912-355-2289	355-2376
Trinity Hospital of Augusta 2803 Wrightsboro Rd # 38 — *TF:* 800-533-3949 ■ *Web:* www.trinityofaugusta.com	Augusta	GA	30909	706-729-6000	729-6454
United Hospice of Atlanta 1626 Jeurgens Ct — *TF:* 800-544-4788	Norcross	GA	30093	404-292-2081	297-4647
VITAS Hospice Care 1575 Northside Dr NW # 470 — *TF:* 800-938-4827 ■ *Web:* www.vitas.com	Atlanta	GA	30309	404-250-1806	843-6510
Wellstar Community Hospice 4040 Hospital W Dr	Austell	GA	30106	770-732-6710	732-6732

HAWAII

Name / Address	City	State	ZIP	Phone	Fax
Hospice Hawaii 860 Iwilei Rd — *Web:* www.hospicehawaii.org	Honolulu	HI	96817	808-924-9255	922-9161
Hospice of Hilo 1011 Waianuenue Ave — *Web:* www.hospiceofhilo.org	Hilo	HI	96720	808-969-1733	969-4863
Saint Francis Hospice Program 24 Puiwa Rd — *Web:* www.stfrancishawaii.org/sfhs	Honolulu	HI	96817	808-595-7566	595-3515

IDAHO

Name / Address	City	State	ZIP	Phone	Fax
Life's Doors Hospice 420 S Orchard St — *Web:* www.lifesdoors.com	Boise	ID	83705	208-344-6500	344-6590

ILLINOIS

Name / Address	City	State	ZIP	Phone	Fax
Advocate Hospice 1441 Branding Ave Suite 200 — *Web:* www.advocatehealth.com	Downers Grove	IL	60515	630-963-6800	963-6877
Blessing Hospice 1415 Vermont St — *TF:* 800-382-8833	Quincy	IL	62301	217-228-5521	223-8231
Carle Hospice 206 A W Anthony Dr — *TF:* 800-239-3620 ■ *Web:* www.carlehomehealthservices.com/hospice	Champaign	IL	61822	217-383-3488	356-8672

	City	State	ZIP	Phone	Fax
CNS Home Health & Hospice 690 E N Ave Suite 100 *Web:* www.cnshomehealth.org	Carol Stream	IL	60188	630-665-7000	665-7371
Family Hospice of Belleville Area 5110 W Main St *Web:* www.familyhospice.org	Belleville	IL	62226	618-277-1800	277-1074
Harbor Light Hospice 800 Roosevelt Rd Bldg C Suite 206 *TF:* 800-419-0542 ■ *Web:* www.hospiceharborlight.com	Glen Ellyn	IL	60137	630-942-0100	942-0118
Heartland Home Health Care & Hospice 4415 Harrison St Suite 403 **Fax Area Code:* 708 ■ *TF:* 888-733-3750 ■ *Web:* www.hcr-manorcare.com	Hillside	IL	60126	888-733-3750	234-2828*
Heartland Hospice 4415 Harrison St Suite 403	Hillside	IL	60162	708-234-2800	234-2828
Horizon Hospice 833 W Chicago Ave *TF:* 866-733-8028 ■ *Web:* www.horizonhospice.org	Chicago	IL	60622	312-733-8900	733-8952
Hospice of Lincolnland 1000 Health Ctr Dr.	Mattoon	IL	61938	217-234-4075	348-6525
Hospice of Northeastern Illinois 405 Lake Zurich Rd. *TF:* 800-425-4444 ■ *Web:* www.hospiceanswers.org	Barrington	IL	60010	847-381-5599	381-1431
Hospice of Southern Illinois 305 S Illinois St *TF:* 800-233-1708	Belleville	IL	62220	618-235-1703	235-2828
Joliet Area Community Hospice 250 Water Stone Cir *TF:* 800-360-1817 ■ *Web:* www.joliethospice.org	Joliet	IL	60431	815-740-4104	740-4107
Little Co of Mary Home Based Services 9800 SW Hwy *Web:* www.lcmh.org	Oak Lawn	IL	60453	708-229-4663	499-5975
Methodist Medical Center of Illinois Hospice Services 221 NE Glen Oak Ave *Web:* www.methodistmedicalcenter.org	Peoria	IL	61636	309-672-5522	672-4602
Midwest Palliative & Hospice CareCenter 2050 Claire Ct *Web:* www.carecenter.org	Glenview	IL	60025	847-467-7423	556-1611
Northern Illinois Hospice Assn 4215 Newburg Rd. *Web:* www.northernillinoishospice.org	Rockford	IL	61108	815-398-0500	398-0588
OSF Hospice 2265 W Altorfer Dr *TF:* 800-446-3009	Peoria	IL	61615	309-683-7703	683-7824
Rainbow Hospice 444 N NW Hwy Suite 145 *Web:* www.rainbowhospice.org	Park Ridge	IL	60068	847-685-9900	685-6390
Unity Hospice 439 E 31st St Suite 213 *TF:* 888-949-1188 ■ *Web:* www.unityhospice.com	Chicago	IL	60616	312-949-1188	949-0158
VITAS Healthcare Corp 600 Holiday Plaza Dr Suite 200 *Web:* www.vitas.com	Matteson	IL	60443	708-748-8777	748-8778

INDIANA

	City	State	ZIP	Phone	Fax
Center for Hospice Care Inc 111 Sunnybrook Ct. *TF:* 800-413-9083 ■ *Web:* www.centerforhospice.org	South Bend	IN	46637	574-243-3100	243-3134
Hosparus Inc 624 E Market St *TF:* 800-895-5633 ■ *Web:* www.hosparus.org	New Albany	IN	47150	812-945-4596	945-4733
Hospice of South Central Indiana 2626 17th St.	Columbus	IN	47201	812-314-8000	314-8151
Hospice of the Calumet Area 600 Superior Ave *Web:* www.hospicecalumet.org	Munster	IN	46321	219-922-2732	922-1947
Saint Vincent Hospice 8450 N Payne Rd Suite 100 *TF:* 888-780-7284 ■ *Web:* www.stvincent.org	Indianapolis	IN	46268	317-338-4040	338-4044

IOWA

	City	State	ZIP	Phone	Fax
Cedar Valley Hospice 2101 Kimball Ave Suite 401 *TF:* 800-617-1972 ■ *Web:* www.cvhospice.org	Waterloo	IA	50702	319-272-2002	272-2071
Hospice of Central Iowa (HCI) 401 Railroad Pl. *TF:* 800-806-9934 ■ *Web:* www.hospiceofcentraliowa.org	West Des Moines	IA	50265	515-333-5810	271-1302
Hospice of North Iowa 232 2nd St SE *TF:* 800-297-4719	Mason City	IA	50401	641-422-6208	422-6244
Hospice of Siouxland 4300 Hamilton Blvd *TF:* 800-383-4545 ■ *Web:* www.hospiceofsiouxland.org	Sioux City	IA	51104	712-233-4100	233-1123

KANSAS

	City	State	ZIP	Phone	Fax
Harry Hynes Memorial Hospice 313 S Market St. *TF:* 800-767-4965 ■ *Web:* www.hynesmemorial.org	Wichita	KS	67202	316-265-9441	265-6066
Hospice Home Health of Olathe Medical Ctr 20333 W 151st St TDB 2 Suite 301 *TF:* 800-467-4451	Olathe	KS	66061	913-324-8515	324-8517
Hospice of Reno County 3 Compound Dr. *TF:* 800-267-6891	Hutchinson	KS	67502	620-665-2473	669-5959
Midland Hospice Care 200 SW Frazier Cir *TF:* 800-491-3691 ■ *Web:* www.midlandcareconnection.org	Topeka	KS	66606	785-232-2044	232-5567

KENTUCKY

	City	State	ZIP	Phone	Fax
Community Hospice 1538 Central Ave. *TF:* 800-926-6184 ■ *Web:* www.communityhospicecares.org	Ashland	KY	41101	606-329-1890	329-0018
Heritage Hospice 120 Enterprise Dr PO Box 1213 *TF:* 800-203-6633 ■ *Web:* www.heritagehospice.com	Danville	KY	40423	859-236-2425	236-6152
Hospice Assn Inc 3419 Wathens Crossing *TF:* 800-466-5348 ■ *Web:* www.hospiceohiovalley.org	Owensboro	KY	42301	270-926-7565	926-1223
Hospice of Lake Cumberland 100 Pkwy Dr *TF:* 800-937-9596	Somerset	KY	42503	606-679-4389	678-0191
Hospice of Southern Kentucky 5872 Scottsville Rd. *TF:* 800-344-9479	Bowling Green	KY	42104	270-782-3402	782-3496
Hospice of the Bluegrass 2312 Alexandria Dr. *TF:* 800-876-6005 ■ *Web:* www.hospicebg.com	Lexington	KY	40504	859-276-5344	223-0490
Lourdes Homecare & Hospice 2855 Jackson St *TF:* 800-870-7460 ■ *Web:* www.elourdes.com	Paducah	KY	42003	270-444-2262	
Saint Anthony's Hospice 2410 S Green St *TF:* 866-380-2326 ■ *Web:* www.stanthonyshospice.org	Henderson	KY	42420	270-826-2326	831-2169

LOUISIANA

	City	State	ZIP	Phone	Fax
Hospice of Acadiana 2600 Johnston St Suite 200 *TF:* 800-738-2226 ■ *Web:* www.hospiceacadiana.com	Lafayette	LA	70503	337-232-1234	232-1297
Hospice of Baton Rouge 9063 Siegen Ln *TF:* 800-349-8833 ■ *Web:* www.hospicebr.org	Baton Rouge	LA	70810	225-767-4673	769-8113
Hospice of South Louisiana 6500 W Main St. *TF General:* 888-893-3829 ■ *Web:* www.glendalehealthcare.com	Houma	LA	70360	985-868-3095	868-3910
North Oaks Hospice PO Box 2668	Hammond	LA	70404	985-230-7620	386-0184

MARYLAND

	City	State	ZIP	Phone	Fax
Carroll Hospice 292 Stoner Ave *TF:* 888-224-2580 ■ *Web:* www.ccgh.com	Westminster	MD	21157	410-871-8000	871-7216
Coastal Hospice & palliative care 2604 Old Ocean City Rd PO Box 1733 *TF:* 800-780-7886 ■ *Web:* www.coastalhospice.org	Salisbury	MD	21804	410-742-8732	548-5669
Heartland Hospice Services 4 E Rolling Cross Rd Suite 307 *TF:* 888-332-6232	Baltimore	MD	21228	410-247-2900	247-2581
Hospice of Baltimore 6601 N Charles St.	Baltimore	MD	21204	443-849-8200	849-6761
Hospice of the Chesapeake 445 Defense Hwy. **Fax Area Code:* 443 ■ *TF:* 800-745-6132 ■ *Web:* www.hospicechesapeake.org	Annapolis	MD	21401	410-987-2003	837-1505*
Montgomery Hospice 1355 Piccard Dr Suite 100 *Web:* www.montgomeryhospice.org	Rockville	MD	20850	301-921-4400	921-4433
Richey Joseph Hospice 838 N Eutaw St *Web:* www.josephricheyhospice.org	Baltimore	MD	21201	410-523-2150	523-1146
Seasons Hospice 6934 Aviation Blvd Suite N. *TF:* 888-523-6000 ■ *Web:* www.seasons.org	Glen Burnie	MD	21061	410-594-9100	689-1869
Stella Maris Hospice Care Program 2300 Dulaney Valley Rd *Web:* www.stellamarisinc.com	Timonium	MD	21093	410-252-4500	560-9693

MASSACHUSETTS

	City	State	ZIP	Phone	Fax
Baystate Visiting Nurse Assn & Hospice 50 Maple St *TF:* 800-249-8298 ■ *Web:* www.baystatehealth.com	Springfield	MA	01102	413-781-5070	781-3342
Community VNA 10 Emory St *TF:* 800-220-0110 ■ *Web:* www.communityvna.com	Attleboro	MA	02703	508-222-0118	226-8939
Hospice & Palliative Care of Cape Cod Inc 765 Attucks Ln *TF:* 800-642-2423 ■ *Web:* www.hospicecapecod.org	Hyannis	MA	02601	508-957-0200	957-0229
Hospice Care 100 Sylvan Rd *TF:* 866-279-7103 ■ *Web:* www.hospicecarema.org	Woburn	MA	01801	781-279-4100	279-4677
Hospice Life Care 113 Hampden St	Holyoke	MA	01040	413-533-3923	536-4513
Hospice of the North Shore 75 Sylvan St # B102 *Web:* www.hns.org	Danvers	MA	01923	978-774-7566	774-4389
Merrimack Valley Hospice 360 Merrimack St Bldg 9 *TF:* 800-933-5593 ■ *Web:* www.merrimackvalleyhospice.org	Lawrence	MA	01843	978-552-4000	552-4401
Old Colony Hospice 1 Credit Union Way *TF:* 800-370-1322 ■ *Web:* www.oldcolonyhospice.org	Randolph	MA	02368	781-341-4145	297-7345
VNA Hospice Alliance 168 Industrial Dr *TF:* 800-244-1060	NorthHampton	MA	01060	413-584-1060	584-9615

MICHIGAN

	City	State	ZIP	Phone	Fax
Angela Hospice Home Care 14100 Newburgh Rd *TF:* 800-467-7423 ■ *Web:* www.angelahospice.org	Livonia	MI	48154	734-464-7810	464-6930
Arbor Hospice & Home Care 2366 Oak Valley Dr. *TF:* 888-992-2273 ■ *Web:* www.arborhospice.org	Ann Arbor	MI	48103	734-662-5999	662-2330
Community Hospice & Home Care Services 6639 Wayne Rd. *TF:* 800-444-0425	Westland	MI	48185	734-522-4244	522-2099
Cranbrook Hospice Care 281 Enterprise Ct Suite 300 *TF:* 800-832-1155	Bloomfield Hills	MI	48302	248-452-5300	334-7064
Genesys Hospice 7280 S State Rd *TF:* 888-943-9690	Goodrich	MI	48438	810-762-4370	762-4110
Good Samaritan Hospice Care 166 E Goodale Ave *TF:* 800-254-5939 ■ *Web:* www.lifespancares.org	Battle Creek	MI	49017	269-660-3600	660-3650
Hospice at Home 4025 Health Pk Ln *TF:* 800-717-3811 ■ *Web:* www.hospiceathomecares.org	Saint Joseph	MI	49085	269-429-7100	428-3499
Hospice Care of Southwest Michigan 222 N Kalamazoo Mall Suite 100 *Web:* www.hospiceswmi.org	Kalamazoo	MI	49007	269-345-0273	345-8522

				Phone	Fax
Hospice of Henry Ford Health System 655 W 13 Mile Rd 1st Fl. *Web:* www.henryford.com	Madison Heights	MI	48071	248-585-5270	585-4210
Hospice of Holland Inc 270 Hoover Blvd. *TF:* 800-255-3522 ■ *Web:* www.hollandhospice.org	Holland	MI	49423	616-396-2972	396-2808
Hospice of Lansing & Ionia Area Hospice 6035 Executive Dr Suite 103. *Web:* www.hospiceoflansing.org	Lansing	MI	48911	517-882-4500	882-3010
Hospice of Michigan 400 Mack Ave *TF:* 888-466-5656 ■ *Web:* www.hom.org	Detroit	MI	48201	313-578-5000	578-6385
Hospice of North Ottawa Community 1515 S DeSpelder St *TF:* 800-670-7991 ■ *Web:* www.noch.org/hospice.html	Grand Haven	MI	49417	616-846-2015	846-7227
Karmanos Cancer Institute Hospice 24601 Northwestern Hwy *TF:* 800-527-6266 ■ *Web:* www.karmanos.org	Southfield	MI	48075	248-827-1592	827-0972
Mid Michigan Hospice 3007 N Saginaw Rd *TF:* 800-852-9350	Midland	MI	48640	989-633-1400	633-1412
Munson Hospice 1105 6th St *TF:* 800-252-2065 ■ *Web:* www.munsonhealthcare.com	Traverse City	MI	49684	231-935-6520	935-9142
Saint Joseph Mercy Home Care & Hospice 806 Airport Blvd *TF:* 888-884-6569	Ann Arbor	MI	48108	734-327-3200	327-3274
Samaritan Care Hospice 24445 Northwestern Hwy Suite 105 *TF:* 800-397-9360 ■ *Web:* www.samaritancarehospice.com	Southfield	MI	48075	248-355-9900	355-5705

MINNESOTA

				Phone	Fax
Allina Hospice & Palliative Care 1055 Westgate Dr Suite 100 *TF:* 800-261-0879 ■ *Web:* www.allina.com	Saint Paul	MN	55114	651-635-9173	628-2999
Fairview Hospice 2450 26th Ave S. *TF:* 800-285-5647 ■ *Web:* www.fairview.org	Minneapolis	MN	55406	612-728-2455	728-2400
Health Partners Hospice of the Lakes 8170 33rd Ave S.	Minneapolis	MN	55425	952-883-6877	883-6883
Hospice of the Twin Cities 10405 6th Ave N Suite 250 *TF:* 800-364-2478 ■ *Web:* www.hospiceofthetwincities.com	Plymouth	MN	55441	763-531-2424	531-2422
Mayo Hospice Program 200 1st St SW *TF:* 800-679-9084	Rochester	MN	55902	507-284-4002	284-0220
North Memorial Home Health & Hospice 3500 France Ave N Suite 101	Robbinsdale	MN	55422	763-520-5770	
Rice Hospice 301 SW Becker Ave *TF:* 800-336-7423	Willmar	MN	56201	320-231-4450	231-4864

MISSISSIPPI

				Phone	Fax
Delta Area Hospice Care Ltd 522 Arnold Ave *TF:* 800-742-2641	Greenville	MS	38701	662-335-7040	335-7027
Hospice Ministries 450 Towne Ctr Blvd *TF:* 800-273-7724 ■ *Web:* www.hospiceministries.org	Ridgeland	MS	39157	601-898-1053	898-4320
North Mississippi Medical Center Hospice 422-A E President St *TF:* 800-852-1610	Tupelo	MS	38801	662-377-3612	377-2537
Sta-Home Hospice 406 Briarwood Dr Suite 500 *TF:* 800-336-6557 ■ *Web:* www.sta-home.org	Jackson	MS	39206	601-991-1933	991-3343

MISSOURI

				Phone	Fax
American Heartland Hospice 2388 Schuetz Rd # C75 *Web:* www.callmyhospice.com	Saint Louis	MO	63146	314-894-8189	894-7334
Hands of Hope Hospice 105 N Far W Dr Suite 100 *TF:* 800-443-1143	Saint Joseph	MO	64506	816-271-7190	271-7672
Kansas City Hospice & Palliative Care 9221 Ward Pkwy Suite 100 *Web:* www.kansascityhospice.org	Kansas City	MO	64114	816-363-2600	523-0068
Odyssey Healthcare of Kansas City 800 E 101st Terr Suite 150 *TF:* 800-334-1980 ■ *Web:* www.odsyhealth.com	Kansas City	MO	64131	816-333-1980	333-2421
Saint John's Hospice Care 1378 E Republic Rd	Springfield	MO	65804	417-820-7550	820-7426
Saint Luke's Home Care & Hospice 3100 Broadway St Suite 1000	Kansas City	MO	64111	816-756-1160	756-0838
SSM Hospice 2 Harbor Bend Ct *TF:* 800-835-1212 ■ *Web:* www.ssmhc.com	Lake Saint Louis	MO	63367	636-695-2050	695-2060
VNA Hospice Care 9450 Manchester Rd Suite 206 *TF:* 800-392-4740 ■ *Web:* www.vnastl.com	Saint Louis	MO	63119	314-918-7171	918-8054

MONTANA

				Phone	Fax
Peace Hospice of Montana 1101 26th St S	Great Falls	MT	59405	406-455-3040	455-3070

NEBRASKA

				Phone	Fax
AseraCare Hospice - Lincoln 1600 S 70th St Suite 201 *TF:* 800-826-3841 ■ *Web:* www.aserahospicelincoln.com	Lincoln	NE	68506	402-488-1363	488-5976
Visiting Nurse Assn 12565 W Ctr Rd Suite 100 *TF:* 800-456-8869 ■ *Web:* www.thevnacares.org	Omaha	NE	68144	402-342-5566	342-9304

NEVADA

				Phone	Fax
Family Home Hospice 1701 W Charleston Blvd Suite 201 *TF:* 800-999-2536	Las Vegas	NV	89102	702-383-0887	383-9826
Nathan Adelson Hospice 4141 Swenson St *TF:* 888-281-8646 ■ *Web:* www.nah.org	Las Vegas	NV	89169	702-733-0320	938-3900
Odyssey HealthCare of Las Vegas Inc 4011-A McLeod Dr *TF:* 877-637-9432 ■ *Web:* www.odsyhealth.com	Las Vegas	NV	89121	702-693-4904	693-4925
Saint Mary's Hospice of Northern Nevada 429 Elm St *TF:* 866-333-8059 ■ *Web:* www.saintmarysreno.org/Medical_Services/DEVCV121226	Reno	NV	89503	775-770-3081	770-6904

NEW HAMPSHIRE

				Phone	Fax
Concord Regional Visiting Nurse Assoc Hospice Program 30 Pillsbury St *TF:* 800-924-8620 ■ *Web:* www.crvna.org	Concord	NH	03301	603-224-4093	228-7360
Home Health & Hospice Care 22 Prospect St *TF:* 800-887-5973 ■ *Web:* www.hhhc.org	Nashua	NH	03060	603-882-2941	883-1515
Seacoast Hospice 10 Hampton Rd *TF:* 800-416-9207 ■ *Web:* www.seacoasthospice.org	Exeter	NH	03833	603-778-7391	772-7692
VNA of Manchester & Southern New Hampshire 33 S Commercial St Suite 401 *TF:* 800-624-6084	Manchester	NH	03101	603-622-3781	641-4074

NEW JERSEY

				Phone	Fax
Center for Hope Hospice 1900 Raritan Rd *Web:* www.centerforhope.com	Scotch Plains	NJ	07076	908-889-7780	889-5172
Compassionate Care Hospice 600 Highland Dr Suite 624 *TF:* 800-844-4774	West Hampton	NJ	08060	609-267-1178	267-7914
Home Health/Van Dyke Hospice 1433 hooper Ave. *TF:* 800-338-3131	Toms River	NJ	08753	732-818-6800	818-6888
Hospice of New Jersey 400 Broadacres Dr 4th Fl *Web:* www.americanhospice.com	Bloomfield	NJ	07003	973-893-0818	893-0828
Hospice Program of Hackensack University Medical Ctr 30 Prospect Ave *Web:* www.humed.com/hospice	Hackensack	NJ	07601	201-342-7766	487-1982
Karen Ann Quinlan Hospice 99 Sparta Ave. *TF:* 800-882-1117 ■ *Web:* www.karenannquinlanhospice.org	Newton	NJ	07860	973-383-0115	383-6889
Lighthouse Hospice 1040 Kings Hwy N # 100 *TF:* 888-345-7742 ■ *Web:* www.lighthousehospice.net	Cherry Hill	NJ	08034	856-414-1155	414-1313
Saint Barnabas Hospice & Palliative Care Ctr 95 Old Short Hills Rd *Web:* www.saintbarnabas.com	West Orange	NJ	07052	973-322-4800	322-4795
Samaritan Hospice 5 Eves Dr Suite 300 *TF:* 800-229-8183 ■ *Web:* www.Samaritanhealthcarenj.org	Marlton	NJ	08053	856-596-1600	596-7881
South Jersey Healthcare HospiceCare 2848 S Delsea Dr Bldg #1 *TF:* 800-584-1515 ■ *Web:* www.sjhealthcare.net	Vineland	NJ	08360	856-696-2010	696-3689
VNA of Central Jersey (VNACJ) 176 Riverside Ave. *TF:* 800-862-3330 ■ *Web:* www.vnacj.org	Red Bank	NJ	07701	800-862-3330	

NEW MEXICO

				Phone	Fax
Mesilla Valley Hospice 299 Montana Ave. *Web:* www.mvhospice.org	Las Cruces	NM	88005	575-523-4700	527-2204
VistaCare Hospice 1515 W Calle Sur St Suite 129 *TF:* 800-658-6844 ■ *Web:* www.vistacare.com	Hobbs	NM	88240	505-392-2060	392-2807
VistaCare Hospice 5639 Jefferson St NE *TF:* 877-946-7723 ■ *Web:* www.vistacare.com	Albuquerque	NM	87109	505-821-5404	821-5449

NEW YORK

				Phone	Fax
Catskill Area Hospice & Palliative Care Inc 1 Birchwood Dr. *TF:* 800-306-3870 ■ *Web:* www.cahpc.org	Oneonta	NY	13820	607-432-6773	432-7741
Community Hospice of Albany 445 New Karner Rd	Albany	NY	12205	518-724-0200	724-0299
East End Hospice 481 Westhampton-Riverhead Rd PO Box 1048 *Web:* www.eeh.org	WestHampton Beach	NY	11978	631-288-8400	288-8492
Good Shepherd Hospice 190 Motor Pkwy 1st Fl *Web:* goodshepherdhospice.chsli.org	Hauppauge	NY	11788	631-648-1255	648-1268
High Peaks Hospice 309 County Rt 47 # 3 *TF:* 877-324-1686	Saranac Lake	NY	12983	518-891-0606	891-0657
HomeCare & Hospice 1225 W State St *TF:* 800-339-7011 ■ *Web:* www.homecare-hospice.org	Olean	NY	14760	716-372-5735	372-4635
Hospicare of Tompkins County 172 E King Rd *Web:* www.hospicare.org	Ithaca	NY	14850	607-272-0212	272-0237
Hospice & Palliative Care of Buffalo 225 Como Pk Blvd *Web:* www.hospicebuffalo.com	Cheektowaga	NY	14227	716-686-1900	686-8181
Hospice Care in Westchester & Putnam Inc 540 White Plains Rd Suite 300 *TF:* 800-298-6341 ■ *Web:* www.vnahv.org	Tarrytown	NY	10591	914-666-4228	666-0378

			Phone	Fax
Hospice Care Inc 4277 Middle Settlement Rd ... New Hartford *TF:* 800-317-5661 ■ *Web:* www.hospicecareinc.com	NY	13413	315-735-6484	793-8852
Hospice Care Network 99 Sunnyside Blvd ... Woodbury *TF:* 800-246-7742 ■ *Web:* www.hospicecarenetwork.org	NY	11797	516-832-7100	832-7160
Hospice Chautauqua County 20 W Fairmount Ave ... Lakewood *Web:* www.hospicechautco.org	NY	14750	716-753-5383	338-1575
Hospice Family Care 550 E Main St ... Batavia *Web:* www.homecare-hospice.org	NY	14020	585-343-7596	343-7629
Hospice of Jefferson County 425 Washington St ... Watertown *Web:* www.jeffhospice.com	NY	13601	315-788-7323	788-9653
Hospice of Orange & Sullivan Counties 800 Stony Brook Ct ... Newburgh *TF:* 800-924-0157 ■ *Web:* www.hospiceoforange.com	NY	12550	845-561-6111	561-2179
Hospice of Saint Lawrence Valley 6805 State Hwy 11 ... Potsdam *Web:* www.seriousillness.org	NY	13676	315-265-3105	265-0323
Hospice of the North Country 43 Durkee St Suite 200 ... Plattsburgh *TF:* 800-639-6430 ■ *Web:* www.hospicenc.org	NY	12901	518-561-8465	561-3182
Hospice of Westchester 311 N St # 204 ... White Plains *Web:* www.hospiceofwestchester.com	NY	10605	914-682-1484	682-9425
Metropolitan Jewish Health System 6323 7th Ave 3rd Fl ... Brooklyn *Web:* www.mjhs.org	NY	11220	718-759-4677	921-0752
Niagara Hospice 4675 Sunset Dr ... Lockport *TF:* 800-339-7011 ■ *Web:* www.niagarahospice.org	NY	14094	716-439-4417	439-6035
Staten Island University Hospice 256 Mason Ave Bldg C ... Staten Island *TF:* 866-799-2233 ■ *Web:* www.siuh.edu	NY	10305	718-226-6450	226-6607
United Hospice of Rockland 11 Stokum Ln ... New City *Web:* www.hospiceofrockland.org	NY	10956	845-634-4974	634-7549
Visiting Nurse Service of New York Hospice Care 1250 Broadway 7th Fl ... New York *Web:* www.vnsny.org	NY	10001	212-609-1900	290-3933
VNS Hospice of Suffolk 505 Main St ... Northport	NY	11768	631-261-7200	261-1985

NORTH CAROLINA

			Phone	Fax
Caldwell Hospice & Palliative Care 902 Kirkwood St NW ... Lenoir *Web:* www.caldwellhospice.org	NC	28645	828-754-0101	757-3335
CarePartners Mountain Area Hospice PO Box 5779 ... Asheville *Web:* www.carepartners.org	NC	28813	828-255-0231	255-2944
FirstHealth Hospice 5 Aviemore Dr ... Pinehurst *Web:* www.firsthealth.org	NC	28374	910-715-6000	715-6032
Four Seasons Hospice & Palliative Care 571 S Allen Rd ... Flat Rock *TF:* 866-466-9734 ■ *Web:* www.fourseasonscfl.org	NC	28731	828-692-6178	233-0351
Hospice & Palliative Care of Cabarrus County 5003 Hospice Ln ... Kannapolis *Web:* www.hpccc.org	NC	28081	704-935-9434	935-9435
Hospice & Palliative CareCenter 101 Hospice Ln ... Winston-Salem *TF:* 888-876-3663 ■ *Web:* www.hospicecarecenter.org	NC	27103	336-768-3972	659-0461
Hospice at Charlotte 1420 E 7th St ... Charlotte *Web:* www.hospiceatcharlotte.com	NC	28204	704-375-0100	375-8623
Hospice at Greensboro 2500 Summit Ave ... Greensboro *Web:* www.hospicegso.org	NC	27405	336-621-2500	621-4516
Hospice of Alamance Caswell 914 Chapel Hill Rd ... Burlington *TF:* 800-588-8879 ■ *Web:* www.hospiceac.org	NC	27215	336-532-0100	532-0060
Hospice of Burke County 1721 Enon Rd ... Valdese *Web:* www.burkehospice.org	NC	28690	828-879-1601	879-3500
Hospice of Cleveland County 951 Wendover Heights Dr ... Shelby *Web:* www.hospicecares.cc	NC	28150	704-487-4677	481-8050
Hospice of Gaston County 258 E Garrison Blvd PO Box 3984 ... Gastonia *Web:* www.gastonhospice.org	NC	28054	704-861-8405	865-0590
Hospice of Randolph County 416 Vision Dr ... Asheboro *Web:* www.hospiceofrandolph.org	NC	27203	336-672-9300	672-0868
Hospice of Rockingham County Inc 2150 NC Hwy 65 PO Box 281 ... Wentworth *Web:* www.hospiceofrockinghamcounty.com	NC	27375	336-427-9022	427-9030
Hospice of Rutherford County PO Box 336 ... Forest City *Web:* www.hospiceofrutherford.com	NC	28043	828-245-0095	248-1035
Hospice of Stanly County 960 N 1st St ... Albemarle *TF:* 800-230-4236	NC	28001	704-983-4216	983-6662
Hospice of the Piedmont 1801 Westchester Dr ... High Point *Web:* www.hospice-careconnection.org	NC	27262	336-889-8446	889-3450
Hospice of Union County 700 W Roosevelt Blvd ... Monroe *Web:* www.houc.org	NC	28110	704-292-2100	292-2190
Hospice of Wake County Inc 1300 St Mary's St 4th Fl ... Raleigh *TF:* 888-900-3959 ■ *Web:* www.hospiceofwake.org	NC	27605	919-828-0890	828-0664
Kitty Askins Hospice Ctr 107 Handley Pk Ct ... Goldsboro *Web:* www.3hc.org	NC	27534	919-735-5887	735-5948
Lower Cape Fear Hospice & Life Care 1414 physicians Dr ... Wilmington *TF:* 800-733-1476 ■ *Web:* www.hospiceandlifecarecenter.org	NC	28401	910-772-5444	796-7901
Palliative CareCenter & Hospice of Catawba Valley 3975 Robinson Rd ... Newton *Web:* www.pchcv.org	NC	28658	828-466-0466	466-8862
Richmond County Hospice 1119 N US Hwy 1 ... Rockingham	NC	28379	910-997-4464	997-4484
Rowan Regional Home Health & Hospice 720 Grove St ... Salisbury *TF:* 888-279-0304	NC	28144	704-637-7645	637-9901
University Hospice PO Box 272 ... Ahoskie	NC	27910	252-332-3392	332-5705

NORTH DAKOTA

			Phone	Fax
Hospice of the Red River Valley 1701 38th St S Suite 101 ... Fargo *TF:* 800-237-4629 ■ *Web:* www.hrrv.org	ND	58103	701-356-1500	356-1592

OHIO

			Phone	Fax
Bridge Home Health & Hospice 15100 Birchaven Ln ... Findlay *TF:* 800-982-3306 ■ *Web:* www.bvhealthsystem.org	OH	45840	419-423-5351	423-8967
FairHope Hospice & Palliative Care Inc 1111 E Main St ... Lancaster *TF:* 800-994-7077 ■ *Web:* www.fairhopehospice.org	OH	43130	740-654-7077	654-6321
Homereach Hospice 3595 Olentangy River Rd ... Columbus *TF:* 800-300-7075	OH	43214	614-566-5377	566-4391
Hospice of Central Ohio 2269 Cherry Valley Rd ... Newark *TF:* 800-804-2505 ■ *Web:* www.hospiceofcentralohio.org	OH	43055	740-344-0311	344-6577
Hospice of Cincinnati 4360 Cooper Rd ... Cincinnati *TF:* 800-691-7255 ■ *Web:* www.hospiceofcincinnati.org	OH	45242	513-891-7700	792-6980
Hospice of Dayton 324 Wilmington Ave ... Dayton *TF:* 800-653-4490 ■ *Web:* www.hospicedayton.org	OH	45420	937-256-4490	256-9802
Hospice of Medina County 797 N Ct St ... Medina *TF:* 800-700-4771 ■ *Web:* www.hospiceofmedina.org	OH	44256	330-722-4771	722-5266
Hospice of Miami County 550 Summit Ave # 101 ... Troy *TF:* 800-372-0009 ■ *Web:* www.homc.org	OH	45373	937-335-5191	335-8841
Hospice of North Central Ohio 1050 Dauch Dr ... Ashland *TF:* 800-952-2207 ■ *Web:* www.hospiceofnorthcentralohio.org	OH	44805	419-281-7107	281-8427
Hospice of Northwest Ohio 30000 E River Rd ... Perrysburg *TF:* 866-661-4001 ■ *Web:* www.hospicenwo.org	OH	43551	419-661-4001	661-4015
Hospice of the Cleveland Clinic 6801 Brecksville Rd Suite 10 ... Independence *TF:* 800-263-0403	OH	44131	216-444-9819	520-1973
Hospice of the Valley 5190 Market St ... Youngstown *TF:* 800-640-5180 ■ *Web:* www.hospiceofthevalley.com	OH	44512	330-788-1992	788-1998
Hospice of the Western Reserve 300 E 185th St ... Cleveland *Web:* www.hospicewr.org	OH	44119	216-383-2222	383-3750
Hospice of Tuscarawas County 201 W 3rd St ... Dover *TF:* 800-947-7284 ■ *Web:* www.myhospice.org	OH	44622	330-343-7605	343-3542
Hospice of Visiting Nurse Service 3358 Ridgewood Rd ... Akron *TF:* 800-335-1455 ■ *Web:* www.vnsa.com	OH	44333	330-665-1455	668-4680
Madison County Home Health Hospice 212 N Main St ... London *TF:* 866-357-4677 ■ *Web:* www.madisoncountyhospital.org	OH	43140	740-845-7550	845-7551
Mercy Medical Center Hospice 7568 Whipple Ave NW ... Canton	OH	44720	330-649-4380	649-4399
New Life Hospice 5255 N Abbe Rd ... Elyria *TF:* 800-770-5767	OH	44035	440-934-1458	934-1567
Seasons of Life Hospice 9511 W Pleasant Valley Rd ... Cleveland	OH	44130	440-743-7330	743-4905
State of the Heart Home Health & Hospice 1350 N Broadway ... Greenville *TF:* 800-417-7535 ■ *Web:* www.stateoftheheartcare.org	OH	45331	937-548-2999	548-7144
Stein Hospice Service 1912 Hayes Ave # 3 ... Sandusky *TF:* 800-625-5269 ■ *Web:* www.steinhospice.org	OH	44870	419-625-5269	625-5761
Universal Home Health & Hospice Care 701 S Main St ... Bellefontaine *TF:* 800-886-5936	OH	43311	937-593-1605	592-1166
Valley Hospice Inc 380 Summit Ave ... Steubenville *TF:* 877-467-7423 ■ *Web:* www.valleyhospice.org	OH	43952	740-284-4440	284-4478
VNA of Cleveland Hospice 2500 E 22nd St ... Cleveland *TF:* 800-862-5253	OH	44115	216-931-1450	694-6355

OKLAHOMA

			Phone	Fax
Good Shepherd Hospice 4350 Will Rogers Pkwy Suite 400 ... Oklahoma City *TF:* 800-687-9808 ■ *Web:* www.goodshepherdhospice.com	OK	73108	405-943-0903	943-0950
Hospice of Oklahoma County 4334 NW Expy Suite 106 ... Oklahoma City *Web:* www.hospiceokcounty.com	OK	73116	405-848-8884	841-4899
Saint Francis Hospice 6600 S Yale Ave Suite 350 ... Tulsa	OK	74136	918-494-6465	491-5899
Trinity Hospice 12121 E 51st St Suite 102 ... Tulsa *TF:* 800-459-9671 ■ *Web:* www.trinityhospice.com	OK	74146	918-254-1727	254-1755

OREGON

			Phone	Fax
Hospice of Bend-La Pine 2075 NE Wyatt Ct ... Bend *Web:* www.partnersbend.org	OR	97701	541-382-5882	382-2960
Legacy Visiting Nurses Assn Hospice PO Box 3426 ... Portland *Web:* www.legacyhealth.org	OR	97208	503-220-1000	225-6398
Lovejoy Hospice 939 SE 8th St ... Grants Pass *TF:* 888-758-8569 ■ *Web:* www.lovejoyhospice.org	OR	97526	541-474-1193	474-3035
Willamette Valley Hospice 1015 3rd St NW ... Salem *TF:* 800-555-2431 ■ *Web:* www.wvh.org	OR	97304	503-588-3600	363-3891

PENNSYLVANIA

	City	State	Zip	Phone	Fax
Berks VNA Hospice Program 1170 Berkshire Blvd *TF:* 800-346-7848 ■ *Web:* www.vnaa.org	Wyomissing	PA	19610	610-378-0481	378-9762
Chandler Hall Hospice 99 Barclay St *TF:* 888-603-1973 ■ *Web:* www.chandlerhall.org	Newtown	PA	18940	215-860-4000	497-0802
Columbia Montour Home VNA Hospice 410 Glenn Ave Suite 200 *Web:* www.cmhhh.org	Bloomsburg	PA	17815	570-784-1723	784-8512
Compassionate Care Hospice 3331 St Rd # 410 *TF:* 800-584-8165	Bensalem	PA	19020	215-245-3525	245-3540
Family Hospice 301 Bellevue Rd *TF:* 800-513-2148 ■ *Web:* www.familyhospice.com	Pittsburgh	PA	15229	412-572-8800	572-8827
Forbes Hospice 115 S Neville St *TF:* 800-381-8080 ■ *Web:* www.wpahs.org	Pittsburgh	PA	15213	412-665-3302	325-7303
Heartland Hospice 4070 Butler Pike Suite 100 *TF:* 800-807-3738	Plymouth Meeting	PA	19462	610-941-6700	941-6440
Holy Redeemer Home Care & Hospice 12265 Townsend Rd Suite 400 *Web:* www.holyredeemer.com	Philadelphia	PA	19154	215-671-9200	671-1950
Hospice Community Care 601 Wyoming Ave *TF:* 877-421-0699 ■ *Web:* www.hospice-homehealth.com	Kingston	PA	18704	570-288-2288	288-7424
Hospice of Central Pennsylvania 1320 Linglestown Rd *TF:* 866-779-7374 ■ *Web:* www.hospiceofcentralpa.org	Harrisburg	PA	17110	717-732-1000	732-5348
Hospice of Lancaster County 685 Good Dr PO Box 4125 *Web:* www.hospiceoflancaster.org	Lancaster	PA	17604	717-295-3900	391-9582
Hospice Saint John 1201 N Church St Bldg B Suite 403 *TF:* 877-438-3511	Hazleton	PA	18202	570-459-6778	453-5202
Lehigh Valley Hospice 2166 S 12th St Suite 401 *TF:* 800-944-4354 ■ *Web:* www.lvhn.org	Allentown	PA	18103	610-969-0300	969-0326
Neighborhood Hospice 795 E Marshall St Suite 204 *TF:* 800-848-1155	West Chester	PA	19380	610-696-6511	344-7064
Samaritan Care Hospice 653 Skippack Pike *TF:* 800-764-6878 ■ *Web:* www.samaritancarehospice.com	Blue Bell	PA	19422	215-653-7310	653-7340
SUN Home Health Services Inc 61 Duke St PO Box 232 *TF:* 888-478-6227 ■ *Web:* www.sunhomehealth.com	Northumberland	PA	17857	570-473-8320	473-3070
VITAS Healthcare Corp of Pennsylvania 1740 Walton Rd Suite 100 *TF:* 800-209-1080 ■ *Web:* www.vitas.com	Blue Bell	PA	19422	610-260-6020	238-4980
VNA Hospice & Palliative Care Ctr 301 Delaware Ave *TF:* 800-936-7671 ■ *Web:* www.vnahospice.org	Olyphant	PA	18447	570-383-5180	383-5189
VNA Hospice Western Pennsylvania 154 Hindman Rd *TF:* 800-245-3042	Butler	PA	16001	724-282-6806	282-1509

RHODE ISLAND

	City	State	Zip	Phone	Fax
Home Hospice Care of Rhode Island 1085 N Main St *TF:* 800-338-6555 ■ *Web:* www.hhcri.org	Providence	RI	02904	401-415-4200	
Visiting Nurse Services of Greater Rhode Island 6 Blackstone Valley Pl Suite 515 *TF:* 800-696-7991 ■ *Web:* www.vnsgri.org	Lincoln	RI	02865	401-769-5670	762-7300

SOUTH CAROLINA

	City	State	Zip	Phone	Fax
Hospice Community Care PO Box 993 *TF:* 800-895-2273 ■ *Web:* www.hospicecommunitycare.org	Rock Hill	SC	29731	803-329-1500	329-5935
Hospice of the Upstate 1835 Rogers Rd *TF:* 800-261-8636 ■ *Web:* www.hospicehouse.net	Anderson	SC	29621	864-224-3358	224-9971
HospiceCare of the Piedmont 408 W Alexander Ave *Web:* www.hospicepiedmont.org	Greenwood	SC	29646	864-227-9393	227-9377
McLeod Hospice 1203 E Cheves St *TF:* 800-768-4556 ■ *Web:* www.mcleodhealth.org	Florence	SC	29506	843-777-2564	777-5135
Mercy Hospice of Horry County PO Box 50640	Myrtle Beach	SC	29579	843-236-2282	347-5535
Open Arms Hospice 1836w Georgia Rd *Web:* www.openarmshospice.org	simtsonville	SC	29680	864-688-1700	688-1705
Palmetto Health Home Care & Hospice 1400 Pickens St *TF:* 800-238-1884 ■ *Web:* www.palmettohealth.org	Columbia	SC	29202	803-296-3100	296-3320

SOUTH DAKOTA

	City	State	Zip	Phone	Fax
Avera McKennan Hospice 4509 Prince of Peace Pl PO Box 5045 *Web:* www1.avera.org/amck/hospice	Sioux Falls	SD	57117	605-322-7705	322-7713

TENNESSEE

	City	State	Zip	Phone	Fax
Adventa Hospice 1423 W Morris Blvd *TF:* 800-659-2633	Morristown	TN	37814	423-587-9484	587-9408
Alive Hospice Inc 1718 Patterson St *TF:* 800-327-1085 ■ *Web:* www.alivehospice.org	Nashville	TN	37203	615-327-1085	321-8902
Hospice of Chattanooga 4411 Oakwood Dr *TF:* 800-267-6828 ■ *Web:* www.hospiceofchattanooga.org	Chattanooga	TN	37416	423-267-6828	892-8301
Methodist Alliance Hospice 6423 Shelby View Dr Suite 103 *TF:* 800-968-8326	Memphis	TN	38134	901-516-1600	380-8170
Trinity Hospice 6141 Walnut Grove Rd *TF:* 800-727-6416 ■ *Web:* www.trinityhospice.com	Memphis	TN	38120	901-767-6767	762-4627

TEXAS

	City	State	Zip	Phone	Fax
American Hospice 1636 N Hampton Rd Suite 220 *TF:* 800-689-1024	DeSoto	TX	75115	972-228-2634	228-1698
AseraCare Hospice - Austin 1212 Palm Valley Blvd *TF:* 800-332-3982 ■ *Web:* www.aserahospiceaustin.com	Round Rock	TX	78664	512-467-7423	218-9288
CHRISTUS Spohn Hospice 6200 Saratoga St Bldg 2 Suite 104 *TF:* 800-341-1368 ■ *Web:* www.christusspohn.org/services_hospice.htm	Corpus Christi	TX	78414	361-994-3450	994-3495
CHRISTUS VNA 4241 Woodcock Dr # A100 *Web:* www.christushomecare.org	San Antonio	TX	78228	210-785-5200	785-5803
Community Hospice of Texas 6100 Western Pl Suite 500 *TF:* 800-226-0373 ■ *Web:* www.chot.org	Fort Worth	TX	76107	817-870-2795	878-3717
Heart'sWay Hospice of Northeast Texas 1306 Pine Tree Rd *TF:* 800-371-1016 ■ *Web:* www.heartswayhospice.org	Longview	TX	75604	903-295-1680	295-1690
Hendrick Hospice Care 1682 Hickory St *TF:* 800-622-8516 ■ *Web:* www.hendrickhospice.org	Abilene	TX	79601	325-677-8516	675-5031
Home Hospice of Grayson County 505 W Ctr St *Web:* www.homehospice.org	Sherman	TX	75090	903-868-9315	893-2772
Hope Hospice 611 N Walnut Ave *Web:* www.hopehospice.net	New Braunfels	TX	78130	830-625-7500	606-1388
Hospice at the Texas Medical Ctr 1905 Holcombe Blvd **Fax:* Admissions ■ *TF:* 800-630-7894 ■ *Web:* www.houstonhospice.org	Houston	TX	77030	713-467-7423	468-0879*
Hospice Austin 4107 Spicewood Springs Rd Suite 100 *TF:* 800-445-3261 ■ *Web:* www.hospiceaustin.org	Austin	TX	78759	512-342-4700	795-9053
Hospice Brazos Valley 502 W 26th St *TF:* 800-824-2326 ■ *Web:* www.hospicebrazosvalley.org	Bryan	TX	77803	979-821-2266	821-0041
Hospice Care Team 1708 N Amburn Rd # C *TF:* 800-545-8738 ■ *Web:* www.hospicecareteam.org	Texas City	TX	77591	409-938-0070	938-1509
Hospice of East Texas 4111 University Blvd *TF:* 800-777-9860 ■ *Web:* www.hospiceofeasttexas.org	Tyler	TX	75701	903-266-3400	566-0291
Hospice of El Paso 1440 Miracle Way *Web:* www.hospiceelpaso.org	El Paso	TX	79925	915-532-5699	532-7822
Hospice of Midland 911 W Texas Ave *TF:* 800-646-6460 ■ *Web:* www.hospiceofmidland.org	Midland	TX	79701	432-682-2855	682-2989
Hospice of San Angelo 36 E Twohig St Suite 1100 *TF:* 800-499-6524	San Angelo	TX	76903	325-658-6524	658-8895
Hospice of South Texas 605 E Locust Ave *TF:* 800-874-6908 ■ *Web:* www.hospiceofsouthtexas.org	Victoria	TX	77901	361-572-4300	570-1147
Hospice of Wichita Falls 4909 Johnson Rd *Web:* www.hospiceofwf.org	Wichita Falls	TX	76310	940-691-0982	687-1294
Hospice Preferred Choice 1235 N Loop W Suite 215 *TF:* 888-646-8696	Houston	TX	77008	713-864-2626	864-9476
VistaCare Hospice 717 N Harwood St Suite 1500 **Fax Area Code:* 317 ■ *TF:* 800-480-9408 ■ *Web:* www.vistacare.com	Dallas	TX	75201	214-922-9711	788-8760*
VITAS Healthcare Corp 2501 Parkview Dr Suite 600 *TF:* 800-953-5855 ■ *Web:* www.vitas.com	Fort Worth	TX	76102	817-870-7000	870-7090
VITAS Healthcare Corp 4848 Loop Central Dr # 650 *TF:* 800-628-8081 ■ *Web:* www.vitas.com	Houston	TX	77081	713-663-7777	663-4990
VITAS Healthcare Corp 5430 Fredericksburg Rd Suite 200 *TF:* 800-938-4827 ■ *Web:* www.vitas.com	San Antonio	TX	78229	210-348-4300	348-4383
VITAS Healthcare Corp in Texas 18333 Egret Bay Suite 550 **Fax Area Code:* 281 ■ *TF:* 800-628-8081 ■ *Web:* www.vitas.com	Houston	TX	77058	713-663-4900	335-3450*

UTAH

	City	State	Zip	Phone	Fax
IHC Home Care 36 S State St Suite A *TF:* 800-527-1118	Salt Lake City	UT	84111	801-977-9900	977-9956

VERMONT

	City	State	Zip	Phone	Fax
Hospice VNA 331 Olcott Dr Suite U-1 *TF:* 800-858-1696 ■ *Web:* www.vnahospicevtnh.org	White River Junction	VT	05001	802-295-2604	295-6896

VIRGINIA

	City	State	Zip	Phone	Fax
Adventa Hospice 154 W 4th St	Salem	VA	24153	540-378-5281	378-6005
Capital Caring 2900 Telestar Ct *TF:* 800-869-2136 ■ *Web:* www.capitalhospice.org	Falls Church	VA	22042	703-538-2065	531-6092
Capital Hospice Inc 6565 Arlington Blvd *Web:* www.capitalhospice.org	Falls Church	VA	22042	703-538-2065	538-2165
Crater Community Hospice 840 W Roslyn Rd Suite E *Web:* www.cratercommunityhospice.org	Colonial Heights	VA	23834	804-526-4300	526-4337
Good Samaritan Hospice 2408 Electric Rd *TF:* 888-466-7809 ■ *Web:* www.goodsamhospice.com	Roanoke	VA	24018	540-776-0198	776-0841

Phone | Fax

Hospice of the Piedmont
675 Peter Jefferson Pkwy Suite 300 ... Charlottesville VA 22911 434-817-6900 245-0187
TF: 800-975-5501 ■ *Web:* www.hopva.org
Hospice of the Rapidan
1200 Sunset Ln # 2320 ... Culpeper VA 22701 540-825-4840 825-7752
TF: 800-676-2012 ■ *Web:* www.hotr.org
Mary Washington Hospice
5012 Southpoint Pkwy ... Fredericksburg VA 22407 540-741-1667 741-3581
TF: 800-257-1667 ■ *Web:* www.marywashingtonhealthcare.com

WASHINGTON

Phone | Fax

Evergreen Hospice Services
12822 124th Ln NE ... Kirkland WA 98034 425-899-1070 899-1033
Web: www.evergreenhospital.org
Hospice of Spokane 121 S Arthur St ... Spokane WA 99202 509-456-0438 458-0359
TF: 888-459-0438 ■ *Web:* www.hospiceofspokane.org
Providence Hospice & Home Care of Snohomish County
2731 Wetmore Ave Suite 500 ... Everett WA 98201 425-261-4800 261-4850
TF: 800-825-0045
Providence Hospice of Seattle
425 Pontius Ave N Suite 300 ... Seattle WA 98109 206-320-4000 320-7333
TF: 888-782-4445 ■ *Web:* www2.providence.org
Providence Sound Home Care & Hospice
PO Box 5008 ... Lacey WA 98509 360-459-8311 493-4657
TF: 800-869-7062
Tri-Cities Chaplaincy 2108 W Entiat Ave ... Kennewick WA 99336 509-783-7416 735-7850
Web: www.tricitieschaplaincy.org
Whatcom Hospice Foundation
2901 Squalicum Pkwy Suite 1C ... Bellingham WA 98225 360-733-1231 788-6858
Web: www.hospicehelp.org

WEST VIRGINIA

Phone | Fax

Hospice Care Corp Rt 92 S PO Box 760 ... Arthurdale WV 26520 304-864-0884 864-6306
TF: 800-350-1161 ■ *Web:* www.hospicecarecorp.org
Hospice of Huntington 1101 6th Ave ... Huntington WV 25701 304-529-4217 523-6051
TF: 800-788-5480 ■ *Web:* www.hospiceofhuntington.org
Hospice of the Panhandle 122 Waverly Ct ... Martinsburg WV 25401 304-264-0406 264-0409
TF: 800-345-6538 ■ *Web:* www.hospiceotp.org
Kanawha Hospice Care 1143 Dunbar Ave ... Dunbar WV 25064 304-768-8523 768-8627
TF: 800-560-8523 ■ *Web:* www.kanawhahospice.org

WISCONSIN

Phone | Fax

AseraCare Hospice - Milwaukee
6737 W Washington Suite 3200 ... West Allis WI 53214 414-607-1782 607-6196
TF: 800-598-5132 ■ *Web:* www.aserahospicemilwaukee.com
Aurora VNA Zilber Family Hospice
1155 N Honey Creek Pkwy ... Wauwatosa WI 53213 414-615-5900 615-5927
TF: 888-206-6955 ■ *Web:* www.aurorahealthcare.org
Beloit Regional Hospice 655 3rd St Suite 200 ... Beloit WI 53511 608-363-7421 363-7426
TF: 877-363-7421 ■ *Web:* www.beloitregionalhospice.com
Gundersen Lutheran at Home HomeCare & Hospice
914 Green Bay St ... La Crosse WI 54601 608-775-8400
TF: 800-776-4456 ■ *Web:* www.gundluth.org
Horizon Home Care & Hospice
8949 N Deerbrook Trail ... Brown Deer WI 53223 414-365-8300 365-8338
TF: 800-468-4660 ■ *Web:* www.hhch.net
Hospice Alliance
10220 Prairie Ridge Blvd ... Pleasant Prairie WI 53158 262-652-4400 652-4516
TF: 800-830-8344 ■ *Web:* www.hospicealliance.net
HospiceCare 5395 E Cheryl Pkwy ... Madison WI 53711 608-276-4660 276-4672
TF: 800-553-4289 ■ *Web:* www.hospicecare.com
Ministry Home Care Hospice Services
611 St Joseph Ave ... Marshfield WI 54449 715-389-3802 387-9950
TF: 866-740-1166 ■ *Web:* www.ministryhomecare.org
Theda Care at Home 3000 E College Ave ... Appleton WI 54915 920-969-0919 969-0020
TF: 800-984-5554 ■ *Web:* www.thedacare.org
Unity Hospice 2366 Oak Ridge Cir ... De Pere WI 54115 920-338-1111 338-8111
TF: 800-990-9249 ■ *Web:* www.unityhospice.org
VITAS Healthcare Corp
2675 N Mayfair Rd Suite 500 ... Wauwatosa WI 53226 414-257-2600 454-3133
TF: 888-821-6500 ■ *Web:* www.vitas.com

WYOMING

Phone | Fax

Central Wyoming Hospice Program
319 S Wilson St ... Casper WY 82601 307-577-4832 577-4841
Web: www.cwhp.org

375 HOSPITAL HOSPITALITY HOUSES

Phone | Fax

American Cancer Society Hope Lodge of Baltimore
636 W Lexington St ... Baltimore MD 21201 410-547-2522 539-8890
TF: 888-227-6333 ■ *Web:* www.cancer.org
American Cancer Society Hope Lodge of Buffalo
197 Summer St ... Buffalo NY 14222 716-882-9244 822-4436
Web: www.cancer.org
American Cancer Society Hope Lodge of Charleston
269 Calhoun St ... Charleston SC 29401 843-958-0930 958-9054
TF: 800-282-4914 ■ *Web:* www.cancer.org
American Cancer Society Hope Lodge of Marshfield
611 W Doege St ... Marshfield WI 54449 715-486-9100 486-9110
Web: www.cancer.org

Phone | Fax

American Cancer Society Hope Lodge of Rochester
411 2nd St NW ... Rochester MN 55901 507-529-4673 529-4666
Web: www.cancer.org
American Cancer Society Hope Lodge of Saint Louis
4215 Lindell Blvd ... Saint Louis MO 63108 314-286-8150 286-8155
Web: www.cancer.org
American Cancer Society Hope Lodge Worcester
7 Oak St ... Worcester MA 01609 508-792-2985 753-3986
Web: www.cancer.org
American Cancer Society Joe Lee Griffin Hope Lodge
1104 Ireland Way ... Birmingham AL 35205 205-558-7860 558-7862
TF: 888-513-9933 ■ *Web:* www.cancer.org
American Cancer Society Joseph S. & Jeannette M. Silber Hope Lodge
11432 Mayfield Rd ... Cleveland OH 44106 216-844-4673 844-2959
Web: www.cancer.org
American Cancer Society McConnell-Raab Hope Lodge
930A Wellness Dr ... Greenville NC 27834 252-695-6143 695-6557
American Cancer Society Winn-Dixie Hope Lodge
1552 Shoup Ct ... Atlanta GA 30033 404-327-9200 327-9808
Web: www.cancer.org
Arbor House 300 Main St ... Lewiston ME 04240 207-795-0111 795-2303
Web: www.cmmc.org
Arizona Transplant House 11600 N 84th St ... Scottsdale AZ 85260 480-609-1324 609-7268
Web: www.aztransplanthouse.org
Atlanta Hospital Hospitality House
1815 S Ponce De Leon Ave NE ... Atlanta GA 30307 404-377-6333 377-6398
Web: www.atlhhh.org
Auxiliary Guest House 313 S Kline St ... Aberdeen SD 57401 605-622-5050 622-5266
Avera Queen of Peace 600 E 6th Ave ... Mitchell SD 57301 605-995-2468 995-2441
Bannister Family House
200 W Arbor Dr Suite 8961 ... San Diego CA 92103 619-543-7977 543-7937
Web: health.ucsd.edu/bannister
Barnes Lodge 4520 Clayton Ave ... Saint Louis MO 63110 314-652-4319 535-2731
TF: 800-551-3492
Baylor Plaza Hotel 3600 Gaston Ave ... Dallas TX 75246 214-820-7000 820-7323
Web: www.baylorhealth.com
Beacon House 1301 N 3rd St ... Marquette MI 49855 906-225-7100 225-4903
Web: www.upbeaconhouse.org
Blount Hospitality House 610 Madison St ... Huntsville AL 35801 256-534-7014 512-5872
Web: www.blounthospitalityhouse.org
Brent's Place 11980 E 16th Ave ... Aurora CO 80010 303-831-4545 831-4567
Web: www.brentsplace.org
Caring House Inc 2625 Pickett Rd ... Durham NC 27705 919-490-5449 493-8044
Web: www.caringhouse.com
Carolyn Scott Rainbow House 7815 Harney St ... Omaha NE 68114 402-955-7815 955-7805
Web: www.childrensomaha.org
Carpenter Hospitality House 121 5th Ave NE ... Hickory NC 28601 828-324-4544 324-6504
Casa Esperanza 1005 Yale NE ... Albuquerque NM 87106 505-277-9880 277-9876
Web: www.casaesperanzanm.org
Children's Hope House
7922 W Jefferson Blvd ... Fort Wayne IN 46804 260-459-8550 459-8551
Children's House at Johns Hopkins
1915 McElderry St ... Baltimore MD 21205 410-614-2560 614-2568
Web: www.childrenshouse.org
Children's Inn at National Institutes Of Health
7 W Dr ... Bethesda MD 20892 301-496-5672 496-4421
TF: 800-644-4660 ■ *Web:* www.childrensinn.org
Children's Miracle Network Family Guest House
1057 Patterson St ... Eugene OR 97401 541-685-1970 685-1962
Conine Clubhouse 921 N 35th Ave ... Hollywood FL 33021 954-986-6323 985-2265
Web: www.jdch.com/conineclubhouse/ConineClubhouse.aspx
Cynthia C. & William E. Perry Pavilion
9400 Turkey Lake Rd ... Orlando FL 32819 321-842-8844 842-8871
Web: www.orlandohealth.com/drpphillipshospital
Danielle House 160 Riverside Dr ... Binghamton NY 13905 607-724-1540 724-1540
Web: www.daniellehouse.org
Devon Nicole House 21 Autumn St 5th Fl ... Boston MA 02215 617-355-8457 730-0223
Web: www.childrenshospital.org/dnh
Edmond J Safra Family Lodge at National Institutes of Health
9000 Rockville Pike Bldg 65 ... Bethesda MD 20892 301-496-6500 594-4589
Web: www.clinicalcenter.nih.gov/familylodge/index.shtml#referrals
Ernest Eugenia Wyatt Guest House
317 Business Loop 70 W ... Columbia MO 65203 573-884-1825 884-2434
Family House Inc 1509 N Knoxville Ave ... Peoria IL 61603 309-685-5300 688-8324
Web: www.familyhousepeoria.org
Fellowship Ctr 1901 Clinch Ave ... Knoxville TN 37916 865-541-1725 544-1760
Fisher House Inc 7323 Hwy 90 W Suite 107 ... San Antonio TX 78227 210-673-7500 673-7579
Web: www.fisherhouseinc.org
Francis Cheney Family Place 2882 State St ... Medford OR 97504 541-789-5876 789-5841
Web: www.asante.org
Friendship Inn PO Box 3423 ... Kansas City KS 66103 816-506-6339
Gary's House 97 State St ... Portland ME 04101 207-535-1320 535-1339
Web: www.mercyhospital.org
Gift of Life Transplant House
705 2nd St SW ... Rochester MN 55902 507-288-7470 281-9888
Web: www.gift-of-life.org
Gorecki Guest House 1406 6th Ave N ... Saint Cloud MN 56303 320-251-2700 255-5803
Web: www.centracare.com
Hanson House 380 E Paseo El Mirador ... Palm Springs CA 92262 760-416-5070 416-5071
Web: www.hansonhouse.org
Holland's Rose 132 Griegos Rd NW ... Albuquerque NM 87107 505-345-2020 345-5464
Web: www.hollandsrose.com
Home Away From Home 2600 E 18th St ... Cheyenne WY 82001 307-633-7212 633-7229
Hope Lodge Hershey Pennsylvania
125 Lucy Ave ... Hummelstown PA 17036 717-533-5111 533-2587
Web: www.cancer.org
Hospital Hospitality House
342 S Limestone St ... Lexington KY 40508 859-254-8998 255-5185
Web: www.hospitalhospitalityhouse.com
Hospital Hospitality House of Louisville
201 E Main St ... Louisville KY 40202 502-625-1360 625-1363
Web: www.hhhlouisville.org

Name / Address	City	State	ZIP	Phone	Fax
Hospital Hospitality House of Richmond Inc 612 E Marshall St PO Box 10090 *Web:* www.hhhrichmond.org	Richmond	VA	23219	804-828-6901	828-6913
Hospital Hospitality House of SW Michigan Inc 527 W S St *Web:* www.hhhkz.org	Kalamazoo	MI	49007	269-341-7811	341-7817
Hospitality Homes PO Box 15265 **Fax Area Code: 617* ■ *TF:* 888-595-4678 ■ *Web:* www.hosp.org	Boston	MA	02115	857-215-4678	582-7980*
Hospitality Homes of Cleveland 12704 Mapleleaf Dr *Web:* www.hospitalityhomes.com	Cleveland	OH	44125	216-518-0404	
Hospitality House of Charlotte PO Box 36891 *Web:* www.hospitalityhouseofcharlotte.org	Charlotte	NC	28236	704-384-6058	316-0349
Hospitality House of Methodist Hospital Foundation 990 Oak Ridge Tpke PO Box 2529 *Web:* www.mmcoakridge.com	Oak Ridge	TN	37830	865-481-5923	481-5403
Hospitality House of Tulsa PO Box 1988 *Web:* www.tulsahospitalityhouse.org	Broken Arrow	OK	74013	918-694-8888	
Hotel Schmotel 2539 E Edison St	Tucson	AZ	85716	520-907-5063	795-3880
Hubbard House The 29 W Miller St *Web:* www.orlandohealth.com	Orlando	FL	32806	407-649-6886	849-6447
Humility of Mary Guest House 427 Caroline Ave	Youngstown	OH	44504	330-480-2206	
Huntington Hospital Hospitality House 2801 S Staunton Rd *Web:* www.huntingtonhospitality.org	Huntington	WV	25702	304-522-1832	522-6706
Immanuel Auxiliary Hospitality House 7105 Newport Ave	Omaha	NE	68152	402-572-2828	572-3942
Inn at Cherry Hill 500 17th Ave *Web:* www.swedish.org	Seattle	WA	98122	206-320-2164	320-3526
Inn at Virginia Mason 1006 Spring St *TF:* 800-283-6453 ■ *Web:* www.innatvirginiamason.com	Seattle	WA	98104	206-583-6453	625-7197
Jenn's House Inc 3250 S Cedar Crest Blvd *Web:* www.jennshouse.org	Emmaus	PA	18049	610-965-1777	965-1777
Kathy's House Inc 600 N 103 St *Web:* www.kathys-house.org	Milwaukee	WI	53226	414-453-8290	453-8292
Kevin Guest House 782 Ellicott St *Web:* www.kevinguesthouse.com	Buffalo	NY	14203	716-882-1818	882-1291
King's Daughters Hospitality House 2221 Central Ave	Ashland	KY	41101	606-326-7730	326-7748
Kohl's House at Children's Memorial Hospital 2422 N Orchard *Web:* www.childrensmemorial.org	Chicago	IL	60614	773-975-8881	880-3602
Lewis Rathbun Ctr 121 Sherwood Rd *Web:* www.lewisrathbuncenter.org	Asheville	NC	28803	828-251-0595	251-0598
Mario Pastega Guest House 3505 NW Samaritan Dr *Web:* www.samhealth.org	Corvallis	OR	97330	541-768-4650	768-5124
Massachusetts General Hospital Beacon House 19 Myrtle St	Boston	MA	02114	617-726-7679	918-5875
Masterson Place 2325 E Yellowstone Hwy	Casper	WY	82609	307-237-5933	237-5939
McDade House of Shreveport 1825 Warrington Pl	Shreveport	LA	71101	318-681-6560	681-6410
McRee Guest House 2721 S Washington	Lansing	MI	48910	517-372-6153	372-6554
Miracle House 80 8th Ave Suite 315 *Web:* www.miraclehouse.org	New York	NY	10011	212-989-7790	367-9281
Molly's House 430 SE Osceola St *Web:* www.mollyshouse.org	Stuart	FL	34994	772-223-6659	223-9990
Munson Manor Hospitality House 1220 Medical Campus Dr *Web:* www.munsonhealthcare.org	Traverse City	MI	49684	231-935-2300	935-2302
Nebraska House 987600 Nebraska Medical Ctr *TF:* 888-805-1115 ■ *Web:* www.nebraskamed.com/transplant	Omaha	NE	68198	402-559-2081	559-9643
Pay It Forward House 719 Somonauk St *Web:* www.payitforwardhouse.org	Sycamore	IL	60178	815-899-1106	
Pete Gross House 525 Minor Ave N *Web:* www.fhcrc.org	Seattle	WA	98109	206-262-1000	262-1500
Prairie Lakes Caring Club House 401 9th Ave *Web:* www.prairielakes.com	Watertown	SD	57201	605-882-7725	882-7720
Quantum House 901 45th St *Web:* www.quantumhouse.org	West Palm Beach	FL	33407	561-494-0515	494-0522
Quincy Hospitality House 1129 Oak St *Web:* www.blessinghospital.org	Quincy	IL	62301	217-228-3022	223-2569
Rathgeber Hospitality House 1615 12th St *Web:* www.rathgeberhospitalityhouse.org	Wichita Falls	TX	76301	940-764-2400	764-2456
Renucci Hospitality House 100 Michigan St NE MC 172	Grand Rapids	MI	49503	616-391-1787	391-9300
Rose Hill Hospitality House 605 26 1/2 Rd	Grand Junction	CO	81506	970-243-7968	
Rosenbaum Family House 1 Medical Ctr Dr PO Box 8228 *Web:* www.wvuhealthcare.com/rosenbaum	Morgantown	WV	26506	304-598-6094	598-6412
Saint Andrew's Lighthouse Inc 1797 Beach Blvd	Jacksonville Beach	FL	32250	904-246-5606	246-9303
Saint Joseph Inn 3310 E Grand	Wichita	KS	67218	316-689-6359	691-6763
Sarah House Inc 100 Roberts Ave *Web:* www.sarahhouse.org	Syracuse	NY	13207	315-475-1747	
Seton Guest Ctr 2131 W 3rd St *Web:* www.stvincentmedicalcenter.com	Los Angeles	CA	90057	213-484-7767	207-5816
Seton League House 3207 Medical Pkwy *Web:* www.seton.net	Austin	TX	78705	512-324-1999	324-1932
Sowers Hospitality House 1701 S 17th St Suite 1H	Lincoln	NE	68502	402-438-2244	438-2426
Stanton Hospitality House 1617 Roxie Ave	Fayetteville	NC	28304	910-323-1771	485-3449
Steven's Hope for Children Inc 1014 W Foothill Blvd Suite B *Web:* www.stevenshope.org	Upland	CA	91786	909-373-0678	981-4578
Sumner Foundation Hospitality House 404 Steam Plant Rd *Web:* www.sumner.org	Gallatin	TN	37066	615-452-4009	452-0066
Sunshine House Guest Lodging 413 N Lilly Rd NE	Olympia	WA	98506	360-493-7940	493-5569
Texoma Medical Center's Reba Ranch House 5016 S US Hwy 75 *Web:* www.texomamedicalcenter.net	Denison	TX	75020	903-416-4000	416-4129
Travis & Beverly Cross Guest Housing Ctr 9320 SW Barnes Rd *TF:* 888-550-1575 ■ *Web:* www.oregon.providence.org	Portland	OR	97225	503-216-1575	216-6283
Tree House at Liberty Hospital 2533 Glenn W Hendren Dr *Web:* www.libertyhospital.org	Liberty	MO	64068	816-883-2088	883-2316
University of Virginia Medical Center Hospital Hospitality House Inc Hospital Box 800703 *Web:* www.healthsystem.virginia.edu	Charlottesville	VA	22908	434-924-2285	924-1590
Veterans Guest House 880 Locust St *Web:* www.veteransguesthouse.org	Reno	NV	89502	775-324-6958	324-6071
Walton Guest House PO Box 14001	Salem	OR	97302	503-561-5279	375-4828
Yaffe House 3700 W 17th Ave	Denver	CO	80204	303-405-4275	405-4276
Zachary & Elizabeth Fisher House 3200 Vine St *Web:* www.fisherhouse.org/houses	Cincinnati	OH	45220	513-475-6571	487-6661

376 HOSPITAL HOSPITALITY HOUSES - RONALD MCDONALD HOUSE

Name / Address	City	State	ZIP	Phone	Fax
Ronald McDonald House 2524 N State St	Jackson	MS	39216	601-981-5683	981-3613
Akron 245 Locust St *Web:* www.akronchildrens.org	Akron	OH	44302	330-253-5400	253-5477
Albany 139 S Lake Ave *Web:* www.rmhcofalbany.org	Albany	NY	12208	518-438-2655	459-6529
Albuquerque 1011 Yale Ave NE *Web:* www.rmhc-nm.org	Albuquerque	NM	87106	505-842-8960	764-0412
Amarillo 1501 Streit Dr	Amarillo	TX	79106	806-358-8177	358-8170
Ann Arbor 1600 Washington Heights *Web:* www.rmh-annarbor.org	Ann Arbor	MI	48104	734-994-4442	994-4919
Atlanta 792 Houston Mill Rd NE *Web:* www.armhc.org	Atlanta	GA	30329	404-315-1133	315-7873
Augusta 938 Greene St *Web:* www.mcghealth.org	Augusta	GA	30901	706-724-5901	722-0884
Austin 1315 Barbara Jordan Blvd *Web:* www.rmhc-austin.org	Austin	TX	78723	512-472-9844	472-5465
Baltimore 635 W Lexington St *Web:* www.rmhbaltimore.com	Baltimore	MD	21201	410-528-1010	727-6177
Bangor 654 State St	Bangor	ME	04401	207-942-9003	990-2984
Bend 1700 NE Purcell Blvd	Bend	OR	97701	541-318-4950	318-4994
Billings 1144 N 30th St	Billings	MT	59101	406-256-8006	256-0130
Birmingham 920 17th St S	Birmingham	AL	35205	205-933-0695	939-0035
Bismarck 609 N 7th St	Bismarck	ND	58501	701-258-8551	258-5076
Boise 101 Warm Springs Ave *Web:* www.rmhidaho.org	Boise	ID	83712	208-336-5478	336-0587
Boston 229 Kent St *Web:* www.ronaldmcdonaldhouseboston.org	Brookline	MA	02446	617-734-3333	734-5239
Buffalo 780 W Ferry St *Web:* www.rmhbuffalo.org	Buffalo	NY	14222	716-883-1177	881-9312
Burlington 16 S Winooski Ave *Web:* www.rmh-vermont.org	Burlington	VT	05401	802-862-4943	862-2175
Calgary 111 W Campus Pl NW *Web:* www.rmhsouthernalberta.org	Calgary	AB	T3B2R6	403-240-3000	240-1277
Camden 550 Mickle Blvd *Web:* www.ronaldhouse-snj.org	Camden	NJ	08103	856-966-4663	966-1190
Chapel Hill 101 Old Mason Farm Rd *Web:* www.chapelhillrmh.net	Chapel Hill	NC	27517	919-913-2040	966-7651
Charleston 81 Gadsden St *Web:* www.charityadvantage.com/RonaldMcdonaldHouse	Charleston	SC	29401	843-723-7957	722-2204
Charleston 302 30th St *Web:* members.citynet.net/rmh	Charleston	WV	25304	304-346-0279	343-8385
Charlottesville 300 9th St SW *Web:* www.avenue.org	Charlottesville	VA	22903	434-295-1885	295-7735
Chattanooga 200 Central Ave *Web:* www.rmhchattanooga.com	Chattanooga	TN	37403	423-778-4300	778-4350
Chicago 622 W Deming Pl *Web:* www.rmhchinorth.org	Chicago	IL	60614	773-348-5322	348-7619
Chicago 845 E 57th St *Web:* www.ronaldmcdonaldhouseuc.org	Chicago	IL	60637	773-324-5437	324-8029
Chicago Tripp Ave PO Box 7002 *Web:* www.rmhccni.org	Hines	IL	60141	708-327-2273	327-6000
Cincinnati 350 Erkenbrecher Ave *Web:* www.rmhcincinnati.org	Cincinnati	OH	42229	513-636-7642	636-4887
Cleveland 10415 Euclid Ave *Web:* www.rmhcleveland.org	Cleveland	OH	44106	216-229-5758	229-0556
Colorado Springs 311 N Logan Ave *Web:* www.rmhcs.org	Colorado Springs	CO	80909	719-471-1814	471-7147
Columbia 1001 E Stadium Blvd *Web:* www.rmhccolumbia.org	Columbia	MO	65201	573-443-7666	499-0131
Columbus 1959 Hamilton Rd *Web:* www.rmhcwga.org	Columbus	GA	31904	706-321-0033	321-0034
Corpus Christi 3402 Fort Worth St *Web:* www.corpuschristirmhc.org	Corpus Christi	TX	78411	361-854-4073	854-9174
Dallas 4707 Bengal St *Web:* www.rmhdallas.com	Dallas	TX	75235	214-631-7354	631-1527

Address	City	State	ZIP	Phone	Fax
Danville 100 N Academy Ave PO Box 300	Danville	PA	17821	570-271-6300	271-8182
Web: www.rmhdanville.org					
Des Moines 1441 Pleasant St	Des Moines	IA	50314	515-243-2111	280-3111
Web: www.rmhdesmoines.org					
Detroit 3911 Beaubien Blvd	Detroit	MI	48201	313-745-5909	993-0399
Web: www.rmhdet.org					
Durham 506 Alexander Ave	Durham	NC	27705	919-286-9305	286-7307
Web: www.ronaldhousedurham.org					
Edmonton 7726 107th St NW	Edmonton	AB	T6E4K3	780-439-5437	433-6201
Web: www.rmhnorthernalberta.org					
El Paso 300 E California St	El Paso	TX	79902	915-542-1522	577-0678
Web: www.rmhc.org					
Falls Church 3312 Gallows Rd	Falls Church	VA	22042	703-698-7080	698-7745
Web: www.rmhc.greaterdc.org					
Fargo 1234 Broadway	Fargo	ND	58102	701-232-3980	234-9582
Web: www.rmhcfargo.org					
Fort Lauderdale 15 SE 15th St	Fort Lauderdale	FL	33316	954-828-1822	828-1824
Fort Myers 16100 Roserush Ct	Fort Myers	FL	33908	239-437-0202	437-3521
Web: www.rmhcswfl.org					
Fort Worth 1004 7th Ave	Fort Worth	TX	76104	817-870-4942	870-0254
Web: www.ftworthrmh.org					
Galveston 301 14th St	Galveston	TX	77550	409-762-8770	762-9902
Web: www.rmhg.org					
Grand Rapids 1323 Cedar St NE	Grand Rapids	MI	49503	616-776-1300	776-0368
Greenville 549 Moye Blvd	Greenville	NC	27834	252-830-0062	830-0298
Greenville 706 Grove Rd	Greenville	SC	29605	864-235-0506	235-2316
Web: www.rmhgreenville.org					
Halifax 1133 Tower Rd	Halifax	NS	B3H2Y7	902-429-4044	429-8650
Web: www.rmhatlantic.ca					
Hamilton 1510 Main St W	Hamilton	ON	L8S1E3	905-521-9983	521-9515
Web: www.rmhhamilton.ca					
Harlingen 1720 Treasure Hills Blvd	Harlingen	TX	78550	956-412-7200	412-6300
Web: www.rmhcrgv.org					
Hershey 745 W Governor Rd	Hershey	PA	17033	717-533-4001	533-1299
Web: www.rmhc-centralpa.org					
Honolulu 1970 Judd Hillside Rd	Honolulu	HI	96822	808-973-5683	955-8794
Houston 1907 Holcombe Blvd	Houston	TX	77030	713-795-3500	795-3595
Web: www.ronaldmcdonaldhousehouston.org					
Huntington 1500 17th St	Huntington	WV	25701	304-529-1122	529-2970
Web: www.mchouse.org					
Indianapolis 435 Limestone St	Indianapolis	IN	46202	317-269-2247	267-0606
Web: www.rmh-indiana.org					
Iowa City 730 Hawkins Dr	Iowa City	IA	52246	319-356-3939	353-6873
Web: www.uihealthcare.com					
Jacksonville 824 Children's Way	Jacksonville	FL	32207	904-807-4663	807-4700
Web: www.rmhjax.org					
Johnson City 418 N State of Franklin Rd	Johnson City	TN	37604	423-975-5437	434-8989
Joplin 3402 S Jackson Ave PO Box 2688	Joplin	MO	64804	417-624-2273	624-0270
Web: www.rmhjoplin.org					
Kansas City 2502 Cherry St	Kansas City	MO	64108	816-842-8321	842-7033
Web: www.rmhckc.org					
Kansas City 2502 Cherry St	Kansas City	MO	64108	816-842-8321	421-7324
Web: www.rmhckc.org					
Knoxville 1705 W Clinch Ave	Knoxville	TN	37916	865-525-7933	525-7942
Web: www.knoxrmhc.org					
Lansing 121 S Holmes St	Lansing	MI	48912	517-485-9303	485-9810
Web: www.sparrow.org/childrenscenter/ccronald.asp					
Las Vegas 2323 Potosi St	Las Vegas	NV	89146	702-252-4663	252-7345
Web: www.rmhlv.com					
Little Rock 1009 Wolfe St	Little Rock	AR	72202	501-374-1956	374-2418
Loma Linda 11365 Anderson St	Loma Linda	CA	92354	909-558-8300	558-0300
Web: www.llrmh.org					
Long Branch 131 Bath Ave	Long Branch	NJ	07740	732-222-8755	222-9363
Web: www.rmh-cnj.org					
Los Angeles 4560 Fountain Ave	Los Angeles	CA	90029	323-644-3000	669-0552
Web: www.larmh.org					
Macon 1160 Forsyth St	Macon	GA	31201	478-746-4090	746-0580
Web: www.ronaldhousecga.org					
Madera 9161 Randall Way	Madera	CA	93638	559-447-6770	447-6778
Web: www.ronald-mcdonaldhouse.com					
Madison 2716 Marshall Ct	Madison	WI	53705	608-232-4660	232-4670
Web: www.rmhcmadison.org					
Marshfield 803 W N St	Marshfield	WI	54449	715-387-5899	389-5991
Web: www.rmhc-marshfield.org					
Memphis 535 Alabama Ave	Memphis	TN	38105	901-529-4055	523-0315
Web: www.rmhmemphis.org					
Miami 1145 NW 14th Terr	Miami	FL	33136	305-324-5683	324-5689
Minneapolis 608 Ontario St SE	Minneapolis	MN	55414	612-331-5752	331-1255
Web: www.rmhmpls.com					
Missoula 3003 Ft Missoula Rd PO Box 1119	Missoula	MT	59804	406-541-7646	541-7642
Web: www.rmhmissoula.org					
Monroe 200 S 3rd St	Monroe	LA	71202	318-387-7933	
Web: www.bayou.com					
Montreal					
3201 ch de la Cote Sainte Catherine	Montreal	QC	H3T1C4	514-731-2871	739-8823
Morgantown 841 Country Club Dr	Morgantown	WV	26505	304-598-0050	599-0780
Web: www.rmhcmgtn.org					
New Brunswick 145 Somerset St	New Brunswick	NJ	08901	732-249-1222	249-1439
Web: www.rmh-cnj.org					
New Haven 501 George St	New Haven	CT	06511	203-777-5683	777-3082
Web: www.ronaldmcdonaldhouse-ct.org					
New Hyde Park 267-07 76th Ave	New Hyde Park	NY	11042	718-343-5683	343-5798
Web: www.rmhlongisland.org					
New Orleans 4403 Canal St	New Orleans	LA	70119	504-486-6668	482-1666
New York 405 E 73rd St	New York	NY	10021	212-639-0100	472-0376
Web: www.rmh-newyork.org					
Norfolk 404 Colley Ave	Norfolk	VA	23507	757-627-5386	622-0534
Web: www.rmhcnorfolk.com					
Oklahoma City 1301 NE 14th St	Oklahoma City	OK	73117	405-424-6873	424-0919
Web: www.rmhokc.org					
Omaha 620 S 38th Ave	Omaha	NE	68105	402-346-9377	346-9468
Web: www.rmhomaha.org					
Orange 383 S Batavia St	Orange	CA	92868	714-639-3600	516-3697
Web: www.ronaldhouseoc.org					
Orlando 2201 Alden Rd	Orlando	FL	32803	407-898-6127	896-3562
Web: www.rmhorlando.com					
Orlando 1630 Kuhl Ave	Orlando	FL	32806	407-581-1289	581-1392
Web: www.rmhorlando.com					
Ottawa 407 Smyth Rd	Ottawa	ON	K1H8M8	613-737-5523	737-5524
Web: www.rmhottawa.com					
Palo Alto 520 Sand Hill Rd	Palo Alto	CA	94304	650-470-6000	470-6018
Web: www.ronaldhouse.net					
Pasadena 763 S Pasadena Ave	Pasadena	CA	91105	626-585-1588	585-1688
Web: www.pasadenarmh.org					
Pensacola 5200 Bayou Blvd	Pensacola	FL	32503	850-477-2273	477-7607
Web: www.rmhpensacola.org					
Philadelphia 3925 Chestnut St	Philadelphia	PA	19104	215-387-8406	386-4977
Web: www.philarmh.org					
Phoenix 501 E Roanoke Ave	Phoenix	AZ	85004	602-264-2654	264-5670
Web: www.rmhcphoenix.com					
Pittsburgh 451 44th St	Pittsburgh	PA	15201	412-362-3400	362-8540
Web: www.rmhcpgh.org					
Portland 250 Brackett St	Portland	ME	04102	207-780-6282	780-0198
Web: www.rmhportlandme.org					
Portland 3440 SW US Veterans Hospital Rd	Portland	OR	97239	971-230-0808	243-2969*
**Fax Area Code:* 503 ■ *Web:* www.rmhcoregon.org					
Portland 2620 N Commercial Ave	Portland	OR	97227	971-230-6700	630-6720
Web: www.rmhcoregon.org					
Providence 45 Gay St	Providence	RI	02905	401-274-4447	751-3730
Web: www.rmhprovidence.org					
Richmond 2330 Monument Ave	Richmond	VA	23220	804-355-6517	358-3153
Web: www.rmhc-richmond.org					
Roanoke 2224 S Jefferson St	Roanoke	VA	24014	540-857-0770	857-9584
Rochester 333 Westmoreland Dr	Rochester	NY	14620	585-442-5437	442-7330
Web: www.ronaldshouse.com					
Sacramento 2555 49th St	Sacramento	CA	95817	916-734-4230	734-4238
Web: www.rmhcnc.org					
Saint Louis 4381 W Pine Blvd	Saint Louis	MO	63108	314-531-6601	531-6353
Web: www.rmhcstl.com					
Saint Louis 3450 Pk Ave	Saint Louis	MO	63104	314-773-1100	773-2053
Web: www.rmhcstl.com					
Saint Petersburg 401 7th Ave S	Saint Petersburg	FL	33701	727-821-8961	897-4836
Sainte-Foy 2747 boul Laurier	Sainte-Foy	QC	G1V2L9	418-651-1771	651-1772
Salt Lake City 935 E S Temple	Salt Lake City	UT	84102	801-363-4663	363-0092
Web: www.rmhslc.org					
San Antonio 227 Lewis St	San Antonio	TX	78212	210-223-6014	223-6138
San Antonio 4803 Sid Katz Dr	San Antonio	TX	78229	210-614-2554	614-2905
Web: www.ronaldmcdonaldhouse-sa.org					
San Antonio 619 W Houston St	San Antonio	TX	78229	210-704-3860	704-3870
Web: www.christussantarosa.org					
San Diego 3101 Berger Ave	San Diego	CA	92123	858-292-7413	292-7357
Web: www.sdmcdonalds.com					
San Francisco 1640 Scott St	San Francisco	CA	94115	415-673-0891	673-1335
Web: www.ronaldhouse-sf.org					
Saskatoon 1011 University Dr	Saskatoon	SK	S7N0K4	306-244-5700	244-3099
Web: www.rmh.sk.ca					
Savannah 4710 Waters Ave	Savannah	GA	31404	912-356-5520	355-6877
Scranton 332 Wheeler Ave	Scranton	PA	18510	570-969-8998	969-8991
Web: www.rmhscranton.org					
Seattle 5130 40th Ave NE	Seattle	WA	98105	206-838-0600	838-0814
Web: www.rmhcseattle.org					
Seattle 5130 40th Ave NE	Seattle	WA	98105	206-838-0600	838-0650
Web: www.rmhcseattle.org					
Sioux Falls 2001 S Norton Ave	Sioux Falls	SD	57105	605-336-6398	339-2638
Spokane 1015 W 5th Ave	Spokane	WA	99204	509-624-0500	624-3267
Web: www.rmhspokane.org					
Springfield 34 Chapin Terr	Springfield	MA	01107	413-794-5683	794-8199
Web: www.ronmcdhouse.com					
Springfield 949 E Primrose St	Springfield	MO	65807	417-886-0225	882-7206
Web: www.ronaldmcdonaldhouse.org					
Tallahassee 712 E 7th Ave	Tallahassee	FL	32303	850-222-0056	222-0086
Web: www.rmhctallahassee.org					
Tampa 35 Columbia Dr	Tampa	FL	33606	813-254-2398	254-8891
Web: www.rmhctampabay.com					
Temple 2415 S 47th St	Temple	TX	76504	254-770-0910	770-1622
Web: www.rmh-temple.com					
Toledo 3883 Monroe St	Toledo	OH	43606	419-471-4663	479-6961
Web: www.rmhctoledo.org					
Topeka 825 SW Buchanan St	Topeka	KS	66606	785-235-6852	235-3170
Web: www.rmhctopeka.org					
Toronto 26 Gerrard St E	Toronto	ON	M5B1G3	416-977-0458	977-8807
Web: www.rmhtoronto.org					

	City	State	Zip	Phone	Fax
Tucson 3838 N Campbell Ave Bld #6	Tucson	AZ	85719	520-326-0060	881-3314
Web: www.rmhctucson.org					
Tulsa 6102 S Hudson Ave	Tulsa	OK	74136	918-496-2727	496-2762
Web: www.rmhtulsa.org					
Washington 3727 14th St NE	Washington	DC	20017	202-529-8204	635-3578
Web: www.rmhc.greaterdc.org					
Wauwatosa 8948 W Watertown Plank Rd	Wauwatosa	WI	53226	414-475-5333	475-6342
Web: www.rmhcmilwaukee.com					
Wilmington 1901 Rockland Rd	Wilmington	DE	19803	302-656-4847	658-6608
TF: 888-656-4847 ■ *Web:* www.rmhde.org					
Winnipeg 566 Bannatyne Ave	Winnipeg	MB	R3A0G7	204-774-4777	774-2160
Web: www.rmh.org					
Winston-Salem 419 S Hawthorne Rd	Winston-Salem	NC	27103	336-723-0228	723-0302
Web: www.wshouse.com					
Ronald McDonald House - Midtown 1110 N Emporia St	Wichita	KS	67214	316-269-4420	269-0665
Web: www.rmhcwichita.org					
Ronald McDonald House - Sleepy Hollow 520 N Rutan	Wichita	KS	67208	316-687-2000	687-6654
Web: www.rmhcwichita.org					
Ronald McDonald House BC 4116 Angus Dr	Vancouver	BC	V6J4H9	604-736-2957	736-5974
Web: www.rmhbc.ca					
Ronald McDonald House Charities (ARMHC)					
Atlanta 5420 Peachtree Dunwoody Rd	Sandy Springs	GA	30342	404-847-0760	250-4992
Web: www.armhc.org					
Dayton 555 Valley St	Dayton	OH	45404	937-224-0047	496-2476
Web: www.rmhdayton.org					
Gainesville 1600 SW 14th St	Gainesville	FL	32608	352-374-4404	335-5325
Web: www.rmhcncf.org					
Reno 323 Maine St	Reno	NV	89502	775-322-4663	322-8670
Web: www.rmhc-reno.com					
Sioux City 2500 Nebraska St	Sioux City	IA	51104	712-255-4084	255-4281
Web: www.ronaldhouse-siouxcity.com					
Springfield 610 N 7th St	Springfield	IL	62702	217-528-3314	528-6084
Web: www.rmhc-centralillinois.org					
Ronald McDonald House Charities of Central New York 1027 E Genesee St	Syracuse	NY	13210	315-476-1027	476-5022
Web: www.cnyronaldmcdonaldhouse.org					
Ronald McDonald House Charities of Central Ohio 711 E Livingston Ave	Columbus	OH	43205	614-227-3700	227-3765
Web: www.rmhc-centralohio.org					
Ronald McDonald House Charities of Denver Inc 1300 E 21st Ave	Denver	CO	80905	303-832-2667	832-3802
Web: www.ronaldhouse.org					
Ronald McDonald House Charities of Kentuckiana (RMHC) 550 S 1st St	Louisville	KY	40202	502-581-1416	581-0037
Web: www.rmhc-kentuckiana.org					
Ronald McDonald House Charities of Nashville					
Nashville 2144 Fairfax Ave	Nashville	TN	37212	615-343-4000	343-4004
Web: www.rmhcnashville.com					
Ronald McDonald House Charities of the Southwest 3413 10th St	Lubbock	TX	79415	806-744-8877	744-3652
Web: www.rmhcsouthwest.com					
Ronald McDonald House of Columbia 2955 Colonial Dr	Columbia	SC	29203	803-254-3181	254-8688
Web: www.rmhcofcolumbia.org					
Ronald McDonald House of Southwestern Ontario 741 Base Line Rd E	London	ON	N6C2R6	519-685-3232	685-0703
TF: 877-848-8188 ■ *Web:* www.rmhlondon.ca					

377 HOSPITALS

SEE ALSO Health Care Providers - Ancillary p. 2005; Health Care Systems p. 2006; Hospices p. 2028; Veterans Nursing Homes - State p. 2760

HOSPITALS - DEVELOPMENTAL DISABILITIES

SEE Developmental Centers p. 1783

377-1 Children's Hospitals

	City	State	Zip	Phone	Fax
Alfred I duPont Hospital for Children 1600 Rockland Rd	Wilmington	DE	19803	302-651-4000	651-4224*
**Fax:* Admitting ■ *Web:* www.nemours.org					
All Children's Hospital 801 6th St S	Saint Petersburg	FL	33701	727-898-7451	767-8546*
**Fax:* Admitting ■ *TF:* 800-456-4543 ■ *Web:* www.allkids.org					
Arkansas Children's Hospital 1 Children's Way	Little Rock	AR	72202	501-364-1100	364-1452
Web: www.archildrens.org					
Arnold Palmer Hospital for Children & Women 92 W Miller St	Orlando	FL	32806	407-649-9111	649-6926
Web: www.orlandohealth.com					
Bradley Hospital 1011 Veterans Memorial Pkwy	East Providence	RI	02915	401-432-1000	432-1500
Web: www.lifespan.org/bradley					
Children's Care Hospital & School 2501 W 26th St	Sioux Falls	SD	57105	605-782-2300	782-2301
TF: 800-584-9294 ■ *Web:* www.cchs.org					
Children's Healthcare of Atlanta at Egleston 1405 Clifton Rd NE	Atlanta	GA	30322	404-785-6000	785-6143*
**Fax:* Admitting ■ *TF:* 800-250-5437 ■ *Web:* www.choa.org					
Children's Healthcare of Atlanta at Scottish Rite 1001 Johnson Ferry Rd NE	Atlanta	GA	30342	404-785-5252	785-4687*
**Fax:* Admitting ■ *TF:* 800-250-5437 ■ *Web:* www.choa.org					
Children's Hospital 200 Henry Clay Ave	New Orleans	LA	70118	504-899-9511	896-9708*
**Fax:* Admitting ■ *TF:* 800-299-9511 ■ *Web:* www.chnola.org					
Children's Hospital & Medical Ctr 8200 Dodge St	Omaha	NE	68114	402-354-5400	955-4046*
**Fax:* Admitting ■ *Web:* www.chsomaha.org					
Children's Hospital & Research Center at Oakland 747 52nd St	Oakland	CA	94609	510-428-3000	450-5884*
**Fax:* Admitting ■ *Web:* www.childrenshospitaloakland.org					
Children's Hospital Boston 300 Longwood Ave	Boston	MA	02115	617-355-6000	
Web: www.childrenshospital.org					
Children's Hospital Central California 9300 Valley Children's Pl	Madera	CA	93638	559-353-3000	353-5161*
**Fax:* Admitting ■ *TF:* 800-548-5435 ■ *Web:* www.childrenscentralcal.org					
Children's Hospital Colorado (CHC) 13123 E 16th Ave	Aurora	CO	80045	720-777-1234	
TF: 800-624-6553 ■ *Web:* www.childrenscolorado.org					
Children's Hospital Medical Center of Akron 1 Perkins Sq	Akron	OH	44308	330-543-1000	543-3146*
**Fax:* Admitting ■ *TF:* 800-262-0333 ■ *Web:* www.akronchildrens.org					
Children's Hospital of Alabama 1600 7th Ave S	Birmingham	AL	35233	205-939-9100	
Children's Hospital of Los Angeles 4650 Sunset Blvd	Los Angeles	CA	90027	323-660-2450	668-1138*
**Fax:* Admitting ■ *Web:* www.childrenshospitalla.org					
Children's Hospital of Michigan 3901 Beaubien Blvd	Detroit	MI	48201	313-745-5437	966-5134*
**Fax:* Admitting ■ *Web:* www.dmc.org					
Children's Hospital of Orange County 455 S Main St	Orange	CA	92868	714-997-3000	289-4559*
**Fax:* Admitting ■ *Web:* www.choc.org					
Children's Hospital of Philadelphia 3400 Civic Ctr Blvd	Philadelphia	PA	19104	215-590-1000	590-1413*
**Fax:* Admitting ■ *Web:* www.chop.edu					
Children's Hospital of Pittsburgh 4401 Penn Ave	Pittsburgh	PA	15224	412-692-5325	692-8500
Web: www.chp.edu					
Children's Hospital of the King's Daughters 601 Children's Ln	Norfolk	VA	23507	757-668-7000	668-8050*
**Fax:* Admitting ■ *Web:* www.chkd.org					
Children's Hospital of Wisconsin 9000 W Wisconsin Ave	Milwaukee	WI	53226	414-266-2000	266-2547*
**Fax:* Admitting ■ *Web:* www.chw.org					
Children's Hospitals & Clinics Minneapolis 2525 Chicago Ave	Minneapolis	MN	55404	612-813-6000	813-6807
Web: www.childrenshc.org					
Children's Hospitals & Clinics Saint Paul 345 N Smith Ave	Saint Paul	MN	55102	651-220-6000	220-5147
Web: www.childrenshc.org					
Children's Institute of Pittsburgh 1405 Shady Ave	Pittsburgh	PA	15217	412-420-2400	420-2200
TF: 877-433-1109 ■ *Web:* www.amazingkids.org					
Children's Medical Center of Dallas 1935 Medical District Dr	Dallas	TX	75235	214-456-7000	456-2197
Web: www.childrens.com					
Children's Medical Ctr 1 Children's Plaza	Dayton	OH	45404	937-641-3000	641-3326*
**Fax:* Admitting ■ *TF:* 800-228-4055 ■ *Web:* www.childrensdayton.org					
Children's Memorial Hospital 2300 Children's Plaza	Chicago	IL	60614	773-880-4000	880-6986*
**Fax:* Admitting ■ *Web:* www.childrensmemorial.org					
Children's Mercy Hospital & Clinics 2401 Gillham Rd	Kansas City	MO	64108	816-234-3000	
TF: 866-512-2168 ■ *Web:* www.cmh.edu					
Children's National Medical Ctr (CNMC) 111 Michigan Ave NW	Washington	DC	20010	202-476-5000	
TF: 800-884-5433 ■ *Web:* www.childrensnational.org					
Children's Specialized Hospital 150 New Providence Rd	Mountainside	NJ	07092	908-233-3720	233-4176
TF: 888-224-5373 ■ *Web:* www.childrens-specialized.org					
Cincinnati Children's Hospital Medical Ctr 3333 Burnet Ave	Cincinnati	OH	45229	513-636-4200	636-3733*
**Fax:* Admitting ■ *TF:* 800-344-2462 ■ *Web:* www.cincinnatichildrens.org					
Cleveland Clinic Children's Hospital for Rehabilitation 2801 ML King Jr Dr	Cleveland	OH	44104	216-721-5400	791-1012
Connecticut Children's Medical Ctr 282 Washington St	Hartford	CT	06106	860-545-9000	545-8560
Web: www.connecticutchildrens.org					
Cook Children's Medical Ctr 801 7th Ave	Fort Worth	TX	76104	682-885-4000	885-4229
Web: www.cookchildrens.org					
Copper Hills Youth Ctr 5899 Rivendell Dr	West Jordan	UT	84081	801-561-3377	569-2959
TF: 800-776-7116 ■ *Web:* www.copperhillsyouthcenter.com					
Covenant Children's Hospital (CCH) 4015 22nd Pl	Lubbock	TX	79410	806-725-0000	723-7189
TF: 800-378-4189 ■ *Web:* www.covenanthealth.org/Facilities/childrenshospital/default					
Crittenton Children's Ctr 10918 Elm Ave	Kansas City	MO	64134	816-765-6600	767-4101
Web: www.saintlukeshealthsystem.org					
CS Mott Children's Hospital 1500 E Medical Ctr Dr	Ann Arbor	MI	48109	734-936-4000	763-7736
TF: 800-211-8181 ■ *Web:* www.med.umich.edu					
Devereux 1291 Stanley Rd NW PO Box 1688	Kennesaw	GA	30156	678-303-5233	443-1531*
**Fax Area Code:* 480 ■ *TF:* 800-342-3357 ■ *Web:* www.devereux.org					
Devereux Cleo Wallace 8405 Church Ranch Blvd	Westminster	CO	80021	303-466-7391	466-0904*
**Fax:* Admitting ■ *TF:* 800-456-2536 ■ *Web:* www.devereux.org					
Devereux Hospital & Children's Center of Florida 8000 Devereux Dr	Melbourne	FL	32940	321-242-9100	259-0786
Driscoll Children's Hospital 3533 S Alameda St	Corpus Christi	TX	78411	361-694-5000	694-5317
TF: 800-324-5683 ■ *Web:* www.driscollchildrens.org					

Phone | Fax

East Tennessee Children's Hospital
2018 Clinch Ave PO Box 15010 Knoxville TN 37901 865-541-8000
Web: www.etch.com

Franciscan Hospital for Children 30 Warren St Boston MA 02135 617-254-3800 779-1119
Web: www.franciscanhospital.org

Gillette Children's Specialty Healthcare
200 E University Ave. Saint Paul MN 55101 651-291-2848 229-3833
TF: 800-719-4040 ■ Web: www.gillettechildrens.org

Gulf Coast Treatment Ctr
1015 Mar-Walt Dr. Fort Walton Beach FL 32547 850-863-4160 863-8576

Hawthorn Ctr 18471 Haggerty Rd Northville MI 48167 248-349-3000 349-8259
TF: 800-434-2340

Helen DeVos Children's Hospital
100 Michigan St NE Grand Rapids MI 49503 616-391-9000 391-3105
Web: www.devoschildrens.org

HSC Pediatric Ctr 1731 Bunker Hill Rd NE Washington DC 20017 202-832-4400 529-1646
TF: 800-226-4444 ■ Web: www.hscpediatriccenter.org

JD McCarty Center for Children with Developmental Disabilities
2002 E Robinson St Norman OK 73071 405-307-2800 307-2801
TF: 800-777-1272 ■ Web: www.jdmc.org

Kennedy Krieger Institute 707 N Broadway Baltimore MD 21205 443-923-9200 923-9425
TF: 800-873-3377 ■ Web: www.kennedykrieger.org

KidsPeace Orchard Hills Campus
5300 Kids Peace Dr Orefield PA 18069 610-799-8800 799-8900*
*Fax: Admitting ■ TF: 800-854-3123 ■ Web: www.kidspeace.org

Larabida Children's Hospital & Research Ctr
6501 S Promontory Dr
E 65th St at Lake Michigan Chicago IL 60649 773-363-6700
Web: www.larabida.org

Le Bonheur Children's Medical Ctr
50 N Dunlap Memphis TN 38103 901-287-5437 572-4568*
*Fax: Admitting ■ Web: www.lebonheur.org/portal/site/lebonheur

Lucile Packard Children's Hospital (LPCH)
725 Welch Rd Palo Alto CA 94304 650-497-8000 497-8968*
*Fax: Admitting ■ TF: 800-995-5724 ■ Web: www.lpch.org

Mary Bridge Children's Hospital & Health Ctr
317 Martin Luther King Jr Way Tacoma WA 98405 253-403-1400 403-1247
TF: 800-552-1419 ■ Web: www.multicare.org

Massachusetts Hospital School 3 Randolph St Canton MA 02021 781-828-2440 821-4086

Medical University of South Carolina Children's Hospital
165 Ashley Ave. Charleston SC 29425 843-792-2300 792-8948
Web: www.musckids.com

Miami Children's Hospital 3100 SW 62nd Ave. Miami FL 33155 305-666-6511 663-8466
TF: 800-432-6837 ■ Web: www.mch.com

Mount Washington Pediatric Hospital
1708 W Rogers Ave Baltimore MD 21209 410-578-8600 466-1715
Web: www.mwph.org

Phoenix Children's Hospital 1919 E Thomas Rd Phoenix AZ 85016 602-546-1000 546-0191
TF: 888-908-5437 ■ Web: www.phoenixchildrens.com

Primary Children's Medical Ctr
100 N Medical Dr Salt Lake City UT 84113 801-662-1000 662-6202*
*Fax: Admitting ■ Web: www.intermountainhealthcare.org

Queens Children's Psychiatric Ctr
74-03 Commonwealth Blvd Bellerose NY 11426 718-264-4506 264-4954

Rady Children's Hospital (RCH)
3020 Children's Way MC 5101 San Diego CA 92123 858-576-1700 966-4934*
*Fax: Library ■ TF: 800-788-9029 ■ Web: www.rchsd.org

Riverview Hospital for Children
915 River Rd. Middletown CT 06457 860-704-4000 704-4032

Saint Christopher's Hospital for Children
Erie Ave & Front St. Philadelphia PA 19134 215-427-5000 427-6825*
*Fax: Admitting ■ Web: www.stchristophershospital.com

Saint Jude Children's Research Hospital (SJCRH)
262 Danny Thomas Pl Memphis TN 38105 901-495-3300 495-5297*
*Fax: Admitting ■ TF: 866-278-5833 ■ Web: www.stjude.org

Saint Louis Children's Hospital
1 Children's Pl Saint Louis MO 63110 314-454-6000 454-2870
TF: 800-678-5437 ■ Web: www.stlouischildrens.org

Searcy Hospital 725 E Coy Smith Hwy Mount Vernon AL 36560 251-662-6700 829-9075

Seattle Children's Hospital
4800 Sand Pt Way NE. Seattle WA 98105 206-987-2000 987-5018*
*Fax: Admitting ■ TF: 866-987-2000 ■ Web: www.seattlechildrens.org

Shriners Hospitals for Children Boston
51 Blossom St Boston MA 02114 617-722-3000 523-1684
TF: 800-255-1916 ■ Web: www.shrinershospitalsforchildren.org

Shriners Hospitals for Children Canada
1529 Cedar Ave Montreal QC H3G1A6 514-842-4464 842-7553
Web: www.shrinershq.org/shc/canada

Shriners Hospitals for Children Chicago
2211 N Oak Pk Ave. Chicago IL 60707 773-622-5400 385-5453*
*Fax: Admitting ■ TF: 888-385-0161 ■ Web: www.shrinershq.org

Shriners Hospitals for Children Cincinnati
3229 Burnet Ave Cincinnati OH 45229 513-872-6000 872-6999
TF: 800-875-8580 ■ Web: www.support.shrinershospitals.org

Shriners Hospitals for Children Erie
1645 W 8th St. Erie PA 16505 814-875-8700 875-8756
TF: 800-873-5437 ■ Web: www.shrinershq.org/shc/erie

Shriners Hospitals for Children Galveston
2900 Rocky Pt Dr Tampa Fl 33607 813-281-0300
Web: www.shrinershq.org/shc/galveston

Shriners Hospitals for Children Greenville
950 W Faris Rd. Greenville SC 29605 864-271-3444 271-4471
Web: www.shrinershospitalsforchildren.org

Shriners Hospitals for Children Honolulu
1310 Punahou St Honolulu HI 96826 808-941-4466 942-8573
TF: 888-888-6314 ■ Web: www.shrinershq.org

Shriners Hospitals for Children Houston
6977 Main St Houston TX 77030 713-797-1616 793-3762*
*Fax: Admitting ■ Web: www.shrinershq.org

Shriners Hospitals for Children Lexington
1900 Richmond Rd. Lexington KY 40502 859-266-2101 268-5636
TF: 800-668-4634 ■ Web: www.shrinershq.org/shc/lexington

Shriners Hospitals for Children Los Angeles
3160 Geneva St Los Angeles CA 90020 213-388-3151 387-7528*
*Fax: Admitting ■ TF: 888-486-5437 ■ Web: www.shrinershq.org/shc/losangeles

Shriners Hospitals for Children Northern California
2425 Stockton Blvd Sacramento CA 95817 916-453-2000 453-2395*
*Fax: Admitting ■ Web: www.shrinershq.org

Shriners Hospitals for Children Philadelphia
3551 N Broad St. Philadelphia PA 19140 215-430-4000 430-4068*
*Fax: Admitting ■ TF: 800-281-4050 ■ Web: www.shrinershq.org

Shriners Hospitals for Children Portland
3101 SW Sam Jackson Pk Rd. Portland OR 97239 503-241-5090 221-3475
Web: www.shrinershq.org

Shriners Hospitals for Children Saint Louis
2001 S Lindbergh Blvd Saint Louis MO 63131 314-432-3600 432-2930
TF: 800-237-5055 ■ Web: www.shrinershq.org

Shriners Hospitals for Children Salt Lake City
Fairfax Rd & Virginia St Salt Lake City UT 84103 801-536-3500 536-3782
TF: 800-313-3745 ■ Web: www.shrinershospitalsforchildren.org

Shriners Hospitals for Children Shreveport
3100 Samford Ave Shreveport LA 71103 318-222-5704 424-7610
Web: www.shrinershospitalsforchildren.org

Shriners Hospitals for Children Spokane
911 W 5th Ave Spokane WA 99204 509-455-7844 623-0474*
*Fax: Admitting ■ Web: www.shrinershq.org

Shriners Hospitals for Children Springfield
516 Carew St Springfield MA 01104 413-787-2000 787-2009
TF: 800-322-5905 ■ Web: www.shrinershq.org

Shriners Hospitals for Children Tampa
12502 N Pine Dr. Tampa FL 33612 813-972-2250 975-7120*
*Fax: Admitting ■ TF: 800-237-5055 ■ Web: www.shrinershq.org/shc/tampa

Shriners Hospitals for Children Twin Cities
2025 E River Pkwy Minneapolis MN 55414 612-596-6100 339-5954
Web: www.shrinershq.org

SSM Cardinal Glennon Children's Hospital
1465 S Grand Blvd Saint Louis MO 63104 314-577-5600
Web: www.cardinalglennon.com

Steven & Alexandra Cohen Children's Medical Center of New York
269-01 76th Ave. New Hyde Park NY 11040 718-470-3000
Web: www.northshorelij.com

Stollery Children's Hospital 8440 112th St Edmonton AB T6G2B7 780-407-8822 407-3301

Streamwood Behavioral Health Ctr
1400 E Irving Pk Rd Streamwood IL 60107 630-837-9000 837-2639
TF: 800-272-7790 ■ Web: www.streamwoodhospital.com

Texas Children's Hospital 6621 Fannin St Houston TX 77030 832-824-1000 825-3386
TF: 800-364-5437 ■ Web: www.texaschildrenshospital.org

Texas Scottish Rite Hospital for Children
2222 Welborn St. Dallas TX 75219 214-559-5000 559-7447
TF: 800-421-1121 ■ Web: www.tsrhc.org

Wolfson Children's Hospital
800 Prudential Dr Jacksonville FL 32207 904-202-8000 202-8173
Web: www.wolfsonchildrens.org

Women's & Children's Hospital of Buffalo
219 Bryant St Buffalo NY 14222 716-878-7000 888-3979*
*Fax: Admitting ■ TF: 800-388-9672 ■ Web: www.wchob.org

Youth Villages Inner Harbour
4685 Dorsett Shoals Rd Douglasville GA 30135 770-852-6333 920-2745
TF: 800-255-8657 ■ Web: www.youthvillages.org

377-2 General Hospitals - Canada

Phone | Fax

Aberbeen Hospital 835 E River Rd New Glasgow NS B2H3S6 902-752-7600 755-2356
Web: www.aberdeenhealthfoundation.com

Arbutus Care Centre 4505 Valley Dr Vancouver BC V6L2L1 604-261-4292 261-7849

Battlefords Union Hospital
1092 107th St. North Battleford SK S9A1Z1 306-446-6600 446-6561

Belleville General Hospital
265 Dundas St E. Belleville ON K8N5A9 613-969-7400 968-8234
TF: 800-483-2811 ■ Web: www.qhc.on.ca

Brandon Regional Health Ctr
150 McTavish Ave E Brandon MB R7A2B3 204-578-4000 578-4937
Web: www.brandonrha.mb.ca

British Columbia's Women's Hospital & Health Centre
4500 Oak St Vancouver BC V6H3N1 604-875-2424 875-3582
TF: 888-300-3088 ■ Web: www.bcwomens.ca

Brockville General Hospital 75 Charles St. Brockville ON K6V1S8 613-345-5649 345-8336
Web: www.bgh-on.ca

Burnaby Hospital 3935 Kincaid St Burnaby BC V5G2X6 604-453-1910 453-1929*
*Fax: Mail Rm ■ Web: www.fraserhealth.ca

Cambridge Memorial Hospital
700 Coronation Blvd. Cambridge ON N1R3G2 519-621-2330 740-4938
Web: www.cmh.org

Campbell River Hospital 375 2nd Ave Campbell River BC V9W3V1 250-287-7111 286-9675

Centenary Health Centre
2867 Ellesmere Rd Scarborough ON M1E4B9 416-284-8131 281-7323

Centre de sante Cloutier-du Rivage
155 Rue Toupin. Cap-de-la-Madeleine QC G8T7W3 819-370-2100 379-9644

Centre de Sante de la MRC de Maskinonge
41 Boul Comtois. Louiseville QC J5V2H8 819-228-2731 228-0425
Web: www.csssm.qc.ca

Centre de sante et de services sociaux de la Saint-Maurice
885 Blvd Ducharme La Tuque QC G9X3C1 819-523-4581 523-7992
Web: www.cssshsm.qc.ca

Centre de Sante Memphremagog
50 Rue St Patrice E. Magog QC J1X3X3 819-843-3381 843-8262

Centre Hospitalier Affilie Pavillon Enfant-Jesus
1401 18th St. Quebec QC G1J1Z4 418-649-0252 649-5920*

Centre Hospitalier Affilie Universitaire de Quebec-Pavillon Saint-Sacrement
1050 ch Sainte-Foy Quebec QC G1S4L8 418-682-7511 682-7877*
*Fax: Admissions ■ Web: www.cha.quebec.qc.ca

Centre Hospitalier Angrignon
8585 Terrasse Champlain LaSalle QC H8P1C1 514-362-1000 362-2812

Name / Address	City	Prov	Postal Code	Phone	Fax
Centre Hospitalier Angrignon 4000 boul Lasalle	Verdun	QC	H4G2A3	514-362-1000	765-7306
Centre Hospitalier Anna-Laberge 200 boul Brisebois	Chateauguay	QC	J6K4W8	450-699-2425	699-2510*
Centre Hospitalier Baie des Chaleurs 419 boul Perron	Maria	QC	G0C1Y0	418-759-3443	759-5333
Centre Hospitalier Beauce-Etchemin 1515 17e rue	Saint-Georges	QC	G5Y4T8	418-228-2031	227-9147*
Centre Hospitalier Chauveau 29 Rue de l'Hopital	Loretteville	QC	G2A2T7	418-842-3651	842-8931
Centre Hospitalier d'Amqui 135 Rue de l'Hopital; *Web:* www.chamqui.com	Amqui	QC	G5J2K5	418-629-2211	629-4498
Centre Hospitalier de la Region de l'Amiante 1717 Rue Notre-Dame N.; *Web:* www.fondationchra.org	Thetford Mines	QC	G6G2V4	418-338-7777	335-7616
Centre Hospitalier de Lachine 650 16th Ave.	Lachine	QC	H8S3N5	514-637-2351	637-2570*
Centre Hospitalier de Rouyn-Noranda 4 9e rue	Rouyn-Noranda	QC	J9X2B2	819-764-5131	764-4211
Centre Hospitalier de Val-d'Or 725 6e rue	Val-d'Or	QC	J9P3Y1	819-825-6711	825-7919
Centre Hospitalier du Centre-de-la-Mauricie 50 118e rue	Shawinigan-Sud	QC	G9P5K1	819-536-7500	536-7687
Centre Hospitalier et Centre de Readaptation Antoine-Labelle 2561 Ch de la Lievre S	Des Ruisseaux	QC	J9L3G3	819-623-1234	440-4376*
Centre Hospitalier Fleury 2180 Fleury St E	Montreal	QC	H2B1K3	514-381-9311	383-5287
Centre Hospitalier Granby 205 boul Leclerc; *Web:* www.santemonteregie.qc.ca	Granby	QC	J2G1T7	450-372-5491	375-8037
Centre Hospitalier Hotel-Dieu d'Amos 622 4e Rue O	Amos	QC	J9T2S2	819-732-3341	732-7054
Centre Hospitalier Hotel-Dieu de Roberval 450 Rue Brassard	Roberval	QC	G8H1B9	418-275-0110	275-6202
Centre Hospitalier Lac Megantic 3569 Rue Laval	Lac-Megantic	QC	G6B1A5	819-583-0330	583-5364
Centre Hospitalier Laurentien 234 Rue St Vincent	Sainte-Agathe-des-Monts	QC	J8C2B8	819-324-4000	324-4001
Centre Hospitalier Le Gardeur 911 montee des Pionniers; *TF:* 888-654-7525 ■ *Web:* www.csss.sudlanaudiere.ca	Terrebonne	QC	J6V2H2	450-654-7525	470-2640
Centre Hospitalier Mount Sinai 5690 Cavendish Blvd	Montreal	QC	H4W1S7	514-369-2222	369-2225
Centre Hospitalier Pierre Boucher 1333 Boul Jacques-Cartier E	Longueuil	QC	J4M2A5	450-468-8111	468-8188
Centre Hospitalier Regional 1750 prom Sunset; *TF:* 800-727-1699	Bathurst	NB	E2A4L7	506-544-3000	544-2329
Centre Hospitalier Regional Baie-Comeau Pavillon Le Royer 635 boul Joliet	Baie-Comeau	QC	G5C1P1	418-589-3701	589-9654
Centre Hospitalier Regional de Lanaudiere 1000 boul Sainte-Anne	Joliette	QC	J6E6J2	450-759-8222	759-5143
Centre Hospitalier Regional de Rimouski 150 Ave Rouleau	Rimouski	QC	G5L5T1	418-723-7851	723-8616
Centre Hospitalier Regional de Sept-Iles 45 Rue Pere Divet	Sept-Iles	QC	G4R3N7	418-962-9761	962-2701
Centre Hospitalier Regional de Trois-Rivieres 731 Rue Sainte-Julie	Trois-Rivieres	QC	G9A1X1	819-697-3333	372-3546
Centre Hospitalier Regional du Grand Portage 75 Rue St Henri	Riviere-du-Loup	QC	G5R2A4	418-868-1010	868-1035
Centre Hospitalier Regional du Suroit 150 Rue St Thomas	Salaberry-de-Valleyfield	QC	J6T6C1	450-371-9920	371-7454
Centre Hospitalier Universitaire de Quebec 2705 Laurier Blvd	Sainte-Foy	QC	G1V4G2	418-656-4141	654-2247
Centre Hospitalier Universitaire de Quebec Pavillon Hotel-Dieu 11 Cote du Palais	Quebec	QC	G1R2J6	418-691-5151	691-5331
Centre Le Jeannois Pavillon Hotel-Dieu d'Alma 300 Boul Champlain S	Alma	QC	G8B5W3	418-669-2000	668-9695
Centre Universitaire de Sante de l'Estrie 580 Rue Bowen S	Sherbrooke	QC	J1G2E8	819-346-1110	822-6780*
Chatham-Kent Health Alliance 80 Grand Ave W PO Box 2030; *Web:* www.ckha.on.ca	Chatham	ON	N7M5L9	519-352-6400	436-2522
Children's Hospital of Eastern Ontario 401 Smyth Rd.; *TF:* 866-736-2436 ■ *Web:* www.cheo.on.ca	Ottawa	ON	K1H8L1	613-737-7600	738-4866
Chilliwack General Hospital 45600 Menholm Rd; *Web:* www.fraserhealth.ca	Chilliwack	BC	V2P1P7	604-795-4141	795-4110
Chinook Regional Hospital Foundation 960 19th St S; *Web:* www.chr.ab.ca	Lethbridge	AB	T1J1W5	403-388-6001	
CHSLD Centre de la Mauricie 1650 6E Ave; *Web:* www.medecinenmauricie.ca	Grand-Mere	QC	G9T2K4	819-533-2500	538-7640
CHU Sainte-Justine 3175 Ch de la Cote-Sainte-Catherine; *Web:* www.chu-sainte-justine.org	Montreal	QC	H3T1C5	514-345-4931	345-4882
Colchester Regional Hospital 207 Willow St.; *TF:* 800-460-2110 ■ *Web:* www.cehha.nshealth.ca	Truro	NS	B2N5A1	902-893-4321	893-5559
Complexe Sante et Services Sociaux Nicolet-Yamaska 675 Rue St Jean-Baptiste	Nicolet	QC	J3T1S4	819-293-2071	293-6160
Concordia Hospital 1095 Concordia Ave; *Web:* www.concordiahospital.mb.ca/hospital/index.html	Winnipeg	MB	R2K3S8	204-667-1560	667-1049
Cornwall Community Hospital 840 McConnell Ave; *Web:* www.cornwallhospital.ca	Cornwall	ON	K6H5S5	613-938-4240	930-4502
Cowichan District Hospital 3045 Gibbins Rd.	Duncan	BC	V9L1E5	250-746-4141	746-4247
Credit Valley Hospital 2200 Eglinton Ave W; *TF:* 877-292-4284 ■ *Web:* www.cvh.on.ca	Mississauga	ON	L5M2N1	905-813-2200	813-4444
CSSS du Lac des Deux-Montagnes 520 Boul Sauve; *Web:* www.moncsss.com	Saint-Eustache	QC	J7R5B1	450-473-6811	473-6966
Cypress Regional Hospital 2004 Saskatchewan Dr; **Fax:* Admitting ■ *Web:* www.cypressrha.ca	Swift Current	SK	S9H5M8	306-778-9400	778-9409*
Dartmouth General Hospital 325 Pleasant St.; *Web:* www.cdha.nshealth.ca	Dartmouth	NS	B2Y3S3	902-465-8539	
Delta Hospital Foundation 5800 Mountain View Blvd.; *Web:* www.deltahospital.com	Delta	BC	V4K3V6	604-940-9695	940-9670
Dr Everett Chalmers Hospital 700 Priestman St; *Web:* www.medicine.dal.ca/tour/hospitals_tour2.htm	Fredericton	NB	E3B5N5	506-452-5400	452-5500
Dr Georges L Dumont Regional Hospital 330 University Ave	Moncton	NB	E1C2Z3	506-862-4000	862-4256
Eagle Ridge Hospital & Health Care Centre 475 Guildford Way; *Web:* www.fraserhealth.ca	Port Moody	BC	V3H3W9	604-461-2022	461-9972
East Kootenay Regional Hospital 13 24th Ave N; *TF:* 866-288-8082 ■ *Web:* www.interiorhealth.ca	Cranbrook	BC	V1C3H9	250-426-5281	426-5285
Edmundston Regional Hospital 275 boul Hebert	Edmundston	NB	E3V4E4	506-739-2200	739-2231
Flin Flon General Hospital 50 Church St PO Box 340	Flin Flon	MB	R8A1N2	204-687-7591	687-8494
Foothills Medical Centre (FMC) 1403 29th St NW; *Web:* www.albertahealthservices.ca	Calgary	AB	T2N2T9	403-670-1110	944-1663
Glace Bay Healthcare Facility (GBHF) 300 S St.; *Web:* www.cbdha.nshealth.ca	Glace Bay	NS	B1A1K9	902-849-5511	842-9775
Grace General Hospital 300 Booth Dr.; *Web:* www.gracehospital.ca	Winnipeg	MB	R3J3M7	204-837-8311	837-0029
Grand River Hospital Kitchener-Waterloo Health Centre 835 King St W PO Box 9056; *Web:* www.grhosp.on.ca	Kitchener	ON	N2G1G3	519-749-4300	749-4208
Greater Niagara General Hospital 5546 Portage Rd; *Web:* www.niagarahealth.on.ca	Niagara Falls	ON	L2E6X2	905-378-4647	358-8435
Grey Bruce Health Services 1800 8th St E PO Box 1800; *Web:* www.gbhs.on.ca	Owen Sound	ON	N4K6M9	519-376-2121	372-3942
Guelph General Hospital 115 Delhi St; *Web:* www.guelphgeneralhospital.com	Guelph	ON	N1E4J4	519-822-5350	822-2170
Hamilton General Hospital 237 Barton St E	Hamilton	ON	L8L2X2	905-527-4322	521-5067
Hamilton Health Sciences 1200 Main St W; *Web:* www.hamiltonhealthsciences.ca	Hamilton	ON	L8N3Z5	905-521-2100	521-5067
Headwaters Health Care Centre 100 Rolling Hills Dr; *Web:* www.headwatershealth.ca	Orangeville	ON	L9W4X9	519-941-2410	942-0483
Health Sciences Centre 820 Sherbrook St; *Web:* www.hsc.mb.ca	Winnipeg	MB	R3A1R9	204-787-3661	787-3341
High River Hospital 560 9th Ave W	High River	AB	T1V1B3	403-652-2200	652-0199
Hopital Brome Missisquoi-Perkins 950 Rue Principale	Cowansville	QC	J2K1K3	450-266-4342	263-8669
Hopital Charles LeMoyne (HCLM) 3120 boul Taschereau; *Web:* www.santemonteregie.qc.ca/hclm/index.fr.html	Greenfield Park	QC	J4V2H1	450-466-5000	466-5038
Hopital d'Argenteuil 145 boul Providence	Lachute	QC	J8H4C7	450-562-3761	566-3316
Hopital de Papineau 500 Rue Belanger; *Web:* www.csssapapineau.qc.ca	Gatineau	QC	J8L2M4	819-986-3341	
Hopital du Haut-Richelieu 920 Boul du Seminaire N	Saint-Jean-sur-Richelieu	QC	J3A1B7	450-359-5000	359-5251
Hopital du Sacre-Coeur de Montreal 5400 Gouin Blvd W	Montreal	QC	H4J1C5	514-338-2222	338-2384
Hopital General de Montreal 1650 Cedar Ave; *Web:* www.muhc.ca/pfv/mgh	Montreal	QC	H3G1A4	514-934-1934	934-8303
Hopital Jean-Talon 1385 Jean-Talon St E	Montreal	QC	H2E1S6	514-495-6767	495-6771
Hopital Jeffery Hale 1250 ch Sainte-Foy	Quebec	QC	G1S2M6	418-683-4471	683-8980
Hopital Laval 2725 ch Sainte-Foy	Sainte-Foy	QC	G1V4G5	418-656-8711	656-4829
Hopital Maisonneuve-Rosemont 5415 de l'Assomption Blvd.	Montreal	QC	H1T2M4	514-252-3400	252-3569
Hopital Regional de Sudbury Emplacement Laurentien 41 Ramsey Lake Rd; *TF:* 866-469-0822 ■ *Web:* www.hrsrh.on.ca	Sudbury	ON	P3E5J1	705-523-7100	523-7112
Hopital Sainte-Anne-de-Beaupre 1100 Rue Montagnards	Beaupre	QC	G0A1E0	418-827-3726	827-3728
Hopital Sainte-Croix 570 Rue Heriot	Drummondville	QC	J2B1C1	819-478-6464	478-6410
Hopital Santa Cabrini Ospedale 5655 Sainte-Zotique St E	Montreal	QC	H1T1P7	514-252-6000	252-6453
Hospital Complex Sagamie The 305 Ave St Vallier CP 5006; *Web:* www.usherbrooke.ca	Chicoutimi	QC	G7H5H6	418-541-1000	541-1168
Hospital Gatineau 909 boul de la Verandrye; *Web:* www.csssgatineau.qc.ca	Gatineau	QC	J8P7H2	819-966-6100	
Hotel Dieu Hospital 166 Brock St.; *Web:* www.hoteldieu.com	Kingston	ON	K7L5G2	613-544-3310	544-9897
Hotel-Dieu d'Arthabaska 5 Rue des Hospitalieres; *Web:* www.hda.ca	Victoriaville	QC	G6P6N2	819-357-2030	357-4314
Hotel-Dieu de Levis 143 Rue Wolfe; *Web:* www.hdl.qc.ca	Levis	QC	G6V3Z1	418-835-7121	835-7200
Hotel-Dieu de Montmagny 350 Boul Tache O.	Montmagny	QC	G5V3R8	418-248-0630	248-0947
Hotel-Dieu de Saint-Jerome 290 Rue Montigny	Saint-Jerome	QC	J7Z5T3	450-431-8200	431-8244
Hotel-Dieu de Sorel 400 Ave Hotel-Dieu	Sorel-Tracy	QC	J3P1N5	450-746-6000	746-6082
Hotel-Dieu Grace Hospital 1030 Ouellette Ave; *Web:* www.hdgh.org	Windsor	ON	N9A1E1	519-973-4411	977-0018
Innisfail Health Centre 5023 42nd St	Innisfail	AB	T4G1A9	403-227-3381	227-7801
James Paton Memorial Hospital 125 Trans Canada Hwy	Gander	NL	A1V1P7	709-256-2500	256-7800
Joseph Brant Memorial Hospital (JBMH) 1230 N Shore Blvd; *Web:* www.jbmh.com	Burlington	ON	L7S1W7	905-632-3730	336-6480
Kelowna General Hospital (KGH) 2268 Pandosy St.; *TF:* 888-877-4442 ■ *Web:* www.interiorhealth.ca	Kelowna	BC	V1Y1T2	250-862-4000	862-4020
Kingston General Hospital 76 Stuart St; *TF:* 800-567-5722 ■ *Web:* www.kgh.on.ca	Kingston	ON	K7L2V7	613-548-3232	548-6042
Kootenay Boundary Regional Hospital 1200 Hospital Bench; *TF:* 866-368-3314 ■ *Web:* www.interiorhealth.ca	Trail	BC	V1R4M1	250-368-3311	364-3422

Hospital / Address	City	Prov	Postal Code	Phone	Fax
Lacombe Hospital & Care Centre 5430 47th Ave	Lacombe	AB	T4L1G8	403-782-3336	782-2818
Web: www.albertahealthservices.ca					
Lake of the Woods District Hospital (LWDH) 21 Sylvan St	Kenora	ON	P9N3W7	807-468-9861	468-3939
Web: www.lwdh.on.ca					
Lakeridge Health Bowmanville 47 Liberty St S	Bowmanville	ON	L1C2N4	905-623-3331	697-4685
Web: www.lakeridgehealth.on.ca					
Lakeridge Health Oshawa 1 Hospital Ct	Oshawa	ON	L1G2B9	905-576-8711	721-4736
TF: 866-338-1778 ■ *Web:* www.lakeridgehealth.on.ca					
Lakeshore General Hospital 160 ch Stillview	Pointe-Claire	QC	H9R2Y2	514-630-2225	630-2371
Web: www.lgh.qc.ca					
Langley Memorial Hospital 22051 Fraser Hwy	Langley	BC	V3A4H4	604-534-4121	534-8283
Web: www.fraserhealth.ca					
Lions Gate Hospital 231 E 15th St	North Vancouver	BC	V7L2L7	604-988-3131	984-5838
TF: 800-984-1131 ■ *Web:* www.vch.ca					
London Health Sciences Centre 800 Commissioners Rd E PO Box 5010	London	ON	N6A5W9	519-685-8500	685-8127
Web: www.lhsc.on.ca					
London Health Sciences Centre Victoria Campus 800 Commissioners Rd E	London	ON	N6C6B5	519-685-8500	685-8127
Web: www.lhsc.on.ca					
Markham Stouffville Hospital *Markham* 381 Church St PO Box 1800	Markham	ON	L3P7P3	905-472-7000	472-7086
Web: www.msh.on.ca					
Medical Clinic Of North Texas 9003 Airport Fwy Suite 300	N. Richland	TX	76180	817-514-5200	514-5210
Web: www.mcnt.com					
Medicine Hat Regional Hospital 666 5th St SW	Medicine Hat	AB	T1A4H6	403-529-8000	529-8998
Misericordia Community Hospital & Health Centre 16940 87th Ave.	Edmonton	AB	T5R4H5	780-735-2000	735-2774
Web: www.caritas.ab.ca					
Mission Memorial Hospital 7324 Hurd St	Mission	BC	V2V3H5	604-826-6261	826-9513
Web: www.fraserhealth.ca					
Moncton Hospital The 135 MacBeath Ave.	Moncton	NB	E1C6Z8	506-857-5111	857-5545
Web: www.serha.ca/moncton_hospital/default.htm					
Montfort Hospital 713 Montreal Rd	Ottawa	ON	K1K0T2	613-746-4621	748-4914
Web: www.hopitalmontfort.com					
Montreal Chest Institute 5655 Sainte-Zotique St E	Montreal	QC	H1T1P7	514-252-6000	252-6453
Montreal Heart Institute 5000 Belanger St E	Montreal	QC	H1T1C8	514-376-3330	593-2540
Web: www.icm-mhi.org					
Moose Jaw Union Hospital 455 Fairford St E	Moose Jaw	SK	S6H1H3	306-694-0200	694-0270
Mount Saint Joseph Hospital 3080 Prince Edward St	Vancouver	BC	V5T3N4	604-874-1141	
Mount Sinai Hospital 600 University Ave	Toronto	ON	M5G1X5	416-596-4200	586-8544*
**Fax:* PR ■ *Web:* www.mountsinai.on.ca					
Nanaimo Regional General Hospital 1200 Dufferin Crescent	Nanaimo	BC	V9S2B7	250-754-2141	755-7633
Norfolk General Hospital 365 W St.	Simcoe	ON	N3Y1T7	519-426-0750	429-6998
Web: www.ngh.on.ca					
North Bay Regional Health Centre 50 College Dr PO Box 2500	North Bay	ON	P1B5A4	705-474-7525	
Web: www.nbgh.on.ca					
North York General Hospital (NYGH) 4001 Leslie St.	North York	ON	M2K1E1	416-756-6000	756-6738*
**Fax:* Hum Res ■ *Web:* www.nygh.on.ca					
Northern Lights Regional Health Centre (NLRHC) 7 Hospital St.	Fort McMurray	AB	T9H1P2	780-791-6161	791-6029
Web: www.albertahealthservices.ca					
Oakville-Trafalgar Memorial Hospital 327 Reynolds St	Oakville	ON	L6J3L7	905-845-2571	338-4636
Web: www.haltonhealthcare.com					
Orillia Soldiers' Memorial Hospital (OSMH) 170 Colborne St W	Orillia	ON	L3V2Z3	705-325-2201	325-7953*
**Fax:* Admissions ■ *Web:* www.osmh.on.ca					
Pas Health Complex Inc 67 1st St W PO Box 240	The Pas	MB	R9A1K4	204-623-6431	623-9239
Peace Arch Hospital 15521 Russell Ave	White Rock	BC	V4B2R4	604-535-4520	541-5820
Web: www.peacearchhospital.com					
Peace River Community Health Centre 10101 68th St.	Peace River	AB	T8S1T6	780-624-7500	624-7552
Web: www.albertahealthservices.ca					
Pembroke Regional Hospital 705 MacKay St	Pembroke	ON	K8A1G8	613-732-2811	732-9986
Web: www.pemreghos.org					
Penticton Regional Hospital (PRH) 550 Carmi Ave	Penticton	BC	V2A3G6	250-492-4000	492-9068
TF: 877-299-3899 ■ *Web:* www.interiorhealth.ca					
Perth-Smiths Falls District Hospital 60 Cornelia St W	Smiths Falls	ON	K7A2H9	613-283-2330	283-8990
Web: www.psfdh.on.ca					
Peter Lougheed Centre 3500 26th Ave NE	Calgary	AB	T1Y6J4	403-943-4555	943-4878
Web: www.calgaryhealthregion.ca					
Peterborough Regional Health Ctr 1 Hospital Dr	Peterborough	ON	K9J7C6	705-743-2121	876-5107
Web: www.prhc.on.ca					
Powell River General Hospital 5000 Joyce Ave.	Powell River	BC	V8A5R3	604-485-3211	485-3245
Web: www.vch.ca					
Prince County Hospital 65 Roy Boapes Ave	Summerside	PE	C1N6M8	902-438-4200	438-4511
Web: www.pchcare.com/inside.cfm					
Prince George Regional Hospital 1475 Edmonton St	Prince George	BC	V2M1S2	250-565-2000	565-2343
Queen Elizabeth Hospital 60 Riverside Dr PO Box 6600	Charlottetown	PE	C1A8T5	902-894-2111	894-2146
Queensway-Carleton Hospital 3045 Baseline Rd.	Ottawa	ON	K2H8P4	613-721-4700	721-2000
Web: www.qch.on.ca					
Red Deer Regional Hospital Centre 3942 50th A Ave	Red Deer	AB	T4N4E7	403-343-4422	343-4866
Web: www.albertahealthservices.ca					
Reseau Sante Kamouraska 1201 6th Ave.	Lapocatiere	QC	G0R1Z0	418-856-7000	856-4737
Reseau Sante Richelieu-Yamaska 2750 boul Laframboise	Saint-Hyacinthe	QC	J2S4Y8	450-771-3333	771-3289
Richmond Hospital 7000 Westminster Hwy	Richmond	BC	V6X1A2	604-278-9711	244-5191
Web: www.richmondhealth.ca					
Ridge Meadows Hospital 11666 Laity St	Maple Ridge	BC	V2X7G5	604-443-7948	
Web: www.fraserhealth.ca					
Rimbey Hospital & Care Centre 5228 50th Ave PO Box 440	Rimbey	AB	T0C2J0	403-843-2271	843-2506
Riverside Campus of Ottawa Hospital 1967 Riverside Dr	Ottawa	ON	K1H7W9	613-738-7100	738-8522
Rockyview General Hospital 7007 14th St SW	Calgary	AB	T2V1P9	403-541-3000	
Ross Memorial Hospital (RMH) 10 Angeline St N	Lindsay	ON	K9V4M8	705-324-6111	328-2817
TF: 800-510-7365 ■ *Web:* www.rmh.org					
Rouge Valley Ajax & Pickering 580 Harwood Ave S	Ajax	ON	L1S2J4	905-683-2320	683-8527
Web: www.rougevalley.ca					
Royal Alexandra Hospital 10240 Kingsway Ave	Edmonton	AB	T5H3V9	780-735-4111	
Web: www.albertahealthservices.ca					
Royal Columbian Hospital 330 E Columbia St	New Westminster	BC	V3L3W7	604-520-4253	520-4827
Web: www.fraserhealth.ca					
Royal Inland Hospital 311 Columbia St.	Kamloops	BC	V2C2T1	250-374-5111	314-2189
Royal University Hospital 103 Hospital Dr	Saskatoon	SK	S7N0W8	306-655-1000	655-3394
Royal Victoria Hospital 201 Georgian Dr	Barrie	ON	L4M6M2	705-728-9802	728-0982
Web: www.rvh.on.ca					
Royal Victoria Hospital 687 Pine Ave W.	Montreal	QC	H3A1A1	514-934-1934	843-1661
Web: www.muhc.ca/pfv/rvh					
Saint Boniface General Hospital (SBGH) 409 Tache Ave Rm D1003	Winnipeg	MB	R2H2A6	204-233-8563	231-0041*
**Fax:* Hum Res ■ *Web:* www.saintboniface.ca					
Saint Catharines General Hospital 142 Queenston St	Saint Catharines	ON	L2R7C6	905-378-4647	684-1468*
**Fax:* Admitting ■ *Web:* www.niagarahealth.on.ca/services					
Saint John Regional Hospital 400 University Ave PO Box 2100	Saint John	NB	E2L4L2	506-648-6000	648-6957
Web: www.ahsc.health.nb.ca					
Saint Joseph's General Hospital 2137 Comox Ave	Comox	BC	V9M1P2	250-339-2242	339-1432
Web: www.sjghcomox.ca					
Saint Joseph's Health Centre					
Guelph 100 Westmount Rd	Guelph	ON	N1H5H8	519-767-3424	767-3445
Web: www.sjhh.guelph.on.ca					
London 268 Grosvenor St	London	ON	N6A4V2	519-646-6100	646-6054
Web: www.sjhc.london.on.ca					
Toronto 30 The Queensway	Toronto	ON	M6R1B5	416-530-6000	530-6603
Web: www.stjoe.on.ca					
Saint Joseph's Healthcare Hamilton 50 Charlton Ave E	Hamilton	ON	L8N4A6	905-522-1155	521-6140
Web: www.stjosham.on.ca					
Saint Joseph's Lifecare Centre 99 Wayne Gretzky Pkwy	Brantford	ON	N3S6T6	519-751-7096	753-7996
Web: www.sjlc.ca					
Saint Mary's General Hospital 911 Queen's Blvd	Kitchener	ON	N2M1B2	519-744-3311	749-6426
Web: www.smgh.ca					
Saint Mary's Hospital Ctr 3830 Lacombe Ave.	Montreal	QC	H3T1M5	514-345-3511	734-2636
Web: www.smhc.qc.ca					
Saint Michael's Hospital 30 Bond St	Toronto	ON	M5B1W8	416-360-4000	864-5870
TF: 800-304-6394 ■ *Web:* www.stmichaelshospital.com					
Saint Paul's Hospital 1702 20th St W	Saskatoon	SK	S7M0Z9	306-655-5000	655-5555
Saint Thomas-Elgin General Hospital 189 Elm St	Saint Thomas	ON	N5R5C4	519-631-2020	631-1825
Web: www.stegh.on.ca					
Saskatoon City Hospital 701 Queen St.	Saskatoon	SK	S7K0M7	306-655-8000	655-8269
Web: www.saskatoonhealthregion.ca					
Sault Area Hospitals 969 Queen St E	Sault Sainte Marie	ON	P6A2C4	705-759-3434	759-3640
Web: www.sah.on.ca					
Scarborough Hospital Birchmount campus 3030 Birchmount Rd.	Scarborough	ON	M1W3W3	416-495-2400	495-2562
Web: www.tsh.to					
Scarborough Hospital General Div 3050 Lawrence Ave E	Scarborough	ON	M1P2V5	416-438-2911	431-8204
Web: www.tsh.to					
Seven Oaks General Hospital 2300 McPhillips St.	Winnipeg	MB	R2V3M3	204-632-7133	697-2106*
**Fax:* PR ■ *Web:* www.sogh.mb.ca					
Sir Mortimer B Davis Jewish General Hospital 3755 Cote Sainte-Catherine	Montreal	QC	H3T1E2	514-340-8222	340-7530
Web: www.jgh.ca					
South Okanagan General Hospital RR 3 7139 362nd Ave	Oliver	BC	V0H1T0	250-498-5000	498-5004
South Shore Regional Hospital 90 Glen Allan Dr	Bridgewater	NS	B4V3S6	902-543-4603	527-5269
Web: www.ssdha.nshealth.ca					
Southlake Regional Health Centre 596 Davis Dr.	Newmarket	ON	L3Y2P9	905-895-4521	830-5972
Web: www.southlakeregional.org					
Stanton Territorial Health Authority (S) 550 Byrne Rd PO Box 10	Yellowknife	NT	X1A2N1	867-669-4224	669-4128
Web: www.stha.ca					
Stratford General Hospital 46 General Hospital Dr	Stratford	ON	N5A2Y6	519-272-8210	271-7137
Web: www.hpha.ca					
Sunnybrook Health Sciences Centre					
Sunnybrook Campus 2075 Bayview Ave	Toronto	ON	M4N3M5	416-480-6100	480-6836
Web: www.sunnybrookandwomens.on.ca					
Women & Babies research program 76 Grenville St.	Toronto	ON	M5S1B2	416-323-6400	323-6274
Web: www.sunnybrook.ca					
Surrey Memorial Hospital 13750 96th Ave.	Surrey	BC	V3V1Z2	604-588-3381	585-5669
Web: www.fraserhealth.ca					

Name / Address	City	State	Postal Code	Phone	Fax
Thunder Bay Regional Health Sciences Centre 980 Olivier Rd *Web:* www.tbrh.net	Thunder Bay	ON	P7B6V4	807-343-7123	684-5890
Timmins & District Hospital 700 Ross Ave E *Web:* www.tadh.com	Timmins	ON	P4N8P2	705-267-2131	360-6045
Toronto General Hospital 200 Elizabeth St *Web:* www.uhn.ca	Toronto	ON	M5G2C4	416-340-3111	340-5191
Toronto Western Hospital 399 Bathurst St *Web:* www.uhn.ca	Toronto	ON	M5T2S8	416-603-2581	603-5434
Trillium Health Centre 100 Queensway W *Web:* www.trilliumhealthcentre.org	Mississauga	ON	L5B1B8	905-848-7100	848-7189
University of Alberta Hospital 8440 112th St *Web:* www.albertahealthservices.ca	Edmonton	AB	T6G2B7	780-407-8822	407-7418
Valley Regional Hospital 150 Exhibition St *Web:* www.avdha.nshealth.ca	Kentville	NS	B4N5E3	902-678-7381	679-1904
Vancouver General Hospital 899 W 12th Ave *Web:* www.vanhosp.bc.ca	Vancouver	BC	V5Z1M9	604-875-4111	875-5701
Vernon Jubilee Hospital 2101 32nd St *TF:* 877-288-5788 ■ *Web:* www.interiorhealth.ca	Vernon	BC	V1T5L2	250-545-2211	545-5602
Victoria General Hospital 2340 Pembina Hwy *Web:* www.vgh.mb.ca	Winnipeg	MB	R3T2E8	204-477-3347	261-0223
Welland County General Hospital 65 3rd St *Web:* www.niagarahealth.on.ca/index2.html	Welland	ON	L3B4W6	905-732-6111	732-2628
West Coast General Hospital 3949 Port Alberni Hwy *Web:* www.viha.ca	Port Alberni	BC	V9Y4S1	250-731-1370	
West Parry Sound Health Centre 6 Albert St *TF:* 866-766-1477 ■ *Web:* www.wpshc.com	Parry Sound	ON	P2A3A4	705-746-9321	746-7364
Western Memorial Regional Hospital 1 Brookfield Ave	Corner Brook	NL	A2H6J7	709-637-5000	637-5410
William Osler Health Centre					
Brampton Memorial Hospital Campus 20 Lynch St *Web:* www.williamoslerhc.on.ca	Brampton	ON	L6W2Z8	905-494-2120	
Etobicoke Hospital Campus 101 Humber College Blvd *Web:* www.williamoslerhc.on.ca	Etobicoke	ON	M9V1R8	416-494-2120	747-8608
Windsor Regional Hospital Metropolitan Campus (WRH) 1995 Lens Ave *Web:* www.wrh.on.ca	Windsor	ON	N8W1L9	519-254-5577	254-3458
Windsor Regional Hospital Western Campus (WRHWC) 1453 Prince Rd **Fax:* Acctg ■ *Web:* www.wrh.on.ca	Windsor	ON	N9C3Z4	519-254-5577	257-5134*
Woodstock General Hospital 270 Riddell St **Fax:* Admitting ■ *Web:* www.wgh.on.ca	Woodstock	ON	N4S6N6	519-421-4211	421-4238*
Yarmouth Regional Hospital (YRH) 60 Vancouver St **Fax:* Admitting ■ *Web:* www.swndha.nshealth.ca/pages/yrh.htm	Yarmouth	NS	B5A2P5	902-742-3541	742-0369*
York Central Hospital 10 Trench St *Web:* www.yorkcentral.com	Richmond Hill	ON	L4C4Z3	905-883-1212	883-2455
Yorkton Regional Health Centre 270 Bradbrooke Dr **Fax:* Admitting ■ *Web:* www.shr.sk.ca	Yorkton	SK	S3N2K6	306-782-2401	786-0413*

377-3 General Hospitals - US

ALABAMA

Name / Address	City	State	ZIP	Phone	Fax
Andalusia Regional Hospital (ARH) 849 S Three Notch St PO Box 760 *Web:* www.andalusiaregional.com	Andalusia	AL	36420	334-222-8466	427-0349
Athens-Limestone Hospital 700 W Market St *Web:* www.alhosp.com	Athens	AL	35611	256-233-9292	233-9562
Baptist Medical Center-Princeton 701 Princeton Ave SW *Web:* www.bhsala.com/princeton/index.asp	Birmingham	AL	35211	205-783-3000	783-3758
Baptist Medical Ctr South 2105 E S Blvd **Fax:* Admitting ■ *Web:* www.baptistfirst.org	Montgomery	AL	36116	334-288-2100	286-3511*
Baptist Shelby Medical Ctr 1000 1st St N *Web:* www.bhsala.com	Alabaster	AL	35007	205-620-8100	620-7003
Brookwood Medical Ctr 2010 Brookwood Medical Ctr Dr *Web:* www.bwmc.com	Birmingham	AL	35209	205-877-1000	877-1919
Bryan W Whitfield Memorial Hospital 105 US Hwy 80 E	Demopolis	AL	36732	334-289-4000	287-2594
Citizens Baptist Medical Ctr (CBMC) 604 Stone Ave PO Box 978 *Web:* www.bhsala.com/home_citizens.cfm?id=38	Talladega	AL	35161	256-362-8111	761-4543
Cooper Green Hospital 1515 6th Ave S *Web:* www.coopergreenmercyhospital.org	Birmingham	AL	35233	205-930-3200	930-3497
Coosa Valley Medical Ctr 315 W Hickory St	Sylacauga	AL	35150	256-208-0087	249-5622
Crestwood Medical Ctr 1 Hospital Dr *Web:* www.crestwoodmedcenter.com	Huntsville	AL	35801	256-882-3100	880-4733
Cullman Regional Medical Ctr (CRMC) 1912 Alabama Hwy 157 PO Box 1108 *Web:* www.crmchospital.com	Cullman	AL	35058	256-737-2000	737-2005
DCH Regional Medical Ctr 809 University Blvd E *Web:* www.dchsystem.com/body.cfm?id=36926	Tuscaloosa	AL	35401	205-759-7111	759-6168
Decatur General Hospital 1201 7th St SE *Web:* www.decaturgeneral.org	Decatur	AL	35601	256-341-2000	341-2557
DeKalb Regional Medical Ctr 200 Medical Ctr Dr *Web:* www.dekalbregional.com	Fort Payne	AL	35968	256-845-3150	997-2512
East Alabama Medical Ctr 2000 Pepperell Pkwy *Web:* www.eamc.org	Opelika	AL	36801	334-749-3411	528-1509
Eliza Coffee Memorial Hospital (ECM) 205 Marengo St *Web:* www.chgroup.org/ecm	Florence	AL	35630	256-768-9191	768-9420
Flowers Hospital 4370 W Main St *TF:* 800-824-6828 ■ *Web:* www.flowershospital.com	Dothan	AL	36305	334-793-5000	793-4613
Gadsden Regional Medical Ctr 1007 Goodyear Ave *Web:* www.gadsdenregional.com	Gadsden	AL	35903	256-494-4000	494-4474
Helen Keller Hospital 1300 S Montgomery Ave *Web:* www.helenkeller.com	Sheffield	AL	35660	256-386-4196	386-4559
Highlands Medical Ctr 380 Woods Cove Rd *Web:* www.highlandsmedcenter.com	Scottsboro	AL	35768	256-259-4444	218-3536
Huntsville Hospital 101 Sivley Rd *Web:* www.huntsvillehospital.org	Huntsville	AL	35801	256-265-1000	265-2585
Jackson Hospital 1725 Pine St **Fax:* Admitting ■ *Web:* www.jackson.org	Montgomery	AL	36106	334-293-8000	293-8108*
Lanier Health Services (LHS) 4800 48th St **Fax:* Admissions ■ *Web:* www.lanierhospital.com	Valley	AL	36854	334-756-1400	756-6698*
Marshall Medical Center South (MMCS) 2505 US Hwy 431 *Web:* www.mmcenters.com/facilities/mmc_south.php	Boaz	AL	35957	256-593-8310	840-3647
Medical Center Enterprise (MCE) 400 N Edwards St *TF:* 800-993-6837 ■ *Web:* www.mcehospital.com	Enterprise	AL	36330	334-347-0584	347-2080
Mobile Infirmary Medical Ctr (MIMC) 5 Mobile Infirmary Cir **Fax:* Admitting ■ *Web:* www.mobileinfirmary.org	Mobile	AL	36607	251-435-2400	435-2543*
Northeast Alabama Regional Medical Ctr 400 E 10th St *Web:* www.rmccares.org	Anniston	AL	36207	256-235-5121	235-5608
Northport Medical Ctr 2700 Hospital Dr *Web:* www.dchsystem.com	Northport	AL	35476	205-333-4500	333-4522
Providence Hospital 6801 Airport Blvd **Fax:* Admitting ■ *Web:* www.providencehospital.org	Mobile	AL	36608	251-633-1000	633-1679*
Quality of Life Health Services Inc 1411 Piedmont Cutoff PO Box 97 *Web:* www.qolhs.org	Gadsden	AL	35902	256-492-0131	
Riverview Regional Medical Ctr 600 S 3rd St *Web:* www.riverviewregional.com	Gadsden	AL	35901	256-543-5200	543-5888
Saint Vincent's East 50 Medical Pk E Dr *Web:* www.stvhs.com/east	Birmingham	AL	35235	205-838-3000	838-3326
Saint Vincent's Hospital 810 St Vincent's Dr	Birmingham	AL	35205	205-939-7000	930-2259*
Southeast Alabama Medical Ctr 1108 Ross Clark Cir *TF:* 800-248-7047 ■ *Web:* www.samc.org	Dothan	AL	36301	334-793-8111	793-8751
Springhill Medical Ctr 3719 Dauphin St **Fax:* Admissions ■ *Web:* www.springhillmedicalcenter.com	Mobile	AL	36608	251-344-9630	461-2439*
Thomas Hospital 750 Morphy Ave *TF:* 800-883-4309 ■ *Web:* www.thomashospital.com	Fairhope	AL	36532	251-928-2375	990-1497
Trinity Medical Ctr 800 Montclair Rd *Web:* www.trinitymedicalonline.com	Birmingham	AL	35213	205-592-1000	592-5927
UAB Hospital 619 S 19th St *Web:* www.health.uab.edu	Birmingham	AL	35294	205-934-9999	934-7779
UAB Medical West 995 9th Ave SW *TF:* 877-481-7001	Bessemer	AL	35022	205-481-7000	481-7595
University of South Alabama Children & Women's Hospital 1700 Ctr St **Fax:* Admitting ■ *Web:* www.southalabama.edu/usacwh	Mobile	AL	36604	251-415-1000	415-1002*
University of South Alabama Medical Ctr 2451 Fillingim St **Fax:* Admitting ■ *Web:* www.southalabama.edu/usamc	Mobile	AL	36617	251-471-7000	471-7275*
Vaughan Regional Medical Ctr 1015 Medical Ctr Pkwy *TF:* 800-498-8461 ■ *Web:* www.vaughanregional.com	Selma	AL	36701	334-418-4100	418-3599
Walker Baptist Medical Ctr 3400 Hwy 78 E *Web:* www.bhsala.com/walker/index.asp	Jasper	AL	35501	205-387-4000	387-4011

ALASKA

Name / Address	City	State	ZIP	Phone	Fax
Alaska Native Medical Ctr (ANMC) 4315 Diplomacy Dr *TF Admitting:* 800-478-6661 ■ *Web:* www.anmc.org	Anchorage	AK	99508	907-563-2662	729-1984
Alaska Regional Hospital 2801 Debarr Rd *Web:* www.alaskaregional.com	Anchorage	AK	99508	907-276-1131	264-1179
Fairbanks Memorial Hospital 1650 Cowles St	Fairbanks	AK	99701	907-452-8181	458-5324
Providence Alaska Medical Ctr 3200 Providence Dr **Fax:* Admitting ■ *Web:* www.providence.org	Anchorage	AK	99508	907-562-2211	261-6007*

ARIZONA

Name / Address	City	State	ZIP	Phone	Fax
Banner Baywood Medical Ctr 6644 E Baywood Ave *Web:* www.bannerhealth.com	Mesa	AZ	85206	480-981-2000	981-4198
Banner Boswell Medical Ctr 10401 W Thunderbird Blvd *Web:* www.bannerhealth.com	Sun City	AZ	85351	623-977-7211	876-5795
Banner Del E Webb Memorial Hospital 14502 W Meeker Blvd *Web:* www.bannerhealth.com	Sun City West	AZ	85375	623-214-4000	214-4105
Banner Desert Medical Ctr 1400 S Dobson Rd *Web:* www.bannerhealth.com	Mesa	AZ	85202	480-512-3000	512-8711
Banner Good Samaritan Medical Ctr 1111 E McDowell Rd *Web:* www.bannerhealth.com	Phoenix	AZ	85006	602-239-2000	239-5160
Banner Mesa Medical Ctr 1010 N Country Club Dr *Web:* www.bannerhealth.com/patients+and+visitors/facilities/arizona/mesa	Mesa	AZ	85201	480-834-1211	461-2090

Hospital / Address	City	State	ZIP	Phone	Fax
Banner Thunderbird Medical Ctr (BTMC) 5555 W Thunderbird Rd — *Web:* www.bannerhealth.com	Glendale	AZ	85306	602-588-5555	865-5930
Carondelet Saint Joseph's Hospital 350 N Wilmot Rd — *Web:* www.carondelet.org	Tucson	AZ	85711	520-873-3968	
Carondelet St. Mary's Hospital 1601 W St Mary's Rd — *Web:* www.carondelet.org/home/hospitals-locations/st.-marys-hospital.aspx	Tucson	AZ	85745	520-872-3000	872-6641
Casa Grande Regional Medical Ctr (CGRMC) 1800 E Florence Blvd — *Web:* www.casagrandehospital.com	Casa Grande	AZ	85122	520-381-6300	381-6435
Chandler Regional Hospital 475 S Dobson Rd — *TF:* 800-350-4677 ■ *Web:* www.chandlerregional.org	Chandler	AZ	85224	480-728-3000	728-3875
Flagstaff Medical Ctr 1200 N Beaver St — *Web:* www.flagstaffmedicalcenter.com	Flagstaff	AZ	86001	928-779-3366	947-3299
Havasu Regional Medical Ctr 101 Civic Ctr Ln — *Web:* www.havasuregional.com	Lake Havasu City	AZ	86403	928-855-8185	505-5744
John C. Lincoln North Mountain Hospital 250 E Dunlap Ave — *Web:* www.jcl.com/content/northmountain	Phoenix	AZ	85020	602-943-2381	944-9610
Kingman Regional Medical Ctr (KRMC) 3269 Stockton Hill Rd — *TF:* 877-757-2101 ■ *Web:* www.azkrmc.com	Kingman	AZ	86409	928-757-2101	757-0604
La Paz Regional Hospital Inc 1200 W Mohave Rd — *Web:* www.lapazhospital.org	Parker	AZ	85344	928-669-9201	
Maricopa Medical Ctr 2601 E Roosevelt St — *Web:* www.mihs.org	Phoenix	AZ	85008	602-344-5011	344-0719
Maryvale Hospital 5102 W Campbell Ave — *Web:* www.abrazohealth.com	Phoenix	AZ	85031	623-848-5000	848-5553
Mayo Clinic Hospital 5777 E Mayo Blvd — *Web:* www.mayoclinic.org/mchospital-sct	Phoenix	AZ	85054	480-515-6296	342-2525
Northwest Medical Ctr (NMC) 6200 N La Cholla Blvd — *Web:* www.northwestmedicalcenter.com	Tucson	AZ	85741	520-742-9000	469-8610
Paradise Valley Hospital 3929 E Bell Rd — *Web:* www.paradisevalleyhospital.com	Phoenix	AZ	85032	602-923-5000	923-5707
Phoenix Baptist Hospital 2000 W Bethany Home Rd — *Web:* www.abrazohealth.com	Phoenix	AZ	85015	602-249-0212	246-5979
Phoenix Memorial Hospital 1201 S 7th Ave	Phoenix	AZ	85007	602-258-5111	824-3383
Saint Joseph's Hospital & Medical Ctr 350 W Thomas Rd — *Web:* www.stjosephs-phx.org	Phoenix	AZ	85013	602-406-3000	406-7143
Saint Luke's Medical Ctr 1800 E Van Buren St — *Web:* www.iasishealthcare.com/hospitals/az_slmed.htm	Phoenix	AZ	85006	602-251-8100	251-8685
Scottsdale Healthcare Osborn 7400 E Osborn Rd — *Web:* www.shc.org	Scottsdale	AZ	85251	480-675-4000	882-4989
Scottsdale Healthcare Shea 9003 E Shea Blvd — *Web:* www.shc.org	Scottsdale	AZ	85260	480-323-3000	323-3510
Tempe Saint Luke's Hospital (TSLH) 1500 S Mill Ave — *Web:* www.tempestlukeshospital.com	Tempe	AZ	85281	480-784-5500	784-5539
Tucson Medical Ctr 5301 E Grant Rd — *TF:* 800-526-5353 ■ *Web:* www.tmcaz.com	Tucson	AZ	85712	520-327-5461	
University Medical Ctr 1501 N Campbell Ave — *Web:* www.azumc.com	Tucson	AZ	85724	520-694-0111	694-4085
University Physicians Healthcare Hospital at Kino Campus (UPH) 2800 E Ajo Way — *Web:* www.uph.org	Tucson	AZ	85713	520-874-2000	874-4042
US Public Health Service Phoenix Indian Medical Ctr 4212 N 16th St	Phoenix	AZ	85016	602-263-1200	263-1618
Yavapai Regional Medical Ctr 1003 Willow Creek Rd — *TF:* 877-843-9762 ■ *Web:* www.yrmc.org	Prescott	AZ	86301	928-445-2700	771-5509
Yuma Regional Medical Ctr 2400 S Ave A — *Web:* www.yumaregional.org	Yuma	AZ	85364	928-344-2000	336-7337

ARKANSAS

Hospital / Address	City	State	ZIP	Phone	Fax
Arkansas Methodist Medical Ctr 900 W KingsFwy — *Web:* www.myammc.org	Paragould	AR	72451	870-239-7000	239-7400
Baptist Health Medical Ctr 3333 Spring Hill Dr — *Web:* www.baptist-health.com	North Little Rock	AR	72117	501-202-3000	202-3813
Baptist Health Medical Ctr-Little Rock 9601 I-630 Exit 7 — **Fax:* Admitting ■ *TF:* 888-227-8478 ■ *Web:* www.baptist-health.org	Little Rock	AR	72205	501-202-2000	202-1226*
Baxter Regional Medical Ctr 624 Hospital Dr — *Web:* www.baxterregional.org	Mountain Home	AR	72653	870-424-1000	424-2444
Conway Regional Hospital 2302 College Ave — *Web:* www.conwayregional.org	Conway	AR	72032	501-329-3831	450-2283
Crittenden Regional Hospital 200 Tyler St — *Web:* www.crittendenregional.org	West Memphis	AR	72301	870-735-1500	732-7710
Helena Regional Medical Ctr 1801 ML King Dr — *Web:* www.helenarmc.com	Helena	AR	72342	870-338-5800	816-3909
Jefferson Regional Medical Ctr (JRMC) 1600 W 40th Ave — *Web:* www.jrmc.org	Pine Bluff	AR	71603	870-541-7100	
Medical Center of South Arkansas 700 W Grove St — *Web:* www.themedcenter.net	El Dorado	AR	71730	870-863-2000	863-5442
Mercy Health System of Northwest Arkansas 2710 Rife Medical Ln — *Web:* www.mercy4u.com/Default.asp	Rogers	AR	72758	479-338-8000	
National Park Medical Ctr 1910 Malvern Ave — *Web:* www.nationalparkmedical.com	Hot Springs National Park	AR	71901	501-321-1000	620-1450
North Arkansas Regional Medical Ctr 620 N Willow St — *Web:* www.narmc.com	Harrison	AR	72601	870-365-2000	365-2034
North metro Medical Ctr 1400 Braden St — *Web:* www.northmetromed.com	Jacksonville	AR	72076	501-985-7000	985-7407
Northwest Medical Ctr 609 W Maple Ave — *Web:* www.northwesthealth.com	Springdale	AR	72764	479-751-5711	757-2908
Ouachita County Medical Ctr (OCMC) 638 California St — *Web:* www.ouachitamedcenter.com	Camden	AR	71701	870-836-1000	836-1358
Saint Bernard's Medical Ctr 225 E Jackson Ave — *Web:* www.sbrmc.com	Jonesboro	AR	72401	870-972-4100	974-5112
Saint Edward Mercy Medical Ctr 7301 Rogers Ave — *Web:* www.stedwardmercy.com	Fort Smith	AR	72903	479-314-6000	314-1770
Saint Joseph's Mercy Health Ctr 300 Werner St — **Fax:* Admitting ■ *Web:* www.saintjosephs.com	Hot Springs	AR	71913	501-622-1000	622-1199*
Saint Mary's Regional Medical Ctr 1808 W Main St — *Web:* www.saintmarysregional.com	Russellville	AR	72801	479-968-2841	968-8189
Saint Vincent Doctors Hospital 6101 St Vincent Cir	Little Rock	AR	72205	501-552-6000	552-5510
Saint Vincent Infirmary Medical Ctr 2 St Vincent Cir	Little Rock	AR	72205	501-552-3000	552-4241
Saline Memorial Hospital 1 Medical Pk Dr — *Web:* www.salinememorial.org	Benton	AR	72015	501-776-6000	776-6019
Southwest Regional Medical Ctr 11401 IH- 30 — *Web:* www.southwestregional.com	Little Rock	AR	72103	501-455-7100	455-7399
Sparks Regional Medical Ctr (SRMC) 1001 Towson Ave — *Web:* www.sparkshealth.com	Fort Smith	AR	72901	479-441-4000	441-5397
UAMS Medical Ctr 4301 W Markham St — **Fax:* Admitting ■ *Web:* www.uams.edu	Little Rock	AR	72205	501-686-7000	526-4282*
White County Medical Ctr 3214 E Race Ave — *TF:* 888-562-7520	Searcy	AR	72143	501-268-6121	380-1011
White River Medical Ctr 1710 Harrison St — *Web:* www.whiteriverhealthsystem.com	Batesville	AR	72501	870-262-1200	262-1458

CALIFORNIA

Hospital / Address	City	State	ZIP	Phone	Fax
Alameda County Medical Center - Fairmont Hospital 15400 Foothill Blvd — *Web:* www.acmedctr.org	San Leandro	CA	94578	510-895-4200	667-7852
Alameda County Medical Center-Highland Campus 1411 E 31st St — *Web:* www.acmedctr.org	Oakland	CA	94602	510-437-4800	535-7722
Alta Bates Summit Medical Ctr (ABSMC) 2450 Ashby Ave — *Web:* www.altabatessummit.org	Berkeley	CA	94705	510-540-4444	204-1883
Alvarado Hospital Medical Ctr 6655 Alvarado Rd — *Web:* www.alvaradohospital.com	San Diego	CA	92120	619-287-3270	229-7020
Anaheim Memorial Medical Ctr 1111 W La Palma Ave — **Fax:* Admitting ■ *Web:* www.memorialcare.com	Anaheim	CA	92801	714-774-1450	999-6027*
Antelope Valley Hospital 1600 W Ave J — *Web:* www.avhospital.org	Lancaster	CA	93534	661-949-5000	949-5510
Arrowhead Regional Medical Ctr 400 N Pepper Ave — *TF:* 877-873-2762 ■ *Web:* www.arrowheadmedcenter.org	Colton	CA	92324	909-580-1000	580-6214
Bakersfield Memorial Hospital 420 34th St — **Fax:* Admitting ■ *Web:* www.bakersfieldmemorial.org	Bakersfield	CA	93301	661-327-1792	327-2426*
Baldwin Park Medical Ctr 1011 Baldwin Pk Blvd — *Web:* www.kaiserpermanente.org	Baldwin Park	CA	91706	626-851-1011	851-5101
Beverly Hospital 309 W Beverly Blvd — *Web:* www.beverly.org	Montebello	CA	90640	323-726-1222	725-4338
Brotman Medical Ctr 3828 Delmas Terr — *Web:* www.brotmanmedicalcenter.com	Culver City	CA	90231	310-836-7000	202-4141
California Hospital Medical Ctr 1401 S Grand Ave — *Web:* www.chmcla.org	Los Angeles	CA	90015	213-748-2411	765-4078
California Pacific Medical Center Davies Campus Castro & Duboce Sts — *Web:* www.cpmc.org	San Francisco	CA	94114	415-600-6000	565-6223
California Pacific Medical Center Pacific Campus 2333 Buchanan St — *Web:* www.cpmc.org	San Francisco	CA	94115	415-563-4321	600-3679
California Pacific Medical Ctr 3700 California St — **Fax:* Admitting ■ *Web:* www.cpmc.org	San Francisco	CA	94118	415-600-6000	750-5007*
Cedars-Sinai Medical Ctr (CSMC) 8700 Beverly Blvd — **Fax:* Admitting ■ *TF:* 800-233-2771 ■ *Web:* www.csmc.edu	Los Angeles	CA	90048	310-423-3277	123-0105*
Centinela Freeman Regional Medical Center Memorial Campus 333 N Prairie Ave — *TF:* 800-455-1933	Inglewood	CA	90301	310-674-7050	419-8273
Centinela Freeman Regional Medical Center-Marina Campus 4650 Lincoln Blvd	Marina del Rey	CA	90292	310-823-8911	574-7854
Centinela Hospital Medical Ctr 555 E Hardy St — *Web:* www.centinelamed.com	Inglewood	CA	90301	310-673-4660	677-0535

Name / Address	City	State	ZIP	Phone	Fax
Citrus Valley Medical Center Inter-Community Campus 210 W San Bernardino Rd *Web:* www.cvhp.com	Covina	CA	91722	626-331-7331	859-5865
Citrus Valley Medical Center-Queen of the Valley Campus 1115 S Sunset Ave *Web:* www.cvhp.org/facilities/fac_qvc.htm	West Covina	CA	91790	626-962-4011	813-7887
City of Hope National Medical Ctr 1500 E Duarte Rd *TF:* 866-434-4673 ■ *Web:* www.cityofhope.org	Duarte	CA	91010	626-256-4673	
Coast Plaza Doctors Hospital Inc 13100 Studebaker Rd *TF:* 866-462-2627 ■ *Web:* www.coastplazahospital.com	Norwalk	CA	90650	562-868-3751	868-3198
Coastal Communities Hospital 2701 S Bristol St *Web:* www.coastalcommhospital.com	Santa Ana	CA	92704	714-754-5454	754-5556
Community Hospital of Long Beach 1720 Termino Ave *Web:* www.chlb.org	Long Beach	CA	90804	562-498-1000	498-4434
Community Hospital of San Bernardino (CHSB) 1805 Medical Ctr Dr *Web:* www.chsb.org	San Bernardino	CA	92411	909-887-6333	806-1035
Community Hospital of the Monterey Peninsula (CHOMP) 23625 Holman Hwy *Web:* www.chomp.org	Monterey	CA	93940	831-624-5311	625-4948
Community Memorial Hospital 147 N Brent St *Web:* www.cmhhospital.com	Ventura	CA	93003	805-652-5011	667-2895
Community Regional Medical Ctr 2823 Fresno St *Web:* www.communitymedical.org	Fresno	CA	93721	559-459-6000	497-1835
Contra Costa Health Services 2500 Alhambra Ave *Web:* www.cchealth.org/medical_center	Martinez	CA	94553	925-370-5000	370-5138
Dameron Hospital Assn (DHA) 525 W Acacia St *Web:* www.dameronhospital.org	Stockton	CA	95203	209-944-5550	461-3108
Desert Regional Medical Ctr 1150 N Indian Canyon Dr *TF:* 800-962-3765 ■ *Web:* www.desertmedctr.com	Palm Springs	CA	92262	760-323-6511	864-9577
Doctors Medical Ctr 1441 Florida Ave *Web:* www.dmc-modesto.com	Modesto	CA	95350	209-578-1211	576-3680
Doctors Medical Ctr 2000 Vale Rd *Web:* www.doctorsmedicalcenter.org	San Pablo	CA	94806	510-970-5000	970-5730
Dominican Hospital (DH) 1555 Soquel Dr *Web:* www.dominicanhospital.org	Santa Cruz	CA	95065	831-462-7682	462-7761
Downey Regional Medical Ctr 11500 Brookshire Ave *TF:* 888-259-4607 ■ *Web:* www.drmci.org	Downey	CA	90241	562-904-5000	904-5309
Eden Medical Ctr (EMC) 20103 Lake Chabot Rd *Web:* www.edenmedicalcenter.org	Castro Valley	CA	94546	510-537-1234	889-6506
Eisenhower Medical Ctr 39000 Bob Hope Dr *Web:* www.emc.org	Rancho Mirage	CA	92270	760-340-3911	773-4396
El Centro Regional Medical Ctr 1415 Ross Ave *Web:* www.ecrmc.org	El Centro	CA	92243	760-339-7100	339-7345
Emanuel Medical Ctr (EMC) 825 Delbon Ave *Web:* www.emanuelmedicalcenter.org	Turlock	CA	95382	209-667-4200	
Enloe Medical Ctr 1531 Esplanade *TF:* 800-822-8102 ■ *Web:* www.enloe.org	Chico	CA	95926	530-332-7300	899-2067
Family Healthcare Network 305 E Ctr Ave *Web:* www.fhcn.org	Visalia	CA	93291	559-737-4700	
Feather River Hospital (FRH) 5974 Pentz Rd *Web:* www.frhosp.org	Paradise	CA	95969	530-877-9361	876-2160
Foothill Presbyterian Hospital 250 S Grand Ave *Web:* www.cvhp.org	Glendora	CA	91741	626-963-8411	857-3274
Fountain Valley Regional Hospital & Medical Ctr 17100 Euclid St *Web:* www.fountainvalleyhospital.com	Fountain Valley	CA	92708	714-966-7200	966-8039
Fremont Medical Ctr 970 Plumas St *Web:* www.frhg.org	Yuba City	CA	95991	530-751-4000	751-4224
Garden Grove Hospital & Medical Ctr 12601 Garden Grove Blvd *Web:* www.gardengrovehospital.com	Garden Grove	CA	92843	714-537-5160	741-3322
Garfield Medical Ctr 525 N Garfield Ave *Web:* www.garfieldmedicalcenter.com	Monterey Park	CA	91754	626-573-2222	571-8972
Glendale Adventist Medical Ctr 1509 Wilson Terr *Web:* www.glendaleadventist.com	Glendale	CA	91206	818-409-8000	546-5600
Glendale Memorial Hospital & Health Ctr 1420 S Central Ave *Web:* www.glendalememorialhospital.org	Glendale	CA	91204	818-502-1900	
Good Samaritan Hospital 2425 Samaritan Dr **Fax:* Admitting ■ *Web:* www.goodsamsanjose.com	San Jose	CA	95124	408-559-2011	559-2675*
Good Samaritan Hospital 1225 Wilshire Blvd *Web:* www.goodsam.org	Los Angeles	CA	90017	213-977-2121	202-7452
Greater El Monte Community Hospital (GEMCH) 1701 Santa Anita Ave *Web:* www.greaterelmonte.com	South El Monte	CA	91733	626-579-7777	350-0368
Harbor-UCLA Medical Ctr 1000 W Carson St *Web:* www.humc.edu	Torrance	CA	90509	310-222-2345	
Hemet Valley Medical Ctr 1117 E Devonshire Ave *Web:* www.valleyhealthsystem.com	Hemet	CA	92543	951-652-2811	765-4988
Henry Mayo Newhall Memorial Hospital 23845 McBean Pkwy *Web:* www.henrymayo.com	Valencia	CA	91355	661-253-8000	253-8897
Hoag Hospital Irvine (HHI) 16200 Sand Canyon Ave *Web:* www.hoag.org	Irvine	CA	92618	949-764-4624	753-2289
Hoag Memorial Hospital Presbyterian 1 Hoag Dr *Web:* www.hoag.org	Newport Beach	CA	92658	949-645-8600	760-5593
Hollywood Presbyterian Medical Ctr 1300 N Vermont Ave *Web:* www.hollywoodpresbyterian.com	Los Angeles	CA	90027	323-913-4800	660-0446
Huntington Memorial Hospital 100 W California Blvd *Web:* www.huntingtonhospital.com	Pasadena	CA	91109	626-397-5000	397-2995
John F Kennedy Memorial Hospital 47-111 Monroe St *Web:* www.jfkmemorialhosp.com	Indio	CA	92201	760-347-6191	775-8014
John Muir Medical Ctr (JMMC) 1601 Ygnacio Valley Rd *Web:* www.johnmuirhealth.com	Walnut Creek	CA	94598	925-939-3000	308-8944
Kaiser Permanente 401 Bicentennial Way *Web:* www.kaisersantarosa.org	Santa Rosa	CA	95403	707-571-4000	571-4556
Kaiser Permanente Fontana Medical Ctr 9961 Sierra Ave	Fontana	CA	92335	909-427-5000	427-4265
Kaiser Permanente Foundation Hospital 9400 E Rosecrans Ave	Bellflower	CA	90706	562-461-3000	461-4341
Kaiser Permanente Harbor City Medical Ctr 25825 S Vermont Ave *TF:* 800-464-4000 ■ *Web:* www.kp.org	Harbor City	CA	90710	310-325-5111	517-2234
Kaiser Permanente Hayward Medical Ctr 27400 Hesperian Blvd *Web:* www.mydoctor.kaiserpermanente.org	Hayward	CA	94545	510-784-4000	784-4722
Kaiser Permanente Hospital 441 N Lakeview Ave *TF:* 800-464-4000	Anaheim	CA	92807	714-279-4000	279-5590
Kaiser Permanente Los Angeles Medical Ctr 4867 Sunset Blvd	Los Angeles	CA	90027	323-783-4011	783-7227
Kaiser Permanente Medical Center San Francisco 2425 Geary Blvd	San Francisco	CA	94115	415-833-2000	833-2571*
Kaiser Permanente Medical Center-Santa Teresa 250 Hospital Pkwy	San Jose	CA	95119	408-972-7000	972-7156*
Kaiser Permanente Medical Center-South Sacramento 6600 Bruceville Rd *TF:* 800-464-4000	Sacramento	CA	95823	916-688-2000	688-2978
Kaiser Permanente Medical Center-West Los Angeles 6041 Cadillac Ave	Los Angeles	CA	90034	323-857-2000	857-2307
Kaiser Permanente Medical Ctr 4647 Zion Ave	San Diego	CA	92120	619-528-5000	528-5317
Kaiser Permanente Medical Ctr 710 Lawrence Expy # 448 *Web:* www.kaisersantaclara.org	Santa Clara	CA	95051	408-236-6400	236-4408
Kaiser Permanente Medical Ctr 1200 El Camino Real *TF:* 800-660-1231 ■ *Web:* www.kp.org	South San Francisco	CA	94080	650-742-2000	742-3046
Kaiser Permanente Panorama City Medical Ctr 13652 Cantara St	Panorama City	CA	91402	818-375-2000	
Kaiser Permanente Riverside Medical Ctr 10800 Magnolia Ave *TF Cust Svc:* 800-464-4000	Riverside	CA	92505	951-353-2000	353-3055
Kaiser Permanente Vallejo Medical Ctr 975 Sereno Dr	Vallejo	CA	94589	707-651-1000	651-2026
Kaiser Permanente Walnut Creek Medical Ctr 1425 S Main St *TF:* 800-464-4000	Walnut Creek	CA	94596	925-295-4000	
Kaweah Delta Hospital 400 W Mineral King Ave *TF:* 800-529-3244 ■ *Web:* www.kaweahdelta.org	Visalia	CA	93291	559-624-2000	635-4021
Kern Medical Ctr 1700 Mt Vernon Ave **Fax:* Admitting ■ *Web:* www.kernmedicalcenter.com	Bakersfield	CA	93306	661-326-2000	326-2934*
La Palma Intercommunity Hospital 7901 Walker St *Web:* www.lapalmaintercommunityhospital.com	La Palma	CA	90623	714-670-7400	670-6287
LAC-University of Southern California Medical Ctr 1200 N State St	Los Angeles	CA	90033	323-226-2622	441-8030
Lakewood Regional Medical Ctr 3700 S St *Web:* www.lakewoodregional.com	Lakewood	CA	90712	562-531-2550	
Lifelong Medical Care Inc PO Box 11247 *Web:* www.lifelongmedical.org	Berkeley	CA	94712	510-981-4100	
Lodi Memorial Hospital 975 S Fairmont Ave *TF:* 800-876-6750 ■ *Web:* www.lodihealth.org	Lodi	CA	95240	209-334-3411	339-7654
Loma Linda University Medical Ctr 11234 Anderson St *TF:* 877-558-6248 ■ *Web:* www.llu.edu/llumc	Loma Linda	CA	92354	909-558-4000	558-0308
Long Beach Memorial Medical Ctr 2801 Atlantic Ave *Web:* www.memorialcare.com	Long Beach	CA	90806	562-933-2000	933-1336
Los Alamitos Medical Ctr 3751 Katella Ave *Web:* www.losalamitosmedctr.com	Los Alamitos	CA	90720	562-598-1311	493-2812
Los Angeles Community Hospital 4081 E Olympic Blvd	Los Angeles	CA	90023	323-267-0477	261-0809
Los Robles Hospital & Medical Ctr (LRHMC) 215 W Janss Rd *Web:* www.losrobleshospital.com	Thousand Oaks	CA	91360	805-497-2727	370-4498
Madera Community Hospital 1250 E Almond Ave *Web:* www.maderahospital.org	Madera	CA	93637	559-675-5555	675-5509
Marian Medical Ctr 1400 E Church St *Web:* www.marianmedicalcenter.org	Santa Maria	CA	93454	805-739-3000	739-3060
Marin General Hospital 250 Bon Air Rd *Web:* www.maringeneral.com	Greenbrae	CA	94904	415-925-7000	925-7933
Memorial Medical Ctr (MMC) 1700 Coffee Rd PO Box 942 **Fax:* Admitting ■ *Web:* www.memorialmedicalcenter.org	Modesto	CA	95355	209-526-4500	521-6986*
Mendocino Coast District Hospital 700 River Dr *Web:* www.mcdh.org	Fort Bragg	CA	95437	707-961-1234	961-4793
Mercy General Hospital 4001 J St *Web:* www.mercygeneral.org	Sacramento	CA	95819	916-453-4545	457-1141
Mercy Hospitals of Bakersfield û Truxtun Campus (MHB) 2215 Truxtun Ave *Web:* www.mercybakersfield.org	Bakersfield	CA	93301	661-632-5000	327-2592
Mercy Medical Center Merced Community Campus 301 E 13th St *Web:* www.mercymercedcares.org	Merced	CA	95340	209-385-7000	385-7062

Name / Address	City	State	ZIP	Phone	Fax
Mercy Medical Center Redding 2175 Rosaline Ave *TF:* 800-521-6377 ■ *Web:* www.mercy.org	Redding	CA	96001	530-225-6000	225-6125
Mercy San Juan Medical Ctr 6501 Coyle Ave *Web:* www.mercysanjuan.org	Carmichael	CA	95608	916-537-5000	537-5111
Methodist Hospital of Sacramento 7500 Hospital Dr *Web:* www.methodistsacramento.org	Sacramento	CA	95823	916-423-3000	423-6045
Methodist Hospital of Southern California 300 W Huntington Dr *TF:* 888-388-2838 ■ *Web:* www.methodisthospital.org	Arcadia	CA	91007	626-898-8000	574-3767
Mission Hospital Regional Medical Center Inc 27700 Medical Ctr Rd. *Web:* www.mission4health.com	Mission Viejo	CA	92691	949-364-1400	
Mount Diablo Medical Ctr 2540 E St *Web:* www.johnmuirhealth.com	Concord	CA	94520	925-682-8200	674-2009
Natividad Medical Ctr (NMC) 1441 Constitution Blvd. *Web:* www.natividad.com	Salinas	CA	93906	831-755-4111	755-6254
North County Health Services 150 Valpreda Rd *Web:* www.nchs-health.org	San Marcos	CA	92069	760-736-6767	736-6782
Northbay Medical Ctr 1200 B Gale Wilson Blvd *TF:* 888-294-3600 ■ *Web:* www.northbay.org	Fairfield	CA	94533	707-429-3600	426-5287
Northeast Valley Health Corp 1172 N Maclay Ave. *Web:* www.nevhc.org	San Fernando	CA	91340	818-898-1388	365-4031
Northern Inyo Hospital 150 Pioneer Ln *TF:* 877-968-2473 ■ *Web:* www.nih.org	Bishop	CA	93514	760-873-5811	872-5836
Northridge Hospital Medical Center-Roscoe Blvd Campus 18300 Roscoe Blvd. *Web:* www.northridgehospital.org	Northridge	CA	91328	818-885-8500	885-5321
O'Connor Hospital 2105 Forest Ave *Web:* www.oconnorhospital.org	San Jose	CA	95128	408-947-2500	947-2819
Olive View Medical Ctr (OVMC) 14445 Olive View Dr. *Web:* www.uclaoliveview.org/ovmc.html	Sylmar	CA	91342	818-364-1555	364-3011
Olympia Medical Ctr 5900 W Olympic Blvd. **Fax Area Code:* 323 ■ *TF:* 800-827-8599 ■ *Web:* www.olympiamc.com	Los Angeles	CA	90036	310-657-5900	932-5163*
Orange Coast Memorial Medical Ctr (OCMMC) 9920 Talbert Ave. *Web:* www.memorialcare.com/orange_coast	Fountain Valley	CA	92708	714-378-7000	378-7079
Oroville Hospital (OH) 2767 Olive Hwy *Web:* www.orovillehospital.com	Oroville	CA	95966	530-533-8500	532-8433
Pacific Clinics 800 S Santa Anita Ave. *Web:* www.pacificclinics.org	Arcadia	CA	91006	626-254-5000	
Pacific Hospital of Long Beach 2776 Pacific Ave. *Web:* www.phlb.org	Long Beach	CA	90806	562-997-2000	
Pamc Ltd 531 W College St *Web:* www.pamc.net	Los Angeles	CA	90012	213-624-8411	687-7136
Parkview Community Hospital Medical Ctr (PCHMC) 3865 Jackson St. *Web:* www.pchmc.org	Riverside	CA	92503	951-688-2211	352-5484
Peninsula Hospital 1501 Trousdale Dr. *Web:* www.mills-peninsula.org	Burlingame	CA	94010	650-696-5400	696-5279
Pioneer Medical Group Inc 17777 Ctr Ct Dr N Suite 400. *Web:* www.pioneermedicalgroup.com	Cerritos	CA	90703	562-229-9452	
Pioneers Memorial Healthcare District (PMHD) 207 W Legion Rd *Web:* www.pmhd.org	Brawley	CA	92227	760-351-3333	344-4401
Pomerado Hospital 15615 Pomerado Rd. *Web:* www.pph.org	Poway	CA	92064	858-613-4000	613-5678
Pomona Valley Hospital Medical Ctr 1798 N Garey Ave. *Web:* www.pvhmc.org	Pomona	CA	91767	909-865-9500	865-9796
Presbyterian Intercommunity Hospital 12401 Washington Blvd *Web:* www.whittierpres.com	Whittier	CA	90602	562-698-0811	698-1728
Providence Holy Cross Medical Ctr 15031 Rinaldi St. *Web:* www.providence.org/LosAngeles/Facilities/Providence_Holy_Cross	Mission Hills	CA	91345	818-365-8051	898-4688
Providence Little Co of Mary *Medical Center Torrance* 4101 Torrance Blvd *TF:* 800-776-5264 ■ *Web:* www2.providence.org	Torrance	CA	90503	310-540-7676	540-8408
Providence Little Co of Mary Medical Center San Pedro 1300 W 7th St. *Web:* www2.providence.org	San Pedro	CA	90732	310-832-3311	514-5314
Providence Saint Joseph Medical Ctr 501 S Buena Vista St *Web:* www2.providence.org/saintjoseph/Pages/default.aspx	Burbank	CA	91505	818-843-5111	
Queen of the Valley Medical Ctr 1000 Trancas St *Web:* www.thequeen.org	Napa	CA	94558	707-252-4411	257-4032
Radiological Assoc of Sacramento Medical Group Inc 1500 Expo Pkwy *Web:* www.radiological.com	Sacramento	CA	95815	916-646-8300	920-4434
Redlands Community Hospital Foundation PO Box 3391 *TF:* 888-397-4999 ■ *Web:* www.redlandshospital.org	Redlands	CA	92373	909-335-5500	
Regional Medical Center of San Jose (RMCSJ) 225 N Jackson Ave. *Web:* www.regionalmedicalsanjose.com	San Jose	CA	95116	408-259-5000	729-2884
Rideout Memorial Hospital 726 4th St. *Web:* www.frhg.org	Marysville	CA	95901	530-749-4300	751-4226
Riverside Community Hospital 4445 Magnolia Ave. *Web:* www.rchc.org	Riverside	CA	92501	951-788-3000	788-3346
Riverside County Regional Medical Ctr 26520 Cactus Ave. *Web:* www.rcrmc.org	Moreno Valley	CA	92555	951-486-4000	486-4260
Ronald Reagan Medical Ctr 757 Westwood Plaza. *Web:* www.uclahealth.org	Los Angeles	CA	90095	310-825-9111	825-7271
Roseville Medical Ctr 1 Medical Plaza *Web:* www.sutterroseville.org	Roseville	CA	95661	916-781-1000	781-1210
Saddleback Memorial Medical Ctr 24451 Health Ctr Dr *Web:* www.memorialcare.com	Laguna Hills	CA	92653	949-837-4500	452-3467
Saint Agnes Medical Ctr 1303 E Herndon Ave *Web:* www.samc.com	Fresno	CA	93720	559-450-3000	450-3990
Saint Bernardine Medical Ctr 2101 N Waterman Ave *Web:* www.stbernardinemedicalcenter.com	San Bernardino	CA	92404	909-883-8711	881-4546
Saint Francis Medical Ctr 3630 E Imperial Hwy. **Fax:* Admitting ■ *Web:* www.stfrancismedicalcenter.org	Lynwood	CA	90262	310-900-8900	900-4505*
Saint Francis Memorial Hospital 900 Hyde St **Fax:* Admitting ■ *Web:* www.saintfrancismemorial.org	San Francisco	CA	94109	415-353-6000	353-6203*
Saint Helena Hospital 10 Woodland Rd **Fax:* Hum Res ■ *Web:* www.sthelenahospital.org	Saint Helena	CA	94574	707-963-3611	967-5626*
Saint John's Hospital & Health Ctr 1328 22nd St *Web:* www.stjohns.org	Santa Monica	CA	90404	310-829-5511	829-8295
Saint John's Regional Medical Ctr 1600 N Rose Ave	Oxnard	CA	93030	805-988-2500	981-4440
Saint Joseph Hospital 1100 W Stewart Dr. *Web:* www.sjo.org	Orange	CA	92868	714-633-9111	744-8784
Saint Joseph Hospital 2700 Dolbeer St. *Web:* www.stjosepheureka.org	Eureka	CA	95501	707-445-8121	269-3897
Saint Joseph's Medical Ctr 1800 N California St. *Web:* www.stjosephscares.org	Stockton	CA	95204	209-943-2000	461-3299
Saint Jude Medical Ctr 101 E Valencia Mesa Dr *Web:* www.stjudemedicalcenter.org	Fullerton	CA	92835	714-871-3280	992-3029
Saint Mary Medical Ctr 1050 Linden Ave *Web:* www.stmarymedicalcenter.org	Long Beach	CA	90813	562-491-9000	436-6378
Saint Mary's Medical Ctr 450 Stanyan St *Web:* www.stmarysmedicalcenter.com	San Francisco	CA	94117	415-668-1000	668-4531
Saint Rose Hospital 27200 Calaroga Ave. *Web:* www.strosehospital.org	Hayward	CA	94545	510-782-6200	887-7421
Saint Vincent Medical Ctr 2131 W 3rd St *Web:* www.stvincentmedicalcenter.com	Los Angeles	CA	90057	213-484-7111	484-9304
Salinas Valley Memorial Hospital (SVMH) 450 E Romie Ln *TF:* 888-755-7864 ■ *Web:* www.svmh.com	Salinas	CA	93901	831-757-4333	753-6296
San Antonio Community Hospital 999 San Bernardino Rd. *Web:* www.sach.org	Upland	CA	91786	909-985-2811	985-7659
San Francisco General Hospital Medical Ctr 1001 Potrero Ave Suite 1E21 *Web:* www.sfghed.ucsf.edu	San Francisco	CA	94110	415-206-8000	206-8440
San Gabriel Valley Medical Ctr 438 W Las Tunas Dr *Web:* www.sgvmc.org	San Gabriel	CA	91776	626-289-5454	570-6555
San Joaquin General Hospital (SJGH) 500 W Hospital Rd **Fax:* Admitting ■ *Web:* www.sjgeneralhospital.com	French Camp	CA	95231	209-468-6000	468-6659*
Santa Barbara Cottage Hospital PO Box 689 *Web:* www.sbch.org	Santa Barbara	CA	93102	805-682-7111	569-7561
Santa Clara Valley Medical Ctr 751 S Bascom Ave *Web:* www.scvmed.org	San Jose	CA	95128	408-885-5000	793-1817
Santa Monica UCLA Medical Ctr 1250 16th St. *Web:* www.uclahealth.org/homepage_sanmon.cfm?id=265	Santa Monica	CA	90404	310-319-4000	319-4821
Santa Rosa Memorial Hospital (SRMH) 1165 Montgomery Dr. *Web:* www.stjosephhealth.org/Facilities/Santa-Rosa-Memorial-Hospital/default.aspx	Santa Rosa	CA	95405	707-546-3210	522-1543
Scripps Green Hospital 10666 N Torrey Pines Rd *TF:* 800-727-4777 ■ *Web:* www.scripps.org	La Jolla	CA	92037	858-455-9100	
Scripps Memorial Hospital-Encinitas 354 Santa Fe Dr *Web:* www.scripps.org/locations/hospitals__scripps-memorial-hospital-encinitas	Encinitas	CA	92024	760-753-6501	633-7356
Scripps Memorial Hospital-La Jolla 9888 Genesee Ave *Web:* www.scripps.org/locations/hospitals__scripps-memorial-hospital-la-jolla	La Jolla	CA	92037	858-457-4123	626-6122
Scripps Mercy Hospital 4077 5th Ave. *Web:* www.scrippshealth.org	San Diego	CA	92103	619-294-8111	686-3530
Sequoia Hospital 170 Alameda Ave *Web:* www.sequoiahospital.org	Redwood City	CA	94062	650-369-5811	367-5288
Seton Medical Ctr 1900 Sullivan Ave. *Web:* www.setonmedicalcenter.org	Daly City	CA	94015	650-992-4000	991-6024
Sharp Chula Vista Medical Ctr 751 Medical Ctr Ct *Web:* www.sharp.com/hospital/index.cfm?id=915	Chula Vista	CA	91911	619-482-5800	482-3535
Sharp Grossmont Hospital (SGH) 5555 Grossmont Ctr Dr *TF:* 800-827-4277 ■ *Web:* www.sharp.com/grossmont/index.cfm	La Mesa	CA	91942	619-740-6000	
Sharp Memorial Hospital 7901 Frost St *Web:* www.sharp.com/hospital/index.cfm?id=919	San Diego	CA	92123	858-939-3400	939-3514
Shasta Regional Medical Ctr (SRMC) 1100 Butte St *Web:* www.shastaregional.com	Redding	CA	96001	530-244-5400	244-5119
Sherman Oaks Hospital & Health Ctr 4929 Van Nuys Blvd *Web:* www.shermanoakshospital.com	Sherman Oaks	CA	91403	818-981-7111	907-4527

	City	State	Zip	Phone	Fax
Sierra Nevada Memorial Hospital 155 Glasson Way *Web:* www.snmh.org	Grass Valley	CA	95945	530-274-6000	274-6614
Sierra View District Hospital (SVDH) 465 W Putnam Ave *Web:* www.sierra-view.com	Porterville	CA	93257	559-784-1110	788-6135
Sierra Vista Regional Medical Ctr (SVRMC) 1010 Murray Ave *TF:* 888-936-7200 ■ *Web:* www.sierravistaregional.com	San Luis Obispo	CA	93405	805-546-7600	546-7892
Simi Valley Hospital (SVH) 2975 N Sycamore Dr **Fax:* Admitting ■ *Web:* www.simivalleyhospital.com	Simi Valley	CA	93065	805-955-6000	526-0837*
Sonora Regional Medical Ctr (SRMC) 1000 Greenly Rd **Fax:* Admitting ■ *TF Compliance:* 877-336-3566 ■ *Web:* www.sonorahospital.org	Sonora	CA	95370	209-536-5000	536-3500*
Summit Medical Ctr 350 Hawthorne Ave *Web:* www.sutterhealth.org	Oakland	CA	94609	510-655-4000	658-8593
Sutter Auburn Faith Community Hospital (SAFH) 11815 Education St *TF:* 800-478-8837 ■ *Web:* www.sutterauburnfaith.org	Auburn	CA	95602	530-888-4500	886-6611
Sutter General Hospital 2801 L St *Web:* www.sutterhealth.org	Sacramento	CA	95816	916-454-2222	733-3791
Sutter Health Sacramento Sierra Region 2801 L St *Web:* www.checksutterfirst.org	Sacramento	CA	95816	916-454-2222	733-8894
Sutter Medical Center of Santa Rosa 3325 Chanate Rd *TF:* 800-651-5111 ■ *Web:* www.suttersantarosa.org	Santa Rosa	CA	95404	707-576-4000	576-4318
Sutter Memorial Hospital 5151 F St *Web:* www.sutterhealth.org	Sacramento	CA	95819	916-454-3333	733-8135
Sutter Solano Medical Ctr (SSMC) 300 Hospital Dr *Web:* www.suttersolano.org	Vallejo	CA	94589	707-554-4444	648-3227
Torrance Memorial Medical Ctr 3330 Lomita Blvd *Web:* www.torrancememorial.org	Torrance	CA	90505	310-325-9110	784-4801
Tri-City Medical Ctr 4002 Vista Way *Web:* www.tricitymed.org	Oceanside	CA	92056	760-724-8411	940-4050
Tri-City Regional Medical Ctr 21530 S Pioneer Blvd *Web:* www.tri-cityrmc.org	Hawaiian Gardens	CA	90716	562-860-0401	924-5871
Tulare Regional Medical Ctr 869 N Cherry *Web:* www.tulareregional.org	Tulare	CA	93274	559-688-0821	685-3835
UC Irvine Healthcare 101 the City Dr S *TF:* 877-824-3627 ■ *Web:* www.healthcare.uci.edu	Orange	CA	92868	714-456-7890	456-7488
UCSF Medical Ctr 505 Parnassus Ave *Web:* www.ucsfhealth.org	San Francisco	CA	94143	415-476-1000	
Ukiah Valley Medical Ctr 275 Hospital Dr *Web:* www.uvmc.org	Ukiah	CA	95482	707-462-3111	463-7384
University of California Davis Medical Ctr 2315 Stockton Blvd **Fax:* Admitting ■ *Web:* www.ucdmc.ucdavis.edu	Sacramento	CA	95817	916-734-2011	734-8080*
University of California San Diego Medical Ctr 200 W Arbor Dr *TF:* 800-926-8273 ■ *Web:* health.ucsd.edu	San Diego	CA	92103	619-543-6222	543-7448
Valley Presbyterian Hospital 15107 Vanowen St *Web:* www.valleypres.org	Van Nuys	CA	91405	818-782-6600	902-3974
Verdugo Hills Hospital 1812 Verdugo Blvd *Web:* www.verdugohillshospital.org	Glendale	CA	91208	818-790-7100	952-4691
West Anaheim Medical Ctr (WAMC) 3033 W Orange Ave *Web:* www.wamc.phcs.us	Anaheim	CA	92804	714-827-3000	229-6813
Western Medical Center Anaheim (WMCA) 1025 S Anaheim Blvd *Web:* www.westernmedanaheim.com	Anaheim	CA	92805	714-533-6220	563-2859
Western Medical Center Santa Ana 1001 N Tustin Ave *TF:* 800-777-7464 ■ *Web:* www.westernmedicalcenter.com	Santa Ana	CA	92705	714-953-3500	953-3613
White Memorial Medical Ctr 1720 Cesar E Chavez Ave *Web:* www.whitememorial.com	Los Angeles	CA	90033	323-268-5000	881-8605
Whittier Hospital Medical Ctr 9080 Colima Rd *TF:* 800-613-4291 ■ *Web:* www.whittierhospital.com	Whittier	CA	90605	562-945-3561	693-6811
Woodland Healthcare 1325 Cottonwood St *Web:* www.woodlandhealthcare.org	Woodland	CA	95695	530-662-3961	666-7948

COLORADO

	City	State	Zip	Phone	Fax
Arkansas Valley Regional Medical Ctr (AVRMC) 1100 Carson Ave *Web:* www.avrmc.org	La Junta	CO	81050	719-384-5412	383-6005
Avista Adventist Hospital 100 Health Pk Dr	Louisville	CO	80027	303-673-1000	673-1048
Boulder Community Hospital (BCH) 1100 Balsam Ave **Fax:* Admitting ■ *Web:* www.bch.org	Boulder	CO	80301	303-440-2273	440-2278*
Denver Health Medical Ctr (DHMC) 777 Bannock St *Web:* www.denverhealth.org	Denver	CO	80204	303-436-6000	436-6243
Exempla Lutheran Medical Ctr 8300 W 38th Ave *Web:* www.exempla.org	Wheat Ridge	CO	80033	303-425-4500	425-8198
Exempla Saint Joseph Hospital 1835 Franklin St *Web:* www.exempla.org	Denver	CO	80218	303-837-7111	837-7123
Littleton Adventist Hospital 7700 S Broadway *Web:* www.mylittletonhospital.org	Littleton	CO	80122	303-730-8900	730-5867
Longmont United Hospital (LUH) 1950 Mountain View Ave *Web:* www.luhcares.org	Longmont	CO	80501	303-651-5111	678-4050
McKee Medical Ctr 2000 N Boise Ave *Web:* www.bannerhealth.com	Loveland	CO	80538	970-669-4640	635-4112
Medical Center of Aurora (MCA) 1501 S Potomac St *Web:* www.auroramed.com	Aurora	CO	80012	303-695-2600	337-9773
Memorial Health System (MHS) *Central* 1400 E Boulder St **Fax:* Admissions ■ *TF:* 800-826-4889 ■ *Web:* www.memorialhealthsystem.com	Colorado Springs	CO	80909	719-365-5000	365-6884*
Mercy Medical Ctr 1010 Three Springs Blvd *TF:* 800-345-2516 ■ *Web:* www.mercydurango.org	Durango	CO	81301	970-247-4311	382-1065
North Colorado Medical Ctr 1801 16th St *Web:* www.bannerhealth.com	Greeley	CO	80631	970-352-4121	350-6644
North Suburban Medical Ctr (NSMC) 9191 Grant St *Web:* www.northsuburban.com	Thornton	CO	80229	303-451-7800	450-4458
OnCure Medical Corp 188 Inverness Dr W Suite 650 *Web:* www.oncure.com	Englewood	CO	80112	303-643-6500	643-6560
Parkview Medical Ctr 400 W 16th St *TF:* 800-543-8984 ■ *Web:* www.parkviewmc.org	Pueblo	CO	81003	719-584-4000	584-4739
Penrose Hospital 2222 N Nevada Ave **Fax:* Admitting ■ *Web:* www.penrosestfrancis.org	Colorado Springs	CO	80907	719-776-5000	776-2442*
Porter Adventist Hospital 2525 S Downing St *Web:* www.porterhospital.org	Denver	CO	80210	303-778-1955	778-5252
Poudre Valley Hospital 1024 S Lemay Ave *TF:* 800-252-5784 ■ *Web:* www.pvhs.org	Fort Collins	CO	80524	970-495-7000	495-7601
Presbyterian-Saint Luke's Medical Ctr 1719 E 19th Ave *Web:* www.pslmc.com	Denver	CO	80218	303-839-6000	869-2428
Rose Medical Ctr 4567 E 9th Ave *TF:* 888-525-1253 ■ *Web:* www.rosemed.com	Denver	CO	80220	303-320-2121	320-2200
Saint Anthony Central Hospital 4231 W 16th Ave *Web:* www.stanthonyhosp.org	Denver	CO	80204	303-629-3511	629-2318
Saint Anthony North Hospital 2551 W 84th Ave *Web:* www.stanthonynorth.org	Westminster	CO	80031	303-426-2151	426-2155
Saint Mary's Hospital & Regional Medical Ctr 2635 N 7th St *TF:* 800-458-3888 ■ *Web:* www.stmarygj.com	Grand Junction	CO	81502	970-244-2273	244-7510
Saint Mary-Corwin Medical Ctr 1008 Minnequa Ave **Fax:* Admitting ■ *TF:* 800-228-4039 ■ *Web:* www.stmarycorwin.org	Pueblo	CO	81004	719-557-4000	557-5529*
San Luis Valley Regional Medical Ctr 106 Blanca Ave *Web:* www.slvrmc.org	Alamosa	CO	81101	719-589-2511	587-1372
Swedish Medical Ctr 501 E Hampden Ave *Web:* www.swedishhospital.com	Englewood	CO	80113	303-788-5000	788-6265
University of Colorado Hospital 12605 E 16th Ave *Web:* www.uch.edu	Aurora	CO	80045	303-848-4011	

CONNECTICUT

	City	State	Zip	Phone	Fax
Bridgeport Hospital 267 Grant St *Web:* www.bridgeporthospital.org	Bridgeport	CT	06610	203-384-3000	384-3215
Bristol Hospital (BH) 41 Brewster Rd *Web:* www.bristolhospital.org	Bristol	CT	06010	860-585-3000	585-3058
Charlotte Hungerford Hospital (CHH) 540 Litchfield St *Web:* www.charlottesweb.hungerford.org	Torrington	CT	06790	860-496-6666	482-8627
Danbury Hospital (DH) 24 Hospital Ave *TF:* 800-516-3658 ■ *Web:* www.danburyhospital.org	Danbury	CT	06810	203-739-6398	731-8030
Greenwich Hospital 5 Perryridge Rd *Web:* www.greenhosp.org	Greenwich	CT	06830	203-863-3000	863-3954
Griffin Hospital 130 Division St *Web:* www.griffinhealth.org	Derby	CT	06418	203-735-7421	732-7569
Hartford Hospital 80 Seymour St *Web:* www.harthosp.org	Hartford	CT	06102	860-545-5000	545-3622
Hospital of Saint Raphael 1450 Chapel St *TF:* 800-662-2366 ■ *Web:* www.srhs.org	New Haven	CT	06511	203-789-3000	867-5235
Johnson Memorial Hospital 201 Chestnut Hill Rd *Web:* www.jmmc.com	Stafford Springs	CT	06076	860-684-4251	684-8165
Lawrence & Memorial Hospital 365 Montauk Ave *TF:* 888-777-9539 ■ *Web:* www.lmhospital.org	New London	CT	06320	860-442-0711	444-3741
Manchester Memorial Hospital 71 Haynes St *Web:* www.echn.org/mmh.htm	Manchester	CT	06040	860-646-1222	522-3404
Middlesex Hospital 28 Crescent St *TF:* 800-664-5031 ■ *Web:* www.middlesexhospital.org	Middletown	CT	06457	860-358-6000	346-5485
Milford Hospital (MH) 300 Seaside Ave *Web:* www.milfordhospital.org	Milford	CT	06460	203-876-4000	876-4198
New Britain General Hospital 100 Grand St *Web:* www.nbgh.org	New Britain	CT	06050	860-224-5011	224-5767
Norwalk Hospital 34 Maple St *TF:* 800-789-4584 ■ *Web:* www.norwalkhospital.org	Norwalk	CT	06856	203-852-2000	855-3780
Saint Francis Hospital & Medical Ctr 114 Woodland St *TF:* 800-993-4312 ■ *Web:* www.stfranciscare.org	Hartford	CT	06105	860-714-4000	714-8038
Saint Mary's Hospital 56 Franklin St *Web:* www.stmh.org	Waterbury	CT	06706	203-709-6000	709-3238
Saint Vincent's Medical Ctr 2800 Main St *TF:* 877-255-7847 ■ *Web:* www.stvincents.org	Bridgeport	CT	06606	203-576-6000	576-5345
Stamford Hospital 30 Shelburne Rd *Web:* www.stamfordhospital.org	Stamford	CT	06904	203-276-1000	
University of Connecticut Health Ctr *John Dempsey Hospital* 263 Farmington Ave *TF:* 800-535-6232 ■ *Web:* www.uchc.edu	Farmington	CT	06030	860-679-2000	679-1255

	City	State	Zip	Phone	Fax
Waterbury Hospital 64 Robbins St *Web:* www.waterburyhospital.org	Waterbury	CT	06721	203-573-6000	573-6161
William W Backus Hospital The 326 Washington St *Web:* www.backushospital.org	Norwich	CT	06360	860-889-8331	823-6329
Windham Community Memorial Hospital (WCMH) 112 Mansfield Ave *Web:* www.windhamhospital.org	Willimantic	CT	06226	860-456-9116	456-6838
Yale-New Haven Hospital 20 York St *Web:* www.ynhh.org	New Haven	CT	06504	203-688-4242	

DELAWARE

	City	State	Zip	Phone	Fax
Bayhealth Medical Ctr 21 W Clarke Ave *TF:* 800-990-4229 ■ *Web:* www.bayhealth.org	Milford	DE	19963	302-430-5738	430-5598
Beebe Medical Ctr 424 Savannah Rd *Web:* www.beebemed.org	Lewes	DE	19958	302-645-3300	645-3405
Christiana Hospital 4755 Ogletown-Stanton Rd **Fax:* Admitting ■ *Web:* www.christianacare.org	Newark	DE	19718	302-733-1000	733-1313*
Kent General Hospital 640 S State St *TF:* 888-761-8300 ■ *Web:* www.bayhealth.org	Dover	DE	19901	302-674-4700	744-7181
Nanticoke Memorial Hospital 801 Middleford Rd *Web:* www.nanticoke.org	Seaford	DE	19973	302-629-6611	629-2493
Saint Francis Hospital 7th & Clayton St *Web:* www.stfrancishealthcare.org	Wilmington	DE	19805	302-421-4100	579-8320

DISTRICT OF COLUMBIA

	City	State	Zip	Phone	Fax
George Washington University Hospital 900 23rd St NW *TF:* 888-449-4677 ■ *Web:* www.gwhospital.com	Washington	DC	20037	202-715-4000	
Georgetown University Hospital 3800 Reservoir Rd NW *Web:* www.gumc.georgetown.edu	Washington	DC	20007	202-784-2000	784-2875
Greater Southeast Community Hospital *United Medical Centre* 1310 Southern Ave SE	Washington	DC	20032	202-574-6000	574-7188
Howard University Hospital 2041 Georgia Ave *Web:* huhealthcare.com	Washington	DC	20060	202-865-6100	865-1360
Providence Hospital 1150 Varnum St NE *Web:* www.provhosp.org	Washington	DC	20017	202-269-7000	269-7160
Sibley Memorial Hospital 5255 Loughboro Rd NW **Fax:* Admissions ■ *Web:* www.sibley.org	Washington	DC	20016	202-537-4000	243-2246*
Washington Hospital Ctr 110 Irving St NW *Web:* www.whcenter.org	Washington	DC	20010	202-877-7000	877-7826

FLORIDA

	City	State	Zip	Phone	Fax
Aventura Hospital 20900 Biscayne Blvd *TF:* 800-523-5772 ■ *Web:* www.aventurahospital.com	Aventura	FL	33180	305-682-7000	682-7105
Baptist Hospital 1000 W Moreno St *Web:* www.ebaptisthealthcare.org	Pensacola	FL	32501	850-434-4011	469-2307
Baptist Hospital of Miami 8900 SW 88th St *TF:* 800-327-2491 ■ *Web:* www.baptisthealth.net	Miami	FL	33176	786-596-1960	596-5960
Baptist Medical Ctr 800 Prudential Dr *TF:* 800-874-8567 ■ *Web:* www.e-baptisthealth.com	Jacksonville	FL	32207	904-202-2000	202-2285
Bay Medical Ctr 615 N Bonita Ave *TF:* 800-422-2418 ■ *Web:* www.baymedical.org	Panama City	FL	32401	850-769-1511	763-8827
BayCare Health System 3231 McMullen-Booth Rd *Web:* www.measehospitals.com	Safety Harbor	FL	34695	727-725-6111	725-6181
Bayfront Medical Ctr 701 6th St S *Web:* www.bayfront.org	Saint Petersburg	FL	33701	727-823-1234	893-6930
Bethesda Memorial Hospital 2815 S Seacrest Blvd *Web:* www.bethesdaweb.com	Boynton Beach	FL	33435	561-737-7733	737-4534
Blake Medical Ctr 2020 59th St W *Web:* www.blakemedicalcenter.com	Bradenton	FL	34209	941-792-6611	798-6209
Boca Raton Regional Hospital 800 Meadows Rd *Web:* www.brch.com	Boca Raton	FL	33486	561-395-7100	955-5040
Brandon Regional Hospital 119 Oakfield Dr *Web:* www.brandonhospital.com	Brandon	FL	33511	813-681-5551	654-7203
Brooksville Regional Hospital 17240 Cortez Blvd *Web:* www.brooksvilleregionalhospital.org	Brooksville	FL	34601	352-796-5111	544-5711
Cape Coral Hospital 636 Del Prado Blvd *Web:* www.leememorial.org	Cape Coral	FL	33990	239-574-2323	574-0079
Capital Regional Medical Ctr (CRMC) 2626 Capital Medical Blvd *Web:* www.capitalregionalmedicalcenter.com	Tallahassee	FL	32308	850-325-5000	325-5198
Central Florida Regional Hospital 1401 W Seminole Blvd *Web:* www.centralfloridaregional.com	Sanford	FL	32771	407-321-4500	324-4790
Charlotte Regional Medical Ctr 809 E Marion Ave *Web:* www.charlotteregional.com	Punta Gorda	FL	33950	941-639-3131	637-2579
Citrus Memorial Hospital 502 W Highland Blvd *Web:* www.citrusmh.com	Inverness	FL	34452	352-726-1551	344-6565
Cleveland Clinic Hospital 2950 Cleveland Clinic Blvd *TF:* 866-293-7866 ■ *Web:* www.my.clevelandclinic.org	Weston	FL	33331	954-689-5000	689-5165
Columbia Hospital 2201 45th St *Web:* www.columbiahospital.com	West Palm Beach	FL	33407	561-842-6141	881-2650
Community Hospital 5637 Marine Pkwy *Web:* www.communityhospitalnpr.com	New Port Richey	FL	34652	727-848-1733	848-5136
Coral Gables Hospital Inc (CGH) 3100 Douglas Rd *Web:* www.coralgableshospital.com	Coral Gables	FL	33134	305-445-8461	441-6879
Coral Springs Medical Ctr 3000 Coral Hills Dr *Web:* www.browardhealth.org	Coral Springs	FL	33065	954-344-3000	344-3146
Delray Medical Ctr (DMC) 5352 Linton Blvd *Web:* www.delraymedicalctr.com	Delray Beach	FL	33484	561-498-4440	495-3103
DeSoto Memorial Hospital Inc 900 N Robert Ave *Web:* www.dmh.org	Arcadia	FL	34266	863-494-3535	494-8400
Doctors Hospital Sarasota 5731 Bee Ridge Rd *Web:* www.doctorsofsarasota.com	Sarasota	FL	34233	941-342-1100	379-8342
Doctors' Hospital 5000 University Dr *Web:* www.baptisthealth.net	Coral Gables	FL	33146	786-308-3000	308-3402
Edward White Hospital 2323 9th Ave N *Web:* www.edwardwhitehospital.com	Saint Petersburg	FL	33713	727-323-1111	328-6135
Fawcett Memorial Hospital 21298 Olean Blvd *Web:* www.fawcetthospital.com	Port Charlotte	FL	33952	941-629-1181	627-6142
Florida Hospital DeLand 701 W Plymouth Ave **Fax:* Admitting ■ *Web:* www.fhdeland.org	DeLand	FL	32720	386-943-4522	943-3674*
Florida Hospital Heartland Medical Ctr 4200 Sun 'N Lake Blvd *Web:* www.flhosp-heartland.org	Sebring	FL	33871	863-453-7511	402-3110
Florida Hospital Oceanside 264 S Atlantic Ave *Web:* www.floridahospitalmemorial.org	Ormond Beach	FL	32176	386-672-4161	231-3323
Florida Hospital Orlando 601 E Rollins St *Web:* www.floridahospital.com	Orlando	FL	32803	407-303-2800	
Florida Hospital Ormond Memorial 875 Sterthaus Ave *TF:* 888-647-0271 ■ *Web:* www.floridahospitalmemorial.org	Ormond Beach	FL	32174	386-676-6086	
Florida Hospital Zephyrhills 7050 Gall Blvd *Web:* www.fhzeph.org	Zephyrhills	FL	33541	813-788-0411	783-6196
Florida Medical Ctr (FMC) 5000 W Oakland Pk Blvd *TF:* 800-222-9355 ■ *Web:* www.floridamedicalctr.com	Fort Lauderdale	FL	33313	954-735-6000	735-0532
Fort Walton Beach Medical Ctr (FWBMC) 1000 Mar-Walt Dr *Web:* www.fwbmc.com	Fort Walton Beach	FL	32547	850-862-1111	862-9149
Gulf Coast Medical Ctr 13681 Doctors Way *TF:* 800-440-4481 ■ *Web:* www.leememorial.org/facilities/gcmcenter.asp	Fort Myers	FL	33912	239-343-1000	768-8379
Gulf Coast Medical Ctr 449 W 23rd St *Web:* www.gcmc-pc.com	Panama City	FL	32405	850-769-8341	747-7107
Halifax Medical Ctr 303 N Clyde Morris Blvd *Web:* www.hfch.org	Daytona Beach	FL	32114	386-254-4000	254-4375
Health Central 10000 W Colonial Dr *Web:* www.healthcentral.org	Ocoee	FL	34761	407-296-1000	253-1675
Health First Cape Canaveral Hospital 701 W Cocoa Beach Cswy *TF:* 888-434-3730 ■ *Web:* www.health-first.org	Cocoa Beach	FL	32931	321-868-8381	434-6103
Helen Ellis Memorial Hospital 1395 S Pinellas Ave *Web:* www.hemh.com	Tarpon Springs	FL	34689	727-942-5000	942-5161
Holmes Regional Medical Ctr 1350 Hickory St *TF:* 888-434-3730 ■ *Web:* www.health-first.org	Melbourne	FL	32901	321-434-7000	434-7283
Holy Cross Hospital 4725 N Federal Hwy *Web:* www.holy-cross.com	Fort Lauderdale	FL	33308	954-771-8000	492-5741
Homestead Hospital 975 Baptist Way *Web:* www.baptisthealth.net	Homestead	FL	33033	786-243-8000	243-8557
Imperial Point Medical Ctr 6401 N Federal Hwy *Web:* www.browardhealth.org	Fort Lauderdale	FL	33308	954-776-8500	776-8520
Indian River Medical Ctr 1000 36th St *TF:* 800-226-4764 ■ *Web:* www.irmc.cc	Vero Beach	FL	32960	772-567-4311	562-5628
Jackson Hospital 4250 Hospital Dr *Web:* www.jacksonhosp.com	Marianna	FL	32446	850-526-2200	482-6374
Jackson Memorial Hospital 1611 NW 12th Ave *Web:* www.jhsmiami.org	Miami	FL	33136	305-585-1111	325-4262
JFK Medical Ctr 5301 S Congress Ave *Web:* www.jfkmc.com	Atlantis	FL	33462	561-965-7300	548-3685
Jupiter Medical Ctr 1210 S Old Dixie Hwy *Web:* www.jupitermed.com	Jupiter	FL	33458	561-747-2234	744-4493
Kendall Regional Medical Ctr 11750 SW 40th St *Web:* www.kendallmed.com	Miami	FL	33175	305-223-3000	229-2481
Lakeland Regional Medical Ctr 1324 Lakeland Hills Blvd PO Box 95448 *Web:* www.lrmc.com	Lakeland	FL	33805	863-687-1100	687-1214
Largo Medical Ctr (LMC) 201 14th St SW *TF:* 800-733-0592 ■ *Web:* www.largomedical.com	Largo	FL	33770	727-588-5200	588-5906
Lawnwood Regional Medical Ctr (LRMC) 1700 S 23rd St *Web:* www.lawnwoodmed.com	Fort Pierce	FL	34950	772-461-4000	460-1353
Lee Memorial Health Systems 2776 Cleveland Ave *Web:* www.leememorial.org	Fort Myers	FL	33901	239-332-1111	336-6170
Leesburg Regional Medical Ctr (LRMC) 600 E Dixie Ave	Leesburg	FL	34748	352-323-5762	323-5009
Lower Keys Medical Ctr 5900 College Rd *Web:* www.lkmc.com	Key West	FL	33040	305-294-5531	294-8065
Manatee County Rural Health Services Inc (MCRHS) 12271 US Hwy 301 PO Box 499 *Web:* www.mcrhs.org	Parrish	FL	34219	941-776-4000	

Hospital	City	State	ZIP	Phone	Fax
Manatee Memorial Hospital 206 2nd St E *Web:* www.manateememorial.com	Bradenton	FL	34208	941-746-5111	745-6862
Martin Memorial Health Systems (MMHS) 200 SE Hospital Ave PO Box 9010 *TF:* 800-362-8677 ■ *Web:* www.mmhs.com	Stuart	FL	34994	772-287-5200	223-5946
Mease Dunedin Hospital 601 Main St *Web:* www.measehospitals.com	Dunedin	FL	34698	727-733-1111	734-6297
Memorial Hospital of Jacksonville 3625 University Blvd S *Web:* www.memorialhospitaljax.com/home/index.dot	Jacksonville	FL	32216	904-399-6111	399-6817
Memorial Hospital of Tampa 2901 W Swann Ave *TF:* 877-898-6080 ■ *Web:* www.memorialhospitaltampa.com	Tampa	FL	33609	813-873-6400	874-8685
Memorial Hospital Pembroke (MHP) 7800 Sheridan St *Web:* www.memorialpembroke.com	Pembroke Pines	FL	33024	954-962-9650	963-8036
Memorial Hospital West 703 N Flamingo Rd *Web:* www.memorialwest.com	Pembroke Pines	FL	33028	954-436-5000	433-7156
Memorial Regional Hospital 3501 Johnson St *Web:* www.memorialregional.com	Hollywood	FL	33021	954-987-2000	985-3412
Mercy Hospital 3663 S Miami Ave *Web:* www.mercymiami.com	Miami	FL	33133	305-854-4400	285-2967
Metropolitan Hospital of Miami 5959 NW 7th St	Miami	FL	33126	305-264-1000	265-6536
Morton Plant Hospital 300 Pinellas St *Web:* www.mortonplant.com	Clearwater	FL	33756	727-462-7000	461-8101
Mount Sinai Medical Ctr 4300 Alton Rd *Web:* www.msmc.com	Miami Beach	FL	33140	305-674-2121	674-2007
Munroe Regional Medical Ctr 1500 SW 1st Ave *Web:* www.munroeregional.com	Ocala	FL	34474	352-351-7200	351-7336
Naples Community Hospital 350 7th St N *Web:* www.nchmd.org	Naples	FL	34102	239-436-5000	436-5914
North Broward Medical Ctr 201 E Sample Rd *Web:* www.browardhealth.org	Pompano Beach	FL	33064	954-941-8300	786-5174
North Florida Regional Medical Ctr 6500 Newberry Rd *Web:* www.nfrmc.com	Gainesville	FL	32605	352-333-4000	333-4800
North Okaloosa Medical Ctr (NOMC) 151 E Redstone Ave *Web:* www.northokaloosa.com	Crestview	FL	32539	850-689-8100	689-8484
North Ridge Medical Ctr 5757 N Dixie Hwy *Web:* www.northridgemedical.com	Fort Lauderdale	FL	33334	954-776-6000	493-5061
North Shore Medical Ctr 1100 NW 95th St *TF:* 800-984-3434 ■ *Web:* www.northshoremedical.com	Miami	FL	33150	305-835-6000	835-6163
Northside Hospital 6000 49th St N *Web:* www.northsidehospital.com	Saint Petersburg	FL	33709	727-521-4411	521-5007
Northwest Medical Ctr (NWMC) 2801 N SR 7 *Web:* www.northwestmed.com	Margate	FL	33063	954-978-4008	984-3721
Oakhill Hospital 11375 Cortez Blvd *Web:* www.oakhillhospital.com	Brooksville	FL	34613	352-596-6632	597-3024
Ocala Regional Medical Ctr (ORMC) 1431 SW 1st Ave *Web:* www.ocalahealthsystem.com/about/ocala-regional-medical-center.dot	Ocala	FL	34478	352-401-1000	401-1198
Orange Park Medical Ctr 2001 Kingsley Ave *Web:* www.orangeparkmedical.com	Orange Park	FL	32073	904-276-8500	213-2536
Orlando Health 1414 Kuhl Ave *Web:* www.orhs.org	Orlando	FL	32806	321-843-7000	
Orlando Regional Medical Ctr (ORMC) 1414 Kuhl Ave **Fax Area Code:* 407 ■ *TF:* 800-424-6998 ■ *Web:* www.orlandohealth.com	Orlando	FL	32806	321-841-5111	649-6845*
Orlando Regional South Seminole Hospital 555 W State Rd 434 *Web:* www.orlandohealth.com/southseminolehospital/index.aspx	Longwood	FL	32750	407-767-1200	767-5801
Osceola Regional Medical Ctr 700 W Oak St *Web:* www.osceolaregional.com	Kissimmee	FL	34741	407-846-2266	518-3616
Osler Medical 930 S Hbr Cy Blvd Suite 101 *Web:* www.oslermedical.com	Melbourne	FL	32901	321-725-5050	725-5975
Pacer Corp 14100 Palmetto Frontage Rd Suite 110 *PINK:* PHLH ■ *Web:* www.pacerco.com	Miami Lakes	FL	33016	305-828-7660	828-2551
Palm Beach Gardens Medical Ctr 3360 Burns Rd *Web:* www.pbgmc.com	Palm Beach Gardens	FL	33410	561-622-1411	694-7160
Palm Springs General Hospital 1475 W 49th St	Hialeah	FL	33012	305-558-2500	558-8679
Palmetto General Hospital (PGH) 2001 W 68th St *TF:* 800-522-5292 ■ *Web:* www.palmettogeneral.com	Hialeah	FL	33016	305-823-5000	364-2173
Palms of Pasadena Hospital 1501 Pasadena Ave S *Web:* www.palmspasadena.com	Saint Petersburg	FL	33707	727-381-1000	341-7629
Palms West Hospital (PWH) 13001 Southern Blvd *TF:* 866-857-3936 ■ *Web:* www.palmswesthospital.com	Loxahatchee	FL	33470	561-798-3300	791-8108
Parrish Medical Ctr 951 N Washington Ave *Web:* www.parrishmed.com	Titusville	FL	32796	321-268-6111	268-6231
Peace River Regional Medical Ctr 2500 Harbor Blvd *TF:* 800-226-4122 ■ *Web:* www.peaceriverregional.com	Port Charlotte	FL	33952	941-766-4122	766-4140
Plantation General Hospital 401 NW 42nd Ave *Web:* www.plantationgeneral.com	Plantation	FL	33317	954-587-5010	587-4597
Putnam Community Medical Ctr Hwy 20 W *Web:* www.pcmcfl.com	Palatka	FL	32177	386-328-5711	325-8178
Raulerson Hospital 1796 Hwy 441 N *Web:* www.raulersonhospital.com	Okeechobee	FL	34972	863-763-2151	824-2991
Regional Medical Center Bayonet Point 14000 Fivay Rd *Web:* www.rmchealth.com	Hudson	FL	34667	727-863-2411	869-5491
Sacred Heart Hospital of Pensacola 5151 N 9th Ave *TF:* 800-874-1026 ■ *Web:* www.sacred-heart.org	Pensacola	FL	32504	850-416-7000	416-6119
Saint Anthony's Hospital 1200 7th Ave N *Web:* www.stanthonys.com	Saint Petersburg	FL	33705	727-825-1000	825-1230
Saint Joseph's Hospital 3001 W ML King Jr Blvd *TF:* 800-347-2676 ■ *Web:* www.sjbhealth.org	Tampa	FL	33607	813-870-4000	870-4639
Saint Lucie Medical Ctr 1800 SE Tiffany Ave *Web:* www.stluciemed.com	Port Saint Lucie	FL	34952	772-335-4000	398-3608
Saint Luke's Hospital 4201 Belfort Rd *Web:* www.mayoclinic.org/stlukes-jax	Jacksonville	FL	32216	904-296-3700	296-4698
Saint Vincent's Medical Ctr 1800 Barrs St *Web:* www.jaxhealth.com	Jacksonville	FL	32204	904-308-7300	308-2992
Sarasota Memorial Hospital 1700 S Tamiami Trail *TF:* 800-764-8255 ■ *Web:* www.smh.com	Sarasota	FL	34239	941-917-9000	917-1716
Sebastian River Medical Ctr 13695 US Hwy 1 *Web:* www.srmcenter.com	Sebastian	FL	32958	772-589-3186	388-3689
Seven Rivers Regional Medical Ctr (SRRMC) 6201 N Suncoast Blvd *Web:* www.srrmc.com	Crystal River	FL	34428	352-795-6560	795-8369
Shands at AGH Hospital 801 SW 2nd Ave	Gainesville	FL	32601	352-733-0111	733-0151
Shands Hospital at the University of Florida 1600 SW Archer Rd *TF:* 800-749-7424 ■ *Web:* www.shands.org	Gainesville	FL	32610	352-265-0111	265-0363
Shands Jacksonville Medical Ctr 655 W 8th St	Jacksonville	FL	32209	904-244-0411	244-2587
South Bay Hospital 4016 Sun City Ctr Blvd *Web:* www.southbayhospital.com	Sun City Center	FL	33573	813-634-3301	634-8712
South Florida Baptist Hospital 301 N Alexander St *Web:* www.sjbhealth.org/home_south.cfm?id=587	Plant City	FL	33563	813-757-1200	757-8209
South Miami Hospital 6200 SW 73rd St **Fax Area Code:* 786 ■ *Web:* www.baptisthealth.net	Miami	FL	33143	305-661-4611	662-5302*
Southwest Florida Regional Medical Center 2727 Winkler Ave *Web:* www.leememorial.org	Fort Myers	FL	33901	239-939-8457	
St Petersburg General Hospital 6500 38th Ave N *TF:* 800-733-0610 ■ *Web:* www.stpetegeneral.com	Saint Petersburg	FL	33710	727-384-1414	341-4889
Tallahassee Memorial Hospital 1300 Miccosukee Rd *Web:* www.tmh.org	Tallahassee	FL	32308	850-431-1155	431-5883
Tampa General Hospital 1 Tampa General Cir *Web:* www.tgh.org	Tampa	FL	33606	813-844-7000	844-4144
Town & Country Hospital 6001 Webb Rd *Web:* www.townandcountryhospital.com	Tampa	FL	33615	813-885-6666	887-5112
University Community Hospital 3100 E Fletcher Ave *Web:* www.uch.org	Tampa	FL	33613	813-971-6000	615-8100
University Community Hospital Carrollwood 7171 N Dale Mabry Hwy *Web:* www.uch.org	Tampa	FL	33614	813-932-2222	558-8011
University Hospital 7201 N University Dr *Web:* www.uhmchealth.com	Tamarac	FL	33321	954-721-2200	724-6575
University of Miami Hospital 1400 NW 12th Ave *Web:* www.cedarsmed.com	Miami	FL	33136	305-325-5511	325-4673
Venice Regional Medical Ctr (VRMC) 540 The Rialto *Web:* www.veniceregional.com	Venice	FL	34285	941-485-7711	483-7699
West Boca Medical Ctr (WBMC) 21644 State Rd 7 *Web:* www.westbocamedctr.com	Boca Raton	FL	33428	561-488-8000	488-8105
West Florida Hospital 8383 N Davis Hwy *Web:* www.westfloridahospital.com	Pensacola	FL	32514	850-494-4000	
Westside Regional Medical Ctr 8201 W Broward Blvd *Web:* www.westsideregional.com	Plantation	FL	33324	954-473-6600	476-3974
Winter Haven Hospital 200 Ave F NE *Web:* www.winterhavenhospital.org	Winter Haven	FL	33881	863-293-1121	297-1867
Winter Park Memorial Hospital 200 N Lakemont Ave *Web:* www.winterparkhospital.com	Winter Park	FL	32792	407-646-7000	646-7639
Wuesthoff Medical Center Rockledge 110 Longwood Ave *TF:* 800-742-9175 ■ *Web:* www.wuesthoff.org	Rockledge	FL	32955	321-636-2211	690-6645

GEORGIA

Hospital	City	State	ZIP	Phone	Fax
Athens Regional Medical Ctr (ARMC) 1199 Prince Ave *Web:* www.armc.org	Athens	GA	30606	706-475-7000	475-6775
Atlanta Medical Ctr 303 Pkwy Dr NE *Web:* www.atlantamedcenter.com	Atlanta	GA	30312	404-265-4000	265-3903
Candler Hospital 5353 Reynolds St *Web:* www.sjchs.org	Savannah	GA	31405	912-819-6000	819-5887
Coffee Regional Medical Ctr (CRMC) 1101 Ocilla Rd *Web:* www.coffeeregional.org	Douglas	GA	31533	912-384-1900	383-5667
Coliseum Medical Ctr 350 Hospital Dr *Web:* www.coliseumhealthsystem.com	Macon	GA	31217	478-765-7000	742-1247
Colquitt Regional Medical Ctr (CRMC) 3131 S Main St PO Box 40 *TF:* 888-262-2762 ■ *Web:* www.colquittregional.com	Moultrie	GA	31768	229-985-3420	890-2541
DeKalb Medical 2701 N Decatur Rd *Web:* www.dekalbmedicalcenter.org	Decatur	GA	30033	404-501-1000	501-1739
Doctors Hospital 3651 Wheeler Rd *Web:* www.doctors-hospital.net	Augusta	GA	30909	706-651-3232	651-2041
Dodge County Hospital 901 Griffin Ave *Web:* www.dodgecountyhospital.com	Eastman	GA	31023	478-448-4000	

Hospital	City	State	Zip	Phone	Fax
East Georgia Regional Medical Ctr (EGRMC) 1499 Fair Rd *Web:* www.eastgeorgiaregional.com	Statesboro	GA	30458	912-486-1000	871-2354
Eastside Medical Ctr 1700 Medical Way *Web:* www.eastsidemedical.com	Snellville	GA	30078	770-979-0200	736-2395
Emory Crawford Long Hospital 550 Peachtree St NE *Web:* www.emoryhealthcare.org	Atlanta	GA	30308	404-686-4411	686-8956
Emory University Hospital 1364 Clifton Rd *Web:* www.emoryhealthcare.org	Atlanta	GA	30322	404-712-2000	686-8500
Fairview Park Hospital 200 Industrial Blvd *Web:* www.fairviewparkhospital.com	Dublin	GA	31021	478-275-2000	272-0211
Floyd Medical Ctr 304 Turner McCall Blvd *Web:* www.floyd.org	Rome	GA	30165	706-509-5000	509-6901
Grady Health System 80 Jesse Hill Jr Dr SE *Web:* www.gradyhealthsystem.org	Atlanta	GA	30303	404-616-1000	616-6828
Gwinnett Medical Center Lawrenceville 1000 Medical Ctr Blvd *Fax Area Code: 770 ■ *Web:* www.gwinnettmedicalcenter.org	Lawrenceville	GA	30046	678-312-1000	682-2257*
Hamilton Medical Ctr 1200 Memorial Dr PO Box 1168 *Web:* www.hamiltonhealth.com	Dalton	GA	30720	706-278-2105	272-6111
Henry Medical Ctr 1133 Eagle's Landing Pkwy *Web:* www.henrymedical.com	Stockbridge	GA	30281	678-604-1000	604-5580
Houston Medical Ctr 1601 Watson Blvd *Web:* www.hhc.org	Warner Robins	GA	31093	478-922-4281	542-7955
Hutcheson Medical Ctr (HMC) 100 Gross Crescent Cir *Web:* www.hutcheson.org	Fort Oglethorpe	GA	30742	706-858-2000	858-2111
John D Archbold Memorial Hospital 915 Gordon Ave *TF:* 800-341-1009 ■ *Web:* www.archbold.org	Thomasville	GA	31792	229-228-2000	551-8741
Meadows Regional Medical Ctr (MRMC) 1 Meadows Pkwy *Web:* www.meadowsregional.org	Vidalia	GA	30474	912-535-5555	538-5366
Medical Center of Central Georgia 777 Hemlock St *Web:* www.mccg.org	Macon	GA	31201	478-633-1000	633-1702
Medical College of Georgia Hospital & Clinics 1120 15th St *TF:* 800-736-2273 ■ *Web:* www.mcghealth.org	Augusta	GA	30912	706-721-0211	721-1416
Medical Ctr The 710 Ctr St *Web:* www.columbusregional.com/ColumbusContentPage.aspx?nd=2053	Columbus	GA	31901	706-571-1000	571-1216
Memorial Health University Medical Ctr 4700 Waters Ave *Web:* www.memorialhealth.com	Savannah	GA	31404	912-350-8000	350-7073
Memorial Hospital of Adel 706 N Parrish Ave *Web:* www.memorialofadel.com	Adel	GA	31620	229-896-8000	896-8001
Newton Medical Ctr 5126 Hospital Dr NE *Web:* www.newtonmedical.com	Covington	GA	30014	770-786-7053	385-4256
North Fulton Hospital 3000 Hospital Blvd *TF:* 877-228-3638 ■ *Web:* www.northfultonregional.com	Roswell	GA	30076	770-751-2500	751-2912
Northeast Georgia Health System Inc (NGHS) 743 Spring St NE *Web:* www.nghs.com	Gainesville	GA	30501	770-535-3553	718-5465
Northside Hospital 1000 Johnson Ferry Rd NE *Web:* www.northside.com	Atlanta	GA	30342	404-851-8000	250-1317
Oconee Regional Medical Ctr 821 N Cobb St *Web:* www.oconeeregional.com	Milledgeville	GA	31061	478-454-3500	454-3555
Palmyra Medical Centers (PMC) 2000 Palmyra Rd *Web:* www.palmyramedicalcenters.com	Albany	GA	31701	229-434-2000	434-2563
Phoebe Putney Memorial Hospital 417 W 3rd Ave *TF:* 877-312-1167 ■ *Web:* www.phoebeputney.com	Albany	GA	31702	229-312-1000	312-4104
Phoebe Sumter Medical Ctr 1048 E Forsyth St *Web:* www.phoebesumter.org	Americus	GA	31709	229-924-6011	924-1014
Piedmont Hospital 1968 Peachtree Rd NW *Web:* www.piedmonthospital.org	Atlanta	GA	30309	404-605-5000	609-6640
Piedmont Newnan Hospital (PNH) 60 Hospital Rd *Web:* www.piedmontnewnan.org	Newnan	GA	30263	770-253-1912	254-3406
Redmond Regional Medical Ctr 501 Redmond Rd *Web:* www.redmondregional.com	Rome	GA	30165	706-291-0291	291-0971
Rockdale Medical Ctr (RMC) 1412 Milstead Ave NE *Web:* www.rockdalemedicalcenter.org	Conyers	GA	30012	770-918-3000	918-3104
Saint Francis Hospital 2122 Manchester Expy *Web:* www.sfhga.com	Columbus	GA	31904	706-596-4000	596-4481
Saint Joseph Hospital 2260 Wrightsboro Rd *Fax: Admitting ■ *Web:* www.stjoshosp.org	Augusta	GA	30904	706-481-7000	481-7826*
Saint Joseph's Hospital 11705 Mercy Blvd *Web:* www.sjchs.org	Savannah	GA	31419	912-819-4100	819-5188
Saint Joseph's Hospital of Atlanta 5665 Peachtree Dunwoody Rd NE *TF:* 800-678-5637 ■ *Web:* www.stjosephsatlanta.org	Atlanta	GA	30342	404-851-7001	851-7339
Saint Mary's Health Care System 1230 Baxter St *TF:* 800-233-7864 ■ *Web:* www.stmarysathens.org	Athens	GA	30606	706-389-3000	354-3197
South Georgia Medical Ctr 2501 N Patterson St *Web:* www.sgmc.org	Valdosta	GA	31602	229-333-1000	259-4136
Southeast Georgia Health System Brunswick Campus 2415 Parkwood Dr *Web:* www.sghs.org	Brunswick	GA	31520	912-466-7000	466-7013
Southern Regional Medical Ctr 11 Upper Riverdale Rd SW *Web:* www.southernregional.com	Riverdale	GA	30274	770-991-8000	909-2030
Spalding Regional Medical Ctr 601 S 8th St *Web:* www.spaldingregionalhosp.com	Griffin	GA	30224	770-228-2721	229-6953
Stephens County Hospital 2003 Falls Rd	Toccoa	GA	30577	706-282-4200	886-8045
Tanner Medical Ctr 705 Dixie St *Web:* www.tanner.org	Carrollton	GA	30117	770-836-9666	838-8483
Tift Regional Medical Ctr 1641 Madison Ave *TF:* 800-648-1935 ■ *Web:* www.tiftregional.com	Tifton	GA	31794	229-382-7120	353-6192
University Health Care System 1350 Walton Way *Web:* www.universityhealth.org	Augusta	GA	30901	706-722-9011	774-4500
Upson Regional Medical Ctr 801 W Gordon St *Web:* www.urmc.org	Thomaston	GA	30286	706-647-8111	646-3310
Wayne Memorial Hospital (WMH) 865 S 1st St *Web:* www.wmhweb.com	Jesup	GA	31545	912-427-6811	530-3495
Wellstar Cobb Hospital 3950 Austell Rd *Web:* www.wellstar.org	Austell	GA	30106	770-732-4000	732-3703
Wellstar Douglas Hospital 8954 Hospital Dr *Web:* www.wellstar.org	Douglasville	GA	30134	770-949-1500	920-6253
Wellstar Kennestone Hospital 677 Church St *Web:* www.wellstar.org	Marietta	GA	30060	770-793-5000	793-5918
West Georgia Medical Ctr 1514 Vernon Rd *TF:* 800-291-4418 ■ *Web:* www.wghs.org	LaGrange	GA	30240	706-882-1411	845-8918

HAWAII

Hospital	City	State	Zip	Phone	Fax
Castle Medical Ctr 640 Ulukahiki St *Web:* www.castlemed.org	Kailua	HI	96734	808-263-5500	263-5143
Hilo Medical Ctr 1190 Waianuenue Ave *Web:* www.hmc.hhsc.org	Hilo	HI	96720	808-974-4700	974-4746
Kaiser Permanente Medical Ctr 3288 Moanalua Rd	Honolulu	HI	96819	808-432-0000	432-7736
Maui Memorial Hospital 221 Mahalani St *Web:* www.mmmc.hhsc.org	Wailuku	HI	96793	808-244-9056	243-4628
Queen's Medical Ctr The 1301 Punchbowl St *Web:* www.queensmedicalcenter.net	Honolulu	HI	96813	808-538-9011	537-7851
Saint Francis Medical Ctr 2230 Liliha St *Web:* www.stfrancishawaii.org/sfhs	Honolulu	HI	96817	808-547-6011	547-6611
Straub Clinic & Hospital 888 S King St *TF:* 800-232-9491 ■ *Web:* www.whawaiipacific.org	Honolulu	HI	96813	808-522-4000	522-4111
Wilcox Memorial Hospital (WMH) 3-3420 Kuhio Hwy *Web:* www.wilcoxhealth.org	Lihue	HI	96766	808-245-1100	245-1171

IDAHO

Hospital	City	State	Zip	Phone	Fax
Eastern Idaho Regional Medical Ctr (EIRMC) 3100 Channing Way *Web:* www.eirmc.com	Idaho Falls	ID	83404	208-529-6111	529-7021
Kootenai Medical Ctr 2003 Lincoln Way *Web:* www.kootenaihealth.org	Coeur d"Alene	ID	83814	208-666-2000	666-3299
Portneuf Medical Ctr 651 Memorial Dr *Web:* www.portmed.org	Pocatello	ID	83201	208-239-1000	239-1934
Saint Alphonsus Regional Medical Ctr 1055 N Curtis Rd *TF:* 877-341-2121 ■ *Web:* www.saintalphonsus.org	Boise	ID	83706	208-367-2121	
Saint Joseph Regional Medical Ctr 415 6th St *Web:* www.sjrmc.org	Lewiston	ID	83501	208-743-2511	799-5528
Saint Luke's Regional Medical Ctr 190 E Bannock St *Web:* www.slrmc.org	Boise	ID	83712	208-381-2222	381-2861
West Valley Medical Ctr 1717 Arlington Ave *TF:* 800-937-8860 ■ *Web:* www.westvalleymedctr.com	Caldwell	ID	83605	208-459-4641	455-3717

ILLINOIS

Hospital	City	State	Zip	Phone	Fax
Adventist Hinsdale Hospital 120 N Oak St *Web:* www.keepingyouwell.com/facilities/hinsdale	Hinsdale	IL	60521	630-856-9000	856-2021
Adventist La Grange Memorial Hospital (ALMH) 5101 S Willow Springs Rd *Web:* www.keepingyouwell.com/Facilities/lagrange	La Grange	IL	60525	708-245-9000	245-5646
Advocate Bethany Hospital 3435 W Van Buren St *Web:* www.advocatehealth.com/beth	Chicago	IL	60624	773-265-7700	265-3605
Advocate BroMenn Medical Ctr (ABMC) 1304 Franklin Ave *Web:* www.advocatehealth.com/bromenn/default.cfm?id=1	Normal	IL	61761	309-454-1400	454-0103
Advocate Christ Medical Ctr 4440 W 95th St *Web:* www.advocatehealth.com	Oak Lawn	IL	60453	708-684-8000	684-5012
Advocate Condell Medical Ctr (ACMC) 801 S Milwaukee Ave *Web:* www.advocatehealth.com/condell	Libertyville	IL	60048	847-362-2900	362-1721
Advocate Good Samaritan Hospital 3815 Highland Ave *Web:* www.advocatehealth.com	Downers Grove	IL	60515	630-275-5900	963-8605
Advocate Good Shepherd Hospital (AGSH) 450 W Hwy 22 PO Box 70014 *Web:* www.advocatehealth.com/gshp	Barrington	IL	60010	847-381-9600	381-8074
Advocate Illinois Masonic Medical Ctr 836 W Wellington Ave *Web:* www.advocatehealth.com	Chicago	IL	60657	773-975-1600	296-5251
Advocate Lutheran General Hospital 1775 W Dempster St *Web:* www.advocatehealth.com	Park Ridge	IL	60068	847-723-2210	723-2285
Advocate South Suburban Hospital (SSUB) 17800 S Kedzie Ave *Web:* www.advocatehealth.com/ssub	Hazel Crest	IL	60429	708-799-8000	213-0100
Advocate Trinity Hospital 2320 E 93rd St *Web:* www.advocatehealth.com/trin	Chicago	IL	60617	773-967-2000	967-4191
Alexian Bros Medical Ctr 800 Biesterfield Rd *Web:* www.alexianbrothershealth.org	Elk Grove Village	IL	60007	847-437-5500	981-5774
Alton Memorial Hospital 1 Memorial Dr *Web:* www.altonmemorialhospital.org	Alton	IL	62002	618-463-7311	463-7723

	City	State	ZIP	Phone	Fax
Anderson Hospital 6800 SR 162 *Web:* www.andersonhospital.org	Maryville	IL	62062	618-288-5711	288-4088
Blessing Hospital Broadway at 11th St *Web:* www.blessinghospital.org	Quincy	IL	62301	217-223-5811	223-6891
Carle Foundation Hospital 611 W Pk St *Web:* www.carle.org	Urbana	IL	61801	217-383-3311	383-3018
Centegra Memorial Medical Ctr 3701 Doty Rd *TF:* 877-236-8347 ■ *Web:* www.centegra.org	Woodstock	IL	60098	815-338-2500	334-3948
Centegra Northern Illinois Medical Ctr 4201 Medical Ctr Dr *Web:* www.centegra.org	McHenry	IL	60050	815-344-5000	759-4387
Central DuPage Hospital 25 N Winfield Rd *TF:* 877-933-1600 ■ *Web:* www.cdh.org	Winfield	IL	60190	630-933-1600	933-2729
CGH Medical Ctr (CGHMC) 100 E LeFevre Rd *Web:* www.cghmc.com	Sterling	IL	61081	815-625-0400	625-4825
Community Hospital of Ottawa 1100 E Norris Dr *Web:* www.chottawa.org	Ottawa	IL	61350	815-433-3100	431-5500
Decatur Memorial Hospital 2300 N Edward St *Web:* www.dmhcares.org	Decatur	IL	62526	217-877-8121	876-2125
Delnor-Community Hospital (DCH) 300 Randall Rd *TF:* 800-835-2696 ■ *Web:* www.delnor.com	Geneva	IL	60134	630-208-3000	208-3478
Edward Hospital 801 S Washington St *Web:* www.edward.org	Naperville	IL	60540	630-355-0450	
Elmhurst Memorial Hospital 155 E Brushill Rd *Web:* www.emhc.org	Elmhurst	IL	60126	630-833-1400	782-7801
Evanston Hospital 2650 Ridge Ave *Web:* www.northshore.org/about-us/organization-profile/#EH	Evanston	IL	60201	847-570-2000	570-2940
FHN Memorial Hospital 1045 W Stephenson St *TF:* 800-747-4131 ■ *Web:* www.fhn.org	Freeport	IL	61032	815-599-6000	599-6868
Franciscan Saint JamesHealth 1423 Chicago Rd *TF:* 800-785-2637 ■ *Web:* www.stjameshospital.org	Chicago Heights	IL	60411	708-756-1000	756-6863
Galesburg Cottage Hospital (GCH) 695 N Kellogg St *Web:* www.cottagehospital.com	Galesburg	IL	61401	309-343-8131	343-2393
Gateway Regional Medical Ctr (GRMC) 2100 Madison Ave *TF:* 800-559-9992 ■ *Web:* www.gatewayregional.net	Granite City	IL	62040	618-798-3000	798-3508
Genesis Medical Center Illini Campus 801 Illini Dr *TF:* 800-250-6020 ■ *Web:* www.genesishealth.com	Silvis	IL	61282	309-792-9363	792-4274
GlenOaks Hospital 701 Winthrop Ave *Web:* www.keepingyouwell.com	Glendale Heights	IL	60139	630-545-8000	545-3920
Gottlieb Memorial Hospital 701 W N Ave *Web:* www.gottliebhospital.org	Melrose Park	IL	60160	708-681-3200	450-5058
Graham Hospital 210 W Walnut St *Web:* www.grahamhospital.org	Canton	IL	61520	309-647-5240	649-5101
Herrin Hospital 201 S 14th St *Web:* www.herrinhospital.org	Herrin	IL	62948	618-942-2171	351-4929
Highland Park Hospital 777 Pk Ave W *Web:* www.northshore.org	Highland Park	IL	60035	847-432-8000	432-9305
Holy Cross Hospital 2701 W 68th St *Web:* www.holycrosshospital.org	Chicago	IL	60629	773-884-9000	884-8001
Holy Family Medical Ctr 100 N River Rd *Web:* www.reshealth.org	Des Plaines	IL	60016	847-297-1800	297-1863
Illinois Valley Community Hospital 925 W St *Web:* www.ivch.org	Peru	IL	61354	815-223-3300	780-3714
Ingalls Memorial Hospital 1 Ingalls Dr *Web:* www.ingalls.org	Harvey	IL	60426	708-333-2300	915-6136
John H Stoger Hospital of Cook County 1901 W Harrison St *Web:* www.ccbhs.org	Chicago	IL	60612	312-864-6000	864-3070
Katherine Shaw Bethea Hospital 403 E 1st St *Web:* www.ksbhospital.com	Dixon	IL	61021	815-288-5531	285-5859
Kishwaukee Community Hospital 1 Kish Hospital Dr *TF:* 800-397-1521 ■ *Web:* www.kishhospital.org	DeKalb	IL	60115	815-756-1521	756-7665
Lake Forest Hospital 660 N Westmoreland Rd *Web:* www.lakeforesthospital.com	Lake Forest	IL	60045	847-234-5600	535-7846
Little Co of Mary Hospital & Health Care Centers 2800 W 95th St *Web:* www.lcmh.org	Evergreen Park	IL	60805	708-422-6200	425-9756
Loretto Hospital 645 S Central Ave *Web:* www.lorettohospital.org	Chicago	IL	60644	773-626-4300	626-2613
Louis A Weiss Memorial Hospital 4646 N Marine Dr *Web:* www.weisshospital.org	Chicago	IL	60640	773-878-8700	564-7287
Loyola University Medical Ctr 2160 S 1st Ave *TF:* 888-584-7888 ■ *Web:* www.luhs.org	Maywood	IL	60153	708-216-9000	216-6791
MacNeal Hospital 3249 S Oak Pk Ave *TF:* 888-622-6325 ■ *Web:* www.macneal.com	Berwyn	IL	60402	708-795-9100	783-3489
Memorial Hospital 4500 Memorial Dr *Web:* www.memhosp.com	Belleville	IL	62226	618-233-7750	257-5658
Memorial Hospital of Carbondale 405 W Jackson St *Web:* www.sih.net	Carbondale	IL	62902	618-549-0721	529-0449
Memorial Medical Ctr 701 N 1st St *Web:* www.memorialmedical.com	Springfield	IL	62781	217-788-3000	788-5591
Mercy Hospital & Medical Ctr (MHMC) 2525 S Michigan Ave *Web:* www.mercy-chicago.org	Chicago	IL	60616	312-567-2000	567-7054
Methodist Hospital of Chicago (MHC) 5025 N Paulina St *Web:* www.methodistchicago.org	Chicago	IL	60640	773-271-9040	989-1321
Methodist Medical Center of Illinois 221 NE Glen Oak Ave *Web:* www.mymethodist.net	Peoria	IL	61636	309-672-5522	672-4230
Metro South Medical Ctr 12935 S Gregory St *Web:* www.metrosouthmedicalcenter.com	Blue Island	IL	60406	708-597-2000	489-7773
Morris Hospital 150 W High St *Web:* www.morrishospital.org	Morris	IL	60450	815-942-2932	942-3154
Mount Sinai Hospital Medical Center of Chicago 1500 S Fairfield St *Web:* www.sinai.org	Chicago	IL	60608	773-542-2000	257-6943
North Shore Skokie Hospital 9600 Gross Pt Rd *Web:* www.northshore.org/emergency-medicine/skokie-hospital	Skokie	IL	60076	847-677-9600	933-6012
Northwest Community Hospital 800 W Central Rd *Web:* www.nch.org	Arlington Heights	IL	60005	847-618-1000	618-5009
Northwestern Memorial Hospital 251 E Huron St *Web:* www.nmh.org	Chicago	IL	60611	312-908-2000	926-8111
Norwegian-American Hospital 1044 N Francisco St *Web:* www.n-ahs.org	Chicago	IL	60622	773-292-8200	278-3531
OSF Saint Anthony Medical Ctr 5666 E State St *TF:* 800-343-3185 ■ *Web:* www.osfsaintanthony.org	Rockford	IL	61108	815-226-2000	395-5449
OSF Saint Francis Medical Ctr 530 NE Glen Oak Ave *TF:* 888-627-5673 ■ *Web:* www.osfsaintfrancis.org	Peoria	IL	61637	309-655-2000	655-2347
OSF Saint Joseph Medical Ctr 2200 E Washington St *Web:* www.osfstjoseph.org	Bloomington	IL	61701	309-662-3311	662-7143
OSF Saint Mary Medical Ctr 3333 N Seminary St *Web:* www.osfstmary.org	Galesburg	IL	61401	309-344-3161	344-9498
Our Lady of Resurrection Medical Ctr 5645 W Addison St *Web:* www.reshealth.org	Chicago	IL	60634	773-282-7000	794-7651
Palos Community Hospital 12251 S 80th Ave *Web:* www.paloscommunityhospital.org	Palos Heights	IL	60463	708-361-4500	923-4620
Passavant Area Hospital (PAH) 1600 W Walnut St *Web:* www.passavanthospital.com	Jacksonville	IL	62650	217-245-9541	479-5613
Pekin Hospital 600 S 13th St *Web:* www.pekinhospital.org	Pekin	IL	61554	309-347-1151	353-0908
Proctor Hospital 5409 N Knoxville Ave *Web:* www.proctor.org	Peoria	IL	61614	309-691-1000	691-4543
Provena Covenant Medical Ctr 1400 W Pk St *TF:* 800-245-6697 ■ *Web:* www.provenacovenant.org	Urbana	IL	61801	217-337-2000	337-4541
Provena Mercy Ctr 1325 N Highland Ave	Aurora	IL	60506	630-859-2222	859-9014
Provena Saint Joseph Hospital 77 N Airlite St *Web:* www.provena.org	Elgin	IL	60123	847-695-3200	931-5511
Provena Saint Joseph Medical Ctr (PSJMC) 333 N Madison St *Web:* www.provena.org/stjoes	Joliet	IL	60435	815-725-7133	741-7579
Provena Saint Mary's Hospital 500 W Ct St *Web:* www.provenastmarys.com	Kankakee	IL	60901	815-937-2490	937-8772
Provena United Samaritans Medical Ctr 812 N Logan Ave *Web:* www.provenausmc.com	Danville	IL	61832	217-443-5000	443-1965
Resurrection Medical Ctr 7435 W Talcott Ave *Web:* www.reshealth.org	Chicago	IL	60631	773-774-8000	594-7971
Riverside Medical Ctr (RMC) 350 N Wall St *Web:* www.riversidehealthcare.org	Kankakee	IL	60901	815-933-1671	935-7823
Rockford Memorial Hospital 2400 N Rockton Ave *Web:* www.rhsnet.org	Rockford	IL	61103	815-971-5000	968-4795
Roseland Community Hospital 45 W 111th St	Chicago	IL	60628	773-995-3000	995-1052
Rush Oak Park Hospital (ROPH) 520 S Maple Ave *Web:* www.oakparkhospital.org	Oak Park	IL	60304	708-383-9300	660-6658
Rush University Medical Ctr 1653 W Congress Pkwy *Web:* www.rush.edu	Chicago	IL	60612	312-942-5000	942-3212
Rush-Copley Medical Ctr (RCMC) 2000 Ogden Ave *TF:* 866-426-7539 ■ *Web:* www.rushcopley.com	Aurora	IL	60504	630-978-6200	978-6888
Saint Alexius Medical Ctr 1555 Barrigton Rd *Web:* www.alexianbrothershealth.org	Hoffman Estates	IL	60169	847-843-2000	490-2570
Saint Anthony's Health Ctr 1 St Anthonys Way *Web:* www.sahc.org	Alton	IL	62002	618-465-2571	465-4569
Saint Anthony's Memorial Hospital 503 N Maple St *Web:* www.stanthonyshospital.org	Effingham	IL	62401	217-342-2121	347-1563
Saint Bernard Hospital & Health Care Ctr 326 W 64th St *Web:* www.stbernardhospital.com	Chicago	IL	60621	773-962-3900	602-3849
Saint Elizabeth Hospital 1431 N Claremont Ave **Fax Area Code:* 312 ■ *Web:* www.reshealth.org	Chicago	IL	60622	773-278-2000	850-5970*
Saint Elizabeth's Hospital 211 S 3rd St *Web:* www.steliz.org	Belleville	IL	62220	618-234-2120	222-4650
Saint Francis Hospital of Evanston 355 Ridge Ave *Web:* www.reshealth.org	Evanston	IL	60202	847-492-4000	316-4500
Saint James Hospital & Health Centers Olympia Fields Campus 20201 S Crawford Ave *Web:* www.stjameshospital.org	Olympia Fields	IL	60461	708-747-4000	503-3270
Saint John's Hospital 800 E Carpenter St *Web:* www.st-johns.org	Springfield	IL	62769	217-544-6464	535-3989
Saint Joseph Hospital & Health Care Ctr 2900 N Lake Shore Dr *Web:* www.reshealth.org	Chicago	IL	60657	773-665-3000	665-3861
Saint Mary of Nazareth Hospital Ctr 2233 W Division St *Web:* www.reshealth.org	Chicago	IL	60622	312-770-2000	770-3391
Saint Mary's Good Samaritan 400 N Pleasant Ave *Web:* www.smgsi.com	Centralia	IL	62801	618-532-6731	436-8024

Hospital	City	State	ZIP	Phone	Fax
Saint Mary's Hospital 1800 E Lake Shore Dr. *Web:* www.stmarys-hospital.com	Decatur	IL	62521	217-464-2966	464-1616
Sarah Bush Lincoln Health Ctr (SBLHC) 1000 Health Ctr Dr PO Box 372 *Web:* www.sarahbush.org	Mattoon	IL	61938	217-258-2525	258-4117
Sherman Health 1425 N Randall Rd *TF:* 800-397-9000 ■ *Web:* www.shermanhealth.com	Elgin	IL	60123	847-742-9800	429-2035
Silver Cross Hospital 1200 Maple Rd *Web:* www.silvercross.org	Joliet	IL	60432	815-740-1100	740-7047
South Shore Hospital (SSH) 8012 S Crandon Ave. *Web:* www.southshorehospital.com	Chicago	IL	60617	773-356-5000	768-8154
Swedish Covenant Hospital 5145 N California Ave. *Web:* www.swedishcovenant.org	Chicago	IL	60625	773-878-8200	878-6152
SwedishAmerican Hospital 1401 E State St *TF:* 800-642-2790 ■ *Web:* www.swedishamerican.org	Rockford	IL	61104	815-968-4400	966-3999
Thorek Memorial Hospital 850 W Irving Pk Rd *Web:* www.thorek.org	Chicago	IL	60613	773-525-6780	975-6703
Touchette Regional Hospital (TRH) 5900 Bond Ave *Web:* www.touchette.org	Centreville	IL	62207	618-332-3060	332-5256
Trinity Medical Ctr West Campus (TMC) 2701 17th St. *Web:* www.trinityqc.com	Rock Island	IL	61201	309-779-2800	779-2303
University of Chicago Medical Ctr 5841 S Maryland Ave *TF:* 888-824-0200 ■ *Web:* www.uchospitals.edu	Chicago	IL	60637	773-702-1000	702-4846
University of Illinois Medical Ctr 1740 W Taylor St *TF:* 866-600-2273 ■ *Web:* uillinoismedcenter.org	Chicago	IL	60612	312-996-3900	996-7049
Vista Medical Ctr 1324 N Sheridan Rd *Web:* www.vistahealth.com	Waukegan	IL	60085	847-360-3000	360-4109
Vista West Ctr 2615 Washington St *Web:* www.vistahealth.com/stmcvmh/index.htm	Waukegan	IL	60085	847-249-3900	360-4109
West Suburban Hospital Medical Ctr 3 Erie Ct *Web:* www.westsub.com	Oak Park	IL	60302	708-383-6200	383-3159
Westlake Hospital 1225 W Lake St *Web:* www.wlhospital.com	Melrose Park	IL	60160	708-681-3000	938-7975

INDIANA

Hospital	City	State	ZIP	Phone	Fax
Bloomington Hospital (BHHS) 601 W 2nd St *Web:* www.bhhs.org	Bloomington	IN	47403	812-336-6821	353-9339
Clark Memorial Hospital (CMH) 1220 Missouri Ave *Web:* www.clarkmemorial.org	Jeffersonville	IN	47130	812-282-6631	283-2688
Columbus Regional Hospital 2400 E 17th St *TF:* 800-841-4938 ■ *Web:* www.crh.org	Columbus	IN	47201	812-379-4441	376-5001
Community Hospital 901 Macarthur Blvd. **Fax:* Admitting ■ *Web:* www.comhs.org	Munster	IN	46321	219-836-1600	836-4073*
Community Hospital Anderson (CHA) 1515 N Madison Ave *TF:* 800-430-4774 ■ *Web:* www.communityanderson.com	Anderson	IN	46011	765-298-4242	298-5848
Community Hospital East 1500 N Ritter Ave	Indianapolis	IN	46219	317-355-1411	355-1668
De Kalb Memorial Hospital Inc PO Box 542 *Web:* www.dekalbmemorial.com	Auburn	IN	46706	260-925-4600	
Deaconess Hospital 600 Mary St. *Web:* www.deaconess.com	Evansville	IN	47747	812-450-5000	450-2155
Elkhart General Hospital 600 E Blvd *Web:* www.egh.org	Elkhart	IN	46514	574-294-2621	523-3495
Fayette Regional Health System (FRHS) 1941 Virginia Ave *Web:* www.fayetteregional.org	Connersville	IN	47331	765-825-5131	827-7886
Floyd Memorial Hospital 1850 State St *TF:* 800-423-1513 ■ *Web:* www.floydmemorial.org	New Albany	IN	47150	812-944-7701	949-5607
Good Samaritan Hospital 520 S 7th St *Web:* www.gshvin.org	Vincennes	IN	47591	812-882-5220	885-3737
Hendricks Regional Health Danville 1000 E Main St. *Web:* www.hendricks.org	Danville	IN	46122	317-745-4451	745-8400
Henry County Memorial Hospital (HCM) 1000 N 16th St *Web:* www.hcmhcares.org	New Castle	IN	47362	765-521-0890	521-1555
Howard Regional Health System Main Campus (HRHS) 3500 S Lafountain St *Web:* www.howardregional.org	Kokomo	IN	46902	765-453-0702	453-8087
Indiana University Hospital 550 N University Blvd *TF:* 800-248-1199 ■ *Web:* www.iuhealth.org	Indianapolis	IN	46202	317-274-5000	274-1088
IU Health Ball Memorial Hospital 2401 W University Ave *Web:* www.iuhealth.org	Muncie	IN	47303	765-747-3111	741-2848
Johnson Memorial Hospital (JMH) 1125 W Jefferson St *Web:* www.johnsonmemorial.org	Franklin	IN	46131	317-736-3300	736-2692
King's Daughters' Hospital 1 King's Daughters' Dr *TF:* 800-272-5341 ■ *Web:* www.kingsdaughtershospital.org	Madison	IN	47250	812-265-5211	265-0680
La Porte Hospital (LPH) 1007 Lincolnway PO Box 250 *TF:* 800-235-6204 ■ *Web:* www.iuhealth.org/laporte	La Porte	IN	46350	219-326-1234	325-5403
Lutheran Hospital of Indiana 7950 W Jefferson Blvd *TF:* 800-444-2001 ■ *Web:* www.lutheranhospital.com	Fort Wayne	IN	46804	260-435-7001	435-7632
Major Hospital 150 W Washington St *Web:* www.majorhospital.com	Shelbyville	IN	46176	317-392-3211	
Margaret Mary Community Hospital Inc 321 Mitchell Ave PO Box 226 *Web:* www.mmch.org	Batesville	IN	47006	812-934-6624	934-5373
Marion General Hospital (MGH) 441 N Wabash Ave *Web:* www.mgh.net	Marion	IN	46952	765-662-4000	651-7351
Memorial Hospital & Health Care Ctr 800 W 9th St *Web:* www.mhhcc.org	Jasper	IN	47546	812-482-2345	482-0302
Memorial Hospital of South Bend 615 N Michigan St *Web:* www.qualityoflife.org	South Bend	IN	46601	574-234-9041	647-3670
Methodist Hospital 600 Grant St *Web:* www.methodisthospitals.org	Gary	IN	46402	219-886-4000	886-4688
Methodist Hospital I-65 at 21st PO Box 1367 *Web:* www.iuhealth.org/methodist	Indianapolis	IN	46206	317-962-1425	962-0304
Parkview Hospital 2200 Randallia Dr. *TF:* 888-856-2522 ■ *Web:* www.parkview.com	Fort Wayne	IN	46805	260-373-4000	
Porter-Valparaiso Hospital Campus 814 La Porte Ave. *Web:* www.porterhealth.org	Valparaiso	IN	46383	219-465-4600	263-7067
Reid Hospital & Health Care Services 1100 Reid Pkwy *Web:* www.reidhosp.com	Richmond	IN	47374	765-983-3000	983-3219
Riverview Hospital 395 Westfield Rd *TF:* 800-523-6001 ■ *Web:* www.riverviewhospital.com	Noblesville	IN	46060	317-773-0760	776-7134
Saint Anthony Medical Ctr 1201 S Main St *Web:* www.stanthonymedicalcenter.com	Crown Point	IN	46307	219-738-2100	757-6242
Saint Anthony Memorial Health Ctr 301 W Homer St *TF:* 888-879-8511 ■ *Web:* www.samhc.org	Michigan City	IN	46360	219-879-8511	877-1409
Saint Catherine Hospital 4321 Fir St *Web:* www.comhs.org	East Chicago	IN	46312	219-392-1700	392-7002
Saint Elizabeth Hospital Medical Ctr 1501 Hartford St *TF:* 800-371-6011 ■ *Web:* www.glhsi.org	Lafayette	IN	47904	765-423-6011	423-6364
Saint Francis Hospital & Health Centers 1600 Albany St *Web:* www.stfrancishospitals.org	Beech Grove	IN	46107	317-787-3311	782-6731
Saint John's Health System 2015 Jackson St. *Web:* www.stjohnshealthsystem.org	Anderson	IN	46016	765-649-2511	646-8504
Saint Joseph Hospital 700 Broadway *TF:* 800-755-5266 ■ *Web:* www.lutheranhealth.net	Fort Wayne	IN	46802	260-425-3000	425-3108
Saint Joseph Regional Medical Center Mishawaka 5215 Holy Cross Pkwy *Web:* www.sjmed.com	Mishawaka	IN	46545	574-335-5000	
Saint Joseph Regional Medical Ctr 801 E La Salle Ave *Web:* www.sjmed.com	South Bend	IN	46617	574-237-7111	237-7077
Saint Margaret Mercy Healthcare Centers 5454 Hohman Ave *Web:* www.smmhc.com	Hammond	IN	46320	219-932-2300	933-2585
Saint Mary Medical Ctr 1500 S Lake Pk Ave. *Web:* www.comhs.org/stmary	Hobart	IN	46342	219-942-0551	947-6037
Saint Mary's Medical Center of Evansville 3700 Washington Ave. *Web:* www.stmarys.org	Evansville	IN	47750	812-485-4000	485-7080
Saint Vincent Indianapolis Hospital 2001 W 86th St. *TF:* 866-338-2345 ■ *Web:* www.stvincent.org	Indianapolis	IN	46260	317-338-2345	338-7005
Schneck Medical Ctr 411 W Tipton St *TF:* 800-234-9222 ■ *Web:* www.schneckmed.org	Seymour	IN	47274	812-522-2349	522-0792
St Vincent Dunn Hospital 1600 23rd St *Web:* www.stvincent.org	Bedford	IN	47421	812-275-3331	276-1211
Terre Haute Regional Hospital (THRH) 3901 S 7th St *TF:* 800-678-8474 ■ *Web:* www.regionalhospital.com	Terre Haute	IN	47802	812-232-0021	237-9514
Union Hospital 1606 N 7th St *Web:* www.myunionhospital.org/index-normal.php	Terre Haute	IN	47804	812-238-7000	238-7113
Urology of Indiana LLC 679 E County Line Rd *Web:* www.urologyin.com	Greenwood	IN	46143	317-885-1250	
Wishard Health Services 1001 W 10th St. *Web:* www.wishard.edu	Indianapolis	IN	46202	317-639-6671	630-7678
Witham Memorial Hospital PO Box 1200 *Web:* www.witham.org	Lebanon	IN	46052	765-485-8000	
Women's Health Partnership PC 11595 N Meridian St Suite 110 *Web:* www.whp.com	Carmel	IN	46032	317-575-7300	575-7333

IOWA

Hospital	City	State	ZIP	Phone	Fax
Allen Memorial Hospital 1825 Logan Ave *Web:* www.allenhospital.org	Waterloo	IA	50703	319-235-3941	235-3906
Broadlawns Medical Ctr 1801 Hickman Rd *TF:* 800-373-2806 ■ *Web:* www.broadlawns.org	Des Moines	IA	50314	515-282-2200	282-8874
Buena Vista Regional Medical Ctr PO Box 309 *TF:* 877-401-8030 ■ *Web:* www.bvrmc.org	Storm Lake	IA	50588	712-732-4030	
Covenant Medical Ctr 3421 W 9th St *Web:* www.covhealth.com	Waterloo	IA	50702	319-272-8000	272-7313
Finley Hospital 350 N Grandview Ave *TF:* 800-582-1891 ■ *Web:* www.finleyhospital.org	Dubuque	IA	52001	563-582-1881	589-2562
Genesis Medical Ctr 1227 E Rusholme St *Web:* www.genesishealth.com	Davenport	IA	52803	563-421-6000	421-6500
Great River Health Systems 1221 S Gear Ave *Web:* www.greatrivermedical.org	West Burlington	IA	52655	319-768-1000	
Great River Medical Ctr 1221 S Gear Ave *Web:* www.greatrivermedical.org	West Burlington	IA	52655	319-768-1000	768-3266
Iowa Lutheran Hospital 700 E University Ave *Web:* www.iowahealth.org	Des Moines	IA	50316	515-263-5227	263-2205

Hospital	City	State	ZIP	Phone	Fax
Iowa Methodist Medical Ctr (IMMC) 1200 Pleasant St. *Web:* www.iowahealth.org/iowa-methodist-medical-center.aspx	Des Moines	IA	50309	515-241-6212	241-5994
Jennie Edmundson Hospital 933 E Pierce St *Web:* www.bestcare.org	Council Bluffs	IA	51503	712-328-6000	396-6288
Keokuk Area Hospital 1600 Morgan St *Web:* www.keokukhealthsystems.org	Keokuk	IA	52632	319-524-7150	524-5317
Marshalltown Medical & Surgical Ctr 3 S 4th Ave *Web:* www.everydaychampions.org	Marshalltown	IA	50158	641-754-5151	754-5181
Mary Greeley Medical Ctr 1111 Duff Ave *Web:* www.mgmc.org	Ames	IA	50010	515-239-2011	239-2007
Mercy Hospital 800 Mercy Dr *Web:* www.alegent.com	Council Bluffs	IA	51503	712-328-5000	325-2425
Mercy Iowa City 500 E Market St *TF:* 800-637-2942 ■ *Web:* www.mercyic.org	Iowa City	IA	52245	319-339-0300	339-3788
Mercy Medical Center North Iowa 1000 4th St SW *TF:* 800-433-3883 ■ *Web:* www.mercynorthiowa.com	Mason City	IA	50401	641-422-7000	422-7827
Mercy Medical Ctr (MMC) 801 5th St *Web:* www.mercysiouxcity.com	Sioux City	IA	51102	712-279-2010	279-2034
Mercy Medical Ctr 1111 6th Ave *TF:* 800-637-2993 ■ *Web:* www.mercydesmoines.org	Des Moines	IA	50314	515-247-3121	247-4259
Mercy Medical Ctr 701 10th St SE *Web:* www.mercycare.org	Cedar Rapids	IA	52403	319-398-6011	398-6912
Mercy Medical Ctr 250 Mercy Dr *Web:* www.mercydubuque.com	Dubuque	IA	52001	563-589-8000	589-8073
Orange City Area Health System 1000 Lincoln Cir SE *TF:* 800-808-6264 ■ *Web:* www.ochealthsystem.org	Orange City	IA	51041	712-737-4984	
Ottumwa Regional Health Ctr (ORHC) 1001 Pennsylvania Ave *TF:* 800-933-6742 ■ *Web:* www.orhc.com	Ottumwa	IA	52501	641-684-2300	684-2324
Saint Luke's Hospital (SLH) 1026 A Ave NE *Web:* www.stlukescr.org	Cedar Rapids	IA	52406	319-369-7211	369-8105
Saint Luke's Regional Medical Ctr 2720 Stone Pk Blvd *TF:* 800-352-4660 ■ *Web:* www.stlukes.org	Sioux City	IA	51104	712-279-3500	279-7958
Trinity Regional Medical Ctr (TRMC) 802 Kenyon Rd *Web:* www.trmc.org	Fort Dodge	IA	50501	515-573-3101	573-8710
University of Iowa Hospitals & Clinics 200 Hawkins Dr *Web:* www.uihealthcare.com	Iowa City	IA	52242	319-356-1616	356-3862

KANSAS

Hospital	City	State	ZIP	Phone	Fax
Central Kansas Medical Ctr 3515 Broadway St *Web:* www.ckmc.org	Great Bend	KS	67530	620-792-2511	786-6298
Coffeyville Regional Medical Ctr 1400 W 4th St *TF:* 800-540-2762 ■ *Web:* www.crmcinc.com	Coffeyville	KS	67337	620-251-1200	252-1651
Hays Medical Ctr (HMC) 2220 Canterbury Dr *TF:* 800-248-0073 ■ *Web:* www.portal.haysmed.com/portal/page?_pageid=43,1&_dad=portal&_schema=PORTAL	Hays	KS	67601	785-650-2759	623-2291
Lawrence Memorial Hospital (LMH) 325 Maine St *TF:* 800-749-4144 ■ *Web:* www.lmh.org	Lawrence	KS	66044	785-505-5000	749-6126
Menorah Medical Ctr 5721 W 119th St *Web:* www.menorahmedicalcenter.com	Overland Park	KS	66209	913-498-6000	345-3716
Mercy Health Center Fort Scott 401 Woodland Hills Blvd *TF:* 888-637-2937 ■ *Web:* www.mercykansas.com/visitorinfo/ftscott/default.asp	Fort Scott	KS	66701	620-223-2200	223-5327
Newman Regional Health 1201 W 12th Ave *Web:* www.newmanrh.org	Emporia	KS	66801	620-343-6800	341-7801
Olathe Medical Ctr 20333 W 151st St *Web:* www.olathehealth.org	Olathe	KS	66061	913-791-4200	791-4313
Overland Park Regional Medical Ctr 10500 Quivira Rd *Web:* www.oprmc.com	Overland Park	KS	66215	913-541-5000	541-5035
Pratt Regional Medical Center Corp 200 Commodore St *TF:* 877-572-2787 ■ *Web:* www.prmc.org	Pratt	KS	67124	620-672-7451	672-2113
Promise Regional Medical Ctr-Hutchinson 1701 E 23rd Ave *TF:* 800-794-7212 ■ *Web:* www.promiseregional.com	Hutchinson	KS	67502	620-665-2000	513-3811
Providence Medical Ctr 8929 Parallel Pkwy	Kansas City	KS	66112	913-596-4000	596-4098
Saint Catherine Hospital (SCH) 401 E Spruce St *Web:* www.stcath-hosp.org	Garden City	KS	67846	620-272-2222	272-2566
Saint Francis Health Ctr 1700 SW 7th St *TF:* 800-444-2954 ■ *Web:* www.stfrancistopeka.org	Topeka	KS	66606	785-295-8000	295-5479
Saint John Hospital Incorporated of Kansas 3500 S 4th St *Web:* www.providence-health.org	Leavenworth	KS	66048	913-680-6000	680-6013
Salina Regional Health Ctr 400 S Santa Fe Ave *Web:* www.srhc.com	Salina	KS	67401	785-452-7000	452-6963
Shawnee Mission Medical Ctr 9100 W 74th St *Web:* www.shawneemission.org	Shawnee Mission	KS	66204	913-676-2000	676-7792
Stormont-Vail Regional Health Ctr 1500 SW 10th Ave *TF:* 800-432-2951 ■ *Web:* www.stormontvail.org	Topeka	KS	66604	785-354-6000	354-6926
University of Kansas Hospital 3901 Rainbow Blvd *Web:* www.kumed.com	Kansas City	KS	66160	913-588-1270	588-1280
Via Christi Hospital in Pittsburg 1102 E Centennial St *Web:* www.via-christi.org	Pittsburg	KS	66762	620-231-6100	232-0493
Via Christi Regional Medical Ctr 929 N St Francis St *Web:* www.via-christi.org	Wichita	KS	67214	316-268-5000	291-7999
Wesley Medical Ctr 550 N Hillside St *TF:* 800-362-0288 ■ *Web:* www.wesleymc.com	Wichita	KS	67214	316-962-2000	962-7076
Western Plains Medical Complex 3001 Ave A *Web:* www.westernplainsmc.com	Dodge City	KS	67801	620-225-8400	225-8403

KENTUCKY

Hospital	City	State	ZIP	Phone	Fax
ARH Regional Medical Ctr 100 Medical Ctr Dr *Web:* www.arh.org	Hazard	KY	41701	606-439-1331	439-6682
Baptist Hospital East 4000 Kresge Way *Web:* www.baptisteast.com	Louisville	KY	40207	502-897-8100	897-8500
Baptist Regional Medical Ctr 1 Trillium Way	Corbin	KY	40701	606-528-1212	523-8726
Central Baptist Hospital 1740 Nicholasville Rd	Lexington	KY	40503	859-275-6100	260-6119
Clark Regional Medical Center Inc PO Box 630 *TF:* 800-568-1216 ■ *Web:* www.clarkregional.org	Winchester	KY	40392	859-745-3500	744-6408
Ephraim McDowell Regional Medical Ctr 217 S 3rd St *TF:* 800-686-4121 ■ *Web:* www.emhealth.org	Danville	KY	40422	859-239-1000	239-6709
Frankfort Regional Medical Ctr 299 King's Daughters Dr *Web:* www.frankfortregional.com	Frankfort	KY	40601	502-875-5240	226-7936
Greenview Regional Hospital 1801 Ashley Cir *Web:* www.greenviewhospital.com	Bowling Green	KY	42104	270-793-1000	793-5205
Hardin Memorial Hospital 913 W Dixie Ave *Web:* www.hmh.net	Elizabethtown	KY	42701	270-737-1212	706-1141
Harlan ARH Hospital 81 Ballpark Rd *Web:* www.arh.org	Harlan	KY	40831	606-573-8100	573-8200
Highlands Regional Medical Ctr 5000 KY Rt 321 *TF:* 800-533-4762 ■ *Web:* www.hrmc.org	Prestonsburg	KY	41653	606-886-8511	886-1316
Jackson Purchase Medical Ctr 1099 Medical Ctr Cir *TF:* 800-251-1099 ■ *Web:* www.jacksonpurchase.com	Mayfield	KY	42066	270-251-4100	251-4507
Jennie Stuart Medical Ctr 320 W 18th St PO Box 400 *TF:* 800-887-5762 ■ *Web:* www.jsmc.org	Hopkinsville	KY	42241	270-887-0100	887-0223
Kindred Hospital Louisville 1313 St Anthony Pl *Web:* www.kindredlouisville.com	Louisville	KY	40204	502-587-7001	587-0060
King's Daughters Medical Ctr 2201 Lexington Ave *Web:* www.kdmc.com	Ashland	KY	41101	606-327-4000	327-7532
Lake Cumberland Regional Hospital 305 Langdon St *Web:* www.lcrh.ky	Somerset	KY	42503	606-679-7441	678-9919
Lourdes Hospital 1530 Lone Oak Rd *Web:* www.ehealthconnection.com/regions/lourdes	Paducah	KY	42003	270-444-2444	444-2980
Meadowview Regional Medical Ctr (MRMC) 989 Medical Pk Dr *Web:* www.meadowviewregional.com	Maysville	KY	41056	606-759-5311	759-5616
Medical Ctr The 250 Pk St *Web:* www.mcbg.org	Bowling Green	KY	42101	270-745-1268	842-0765
Methodist Hospital 1305 N Elm St *TF:* 800-467-7766 ■ *Web:* www.methodisthospital.net	Henderson	KY	42420	270-827-7700	827-7402
Middlesboro Appalachian Regional Hospital 3600 W Cumberland Ave *Web:* www.arh.org/middlesboro	Middlesboro	KY	40965	606-242-1100	248-1018
Muhlenberg Community Hospital 440 Hopkinsville St *Web:* www.mchky.org	Greenville	KY	42345	270-338-8000	338-8278
Murray-Calloway County Hospital 803 Poplar St *Web:* www.murrayhospital.org	Murray	KY	42071	270-762-1100	767-3600
Norton Audubon Hospital 1 Audobon Plaza Dr *Web:* www.nortonhealthcare.com	Louisville	KY	40217	502-636-7111	636-7216
Norton Hospital 200 E Chestnut St *Web:* www.nortonhealthcare.com	Louisville	KY	40202	502-629-8000	629-6060
Norton Suburban Hospital 4001 Dutchmans Ln *Web:* www.nortonhealthcare.com	Louisville	KY	40207	502-893-1000	899-6131
Our Lady of Bellefonte Hospital 1000 St Christopher Dr *Web:* www.olbh.com	Ashland	KY	41101	606-833-3333	833-3593
Owensboro Medical Health Systems (OMHS) 811 E Parish Ave PO Box 20007 *TF:* 877-888-6647 ■ *Web:* www.omhs.org	Owensboro	KY	42303	270-688-2000	688-1492
Pikeville Medical Ctr 911 Bypass Rd *Web:* www.medicalleader.org	Pikeville	KY	41501	606-437-3500	432-9479
Pineville Community Hospital 850 Riverview Ave	Pineville	KY	40977	606-337-3051	337-4284
Regional Medical Ctr 900 Hospital Dr *TF:* 800-998-5100 ■ *Web:* www.troverfoundation.org/about/about_rmc	Madisonville	KY	42431	270-825-5100	825-5204
Saint Claire Regional Medical Ctr 222 Medical Cir *Web:* www.st-claire.org	Morehead	KY	40351	606-783-6500	783-6503
Saint Elizabeth Healthcare - Covington 1500 James Simpson Jr Way *Web:* www.stelizabeth.com	Covington	KY	41011	859-655-8800	
Saint Joseph Hospital 1 St Joseph Dr **Fax:* Admitting ■ *Web:* www.sjhlex.org	Lexington	KY	40504	859-313-1000	313-3000*
Saint Joseph Hospital East 150 N Eagle Creek Dr *Web:* www.sjhlex.org	Lexington	KY	40509	859-967-5000	967-5332

	City	State	Zip	Phone	Fax
Saint Luke Hospital West 7380 Turfway Rd *TF:* 800-345-7151	Florence	KY	41042	859-212-5200	212-4411
Saints Mary & Elizabeth Hospital 1850 Bluegrass Ave *Web:* www.jhsmh.org	Louisville	KY	40215	502-361-6000	361-6799
Taylor Regional Hospital 1700 Old Lebanon Rd *Web:* www.tchosp.org	Campbellsville	KY	42718	270-465-3561	465-3465
TJ Samson Community Hospital 1301 N Race St *TF:* 800-651-5635 ■ *Web:* www.tjsamson.org	Glasgow	KY	42141	270-651-4444	651-4848
UK Good Samaritan Hospital 310 S Limestone St *Web:* www.samaritanhospital.com	Lexington	KY	40508	859-252-6612	226-7154
University of Kentucky Chandler Medical Ctr 800 Rose St *Web:* www.mc.uky.edu	Lexington	KY	40536	859-323-5000	323-2044
University of Louisville Hospital 530 S Jackson St *Web:* www.uoflhealthcare.org	Louisville	KY	40202	502-562-3000	562-4368
Western Baptist Hospital (WBH) 2501 Kentucky Ave	Paducah	KY	42003	270-575-2100	575-2164
Whitesburg Appalachian Regional Hospital (ARH) 240 Hospital Rd *Web:* www.arh.org/Whitesburg/default.php	Whitesburg	KY	41858	606-633-3500	633-3652
Williamson ARH Hospital 260 Hospital Dr *TF:* 800-283-9375 ■ *Web:* www.arh.org/Williamson	South Williamson	KY	41503	606-237-1700	237-1701

LOUISIANA

	City	State	Zip	Phone	Fax
American Legion Hospital 1305 Crowley Rayne Hwy *Web:* www.alh.org	Crowley	LA	70526	337-783-3222	788-6413
Baton Rouge General Medical Ctr (BRGMC) 3600 Florida Blvd *Fax: Admissions ■ *Web:* www.brgeneral.org	Baton Rouge	LA	70806	225-387-7000	381-6165*
CHRISTUS Bossier Medical Ctr 2105 Airline Dr *Web:* www.christushealth.org	Bossier City	LA	71111	318-848-8000	681-4215
CHRISTUS Schumpert Highland 1453 E Bert Kouns *Web:* www.christusschumpert.org/maphighland.htm	Shreveport	LA	71105	318-798-4300	798-4375
CHRISTUS Schumpert St Mary Place 1 St Mary Pl *Web:* www.christusschumpert.org	Shreveport	LA	71101	318-681-4500	681-4177
Dauterive Hospital 600 N Lewis St *Web:* www.dauterivehospital.com	New Iberia	LA	70563	337-365-7311	374-4104
EA Conway Medical Ctr 4864 Jackson St *Web:* www.conway.lsuhsc.edu	Monroe	LA	71201	318-330-7000	330-7591
Earl K Long Medical Ctr 5825 Airline Hwy	Baton Rouge	LA	70805	225-358-1000	
East Jefferson General Hospital (EJGH) 4200 Houma Blvd *TF:* 866-280-7737 ■ *Web:* www.ejgh.org	Metairie	LA	70006	504-454-4000	456-8151
Glenwood Regional Medical Ctr 503 McMillan Rd *Web:* www.grmc.com	West Monroe	LA	71291	318-329-4200	329-4710
Homer Memorial Hospital 620 E College St *Web:* www.homerhospital.com	Homer	LA	71040	318-927-2024	
Huey P Long Medical Ctr 352 Hospital Blvd PO Box 5352 *Web:* www.lsuhsc.edu/hcsd/hpl	Pineville	LA	71361	318-448-0811	473-6360
Iberia Medical Ctr (IMC) 2315 E Main St *Web:* www.iberiamedicalcenter.com	New Iberia	LA	70560	337-364-0441	374-7641
Kenner Regional Medical Ctr 180 W Esplanade Ave *Web:* www.kennerregional.com	Kenner	LA	70065	504-468-8600	464-8600
Lady of The Sea General Hospital (LOSGH) 200 W 134th Pl *Web:* www.losgh.org	Cut Off	LA	70345	985-632-6401	632-8263
Lafayette General Medical Ctr 1214 Coolidge Blvd *Web:* www.lafayettegeneral.org	Lafayette	LA	70505	337-289-7991	289-8671
Lake Charles Memorial Health System (LCMH) 1701 Oak Pk Blvd *Web:* www.lcmh.com	Lake Charles	LA	70601	337-494-3000	494-3299
Lakeview Regional Medical Ctr 95 E Fairway Dr *Web:* www.lakeviewregional.com	Covington	LA	70433	985-867-3800	867-4449
Lane Regional Medical Ctr 6300 Main St *Web:* www.lanermc.org	Zachary	LA	70791	225-658-4000	658-4234
Leonard J Chabert Medical Ctr 1978 Industrial Blvd	Houma	LA	70363	985-873-2200	873-1262
Louisiana State University Health Sciences Ctr (LSUHSC) 1501 Kings Hwy PO Box 33932 *Web:* www.lsuhscshreveport.edu/LSUHealthShreveport/LSUHealthShreveport.aspx	Shreveport	LA	71130	318-675-5000	675-5666
Minden Medical Ctr 1 Medical Plaza *Web:* www.mindenmedicalcenter.com	Minden	LA	71055	318-377-2321	371-5606
Natchitoches Parish Hospital 501 Keyser Ave *Web:* www.natchitocheshospital.org	Natchitoches	LA	71457	318-214-4200	214-4455
North Oaks Health System (NOHS) PO Box 2668 *Web:* www.northoaks.org/index.php	Hammond	LA	70404	985-345-2700	230-6482
Northern Louisiana Medical Ctr 401 E Vaughn St *Web:* www.northernlouisianamedicalcenter.com	Ruston	LA	71270	318-254-2100	254-2728
NorthShore Regional Medical Ctr (NRMC) 100 Medical Ctr Dr *Web:* www.ochsner.org/locations/north_shore	Slidell	LA	70461	985-649-7070	646-5552
Ochsner Clinic Foundation Hospital 1514 Jefferson Hwy *TF:* 800-928-6247 ■ *Web:* www.ochsner.org	New Orleans	LA	70121	504-842-3000	842-2152
Ochsner Medical Center Baton Rouge 17000 Medical Ctr Dr *Fax: Admissions ■ *Web:* www.ochsner.org	Baton Rouge	LA	70816	225-752-2470	755-4891*
Ochsner Medical Center West Bank 2500 Belle Chasse Hwy *Web:* www.ochsner.org	Gretna	LA	70056	504-392-3131	391-5490
Opelousas General Health System 1233 Wayne Gilmore Cir *Web:* www.opelousasgeneral.com	Opelousas	LA	70570	337-948-3011	948-5126
Our Lady of Lourdes Regional Medical Ctr 4801 Ambassador Caffery Pkwy *Web:* www.lourdes.net	Lafayette	LA	70508	337-289-2000	289-2574
Our Lady of the Lake Regional Medical Ctr 5000 Hennessy Blvd *Fax: Admissions ■ *Web:* www.ololrmc.com	Baton Rouge	LA	70808	225-765-6565	765-5290*
Rapides Regional Medical Ctr 211 4th St *Web:* www.rapidesregional.com	Alexandria	LA	71301	318-473-3000	449-7575
Saint Francis Medical Ctr 309 Jackson St *Web:* www.stfran.com	Monroe	LA	71201	318-327-4000	327-4142
Saint Francis North Hospital 3421 Medical Pk Dr *Web:* www.stfran.com	Monroe	LA	71203	318-388-1946	388-7878
Saint Patrick Hospital of Lake Charles 524 Dr Michael DeBakey Dr *Web:* www.stpatrickhospital.org	Lake Charles	LA	70601	337-436-2511	491-7157
Saint Tammany Parish Hospital 1202 S Tyler St *Web:* www.stph.org	Covington	LA	70433	985-898-4000	898-4491
Savoy Medical Ctr 801 Poinciana Ave *Web:* www.savoymedical.com	Mamou	LA	70554	337-468-5261	468-3342
Slidell Memorial Hospital (SMH) 1001 Gause Blvd *Web:* www.smhplus.org	Slidell	LA	70458	985-643-2200	649-8626
Teche Regional Medical Ctr 1125 Marguerite St *Web:* www.techeregional.com	Morgan City	LA	70380	985-384-2200	380-4546
Terrebonne General Medical Ctr (TGMC) 8166 Main St *TF:* 800-456-9121 ■ *Web:* www.tgmc.com	Houma	LA	70360	985-873-4141	873-4640
Thibodaux Regional Medical Ctr (TRMC) 602 N Acadia Rd *TF:* 800-822-8442	Thibodaux	LA	70301	985-493-4704	446-5033
Touro Infirmary 1401 Foucher St *Web:* www.touro.com	New Orleans	LA	70115	504-897-7011	897-8769
Tulane Medical Ctr (TMC) 1415 Tulane Ave *TF:* 800-588-5800 ■ *Web:* www.tulanehealthcare.com	New Orleans	LA	70112	504-588-5263	988-7973
University Hospital (MCLNO) 2021 Perdido St *Web:* www.mclno.org/mclno/menu	New Orleans	LA	70112	504-903-3000	903-6207
University Medical Ctr 2390 W Congress St	Lafayette	LA	70506	337-261-6000	261-6003
West Calcasieu Cameron Hospital 701 E Cypress St *Fax: Administration ■ *Web:* www.wcch.com	Sulphur	LA	70663	337-527-7034	527-4163*
West Jefferson Medical Ctr 1101 Medical Ctr Blvd *Web:* www.wjmc.org	Marrero	LA	70072	504-349-1134	349-6299
Willis-Knighton Medical Ctr (WKMC) 2600 Greenwood Rd *Web:* www.wkhs.com/Home.aspx	Shreveport	LA	71103	318-212-4000	212-4956

MAINE

	City	State	Zip	Phone	Fax
Aroostook Medical Ctr The (TAMC) 140 Academy St *Web:* www.tamc.org	Presque Isle	ME	04769	207-768-4000	768-4116
Central Maine Medical Ctr 300 Main St *Web:* www.cmmc.org	Lewiston	ME	04240	207-795-0111	795-2303
Eastern Maine Medical Ctr 489 State St *Web:* www.emmc.org	Bangor	ME	04401	207-973-7000	973-7348
Franklin Community Health Network 111 Franklin Health Commons *TF:* 800-398-6031 ■ *Web:* www.fchn.org	Farmington	ME	04938	207-778-6031	778-2548
Maine General Medical Ctr (MGMC) *Augusta* 6 E Chestnut St *Web:* www.mainegeneral.org	Augusta	ME	04330	207-626-1000	626-1549
Maine Medical Ctr 22 Bramhall St *Web:* www.mmc.org	Portland	ME	04102	207-871-0111	662-6027
Brighton Campus 335 Brighton Ave *Web:* www.mmc.org/mmc_body.cfm?id=2291	Portland	ME	04102	207-662-8000	662-8198
Mercy Hospital 144 State St *TF:* 800-293-6583 ■ *Web:* www.mercyhospital.org	Portland	ME	04101	207-879-3000	879-3429
Mid Coast Hospital 123 Medical Ctr Dr *TF:* 877-729-0181 ■ *Web:* www.midcoasthealth.com	Brunswick	ME	04011	207-729-0181	373-6195
Miles Memorial Hospital 35 Miles St *Web:* www.mileshealthcare.org	Damariscotta	ME	04543	207-563-1234	563-3717
Northern Maine Medical Ctr (NMMC) 194 E Main St *Web:* www.nmmc.org	Fort Kent	ME	04743	207-834-3155	834-2949
Penobscot Bay Medical Ctr 4 Glen Cove Dr # 101 *Web:* www.penbayhealthcare.org	Rockport	ME	04856	207-596-8000	593-5287
Saint Joseph Hospital 360 Broadway PO Box 403 *Web:* www.stjoseph-me.org	Bangor	ME	04402	207-262-1000	262-1240
Saint Mary's Regional Medical Ctr PO Box 291 *Web:* www.stmarysmaine.com	Lewiston	ME	04243	207-777-8100	777-8800
Southern Maine Medical Ctr (SMMC) 1 Medical Ctr Dr PO Box 626 *Web:* www.smmc.org	Biddeford	ME	04005	207-283-7000	283-7020

MARYLAND

				Phone	Fax
Anne Arundel Medical Ctr 2001 Medical Pkwy *Web:* www.aahs.org	Annapolis	MD	21401	443-481-1000	481-1313
Baltimore Washington Medical Ctr 301 Hospital Dr *Web:* www.mybwmc.org	Glen Burnie	MD	21061	410-787-4000	766-4036
Braddock Hospital 12500 Willowbrook Rd *Web:* www.wmhs.com	Cumberland	MD	21502	240-964-7000	
Carroll Hospital Ctr 200 Memorial Ave *Web:* www.ccgh.com	Westminster	MD	21157	410-848-3000	871-7474
Civista Medical Ctr 701 E Charles St *TF:* 800-422-8585	La Plata	MD	20646	301-609-4000	609-4037
Doctors Community Hospital (DCH) 8118 Good Luck Rd *Web:* www.dchweb.org	Lanham	MD	20706	301-552-8118	552-9306
Franklin Square Hospital Ctr 9000 Franklin Sq Dr *Web:* www.medstarhealth.org	Baltimore	MD	21237	443-777-7000	777-7904
Frederick Memorial Hospital 400 W 7th St **Fax:* Admitting ■ *Web:* www.fmh.org	Frederick	MD	21701	240-566-3300	566-3666*
Good Samaritan Hospital of Maryland 5601 Loch Raven Blvd *Web:* www.medstarhealth.org	Baltimore	MD	21239	410-532-8000	532-4599
Greater Baltimore Medical Ctr (GBMC) 6701 N Charles St *Web:* www.gbmc.org	Baltimore	MD	21204	443-849-2000	849-8679
Harbor Hospital Ctr 3001 S Hanover St *Web:* www.harborhospital.org	Baltimore	MD	21225	410-350-3200	354-4440
Harford Memorial Hospital 501 S Union Ave *Web:* www.uchs.org	Havre de Grace	MD	21078	443-843-5000	
Holy Cross Hospital 1500 Forest Glen Rd *Web:* www.holycrosshealth.org	Silver Spring	MD	20910	301-754-7000	754-7012
Howard County General Hospital 5755 Cedar Ln *Web:* www.hcgh.org	Columbia	MD	21044	410-740-7890	740-7610
Johns Hopkins Bayview Medical Ctr 4940 Eastern Ave *Web:* www.hopkinsbayview.org	Baltimore	MD	21224	410-550-0100	550-7996
Johns Hopkins Hospital The (JHH) 600 N Wolfe St *Web:* www.hopkinsmedicine.org/the_johns_hopkins_hospital/index.html	Baltimore	MD	21287	410-955-5000	502-5392
Laurel Regional Hospital (LRH) 7300 Van Dusen Rd *Web:* www.dimensionshealth.org/website/c/lrh	Laurel	MD	20707	301-725-4300	497-7953
Maryland General Hospital 827 Linden Ave *Web:* www.marylandgeneral.org	Baltimore	MD	21201	410-225-8000	462-5834
Memorial Hospital at Easton (MHE) 219 S Washington St *Web:* www.shorehealth.org/services/mhe	Easton	MD	21601	410-822-1000	822-7834
Mercy Medical Ctr (MMC) 345 St Paul Pl *TF:* 800-636-3729 ■ *Web:* www.mdmercy.com	Baltimore	MD	21202	410-332-9000	962-1303
Meritus Health 11116 Medical Campus Rd *TF:* 800-735-2258 ■ *Web:* www.meritushealth.com	Hagerstown	MD	21742	301-790-8000	
Montgomery General Hospital 18101 Prince Philip Dr *Web:* www.montgomerygeneral.com	Olney	MD	20832	301-774-8882	774-8886
Northwest Hospital Ctr 5401 Old Ct Rd *TF:* 800-654-4677 ■ *Web:* www.lifebridgehealth.org	Randallstown	MD	21133	410-521-2200	521-7977
Peninsula Regional Medical Ctr 100 E Carroll St *TF:* 800-543-7780 ■ *Web:* www.peninsula.org	Salisbury	MD	21801	410-546-6400	543-7102
Prince George's Hospital Ctr 3001 Hospital Dr *Web:* www.dimensionshealth.org	Cheverly	MD	20785	301-618-2000	618-3966
Saint Agnes HealthCare 900 S Caton Ave *TF:* 800-875-8750 ■ *Web:* www.stagnes.org	Baltimore	MD	21229	410-368-6000	368-2109
Saint Joseph Medical Ctr (SJMC) 7601 Osler Dr	Towson	MD	21204	410-337-1000	337-4860
Saint Mary's Hospital 25500 Pt Lookout Rd *TF:* 800-222-1764 ■ *Web:* www.stmaryshospitalmd.org	Leonardtown	MD	20650	301-475-8981	475-5388
Shady Grove Adventist Hospital 9901 Medical Ctr Dr *Web:* www.adventisthealthcare.com/SGAH	Rockville	MD	20850	301-279-6000	217-5301
Sinai Hospital of Baltimore 2401 W Belvedere Ave *TF:* 800-444-8233 ■ *Web:* www.sinai-balt.com	Baltimore	MD	21215	410-601-9000	601-8356
Southern Maryland Hospital Ctr 7503 Surratts Rd **Fax:* Admissions ■ *Web:* www.southernmarylandhospital.com	Clinton	MD	20735	301-868-8000	868-5015*
Suburban Hospital 8600 Old Georgetown Rd *Web:* www.suburbanhospital.org	Bethesda	MD	20814	301-896-3100	897-1330
Total Health Care Inc 1501 Division St *Web:* www.totalhealthcare.org	Baltimore	MD	21217	410-383-8300	728-4412
Union Hospital 106 Bow St *Web:* www.uhcc.com	Elkton	MD	21921	410-398-4000	620-1494
Union Memorial Hospital 201 E University Pkwy *Web:* www.unionmemorial.org	Baltimore	MD	21218	410-554-2000	554-2652
University of Maryland Medical Ctr 22 S Greene St *TF:* 800-787-6363 ■ *Web:* www.umm.edu/center	Baltimore	MD	21201	410-328-8667	
Upper Chesapeake Medical Ctr 500 Upper Chesapeake Dr *Web:* www.uchs.org/hospitals/upperchesapeake.cfm	Bel Air	MD	21014	443-643-1000	
Washington Adventist Hospital 7600 Carroll Ave *Web:* www.adventisthealthcare.com	Takoma Park	MD	20912	301-891-7600	891-5991
Western Maryland Health System Memorial Campus 600 Memorial Ave *TF:* 877-852-7400 ■ *Web:* www.wmhs.com	Cumberland	MD	21502	301-777-4000	723-4045

MASSACHUSETTS

				Phone	Fax
Anna Jaques Hospital (AJH) 25 Highland Ave *Web:* www.ajh.org	Newburyport	MA	01950	978-463-1000	463-1250
Baystate Franklin Medical Ctr 164 High St *Web:* www.baystatehealth.com	Greenfield	MA	01301	413-773-0211	
Baystate Medical Ctr 759 Chestnut St *Web:* www.baystatehealth.com/Baystate	Springfield	MA	01199	413-784-0000	794-2722
Berkshire Medical Ctr 725 N St *Web:* www.berkshirehealthsystems.com/location_services.asp?ID=509	Pittsfield	MA	01201	413-447-2000	447-2206
Beth Israel Deaconess Medical Ctr (BIDMC) 330 Brookline Ave *TF:* 800-667-5356 ■ *Web:* www.bidmc.org	Boston	MA	02215	617-667-7000	754-2224
Beverly Hospital 85 Herrick St *Web:* www.beverlyhospital.com	Beverly	MA	01915	978-922-3000	921-7010
Boston Medical Ctr 1 Boston Medical Ctr Pl *Web:* www.bmc.org	Boston	MA	02118	617-638-8000	638-6905
Brockton Hospital 680 Centre St *Web:* www.signature-healthcare.org	Brockton	MA	02302	508-941-7000	941-6201
Cambridge Hospital 1493 Cambridge St *Web:* www.challiance.org	Cambridge	MA	02139	617-498-1000	665-1003
Cape Cod Hospital 27 Pk St *Web:* www.capecodhealth.org/capecodhospital	Hyannis	MA	02601	508-771-1800	862-7337
Caritas Carney Hospital 2100 Dorchester Ave *Web:* www.healthcaresource.com/CARNEY	Boston	MA	02124	617-296-4000	296-4033
Caritas Norwood Hospital 800 Washington St *TF:* 800-664-3884 ■ *Web:* www.caritaschristi.org/Norwood/Home_Page/Norwood_Home_Page	Norwood	MA	02062	781-769-4000	278-6810
Charlton Memorial Hospital 363 Highland Ave *Web:* www.southcoast.org	Fall River	MA	02720	508-679-3131	679-7692
Cooley Dickinson Hospital 30 Locust St *Web:* www.cooley-dickinson.org	NorthHampton	MA	01060	413-582-2000	582-2867
Emerson Hospital 133 Old Rd To 9 Acre Corner *Web:* www.emersonhospital.org	Concord	MA	01742	978-369-1400	287-3655
Falmouth Hospital 100 Ter Heun Dr *Web:* www.capecodhealth.org	Falmouth	MA	02540	508-548-5300	457-3576
Faulkner Hospital 1153 Centre St *Web:* www.faulknerhospital.org	Jamaica Plain	MA	02130	617-983-7000	524-8663
Good Samaritan Medical Ctr 235 N Pearl St *Web:* www.caritaschristi.org	Brockton	MA	02301	508-427-3000	427-3010
Harrington Memorial Hospital (HMH) 100 S St *Web:* www.harringtonhospital.org	Southbridge	MA	01550	508-765-9771	765-3147
HealthAlliance Leominster Hospital 60 Hospital Rd *Web:* www.umassmemorial.org/healthalliancehp.cfm?id=9	Leominster	MA	01453	978-466-2000	466-2200
Heywood Hospital 242 Green St *Web:* www.heywood.org	Gardner	MA	01440	978-632-3420	630-6529
Holy Family Hospital 70 E St *Web:* www.caritaschristi.org	Methuen	MA	01844	978-687-0151	688-7689
Holyoke Medical Ctr 575 Beech St *Web:* www.holyokehealth.com	Holyoke	MA	01040	413-534-2500	534-2633
Jordan Hospital 275 Sandwich St *TF:* 800-256-7326 ■ *Web:* www.jordanhospital.org	Plymouth	MA	02360	508-746-2000	830-1131
Lahey Clinic Foundation Inc 41 Mall Rd *TF:* 800-524-3955 ■ *Web:* www.lahey.org	Burlington	MA	01805	781-744-8000	
Lawrence General Hospital 1 General St *Web:* www.lawrencegeneral.org	Lawrence	MA	01842	978-683-4000	946-8199
Lawrence Memorial Hospital of Medford 170 Governors Ave *Web:* www.hallmarkhealth.org	Medford	MA	02155	781-306-6000	306-6361
Lowell General Hospital (LGH) 295 Varnum Ave *Web:* www.lowellgeneral.org	Lowell	MA	01854	978-937-6000	937-6103
Massachusetts General Hospital 55 Fruit St *Web:* www.massgeneral.org	Boston	MA	02114	617-726-2000	726-2093
Melrose-Wakefield Hospital 585 Lebanon St *Web:* www.hallmarkhealth.org	Melrose	MA	02176	781-979-3000	979-3015
Mercy Medical Ctr 271 Carew St *Web:* www.mercycares.com	Springfield	MA	01104	413-748-9000	781-7217
Merrimack Valley Hospital 140 Lincoln Ave *Web:* www.merrimackvalleyhospital.com	Haverhill	MA	01830	978-374-2000	521-8138
MetroWest Medical Ctr 115 Lincoln St *Web:* www.mwmc.com	Framingham	MA	01702	508-383-1000	383-1166
Leonard Morse Campus 67 Union St *Web:* www.mwmc.com	Natick	MA	01760	508-650-7000	650-7777
Milford Regional Medical Ctr 14 Prospect St *Web:* www.milfordregional.org	Milford	MA	01757	508-473-1190	473-2744
Milton Hospital 199 Reedsdale Rd *Web:* www.miltonhospital.org	Milton	MA	02186	617-696-4600	313-1565
Morton Hospital & Medical Ctr 88 Washington St *Web:* www.mortonhospital.org	Taunton	MA	02780	508-828-7000	824-6947
Mount Auburn Hospital (MAH) 330 Mt Auburn St *Web:* www.mountauburnhospital.org	Cambridge	MA	02138	617-492-3500	499-5654
New England Baptist Hospital 125 Parker Hill Ave *TF:* 800-340-6324 ■ *Web:* www.nebh.org	Boston	MA	02120	617-754-5800	754-6397
Newton-Wellesley Hospital 2014 Washington St *Web:* www.nwh.org	Newton	MA	02462	617-243-6000	243-6954
North Adams Regional Hospital (NARH) 71 Hospital Ave *Web:* www.nbhealth.org	North Adams	MA	01247	413-664-5000	664-5197
North Shore Medical Ctr 81 Highland Ave *Web:* www.nsmc.partners.org	Salem	MA	01970	978-741-1200	
Quincy Medical Ctr 114 Whitwell St *Web:* www.quincymc.org	Quincy	MA	02169	617-773-6100	376-1604
Saint Anne's Hospital 795 Middle St *Web:* www.caritaschristi.org	Fall River	MA	02721	508-674-5600	235-5647

				Phone	Fax
Saint Elizabeth's Medical Ctr 736 Cambridge St. *Web:* www.caritaschristi.org	Brighton	MA	02135	617-789-3000	562-7568
Saint Luke's Hospital of New Bedford 101 Page St *TF:* 800-245-8537 ■ *Web:* www.southcoast.org/stlukes	New Bedford	MA	02740	508-997-1515	979-8115
Saint Vincent Hospital-Worcester Medical Ctr 123 Summer St. *TF:* 800-370-6300 ■ *Web:* www.stvincenthospital.com	Worcester	MA	01608	508-363-5000	363-5387
Saints Memorial Medical Ctr (SMMC) 1 Hospital Dr *Web:* www.saintsmedicalcenter.com	Lowell	MA	01852	978-458-1411	934-8566
South Shore Hospital 55 Fogg Rd *TF:* 800-472-3434 ■ *Web:* www.sshosp.org	South Weymouth	MA	02190	781-340-8000	337-3768
Southboro Medical Group Inc 24 Newton St *Web:* www.southboromedical.com	Southborough	MA	01772	508-481-5500	460-3221
Sturdy Memorial Hospital 211 Pk St *Web:* www.sturdymemorial.org	Attleboro	MA	02703	508-222-5200	236-8409
Tufts Medical Ctr (TMC) 800 Washington St. *TF:* 866-636-5001 ■ *Web:* www.tuftsmedicalcenter.org/default	Boston	MA	02111	617-636-5000	636-7623
UMass Memorial Medical Ctr					
Memorial Campus 119 Belmont St *Web:* www.umassmemorial.org	Worcester	MA	01605	508-334-1000	334-5049
University Campus 55 Lake Ave N. *Web:* www.umassmemorial.org	Worcester	MA	01655	508-334-1000	856-1825
Union Hospital 500 Lynnfield St	Lynn	MA	01904	781-581-9200	477-3840
Upham's Corner Health Center 500 Columbia Rd *Web:* www.uphamscornerhealthctr.com	Dorchester	MA	02125	617-287-8000	282-8625
Whidden Memorial Hospital 103 Garland St *Web:* www.challiance.org	Everett	MA	02149	617-389-6270	389-3883
Winchester Hospital 41 Highland Ave. *Web:* www.winchesterhospital.org	Winchester	MA	01890	781-729-9000	756-2923

MICHIGAN

				Phone	Fax
Allegan General Hospital 555 Linn St *Web:* www.aghosp.org	Allegan	MI	49010	269-673-8424	673-3900
Allegiance Health 205 N E Ave *TF:* 800-872-6480 ■ *Web:* www.foote.com	Jackson	MI	49201	517-788-4800	788-4829
Alpena Regional Medical Ctr 1501 W Chisholm St *TF:* 800-556-8842 ■ *Web:* www.alpenaregionalmedicalcenter.org	Alpena	MI	49707	989-356-7000	356-7305
Battle Creek Health System					
Main Campus 300 N Ave. *Web:* www.bchealth.com	Battle Creek	MI	49008	269-966-8000	966-8010
Bay Regional Medical Ctr (BRMC) 1900 Columbus Ave. *TF:* 800-656-3950 ■ *Web:* www.bayregional.org	Bay City	MI	48708	989-894-3000	894-3808
Bixby Medical Ctr 818 Riverside Ave *Web:* www.promedica.org	Adrian	MI	49221	517-263-0711	263-1839
Bon Secours Hospital 468 Cadieux Rd *Web:* www.bonsecourscottage.org	Grosse Pointe	MI	48230	313-343-1000	343-1185
Borgess Medical Ctr 1521 Gull Rd *Web:* www.borgess.com	Kalamazoo	MI	49048	269-226-7000	226-5966
Botsford Hospital 28050 Grand River Ave. *Web:* www.botsford.org	Farmington Hills	MI	48336	248-471-8000	471-8896
Bronson Methodist Hospital 601 John St *TF:* 800-276-6766 ■ *Web:* www.bronsonhealth.com	Kalamazoo	MI	49007	269-341-7654	341-8314
Chelsea Community Hospital 775 S Main St. *Web:* www.cch.org	Chelsea	MI	48118	734-475-1311	475-4066
Community Health Center of Branch County (CHCBC) 274 E Chicago St *TF:* 888-774-1471 ■ *Web:* www.chcbc.com	Coldwater	MI	49036	517-279-5400	279-8830
Cottage Hospital 159 Kercheval Ave *Web:* www.bonsecourscottage.org	Grosse Pointe Farms	MI	48236	313-640-1000	640-2507
Covenant Medical Center Cooper 700 Cooper Ave *Fax: Admitting ■ *Web:* www.covenanthealthcare.com	Saginaw	MI	48602	989-583-7080	583-6314*
Covenant Medical Center Harrison 1447 N Harrison St. *Web:* www.covenanthealthcare.com	Saginaw	MI	48602	989-583-4803	583-4784
Crittenton Hospital 1101 W University Dr *Web:* www.crittenton.com	Rochester Hills	MI	48307	248-652-5000	652-5424
Detroit Receiving Hospital & University Health Ctr 4201 St Antoine Blvd *Web:* www.drhuhc.org	Detroit	MI	48201	313-745-3100	745-3455
Dickinson County Healthcare System 1721 S Stephenson Ave *Web:* www.dchs.org	Iron Mountain	MI	49801	906-774-1313	776-5427
Doctors Hospital Of Michigan 461 W Huron St. *Web:* www.dhofm.com	Pontiac	MI	48341	248-857-7200	857-6801
Eaton Rapids Medical Ctr 1500 S Main St. *Web:* www.eatonrapidsmedicalcenter.org	Eaton Rapids	MI	48827	517-663-2671	663-4920
Emergency Physicians Medical Group Pc Inc 2000 Green Rd Suite 300 *Web:* www.epmgpc.com	Ann Arbor	MI	48105	734-995-3764	995-2913
Garden City Hospital (GCH) 6245 Inkster Rd. *Web:* www.gchosp.org	Garden City	MI	48135	734-421-3300	421-3342
Genesys Regional Medical Ctr 1 Genesys Pkwy *TF:* 888-606-6556 ■ *Web:* www.genesys.org	Grand Blanc	MI	48439	810-606-5000	606-6605
Hackley Hospital 1700 Clinton St. *TF:* 800-825-4677 ■ *Web:* www.hackley.org	Muskegon	MI	49442	231-726-3511	722-0739
Harper University Hospital 3990 John R St *Web:* www.harperhospital.org	Detroit	MI	48201	313-745-8040	745-1520
Henry Ford Bi-County Hospital 13355 E Ten-Mile Rd *TF:* 800-423-1948	Warren	MI	48089	586-759-7300	759-7357
Henry Ford Hospital 2799 W Grand Blvd *TF:* 800-999-4340 ■ *Web:* www.henryfordhealth.org	Detroit	MI	48202	313-916-2600	916-8200
Henry Ford Macomb Hospital 15855 19-Mile Rd *Web:* www.henryfordmacomb.com	Clinton Township	MI	48038	586-263-2300	263-2255
Henry Ford Wyandotte Hospital 2333 Biddle Ave *Web:* www.henryfordwyandotte.com	Wyandotte	MI	48192	734-284-2400	246-6904
Holland Community Hospital 602 Michigan Ave *Web:* www.hoho.org	Holland	MI	49423	616-392-5141	394-3528
Hurley Medical Ctr 1 Hurley Plaza *TF:* 800-336-8999 ■ *Web:* www.hurleymc.com	Flint	MI	48503	810-257-9000	762-6585
Huron Valley Sinai Hospital (HVSH) 1 William Carls Dr *Web:* www.hvsh.org	Commerce	MI	48382	248-937-3300	937-3378
Ingham Regional Medical Ctr 401 W Greenlawn Ave. *Web:* www.irmc.org	Lansing	MI	48910	517-975-6000	334-2939
Lakeland Medical Center-Niles 31 N St Joseph Ave. *Web:* www.lakelandhealth.org	Niles	MI	49120	269-683-5510	683-2337
Lapeer Regional Hospital 1375 N Main St *Web:* www.lapeerregional.org	Lapeer	MI	48446	810-667-5500	667-5582
Marquette General Hospital 580 W College Ave *Web:* www.mgh.org	Marquette	MI	49855	906-228-9440	225-3084
McKenzie Memorial Hospital 120 N Delaware St *Web:* www.mckenziehospital.org	Sandusky	MI	48471	810-648-3770	
McLaren Regional Medical Ctr 401 S Ballenger Hwy *TF:* 800-821-6517 ■ *Web:* www.mclaren.org	Flint	MI	48532	810-342-2000	342-2428
Memorial Healthcare Ctr 826 W King St *TF:* 800-206-8706 ■ *Web:* www.memorialhealthcare.org	Owosso	MI	48867	989-723-5211	725-7902
Mercy General Health Partners					
Mercy Campus 1500 E Sherman Blvd *Web:* www.mghp.com	Muskegon	MI	49443	231-672-9341	672-3074
Muskegon Campus 1700 Oak Ave. *Web:* www.mghp.com	Muskegon	MI	49442	231-672-3311	672-6255
Mercy Hospital Cadillac 400 Hobart St *Web:* www.munsonhealthcare.org	Cadillac	MI	49601	231-876-7520	
Mercy Memorial Hospital (MMH) 718 N Macomb St *Web:* www.mercymemorial.org	Monroe	MI	48162	734-240-8400	240-4424
Metro Health Hospital 1919 Boston St SE *TF:* 800-968-0051 ■ *Web:* www.metrohealth.net	Grand Rapids	MI	49506	616-252-7200	252-7307
MidMichigan Medical Ctr 4005 Orchard Dr *Web:* www.midmichigan.org	Midland	MI	48670	989-839-3000	839-1399
Mount Clemens General Hospital 1000 Harrington Blvd *Web:* www.mcrmc.org	Mount Clemens	MI	48043	586-493-8000	493-8700
Munson Medical Ctr 1105 6th St. *Web:* www.munsonhealthcare.org	Traverse City	MI	49684	231-935-5000	
Northern Michigan Hospital 416 Connable Ave. *TF:* 800-748-0466 ■ *Web:* www.northernhealth.org	Petoskey	MI	49770	231-487-4000	487-7703
Oakwood Annapolis Hospital 33155 Annapolis Rd *Web:* www.oakwood.org	Wayne	MI	48184	734-467-4000	467-4017
Oakwood Heritage Hospital 10000 Telegraph Rd. *Web:* www.oakwood.org	Taylor	MI	48180	313-295-5000	295-5085
Oakwood Hospital & Medical Ctr 18101 Oakwood Blvd *TF:* 800-543-9355 ■ *Web:* www.oakwood.org	Dearborn	MI	48124	313-593-7000	436-2042
Oakwood Southshore Medical Ctr 5450 Fort St *Web:* www.oakwood.org	Trenton	MI	48183	734-671-3800	671-3891
POH Regional Medical Ctr 50 N Perry St *Web:* www.pohregional.org	Pontiac	MI	48342	248-338-5000	338-5667
Port Huron Hospital (PHH) 1221 Pine Grove Ave *Web:* www.porthuronhospital.org	Port Huron	MI	48060	810-987-5000	985-2675
Providence Hospital 16001 W Nine-Mile Rd. *Web:* www.providence-hospital.org	Southfield	MI	48075	248-849-3000	849-5399
Saint John Hospital & Medical Ctr 22101 Moross Rd. *Web:* www.stjohnprovidence.org/stjohnhospital	Detroit	MI	48236	313-343-4000	343-3607
Saint John Macomb Hospital 11800 E 12-Mile Rd *Web:* www.stjohnprovidence.org	Warren	MI	48093	586-573-5000	573-5541
Saint John Macomb-Oakland Hospital					
Oakland Ctr 27351 Dequindre Rd *Web:* www.stjohnprovidence.org/macomb	Madison Heights	MI	48071	248-967-7000	967-7619
Saint Joseph Mercy Ann Arbor 5301 McAuley Dr *Web:* www.stjoeshealth.org	Ypsilanti	MI	48197	734-712-3456	712-3855
Saint Joseph Mercy Hospital Port Huron 2601 Electric Ave *Web:* www.mymercy.us/welcom-port-huron	Port Huron	MI	48060	810-985-1500	985-1579
Saint Joseph Mercy Oakland 44405 Woodward Ave. *Web:* www.stjoesoakland.org	Pontiac	MI	48341	248-858-3000	858-3155
Saint Mary Mercy Hospital 36475 Five-Mile Rd *TF:* 800-464-7492 ■ *Web:* www.stmarymercy.org	Livonia	MI	48154	734-655-4800	655-3093
Saint Mary's Health Care 200 Jefferson St SE *Web:* www.smhealthcare.org	Grand Rapids	MI	49503	616-752-6090	752-4464
Saint Mary's Hospital (STMH) 800 S Washington Ave	Saginaw	MI	48601	989-907-8115	
Scheurer Hospital Inc 170 N Caseville Rd. *TF:* 800-208-9060 ■ *Web:* www.scheurer.org	Pigeon	MI	48755	989-453-3223	453-2411
Sinai Grace Hospital 6071 W Outer Dr *TF:* 888-362-2500 ■ *Web:* www.sinaigrace.org	Detroit	MI	48235	313-966-3300	966-3160

	City	State	Zip	Phone	Fax
Southwestern Medical Clinic PC 8008 M-139 Web: www.swmc.org	Berrien Springs	MI	49102	269-471-1700	471-1975
Sparrow Health System 1215 E Michigan Ave TF: 800-772-7769 ■ Web: www.sparrow.org	Lansing	MI	48912	517-364-1000	364-5050
Spectrum Health Blodgett Campus 100 Michigan St NE TF: 866-989-7999 ■ Web: www.spectrum-health.org	Grand Rapids	MI	49503	616-774-7444	391-1883
St John Detroit Riverview Ctr 7733 E Jefferson Ave Web: www.stjohnprovidence.org/DetroitRiverView	Detroit	MI	48214	313-499-4000	
Three Rivers Health 701 S Health Pkwy Web: www.threeriversheath.org	Three Rivers	MI	49093	269-278-1145	273-9703
University Hospital 1500 E Medical Ctr Dr Web: www.med.umich.edu	Ann Arbor	MI	48109	734-936-4000	936-9437
War Memorial Hospital (WMH) 500 Osborn Blvd Web: www.warmemorialhospital.org	Sault Sainte Marie	MI	49783	906-635-4460	635-4467
William Beaumont Hospital Troy 44201 Dequindre Rd TF: 800-482-8767 ■ Web: www.beaumont.edu	Troy	MI	48085	248-828-5000	964-8840

MINNESOTA

	City	State	Zip	Phone	Fax
Abbott Northwestern Hospital 800 E 28th St Web: www.abbottnorthwestern.com	Minneapolis	MN	55407	612-863-4000	863-5667
Affiliated Community Medical Centers (ACMC) 101 Willmar Ave SW TF: 888-225-6580 ■ Web: www.acmc.com	Willmar	MN	56201	320-231-5000	
Cambridge Medical Ctr (CMC) 701 S Dellwood St TF: 800-252-4133 ■ Web: www.cambridgemedicalcenter.com	Cambridge	MN	55008	763-689-7700	689-7941
Douglas County Hospital (DCH) 111 17th Ave E Web: www.dchospital.com	Alexandria	MN	56308	320-762-1511	762-6120
Essentia Health 502 E 2nd St Web: www.essentiahealth.org	Duluth	MN	55805	218-786-8376	786-5892
Fairview Ridges Hospital - Burnsville 201 Nicollet Blvd Web: www.fairview.org	Burnsville	MN	55337	952-892-2000	
Fairview Southdale Hospital 6401 France Ave S Web: www.fairview.org/Hospitals/Southdale/index.htm	Edina	MN	55435	952-924-5000	924-5382
Fairview University Medical Center Mesabi 750 E 34th St TF: 888-870-8626 ■ Web: www.range.fairview.org	Hibbing	MN	55746	218-262-4881	362-6619
Glacial Ridge Hospital Foundation Inc 10 4th Ave SE TF: 866-667-4747 ■ Web: www.glacialridge.org	Glenwood	MN	56334	320-634-4521	634-2269
Hennepin County Medical Ctr (HCMC) 701 Pk Ave Web: www.hcmc.org	Minneapolis	MN	55415	612-873-3000	904-4214
Immanuel-Saint Joseph's Hospital 1025 Marsh St TF: 800-327-3721 ■ Web: www.isj-mhs.net	Mankato	MN	56001	507-625-4031	345-2908
Lake Region Hospital 712 S Cascade St TF: 800-439-6424 ■ Web: www.lrhc.org	Fergus Falls	MN	56537	218-736-8000	736-8765
Mayo Clinic 200 1st St SW Web: www.mayo.edu	Rochester	MN	55905	507-284-2511	284-0574
Mayo Clinic Health System Austin 1000 1st Dr NW TF: 888-609-4065 ■ Web: www.mayohealthsystem.org	Austin	MN	55912	507-433-7351	434-1992
Mercy Hospital 4050 Coon Rapids Blvd Web: www.allinamercy.org	Coon Rapids	MN	55433	763-236-6000	236-8124
Methodist Hospital 6500 Excelsior Blvd Web: www.parknicollet.com	Saint Louis Park	MN	55426	952-993-5000	993-5273
Mille Lacs Health System 200 Elm St N TF: 877-535-3154 ■ Web: www.millelacshealth.com	Onamia	MN	56359	320-532-3154	
North Country Regional Hospital 1300 Anne St NW Web: www.nchs.com	Bemidji	MN	56601	218-751-5430	333-5880
North Memorial Health Care 3300 Oakdale Ave N Web: www.northmemorial.com	Robbinsdale	MN	55422	763-520-5200	520-1454
Regions Hospital 640 Jackson St Web: www.regionshospital.com	Saint Paul	MN	55101	651-254-3456	254-2194
Rice Memorial Hospital 301 Becker Ave SW Web: www.ricehospital.com	Willmar	MN	56201	320-235-4543	231-4869
Ridgeview Medical Ctr (RMC) 500 S Maple St TF: 800-967-4620 ■ Web: www.ridgeviewmedical.org	Waconia	MN	55387	952-442-2191	442-6524
Rochester Methodist Hospital 201 W Ctr St Web: www.mayoclinic.org/methodisthospital	Rochester	MN	55902	507-286-7890	266-7467
Saint Cloud Hospital 1406 6th Ave TF: 800-835-6652 ■ Web: www.centracare.com	Saint Cloud	MN	56303	320-251-2700	255-5711
Saint John's Hospital 1575 Beam Ave TF: 866-257-4411 ■ Web: www.healtheast.org	Maplewood	MN	55109	651-232-7000	232-7697
Saint Joseph's Hospital 45 W 10th St Web: www.healtheast.org	Saint Paul	MN	55102	651-232-3000	232-3518
Saint Joseph's Medical Ctr 523 N 3rd St *Fax: Admitting ■ TF: 888-829-2861 ■ Web: www.brainerdlakeshealth.org	Brainerd	MN	56401	218-828-7362	828-3103*
Saint Luke's Hospital & Regional Trauma Ctr 915 E 1st St TF: 800-321-3790 ■ Web: www.slhduluth.com	Duluth	MN	55805	218-249-5555	249-3090
Saint Mary's Hospital 1216 2nd St SW Web: www.mayoclinic.org/saintmaryshospital	Rochester	MN	55902	507-255-5123	255-3125
Saint Mary's Medical Ctr 407 E 3rd St Web: www.smdc.org	Duluth	MN	55805	218-786-4000	786-4734
St Paul Heart Clinic Pa 225 Smith Ave N Web: www.stphc.com	Saint Paul	MN	55102	651-292-0616	726-7256
United Hospital 333 N Smith Ave TF: 800-869-1320 ■ Web: www.unitedhospital.com	Saint Paul	MN	55102	651-241-8000	241-5189
Unity Hospital 550 Osborne Rd Web: www.mercyunity.com/ahs/mercyunity.nsf	Fridley	MN	55432	763-236-4111	236-4120
University of Minnesota Medical Center Fairview *Riverside Campus* 2450 Riverside Ave TF: 888-702-4073 ■ Web: www.uofmmedicalcenter.org	Minneapolis	MN	55454	612-273-3000	273-4098
University of Minnesota Medical Center Fairview - University Campus 500 Harvard St TF: 800-688-5252 ■ Web: www.uofmmedicalcenter.org	Minneapolis	MN	55455	612-273-3000	273-1919
Virginia Regional Medical Ctr (VRMC) 901 9th St N TF: 866-441-3340 ■ Web: www.vrmc.org	Virginia	MN	55792	218-741-3340	749-9427

MISSISSIPPI

	City	State	Zip	Phone	Fax
Baptist Medical Ctr 1225 N State St *Fax: Admitting ■ TF: 800-948-6262 ■ Web: www.mbhs.org	Jackson	MS	39202	601-968-1000	968-1149*
Baptist Memorial Hospital DeSoto 7601 Southcrest Pkwy Web: www.bmhcc.org	Southaven	MS	38671	662-772-4000	772-2111
Baptist Memorial Hospital Golden Triangle 2520 5th St N TF: 800-544-8762 ■ Web: www.bmhcc.org	Columbus	MS	39703	662-244-1000	244-1651
Baptist Memorial Hospital North Mississippi 2301 S Lamar Blvd Web: www.bmhcc.org	Oxford	MS	38655	662-232-8100	232-8391
Baptist Memorial Hospital Union County 200 Hwy 30 W Web: www.bmhcc.org/facilities/newalbany	New Albany	MS	38652	662-538-7631	538-2591
Biloxi Regional Medical Ctr 150 Reynoir St Web: www.biloxiregional.net/default.aspx	Biloxi	MS	39530	228-432-1571	436-1205
Bolivar Medical Ctr 901 Hwy 8 E PO Box 1380 Web: www.bolivarmedical.com	Cleveland	MS	38732	662-846-2496	846-2380
Central Mississippi Medical Ctr 1850 Chadwick Dr TF: 800-844-0919 ■ Web: www.centralmississippimedicalcenter.com	Jackson	MS	39204	601-376-1000	376-2821
Crossgates River Oaks Hospital 350 Crossgates Blvd Web: www.crossgatesriveroaks.com	Brandon	MS	39042	601-825-2811	824-8519
Delta Regional Medical Ctr (DRMC) 1400 E Union St Web: www.deltaregional.com	Greenville	MS	38703	662-378-3783	334-2189
Forrest General Hospital 6051 US Hwy 49 Web: www.forrestgeneral.com	Hattiesburg	MS	39402	601-288-7000	288-4441
George County Hospital PO Box 607 Web: www.georgeregional.com	Lucedale	MS	39452	601-947-3161	
Gilmore Memorial Regional Medical Ctr (GMRMC) 1105 Earl Frye Blvd Web: www.gilmorehealth.com	Amory	MS	38821	662-256-7111	256-6007
Greenwood Leflore Hospital 1401 River Rd Web: www.glh.org	Greenwood	MS	38930	662-459-7000	459-2719
Grenada Lake Medical Ctr (GLMC) 960 Avent Dr Web: www.glmc.net	Grenada	MS	38901	662-227-7000	227-7021
Jeff Anderson Regional Medical Ctr 2124 14th St Web: www.jarmc.org	Meridian	MS	39301	601-553-6000	553-6144
King's Daughters Medical Ctr 427 Hwy 51 N	Brookhaven	MS	39601	601-833-6011	833-2791
Magnolia Regional Health Ctr 611 Alcorn Dr Web: www.mrhc.org	Corinth	MS	38834	662-293-1000	293-7667
Memorial Hospital at Gulfport 4500 13th St Web: www.gulfportmemorial.com	Gulfport	MS	39501	228-867-4000	865-3098
Natchez Regional Medical Ctr 54 Sergeant S Prentiss Dr Web: www.natchezregional.com	Natchez	MS	39120	601-443-2100	445-0362
North Mississippi Medical Ctr 830 S Gloster St Web: www.nmhs.net/tupelo	Tupelo	MS	38801	662-377-3000	377-3564
Northwest Mississippi Regional Medical Ctr 1970 Hospital Dr Web: www.northwestregional.com	Clarksdale	MS	38614	662-627-3211	627-5440
Oktibbeha County Hospital 400 Hospital Rd Web: www.och.org	Starkville	MS	39759	662-323-4320	
River Oaks Hospital 1030 River Oaks Dr Web: www.riveroakshospital.org	Jackson	MS	39232	601-932-1030	936-2263
River Region Medical Ctr 2100 Hwy 61 N Web: www.riverregion.com	Vicksburg	MS	39183	601-631-2131	883-5196
River Region West Campus 1111 N Frontage Rd TF: 800-548-2419 ■ Web: www.riverregion.com	Vicksburg	MS	39180	601-636-2611	631-6094
Rush Foundation Hospital 1314 19th Ave Web: www.rushhealthsystems.org	Meridian	MS	39301	601-483-0011	703-4427
Saint Dominic-Jackson Memorial Hospital 969 Lakeland Dr Web: www.stdom.com	Jackson	MS	39216	601-200-2000	200-6800
Singing River Hospital 2809 Denny Ave Web: www.mysrhs.com	Pascagoula	MS	39581	228-809-5000	809-5064
South Central Regional Medical Ctr (SCRMC) 1220 Jefferson St Web: www.scrmc.com	Laurel	MS	39440	601-426-4000	
Southwest Mississippi Regional Medical Ctr 215 Marion Ave Web: www.smrmc.com	McComb	MS	39648	601-249-5500	249-1709
University of Mississippi Medical Ctr 2500 N State St Web: www.umc.edu	Jackson	MS	39216	601-984-1000	984-4125
Wesley Medical Ctr 5001 Hardy St TF: 800-622-8892 ■ Web: www.wesley.com	Hattiesburg	MS	39402	601-268-8000	268-5008

MISSOURI

	City	State	Zip	Phone	Fax
Audrain Medical Ctr 620 E Monroe St TF: 800-748-7098 ■ Web: www.audrainmedicalcenter.com	Mexico	MO	65265	573-582-5000	582-3700

				Phone	Fax
Barnes-Jewish Hospital 1 Barnes-Jewish Hospital Plaza *Web:* www.barnesjewish.org	Saint Louis	MO	63110	314-362-5000	362-3725
Barnes-Jewish Saint Peters Hospital 10 Hospital Dr *Web:* www.bjc.org	Saint Peters	MO	63376	636-447-6600	916-9414
Boone Hospital Ctr 1600 E Broadway *Web:* www.boone.org	Columbia	MO	65201	573-815-8000	815-2638
Bothwell Regional Health Ctr 601 E 14th St *Web:* www.brhc.org	Sedalia	MO	65302	660-826-8833	
Capital Region Medical Ctr 1125 Madison St *Web:* www.crmc.org	Jefferson City	MO	65101	573-632-5000	632-5880
Centerpoint Medical Ctr 19600 E 39th St *Web:* www.centerpointmedical.com	Independence	MO	64057	816-698-7000	698-7003
Christian Hospital Northeast 11133 Dunn Rd **Fax:* Admissions ■ *Web:* www.christianhospital.org	Saint Louis	MO	63136	314-355-2300	653-4408*
Columbia Regional Hospital 404 Keene St *Web:* www.columbiaregional.org	Columbia	MO	65201	573-875-9200	449-7588
Cox Hospital North 1423 N Jefferson Ave *Web:* www.coxhealth.com	Springfield	MO	65802	417-269-3000	269-8204
Cox Hospital South 3801 S National Ave *Web:* www.coxhealth.com	Springfield	MO	65807	417-269-6000	269-4108
DesPeres Hospital 2345 Dougherty Ferry Rd *TF:* 888-457-5203 ■ *Web:* www.despereshospital.com	Saint Louis	MO	63122	314-966-9100	966-9274
Freeman Health System 1102 W 32nd St *Web:* www.freemanhealth.com	Joplin	MO	64804	417-347-1111	
Golden Valley Memorial Hospital 1600 N 2nd St *TF:* 800-748-7681 ■ *Web:* www.gvmh.org	Clinton	MO	64735	660-885-5511	885-8496
Hannibal Regional Hospital 6500 Hospital Dr *Web:* www.hrhonline.org	Hannibal	MO	63401	573-248-1300	248-5264
Heartland Hospital East 5325 Faraon St *TF:* 800-443-1143 ■ *Web:* www.heartland-health.com	Saint Joseph	MO	64506	816-271-6000	271-6659
Jefferson Regional Medical Ctr (JRMC) Hwy 61 S PO Box 350 *Web:* www.jeffersonmemorial.org	Crystal City	MO	63019	636-933-1000	933-1119
Kindred Hospital - Saint Louis 4930 Lindell Blvd *Web:* www.kindredstlouis.com	Saint Louis	MO	63108	314-361-8700	361-1210
Lake Regional Health System 54 Hospital Dr *Web:* www.lakeregional.com	Osage Beach	MO	65065	573-348-8000	348-8309
Liberty Hospital 2525 Glenn Hendren Dr *TF:* 888-610-7084 ■ *Web:* www.libertyhospital.org	Liberty	MO	64068	816-781-7200	792-7117
Mineral Area Regional Medical Ctr (WARMC) 1212 Weber Rd *Web:* www.mineralarearegional.com	Farmington	MO	63640	573-756-4581	756-6007
Missouri Baptist Hospital of Sullivan 751 Sappington Bridge Rd *TF:* 866-888-8918 ■ *Web:* www.missouribaptistsullivan.org	Sullivan	MO	63080	573-468-4186	860-2696
Missouri Baptist Medical Ctr 3015 N Ballas Rd **Fax Area Code:* 314 ■ *TF:* 800-392-0936 ■ *Web:* www.missouribaptist.org	Saint Louis	MO	63131	341-996-5000	996-5373*
Missouri Delta Medical Ctr 1019 N Main St *Web:* www.missouridelta.com	Sikeston	MO	63801	573-471-1600	472-7606
North Kansas City Hospital 2800 Clay Edwards Dr *Web:* www.nkch.org	North Kansas City	MO	64116	816-691-2000	346-7020
Ozarks Medical Ctr 1100 N Kentucky Ave *Web:* www.ozarksmedicalcenter.com	West Plains	MO	65775	417-256-9111	257-6770
Parkland Health Ctr 1101 W Liberty St *Web:* www.parklandhealthcenter.org	Farmington	MO	63640	573-756-6451	760-8354
Poplar Bluff Regional Medical Center South Campus 621 WPine Blvd *TF:* 800-327-0275 ■ *Web:* www.poplarbluffregional.com	Poplar Bluff	MO	63901	573-686-4111	727-7462
Poplar Bluff Regional Medical Ctr 2620 N Westwood Blvd *TF:* 800-327-0275 ■ *Web:* www.poplarbluffregional.com	Poplar Bluff	MO	63901	573-785-7721	727-2498
Research Medical Ctr 2316 E Meyer Blvd	Kansas City	MO	64132	816-276-4000	276-4387
Saint Alexius Hospital *Broadway Campus* 3933 S Broadway *Web:* www.stalexiushospital.com	Saint Louis	MO	63118	314-865-3333	865-7938
Forest Park Campus 6150 Oakland Ave *TF:* 877-249-8557 ■ *Web:* www.stalexiushospital.com	Saint Louis	MO	63139	314-865-7000	865-3337
Saint Anthony's Medical Ctr 10010 Kennerly Rd *Web:* www.stanthonysmedcenter.com	Saint Louis	MO	63128	314-525-1000	525-1228
Saint Francis Medical Ctr 211 St Francis Dr *Web:* www.sfmc.net	Cape Girardeau	MO	63703	573-331-3000	331-5009
Saint John's Hospital 1235 E Cherokee St *Web:* www.stjohns.com	Springfield	MO	65804	417-885-2000	820-2288
Saint John's Mercy Medical Ctr 615 S New Ballas Rd *Web:* www.stjohnsmercy.org	Saint Louis	MO	63141	314-251-6000	251-6910
Saint John's Regional Medical Ctr 2727 McClelland Blvd *Web:* www.stj.com	Joplin	MO	64804	417-781-2727	625-2910
Saint Joseph Health Ctr 1000 Carondelet Dr *Web:* www.carondelethealth.org	Kansas City	MO	64114	816-942-4400	943-3131
Saint Louis University Hospital 3635 Vista Ave *Web:* www.sluhospital.com	Saint Louis	MO	63110	314-577-8000	577-8003
Saint Luke's Hospital 232 S Woods Mill Rd *Web:* www.stlukes-stl.com	Chesterfield	MO	63017	314-434-1500	205-6865
Saint Luke's Hospital 4401 Wornall Rd *Web:* www.saintlukeshealthsystem.org	Kansas City	MO	64111	816-932-2000	932-5990
Saint Mary's Health Ctr (SMHC) 100 St Marys Medical Plaza *Web:* www.lethealingbegin.com	Jefferson City	MO	65101	573-761-7000	636-5733
Saint Mary's Health Ctr 6420 Clayton Rd *TF:* 800-468-7642 ■ *Web:* www.ssmhealth.com	Richmond Heights	MO	63117	314-768-8000	768-8011
Saint Mary's Medical Ctr 201 NW Rd Mize Rd *Web:* www.stmaryskc.com	Blue Springs	MO	64014	816-228-5900	655-5408
Skaggs Community Health Ctr 261 Skaggs Rd *Web:* www.skaggs.net	Branson	MO	65616	417-335-7000	334-1505
Southeast Missouri Hospital (SMH) 1701 Lacey St *TF:* 800-800-5123 ■ *Web:* www.sehealth.org	Cape Girardeau	MO	63701	573-334-4822	651-5850
SSM Saint Joseph Health Ctr 300 1st Capitol Dr *Web:* www.ssmhealth.com	Saint Charles	MO	63301	636-949-7077	
SSM Saint Joseph Hospital of Kirkwood 525 Couch Ave *Web:* www.stjosephkirkwood.com	Kirkwood	MO	63122	314-966-1500	966-1681
St John's Health System 1235 E Cherokee *TF:* 800-909-8326 ■ *Web:* www.stjohns.net	Springfield	MO	65804	417-820-2000	820-6996
Truman Medical Center Hospital Hill 2301 Holmes St *Web:* www.trumed.org	Kansas City	MO	64108	816-404-1000	404-2828
Twin Rivers Regional Medical Ctr (TRRMC) 1301 1st St *Web:* www.twinriversregional.com	Kennett	MO	63857	573-888-4522	888-5525
University Hospital 1 Hospital Dr *Web:* www.muhealth.org	Columbia	MO	65212	573-882-4141	884-4174
US Medical Center for Federal Prisoners 1900 W Sunshine St *Web:* www.bop.gov	Springfield	MO	65807	417-862-7041	837-1711

MONTANA

				Phone	Fax
Benefis Health Care *West Campus* 1101 26th St S *Web:* www.benefis.org	Great Falls	MT	59405	406-455-5000	455-2189
Benefis Healthcare *East Campus* 1101 26th St S *Web:* www.benefis.org	Great Falls	MT	59405	406-761-1200	455-4587
Billings Clinic 2800 10th Ave N *TF:* 800-332-7156 ■ *Web:* www.billingsclinic.com	Billings	MT	59101	406-657-4000	238-2785
Bozeman Deaconess Hospital 915 Highland Blvd *Web:* www.bozemandeaconess.org	Bozeman	MT	59715	406-585-5000	585-1070
Community Medical Ctr 2827 Fort Missoula Rd *Web:* www.communitymed.org	Missoula	MT	59804	406-728-4100	327-4501
Holy Rosary Healthcare 2600 Wilson St *TF:* 800-843-3820 ■ *Web:* www.holyrosaryhealthcare.org	Miles City	MT	59301	406-233-2600	233-4214
Kalispell Regional Medical Ctr 310 Sunnyview Ln *TF:* 800-228-1574 ■ *Web:* www.nwhc.org	Kalispell	MT	59901	406-752-5111	756-2703
Livingston Healtcare 504 S 13th St *Web:* www.livingstonhealthcare.org	Livingston	MT	59047	406-222-3541	222-5099
Saint James Healthcare 400 S Clark St *Web:* www.stjameshealthcare.org	Butte	MT	59701	406-723-2500	723-2443
Saint Patrick Hospital 500 W Broadway St *Web:* www.saintpatrick.org	Missoula	MT	59802	406-543-7271	329-5693
Saint Peter's Hospital 2475 Broadway *Web:* www.stpetes.org	Helena	MT	59601	406-442-2480	444-2389
Saint Vincent Healthcare 1233 N 30th St *Web:* www.svh-mt.org	Billings	MT	59101	406-657-7000	237-3078
St Johns Lutheran Hospital Inc 350 Louisiana Ave *Web:* www.sjlh.org	Libby	MT	59923	406-293-0100	293-7931
St Luke Community Hospital (inc) 107 6th Ave SW *Web:* www.stlukehealthnet.org	Ronan	MT	59864	406-676-4441	

NEBRASKA

				Phone	Fax
Bergen Mercy Medical Ctr 7500 Mercy Rd *Web:* www.alegent.com	Omaha	NE	68124	402-398-6060	398-6920
Bryan LGH Medical Center East 1600 S 48th St *TF:* 800-742-7844 ■ *Web:* www.bryanlgh.org	Lincoln	NE	68506	402-489-0200	481-8306
Bryan LGH Medical Center West 2300 S 16th St *Web:* www.bryanlgh.org	Lincoln	NE	68502	402-475-1011	
Creighton University Medical Ctr 601 N 30th St *Web:* www.creighton.edu	Omaha	NE	68131	402-449-4000	449-5020
Faith Regional Health Services 2700 W Norfolk Ave *Web:* www.frhs.org	Norfolk	NE	68701	402-371-4880	644-7468
Fremont Area Medical Ctr 450 E 23rd St *Web:* www.famc.org	Fremont	NE	68025	402-721-1610	727-3656
Good Samaritan Hospital 10 E 31st St *TF:* 800-658-4250 ■ *Web:* www.gshs.org	Kearney	NE	68847	308-865-7100	865-2913
Great Plains Regional Medical Ctr (GPRMC) 601 W Leota St PO Box 1167 *TF:* 800-662-0011 ■ *Web:* www.gprmc.com	North Platte	NE	69101	308-696-8000	535-3410
Immanuel Medical Ctr 6901 N 72nd St *Web:* www.alegent.com	Omaha	NE	68122	402-572-2121	572-3177
Mary Lanning Memorial Hospital 715 N St Joseph Ave *Web:* www.mlmh.org	Hastings	NE	68901	402-463-4521	461-5321
Midlands Community Hospital 11111 S 84th St *Web:* www.alegent.com/body.cfm?id=2676	Papillion	NE	68046	402-593-3000	593-3100

	City	State	Zip	Phone	Fax
Nebraska Medical Ctr The 4350 Dewey Ave. *Web:* www.nebraskamed.com	Omaha	NE	68105	402-552-2000	552-3267
Nebraska Methodist Hospital 8303 Dodge St *Web:* www.bestcare.org	Omaha	NE	68114	402-390-4000	354-8735
Regional West Medical Ctr 4021 Ave B *Web:* www.rwmc.net	Scottsbluff	NE	69361	308-635-3711	630-1815
Saint Elizabeth Regional Medical Ctr 555 S 70th St *Web:* www.saintelizabethonline.com	Lincoln	NE	68510	402-219-8000	219-8973
Saint Francis Medical Ctr (SFMC) 2620 W Faidley Ave *TF:* 800-353-4896 ■ *Web:* www.saintfrancisgi.org/index2.php	Grand Island	NE	68803	308-384-4600	398-5589
University of Nebraska Medical Ctr 600 S 42nd St. *TF:* 800-642-1095 ■ *Web:* www.unmc.edu	Omaha	NE	68198	402-559-7416	559-7866

NEVADA

	City	State	Zip	Phone	Fax
Carson Tahoe Hospital 1600 Medical Pkwy *Web:* www.carsontahoehospital.com	Carson City	NV	89703	775-882-1361	887-4580
Desert Springs Hospital Medical Ctr 2075 E Flamingo Rd *Web:* www.desertspringshospital.net	Las Vegas	NV	89119	702-733-8800	369-7836
MountainView Hospital 3100 N Tenaya Way *Web:* www.mountainview-hospital.com	Las Vegas	NV	89128	702-255-5000	255-5074
Northern Nevada Medical Ctr 2375 E Prater Way *Web:* www.northernnvmed.com	Sparks	NV	89434	775-331-7000	356-4986
Renown Regional Medical Ctr 1155 Mill St *Web:* www.renown.org	Reno	NV	89502	775-982-4100	982-4111
Saint Mary's Regional Medical Ctr 235 W 6th St. *Web:* www.saintmarysreno.com	Reno	NV	89503	775-770-3000	770-3621
Saint Rose Dominican Hospital *Rose de Lima Campus* 102 E Lake Mead Dr *Web:* www.strosecares.com	Henderson	NV	89015	702-564-2622	616-7549
Summerlin Hospital Medical Ctr 657 Town Ctr Dr *Web:* www.summerlinhospital.org	Las Vegas	NV	89144	702-233-7000	
Sunrise Hospital & Medical Ctr 3186 S Maryland Pkwy *Web:* www.sunrisehospital.com	Las Vegas	NV	89109	702-731-8000	731-8668
University Medical Ctr 1800 W Charleston Blvd *Web:* www.umc-cares.org	Las Vegas	NV	89102	702-383-2000	383-2067
Valley Hospital Medical Ctr 620 Shadow Ln *Web:* www.valleyhospital.net	Las Vegas	NV	89106	702-388-4000	388-4636

NEW HAMPSHIRE

	City	State	Zip	Phone	Fax
Catholic Medical Ctr (CMC) 100 McGregor St. *TF:* 800-437-9666 ■ *Web:* www.catholicmedicalcenter.org	Manchester	NH	03102	603-668-3545	663-6989
Cheshire Medical Ctr 590 Ct St. *Web:* www.cheshire-med.com	Keene	NH	03431	603-352-4111	354-5402
Concord Hospital 250 Pleasant St *Web:* www.concordhospital.org	Concord	NH	03301	603-225-2711	228-7020
Dartmouth-Hitchcock Medical Ctr 1 Medical Ctr Dr *Web:* www.dhmc.org	Lebanon	NH	03756	603-650-5000	650-8765
Elliot Hospital 1 Elliot Way Suite 100 *Web:* www.elliothospital.org	Manchester	NH	03103	603-627-1669	624-2297
Exeter Hospital 5 Alumni Dr *Web:* www.exeterhospital.com	Exeter	NH	03833	603-580-6668	580-6592
Frisbie Memorial Hospital 15 Whitehall Rd *Web:* www.frisbiehospital.com	Rochester	NH	03867	603-332-5211	335-8488
Lakes Region General Hospital 80 Highland St. *Web:* www.lrgh.org	Laconia	NH	03246	603-524-3211	527-2887
Parkland Medical Ctr 1 Parkland Dr *Web:* www.parklandmedicalcenter.com	Derry	NH	03038	603-432-1500	421-2111
Portsmouth Regional Hospital 333 Borthwick Ave *TF:* 800-685-8282 ■ *Web:* www.portsmouthhospital.com	Portsmouth	NH	03801	603-436-5110	431-3783
Saint Joseph Hospital 172 Kinsley St *TF:* 877-899-6345 ■ *Web:* www.stjosephhospital.com	Nashua	NH	03060	603-882-3000	889-1651
Southern New Hampshire Medical Ctr 8 Prospect St PO Box 2014 *Web:* www.formsweb.snhmc.org	Nashua	NH	03061	603-577-2000	577-5630
Speare Memorial Hospital Assn 16 Hospital Rd *Web:* www.spearehospital.com	Plymouth	NH	03264	603-536-1120	536-1083
Wentworth-Douglass Hospital 789 Central Ave. *TF:* 877-201-7100 ■ *Web:* www.wdhospital.com	Dover	NH	03820	603-742-5252	740-2242

NEW JERSEY

	City	State	Zip	Phone	Fax
Atlanticare Regional Medical Ctr 1925 Pacific Ave *Web:* www.atlanticare.org	Atlantic City	NJ	08401	609-344-4081	569-7020
Bayshore Community Hospital 727 N Beers St *Web:* www.bchs.com	Holmdel	NJ	07733	732-739-5900	739-5887
Bergen Regional Medical Ctr 230 E Ridgewood Ave *Web:* www.bergenregional.com	Paramus	NJ	07652	201-967-4000	967-4277
Cape Regional Medical Ctr Inc (CRMC) 2 Stone Harbor Blvd *Web:* www.caperegional.com	Cape May Court House	NJ	08210	609-463-2000	465-9391
Capital Health System at Fuld 750 Brunswick Ave *Web:* www.capitalhealth.org	Trenton	NJ	08638	609-394-6000	394-6687
Capital Health System at Mercer 446 Bellevue Ave *Web:* www.capitalhealth.org	Trenton	NJ	08618	609-394-4000	394-4032
CentraState Medical Ctr 901 W Main St *Web:* www.centrastate.com	Freehold	NJ	07728	732-431-2000	462-5129
Chilton Hospital 97 W Pkwy *Web:* www.chiltonmemorial.org	Pompton Plains	NJ	07444	973-831-5000	831-5183
Christ Hospital 176 Palisade Ave *Web:* www.christhospital.org	Jersey City	NJ	07306	201-795-8200	795-8758
Clara Maass Medical Ctr 1 Clara Maass Dr *Web:* www.saintbarnabas.com	Belleville	NJ	07109	973-450-2000	450-0181
Columbus Hospital 495 N 13th St	Newark	NJ	07107	973-268-1400	268-1523
Community Medical Ctr (CMC) 99 Hwy 37 W *TF:* 888-724-7123 ■ *Web:* www.sbhcs.com/hospitals/community_medical/index.html	Toms River	NJ	08755	732-240-8000	557-8935
Cooper University Hospital 3 Cooper Plaza *TF:* 800-826-6737 ■ *Web:* www.cooperhealth.org	Camden	NJ	08103	856-342-2000	342-3299
East Orange General Hospital 300 Central Ave *Web:* www.evh.org	East Orange	NJ	07017	973-672-8400	
Englewood Hospital & Medical Ctr 350 Engle St *Web:* www.englewoodhospital.com	Englewood	NJ	07631	201-894-3000	894-1345
Hackensack University Medical Ctr 30 Prospect Ave *Web:* www.humed.com	Hackensack	NJ	07601	201-996-2000	489-7275
Hoboken University Medical Ctr 308 Willow Ave. *Web:* www.hobokenumc.com	Hoboken	NJ	07030	201-418-1000	418-1428
Holy Name Hospital 718 Teaneck Rd *Web:* www.holyname.org	Teaneck	NJ	07666	201-833-3000	833-3230
Hunterdon Medical Ctr 2100 Westcott Dr *Web:* www.hunterdonhealthcare.org	Flemington	NJ	08822	908-788-6100	788-6111
Irvington General Hospital 832 Chancellor Ave. *Web:* www.saintbarnabas.com	Irvington	NJ	07111	973-399-6000	373-0799
Jersey City Medical Ctr 355 Grand St. *Web:* www.libertyhealth.org	Jersey City	NJ	07302	201-915-2000	915-2559
Jersey Shore University Medical Ctr 1945 Rt 33 *TF:* 800-560-9990 ■ *Web:* www.jerseyshoreuniversitymedicalcenter.com	Neptune	NJ	07753	732-775-5500	776-4836
JFK Medical Ctr 65 James St *Web:* www.jfkmc.org	Edison	NJ	08818	732-321-7000	549-8532
Kennedy Health System-Cherry Hill 2201 Chapel Ave W *Web:* www.kennedyhealth.org	Cherry Hill	NJ	08002	856-488-6789	488-6526
Kimball Medical Ctr 600 River Ave *Web:* www.saintbarnabas.com	Lakewood	NJ	08701	732-363-1900	886-4406
Lifeline Medical Assoc LLC PO Box 34175 *Fax Area Code: 973 ■ *Web:* www.lma-llc.com	Newark	NJ	07189	800-845-2785	316-0307*
Lourdes Medical Center of Burlington County 218-A Sunset Rd *Web:* www.lourdesnet.org/burlington	Willingboro	NJ	08046	609-835-2900	835-3061
Meadowlands Hospital Medical Ctr 55 Meadowland Pkwy *Web:* www.libertyhealth.org	Secaucus	NJ	07096	201-392-3100	392-3527
Memorial Hospital of Salem County 310 Woodstown Rd. *Web:* www.mhschealth.com	Salem	NJ	08079	856-935-1000	935-3175
Monmouth Medical Ctr 300 2nd Ave *TF:* 888-661-7484 ■ *Web:* www.saintbarnabas.com	Long Branch	NJ	07740	732-222-5200	923-7544
Morristown Medical Ctr 100 Madison Ave *Web:* www.atlantichealth.org	Morristown	NJ	07960	973-971-5000	290-7010
Mountainside Hospital 1 Bay Ave *Web:* www.atlantichealth.org	Montclair	NJ	07042	973-429-6000	429-6209
Muhlenberg Regional Medical Ctr Park Ave & Randolph Rd. *Web:* www.muhlenberg.com/index.htm	Plainfield	NJ	07061	908-668-2000	226-4517
Newark Beth Israel Medical Ctr 201 Lyons Ave *Web:* www.saintbarnabas.com	Newark	NJ	07112	973-926-7000	923-2886
Newton Memorial Hospital (NMH) 175 High St. *Web:* www.nmhnj.org	Newton	NJ	07860	973-383-2121	383-8973
Ocean Medical Ctr (OMC) 425 Jack Martin Blvd. *TF:* 800-560-9990 ■ *Web:* www.oceanmedicalcenter.com/OMC	Brick	NJ	08724	732-840-2200	840-3284
Our Lady of Lourdes Medical Ctr 1600 Haddon Ave *Web:* www.lourdesnet.org	Camden	NJ	08103	856-757-3500	757-3611
Overlook Medical Ctr 99 Beauvoir Ave *Web:* www.atlantichealth.org	Summit	NJ	07902	908-522-2000	273-5134
Palisades Medical Ctr 7600 River Rd *Fax: Admitting ■ *Web:* www.palisadesmedical.org	North Bergen	NJ	07047	201-854-5000	854-5272*
Pascack Valley Hospital 250 Old Hook Rd. *Fax: Admitting ■ *Web:* www.pvhospital.org	Westwood	NJ	07675	201-358-3000	358-3624*
Raritan Bay Medical Ctr 530 New Brunswick Ave *Fax: Hum Res ■ *Web:* www.rbmc.org	Perth Amboy	NJ	08861	732-442-3700	293-2297*
Riverview Medical Ctr 1 Riverview Plaza *Web:* www.meridianhealth.com/rmc.cfm/index.cfm	Red Bank	NJ	07701	732-741-2700	224-8408
Robert Wood Johnson University Hospital 1 Robert Wood Johnson Pl. *TF:* 888-637-9584 ■ *Web:* www.rwjuh.edu	New Brunswick	NJ	08901	732-828-3000	937-8730
Robert Wood Johnson University Hospital at Rahway (RWJUHR) 865 Stone St. *Web:* www.rwjuhr.com	Rahway	NJ	07065	732-381-4200	499-6337
RWJ University Hospital at Hamilton 1 Hamilton Health Pl. *Web:* www.rwjhamilton.org	Hamilton	NJ	08690	609-586-7900	584-6429
Saint Barnabas Medical Ctr 94 Old Short Hills Rd *Fax: Admitting ■ *TF:* 888-724-7123 ■ *Web:* www.saintbarnabas.com	West Orange	NJ	07052	973-322-5000	322-8790*
Saint Clare's Hospital 25 Pocono Rd *Web:* www.saintclares.org	Denville	NJ	07834	973-625-6000	625-6184

	City	State	Zip	Phone	Fax
Saint Francis Medical Ctr 601 Hamilton Ave *TF:* 800-950-2549 ■ *Web:* www.stfrancismedical.com	Trenton	NJ	08629	609-599-5000	695-2744
Saint James Hospital of Newark 155 Jefferson St *Web:* www.cathedralhealth.org	Newark	NJ	07105	973-589-1300	465-2590
Saint Joseph's Regional Medical Ctr 703 Main St *Web:* www.stjosephshealth.org	Paterson	NJ	07503	973-754-2000	754-2208
Saint Mary's Hospital (SMH) 350 Blvd *Web:* www.smh-passaic.org	Passaic	NJ	07055	973-365-4300	470-0184
Saint Michael's Medical Ctr 268 Dr ML King Jr Blvd *Web:* www.cathedralhealth.org	Newark	NJ	07102	973-877-5000	
Saint Peter's University Hospital 254 Easton Ave **Fax:* Admitting ■ *Web:* www.saintpetershcs.com	New Brunswick	NJ	08901	732-745-8600	247-8159*
Shore Memorial Hospital 1 E New York Ave *Web:* www.shorememorial.org	Somers Point	NJ	08244	609-653-3500	927-8172
SJH Elmer Hospital 501 W Front St *Web:* www.sjhealthcare.net	Elmer	NJ	08318	856-363-1000	358-3476
SJH Regional Medical Ctr (SJHRMC) 1505 W Sheman Ave *Web:* www.sjhealthcare.net	Vineland	NJ	08360	856-641-8000	451-7903
Somerset Medical Ctr (SMC) 110 Rehill Ave *Web:* www.somersetmedicalcenter.com	Somerville	NJ	08876	908-685-2200	685-2894
Southern Jersey Family Medical Centers Inc 1 White Horse Ctr *Web:* www.sjfmc.org	Hammonton	NJ	08037	609-567-0434	
Southern Ocean County Hospital 1140 Rt 72 W	Manahawkin	NJ	08050	609-978-9639	978-8920
St Joseph's Wayne Hospital 224 Hamburg Tpke *Web:* www.stjosephshealth.org	Wayne	NJ	07470	973-942-6900	389-4010
Trinitas Hospital 225 Williamson St *Web:* www.trinitashospital.com	Elizabeth	NJ	07207	908-994-5000	994-5756
Underwood-Memorial Hospital 509 N Broad St *Web:* www.umhospital.org	Woodbury	NJ	08096	856-845-0100	845-5322
Union Hospital 1000 Galloping Hill Rd *Web:* www.sbhcs.com	Union	NJ	07083	908-687-1900	851-7281
University Medical Center at Princeton (UMCP) 253 Witherspoon St *TF:* 866-460-4776 ■ *Web:* www.princetonhcs.org/default.aspx?p=7560	Princeton	NJ	08540	609-497-4000	497-4977
University of Medicine & Dentistry of New Jersey *The University Hospital* 150 Bergen St C- 431 *Web:* www.theuniversityhospital.com	Newark	NJ	07103	973-972-4300	972-6932
Valley Health System 223 N Van Dien Ave *TF:* 800-825-5391 ■ *Web:* www.valleyhealth.com	Ridgewood	NJ	07450	201-447-8000	
Virtua Voorhees 101 Carnie Blvd *Web:* www.virtua.org	Voorhees	NJ	08043	856-325-3328	
Virtua-Memorial Hospital Burlington County 175 Madison Ave *Web:* www.virtua.org	Mount Holly	NJ	08060	609-267-0700	702-9751
Warren Hospital 185 Roseberry St *Web:* www.warrenhospital.org	Phillipsburg	NJ	08865	908-859-6700	213-1139
West Jersey Hospital Berlin 100 Townsend Ave *Web:* www.virtua.org	Berlin	NJ	08009	856-322-3000	322-3201
West Jersey Hospital Marlton 90 Brick Rd *Web:* www.virtua.org/page.cfm?id=about_loc_marlton	Marlton	NJ	08053	856-355-6000	355-6201

NEW MEXICO

	City	State	Zip	Phone	Fax
Albuquerque Regional Medical Ctr 601 ML King Jr Dr	Albuquerque	NM	87102	505-727-8000	727-7888
Carlsbad Medical Ctr 2430 W Pierce St *Web:* www.carlsbadmedicalcenter.com	Carlsbad	NM	88220	505-887-4100	887-4256
Eastern New Mexico Medical Ctr 405 W Country Club Rd *TF:* 800-437-9275 ■ *Web:* www.enmmc.com	Roswell	NM	88201	505-622-8170	624-8726
Gallup Indian Medical Ctr 516 E Nizhoni Blvd PO Box 1337	Gallup	NM	87301	505-722-1000	722-1397
Gila Regional Medical Ctr 1313 E 32nd St *Web:* www.grmc.org	Silver City	NM	88061	505-538-4000	538-9714
Lea Regional Medical Ctr 5419 N Lovington Hwy **Fax Area Code:* 505 ■ *TF:* 877-492-8001 ■ *Web:* www.learegionalmedical.com	Hobbs	NM	88240	575-492-5000	492-5505*
Lovelace Medical Ctr 5400 Gibson Blvd SE *TF:* 800-877-7526 ■ *Web:* www.lovelace.com	Albuquerque	NM	87108	505-262-7000	262-7729
Memorial Medical Ctr 2450 S Telshor Blvd *TF:* 800-829-8641 ■ *Web:* www.mmclc.org	Las Cruces	NM	88011	575-522-8641	521-5013
MountainView Regional Medical Ctr 4311 E Lohman Ave *TF:* 877-999-7604 ■ *Web:* www.mountainviewregional.com	Las Cruces	NM	88001	575-556-7600	556-7619
Nor-Lea General Hospital Inc 1600 N Main Ave *Web:* www.nlgh.org	Lovington	NM	88260	575-396-6611	
Plains Regional Medical Ctr 2100 N ML King Blvd *TF:* 800-221-3706 ■ *Web:* www.phs.org	Clovis	NM	88101	505-769-2141	769-7337
Presbyterian Espanola Hospital 1010 Spruce St *Web:* www.phs.org/espanola	Espanola	NM	87532	505-753-7111	367-0257
Presbyterian Hospital 1100 Central Ave SE *TF:* 800-841-1861 ■ *Web:* www.phs.org	Albuquerque	NM	87106	505-841-1234	841-1861
Presbyterian Kaseman Hospital 8300 Constitution Ave NE *TF:* 800-432-4600 ■ *Web:* www.phs.org	Albuquerque	NM	87110	505-291-2000	291-2983
Rehoboth McKinley Christian Hospital 1900 Redrock Dr *Web:* www.rmch.org	Gallup	NM	87301	505-863-7000	863-5806
Saint Vincent Regional Medical Ctr 455 St Michael's Dr *Web:* www.stvin.org	Santa Fe	NM	87505	505-983-3361	820-5210
San Juan Regional Medical Ctr 801 W Maple St *Web:* www.sanjuanregional.com	Farmington	NM	87401	505-325-5011	599-6249
University Hospital 2211 Lomas Blvd NE **Fax:* Admitting ■ *Web:* www.hospitals.unm.edu	Albuquerque	NM	87106	505-272-2111	272-0122*

NEW YORK

	City	State	Zip	Phone	Fax
Adirondack Medical Ctr 2233 SR-86 PO Box 471 *Web:* www.amccares.org	Saranac Lake	NY	12983	518-891-4141	891-1191
Albany Medical Ctr 47 New Scotland Ave *Web:* www.amc.edu	Albany	NY	12208	518-262-3125	262-3398
Albany Memorial Hospital 600 Northern Blvd *Web:* www.nehealth.com	Albany	NY	12204	518-471-3221	449-4410
Alice Hyde Medical Ctr 133 Pk St *Web:* www.alicehyde.com	Malone	NY	12953	518-483-3000	481-2320
Arnot Ogden Medical Ctr 600 Roe Ave *Web:* www.aomc.org	Elmira	NY	14905	607-737-4100	737-4447
Auburn Memorial Hospital 17 Lansing St *Web:* www.auburnhospital.org	Auburn	NY	13021	315-255-7011	255-7382
Aurelia Osborn Fox Memorial Hospital 1 Norton Ave *Web:* www.aofoxhospital.com	Oneonta	NY	13820	607-432-2000	431-5006
Bassett Healthcare Network 1 Atwell Rd *TF:* 800-227-7388 ■ *Web:* www.bassett.org	Cooperstown	NY	13326	607-547-3456	547-3921
Bellevue Hospital Ctr 462 1st Ave	New York	NY	10016	212-562-4141	562-4036
Beth Israel Medical Ctr 1st Ave & 16th St *Web:* www.bethisraelny.org	New York	NY	10003	212-420-2000	844-1565
Kings Highway Div 3201 Kings Hwy *Web:* www.bethisraelny.org	Brooklyn	NY	11239	718-252-3000	951-2726
Bon Secours Community Hospital 160 E Main St *Web:* www.bonsecourscommunityhosp.org	Port Jervis	NY	12771	845-858-7000	858-7415
Brookdale University Hospital & Medical Ctr 1 Brookdale Plaza *Web:* www.brookdalehospital.org	Brooklyn	NY	11212	718-240-5000	240-5042
Brookhaven Memorial Hospital Medical Ctr 101 Hospital Rd *Web:* www.brookhavenhospital.org	Patchogue	NY	11772	631-654-7100	447-3714
Brooklyn Hospital Ctr 121 DeKalb Ave *Web:* www.tbh.org	Brooklyn	NY	11201	718-250-8000	250-8902
Brooks Memorial Hospital 529 Central Ave *TF:* 800-366-0717 ■ *Web:* www.brookshospital.org	Dunkirk	NY	14048	716-366-1111	363-7288
Brunswick Hospital Ctr 366 Broadway *Web:* www.brunswickhospital.com	Amityville	NY	11701	631-789-7421	789-4929
Buffalo General Hospital 100 High St *TF:* 800-242-0055 ■ *Web:* www.kaleidahealth.org	Buffalo	NY	14203	716-859-5600	859-3323
Catskill Regional Medical Ctr 68 Harris-Bushville Rd PO Box 800 *TF:* 800-633-3413 ■ *Web:* www.crmcny.org	Harris	NY	12742	845-794-3300	794-3240
Cayuga Medical Ctr 101 Dates Dr *Web:* www.cayugamed.org	Ithaca	NY	14850	607-274-4011	274-4527
Claxton-Hepburn Medical Ctr 214 King St **Fax:* Hum Res ■ *Web:* www.chmed.org	Ogdensburg	NY	13669	315-393-3600	393-8506*
Clifton Springs Hospital & Clinic 2 Coulter Rd *Web:* www.cliftonspringshospital.com	Clifton Springs	NY	14432	315-462-9561	462-3492
Columbia Memorial Hospital 71 Prospect Ave *Web:* www.columbiamemorial.com	Hudson	NY	12534	518-828-7601	828-8525
Coney Island Hospital 2601 Ocean Pkwy *Web:* www.ci.nyc.ny.us/html/hhc/html/facilities/coneyisland.shtml	Brooklyn	NY	11235	718-616-3000	616-4512
Corning Hospital 176 Denison Pkwy E *TF:* 800-295-1122 ■ *Web:* www.corninghospital.com	Corning	NY	14830	607-937-7200	937-7693
Cortland Regional Medical Ctr (CRMC) 134 Homer Ave PO Box 2010 *Web:* www.cortlandregional.org	Cortland	NY	13045	607-756-3500	756-3590
Crouse Hospital 736 Irving Ave *Web:* www.crouse.org	Syracuse	NY	13210	315-470-7111	470-7014
CVPH Medical Ctr (CPVH) 75 Beekman St *Web:* www.cvph.org	Plattsburgh	NY	12901	518-561-2000	561-0881
De Graff Memorial Hospital 445 Tremont St *Web:* www.kaleidahealth.org	North Tonawanda	NY	14120	716-694-4500	690-2300
Eastern Long Island Hospital Assn The 201 Manor Pl *Web:* www.elih.org	Greenport	NY	11944	631-477-1000	
Ellis Hospital 1101 Nott St *TF:* 888-355-4746 ■ *Web:* www.ellismedicine.org/Home/EllisHospitalMain.aspx	Schenectady	NY	12308	518-243-4000	243-4668
Elmhurst Hospital Ctr 79-01 Broadway	Elmhurst	NY	11373	718-334-4000	334-5161
Erie County Medical Ctr 462 Grider St *Web:* www.ecmc.edu	Buffalo	NY	14215	716-898-3000	898-5178
Faxton Saint Luke's Healthcare *Faxton Campus* 1676 Sunset Ave *Web:* www.faxtonstlukes.com	Utica	NY	13502	315-624-6000	624-4418
Saint Luke's Campus 1656 Champlin Ave *Web:* www.faxtonstlukes.com	New Hartford	NY	13413	315-624-6000	624-6269
FF Thompson Hospital 350 Parrish St *Web:* www.thompsonhealth.com	Canandaigua	NY	14424	585-396-6000	396-6481
Flushing Hospital Medical Ctr 4500 Parsons Blvd *Web:* www.flushinghospital.org	Flushing	NY	11355	718-670-5000	670-3077
Forest Hills Hospital (FHH) 102-01 66th Rd *Web:* www.northshorelij.com/NSLIJ/Forest+Hills+Hospital	Forest Hills	NY	11375	718-830-4000	830-4168
Franklin Hospital 900 Franklin Ave *Web:* www.northshorelij.com/body.cfm?ID=58	Valley Stream	NY	11580	516-256-6000	256-6503

				Phone	Fax
Geneva General Hospital 196 N St *Web:* www.flhealth.org	Geneva	NY	14456	315-787-4000	
Glen Cove Hospital 101 St Andrews Ln *Web:* www.northshorelij.com/body.cfm?ID=53	Glen Cove	NY	11542	516-674-7300	674-7588
Glens Falls Hospital 100 Pk St *TF:* 800-836-3151 ■ *Web:* www.glensfallshospital.org	Glens Falls	NY	12801	518-926-1000	926-1919
Good Samaritan Hospital 255 Lafayette Ave *Web:* www.goodsamhosp.org	Suffern	NY	10901	845-368-5000	368-5430
Harlem Hospital Ctr 506 Lenox Ave	New York	NY	10037	212-939-1000	939-1974
Highland Hospital of Rochester 1000 S Ave *Web:* www.stronghealth.com	Rochester	NY	14620	585-473-2200	341-8350
Hudson Valley Hospital Ctr 1980 Crompond Rd *Web:* www.hvhc.org	Cortlandt Manor	NY	10567	914-737-9000	
Huntington Hospital 270 Pk Ave *Web:* www.hunthosp.org	Huntington	NY	11743	631-351-2000	351-2586
Interfaith Medical Ctr 1545 Atlantic Ave *Web:* www.interfaithmedical.com	Brooklyn	NY	11213	718-613-4000	613-4101
Ira Davenport Memorial Hospital Inc 7571 State Rte 54 *Web:* www.davenportandtaylor.org	Bath	NY	14810	607-776-8500	
Jacobi Medical Ctr 1400 Pelham Pkwy S *Web:* www.nyc.gov/html/hhc/jacobi/home.html	Bronx	NY	10461	718-918-8141	918-4607
Jamaica Hospital Medical Ctr 8900 Van Wyck Expy *Web:* www.jamaicahospital.org	Jamaica	NY	11418	718-206-6000	657-0545
John T Mather Memorial Hospital 75 N Country Rd *Web:* www.matherhospital.org	Port Jefferson	NY	11777	631-473-1320	473-7367
Kenmore Mercy Hospital 2950 Elmwood Ave *Web:* www.chsbuffalo.org/body.cfm?id=49	Kenmore	NY	14217	716-879-6100	447-6090
Kings County Hospital Ctr 451 Clarkson Ave *Web:* www.home.nyc.gov	Brooklyn	NY	11203	718-245-3131	613-8019
Kingsbrook Jewish Medical Ctr 585 Schenectady Ave *Web:* www.kingsbrook.org	Brooklyn	NY	11203	718-604-5000	604-5243
Lawrence Hospital 55 Palmer Ave *Web:* www.lawrencehealth.org	Bronxville	NY	10708	914-787-1000	787-3113
Lenox Hill Hospital 100 E 77th St *Web:* www.lenoxhillhospital.org	New York	NY	10021	212-434-2000	434-3205
Lincoln Medical & Mental Health Ctr 234 E 149th St	Bronx	NY	10451	718-579-5000	579-5319
Little Falls Hospital 140 Burwell St *Web:* www.bassett.org	Little Falls	NY	13365	315-823-1000	823-2516
Lockport Memorial Hospital 521 E Ave	Lockport	NY	14094	716-514-5700	514-5783
Long Beach Medical Ctr 455 E Bay Dr *Web:* www.lbmc.org	Long Beach	NY	11561	516-897-1000	897-1214
Long Island College Hospital (LICH) 339 Hicks St *TF:* 888-445-0338 ■ *Web:* www.downstate.edu/lich	Brooklyn	NY	11201	718-780-1000	780-1365
Long Island Jewish Medical Ctr 270-05 76th Ave *Web:* www.lij.edu	New Hyde Park	NY	11040	718-470-7000	962-6759
Lutheran Medical Ctr (LHC) 150 55th St *Web:* www.lmcmc.com	Brooklyn	NY	11220	718-630-7000	630-8228
Maimonides Medical Ctr (MMC) 4802 10th Ave *Web:* www.maimonidesmed.org	Brooklyn	NY	11219	718-283-6000	635-8157
Mercy Hospital of Buffalo 565 Abbott Rd *Web:* www.chsbuffalo.org	Buffalo	NY	14220	716-826-7000	828-2700
Mercy Medical Ctr 1000 N Village Ave PO Box 9024 *Web:* www.mercymedicalcenter.chsli.org	Rockville Centre	NY	11571	516-705-2525	705-1406
Metropolitan Hospital Ctr 1901 1st Ave	New York	NY	10029	212-423-6262	423-8538
Millard Fillmore Gates Circle Hospital 3 Gates Cir *Web:* gates.kaleidahealth.org	Buffalo	NY	14209	716-887-4600	887-4339
Montefiore Medical Ctr 111 E 210th St *Web:* www.montefiore.org	Bronx	NY	10467	718-920-4321	920-8543
Mount Saint Mary's Hospital 5300 Military Rd *Web:* www.msmh.org	Lewiston	NY	14092	716-297-4800	298-2001
Mount Sinai Medical Ctr The 1 Gustave L Levy Pl *Web:* www.mountsinai.org	New York	NY	10029	212-241-6500	731-3418
Mount Sinai of Queens 25-10 30th Ave *Web:* www.mshq.org	Astoria	NY	11102	718-932-1000	278-1786
Mount Vernon Hospital 12 N 7th Ave *Web:* www.ssmc.org/homepagemv.cfm?id=45	Mount Vernon	NY	10550	914-664-8000	664-2113
Nassau University Medical Ctr 2201 Hempstead Tpke *Web:* www.ncmc.edu	East Meadow	NY	11554	516-572-0123	572-6252
New Island Hospital 4295 Hempstead Tpke *Web:* www.newislandhospital.org	Bethpage	NY	11714	516-579-6000	579-0417
New York Community Hospital 2525 Kings Hwy *Web:* www.nych.com	Brooklyn	NY	11229	718-692-5300	692-8454
New York Downtown Hospital 170 William St *Web:* www.downtownhospital.org	New York	NY	10038	212-312-5000	312-5977
New York Hospital Medical Center of Queens 56-45 Main St *Web:* www.nyhq.org	Flushing	NY	11355	718-670-2000	661-7704
New York Methodist Hospital 506 6th St *Web:* www.nym.org	Brooklyn	NY	11215	718-780-3000	780-5975
New York Presbyterian Hospital 525 E 68th St *Web:* www.nyp.org	New York	NY	10021	212-746-5454	746-4293
Newark-Wayne Community Hospital 1250 Driving Pk Ave *Web:* www.rochestergeneral.org	Newark	NY	14513	315-332-2427	332-2371
Niagara Falls Memorial Medical Ctr 621 10th St *Web:* www.nfmmc.org	Niagara Falls	NY	14302	716-278-4000	278-4054
North Central Bronx Hospital 3424 Kossuth Ave	Bronx	NY	10467	718-519-5000	519-3172
North Fork Radiology PC 1333 Roanoke Ave Suite 202 *Web:* www.northforkrad.com	Riverhead	NY	11901	631-727-2755	
North Shore University Hospital 888 Old Country Rd *Web:* www.northshorelij.com	Plainview	NY	11803	516-719-3000	719-2719
North Shore University Hospital 300 Community Dr *Web:* www.northshorelij.com/body.cfm?ID=51	Manhasset	NY	11030	516-562-0100	562-4545
Northern Westchester Hospital 400 E Main St *Web:* www.nwhc.net	Mount Kisco	NY	10549	914-666-1200	666-1055
Nyack Hospital 160 N Midland Ave *Web:* www.nyackhospital.org	Nyack	NY	10960	845-348-2000	348-3040
NYU Langone Medical Ctr 550 1st Ave *Web:* www.med.nyu.edu	New York	NY	10016	212-263-7300	263-8460
Olean General Hospital 515 Main St *Web:* www.ogh.org	Olean	NY	14760	716-373-2600	375-6394
Oneida Healthcare Ctr 321 Genesee St *Web:* www.oneidahealthcare.org	Oneida	NY	13421	315-363-6000	361-2043
Orange Regional Medical Ctr 60 Prospect Ave *Web:* www.ormc.org	Middletown	NY	10940	845-343-2424	342-7514
Arden Hill Campus 4 Harriman Dr *Web:* www.ormc.org	Goshen	NY	10924	845-294-5441	294-2105
Oswego Hospital 110 W 6th St *Web:* www.oswegohealth.org/ohny/oh.tpl	Oswego	NY	13126	315-349-5511	349-5732
Our Lady of Lourdes Memorial Hospital 169 Riverside Dr *Web:* www.lourdes.com	Binghamton	NY	13905	607-798-5111	798-7681
Our Lady of Mercy Medical Ctr 600 E 233rd St *Web:* www.montefiore.org/northdivision	Bronx	NY	10466	718-920-9901	920-6829
Park Ridge Hospital 1555 Long Pond Rd *Web:* www.unityhealth.org/parkridge.asp	Rochester	NY	14626	585-723-7000	368-3888
Parkway Hospital 70-35 113th St	Forest Hills	NY	11375	718-990-4100	261-2812
Peconic Bay Medical Ctr 1300 Roanoke Ave *Web:* www.peconicbaymedicalcenter.org	Riverhead	NY	11901	631-548-6000	548-6048
Peninsula Hospital Ctr (PHC) 51-15 Beach Ch Dr	Far Rockaway	NY	11691	718-734-2000	734-2993
Phelps Memorial Hospital Ctr (PMHC) 701 N Broadway Rte 9 *Web:* www.phelpshospital.org	Sleepy Hollow	NY	10591	914-366-3000	366-1017
Prohealth Care Assoc LLP 2800 Marcus Ave *Web:* www.prohealthcare.com	New Hyde Park	NY	11042	516-622-6000	
Putnam Hospital Ctr 670 Stoneleigh Ave *Web:* www.health-quest.org	Carmel	NY	10512	845-279-5711	279-7482
Queens Hospital Ctr 82-68 164th St	Jamaica	NY	11432	718-883-3000	883-6116
Richmond University Medical Ctr 355 Bard Ave	Staten Island	NY	10310	718-818-1234	818-3714
Rochester General Health System (RGHS) 1425 Portland Ave *TF:* 877-922-5465 ■ *Web:* www.rochestergeneral.org	Rochester	NY	14621	585-922-4000	922-5105
Rome Memorial Hospital 1500 N James St *Web:* www.romehosp.org	Rome	NY	13440	315-338-7000	338-7695
Saint Barnabas Hospital 4422 3rd Ave *Web:* www.stbarnabashospital.org	Bronx	NY	10457	718-960-9000	960-5704
Saint Catherine of Siena Medical Ctr 50 Rt 25 A *Web:* www.stcatherinemedicalcenter.org	Smithtown	NY	11787	631-862-3000	862-3105
Saint Clare's Hospital of Schenectady 600 McClellan St	Schenectady	NY	12304	518-382-2000	347-5409
Saint Elizabeth Medical Ctr 2209 Genesee St *Web:* www.stemc.org	Utica	NY	13501	315-798-8100	798-8344
Saint Francis Hospital & Health Centers 241 N Rd *Web:* www.sfhhc.org	Poughkeepsie	NY	12601	845-483-5000	485-3762
Saint James Mercy Hospital 411 Canisteo St *Web:* www.stjamesmercy.org	Hornell	NY	14843	607-324-8000	324-8115
Saint John's Riverside Hospital *ParkCare Pavilion* 2 Pk Ave *Web:* www.riversidehealth.org	Yonkers	NY	10703	914-964-7300	964-7704
Saint Joseph Hospital 2605 Harlem Rd *Web:* www.chsbuffalo.org	Cheektowaga	NY	14225	716-891-2400	891-2616
Saint Joseph's Hospital 555 E Market St *Web:* www.stjosephs.org	Elmira	NY	14901	607-733-6541	737-7837
Saint Joseph's Hospital Health Ctr 301 Prospect Ave *TF:* 888-785-6371 ■ *Web:* www.sjhsyr.org	Syracuse	NY	13203	315-448-5111	448-6161
Saint Joseph's Medical Ctr (SJMC) 127 S Broadway	Yonkers	NY	10701	914-378-7000	378-7130
Saint Luke's Cornwall Hospital *Cornwall Campus* 19 Laurel Ave *Web:* www.stlukescornwallhospital.org	Cornwall	NY	12518	845-534-7711	458-4811
Newburgh Campus 70 Dubois St *Web:* www.stlukescornwallhospital.org	Newburgh	NY	12550	845-561-4400	568-2919
Saint Luke's-Roosevelt Hospital Ctr 1111 Amsterdam Ave *Web:* www.slrhc.org	New York	NY	10025	212-523-4000	523-1981
Saint Mary's Hospital 427 Guy Pk Ave *Web:* www.smha.org	Amsterdam	NY	12010	518-842-1900	841-7158
Saint Mary's Hospital 1300 Massachusetts Ave **Fax:* Mktg ■ *Web:* www.setonhealth.org	Troy	NY	12180	518-268-5000	268-4985*
Saint Peter's Health Care Services 315 S Manning Blvd *Web:* www.sphcs.org	Albany	NY	12208	518-454-1550	
Saint Vincent's Midtown Hospital 415 W 51st St *Web:* www.svcmc.org/midtown	New York	NY	10019	212-586-1500	459-8127
Samaritan Hospital 2215 Burdett Ave *Web:* www.nehealth.com	Troy	NY	12180	518-271-3300	271-3203

				Phone	Fax
Samaritan Medical Ctr 830 Washington St *TF:* 877-888-6138 ■ *Web:* www.samaritanhealth.com	Watertown	NY	13601	315-785-4000	785-4343
Saratoga Hospital 211 Church St *Web:* www.saratogahospital.org/index.cfm	Saratoga Springs	NY	12866	518-587-3222	580-4285
Sisters of Charity Hospital of Buffalo 2157 Main St *Web:* www.chsbuffalo.org/body.cfm?id=53	Buffalo	NY	14214	716-862-2000	862-1899
Sound Shore Medical Center of Westchester 16 Guion Pl *Web:* www.ssmc.org	New Rochelle	NY	10802	914-632-5000	632-1976
South Nassau Communities Hospital 1 Healthy Way *Web:* www.southnassau.org	Oceanside	NY	11572	516-632-3000	336-2922
Southampton Hospital 240 Meeting House Ln *Web:* www.southamptonhospital.org	SouthHampton	NY	11968	631-726-8200	726-8666
Southside Hospital 301 E Main St *Web:* www.northshorelij.com/NSLIJ/Southside+Hospital	Bay Shore	NY	11706	631-968-3000	968-3315
Staten Island University Hospital 475 Seaview Ave *Web:* www.siuh.edu	Staten Island	NY	10305	718-226-9000	226-8966
Stony Brook University Hospital (SBUH) 101 Nicolls Rd *Web:* www.stonybrookhospital.com	Stony Brook	NY	11794	631-444-4000	444-6649
Strong Memorial Hospital *University of Rochester Medical Ctr* 601 Elmwood Ave *Web:* www.stronghealth.com/about/hospitals/smh.cfm	Rochester	NY	14642	585-275-2100	273-1118
Syosset Hospital 221 Jericho Tpke *Web:* www.northshorelij.com/body.cfm?ID=62	Syosset	NY	11791	516-496-6400	496-6487
United Medical Assoc Pllc 8714 5th Ave *Web:* www.allergy-uma.com	Brooklyn	NY	11209	718-748-2900	
United Memorial Medical Ctr 127 N St *Web:* www.ummc.org	Batavia	NY	14020	585-343-6030	344-7434
University Hospital of Brooklyn 450 Clarkson Ave *Web:* www.uhb.org	Brooklyn	NY	11203	718-270-1000	221-6307
University Hospital SUNY Upstate Medical University 750 E Adams St *TF:* 877-464-5540 ■ *Web:* www.upstate.edu/uh	Syracuse	NY	13210	315-464-5540	464-4841
Upstate University Hospital at Community General 4900 Broad Rd *Web:* www.cgh-home.org	Syracuse	NY	13215	315-492-5011	492-5418
Vassar Bros Medical Ctr 45 Reade Pl *Web:* www.health-quest.org	Poughkeepsie	NY	12601	845-454-8500	437-3120
Victory Memorial Hospital 699 92nd St *Web:* www.vmhny.org	Brooklyn	NY	11228	718-567-1579	
Westchester Medical Ctr 100 Woods Rd *Web:* www.worldclassmedicine.com	Valhalla	NY	10595	914-493-7000	
White Plains Hospital Ctr 41 E Post Rd *Web:* www.wphospital.org	White Plains	NY	10601	914-681-0600	681-2902
Winthrop University Hospital 259 1st St *Web:* www.winthrop.org	Mineola	NY	11501	516-663-0333	663-2953
Woodhull Medical & Mental Health Ctr 760 Broadway	Brooklyn	NY	11206	718-963-8000	963-8999

NORTH CAROLINA

				Phone	Fax
Alamance Regional Medical Ctr 1240 Huffman Mill Rd *Web:* www.armc.com	Burlington	NC	27215	336-538-7000	538-7425
Albemarle Hospital 1144 N Rd St *Web:* www.albemarlehealth.org	Elizabeth City	NC	27909	252-335-0531	384-4654
Annie Penn Hospital 618 S Main St *Web:* www.mosescone.com	Reidsville	NC	27320	336-951-4000	951-4561
Beaufort Regional Health System 628 E 12th St *Web:* www.beaufortregionalhealthsystem.org	Washington	NC	27889	252-975-4100	
Betsy Johnson Regional Hospital 800 Tilghman Dr PO Box 1706 *Web:* www.bjrh.org	Dunn	NC	28334	910-892-7161	891-6030
Caldwell Memorial Hospital 321 Mulberry St SW *Web:* www.caldwellmemorial.org	Lenoir	NC	28645	828-757-5100	757-5512
Cape Fear Hospital 5301 Wrightsville Ave *Web:* www.nhhn.org	Wilmington	NC	28403	910-452-8100	452-8121
Cape Fear Valley Medical Ctr (CFVMC) 1638 Owen Dr PO Box 2000 *Web:* www.capefearvalley.com	Fayetteville	NC	28304	910-609-4000	609-6160
CarolinaEast Health System 2000 Neuse Blvd *Web:* www.carolinaeasthealth.com	New Bern	NC	28561	252-633-8111	633-8144
Carolinas Medical Center Mercy 2001 Vail Ave *Web:* www.carolinas.org	Charlotte	NC	28207	704-379-5000	304-5695
Carolinas Medical Center Union (CMCU) 600 Hospital Dr *Web:* www.cmcunion.org	Monroe	NC	28112	704-283-3100	296-4175
Carolinas Medical Center-NorthEast 920 Church St N *TF:* 800-575-1275 ■ *Web:* www.northeastmedical.org	Concord	NC	28025	704-403-1275	403-3000
Carolinas Medical Center-University 8800 N Tryon St *Web:* www.carolinas.org	Charlotte	NC	28262	704-863-6000	863-6236
Carolinas Medical Ctr 1000 Blythe Blvd *Web:* www.carolinashealthcare.org	Charlotte	NC	28203	704-355-2000	355-5577
Carteret General Hospital 3500 Arendell St PO Drawer 1619 *Web:* www.ccgh.org	Morehead City	NC	28557	252-808-6000	808-6985
Catawba Valley Medical Ctr 810 Fairgrove Church Rd SE *Web:* www.catawbavalleymedical.org	Hickory	NC	28602	828-326-3000	326-3371
Central Carolina Hospital 1135 Carthage St *TF:* 800-292-2262 ■ *Web:* www.centralcarolinahosp.com	Sanford	NC	27330	919-774-2100	774-2295
Cleveland Regional Medical Ctr (CRMC) 201 E Grover St *Web:* www.clevelandregional.org	Shelby	NC	28150	704-487-3000	487-3790
Columbus Regional Healthcare System 500 Jefferson St *Web:* www.cchospital.com	Whiteville	NC	28472	910-642-8011	642-9305
Davis Regional Medical Ctr 218 Old Mocksville Rd PO box 1823 *Web:* www.davisregional.com	Statesville	NC	28625	704-873-0281	838-7287
Duke Health Raleigh Hospital 3400 Wake Forest Rd *Web:* www.dukeraleighhospital.org	Raleigh	NC	27609	919-954-3000	954-3900
Duke University Hospital 2301 Erwin Rd *Web:* www.dukehealth.org	Durham	NC	27710	919-684-8111	
Durham Regional Hospital 3643 N Roxboro Rd *Web:* www.durhamregional.org	Durham	NC	27704	919-470-4000	470-6147
Forsyth Medical Ctr 3333 Silas Creek Pkwy *Web:* www.forsythmedicalcenter.org	Winston-Salem	NC	27103	336-718-5000	718-9258
Frye Regional Medical Ctr (FRMC) 420 N Ctr St *Web:* www.fryemedctr.com	Hickory	NC	28601	828-315-5000	315-3901
Gaston Memorial Hospital 2525 Ct Dr *Web:* www.gastonhealthcare.org	Gastonia	NC	28054	704-834-2000	834-2500
Grace Hospital 2201 S Sterling St *TF:* 866-687-2747 ■ *Web:* www.blueridgehealth.org/grace-hospital.html	Morganton	NC	28655	828-580-5000	580-5509
Halifax Regional Medical Ctr 250 Smith Church Rd *Web:* www.halifaxmedicalcenter.org	Roanoke Rapids	NC	27870	252-535-8011	535-8466
Harris Regional Hospital 68 Hospital Rd *TF:* 800-496-2362 ■ *Web:* www.westcare.org	Sylva	NC	28779	828-586-7000	586-7467
Heritage Hospital 111 Hospital Dr *Web:* www.uhseast.com/heritage/dynamic-detail.aspx?id=430	Tarboro	NC	27886	252-641-7700	641-7484
High Point Regional Health System (HPRHS) 601 N Elm St PO Box HP-5 *TF:* 800-367-7066 ■ *Web:* www.highpointregional.com	High Point	NC	27262	336-878-6000	878-6158
Highsmith-Rainey Memorial Hospital 150 Robeson St	Fayetteville	NC	28301	910-609-1000	609-1046
Hugh Chatham Memorial Hospital 180 Parkwood Dr PO Box 560 *Web:* www.hughchatham.org	Elkin	NC	28621	336-527-7000	526-6056
Iredell Memorial Hospital 557 Brookdale Dr *Web:* www.iredellmemorial.org	Statesville	NC	28677	704-873-5661	872-7924
Johnston Memorial Hospital 509 N Bright Leaf Blvd *Web:* www.johnstonmemorial.org	Smithfield	NC	27577	919-934-8171	989-7297
Kernodle Clinic Inc 1234 Huffman Mill Rd *Web:* www.kernodle.com	Burlington	NC	27215	336-538-1234	
Lake Norman Regional Medical Ctr 171 Fairview Rd *Web:* www.lnrmc.com	Mooresville	NC	28117	704-660-4000	660-4005
Lenoir Memorial Hospital 100 Airport Rd *Web:* www.lenoirmemorial.org	Kinston	NC	28501	252-522-7171	522-7007
Margaret R Pardee Memorial Hospital 800 N Justice St *Web:* www.pardeehospital.org	Hendersonville	NC	28791	828-696-1000	696-1128
Maria Parham Medical Ctr 566 Ruin Creek Rd PO Box 59 *Web:* www.mphosp.org	Henderson	NC	27536	252-438-4143	436-1114
Mid Carolina Cardiology PA 1718 E Fourth St Suite 501 *Web:* www.mccardiology.com	Charlotte	NC	28204	704-343-9800	347-2011
Moore Regional Hospital 155 Memorial Dr PO Box 3000 *TF:* 800-672-6072 ■ *Web:* www.firsthealth.org	Pinehurst	NC	28374	910-715-1000	715-1462
Morehead Memorial Hospital 117 E King's Hwy *Web:* www.morehead.org	Eden	NC	27288	336-623-9711	623-7660
Moses H Cone Memorial Hospital 1200 N Elm St *TF:* 866-391-2734 ■ *Web:* www.mosescone.com	Greensboro	NC	27401	336-832-7000	832-8192
Nash Health Care Systems (NHCS) 2460 Curtis Ellis Dr *Web:* www.nhcs.org	Rocky Mount	NC	27804	252-443-8000	443-8877
New Hanover Regional Medical Ctr 2131 S 17th St *TF:* 877-228-8135 ■ *Web:* www.nhrmc.org	Wilmington	NC	28401	910-343-7000	343-7220
Northern Hospital of Surry County 830 Rockford St *Web:* www.northernhospital.com	Mount Airy	NC	27030	336-719-7000	719-0302
Onslow Memorial Hospital 317 Western Blvd *Web:* www.onslow.org	Jacksonville	NC	28541	910-577-2345	577-2246
Pender Memorial Hospital 507 E Fremont St *Web:* www.pendermemorial.org	Burgaw	NC	28425	910-259-5451	259-6182
Pitt County Memorial Hospital 2100 Stantonsburg Rd *Web:* www.uhseast.com	Greenville	NC	27835	252-847-4100	847-5147
Presbyterian Hospital Charlotte 200 Hawthorne Ln *Web:* www.presbyterian.org	Charlotte	NC	28204	704-384-4000	384-5600
Randolph Hospital 364 White Oak St PO Box 1048 *Web:* www.randolphhospital.org	Asheboro	NC	27204	336-625-5151	626-7664
Rex Healthcare 4420 Lake Boone Trail *Web:* www.rexhealth.com	Raleigh	NC	27607	919-783-3100	781-7192
Richmond Memorial Hospital 925 Long Dr *Web:* www.firsthealth.org	Rockingham	NC	28379	910-417-3000	417-3709
Roanoke-Chowan Hospital 500 S Academy St *Web:* www.uhseast.com	Ahoskie	NC	27910	252-209-3148	209-3146

	City	State	Zip	Phone	Fax
Rowan Regional Medical Ctr (RRMC) 612 Mocksville Ave. *Web:* www.rowan.org	Salisbury	NC	28144	704-210-5000	210-5498
Rutherford Hospital 288 S Ridgecrest Ave *Web:* www.rutherfordhosp.org	Rutherfordton	NC	28139	828-286-5000	286-5207
Saint Joseph's Hospital 428 Biltmore Ave	Asheville	NC	28801	828-213-1111	213-0763
Sampson Regional Medical Ctr 607 Beaman St *Web:* www.sampsonrmc.org	Clinton	NC	28328	910-592-8511	590-2321
Scotland Memorial Hospital 500 Lauchwood Dr *Web:* www.scotlandhealth.org	Laurinburg	NC	28352	910-291-7000	291-7499
Southeastern Regional Medical Ctr 300 W 27th St. *Web:* www.srmc.org	Lumberton	NC	28358	910-671-5000	671-5200
Stanly Memorial Hospital 301 Yadkin St *Web:* www.stanly.org	Albemarle	NC	28001	704-984-4000	983-3562
Thomasville Medical Ctr 207 Old Lexington Rd. *TF:* 800-880-0110 ■ *Web:* www.thomasvillemedicalcenter.org	Thomasville	NC	27360	336-472-2000	476-2534
Triangle Orthopedic Assoc PA 120 William Penn Plaza *TF:* 800-359-3053 ■ *Web:* www.triangleortho.com	Durham	NC	27704	919-220-5255	220-0520
University of North Carolina Health Care (UNCHC) 101 Manning Dr *Web:* www.unchealthcare.org	Chapel Hill	NC	27514	919-966-4131	966-7772
Valdese General Hospital (VGH) 720 Malcolm Blvd *Web:* www.blueridgehealth.org/valdese-hospital.html	Valdese	NC	28690	828-874-2251	879-7544
Wake Forest University Baptist Medical Ctr Medical Ctr Blvd. *Web:* www.wakehealth.edu	Winston-Salem	NC	27157	336-716-2011	716-2067
WakeMed Raleigh Campus 3000 New Bern Ave. *Web:* www.wakemed.org	Raleigh	NC	27610	919-350-7000	350-8868
Watauga Medical Ctr 336 Deerfield Rd *Web:* www.apprhs.org	Boone	NC	28607	828-262-4100	262-4103
Wayne Memorial Hospital 2700 Wayne Memorial Dr. *Web:* www.waynehealth.org	Goldsboro	NC	27534	919-736-1110	731-6966
Wesley Long Community Hospital 501 N Elam Ave *Web:* www.mosescone.com/body.cfm?id=41	Greensboro	NC	27403	336-832-1000	832-1742
Wilkes Regional Medical Ctr 1370 W D St PO Box 609 *Web:* www.wilkesregional.com	North Wilkesboro	NC	28659	336-651-8100	651-8465
Wilson Medical Ctr 1705 SW Tarboro St *Web:* www.wilmed.org	Wilson	NC	27893	252-399-8040	399-8778

NORTH DAKOTA

	City	State	Zip	Phone	Fax
Altru Hospital 1200 S Columbia Rd *TF:* 800-732-4277 ■ *Web:* www.altru.org	Grand Forks	ND	58201	701-780-5000	780-5238
Medcenter One Hospital 300 N 7th St *TF:* 800-932-8758 ■ *Web:* www.medcenterone.com	Bismarck	ND	58501	701-323-6000	323-5221
Saint Joseph's Hospital & Health Ctr 30 7th St SW *TF:* 800-446-6215 ■ *Web:* www.stjoeshospital.org	Dickinson	ND	58601	701-456-4000	456-4800
St Alexius Medical Ctr 900 E Broadway Ave *TF:* 877-530-5550 ■ *Web:* www.alexius.org	Bismarck	ND	58501	701-224-7000	530-8984
Trinity Hospital Saint Joseph's 1 W Burdick Expy *TF:* 800-247-1316 ■ *Web:* www.trinityhealth.org	Minot	ND	58701	701-857-5000	857-5117
Trinity Medical Ctr 1 Burdick Expy W PO Box 5020 *Web:* www.trinityhealth.org	Minot	ND	58702	701-857-5000	857-5117

OHIO

	City	State	Zip	Phone	Fax
Adena Regional Medical Ctr 272 Hospital Rd *Web:* www.adena.org	Chillicothe	OH	45601	740-779-7500	779-7934
Affinity Medical Ctr 875 8th St NE *TF:* 800-346-4869 ■ *Web:* www.affinitymedicalcenter.com	Massillon	OH	44646	330-832-8761	837-6871
Akron General Medical Ctr 400 Wabash Ave **Fax:* Admitting ■ *TF:* 800-221-4601 ■ *Web:* www.akrongeneral.org	Akron	OH	44307	330-344-6000	344-1752*
Alliance Community Hospital (ACH) 200 E State St *Web:* www.achosp.org	Alliance	OH	44601	330-596-6000	596-7079
Ashtabula County Medical Ctr (ACMC) 2420 Lake Ave *Web:* www.acmchealth.org	Ashtabula	OH	44004	440-997-2262	997-6644
Atrium Medical Ctr 1 Medical Ctr Dr *TF:* 800-338-4057 ■ *Web:* www.atriummedcenter.org	Middletown	OH	45005	513-424-2111	
Aultman Hospital 2600 6th St SW *Web:* www.aultman.com	Canton	OH	44710	330-452-9911	438-6356
Bethesda Hospital 2951 Maple Ave *TF:* 800-322-4762	Zanesville	OH	43701	740-454-4000	454-4781
Bethesda North Hospital 10500 Montgomery Rd *Web:* www.trihealth.com	Cincinnati	OH	45242	513-745-1111	745-1441
Blanchard Valley Hospital 1900 S Main St *Web:* www.bvhealthsystem.org	Findlay	OH	45840	419-423-4500	423-5358
Bryan Hospital 433 W High St *Web:* www.chwchospital.com/default.asp	Bryan	OH	43506	419-636-1131	636-3100
Charles F Kettering Memorial Hospital 3535 Southern Blvd *Web:* www.kmcnetwork.org	Kettering	OH	45429	937-298-4331	395-8423
Christ Hospital 2139 Auburn Ave *TF:* 800-527-8919	Cincinnati	OH	45219	513-585-2000	585-3300
Clermont Mercy Hospital 3000 Hospital Dr	Batavia	OH	45103	513-732-8200	732-8550
Cleveland Clinic 9500 Euclid Ave. *TF:* 800-223-2273 ■ *Web:* www.my.clevelandclinic.org	Cleveland	OH	44195	216-444-2200	444-0271
Clinton Memorial Hospital (CMH) 610 W Main St PO Box 600 *TF:* 800-803-9648 ■ *Web:* www.cmhregional.com	Wilmington	OH	45177	937-382-6611	382-6633
Community Hospital 2615 E High St *Web:* www.community-mercy.org	Springfield	OH	45505	937-325-0531	328-9600
Coshocton County Memorial Hospital Assn Inc PO Box 1330 *TF:* 888-688-5919 ■ *Web:* www.ccmh.com	Coshocton	OH	43812	740-622-6411	623-4095
Deaconess Hospital 311 Straight St. *TF:* 800-398-5699 ■ *Web:* www.deaconess-healthcare.com	Cincinnati	OH	45219	513-559-2100	475-5251
Doctors Hospital 5100 W Broad St. **Fax:* Admitting ■ *Web:* www.ohiohealth.com/facilities/doctors	Columbus	OH	43228	614-544-4000	544-1762*
Doctors Hospital of Stark County 400 Austin Ave NW. *Web:* www.drshospital.com	Massillon	OH	44646	330-837-7200	830-1616
East Liverpool City Hospital (ELCH) 425 W 5th St. *Web:* www.elch.org	East Liverpool	OH	43920	330-385-7200	386-2074
East Ohio Regional Hospital (EORH) 90 N 4th St *Web:* www.eorh-online.com	Martins Ferry	OH	43935	740-633-1100	633-4512
EMH Regional Medical Ctr 630 E River St *Web:* www.emh-healthcare.org	Elyria	OH	44035	440-329-7500	329-7507
Euclid Hospital 18901 Lake Shore Blvd *Web:* www.euclidhospital.org	Euclid	OH	44119	216-531-9000	692-7488
Fairfield Medical Ctr (FMC) 401 N Ewing St *TF:* 800-548-2627 ■ *Web:* www.fmchealth.org	Lancaster	OH	43130	740-687-8000	687-8115
Fairview Hospital 18101 Lorain Ave. *TF:* 800-323-8434 ■ *Web:* www.fairviewhospital.org	Cleveland	OH	44111	216-476-7000	476-4064
Firelands Regional Medical Ctr 1111 hayes Ave. *TF:* 800-342-1177 ■ *Web:* www.firelands.com	Sandusky	OH	44870	419-557-7400	557-6977
Fisher-Titus Medical Ctr (FTMC) 272 Benedict Ave *TF:* 800-589-3862 ■ *Web:* www.ftmc.com	Norwalk	OH	44857	419-668-8101	663-6036
Flower Hospital 5200 Harroun Rd. *Web:* www.promedica.org	Sylvania	OH	43560	419-824-1444	882-2342
Fort Hamilton Hospital 630 Eaton Ave *Web:* www.khnetwork.org/fort_hamilton	Hamilton	OH	45013	513-867-2000	867-2119
Good Samaritan Hospital 375 Dixmyth Ave *Web:* www.trihealth.com	Cincinnati	OH	45220	513-872-1400	872-1190
Good Samaritan Hospital 2222 Philadelphia Dr *Web:* www.goodsamdayton.org	Dayton	OH	45406	937-278-2612	276-8219
Good Samaritan Medical & Rehabilitation Ctr 800 Forest Ave *TF:* 800-322-4762	Zanesville	OH	43701	740-454-5843	
Grandview Medical Ctr 405 W Grand Ave. *Web:* www.kmcnetwork.org	Dayton	OH	45405	937-226-3200	226-3382
Grant Medical Ctr 111 S Grant Ave *Web:* www.ohiohealth.com	Columbus	OH	43215	614-566-9000	566-8043
Greene Memorial Hospital 1141 N Monroe Dr. *Web:* www.greenehealth.org/gmh	Xenia	OH	45385	937-352-2000	376-7381
Hillcrest Hospital 6780 Mayfield Rd. *Web:* www.hillcresthospital.org	Mayfield Heights	OH	44124	440-312-4500	
Holzer Health Systems 100 Jackson Pike *Web:* www.holzer.org	Gallipolis	OH	45631	740-446-5000	446-5522
Huron Hospital 13951 Terr Rd *Web:* www.huronhospital.org	East Cleveland	OH	44112	216-761-3300	761-7476
Jewish Hospital 4777 E Galbraith Rd *Web:* www.jewishhospitalcincinnati.com	Cincinnati	OH	45236	513-686-3000	686-3003
Kaiser Permanente Parma Medical Ctr 12301 Snow Rd *TF:* 800-524-7372	Parma	OH	44130	216-362-2000	362-2093
Knox Community Hospital 1330 Coshocton Rd *Web:* www.knoxcommhosp.org	Mount Vernon	OH	43050	740-393-9000	399-3130
Lake Hospital System (LHS) 10 E Washington St	Painesville	OH	44077	440-354-2400	354-1994
Lakewood Hospital 14519 Detroit Ave *TF:* 800-521-3955 ■ *Web:* www.lakewoodhospital.org	Lakewood	OH	44107	216-521-4200	529-7161
Licking Memorial Hospital 1320 W Main St *Web:* www.lmhealth.org	Newark	OH	43055	740-348-4000	348-4106
Lima Memorial Hospital 1001 Bellefontaine Ave. *Web:* www.limamemorial.org	Lima	OH	45804	419-228-3335	226-5013
Lutheran Hospital 1730 W 25th St *Web:* www.lutheranhospital.org	Cleveland	OH	44113	216-696-4300	363-2082
Marietta Memorial Hospital 401 Matthew St. *TF:* 800-523-3977 ■ *Web:* www.mmhospital.org	Marietta	OH	45750	740-374-1400	374-1787
Marion General Hospital (MGH) 1000 McKinley Pk Dr *Web:* www.mariongeneral.com	Marion	OH	43302	740-383-8400	383-8880
Marymount Hospital 12300 McCracken Rd. *Web:* www.marymount.org	Garfield Heights	OH	44125	216-581-0500	587-8882
Medcentral Health System Mansfield Hospital 335 Glessner Ave *Web:* www.medcentral.org	Mansfield	OH	44903	419-526-8000	521-7960
Medical College of Ohio Hospital 3000 Arlington Ave. *TF:* 800-321-8383	Toledo	OH	43614	419-383-4000	383-3850
Medina General Hospital 1000 E Washington St *TF:* 877-792-1001 ■ *Web:* www.medinahospital.org	Medina	OH	44256	330-725-1000	721-4906
Memorial Hospital 715 S Taft Ave *Web:* www.fremontmemorial.org	Fremont	OH	43420	419-332-7321	332-5875
Mercer County Joint Township Community Hospital 800 W Main St. *TF:* 888-844-2341 ■ *Web:* www.mercer-health.com	Coldwater	OH	45828	419-678-2341	
Mercy Hospital Anderson 7500 State Rd	Cincinnati	OH	45255	513-624-4500	624-3299
Mercy Hospital Fairfield 3000 Mack Rd *Web:* www.ehealthconnection.com	Fairfield	OH	45014	513-870-7000	870-7065

Name / Address	City	State	ZIP	Phone	Fax
Mercy Hospital Mount Airy 2446 Kipling Ave *Web:* www.e-mercy.com	Cincinnati	OH	45239	513-981-6329	853-7865
Mercy Hospital Western Hills 3131 Queen City Ave *Web:* e-mercy.com	Cincinnati	OH	45238	513-389-5000	389-5201
Mercy Medical Ctr 1343 N Fountain Blvd	Springfield	OH	45501	937-390-5000	390-5527
Mercy Medical Ctr 1320 Mercy Dr NW *TF:* 800-999-8662 ■ *Web:* www.cantonmercy.org	Canton	OH	44708	330-489-1000	489-1312
Mercy Regional Medical Ctr 3700 Kolbe Rd *Web:* www.mercyonline.org	Lorain	OH	44053	440-960-4000	
MetroHealth Medical Ctr 2500 MetroHealth Dr *TF:* 800-554-5251 ■ *Web:* www.metrohealth.org	Cleveland	OH	44109	216-778-7800	
Miami Valley Hospital 1 Wyoming St *TF:* 866-608-3463 ■ *Web:* www.miamivalleyhospital.com	Dayton	OH	45409	937-208-8000	208-2225
Mount Carmel Saint Ann's Hospital 500 S Cleveland Ave *Web:* www.mountcarmelhealth.com	Westerville	OH	43081	614-898-4000	898-8668
Mount Carmel West Hospital 793 W State St *TF:* 800-225-9344 ■ *Web:* www.mountcarmelhealth.com/84.cfm	Columbus	OH	43222	614-234-5000	234-5740
Northside Medical Ctr (NMC) 500 Gypsy Ln *Web:* www.northsidemedicalcenter.net/Pages/home.aspx	Youngstown	OH	44501	330-884-1000	884-2589
Ohio State University Medical Ctr 410 W 10th Ave *Web:* www.medicalcenter.osu.edu	Columbus	OH	43210	614-293-8652	293-5677
Ohio State University Medical Ctr The 410 W 10th Ave *TF:* 800-293-5123 ■ *Web:* www.medicalcenter.osu.edu	Columbus	OH	43210	614-293-8652	257-3439
Parma Community General Hospital (PCGH) 7007 Powers Blvd *TF:* 866-699-7244 ■ *Web:* www.parmahospital.org	Parma	OH	44129	440-743-3000	743-4386
ProMedica 2142 N Cove Blvd **Fax:* Admitting ■ *Web:* www.promedica.org	Toledo	OH	43606	419-291-5437	291-6901*
Riverside Methodist Hospital 3535 Olentangy River Rd *TF:* 800-837-7555 ■ *Web:* www.ohiohealth.com/facilities/riverside	Columbus	OH	43214	614-566-5000	566-6760
Robinson Memorial Hospital 6847 N Chestnut St *Web:* www.robinsonmemorial.org	Ravenna	OH	44266	330-297-0811	297-2949
Saint Anne Mercy Hospital 3404 W Sylvania Ave *Web:* www.mercyweb.org	Toledo	OH	43623	419-407-2663	407-3888
Saint Charles Mercy Hospital 2600 Navarre Ave *TF:* 800-692-6363 ■ *Web:* www.mercyweb.org	Oregon	OH	43616	419-696-7200	696-7328
Saint Luke's Hospital 5901 Monclova Rd *Web:* www.stlukeshospital.com	Maumee	OH	43537	419-893-5911	891-8037
Saint Rita's Medical Ctr (SRMC) 730 W Market St *TF:* 800-232-7762 ■ *Web:* www.ehealthconnection.com/regions/st_ritas	Lima	OH	45801	419-227-3361	226-9750
Saint Thomas Hospital 444 N Main St *Web:* www.summahealth.org	Akron	OH	44310	330-375-3000	375-3050
Saint Vincent Charity Hospital (SVCH) 2351 E 22nd St *TF:* 877-861-3550 ■ *Web:* www.stvincentcharity.com	Cleveland	OH	44115	216-861-6200	363-2519
Saint Vincent Mercy Medical Ctr 2213 Cherry St *Web:* www.mercyweb.org	Toledo	OH	43608	419-321-3232	251-3810
Salem Community Hospital 1995 E State St *Web:* www.salemhosp.com	Salem	OH	44460	330-332-1551	332-7691
South Pointe Hospital 20000 Harvard Rd *Web:* www.southpointehospital.org	Warrensville Heights	OH	44122	216-491-6000	491-7193
Southeastern Ohio Regional Medical Ctr 1341 Clark St *Web:* www.seormc.org	Cambridge	OH	43725	740-439-8000	439-8175
Southern Ohio Medical Ctr (SOMC) 1805 27th St *Web:* www.somc.org	Portsmouth	OH	45662	740-354-5000	353-2981
Southwest General Health Ctr 18697 Bagley Rd *Web:* www.swgeneral.com	Middleburg Heights	OH	44130	440-816-8000	816-5348
St Joseph Health Ctr 667 Eastland Ave SE *Web:* www.ehealthconnection.com	Warren	OH	44484	330-841-4000	841-4019
Summa Barberton Hospital 155 5th St NE *TF:* 877-227-8745 ■ *Web:* www.barbhosp.com	Barberton	OH	44203	330-615-3000	848-7820
Trinity Medical Center West 4000 Johnson Rd *Web:* www.trinityhealth.com	Steubenville	OH	43952	740-264-8000	283-7104
Trumbull Memorial Hospital (TMH) 1350 E Market St *Web:* www.trumbullmemorial.net/Pages/home.aspx	Warren	OH	44482	330-841-9011	841-9281
Union Hospital 659 Blvd *Web:* www.unionhospital.org	Dover	OH	44622	330-343-3311	364-0951
University Hospital 234 Goodman St *Web:* www.universityhospital.uchealth.com	Cincinnati	OH	45219	513-584-1000	584-3779
University Hospital Bedford Medical Ctr 44 Blaine Ave *Web:* www.uhhospitals.org	Bedford	OH	44146	440-735-3900	735-3631
University Hospitals of Cleveland 11100 Euclid Ave *TF:* 866-844-2273 ■ *Web:* www.uhhospitals.org	Cleveland	OH	44106	216-844-1000	844-2525
Upper Valley Medical Ctr (UVMC) 3130 N County Rd 25-A *TF:* 866-608-3463 ■ *Web:* www.uvmc.com	Troy	OH	45373	937-440-4000	440-7337
Wayne HealthCare 835 Sweitzer St *Web:* www.waynehospital.com	Greenville	OH	45331	937-547-5704	547-5793
Wilson Memorial Hospital 915 W Michigan St *TF:* 800-589-9641 ■ *Web:* www.wilsonhospital.com	Sidney	OH	45365	937-498-2311	497-8251
Wood County Hospital 950 W Wooster St *Web:* www.woodcountyhospital.org	Bowling Green	OH	43402	419-354-8900	354-8957

OKLAHOMA

Name / Address	City	State	ZIP	Phone	Fax
Children's Hospital at OU Medical Ctr The 1200 N Everett Dr *Web:* www.oumedicine.com	Oklahoma City	OK	73104	405-271-5656	271-1773
Claremore Regional Hospital LLC 1202 N Muskogee Pl *Web:* www.claremoreregHospital.com	Claremore	OK	74017	918-341-2556	
Comanche County Memorial Hospital 3401 NW Gore Blvd *Web:* www.memorialhealthsource.com	Lawton	OK	73505	580-355-8620	585-5458
Duncan Regional Hospital 1407 Whisenant Dr *Web:* www.duncanregional.com	Duncan	OK	73533	580-252-5300	251-8559
Grady Memorial Hospital 2220 Iowa Ave *Web:* www.gradymem.org	Chickasha	OK	73018	405-224-2300	779-2413
Hillcrest Medical Ctr 1120 S Utica Ave *Web:* www.hillcrest.com	Tulsa	OK	74104	918-579-1000	584-0840
INTEGRIS Baptist Medical Ctr 3300 NW Expy **Fax:* Admitting ■ *Web:* www.integrisok.com	Oklahoma City	OK	73112	405-949-3011	949-3998*
INTEGRIS Baptist Regional Health Ctr 200 2nd Ave SW *TF:* 888-951-2277 ■ *Web:* www.integrisok.com	Miami	OK	74355	918-542-6611	540-7605
INTEGRIS Bass Baptist Health Ctr 600 S Monroe St *TF:* 888-951-2277 ■ *Web:* www.integrisok.com/enid	Enid	OK	73701	580-233-2300	548-1553
INTEGRIS Southwest Medical Ctr 4401 S Western St *TF:* 888-951-2255 ■ *Web:* www.integrisok.com/southwest	Oklahoma City	OK	73109	405-636-7000	636-7702
Jackson County Memorial Hospital 1200 E Pecan St *TF:* 800-250-9965 ■ *Web:* www.jcmh.com	Altus	OK	73521	580-379-5000	481-2345
Jane Phillips Medical Ctr 3500 SE Frank Phillips Blvd *TF:* 800-824-8854 ■ *Web:* www.jpmc.org	Bartlesville	OK	74006	918-333-7200	331-1529
McAlester Regional Health Ctr 1 Clark Bass Blvd *Web:* www.mrhcok.com	McAlester	OK	74501	918-426-1800	421-8066
Medical Center of Southeastern Oklahoma 1800 University Blvd *TF:* 888-280-6276 ■ *Web:* www.mymcso.com	Durant	OK	74701	580-924-3080	924-0422
Mercy Health Ctr (MHC) 4300 W Memorial Rd *Web:* www.mercyok.net/mhc/default.asp	Oklahoma City	OK	73120	405-755-1515	936-5794
Mercy Memorial Health Ctr (MMHC) 1011 14th Ave NW *Web:* www.mercyok.net	Ardmore	OK	73401	580-223-5400	220-6580
Midwest Regional Medical Ctr 2825 Parklawn Dr *Web:* www.midwestregional.com	Midwest City	OK	73110	405-610-4411	610-1380
Muskogee Regional Medical Ctr 300 Rockefeller Dr *Web:* www.muskogeeregionalmedical.com	Muskogee	OK	74401	918-682-5501	684-2552
Norman Regional Hospital 901 N Porter St *Web:* www.normanregional.com	Norman	OK	73071	405-307-1000	307-1076
OSU Medical Ctr 744 W 9th St *TF:* 800-876-5664 ■ *Web:* www.osumc.net	Tulsa	OK	74127	918-599-1000	599-5892
OU Medical Center Edmond 1 S Bryant St *Web:* www.oumedicine.com	Edmond	OK	73034	405-341-6100	359-5500
Ponca City Medical Ctr 1900 N 14th St *Web:* www.poncamedcenter.com	Ponca City	OK	74601	580-765-3321	765-0341
Saint Anthony Hospital 1000 N Lee St *TF:* 800-227-6964 ■ *Web:* www.saintsok.com	Oklahoma City	OK	73101	405-272-7000	272-6592
Saint Anthony South 2129 SW 59th St *Web:* www.saintsok.com	Oklahoma City	OK	73119	405-685-6671	680-4149
Saint Francis Hospital 6161 S Yale Ave *TF:* 800-888-9599 ■ *Web:* www.saintfrancis.com	Tulsa	OK	74136	918-494-2200	494-1426
Saint John Medical Ctr (SJMC) 1923 S Utica Ave	Tulsa	OK	74104	918-744-2345	744-2527
Saint Mary's Regional Medical Ctr 305 S 5th St *Web:* www.stmarysregional.com	Enid	OK	73701	580-233-6100	249-3982
SouthCrest Hospital 8801 S 101st E Ave *Web:* www.southcresthospital.com	Tulsa	OK	74133	918-294-4000	294-4809
Southwestern Medical Ctr (SWMC) 5602 SW Lee Blvd *Web:* www.southwesternmedcenter.com	Lawton	OK	73505	580-531-4700	531-4702
Stillwater Medical Ctr 1323 W 6th St *Web:* www.stillwater-medical.org	Stillwater	OK	74074	405-372-1480	372-9552
Unity Health Ctr 1102 W MacArthur St *Web:* www.unityhealthcenter.com	Shawnee	OK	74804	405-273-2270	878-8101
Valley View Regional Hospital 430 N Monte Vista St *Web:* www.valleyviewregional.com	Ada	OK	74820	580-332-2323	421-6060

OREGON

Name / Address	City	State	ZIP	Phone	Fax
Adventist Medical Ctr 10123 SE Market St *Web:* www.adventisthealthnw.com	Portland	OR	97216	503-257-2500	261-6638
Bay Area Hospital 1775 Thompson Rd *Web:* www.bayareahospital.org	Coos Bay	OR	97420	541-269-8111	267-7057
Good Samaritan Regional Medical Ctr 3600 NW Samaritan Dr *TF:* 888-872-0760 ■ *Web:* www.samhealth.org/shs_facilities/gsrmc	Corvallis	OR	97330	541-757-5111	768-4776
Holy Rosary Medical Ctr 351 SW 9th St *TF:* 877-225-4762 ■ *Web:* www.holyrosary-ontario.org	Ontario	OR	97914	541-881-7000	881-7184
Kaiser Permanente Medical Ctr 10180 SE Sunnyside Rd *TF:* 800-813-2000	Clackamas	OR	97015	503-652-2880	571-2671
Legacy Emanuel Hospital & Health Ctr 2801 N Gantenbein Ave *TF:* 800-422-2509 ■ *Web:* www.legacyhealth.org	Portland	OR	97227	503-413-2200	413-2428
Legacy Good Samaritan Hospital 1015 NW 22nd Ave *TF:* 800-733-9959 ■ *Web:* www.legacyhealth.org	Portland	OR	97210	503-229-7711	413-6347

				Phone	Fax
Legacy Meridian Park Hospital 19300 SW 65th Ave *Web:* www.legacyhealth.org	Tualatin	OR	97062	503-692-1212	692-2478
McKenzie-Willamette Hospital 1460 G St *Web:* www.mckweb.com	Springfield	OR	97477	541-726-4400	726-4540
Mercy Medical Ctr (MMC) 2700 Stewart Pkwy *Web:* www.mercyrose.org	Roseburg	OR	97470	541-673-0611	677-4848
Oregon Health & Science University Hospital 3181 SW Sam Jackson Pk Rd *Web:* www.ohsu.edu	Portland	OR	97239	503-494-8311	494-3400
Providence Medford Medical Ctr 1111 Crater Lake Ave *TF:* 877-541-0588 ■ *Web:* www.oregon.providence.org	Medford	OR	97504	541-732-5000	732-5872
Providence Portland Medical Ctr 4805 NE Glisan St *TF:* 800-833-8899 ■ *Web:* www.oregon.providence.org	Portland	OR	97213	503-215-1111	215-6858
Providence Saint Vincent Medical Ctr 9205 SW Barnes Rd Suite 20 *TF:* 800-677-6752 ■ *Web:* www.oregon.providence.org	Portland	OR	97225	503-216-2401	216-4041
Rogue Valley Medical Ctr 2825 E Barnett Rd *TF:* 800-944-7073 ■ *Web:* www.asante.org	Medford	OR	97504	541-789-7000	789-5931
Sacred Heart Medical Ctr 1255 Hilyard St *TF:* 800-288-7444 ■ *Web:* www.peacehealth.org	Eugene	OR	97401	541-686-7300	686-3699
Saint Charles Medical Ctr 2500 NE Neff Rd *Web:* www.scmc.org	Bend	OR	97701	541-382-4321	388-7723
Salem Hospital 665 Winter St SE *TF:* 800-876-1718 ■ *Web:* www.salemhealth.org	Salem	OR	97301	503-370-5200	561-4844
Samaritan Albany General Hospital 1046 6th Ave SW *Web:* www.samhealth.org	Albany	OR	97321	541-812-4000	812-4449
Sky Lakes Medical Ctr 2865 Daggett Ave *Web:* www.skylakes.org	Klamath Falls	OR	97601	541-882-6311	274-6725
Tuality Community Hospital 335 SE 8th Ave *Web:* www.tuality.org	Hillsboro	OR	97123	503-681-1111	681-1608
Willamette Falls Hospital 1500 Division St *Web:* www.willamettefallshospital.org	Oregon City	OR	97045	503-656-1631	650-6807

PENNSYLVANIA

				Phone	Fax
Abington Memorial Hospital 1200 Old York Rd *Web:* www.amh.org	Abington	PA	19001	215-481-2000	481-4014
Albert Einstein Medical Ctr 5501 Old York Rd *TF:* 800-346-7834 ■ *Web:* www.einstein.edu	Philadelphia	PA	19141	215-456-7010	456-6242
Alle-Kiski Medical Ctr 1301 Carlisle St *Web:* www.wpahs.org	Natrona Heights	PA	15065	724-224-5100	226-7490
Allegheny General Hospital 320 E N Ave *Web:* www.wpahs.org/agh/index.html	Pittsburgh	PA	15212	412-359-3131	359-4108
Altoona Regional Health System Altoona Hospital 620 Howard Ave *TF:* 800-946-1902 ■ *Web:* www.altoonaregional.org	Altoona	PA	16601	814-889-2011	889-7808
Altoona Regional Health System Bon Secours Campus 2500 7th Ave *Web:* www.altoonaregional.org	Altoona	PA	16602	814-944-1681	889-7808
Aria Health Bucks County Campus 380 N Oxford Valley Rd *Web:* www.ariahealth.org	Langhorne	PA	19047	215-949-5000	949-5105
Aria Health System *Frankford Campus* 4900 Frankford Ave *Web:* www.ariahealth.org	Philadelphia	PA	19124	215-831-2000	831-2331
Armstrong County Memorial Hospital (ACMH) 1 Nolte Dr *Web:* www.acmh.org	Kittanning	PA	16201	724-543-8500	543-8704
Berwick Hospital Ctr The 701 E 16th St *Web:* www.berwick-hospital.com	Berwick	PA	18603	570-759-5000	759-3473
Bradford Regional Medical Ctr 600 IH- Pkwy *Web:* www.brmc.com	Bradford	PA	16701	814-368-4143	368-5722
Brandywine Hospital 201 Reeceville Rd *Web:* www.brandywinehospital.com	Coatesville	PA	19320	610-383-8000	383-8360
Bryn Mawr Hospital 130 S Bryn Mawr Ave *Web:* www.mainlinehealth.org/bmh	Bryn Mawr	PA	19010	610-526-3000	526-4488
Butler Health System 1 Hospital Way *Web:* www.butlerhealthsystem.org	Butler	PA	16001	724-283-6666	284-4645
Canonsburg General Hospital 100 Medical Blvd *Web:* www.wpahs.org/cgh	Canonsburg	PA	15317	724-745-6100	873-5876
Carlisle Regional Medical Ctr 361 Alexander Spring Rd	Carlisle	PA	17015	717-249-1212	249-0770
Central Montgomery Medical Ctr 100 Medical Campus Dr *Web:* www.cmmc-uhs.com	Lansdale	PA	19446	215-368-2100	361-4933
Chambersburg Hospital 112 N 7th St *Web:* www.summithealth.org	Chambersburg	PA	17201	717-267-3000	267-7704
Charles Cole Memorial Hospital 1001 E 2nd St *Web:* www.charlescolehospital.com	Coudersport	PA	16915	814-274-9300	274-0884
Chester County Hospital 701 E Marshall St **Fax:* Admitting ■ *Web:* www.cchosp.com	West Chester	PA	19380	610-431-5000	430-2958*
Chestnut Hill Hospital 8835 Germantown Ave *Web:* www.chh.org	Philadelphia	PA	19118	215-248-8200	248-8330
Clarion Hospital (CH) 1 Hospital Dr *TF:* 800-522-0505 ■ *Web:* www.clarionhospital.org	Clarion	PA	16214	814-226-9500	226-1224
Clearfield Hospital 809 Tpke Ave PO Box 992 *TF:* 888-313-0082 ■ *Web:* www.clearfieldhosp.org	Clearfield	PA	16830	814-765-5341	768-2421
Community Medical Ctr (CMC) 1800 Mulberry St *Web:* www.cmccare.org	Scranton	PA	18510	570-969-8000	969-8951
Crozer-Chester Medical Ctr (CCMC) 1 Medical Ctr Blvd *Web:* www.crozer.org	Upland	PA	19013	610-447-2000	447-2234
Delaware County Memorial Hospital 501 N Lansdowne Ave *Web:* www.crozer.org	Drexel Hill	PA	19026	610-284-8100	284-8993
Divine Providence Hospital 1100 Grampian Blvd	Williamsport	PA	17701	570-326-8181	326-8000
Doylestown Hospital 595 W State St *Web:* www.dh.org	Doylestown	PA	18901	215-345-2200	345-2532
DuBois Regional Medical Ctr 100 Hospital Ave *Web:* www.drmc.org	Du Bois	PA	15801	814-371-2200	375-3562
Easton Hospital 250 S 21st St *Web:* www.easton-hospital.com	Easton	PA	18042	610-250-4000	250-4078
Einstein at Elkins Park 60 E Township Line Rd *Web:* www.einstein.edu/facilities/article10068.html	Elkins Park	PA	19027	215-663-6000	663-6002
Elk Regional Health Ctr 763 Johnsonburg Rd *TF:* 877-391-6800 ■ *Web:* www.elkregional.org	Saint Marys	PA	15857	814-788-8000	788-8040
Ellwood City Hospital 724 Pershing St *Web:* www.echospital.org	Ellwood City	PA	16117	724-752-0081	752-0966
Ephrata Community Hospital 169 Martin Ave PO Box 1002 *Web:* www.ephratahospital.org	Ephrata	PA	17522	717-733-0311	738-6675
Evangelical Community Hospital 1 Hospital Dr *Web:* www.evanhospital.com	Lewisburg	PA	17837	570-522-2000	522-2500
Forbes Regional Hospital 2570 Haymaker Rd *Web:* www.wpahs.org	Monroeville	PA	15146	412-858-2000	858-2088
Frick Hospital 508 S Church St	Mount Pleasant	PA	15666	724-547-1500	542-1815
Geisinger Medical Ctr 100 N Academy Ave *Web:* www.geisinger.org	Danville	PA	17822	570-271-6211	271-6927
Geisinger South Wilkes-Barre (GSWB) 25 Church St *Web:* www.geisinger.org	Wilkes-Barre	PA	18765	570-808-3100	831-8989
Geisinger Wyoming Valley Medical Ctr 1000 E Mountain Dr *Web:* www.geisinger.org	Wilkes-Barre	PA	18711	570-826-7300	826-7387
Gettysburg Hospital 147 Gettys St PO Box 3786 *Web:* www.wellspan.org/body.cfm?id=30	Gettysburg	PA	17325	717-334-2121	338-3245
Gnaden Huetten Memorial Hospital 211 N 12th St *Web:* www.ghmh.org	Lehighton	PA	18235	610-377-1300	377-7000
Good Samaritan Hospital (GSH) 252 S 4th St *Web:* www.gshleb.org	Lebanon	PA	17042	717-270-7500	272-4716
Good Samaritan Regional Medical Ctr 700 E Norwegian St *Web:* www.gsrmc.com	Pottsville	PA	17901	570-621-4636	622-7950
Grand View Hospital 700 Lawn Ave *Web:* www.gvh.org	Sellersville	PA	18960	215-453-4000	453-9151
Grove City Medical Ctr (GCMC) 631 N Broad St Ext *TF:* 877-459-5455 ■ *Web:* www.gcmcpa.org	Grove City	PA	16127	724-450-7000	450-7179
Hahnemann University Hospital 230 N Broad St **Fax:* Admitting ■ *Web:* www.hahnemannhospital.com	Philadelphia	PA	19102	215-762-7000	762-3272*
Hanover Hospital 300 Highland Ave *TF:* 800-673-2426 ■ *Web:* www.hanoverhospital.org	Hanover	PA	17331	717-637-3711	633-3534
Harrisburg Hospital 111 S Front St *TF:* 888-782-5678 ■ *Web:* www.pinnaclehealth.org	Harrisburg	PA	17101	717-782-3131	782-5536
Hazleton General Hospital 700 E Broad St *Web:* www.ghha.org	Hazleton	PA	18201	570-450-4357	501-6203
Heart of Lancaster Regional Medical Ctr 1500 Highland Dr *Web:* www.heartoflancaster.com	Lititz	PA	17543	717-625-5000	625-5672
Holy Redeemer Hospital & Medical Ctr 1648 Huntingdon Pike *TF:* 800-818-4747 ■ *Web:* www.holyredeemer.com	Meadowbrook	PA	19046	215-947-3000	938-2023
Holy Spirit Hospital 503 N 21st St *Web:* www.hsh.org	Camp Hill	PA	17011	717-763-2100	763-2183
Hospital of the University of Pennsylvania 3400 Spruce St *Web:* www.pennhealth.com/hup	Philadelphia	PA	19104	215-662-4000	662-3645
Indiana Regional Medical Ctr 835 Hospital Rd *Web:* www.indianarmc.org	Indiana	PA	15701	724-357-7000	357-7449
JC Blair Memorial Hospital 1225 Warm Springs Ave *Web:* www.jcblair.org	Huntingdon	PA	16652	814-643-2290	643-9718
Jeanes Hospital 7600 Central Ave *Web:* www.jeanes.com	Philadelphia	PA	19111	215-728-2000	728-3365
Jefferson Regional Medical Ctr 565 Coal Valley Rd PO Box 18119 *Web:* www.jeffersonregional.com	Pittsburgh	PA	15236	412-469-5000	469-7062
Lancaster General Hospital 555 N Duke St *Web:* www.lancastergeneralhealth.org	Lancaster	PA	17604	717-290-5511	291-9657
Lancaster Regional Medical Ctr 250 College Ave *Web:* www.lancaster-regional.com	Lancaster	PA	17603	717-291-8211	291-8090
Lankenau Medical Ctr 100 E Lancaster Ave *Web:* www.mainlinehealth.org/lh	Wynnewood	PA	19096	610-645-2000	645-8007
Latrobe Area Hospital 121 W 2nd Ave *Web:* www.lah.com	Latrobe	PA	15650	724-537-1000	532-6073
Lehigh Valley Hospital 1200 S Cedar Crest Blvd *TF:* 800-548-7247 ■ *Web:* www.lvh.com	Allentown	PA	18103	610-402-8000	402-1696
Lehigh Valley Hospital Muhlenberg 2545 Schoenersville Rd **Fax Area Code:* 610 ■ *TF:* 800-548-7247 ■ *Web:* www.lvhn.org	Bethlehem	PA	18017	484-884-2200	402-8061*
Lewistown Hospital 400 Highland Ave *TF:* 800-248-0505 ■ *Web:* www.lewistownhospital.org	Lewistown	PA	17044	717-248-5411	242-7132

Hospital	City	State	Zip	Phone	Fax
Lower Bucks Hospital 501 Bath Rd	Bristol	PA	19007	215-785-9200	785-9175
Web: www.lowerbuckshospital.org					
Marian Community Hospital (MCH)					
100 Lincoln Ave	Carbondale	PA	18407	570-281-1000	282-7177
Web: www.marianhospital.org/welcome.php					
Meadville Medical Ctr (MMC) 751 Liberty St	Meadville	PA	16335	814-333-5000	333-9456
TF: 800-283-8321 ■ *Web:* www.mmchs.org					
Medical Ctr The 1000 Dutch Ridge Rd	Beaver	PA	15009	724-728-7000	773-8210
Memorial Hospital 325 S Belmont St	York	PA	17405	717-843-8623	849-5329
TF: 800-436-4326 ■ *Web:* www.mhyork.org					
Memorial Medical Ctr 1086 Franklin St	Johnstown	PA	15905	814-534-9000	539-0264
Web: www.conemaugh.org					
Mercy Hospital of Philadelphia					
501 S 54th St	Philadelphia	PA	19143	215-748-9000	748-9339
Web: www.mercyhealth.org					
Mercy Hospital of Pittsburgh					
1400 Locust St	Pittsburgh	PA	15219	412-232-8111	232-7380
Web: www.mercylink.org					
Mercy Suburban Hospital (MSH)					
2701 De Kalb Pike	Norristown	PA	19401	610-278-2000	272-4642
Web: www.mercyhealth.org/suburban					
Methodist Hospital 2301 S Broad St	Philadelphia	PA	19148	215-952-9000	952-9933
Web: www.jeffersonhospital.org/methodist					
Millcreek Community Hospital 5515 Peach St	Erie	PA	16509	814-864-4031	868-8249
Web: www.millcreekcommunityhospital.com					
Monongahela Valley Hospital					
1163 Country Club Rd	Monongahela	PA	15063	724-258-1000	258-1850
Web: www.monvalleyhospital.com					
Montgomery Hospital 1301 Powell St	Norristown	PA	19401	610-270-2000	270-2789
Web: www.montgomeryhospital.org					
Moses Taylor Hospital 700 Quincy Ave	Scranton	PA	18510	570-340-2100	969-2629
Web: www.mth.org					
Mount Nittany Medical Ctr					
1800 E Pk Ave	State College	PA	16803	814-231-7000	231-7200
TF: 866-757-2317 ■ *Web:* www.mountnittany.org					
Nazareth Hospital 2601 Holme Ave	Philadelphia	PA	19152	215-335-6000	335-6363
Web: www.mercyhealth.org/nazareth					
Northeastern Hospital School of Nursing					
2301 E Allegheny Ave	Philadelphia	PA	19134	215-926-3145	
Web: www.nehson.templehealth.org					
Ohio Valley General Hospital					
25 Heckel Rd Kennedy Township	McKees Rocks	PA	15136	412-777-6161	777-6131
Web: www.ohiovalleyhospital.org					
Paoli Hospital (PH) 255 W Lancaster Ave	Paoli	PA	19301	610-648-1000	647-0450
Web: www.mainlinehealth.org/ph					
Penn Presbyterian Medical Ctr (PPMC)					
39th & Market Sts	Philadelphia	PA	19104	215-662-8000	662-9212
TF: 800-789-7366 ■ *Web:* www.pennmedicine.org/presby					
Penn State Milton S Hershey Medical Ctr					
500 University Dr	Hershey	PA	17033	717-531-8521	531-4162
Web: www.hmc.psu.edu					
Pennsylvania Hospital 800 Spruce St	Philadelphia	PA	19107	215-829-3000	829-6363
TF: 800-789-7366 ■ *Web:* www.pennmedicine.org					
Phoenixville Hospital 140 Nutt Rd	Phoenixville	PA	19460	610-983-1000	983-1488
Web: www.phoenixvillehospital.com					
Pinnacle Health Hospital at Community General					
4300 Londonderry Rd	Harrisburg	PA	17109	717-652-3000	782-5911
TF: 888-782-5678 ■ *Web:* www.pinnaclehealth.org/body.cfm?id=770					
Pocono Medical Ctr 206 E Brown St	East Stroudsburg	PA	18301	570-421-4000	476-3469
Web: www.poconohealthsystem.org					
Pottstown Memorial Medical Ctr (PMMC)					
1600 E High St	Pottstown	PA	19464	610-327-7000	327-7432
Web: www.pottstownmemorial.com					
Pottsville Hospital & Warne Clinic					
420 S Jackson St	Pottsville	PA	17901	570-621-5000	622-8221
Punxsutawney Area Hospital Inc (PAH)					
81 Hillcrest Dr	Punxsutawney	PA	15767	814-938-1800	938-1453
Web: www.pah.org					
Reading Hospital & Medical Ctr PO Box 16052	Reading	PA	19612	610-988-8000	988-5192
Web: www.readinghospital.org					
Regional Hospital of Scranton					
746 Jefferson Ave	Scranton	PA	18510	570-348-7100	348-7639
Web: www.regionalhospitalofscranton.net					
Riddle Memorial Hospital 1068 W Baltimore Pike	Media	PA	19063	484-227-9400	891-3592*
**Fax Area Code:* 610 ■ *TF:* 866-225-5654 ■ *Web:* www.riddlehospital.org					
Robert Packer Hospital 1 Guthrie Sq	Sayre	PA	18840	570-888-6666	882-5091
TF: 888-448-8474 ■ *Web:* www.guthrie.org					
Roxborough Memorial Hospital (RMH)					
5800 Ridge Ave	Philadelphia	PA	19128	215-483-9900	487-4221
Web: www.roxboroughmemorial.com					
Sacred Heart HealthCare System 421 Chew St	Allentown	PA	18102	610-776-4500	
TF: 800-694-4777 ■ *Web:* www.shh.org					
Saint Clair Hospital 1000 Bower Hill Rd	Pittsburgh	PA	15243	412-561-4900	572-6580
Web: www.stclair.org					
Saint Joseph Medical Ctr 2500 Bernville Rd	Reading	PA	19605	610-378-2000	378-2798
Web: www.thefutureofhealthcare.org					
Saint Mary Medical Ctr					
1201 Langhorne-Newtown Rd	Langhorne	PA	19047	215-710-2000	710-5971
Web: www.stmaryhealthcare.org					
Saint Vincent Health Ctr 232 W 25th St	Erie	PA	16544	814-452-5000	455-1724
Web: www.saintvincenthealth.com					
Sewickley Valley Hospital 720 Blackburn Rd	Sewickley	PA	15143	412-741-6600	749-7400
Web: www.heritagevalley.org					
Sharon Regional Health System 740 E State St	Sharon	PA	16146	724-983-3911	983-3958
TF: 866-228-1055 ■ *Web:* www.sharonregional.com					
Soldiers + Sailors Memorial Hospital					
32-36 Central Ave	Wellsboro	PA	16901	570-723-7764	724-2126
TF: 800-808-5287 ■ *Web:* www.laurelhs.org					
Somerset Hospital 225 S Ctr Ave	Somerset	PA	15501	814-443-5000	443-4937
Web: www.somersethospital.com					
St Joseph's Hospital					
16th St at Girard Ave	Philadelphia	PA	19130	215-787-9000	787-2115
Web: www.nphs.com					
Sunbury Community Hospital (SCH) 350 N 11th St	Sunbury	PA	17801	570-286-3333	286-3500
Web: www.sunburyhospital.com					
Taylor Hospital 175 E Chester Pike	Ridley Park	PA	19078	610-595-6000	595-6198
Web: www.crozer.org					
Temple University Hospital					
3401 N Broad St	Philadelphia	PA	19140	215-707-2000	707-3679
Web: www.tuh.templehealth.org					
Temple University Hospital Episcopal Campus					
100 E Lehigh Ave	Philadelphia	PA	19125	215-707-1200	707-0953
Web: www.episcopal.templehealth.org					
Thomas Jefferson University Hospital					
111 S 11th St	Philadelphia	PA	19107	215-955-6000	955-6464
Web: www.jeffersonhospital.org					
Uniontown Hospital (UH) 500 W Berkeley St	Uniontown	PA	15401	724-430-5000	430-3342
TF: 800-843-3121 ■ *Web:* www.uniontownhospital.com					
University of Pittsburgh Medical Ctr (UPMC)					
Horizon 110 N Main St	Greenville	PA	16125	724-588-2100	588-8902
TF: 888-447-1122 ■ *Web:* www.upmc.com					
Northwest 100 Fairfield Dr	Seneca	PA	16346	814-676-7600	676-7150
Web: www.upmc.com					
Passavant 9100 Babcock Blvd	Pittsburgh	PA	15237	412-367-6700	367-5498*
Web: www.upmc.com/HospitalsFacilities/Hospitals/UPMCPassavant/Pages/passavant.aspx					
Saint Margaret 815 Freeport Rd	Pittsburgh	PA	15215	412-784-4000	784-5384
Web: www.upmc.com					
Shadyside 5230 Centre Ave	Pittsburgh	PA	15232	412-623-2121	
Web: www.upmc.com					
South Side 2000 Mary St	Pittsburgh	PA	15203	412-488-5550	488-5748
Web: www.upmc.com/Hospitals.htm					
UPMC Hamot 201 State St	Erie	PA	16550	814-877-6000	877-6104
Web: www.hamot.org					
UPMC McKeesport 1500 5th Ave	McKeesport	PA	15132	412-664-2000	664-2309
Web: www.upmc.com					
UPMC Presbyterian 200 Lothrop St	Pittsburgh	PA	15213	412-648-6000	647-3496
Web: www.upmc.com					
Warren General Hospital 2 Crescent Pk W	Warren	PA	16365	814-723-3300	723-2248
Web: www.wgh.org					
Washington Hospital The 155 Wilson Ave	Washington	PA	15301	724-225-7000	222-7316
Web: www.washingtonhospital.org					
Wayne Memorial Hospital (WMH) 601 Pk St	Honesdale	PA	18431	570-253-8100	253-7312
Web: www.wmh.org					
Western Pennsylvania Hospital					
4800 Friendship Ave	Pittsburgh	PA	15224	412-578-5000	578-4321
Web: www.wpahs.org/wph/index.html					
Westmoreland Regional Hospital					
532 W Pittsburgh St	Greensburg	PA	15601	724-832-4000	830-8573
Web: www.westmoreland.org					
Wilkes-Barre General Hospital					
575 N River St	Wilkes-Barre	PA	18764	570-829-8111	552-3030*
**Fax:* Admitting ■ *Web:* www.wvhcs.org					
Williamsport Hospital & Medical Ctr					
777 Rural Ave	Williamsport	PA	17701	570-321-1000	
Web: www.susquehannahealth.org					
York Hospital 1001 S George St	York	PA	17405	717-851-2345	851-3020
Web: www.wellspan.org					

RHODE ISLAND

Hospital	City	State	Zip	Phone	Fax
Kent Hospital 455 Toll Gate Rd	Warwick	RI	02886	401-737-7000	736-1000
Web: www.kentri.org					
KOCH EYE Assoc 566 Toll Gate Rd	Warwick	RI	02886	401-738-4800	738-8153
Web: www.kocheye.com					
Landmark Medical Ctr 115 Cass Ave	Woonsocket	RI	02895	401-769-4100	766-5488
TF: 800-722-0175 ■ *Web:* www.landmarkmedical.org					
Memorial Hospital of Rhode Island					
111 Brewster St	Pawtucket	RI	02860	401-729-2000	722-0198
Web: www.mhriweb.org					
Miriam Hospital The 164 Summit Ave	Providence	RI	02906	401-793-2500	793-7587
Web: www.lifespan.org/partners/tmh					
Newport Hospital (NH) 11 Friendship St	Newport	RI	02840	401-846-6400	848-6003
Web: www.lifespan.org/newport					
Our Lady of Fatima Hospital					
200 High Service Ave	North Providence	RI	02904	401-456-3000	456-3028
Web: www.saintjosephri.com					
Rhode Island Hospital 593 Eddy St	Providence	RI	02903	401-444-4000	444-4218
Web: www.rhodeislandhospital.org					
Roger Williams Medical Ctr					
825 Chalkstone Ave	Providence	RI	02908	401-456-2000	456-2029
Web: www.rwmc.com					
South County Hospital 100 Kenyon Ave	Wakefield	RI	02879	401-782-8000	789-9765
Web: www.schospital.com					
Westerly Hospital 25 Wells St	Westerly	RI	02891	401-596-6000	348-3670
TF: 800-933-5960 ■ *Web:* www.westerlyhospital.org					

SOUTH CAROLINA

Hospital	City	State	Zip	Phone	Fax
Aiken Regional Medical Centers					
302 University Pkwy	Aiken	SC	29801	803-641-5000	641-5690
TF: 800-245-3679 ■ *Web:* www.aikenregional.com					
AnMed Health 800 N Fant St	Anderson	SC	29621	864-512-1000	260-3750
Web: www.anmed.com					
Beaufort Memorial Hospital 955 Ribaut Rd	Beaufort	SC	29902	843-522-5200	522-5671
TF: 877-532-6472 ■ *Web:* www.bmhsc.org					
Bon Secours Saint Francis Hospital					
2095 Henry Tecklenburg Dr	Charleston	SC	29414	843-402-1000	402-1769
Web: www.ropersaintfrancis.com					

Name / Address	City	State	ZIP	Phone	Fax
Carolina Pines Regional Medical Ctr 1304 W Bobo Newsome Hwy *Web:* www.cprmc.com	Hartsville	SC	29550	843-339-2100	339-4116
Carolinas Hospital System 805 Pamplico Hwy *Web:* www.carolinashospital.com	Florence	SC	29505	843-674-5000	674-2519
Colleton Medical Ctr (CMC) 501 Robertson Blvd *Web:* www.colletonmedical.com	Walterboro	SC	29488	843-782-2000	549-0246
Conway Medical Ctr 300 Singleton Ridge Rd *Web:* www.conwaymedicalcenter.com	Conway	SC	29526	843-347-7111	347-8056
Georgetown Memorial Hospital PO Box 421718 *Web:* www.georgetownhospitalsystem.org	Georgetown	SC	29442	843-527-7000	520-7887
Grand Strand Regional Medical Ctr 809 82nd Pkwy *TF:* 800-222-1859 ■ *Web:* www.grandstrandmed.com	Myrtle Beach	SC	29572	843-692-1000	692-1109
Greenville Memorial Hospital 701 Grove Rd *Web:* www.ghs.org	Greenville	SC	29605	864-455-7000	455-8921
Hilton Head Regional Medical Ctr 25 Hospital Ctr Blvd **Fax:* Admitting ■ *Web:* www.hiltonheadmedctr.com	Hilton Head Island	SC	29926	843-681-6122	689-3670*
KershawHealth Medical Ctr 1315 Roberts St PO Box 7003 *Web:* www.kershawhealth.org	Camden	SC	29020	803-432-4311	713-6380
Lexington Medical Ctr 2720 Sunset Blvd *Web:* www.lexmed.com	West Columbia	SC	29169	803-791-2000	791-2660
Marion County Medical Ctr PO Box 1150 *Web:* www.marioncountymedical.com	Marion	SC	29571	843-431-2000	431-2414
Mary Black Memorial Hospital 1700 Skylyn Dr *Web:* www.maryblackhospital.org	Spartanburg	SC	29307	864-573-3000	573-3240
McLeod Medical Center Dillon 301 E Jackson St *Web:* www.mcleodhealth.org	Dillon	SC	29536	843-774-4111	774-1563
McLeod Regional Medical Ctr 555 E Cheves St *Web:* www.mcleodhealth.org	Florence	SC	29506	843-777-2000	777-5465
Medical University of South Carolina Medical Ctr 171 Ashley Ave *TF:* 800-424-6872 ■ *Web:* www.musc.edu	Charleston	SC	29425	843-792-2300	792-3126
Oconee Medical Ctr (OMC) 298 Memorial Dr *Web:* www.oconeemed.org	Seneca	SC	29672	864-882-3351	882-3711
Palmetto Health Baptist Columbia 1330 Taylor St *Web:* www.palmettohealth.org	Columbia	SC	29221	803-296-5010	296-5462
Palmetto Health Baptist Medical Center Easley 200 Fleetwood Dr *Web:* www.palmettohealth.org	Easley	SC	29640	864-442-7200	442-7521
Palmetto Health Richland 5 Richland Medical Pk *Web:* www.palmettohealth.org/facilities/richland	Columbia	SC	29203	803-434-7000	434-3571
Piedmont Medical Ctr 222 S Herlong Ave *Web:* www.piedmonthealth.com	Rock Hill	SC	29732	803-329-1234	329-0979
Providence Hospitals 2435 Forest Dr *Web:* www.providencehospitals.com	Columbia	SC	29204	803-256-5300	256-5935
Regional Medical Center of Orangeburg & Calhoun Counties 3000 St Matthews Rd *TF:* 800-476-3377	Orangeburg	SC	29118	803-395-2200	395-2304
Roper Hospital 316 Calhoun St *Web:* www.ropersaintfrancis.com	Charleston	SC	29401	843-724-2000	724-2995
Saint Francis Hospital 1 St Francis Dr	Greenville	SC	29601	864-255-1000	255-1137*
Self Regional Hospital 1325 Spring St *Web:* www.selfregional.org	Greenwood	SC	29646	864-725-4111	725-4260
Spartanburg Regional Medical Ctr (SRMC) 101 E Wood St *TF:* 800-868-8784 ■ *Web:* www.spartanburgregional.com/Pages/Home.aspx	Spartanburg	SC	29303	864-560-6000	560-6035
Springs Memorial Hospital 800 W Meeting St *TF:* 800-488-2567 ■ *Web:* www.springsmemorial.com	Lancaster	SC	29720	803-286-1214	
Trident Medical Ctr 9330 Medical Plaza Dr *TF:* 877-300-6062 ■ *Web:* www.tridenthealthsystem.com	Charleston	SC	29406	843-797-7000	847-4086
Tuomey Regional Medical Ctr 129 N Washington St *Web:* www.tuomey.com	Sumter	SC	29150	803-774-9000	774-9489
Upstate Carolina Medical Ctr 1530 N Limestone St *Web:* www.upstatecarolina.org	Gaffney	SC	29340	864-487-4271	489-0585
Wallace Thomson Hospital 322 W S St *TF:* 800-277-5633 ■ *Web:* www.wallacethomson.com	Union	SC	29379	864-427-0351	429-2653

SOUTH DAKOTA

Name / Address	City	State	ZIP	Phone	Fax
Avera McKennan Hospital & University Health Ctr 1325 S Cliff Ave PO Box 5045 **Fax:* Admitting ■ *Web:* www.avera.org/mckennan/index.aspx	Sioux Falls	SD	57117	605-322-8000	322-7823*
Avera Queen of Peace Hospital 525 N Foster St *TF:* 888-531-1685 ■ *Web:* www.avera.org/queen-of-peace	Mitchell	SD	57301	605-995-2000	995-2441
Avera Sacred Heart Hospital (ASHH) 501 Summit St *Web:* www.avera.org/sacred-heart/index.aspx	Yankton	SD	57078	605-668-8000	665-8840
Avera Saint Luke's Hospital 305 S State St *TF:* 800-225-8537 ■ *Web:* www.avera.org/st-lukes-hospital/index.aspx	Aberdeen	SD	57401	605-622-5000	622-5127
Huron Regional Medical Ctr (HRMC) 172 4th St SE *Web:* www.huronregional.org	Huron	SD	57350	605-353-6200	353-6300
Mobridge Regional Hospital Inc PO Box 580 *Web:* www.mobridgehospital.org	Mobridge	SD	57601	605-845-3692	
Prairie Lakes Hospital & Care Ctr 401 9th Ave NW *TF:* 877-917-7547 ■ *Web:* www.prairielakes.com	Watertown	SD	57201	605-882-7000	882-7607
Rapid City Regional Health 353 Fairmont Blvd *Web:* www.regionalhealth.com	Rapid City	SD	57701	605-719-1000	719-8988
Saint Mary's Healthcare Ctr 801 E Sioux Ave *Web:* www.st-marys.com	Pierre	SD	57501	605-224-3100	224-3439
Sanford USD Medical Ctr 1305 W 18th St *Web:* www.sanfordhealth.org	Sioux Falls	SD	57117	605-333-1000	333-1531

TENNESSEE

Name / Address	City	State	ZIP	Phone	Fax
Athens Regional Medical Ctr 1114 W Madison Ave *Web:* www.athensrmc.com	Athens	TN	37303	423-745-1411	744-3362
Baptist Hospital 2000 Church St *Web:* www.baptist-hosp.org	Nashville	TN	37236	615-284-5555	284-1592
Baptist Memorial Hospital Memphis 6019 Walnut Grove Rd *Web:* www.baptistonline.org	Memphis	TN	38120	901-226-5000	226-5618
Baptist Memorial Hospital Union City 1201 Bishop St *Web:* www.baptistonline.org/facilities/unioncity	Union City	TN	38261	731-885-2410	884-8603
Blount Memorial Hospital 907 E Lamar Alexander Pkwy *Web:* www.blountmemorial.org	Maryville	TN	37804	865-983-7211	981-2333
Bristol Regional Medical Ctr 1 Medical Pk Blvd *Web:* www.wellmont.org/Facilities/Bristol/WBRMC/wbrmc.html	Bristol	TN	37620	423-968-1121	844-4204
Centennial Medical Ctr 2300 Patterson St *Web:* www.centennialmedicalcenter.com	Nashville	TN	37203	615-342-1000	342-1045
Claiborne County Hospital & Nursing Home 1850 Old Knoxville Rd *TF:* 855-884-8336 ■ *Web:* www.claibornehospital.org	Tazewell	TN	37879	423-626-4211	
Cookeville Regional Medical Ctr (CRMC) 1 Medical Ctr Blvd *Web:* www.crmchealth.org	Cookeville	TN	38501	931-528-2541	526-8814
Cumberland Medical Ctr (CMC) 421 S Main St *Web:* www.cmchealthcare.org	Crossville	TN	38555	931-484-9511	707-8148
Delta Medical Ctr (DMC) 3000 Getwell Rd *Web:* www.deltamedcenter.com	Memphis	TN	38118	901-369-8100	369-4603
Dyersburg Regional Medical Ctr 400 E Tickle St *Web:* www.dyersburgregionalmc.com	Dyersburg	TN	38024	731-285-2410	285-9545
Erlanger Medical Ctr 975 E 3rd St *TF:* 877-778-7001 ■ *Web:* www.erlanger.org	Chattanooga	TN	37403	423-778-7000	778-8068
Fort Sanders Regional Medical Ctr 1901 W Clinch Ave *Web:* www.fsregional.com	Knoxville	TN	37916	865-541-1111	541-1262
Gateway Medical Ctr (GMC) 651 Dunlop Ln *Web:* www.todaysgateway.com/Pages/home.aspx	Clarksville	TN	37043	931-502-1000	551-1027
Harton Regional Medical Ctr 1801 N Jackson St *TF:* 800-388-4278 ■ *Web:* www.hartonmedicalcenter.com	Tullahoma	TN	37388	931-393-3000	393-7855
HCA Southern Hills Medical Ctr 391 Wallace Rd *Web:* www.southernhills.com	Nashville	TN	37211	615-781-4000	781-4113
Henry County Medical Ctr 301 Tyson Ave *Web:* www.hcmc-tn.org	Paris	TN	38242	731-642-1220	642-9588
Holston Valley Hospital & Medical Ctr 130 W Ravine Rd *Web:* www.wellmont.org	Kingsport	TN	37660	423-224-4000	224-5037
Horizon Medical Ctr 111 Hwy 70 E *Web:* www.horizonmedctr.com	Dickson	TN	37055	615-446-0446	441-2514
Indian Path Medical Ctr 2000 Brookside Dr *Web:* www.msha.com/facility.cfm?id=50	Kingsport	TN	37660	423-392-7000	857-7109
Jackson-Madison County General Hospital 620 Skyline Dr *Web:* www.wth.net	Jackson	TN	38301	731-541-5000	541-3157
Johnson City Medical Ctr 400 N State of Franklin Rd *Web:* www.jcmc.com	Johnson City	TN	37604	423-431-6111	431-3077
Lakeway Regional Hospital (LRH) 726 McFarland St *Web:* www.lakewayregionalhospital.com	Morristown	TN	37814	423-522-6000	587-8548
Laughlin Memorial Hospital 1420 Tusculum Blvd *Web:* www.laughlinmemorial.org	Greeneville	TN	37745	423-787-5000	787-5083
Livingston Regional Hospital 315 Oak St *Web:* www.livingston-hospital.com	Livingston	TN	38570	931-823-5611	403-2334
Maury Regional Hospital 1224 Trotwood Ave *TF:* 800-355-8718 ■ *Web:* www.mauryregional.com	Columbia	TN	38401	931-381-1111	
Memorial Hospital 2525 Desales Ave *Web:* www.memorial.org	Chattanooga	TN	37404	423-495-2525	495-7726
Memorial North Park Hospital 2051 Hamill Rd *Web:* www.memorial.org	Hixson	TN	37343	423-495-7100	495-7388
Methodist Hospital South (MHS) 1300 Wesley Dr *Web:* www.methodisthealth.org/methodist	Memphis	TN	38116	901-516-3700	516-3085
Methodist Medical Center of Oak Ridge 990 Oak Ridge Tpke *Web:* www.mmcoakridge.com	Oak Ridge	TN	37831	865-835-1000	835-4054
Methodist North Hospital 3960 New Covington Pike *Web:* www.methodisthealth.org	Memphis	TN	38128	901-516-5200	516-5323
Middle Tennessee Medical Ctr 400 N Highland Ave *TF:* 800-596-3455 ■ *Web:* www.mtmc.org	Murfreesboro	TN	37130	615-849-4100	396-4659
Nashville General Hospital 1818 Albion St *Web:* www.nashville.gov/general_hospital	Nashville	TN	37208	615-341-4000	341-4493
Northcrest Medical Ctr 100 Northcrest Dr *Web:* www.northcrest.com	Springfield	TN	37172	615-384-2411	384-1509
Parkridge East Hospital 941 Spring Creek Rd *TF:* 800-605-1527 ■ *Web:* www.parkridgeeasthospital.com	Chattanooga	TN	37412	423-894-7870	855-3648
Parkridge Medical Ctr 2333 McCallie Ave *Web:* www.parkridgemedicalcenter.com	Chattanooga	TN	37404	423-698-6061	493-1208
Parkwest Medical Ctr 9352 Pk W Blvd *Web:* www.covenanthealth.com	Knoxville	TN	37923	865-373-1000	373-1012

			Phone	Fax
Premier Medical Group Pc 1850 Business Pk Dr PO Box 3799 ... Clarksville Web: www.premiermed.com	TN	37043	931-245-7000	
Regional Hospital of Jackson 367 Hospital Blvd ... Jackson TF: 800-454-9970	TN	38305	731-661-2000	661-2187
Regional Medical Center at Memphis 877 Jefferson Ave ... Memphis Web: www.the-med.org	TN	38103	901-545-7100	545-7037
Roane Medical Ctr 412 Devonia St ... Harriman Web: www.covenanthealth.com	TN	37748	865-882-1323	882-4343
Saint Francis Hospital 5959 Pk Ave ... Memphis TF: 866-904-6871 ■ Web: www.saintfrancishosp.com/en-US/Pages/default.aspx	TN	38119	901-765-1000	765-1799
Saint Mary's Medical Ctr 900 E Oak Hill Ave ... Knoxville Web: www.ehealthconnection.com/regions/tennessee	TN	37917	865-545-8000	545-6732
Saint Thomas Hospital 4220 Harding Rd ... Nashville Web: www.stthomas.org	TN	37205	615-222-2111	222-6502
Skyline Madison Campus 500 Hospital Dr ... Madison Web: www.skylinemadison.com	TN	37115	615-769-5000	860-6378
Skyline Medical Ctr 3441 Dickerson Pike ... Nashville TF: 800-690-0096 ■ Web: www.skylinemedicalcenter.com	TN	37207	615-769-2000	769-7102
SkyRidge Medical Ctr 2305 Chambliss Ave ... Cleveland Web: www.skyridgemedicalcenter.net	TN	37311	423-559-6000	559-6653
Summit Medical Ctr 5655 Frist Blvd ... Hermitage Web: www.summitmedctr.com	TN	37076	615-316-3000	316-4912
Sumner Regional Medical Ctr 555 Hartsville Pike ... Gallatin TF: 800-728-4217 ■ Web: www.sumner.org	TN	37066	615-452-4210	328-5523
Takoma Regional Hospital 401 Takoma Ave ... Greeneville Web: www.takoma.org	TN	37743	423-639-3151	636-2374
University Medical Ctr 1411 W Baddour Pkwy ... Lebanon Web: www.hma.com	TN	37087	615-444-8262	449-1215
University of Tennessee Medical Ctr 1924 Alcoa Hwy ... Knoxville Web: www.utmedicalcenter.org	TN	37920	865-544-9000	544-9429
Vanderbilt University Medical Ctr 1215 21st Ave S ... Nashville Web: www.mc.vanderbilt.edu	TN	37232	615-322-5000	343-7317
Williamson Medical Ctr (WMC) 4321 Carothers Pkwy ... Franklin Web: www.williamsonmedicalcenter.org	TN	37067	615-435-5000	435-5161
Woods Memorial Hospital 886 Hwy 411 N ... Etowah Web: www.woodshospital.com	TN	37331	423-263-3600	

TEXAS

			Phone	Fax
Abilene Regional Medical Ctr 6250 S Hwy 83-84 ... Abilene Web: www.abileneregional.com	TX	79606	325-428-1000	428-1029
Arlington Memorial Hospital 800 W Randol Mill Rd ... Arlington Web: www.texashealth.org	TX	76012	817-548-6100	548-6357
Baptist Medical Ctr 111 Dallas St ... San Antonio Web: www.baptisthealthsystem.com	TX	78205	210-297-7000	297-0700
Baylor All Saints Medical Ctr 1400 8th Ave ... Fort Worth Web: www.baylorhealth.com/locations/allsaints	TX	76104	817-926-2544	927-6226
Baylor Medical Center at Garland 2300 Marie Curie Blvd ... Garland Web: www.baylorhealth.com/Locations/garland	TX	75042	972-487-5000	485-3051
Baylor Medical Center at Irving 1901 N MacArthur Blvd ... Irving Web: www.baylorhealth.com/PhysiciansLocations/Irving	TX	75061	972-579-8100	579-5254
Baylor Regional Medical Center at Grapevine 1650 W College St ... Grapevine TF: 800-422-9567 ■ Web: www.baylorhealth.com	TX	76051	817-488-7546	329-4812
Baylor University Medical Ctr at Dallas 3500 Gaston Ave ... Dallas Web: www.baylorhealth.com	TX	75246	214-820-0111	820-2411
Bayshore Medical Ctr 4000 Spencer Hwy ... Pasadena Web: www.bayshoremedical.com	TX	77504	713-359-2000	359-1004
Ben Taub General Hospital 1504 Taub Loop ... Houston Web: www.hchdonline.com	TX	77030	713-873-2000	873-2305
Brackenridge Hospital 601 E 15th St ... Austin Web: www.seton.net	TX	78701	512-324-7000	324-7051
Brazosport Regional Health System (BRHS) 100 Medical Dr ... Lake Jackson Web: www.brhstx.org	TX	77566	979-297-4411	297-6905
Brownwood Regional Medical Ctr 1501 Burnet Dr ... Brownwood Web: www.brmc-cares.com	TX	76801	325-646-8541	646-5459
Central Texas Medical Ctr (CTMC) 1301 Wonder World Dr ... San Marcos TF: 800-508-8515 ■ Web: www.ctmc.org	TX	78666	512-353-8979	753-3598
CHRISTUS Hospital - St Elizabeth 2830 Calder St ... Beaumont Web: www.christushospital.org	TX	77702	409-892-7171	924-3959
CHRISTUS Saint John Hospital 18300 St John Dr ... Nassau Bay Web: www.christusstjohn.org	TX	77058	281-333-5503	333-8891
CHRISTUS Saint Mary Hospital 3600 Gates Blvd PO Box 3696 ... Port Arthur Web: www.christushospital.org	TX	77642	409-985-7431	989-1033
CHRISTUS Saint Michael Health System 2600 St Michael Dr ... Texarkana Web: www.christusstmichael.org	TX	75503	903-614-1000	614-2212
CHRISTUS Santa Rosa Hospital 333 N Santa Rosa St ... San Antonio Web: www.christussantarosa.org	TX	78207	210-704-2011	704-3632
CHRISTUS Spohn Hospital Corpus Christi Shoreline 600 Elizabeth St 3rd Fl ... Corpus Christi Web: www.christushealth.org	TX	78404	361-881-3640	881-3149
CHRISTUS Spohn Hospital Corpus Christi-South 5950 Saratoga Blvd ... Corpus Christi Web: www.christusspohn.org	TX	78414	361-985-5000	985-5173
CHRISTUS Spohn Hospital Kleberg 1311 General Cavazos Blvd ... Kingsville Web: www.christusspohn.org	TX	78363	361-595-1661	595-5005
CHRISTUS Spohn Hospital Memorial 2606 Hospital Blvd ... Corpus Christi Web: www.christusspohn.org	TX	78405	361-902-4000	902-4968
Citizens Medical Ctr 2701 Hospital Dr ... Victoria Web: www.citizensmedicalcenter.org	TX	77901	361-573-9181	572-5070
Clear Lake Regional Medical Ctr 500 W Medical Ctr Blvd ... Webster Web: www.clearlakermc.com	TX	77598	281-332-2511	338-3352
Cleveland Regional Medical Ctr 300 E Crockett St ... Cleveland Web: www.clevelandregionalmedicalcenter.com	TX	77327	281-593-1811	432-4370
College Station Medical Ctr 1604 Rock Prairie Rd ... College Station Web: www.csmedcenter.com	TX	77845	979-764-5100	696-7373
Conroe Regional Medical Ctr 504 Medical Ctr Blvd ... Conroe TF: 888-633-2687 ■ Web: www.conroeregional.com	TX	77304	936-539-1111	539-5620
Corpus Christi Medical Center Bay Area 7101 S Padre Island Dr ... Corpus Christi Web: www.ccmedicalcenter.com	TX	78412	361-761-1200	761-3670
Corpus Christi Medical Ctr 13725 NW Blvd ... Corpus Christi Web: www.ccmedicalcenter.com	TX	78410	361-767-4300	761-1501
Covenant Medical Ctr 3615 19th St ... Lubbock Web: www.covenanthealth.org	TX	79410	806-725-1011	723-7188
Covenant Medical Lakeside 4000 24th St ... Lubbock Web: www.covenanthealth.com	TX	79410	806-725-6000	723-6574
Cypress Fairbanks Medical Ctr 10655 Steepletop Dr ... Houston Web: www.cyfairhospital.com	TX	77065	281-890-4285	890-5341
Dallas Regional Medical Ctr (DRMC) 1011 N Galloway Ave ... Mesquite *Fax Area Code: 972 ■ Web: www.dallasregionalmedicalcenter.com	TX	75149	214-320-7000	289-9468*
Del Sol Medical Ctr 10301 Gateway W ... El Paso Web: www.laspalmasdelsolhealthcare.com/home.aspx	TX	79925	915-595-9000	595-7224
Denton Regional Medical Ctr 3535 S I-35 E ... Denton Web: www.dentonregional.com	TX	76210	940-384-3535	384-4700
Detar Hospital Navarro 506 E San Antonio St ... Victoria Web: www.detar.com	TX	77901	361-575-7441	788-6114
Detar Hospital North 101 Medical Dr ... Victoria Web: www.detar.com	TX	77904	361-573-6100	788-2693
Doctors Hospital at White Rock Lake 9440 Poppy Dr ... Dallas Web: www.doctorshospitaldallas.com	TX	75218	214-324-6100	324-0612
Doctors Hospital of Laredo 10700 McPherson Rd ... Laredo Web: www.doctorshosplaredo.com	TX	78045	956-523-2000	523-0444
East Houston Regional Medical Ctr 13111 E Fwy ... Houston Web: www.easthoustonrmc.com	TX	77015	713-393-2000	393-2714
East Texas Medical Center Athens 2000 S Palestine St ... Athens Web: www.etmc.org	TX	75751	903-676-1000	676-3337
East Texas Medical Center Tyler 1000 S Beckham Ave ... Tyler Web: www.etmc.org	TX	75701	903-597-0351	535-6334
Edinburg Regional Medical Ctr (ERMC) 1102 W Trenton Rd ... Edinburg TF: 800-465-5585 ■ Web: www.southtexashealthsystem.com	TX	78539	956-388-6000	388-6020
Fort Duncan Regional Medical Ctr 3333 N Foster Maldonado Blvd ... Eagle Pass *Fax: Admissions ■ Web: www.fortduncanmedicalcenter.com	TX	78852	830-773-5321	872-2549*
Good Shepherd Medical Ctr 700 E Marshall Ave ... Longview Web: www.gsmc.org	TX	75601	903-315-2000	315-2479
Gulf Coast Medical Ctr (GCMC) 10141 US 59 Rd ... Wharton Web: www.gulfcoastmedical.com	TX	77488	979-532-2500	282-6190
Harris Methodist Fort Worth 1301 Pennsylvania Ave ... Fort Worth Web: www.texashealth.org	TX	76104	817-882-2000	882-3169
Harris Methodist Southwest 6100 Harris Pkwy ... Fort Worth Web: www.texashealth.org	TX	76132	817-346-5050	433-6574
Harris Methodist-HEB 1600 Hospital Pkwy ... Bedford Web: www.texashealth.org	TX	76022	817-685-4000	685-4890
Hendrick Health System 1900 Pine St ... Abilene Web: www.hendrickhealth.org	TX	79601	325-670-2000	670-2209
Hillcrest Baptist Medical Ctr 3000 Herring Ave ... Waco Web: www.hillcrest.net	TX	76708	254-202-2000	202-8978
Houston Northwest Medical Ctr 710 FM 1960 W ... Houston Web: www.hnmc.com	TX	77090	281-440-1000	440-2666
Huguley Memorial Medical Ctr 11801 S Fwy ... Burleson Web: www.huguley.org	TX	76028	817-293-9110	568-1298
Hunt Regional Healthcare 4215 Joe Ramsey Blvd ... Greenville TF: 800-984-9223 ■ Web: www.hmhd.org	TX	75401	903-408-5000	408-1609
Huntsville Memorial Hospital 110 Memorial Hospital Dr ... Huntsville Web: www.huntsvillememorial.com	TX	77340	936-291-3411	291-4373
John Peter Smith Hospital 1500 S Main St ... Fort Worth Web: www.jpshealthnet.org	TX	76104	817-921-3431	927-1604
Kingwood Medical Ctr 22999 US Hwy 59 ... Kingwood Web: www.kingwoodmedical.com	TX	77339	281-348-8000	348-8010

Hospital	City	State	ZIP	Phone	Fax
Knapp Medical Ctr (KMC) 1401 E 8th St PO Box 1110 *Web:* www.knappmed.org	Weslaco	TX	78596	956-968-8567	969-2293
Lake Pointe Medical Ctr (LPMC) 6800 Scenic Dr *Web:* www.lakepointemedical.com	Rowlett	TX	75088	972-412-2273	412-3276
Laredo Medical Ctr (LMC) 1700 E Saunders Ave *Web:* www.laredomedical.com	Laredo	TX	78041	956-796-5000	796-3175
Las Colinas Medical Ctr 6800 N MacArthur Blvd *Web:* www.lascolinasmedical.com	Irving	TX	75039	972-969-2000	969-2080
Las Palmas Medical Ctr 1801 N Oregon St *Web:* www.laspalmasdelsolhealthcare.com	El Paso	TX	79902	915-521-1200	544-5203
Live centre speciality 1111 Gallagher Dr *Web:* www.cshsherman.org	Sherman	TX	75090	903-870-7000	870-7599
Longview Regional Medical Ctr 2901 N 4th St *Web:* www.longviewregional.com	Longview	TX	75605	903-758-1818	758-5167
Mainland Medical Ctr 6801 Emmett Lowry Expy *Web:* www.mainlandmedical.com	Texas City	TX	77591	409-938-5000	938-5001
McAllen Medical Ctr 301 W Expy 83 *Web:* www.southtexashealthsystem.com	McAllen	TX	78503	956-632-4000	632-4010
Medical Center Hospital (MCH) 500 W 4th St *Web:* www.medicalcenterhealthsystem.com	Odessa	TX	79761	432-640-4000	640-1118
Medical Center of Arlington (MCA) 3301 Matlock Rd *Web:* www.medicalcenterarlington.com	Arlington	TX	76015	817-465-3241	472-4878
Medical Center of Lewisville 500 W Main St *Web:* www.lewisvillemedical.com	Lewisville	TX	75057	972-420-1000	353-1789
Medical Center of McKinney 4500 Medical Ctr Dr *Web:* www.medicalcenterofmckinney.com/home/index.dot	McKinney	TX	75069	972-547-8000	547-8042
Medical Center of Plano The 3901 W 15th St *Web:* www.themedicalcenterofplano.com	Plano	TX	75075	972-596-6800	519-1409
Medical Center of Southeast Texas The 2555 Jimmy Johnson Blvd *Web:* www.medicalcentersetexas.com	Port Arthur	TX	77640	409-724-7389	853-5910
Medical City Hospital 7777 Forest Ln *Web:* www.medicalcityhospital.com	Dallas	TX	75230	972-566-7000	566-5867
Memorial Hermann - Texas Medical Ctr 6411 Fannin St *Web:* www.memorialhermann.org	Houston	TX	77030	713-704-4000	704-5872
Memorial Hermann Baptist Beaumont Hospital 3080 College St *Web:* www.mhbh.org	Beaumont	TX	77701	409-212-5000	212-5001
Memorial Hermann Baptist Hospital 3080 College St *Web:* www.mhbh.org	Beaumont	TX	77701	409-212-5000	212-5022
Memorial Hermann Baptist Orange Hospital 608 Strickland Dr *Web:* www.mhbh.org	Orange	TX	77630	409-883-9361	883-1223
Memorial Hermann Katy Hospital 23900 Katy Fwy *Web:* www.memorialhermann.org/locations/K.html	Katy	TX	77494	281-644-7000	644-7090
Memorial Hermann Memorial City Hospital 921 Gessner Rd *TF:* 800-392-6370 ■ *Web:* www.memorialhermann.org	Houston	TX	77024	713-242-3000	242-4096
Memorial Hermann Southwest Hospital 7600 Beechnut St *Web:* www.memorialhermann.org	Houston	TX	77074	713-456-5000	456-8363
Memorial Medical Center of East Texas 1201 W Frank Ave *TF:* 800-348-5969 ■ *Web:* www.mymemorialhealth.org	Lufkin	TX	75904	936-634-8111	639-7004
Mesquite Community Hospital 3500 I-30 *Web:* www.mchtx.com	Mesquite	TX	75150	972-698-3300	698-2133
Methodist Charlton Medical Ctr 3500 W Wheatland Rd *Web:* www.methodisthealthsystem.org/facil_cmh.html	Dallas	TX	75237	214-947-7777	947-7525
Methodist Dallas Medical Ctr 1441 N Beckley Ave *Web:* www.methodisthealthsystem.org	Dallas	TX	75203	214-947-8181	947-3403
Methodist Hospital 6565 Fannin St *Web:* www.methodisthealth.com	Houston	TX	77030	713-790-3311	790-2605
Methodist Hospital 7700 Floyd Curl Dr *Web:* www.mh.sahealth.com	San Antonio	TX	78229	210-575-4000	575-4410
Methodist Hospital System The 6447 Main St *Web:* www.methodisthealth.com	Houston	TX	77030	713-790-0790	790-2605
Methodist Richardson Medical Ctr 401 W Campbell Rd *Web:* www.richardsonregional.com	Richardson	TX	75080	972-498-4000	498-4931
Metroplex Hospital 2201 S Clear Creek Rd *Web:* www.mplex.org	Killeen	TX	76549	254-526-7523	526-3483
Metropolitan Methodist Hospital 1310 McCullough Ave *Web:* sahealth.com	San Antonio	TX	78212	210-757-2200	757-2915
Midland Memorial Hospital 2200 W Illinois Ave *TF:* 800-833-2916 ■ *Web:* www.midland-memorial.com	Midland	TX	79701	432-685-1111	685-4970
Mission Regional Medical Ctr 900 S Bryan Rd *Web:* www.missionhospital.com	Mission	TX	78572	956-580-9000	580-9103
Mother Frances Hospital 800 E Dawson St *Web:* www.tmfhs.org	Tyler	TX	75701	903-593-8441	525-1201
Nacogdoches Medical Ctr 4920 NE Stallings Dr *TF:* 800-539-2772 ■ *Web:* www.nacmedicalcenter.com	Nacogdoches	TX	75965	936-569-9481	568-3400
Nacogdoches Memorial Hospital 1204 N Mound St *Web:* www.nacmem.org	Nacogdoches	TX	75961	936-564-4611	568-8588
Navarro Regional Hospital (NRH) 3201 W Hwy 22 *Web:* www.navarrohospital.com	Corsicana	TX	75110	903-654-6800	654-6955
Nix Medical Ctr 414 Navarro St *Web:* www.nixhealth.com	San Antonio	TX	78205	210-271-1800	271-2023
North Hills Hospital 4401 Booth Calloway Rd *Web:* www.northhillshospital.com	North Richland Hills	TX	76180	817-255-1000	255-1991

Hospital	City	State	ZIP	Phone	Fax
Northeast Baptist Hospital 8811 Village Dr *Web:* www.baptisthealthsystem.com	San Antonio	TX	78217	210-297-2000	297-0200
Northeast Medical Center Hospital 18951 Memorial N *Web:* www.memorialhermann.org	Humble	TX	77338	281-540-7700	540-7846
Northeast Methodist Hospital 12412 Judson Rd *Web:* www.sahealth.com	San Antonio	TX	78233	210-757-7000	757-5072
Northwest Texas Hospital 1501 S Coulter *Web:* www.nwtexashealthcare.com	Amarillo	TX	79106	806-354-1000	354-1122
OakBend Medical Ctr 1705 Jackson St *Web:* www.oakbendmedcenter.org	Richmond	TX	77469	281-342-2000	341-3056
Palestine Regional Medical Ctr 2900 S Loop 256 *Web:* www.palestineregional.com	Palestine	TX	75801	903-731-1000	731-2236
Pampa Regional Medical Ctr 1 Medical Plaza *Web:* www.prmctx.com	Pampa	TX	79065	806-665-3721	665-2361
Paris Regional Medical Center 820 Clarksville St *Web:* www.parisrmc.com	Paris	TX	75460	903-785-4521	737-3848
Parkland Health & Hospital System 5201 Harry Hines Blvd **Fax:* Admitting ■ *Web:* www.parklandhospital.com	Dallas	TX	75235	214-590-8000	590-2713*
Peterson Regional Medical Ctr 551 Hill Country Dr *Web:* www.petersonrmc.com	Kerrville	TX	78028	830-896-4200	258-7833
Plaza Medical Ctr 900 8th Ave *Web:* www.plazamedicalcenter.com	Fort Worth	TX	76104	817-336-2100	347-5796
Presbyterian Hospital of Dallas 8200 Walnut Hill Ln *Web:* www.texashealth.org	Dallas	TX	75231	214-345-6789	345-4603
Providence Healthcare Network 6901 Medical Pkwy *Web:* www.providence.net	Waco	TX	76712	254-751-4000	751-4769
Providence Memorial Hospital (PMH) 2001 N Oregon St *Web:* www.sphn.com/en-us/aboutus/pages/providence%20memorial%20hospital.aspx	El Paso	TX	79902	915-577-6011	577-6549
Rio Grande Regional Hospital 101 E Ridge Rd *Web:* www.riohealth.com	McAllen	TX	78503	956-632-6000	632-6621
Saint Anthony's Baptist Health System 1600 Wallace Blvd *Web:* www.bsahs.org	Amarillo	TX	79106	806-212-2000	212-2919
Saint David's Medical Ctr 919 E 32nd St *Web:* www.stdavids.com	Austin	TX	78705	512-476-7111	544-8102
Saint David's North Austin Medical Ctr 12221 N Mopac Expy *TF:* 888-356-5315 ■ *Web:* www.stdavids.com	Austin	TX	78758	512-901-1000	901-1995
Saint David's South Austin Medical Ctr 901 W Ben White Blvd *Web:* www.stdavids.com	Austin	TX	78704	512-447-2211	448-7326
Saint Joseph Medical Ctr 1401 St Joseph Pkwy *Web:* www.sjmctx.com	Houston	TX	77002	713-757-1000	657-7123
Saint Joseph Regional Health Ctr 2801 Franciscan Dr *Web:* www.st-joseph.org	Bryan	TX	77802	979-776-3777	774-4590
Saint Luke's Episcopal Hospital (SLEH) 6720 Bertner Ave *Web:* www.stlukestexas.com/index.cfm	Houston	TX	77030	832-355-1000	355-6812
Saint Paul University Hospital 5909 Harry Hines Blvd *Web:* www.utsouthwestern.edu/utsw/home/pc/universityhospitals/index.html	Dallas	TX	75390	214-645-5555	634-7087
San Angelo Community Medical Ctr 3501 Knickerbocker Rd *Web:* www.sacmc.com	San Angelo	TX	76904	325-949-9511	947-6550
San Jacinto Methodist Hospital (SJMH) 4401 Garth Rd **Fax:* Admitting ■ *Web:* www.methodisthealth.com/sjmh.cfm?id=36844	Baytown	TX	77521	281-420-8600	420-8672*
Scott & White Memorial Hospital 2401 S 31st St *TF:* 800-792-3710 ■ *Web:* www.sw.org	Temple	TX	76508	254-724-2111	724-2786
Seton Medical Ctr 1201 W 38th St *Web:* www.seton.net	Austin	TX	78705	512-324-1000	324-1924
Shannon Medical Ctr (SMC) 120 E Harris Ave *TF:* 888-653-6741 ■ *Web:* www.shannonhealth.com	San Angelo	TX	76903	325-653-6741	658-8295
Sierra Medical Ctr 1625 Medical Ctr Dr *Web:* www.sphn.com/en-US/Pages/default.aspx	El Paso	TX	79902	915-747-4000	
Southeast Baptist Hospital 4214 E Southcross Blvd *Web:* www.baptisthealthsystem.com	San Antonio	TX	78222	210-297-3000	297-0300
Southwest General Hospital (SGH) 7400 Barlite Blvd *Web:* www.swgeneralhospital.com	San Antonio	TX	78224	210-921-2000	921-3508
Spring Branch Medical Ctr (SBMC) 8850 Long Pt St *Web:* www.sbmchealthcare.com	Houston	TX	77055	713-467-6555	722-3771
St David's Round Rock Medical Ctr 2400 Round Rock Ave *Web:* www.stdavids.com	Round Rock	TX	78681	512-341-1000	238-1799
Texas Health Presbyterian Hospital Denton 3000 N I-35 *Web:* www.texashealth.org	Denton	TX	76201	940-898-7000	898-7071
Texas Health Presbyterian Hospital-WNJ Therapy Services 500 N Highland Ave *Web:* www.wnj.org	Sherman	TX	75092	903-870-4611	870-4409
Texas Healthcare PLLC 2821 Lackland Rd Suite 300 *Web:* www.txhealthcare.com	Fort Worth	TX	76116	817-378-3640	740-8516
Texoma Medical Ctr 5016 S US Hwy 75 *Web:* www.texomamedicalcenter.net	Denison	TX	75020	903-416-4000	416-4129
Titus Regional Medical Ctr 2001 N Jefferson Ave *Web:* www.titusregional.com	Mount Pleasant	TX	75455	903-577-6000	577-6027

Hospital	City	State	ZIP	Phone	Fax
Tomball Regional Hospital (TRMC) 605 Holderrieth St	Tomball	TX	77375	281-401-7500	
Web: www.tomballhospital.org					
Trinity Medical Ctr (TMC) 4343 N Josey Ln	Carrollton	TX	75010	972-492-1010	492-9028
Twelve Oaks Medical Ctr 6700 Belaire Blvd	Houston	TX	77074	713-774-7611	778-2616
Web: www.twelveoaksmedicalcenter.com					
United Regional Health Care System *Eleventh Street Campus* 1600 11th St	Wichita Falls	TX	76301	940-764-7000	764-3041
Web: www.unitedregional.org					
United Regional Hospital *Eighth Street Campus* 1600 8th St 2nd Fl	Wichita Falls	TX	76301	940-764-7000	764-3041
Web: www.unitedregional.org					
University Hospital 4502 Medical Dr	San Antonio	TX	78229	210-358-4000	358-2837
TF: 800-256-2311 ■ *Web:* www.universityhealthsystem.com					
University Medical Center of El Paso (UMCEP) 4815 Alameda Ave	El Paso	TX	79905	915-544-1200	521-7612
Web: www.umcelpaso.org					
University Medical Ctr 602 Indiana Ave	Lubbock	TX	79415	806-775-8200	775-8611
Web: www.umchealthsystem.com					
University of Texas Health Center at Tyler (UTHCT) 11937 US Hwy 271	Tyler	TX	75708	903-877-7777	877-7759
Web: www.uthct.edu					
University of Texas Medical Branch Hospitals 301 University Blvd	Galveston	TX	77555	409-772-1011	772-5119
Web: www.utmb.edu					
Valley Baptist Medical Center Brownsville 1040 W Jefferson St	Brownsville	TX	78520	956-544-1400	541-0712*
**Fax:* Hum Res ■ *Web:* www.valleybaptist.net/brownsville					
Valley Baptist Medical Center Harlingen 2101 Pease St	Harlingen	TX	78550	956-389-1100	389-1632
Web: www.valleybaptist.net					
Valley Regional Medical Ctr 100-A E Alton Gloor Blvd	Brownsville	TX	78526	956-350-7000	350-7111
Web: www.valleyregionalmedicalcenter.com					
Wadley Regional Medical Ctr 1000 Pine St	Texarkana	TX	75501	903-798-8000	
Web: www.wadleyhealth.com					
West Houston Medical Ctr 12141 Richmond Ave	Houston	TX	77082	281-558-3444	596-5989
TF: 800-558-7619					
Woodland Heights Medical Ctr 505 S John Redditt Dr	Lufkin	TX	75904	936-634-8311	637-8600
Web: www.woodlandheights.net					
Zale Lipshy University Hospital 5151 Harry Hines Blvd	Dallas	TX	75390	214-645-5555	545-4648*
**Fax:* Admitting ■ *Web:* www.utsouthwestern.edu					

UTAH

Hospital	City	State	ZIP	Phone	Fax
American Fork Hospital 170 N 1100 E	American Fork	UT	84003	801-763-3300	855-3548
Web: www.intermountainhealthcare.org					
Davis Hospital & Medical Ctr (DHMC) 1600 W Antelope Dr	Layton	UT	84041	801-807-1000	807-7610
TF: 877-898-6080 ■ *Web:* www.davishospital.com					
Dixie Regional Medical Ctr 1380 E Medical Ctr Dr	Saint George	UT	84790	435-251-1000	251-2115
Web: www.intermountainhealthcare.org					
Intermountain Healthcare Logan Regional Hospital 500 E 1400 N	Logan	UT	84341	435-716-1000	716-5409
Web: www.intermountainhealthcare.org					
Lakeview Hospital 630 E Medical Dr	Bountiful	UT	84010	801-292-6231	299-2534
Web: www.lakeviewhospital.com					
LDS Hospital 8th Ave & C St	Salt Lake City	UT	84143	801-408-1100	408-1665
TF: 888-301-3880					
McKay-Dee Hospital Ctr 4401 S Harrison Blvd	Ogden	UT	84403	801-627-2800	387-3725
Web: www.intermountainhealthcare.org/hospitals/mckaydee/Pages/home.aspx					
Mountain View Hospital 1000 E 100 N	Payson	UT	84651	801-465-7000	465-7170
Web: www.mvhpayson.com					
Ogden Regional Medical Ctr 5475 Adams Ave Pkwy	Ogden	UT	84405	801-479-2111	479-2091
TF: 800-237-9194 ■ *Web:* www.ogdenregional.com					
Pioneer Valley Hospital 3460 S Pioneer Pkwy	West Valley City	UT	84120	801-964-3100	964-3247
Web: www.pioneervalleyhospital.com					
Saint Mark's Hospital 1200 E 3900 S	Salt Lake City	UT	84124	801-268-7111	270-3489
Web: www.stmarkshospital.com					
Salt Lake Regional Medical Ctr 1050 E S Temple	Salt Lake City	UT	84102	801-350-4111	350-4522
Web: www.saltlakeregional.com					
University of Utah Hospital & Clinics 50 N Medical Dr	Salt Lake City	UT	84132	801-581-2121	585-5280
Web: www.med.utah.edu					
Utah Valley Regional Medical Ctr 1034 N 500 W	Provo	UT	84604	801-373-7850	357-7780
Web: www.intermountainhealthcare.org/xp/public/uvrmc					

VERMONT

Hospital	City	State	ZIP	Phone	Fax
Brattleboro Memorial Hospital Inc 17 Belmont Ave Suite 1	Brattleboro	VT	05301	802-257-0341	257-8869
TF: 866-972-5266 ■ *Web:* www.bmhvt.org					
Central Vermont Medical Ctr (CVMC) 130 Fisher Rd	Berlin	VT	05602	802-229-9121	371-4401
Web: www.cvmc.org					
Copley Hospital Inc 528 Washington Hwy	Morrisville	VT	05661	802-888-8888	
Web: www.copleyvt.org					
Fletcher Allen Health Care Medical Center Campus (FAHC) 111 Colchester Ave	Burlington	VT	05401	802-847-0000	847-5252
TF: 800-358-1144 ■ *Web:* www.fahc.org					
Northwestern Medical Ctr 133 Fairfield St	Saint Albans	VT	05478	802-524-5911	524-1088
Web: www.northwesternmedicalcenter.org					
Rutland Regional Medical Ctr 160 Allen St	Rutland	VT	05701	802-775-7111	747-1620
TF: 800-649-2187 ■ *Web:* www.rrmc.org					
Southwestern Vermont Medical Ctr 100 Hospital Dr	Bennington	VT	05201	802-442-6361	447-5013
TF: 800-543-1624 ■ *Web:* www.svhealthcare.org/hospital					
Springfield Hospital 25 Ridgewood Rd PO Box 2003	Springfield	VT	05156	802-885-2151	885-7357
Web: www.springfieldhospital.org					

VIRGINIA

Hospital	City	State	ZIP	Phone	Fax
Alleghany Regional Hospital 1 ARH Ln PO Box 7	Low Moor	VA	24457	540-862-6011	862-6589
Web: www.alleghanyregional.com					
Augusta Medical Ctr (AMC) 78 Medical Ctr Dr PO Box 1000	Fishersville	VA	22939	540-932-4000	932-4809
TF: 800-932-0262 ■ *Web:* www.augustahealth.com					
Bon Secours DePaul Medical Ctr 150 Kingsley Ln	Norfolk	VA	23505	757-489-5000	889-5837
Web: www.bonsecourshamptonroads.com					
Bon Secours Maryview Medical Ctr 3636 High St	Portsmouth	VA	23707	757-398-2200	398-2157*
**Fax:* Admitting ■ *Web:* www.bonsecourshamptonroads.com/facilities/maryview.html					
Bon Secours Memorial Regional Medical Ctr 8260 Atlee Rd	Mechanicsville	VA	23116	804-764-6000	764-6420
TF: 888-455-3766 ■ *Web:* www.bonsecours.org/richmond/mrmc.htm					
Bon Secours Saint Mary's Hospital 5801 Bremo Rd	Richmond	VA	23226	804-285-2011	285-8327
TF: 800-472-2011 ■ *Web:* www.bonsecours.org/richmond/smary.htm					
Buchanan General Hospital (BGH) 1535 Slate Creek Rd	Grundy	VA	24614	276-935-1000	935-1354
Web: www.bgh.org					
Carilion New River Valley Medical Ctr 2900 Lamb Cir	Christiansburg	VA	24073	540-731-2000	731-2505
TF: 800-432-7874 ■ *Web:* www.carilionclinic.org					
Carilion Roanoke Community Hospital (CRCH) 101 Elm Ave SE	Roanoke	VA	24013	540-985-8000	224-4537
Web: www.carilionclinic.org/Carilion/Carilion+Roanoke+Community+Hospital					
Carilion Roanoke Memorial Hospital 1906 Belleview Ave	Roanoke	VA	24014	540-981-7000	981-7670
Web: www.carilionclinic.org					
Chesapeake General Hospital 736 Battlefield Blvd N	Chesapeake	VA	23320	757-312-6100	312-6184
Web: www.chesapeakehealth.com					
CJW Medical Ctr 7101 Jahnke Rd	Richmond	VA	23225	804-320-3911	323-8049
TF: 800-468-6620 ■ *Web:* www.cjwmedical.com					
Community Memorial Healthcenter 412 Bracey Ln	South Hill	VA	23970	434-447-3151	774-2401
Web: www.cmh-sh.org					
Culpeper Memorial Hospital Inc PO Box 592	Culpeper	VA	22701	540-829-4100	
TF: 800-232-4264 ■ *Web:* www.culpeperhospital.com					
Danville Regional Medical Ctr 142 S Main St	Danville	VA	24541	434-799-2100	799-2260
TF: 800-688-3762 ■ *Web:* www.danvilleregional.org					
Fauquier Hospital 500 Hospital Dr	Warrenton	VA	20186	540-316-5000	349-0572
Web: www.fauquierhospital.org					
Halifax Regional Health System (HRHS) 2204 Wilborn Ave	South Boston	VA	24592	434-517-3100	517-3626
Web: www.hrhs.org					
Henrico Doctor's Hospital 1602 Skipwith Rd	Richmond	VA	23229	804-289-4500	289-4801
Web: www.henricodoctorshospital.com					
Inova Alexandria Hospital 4320 Seminary Rd	Alexandria	VA	22304	703-504-3000	504-3700
Web: www.inova.com					
Inova Fair Oaks Hospital 3600 Joseph Siewick Dr	Fairfax	VA	22033	703-391-3600	391-3273
Web: www.inova.org					
Inova Fairfax Hospital 3300 Gallows Rd	Falls Church	VA	22042	703-776-4001	776-3623
Web: www.inova.org					
Inova Mount Vernon Hospital 2501 Parkers Ln	Alexandria	VA	22306	703-664-7000	664-7235
Web: www.inova.org					
John Randolph Medical Ctr 411 W Randolph Rd PO Box 971	Hopewell	VA	23860	804-541-1600	452-3699
TF: 800-999-0374 ■ *Web:* www.johnrandolphmedicalcenter.com					
Johnston Memorial Hospital (JMH) 351 Ct St NE	Abingdon	VA	24210	276-676-7000	676-2631
Web: www.jmh.org					
Lewis-Gale Medical Ctr 1900 Electric Rd	Salem	VA	24153	540-776-4000	776-4785
TF: 800-543-5660 ■ *Web:* www.lewis-gale.com					
Lynchburg General Hospital 1901 Tate Springs Rd	Lynchburg	VA	24501	434-947-3000	947-3271
Martha Jefferson Hospital (MJH) 459 Locust Ave	Charlottesville	VA	22902	434-982-7000	982-7324
TF: 888-652-6663 ■ *Web:* www.marthajefferson.org					
Mary Immaculate Hospital 2 Bernardine Dr	Newport News	VA	23602	757-886-6000	886-6751
Web: www.bshsi.com					
Mary Washington Hospital 1001 Sam Perry Blvd	Fredericksburg	VA	22401	540-741-1100	741-1420
TF: 800-468-1092 ■ *Web:* www.marywashingtonhealthcare.com					
Memorial Hospital 320 Hospital Dr	Martinsville	VA	24115	276-666-7200	666-7600
Web: www.martinsvillehospital.org					
Montgomery Regional Hospital 3700 S Main St	Blacksburg	VA	24060	540-951-1111	953-5295
Web: www.mrhospital.com					
Northern Virginia Community Hospital 601 S Carlin Springs Rd	Arlington	VA	22204	703-671-1200	578-2075
Web: www.nvchospital.com					
Norton Community Hospital (NCH) 100 15th St NW	Norton	VA	24273	276-679-9600	679-9664
Web: www.msha.com					
Potomac Hospital 2300 Opitz Blvd	Woodbridge	VA	22191	703-670-1313	670-7643
Web: www.potomachospital.com					

	City	State	Zip	Phone	Fax
Prince William Hospital 8700 Sudly Rd *Web:* www.pwhs.org	Manassas	VA	20110	703-369-8000	369-8010
Reston Hospital Ctr 1850 Town Ctr Pkwy *TF:* 800-695-9426 ■ *Web:* www.restonhospital.com	Reston	VA	20190	703-689-9000	689-0840
Retreat Hospital 2621 Grove Ave *TF:* 800-235-9091 ■ *Web:* www.henricodoctors.com	Richmond	VA	23220	804-254-5100	254-5187
Riverside Regional Medical Ctr 500 J Clyde Morris Blvd	Newport News	VA	23601	757-594-2000	594-2084
Rockingham Memorial Hospital (RMH) 2010 Health Campus Dr *TF:* 800-433-4580 ■ *Web:* www.rmhonline.com	Harrisonburg	VA	22801	540-689-1000	
Sentara Careplex Hospital 3000 Colliseum Dr *TF:* 800-736-8272 ■ *Web:* www.sentara.com	Hampton	VA	23666	757-736-1000	736-2659
Sentara Leigh Hospital 830 Kempsville Rd *Web:* www.sentara.com/hospitals	Norfolk	VA	23502	757-261-6000	461-6796
Sentara Norfolk General Hospital 600 Gresham Dr **Fax:* Admitting ■ *Web:* www.sentara.com/hospitals	Norfolk	VA	23507	757-388-3000	388-4319*
Sentara Obici Hospital 2800 Godwin Blvd *TF:* 800-237-5788 ■ *Web:* www.sentara.com	Suffolk	VA	23434	757-934-4000	934-4284
Sentara Virginia Beach General Hospital 1060 First Colonial Rd *TF:* 800-736-8272 ■ *Web:* www.sentara.com/hospitals	Virginia Beach	VA	23454	757-395-8000	395-6106
Sentara Williamsburg Regional Medical Ctr 100 Sentara Cir *Web:* www.sentara.com	Williamsburg	VA	23188	757-984-6000	984-8145
Shore Memorial Hospital 9507 Hospital Ave PO Box 17 *TF:* 800-834-7035 ■ *Web:* www.shorehealthservices.org	Nassawadox	VA	23413	757-414-8000	414-8633
Smyth County Community Hospital 565 Radio Hill Rd *Web:* www.scchosp.org	Marion	VA	24354	276-782-1234	782-1438
Southampton Memorial Hospital 100 Fairview Dr *Web:* www.smhfranklin.com	Franklin	VA	23851	757-569-6100	569-6390
Southside Community Hospital (SCH) 800 Oak St *Web:* www.sch.centrahealth.com	Farmville	VA	23901	434-392-8811	392-7654
Southside Regional Medical Ctr 801 S Adams St *TF:* 866-434-9101 ■ *Web:* www.srmconline.com	Petersburg	VA	23803	804-862-5000	862-5948
Tidewater Physicians Multispecialty Group PC 860 Omni Blvd Suite 304 *TF:* 877-299-3701 ■ *Web:* www.tpmgpc.com	Newport News	VA	23606	757-232-8764	232-8865
Twin County Regional Hospital 200 Hospital Dr *TF:* 800-295-3342 ■ *Web:* www.tcrh.org	Galax	VA	24333	276-236-8181	236-1715
University of Virginia Health System 1215 Lee St *TF:* 800-251-3627 ■ *Web:* www.healthsystem.virginia.edu/toplevel/home/home.cfm	Charlottesville	VA	22908	434-924-0211	982-3759
Virginia Baptist Hospital 3300 Rivermont Ave *TF:* 800-423-5535 ■ *Web:* www.centrahealth.com	Lynchburg	VA	24503	434-947-4000	947-7448
Virginia Hospital Ctr 1701 N George Mason Dr *Web:* www.virginiahospitalcenter.com	Arlington	VA	22205	703-558-5000	558-6583
Winchester Medical Ctr 1840 Amherst St *Web:* www.valleyhealthlink.com	Winchester	VA	22601	540-536-8000	536-8606

WASHINGTON

	City	State	Zip	Phone	Fax
Auburn Regional Medical Ctr 202 N Division St Plaza 1 *TF:* 800-303-7713 ■ *Web:* www.auburnregional.com	Auburn	WA	98001	253-833-7711	939-2376
Capital Medical Ctr 3900 Capital Mall Dr SW *TF:* 888-677-9757 ■ *Web:* www.capitalmedical.com	Olympia	WA	98502	360-754-5858	956-2574
Deaconess Medical Ctr 800 W 5th Ave *Web:* www.deaconess-spokane.org	Spokane	WA	99204	509-458-5800	473-7286
Eastside Hospital 2700 152nd Ave NE *Web:* www.ghc.org	Redmond	WA	98052	425-883-5151	883-5638
Evergreen Hospital Medical Ctr 12040 NE 128th St *Web:* www.evergreenhospital.org	Kirkland	WA	98034	425-899-1000	899-2624
Good Samaritan Hospital (GSH) 407 14th Ave SE *Web:* www.multicare.org/goodsam	Puyallup	WA	98372	253-697-4000	697-5656
Grays Harbor Community Hospital 920 Anderson Dr *Web:* www.ghchwa.org	Aberdeen	WA	98520	360-532-8330	537-5039
Harrison Memorial Hospital 2520 Cherry Ave *Web:* www.harrisonhospital.org	Bremerton	WA	98310	360-377-3911	792-6515
Highline Medical Ctr 16251 Sylvester Rd SW *Web:* www.hchnet.org	Burien	WA	98166	206-244-9970	246-5385
Kadlec Regional Medical Ctr 888 Swift Blvd *TF:* 800-780-6067 ■ *Web:* www.kadlecmed.org	Richland	WA	99352	509-946-4611	942-2679
Kennewick General Hospital (KGH) 900 S Auburn St *Web:* www.kennewickgeneral.com	Kennewick	WA	99336	509-586-6111	586-5892
Legacy Salmon Creek Hospital 2211 NE 139th St *TF:* 877-397-9727 ■ *Web:* www.legacyhealth.org	Vancouver	WA	98686	360-487-1000	487-3459
Lourdes Medical Ctr 520 N 4th Ave *Web:* www.lourdeshealth.net	Pasco	WA	99301	509-547-7704	546-2291
Northwest Hospital & Medical Ctr 1550 N 115th St *TF:* 877-694-4677 ■ *Web:* www.nwhospital.org	Seattle	WA	98133	206-364-0500	368-1949
Olympic Medical Ctr 939 Caroline St *TF:* 888-362-6260 ■ *Web:* www.olympicmedical.org	Port Angeles	WA	98362	360-417-7000	417-7333
Overlake Hospital Medical Ctr 1035 116th Ave NE *Web:* www.overlakehospital.org	Bellevue	WA	98004	425-688-5000	688-5087
PeaceHealth St Joseph Medical Ctr 2901 Squalicum Pkwy *TF:* 800-541-7209 ■ *Web:* www.peacehealth.org	Bellingham	WA	98225	360-734-5400	738-6393
Peninsula Community Health Services PO Box 960 *Web:* www.pchsweb.org	Bremerton	WA	98337	360-377-3776	373-2096
Proliance Surgeons Inc 805 Madison Suite 901 *Web:* www.proliancesurgeons.com	Seattle	WA	98101	206-264-8100	
Providence Centralia Hospital 914 S Scheuber Rd *TF:* 877-736-2803 ■ *Web:* www.providence.org/swsa/facilities/Centralia_Hospital/default.htm	Centralia	WA	98531	360-736-2803	330-8614
Providence Everett Medical Ctr *Colby Campus* 1321 Colby Ave *Web:* www2.providence.org	Everett	WA	98201	425-261-2000	261-4030
Providence Holy Family Hospital 5633 N Lidgerwood St *Web:* www2.providence.org	Spokane	WA	99208	509-482-0111	482-2456
Providence Regional Medical Center Everett 916 Pacific Ave *Web:* www2.providence.org	Everett	WA	98201	425-261-2000	261-4051
Providence Sacred Heart Medical Ctr 101 W 8th Ave *TF:* 800-442-8534 ■ *Web:* www2.providence.org/spokane	Spokane	WA	99204	509-455-3131	474-4925
Providence Saint Peter Hospital (PSPH) 413 Lilly Rd NE *TF:* 888-492-9480 ■ *Web:* www2.providence.org	Olympia	WA	98506	360-491-9480	493-4277
Providence St Mary Medical Ctr 401 W Poplar St PO Box 1477 *TF:* 800-452-3320 ■ *Web:* www2.providence.org	Walla Walla	WA	99362	509-525-3320	522-5950
Qualis Health PO Box 33400 *TF:* 800-949-7536 ■ *Web:* www.qualishealth.org	Seattle	WA	98133	206-364-9700	368-2419
Saint Francis Hospital 34515 9th Ave S	Federal Way	WA	98003	253-838-9700	944-7913
Saint John Medical Ctr 1615 Delaware St PO Box 3002 *Web:* www.peacehealth.org	Longview	WA	98632	360-414-2000	
Saint Joseph Medical Ctr (SJMC) 1717 S J St *Web:* www.fhshealth.org	Tacoma	WA	98405	253-627-4101	426-6260
Skagit Valley Hospital 1415 E Kincaid St *Web:* www.skagitvalleyhospital.org	Mount Vernon	WA	98273	360-424-4111	428-2416
Southwest Washington Medical Ctr (SWMC) 400 NE Mother Joseph Pl PO Box 1600 *Web:* www.swmedicalcenter.com	Vancouver	WA	98664	360-514-2000	514-2006
Swedish Medical Ctr Cherry Hill Campus 500 17th Ave *Web:* www.swedish.org	Seattle	WA	98122	206-320-2000	320-2140
Swedish Medical Ctr First Hill 747 Broadway *Web:* www.swedish.org	Seattle	WA	98122	206-386-6000	386-2277
Swedish Medical Ctr/Edmonds 21601 76th Ave W *Web:* www.swedish.org	Edmonds	WA	98026	425-640-4000	640-4010
Tacoma General Hospital 315 MLK Jr Way *TF:* 800-552-1419 ■ *Web:* www.multicare.org	Tacoma	WA	98405	253-403-1000	403-1180
University of Washington Medical Ctr 1959 NE Pacific St *Web:* www.washington.edu	Seattle	WA	98195	206-548-3300	598-2343
Valley Hospital & Medical Ctr (VHMC) 12606 E Mission Ave *Web:* www.spokanevalleyhospital.com/Pages/home.aspx	Spokane Valley	WA	99216	509-924-6650	462-0502
Valley Medical Ctr 400 S 43rd St **Fax Area Code:* 206 ■ *TF:* 800-540-1814 ■ *Web:* www.valleymed.org	Renton	WA	98055	425-228-3450	575-2593*
Virginia Mason Medical Ctr 925 Seneca St *Web:* www.virginiamason.org	Seattle	WA	98101	206-624-1144	223-6976
Yakima Regional Medical & Heart Ctr 110 S 9th Ave *Web:* www.yakimaregional.org	Yakima	WA	98902	509-575-5000	454-6193
Yakima Valley Memorial Hospital 2811 Tieton Dr *Web:* www.yakimamemorial.org	Yakima	WA	98902	509-575-8000	574-5800

WEST VIRGINIA

	City	State	Zip	Phone	Fax
Beckley Appalachian Regional Hospital 306 Stanaford Rd *Web:* www.arh.org	Beckley	WV	25801	304-255-3000	255-3544
Bluefield Regional Medical Ctr (BRMC) 500 Cherry St *Web:* www.bluefieldregional.net/Pages/home.aspx	Bluefield	WV	24701	304-327-1100	327-1075
Cabell Huntington Hospital 1340 Hal Greer Blvd *Web:* www.cabellhuntington.org	Huntington	WV	25701	304-526-2000	526-2008
Camden-Clark Memorial Hospital (CCMH) 800 Garfield Ave *TF:* 800-422-6437 ■ *Web:* www.ccmh.org	Parkersburg	WV	26101	304-424-2111	424-2782
Charleston Area Medical Ctr 501 Morris St *Web:* www.camc.org	Charleston	WV	25301	304-388-5432	388-3604
City Hospital 2500 Hospital Dr *Web:* www.wvuh.org	Martinsburg	WV	25401	304-264-1000	264-1255
Davis Memorial Hospital 812 Gorman Ave *Web:* www.davishealthsystem.org	Elkins	WV	26241	304-636-3300	637-3184
Fairmont General Hospital (FGH) 1325 Locust Ave *Web:* www.fghi.com	Fairmont	WV	26554	304-367-7100	367-7167
Grafton City Hospital Inc 500 Market St *Web:* www.graftonhospital.com	Grafton	WV	26354	304-265-0400	
Greenbrier Valley Medical Ctr 202 Maplewood Ave *Web:* www.gvmc.com	Ronceverte	WV	24970	304-647-4411	647-6010
Logan Regional Medical Ctr 20 Hospital Dr *Web:* www.loganregionalmedicalcenter.com	Logan	WV	25601	304-831-1101	831-1871
Monongalia General Hospital 1200 JD Anderson Dr *TF:* 800-992-7600 ■ *Web:* www.monhealthsys.org	Morgantown	WV	26505	304-598-1200	598-1987

Hospital	City	State	ZIP	Phone	Fax
Ohio Valley Medical Center 2000 Eoff St *Web:* www.ovmc-online.com	Wheeling	WV	26003	304-234-0123	234-8229
Pleasant Valley Hospital 2520 Valley Dr *Web:* www.pvalley.org	Point Pleasant	WV	25550	304-675-4340	675-5243
Princeton Community Hospital 122 12th St *Web:* www.pchonline.org	Princeton	WV	24740	304-487-7000	487-2161
Raleigh General Hospital 1710 Harper Rd *Web:* www.raleighgeneral.com	Beckley	WV	25801	304-256-4100	256-4009
Reynolds Memorial Hospital (RMH) 800 Wheeling Ave *Web:* www.reynoldsmemorial.com	Glen Dale	WV	26038	304-845-3211	843-3202
Saint Francis Hospital 333 Laidley St *Web:* www.stfrancishospital.com	Charleston	WV	25301	304-347-6500	347-6885
Saint Joseph's Hospital 1824 Murdock Ave *Web:* www.stjosephs-hospital.com	Parkersburg	WV	26101	304-424-4111	424-4807
Saint Mary's Medical Ctr 2900 1st Ave *TF:* 800-978-6279 ■ *Web:* www.st-marys.org	Huntington	WV	25701	304-526-1234	526-1538
Stonewall Jackson Memorial Hospital (SJMH) 230 Hospital Plaza *Web:* www.stonewalljacksonhospital.com/getpage.php?name=index	Weston	WV	26452	304-269-8000	269-8090
Thomas Memorial Hospital 4605 MacCorkle Ave SW *Web:* www.thomaswv.org	South Charleston	WV	25309	304-766-3600	766-3477
United Hospital Ctr 3 Hospital Plaza *Web:* www.uhcwv.org	Clarksburg	WV	26301	304-624-2121	624-2909
Weirton Medical Ctr 601 Colliers Way *TF:* 800-243-4962 ■ *Web:* www.weirtonmedical.com	Weirton	WV	26062	304-797-6000	797-6176
West Virginia University Hospitals 1 Medical Ctr Dr *Web:* www.wvuhealthcare.com	Morgantown	WV	26506	304-598-4200	598-4124
Wetzel County Hospital 3 E Benjamin Dr *Web:* www.wetzelcountyhospital.com	New Martinsville	WV	26155	304-455-8000	455-4259
Wheeling Hospital 1 Medical Pk *Web:* www.wheelinghospital.com	Wheeling	WV	26003	304-243-3000	243-3060

WISCONSIN

Hospital	City	State	ZIP	Phone	Fax
Appleton Medical Ctr 1818 N Meade St *TF:* 800-236-4101 ■ *Web:* www.thedacare.org	Appleton	WI	54911	920-731-4101	738-6319
Aspirus Wausau Hospital 333 Pine Ridge Blvd *TF:* 800-283-2881 ■ *Web:* www.aspirus.org	Wausau	WI	54401	715-847-2121	847-2108
Aurora Lakeland Medical Ctr (ALMC) W3985 County Rd NN *Web:* www.aurorahealthcare.org	Elkhorn	WI	53121	262-741-2000	741-2759
Aurora Sinai Medical Ctr 945 N 12th St *TF:* 888-414-7762 ■ *Web:* www.aurorahealthcare.org	Milwaukee	WI	53201	414-219-2000	219-6735
Bay Area Medical Ctr 3100 Shore Dr *TF:* 888-788-2070 ■ *Web:* www.bamc.com	Marinette	WI	54143	715-735-6621	735-8080
Beaver Dam Community Hospital 707 S University Ave *Web:* www.bdch.com	Beaver Dam	WI	53916	920-887-7181	887-7973
Bellin Hospital 744 S Webster Ave *Web:* www.bellin.org	Green Bay	WI	54301	920-433-3500	431-5568
Beloit Memorial Hospital 1969 W Hart Rd *TF:* 800-637-2641 ■ *Web:* www.beloithealthsystem.org	Beloit	WI	53511	608-363-5724	363-5702
Columbia Saint Mary's Hospital 2025 E Newport Ave *Web:* www.columbia-stmarys.com	Milwaukee	WI	53211	414-961-3300	961-8712
Community Memorial Hospital (CMH) W 180 N 8085 Town Hall Rd *Web:* www.communitymemorial.com	Menomonee Falls	WI	53051	262-251-1000	253-7169
Elmbrook Memorial Hospital (EMH) 19333 W N Ave *Web:* www.mywheaton.org/locations/elmbrook_memorial/index.asp	Brookfield	WI	53045	262-785-2000	785-2485
Fort Atkinson Memorial Hospital 611 Sherman Ave E *Web:* www.forthealthcare.com	Fort Atkinson	WI	53538	920-568-5000	568-5412
Franciscan Skemp Health Care 700 W Ave S	La Crosse	WI	54601	608-785-0940	791-9429
Froedtert Hospital 9200 W Wisconsin Ave *Web:* www.froedtert.com	Milwaukee	WI	53226	414-259-3000	805-7790
Gundersen Lutheran Medical Ctr 1910 S Ave *TF:* 800-362-9567 ■ *Web:* www.gundluth.org	La Crosse	WI	54601	608-785-0530	775-6334
Holy Family Memorial Medical Ctr 2300 Western Ave PO Box 1450 *TF:* 800-994-3662 ■ *Web:* www.hfmhealth.org	Manitowoc	WI	54220	920-320-2011	
Kenosha Medical Ctr 6308 8th Ave *TF:* 800-994-6610 ■ *Web:* www.uhsi.org	Kenosha	WI	53143	262-656-2011	656-2124
Lakeview Medical Ctr 1100 N Main St *Web:* www.lakeviewmedical.com	Rice Lake	WI	54868	715-234-1515	236-6342
Mayo Foundation for Medical Education & Research 1221 Whipple St PO Box 4105 *Web:* www.mayohealthsystem.org	Eau Claire	WI	54702	715-838-3219	838-3268
Memorial Medical Ctr 1615 Maple Ln *Web:* www.ashlandmmc.com	Ashland	WI	54806	715-685-5500	685-5118
Mercy Hospital & Trauma Ctr 1000 Mineral Pt Ave *TF:* 800-756-4147 ■ *Web:* www.mercyhealthsystem.com	Janesville	WI	53548	608-756-6000	756-6236
Mercy Medical Ctr (MMC) 500 S Oakwood Rd *TF:* 800-242-5650 ■ *Web:* www.affinityhealth.org/object/mercy-medical-center-visitor-guidelines.html	Oshkosh	WI	54904	920-236-2000	223-0508
Meriter Hospital 202 S Pk St *TF:* 800-261-4449 ■ *Web:* www.meriter.com/mhs/index.htm	Madison	WI	53715	608-267-6000	267-6645
Ministry Saint Joseph's Hospital (MSJH) 611 St Joseph Ave *Web:* www.ministryhealth.org/SJH/home.nws	Marshfield	WI	54449	715-387-1713	389-3939
Monroe Clinic Hospital 515 22nd Ave *TF:* 800-338-0568 ■ *Web:* www.monroeclinic.org	Monroe	WI	53566	608-324-2000	324-1114
Oconomowoc Memorial Hospital 791 Summit Ave *TF:* 800-242-0313 ■ *Web:* www.prohealthcare.org	Oconomowoc	WI	53066	262-569-9400	569-0336
Prairie Du Chien Memorial Hospital 705 E Taylor St *Web:* www.pdcmemorialhospital.org	Prairie Du Chien	WI	53821	608-357-2000	
Richland Hospital Inc The 333 E 2nd St *TF:* 888-467-7485 ■ *Web:* www.richlandhospital.com	Richland Center	WI	53581	608-647-6321	647-6325
Sacred Heart Hospital 900 W Clairemont Ave *TF:* 888-445-4554 ■ *Web:* www.sacredhearteauclaire.org	Eau Claire	WI	54701	715-839-4121	839-8417
Saint Elizabeth Hospital 1506 S Oneida St *TF:* 800-223-7332 ■ *Web:* www.affinityhealth.org	Appleton	WI	54915	920-738-2000	831-8948
Saint Joseph's Community Hospital 3200 Pleasant Valley Rd *Web:* www.stjosephswb.com/homepage.cfm?id=463	West Bend	WI	53095	262-334-5533	335-8152
Saint Joseph's Hospital 2661 County Hwy I *TF:* 877-723-1811 ■ *Web:* www.stjoeschipfalls.com	Chippewa Falls	WI	54729	715-723-1811	726-3204
Saint Luke's Medical Ctr 2900 W Oklahoma Ave *Web:* www.aurorahealthcare.org/facilities	Milwaukee	WI	53215	414-649-6000	649-8386
Saint Mary's Hospital 2323 N Lake Dr *Web:* www.columbia-stmarys.com	Milwaukee	WI	53211	414-291-1000	
Saint Mary's Hospital 2251 N Shore Dr *TF Cust Svc:* 800-578-0840 ■ *Web:* www.ministryhealth.org	Rhinelander	WI	54501	715-361-2000	361-2011
Saint Mary's Hospital Medical Ctr 707 S Mills St *Web:* www.stmarysmadison.com	Madison	WI	53715	608-251-6100	258-6731
Saint Mary's Hospital Ozaukee 13111 N Port Washington Rd *TF:* 800-848-2844 ■ *Web:* www.columbia-stmarys.com	Mequon	WI	53097	262-243-7300	
Saint Mary's Medical Ctr 1726 Shawano Ave *TF:* 800-666-5606 ■ *Web:* www.stmgb.org	Green Bay	WI	54303	920-498-4200	498-1861
Saint Michael's Hospital 900 Illinois Ave *Web:* www.ministryhealth.org	Stevens Point	WI	54481	715-346-5000	346-5088
Saint Nicholas Hospital 3100 Superior Ave *TF:* 800-472-6710 ■ *Web:* www.stnicholashospital.org	Sheboygan	WI	53081	920-459-8300	452-8336
Saint Vincent Hospital 835 S Van Buren St *TF:* 800-236-3030 ■ *Web:* www.stvincenthospital.org	Green Bay	WI	54301	920-433-0111	431-3215
Southwest Health Center Inc 1400 Eastside Rd *Web:* www.southwesthealth.org	Platteville	WI	53818	608-348-2331	
St Agnes Hospital 430 E Division St *TF:* 800-922-3400 ■ *Web:* www.agnesian.com	Fond du Lac	WI	54935	920-929-2300	926-4866
Stoughton Hospital 900 Ridge St *Web:* www.stoughtonhospital.com	Stoughton	WI	53589	608-873-6611	873-2355
Theda Clark Medical Ctr 130 2nd St *TF:* 800-236-3122 ■ *Web:* www.thedacare.org	Neenah	WI	54956	920-729-3100	729-3167
University of Wisconsin Hospital & Clinics 600 Highland Ave *TF:* 800-323-8942 ■ *Web:* www.uwhealth.org	Madison	WI	53792	608-263-6400	263-9830
Waukesha Memorial Hospital 725 American Ave *TF:* 800-326-2011 ■ *Web:* www.prohealthcare.org	Waukesha	WI	53188	262-928-1000	544-4995
West Allis Memorial Hospital 8901 W Lincoln Ave 2nd Fl *Web:* www.aurorahealthcare.org	West Allis	WI	53227	414-328-6000	328-8536
Wheaton Franciscan - Saint Joseph 5000 W Chambers St *Web:* www.mywheaton.org	Milwaukee	WI	53210	414-447-2000	
Wheaton Franciscan Healthcare 1320 Wisconsin Ave *TF:* 800-526-9309 ■ *Web:* www.mywheaton.org	Racine	WI	53403	262-636-2011	687-2115
All Saints 3801 Spring St *TF:* 800-526-9309 ■ *Web:* www.allsaintshealth.com	Racine	WI	53405	262-687-4011	687-5116
Wheaton Franciscan Healthcare - St. Francis 3237 S 16th St *Web:* www.mywheaton.org	Milwaukee	WI	53215	414-647-5000	647-5565

WYOMING

Hospital	City	State	ZIP	Phone	Fax
Campbell County Memorial Hospital 501 S Burma PO Box 3011 *Fax: Hum Res ■ *TF Hum Res:* 800-208-2043 ■ *Web:* www.ccmh.net	Gillette	WY	82717	307-688-1000	688-1516*
Cheyenne Regional Medical Ctr (CRMC) 214 E 23rd St *Web:* www.crmcwy.org	Cheyenne	WY	82001	307-634-2273	633-3569
Ivinson Memorial Hospital 255 N 30th St *TF:* 800-854-1115 ■ *Web:* www2.ivinsonhospital.org	Laramie	WY	82072	307-742-2141	742-2150
Memorial Hospital of Sweetwater County 1200 College Dr *TF:* 800-307-3711 ■ *Web:* www.minershospital.com	Rock Springs	WY	82901	307-362-3711	352-8180
Riverton Memorial Hospital LLC 2100 W Sunset Dr *TF:* 800-967-1646 ■ *Web:* www.riverton-hospital.com	Riverton	WY	82501	307-856-4161	857-3571
Sheridan Memorial Hospital 1401 W 5th St *Web:* www.sheridanhospital.org	Sheridan	WY	82801	307-672-1000	672-1007
Wyoming Medical Ctr 1233 E 2nd St *TF:* 800-822-7201 ■ *Web:* www.wmcnet.org	Casper	WY	82601	307-577-7201	237-1703

377-4 Military Hospitals

Hospital	City	State	ZIP	Phone	Fax
Bayne-Jones Army Community Hospital 1585 3rd St Bldg 285	Fort Polk	LA	71459	337-531-3118	531-3050
Brooke Army Medical Ctr 3851 Roger Brook Dr Bldg 3600	Fort Sam Houston	TX	78234	210-916-6141	916-2100

				Phone	Fax
Charleston Naval Hospital 3600 Rivers Ave	North Charleston	SC	29405	843-743-7000	743-7259
Web: www.med.navy.mil/sites/chas/Pages/default.aspx					
Colonel Florence A Blanchfield Army Community Hospital 650 Joel Dr	Fort Campbell	KY	42223	270-798-8400	798-8812
Darnall Army Community Hospital Bldg 36000	Fort Hood	TX	76544	254-288-8000	288-8827
TF: 800-611-2875					
David Grant US Air Force Medical Ctr 101 Bodin Cir	Travis AFB	CA	94535	707-423-7300	423-7416
TF: 800-264-3462					
Dewitt Army Community Hospital 9501 Farrell Rd Suite GC11	Fort Belvoir	VA	22060	703-805-0510	805-0219
Dwight David Eisenhower Army Medical Ctr (DDAMC) 300 Hospital Rd	Fort Gordon	GA	30905	706-787-5811	787-5342*
**Fax:* Admitting ■ *Web:* www.ddeamc.amedd.army.mil					
Ehrling Bergquist US Air Force Hospital 2501 Capehart Rd	Offutt AFB	NE	68113	402-294-9760	294-2816
Evans Army Community Hospital 1650 Cochran Cir	Fort Carson	CO	80913	719-526-7000	526-3726
Web: www.evans.amedd.army.mil					
General Leonard Wood Army Community Hospital 126 Missouri Ave	Fort Leonard Wood	MO	65473	573-596-1490	596-0035
Web: www.glwach.amedd.army.mil					
Ireland Army Community Hospital 851 Ireland Loop	Fort Knox	KY	40121	502-624-9333	624-9604
Irwin Army Community Hospital 600 Caisson Hill Rd	Fort Riley	KS	66442	785-239-7000	239-7405
Keller Army Community Hospital 900 Washington Rd	West Point	NY	10996	845-938-3305	938-5164
Web: www.usma.edu/meddac					
Kimbrough Ambulatory Care Ctr 2480 Lewellyn Ave	Fort Meade	MD	20755	301-677-8392	677-8499
Lyster Army Health Clinic 301 Andrews St	Fort Rucker	AL	36362	334-255-7999	255-7710
Madigan Army Medical Ctr 9040 Jackson Ave	Tacoma	WA	98431	253-968-1110	968-1633*
Martin Army Community Hospital 7950 Martin Loop Bldg 9200	Fort Benning	GA	31905	706-544-2041	544-2407
McDonald Army Community Hospital 576 Jefferson Ave	Fort Eustis	VA	23604	757-878-7500	878-7661
TF: 800-304-9863					
Moncrief Army Community Hospital 4500 Stuart St PO Box 500	Fort Jackson	SC	29207	803-751-2160	751-2471
National Naval Medical Ctr 8901 Wisconsin Ave	Bethesda	MD	20889	301-295-4611	295-6521
Web: www.dcmilitary.com/baseguides					
Naval Health Clinic Great Lakes 3001-A 6th St	Great Lakes	IL	60088	847-688-4560	688-5752
Naval Hospital 2080 Child St	Jacksonville	FL	32214	904-542-7300	542-7281
Naval Hospital 100 Brewster Blvd	Camp Lejeune	NC	28547	910-450-4300	450-4012
Web: www.med.navy.mil/sites/nhcl/Pages/default.aspx					
Naval Hospital Bremerton 1 Boone Rd	Bremerton	WA	98312	360-475-4000	
TF: 800-422-1383 ■ *Web:* www.med.navy.mil					
Naval Hospital Pensacola 6000 W Hwy 98	Pensacola	FL	32512	850-505-6601	505-6213
Web: www.med.navy.mil					
Naval Medical Center Portsmouth 620 John Paul Jones Cir Bldg 3 Suite 1400	Portsmouth	VA	23708	757-953-0422	953-0477
Web: www-nmcp.med.navy.mil					
Naval Medical Center San Diego 34800 Bob Wilson Dr	San Diego	CA	92134	619-532-6400	
Web: www.med.navy.mil					
Raymond W Bliss Army Health Ctr 45001 Winrow St	Fort Huachuca	AZ	85613	520-533-9200	
Tripler Army Medical Ctr 1 Jarrett White Rd Tripler AMC	Honolulu	HI	96859	808-433-6661	433-4899
Web: www.tamc.amedd.army.mil					
US Air Force 10th Medical Group 4102 Pinion Dr Suite 100	Usaf Academy	CO	80840	719-333-5111	333-5600
US Air Force 2nd Medical Group 243 Curtiss Rd	Barksdale AFB	LA	71110	318-456-6004	456-6112
US Air Force 355th Medical Group 4175 S Alamo Ave	Davis-Monthan AFB	AZ	85707	520-228-3900	228-2901
US Air Force 375th Medical Group 310 W Losey St	Scott AFB	IL	62225	618-256-7500	256-7613
US Air Force 42nd Medical Group Hospital 300 S Twining St	Maxwell AFB	AL	36112	334-953-7805	953-7270
US Air Force 56th Medical Group 7219 N Litchfield Rd	Luke AFB	AZ	85309	623-856-9100	
US Air Force 6th Medical Group 8415 Bayshore Blvd	MacDill AFB	FL	33621	813-828-2273	828-5283
US Air Force 74th Medical Group 4881 Sugar Maple Dr	Wright-Patterson AFB	OH	45433	937-257-9183	656-1767
TF: 800-941-4501					
US Air Force 82nd Medical Group 149 Hart St	Sheppard AFB	TX	76311	940-676-2010	676-6416
Web: www.sheppard.af.mil					
US Air Force 89th Medical Group 1050 W Perimeter	Andrews AFB	MD	20762	240-857-5911	857-8205
US Air Force 96th Medical Group 307 Boatner Rd Suite 114	Eglin AFB	FL	32542	850-883-8242	883-8222
US Air Force Hospital 1st Medical Group 45 Pine Rd	Langley AFB	VA	23665	757-764-6969	764-9845
US Air Force Medical Center Keesler 81st Medical Group 301 Fisher St	Keesler AFB	MS	39534	228-377-6550	377-9748
Web: www.keesler.af.mil					
Wilford Hall US Air Force Medical Ctr 2200 Bergquist Dr Suite 1 59MDW	Lackland AFB	TX	78236	210-292-7100	292-7983
William Beaumont Army Medical Ctr 5005 N Piedras St	El Paso	TX	79920	915-569-2121	569-2874
Winn Army Community Hospital 1061 Harmon Ave	Fort Stewart	GA	31314	912-435-6837	370-6546
Womack Army Medical Ctr Bldg 4-2817 Reilly Rd	Fort Bragg	NC	28310	910-907-6000	907-8473
Web: www.wamc.amedd.army.mil					

377-5 Psychiatric Hospitals

Listings Here Include State Psychiatric Facilities As Well As Private Psychiatric Hospitals.

				Phone	Fax
Adventist Behavioral Health 14901 Broschart Rd	Rockville	MD	20850	301-251-4500	424-3841
TF: 800-204-8600 ■ *Web:* www.adventistbehavioralhealth.com					
Alaska Psychiatric Institute 3700 Piper St	Anchorage	AK	99508	907-269-7100	269-7128
Web: www.health.hss.state.ak.us					
Allentown State Hospital 1600 Hanover Ave	Allentown	PA	18109	610-740-3200	740-3413
TF: 800-256-3571					
Alton Mental Health Ctr 4500 College Ave	Alton	IL	62002	618-474-3200	474-3807
Ancora Psychiatric Hospital 301 Spring Garden Rd	Ancora	NJ	08037	609-561-1700	561-2509
Andrew McFarland Mental Health Ctr 901 Southwind Rd	Springfield	IL	62703	217-786-6900	786-7167
Appalachian Behavioral Healthcare 100 Hospital Dr	Athens	OH	45701	740-594-5000	594-3006
Arizona State Hospital 2500 E Van Buren St	Phoenix	AZ	85008	602-244-1331	220-6292
TF: 877-588-5163					
Arkansas State Hospital 4313 W Markham St	Little Rock	AR	72205	501-686-9000	686-9483
Atascadero State Hospital 10333 S Camino Real	Atascadero	CA	93422	805-468-2000	466-6011
Aurora Las Encinas Hospital 2900 E Del Mar Blvd	Pasadena	CA	91107	626-795-9901	792-2919
TF: 800-792-2345 ■ *Web:* www.lasencinashospital.com					
Austin State Hospital 4110 Guadalupe St	Austin	TX	78751	512-452-0381	419-2163
Banner Behavioral Health Hospital 7575 E Earll Dr	Scottsdale	AZ	85251	480-941-7500	994-5558
TF: 800-254-4357 ■ *Web:* www.bannerhealth.com					
Belmont Center for Comprehensive Treatment 4200 Monument Rd	Philadelphia	PA	19131	215-877-2000	581-9141*
**Fax:* Admissions ■ *Web:* www.einstein.edu					
Big Spring State Hospital 1901 N Hwy 87	Big Spring	TX	79720	432-267-8216	268-7263
Brainerd Regional Human Services Ctr 11800 State Hwy 18	Brainerd	MN	56401	218-828-2201	828-2207
Web: www.dhs.state.mn.us/SOS/default.htm					
Brentwood A Behavioral Health Co 1006 Highland Ave	Shreveport	LA	71101	318-678-7500	227-9296
TF: 877-678-7500					
Bridgewater State Hospital 20 Administration Rd	Bridgewater	MA	02324	508-279-4500	279-4832
Bronx Psychiatric Ctr 1500 Waters Pl	Bronx	NY	10461	718-931-0600	862-4858
Broughton Hospital 1000 S Sterling St	Morganton	NC	28655	828-433-2111	433-2292
Bryce Hospital 200 University Blvd	Tuscaloosa	AL	35401	205-759-0799	759-0895
BryLin Hospitals 1263 Delaware Ave	Buffalo	NY	14209	716-886-8200	886-1986
TF: 800-727-9546 ■ *Web:* www.brylin.com					
Buffalo Psychiatric Ctr 400 Forest Ave	Buffalo	NY	14213	716-885-2261	885-4852
Web: www.omh.state.ny.us					
Butler Hospital 345 Blackstone Blvd	Providence	RI	02906	401-455-6200	455-6532*
**Fax:* Admitting ■ *Web:* www.butler.org					
Capital District Psychiatric Ctr 75 New Scotland Ave	Albany	NY	12208	518-447-9611	434-0041
Caro Ctr 2000 Chambers Rd	Caro	MI	48723	989-673-3191	673-6749
Carrier Clinic 252 County Rd 601	Belle Mead	NJ	08502	908-281-1000	281-1680
TF: 800-933-3579 ■ *Web:* www.carrier.org					
Catawba Hospital PO Box 200	Catawba	VA	24070	540-375-4200	375-4394
Web: www.catawba.dmhmrsas.virginia.gov					
Cedar Springs Behavioral Health System 2135 Southgate Rd	Colorado Springs	CO	80906	719-633-4114	578-0857
TF: 800-888-1088					
Cedarcrest Hospital 525 Russell Rd	Newington	CT	06111	860-666-4613	666-7642
CenterPointe Hospital 5931 Hwy 94 S	Saint Charles	MO	63304	636-441-7300	447-6001
TF: 800-345-5407 ■ *Web:* www.centerpointhospital.com					
Central Louisiana State Hospital PO Box 5031	Pineville	LA	71361	318-484-6200	484-6501
TF: 866-666-8335					
Central State Hospital 620 Broad St	Milledgeville	GA	31061	478-445-4575	445-6034
Web: www.centralstatehospital.org					
Central State Hospital 26317 W Washington St	Petersburg	VA	23803	804-524-7000	524-7069
Web: www.csh.dmhmrsas.virginia.gov					
Central State Hospital 10510 LaGrange Rd	Louisville	KY	40223	502-253-7000	253-7044
Central Washington Hospital 1201 S Miller St	Wenatchee	WA	98801	509-662-1511	665-6132
TF: 800-365-6428 ■ *Web:* www.cwhs.com					
Cherry Hospital 201 Stevens Mill Rd	Goldsboro	NC	27530	919-731-3200	731-3785
Chester Mental Health Ctr 1315 Lehman Dr PO Box 31	Chester	IL	62233	618-826-4571	826-3229
Chicago Lakeshore Hospital 4840 N Marine Dr	Chicago	IL	60640	773-878-9700	907-4607
TF Cust Svc: 800-888-0560 ■ *Web:* www.chicagolakeshorehospital.com					
Chicago-Read Mental Health Ctr 4200 N Oak Pk Ave	Chicago	IL	60634	773-794-4000	794-4046
Choate Mental Health & Developmental Ctr 1000 N Main St	Anna	IL	62906	618-833-5161	833-4191
Clarks Summit State Hospital 1451 Hillside Dr	Clarks Summit	PA	18411	570-586-2011	587-7415
Clifton T Perkins Hospital Ctr 8450 Dorsey Run Rd	Jessup	MD	20794	410-724-3000	724-3009
Coastal Harbor Treatment Ctr 1150 Cornell Ave	Savannah	GA	31406	912-354-3911	355-1336
College Hospital 10802 College Pl	Cerritos	CA	90703	562-924-9581	809-0981
TF: 800-352-3301 ■ *Web:* www.collegehospitals.com					
College Hospital Costa Mesa 301 Victoria St	Costa Mesa	CA	92627	949-642-2734	574-3320
TF: 800-773-8001 ■ *Web:* www.collegehospitals.com					
Colorado Mental Health Institute at Fort Logan (CMHIFL) 3520 W Oxford Ave	Denver	CO	80236	303-866-7066	866-7101*
Web: www.colorado.gov/cs/Satellite/CDHS-BehavioralHealth/CBON/1251580627038					

Name / Address	City	State	Zip	Phone	Fax
Colorado Mental Health Institute at Pueblo (CMHIP) 1600 W 24th St. *Web:* www.colorado.gov	Pueblo	CO	81003	719-546-4000	546-4484
Community Behavioral Health Hospital 1801 W Alcott Ave PO Box 478	Fergus Falls	MN	56537	218-332-5001	739-1329
Connecticut Valley Hospital 1000 Silver St.	Middletown	CT	06457	860-262-5000	262-5989
Creedmoor Psychiatric Ctr 80-45 Winchester Blvd	Queens Village	NY	11427	718-464-7500	264-3635
Danville State Hospital 200 State Hospital Dr *TF:* 888-796-3476	Danville	PA	17821	570-271-4500	271-4694
Del Amo Hospital 23700 Camino Del Sol *TF:* 800-824-4936 ■ *Web:* www.delamohospital.com	Torrance	CA	90505	310-530-1151	539-5061
Delaware Psychiatric Ctr 1901 N Dupont Hwy Main Bldg *TF:* 800-652-2929 ■ *Web:* dhss.delaware.gov	New Castle	DE	19720	302-255-9399	255-4428
Dominion Hospital 2960 Sleepy Hollow Rd *TF:* 800-950-6463 ■ *Web:* www.dominionhospital.com	Falls Church	VA	22044	703-536-2000	533-9650
Dorothea Dix Hospital (DDH) 820 S Boylan Ave *Web:* www.ncdhhs.gov/dsohf/services/dix/index.htm	Raleigh	NC	27699	919-733-5540	
Dorothea Dix Psychiatric Ctr 656 State St.	Bangor	ME	04401	207-941-4000	941-4062
East Central Regional Hospital *Augusta* 3405 Mike Padgett Hwy *Web:* www.augustareg.dhr.state.ga.us	Augusta	GA	30906	706-792-7000	792-7030
East Louisiana State Hospital PO Box 498	Jackson	LA	70748	225-634-0100	634-4345
East Mississippi State Hospital 4555 Highland Pk Dr *Web:* www.emsh.state.ms.us	Meridian	MS	39307	601-482-6186	483-5543
Eastern Louisiana Mental Health System Greenwell Springs Campus 23260 Greenwell Springs Rd PO Box 549	Greenwell Springs	LA	70739	225-262-2400	261-9080
Eastern State Hospital 627 W 4th St.	Lexington	KY	40508	859-246-7000	246-7018*
Eastern State Hospital (ESH) 4601 Ironbound Rd. *Web:* www.esh.dmhmrsas.virginia.gov	Williamsburg	VA	23188	757-253-5161	253-5065
Elgin Mental Health Ctr 750 S State St.	Elgin	IL	60123	847-742-1040	429-4938
Elmira Psychiatric Ctr 100 Washington St	Elmira	NY	14901	607-737-4711	737-9080
Essex County Hospital Ctr 125 Fairview Ave	Cedar Grove	NJ	07009	973-228-8000	228-0674
Evansville State Hospital 3400 Lincoln Ave	Evansville	IN	47714	812-469-6800	469-6868
Fair Oaks Hospital 5440 Linton Blvd	Delray Beach	FL	33484	561-495-1000	495-3796
Fairfax Hospital 10200 NE 132nd St *TF:* 800-435-7221 ■ *Web:* www.fairfaxhospital.com	Kirkland	WA	98034	425-821-2000	821-9010
Fairmount Behavioral Health System 561 Fairthorne Ave *TF:* 800-235-0200 ■ *Web:* www.fairmountbhs.com	Philadelphia	PA	19128	215-487-4000	483-8187
Florida State Hospital PO Box 1000 *TF:* 800-663-7020	Chattahoochee	FL	32324	850-663-7001	663-7303
Fort Lauderdale Hospital 1601 E Las Olas Blvd *TF:* 800-585-7527 ■ *Web:* www.fortlauderdalehospital.org	Fort Lauderdale	FL	33301	954-463-4321	525-2584
Four Winds Hospital 800 Cross River Rd. *TF:* 800-528-6624 ■ *Web:* www.fourwindshospital.com	Katonah	NY	10536	914-763-8151	763-9597
Friends Hospital 4641 Roosevelt Blvd *TF:* 800-889-0548 ■ *Web:* www.friendshospitalonline.org	Philadelphia	PA	19124	215-831-4600	831-7859
Fulton State Hospital 600 E 5th St *Web:* www.dmh.missouri.gov	Fulton	MO	65251	573-592-4100	592-3000
GEO Care South Florida State Hospital 800 E Cypress Dr	Pembroke Pines	FL	33025	954-392-3000	392-4304
Georgia Regional Hospital at Atlanta 3073 Panthersville Rd. *Fax:* Hum Res ■ *Web:* www.atlantareg.dhr.state.ga.us/JobAnnouncements.html	Atlanta	GA	30034	404-212-4617	243-2740*
Georgia Regional Hospital at Savannah 1915 Eisenhower Dr	Savannah	GA	31406	912-356-2011	356-2691
Gracie Square Hospital (GSH) 420 E 76th St *Web:* www.nygsh.org	New York	NY	10021	212-988-4400	434-5373
Greater Binghamton Health Ctr 425 Robinson St.	Binghamton	NY	13904	607-724-1391	773-4387
Green Oaks Hospital 7808 Clodus Fields Dr *TF:* 800-866-6554 ■ *Web:* www.greenoakspsych.com	Dallas	TX	75251	972-991-9504	789-1865
Greystone Park Psychiatric Hospital 1 Central Ave	Greystone Park	NJ	07950	973-538-1800	993-8782*
Griffin Memorial Hospital PO Box 151 *TF:* 877-580-5044	Norman	OK	73070	405-321-4880	573-6652
H Douglas Singer Mental Health & Development Ctr 4402 N Main St	Rockford	IL	61103	815-987-7096	987-7581
Hagedorn Psychiatric Hospital 200 Sanitorium Rd	Glen Gardner	NJ	08826	908-537-2141	537-3149
Hamilton Center Inc PO Box 4323 *TF:* 800-742-0787 ■ *Web:* www.hamiltoncenter.org	Terre Haute	IN	47804	812-231-8323	
Hampstead Hospital 218 E Rd *Web:* www.hampsteadhospital.com	Hampstead	NH	03841	603-329-5311	329-4746
Harris County Psychiatric Ctr 2800 S MacGregor Way *Web:* hcpc.uth.tmc.edu	Houston	TX	77021	713-741-5000	741-5939
Hartgrove Hospital 5730 W Roosevelt Rd *TF:* 800-478-4783 ■ *Web:* hartgrovehospital.com	Chicago	IL	60629	773-722-3113	413-1805
Havenwyck Hospital 1525 University Dr *Fax:* Admitting ■ *TF:* 800-401-2727	Auburn Hills	MI	48326	248-373-9200	373-9077*
Hawaii State Hospital 45-710 Keaahala Rd.	Kaneohe	HI	96744	808-247-2191	247-7335
Heartland Behavioral Healthcare 3000 S Erie St.	Massillon	OH	44646	330-833-3135	833-6564
Hill Crest Behavioral Health Services 6869 5th Ave S *TF:* 800-292-8553	Birmingham	AL	35212	205-833-9000	838-2080
Holliswood Hospital 87-37 Palermo St *Fax:* Admitting ■ *TF:* 800-486-3005	Holliswood	NY	11423	718-776-8181	776-8572*
Holly Hill Hospital 3019 Falstaff Rd *TF:* 800-422-1840 ■ *Web:* www.hollyhillhospital.com	Raleigh	NC	27610	919-250-7000	231-3231
Horsham Clinic 722 E Butler Pike *Fax:* Admissions ■ *TF:* 800-237-4447 ■ *Web:* www.horshamclinic.com	Ambler	PA	19002	215-643-7800	654-1148*
Hudson River Psychiatric Ctr 10 Ross Cir. *TF:* 800-871-7910	Poughkeepsie	NY	12601	845-452-8000	452-8040
Intracare Medical Center Hospital 7601 Fannin St *Web:* www.intracarehospital.com	Houston	TX	77054	713-790-0949	790-0456
Jewish Hospital & St Mary's HealthCare 2020 Newburg Rd *TF:* 800-451-3637 ■ *Web:* www.jhsmh.org	Louisville	KY	40205	502-451-3330	479-4350
John J Madden Mental Health Ctr 1200 S 1st Ave	Hines	IL	60141	708-338-7400	338-7057
John Umstead Hospital 1003 12th St	Butner	NC	27509	919-575-7211	575-7013
Kalamazoo Psychiatric Hospital 1312 Oakland Dr.	Kalamazoo	MI	49008	269-337-3000	337-3007*
Kerrville State Hospital 721 Thompson Dr.	Kerrville	TX	78028	830-896-2211	792-4926
Kingsboro Psychiatric Ctr 681 Clarkson Ave	Brooklyn	NY	11203	718-221-7000	221-7633*
Lakeshore Mental Health Institute 5908 Lyons View Dr	Knoxville	TN	37919	865-584-1561	450-5203
Lakeside Behavioral Health System 2911 Brunswick Rd.	Bartlett	TN	38133	901-377-4700	373-0912
Langley Porter Psychiatric Institute 401 Parnassus Ave *Web:* www.psych.ucsf.edu	San Francisco	CA	94143	415-476-7000	476-7320
Larned State Hospital RR 3 PO Box 89	Larned	KS	67550	620-285-2131	285-4359*
Lincoln Regional Ctr PO Box 94949	Lincoln	NE	68509	402-471-4444	479-5124
Logansport State Hospital 1098 SR 25 S	Logansport	IN	46947	574-722-4141	735-3414
Madison State Hospital 711 Green Rd	Madison	IN	47250	812-265-2611	265-7260
McLean Hospital 115 Mill St *Web:* www.mclean.harvard.edu	Belmont	MA	02478	617-855-2000	855-3735
Meadows Psychiatric Ctr 132 Meadows Dr *TF:* 800-641-7529 ■ *Web:* www.themeadows.org	Centre Hall	PA	16828	814-364-2161	364-9742
Meadowview Psychiatric Hospital 595 County Ave	Secaucus	NJ	07094	201-319-3660	319-3616
Memorial Hermann Prevention & Recovery Ctr (MHPARC) 3043 Gessner *TF:* 800-464-7272 ■ *Web:* www.mhparc.org	Houston	TX	77080	713-329-7300	939-7272
Mendota Mental Health Institute 301 Troy Dr *Web:* www.dhs.wisconsin.gov	Madison	WI	53704	608-301-1000	301-1358
Menninger Clinic 2801 Gessner Dr PO Box 809045 *TF:* 800-351-9058 ■ *Web:* www.menningerclinic.com	Houston	TX	77080	713-275-5000	275-5107
Mental Health Institute 2277 Iowa Ave	Independence	IA	50644	319-334-2583	334-5252
MeritCare South University 1720 S University Dr	Fargo	ND	58103	701-280-4150	280-4819
Metropolitan Saint Louis Psychiatric Ctr 5351 Delmar Blvd.	Saint Louis	MO	63112	314-877-0500	877-0553
Metropolitan State Hospital 11401 Bloomfield Ave.	Norwalk	CA	90650	562-863-7011	868-6920
Middle Tennessee Mental Health Institute 221 Stewarts Ferry Pike *TF:* 800-575-3506	Nashville	TN	37214	615-902-7400	902-7541
Milwaukee County Mental Health Complex 9455 Watertown Plank Rd.	Milwaukee	WI	53226	414-257-6995	257-8139*
Mississippi State Hospital PO Box 157A *Web:* www.msh.state.ms.us	Whitfield	MS	39193	601-351-8000	351-8228
Moccasin Bend Mental Health Institute 100 Moccasin Bend Rd.	Chattanooga	TN	37405	423-265-2271	785-3333
Mohawk Valley Psychiatric Ctr 1400 Noyes St. *TF:* 800-584-8640	Utica	NY	13502	315-738-3800	738-4414
Montana State Hospital 300 Garnet Way	Warm Springs	MT	59756	406-693-7000	693-7069
Napa State Hospital 2100 Napa-Vallejo Hwy.	Napa	CA	94558	707-253-5000	253-5513
New Hampshire Hospital 36 Clinton St.	Concord	NH	03301	603-271-5200	271-5395
New Mexico Behavioral Health Institute 3695 Hot Springs Blvd *Fax:* Admissions ■ *TF:* 800-446-5970	Las Vegas	NM	87701	505-454-2100	454-2211*
Norfolk Regional Ctr PO Box 1209	Norfolk	NE	68702	402-370-3400	370-3194
Norristown State Hospital 1001 Sterigere St	Norristown	PA	19401	610-313-1000	313-1013
North Coast Behaviorial Health Care System *North Campus* 1708 Southpoint Dr.	Cleveland	OH	44109	216-787-0500	787-0446
North Dakota State Hospital 2605 Cir Dr.	Jamestown	ND	58401	701-253-3650	253-3999
Northcoast Behavioral Healthcare System *South Campus* 1756 Sagamore Rd PO Box 305	Northfield	OH	44067	330-467-7131	467-2420
Northwest Center for Behavioral Health PO Box 1	Fort Supply	OK	73841	580-766-2311	766-2017
Northwest Georgia Regional Hospital 1305 Redmond Cir	Rome	GA	30165	706-295-6246	802-5454
Northwest Missouri Psychiatric Rehabilitation Ctr 3505 Frederick Ave.	Saint Joseph	MO	64506	816-387-2300	387-2329*
Oklahoma Forensic Ctr PO Box 69	Vinita	OK	74301	918-256-7841	256-4491
Oregon State Hospital 2600 Ctr St NE.	Salem	OR	97301	503-945-2800	945-2807
Osawatomie State Hospital 500 State Hospital Dr	Osawatomie	KS	66064	913-755-7000	755-7328*
Patton State Hospital 3102 E Highland Ave	Patton	CA	92369	909-425-7000	425-6370*
Peachford Behavioral Health System (PBHS) 2151 Peachford Rd *TF:* 866-897-3224 ■ *Web:* www.peachfordhospital.com	Atlanta	GA	30338	770-455-3200	455-2362
Pembroke Hospital 199 Oak St *TF:* 800-222-2237	Pembroke	MA	02359	781-826-8161	826-2061
Peninsula Hospital 2347 Jones Bend Rd *Fax:* Admitting ■ *TF:* 800-526-8215	Louisville	TN	37777	865-970-9800	970-6317*
Pilgrim Psychiatric Ctr 998 Crooked Hill Rd	West Brentwood	NY	11717	631-761-3500	761-2600
Pine Rest Christian Mental Health Services 300 68th St SE PO Box 165 *Fax:* Hum Res ■ *TF:* 800-678-5500 ■ *Web:* www.pinerest.org	Grand Rapids	MI	49501	616-455-5000	831-2608*
Poplar Springs Hospital 350 Poplar Dr PO Box 3060 *Fax:* Admitting ■ *Web:* www.poplarsprings.com	Petersburg	VA	23805	804-733-6874	862-6322*
Psychiatric Institute of Washington 4228 Wisconsin Ave NW *TF:* 800-369-2273 ■ *Web:* www.psychinstitute.com	Washington	DC	20016	202-885-5600	885-5614
Research Psychiatric Ctr 2323 E 63rd St.	Kansas City	MO	64130	816-444-8161	333-4495
Retreat Healthcare PO Box 803 *Fax:* Admissions ■ *TF:* 800-345-5550 ■ *Web:* www.retreathealthcare.org	Brattleboro	VT	05302	802-257-7785	258-3791*

	City	State	ZIP	Phone	Fax
Richard H Hutchings Psychiatric Ctr 620 Madison St	Syracuse	NY	13210	315-426-3600	426-7751
Richmond State Hospital (RSH) 498 NW 18th St	Richmond	IN	47374	765-966-0511	966-4593
Web: www.in.gov/fssa/dmha/6914.htm					
Ridge Behavioral Health System 3050 Rio Dosa Dr	Lexington	KY	40509	859-269-2325	268-6451
TF: 800-753-4673 ■ *Web:* www.ridgebhs.com					
River Park Hospital 1230 6th Ave	Huntington	WV	25701	304-526-9111	526-9140
TF: 800-992-9101 ■ *Web:* www.riverparkhospital.net					
Riverview Psychiatric Ctr 250 Arsenal St	Augusta	ME	04330	207-287-7200	287-7127
Rochester Psychiatric Ctr 1111 Elmwood Ave	Rochester	NY	14620	585-241-1200	241-1424
Rockland Psychiatric Ctr 140 Old Orangeburg Rd	Orangeburg	NY	10962	845-359-1000	365-5569*
Rogers Memorial Hospital Inc 34700 Valley Rd	Oconomowoc	WI	53066	262-646-4411	646-3158
TF: 800-767-4411 ■ *Web:* www.rogershospital.org					
Rusk State Hospital PO Box 318	Rusk	TX	75785	903-683-3421	683-7101
Saint Elizabeths Hospital 2700 ML King Jr Ave SE	Washington	DC	20032	202-562-4000	645-7494
Saint Peter Regional Treatment Ctr 100 Freeman Dr	Saint Peter	MN	56082	507-931-7100	931-7711
San Antonio State Hospital 6711 S Braunfels Ave	San Antonio	TX	78223	210-532-8811	531-8171*
San Diego County Psychiatric Hospital 3853 Rosecrans St	San Diego	CA	92110	619-692-8232	542-4060
Web: www.sgcounty.gov					
Searcy Hospital 725 E Coy Smith Hwy	Mount Vernon	AL	36560	251-662-6700	829-9075
Seton Shoal Creek Hospital 3501 Mills Ave	Austin	TX	78731	512-324-2000	324-2003
Web: www.seton.net					
Sharp-Mesa Vista Hospital 7850 Vista Hill Ave	San Diego	CA	92123	858-278-4110	715-8703
Web: www.sharp.com					
Sheppard Pratt at Ellicott City 4100 College Ave PO Box 836	Ellicott City	MD	21041	443-364-5500	
Web: www.sheppardpratt.org					
Sheppard Pratt Health System (SPHS) 6501 N Charles St	Baltimore	MD	21285	410-938-3000	938-3828*
**Fax:* Admissions ■ *TF:* 800-627-0330 ■ *Web:* www.sheppardpratt.org					
South Beach Psychiatric Ctr 777 Seaview Ave	Staten Island	NY	10305	718-667-2300	667-2344
South Florida Evaluation & Treatment Ctr 2200 NW 7th Ave	Miami	FL	33127	305-637-2500	637-2650
South Oaks Hospital 400 Sunrise Hwy	Amityville	NY	11701	631-264-4000	264-5259
Southeast Louisiana Hospital 23515 Hwy 190	Mandeville	LA	70448	985-626-6300	626-6490*
Southeast Missouri Mental Health Ctr 1010 W Columbia St	Farmington	MO	63640	573-218-6792	218-6785
Southwest Behavioral Health Services Inc 3450 N 3rd St	Phoenix	AZ	85012	602-257-9339	265-8377
Web: www.sbhservices.org					
Southwestern Virginia Mental Health Institute 340 Bagley Cir	Marion	VA	24354	276-783-1200	783-1216*
**Fax:* Admitting ■ *Web:* www.swvmhi.dmhmrsas.virginia.gov					
Spring Grove Hospital Ctr 55 Wade Ave	Catonsville	MD	21228	410-402-6000	402-7983
TF: 866-734-3337 ■ *Web:* www.springgrove.com					
Spring Harbor Hospital 123 Andover Rd	Westbrook	ME	04092	207-761-2200	761-2108
TF: 888-524-0080 ■ *Web:* www.springharbor.org					
Springfield Hospital Ctr 6655 Sykesville Rd	Sykesville	MD	21784	410-970-7000	970-7024*
**Fax:* Hum Res ■ *TF:* 800-333-7564					
State Hospital South PO Box 400	Blackfoot	ID	83221	208-785-1200	785-8516
Summit Behavioral Healthcare 1101 Summit Rd	Cincinnati	OH	45237	513-948-3600	948-3080
Taunton State Hospital 60 Hodges Ave	Taunton	MA	02780	508-977-3000	977-3751
Terrell State Hospital 1200 E Brin St	Terrell	TX	75160	972-563-6452	551-8302*
Thomas B Finan Ctr 10102 Country Club Rd SE PO Box 1722	Cumberland	MD	21501	301-777-2405	777-2364
TF: 888-854-0035					
Timberlawn Mental Health System 4600 Samuell Blvd	Dallas	TX	75228	214-381-7181	388-6453
TF: 800-426-4944 ■ *Web:* www.timberlawn.com					
Tinley Park Mental Health Ctr 7400 W 183rd St	Tinley Park	IL	60477	708-614-4000	614-4495
Torrance State Hospital 121 Longview Dr PO Box 111	Torrance	PA	15779	724-459-8000	459-1212*
**Fax:* Admitting ■ *TF:* 866-816-9212 ■ *Web:* www.dpw.state.pa.us/foradults/statehospitals/torrancestatehospital/index.htm					
Trenton Psychiatric Hospital PO Box 7500	West Trenton	NJ	08628	609-633-1500	396-5701
Twin Valley Behavioral Healthcare 2200 W Broad St	Columbus	OH	43223	614-752-0333	752-0385
UCLA Neuropsychiatric Institute & Hospital 760 Westwood Plaza	Los Angeles	CA	90095	310-825-0511	794-5098*
**Fax:* Admitting ■ *Web:* www.semel.ucla.edu					
University Behavioral Ctr 2500 Discovery Dr	Orlando	FL	32826	407-281-7000	282-7012
TF: 800-999-0807					
Utah State Hospital 1300 E Ctr St	Provo	UT	84606	801-344-4400	344-4225
Web: www.ush.utah.gov					
Walter P Reuther Psychiatric Hospital 30901 Palmer Rd	Westland	MI	48186	734-367-8400	722-5562*
Warren State Hospital 33 Main Dr	North Warren	PA	16365	814-723-5500	726-4377
Wernersville State Hospital PO Box 300	Wernersville	PA	19565	610-670-4173	670-4101
West Oaks Hospital 6500 Hornwood Dr	Houston	TX	77074	713-995-0909	778-5253
Westborough State Hospital Lyman St PO Box 288	Westborough	MA	01581	508-616-2100	616-2875*
Western Mental Health Institute 11100 Hwy 64 W	Bolivar	TN	38008	731-228-2000	658-2783
TF: 800-548-0635					
Western Missouri Mental Health Ctr 1000 E 24th St	Kansas City	MO	64108	816-512-7000	512-7509
Western State Hospital 2400 Russellville Rd	Hopkinsville	KY	42241	270-889-6025	886-4487
TF: 800-449-1189					
Western State Hospital 1301 Richmond Ave	Staunton	VA	24401	540-332-8000	332-8197
Web: www.healthsystem.virginia.edu					
Western State Hospital 9601 Steilacoom Blvd SW	Tacoma	WA	98498	253-582-8900	756-2963
Westwood Lodge Hospital 45 Clapboardtree St	Westwood	MA	02090	781-762-7764	762-0550
TF: 800-222-2237					
Wichita Falls State Hospital PO Box 300	Wichita Falls	TX	76307	940-692-1220	689-5538
William R Sharpe Jr Hospital 936 Sharpe Hospital Rd	Weston	WV	26452	304-269-1210	269-6235
William S Hall Psychiatric Institute 1800 Colonial Dr	Columbia	SC	29202	803-898-1693	898-2048
Willmar Regional Treatment Ctr 1550 Hwy 71 NE	Willmar	MN	56201	320-231-5100	231-5329
TF: 800-657-3898					
Winnebago Mental Health Institute (WMHI) 1300 S Dr PO Box 9	Winnebago	WI	54985	920-235-4910	237-2047
Web: www.dhs.wisconsin.gov/mh_winnebago					
Wyoming State Hospital (WSH) 831 Hwy 150 S	Evanston	WY	82930	307-789-3464	789-7213
Web: www.health.wyo.gov/statehospital/index.html					
Bellevue Hospital Ctr 462 1st Ave	New York	NY	10016	212-562-4141	562-4036
Lincoln Medical & Mental Health Ctr 234 E 149th St	Bronx	NY	10451	718-579-5000	579-5319

377-6 Rehabilitation Hospitals

	City	State	ZIP	Phone	Fax
Allied Services Rehabilitation Hospital 475 Morgan Hwy	Scranton	PA	18508	570-348-1300	341-4548
Web: www.allied-services.org					
Bacharach Institute for Rehabilitation 61 W Jimmie Leads Rd	Pomona	NJ	08240	609-652-7000	652-7487
Web: www.bacharach.org					
Baptist Health Rehabilitation Institute of Arkansas 9601 IH- 630	Little Rock	AR	72205	501-202-7000	202-7259*
Baptist Rehabilitation Germantown 2100 Exeter Rd	Germantown	TN	38138	901-757-1350	757-3496
Web: www.baptistonline.org					
Baylor Institute for Rehabilitation 909 N Washington Ave	Dallas	TX	75246	214-820-9300	818-8177
TF: 800-242-2334 ■ *Web:* www.baylorhealth.com					
Brooks Rehabilitation Hospital 3599 University Blvd S	Jacksonville	FL	32216	904-858-7600	858-7610
TF: 800-487-7342 ■ *Web:* www.brookshealth.org					
Bryn Mawr Rehabilitation Hospital 414 Paoli Pike	Malvern	PA	19355	610-251-5400	889-0943
TF: 888-734-2241 ■ *Web:* www.mainlinehealth.org/bmr					
Burke Rehabilitation Hospital 785 Mamaroneck Ave	White Plains	NY	10605	914-597-2500	597-0787
TF: 888-992-8753 ■ *Web:* www.burke.org					
Cardinal Hill Healthcare System 2050 Versailles Rd	Lexington	KY	40504	859-254-5701	255-9303*
**Fax:* Admitting ■ *TF:* 800-843-1408 ■ *Web:* www.cardinalhill.org					
Central Georgia Rehabilitation Hospital 3351 Northside Dr	Macon	GA	31210	478-201-6500	471-6536
Web: www.centralgarehab.com					
Charlotte Institute of Rehabilitation 1100 Blythe Blvd	Charlotte	NC	28203	704-355-4300	355-4231
TF: 800-634-2256 ■ *Web:* www.carolinas.org/services/rehab/cir					
Craig Hospital 3425 S Clarkson St	Englewood	CO	80113	303-789-8000	789-8219
Web: www.craighospital.org					
Crotched Mountain Rehabilitation Ctr 1 Verney Dr	Greenfield	NH	03047	603-547-3311	547-3232
Web: www.cmf.org					
Drake Ctr 151 W Galbraith Rd	Cincinnati	OH	45216	513-948-2500	948-2501
TF: 800-948-0003 ■ *Web:* www.drakecenter.uchealth.com					
Edwin Shaw Rehab 1621 Flickinger Rd	Akron	OH	44312	330-784-8229	784-1968
Elks Rehabilitation Hospital 600 N Robbins Rd	Boise	ID	83702	208-489-4444	489-4005
TF: 800-835-4514 ■ *Web:* www.idahoelksrehab.org					
Fairlawn Rehabilitation Hospital 189 May St	Worcester	MA	01602	508-791-6351	753-2087
Web: www.fairlawnrehab.org					
Frazier Rehabilitation Institute 220 Abraham Flexner Way	Louisville	KY	40202	502-582-7400	582-7477
Gaylord Hospital Gaylord Farms Rd PO Box 400	Wallingford	CT	06492	203-284-2800	284-2894
TF: 866-429-5673 ■ *Web:* www.gaylord.org					
Goddard Rehabilitation & Nursing Ctr 909 Sumner St	Stoughton	MA	02072	781-297-8200	297-8300
Web: www.goddardnursing.com					
Good Shepherd Rehabilitation Hospital 501 St John St	Allentown	PA	18103	610-776-3120	776-3503*
**Fax:* Admitting ■ *TF:* 877-724-2247 ■ *Web:* www.goodshepherdrehab.org					
Harmon Medical & Rehabilitation Hospital 2170 E Harmon Ave	Las Vegas	NV	89119	702-794-0100	794-0041
HealthSouth Bakersfield Rehabilitation Hospital 5001 Commerce Dr	Bakersfield	CA	93309	661-323-5500	633-5254
HealthSouth Braintree Rehabilitation Hospital 250 Pond St	Braintree	MA	02184	781-348-2500	356-2748
TF: 800-997-3422 ■ *Web:* www.braintreerehabhospital.com					
HealthSouth Chattanooga Rehabilitation Hospital 2412 McCallie Ave	Chattanooga	TN	37404	423-697-9129	697-9124*
**Fax:* Admissions ■ *TF:* 800-763-5189 ■ *Web:* www.healthsouth.com					
HealthSouth City View Rehabilitation Hospital 6701 Oakmont Blvd	Fort Worth	TX	76132	817-370-4700	370-4986
HealthSouth Deaconess Rehabilitation Hospital 4100 Covert Ave	Evansville	IN	47714	812-476-9983	476-4270
TF: 800-677-3422					
HealthSouth Harmarville Rehabilitation Hospital 320 Guys Run Rd PO Box 11460	Pittsburgh	PA	15238	412-828-1300	828-6954*

				Phone	Fax
HealthSouth Hospital of Pittsburgh 2380 McGinley Rd	Monroeville	PA	15146	412-856-2554	856-9320
TF: 877-937-7342 ■ *Web:* www.healthsouth.com					
HealthSouth Houston Rehabilitation Institute 17506 Red Oak Dr	Houston	TX	77090	281-580-1212	580-6714
Web: www.healthsouthhospitalofhouston.com					
HealthSouth Humble Rehabilitation Hospital 19002 McKay Dr.	Humble	TX	77338	281-319-9541	446-8022
Web: www.healthsouthhumble.com					
HealthSouth Lakeshore Rehabilitation Hospital 3800 Ridgeway Dr	Homewood	AL	35209	205-868-2025	868-2007
Web: www.healthsouth.com					
HealthSouth MountainView Regional Rehabilitation Hospital 1160 Van Voorhis Rd	Morgantown	WV	26505	304-598-1100	598-1103
TF: 800-388-2451 ■ *Web:* www.healthsouthmountainview.com					
HealthSouth Nittany Valley Rehabilitation Hospital 550 W College Ave	Pleasant Gap	PA	16823	814-359-3421	359-5898
TF: 800-842-6026 ■ *Web:* www.nittanyvalleyrehab.com					
HealthSouth North Louisiana Rehabilitation Hospital 1401 Ezell St.	Ruston	LA	71270	318-251-5392	251-1594
TF: 800-765-4772 ■ *Web:* www.rustonhealthsouth.com					
HealthSouth Plano Rehabilitation Hospital 2800 W 15th St.	Plano	TX	75075	972-612-9000	423-4293
HealthSouth Reading Rehabilitation Hospital 1623 Morgantown Rd	Reading	PA	19607	610-796-6000	796-6306
TF: 800-755-8027					
HealthSouth Rehabilitation Hospital of Albuquerque 7000 Jefferson St NE	Albuquerque	NM	87109	505-344-9478	345-6722
Web: www.healthsouthnewmexico.com					
HealthSouth Rehabilitation Hospital of Altoona 2005 Valley View Blvd	Altoona	PA	16602	814-944-3535	944-6160
TF: 800-873-4220 ■ *Web:* www.healthsouthaltoona.com					
HealthSouth Rehabilitation Hospital of Arlington 3200 Matlock Rd	Arlington	TX	76015	817-468-4000	468-3055
Web: www.healthsoutharlington.com					
HealthSouth Rehabilitation Hospital of Austin 1215 Red River	Austin	TX	78701	512-474-5700	
TF: 800-765-4772					
HealthSouth Rehabilitation Hospital of Beaumont 3340 Plaza 10 Blvd.	Beaumont	TX	77707	409-835-0835	835-1401
Web: www.healthsouthbeaumont.com					
HealthSouth Rehabilitation Hospital of Columbia 2935 Colonial Dr	Columbia	SC	29203	803-254-7777	401-1414
Web: www.healthsouthcolumbia.com					
HealthSouth Rehabilitation Hospital of Erie 143 E 2nd St.	Erie	PA	16507	814-878-1274	878-1399
TF: 800-234-4574					
HealthSouth Rehabilitation Hospital of Fayetteville 153 E Monte Painter Dr	Fayetteville	AR	72703	479-444-2200	444-2390
Web: www.healthsouth.com					
HealthSouth Rehabilitation Hospital of Florence 900 E Cheves St.	Florence	SC	29506	843-673-7122	678-3767
Web: www.healthsouthflorence.com					
HealthSouth Rehabilitation Hospital of Fort Smith 1401 S J St.	Fort Smith	AR	72901	479-785-8513	785-8599
Web: www.healthsouthfortsmith.com					
HealthSouth Rehabilitation Hospital of Fort Worth 1212 W Lancaster	Fort Worth	TX	76102	817-289-3103	335-1202
Web: www.healthsouthfortworth.com					
HealthSouth Rehabilitation Hospital of Jonesboro 1201 Fleming Ave.	Jonesboro	AR	72401	870-932-0440	932-6792
Web: www.healthsouthjonesboro.com					
HealthSouth Rehabilitation Hospital of Kingsport 113 Cassel Dr.	Kingsport	TN	37660	423-246-7240	246-3441
TF: 800-454-7422 ■ *Web:* www.healthsouthkingsport.com					
HealthSouth Rehabilitation Hospital of Largo 901 N Clearwater-Largo Rd.	Largo	FL	33770	727-586-2999	588-3404
HealthSouth Rehabilitation Hospital of Memphis 4100 Austin Peay Hwy	Memphis	TN	38128	901-213-5500	729-5171
TF: 800-363-7342 ■ *Web:* www.healthsouthnorthmemphis.com					
HealthSouth Rehabilitation Hospital of Montgomery 4465 Narrow Ln Rd.	Montgomery	AL	36116	334-284-7700	281-5136
HealthSouth Rehabilitation Hospital of New Jersey 14 Hospital Dr	Toms River	NJ	08755	732-505-5037	244-7829*
HealthSouth Rehabilitation Hospital of North Alabama 107 Governors Dr.	Huntsville	AL	35801	256-535-2300	428-2608
HealthSouth Rehabilitation Hospital of Sarasota 3251 Proctor Rd	Sarasota	FL	34231	941-921-8600	922-6228
HealthSouth Rehabilitation Hospital of Tallahassee 1675 Riggins Rd.	Tallahassee	FL	32308	850-656-4863	656-4892
Web: www.healthsouthtallahassee.com					
HealthSouth Rehabilitation Hospital of Texarkana 515 W 12th St.	Texarkana	TX	75501	903-735-5011	793-0899
Web: www.healthsouthtexarkana.com					
HealthSouth Rehabilitation Hospital of Tyler 3131 Troup Hwy	Tyler	TX	75701	903-510-7000	510-7005
HealthSouth Rehabilitation Hospital of Utah 8074 S 1300 E	Sandy	UT	84094	801-565-6666	565-6576
Web: www.healthsouthutah.com					
HealthSouth Rehabilitation Institute of Tucson 2650 N Wyatt Dr	Tucson	AZ	85750	520-325-1300	322-4400
Web: www.rehabinstituteoftucson.com					
HealthSouth Riosa 9119 Cinnamon Hill	San Antonio	TX	78240	210-691-0737	558-1297
Web: www.hsriosa.com					
HealthSouth Sea Pines Rehabilitation Hospital 101 E Florida Ave	Melbourne	FL	32901	321-984-4662	984-4627
Web: www.healthsouthseapines.com					
HealthSouth Sunrise Rehabilitation Hospital 4399 Nob Hill Rd	Sunrise	FL	33351	954-749-0300	746-1378
HealthSouth Treasure Coast Rehabilitation Hospital 1600 37th St.	Vero Beach	FL	32960	772-778-2100	562-9763
HealthSouth Tustin Rehabilitation Hospital 14851 Yorba St.	Tustin	CA	92780	714-832-9200	734-4851

				Phone	Fax
Hebrew Rehabilitation Ctr (HRC) 1200 Centre St	Roslindale	MA	02131	617-325-8000	363-8911
Web: www.hebrewseniorlife.org					
Hillside Rehabilitation Hospital (HRH) 8747 Squires Ln NE	Warren	OH	44484	330-841-3700	841-3647
Web: www.hillsiderehabhospital.net					
Hospital for Special Care 2150 Corbin Ave.	New Britain	CT	06053	860-223-2761	827-4849
Web: www.hfsc.org					
Howard Regional Health System West Campus Specialty Hospital 829 N Dixon Rd	Kokomo	IN	46901	765-452-6700	452-7470
Web: www.howardregional.org					
James H & Cecile C Quillen Rehabilitation Hospital 2511 Wesley St.	Johnson City	TN	37601	423-283-0700	283-0906
Web: www.msha.com					
JFK Johnson Rehabilitation Institute 65 James St	Edison	NJ	08818	732-321-7733	632-1671
Web: www.njrehab.org					
John Heinz Institute of Rehabilitation Medicine 150 Mundy St.	Wilkes-Barre	PA	18702	570-826-3800	826-3898
TF: 877-727-3422					
Kansas Rehabilitation Hospital 1504 SW 8th St.	Topeka	KS	66606	785-235-6600	232-8545
Web: www.kansasrehab.com					
Kentfield Rehabilitation Hospital 1125 Sir Francis Drake Blvd	Kentfield	CA	94904	415-456-9680	485-3622*
**Fax:* Admissions ■ *Web:* www.kentfieldrehab.com					
Kernan Hospital 2200 Kernan Dr	Baltimore	MD	21207	410-448-2500	448-2859
Web: www.kernan.org					
Laguna Honda Hospital & Rehabilitation Ctr 375 Laguna Honda Blvd	San Francisco	CA	94116	415-759-2300	759-2374
Madonna Rehabilitation Hospital 5401 S St	Lincoln	NE	68506	402-489-7102	486-8368
TF: 800-676-5448 ■ *Web:* www.madonna.org					
Magee Rehabilitation Hospital 1513 Race St	Philadelphia	PA	19102	215-587-3000	568-3736
TF: 800-966-2433 ■ *Web:* www.mageerehab.org					
Marianjoy Rehabilitation Hospital 26 W 171 Roosevelt Rd	Wheaton	IL	60187	630-462-4000	462-4442
TF: 800-462-2371 ■ *Web:* www.marianjoy.org					
Mary Free Bed Rehabilitation Hospital 235 Wealthy St SE	Grand Rapids	MI	49503	616-242-0300	454-3939
TF: 800-528-8989 ■ *Web:* www.maryfreebed.com					
Methodist Rehabilitation Ctr 1350 E Woodrow Wilson Dr	Jackson	MS	39216	601-981-2611	364-3465*
**Fax:* Admitting ■ *TF:* 800-223-6672 ■ *Web:* www.mmrcrehab.org					
Mid-America Rehabilitation Hospital 5701 W 110th St.	Overland Park	KS	66211	913-491-2400	338-3762
Missouri Rehabilitation Ctr 600 N Main St	Mount Vernon	MO	65712	417-466-3711	461-5775
Web: www.muhealth.org					
Montgomery Rehab Hospital Of Chestnut Hill 8601 Stenton Ave	Wyndmoor	PA	19038	215-233-6200	233-6339
Web: www.montrehab.com					
National Rehabilitation Hospital 102 Irving St NW	Washington	DC	20010	202-877-1000	829-5180
Web: www.nrhrehab.org					
New England Rehabilitation Hospital of Portland 335 Brighton Ave	Portland	ME	04102	207-775-4000	662-8446
Web: www.mainehealth.org/mmc_body.cfm?id=2169					
New England Rehabilitation Hospital of Woburn 2 Rehabilitation Way	Woburn	MA	01801	781-935-5050	935-3555
Web: www.newenglandrehab.com					
Northeast Rehabilitation Hospital 70 Butler St	Salem	NH	03079	603-893-2900	893-1628
TF: 800-825-7292 ■ *Web:* www.northeastrehab.com					
Pinecrest Rehabilitation Hospital 5360 Linton Blvd	Delray Beach	FL	33484	561-495-0400	499-6812
Web: www.pinecrestrehab.com					
Rancho Los Amigos National Rehabilitation Ctr 7601 E Imperial Hwy.	Downey	CA	90242	562-401-7111	401-7022*
**Fax:* Admitting ■ *TF:* 877-726-2461 ■ *Web:* www.rancho.org					
Rehabilitation Hospital of Indiana 4141 Shore Dr	Indianapolis	IN	46254	317-329-2000	329-2600
TF: 800-933-0123 ■ *Web:* www.rhin.com					
Rehabilitation Hospital of New Mexico 505 Elm St	Albuquerque	NM	87102	505-727-4700	727-4793
Rehabilitation Hospital of the Pacific 226 N Kuakini St.	Honolulu	HI	96817	808-531-3511	544-3335
TF: 800-973-4226 ■ *Web:* www.rehabhospital.org					
Rehabilitation Institute of Chicago 345 E Superior St	Chicago	IL	60611	312-238-1000	238-1369*
**Fax:* Admitting ■ *TF Admitting:* 800-354-7342 ■ *Web:* www.ric.org					
Rehabilitation Institute of Michigan 261 Mack Blvd	Detroit	MI	48201	313-745-1203	966-8294
Web: www.rimrehab.org					
Roosevelt Warm Springs Institute for Rehabilitation 6135 Roosevelt Hwy	Warm Springs	GA	31830	706-655-5000	655-5258*
**Fax:* Admissions ■ *Web:* www.rooseveltrehab.org					
Sacred Heart Rehabilitation Institute 2323 N Lake Dr.	Milwaukee	WI	53211	414-298-6700	298-6751
Saint Catherine's Rehabilitation Hospital 1050 NE 125th St	North Miami	FL	33161	305-891-8850	891-3361
Saint Lawrence Rehabilitation Ctr 2381 Lawrenceville Rd	Lawrenceville	NJ	08648	609-896-9500	895-0242
Web: www.slrc.org					
Saint Luke's Rehabilitation Institute 711 S Cowley St	Spokane	WA	99202	509-838-4771	473-6978
Web: www.st-lukes.org					
Saint Vincent Rehabilitation Hospital 2201 Wildwood Ave	Sherwood	AR	72120	501-834-1800	834-2227
San Joaquin Valley Rehabilitation Hospital 7173 N Sharon Ave.	Fresno	CA	93720	559-436-3600	436-3606
Web: www.sanjoaquinrehab.com					
Santa Rosa Memorial Hospital - Sotoyome Campus 151 Sotoyome St	Santa Rosa	CA	95405	707-543-2500	525-8413*

Name / Address	City	State	ZIP	Phone	Fax
Schwab Rehabilitation Hospital & Care Network 1401 S California Blvd	Chicago	IL	60608	773-522-2010	522-1177*
Shadyside Nursing & Rehabilitation Ctr 5609 5th Ave.	Pittsburgh	PA	15232	412-362-3500	362-1951
Shaughnessy-Kaplan Rehabilitation Hospital Dove Ave. *Web:* www.nsmc.partners.org/whoweare/skrh1.html	Salem	MA	01970	978-745-9000	741-1967
Shepherd Ctr 2020 Peachtree Rd NE *Web:* www.shepherd.org	Atlanta	GA	30309	404-352-2020	350-7341
Sierra Providence Physical Rehabilitation Hospital 1740 Curie Dr. *TF:* 800-999-8392 ■ *Web:* www.sphn.com	El Paso	TX	79902	915-544-3399	541-7714
Siskin Hospital for Physical Rehabilitation 1 Siskin Plaza *TF:* 800-474-7546 ■ *Web:* www.siskinrehab.org	Chattanooga	TN	37403	423-634-1200	634-1209
Southern Indiana Rehabilitation Hospital 3104 Blackiston Blvd *TF:* 800-737-7090 ■ *Web:* www.sirh.org	New Albany	IN	47150	812-941-8300	941-6276
Southern Kentucky Rehabilitation Hospital 1300 Campbell Ln *TF:* 800-989-5775 ■ *Web:* www.skyrehab.com	Bowling Green	KY	42104	270-782-6900	782-7228
Spalding Rehabilitation Hospital 900 Potomac St *TF:* 800-367-3309 ■ *Web:* www.spaldingrehab.com	Aurora	CO	80011	303-367-1166	360-8208
Spaulding Rehabilitation Hospital 125 Nashua St *Web:* www.spauldingrehab.org	Boston	MA	02114	617-573-7000	573-7009
SSM Rehabilitation Hospital 6420 Clayton Rd. *TF:* 800-818-9494 ■ *Web:* www.ssm-select.com	Saint Louis	MO	63117	314-768-5300	768-5355
Sunnyview Rehabilitation Hospital 1270 Belmont Ave. **Fax:* Admitting ■ *Web:* www.nehealth.com	Schenectady	NY	12308	518-382-4500	382-4533*
Thoms Rehabilitation Hospital 68 Sweeten Creek Rd *TF:* 800-627-1533 ■ *Web:* www.thoms.org	Asheville	NC	28803	828-274-2400	274-9452
TIRR Memorial Hermann Hospital 1333 Moursund St *TF:* 800-447-3422 ■ *Web:* www.memorialhermann.org	Houston	TX	77030	713-799-5000	799-7095
Trinity Neurological Rehabilitation Ctr 1400 Lindberg Dr	Slidell	LA	70458	985-641-4985	646-0793
Via Christi Rehabilitation Ctr 1151 N Rock Rd *TF:* 800-667-4241 ■ *Web:* www.viachristi.org	Wichita	KS	67206	316-634-3400	634-1141
Walton Rehabilitation Hospital 1355 Independence Dr *TF:* 866-492-5866 ■ *Web:* www.wrh.org	Augusta	GA	30901	706-724-7746	724-5752
Warm Springs Rehabilitation Hospital of San Antonio 5101 Medical Dr. *TF:* 800-451-1350 ■ *Web:* www.warmsprings.org	San Antonio	TX	78229	210-595-2380	614-0649
Warm Springs Specialty Hospital 200 Memorial Dr *TF:* 800-792-9276 ■ *Web:* www.warmsprings.org	Luling	TX	78648	830-875-8400	875-5029
Wesley Rehabilitation Hospital 8338 W 13th St N	Wichita	KS	67212	316-729-9999	729-8888
Youville Hospital & Rehabilitation Ctr 1575 Cambridge St. *Web:* www.youville.org	Cambridge	MA	02138	617-876-4344	547-5501

377-7 Specialty Hospitals

Name / Address	City	State	ZIP	Phone	Fax
Barbara Ann Karmanos Cancer Institute 4100 John R St *TF:* 800-527-6266 ■ *Web:* www.karmanos.org	Detroit	MI	48201	313-833-0710	831-6535
Bascom Palmer Eye Institute 900 NW 17th St *TF:* 800-329-7000 ■ *Web:* www.bascompalmer.org/site	Miami	FL	33136	305-326-6000	326-6374
Beckman Research Institute of City of Hope 1500 E Duarte Rd *TF:* 800-826-4673 ■ *Web:* www.cityofhope.org/research/beckman-research-institute	Duarte	CA	91010	626-359-8111	930-5486
Bone & Joint Hospital 1111 N Dewey Ave. **Fax:* Admitting ■ *Web:* www.boneandjoint.com	Oklahoma City	OK	73103	405-272-9671	552-9170*
Bordeaux Long-Term Care 1414 County Hospital Rd *Web:* www.bordeauxltc.org	Nashville	TN	37218	615-862-7000	862-6960
Brigham & Women's Hospital 75 Francis St **Fax:* Admitting ■ *TF:* 800-722-5520 ■ *Web:* www.brighamandwomens.org	Boston	MA	02115	617-732-5500	264-5181*
Callahan Eye Foundation Hospital 1720 University Blvd **Fax:* Admitting ■ *Web:* www.health.uab.edu	Birmingham	AL	35233	205-325-8100	325-8587*
Calvary Hospital 1740 Eastchester Rd **Fax:* Hum Res ■ *Web:* www.calvaryhospital.org	Bronx	NY	10461	718-863-6900	518-2690*
Coler-Goldwater Specialty Hospital & Nursing Facility 1 Main St Franklin D Roosevelt Island *Web:* www.nyc.gov	New York	NY	10044	212-318-8000	318-4370
Cornerstone Hospital of Austin 4207 Burnet Rd.	Austin	TX	78756	512-706-1900	706-1901
Dana-Farber Cancer Institute 44 Binney St. **Fax:* PR ■ *TF:* 800-757-3324 ■ *Web:* www.dana-farber.org	Boston	MA	02115	617-632-3000	632-5520*
Deborah Heart & Lung Ctr 200 Trenton Rd *Web:* www.deborah.org	Browns Mills	NJ	08015	609-893-6611	893-1213
Delaware Hospital for the Chronically Ill 100 Sunnyside Rd	Smyrna	DE	19977	302-233-1000	223-1549*
Dermatology Assoc of Atlanta 5555 Pchtrdnwyd Suite 190 *TF:* 800-233-0706 ■ *Web:* www.dermatlanta.com	Atlanta	GA	30342	404-256-4457	256-1145
Doheny Eye Institute 1450 San Pablo St *TF:* 800-872-2273 ■ *Web:* www.usc.edu/hsc/doheny	Los Angeles	CA	90033	323-442-6300	442-6338
Eleanor Slater Hospital 111 Howard Ave PO Box 8269	Cranston	RI	02920	401-462-3666	462-3679
Eye & Ear Clinic of Charleston 1306 Kanawha Blvd E *Web:* www.wvha.com/web/eye.ear	Charleston	WV	25301	304-343-4371	353-0215
Fox Chase Cancer Ctr 333 Cottman Ave *TF:* 888-369-2427 ■ *Web:* www.fccc.edu	Philadelphia	PA	19111	215-728-6900	728-2682
Georgia Cancer Specialists Pc (GCS) 1872 Montreal Rd. *Web:* www.gacancer.com	Tucker	GA	30084	770-496-9443	496-9490
H Lee Moffitt Cancer Center & Research Institute University of S Florida 12902 Magnolia Dr. *TF:* 800-456-3434 ■ *Web:* www.moffittcancercenter.com	Tampa	FL	33612	813-972-4673	745-8495
Healtheast Bethesda Rehabilitation Hosopital 559 Capitol Blvd. *Web:* www.healtheast.org	Saint Paul	MN	55103	651-232-2000	232-2118
HealthSouth Rehabilitation Hospital of York 1850 Normandie Dr *Web:* www.healthsouth.com	York	PA	17408	717-767-6941	764-1341
Hebrew Hospital Home Continuum of Care 61 Grasslands Rd. *Web:* www.hebrewhospitalhome.org	Valhalla	NY	10595	914-681-8400	
Hospice of Washington County Inc 747 Northern Ave *Web:* www.hwc-md.org	Hagerstown	MD	21742	301-791-6360	791-6579
Hospital for Special Surgery 535 E 70th St *Web:* www.hss.edu	New York	NY	10021	212-606-1000	606-1930
Hughston Orthopedic Hospital 100 Frist Ct. *TF:* 866-484-4786	Columbus	GA	31908	706-494-2100	494-2446
James Cancer Hospital & Solove Research Institute The 300 W 10th Ave *Web:* www.cancer.osu.edu	Columbus	OH	43210	614-293-8000	293-3132
Jewish Memorial Hospital & Rehabilitation Ctr (JMHRC) 59 Townsend St *TF:* 800-564-5868 ■ *Web:* www.jmhrc.com	Boston	MA	02119	617-989-8315	989-8207
Kapiolani Medical Center for Women & Children (KMCWC) 1319 Punahou St **Fax:* Admitting ■ *Web:* www.kapiolani.org/women-and-children/default.aspx	Honolulu	HI	96826	808-983-6000	983-6173*
Kindred Hospital Atlanta 705 Juniper St *Web:* www.kindredatlanta.com	Atlanta	GA	30308	404-873-2871	873-4516
Kindred Hospital Dallas 9525 Greenville Ave *Web:* www.khdallas.com	Dallas	TX	75243	214-355-2600	355-2630
Kindred Hospital Fort Worth Southwest 7800 Oakmont Blvd *Web:* www.kindredhospitalfwsw.com	Fort Worth	TX	76132	817-346-0094	263-4071
Kindred Hospital Kansas City 8701 Troost Ave *Web:* www.kindredhospitalkc.com	Kansas City	MO	64131	816-995-2000	995-2171
Kindred Hospital Northeast Braintree 2001 Washington St.	Braintree	MA	02184	781-848-2600	849-3290
Kindred Hospital Park View 1400 State St.	Springfield	MA	01109	413-787-6700	726-6110
Lake Taylor Transitional Hospital 1309 Kempsville Rd *Web:* www.laketaylor.org/index.php	Norfolk	VA	23502	757-461-5001	461-4282
Lawrence F Quigley Memorial Hospital 91 Crest Ave.	Chelsea	MA	02150	617-884-5660	884-1162
Leahi Hospital 3675 Kilauea Ave. *Web:* www.hhsc.org	Honolulu	HI	96816	808-733-8000	733-7914
Life Care Hospital of Pittsburgh 225 Penn Ave	Pittsburgh	PA	15221	412-247-2424	247-2333
Lombardi Comprehensive Cancer Center at Georgetown University 3800 Reservoir Rd NW *Web:* lombardi.georgetown.edu	Washington	DC	20007	202-444-2198	444-9429
Los Angeles County Central Jail Clinic 441 Bauchet St	Los Angeles	CA	90012	213-974-4984	625-7361
Magee-Womens Hospital 300 Halket St *Web:* www.magee.edu	Pittsburgh	PA	15213	412-641-1000	641-4343
Mary Rutan Hospital 205 E Palmer Rd. *Web:* www.maryrutan.org	Bellefontaine	OH	43311	937-592-5015	592-0207
Massachusetts Eye & Ear 243 Charles St **Fax:* Admitting ■ *Web:* www.masseyeandear.org	Boston	MA	02114	617-523-7900	573-4017*
Matheny Medical & Educational Ctr 65 Highland Ave *Web:* www.matheny.org	Peapack	NJ	07977	908-234-0011	719-2137
MD Anderson Cancer Ctr 1515 Holcombe Blvd **Fax:* Admitting ■ *TF:* 800-889-2094 ■ *Web:* www.mdanderson.org	Houston	TX	77030	713-792-2121	794-4915*
Memorial Sloan-Kettering Cancer Ctr 1275 York Ave. **Fax:* Admitting ■ *TF:* 800-525-2225 ■ *Web:* www.mskcc.org	New York	NY	10065	212-639-2000	432-2331*
Miami Heart Institute 4701 N Meridian Ave *Web:* www.msmc.com	Miami Beach	FL	33140	305-672-1111	674-3006
Midwestern Regional Medical Ctr (MRMC) 2520 Elisha Ave *TF:* 800-322-9183 ■ *Web:* www.cancercenter.com	Zion	IL	60099	847-872-4561	872-1591
Monroe Community Hospital 435 E Henrietta Rd **Fax:* Admitting ■ *Web:* www.monroehosp.org	Rochester	NY	14620	585-760-6500	760-6026*
National Jewish Medical & Research Ctr 1400 Jackson St PO Box 17169 *TF:* 877-225-5654 ■ *Web:* www.nationaljewish.org	Denver	CO	80206	303-388-4461	
New York Eye & Ear Infirmary 310 E 14th St *TF:* 800-449-4673 ■ *Web:* www.nyee.edu	New York	NY	10003	212-979-4000	228-0664
New York University Hospital for Joint Diseases (HJD) 301 E 17th St *TF:* 800-372-2887 ■ *Web:* www.hjd.med.nyu.edu	New York	NY	10003	212-598-6022	260-1203
Norris Comprehensive Cancer Center & Hospital 1441 Eastlake Ave. *TF:* 800-522-6237 ■ *Web:* www.ccnt.hsc.usc.edu	Los Angeles	CA	90033	323-865-9031	865-3868
Oak Forest Hospital of Cook County 15900 S Cicero Ave	Oak Forest	IL	60452	708-687-7200	687-7979
Oaks Treatment Ctr 1407 W Stassney Ln. *TF:* 800-843-6257 ■ *Web:* www.theoakstc.com	Austin	TX	78745	512-464-0448	
Odessa Regional Medical Ctr 520 E 6th St *TF:* 877-898-6080 ■ *Web:* www.odessaregionalmedicalcenter.com	Odessa	TX	79761	432-582-8000	

	City	State	ZIP	Phone	Fax
Orthopaedic Hospital 2400 S Flower St. *Web:* www.orthohospital.org	Los Angeles	CA	90007	213-742-1000	741-8338
Phillips Eye Institute 2215 Pk Ave S **Fax:* Admitting ■ *Web:* www.allina.com	Minneapolis	MN	55404	612-775-8800	870-0315*
Piedmont Geriatric Hospital 5001 E Patrick Henry Hwy PO Box 427	Burkeville	VA	23922	434-767-4401	767-4500
Presbyterian Orthopaedic Hospital 1901 Randolph Rd *Web:* www.presbyterian.org	Charlotte	NC	28207	704-316-2000	316-1803
Princess Margaret Hospital 610 University Ave *Web:* www.uhn.ca	Toronto	ON	M5G2M9	416-946-2000	
River Oaks East-Woman's Pavilion 1026 N Flowood Dr	Flowood	MS	39208	601-932-1000	932-4138*
Roswell Park Cancer Institute 666 Elm St *TF:* 877-275-7724 ■ *Web:* www.roswellpark.org	Buffalo	NY	14263	716-845-2300	845-8335
Runnells Specialized Hospital of Union County 40 Watchung Way *Web:* www.ucnj.org/government/runnells-specialized-hospital	Berkeley Heights	NJ	07922	908-771-5700	771-0376
Saint Francis Health Care Ctr (SFHCC) 401 N Broadway St *TF:* 800-248-2552	Green Springs	OH	44836	419-639-2626	639-6225
Saint Francis Hospital 100 Port Washington Blvd *Web:* www.stfrancisheartcenter.com	Roslyn	NY	11576	516-562-6000	562-6909
Saint Jude Children's Research Hospital (SJCRH) 262 Danny Thomas Pl **Fax:* Admitting ■ *TF:* 866-278-5833 ■ *Web:* www.stjude.org	Memphis	TN	38105	901-495-3300	495-5297*
Saint Vincent Women's Hospital 8111 Township Line Rd **Fax:* Admitting ■ *TF:* 877-664-4076 ■ *Web:* www.stvincent.org	Indianapolis	IN	46260	317-415-8111	415-7587*
Samuel Mahelona Memorial Hospital 4800 Kawaihau Rd *Web:* www.smmh.hhsc.org	Kapaa	HI	96746	808-822-4961	823-4100
Select Specialty Hospital Houston Heights 1917 Ashland St	Houston	TX	77008	713-861-6161	802-8653
Sidney Kimmel Comprehensive Cancer Center at Johns Hopkins 401 N Broadway The Harry & Jeanette Weinberg Bldg Suite 1100 *Web:* www.hopkinsmedicine.org	Baltimore	MD	21231	410-955-5222	955-6787
Siteman Cancer Ctr 4921 Parkview Pl *TF:* 800-600-3606 ■ *Web:* www.siteman.wustl.edu	Saint Louis	MO	63110	314-362-5196	
Specialty Hospital Jacksonville 4901 Richard St *TF:* 800-378-9497 ■ *Web:* www.specialtyhospitaljax.com	Jacksonville	FL	32207	904-737-3120	730-5991
Stanford Cancer Ctr 875 Lake Blake Wilbur Dr *Web:* www.cancer.stanford.edu	Stanford	CA	94305	650-498-6000	725-9113
Stony Point Surgical Ctr 8700 Stony Pt Pkwy *TF:* 800-328-7334 ■ *Web:* www.stonypointsc.com	Richmond	VA	23235	804-775-4500	643-3542
Straith Hospital for Special Surgery 23901 Lahser Rd	Southfield	MI	48034	248-357-3360	357-0915
Tewksbury Hospital 365 E St **Fax:* Mail Rm ■ *Web:* www.mass.gov/dph/hosp/th.htm	Tewksbury	MA	01876	978-851-7321	851-5648*
Texas Center for Infectious Diseases 2303 SE Military Dr *TF:* 800-839-5864	San Antonio	TX	78223	210-534-8857	531-4502
Texas Orthopedic Hospital 7401 Main St *TF:* 800-678-4501 ■ *Web:* www.texasorthopedic.com	Houston	TX	77030	713-799-8600	794-3580
UC Davis Cancer Ctr 4501 X St *TF:* 800-362-5566 ■ *Web:* www.ucdmc.ucdavis.edu/cancer	Sacramento	CA	95817	916-734-5800	703-5067
University of Michigan Trauma Burn Ctr 1500 E Medical Ctr Dr Rm 1C435-UH PO Box 0033	Ann Arbor	MI	48109	734-936-9673	936-9657
University Specialty Hospital 601 S Charles St	Baltimore	MD	21230	410-547-8500	752-2920
Vanderbilt-Ingram Cancer Ctr 691 Preston Bldg *Web:* www.vicc.org	Nashville	TN	37232	615-936-1793	936-5879
Veterans Home & Hospital 287 W St	Rocky Hill	CT	06067	860-529-2571	721-5979*
Villa Feliciana Chronic Disease Hospital 5002 Hwy 10	Jackson	LA	70748	225-634-4000	634-4191
Wills Eye 840 Walnut St *Web:* www.willseye.org	Philadelphia	PA	19107	215-928-3000	928-0634
Woman's Hospital 9050 Airlines Hwy *Web:* www.womans.org	Baton Rouge	LA	70815	225-927-1300	924-8110
Woman's Hospital of Texas 7600 Fannin St *Web:* www.womanshospital.com	Houston	TX	77054	713-790-1234	790-0469
Women & Infants Hospital of Rhode Island 101 Dudley St *Web:* www.womenandinfants.org	Providence	RI	02905	401-274-1100	453-7666
Women's & Children's Hospital (WCH) 4600 Ambassador Caffery Pkwy *Web:* www.womens-childrens.com	Lafayette	LA	70508	337-521-9100	521-9102
Women's Christian Assn Hospital 207 Foote Ave **Fax:* Admitting ■ *Web:* www.wcahospital.org	Jamestown	NY	14701	716-487-0141	644-8144*

377-8 Veterans Hospitals

Listings For Veterans Hospitals Are Organized By States, And Then By City Names Within Those Groupings.

	City	State	ZIP	Phone	Fax
Veterans Affairs Medical Ctr 700 S 19th St	Birmingham	AL	35233	205-933-8101	933-4498*
VA Central Alabama Veterans Health Care System 215 Perry Hill Rd *TF:* 800-214-8387	Montgomery	AL	36109	334-272-4670	260-4115
Veterans Affairs Medical Ctr 3701 Loop Rd E *TF:* 888-269-3045	Tuscaloosa	AL	35404	205-554-2000	554-2077
Veterans Affairs Medical Ctr 2400 Hospital Rd *TF:* 800-214-8387	Tuskegee	AL	36083	334-727-0550	724-6825
Carl T Hayden Veterans Affairs Medical Ctr 650 E Indian School Rd	Phoenix	AZ	85012	602-277-5551	222-6435
Veterans Affairs Medical Ctr 500 Hwy 89 N *TF:* 800-949-1005	Prescott	AZ	86313	928-445-4860	776-6098
Southern Arizona Veterans Healthcare System 3601 S 6th Ave **Fax:* Admissions ■ *TF:* 800-470-8262	Tucson	AZ	85723	520-792-1450	629-4969*
Veterans Affairs Medical Ctr 1100 N College Ave *TF:* 800-691-8387	Fayetteville	AR	72703	479-443-4301	444-5089
Veterans Affairs Medical Ctr 4300 W 7th St	Little Rock	AR	72205	501-257-1000	257-5404
Veterans Affairs Medical Ctr 2615 E Clinton Ave	Fresno	CA	93703	559-225-6100	
Jerry L Pettis Memorial Veterans Affairs Medical Ctr 11201 Benton St **Fax:* Admitting ■ *TF:* 800-827-1000 ■ *Web:* www.lomalinda.va.gov	Loma Linda	CA	92357	909-825-7084	422-3140*
Veterans Affairs Long Beach Medical Ctr 5901 E 7th St *TF:* 888-769-8387 ■ *Web:* www.longbeach.va.gov	Long Beach	CA	90822	562-826-8000	826-5906
VA Greater Los Angeles Healthcare System 11301 Wilshire Blvd *Web:* www.losangeles.va.gov	Los Angeles	CA	90073	310-478-3711	268-3494
Sepulveda Veterans Affairs Medical Ctr 16111 Plummer St *TF:* 800-827-1000	North Hills	CA	91343	818-891-7711	
Veterans Affairs Medical Ctr 3801 Miranda Ave *Web:* www.paloalto.va.gov	Palo Alto	CA	94304	650-493-5000	852-3228
Veterans Affairs Medical Ctr 3350 La Jolla Village Dr *TF:* 800-331-8387	San Diego	CA	92161	858-552-8585	
San Francisco VA Medical Ctr 4150 Clement St *Web:* www2.va.gov	San Francisco	CA	94121	415-221-4810	750-2177
Veterans Affairs Medical Ctr 1055 Clermont St **Fax:* Mail Rm ■ *TF:* 888-336-8262	Denver	CO	80220	303-399-8020	393-4656*
Veterans Affairs Medical Ctr 2121 N Ave	Grand Junction	CO	81501	970-242-0731	244-1323
Veterans Affairs Connecticut Health Care System 950 Campbell Ave	West Haven	CT	06516	203-932-5711	937-4964
Veterans Affairs Medical Ctr 1601 Kirkwood Hwy *TF:* 800-450-8262	Wilmington	DE	19805	302-994-2511	
Veterans Affairs Medical Ctr 50 Irving St NW	Washington	DC	20422	202-745-8000	745-2278*
Veterans Affairs Medical Ctr 10000 Bay Pines Blvd *TF:* 888-820-0230 ■ *Web:* www2.va.gov	Bay Pines	FL	33744	727-398-6661	398-9442
Malcom Randall VAMC NF/SGVHS 1601 SW Archer Rd **Fax:* Mail Rm ■ *TF:* 800-324-8387 ■ *Web:* www2.va.gov/directory/guide/facility.asp?id=54	Gainesville	FL	32608	352-376-1611	374-6113*
Veterans Affairs Medical Ctr 619 S Marion Ave	Lake City	FL	32025	386-755-3016	758-6005
Veterans Affairs Medical Ctr 1201 NW 16th St **Fax:* Admitting ■ *TF:* 888-276-1785	Miami	FL	33125	305-324-4455	575-3420*
Veterans Affairs Medical Ctr 13000 Bruce B Downs Blvd *Web:* www.va.gov	Tampa	FL	33612	813-972-2000	910-3020
Veterans Affairs Medical Ctr 7305 N Military Trail *TF:* 800-972-8262	West Palm Beach	FL	33410	561-422-8262	422-8613
Veterans Affairs Medical Ctr 1 Freedom Way **Fax:* Admitting ■ *TF:* 800-836-5561	Augusta	GA	30904	706-733-0188	481-6726*
Veterans Affairs Medical Ctr 1670 Clairmont Rd *TF:* 800-944-9726	Decatur	GA	30033	404-321-6111	
Carl Vinson Veterans Affairs Medical Ctr 1826 Veterans Blvd **Fax:* Mail Rm ■ *TF:* 800-595-5229	Dublin	GA	31021	478-272-1210	277-2717*
Veterans Affairs Medical Ctr 500 W Fort St **Fax:* Admitting ■ *TF:* 866-437-5093	Boise	ID	83702	208-422-1000	422-1148*
Veterans Affairs Medical Ctr 820 S Damen Ave *TF:* 888-569-5282 ■ *Web:* www.chicago.va.gov	Chicago	IL	60612	312-569-8387	
Veterans Affairs Medical Ctr 1900 E Main St *TF:* 800-320-8387 ■ *Web:* www2.va.gov	Danville	IL	61832	217-554-3000	554-4552
Edward Hines Jr Veterans Affairs Hospital 5000 S 5th Ave PO Box 5000 *Web:* www.hines.va.gov	Hines	IL	60141	708-202-8387	202-2506
Veterans Affairs Medical Ctr 2401 W Main St	Marion	IL	62959	618-997-5311	993-4148*
Veterans Affairs Medical Ctr 3001 Green Bay Rd **Fax Area Code:* 224 ■ *TF:* 800-393-0865	North Chicago	IL	60064	847-688-1900	610-3280*
Veterans Affairs Medical Ctr 2121 Lake Ave *TF:* 800-360-8387	Fort Wayne	IN	46805	260-426-5431	460-1332
Veterans Affairs Medical Ctr 1481 W 10th St *TF:* 888-878-6889 ■ *Web:* www1.va.gov/directory/guide/facility.asp?ID=62	Indianapolis	IN	46202	317-988-4498	
Veterans Affairs Medical Ctr 1700 E 38th St **Fax:* Admitting ■ *TF:* 800-498-8792	Marion	IN	46953	765-674-3321	677-3188*
Veterans Affairs Medical Ctr 3600 30th St *TF:* 800-294-8387 ■ *Web:* www2.va.gov	Des Moines	IA	50310	515-699-5999	699-5862
Veterans Affairs Medical Ctr 200 Hawkins Dr # S209 *Web:* www.iowa-city.med.va.gov	Iowa City	IA	52242	319-338-0581	339-7171
Veterans Affairs Medical Ctr 1515 W Pleasant St Bldg 1 *TF:* 800-816-8878 ■ *Web:* www.centraliowa.va.gov	Knoxville	IA	50138	641-842-3101	828-5066

Name / Address	City	State	ZIP	Phone	Fax
Dwight D Eisenhower Veterans Affairs Medical Ctr					
4101 S 4th St	Leavenworth	KS	66048	913-682-2000	758-4233
TF: 800-952-8387					
Colmery-O'Neil Veterans Affairs Medical Ctr					
2200 SW Gage Blvd	Topeka	KS	66622	785-350-3111	350-4336
TF: 800-574-8387					
Veterans Affairs Medical Ctr					
5500 E Kellogg St	Wichita	KS	67218	316-685-2221	651-3666
TF: 888-878-6881					
Veterans Affairs Medical Center Lexington					
1101 Veterans Dr	Lexington	KY	40502	859-233-4511	281-4953*
Veterans Affairs Medical Ctr 800 Zorn Ave	Louisville	KY	40206	502-287-4000	287-6954*
New Orleans Veteran Affairs Outpatient Clinic					
1601 Perdido St PO Box 60011	New Orleans	LA	70112	504-412-3700	310-6300
TF: 800-935-8387 ■ *Web:* www.neworleans.va.gov					
Alexandria Veterans Affairs Medical Ctr					
2495 Shreveport Hwy 71 N	Pineville	LA	71360	318-473-0010	483-5093*
**Fax:* Hum Res ■ *TF:* 800-375-8387 ■ *Web:* www.alexandria.va.gov					
Overton Brooks Veterans Affairs Medical Ctr					
510 E Stoner Ave	Shreveport	LA	71101	318-221-8411	990-5556
TF: 800-863-7441 ■ *Web:* www.shreveport.va.gov					
Togus VA Medical Ctr 1 VA Ctr	Augusta	ME	04330	207-623-8411	623-5792*
**Fax:* Admissions ■ *TF:* 877-421-8263					
Veterans Affairs Medical Ctr					
10 N Greene St	Baltimore	MD	21201	410-605-7000	605-7904
TF: 800-463-6295					
Edith Nourse Rogers Memorial Veterans Hospital					
200 Springs Rd	Bedford	MA	01730	781-275-7500	687-3537
Veterans Affairs Medical Ctr 940 Belmont St	Brockton	MA	02301	508-583-4500	
Web: www2.va.gov					
Veterans Affairs Medical Ctr					
150 S Huntington Ave	Jamaica Plain	MA	02130	617-232-9500	278-4410
Web: www.va.gov					
North Hampton Veterans Affairs Medical Ctr					
421 N Main St	Leeds	MA	01053	413-584-4040	582-3185*
Veterans Affairs Medical Ctr					
2215 Fuller Rd	Ann Arbor	MI	48105	734-769-7100	761-5398*
Veterans Affairs Medical Ctr					
5500 Armstrong Rd	Battle Creek	MI	49037	269-966-5600	223-5678*
**Fax:* Admissions ■ *TF:* 888-214-1247					
Veterans Affairs Medical Ctr 4646 John R St	Detroit	MI	48201	313-576-1000	576-1025
Oscar G Johnson Veterans Affairs Medical Ctr					
325 E 'H' St	Iron Mountain	MI	49801	906-774-3300	779-3108
TF: 800-215-8262 ■ *Web:* www.ironmountain.va.gov					
Paragon Health Pc 2318 Gull Rd Suite B	Kalamazoo	MI	49048	269-341-4554	381-3063
Web: www.paragonhealthpc.com					
Veterans Affairs Medical Ctr 1500 Weiss St	Saginaw	MI	48602	989-497-2500	321-4903*
**Fax:* Hum Res ■ *Web:* www2.va.gov					
Veterans Affairs Medical Ctr					
1 Veterans Dr	Minneapolis	MN	55417	612-725-2000	467-5531*
**Fax:* Admitting ■ *TF:* 866-414-5058					
Veterans Affairs Medical Ctr					
4801 Veterans Dr	Saint Cloud	MN	56303	320-252-1670	255-6494*
**Fax:* Mail Rm ■ *TF:* 800-247-1739					
Veterans Affairs Medical Ctr					
1500 E Woodrow Wilson Dr	Jackson	MS	39216	601-362-4471	368-3811*
Harry S Truman Memorial Veterans Hospital					
800 Hospital Dr	Columbia	MO	65201	573-814-6000	814-6600
Veterans Affairs Medical Ctr					
4801 E Linwood Blvd	Kansas City	MO	64128	816-861-4700	922-3331*
**Fax:* Hum Res ■ *TF:* 800-525-1483					
John J Pershing Veterans Affairs Medical Ctr					
1500 N Westwood Blvd	Poplar Bluff	MO	63901	573-686-4151	778-4559
Veterans Affairs Hospital					
3687 Veterans Dr	Fort Harrison	MT	59636	406-442-6410	447-7904
Veterans Affairs Medical Ctr					
2201 N Broadwell Ave	Grand Island	NE	68803	308-382-3660	385-2712*
**Fax:* Admissions ■ *TF:* 866-580-1810					
Veterans Affairs Medical Ctr 600 S 70th St	Lincoln	NE	68510	402-489-3802	486-7840
TF: 866-851-6052					
Veterans Affairs Medical Ctr					
4101 Woolworth Ave	Omaha	NE	68105	402-346-8800	997-5635*
**Fax:* Admitting ■ *TF:* 800-451-5796					
Sierra NV Healthcare Systems (VA Medical Ctr)					
1000 Locust St	Reno	NV	89502	775-786-7200	328-1464*
**Fax:* Mail Rm ■ *TF:* 888-838-6256					
Veterans Affairs Medical Ctr 718 Smyth Rd	Manchester	NH	03104	603-624-4366	626-6576
TF: 800-892-8384					
East Orange Campus of the VA New Jersey Health Care System					
385 Tremont Ave	East Orange	NJ	07018	973-676-1000	395-7148*
**Fax:* Hum Res ■ *Web:* www1.va.gov/visns/visn03/eorginfo.asp					
Veterans Affairs Medical Ctr 151 Knollcroft Rd	Lyons	NJ	07939	908-647-0180	604-5245*
**Fax:* Admissions ■ *Web:* www.va.gov					
Veterans Affairs Medical Ctr					
1501 San Pedro Dr SE	Albuquerque	NM	87108	505-265-1711	256-2855
Stratton Veterans Affairs Medical Ctr					
113 Holland Ave	Albany	NY	12208	518-626-5000	626-6709*
**Fax:* Admitting ■ *TF:* 800-223-4810 ■ *Web:* www.albany.va.gov					
Veterans Affairs Medical Ctr					
222 Richmond Ave	Batavia	NY	14020	585-297-1000	344-3300
Bath Veterans Affairs Medical Ctr					
76 Veterans Ave	Bath	NY	14810	607-664-4000	664-4915*
**Fax:* Admissions ■ *TF:* 877-845-3247 ■ *Web:* www.bath.va.gov					
James J Peters Veterans Affairs Medical Ctr					
130 W Kingsbridge Rd	Bronx	NY	10468	718-584-9000	741-4571
Veterans Affairs Medical Ctr 800 Poly Pl	Brooklyn	NY	11209	718-836-6600	567-4029*
Veterans Affairs Medical Ctr 3495 Bailey Ave	Buffalo	NY	14215	716-834-9200	862-8533
TF: 800-532-8387					
Veterans Affairs Medical Ctr					
400 Fort Hill Ave	Canandaigua	NY	14424	585-394-2000	393-8328
TF: 800-204-9917					
Castle Point Campus Rt 9D	Castle Point	NY	12511	845-831-2000	838-5193
Web: www2.va.gov					
VA Hudson Valley Health Care System					
Montrose Campus					
2094 Albany Post Rd PO Box 100	Montrose	NY	10548	914-737-4400	788-4244
TF: 800-269-8749 ■ *Web:* www.hudsonvalley.va.gov					
Veterans Affairs Medical Ctr 423 E 23rd St	New York	NY	10010	212-686-7500	951-3375
Veterans Affairs Medical Ctr					
79 Middleville Rd	Northport	NY	11768	631-261-4400	754-7952*
**Fax:* Admissions ■ *TF:* 800-827-1000					
Veterans Affairs Medical Ctr 800 Irving Ave	Syracuse	NY	13210	315-425-4400	425-4375*
**Fax:* Admitting ■ *TF:* 800-792-4334					
Veterans Affairs Medical Ctr					
1100 Tunnel Rd	Asheville	NC	28805	828-298-7911	299-2502
TF: 800-932-6408					
Veterans Affairs Medical Ctr 508 Fulton St	Durham	NC	27705	919-286-0411	286-6825
Veterans Affairs Medical Ctr					
2300 Ramsey St	Fayetteville	NC	28301	910-488-2120	
TF: 800-771-6106					
WG Bill Hefner Veterans Affairs Medical Ctr					
1601 Brenner Ave	Salisbury	NC	28144	704-638-9000	638-3866*
**Fax:* Admissions ■ *TF:* 800-469-8262					
Veterans Affairs Medical Ctr 2101 Elm St N	Fargo	ND	58102	701-232-3241	239-3729
TF: 800-410-9723					
Veterans Affairs Medical Ctr					
17273 SR-104	Chillicothe	OH	45601	740-773-1141	772-7160
TF: 800-827-1000					
Veterans Affairs Medical Ctr 3200 Vine St	Cincinnati	OH	45220	513-475-6571	487-6661
TF: 888-267-7873 ■					
Web: www.fisherhouse.org/houses/house-locations/#Ohio					
Louis Stokes Cleveland Veterans Affairs Medical Ctr					
10701 E Blvd	Cleveland	OH	44106	216-791-3800	707-5973
TF: 888-350-3100 ■ *Web:* www.cleveland.med.va.gov					
Veterans Affairs Medical Ctr 4100 W 3rd St	Dayton	OH	45428	937-268-6511	262-3383
Veterans Affairs Medical Ctr					
1011 Honor Heights Dr	Muskogee	OK	74401	918-683-3261	577-3664*
Veterans Affairs Medical Ctr					
921 NE 13th St	Oklahoma City	OK	73104	405-456-1000	456-5132
TF: 866-835-5273					
Veterans Affairs Medical Ctr					
3710 SW US Veterans Hospital Rd	Portland	OR	97239	503-220-8262	402-2909*
**Fax:* Admissions ■ *TF:* 888-233-8305					
Veterans Affairs Medical Ctr					
913 NW Garden Valley Blvd	Roseburg	OR	97470	541-440-1000	440-1225
Web: www2.va.gov					
James E Van Zandt Veterans Affairs Medical Ctr					
2907 Pleasant Valley Blvd	Altoona	PA	16602	814-943-8164	940-7898
TF: 877-626-2500					
Veterans Affairs Medical Ctr					
325 New Castle Rd	Butler	PA	16001	724-287-4781	477-5019*
**Fax:* Hum Res ■ *TF:* 800-362-8262					
Veterans Affairs Medical Ctr					
1400 Black Horse Hill Rd	Coatesville	PA	19320	610-384-7711	383-0207
TF: 800-290-6172					
Veterans Affairs Medical Ctr 135 E 38th St	Erie	PA	16504	814-868-8661	860-2211
TF: 800-274-8387					
Veterans Affairs Medical Ctr					
1700 S Lincoln Ave	Lebanon	PA	17042	717-272-6621	228-5944*
**Fax:* Admissions ■ *TF:* 800-409-8771					
Veterans Affairs Medical Ctr					
3900 Woodland Ave	Philadelphia	PA	19104	215-823-5800	823-5839*
**Fax:* Admissions ■ *TF:* 800-949-1001 ■ *Web:* www.philadelphia.va.gov					
Veterans Affairs Medical Ctr					
University Dr C	Pittsburgh	PA	15240	412-688-6000	688-6932
TF: 866-482-7488 ■ *Web:* www.va.gov/pittsburgh					
Veterans Affairs Medical Ctr					
7180 Highland Dr	Pittsburgh	PA	15206	866-482-7488	365-5105*
**Fax Area Code:* 412 ■ *TF:* 866-482-7488 ■ *Web:* www.va.gov/pittsburgh/highland.htm					
Veterans Affairs Medical Ctr					
1111 E End Blvd	Wilkes-Barre	PA	18711	570-824-3521	
TF: 877-928-2621					
Veterans Affairs Medical Ctr					
830 Chalkstone Ave	Providence	RI	02908	401-273-7100	861-2396*
**Fax:* Hum Res ■ *TF:* 866-590-2976 ■ *Web:* www.va.gov					
Ralph H Johnson Veterans Affairs Medical Ctr					
109 Bee St	Charleston	SC	29401	843-577-5011	
Veterans Affairs Medical Ctr					
6439 Garners Ferry Rd	Columbia	SC	29209	803-776-4000	695-6799*
**Fax:* Mail Rm ■ *Web:* www.va.gov/columbiasc					
Veterans Affairs Medical Ctr					
113 Comanche Rd	Fort Meade	SD	57741	605-347-7000	720-7099
TF: 800-743-1070					
Veterans Affairs Medical Ctr					
500 N 5th St	Hot Springs	SD	57747	605-745-2000	745-2097*
Royal C Johnson Veterans Memorial Hospital					
2501 W 22nd St	Sioux Falls	SD	57105	605-336-3230	333-6872
TF: 800-316-8387					
Veterans Affairs Medical Ctr					
1030 Jefferson Ave	Memphis	TN	38104	901-523-8990	577-7533*
**Fax:* Admissions ■ *TF:* 800-636-8262					
James H Quillen Veterans Affairs Medical Ctr					
Corner of Lamont & Veterans Way					
PO Box 4000	Mountain Home	TN	37684	423-926-1171	979-3519
TF: 877-573-3529 ■ *Web:* www.mountainhome.va.gov					
Alvin C York Medical Ctr					
3400 Lebanon Pike	Murfreesboro	TN	37129	615-867-6000	867-5802*
**Fax:* Admitting ■ *TF:* 800-876-7093					
Veterans Affairs Medical Ctr					
1310 24th Ave S	Nashville	TN	37212	615-327-4751	
TF: 800-228-4973 ■ *Web:* www.va.gov					
Thomas E Creek Veterans Affairs Medical Ctr					
6010 Amarillo Blvd W	Amarillo	TX	79106	806-355-9703	
TF: 800-687-8262					
Veterans Affairs Medical Ctr					
300 Veterans Blvd	Big Spring	TX	79720	432-263-7361	268-5017*

	City	State	Zip	Phone	Fax
Veterans Affairs Medical Ctr 1201 E 9th St TF: 800-924-8387 ■ Web: www2.va.gov	Bonham	TX	75418	903-583-2111	583-6692
VA Medical Ctr 4500 S Lancaster Rd TF: 800-849-3597 ■ Web: www.northtexas.va.gov	Dallas	TX	75216	214-742-8387	857-1171
Veterans Affairs Medical Ctr 2002 Holcombe Blvd TF: 800-553-2278 ■ Web: www.houston.med.va.gov	Houston	TX	77030	713-791-1414	794-7218
Audie L Murphy Memorial Veterans Hospital 7400 Merton Minter St	San Antonio	TX	78229	210-617-5300	
Central Texas Veterans Health Care System 1901 Veterans Memorial Dr TF: 800-423-2111 ■ Web: www2.va.gov	Temple	TX	76504	254-778-4811	743-0691
Veterans Affairs Medical Ctr 4800 Memorial Dr	Waco	TX	76711	254-752-6581	297-3077
Veterans Affairs Medical Ctr 500 S Foothill Dr TF: 800-827-1000 ■ Web: www.va.gov/visn19/slc.htm	Salt Lake City	UT	84148	801-582-1565	582-1565
White River Junction Veterans Affairs Medical Ctr 215 N Main St TF: 866-687-8387 ■ Web: www.whiteriver.va.gov	White River Junction	VT	05009	802-295-9363	296-5138
Veterans Affairs Medical Ctr 100 Emancipation Dr Web: www.va.gov	Hampton	VA	23667	757-728-3100	
Hunter Holmes McGuire Veterans Affairs Medical Ctr 1201 Broad Rock Blvd TF: 800-784-8381	Richmond	VA	23249	804-675-5000	
Veterans Affairs Medical Ctr 1970 Roanoke Blvd	Salem	VA	24153	540-982-2463	983-1093*
Veterans Affairs Puget Sound Medical Ctr 1660 S Columbian Way *Fax: Admitting ■ TF: 800-329-8387 ■ Web: www.puget-sound.med.va.gov	Seattle	WA	98108	206-762-1010	764-2270*
Veterans Affairs Medical Ctr 4815 N Assembly St	Spokane	WA	99205	509-434-7000	434-7131*
Veterans Affairs Medical Ctr 77 Wainwright Dr	Walla Walla	WA	99362	509-525-5200	526-6207*
Veterans Affairs Medical Ctr 200 Veterans Ave Web: www1.va.gov	Beckley	WV	25801	304-255-2121	255-2431
Louis A Johnson Veterans Affairs Medical Ctr 1 Medical Ctr Dr	Clarksburg	WV	26301	304-623-3461	626-7724
Veterans Affairs Medical Ctr 1540 Spring Valley Dr	Huntington	WV	25704	304-429-6741	429-0270
Veterans Affairs Medical Ctr 510 Butler Ave	Martinsburg	WV	25405	304-263-0811	264-3990
Veterans Affairs Medical Ctr 2500 Overlook Terr TF: 888-478-8321 ■ Web: www.madison.va.gov	Madison	WI	53705	608-256-1901	280-7116
Veterans Affairs Medical Ctr 5000 W National Ave *Fax: Admitting ■ TF: 888-469-6614	Milwaukee	WI	53295	414-384-2000	382-5388*
Tomah Veterans Affairs Medical Ctr 500 E Veterans St *Fax: Admissions ■ TF: 800-872-8662 ■ Web: www.visn12.med.va.gov/tomah	Tomah	WI	54660	608-372-3971	372-1692*
Veterans Affairs Medical Ctr 1898 Fort Rd *Fax: Admissions ■ TF: 800-370-0250	Sheridan	WY	82801	307-672-3473	672-1900*

378 HOT TUBS, SPAS, WHIRLPOOL BATHS

	City	State	Zip	Phone	Fax
Alaglass Pools 165 Sweet Bay Rd TF: 877-655-7179 ■ Web: www.alaglass.com	Saint Matthews	SC	29135	803-655-7179	655-5680
Almost Heaven Group HC 67 PO Box 539 BB Web: www.almostheaven.net	Renick	WV	24966	304-497-2610	
Atlantic Spas & Billiards 8721 Glenwood Ave TF: 800-849-8827	Raleigh	NC	27617	919-783-7447	783-0146
Baker Mfg Corp 7460 Chancellor Dr TF: 800-881-2284	Orlando	FL	32809	407-816-9559	857-9240
Bath-Tec Inc PO Box 1118 TF: 800-526-3301 ■ Web: www.bathtec.com	Ennis	TX	75120	972-646-5279	646-5688
Bathroom World Mfg Co 4160 NE 6th Ave TF: 800-566-0541 ■ Web: www.bathroomworld.com	Fort Lauderdale	FL	33334	954-566-0451	561-8510
Best Bath Systems 723 Garber St TF: 866-333-8657 ■ Web: www.best-bath.com	Caldwell	ID	83605	208-342-6823	333-8657
Cal Spas Inc 1462 E Ninth St TF: 800-225-7727 ■ Web: www.calspas.com	Pomona	CA	91766	909-623-8781	620-0751
Cameo Marble 540 Central Ct TF: 800-447-8558	New Albany	IN	47150	812-944-5055	944-5236
Clarke Products Inc 1207 S White's Chapel Blvd Suite 150 *Fax Area Code: 817 ■ TF: 800-426-8964 ■ Web: www.clarkeproducts.com	Southlake	TX	76092	972-660-1992	416-4204*
Coleman Spas Inc 25605 S Arizona Ave Web: www.colemanspas.com	Chandler	AZ	85248	480-895-0598	895-7849
Dimension One Spas 2611 Business Pk Dr TF: 800-345-7727 ■ Web: www.d1spas.com	Vista	CA	92081	760-727-7727	734-4225
Galaxy Aquatics Inc 1075 W Sam Houston Pkwy N Suite 210 Web: www.galaxy-aquatics.com	Houston	TX	77043	713-464-0303	464-0399
Gatsby Spas Inc 1003 S Alexander St PO Box 5457 TF: 800-393-7727	Plant City	FL	33563	813-754-4122	752-5716
Hydra Baths 2100 S Fairview St TF: 800-854-8680 ■ Web: www.hydrabaths.com	Santa Ana	CA	92704	714-556-9133	708-0632
Hydro Systems Inc 29132 Ave Paine TF: 800-747-9990 ■ Web: www.hydrosystem.com	Valencia	CA	91355	661-775-0686	775-0668
Jason International Inc 8328 MacArthur Dr TF: 800-255-5766 ■ Web: www.jasoninternational.com	North Little Rock	AR	72118	501-771-4477	771-2333
Kallista Inc 1227 N 8th St Suite 2 TF Cust Svc: 888-452-5547 ■ Web: www.kallista.com	Sheboygan	WI	53081	920-457-4441	803-4867
Koral Industries Inc 1504 S Kaufman St TF: 800-627-2441 ■ Web: www.koralco.com	Ennis	TX	75119	972-875-6555	875-9558
Marquis Spas Corp 596 Hoffman Rd TF: 800-275-0888 ■ Web: www.marquisspas.com	Independence	OR	97351	503-838-0888	838-3849
Master Spas Inc 6927 Lincoln Pkwy TF: 800-860-7727 ■ Web: www.masterspas.com	Fort Wayne	IN	46804	260-436-9100	432-7935
Oasis Industries Inc 1600 Mountain St TF: 800-323-2748	Aurora	IL	60505	630-898-3500	375-1500
Plastic Development Co Inc PO Box 4007 TF: 800-451-1420 ■ Web: www.pdcspas.com	Williamsport	PA	17701	570-323-3060	323-8485
Royal Baths Mfg Co 14635 Chrisman Rd TF: 800-826-0074 ■ Web: www.royalbaths.com	Houston	TX	77039	281-442-3400	442-1455
Spa Manufacturers 6060 Ulmerton Rd TF: 877-530-9493 ■ Web: www.spamanufacturers.com	Clearwater	FL	33760	727-530-9493	539-8151
Spurlin Industries Inc 625 Main St TF: 800-749-4475 ■ Web: www.spurlinindustries.com	Palmetto	GA	30268	770-463-1644	463-2932
Thermo Spas Inc 155 E St TF: 800-876-0158 ■ Web: www.thermospas.com	Wallingford	CT	06492	203-265-6133	265-7133
Twirl Jet Spas Inc 3990 Industrial Ave TF: 800-854-4890 ■ Web: www.twirljetspas.com	Hemet	CA	92545	951-766-4306	766-4310
Watertech Whirlpool Bath & Spa 2507 Plymouth Rd TF: 800-289-8827 ■ Web: www.watertechtn.com	Johnson City	TN	37601	423-926-1470	926-6438
Watkins Mfg Corp 1280 Pk Ctr Dr TF: 800-999-4688 ■ Web: www.hotspring.com	Vista	CA	92083	760-598-6464	598-8910

379 HOTEL RESERVATIONS SERVICES

	City	State	Zip	Phone	Fax
AC Central Reservations Inc 201 Tilton Rd London Sq Mall Suite 17B TF: 888-227-6667 ■ Web: www.acrooms.com	Northfield	NJ	08225	609-383-8880	383-8801
Accommodations Plus 4230 Merrick Rd TF Cust Svc: 800-733-7666 ■ Web: www.hotelexpress.com	Massapequa	NY	11758	718-751-4000	995-6099
Advance Reservations Inn Arizona PO Box 950 TF: 800-456-0682 ■ Web: www.azres.com	Tempe	AZ	85280	480-990-0682	990-3390
Advanced Reservation Systems Inc 1059 1st Ave TF: 800-434-7894 ■ Web: www.aresdirect.com	San Diego	CA	92101	619-238-0900	374-2085
Alaska Sourdough Bed & Breakfast Assn 889 Cardigan Cir	Anchorage	AK	99503	907-563-6244	743-0664
Alberta Express Reservations PO Box 6295 TF: 800-884-8803	Drayton Valley	AB	T7A1R7	780-621-2855	542-6505
All Around the Town 270 Lafayette St Suite 804 TF: 800-443-3800 ■ Web: www.newyorkcitybestbb.com	New York	NY	10012	212-334-2655	334-2654
Alliance Reservations Network 14435 N 7th St Suite 300-B TF Cust Svc: 800-892-2108 ■ Web: www.reservetravel.com	Phoenix	AZ	85022	602-952-2106	224-9896
Anchorage Alaska Bed & Breakfast Assn (AABBA) PO Box 242623 TF: 888-584-5147 ■ Web: www.anchorage-bnb.com	Anchorage	AK	99524	907-272-5909	277-4034
Annapolis Accommodations 41 Maryland Ave TF: 800-715-1000 ■ Web: www.stayannapolis.com	Annapolis	MD	21401	410-280-0900	263-1703
Atlantic City Toll-Free Reservations PO Box 665 TF: 800-833-7070	Northfield	NJ	08225	609-646-7070	646-8655
B & B Agency of Boston 47 Commercial Wharf # 3 TF: 800-248-9262 ■ Web: www.boston-bnbagency.com	Boston	MA	02110	617-720-3540	523-5761
Barclay International Group 6800 Jericho Tpke TF: 800-845-6636 ■ Web: www.barclayweb.com	Syosset	NY	11791	516-364-0064	364-4468
Bed & Breakfast Accommodations Ltd PO Box 12011 TF: 877-893-3233 ■ Web: bedandbreakfastdc.com	Washington	DC	20005	202-328-3510	332-3885
Bed & Breakfast Assn of Downtown Toronto PO Box 190 Stn B Web: www.bnbinfo.com	Toronto	ON	M5T2W1	416-410-3938	483-8822
Bed & Breakfast Assoc Bay Colony Ltd 453 Beacon St PO Box 57166 TF: 888-486-6018 ■ Web: www.bnbboston.com	Boston	MA	02115	781-449-5302	455-6745
Bed & Breakfast Atlanta 790 N Ave Suite 202 TF: 800-967-3224 ■ Web: www.bedandbreakfastatlanta.com	Atlanta	GA	30306	404-875-0525	876-6544
Bed & Breakfast Cape Cod PO Box 1312 TF: 800-541-6226 ■ Web: www.bedandbreakfastcapecod.com	Orleans	MA	02653	508-255-3824	240-0599
Bed & Breakfast Directory for San Diego PO Box 3292	San Diego	CA	92103	619-297-3130	299-6213
Bed & Breakfast Homes of Toronto Assn 287 Humberside Ave Web: www.bbcanada.com/associations/toronto2	Toronto	ON	M6P1L4	416-769-2028	
Bed & Breakfast of Hawaii 5031 Haleilio Rd TF: 800-733-1632 ■ Web: www.bandb-hawaii.com	Kapaa	HI	96746	808-822-7771	822-2723
Bed & Breakfast of Philadelphia PO Box 21 TF: 800-448-3619 ■ Web: www.bnbphiladelphia.com	Devon	PA	19333	610-687-3565	995-9524
Bed & Breakfast Reservations 11A Beach Rd TF: 800-832-2632 ■ Web: www.bbreserve.com	Gloucester	MA	01930	978-281-9505	281-9426
Bed & Breakfast San Francisco PO Box 420009 TF: 800-452-8249 ■ Web: www.bbsf.com	San Francisco	CA	94142	415-899-0060	899-9923
Best Canadian Bed & Breakfast Network 1064 Balfour Ave	Vancouver	BC	V6H1X1	604-738-7207	
Branson's Best Reservations 165 Expy Ln TF: 800-800-2019 ■ Web: www.bransonbest.com	Branson	MO	65616	417-339-2204	339-4051
Branson/Lakes Area Lodging Assn PO Box 430 TF: 888-238-6782 ■ Web: www.bransonarealodging.com	Branson	MO	65615	417-332-1400	239-1400
Capital Area Bed & Breakfast Network 4938 Hampden Ln TF: 888-549-3415	Bethesda	MD	20814	703-549-3415	
Capitol Reservations 1730 Rhode Island Ave NW Suite 1210 TF: 800-847-4832 ■ Web: www.visitdc.com	Washington	DC	20036	202-452-1270	452-0537

	City	State	ZIP	Phone	Fax
Central Reservation Service					
200 Lookout Pl Suite 150	Maitland	FL	32751	407-740-6442	740-8222
TF: 800-555-7555 ■ *Web:* www.reservation-services.com					
Central Reservation Service of New England Inc					
300 Terminal C					
Logan International Airport	East Boston	MA	02128	617-569-3800	561-4840
TF: 800-332-3026					
Colonial Williamsburg Reservation Ctr					
506 N Henry St	Williamsburg	VA	23185	757-253-2277	565-8797
TF: 800-447-8679 ■ *Web:* www.history.org					
Colorado Resort Services					
2955 Village Dr	Steamboat Springs	CO	80487	970-879-7654	879-3027
TF: 800-525-7654 ■ *Web:* www.crs-steamboat.com					
Equity Corporate Housing					
100 Northwoods Village Dr	Casy	NC	27513	919-468-5611	468-5499
TF: 800-533-2370 ■ *Web:* www.equitycorporatehousing.com					
Eugene Area Bed & Breakfast Assn					
South Willamette Bed & Breakfast Assn					
1006 Taylor St	Eugene	OR	97402	541-302-3014	
TF: 866-302-3014 ■ *Web:* www.southwillamettebedandbreakfasts.com					
Florida SunBreak 90 Alton Rd Suite 16	Miami Beach	FL	33139	305-532-1516	532-0564
TF: 800-786-2732 ■ *Web:* www.zilbert.com					
Gites et Auberges du Passant					
4545 Pierre-De Coubertin Ave					
CP 1000 Succursale M	Montreal	QC	H1V3R2	514-252-3138	252-3173
Web: www.giteetaubergedupassant.com					
Greater Miami & the Beaches Hotel Assn (GMBHA)					
1674 Meridian Ave Suite 420	Miami Beach	FL	33139	305-531-3553	531-8954
TF: 800-531-3553 ■ *Web:* www.gmbha.org					
Greater New Orleans Hotel & Lodging Assn					
203 Carondelet St Suite 415	New Orleans	LA	70130	504-525-2264	525-9327
Web: www.gnohla.com					
Greek Hotel & Cruise Reservation Ctr					
17280 Newhope St Suite 18	Fountain Valley	CA	92708	714-429-7962	641-0303
TF: 800-736-5717 ■ *Web:* www.greekhotels.com					
Greenville Area Central Reservations					
PO Box 10527	Greenville	SC	29603	864-233-0461	421-0005
TF: 800-351-7180					
Gulf Coast Hotel Reservations PO Box 116	Biloxi	MS	39533	228-374-8680	388-8117
TF General: 888-388-1006					
Hawaii's Best Bed & Breakfasts 571 Pauku St	Kailua	HI	96734	808-263-3100	262-5030
TF: 800-262-9912 ■ *Web:* www.bestbnb.com					
Hilton Head Vacation Rentals					
430 William Hilton Pkwy Suite 504	Hilton Head Island	SC	29926	843-689-3010	689-3011
TF: 800-732-7671 ■ *Web:* www.800beachme.com					
Historic Charleston Bed & Breakfast Reservations Service					
57 Broad St	Charleston	SC	29401	843-722-6606	722-9589
TF: 800-743-3583 ■ *Web:* www.historiccharlestonbedandbreakfast.com					
Hot Rooms 1 E Erie St Suite 225	Chicago	IL	60611	773-468-7666	649-0559*
**Fax Area Code:* 312 ■ *TF:* 800-468-3500 ■ *Web:* www.hotrooms.com					
Hotel Locators.com 919 Garnet Ave Suite 216	San Diego	CA	92109	858-581-1315	581-1730
TF: 800-576-0003					
HotelNetDiscount.com					
3070 Windward Plaza Suite F-302	Alpharetta	GA	30005	770-664-1316	664-1507
Web: www.hotelnetdiscount.com					
Hotels.com LP 10440 N Central Expy Suite 800	Dallas	TX	75231	800-246-8357	
NASDAQ: EXPE ■ *TF Sales:* 800-246-8357 ■ *Web:* www.hotels.com					
Jackson Hole Central Reservations (JHCR)					
140 E Broadway Suite 24 PO Box 2618	Jackson	WY	83001	307-733-4005	733-1286
TF: 888-838-6606 ■ *Web:* www.jacksonholewy.com					
Jackson Hole Resort Reservations LLC					
PO Box 12739	Jackson	WY	83002	307-733-6331	733-4728
TF: 800-329-9205 ■ *Web:* www.jacksonholeres.com					
Key West Key 726 Passover Ln	Key West	FL	33040	305-294-4357	294-2974
TF: 800-881-7321 ■ *Web:* www.keywestkey.com					
Know Before You Go Reservations					
8000 international Dr	orlando	FL	32819	407-352-9813	396-8404
TF: 800-749-1993 ■ *Web:* www.knowbeforeugo.com					
Leading Hotels of the World 99 Pk Ave	New York	NY	10016	212-515-5600	515-5899
TF: 800-223-6800 ■ *Web:* www.lhw.com					
Luxe Worldwide Hotels					
11461 W Sunset Blvd	Los Angeles	CA	90049	310-440-3090	440-0821
TF: 866-589-3411 ■ *Web:* www.luxehotels.com					
Martha's Vineyard & Nantucket Reservations					
73 Lagoon Pond Rd	Vineyard Haven	MA	02568	508-693-7200	693-1878
TF: 800-649-5671 ■ *Web:* www.mvreservations.com					
Myrtle Beach Reservation Service					
1551 21st Ave N Suite 20	Myrtle Beach	SC	29577	800-626-7477	448-8143*
**Fax Area Code:* 843 ■ *TF:* 800-626-7477 ■ *Web:* www.mbhospitality.org					
Nantucket Accommodations					
4 Dennis Dr PO Box 217	Nantucket	MA	02554	508-228-9559	325-7009
Web: www.nantucketaccommodation.com					
New Otani North America Reservation Ctr					
120 S Los Angeles St	Los Angeles	CA	90012	213-629-1200	473-1416
TF Cust Svc: 800-421-8795 ■ *Web:* www.kyotogranthotel.com					
Ocean City Hotel-Motel-Restaurant Assn					
PO Box 340	Ocean City	MD	21843	410-289-6733	289-5645
TF: 800-626-2326 ■ *Web:* www.ocvisitor.com					
Pacific Reservation Service PO Box 20703	Seattle	WA	98109	206-439-7677	431-0932
TF: 800-684-2932 ■ *Web:* www.seattlebedandbreakfast.com					
Private Lodging Service 1489 Crest Rd	Cleveland	OH	44121	216-291-1209	
Quikbook 381 Pk Ave S 3rd Fl	New York	NY	10016	212-779-7666	779-6120
TF: 800-789-9887 ■ *Web:* www.quikbook.com					
Reservations USA 2713 N Pkwy	Pigeon Forge	TN	37863	865-453-6618	453-7484
TF: 800-251-4444 ■ *Web:* www.lodging4u.com					
Resort 2 Me 2600 Garden Rd Suite 111	Monterey	CA	93940	831-642-6622	642-6641
TF: 800-757-5646 ■ *Web:* www.resort2me.com					
RSVP Martha's Vineyard PO Box 2042	Oak Bluffs	MA	02557	508-693-9371	696-0431
TF: 866-778-7689 ■ *Web:* www.rsvpmarthasvineyard.com					
San Diego Concierge 4379 30th St Suite 4	San Diego	CA	92104	619-280-4121	280-4119
TF: 800-979-9091 ■ *Web:* www.sandiegoconcierge.com					
San Diego Hotel Collection					
1550 Hotel Cir N	San Diego	CA	92108	619-881-4700	881-4701
San Francisco Reservations					
360 22nd St Suite 300	Oakland	CA	94612	510-628-4444	628-9025
TF: 800-677-1550 ■ *Web:* www.hotelres.com					
Scottsdale Resort Accommodations					
7339 E Evans Rd Suite 100	Scottsdale	AZ	85260	480-515-2300	505-7878
TF: 888-868-4378 ■ *Web:* www.scottsdale-resorts.com					
Seattle Super Saver 701 Pike St Suite 800	Seattle	WA	98101	702-939-2525	
TF: 800-205-3315 ■ *Web:* www.seattlesupersaver.com					
Southern Arizona Lodging & Resort Assn					
3305 N Swan Rd Suite 109	Tucson	AZ	85712	520-299-6787	299-6431
Web: www.acfchefsarizona.org					
Stay Aspen Snowmass 425 Rio Grande Pl	Aspen	CO	81611	970-925-9000	925-9008
TF: 800-670-0792 ■ *Web:* www.stayaspensnowmass.com					
Travel Planners Inc 381 Pk Ave S	New York	NY	10016	212-532-1660	532-1556
TF: 800-221-3531 ■ *Web:* www.tphousing.com					
Travelworm Inc					
6280 S Valley View Blvd Suite 502	Las Vegas	NV	89118	702-948-4395	
Web: www.travelworm.com					
Turbotrip.com 4124 S McCann Ct	Springfield	MO	65804	800-473-7829	864-8811*
**Fax Area Code:* 417 ■ *TF:* 800-473-7829 ■ *Web:* www.turbotrip.com					
USA Hotel Guide					
11300 Federal Hwy Suite 3	North Palm Beach	FL	33408	561-227-2181	882-3954
TF: 888-729-7705 ■ *Web:* www.usahotelguide.com					
Utell 8350 N Central Expy Suite 1900	Dallas	TX	75206	214-234-4000	234-4040
TF: 800-223-6510 ■ *Web:* www.utell.com					
Vacation Co					
42 New Orleans Rd Suite 102	Hilton Head Island	SC	29928	843-686-6100	686-3255
TF: 800-845-7018					
Van Voast House Bed & Breakfast Homes					
1353 Union St	Schenectady	NY	12308	518-393-1634	
TF: 800-810-4948 ■ *Web:* www.bandbreservations.com					
Washington DC Accommodations					
2201 Wisconsin Ave NW Suite C-120	Washington	DC	20007	202-289-2220	338-1365
TF: 800-503-3330 ■ *Web:* www.wdcahotels.com					
Winter Park Resort					
85 Parsenn Rd PO Box 36	Winter Park	CO	80482	970-726-5514	726-1690
TF: 800-525-3538 ■ *Web:* www.winterpark.travel					
Worldhotels 152 W 57th St 6th Fl	New York	NY	10019	212-956-0200	956-2555
Web: www.worldhotels.com					
WorldRes Ltd 15333 N Pima Rd Suite 245	Scottsdale	AZ	85260	480-946-5100	946-0450
Web: www.worldres.com					
Xanterra South Rim LLC					
10 Albright St PO Box 699	Grand Canyon	AZ	86023	928-638-2631	638-9810
Web: www.grandcanyonlodges.com					

380 HOTELS - CONFERENCE CENTER

	City	State	ZIP	Phone	Fax
Aberdeen Woods Conference Ctr					
201 Aberdeen Pkwy	Peachtree City	GA	30269	770-487-2666	487-1063
TF: 800-285-6338 ■ *Web:* www.awcc.com					
ACE Conference Ctr 800 Ridge Pike	Lafayette Hill	PA	19444	610-825-8000	940-4343
TF: 800-523-0090 ■ *Web:* www.aceconferencecenter.com					
Airlie Conference Ctr 6809 Airlie Rd	Warrenton	VA	20187	540-347-1300	341-3207
TF: 800-288-9573 ■ *Web:* www.airlie.com					
Aspen Wye River Conference Ctr					
600 River House Ln	Queenstown	MD	21658	410-827-7400	827-9295
Web: www.marriott.com					
Babson Executive Conference Ctr					
1 Executive Education Cir Babson Pk	Wellesley	MA	02457	781-239-4000	239-4026
Web: www.aramarkharrisonlodging.com/properties					
Banff Centre The					
107 Tunnel Mountain Dr PO Box 1020	Banff	AB	T1L1H5	403-762-6100	762-6444
TF: 800-884-7574 ■ *Web:* www.banffcentre.ca					
Burkshire Marriott Conference Hotel					
10 W Burke Ave	Towson	MD	21204	410-324-8100	616-3749
TF: 800-435-5986 ■ *Web:* www.marriott.com					
Chattanoogan The 1201 Broad St	Chattanooga	TN	37402	423-756-3400	756-3404
TF: 877-756-1684 ■ *Web:* www.chattanooganhotel.com					
Chauncey Conference Ctr					
660 Rosedale Rd PO Box 6652	Princeton	NJ	08541	609-921-3600	683-4958
Web: www.acc-chaunceyconferencecenter.com					
Cheyenne Mountain Conference Resort					
3225 Broadmoor Valley Rd	Colorado Springs	CO	80906	719-538-4000	576-4186
TF: 800-428-8886 ■ *Web:* www.cheyennemountain.com					
Clarion Hotel & Conference Center Antietam Creek					
901 Dual Hwy	Hagerstown	MD	21740	301-733-5100	733-9192
TF: 888-528-6738 ■ *Web:* www.clarionhagerstown.com					
Conference Center at Marlboro					
280 Locke Dr	Marlborough	MA	01752	508-263-5500	624-0130
Conference Center at NorthPointe					
9243 Columbus Pike	Lewis Center	OH	43035	614-880-4300	880-4167
TF: 866-233-9393 ■ *Web:* www.conferencecenteratnorthpointe.com					
Cook Hotel & Conference Ctr					
3848 W Lakeshore Dr	Baton Rouge	LA	70808	225-383-2665	383-4200
TF: 866-610-2665 ■ *Web:* www.thecookhotel.com					
Country Springs Hotel & Conference Ctr					
2810 Golf Rd	Pewaukee	WI	53072	262-547-0201	547-0207
TF: 800-247-6640 ■ *Web:* www.countryspringshotel.com					
Delta Sherbrooke Hotel & Conference Centre					
2685 Rue King O	Sherbrooke	QC	J1L1C1	819-822-1989	822-8990
TF: 800-268-1133 ■ *Web:* www.deltahotels.com					
Dodgertown Sports & Conference Ctr					
3901 26th St	Vero Beach	FL	32960	772-569-4900	562-5199
TF: 866-656-4900 ■ *Web:* www.dodgertownverobeach.com					
Dolce Hayes Mansion 200 Edenvale Ave	San Jose	CA	95136	408-226-3200	362-2377
TF: 866-981-3300 ■ *Web:* www.dolce-hayes-mansion-hotel.com					
Doubletree Hotel & Executive Meeting Center Somerset					
200 Atrium Dr	Somerset	NJ	08873	732-469-2600	469-4617
TF: 800-222-8733 ■ *Web:* www.doubletreesomerset.com					
Dover Downs Hotel & Casino 1131 N DuPont Hwy	Dover	DE	19901	302-674-4600	857-2198
TF: 800-711-5882 ■ *Web:* www.doverdowns.com					

				Phone	Fax
Edith Macy Conference Ctr 550 Chappaqua Rd	Briarcliff Manor	NY	10510	914-945-8000	945-8009
TF: 800-442-6229 ■ Web: www.edithmacy.com					
Emory Conference Center Hotel 1615 Clifton Rd	Atlanta	GA	30329	404-712-6000	712-6025
TF: 800-933-6679 ■ Web: www.emoryconferencecenter.com					
Evergreen Marriott Conference Resort 4021 Lakeview Dr	Stone Mountain	GA	30083	770-879-9900	465-3264
TF: 800-228-9290 ■ Web: www.evergreenresort.com					
Fogelman Executive Conference Ctr 330 Innovation Dr University of Memphis	Memphis	TN	38152	901-678-3700	678-5329
Web: www.wilsonhotels.com					
Founders Inn 5641 Indian River Rd	Virginia Beach	VA	23464	757-424-5511	366-0613
TF: 800-926-4466 ■ Web: www.foundersinn.com					
Four Points by Sheraton Norwood Hotel & Conference Ctr 1125 Boston-Providence Tpke (Rt 1)	Norwood	MA	02062	781-769-7900	551-3552
Web: www.fourpointsnorwood.com					
Georgetown University Hotel & Conference Ctr 3800 Reservoir Rd NW	Washington	DC	20057	202-687-3200	687-3297
TF: 800-228-9290 ■ Web: www.acc-guhotelandconferencecenter.com					
Glen Cove Mansion Hotel & Conference Ctr 200 Dosoris Ln	Glen Cove	NY	11542	516-671-6400	705-0147
TF: 877-782-9426 ■ Web: www.glencovemansion.com					
Grandover Resort & Conference Ctr 1000 Club Rd	Greensboro	NC	27407	336-294-1800	856-9991
TF: 800-472-6301 ■ Web: www.grandoverresort.com					
H Hotel The 111 W Main St	Midland	MI	48642	989-839-0500	837-6000
TF: 877-645-3643 ■ Web: www.marriott.com/property/propertypage/MBSAC					
Hamilton Park Hotel & Conference Ctr 175 Pk Ave	Florham Park	NJ	07932	973-377-2424	377-9560
TF: 800-321-6000 ■ Web: www.hamiltonparkhotel.com					
Hickory Ridge Marriott Conference Hotel 1195 Summerhill Dr	Lisle	IL	60532	630-971-5000	971-6956
TF: 800-334-0344 ■ Web: www.marriott.com					
Hilton Scranton & Conference Ctr 100 Adams Ave	Scranton	PA	18503	570-343-3000	343-8415
TF: 800-445-8667 ■ Web: www.hilton.com					
Hilton University of Florida Conference Ctr 1714 SW 34th St	Gainesville	FL	32607	352-371-3600	371-0306
TF: 800-774-1500 ■ Web: www1.hilton.com					
Hotel at Auburn University & Dixon Conference Ctr The 241 S College St	Auburn	AL	36830	334-821-8200	826-8746
TF: 800-228-2876 ■ Web: www.auhcc.com					
Hotel Roanoke & Conference Ctr 110 Shenandoah Ave	Roanoke	VA	24016	540-985-5900	853-8264
TF: 866-594-4722 ■ Web: www.hotelroanoke.com					
IBM Palisades Conference Ctr 334 Rt 9 W	Palisades	NY	10964	845-732-6000	732-6175
TF: 800-426-0889 ■ Web: www.dolce-ibm-palisades.com					
Inn at Aspen 38750 Hwy 82	Aspen	CO	81611	970-925-1500	925-9037
TF: 800-952-1515					
Inn at Virginia Tech & Skelton Conference Ctr 901 Prices Fork Rd MS 0104	Blacksburg	VA	24061	540-231-8000	231-0146
TF: 877-200-3360 ■ Web: www.innatvirginiatech.com					
InterContinental Hotel Cleveland 9801 Carnegie Ave	Cleveland	OH	44106	216-707-4100	707-4101
TF: 877-707-8999 ■ Web: www.ichotelsgroup.com/intercontinental/en/gb/locations/overview/cleveland					
James L Allen Ctr 2169 Campus Dr	Evanston	IL	60208	847-864-9270	491-4323
John Hancock Hotel & Conference Ctr 40 Trinity Pl	Boston	MA	02116	617-933-7700	933-7709
Web: www.jhcenter.com					
Kingbridge Centre The 12750 Jane St	King City	ON	L7B1A3	905-833-3086	833-3075
TF: 800-827-7221 ■ Web: www.kingbridgecentre.com					
Kingsgate Marriott Conference Center at the University of Cincinnati 151 Goodman St	Cincinnati	OH	45219	513-487-3800	487-3810
TF: 800-228-9290 ■ Web: www.marriott.com/hotels/travel/cvgkg					
Lakeway Inn & Resort 101 Lakeway Dr	Austin	TX	78734	512-261-6600	261-7311
TF: 800-525-3929 ■ Web: www.lakewayresortandspa.com					
Lodge & Spa at Breckenridge 112 Overlook Dr	Breckenridge	CO	80424	970-453-9300	453-0625
TF: 800-736-1607 ■ Web: www.thelodgeatbreck.com					
Marietta Conference Center & Resort 500 Powder Springs St	Marietta	GA	30064	770-427-2500	819-3224*
*Fax Area Code: 678 ■ TF: 888-685-2500 ■ Web: www1.hilton.com					
Marriott Montgomery Prattville at Capitol Hill 2500 Legends Cir	Prattville	AL	36066	334-290-1235	290-2222
TF: 888-250-3767 ■ Web: www.marriott.com					
Millennium Broadway Hotel New York 145 W 44th St	New York	NY	10036	212-768-4400	768-0847
TF: 800-622-5569 ■ Web: www.millenniumhotels.com					
National Center for Employee Development (NCED) 2701 E Imhoff Rd	Norman	OK	73071	405-366-4420	366-4319
TF: 866-438-6233 ■ Web: www.nced.com					
NAV Canada Training & Conference Ctr 1950 Montreal Rd	Cornwall	ON	K6H6L2	613-563-3710	936-5157
TF: 877-832-6416 ■ Web: www.navcanada.ca					
New England Ctr 15 Strafford Ave University of New Hampshire	Durham	NH	03824	603-862-2801	862-0692
TF: 800-590-4334 ■ Web: www.newenglandcenter.com					
North Maple Inn at Basking Ridge 300 N Maple Ave	Basking Ridge	NJ	07920	908-953-3000	953-3100
TF: 866-775-0277 ■ Web: www.dolce-basking-ridge-hotel.com					
Northland Inn & Executive Conference Ctr The 7025 Northland Dr	Minneapolis	MN	55428	763-536-8300	535-8221
TF: 800-441-6422 ■ Web: www.northlandinn.com					
Oak Brook Hills Marriott Resort 3500 Midwest Rd	Oak Brook	IL	60523	630-850-5555	850-5569
TF: 800-445-3315 ■ Web: www.marriott.com/property/propertypage/CHIMC					
Oak Ridge Conference Ctr 1 Oak Ridge Dr	Chaska	MN	55318	952-368-3100	368-1488
TF Sales: 800-737-9588 ■ Web: www.oakridgeconference.com					
Paul J Rizzo Conference Ctr Rizzo Conference Ctr 150 DuBose House Ln	Chapel Hill	NC	27517	919-913-2098	913-2099
Web: www.rizzoconferencecenter.com					
Penn Stater Conference Center Hotel 215 Innovation Blvd	State College	PA	16803	814-863-5000	863-5002
TF: 800-233-7505 ■ Web: www.pshs.psu.edu					
R David Thomas Executive Conference Ctr (RDTC) 1 Science Dr PO Box 90344	Durham	NC	27708	919-660-6400	660-3607
Web: www.fuqua.duke.edu/admin/rdtc					
Ramada Oasis Convention Ctr 2546 N Glenstone	Springfield	MO	65803	417-866-5253	866-5292
TF: 888-532-4338 ■ Web: www.ramadaoasis.com					
Renaissance Portsmouth Hotel & Waterfront Conference Ctr 425 Water St	Portsmouth	VA	23704	757-673-3000	673-3030
TF: 888-839-1775 ■ Web: www.renaissancenavigator.com/hotels/navigator/orfpt					
Renaissance Tulsa Hotel & Convention Ctr 6808 S 107th E Ave	Tulsa	OK	74133	918-307-2600	307-2907
Web: www.renaissancehotel.com					
San Ramon Valley Conference Ctr 3301 Crow Canyon Rd	San Ramon	CA	94583	925-866-7500	866-7378
TF: 800-521-4335 ■ Web: www.sanramonvalleyconferencecenter.com					
Saratoga Hilton 534 Broadway	Saratoga Springs	NY	12866	518-584-4000	584-7430
TF: 866-773-7070 ■ Web: www.hilton.com					
Scottsdale Resort & Conference Ctr 7700 E McCormick Pkwy	Scottsdale	AZ	85258	480-991-9000	596-7428
TF: 800-528-0293 ■ Web: www.scottsdale-resort.com					
Skamania Lodge 1131 SW Skamania Lodge Way PO Box 189	Stevenson	WA	98648	509-427-7700	427-2547
TF: 800-221-7117 ■ Web: www.skamania.com					
Spencer Conference Centre 551 Windermere Rd	London	ON	N5X2T1	519-679-4546	645-0733
TF: 800-983-6523 ■ Web: www.dolce-spencer-leadership-centre-hotel.com					
Talaris Conference Ctr 4000 NE 41st St	Seattle	WA	98105	206-268-7000	268-7001
Web: www.talarisconferencecenter.com					
University Inn & Conference Ctr 2402 N Forest Rd	Amherst	NY	14226	716-636-7500	636-8296
TF: 800-537-8483 ■ Web: www.universityinn.com					
University of Maryland University College Marriott Conference Center Hotel 3501 University Blvd E	Adelphi	MD	20783	301-985-7303	985-7517
TF: 800-727-8622 ■ Web: www.marriott.com					
University Place Conference Center & Hotel-Indianapolis 850 W Michigan St	Indianapolis	IN	46202	317-269-9000	231-5168
TF: 800-627-2700 ■ Web: www.universityplace.iupui.edu					
University Plaza Hotel & Convention Ctr 333 John Q Hammons Pkwy	Springfield	MO	65806	417-864-7333	831-5893
TF: 800-465-4329 ■ Web: www.upspringfield.com					
Valley Forge Scanticon Hotel & Conference Ctr 1210 First Ave	King of Prussia	PA	19406	610-265-1500	768-0183
TF: 800-333-3333 ■ Web: www.scanticonvalleyforge.com					
Whispering Woods Hotel & Conference Ctr 11200 Goodman Rd	Olive Branch	MS	38654	662-895-2941	895-1590
Web: www.wwconferencecenter.com					
White Oaks Conference Resort & Spa 253 Taylor Rd SS4	Niagara-on-the-Lake	ON	L0S1J0	905-688-2550	688-2220
TF Resv: 800-263-5766 ■ Web: www.whiteoaksresort.com					
Woodlands Resort & Conference Ctr The 2301 N Millbend Dr	The Woodlands	TX	77380	281-367-1100	364-6275
TF Resv: 800-433-2624 ■ Web: www.woodlandsresort.com					
Wyndham Peachtree Conference Ctr 2443 Hwy 54 W	Peachtree City	GA	30269	770-487-2000	487-4428
TF: 800-996-3426 ■ Web: www.wyndham.com					
Chaminade 1 Chaminade Ln	Santa Cruz	CA	95065	831-475-5600	476-4798
TF: 800-283-6569 ■ Web: www.chaminade.com					
Resort at Squaw Creek 400 Squaw Creek Rd PO Box 3333	Olympic Valley	CA	96146	530-583-6300	581-6632
TF: 800-327-3353 ■ Web: www.squawcreek.com					
Heritage Hotel 522 Heritage Rd	Southbury	CT	06488	203-264-8200	264-5035
TF: 800-932-3466 ■ Web: www.heritagesouthbury.com					
Chateau Elan Resort & Conference Ctr 100 Rue Charlemagne	Braselton	GA	30517	678-425-0900	425-6000
TF: 800-233-9463 ■ Web: www.chateauelan.com					
Crystal Mountain Resort 12500 Crystal Mountain Dr	Thompsonville	MI	49683	231-378-2000	378-2998
TF: 800-968-7686 ■ Web: www.crystalmountain.com					
Doral Arrowwood Conference Resort 975 Anderson Hill Rd	Rye Brook	NY	10573	914-939-5500	323-5500
TF: 800-223-6725 ■ Web: www.arrowwood.com					
Hidden Valley Resort & Conference Ctr 1 Craighead Dr PO Box 4420	Hidden Valley	PA	15502	814-443-8000	443-1907
TF: 800-458-0175 ■ Web: www.hiddenvalleyresort.com					
Snowbird Ski & Summer Resort Hwy 210 PO Box 929000	Snowbird	UT	84092	801-742-2222	947-8227
TF: 800-453-3000 ■ Web: www.snowbird.com					
Stoweflake Mountain Resort & Spa 1746 Mountain Rd PO Box 369	Stowe	VT	05672	802-253-7355	253-6858
TF: 800-253-2232 ■ Web: www.stoweflake.com					
Kingsmill Resort & Spa 1010 Kingsmill Rd	Williamsburg	VA	23185	757-253-1703	253-8246
TF: 800-832-5665 ■ Web: www.kingsmill.com					
Lansdowne Resort 44050 Woodridge Pkwy	Leesburg	VA	20176	703-729-8400	729-4096
TF: 800-541-4801 ■ Web: www.lansdowneresort.com					
Lakeview Golf Resort &Spa 1 Lakeview Dr	Morgantown	WV	26508	304-594-1111	594-9472
TF: 800-624-8300 ■ Web: www.lakeviewresort.com					

381 HOTELS - FREQUENT STAY PROGRAMS

				Phone	Fax
AmericaÆs Best Inns & Suites 50 Glenlake Pkwy Suite 350	Atlanta	GA	30328	770-393-2662	
TF: 800-237-8466 ■ Web: www.americasbestinns.com					
AmericInn Inn-Pressive Club 250 Lake Dr E	Chanhassen	MN	55317	952-294-5000	294-5001
TF: 800-634-3444 ■ Web: www.americinn.com					

Phone | Fax

Baymont Guest Ovations Program
100 E Wisconsin Ave .... Milwaukee WI 53202 414-905-2000 905-2957
TF: 866-464-2321 ■ *Web:* www.baymontinns.com
CHIP Hospitality Traveller's Reward Program
1600-1030 W Georgia St .... Vancouver BC V6E2Y3 604-646-2447 689-8167
TF: 800-431-0070
ClubHouse Rewards Program
3211 W Sencore Dr .... Sioux Falls SD 57107 605-361-4395 334-8480
Web: www.clubhouseinn.com
Concorde Hotels International Prestige Card
1 Penn Plaza Suite 2127 .... New York NY 10119 212-935-1045 752-8916
TF: 800-888-4747 ■ *Web:* www.concorde-hotels.com
Country Hearth Inn Country Club
4243 Don Woody Club Dr Suite 200 .... Atlanta GA 30350 770-393-2662
TF: 888-635-2582 ■ *Web:* www.countryhearth.com/countryclub
Delta Hotels Privilege Program
1133 Regent St Suite 109 .... Fredericton NB E3B3Z2 416-874-2000 874-2001
TF: 888-321-3358 ■ *Web:* www.deltahotels.com/privilege
Drury Inns Gold Key Club PO Box 910 .... Cape Girardeau MO 63702 800-325-0581 334-6440*
**Fax Area Code:* 573 ■ *TF:* 800-325-0581 ■ *Web:* www.drurygoldkey.com
Fairmont President's Club
650 California St 12th Fl .... San Francisco CA 94108 415-772-7800 772-7805
TF: 800-663-7575 ■ *Web:* www.fpcnews.com
Homestead Studio Suites Hotels SuiteOffers Program
100 Dunbar St .... Spartanburg SC 29306 864-573-1600 980-2311*
**Fax Area Code:* 770 ■ *Web:* www.homesteadhotels.com
Hospitality International INNcentive Card Program
1726 Montreal Cir .... Tucker GA 30084 800-247-4677 270-1077*
**Fax Area Code:* 770 ■ *TF:* 800-247-4677 ■ *Web:* www.bookroomsnow.com/inncentive.asp
Hyatt Gold Passport Program
9805 Q St PO Box 27089 .... Omaha NE 68127 800-544-9288 593-4030*
**Fax Area Code:* 402 ■ *TF:* 800-522-1100 ■ *Web:* www.goldpassport.com
La Quinta Returns Club PO Box 2636 .... San Antonio TX 78299 800-642-4258 616-7616*
**Fax Area Code:* 210 ■ *TF:* 800-642-4258 ■ *Web:* www.lq.com
Leaders Club Services
Leading Hotels of the World 99 Pk Ave .... New York NY 10016 212-515-5600 515-5770
TF Resv: 800-223-6800 ■ *Web:* www.lhw.com/leaders_club
Lees Elite Club 130 N State St .... North Vernon IN 47265 812-346-5072 346-7521
TF: 800-733-5337 ■ *Web:* www.leesinn.com
Marriott Hotels Rewards Program
310 Bearcat Dr .... Salt Lake City UT 84115 800-249-0800 468-4033*
**Fax Area Code:* 801 ■ *TF Sales:* 800-450-4442 ■ *Web:* www.marriott.com/rewards
Masters Inn Preferred Guest Program
4200 Hwy 21 N .... Garden City GA 31408 912-964-4344 964-4144
TF: 800-358-6122 ■ *Web:* www.mastersinn.com
Omni Hotels Select Guest Loyalty Program
11819 Miami St 3rd Fl .... Omaha NE 68164 800-367-6664
TF Cust Svc: 877-440-6664 ■ *Web:* www.omnihotels.com/SelectGuestProgram.aspx
Prince Preferred Guest Program
100 Holomoana St .... Honolulu HI 96815 800-774-6234 943-4158*
**Fax Area Code:* 808 ■ *TF:* 800-774-6234 ■ *Web:* www.princepreferred.com
Priority Club Rewards PO Box 30320 .... Salt Lake City UT 84130 800-272-9273 725-8232
TF: 888-211-9874 ■ *Web:* www.ichotelsgroup.com
Sandals Life Style 4950 SW 72nd Ave .... Miami FL 33155 305-284-1300 667-8996
TF: 888-726-3257 ■ *Web:* www.sandals.com/ssg/index.cfm
Starwood Hotels Preferred Guest Program
111 Westchester Ave .... White Plains NY 10604 512-834-2426 834-0656
TF: 888-625-4988 ■ *Web:* www.starwoodhotels.com
TripRewards PO Box 4888 .... Aberdeen SD 57402 866-996-7937 306-0671*
**Fax Area Code:* 800 ■ *TF:* 866-996-7937
Wyndham ByRequest Program 2001 Bryan St .... Dallas TX 75201 214-863-1000 863-1342
TF: 800-347-7559 ■ *Web:* www.wyndham.com

382 HOTELS & HOTEL COMPANIES

SEE ALSO Casino Companies p. 1557; Corporate Housing p. 1764; Hotel Reservations Services p. 2078; Hotels - Conference Center p. 2079; Hotels - Frequent Stay Programs p. 2080; Resorts & Resort Companies p. 2542

Phone | Fax

1859 Historic Hotels Ltd PO Box 59 .... Galveston TX 77553 409-763-8536 763-5304
Web: www.1859historichotels.com
1886 Crescent Hotel & Spa
75 Prospect Ave .... Eureka Springs AR 72632 479-253-9766 253-5296
TF: 877-342-9766 ■ *Web:* www.crescent-hotel.com
21c Museum Hotel 700 W Main St .... Louisville KY 40202 502-217-6300 217-6400
TF: 877-217-6400 ■ *Web:* www.21chotel.com
5 Calgary Downtown Suites Hotel
618 5th Ave SW .... Calgary AB T2P0M7 403-263-0520 298-4888
TF: 877-890-7666 ■ *Web:* www.5calgary.com
500 West Hotel 500 W Broadway .... San Diego CA 92101 619-234-5252 234-5272
TF: 866-500-7533 ■ *Web:* www.500westhotelsd.com
70 Park Avenue Hotel 70 Pk Ave at 38th St .... New York NY 10016 212-973-2400 973-2401
TF: 877-707-2752 ■ *Web:* www.70parkave.com
Abraham Lincoln the - A Wyndham Historic Hotel
100 N 5th St .... Reading PA 19601 610-372-3700 372-2966
TF: 877-999-3223
Acadia Inn 98 Eden St .... Bar Harbor ME 04609 207-288-3500 288-8428
TF: 800-638-3636 ■ *Web:* www.acadiainn.com
Acapulco Hotel & Resort
2505 S Atlantic Ave .... Dayton Beach Shores FL 32118 386-761-2210 761-2216
TF: 800-245-3580 ■ *Web:* www.daytonahotels.com/Acapulco/index.php
Accent Inns Vancouver Airport
10551 St Edwards Dr .... Richmond BC V6X3L8 604-273-3311 273-9522
TF: 800-663-0298 ■ *Web:* www.accentinns.com/locations/airport.htm
Accent Inns Vancouver-Burnaby
3777 Henning Dr .... Burnaby BC V5C6N5 604-473-5000 473-5095
TF: 800-663-0298 ■ *Web:* www.accentinns.com/locations/burnaby.htm

Phone | Fax

Accor North America
4001 International Pkwy .... Carrollton TX 75007 972-360-9000 360-5821
TF: 800-557-3435 ■ *Web:* www.accor-na.com
Accor North America Business & Leisure Div
Novotel 4001 International Pkwy .... Carrollton TX 75007 972-360-9000 360-2821
Web: www.accor-na.com/accor/abl.asp
Sofitel 4001 International Pkwy .... Carrollton TX 75007 972-360-9000 360-2821
Web: www.accor-na.com/accor/abl.asp
Accor North America Economy Lodging Div
Motel 6 4001 International Pkwy .... Carrollton TX 75007 972-360-9000 360-2821
TF: 800-466-8356 ■ *Web:* www.motel6.com
Red Roof Inn 4001 International Pkwy .... Carrollton TX 75007 972-360-9000 360-2821
TF: 800-733-7663 ■ *Web:* www.redroof.com
Studio 6 4001 International Pkwy .... Carrollton TX 75007 972-360-9000 360-2821
TF: 800-466-8356 ■ *Web:* www.staystudio6.com
Acqua Hotel 555 Redwood Hwy .... Mill Valley CA 94941 415-380-0400 380-9696
TF: 800-662-9555 ■ *Web:* www.marinhotels.com
Acqualina 17875 Collins Ave .... Sunny Isles Beach FL 33160 305-918-8000 918-8100
Web: www.acqualinaresort.com
Adam's Mark Hotels & Resorts
11330 Olive Blvd .... Saint Louis MO 63141 314-567-9000 567-3186
Web: www.adamsmark.com
Adams Oceanfront Resort 4 Read St .... Dewey Beach DE 19971 302-227-3030 227-1034
TF: 800-448-8080 ■ *Web:* www.adamsoceanfront.com
Admiral Fell Inn
888 S Broadway Historic Fell's Pt .... Baltimore MD 21231 410-522-7377 522-0707
TF: 866-583-4162 ■ *Web:* www.admiralfell.com
Admiral Hotel 2 Baltimore Ave .... Rehoboth Beach DE 19971 302-227-2103 227-3620
TF: 888-882-4188 ■ *Web:* www.admiralrehoboth.com
Adolphus The 1321 Commerce St .... Dallas TX 75202 214-742-8200 651-3588
TF: 800-221-9083 ■ *Web:* www.hoteladolphus.com
Adventureland Inn I-80 & Hwy 65 .... Des Moines IA 50316 515-265-7321 265-3506
TF: 800-910-5382 ■ *Web:* www.adventurelandpark.com
Affina Dumont 150 E 34th St .... New York NY 10016 212-481-7600 889-8856
TF: 866-233-4642 ■ *Web:* www.affinia.com
Affinia 50 155 E 50th St .... New York NY 10022 212-751-5710 753-1468
TF: 866-246-2203 ■ *Web:* www.affinia.com
Affinia Chicago 166 E Superior St .... Chicago IL 60611 312-787-6000 787-6133
TF: 866-246-2203 ■ *Web:* www.affinia.com
Affinia Gardens 215 E 64th St .... New York NY 10065 212-355-1230 758-7858
TF: 800-637-8483 ■ *Web:* www.affinia.com
Affinia Manhattan 371 7th Ave .... New York NY 10001 212-563-1800 643-8028
TF: 866-246-2203 ■ *Web:* www.affinia.com
Airport Regency Hotel 1000 NW Lejeune Rd .... Miami FL 33126 305-441-1600 443-0766
TF: 800-367-1039 ■ *Web:* www.airportregencyhotel.com
Airport Settle Inn 2620 S Packerland Dr .... Green Bay WI 54313 920-499-1900 499-1973
TF: 800-688-9052 ■ *Web:* www.settle-inn.com
Airtel Plaza Hotel 7277 Valjean Ave .... Van Nuys CA 91406 818-997-7676 785-8864
TF: 800-224-7835 ■ *Web:* www.airtelplaza.com
Ala Moana Hotel 410 Atkinson Dr .... Honolulu HI 96814 808-955-4811 944-6839
TF: 800-367-6025 ■
Web: www.outrigger.com/hotels-resorts/hawaiian-islands/oahu-waikiki/ala-moana-hotel
Alamo Inn 2203 E Commerce St .... San Antonio TX 78203 210-227-2203 222-2860
TF: 888-222-7666 ■ *Web:* www.alamoinnsa.com
Albert at Bay Suite Hotel 435 Albert St .... Ottawa ON K1R7X4 613-238-8858 238-1433
TF: 800-267-6644 ■ *Web:* www.albertatbay.com
Alberta Place Suite Hotel 10049 103rd St .... Edmonton AB T5J2W7 780-423-1565 426-6260
TF Cust Svc: 800-661-3982 ■ *Web:* www.albertaplace.com
Albion Hotel 1650 James Ave .... Miami Beach FL 33139 305-913-1000 674-0507
TF General: 888-665-0008 ■ *Web:* www.rubellhotels.com
Alex The 205 E 45th St .... New York NY 10017 212-867-5100 867-7878
Web: www.thealexhotel.com
Alexander Hotel 5225 Collins Ave .... Miami Beach FL 33140 305-865-6500 341-6555
TF: 800-327-6121 ■ *Web:* www.alexanderhotel.com
Alexander Palms Court 715 S St .... Key West FL 33040 305-296-6413 292-3975
TF: 800-858-1943 ■ *Web:* www.alexanderpalms.com
Alexis Hotel 1007 1st Ave .... Seattle WA 98104 206-624-4844 621-9009
TF: 800-264-8482 ■ *Web:* www.alexishotel.com
Algonquin Hotel 59 W 44th St .... New York NY 10036 212-840-6800 944-1419
Web: www.thealgonquin.net
All Seasons Motor Inn 1199 Main St .... South Yarmouth MA 02664 508-394-7600 398-7160
TF: 800-527-0359 ■ *Web:* www.allseasons.com
Alpenhof Lodge
3255 W Village Dr PO Box 288 .... Teton Village WY 83025 307-733-3242 739-1516
TF: 800-732-3244 ■ *Web:* www.alpenhoflodge.com
ALT Hotel 1200 Germain-des-Pres Ave .... Sainte-Foy QC G1V3M7 418-658-1224 658-8846
TF: 800-463-5253 ■ *Web:* www.quebec.althotels.ca/en
Alta Peruvian Lodge PO Box 8017 .... Alta UT 84092 801-742-3000 742-3007
TF: 800-453-8488 ■ *Web:* www.altaperuvian.com
Alta Vista Hotel & Conference Ctr
260 Goodwin Crest Dr .... Birmingham AL 35209 205-290-8000 290-8001
TF: 888-290-8099 ■ *Web:* www.altavistahotel.com
Amalfi Hotel Chicago 20 W Kinzie St .... Chicago IL 60610 312-395-9000 395-9001
TF: 877-262-5341 ■ *Web:* www.amalfihotelchicago.com
Amarillo Ritz Plaza Hotel 7909 I-40 E .... Amarillo TX 79118 806-373-3303 373-3353
TF: 800-274-5315 ■ *Web:* www.ritzcarlton.com
Ambassador Hotel 3100 I-40 W .... Amarillo TX 79102 806-358-6161 358-9869
TF: 800-817-0521 ■ *Web:* www.ambassadoramarillo.com
Ambassador Hotel 2308 W Wisconsin Ave .... Milwaukee WI 53233 414-342-8400 345-5001
Web: www.ambassadormilwaukee.com
Ambassador Hotel 535 Tchoupitoulas St .... New Orleans LA 70130 504-527-5271 599-2107
TF: 800-455-3417 ■ *Web:* www.neworleansboutiquehotels.com
Ambrosia House Tropical Lodging
622 Fleming St .... Key West FL 33040 305-296-9838 296-2425
TF: 800-535-9838 ■ *Web:* www.ambrosiakeywest.com
America's Best Franchising Inc
50 Glen Lake Pkwy NE Suite 350 .... Atlanta GA 30328 770-393-2662 393-2480
TF: 800-432-7992 ■ *Web:* www.buckheadamerica.com

			Phone	Fax
America's Best Inns & Suites 50 Glen Lake Pkwy NE Suite 350 .... Atlanta *TF:* 800-432-7992 ■ *Web:* www.americasbestinns.com	GA	30328	770-393-2662	393-2480
Country Hearth Inn & Suites 50 Glenlake Pkwy # 350 .... Atlanta *TF:* 800-432-7992 ■ *Web:* www.countryhearth.com	GA	30328	770-393-2662	393-2480
Americas Best Value & Suites Cypress Tree Inn 2227 N Fremont St .... Monterey *TF:* 800-446-8303 ■ *Web:* www.cypresstreeinn.com	CA	93940	831-372-7586	372-2940
AmericInn International LLC 250 Lake Dr E .... Chanhassen *TF Resv:* 800-396-5007 ■ *Web:* www.americinn.com	MN	55317	952-294-5000	294-5001
Ameristar Casino & Hotel 3200 N Ameristar Dr .... Kansas City **Fax:* Mktg ■ *TF:* 800-499-4961 ■ *Web:* www.ameristar.com	MO	64161	816-414-7000	414-7221*
Ameritel Inn Boise Towne Square 7965 W Emerald St .... Boise *TF:* 800-600-6001 ■ *Web:* www.ameritelinns.com	ID	83704	208-378-7000	378-7040
Ameritel Inn Pocatello 1440 Pocatello Bench Rd .... Pocatello *TF:* 800-600-6001 ■ *Web:* www.ameritelinns.com	ID	83201	208-234-7500	234-0000
Amsterdam Court Hotel 226 W 50th St .... New York *TF:* 888-664-6835 ■ *Web:* www.nychotels.com	NY	10019	212-459-1000	262-4170
Amway Grand Plaza Hotel 187 Monroe Ave NW .... Grand Rapids *TF:* 800-253-3590 ■ *Web:* www.amwaygrand.com	MI	49503	616-774-2000	776-6489
Anaheim Plaza Hotel & Suites 1700 S Harbor Blvd .... Anaheim *TF:* 800-631-4144 ■ *Web:* www.anaheimplazahotel.com	CA	92802	714-772-5900	772-8386
Anastasia Inn 218 Anastasia Blvd .... Saint Augustine *TF:* 888-226-6181 ■ *Web:* www.anastasiainn.com	FL	32080	904-825-2879	825-2724
Anchor-In 1 S St .... Hyannis *Web:* www.anchorin.com	MA	02601	508-775-0357	775-1313
Anchorage Inn 26 Vendue Range .... Charleston *TF:* 800-421-2952 ■ *Web:* www.anchoragencharleston.com	SC	29401	843-723-8300	723-9543
Anchorage Uptown Suites 234 E 2nd Ave .... Anchorage *TF:* 866-764-3460 ■ *Web:* www.anchorageuptownsuites.com	AK	99501	907-279-4232	279-4231
Andaluz 125 2nd St NW .... Albuquerque *TF:* 877-987-9090 ■ *Web:* www.hotelandaluz.com	NM	87102	505-242-9090	242-8664
Andaz San Diego 600 F St .... San Diego *TF:* 877-489-4489 ■ *Web:* sandiego.andaz.hyatt.com/hyatt/hotels/index.jsp?null	CA	92101	619-849-1234	531-7955
Andrews Hotel 624 Post St .... San Francisco *TF:* 800-926-3739 ■ *Web:* www.andrewshotel.com	CA	94109	415-563-6877	928-6919
Angler's Inn 265 N Millward .... Jackson *TF:* 800-867-4667 ■ *Web:* www.anglersinn.net	WY	83001	307-733-3682	733-8662
Ansonborough Inn 21 Hasell St .... Charleston *TF:* 800-522-2073 ■ *Web:* www.ansonboroughinn.com	SC	29401	843-723-1655	577-6888
Antler Inn 43 W Pearl St PO Box 575 .... Jackson *TF:* 800-483-8667 ■ *Web:* www.townsquareinns.com	WY	83001	307-733-2535	733-4158
Apollo Park Executive Suites 805 S Cir Dr Suite 2B .... Colorado Springs *TF:* 800-279-3620 ■ *Web:* www.apollopark.com	CO	80910	719-634-0286	635-1539
Apple Tree Inn 9508 N Division St .... Spokane *TF:* 800-323-5796 ■ *Web:* www.appletreeinnmotel.com	WA	99218	509-466-3020	467-4377
Applewood Manor Inn 62 Cumberland Cir .... Asheville *TF:* 800-442-2197 ■ *Web:* www.applewoodmanor.com	NC	28801	828-254-2244	254-0899
Aqua Bamboo 2425 Kuhio Ave .... Honolulu *TF:* 866-406-2782 ■ *Web:* www.aquaresorts.com	HI	96815	808-922-7777	922-9473
Aqua Coconut Plaza Hotel 450 Lewers St .... Honolulu *TF:* 877-997-6667 ■ *Web:* www.aquaresorts.com	HI	96815	808-923-8828	923-3473
Aqua Hotel & Lounge 1530 Collins Ave .... Miami Beach *Web:* www.aquamiami.com	FL	33139	305-538-4361	673-8109
Aqua Island Colony 445 Seaside Ave .... Honolulu *TF:* 800-367-5004 ■ *Web:* www.aquaresorts.com	HI	96815	808-923-2345	921-7105
Aqua Waikiki Wave 2299 Kuhio Ave .... Honolulu *TF:* 866-406-2782 ■ *Web:* www.aquaresorts.com	HI	96815	808-922-1262	922-5048
ARC the Hotel Ottawa 140 Slater St .... Ottawa *TF:* 800-699-2516 ■ *Web:* www.arcthehotel.com	ON	K1P5H6	613-238-2888	235-8421
Arena Hotel 817 The Alameda .... San Jose *TF:* 800-954-6835 ■ *Web:* www.pacifichotels.com	CA	95126	408-294-6500	294-6585
Argonaut Hotel 495 Jefferson St .... San Francisco *TF:* 866-415-0704 ■ *Web:* www.argonauthotel.com	CA	94109	415-563-0800	563-2800
Arizona Inn 2200 E Elm St .... Tucson *TF:* 800-933-1093 ■ *Web:* www.arizonainn.com	AZ	85719	520-325-1541	881-5830
Arosa Suites Hotel 163 McLaren St .... Ottawa *TF:* 866-238-6783 ■ *Web:* www.arosaresidences.com	ON	K2P2G4	613-238-6783	238-5080
Ascot Inn 1025 S Tryon St .... Charlotte *TF:* 800-333-9417 ■ *Web:* www.boonelodging.com/ascot.html	NC	28203	704-377-3611	
Ashland Springs Hotel 212 E Main St .... Ashland *TF:* 888-795-4545 ■ *Web:* www.ashlandspringshotel.com	OR	97520	541-488-1700	488-0240
Ashmore Inn & Suites 4019 S Loop 289 .... Lubbock *TF:* 800-785-0061 ■ *Web:* www.ashmoreinn.com	TX	79423	806-785-0060	785-6001
Ashton Hotel 610 Main St .... Fort Worth *Web:* www.slh.com	TX	76102	817-332-0100	332-0110
Assiniboine Gordon Inn on the Park 1975 Portage Ave .... Winnipeg *Web:* www.gordonhotels.com/assiniboine.htm	MB	R3J0J9	204-888-4806	897-9870
Associated Hotels LLC 29 S La Salle St Suite 705 .... Chicago *Web:* www.associatedhotelsllc.com	IL	60603	312-782-6008	782-2356
Asticou Inn 15 Peabody Dr .... Northeast Harbor *TF:* 800-258-3373 ■ *Web:* www.asticou.com	ME	04662	207-276-3344	276-3373
Aston Hotels & Resorts 2155 Kalakaua Ave Suite 500 .... Honolulu *TF:* 800-775-4228 ■ *Web:* www.resortquesthawaii.com	HI	96815	808-931-1400	931-1414
Astor Crowne Plaza 739 Canal St .... New Orleans *TF:* 888-696-4806 ■ *Web:* www.astorneworleans.com	LA	70130	504-962-0500	962-0503
Astor Hotel The 924 E Juneau Ave .... Milwaukee *TF:* 800-558-0200 ■ *Web:* www.theastorhotel.com	WI	53202	414-271-4220	271-6370
Atheneum Suite Hotel & Conference Ctr 1000 Brush Ave .... Detroit *TF:* 800-772-2323 ■ *Web:* www.atheneumsuites.com	MI	48226	313-962-2323	962-2424
Atlantic Eyrie Lodge 6 Norman Rd .... Bar Harbor *TF:* 800-422-2883 ■ *Web:* www.atlanticeyrielodge.com	ME	04609	207-288-9786	288-8500
Atlantic Palace Suites Hotel 1507 Boardwalk .... Atlantic City *TF:* 800-527-8483 ■ *Web:* www.atlanticpalacesuites.com	NJ	08401	609-344-1200	345-0673
Atlantic Sands Hotel 101 N Boardwalk .... Rehoboth Beach *TF:* 800-422-0600 ■ *Web:* www.atlanticsandshotel.com	DE	19971	302-227-2511	227-9476
Atlantic The 601 N Fort Lauderdale Beach Blvd .... Fort Lauderdale *TF:* 877-567-8020 ■ *Web:* www.atlantichotelfl.com	FL	33304	954-567-8020	567-8040
Atrium Hotel 18700 MacArthur Blvd .... Irvine *TF:* 800-854-3012 ■ *Web:* www.atriumhotel.com	CA	92612	949-833-2770	757-1228
Auberge du Soleil 180 Rutherford Hill Rd .... Rutherford *TF:* 800-348-5406 ■ *Web:* www.aubergedusoleil.com	CA	94573	707-963-1211	963-8764
Auberge du Vieux-Port 97 de la Commune E .... Montreal *TF:* 888-660-7678 ■ *Web:* www.aubergeduvieuxport.com	QC	H2Y1J1	514-876-0081	876-8923
Auberge Saint-Antoine 8 St Antoine St .... Quebec *TF:* 888-692-2211 ■ *Web:* www.saint-antoine.com	QC	G1K4C9	418-692-2211	692-1177
Aurora Inn 51 Holland Ave .... Bar Harbor *TF:* 800-841-8925 ■ *Web:* www.aurorainn.com	ME	04609	207-288-3771	
Austin Hotel & Spa 305 Malvern Ave .... Hot Springs *TF:* 877-623-6697 ■ *Web:* www.theaustinhotel.com	AR	71901	501-623-6600	624-7160
Avalon Beverly Hills 9400 W Olympic Blvd .... Beverly Hills *TF:* 800-670-6183 ■ *Web:* www.avalonbeverlyhills.com	CA	90212	310-277-5221	277-4928
Avalon Corporate Furnished Apartments 1553 Empire Blvd .... Webster *TF:* 800-934-9763 ■ *Web:* www.rochesterfurnished.com	NY	14580	585-671-4421	671-9771
Avalon Hotel 16 W 10th St .... Erie *TF:* 800-822-5011 ■ *Web:* www.avalonerie.com	PA	16501	814-459-2220	459-2322
Avalon Hotel & Spa 4650 SW Macadam Ave .... Portland *TF:* 888-556-4402 ■ *Web:* www.avalonhotelandspa.com	OR	97239	503-802-5800	802-5820
Avalon Majestic 700 Ocean Dr .... Miami Beach *TF:* 800-933-3306 ■ *Web:* www.southbeachhotels.com	FL	33139	305-538-0133	534-0258
Avendra LLC 702 King Farm Blvd Suite 600 .... Rockville *Web:* www.avendra.com	MD	20850	301-825-0500	825-0497
Avenue Inn & Spa 33 Wilmington Ave .... Rehoboth Beach *TF:* 800-433-5870 ■ *Web:* www.avenueinn.com	DE	19971	302-226-2900	226-7549
Avenue Plaza Resort 2111 St Charles Ave .... New Orleans *TF:* 800-251-8736 ■ *Web:* www.avenueplazaresort.com	LA	70130	504-566-1212	525-6899
Bahama House 2001 S Atlantic Ave .... Daytona Beach Shores *TF:* 800-571-2001 ■ *Web:* www.daytonabahamahouse.com	FL	32118	386-248-2001	248-0991
Balance Rock Inn 21 Albert Meadow .... Bar Harbor *TF:* 800-753-0494 ■ *Web:* www.balancerockinn.com	ME	04609	207-288-2610	288-5534
Balboa Park Inn 3402 Pk Blvd .... San Diego *TF:* 800-938-8181 ■ *Web:* www.balboaparkinn.com	CA	92103	619-298-0823	294-8070
Balmoral Inn 120 Balmoral Ave .... Biloxi *TF:* 800-393-9131 ■ *Web:* www.balmoralinn.com	MS	39531	228-388-6776	388-5450
Bar Harbor Hotel-Bluenose Inn 90 Eden St .... Bar Harbor *TF:* 800-445-4077 ■ *Web:* www.bluenoseinn.com	ME	04609	207-288-3348	288-2183
Barcelo Crestline Corp 3950 University Dr Suite 301 .... Fairfax *Web:* www.barcelocrestline.com	VA	22030	571-529-6000	529-6050
Barclay Hotel 1348 Robson St .... Vancouver *Web:* www.barclayhotel.com	BC	V5E1C5	604-688-8850	688-2534
Barnstead Inn 349 Bonnet St .... Manchester Center *TF:* 800-331-1619 ■ *Web:* www.barnsteadinn.com	VT	05255	802-362-1619	362-0688
Baronne Plaza Hotel 201 Baronne St .... New Orleans *TF:* 888-756-0083 ■ *Web:* www.baronneplaza.com	LA	70112	504-522-0083	522-0053
Barrington Hotel & Suites 263 Shepherd of the Hills Expy .... Branson *TF:* 800-760-8866 ■ *Web:* www.barringtonhotel.com	MO	65616	417-334-8866	336-2585
Bavarian Inn PO Box 152 .... Custer *TF:* 800-657-4312 ■ *Web:* www.bavarianinnsd.com	SD	57730	605-673-2802	673-4777
Bay Club Hotel & Marina 2131 Shelter Island Dr .... San Diego *TF:* 800-672-0800 ■ *Web:* www.bayclubhotel.com	CA	92106	619-224-8888	225-1604
Bay Harbor Inn & Suites *Daddy O Miami* 9660 E Bay Harbor Dr .... Bay Harbor Island *Web:* www.daddyohotel.com/miami	FL	33154	305-868-4141	675-6488
Bay Park Hotel 1425 Munras Ave .... Monterey *TF Resv:* 800-338-3564 ■ *Web:* www.bayparkhotel.com	CA	93940	831-649-1020	373-4258
Bayfront Inn 138 Avenida Menendez .... Saint Augustine *TF:* 800-558-3455 ■ *Web:* www.bayfrontinn.com	FL	32084	904-824-1681	829-8721
Bayfront Inn on Fifth 1221 5th Ave S .... Naples *TF:* 800-382-7941 ■ *Web:* www.bayfrontinnnaples.com	FL	34102	239-649-5800	649-0523
Baymont Inn Suites 5805 Pacific Hwy E .... Tacoma *TF:* 800-422-3051 ■ *Web:* www.baymottacoma.com	WA	98424	253-922-2500	922-6443
Beach Haven Inn 4740 Mission Blvd .... San Diego *TF:* 800-831-6323 ■ *Web:* www.beachhaveninn.com	CA	92109	858-272-3812	272-3532
Beach House Suites by the Don Cesar 3860 Gulf Blvd .... Saint Pete Beach *TF:* 800-282-1116 ■ *Web:* www.beachhousesuites.com	FL	33706	727-363-0001	363-5055
Beach Plaza Hotel 625 N Atlantic Blvd .... Fort Lauderdale *TF:* 800-451-4711 ■ *Web:* www.hotelbeachplaza.com	FL	33304	954-566-7631	537-9358
Beachcomber Hotel 1340 Collins Ave .... Miami Beach *Web:* www.beachcombermiami.com	FL	33139	305-531-3755	673-8609
Beacher's Lodge 6970 US Hwy A1A S .... Saint Augustine *TF:* 800-527-8849 ■ *Web:* www.beacherslodge.com	FL	32080	904-471-8849	471-3002
Beacon Hotel 720 Ocean Dr .... Miami Beach *TF:* 877-674-8200 ■ *Web:* www.beacon-hotel.com	FL	33139	305-674-8200	674-8976
Beacon Hotel & Corporate Quarters 1615 Rhode Island Ave NW .... Washington *TF:* 800-821-4367 ■ *Web:* www.capitalhotelswdc.com/BeaconHotelWDC_com	DC	20036	202-296-2100	331-0227
Beaver Creek Lodge 26 Avon Dale Ln .... Beaver Creek *TF:* 800-525-7280 ■ *Web:* www.beavercreeklodge.net	CO	81620	970-845-9800	845-8242
Beechwood Hotel 363 Plantation St .... Worcester *TF:* 800-344-2589 ■ *Web:* www.beechwoodhotel.com	MA	01605	508-754-5789	752-2060
Beekman Tower Hotel 3 Mitchell Pl .... New York *TF:* 866-298-4606 ■ *Web:* www.thebeekmanhotel.com	NY	10017	212-355-7300	753-9366

Phone Fax

Bel Age 1020 N San Vicente Blvd ... West Hollywood CA 90069 310-854-1111
TF: 866-282-4560 ■ *Web:* www.belagehotel.com
Belden-Stratford Hotel 2300 N Lincoln Pk W ... Chicago IL 60614 773-281-2900 880-2039
TF: 866-589-3411 ■ *Web:* www.beldenstratford.com
Bell Tower Hotel 300 S Thayer St ... Ann Arbor MI 48104 734-769-3010 769-4339
TF: 800-562-3559 ■ *Web:* www.belltowerhotel.com
Bell Tower Inn 1235 2nd St SW ... Rochester MN 55902 507-289-2233 289-2233
TF: 800-448-7583 ■ *Web:* www.rochesterlodging.com
Bellasera Hotel 221 9th St S ... Naples FL 34102 239-649-7333 649-6233
TF: 888-612-1115 ■ *Web:* www.bellaseranaples.com
Bellevue Club Hotel 11200 SE 6th St ... Bellevue WA 98004 425-454-4424 688-3101
TF: 800-579-1110 ■ *Web:* www.bellevueclub.com
Bellmoor The 6 Christian St ... Rehoboth Beach DE 19971 866-899-2779 227-0323*
*Fax Area Code: 302 ■ *TF:* 800-425-2355 ■ *Web:* www.thebellmoor.com
Belvedere Hotel 319 W 48th St ... New York NY 10036 212-245-7000 245-4455
TF: 888-468-3558 ■ *Web:* www.newyorkhotel.com
BEN LOMOND SUITES LLC 2510 Washington Blvd ... Ogden UT 84401 801-627-1900 394-5342
TF: 877-627-1900 ■ *Web:* www.benlomondsuites.com
Benchmark Hospitality International
4 Waterway Sq Suite 300 ... The Woodlands TX 77380 281-367-5757 367-1407
Web: www.benchmark-hospitality.com
Bendel Executive Suites 213 Bendel Rd ... Lafayette LA 70503 337-261-0604 233-4296
TF: 800-990-5708 ■ *Web:* www.bendelexec.com
Benjamin The 125 E 50th St ... New York NY 10022 212-715-2500 715-2525
TF: 866-233-4642 ■ *Web:* www.thebenjamin.com
Bennett Enterprises Inc PO Box 670 ... Perrysburg OH 43552 419-874-1933 874-0198
Web: www.bennett-enterprises.com
Benson The 309 SW Broadway ... Portland OR 97205 503-228-2000 471-3920
TF: 800-426-0670 ■ *Web:* www.bensonhotel.com
Bentley Beach Hotel 101 Ocean Dr ... Miami Beach FL 33139 305-938-4600 938-4601
TF: 866-236-8539 ■ *Web:* www.thebentleybeachhotel.com
Bentley Hotel 510 Ocean Dr ... Miami Beach FL 33139 305-538-1700 532-4865
TF: 866-236-8539 ■ *Web:* www.thebentleyhotel.com
Bentley Hotel New York 500 E 62nd St ... New York NY 10021 212-644-6000 207-4800
TF: 888-664-6235 ■ *Web:* www.hotelbentleynewyork.com
Berkeley Hotel The 1200 E Cary St ... Richmond VA 23219 804-780-1300 648-4728
TF: 888-780-4422 ■ *Web:* www.berkeleyhotel.com
Bernards Inn 27 Mine Brook Rd ... Bernardsville NJ 07924 908-766-0002 766-4604
TF: 888-766-0002 ■ *Web:* www.bernardsinn.com
Bernardus Lodge 415 Carmel Valley Rd ... Carmel Valley CA 93924 831-658-3400 659-8657
TF: 888-648-9463 ■ *Web:* www.bernardus.com
Best Rest Inn 1206 W 2100 S ... Ogden UT 84401 801-393-8644 399-0954
TF: 800-343-8644
Best Western Chincoteague Island
7105 Maddox Blvd ... Chincoteague Island VA 23336 757-336-6557 336-6558
TF: 800-553-6117 ■ *Web:* www.bestwestern.com
Best Western International Inc
6201 N 24th Pkwy ... Phoenix AZ 85016 602-957-4200 957-5942*
*Fax: Mktg ■ *TF:* 800-528-1234 ■ *Web:* www.bestwestern.com
Best Western Laguna Brisas Spa Hotel
1600 S Coast Hwy ... Laguna Beach CA 92651 949-497-7272 497-8306
TF: 877-503-1461 ■ *Web:* www.lagunabrisas.com
Best Western the Academy Hotel
8110 N Academy Blvd ... Colorado Springs CO 80920 719-598-5770 598-5965
TF: 800-766-8524 ■ *Web:* www.theacademyhotel.com
Best Western Victorian Inn 487 Foam St ... Monterey CA 93940 831-373-8000 655-8174
TF: 800-232-4141 ■ *Web:* www.victorianinn.com
Betsy Hotel 1440 Ocean Dr ... Miami Beach FL 33139 305-531-6100 531-9009
TF: 866-792-3879 ■ *Web:* www.thebetsyhotel.com
Beverly Garland Holiday Inn The
4222 Vineland Ave ... North Hollywood CA 91602 818-980-8000 766-0112
TF: 800-238-3759 ■ *Web:* www.beverlygarland.com
Beverly Heritage Hotel 1820 Barber Ln ... Milpitas CA 95035 408-943-9080 432-8617
TF: 800-443-4455 ■ *Web:* www.beverlyheritage.com
Beverly Hills Hotel 9641 Sunset Blvd ... Beverly Hills CA 90210 310-276-2251 887-2887
TF: 800-283-8885 ■ *Web:* www.thebeverlyhillshotel.com
Beverly Hilton 9876 Wilshire Blvd ... Beverly Hills CA 90210 310-274-7777 285-1313
TF: 800-445-8667 ■ *Web:* www.beverlyhilton.com
Beverly Wilshire - A Four Seasons Hotel
9500 Wilshire Blvd ... Beverly Hills CA 90212 310-275-5200 274-2851
TF: 800-545-4000 ■ *Web:* www.fourseasons.com/beverlywilshire
Bienville House Hotel 320 Decatur St ... New Orleans LA 70130 504-529-2345 525-6079
TF: 800-535-7836 ■ *Web:* www.bienvillehouse.com
Bill's Gamblin' Hall & Saloon
3595 S Las Vegas Blvd ... Las Vegas NV 89109 702-737-2100 894-9954
TF: 866-245-5748 ■ *Web:* www.billslasvegas.com
Billings C'mon Inn Hotel 2020 Overland Ave ... Billings MT 59102 406-655-1100 652-7672
TF: 800-655-1170 ■ *Web:* www.cmoninn.com
Billings Hotel & Convention Ctr
1223 Mullowney Ln ... Billings MT 59101 406-248-7151 259-5338
TF: 800-537-7286 ■ *Web:* www.billingshotel.net
Biltmore Greensboro Hotel
111 W Washington St ... Greensboro NC 27401 336-272-3474 275-2523
TF: 800-332-0303 ■ *Web:* www.biltmorehotelgreensboro.com
Biltmore Hotel & Suites
2151 Laurelwood Rd ... Santa Clara CA 95054 408-988-8411 988-0225
TF: 800-255-9925 ■ *Web:* www.hotelbiltmore.com
Biltmore Hotel Oklahoma
401 S Meridian Ave ... Oklahoma City OK 73108 405-947-7681 947-4253
TF: 800-522-6620 ■ *Web:* www.biltmoreokc.com
Biltmore Suites 205 W Madison St ... Baltimore MD 21201 410-728-6550 728-5829
TF: 800-868-5064 ■ *Web:* www.biltmoresuites.com
Black Swan Inn 746 E Ctr St ... Pocatello ID 83201 208-233-3051 478-8516
Web: www.blackswaninn.com
Blackfoot Inn 5940 Blackfoot Trail SE ... Calgary AB T2H2B5 403-252-2253 252-3574
TF: 800-661-1151 ■ *Web:* www.blackfootinn.com
Blackwell The 2110 Tuttle Pk Pl ... Columbus OH 43210 614-247-4000 247-4040
TF: 866-247-4003 ■ *Web:* www.theblackwell.com
Blakely New York 136 W 55th St ... New York NY 10019 212-245-1800 582-8332
TF: 800-735-0710 ■ *Web:* www.blakelynewyork.com
Blantyre 16 Blantyre Rd PO Box 995 ... Lenox MA 01240 413-637-3556 637-4282
Blondell Hotel & Antiques 1406 2nd St S W ... Rochester MN 55902 507-282-9444 282-8683
TF: 800-441-5209 ■ *Web:* www.blondell.com

Blue Horizon Hotel 1225 Robson St ... Vancouver BC V6E1C3 604-688-1411 688-4461
TF: 800-663-1333 ■ *Web:* www.bluehorizonhotel.com
Blue Moon Hotel 944 Collins Ave ... Miami Beach FL 33139 305-673-2262 534-1546
TF: 800-724-1623 ■ *Web:* www.bluemoonhotel.com
Blue Parrot Inn 916 Elizabeth St ... Key West FL 33040 305-296-0033 296-5697
TF: 800-231-2473 ■ *Web:* www.blueparrotinn.com
Bluenose Inn & Suites 636 Bedford Hwy ... Halifax NS B3M2L8 902-443-3171 443-9368
TF: 800-565-2301
Boardwalk Inn 5757 Palm Blvd ... Isle of Palms SC 29451 843-886-6000 886-2060
TF: 800-845-8880 ■ *Web:* www.wilddunes.com/accommodations.php
Boardwalk Plaza Hotel 2 Olive Ave ... Rehoboth Beach DE 19971 302-227-7169 227-0561
TF: 800-332-3224 ■ *Web:* www.boardwalkplaza.com
Bodega Bay Lodge 103 Coast Hwy 1 ... Bodega Bay CA 94923 707-875-3525 875-2428*
*Fax: Resv ■ *TF Resv:* 888-875-2250 ■ *Web:* www.bodegabaylodge.com
Bohemian Hotel Celebration 700 Bloom St ... Celebration FL 34747 407-566-6000 566-1844
TF: 888-249-4007 ■ *Web:* www.celebrationhotel.com
Bond Place Hotel 65 Dundas St E ... Toronto ON M5B2G8 416-362-6061 360-6406
TF: 800-268-9390
Boone Tavern Hotel of Berea College
100 S Main St ... Berea KY 40403 859-985-3700 985-3715
TF: 800-366-9358 ■ *Web:* www.boonetavernhotel.com
Borgata Hotel Casino & Spa
1 Borgata Way ... Atlantic City NJ 08401 609-317-1000 317-1035
TF: 866-692-6742 ■ *Web:* www.theborgata.com
Boston Harbor Hotel 70 Rowes Wharf ... Boston MA 02110 617-439-7000 330-9450
TF: 800-752-7077 ■ *Web:* www.bhh.com
Boston Park Plaza Hotel & Towers 50 Pk Plaza ... Boston MA 02116 617-426-2000 426-5545
TF: 800-225-2008 ■ *Web:* www.bostonparkplaza.com
Boulder Mountain Lodge
91 Four-Mile Canyon Rd ... Boulder CO 80302 303-444-0882 541-0665
TF: 800-458-0882 ■ *Web:* www.boulderguide.com/Lodge
Bourbon Orleans - A Wyndham Historic Hotel
717 Orleans St ... New Orleans LA 70116 504-523-2222 571-4666
TF: 866-527-1380 ■ *Web:* www.bourbonorleans.com
Bradley Boulder Inn 2040 16th St ... Boulder CO 80302 303-545-5200 440-6740
TF: 800-858-5811 ■ *Web:* www.thebradleyboulder.com
Bradley Inn 3063 Bristol Rd ... New Harbor ME 04554 207-677-2105 677-3367
TF: 800-942-5560 ■ *Web:* www.bradleyinn.com
Brandywine Suites Hotel 707 N King St ... Wilmington DE 19801 302-656-9300 656-2459
TF: 800-756-0070
Brazilian Court The 301 Australian Ave ... Palm Beach FL 33480 561-655-7740 655-0801
TF: 800-552-0335 ■ *Web:* www.thebraziliancourt.com
Breakers at Waikiki The 250 Beach Walk ... Waikiki HI 96815 808-923-3181 923-7174
TF: 800-426-0494 ■ *Web:* www.breakers-hawaii.com
Breakers Hotel & Suites 105 2nd St ... Rehoboth Beach DE 19971 302-227-6688 227-2013
TF: 800-441-8009 ■ *Web:* www.thebreakershotel.com
Breakwater Inn 1711 Glacier Ave ... Juneau AK 99801 907-586-6303 463-4820
TF: 800-544-2250 ■ *Web:* www.breakwaterinn.com
Breckinridge Inn 2800 Breckinridge Ln ... Louisville KY 40220 502-456-5050 451-1577
Web: www.breckinridgeinn.com
Brent House Hotel 1512 Jefferson Hwy ... New Orleans LA 70118 504-842-4140 842-4160
TF: 800-535-3986 ■ *Web:* www.brenthouse.com
Bridgewater Hotel 723 1st Ave ... Fairbanks AK 99701 907-452-6661 452-6126
TF: 800-528-4916 ■ *Web:* www.fountainheadhotels.com
Bristol Hotel 1055 1st Ave ... San Diego CA 92101 619-232-6141 232-0118
TF: 800-662-4477 ■ *Web:* www.bristolhotelsandiego.com
Broadway Inn 264 W 46th St ... New York NY 10036 212-997-9200 768-2807
TF: 800-826-6300 ■ *Web:* www.broadwayinn.com
Brookfield Suites Hotel & Convention Ctr
1200 S Moorland Rd ... Brookfield WI 53008 262-782-2900 796-9159
TF resv: 800-444-6404 ■ *Web:* www.brookfieldhotel.com
Brookshire Suites 120 E Lombard St ... Baltimore MD 21202 410-625-1300 625-0912
TF: 866-583-4162 ■ *Web:* www.brookshiresuites.com
Brookstown Inn 200 Brookstown Ave ... Winston-Salem NC 27101 336-725-1120 773-0147
TF: 800-845-4262 ■ *Web:* www.brookstowninn.com
Brookstreet Hotel 525 Legget Dr ... Ottawa ON K2K2W2 613-271-1800 271-1850
TF: 888-826-2220 ■ *Web:* www.brookstreethotel.com
Brown County Inn 51 State Rd 46 ... Nashville IN 47448 812-988-2291 988-8312
TF: 800-772-5249 ■ *Web:* www.browncountyinn.com
Brown Hotel The 335 W Broadway St ... Louisville KY 40202 502-583-1234 587-7006
TF: 888-387-0498 ■ *Web:* www.thebrownhotel.com
Brown Palace Hotel 321 17th St ... Denver CO 80202 303-297-3111 312-5900
TF: 800-321-2599 ■ *Web:* www.brownpalace.com
Brown's Wharf Inn 121 Atlantic Ave ... Boothbay Harbor ME 04538 207-633-5440 633-5440
TF: 800-334-8110 ■ *Web:* www.brownswharfinn.com
Bryant Park Hotel 40 W 40th St ... New York NY 10018 212-869-0100 869-4446
Web: www.bryantparkhotel.com
Buckingham Hotel 101 W 57th St ... New York NY 10019 212-246-1500 262-0698
TF: 866-589-3411
Buckrail Lodge 110 E Karns Ave PO Box 23 ... Jackson WY 83001 307-733-2079 734-1663
Web: www.buckraillodge.com
Budget Host International
2307 Roosevelt Dr ... Arlington TX 76016 817-861-6088 861-6089
Web: www.budgethost.com
Budget Suites of America
4640 S Eastern Ave ... Las Vegas NV 89119 702-456-1606 456-8647
Web: www.budgetsuites.com
Buena Vista Suites 8203 World Ctr Dr ... Orlando FL 32821 407-239-8588 239-1401
TF Resv: 800-537-7737 ■ *Web:* www.thecaribeorlando.com
Burlage Hotels Assoc LLC
809 Atlantic Ave ... Virginia Beach VA 23451 757-491-2700 428-3790
TF: 800-344-4473 ■ *Web:* www.vbhotels.com
Burnside Hotel 739 Windmill Rd ... Dartmouth NS B3B1C1 902-468-7117 468-1770
TF: 800-830-4656 ■ *Web:* www.burnsidehotel.ca
Burnsley Hotel 1000 Grant St ... Denver CO 80203 303-830-1000 830-7676
TF: 800-231-3915 ■ *Web:* www.burnsley.com
Business Inn 180 MacLaren St ... Ottawa ON K2P0L3 613-232-1121 232-8143
TF: 800-363-1777 ■ *Web:* www.thebusinessinn.com
C'mon Inn Grand Forks 3051 32nd Ave S ... Grand Forks ND 58201 701-775-3320 780-8141
TF: 800-255-2323 ■ *Web:* www.cmoninn.com

	City	State	Zip	Phone	Fax
Caesars Indiana Casino Hotel 11999 Avenue of the Emperors *TF:* 877-237-6626 ■ *Web:* www.harrahs.com	Elizabeth	IN	47117	812-969-6000	969-6632
Caesars Palace Las Vegas 3655 Las Vegas Blvd S *TF:* 877-796-2096 ■ *Web:* www.parislasvegas.com	Las Vegas	NV	89109	702-946-7000	866-1700
Camberley Hotel Co 4405 Northside Pkwy Suite 2124 *TF:* 800-555-8000 ■ *Web:* www.camberleyhotels.com	Atlanta	GA	30327	404-261-9600	261-4278
Cambridge Suites Hotel Halifax 1583 Brunswick St *TF:* 800-565-1263 ■ *Web:* www.cambridgesuiteshalifax.com	Halifax	NS	B3J3P5	902-420-0555	420-9379
Cambridge Suites Hotel Toronto 15 Richmond St E *TF:* 800-463-1990 ■ *Web:* www.cambridgesuitestoronto.com	Toronto	ON	M5C1N2	416-368-1990	601-3751
Camino Real El Paso 101 S El Paso St *TF:* 800-901-2300 ■ *Web:* www.caminoreal.com	El Paso	TX	79901	915-534-3000	534-3024
Campus Inn & Suites 390 E Broadway *TF:* 877-313-4137 ■ *Web:* www.campus-inn.com	Eugene	OR	97401	541-343-3376	485-9392
Canad Inns - Club Regent Casino Hotel 1415 Regent Ave W *TF:* 888-332-2623 ■ *Web:* www.canadinns.com	Winnipeg	MB	R2C3B2	204-667-5560	667-5913
Canad Inns Fort Garry 1824 Pembina Hwy *TF:* 888-332-2623 ■ *Web:* www.canadinns.com	Winnipeg	MB	R3C2G2	204-261-7450	261-5433
Canad Inns Garden City 2100 McPhillips St *TF:* 888-332-2623 ■ *Web:* www.canadinns.com	Winnipeg	MB	R2V3T9	204-633-0024	697-3377
Canad Inns Polo Park 1405 St Matthews Ave *TF:* 888-332-2623 ■ *Web:* www.canadinns.com	Winnipeg	MB	R3G0K5	204-775-8791	783-4039
Canal Park Lodge 250 Canal Pk Dr *TF:* 800-777-8560 ■ *Web:* www.canalparklodge.com	Duluth	MN	55802	218-279-6000	279-4055
Canandaigua Inn on the Lake 770 S Main St *TF:* 800-228-2801 ■ *Web:* www.theinnonthelake.com	Canandaigua	NY	14424	585-394-7800	394-5003
Cannery Casino & Hotel The *Cannery Casino Resorts LLC* 2121 E Craig Rd *TF:* 866-999-4899 ■ *Web:* www.cannerycasinos.com	North Las Vegas	NV	89030	702-507-5700	507-5750
Canoe Bay RR 2 PO Box 28 *Web:* www.canoebay.com	Chetek	WI	54728	715-924-4594	924-2078
Cape Cod Irish Village 512 Rt 28 *TF:* 800-244-9692 ■ *Web:* www.capecod-irishvillage.com	West Yarmouth	MA	02673	508-771-0100	
Cape Point Hotel Rte 28 *TF:* 800-323-9505 ■ *Web:* www.capepointhotel.com	West Yarmouth	MA	02673	508-778-1500	778-5516
Capital Hill Hotel & Suites 88 Albert St *TF:* 800-463-7705 ■ *Web:* www.capitalhill.com	Ottawa	ON	K1P5E9	613-235-1413	235-6047
Capital Hotel 111 W Markham St *TF:* 877-637-0037 ■ *Web:* www.thecapitalhotel.com	Little Rock	AR	72201	501-374-7474	370-7091
Capitol Hill Suites 200 C St SE *TF:* 888-627-7811 ■ *Web:* www.capitolhillsuites.com	Washington	DC	20003	202-543-6000	547-2608
Capitol Plaza Hotel & Conference Ctr 100 State St *TF:* 800-274-5252 ■ *Web:* www.capitolplaza.com	Montpelier	VT	05602	802-223-5252	229-5427
Capitol Plaza Hotel Jefferson City 415 W McCarty St *TF:* 800-338-8088 ■ *Web:* www.capitolplazajeffersoncity.com	Jefferson City	MO	65101	573-635-1234	635-4565
Captain Bartlett Inn 1411 Airport Way *TF:* 800-544-7528	Fairbanks	AK	99701	907-452-1888	452-7674
Captain Daniel Stone Inn 10 Water St *TF:* 877-573-5151 ■ *Web:* www.captaindanielstoneinn.com	Brunswick	ME	04011	207-725-9898	373-1857
Caribe Royale Orlando All-Suites Hotel & Convention Ctr 8101 World Ctr Dr *TF Resv:* 800-823-8300 ■ *Web:* www.thecaribeorlando.com	Orlando	FL	32821	407-238-8000	238-8050
Carlson Hotels Worldwide 701 Carlson Pkwy *Web:* www.carlsonhotels.com	Minneapolis	MN	55305	763-212-5000	
Country Inns & Suites by Carlson 11340 Blondo St Suite 100 *TF:* 800-600-7275 ■ *Web:* www.countryinns.com	Omaha	MN	68164	800-600-7275	
Carlson Hotels Worldwide Inc *Regent International Hotels* 11340 Blondo St *TF:* 800-545-4000 ■ *Web:* www.regenthotels.com	Omaha	NE	68164	800-545-4000	
Carlton Arms 160 E 25th St *Web:* www.carltonarms.com	New York	NY	10010	212-679-0680	
Carlton on Madison Ave 88 Madison Ave *TF:* 800-542-1502 ■ *Web:* www.carltonhotelny.com	New York	NY	10016	212-532-4100	696-9758
Carlyle Suites Hotel 1731 New Hampshire Ave NW *TF:* 800-964-5377 ■ *Web:* www.carlylesuites.com	Washington	DC	20009	202-234-3200	387-0085
Carlyle The 35 E 76th St *TF:* 800-227-5737 ■ *Web:* www.thecarlyle.com	New York	NY	10021	212-744-1600	717-4682
Carmel River Inn 26600 Oliver Rd *TF:* 800-882-8142 ■ *Web:* www.carmelriverinn.com	Carmel	CA	93923	831-624-1575	624-0290
Carnegie Hotel 1216 W State of Franklin Rd *TF:* 866-757-8277 ■ *Web:* www.carnegiehotel.com	Johnson City	TN	37604	423-979-6400	979-6424
Carolina Inn 211 Pittsboro St *TF:* 800-962-8519 ■ *Web:* www.carolinainn.com	Chapel Hill	NC	27516	919-933-2001	962-3400
Carousel Beachfront Hotel & Suites 11700 Coastal Hwy *TF:* 800-641-0011 ■ *Web:* www.carouselhotel.com	Ocean City	MD	21842	410-524-1000	524-7766
Carousel Inn & Suites 1530 S Harbor Blvd *TF:* 800-854-6767 ■ *Web:* www.carouselinnandsuites.com	Anaheim	CA	92802	714-758-0444	772-9960
Cartier Place Suite Hotel 180 Cooper St *TF:* 800-236-8399 ■ *Web:* www.suitedreams.com	Ottawa	ON	K2P2L5	613-236-5000	238-3842
Casa de Estrellas 310 E Marcy St *Web:* www.estrellashotelsantafe.com	Santa Fe	NM	87501	505-795-0278	989-7381
Casa Grande Suite Hotel 834 Ocean Dr *TF:* 866-420-2272 ■ *Web:* www.casagrandesuitehotel.com	Miami Beach	FL	33139	305-672-7003	673-3669
Casa Madrona Hotel 801 Bridgeway *TF:* 800-567-9524 ■ *Web:* www.casamadrona.com	Sausalito	CA	94965	415-332-0502	288-0502
Casa Monica Hotel 95 Cordova St *TF:* 888-472-6312 ■ *Web:* www.casamonica.com	Saint Augustine	FL	32084	904-827-1888	819-6065
Casa Munras Hotel 700 Munras Ave *TF:* 800-222-2558 ■ *Web:* www.hotelcasamunras.com	Monterey	CA	93940	831-375-2411	375-1365
Casa Sirena Hotel & Marina 3605 Peninsula Rd *TF:* 800-447-3529	Oxnard	CA	93035	805-985-6311	985-4329
Casa Via Mar Inn & Tennis Club 377 W Ch Islands Blvd *TF:* 800-992-5522 ■ *Web:* www.casaviamar.com	Port Hueneme	CA	93041	805-984-6222	984-9490
Casablanca Hotel 147 W 43rd St *TF:* 888-922-7225 ■ *Web:* www.casablancahotel.com	New York	NY	10036	212-869-1212	391-7585
Cascades Inn 3226 Shepherd of the Hills Expy *TF:* 800-588-8424 ■ *Web:* www.cascadesinn.com	Branson	MO	65616	417-335-8424	334-1927
Casino Aztar Hotel 421 NW Riverside Dr *TF:* 800-544-0120 ■ *Web:* www.casinoaztar.com	Evansville	IN	47708	812-433-4444	433-4384
Castle in the Sand Hotel 3701 Atlantic Ave *TF:* 800-552-7263 ■ *Web:* www.castleinthesand.com	Ocean City	MD	21842	410-289-6846	289-9446
Castle Inn & Suites 1734 S Harbor Blvd *TF:* 800-521-5653 ■ *Web:* www.castleinn.com	Anaheim	CA	92802	714-774-8111	956-4736
Castle on the Hudson 400 Benedict Ave *TF:* 800-616-4487 ■ *Web:* www.castleonthehudson.com	Tarrytown	NY	10591	914-631-1980	631-4612
Cathedral Hill Hotel 1101 Van Ness Ave *TF:* 800-622-0855	San Francisco	CA	94109	415-776-8200	441-2841
Cavalier Hotel 1320 Ocean Dr *Web:* www.cavaliermiami.com	Miami Beach	FL	33139	305-531-3555	531-5543
Centennial Hotel 96 Pleasant St *TF:* 800-360-4839 ■ *Web:* www.thecentennialhotel.com	Concord	NH	03301	603-225-7102	225-5031
Center Court Historic Inn & Cottages 915 Ctr St *TF:* 800-797-8787 ■ *Web:* www.centercourtkw.com	Key West	FL	33040	305-296-9292	296-2561
Century Hotel South Beach 140 Ocean Dr *TF:* 877-659-8855 ■ *Web:* www.centurysouthbeach.com	Miami Beach	FL	33139	305-674-8855	538-5733
Century House The 997 New Loudon Rd PO Box 1100 *TF:* 888-674-6873 ■ *Web:* www.thecenturyhouse.com	Latham	NY	12110	518-785-0931	782-2578
Century Plaza Hotel & Spa 1015 Burrard St *TF:* 800-663-1818 ■ *Web:* www.century-plaza.com	Vancouver	BC	V6Z1Y5	604-687-0575	682-5790
Century Suites Hotel 300 SR-446 *TF:* 800-766-5446 ■ *Web:* www.centurysuites.com	Bloomington	IN	47401	812-336-7777	336-0436
Chamberlain West Hollywood 1000 Westmount Dr *TF:* 800-201-9637 ■ *Web:* www.chamberlainwesthollywood.com	West Hollywood	CA	90069	310-657-7400	854-6744
Chambers Hotel 15 W 56th St *TF:* 866-204-5656 ■ *Web:* www.chambersnyc.com	New York	NY	10019	212-974-5656	974-5657
Chancellor Hotel on Union Square 433 Powell St *TF:* 800-428-4748 ■ *Web:* www.chancellorhotel.com	San Francisco	CA	94102	415-362-2004	362-1403
Chandler Inn 26 Chandler St *TF:* 800-842-3450 ■ *Web:* www.chandlerinn.com	Boston	MA	02116	617-482-3450	542-3428
Channel Inn Hotel 650 Water St SW *TF:* 800-368-5668 ■ *Web:* www.channelinn.com	Washington	DC	20024	202-554-2400	863-1164
Charles Hotel Harvard Square 1 Bennett St *TF:* 800-882-1818 ■ *Web:* www.charleshotel.com	Cambridge	MA	02138	617-864-1200	864-5715
Charles Inn 20 Broad St *Web:* www.thecharlesinn.com	Bangor	ME	04401	207-992-2820	992-2826
Charleston Place 205 Meeting St *TF:* 800-611-5545 ■ *Web:* www.charlestonplace.com	Charleston	SC	29401	843-722-4900	722-0728
Charter at Beaver Creek 120 Offerson Rd PO Box 5310 *TF:* 800-525-6660 ■ *Web:* www.thecharter.com	Avon	CO	81620	970-949-6660	949-6709
Charter One Hotels & Resorts Inc 2032 Hillview St *Web:* www.charteronehotels.com	Sarasota	FL	34239	941-364-9224	921-5246
Chase Hotel at Palm Springs 200 W Arenas Rd *TF:* 877-532-4273 ■ *Web:* www.chasehotelpalmsprings.com	Palm Springs	CA	92262	760-320-8866	323-1501
Chase Park Plaza 212 N Kingshighway Blvd *TF resv:* 877-587-2427 ■ *Web:* www.chaseparkplaza.com	Saint Louis	MO	63108	314-633-3000	633-3077
Chateau Bonne Entente 3400 ch Sainte-Foy *Web:* www.chateaubonneentente.com	Sainte-Foy	QC	G1X1S6	418-653-5221	653-3098
Chateau du Sureau 48688 Victoria Ln PO Box 577 *Web:* www.chateausureau.com	Oakhurst	CA	93644	559-683-6860	683-0800
Chateau Dupre Hotel 2119 Decatur St *TF:* 800-211-3447 ■ *Web:* www.neworleansfinehotels.com	New Orleans	LA	70116	504-569-0600	569-0606
Chateau Hotel & Conference Ctr The 1601 Jumer Dr *TF:* 866-690-4006 ■ *Web:* www.chateauhotel.biz	Bloomington	IL	61704	309-662-2020	662-6522
Chateau Louis Hotel & Conference Centre 11727 Kingsway *TF:* 800-661-9843 ■ *Web:* www.chateaulouis.com	Edmonton	AB	T5G3A1	780-452-7770	454-3436
Chateau Marmont Hotel 8221 Sunset Blvd *TF:* 800-242-8328 ■ *Web:* www.chateaumarmont.com	Hollywood	CA	90046	323-656-1010	655-5311
Chateau on the Lake 415 N State Hwy 265 *TF:* 888-333-5253 ■ *Web:* www.chateauonthelakebranson.com	Branson	MO	65616	417-334-1161	339-5566
Chateau Sonesta Hotel New Orleans 800 Iberville St *TF:* 800-766-3782 ■ *Web:* www.sonesta.com	New Orleans	LA	70112	504-586-0800	586-1987
Chateau Vaudreuil Suites Hotel 21700 Rt Transcanada Hwy *TF:* 800-363-7896 ■ *Web:* www.chateau-vaudreuil.com	Vaudreuil-Dorion	QC	J7V8P3	450-455-0955	455-6617
Chateau Versailles 1659 Sherbrooke St W *TF:* 888-933-8111 ■ *Web:* www.chateauversaillesmontreal.com	Montreal	QC	H3H1E3	514-933-3611	933-7102
Chelsea Savoy Hotel 204 W 23rd St *TF:* 866-929-9353 ■ *Web:* www.chelseasavoynyc.com	New York	NY	10011	212-929-9353	741-6309
Cheshire The 6300 Clayton Rd *TF:* 866-631-3408 ■ *Web:* www.cheshirestl.com	Saint Louis	MO	63117	314-647-7300	647-0442
Chesterfield Hotel 855 Collins Ave *TF:* 877-762-3477 ■ *Web:* www.thechesterfieldhotel.com	Miami Beach	FL	33139	305-531-5831	535-9665
Chesterfield Hotel 363 Cocoanut Row *TF:* 800-243-7871 ■ *Web:* www.chesterfieldpb.com	Palm Beach	FL	33480	561-659-5800	659-6707
Chestnut Hill Hotel 8229 Germantown Ave *TF:* 800-628-9744 ■ *Web:* www.chestnuthillhotel.com	Philadelphia	PA	19118	215-242-5905	242-8778

Name / Address	City	State	Zip	Phone	Fax
Chiltern Inn 3 Cromwell Harbor Rd	Bar Harbor	ME	04609	207-288-0114	288-0124
TF: 800-404-0114 ■ *Web:* www.chilterninn.com					
Chimo Hotel 1199 Joseph Cyr St	Gloucester	ON	K1J7T4	613-744-1060	744-7076
TF: 800-387-9779 ■ *Web:* www.chimohotel.com					
Choice Hotels International Inc 10750 Columbia Pike	Silver Spring	MD	20901	301-592-5000	592-6157
NYSE: CHH ■ *TF:* 800-424-6423 ■ *Web:* www.choicehotels.com					
Rodeway Inns 10750 Columbia Pike	Silver Spring	MD	20901	301-592-5000	592-6157
TF: 800-424-6423 ■ *Web:* www.choicehotels.com					
Chrysalis Inn & Spa 804 10th St	Bellingham	WA	98225	360-756-1005	647-0342
TF: 888-808-0005 ■ *Web:* www.thechrysalisinn.com					
Churchill Hotel 1914 Connecticut Ave NW	Washington	DC	20009	202-797-2000	462-0944
TF: 800-424-2464 ■ *Web:* www.thechurchillhotel.com					
Cincinnatian Hotel 601 Vine St	Cincinnati	OH	45202	513-381-3000	651-0256
TF: 800-942-9000 ■ *Web:* www.cincinnatianhotel.com					
Circa39 Hotel 3900 Collins Ave	Miami Beach	FL	33140	305-538-4900	538-4998
TF: 877-247-2239 ■ *Web:* www.circa39.com					
Citadel Halifax Hotel 1960 Brunswick St	Halifax	NS	B3J2G7	902-422-1391	429-6672
TF: 800-565-7162 ■ *Web:* www.citadelhalifax.com					
City Suites Hotel 933 W Belmont Ave	Chicago	IL	60657	773-404-3400	404-3405
TF: 800-248-9108 ■ *Web:* www.chicagocitysuites.com					
Civic Plaza Hotel 505 Pine St	Abilene	TX	79601	325-676-0222	676-0513
TF: 800-588-0222 ■ *Web:* www.civicplazahotel.com					
CJ Grand Hotel & Spa 67585 Hacienda Ave	Desert Hot Springs	CA	92240	760-329-4488	329-4570
Web: www.cjgrandhotel.com					
Clarendon Hotel & Suites 401 W Clarendon Ave	Phoenix	AZ	85013	602-252-7363	274-9009
Web: www.theclarendon.net					
Clarion Collection Sundance Plaza Hotel 3050 University Pkwy	Winston-Salem	NC	27105	336-723-2911	714-4578
Web: www.clarionhotel.com					
Clayton on the Park 8025 Bonhomme Ave	Clayton	MO	63105	314-725-9990	721-8588
TF: 800-323-7500					
Cleftstone Manor 92 Eden St	Bar Harbor	ME	04609	207-288-8086	288-2089
TF: 888-288-4951 ■ *Web:* www.cleftstone.com					
Cliff House at Pikes Peak 306 Canyon Ave	Manitou Springs	CO	80829	719-785-1000	685-3913
TF: 888-212-7000 ■ *Web:* www.thecliffhouse.com					
Clift The 495 Geary St	San Francisco	CA	94102	415-775-4700	441-4621
TF Cust Svc: 800-652-5438					
Clinton Inn Hotel 145 Dean Dr	Tenafly	NJ	07670	201-871-3200	871-3435
TF: 800-275-4411 ■ *Web:* www.clinton-inn.com					
Clocktower Inn Hotel 181 E Santa Clara St	Ventura	CA	93001	805-652-0141	643-1432
TF: 800-727-1027 ■ *Web:* www.clocktowerinn.com					
ClubHouse Hotel & Suites Sioux Falls 2320 S Louise Ave	Sioux Falls	SD	57106	605-361-8700	361-5950
TF: 800-258-2466 ■ *Web:* siouxfalls.clubhouseinn.com					
Coachman Inn 32959 SR-Hwy 20	Oak Harbor	WA	98277	360-675-0727	675-1419
TF: 800-635-0043 ■ *Web:* www.thecoachmaninn.com					
Coast Edmonton House Suite Hotel 10205 100 Ave	Edmonton	AB	T5J4B5	780-420-4000	420-4364
TF: 800-716-6199 ■ *Web:* www.coasthotels.com					
Coastal Hotel Group 18525 36th Ave S	Seattle	WA	98188	206-388-0400	388-0400
Web: www.coastalhotels.com					
Coastal Inn Concorde 379 Windmill Rd	Dartmouth	NS	B3A1J6	902-465-7777	465-3956
TF: 800-565-1565 ■ *Web:* www.coastalinns.com/halifax.php					
Coastal Inns Inc 515 Kennedy St Unit 5	Dieppe	NB	E1A7R9	506-859-2486	857-1791
TF: 800-665-7829 ■ *Web:* www.coastalinns.com					
Cocca's Inn & Suites Corner of Wolf Rd & Central Ave	Albany	NY	12205	518-459-2240	459-9758
TF: 888-426-2227 ■ *Web:* www.coccas.com					
Cohasset Harbor Inn 124 Elm St	Cohasset	MA	02025	781-383-6650	383-2872
TF: 800-252-5287					
Colby Hill Inn 33 The Oaks PO Box 779	Henniker	NH	03242	603-428-3281	428-9218
TF: 800-531-0330 ■ *Web:* www.colbyhillinn.com					
Colcord Hotel 15 N Robinson Ave	Oklahoma City	OK	73102	405-601-4300	208-4399
TF: 866-781-3800 ■ *Web:* www.colcordhotel.com					
Colgate Inn 1 Payne St	Hamilton	NY	13346	315-824-2300	824-4500
Web: www.colgateinn.com					
Collegiate Village Inn 2121 W Tennessee St	Tallahassee	FL	32304	850-576-6121	576-3508
Collier Development Co Inc PO Box 648	Pigeon Forge	TN	37868	865-453-2526	453-2564
TF: 888-482-7829 ■ *Web:* www.smokymountainresorts.com					
Colonnade Hotel 120 Huntington Ave	Boston	MA	02116	617-424-7000	424-1717
TF: 800-962-3030 ■ *Web:* www.colonnadehotel.com					
Colony Hotel 155 Hammon Ave	Palm Beach	FL	33480	561-655-5430	832-7318
TF: 800-521-5525 ■ *Web:* www.thecolonypalmbeach.com					
Colony Hotel & Cabana Club 525 E Atlantic Ave	Delray Beach	FL	33483	561-276-4123	276-0123
Web: www.thecolonyhotel.com					
Colony South Hotel 7401 Surratts Rd	Clinton	MD	20735	301-856-4500	868-1439
TF: 800-537-1147 ■ *Web:* www.colonysouth.com					
Columbia Gorge Hotel 4000 Westcliff Dr	Hood River	OR	97031	541-386-5566	386-9141
TF: 800-345-1921 ■ *Web:* www.columbiagorgehotel.com					
Columbia Hospitality 2223 Alaskan Way Suite 200	Seattle	WA	98121	206-239-1800	239-1801
Web: www.columbiahospitality.com					
Columbia Sussex Corp 207 Grandview Dr	Fort Mitchell	KY	41017	859-331-0091	578-1190
Web: www.columbiasussex.com					
Columns The 3811 St Charles Ave	New Orleans	LA	70115	504-899-9308	899-8170
TF: 800-445-9308 ■ *Web:* www.thecolumns.com					
Comfort Inn & Suites Milwaukee 916 E State St	Milwaukee	WI	53202	414-276-8800	765-1919
TF: 888-522-9472 ■ *Web:* www.choicehotels.com					
Commander Hotel 1401 Atlantic Ave	Ocean City	MD	21842	410-289-6166	289-3998
TF: 888-289-6166 ■ *Web:* www.commanderhotel.com					
Commonwealth Park Suites Hotel 901 Bank St	Richmond	VA	23219	804-343-7300	343-1025
TF: 888-343-7301 ■ *Web:* www.commonwealthparksuites.com					
Conch House Heritage Inn 625 Truman Ave	Key West	FL	33040	305-293-0020	293-8447
TF: 800-207-5806 ■ *Web:* www.conchhouse.com					
Conch House Marina Resort 57 Comares Ave	Saint Augustine	FL	32080	904-829-8646	829-5414
TF: 800-940-6256 ■ *Web:* www.conch-house.com					

Name / Address	City	State	Zip	Phone	Fax
Concourse Hotel & Conference Ctr 4300 International Gateway	Columbus	OH	43219	614-237-2515	237-6134
TF: 800-541-4574 ■ *Web:* www.theconcoursehotel.com					
Congress Plaza Hotel & Convention Ctr 520 S Michigan Ave	Chicago	IL	60605	312-427-3800	427-3972
TF: 800-635-1666 ■ *Web:* www.congressplazahotel.com					
Conrad Miami 1395 Brickell Ave	Miami	FL	33131	305-503-6500	503-6599
Web: www.miami.conradmeetings.com					
Continental Bayside Hotel 146 Biscayne Blvd	Miami	FL	33132	305-358-4555	371-5253
TF: 800-742-6331 ■ *Web:* www.continentalhotelbayside.com					
Cooper Cos Cooper Hotels Div 1661 arrionbrainner Dr Suite 200	Memphis	TN	38120	901-725-9631	274-9169
Web: www.cooperhotels.com					
Cooper Cos CSS Hotels Div 1407 Union Ave Suite 400	Memphis	TN	38104	901-725-9631	274-9169
Web: www.cooperhotels.com					
Copley Square Hotel 47 Huntington Ave	Boston	MA	02116	617-536-9000	267-3547
TF: 800-225-7062 ■ *Web:* www.copleysquarehotel.com					
Coral Reef Resort 5800 Gulf Blvd	Saint Pete Beach	FL	33706	727-363-1604	363-6434
TF: 800-352-4874 ■ *Web:* www.vrivacations.com					
Cornhusker Hotel The 333 S 13th St	Lincoln	NE	68508	402-474-7474	474-1847
TF: 866-706-7706 ■ *Web:* www.marriott.com					
Cosmopolitan Hotel 125 Chambers St	New York	NY	10007	212-566-1900	566-6909
TF: 888-895-9400 ■ *Web:* www.cosmohotel.com					
Cosmopolitan Hotel Toronto 8 Colborne St	Toronto	ON	M5E1E1	416-350-2000	350-2460
TF: 800-958-3488 ■ *Web:* www.cosmotoronto.com					
Country Hearth 3450 S Clack St	Abilene	TX	79606	325-695-7700	698-0546
TF: 800-676-7262 ■ *Web:* www.countryhearthabilene.com					
Country Inn at the Mall 936 Stillwater Ave	Bangor	ME	04401	207-941-0200	942-1167
TF: 800-244-3961 ■ *Web:* www.countryinnatthemall.net					
Country Inn Lake Resort 1332 Airport Rd	Hot Springs	AR	71913	501-767-3535	
TF: 800-822-7402 ■ *Web:* www.countryinnlakeresort.com					
Courtyard Fort Lauderdale Beach 440 Seabreeze Blvd	Fort Lauderdale	FL	33316	954-524-8733	467-7489
TF: 888-236-2427 ■ *Web:* www.marriott.com/courtyard/travel.mi					
Courtyard mariott Waikki Beach The 400 Royal Hawaiian Ave	Honolulu	HI	96815	808-954-4000	954-4047
TF: 866-346-4679					
Cove Inn 900 Broad Ave S	Naples	FL	34102	239-262-7161	261-6905
TF: 800-255-4365 ■ *Web:* www.bestof.net					
Cowboy Village Resort 120 S Flat Creek Dr PO Box 38	Jackson	WY	83001	307-733-3121	739-1955
TF: 800-962-4988 ■ *Web:* www.townsquareinns.com/cowboy-village					
Cozy Country Inn 103 Frederick Rd	Thurmont	MD	21788	301-271-4301	271-3107
Web: www.cozyvillage.com					
Craftsman Inn 7300 E Genesee St	Fayetteville	NY	13066	315-637-8000	637-2440
TF: 800-797-4464 ■ *Web:* www.craftsmaninn.com					
Creekside Inn 3400 El Camino Real	Palo Alto	CA	94306	650-493-2411	493-6787
TF: 866-589-3411 ■ *Web:* www.greystonehotels.com					
Crescent Hotel 403 N Crescent Dr	Beverly Hills	CA	90210	310-247-0505	247-9053
TF: 800-451-1566 ■ *Web:* www.crescentbh.com					
Crest Hotel & Suites 1670 James Ave	Miami Beach	FL	33139	305-531-0321	531-8180
TF: 800-531-3880 ■ *Web:* www.crestgrouphotels.com					
Crockett Hotel 320 Bonham St	San Antonio	TX	78205	210-225-6500	225-6251
TF: 800-292-1050 ■ *Web:* www.crocketthotel.com					
Cross Creek Resort 3815 Pennsylvania 8	Titusville	PA	16354	814-827-9611	827-2062
TF: 800-461-3173 ■ *Web:* www.crosscreekresort.com					
Crown American Hotels Co Pasquerilla Plaza	Johnstown	PA	15907	814-533-4600	535-9323
Web: www.crownamericanhotels.com					
Crown Reef Resort 2913 S Ocean Blvd	Myrtle Beach	SC	29577	843-626-8077	916-0735
TF: 877-435-9125 ■ *Web:* www.crownreef.com					
Crowne Plaza Campbell House 1375 Harrodsburg Rd	Lexington	KY	40504	859-255-4281	254-4368
TF Resv: 800-227-6963 ■ *Web:* www.crowneplaza.com					
Crystal Beach Suites & Health Club 6985 Collins Ave	Miami Beach	FL	33141	305-865-9555	866-3514
TF: 800-435-0766 ■ *Web:* www.crystalbeachsuites.com					
Crystal Inn Gulfport 9379 Canal Rd	Gulfport	MS	39503	228-822-9600	822-0666
TF: 888-822-9600 ■ *Web:* www.crystalinns.com					
Crystal Inn Salt Lake City Downtown 230 W 500 S	Salt Lake City	UT	84101	801-328-4466	328-4072
TF: 800-366-4466 ■ *Web:* www.crystalinns.com/slcdt.html					
Curtis The 1405 Curtis St	Denver	CO	80202	303-571-0300	825-4301
TF: 800-525-6651 ■ *Web:* www.thecurtis.com					
Custom Hotel 8639 Lincoln Blvd	Los Angeles	CA	90045	310-645-0400	645-0700
TF: 877-287-8601 ■ *Web:* www.jdvhotels.com					
Cypress Hotel 10050 S DeAnza Blvd	Cupertino	CA	95014	408-253-8900	253-3800
TF: 800-499-1408 ■ *Web:* www.thecypresshotel.com					
Dahlmann Campus Inn 615 E Huron St	Ann Arbor	MI	48104	734-769-2200	769-6222
TF: 800-666-8693 ■ *Web:* www.campusinn.com					
Dallas Plaza Hotel 1011 S Akard St	Dallas	TX	75215	214-421-1083	428-6827
Dan'l Webster Inn 149 Main St	Sandwich	MA	02563	508-888-3622	888-5156
TF: 800-444-3566 ■ *Web:* www.danlwebsterinn.com					
Dauphine Orleans Hotel 415 Dauphine St	New Orleans	LA	70112	504-586-1800	586-1409
TF: 800-521-7111 ■ *Web:* www.dauphineorleans.com					
Davenport Hotel The 10 S Post St	Spokane	WA	99201	509-455-8888	624-4455
TF: 800-899-1482 ■ *Web:* www.thedavenporthotel.com					
David William Hotel 700 Biltmore Way	Coral Gables	FL	33134	305-445-7821	913-1933
TF: 800-757-8073 ■ *Web:* www.davidwilliamhotel.com					
Davidson Hotel Co 3340 Players Club Suite 200	Memphis	TN	38125	901-761-4664	761-4664
Web: www.davidsonhotels.com					
Days Hotel New York City Broadway 215 W 94th St Broadway	New York	NY	10025	212-866-6400	866-1357
TF: 800-834-2972 ■ *Web:* www.daysinn.com					
Daytona Beach Resort & Conference Ctr 2700 N Atlantic Ave	Daytona Beach	FL	32118	386-672-3770	673-7262
TF: 800-654-6216 ■ *Web:* www.daytonabeachresort.com					
Daytona Inn Beach Resort 219 S Atlantic Ave	Daytona Beach	FL	32118	386-252-3626	255-3680
TF: 800-874-1822 ■ *Web:* www.bsrresorts.com					

Name / Address	City	State	ZIP	Phone	Fax
Dearborn Inn the - A Marriott Hotel 20301 Oakwood Blvd — TF: 800-228-9290 ■ Web: www.marriotthotels.com/DTWDI	Dearborn	MI	48124	313-271-2700	271-2700
Deer Haven Inn 740 Crocker Ave — *Fax Area Code: 831 ■ TF: 800-525-3373 ■ Web: www.monterey.com/mcp/deerhaven/index.html	Pacific Grove	CA	93950	800-935-9960	655-5048*
Deer Path Inn 255 E Illinois Rd — TF: 800-788-9480 ■ Web: www.dpihotel.com	Lake Forest	IL	60045	847-234-2280	234-3352
Del Monte Lodge Renaissance Rochester Hotel & Spa The 41 N Main St — TF: 866-237-5979 ■ Web: www.marriott.com/hotels/travel/rocdl	Pittsford	NY	14534	585-381-9900	381-9825
DELAMAR Greenwich Harbor 500 Steamboat Rd — TF: 866-335-2627 ■ Web: www.slh.com	Greenwich	CT	06830	203-661-9800	661-2513
Delano Hotel 1685 Collins Ave — TF: 800-697-1791 ■ Web: www.delano-hotel.com	Miami Beach	FL	33139	305-672-2000	532-0099
Delta Holding Inc 600 Horizon Dr — Web: www.designandsupply.com	Chalfont	PA	18914	215-997-8850	997-8837
Delta King Riverboat Hotel 1000 Front St — TF: 800-825-5464 ■ Web: www.deltaking.com	Sacramento	CA	95814	916-444-5464	447-5959
Denihan Hospitality Group LLC (DHG) *Affinia Hotels* 551 5th Ave — TF: 866-246-2203 ■ Web: www.affinia.com	New York	NY	10176	212-465-3700	465-3697
DePalma Hotel Corp 700 Highlander Blvd Suite 400 — Web: www.depalmahotels.com	Arlington	TX	76015	817-557-1811	557-4333
Desert Inn Resort 900 N Atlantic Ave — TF: 800-826-1711 ■ Web: www.desertinnresort.com	Daytona Beach	FL	32118	386-258-6555	238-1635
Desmond Albany 660 Albany-Shaker Rd — TF: 800-448-3500 ■ Web: www.desmondhotelsalbany.com	Albany	NY	12211	518-869-8100	869-7659
Desmond Great Valley 1 Liberty Blvd — TF: 800-575-1776 ■ Web: www.desmondgv.com	Malvern	PA	19355	610-296-9800	889-9869
Diamond Head Inn 605 Diamond St — TF: 888-478-7829 ■ Web: www.diamond-head-inn.pacificahost.com	San Diego	CA	92109	858-273-1900	273-8532
Dimension Development Co Inc 401 Keyser Ave — Web: www.dimdev.com	Natchitoches	LA	71457	318-352-8238	352-8276
Dinah's Garden Hotel 4261 El Camino Real — TF: 800-227-8220 ■ Web: www.dinahshotel.com	Palo Alto	CA	94306	650-493-4542	856-4713
Disney's Paradise Pier Hotel 1717 S Disneyland Dr — Web: www.disneyworld.disney.go.com	Anaheim	CA	92802	714-999-0990	776-5763
Disney's Saratoga Springs Resort & Spa 1960 Broadway St — Web: disneyworld.disney.go.com/resorts/saratoga-springs-resort-and-spa	Lake Buena Vista	FL	32830	407-827-1100	827-4444
Disneyland Hotel 1150 Magic Way — Web: www.disneyland.disney.go.com	Anaheim	CA	92802	714-778-6600	956-6597
Dockers Inn 3060 Green Mountain Dr — TF: 800-324-8748 ■ Web: www.dockersinn.com	Branson	MO	65616	417-334-3600	334-8166
Dolphin Beach Resort 4900 Gulf Blvd — TF: 800-237-8916 ■ Web: www.dolphinbeach.com	Saint Pete Beach	FL	33706	727-360-7011	367-5909
Dolphin Inn 1705 Atlantic Ave — TF: 800-365-3467 ■ Web: www.vbeach.com/hotels/dolphin.htm	Virginia Beach	VA	23451	757-491-1420	425-8390
Don Hall's Guesthouse 1313 W Washington Ctr Rd — TF: 800-348-1999 ■ Web: www.donhalls.com	Fort Wayne	IN	46825	260-489-2524	489-7067
Donatello The 501 Post St — TF: 800-258-2366 ■ Web: www.clubdonatello.org	San Francisco	CA	94102	415-441-7100	441-7100
Doral Tesoro Hotel & Golf Club 3300 Championship Pkwy — TF: 866-983-7676 ■ Web: www.marriott.com	Fort Worth	TX	76177	817-961-0800	497-3011
Doubletree Claremont 555 W Foothill Blvd — TF: 800-222-8733 ■ Web: www.doubletree1.hilton.com	Claremont	CA	91711	909-626-2411	624-0756
Doubletree Hotel Downtown Wilmington Legal District 700 N King St — TF: 800-222-8733 ■ Web: www.doubletree1.hilton.com	Wilmington	DE	19801	302-655-0400	655-0430
Doubletree Inn at the Colonnade 4 W University Pkwy — Web: www.doubletree1.hilton.com/en_US	Baltimore	MD	21218	410-235-5400	235-5572
Doubletree Marina Hotel 2800 Via Cabrillo Marina — TF: 800-222-8733	San Pedro	CA	90731	310-514-3344	514-8945
Doubletree North Shore Hotel 9599 Skokie Blvd — Web: www.doubletree1.hilton.com	Skokie	IL	60077	847-679-7000	679-0904
Downtown Erie Hotel 18 W 18th St — Web: www.downtownneriehotel.com	Erie	PA	16501	814-456-2961	456-7067
Drake Hotel The 140 E Walton Pl — TF: 800-553-7253 ■ Web: www.thedrakehotel.com	Chicago	IL	60611	312-787-2200	787-1431
Drawbridge Hotel & Convention Ctr 2477 Royal Dr — TF Resv: 800-354-9793	Fort Mitchell	KY	41017	859-341-2800	
Dream 210 W 55th St — TF: 866-437-3266 ■ Web: www.dreamny.com	New York	NY	10019	212-247-2000	581-2248
Driftwood Lodge 435 Willoughby Ave — TF: 800-544-2239 ■ Web: www.driftwoodalaska.com	Juneau	AK	99801	907-586-2280	586-1034
Driftwood on the Oceanfront 1600 N Ocean Blvd — TF: 800-942-3456 ■ Web: www.driftwoodlodge.com	Myrtle Beach	SC	29578	843-448-1544	448-2917
Driftwood Shores Resort 88416 1st Ave — TF: 800-422-5091 ■ Web: www.driftwoodshores.com	Florence	OR	97439	541-997-8263	997-3253
Driskill Hotel 604 Brazos St — TF: 800-252-9367 ■ Web: www.driskillhotel.com	Austin	TX	78701	512-474-5911	474-2214
Drury Inns Inc 721 Emerson Rd Suite 400 — TF: 800-378-7946 ■ Web: www.druryhotels.com	Saint Louis	MO	63141	314-429-2255	429-2255
Pear Tree Inns 721 Emerson Rd Suite 400 — Web: www.druryhotels.com	Saint Louis	MO	63141	314-429-2255	429-5166
Duane Street Hotel 130 Duane St — TF: 866-589-3411 ■ Web: www.duanestreethotel.com	New York	NY	10013	212-964-4600	964-4800
Dude Rancher Lodge 415 N 29th St — TF: 800-221-3302 ■ Web: www.duderancherlodge.com	Billings	MT	59101	406-259-5561	259-0095
Duke Towers Residential Suites 807 W Trinity Ave — TF: 866-385-3869 ■ Web: www.duketower.com	Durham	NC	27701	919-687-4444	683-1215
Duke's 8th Avenue Hotel 630 W 8th Ave — TF: 800-478-4837 ■ Web: www.dukesalaskahotel.com	Anchorage	AK	99501	907-274-6213	272-6308
Dunes Manor Hotel 2800 Baltimore Ave — TF: 800-523-2888 ■ Web: www.dunesmanor.com	Ocean City	MD	21842	410-289-1100	289-4905
Dunhill Hotel 237 N Tryon St — TF: 800-354-4141 ■ Web: www.dunhillhotel.com	Charlotte	NC	28202	704-332-4141	376-4117
Dylan Hotel 52 E 41st St — TF: 866-553-9526 ■ Web: www.dylanhotel.com	New York	NY	10017	212-338-0500	338-0569
Dynasty Suites 3735 Iowa Ave — TF: 800-842-7899 ■ Web: www.dynastysuites.com	Riverside	CA	92507	951-369-8200	341-6486
Eagle Mountain House 179 Carter Notch Rd PO Box 804 — TF: 800-966-5779 ■ Web: www.eaglemt.com	Jackson	NH	03846	603-383-9111	383-0854
Eagles Landing Hotel 12840 188th Ave SW — TF: 800-370-8205 ■ Web: www.luckyeagle.com	Rochester	WA	98579	360-273-8640	273-8670
East Canyon Hotel & Spa 288 E Camino Monte Vista — TF: 877-324-6835 ■ Web: www.eastcanyonps.com	Palm Springs	CA	92262	760-320-1928	320-0599
Eastgate Tower 222 E 39th St — TF: 866-233-4642 ■ Web: www.affinia.com	New York	NY	10016	212-687-8000	490-2634
Eastland Park Hotel 157 High St — TF: 888-671-8008 ■ Web: www.eastlandparkhotel.com	Portland	ME	04101	207-775-5411	775-2872
Eden House 1015 Fleming St — TF: 800-533-5397 ■ Web: www.edenhouse.com	Key West	FL	33040	305-296-6868	294-1221
Edgewater Beach Hotel 1901 Gulf Shore Blvd N — TF: 888-564-1308 ■ Web: www.edgewaternaples.com	Naples	FL	34102	239-403-2000	403-2100
Edgewater Hotel 2411 Alaskan Way Pier 67 — TF: 800-624-0670 ■ Web: www.edgewaterhotel.com	Seattle	WA	98121	206-728-7000	441-4119
Edgewater Resort 200 Edgewater Cir — TF: 800-234-3687	Hot Springs	AR	71913	501-767-3311	
Edgewater Resort & Waterpark 2400 London Rd — TF: 800-777-7925 ■ Web: www.duluthwaterpark.com	Duluth	MN	55812	218-728-3601	728-3727
Edgewater The 666 Wisconsin Ave — TF: 800-922-5512 ■ Web: www.theedgewater.com	Madison	WI	53703	608-256-9071	256-0910
Edison Walthall Hotel 225 E Capitol St — TF: 800-932-6161 ■ Web: www.edisonwalthallhotel.com	Jackson	MS	39201	601-948-6161	948-0088
Edmonds Harbor Inn & Suites 130 W Dayton — TF: 800-441-8033 ■ Web: www.bestwestern.com	Edmonds	WA	98020	425-771-5021	672-2880
EF Lane Hotel 30 Main St — TF: 888-300-5056 ■ Web: www.eflane.com	Keene	NH	03431	603-357-7070	357-7075
Eisenhower Inn & Conference Ctr 2634 Emmitsburg Rd — TF: 800-776-8349 ■ Web: www.eisenhower.com	Gettysburg	PA	17325	717-334-8121	334-6066
El Rey Inn 1862 Cerillos Rd — TF: 800-521-1349 ■ Web: www.elreyinnsantafe.com	Santa Fe	NM	87505	505-982-1931	989-9249
El Tovar Hotel 10 Albright St PO Box 699 — TF: 888-297-2757 ■ Web: www.grandcanyonlodges.com/el-tovar-409.html	Grand Canyon	AZ	86023	928-638-2631	638-2855
Elan Hotel 8435 Beverly Blvd — TF: 866-203-2212 ■ Web: www.greystonehotels.com	Los Angeles	CA	90048	323-658-6663	658-6640
Elbow River Casino (ERC) 218 18th Ave SE — TF: 800-661-1463 ■ Web: www.elbowrivercasino.com	Calgary	AB	T2G5P9	403-289-8880	290-1457
Eldorado Hotel 309 W San Francisco St — TF: 800-955-4455 ■ Web: www.eldoradohotel.com	Santa Fe	NM	87501	505-988-4455	995-4543
Eldridge Hotel 701 Massachusetts St — TF: 800-527-0909 ■ Web: www.eldridgehotel.com	Lawrence	KS	66044	785-749-5011	749-4512
Eliot Hotel The 370 Commonwealth Ave — TF: 800-443-5468 ■ Web: www.eliothotel.com	Boston	MA	02215	617-267-1607	536-9114
Elk Country Inn 480 W Pearl St PO Box 1255 — Web: www.townsquareinns.com	Jackson	WY	83001	307-733-2364	733-4465
Elvis Presley's Heartbreak Hotel 3677 Elvis Presley Blvd — TF: 877-777-0606 ■ Web: www.elvis.com	Memphis	TN	38116	901-332-1000	332-2107
Embarcadero Resort Hotel & Marina 1000 SE Bay Blvd — TF: 800-547-4779 ■ Web: www.embarcadero-resort.com	Newport	OR	97365	541-265-8521	265-7844
Embassy Hotel 610 Polk St — Web: www.theembassyhotelsf.com	San Francisco	CA	94102	415-673-1404	474-4188
Embassy Hotel & Suites 25 Cartier St — TF: 800-661-5495 ■ Web: www.embassyhotelottawa.com	Ottawa	ON	K2P1J2	613-237-2111	563-1353
Embassy West Hotel 1400 Carling Ave — TF: 800-267-8696 ■ Web: www.embassywesthotel.com	Ottawa	ON	K1Z7L8	613-729-4331	729-1600
Emerald Queen Hotel & Casino 5700 Pacific Hwy E — TF: 888-820-3555 ■ Web: www.emeraldqueencasino.com	Tacoma	WA	98424	253-922-3555	922-3550
Emerson Resort & Spa 5368 Rt 28 — TF: 877-688-2828 ■ Web: www.emersonresortandspa.com	Mount Tremper	NY	12457	845-688-7900	688-2789
Emory Inn 1641 Clifton Rd NE — TF: 800-933-6679 ■ Web: www.emoryconferencecenter.com/accom.html	Atlanta	GA	30329	404-712-6720	712-6701
Empire Landmark Hotel & Conference Centre 1400 Robson St — TF: 800-830-6144 ■ Web: www.empirelandmarkhotel.com	Vancouver	BC	V6G1B9	604-687-0511	687-2801
Empress Hotel 7766 Fay Ave — TF: 888-369-9900 ■ Web: www.empress-hotel.com	La Jolla	CA	92037	858-454-3001	454-6387
Enclave Suites of Orlando 6165 Carrier Dr — TF: 800-457-0077 ■ Web: www.enclavesuites.com	Orlando	FL	32819	407-351-1155	351-2001
Essex House Hotel & Convention Ctr 44916 N 10th St W — TF: 800-843-7739	Lancaster	CA	93534	661-948-0961	945-3821
Ethan Allen Hotel 21 Lake Ave Ext — TF: 800-742-1776 ■ Web: www.ethanallenhotel.com	Danbury	CT	06811	203-744-1776	791-9673
Euro-Suites Hotel 501 Chestnut Ridge Rd — TF: 800-678-1837 ■ Web: www.euro-suites.com	Morgantown	WV	26505	304-598-1000	599-2736
Evergreen Lodge 250 S Frontage Rd W — TF: 800-284-8245 ■ Web: www.evergreenvail.com	Vail	CO	81657	970-476-7810	476-4504
Ewa Hotel Waikiki 2555 Cartwright Rd — TF: 800-359-8639 ■ Web: www.ewahotel.com	Honolulu	HI	96815	808-922-1677	923-8538
Executive Hotel Vintage Court 650 Bush St — TF resv: 800-654-1100 ■ Web: www.executivehotels.com	San Francisco	CA	94108	415-392-4666	433-4065
Executive Inn 978 Phillips Ln — TF: 800-626-2706	Louisville	KY	40209	502-367-6161	367-6161
Executive Inn Evansville 600 Walnut St — TF: 877-424-0888 ■ Web: www.executiveinnevansville.com	Evansville	IN	47708	812-424-8000	424-8999

Phone Fax

Executive Inn Group Corp
Executive Hotels & Resorts
1080 Howe St 8th Fl — Vancouver BC V6Z2T1 604-642-5250 642-5255
TF: 866-642-6888 ■ *Web:* www.executivehotels.net

Executive Inn Rivermont 1 Executive Blvd — Owensboro KY 42301 270-926-8000 926-8000
TF: 800-626-1936

Executive Pacific Plaza Hotel 400 Spring St — Seattle WA 98104 206-623-3900 623-2059
TF: 888-388-3932 ■
Web: www.executivehotels.net/downtownseattlehotel/s_seattle_home.cgi

Executive Suite Hotel 4360 Spenard Rd — Anchorage AK 99517 907-243-6366 248-2161
TF: 800-770-6366 ■ *Web:* www.executivesuitehotel.com

Executive West Hotel 830 Phillips Ln — Louisville KY 40209 502-367-2251 367-2251
TF: 800-626-2708

Expressway Hotels 4303 17th Ave S — Fargo ND 58103 701-235-3141 239-4303
TF: 877-239-4303 ■ *Web:* www.expresswayhotels.com/FargoInn.htm

Expressway Suites 180 E Bismarck Expy — Bismarck ND 58504 701-222-3311 222-3311
TF: 888-774-5566 ■ *Web:* www.expresswayhotels.com/BisSuites.htm

Extended Stay Hotels
c/o HVM LLC 100 Dunbar St — Spartanburg SC 29306 864-573-1600 573-1695
Web: www.extendedstayhotels.com
Crossland Economy Studios 100 Dunbar St — Spartanburg SC 29306 864-573-1600 573-1695
TF: 800-804-3724 ■ *Web:* www.crosslandstudios.com
Extended Stay Deluxe Studios
100 Dunbar St — Spartanburg SC 29306 864-573-1600 573-1695
TF: 800-804-3724 ■ *Web:* www.extendedstaydeluxe.com
Extended StayAmerica 100 Dunbar St — Spartanburg SC 29306 864-573-1600 573-1695
TF: 800-804-3724 ■ *Web:* www.extendedstayamerica.com
Homestead Studio Suites Hotels
100 Dunbar St — Spartanburg SC 29306 864-573-1600 573-1695
TF: 800-804-3724 ■ *Web:* www.homesteadhotels.com
StudioPLUS Deluxe Studios 100 Dunbar St — Spartanburg SC 29306 864-573-1600 573-1695
TF: 800-804-3724 ■ *Web:* www.studioplus.com

Fairbanks Golden Nugget Hotel 900 Noble St — Fairbanks AK 99701 907-452-5141 452-5458
Web: www.golden-nuggethotel.com

Fairbanks Princess Riverside Lodge
4477 Pikes Landing Rd — Fairbanks AK 99709 907-455-4477 455-4476
TF: 800-426-0500 ■ *Web:* www.princesslodges.com

Fairmont Hotels & Resorts Inc
100 Wellington St W TD Centre Suite 1600 — Toronto ON M5K1B7 416-874-2600 874-2601
TF: 800-866-5577 ■ *Web:* www.fairmont.com

Fairmount Hotel The 401 S Alamo St — San Antonio TX 78205 210-224-8800 475-0082
TF: 800-996-3426 ■ *Web:* www.thefairmounthotel-sanantonio.com

Falmouth Inn 824 Main St — Falmouth MA 02540 508-540-2500 540-9256
TF: 800-255-4157 ■ *Web:* www.falmouthinn.com

Family Inn 208 S Old County Rd — Branson MO 65616 417-334-2113 334-2234
Web: www.myfamilyinn.com

Family Inns of America Inc 3144 Pkwy — Pigeon Forge TN 37863 865-453-4988 453-0220
TF: 800-251-9752 ■ *Web:* www.familyinnsofamerica.com

Fargo C'mon Inn Hotel 4338 20th Ave SW — Fargo ND 58103 701-277-9944 277-9117
TF: 800-334-1570 ■ *Web:* www.cmoninn.com

Fearrington House
2000 Fearrington Village Ctr — Pittsboro NC 27312 919-542-2121 542-4202
Web: www.fearrington.com

Federal Square Inn & Extended Stay
8781 Madison Blvd — Madison AL 35758 256-772-8470 772-0620
TF: 800-458-1639 ■ *Web:* www.federalsquare.com

Fenwick Inn 13801 Coastal Hwy — Ocean City MD 21842 410-250-1100 250-0087
TF: 800-492-1873 ■ *Web:* www.fenwickinn.com

Fiesta Henderson Casino Hotel
777 W Lake Mead Pkwy — Henderson NV 89015 702-558-7000 567-7373
TF: 888-899-7770 ■ *Web:* www.fiestahendersonlasvegas.com

Fiesta Resort Conference Ctr 2100 S Priest Dr — Tempe AZ 85282 480-967-1441 967-0224
TF: 800-528-6481 ■ *Web:* www.fiestainnresort.com

Fifteen Beacon Hotel 15 Beacon St — Boston MA 02108 617-670-1500 670-6925
TF: 877-982-3226 ■ *Web:* www.xvbeacon.com

Fifth Season Inn 2219 S Waldron Rd — Fort Smith AR 72903 479-452-4880 452-8653
TF: 877-452-4880 ■ *Web:* www.hotelpureseasonsinn.com

Figueroa Hotel 939 S Figueroa St — Los Angeles CA 90015 213-627-8971 689-0305
TF: 800-421-9092 ■ *Web:* www.figueroahotel.com

Fiksdal Hotel & Suites 1215 2nd St SW — Rochester MN 55902 507-288-2671 285-9325*
**Fax:* Resv ■ *TF:* 800-366-3451 ■ *Web:* www.fiksdalhotel.com

Findlay Inn & Conference Ctr
200 E Main Cross St — Findlay OH 45840 419-422-5682 422-5581
TF Cust Svc: 800-825-1455 ■ *Web:* www.findlayinn.com

Fireside Inn & Suites 25 Airport Rd — West Lebanon NH 03784 603-298-5906 298-0340
TF: 877-258-5900 ■ *Web:* www.afiresideinn.com

First Gold Hotel 270 Main St — Deadwood SD 57732 605-578-9777 578-3979
TF: 800-274-1876 ■ *Web:* www.firstgold.com

First Interstate Inn 20 SE Wyoming Blvd — Casper WY 82609 307-234-9125 265-0264
TF: 800-462-4667 ■ *Web:* www.1stinns.com

Fisherman's Wharf Inn
22 Commercial St — Boothbay Harbor ME 04538 207-633-5090 633-5092
TF: 800-628-6872

Fitger's Inn 600 E Superior St — Duluth MN 55802 218-722-8826 722-8826
Web: www.fitgers.com

Fitzgerald Hotel 620 Post St — San Francisco CA 94109 415-775-8100 775-1278
TF: 800-334-6835 ■ *Web:* www.fitzgeraldhotel.com

Fitzgerald's Casino & Hotel Las Vegas
301 Fremont St — Las Vegas NV 89101 702-388-2400 388-2183
TF: 800-274-5825 ■ *Web:* www.fitzgeraldslasvegas.com

Fitzpatrick Manhattan Hotel
687 Lexington Ave — New York NY 10022 212-355-0100 355-1371
TF: 800-367-7701 ■ *Web:* www.fitzpatrickhotels.com

Flagship All Suites Resort
60 N Maine Ave — Atlantic City NJ 08401 609-343-7447 347-9597
TF: 800-647-7890 ■ *Web:* www.fantasearesorts.com

Flagship Hotel Over the Water
2501 Seawall Blvd — Galveston TX 77550 409-762-9000 762-9040
TF: 800-392-6542

Flatotel International 135 W 52nd St — New York NY 10019 212-887-9400 887-9795
TF: 800-352-8683 ■ *Web:* www.flatotel.com

Phone Fax

Foley House Inn 14 W Hull St Chippewa Sq — Savannah GA 31401 912-232-6622 231-1218
TF: 800-647-3708 ■ *Web:* www.foleyinn.com

Foot of the Mountain Motel
200 W Arapahoe Ave — Boulder CO 80302 303-442-5688 442-5719
TF: 866-773-5489 ■ *Web:* www.footofthemountainmotel.com

Foothills Inn 1625 N La Crosse St — Rapid City SD 57701 605-348-5640 348-0073
TF: 877-428-5666 ■ *Web:* www.thefoothillsinn.com

Fort Collins Mulberry Inn
4333 E Mulberry St — Fort Collins CO 80524 970-493-9000 224-9636
TF: 800-234-5548 ■ *Web:* www.mulberry-inn.com

Fort Garry The 222 Broadway — Winnipeg MB R3C0R3 204-942-8251 956-2351
TF: 800-665-8088 ■ *Web:* www.fortgarryhotel.com

Fort Marcy Hotel Suites 320 Artist Rd — Santa Fe NM 87501 505-988-2800 992-1804
TF: 800-745-9910 ■ *Web:* www.allseasonsresortlodging.com

Forum Motor Inn
800-814 Atlantic Ave PO Box 448 — Ocean City NJ 08226 609-399-8700 399-8704
Web: www.theforuminoc.homestead.com

Four Points by Sheraton Charlotte
315 E Woodlawn Rd — Charlotte NC 28217 704-522-0852 522-1634
TF: 800-368-7764 ■ *Web:* www.starwoodhotels.com

Four Queens Hotel & Casino 202 Fremont St — Las Vegas NV 89101 702-385-4011 387-5133
TF: 800-634-6045 ■ *Web:* www.fourqueens.com

Four Sails Resort Hotel
3301 Atlantic Ave — Virginia Beach VA 23451 757-491-8100 491-0573
TF: 800-227-4213 ■ *Web:* www.foursails.com

Four Seasons Hotels Inc 1165 Leslie St — Toronto ON M3C2K8 416-449-1750 441-4374
CVE: FSH.SV ■ *TF:* 800-332-3442 ■ *Web:* www.fourseasons.com

Francis Marion Hotel The 387 King St — Charleston SC 29403 843-722-0600 853-2186
TF: 877-756-2121 ■ *Web:* www.francismarionhotel.com

Franklin The 164 E 87th St — New York NY 10128 212-369-1000 369-8000
Web: www.franklinhotel.com

French Quarter Suites Hotel
1119 N Rampart St — New Orleans LA 70116 504-524-7725 522-9716
Web: www.frenchquartersuites.com

Galleria Park Hotel 191 Sutter St — San Francisco CA 94104 415-781-3060 433-4409
Web: www.galleriapark.com

Galt House Hotel 140 N 4th St — Louisville KY 40202 502-589-5200 589-3444
TF: 800-626-1814 ■ *Web:* www.galthouse.com

Garden City Hotel 45 7th St — Garden City NY 11530 516-747-3000 747-1414
TF: 800-547-0400 ■ *Web:* www.gardencityhotel.com

Garden Court Hotel 520 Cowper St — Palo Alto CA 94301 650-322-9000 324-3609
TF: 800-824-9028 ■ *Web:* www.gardencourt.com

Garden District Hotel
Clarion Collection New Orleans
2203 St Charles Ave — New Orleans LA 70130 504-566-1200 581-1352
TF: 800-230-4134 ■ *Web:* www.thegardendistricthotel.com

Garden Place Hotel 6615 Transit Rd — Williamsville NY 14221 716-635-9000 635-9098
TF: 877-456-6036 ■ *Web:* www.salvatores.net/garden_place/index.html

Gardens Hotel 526 Angela St — Key West FL 33040 305-294-2661 292-1007
TF: 800-526-2664 ■ *Web:* www.gardenshotel.com

Gardner Hotel 311 E Franklin Ave — El Paso TX 79901 915-532-3661
Web: www.gardnerhotel.com

Garfield Suites Hotel 2 Garfield Pl — Cincinnati OH 45202 513-421-3355 421-3729
TF: 800-367-2155 ■ *Web:* www.garfieldsuiteshotel.com

Garrett's Desert Inn 311 Old Santa Fe Trail — Santa Fe NM 87501 505-982-1851 989-1647
TF: 800-888-2145 ■ *Web:* www.garrettsdesertinn.com

Gaslamp Plaza Suites 520 E St — San Diego CA 92101 619-232-9500 238-9945
TF: 800-874-8770 ■ *Web:* www.gaslampplaza.com

Gastonian The 220 E Gaston St — Savannah GA 31401 912-232-2869 232-0710
TF: 800-322-6603 ■ *Web:* www.gastonian.com

Gateways Inn 51 Walker St — Lenox MA 01240 413-637-2532 637-1432
TF: 888-492-9466 ■ *Web:* www.gatewaysinn.com

Gaylord Entertainment Co 1 Gaylord Dr — Nashville TN 37214 615-316-6000 316-6060
NYSE: GET ■ *Web:* www.gaylordentertainment.com

Gaylord Opryland Hotel & Convention Ctr
2800 Opryland Dr — Nashville TN 37214 615-889-1000 885-3054
Web: www.gaylordhotels.com

General Morgan Inn 111 N Main St — Greeneville TN 37743 423-787-1000 787-1001
TF: 800-223-2679 ■ *Web:* www.generalmorganinn.com

Genesee Grande Hotel 1060 E Genesee St — Syracuse NY 13210 315-476-4212 471-4663
TF: 800-365-4663 ■ *Web:* www.geneseegrande.com

Geneva on the Lake 1001 Lochland Rd — Geneva NY 14456 315-789-7190 789-0322
TF: 800-343-6382 ■ *Web:* www.genevaonthelake.com

George Washington University Inn
824 New Hampshire Ave NW — Washington DC 20037 202-337-6620 298-7499
TF: 800-426-4455 ■ *Web:* www.gwuinn.com

Georgetown Inn 1310 Wisconsin Ave — Washington DC 20007 202-333-8900 625-1744
TF: 888-587-2388 ■ *Web:* www.georgetowninn.com

Georgian Court Hotel 773 Beatty St — Vancouver BC V6B2M4 604-682-5555 682-8830
TF: 800-663-1155 ■ *Web:* www.georgiancourthotelvancouver.com

Georgian Hotel 1415 Ocean Ave — Santa Monica CA 90401 310-395-9945 451-3374
TF: 800-538-8147 ■ *Web:* www.georgianhotel.com

Georgian Resort 384 Canada St — Lake George NY 12845 518-668-5401 668-5870
TF: 800-525-3436 ■ *Web:* www.georgianresort.com

Georgian Terrace Hotel 659 Peachtree St NE — Atlanta GA 30308 404-897-1991 724-9116
TF: 800-651-2316 ■ *Web:* www.thegeorgianterrace.com

Gershwin Hotel 7 E 27th St — New York NY 10016 212-545-8000 684-5546
Web: www.gershwinhotel.com

Gideon Putnam Resort & Spa
24 Gideon Putnam Rd — Saratoga Springs NY 12866 518-584-3000 584-1354
TF: 866-890-4171 ■ *Web:* www.gideonputnam.com

Glacier Bay Country Inn 35 Tong Rd — Gustavus AK 99826 907-697-2288 697-2289
TF: 800-628-0912 ■ *Web:* www.glacierbayalaska.com

Glass House Inn 3202 W 26th St — Erie PA 16506 814-833-7751 833-4222
TF: 800-956-7222 ■ *Web:* www.glasshouseinn.com

Glen Grove Suites 2837 Yonge St — Toronto ON M4N2J6 416-489-8441 440-3065
TF: 800-565-3024 ■ *Web:* www.glengrove.com

Glendorn 1000 W Corydon St — Bradford PA 16701 814-362-6511 368-9923
TF: 800-843-8568 ■ *Web:* www.glendorn.com

Glenerin Inn The 1695 The Collegeway — Mississauga ON L5L3S7 905-828-6103 828-0891
TF: 877-991-9971 ■ *Web:* www.glenerininn.com

				Phone	Fax
Glenmore Inn 2720 Glenmore Trail SE *TF:* 800-661-3163 ■ *Web:* www.glenmoreinn.com	Calgary	AB	T2C2E6	403-279-8611	236-8035
Glidden House 1901 Ford Dr *TF:* 800-759-8358 ■ *Web:* www.gliddenhouse.com	Cleveland	OH	44106	216-231-8900	231-2130
Glorietta Bay Inn 1630 Glorietta Blvd *TF:* 800-283-9383 ■ *Web:* www.gloriettabayinn.com	Coronado	CA	92118	619-435-3101	435-6182
Goldbelt Hotel Juneau 51 Egan Dr *TF:* 888-478-6909 ■ *Web:* www.goldbelt.com/subsidiaries/GBHJ.html	Juneau	AK	99801	907-586-6900	463-3567
Golden Eagle Resort 511 Mountain Rd PO Box 1090 *TF:* 800-626-1010 ■ *Web:* www.goldeneagleresort.com	Stowe	VT	05672	802-253-4811	253-2561
Golden Hotel The 800 11th St *TF:* 800-233-7214 ■ *Web:* www.thegoldenhotel.com	Golden	CO	80401	303-279-0100	279-9353
Goldener Hirsch Inn 7570 Royal St E *TF Cust Svc:* 800-252-3373 ■ *Web:* www.goldenerhirschinn.com	Park City	UT	84060	435-649-7770	649-7901
Good-Nite Inn Fremont 4135 Cushing Pkwy *TF:* 800-648-3466 ■ *Web:* www.goodnite.com	Fremont	CA	94538	510-656-9307	656-9110
Gouverneur Hotel Montreal (Place-Dupuis) 1415 St Hubert St *TF:* 888-910-1111 ■ *Web:* www.gouverneur.com	Montreal	QC	H2L3Y9	888-910-1111	
Gouverneur Hotels 1000 Sherbrooke St W Suite 2300 *Web:* www.gouverneur.com	Montreal	QC	H3A3R3	514-875-8822	875-0988
Governor Calvert House 58 State Cir *TF:* 800-847-8882 ■ *Web:* www.historicinnsofannapolis.com	Annapolis	MD	21401	410-263-2641	268-8041
Governor Hotel 621 S Capitol Way *TF:* 877-352-7701 ■ *Web:* www.olywagov.com	Olympia	WA	98501	360-352-7700	943-9349
Governor Hotel 614 SW 11th Ave *TF:* 800-554-3456 ■ *Web:* www.governorhotel.com	Portland	OR	97205	503-224-3400	241-2122
Governor's House Hotel & Conference Ctr 2705 E S Blvd *TF:* 866-535-5392	Montgomery	AL	36116	334-288-2800	288-6472
Governor's Inn 700 W Sioux Ave *TF:* 888-315-2378 ■ *Web:* www.govinn.com	Pierre	SD	57501	605-224-4200	
Governor's Inn 210 Richards Blvd *TF:* 800-999-6689 ■ *Web:* www.governorsinnhotel.com	Sacramento	CA	95814	916-448-7224	448-7382
Governors Inn 209 S Adams St *Web:* www.thegovinn.com	Tallahassee	FL	32301	850-681-6855	222-3105
Grafton on Sunset 8462 W Sunset Blvd *TF:* 800-821-3660 ■ *Web:* www.graftononsunset.com	West Hollywood	CA	90069	323-654-4600	654-5918
Gramercy Park Hotel 2 Lexington Ave *TF:* 866-784-1300 ■ *Web:* www.gramercyparkhotel.com	New York	NY	10010	212-920-3300	673-5890
Grand America Hotel 555 S Main St *TF:* 800-621-4505 ■ *Web:* www.grandamerica.com	Salt Lake City	UT	84111	801-258-6000	258-6911
Grand Beach Inn (GBI) 198 E Grand Ave *TF:* 800-834-9696 ■ *Web:* www.oobme.com/Grand/gbihome.html	Old Orchard Beach	ME	04064	207-934-4621	934-3435
Grand Country Inn Grand Country Sq 1945 W Hwy 76 *TF:* 800-514-1088 ■ *Web:* www.grandcountry.com/hotel.asp	Branson	MO	65616	417-335-3535	336-6286
Grand Del Mar 5300 Grand Del Mar Ct *Web:* www.thegranddelmar.com	San Diego	CA	92130	858-314-2000	314-2001
Grand Gateway Hotel 1721 N LaCrosse St *TF:* 866-742-1300 ■ *Web:* www.grandgatewayhotel.com	Rapid City	SD	57701	605-342-8853	342-0663
Grand Hotel & Suites Toronto 225 Jarvis St *TF:* 877-324-7263 ■ *Web:* www.grandhoteltoronto.com	Toronto	ON	M5B2C1	416-863-9000	863-1100
Grand Hotel Edmonton 10266 103rd St *TF:* 888-422-6365 ■ *Web:* www.edmontongrandhotel.com	Edmonton	AB	T5J0Y8	780-422-6365	425-9070
Grand Hotel Minneapolis The 615 2nd Ave S *TF:* 866-843-4726 ■ *Web:* www.grandhotelminneapolis.com	Minneapolis	MN	55402	612-288-8888	373-0407
Grand Hotel The State Hwy 64 PO Box 3319 *TF:* 866-634-7263 ■ *Web:* www.the-grand-hotel-grand-canyon.pacificahost.com	Grand Canyon	AZ	86023	928-638-3333	638-3131
Grand Oaks Hotel 2315 Green Mountain Dr *TF:* 800-553-6423 ■ *Web:* www.grandoakshotel.net	Branson	MO	65615	417-336-6423	334-6264
Grand Summit Hotel 570 Springfield Ave *TF:* 800-346-0773	Summit	NJ	07901	908-273-3000	273-4228
Grande Colonial 910 Prospect St *Web:* www.thegrandecolonial.com	La Jolla	CA	92037	858-454-2181	454-5679
Grant Plaza Hotel 465 Grant Ave *TF:* 800-472-6899 ■ *Web:* www.grantplaza.com	San Francisco	CA	94108	415-434-3883	434-3886
Granville Island Hotel 1253 Johnston St **Fax:* Admin ■ *TF Resv:* 800-663-1840 ■ *Web:* www.granvilleislandhotel.com	Vancouver	BC	V6H3R9	604-683-7373	683-3061*
Graves 601 Hotel 601 1st Ave N *TF:* 866-523-1100 ■ *Web:* www.graves601hotel.com	Minneapolis	MN	55403	612-677-1100	677-1200
Graycote Inn 40 Holland Ave *Web:* www.graycoteinn.com	Bar Harbor	ME	04609	207-288-3044	288-2719
Great Divide Lodge 550 Village Rd PO Box 8059 *TF:* 888-906-5698 ■ *Web:* www.breckresorts.com	Breckenridge	CO	80424	970-547-5550	453-0212
Green Harbor Resort 182 Baxter Ave *Web:* www.greenharborresort.com	West Yarmouth	MA	02673	508-771-1126	771-0701
Green Mountain Inn 18 Main St PO Box 60 *TF:* 800-253-7302 ■ *Web:* www.greenmountaininn.com	Stowe	VT	05672	802-253-7301	253-5096
Green Park Inn 9239 Valley Blvd *TF:* 800-852-2462 ■ *Web:* www.greenparkinn.com	Blowing Rock	NC	28605	828-295-3141	
Greenwood Inn & Suites Calgary 3515 26th St NE *TF:* 888-233-6730 ■ *Web:* www.greenwoodinn.ca	Calgary	AB	T1Y7E3	403-250-8855	250-8050
Greenwood Inn & Suites Edmonton 4485 Gateway Blvd *TF:* 888-233-6730 ■ *Web:* www.greenwoodinn.ca	Edmonton	AB	T6H5C3	780-431-1100	437-3455
Greenwood Inn & Suites Winnipeg 1715 Wellington Ave *TF:* 888-233-6730 ■ *Web:* www.greenwoodinn.ca	Winnipeg	MB	R3H0G1	204-775-9889	775-4576
Grey Bonnet Inn 831 Rt 100 N *TF:* 800-342-2086 ■ *Web:* www.greybonnetinn.com	Killington	VT	05751	802-775-2537	775-3371
Greyfield Inn 6 N 2nd St # 300 *TF:* 888-241-6408 ■ *Web:* www.greyfieldinn.com	Fernandina Beach	FL	32034	904-261-6408	321-0666
Grove Hotel The 245 S Capitol Blvd *TF:* 888-961-5000 ■ *Web:* www.grovehotelboise.com	Boise	ID	83702	208-333-8000	333-8800
Grove Isle Hotel & Spa 4 Grove Isle Dr *TF:* 800-884-7683 ■ *Web:* www.groveisle.com	Coconut Grove	FL	33133	305-858-8300	858-5908
Guest Inn 2533 N Piccoli Rd	Stockton	CA	95215	209-931-6675	931-8351
Guest Lodge at Cooper Aerobic Center Clinic 12230 Preston Rd *TF:* 800-444-5187 ■ *Web:* www.cooperaerobics.com/hotel	Dallas	TX	75230	972-386-0306	386-5415
GuestHouse International LLC 130 Maple Dr N **Fax Area Code:* 770 ■ *TF:* 800-214-8378 ■ *Web:* www.guesthouseintl.com	Hendersonville	TN	37075	615-264-8000	951-0307*
Habana Inn 2200 NW 40th St *TF:* 800-988-2221 ■ *Web:* www.habanainn.com	Oklahoma City	OK	73112	405-528-2221	528-0496
Habitat Suites 500 E Highland Mall Blvd *TF:* 800-535-4663 ■ *Web:* www.habitatsuites.com	Austin	TX	78752	512-467-6000	452-6712
Hacienda Hotel 525 N Sepulveda Blvd *TF:* 800-421-5900 ■ *Web:* www.haciendahotel.com	El Segundo	CA	90245	310-615-0015	615-0217
Hacienda The at Hotel Santa Fe 1501 Paseo del Peralta *TF:* 866-589-3411 ■ *Web:* www.hotelsantafe.com/the_hacienda	Santa Fe	NM	87501	505-982-1200	955-7835
Halekulani Hotel 2199 Kalia Rd *TF:* 800-367-2343 ■ *Web:* www.halekulani.com	Honolulu	HI	96815	808-923-2311	926-8004
Half Moon Bay Lodge & Conference Ctr 2400 S Cabrillo Hwy *TF:* 800-710-0778 ■ *Web:* www.halfmoonbaylodge.com	Half Moon Bay	CA	94019	650-726-9000	726-7951
Halifax Marriott Harborfront Hotel 1919 Upper Water St *TF:* 866-425-4329 ■ *Web:* www.marriott.com/hotels/travel/yhzmc-halifax-marriott-harbourfront-hotel	Halifax	NS	B3J3J5	902-421-1700	422-5805
Halliburton House Inn 5184 Morris St *TF:* 888-512-3344 ■ *Web:* www.thehalliburton.com	Halifax	NS	B3J1B3	902-420-0658	423-2324
Hallmark Inns & Resorts 15455 Hallmark Dr Suite 200 *TF:* 888-448-4449 ■ *Web:* www.hallmarkinns.com	Lake Oswego	OR	97035	503-436-1566	436-0324
Hampshire Hotels & Resorts LLC 1251 Avenue of the Americas Suite 934 *Web:* www.hampshirehotels.com	New York	NY	10020	212-474-9800	474-9801
Handlery Union Square Hotel 351 Geary St *TF:* 800-843-4343 ■ *Web:* www.handlery.com	San Francisco	CA	94102	415-781-7800	781-0216
Hanover Inn 2 S Main St *TF:* 800-443-7024 ■ *Web:* www.hanoverinn.com	Hanover	NH	03755	603-643-4300	643-4433
Harbor Court Hotel 165 Steuart St *TF:* 800-346-0555 ■ *Web:* www.harborcourthotel.com	San Francisco	CA	94105	415-882-1300	882-1313
Harbor Court Hotel 550 Light St *TF:* 800-824-0076 ■ *Web:* www.harborcourt.com	Baltimore	MD	21202	410-234-0550	659-5925
Harbor House 28 Pier 21 *TF:* 800-874-3721 ■ *Web:* www.harborhousepier21.com	Galveston	TX	77550	409-763-3321	765-6421
Harbor View Hotel 131 N Water St Martha's Vineyard PO Box 7 *TF:* 800-225-6005 ■ *Web:* www.harbor-view.com	Edgartown	MA	02539	508-627-7000	627-8417
Harborside Hotel & Marina 55 W St *TF:* 800-328-5033 ■ *Web:* www.theharborsidehotel.com	Bar Harbor	ME	04609	207-288-5033	288-3661
Harborside Inn 1 Christie's Landing *TF:* 800-427-9444 ■ *Web:* www.newportharborsideinn.com	Newport	RI	02840	401-846-6600	849-8510
Harborside Inn of Boston 185 State St *TF:* 888-723-7565 ■ *Web:* www.harborsideinnboston.com	Boston	MA	02109	617-723-7500	670-6015
Hard Rock Hotel San Diego 207 5th Ave *TF:* 866-751-7625 ■ *Web:* www.hardrockhotelsd.com	San Diego	CA	92101	619-702-3000	702-3007
Harrah's Entertainment Inc 1 Harrah's Ct *TF:* 800-442-6443 ■ *Web:* www.totalrewards.com/brands/harrahs/hotel-casinos/harrahs-brand.shtml	Las Vegas	NV	89119	702-407-6000	407-6022
Harrah's Reno 219 N Ctr St *TF:* 800-736-6427 ■ *Web:* www.harrahsreno.com	Reno	NV	89501	775-788-3044	788-3703
Harraseeket Inn 162 Main St *TF:* 800-342-6423 ■ *Web:* www.harraseeketinn.com	Freeport	ME	04032	207-865-9377	865-1684
Harrison Plaza Suite Hotel 409 S Cole Rd *TF:* 800-376-3608 ■ *Web:* www.harrisonhotelboise.com	Boise	ID	83709	208-375-7666	376-3608
Hartness House Inn 30 Orchard St *TF:* 800-732-4789 ■ *Web:* www.hartnesshouse.com	Springfield	VT	05156	802-885-2115	885-2207
Harvard Square Hotel 110 Mt Auburn St Harvard Sq *TF:* 800-458-5886 ■ *Web:* www.hotelsinharvardsquare.com	Cambridge	MA	02138	617-864-5200	864-2409
Harvest Inn 1 Main St *TF:* 800-950-8466 ■ *Web:* www.harvestinn.com	Saint Helena	CA	94574	707-963-9463	963-4402
Hassayampa Inn 122 E Gurley St *TF Cust Svc:* 800-322-1927 ■ *Web:* www.hassayampainn.com	Prescott	AZ	86301	928-778-9434	445-8590
Hastings House Country House Hotel 160 Upper Ganges Rd *TF:* 800-661-9255 ■ *Web:* www.hastingshouse.com	Salt Spring Island	BC	V8K2S2	250-537-2362	537-5333
Havana Libre Beach Resort *Red South Beach* 3010 Collins Ave *TF:* 800-528-0823	Miami Beach	FL	33140	305-531-7742	532-6158
Hawaiian Inn 2301 S Atlantic Ave *TF:* 800-457-0077 ■ *Web:* www.hawaiianinn.com	Daytona Beach Shores	FL	32118	386-255-5411	253-1209
Hawthorn Park Hotel 2431 N Glenstone Ave	Springfield	MO	65803	417-831-3131	831-9786
Hawthorne Hotel 18 Washington Sq W *TF:* 800-729-7829 ■ *Web:* www.hawthornehotel.com	Salem	MA	01970	978-744-4080	745-9842
Hawthorne Inn & Conference Ctr 420 High St *TF:* 877-777-3099 ■ *Web:* www.wakehealth.edu	Winston-Salem	NC	27101	336-777-3000	777-3282
Hay-Adams Hotel 800 16th St NE *TF:* 800-424-5054 ■ *Web:* www.hayadams.com	Washington	DC	20006	202-638-6600	638-2716
Haywood Park Hotel 1 Battery Pk Ave *TF:* 800-228-2522 ■ *Web:* www.haywoodpark.com	Asheville	NC	28801	828-252-2522	253-0481
Hazelton Hotel The 118 Yorkville Ave *TF:* 866-473-6301 ■ *Web:* www.thehazeltonhotel.com	Toronto	ON	M5R1C2	416-963-6300	963-6399
Heartland Inn Cedar Rapids 3315 Southgate Ct SW *TF:* 800-334-3277 ■ *Web:* www.heartlandinns.com	Cedar Rapids	IA	52404	319-362-9012	362-9694
Heartland Inn Dubuque West 4025 McDonald Dr *TF:* 800-334-3277 ■ *Web:* www.heartlandinns.com	Dubuque	IA	52003	563-582-3752	582-0113
Heartland Inns of America 1027 Peoples Sq *Web:* www.heartlandinns.com	Waterloo	IA	50702	319-235-1025	

Name / Address	City	State	Zip	Phone	Fax
Heathman Hotel 1001 SW Broadway *TF:* 800-551-0011 ■ *Web:* www.heathmanhotel.com	Portland	OR	97205	503-241-4100	790-7110
Heathman Lodge 7801 NE Greenwood Dr. *TF:* 888-475-3100 ■ *Web:* www.heathmanlodge.com	Vancouver	WA	98662	360-254-3100	254-6100
Helmsley Carlton House Hotel 680 Madison Ave *TF:* 800-221-4982 ■ *Web:* www.helmsleycarltonhouse.com	New York	NY	10021	212-838-3000	753-8575
Helmsley Enterprises Inc 230 Pk Ave Suite 659 *Web:* www.helmsleyhotels.com	New York	NY	10169	212-679-3600	953-2180
Helmsley Middletowne Hotel 148 E 48th St *TF:* 800-221-4982 ■ *Web:* www.helmsleymiddletowne.com	New York	NY	10017	212-755-3000	832-0261
Helmsley Park Lane Hotel 36 Central Pk S. *TF:* 800-221-4982 ■ *Web:* www.helmsleyparklane.com	New York	NY	10019	212-371-4000	750-7279
Helmsley Sandcastle Hotel 1540 Ben Franklin Dr *TF:* 800-225-2181 ■ *Web:* www.helmsleysandcastle.com	Sarasota	FL	34236	941-388-2181	388-2655
Hemstreet Development Corp 16100 NW Cornell Rd Suite 100. *TF Resv:* 800-443-7777 ■ *Web:* www.valuinn.com	Beaverton	OR	97006	503-531-4000	531-4001
Henley Park Hotel 926 Massachusetts Ave NW *TF:* 800-222-8474 ■ *Web:* www.henleypark.com	Washington	DC	20001	202-638-5200	638-6740
Henlopen Hotel 511 N Boardwalk *TF:* 800-441-8450 ■ *Web:* www.henlopenhotel.com	Rehoboth Beach	DE	19971	302-227-2551	227-8147
Heritage Hotel 234 3rd Ave N *Web:* www.theheritagehi.com	Saint Petersburg	FL	33701	727-822-4814	823-1644
Heritage Inn The 1350 Richmond Rd *TF:* 800-552-5571	Williamsburg	VA	23185	757-229-2455	229-0122
Heritage Inn The 34521 Postal Ln *TF Resv:* 800-669-9399 ■ *Web:* www.heritageinnandgolf.com	Lewes	DE	19958	302-644-0600	644-8522
Hermitage Hotel 231 6th Ave N *TF:* 888-888-9414 ■ *Web:* www.thehermitagehotel.com	Nashville	TN	37219	615-244-3121	254-6909
Hermosa Inn 5532 N Palo Cristi Rd *TF:* 800-241-1210 ■ *Web:* www.hermosainn.com	Paradise Valley	AZ	85253	602-955-8614	955-8299
Hershey Lodge W Chocolate Ave & University Dr *TF:* 800-533-3131 ■ *Web:* www.hersheylodge.com	Hershey	PA	17033	717-533-3311	533-9642
Heyde Hospitality Inc 345 Frenette Dr. *Web:* www.heydecompanies.com	Chippewa Falls	WI	54729	715-726-9237	723-1205
HI Development Corp 111 W Fortune St *Web:* www.hidevelopment.com	Tampa	FL	33602	813-229-6686	223-9734
High Hotels Ltd 1853 William Penn Way PO Box 10008 *Web:* www.highhotels.com	Lancaster	PA	17605	717-293-4446	293-4470
Highlander Inn 2 Highlander Way *TF:* 800-548-9248 ■ *Web:* www.highlanderinn.com/inn.html	Manchester	NH	03103	603-625-6426	625-6466
Hilgard House Hotel & Suites 927 Hilgard Ave *TF:* 800-826-3934 ■ *Web:* www.hilgardhouse.com	Los Angeles	CA	90024	310-208-3945	208-1972
Hilltop Inn of Vermont 3472 Airport Rd. *Web:* www.hilltopinnvt.net	Montpelier	VT	05602	802-229-5766	229-5766
Hilton Hotels Corp 9336 Civic Ctr Dr *TF:* 800-445-8667 ■ *Web:* www.hilohotels.net	Beverly Hills	CA	90210	310-278-4321	205-4613
Historic Bullock Hotel 633 Main St. *TF:* 800-336-1876 ■ *Web:* www.historicbullock.com	Deadwood	SD	57732	605-578-1745	578-1382
Historic French Market Inn 501 Rue Decatur *TF:* 888-538-5651 ■ *Web:* www.frenchmarketinn.com	New Orleans	LA	70130	504-561-5621	569-0619
Historic Inns of Annapolis 58 State Cir *TF:* 800-847-8882 ■ *Web:* www.historicinnsofannapolis.com	Annapolis	MD	21401	410-263-2641	268-3613
HLC Hotels Inc 7080 Abercorn St PO Box 13069 *Web:* www.hlchotels.com	Savannah	GA	31416	912-352-4493	352-0314
Holiday Inn 301 Government St *TF:* 888-465-4329 ■ *Web:* www.holidayinn.com	Mobile	AL	36602	251-694-0100	694-0160
Holiday Inn Express DFW North 4550 W John Carpenter Fwy. *TF:* 888-465-4329 ■ *Web:* www.hiexpress.com	Irving	TX	75063	972-929-4499	929-0774
Holiday Inn Express Vancouver 2889 E Hastings St. *TF:* 877-709-7666 ■ *Web:* www.hievancouver.com	Vancouver	BC	V5K2A1	604-254-1000	253-1234
Hollow Inn 278 S Main St. *TF:* 800-998-9444 ■ *Web:* www.hollowinn.com	Barre	VT	05641	802-479-9313	476-5242
Hollywood Roosevelt Hotel 7000 Hollywood Blvd *TF:* 800-950-7667 ■ *Web:* www.hollywoodroosevelt.com	Hollywood	CA	90028	323-466-7000	462-8056
Hollywood Standard Hotel 8300 Sunset Blvd *Web:* www.standardhotels.com	West Hollywood	CA	90069	323-650-9090	650-2820
Homestead Inn 420 Field Pt Rd. *Web:* www.homesteadinn.com	Greenwich	CT	06830	203-869-7500	869-7502
Horton Grand Hotel 311 Island Ave *TF:* 800-542-1886 ■ *Web:* www.hortongrand.com	San Diego	CA	92101	619-544-1886	239-3823
Hospitality Inn 4400 S 27th St *TF:* 800-825-8466 ■ *Web:* www.hospitalityinn.com	Milwaukee	WI	53221	414-282-8800	282-7713
Hospitality Inn 3709 NW 39th St.	Oklahoma City	OK	73112	405-942-7730	948-6238
Hospitality International Inc 1726 Montreal Cir *TF:* 800-251-1962 ■ *Web:* www.bookroomsnow.com	Tucker	GA	30084	770-270-1180	270-1077
Downtowner Inns 1726 Montreal Cir *TF:* 800-251-1962 ■ *Web:* www.bookroomsnow.com	Tucker	GA	30084	770-270-1180	270-1077
Master Hosts Inns & Resorts 1726 Montreal Cir *TF:* 800-247-4677 ■ *Web:* www.bookroomsnow.com	Tucker	GA	30084	770-270-1180	270-1077
Passport Inn 1726 Montreal Cir. *TF:* 800-251-1962 ■ *Web:* www.bookroomsnow.com	Tucker	GA	30084	770-270-1180	270-1077
Red Carpet Inn 1726 Montreal Cir *TF:* 800-251-1962 ■ *Web:* www.bookroomsnow.com	Tucker	GA	30084	770-270-1180	270-1077
Scottish Inns 1726 Montreal Cir *TF:* 800-251-1962 ■ *Web:* www.bookroomsnow.com	Tucker	GA	30084	770-270-1180	270-1077
Hospitality Suites Resort 409 N Scottsdale Rd *TF:* 800-445-5115 ■ *Web:* www.hospitalitysuites.com	Scottsdale	AZ	85257	480-949-5115	941-8014
Host Airport Hotel 6945 Airport Blvd *TF:* 800-903-4678 ■ *Web:* www.hostairporthotel.com	Sacramento	CA	95837	916-922-8071	929-8636
Hostmark Hospitality Group 1300 E Woodfield Rd # 400 *Web:* www.hostmark.com	Schaumburg	IL	60173	847-517-9100	517-9797
Hot Springs Hotel & Spa 135 Central Ave *TF:* 888-624-5521 ■ *Web:* www.springshotelandspa.com	Hot Springs	AR	71901	501-624-5521	624-4635
Hotel & Suites Normandin 4700 Pierre-Bertrand Blvd *TF:* 800-463-6721 ■ *Web:* www.hotelnormandin.com	Quebec	QC	G2J1A4	418-622-1611	622-9277
Hotel 1000 1000 1st Ave *TF:* 877-315-1088 ■ *Web:* www.hotel1000seattle.com	Seattle	WA	98104	206-957-1000	337-9457
Hotel 140 140 Clarendon St *TF:* 800-714-0140 ■ *Web:* www.hotel140.com	Boston	MA	02118	617-585-5600	585-5699
Hotel 43 981 Grove St. *TF:* 800-243-4622 ■ *Web:* www.hotel43.com	Boise	ID	83702	208-342-4622	344-5751
Hotel 71 71 St Pierre St *TF:* 888-692-1171 ■ *Web:* www.hotel71.ca	Quebec City	QC	G1K4A4	418-692-1171	692-0669
Hotel 71 Chicago 71 E Wacker Dr. *TF:* 888-621-4005 ■ *Web:* www.hotel71.com	Chicago	IL	60601	312-346-7100	346-1721
Hotel Acadia 43 Sainte-Ursule St *TF:* 800-463-0280 ■ *Web:* www.hotelsvieuxquebec.com/en/hotel/hotel-acadia	Old-Quebec	QC	G1R4E4	418-694-0280	694-0458
Hotel Adagio 550 Geary St *TF:* 800-228-8830 ■ *Web:* www.jdvhotels.com	San Francisco	CA	94102	415-775-5000	775-9388
Hotel Alex Johnson 523 6th St. *TF:* 800-888-2539 ■ *Web:* www.alexjohnson.com	Rapid City	SD	57701	605-342-1210	342-7436
Hotel Allegro Chicago 171 W Randolph St *TF:* 800-643-1500 ■ *Web:* www.allegrochicago.com	Chicago	IL	60601	312-236-0123	236-3440
Hotel Amarano Burbank The 322 N Pass Ave *TF:* 888-956-1900 ■ *Web:* www.hotelamarano.com	Burbank	CA	91505	818-842-8887	260-8999
Hotel Ambassadeur 321 Sainte-Anne Blvd. *TF:* 800-363-4619 ■ *Web:* www.hotelambassadeur.ca	Beauport	QC	G1E3L4	418-666-2828	666-2775
Hotel Ambassador 1324 S Main St. *TF:* 888-408-8282 ■ *Web:* www.hotelambassador-tulsa.com	Tulsa	OK	74119	918-587-8200	587-8208
Hotel Andalucia 31 W Carrillo St *TF:* 877-468-3515 ■ *Web:* www.andaluciasb.com	Santa Barbara	CA	93101	805-884-0300	884-8153
Hotel Andra 2000 4th Ave *TF:* 877-448-8600 ■ *Web:* www.hotelandra.com	Seattle	WA	98121	206-448-8600	441-7140
Hotel Andrew Jackson 919 Royal St *TF:* 800-654-0224 ■ *Web:* www.andrewjacksonhotel.com	New Orleans	LA	70116	504-561-5881	596-6769
Hotel Angeleno 170 N Church Ln *TF:* 866-264-3536 ■ *Web:* www.jdvhotels.com/angeleno	Los Angeles	CA	90049	310-476-6411	472-1157
Hotel Astor 956 Washington Ave *TF:* 800-270-4981 ■ *Web:* www.hotelastor.com	Miami Beach	FL	33139	305-531-8081	531-3193
Hotel at Old Town Wichita 830 E 1st St *TF:* 877-265-3869 ■ *Web:* www.hotelatoldtown.com	Wichita	KS	67202	316-267-4800	267-4840
Hotel at Terminal City Club The 837 W Hastings St *TF:* 888-253-8777 ■ *Web:* www.tctowerhotel.com	Vancouver	BC	V6C1B6	604-681-4121	488-8604
Hotel Avante 860 E El Camino Real *TF:* 800-538-1600 ■ *Web:* www.jdvhotels.com/hotels/avante	Mountain View	CA	94040	650-940-1000	968-7870
Hotel Baronette 27790 Novi Rd *TF:* 800-395-9009 ■ *Web:* www.hotelbaronette.com	Novi	MI	48377	248-349-7800	349-7467
Hotel Beacon 2130 Broadway *TF:* 800-572-4969 ■ *Web:* www.beaconhotel.com	New York	NY	10023	212-787-1100	724-0839
Hotel Bedford 118 E 40th St *TF:* 800-221-6881 ■ *Web:* www.bedfordhotel.com	New York	NY	10016	212-697-4800	697-1093
Hotel Bel-Air 701 Stone Canyon Rd. *TF:* 800-648-4097 ■ *Web:* www.hotelbelair.com	Los Angeles	CA	90077	310-472-1211	276-2251
Hotel Bethlehem 437 Main St. *TF:* 800-333-3333 ■ *Web:* www.radisson.com	Bethlehem	PA	18018	610-625-5000	625-2218
Hotel Bijou 111 Mason St *TF:* 800-771-1022 ■ *Web:* www.jdvhotels.com	San Francisco	CA	94102	415-771-1200	346-3196
Hotel Boulderado 2115 13th St *TF:* 800-433-4344 ■ *Web:* www.boulderado.com	Boulder	CO	80302	303-442-4344	442-4378
Hotel Britton *Good Hotel* 112 7th St. *TF:* 800-444-5819 ■ *Web:* www.i-hotels.com	San Francisco	CA	94104	415-621-7001	621-4069
Hotel Burnham 1 W Washington St. *TF:* 877-294-9712 ■ *Web:* www.burnhamhotel.com	Chicago	IL	60602	312-782-1111	782-0899
Hotel Captain Cook 939 W 5th Ave *TF:* 800-843-1950 ■ *Web:* www.captaincook.com	Anchorage	AK	99501	907-276-6000	343-2298
Hotel Carlton 1075 Sutter St *TF:* 800-738-7477 ■ *Web:* www.jdvhotels.com	San Francisco	CA	94109	415-673-0242	929-8788
Hotel Casa del Mar 1910 Ocean Way *TF:* 800-898-6999 ■ *Web:* www.hotelcasadelmar.com	Santa Monica	CA	90405	310-581-5533	581-5503
Hotel Chateau Bellevue 16 Rue de la Porte *TF:* 877-849-1877 ■ *Web:* www.vieux-quebec.com	Quebec	QC	G1R4M9	418-692-2573	692-4876
Hotel Chateau Laurier 1220 Pl George-V Ouest *TF:* 877-522-8108 ■ *Web:* www.vieux-quebec.com/fr/laurier	Quebec	QC	G1R5B8	418-522-8108	524-8768
Hotel Chelsea 944 Washington Ave *Web:* www.thehotelchelsea.com	Miami Beach	FL	33139	305-534-4069	672-6712
Hotel Clarendon 57 Rue Sainte-Anne *TF:* 888-222-3304 ■ *Web:* www.hotelclarendon.com	Quebec	QC	G1R3X4	418-692-2480	692-4652
Hotel Classique 2815 Laurier Blvd *TF:* 800-463-1885 ■ *Web:* www.hotelclassique.com	Sainte-Foy	QC	G1V4H3	418-658-2793	658-6816
Hotel Colorado 526 Pine St. *TF:* 800-544-3998 ■ *Web:* www.hotelcolorado.com	Glenwood Springs	CO	81601	970-945-6511	945-7030
Hotel Commonwealth 500 Commonwealth Ave. *TF:* 866-784-4000 ■ *Web:* www.hotelcommonwealth.com	Boston	MA	02215	617-933-5000	266-6888
Hotel Congress 311 E Congress St. *TF:* 800-722-8848 ■ *Web:* www.hotelcongress.com	Tucson	AZ	85701	520-622-8848	792-6366
Hotel Contessa 306 W Market St *TF:* 866-435-0900 ■ *Web:* www.thehotelcontessa.com	San Antonio	TX	78205	210-229-9222	229-9228
Hotel Crescent Court 400 Crescent Ct. *Web:* www.crescentcourt.com	Dallas	TX	75201	214-871-3200	871-3272
Hotel de Anza 233 W Santa Clara St *TF:* 800-843-3700 ■ *Web:* www.hoteldeanza.com	San Jose	CA	95113	408-286-1000	286-0500
Hotel de la Montagne 1430 de la Montagne St. *TF:* 800-361-6262 ■ *Web:* www.hoteldelamontagne.com	Montreal	QC	H3G1Z5	514-288-5656	288-9658

				Phone	Fax
Hotel Deca 4507 Brooklyn Ave NE	Seattle	WA	98105	206-634-2000	
TF: 800-899-0251 ■ *Web:* www.hoteldeca.com					
Hotel Del Sol 3100 Webster St.	San Francisco	CA	94123	415-921-5520	931-4137
TF: 877-433-5765 ■ *Web:* www.jdvhotels.com					
Hotel Deluxe 729 SW 15th Ave	Portland	OR	97205	503-219-2094	219-2095
TF: 866-895-2094 ■ *Web:* www.hoteldeluxeportland.com					
Hotel Derek 2525 W Loop S	Houston	TX	77027	713-961-3000	297-4392
TF: 866-292-4100 ■ *Web:* www.hotelderek.com					
Hotel DeVille/Baymont Inn					
319 W Miller St	Jefferson City	MO	65109	573-636-5231	636-5260
TF: 800-392-3366 ■ *Web:* www.devillehotel.com					
Hotel Drisco 2901 Pacific Ave	San Francisco	CA	94115	415-346-2880	567-5537
TF: 800-634-7277 ■ *Web:* www.jdvhotels.com/hotels/sanfrancisco/drisco					
Hotel du Fort 1390 du Fort St	Montreal	QC	H3H2R7	514-938-8333	938-2078
TF: 800-565-6333 ■ *Web:* www.hoteldufort.com					
Hotel du Pont 11th & Market Sts.	Wilmington	DE	19801	302-594-3100	594-3108
TF: 800-441-9019 ■ *Web:* www.hoteldupont.com					
Hotel Durant 2600 Durant Ave.	Berkeley	CA	94704	510-845-8981	486-8336
TF: 800-238-7268 ■ *Web:* www.jdvhotels.com					
Hotel Edison 228 W 47th St.	New York	NY	10036	212-840-5000	596-6868
TF: 800-637-7070 ■ *Web:* www.edisonhotelnyc.com					
Hotel Elysee 60 E 54th St	New York	NY	10022	212-753-1066	980-9278
TF: 800-535-9733 ■ *Web:* www.elyseehotel.com					
Hotel Encanto de Las Cruces					
755 Avenida de Mesilla.	Las Cruces	NM	88005	575-526-8311	527-2015
TF: 888-846-6741 ■ *Web:* www.hamptoninn1.hilton.com					
Hotel Fort Des Moines 1000 Walnut St	Des Moines	IA	50309	515-243-1161	243-4317
TF: 800-532-1466 ■ *Web:* www.hotelfortdm.com					
Hotel Galvez - A Wyndham Historic Hotel					
2024 Seawall Blvd	Galveston	TX	77550	409-765-7721	765-5623
TF: 800-996-3426 ■ *Web:* www.wyndham.com					
Hotel Gault 449 Rue Sainte-Helene St	Montreal	QC	H2Y2K9	514-904-1616	304-1717
TF: 866-904-1616 ■ *Web:* www.hotelgault.com					
Hotel George 15 E St NW.	Washington	DC	20001	202-347-4200	347-4213
TF: 800-576-8831 ■ *Web:* www.hotelgeorge.com					
Hotel Giraffe 365 Pk Ave S at 26th St	New York	NY	10016	212-685-7700	685-7771
TF: 877-296-0009 ■ *Web:* www.hotelgiraffe.com					
Hotel Grand Pacific 463 Belleville St.	Victoria	BC	V8V1X3	250-386-0450	380-4475
TF: 800-663-7550 ■ *Web:* www.hotelgrandpacific.com					
Hotel Grand Victorian 2325 W Hwy 76	Branson	MO	65616	417-336-2935	336-1932
TF: 800-324-8751 ■ *Web:* www.luxehotels.com					
Hotel Granduca 1080 Uptown Pk Blvd	Houston	TX	77056	713-418-1000	418-1001
TF: 888-472-6382 ■ *Web:* www.granducahouston.com					
Hotel Griffon 155 Steuart St.	San Francisco	CA	94105	415-495-2100	495-3522
TF: 800-321-2201 ■ *Web:* www.greystonehotels.com/hotelgriffon					
Hotel Group The (THG) 110 James St Suite 102	Edmonds	WA	98020	425-771-1788	672-8280
Web: www.thehotelgroup.com					
Hotel Helix 1430 Rhode Island Ave NW	Washington	DC	20005	202-462-9001	332-3519
Web: www.hotelhelix.com					
Hotel Highland 1023 20th St S	Birmingham	AL	35205	205-933-9555	933-6918
TF Cust Svc: 800-255-7304					
Hotel Huntington Beach 7667 Ctr Ave	Huntington Beach	CA	92647	714-891-0123	
TF: 877-891-0123 ■ *Web:* www.hotelhb.com					
Hotel Icon 220 Main St	Houston	TX	77002	713-224-4266	223-3223
TF: 800-970-4266 ■ *Web:* www.hotelicon.com					
Hotel Jerome 330 E Main St	Aspen	CO	81611	970-920-1000	925-2784
TF: 800-331-7213 ■ *Web:* www.hoteljerome.com					
Hotel Kabuki San Francisco					
1625 Post St.	San Francisco	CA	94115	415-922-3200	614-5498
TF: 800-533-4567 ■ *Web:* www.jdvhotels.com/hotels/kabuki					
Hotel La Jolla 7955 La Jolla Shores Dr	La Jolla	CA	92037	858-459-0261	459-7649
TF: 800-666-0261 ■ *Web:* www.hotellajolla.com					
Hotel La Rose 308 Wilson St.	Santa Rosa	CA	95401	707-579-3200	579-3247
TF: 800-527-6738 ■ *Web:* www.hotellarose.com					
Hotel Lawrence 302 S Houston St	Dallas	TX	75202	214-761-9090	761-0740
TF: 877-396-0334 ■ *Web:* www.hotellawrence.com					
Hotel Le Bleu 370 4th Ave.	Brooklyn	NY	11215	718-625-1500	625-2600
TF: 866-427-6073 ■ *Web:* www.hotellebleu.com					
Hotel Le Cantlie Suites					
1110 Sherbrooke St W	Montreal	QC	H3A1G9	514-842-2000	844-7808
TF: 800-567-1110 ■ *Web:* www.hotelcantlie.com					
Hotel Le Capitole 972 St Jean St	Quebec	QC	G1R1R5	418-694-4040	694-9924
TF: 800-363-4040 ■ *Web:* www.lecapitole.com					
Hotel Le Clos Saint-Louis 69 St Louis St	Quebec	QC	G1R3Z2	418-694-1311	694-9411
TF: 800-461-1311 ■ *Web:* www.clossaintlouis.com					
Hotel Le Germain 2050 Mansfield St	Montreal	QC	H3A1Y9	514-849-2050	849-1437
TF: 877-333-2050 ■ *Web:* www.germainmontreal.com					
Hotel Le Germain Toronto 30 Mercer St	Toronto	ON	M5V1H3	416-345-9500	345-9501
TF: 866-345-9501 ■ *Web:* www.germaintoronto.com					
Hotel le Gite 5160 Wilfrid-Hamel Blvd W	Quebec	QC	G2E2G8	418-871-8899	872-8533
TF: 800-363-4906 ■					
Web: www.secure9.securewebexchange.com/hotellegite.com/en/index.php					
Hotel le Priori 15 du Sault-au-Matelot St	Quebec	QC	G1K3Y7	418-692-3992	692-0883
TF: 800-351-3992 ■ *Web:* www.hotellepriori.com					
Hotel Le Soleil 567 Hornby St.	Vancouver	BC	V6C2E8	604-632-3000	632-3001
TF: 877-632-3030 ■ *Web:* www.hotellesoleil.com					
Hotel Le St-James 355 St Jacques St	Montreal	QC	H2Y1N9	514-841-3111	841-1232
TF: 866-841-3111 ■ *Web:* www.hotellestjames.com					
Hotel Lombardy 2019 Pennsylvania Ave NW	Washington	DC	20006	202-828-2600	872-0503
TF: 800-424-5486 ■ *Web:* www.hotellombardy.com					
Hotel Lord-Berri 1199 Berri St	Montreal	QC	H2L4C6	514-845-9236	849-9855
TF: 888-363-0363 ■ *Web:* www.lordberri.com					
Hotel Los Gatos 210 E Main St	Los Gatos	CA	95030	408-335-1700	335-1750
TF: 866-335-1700 ■ *Web:* www.jdvhotels.com					
Hotel Lucia 400 SW Broadway	Portland	OR	97205	503-225-1717	225-1919
TF: 877-225-1717 ■ *Web:* www.hotellucia.com					
hotel Lumen 6101 Hillcrest Ave.	Dallas	TX	75205	214-219-2400	219-2402
TF: 800-908-1140 ■ *Web:* www.hotellumen.com					
Hotel Lusso 1 N Post St	Spokane	WA	99201	509-747-9750	747-9751
TF: 800-525-4800 ■ *Web:* www.hotellusso.com					
Hotel Madera 1310 New Hampshire Ave NW	Washington	DC	20036	202-296-7600	293-2476
TF: 800-368-5691 ■ *Web:* www.hotelmadera.com					
Hotel Majestic 1500 Sutter St.	San Francisco	CA	94109	415-441-1100	673-7331
TF: 800-869-8966 ■ *Web:* www.thehotelmajestic.com					
Hotel Manoir Victoria 44 Cote du Palais.	Quebec	QC	G1R4H8	418-692-1030	692-3822
TF: 800-463-6283 ■ *Web:* www.manoir-victoria.com					
Hotel Maritime Plaza 1155 Guy St	Montreal	QC	H3H2K5	514-932-1411	932-0446
TF: 800-363-6255 ■ *Web:* www.hotelmaritime.com					
Hotel Mark Twain 345 Taylor St	San Francisco	CA	94102	415-673-2332	673-0529
TF: 877-854-4106 ■ *Web:* www.hotelmarktwain.com					
Hotel Marlowe Cambridge					
25 Edwind H Land Blvd	Cambridge	MA	02141	617-868-8000	868-8001
TF: 800-825-7040 ■ *Web:* www.hotelmarlowe.com					
Hotel Max 620 Stewart St.	Seattle	WA	98101	206-728-6299	443-5754
TF: 866-833-6299 ■ *Web:* www.hotelmaxseattle.com					
Hotel Mead 451 E Grand Ave.	Wisconsin Rapids	WI	54494	715-423-1500	423-1510
TF: 800-843-6323 ■ *Web:* www.hotelmead.com					
Hotel Mela 120 W 44th St	New York	NY	10036	212-710-7000	704-9680
TF: 877-452-6352 ■ *Web:* www.hotelmela.com					
Hotel Metro 411 E Mason St	Milwaukee	WI	53202	414-272-1937	223-1158
TF: 877-638-7620 ■ *Web:* www.hotelmetro.com					
Hotel Milano 55 5th St.	San Francisco	CA	94103	415-543-8555	543-8555
TF: 800-398-7555 ■ *Web:* www.hotelmilanosf.com					
Hotel Monaco Chicago 225 N Wabash Ave.	Chicago	IL	60601	312-960-8500	960-1883
TF: 800-397-7661 ■ *Web:* www.monaco-chicago.com					
Hotel Monaco Denver 1717 Champa St.	Denver	CO	80202	303-296-1717	296-1818
TF: 800-397-5380 ■ *Web:* www.monaco-denver.com					
Hotel Monaco Portland					
506 SW Washington at 5th Ave.	Portland	OR	97204	503-222-0001	222-0004
TF: 866-861-9514 ■ *Web:* www.monaco-portland.com					
Hotel Monaco Salt Lake City					
15 W 200 S.	Salt Lake City	UT	84101	801-595-0000	532-8500
TF: 877-294-9710 ■ *Web:* www.monaco-saltlakecity.com					
Hotel Monaco San Francisco					
501 Geary St.	San Francisco	CA	94102	415-292-0100	292-0111
TF: 866-622-5284 ■ *Web:* www.monaco-sf.com					
Hotel Monaco Seattle 1101 4th Ave	Seattle	WA	98101	206-621-1770	621-7779
TF: 800-715-6513 ■ *Web:* www.monaco-seattle.com					
Hotel Monte Vista 100 N San Francisco St	Flagstaff	AZ	86001	928-779-6971	779-2904
TF: 800-545-3068 ■ *Web:* www.hotelmontevista.com					
Hotel Monteleone 214 Royal St.	New Orleans	LA	70130	504-523-3341	681-4413
TF: 800-535-9595 ■ *Web:* www.hotelmonteleone.com					
Hotel Montgomery 211 S 1st St.	San Jose	CA	95113	408-282-8800	282-8850
TF: 866-823-0530 ■ *Web:* www.jdvhotels.com/montgomery					
Hotel Monticello					
1075 Thomas Jefferson St NW	Washington	DC	20007	202-337-0900	333-6526
TF: 800-388-2410 ■ *Web:* www.monticellohotel.com					
Hotel Montreal Centrale 1586 St Hubert St	Montreal	QC	H2L3Z3	514-843-5739	904-0888
TF: 866-878-5739 ■ *Web:* www.hotelmontrealcentrale.com					
Hotel Murano 1320 Broadway Plaza	Tacoma	WA	98402	253-238-8000	591-4105
TF: 888-862-3255 ■ *Web:* www.hotelmuranotacoma.com					
Hotel Nikko San Francisco 222 Mason St	San Francisco	CA	94102	415-394-1111	394-1106
TF: 800-645-5687 ■ *Web:* www.hotelnikkosf.com					
Hotel Northampton 36 King St	NorthHampton	MA	01060	413-584-3100	584-9455
TF: 800-547-3529 ■ *Web:* www.hotelnorthampton.com					
Hotel Ocean 1230 Ocean Dr.	Miami Beach	FL	33139	305-672-2579	672-7665
TF: 800-783-1725 ■ *Web:* www.hotelocean.com					
Hotel Oceana					
Oceana Santa Monica 849 Ocean Ave	Santa Monica	CA	90403	310-393-0486	458-1182
TF: 800-777-0758 ■ *Web:* www.hoteloceanasantamonica.com					
Santa Barbara 202 W Cabrillo Blvd	Santa Barbara	CA	93101	805-965-4577	965-9937
TF: 800-965-9776 ■ *Web:* www.hoteloceanasantabarbara.com					
Hotel Omni Mont-Royal 1050 Sherbrooke St W	Montreal	QC	H3A2R6	514-284-1110	845-3025
TF: 800-843-6664 ■ *Web:* www.omnihotels.com					
Hotel Orrington 1710 Orrington Ave	Evanston	IL	60201	847-866-8700	866-8724
TF: 888-677-4648 ■ *Web:* www.hotelorrington.com					
Hotel Pacific 300 Pacific St.	Monterey	CA	93940	831-373-5700	373-6921
TF: 800-554-5542 ■ *Web:* www.hotelpacific.com					
Hotel Palomar Arlington 1121 N 19th St	Arlington	VA	22209	703-351-9170	351-9175
TF: 866-505-1001 ■ *Web:* www.hotelpalomar-arlington.com					
Hotel Palomar Dallas 5300 E Mockingbird Ln.	Dallas	TX	75206	214-520-7969	520-8025
TF: 888-253-9030 ■ *Web:* www.hotelpalomar-dallas.com					
Hotel Palomar San Francisco 12 4th St.	San Francisco	CA	94103	415-348-1111	348-0302
TF: 877-294-9711 ■ *Web:* www.hotelpalomar-sf.com					
Hotel Parisi 1111 Prospect	La Jolla	CA	92037	858-454-1511	454-1531
TF: 877-472-7474 ■ *Web:* www.hotelparisi.com					
Hotel Park City (HPC) 2001 Pk Ave	Park City	UT	84060	435-200-2000	940-5001
TF: 888-999-0098 ■ *Web:* www.hotelparkcity.com					
Hotel Pere Marquette 501 Main St.	Peoria	IL	61602	309-637-6500	637-6500
TF: 800-447-1676 ■ *Web:* www.hotelperemarquette.com					
Hotel Phillips 106 W 12th St.	Kansas City	MO	64105	816-221-7000	221-3477
TF: 800-433-1426 ■ *Web:* www.hotelphillips.com					
Hotel Plaza Athenee 37 E 64th St	New York	NY	10065	212-734-9100	772-0958
TF: 800-447-8800 ■ *Web:* www.plaza-athenee.com					
Hotel Plaza Quebec 3031 Laurier Blvd.	Sainte-Foy	QC	G1V2M2	418-658-2727	658-6587
TF: 800-567-5276 ■ *Web:* www.hotelsjaro.com/plazaquebec/index-en.aspx					
Hotel Plaza Real 125 Washington Ave	Santa Fe	NM	87501	505-988-4900	983-9322
TF: 877-901-7666					
Hotel Provincial 1024 Rue Chartres	New Orleans	LA	70116	504-581-4995	581-1018
TF: 800-535-7922 ■ *Web:* www.hotelprovincial.com					
Hotel PUR 395 Rue de la Couronne	Quebec City	QC	G1K7X4	418-647-2611	640-0666
Web: www.hotelpur.com					
Hotel Quartier 2955 Laurier Blvd.	Quebec	QC	G1V2M2	418-650-1616	650-6611
TF: 888-818-5863 ■ *Web:* www.hotelquartier.com					
Hotel Queen Mary 1126 Queens Hwy.	Long Beach	CA	90802	562-435-3511	437-4531
TF: 877-342-0738 ■ *Web:* www.queenmary.com					
Hotel Rex 562 Sutter St	San Francisco	CA	94102	415-433-4434	433-3695
TF: 800-433-4434 ■ *Web:* www.jdvhotels.com/hotels/rex					
Hotel Rodney 142 2nd St.	Lewes	DE	19958	302-645-6466	645-7196
TF: 800-824-8754 ■ *Web:* www.hotelrodneydelaware.com					
Hotel Roger Williams 131 Madison Ave	New York	NY	10016	212-448-7000	448-7007
TF Resv: 888-448-7788 ■ *Web:* www.hotelrogerwilliams.com					

	City	State	Zip	Phone	Fax
Hotel Rouge 1315 16th St NW	Washington	DC	20036	202-232-8000	667-9827
TF: 800-738-1202 ■ *Web:* www.rougehotel.com					
Hotel Royal Palace					
775 Honore Mercier Ave	Quebec City	QC	G1R6A5	418-694-2000	380-2553
TF: 800-567-5276 ■ *Web:* www.hotelsjaro.com/palaceroyal/index-en.aspx					
Hotel Royal Plaza					
1905 Hotel Plaza Blvd	Lake Buena Vista	FL	32830	407-828-2828	827-3977
TF: 800-248-7890 ■ *Web:* www.royalplaza.com					
Hotel Ruby Foo's 7655 Decarie Blvd	Montreal	QC	H4P2H2	514-731-7701	731-7158
TF: 800-361-5419 ■ *Web:* www.hotelrubyfoos.com					
Hotel Saint Francis 210 Don Gaspar Ave	Santa Fe	NM	87501	505-983-5700	989-7690
TF: 800-529-5700 ■ *Web:* www.hotelstfrancis.com					
Hotel Saint Germain 2516 Maple Ave	Dallas	TX	75201	214-871-2516	871-0740
TF: 800-683-2516 ■ *Web:* www.hotelstgermain.com					
Hotel Saint Marie 827 Toulouse St	New Orleans	LA	70112	504-561-8951	571-2802
TF: 800-366-2743 ■ *Web:* www.hotelstmarie.com					
Hotel Saint Pierre 911 Burgundy St	New Orleans	LA	70116	504-524-4401	593-9425
TF Resv: 800-225-4040 ■ *Web:* www.frenchquarterinns.com					
Hotel Saint Regis Detroit 3071 W Grand Blvd	Detroit	MI	48202	313-873-3000	875-2035
Web: www.hotelstregisdetroit.com					
Hotel San Carlos 202 N Central Ave	Phoenix	AZ	85004	602-253-4121	253-6668
TF: 866-253-4121 ■ *Web:* www.hotelsancarlos.com					
Hotel Santa Barbara 533 State St	Santa Barbara	CA	93101	805-957-9300	962-2412
TF: 888-259-7700 ■ *Web:* www.hotelsantabarbara.com					
Hotel Santa Fe 1501 Paseo de Peralta	Santa Fe	NM	87501	505-982-1200	984-2211
TF: 800-825-9876 ■ *Web:* www.hotelsantafe.com					
Hotel Saranac The 100 Main St	Saranac Lake	NY	12983	518-891-2200	891-5664
TF: 800-937-0211 ■ *Web:* www.hotelsaranac.com					
Hotel Sax Chicago 333 N Dearborn St	Chicago	IL	60610	312-245-0333	923-2458
TF: 877-569-3742 ■ *Web:* www.thompsonhotels.com					
Hotel Sepia 3135 ch St-Louis	Sainte-Foy	QC	G1W1R9	418-653-4941	653-0774
TF: 800-463-6603 ■ *Web:* www.hotelsepia.ca					
Hotel Shelley 844 Collins Ave	Miami Beach	FL	33139	305-531-3341	674-0811
TF: 877-762-3477 ■ *Web:* www.hotelshelley.com					
Hotel Solamar 435 6th Ave	San Diego	CA	92101	619-819-9500	923-2864
TF: 877-230-0300 ■ *Web:* www.hotelsolamar.com					
Hotel Strasburg The 213 S Holliday St	Strasburg	VA	22657	540-465-9191	465-4788
TF: 800-348-8327 ■ *Web:* www.hotelstrasburg.com					
Hotel Teatro 1100 14th St	Denver	CO	80202	303-228-1100	228-1101
TF: 888-727-1200 ■ *Web:* www.hotelteatro.com					
Hotel The 801 Collins Ave	Miami Beach	FL	33139	305-531-2222	531-3222
TF: 800-727-5236 ■ *Web:* www.thehotelofsouthbeach.com					
Hotel Triton 342 Grant Ave	San Francisco	CA	94108	415-394-0500	394-0555
TF: 800-800-1299 ■ *Web:* www.hoteltriton.com					
Hotel Universel 2300 ch Sainte-Foy	Sainte-Foy	QC	G1V1S5	418-653-5250	653-4486
TF: 800-463-4495 ■ *Web:* www.hoteluniversel.qc.ca					
Hotel Utica 102 Lafayette St	Utica	NY	13502	315-724-7829	733-7663
TF: 877-906-1912 ■ *Web:* www.hotelutica.com					
Hotel Val-des-Neiges					
201 Val-des-Neiges St Mont Sainte-Anne	Beaupre	QC	G0A1E0	418-827-5711	827-5997
TF: 888-222-3305 ■ *Web:* www.hotelvaldesneiges.com/en					
Hotel Valencia Santana Row 355 Santana Row	San Jose	CA	95128	408-551-0010	551-0550
TF: 866-842-0100 ■ *Web:* www.hotelvalencia-santanarow.com					
Hotel Valley Ho 6850 Main St	Scottsdale	AZ	85251	480-248-2000	248-2002
TF: 866-882-4484 ■ *Web:* www.hotelvalleyho.com					
Hotel Victoria 56 Yonge St	Toronto	ON	M5E1G5	416-363-1666	363-7327
TF: 800-363-8228 ■ *Web:* www.hotelvictoria-toronto.com					
Hotel Viking 1 Bellevue Ave	Newport	RI	02840	401-847-3300	848-4864
TF: 800-556-7126 ■ *Web:* www.hotelviking.com					
Hotel Vintage Park 1100 5th Ave	Seattle	WA	98101	206-624-8000	623-0568
TF: 800-853-3914 ■ *Web:* www.hotelvintagepark.com					
Hotel Vintage Plaza 422 SW Broadway	Portland	OR	97205	503-228-1212	228-3598
TF: 800-263-2305 ■ *Web:* www.vintageplaza.com					
Hotel Vitale 8 Mission St	San Francisco	CA	94105	415-278-3700	278-3750
TF: 888-890-8688 ■ *Web:* www.hotelvitale.com					
Hotel Wales 1295 Madison Ave	New York	NY	10128	212-876-6000	860-7000
TF: 866-925-3746					
Hotel Washington 515 15th St NW	Washington	DC	20004	202-661-2400	
TF: 800-424-9540 ■ *Web:* www.wwashingtondc.com					
Hotel Weatherford The 23 N Leroux St	Flagstaff	AZ	86001	928-779-1919	773-8951
Web: www.weatherfordhotel.com					
Hotel Windsor					
1700 Benjamin Franklin Pkwy	Philadelphia	PA	19103	215-981-5678	981-5684
Web: www.windsorhotel.com					
Hotel Wolcott 4 W 31st St	New York	NY	10001	212-268-2900	563-0096
Web: www.wolcott.com					
Hotel XIXe Siecle					
Lhotel 262 St Jacques St W	Vieux Montreal	QC	H2Y1N1	514-985-0019	985-0059
TF: 877-553-0019 ■ *Web:* www.lhotelmontreal.com					
Hotel ZaZa Dallas 2332 Leonard St	Dallas	TX	75201	214-468-8399	468-8397
TF: 800-597-8399 ■ *Web:* www.hotelzaza.com					
Hotel ZaZa Houston 5701 Main St	Houston	TX	77005	713-526-1991	526-0359
TF Resv: 888-880-3244 ■ *Web:* www.hotelzaza.com/Houston					
Houston Grand Plaza Hotel 8686 Kirby Dr	Houston	TX	77054	713-748-3221	796-9371
Web: www.houstongrandplaza.com					
HTH Corp 2490 Kalakaua Ave	Honolulu	HI	96815	808-922-1233	923-2566*
**Fax:* Sales ■ *TF:* 800-367-6060 ■ *Web:* www.hthcorp.com					
Hummingbird Hill Cabin Village 1785 Hwy 105	Boone	NC	28607	828-264-1000	262-0073
TF: 800-334-5605 ■ *Web:* www.hummingbirdhillcabins.com					
Humphrey's Half Moon Inn & Suites					
2303 Shelter Island Dr	San Diego	CA	92106	619-224-3411	224-3478
TF: 800-542-7400 ■ *Web:* www.halfmooninn.com					
Huntington Hotel & Nob Hill Spa					
1075 California St	San Francisco	CA	94108	415-474-5400	474-6227
TF: 800-227-4683 ■ *Web:* www.huntingtonhotel.com					
Hyannis Holiday Motel 131 Ocean St	Hyannis	MA	02601	508-775-1639	775-1672
TF: 800-423-1551 ■ *Web:* www.hyannisholiday.com					
Hyannis Travel Inn 18 N St	Hyannis	MA	02601	508-775-8200	775-8201
TF: 800-352-7190 ■ *Web:* www.hyannistravelinn.com					
Hyatt Carmel Highlands 120 Highlands Dr	Carmel	CA	93923	831-624-3801	626-1574
TF: 800-682-4811 ■ *Web:* www.highlandsinn.hyatt.com/hyatt/hotels					
Hyatt Hotels Corp 71 S Wacker Dr	Chicago	IL	60606	312-750-1234	750-8597*
**Fax:* Mktg ■ *TF:* 888-591-1234 ■ *Web:* www.hyatt.com					
Grand Hyatt Hotels 71 S Wacker Dr	Chicago	IL	60606	312-750-1234	780-5289*
**Fax:* Mktg ■ *TF Resv:* 800-233-1234 ■ *Web:* www.hyatt.com					
Hyatt Place Hotels 71 S Wacker Dr	Chicago	IL	60606	312-750-1234	780-5289
TF Cust Svc: 888-492-8847 ■ *Web:* www.hyatt.com/hyatt/place					
Hyatt Regency Hotels 71 S Wacker Dr	Chicago	IL	60606	312-750-1234	780-5289*
**Fax:* Mktg ■ *TF Resv:* 800-233-1234 ■ *Web:* www.hyatt.com					
Hyatt Summerfield Suites 71 S Wacker Dr	Chicago	IL	60606	312-750-1234	780-5289
Web: www.hyatt.com/hyatt/summerfield					
Park Hyatt Hotels 71 S Wacker Dr	Chicago	IL	60606	312-750-1234	780-5289*
**Fax:* Mktg ■ *TF Resv:* 800-233-1234 ■ *Web:* www.hyatt.com					
Iberville Suites The 910 Iberville St	New Orleans	LA	70112	504-523-2400	524-1321
TF: 866-229-4351 ■ *Web:* www.ibervillesuites.com					
Ilikai Hotel & Suites 1777 Ala Moana Blvd	Honolulu	HI	96815	808-949-3811	947-0892
TF: 866-769-8814 ■ *Web:* www.ilikaihotel.com					
Imperial of Waikiki 205 Lewers St	Honolulu	HI	96815	808-923-1827	921-7586
TF: 800-347-2582 ■ *Web:* www.imperialofwaikiki.com					
Imperial Swan Hotel 7050 S Kirkman Rd	Orlando	FL	32819	407-351-2000	363-1835
TF: 800-327-3808 ■ *Web:* www.imperialswanorlando.com					
Indian Creek Hotel 2727 Indian Creek Dr	Miami Beach	FL	33140	305-531-2727	531-5651
TF: 800-491-2772 ■ *Web:* www.indiancreekhotelmb.com					
Indiana Memorial Union Board					
900 E 7th St Rm 270	Bloomington	IN	47405	812-855-4682	
Web: www.imu.indiana.edu					
Indigo Inn 1 Maiden Ln	Charleston	SC	29401	843-577-5900	577-0378
TF: 800-845-7639 ■ *Web:* www.indigoinn.com					
Ingleside Inn 200 W Ramon Rd	Palm Springs	CA	92264	760-325-0046	325-0710
TF: 800-772-6655 ■ *Web:* www.inglesideinn.com					
Inlet Tower Suites 1200 L St	Anchorage	AK	99501	907-276-0110	258-4914
TF: 800-544-0786 ■ *Web:* www.inlettower.com					
Inn & Spa at Loretto 211 Old Santa Fe Trail	Santa Fe	NM	87501	505-988-5531	984-7968
TF: 800-727-5531 ■ *Web:* www.innatloretto.com					
Inn at Camachee Harbor					
201 Yacht Club Dr	Saint Augustine	FL	32084	904-825-0003	825-0048
TF: 800-688-5379 ■ *Web:* www.camacheeinn.com					
Inn at Essex 70 Essex Way	Essex Junction	VT	05452	802-878-1100	878-0063
TF: 800-727-4295 ■ *Web:* www.vtculinaryresort.com					
Inn at Gig Harbor 3211 56th St NW	Gig Harbor	WA	98335	253-858-1111	851-5402
TF: 800-795-9980 ■ *Web:* www.innatgigharbor.com					
Inn at Harbour Town					
7 Lighthouse Ln	Hilton Head Island	SC	29928	843-363-8100	363-8155
TF Cust Svc: 888-807-6873 ■					
Web: www.seapines.com/accommodations/inn_at_harbour_town.cfm					
Inn at Harvard 1201 Massachusetts Ave	Cambridge	MA	02138	617-491-2222	520-3711
TF: 800-458-5886 ■ *Web:* www.hotelsinharvardsquare.com					
Inn at Henderson's Wharf 1000 Fell St	Baltimore	MD	21231	410-522-7777	522-7087
TF: 800-522-2088 ■ *Web:* www.hendersonswharf.com					
Inn at Jarrett Farm 38009 US Hwy 75 N	Ramona	OK	74061	918-371-1200	371-1300
TF: 877-371-1200 ■ *Web:* www.jarrettfarm.com					
Inn at Lambertville Station					
11 Bridge St	Lambertville	NJ	08530	609-397-4400	397-9744
TF: 800-524-1091 ■ *Web:* www.lambertvillestation.com					
Inn at Langley 400 1st St PO Box 835	Langley	WA	98260	360-221-3033	221-3033
TF: 800-843-3779 ■ *Web:* www.innatlangley.com					
Inn at Little Washington					
Middle & Main St PO Box 300	Washington	VA	22747	540-675-3800	675-3100
Web: www.theinnatlittlewashington.com					
Inn at Longshore 260 Compo Rd S	Westport	CT	06880	203-226-3316	226-5723
Web: www.innatlongshore.com					
Inn at Mayo Clinic 4420 Mary Brigh Dr	Jacksonville	FL	32224	904-992-9992	992-4463
TF: 888-255-4458 ■ *Web:* www.mayoclinic.org					
Inn at Montchanin Village					
528 Montchanin Rd	Wilmington	DE	19710	302-888-2133	888-0389
TF: 800-269-2473 ■ *Web:* www.montchanin.com					
Inn at Montpelier The 147 Main St	Montpelier	VT	05602	802-223-2727	223-0722
Web: www.innatmontpelier.com					
Inn at Morro Bay 60 State Pk Rd	Morro Bay	CA	93442	805-772-5651	772-4779
TF: 800-321-9566 ■ *Web:* www.innatmorrobay.com					
Inn at Mystic 3 Williams Ave PO Box 216	Mystic	CT	06355	860-536-9604	572-1635
TF: 800-237-2415 ■ *Web:* www.innatmystic.com					
Inn at National Hall 2 Post Rd W	Westport	CT	06880	203-221-1351	221-0276
TF: 800-628-4255 ■ *Web:* www.innatnationalhall.com					
Inn at Nichols Village					
1101 Northern Blvd	South Abington Twp	PA	18411	570-587-1135	586-7140
TF: 800-642-2215 ■ *Web:* www.nicholsvillage.com					
Inn at Otter Crest 301 Otter Crest Loop	Otter Rock	OR	97369	541-765-2111	765-2047
TF: 800-452-2101 ■ *Web:* www.innatottercrest.com					
Inn at Oyster Point					
425 Marina Blvd	South San Francisco	CA	94080	650-737-7633	737-0795
TF: 800-642-2720 ■ *Web:* www.innatoysterpoint.com					
Inn at Pelican Bay 800 Vanderbilt Beach Rd	Naples	FL	34108	239-597-8777	597-8012
TF: 800-597-8770 ■ *Web:* www.innatpelicanbay.com					
Inn at Perry Cabin 308 Watkins Ln	Saint Michaels	MD	21663	410-745-2200	745-3348
TF: 800-722-2949 ■ *Web:* www.perrycabin.com					
Inn at Queen Anne 505 1st Ave N	Seattle	WA	98109	206-282-7357	217-9719
TF: 800-952-5043 ■ *Web:* www.innatqueenanne.com					
Inn at Reading The 1040 N Pk Rd	Wyomissing	PA	19610	610-372-7811	372-4545
TF: 800-383-9713 ■ *Web:* www.innatreading.com					
Inn at Saint John 939 Congress St	Portland	ME	04102	207-773-6481	756-7629
TF: 800-636-9127 ■ *Web:* www.innatstjohn.com					
Inn at Saint Mary's 53993 US Hwy 31-33 N	South Bend	IN	46637	574-232-4000	289-0986
TF: 800-947-8627 ■ *Web:* www.innatsaintmarys.com					
Inn at Sawmill Farm The					
7 Crosstown Rd PO Box 367	West Dover	VT	05356	802-464-8131	464-1130
TF: 800-493-1133 ■ *Web:* www.theinnatsawmillfarm.com					
Inn at Spanish Head 4009 SW Hwy 101	Lincoln City	OR	97367	541-996-2161	996-4089
TF: 800-452-8127 ■ *Web:* www.spanishhead.com					
Inn at Tallgrass The 2280 N Tara Cir	Wichita	KS	67226	316-684-3466	685-3466
TF: 800-684-3466 ■ *Web:* www.theinnattallgrass.com					
Inn at the Ballpark 1520 Texas Ave	Houston	TX	77002	713-228-1520	228-1555
TF: 866-406-1520 ■ *Web:* www.innattheballpark.com					

	City	State	Zip	Phone	Fax
Inn at the Market 86 Pine St	Seattle	WA	98101	206-443-3600	448-0631
TF: 800-446-4484 ■ *Web:* www.innatthemarket.com					
Inn at the Opera 333 Fulton St	San Francisco	CA	94102	415-863-8400	861-0821
TF: 800-325-2708 ■ *Web:* www.innattheopera.com					
Inn At The Quay 900 Quayside Dr	New Westminster	BC	V3M6G1	604-520-1776	520-5645
TF: 800-663-2001 ■ *Web:* www.innatwestminsterquay.com					
Inn at The Tides The 800 Coast Hwy 1 PO Box 640	Bodega Bay	CA	94923	707-875-2751	875-2669
TF: 800-541-7788 ■ *Web:* www.innatthetides.com					
Inn at Union Square 440 Post St	San Francisco	CA	94102	415-397-3510	989-0529
TF: 800-288-4346 ■ *Web:* www.greystonehotels.com					
Inn by the Lake 3300 Lake Tahoe Blvd	South Lake Tahoe	CA	96150	530-542-0330	541-6250
TF: 800-877-1466 ■ *Web:* www.innbythelake.com					
Inn of Chicago Magnificent Mile 162 E Ohio St	Chicago	IL	60611	312-787-3100	573-3159
TF: 800-557-2378 ■ *Web:* www.innofchicago.com					
Inn of Long Beach 185 Atlantic Ave	Long Beach	CA	90802	562-435-3791	436-7510
TF: 800-230-7500 ■ *Web:* www.innoflongbeach.com					
Inn of the Anasazi 113 Washington Ave	Santa Fe	NM	87501	505-988-3030	988-3277
TF: 800-688-8100 ■ *Web:* www.innoftheanasazi.com					
Inn of the Governors 101 W Alameda St	Santa Fe	NM	87501	505-982-4333	989-9149
TF: 800-234-4534 ■ *Web:* www.innofthegovernors.com					
Inn of the Six Mountains 2617 Killington Rd	Killington	VT	05751	802-422-4302	422-4321
TF: 800-228-4676 ■ *Web:* www.sixmountains.com					
Inn on Biltmore Estate 1 Antler Hill Rd	Asheville	NC	28803	828-225-1600	225-1680
TF: 800-411-3812 ■ *Web:* www.biltmore.com					
Inn on Bourbon - A Ramada Plaza Hotel 541 Bourbon St	New Orleans	LA	70130	504-524-7611	568-9427
TF: 800-535-7891 ■ *Web:* www.innonbourbon.com					
Inn on Fifth 699 5th Ave S	Naples	FL	34102	239-403-8777	403-8778
TF: 888-403-8778 ■ *Web:* www.innonfifth.com					
Inn on Gitche Gumee 8517 Congdon Blvd	Duluth	MN	55804	218-525-4979	
TF: 800-317-4979 ■ *Web:* www.innongitchegumee.com					
Inn on Lake Superior 350 Canal Pk Dr	Duluth	MN	55802	218-726-1111	727-3976
TF: 888-668-4352 ■ *Web:* www.theinnonlakesuperior.com					
Inn on Mount Ada 398 Wrigley Rd PO Box 2560	Avalon	CA	90704	310-510-2030	510-2237
TF: 800-608-7669 ■ *Web:* www.innonmtada.com					
Inn on the Alameda 303 E Alameda St	Santa Fe	NM	87501	505-984-2121	986-8325
TF: 888-984-2121 ■ *Web:* www.innonthealameda.com					
Inn on the Beach 1615 S Atlantic Ave	Daytona Beach	FL	32118	386-255-0921	255-3849
TF: 800-874-0975 ■ *Web:* www.innonthebeach.com					
Inn on the Creek 295 N Millward Ave PO Box 445	Jackson	WY	83001	307-739-1565	734-9116
TF: 800-669-9534 ■ *Web:* www.innonthecreek.com					
Inn on the Paseo 630 Paseo de Peralta	Santa Fe	NM	87501	505-984-8200	955-7835
TF: 800-457-9045 ■ *Web:* www.innonthepaseo.com					
Inns at Mill Falls 312 Daniel Webster Hwy	Meredith	NH	03253	800-622-6455	279-6797*
**Fax Area Code:* 603 ■ *TF:* 800-622-6455 ■ *Web:* www.millfalls.com					
Inns of America Suites 755 Raintree Dr	Carlsbad	CA	92009	760-438-6661	431-9212
TF Resv: 800-826-0778 ■ *Web:* www.innsofamerica.com					
InnSuites Hospitality Trust InnSuites Hotels & Suites 1625 E Northern Ave Suite 102	Phoenix	AZ	85020	520-622-3000	678-0281*
**Fax Area Code:* 602 ■ *TF:* 800-842-4242 ■ *Web:* www.innsuites.com					
InnSuites Hotel Flagstaff/Grand Canyon 1008 E Rt 66	Flagstaff	AZ	86001	928-774-7356	556-0130
TF: 800-898-9124 ■ *Web:* www.hotelaspenflagstaff.com					
InnSuites Hotel Tempe/Phoenix Airport 1651 W Baseline Rd	Tempe	AZ	85283	480-897-7900	491-1008
TF: 800-841-4242 ■ *Web:* www.innsuites.com/tempe					
InnSuites Hotel Tucson City Ctr 475 N Granada Ave	Tucson	AZ	85701	520-622-3000	623-8922
TF: 888-784-8324 ■ *Web:* www.innsuites.com/tucson_citycenter					
InterContinental Hotels Group 3315 Peachtree Rd N E	Atlanta	GA	30326	404-946-9000	946-9001
Web: www.ichotelsgroup.com					
InterContinental Hotels Group (IHG) 3 Ravinia Dr Suite 100	Atlanta	GA	30346	770-604-2000	604-5403
Web: www.ihgplc.com					
Crowne Plaza Hotels & Resorts 3 Ravinia Dr Suite 2900	Atlanta	GA	30346	770-604-2000	604-5403
Holiday Inn Express 3 Ravinia Dr Suite 100	Atlanta	GA	30346	770-604-2000	604-5403
Web: www.ihgplc.com/index.asp?pageid=410					
Holiday Inn Hotels & Resorts 3 Ravinia Dr Suite 100	Atlanta	GA	30346	770-604-2000	604-5403
Web: www.ihgplc.com/index.asp?pageid=409					
Hotel Indigo 3 Ravinia Dr Suite 100	Atlanta	GA	30346	704-604-2000	604-5403*
**Fax Area Code:* 770 ■ *Web:* www.ihgplc.com					
Staybridge Suites 3 Ravinia Dr Suite 100	Atlanta	GA	30346	770-604-2000	604-5403
TF: 800-465-4329 ■ *Web:* www.ihgplc.com					
International Hotel 20 2nd Ave SW	Rochester	MN	55902	507-328-8000	285-2701
TF: 800-940-6811 ■ *Web:* www.internationalhotelmn.com					
International Hotel of Calgary 220 4th Ave SW	Calgary	AB	T2P0H5	403-265-9600	290-7879
TF: 800-661-8627 ■ *Web:* www.inernationalhotel.ca					
International House Hotel 221 Camp St	New Orleans	LA	70130	504-553-9550	553-9560
TF: 800-633-5770 ■ *Web:* www.ihhotel.com					
Interstate Hotels & Resorts Inc 4501 N Fairfax Dr	Arlington	VA	22033	703-387-3100	387-3101
NYSE: IHR ■ *Web:* www.ihrco.com					
Iroquois New York 49 W 44th St	New York City	NY	10036	212-840-3080	719-0006
TF: 800-332-7220 ■ *Web:* www.iroquoisny.com					
Island Hotel The 690 Newport Ctr Dr	Newport Beach	CA	92660	949-759-0808	759-0568
TF: 866-554-4620 ■ *Web:* www.islandhotel.com					
Jack London Inn 444 Embarcadero W	Oakland	CA	94607	510-444-2032	834-3074
TF: 800-549-8780 ■ *Web:* www.jacklondoninn.com					
Jackson Hole Lodge 420 W Broadway PO Box 1805	Jackson	WY	83001	307-733-2992	739-2144
TF: 800-604-9404 ■ *Web:* www.jacksonholelodge.com					
Jailhouse Inn 13 Marlborough St	Newport	RI	02840	401-847-4638	849-0605
TF: 800-427-9444 ■ *Web:* www.historicinnsofnewport.com					
James Chicago The 55 E Ontario	Chicago	IL	60611	312-337-1000	337-7217
TF: 888-526-3778 ■ *Web:* www.jameshotels.com					
James Gettys Hotel 27 Chambersburg St	Gettysburg	PA	17325	717-337-1334	334-2103
TF: 888-900-5275 ■ *Web:* www.jamesgettyshotel.com					
Jared Coffin House 29 Broad St	Nantucket	MA	02554	508-228-2400	228-8549
TF Cust Svc: 800-248-2405 ■ *Web:* www.jaredcoffinhouse.com					
Jefferson Hotel 101 W Franklin St	Richmond	VA	23220	804-788-8000	225-0334
TF: 800-424-8014 ■ *Web:* www.jeffersonhotel.com					
JHM Hotels Inc 60 Pointe Cir	Greenville	SC	29515	864-232-9944	232-6931*
**Fax:* PR ■ *TF:* 800-763-1100 ■ *Web:* www.jhmhotels.com					
John Q Hammons Hotel Management LLC 300 S John Q Hammons Pkwy #900	Springfield	MO	65806	417-864-4300	873-3540
Web: www.jqhhotels.com					
Joie de Vivre Hospitality Inc 530 Bush St Suite 501	San Francisco	CA	94108	415-835-0300	835-0317
TF: 800-738-7477 ■ *Web:* www.jdvhotels.com					
Jolly Hotel Madison Towers 22 E 38th St	New York	NY	10016	212-802-0600	447-0747
TF: 800-221-2626 ■ *Web:* www.jollymadison.com					
Jolly Roger Inn 640 W Katella Ave	Anaheim	CA	92802	714-782-7500	772-2308
TF: 888-296-5986 ■ *Web:* www.jollyrogerhotel.com					
Jorgenson's Inn & Suites 1714 11th Ave	Helena	MT	59601	406-442-1770	449-0155
TF: 800-272-1770 ■ *Web:* www.jorgensonsinn.com					
Juniper Inn 1315 N 27th St	Billings	MT	59101	406-245-4128	
TF: 800-826-7530					
Jury's Boston Hotel 350 Stuart St	Boston	MA	02116	617-266-7200	266-7203
TF: 800-423-6953 ■ *Web:* www.doylecollection.com					
Kahala Mandarin Oriental Hotel Hawaii Resort 5000 Kahala Ave	Honolulu	HI	96816	808-739-8888	739-8800
TF: 800-367-2525 ■ *Web:* www.kahalaresort.com					
Kawada Hotel 200 S Hill St	Los Angeles	CA	90012	213-621-4455	687-4455
TF: 800-752-9232 ■ *Web:* www.kawadahotel.com					
Kawailoa Development Co LP 1571 Poipu Rd Suite 307 PO Box 369	Koloa	HI	96756	808-742-6300	742-7197
Web: www.kawailoa.com					
Kellogg Hotel & Conference Ctr 55 S Harrison Rd Michigan State University Campus	East Lansing	MI	48824	517-432-4000	353-1872
TF: 800-875-5090 ■ *Web:* www.hfs.msu.edu/kellogg					
Kelly Inns Ltd 3205 W Sencore Dr	Sioux Falls	SD	57107	605-965-1440	965-1450
TF: 800-635-3559 ■ *Web:* www.kellyinns.com					
Kensington Court Ann Arbor 610 Hilton Blvd	Ann Arbor	MI	48108	734-761-7800	761-1040
TF Orders: 800-344-7829 ■ *Web:* www.kcourtaa.com					
Kensington Park Hotel 450 Post St	San Francisco	CA	94102	415-788-6400	399-9484
TF: 800-553-1900 ■ *Web:* www.kensingtonparkhotel.com					
Kensington Riverside Inn 1126 Memorial Dr NW	Calgary	AB	T2N3E3	403-228-4442	228-9608
TF: 877-313-3733 ■ *Web:* www.kensingtonriversideinn.com					
Kent The 1131 Collins Ave	Miami Beach	FL	33139	305-604-5068	531-0720
TF: 866-826-5368 ■ *Web:* www.thekenthotel.com					
Keswick Hall 701 Club Dr	Keswick	VA	22947	434-979-3440	977-4171
TF: 800-274-5391 ■ *Web:* www.keswick.com					
Key Lime Inn 725 Truman Ave	Key West	FL	33040	305-294-5229	294-9623
TF: 800-549-4430 ■ *Web:* www.historickeywestinns.com					
Keystone Lodge & Spa 22010 US Hwy 6	Keystone	CO	80435	866-990-9491	
TF: 866-990-9491 ■ *Web:* www.preferredhotels.com					
Killington Grand Resort Hotel & Conference Ctr 4763 Killington Rd	Killington	VT	05751	802-422-5001	422-1399
TF: 800-621-6867 ■ *Web:* www.killington.com					
Kimball Terrace Inn 10 Huntington Rd	Northeast Harbor	ME	04662	207-276-3383	276-4102
TF: 800-454-6225 ■ *Web:* www.kimballterraceinn.com					
Kimberly Hotel 145 E 50th St	New York	NY	10022	212-755-0400	750-0113
TF: 800-683-0400 ■ *Web:* www.kimberlyhotel.com					
Kimpton Hotel & Restaurant Group LLC 222 Kearny St Suite 200	San Francisco	CA	94108	415-397-5572	296-8031
TF: 800-546-2686 ■ *Web:* www.kimptonhotels.com					
King Kamehameha's Kona Beach Hotel 75-5660 Palani Rd	Kailua-Kona	HI	96740	808-329-2911	329-4602
TF: 800-367-2111 ■ *Web:* www.konabeachhotel.com					
King Pacific Lodge 255 W 1st St Suite 214	North Vancouver	BC	V7M3G8	604-987-5452	987-5472
TF: 888-592-5464 ■ *Web:* www.kingpacificlodge.com					
Kings Island Resort & Conference Ctr 5691 Kings Island Dr	Mason	OH	45040	513-398-0115	398-1095
TF: 800-704-2439 ■ *Web:* www.kingsislandresort.com					
Kinseth Hotel Corp 2 Quail Creek Cir	North Liberty	IA	52317	319-626-5600	
Web: www.kinseth.com					
Kitano New York 66 Pk Ave E 38th St	New York	NY	10016	212-885-7000	885-7100
TF: 800-548-2666 ■ *Web:* www.kitano.com					
Knickerbocker on The Lake The 1028 E Juneau Ave	Milwaukee	WI	53202	414-276-8500	276-3668
Web: www.knickerbockeronthelake.com					
Knights Inn 620 York St	Williamsburg	VA	23185	757-220-0960	220-1531
TF: 800-446-9222 ■ *Web:* www.knightsinnwilliamsburgva.com					
Knob Hill Inn 960 N Main St PO Box 800	Ketchum	ID	83340	208-726-8010	726-2712
TF: 800-526-8010 ■ *Web:* www.knobhillinn.com					
Koko Inn 5201 Ave Q	Lubbock	TX	79412	806-747-2591	747-2591
TF: 800-782-3254 ■ *Web:* www.lubbockhospitality.net/Koko					
Kona Kai Resort 1551 Shelter Island Dr	San Diego	CA	92106	619-221-8000	819-8101
TF: 800-566-2524 ■ *Web:* www.resortkonakai.com					
Kyoto Grand Hotel & Gardens 120 S Los Angeles St	Los Angeles	CA	90012	213-629-1200	622-0980
TF: 800-639-6826 ■ *Web:* www.kyotograndhotel.com					
L' Appartement Hotel 455 Sherbrooke W	Montreal	QC	H3A1B7	514-284-3634	287-1431
TF: 800-363-3010 ■ *Web:* www.appartementhotel.com					
L'Enfant Plaza Hotel 480 L'Enfant Plaza SW	Washington	DC	20024	202-484-1000	646-4456
TF: 800-635-5065 ■ *Web:* www.lenfantplazahotel.com					
L'Ermitage Beverly Hills Hotel 9291 Burton Way	Beverly Hills	CA	90210	310-278-3344	278-8247
TF: 877-235-7582 ■ *Web:* www.lermitagebh.com					

				Phone	Fax
L'Hotel du Vieux-Quebec 1190 St Jean St	Quebec	QC	G1R1S6	418-692-1850	692-5637
TF: 800-361-7787 ■ *Web:* www.hvq.com					
L'Hotel Quebec 3115 des Hotels Ave	Sainte-Foy	QC	G1W3Z6	418-658-5120	658-4504
TF: 800-567-5276 ■ *Web:* www.hotelsjaro.com					
La Colombe D'Or Inn 3410 Montrose Blvd	Houston	TX	77006	713-524-7999	524-8923
Web: www.lacolombedor.com					
La Fonda 100 E San Francisco St	Santa Fe	NM	87501	505-982-5511	988-2952
TF: 800-523-5002 ■ *Web:* www.lafondasantafe.com					
La Pensione Hotel 606 W Date St	San Diego	CA	92101	619-236-8000	236-8088
TF: 800-232-4683 ■ *Web:* www.lapensionehotel.com					
La Playa Hotel & Cottages-by-the-Sea PO Box 900	Carmel	CA	93921	831-624-6476	624-7966
TF: 800-582-8900 ■ *Web:* www.laplayahotel.com					
La Posada Hotel & Suites 1000 Zaragoza St	Laredo	TX	78040	956-722-1701	726-8524
TF: 800-444-2099 ■ *Web:* www.laposada.com					
La Quinta Inn & Suites Secaucus Meadowlands 350 Lighting Way	Secaucus	NJ	07094	201-863-8700	863-6209
TF: 800-531-5900 ■ *Web:* www.7719.lq.com/lq/index.jsp					
La Valencia Hotel 1132 Prospect St	La Jolla	CA	92037	858-454-0771	456-3921
TF: 800-451-0772 ■ *Web:* www.lavalencia.com					
Lafayette Hotel 600 St Charles Ave	New Orleans	LA	70130	504-524-4441	523-7327
TF: 800-366-2743 ■ *Web:* www.lafayettehotelneworleans.com					
Lafayette Hotel 101 Front St	Marietta	OH	45750	740-373-5522	373-4684
TF: 800-331-9336 ■ *Web:* www.lafayettehotel.com					
Lafayette Hotel & Suites San Diego 2223 El Cajon Blvd	San Diego	CA	92104	619-296-2101	296-0512
TF: 800-468-3531 ■ *Web:* www.lafayettehotelsd.com					
Lafayette Park Hotel 3287 Mt Diablo Blvd	Lafayette	CA	94549	925-283-3700	284-1621
TF: 800-368-2468 ■ *Web:* www.lafayetteparkhotel.com					
Lake Louise Inn 210 Village Rd PO Box 209	Lake Louise	AB	T0L1E0	403-522-3791	522-2018
TF: 800-661-9237 ■ *Web:* www.lakelouiseinn.com					
Lake Lure Inn & Spa The 2771 Memorial Hwy PO Box 10	Lake Lure	NC	28746	828-625-2526	625-9655
TF: 888-434-4970 ■ *Web:* www.lakelure.com					
Lake Merritt Hotel & Apartments 1800 Madison St	Oakland	CA	94612	510-832-2300	832-7150
TF: 800-933-4683 ■ *Web:* www.lakemerritthotel.com					
Lake Placid Lodge 144 Lodge Way	Lake Placid	NY	12946	518-523-2700	523-1124
TF: 877-523-2700 ■ *Web:* www.lakeplacidlodge.com					
Lake San Marcos Resort & Country Club 1025 La Bonita Dr	Lake San Marcos	CA	92078	760-744-0120	744-0748
TF: 800-447-6556 ■ *Web:* www.lakesanmarcosresort.com					
Lakeside Inn 100 N Alexander St	Mount Dora	FL	32757	352-383-4101	385-1615
TF: 800-556-5016 ■ *Web:* www.lakeside-inn.com					
Lakeview on the Lake 8696 E Lake Rd	Erie	PA	16511	814-899-6948	
TF: 888-558-8439 ■ *Web:* www.lakevieweerie.com					
Lamothe House Hotel 621 Esplanade Ave	New Orleans	LA	70116	504-947-1161	218-4297
TF: 800-367-5858 ■ *Web:* www.lamothehouse.com					
Lamp Post Inn 2424 E Stadium Blvd	Ann Arbor	MI	48104	734-971-8000	971-7483
Web: www.lamppostinn.com					
Lamplighter Inn & Suites South 1772 S Glenstone Ave	Springfield	MO	65804	417-882-1113	882-8869
TF: 800-749-7275 ■ *Web:* www.lamplighter-sgf.com					
Lancaster Hotel 701 Texas St	Houston	TX	77002	713-228-9500	223-4528
TF: 800-231-0336 ■ *Web:* www.thelancaster.com					
Landmark Inn 230 N Front St	Marquette	MI	49855	906-228-2580	228-5676
TF: 800-752-6362 ■ *Web:* www.thelandmarkinn.com					
Lane Hospitality 1 Ln Ctr 1200 Shermer Rd	Northbrook	IL	60062	847-498-6650	498-6808
Web: www.lanehospitality.com					
Langdon Hall Country House Hotel & Spa 1 Langdon Dr	Cambridge	ON	N3H4R8	519-740-2100	740-8161
TF: 800-268-1898 ■ *Web:* www.langdonhall.ca					
Langham Boston The 250 Franklin St	Boston	MA	02110	617-451-1900	423-2844
TF: 800-791-7781 ■ *Web:* www.langhamhotels.com					
Lantern Lodge Motor Inn 411 N College St	Myerstown	PA	17067	717-866-6536	866-8857
TF: 800-262-5564 ■ *Web:* www.thelanternlodge.com					
LaPlaya Resort & Suites 2500 N Atlantic Ave	Daytona Beach Shores	FL	32118	386-672-0990	
Web: www.daytonahotels.com					
Larkspur Hotels & Restaurants Inc 125 E Sir Francis Drake Blvd Suite 200	Larkspur	CA	94939	415-945-5000	945-5001
Web: www.larkspurhotels.com					
LaSalle Hotel 120 S Main St	Bryan	TX	77803	979-822-2000	779-4343
TF: 866-822-2000 ■ *Web:* www.lasalle-hotel.com					
LaSalle Hotel Properties 3 Bethesda Metro Ctr Suite 1200	Bethesda	MD	20814	301-941-1500	941-1553
NYSE: LHO ■ *Web:* www.lasallehotels.com					
Latham Hotel Center City 135 S 17th St	Philadelphia	PA	19103	215-563-7474	568-0110
TF: 877-528-4261 ■ *Web:* www.lathamhotel.com					
Laurel Inn 444 Presidio Ave	San Francisco	CA	94115	415-567-8467	928-1866
TF: 800-552-8736 ■ *Web:* www.jdvhotels.com/hotels/sanfrancisco/laurel_inn					
Le Chamois 4557 Blackcomb Way	Whistler	BC	V0N1B4	604-932-8700	932-4486
TF: 888-560-9453 ■ *Web:* www.lechamoiswhistlerhotel.com					
Le Meridian 20 Sidney St	Cambridge	MA	02139	617-577-0200	494-8366
TF: 800-754-7130					
Le Meridien Chambers Minneapolis 901 Hennepin Ave	Minneapolis	MN	55403	612-767-6900	767-6801
TF: 800-543-4300 ■ *Web:* www.lemeridienchambers.com					
Le Merigot - A JW Marriott Beach Hotel & Spa 1740 Ocean Ave	Santa Monica	CA	90401	310-395-9700	395-9200
TF: 888-539-7899 ■ *Web:* www.marriott.com					
Le Montrose Suite Hotel 900 Hammond St	West Hollywood	CA	90069	310-855-1115	657-9192
TF: 800-776-0666 ■ *Web:* www.lemontrose.com					
Le Nouvel Montreal Hotel & Spa 1740 Rene-Levesque Blvd W	Montreal	QC	H3H1R3	514-931-8841	931-5581
TF: 800-363-6063 ■ *Web:* www.lenouvelhotel.com					
Le Parc Suite Hotel 733 N W Knoll Dr	West Hollywood	CA	90069	310-855-8888	659-7812
TF: 800-578-4837 ■ *Web:* www.leparcsuites.com					
Le Pavillon Hotel 833 Poydras St	New Orleans	LA	70112	504-581-3111	620-4130
Web: www.lepavillon.com					
Le Place D'armes Hotel & Suites 55 St Jacques St W	Old Montreal	QC	H2Y3X2	514-842-1887	842-6469
TF: 888-450-1887 ■ *Web:* www.hotelplacedarmes.com					
Le Port-Royal Hotel & Suites 144 St Pierre St	Quebec	QC	G1K8N8	418-692-2777	692-2778
TF: 866-417-2777 ■ *Web:* www.leportroyal.com					
Le Richelieu Hotel 1234 Chartres St	New Orleans	LA	70116	504-529-2492	524-8179
TF: 800-535-9653 ■ *Web:* www.lerichelieuhotel.com					
Le Saint Sulpice 414 Rue St Sulpice	Montreal	QC	H2Y2V5	514-288-1000	288-0077
TF: 877-785-7423 ■ *Web:* www.lesaintsulpice.com					
Lees Inns of America Inc 130 N State St	North Vernon	IN	47265	812-346-5072	346-7521
TF Resv: 800-733-5337 ■ *Web:* www.leesinn.com					
Leisure Group of Cos					
Leisure Hotel Corp 4501 College Blvd Suite 275	Leawood	KS	66211	913-905-1460	905-1461
Web: www.leisurehotel.com					
Leland The 400 Bagley St	Detroit	MI	48226	313-962-2300	962-1045
Lenox Hotel 61 Exeter St	Boston	MA	02116	617-536-5300	267-1237
TF: 800-225-7676 ■ *Web:* www.lenoxhotel.com					
Leola Village Inn & Suites 38 Deborah Dr	Leola	PA	17540	717-656-7002	656-7648
TF: 877-669-5094 ■ *Web:* www.leolavillage.com					
Les Mars Hotel 27 N St	Healdsburg	CA	95448	707-433-4211	433-4611
TF: 877-431-1700 ■ *Web:* www.hotellesmars.com					
Les Suites Hotel Ottawa 130 Besserer St	Ottawa	ON	K1N9M9	613-232-2000	232-1242
TF: 866-682-0879 ■ *Web:* www.les-suites.com					
Lexington George Washington Inn & Conference Cente 500 Merrimac Trail	Williamsburg	VA	23185	757-220-1410	259-5500
TF: 866-787-4494 ■ *Web:* www.lexingtonhotelwilliamsburg.com					
Library Hotel 299 Madison Ave	New York	NY	10017	212-983-4500	499-9099
TF: 877-793-7323 ■ *Web:* www.libraryhotel.com					
Lighthouse Club Hotel 201 60th St	Ocean City	MD	21842	410-524-5400	524-3928
TF: 888-371-5400					
Lighthouse Inn 6 Guthrie Pl	New London	CT	06320	860-443-8411	443-8411
TF: 888-600-5681 ■ *Web:* www.lighthouseinn-ct.com					
Lighthouse Lodge & Suites 1150 & 1249 Lighthouse Ave	Pacific Grove	CA	93950	831-655-2111	655-4922
TF: 800-858-1249 ■ *Web:* www.lhls.com					
Lily Leon Hotel 855 Collins Ave	Miami Beach	FL	33139	305-535-9900	535-9665
TF: 877-762-3477 ■ *Web:* www.lilyleonhotel.com					
Linden Row Inn 100 E Franklin St	Richmond	VA	23219	804-783-7000	648-7504
TF: 800-348-7424 ■ *Web:* www.lindenrowinn.com					
Listel Hotel The 1300 Robson St	Vancouver	BC	V6E1C5	604-684-8461	684-7092
TF: 800-663-5491 ■ *Web:* www.thelistelhotel.com					
Litchfield Plantation 24 Avenue of the Oaks	Pawleys Island	SC	29585	843-237-4286	237-1688
TF: 800-869-1410 ■ *Web:* www.litchfieldplantation.com					
Little America Hotel & Resort Cheyenne 2800 W Lincolnway	Cheyenne	WY	82009	307-775-8400	775-8425
TF: 888-709-8384 ■ *Web:* www.cheyenne.littleamerica.com					
Little America Hotel & Towers Salt Lake City 500 S Main St	Salt Lake City	UT	84101	801-363-6781	596-5911
TF: 800-453-9450 ■ *Web:* www.littleamerica.com					
Little America Hotel Flagstaff 2515 E Butler Ave	Flagstaff	AZ	86004	928-779-2741	779-7983
TF: 800-352-4386 ■ *Web:* www.littleamerica.com/flagstaff					
Little Inn by the Sea 4546 El Mar Dr	Lauderdale-by-the-Sea	FL	33308	877-563-1939	938-9354*
**Fax Area Code:* 954 ■ *TF:* 800-492-0311 ■ *Web:* www.alittleinnhotel.com					
Little Nell The 675 E Durant Ave	Aspen	CO	81611	970-920-4600	920-4670
TF: 888-843-6355 ■ *Web:* www.thelittlenell.com					
Lodge & Spa at Breckenridge 112 Overlook Dr	Breckenridge	CO	80424	970-453-9300	453-0625
TF: 800-736-1607 ■ *Web:* www.thelodgeatbreck.com					
Lodge & Spa at Cordillera 2205 Cordillera Way	Edwards	CO	81632	970-926-2200	926-2486
TF: 800-877-3529 ■ *Web:* www.cordilleralodge.com					
Lodge at the Mountain Village 1415 Lowell Ave	Park City	UT	84060	435-649-0800	649-1464
TF: 888-727-5248					
Lodge Hotel & Conference Ctr 900 Spruce Hills Dr	Bettendorf	IA	52722	563-359-7141	359-7141
TF: 866-690-4006 ■ *Web:* www.lodgehotel.com					
Lodge of the Ozarks 3431 W 76 Country Blvd	Branson	MO	65616	417-334-7535	334-6861
TF: 800-213-2584 ■ *Web:* www.bransonlodging.net					
Lodge on the Desert 306 N Alvernon Way	Tucson	AZ	85711	520-320-2000	327-5834
TF: 877-498-6776 ■ *Web:* www.lodgeonthedesert.com					
LodgeWorks LP 8100 E 22nd St Bldg 500	Wichita	KS	67226	316-681-5100	681-0905
Web: www.lodgeworks.com					
Sierra Suites 8100 E 22nd St Bldg 500	Wichita	KS	67226	316-681-5100	681-0905
TF Resv: 888-695-7608 ■ *Web:* www.lodgeworks.com					
Lodgian Inc 2002 Summit Blvd Suite 300	Atlanta	GA	30319	404-364-9400	812-3102
NYSE: LGN ■ *Web:* www.lodgian.com					
Lodging Unlimited Inc 344 Willowbrook Ln	West Chester	PA	19382	610-436-8400	436-8861
Web: www.lodgingunlimited.com					
Loews Hotels 667 Madison Ave	New York	NY	10021	212-521-2000	521-2994
TF: 800-235-6397 ■ *Web:* www.loewshotels.com					
Lofts Hotel & Suites 55 E Nationwide Blvd	Columbus	OH	43215	614-461-2663	461-2630
TF: 800-735-6387 ■ *Web:* www.55lofts.com					
Lombardy the Hotel 111 E 56th St	New York	NY	10022	212-753-8600	754-5683
TF: 800-223-5254 ■ *Web:* www.lombardyhotel.com					
Lone Oak Lodge 2221 N Fremont St	Monterey	CA	93940	831-372-4924	372-4985
TF: 800-283-5663 ■ *Web:* www.loneoaklodge.com					
Long House Alaskan Hotel 4335 Wisconsin St	Anchorage	AK	99517	907-243-2133	243-6060
TF: 888-243-2133 ■ *Web:* www.longhousehotel.com					
Longhouse Hospitality 4770 S Atlanta Rd	Smyrna	GA	30080	404-350-9990	350-6106
TF Resv: 800-526-3766 ■ *Web:* www.longhousehospitality.com					
Crestwood Suites Extended Stay Hotels 4770 S Atlanta Rd Suite 200	Smyrna	GA	30080	404-350-9990	350-8660
Web: www.crestwoodsuites.com					
Jameson Inns 4770 S Atlanta Rd	Smyrna	GA	30080	404-350-9990	350-6106
TF: 800-526-3766 ■ *Web:* www.jamesoninns.com					

	City	State	ZIP	Phone	Fax
Lodge America 4700 S Atlanta Rd *Web:* www.lodgeamerica.com	Smyrna	GA	30080	404-350-9990	350-2240
Signature Inns 4770 S Atlanta Rd *Web:* www.signatureinns.com	Smyrna	GA	30080	404-350-9990	601-6106
Sun Suites Extended Stay Hotels 4770 S Atlanta Rd Suite 200 *Web:* www.sunsuites.com	Smyrna	GA	30080	404-350-9990	350-8660
Lonsdale Quay Hotel 123 Carrie Cates Ct *TF:* 800-836-6111 ■ *Web:* www.lonsdalequayhotel.com	North Vancouver	BC	V7M3K7	604-986-6111	986-8782
Lookout Inn 6901 Lookout Rd *TF:* 800-530-1513 ■ *Web:* www.lookoutinnguesthouse.com	Boulder	CO	80301	303-530-1513	530-4573
Lord Elgin Hotel 100 Elgin St *TF:* 800-267-4298 ■ *Web:* www.lordelginhotel.ca	Ottawa	ON	K1P5K8	613-235-3333	235-3223
Lord Nelson Hotel & Suites 1515 S Pk St *TF:* 800-565-2020 ■ *Web:* www.lordnelsonhotel.com	Halifax	NS	B3J2L2	902-423-6331	423-7148
Lord Stanley Suites on the Park 1889 Alberni St *TF:* 888-767-7829 ■ *Web:* www.lordstanley.com	Vancouver	BC	V6G3G7	604-688-9299	688-9297
Los Angeles Athletic Club 431 W 7th St *TF:* 800-421-8777 ■ *Web:* www.laac.com	Los Angeles	CA	90014	213-625-2211	689-1194
Los Willows Inn & Spa 530 Stewart Canyon Rd *TF:* 888-731-9400 ■ *Web:* www.loswillows.com	Fallbrook	CA	92028	760-731-9400	728-3622
Lowell Hotel The 28 E 63rd St *TF:* 800-221-4444 ■ *Web:* www.lowellhotel.com	New York	NY	10065	212-838-1400	319-4230
Lowell Inn 102 N 2nd St *TF:* 888-569-3554 ■ *Web:* www.lowellinn.com	Stillwater	MN	55082	651-439-1100	439-0253
LQ Management LLC 909 Hidden Ridge Suite 600 *TF:* 866-832-6574 ■ *Web:* www.lq.com	Irving	TX	75038	214-492-6600	492-6785
La Quinta Inn & Suites 909 Hidden Ridge Suite 600 *Fax: Mktg ■ *TF:* 877-204-9204 ■ *Web:* www.lq.com	Irving	TX	75038	214-492-6600	492-6785*
Lubbock Inn 3901 19th St *TF:* 800-545-8226 ■ *Web:* www.lubbockinn.com	Lubbock	TX	79410	806-792-5181	792-1319
Luxe Hotel Rodeo Drive 360 N Rodeo Dr *TF:* 800-468-3541 ■ *Web:* www.luxehotels.com	Beverly Hills	CA	90210	310-273-0300	859-8730
Luxe Hotel Sunset Blvd 11461 Sunset Blvd *TF:* 800-468-3541 ■ *Web:* www.luxehotels.com	Los Angeles	CA	90049	310-476-6571	471-6310
Luxe Worldwide Hotels 11461 W Sunset Blvd *TF:* 866-589-3411 ■ *Web:* www.luxehotels.com	Los Angeles	CA	90049	310-440-3090	440-0821
MacArthur Place 29 E MacArthur St *TF:* 800-722-1866 ■ *Web:* www.macarthurplace.com	Sonoma	CA	95476	707-938-2929	933-9833
Madison Concourse Hotel & Governors Club 1 W Dayton St *TF:* 800-356-8293 ■ *Web:* www.concoursehotel.com	Madison	WI	53703	608-257-6000	257-5280
Madison Hotel 79 Madison Ave *TF:* 888-636-7447 ■ *Web:* www.slh.com	Memphis	TN	38103	901-333-1200	333-1299
Madison Hotel The 1 Convent Rd *TF:* 800-526-0729 ■ *Web:* www.themadisonhotel.com	Morristown	NJ	07960	973-285-1800	540-8566
Madison the - A Loews Hotel 1177 15th St NW *TF:* 866-563-9792 ■ *Web:* www.loewshotels.com	Washington	DC	20005	202-862-1600	785-1255
Magnolia Hotel & Spa The 623 Courtney St *TF:* 877-624-6654 ■ *Web:* www.magnoliahotel.com	Victoria	BC	V8W1B8	250-381-0999	381-0988
Magnolia Hotel Dallas 1401 Commerce St *TF:* 888-915-1110 ■ *Web:* www.magnoliahotels.com	Dallas	TX	75201	214-915-6500	253-0053
Magnolia Hotel Denver 818 17th St *TF:* 888-915-1110 ■ *Web:* www.magnoliahoteldenver.com	Denver	CO	80202	303-607-9000	607-0101
Magnolia Hotel Houston 1100 Texas Ave *TF:* 888-915-1110 ■ *Web:* www.magnoliahotelhouston.com	Houston	TX	77002	713-221-0011	221-0022
Main Street Inn 2200 Main St *TF:* 800-471-3001 ■ *Web:* www.mainstreetinn.com	Hilton Head Island	SC	29926	843-681-3001	681-5541
Main Street Station Hotel & Casino 200 N Main St *TF:* 800-713-8933 ■ *Web:* www.mainstreetcasino.com	Las Vegas	NV	89101	702-387-1896	386-4421
Maison 140 Beverly Hills 140 Lasky Dr *TF:* 800-670-6182 ■ *Web:* www.maison140beverlyhills.com	Beverly Hills	CA	90212	310-281-4000	281-4001
Maison Dupuy Hotel 1001 Toulouse St *TF:* 800-535-9177 ■ *Web:* www.maisondupuy.com	New Orleans	LA	70112	504-586-8000	648-6180
Majestic Hotel 528 W Brompton *TF:* 800-727-5108 ■ *Web:* www.majestic-chicago.com	Chicago	IL	60657	773-404-3499	404-3495
Malaga Inn 359 Church St *TF:* 800-235-1586 ■ *Web:* www.malagainn.com	Mobile	AL	36602	251-438-4701	438-4701
Malibu Beach Inn 22878 Pacific Coast Hwy *TF:* 800-462-5428 ■ *Web:* www.malibubeachinn.com	Malibu	CA	90265	310-456-6444	456-1499
Mandarin Oriental Hotel Group (USA) 345 California St Suite 1250 *Web:* www.mandarinoriental.com	San Francisco	CA	94104	415-772-8800	782-3778
Mandarin Oriental Miami 500 Brickell Key Dr *TF:* 800-526-6566 ■ *Web:* www.mandarinoriental.com	Miami	FL	33131	305-913-8288	913-8300
Mandarin Oriental New York 80 Columbus Cir *TF:* 866-801-8880 ■ *Web:* www.mandarinoriental.com	New York	NY	10023	212-805-8800	805-8888
Mandarin Oriental San Francisco 222 Sansome St *TF:* 800-526-6566 ■ *Web:* www.mandarinoriental.com	San Francisco	CA	94104	415-276-9888	433-0289
Mandarin Oriental Washington DC 1330 Maryland Ave SW *TF:* 888-888-1778 ■ *Web:* www.mandarinoriental.com	Washington	DC	20024	202-554-8588	554-8999
Manor House Inn 106 W St *TF:* 800-437-0083 ■ *Web:* www.barharbormanorhouse.com	Bar Harbor	ME	04609	207-288-3759	288-2974
Mansfield The 12 W 44th St *TF:* 800-255-5167 ■ *Web:* www.mansfieldhotel.com	New York	NY	10036	212-277-8700	764-4477
Mansion on Forsyth Park 700 Drayton St *TF:* 888-711-5114 ■ *Web:* www.mansiononforsythpark.com	Savannah	GA	31401	912-238-5158	238-5146
Mansion on Turtle Creek 2821 Turtle Creek Blvd *TF:* 800-527-5432 ■ *Web:* www.mansiononturtlecreek.com	Dallas	TX	75219	214-559-2100	528-4187
Mansion View Inn & Suites 529 S 4th St *TF:* 800-252-1083 ■ *Web:* www.mansionview.com	Springfield	IL	62701	217-544-7411	544-6211
Maple Hill Farm Bed & Breakfast Inn 11 Inn Rd *TF:* 800-622-2708 ■ *Web:* www.maplebb.com	Hallowell	ME	04330	207-622-2708	622-0655
Marcus Corp 100 E Wisconsin Ave *NYSE: MCS* ■ *TF:* 800-274-0099 ■ *Web:* www.marcuscorp.com	Milwaukee	WI	53202	414-905-1000	905-2129
Marcus Hotels & Resorts 100 E Wisconsin Ave Suite 1950 *Web:* www.marcushotels.com	Milwaukee	WI	53202	414-905-1200	905-2250
Marina Del Mar Resort & Marina 527 Caribbean Dr *TF:* 800-451-3483 ■ *Web:* www.marinadelmarkeylargo.com	Key Largo	FL	33037	305-451-4107	451-1891
Marina Inn at Grande Dunes 8121 Amalfi Pl *TF resv:* 877-913-1333 ■ *Web:* www.marinainnatgrandedunes.com	Myrtle Beach	SC	29572	843-913-1333	913-1334
Marine Surf Waikiki Hotel 364 Seaside Ave *TF:* 800-230-4134	Honolulu	HI	96815	808-931-2424	931-2454
Mariner's Point Resort of Cape Cod 425 Grand Ave *Web:* www.marinerspointresort.com	Falmouth	MA	02540	508-457-0300	
Mark I Guest Suites 4321 Hale Pkwy	Denver	CO	80220	303-886-1579	
Mark Spencer Hotel 409 SW 11th Ave *TF:* 800-548-3934 ■ *Web:* www.markspencer.com	Portland	OR	97205	503-224-3293	223-7848
Mark Twain Hotel 225 NE Adams St *TF:* 866-325-6351 ■ *Web:* www.marktwainhotel.com	Peoria	IL	61602	309-676-3600	636-6259
Market Pavilion Hotel 225 E Bay St *TF:* 877-440-2250 ■ *Web:* www.marketpavilion.com	Charleston	SC	29401	843-723-0500	723-4320
Maron Hotel & Suites 42 Lake Ave Ext Mill Plain Rd *Web:* www.maronhotel.com	Danbury	CT	06811	203-791-2200	791-2201
MarQueen Hotel 600 Queen Anne Ave N *TF:* 888-445-3076 ■ *Web:* www.marqueen.com	Seattle	WA	98109	206-282-7407	283-1499
Marquesa Hotel 600 Fleming St *TF:* 800-869-4631 ■ *Web:* www.marquesa.com	Key West	FL	33040	305-292-1919	294-2121
Marquette Hotel The 710 Marquette Ave *TF:* 800-328-4782 ■ *Web:* www.marquettehotel.com	Minneapolis	MN	55402	612-333-4545	288-2188
Marriott Charleston Hotel 170 Lockwood Blvd *TF:* 888-236-2427 ■ *Web:* www.marriott.com	Charleston	SC	29403	843-723-3000	723-0276
Marriott Columbus 800 Front Ave *TF:* 800-445-9261 ■ *Web:* www.marriott.com	Columbus	GA	31901	706-324-1800	576-4413
Marriott International Inc 1 Marriott Dr *NYSE: MAR* ■ *Fax: Mail Rm ■ *Web:* www.marriott.com	Washington	DC	20058	301-380-3000	380-3008*
Ritz-Carlton Hotel Co LLC 4445 Willard Ave Suite 800 *TF:* 800-241-3333 ■ *Web:* www.ritzcarlton.com	Chevy Chase	MD	20815	301-547-4700	547-4740
Marseilles Hotel 1741 Collins Ave *TF:* 800-327-4739 ■ *Web:* www.marseilleshotel.com	Miami Beach	FL	33139	305-538-5711	673-1006
Martha Washington Hotel & Spa The 150 W Main St *TF:* 888-999-8078 ■ *Web:* www.marthawashingtoninn.com	Abingdon	VA	24210	276-628-3161	628-8885
Maryland Inn 16 Church Cir *TF:* 800-847-8882 ■ *Web:* www.historicinnsofannapolis.com	Annapolis	MD	21401	410-263-2641	268-3613
Matrix Hotel 10001 107th St *TF:* 866-456-8150 ■ *Web:* www.matrixedmonton.com	Edmonton	AB	T5J1J1	780-429-2861	426-7225
Maumee Bay Lodge & Conference Ctr 1750 Pk Rd Suite 2 *TF:* 800-282-7275 ■ *Web:* www.maumeebaystateparklodge.com	Oregon	OH	43616	419-836-1466	836-2438
Maxwell Hotel 386 Geary St *TF:* 800-553-1900 ■ *Web:* www.hotelfranksf.com	San Francisco	CA	94102	415-986-2000	397-2447
Mayfair Hotel & Spa 3000 Florida Ave *TF:* 800-433-4555 ■ *Web:* www.mayfairhotelandspa.com	Coconut Grove	FL	33133	305-441-0000	447-9173
Mayfield Inn & Suites 16615 109th Ave *TF:* 800-661-9804 ■ *Web:* www.mayfieldinnedmonton.com	Edmonton	AB	T5P4K8	780-484-0821	481-3923
Mayflower Inn 118 Woodbury Rd PO Box 1288 *Web:* www.mayflowerinn.com	Washington	CT	06793	860-868-9466	868-1497
Mayflower Park Hotel 405 Olive Way *TF:* 800-426-5100 ■ *Web:* www.mayflowerpark.com	Seattle	WA	98101	206-623-8700	382-6996
McCamly Plaza Hotel 50 Capital Ave SW *Web:* www.mccamlyplazahotel.com	Battle Creek	MI	49017	269-963-7050	
McKinley Grand Hotel 320 Market Ave S *TF:* 877-454-5008 ■ *Web:* www.mckinleygrandhotel.com	Canton	OH	44702	330-454-5000	454-5494
McLure House Hotel & Conference Ctr 1200 Market St *Web:* www.mclurehotel.com	Wheeling	WV	26003	304-232-0300	233-1653
MCM Elegante Suites 4250 Ridgemont Dr *TF:* 888-897-9644 ■ *Web:* www.mcmelegantesuites.com	Abilene	TX	79606	325-698-1234	698-2771
Mediterranean Inn 425 Queen Anne Ave N *TF:* 866-525-4700 ■ *Web:* www.mediterranean-inn.com	Seattle	WA	98109	206-428-4700	428-4699
Meeting Street Inn 173 Meeting St *TF:* 800-842-8022 ■ *Web:* www.meetingstreetinn.com	Charleston	SC	29401	843-723-1882	577-0851
Melrose Hotel Washington DC The 2430 Pennsylvania Ave NW *Web:* www.melrosehotel.com	Washington	DC	20037	202-955-6400	955-5765
Mendocino Hotel & Garden Suites 45080 Main St *TF:* 800-548-0513 ■ *Web:* www.mendocinohotel.com	Mendocino	CA	95460	707-937-0511	937-0513
Menger Hotel 204 Alamo Plaza *TF:* 800-345-9285 ■ *Web:* www.mengerhotel.com	San Antonio	TX	78205	210-223-4361	228-0022
Mercer Hotel 147 Mercer St *TF:* 888-918-6060 ■ *Web:* www.mercerhotel.com	New York	NY	10012	212-966-6060	965-3838
Mercury Resort 100 Collins Ave *TF:* 877-786-2732 ■ *Web:* www.mercuryresort.com	Miami Beach	FL	33139	305-398-3000	398-3001
Meridian Plaza Resort 2310 N Ocean Blvd *TF:* 800-323-3011 ■ *Web:* www.meridianplaza.com	Myrtle Beach	SC	29577	843-626-4734	448-4569
Metropolitan Hotel Toronto 108 Chestnut St *TF:* 800-668-6600 ■ *Web:* www.metropolitan.com/toronto	Toronto	ON	M5G1R3	416-977-5000	977-9513
Metropolitan Hotel Vancouver 645 Howe St *TF:* 800-667-2300 ■ *Web:* www.metropolitan.com/vanc	Vancouver	BC	V6C2Y9	604-687-1122	643-7267
Metterra Hotel on Whyte 10454 82nd Ave *TF:* 866-465-8150 ■ *Web:* www.metterra.com	Edmonton	AB	T6E4Z7	780-465-8150	465-8174
Meyer Crest Ltd 2515 Pk Marina Dr Suite 201 *TF:* 800-626-1900 ■ *Web:* www.meyercrest.com	Redding	CA	96001	530-242-2010	247-3982

	City	State	Zip	Phone	Fax
Meyer Jabara Hotels 1601 Belvedere Rd Suite 407 S *Web:* www.meyerjabarahotels.com	West Palm Beach	FL	33406	561-689-6602	689-4363
Miami International Airport Hotel NW 20th St & Le Jeune Rd PO Box 660708 *TF:* 800-327-1276 ■ *Web:* www.miahotel.com	Miami	FL	33122	305-871-4100	871-0801
Michelangelo Hotel 152 W 51st St *TF:* 800-237-0990 ■ *Web:* www.michelangelohotel.com	New York	NY	10019	212-765-1900	541-6604
Midtown Hotel 220 Huntington Ave *TF:* 800-343-1177 ■ *Web:* www.midtownhotel.com	Boston	MA	02115	617-262-1000	262-8739
Mill Street Inn 75 Mill St *TF:* 800-392-1316 ■ *Web:* www.millstreetinn.com	Newport	RI	02840	401-849-9500	848-5131
Mill Valley Inn 165 Throckmorton Ave *TF:* 800-595-2100 ■ *Web:* www.marinhotels.com	Mill Valley	CA	94941	415-389-6608	389-5051
Mills House Hotel 115 Meeting St *TF:* 800-874-9600 ■ *Web:* www.millshouse.com	Charleston	SC	29401	843-577-2400	722-0623
Milner Hotel Boston 78 Charles St S *TF:* 800-453-1731 ■ *Web:* www.milner-hotels.com	Boston	MA	02116	617-426-6220	350-0360
Milner Hotels Inc 1538 Centre St *TF:* 877-645-6377 ■ *Web:* www.milner-hotels.com	Detroit	MI	48226	313-963-3950	962-0410
Minto Place Suite Hotel 185 Lyons St N *TF:* 800-267-3377 ■ *Web:* www.minto.com	Ottawa	ON	K1R5C1	613-232-2200	232-6962
Mira Monte Inn & Suites 69 Mt Desert St *TF:* 800-553-5109 ■ *Web:* www.miramonte.com	Bar Harbor	ME	04609	207-288-4263	288-3115
Mirabeau Park Hotel 1100 N Sullivan Rd *Web:* www.mirabeauparkhotel.com	Spokane Valley	WA	99037	509-924-9000	922-4965
Miramar Hotel at Waikiki 2345 Kuhio St *TF:* 800-367-2303 ■ *Web:* www.miramarwaikiki.com	Honolulu	HI	96815	808-922-2077	926-3217
Mirbeau Inn & Spa 851 W Genesee St *TF:* 877-647-2328 ■ *Web:* www.mirbeau.com	Skaneateles	NY	13152	315-685-5006	685-5150
Mission Inn 3649 Mission Inn Ave *TF:* 800-843-7755 ■ *Web:* www.missioninn.com	Riverside	CA	92501	951-784-0300	683-1342
Misty Harbor & Barefoot Beach Resort 118 Weirs Rd *TF:* 800-336-4789 ■ *Web:* www.mistyharbor.com	Gilford	NH	03249	603-293-4500	293-0493
Miyako Hotel Los Angeles 328 E 1st St *TF:* 800-228-6596 ■ *Web:* www.miyakoinn.com	Los Angeles	CA	90012	213-617-2000	617-2700
MMI Hotel Group PO Box 320009 *Web:* www.mmihotelgroup.com	Jackson	MS	39232	601-936-3666	939-5685
MODA Hotel 900 Seymour St *TF:* 877-683-5522 ■ *Web:* www.modahotel.ca	Vancouver	BC	V6B3L9	604-683-4251	683-4256
Moderne Hotel The 243 W 55th St *TF:* 888-664-6235	New York	NY	10019	212-397-6767	397-8787
Mojave A Desert Resort 73721 Shadow Mountain Dr *TF Resv:* 800-391-1104 ■ *Web:* www.resortmojave.com	Palm Desert	CA	92260	760-346-6121	674-9072
Molokai Lodge & Beach Village 100 Maunaloa Hwy *TF:* 888-627-8082	Maunaloa	HI	96770	808-552-2741	552-2773
Monarch Hotel & Conference Ctr 12566 SE 93rd Ave *TF:* 800-492-8700 ■ *Web:* www.monarchhotel.cc	Clackamas	OR	97015	503-652-1515	652-7509
Mondrian Hotel 8440 Sunset Blvd *TF:* 800-525-8029 ■ *Web:* www.morganshotelgroup.com	West Hollywood	CA	90069	323-650-8999	650-5215
Monmouth Plantation 36 Melrose Ave *TF:* 800-828-4531 ■ *Web:* www.monmouthplantation.com	Natchez	MS	39120	601-442-5852	446-7762
Monte Carlo Inn-Airport Suites 5 Derry Rd *TF:* 800-363-6400 ■ *Web:* www.montecarloinns.com	Mississauga	ON	L5T2H8	905-564-8500	564-8400
Monterey Bay Inn 242 Cannery Row *TF:* 800-424-6242 ■ *Web:* www.montereybayinn.com	Monterey	CA	93940	831-373-6242	655-8174
Monterey Hotel 406 Alvarado St *TF:* 800-727-0960 ■ *Web:* www.montereyhotel.com	Monterey	CA	93940	831-375-3184	373-2899
Monterey Inn Resort & Conference Centre 2259 Prince of Wales Dr *TF:* 800-565-1311 ■ *Web:* www.montereyinn.com	Ottawa	ON	K2E6Z8	613-288-3500	226-5900
Monterey Plaza Hotel & Spa 400 Cannery Row *TF:* 800-334-3999 ■ *Web:* www.woodsidehotels.com	Monterey	CA	93940	831-646-1700	646-0285
Monticello Inn 127 Ellis St *Fax Area Code: 415 ■ *TF:* 866-823-4669 ■ *Web:* www.monticelloinn.com	San Francisco	CA	94102	866-778-6169	398-2650*
Moody Gardens Hotel 7 Hope Blvd *TF:* 888-388-8484 ■ *Web:* www.moodygardenshotel.com	Galveston	TX	77554	409-741-8484	683-4937
Moorpark Hotel 4241 Moorpark Ave *TF:* 877-740-6622 ■ *Web:* www.jdvhotels.com/hotels/moorpark	San Jose	CA	95129	408-864-0300	864-0350
Morgans Hotel 237 Madison Ave *TF:* 800-334-3408 ■ *Web:* www.morganshotel.com	New York	NY	10016	212-686-0300	779-8352
Morgans Hotel Group Co 475 10th Ave *NASDAQ: MHGC* ■ *TF:* 800-697-1791 ■ *Web:* www.morganshotelgroup.com	New York	NY	10018	212-277-4100	277-4260
Morris Inn Notre Dame Ave University of Notre Dame *Web:* www.morrisinn.nd.edu	Notre Dame	IN	46556	574-631-2000	631-2340
Morrison-Clark Inn 1101 11th St NW *TF:* 800-222-8474 ■ *Web:* www.morrisonclark.com	Washington	DC	20001	202-898-1200	289-8576
Mosaic Hotel 125 S Spalding Dr *TF:* 800-463-4466 ■ *Web:* www.mosaichotel.com	Beverly Hills	CA	90212	310-278-0303	278-1728
Mosser Hotel 54 4th St *TF:* 800-227-3804 ■ *Web:* www.themosser.com	San Francisco	CA	94103	415-986-4400	495-7653
Motel 6 Wichita 465 S Webb Rd *TF:* 800-466-8356 ■ *Web:* www.motel6.com	Wichita	KS	67207	316-684-6363	684-6363
Mount View Hotel & Spa 1457 Lincoln Ave *TF:* 800-816-6877 ■ *Web:* www.mountviewhotel.com	Calistoga	CA	94515	707-942-6877	942-6904
Mountain Haus 292 E Meadow Dr *TF:* 800-237-0922 ■ *Web:* www.mountainhaus.com	Vail	CO	81657	970-476-2434	476-3007
Mountain Lake Hotel 115 Hotel Cir *TF:* 800-346-3334 ■ *Web:* www.mtnlakehotel.com	Pembroke	VA	24136	540-626-7121	626-7172
Mountain Springs Cabins PO Box 6922 *Web:* www.mtnsprings.com	Asheville	NC	28816	828-665-1004	667-1581
Mountain Villas 9525 W Skyline Pkwy *TF:* 866-688-4552 ■ *Web:* www.mtvillas.com	Duluth	MN	55810	218-624-5784	624-1949
Movie Colony Hotel 726 N Indian Canyon Dr *TF:* 888-953-5700 ■ *Web:* www.moviecolonyhotel.com	Palm Springs	CA	92262	760-320-6340	320-1640
Mulberry Inn 601 E Bay St *TF:* 877-468-1200 ■ *Web:* www.savannahhotel.com	Savannah	GA	31401	912-238-1200	236-2184
Muse The 130 W 46th St *TF:* 877-692-6873 ■ *Web:* www.themusehotel.com	New York	NY	10036	212-485-2400	485-2789
Mutiny Hotel 2951 S Bayshore Dr *TF:* 888-868-8469 ■ *Web:* www.mutinyhotel.com	Miami	FL	33133	305-441-2100	441-2822
Napa River Inn 500 Main St *TF:* 877-251-8500 ■ *Web:* www.napariverinn.com	Napa	CA	94559	707-251-8500	251-8504
Nassau Inn The 10 Palmer Sq *TF:* 800-862-7728 ■ *Web:* www.nassauinn.com	Princeton	NJ	08542	609-921-7500	921-9385
Nathan Hale Inn & Conference Ctr 855 Bolton Rd *Web:* www.nathanhaleinn.com	Storrs	CT	06268	860-427-7888	427-7850
National Hotel 1677 Collins Ave *TF:* 800-327-8370 ■ *Web:* www.nationalhotel.com	Miami Beach	FL	33139	305-532-2311	534-1426
Nativo Lodge Hotel 6000 Pan American Fwy NE *TF:* 888-628-4861 ■ *Web:* www.hhandr.com	Albuquerque	NM	87109	505-798-4300	798-4305
New Haven Hotel 229 George St *TF:* 800-644-6835 ■ *Web:* www.newhavenhotel.com	New Haven	CT	06510	203-498-3100	498-0911
New Haven Premier Suites Hotel 3 Long Wharf Dr *TF:* 866-458-0232 ■ *Web:* www.newhavensuites.com	New Haven	CT	06511	203-777-5337	777-2808
New Orleans Fine Hotels 301 Magazine St *TF:* 800-510-3450 ■ *Web:* www.neworleansfinehotels.com	New Orleans	LA	70130	800-510-3450	
New Otani Kaimana Beach Hotel 2863 Kalakaua Ave *TF:* 800-356-8264 ■ *Web:* www.kaimana.com	Honolulu	HI	96815	808-923-1555	922-9404
New World Inn Hwy 30 & 81 S *TF:* 800-433-1492 ■ *Web:* www.newworldinncc.com	Columbus	NE	68601	402-564-1492	563-3989
New York Helmsley Hotel 212 E 42nd St *TF:* 800-221-4982 ■ *Web:* www.newyorkhelmsley.com	New York	NY	10017	212-490-8900	986-4792
New York Palace Hotel 455 Madison Ave *TF:* 800-697-2522 ■ *Web:* www.newyorkpalace.com	New York	NY	10022	212-888-7000	303-6000
New York's Hotel Pennsylvania 401 7th Ave *TF:* 800-223-8585 ■ *Web:* www.hotelpenn.com/thehotel.html	New York	NY	10001	212-736-5000	502-8712
New Yorker Hotel 481 8th Ave *TF:* 800-764-4680 ■ *Web:* www.newyorkerhotel.com	New York	NY	10001	212-971-0101	629-6536
Newport Bay Club & Hotel 337 Thames St PO Box 1440 *Web:* www.newportbayclub.com	Newport	RI	02840	401-849-8600	846-6857
Newport Beach Hotel & Suites 1 Wave Ave *TF:* 800-655-1778 ■ *Web:* www.newportbeachhotelandsuites.com	Middletown	RI	02842	401-846-0310	847-2621
Newport Beachside Hotel & Resort 16701 Collins Ave *TF:* 800-327-5476 ■ *Web:* www.newportbeachsideresort.com	Miami Beach	FL	33160	305-949-1300	956-2733
Newport Harbor Hotel & Marina 49 America's Cup Ave *TF:* 800-955-2558 ■ *Web:* www.thenewport-hotel.com	Newport	RI	02840	401-847-9000	849-6380
Nine Zero Hotel 90 Tremont St *TF:* 866-646-9937 ■ *Web:* www.ninezero.com	Boston	MA	02108	617-772-5800	772-5810
Nittany Lion Inn 200 W Pk Ave *TF:* 800-233-7505 ■ *Web:* www.pshs.psu.edu	State College	PA	16803	814-865-8500	865-8501
Noble House Hotels & Resorts 600 6th St S *Web:* www.noblehousehotels.com	Bellevue	WA	98033	425-827-8737	827-6707
Norwood Hotel 112 Marion St *TF:* 888-888-1878 ■ *Web:* www.norwood-hotel.com	Winnipeg	MB	R2H0T1	204-233-4475	231-1910
O Henry Hotel 624 Green Valley Rd *TF:* 800-965-8259 ■ *Web:* www.ohenryhotel.com	Greensboro	NC	27408	336-854-2000	854-2223
O Hotel 819 S Flower St *Web:* www.ohotelgroup.com	Los Angeles	CA	90017	213-623-9904	614-8010
O'Neill Hotels & Resorts Management Ltd 401 W Georgia St Suite 1690 *Web:* www.oneillhotels.com	Vancouver	BC	V6B5A1	604-684-0444	684-0482
Oak Meadow Lodge 11503 Browning Rd *TF:* 800-933-1920	Evansville	IN	47725	812-867-6431	867-6400
Oberlin Inn 7 N Main St *TF:* 800-376-4173 ■ *Web:* www.oberlininn.com	Oberlin	OH	44074	440-775-1111	775-6356
Occidental Hotels & Resorts 6303 Blue Lagoon Dr Suite 250 *TF:* 800-858-2258 ■ *Web:* www.occidentalhotels.com	Miami	FL	33126	305-262-5909	262-5570
Ocean Five Hotel 436 Ocean Dr *TF:* 866-666-0505 ■ *Web:* www.oceanfive.com	Miami Beach	FL	33139	305-532-7093	534-7353
Ocean Forest Plaza 5523 N Ocean Blvd *TF:* 800-522-0818 ■ *Web:* www.sandsresorts.com	Myrtle Beach	SC	29577	843-497-0044	497-3051
Ocean Hospitalities Inc 1000 Market St Bldg 1 Suite 300 *Web:* www.oceanhospitalities.com	Portsmouth	NH	03801	603-559-2100	559-2195
Ocean Key Resort 424 Atlantic Ave *TF:* 800-955-9700 ■ *Web:* www.vsaresorts.com	Virginia Beach	VA	23451	757-425-2200	491-1186
Ocean Pointe Suites at Key Largo 500 Burton Dr *TF:* 800-882-9464 ■ *Web:* www.providentresorts.com/ocean-pointe-suites	Tavernier	FL	33070	305-853-3000	853-3007
Ocean Resort Hotel Waikiki 175 Paoakalani Ave *Web:* www.castleresorts.com	Honolulu	HI	96815	808-922-3861	922-3773
Ocean Sky Hotel & Resort 4060 Galt Ocean Dr *TF:* 800-678-9022 ■ *Web:* www.oceanskyresort.com	Fort Lauderdale	FL	33308	954-565-6611	564-7730
Ocean Walk Resort 300 N Atlantic *TF:* 888-743-2323 ■ *Web:* www.oceanwalk.com	Daytona Beach	FL	32118	386-323-4800	323-4810
Oceancliff Hotel & Resort 65 Ridge Rd *Web:* www.newportexperience.com	Newport	RI	02840	401-841-8868	849-3927
Ocotillo Lodge 1111 E Palm Canyon Dr *TF:* 800-777-1818 ■ *Web:* www.ocotillolodge.com	Palm Springs	CA	92264	760-416-0678	416-0599
OHANA Waikiki Beachcomber Hotel 2300 Kalakaua Ave *TF:* 877-317-5757 ■ *Web:* www.outrigger.com	Honolulu	HI	96815	808-922-4646	923-4889
Old City House Inn 115 Cordova St *Web:* www.oldcityhouse.com	Saint Augustine	FL	32084	904-826-0113	
Old Mill Toronto Inn & Spa 21 Old Mill Rd *TF:* 866-653-6455	Toronto	ON	M8X1G5	416-236-2641	236-2749

Name / Address	City	State	ZIP	Phone	Fax
Olympic Corporate Suites 400 Village Gardens SW *Web:* www.olympicsuites.com	Calgary	AB	T3H2L1	403-355-5175	697-3265
Omni Hotels 420 Decker Dr Suite 200 *Fax: Mktg ■ *TF:* 800-843-6664 ■ *Web:* www.omnihotels.com	Irving	TX	75062	972-730-6664	871-5665*
Omni La Mansion del Rio 112 College St *TF:* 800-292-7300 ■ *Web:* www.omnihotels.com	San Antonio	TX	78205	210-518-1000	226-0389
One Washington Circle Hotel 1 Washington Cir NW *TF:* 800-424-9671 ■ *Web:* www.thecirclehotel.com	Washington	DC	20037	202-872-1680	887-4989
Onyx Hotel 155 Portland St *TF:* 866-660-6699 ■ *Web:* www.onyxhotel.com	Boston	MA	02114	617-557-9955	557-0005
Opus Hotel 322 Davie St *TF:* 866-642-6787 ■ *Web:* www.opushotel.com	Vancouver	BC	V6B5Z6	604-642-6787	642-6780
Opus Hotel Montreal 10 Sherbrooke St W *TF:* 866-744-6346 ■ *Web:* www.opushotel.com	Montreal	QC	H2X4C9	514-843-6000	843-6810
Orchard Garden Hotel 466 Bush St *TF:* 888-717-2881 ■ *Web:* www.theorchardgardenhotel.com	San Francisco	CA	94108	415-399-9807	393-9917
Orchard Hotel 665 Bush St *TF:* 888-717-2881 ■ *Web:* www.theorchardhotel.com	San Francisco	CA	94108	415-362-8878	362-8088
Orchards Hotel The 222 Adams Rd *TF:* 800-225-1517 ■ *Web:* www.orchardshotel.com	Williamstown	MA	01267	413-458-9611	458-3273
Orchards Inn of Sedona 254 Hwy N 89 A *TF:* 800-474-7719 ■ *Web:* www.orchardsinn.com	Sedona	AZ	86336	928-282-2405	282-5710
Orient Express Hotels Inc 1114 Avenue of the Americas 30th Fl *NYSE: OEH* ■ *TF:* 800-237-1236 ■ *Web:* www.orient-express.com	New York	NY	10036	212-302-5055	302-5203
Orlando The 8384 W 3rd St *TF:* 800-624-6835 ■ *Web:* www.theorlando.com	Los Angeles	CA	90048	323-658-6600	653-3464
Outrigger Enterprises Group 2375 Kuhio Ave *TF:* 800-462-6262 ■ *Web:* www.outrigger.com	Honolulu	HI	96815	808-921-6941	922-8509
OHANA Hotels & Resorts 2375 Kuhio Ave. *TF:* 866-254-1605 ■ *Web:* www.ohanahotelsoahu.com	Honolulu	HI	96815	866-254-1605	
Outrigger Lodging Services LP 16000 Ventura Blvd Suite 1010 *Web:* www.outriggerlodging.com	Encino	CA	91436	818-905-8280	905-7786
Outrigger Waikiki on the Beach 2335 Kalakaua Ave *TF:* 800-688-7444 ■ *Web:* www.outrigger.com	Honolulu	HI	96815	808-923-0711	921-9749
Overlook Lodge PO Box 351 *Web:* www.visitbearmountain.com	Bear Mountain	NY	10911	845-786-2731	786-2543
Owyhee Plaza Hotel 1109 Main St *TF:* 800-233-4611 ■ *Web:* www.owyheeplaza.com	Boise	ID	83702	208-343-4611	336-3860
Oxford Hotel 1600 17th St *TF:* 800-228-5838 ■ *Web:* www.theoxfordhotel.com	Denver	CO	80202	303-628-5400	628-5413
Oxford Palace 745 S Oxford Ave *TF:* 800-532-7887 ■ *Web:* www.oxfordhotel.com	Los Angeles	CA	90005	213-389-8000	389-8500
Oxford Suites Boise 1426 S Entertainment Ave *TF:* 888-322-8001 ■ *Web:* www.oxfordsuitesboise.com	Boise	ID	38709	208-322-8000	322-8002
Oxford Suites Spokane Valley 15015 E Indiana Ave *TF:* 866-668-7848 ■ *Web:* www.oxfordsuitesspokanevalley.com	Spokane Valley	WA	99216	509-847-1000	847-1001
Oxford Suites Spokane-Downtown 115 W N River Dr *TF:* 800-774-1877 ■ *Web:* www.oxfordsuitesspokane.com	Spokane	WA	99201	509-353-9000	353-9164
Oyster Point Hotel The 146 Bodman Pl *TF:* 800-345-3484 ■ *Web:* www.theoysterpointhotel.com	Red Bank	NJ	07701	732-530-8200	747-1875
Pace's Lodging Corp 4265 45th St S Suite 200 *Web:* www.propertyresourcesgroup.com	Fargo	ND	58104	701-281-9500	281-9501
Pacific Beach Hotel 2490 Kalakaua Ave *TF:* 800-367-6060 ■ *Web:* www.pacificbeachhotel.com	Honolulu	HI	96815	808-922-1233	922-0129
Pacific Edge Hotel 647 S Coast Hwy *Web:* www.pacificedgehotel.com	Laguna Beach	CA	92651	949-494-8566	
Pacific Inn 600 Marina Dr *TF:* 866-466-0300 ■ *Web:* www.pacificinn-sb.com	Seal Beach	CA	90740	562-493-7501	596-3448
Pacific Inn Resort & Conference Centre 1160 King George Hwy *TF:* 800-667-2248 ■ *Web:* www.pacificinn.com	Surrey	BC	V4A4Z2	604-535-1432	531-6979
Pacific Shores Inn 4802 Mission Blvd *TF:* 888-478-7829 ■ *Web:* www.pacific-shores-inn.pacificahost.com	San Diego	CA	92109	858-483-6300	483-9276
Pacific Terrace Hotel 610 Diamond St *TF:* 800-344-3370 ■ *Web:* www.pacificterrace.com	San Diego	CA	92109	858-581-3500	274-2534
Pacifica Coast Hotels 1785 Hancock St # 100 *Web:* www.pacificahost.com	San Diego	CA	92110	619-296-9000	296-9080
Pagoda Hotel 1525 Rycroft St *TF:* 800-367-6060 ■ *Web:* www.pagodahotel.com	Honolulu	HI	96814	808-941-6611	955-5067
Painted Buffalo Inn 400 W Broadway PO Box 2547 *TF:* 800-288-3866 ■ *Web:* www.paintedbuffaloinn.com	Jackson	WY	83001	307-733-4340	733-7953
Palace Casino 158 Howard Ave *Fax: Mktg ■ *TF:* 800-725-2239 ■ *Web:* www.palacecasinoresort.com	Biloxi	MS	39530	228-432-8888	386-2314*
Palace Hotel 2 New Montgomery St *Web:* www.sfpalace.com	San Francisco	CA	94105	415-512-1111	543-0671
Palmer House Hilton 17 E Monroe St *TF:* 800-445-8667 ■ *Web:* www.hiltonfamilychicago.com	Chicago	IL	60603	312-726-7500	917-1707
Palmer Inn The 3499 Rt 1 S *TF:* 800-688-2500 ■ *Web:* www.palmerinnprinceton.com	Princeton	NJ	08640	609-452-2500	452-1371
Palo Verde Inn & Suites 5251 S Julian Dr *TF:* 800-272-6232 ■ *Web:* www.paloverdeinn.com	Tucson	AZ	85706	520-294-5250	889-1982
Palos Verdes Inn 1700 S Pacific Coast Hwy *TF:* 800-421-9241 ■ *Web:* www.palosverdesinn.com	Redondo Beach	CA	90277	310-316-4211	316-4863
Pan Pacific Hotel Vancouver 999 Canada Pl Suite 300 *TF:* 800-937-1515 ■ *Web:* www.panpacific.com	Vancouver	BC	V6C3B5	604-662-8111	685-8690
Pan Pacific Seattle 2125 Terry Ave *Web:* www.panpacific.com	Seattle	WA	98121	206-264-8111	654-5049
Pantages Hotel 200 Victoria St *TF:* 866-852-1777 ■ *Web:* www.pantageshotel.com	Toronto	ON	M5E1E1	416-362-1777	214-5618
Par-A-Dice Hotel 21 Blackjack Blvd *TF:* 800-727-2342 ■ *Web:* www.paradicecasino.com	East Peoria	IL	61611	309-699-7711	699-9317
Paradise Inn The 819 Simonton St *TF:* 800-888-9648 ■ *Web:* www.theparadiseinn.com	Key West	FL	33040	305-293-8007	293-0807
Paragon Hotel Corp 5333 N 7th St Suite A-100 *Web:* www.paragonhotels.com	Phoenix	AZ	85014	602-248-0811	279-6765
Paramount Hotel 724 Pine St *TF:* 800-663-1144 ■ *Web:* www.paramounthotelseattle.com	Seattle	WA	98101	206-292-9500	292-8610
Paramount Hotel 235 W 46th St *TF:* 888-741-5600 ■ *Web:* www.solmelia.com	New York	NY	10036	212-764-5500	354-5237
Paramount Hotel 808 SW Taylor St *TF:* 866-760-3174 ■ *Web:* www.portlandparamount.com	Portland	OR	97205	503-223-9900	223-7900
Paramount Hotel Group 710 Rt 46 E Suite 206 *Web:* www.paramounthotelgroup.com	Fairfield	NJ	07004	973-882-0505	882-0043
Parc 55 Hotel 55 Cyril Magnin St *Web:* www.parc55hotel.com	San Francisco	CA	94102	415-392-8000	403-6602
Paris Las Vegas 3655 Las Vegas Blvd S *TF:* 877-603-4386 ■ *Web:* www.totalrewards.com	Las Vegas	NV	89109	702-946-7000	946-4259
Park Central Hotel 1010 Houston St *TF:* 800-848-7275 ■ *Web:* www.parkcentralhotel.com	Fort Worth	TX	76102	817-336-2011	336-2011
Park Central New York 870 7th Ave *TF:* 800-346-1359 ■ *Web:* www.parkcentralny.com	New York	NY	10019	212-247-8000	707-5557
Park Central The 640 Ocean Dr *TF:* 800-727-5236 ■ *Web:* www.theparkcentral.com	Miami Beach	FL	33139	305-538-1611	534-7520
Park Lane Hotel at Four Seasons 3005 High Pt Rd *TF:* 800-942-6556 ■ *Web:* www.park-lane-hotel.com	Greensboro	NC	27403	336-294-4565	294-0572
Park Plaza Hotel Oakland 150 Hegenberger Rd *TF:* 800-635-5301 ■ *Web:* www.parkplazaoakland.com	Oakland	CA	94621	510-635-5300	635-9661
Park Shore Waikiki Hotel 2586 Kalakaua Ave. *TF:* 866-282-4773 ■ *Web:* www.parkshorewaikiki.com	Honolulu	HI	96815	808-923-0411	923-0311
Park South Hotel 122 E 28th St *TF:* 800-315-4642 ■ *Web:* www.parksouthhotel.com	New York	NY	10016	212-448-0888	448-0811
Park Vista Resort Hotel 705 Cherokee Orchard Rd PO Box 30 *TF:* 800-421-7275 ■ *Web:* www.parkvista.com	Gatlinburg	TN	37738	865-436-9211	430-7533
Parkway Inn 125 N Jackson St PO Box 494 *TF:* 800-247-8390 ■ *Web:* www.parkwayinn.com	Jackson	WY	83001	307-733-3143	733-0955
Parkway Plaza Hotel 123 W E St *TF:* 800-270-7829 ■ *Web:* www.parkwayplaza.net	Casper	WY	82601	307-235-1777	235-8068
Partridge Inn 2110 Walton Way *TF:* 800-476-6888 ■ *Web:* www.partridgeinn.com	Augusta	GA	30904	706-737-8888	731-0826
Paso Robles Inn 1103 Spring St *TF:* 800-676-1713 ■ *Web:* www.pasoroblesinn.com	Paso Robles	CA	93446	805-238-2660	238-4707
Peabody Hotel Group 5118 Pk Ave Suite 245 *Web:* www.peabodyhotelgroup.com	Memphis	TN	38117	901-762-5400	762-5464
Peabody Little Rock The 3 Statehouse Plaza *TF:* 800-527-1745 ■ *Web:* www.peabodylittlerock.com	Little Rock	AR	72201	501-906-4000	375-4721
Peabody Memphis 149 Union Ave *TF:* 800-833-2548 ■ *Web:* www.peabodymemphis.com	Memphis	TN	38103	901-529-4000	529-3600
Peabody Orlando 9801 International Dr *TF:* 800-732-2639 ■ *Web:* www.peabodyorlando.com	Orlando	FL	32819	407-352-4000	351-9177
Peacock Suites 1745 S Anaheim Blvd *TF:* 800-522-6401 ■ *Web:* www.shellhospitality.com	Anaheim	CA	92805	714-535-8255	535-8914
Pearl Hotel The 1410 Rosecrans St *TF:* 877-732-7573 ■ *Web:* www.thepearlsd.com	San Diego	CA	92106	619-226-6100	226-6161
Peery Hotel 110 W 300 S *TF:* 800-331-0073 ■ *Web:* www.peeryhotel.com	Salt Lake City	UT	84101	801-521-4300	575-5014
Pegasus International Hotel 501 Southard St *TF:* 800-397-8148 ■ *Web:* www.pegasuskeywest.com	Key West	FL	33040	305-294-9323	294-4741
Pelham Hotel 444 Common St *TF:* 888-211-3447 ■ *Web:* www.thepelhamhotel.com	New Orleans	LA	70130	504-522-4444	539-9010
Penguin Hotel 1418 Ocean Dr *TF:* 800-235-3296 ■ *Web:* www.penguinhotel.com	Miami Beach	FL	33139	305-534-9334	604-0350
Peninsula Beverly Hills 9882 S Santa Monica Blvd *TF:* 800-462-7899 ■ *Web:* www.peninsula.com	Beverly Hills	CA	90212	310-551-2888	788-2319
Peninsula Chicago 108 E Superior St *TF:* 866-288-8889 ■ *Web:* www.peninsula.com	Chicago	IL	60611	312-337-2888	751-2888
Peninsula New York 700 5th Ave *TF:* 800-262-9467 ■ *Web:* www.newyork.peninsula.com	New York	NY	10019	212-956-2888	903-3949
Penn Tower Hotel 399 S 34th St	Philadelphia	PA	19104	215-387-8333	386-8306
Penn's View Hotel 14 N Front St *TF:* 800-331-7634 ■ *Web:* www.pennsviewhotel.com	Philadelphia	PA	19106	215-922-7600	922-7642
Petite Auberge 863 Bush St *TF:* 800-365-3004 ■ *Web:* www.jdvhotels.com/petite_auberge	San Francisco	CA	94108	415-928-6000	673-7214
Pfister Hotel 424 E Wisconsin Ave *TF:* 800-558-8222 ■ *Web:* www.pfisterhotel.com	Milwaukee	WI	53202	414-273-8222	273-5025
Phillips Beach Plaza Hotel 1301 Atlantic Ave *TF:* 800-492-5834 ■ *Web:* www.phillipsbeachplaza.com	Ocean City	MD	21842	410-289-9121	289-3041
Phoenix Grand Hotel Salem 201 Liberty St SE *TF:* 877-540-7800 ■ *Web:* www.grandhotelsalem.com	Salem	OR	97301	503-540-7800	540-7830
Phoenix Hotel 601 Eddy St *TF:* 800-248-9466 ■ *Web:* www.jdvhotels.com/phoenix	San Francisco	CA	94109	415-776-1380	885-3109
Phoenix Park Hotel 520 N Capitol St *TF:* 800-824-5419 ■ *Web:* www.phoenixparkhotel.com	Washington	DC	20001	202-638-6900	393-3236
Piccadilly Inn Airport 5115 E McKinley Ave *TF:* 800-468-3587 ■ *Web:* www.piccadillyinn.com	Fresno	CA	93727	559-251-6000	251-6956
Piccadilly Inn Express 5113 E McKinley Ave *TF:* 800-445-2428 ■ *Web:* www.piccadillyinn.com	Fresno	CA	93727	559-456-1418	456-4643
Piccadilly Inn Shaw 2305 W Shaw Ave *TF:* 800-468-3587 ■ *Web:* www.piccadillyinn.com	Fresno	CA	93711	559-226-3850	226-2448
Piccadilly Inn University 4961 N Cedar St *TF:* 800-468-3587 ■ *Web:* www.piccadillyinn.com	Fresno	CA	93726	559-224-4200	227-2382
Pickwick Grand Heritage Hotel 85 5th St *TF:* 800-227-3282 ■ *Web:* www.thepickwickhotel.com	San Francisco	CA	94103	415-421-7500	243-8066
Pier 5 Hotel 711 Eastern Ave *TF:* 866-583-4162 ■ *Web:* www.thepier5.com	Baltimore	MD	21202	410-539-2000	783-1787
Pier Pointe Resort 4320 El Mar Dr *TF:* 800-331-6384	Lauderdale-by-the-Sea	FL	33308	954-776-5121	491-9084

Name / Address	City	State	Zip	Phone	Fax
Pierpont Inn 550 Sanjon Rd	Ventura	CA	93001	805-643-6144	643-9167
TF: 800-285-4667 ■ *Web:* www.pierpontinn.com					
Pierre The 5th Ave at 61st St	New York	NY	10021	212-838-8000	940-8109
Web: www.tajhotels.com					
Pillars Hotel at New River Sound 111 N Birch Rd	Fort Lauderdale	FL	33304	954-467-9639	763-2845
TF: 800-800-7666 ■ *Web:* www.pillarshotel.com					
Pine Crest Inn 85 Pine Crest Ln	Tryon	NC	28782	828-859-9135	859-9136
TF: 800-633-3001 ■ *Web:* www.pinecrestinn.com					
Pines Lodge 141 Scott Hill Rd	Avon	CO	81620	970-845-7900	845-7809
TF Resv: 800-859-8242 ■ *Web:* www.pineslodge.rockresorts.com					
Pisgah Inn PO Box 749	Waynesville	NC	28786	828-235-8228	648-9719
Web: www.pisgahinn.com					
Pitcher Inn 275 Main St PO Box 347	Warren	VT	05674	802-496-6350	496-6354
TF: 888-867-4824 ■ *Web:* www.pitcherinn.com					
Place D'Armes Hotel 625 St Ann St	New Orleans	LA	70116	504-524-4531	571-2803
TF: 800-366-2743 ■ *Web:* www.placedarmes.com					
Place Louis Riel All-Suite Hotel 190 Smith St	Winnipeg	MB	R3C1J8	204-947-6961	947-3029
TF: 800-665-0569 ■ *Web:* www.placelouisriel.com					
Plains Hotel The 1600 Central Ave	Cheyenne	WY	82001	307-638-3311	635-2022
TF: 866-275-2467 ■ *Web:* www.theplainshotel.com					
Plantation Inn of New England 295 Burnett Rd	Chicopee	MA	01020	413-592-8200	592-9671
TF: 800-248-8495 ■ *Web:* www.plantation-inn.com					
Planters Inn 112 N Market St	Charleston	SC	29401	843-722-2345	577-2125
TF: 800-845-7082 ■ *Web:* www.plantersinn.com					
Planters Inn 29 Abercorn St	Savannah	GA	31401	912-232-5678	232-8893
TF: 800-554-1187 ■ *Web:* www.plantersinnsavannah.com					
Platinum Hotel 211 E Flamingo Rd	Las Vegas	NV	89169	702-365-5000	636-2500
TF: 877-211-9111 ■ *Web:* www.theplatinumhotel.com					
Plaza 500 Hotel 500 W 12th Ave	Vancouver	BC	V5Z1M2	604-873-1811	873-5103
TF: 800-473-1811					
Plaza Hotel & Apartments 1007 N Cass St	Milwaukee	WI	53202	414-276-2101	276-0404
TF: 800-340-9590 ■ *Web:* www.shorelinerealestate.com					
Plaza Hotel & Casino 1 Main St PO Box 760	Las Vegas	NV	89101	702-386-2110	382-8281
TF: 800-634-6575 ■ *Web:* www.plazahotelcasino.com					
Plaza Inn 900 Medical Arts NE	Albuquerque	NM	87102	505-243-5693	843-6229
TF: 800-237-1307 ■ *Web:* www.plazainnabq.com					
Plaza on the River Resort Club Hotel 121 W St	Reno	NV	89501	775-786-2200	786-4861
TF: 800-628-5974					
Plaza Square Motor Lodge 2255 Central Blvd	Brownsville	TX	78520	956-546-5104	548-0243
Plaza Suite Hotel Resort 620 S Peters St	New Orleans	LA	70130	504-524-9500	524-2135
TF: 800-770-6721 ■ *Web:* www.plazaresort.com					
Plaza Suites Silicon Valley 3100 Lakeside Dr	Santa Clara	CA	95054	408-748-9800	748-1476
TF: 800-345-1554 ■ *Web:* www.theplazasuites.com					
Plim Plaza Hotel 109 Atlantic Ave # 1	Ocean City	MD	21842	410-289-6181	289-0714
TF: 800-837-3587 ■ *Web:* www.ocmdhotels.com					
Plump Jack's Squaw Valley Inn 1920 Squaw Valley Rd PO Box 2407	Olympic Valley	CA	96146	530-583-1576	583-1734
TF: 800-323-7666 ■ *Web:* www.plumpjacksquawvalleyinn.com					
Point Plaza Suites & Conference Hotel 950 J Clyde Morris Blvd	Newport News	VA	23601	757-599-4460	599-4336
TF: 800-841-1112 ■ *Web:* www.pointplazasuites.com					
Pollard The 2 N Broadway PO Box 650	Red Lodge	MT	59068	406-446-0001	446-0002
TF: 800-765-5273 ■ *Web:* www.thepollard.com					
Pontchartrain Hotel 2031 St Charles Ave	New Orleans	LA	70140	504-524-0581	529-1165
TF: 800-777-6193 ■ *Web:* www.pontchartrainhotel.com					
Port-O-Call Hotel 1510 Boardwalk	Ocean City	NJ	08226	609-399-8812	399-0387
TF: 800-334-4546 ■ *Web:* www.portocallhotel.com					
Portland Harbor Hotel 468 Fore St	Portland	ME	04101	207-775-9090	775-9990
TF: 888-798-9090 ■ *Web:* www.portlandharborhotel.com					
Portland Regency Hotel 20 Milk St	Portland	ME	04101	207-774-4200	775-2150
TF: 800-727-3436 ■ *Web:* www.theregency.com					
Portofino Hotel & Yacht Club 260 Portofino Way	Redondo Beach	CA	90277	310-379-8481	372-7329
TF: 800-468-4292 ■ *Web:* www.hotelportofino.com					
Portofino Inn & Suites Anaheim 1831 S Harbor Blvd	Anaheim	CA	92802	714-782-7600	782-7619
TF: 888-297-7143 ■ *Web:* www.portofinoinnanaheim.com					
Portola Plaza Hotel 2 Portola Plaza	Monterey	CA	93940	831-649-4511	649-4511
TF: 866-711-1534 ■ *Web:* www.portolahotel.com					
Post Hotel The 200 Pipestone Rd PO Box 69	Lake Louise	AB	T0L1E0	403-522-3989	522-3966
TF: 800-661-1586 ■ *Web:* www.posthotel.com					
Prairie Hotel 700 Prairie Pk Ln PO Box 5210	Yelm	WA	98597	360-458-8300	458-8301
Web: www.prairiehotel.com					
Preferred Hotel Group 311 S Wacker Dr Suite 1900	Chicago	IL	60606	312-542-9380	913-5124
Web: www.preferredhotelgroup.com					
Preferred Hotels & Resorts Worldwide Inc 311 S Wacker Dr Suite 1900	Chicago	IL	60606	312-913-0400	913-0444
TF: 800-323-7500 ■ *Web:* www.preferredhotels.com					
Sterling Hotels Corp 311 S Wacker Dr Suite 1900	Chicago	IL	60606	312-913-0400	913-5124
Web: www.sterlinghotels.com					
Summit Hotels & Resorts 311 S Wacker Dr Suite 1900	Chicago	IL	60606	312-913-0400	913-5124
TF: 800-457-4000 ■ *Web:* www.summithotels.com					
Premier Hotel The 133 W 44th St	New York	NY	10036	212-789-7670	789-7673
TF: 800-622-5569 ■ *Web:* www.premierhotel.com					
Premier Suites 11601 W Markham Rd Suite D	Little Rock	AR	72211	501-221-7378	219-1920
TF: 800-735-2955 ■ *Web:* www.premiersuites.com					
Prescott Hotel 545 Post St	San Francisco	CA	94102	415-563-0303	563-6831
TF: 800-283-7322 ■ *Web:* www.prescotthotel.com					
President Abraham Lincoln Hotel & Conference Ctr (PALHACC) 701 E Adams St	Springfield	IL	62701	217-544-8800	544-9607
TF: 866-788-1860 ■ *Web:* www.presidentabrahamlincolnhotel.com					
President Hotel 1423 Collins Ave	Miami Beach	FL	33139	305-538-2882	604-0350
TF: 800-235-3296 ■ *Web:* www.penguinhotel.com					
Priced Rite Suites 2327 University Ave	Green Bay	WI	54302	920-469-2130	
Web: www.pricedritesuites.com					
Prince Conti Hotel 830 Conti St	New Orleans	LA	70112	504-529-4172	636-1046
TF: 800-366-2743 ■ *Web:* www.princecontihotel.com					
Prince George Hotel The 1725 Market St	Halifax	NS	B3J3N9	902-425-1986	429-6048
TF: 800-565-1567 ■ *Web:* www.princegeorgehotel.com					
Princess Bayside Beach Hotel & Golf Ctr 4801 Coastal Hwy	Ocean City	MD	21842	410-723-2900	723-0207
TF: 800-854-9785 ■ *Web:* www.princessbayside.com					
Princess Royale Oceanfront Hotel & Conference Ctr 9100 Coastal Hwy	Ocean City	MD	21842	410-524-7777	524-1623
TF: 800-476-9253 ■ *Web:* www.princessroyale.com					
Priory The 614 Pressley St	Pittsburgh	PA	15212	412-231-3338	231-4838
Web: www.thepriory.com					
Prospector Hotel 375 Whittier St	Juneau	AK	99801	907-586-3737	586-1204
TF: 800-331-2711 ■ *Web:* www.prospectorhotel.com					
Providence Biltmore Hotel Kennedy Plaza 11 Dorrance St	Providence	RI	02903	401-421-0700	455-3050
TF: 800-294-7709 ■ *Web:* www.providencebiltmore.com					
Publick House Historic Resort 295 Main St Rt 131	Sturbridge	MA	01566	508-347-3313	347-5073
TF Cust Svc: 800-782-5425 ■ *Web:* www.publickhouse.com					
Puffin Inn 4400 Spenard Rd	Anchorage	AK	99517	907-243-4044	248-6853
TF: 800-478-3346 ■ *Web:* www.puffininn.net					
Quail Run Lodge 1130 Bob Harman Rd	Savannah	GA	31408	912-964-1421	966-5646
TF: 800-627-7035 ■ *Web:* www.quailrunlodge.com					
Quaintance-Weaver Inc 324 W Wendover Ave	Greensboro	NC	27408	336-370-0966	370-0965
Web: www.qwrh.com					
Quality Inn Flamingo 1300 N Stone Ave	Tucson	AZ	85705	520-770-1910	770-0750
Web: www.flamingohoteltucson.com					
Quality Inn Halifax Airport Hotel 60 Sky Blvd Halifax International Airport	Goffs	NS	B2T1K3	902-873-3000	873-3001
TF: 800-667-3333 ■ *Web:* www.airporthotelhalifax.com					
Quality Inn West Harvest 17803 Stony Plain Rd	Edmonton	AB	T5S1B4	780-484-8000	486-6060
TF: 800-661-6993 ■ *Web:* www.westharvest.ca					
Quarterage Hotel 560 Westport Rd	Kansas City	MO	64111	816-931-0001	931-8891
TF: 800-942-4233 ■ *Web:* www.quarteragehotel.com					
Quebec Inn 7175 Blvd Hamel Ouest	Quebec City	QC	G2G1B6	418-872-9831	872-1336
TF: 800-567-5276 ■ *Web:* www.hotelsjaro.com/quebecinn/index-en.aspx					
Queen & Crescent Hotel 344 Camp St	New Orleans	LA	70130	504-587-9700	587-9701
TF: 800-455-3417 ■ *Web:* www.neworleansboutiquehotels.com					
Queen Anne Hotel 1590 Sutter St	San Francisco	CA	94109	415-441-2828	775-5212
TF: 800-227-3970 ■ *Web:* www.queenanne.com					
Queen Kapiolani Hotel 150 Kapahulu Ave	Honolulu	HI	96815	808-922-1941	922-2694
TF: 800-367-2317 ■ *Web:* www.queenkapiolani.com					
Quimby House Inn 109 Cottage St	Bar Harbor	ME	04609	207-288-5811	
TF: 800-344-5811 ■ *Web:* www.quimbyhouse.com					
Quincy Hotel 1823 L St NW	Washington	DC	20036	202-223-4320	293-4977
TF: 800-424-2970 ■ *Web:* www.thequincy.com					
Rabbit Hill Inn 48 Lower Waterford Rd PO Box 55	Lower Waterford	VT	05848	802-748-5168	748-8342
TF: 800-762-8669 ■ *Web:* www.rabbithillinn.com					
Radisson Butler Blvd 4700 Salisbury Rd	Jacksonville	FL	32256	904-281-9700	281-1957
TF: 888-201-1718 ■ *Web:* www.radisson.com					
Radisson Chicago-O'Hare Hotel 1450 E Touhy Ave	Des Plaines	IL	60018	847-296-8866	296-8268
TF: 888-201-1718 ■ *Web:* www.radisson.com					
Radisson Hotel Bloomington Mall of America 1700 American Blvd E	Bloomington	MN	55425	952-854-8700	854-8701
TF Resv: 800-967-9033 ■ *Web:* www.radisson.com/bloomington-hotel-mn-55425/mnblmmal					
Radisson Hotel Gateway Seattle-Tacoma Airport 18118 International Blvd	Seattle	WA	98188	206-244-6666	244-6679
Web: www.radisson.com					
Radisson Milwaukee North Shore 7065 N Port Washington Rd	Milwaukee	WI	53217	414-351-6960	351-5194
TF: 800-395-7046 ■ *Web:* www.radisson.com					
Radnor Hotel 591 E Lancaster Ave	Saint Davids	PA	19087	610-688-5800	341-3299
TF: 800-537-3000 ■ *Web:* www.radnorhotel.com					
Raffaello Hotel 201 E Delaware Pl	Chicago	IL	60611	312-943-5000	924-9158
Web: www.chicagoraffaello.com					
Ramada Plaza & Conference Ctr 4900 Sinclair Rd	Columbus	OH	43229	614-846-0300	847-1022
TF: 800-272-6232 ■ *Web:* www.ramada.com					
Ranch at Steamboat 1800 Ranch Rd	Steamboat Springs	CO	80487	970-879-3000	879-5409
TF: 800-525-2002 ■ *Web:* www.ranch-steamboat.com					
Ranch Inn 45 E Pearl St	Jackson	WY	83001	307-733-6363	733-0623
TF: 800-348-5599 ■ *Web:* www.ranchinn.com					
Rancho Alegre Lodge 3600 S Pk Loop Rd PO Box 998	Jackson	WY	83001	307-733-7988	734-0254
Web: www.ranchoalegre.com					
Rancho de San Juan 3420 US 285	Espanola	NM	87532	505-753-6818	753-6818
Web: www.ranchodesanjuan.com					
Raphael Kansas City 325 Ward Pkwy	Kansas City	MO	64112	816-756-3800	802-2131
TF: 800-821-5343 ■ *Web:* www.raphaelkc.com					
Red Jacket Beach Resort 1 S Shore Dr	South Yarmouth	MA	02664	508-398-6941	898-1214
TF: 800-227-3263 ■ *Web:* www.redjacketresorts.com					
Red Lion Hotels Corp 201 W N River Dr Suite 100	Spokane	WA	99201	509-459-6100	325-7324
NYSE: RLH ■ *TF Resv:* 800-325-4000 ■ *Web:* www.redlion.com					
WestCoast Hotel Partners					
Red Lion Hotel Corp 201 W N River Dr Suite 100	Spokane	WA	99201	509-459-6100	325-7324
TF: 800-325-4000 ■ *Web:* www.westcoast.rdln.com					
Red Lion Inn 30 Main St PO Box 954	Stockbridge	MA	01262	413-298-5545	298-5130
Web: www.redlioninn.com					
Redstone Inn 82 Redstone Blvd	Redstone	CO	81623	970-963-2526	963-2527
TF: 800-748-2524 ■ *Web:* www.redstoneinn.com					
Redstone Inn & Suites 504 Bluff St	Dubuque	IA	52001	563-582-1894	
Web: www.theredstoneinn.com					

Phone | Fax

Regal Sun Resort at Walt Disney World Village
1850 Hotel Plaza Blvd. Lake Buena Vista FL 32830 407-828-4444 828-8192
TF: 800-624-4109 ■ *Web:* www.wyndhamlakebuenavista.com

Regency Fairbanks Hotel 95 10th Ave Fairbanks AK 99701 907-459-2700 452-6505
TF: 800-478-1320 ■ *Web:* www.regencyfairbankshotel.com

Regency House Hotel 140 Rt 23 N. Pompton Plains NJ 07444 973-696-0900 696-0201
Web: www.regencyhousehotel.com

Regency Suites Calgary 610 4th Ave SW Calgary AB T2P0K1 403-231-1000 231-1012
TF: 800-468-4044 ■ *Web:* www.regencycalgary.com

Regency Suites Hotel Midtown Atlanta
975 W Peachtree St Atlanta GA 30309 404-876-5003 817-7511
TF: 800-642-3629 ■ *Web:* www.regencysuites.com

Remington Hotel Corp
14185 Dallas Pkwy Suite 1150 Dallas TX 75254 972-980-2700 392-1929
Web: www.remingtonhospitalityservices.com

Remington Suite Hotel 220 Travis St. Shreveport LA 71101 318-425-5000 425-5011
TF: 800-444-6750 ■ *Web:* www.remingtonsuite.com

Rennaissance Syracuse 701 E Genesee St Syracuse NY 13210 315-479-7000 472-2700
TF: 800-468-3571

Residence & Conference Centre - Toronto
1760 Finch Ave E Toronto ON M2J5G3 416-491-8811 491-0486
TF: 877-225-8664 ■ *Web:* www.residenceconferencecentre.com/toronto

Residences on Georgia
101-1288 W Georgia St Vancouver BC V6E4R3 604-891-6101 891-6103
Web: www.respal.com

Resort at Port Ludlow 1 Heron Rd. Port Ludlow WA 98365 360-437-7000 437-7410
TF: 877-805-0868 ■ *Web:* www.portludlowresort.com

ResortQuest Waikiki Circle Hotel
2464 Kalakaua Ave Honolulu HI 96815 808-923-1571 926-8024
TF: 866-774-2924 ■ *Web:* www.astonhotels.com

Rhett House Inn 1009 Craven St. Beaufort SC 29902 843-524-9030 524-1310
TF: 888-480-9530 ■ *Web:* www.rhetthouseinn.com

Richfield Hospitality Services
7600 E Orchard Rd Suite 230-S Greenwood Village CO 80111 303-220-2000 220-2120
Web: www.richfield.com

Richmond Hill Inn 87 Richmond Hill Dr Asheville NC 28806 828-252-7313 252-8726
TF: 888-742-4554 ■ *Web:* www.richmondhillinn.com

Richmond The 1757 Collins Ave Miami Beach FL 33139 305-538-2331 531-9021
TF: 800-327-3163 ■ *Web:* www.richmondhotel.com

Rittenhouse Hotel 210 W Rittenhouse Sq Philadelphia PA 19103 215-546-9000 732-3364
TF: 800-635-1042 ■ *Web:* www.rittenhousehotel.com

Ritz Milner Hotel 813 S Flower St Los Angeles CA 90017 213-627-6981 623-9751
TF: 800-827-0411 ■ *Web:* www.milner-hotels.com/la.html

Ritz-Carlton Dallas 2121 McKinney Ave Dallas TX 75201 214-922-0200 720-7575
TF: 800-960-7082 ■ *Web:* www.ritzcarlton.com

Riu Hotel Florida Beach 3101 Collins Ave Miami FL 33140 305-673-5333 673-9335
TF: 888-666-8816 ■ *Web:* www.riu.com

River Inn 924 25th St NW Washington DC 20037 202-337-7600 337-6520
TF: 800-424-2741 ■ *Web:* www.theriverinn.com

River Street Inn 124 E Bay St Savannah GA 31401 912-234-6400 234-1478
TF: 800-253-4229 ■ *Web:* www.riverstreetinn.com

River's Edge Resort Cottages 4200 Boat St. Fairbanks AK 99709 907-474-0286 474-3665
TF: 800-770-3343 ■ *Web:* www.riversedge.net

Riveredge Resort Hotel 17 Holland St Alexandria Bay NY 13607 315-482-9917 482-5010
TF: 800-365-6987 ■ *Web:* www.riveredge.com

RiverPlace Hotel 1510 SW Harbor Way Portland OR 97201 503-228-3233 295-6167
TF: 800-227-1333 ■ *Web:* www.larkspurhotels.com/collection/riverplace

Riverside Hotel 620 E Las Olas Blvd. Fort Lauderdale FL 33301 954-467-0671 462-2148
TF: 800-325-3280 ■ *Web:* www.riversidehotel.com

Riverside Inn 1 Fountain Ave. Cambridge Springs PA 16403 814-398-4645 398-8161
TF: 800-964-5173 ■ *Web:* www.theriversideinn.com

Riverstone Billings Inn 880 N 29th St. Billings MT 59101 406-252-6800 252-6800
TF: 800-231-7782 ■ *Web:* www.billingsinn.com

Riverview Plaza Hotel 64 S Water St. Mobile AL 36602 251-438-4000 415-0123
Web: www.riverviewmobile.com

Riviera Hotel 1431 Robson St Vancouver BC V6G1C1 604-685-1301 685-1335
TF: 888-699-5222 ■ *Web:* www.rivieraonrobson.com

Road King Inn Columbia Mall
3300 30th Ave S Grand Forks ND 58201 701-746-1391 746-8586
TF: 800-707-1391 ■ *Web:* www.roadkinginn.com

Robert Treat Hotel 50 Pk Pl Newark NJ 07102 973-622-1000 622-6410
TF: 800-569-2300 ■ *Web:* www.rthotel.com

Roberts Mayfair the - A Wyndham Historic Hotel
806 St Charles St Saint Louis MO 63101 314-421-2500 421-6254
TF: 800-996-3426 ■ *Web:* www.wyndham.com

Rock View Resort 1049 Parkview Dr Hollister MO 65672 417-334-4678 334-1808
TF: 800-375-9530 ■ *Web:* www.rockviewresort.com

Rocklin Park Hotel 5450 China Garden Rd Rocklin CA 95677 916-630-9400 630-9448
TF: 888-630-9400 ■ *Web:* www.rocklinpark.com

Rodeway Inn & Suites 3033 Hilton Dr. Bossier City LA 71111 318-747-2400 747-6822
TF: 800-424-6423 ■ *Web:* www.rodewayinn.com

Roger Sherman Inn 195 Oenoke Ridge New Canaan CT 06840 203-966-4541 966-0503
Web: www.rogershermaninn.com

Roger Smith Hotel 501 Lexington Ave New York NY 10017 212-755-1400 758-4061
TF: 800-445-0277 ■ *Web:* www.rogersmith.com

Room Mate Waldorf 860 Ocean Dr Miami Beach FL 33139 305-531-7684 672-6836
TF: 800-933-2322 ■ *Web:* www.room-matehotels.com

Roosevelt Hotel 45 E 45th St New York NY 10017 212-661-9600 885-6161
TF: 888-833-3969 ■ *Web:* www.therooseveltvhotel.com

Rose Hotel 807 Main St. Pleasanton CA 94566 925-846-8802 846-2272
TF: 800-843-9540 ■ *Web:* www.rosehotel.net

Rosedale on Robson Suite Hotel
838 Hamilton St Vancouver BC V6B6A2 604-689-8033 689-4426
TF: 800-661-8870 ■ *Web:* www.rosedaleonrobson.com

Rosellen Suites at Stanley Park
2030 Barclay St Vancouver BC V6G1L5 604-689-4807 684-3327
TF: 888-317-6648 ■ *Web:* www.rosellensuites.com

Rosen Centre Hotel 9840 International Dr Orlando FL 32819 407-996-9840 996-0865
TF: 800-204-7234 ■ *Web:* www.rosencentre.com

Rosen Plaza Hotel 9700 International Dr Orlando FL 32819 407-996-9700 354-5774
TF: 800-366-9700 ■ *Web:* www.rosenplaza.com

Rosen Shingle Creek 9939 Universal Blvd. Orlando FL 32819 407-996-9939 996-9938
TF: 866-996-9939 ■ *Web:* www.rosenshinglecreek.com

Roslyn Claremont Hotel 1221 Old Northern Blvd Roslyn NY 11576 516-625-2700 625-2731
TF: 800-626-9005 ■ *Web:* www.roslynclaremonthotel.com

Rough Creek Lodge 5165 County Rd 2013 Glen Rose TX 76043 254-965-3700 918-2571
TF: 877-907-0754 ■ *Web:* www.roughcreek.com

Royal Garden at Waikiki Hotel
440 Olohana St. Honolulu HI 96815 808-943-0202 946-8777
TF: 800-367-5666 ■ *Web:* www.royalgardens.com

Royal Holiday Beach Resort 1988 Beach Blvd. Biloxi MS 39531 228-388-7553 388-8959
TF Resv: 800-874-0402 ■ *Web:* www.holidaybeachresort.com

Royal Hotel South Beach
763 Pennsylvania Ave. Miami Beach FL 33139 305-673-9009 673-9244
TF: 888-394-6835 ■ *Web:* www.royalhotelsouthbeach.com

Royal Palm Resort Hotel 1545 Collins Ave. Miami Beach FL 33139 786-276-0100
Web: www.royalpalmmiamibeach.com

Royal Plaza Hotel 425 E Main Rd. Middletown RI 02842 401-846-3555 846-3666
TF: 800-825-7072

Royal Regency Hotel 165 Tuckahoe Rd Yonkers NY 10710 914-476-6200 375-7017
TF: 800-215-3858 ■ *Web:* www.royalregencyhotelny.com

Royal Sonesta Hotel Boston
40 Edwin H Land Blvd Cambridge MA 02142 617-806-4200 806-4232
TF: 800-766-3782 ■ *Web:* www.sonesta.com/boston

Royal Sonesta Hotel New Orleans
300 Bourbon St New Orleans LA 70130 504-586-0300 586-0335
TF: 800-766-3782 ■ *Web:* www.sonesta.com/neworleans_royal

Royal Suite Lodge 3811 Minnesota Dr. Anchorage AK 99503 907-563-3114 563-4296
TF: 800-282-3114

Royal Sun Inn 1700 S Palm Canyon Dr Palm Springs CA 92264 760-327-1564 323-9092
TF: 800-619-4786 ■ *Web:* www.royalsuninn.com

Royal Towers Hotel & Casino
140 6th St. New Westminster BC V3M1J4 604-524-3777 524-6673
TF: 800-663-0202 ■ *Web:* www.royaltowers.com

Royalton Hotel 44 W 44th St. New York NY 10036 212-869-4400 869-8965
TF: 800-606-6090 ■ *Web:* www.royaltonhotel.com

Roycroft Inn 40 S Grove St East Aurora NY 14052 716-652-5552 655-5345
TF: 888-652-5552 ■ *Web:* www.roycroftinn.com

Rushmore View Inn 610 Hwy 16A Keystone SD 57751 605-666-4466 666-4425
TF: 800-888-2603 ■ *Web:* www.rushmoreviewinn.com

Saddleridge 44 Meadows Ln Beaver Creek CO 81620 970-754-5450 845-5459
TF: 800-859-8242

Sage Hospitality Resources LLC
1575 Welton St Suite 300 Denver CO 80202 303-595-7200 595-7219
Web: www.sagehospitality.com

Saint Ann/Marie Antoinette Hotel
717 Conti St New Orleans LA 70130 504-525-2300 524-8925
TF: 800-935-8740 ■ *Web:* www.hotellemarais.com

Saint Anthony the - A Wyndham Historic Hotel
300 E Travis St San Antonio TX 78205 210-227-4392 227-0915
TF: 800-996-3426 ■ *Web:* www.wyndham.com

Saint Clair Inn 500 N Riverside Ave Saint Clair MI 48079 810-329-2222 329-7664
TF: 800-482-8327 ■ *Web:* www.stclairinn.com

Saint Gregory Luxury Hotel & Suites
2033 M St NW Washington DC 20036 202-530-3600 466-6770
TF: 800-829-5034 ■ *Web:* www.capitalhotelswdc.com

Saint James Hotel 330 Magazine St. New Orleans LA 70130 504-304-4000 304-4444
TF: 888-856-4485 ■ *Web:* www.saintjameshotel.com

Saint Louis Hotel 730 Bienville St New Orleans LA 70130 504-581-7300 200-3112
TF Cust Svc: 800-535-9111 ■ *Web:* www.stlouishotel.com

Saint Michaels Harbour Inn & Marina
101 N Harbor Rd. Saint Michaels MD 21663 410-745-9001 745-9150
TF: 800-955-9001 ■ *Web:* www.harbourinn.com

Saint Paul Hotel 350 Market St. Saint Paul MN 55102 651-292-9292 228-9506
TF: 800-292-9292 ■ *Web:* www.saintpaulhotel.com

Saint Regis Hotel 602 Dunsmuir St Vancouver BC V6B1Y6 604-681-1135 683-1126
TF: 800-770-7929 ■ *Web:* www.stregishotel.com

Saint Regis Hotel Winnipeg 285 Smith St Winnipeg MB R3C1K1 204-942-0171 943-3077
TF: 800-663-7344 ■ *Web:* www.stregishotel.net

Saint Tropez Hotel
Rumor 455 E Harmon Ave Las Vegas NV 89109 702-369-5400 369-8901
TF: 877-997-8667 ■ *Web:* www.rumorvegas.com

Sainte Claire The 302 S Market St. San Jose CA 95113 408-295-2000 977-0403
TF Resv: 866-870-0726 ■ *Web:* www.larkspurhotels.com

Salisbury Hotel 123 W 57th St New York NY 10019 212-246-1300 977-7752
TF: 888-692-5757 ■ *Web:* www.nycsalisbury.com

San Carlos Hotel 150 E 50th St. New York NY 10022 212-755-1800 688-9778
TF: 800-722-2012 ■ *Web:* www.sancarloshotel.com

San Joaquin Hotel 1309 W Shaw Ave. Fresno CA 93711 559-225-1309 225-6021
TF: 800-775-1309 ■ *Web:* www.sjhotel.com

Sandalwood Hotel & Suites
5050 Orbitor Dr Mississauga ON L4W4X2 905-238-9600 238-8502
TF: 800-387-3355 ■ *Web:* www.sandalwoodhotel.com

Sandman Hotels Inns & Suites
1755 W Broadway Suite 310 Vancouver BC V6J4S5 604-730-6600 730-4645
Web: www.sandmanhotels.com

Sands Beach Club All-Suite Resort Hotel
201 74th Ave. Myrtle Beach SC 29572 843-449-1531 449-4021
TF: 800-726-3783 ■ *Web:* www.sandsresorts.com

Sands Central Inn 1525 Central Ave. Hot Springs AR 71901 501-624-1258 624-2800

Sands Ocean Club Resort 9550 Shore Dr Myrtle Beach SC 29572 843-449-6461 449-1837
TF: 800-845-6701 ■ *Web:* www.sandsresorts.com

Sands Regency Casino Hotel 345 N Arlington Ave Reno NV 89501 775-348-2200 348-2278*
*Fax: Hum Res ■ *TF Resv:* 800-648-3553 ■ *Web:* www.sandsregency.com

Sandwich Lodge & Resort
54 Rt 6A - Old King's Hwy PO Box 1038. Sandwich MA 02563 508-888-2275 888-8102
TF: 800-282-5353 ■ *Web:* www.sandwichlodge.com

Sandy Point Inn
Boulder Twin Lakes Inn 6485 Twin Lakes Rd Boulder CO 80301 303-530-2939 530-9101
TF: 800-322-2939 ■ *Web:* www.twinlakesinnboulder.com

Sanibel Inn 937 E Gulf Dr. Sanibel FL 33957 239-472-3181 472-5234
TF: 866-565-5480 ■ *Web:* www.sanibelcollection.com

Name / Address	City	State	Zip	Phone	Fax
Santa Barbara Inn 901 E Cabrillo Blvd *TF:* 800-231-0431 ■ *Web:* www.santabarbarainn.com	Santa Barbara	CA	93103	805-966-2285	966-6584
Santa Maria Inn 801 S Broadway *TF:* 800-462-4276 ■ *Web:* www.santamariainn.com	Santa Maria	CA	93454	805-928-7777	928-5690
Saratoga Hilton 534 Broadway *TF:* 866-773-7070 ■ *Web:* www.hilton.com	Saratoga Springs	NY	12866	518-584-4000	584-7430
Satellite Hotel 411 Lakewood Cir *TF:* 800-423-8409	Colorado Springs	CO	80910	719-596-6800	570-4499
Saunders Hotel Group Ltd 240 Newbury St *Web:* www.saundershotelgroup.net	Boston	MA	02116	617-425-0900	425-0901
Savoy on South Beach 425 Ocean Dr *TF:* 800-237-2869 ■ *Web:* www.savoymiami.com	Miami Beach	FL	33139	305-532-0200	534-7436
Savoy Suites Georgetown 2505 Wisconsin Ave NW *TF:* 800-944-5377 ■ *Web:* www.savoysuites.com	Washington	DC	20007	202-337-9700	337-3644
Scotsman Inn West 5922 W Kellogg St *TF:* 800-950-7268 ■ *Web:* www.scotsmaninn.com	Wichita	KS	67209	316-943-3800	943-3800
Sea Chambers Motel 67 Shore Rd *Web:* www.seachambers.com	Ogunquit	ME	03907	207-646-9311	646-0938
Sea Gull Motel on the Beach 2613 Atlantic Ave *TF:* 888-871-4855 ■ *Web:* www.seagullinn.net	Virginia Beach	VA	23451	757-425-5711	425-5710
Sea Ranch Lodge 60 Sea Walk Dr PO Box 44 *TF:* 800-732-7262 ■ *Web:* www.searanchlodge.com	The Sea Ranch	CA	95497	707-785-2371	785-2917
Sea Turtle Inn 1 Ocean Blvd *TF:* 800-874-6000	Atlantic Beach	FL	32233	904-249-7402	247-1517
Sea View Hotel 9909 Collins Ave *TF:* 800-447-1010 ■ *Web:* www.seaview-hotel.com	Bal Harbour	FL	33154	305-866-4441	866-1898
Seacoast Suites Hotel 5101 Collins Ave *TF:* 800-969-6329 ■ *Web:* www.seacoastsuites.com	Miami Beach	FL	33140	305-865-5152	868-4090
Seafarer of Chatham 2079 Main St *TF:* 800-786-2772	Chatham	MA	02633	508-432-1739	432-8969
Seaport Hotel & World Trade Ctr 1 Seaport Ln *TF:* 877-732-7678 ■ *Web:* www.seaportboston.com	Boston	MA	02210	617-385-4000	385-4001
Seaport Marina Hotel 6400 E Pacific Coast Hwy *Web:* www.seaportmarinahotel.com	Long Beach	CA	90803	562-434-8451	598-6028
Seascape Resort Monterey Bay 1 Seascape Resort Dr *TF:* 866-589-3411 ■ *Web:* www.seascaperesort.com	Aptos	CA	95003	831-688-6800	685-0615
Seaside Inn 541 E Gulf Dr *TF:* 866-565-5092 ■ *Web:* www.sanibelcollection.com	Sanibel Island	FL	33957	239-472-1400	
Seattle Convention Center Pike Street 1011 Pike St *Web:* homewoodsuites1.hilton.com/en_US/hw/index.do	Seattle	WA	98101	206-682-8282	682-5315
Seelbach Hilton Louisville 500 S 4th St *TF:* 800-333-3399 ■ *Web:* www.seelbachhilton.com	Louisville	KY	40202	502-585-3200	585-9239
Senate Luxury Suites 900 SW Tyler St *TF:* 800-488-3188 ■ *Web:* www.senatesuites.com	Topeka	KS	66612	785-233-5050	233-1614
Seneca Hotel & Suites The 200 E Chestnut St *TF:* 800-800-6261 ■ *Web:* www.senecahotel.com	Chicago	IL	60611	312-787-8900	988-4438
Serene Hotel & Suites 12004 Coastal Hwy *TF:* 800-542-4444 ■ *Web:* www.serenehotel.com	Ocean City	MD	21842	410-250-4000	250-9014
Serrano Hotel 405 Taylor St *TF:* 866-289-6561 ■ *Web:* www.serranohotel.com	San Francisco	CA	94102	415-885-2500	474-4879
Setai The 2001 Collins Ave *TF:* 888-625-7500 ■ *Web:* www.setai.com	Miami Beach	FL	33139	305-520-6000	
Seven Gables Inn 26 N Meramec Ave *TF:* 800-433-6590 ■ *Web:* www.sevengablesinn.com	Saint Louis	MO	63105	314-863-8400	863-8846
Shades of Green on Walt Disney World Resort 1950 W Magnolia Palm Dr *TF:* 888-593-2242 ■ *Web:* www.shadesofgreen.org	Lake Buena Vista	FL	32830	407-824-3400	824-3665
Shaner Hotel Group 1965 Waddle Rd **Fax:* Hum Res ■ *Web:* www.shanercorp.com	State College	PA	16803	814-234-4460	278-7288*
Shelborne Beach Resort The 1801 Collins Ave *TF:* 800-327-8757 ■ *Web:* www.shelborne.com	Miami Beach	FL	33139	305-531-1271	531-2206
Shelburne Murray Hill 303 Lexington Ave *TF:* 866-233-4642 ■ *Web:* www.affinia.com	New York	NY	10016	212-689-5200	779-7068
Shephard's Beach Resort 619 S Gulfview Blvd *TF:* 800-237-8477 ■ *Web:* www.shephards.com	Clearwater Beach	FL	33767	727-441-6875	442-7321
Sheraton Colonial Hotel & Golf Club Boston North 1 Audubon Rd *Web:* www.starwoodhotels.com	Wakefield	MA	01880	781-245-9300	245-9300
Sheraton Delfina Santa Monica 530 W Pico Blvd *TF:* 888-627-8532 ■ *Web:* www.sheratondelfina.com	Santa Monica	CA	90405	310-399-9344	399-2504
Sheraton Detroit Riverside 2 Washington Blvd *TF:* 866-837-4212 ■ *Web:* www.starwoodhotels.com	Detroit	MI	48226	313-965-0200	262-5415
Sheraton Gateway Hotel Los Angeles 6101 W Century Blvd *TF:* 800-325-3535 ■ *Web:* www.sheratonlosangeles.com	Los Angeles	CA	90045	310-642-1111	645-1414
Sheridan Pond Executive Suites 8130 S Lakewood Pl *Web:* www.sheridanpond.com	Tulsa	OK	74137	918-481-6598	492-6644
Sherry-Netherland Hotel 781 5th Ave *TF:* 877-743-7710 ■ *Web:* www.sherrynetherland.com	New York	NY	10022	212-355-2800	319-4306
Shilo Inn Hotel Salt Lake City 206 S W Temple *TF:* 800-222-2244 ■ *Web:* www.shiloinns.com	Salt Lake City	UT	84101	801-521-9500	359-6527
Shilo Inn Suites Hotel Portland Airport 11707 NE Airport Way *TF:* 800-222-2244 ■ *Web:* www.shiloinns.com	Portland	OR	97220	503-252-7500	254-0794
Shilo Inn Suites Salem 3304 Market St *TF:* 800-222-2244 ■ *Web:* www.shiloinns.com	Salem	OR	97303	503-581-4001	399-9385
Shilo Inns Suites Hotels 11600 SW Shilo Ln **Fax:* Mktg ■ *TF:* 800-222-2244 ■ *Web:* www.shiloinns.com	Portland	OR	97225	503-641-6565	644-0868*
Shore Club 1901 Collins Ave *Web:* www.shoreclub.com	Miami	FL	33139	305-695-3100	695-3299
Shoreham Hotel 33 W 55th St *TF:* 800-553-3347 ■ *Web:* www.shorehamhotel.com	New York	NY	10019	212-247-6700	765-9741
Shores Resort & Spa The 2637 S Atlantic Ave *TF:* 866-396-2217 ■ *Web:* www.shoresresort.com	Daytona Beach Shores	FL	32118	386-767-7350	760-3651
Shutters on the Beach 1 Pico Blvd *TF:* 800-334-9000 ■ *Web:* www.shuttersonthebeach.com	Santa Monica	CA	90405	310-458-0030	458-4589
Siena Hotel 1505 E Franklin St *TF:* 800-223-7379 ■ *Web:* www.sienahotel.com	Chapel Hill	NC	27514	919-929-4000	968-8527
Silver Cloud Hotel Seattle Broadway 1100 Broadway *TF:* 800-590-1801 ■ *Web:* www.silvercloud.com	Seattle	WA	98122	206-325-1400	324-1995
Silver Cloud Inn Seattle-Lake Union 1150 Fairview Ave N *TF:* 800-330-5812 ■ *Web:* www.scinns.com	Seattle	WA	98109	206-447-9500	812-4900
Silver Cloud Inn University District 5036 25th Ave NE *TF:* 800-205-6940 ■ *Web:* www.silvercloud.com	Seattle	WA	98105	206-526-5200	522-1450
Silver King Hotel 1485 Empire Ave *TF:* 800-331-8652 ■ *Web:* www.allseasonsresortlodging.com	Park City	UT	84060	435-649-5500	649-6647
Silver Smith Hotel & Suites 10 S Wabash Ave *TF:* 800-979-0084 ■ *Web:* www.silversmithchicagohotel.com	Chicago	IL	60603	312-372-7696	372-7320
Silverdale Beach Hotel 3073 NW Bucklin Hill Rd *TF:* 800-544-9799 ■ *Web:* www.silverdalebeachhotel.com	Silverdale	WA	98383	360-698-1000	692-0932
Silvertree Hotel 100 Elbert Ln *TF:* 800-525-9402 ■ *Web:* www.silvertreehotel.com	Snowmass Village	CO	81615	970-923-3520	923-5192
Simonton Court Historic Inn & Cottages 320 Simonton St *TF:* 800-944-2687 ■ *Web:* www.simontoncourt.com	Key West	FL	33040	305-294-6386	293-8447
Sir Francis Drake Hotel 450 Powell St *TF:* 800-227-5480 ■ *Web:* www.sirfrancisdrake.com	San Francisco	CA	94102	415-392-7755	391-8719
Sise Inn 40 Ct St *TF:* 877-747-3466 ■ *Web:* www.siseinn.com	Portsmouth	NH	03801	603-433-1200	431-0200
Sixth Avenue Inn 2000 6th Ave *TF:* 800-648-6440 ■ *Web:* www.sixthaveinn.com	Seattle	WA	98121	206-441-8300	441-9903
Sky Hotel 709 E Durant Ave *TF:* 800-882-2582 ■ *Web:* www.theskyhotel.com	Aspen	CO	81611	970-925-6760	925-6778
Skyline Hotel 725 10th Ave *TF:* 800-433-1982 ■ *Web:* www.skylinehotelny.com	New York	NY	10019	212-586-3400	582-4604
Smoky Shadows Motel & Conference Ctr 4215 Pkwy *TF:* 800-282-2121 ■ *Web:* www.smokyshadows.com	Pigeon Forge	TN	37863	865-453-7155	453-0308
Snell House 21 Atlantic Ave *TF:* 866-763-5524 ■ *Web:* www.snellhouse.com	Bar Harbor	ME	04609	207-288-8004	
Snowbird Mountain Lodge 4633 Santeetlah Rd *TF:* 800-941-9290 ■ *Web:* www.snowbirdlodge.com	Robbinsville	NC	28771	828-479-3433	479-3473
Snowy Owl Inn 4 Village Rd *TF:* 800-766-9969 ■ *Web:* www.snowyowlinn.com	Waterville Valley	NH	03215	603-236-8383	236-4890
Sofia Hotel 150 W Broadway *TF:* 800-826-0009 ■ *Web:* www.thesofiahotel.com	San Diego	CA	92101	619-234-9200	544-9879
SoHo Grand Hotel 310 W Broadway *TF:* 800-965-3000 ■ *Web:* www.sohogrand.com	New York	NY	10013	212-965-3000	965-3200
SoHo Metropolitan Hotel 318 Wellington St W *TF:* 866-764-6638 ■ *Web:* www.metropolitan.com/soho	Toronto	ON	M5V3T4	416-599-8800	599-8801
Somerset Hills Hotel 200 Liberty Corner Rd *TF:* 800-688-0700 ■ *Web:* www.shh.com	Warren	NJ	07059	908-647-6700	647-8053
Somerset Inn 2601 W Big Beaver Rd *TF:* 800-228-8769 ■ *Web:* www.somersetinn.com	Troy	MI	48084	248-643-7800	643-2296
Sonesta Hotel & Suites Coconut Grove 2889 McFarlane Rd *TF:* 800-766-3782 ■ *Web:* www.sonesta.com/coconut_grove	Coconut Grove	FL	33133	305-529-2828	529-2008
Song of the Sea 863 E Gulf Dr *TF:* 866-565-5101 ■ *Web:* www.sanibelcollection.com	Sanibel Island	FL	33957	239-472-2220	
Soniat House 1133 Chartres St *TF:* 800-544-8808 ■ *Web:* www.soniathouse.com	New Orleans	LA	70116	504-522-0570	522-7208
Sophie Station Suites 1717 University Ave *TF:* 800-528-4916 ■ *Web:* www.fountainheadhotels.com	Fairbanks	AK	99709	907-479-3650	479-7951
Sorrento Hotel 900 Madison St *TF:* 800-426-1265 ■ *Web:* www.hotelsorrento.com	Seattle	WA	98104	206-622-6400	343-6155
South Beach Marina Inn & Vacation Rentals 232 S Sea Pines Dr *TF:* 800-367-3909 ■ *Web:* www.sbinn.com	Hilton Head Island	SC	29928	843-671-6498	671-7495
South Pier Inn on the Canal 701 Lake Ave S *TF:* 800-430-7437 ■ *Web:* www.southpierinn.com	Duluth	MN	55802	218-786-9007	786-9015
South Seas Hotel 1751 Collins Ave *TF:* 800-345-2678 ■ *Web:* www.southseashotel.com	Miami Beach	FL	33139	305-538-1411	532-9477
Southampton Inn 91 Hill St *TF:* 800-832-6500 ■ *Web:* www.southamptoninn.com	SoutHampton	NY	11968	631-283-6500	283-6559
Southernmost Hotel 1319 Duval St *TF:* 888-782-9722 ■ *Web:* www.southernmostresorts.com	Key West	FL	33040	305-296-6577	294-8272
Southernmost On the Beach 508 S St *TF:* 800-354-4455 ■ *Web:* www.southernmostresorts.com	Key West	FL	33040	305-296-5611	294-2108
Southfork Hotel 1600 N Central Expy *TF:* 877-386-4383 ■ *Web:* www.southforkhotel.com	Plano	TX	75074	972-578-8555	
Southway Inn 2431 Bank St *TF:* 877-688-4929 ■ *Web:* www.southway.com	Ottawa	ON	K1V8R9	613-737-0811	737-3207
Spindrift Inn 652 Cannery Row *TF:* 800-841-1879 ■ *Web:* www.spindriftinn.com	Monterey	CA	93940	831-646-8900	655-8174
Spring Creek Ranch 1800 Spirit Dance Rd *TF:* 800-443-6139 ■ *Web:* www.springcreekranch.com	Jackson	WY	83001	307-733-8833	733-1964
St James Hotel 406 Main St *TF:* 800-252-1875 ■ *Web:* www.st-james-hotel.com	Red Wing	MN	55066	651-388-2846	388-5226
St Julien Hotel & Spa 900 Walnut St *TF:* 877-303-0900 ■ *Web:* www.stjulien.com	Boulder	CO	80302	720-406-9696	406-9668
Stamford Suites 720 Bedford St *TF:* 866-394-4365 ■ *Web:* www.stamfordsuites.com	Stamford	CT	06901	203-359-7300	359-7304
Stanford Court - A Renaissance Hotel 905 California St *Web:* www.renaissancehotel.com/sfosc	San Francisco	CA	94108	415-989-3500	391-0513
Stanley Hotel 333 Wonderview Ave *TF:* 800-976-1377 ■ *Web:* www.stanleyhotel.com	Estes Park	CO	80517	970-586-3371	586-4964

Phone Fax

Stanyan Park Hotel 750 Stanyan St . . . San Francisco CA 94117 415-751-1000 668-5454
Web: www.stanyanpark.com

Star Island Resort
5000 Avenue of the Stars . . . Kissimmee FL 34746 407-997-8000 997-5252
TF: 800-513-2820 ■ *Web:* www.star-island.com

Starwood Hotels & Resorts Worldwide Inc
1111 Westchester Ave. . . . White Plains NY 10604 914-640-8100 640-8310
NYSE: HOT ■ *TF Cust Svc:* 877-443-4585 ■ *Web:* www.starwoodhotels.com

Four Points by Sheraton
1111 Westchester Ave . . . White Plains NY 10604 914-640-8100 640-8310
TF Cust Svc: 877-443-4585 ■ *Web:* www.starwoodhotels.com

Sheraton Hotels & Resorts
1111 Westchester Ave . . . White Plains NY 10604 914-640-8100 640-8310
TF: 888-625-5144 ■ *Web:* www.starwoodhotels.com

Westin Hotels & Resorts
1111 Westchester Ave . . . White Plains NY 10604 914-640-8100 640-8310
TF: 877-443-4585 ■ *Web:* www.starwoodhotels.com

State Plaza Hotel 2117 E St NW. . . . Washington DC 20037 202-861-8200 659-8601
TF: 800-424-2859 ■ *Web:* www.stateplaza.com

Staten Island Hotel 1415 Richmond Ave . . . Staten Island NY 10314 718-698-5000 354-7071
TF: 800-230-4134 ■ *Web:* www.statenislandhotel.com

Sterling Hotel 1300 H St . . . Sacramento CA 95814 916-448-1300 448-8066
TF: 800-365-7660 ■ *Web:* www.sterlinghotel.com

Stockyards Hotel 109 E Exchange Ave . . . Fort Worth TX 76106 817-625-6427 624-2571
TF: 800-423-8471 ■ *Web:* www.stockyardshotel.com

Stone Castle Hotel & Conference Ctr The
3050 Green Mountain Dr . . . Branson MO 65616 417-335-4700 335-3906
TF: 800-677-6906 ■ *Web:* www.bransonsettleinn.com

Stonebridge Inn
300 Carriage Way PO Box 5008 . . . Snowmass Village CO 81615 970-923-2420 923-5889
TF: 800-922-7242 ■ *Web:* www.stonebridgeinn.com

Stonehedge Inn 160 Pawtucket Blvd . . . Tyngsboro MA 01879 978-649-4400 649-9256
TF: 800-648-7070 ■ *Web:* www.stonehedgeinnandspa.com

Stoneleigh Hotel 2927 Maple Ave . . . Dallas TX 75201 214-871-7111 871-9379
TF: 800-255-9299 ■ *Web:* www.stoneleighhotel.com

Stonewall Jackson Hotel & Conference Ctr
24 S Market St . . . Staunton VA 24401 540-885-4848 885-4840
TF: 866-880-0024 ■ *Web:* www.stonewalljacksonhotel.com

Stoney Creek Inn 101 Mariner's Way . . . East Peoria IL 61611 309-694-1300 694-9303
TF: 800-659-2220 ■ *Web:* www.stoneycreekinn.com

Strater Hotel 699 Main Ave . . . Durango CO 81301 970-247-4431 259-2208
TF: 800-247-4431 ■ *Web:* www.strater.com

Stratford Hotel 242 Powell St . . . San Francisco CA 94102 415-397-7080 397-7087
TF: 888-504-6835 ■ *Web:* www.hotelstratford.com

Strathallan Hotel 550 E Ave . . . Rochester NY 14607 585-461-5010 461-2503
TF: 800-678-7284 ■ *Web:* www.strathallan.com

Strathcona Hotel 60 York St . . . Toronto ON M5J1S8 416-363-3321 363-4679
TF: 800-268-8304 ■ *Web:* www.thestrathconahotel.com

Strathcona Hotel The 919 Douglas St . . . Victoria BC V8W2C2 250-383-7137 383-6893
TF: 800-663-7476 ■ *Web:* www.strathconahotel.com

Sturbridge Host Hotel & Conference Ctr
366 Main St . . . Sturbridge MA 01566 508-347-7393 347-3944
TF: 800-582-3232 ■ *Web:* www.sturbridgehosthotel.com

Sugar Magnolia 804 Edgewood Ave NE . . . Atlanta GA 30307 404-222-0226 681-1067
Web: www.sugarmagnoliabb.com

Suites at Fisherman's Wharf
2655 Hyde St . . . San Francisco CA 94109 415-771-0200 346-8058
TF: 800-227-3608 ■ *Web:* www.shellhospitality.com

Suites Hotel in Canal Park The 325 Lake Ave S . . . Duluth MN 55802 218-727-4663 722-0572
TF: 877-766-2665 ■ *Web:* www.thesuitesduluth.com

Summit Lodge & Spa 4359 Main St . . . Whistler BC V0N1B4 604-932-2778 932-2716
TF: 888-913-8811 ■ *Web:* www.summitlodge.com

Sun Viking Lodge
2411 S Atlantic Ave. . . . Daytona Beach Shores FL 32118 386-252-6252 252-5463
TF: 800-874-4469 ■ *Web:* www.sunviking.com

Sunburst Hospitality Corp
10770 Columbia Pike Suite 200 . . . Silver Spring MD 20901 301-592-3800 592-3830
Web: www.snbhotels.com

Sundial Boutique Hotel
4340 Sundial Crescent . . . Whistler BC V0N1B4 604-932-2321 935-0554
TF: 800-661-2321 ■ *Web:* www.sundialhotel.com

Sunrise Suites Resort Key West
3685 Seaside Dr. . . . Key West FL 33040 305-296-6661 296-6665
TF: 877-629-5252 ■ *Web:* www.sunrisesuiteskeywest.com

Sunset Inn Travel Apartments
1111 Burnaby St . . . Vancouver BC V6E1P4 604-688-2474 669-3340
TF: 800-786-1997 ■ *Web:* www.sunsetinn.com

Sunset Marquis Hotel & Villas
1200 N Alta Loma Rd . . . West Hollywood CA 90069 310-657-1333 652-5300
TF: 800-858-9758 ■ *Web:* www.sunsetmarquis.com

Sunset Tower Hotel 8358 Sunset Blvd . . . West Hollywood CA 90069 323-654-7100 654-9287
TF: 800-225-2637 ■ *Web:* www.sunsettowerhotel.com

Surf & Sand Resort 1555 S Coast Hwy. . . . Laguna Beach CA 92651 949-497-4477 494-2897
TF: 888-869-7569 ■ *Web:* www.surfandsandresort.com

Surfsand Resort 148 W Gower Rd. . . . Cannon Beach OR 97110 503-436-2274 436-9116
TF: 800-547-6100 ■ *Web:* www.surfsand.com

Surfside Inn 1211 Atlantic Ave. . . . Virginia Beach VA 23451 757-428-1183 428-2243
TF: 800-437-2497 ■ *Web:* www.virginiabeachsurfside.com

Surrey Hotel 20 E 76th St. . . . New York NY 10021 212-288-3700 628-1549
TF: 866-233-4642 ■ *Web:* www.affinia.com

Sutton Place Hotel Chicago 21 E Bellevue Pl . . . Chicago IL 60611 312-266-2100 266-2103
TF: 800-606-8188 ■ *Web:* www.suttonplace.com/Chicago

Sutton Place Hotel Edmonton 10235 101st St. . . . Edmonton AB T5J3E9 780-428-7111 441-3098
TF: 800-263-9030 ■ *Web:* www.edmonton.suttonplace.com

Sutton Place Hotel Toronto 955 Bay St . . . Toronto ON M5S2A2 416-924-9221 924-1778
TF: 866-378-8866 ■ *Web:* www.toronto.suttonplace.com

Sutton Place Hotel Vancouver
845 Burrard St . . . Vancouver BC V6Z2K6 604-682-5511 642-2926
TF: 800-961-7555 ■ *Web:* www.vancouver.suttonplace.com

Swag The 2300 Swag Rd . . . Waynesville NC 28785 828-926-0430 926-2036
TF: 800-789-7672 ■ *Web:* www.theswag.com

Phone Fax

Sweden House 4605 E State St . . . Rockford IL 61108 815-398-4130 398-9203
TF: 800-230-4134

Taj Boston 15 Arlington St . . . Boston MA 02116 617-536-5700 536-1335
TF: 877-482-5267 ■ *Web:* www.tajhotels.com

Taj Campton Place 340 Stockton St. . . . San Francisco CA 94108 415-781-5555 955-5536
TF: 800-235-4300 ■ *Web:* www.tajhotels.com

Talbott Hotel 20 E Delaware Pl . . . Chicago IL 60611 312-944-4970 944-7241
TF: 800-825-2688 ■ *Web:* www.talbotthotel.com

Tarsadia Hotels
620 Newport Ctr Dr 14th Fl. . . . Newport Beach CA 92660 949-610-8000 610-8001
Web: www.tarsadia.com

Tazewell Hotel & Suites 245 Granby St . . . Norfolk VA 23510 757-623-6200 457-1516
Web: www.thetazewell.com

Teton Mountain Lodge & Spa
3385 Cody Ln PO Box 564 . . . Teton Village WY 83025 307-734-7111 734-7999
TF: 800-631-6271 ■ *Web:* www.tetonlodge.com

Tharaldson Motels Inc 1202 Westrac Dr. . . . Fargo ND 58103 701-235-1060 232-6487
Web: www.tharaldson.com

Thayer Hotel 674 Thayer Rd . . . West Point NY 10996 845-446-4731 446-0338
TF: 800-247-5047 ■ *Web:* www.thethayerhotel.com

TheßDupont CircleßHotel
1500 New Hampshire Ave NW . . . Washington DC 20036 202-483-6000 328-3265
TF: 800-423-6953 ■ *Web:* www.doylecollection.com

Tickle Pink Inn at Carmel Highlands
155 Highland Dr. . . . Carmel CA 93923 831-624-1244 626-9516
TF: 800-635-4774 ■ *Web:* www.ticklepinkinn.com

Tides The 1220 Ocean Dr. . . . Miami Beach FL 33139 305-604-5070 604-5180
TF: 800-439-4095 ■ *Web:* www.tidessouthbeach.com

Tidewater Inn & Conference Ctr 101 E Dover St . . . Easton MD 21601 410-822-1300 820-8847
TF: 800-237-8775 ■ *Web:* www.tidewaterinn.com

Timbers Hotel The 4411 Peoria St . . . Denver CO 80239 303-373-1444 373-1975
TF: 800-844-9404 ■ *Web:* www.timbersdenver.com

Time The 224 W 49th St. . . . New York NY 10019 212-246-5252 245-2305
TF: 877-846-3692 ■ *Web:* www.thetimeny.com

Times Hotel & Suites
6515 Wilfrid-Hamel Blvd . . . L'Ancienne-Lorette QC G2E5W3 418-877-7788 877-3333
Web: timeshotel.ca

Tivoli Lodge 386 Hanson Ranch Rd . . . Vail CO 81657 970-476-5615 476-6601
TF: 800-451-4756 ■ *Web:* www.tivolilodge.com

Topaz Hotel 1733 N St NW. . . . Washington DC 20036 202-393-3000 785-9581
TF: 800-424-2950 ■ *Web:* www.topazhotel.com

Tower Beverly Hills The 1224 Beverwil Dr . . . Los Angeles CA 90035 310-277-2800 277-5470
TF: 800-421-3212 ■ *Web:* www.thetowerbeverlyhills.com

TOWER23 Hotel 4551 Ocean Blvd . . . San Diego CA 92109 858-270-2323
TF: 866-869-3723 ■ *Web:* www.tower23hotel.com

Town & Country Inn 20 SR 2 PO Box 220 . . . Gorham NH 03581 603-466-3315 466-3315
TF: 800-325-4386 ■ *Web:* www.townandcountryinn.com

Town & Country Inn & Conference Ctr
2008 Savannah Hwy. . . . Charleston SC 29407 843-571-1000 766-9444
TF General: 800-334-6660 ■ *Web:* www.palacehospitality.com

Town Inn Suites 620 Church St. . . . Toronto ON M4Y2G2 416-964-3311 924-9466
TF: 800-387-2755 ■ *Web:* www.towninn.com

TownHouse Inn 1411 10th Ave S. . . . Great Falls MT 59405 406-761-4600 761-7603
TF: 800-442-4667

Townsend Hotel 100 Townsend St . . . Birmingham MI 48009 248-642-7900 645-9061
TF: 800-548-4172 ■ *Web:* www.townsendhotel.com

Townsend Manor Inn 714 Main St. . . . Greenport NY 11944 631-477-2000
Web: www.townsendmanorinn.com

Tradewinds Carmel
Mission St at 3rd Ave . . . Carmel-by-the-Sea CA 93921 831-624-2776 624-0634
TF: 800-624-6665 ■ *Web:* www.tradewindscarmel.com

TradeWinds Sandpiper Hotel & Suites
6000 Gulf Blvd . . . Saint Pete Beach FL 33706 727-360-5551 363-2367
TF: 800-237-0707

Trans World Corp (TWC) 545 5th Ave Suite 940 . . . New York NY 10017 212-983-3355 983-8129
PINK: TWOC ■ *Web:* www.transwc.com

Travelodge Virginia Beach
1909 Atlantic Ave . . . Virginia Beach VA 23451 757-425-0650 425-8898
TF: 800-578-7878 ■ *Web:* www.travelodge.com

Traymore Hotel 2445 Collins Ave . . . Miami Beach FL 33140 305-534-7111 538-2632
TF: 800-445-1512 ■ *Web:* www.traymorehotel.com

Tremont Chicago 100 E Chestnut St. . . . Chicago IL 60611 312-751-1900 751-8691
TF: 800-621-8133 ■ *Web:* www.tremontchicago.com

Tremont House - A Wyndham Historic Hotel The
2300 Ship Mechanic Row. . . . Galveston TX 77550 409-763-0300 763-1539
Web: www.wyndham.com

Tremont Plaza Hotel Baltimore
222 St Paul Pl. . . . Baltimore MD 21202 410-727-2222 685-4215
TF: 800-873-6668 ■ *Web:* www.tremontplazahotel.com

Trianon Old Naples 955 7th Ave S . . . Naples FL 34102 239-435-9600 261-0025
TF: 877-482-5228 ■ *Web:* www.trianon.com

Tribeca Grand Hotel
2 Avenue of the Americas . . . New York NY 10013 212-519-6600 519-6700
TF: 800-965-3000 ■ *Web:* www.tribecagrand.com

Trigild Inc 12707 High Bluff Dr Suite 300 . . . San Diego CA 92130 858-720-6700 720-6707
Web: www.trigild.com

Tropical Winds Oceanfront Hotel
1398 N Atlantic Ave . . . Daytona Beach FL 32118 386-258-1016 255-6462
TF: 800-245-6099

Tropicana Inn & Suites 1540 S Harbor Blvd . . . Anaheim CA 92802 714-635-4082 635-1535
TF: 800-828-4898 ■ *Web:* www.bei-hotels.com

Truman Hotel & Conference Ctr
1510 Jefferson St . . . Jefferson City MO 65109 573-635-7171 635-8006
TF: 800-272-6232 ■ *Web:* www.trumanjeffersoncity.com

Trump International Hotel & Tower
1 Central Pk W . . . New York NY 10023 212-299-1000 299-1150
TF: 888-448-7867 ■ *Web:* www.trumpintl.com

Tugboat Inn
80 Commercial St PO Box 267. . . . Boothbay Harbor ME 04538 207-633-4434 633-5892
TF: 800-248-2628 ■ *Web:* www.tugboatinn.com

TWELVE Atlantic Station 361 17th St. . . . Atlanta GA 30363 404-961-1212 961-1221
Web: www.twelvehotels.com

Name / Address	City	State	Zip	Phone	Fax
TWELVE Centennial Park 400 W Peachtree St *Web:* www.twelvehotels.com	Atlanta	GA	30308	404-418-1212	418-1221
Twin Farms Stage Rd PO box 115 *TF:* 800-894-6327 ■ *Web:* www.twinfarms.com	Barnard	VT	05031	802-234-9999	234-9990
Twin Palms Hotel 225 Apache Blvd *TF:* 800-367-0835 ■ *Web:* www.twinpalmshotel.com	Tempe	AZ	85281	480-967-9431	303-6602
UMass Hotel at the Campus Ctr 1 Campus Ctr Way	Amherst	MA	01003	413-549-6000	545-1210
Umstead Hotel & Spa 100 Woodland Pond *TF:* 866-877-4141 ■ *Web:* www.theumstead.com	Cary	NC	27513	919-447-4000	447-4100
Union Station - A Wyndham Historic Hotel 1001 Broadway St *TF:* 800-996-3426 ■ *Web:* www.wyndham.com	Nashville	TN	37203	615-726-1001	248-3554
University Inn Seattle 4140 Roosevelt Way NE *TF:* 800-733-3855 ■ *Web:* www.universityinnseattle.com	Seattle	WA	98105	206-632-5055	547-4937
University Place 310 SW Lincoln St *TF:* 866-845-4647 ■ *Web:* www.pdx.edu/cegs/university-place-hotel-conference-center	Portland	OR	97201	503-221-0140	226-6260
University Plaza Hotel & Conference Ctr 3110 Olentangy River Rd *TF:* 877-677-5292 ■ *Web:* www.universityplazaosu.com	Columbus	OH	43202	614-267-7461	263-5299
University Plaza Hotel & Convention Ctr 333 John Q Hammons Pkwy *TF:* 800-465-4329 ■ *Web:* www.upspringfield.com	Springfield	MO	65806	417-864-7333	831-5893
US Grant The 326 Broadway *TF:* 800-237-5029 ■ *Web:* www.usgrant.net	San Diego	CA	92101	619-232-3121	232-3626
US Suites 4970 Windplay Dr C1 *TF Cust Svc:* 800-877-8483 ■ *Web:* www.ussuites.com	El Dorado Hills	CA	95762	916-941-7970	
Valley Park Hotel 2404 Stevens Creek Blvd *TF:* 800-954-6835 ■ *Web:* www.pacifichotels.com/valley/index.html	San Jose	CA	95128	408-293-5000	293-5287
Valley River Inn 1000 Valley River Way *TF:* 800-543-8266 ■ *Web:* www.valleyriverinn.com	Eugene	OR	97401	541-743-1000	683-5121
Vancouver Extended-Stay Suites 1288 W Georgia St Suite 101 *Web:* www.vancouverextendedstay.com	Vancouver	BC	V6E4R3	604-891-6181	891-6151
Vanderbilt Grace 41 Mary St *TF:* 888-826-4255 ■ *Web:* www.vanderbiltgrace.com	Newport	RI	02840	401-846-6200	847-7689
Varscona Hotel 8208 106th St *TF:* 888-515-3355 ■ *Web:* www.varscona.com	Edmonton	AB	T6E6R9	780-434-6111	439-1195
Velvet Cloak Inn The 1505 Hillsborough St *TF:* 800-334-4372 ■ *Web:* www.velvetcloakinn.com	Raleigh	NC	27605	919-828-0333	828-2656
Viceroy Palm Springs 415 S Belardo Rd *TF:* 800-237-3687 ■ *Web:* www.viceroypalmsprings.com	Palm Springs	CA	92262	760-320-4117	323-3303
Viceroy Santa Monica 1819 Ocean Ave *TF:* 800-670-6185 ■ *Web:* www.viceroyhotelsandresorts.com	Santa Monica	CA	90401	310-260-7500	260-7515
Victoria Inn Winnipeg 1808 Wellington Ave *TF:* 877-842-4667 ■ *Web:* www.vicinn.com	Winnipeg	MB	R3H0G3	204-786-4801	786-1329
Victoria Regent Hotel The 1234 Wharf St *TF:* 800-663-7472 ■ *Web:* www.victoriaregent.com	Victoria	BC	V8W3H9	250-386-2211	386-2622
Victorian Condo-Hotel & Conference Ctr 6300 Seawall Blvd *TF:* 800-231-6363 ■ *Web:* www.victoriancondo.com	Galveston	TX	77551	409-740-3555	741-1676
Villa Florence 225 Powell St *TF:* 866-823-4669 ■ *Web:* www.larkspurhotels.com	San Francisco	CA	94102	415-397-7700	397-1006
Villa Royale Inn 1620 Indian Trail *TF:* 800-245-2314 ■ *Web:* www.villaroyale.com	Palm Springs	CA	92264	760-327-2314	322-3794
Village Latch Inn 101 Hill St PO Box 3000 *Web:* www.villagelatch.com	SouthHampton	NY	11968	631-283-2160	283-3236
Village Suites at Ashland Hills 2525 Ashland St *TF:* 800-547-4747 ■ *Web:* www.windmillinns.com	Ashland	OR	97520	541-482-8310	488-1783
Villagio Inn & Spa 6481 Washington St *TF:* 800-351-1133 ■ *Web:* www.villagio.com	Yountville	CA	94599	707-944-8877	944-8855
Villas de Santa Fe 400 Griffin St *TF:* 800-869-6790 ■ *Web:* www.villasdesantafe.com	Santa Fe	NM	87501	505-988-3000	988-4700
Villas on the Bay 105 Marine St *Web:* www.thevillas.com	Saint Augustine	FL	32084	904-599-7301	
Vincci Avalon Hotel 16 E 32nd St *TF:* 888-442-8256 ■ *Web:* www.avalonhotelnyc.com	New York	NY	10016	212-299-7000	299-7001
Vintage Inn Napa Valley 6541 Washington St *TF Cust Svc:* 800-351-1133 ■ *Web:* www.vintageinn.com	Yountville	CA	94599	707-944-1112	944-1617
Vintners Inn 4350 Barnes Rd *TF:* 800-421-2584 ■ *Web:* www.vintnersinn.com	Santa Rosa	CA	95403	707-575-7350	575-1426
Virginian Lodge 750 W Broadway PO Box 1052 *TF:* 800-262-4999 ■ *Web:* www.virginianlodge.com	Jackson Hole	WY	83001	307-733-2792	733-9513
Virginian Suites 1500 Arlington Blvd *TF:* 800-275-2866 ■ *Web:* www.virginiansuites.com	Arlington	VA	22209	703-522-9600	525-4462
Viscount Gort Hotel 1670 Portage Ave *TF:* 800-665-1122 ■ *Web:* www.viscount-gort.com	Winnipeg	MB	R3J0C9	204-775-0451	772-2161
Viscount Suite Hotel 4855 E Broadway Blvd *TF Resv:* 800-527-9666 ■ *Web:* www.viscountsuite.com	Tucson	AZ	85711	520-745-6500	790-5114
Vista Host Inc 10370 Richmond Ave Suite 150 *TF:* 800-688-4782 ■ *Web:* www.vistahost.com	Houston	TX	77042	713-267-5800	267-5820
Voyageur Inn 200 Viking Dr *TF:* 800-444-4493 ■ *Web:* www.voyageurinn.net	Reedsburg	WI	53959	608-524-6431	524-0036
Voyageur Lakewalk Inn 333 E Superior St *TF:* 800-258-3911 ■ *Web:* www.voyageurlakewalkinn.com	Duluth	MN	55802	218-722-3911	722-3124
Waikiki Gateway Hotel 2070 Kalakaua Ave *TF:* 800-247-1903 ■ *Web:* www.waikikigateway.com	Honolulu	HI	96815	808-955-3741	955-1313
Waikiki Joy Hotel *Aston Waikiki Joy Hotel* 320 Lewers St *TF:* 800-321-2558 ■ *Web:* www.aston-hotels.com	Honolulu	HI	96815	808-923-2300	924-4010
Waikiki Parc Hotel 2233 Helumoa Rd *TF:* 800-422-0450 ■ *Web:* www.waikikiparc.com	Honolulu	HI	96815	808-921-7272	923-1336
Waikiki Resort Hotel 2460 Koa Ave *TF:* 800-367-5116 ■ *Web:* www.waikikiresort.com	Honolulu	HI	96815	808-922-4911	922-9468
Waldorf Towers The 100 E 50th St *TF:* 800-925-3673 ■ *Web:* www.waldorfnewyork.com	New York	NY	10022	212-355-3100	872-4799
Waldorf-Astoria 301 Pk Ave *TF:* 800-925-3673 ■ *Web:* www.hilton.com/en/hi/waldorf	New York	NY	10022	212-355-3000	872-7272
Warwick Denver Hotel 1776 Grant St *TF:* 800-525-2888 ■ *Web:* www.warwickdenver.com	Denver	CO	80203	303-861-2000	832-0320
Warwick Melrose Hotel 3015 Oak Lawn Ave *TF:* 800-521-7172 ■ *Web:* www.warwickmelrosedallas.com	Dallas	TX	75219	214-521-5151	521-2470
Warwick New York Hotel 65 W 54th St **Fax:* Sales ■ *TF:* 800-223-4099 ■ *Web:* www.warwickhotelny.com	New York	NY	10019	212-247-2700	247-2725*
Warwick Regis Hotel San Francisco 490 Geary St *TF:* 800-827-3447 ■ *Web:* www.warwicksf.com	San Francisco	CA	94102	415-928-7900	441-8788
Warwick Seattle Hotel 401 Lenora St *TF:* 800-426-9280 ■ *Web:* www.warwickwa.com	Seattle	WA	98121	206-443-4300	448-1662
Washington Court Hotel 525 New Jersey Ave NW *TF:* 800-321-3010 ■ *Web:* www.washingtoncourthotel.com	Washington	DC	20001	202-628-2100	879-7918
Washington Duke Inn & Golf Club 3001 Cameron Blvd *TF:* 800-443-3853 ■ *Web:* www.washingtondukeinn.com	Durham	NC	27705	919-490-0999	688-0105
Washington Inn 495 10th St *Web:* www.thewashingtoninn.com	Oakland	CA	94607	510-452-1776	452-4436
Washington Plaza Hotel 10 Thomas Cir NW Massachusetts Ave at 14th St *TF:* 800-424-1140 ■ *Web:* www.washingtonplazahotel.com	Washington	DC	20005	202-842-1300	371-9602
Washington Square Hotel 103 Waverly Pl *TF:* 800-222-0418 ■ *Web:* www.washingtonsquarehotel.com	New York	NY	10011	212-777-9515	979-8373
Washington Suites 100 S Reynolds St *TF:* 877-736-2500 ■ *Web:* www.washingtonsuitesalexandria.com	Alexandria	VA	22304	703-370-9600	370-0467
Washington Suites Georgetown 2500 Pennsylvania Ave NW *TF:* 877-736-2500 ■ *Web:* www.washingtonsuitesgeorgetown.com	Washington	DC	20037	202-333-8060	338-3818
Waterfront Hotel 10 Washington St *TF:* 888-842-5333 ■ *Web:* www.jdvhotels.com	Oakland	CA	94607	510-836-3800	832-5695
Waters Edge Hotel 25 Main St *TF:* 800-738-7477 ■ *Web:* www.marinhotels.com	Tiburon	CA	94920	415-789-5999	789-5888
Watertown Seattle 4242 Roosevelt Way NE *TF:* 866-944-4242 ■ *Web:* www.watertownseattle.com	Seattle	WA	98105	206-826-4242	315-4242
Wauwinet The 120 Wauwinet Rd PO Box 2580 *TF:* 800-426-8718 ■ *Web:* www.wauwinet.com	Nantucket	MA	02584	508-228-0145	228-6712
WB Johnson Properties 100 W Paces Ferry Rd	Atlanta	GA	30305	404-237-7300	365-9800
Weber's Inn 3050 Jackson Rd *TF Resv:* 800-443-3050 ■ *Web:* www.webersinn.com	Ann Arbor	MI	48103	734-769-2500	769-4743
Wedgewood Hotel 845 Hornby St *TF:* 800-663-0666 ■ *Web:* www.wedgewoodhotel.com	Vancouver	BC	V6Z1V1	604-689-7777	608-5348
Wedgewood Resort Hotel 212 Wedgewood Dr *TF:* 800-528-4916 ■ *Web:* www.fountainheadhotels.com	Fairbanks	AK	99701	907-452-1442	451-8184
Wellington Hotel 871 7th Ave *TF:* 800-652-1212 ■ *Web:* www.wellingtonhotel.com	New York	NY	10019	212-247-3900	956-2381
Wellington Resort 551 Thames St *Web:* www.wellingtonresort.com	Newport	RI	02840	401-849-1770	847-6250
Wentworth Mansion 149 Wentworth St *TF:* 888-466-1886 ■ *Web:* www.wentworthmansion.com	Charleston	SC	29401	843-853-1886	720-5290
Western States Lodging 1018 W Atherton Dr *Web:* www.westernstateslodging.com	Taylorsville	UT	84107	801-269-0700	269-1512
Westford Regency Inn & Conference Ctr 219 Littleton Rd *TF:* 800-543-7801 ■ *Web:* www.westfordregency.com	Westford	MA	01886	978-692-8200	692-7403
Westgate Branson Woods 2201 Roark Valley Rd *TF:* 800-935-2345 ■ *Web:* www.wgbransonwoods.com	Branson	MO	65616	417-332-3550	334-0834
Westgate Hotel The 1055 2nd Ave *TF:* 800-522-1564 ■ *Web:* www.westgatehotel.com	San Diego	CA	92101	619-238-1818	557-3737
Westgate Painted Mountain Country Club 6302 E McKellips Rd *TF:* 888-433-3707 ■ *Web:* www.wgpaintedmountain.com	Mesa	AZ	85215	480-654-3611	654-3613
Westin San Francisco Market Street 50 3rd St *TF:* 888-627-8561 ■ *Web:* www.starwoodhotels.com	San Francisco	CA	94103	415-974-6400	543-8268
Westmark Hotels Inc 300 Elliott Ave W *TF:* 800-544-0970 ■ *Web:* www.westmarkhotels.com	Seattle	WA	98119	206-301-5223	285-7152
Westmont Hospitality Group Inc 5090 Explorer Dr Suite 700 *Web:* www.whg.com	Mississauga	ON	L4W4T9	905-629-3400	624-7805
Westmont Hospitality Group Inc 5847 San Felipe St Suite 4650 *Web:* www.whg.com	Houston	TX	77057	713-782-9100	782-9600
Westport Inn The 1595 Post Rd E *TF:* 800-446-8997 ■ *Web:* www.westportinn.com	Westport	CT	06880	203-418-2500	254-8439
Wheatleigh 11 Hawthorne Rd *Web:* www.wheatleigh.com	Lenox	MA	01240	413-637-0610	637-4507
White Barn Inn 37 Beach Ave PO Box 560C *Web:* www.whitebarninn.com	Kennebunk	ME	06046	207-967-2321	967-1100
White Elephant Inn & Cottages 50 Easton St *TF:* 800-475-2637 ■ *Web:* www.whiteelephanthotel.com	Nantucket	MA	02554	508-228-2500	325-1195
White Inn The 52 E Main St *TF:* 888-373-3664 ■ *Web:* www.whiteinn.com	Fredonia	NY	14063	716-672-2103	672-2107
White Lodging Services Inc 701 E 83rd Ave *Web:* www.whitelodging.com	Merrillville	IN	46410	219-472-2900	756-2902
White Swan Inn 845 Bush St *TF:* 800-999-9570 ■ *Web:* www.jdvhotels.com	San Francisco	CA	94108	415-775-1755	775-5717
Whitehall Hotel 105 E Delaware Pl *TF Resv:* 866-753-4081 ■ *Web:* www.thewhitehallhotel.com	Chicago	IL	60611	312-944-6300	944-8552
Whitelaw Hotel 808 Collins Ave *Web:* www.whitelawhotel.com	Miami Beach	FL	33139	305-398-7000	398-7010
Whitney Hotel 700 Woodrow St *TF:* 800-637-4008 ■ *Web:* www.whitneyhotel.com	Columbia	SC	29205	803-252-0845	771-0495
Whitney the - A Wyndham Historic Hotel 610 Poydras St *TF:* 800-996-3426 ■ *Web:* www.wyndham.com	New Orleans	LA	70130	504-581-4222	207-0101
Wickaninnish Inn 500 Osprey Ln PO Box 250 **Fax:* Resv ■ *TF:* 800-333-4604 ■ *Web:* www.wickinn.com	Tofino	BC	V0R2Z0	250-725-3100	725-3110*

Phone *Fax*

Wild Palms Hotel 910 E Fremont Ave .... Sunnyvale CA 94087 408-738-0500 736-8302
TF: 866-470-7062 ■ *Web:* www.jdvhotels.com

Williamsburg Hospitality House
415 Richmond Rd .... Williamsburg VA 23185 757-229-4020 220-1560
TF: 800-932-9192 ■ *Web:* www.williamsburghosphouse.com

Williamsburg Lodge 310 S England St .... Williamsburg VA 23185 757-229-1000 220-7799
TF Cust Svc: 800-447-8679 ■ *Web:* www.williamsburglodge.com

Willows Historic Palm Springs Inn
412 W Tahquitz Canyon Way .... Palm Springs CA 92262 760-320-0771 320-0780
TF: 800-966-9597 ■ *Web:* www.thewillowspalmsprings.com

Willows Hotel 555 W Surf St .... Chicago IL 60657 773-528-8400 528-8483
TF: 800-787-3108 ■ *Web:* www.willowshotelchicago.com

Willows Lodge 14580 NE 145th St .... Woodinville WA 98072 425-424-3900 424-2585
TF: 877-424-3930 ■ *Web:* www.willowslodge.com

Wilshire Grand Hotel & Ctr
930 Wilshire Blvd .... Los Angeles CA 90017 213-688-7777 612-3987
TF: 888-773-2888 ■ *Web:* www.wilshiregrand.com

Wilson Hotel Management Co Inc
8700 Trail Lake Dr W Suite 300 .... Memphis TN 38125 901-346-8800 346-5808
TF: 800-945-7661 ■ *Web:* www.wilsonhotels.com

Windmill Inn at Saint Philip's Plaza Tucson
4250 N Campbell Ave .... Tucson AZ 85718 520-577-0007 577-0045
TF: 800-547-4747 ■ *Web:* www.windmillinns.com

Windsor Arms Hotel 18 St Thomas St .... Toronto ON M5S3E7 416-971-9666 921-9121
TF: 877-999-2767 ■ *Web:* www.windsorarmshotel.com

Windsor Capital Group Inc
3000 Ocean Pk Blvd Suite 3010 .... Santa Monica CA 90405 310-566-1100 566-1199
Web: www.wcghotels.com

Windsor Court Hotel 300 Gravier St .... New Orleans LA 70130 504-523-6000 596-4513
TF: 800-262-2662 ■ *Web:* www.windsorcourthotel.com

Windsor Hotel 125 W Lamar St .... Americus GA 31709 229-924-1555 924-1555
TF: 888-297-9567 ■ *Web:* www.windsor-americus.com

Winegardner & Hammons Inc 4243 Hunt Rd .... Cincinnati OH 45242 513-891-1066 794-2590
Web: www.whihotels.com

Wonder View Inn & Suites
50 Eden St PO Box 25 .... Bar Harbor ME 04609 207-288-3358 288-2005
TF: 888-439-8439 ■ *Web:* www.wonderviewinn.com

Woodfin Suite Hotels LLC
12671 High Bluff Dr Suite 300 .... San Diego CA 92130 858-794-2338 794-2348
TF: 800-237-8811 ■ *Web:* www.thehardagegroup.com

Woodloch Pines Inc 731 Welcome Lake Rd .... Hawley PA 18428 570-685-8000 685-8093
TF: 800-966-3562 ■ *Web:* www.woodloch.com

Woodmark Hotel on Lake Washington
1200 Carillon Pt .... Kirkland WA 98033 425-822-3700 822-3699
TF: 800-822-3700 ■ *Web:* www.thewoodmark.com

Wort Hotel 50 N Glenwood .... Jackson WY 83001 307-733-2190 733-2067
TF Cust Svc: 800-322-2727 ■ *Web:* www.worthotel.com

Wyndham Blake Chicago 500 S Dearborn St .... Chicago IL 60605 312-986-1234 939-2468
Web: www.hotelblake.com

Wyndham Hotel Group
AmeriHost Inn 1 Sylvan Way .... Parsippany NJ 07054 973-428-9700
TF Resv: 800-996-3426 ■ *Web:* www.wyndham.com
Baymont Inn & Suites PO Box 5090 .... Aberdeen SD 57401 888-288-5090
TF: 888-288-5090 ■ *Web:* www.baymontinns.com
Days Inn 1 Sylvan Way .... Parsippany NJ 07054 973-753-6600
TF Resv: 800-329-7466 ■ *Web:* www.daysinn.com
Howard Johnson International Inc
1 Sylvan Way .... Parsippany NJ 07054 973-753-6600
TF Resv: 800-446-4656 ■ *Web:* www.hojo.com
Knights Inn 1 Sylvan Way .... Parsippany NJ 07054 888-288-5093
TF: 888-288-5093 ■ *Web:* www.knightsinn.com
Ramada 1 Sylvan Way .... Parsippany NJ 07054 973-753-6600
TF Resv: 800-272-6232 ■ *Web:* www.ramada.com
Super 8 1 Sylvan Way .... Parsippany NJ 07054 973-753-6600
TF Resv: 800-800-8000 ■ *Web:* www.super8.com
Travelodge 1 Sylvan Way .... Parsippany NJ 07054 973-753-6600
TF Resv: 800-578-7878 ■ *Web:* www.travelodge.com
Wingate by Wyndham 1 Sylvan Way .... Parsippany NJ 07054 973-428-9700
TF Resv: 800-228-1000 ■ *Web:* www.wyndham.com
Wyndham Vacation Resorts
8427 S Park Cir Suite 500 .... Orlando FL 32819 800-251-8736
TF Resv: 888-884-4321 ■ *Web:* www.wyndhamvacationresorts.com

Wyndham Worldwide Corp
Wyndham Hotel Group 22 Sylvan Way .... Parsippany NJ 07054 973-428-9700 753-6000
NYSE: WYN ■ *Web:* www.wyndhamworldwide.com

Wynfrey Hotel 1000 Riverchase Galleria .... Birmingham AL 35244 205-987-1600 988-4597
TF: 800-996-3739 ■ *Web:* www.wynfrey.com

Wyoming Inn of Jackson Hole The
930 W Broadway PO Box 8820 .... Jackson WY 83001 307-734-0035 734-0037
TF: 800-844-0035 ■ *Web:* www.wyominginn.com

Yankee Inn 461 Pittsfield Lenox Rd .... Lenox MA 01240 413-499-3700 499-3634
TF: 800-835-2364 ■ *Web:* www.yankeeinn.com

Yankee Peddler Inn 113 Touro St .... Newport RI 02840 401-846-1323 849-0426
TF: 800-427-9444 ■ *Web:* www.historicinnsofnewport.com

Yarmouth Resort Rte 28 .... West Yarmouth MA 02673 508-775-5155
Web: www.yarmouthresort.com

Yarrow Hotel & Conference Ctr 1800 Pk Ave .... Park City UT 84060 435-649-7000 645-7007
TF: 800-927-7694 ■ *Web:* www.yarrowhotelparkcity.com

Yogo Inn 211 E Main St .... Lewistown MT 59457 406-535-8721 535-8969
TF: 800-860-9646 ■ *Web:* www.yogoinn.com

York Hotel 940 Sutter St .... San Francisco CA 94109 415-885-6800 885-2115
TF: 800-553-1900 ■ *Web:* www.yorkhotel.com

Yorktowne Hotel 48 E Market St .... York PA 17401 717-848-1111 854-7678
TF: 800-233-9324 ■ *Web:* www.yorktowne.com

Deerfoot Inn & Casino 1000 11500 35th St SE .... Calgary AB T2Z3W4 403-236-7529 252-4767
TF: 877-236-5225 ■ *Web:* www.deerfootinn.com

Coast Hotels & Resorts Canada
1090 W Georgia St .... Vancouver BC V6E3V7 604-682-7982 682-8942
Web: www.coasthotels.com

Phone *Fax*

Fairmont Hotels & Resorts Inc
1 Beach St .... San Francisco CA 94133 415-772-7800 772-7805
Web: www.fairmont.com

Leisure Sports Inc
7077 Koll Ctr Pkwy Suite 110 .... Pleasanton CA 94566 925-600-1966 600-1144
Web: www.leisuresportsinc.com

Pan Pacific Hotels & Resorts
500 Post St .... San Francisco CA 94102 415-732-7747 732-5800
TF: 800-327-8585 ■ *Web:* www.panpacific.com

Destination Hotels & Resorts Inc
10333 E Dry Creek Rd Suite 450 .... Englewood CO 80112 303-799-3830 799-6011
TF: 800-633-8347 ■ *Web:* www.destinationhotels.com

Millennium Hotels & Resorts (MHR)
6560 Greenwood Plaza Blvd
Suite 300 .... Greenwood Village CO 80111 303-779-2000 779-2001
Web: www.millenniumhotels.com

Janus Hotels & Resorts Inc
2300 Corporate Blvd NW Suite 232 .... Boca Raton FL 33431 561-997-2325 997-5331
Web: www.janushotels.com

Rosen Hotels & Resorts Inc
9840 International Dr .... Orlando FL 32819 407-996-9840 996-0865
TF: 800-204-7234 ■ *Web:* www.rosenhotels.com

Castle Group Inc
Castle Resorts & Hotels
500 Ala Moana Blvd
Suite 555 3 Waterfront Plaza .... Honolulu HI 96813 808-524-0900 521-9994
TF: 800-733-7753 ■ *Web:* www.castleresorts.com
Outrigger Hotels & Resorts 2375 Kuhio Ave .... Honolulu HI 96815 808-921-6941 926-4368*
**Fax:* Sales ■ *TF:* 800-688-7444 ■ *Web:* www.outrigger.com

Harrah's Joliet 151 N Joliet St .... Joliet IL 60432 815-740-7800 740-2223
TF: 800-427-7247 ■ *Web:* www.harrahsjoliet.com

Ameristar Casino Hotel Council Bluffs
2200 River Rd .... Council Bluffs IA 51501 712-328-8888 329-6984*
**Fax:* Mktg ■ *TF:* 866-667-3386 ■ *Web:* www.ameristarcasinos.com

Harrah's Council Bluffs 2701 23rd Ave .... Council Bluffs IA 51501 712-329-6000 329-6491
TF: 888-598-8451 ■ *Web:* www.harrahscouncilbluffs.com

Prairie Band Casino & Resort 12305 150th Rd .... Mayetta KS 66509 785-966-7777 966-7799
TF: 888-727-4946 ■ *Web:* www.pbpgaming.com

Boomtown Hotel Casino 300 Riverside Dr .... Bossier City LA 71111 318-746-0711 226-9434
TF: 877-862-4428 ■ *Web:* www.boomtownbossier.com

Sam's Town Hotel & Casino Shreveport
315 Clyde Fant Pkwy .... Shreveport LA 71101 318-424-7777 424-5658
TF: 877-429-0711 ■ *Web:* www.samstownshreveport.com

Sonesta International Hotels Corp
116 Huntington Ave 9th Fl .... Boston MA 02116 617-421-5400 421-5402
NASDAQ: SNSTA ■ *TF:* 800-766-3782 ■ *Web:* www.sonesta.com

Carlson
Radisson Hotels & Resorts
701 Carlson Pkwy .... Minnetonka MN 55305 763-212-5000
TF: 800-333-3333 ■ *Web:* www.carlson.com

Bally's Casino Tunica
1450 Bally's Blvd Casino Ctr .... Robinsonville MS 38664 662-357-1500 357-1756
TF: 800-382-2559 ■ *Web:* www.ballystunica.com

Hard Rock Hotel & Casino Biloxi
777 Beach Blvd .... Biloxi MS 39530 228-374-7625 276-7655
TF: 877-877-6256 ■ *Web:* www.hardrockbiloxi.com

Harrah's Saint Louis Casino & Hotel
777 Casino Ctr Dr .... Maryland Heights MO 63043 314-770-8100 770-8399
TF: 800-427-7247 ■ *Web:* www.harrahsstlouis.com

Arizona Charlie's Boulder Casino & Hotel
4575 Boulder Hwy .... Las Vegas NV 89121 702-951-9000 951-1046
TF: 800-362-4040 ■ *Web:* www.arizonacharliesboulder.com

Arizona Charlie's Decatur Casino & Hotel
740 S Decatur Blvd .... Las Vegas NV 89107 702-258-5111 258-5192
TF: 888-236-8645 ■ *Web:* www.arizonacharliesdecatur.com

Binion's Horseshoe Hotel & Casino
128 Fremont St .... Las Vegas NV 89101 702-382-1600 384-1574
TF: 800-237-6537 ■ *Web:* www.binions.com

Boulder Station Hotel & Casino
4111 Boulder Hwy .... Las Vegas NV 89121 702-432-7777 432-7744
TF: 800-683-7777 ■ *Web:* www.boulderstation.com

California Hotel & Casino 12 E Ogden Ave .... Las Vegas NV 89101 702-385-1222 388-2660
TF: 800-634-6505 ■ *Web:* www.thecal.com

Casino Royale Hotel 3411 Las Vegas Blvd S .... Las Vegas NV 89109 702-737-3500 650-4743
TF: 800-854-7666 ■ *Web:* www.casinoroyalehotel.com

Circus Circus Hotel & Casino Reno
500 N Sierra St .... Reno NV 89503 775-329-0711 328-9652
TF: 800-648-5010 ■ *Web:* www.circusreno.com

Circus Circus Hotel Casino & Theme Park Las Vegas
2880 Las Vegas Blvd S .... Las Vegas NV 89109 702-734-0410 794-3816
TF Resv: 800-634-3450 ■ *Web:* www.circuscircus.com

Colorado Belle Hotel & Casino
2100 S Casino Dr .... Laughlin NV 89029 702-298-4000 298-3697*
**Fax:* Hum Res ■ *TF Resv:* 877-460-0777 ■ *Web:* www.coloradobelle.com

El Cortez Hotel & Casino 600 E Fremont St .... Las Vegas NV 89101 702-385-5200 474-3633
TF: 800-634-6703 ■ *Web:* www.elcortezhotelcasino.com

Eldorado Hotel Casino 345 N Virginia St .... Reno NV 89501 775-786-5700 322-7124
TF Resv: 800-879-8879 ■ *Web:* www.eldoradoreno.com

Excalibur Hotel & Casino
3850 Las Vegas Blvd S PO Box 96776 .... Las Vegas NV 89109 702-597-7777 597-7009
TF: 877-750-5464 ■ *Web:* www.excalibur.com

Fitzgeralds Casino & Hotel Reno
255 N Virginia St PO Box 40130 .... Reno NV 89504 775-785-3300 785-3318
TF: 800-535-5825

Fremont Hotel & Casino 200 Fremont St .... Las Vegas NV 89101 702-385-3232 385-6270
TF: 800-634-6460 ■ *Web:* www.fremontcasino.com

Gold Coast Hotel & Casino
4000 W Flamingo Rd .... Las Vegas NV 89103 702-367-7111 367-8575
TF: 800-331-5334 ■ *Web:* www.goldcoastcasino.com

Green Valley Ranch Resort Casino & Spa
2300 Paseo Verde Pkwy .... Henderson NV 89052 702-617-7777 617-7778
TF: 866-617-0777 ■ *Web:* www.greenvalleyranchresort.com

Imperial Palace Hotel & Casino
3535 Las Vegas Blvd S .... Las Vegas NV 89109 702-731-3311 735-8328
TF: 800-634-6441 ■ *Web:* www.imperialpalace.com

Las Vegas Club Hotel & Casino (LVC)
18 E Fremont St .... Las Vegas NV 89101 702-385-1664 380-5793
TF: 800-634-6532 ■ *Web:* www.vegasclubcasino.net

Las Vegas Sands Corp 3355 Las Vegas Blvd S .... Las Vegas NV 89109 702-414-1000 414-4884
NYSE: LVS ■ *Web:* www.lasvegassands.com

Luxor Hotel & Casino 3900 Las Vegas Blvd S .... Las Vegas NV 89119 702-262-4000 262-4404

Phone Fax

TF Resv: 800-288-1000 ■ *Web:* www.luxor.com

Orleans Las Vegas Hotel & Casino
4500 W Tropicana Ave .... Las Vegas NV 89103 702-365-7111 365-7500
TF: 800-675-3267 ■ *Web:* www.orleanscasino.com

Palace Station Hotel & Casino
2411 W Sahara Ave .... Las Vegas NV 89102 702-367-2411 367-2478
TF: 800-634-3101 ■ *Web:* www.palacestation.com

Peppermill Hotel & Casino 2707 S Virginia St .... Reno NV 89502 775-826-2121 826-7041
TF: 800-648-6992 ■ *Web:* www.peppermillreno.com

Railroad Pass Hotel & Casino
2800 S Boulder Hwy .... Henderson NV 89002 702-294-5000 294-0092
TF: 800-654-0877 ■ *Web:* www.railroadpass.com

Red Rock Resort Spa & Casino
11011 W Charleston Blvd .... Las Vegas NV 89135 702-797-7777 797-7890
TF: 866-767-7773 ■ *Web:* www.redrocklasvegas.com

Sam's Town Hotel & Gambling Hall
5111 Boulder Hwy .... Las Vegas NV 89122 702-456-7777 454-8107
TF: 800-897-8696 ■ *Web:* www.samstownlv.com

South Point Hotel & Casino
9777 Las Vegas Blvd S .... Las Vegas NV 89183 702-796-7111 797-8041
TF: 866-796-7111 ■ *Web:* www.southpointcasino.com

Stratosphere Tower Hotel & Casino
2000 S Las Vegas Blvd .... Las Vegas NV 89104 702-380-7777 383-4755*
**Fax:* Sales ■ *TF:* 800-998-6937 ■ *Web:* www.stratospherehotel.com

Suncoast Hotel & Casino 9090 Alta Dr .... Las Vegas NV 89145 702-636-7111 636-7288
TF: 877-677-7111 ■ *Web:* www.suncoastcasino.com

Sunset Station Hotel & Casino
1301 W Sunset Rd .... Henderson NV 89014 702-547-7777 547-7744
TF: 888-786-7389 ■ *Web:* www.sunsetstation.com

Tuscany Suites & Casino 255 E Flamingo Rd .... Las Vegas NV 89109 702-893-8933 947-5994
TF Resv: 877-887-2261 ■ *Web:* www.tuscanylv.com

Whiskey Pete's Hotel & Casino 100 W Primm Blvd .... Primm NV 89019 702-386-7867 679-5195
TF: 800-386-7867 ■ *Web:* www.primmvalleyresorts.com

Wynn Las Vegas 3131 Las Vegas Blvd S .... Las Vegas NV 89109 702-770-7000 770-1571
TF: 877-321-9966 ■ *Web:* www.wynnlasvegas.com

Dolce International 28 W Grand Ave .... Montvale NJ 07645 201-307-8700 307-8837
TF: 888-993-6523 ■ *Web:* www.dolce.com

Le Meridien 1111 Westchester Ave .... White Plains NY 10604 914-640-8100 640-8310
TF: 888-625-5144 ■ *Web:* www.starwoodhotels.com/lemeridien

Saint Regis Hotels & Resorts
1111 Westchester Ave .... White Plains NY 10604 914-640-8100 640-8310
Web: www.starwoodhotels.com

Delta Hotels Ltd 70 University Ave 11th Fl .... Toronto ON M5J2M4 416-874-2000 874-2001
TF: 800-268-1133 ■ *Web:* www.deltahotels.com

Hershey Entertainment & Resorts Co
27 W Chocolate Ave .... Hershey PA 17033 717-534-3131 534-3324
TF: 800-437-7439 ■ *Web:* www.hersheypa.com

Quorum Hotels & Resorts
5429 Lyndon B Johnson Fwy #625 .... Dallas TX 75240 972-458-7265 991-5647
Web: www.quorumhotels.com

Rosewood Hotels & Resorts
500 Crescent Ct Suite 300 .... Dallas TX 75201 214-880-4200 880-4201
TF: 888-767-3966 ■ *Web:* www.rosewoodhotels.com

Little America Hotels & Resorts
500 S Main St .... Salt Lake City UT 84101 801-363-6781 596-5911
TF Resv: 800-453-9450 ■ *Web:* www.littleamerica.com

Crestline Hotels & Resorts
8405 Greensboro Dr Suite 500 .... McLean VA 22102 571-382-1800 382-1860
Web: www.crestlinehotels.com

Coast Hotels & Resorts USA
2003 Western Ave Suite 500 .... Seattle WA 98121 206-826-2700 826-2701
Web: www.coasthotels.com

383 ICE - MANUFACTURED

Phone Fax

CV Ice Co Inc 83796 Date Ave .... Indio CA 92201 760-347-3529 347-3529
Web: www.cvice.com

Dusing Bros Ice Mfg Co 3607 Dixie Hwy .... Elsmere KY 41018 859-727-2720 727-2780

Hanover Foods Corp 1550 York St PO Box 334 .... Hanover PA 17331 717-632-6000 632-6681
TF: 800-888-4646 ■ *Web:* www.hanoverfoods.com

Happy Ice LLC 900 Turk Hill Rd .... Fairport NY 14450 585-388-0300 388-0185
Web: www.happyice.com

Herrin Bros Co PO Box 5291 .... Charlotte NC 28299 704-332-2193 376-3408

House of Flavors Inc 110 N William St .... Ludington MI 49431 231-845-7369 845-3990
TF: 800-930-7740 ■ *Web:* www.houseofflavors.com

Icemakers Inc PO Box 321755 .... Birmingham AL 35232 205-591-2791 591-2389
TF: 800-467-2181 ■ *Web:* www.icemakers.net

Lansdowne Beverage Inc
500 E Baltimore Pike .... Lansdowne PA 19050 610-623-7000 623-7000
Web: www.lansdownebeverage.com

Pelican Ice & Cold Storage Inc PO Box 2131 .... Kenner LA 70063 504-525-4193 733-1271

Reddy Ice Holdings Inc
8750 N Central Expy Suite 1800 .... Dallas TX 75231 214-526-6740 528-0995
NYSE: FRZ ■ *TF:* 800-683-4423 ■ *Web:* www.reddyice.com

384 ICE CREAM & DAIRY STORES

Phone Fax

All American Frozen Yogurt & Ice Cream Shops
812 SW Washington St Suite 1100 .... Portland OR 97205 503-224-6199 224-5042
Web: www.allamericanicecream.com

Amy's Ice Creams 3500 Guadalupe St .... Austin TX 78705 512-458-6895 458-4971
Web: www.amysicecreams.com

Bahama Buck's Original Shaved Ice Co
5123 69th St .... Lubbock TX 79424 806-771-2189 771-2190
Web: www.bahamabucks.com

Baskin-Robbins Inc 130 Royall St .... Canton MA 02021 781-737-3000
TF: 800-859-5339 ■ *Web:* www.baskinrobbins.com

Ben & Jerry's Homemade Inc
30 Community Dr .... South Burlington VT 05403 802-846-1500 846-1556
Web: www.benjerry.com

Braum's Ice Cream & Dairy Stores
3000 NE 63rd St PO Box 25429 .... Oklahoma City OK 73121 405-478-1656 475-2460
TF: 877-274-4197 ■ *Web:* www.braums.com

Bruster's Ice Cream Inc
1525 Riverside Dr .... Bridgewater PA 15009 724-774-4155 774-6384
Web: www.brusters.com

Carvel Franchising
200 Glenridge Pt Pkwy Suite 200 .... Atlanta GA 30342 404-255-3250 255-4978
TF: 800-227-8353 ■ *Web:* www.carvel.com

Cloverland Green Spring Dairy Inc
2701 Loch Raven Rd .... Baltimore MD 21218 410-235-4477 889-3690
TF Orders: 800-876-6455 ■ *Web:* www.cloverlanddairy.com

Cold Stone Creamery Inc
9311 E Via De Ventura .... Scottsdale AZ 85258 480-362-4800 362-4812
TF Cust Svc: 866-464-9467 ■ *Web:* www.coldstonecreamery.com

Dairy Queen 7505 Metro Blvd .... Minneapolis MN 55439 952-830-0200 830-0480
TF: 800-679-6556 ■ *Web:* www.dairyqueen.com

Freshens Quality Brands 1750 The Exchange .... Atlanta GA 30339 678-627-5400 627-5454
TF: 800-633-4519 ■ *Web:* www.freshens.com

High's Of Baltimore Inc 7477 New Ridge Rd .... Hanover MD 21076 410-859-3636 859-3527
Web: www.highsdairystores.com

Kilwin's Quality Confections
355 N Division Rd .... Petoskey MI 49770 231-347-3800 347-6951
TF: 800-454-5946 ■ *Web:* www.kilwins.com

Newport Creamery Inc 35 Stockanosset Rd .... Cranston RI 02920 401-946-4000 946-4392
Web: www.newportcreamery.com

Rita's Water Ice Franchise Co LLC
1210 Northbrook Dr .... Trevose PA 19053 215-876-9300
TF: 800-677-7482 ■ *Web:* www.ritasice.com

Royal Crest Dairy Inc 350 S Pearl St .... Denver CO 80209 303-777-2227 744-9173
Web: www.royalcrestdairy.com

Stewart's Shops PO Box 435 .... Saratoga Springs NY 12866 518-581-1000 581-1209
Web: www.stewartshops.com

TCBY Enterprises Inc
2855 E Cottonwood Pkwy Suite 400 .... Salt Lake City UT 84121 801-736-5600 736-5970
TF: 888-900-8229 ■ *Web:* www.tcby.com

385 IMAGING EQUIPMENT & SYSTEMS - MEDICAL

SEE ALSO Medical Instruments & Apparatus - Mfr p. 2227

Phone Fax

Agfa Corp 100 Challenger Rd .... Ridgefield Park NJ 07660 201-440-2500 342-4742
TF: 800-581-2432 ■ *Web:* www.agfa.com/usa

Alpine Solutions Inc
3222 Corte Malpaso Suite 204 .... Camarillo CA 93012 805-388-1699 388-2373
Web: www.alpinesolutionsinc.com

Applied Precision Inc (API) 1040 12th Ave NW .... Issaquah WA 98027 425-557-1000 557-1055
TF: 800-862-5166 ■ *Web:* www.api.com

Bioscan Inc 4590 MacArthur Blvd NW .... Washington DC 20007 202-338-0974 333-8514
TF: 800-255-7226 ■ *Web:* www.bioscan.com

BrainLAB Inc
3 Westbrook Corp Ctr Suite 400 .... Westchester IL 60154 708-409-1343 409-1619
TF: 800-784-7700 ■ *Web:* www.brainlab.com

CIVCO Medical Instruments 102 1st St .... Kalona IA 52247 319-656-4447 656-4451
TF: 800-445-6741 ■ *Web:* www.civcomedical.com

Clarient Inc 31 Columbia .... Aliso Viejo CA 92656 949-425-5700 425-5701
NASDAQ: CLRT ■ *TF:* 888-443-3310 ■ *Web:* www.clarientinc.com

Del Global Technologies Corp 1 Commerce Pk .... Valhalla NY 10595 914-686-3650 686-3650

Dent-X Corp 250 Clearbrook Rd Suite 240 .... Elmsford NY 10523 914-592-6100 592-6148
TF: 800-592-6666 ■ *Web:* www.imageworkscorporation.com/dentalproducts

Dentsply International Inc
221 W Philadelphia St PO Box 872 .... York PA 17405 717-845-7511 849-4762
NASDAQ: XRAY ■ *TF:* 800-877-0020 ■ *Web:* www.dentsply.com

Digirad Corp 13950 Stowe Dr .... Poway CA 92064 858-726-1600 726-1700
NASDAQ: DRAD ■ *TF:* 800-947-6134 ■ *Web:* www.digirad.com

Dornier MedTech America Inc
1155 Roberts Blvd .... Kennesaw GA 30144 770-426-1315 426-6115
TF: 800-367-6437 ■ *Web:* www.dornier.com

Eastman Kodak Co 343 State St .... Rochester NY 14650 585-724-4000 724-0663
NYSE: EK ■ *Web:* www.kodak.com

Fonar Corp 110 Marcus Dr .... Melville NY 11747 631-694-2929 390-7766
NASDAQ: FONR ■ *Web:* www.fonar.com

GE Healthcare 3000 N Grandview Blvd .... Waukesha WI 53188 262-544-3011 548-2443
TF: 800-558-5102 ■ *Web:* www.gehealthcare.com

Given Imaging Ltd
3950 Shackleford Rd Suite 500 .... Duluth GA 30096 770-662-0870 662-0510
NASDAQ: GIVN ■ *Web:* www.givenimaging.com

Hitachi Medical Systems America Inc
1959 Summit Commerce Pk .... Twinsburg OH 44087 330-425-1313 425-1410
TF: 800-800-3106 ■ *Web:* www.hitachimed.com

Hologic Inc 35 Crosby Dr .... Bedford MA 01730 781-999-7300 280-0669
NASDAQ: HOLX ■ *TF:* 800-343-9729 ■ *Web:* www.hologic.com

Holorad 2929 S Main St .... Salt Lake City UT 84115 801-983-6075 802-8004
Web: www.holorad.com

iCAD Inc 4 Townsend W Suite 17 .... Nashua NH 03063 603-882-5200 880-3843
NASDAQ: ICAD ■ *TF:* 866-280-2239 ■ *Web:* www.icadmed.com

ImageWorks 250 Clearbrook Rd .... Elmsford NY 10523 914-592-6100 592-6148
TF: 800-592-6666 ■ *Web:* www.imageworkscorporation.com

Imaging Diagnostic Systems Inc
6531 NW 18th Ct .... Plantation FL 33313 954-581-9800 581-0555
TF: 800-992-9008 ■ *Web:* www.imds.com

	City	State	Zip	Phone	Fax
IRIS International Inc 9172 Eton Ave *NASDAQ: IRIS* ■ *TF:* 800-776-4747 ■ *Web:* www.proiris.com	Chatsworth	CA	91311	818-709-1244	700-9661
ITT Night Vision & Imaging 7635 Plantation Rd *TF:* 800-448-8678 ■ *Web:* www.nightvision.com	Roanoke	VA	24019	540-563-0371	362-4979
Konica Minolta Medical Imaging 411 Newark Pompton Tpke *Web:* konicaminolta.us	Wayne	NJ	07470	973-633-1500	523-7408
Medrad Inc 1 Medrad Dr **Fax:* Cust Svc ■ *TF Cust Svc:* 800-633-7237 ■ *Web:* www.medrad.com	Indianola	PA	15051	412-767-2400	767-4120*
Merge Emed Inc 6737 W Washington St Suite 2250 *NASDAQ: MRGE* ■ *TF:* 877-446-3743	Milwaukee	WI	53214	414-977-4000	977-4200
Neoprobe Corp 425 Metro Pl N Suite 300 *TF:* 800-793-0079 ■ *Web:* www.neoprobe.com	Dublin	OH	43017	614-793-7500	793-7520
Nichols Institute Diagnostics 1311 Calle Batido *TF:* 800-286-4643	San Clemente	CA	92673	949-940-7200	940-7271
Novadaq Technologies Inc 2585 Skymark Ave Suite 306 *TF:* 888-728-4368 ■ *Web:* www.novadaq.com	Mississauga	ON	L4W4L5	905-629-3822	629-0282
One Call Medical Inc (OCM) 20 Waterview Blvd PO Box 614 *TF:* 800-872-2875 ■ *Web:* www.onecallmedical.com	Parsippany	NJ	07054	973-257-1000	257-0044
PerkinElmer Inc 45 William St *NYSE: PKI* ■ *Web:* www.perkinelmer.com	Wellesley	MA	02481	781-237-5100	237-9386
Philips Global PACS 5000 Marina Blvd Suite 100 *TF Cust Svc:* 877-328-2808 ■ *Web:* www.healthcare.philips.com	Brisbane	CA	94005	650-866-4100	228-5580
Philips Medical Systems 3000 Minuteman Rd *TF:* 800-934-7372 ■ *Web:* www.medical.philips.com	Andover	MA	01810	978-659-3000	689-8295
Precision Optics Corp Inc 22 E Broadway *TF:* 800-447-2812 ■ *Web:* www.poci.com	Gardner	MA	01440	978-630-1800	630-1487
S & S Technology 10625 Telge Rd *TF:* 800-231-1747 ■ *Web:* www.ssxray.com	Houston	TX	77095	281-815-1300	815-1444
Shimadzu Medical Systems 20101 S Vermont Ave *TF:* 800-228-1429 ■ *Web:* www.shimadzumed.com	Torrance	CA	90502	310-217-8855	217-0661
Siemens Medical Solutions Inc 51 Valley Stream Pkwy *TF:* 866-872-9745 ■ *Web:* www.medical.siemens.com	Malvern	PA	19355	610-448-6300	219-3124
Siemens Medical Solutions Ultrasound Div 1230 Shorebird Way *TF:* 800-422-8766	Mountain View	CA	94043	650-969-9112	
Siemens Molecular Imaging Inc 810 Innovation Dr *TF:* 800-841-7226 ■ *Web:* www.medical.siemens.com	Knoxville	TN	37932	865-218-2000	218-3000
SonoSite Inc 21919 30th Dr SE *NASDAQ: SONO* ■ *TF:* 888-482-9449 ■ *Web:* www.sonosite.com	Bothell	WA	98021	425-951-1200	951-1201
Stereotaxis Inc 4320 Forest Pk Ave *NASDAQ: STXS* ■ *TF:* 866-646-2346 ■ *Web:* www.stereotaxis.com	Saint Louis	MO	63108	314-678-6100	678-6159
Swissray International Inc 1180 McLester St Unit 2 *TF:* 800-903-5543 ■ *Web:* www.swissray.com	Elizabeth	NJ	07201	908-353-0971	353-1237
Topcon Medical Systems Inc 111 Bauer Dr *TF:* 800-223-1130 ■ *Web:* www.topconmedical.com	Oakland	NJ	07436	201-599-5100	599-5250
Toshiba America Inc 1251 Avenue of the Americas Suite 4100 *TF:* 800-457-7777 ■ *Web:* www.toshiba.com	New York	NY	10020	212-596-0600	593-3875
Toshiba America Medical Systems Inc 2441 Michelle Dr *TF Cust Svc:* 800-521-1968 ■ *Web:* www.medical.toshiba.com	Tustin	CA	92780	714-730-5000	730-4022
Varian Medical Systems Inc 3100 Hansen Way *NYSE: VAR* ■ **Fax:* Hum Res ■ *TF:* 800-544-4636 ■ *Web:* www.varian.com	Palo Alto	CA	94304	650-493-4000	424-4820*
Vision-Sciences Inc 40 Ramland Rd S *NASDAQ: VSCI* ■ *TF:* 800-874-9975 ■ *Web:* www.visionsciences.com	Orangeburg	NY	10962	845-365-0600	365-0620
Wolf X-Ray Corp 100 W Industry Ct *TF Cust Svc:* 800-356-9729 ■ *Web:* www.wolfxray.com	Deer Park	NY	11729	631-242-9729	925-5003

386 IMAGING SERVICES - DIAGNOSTIC

	City	State	Zip	Phone	Fax
Alliance Imaging Inc 100 Bayview Cir Suite 400 **Fax Area Code:* 888 ■ *TF:* 800-544-3215 ■ *Web:* www.alliancehealthcareservices-us.com	Newport Beach	CA	92660	800-544-3215	662-2730*
Center for Diagnostic Imaging 5775 Wayzata Blvd Suite 400 *TF:* 877-566-6500 ■ *Web:* www.cdiradiology.com	Saint Louis Park	MN	55416	952-543-6500	847-1152
InfiMed Inc 121 Metropolitan Dr *TF:* 800-825-8845 ■ *Web:* www.infimed.com	Liverpool	NY	13088	315-453-4545	453-4550
InSight Health Services Corp 26250 Enterprise Ct Suite 100 *TF:* 800-874-8634 ■ *Web:* www.insighthealth.com	Lake Forest	CA	92630	949-282-6000	452-0203
Medical Resources Inc 1455 Broad St *TF:* 800-537-7272	Bloomfield	NJ	07003	973-707-1100	707-1118
Medquest Assoc Inc 3480 Preston Ridge Rd Suite 600 *Web:* www.mqimaging.com	Alpharetta	GA	30005	678-992-7200	

387 INCENTIVE PROGRAM MANAGEMENT SERVICES

SEE ALSO Conference & Events Coordinators p. 1700

Many Of The Companies Listed Here Provide Travel As A Reward For Employees Or Corporate Customers In Order To Boost Sales Or Employee Performance. Most Of These Companies Are Members Of The Society Of Incentive & Travel Executives. Some Of The Companies Listed Offer Merchandise Or Other Types Of Incentives As Well.

	City	State	Zip	Phone	Fax
ADI Meetings & Incentives Inc 1223 E Broadway Rd *TF:* 800-944-2359 ■ *Web:* www.adimi.com	Tempe	AZ	85282	480-350-9090	350-9393
Amorde Incentive Marketing 33161 Camino Capistrano Suite L	San Juan Capistrano	CA	92675	949-388-7078	388-7082
Beatty Group International 9800 Beaverton Hillsdale # 105 *TF:* 800-285-6215 ■ *Web:* www.beattygroup.com	Beaverton	OR	97005	503-644-3340	644-2219
Brickell Incentives 569 Central Dr Suite 103 *Web:* www.brickellincentives.com	Virginia Beach	VA	23454	757-233-0076	368-0387
Don Jagoda Assoc Inc 100 Marcus Dr *Web:* www.dja.com	Melville	NY	11747	631-454-1800	454-1834
Eaton Incentives Inc 271 US Hwy 46 # H212-2 *Web:* www.eatonincentives.com	Fairfield	NJ	07004	973-882-7700	882-9825
Fennell Promotions Inc 951 Hornet Dr **Fax Area Code:* 800 ■ *TF:* 800-495-9765 ■ *Web:* www.fennellpromotions.com	Hazelwood	MO	63042	314-592-3300	495-9845*
Fields Group Inc 9124 Technology Dr *TF:* 800-600-2969 ■ *Web:* www.thefieldsgroupinc.com	Fishers	IN	46038	317-578-4414	578-4411
Fox Premier Meetings & Incentives 2150 S Washburn St *TF:* 800-236-5095 ■ *Web:* www.gofoxpremier.com	Oshkosh	WI	54904	920-236-8030	236-8006
Fraser & Hoyt Group Incentive Div 1505 Barrington St Suite 107 *TF:* 800-565-8747 ■ *Web:* www.fraserhoyt.com/incentives.asp	Halifax	NS	B3J3K5	902-421-1113	422-2040
Global Incentives Inc 2120 Main St Suite 130 *TF:* 800-292-7348 ■ *Web:* www.globalinc.net	Huntington Beach	CA	92648	714-960-2300	536-5308
Impact Incentives & Meetings Inc 23 vreland Rd Suite 203 Suite 204 *Web:* www.impactincentives.com	Florham Park	NJ	07932	973-952-9052	952-1024
Incentive Solutions 2337 Perimeter Pk Dr Suite 220 *TF:* 800-463-5836 ■ *Web:* www.incentivesolutions.com	Atlanta	GA	30341	770-457-4597	457-4994
Incentive Travel & Meetings (ITM) 970 Clementstone Dr Suite 100 *Web:* www.usaitm.com	Atlanta	GA	30342	404-252-2728	252-8328
Incentive Travel Services Inc 805 Peachtree St NE Suite 602	Atlanta	GA	30308	404-872-6165	872-6695
Incentives Unlimited 1200 Woodruff Rd Suite C-27 *Web:* www.incentivesunlimited.com	Greenville	SC	29607	864-458-7694	458-7698
ITAGroup 4800 Westown Pkwy *TF:* 800-257-1985 ■ *Web:* www.itagroup.com	West Des Moines	IA	50266	515-224-3400	224-3552
LMS Meetings & Incentives 300 Corporate Pointe Suite 310	Culver City	CA	90230	310-641-4222	641-5222
Maritz Travel û Boston 17 Columbia St *Web:* www.maritz.com	Swampscott	MA	01907	781-584-5600	
Marketing Innovators International Inc 9701 W Higgins Rd **Fax Area Code:* 847 ■ *TF:* 800-543-7373 ■ *Web:* www.marketinginnovators.com	Rosemont	IL	60018	800-543-7373	696-3194*
Maxcel Co 6600 LBJ Fwy Suite 109 *Web:* www.maxcel.net	Dallas	TX	75240	972-644-0880	680-2488
MotivAction 16355 36th Ave N Suite 100 *TF:* 800-326-2226 ■ *Web:* www.motivaction.com	Minneapolis	MN	55446	763-525-5200	525-5300
Motivation Through Incentives Inc 10400 W 103 St Suite 10 *TF:* 800-826-3464 ■ *Web:* www.miinc.com	Overland Park	KS	66214	816-942-0122	942-2252
Performance Strategies Inc 6862 Hillsdale Ct *Web:* www.performancestrategies.com	Indianapolis	IN	46250	317-842-0393	578-4711
Premier Incentives Inc 6 Admiral's Ln *TF:* 877-271-5622 ■ *Web:* www.premierincentives.com	Salem	MA	01970	978-607-0135	607-0136
PROVIDENT TRAVEL 15 W Central Pkwy *TF:* 888-301-3866 ■ *Web:* www.providenttravel.com	Cincinnati	OH	45202	513-763-3070	763-3071
Sperry & Hutchinson Co Inc 1625 S Congress Ave	Delray Beach	FL	33445	561-454-7600	265-2493
Student Advantage LLC 280 Summer St *TF:* 800-333-2920 ■ *Web:* www.studentadvantage.com	Boston	MA	02210	617-912-2011	912-2012
Travel Marketing Inc PO Box 91545 *Web:* www.travelmarketing.org	Portland	OR	97291	503-222-1020	645-2611
United Incentives Inc 131 N 3rd St *TF:* 800-431-8497 ■ *Web:* www.unitedincentives.com	Philadelphia	PA	19106	215-625-2700	625-2502
Universal Odyssey Inc 1601 Dove St Suite 260 *Web:* www.universalodyssey.com	Newport Beach	CA	92660	949-263-1222	263-0983
USMotivation 7840 Roswell Rd Bldg 100 3rd Fl *TF:* 800-476-0496 ■ *Web:* www.usmotivation.com	Atlanta	GA	30350	770-290-4700	290-4701
Vertrue Inc 20 Glover Ave *TF:* 800-374-6135 ■ *Web:* www.vertrue.com	Norwalk	CT	06850	203-324-7635	674-7080
Viktor Incentives & Meetings 4020 Copper View Suite 130 *TF:* 800-748-0478 ■ *Web:* www.viktorwithak.com	Traverse City	MI	49684	231-947-0882	947-2532

388 INDUSTRIAL EQUIPMENT & SUPPLIES (MISC) - WHOL

	City	State	Zip	Phone	Fax
A.a. Anderson & Co Inc PO Box 523 *Web:* www.aaaco.com	Brookfield	WI	53008	262-784-3340	784-9749
AaronEquipment Co Inc 735 E Green St PO Box 80 *TF:* 800-492-2766 ■ *Web:* www.aaronequipment.com	Bensenville	IL	60106	630-350-2200	350-9047
Abatix Corp 2400 Skyline Dr Suite 400 *NASDAQ: ABIX* ■ *TF:* 800-426-3983 ■ *Web:* www.abatix.com	Mesquite	TX	75149	214-381-0322	388-0443
Accurate Air Engineering Inc 16207 Carmennita Rd *TF:* 800-438-5577 ■ *Web:* www.accurateair.com	Cerritos	CA	90703	562-484-6370	484-6371

Company	City	State	Zip	Phone	Fax
ACG Direct 14660 23-Mile Rd *TF:* 800-968-7101	Shelby Township	MI	48315	586-247-7100	247-6602
Adco Mfg Inc 2170 Academy Ave *Web:* www.adcomfg.com	Sanger	CA	93657	559-875-5563	875-7665
AIM Supply Co 7337 Bryan Dairy Rd *TF:* 800-999-0125 ■ *Web:* www.aimsupply.com	Largo	FL	33777	727-544-6114	544-6211
Aimco 10000 SE Pine St *TF:* 800-852-1368 ■ *Web:* www.aimco-global.com	Portland	OR	97216	503-255-7364	254-0036
Airgas Inc 259 N Radnor-Chester Rd Suite 100 *NYSE: ARG* ■ *TF:* 800-255-2165 ■ *Web:* www.airgas.com	Radnor	PA	19087	610-687-5253	687-1052
Airgas Inc 6055 Rockside Woods Blvd **Fax Area Code:* 440 ■ *Web:* www.airgas.com	Independence	OH	44131	216-642-6600	232-7799*
Airgas North Central 1801 Marinette Ave *Web:* www.airgas.com	Marinette	WI	54143	715-732-7950	732-7940
Alamo Iron Works Inc 943 AT&T Ctr Pkwy PO Box 231 *TF Cust Svc:* 800-292-7817 ■ *Web:* www.aiwnet.com	San Antonio	TX	78219	210-223-6161	704-8351
Ames Supply Co 1936 University Ln *TF:* 800-323-3856 ■ *Web:* www.amessupply.com	Lisle	IL	60532	630-964-2440	964-0497
Applied Industrial Technologies Inc One Applied Plaza Eulid Ave *NYSE: AIT* ■ *Web:* www.applied.com	Cleveland	OH	44115	216-426-4000	426-4845
Associated Packaging Inc 435 Calvert Dr *Web:* www.associatedpackaging.com	Gallatin	TN	37066	615-452-2131	452-7790
Atlantic Lift Truck Inc 2945 Whittington Ave *TF:* 800-638-4566 ■ *Web:* www.atlanticlift.com	Baltimore	MD	21230	410-644-7777	
Austin Pump & Supply Co PO Box 17037 *TF:* 800-252-9692 ■ *Web:* www.austinpump.com	Austin	TX	78760	512-442-2348	442-2932
Barnes Distribution 1301 E 9th St Suite 700 *TF:* 800-726-9626 ■ *Web:* www.barnesdistribution.com	Cleveland	OH	44114	216-416-7200	430-6903
Bearing Distributors Inc 8000 Hub Pkwy *TF:* 888-435-7234 ■ *Web:* www.bdi-usa.com	Cleveland	OH	44125	216-642-9100	642-9573
Bearing Headquarters Co 2550 S 25th Ave *Web:* www.bearingheadquarters.com	Broadview	IL	60155	708-681-4400	681-4462
Bearings & Drives Inc 607 Lower Poplar St PO Box 4325 *Web:* www.bearingsdrives.com	Macon	GA	31208	478-746-7623	742-7836
Berendsen Fluid Power 401 S Boston Ave Suite 1200 *TF:* 800-360-2327 ■ *Web:* www.bfpna.com	Tulsa	OK	74103	918-592-3781	581-5080
Brake Supply Co Inc 5501 Foundation Blvd *TF:* 800-457-5788 ■ *Web:* www.brake.com	Evansville	IN	47725	812-467-1000	429-9493
Brauer Material Handling Systems Inc 226 Molly Walton Dr *TF:* 800-645-6083 ■ *Web:* www.braueronline.com	Hendersonville	TN	37075	615-859-2930	859-2937
Briggs Equipment 10540 N Stemmons Fwy Suite 1525 *TF:* 800-606-1833 ■ *Web:* www.briggsequipment.com	Dallas	TX	75220	214-630-0808	631-3560
Briggs Industrial Equipment 10550 N Stemmons Fwy *TF:* 800-606-1833 ■ *Web:* www.briggsindustrial.com	Dallas	TX	75220	214-630-0808	631-3560
C & H Distributors LLC 770 S 70th St **Fax Area Code:* 800 ■ *TF Sales:* 800-558-9966 ■ *Web:* www.chdist.com	Milwaukee	WI	53214	414-443-1700	336-1331*
Canadian Bearings Ltd 1600 Drew Rd *TF:* 800-229-2327 ■ *Web:* www.canadianbearings.com	Mississauga	ON	L5S1S5	905-670-6700	670-0459
Carolina Material Handling Services Inc PO Box 6 *TF:* 800-922-6709 ■ *Web:* www.cmhservices.net	Columbia	SC	29202	803-695-0149	783-1659
Cascade Machinery & Electric Inc 4600 E Marginal Way S PO Box 3575 *TF:* 800-289-0500 ■ *Web:* www.cascade-machinery.com	Seattle	WA	98124	206-762-0500	767-5122
Cee Kay Supply Co 5835 Manchester Ave *Web:* www.ceekay.com	Saint Louis	MO	63110	314-644-3500	644-4336
Central Power Systems & Services 9200 W Liberty Dr **Fax:* Sales ■ *Web:* www.cpower.com	Liberty	MO	64068	816-781-8070	781-2207*
Certified Slings & Supply Inc PO Box 180127 *Web:* www.certifiedslings.com	Casselberry	FL	32718	407-331-6677	260-9196
Cisco-Eagle 2120 Valley View Ln *TF:* 800-877-3861 ■ *Web:* www.cisco-eagle.com	Dallas	TX	75234	972-406-9330	406-9577
CMC Construction Services 9103 E Almeda Rd *TF:* 877-297-9111 ■ *Web:* www.cmcconstructionservices.com	Houston	TX	77054	713-799-1150	799-8431
Connell Gatco Co 200 Connell Dr *TF:* 800-233-3240 ■ *Web:* www.connellco.com/GATCO.htm	Berkeley Heights	NJ	07922	908-673-3700	673-3800
Conveyco Technologies Inc PO Box 1000 *TF:* 800-229-8215 ■ *Web:* www.conveyco.com	Bristol	CT	06011	860-589-8215	583-1384
Crane Engineering Inc 707 Ford St PO Box 38 *Web:* www.craneengineering.net	Kimberly	WI	54136	920-733-4425	733-0211
Cross Co 4400 Piedmont Pkwy *TF:* 800-472-2767 ■ *Web:* www.crossco.com	Greensboro	NC	27410	336-856-6000	856-6999
Cummins Southern Plains Inc PO Box 90027 *TF:* 800-516-4354 ■ *Web:* www.cummins-sp.com	Arlington	TX	76004	817-640-6801	640-6852
Cvg International America Inc 7200 NW 19th St Suite 110 *Web:* www.cvgin.com	Miami	FL	33126	305-470-8100	470-8199
Daily Equipment Co PO Box 98209 *Web:* www.dailyeq.com	Jackson	MS	39298	601-932-6011	932-2311
Deacon Industrial Supply Co Inc 165 Boro Line Rd *Web:* www.deaconind.com	King of Prussia	PA	19406	610-265-5322	265-6470
Deleet Merchandising Corp 26 Blanchard St *Web:* www.prisco.com	Newark	NJ	07105	973-589-7800	589-3225
Detroit Pump & Mfg Co 450 Fair St Bldg D *TF:* 800-686-1662 ■ *Web:* www.detroitpump.com	Ferndale	MI	48220	248-544-4242	544-4141
DoALL Co 1480 S Wolf Rd *Web:* www.doall.com	Wheeling	IL	60090	847-495-6800	484-2045
Drago Supply Co 740 Houston Ave **Fax:* Sales ■ *Web:* www.dragosupply.com	Port Arthur	TX	77640	409-983-4911	982-8240*
Dueco N4 W22610 Bluemound Rd *TF:* 800-558-4004 ■ *Web:* www.dueco.com	Waukesha	WI	53186	262-547-8500	547-8407
Duncan Industrial Solutions 3450 S MacArthur Blvd *TF:* 800-375-9470 ■ *Web:* www.duncanindustrial.com	Oklahoma City	OK	73179	405-688-2300	
Duo-Fast Carolinas Inc 1923 John Crossland Jr Dr *Web:* www.duofast.net	Charlotte	NC	28208	704-377-5721	377-2368
DXP Enterprises Inc 7272 Pinemont Dr *NASDAQ: DXPE* ■ *TF:* 877-996-4700 ■ *Web:* www.dxpe.com	Houston	TX	77040	713-996-4700	996-4701
E & M Electric & Machinery Inc 126 Mill St *TF:* 866-693-2636 ■ *Web:* www.enm.com	Healdsburg	CA	95448	707-473-3100	473-3191
Eastern Lift Truck Co Inc 549 E Linwood Ave *TF:* 866-980-7175 ■ *Web:* www.easternlifttruck.com	Maple Shade	NJ	08052	856-779-8880	482-8804
Edgen Corp 18444 Highland Rd *TF:* 866-334-3648 ■ *Web:* www.edgenmurray.com	Baton Rouge	LA	70809	225-756-9868	756-9868
Ellison Machinery Co 9912 S Pioneer Blvd *TF:* 800-358-4828 ■ *Web:* www.ellisontechnologies.com	Santa Fe Springs	CA	90670	562-949-8311	949-9091
Endries International Inc 714 W Ryan St PO Box 69 *TF:* 800-852-5821 ■ *Web:* www.endries.com	Brillion	WI	54110	920-756-5381	756-3772
Engman-Taylor Co Inc (ETCO) W142 N9351 Fountain Blvd *TF:* 800-236-1975 ■ *Web:* www.engman-taylor.com	Menomonee Falls	WI	53051	262-255-9300	255-6512
Enpro Inc 121 S Lombard Rd *TF:* 800-323-2416 ■ *Web:* www.enproinc.com	Addison	IL	60101	630-629-3504	629-3512
Exterran 16666 Northchase Dr *NYSE: HC* ■ **Fax Area Code:* 214 ■ *TF Sales:* 800-522-9270 ■ *Web:* www.exterran.com	Houston	TX	77060	281-836-7000	378-5091*
Fairmont Supply Co 1001 Consol Energy Dr *Web:* www.fairmontsupply.com	Canonsburg	PA	15317	724-514-3900	261-5310
FCx Performance 3000 E 14th Ave *TF:* 800-253-6223 ■ *Web:* www.fcxperformance.com	Columbus	OH	43219	614-253-1996	253-2033
Flexlink Systems Inc 6580 Snowdrift Rd Suite 200 *Web:* www.flexlink.com	Allentown	PA	18106	610-973-8200	973-8345
Florida Detroit Diesel-Allison Inc 5040 University Blvd W *TF:* 888-812-4440 ■ *Web:* www.fdda.com	Jacksonville	FL	32216	904-737-7330	733-5871
Forklifts of Minnesota Inc 2201 W 94th St *TF:* 800-752-4300 ■ *Web:* www.forkliftsofmn.com	Bloomington	MN	55431	952-887-5400	881-3030
FUJIFILM Graphic System USA Inc 200 Summit Lake Dr *TF:* 800-755-3854 ■ *Web:* www.fujifilmgs.com	Valhalla	NY	10595	914-749-4800	749-4899
FW Webb Co 160 Middlesex Tpke *TF:* 800-453-1100 ■ *Web:* www.fwwebb.com	Bedford	MA	02118	781-272-6600	275-3354
Gaffney-Kroese Supply Corp 60 Kingsbridge Rd *Web:* www.gaffneykroese.com	Piscataway	NJ	08854	732-885-9000	885-9555
Gas Equipment Co 1440 Lakes Pkwy Suite 300 *TF:* 800-241-4155	Lawrenceville	GA	30043	770-995-1131	995-1216
General Tool & Supply Co Inc 2705 NW Nicolai St *TF:* 800-783-3411 ■ *Web:* www.generaltool.com	Portland	OR	97210	503-226-3411	778-5518
Geneva Scientific Inc 11 N Batavia Ave *TF:* 800-338-2697 ■ *Web:* www.barcoproducts.com	Batavia	IL	60510	630-879-0084	879-8687
Genuine Parts Co 2999 Cir 75 Pkwy *NYSE: GPC* ■ *Web:* www.genpt.com	Atlanta	GA	30339	770-953-1700	956-2211
Gerotech Inc 29220 Commerce Dr *Web:* www.gerotechinc.com	Flat Rock	MI	48134	734-379-7788	379-2244
Glatt Air Techniques Inc 20 Spear Rd *Web:* www.glattair.com	Ramsey	NJ	07446	201-825-8700	825-0389
Gosiger Inc 108 McDonough St *TF:* 800-888-4188 ■ *Web:* www.gosiger.com	Dayton	OH	45402	937-228-5174	228-5189
H G Makelim Co 219 Shaw Rd *TF:* 800-471-0590 ■ *Web:* www.hgmakelim.com	South San Francisco	CA	94080	650-873-4757	872-5438
Ha Metzger Inc 550 Grand St *TF:* 800-746-2332 ■ *Web:* www.hametzger.com	Jersey City	NJ	07302	201-332-9900	332-0303
Hagemeyer North America Inc 1460 Tobias Gadson Blvd *TF:* 800-752-0007 ■ *Web:* www.hagemeyerna.com	Charleston	SC	29407	843-745-2400	745-6942
Haggard & Stocking Assoc 5318 Victory Dr *TF:* 800-622-4824 ■ *Web:* www.haggard-stocking.com	Indianapolis	IN	46203	317-788-4661	788-1645
Hahn Systems Co Inc 5762 W 74th St *TF:* 800-589-3796 ■ *Web:* www.hahnsystems.com	Indianapolis	IN	46278	317-243-3796	244-9079
Harrington Industrial Plastics LLC 14480 Yorba Ave *TF:* 800-669-8641 ■ *Web:* www.harringtonplastics.com	Chino	CA	91710	909-597-8641	597-9826
HD Supply Waterworks Ltd 200 W Hwy Suite 620 *TF:* 800-817-5355 ■ *Web:* www.waterworks.hdsupply.com	Waco	TX	76714	254-772-5355	772-5716
Herc-U-Lift Inc 5655 Hwy 12 W PO Box 69 *TF:* 800-362-3500 ■ *Web:* www.herculift.com	Maple Plain	MN	55359	763-479-2501	479-2296
Hope Group 70 Bearfoot Rd *Web:* www.thehopegroup.com	Northborough	MA	01532	508-393-7660	393-8203
Hughes Machinery Co 8820 Bond St *Web:* www.hughesmachinery.com	Overland Park	KS	66214	913-492-0355	492-1420
Hull Lift Truck Inc 28747 Old US 33 W *TF:* 800-860-4855 ■ *Web:* www.hulllifttruck.com	Elkhart	IN	46516	574-293-8651	293-9769
Hydraulics International Inc 9201 Independence Ave *Web:* www.hiinet.com	Chatsworth	CA	91311	818-998-1231	718-2459
IBT Inc 9400 W 55th St *TF:* 800-332-2114 ■ *Web:* www.ibtinc.com	Merriam	KS	66203	913-677-3151	677-3752
Illinois Auto Electric Co 700 Enterprise St *TF:* 800-683-9312 ■ *Web:* www.illinoisautoelectric.com	Aurora	IL	60504	630-862-3300	862-3137
Indeck Power Equipment Co 1111 Willis Ave *TF:* 800-446-3325 ■ *Web:* www.indeck.com	Wheeling	IL	60090	847-541-8300	541-9984
Indoff Inc 11816 Lackland Rd *TF:* 800-486-7867 ■ *Web:* www.indoff.com	Saint Louis	MO	63146	314-997-1122	812-3932

Company	City	State	Zip	Phone	Fax
Industrial Controls Distributors Inc (ICD) 1776 Bloomsbury Ave *TF Sales:* 800-281-4788 ■ *Web:* www.industrialcontrolsonline.com	Wanamassa	NJ	07712	732-918-9000	922-4417
Industrial Diesel Inc 8705 Harmon Rd *TF:* 800-323-3659 ■ *Web:* www.industrialdiesel.net	Fort Worth	TX	76177	817-232-1071	232-0354
Industrial Services of America Inc 7100 Grade Ln *NASDAQ: IDSA* ■ *TF:* 800-824-2144 ■ *Web:* www.isa-inc.com	Louisville	KY	40213	502-368-1661	368-1440
Industrial Supply Solutions Inc 520 Elizabeth St *TF:* 800-346-5341 ■ *Web:* www.issimro.com	Charleston	WV	25311	304-346-5341	346-5347
J. H. Bennett & Co Inc PO Box 8028 *TF:* 800-837-5426 ■ *Web:* www.jhbennett.com	Novi	MI	48376	248-596-5100	596-0640
Jabo Supply Corp 5164 County Rd 64/66 *TF:* 800-334-5226 ■ *Web:* www.jabosupply.com	Huntington	WV	25705	304-736-8333	736-8551
Jefferds Corp 652 Winfield Rd PO Box 757 *TF:* 800-735-8111 ■ *Web:* www.jefferds.com	Saint Albans	WV	25177	304-755-8111	755-7544
Kaman Industrial Technologies Inc 1 Waterside Crossing *TF:* 800-526-2626 ■ *Web:* www.kamandirect.com	Windsor	CT	06095	860-687-5000	687-5170
Kemper Equipment Inc 5051 Horseshoe Pike *Web:* www.kemperequipment.com	Honey Brook	PA	19344	610-273-2066	273-3537
Kennametal Inc 1600 Technology Way PO Box 231 *NYSE: KMT* ■ *TF Cust Svc:* 800-446-7738 ■ *Web:* www.kennametal.com	Latrobe	PA	15650	724-539-5000	539-8787
Kimball Midwest 4800 Robert Rd *TF:* 800-233-1294 ■ *Web:* www.kimballmidwest.com	Columbus	OH	43228	614-219-6100	219-6101
Kinecor 2200 52nd Ave *TF:* 866-546-3267 ■ *Web:* www.kinecor.com	Lachine	QC	H8T2Y3	514-636-3333	636-7777
Knickerbocker Russell Co Inc 4759 Campbells Run *Web:* www.knickerbockerrussell.com	Pittsburgh	PA	15205	412-494-9233	787-7991
Kramer Air Tool Sales & Service Inc 23149 Commerce Dr *Web:* www.krameairtool.com	Farmington Hills	MI	48335	248-442-8550	442-8555
Lawson Products Inc 1666 E Touhy Ave *NASDAQ: LAWS* ■ **Fax:* Sales ■ *TF:* 800-323-6312 ■ *Web:* www.lawsonproducts.com	Des Plaines	IL	60018	847-827-9666	296-6309*
Lewis Goetz & Co Inc 1571 Grandview Ave *TF:* 800-562-8002 ■ *Web:* www.lewis-goetz.com	Paulsboro	NJ	08066	856-579-1421	579-1429
Lewis-Goetz & Co Inc 650 Washington Rd Suite 210 *TF:* 800-289-1236 ■ *Web:* www.lewis-goetz.com	Pittsburgh	PA	15228	412-341-7100	341-7192
Lipten Co LLC 28054 Ctr Oaks Ct *TF:* 800-860-0790 ■ *Web:* www.lipten.com	Wixom	MI	48393	248-374-8910	374-8906
Lister-Petter Americas Inc 815 E 56 Hwy *TF:* 800-888-3512 ■ *Web:* www.lister-petter.com	Olathe	KS	66061	913-764-3512	764-5493
Livingston & Haven 11529 Wilmar Blvd PO Box 7207 *Web:* www.lhtech.com	Charlotte	NC	28273	704-588-3670	504-2530
Logan Corp 555 7th Ave *TF:* 888-853-4751 ■ *Web:* www.logancorp.com	Huntington	WV	25706	304-526-4700	526-4747
M & L Industries Inc 1210 St Charles St *TF:* 800-969-0068 ■ *Web:* www.mlind.net	Houma	LA	70360	985-876-2280	872-9596
Mac-Gray Corp 404 Wyman St Suite 404 *NYSE: TUC* ■ *TF:* 866-613-4411 ■ *Web:* www.macgray.com	Waltham	MA	02451	781-487-7600	487-7601
Machine & Welding Supply Co 1660 Hwy 301 S PO Box 1708 *Web:* www.mwsc.com	Dunn	NC	28335	910-892-4016	892-3575
Machinery Sales Co 17253 Chestnut St *TF:* 800-588-8111 ■ *Web:* www.mchysales.com	City of Industry	CA	91748	626-581-9211	581-9277
Machinery Systems Inc 614 E State Pkwy *TF:* 800-347-8085 ■ *Web:* www.machsys.com	Schaumburg	IL	60173	847-882-8085	882-2894
Mack Boring & Parts Co PO Box 3116 *Web:* www.mackboring.com	Union	NJ	07083	908-964-0700	964-8475
Mahar Tool Supply Co Inc 112 Williams St *TF:* 800-456-2427 ■ *Web:* www.mahartool.com	Saginaw	MI	48602	989-799-5530	799-0830
Mannings USA Inc PO Box 896 *TF:* 800-447-4473 ■ *Web:* www.manningsusa.com	Dover	NJ	07802	973-537-1576	
Martin Supply Co 200 Appleton Ave *TF:* 800-828-8116 ■ *Web:* www.mscoinc.com	Sheffield	AL	35660	256-383-3131	389-9447
Material Handling Services LLC PO Box 40303 *TF:* 800-466-3871 ■ *Web:* www.materialshandlingservices.com	Nashville	TN	37204	615-383-4498	383-4498
McCall Handling Co 8801 Wise Ave Suite 200 *TF:* 888-870-0685 ■ *Web:* www.mccallhandling.com	Baltimore	MD	21222	410-388-2600	244-7222
McGuffy Industries Inc 18635 Telge Rd *TF:* 800-365-6955 ■ *Web:* www.mcguffygroup.com	Cypress	TX	77429	281-255-6955	
McKinley Equipment Corp 17611 Armstrong Ave *TF:* 800-770-6094 ■ *Web:* www.mckinleyequipment.com	Irvine	CA	92614	949-261-9222	250-7301
Medart Inc 124 Manufacturers Dr **Fax Area Code:* 888 ■ *TF:* 800-888-7181 ■ *Web:* www.medartinc.com	Arnold	MO	63010	636-282-2300	510-3100*
MEE Material Handling Equipment 11721 W Carmen Ave *TF:* 800-242-5452 ■ *Web:* www.meelift.com	Milwaukee	WI	53225	414-353-3300	353-6327
Minnesota Supply Co Inc 6470 Flying Cloud Dr *TF:* 800-869-1058 ■ *Web:* www.mnsupply.com	Eden Prairie	MN	55344	952-828-7300	828-7301
Mitsubishi International Corp 655 3rd Ave *Web:* www.micusa.com	New York	NY	10017	212-605-2000	
Modern Group Ltd 2501 Durham Rd *TF:* 800-223-3827 ■ *Web:* www.moderngroup.com	Bristol	PA	19007	215-943-9100	943-4978
Motion Industries Inc 1605 Alton Rd *TF:* 800-526-9328 ■ *Web:* www.motion-industries.com	Birmingham	AL	35210	205-956-1122	951-1172
MSC Industrial Direct Co 75 Maxess Rd *NYSE: MSM* ■ **Fax Area Code:* 800 ■ *TF:* 800-645-7270 ■ *Web:* www.mscdirect.com	Melville	NY	11747	516-812-2000	255-5067*
Multiquip Inc 18910 Wilmington Ave *TF:* 800-421-1244 ■ *Web:* www.multiquip.com	Carson	CA	90746	310-537-3700	537-3927
Nachi Robotic Systems Inc 22285 Roethel Dr *Web:* www.nachirobotics.com	Novi	MI	48375	248-305-6545	305-6542
National Welders Supply Co Inc 810 Gesco St *TF:* 800-866-4422 ■ *Web:* www.nwsco.com	Charlotte	NC	28208	704-333-5475	342-0260
NC Machinery Co 17025 W Valley Hwy *TF:* 800-562-4735 ■ *Web:* www.ncmachinery.com	Tukwila	WA	98188	425-251-9800	251-5886
Nebraska Machinery Co Inc 3501 S Jeffers St PO Box 809 *TF:* 800-494-9560 ■ *Web:* www.nebraska-machinery.com	North Platte	NE	69103	308-532-3100	532-3173
Nelson-Jameson Inc 2400 E 5th St PO Box 647 *TF:* 800-826-8302 ■ *Web:* www.nelsonjameson.com	Marshfield	WI	54449	715-387-1151	387-8746
New England Industrial Truck Inc 195 Wildwood Ave *Web:* www.neit.com	Woburn	MA	01801	781-935-9105	938-3879
Newman's Inc 1300 Gazin St *TF:* 800-231-3505 ■ *Web:* www.newcovalves.com	Houston	TX	77020	713-675-8631	675-1589
NSC International 7090 Central Ave **Fax Area Code:* 800 ■ *TF:* 800-643-1520 ■ *Web:* www.binding.com	Hot Springs	AR	71913	501-525-0133	960-2727*
Nu-Life Environmental Inc PO Box 1527 *TF:* 800-654-1752 ■ *Web:* www.nulifeenv.com	Easley	SC	29641	864-295-2183	295-2707
O Berk Co 3 Milltown Ct *TF:* 800-631-7392 ■ *Web:* www.oberk.com	Union	NJ	07083	908-851-9500	851-9367
Ohio Transmission & Pump Co 1900 Rimrock Rd *TF:* 800-837-6827 ■ *Web:* www.otpnet.com	Columbus	OH	43219	614-342-6123	342-6490
Pacific Power Products 600 S 56th Pl *TF:* 800-882-3860 ■ *Web:* www.pacificdda.com	Ridgefield	WA	98642	360-887-7400	887-7401
Pearce Industries Inc PO Box 35068 *Web:* www.wpi.com	Houston	TX	77235	713-723-1050	551-0454
Peerless Supply Inc PO Box 3307 *Web:* www.peerless-supply.com	Des Moines	IA	50316	515-265-9905	265-4385
Phenix Supply Co 5330 Dividend Dr *TF:* 800-688-3032 ■ *Web:* www.phenixsupply.com	Decatur	GA	30035	770-981-2800	981-6462
Piping & Equipment Inc 9100 Canniff St *TF:* 800-364-9384 ■ *Web:* www.pipingequipment.com	Houston	TX	77017	713-947-9393	948-9559
Pitman Co 721 Union Blvd *TF:* 800-631-3128 ■ *Web:* www.pitmanco.com	Totowa	NJ	07512	973-812-0400	812-1630
Poclain Hydraulics Inc PO Box 801 *Web:* www.poclain-hydraulics.com	Sturtevant	WI	53177	262-321-0676	554-4860
Power & Pumps Inc 803 N Myrtle Ave *TF:* 800-226-5050 ■ *Web:* www.powerandpumps.com	Jacksonville	FL	32204	904-356-5881	356-8717
Precision Industries Inc 4611 S 96th St *TF:* 800-373-7777 ■ *Web:* www.precisionind.com	Omaha	NE	68127	402-593-7000	593-7054
Premier Equipment Inc 990 Sunshine Ln *Web:* www.premierequipment.com	Altamonte Springs	FL	32714	407-786-2000	786-2001
Production Tool Supply 8655 E Eight Mile Rd **Fax:* Sales ■ *TF:* 800-366-3600 ■ *Web:* www.pts-tools.com	Warren	MI	48089	586-755-7770	755-2151*
R & M Energy Systems 301 Premier Rd *TF Sales:* 800-858-4158 ■ *Web:* www.rmenergy.com	Borger	TX	79008	806-274-5293	274-3418
R B M Co 2700 Texas Ave PO Box 12 *TF:* 800-521-5656 ■ *Web:* www.rbmcompany.com	Knoxville	TN	37901	865-524-8621	546-7326
Red Ball Oxygen Co Inc PO Box 7316 *TF:* 800-325-4578 ■ *Web:* www.redballoxygen.com	Shreveport	LA	71137	318-425-3211	425-6310
Rem Sales Inc 910 Gay Hill Rd *TF:* 800-808-1020 ■ *Web:* www.remsales.com	Windsor	CT	06095	860-687-3400	687-3401
Remstar International Inc 41 Eisenhower Dr *TF:* 800-234-3654 ■ *Web:* www.kardexremstar.com	Westbrook	ME	04092	207-854-1861	854-1610
Renishaw Inc 5277 Trillium Blvd *Web:* www.renishaw.com	Hoffman Estates	IL	60192	847-286-9953	286-9974
Rex Supply Co 3715 Harrisburg Blvd *TF:* 800-369-0669 ■ *Web:* www.rex-supply.com	Houston	TX	77003	713-222-2251	225-5739
RHM Fluid Power Inc 375 Manufacturers Dr *Web:* www.rhmfluidpower.com	Westland	MI	48186	734-326-5400	326-0339
Richards G.e. Graphic Supplies Midwest Inc PO Box 339 *TF:* 800-233-0410 ■ *Web:* www.gerichards.com	Landisville	PA	17538	717-898-3151	898-9083
Riekes Equipment Co PO Box 3392 *TF:* 800-856-0931 ■ *Web:* www.riekesequipment.com	Omaha	NE	68103	402-593-1181	593-9295
Road Builders Machinery & Supply Co Inc 1001 S 7th St *Web:* www.roadbuildersmachinery.com	Kansas City	KS	66105	913-371-3822	371-3870
Robert Dietrick Co Inc PO Box 605 *Web:* www.rd-co.com	Fishers	IN	46038	317-842-1991	842-2698
Robert E Morris Co 910 Gay Hill Rd *TF:* 800-223-0785 ■ *Web:* www.robertemorris.com	Windsor	CT	06095	860-687-3300	687-3301
RS Hughes Co Inc 10639 Glenoaks Blvd *TF:* 877-774-8443 ■ *Web:* www.rshughes.com	Pacoima	CA	91331	818-686-9111	686-1973
Ryan Herco Products Corp 3010 N San Fernando Blvd *TF:* 800-848-1141 ■ *Web:* www.ryanherco.com	Burbank	CA	91504	818-841-1141	973-2600
S&K /Air Power 317 Dewitt Ave E PO Box 1279 *Web:* www.skairpower.com	Mattoon	IL	61938	217-258-8500	258-8571
S. J. Smith Co Inc 3707 W River Dr *Web:* www.sjsmith.com	Davenport	IA	52802	563-263-1829	324-1336
S.l.c. Meter Service Inc 10375 Dixie Hwy *TF:* 800-433-4332 ■ *Web:* www.slcmeter.com	Davisburg	MI	48350	248-625-0667	625-8650
Service Motor Co PO Box 170 *Web:* www.servicemotor.com	Dale	WI	54931	920-779-4311	667-5330
Shively Bros Inc 2919 S Grand Travers St PO Box 1520 *TF:* 800-530-9352 ■ *Web:* www.shivelybros.com	Flint	MI	48501	810-232-7401	232-3219
Smith Power Products Inc 3065 W California Ave *TF:* 800-658-5352 ■ *Web:* www.smithpowerproducts.com	Salt Lake City	UT	84104	801-415-5000	415-5700
Sooner Pipe LLC 1331 Lamar St Suite 970 4 Houston Ctr *TF:* 800-888-9161 ■ *Web:* www.soonerpipe.com	Houston	TX	77010	713-759-1200	759-0442
Southern Pump & Tank Co 4800 N Graham St *TF Cust Svc:* 800-477-2826 ■ *Web:* www.southernpump.com	Charlotte	NC	28269	704-596-4373	599-7700
Stanley M Proctor Co 2016 Midway Dr *TF:* 800-352-0123 ■ *Web:* www.stanleyproctor.com	Twinsburg	OH	44087	330-425-7814	425-3222
Star CNC Machine Tool Corp 123 Powerhouse Rd *TF:* 800-377-4006 ■ *Web:* www.starcnc.com	Roslyn Heights	NY	11577	516-484-0500	484-5820

Company	City	State	Zip	Phone	Fax
Strategic Distribution Inc 1414 Radcliffe St Suite 300 *NASDAQ: STRD* ■ *TF:* 800-322-2644 ■ *Web:* www.sdi.com	Bristol	PA	19007	215-633-1900	633-4426
Swift Industrial Power Inc 10917 McBride Ln *Web:* www.swiftpower.com	Knoxville	TN	37932	865-966-9758	
Tate Engineering Systems Inc 1560 Caton Ctr Dr *TF:* 800-800-8283 ■ *Web:* www.tate.com	Baltimore	MD	21227	410-242-8800	242-7777
Teeco Products Inc 16881 Armstrong Ave *TF:* 800-854-3463 ■ *Web:* www.teecoproducts.com	Irvine	CA	92606	949-261-6295	474-8663
Tencarva Machinery Co Inc 12200 Wilfong Ct *Web:* www.tencarva.com	Midlothian	VA	23112	804-639-4646	639-2400
Texas Process Equipment Co 5215 Ted St *TF:* 800-828-4114 ■ *Web:* www.texasprocess.com	Houston	TX	77040	713-460-5555	460-4807
Total Equipment Co 400 5th Ave *Web:* www.totalequipment.com	Coraopolis	PA	15108	412-269-0999	269-0262
Tox-Pressotechnik LLC 4250 Weaver Pkwy *Web:* www.tox-us.com	Warrenville	IL	60555	630-393-0300	393-6800
Travers Tool Co Inc 128-15 26th Ave **Fax Area Code:* 800 ■ *TF Cust Svc:* 800-221-0270 ■ *Web:* www.travers.com	Flushing	NY	11354	718-886-7200	722-0703*
Turck Inc 3000 Campus Dr *Web:* www.turck.com	Minneapolis	MN	55441	763-553-7300	553-0708
Ulvac Technologies Inc 401 Griffin Brook Dr *TF:* 800-998-5822 ■ *Web:* www.ulvac.com	Methuen	MA	01844	978-686-7550	689-6300
Valtra Inc 7141 Paramount Blvd *TF:* 800-989-5244 ■ *Web:* www.valtrainc.com	Pico Rivera	CA	90660	562-949-8625	
Vellano Bros Inc 7 Hemlock St *TF:* 800-342-9855 ■ *Web:* www.vellano.com	Latham	NY	12110	518-785-5537	785-5578
Voto Manufacturers Sales Co 500 N 3rd St PO Box 1299 *TF:* 800-848-4010 ■ *Web:* www.votosales.com	Steubenville	OH	43952	740-282-3621	282-5441
W W Engine & Supply Inc PO Box 68 *TF:* 800-248-6225 ■ *Web:* www.wwengine.com	Kylertown	PA	16847	814-345-5693	245-6026
Werres Corp 807 E S St **Fax:* Sales ■ *TF:* 800-638-6563 ■ *Web:* www.werres.com	Frederick	MD	21701	301-620-4000	662-1028*
Wilson Supply Co 1302 Conti St *NYSE: SOB* ■ *TF:* 800-228-3194 ■ *Web:* www.iwilson.com	Houston	TX	77002	713-237-3700	237-3433
Windsor Factory Supply Ltd 730 N Service Rd *TF:* 800-387-2659 ■ *Web:* www.wfsltd.com	Windsor	ON	N8X3J3	519-966-2202	966-2740
Wolseley Industrial Products Group 680 Davenport Rd *TF:* 888-447-4123 ■ *Web:* www.wolseleyinc.ca	Waterloo	ON	N2V2C3	519-885-6500	747-4133
Yamazen Inc 735 E Remington Rd *TF:* 800-882-8558 ■ *Web:* www.yamazen.com	Schaumburg	IL	60173	847-490-8130	490-3192
Yanmar America Corp 101 International Parkwy *Web:* www.yanmar.com	Adairsville	GA	30103	770-877-9894	877-9009
Zatkoff Seals & Packings 23230 Industrial Pk Dr *TF:* 800-967-3257 ■ *Web:* www.zatkoff.com	Farmington Hills	MI	48335	248-478-2400	478-3392
Zuckerman-Honickman Inc 191 S Gulph Rd *TF:* 800-523-1475 ■ *Web:* www.zh-inc.com	King of Prussia	PA	19406	610-962-0100	962-1080

389 INDUSTRIAL MACHINERY, EQUIPMENT, & SUPPLIES

SEE ALSO Conveyors & Conveying Equipment p. 1762; Food Products Machinery p. 1873; Furnaces & Ovens - Industrial Process p. 1893; Machine Shops p. 2190; Material Handling Equipment p. 2221; Packaging Machinery & Equipment p. 2331; Paper Industries Machinery p. 2337; Printing & Publishing Equipment & Systems p. 2454; Rolling Mill Machinery p. 2628; Textile Machinery p. 2707; Woodworking Machinery p. 2779

Company	City	State	Zip	Phone	Fax
3G Tech Inc 6910 Hayvenhurst Ave Suite 100 *Web:* www.gggtech.com	Van Nuys	CA	91406	818-510-4709	510-4716
ABB Inc 501 Merritt 7 *TF Prod Info:* 800-626-4999 ■ *Web:* www.abb.us	Norwalk	CT	06851	203-750-2200	435-7365
Accu Therm Inc PO Box 249 *TF:* 888-925-4332 ■ *Web:* www.accutherm.com	Monroe City	MO	63456	573-735-1060	735-1066
Acme Electric N85 W12545 Westbrook Crossing **Fax Area Code:* 262 ■ *TF:* 800-334-5214 ■ *Web:* www.acmepowerdist.com	Menomonee Falls	WI	53051	910-738-1121	293-7022*
Acorn Gencon Plastics Inc 13818 Oaks Ave *Web:* www.whitehallmfg.com	Chino	CA	91710	909-591-8461	
Adept Technology Inc 5960 Inglewood Dr *NASDAQ: ADEP* ■ *TF:* 800-292-3378 ■ *Web:* www.adept.com	Pleasanton	CA	94588	925-245-3400	960-0452
Advance Ross Electronics Corp 3000 E Marshall Ave *Web:* www.ppcesp.com	Longview	TX	75601	903-758-3395	758-6487
Advanced Assembly Automation 313 Mound St *Web:* www.assembly-testww.com	Dayton	OH	45402	937-222-3030	222-2931
Advent Design Corp Canal St & Jefferson Ave *TF:* 800-959-0310 ■ *Web:* www.adventdesign.com	Bristol	PA	19007	215-781-0500	781-0508
Aeroglide Corp 100 Aeroglide Dr *TF:* 800-722-7483 ■ *Web:* www.aeroglide.com	Cary	NC	27511	919-851-2000	851-6029
Airtech International Inc 5700 Skylab Rd *Web:* www.airtechintl.com	Huntington Beach	CA	92647	714-899-8100	899-8179
Alemite LLC 1057-521 Corporate Ctr Dr Suite 100 *TF:* 800-267-8022 ■ *Web:* www.alemite.com	Fort Mill	SC	29715	803-802-0001	802-0198
Allen-Sherman-Hoff Co 457 Creamery Way	Exton	PA	19341	484-875-1600	875-2080
Allentown Equipment 421 Schantz Rd *TF:* 800-553-3414 ■ *Web:* www.allentownequipment.com	Allentown	PA	18104	610-398-0451	391-1934
Allentown Inc PO Box 698 *Web:* www.allentowninc.com	Allentown	NJ	08501	609-259-7951	259-0772
American Baler Co 800 E Centre St *TF:* 800-843-7512 ■ *Web:* www.americanbaler.com	Bellevue	OH	44811	419-483-5790	483-3815
AO Smith Water Products Co 500 Tennessee Waltz Pkwy **Fax Area Code:* 615 ■ *TF:* 800-527-1953 ■ *Web:* www.hotwater.com	Ashland City	TN	37015	800-527-1953	792-2163*
Apache Stainless Equipment Corp 200 W Industrial Dr PO Box 538 *TF:* 800-444-0398 ■ *Web:* www.apachestainless.com	Beaver Dam	WI	53916	920-887-3721	887-0206
Assembly Technology & Test 400 Florence St *Web:* www.assembly-testww.com	Saginaw	MI	48602	989-791-6400	791-6486
Ats Systems Oregon Inc 2121 NE Jack London St *Web:* www.atsautomation.com	Corvallis	OR	97330	541-758-3329	758-9022
Auto Chlor System 450 Ferguson Dr *Web:* www.autochlor.net	Mountain View	CA	94043	650-967-3085	
Azon USA Inc 643 W Crosstown Pkwy *TF:* 800-788-5942 ■ *Web:* www.azonintl.com	Kalamazoo	MI	49008	269-385-5942	373-6195
Bauer-Pileco 111 Berry Rd PO Box 16099 *TF:* 800-474-5326 ■ *Web:* www.pileco.com	Houston	TX	77222	713-691-3000	691-0089
Besser Co 801 Johnson St *TF:* 800-530-9980 ■ *Web:* www.besser.com	Alpena	MI	49707	989-354-4111	354-3120
Besser Lithibar Co 13521 Quality Dr *TF:* 800-626-0415 ■ *Web:* www.besser.com	Holland	MI	49424	616-399-5215	399-4026
Billco Mfg Inc 100 Halstead Blvd *Web:* www.billco-mfg.com	Zelienople	PA	16063	724-452-7390	452-0217
Blower Application Co Inc N 114 W 19125 Clinton Dr *TF:* 800-959-0880 ■ *Web:* www.bloapco.com	Germantown	WI	53022	262-255-5580	255-3446
Burke E Porter Machinery Co 730 Plymouth Ave NE *Web:* www.bepco.com	Grand Rapids	MI	49505	616-459-9531	459-1032
Cantwell Machinery Co 3180 Valleyview Dr PO Box 44130 *Web:* www.cantwellmachinery.com	Columbus	OH	43204	614-276-5171	279-6287
CHA Industries 4201 Business Ctr Dr **Fax:* Sales ■ *Web:* www.chaindustries.com	Fremont	CA	94538	510-683-8554	683-3848*
Charles Ross & Son Co 710 Old Willets Path *TF:* 800-243-7677 ■ *Web:* www.mixers.com	Hauppauge	NY	11788	631-234-0500	234-0691
Chemineer Inc 5870 Poe Ave **Fax:* Sales ■ *TF:* 800-643-0641 ■ *Web:* www.chemineer.com	Dayton	OH	45414	937-454-3200	454-3379*
Chemithon Corp 5430 W Marginal Way SW *Web:* www.chemithon.com	Seattle	WA	98106	206-937-9954	932-3786
Chief Automotive Systems Inc 1924 E 4th St **Fax:* Mktg ■ *TF:* 800-445-9262 ■ *Web:* www.chiefautomotive.com	Grand Island	NE	68801	308-384-9747	384-8966*
Clean Diesel Technologies Inc 4567 Telephone Rd Suite 206 *NASDAQ: CDTID* ■ **Fax Area Code:* 905 ■ *TF:* 800-661-9963 ■ *Web:* www.cdti.com	Ventura	CA	93003	805-639-9458	707-7746*
Clemco Industries Corp l Cable Car Dr **Fax Area Code:* 800 ■ *Web:* www.clemcoindustries.com	Washington	MO	63090	636-239-0300	726-7559*
Cma Dishmachines 12700 Knott St *TF:* 800-854-6417 ■ *Web:* www.cmadishmachines.com	Garden Grove	CA	92841	714-898-8781	891-9836
Cohesant Inc 23400 Commerce Pk *PINK: COHY* ■ *Web:* www.cohesant.com	Beachwood	OH	44122	216-910-1700	
Comau Pico 21000 Telegraph Rd *Web:* www.comaupico.com	Southfield	MI	48034	248-353-8888	368-2511
Concept Packaging Group 6 Nesbitt Dr *TF:* 800-868-4808 ■ *Web:* www.concept-pkg.com	Inman	SC	29349	864-578-0085	578-4755
Concrete Forming Equipment & Engineering Corp (CFEE) 305 S New Albany Ave *TF:* 800-590-2448	Sellersberg	IN	47172	812-246-8088	246-8833
Corotec Corp 145 Hyde Rd *TF:* 800-423-0348 ■ *Web:* www.corotec.com	Farmington	CT	06032	860-678-0038	674-5229
CUNO Inc 400 Research Pkwy *TF:* 800-243-6894 ■ *Web:* www.cuno.com	Meriden	CT	06450	203-237-5541	238-8701
Davis-Ulmer Sprinkler Co Inc 1 Commerce Dr *TF:* 877-691-3200 ■ *Web:* www.davisulmer.com	Amherst	NY	14228	716-691-3200	691-1230
Despatch Industries Inc 8860 207th St W *Web:* www.despatch.com	Lakeville	MN	55044	952-469-5424	469-4513
Diamond Power International Inc 2600 E Main St *TF:* 800-848-5086 ■ *Web:* www.diamondpower.com	Lancaster	OH	43130	740-687-6500	687-4229
Dings Co 4740 W Electric Ave *Web:* www.dingsbrakes.com	Milwaukee	WI	53219	414-672-7830	672-7830
Dom-Ex LLC 109 Grant St PO Box 877 *Web:* www.dom-ex.com	Hibbing	MN	55746	218-262-6116	263-8611
Donaldson Co Inc 1400 W 94th St *NYSE: DCI* ■ *Web:* www.donaldson.com	Bloomington	MN	55431	952-887-3131	887-3155
Dorr-Oliver Eimco USA Inc 2850 S Decker Lake Dr *TF:* 800-257-0552 ■ *Web:* www.glv.com	Salt Lake City	UT	84119	801-526-2000	526-2543
Dresser-Rand West8 Tower Suite 1000 10205 Westheimer Rd *NYSE: DRC* ■ *Web:* www.dresser-rand.com	Houston	TX	77042	713-354-6100	354-6110
Dynamic Mfg Inc 1930 N Mannheim Rd *Web:* www.dynamicmanufacturinginc.com	Melrose Park	IL	60160	708-343-8753	343-8768
Easom Automation Systems Inc 32471 Industrial Dr *Web:* www.easomeng.com	Madison Heights	MI	48071	248-307-0650	307-0701
Ecodyne Ltd 4475 Corporate Dr *TF:* 888-326-3963 ■ *Web:* www.ecodyne.com	Burlington	ON	L7L5T9	905-332-1404	332-6726
EFD Induction Inc 31511 Dequindre Rd *Web:* www.efd-induction.com	Madison Heights	MI	48071	248-658-0700	658-0701
Elliott Tape Inc 1882 Pond Run *Web:* www.egitape.com	Auburn Hills	MI	48326	248-475-2000	475-5893

Company	City	State	Zip	Phone	Fax
Enerflex Systems Ltd 1331 Macleod Trail SE Suite 904 *TSX: EFX* ■ *TF:* 800-242-3178 ■ *Web:* www.enerflex.com	Calgary	AB	T2GOK3	403-387-6377	
Energy Sciences Inc 42 Industrial Way *Web:* www.ebeam.com	Wilmington	MA	01887	978-694-9000	694-9046
Engis Corp 105 W Hintz Rd *TF:* 800-993-6447 ■ *Web:* www.engis.com	Wheeling	IL	60090	847-808-9400	808-9430
Enterprise Co 616 S Santa Fe St *Web:* www.enterpriseco.com	Santa Ana	CA	92705	714-835-0541	543-2856
Entwistle Co The 6 Bigelow St *Web:* www.entwistleco.com	Hudson	MA	01749	508-481-4000	481-4004
Equipment Mfg Corp (EMC) 14930 Marquardt Ave *TF:* 888-833-9000 ■ *Web:* www.equipmentmanufacturing.com	Santa Fe Springs	CA	90670	562-623-9394	623-9342
Facilitec USA Inc 2410 Vantage Dr *TF:* 800-284-8273 ■ *Web:* www.facilitec-corp.com	Elgin	IL	60124	800-284-8273	
FANUC Robotics North America Inc 3900 W Hamlin Rd *TF:* 800-477-6268 ■ *Web:* www.fanucrobotics.com	Rochester Hills	MI	48309	248-377-7000	377-7832
Farrel Corp 25 Main St *TF:* 800-800-7290 ■ *Web:* www.farrel.com	Ansonia	CT	06401	203-736-5500	735-6267
Fluid Management Inc 1023 S Wheeling Rd *TF:* 800-462-2466 ■ *Web:* www.fluidman.com	Wheeling	IL	60090	847-537-0880	537-3221
Formaloy Corp 1080 W Jefferson St	Morton	IL	61550	309-266-5381	263-0366
Forward Technology Industries Inc 3050 Ranchview Ln N *TF Cust Svc:* 800-307-6040 ■ *Web:* www.forwardtech.com	Minneapolis	MN	55447	763-559-1785	559-3929
Foster Wheeler Energy International Inc Perryville Corporate Pk *Web:* www.fwc.com	Clinton	NJ	08809	908-730-4000	730-5315
French Oil Mill Machinery Co 1035 W Greene St *Web:* www.frenchoil.com	Piqua	OH	45356	937-773-3420	773-3424
Fusion Inc 4658 E 355th St *TF:* 800-626-9501 ■ *Web:* www.fusion-inc.com	Willoughby	OH	44094	440-946-3300	942-9083
Galbreath Inc 461 E Rosser Dr *TF:* 800-285-0666 ■ *Web:* www.galbreath-inc.com	Winamac	IN	46996	574-946-6631	946-4579
Gamajet Cleaning Systems Inc 604 Jeffers Cir *TF Sales:* 877-426-2538 ■ *Web:* www.gamajet.com	Exton	PA	19341	610-408-9940	408-9945
GEA Niro Inc 9165 Rumsey Rd *TF:* 800-446-4231 ■ *Web:* www.niroinc.com	Columbia	MD	21045	410-997-8700	997-5021
General Equipment Co 620 Alexander Dr SW PO Box 334 *TF Cust Svc:* 800-533-0524 ■ *Web:* www.generalequip.com	Owatonna	MN	55060	507-451-5510	451-5511
Genmark Automation Inc 1201 Cadillac Ct *TF:* 866-467-6268 ■ *Web:* www.genmarkautomation.com	Milpitas	CA	95035	408-678-8500	942-7561
George Koch Sons LLC 10 S 11th Ave **Fax:* Sales ■ *TF:* 888-873-5624 ■ *Web:* www.kochllc.com	Evansville	IN	47744	812-465-9600	465-9676*
Gerber Scientific Inc 24 Industrial Pk Rd W *NYSE: GRB* ■ *Web:* www.gerberscientific.com	Tolland	CT	06084	860-870-2890	870-2891
Glastender Inc 5400 N Michigan Rd *TF:* 800-748-0423 ■ *Web:* www.glastender.com	Saginaw	MI	48604	989-752-4275	752-4444
Globe Products Inc 5051 Kitridge Rd *Web:* www.globe-usa.com	Dayton	OH	45424	937-233-0233	233-5290
Glunt Industries Inc 319 N River Rd NW *Web:* www.glunt.com	Warren	OH	44483	330-399-7585	393-0387
GLV Inc 2001 Mc Gill College Suite 2100 2nd Fl *TSE: GLV.B* ■ *Web:* www.glv.com	Montreal	QC	H3A1G1	514-284-2224	284-2225
Gougler Industries Inc 705 Lake St *TF:* 800-527-2282 ■ *Web:* www.gougler.com	Kent	OH	44240	330-673-5821	673-5824
Graham Corp 20 Florence Ave *AMEX: GHM* ■ *TF Orders:* 800-828-8150 ■ *Web:* www.graham-mfg.com	Batavia	NY	14020	585-343-2216	343-1097
Gregory Poole Equipment Co 4807 Beryl Rd PO Box 469 *TF:* 800-451-7278 ■ *Web:* www.gregorypoole.com	Raleigh	NC	27606	919-828-0641	890-4389
Grenzebach Corp 10 Herring Rd *Web:* www.grenzebach.com	Newnan	GA	30265	770-253-4980	253-5189
Guzzler Mfg Inc 1621 S Illinois St **Fax:* Sales ■ *Web:* www.guzzler.com	Streator	IL	61364	815-672-3171	672-2779*
Hamon Research-Cottrell Inc 58 E Main St *TF:* 800-722-7580 ■ *Web:* www.hamon-researchcottrell.com	Somerville	NJ	08876	908-685-4000	333-2152
Harrington Hoists Inc 401 W End Ave *TF:* 800-233-3010 ■ *Web:* www.harringtonhoists.com	Manheim	PA	17545	717-665-2000	665-2861
Helgesen Industries Inc 7261 Hwy 60 W *TF:* 866-628-9488 ■ *Web:* www.helgesen.com	Hartford	WI	53027	262-673-4444	709-4409
Hfw Industries Inc 196 Philadelphia St PO Box 8 *Web:* www.hfwindustries.com	Buffalo	NY	14207	716-875-3380	875-3385
Hirotec America Inc 4567 Glenmeade Ln *Web:* www.hirotecamerica.com	Auburn Hills	MI	48326	248-836-5100	836-5101
Holtec International Inc 1001 N US Hwy 1 Suite 204 *Web:* www.holtecinternational.com	Jupiter	FL	33477	856-797-0900	797-0909
Hosokawa Micron Powder Systems 10 Chatham Rd *Web:* www.hosokawamicron.com	Summit	NJ	07901	908-273-6360	273-6344
Hosokawa Polymer Systems 63 Fuller Way *TF:* 800-233-6112 ■ *Web:* www.polysys.com	Berlin	CT	06037	860-828-0541	829-1313
Husky Injection Molding Systems Ltd 500 Queen St S *TSX: HKY* ■ *Web:* www.husky.ca	Bolton	ON	L7E5S5	905-951-5000	951-5384
Hydro-Thermal Corp 400 Pilot Ct *TF:* 800-952-0121 ■ *Web:* www.hydro-thermal.com	Waukesha	WI	53188	262-548-8900	548-8908
Illinois Tool Works Inc (ITW) 3600 W Lake Ave *NYSE: ITW* ■ *TF:* 800-724-6166 ■ *Web:* www.itwinc.com	Glenview	IL	60026	847-724-7500	657-4261
Industrial Fabricators Inc 403 N Cemetery St	Thorp	WI	54771	715-669-5512	669-5514
ITW United Silicone 4471 Walden Ave *Web:* www.unitedsilicone.com	Lancaster	NY	14086	716-681-8222	681-8789
Jesco-Wipco Industries Inc 950 Anderson Rd PO Box 388 *TF:* 888-463-1246 ■ *Web:* www.jescoonline.com	Litchfield	MI	49252	517-542-2903	542-2501
John Dusenbery Co Inc 220 Franklin Rd *Web:* www.dusenbery.com	Randolph	NJ	07869	973-366-7500	366-7453
Jv Mfg Inc 701 Butterfield Coach Rd PO Box 229 *TF:* 800-678-7320 ■ *Web:* www.cram-a-lot.com	Springdale	AR	72765	479-751-7320	872-0037
K & B Machine Works Inc 212 Redmond Rd PO Box 10265 *TF:* 800-256-1526 ■ *Web:* www.kb-machine.com	Houma	LA	70363	985-868-6730	868-6036
Kanematsu USA Inc 75 Rockefeller Plaza 22nd Fl *Web:* www.kanematsuusa.com	New York	NY	10019	212-704-9400	704-9483
Kawasaki Robotics Inc 28140 Lakeview Dr *Web:* www.kawasakirobotics.com	Wixom	MI	48393	248-446-4100	446-4200
KJ Brewco Collision Repair Systems Inc 309 Exchange Ave *TF:* 800-582-5215 ■ *Web:* www.kansasjack.com	Conway	AR	72032	501-450-1500	450-2085
Kobelco Stewart Bolling Inc (KSBI) 1600 Terex Rd *TF:* 800-464-0064 ■ *Web:* www.ksbiusa.com	Hudson	OH	44236	330-655-3111	656-2982
Koch Membrane Systems Inc 850 Main St *TF:* 800-343-0499 ■ *Web:* www.kochmembrane.com	Wilmington	MA	01887	978-694-7000	657-5208
Koch-Glitsch Inc 4111 E 37th St N *Web:* www.koch-glitsch.com	Wichita	KS	67220	316-828-5110	828-5263
Kois Bros Equipment Co Inc 5200 Colorado Blvd *TF:* 800-672-6010 ■ *Web:* www.koisbrothers.com	Commerce City	CO	80022	303-298-7370	298-8527
Komatsu America Industries LLC 1701 W Golf Rd Suite 300 *Web:* www.komatsupress.com	Rolling Meadows	IL	60008	847-437-3888	437-1811
Komline-Sanderson Engineering Corp 12 Holland Ave *TF:* 800-225-5457 ■ *Web:* www.komline.com	Peapack	NJ	07977	908-234-1000	234-9487
Lapoint Industries Inc PO Box 1970 *Web:* www.strainrite.com	Auburn	ME	04211	207-777-3100	777-3177
Lawton Industries Inc 4353 Pacific St *TF:* 800-692-2600 ■ *Web:* www.lawtonindustries.com	Rocklin	CA	95677	916-624-7894	624-7898
Ldi Industries Inc PO Box 1810 *Web:* www.ldi-industries.com	Manitowoc	WI	54221	920-682-6877	684-7210
Lee Industries Inc 50 W Pine St *Web:* www.leeind.com	Philipsburg	PA	16866	814-342-0461	342-5660
Lesman Instrument Co 135 Bernice Dr *TF:* 800-953-7626 ■ *Web:* www.lesman.com	Bensenville	IL	60106	630-595-8400	595-2386
Leviathan Corp 20 Jay St *Web:* www.leviathancorp.com	Brooklyn	NY	11201	718-701-5718	701-5745
Lightnin 135 Mt Read Blvd *Web:* www.lightninmixers.com	Rochester	NY	14611	585-436-5550	436-5589
Ligon Industries LLC 1927 1st Ave N 5th Fl *Web:* www.ligonindustries.com	Birmingham	AL	35203	205-322-3302	322-3188
Lincoln Industrial Corp 1 Lincoln Way **Fax Area Code:* 800 ■ **Fax:* Cust Svc ■ *Web:* www.lincolnindustrial.com	Saint Louis	MO	63120	314-679-4200	424-5359*
Littleford Day Inc 7451 Empire Dr *TF:* 800-365-8555 ■ *Web:* www.littleford.com	Florence	KY	41042	859-525-7600	525-1446
Lmt USA Inc 1081 S Northpoint Blvd **Fax Area Code:* 630 ■ *TF:* 800-225-0852 ■ *Web:* www.lmtfette.com	Waukegan	IL	60085	800-225-0852	969-5492*
Lynch Systems Inc 601 Independent St *TF:* 800-428-6333	Bainbridge	GA	39817	229-248-2345	243-0987
M-b Cos Inc Of Wisconsin 1615 Wisconsin Ave PO Box 200 *TF:* 800-558-5800 ■ *Web:* www.m-bco.com	New Holstein	WI	53061	920-898-4203	898-4588
Marathon Equipment Co 950 County Hwy 9 S PO Box 1798 *TF Mktg:* 800-269-7237 ■ *Web:* www.marathon-equipment.com	Vernon	AL	35592	205-695-9105	695-8813
Mark-Costello Co The 1145 E Dominguez St *Web:* www.mark-costello.com	CARSON	CA	90746	310-637-1851	762-2330
Maruka USA Inc 400 Commons Way *Web:* www.marukausa.com	Rockaway	NJ	07866	973-983-1000	983-8647
Material Handling Supply Inc 15 Old Salem Rd *TF:* 877-647-9320 ■ *Web:* www.mhslift.com	Gloucester City	NJ	08030	856-541-1290	456-1245
Materials Transportation Co (MTC) 1408 S Commerce PO Box 1358 *TF:* 800-433-3110 ■ *Web:* www.mtcworldwide.com	Temple	TX	76503	254-298-2900	771-0287
McCarty Equipment Co Ltd 1103 Industrial Blvd PO Box 1841 *Web:* www.mccartyequipment.com	Abilene	TX	79604	325-691-5558	691-5453
McKesson Automation Corp 500 Cranberry Wood Dr *TF:* 800-700-8737 ■ *Web:* www.robot-rx.com	Cranberry Township	PA	16066	724-741-8000	741-8002
McNeil & NRM Inc 96 E Crosier St *TF:* 800-669-2525 ■ *Web:* www.mcneilnrm.com	Akron	OH	44311	330-253-2525	253-5612
MEGTEC Systems Inc 830 Prosper Rd *TF Cust Svc:* 800-558-5535 ■ *Web:* www.megtec.com	De Pere	WI	54115	920-336-5715	336-3404
Met-Pro Corp 160 Cassell Rd PO Box 144 *NYSE: MPR* ■ *TF:* 800-722-3267 ■ *Web:* www.met-pro.com	Harleysville	PA	19438	215-723-6751	723-6758
Met-Pro Corp Mefiag Div 1550 Industrial Dr *Web:* www.met-pro.com	Owosso	MI	48867	989-725-8184	729-1013
Metem Corp 700 Parsippany Rd *Web:* www.metem.com	Parsippany	NJ	07054	973-887-6635	887-1755
MFRI Inc 7720 N Lehigh Ave *NASDAQ: MFRI* ■ *Web:* www.mfri.com	Niles	IL	60714	847-966-1000	966-8563
Michigan Fluid Power Inc 4556 Spartan Industrial Dr SW *Web:* www.mifp.com	Grandville	MI	49418	616-538-5700	538-0888
Michigan Wheel Corp 1501 Buchanan Ave SW *TF:* 800-369-4335 ■ *Web:* www.miwheel.com	Grand Rapids	MI	49507	616-452-6941	247-0227
Mico Inc 1911 Lee Blvd *TF:* 800-477-6426 ■ *Web:* www.mico.com	North Mankato	MN	56003	507-625-6426	625-3212
Micro-Poise Measurment Systems LLC 1624 Englewood Ave *Web:* www.micropoise.com	Akron	OH	44305	330-784-1251	798-0250
Milacron Inc 3010 Disney St *NYSE: MZ* ■ *Web:* www.milacron.com	Cincinnati	OH	45209	513-487-5000	487-5086
Minuteman International Inc 111 S Rohlwing Rd *TF:* 800-323-9420 ■ *Web:* www.minutemanintl.com	Addison	IL	60101	630-627-6900	627-1130

Phone Fax

Mississippi Welders Supply Co
5150 W 6th St PO Box 1036 . . . . Winona MN 55987 507-454-5231 454-8104
TF: 800-657-4422 ■ *Web:* www.mwsco.com

Monroe Environmental Corp 810 W Front St . . . . Monroe MI 48161 734-242-7654 242-5275
TF: 800-992-7707 ■ *Web:* www.monroeenvironmental.com

Moody-Price LLC PO Box 260044 . . . . Baton Rouge LA 70826 225-767-7755 763-6005
TF: 800-272-9832 ■ *Web:* www.moodyprice.com

Morrell Inc 333 Bald Mountain Rd . . . . Auburn Hills MI 48326 248-373-1600 373-0612
Web: www.morrellinc.com

Mueller Graphic Supply Inc
11475 W Thdore Trcker Way . . . . Milwaukee WI 53214 414-475-0990 475-0454
Web: www.muellergraphics.com

Mueller Steam Specialty 1491 NC Hwy 20 W . . . . Saint Pauls NC 28384 910-865-8241 865-8245
TF: 800-334-6259 ■ *Web:* www.muellersteam.com

National Super Service Co Inc
3115 Frenchman Rd . . . . Toledo OH 43607 419-531-2121 531-3761
TF Cust Svc: 800-677-1663 ■ *Web:* www.nss.com

Netzsch Inc 119 Pickering Way . . . . Exton PA 19341 610-363-8010 363-0971
Web: www.netzschusa.com

Neumayer Equipment Co Inc
5060 Arsenal St . . . . Saint Louis MO 63139 314-772-4501 772-2311
TF: 800-843-4563 ■ *Web:* www.neumayerequipment.com

New 9 Inc 1411 Michigan St Ne . . . . Grand Rapids MI 49503 616-459-8274 459-3390
Web: www.gwiengineering.com

Nexen Group Inc 560 Oak Grove Pkwy . . . . Vadnais Heights MN 55127 651-484-5900 286-1099
Web: www.nexengroup.com

Nilfisk-Advance Group 14600 21st Ave N . . . . Plymouth MN 55447 763-745-3500 745-3718*
**Fax:* Cust Svc ■ *TF Cust Svc:* 800-989-2235 ■ *Web:* www.nilfisk-advance.com

Nordson Corp 28601 Clemens Rd . . . . Westlake OH 44145 440-892-1580 892-9507
NASDAQ: NDSN ■ *TF:* 800-321-2881 ■ *Web:* www.nordson.com

North Light Color Inc 5008 Hillsboro Ave N . . . . New Hope MN 55428 763-531-8222 531-8224
Web: www.northlightcolor.com

Norwood Kingsley Machine Co
2538 Wisconsin Ave . . . . Downers Grove IL 60515 630-968-0647 968-7672
TF: 800-626-3464 ■ *Web:* www.kingsleymachine.com

Oil & Gas Equipment Corp 4910 E Main St . . . . Farmington NM 87402 505-327-9624 327-5459
Web: www.ogequip.com

Oscar Wilson Engines & Parts Inc
826 Lone Star Dr . . . . O Fallon MO 63366 636-978-1313 873-6720*
**Fax Area Code:* 800 ■ *TF:* 800-873-6721 ■ *Web:* www.oscar-wilson.com

Pall Corp 2200 Northern Blvd . . . . East Hills NY 11548 516-484-5400 801-9754
NYSE: PLL ■ *TF:* 800-645-6532 ■ *Web:* www.pall.com

Parker Industries Inc 1650 Sycamore Ave . . . . Bohemia NY 11716 631-567-1000 567-1355
Web: www.parkerind.com

Parkson Corp
1401 W Cyperess Creek Rd . . . . Fort Lauderdale FL 33309 954-974-6610 974-6182
Web: www.parkson.com

Paul Mueller Co 1600 W Phelps St . . . . Springfield MO 65802 417-831-3000 831-3528
TF: 800-641-2830 ■ *Web:* www.muel.com

PDQ Mfg Inc 1698 Scheuring Rd . . . . De Pere WI 54115 920-983-8333 983-8330
TF: 800-227-3373 ■ *Web:* www.pdqinc.com

Peach State Integrated Technologies Inc
3005 Business Pk Dr . . . . Norcross GA 30071 678-327-2000 327-2030
TF: 800-998-6517 ■ *Web:* www.peachstate.com

Peerless Mfg Co 14651 N Dallas Pkwy Suite 500 . . . . Dallas TX 75254 214-357-6181 351-0194
NASDAQ: PMFG ■ *TF:* 877-879-7634 ■ *Web:* www.peerlessmfg.com

Pengate Handling Systems Inc 3 Interchange Pl . . . . York PA 17406 717-764-3050 764-5854
Web: www.pengate.com

Permadur Industries Inc 186 Rt 206 S . . . . Hillsborough NJ 08844 908-359-9767 359-9773
TF: 800-392-0146 ■ *Web:* www.permadur.com

Perry Videx LLC PO Box 10 . . . . Hainesport NJ 08036 609-267-1600 267-4499
Web: www.perryvidex.com

Peterson Machine Tool Inc
1100 N Union St . . . . Council Grove KS 66846 620-767-6721 676-6415
TF: 800-835-3528 ■ *Web:* www.petersonmachine.com

Pfaudler Inc 1000 W Ave . . . . Rochester NY 14611 585-235-1000 235-6393
Web: www.pfaudler.com

Phillips Machine Service Inc 367 George St . . . . Beckley WV 25801 304-255-0537 253-6198
TF: 800-733-1521 ■ *Web:* www.phillipsmachine.com

Phoenix Process Equipment Co
2402 Watterson Trial . . . . Louisville KY 40299 502-499-6198 499-1079
Web: www.dewater.com

Pioneer/Eclipse Corp 1 Eclipse Rd . . . . Sparta NC 28675 336-372-8080 372-2895
TF Cust Svc: 800-367-3550 ■ *Web:* www.pioneer-eclipse.com

Pipe & Tube Supply Inc
1407 N Cypress . . . . North Little Rock AR 72114 501-372-6556 372-7694
Web: www.pipeandtubesupply.com

Powerboss Inc 175 Anderson St . . . . Aberdeen NC 28315 910-944-2105 944-7409

PPT Vision Inc 12988 Valleyview Rd . . . . Eden Prairie MN 55344 952-996-9500 996-9501
Web: www.pptvision.com

Premier Safety & Service Inc
2 Industrial Pk Dr . . . . Oakdale PA 15071 724-693-8699 693-8698
TF: 800-828-1080 ■ *Web:* www.premiersafety.com

Psb Industries Inc PO Box 1318 . . . . Erie PA 16512 814-452-4536 455-9082
Web: www.psbindustries.com

PTI Technologies Inc 501 Del Norte Blvd . . . . Oxnard CA 93030 805-604-3700 604-3701
TF: 800-331-2701 ■ *Web:* www.ptitechnologies.com

Pullman/Holt Corp 10702 N 46th St . . . . Tampa FL 33617 813-971-2223 971-6090
TF: 800-237-7582 ■ *Web:* www.pullman-holt.com

Quipp Inc 4800 NW 157th St . . . . Miami FL 33014 305-623-8700 623-0980
TF: 800-345-9680 ■ *Web:* www.quipp.com

R&r Products Inc 3334 E Milber St . . . . Tucson AZ 85714 520-889-3593 294-1045
TF: 800-528-3446 ■ *Web:* www.rrproducts.com

R-V Industries Inc 584 Poplar Rd . . . . Honey Brook PA 19344 610-273-2457 273-3361*
**Fax:* Sales ■ *Web:* www.rvii.com

Retech Systems LLC 100 Henry Stn Rd . . . . Ukiah CA 95482 707-462-6522 467-1708
Web: www.retechinc.com

Roberts Sinto Corp 3001 W Main St . . . . Lansing MI 48917 517-371-2460 371-4930
Web: www.robertssinto.com

Rockford Industrial Welding Supply Inc
4646 Linden Rd PO Box 5404 . . . . Rockford IL 61125 815-226-1900 226-5617
TF: 800-226-1904 ■ *Web:* www.riws.com

Phone Fax

Rotary Lift 2700 Lanier Dr . . . . Madison IN 47250 812-273-1622 273-3404
TF: 800-445-5438 ■ *Web:* www.rotarylift.com

SAES Pure Gas Inc 4175 Santa Fe Rd . . . . San Luis Obispo CA 93401 805-541-9299 541-9399
Web: www.saespuregas.com

Salem Tools Inc 1602 Midland Rd PO Box 1509 . . . . Salem VA 24153 540-389-0233 375-3807
TF: 800-390-4348 ■ *Web:* www.salemtools.com

Salvagnini America Inc 27 Bicentennial Ct . . . . Hamilton OH 45015 513-874-8284 874-2229
Web: www.salvagnini.com

Schutte & Koerting LLC 2510 Metropolitan . . . . Trevose PA 19053 215-639-0900 639-1597
TF: 800-752-8558 ■ *Web:* www.s-k.com

Scott Fetzer Co 28800 Clemens Rd . . . . Westlake OH 44145 440-892-3000 892-3060

Sellers Equipment Inc 400 N Chicago . . . . Salina KS 67701 785-823-6378 823-8083
Web: www.sellerstractor.com

Senior Flexonics Inc Metal Bellows Div
1075 Providence Hwy . . . . Sharon MA 02067 781-784-1400 784-1405
Web: www.metalbellows.com

Sentry Equipment & Erectors Inc
13150 E Lynchburg Salem Tpke . . . . Forest VA 24551 434-525-0769 525-1701
Web: www.sentryequipment.com

Shop-Vac Corp 2323 Reach Rd . . . . Williamsport PA 17701 570-326-0502 321-7089
Web: www.shopvac.com

Sjf Material Handling Equipment
211 Baker Ave . . . . Winsted MN 55395 320-485-2824 485-2832
TF: 800-598-5532 ■ *Web:* www.sjf.com

SPX - Midwest Service Ctr 611 Sugar Creek Rd . . . . Delavan WI 53115 262-728-1900 728-4950
TF: 800-252-5200 ■ *Web:* www.spxpe.com

Sterling Production Control Units
2280 W Dorothy Ln . . . . Dayton OH 45439 937-299-5594 299-3843
TF: 800-968-7728 ■ *Web:* www.sterlingpcu.com

STI Electronics Inc
261 Palmer Rd 261 Palmer Rd . . . . Madison AL 35758 256-461-9191 461-7524
TF: 888-650-3006 ■ *Web:* www.solderingtech.com

Stopol Inc 31005 Bainbridge Rd . . . . Solon OH 44139 440-498-4000 498-4001
Web: www.stopol.com

Strasbaugh 825 Buckley Rd . . . . San Luis Obispo CA 93401 805-541-6424 541-6425
Web: www.strasbaugh.com

Super Products LLC 17000 W Cleveland Ave . . . . New Berlin WI 53151 262-784-7100 784-9561
TF: 800-837-9711 ■ *Web:* www.superproductscorp.com

Superior Crane Corp (SCC)
208 Wilmont Dr PO Box 1464 . . . . Waukesha WI 53189 262-542-0099 542-7767
Web: www.superiorcrane.com

Swiss Precision Instruments Inc
11450 Markon Dr . . . . Garden Grove CA 92842 714-799-1555 842-5164*
**Fax Area Code:* 800 ■ *TF:* 888-774-8200 ■ *Web:* www.swissprec.com

Synventive Molding Solutions Inc
10 Centennial Dr . . . . Peabody MA 01960 978-750-8065 646-3600
TF: 800-367-5662 ■ *Web:* www.synventive.com

TCM Fork Lift Trucks 7950 Blankenship Dr . . . . Houston TX 77055 713-681-8888 681-8899

Tennant Co 701 N Lilac Dr . . . . Minneapolis MN 55422 763-540-1200 540-1437
NYSE: TNC ■ *TF Cust Svc:* 800-553-8033 ■ *Web:* www.tennantco.com

Thermotron Industries Co 291 Kollen Pk Dr . . . . Holland MI 49423 616-393-4580 392-5643
Web: www.thermotron.com

Thomas Engineering Inc
575 W Central Rd . . . . Hoffman Estates IL 60195 847-358-5800 358-5817
TF: 800-634-9910 ■ *Web:* www.thomaseng.com

Thompson International Inc PO Box 57 . . . . Henderson KY 42420 270-826-3751 826-3881
Web: www.thompsoninternational.com

Timesavers Inc 11123 89th Ave N . . . . Maple Grove MN 55369 763-488-6600 488-6601
TF: 800-537-3611 ■ *Web:* www.timesaversinc.com

Tool Smith Co Inc
1300 4th Ave S PO Box 2384 . . . . Birmingham AL 35233 205-323-2576 323-9060
TF: 800-317-8665 ■ *Web:* www.toolsmith.ws

Tulsa Rig Iron Inc 4457 W 151st PO Box 880 . . . . Kiefer OK 74041 918-321-3330 321-3339
Web: www.tulsarigiron.com

Unified Brands Inc 525 S Coldwater Rd . . . . Weidman MI 48893 989-644-3331 634-5369*
**Fax Area Code:* 800 ■ *TF:* 800-621-8560 ■ *Web:* www.unifiedbrands.net

Universal Machine & Engineering Corp
645 Old Reading Pike . . . . Stowe PA 19464 610-323-1810 323-9756
Web: www.umc-oscar.com

USM Corp 32 Stevens St . . . . Haverhill MA 01830 978-374-0303 521-5519
TF: 800-343-0772 ■ *Web:* www.usmcorporation.com

Vactor Mfg Inc 1621 S Illinois St . . . . Streator IL 61364 815-672-3171 672-2779*
**Fax:* Sales ■ *Web:* www.vactor.com

Vacudyne Inc 375 E Joe Orr Rd . . . . Chicago Heights IL 60411 708-757-5200 757-7180
TF: 800-459-9591 ■ *Web:* www.vacudyne.com

Van Air Systems Inc 2950 Mechanic St . . . . Lake City PA 16423 814-774-2631 774-3482
TF: 800-840-9906 ■ *Web:* www.vanairsystems.com

Van Dam Machine Corp 81-B Walsh Dr . . . . Parsippany NJ 07054 973-257-7050 257-7398
Web: www.vandammachine.com

Vermeer Midsouth Inc 1200 Vermeer Cv . . . . Cordova TN 38018 901-758-1928 758-1929
TF: 800-264-4123 ■ *Web:* www.vermeermidsouth.com

VFP Fire Systems 1301 L'Orient St . . . . Saint Paul MN 55117 651-558-3300 558-3310
TF: 800-229-6263 ■ *Web:* www.vfpfire.com

Videojet Technologies Inc 1500 Mittel Blvd . . . . Wood Dale IL 60191 630-860-7300 616-3657*
**Fax:* Mktg ■ *TF Cust Svc:* 800-843-3610 ■ *Web:* www.videojet.com

Vulcan Engineering Co
1 Vulcan Dr Helena Industrial Pk . . . . Helena AL 35080 205-663-0732 663-9103
Web: www.vulcangroup.com

W M Sprinkman Corp
4234 Courtney Rd PO Box 390 . . . . Franksville WI 53126 262-835-2390 835-4325
TF: 800-816-1610 ■ *Web:* www.sprinkman.com

Wastequip Inc 25800 Science Pk Dr Suite 140 . . . . Cleveland OH 44122 216-292-2554 292-0625
TF: 800-248-7717 ■ *Web:* www.wastequip.com

Welex Inc 1600 Union Meeting Rd . . . . Blue Bell PA 19422 215-542-8000 542-9841
Web: www.welex.com

Western Hydro Corp 3449 Enterprise Ave . . . . Hayward CA 94545 510-783-9166 732-0250
TF: 800-972-5945 ■ *Web:* www.westernhydro.com

WH Bagshaw Co Inc 1 Pine St Ext PO Box 766 . . . . Nashua NH 03061 603-883-7758 882-2651
TF: 800-343-7467 ■ *Web:* www.whbagshaw.com

Williams Form Engineering Corp
8165 Graphic Dr . . . . Belmont MI 49306 616-866-0815 866-1810
Web: www.williamsform.com

	City	State	Zip	Phone	Fax
Williams Patent Crusher & Pulverizer Co 2701 N Broadway *Web:* www.williamscrusher.com	Saint Louis	MO	63102	314-621-3348	436-2639
Windsor Industries Inc 1351 W Stanford Ave *TF:* 800-444-7654 ■ *Web:* www.windsorind.com	Englewood	CO	80110	303-762-1800	865-2800
Wood Group Pratt & Whitney Industrial Turbine Services LLC 1460 Blue Hills Ave PO Box 45 *Web:* www.wgpwllc.com	Bloomfield	CT	06002	860-286-4600	769-7337
World Market Supply Inc 10842 Galt Indus Blvd *TF:* 800-580-5582 ■ *Web:* www.worldmarketsupply.com	Saint Louis	MO	63132	314-426-0026	423-3365
Wright Metal Products Inc 378 Neely Ferry Rd *Web:* www.wrightmetalproducts.com	Simpsonville	SC	29680	864-688-6540	
Yale Carolinas Inc (YCI) 9839 S Tryon St PO Box 32457 *TF:* 800-844-1454 ■ *Web:* www.yalecarolinas.com	Charlotte	NC	28232	704-588-6930	588-6047
Young Welding Supply Inc 101 E 1st St PO Box 700 *Web:* www.youngwelding.com	Sheffield	AL	35660	256-383-5429	383-1385

390 INFORMATION RETRIEVAL SERVICES (GENERAL)

SEE ALSO Investigative Services p. 2128

	City	State	Zip	Phone	Fax
Amigos Library Services 14400 Midway Rd *TF:* 800-843-8482 ■ *Web:* www.amigos.org	Dallas	TX	75244	972-851-8000	991-6061
Binary Group Inc 1911 Fort Myer Dr Suite 300 *Web:* www.binarygroup.com	Arlington	VA	22209	571-480-4444	480-4445
BurrellesLuce 75 E Northfield Rd *TF:* 800-631-1160 ■ *Web:* www.burrellesluce.com	Livingston	NJ	07039	973-992-6600	992-7675
Cal Info 316 W 2nd St Suite 1102 *TF:* 877-687-8710 ■ *Web:* www.calinfo.net	Los Angeles	CA	90012	213-687-8710	687-8778
Chemical Abstracts Service (CAS) 2540 Olentangy River Rd *TF:* 800-848-6538 ■ *Web:* www.info.cas.org	Columbus	OH	43202	614-447-3600	447-3713
Data Transmission Network Corp 9110 W Dodge Rd Suite 200 *TF:* 800-485-4000 ■ *Web:* www.dtn.com	Omaha	NE	68114	402-390-2328	390-7188
DataWorld Inc 15120 Enterprise Ct *TF:* 800-368-5754 ■ *Web:* www.dataworld.com	Chantilly	VA	20151	703-227-9680	803-3299
Dialog Corp 11000 Regency Pkwy Suite 10 *TF:* 800-334-2564 ■ *Web:* www.dialog.com	Cary	NC	27511	919-462-8600	468-9890
Digital Datavoice Corp (DDV) 1210 Northland Dr Suite 160 *Web:* www.ddvc.com	Mendota Heights	MN	55120	651-452-0300	452-5470
EBSCO Information Services PO Box 1943 *TF:* 800-758-5995 ■ *Web:* www.ebsco.com	Birmingham	AL	35201	205-991-6600	991-1264
Environmental Data Resources Inc 440 Wheelers Farms Rd **Fax Area Code:* 800 ■ *TF:* 800-352-0050 ■ *Web:* www.edrnet.com	Milford	CT	06460	203-783-0300	231-6802*
eScreen Inc 7500 W 110th St Suite 500 *TF:* 800-881-0722 ■ *Web:* www.escreen.com	Overland Park	KS	66210	913-327-5915	327-8606
FOI Services Inc 704 Quince Orchard Rd Suite 275 *Web:* www.foiservices.com	Gaithersburg	MD	20878	301-975-9400	975-0702
FOIA Group Inc (FGI) 1259 Connecticut Ave NW Suite 200 **Fax Area Code:* 202 ■ *TF:* 888-461-7951 ■ *Web:* www.foia.com	Washington	DC	20036	888-461-7951	347-8419*
Franchise Information Services Inc 4300 Wilson Blvd Suite 480 *TF:* 800-485-9570 ■ *Web:* www.frandata.com	Arlington	VA	22203	703-740-4700	
Healthcare Management Systems Inc (HMS) 3102 W End Ave Suite 400 *TF:* 800-383-3317 ■ *Web:* www.hmstn.com	Nashville	TN	37203	615-383-7300	383-6093
Infotrieve Inc 11755 Wilshire Blvd 19th Fl *TF:* 800-422-4633 ■ *Web:* www.infotrieve.com	Los Angeles	CA	90025	310-445-3001	445-3003
infoUSA Inc 5711 S 86th Cir **Fax:* Sales ■ *TF:* 800-321-0869 ■ *Web:* www.infousa.com	Omaha	NE	68127	402-593-4500	331-1505*
LexisNexis Martindale-Hubbell 121 Chanlon Rd **Fax Area Code:* 908 ■ **Fax:* Sales ■ *TF:* 800-526-4902 ■ *Web:* www.martindale.com	New Providence	NJ	07974	800-526-4902	665-3593*
MarketResearch.com 11200 Rockville Pike Suite 504 *Web:* www.marketresearch.com	Rockville	MD	20852	240-747-3000	747-3004
National Technical Information Service (NTIS) 5285 Port Royal Rd *TF Orders:* 800-553-6847 ■ *Web:* www.ntis.gov	Springfield	VA	22161	703-605-6000	605-6900
NERAC Inc 1 Technology Dr *Web:* www.nerac.com	Tolland	CT	06084	860-872-7000	875-1749
Newsbank Inc 5801 Pelican Bay Blvd # 600 *TF:* 800-243-7694 ■ *Web:* www.newsbank.com	Naples	FL	34108	239-263-6004	263-3004
Omitron Inc 7051 Muirkirk Meadows Dr Suite A *Web:* www.omitron.com	Beltsville	MD	20705	301-474-1700	345-4594
Ovid Technologies Inc 333 7th Ave 20th Fl *TF:* 800-950-2035 ■ *Web:* www.ovid.com	New York	NY	10001	646-674-6300	674-6301
Questia Media America Inc 24 Greenway Plaza Suite 1050 *TF:* 888-950-2580 ■ *Web:* www.questia.com	Houston	TX	77046	713-358-2500	358-2601
Research on Demand Inc PO Box 479 **Fax Area Code:* 877 ■ *TF:* 800-200-4095 ■ *Web:* www.researchondemand.com	Santa Barbara	CA	93102	805-963-4095	564-4878*
Research Wizard of Tulsa City-County Library 400 Civic Ctr *Web:* www.researchwizard.org	Tulsa	OK	74103	918-596-7991	596-2598
Scott Enterprises Inc 2225 Downs Dr 6th Fl Exce Suites *TF:* 877-866-3445 ■ *Web:* www.scottenterprises.org	Erie	PA	16509	814-868-9500	866-0463
Sopheon Corp 3050 Metro Dr Suite 200 *TF:* 800-367-8358 ■ *Web:* www.sopheon.com	Minneapolis	MN	55425	952-851-7500	851-7599
Strategic Staffing Solutions Inc 645 Griswold St Suite 2900 *TF:* 888-738-3261 ■ *Web:* www.strategicstaff.com	Detroit	MI	48226	313-965-1110	965-9967
Sutherland Global Services 1160 Pittsford-Victor Rd *Web:* www.sutherlandglobal.com	Pittsford	NY	14534	585-586-5757	784-2154
Tele Atlas North America Inc 11 Lafayette St *Web:* www.teleatlas.com	Lebanon	NH	03766	603-643-0330	653-0249
Thomson Financial 22 Thomson Pl **Fax:* Hum Res ■ *TF:* 888-837-4636 ■ *Web:* www.thomsonreuters.com	Boston	MA	02210	617-856-2000	856-5601*
TTS LLC 2595 Dallas Pkwy Suite 300 *Web:* www.tts-us.com	Frisco	TX	75034	214-778-0800	778-0880
Video Monitoring Services of America Inc 6430 W Sunset Blvd Suite 400 *Web:* www.vidmon.com	Los Angeles	CA	90028	323-993-0111	467-7540
West Group 610 Opperman Dr *TF Cust Svc:* 800-328-4880 ■ *Web:* www.west.thomson.com	Eagan	MN	55123	651-687-7000	687-7551

391 INK

	City	State	Zip	Phone	Fax
AJ Daw Printing Ink Co 3559 Greenwood Ave *TF:* 800-432-9465	Los Angeles	CA	90040	323-723-3253	723-3253
Bomark Inks Inc 601 S 6th Ave *TF:* 800-323-5174 ■ *Web:* www.bomarkinks.com	City of Industry	CA	91746	626-968-1666	330-2373
Braden Sutphin Ink Co 3650 E 93rd St *TF:* 800-289-6872 ■ *Web:* www.bsink.com	Cleveland	OH	44105	216-271-2300	271-0515
Central Ink Corp 1100 Harvester Rd *TF:* 800-345-2541 ■ *Web:* www.cicink.com	West Chicago	IL	60185	630-231-6500	231-6554
Color Converting Industries Co 3535 SW 56th St *TF:* 800-728-8200 ■ *Web:* www.color-converting.com	Des Moines	IA	50321	515-471-2100	471-2202
Color Resolutions International 575 Quality Blvd *TF:* 800-346-8570 ■ *Web:* www.colorresolutions.com	Fairfield	OH	45014	513-552-7200	552-1588
Cudner & O'Connor Co 4035 W Kinzie St *Web:* www.candocinks.com	Chicago	IL	60624	773-826-0200	826-0477
Formulabs Inc 529 W 4th Ave *TF:* 800-642-2345 ■ *Web:* www.formulabs.com	Escondido	CA	92025	760-741-2345	740-0593
Gans Ink & Supply Co Inc 1441 Boyd St *TF:* 800-372-7410 ■ *Web:* www.gansink.com	Los Angeles	CA	90033	323-264-2200	264-2916
Graphic Sciences Inc 7515 NE Ambassador Pl Suite L *TF:* 888-546-4465	Portland	OR	97220	503-460-0203	460-0225
Independent Ink Inc 13700 Gramercy Pl *TF:* 800-446-5538 ■ *Web:* www.independentink.com	Gardena	CA	90249	310-523-4657	329-0943
International Coatings Co 13929 166th St *TF:* 800-423-4103 ■ *Web:* www.iccink.com	Cerritos	CA	90703	562-926-1010	926-9486
Kerley Ink Engineers Inc 2700 S 12th Ave *Web:* www.kerleyink.com	Broadview	IL	60155	708-344-1295	865-5759
Keystone Printing Ink Co 2700 Roberts Ave *TF:* 800-523-0111 ■ *Web:* www.keystoneink.com	Philadelphia	PA	19129	215-228-8100	228-4743
Lakeland Laboratories Alfa Ink Div 655 Washington Ave	Carlstadt	NJ	07072	201-939-1122	939-3328
Matsui International Co Inc 1501 W 178th St *TF:* 800-359-5679 ■ *Web:* www.matsui-color.com	Gardena	CA	90248	310-767-7812	767-7836
Miller-Cooper Co 5187 Merriam Dr *TF:* 800-289-6246 ■ *Web:* www.mcink.com	Merriam	KS	66203	913-312-5020	312-5033
Nazdar 8501 Hedge Ln Terr *TF:* 800-767-9942 ■ *Web:* www.nazdar.com	Shawnee	KS	66227	913-422-1888	422-2296
Nor-Cote International Inc 506 Lafayette Ave *TF:* 800-488-9180 ■ *Web:* www.norcote.com	Crawfordsville	IN	47933	765-362-9180	364-5408
Polypore Inc 4601 S 3rd Ave	Tucson	AZ	85714	520-889-3306	741-9647
Polytex Environmental Inks Ltd 820 E 140th St *Web:* www.polytexink.com	Bronx	NY	10454	718-402-2000	402-2000
Sensient Technologies Corp 777 E Wisconsin Ave 11th Fl *NYSE:* SXT ■ *TF:* 800-558-9892 ■ *Web:* www.sensient-tech.com	Milwaukee	WI	53202	414-271-6755	347-4783
Sericol Inc 1101 W Cambridge Dr *TF:* 800-737-4265 ■ *Web:* www.sericol.com	Kansas City	KS	66103	913-342-4060	342-4752
Spectrachem Corp 10 Dell Glen Ave Suite 3A *TF:* 800-524-2806	Lodi	NJ	07644	973-253-3553	253-3663
Sun Chemical Corp 35 Waterview Blvd *Web:* www.sunchemical.com	Parsippany	NJ	07054	973-404-6000	404-6001
Superior Printing Ink Co Inc 100 N St *Web:* www.superiorink.com	Teterboro	NJ	07608	201-478-5600	478-5650
Toyo Ink America LLC 710 W Belden *TF:* 800-227-8696 ■ *Web:* www.toyoink.com	Addison	IL	60101	630-930-5100	628-1769
US Ink Corp 651 Garden St **Fax:* Mktg ■ *TF:* 800-423-8838 ■ *Web:* www.usink.com	Carlstadt	NJ	07072	201-935-8666	933-3728*
Van Son Holland Ink Corp of America 888 weatherend Hwy *TF:* 800-645-4182 ■ *Web:* www.vansonink.com	hauppauge	NY	11788	800-645-4182	442-8744
Wikoff Color Corp 1886 Merritt Rd *Web:* www.wikoff.com	Fort Mill	SC	29715	803-548-2210	548-5728

392 INSULATION & ACOUSTICAL PRODUCTS

	City	State	Zip	Phone	Fax
Anco Products Inc (API) 2500 S 17th St *TF:* 800-837-2626 ■ *Web:* www.ancoproductsinc.com	Elkhart	IN	46517	574-293-5574	295-6235
Applegate Insulation Mfg Inc 1000 Highview Dr *TF:* 800-627-7536 ■ *Web:* www.applegateinsulation.com	Webberville	MI	48892	517-521-3545	521-3597
CertainTeed Corp 750 E Swedesford Rd *TF Prod Info:* 800-782-8777 ■ *Web:* www.certainteed.com	Valley Forge	PA	19482	610-341-7000	341-7797
Claremont Sales Corp 35 Winsome Dr PO Box 430 *TF:* 800-222-4448 ■ *Web:* claremontcorporation.com	Durham	CT	06422	860-349-4499	349-7977
CTA Acoustics Inc 100 CTA Blvd PO Box 448 *Web:* www.ctaacoustics.com	Corbin	KY	40702	606-528-8050	528-8074
Dryvit Systems Inc 1 Energy Way *TF:* 800-556-7752 ■ *Web:* www.dryvit.com	West Warwick	RI	02893	401-822-4100	822-4510
F Rodgers Corp 7901 National Dr *Web:* www.frodgers.com	Livermore	CA	94550	925-960-2300	960-2301

	City	State	Zip	Phone	Fax
Fibrex Insulations Inc 561 Scott Rd PO Box 2079 **Fax:* Cust Svc ■ *TF Cust Svc:* 800-265-7514 ■ *Web:* www.fibrex.org	Sarnia	ON	N7T8G3	519-336-7770	336-7770*
Hi-Temp Insulation Inc 4700 Calle Alto *Web:* www.hi-tempinsulation.com	Camarillo	CA	93012	805-484-2774	484-7551
Industrial Acoustics Co Inc 1160 Commerce Ave *Web:* www.industrialacoustics.com	Bronx	NY	10462	718-931-8000	863-1138
Industrial Insulation Group LLC (IIG) 2100 Line St **Fax Area Code:* 912 ■ *TF:* 800-334-7997 ■ *Web:* www.iig-llc.com	Brunswick	GA	31520	800-334-7997	267-6096*
Isolatek International Inc 41 Furnace St *TF:* 800-631-9600 ■ *Web:* www.cafco.com	Stanhope	NJ	07874	973-347-1200	347-5131
ITW Insulation Systems 1370 E 40th St Suite 1 Bldg 7 **Fax Area Code:* 713 ■ *TF:* 800-231-1024 ■ *Web:* www.itwinsulation.com	Houston	TX	77022	800-231-1024	691-7492*
Johns Manville Corp 717 17th St PO Box 5108 **Fax:* PR ■ *TF Prod Info:* 800-654-3103 ■ *Web:* www.jm.com	Denver	CO	80217	303-978-2000	978-2041*
Johns Manville International Group Inc 717 17th St PO Box 5108 **Fax:* PR ■ *TF:* 800-654-3101 ■ *Web:* www.jm.com	Denver	CO	80217	303-978-2000	978-2041*
Knauf Insulation 1 Knauf Dr *TF:* 800-825-4434 ■ *Web:* www.knaufinsulation.com	Shelbyville	IN	46176	317-398-4434	398-3675
MIT International 9000 Railwood Dr *TF:* 800-275-6679 ■ *Web:* www.insulpad.com	Houston	TX	77078	713-675-0075	675-8393
Molded Acoustical Products of Easton Inc 3 Danforth Dr *Web:* www.map-easton.com	Easton	PA	18045	610-253-7135	253-1664
Nu-Wool Co Inc 2472 Port Sheldon Rd *TF:* 800-748-0128 ■ *Web:* www.nuwool.com	Jenison	MI	49428	616-669-0100	669-2370
Owens Corning 1 Owens Corning Pkwy *Web:* www.owenscorning.com	Toledo	OH	43659	419-248-8000	325-1538
Pittsburgh Corning Corp 800 Presque Isle Dr *TF:* 800-245-1217 ■ *Web:* www.pittsburghcorning.com	Pittsburgh	PA	15239	724-327-6100	387-3806
Premier Mfg Corp 12117 Bennington Ave *Web:* www.premiermfg.com	Cleveland	OH	44135	216-941-9700	941-9719
Rock Wool Mfg Co 1400 7th Ct PO Box 506 *TF Sales:* 800-874-7625 ■ *Web:* www.deltainsulation.com	Leeds	AL	35094	205-699-6121	699-3132
S & S Industries Inc PO Box 17087 *TF:* 800-445-6505	Nashville	TN	37217	615-754-8000	754-8011
Scott Industries Inc 1573 Hwy 136 W PO Box 7 *TF:* 800-951-9276 ■ *Web:* www.scott-mfg.com	Henderson	KY	42419	270-831-2037	831-2039
Sloss Industries Corp 3500 35th Ave N **Fax:* Sales ■ *Web:* www.walterenergy.com	Birmingham	AL	35207	205-808-7803	808-7715*
Soundcoat Co Inc 1 Burt Dr *TF:* 800-394-8913 ■ *Web:* www.soundcoat.com	Deer Park	NY	11729	631-242-2200	242-2246
Thermafiber Inc 3711 W Mill St *TF:* 888-834-2371 ■ *Web:* www.thermafiber.com	Wabash	IN	46992	260-563-2111	563-8979
Thermoguard Insulation Co N 125 Dyer Rd *TF:* 800-541-0579 ■ *Web:* www.thermoguard.net	Spokane	WA	99212	509-535-4600	535-8519
Thermwell Products Co 420 Rt 17 S *TF:* 800-526-5265 ■ *Web:* www.frostking.com	Mahwah	NJ	07430	201-684-4400	684-1214
TIGHITCO Inc 1375 Seaboard Industrial Blvd *TF:* 800-223-1205 ■ *Web:* www.tighitco.com	Atlanta	GA	30318	404-355-1205	351-4458
Transco Products Inc 55 E Jackson Blvd Suite 2100 *Web:* www.transcoproducts.com	Chicago	IL	60604	312-427-2818	427-4975
Transonic Inc 2824 N Sylvania Ave	Fort Worth	TX	76111	817-831-3119	831-3110
Unifrax Corp 2351 Whirlpool St **Fax:* Cust Svc ■ *Web:* www.unifrax.com	Niagara Falls	NY	14305	716-278-3800	278-3904*
USG Interiors Inc 125 S Franklin St *TF:* 800-621-9622	Chicago	IL	60606	312-606-4000	606-4093
Ward Process Inc 6 October Hill Rd *Web:* www.aapusa.com	Holliston	MA	01746	508-429-1165	429-8543

393 INSURANCE AGENTS, BROKERS, SERVICES

	City	State	Zip	Phone	Fax
Affinion Group Inc 6 High Ridge Pk *TF:* 800-251-2148 ■ *Web:* www.affiniongroup.com	Stamford	CT	06905	203-956-1000	956-1005
Agency Software Inc 215 W Commerce Dr *TF:* 800-342-7327 ■ *Web:* www.agencysoftware.com	Hayden Lake	ID	83835	208-762-7188	762-1265
Amfed Cos LLC 576 Highland Colony Pkwy *TF:* 800-264-8085 ■ *Web:* www.amfed.com	Ridgeland	MS	39157	601-853-4949	853-2727
ANCO Insurance 1733 Briarcrest Dr PO Box 3889 *TF:* 800-749-1733 ■ *Web:* www.anco.com	Bryan	TX	77802	979-776-2626	776-1308
Andreini & Co 220 W 20th Ave *TF:* 800-969-2522 ■ *Web:* www.andreini.com	San Mateo	CA	94403	650-573-1111	378-4361
Aon Risk Services Inc 200 E Randolph St **Fax Area Code:* 847 ■ *TF:* 800-432-3672 ■ *Web:* www.aon.com	Chicago	IL	60601	312-381-4000	953-5390*
Arthur J Gallagher & Co 2 Pierce Pl *NYSE: AJG* ■ *Web:* www.ajg.com	Itasca	IL	60143	630-773-3800	285-4000
Arthur J. Glatfelter Agency Inc PO Box 2726 *TF:* 800-233-1957 ■ *Web:* www.glatfelters.com	York	PA	17405	717-741-0911	741-4160
Associated Agencies Inc 1701 Golf Rd Tower 3 Suite 700 *TF:* 800-443-2827 ■ *Web:* www.assocagencies.com	Rolling Meadows	IL	60008	847-427-8400	427-3559
Automobile Protection Corp 6010 Atlantic Blvd *TF Cust Svc:* 800-458-7071 ■ *Web:* www.easycare.com	Norcross	GA	30071	770-394-6610	394-2129
Berkley Risk Administrators Co LLC 222 S 9th St Suite 1300 *TF:* 800-640-0345 ■ *Web:* www.berkleyrisk.com	Minneapolis	MN	55402	612-766-3000	766-3099
BMI Financial Group Inc 1320 S Dixie Hwy 6th Fl *Web:* www.bmicos.com	Coral Gables	FL	33146	305-443-2898	442-8486
Body-Borneman Insurance PO Box 584 *TF:* 800-326-5290 ■ *Web:* www.body-borneman.com	Boyertown	PA	19512	610-367-1100	367-1140
Bogart & Brownell 7529 Standish Pl Suite 320 *Web:* www.bogartandbrownell.com	Rockville	MD	20855	301-654-5000	444-4510
Bollinger Insurance 101 JFK Pkwy *TF:* 800-526-1379 ■ *Web:* www.bollingerinsurance.com	Short Hills	NJ	07078	973-467-0444	921-2876
Bolton & Co 245 S Los Robles Ave Suite 105 *TF:* 888-700-1444 ■ *Web:* www.boltonco.com	Pasadena	CA	91101	626-799-7000	441-3233
Brinckerhoff & Neuville Inc PO Box 424 *Web:* www.bninsurancegroup.com	Fishkill	NY	12524	845-896-4700	897-5110
Brown & Brown Agency of Insurance Professionals Inc 208 N Mill *Web:* www.bbinsurance.com	Pryor	OK	74361	918-825-3295	825-2727
Brown & Brown Inc 220 S Ridgewood Ave *NYSE: BRO* ■ *TF:* 800-877-2769	Daytona Beach	FL	32114	386-252-9601	239-5729
BWD Group LLC 113 S Service Rd BWD Plaza *Web:* www.bwdgroup.com	Jericho	NY	11753	516-327-2700	327-2800
CalSurance 681 S Parker St Suite 300 *TF:* 800-762-7800 ■ *Web:* www.calsurance.com	Orange	CA	92868	714-939-0800	939-1641
Casswood Insurance Agency Ltd 5 Executive Pk Dr *TF:* 800-972-2242 ■ *Web:* www.casswood.com	Clifton Park	NY	12065	518-373-8700	373-8799
CBCA Administrators Inc 4150 International Plaza Suite 900 **Fax:* Hum Res ■ *TF:* 800-759-0101 ■ *Web:* www.cbca.com	Fort Worth	TX	76109	817-737-1700	731-5777*
CBIZ Benefits & Insurance Services of Maryland Inc 44 Baltimore St **Fax:* Sales ■ *TF Cust Svc:* 800-624-0954 ■ *Web:* www.cbiz.com	Cumberland	MD	21502	301-777-1500	724-3953*
Charles L Crane Agency Co 100 N Broadway Suite 900 *Web:* www.craneagency.com	Saint Louis	MO	63102	314-241-8700	444-4970
Citizens Clair Insurance Group 2 W Lafayette St Suite 400 *TF:* 800-220-3008	Norristown	PA	19401	484-530-6700	530-6700
Coalition America Inc 2 Concourse Pkwy NE # 300 *Web:* www.coalitionamerica.com	Atlanta	GA	30328	404-459-7201	459-6645
Commerce Insurance Services Inc 1701 Rt 70 E Commerce Atrium **Fax Area Code:* 856 ■ *TF:* 888-751-9000	Cherry Hill	NJ	08034	877-396-3800	795-9783*
Crawford & Co 1001 Summit Blvd PO Box 5047 *NYSE: CRD.B* ■ **Fax:* Mktg ■ *TF:* 800-241-2541 ■ *Web:* www.us.crawfordandcompany.com	Atlanta	GA	30319	404-256-0830	847-4028*
Cross Financial Corp 74 Gilman Rd PO Box 1388 *TF:* 800-999-7345 ■ *Web:* www.crossagency.com	Bangor	ME	04401	207-947-7345	941-0849
Cumbre Inc 3333 Concours Suite 5100 *TF:* 800-998-7986 ■ *Web:* www.cumbreinc.com	Ontario	CA	91764	909-484-2456	484-2491
Custard Insurance Adjusters Inc PO Box 921329 *TF:* 800-457-3390 ■ *Web:* www.custard.com	Norcross	GA	30010	770-263-6800	368-3375
Daniel & Henry Co 1001 Highlands Plaza Dr W Suite 500 *Web:* www.danielandhenry.com	Saint Louis	MO	63110	314-421-1525	444-1990
Detwiler Mitchell & Co 150 Federal St *Web:* www.dmcos.com	Boston	MA	02110	617-451-0100	747-0800
Eagan Insurance Agency Inc 2629 N Cswy Blvd *TF:* 888-882-9600 ■ *Web:* www.eaganins.com	Metairie	LA	70002	504-836-9600	836-9621
Encore Insurance Group 201 N Broadway St *TF:* 866-341-2674 ■ *Web:* www.encoreinsgroup.com	Greensburg	IN	47240	812-663-5151	663-8483
Endurance Specialty Holdings Ltd 767 Third Ave 5th Fl *NYSE: ENH* ■ *Web:* www.endurance.bm	New York	NY	10017	212-209-6500	209-6501
Entertainment Brokers International 10940 Wilshire Blvd Suite 1 *TF:* 888-799-6642 ■ *Web:* www.ebi-ins.com	Los Angeles	CA	90024	310-824-0111	824-5733
Esurance Inc 747 Front St 4th Fl *TF:* 800-926-6012 ■ *Web:* www.esurance.com	San Francisco	CA	94111	415-875-4500	875-4501
First Acceptance Corp 3813 Green Hills Village Dr *NYSE: FAC* ■ *TF:* 800-321-0899 ■ *Web:* www.firstacceptancecorp.com	Nashville	TN	37215	615-327-4888	844-2835
First Security Co Inc PO Box 2205 *TF:* 800-829-6549 ■ *Web:* www.1security.net	Hickory	NC	28603	828-322-4171	322-5094
Fortun Insurance Agency Inc 365 Palermo Ave *TF:* 877-643-2055 ■ *Web:* www.fortuninsurance.com	Coral Gables	FL	33134	305-445-3535	447-9478
Frank Crystal & Co 32 Old Slip 17th Fl *TF:* 800-221-5830 ■ *Web:* www.frankcrystal.com	New York	NY	10005	212-344-2444	504-5989
Fred A Moreton & Co 709 E S Temple *TF:* 800-594-8949 ■ *Web:* www.famoreton.com	Salt Lake City	UT	84102	801-531-1234	531-6117
Fred Loya Insurance 1800 Lee Trevino Suite 201 **Fax Area Code:* 800 ■ *TF:* 800-554-0595 ■ *Web:* www.fredloya.com	El Paso	TX	79936	915-590-5692	387-8220*
Frederick Mutual Insurance Co PO Box 608 *Web:* www.fredmut.com	Frederick	MD	21705	301-663-9522	662-2053
Frenkel & Co Inc 350 Hudson St *TF:* 800-373-6535 ■ *Web:* www.frenkel.com	New York	NY	10014	212-488-0200	488-1800
Fringe Benefits Management Co 3101 Sessions Rd *TF:* 800-872-0345 ■ *Web:* www.fbmc.com	Tallahassee	FL	32303	850-425-6200	425-6220
Frontier Adjusters of America Inc 4745 N 7th St **Fax Area Code:* 800 ■ *TF:* 800-528-1187 ■ *Web:* www.frontieradjusters.com	Phoenix	AZ	85014	602-264-1061	553-4799*
Gallagher Healthcare Insurance Services Inc 9821 Katy Fwy # 700 *TF:* 800-733-4474 ■ *Web:* www.ajg.com	Houston	TX	77024	713-461-4000	461-4334

Name / Address	City	State	ZIP	Phone	Fax
Gebco Insurance Assoc 8600 LaSalle Rd Suite 338 TF: 800-464-3226 ■ Web: www.gogebco.com	Towson	MD	21286	410-339-6780	339-6789
Graham Co 30 S 15th St # 2400 TF: 888-472-4262 ■ Web: www.grahamco.com	Philadelphia	PA	19102	215-567-6300	751-9518
Great American Custom Insurance Services Inc 725 S Figueroa St Web: www.gamcustom.com	Los Angeles	CA	90017	213-430-4300	629-8223
Haas & Wilkerson Inc PO Box 2946 TF: 800-821-7703 ■ Web: www.hwins.com	Shawnee Mission	KS	66205	913-432-4400	432-6159
Herbert H. Landy Insurance Agency Inc 75 2nd Ave Suite 410 *Fax Area Code: 781 ■ TF: 800-336-5422 ■ Web: www.landy.com	Needham	MA	02494	800-336-5422	449-7908*
Hibbs Hallmark & Co 501 Shelley Dr TF: 800-765-6767 ■ Web: www.hibbshallmark.com	Tyler	TX	75701	903-561-8484	581-5988
Holmes Murphy & Assoc Inc 3001 Westown Pkwy TF: 800-247-7756 ■ Web: www.holmesmurphy.com	West Des Moines	IA	50266	515-223-6800	223-6944
Horton Group The 10320 Orland Pkwy Web: www.thehortongroup.com	Orland Park	IL	60467	708-845-3000	845-3001
Housing Authority Risk Retention Group Inc PO Box 189 TF: 800-873-0242 ■ Web: www.housingcenter.com	Cheshire	CT	06410	203-272-8220	271-2265
Hub International Ltd 1065 Avenue of the Americas TF: 800-456-5293 ■ Web: www.hubinternational.com	New York	NY	10018	212-338-2000	338-2100
HUB International Ltd 55 E Jackson Blvd NYSE: HBG ■ TF: 800-432-2558 ■ Web: www.hubinternational.com	Chicago	IL	60604	877-402-6601	
Hull & Co Inc 2150 S Andrews Ave *Fax Area Code: 866 ■ TF: 877-409-4855 ■ Web: www.hullco.com	Fort Lauderdale	FL	33316	954-527-4855	449-8449*
Hylant Group 811 Madison Ave TF: 800-449-5268 ■ Web: www.hylant.com	Toledo	OH	43624	419-255-1020	255-7557
IMA Financial Group Inc 8200 E 32nd St N PO Box 2992 TF: 800-333-8913 ■ Web: www.imacorp.com	Wichita	KS	67226	316-267-9221	266-6254
Insurance Services Office Inc (ISO) 545 Washington Blvd *Fax: Hum Res ■ TF: 800-888-4476 ■ Web: www.iso.com	Jersey City	NJ	07310	201-469-2000	748-1472*
Insurance.com Insurance Agency LLC 29001 Solon Rd TF: 866-533-0227 ■ Web: www.insurance.com	Solon	OH	44139	440-264-1120	498-1875
Interstate National Dealer Services Inc 6120 Power Ferry Rd Suite 200 Web: www.inds.com	Atalnta	GA	30339	678-394-3500	
InterWest Insurance Services Inc 3636 American River Dr TF: 800-444-4134 ■ Web: www.iwins.com	Sacramento	CA	95864	916-488-3100	488-3492
J Smith Lanier & Co 300 W 10th St TF: 800-226-4522 ■ Web: www.jsmithlanier.com	West Point	GA	31833	706-645-2211	643-0606
Jas. D. Collier & Co 606 S Mendenhall Rd Suite 200 *Fax Area Code: 901 ■ TF: 866-600-2655 ■ Web: www.collierinsurance.com	Memphis	TN	38117	800-511-1548	529-2916*
John L Wortham & Son LP 2727 Allen Pkwy Web: www.worthaminsurance.com	Houston	TX	77019	713-526-3366	526-2757
Johns Eastern Co Inc PO Box 4175 TF: 800-767-9480 ■ Web: www.johnseastern.com	Sarasota	FL	34230	941-907-3100	907-7227
Keenan & Assoc 2355 Crenshaw Blvd Suite 200 PO Box 4328 TF: 800-654-8102 ■ Web: www.keenanassoc.com	Torrance	CA	90510	310-212-3344	328-6793
Kelter-Alliant Insurance Services Inc 101 Southfield TF: 800-888-9088	Birmingham	MI	48009	248-540-3131	540-2002
Kraus-Anderson Insurance 420 Gateway Blvd TF: 800-207-9261 ■ Web: www.kainsurance.com	Burnsville	MN	55337	952-707-8200	890-0535
Land Title Guarantee Co Inc 3033 E 1st Ave Suite 600 PO Box 5440 Web: www.ltgc.com	Denver	CO	80217	303-321-1880	322-7603
Landry harris & Co 600 Jefferson St Suite 200 PO Box 2456 Web: www.landryharris.com	Lafayette	LA	70501	337-266-2150	266-2151
Lawley Service Insurance 361 Delaware Ave TF Cust Svc: 800-860-5741 ■ Web: www.lawleyinsurance.com	Buffalo	NY	14202	716-849-8618	849-9291
Lawson Hawks Insurance Assoc 1091 N Shoreline Blvd Suite 200 PO Box 39 Web: www.lawson-hawks.com	Mountain View	CA	94042	650-964-8000	964-0816
Le Mars Insurance Co PO Box 1608 TF: 800-545-6480 ■ Web: www.lemm.com	Le Mars	IA	51031	712-546-7847	
Leavitt Group 216 S 200 W PO Box 130 Web: www.leavitt.com	Cedar City	UT	84720	435-586-6553	586-1510
Lewer Agency Inc 4534 Wornall Rd TF: 800-821-7715 ■ Web: www.lewer.com	Kansas City	MO	64111	816-753-4390	561-6840
Lockton Cos 444 W 47th St Suite 900 Web: www.lockton.com	Kansas City	MO	64112	816-960-9000	960-9099
Loomis Co 850 N Pk Rd TF: 800-782-0392 ■ Web: www.loomisco.com	Wyomissing	PA	19610	610-374-4040	374-6578
Lovitt & Touche Inc 7202 E Rosewood St TF: 800-426-2756 ■ Web: www.lovitt-touche.com	Tucson	AZ	85710	520-722-3000	722-7245
Managed Care of America Inc 1910 Cochran Rd Suite 605 TF: 800-922-4966 ■ Web: www.mcoa.com	Pittsburgh	PA	15220	412-922-2803	
Managed HealthCare Northwest Inc 1120 NW 20th Ave Suite 200 Web: www.mhninc.com	Portland	OR	97209	503-413-5800	413-5801
Marsh Saldana 701 Ponce de Leon Ave Web: www.saldana.net	San Juan	PR	00907	787-721-2600	721-1093
Marshall & Sterling Inc 110 Main St TF: 800-333-3766 ■ Web: www.marshallsterling.com	Poughkeepsie	NY	12601	845-454-0800	454-0880
MCA Administrators Inc 820 Parish St Web: www.mcoa.com	Pittsburgh	PA	15220	412-922-0780	922-3071
McGriff Seibels & Williams Inc 2211 7th Ave S PO Box 10265 TF: 800-476-2211 ■ Web: www.mcgriff.com	Birmingham	AL	35202	205-252-9871	581-9293
McLaughlin Co The 9210 Corporate Blvd Suite 250 Web: www.mclaughlin-online.com	Rockville	MD	20850	202-293-5566	857-8355
Mesirow Financial Insurance Services Div 353 N Clark St TF: 888-973-2323 ■ Web: www.mesirowfinancial.com	Chicago	IL	60654	312-595-6200	
Minnesota Lawyers Mutual Insurance Co 333 S 7th St Suite 2200 TF: 800-422-1370 ■ Web: www.mlmins.com	Minneapolis	MN	55402	800-422-1370	305-1510
Morstan General Agency Inc 600 Community Dr PO Box 4500 Web: www.morstan.com	Manhasset	NY	11030	516-488-4747	437-5050
MSI Benefits Group Inc 245 Townpark Dr Suite 100 Web: www.msibenefitsgroup.com	Kennesaw	GA	30144	770-425-1231	425-4722
Multiplan inc 115 5th Ave Web: www.multiplan.com	New York	NY	10003	212-780-2000	780-0420
National Catastrophe Adjusters Inc (NCA) 9725 Windermere Blvd *Fax Area Code: 317 ■ TF: 800-968-4456 ■ Web: www.ncagroup.com	Fishers	IN	46037	407-215-1020	915-8889*
NCCI Holdings Inc 901 Peninsula Corporate Cir TF Cust Svc: 800-622-4123 ■ Web: www.ncci.com	Boca Raton	FL	33487	561-893-1000	893-1191
Nevada Title Co 2500 N Buffalo Dr Suite 150 Web: www.nevadatitle.com	Las Vegas	NV	89128	702-251-5000	
NIA Group Inc 66 N State Rt 17 *Fax Area Code: 866 ■ TF: 800-642-0106 ■ Web: www.niagroup.com	Paramus	NJ	07652	201-845-6600	795-1158*
Northwest Administrators Inc 2323 Eastlake Ave E TF: 800-552-7334	Seattle	WA	98102	206-329-4900	726-3209
Northwest Insurance Network Inc 330 S Wells St 16th Fl Web: www.northwestinsurance.com	Chicago	IL	60606	312-427-1777	
Oryx Insurance Brokerage Inc 2 Ct St *Fax Area Code: 888 ■ Web: www.oryxinsurance.com	Binghamton	NY	13901	607-724-0173	462-6799*
Oswald Cos 1360 E 9th St Suite 600 TF: 800-466-0468 ■ Web: www.oswaldcompanies.com	Cleveland	OH	44114	216-367-8787	241-4520
Otis-Magie Insurance Agency Inc 227 W 1st St Suite 900 PO Box 137 TF: 800-241-2425 ■ Web: www.otismagie.com	Duluth	MN	55801	218-722-7753	722-7756
Parker Smith & Feek Inc 2233 112th Ave NE TF Cust Svc: 800-457-0220 ■ Web: www.psfinc.com	Bellevue	WA	98004	425-709-3600	709-7460
POMCO 2425 James St TF: 800-934-2459 ■ Web: www.pomcogroup.com	Syracuse	NY	13206	315-432-9171	432-9171
Proctor Financial Inc 200 Kirts Blvd Suite 100 TF: 800-521-6800 ■ Web: www.pfic.com	Troy	MI	48084	248-269-5700	269-5735
Professional Risk Solutions LLC 285 Davidson Ave Web: www.prsbrokers.com	Somerset	NJ	08873	732-764-1000	
Protegrity Services Inc PO Box 914700 TF: 800-883-4000 ■ Web: www.protegritynow.com	Longwood	FL	32791	407-788-1717	788-0812
Rampart Brokerage Corp 1983 Marcus Ave Suite C130 TF: 800-772-6727 ■ Web: www.rampartinsurance.com	Lake Success	NY	11042	516-538-7000	390-3555
RC Knox & Co 1 Goodwin Sq 24th Fl TF: 800-742-2765 ■ Web: www.rcknox.com	Hartford	CT	06103	860-524-7600	240-1599
Regional Reporting Inc (RRI) 90 John St Suite 702 Web: www.regionalreporting.com	New York	NY	10038	212-964-5973	608-5074
Reid Jones McRorie & Williams Inc PO Box 18527 TF: 800-785-2604 ■ Web: www.rjmw.com	Charlotte	NC	28218	704-537-0012	
Robert J Hanafin Inc 204 Washington Ave PO Box 509 Web: www.rjhanafin.com	Endicott	NY	13760	607-754-3500	754-9797
Robertson Ryan & Assoc Inc 330 E Kilbourn Ave 2 Plaza E Suite 650	Milwaukee	WI	53202	414-271-3575	271-0196
Rutherfoord Thomas Inc 1 S Jefferson St TF: 800-283-1478 ■ Web: www.rutherfoord.com	Roanoke	VA	24011	540-982-3511	342-9747
Scott Danahy Naylon Co Inc (SDN) 300 SPINDRIFT DR Web: www.scottdanahynaylon.com	BUFFALO	NY	14221	716-633-3400	633-4306
Security State Agency-aitkin PO Box 347 TF: 888-335-9881 ■ Web: www.ssbmn.com	Aitkin	MN	56431	218-927-3712	927-4481
Seitlin 9800 NW 41st St Suite 300 TF: 800-677-7348 ■ Web: www.seitlin.com	Miami	FL	33178	305-591-0090	593-6993
Selectquote Insurance Services 595 Market St FL 6 *Fax Area Code: 800 ■ TF: 877-492-3988 ■ Web: www.selectquote.com	San Francisco	CA	94105	415-543-7338	136-7000*
Senior Market Sales Inc (SMS) 8420 W Dodge Rd 5th Fl TF: 800-786-5566 ■ Web: www.seniormarketsales.com	Omaha	NE	68114	402-397-3311	397-0455
SilverStone Group 11516 Miracle Hills Dr Suite 102 TF: 800-288-5501 ■ Web: www.silverstonegroup.com	Omaha	NE	68154	402-964-5400	964-5454
Simkiss Cos 2 Paoli Office Pk PO Box 1787 Web: www.simkiss.com	Paoli	PA	19301	610-727-5300	727-5414
Stallings Crop Insurance Corp PO Box 6100 TF: 800-721-7099 ■ Web: www.stallingscrop.com	Lakeland	FL	33807	863-647-2747	
Standard Insurance Agency Corp 620 W Pipeline Web: www.siatexas.com	Hurst	TX	76053	817-285-1800	
Star Casualty Insurance Co 3750 W Flagler St TF: 888-511-7722 ■ Web: www.starcasualty.com	Miami	FL	33134	305-442-2276	476-8586
Starkweather & Shepley Inc 60 Catamore Blvd TF: 800-854-4625 ■ Web: www.starkweathershepley.com	East Providence	RI	02914	401-435-3600	438-0150
Sullivan Curtis Monroe 1920 Main St TF: 800-427-3253 ■ Web: www.sullivancurtismonroe.com	Irvine	CA	92614	949-250-7172	852-9762
Tanenbaum-Harber Co Inc 320 W 57th St 2nd Fl Web: www.tanhar.com	New York	NY	10019	212-603-0200	262-9470

				Phone	Fax
Transguard Insurance Co of America Inc 215 S Human Blvd *Web:* www.transguard.com	Naperville	IL	60563	630-864-3500	
U S Risk Insurance Group Inc 10210 N Central Expy *TF:* 800-926-9155 ■ *Web:* www.usrisk.com	Dallas	TX	75231	214-265-7090	739-1421
UIC Inc 1 Pk Way 3rd Fl *Web:* www.uici.com	Upper Saddle River	NJ	07458	201-661-5010	221-7529
United Underwriters Inc PO Box 971000 *Web:* www.uuinsurance.com	Orem	UT	84097	801-226-2662	229-2662
USG Insurance Service Inc 14499 N Dale Mabry Hwy *Web:* www.usgins.com	Tampa	FL	33618	813-961-1300	961-0768
USI Holdings Corp 555 Pleasantville Rd Suite 160 S **Fax Area Code:* 610 ■ *Web:* www.usi.biz	Briarcliff Manor	NY	10510	914-749-8500	537-4500*
Van Dyk Group Inc The 12800 Long Beach Blvd *TF:* 800-222-0131 ■ *Web:* www.vandykgroup.com	Beach Haven	NJ	08008	609-492-1511	492-7643
Van Gilder Insurance Corp 700 Broadway Suite 1000 *TF:* 800-873-8500 ■ *Web:* www.vgic.com	Denver	CO	80204	303-837-8500	831-5295
Van Zandt Emrich & Cary Inc 12401 Plantside Dr *TF:* 800-928-7355 ■ *Web:* www.vzecins.com	Louisville	KY	40299	502-456-2001	454-5137
VanBeurden Insurance Services Inc 1600 Draper St PO Box 67 *Web:* www.vanbeurden.com	Kingsburg	CA	93631	559-897-2975	897-4070
Wallace Welch Willingham 300 First Ave S 5th Fl *TF:* 800-783-5085 ■ *Web:* www.wiseleymarineinsurance.com	Saint Petersbu	FL	33701	727-522-7777	521-2902
Weaver Bros Insurance Assoc Inc 7315 Wisconsin Ave Suite 900 E *Web:* www.weaverbros.com	Bethesda	MD	20814	301-986-4400	986-4422
Wells Fargo Insurance Inc 600 S Hwy 169 12th Fl *TF:* 800-328-2791 ■ *Web:* www.wellsfargo.com	Saint Louis Park	MN	55426	612-667-5600	667-2680
Wharton Group 101 S Livingston Ave *TF:* 800-521-2725 ■ *Web:* www.whartoninsurance.com	Livingston	NJ	07039	973-992-5775	992-6660
William Gallagher Assoc Investment Services Group Inc (WGA) 470 Atlantic Ave *Web:* www.wgains.com	Boston	MA	02210	617-261-6700	
Willis Group Holdings Ltd 200 Liberty St 1 World Financial Ctr *NYSE: WSH* ■ *TF:* 800-234-8596 ■ *Web:* www.willis.com	New York	NY	10281	212-915-8888	915-8511
XL Environmental Inc PO Box 636 *Web:* www.xlenvironmental.com	Exton	PA	19341	610-968-9500	458-8667
York Stb Inc 2170 W State Rd 434 *TF:* 877-927-2255 ■ *Web:* www.yorkisg.com	Longwood	FL	32779	407-618-1172	

394 INSURANCE COMPANIES

SEE ALSO Home Warranty Services p. 2026; Viatical Settlement Companies p. 2762

394-1 Animal Insurance

				Phone	Fax
Ark Agency Animal Insurance Services 310 Washburne Ave *TF:* 800-328-8894 ■ *Web:* www.arkagency-naha.com	Paynesville	MN	56362	320-243-7250	243-7224
Canadian Livestock Insurance 480 University Ave Suite 412 *TF:* 800-727-1502 ■ *Web:* www.cdnlivestock.com	Toronto	ON	M5G1V2	416-510-8191	510-8186
Equisport Agency Inc 2306 Eastways Rd *TF:* 800-432-1215 ■ *Web:* www.equisportagency.com	Bloomfield Hills	MI	48304	248-644-1215	644-1404
Henry Equestrian Insurance Brokers 28 Victoria St *TF:* 800-363-6437 ■ *Web:* www.hep.ca	Aurora	ON	L4G3L6	905-727-1144	727-4986
Merry Rama Insurance 4236 County Hwy 18 *Web:* www.cattlexchange.com/insurance.htm	Delhi	NY	13753	607-746-2226	746-2911
Pet's Health Plan 3840 Greentree Ave SW *TF:* 877-592-7387 ■ *Web:* www.petshealthplan.com	Canton	OH	44706	330-484-8179	484-8081
Veterinary Pet Insurance Inc 3060 Saturn St **Fax Area Code:* 714 ■ *TF:* 877-263-6002 ■ *Web:* www.petinsurance.com	Brea	CA	92821	800-872-7387	989-0533*

394-2 Life & Accident Insurance

				Phone	Fax
Acacia Life Insurance Co 7315 Wisconsin Ave **Fax:* Cust Svc ■ *TF:* 800-444-1889 ■ *Web:* www.unificompanies.com	Bethesda	MD	20814	301-280-1000	280-1451*
Acacia National Life 7315 Wisconsin Ave *TF:* 800-444-1889 ■ *Web:* www.unificompanies.com	Bethesda	MD	20814	301-280-1000	280-1451
Advance Insurance Co of Kansas 1133 SW Topeka Blvd *TF:* 800-530-5989 ■ *Web:* www.advanceinsurance.com	Topeka	KS	66629	785-273-9804	273-6121
Aegon Special Markets Group Inc 20 Moores Rd *TF:* 800-523-7900 ■ *Web:* www.aegonsmg.com	Frazer	PA	19355	610-648-5000	648-5348
Aetna Inc 151 Farmington Ave *NYSE: AET* ■ *TF:* 800-872-3862 ■ *Web:* www.aetna.com	Hartford	CT	06156	860-273-0123	273-8909
AIG American General 3051 Hollis Dr *TF:* 800-528-2011	Springfield	IL	62704	217-541-7700	
AIG American General 2727 A Allen Pkwy *TF:* 800-231-3655 ■ *Web:* www.aigag.com	Houston	TX	77019	713-522-1111	831-3028
Alfa Life Insurance Corp *Alfa Corp* 2108 E S Blvd PO Box 11000	Montgomery	AL	36116	334-288-3900	613-4709
Allegiance Life Insurance Co 1 Horace Mann Plaza *NYSE: HMN* ■ *TF:* 800-999-1030 ■ *Web:* www.horacemans.com	Springfield	IL	62715	217-789-2500	788-5161
Alliant Insurance Services Inc 1301 Dove St *Web:* www.alliantinsurance.com	Newport Beach	CA	92660	949-756-0271	756-2713
Allianz Life Insurance Co of North America 5701 Golden Hills Dr **Fax:* Mktg ■ *TF:* 800-328-5600 ■ *Web:* www.allianzlife.com	Minneapolis	MN	55416	763-765-6500	582-6407*
Allstate Life Insurance Co 3100 Sanders Rd Allstate W Plaza *TF Cust Svc:* 800-366-1411 ■ *Web:* www.allstate.com	Northbrook	IL	60062	847-402-5000	
Allstate Life Insurance Co of New York PO Box 80469 *TF:* 800-347-5433	Lincoln	NE	68501	800-347-5433	255-1329
Amalgamated Life Insurance Co 730 Broadway *Web:* www.amalgamatedlife.com	New York	NY	10003	212-539-5000	
American Amicable Life Insurance Co PO Box 2549 *TF:* 800-736-7311 ■ *Web:* www.americanamicable.com	Waco	TX	76702	254-297-2777	297-2757
American Community Mutual Insurance Co 39201 Seven-Mile Rd *TF:* 800-991-2642 ■ *Web:* www.american-community.com	Livonia	MI	48152	734-591-9000	591-4628
American Equity Investment Life Insurance Co 6000 Westown Pkwy *NYSE: AEL* ■ *TF:* 888-221-1234 ■ *Web:* www.american-equity.com	West Des Moines	IA	50266	515-221-0002	221-9947
American Family Life Assurance Co of Columbus (AFLAC) 1932 Wynnton Rd **Fax Area Code:* 800 ■ **Fax:* Cust Svc ■ *TF Cust Svc:* 800-992-3522 ■ *Web:* www.aflac.com	Columbus	GA	31999	706-323-3431	448-8922*
American Family Life Insurance Co 6000 American Pkwy *TF:* 888-428-5433 ■ *Web:* www.amfam.com	Madison	WI	53783	608-249-2111	243-4921
American Family Mutual Insurance Co 6000 American Pkwy **Fax:* Hum Res ■ *TF Cust Svc:* 800-374-0008 ■ *Web:* www.amfam.com	Madison	WI	53783	608-249-2111	243-4921*
American Fidelity Assurance Co 2000 N Classen Blvd *TF:* 800-654-8489 ■ *Web:* www.afadvantage.com	Oklahoma City	OK	73106	405-523-2000	523-5645
American Fidelity Life Insurance Co 4060 Barrancas Ave *Web:* www.americanfidelitylifeins.com	Pensacola	FL	32507	850-456-7401	453-5440
American Foreign Service Protective Assn 1716 N St NW *Web:* www.afspa.org	Washington	DC	20036	202-833-4910	833-4918
American Income Life Insurance Co (AIL) 1200 Wooded Acres *TF:* 800-433-3405 ■ *Web:* www.ailins.com	Waco	TX	76710	254-761-6400	761-5724
American National Insurance Co 1 Moody Plaza *NASDAQ: ANAT*	Galveston	TX	77550	409-763-4661	763-4545
American Progressive Life & Health Insurance Co of New York 6 International Dr Suite 190 *TF:* 800-332-3377 ■ *Web:* www.uafc.com	Rye Brook	NY	10573	914-934-8300	934-9123
American Republic Insurance Co 601 6th Ave *TF Cust Svc:* 800-247-2190 ■ *Web:* www.americanrepublic.com	Des Moines	IA	50309	515-245-2000	247-2435
American Standard Insurance Co of Wisconsin 6000 American Pkwy *TF:* 800-692-6326 ■ *Web:* www.amfam.com	Madison	WI	53783	608-249-2111	
American United Life Insurance Co 1 American Sq PO Box 6010 *TF:* 800-537-6442 ■ *Web:* www.aul.com	Indianapolis	IN	46206	317-285-1877	285-1855
Americo Financial Life & Annuity Insurance Co PO Box 410288 *TF:* 800-231-0801 ■ *Web:* www.americo.com	Kansas City	MO	64141	800-231-0801	
Ameritas Direct 5900 'O' St *TF:* 800-552-3553 ■ *Web:* www.ameritasdirect.com	Lincoln	NE	68510	402-467-1122	467-7935
Ameritas Life Insurance Corp 5900 'O' St **Fax:* Hum Res ■ *TF:* 800-283-9588 ■ *Web:* www.ameritas.com	Lincoln	NE	68510	402-467-1122	467-7935*
Ameritas Variable Life Insurance Co 5900 'O' St **Fax:* Hum Res ■ *TF:* 800-634-8353 ■ *Web:* www.overturelife.com	Lincoln	NE	68510	402-467-1122	467-7935*
Amica Life Insurance Co PO Box 6008 **Fax Area Code:* 401 ■ *TF:* 800-992-6422 ■ *Web:* www.amica.com	Providence	RI	02940	800-242-6422	333-9360*
Annuity Investors Life Insurance Co 525 Vine St 7th Fl *TF:* 800-789-6771	Cincinnati	OH	45202	513-357-3300	357-3397
Anthem Life Insurance Co 6740 N High St Suite 200 *TF:* 800-551-7265 ■ *Web:* www.anthem.com	Worthington	OH	43085	614-436-0688	
Assurant Employee Benefits 2323 Grand Blvd *TF:* 800-733-7879 ■ *Web:* www.assurantemployeebenefits.com	Kansas City	MO	64108	816-474-2345	881-8996
Assurant Life Insurance Co 308 Maltbie St Suite 200 *TF:* 800-745-7100 ■ *Web:* www.assurant.com	Syracuse	NY	13204	315-451-0066	453-2343
Aurora National Life Assurance Co PO Box 4490 **Fax Area Code:* 860 ■ *TF:* 800-265-2652 ■ *Web:* www.auroralife.com	Hartford	CT	06147	800-265-2652	513-5390*
AUSA Life Insurance Co Inc 4333 Edgewood Rd NE *TF Cust Svc:* 800-625-4213	Cedar Rapids	IA	52499	319-398-8511	369-2209
Auto-Owners Life Insurance Co 6101 Anacapri Blvd *TF:* 800-288-8740 ■ *Web:* www.auto-owners.com	Lansing	MI	48917	517-323-1200	323-8796
AXA Equitable Life Insurance Co 1290 Avenue of the Americas *TF:* 888-855-5100 ■ *Web:* www.axa-equitable.com	New York	NY	10104	212-554-1234	
Baltimore Life Cos 10075 Red Run Blvd **Fax:* Claims ■ *TF:* 800-628-5433 ■ *Web:* www.baltlife.com	Owings Mills	MD	21117	410-581-6600	654-0786*
Bankers Fidelity Life Insurance Co 4370 Peachtree Rd *NASDAQ: AAME* ■ **Fax:* Sales ■ *TF:* 800-241-1439 ■ *Web:* www.bflic.com	Atlanta	GA	30319	404-266-5500	266-5699*

	City	State	Zip	Phone	Fax
Bankers Insurance Co 11101 Roosevelt Blvd N	Saint Petersburg	FL	33716	727-823-4000	898-1511
TF: 800-627-0000 ■ *Web:* www.bankersinsurance.com					
Bankers Insurance LLC 4490 Cox Rd	Glen Allen	VA	23060	804-497-3634	643-6308
Web: www.bankersinsurance.net					
Bankers Life & Casualty Co 600 W Chicago Ave	Chicago	IL	60654	312-396-6000	324-5060
TF: 800-621-3724 ■ *Web:* www.bankerslife.com					
Banner Life Insurance Co 1701 Research Blvd	Rockville	MD	20850	301-279-4800	294-6961
TF: 800-638-8428 ■ *Web:* www.lgamerica.com					
Beneficial Financial Group 55 N 300 W	Salt Lake City	UT	84145	801-933-1100	884-6218*
**Fax Area Code:* 800 ■ **Fax:* Cust Svc ■ *TF:* 800-233-7979 ■ *Web:* www.beneficialfinancialgroup.com					
Benevolent Life Insurance Co Inc 1624 Milam St	Shreveport	LA	71103	318-425-1522	221-1761
TF: 800-435-1522					
Berkshire Hathaway Life Insurance Co of Nebraska 3024 Harney St	Omaha	NE	68131	402-536-3100	536-3030
TF: 800-786-6426 ■ *Web:* www.brkdirect.com					
Berkshire Life Insurance Co of America 700 S St	Pittsfield	MA	01201	413-499-4321	499-4831
TF: 800-819-2468 ■ *Web:* www.berkshirelife.com					
Best Life & Health Insurance Co 2505 McCabe Way	Irvine	CA	92630	949-253-4080	222-1004
Web: www.bestlife.com					
Booker T Washington Insurance Co 1728 3rd Ave N	Birmingham	AL	35203	205-328-5454	251-6873
TF: 800-228-4180					
Boston Mutual Life Insurance Co 120 Royall St	Canton	MA	02021	781-828-7000	770-0490
TF: 800-669-2668 ■ *Web:* www.bostonmutual.com					
Bristol West Insurance Group 5701 Stirling Rd PO Box 229080	Davie	FL	33314	954-316-5200	316-5275
Web: www.bristolwest.com					
Central Security Life Insurance Co 2175 N Glenville Dr PO Box 833879	Richardson	TX	75082	972-699-2770	699-2788
TF: 866-629-2677 ■ *Web:* www.cslic.com					
Central States Health & Life Co of Omaha 1212 N 96th St	Omaha	NE	68114	402-397-1111	399-3497
TF: 800-541-2363 ■ *Web:* www.cso.com					
CIGNA Reinsurance 900 Cottage Grove Rd	Hartford	CT	06152	860-226-6000	226-4566
TF: 888-244-6237					
Cincinnati Life Insurance Co PO Box 145496	Cincinnati	OH	45250	513-870-2000	870-2911
TF Cust Svc: 800-783-4479 ■ *Web:* www.cinfin.com					
Citizens Insurance Co of America 400 E Anderson Ln	Austin	TX	78752	512-836-9730	836-9785
TF: 800-880-5044 ■ *Web:* www.citizensinc.com					
Citizens Security Life Insurance Co PO Box 436149	Louisville	KY	40253	502-244-2420	244-2439
TF: 800-843-7752 ■ *Web:* www.citizenssecuritylife.com					
Colonial Life & Accident Insurance Co 1200 Colonial Life Blvd	Columbia	SC	29210	803-798-7000	731-2618
TF: 800-325-4368 ■ *Web:* www.coloniallife.com					
Colonial Penn Life Insurance Co 399 Market St	Philadelphia	PA	19181	215-928-8000	
TF: 800-523-9100 ■ *Web:* www.colonialpenn.com					
Columbus Life Insurance Co 400 E 4th St PO Box 5737	Cincinnati	OH	45201	513-361-6700	361-6939
TF: 800-677-8383 ■ *Web:* www.columbuslife.com					
Companion Life Insurance Co 7909 Parklane Rd Suite 200	Columbia	SC	29223	803-735-1251	735-0736
TF: 800-753-0404 ■ *Web:* www.companionlife.com					
Concord Group Insurance Cos 4 Bouton St	Concord	NH	03301	603-224-4086	225-5268*
**Fax:* Hum Res ■ *TF:* 800-852-3380 ■ *Web:* www.concordgroupinsurance.com					
Conseco Annuity Assurance Co 11815 N Pennsylvania St	Carmel	IN	46032	317-817-6100	817-5704
TF: 800-541-2254 ■ *Web:* www.conseco.com					
Conseco Health Insurance Co 11815 N Pennsylvania St	Carmel	IN	46932	317-817-6100	817-5704
TF: 800-541-2254 ■ *Web:* www.conseco.com					
Conseco Life Insurance Co 11815 N Pennsylvania St	Carmel	IN	46032	317-817-6100	817-6721
Web: www.conseco.com					
Conseco Senior Health Insurance Co 11825 N Pennsylvania St PO Box 1980	Carmel	IN	46032	317-817-6100	817-6721
TF: 877-454-5824 ■ *Web:* www.conseco.com					
Conseco Variable Insurance Co 11815 N Pennsylvania St	Carmel	IN	46032	317-817-6100	817-6721
Web: www.conseco.com					
Continental Assurance Co 333 S Wabash Ave	Chicago	IL	60604	312-822-5000	822-6419
TF: 800-262-2000 ■ *Web:* www.cna.com					
COUNTRY Insurance & Financial Services 1705 Towanda Ave	Bloomington	IL	61701	309-557-3000	821-2501
TF: 888-211-2555 ■ *Web:* www.countryfinancial.com					
Crump Insurance Services Inc 105 Eisenhower Pkwy	Roseland	NJ	07068	973-461-2100	461-2128
TF: 888-305-2191 ■ *Web:* www.crump.com					
Epic Life Insurance Co 1765 W Broadway	Madison	WI	53713	608-223-2100	223-2159
TF Sales: 800-236-8809 ■ *Web:* www.epiclife.com					
Equitable Distributors Inc 1290 Avenue of the Americas	New York	NY	10104	212-554-1234	314-3141
TF: 888-855-5100 ■ *Web:* www.axa-equitable.com					
Equitable Life & Casualty Insurance Co 3 Triad Ctr Suite 200	Salt Lake City	UT	84180	801-521-2500	579-3715
TF Cust Svc: 800-352-5150 ■ *Web:* www.equilife.com					
Erie Family Life Insurance Co 100 Erie Insurance Pl	Erie	PA	16530	814-870-2000	870-2095
TF: 800-458-0811 ■ *Web:* www.erieinsurance.com					
Farm Bureau Life Insurance Co 5400 University Ave	West Des Moines	IA	50266	515-225-5400	226-6053*
**Fax:* Hum Res ■ *TF:* 800-247-4170 ■ *Web:* www.fbfs.com					
Farm Family Life Insurance Co PO Box 656	Albany	NY	12201	518-431-5000	
TF: 800-948-3276 ■ *Web:* www.farmfamily.com					
Farmers New World Life Insurance 3003 77th Ave SE	Mercer Island	WA	98040	206-232-8400	236-6642
Federal Life Insurance Co Mutual 3750 W Deerfield Rd Suite A	Riverwoods	IL	60015	847-520-1900	520-1916
TF: 800-233-3750 ■ *Web:* www.federallife.com					
Federated Life Insurance Co 121 E Pk Sq PO Box 328	Owatonna	MN	55060	507-455-5200	444-6778
TF: 800-533-0472 ■ *Web:* www.federatedinsurance.com					
Federated Mutual Insurance Co 129 E Broadway St	Owatonna	MN	55060	507-455-5200	455-7808
TF: 800-533-0472 ■ *Web:* www.federatedinsurance.com					
FEDUSA 1839 N Pine Island Rd	Plantation	FL	33322	954-475-0182	475-1058
Web: www.fedusa.com					
FIC Insurance Group 6500 River Pl Blvd Bldg 1	Austin	TX	78730	512-404-5000	
TF: 800-925-6000					
Fidelity & Guaranty Life Insurance Co PO Box 1137	Baltimore	MD	21203	410-895-0100	895-0100
TF Sales: 800-445-6758 ■ *Web:* www.omfn.com					
First Investors Life Insurance Co Raritan Plaza 1 PO Box 7836	Edison	NJ	08818	732-855-2500	510-4209
TF: 800-832-7783 ■ *Web:* www.firstinvestorslife.com					
First UNUM Life Insurance Co 2211 Congress St	Portland	ME	04122	800-658-8686	328-8977*
**Fax Area Code:* 212 ■ *TF:* 800-658-8686 ■ *Web:* www.unum.com					
Forethought Financial Services Inc Forethought Ctr	Batesville	IN	47006	800-881-2430	934-8564*
**Fax Area Code:* 812 ■ *TF:* 800-881-2430 ■ *Web:* www.forethought.com					
Fremont Life Insurance Co PO Box 410288	Kansas City	MO	64141	816-391-2000	391-2100
TF: 800-243-4651					
General Reinsurance Corp 695 E Main St Financial Ctr	Stamford	CT	06901	203-328-5000	328-6423
TF: 800-431-9994 ■ *Web:* www.genre.com					
Genworth Financial Inc 6620 W Broad St	Richmond	VA	23230	804-484-3821	484-7198
NYSE: GNW ■ *TF:* 888-436-9678 ■ *Web:* www.genworth.com					
Gerber Life Insurance Co 1311 Mamaroneck Ave	White Plains	NY	10605	914-272-4000	272-4099
TF: 800-704-2180 ■ *Web:* www.gerberlife.com					
Grange Life Insurance Co 671 S Front St	Columbus	OH	43216	614-445-2900	445-2337
TF: 800-422-0550					
Great American Life Assurance Co of Puerto Rico Inc PO Box 363786	San Juan	PR	00936	787-758-4888	766-1985
TF: 800-980-7651 ■ *Web:* www.galifepr.com					
Great Southern Life Insurance Co PO Box 410288	Kansas City	MO	64141	800-231-0801	
TF: 800-231-0801 ■ *Web:* www.greatsouthern.com					
Great-West Life & Annuity Insurance Co 8515 E Orchard Rd	Greenwood Village	CO	80111	303-737-3000	737-3198
TF: 800-537-2033 ■ *Web:* www.greatwest.com					
Great-West Life Assurance Co 100 Osborne St	Winnipeg	MB	R3C3A5	204-946-1190	946-4129*
**Fax:* Investor Rel ■ *TF:* 800-990-6654 ■ *Web:* www.gwl.ca					
Group Variable Universal Life Insurance (GVUL) 190 Carondelet Plaza	Saint Louis	MO	63105	800-685-0124	862-5171*
**Fax Area Code:* 314 ■ *TF:* 800-685-0124 ■ *Web:* www.metlife.com					
Guarantee Trust Life Insurance Co 1275 Milwaukee Ave	Glenview	IL	60025	847-699-0600	699-2355
TF: 800-338-7452 ■ *Web:* www.gtlic.com					
Guardian Investor Services LLC 7 Hanover Sq	New York	NY	10004	212-598-8000	919-2170
TF: 800-221-3253 ■ *Web:* www.guardianinvestor.com					
Guardian Life Insurance Co of America 7 Hanover Sq	New York	NY	10004	212-598-8000	919-2762*
**Fax:* Hum Res ■ *TF:* 888-482-7342 ■ *Web:* www.guardianlife.com					
GuideOne Mutual Insurance Co 1111 Ashworth Rd	West Des Moines	IA	50265	515-267-5000	267-5530*
**Fax:* Hum Res ■ *TF:* 877-448-4331 ■ *Web:* www.guideone.com					
Hannover Life Reassurance Co of America 800 N Magnolia Ave Suite 1400	Orlando	FL	32803	407-649-8411	649-8322
TF: 800-327-1910 ■ *Web:* www.hlramerica.com					
Hanover Insurance Group Inc The 440 Lincoln St	Worcester	MA	01653	508-855-1000	853-6332
TF: 800-628-0250 ■ *Web:* www.hanover.com					
Harleysville Life Insurance Co 1440 Pennbrook Pkwy	Lansdale	PA	19446	800-222-1981	
TF: 800-222-1981 ■ *Web:* www.harleysville.com					
Harleysville Mutual Insurance Co 355 Maple Ave	Harleysville	PA	19438	215-256-5000	256-5601
TF: 800-523-6344 ■ *Web:* www.harleysville.com					
Hartford Life & Accident Insurance Co 200 Hopmeadow St	Simsbury	CT	06089	860-547-5000	
TF: 800-833-5575 ■ *Web:* www.thehartford.com					
Harvey Watt & Co 475 N Central Ave	Atlanta	GA	30354	404-767-7501	761-8326
TF: 800-241-6103 ■ *Web:* www.harveywatt.com					
Hcc Life Insurance Co 225 Townpark Dr Suite 145	Kennesaw	GA	30144	770-973-9851	973-9854
TF: 800-447-0460 ■ *Web:* www.hcclife.com					
HealthExtras Inc 800 King Farm Blvd	Rockville	MD	20850	301-548-2900	
NASDAQ: HLEX ■ *TF:* 800-323-6640 ■ *Web:* www.healthextras.com					
HM Benefits Administrators 5th Ave Pl 120 5th Ave	Pittsburgh	PA	15222	412-544-2000	
TF: 800-833-1115 ■ *Web:* www.highmarklife.com					
Horace Mann Insurance Co 1 Horace Mann Plaza	Springfield	IL	62715	217-789-2500	788-5161
TF: 800-999-1030 ■ *Web:* www.horacemann.com					
Horace Mann Life Insurance Co 1 Horace Mann Plaza	Springfield	IL	62715	217-789-2500	788-5161
TF: 800-999-1030 ■ *Web:* www.horacemann.com					
Hudson Health Plan Inc 303 S Broadway Suite 321	Tarrytown	NY	10591	914-631-1611	631-1746
TF: 800-339-4557 ■ *Web:* www.hudsonhealthplan.org					
Humana Inc 500 W Main St	Louisville	KY	40202	502-580-1000	580-3690
NYSE: HUM ■ *TF:* 800-486-2620 ■ *Web:* www.humana.com					

Company / Address	City	State	ZIP	Phone	Fax
Illinois Mutual Life Insurance Co 300 SW Adams St *TF:* 800-380-6688 ■ *Web:* www.illinoismutual.com	Peoria	IL	61634	309-674-8255	674-8637
Independence Holding Co 96 Cummings Pt Rd *NYSE: IHC* ■ *Web:* www.independenceholding.com	Stamford	CT	06902	203-358-8000	348-3103
Indiana Farm Bureau Insurance Co 225 S E St PO Box 1250 **Fax:* Sales ■ *TF:* 800-723-3276 ■ *Web:* www.infarmbureau.com	Indianapolis	IN	46206	317-692-7200	692-7185*
Indianapolis Life Insurance Co 9200 N Meridian St **Fax Area Code:* 317 ■ *TF:* 800-457-3557	Indianapolis	IN	46240	800-831-4380	927-6510*
Industrial Alliance Insurance & Financial Services 1080 Grande Allee W PO Box 1907 Stn Therminus *TF:* 800-463-6236 ■ *Web:* www.inalco.com	Quebec City	QC	G1K7M3	418-684-5000	684-5106
Ing Life Insurance & Annuity Co 1 Orange Way *TF:* 866-726-4646 ■ *Web:* www.ingretirementplans.com	Windsor	CT	06095	866-726-4646	
Insurance Marketing Agencies Inc 306 Main St *TF:* 800-891-1226 ■ *Web:* www.imaagency.com	Worcester	MA	01608	508-753-7233	754-0487
Investors Heritage Life Insurance Co (IHLIC) 200 Capital Ave PO Box 717 *TF:* 800-422-2011 ■ *Web:* www.investorsheritage.com	Frankfort	KY	40602	502-223-2361	875-7084
Investors Life Insurance Co of Indiana 6500 River Pl Blvd Bldg 1 *TF:* 800-925-6000	Austin	TX	78730	512-404-5000	404-5210
Investors Life Insurance Co of North America 6500 River Pl Blvd Bldg 1 *TF:* 800-925-6000	Austin	TX	78730	512-404-5000	404-5210
Investors Partner Life Insurance Co PO Box 111 *TF:* 800-732-5543	Boston	MA	02117	617-572-6000	572-7756
Jackson National Life Insurance Co 1 Corporate Way *TF:* 800-644-4565 ■ *Web:* www.jackson.com	Lansing	MI	48951	517-381-5500	
John Hancock Life Insurance Co 1 John Hancock Way Suite 1101 *Web:* www.johnhancock.com	Boston	MA	02117	617-572-6000	
John Hancock New York 100 Summit Lake Dr 2nd Fl *TF:* 800-551-2078 ■ *Web:* www.johnhancock.com	Valhalla	NY	10595	914-773-0708	773-0709
John Hancock Variable Life Insurance Co 601 Congress St *TF:* 800-732-5543 ■ *Web:* www.johnhancock.com	Boston	MA	02210	617-572-6000	572-7756
Kanawha Insurance Co 322 S Main St *TF:* 800-635-4252 ■ *Web:* www.kanawha.com	Lancaster	SC	29720	803-283-5300	283-5676
Lafayette Life Insurance Co 1905 Teal Rd *TF:* 800-243-6631 ■ *Web:* www.llic.com	Lafayette	IN	47905	765-477-7411	477-3349
Liberty National Life Insurance Co PO Box 2612 *TF:* 800-333-0637 ■ *Web:* www.libertynational.com	Birmingham	AL	35202	205-325-4979	325-4909
Life Insurance Co of Alabama 302 Broad St *TF:* 800-226-2371 ■ *Web:* www.licoa.com	Gadsden	AL	35901	256-439-3306	543-0019
Life Insurance Co of the Southwest 15455 Dallas Pkwy Suite 800 **Fax Area Code:* 214 ■ *TF:* 800-579-2878 ■ *Web:* www.lifeofsouthwest.com	Dallas	TX	75001	800-579-2878	638-9162*
Life Investors Insurance Co of America 4333 Edgewood Rd NE **Fax Area Code:* 800 ■ **Fax:* Cust Svc ■ *TF:* 800-625-4213	Cedar Rapids	IA	52499	319-398-8511	235-4782*
Lincoln Heritage Life Insurance Co 4343 E Camelback Rd Suite 400 PO Box 29045 *TF:* 800-438-8181 ■ *Web:* www.lhlic.com	Phoenix	AZ	85018	602-957-1650	840-0969
Lincoln National Life Insurance Co 1300 S Clinton St **Fax:* Hum Res ■ *TF:* 800-454-6265 ■ *Web:* www.lfg.com	Fort Wayne	IN	46802	260-455-2000	455-4268*
London Insurance Group Corp PO Box 29045 **Fax Area Code:* 602 ■ *TF:* 800-433-8181 ■ *Web:* www.lhlic.com	Phoenix	AZ	85038	800-433-8181	840-0969*
London Life Insurance Co 255 Dufferin Ave *TF:* 800-990-6654 ■ *Web:* www.londonlife.com	London	ON	N6A4K1	519-432-5281	435-7555
Louisiana Dealer Services Insurance Inc PO Box 83480 *Web:* www.theldsgroup.com	Baton Rouge	LA	70884	225-769-9923	769-9112
Loyal American Life Insurance Co *Great American Financial Resources Inc* PO Box 559004 **Fax Area Code:* 512 ■ *TF:* 800-633-6752 ■ *Web:* www.gafri.com	Austin	TX	78755	800-633-6752	302-0913*
Madison National Life Insurance Co Inc PO Box 5008 *TF:* 800-356-9601 ■ *Web:* www.madisonlife.com	Madison	WI	53705	608-830-2000	830-2700
Manulife Financial 200 Bloor St E *Web:* www.manulife.ca	Toronto	ON	M4W1E5	416-926-3000	926-5410
Manulife Mutual Funds 200 Bloor St E N Tower 3 *TF:* 888-588-7999 ■ *Web:* www.manulife.ca	Toronto	ON	M4W1E5	888-588-7999	
Medico Group 1515 S 75th St *TF:* 800-228-6080 ■ *Web:* www.gomedico.com	Omaha	NE	68124	402-391-6900	391-6489
Medico Life Insurance Co 1515 S 75th St *TF:* 800-228-6080	Omaha	NE	68124	402-391-6900	391-6489
MEGA Life & Health Insurance Co 9151 Grapevine Hwy **Fax Area Code:* 800 ■ **Fax:* Cust Svc ■ *TF:* 800-527-2845 ■ *Web:* www.megainsurance.com	North Richland Hills	TX	76180	817-255-3100	343-3702*
Merrill Lynch Life Insurance Co 4804 Deer Lake Dr E **Fax:* Hum Res ■ *TF:* 800-535-5549	Jacksonville	FL	32246	904-218-7000	218-7205*
MetLife Inc 200 Pk Ave *NYSE: MET* ■ *TF:* 800-638-5433 ■ *Web:* www.metlife.com	New York	NY	10166	212-578-2211	578-3320
MetLife Investors Insurance Co 5 Pk Plaza Suite 1900 *TF:* 800-848-3854 ■ *Web:* www.metlifeinvestors.com	Irvine	CA	92614	949-629-1300	629-1687
Metropolitan Life Insurance Co 2701 Queens Plaza N Met Life Plaza **Fax:* Mail Rm ■ *TF:* 800-638-5433 ■ *Web:* www.metlife.com	Long Island City	NY	11101	212-578-2211	689-1980*
Mid-Century Insurance Co 4680 Wilshire Blvd *TF:* 888-516-5656 ■ *Web:* www.farmers.com	Los Angeles	CA	90010	323-932-3200	932-3101
Mid-West National Life Ins Co of Tennessee 9151 Grapevine Hwy **Fax Area Code:* 888 ■ *TF:* 800-733-1110 ■ *Web:* www.midwestlife.com	North Richland Hills	TX	76182	800-733-1110	377-4391*
Midland National Life Insurance Co 1 Midland Plaza *TF:* 800-923-3223	Sioux Falls	SD	57193	605-335-5700	335-3621
MML Bay State Life Insurance Co 100 Bright Meadow Blvd *Web:* www.massmutual.com	Enfield	CT	06082	860-562-1000	
Modern Woodmen of America 1701 1st Ave *TF:* 800-447-9811 ■ *Web:* www.modern-woodmen.org	Rock Island	IL	61201	309-786-6481	793-5547
Monumental Life Insurance Co 2 E Chase St *TF:* 800-638-3080 ■ *Web:* www.monlife.com	Baltimore	MD	21202	410-685-2900	347-8653
Motorists Life Insurance Co 471 E Broad St *Web:* www.motoristsmutual.com	Columbus	OH	43215	614-225-8211	225-8365
Munich American Reassurance Co PO Box 3210 *Web:* www.marclife.com	Atlanta	GA	30302	770-394-5665	394-7744
Mutual Insurance Co of Arizona PO Box 33180 *TF:* 800-352-0402 ■ *Web:* www.mica-insurance.com	Phoenix	AZ	85067	602-956-5276	468-1710
Mutual of America Life Insurance Co 320 Pk Ave **Fax:* Mail Rm ■ *TF:* 800-468-3785 ■ *Web:* www.mutualofamerica.com	New York	NY	10022	212-224-1600	224-2500*
Mutual of Detroit Insurance Co 333 Plymouth Rd *TF:* 866-453-8510 ■ *Web:* www.mutualofdetroit.com	Plymouth	MI	48170	734-453-8500	453-2610
Mutual of Omaha Insurance Co Mutual of Omaha Plaza *TF:* 800-775-6000 ■ *Web:* www.mutualofomaha.com	Omaha	NE	68175	402-342-7600	351-2775
Mutual Trust Life Insurance Co 1200 Jorie Blvd *TF:* 800-323-7320 ■ *Web:* www.mutualtrust.com	Oak Brook	IL	60522	630-990-1000	990-7083
National Guardian Life Insurance Co PO Box 1191 *TF:* 800-548-2962	Madison	WI	53701	608-257-5611	257-4308
National Mutual Benefit 6522 Grand Teton Plaza *TF:* 800-779-1936 ■ *Web:* www.nmblife.org	Madison	WI	53719	608-833-1936	833-8714
National Security Life & Accident Insurance Co PO Box 149151 *TF:* 800-880-5044	Austin	TX	78714	512-837-7100	836-9785
National Western Life Insurance Co 850 E Anderson Ln *NASDAQ: NWLIA* ■ **Fax:* Hum Res ■ *TF:* 800-531-5442 ■ *Web:* www.nationalwesternlife.com	Austin	TX	78752	512-836-1010	719-0104*
Nationwide Life & Annuity Insurance Co 1 nationwide pl **Fax:* Hum Res ■ *TF:* 800-882-2822 ■ *Web:* www.nationwide.com	columbus	OH	43215	614-249-7111	249-2205*
Nationwide Life Insurance Co 5100 Rings Rd *TF:* 800-543-3747	Dublin	OH	43017	614-249-7111	249-2235
Nationwide Provident 1000 Chesterbrook Blvd *TF:* 800-523-4681	Berwyn	PA	19312	610-889-1717	407-1322
New England Financial 501 Boylston St *TF:* 800-388-4000 ■ *Web:* www.nef.metlife.com	Boston	MA	02116	800-388-4000	
New England Life Insurance Co 501 Boylston St **Fax:* Hum Res ■ *TF:* 800-388-4000	Boston	MA	02116	617-578-2000	536-2393*
New York Life Insurance & Annuity Corp 51 Madison Ave **Fax:* Hum Res ■ *TF:* 800-598-2019	New York	NY	10010	212-576-7000	447-4292*
New York Life Insurance Co 51 Madison Ave *Web:* www.newyorklife.com	New York	NY	10010	212-576-7000	448-1646
Nippon Life Insurance Co of America 521 5th Ave 5th Fl *TF:* 877-252-7174 ■ *Web:* www.nlia.com	New York	NY	10175	212-682-3000	682-3002
North American Co for Life & Health Insurance 525 W Van Buren St *TF:* 800-800-3656 ■ *Web:* www.nacolah.com	Chicago	IL	60607	312-648-7600	648-7765
North Carolina Mutual Life Insurance Co 411 W Chapel Hill St *TF:* 800-626-1899 ■ *Web:* www.ncmutuallife.com	Durham	NC	27701	919-682-9201	683-1694
Ohio National Life Insurance Co 1 Financial Way Suite 100 *TF:* 800-366-6654 ■ *Web:* www.ohionational.com	Cincinnati	OH	45242	513-794-6100	794-4730
Ohio State Life Insurance Co PO Box 410288 *TF:* 800-752-1387 ■ *Web:* www.ohiostatelife.com	Kansas City	MO	64141	800-752-1387	
Old American Insurance Co 3520 Broadway *TF:* 800-733-6242 ■ *Web:* www.oaic.com	Kansas City	MO	64111	816-753-4900	753-4902
OneAmerica Financial Partners Inc 1 American Sq PO Box 368 **Fax:* Hum Res ■ *Web:* www.oneamerica.com	Indianapolis	IN	46206	317-285-1111	285-1931*
Oxford Life Insurance Co 2721 N Central Ave *TF Cust Svc:* 800-528-0463 ■ *Web:* www.oxfordlife.com	Phoenix	AZ	85004	602-263-6666	277-5901
Ozark National Life Insurance Inc 500 E 9th St *Web:* www.ozark-national.com	Kansas City	MO	64106	816-842-6300	842-8373
Pacific Guardian Life Insurance Co Ltd 1440 Kapiolani Blvd Suite 1700 *TF:* 800-367-5354 ■ *Web:* www.pacificguardian.com	Honolulu	HI	96814	808-955-2236	942-1284
Pacific Life Insurance Co 700 Newport Ctr Dr **Fax:* Hum Res ■ *TF:* 800-800-7646 ■ *Web:* www.pacificlife.com	Newport Beach	CA	92660	949-219-3011	219-3483*
Pan-American Life Insurance Co 601 Poydras St *TF Life Ins:* 877-939-4550 ■ *Web:* www.panamericanlife.com	New Orleans	LA	70130	504-566-1300	566-3381
Partner Reinsurance Co of the US 1 Greenwich Plaza *TF:* 800-261-3164 ■ *Web:* www.partnerre.com	Greenwich	CT	06830	203-485-4200	485-4300
Paul Revere Life Insurance Co 18 Chestnut St **Fax:* Hum Res ■ *TF:* 800-799-0990	Worcester	MA	01608	508-799-4441	751-7079*

Phone | Fax

Pekin Life Insurance Co 2505 Ct St .... Pekin IL 61558 309-346-1161 346-8512
TF: 800-322-0160 ■ Web: www.pekininsurance.com

Penn Insurance & Annuity Co 600 Dresher Rd .... Horsham PA 19044 215-956-8000 956-7699
TF Cust Svc: 800-523-0650 ■ Web: www.pennmutual.com

Penn Mutual Life Insurance Co 600 Dresher Rd .... Horsham PA 19044 215-956-8000 956-7699
TF Cust Svc: 800-523-0650 ■ Web: www.pennmutual.com

Penn Treaty Network America Insurance Co
3440 Lehigh St .... Allentown PA 18103 610-965-2222 967-4616
TF: 800-222-3469 ■ Web: www.penntreaty.com

Physicians Life Insurance Co 2600 Dodge St .... Omaha NE 68131 402-633-1000 633-1096
TF: 800-228-9100

Physicians Mutual Insurance Co 2600 Dodge St .... Omaha NE 68131 402-633-1000 633-1096
TF: 800-228-9100 ■ Web: www.physiciansmutual.com

Pioneer Mutual Life Insurance Co (PML)
101 N 10th St .... Fargo ND 58102 701-297-5700 297-5772
TF: 800-279-2008 ■ Web: www.oneamerica.com

Presidential Life Insurance Co 69 Lydecker St .... Nyack NY 10960 845-358-2300 353-0273
TF: 800-926-7599 ■ Web: www.presidentiallife.com

Pro Assurance Corp
1250 23rd St NW Suite 250 .... Washington DC 20037 202-969-1866 969-1881
TF: 800-613-3615 ■ Web: www.proassurance.com

Property-Owners Insurance Co PO Box 30660 .... Lansing MI 48909 517-323-1200 323-8796
TF: 800-288-8740

Protective Life & Annuity Insurance Co
2801 Hwy 280 S .... Birmingham AL 35223 205-879-9230 268-3196
TF: 800-866-3555 ■ Web: www.protective.com

Protective Life Insurance Co
2801 Hwy 280 S .... Birmingham AL 35223 205-879-9230 268-3196
TF: 800-866-3555 ■ Web: www.protective.com

Provident American Insurance Co Inc
10501 N Central Expy Suite 200 .... Dallas TX 75231 214-696-9091 696-4756
TF: 800-933-9456 ■ Web: www.providentamerican.com

Prudential Financial Inc 751 Broad St .... Newark NJ 07102 973-802-6000 367-6476
NYSE: PRU ■ TF: 800-843-7625 ■ Web: www.prudential.com

RBC Liberty Insurance PO Box 789 .... Greenville SC 29602 864-609-8111 609-3581
TF: 800-551-8354 ■ Web: www.rbcinsurance.com

Reliable Life Insurance Co
100 King St W PO Box 557 .... Hamilton ON L8N3K9 905-523-5587 551-1704*
*Fax Area Code: 866 ■ *Fax: Claims ■ TF: 800-465-0661 ■ Web: www.reliablelifeinsurance.com

Reliance Standard Life Insurance
2001 Market St Suite 1500 .... Philadelphia PA 19103 267-256-3500 256-3531*
*Fax: Sales ■ TF: 800-351-7500 ■ Web: www.rsli.com

Reserve National Insurance Co
6100 NW Grand Blvd .... Oklahoma City OK 73118 405-848-7931 254-2111
TF: 800-654-9106 ■ Web: www.reservenational.com

Savings Bank Life Insurance Co of Massachusetts The (SBLI)
1 Linscott Rd .... Woburn MA 01801 781-938-3500 938-3718
Web: www.sbli.com

Security Benefit Life Insurance Co
1 Security Benefit Pl .... Topeka KS 66636 785-438-3000 438-5177*
*Fax: Cust Svc ■ TF: 800-888-2461 ■ Web: www.securitybenefit.com

Security Life Insurance Co of America
10901 Red Cir Dr .... Minnetonka MN 55343 952-544-2121 945-3419
TF: 800-328-4667 ■ Web: www.securitylife.com

Security Mutual Life Insurance Co of New York
PO Box 1625 .... Binghamton NY 13902 607-723-3551 722-0598*
*Fax: Cust Svc ■ TF: 800-346-7171 ■ Web: www.smlny.com

Security National Financial Corp (SNFC)
5300 S 360 W Suite 250 PO Box 57250 .... Salt Lake City UT 84123 801-264-1060 265-9882
NASDAQ: SNFCA ■ TF: 800-574-7117 ■ Web: www.securitynational.com

Sentry Life Insurance Co 1800 N Pt Dr .... Stevens Point WI 54481 715-346-6000 346-7283
TF: 800-373-6879 ■ Web: www.sentry.com

Sequoia Insurance Co
31 Upper Ragsdale Dr PO Box 1510 .... Monterey CA 93940 831-333-9880 632-5246*
*Fax Area Code: 866 ■ TF: 888-704-1384 ■ Web: www.sequoiains.com

Settlers Life Insurance Co 1969 Lee Hwy # U1 .... Bristol VA 24201 276-645-4300 645-4399
TF: 800-523-2650 ■ Web: www.settlerslife.com

Shelter Life Insurance Co 1817 W Broadway .... Columbia MO 65218 573-445-8441 445-3199
TF Claims: 800-743-5837

Shenandoah Life Insurance Co
2301 Brambleton Ave .... Roanoke VA 24015 540-985-4400 985-4444
TF: 800-848-5433 ■ Web: www.shenlife.com

Southern Farm Bureau Life Insurance Co
PO Box 78 .... Jackson MS 39205 601-981-7422 366-5808*
*Fax: Hum Res ■ Web: www.sfbli.com

Southwestern Life Insurance Co
8710 Freeport Pkwy Suite 150 .... Irving TX 75063 800-792-4368 333-7833*
*Fax Area Code: 803 ■ TF: 800-792-4368

Standard Life & Accident Insurance Co
PO Box 1800 .... Galveston TX 77553 888-350-1488 621-3096*
*Fax Area Code: 409 ■ *Fax: Cust Svc ■ TF: 888-350-1488

Standard Life Insurance Co of Indiana
10689 N Pennsylvania St .... Indianapolis IN 46280 317-574-6201 574-6278*
*Fax: Mktg ■ TF: 800-222-3216 ■ Web: www.standardagents.com

Standard Security Life Insurance Co of New York
485 Madison Ave 14th Fl .... New York NY 10022 212-355-4141 644-5786
Web: www.sslicny.com

State Farm Life & Accident Assurance Co
1 State Farm Plaza .... Bloomington IL 61710 309-766-2311 763-8777*
*Fax: Mktg ■ Web: www.statefarm.com

State Farm Life Insurance Co
1 State Farm Plaza .... Bloomington IL 61710 309-766-2311 766-2621*
*Fax: Hum Res ■ Web: www.statefarm.com/insuranc/life/life.htm

State Life Insurance Co
1 American Sq PO Box 368 .... Indianapolis IN 46206 317-285-2300 285-2380
Web: www.oneamerica.com/Home

Sun Life Assurance Co of Canada
1 Sun Life Executive Pk PO Box 9133 .... Wellesley Hills MA 02481 781-237-6030 431-4959*
*Fax: Hum Res ■ TF: 800-786-5433 ■ Web: www.sunlife.com/us

SunAmerica Annuity & Life Insurance Co
21650 Oxnard St .... Woodland Hills CA 91367 888-502-2900
TF: 888-502-2900 ■ Web: www.sunamerica.com

Phone | Fax

Sunset Life Insurance Co of America
PO Box 219139 .... Kansas City MO 64121 800-678-6898 753-4902*
*Fax Area Code: 816 ■ TF: 800-678-6898 ■ Web: www.sunsetlife.com

Texas Life Insurance Co PO Box 830 .... Waco TX 76703 254-752-6521 754-7629
TF: 800-283-9233 ■ Web: www.texaslife.com

Thrivent Financial for Lutherans
4321 N Ballard Rd .... Appleton WI 54919 920-734-5721 628-4757
TF: 800-847-4836 ■ Web: www.thrivent.com

TIAA-CREF 730 Third Ave .... New York NY 10017 212-490-9000 913-2803
TF: 866-842-2442 ■ Web: www.tiaa-cref.org

Transamerica Occidental Life Insurance Co
1150 S Olive St .... Los Angeles CA 90015 213-742-2111 741-7939*
*Fax: Mail Rm ■ TF Cust Svc: 800-852-4678

Travelers Indemnity Co 1 Tower Sq .... Hartford CT 06183 860-277-0111 277-1970*
*Fax: Hum Res ■ Web: www.travelers.com

Trustmark Insurance Co 400 Field Dr .... Lake Forest IL 60045 847-615-1500 615-3910
TF: 800-877-9077 ■ Web: www.trustmarkinsurance.com

United American Insurance Co Inc
PO Box 8080 .... McKinney TX 75070 972-529-5085 569-3709
TF: 800-331-2512 ■ Web: www.unitedamerican.com

United Heritage Life Insurance Co
PO Box 7777 .... Meridian ID 83680 208-493-6100 466-0825
TF: 800-657-6351 ■ Web: www.unitedheritage.com

United Insurance Holdings Corp
360 Central Ave Suite 900 .... Saint Petersburg FL 33701 800-295-8016 499-2531*
OTC: UIHC ■ *Fax Area Code: 469 ■ TF: 800-295-8016 ■ Web: www.upcic.com

United Investors Life Insurance Co
2001 3rd Ave S .... Birmingham AL 35233 205-325-4300 325-2092*
*Fax: Cust Svc ■ TF: 800-318-4542 ■ Web: www.uilic.com

United Life Insurance Co PO Box 73909 .... Cedar Rapids IA 52407 319-399-5700 399-5499
TF: 800-332-7977 ■ Web: www.unitedfiregroup.com

United of Omaha Life Insurance Co
Mutual of Omaha Plaza .... Omaha NE 68175 402-342-7600 351-2775
TF: 800-775-6000 ■ Web: www.mutualofomaha.com

United Security Life Insurance Co of Illinois (inc)
6640 S Cicero Ave .... Bedford Park IL 60638 847-298-1400 475-6121*
*Fax Area Code: 708 ■ Web: www.unitedsecuritylandh.com

United World Life Insurance Co
Mutual of Omaha Plaza .... Omaha NE 68175 402-342-7600 351-2775
TF: 800-775-6000 ■ Web: www.mutualofomaha.com

Unity Mutual Life Insurance Co 507 Plum St .... Syracuse NY 13204 315-448-7000 448-7100
TF: 800-836-7100 ■ Web: www.unity-life.com

USAA Life Insurance Co (USAA)
9800 Fredericksburg Rd .... San Antonio TX 78288 210-498-8000 531-8877*
*Fax Area Code: 800 ■ *Fax: Sales ■ TF: 800-531-8000 ■ Web: www.usaa.com

USAble Life Insurance Co
400 W Capitol Ave 15th Fl .... Little Rock AR 72201 800-370-5856 235-8500*
*Fax Area Code: 501 ■ TF: 800-370-5856 ■ Web: www.usablelife.com

Utica National Insurance Group
180 Genesee St .... New Hartford NY 13413 315-734-2000 734-2680
TF: 800-274-1914 ■ Web: www.uticanational.com

Utica National Life Insurance Co
180 Genesee St .... New Hartford NY 13413 315-734-2000 734-2680
TF: 800-274-1914 ■ Web: www.uticanational.com

Variable Annuity Life Insurance Co (VALIC)
2929 Allen Pkwy .... Houston TX 77019 713-522-1111 831-4317*
*Fax: Cust Svc ■ TF: 800-633-8960 ■ Web: www.valic.com

Washington National Insurance Co
11815 N Pennsylvania St .... Carmel IN 46032 800-933-9301 817-4431*
*Fax Area Code: 317 ■ *Fax: Claims ■ TF: 800-933-9301

Wawanesa Life Insurance Co
191 Broadway Suite 900 .... Winnipeg MB R3C3P1 204-985-0684
Web: www.wawanesalife.com

West Coast Life Insurance Co
343 Sansome St .... San Francisco CA 94104 415-591-8200 433-9477
TF: 800-366-9378 ■ Web: www.westcoastlife.com

Western & Southern Life Insurance Co
400 Broadway .... Cincinnati OH 45202 513-629-1800 629-1212*
*Fax: Hum Res ■ TF: 800-333-5222 ■ Web: www.westernsouthernlife.com

Western Fraternal Life Assn
1900 1st Ave NE .... Cedar Rapids IA 52402 319-363-2653 363-8806
TF: 877-935-2467 ■ Web: www.wflains.com

Western United Life Assurance Co
929 W Sprague Ave PO Box 2290 .... Spokane WA 99210 509-835-2500 835-2468
TF: 800-247-2045 ■ Web: www.wula.com

Western-Southern Life Assurance Co
400 Broadway .... Cincinnati OH 45202 513-629-1800 629-1212
TF: 800-333-5222 ■ Web: www.westernsouthernlife.com

William Penn Life Insurance Co of New York
100 Quentin Roosevelt Blvd .... Garden City NY 11530 516-794-3700 229-3004*
*Fax: Hum Res ■ TF: 800-346-4773 ■ Web: www.lgamerica.com

Woman's Life Insurance Society
1338 Military St PO Box 5020 .... Port Huron MI 48061 810-985-5191 985-6970
TF: 800-521-9292 ■ Web: www.womanslife.org

Woodmen of the World/Omaha Woodmen Life Insurance Society
1700 Farnam St .... Omaha NE 68102 402-342-1890 271-7269
TF: 800-225-3108 ■ Web: www.woodmen.com

394-3 Medical & Hospitalization Insurance

Companies Listed Here Provide Managed Care And/Or Traditional Hospital And Medical Service Plans To Individuals And/Or Groups. Managed Care Companies Typically Offer Plans As Health Maintenance Organizations (Hmos), Preferred Provider Organizations (Ppos), Exclusive Provider Organizations (Epos), And/Or Point Of Service (Pos) Plans. Other Types Of Hospital And Medical Service Plans Offered By Companies Listed Here Include Indemnity Plans And Medical Savings Accounts.

Phone | Fax

AARP Health Care Options PO Box 1017 .... Montgomeryville PA 18936 800-523-5800 391-6259*
*Fax Area Code: 610 ■ TF: 800-523-5800 ■ Web: www.aarphealthcare.com

Aetna Inc 151 Farmington Ave .... Hartford CT 06156 860-273-0123 273-8909
NYSE: AET ■ TF: 800-872-3862 ■ Web: www.aetna.com

Phone Fax

Aetna US Healthcare Inc 980 Jolly Rd . . . . Blue Bell PA 19422 800-962-6842 775-6775*
Fax Area Code: 215 ■ **Fax:* Hum Res ■ *TF:* 800-962-6842 ■ *Web:* www.aetna.com

Alberta Blue Cross 10009 108th St NW. . . . . Edmonton AB T5J3C5 780-498-8100 425-4627
TF: 800-661-6995 ■ *Web:* www.ab.bluecross.ca

Alliance PPO LLC 4 Taft Ct . . . . Rockville MD 20850 301-762-8205 545-5389*
**Fax:* Hum Res ■ *TF:* 800-544-2853 ■ *Web:* www.mamsiunitedhealthcare.com

Altius Health Plans
10421 S Jordan Gateway Suite 400 . . . . .South Jordan UT 84095 801-355-1234 323-6400
TF: 800-365-1334 ■ *Web:* www.altius.coventryhealthcare.com

American Community Mutual Insurance Co
39201 Seven-Mile Rd. . . . . Livonia MI 48152 734-591-9000 591-4628
TF: 800-991-2642 ■ *Web:* www.american-community.com

American Specialty Health Plans
10221 Wateridge Cir. . . . . San Diego CA 92121 619-297-8100 237-3810
TF: 800-848-3555 ■ *Web:* www.ashcompanies.com

Americhoice Corp 8045 Leesburg Pike 6th Fl . . . . Vienna VA 22182 703-506-3555 506-3556
Web: www.americhoice.com

AMERIGROUP Corp 4425 Corporation Ln . . . . Virginia Beach VA 23462 757-490-6900 518-3600
NYSE: AGP ■ *TF:* 800-600-4441 ■ *Web:* www.realsolutions.com

Ameritas Managed Dental Plan Inc 5900 'O' St. . . . . . . Lincoln NE 68510 402-467-1122 467-7338
TF: 800-404-8019 ■ *Web:* www.group.ameritas.com

Anthem Blue Cross & Blue Shield
2015 Staples Mill Rd . . . . Richmond VA 23230 804-354-7000 354-3897
TF: 800-451-1527 ■ *Web:* www.anthem.com

Anthem Blue Cross & Blue Shield of Connecticut
370 Bassett Rd . . . . North Haven CT 06473 203-239-4911 239-8495
TF: 800-922-1742 ■ *Web:* www.anthem.com

Anthem Blue Cross & Blue Shield of Maine
2 Gannett Dr. . . . . South Portland ME 04106 207-822-7272 822-7375
TF Cust Svc: 800-482-0966 ■ *Web:* www.anthem.com

Anthem Blue Cross & Blue Shield of Nevada
9133 W Russell Rd. . . . . Las Vegas NV 89148 702-228-2583 228-1259
TF: 800-992-6907

Anthem Blue Cross & Blue Shield of the Midwest
1351 William Howard Taft Rd . . . . Cincinnati OH 45204 513-872-8100 872-8174
TF: 888-426-8436

Anthem Blue Cross Blue Shield Colorado
700 Broadway. . . . . .Denver CO 80273 303-831-2131 830-0887
TF: 800-654-9338 ■ *Web:* www.anthem.com

Arkansas Blue Cross Blue Shield
PO Box 2181 . . . . Little Rock AR 72203 501-378-2000 378-2969
TF: 800-238-8379 ■ *Web:* www.arkbluecross.com

AvMed 4300 NW 89th Blvd. . . . . .Gainesville FL 32606 352-372-8400 337-8575*
**Fax:* Hum Res ■ *TF:* 800-346-0231 ■ *Web:* www.avmed.org

Blue Care Network of Michigan
20500 Civic Ctr Dr . . . . Southfield MI 48076 248-799-6400 799-6969*
**Fax:* Cust Svc ■ *TF:* 800-662-6667 ■ *Web:* www.mibcn.com

Blue Cross & Blue Shield of Alabama
450 Riverchase Pkwy E. . . . . Birmingham AL 35244 205-988-2200 220-2902*
**Fax:* Hum Res ■ *TF:* 800-292-8868 ■ *Web:* www.bcbsal.org

Blue Cross & Blue Shield of Florida Inc
PO Box 1798 . . . . Jacksonville FL 32231 904-905-7864 905-8126*
**Fax:* Hum Res ■ *TF Sales:* 877-465-1125 ■ *Web:* www3.bcbsfl.com

Blue Cross & Blue Shield of Kansas City
2301 Main St . . . . Kansas City MO 64108 816-395-2222 395-2726*
**Fax:* Hum Res ■ *TF:* 800-892-6048 ■ *Web:* www.bluekc.com

Blue Cross & Blue Shield of Michigan
600 Lafayette Blvd E. . . . . Detroit MI 48226 313-225-9000 225-5629*
**Fax:* Hum Res ■ *Web:* www.bcbsm.com

Blue Cross & Blue Shield of Mississippi
PO Box 1043 . . . . .Jackson MS 39215 601-932-3704 939-7035
TF: 800-222-8046 ■ *Web:* www.bcbsms.com

Blue Cross & Blue Shield of Montana
560 N Pk Ave PO Box 4309 . . . . Helena MT 59604 406-437-5000 442-6946*
**Fax:* Hum Res ■ *TF:* 800-447-7828 ■ *Web:* www.bcbsmt.com

Blue Cross & Blue Shield of Nebraska
1919 Aksarben Dr PO Box 3248. . . . . Omaha NE 68180 402-982-7000
TF: 800-422-2763 ■ *Web:* www.nebraskablue.com

Blue Cross & Blue Shield of New Mexico
PO Box 27630 . . . . Albuquerque NM 87125 505-291-3500 816-5011
TF: 800-835-8699 ■ *Web:* www.bcbsnm.com

Blue Cross & Blue Shield of North Carolina
1965 Ivory Creek Blvd . . . . Durham NC 27702 919-489-7431 765-3521*
**Fax:* Hum Res ■ *TF Cust Svc:* 800-446-8053 ■ *Web:* www.bcbsnc.com

Blue Cross & Blue Shield of Oklahoma
1215 S Boulder Ave . . . . Tulsa OK 74119 918-560-3500 560-3060
TF Cust Svc: 800-942-5837 ■ *Web:* www.bcbsok.com

Blue Cross & Blue Shield of Rhode Island
500 Exchange St. . . . . Providence RI 02903 401-459-1000 459-1996
TF: 800-637-3718 ■ *Web:* www.bcbsri.com

Blue Cross & Blue Shield of South Carolina
4100 Percival Rd . . . . Columbia SC 29229 803-788-0222
TF: 800-288-2227 ■ *Web:* www.southcarolinablues.com

Blue Cross & Blue Shield of Texas Inc
1001 E Lookout Dr . . . . Richardson TX 75082 972-766-6900 766-6060
TF: 800-521-2227 ■ *Web:* www.bcbstx.com

Blue Cross & Blue Shield of Vermont
445 Industrial Ln . . . . Montpelier VT 05602 802-223-6131 223-4229*
**Fax:* Hum Res ■ *TF Cust Svc:* 800-247-2583 ■ *Web:* www.bcbsvt.com

Blue Cross & Blue Shield of Western New York
PO Box 80 . . . . Buffalo NY 14240 716-887-6900 887-7912
TF: 800-888-0757 ■ *Web:* www.healthnowny.com

Blue Cross & Blue Shield of Western New York Inc
257 W Genesee St PO Box 80. . . . . Buffalo NY 14240 716-884-2800 887-7912*
**Fax:* Cust Svc ■ *TF:* 800-544-2583 ■ *Web:* www.healthnowny.com

Blue Cross Blue Shield of Arizona
2444 W Las Palmaritas Dr . . . . Phoenix AZ 85021 602-864-4400 864-4041*
**Fax:* Cust Svc ■ *TF:* 800-232-2345 ■ *Web:* www.bcbsaz.com

Blue Cross Blue Shield of Delaware
PO Box 1991 . . . . Wilmington DE 19899 302-421-3000 421-3110*
**Fax:* Mktg ■ *TF:* 800-633-2563 ■ *Web:* www.bcbsde.com

Blue Cross Blue Shield of Georgia
3350 Peachtree Rd NE . . . . Atlanta GA 30326 404-842-8000 842-8010
TF Cust Svc: 800-441-2273 ■ *Web:* www.bcbsga.com

Blue Cross Blue Shield of Illinois
300 E Randolph St . . . . Chicago IL 60601 312-653-6000 938-8847*
**Fax:* Hum Res ■ *Web:* www.bcbsil.com

Blue Cross Blue Shield of Kansas
1133 SW Topeka Blvd. . . . . Topeka KS 66629 785-291-7000 291-6544
TF: 800-432-0216 ■ *Web:* www.bcbsks.com

Blue Cross Blue Shield of Louisiana
5525 Reitz Ave . . . . Baton Rouge LA 70898 225-295-3307 295-2054
TF: 800-599-2583 ■ *Web:* www.bcbsla.com

Blue Cross Blue Shield of Massachusetts
401 Pk Dr . . . . Boston MA 02215 800-262-2583 246-4832*
**Fax Area Code:* 617 ■ **Fax:* PR ■ *TF:* 800-262-2583 ■ *Web:* www.bluecrossma.com

Blue Cross Blue Shield of Minnesota
3535 Blue Cross Rd . . . . Saint Paul MN 55122 651-662-8000 662-2727
TF: 800-382-2000 ■ *Web:* www.bluecrossmn.com

Blue Cross Blue Shield of North Dakota
4510 13th Ave S . . . . Fargo ND 58121 701-282-1100 277-2216*
**Fax:* Hum Res ■ *TF:* 800-342-4718 ■ *Web:* www.bcbsnd.com

Blue Cross Blue Shield of Tennessee
801 Pine St. . . . . Chattanooga TN 37402 423-755-5600
TF: 800-565-9140 ■ *Web:* www.bcbst.com

Blue Cross Blue Shield of Wyoming
4000 House Ave . . . . Cheyenne WY 82001 307-634-1393 778-8582
TF: 800-851-9145 ■ *Web:* www.bcbswy.com

Blue Cross of California
21555 Oxnard St. . . . . Woodland Hills CA 91365 818-703-2345 703-2848
TF: 800-999-3643 ■ *Web:* www.anthem.com

Blue Cross of Idaho 3000 E Pine Ave. . . . . Meridian ID 83642 208-345-4550 331-7311
TF: 800-274-4018 ■ *Web:* www.bcidaho.com

Blue Cross of Northeastern Pennsylvania
19 N Main St . . . . Wilkes-Barre PA 18711 570-200-4300 200-6710
TF Cust Svc: 800-829-8599 ■ *Web:* www.bcnepa.com

Blue Shield of California 50 Beale St . . . . San Francisco CA 94105 415-229-5000 229-6222*
**Fax:* Hum Res ■ *Web:* www.blueshieldca.com

Capital Blue Cross 2500 Elmerton Ave. . . . . Harrisburg PA 17110 610-820-2700
TF Cust Svc: 800-958-5558 ■ *Web:* www.capbluecross.com

Capital BlueCross
2500 Elmerton Ave PO Box 779519 . . . . Harrisburg PA 17177 800-962-2242 541-6915*
**Fax Area Code:* 717 ■ *TF:* 800-962-2242 ■ *Web:* www.capbluecross.com

Capital District Physicians' Health Plan
500 Patroon Creek Blvd . . . . Albany NY 12206 518-641-3000 641-3507
TF: 888-258-0477 ■ *Web:* www.cdphp.com

Capital Health Plan PO Box 15349 . . . . Tallahassee FL 32317 850-383-3333 383-3339
TF: 800-390-1434 ■ *Web:* www.capitalhealth.com

CareFirst BlueCross BlueShield
10455 Mill Run Cir. . . . . Owings Mills MD 21117 410-581-3000 998-5576
Web: www.carefirst.com

Carelink Health Plans
500 Virginia St E Suite 400. . . . . Charleston WV 25301 304-348-2900 348-2064
TF: 800-348-2922 ■ *Web:* www.chcwestvirginia.coventryhealthcare.com

Centene Corp 7700 Forsyth Blvd. Saint Louis MO 63105 314-725-4477 725-2065
NYSE: CNC ■ *TF:* 800-225-2573 ■ *Web:* www.centene.com

Central Reserve Life Insurance Co
17800 Royalton Rd. . . . . Strongsville OH 44136 440-572-2400 572-8380
TF: 800-321-3997 ■ *Web:* www.centralreserve.com

Chiropractic Health Plan of California
PO Box 190 . . . . Clayton CA 94517 925-672-0106 844-3124
TF: 800-995-2442 ■ *Web:* www.chpc.com

CIGNA Healthcare 900 Cottage Grove Rd. . . . . Hartford CT 06152 860-226-6000
TF: 800-832-3211 ■ *Web:* www.cigna.com/health

CIGNA Healthcare of North Carolina Inc
701 Corporate Ctr Dr . . . . Raleigh NC 27607 919-854-7000 854-7101*
**Fax:* Hum Res ■ *TF:* 800-849-9300 ■ *Web:* www.cigna.com

Community Care 218 W 6th St . . . . Tulsa OK 74119 918-594-5200 594-5209
TF: 800-278-7563 ■ *Web:* www.ccok.com

CompBenefits Corp 100 Mansell Ct E Suite 400 . . . . Roswell GA 30076 770-552-7101 998-6871*
**Fax:* Cust Svc ■ *TF:* 800-633-1262 ■ *Web:* www.compbenefits.com

Comprehensive Health Services Inc
8229 Boone Blvd Suite 700 . . . . Vienna VA 22182 703-760-0700 760-0894
TF: 800-638-8083 ■ *Web:* www.chsmedical.com

ConnectiCare Inc 175 Scott Swamp Rd . . . . Farmington CT 06032 860-674-5700 674-5728
TF Cust Svc: 800-251-7722 ■ *Web:* www.connecticare.com

Coventry Health Care Inc
6705 Rockledge Dr Suite 900. . . . . Bethesda MD 20817 301-581-0600 581-0600*
NYSE: CVH ■ **Fax:* Hum Res ■ *TF:* 800-843-7421 ■ *Web:* www.coventryhealthcare.com

Coventry Health Care of Delaware Inc
750 Prides Crossing Suite 200. . . . . Newark DE 19713 800-833-7423
TF: 877-843-1942 ■ *Web:* www.chcdelaware.coventryhealthcare.com

Coventry Health Care of Georgia Inc
1100 Cir 75 Pkwy Suite 1400. . . . . Atlanta GA 30339 678-202-2100
TF: 800-470-2004 ■ *Web:* www.chcnorthcarolina.coventryhealthcare.com

Coventry Health Care of Iowa Inc
4600 Westown Pkwy
Regency 6 Suite 200. . . . . West Des Moines IA 50266 515-225-1234 223-0097
TF: 800-470-6352 ■ *Web:* www.chciowa.com

Coventry Health Care of Kansas Inc
8320 Ward Pkwy Suite 700. . . . . Kansas City MO 64114 816-221-8400 221-7709
TF: 800-468-1442 ■ *Web:* www.chckansas.com

Coventry Health Care of Louisiana Inc
3838 N Cswy Blvd Suite 3350 . . . . Metairie LA 70002 504-834-0840 834-2694
TF: 800-245-8327 ■ *Web:* www.chclouisiana.com

Coventry Health Care of Nebraska Inc
13305 Birch Dr Suite 100. . . . . Omaha NE 68164 402-498-9030 498-9706
TF: 800-471-0420 ■ *Web:* www.chcnebraska.com

Dakotacare 1323 S Minnesota Ave . . . . Sioux Falls SD 57105 605-334-4000 336-0270
TF: 800-325-5598 ■ *Web:* www.dakotacare.com

Davis Vision Inc 159 Express St. . . . . Plainview NY 11803 516-932-9500 328-4761*
**Fax Area Code:* 888 ■ **Fax:* Claims ■ *TF:* 800-328-4728 ■ *Web:* www.davisvision.com

Dean Health Insurance Inc 1277 Deming Way. . . . . Madison WI 53717 608-836-1400 827-4212
TF: 800-279-1301 ■ *Web:* www.deancare.com

Phone Fax

Delta Dental Insurance Co
1000 Mansell Exchange W PO Box 1809 Alpharetta GA 30023 770-645-8700 518-4757
TF: 800-521-2651 ■ *Web:* www.deltadentalins.com

Delta Dental Insurance Co of Alaska
PO Box 1809 Alpharetta GA 30023 800-521-2651
TF: 800-521-2651 ■ *Web:* www.deltadentalins.com

Delta Dental of Alabama
1000 Mansell Exchange W
Bldg 100 Suite 100 Alpharetta GA 30022 770-645-8700 518-4757
TF: 800-422-4234 ■ *Web:* www.deltadentalins.com

Delta Dental of Arizona PO Box 43026 Phoenix AZ 85080 800-352-6132 588-3636*
**Fax Area Code:* 602 ■ *TF:* 800-352-6132 ■ *Web:* www.deltadentalaz.com

Delta Dental of Arkansas
1513 Country Club Rd PO Box 15965 Sherwood AR 72120 501-835-3400 835-2733
TF: 800-462-5410 ■ *Web:* www.deltadentalar.com

Delta Dental of Colorado
4582 S Ulster St Suite 800 Denver CO 80237 303-741-9300 741-9338
TF: 800-233-0860 ■ *Web:* www.deltadentalco.com

Delta Dental of Connecticut PO Box 222 Parsippany NJ 07054 973-285-4000 285-4141
TF: 800-346-5377

Delta Dental of Delaware 1 Delta Dr Mechanicsburg PA 17055 717-766-8500 691-6653
TF: 800-932-0783 ■ *Web:* www.midatlanticdeltadental.com

Delta Dental of Florida
1000 Mansell Exchange W
Bldg 100 Suite 100 Alpharetta GA 30022 800-422-4234
TF: 800-422-4234 ■ *Web:* www.deltadentalins.com/fl_indiv

Delta Dental of Georgia PO Box 1803 Alpharetta GA 30023 800-422-4234
TF: 800-422-4234 ■ *Web:* www.deltadentalins.com

Delta Dental of Idaho
555 E Parkcenter Blvd PO Box 2870 Boise ID 83706 208-489-3580 344-4649
TF: 800-356-7586 ■ *Web:* www.deltadentalid.com

Delta Dental of Indiana PO Box 30416 Lansing MI 48909 800-524-0149
TF: 800-524-0149 ■ *Web:* www.deltadentalin.com

Delta Dental of Iowa 2401 SE Tones Dr Suite 13 Ankeny IA 50021 515-261-5500 261-5577
TF: 800-532-1514 ■ *Web:* www.deltadentalia.com

Delta Dental of Kansas PO Box 49198 Wichita KS 67201 316-264-4511 462-3392
TF: 800-234-3375 ■ *Web:* www.deltadentalks.com

Delta Dental of Kentucky PO Box 242810 Louisville KY 40224 502-736-5000 736-4839
TF: 800-955-2030 ■ *Web:* www.ddpky.com

Delta Dental of Louisiana PO Box 1803 Alpharetta GA 30023 800-422-4234
TF: 800-422-4234 ■ *Web:* www.deltadentalins.com

Delta Dental of Maine PO Box 2002 Concord NH 03302 603-223-1000 223-1199
TF: 800-537-1715 ■ *Web:* www.nedelta.com

Delta Dental of Maryland 1 Delta Dr Mechanicsburg PA 17055 717-766-8500 691-6653
TF: 800-932-0783 ■ *Web:* www.deltadentalins.com

Delta Dental of Massachusetts 465 Medford St Boston MA 02129 617-886-1000 886-1199
TF Cust Svc: 800-872-0500 ■ *Web:* www.deltamass.com

Delta Dental of Michigan PO Box 30416 Lansing MI 48909 800-524-0149
TF: 800-524-0149 ■ *Web:* www.deltadentalmi.com

Delta Dental of Minnesota PO Box 330 Minneapolis MN 55440 651-406-5900
TF: 800-553-9536 ■ *Web:* www.deltadentalmn.org

Delta Dental of Mississippi PO Box 1803 Alpharetta GA 30023 800-422-4234
TF: 800-422-4234 ■ *Web:* www.deltadentalins.com

Delta Dental of Missouri
12399 Gravois Rd # 2 Saint Louis MO 63127 314-656-3000 656-2900
TF: 800-392-1167 ■ *Web:* www.deltadentalmo.com

Delta Dental of Montana PO Box 1803 Alpharetta GA 30023 800-422-4234
TF: 800-422-4234 ■ *Web:* www.deltadentalins.com

Delta Dental of Nevada PO Box 1803 Alpharetta GA 30023 800-422-4234
TF: 800-422-4234

Delta Dental of New Hampshire
1 Delta Dr PO Box 2002 Concord NH 03302 603-223-1000 223-1129*
**Fax:* Cust Svc ■ *TF:* 800-537-1715 ■ *Web:* www.nedelta.com

Delta Dental of New Jersey
1639 State Rt 10 Parsippany NJ 07054 973-285-4000 285-4170
TF: 800-346-5377 ■ *Web:* www.deltadentalnj.org

Delta Dental of New Mexico
2500 Louisiana Blvd NE Suite 600 Albuquerque NM 87110 505-883-4777 883-7444
TF: 800-999-0963 ■ *Web:* www.deltadentalnm.com

Delta Dental of New York 1 Delta Dr Mechanicsburg PA 17055 717-766-8500 691-6653
TF: 800-932-0783 ■ *Web:* www.deltadentalins.com

Delta Dental of North Carolina
343 E Six Forks Rd # 180 Raleigh NC 27609 919-832-6015 832-6061
TF: 800-662-8856

Delta Dental of Ohio PO Box 30416 Lansing MI 48909 800-524-0149
TF: 800-524-0149 ■ *Web:* www.deltadentaloh.com

Delta Dental of Oklahoma
16 NW 63rd St Suite 301 Oklahoma City OK 73116 405-607-2100 607-2190
TF: 800-522-0188 ■ *Web:* www.deltadentalok.org

Delta Dental of Pennsylvania
1 Delta Dr Mechanicsburg PA 17055 800-932-0783
TF: 800-932-0783 ■ *Web:* www2.midatlanticdeltadental.com

Delta Dental of Rhode Island
10 Charles St Providence RI 02904 401-752-6000 752-6060*
**Fax:* Cust Svc ■ *TF:* 800-598-6684 ■ *Web:* www.deltadentalri.com

Delta Dental of South Carolina
PO Box 8690 Saint Louis MO 63126 314-656-3000 656-2900
TF: 800-392-1167

Delta Dental of South Dakota
720 N Euclid Ave PO Box 1157 Pierre SD 57501 605-224-7345 224-0909
TF: 800-627-3961 ■ *Web:* www.deltadentalsd.com

Delta Dental of Tennessee 240 Venture Cir Nashville TN 37228 615-255-3175 244-8108
TF Cust Svc: 800-223-3104 ■ *Web:* www.deltadentaltn.com

Delta Dental of Texas PO Box 1803 Alpharetta GA 30023 800-422-4234
TF: 800-422-4234 ■ *Web:* www.deltadentalins.com

Delta Dental of Utah PO Box 1803 Alpharetta GA 30023 800-422-4234
TF: 800-422-4234 ■ *Web:* www.deltadentalins.com

Delta Dental of Virginia 4818 Starkey Rd Roanoke VA 24014 540-989-8000 725-3890
TF: 800-367-3531 ■ *Web:* www.deltadentalva.com

Delta Dental of West Virginia
1 Delta Dr Mechanicsburg PA 17055 717-766-8500 691-6653
TF: 800-932-0783 ■ *Web:* www.deltadentalins.com

Phone Fax

Delta Dental of Wisconsin
2801 Hoover Rd PO Box 828 Stevens Point WI 54481 715-344-6087 344-2446
TF: 800-236-3713 ■ *Web:* www.deltadentalwi.com

Delta Dental of Wyoming
320 W 25th St Suite 100 Cheyenne WY 82001 307-632-3313 632-7309
TF: 800-735-3379

Delta Dental Plan of Minnesota
PO Box 330 Minneapolis MN 55440 651-406-5903
TF: 800-448-3815 ■ *Web:* www.deltadentalmn.org

Empire Deluxe PPO 11 W 42nd St New York NY 10036 212-476-1000 476-1281*
**Fax:* Hum Res ■ *TF:* 800-261-5962 ■ *Web:* www.empireblue.com

Excellus BlueCross BlueShield PO Box 22999 Rochester NY 14692 585-454-1700 238-4400
TF: 800-278-1247 ■ *Web:* www.excellusbcbs.com

Excellus BlueCross BlueShield of Central New York
333 Butternut Dr Syracuse NY 13214 315-671-6400 448-4922*
**Fax:* Cust Svc ■ *TF:* 800-633-6066 ■ *Web:* www.excellusbcbs.com

EyeMed Vision Care 4000 Luxottica Pl Mason OH 45040 888-439-3633 765-6050*
**Fax Area Code:* 513 ■ *TF:* 866-939-3633 ■ *Web:* www.eyemedvisioncare.com

Fallon Community Health Plan Inc
10 Chestnut St # 7 Worcester MA 01608 508-799-2100 754-1931
TF: 800-333-2535 ■ *Web:* www.fchp.org

First Choice Health Plan
600 University St Suite 1400 Seattle WA 98101 206-268-2406 667-8062*
**Fax:* Cust Svc ■ *TF:* 800-467-5281 ■ *Web:* www.fchn.com

First Priority Health 19 N Main St Wilkes-Barre PA 18711 800-822-8753 200-6730*
**Fax Area Code:* 570 ■ *TF:* 800-822-8753 ■ *Web:* www.bcnepa.com

Geisinger Health Plan 100 N Academy Ave Danville PA 17822 570-271-8760 271-5268
TF: 800-447-4000 ■ *Web:* www.thehealthplan.com

Golden Rule Insurance Co 7440 Woodlands Indianapolis IN 46278 317-297-4123 298-0875
TF Cust Svc: 800-657-8205 ■ *Web:* www.goldenrule.com

Group Health Co-op
320 Westlake Ave N Suite 100 Seattle WA 98109 206-448-5600 448-2137
TF: 888-901-4636 ■ *Web:* www.ghc.org

Group Health Plan Inc (GHJP)
550 Maryville Centre Dr Suite 300 St. Louis MO 63141 314-506-1700 506-1958
TF: 800-743-3901 ■ *Web:* www.chcmissouri.coventryhealthcare.com

Hanover Insurance Co 440 Lincoln St Worcester MA 01653 508-855-1000 853-6332
TF: 800-853-0456 ■ *Web:* www.hanover.com

Harvard Pilgrim Health Care Inc
93 Worcester St Wellesley MA 02481 617-509-1000 509-2515
TF: 888-888-4742 ■ *Web:* www.harvardpilgrim.org

Hawaii Dental Service
700 Bishop St Suite 700 Honolulu HI 96813 808-521-1431 529-9368
TF: 800-232-2533

Hawaii Medical Service Assn
818 Keeaumoku St Honolulu HI 96822 808-948-6111 948-5567*
**Fax:* Cust Svc ■ *TF:* 800-776-4672 ■ *Web:* www.hmsa.com

Health Alliance Plan 2850 W Grand Blvd Detroit MI 48202 313-872-8100 664-8404*
**Fax:* Hum Res ■ *TF:* 800-422-4641 ■ *Web:* www.hap.org

Health Net Inc 21650 Oxnard St Woodland Hills CA 91367 818-676-6000 676-5166*
NYSE: HNT ■ **Fax:* Hum Res ■ *TF:* 800-848-4747 ■ *Web:* www.health.net

Health Plan of Nevada Inc PO Box 15645 Las Vegas NV 89114 702-242-7200 242-7920
Web: www.healthplanofnevada.com

Health Plan of Upper Ohio Valley Inc
52160 E Lawn Saint Clairsville OH 43950 740-695-3585 695-5297
TF: 800-624-6961 ■ *Web:* www.healthplan.org

HealthAmerica Pennsylvania Inc
3721 Tecport Dr Harrisburg PA 17111 717-540-4260 671-2407*
**Fax:* Hum Res ■ *TF:* 800-788-6445 ■ *Web:* www.healthamerica.cvty.com

HealthCare USA 10 S Broadway Suite 1200 Saint Louis MO 63102 314-241-5300 241-8010
TF: 800-213-7792 ■
Web: www.chcmedicaid-missouri.coventryhealthcare.com

HealthPartners Inc PO Box 1309 Minneapolis MN 55440 952-883-5000 967-5666*
**Fax:* Cust Svc ■ *TF:* 800-883-2177 ■ *Web:* www.healthpartners.com

Healthplex Inc 333 Earl Ovington Blvd Uniondale NY 11553 516-794-3000 794-3186
TF Cust Svc: 800-468-0608 ■ *Web:* www.healthplex.com

HealthPlus of Michigan 2050 S Linden Rd Flint MI 48532 810-230-2000 230-2208
TF: 800-332-9161 ■ *Web:* www.healthplus.com

Heritage Summit HealthCare of Florida Inc
PO Box 2928 Lakeland FL 33806 863-665-6629 665-5177
TF: 800-282-7644 ■ *Web:* www.summitholdings.com

Highmark Inc 120 5th Ave Pl Pittsburgh PA 15222 412-544-7000 544-8368*
**Fax:* Hum Res ■ *TF:* 800-662-0849 ■ *Web:* www.highmark.com

HIP Health Plans 7 W 34th St55 Water St New York NY 10041 646-447-5000
TF: 800-447-8255 ■ *Web:* www.hipusa.com

Horizon Blue Cross Blue Shield of New Jersey
949 Raymond Blvd Newark NJ 07105 973-466-4000 466-4317
TF: 800-466-2583 ■ *Web:* www.horizon-bcbsnj.com

Humana Inc 500 W Main St Louisville KY 40202 502-580-1000 580-3690
NYSE: HUM ■ *TF:* 800-486-2620 ■ *Web:* www.humana.com

Humana Military Healthcare Services
500 W Main St Louisville KY 40201 502-580-3200 580-2000
TF: 800-964-5482 ■ *Web:* www.humana-military.com

Independence Blue Cross 1901 Market St Philadelphia PA 19103 215-241-2400 241-3237*
**Fax:* Hum Res ■ *TF:* 800-227-3114 ■ *Web:* www.ibx.com

Independent Health 511 Farber Lakes Dr Buffalo NY 14221 716-631-3001 631-2346*
**Fax:* Hum Res ■ *TF:* 800-247-1466 ■ *Web:* www.independenthealth.com

Intermountain Healthcare
4646 W Lake Pk Blvd PO Box 30192 Salt Lake City UT 84130 801-442-5000 442-3327*
**Fax:* Hum Res ■ *TF:* 800-538-5038 ■ *Web:* www.intermountainhealthcare.org

Kaiser Foundation Health Plan & Hospitals Inc
1 Kaiser Plaza 27th Fl Oakland CA 94612 510-271-5660 271-5820
Web: www.kp.org

Kaiser Foundation Health Plan Inc
1 Kaiser Plaza 27th Fl Oakland CA 94612 510-271-5800 271-6493
TF: 800-464-4000

Kaiser Permanente 1 Kaiser Plaza 27th Fl Oakland CA 94612 510-271-5910 271-2383
TF: 800-464-4000 ■ *Web:* www.kaiserpermanente.org

Kaiser Permanente Colorado Denver/Boulder
2500 S Havanna Aurora CO 80014 303-338-3800 338-3444
TF: 800-632-9700

Phone Fax

Kaiser Permanente Georgia
3495 Piedmont Rd NE Piedmont Ctr Bldg 9 .... Atlanta GA 30305 404-364-7000 364-4794*
*Fax: PR ■ TF: 800-611-1811

Kaiser Permanente Hawaii 711 Kapiolani Blvd .... Honolulu HI 96813 808-432-5955 432-5070
TF: 800-966-5955

Kaiser Permanente Northwest
500 NE Multnomah St Suite 100 .... Portland OR 97232 503-813-2800 813-4733*
*Fax: Hum Res ■ TF Cust Svc: 800-813-2000 ■ Web: www.kp.org

Kanawha Insurance Co 322 S Main St .... Lancaster SC 29720 803-283-5300 283-5676
TF: 800-635-4252 ■ Web: www.kanawha.com

Long Term Preferred Care Inc
800 Crescent Ctr Dr Suite 200 .... Franklin TN 37067 800-742-1110 764-5632*
*Fax Area Code: 615 ■ TF: 800-742-1110

Lovelace Health Plan
4101 Indian School Rd NE .... Albuquerque NM 87110 505-262-7363 262-7987*
*Fax: Hum Res ■ TF Hum Res: 800-877-7526 ■ Web: www.lovelacehealthplan.com

MAMSI Life & Health Insurance Co 4 Taft Ct .... Rockville MD 20850 301-762-8205 545-5389*
*Fax: Hum Res ■ TF: 800-544-2853 ■ Web: www.mamsiunitedhealthcare.com

MEDICA 401 Carlson Pkwy .... Minnetonka MN 55305 952-992-2900 992-3700*
*Fax: Sales ■ TF Cust Svc: 800-952-3455 ■ Web: www.medica.com

Medical Mutual of Ohio 2060 E 9th St .... Cleveland OH 44115 216-687-7000 687-6444*
*Fax: Hum Res ■ TF: 800-700-2583 ■ Web: www.medmutual.com

Memorial Health Partners
7135 Hodgson Memorial Dr Suite 13 .... Savannah GA 31406 912-350-6608 350-6420
TF: 800-566-6710 ■ Web: www.memorialhealth.com

MetLife Inc 200 Pk Ave .... New York NY 10166 212-578-2211 578-3320
NYSE: MET ■ TF: 800-638-5433 ■ Web: www.metlife.com

Molina Healthcare Inc
200 Oceangate Suite 100 .... Long Beach CA 90802 562-435-3666 437-7235
NYSE: MOH ■ TF: 888-562-5442 ■ Web: www.molinahealthcare.com

Mountain State Blue Cross & Blue Shield
700 Market St .... Parkersburg WV 26102 304-424-7700 424-7730
TF: 800-344-5514 ■ Web: www.msbcbs.com

MVP Health Care 625 State St .... Schenectady NY 12305 518-370-4793 388-2603*
*Fax: Hum Res ■ TF: 800-777-4793 ■ Web: www.mvphealthcare.com

Nationwide Health Plans 5525 Parkcenter Cir .... Dublin OH 43017 614-854-3001
TF: 800-372-0713 ■ Web: www.nationwidehealthplans.com

Neighborhood Health Partnership Inc
7600 NW 19th St # 200 .... Miami FL 33126 305-715-2200 715-2220
TF: 800-354-0222 ■ Web: www.neighborhood-health.com

Northeast Delta Dental 1 Delta Dr PO Box 2002 .... Concord NH 03302 603-223-1000 223-1199
TF: 800-537-1715 ■ Web: www.nedelta.com

ODS Cos 601 SW 2nd Ave .... Portland OR 97204 503-228-6554 243-3895
TF: 800-852-5195 ■ Web: www.odscompanies.com

Optima Health 4417 Corporation Ln .... Virginia Beach VA 23462 757-552-7400 687-6111
Web: www.optimahealth.com

Optima Health Services Inc
707 60th St Ct E Suite C .... Bradenton FL 34208 941-747-1585 745-1387
TF: 800-841-1585

Oxford Health Plans (NH) Inc 10 Tara Blvd .... Nashua NH 03062 603-891-7000 891-7050
TF: 800-889-7630

Oxford Health Plans (NJ) Inc
111 Wood Ave 2nd Fl .... Iselin NJ 08830 732-623-1000 623-1900
TF: 800-201-6920

Oxford Health Plans LLC 48 Monroe Tpke .... Trumbull CT 06611 203-459-9100 459-6464
TF: 800-444-6222 ■ Web: www.oxhp.com

Pacific Union Dental 2300 Clayton Rd # 1000 .... Concord CA 94520 925-363-6000 363-6099
TF: 800-999-3367 ■ Web: www.pacificuniondental.com

PacifiCare Dental & Vision Administrators
PO Box 25187 .... Santa Ana CA 92704 800-622-6388 228-3384*
*Fax: Cust Svc ■ TF: 800-622-6388 ■ Web: www.pacificare-dental.com

PacifiCare of Arizona PO Box 52078 .... Phoenix AZ 85072 602-244-8200 681-7545
TF: 800-347-8600

PacifiCare of Oregon
5 Centerpointe Dr Suite 600 .... Lake Oswego OR 97035 800-922-1444 603-7373*
*Fax Area Code: 503 ■ *Fax: Hum Res ■ TF: 800-922-1444

Pacificare of Texas 6200 NW Pkwy .... San Antonio TX 78249 210-474-5000
TF: 800-624-7272

Paramount Health Care 1901 Indian Wood Cir .... Maumee OH 43537 419-887-2525 887-2034*
*Fax: Hum Res ■ TF: 800-462-3589 ■ Web: www.paramounthealthcare.com

Physicians Plus Insurance Corp
22 E Mifflin St Suite 200 .... Madison WI 53701 608-282-8900 258-1908*
*Fax: Hum Res ■ TF: 800-545-5015 ■ Web: www.pplusic.com

PPOM 28588 Northwestern Hwy .... Southfield MI 48034 248-357-7766 357-3169*
*Fax: Cust Svc ■ TF: 800-831-1166

Precis Inc PO Box 3030 .... Rancho Santa Fe CA 92067 866-694-0395
TF: 866-694-0395 ■ Web: www.precis-inc.com

Preferred CommunityChoice PPO 218 W 6th St .... Tulsa OK 74119 918-594-5200 594-5210
TF: 800-884-4776 ■ Web: www.ccok.com

Preferred Health Systems Inc
8535 E 21st St N .... Wichita KS 67206 316-609-2345 609-2481
TF: 800-990-0345 ■ Web: www.phsystems.com

Premera Blue Cross
7001 220th St SW .... Mount Lake Terrace WA 98043 425-918-4000
TF Cust Svc: 800-722-1471 ■ Web: www.premera.com

Premera Blue Cross Blue Shield of Alaska
2550 Denali St Suite 1404 .... Anchorage AK 99503 907-258-5065
TF Cust Svc: 800-508-4722

Priority Health 1231 E Beltline NE .... Grand Rapids MI 49525 616-942-0954 942-0145
TF: 800-942-0954 ■ Web: www.priorityhealth.com

Prison Health Services
105 Westpark Dr Suite 200 .... Brentwood TN 37027 615-373-3100 729-0069*
*Fax Area Code: 888 ■ TF: 800-729-0069 ■ Web: www.phscorrections.com

Provident American Insurance Co Inc
10501 N Central Expy Suite 200 .... Dallas TX 75231 214-696-9091 696-4756
TF: 800-933-9456 ■ Web: www.providentamerican.com

Regence Blue Cross Blue Shield of Oregon
PO Box 1071 .... Portland OR 97207 503-225-5221 225-5274*
*Fax: Hum Res ■ TF: 888-734-3623 ■ Web: www.regence.com

Regence BlueCross BlueShield of Utah
2890 E Cottonwood Pkwy .... Salt Lake City UT 84121 801-333-2100 333-6506*
*Fax: Hum Res ■ TF Cust Svc: 800-624-6519 ■ Web: www.regence.com

Phone Fax

Rocky Mountain Health Plans
2775 Crossroads Blvd PO Box 10600 .... Grand Junction CO 81502 970-244-7760 244-7880
TF: 800-843-0719 ■ Web: www.rmhmo.org

SafeGuard Health Enterprises Inc
95 Enterprise Suite 100 .... Aliso Viejo CA 92656 949-425-4300 425-4565
TF: 800-880-1800 ■ Web: www.safeguard.net

Sagamore Health Network
11555 N Meridian St Suite 400 .... Carmel IN 46032 317-573-2886 573-2875
TF: 800-364-3469 ■ Web: www.sagamorehn.com

Scott & White Health Plan 2401 S 31st St .... Temple TX 76508 254-298-3000 298-3011
TF: 800-321-7947 ■ Web: www.sw.org

Spectera Inc 2811 Lord Baltimore Dr .... Baltimore MD 21244 410-265-6084 265-6260
TF: 800-638-3120 ■ Web: www.spectera.com

Spectera Vision
100 Corporate Pt Suite 380 .... Culver City CA 90230 310-242-6200 242-6222
TF: 800-305-0230 ■ Web: www.spectera.com/vision.html

Tufts Associated Health Plans Inc
333 Wyman St .... Waltham MA 02451 781-466-9400 466-8583
TF: 800-462-0224 ■ Web: www.tuftshealthplan.com

Union Pacific Railroad Employees' Health Systems
1040 N 2200 W .... Salt Lake City UT 84116 801-595-4300 595-4399
TF: 800-547-0421 ■ Web: www.uphealth.com

United American Healthcare Corp
303 E Wacker Dr Suite 1200 .... Chicago IL 60601 313-393-4571 393-3394
NASDAQ: UAHC

UnitedHealth Group Inc 9900 Bren Rd E .... Minnetonka MN 55343 952-936-1300 992-5210*
NYSE: UNH ■ *Fax: Hum Res ■ TF: 800-328-5979 ■ Web: www.unitedhealthgroup.com

UnitedHealthcare 9900 Bren Rd E .... Minnetonka MN 55343 952-936-1300 992-5210*
*Fax: Hum Res ■ TF: 800-328-5979 ■ Web: www.uhc.com

Unity Health Insurance 840 Carolina St .... Sauk City WI 53583 608-643-2491 643-2564
TF: 800-362-3308 ■ Web: www.unityhealth.com

Univera Healthcare 205 Pk Club Ln .... Buffalo NY 14221 716-847-1480 857-4543*
*Fax: Hum Res ■ TF: 800-628-8451 ■ Web: www.univerahealthcare.com

Universal Care Inc 1600 E Hill St .... Signal Hill CA 90755 562-424-6200
TF: 800-635-6668 ■ Web: www.universalcare.com

USA Managed Care Organization
7301 N 16th St Suite 201 .... Phoenix AZ 85020 800-872-0020 861-2805*
*Fax Area Code: 602 ■ TF: 800-872-0020 ■ Web: www.usamco.com

Valley Health Plan Inc 2270 Eastridge Ctr .... Eau Claire WI 54701 715-836-1254 836-1298
TF: 800-472-5411 ■ Web: www.valleyhealth.biz

Vision Service Plan (VSP)
3333 Quality Dr .... Rancho Cordova CA 95670 916-851-5000 851-4852
TF Cust Svc: 800-852-7600 ■ Web: www.vsp.com

Vytra Health Plans 395 N Service Rd .... Melville NY 11747 631-694-4000 694-5787*
*Fax: Hum Res ■ TF: 800-448-2527 ■ Web: www.vytra.com

Washington Dental Service 9706 4th Ave NE .... Seattle WA 98115 206-522-1300 524-0913
TF: 800-367-4104 ■ Web: www.deltadentalwa.com

WellCare Group Inc 8735 Henderson Rd Rm 4 .... Tampa FL 33634 813-290-6200 675-2929
NYSE: WCG ■ TF: 866-765-4385 ■ Web: www.wellcare.com

WellCare of New York 1404 Rt 300 .... Newburgh NY 12550 800-288-5441 566-6056*
*Fax Area Code: 845 ■ *Fax: Cust Svc ■ TF: 800-288-5441 ■ Web: www.wellcare.com/HealthPlans/NewYork/Home.aspx

Wellmark Blue Cross & Blue Shield of Iowa
636 Grand Ave .... Des Moines IA 50309 515-245-4500 245-4698*
*Fax: Hum Res ■ TF: 800-526-8995 ■ Web: www.wellmark.com

Wellmark Inc 636 Grand Ave .... Des Moines IA 50309 515-245-4500 245-4698
TF: 800-362-1697 ■ Web: www.wellmark.com

394-4 Property & Casualty Insurance

Phone Fax

Acadia Insurance Co
1 Acadia Commons 250 County Rd PO Box 9010 ...... Westbrook ME 04098 207-772-4300 772-6104
TF: 800-773-4300 ■ Web: www.acadiainsurance.com

Access Management Group
1100 Northmeadow Pkwy Suite 114 .... Roswell GA 30076 770-777-6890 777-6916
Web: www.accessmgt.com

Accident Fund Co
232 S Capitol Ave PO Box 40790 .... Lansing MI 48901 517-342-4200 367-1492*
*Fax: Mktg ■ TF Mktg: 888-276-0327 ■ Web: www.accidentfund.com

ACE USA 436 Walnut St PO Box 1000 .... Philadelphia PA 19106 215-640-1000 640-2489
Web: www.aceusa.com

Acuity Insurance 2800 S Taylor Dr PO Box 58 .... Sheboygan WI 53082 920-458-9131 458-1618
Web: www.acuity.com

Addison Insurance Co
118 2nd Ave SE PO Box 73909 .... Cedar Rapids IA 52401 319-399-5700 399-5499
TF: 800-332-7977 ■ Web: www.unitedfiregroup.com

Admiral Insurance Co 1255 Caldwell Rd .... Cherry Hill NJ 08034 856-429-9200 429-8611
Web: www.admiralins.com

Aegis Security Inc PO Box 3153 .... Harrisburg PA 17105 717-657-9671 657-0340
TF: 800-233-2160 ■ Web: www.aegisfirst.com

Affirmative Insurance Services Inc
6640 S Cicero Ave PO Box 488 .... Bedford Park IL 60638 815-467-8731

Ag States Agency 5500 Cenex Dr .... Inver Grove Heights MN 55077 651-355-3700 355-6359
TF: 800-548-1494 ■ Web: www.agstatesgroup.com

Agricultural Workers Mutual Auto Insurance Co
PO Box 88 .... Fort Worth TX 76101 817-831-9900 831-7565
TF: 800-772-7424 ■ Web: www.agworkers.com

Alfa General Insurance Corp
2108 E S Blvd PO Box 11000 .... Montgomery AL 36116 334-288-0375 288-0905
Web: www.alfains.com

Allegiance Insurance Co
1 Horace Mann Plaza .... Springfield IL 62715 217-789-2500 788-5161
NYSE: HMN ■ TF: 800-999-1030

Allianz Insurance Co 2350 Empire Ave .... Burbank CA 91504 818-260-7500 260-7207
TF: 800-421-0504 ■ Web: www.aic-allianz.com

ALLIED Group Inc 1100 Locust St .... Des Moines IA 50391 515-508-4211 280-4904
TF: 800-532-1436 ■ Web: www.alliedinsurance.com

Allied Insurance 1601 Exposition Blvd .... Sacramento CA 95815 916-924-4000 925-4933*
*Fax: Claims ■ TF: 800-552-2437 ■ Web: www.alliedinsurance.com

Allstate Insurance Co
2775 Sanders Rd Allstate Plaza .... Northbrook IL 60062 847-402-5000 836-3998*
*Fax: Hum Res ■ TF: 800-366-2958 ■ Web: www.allstate.com

Company	City	State	ZIP	Phone	Fax
American Agricultural Insurance Co 1501 E Woodfield Rd Suite 300 W *Web:* www.aaic.com	Schaumburg	IL	60173	847-969-2900	969-2752
American Commerce Insurance Co 3590 Twin Creeks Dr. *TF:* 800-848-2945 ■ *Web:* www.acilink.com	Columbus	OH	43204	614-308-3366	308-3365
American Family Mutual Insurance Co 6000 American Pkwy **Fax:* Hum Res ■ *TF Cust Svc:* 800-374-0008 ■ *Web:* www.amfam.com	Madison	WI	53783	608-249-2111	243-4921*
American Hardware Mutual Insurance Co PO Box 15440 **Fax:* Hum Res ■ *TF:* 800-227-4663	Minneapolis	MN	55440	952-935-1400	930-7348*
American Home Assurance Co 180 Maiden Ln **Fax:* Mail Rm ■ *Web:* www.aig.com	New York	NY	10038	212-770-7000	943-1125*
American Manufacturers Mutual Insurance Co 1 Kemper Dr *TF:* 800-833-0355	Long Grove	IL	60049	847-320-2000	320-5624
American Modern Home Insurance Co PO Box 5323 *TF:* 800-543-2644 ■ *Web:* www.amig.com	Cincinnati	OH	45201	513-943-7200	943-7368
American National Property & Casualty Co 1949 E Sunshine St **Fax:* Hum Res ■ *TF:* 800-333-2860 ■ *Web:* www.anpac.com	Springfield	MO	65899	417-887-0220	887-2814*
American Protection Insurance Co 1 Kemper Dr *TF:* 800-833-0355	Long Grove	IL	60049	847-320-2000	320-5624
American Road Insurance Co 4 Pk Ln Blvd Suite 460 *TF:* 800-234-2722	Dearborn	MI	48126	313-845-5850	845-7367
American Southern Insurance Co 3715 Northside Pkwy NW Bldg 400 8th Fl *TF:* 800-241-1172 ■ *Web:* www.amsou.com	Atlanta	GA	30327	404-266-9599	266-8327
AMERISAFE Inc 2301 Hwy 190 W *NASDAQ: AMSF* ■ *TF:* 800-256-9052 ■ *Web:* www.amerisafe.com	DeRidder	LA	70634	337-463-9052	463-7298
Amerisure Insurance Co 26777 Halsted Rd # 200 *TF:* 800-257-1900 ■ *Web:* www.amerisure.com	Farmington Hills	MI	48331	248-615-9000	615-8548
Amica Mutual Insurance Co 100 Amica Way **Fax Area Code:* 401 ■ *TF:* 800-652-6422 ■ *Web:* www.amica.com	Lincoln	RI	02865	800-652-6422	334-4241*
Applied Underwriters Inc PO Box 3648 **Fax Area Code:* 877 ■ *TF Cust Svc:* 877-234-4420 ■ *Web:* www.auw.com	Omaha	NE	68103	415-656-5000	234-4425*
Arbella Indemnity Insurance Co 1100 Crown Colony Dr PO Box 699103 *TF:* 800-972-5348 ■ *Web:* www.arbella.com	Quincy	MA	02269	617-328-2800	328-2970
Arbella Mutual Insurance Co 1100 Crown Colony Dr *TF:* 800-972-5348 ■ *Web:* www.arbella.com	Quincy	MA	02169	617-328-2800	328-2970
Armed Forces Insurance Exchange (AFI) PO Box G *TF:* 800-828-7732 ■ *Web:* www.afi.org	Fort Leavenworth	KS	66027	913-651-5000	727-4686
Armour Risk Management Inc 1735 Market St Suite 3000 **Fax:* Mail Rm ■ *Web:* www.armour-risk.com/Armour_US.html	Philadelphia	PA	19103	215-665-5000	665-5099*
Assn Casualty Insurance Co *Columbia Insurance Group Inc* 3420 Executive Ctr Suite 200 PO Box 9728 *TF:* 800-252-9641	Austin	TX	78766	512-345-7500	345-1972
Associated Industries Of Massachusetts Mutual Insurance Com PO Box 4070 *Web:* www.aimmutual.com	Burlington	MA	01803	781-221-1600	270-5599
AssuranceAmerica Corp 5500 I- N Pkwy Suite 600 *TF:* 800-450-7857 ■ *Web:* www.assuranceamerica.com	Atlanta	GA	30328	770-952-0200	952-0258
Asurion Marketing Services 648 Grassmere Pk Dr Suite 300 *Web:* www.asurion.com	Nashville	TN	37211	615-837-3000	837-3001
Atlantic Mutual Insurance Co 100 Wall St	New York	NY	10005	212-943-1800	428-6577*
Auto-Owners Insurance Co 6101 Anacapri Blvd *TF:* 800-346-0346 ■ *Web:* www.auto-owners.com	Lansing	MI	48917	517-323-1200	323-8796
Avemco Insurance Co 411 Aviation Way *TF:* 800-874-9125 ■ *Web:* www.avemco.com	Frederick	MD	21701	301-694-5700	694-4376
AXA Canada Inc 2020 University St Suite 700 *TF:* 800-361-1594	Montreal	QC	H3A2A5	514-282-1914	282-9588
Baldwin & Lyons Inc 1099 N Meridian St Suite 700 *NASDAQ: BWINB* ■ *TF:* 800-231-6024 ■ *Web:* www.baldwinandlyons.com	Indianapolis	IN	46204	317-636-9800	632-9444
Bankers Insurance Co 11101 Roosevelt Blvd N *TF:* 800-627-0000 ■ *Web:* www.bankersinsurance.com	Saint Petersburg	FL	33716	727-823-4000	898-1511
Berkshire Hathaway Group (BHG) 3024 Harney St *TF:* 800-786-6426 ■ *Web:* www.brkdirect.com	Omaha	NE	68131	402-536-3100	536-3030
Berkshire Hathaway Homestates Cos (BHHC) PO Box 2048 **Fax Area Code:* 402 ■ *TF:* 888-495-8949 ■ *Web:* www.bhhc.com	Omaha	NE	68103	888-495-8949	393-7619*
Bituminous Insurance Cos 320 18th St *TF:* 800-475-4477 ■ *Web:* www.bituminousinsurance.com	Rock Island	IL	61201	309-786-5401	786-3847
Brotherhood Mutual Insurance Co (BMI) 6400 Brotherhood Way PO Box 2589 *TF Cust Svc:* 800-333-3735 ■ *Web:* www.brotherhoodmutual.com	Fort Wayne	IN	46825	260-482-8668	483-7525
Brown & Brown Insurance PO Box 1718 *TF:* 800-562-8171 ■ *Web:* www.bbtacoma.com	Tacoma	WA	98401	253-396-5500	396-4500
California Automobile Insurance Co 4484 Wilshire Blvd *TF:* 800-431-6654 ■ *Web:* www.marketinginsurance.com	Los Angeles	CA	90010	323-937-1060	857-4936
California Casualty Insurance Group 1900 Alameda De Las Pulgas *TF:* 800-288-7765 ■ *Web:* www.calcas.com	San Mateo	CA	94403	650-574-4000	572-4608
Canada Life Assurance Co The 330 University Ave *TF:* 888-252-1847 ■ *Web:* www.canadalife.com	Toronto	ON	M5G1R8	416-597-1456	597-6520
Canal Insurance Co 400 E Stone Ave PO Box 7 *TF:* 800-452-6911 ■ *Web:* www.canal-ins.com	Greenville	SC	29601	864-242-5365	232-5707
Capitol Indemnity Corp 1600 Aspen Commons *TF:* 800-475-4450 ■ *Web:* www.capitolindemnity.com	Middleton	WI	53562	608-829-4200	829-7419
Capitol Insurance Cos 1600 Aspen Commons *TF:* 800-475-4450	Middleton	WI	53562	608-829-4852	
Carolina Casualty Insurance Co 4600 Touchton Rd E Bldg 100 Suite 400 *TF:* 800-874-8053 ■ *Web:* www.carolinacas.com	Jacksonville	FL	32246	904-363-0900	363-8098
Central Insurance Cos 800 S Washington St **Fax:* Claims ■ *TF:* 800-736-7000 ■ *Web:* www.central-insurance.com	Van Wert	OH	45891	419-238-1010	238-7626*
Century-National Insurance Co 12200 Sylvan St PO Box 3999 *TF Cust Svc:* 800-894-8384 ■ *Web:* www.cnico.com	North Hollywood	CA	91606	818-760-0880	509-1526
Chubb & Son 15 Mountain View Rd *TF:* 800-252-4670 ■ *Web:* www.chubb.com	Warren	NJ	07059	908-903-2000	903-2027
Chubb Group of Insurance Cos 15 Mountain View Rd *Web:* www.chubb.com	Warren	NJ	07059	908-903-2000	903-2027
Church Mutual Insurance Co 3000 Schuster Ln *TF:* 800-542-3465 ■ *Web:* www.churchmutual.com	Merrill	WI	54452	715-536-5577	539-4650
Cincinnati Indemnity Co 6200 S Gilmore Rd	Fairfield	OH	45014	513-870-2000	870-2093
Cincinnati Insurance Co 6200 S Gilmore Rd *Web:* www.cinfin.com	Fairfield	OH	45014	513-870-2000	870-2093
Civil Service Employees Insurance Co 50 California St Suite 2550 *TF:* 800-282-6848 ■ *Web:* www.cseinsurance.com	San Francisco	CA	94111	925-817-6300	817-6383
CNA 40 Wall St **Fax:* Hum Res ■ *TF:* 800-331-6053 ■ *Web:* www.cna.com	New York	NY	10005	212-440-3000	440-7909*
CNA Insurance Co 333 S Wabash Ave *TF:* 800-262-2000 ■ *Web:* www.cna.com	Chicago	IL	60604	312-822-5000	822-6419
Colorado Farm Bureau Mutual Insurance Co PO Box 5647 *TF:* 888-997-7683 ■ *Web:* www.cfbmic.com	Denver	CO	80217	303-749-7500	749-7748
Commerce Insurance Co 211 Main St *TF:* 800-221-1605 ■ *Web:* www.commerceinsurance.com	Webster	MA	01570	508-943-9000	949-4921
Commerce West Insurance Co 6130 Stoneridge Mall Road, 4th Fl PO Box 8006 **Fax Area Code:* 925 ■ *TF:* 800-244-1545 ■ *Web:* www.commercewest.net	Pleasanton	CA	94588	800-244-1545	734-1789*
Community Assn Underwriters of America (CAU) 2 Caufield Pl *Web:* www.cauinsure.com	Newtown	PA	18940	267-757-7100	757-7410
Concord Group Insurance Cos 4 Bouton St **Fax:* Hum Res ■ *TF:* 800-852-3380 ■ *Web:* www.concordgroupinsurance.com	Concord	NH	03301	603-224-4086	225-5268*
Continental Casualty Co 333 S Wabash Ave. *TF:* 800-262-2000 ■ *Web:* www.cna.com	Chicago	IL	60685	312-822-5000	822-6419
Continental Western Group 11201 Douglas Ave. **Fax:* Hum Res ■ *TF:* 800-235-2942 ■ *Web:* www.cwgins.com	Urbandale	IA	50322	515-473-3000	473-3021*
Cornhusker Casualty Co PO Box 2048 **Fax Area Code:* 415 ■ *TF:* 800-488-2930 ■ *Web:* www.bhhc.com	Omaha	NE	68103	402-393-7255	675-5542*
Country Mutual Insurance Co 1701 Towanda Ave *TF Cust Svc:* 888-211-2555 ■ *Web:* www.countryfinancial.com	Bloomington	IL	61701	309-557-3000	821-5459
Crum & Forster Insurance Inc 305 Madison Ave PO Box 1973 **Fax:* Hum Res ■ *TF:* 800-227-3745 ■ *Web:* www.cfins.com	Morristown	NJ	07962	973-490-6600	490-6600*
Cumberland Insurance Group 633 Shiloh Pike *TF:* 800-232-6992 ■ *Web:* www.cumberlandgroup.com	Bridgeton	NJ	08302	856-451-4050	451-7564
Cumberland Mutual Fire Insurance Co 633 Shiloh Pike *TF:* 800-232-6992	Bridgeton	NJ	08302	856-451-4050	455-8468
Dairyland Insurance Co 1800 N Pt Dr **Fax:* Sales ■ *TF Sales:* 800-532-2525 ■ *Web:* www.sentryinsurance.com	Stevens Point	WI	54481	715-346-6000	346-7266*
DCAP Group Inc 1154 Broadway *NASDAQ: KINS* ■ *Web:* www.kingstonecompanies.com	Hewlett	NY	11557	516-374-7600	295-7216
Donegal Mutual Insurance Co 1195 River Rd PO Box 302 *TF:* 800-877-0600 ■ *Web:* www.donegalgroup.com	Marietta	PA	17547	717-426-1931	426-7033
Dorinco Reinsurance Co 1320 Waldo Ave. *TF:* 800-225-1350 ■ *Web:* www.dorinco.com	Midland	MI	48642	989-636-0047	638-9963
Economical Insurance Group The 111 Westmount Rd S PO Box 2000 *TF:* 800-265-2180 ■ *Web:* www.economicalinsurance.com	Waterloo	ON	N2J4S4	519-570-8200	570-8389
Endurance Reinsurance Corp of America 750 Third Ave Fl 18 & 19 *Web:* www.endurancereusa.com	New York	NY	10017	212-471-2800	471-1748
Erie Indemnity Co *Erie Insurance Group* 100 Erie Insurance Pl. *NASDAQ: ERIE* ■ **Fax:* Mail Rm ■ *TF:* 800-458-0811 ■ *Web:* www.erieinsurance.com	Erie	PA	16530	814-870-2000	870-3126*
Erie Insurance Exchange 100 Erie Insurance Pl *TF:* 800-458-0811 ■ *Web:* www.erieinsurance.com	Erie	PA	16530	814-870-2000	870-3126
Erie Insurance Property & Casualty Co 100 Erie Insurance Pl *TF:* 800-458-0811 ■ *Web:* www.erieinsurance.com	Erie	PA	16530	814-870-2000	870-4408
Everest Reinsurance Co 477 Martinsville Rd *TF:* 800-269-6660 ■ *Web:* www.everestregroup.com	Liberty Corner	NJ	07938	908-604-3000	604-3450
Factory Mutual Insurance Co 270 Central Ave PO Box 7500 *TF:* 800-343-7722 ■ *Web:* www.fmglobal.com	Johnston	RI	02919	401-275-3000	275-3029
Farm Family Casualty Insurance Co PO Box 656 *TF:* 800-843-3276 ■ *Web:* www.farmfamily.com	Albany	NY	12201	518-431-5000	
Farmers Alliance Mutual Insurance Co 1122 N Main PO Box 1401 *TF:* 800-362-1075 ■ *Web:* www.fami.com	McPherson	KS	67460	620-241-2200	241-5482
Farmers Automobile Insurance Assn (FAIA) 2505 Ct St *TF:* 800-322-0160	Pekin	IL	61558	309-346-1161	346-8512
Farmers Insurance Exchange 4680 Wilshire Blvd **Fax:* Hum Res ■ *TF:* 888-516-5656 ■ *Web:* www.farmers.com	Los Angeles	CA	90010	323-932-3200	932-7496*

				Phone	Fax
Farmers Mutual Hail Insurance Co of Iowa 6785 Westown Pkwy *TF:* 800-247-5248 ■ *Web:* www.fmh.com	West Des Moines	IA	50266	515-282-9104	282-1220
Farmers Mutual Insurance Co of Nebraska 1220 Lincoln Mall *TF:* 800-742-7433 ■ *Web:* www.fmne.com	Lincoln	NE	68508	402-434-8300	434-8385
Farmers Union Mutual Insurance Co PO Box 2020 *TF:* 800-366-6338	Jamestown	ND	58402	701-252-2701	252-0404
FCCI Insurance Group 6300 University Pkwy PO Box 58004 *TF:* 800-226-3224 ■ *Web:* www.fcci-group.com	Sarasota	FL	34232	941-907-3224	907-2709
Federated Mutual Insurance Co 129 E Broadway St *TF:* 800-533-0472 ■ *Web:* www.federatedinsurance.com	Owatonna	MN	55060	507-455-5200	455-7808
FEDUSA 1839 N Pine Island Rd *Web:* www.fedusa.com	Plantation	FL	33322	954-475-0182	475-1058
Fhm Insurance Co 4601 Touchton Rd East Bldg 300, Suite 3150 *TF:* 800-393-0001 ■ *Web:* www.fhmic.com	Jacksonville	FL	32246	904-724-9890	724-9889
FIC Insurance Group 6500 River Pl Blvd Bldg 1 *TF:* 800-925-6000	Austin	TX	78730	512-404-5000	
Financial Indemnity Co 21650 Oxnard St Suite 1800 *TF:* 800-777-4342	Woodland Hills	CA	91367	818-313-8500	340-4881
Fireman's Fund Insurance Co 777 San Marin Dr **Fax:* Mail Rm ■ *TF:* 866-386-3932 ■ *Web:* www.firemansfund.com	Novato	CA	94998	415-899-2000	899-3600*
Fireman's Fund McGee Marine Underwriters 75 Wall St *TF:* 800-235-6029 ■ *Web:* www.firemansfund.com	New York	NY	10005	212-524-8600	524-9446
First Insurance Co of Hawaii Ltd 1100 Ward Ave PO Box 2866 *TF:* 800-272-5202 ■ *Web:* www.ficoh.com	Honolulu	HI	96803	808-527-7777	527-3200
Firstcomp Insurance Co 222 S 15TH St StE Suite 1500N **Fax Area Code:* 866 ■ *TF:* 888-500-3344 ■ *Web:* www.firstcomp.com	Omaha	NE	68102	888-500-3344	338-2667*
Florida Family Insurance Services LLC 27599 Riverview Ctr Blvd Suite 100 PO Box 136001 *TF:* 888-850-4663 ■ *Web:* www.flfamily.com	Bonita Springs	FL	34136	239-495-4700	948-7381
Florida Farm Bureau Casualty Insurance Co 5700 SW 34th St *Web:* www.ffbic.com	Gainesville	FL	32608	352-378-1321	374-1577
Florida Farm Bureau General Insurance Co 5700 SW 34th St *Web:* www.ffbic.com	Gainesville	FL	32608	352-378-1321	374-1577
Florida Farm Bureau Insurance Cos 5700 SW 34th St *Web:* www.ffbic.com	Gainesville	FL	32608	352-378-1321	374-1577
Foremost Insurance Co 5600 Beech Tree Ln *TF:* 800-532-4221 ■ *Web:* www.foremost.com	Caledonia	MI	49316	800-532-4221	
Frankenmuth Insurance 1 Mutual Ave *TF:* 800-234-4433 ■ *Web:* www.fmins.com	Frankenmuth	MI	48787	989-652-6121	652-3588
Franklin Mutual Insurance Co 5 Broad St *TF:* 800-842-0551 ■ *Web:* www.fmiweb.com	Branchville	NJ	07826	973-948-3120	948-7190
Frontier Insurance Group Inc 146 Rock Hill Dr **Fax:* Mktg ■ *Web:* www.frontier.com	Rock Hill	NY	12775	845-794-3600	796-1906*
GAINSCO County Mutual Insurance Co PO Box 199023	Dallas	TX	75219	972-629-4301	629-4335
GEICO Casualty Co 1 GEICO Plaza *TF:* 800-841-3000 ■ *Web:* www.geico.com	Washington	DC	20076	301-986-2300	986-3225
GEICO General Insurance Co 1 GEICO Plaza *TF:* 800-841-3000 ■ *Web:* www.geico.com	Washington	DC	20076	301-986-2300	986-2851
Gemini Insurance Co 200 W Madison St Suite 2700	Chicago	IL	60606	312-553-4413	553-4416
General Casualty Co of Wisconsin 1 General Dr **Fax:* Hum Res ■ *TF:* 800-362-5448 ■ *Web:* www.generalcasualty.com	Sun Prairie	WI	53596	608-837-4440	825-5125*
General Reinsurance Corp 695 E Main St Financial Ctr *TF:* 800-431-9994 ■ *Web:* www.genre.com	Stamford	CT	06901	203-328-5000	328-6423
General Star National Insurance Co 695 E Main St Financial Ctr *TF:* 800-431-9994 ■ *Web:* www.generalstar.com	Stamford	CT	06901	203-328-5000	328-6423
Georgia Casualty & Surety Co *Columbia Insurance Group Inc* 4370 Peachtree Rd NE Suite 200 **Fax Area Code:* 800 ■ *TF:* 800-767-4080	Atlanta	GA	30319	404-442-1100	682-9930*
Germania Farm Mutual Insurance Assn 507 Hwy 290 E *TF:* 800-392-2202 ■ *Web:* www.germania-ins.com	Brenham	TX	77833	979-836-5224	836-1977
Globe Indemnity Co 9300 Arrowpoint Blvd *TF Cust Svc:* 800-523-5451	Charlotte	NC	28273	704-522-2000	522-3200
Golden Eagle Insurance Corp 525 B St **Fax:* Claims ■ *TF:* 800-688-8661 ■ *Web:* www.goldeneagle-ins.com	San Diego	CA	92101	619-744-6000	744-6511*
Government Employees Insurance Co (GEICO) 1 GEICO Plaza *TF:* 800-841-3000 ■ *Web:* www.geico.com	Washington	DC	20076	301-986-3000	718-5239
Grain Dealers Mutual Insurance Co 6201 Corporate Dr *TF:* 800-428-7081 ■ *Web:* www.graindealers.com	Indianapolis	IN	46278	317-388-4500	295-9434
Grange Guardian 650 S Front St **Fax:* Hum Res ■ *TF:* 800-422-0550	Columbus	OH	43206	614-445-2900	445-2695*
Grange Mutual Casualty Co 650 S Front St **Fax:* Mktg ■ *TF:* 800-422-0550	Columbus	OH	43206	614-445-2900	445-2337*
Graphic Arts Mutual Insurance Co PO Box 530 *TF:* 800-274-1914 ■ *Web:* www.uticanational.com	Utica	NY	13503	315-734-2000	734-2680
Great American Insurance Co 580 Walnut St *Web:* www.greatamericaninsurance.com	Cincinnati	OH	45202	513-369-5000	
Great Central Insurance Co 3625 N Sheridan Rd *TF:* 800-447-1972	Peoria	IL	61633	309-688-8571	688-2738
Great Northern Insurance Co 15 Mountain View Rd *TF Cust Svc:* 800-252-4670 ■ *Web:* www.chubb.com	Warren	NJ	07059	908-903-2000	903-2027
Great West Casualty Co 1100 W 29th St **Fax:* Claims ■ *TF:* 800-228-8602	South Sioux City	NE	68776	402-494-2411	494-7480*
Grinnell Mutual Reinsurance Co 4215 Hwy 146 PO Box 790 *TF:* 800-362-2041 ■ *Web:* www.grinnellmutual.com	Grinnell	IA	50112	641-269-8000	236-2840
GuideOne Insurance Co 1111 Ashworth Rd **Fax:* Hum Res ■ *TF:* 877-448-4331 ■ *Web:* www.guideone.com	West Des Moines	IA	50265	515-267-5000	267-5730*
GuideOne Mutual Insurance Co 1111 Ashworth Rd **Fax:* Hum Res ■ *TF:* 877-448-4331 ■ *Web:* www.guideone.com	West Des Moines	IA	50265	515-267-5000	267-5530*
GuideOne Specialty Mutual Insurance Co 1111 Ashworth Rd **Fax:* Hum Res ■ *TF:* 877-448-4331 ■ *Web:* www.guideone.com	West Des Moines	IA	50265	515-267-5000	267-5730*
Hagerty Insurance Agency LLC 141 River's Edge Dr Suite 200 PO Box 1303 *TF:* 877-922-9701 ■ *Web:* www.hagerty.com	Traverse City	MI	49684	231-947-6868	941-8227
Hanover Insurance Co 440 Lincoln St *TF:* 800-853-0456 ■ *Web:* www.hanover.com	Worcester	MA	01653	508-855-1000	853-6332
Harco National Insurance Co PO Box 68309 *TF:* 800-448-4642	Schaumburg	IL	60168	847-321-4800	321-4810
Harleysville Atlantic Insurance Co 5901 Peachtree Dunwoody Rd NE Suite A-100 *TF:* 866-574-5272 ■ *Web:* www.harleysvillegroup.com	Atlanta	GA	30328	770-391-1992	391-4364
Harleysville Insurance Co 7900 W 78th St Suite 400 *TF:* 800-727-5353 ■ *Web:* www.harleysvilleinsurance.com	Edina	MN	55439	952-829-1400	829-1487
Harleysville Insurance Co of New Jersey 224 Strawbridge Dr Suite 301 **Fax:* Claims ■ *TF:* 888-595-9876 ■ *Web:* www.harleysvillegroup.com	Moorestown	NJ	08057	856-642-1646	642-9415*
Harleysville Insurance Co of New York 120 Washington St **Fax:* Hum Res ■ *TF:* 800-962-1006 ■ *Web:* www.harleysville.com	Watertown	NY	13601	315-782-1160	782-4571*
Harleysville Lake States Insurance Co 12935 S W Bay Shore Dr PO Box 352 *TF:* 800-968-2090 ■ *Web:* www.harleysville.com	Traverse City	MI	49685	231-946-6390	946-0443
Harleysville Pennland Insurance Co 355 Maple Ave **Fax:* Hum Res ■ *TF:* 800-523-6344 ■ *Web:* www.harleysvillegroup.com	Harleysville	PA	19438	215-256-5000	256-5602*
Harleysville Preferred Insurance Co 355 Maple Ave **Fax:* Hum Res ■ *TF:* 800-523-6344 ■ *Web:* www.harleysvillegroup.com	Harleysville	PA	19438	215-256-5000	256-5602*
Harleysville Worcester Insurance Co 120 Front St Suite 400 **Fax:* Hum Res ■ *TF:* 800-225-7387 ■ *Web:* www.harleysvillegroup.com	Worcester	MA	01608	508-751-8100	753-9366*
Hartford Accident & Indemnity Co 1 Hartford Plaza *Web:* www.thehartford.com	Hartford	CT	06115	860-547-5000	547-5392
Hartford Casualty Insurance Co 1 Hartford Plaza *Web:* www.thehartford.com	Hartford	CT	06115	860-547-5000	
Hartford Fire Insurance Co 1 Hartford Plaza *Web:* www.thehartford.com	Hartford	CT	06115	860-547-5000	
Hartford Steam Boiler Inspection & Insurance Co The (HSB) 1 State St PO Box 5024 **Fax Area Code:* 860 ■ *TF:* 800-472-1866 ■ *Web:* www.hsb.com	Hartford	CT	06102	800-472-1866	722-5106*
Hartford's Omni Auto Plan PO Box 105440 **Fax Area Code:* 800 ■ *TF:* 800-777-6664 ■ *Web:* www.thehartford.com	Atlanta	GA	30348	770-952-4500	983-3633*
Hingham Mutual Fire Insurance Co 230 Beal St *TF:* 800-341-8200 ■ *Web:* www.hinghammutual.com	Hingham	MA	02043	781-749-0841	749-4477
Home-Owners Insurance Co 6101 Anacapri Blvd *TF:* 800-288-8740	Lansing	MI	48909	517-323-1200	323-8796
Hortica Insurance 1 Horticultural Ln PO Box 428 *TF:* 800-851-7740 ■ *Web:* www.hortica-insurance.com	Edwardsville	IL	62025	618-656-4240	656-7581
HSB Group Inc 1 State St PO Box 5024 *TF:* 800-472-1866 ■ *Web:* www.hsb.com	Hartford	CT	06102	860-722-1866	722-5106
ICW Group 11455 El Camino Real *TF:* 800-877-1111 ■ *Web:* www.icwgroup.com	San Diego	CA	92130	858-350-2400	350-2592
IMT Group The PO Box 1336 *TF:* 800-274-3531 ■ *Web:* www.imtins.com	Des Moines	IA	50305	515-327-2777	372-2892
Indiana Farmers Mutual Insurance Co 10 W 106th St *TF:* 800-666-6460 ■ *Web:* www.indianafarmers.com	Indianapolis	IN	46290	317-846-4211	848-8629
Infinity Insurance Co PO Box 830189 **Fax:* Hum Res ■ *TF:* 800-782-2040 ■ *Web:* www.infinity-insurance.com	Birmingham	AL	35283	205-870-4000	803-8406*
ING Canada Inc 700 University Ave Suite 1500 **Fax:* Claims ■ *TF:* 877-341-1464	Toronto	ON	M5G0A1	416-341-1464	941-5320*
Injured Workers Insurance Fund 8722 Loch Raven Blvd *TF:* 800-264-4943 ■ *Web:* www.iwif.com	Towson	MD	21286	410-494-2000	494-2154
Insurance Co of the West 11455 El Camino Real *TF:* 800-877-1111 ■ *Web:* www.icwgroup.com	San Diego	CA	92130	858-350-2400	350-2616
Investors Underwriting Managers Inc 310 Hwy 35S *TF:* 800-243-6869 ■ *Web:* www.investorsunderwriters.com	Red Bank	NJ	07701	732-224-0500	741-2266
James A Scott & Son Inc PO Box 10489 *TF:* 800-365-0101 ■ *Web:* www.scottins.com	Lynchburg	VA	24506	434-832-2100	832-2190
Keen Battle Mead & Co (KBMCO) 7850 NW 146th St Suite 200 PO BOX 171870 *Web:* www.kbmco.com/index.php	Hialeah	FL	33016	305-558-1101	822-4722
Kentucky Farm Bureau Mutual Insurance Co 9201 Bunsen Pkwy	Louisville	KY	40220	502-495-5000	495-5177
Kingsway Financial Services Inc 45 St Clair Ave W Suite 400 *NYSE: KFS* ■ *TF:* 800-265-5458 ■ *Web:* www.kingsway-financial.com	Toronto	ON	M4V1K9	416-848-1171	848-1171

Company	City	State	ZIP	Phone	Fax
Koch Supply & Trading LP 4111 E 37th St N *TF:* 800-245-2243 ■ *Web:* www.kochoil.com	Wichita	KS	67220	316-828-5500	828-5752
Leader Insurance Co 5205 N O'Connor Blvd Suite 700 *TF:* 877-953-2337	Irving	TX	75039	877-953-2337	532-3379
Legion Insurance 1 Logan Sq Suite 1400 *TF:* 800-255-6738 ■ *Web:* www.legioninsurance.com	Philadelphia	PA	19103	215-963-1200	963-7575
Lexington Insurance Co Inc 100 Summer St *TF:* 800-355-4891 ■ *Web:* www.lexingtoninsurance.com	Boston	MA	02110	617-330-1100	355-4891
Liberty Mutual Group 175 Berkeley St *Web:* www.libertymutual.com	Boston	MA	02117	617-357-9500	
Lititz Mutual Insurance Co 2 N Broad St PO Box 900 *TF:* 800-626-4751 ■ *Web:* www.lititzmutual.com	Lititz	PA	17543	717-626-4751	626-0970
Lumbermen's Underwriting Alliance 2501 N Military Trail **Fax:* Hum Res ■ *TF:* 800-327-0630 ■ *Web:* www.lumbermensunderwriting.com	Boca Raton	FL	33431	561-994-1900	997-9489*
Lykes Insurance Inc PO Box 2879 *TF:* 800-243-0491 ■ *Web:* www.lykesinsurance.com	Tampa	FL	33601	813-223-3911	221-1857
Lynn Insurance Group 1905 NW Corporate Blvd *TF:* 800-327-0630	Boca Raton	FL	33431	561-994-1900	994-8362
Magna Carta Co 1 Pk Ave *TF:* 888-663-7275 ■ *Web:* www.mcarta.com	New York	NY	10016	212-591-9500	591-9600
Main Street America Group 55 W St *TF:* 800-258-5310 ■ *Web:* www.msagroup.com	Keene	NH	03431	603-352-4000	358-1173
Manuel Lujan Insurance Inc 4801 Indian School Rd NE *TF:* 888-652-7771 ■ *Web:* www.manuellujan.com	Albuquerque	NM	87110	505-266-7771	255-8140
MAPFRE USA Corp 211 Main St *TF:* 800-922-8276 ■ *Web:* www.commerceinsurance.com	Webster	MA	01570	800-922-8276	
Markel Insurance Co 4600 Cox Rd *TF:* 800-431-1270	Glen Allen	VA	23060	804-527-2700	965-1689
Mendota Insurance Co PO Box 64586 *TF:* 800-422-0792 ■ *Web:* www.mendota-insurance.com	Saint Paul	MN	55164	651-468-2910	
Mercer Insurance Group Inc 10 N Hwy 31 PO Box 278 *TF:* 800-223-0534 ■ *Web:* www.mercerins.com	Pennington	NJ	08534	609-737-0426	737-8719
Merchants Insurance Group 250 Main St *TF:* 800-462-1077 ■ *Web:* www.merchantsgroup.com	Buffalo	NY	14202	716-849-3333	849-3246
Mercury Casualty Co 555 W Imperial Hwy	Brea	CA	92821	714-671-6600	671-6603*
Mercury General Corp 4484 Wilshire Blvd *NYSE:* MCY ■ *TF:* 800-431-6654 ■ *Web:* www.mercuryinsurance.com	Los Angeles	CA	90010	323-937-1060	857-7116
Mercury Insurance Co 555 W Imperial Hwy	Brea	CA	92821	714-671-6600	671-6603*
MetLife Auto & Home Insurance Co 700 Quaker Ln *TF:* 800-422-4272 ■ *Web:* www.metlife.com	Warwick	RI	02886	401-827-2400	827-2358
Michigan Millers Mutual Insurance Co 2425 E Grand River Ave # 2 *TF:* 800-888-1914 ■ *Web:* www.michiganmillers.com	Lansing	MI	48912	517-482-6211	482-6245
Mico Insurance Co 471 E Broad St *TF:* 800-876-6426	Columbus	OH	43215	614-225-8211	225-8350
Mid-Century Insurance Co 4680 Wilshire Blvd *TF:* 888-516-5656 ■ *Web:* www.farmers.com	Los Angeles	CA	90010	323-932-3200	932-3101
Mid-Continent Casualty Co PO Box 1409 **Fax:* Hum Res ■ *TF:* 800-722-4994	Tulsa	OK	74101	918-587-7221	588-1293*
Middlesex Insurance Co Inc 3 Carlisle Rd *TF:* 800-225-1390	Westford	MA	01886	978-392-7000	392-7033
Middlesex Mutual Assurance Co 213 Ct St PO Box 891 **Fax:* Hum Res ■ *TF:* 800-622-3780 ■ *Web:* www.middlesexmutual.com	Middletown	CT	06457	860-347-4621	638-5260*
Midwest Employers Casualty Co 14755 N Outer 40 Dr Suite 300 *TF:* 877-975-2667 ■ *Web:* www.mwecc.com	Chesterfield	MO	63017	636-449-7000	449-7199
Millers First Insurance Co 111 E 4th St **Fax:* Cust Svc ■ *TF:* 800-558-0500 ■ *Web:* www.millersfirst.com	Alton	IL	62002	618-463-3636	463-2612*
Millers Mutual Insurance Assn 111 E 4th St **Fax:* Cust Svc ■ *TF:* 800-558-0500	Alton	IL	62002	618-463-3636	463-2612*
Montgomery Mutual Insurance Co 13830 Ballantyne Corporate Pl Suite 300 **Fax:* Hum Res ■ *TF:* 800-561-0178 ■ *Web:* www.montgomery-ins.com	Charlotte	NC	28277	704-759-7661	544-2971*
Motorists Mutual Insurance Co 471 E Broad St *Web:* www.motoristsmutual.com	Columbus	OH	43215	614-225-8211	225-8407
Mutual of Enumclaw Insurance Co 1460 Wells St *TF:* 800-366-5551 ■ *Web:* www.mutualofenumclaw.com	Enumclaw	WA	98022	360-825-2591	825-6885
National American Insurance Co Of California (NAICO) 1010 Manvel Ave *TF:* 800-822-7802 ■ *Web:* www.naico.com	Chandler	OK	74834	405-258-0804	258-4574
National Farmers Union Property & Casualty Co 5619 DTC Pkwy Suite 300 *TF:* 800-669-0622 ■ *Web:* www.nfuic.com	Greenwood Village	CO	80111	303-337-5500	200-7134
National Fire & Marine Insurance Co 3024 Harney St *Web:* www.nationalindemnity.com	Omaha	NE	68131	402-536-3000	916-3030
National Grange Mutual Insurance Co 55 W St *TF:* 800-258-5310	Keene	NH	03431	603-352-4000	358-1173
National Indemnity Co 3024 Harney St *Web:* www.nationalindemnity.com	Omaha	NE	68131	402-536-3000	536-3030
National Interstate Corp 3250 IH- Dr *NASDAQ:* NATL ■ *TF:* 800-929-1500 ■ *Web:* www.nationalinterstate.com	Richfield	OH	44286	330-659-8900	659-8901
National Union Fire Insurance Co of Pittsburgh Pennsylvania 180 Maiden Ln **Fax:* Mail Rm ■ *TF:* 877-520-4636 ■ *Web:* www.aig.com	New York	NY	10270	212-770-7000	943-1125*
Nationwide Mutual Fire Insurance Co 1 Nationwide Plaza *TF:* 877-669-6877 ■ *Web:* www.nationwide.com	Columbus	OH	43215	614-249-7111	961-3064
Nationwide Mutual Insurance Co 1 Nationwide Plaza **Fax:* Cust Svc ■ *TF:* 877-669-6877 ■ *Web:* www.nationwide.com	Columbus	OH	43215	614-249-7111	961-3064*
Nautilus Insurance Co 7273 E Butherus Dr *TF:* 800-842-8972 ■ *Web:* www.nautilusagents.com	Scottsdale	AZ	85260	480-951-0905	951-9730
Navigator's Management Co Inc 1 Penn Plaza *Web:* www.navg.com	New York	NY	10119	212-244-2333	244-4077
Nevada General Insurance Co 5685 Spring Mountain Rd PO Box 30367 *TF:* 800-234-2886 ■ *Web:* www.nvgeneral.com	Las Vegas	NV	89146	702-367-9616	222-2040
New Era Life Insurance Co PO Box 4884 *TF:* 800-552-7879 ■ *Web:* www.neweralife.com	Houston	TX	77210	281-368-7200	386-7286
New Jersey Manufacturers Insurance Co 301 Sullivan Way *TF:* 800-232-6600 ■ *Web:* www.njm.com	West Trenton	NJ	08628	609-883-1300	771-0384
New Mexico Mutual Casualty Co PO Box 27825 *TF:* 800-788-8851 ■ *Web:* www.nmmcc.com	Albuquerque	NM	87125	505-345-7260	345-0816
New York Central Mutual Fire Insurance Co (NYCM) 1899 Central Plaza E *TF:* 800-234-6926 ■ *Web:* www.nycm.com	Edmeston	NY	13335	607-965-8321	965-2712
Nobel Insurance 12225 Greenville Ave Suite 750 *TF:* 800-766-6235 ■ *Web:* www.nobelinsurance.com	Dallas	TX	75243	972-644-0434	644-0424
North American Specialty Insurance Co 650 Elm St 6th Fl *TF:* 800-542-9200	Manchester	NH	03101	603-644-6600	644-6613
North Carolina Farm Bureau Mutual Insurance Co (NCFBMIC) PO Box 27427 *Web:* www.ncfbins.com	Raleigh	NC	27611	919-782-1705	783-3593
Northern Security Insurance Co PO Box 188 *TF:* 800-451-5000 ■ *Web:* www.vermontmutual.com	Montpelier	VT	05601	802-223-2341	229-7646
Northland Insurance Co 385 Washington St # Sbo3m *TF:* 800-237-9334 ■ *Web:* www.northlandins.com	Saint Paul	MN	55102	651-310-4100	310-4949
Northwestern Pacific Indemnity Co 15 Mountain View Rd *TF Claims:* 800-252-4670 ■ *Web:* www.chubb.com	Warren	NJ	07059	908-903-2000	903-2027
Odyssey Re Holdings Corp 300 1st Stamford Pl *NYSE:* ORH ■ *TF:* 866-246-9945 ■ *Web:* www.odysseyre.com	Stamford	CT	06902	203-977-8000	356-0196
Ohio Casualty Insurance Co 9450 Seward Rd *TF:* 800-843-6446	Fairfield	OH	45014	513-603-2400	867-3215
Ohio Farmers Insurance Co 1 Pk Cir *TF:* 800-243-0210	Westfield Center	OH	44251	330-887-0101	887-0840
Ohio Indemnity Co 250 E Broad St 7th Fl *TF:* 800-628-8581 ■ *Web:* www.ohioindemnity.com	Columbus	OH	43215	614-228-1601	228-5552
Oklahoma Farm Bureau Mutual Insurance Co (OFB) 2501 N Stiles Ave *Web:* www.okfarmbureau.org	Oklahoma City	OK	73105	405-523-2300	523-2362
Oklahoma Surety Co 1437 S Boulder Ave Suite 200 *TF:* 800-722-4994	Tulsa	OK	74119	918-587-7221	588-1298
Old Dominion Insurance Co 4601 Touchton Rd E Suite 330 PO Box 16100 *TF:* 800-226-0875	Jacksonville	FL	32245	904-642-3000	730-9217
Old Republic Insurance Co PO Box 789	Greensburg	PA	15601	724-834-5000	834-4025
Omaha Property & Casualty Insurance Co 3316 Farnam St *TF:* 800-788-9488 ■ *Web:* www.mutualofomaha.com	Omaha	NE	68131	402-342-7600	351-2650
OneBeacon Insurance Group 601 Carlson Pkwy Suite 600 *TF:* 800-327-6286 ■ *Web:* www.onebeacon.com	Canton	MA	55305	781-332-7000	332-7904
Oregon Mutual Insurance Co PO Box 808 *TF:* 800-888-2141 ■ *Web:* www.ormutual.com	McMinnville	OR	97128	503-472-2141	565-3846
Oregon Mutual Insurance Group PO Box 808 *TF:* 800-888-2141 ■ *Web:* www.ormutual.com	McMinnville	OR	97128	503-472-2141	565-3846
Owners Insurance Co 6101 Anacapri Blvd *TF:* 800-288-8740	Lansing	MI	48917	517-323-1200	323-8796
Pacific Specialty Insurance Co 3601 Haven Ave **Fax Area Code:* 650 ■ *TF:* 800-962-1172 ■ *Web:* www.pacificspecialty.com	Menlo Park	CA	94025	800-962-1172	780-4820*
Peerless Insurance Co 62 Maple Ave *TF:* 800-542-5385 ■ *Web:* www.peerless-ins.com	Keene	NH	03431	603-352-3221	352-6055
Pekin Insurance Co 2505 Ct St *TF:* 800-322-0160 ■ *Web:* www.pekininsurance.com	Pekin	IL	61558	309-346-1161	346-8512
Penn Millers Insurance Co 72 N Franklin St PO Box P *NASDAQ:* PMIC ■ **Fax Area Code:* 570 ■ *TF:* 800-233-8347 ■ *Web:* www.pennmillers.com	Wilkes-Barre	PA	18773	800-233-8347	822-2165*
Penn National Insurance Co 2 N 2nd St Penn National Plaza *TF:* 800-388-4764 ■ *Web:* www.pennnationalinsurance.com	Harrisburg	PA	17101	717-234-4941	255-6850
Penn-America Insurance Co 3 Bala Plaza *Web:* www.penn-america.com	Bala Cynwyd	PA	19004	215-443-3600	443-3604
Pennsylvania Manufacturers Assn Insurance Co 380 Sentry Pkwy **Fax:* Mail Rm ■ *TF:* 800-222-2749	Blue Bell	PA	19422	610-397-5000	397-5366*
Permanent General Cos PO Box 305054 *TF:* 800-280-1466 ■ *Web:* www.pgac.com	Nashville	TN	37230	800-280-1466	467-8767
Pharmacists Mutual Insurance Co 808 US Hwy 18 W PO Box 370 *TF:* 800-247-5930 ■ *Web:* www.phmic.com/Default.aspx	Algona	IA	50511	515-295-2461	295-9306
Philadelphia Contributionship Insurance Co 212 S 4th St *TF:* 800-346-9229 ■ *Web:* www.contributionship.com	Philadelphia	PA	19106	215-627-1752	627-8303
Philadelphia Insurance Cos 1 Bala Plaza Suite 100 *TF:* 800-525-7662 ■ *Web:* www.phly.com	Bala Cynwyd	PA	19004	610-617-7900	617-7940
Pinnacol Assurance 7501 E Lowry Blvd *TF:* 800-873-7242 ■ *Web:* www.pinnacol.com	Denver	CO	80230	303-361-4000	361-5000
Preferred Employers Group Inc 10800 Biscayne Blvd 10th Fl *TF:* 800-433-5755 ■ *Web:* www.preferredemployers.com	Miami	FL	33161	305-893-4040	893-8659
Preferred Employers Insurance Co PO Box 85478 *TF Cust Svc:* 888-472-9001 ■ *Web:* www.preferredworkcomp.com	San Diego	CA	92186	619-688-3900	688-3913

Company / Address	City	State	ZIP	Phone	Fax
Preferred Mutual Insurance Co 1 Preferred Way	New Berlin	NY	13411	607-847-6161	847-8046*
*Fax: Mail Rm ■ TF: 800-333-7642 ■ Web: www.pminsco.com					
Princeton Excess & Surplus Lines Insurance Co 555 College Rd E	Princeton	NJ	08543	609-243-4200	243-4257
TF: 800-255-5676					
Princeton Insurance Co 746 Alexander Rd PO Box 5322	Princeton	NJ	08540	609-452-9404	734-8461
TF: 800-334-0588 ■ Web: www.princetoninsurance.com					
Progressive Casualty Insurance Co 6300 Wilson Mills Rd Campus E	Mayfield Village	OH	44143	440-461-5000	446-5372
TF: 800-321-9843 ■ Web: www1.progressive.com					
Providence Mutual Fire Insurance Co 340 E Ave	Warwick	RI	02886	401-827-1800	822-1789
TF: 877-763-1800 ■ Web: www.providencemutual.com					
Prudential Financial Inc 751 Broad St	Newark	NJ	07102	973-802-6000	367-6476
NYSE: PRU ■ TF: 800-843-7625 ■ Web: www.prudential.com					
PXRE Reinsurance Co 399 Thornall St 14th Fl	Edison	NJ	08837	732-906-8100	906-9157
QBE Reinsurance Corp 88 Pine St Wall St Plaza 16th Fl	New York	NY	10005	212-422-1212	422-1313
Web: www.qbe.com/americas/index.html					
Quincy Mutual Fire Insurance Co 57 Washington St	Quincy	MA	02169	617-472-8770	899-7790*
*Fax Area Code: 800 ■ TF: 800-899-1116 ■ Web: www.quincymutual.com					
Republic Western Insurance Co 2721 N Central Ave	Phoenix	AZ	85004	602-263-6755	745-6436
TF Claims: 800-528-7134 ■ Web: www.repwest.com					
Risk Planners Inc (RPI) PO Box 240	Minneapolis	MN	55440	952-914-5777	914-5778
TF: 800-328-7475 ■ Web: www.riskplanners.com					
RLI Insurance Co 9025 N Lindbergh Dr	Peoria	IL	61615	309-692-1000	692-1068
TF: 800-331-4929 ■ Web: www.rlicorp.com					
Royal & SunAlliance Insurance Co of Canada (RSA) 10 Wellington St E	Toronto	ON	M5E1L5	416-366-7511	367-9869
TF: 800-268-8406 ■ Web: www.rsagroup.ca					
RTW Inc 8500 Normandale Lake Blvd Suite 1400 PO Box 390327	Bloomington	MN	55437	952-893-0403	893-3700
NASDAQ: RTWI ■ TF Sales: 800-789-2242 ■ Web: www.rtwi.com					
Rural Mutual Insurance Co Inc 1241 John Q Hammons Dr PO Box 5555	Madison	WI	53705	608-836-5525	828-5582
TF: 800-362-7881 ■ Web: www.ruralins.com					
Safe Auto Insurance Co 226 N 5th St	Columbus	OH	43215	614-231-0200	231-4690
TF: 800-723-3288 ■ Web: www.safeauto.com					
Safeco Insurance Co of America 1001 4th Ave	Seattle	WA	98184	206-545-5000	925-0165*
*Fax: Hum Res ■ Web: www.safeco.com					
Safety Insurance Group Inc 20 Custom House St	Boston	MA	02110	617-951-0600	
NASDAQ: SAFT ■ Web: www.safetyinsurance.com					
Safeway Insurance Group 790 Pasquinelli Dr	Westmont	IL	60559	630-887-8300	887-8975*
*Fax: Hum Res ■ TF: 800-273-0300 ■ Web: www.safewayinsurance.com					
Sagamore Insurance Co 1099 N Meridian St Suite 700	Indianapolis	IN	46204	800-317-9402	511-5087
TF: 800-317-9402 ■ Web: www.sagamoreinsurance.com					
Savers Property & Casualty Insurance Co 26255 American Dr	Southfield	MI	48034	248-358-1100	358-1614
TF: 800-482-2726 ■ Web: www.meadowbrookinsgrp.com/savers.html					
Scottsdale Insurance Co 8877 N Gainey Ctr Dr	Scottsdale	AZ	85258	480-365-4000	483-6752
TF: 800-423-7675 ■ Web: www.scottsdaleins.com					
Secura Insurance Cos PO Box 819	Appleton	WI	54912	920-739-3161	739-6795
TF: 800-558-3405 ■ Web: www.secura.net					
Seibels Bruce Group Inc 1501 Lady St PO Box 1	Columbia	SC	29201	877-734-2357	748-8394*
*Fax Area Code: 803 ■ *Fax: Hum Res ■ TF: 800-525-8835 ■ Web: www.seibels.com					
Selective Insurance Co of America 40 Wantage Ave	Branchville	NJ	07890	973-948-3000	948-0292*
*Fax: Hum Res ■ TF: 800-777-9656 ■ Web: www.selective.com					
Selective Way Insurance Co 40 Wantage Ave	Branchville	NJ	07890	973-948-3000	948-0292*
*Fax: Hum Res ■ TF: 800-777-9656 ■ Web: www.selective.com					
Seneca Insurance Co Inc 160 Water St 16th Fl	New York	NY	10038	212-344-3000	344-4545
Web: www.senecainsurance.com					
Sentry Insurance A Mutual Co 1800 N Pt Dr	Stevens Point	WI	54481	715-346-6000	346-6770*
*Fax: Hum Res ■ Web: www.sentry.com					
Shelter Mutual Insurance Co 1817 W Broadway	Columbia	MO	65218	573-445-8441	446-7318
TF: 800-743-5837					
Signature Group The 200 N Martingale Rd	Schaumburg	IL	60173	847-605-3000	605-4835*
*Fax: Hum Res ■ TF: 800-621-0393					
Signet Star Reinsurance Co 475 Steamboat Rd	Greenwich	CT	06830	203-542-3800	542-3290
Sompo Japan Insurance Co of America 2 World Financial Ctr 225 Liberty St 43rd Fl	New York	NY	10281	212-416-1200	
TF: 800-444-6870 ■ Web: www.sompo-japan-us.com					
Southern Farm Bureau Casualty Insurance Co 1800 E County Line Rd Suite 400	Ridgeland	MS	39157	601-957-7777	957-4329
TF: 800-272-7977 ■ Web: www.sfbcic.com					
Southern United Fire Insurance Co PO Box 190429	Mobile	AL	36619	251-661-8008	662-6562
Web: www.southernunited.com					
Southern-Owners Insurance Co 6101 Anacapri Blvd	Lansing	MI	48917	517-323-1200	323-8796
TF: 800-288-8740					
SS Nesbitt & Co Inc 2501 20th Pl S Suite 425	Birmingham	AL	35223	205-870-1316	870-3328
Web: www.ssnesbitt.com					
Star Insurance Co 26255 American Dr	Southfield	MI	48034	248-358-1100	358-1614
TF: 800-482-2726 ■ Web: www.meadowbrook.com/star.html					
State Auto Insurance Cos 518 E Broad St	Columbus	OH	43215	614-464-5000	
Web: www.state-auto-ins.com					
State Auto National Insurance Co 518 E Broad St	Columbus	OH	43215	614-464-5000	464-5341*
*Fax: Hum Res ■ TF: 800-444-9950 ■ Web: www.stateauto.com					
State Auto Property & Casualty Insurance Co 518 E Broad St	Columbus	OH	43215	614-464-5000	464-5341*
*Fax: Hum Res ■ TF: 800-444-9950 ■ Web: www.stateauto.com					
State Automobile Mutual Insurance Co 518 E Broad St	Columbus	OH	43215	614-464-5000	464-5341*
*Fax: Hum Res ■ TF: 800-444-9950 ■ Web: www.stateauto.com					
State Compensation Insurance Fund 1275 Market St	San Francisco	CA	94103	415-565-1234	565-3127
TF: 866-721-3498 ■ Web: www.statefundca.com					
State Farm Fire & Casualty Co 1 State Farm Plaza	Bloomington	IL	61710	309-766-2311	763-8777*
State Farm General Insurance Co 1 State Farm Plaza	Bloomington	IL	61710	309-766-2311	766-3621
Web: www.statefarm.com					
State Farm Indemnity Co 1 State Farm Plaza	Bloomington	IL	61710	309-766-2311	763-8777*
State Farm Insurance 333 First Commerce Dr	Aurora	ON	L4G8A4	905-750-4100	750-4716
Web: www.statefarm.ca					
State Farm Mutual Automobile Insurance Co 1 State Farm Plaza	Bloomington	IL	61710	309-766-2311	763-8777*
*Fax: Mktg ■ Web: www.statefarm.com					
STOPS Inc 8855 Grissom Pkwy	Titusville	FL	32780	321-383-0499	383-4116*
*Fax Area Code: 800 ■ TF: 800-487-0521 ■ Web: www.stopsinc.com					
Stratford Insurance Co 400 Parson's Pond Dr	Franklin Lakes	NJ	07417	201-847-8600	847-1010
Web: www.westernworld.com					
Swiss Re America Corp 175 King St	Armonk	NY	10504	914-828-8000	828-7000
TF: 877-794-7773 ■ Web: www.swissre.com					
Texas Mutual Insurance Co 6210 E Hwy 290	Austin	TX	78723	512-224-3800	224-3889
TF: 888-532-5246 ■ Web: www.texasmutual.com					
Toa Reinsurance Co of America 177 Madison Ave PO Box 1930	Morristown	NJ	07962	973-898-9480	898-9495
TF: 800-898-7977 ■ Web: www.toare.com					
Tokio Marine Life 230 Pk Ave	New York	NY	10169	212-297-6600	297-6062
TF: 800-628-2796 ■ Web: www.tokiomarine.us					
Topa Insurance Corp 1800 Avenue of the Stars	Los Angeles	CA	90067	310-201-0451	843-9409
TF: 800-949-6505 ■ Web: www.topains.com					
Tower Group Inc 120 Broadway 14th Fl	New York	NY	10271	212-655-2000	655-2199
NASDAQ: TWGP ■ TF: 877-883-6599 ■ Web: www.twrgrp.com					
Transatlantic Reinsurance Co 80 Pine St	New York	NY	10005	212-365-2200	365-2360
Web: www.transre.com					
Transcontinental Insurance Co 333 S Wabash Ave CNA Ctr	Chicago	IL	60604	312-822-5000	822-6419
TF: 800-262-2000 ■ Web: www.cna.com					
Transportation Insurance Co 333 S Wabash Ave	Chicago	IL	60604	312-822-5000	822-6419
TF: 800-262-2000 ■ Web: www.cna.com					
Travelers Indemnity Co 1 Tower Sq	Hartford	CT	06183	860-277-0111	277-1970*
*Fax: Hum Res ■ Web: www.travelers.com					
Tri-State Insurance Co of Minnesota 10 Roundwind Rd PO Box 500	Luverne	MN	56156	507-283-9561	232-9925*
*Fax Area Code: 800 ■ TF: 800-533-0303 ■ Web: www.cwgcollectorcar.com					
ULLICO Casualty Co 1625 I St NW	Washington	DC	20006	202-682-0900	682-4911
TF: 800-431-5425 ■ Web: www.ullico.com					
Unigard Security Insurance Co 15805 NE 24th St	Bellevue	WA	98008	425-945-5906	
TF: 800-777-1757 ■ Web: www.unigard.com					
Union National Fire Insurance Co 3636 S Sherwood Forest Blvd	Baton Rouge	LA	70816	225-292-7600	292-7614
TF: 800-765-0550					
Union Standard Insurance Co 122 W Carpenter Fwy Suite 350	Irving	TX	75039	972-719-2400	719-2401
TF: 800-444-0049 ■ Web: www.usic.com					
United Educators Insurance A Reciprocal Risk Retention Group 2 Wisconsin Cir 4th Fl	Chevy Chase	MD	20815	301-907-4908	907-4830
TF: 800-346-7877 ■ Web: www.ue.org					
United Fire & Casualty Co 118 Second Ave SE	Cedar Rapids	IA	52407	319-399-5700	399-5499
NASDAQ: UFCS ■ TF: 800-332-7977 ■ Web: www.unitedfiregroup.com					
United Heartland Inc PO Box 3026	Milwaukee	WI	53201	262-787-7700	787-7701
TF: 800-258-2667 ■ Web: www.unitedheartland.biz					
United National Group 3 Bala Plaza E Suite 300	Bala Cynwyd	PA	19004	610-664-1500	660-8882
TF: 800-333-0352 ■ Web: www.unitednat.com					
United National Insurance Co 3 Bala Plaza E Suite 300	Bala Cynwyd	PA	19004	610-664-1500	660-8882
TF: 800-333-0352 ■ Web: www.unitednat.com					
Universal Insurance Holding Inc (UIH) 1110 W Commerical Blvd Suite 100	Fort Lauderdale	FL	33309	954-958-1200	958-1201
AMEX: UVE ■ Web: www.universalinsuranceholdings.com					
USA Workers' Injury Network 916 S Capital of Texas Hwy	Austin	TX	78746	512-306-0201	328-6785
TF Cust Svc: 800-872-0820 ■ Web: www.usamco.com					
USAA Property & Casualty Insurance Group 9800 Fredericksburg Rd	San Antonio	TX	78288	800-531-8169	531-8877
TF: 800-531-8169 ■ Web: www.usaa.com/inet/pages/newsroom_factsheets_pnc					
Utica First Insurance Co 5981 Airport Rd	Oriskany	NY	13424	315-736-8211	768-4408
TF: 800-456-4556 ■ Web: www.uticafirst.com					
Utica National Insurance Group 180 Genesee St	New Hartford	NY	13413	315-734-2000	734-2680
TF: 800-274-1914 ■ Web: www.uticanational.com					
Valley Forge Insurance Co 100 CNA Dr	Nashville	TN	37214	615-871-1400	886-1883
TF: 800-437-8854					
Vermont Mutual Insurance Co 89 State St PO Box 188	Montpelier	VT	05601	802-223-2341	229-7646
TF: 800-451-5000 ■ Web: www.vermontmutual.com					
Victoria Insurance 22901 Millcreek Blvd	Cleveland	OH	44122	440-461-3461	461-0958
TF: 800-888-8424 ■ Web: www.victoriainsurance.com					
Vigilant Insurance Co 15 Mountain View Rd	Warren	NJ	07059	908-903-2000	903-2027
TF: 800-252-4670 ■ Web: www.chubd.com					

Phone | Fax

Viking Insurance
1800 N Pt Dr PO Box 8026 ... Stevens Point WI 54481 800-334-0090 346-9040*
*Fax Area Code: 715 ■ TF: 800-462-6342 ■ Web: www.vikinginsurance.com

Wawanesa Insurance 191 Broadway ... Winnipeg MB R3C3P1 204-985-3923 942-7724
Web: www.wawanesa.com

West Bend Mutual Insurance Co
1900 S 18th Ave ... West Bend WI 53095 262-334-5571 338-7293
TF: 800-236-5010 ■ Web: www.thesilverlining.com

Western Agricultural Insurance Co
325 S Higley Rd ... Higley AZ 85236 480-635-3600 854-8861*
*Fax Area Code: 866 ■ TF Cust Svc: 800-727-7868

Western Mutual Insurance Co
27489 Agoura Rd ... Agoura Hills CA 91301 800-927-2142 838-0144*
*Fax Area Code: 949 ■ TF: 800-927-2142 ■ Web: www.westernmutual.com

Western National Mutual Insurance Co
5350 W 78th St ... Edina MN 55439 952-835-5350 921-3159*
*Fax: Hum Res ■ TF: 800-862-6070 ■ Web: www.wnins.com

Western Reserve Group The 1685 Cleveland Rd ... Wooster OH 44691 330-262-9060 262-3259*
*Fax: Hum Res ■ TF: 800-362-0426 ■ Web: www.wrg-ins.com

Westfield Insurance Co
1 Pk Cir PO Box 5001 ... Westfield Center OH 44251 800-243-0210 887-0840*
*Fax Area Code: 330 ■ TF: 800-243-0210 ■ Web: www.westfieldinsurance.com

Westfield National Insurance Co
PO Box 5001 ... Westfield Center OH 44251 330-887-0101 887-0840
TF: 800-368-3530 ■ Web: www.westfieldgrp.com

Windham Injury Management Group Inc
500 N Comercial St Suite 301 ... Manchester NH 03101 603-626-5789 626-6717
Web: www.windhamgroup.com

Wisconsin Reinsurance Corp 2810 City View Dr ... Madison WI 53707 608-242-4500 242-4514
TF: 800-939-9473 ■ Web: www.thewrcgroup.com

XL Reinsurance America Inc 70 Sea View Ave ... Stamford CT 06902 203-964-5200 964-0763
Web: www.xlre.com

Zenith Insurance Co PO Box 9055 ... Van Nuys CA 91409 818-713-1000 883-3363
TF: 800-448-4356 ■ Web: www.thezenith.com

Zenithstar Insurance Co
Zenith Insurance Co
1101 Capital of Texas Hwy S Bldg J
PO Box 163510 ... Austin TX 78746 512-306-1700 327-6497
TF: 800-841-3987 ■ Web: www.thezenith.com

394-5 Surety Insurance

Phone | Fax

ACMAT Corp 233 Main St ... New Britain CT 06050 860-229-9000 229-1111
Web: www.acmatcorp.com

Acstar Insurance Co 233 Main St ... New Britain CT 06050 860-224-2000 229-1111
Web: www.acstarins.com

Admiral Insurance Co 1255 Caldwell Rd ... Cherry Hill NJ 08034 856-429-9200 429-8611
Web: www.admiralins.com

AMBAC Assurance Corp
1 State St Plaza 15th Fl ... New York NY 10004 212-668-0340 509-9190
TF: 800-221-1854 ■ Web: www.ambac.com

American Home Assurance Co 180 Maiden Ln ... New York NY 10038 212-770-7000 943-1125*
*Fax: Mail Rm ■ Web: www.aig.com

American Physicians Insurance Co (API)
1301 S Capitol of Texas Hwy Suite C-300 ... Austin TX 78746 512-328-0888 314-4398
TF: 800-252-3628 ■ Web: www.api-c.com

American Public Life Insurance Co
2305 Lakeland Dr PO Box 925 ... Jackson MS 39205 601-936-6600 936-2157
TF: 800-256-8606 ■ Web: ampublic.com

Assurant Solutions 260 IH- N Cir SE ... Atlanta GA 30339 770-763-1000 859-4403
Web: www.assurantsolutions.com

Assured Guaranty Corp 31 W 52nd St ... New York NY 10019 212-974-0100 581-3268
Web: www.assuredguaranty.com

Balboa Life & Casualty Insurance Co
3349 Michelson Dr Suite 200 ... Irvine CA 92612 949-222-8000 222-8716
TF: 800-854-6115 ■ Web: www.balboainsurance.com

Catholic Mutual Group 10843 Old Mill Rd ... Omaha NE 68154 402-551-8765 551-2943
TF: 800-228-6108 ■ Web: www.catholicmutual.org

Central Insurance Cos 800 S Washington St ... Van Wert OH 45891 419-238-1010 238-7626*
*Fax: Claims ■ TF: 800-736-7000 ■ Web: www.central-insurance.com

Central States Indemnity Co of Omaha
1212 N 96th St ... Omaha NE 68114 800-445-6500 997-8010*
*Fax Area Code: 402 ■ TF: 888-439-9440 ■ Web: www.csi-omaha.com

Century Insurance Group
465 Cleveland Ave ... Westerville OH 43082 614-895-2000 895-7036
TF: 800-878-7389 ■ Web: www.meadowbrook.com

Chubb Specialty Insurance 82 Hopmeadow St ... Simsbury CT 06070 860-408-2000 408-2002
TF: 800-432-8168 ■ Web: www.chubb.com

Cincinnati Casualty Co 6200 S Gilmore Rd ... Fairfield OH 45014 513-870-2000 870-2066

CMG Mortgage Insurance Co
22 4th St # 13 ... San Francisco CA 94103 415-284-2500 981-4601
TF: 800-909-4264 ■ Web: www.cmgmi.com

CNA 40 Wall St ... New York NY 10005 212-440-3000 440-7909*
*Fax: Hum Res ■ TF: 800-331-6053 ■ Web: www.cna.com

CNA Surety Corp 333 S Wabash Ave ... Chicago IL 60604 312-822-5000 822-6419
NYSE: SUR ■ TF: 877-672-6115 ■ Web: www.cnasurety.com

Connecticut Medical Insurance Co (CMIC)
80 Glastonbury Blvd, Third Fl PO Box 71 ... Glastonbury CT 06033 860-633-7788 633-8237
TF: 800-228-0287 ■ Web: www.ctmed.com

Copic Insurance Co 7351 Lowry Blvd ... Denver CO 80230 720-858-6000 858-6001
TF: 800-421-1834 ■ Web: www.callcopic.com/cic

Cumberland Casualty & Surety Co
4311 W Waters Ave Suite 401 ... Tampa FL 33614 813-885-2112 594-3323
TF: 800-723-0171 ■ Web: www.cumberlandtech.com

Dentists Insurance Co 1201 K St 17th Fl ... Sacramento CA 95814 916-443-4501 498-6162
Web: www.thedentists.com

Doctors' Co The 185 Greenwood Rd ... Napa CA 94558 707-226-0100 226-0165
TF: 800-421-2368 ■ Web: www.thedoctors.com

Phone | Fax

Euler Hermes ACI
800 Red Brook Blvd 4th Fl ... Owings Mills MD 21117 410-753-0753 554-0883
TF: 877-883-3224

Everest Reinsurance Co
477 Martinsville Rd ... Liberty Corner NJ 07938 908-604-3000 604-3450
TF: 800-269-6660 ■ Web: www.everestregroup.com

Federated Mutual Insurance Co
129 E Broadway St ... Owatonna MN 55060 507-455-5200 455-7808
TF: 800-533-0472 ■ Web: www.federatedinsurance.com

Financial Guaranty Insurance Co
125 Pk Ave 6th Fl ... New York NY 10017 212-312-3000 312-3231
TF: 800-352-0001 ■ Web: www.fgic.com

Fireman's Fund Insurance Co 777 San Marin Dr ... Novato CA 94998 415-899-2000 899-3600*
*Fax: Mail Rm ■ TF: 866-386-3932 ■ Web: www.firemansfund.com

First Insurance Co of Hawaii Ltd
1100 Ward Ave PO Box 2866 ... Honolulu HI 96803 808-527-7777 527-3200
TF: 800-272-5202 ■ Web: www.ficoh.com

First Professionals Insurance Co Inc (FPIC)
1000 Riverside Ave Suite 800 ... Jacksonville FL 32204 904-354-5910 358-6728
TF: 800-741-3742 ■ Web: www.fpicmedmal.com

First Southeast Insurance Services Inc
2430 Mall Dr Suite 280 ... Charleston SC 29406 843-529-5470 403-1454*
*Fax Area Code: 866 ■ TF: 877-590-4284 ■ Web: www.firstseinsurance.com

Genworth Financial Inc 6620 W Broad St ... Richmond VA 23230 804-484-3821 484-7198
NYSE: GNW ■ TF: 888-436-9678 ■ Web: www.genworth.com

Genworth Mortgage Insurance Corp
6601 Six Forks Rd ... Raleigh NC 27615 919-846-4100 846-4434
TF: 800-334-9270 ■ Web: www.mortgageinsurance.genworth.com

Great American Insurance Co 580 Walnut St ... Cincinnati OH 45202 513-369-5000
Web: www.greatamericaninsurance.com

Hartford Underwriters Insurance Co
1 Hartford Plaza ... Hartford CT 06115 860-547-5000
Web: www.thehartford.com

Heritage Insurance Managers Inc
PO Box 659570 ... San Antonio TX 78265 210-829-7467 822-4113

ICI Mutual Insurance Co PO Box 730 ... Burlington VT 05402 802-863-0096 660-4320
TF: 800-332-5564 ■ Web: www.sbtinsurance.com

Illinois State Medical Inter-Insurance Exchange (ISMIE)
20 N Michigan Ave Suite 700 ... Chicago IL 60602 312-782-2749 782-2023
TF: 800-782-4767 ■ Web: www.ismie.com

Indemnity Co of California
17780 Fitch Suite 200 ... Irvine CA 92614 949-263-3300 553-8149
TF: 800-782-1546 ■ Web: www.inscodico.com

Insco Dico Group 17780 Fitch Suite 200 ... Irvine CA 92614 949-263-3300 553-8149
TF: 800-782-1546 ■ Web: www.inscodico.com

Insurance Co of the West
11455 El Camino Real ... San Diego CA 92130 858-350-2400 350-2616
TF: 800-877-1111 ■ Web: www.icwgroup.com

International Fidelity Insurance Co
1111 Raymond Blvd ... Newark NJ 07102 973-624-7200 624-9048
TF: 800-333-4167 ■ Web: www.ific.com

JP Everhart & Co
1840 N Greenville Ave Suite 178 ... Richardson TX 75081 972-808-9001 808-9012
Web: www.texasnotaryonline.com

Kansas Bankers Surety Co 1220 SW Executive Dr ... Topeka KS 66615 785-228-0000 228-0079

Kansas Medical Mutual Insurance Co (KaMMCO)
623 SW 10th Ave Suite 200 ... Topeka KS 66612 785-232-2224 232-4704
TF: 800-232-2259 ■ Web: www.kammco.com

Lexington Insurance Co Inc 100 Summer St ... Boston MA 02110 617-330-1100 355-4891
TF: 800-355-4891 ■ Web: www.lexingtoninsurance.com

Life of the South Insurance Co
10151 Deerwood Pk Blvd Bldg 100 ... Jacksonville FL 32256 904-350-9660 354-4525
TF: 800-888-2738 ■ Web: www.life-south.com

Louisiana Medical Mutual Insurance Co
1 Galleria Blvd Suite 700 ... Metairie LA 70001 504-831-3756 841-5300
TF: 800-452-2120 ■ Web: www.lammico.com

MBIA Insurance Corp 113 King St ... Armonk NY 10504 914-273-4545 765-3163
TF: 800-765-6242 ■ Web: www.mbia.com

Media/Professional Insurance Inc
2300 Main St Suite 800 ... Kansas City MO 64108 816-471-6118 471-6119
TF: 866-282-0565 ■ Web: www.mediaprof.com

Medical Assurance Inc
100 Brookwood Pl Suite 300 ... Birmingham AL 35209 205-877-4400 802-4799
NYSE: PRA ■ TF Cust Svc: 800-282-6242 ■ Web: www.proassurance.com

Medical Liability Mutual Insurance Co (MLMIC)
2 Pk Ave 25th Fl ... New York NY 10016 212-576-9800 725-0916
TF: 800-275-6564 ■ Web: www.mlmic.com

Medical Mutual Group 700 Spring Forest Rd ... Raleigh NC 27609 919-872-7117 878-7550
TF: 800-662-7917 ■ Web: www.medicalmutualgroup.com

Medical Mutual Insurance Co of Maine
1 City Ctr # 9 ... Portland ME 04101 207-775-2791 775-6576
TF: 800-942-2791 ■ Web: www.medicalmutual.com

Medical Mutual Liability Insurance Society of Maryland
225 International Cir PO Box 8016 ... Hunt Valley MD 21030 410-785-0050 785-2631
TF: 800-492-0193 ■ Web: www.medicalmutualofmd.com

Medical Protective Co 5814 Reed Rd ... Fort Wayne IN 46885 260-485-9622 398-6726*
*Fax Area Code: 800 ■ TF: 800-463-3776 ■ Web: www.medpro.com

Mortgage Guaranty Insurance Corp
270 E Kilbourn Ave ... Milwaukee WI 53202 414-347-6480 347-6696
TF: 800-558-9900 ■ Web: www.mgic.com

National Union Fire Insurance Co of Pittsburgh Pennsylvania
180 Maiden Ln ... New York NY 10270 212-770-7000 943-1125*
*Fax: Mail Rm ■ TF: 877-520-4636 ■ Web: www.aig.com

NCMIC Insurance Co 14001 University Ave ... Clive IA 50325 515-313-4500 996-2642*
*Fax Area Code: 800 ■ TF: 800-769-2000 ■ Web: www.ncmic.com

Nobel Insurance 12225 Greenville Ave Suite 750 ... Dallas TX 75243 972-644-0434 644-0424
TF: 800-766-6235 ■ Web: www.nobelinsurance.com

Norcal Mutual Insurance Co Inc
560 Davis St ... San Francisco CA 94111 415-397-9700 835-0800
TF: 800-652-1051 ■ Web: www.norcalmutual.com

Northwest Physicians Mutual Insurance Co
2965 Ryan Dr SE ... Salem OR 97301 503-371-8228 371-0087
TF: 800-243-3503 ■ Web: www.npmic.com

Phone Fax

Oklahoma Surety Co 1437 S Boulder Ave Suite 200 . . . . Tulsa OK 74119 918-587-7221 588-1298
TF: 800-722-4994

Old Republic Insured Automotive Services Inc
8282 S Memorial Dr . . . . Tulsa OK 74133 918-307-1000 874-9559*
**Fax Area Code:* 800 ■ *TF:* 800-331-4065 ■ *Web:* www.orias.com

Old Republic Surety
445 S Moorlands Rd Suite 301 . . . . Brookfield WI 53005 262-797-2640 797-9495
TF: 800-217-1792 ■ *Web:* www.orsurety.com

Pekin Life Insurance Co 2505 Ct St . . . . Pekin IL 61558 309-346-1161 346-8512
TF: 800-322-0160 ■ *Web:* www.pekininsurance.com

Penn National Insurance Co
2 N 2nd St Penn National Plaza . . . . Harrisburg PA 17101 717-234-4941 255-6850
TF: 800-388-4764 ■ *Web:* www.pennnationalinsurance.com

Pennsylvania Medical Society Liability Insurance Co (PMSLIC)
1700 Bent Creek Blvd PO Box 2080 . . . . Mechanicsburg PA 17050 717-791-1212 796-8080
TF: 800-445-1212 ■ *Web:* www.pmslic.com

PMI Mortgage Insurance Co 3003 Oak Rd . . . . Walnut Creek CA 94597 925-658-7878 658-6940
TF: 800-288-1970 ■ *Web:* www.pmi-us.com

Podiatry Insurance Co of America
110 Westwood Pl Suite 100 . . . . Brentwood TN 37027 615-371-8776 846-9486
TF: 866-742-2477 ■ *Web:* www.picagroup.com

Pre-Paid Legal Services Inc 1 Pre-Paid Way . . . . Ada OK 74820 580-436-1234 436-7565*
NYSE: PPD ■ **Fax:* Cust Svc ■ *TF:* 800-654-7757 ■ *Web:* www.prepaidlegal.com

Princeton Insurance Co
746 Alexander Rd PO Box 5322 . . . . Princeton NJ 08540 609-452-9404 734-8461
TF: 800-334-0588 ■ *Web:* www.princetoninsurance.com

Pro Assurance 20 Allen Ave Suite 420 . . . . Saint Louis MO 63119 314-961-7700 918-0530

ProMutual Group 101 Arch St 4th Fl . . . . Boston MA 02110 617-330-1755 330-1748
TF: 800-225-6168 ■ *Web:* www.promutualgroup.com

Protective Insurance Co PO Box 7099 . . . . Indianapolis IN 46207 317-636-9800 632-9444
TF: 800-644-5501 ■ *Web:* www.baldwinandlyons.com

Radian Asset Assurance Inc
The Radian Group Inc 335 Madison Ave 25th Fl . . . . New York NY 10017 212-983-3100 682-5377
TF: 877-337-4925 ■ *Web:* www.radian.biz

Radian Group Inc 1601 Market St . . . . Philadelphia PA 19103 215-564-6600
NYSE: RDN ■ *TF:* 800-523-1988 ■ *Web:* www.radian.biz

Reciprocal of America 4200 Innslake Dr . . . . Glen Allen VA 23060 804-747-8600 270-5281

Republic Mortgage Insurance Co
101 N Cherry St # 101 . . . . Winston-Salem NC 27101 336-661-0015 661-3275
TF: 800-999-7642 ■ *Web:* www.rmic.com

RLI Insurance Co 9025 N Lindbergh Dr . . . . Peoria IL 61615 309-692-1000 692-1068
TF: 800-331-4929 ■ *Web:* www.rlicorp.com

Rose & Kiernan Inc 99 Troy Rd . . . . East Greenbush NY 12061 518-244-4245 244-4262
Web: www.rkinsurance.com

SAFECO Surety 1001 4th Ave Suite 1700 . . . . Seattle WA 98154 206-473-3799 376-6533*
**Fax Area Code:* 425 ■ *Web:* www.safeco.com/surety/default.asp

Securities Investors Protection Corp
805 15th St NW Suite 800 . . . . Washington DC 20005 202-371-8300 371-6728
Web: www.sipc.org

State Volunteer Mutual Insurance Co
101 W Pk Dr Suite 300 . . . . Brentwood TN 37027 615-377-1999 370-1343
TF: 800-342-2239 ■ *Web:* www.svmic.com

Surety Group Inc
3715 Northside PkwyNW Suite 1-315 . . . . Atlanta GA 30327 404-352-8211 351-3237
TF: 800-486-8211 ■ *Web:* www.suretygroup.com

Texas Hospital Insurance Exchange
8310 N Capital of Texas Hwy Bldg 1 Suite 550 . . . . Austin TX 78752 512-451-5775 451-3101
TF: 800-792-0060 ■ *Web:* www.thie.com

Texas Lawyers Insurance Exchange (TLIE)
900 Congress Ave Suite 500 . . . . Austin TX 78701 512-480-9074 482-8738
Web: www.tlie.org

Transamerica 520 Pk Ave . . . . Baltimore MD 21201 410-685-5500 685-6500
TF: 800-233-4624 ■ *Web:* www.aegonusa.com

Transatlantic Reinsurance Co 80 Pine St . . . . New York NY 10005 212-365-2200 365-2360
Web: www.transre.com

Travelers Indemnity Co 1 Tower Sq . . . . Hartford CT 06183 860-277-0111 277-1970*
**Fax:* Hum Res ■ *Web:* www.travelers.com

Triad Guaranty Insurance Corp
101 S Stratford Rd . . . . Winston-Salem NC 27104 336-723-1282 723-2824
TF Cust Svc: 888-691-8074 ■ *Web:* www.tgic.com

Tudor Insurance Co
400 Parson's Pond Dr . . . . Franklin Lakes NJ 07417 201-847-8600 847-1010

ULLICO Casualty Co 1625 I St NW . . . . Washington DC 20006 202-682-0900 682-4911
TF: 800-431-5425 ■ *Web:* www.ullico.com

United Guaranty Corp (UGC) 230 N Elm St . . . . Greensboro NC 27401 336-373-0232 230-1946*
**Fax:* Hum Res ■ *TF:* 800-334-8966 ■ *Web:* www.ugcorp.com

United National Group
3 Bala Plaza E Suite 300 . . . . Bala Cynwyd PA 19004 610-664-1500 660-8882
TF: 800-333-0352 ■ *Web:* www.unitednat.com

United States Liability Insurance Group
1190 Devon Pk Dr PO Box 6700 . . . . Wayne PA 19087 610-688-2535 688-4391
TF: 800-523-5545 ■ *Web:* www.usli.com

Universal Surety of America
950 Echo Ln Suite 250 . . . . Houston TX 77024 713-722-4601
TF: 800-392-9697 ■ *Web:* www.universalsurety.com

Utica National Insurance Group
180 Genesee St . . . . New Hartford NY 13413 315-734-2000 734-2680
TF: 800-274-1914 ■ *Web:* www.uticanational.com

Victor O Schinnerer & Co Inc
2 Wisconsin Cir Suite 1100 . . . . Chevy Chase MD 20815 301-961-9800 951-5444
TF: 888-867-9327 ■ *Web:* www.schinnerer.com

Vision Financial Corp PO Box 506 . . . . Keene NH 03431 603-357-1450 357-0250
TF: 800-793-0223 ■ *Web:* www.visfin.com

Western World Insurance Co
400 Parson's Pond Dr . . . . Franklin Lakes NJ 07417 201-847-8600 847-1010
Web: www.westernworld.com

Western World Insurance Group Inc
400 Parson's Pond Dr . . . . Franklin Lakes NJ 07417 201-847-8600 847-1010
Web: www.westernworld.com

XL Specialty Insurance Co
20 N Martingale Rd Suite 200 . . . . Schaumburg IL 60173 847-517-2990 517-5240
TF: 800-394-3909

Zurich North America 1400 American Ln . . . . Schaumburg IL 60196 847-605-6000 962-2567*
**Fax Area Code:* 877 ■ **Fax:* Claims ■ *TF:* 800-382-2150 ■ *Web:* www.zurichna.com

394-6 Title Insurance

Most Title Insurance Companies Also Provide Other Real Estate Services Such As Escrow, Flood Certification, Appraisals, Etc.

Phone Fax

Alamo Title Insurance 601 Riverside Ave . . . . Jacksonville FL 32204 904-854-8100
TF Mktg: 888-866-3684 ■ *Web:* www.alamotitle.com

AmeriPoint Title Inc
10101 Reunion Pl Suite 250 . . . . San Antonio TX 78216 210-340-2921 340-9640
Web: www.ameripointtitle.com

Attorney's Title Insurance Fund Inc
6545 Corporate Ctr Blvd . . . . Orlando FL 32822 407-240-3863 240-1106
TF: 800-336-3863 ■ *Web:* www.thefund.com

Chicago Title & Trust Co 171 N Clark St . . . . Chicago IL 60601 312-223-2000 223-5627*
**Fax:* Hum Res ■ *TF:* 800-621-1919 ■ *Web:* www.ctic.com

Chicago Title Insurance Co of Oregon
10135 SE Sunnyside Rd Suite 130 . . . . Clackamas OR 97015 503-653-7300 653-7833
Web: www.ctic.com

Commerce Title Co 1461 E Cooley Dr Suite 280 . . . . Colton CA 92324 909-430-3218 433-0816
TF: 800-244-4322 ■ *Web:* www.commercetitlecompany.com

Commonwealth Land Title Insurance Co
601 Riverside Ave . . . . Jacksonville FL 32204 888-866-3684
TF: 888-866-3684 ■ *Web:* www.cltic.com

Community Title & Escrow Ltd
2600 State St Bldg D . . . . Alton IL 62002 618-466-7755 466-7782
TF: 800-854-4049 ■ *Web:* www.communitytitle.net

Dakota Homestead Title Insurance Co
315 S Phillips Ave . . . . Sioux Falls SD 57104 605-336-0388 336-5649
TF: 800-425-0388

Fidelity National Title Group Inc
601 Riverside Ave . . . . Jacksonville FL 32204 904-854-8100 357-1007
TF: 888-866-3684 ■ *Web:* www.fntg.com

Fidelity National Title Insurance Co
10010 San Pedro Blvd Suite 700 . . . . San Antonio TX 78216 210-340-0456 336-2460
Web: www.fntic.com

Fidelity National Title Insurance Co of Oregon
900 SW 5th Ave Mezzanine Level . . . . Portland OR 97204 503-223-8338 796-6611
Web: www.fntic.com

First American Corp 1 First American Way . . . . Santa Ana CA 92707 714-558-3211 800-3135
NYSE: FAF ■ *TF:* 800-854-3643 ■ *Web:* www.firstam.com

Gracy Title Co 524 N Lamar Blvd Suite 200 . . . . Austin TX 78703 512-472-8421 478-6038
Web: www.gracytitle.com

Greater Illinois Title Co
120 N La Salle St Suite 900 . . . . Chicago IL 60602 312-236-7300 236-0284
Web: www.gitc.com

Hanover Insurance Co 440 Lincoln St . . . . Worcester MA 01653 508-855-1000 853-6332
TF: 800-853-0456 ■ *Web:* www.hanover.com

LandAmerica OneStop Inc
600 Clubhouse Dr . . . . Moon Township PA 15108 412-507-2000 296-0095*
**Fax Area Code:* 866 ■ *TF:* 866-226-8616 ■ *Web:* www.landam.com

Lawyers Title Co 251 S Lake Ave Suite 400 . . . . Pasadena CA 91101 626-304-2700 795-0875
TF: 800-347-7800

Lawyers Title Insurance Corp
601 Riverside Ave . . . . Jacksonville FL 32204 888-866-3684
TF: 888-866-3684 ■ *Web:* www.ltic.com

Meridian Title Corp 202 S Michigan St . . . . South Bend IN 46601 574-232-5845 289-1514
TF: 800-777-1574 ■ *Web:* www.meridiantitle.com

Mississippi Valley Title Insurance Co
315 Tom Bigbee St . . . . Jackson MS 39201 601-969-0222 969-2215
TF: 800-647-2124 ■ *Web:* www.mvt.com

Monroe Title Insurance Corp 47 W Main St . . . . Rochester NY 14614 585-232-4950 232-4988
TF: 800-966-6763 ■ *Web:* www.monroetitle.com

North American Title Co
2185 N California Blvd Suite 575 . . . . Walnut Creek CA 94596 925-935-5599 933-4851
TF: 800-869-3434 ■ *Web:* www.nat.com/nationalsite/default.asp

Old Republic National Title Insurance Co
400 2nd Ave S . . . . Minneapolis MN 55401 612-371-1111 371-1129
TF: 800-328-4441 ■ *Web:* www.oldrepnatl.com

Pacific Northwest Title (PNWT) 215 Columbia St . . . . Seattle WA 98104 206-622-1040 343-1334
TF: 800-634-5544 ■ *Web:* www.pnwt.com

Placer Title Co 2394 Fair Oaks Blvd . . . . Sacramento CA 95825 916-973-1002 482-3049
Web: www.placertitle.com

Rattikin Title Co 201 Main St Suite 800 . . . . Fort Worth TX 76102 817-332-1171 882-9886

Southland Title Co 7530 N Glenoaks Blvd . . . . Burbank CA 91504 818-767-2000 768-5250
TF: 800-747-7777 ■ *Web:* www.southlandtitle.com

Stewart Information Services Corp
1980 Post Oak Blvd Suite 800 . . . . Houston TX 77056 713-625-8100 552-9523
NYSE: STC ■ *TF:* 800-729-1900 ■ *Web:* www.stewart.com

Stewart REI Data Inc
1980 Post Oak Blvd Suite 800 . . . . Houston TX 77056 800-783-9278 705-9377*
**Fax Area Code:* 630 ■ *TF:* 888-534-4461 ■ *Web:* www.stewart.com

Stewart Title & Trust of Phoenix
244 W Osborn Rd . . . . Phoenix AZ 85013 602-248-8444 776-6251*
**Fax:* Cust Svc ■ *Web:* www.stewartaz.com

Stewart Title Co 1980 Post Oak Blvd Suite 800 . . . . Houston TX 77056 713-625-8100 552-9523
TF: 800-729-1900 ■ *Web:* www.stewart.com

Stewart Title Guaranty Co
1980 Post Oak Blvd Suite 800 . . . . Houston TX 77056 713-625-8100 552-9523
TF: 800-729-1900 ■ *Web:* www.stewart.com

Ticor Title Insurance Co
203 N LaSalle St Suite 2200 . . . . Chicago IL 60601 312-621-5000 621-5123
TF: 800-879-1167 ■ *Web:* www.ticortitle.com

Title Guaranty of Hawaii Inc 235 Queen St . . . . Honolulu HI 96813 808-533-6261 521-0210
TF: 800-548-2429 ■ *Web:* www.tghawaii.com

Title Resources Guaranty Co
8111 LBJ Fwy Suite 1200 . . . . Dallas TX 75251 972-644-6500 644-8141
TF: 800-526-8018 ■ *Web:* www.trgc.com

394-7 Travel Insurance

Most Of The Companies Listed Here Are Insurance Agencies And Brokerages That Specialize In Selling Travel Insurance Policies, Rather Than The Insurers Who Underwrite The Policies.

	City	State	Zip	Phone	Fax
Access America 2805 N Parham Rd TF: 800-729-6021 ■ Web: www.accessamerica.com	Richmond	VA	23294	804-285-3300	673-1586
All Aboard Benefits 6162 E Mockingird Ln Suite 104 TF: 800-462-2322 ■ Web: www.allaboardbenefits.com	Dallas	TX	75214	214-821-6677	821-6676
Continental Assurance Co 333 S Wabash Ave TF: 800-262-2000 ■ Web: www.cna.com	Chicago	IL	60604	312-822-5000	822-6419
CSA Travel Protection 5454 Ruffin Rd *Fax Area Code: 800 ■ TF: 800-873-9855 ■ Web: www.csatravelprotection.com	San Diego	CA	92123	858-810-2000	336-6409*
Gateway Insurance Co PO Box 440400 TF: 800-779-3600 ■ Web: www.gicauto.com	Saint Louis	MO	63144	314-373-3333	373-4444
Highway To Health Inc 1 Radnor Corporate Ctr Suite 100 TF: 888-243-2358 ■ Web: www.hthtravelinsurance.com	Radnor	PA	19087	610-254-8700	254-8797
Ingle International 460 Richmond St W Suite 701 TF: 800-360-3234 ■ Web: www.ingle-health.com	Toronto	ON	M5V1Y1	416-640-7863	730-1878
Insurance Consultants International 7405 Campstool Dr Suite 101 TF: 800-576-2674 ■ Web: www.globalhealthinsurance.com	Colorado Springs	CO	80922	719-573-9080	
International SOS Assistance Inc 3600 Horizon Blvd Suite 300 TF: 800-523-8930 ■ Web: www.internationalsos.com	Trevose	PA	19053	215-244-1500	942-8298
Lloyd's America Inc 25 W 53rd St 14th Fl Web: www.lloyds.com	New York	NY	10036	212-382-4060	382-4070
Pan-American Life Insurance Co 601 Poydras St TF Life Ins: 877-939-4550 ■ Web: www.panamericanlife.com	New Orleans	LA	70130	504-566-1300	566-3381
Titan Insurance Co 901 Wilshire Dr Suite 550 *Fax Area Code: 877 ■ TF: 800-347-7930 ■ Web: www.titanauto.com	Troy	MI	48084	800-775-4642	295-2923*
Travel Guard International 3300 Business Pk Dr *Fax Area Code: 800 ■ TF: 800-826-1300 ■ Web: www.travelguard.com	Stevens Point	WI	54482	715-345-0505	955-8785*
Travel Insured International 52-S Oakland Ave PO Box 280568 TF: 800-243-3174 ■ Web: www.travelinsured.com	East Hartford	CT	06128	860-528-7663	528-8005
Virginia Risk Co 9200 Keystone Crossing Suite 300 *Fax: Claims ■ TF: 800-523-6944 ■ Web: www.virginiarisk.com	Indianapolis	IN	46240	317-818-2089	575-2659*
Wallach & Co Inc 107 W Federal St TF: 800-237-6615 ■ Web: www.wallach.com	Middleburg	VA	20117	540-687-3166	687-3172
World Access Inc 2805 N Parham Rd TF: 800-628-4908 ■ Web: www.worldaccess.com	Richmond	VA	23294	804-285-3300	673-1586

395 INTERCOM EQUIPMENT & SYSTEMS

	City	State	Zip	Phone	Fax
Anacom General Corp 1240 S Claudina St *Fax: Sales ■ TF: 800-955-9540 ■ Web: www.anacom-medtek.com	Anaheim	CA	92805	714-774-8484	774-7388*
Clear-Com USA 850 Marina Village Pkwy Web: www.clearcom.com	Alameda	CA	94501	510-337-6600	
Clever Devices Ltd 137 Commercial St TF: 800-872-6129 ■ Web: www.cleverdevices.com	Plainview	NY	11803	516-433-6100	433-5088
Crest Healthcare Supply 195 3rd St TF: 800-328-8908 ■ Web: www.cresthealthcare.com	Dassel	MN	55325	320-275-3382	275-2306
David Clark Co Inc 360 Franklin St *Fax: Sales ■ TF Cust Svc: 800-298-6235 ■ Web: www.davidclark.com	Worcester	MA	01615	508-751-5800	753-5827*
Lee Dan Communications Inc 155 Adams Ave TF: 800-231-1414 ■ Web: www.leedan.com	Hauppauge	NY	11788	631-231-1414	231-1498

396 INTERIOR DESIGN

	City	State	Zip	Phone	Fax
Building Service Inc (BSI) 11925 W Carmen Ave TF: 866-353-3600 ■ Web: www.buildingservice.com	Milwaukee	WI	53225	414-353-3600	353-6060
Cole Martinez Curtis & Assoc 4040 Del Rey Ave # 7 Web: www.cmcadesign.com	Marina del Rey	CA	90292	310-827-7200	822-5803
Commercial Furniture Interiors Inc 1135 Spruce Dr Web: www.cfioffice.com	Mountainside	NJ	07092	908-518-1670	654-8436
Curran Assoc 737 Miami Cir NE TF: 800-241-0178 ■ Web: www.curran-aat.com	Atlanta	GA	30324	404-237-4246	237-4246
Decorating Den Systems Inc 8659 Commerce Dr TF: 800-332-3367 ■ Web: www.decoratingden.com	Easton	MD	21601	410-822-9001	
Erik Johnson & Assoc 758 N Larrabee Suite 415 Web: www.erikjohnsonassociates.com	Chicago	IL	60654	312-644-2202	645-5883
Gary Raub Assoc PO Box 26835	San Diego	CA	92196	858-565-2775	565-9035
H Chambers Co 1010 N Charles St	Baltimore	MD	21201	410-727-4535	727-6982
Hubbuch & Co 324 W Main St Web: www.hubbuch.com	Louisville	KY	40202	502-583-2713	582-7375
Interior Space International (ISI) *Epstein* 600 W Fulton Web: www.epsteinglobal.com	Chicago	IL	60661	312-454-9100	559-1217
Kay Green Design Inc 859 Outer Rd TF: 800-226-5186 ■ Web: www.kaygreendesign.com	Orlando	FL	32814	407-246-7155	426-7873
Mancini Duffy 1350 Avenue of the Americas 2nd Fl Web: www.manciniduffy.com	New York	NY	10019	212-938-1260	
Merida Meridian Inc 643 Summer St TF: 800-345-2200 ■ Web: www.meridameridian.com	Boston	MA	02210	800-345-2200	
MGM Mirage Design Group Inc 3260 Industrial Rd TF: 800-477-5110	Las Vegas	NV	89109	702-792-4600	792-4790
Miller/Zell Inc 4715 Frederick Dr SW Web: www.millerzell.com	Atlanta	GA	30336	404-691-7400	699-2189
Niermann Weeks Co Inc 760 Generals Hwy Web: www.niermannweeks.com	Millersville	MD	21108	410-923-0123	923-0647
Omnifics Inc 5845 Richmond Hwy Suite 300 Web: www.omnifics.com	Alexandria	VA	22303	703-548-4040	836-8159
Philpotts 40 S School St Suite 200 Web: www.philpotts.net	Honolulu	HI	96813	808-523-6771	521-9569
Ravenswood Studio Inc 6900 N Central Pk Ave Web: www.ravenswoodstudio.com	Lincolnwood	IL	60712	847-679-2800	679-2805
Rucker Fuller Co 333 Pine St Suite 100 Web: www.ruckerfuller.com	San Francisco	CA	94104	415-445-3000	445-3001
Sloan Accoustics Inc 38 Fairfield Pl PO Box 2845 Web: www.sloanandcompany.com	Caldwell	NJ	07006	973-227-3555	227-8731
TriMark Raygal 2719 White Rd Web: www.trimarkusa.com	Irvine	CA	92614	949-474-1000	474-7298
Veenendaalcave Inc 1170 Peachtree St NE Web: www.vcave.com	Atlanta	GA	30309	404-881-1811	876-1289
Villa Lighting Supply Inc 2929 Chouteau Ave TF: 800-325-0963 ■ Web: www.villalighting.com	Saint Louis	MO	63103	314-531-2600	531-8720
Vladimir Kagan Design Group 1185 Pk Ave Suite 14G Web: www.vladimirkagan.com	New York	NY	10128	212-289-0031	289-0031
Wilson Office Interiors 1444 Oak Lawn Ave Suite 545 Web: www.wilsonoi.com	Dallas	TX	75207	972-488-4100	488-8815

397 INTERNET BACKBONE PROVIDERS

Companies That Are, In Effect, Internet Service Providers For Internet Service Providers (Isps).

	City	State	Zip	Phone	Fax
AboveNet Communications Inc 360 Hamilton Ave TF: 866-859-6971 ■ Web: www.abovenet.com	White Plains	NY	10601	914-421-6700	421-6777
BT Americas Inc 2160 E Grand Ave TF: 888-767-2988 ■ Web: www.globalservices.bt.com	El Segundo	CA	90245	408-330-2700	330-2701
Cogent Communications Group Inc 1015 31st St NW NASDAQ: CCOI ■ TF: 877-875-4432 ■ Web: www.cogentco.com	Washington	DC	20007	202-295-4200	338-8798
IDT Corp 520 Broad St NYSE: IDT ■ TF: 800-225-5438 ■ Web: www.idt.net	Newark	NJ	07102	973-438-1000	438-1453
iPass Inc 3800 Bridge Pkwy NASDAQ: IPAS ■ TF: 877-674-7277 ■ Web: www3.ipass.com	Redwood Shores	CA	94065	650-232-4100	232-4111
Level 3 Communications Inc 1025 Eldorado Blvd NASDAQ: LVLT ■ TF: 877-453-8353 ■ Web: www.level3.com	Broomfield	CO	80021	720-888-1000	
nFrame Inc 701 Congressional Blvd Suite 100 TF: 888-223-8633 ■ Web: www.nframe.com	Carmel	IN	46032	317-805-3759	805-3757
SAVVIS Inc 1 Savvis Pkwy NASDAQ: SVVS ■ TF: 800-728-8471 ■ Web: www.savvis.net	Town & Country	MO	63017	314-628-7000	
SunGard Availability Services 680 E Swedesford Rd *Fax Area Code: 610 ■ TF: 800-468-7483 ■ Web: www.sungardas.com	Wayne	PA	19087	484-582-2000	225-1120*
Verio Inc 8005 S Chester St Suite 200 TF Sales: 800-438-8374 ■ Web: www.verio.com	Centennial	CO	80112	561-912-2555	
Verizon Business 1 Verizon Way TF Cust Svc: 866-232-4282 ■ Web: www.verizonbusiness.com	Basking Ridge	NJ	07920	800-339-9911	
XO Communications Inc 13865 Sunrise Valley Dr TF: 800-900-6398 ■ Web: www.xo.com	Herndon	VA	20171	703-547-2000	547-2881

398 INTERNET BROADCASTING

	City	State	Zip	Phone	Fax
Atom Entertainment Inc 225 Bush St Suite 1200 Web: www.atomentertainment.com	San Francisco	CA	94104	415-503-2400	
Audible Inc 1 Washington Pk TF: 888-283-5051 ■ Web: www.audible.com	Newark	NJ	07102	973-820-0400	890-2442
IA Global Inc 101 California St Suite 2450 PINK: IAGI ■ Web: www.iaglobalinc.com	San Francisco	CA	94111	415-946-8828	946-8801
Live365 Inc 950 Tower Ln Suite 400 Web: www.live365.com	Foster City	CA	94404	650-345-7400	345-7497
Nstreams Technologies Inc 209 E Java Dr Web: www.nstreams.com	Sunnyvale	CA	94089	408-734-8889	734-8886
OMT Inc 1555 Dublin Ave Unit 1 TF: 888-665-6501 ■ Web: www.omt.net	Winnipeg	MB	R3E3M8	204-786-3994	783-5805
ON24 Inc 201 3rd St # 3 Web: www.on24.com	San Francisco	CA	94103	415-369-8000	369-8388
Trailervision Studios 6 Vista Rd Web: www.trailervision.com	Bolton West	QC	J0E2T0	450-242-2927	242-2313
Yahoo! LAUNCH 701 1st Ave Web: www.new.music.yahoo.com	Sunnyvale	CA	94089	408-349-3300	349-3301
@Com Technology LLC 1353 Pine St Suite E TF: 877-888-4424 ■ Web: www.atcomtechnology.com	Walnut Creek	CA	94596	877-888-4424	

399 INTERNET DOMAIN NAME REGISTRARS

	City	State	Zip	Phone	Fax
123 Registration.com PO Box 2600 Web: www.123-registration.com	Sarasota	FL	34230	941-365-5225	954-5771
4Domains.com 77-670 Springfield Ln Suite 11B TF: 877-777-6263 ■ Web: www.4domains.com	Palm Desert	CA	92211	760-360-4600	772-3654

				Phone	Fax
AITDomains.com 421 Maiden Ln	Fayetteville	NC	28301	877-549-2881	321-1390*
*Fax Area Code: 910 ■ TF: 877-549-2881 ■ Web: www.aitdomains.com					
Alldomains.com 391 N Ancestor Pl Suite 150	Boise	ID	83704	208-685-1888	685-1891
TF: 800-561-5131 ■ Web: www.alldomains.com					
Best Registration Services Inc 1418 S 3rd St	Louisville	KY	40208	502-637-4528	636-9157
TF: 800-977-3475 ■ Web: www.bestregistrar.com					
CVO.ca Corp 43 Auriga Dr	Nepean	ON	K2E7Y8	613-768-5127	820-0777
Web: www.cvo.ca					
directNIC 650 Poydras St Suite 1150	New Orleans	LA	70130	504-679-5170	566-0484
Web: www.directnic.com					
Domain Registration Services PO Box 447	Palmyra	NJ	08065	888-339-9001	922-4961*
*Fax Area Code: 215 ■ TF: 888-339-9001 ■ Web: www.dotearth.com					
Domain-It! 9525 Kenwood Rd Suite 328	Cincinnati	OH	45242	513-351-4222	351-8222
TF: 866-927-3624 ■ Web: www.domainit.com					
DomainPeople Inc 550 Burrard St Suite 200, Bentall Tower 5	Vancouver	BC	V6C2B5	604-639-1680	688-9013
TF: 877-734-3667 ■ Web: www.domainpeople.com					
DomainRegistry.com Inc 3554 Hulmeville Rd Suite 108	Bensalem	PA	19020	215-244-6700	244-6605
Web: www.domainregistry.com					
Domainsatcost.ca 43 Auriga Dr	Ottawa	ON	K2E7Y8	613-768-5125	820-0777
Web: www.domainsatcost.ca					
Dotster Inc 11807 NE 99th St Suite 1100	Vancouver	WA	98682	360-253-2210	253-4234
Web: www.dotster.com					
Dynadot LLC PO Box 345	Belmont	CA	94401	650-585-1961	869-2893*
*Fax Area Code: 415 ■ TF Cust Svc: 866-652-2039 ■ Web: www.dynadot.com					
easyDNS 219 Dufferin St Suite 304A	Toronto	ON	M6K3J1	416-535-8672	535-0237
TF: 888-677-4741 ■ Web: www.web.easydns.com					
EnCirca Inc 400 W Cummings Pk Suite 1725-307	Woburn	MA	01801	800-366-1336	823-8911*
*Fax Area Code: 781 ■ TF: 800-366-1336 ■ Web: www.encirca.biz					
eNom Inc 5808 Lake Washington Blvd Suite 300	Kirkland	WA	98033	425-974-4689	974-4796*
*Fax: Acctg ■ Web: www.enom.com					
Go Daddy Group Inc 14455 N Hayden Rd Suite 219	Scottsdale	AZ	85260	480-505-8899	505-8844
Web: www.godaddy.com					
iHoldings.com Inc 13205 SW 137th Ave Suite 133	Miami	FL	33186	305-971-3440	675-2830
Misk 973 Main St Suite B	Fishkill	NY	12524	845-896-4602	510-1878
Web: www.misk.com					
Mobile Name Services 2002 156th Ave NE Suite 300	Bellevue	WA	98007	425-274-4500	974-4791
Moniker Online Services LLC 20 SW 27th Ave Suite 201	Pompano Beach	FL	33069	954-984-0923	
TF: 800-841-7686 ■ Web: www.moniker.com					
Name.com LLC 2500 E 2nd Ave 2 Fl Suite 300	Denver	CO	80206	720-249-2374	399-3167*
*Fax Area Code: 303 ■ Web: www.name.com					
Namesbeyond.com 922 S Woodbourne Rd Suite 122	Levittown	PA	19057	267-573-1142	321-1970*
*Fax Area Code: 215 ■ TF: 877-227-8870 ■ Web: www.namesbeyond.com					
NameSecure LLC PO Box 27096	Concord	CA	94527	925-609-1111	609-1112
TF: 800-299-1288 ■ Web: www.namesecure.com					
Network Solutions LLC 13861 Sunrise Valley Dr Suite 300	Herndon	VA	20171	703-742-0400	742-3386
TF: 800-638-9759 ■ Web: www.networksolutions.com					
Register.com Inc 575 8th Ave 11th Fl	New York	NY	10018	212-798-9100	594-9448
TF: 800-899-9724 ■ Web: www.register.com					
RegisterNames Inc PO Box 821066	Vancouver	WA	98682	360-253-2210	462-4832*
*Fax Area Code: 603 ■ TF: 888-295-7227 ■ Web: www.registernames.com					
Simply Named Inc 1829 US Hwy 64	Marion	AR	72364	800-815-1654	
TF: 800-815-1654 ■ Web: www.simplynamed.com					
Spirit Telecom 1500 Hampton St Suite 101	Columbia	SC	29201	803-771-7476	771-7436
TF: 800-333-2949 ■ Web: www.spirittelecom.com					
Tiger Technologies LLC PO Box 7596	Berkeley	CA	94707	510-527-3131	539-5032*
*Fax Area Code: 866 ■ Web: www.tigertech.net					
Webnames.ca Inc 21 Water St 5th Fl	Vancouver	BC	V6B1A!	866-221-7878	633-3174*
*Fax Area Code: 604 ■ TF Cust Svc: 866-221-7878 ■ Web: www.webnames.ca					

400 INTERNET SEARCH ENGINES, PORTALS, DIRECTORIES

				Phone	Fax
555-1212.com Inc PO Box 3713	Truckee	CA	96160	415-288-2440	
Web: www.555-1212.com					
About Inc 1440 Broadway 19th Fl	New York	NY	10018	212-204-4000	204-1521
Web: www.about.com					
Adknowledge Inc 4600 Madison Ave 10th Fl	Kansas City	FL	64112	816-931-1771	
TF: 888-882-3178 ■ Web: www.miva.com/us					
America Online Inc (AOL) 22000 AOL Way	Dulles	VA	20166	703-265-1000	265-5769
TF Orders: 888-265-8002 ■ Web: www.aol.com					
Ancestry.com 360 W 4800 N	Provo	UT	84606	801-705-7000	705-7001
TF Cust Svc: 800-262-3787 ■ Web: www.ancestry.com					
Artcyclopedia 51 Tuscany Hills Terr NW	Calgary	AB	T3L2G7	403-547-9692	547-1506
Web: www.artcyclopedia.com					
ARTISTdirect Inc 10900 Wilshire Blvd Suite 1400	Los Angeles	CA	90024	323-634-4000	634-4299
Web: www.artistdirect.com					
Ask.com 555 12th St Suite 500	Oakland	CA	94607	510-985-7400	985-7410
Web: www.ask.com					
Bankrate Inc 11760 US Hwy 1 Suite 200	North Palm Beach	FL	33408	561-630-2400	625-4540
NYSE: RATE ■ TF: 800-243-7720 ■ Web: www.bankrate.com					
Bio.com 1900 Powell St Suite 230	Emeryville	CA	94608	510-601-7194	601-1862
Web: www.bio.com					
BioSpace Inc 564 Market St	San Francisco	CA	94104	732-528-3688	659-0111*
*Fax Area Code: 239 ■ TF: 888-246-7722 ■ Web: www.biospace.com					
Buyer's Index Wired Markets Inc 1045 Via Mil Cumbres	Solana Beach	CA	92075	858-793-0085	793-0629
Web: www.buyersindex.com					
CEOExpress Co 1 Broadway 14th Fl	Cambridge	MA	02142	617-482-1200	225-4440
Web: www.ceoexpress.com					
CityGrid Media 8833 W Sunset Blvd	West Hollywood	CA	90069	877-312-9686	
TF: 800-611-4827 ■ Web: www.citysearch.com					
CNET Search.com CNET Networks Inc 235 Second St	San Francisco	CA	94105	415-344-2000	344-1219
Web: www.cnet.com					
Congress.Org 77 K St NE	Washington	DC	20002	202-650-6878	
Web: www.congress.org					
Dine.com 445 Sherman Ave Suite C	Palo Alto	CA	94306	650-847-3100	324-9379
Web: www.dine.com					
Dogpile 601 108th Ave NE Suite 1200	Bellevue	WA	98004	425-201-6100	201-6150
Web: www.dogpile.com					
Domainsearch.com 9525 Kenwood Rd Suite 328	Cincinnati	OH	45242	513-351-4222	351-8222
TF Cust Svc: 866-927-3624 ■ Web: www.domainsearch.com					
EarthCam Inc 84 Kennedy St	Hackensack	NJ	07601	201-488-1111	488-1119
Web: www.earthcam.com					
Encyclopedia.com 360 N Michigan Ave Suite 1320	Chicago	IL	60601	312-782-3900	782-3901
Web: www.encyclopedia.com					
Essential Links Essentix Inc 13807 SE McLoughlin Suite 626	Portland	OR	97222	503-659-0707	659-0700
TF: 800-401-6970 ■ Web: www.el.com					
Excite 1 Bridge St Suite 42	Irvington	NY	10053	914-591-2000	591-0205
Web: www.excite.com					
Fact Monster Pearson Education 501 Boylston St Suite 900	Boston	MA	02116	800-498-3264	
TF: 800-498-3264 ■ Web: www.factmonster.com					
Federal Resources for Educational Excellence (FREE) 400 Maryland Ave SW Rm 7W114	Washington	DC	20202	202-401-3000	401-0596
TF: 800-872-5327 ■ Web: www.ed.gov/free					
FindLaw 610 Opperman Dr	Eagan	MN	55123	651-687-6393	392-6206*
*Fax Area Code: 800 ■ Web: www.findlaw.com					
Fine Arts Museums of San Francisco 50 Hagiwara Tea Garden Dr	San Francisco	CA	94118	415-750-3600	
Web: deyoung.famsf.org					
Genealogy.com 360 W 4800 N	Provo	UT	84606	801-705-7000	705-7001
TF: 800-262-3787 ■ Web: www.genealogy.com					
Google Inc 1600 Amphitheatre Pkwy	Mountain View	CA	94043	650-253-0000	253-0001
NASDAQ: GOOG ■ Web: www.google.com					
GourmetSpot StartSport Mediaworks Inc 1840 Oak Ave	Evanston	IL	60201	847-866-1830	866-1880
Web: www.gourmetspot.com					
GovSpot StartSpot Mediaworks Inc 1840 Oak Ave	Evanston	IL	60201	847-866-1830	866-1880
Web: www.govspot.com					
Great Web Sites for Kids American Library Assn 50 E Huron St	Chicago	IL	60611	312-944-6780	
TF: 800-545-2433 ■ Web: www.ala.org/parentspage/greatsites					
HighBeam Research Inc 65 E Wacker Pl Suite 400	Chicago	IL	60601	312-782-3900	782-3901
Web: www.highbeam.com					
Hollywood Media Corp 2255 Glades Rd Suite 221A	Boca Raton	FL	33431	561-998-8000	998-2974
NASDAQ: HOLL ■ TF: 888-861-8898 ■ Web: www.hollywoodmedia.com					
HotBot 100 5th Ave	Waltham	MA	02451	781-370-2700	370-2600
Web: www.hotbot.com					
Hotelrooms.com Inc 108-18 Queens Blvd	Forest Hills	NY	11375	718-730-6000	261-4598
TF: 800-486-7000 ■ Web: www.hotelrooms.com					
HowStuffWorks Inc 3350 Peachtree Rd NE # 1500	Atlanta	GA	30326	404-760-4729	
Web: www.howstuffworks.com					
ImproveNet Inc 14023 Denver W Pkwy Suite 200	Golden	CO	80401	303-963-7200	980-3003
TF: 800-474-1596 ■ Web: www.improvenet.com					
Information Outpost LLC 42 Holmes St	Mystic	CT	06355	860-536-0028	
Web: www.informationoutpost.com					
Information Please Pearson Education 501 Boylston St Suite 900	Boston	MA	02116	800-498-3264	
TF: 800-498-3264 ■ Web: www.infoplease.com					
InfoSpace Inc 601 108th Ave NE Suite 1200	Bellevue	WA	98004	425-201-6100	201-6150
NASDAQ: INSP ■ Web: www.infospaceinc.com					
Internet Archive 300 Funston Ave	San Francisco	CA	94118	415-561-6767	840-0391
Web: www.archive.org					
Internet Public Library University of Michigan School of Information 304 W Hall	Ann Arbor	MI	48109	734-763-2285	764-2475
Web: www.ipl.org					
Jayde.com iEntry Inc 2549 Richmond Rd 2nd Fl	Lexington	KY	40509	859-514-2720	219-9065
Web: www.jayde.com					
Law Engine c/o Goldberger & Assoc 920 Kline St Suite 304	La Jolla	CA	92037	858-456-1234	454-3375
Web: www.thelawengine.com					
Law.com Inc 10 United Nations Plaza 3rd Fl	San Francisco	CA	94102	800-903-9872	558-9380*
*Fax Area Code: 415 ■ TF: 800-903-9872 ■ Web: www.law.com					
Library of Congress The 101 Independence Ave SE	Washington	DC	20540	202-707-5000	707-5844
Web: www.loc.gov					
LookSmart Ltd 55 Second St Suite 700	San Francisco	CA	94105	415-348-7000	348-7050
NASDAQ: LOOK ■ TF: 877-512-5665 ■ Web: www.looksmart.com					
Lycos Inc 100 5th Ave	Waltham	MA	02451	781-370-2700	370-2600
Web: www.lycos.com					
MagPortal.com 275 Bryn Mawr Ave Suite M14	Bryn Mawr	PA	19010	610-581-7702	
Web: www.magportal.com					
MetaCrawler 601 108th Ave NE Suite 1200	Bellevue	WA	98004	425-201-6100	201-6150
TF: 866-438-4677 ■ Web: www.metacrawler.com					
MindEdge Inc 1601 Trapelo Rd Suite 170	Waltham	MA	02451	781-250-1805	250-1810
TF: 877-592-8000 ■ Web: www.mindedge.com					

	City	State	ZIP	Phone	Fax
MP3.com Inc 235 2nd St.	San Francisco	CA	94105	415-344-2000	395-9207
Web: www.mp3.com					
MyFamily.com Inc 360 W 4800 North	Provo	UT	84604	801-705-7000	705-7001
TF: 800-262-3787 ■ *Web:* www.myfamily.com					
Nerd World Media					
8 New England Executive Pk.	Burlington	MA	01803	781-272-6599	852-5375
Web: www.headlines.nerdworld.com					
NewsHub 96 Mowat Ave	Toronto	ON	M6K3M1	416-535-0123	531-5584
TF: 800-371-6992 ■ *Web:* www.newshub.com					
Nursing Ctr 323 Norristown Rd Suite 200	Ambler	PA	19002	215-646-8700	654-2585
TF: 800-346-7844 ■ *Web:* www.nursingcenter.com					
Pulp & Paper Network LLC 225 N Franklin Tpke	Ramsey	NJ	07446	201-818-8632	818-8720
Web: www.pulpandpaper.net					
Quickbrowse.com Inc 935 4th St	Miami Beach	FL	33139	305-604-9500	468-6282
Quoteland.com Inc PO Box 600250.	Newtonville	MA	02460	617-283-9296	235-0084*
**Fax Area Code:* 781 ■ *Web:* www.quoteland.com					
Rhapsody.com 500 3rd St.	San Francisco	CA	94107	415-934-2000	934-6720
TF: 866-311-0228 ■ *Web:* www.rhapsody.com					
RootsWeb.com 360 W 4800 N	Provo	UT	84606	801-705-7000	705-7001
TF: 800-262-3787 ■ *Web:* www.rootsweb.com					
ServiceMagic Inc 14023 Denver W Pkwy Suite 200.	Golden	CO	80401	303-963-7200	980-3003
TF: 800-474-1596 ■ *Web:* www.servicemagic.com					
ShoppingSpot 1840 Oak Ave	Evanston	IL	60201	847-866-1830	866-1880
Web: www.shoppingspot.com					
StartSpot Mediaworks Inc					
820 Davis St Suite 403	Evanston	IL	60201	847-475-0354	866-1880
Web: www.startspot.com					
Tours.com Inc 490 Post St Suite 1701	San Francisco	CA	94102	415-332-7916	332-7980
Web: www.tours.com					
Tucows Inc 96 Mowat Ave	Toronto	ON	M6K3M1	416-535-0123	531-5584
TF: 800-371-6992 ■ *Web:* www.tucowsinc.com					
US/Canadian Parks					
About.com Inc 1440 Broadway 20th Fl	New York	NY	10018	212-204-4000	
Web: www.usparks.about.com					
USGS Education					
United States Geological Survey					
12201 Sunrise Valley Dr MS 801	Reston	VA	20192	703-648-4000	648-4454
Web: education.usgs.gov					
WebCrawler 601 108th Ave NE Suite 1200	Bellevue	WA	98004	425-201-6100	201-6150
Web: www.webcrawler.com					
Wired News 660 3rd St	San Francisco	CA	94107	415-276-8400	276-8500
Yahoo! Inc 701 1st Ave	Sunnyvale	CA	94089	408-349-3300	349-3301
NASDAQ: YHOO ■ *Web:* www.pressroom.yahoo.net					
Yahoo! Search Marketing					
74 N Pasadena Ave 3rd Fl.	Pasadena	CA	91103	626-685-5600	685-5601
TF: 888-811-4686					
Yahooligans! 701 1st Ave	Sunnyvale	CA	94089	408-349-3300	349-3301
Web: www.kids.yahoo.com					
YELLOWPAGES.com LLC 208 S Akard Suite 1825	Dallas	TX	75202	866-329-7118	
TF: 866-329-7118 ■ *Web:* www.yellowpages.com					

401 INTERNET SERVICE PROVIDERS (ISPS)

	City	State	ZIP	Phone	Fax
711.NET Inc 2063 N Lecanto Hwy	Lecanto	FL	34461	866-558-6778	
TF: 866-558-6778					
ABT Internet Inc					
525 Northern Blvd Suite 302	Great Neck	NY	11021	516-829-5484	829-2955
TF: 800-367-3414 ■ *Web:* www.abt.net					
Access US 712 N 2nd St Suite 300	Saint Louis	MO	63102	314-655-7700	655-7701
TF: 800-638-6373 ■ *Web:* www.accessus.net					
America Online Inc (AOL) 22000 AOL Way	Dulles	VA	20166	703-265-1000	265-5769
TF Orders: 888-265-8002 ■ *Web:* www.aol.com					
Aplus.net Internet Services					
10350 Barnes Canyon Rd.	San Diego	CA	92121	858-410-6929	
TF: 877-275-8763 ■ *Web:* www.aplus.net					
AT & T Inc 175 E Houston St	San Antonio	TX	78205	210-821-4105	351-2274*
NYSE: T ■ **Fax:* Hum Res ■ *TF:* 888-875-6388 ■ *Web:* www.att.com					
Aurora Cable Internet 350 Industrial Pkwy S	Aurora	ON	L4G3H3	905-727-1981	
Cable One Inc 1314 N 3rd St 3rd Fl.	Phoenix	AZ	85004	602-364-6000	364-6010
Web: www.cableone.net					
Cayuse Networks Inc 3019 117th Ave Ct E	Edgewood	WA	98372	888-245-9691	
TF: 888-245-9691 ■ *Web:* www.outlandhosting.com					
ChristianLiving.net					
1302 Clear Springs Trace	Louisville	KY	40223	888-772-7355	515-3710*
**Fax Area Code:* 502 ■ *TF Tech Supp:* 877-486-2660 ■ *Web:* www.christianliving.net					
Cincinnati Bell Inc 221 E 4th St.	Cincinnati	OH	45202	513-397-9900	241-1264
NYSE: CBB ■ *TF:* 800-422-1199 ■ *Web:* www.cincinnatibell.com					
ClearSail Communications LLC 3950 Braxton Dr	Houston	TX	77063	713-230-2800	378-7550
TF: 888-905-0888 ■ *Web:* www.clearsail.net					
Covad Communications Group Inc					
110 Rio Robles	San Jose	CA	95134	408-952-6400	952-7687
TF Tech Supp: 888-642-6823 ■ *Web:* www.covad.com					
Direct Internet Access					
141 Desiard St PO Box 7263	Monroe	LA	71201	800-296-2249	835-2121*
**Fax Area Code:* 888 ■ *TF:* 800-296-2249 ■ *Web:* www.directinternet.net					
DSLextreme.com 20847 Sherman Way.	Winnetka	CA	91306	818-902-4821	206-0326
TF: 800-774-3379 ■ *Web:* www.dslextreme.com					
EarthLink Inc 1375 Peachtree St NE	Atlanta	GA	30309	404-815-0770	888-9210*
NASDAQ: ELNK ■ **Fax:* Sales ■ *TF:* 800-332-4892 ■ *Web:* www.earthlink.net					
Expedient 1810 Parish St.	Pittsburgh	PA	15220	412-316-7800	316-7899
TF: 800-969-0099 ■ *Web:* www.expedient.com					
Friendfinder networks inc					
6800 Broken Sound Pkwy Suite 200.	Boca Raton	FL	33487	561-912-7000	912-7038
Web: www.ffn.com					
Frontline Communications PO Box 98	Orangeburg	NY	10962	888-376-6854	680-6541*
**Fax Area Code:* 845 ■ **Fax:* Sales ■ *TF:* 888-376-6854 ■ *Web:* www.frontline.net					
HughesNet 11717 Exploration Ln.	Germantown	MD	20876	301-428-5500	428-1868
TF: 800-347-3292 ■ *Web:* www.hughesnet.com					
Internet America Inc					
350 N St Paul St 1 Dallas Ctr Suite 3000	Dallas	TX	75201	214-861-2662	861-2663
TF: 800-232-4335 ■ *Web:* www.internetamerica.com					
Ionix Internet 266 Sutter St.	San Francisco	CA	94108	415-288-9940	288-9942
TF: 888-884-6649 ■ *Web:* www.ionix.net					
iSelect Internet Inc 1011 E Pine Suite 3	Lodi	CA	95240	209-334-0496	837-1427*
**Fax Area Code:* 877 ■ *TF:* 888-677-8679 ■ *Web:* www.iselect.net					
J2 Interactive LLC 2 13th St.	Charlestown	MA	02129	617-241-7266	241-8636
Web: www.j2-interactive.com					
MichTel Communications LLC 10 W Huron St.	Pontiac	MI	48343	248-771-5000	776-1383
TF: 888-244-6381 ■ *Web:* www.michtel.com					
Millenicom Inc					
1500 NW Bethany Blvd Suite 200.	Beaverton	OR	97006	800-996-1285	
TF: 888-925-4221 ■ *Web:* www.millenicom.com					
Net Access Corp 9 Wing Dr	Cedar Knolls	NJ	07927	973-590-5000	590-5080
TF: 800-638-6336 ■ *Web:* www.nac.net					
NetZero Inc 21301 Burbank Blvd	Woodland Hills	CA	91367	818-287-3000	287-3001
TF: 888-340-0029 ■ *Web:* www.netzero.net					
NeuStar Inc 21575 Ridgetop Cir	Sterling	VA	20166	571-434-5400	434-5459
NYSE: NSR ■ *TF:* 855-638-2677 ■ *Web:* www.neustar.biz					
New Edge Networks					
3000 Columbia House Blvd Suite 106	Vancouver	WA	98661	360-693-9009	
TF: 877-725-3343 ■ *Web:* www.newedgenetworks.com					
Newsguy Inc 824 Roosevelt Trail Suite 272	Windham	ME	04062	866-487-3638	720-7630*
**Fax Area Code:* 408 ■ *TF:* 866-487-3638 ■ *Web:* www.newsguy.com					
Nova Internet Services Inc					
12225 Greenville Ave Suite 230	Dallas	TX	75243	214-904-9600	357-1431
TF: 877-668-2663 ■ *Web:* www.novaone.net					
Novatrope Inc					
150 Professional Ctr Suite H	Rohnert Park	CA	94928	800-603-3022	
TF: 800-603-3022 ■ *Web:* www.connectto.net					
ProtoSource Network 2511 W Shaw Ave Suite 102.	Fresno	CA	93711	559-486-8638	490-8630
TF: 866-490-8600 ■ *Web:* www.psnw.com					
Road Runner Group					
13241 Woodland Pk Rd 60 columbus Cir.	Newyork	NY	10023	703-345-2400	961-1157*
NYSE: TWC ■ **Fax Area Code:* 716 ■ *TF:* 800-950-2266 ■ *Web:* www.timewarnercable.com					
ServUsa Internet 305 S Main St.	Laurinburg	NC	28352	910-276-1633	
Speakeasy Inc 1201 Western St	Seattle	WA	98121	206-728-9770	728-1500
TF: 800-556-5829 ■ *Web:* www.speakeasy.net					
TOAST.net 4841 Monroe St Suite 307	Toledo	OH	43623	419-292-2200	474-1762
TF: 888-862-7863 ■ *Web:* www.toast.net					
True Vine Online 50 Damsite Rd.	Center Barnstead	NH	03225	877-878-3846	
TF: 877-878-3846 ■ *Web:* www.truevine.net					
United Online Inc 21301 Burbank Blvd.	Woodland Hills	CA	91367	818-287-3000	287-3001
NASDAQ: UNTD ■ *Web:* www.unitedonline.net					
Verio Inc 8005 S Chester St Suite 200.	Centennial	CO	80112	561-912-2555	
TF Sales: 800-438-8374 ■ *Web:* www.verio.com					
Verizon Business 1 Verizon Way.	Basking Ridge	NJ	07920	800-339-9911	
TF Cust Svc: 866-232-4282 ■ *Web:* www.verizonbusiness.com					
VIA NET.WORKS Inc 3575 Piedmont Rd Suite 710	Atlanta	GA	30305	404-926-3611	926-3612
TF: 800-749-1706 ■ *Web:* www.vianetworks.com					
WorldGate Communications Inc					
3800 Horizon Blvd Suite 103	Trevose	PA	19053	215-354-5100	354-1040
PINK: WGAT ■ *Web:* www.ojoservices.com					
ZDial Inc 119 High St PO Box 626	West Chester	PA	19380	610-692-9205	356-2250*
**Fax Area Code:* 302 ■ *TF:* 888-737-1001 ■ *Web:* www.zdial.com					

402 INVENTORY SERVICES

	City	State	ZIP	Phone	Fax
Douglas-Guardian Services Corp					
14800 St Mary's Ln.	Houston	TX	77079	281-531-0500	531-1777
TF: 800-255-0552 ■ *Web:* www.douglasguardian.com					
MSI Inventory Service Corp PO Box 230129	Flowood	MS	39232	601-939-0130	939-0061
TF: 800-820-1460 ■ *Web:* www.msi-inv.com					
Mst Steel Corp 24417 Groesbeck Hwy	Warren	MI	48089	586-773-5460	773-5486
Web: www.mststeel.com					
WIS International 3770 Nashua Dr Suite 5.	Mississauga	ON	L4V1M6	905-677-1947	677-1945
TF: 800-268-6848 ■ *Web:* www.wis.ca					

403 INVESTIGATIVE SERVICES

SEE ALSO Information Retrieval Services (General) p. 2110; Public Records Search Services p. 2459; Security & Protective Services p. 2650

	City	State	ZIP	Phone	Fax
Advanced Investigations Inc					
24 NW Racetrack Rd.	Fort Walton Beach	FL	32547	850-863-3997	864-1733
Alliance Investigations LLC					
240 S Montezuma St Suite 100	Prescott	AZ	86303	928-717-1196	717-1366
TF: 800-717-1196 ■ *Web:* www.arizona-pi.com					
American Professional Services Inc					
111 Harrison Ave	Oklahoma City	OK	73104	405-636-4222	632-7667
TF: 800-219-9120 ■ *Web:* www.americanpi.net					
ASK Services Inc 42180 Ford Rd Suite 101	Canton	MI	48187	734-983-9040	983-9041
TF: 888-416-1313 ■ *Web:* www.ask-services.com					
Bombet Cashio & Assoc					
11220 N Harrells Ferry Rd	Baton Rouge	LA	70816	225-275-0796	272-3631
TF: 800-256-5333 ■ *Web:* www.bombet.com					
Bontecou Investigative Services Inc					
235 E Broadway	Jackson	WY	83001	307-733-2637	733-5873
TF: 877-733-2639 ■ *Web:* www.wyominginvestigator.com					
Brabston Legal Investigations Inc					
3746 Halls Mills Rd	Mobile	AL	36693	251-666-5666	661-8807
Capitol Detective Agency 2922 N 18th Pl	Phoenix	AZ	85016	602-264-9771	264-9814
TF: 800-346-0347 ■ *Web:* www.capitoldetective.com					
Cleveland Process Support					
40 Front St PO Box 5358	Central Point	OR	97502	541-665-5162	665-5182

	City	State	Zip	Phone	Fax
Confidential Services PO Box 91034	Columbus	OH	43209	614-252-4646	252-4669
TF: 800-752-4581					
DataTrace Investigations Inc PO Box 95322	South Jordan	UT	84095	801-253-2400	253-2478
TF: 800-748-5335 ■ *Web:* www.datatraceonline.com					
DCS Information Systems Inc 500 N Central Expy Suite 280	Plano	TX	75074	972-422-3600	422-3621
TF: 800-299-3647 ■ *Web:* www.dcsinfosys.com					
Donan Engineering Co Inc 11321 Plantside Dr	Louisville	KY	40299	502-267-6936	267-6973
TF: 800-482-5611 ■ *Web:* www.donan.com					
Douglas Baldwin & Assoc PO Box 1249	La Canada	CA	91012	818-952-4433	790-4622
TF: 800-392-3950 ■ *Web:* www.baldwinpi.com					
EX-CEL Investigations PO Box 22124	Saint Petersburg	FL	33742	727-527-5440	527-2442
Web: www.ex-celpi.com					
Gietzen & Assoc Inc 1302 N Marion St	Tampa	FL	33602	813-223-3233	223-9717
TF: 888-779-2345 ■ *Web:* www.gietzen.com					
Gold Coast Agency Inc PO Box 51465	Sparks	NV	89435	775-324-1161	324-1163
Graymark Security Group 7301 NW 4th St Suite 110	Fort Lauderdale	FL	33317	954-581-5575	581-5750
TF: 800-881-3242 ■ *Web:* www.graymarksecurity.com					
Gregg Investigations Inc 222 S Hamilton # 17	Madison	WI	53703	608-256-1074	755-5853
TF: 800-866-1976 ■ *Web:* www.gregginvestigations.com					
Hrodey & Assoc 114 W Calhoun St	Woodstock	IL	60098	815-337-4636	337-4638
Web: www.hrodey.com					
ID Investigators & Adjustors Inc 31225 La Baya Dr Suite 111	Westlake Village	CA	91362	818-991-1122	991-3703
Web: www.idinvestigations.com					
International Investigators Inc 3216 N Pennsylvania St	Indianapolis	IN	46205	317-925-1496	926-1177
TF: 800-403-8111 ■ *Web:* www.iiiweb.net					
Internet Crimes Group Inc PO Box 3599	Princeton	NJ	08543	609-806-5000	806-5001
Web: www.icginc.com					
Intra-Lex Investigations Inc 505 6th St Suite 202	Sioux City	IA	51101	712-233-1639	255-1127
Investigative Services Inc 4381 S 153rd Cir	Omaha	NE	68137	402-894-5625	896-0621
Kessler International 45 Rockefeller Plaza Suite 2000	New York	NY	10111	212-286-9100	730-2433
TF: 800-932-2221 ■ *Web:* www.investigation.com					
MacIntire & Assoc Inc 3906 W Ina Rd Suite 316	Tucson	AZ	85741	520-622-2737	363-6143*
**Fax Area Code:* 866 ■ *TF:* 800-641-2737					
Michael Ramey & Assoc Inc PO Box 744	Danville	CA	94526	925-820-8900	820-8082
TF: 800-321-0505 ■ *Web:* www.rameypi.com					
North Winds Investigations Inc PO Box 1654	Rogers	AR	72757	479-925-1612	925-2819
TF: 800-530-4514					
Northwest Location Services Inc PO Box 948	Wauna	WA	98395	253-858-1984	238-0022
TF: 800-916-3724 ■ *Web:* www.nwlocation.com					
Owens & Assoc Investigations 2245 San Diego Ave Suite 225	San Diego	CA	92110	619-297-1343	297-7622
TF: 800-297-1343 ■ *Web:* www.owenspi.com					
PADIC Inc 1609 E Broadway	Gainesville	TX	76240	940-665-6130	665-7486
TF: 800-679-5727 ■ *Web:* www.padic.com					
Palmer Investigative Services 624 W Gurley St Suite A	Prescott	AZ	86305	928-778-2951	445-7204
TF: 800-280-2951 ■ *Web:* www.palmerinvestigative.com					
PI & Information Services LLC PO Box 157	Beaverton	OR	97075	503-643-4274	643-5474
Web: www.pi-info.com					
Research Assoc Inc 27999 Clemens Rd	Cleveland	OH	44145	440-892-9439	892-9439
TF: 800-255-9693 ■ *Web:* www.researchassociatesinc.com					
Rick Johnson & Assoc of Colorado 1649 Downing St	Denver	CO	80218	303-296-2200	296-3038
TF: 800-530-2300 ■ *Web:* www.denverpi.com					
Shawver & Assoc 6262 Weber Rd Suite 112	Corpus Christi	TX	78413	361-880-8968	880-8971
TF: 800-364-2333 ■ *Web:* www.stxpi.com					
Southern Research Co Inc 2850 Centenary Blvd	Shreveport	LA	71104	318-227-9700	424-1801
TF: 888-772-6952 ■ *Web:* www.southernresearchinc.com					
Specialized Investigations 14530 Delano St	Van Nuys	CA	91411	818-909-9607	782-3012
TF: 800-714-3728 ■ *Web:* www.specialpi.com					
State Information Bureau 842 E Pk Ave	Tallahassee	FL	32301	850-561-3990	561-3995
TF: 800-881-1742 ■ *Web:* www.sibflorida.com					
Stewart & Assoc Inc 50 W Douglas St Suite 1200	Freeport	IL	61032	815-235-3807	235-1290
TF: 800-442-3807 ■ *Web:* www.bwstewart.com					
Vericon Resources Inc 3550 Engineering Dr Suite 225	Noncross	GA	30092	770-457-9922	457-5006
TF: 800-795-3784 ■ *Web:* www.vericon.com					
VISTA Inc 29516 Southfield Rd Suite 104	Southfield	MI	48076	248-559-3500	559-4757
TF: 888-873-8478					
VTS Investigations LLC 7 S State St	Elgin	IL	60123	847-888-4464	888-8588
TF: 800-538-4464 ■ *Web:* www.pichicago.com					
Wood & Tait Inc 64-5249 Kauakea Rd	Kamuela	HI	96743	808-885-5090	630-0500*
**Fax Area Code:* 888 ■ *TF:* 800-774-8585 ■ *Web:* www.woodtait.com					

404 INVESTMENT ADVICE & MANAGEMENT

SEE ALSO Commodity Contracts Brokers & Dealers p. 1668; Investment Guides - Online p. 2133; Mutual Funds p. 2295; Securities Brokers & Dealers p. 2646

	City	State	Zip	Phone	Fax
300 North Capital LLC 300 N Lake Ave Suite 1120	Pasadena	CA	91101	626-449-8500	356-0533
Web: www.300northcapital.com					
Acadian Asset Management Inc 2 International Way	Boston	MA	02110	617-850-3500	850-3501
TF: 800-946-0166 ■ *Web:* www.acadian-asset.com					
Advent Capital Management LLC 1065 Avenue of the Americas 31st Fl	New York	NY	10018	212-482-1600	480-9655
TF: 888-523-8368 ■ *Web:* www.adventcap.com					
AEW Capital Management LP 225 Franklin St # 2600	Boston	MA	02110	617-261-9000	261-9555
Web: www.aew.com					
AGF Management Ltd 66 Wellington St W 31st Fl	Toronto	ON	M5K1E9	905-214-8203	214-8243
TF: 800-268-8583 ■ *Web:* www.agf.com					
AllianceBernstein Holding LP (AB) 1345 Avenue of the Americas	New York	NY	10105	212-486-5800	969-2229*
**Fax:* Hum Res ■ *TF Cust Svc:* 800-221-5672 ■ *Web:* www.alliancecapital.com					
Allianz Global Investors of America LP 680 Newport Ctr Dr Suite 250	Newport Beach	CA	92660	949-219-2200	
Web: www.allianzinvestors.com					
Allianz of America Inc 55 Green Farms Rd PO Box 5160	Westport	CT	06881	203-221-8500	341-5722
Web: www.azoa.com					
American Century Investments Inc 4500 Main St PO Box 419200	Kansas City	MO	64111	816-531-5575	340-7962*
**Fax:* Cust Svc ■ *TF:* 800-345-2021 ■ *Web:* www.americancentury.com					
Amerindo Investment Advisors Inc 1 Embarcadero Ctr Suite 2310	San Francisco	CA	94111	415-362-0292	362-0533
TF: 888-832-4386					
Ameriprise Financial Inc 55 Ameriprise Financial Ctr	Minneapolis	MN	55474	612-671-3131	671-8880
NYSE: AMP ■ *TF:* 800-328-8300 ■ *Web:* www.ameriprise.com					
Ameriprise Financial Services Inc 70100 Ameriprise Financial Ctr	Minneapolis	MN	55474	612-671-3131	671-8880
TF: 800-862-7919 ■ *Web:* www.ameriprise.com					
Amivest Capital Management 703 Market St 18th Fl	San Francisco	CA	94103	415-541-7744	541-9760
TF: 800-541-7774 ■ *Web:* www.wrapmanager.com					
AMR Investment Services Inc PO Box 619003 MD 2450	DFW Airport	TX	75261	817-967-3509	967-0768
TF: 800-967-9009 ■ *Web:* www.aafunds.com					
AmSouth Investment Services Inc (AIS) 250 Riverchase Pkwy E 5th Fl	Hoover	AL	35244	866-512-3479	560-7923*
**Fax Area Code:* 205 ■ *TF:* 800-316-4009 ■ *Web:* www.regions.com					
Analytic Investors LLC 555 W Fifth St 50th Fl	Los Angeles	CA	90013	213-688-3015	688-8856
TF: 800-618-1872 ■ *Web:* www.aninvestor.com					
Appleton Partners Inc 45 Milk St FL 8	Boston	MA	02109	617-338-0700	338-2379
TF: 800-338-0745 ■ *Web:* www.appletonpartners.com					
Ascend One Corp 8930 Stanford Blvd	Columbia	MD	21045	410-910-1735	910-2739
TF: 800-227-3123 ■ *Web:* www.ascendone.com					
Atalanta/Sosnoff Capital LLC 101 Pk Ave 6th Fl	New York	NY	10178	212-867-5000	922-1820
Web: www.atalantasosnoff.com					
Atlanta Capital Management Co LLC 1075 Peachtree St NW Suite 2100	Atlanta	GA	30309	404-876-9411	872-1672
Web: www.atlcap.com					
Atlantic Trust 100 E Pratt St Suite 2550	Baltimore	MD	21202	410-539-4660	539-4661
TF: 888-880-1621 ■ *Web:* www.atlantictrust.com					
AXA Rosenberg Investment Management LLC 4 Orinda Way Bldg E	Orinda	CA	94563	925-254-6464	253-0141
Web: www.axarosenberg.com					
Ayco Co LP 1 Wall St	Albany	NY	12205	518-464-2000	464-2122
Web: www.ayco.com					
Babson Capital Management Co 470 Atlantic Ave	Boston	MA	02210	617-225-3800	225-3801
TF: 877-766-0014 ■ *Web:* www.babsoncapital.com					
Bahl & Gaynor Inc 212 E 3rd St Suite 200	Cincinnati	OH	45202	513-287-6100	287-6110
TF: 800-341-1810 ■ *Web:* www.bahl-gaynor.com					
Bailard Biehl & Kaiser Group 950 Tower Ln Suite 1900	Foster City	CA	94404	650-571-5800	573-7128
TF: 800-882-8383 ■ *Web:* www.bailard.com					
Bank of America Charitable Foundation 100 N Tryon St	Charlotte	NC	28255	800-218-9946	622-3469*
**Fax Area Code:* 415 ■ *TF:* 888-488-9802 ■ *Web:* www.bankofamerica.com/foundation					
Baring Asset Management Co Inc 470 Atlantic Ave Independence Wharf	Boston	MA	02110	617-946-5200	946-5400
TF: 800-533-7432 ■ *Web:* www.barings.com					
Barrow Hanley Mewhinney & Strauss LLC 2200 Ross Ave 31st Fl	Dallas	TX	75201	214-665-1900	665-1933*
**Fax:* Mktg ■ *Web:* www.barrowhanley.com					
Bartlett & Co 600 Vine St # 2100	Cincinnati	OH	45202	513-621-4612	621-6462
TF: 800-800-4612 ■ *Web:* www.bartlett1898.com					
Batterymarch Financial Management Inc 200 Clarendon St	Boston	MA	02116	617-266-8300	266-0633
Web: www.batterymarch.com					
Bessemer Trust Co 630 5th Ave 6th Fl	New York	NY	10111	212-708-9100	265-5826
Web: www.bessemer.com					
BlackRock Inc 40 E 52nd St 25th Fl	New York	NY	10055	212-754-5560	
NYSE: BLK ■ *Web:* www2.blackrock.com					
Boston Advisors Inc One Liberty Sq 10th Fl	Boston	MA	02109	617-348-3100	348-0081
TF: 800-523-5903 ■ *Web:* www.bostonadvisors.com					
Boston Financial Data Services 2000 Crown Colony Dr	Quincy	MA	02169	617-483-5000	483-2209
TF: 888-772-2337 ■ *Web:* www.bostonfinancial.com					
Brandes Investment Partners LP 11988 El Camino Real Suite 500	San Diego	CA	92130	858-755-0239	755-0916
TF: 800-237-7119 ■ *Web:* www.brandes.com					
Brandywine Global Investment Management LLC 2929 Arch St 8th Fl	Philadelphia	PA	19104	215-609-3500	609-3501
TF: 800-348-2499 ■ *Web:* www.brandywineglobal.com					
Bridgewater Assoc Inc 1 Glendinning Pl	Westport	CT	06880	203-226-3030	291-7300
Web: www.bridgewaterassociates.com					
Brown Bros Harriman & Co 140 Broadway	New York	NY	10005	212-483-1818	493-7287*
**Fax:* Hum Res ■ *Web:* www.bbh.com					
Brown Capital Management Inc 1201 N Calvert St	Baltimore	MD	21202	410-837-3234	837-6525
TF: 800-809-3863 ■ *Web:* www.browncapital.com					

				Phone	Fax
Broyhill Asset Management LLC					
800 Golfview Pk PO Box 500	Lenoir	NC	28645	828-758-6100	758-8919
TF: 888-818-4455 ■ *Web:* www.broyhillasset.com					
Cadence Capital Management					
265 Franklin St 11th Fl	Boston	MA	02110	617-624-3500	624-3591
TF: 800-298-2194 ■ *Web:* www.cadencecapital.com					
Calamos Asset Management Inc					
2020 Calamos Ct	Naperville	IL	60563	630-245-7200	245-6335
NASDAQ: CLMS ■ *TF:* 800-582-6959 ■ *Web:* www.calamos.com					
Callan Assoc Inc					
101 California St Suite 3500	San Francisco	CA	94111	415-974-5060	291-4014
TF: 800-227-3288 ■ *Web:* www.callan.com					
Cambiar Investors Inc 2401 E 2nd Ave Suite 500	Denver	CO	80206	303-302-9000	302-9050
TF: 888-673-9950 ■ *Web:* www.cambiar.com					
Capital Group Cos Inc 333 S Hope St	Los Angeles	CA	90071	213-486-9200	486-9217
TF: 800-421-8511 ■ *Web:* www.capgroup.com					
Capital Growth Management LP					
1 International Pl 45th Fl	Boston	MA	02110	617-737-3225	261-0572
TF: 800-334-6440 ■ *Web:* www.cgmfunds.com					
Capital Research & Management Co (CRMC)					
333 S Hope St	Los Angeles	CA	90071	213-486-9200	486-9217
Web: www.capgroup.com/about_us/our_history.html					
Cargill Asset Investment & Finance Group					
12700 Whitewater Dr	Minnetonka	MN	55343	952-984-3444	984-3900
TF: 800-227-4455 ■ *Web:* www.cargill.com					
Churchill Corporate Services 56 Utter Ave	Hawthorne	NJ	07506	973-636-9400	636-0179
TF: 800-941-7458 ■ *Web:* www.furnishedhousing.com					
CI Fund Management Inc 151 Yonge St 11th Fl	Toronto	ON	M5C2W7	416-364-1145	364-6299
TSX: CIX ■ *TF:* 800-268-9374 ■ *Web:* www.ci.com					
Cincinnati Asset Management Inc					
4350 Glndl Milford Rd 1	Cincinnati	OH	45242	513-554-8500	
Web: www.cambonds.com					
Citigroup Asset Management 153 E 53rd St	New York	NY	10022	212-559-9124	793-5906
Clark Capital Management Group Inc (CCMG)					
1650 Market St 1 Liberty Pl 53rd Fl	Philadelphia	PA	19103	215-569-2224	569-3639
TF: 800-766-2264 ■ *Web:* www.ccmg.com					
Cohen & Steers Inc 280 Pk Ave 10th Fl	New York	NY	10017	212-832-3232	832-3498*
NYSE: CNS ■ **Fax:* Mktg ■ *TF:* 800-330-7348 ■ *Web:* www.cohenandsteers.com					
Colony Capital Management					
3340 Peachtree Rd NW Suite 1755	Atlanta	GA	30326	404-365-5050	365-5070
TF: 877-365-5050 ■ *Web:* www.colonycapital.com					
Columbia Funds Distributor Inc 1 Fincial Ctr	Boston	MA	02111	617-426-3750	
TF: 800-225-2365					
Columbia Management Assoc Inc 1 Financial Ctr	Boston	MA	02111	617-426-3750	330-9701
TF: 800-225-2365 ■ *Web:* www.columbiamanagement.com					
Columbia Management Group 1 Financial Ctr	Boston	MA	02111	617-426-3750	261-7350
TF: 800-225-2365 ■ *Web:* www.columbiamanagement.com					
Columbus Circle Investors Inc (CCI)					
1 Stn Pl Metro Ctr 8th Fl	Stamford	CT	06902	203-353-6000	406-5479
TF: 888-826-5247 ■ *Web:* www.columbuscircle.com					
Commonwealth Financial Network 29 Sawyer Rd	Waltham	MA	02453	781-736-0700	316-8357*
**Fax Area Code:* 866 ■ *TF:* 800-237-0081 ■ *Web:* www.commonwealth.com					
Connell Technologies Co LLC					
350 Lindbergh Ave	Livermore	CA	94550	925-455-6790	455-6791
TF: 888-301-0300 ■ *Web:* www.connellco.com					
Conning Asset Management Co					
1 Financial Plaza	Hartford	CT	06103	860-299-2000	299-2479
Web: www.conning.com/asset					
Consulting Services Group LLC					
6075 Poplar Ave Suite 700	Memphis	TN	38119	901-761-8080	682-4090
Web: www.csgllc.com					
Cooke & Bieler LP					
1700 Market St Suite 3222	Philadelphia	PA	19103	215-567-1101	567-1681
Web: www.cooke-bieler.com					
Cramer Rosenthal Mcglynn LLC					
520 Madison Ave FL 32	New York	NY	10022	212-838-3830	644-8291
Web: www.crmllc.com					
Creative Financial Group (CFG)					
16 Campus Blvd	Newtown Square	PA	19073	610-325-6100	325-6240
Web: www.creativefinancialgroup.com					
Crown Financial Ministries					
601 Broad St SE	Gainesville	GA	30501	770-534-1000	244-7519*
**Fax Area Code:* 678 ■ *TF:* 800-722-1976 ■ *Web:* www.crown.org					
Dalton Greiner Hartman Maher & Co LLC					
565 5th Ave Suite 2101	New York	NY	10017	212-557-2445	557-4898
Web: www.dghm.com					
DDJ Capital Management LLC					
130 Turner St Bldg 3 Suite 600	Waltham	MA	02453	781-283-8500	283-8555
Web: www.ddjcap.com					
Dean Investment Assoc					
Kettering Tower Suite 2480	Dayton	OH	45423	937-222-0282	227-9304
TF: 800-327-3656 ■ *Web:* www.chdean.com					
Denver Investment Advisors LLC					
1225 17th St 26th Fl	Denver	CO	80202	303-312-5000	312-4900
Web: www.denveria.com					
Depository Trust Co 55 Water St 22nd Fl	New York	NY	10041	212-855-1000	855-8440
Web: www.dtcc.com					
Dimeo Schneider & Assoc LLC					
500 W Madision St # 3855	Chicago	IL	60661	312-853-1000	853-3352
Web: www.dimeoschneider.com					
Diversfield Investment Advisors Inc					
440 Mamaroneck Ave	Harrison	NY	10528	914-627-3000	697-3743
Web: www.divinvest.com					
Dodge & Cox 555 California St 40th Fl	San Francisco	CA	94104	415-981-1710	986-8126
TF: 800-621-3979 ■ *Web:* www.dodgeandcox.com					
Driehaus Capital Management Inc 25 E Erie St	Chicago	IL	60611	312-587-3800	587-3840
TF: 800-688-8819 ■ *Web:* www.driehaus.com					
Dwight Asset Management Co					
100 Bank St Suite 800	Burlington	VT	05401	802-383-4000	862-2513
Web: www.dwight.com					
Eagle Asset Management					
880 Carillon Pkwy	Saint Petersburg	FL	33716	727-573-2453	567-8020*
**Fax:* Mktg ■ *TF:* 800-237-3101 ■ *Web:* www.eagleasset.com					
Earnest Partners LLC					
1180 Peachtree St Suite 2300	Atlanta	GA	30309	404-815-8772	815-8948
TF: 800-322-0068 ■ *Web:* www.earnestpartners.com					
Eaton Vance Corp 2 International Pl	Boston	MA	02110	617-482-8260	482-2396*
NYSE: EV ■ **Fax:* Cust Svc ■ *TF:* 800-225-6265 ■ *Web:* www.eatonvance.com					
Edgar Lomax Co 6564 Loisdale Ct Suite 310	Springfield	VA	22150	703-719-0026	
TF: 866-205-0524 ■ *Web:* www.edgarlomax.com					
Epoch Investment Partners Inc					
640 5th Ave 18th Fl	New York	NY	10019	212-303-7200	202-4948
NASDAQ: EPHC ■ *Web:* www.eipny.com					
Essex Investment Management Co LLC					
125 High St 29th Fl	Boston	MA	02110	617-342-3200	342-3280
TF: 800-342-3202 ■ *Web:* www.essexinvest.com					
Estrada Hinojosa & Co Inc 1717 Main St LB47	Dallas	TX	75201	214-658-1670	658-1671
TF: 800-676-5352 ■ *Web:* www.estradahinojosa.com					
Fayez Sarofim & Co 2 Houston Ctr Suite 2907	Houston	TX	77010	713-654-4484	654-8184
TF: 800-288-7125 ■ *Web:* www.sarofim.com					
Fcm Investments 2200 Ross Ave Suite 4600w	Dallas	TX	75201	214-665-6900	665-6940
Web: www.fcminvest.com					
Federated Investors					
1001 Liberty Ave					
Federated Investors Tower	Pittsburgh	PA	15222	412-288-1900	288-6751*
NYSE: FII ■ **Fax:* Hum Res ■ *TF:* 800-245-0242 ■ *Web:* www.federatedinvestors.com					
Fidelity Investments Institutional Services Co Inc					
82 Devonshire St	Boston	MA	02109	617-563-7000	
TF: 800-343-3548 ■ *Web:* www.fidelity.com					
Fiduciary Capital Management Inc					
PO Box 80	Wallingford	CT	06492	203-269-0440	269-6440
Web: www.fcmstablevalue.com					
Fiduciary Management Assoc LLC					
55 W Monroe St Suite 2550	Chicago	IL	60603	312-930-6850	641-2511
Web: www.fmausa.com					
Fiduciary Management Inc of Milwaukee					
100 E Wisconsin Ave Suite 2200	Milwaukee	WI	53202	414-226-4545	226-4522
Web: www.fiduciarymgt.com					
First Allied Securities Inc					
311 S Wacker Dr Suite 6150	Chicago	IL	60606	312-377-5300	377-5314
TF: 800-474-0900 ■ *Web:* www.advancedequities.com					
First Pacific Advisors Inc					
11400 W Olympic Blvd Suite 1200	Los Angeles	CA	90064	310-473-0225	996-5450
TF: 800-982-4372 ■ *Web:* www.fpafunds.com					
Fischer Francis Trees & Watts Inc					
200 Pk Ave 11th Fl	New York	NY	10166	212-681-3000	681-3250
TF: 888-367-3389 ■ *Web:* www.fftw.com					
Fisher Investments 13100 Skyline Blvd	Woodside	CA	94062	650-851-3334	851-3514
TF: 800-851-8845 ■ *Web:* www.fi.com					
FMR Corp 82 Devonshire St	Boston	MA	02109	617-563-7000	
TF: 800-522-7297 ■ *Web:* www.fidelity.com					
Forest Investment Assoc					
15 Piedmont Ctr Suite 1250	Atlanta	GA	30305	404-261-9575	261-9574
Web: www.forestinvest.com					
Founders Asset Management LLC					
210 University Blvd Suite 800	Denver	CO	80206	303-394-4404	394-7870
TF: 800-525-2440 ■ *Web:* www.founders.com					
Franklin Resources Inc					
1 Franklin Pkwy Bdge 970 1st Fl	San Mateo	CA	94403	650-312-2000	312-3655*
NYSE: BEN ■ **Fax:* Hum Res ■ *TF:* 800-632-2301 ■ *Web:* www.franklintempleton.com					
Freedom Capital LLC 155 Federal St 16th Fl	Boston	MA	02110	617-722-4700	722-4714
Fundquest Inc 125 High St FL 13	Boston	MA	02110	617-526-7300	526-7377
Web: www.fundquest.com					
Gannett Welsh & Kotler LLC					
222 Berkeley St 15th Fl	Boston	MA	02116	617-236-8900	236-1815
TF: 800-225-4236 ■ *Web:* www.gwkinc.com					
Gartmore Morley Financial Services Inc					
1300 SW 5th Ave Suite 3300	Portland	OR	97201	503-484-9300	
Gemini Fund Services LLC 450 Wireless Blvd	Hauppauge	NY	11788	631-470-2600	951-0573
Web: www.geminifund.com					
Glenmede Trust Co					
1650 Market St Suite 1200	Philadelphia	PA	19103	215-419-6000	419-6199
TF: 800-966-3200 ■ *Web:* www.glenmede.com					
Goldman Sachs Asset Management (GSAM) 200 W St	New York	NY	10282	212-902-1000	
TF: 800-526-7384 ■ *Web:* www.goldmansachs.com					
Goode Investment Management Inc					
50 Public Sq Suite 1700	Cleveland	OH	44113	216-771-9000	771-1949
Web: www.goodeinvestment.com					
Grantham Mayo Van Otterloo & Co LLC (GMO)					
40 Rowes Wharf	Boston	MA	02110	617-330-7500	261-0134
Web: www.gmo.com					
Graybill Bartz & Thompson 568 S Spring Rd	Elmhurst	IL	60126	630-941-9460	832-3491
Web: www.graybillbartz.com					
Greenhill & Co Inc 300 Pk Ave 23rd Fl	New York	NY	10022	212-389-1500	389-1700
NYSE: GHL ■ *Web:* www.greenhill-co.com					
Guardian Investor Services LLC 7 Hanover Sq	New York	NY	10004	212-598-8000	919-2170
TF: 800-221-3253 ■ *Web:* www.guardianinvestor.com					
H A M Media Group 305 Madison St Suite 3016	New York	NY	10017	212-297-2575	297-2576
Web: www.hammedia.com					
Hamilton Advisors Inc 373 Stanwich Rd	Greenwich	CT	06830	203-629-1112	629-1469
Web: www.hamiltonadvisors.com					
Harris Assoc LP 2 N La Salle St Suite 500	Chicago	IL	60602	312-621-0600	621-0372
TF: 800-731-0700 ■ *Web:* www.harrisassoc.com					
HD Vest Financial Services					
6333 N State Hwy 161 4th Fl	Irving	TX	75038	972-870-6000	870-6128
TF: 800-821-8254 ■ *Web:* www.hdvest.com					
Heaton Adams & Co 333 W 4th St	Waterloo	IA	50701	319-232-1943	235-6664
Web: www.heatonadams.com					
Henderson Global Investors					
1 Financial Plaza FL 19	Hartford	CT	06103	860-723-8600	
TF: 888-832-6774 ■ *Web:* www.henderson.com					
Holland Capital Management LP					
1 N Wacker Dr Suite 700	Chicago	IL	60606	312-553-4830	553-4848
TF: 800-522-2711 ■ *Web:* www.hollandcap.com					
Houston Trust Co 1001 Fannin St Suite 700	Houston	TX	77002	713-651-9400	651-9402
Web: www.houstontrust.com					

Company / Address	City	State	Zip	Phone	Fax
Howland Capital Management Inc 75 Federal St Suite 1100 *Web:* www.howlandcapital.com	Boston	MA	02110	617-357-9110	357-5540
HSBC Asset Management Inc 452 5th Ave. *TF:* 800-975-4722 ■ *Web:* www.banking.us.hsbc.com	New York	NY	10018	212-525-5000	
Hughes Capital Management Inc 916 Prince St 3rd Fl	Alexandria	VA	22314	703-684-7222	684-7799
Hyperion Capital Management Inc 200 Vessey St 3 World Financial Ctr. *TF:* 800-497-3746 ■ *Web:* www.us.brookfieldim.com	New York	NY	10281	212-549-8400	549-8300
ICM Asset Management Inc 601 W Main Ave Suite 600 *TF:* 800-488-4075 ■ *Web:* www.icmasset.com	Spokane	WA	99201	509-455-3588	777-0999
IGM Financial Inc 447 Portage Ave 1 Canada Ctr *TF:* 888-746-6344 ■ *Web:* www.investorsgroup.com	Winnipeg	MB	R3C3B6	204-943-0361	956-7688
Integral Group LLC The 60 Piedmont Ave Ne. *Web:* www.integral-online.com	Atlanta	GA	30303	404-224-1860	224-1899
InvestAmerica Investment Advisors Inc 101 2nd St SE Suite 800 *Web:* www.investamericaventure.com	Cedar Rapids	IA	52401	319-363-8249	363-9683
Investment Counselors of Maryland LLC 803 Cathedral St. *Web:* www.icomd.com	Baltimore	MD	21201	410-539-3838	625-9016
Investor Growth Capital Inc 1 Rockefeller Plaza Suite 2801 *Web:* www.investorab.com	New York	NY	10020	212-515-9000	212-9009
IXIS Asset Management North America LP 399 Boylston St *TF:* 800-225-5478 ■ *Web:* www.ixis-amna.com	Boston	MA	02116	617-449-2100	247-1447
J & W Seligman & Co Inc 100 Pk Ave. *TF:* 800-221-7844 ■ *Web:* www.seligman.com	New York	NY	10017	212-850-1864	922-5742
James M Davidson & Co 20 N Waterloo Rd *Web:* www.davidsoncapmgt.com	Devon	PA	19333	610-687-6540	687-4855
Jones & Roth PC 432 W 11th Ave PO Box 10086 *Web:* www.jrcpa.com	Eugene	OR	97401	541-687-2320	485-0960
Jones Heward Investment Counsel Inc 77 King St W Suite 4200 *Web:* www.assetmanagement.bmo.com	Toronto	ON	M5K1J5	416-359-5000	359-5040
JPMorgan Fleming Asset Management PO Box 8528 **Fax Area Code:* 816 ■ *TF:* 800-348-4782 ■ *Web:* www.jpmorganfunds.com	Boston	MA	02266	800-480-4111	471-3053*
Karr Barth Assoc Inc 40 Monument Rd *Web:* www.karr-barthassociates.com	Bala Cynwyd	PA	19004	610-660-4459	
Killen Group Inc 1189 Lancaster Ave *TF:* 877-454-5536 ■ *Web:* www.thekillengroup.com	Berwyn	PA	19312	610-296-7222	296-3168
Kopp Investment Advisors Inc 7701 France Ave S Suite 500 *TF:* 800-333-9128 ■ *Web:* www.koppfunds.com	Edina	MN	55435	952-841-0400	841-0411
Laird Norton Tyee 801 2nd Ave Suite 1600 *TF:* 800-426-5105 ■ *Web:* www.lntyee.com	Seattle	WA	98104	206-464-5100	464-5267
Lazard Middle Market LLC 225 S 6th St 46 Fl. *Web:* www.agio.com	Minneapolis	MN	55402	612-339-0500	339-0507
Lcg Assoc Inc 400 Galleria Pkwy SE *Web:* www.lcgassociates.com	Atlanta	GA	30339	770-644-0100	644-0105
Leerink Swann & Co 1 Federal St 37th Fl. *TF:* 800-808-7525 ■ *Web:* www.leerink.com	Boston	MA	02110	617-248-1601	918-4900
Loomis Sayles & Co Inc LP 1 Financial Ctr. *TF:* 800-343-2029 ■ *Web:* www.loomissayles.com	Boston	MA	02111	617-482-2450	423-3065
Lord Abbett & Co 90 Hudson St **Fax Area Code:* 212 ■ *TF:* 888-522-2388 ■ *Web:* www.lordabbett.com	Jersey City	NJ	07302	201-827-2000	888-4405*
M & I Wealth Management 111 E Kilbourn Ave. *TF:* 800-342-2265 ■ *Web:* www.mibank.com	Milwaukee	WI	53202	414-287-8700	287-7025
Mackenzie Financial Corp 180 Queen St W. *TF:* 888-653-7070 ■ *Web:* www.mackenziefinancial.com	Toronto	ON	M5V3K1	416-922-5322	922-5660
Madison Investment Advisors Inc 550 Science Dr *TF:* 800-767-0300 ■ *Web:* www.madisonadv.com	Madison	WI	53711	608-274-0300	274-7905
Manning & Napier Advisors Inc 290 Woodcliff Dr. *TF:* 800-444-6885 ■ *Web:* www.manning-napier.com	Fairport	NY	14450	585-325-6880	325-1984
Marvin & Palmer Assoc Inc 1201 N Market St Suite 2300 *Web:* www.marvinandpalmer.com	Wilmington	DE	19801	302-573-3570	573-6772
Maryanov Madsen Gordon & Campbell CPA 801 E Tahquitz Canyon Way, Suite 200 PO Box 1826 *Web:* www.mmgccpa.com	Palm Springs	CA	92263	760-320-6642	327-6854
McAdams Wright Ragen Inc 925 4th Ave Suite 3900 *TF:* 888-567-6297 ■ *Web:* www.mwrinc.com	Seattle	WA	98104	206-664-8850	470-3512
McGlinn Capital Management 850 N Wyomissing Blvd *TF:* 800-783-1478	Wyomissing	PA	19610	610-374-5125	371-1116
McMorgan & Co LLC 1 Front St Suite 500 *Web:* www.nylim.com/portal/site/McMorgan	San Francisco	CA	94111	415-788-9300	616-9386
MD Sass Investor Services Inc 1185 Avenue of the Americas 18th Fl *Web:* www.mdsass.com	New York	NY	10036	212-730-2000	764-0381
Mellon Capital Management Corp 50 Fremont St Suite 3900. *Web:* www.mcm.com	San Francisco	CA	94105	415-546-6056	777-5699
MFS Investment Management 500 Boylston St. **Fax Area Code:* 877 ■ *TF:* 800-637-2929 ■ *Web:* www.mfs.com	Boston	MA	02116	617-954-5000	654-3203*
MidMark Capital 177 Madison Ave *Web:* www.midmarkcapital.com	Morristown	NJ	07960	973-971-9960	971-9963
Mitchell & Titus LLP 1 Battery Pk Plaza 27th Fl. *Web:* www.mitchelltitus.com	New York	NY	10004	212-709-4500	709-4680
Moody Aldrich Partners LLC 18 Sewall St *Web:* www.moodyaldrich.com	Marblehead	MA	01945	781-639-2750	639-2751
Moody's Corp 250 Greenwich St 7 World Trade Ctr. *NYSE: MCO* ■ *Web:* www.moodys.com	New York	NY	10007	212-553-0300	553-5376
Moore Capital Management Inc 1251 Avenue of the Americas 53rd Fl *Web:* www.moorecap.com	New York	NY	10020	212-782-7000	782-7576
Morgan Stanley Dean Witter Realty Inc 2 Penn Plaza Frnt 2. *Web:* www.morganstanleysmithbarney.com	New York	NY	10121	212-613-6700	613-6825
Morningstar Inc 22 W Washington St. *NASDAQ: MORN* ■ *TF Orders:* 800-735-0700 ■ *Web:* www.corporate.morningstar.com	Chicago	IL	60606	312-696-6000	696-6009
National Financial Partners Corp (NFP) 340 Madison Ave 20th Fl *NYSE: NFP* ■ *Web:* www.nfp.com	New York	NY	10173	212-301-4000	301-4001
Navellier Securities Corp 1 E Liberty St 3rd Fl. *TF:* 800-887-8671 ■ *Web:* www.navellier.com	Reno	NV	89501	775-785-2300	785-2321
NCM Capital Management Group Inc 2634 Durham Chapel Hill Blvd Suite 206 **Fax:* Mktg ■ *Web:* www.ncmcapital.com	Durham	NC	27707	919-688-0620	683-1352*
Nelson Benson & Zellmer Inc 3200 Cherry Creek S Dr Suite 730 *Web:* www.investmenttrust.com	Denver	CO	80209	303-778-6800	778-7931
Neuberger Berman LLC 605 3rd Ave *TF:* 800-223-6448 ■ *Web:* www.nb.com	New York	NY	10158	212-476-9000	476-9090
Northern Trust Co of Connecticut 300 Atlantic St Suite 400 *TF:* 800-722-4609 ■ *Web:* www.ntrs.com	Stamford	CT	06901	203-977-7000	356-9341
Odlum Brown Ltd 250 Howe St Suite 1100 *TF:* 866-636-8222 ■ *Web:* www.odlumbrown.com	Vancouver	BC	V6C3S9	604-669-1600	844-5342
Pacific Investment Management Co LLC 840 Newport Ctr Dr. *TF:* 800-387-4626 ■ *Web:* www.pimco.com	Newport Beach	CA	92660	949-720-6000	720-1376
Payden & Rygel 333 S Grand Ave. *TF:* 800-572-9336 ■ *Web:* www.payden.com	Los Angeles	CA	90071	213-625-1900	628-8488
Peninsula Asset Management Inc 1111 3rd Ave W Suite 340 *TF:* 800-269-6417 ■ *Web:* www.peninsulaasset.com	Bradenton	FL	34205	941-748-8680	748-2654
Placemark Investments Inc 16633 Dallas Pkwy Suite 700 *Web:* www.placemark.com	Addison	TX	75001	972-404-8100	404-4505
Ppm America Inc 225 W Wacker Dr Suite 1200 *Web:* www.ppmamerica.com	Chicago	IL	60606	312-634-2500	634-0050
Prime Buchholz & Assoc Inc 25 Chestnut St *Web:* www.primebuchholz.com	Portsmouth	NH	03801	603-433-1143	433-8661
Primerica Financial Services 3120 Breckinridge Blvd **Fax:* PR ■ *TF:* 800-257-4725 ■ *Web:* www.primerica.com	Duluth	GA	30099	770-381-1000	564-6110*
Progress Investment Management Co 33 New Montgomery St Suite 1900 *Web:* www.progressinvestment.com	San Francisco	CA	94105	415-512-3480	512-3475
Prudential Financial Inc 751 Broad St *NYSE: PRU* ■ *TF:* 800-843-7625 ■ *Web:* www.prudential.com	Newark	NJ	07102	973-802-6000	367-6476
Pugh Capital Management Inc 1414 31st Ave S Suite 302 **Fax Area Code:* 206 ■ *Web:* www.pughcapital.com	Seattle	WA	98144	404-872-3200	322-3025*
Putnam Investments 30 Dan Rd PO Box 8383 *TF:* 888-478-8626 ■ *Web:* www.putnam.com	Boston	MA	02021	617-292-1000	
PVG Asset Management Corp 24918 Genesee Trail Rd *TF:* 800-777-0818 ■ *Web:* www.pvgassetmanagement.com	Golden	CO	80401	303-526-0548	526-1391
Pzena Investment Management Inc 120 W 45th St 20th Fl. *NYSE: PZN* ■ *Web:* www.pzena.com	New York	NY	10036	212-355-1600	308-0010
Qci Asset Management 40A Grove St. *TF:* 800-836-3960 ■ *Web:* www.e-qci.com	Pittsford	NY	14534	585-218-2060	218-2013
RBC Global Asset Management 100 S 5th St Suite 2300 *TF Cust Svc:* 800-553-2143 ■ *Web:* www.voyageur.net	Minneapolis	MN	55402	612-376-7000	376-7007
RCM 555 Mission St *Web:* www.rcm.com	San Francisco	CA	94105	415-954-5474	954-8200
Reed Conner & Birdwell Inc 11111 Santa Monica Blvd Suite 1700. *TF:* 877-478-4722 ■ *Web:* www.rcbinvest.com	Los Angeles	CA	90025	310-478-4005	478-8496
Retirement System Group Inc 150 E 42nd St 27th Fl. *TF:* 800-446-7774 ■ *Web:* www.rsgroup.com	New York	NY	10017	212-503-0100	503-0198
Rhumbline Advisers Corp 30 Rowes Wharf Suite 350 *Web:* www.rhumblineadvisers.com	Boston	MA	02110	617-345-0434	345-0675
Rice Hall James & Assoc LLC 600 W Broadway Suite 1000. *Web:* www.ricehalljames.com	San Diego	CA	92101	619-239-9005	
RNC Genter Capital Management 11601 Wilshire Blvd 25th Fl. *TF:* 800-877-7624 ■ *Web:* www.rncgenter.com	Los Angeles	CA	90025	310-477-6543	479-6406
Roffman Miller Assoc Inc 1835 Market St Suite 500. *TF:* 800-995-1030 ■ *Web:* www.roffmanmiller.com	Philadelphia	PA	19103	215-981-1030	981-0146
Rogerscasey LLC 1 Parklands Dr *Web:* www.rogerscasey.com	Darien	CT	06820	203-656-5900	656-2233
Ronald Blue & Co LLC 300 Colonial Ctr Pkwy Suite 300 *TF:* 800-841-0362 ■ *Web:* www.ronblue.com	Roswell	GA	30076	770-280-6000	280-6001
Rosenblum-silverman-sutton Sf Inc 1388 Sutter St Suite 725. *Web:* www.rssic.com	San Francisco	CA	94109	415-771-4500	771-0542
Rothschild North America Inc 1251 Avenue of the Americas 51st Fl *Web:* www.us.rothschild.com	New York	NY	10020	212-403-3500	403-3501
Royce & Assoc LLC 1414 Avenue of the Americas 9th Fl *TF:* 800-348-1414 ■ *Web:* www.roycefunds.com	New York	NY	10019	212-486-1445	752-8875

Phone | Fax

RREEF 101 California St 26th Fl — San Francisco CA 94111 — 415-781-3300 — 986-6248
TF: 800-222-5885 ■ *Web:* www.rreef.com
RS Investment Management Co LLC
388 Market St Suite 1700 — San Francisco CA 94111 — 415-591-2700
Web: www.rsim.com
Ruane Cunniff & Goldfarb Inc
767 5th Ave Suite 4701 — New York NY 10153 — 212-832-5280 — 832-5298
Russell Investment Group 909 A St — Tacoma WA 98402 — 800-787-7354 — 594-1889*
**Fax Area Code:* 253 ■ **Fax:* Mktg ■ *TF:* 800-787-7354 ■ *Web:* www.russell.com
Russell Investments 1301 Second Ave 18th Fl — Seattle WA 98101 — 206-505-7877
TF: 800-426-7969 ■ *Web:* www.russell.com
Saybrook Capital LLC
401 Wilshire Blvd Suite 850 — Santa Monica CA 90401 — 310-899-9200 — 899-9101
Web: www.saybrook.net
SCM Advisors LLC
909 Montgomery St Suite 500 — San Francisco CA 94133 — 415-486-6500 — 486-6783
TF: 800-828-1212 ■ *Web:* www.scmadv.com
Sears Investment Management Co
3333 Beverly Rd — Hoffman Estates IL 60179 — 847-286-4766 — 286-4785
SEI Investments Co 1 Freedom Valley Dr — Oaks PA 19456 — 610-676-1000 — 676-4160*
NASDAQ: SEIC ■ **Fax:* Hum Res ■ *TF:* 800-342-5734 ■ *Web:* www.seic.com
Signalert Corp 150 Great Neck Rd Suite 301 — Great Neck NY 11021 — 516-829-6444 — 829-9366
TF: 800-829-6229 ■ *Web:* www.systemsandforecasts.com
Silver Lake Technology Management LLC
2775 Sand Hill Rd Suite 100 — Menlo Park CA 94025 — 650-233-8120 — 233-8125
Web: www.silverlake.com
Simms Capital Management Inc
107 Elm St Suite 401 — Stamford CT 06902 — 203-252-5700 — 252-5742
TF: 888-258-6365 ■ *Web:* www.simmscapital.com
Sit Investment Assoc Inc
80 S 8th St 3300 IDS Ctr — Minneapolis MN 55402 — 612-332-3223 — 332-1911
Web: www.sitinvest.com
SKBA Capital Management
44 Montgomery St Suite 3500 — San Francisco CA 94104 — 415-989-7852 — 989-2114
Web: www.skba.com
Smith Barney Consulting Group
222 Delaware Ave 7th Fl — Wilmington DE 19801 — 302-888-4100 — 888-4199
Smith Graham & Co 600 Travis St Suite 6900 — Houston TX 77002 — 713-227-1100 — 223-0844
TF: 800-739-4470 ■ *Web:* www.smith-graham.com
Smith Graham & Co Investment Advisors LP
600 Travis St Suite 6900 — Houston TX 77002 — 713-292-2105 — 223-0844
TF: 800-739-4470 ■ *Web:* www.smithgraham.com
Standard & Poor's 55 Water St 45th Fl — New York NY 10041 — 212-438-2000 — 438-3958*
**Fax:* Sales ■ *TF Cust Svc:* 800-344-3014 ■ *Web:* www.standardandpoors.com
Standish Mellon 1 Boston Pl — Boston MA 02108 — 617-248-6000 — 248-6050
Web: www.standishmellon.com
StarMine Corp 49 Stevenson St 8th Fl — San Francisco CA 94105 — 415-777-1147 — 536-0130
State Street Global Advisors 1 Lincoln St — Boston MA 02111 — 617-786-3000 — 654-6012
Web: www.ssga.com
Sterling Capital Management
2 Morrocroft Ctr 4064 Colony Rd Suite 300 — Charlotte NC 28211 — 704-372-8670 — 376-8127
TF Cust Svc: 800-627-1156 ■ *Web:* www.sterling-capital.com
Swarthmore Group 1717 Arch St Suite 3810 — Philadelphia PA 19103 — 215-557-9300 — 557-9305
Web: www.swarthmoregroup.com
Systematic Financial Management LP
300 Frank W Burr Blvd 7th Fl
Glenpoint Ctr E 7th Fl — Teaneck NJ 07666 — 201-928-1982 — 928-1984
TF: 800-258-0497 ■ *Web:* www.sfmlp.com
T Rowe Price Assoc Inc 100 E Pratt St — Baltimore MD 21202 — 410-345-2000 — 345-6244*
**Fax:* Cust Svc ■ *TF:* 800-638-7890 ■ *Web:* www.corporate.troweprice.com/ccw/home.do
Thompson Siegel & Walmsley Inc
6806 Paragon Pl Suite 300 — Richmond VA 23230 — 804-353-4500 — 353-0925
TF: 800-697-1056 ■ *Web:* www.tswinvest.com
Todd Investment Advisors Inc
101 S 5th St Suite 3160 — Louisville KY 40202 — 502-585-3121 — 585-4203
TF: 888-544-8633 ■ *Web:* www.toddinvestment.com
Tom Johnson Investment Management Inc
204 N Robinson St Suite 2900 — Oklahoma City OK 73102 — 405-236-2111 — 236-2008
Web: www.tjim.com
Torch Energy Advisors Inc (TEAI)
1331 Lamar Ave Suite 1450 — Houston TX 77010 — 713-650-1246 — 655-1866
TF: 800-324-8672 ■ *Web:* www.teai.com
Transamerica Investment Management
11111 Santa Monica Blvd Suite 820 — Los Angeles CA 90025 — 310-996-3200 — 477-9767
TF: 866-846-1800 ■ *Web:* www.transamerica.com
Transmarket Group LLC
550 W Jackson Blvd Suite 1300 — Chicago IL 60661 — 312-284-5500 — 284-5650
Web: www.transmarketgroup.com
Trimaran Fund Management LLC
1325 Avenue of the Americas — New York NY 10019 — 212-616-3700 — 616-3701
Web: www.trimarancapital.com
Trusco Capital Management Inc
50 Hurt Plaza Suite 1400 — Atlanta GA 30303 — 404-586-6450 — 575-2978
Web: www.truscocapital.com
Tsg Equity Partners LLC 636 Great Rd — Stow MA 01775 — 978-461-9900 — 461-9909
Web: www.tsgequity.com
Turner Investment Partners Inc
1205 Westlakes Dr Suite 100 — Berwyn PA 19312 — 484-329-2300 — 251-0732*
**Fax Area Code:* 610 ■ *Web:* www.turnerinvestments.com
UBS Global Asset Management Inc 51 W 52 St — New York NY 10019 — 212-882-5000 — 882-5472
Web: www.us.ubs-globalam.com
UNC Partners 54 Burroughs St — Boston MA 02130 — 617-522-2160 — 522-2176
Web: www.uncpartners.com
US Global Investors Inc
7900 Callaghan Rd — San Antonio TX 78229 — 210-308-1234 — 308-1223
NASDAQ: GROW ■ *TF:* 800-873-8637 ■ *Web:* www.usfunds.com
US Trust Corp 11 W 54th St — New York NY 10019 — 212-852-1000 — 852-3852
TF: 800-878-7878 ■ *Web:* www.ustrust.com
USAA Investment Management
9800 Fredericksburg Rd PO Box 659453 — San Antonio TX 78288 — 210-498-8777 — 292-8177*
**Fax Area Code:* 800 ■ *TF:* 800-531-8722 ■ *Web:* www.usaa.com
Value Line Asset Management 220 E 42nd St — New York NY 10017 — 212-907-1500 — 818-9781
TF: 800-634-3583 ■ *Web:* www.valueline.com

Value Line Inc 220 E 42nd St — New York NY 10017 — 212-907-1500 — 818-9747
NASDAQ: VALU ■ *TF Cust Svc:* 800-634-3583 ■ *Web:* www.valueline.com
Vanguard Group 455 Devon Pk Dr — Wayne PA 19087 — 610-669-1000 — 669-6551
TF: 800-662-7447 ■ *Web:* www.vanguard.com
Veritas Capital Fund LP
590 Madison Ave 41st Fl — New York NY 10022 — 212-415-6700 — 688-9411
Web: www.veritascapital.com
Vontobel Asset Management Inc
1540 Broad way Ave 38th Fl — New York NY 10036 — 212-415-7000 — 415-7087
TF Cust Svc: 800-445-8872 ■ *Web:* www.vusa.com
Waddell & Reed Financial Inc
6300 Lamar Ave — Overland Park KS 66202 — 913-236-2000 — 236-5044
NYSE: WDR ■ *TF:* 888-923-3355 ■ *Web:* www.waddell.com
Washington Capital Management Inc
1301 5th Ave Suite 3100 — Seattle WA 98101 — 206-382-0825 — 382-0950
Web: www.wcmadvisors.com
Wasmer Schroeder & Co Inc
600 5th Ave S Suite 210 — Naples FL 34102 — 239-263-6877 — 263-8146
Web: www.wasmerschroeder.com
Wedge Capital Management LLP
301 S College St Suite 2920 — Charlotte NC 28202 — 704-334-6475 — 334-3542
Web: www.wedgecapital.com
Wellington Management Co LLP 75 State St — Boston MA 02109 — 617-951-5000 — 951-5250
Web: www.wellington.com
Wellington West Capital Inc
400 - 200 Waterfront Dr Suite 400 — Winnipeg MB R3B3P1 — 204-925-2250 — 942-6194
TF: 800-461-6314 ■ *Web:* www.wellwest.ca
Wentworth Hauser & Violich
301 Battery St — San Francisco CA 94111 — 415-981-6911 — 288-6153
TF: 800-204-2650 ■ *Web:* www.whv.com
Wescap Management Group Inc
1314 W Glenoaks Blvd — Glendale CA 91201 — 818-563-5170 — 563-5174
TF: 800-820-2453 ■ *Web:* www.wescapgroup.com
Whi Capital Partners
191 N Wacker Dr Suite 1500 — Chicago IL 60606 — 312-621-0590 — 604-2271
Web: www.whicapital.com
Wilshire Assoc Inc
1299 Ocean Ave Suite 700 — Santa Monica CA 90401 — 310-451-3051 — 458-0520
Web: www.wilshire.com
Woodbury Financial Services Inc
500 Bielenberg Dr PO Box 64284 — Saint Paul MN 55164 — 651-738-4000
TF: 800-800-2638 ■ *Web:* www.woodburyfinancial.com
WP Stewart & Co Ltd 527 Madison Ave 20th Fl — New York NY 10022 — 212-750-8585 — 980-8039
PINK: WPSL ■ *TF:* 888-695-4092 ■ *Web:* www.wpstewart.com
Wright Investors' Service
440 Wheelers Farms Rd — Milford CT 06461 — 203-783-4400 — 783-4401
TF: 800-232-0013 ■ *Web:* www.wisi.com
Yacktman Asset Management Co
6300 Bridgepoint Pkwy Bldg 1 Suite 320 — Austin TX 78730 — 512-767-6700
TF: 800-356-6356 ■ *Web:* www.yacktman.com

405 INVESTMENT COMPANIES - SMALL BUSINESS

The Companies Listed Here Conform To The Small Business Administration's Standards For Investing.

Phone | Fax

Anthem Capital Management LLC
1414 Key Hwy Suite 300 — Baltimore MD 21230 — 410-625-1510 — 625-1735
Web: www.anthemcapital.com
Argentum Group The 60 Madison Ave Suite 701 — New York NY 10010 — 212-949-6262 — 949-8294
Web: www.argentumgroup.com
Atalanta Investment Co Inc
PO Box 7718 — Incline Village NV 89452 — 775-833-1836 — 833-1890
Bankoh Investment Services Inc
130 Merchant St Suite 850 — Honolulu HI 96813 — 808-537-8500 — 538-4891
Web: www.boh.com
Brynwood Partners LP
8 Sound Shore Dr Suite 265 — Greenwich CT 06830 — 203-622-1790 — 622-0559
Web: www.brynwoodpartners.com
Capital Access Network Inc
2 Overhill Rd Suite 410 — Scarsdale NY 10583 — 914-725-9301 — 725-9312
Web: www.advanceme.com
Capital for Business Inc
11 S Meramec Ave Suite 1430 — Saint Louis MO 63105 — 314-746-7427 — 746-8739
Web: www.capitalforbusiness.com
Center for Innovation
University of N Dakota PO Box 8372 — Grand Forks ND 58202 — 701-777-3132 — 777-2339
Web: www.innovators.net
CIP Capital LP 1200 Liberty Ridge Dr Suite 300 — Wayne PA 19087 — 610-964-7860 — 964-8136
Cypress Group LLC 437 Madison Ave 33rd Fl — New York NY 10022 — 212-705-0150 — 705-0199
Web: www.cypressgp.com
El Dorado Ventures 2884 Sand Hill Rd — Menlo Park CA 94025 — 650-854-1200 — 854-1202
Web: www.eldorado.com
Elliott Management 712 5th Ave — New York NY 10019 — 212-974-6000 — 586-9431
Web: www.elliottmgmt.com
Enterprise Venture Capital Corp of Pennsylvania
245 Market St # 200 — Johnstown PA 15901 — 814-535-7597 — 535-8677
Eos Partners LP 320 Pk Ave 9th Fl — New York NY 10022 — 212-832-5800 — 832-5815
Web: www.eospartners.com
Federal Farm Credit Banks Funding Corp
10 Exchange Pl Suite 1401 — Jersey City NJ 07302 — 201-200-8000 — 200-8156
Web: www.farmcredit-ffcb.com
Forrest Binkley & Brown (FBB)
19800 MacArthur Blvd Suite 690 — Irvine CA 92612 — 949-222-1987 — 222-1988
Web: www.fbbvc.com
Galliard Capital Management Inc
800 La Salle Ave Suite 1100 — Minneapolis MN 55402 — 612-667-3210 — 667-3223
TF: 800-717-1617 ■ *Web:* www.galliard.com
GamePlan Financial Marketing LLC
300 ParkBrooke Pl Suite 200 — Woodstock GA 30189 — 770-517-2765 — 517-0649
TF Cust Svc: 800-886-4757 ■ *Web:* www.gameplanfinancial.com

Company	City	State	ZIP	Phone	Fax
Gemini Investors LLC 20 William St Suite 250 *Web:* www.gemini-investors.com	Wellesley	MA	02481	781-237-7001	237-7233
Hornor Townsend & Kent Inc (HTK) 600 Dresher Rd. *Web:* www.pennmutual.com/htkwebsite/home.action	Horsham	PA	19044	215-956-8108	956-7750
Impact Seven Inc 147 Lake Almena Dr. *TF:* 800-685-9353 ■ *Web:* www.impactseven.org	Almena	WI	54805	715-357-3334	357-6233
Inverness Management LLC 630 5th Ave *Web:* www.invernessmanagement.com	New York	NY	10111	212-632-3415	
Kansas City Equity Partners 233 W 47th St. *Web:* www.kcep.com	Kansas City	MO	64112	816-960-1771	960-1777
Kansas Venture Capital Inc 6700 Antioch Plaza Suite 460 *Web:* www.kvci.com	Overland Park	KS	66204	913-262-7117	262-3509
Kentucky Highlands Investment Corp 362 Old Whitley Rd. *Web:* www.khic.org	London	KY	40744	606-864-5175	864-5194
Kline Hawkes & Co 11726 San Vicente Blvd Suite 300 *Web:* www.klinehawkes.com	Los Angeles	CA	90049	310-442-4700	442-4707
MACC Private Equities Inc 101 2nd St SE Suite 800 *NASDAQ: MACC*	Cedar Rapids	IA	52401	319-363-8249	363-9683
Marwit Capital LLC 100 Bayview Cir Suite 550 *Web:* www.marwit.com	Newport Beach	CA	92660	949-861-3636	861-3637
Mason Wells 411 E Wisconsin Ave Suite 1280 *TF:* 800-342-2265 ■ *Web:* www.masonwells.com	Milwaukee	WI	53202	414-727-6400	727-6410
MorAmerica Capital Corp 101 2nd St SE Suite 800	Cedar Rapids	IA	52401	319-363-8249	363-9683
Mountain Ventures Inc PO Box 1738	London	KY	40743	606-864-5175	864-5194
MVP Capital Partners 201 King of Prussia Rd Suite 240 *Web:* www.meridian-venture.com	Radnor	PA	19087	610-254-2999	254-2996
Northern Pacific Capital Corp PO Box 1658	Portland	OR	97207	503-241-1255	299-6653
Novus Ventures LP 20111 Stevens Creek Blvd Suite 130 *Web:* www.novusventures.com	Cupertino	CA	95014	408-252-3900	252-1713
Physical Optics Corp 20600 Gramercy Pl *Web:* www.poc.com	Torrance	CA	90501	310-320-3088	320-4667
RFE Investment Partners 36 Grove St *Web:* www.rfeip.com	New Canaan	CT	06840	203-966-2800	966-3109
River Cities Capital Funds 221 E 4th St Suite 2400 *Web:* www.rccf.com	Cincinnati	OH	45202	513-621-9700	579-8939
Seacoast Capital Partners 55 Ferncroft Rd *Web:* www.seacoastcapital.com	Danvers	MA	01923	978-750-1351	750-1301
Sorrento Assoc Inc 12250 El Camino Real Suite 100 *Web:* www.sorrentoventures.com	San Diego	CA	92130	858-792-2700	792-5070
Stonehenge Capital Co LLC 236 3rd St *Web:* www.stonehengecapital.com	Baton Rouge	LA	70801	225-408-3000	408-3090
TPG Capital LP 301 Commerce St Suite 3300 *Web:* www.tpg.com	Fort Worth	TX	76102	817-871-4000	871-4010
UMB Capital Corp 1010 Grand Blvd *TF:* 800-821-2171 ■ *Web:* www.umb.com	Kansas City	MO	64106	816-860-7914	860-7143
Vestor Partners LP 607 Cerrillos Rd Suite D2 *Web:* www.vestor.com	Santa Fe	NM	87505	505-988-9100	988-1958
Virginia Capital Partners LLC 1801 Libbie Ave Suite 201 *Web:* www.vacapital.com	Richmond	VA	23226	804-648-4802	648-4809
Waterside Capital Corp 3092 Brickhouse Rd Suite 800 *NASDAQ: WSCC* ■ *Web:* www.watersidecapital.com	Virginia Beach	VA	23452	757-626-1111	626-0114
White Pines Ventures LLC 900 Victors Way Suite 280 *Web:* www.whitepines.com	Ann Arbor	MI	48108	734-747-9401	747-9704
Windward Capital Partners LP 712 5th Ave 21st Fl. **Fax Area Code:* 212	New York	NY	10019	646-378-2151	382-6534*
Xspand 115 S Jefferson Rd Bldg D-1 *TF:* 866-267-4811 ■ *Web:* www.xspand.com	Whippany	NJ	07981	973-793-4811	793-2372

406 INVESTMENT COMPANIES - SPECIALIZED SMALL BUSINESS

Companies Listed Here Conform To The Small Business Administration's Requirements For Investment In Minority Companies.

Company	City	State	ZIP	Phone	Fax
Al Copeland Investments Inc 1001 Harimaw Ct S. *TF:* 800-401-0401 ■ *Web:* www.alcopeland.com	Metairie	LA	70001	504-830-1000	832-8918
Arlington Capital Partners 5425 Wisconsin Ave Suite 200 *Web:* www.arlingtoncap.com	Chevy Chase	MD	20815	202-337-7500	337-7525
Associated Southwest Investors Inc 6501 Americas Pkwy NE Suite 210	Albuquerque	NM	87110	505-247-4050	888-5244
Bastion Capital Corp 1901 Avenue of the Stars Suite 470	Los Angeles	CA	90067	310-788-5700	277-7582
Brentwood Assoc 11150 Santa Monica Blvd Suite 1200 *Web:* www.brentwood.com	Los Angeles	CA	90025	310-477-6611	477-1011
Brown Gibbons Lang & Co LLC 1111 Superior Ave Suite 900 *Web:* www.bglco.com	Cleveland	OH	44114	216-920-6612	241-7417
Burney Co 121 Rowell Ct *Web:* www.burney.com	Falls Church	VA	22046	703-241-5611	531-0417
Capricorn Management LLC 30 E Elm St *Web:* www.capricornholdings.com	Greenwich	CT	06830	203-861-6600	861-6671
Castle Harlan Inc 150 E 58th St *Web:* www.castleharlan.com	New York	NY	10155	212-644-8600	207-8042
Clayton Dubilier & Rice Inc 375 Pk Ave 18th Fl *Web:* www.cdr-inc.com	New York	NY	10152	212-407-5200	407-5252
Community Mortgage Corp 142 Timber Creek Dr. *Web:* www.communitymtg.com	Cordova	TN	38018	901-759-4400	758-0503
Continental SBIC 4141 N Henderson Rd Suite 8	Arlington	VA	22203	703-527-5200	527-3700
Cypress Sharpridge Investments Inc 437 Madison Ave Fl 33 *NYSE: CYS* ■ *Web:* www.cypresssharpridge.com	New York	NY	10022	212-612-3210	705-0199
Far East Capital Corp 350 S Grand Ave *TF:* 800-753-8449	Los Angeles	CA	90071	213-687-1260	626-3884
First American Capital Funding 10101 Slater Ave Suite 214	Fountain Valley	CA	92708	714-965-7190	965-7193
First County Capital Inc 40-48 Ming St Suite 301	Flushing	NY	11354	718-461-1778	461-1835
Fulcrum Capital Group 10940 Wilshire Blvd Suite 1626 *Web:* www.fulcrumventures.com	Los Angeles	CA	90024	310-443-4281	443-4282
Goldner Hawn Johnson & Morrison Inc (GHJ&M) 90 S 7th St 3700 Wells Fargo Ctr *Web:* www.ghjm.com	Minneapolis	MN	55402	612-338-5912	338-2860
Greater Philadelphia Venture Capital Corp Inc 351 E Conestoga Rd	Wayne	PA	19087	610-688-6829	254-8958
HIG Capital Management Inc 1450 Brickell Ave 31st Fl *Web:* www.higcapital.com	Miami	FL	33131	305-379-2322	379-2013
Ibero American Investors Corp 104 Scio St *Web:* www.iberoinvestors.com	Rochester	NY	14604	585-262-3440	262-3441
Littlejohn & Co LLC 8 Sound Shore Dr Suite 303 *Web:* www.littlejohnllc.com	Greenwich	CT	06830	203-552-3500	552-3550
Madison Capital Partners Corp 500 W Madison St Suite 3890 *Web:* www.madisoncapitalpartners.net	Chicago	IL	60661	312-277-0156	277-0163
MCG Global LLC 300 Long Beach Blvd Suite 13 *Web:* www.mcgglobal.com	Stratford	CT	06615	203-386-0615	386-0771
Medallion Capital 3000 W County Rd 42 Suite 301 *Web:* www.medallionfinancial.com	Burnsville	MN	55337	952-831-2025	831-2945
Milestone Growth Fund 401 2nd Ave S Suite 1032 *Web:* www.milestonegrowth.com	Minneapolis	MN	55401	612-338-0090	338-1172
Milestone Merchant Partners LLC 1775 I St NW Suite 800 *Web:* www.milestonecap.com	Washington	DC	20006	202-367-3000	367-3001
MMG Ventures LP 826 E Baltimore St *Web:* www.mmggroup.com	Baltimore	MD	21202	410-659-7850	333-2552
Nca Partners Inc 1200 Westlake Ave N Suite 600 *Web:* www.nwcap.com	Seattle	WA	98109	206-689-5615	689-5614
Nitze-Stagen & Co Inc 2401 Utah Ave S Suite 305 *Web:* www.nitze-stagen.com	Seattle	WA	98134	206-467-0420	467-0423
Opportunity Capital Corp 2201 Walnut Ave Suite 210 *Web:* www.opportunitycapitalpartners.com	Fremont	CA	94538	510-795-7000	494-5439
Pierre Funding Corp 805 3rd Ave 19th Fl.	New York	NY	10022	212-888-1515	687-0659
Polestar Capital Inc 180 N Michigan Ave Suite 1905 *Web:* www.polestarvc.com	Chicago	IL	60601	312-984-9090	984-9877
Princeton Financial Systems LLC 600 College Rd E *Web:* www.pfs.com	Princeton	NJ	08540	609-987-2400	987-9320
Smith affiliated capital (SAC) 800 3rd Ave 12th Fl *TF:* 888-387-3298 ■ *Web:* www.smithcapital.com	New York	NY	10022	212-644-9440	644-1979
West Tennessee Venture Capital Corp 5 N 3rd St Suite 2001	Memphis	TN	38103	901-523-1884	527-6091

407 INVESTMENT GUIDES - ONLINE

SEE ALSO Buyer's Guides - Online p. 1551

Company	City	State	ZIP	Phone	Fax
BigCharts Inc 123 N 3rd St Suite 300 *Web:* www.bigcharts.marketwatch.com	Minneapolis	MN	55401	612-338-0049	338-0069
Briefing.com Inc 555 Airport Blvd # 150 *TF:* 800-752-3013 ■ *Web:* www.briefing.com	Burlingame	CA	94010	650-347-2220	347-2223
EarningsWhispers.com c/o WebTools LLC 113 W Main St Suite 8 *Web:* www.earningswhispers.com	Jackson	MO	63755	573-243-2734	243-2331
EDGAR Online Inc 11200 Rockville Pike Suite 310 *NASDAQ: EDGR* ■ **Fax:* Cust Svc ■ *TF:* 800-416-6651 ■ *Web:* www.edgar-online.com	Rockville	MD	20852	301-287-0300	287-0390*
eSignal 3955 Salt Way *TF:* 800-367-4670 ■ *Web:* www.esignal.com	Hayward	CA	94545	510-266-6000	266-6100
FactSet Research Systems Inc 601 Merritt 7 3rd Fl *NYSE: FDS* ■ *TF:* 877-322-8738 ■ *Web:* www.factset.com	Norwalk	CT	06851	203-810-1000	810-1000
Harris myCFO Inc 2200 Geng Rd Suite 100 *TF:* 877-692-3609 ■ *Web:* www.harrismycfo.com	Palo Alto	CA	94303	650-210-5000	210-5010
Hoover's Inc 5800 Airport Blvd *TF:* 800-486-8666 ■ *Web:* www.hoovers.com	Austin	TX	78752	512-374-4500	374-4501
InvestorPlace.com c/o Phillips Investment Resources LLC 2420A Gehman Ln **Fax Area Code:* 301 ■ *TF:* 800-219-8592 ■ *Web:* www.investorplace.com	Lancaster	PA	17602	800-219-8592	762-6776*
IPO Monitor 5200 W Century Blvd Suite 470 **Fax Area Code:* 310 ■ *TF:* 800-266-0126 ■ *Web:* www.ipomonitor.com	Los Angeles	CA	90045	800-266-0126	642-6933*

	City	State	Zip	Phone	Fax
Motley Fool Inc 2000 Duke St 4th Fl *Web:* www.fool.com	Alexandria	VA	22314	703-838-3665	254-1999
Stockwatch 700 W Georgia St PO Box 10371 *TF:* 800-268-6397 ■ *Web:* www.stockwatch.com	Vancouver	BC	V7Y1J6	604-687-1500	687-0541
TheStreet.com Inc 14 Wall St 15th Fl *NASDAQ: TST* ■ *TF:* 800-562-9571 ■ *Web:* www.thestreet.com	New York	NY	10005	212-321-5000	321-5016
Yahoo! Finance 701 1st Ave *Web:* finance.yahoo.com	Sunnyvale	CA	94089	408-349-3300	349-3301

408 INVESTMENT (MISC)

SEE ALSO Banks - Commercial & Savings p. 1506; Commodity Contracts Brokers & Dealers p. 1668; Franchises p. 1884; Investment Guides - Online p. 2133; Mortgage Lenders & Loan Brokers p. 2254; Mutual Funds p. 2295; Investment Newsletters p. 2303; Real Estate Investment Trusts (REITs) p. 2523; Royalty Trusts p. 2628; Securities Brokers & Dealers p. 2646; Venture Capital Firms p. 2754

	City	State	Zip	Phone	Fax
ABRY Partners LLC 111 Huntington Ave 30th Fl. *TF:* 800-578-2279 ■ *Web:* www.abry.com	Boston	MA	02199	617-859-2959	859-7205
Acacia Research Corp 500 Newport Ctr Dr Suite 700 *NASDAQ: ACTG* ■ *Web:* www.acaciaresearch.com	Newport Beach	CA	92660	949-480-8300	480-8301
Adams Express Co 7 St Paul St Suite 1140 *NYSE: ADX* ■ *TF:* 800-638-2479 ■ *Web:* www.adamsexpress.com	Baltimore	MD	21202	410-752-5900	659-0080
AEA Investors Inc 55 E 52nd St 35th FL *Web:* www.aeainvestors.com	New York	NY	10055	212-644-5900	888-1459
Anschutz Corp 555 17th St Suite 2400	Denver	CO	80202	303-298-1000	298-8881
Bancroft Fund Ltd 65 Madison Ave Suite 550 *AMEX: BCV* ■ *Web:* www.bancroftfund.com	Morristown	NJ	07960	973-631-1177	631-1313
Barry S. Nussbaum Co Inc 13151 Emily Rd Suite 250 *Web:* www.bncrealestate.com	Dallas	TX	75240	972-437-9900	437-9377
BKF Capital Group Inc 225 NE Mizner Blvd Suite 400 *NYSE: BKF* ■ *Web:* www.bkfcapital.com	Boca Raton	FL	33432	561-362-4199	362-4722
CC Industries Inc 222 N La Salle St Suite 1000	Chicago	IL	60601	312-855-4000	236-7074
Central Securities Corp 630 5th Ave Suite 820 *AMEX: CET* ■ *TF:* 866-593-2507 ■ *Web:* www.centralsecurities.com	New York	NY	10111	212-698-2020	
Cerberus Capital Management LP 299 Pk Ave *Web:* www.cerberuscapital.com	New York	NY	10171	212-891-2100	
Columbia Ventures Corp 203 SE Pk Plaza Dr Suite 270 *TF:* 866-204-0747 ■ *Web:* www.colventures.com	Vancouver	WA	98684	360-816-1840	816-1841
Counsel Corp 1211 Avenue of the Americas Suite 2902 *TSX: CXS* ■ *TF:* 800-879-9548 ■ *Web:* www.crexusinvestment.com	New York	NY	10036	212-696-0100	696-9809
Dundee Wealth Management Inc 1 Adelaide St E *TSE: DW* ■ *TF:* 888-292-3847 ■ *Web:* www.dundeewealth.com	Toronto	ON	M5C2V9	416-350-3250	350-5105
Energy Savings Income Fund *Energy Savings LP* 100 King St W Suite 2630 PO Box 355 *TSX: SIF.UN* ■ *TF:* 877-657-3902 ■ *Web:* www.energysavings.com	Toronto	ON	M5X1E1	416-367-2998	367-4749
Enerplus Resources Fund 333 7th Ave SW Suite 3000 *TSE: ERF* ■ *TF:* 800-319-6462 ■ *Web:* www.enerplus.com	Calgary	AB	T2P2Z1	403-298-2200	298-2211
Enstar Group Inc 7035 Halcyon Pk Dr *Web:* www.enstargroup.com	Montgomery	AL	36117	334-834-5483	834-2530
Eureka Growth Capital 1717 Arch St 3420 Bell Atlantic Tower *Web:* www.eurekagrowth.com	Philadelphia	PA	19103	267-238-4200	238-4201
Fairmont Capital Inc 3350 E Birch St Suite 206 *Web:* www.fairmontcapital.com	Brea	CA	92821	714-524-4770	524-4775
Fairview Capital Partners Inc 10 Stanford Dr *Web:* www.fairviewcapital.com	Farmington	CT	06032	860-674-8066	678-5108
Fidelity Investments Charitable Gift Fund PO Box 55158 **Fax Area Code: 617* ■ *TF:* 800-682-4438 ■ *Web:* www.charitablegift.org	Boston	MA	02205	800-682-4438	476-7206*
Forstmann Little & Co 767 5th Ave 44th Fl *Web:* www.forstmannlittle.com	New York	NY	10153	212-355-5656	759-9059
Fremont Group Inc 199 Fremont St *Web:* www.fremontgroup.com	San Francisco	CA	94105	415-284-8500	284-8191
Gain Capital Security Inc 27600 Chagrin Blvd *TF:* 800-222-5520 ■ *Web:* www.gainsecurities.com	Cleveland	OH	44122	216-765-8500	765-8073
General American Investors Co Inc 450 Lexington Ave Suite 3300 *NYSE: GAM* ■ *TF:* 800-436-8401 ■ *Web:* www.generalamericaninvestors.com	New York	NY	10017	212-916-8400	916-8490
Golden Gate Capital LP 1 Embarcadero Ctr FL 39 *Web:* www.goldengatecap.com	San Francisco	CA	94111	415-627-4500	983-2701
Gores Technology Group 10877 Wilshire Blvd Suite 1805 *Web:* www.gores.com	Los Angeles	CA	90024	310-209-3010	209-3310
Gould Investors LP 60 Cutter Mill Rd Suite 303	Great Neck	NY	11021	516-466-3100	466-3132
Haverford Trust Co 3 Radnor Corp Ctr Suite 450 *TF:* 888-995-1979 ■ *Web:* www.haverfordtrust.com	Radnor	PA	19087	610-995-8700	995-8796
Hellman & Friedman LLC 1 Maritime Plaza 12th FL *Web:* www.hf.com	San Francisco	CA	94111	415-788-5111	788-0176
Henry Crown & Co 222 N La Salle St Suite 2000	Chicago	IL	60601	312-236-6300	899-5039
Highland Capital Management LP 13455 Noel Rd 2 Galleria Tower Suite 800 *Web:* www.hcmlp.com	Dallas	TX	75240	972-628-4100	628-4147
Hillman Co 330 Grant St Suite 1900 *TF All:* 800-445-5626	Pittsburgh	PA	15219	412-281-2620	338-3520
HM Capital Partners LLC 200 Crescent Ct Suite 1600 *Web:* www.hmcapital.com	Dallas	TX	75201	214-740-7300	720-7888
Hold Bros On-Line Investment Services Inc 525 Washington Blvd 14th Fl *Web:* www.holdbrothers.com	Jersey City	NJ	07310	201-499-8700	499-8750
HomeVestors of America Inc 6500 Greenville Ave Suite 400 *TF:* 800-442-8937 ■ *Web:* www.homevestors.com	Dallas	TX	75206	972-761-0046	761-9022
ICV Capital Partners LLC 666 3rd Ave 29th Fl *Web:* www.icvcapital.com	New York	NY	10017	212-455-9600	455-9603
InvestPrivate.com 500 5th Ave 54th Fl *TF:* 877-669-4732 ■ *Web:* www.investprivate.com	New York	NY	10110	212-739-7700	655-0140
JII Partners Inc 450 Lexington Ave 31st Fl *Web:* www.jllpartners.com	New York	NY	10017	212-286-8600	286-8626
Kunath Karren Rinne & Atkin LLC 1000 2nd Ave Suite 4000 *Web:* www.kkra.com	Seattle	WA	98104	206-621-7400	343-3085
Lion Chemical Capital LLC 535 Madison Ave 4th Fl *Web:* www.lionchemicalcapital.com	New York	NY	10022	212-355-5500	355-6283
Liquidnet Holdings Inc 498 7th Ave 12th Fl *Web:* www.liquidnet.com	New York	NY	10018	646-674-2000	674-2003
Main Street Capital Corp 1300 Post Oak Blvd *NYSE: MAIN* ■ *Web:* www.mainstcapital.com	Houston	TX	77056	713-350-6000	350-6042
MassMutual Financial Group 1295 State St *TF:* 800-272-2216 ■ *Web:* www.massmutual.com	Springfield	MA	01111	800-272-2216	
McCown De Leeuw & Co (MDC) 950 Tower Ln Suite 800 *Web:* www.mdcpartners.com	Foster City	CA	94404	650-854-6000	854-0853
MidCoast Financial Inc 1926 10th Ave N Suite 400 *TF:* 800-444-5626	Lake Worth	FL	33461	561-540-6224	540-4226
Moors & Cabot Inc 111 Devonshire St *TF:* 800-426-0501 ■ *Web:* www.moorscabot.com	Boston	MA	02109	617-426-0500	426-9608
Pembina Pipeline Corp 700 9th Ave SW Suite 2000 *TSX: PIF.UN* ■ *TF:* 888-428-3222 ■ *Web:* www.pembina.com	Calgary	AB	T2P3V4	403-231-7500	237-0254
Pennsylvania Early Stage Partners 435 Devon Pk Dr Suite 801 *Web:* www.novitascapital.com	Wayne	PA	19087	610-293-4075	254-4240
Petroleum & Resources Corp 7 St Paul St Suite 1140 *NYSE: PEO* ■ *TF:* 800-638-2479 ■ *Web:* www.peteres.com	Baltimore	MD	21202	410-752-5900	659-0080
Platinum Equity Holdings (PEH) *Platinum Equity LLC* 360 N Crescent Dr *Web:* www.platinumequity.com	Beverly Hills	CA	90210	310-712-1850	712-1848
Provender Capital Group LLC 17 State St	New York	NY	10004	212-271-8888	271-8875
Rand Capital Corp 2200 Rand Bldg *NASDAQ: RAND* ■ *Web:* www.randcapital.com	Buffalo	NY	14203	716-853-0802	854-8480
Rodman & Renshaw Capital Group Inc 1251 Avenue of the Americas 20th Fl *NASDAQ: RODM* ■ *Web:* www.rodmanandrenshaw.com	New York	NY	10020	212-356-0500	581-5690
Safeguard International Fund LP 435 Devon Pk Dr Bldg 400 *Web:* www.safeguardintl.com	Wayne	PA	19087	610-293-0838	293-0854
SCP Private Equity Partners 1200 Liberty Ridge Dr Suite 300 *Web:* www.scppartners.com	Wayne	PA	19087	610-995-2900	975-9546
Sequoia Equities Inc 1777 Botelho Dr Suite 300 *Web:* www.experiencesequoia.com	Walnut Creek	CA	94596	925-945-0900	256-3780
Smith Whiley & Co 242 Trumbull St 8th Fl *Web:* www.smithwhiley.com	Hartford	CT	06103	860-548-2513	548-2518
Spell Capital Partners LLC 222 S 9th St Suite 2880 *Web:* www.spellcapital.com	Minneapolis	MN	55402	612-371-9650	371-9651
St Johns Wealth Management 10060 Skinner Lake Dr Suite 501 *TF:* 800-992-3150 ■ *Web:* www.stjohnsinvestment.com	Jacksonville	FL	32246	904-399-0662	346-0047
Superior Plus Income Fund 840-7 Ave SW Suite 1400 *TF:* 866-490-7587 ■ *Web:* www.superiorplus.ca	Calgary	AB	T2P3G2	403-218-2970	218-2973
Technology Ventures Corp 1155 University Blvd SE *Web:* www.techventures.org	Albuquerque	NM	87106	505-246-2882	246-2891
Thomas H Lee Partners 100 Federal St Suite 3500 *TF:* 800-227-1050 ■ *Web:* www.thl.com	Boston	MA	02110	617-227-1050	227-3514
Thomas Properties Group Inc 515 S Flower St 6th Fl *NASDAQ: TPGI* ■ *Web:* www.tpgre.com	Los Angeles	CA	90071	213-613-1900	633-4760
Tracinda Corp 150 Rodeo Dr Suite 250	Beverly Hills	CA	90212	310-271-0638	271-3416
Vulcan Inc 505 5th Ave S Suite 900 *Web:* www.vulcan.com	Seattle	WA	98104	206-342-2000	342-3000
Welsh Carson Anderson & Stowe 320 Pk Ave Suite 2500 *Web:* www.welshcarson.com	New York	NY	10022	212-893-9500	
Yucaipa Cos LLC 9130 W Sunset Blvd	Los Angeles	CA	90069	310-789-7200	789-7201

409 JANITORIAL & CLEANING SUPPLIES - WHOL

	City	State	Zip	Phone	Fax
AmSan 3031 N Andrews Ave *Web:* www.amsan.com	Pompano Beach	FL	33064	954-972-1700	247-4318

	City	State	ZIP	Phone	Fax
Brady Industries Inc 7055 Lindell Rd *TF:* 800-293-4698 ■ *Web:* www.bradyindustries.com	Las Vegas	NV	89118	702-876-3990	876-1580
EXSL/Ultra Labs Inc 30921 Wiegman Rd	Hayward	CA	94544	510-324-4567	324-8881
Fitch Co 2201 Russell St *TF:* 800-933-4824 ■ *Web:* www.fitchco.com	Baltimore	MD	21230	410-539-1953	727-2244
HP Products Corp 4220 Saguaro Trail *TF:* 800-382-5326 ■ *Web:* www.hpproducts.com	Indianapolis	IN	46268	317-298-9950	293-0459
I Janvey & Sons Inc 218 Front St *Web:* www.janvey.com	Hempstead	NY	11550	516-489-9300	486-3927
Industrial Soap Co 722 S Vandeventer Ave *Web:* www.industrialsoap.com	Saint Louis	MO	63110	314-241-6363	533-5556
Kellermeyer Co 475 W Woodland Cir *TF:* 800-445-7415 ■ *Web:* www.kellermeyer.com	Bowling Green	OH	43402	419-255-3022	255-2752
Kenway Distributors Inc 6320 Strawberry Ln *Web:* www.kenway.net	Louisville	KY	40214	502-367-2201	368-5519
Rose Products & Services Inc 545 Stimmel Rd *TF:* 800-264-1568	Columbus	OH	43223	614-443-7647	443-2771
Sani-Clean Distributors 470 Riverside St	Portland	ME	04103	207-797-8240	878-3513

410 JEWELERS' FINDINGS & MATERIALS

	City	State	ZIP	Phone	Fax
Ampex Casting Corp 23 W 47th St 4th Fl	New York	NY	10036	212-719-1318	719-3493
ARC Traders Inc PO Box 3429 *TF:* 800-528-2374	Scottsdale	AZ	85271	480-945-0769	946-9089
BA Ballou & Co Inc 800 Waterman Ave *TF:* 800-729-3347 ■ *Web:* www.ballou.com	East Providence	RI	02914	401-438-7000	434-3336
Craftstones PO Box 847 *Web:* www.craftstones.com	Ramona	CA	92065	760-789-1620	789-3432
David H Fell & Co Inc 6009 Bandini Blvd *TF:* 800-822-1996 ■ *Web:* www.dhfco.com	Commerce	CA	90040	323-722-9992	722-6567
Findings Inc 160 Water St *TF:* 800-343-0806 ■ *Web:* www.findingsinc.net	Keene	NH	03431	603-352-3717	352-5535
James A Murphy & Son Inc PO Box 3006 *TF:* 800-422-3237	South Attleboro	MA	02703	508-761-5060	761-4580
Kahan Jewelry Corp 36 W 47th St Rm 308	New York	NY	10036	212-719-1055	944-1715
Karbra Co 131 W 35th St 8th Fl *TF:* 800-527-2721	New York	NY	10001	212-736-9300	736-9303
Krohn Industries Inc 303 Veterans Blvd *TF:* 800-526-6299	Carlstadt	NJ	07072	201-933-9696	933-9684
Lazare Kaplan International Inc 19 W 44th St 16th Fl *AMEX:* LKI ■ *TF Cust Svc:* 800-554-3325 ■ *Web:* www.lazarediamonds.com	New York	NY	10036	212-972-9700	972-8561
Lee's Mfg Co 160 Niantic Ave *TF:* 800-821-1700 ■ *Web:* www.leesmfg.com	Providence	RI	02907	401-353-1740	353-0740
Magic Novelty Inc 308 Dyckman St *Web:* www.magicnovelty.com	New York	NY	10034	212-304-2777	567-2809
MS Co 61 School St *TF:* 800-675-4657 ■ *Web:* www.mscompany.net	Attleboro	MA	02703	508-222-1700	222-6449
Paul H Gesswein & Co 255 Hancock Ave *TF:* 800-544-2043 ■ *Web:* www.gesswein.com	Bridgeport	CT	06605	203-366-5400	366-3953
Providence Chain 225 Carolina Ave *TF:* 800-783-1499	Providence	RI	02905	401-781-1330	941-7932
Romanoff International Supply Corp 9 Deforest St *TF Cust Svc:* 800-221-7448 ■ *Web:* www.romanoff.com	Amityville	NY	11701	631-842-2400	842-0028
Stuller Settings Inc PO Box 87777 *TF:* 800-877-7777 ■ *Web:* www.stuller.com	Lafayette	LA	70598	800-877-7777	444-4741
Victors 3-D Inc 25 Brook Ave *TF:* 800-322-9008 ■ *Web:* www.victorssettings.com	Maywood	NJ	07607	201-845-4433	712-0818
William Goldberg Diamond Corp 589 5th Ave *Web:* www.williamgoldberg.com	New York	NY	10017	212-980-4343	980-6120

411 JEWELRY - COSTUME

	City	State	ZIP	Phone	Fax
1928 Jewelry Co 3000 W Empire Ave *TF:* 800-227-1928 ■ *Web:* www.1928.com	Burbank	CA	91504	818-841-1928	526-4558
A & Z Hayward Co 655 Waterman Ave *TF:* 800-556-7462 ■ *Web:* www.azhayward.com	East Providence	RI	02914	401-438-0550	438-6970
Alan Jewelry Co Inc 1 Baker St	Providence	RI	02905	401-785-0900	461-8715
American Ring Co Inc 19 Grosvenor Ave	East Providence	RI	02914	401-438-9060	438-3806
Arden Jewelry Mfg Co 10 Industrial Ln *Web:* www.ardenjewelry.com	Johnston	RI	02919	401-274-9800	273-1862
Bazar Inc Sales Co 793 Waterman Ave	East Providence	RI	02914	401-434-2595	434-0814
C & J Jewelry Co Inc 100 Dupont Dr *TF:* 800-556-7494 ■ *Web:* www.candjjewelry.com	Providence	RI	02907	401-944-2200	944-7915
Carolee Designs Inc 19 E Elm St *TF:* 800-227-6533 ■ *Web:* www.carolee.com	Greenwich	CT	06830	203-629-1139	629-1872
Donald Bruce & Co 3600 N Talman Ave	Chicago	IL	60618	773-477-8100	477-6293
Foster grant International 500 George Washington Hwy *TF:* 800-388-0258	Smithfield	RI	02917	401-231-3800	231-4625
Gem-Craft Inc 1420 Elmwood Ave	Cranston	RI	02910	401-854-1200	854-1204
Imperial-Deltah Inc 795 Waterman Ave *TF:* 800-556-7738	East Providence	RI	02914	401-434-2250	434-0814
Jewelry Fashions Inc 520 8th Ave 12th Fl	New York	NY	10018	212-947-7700	564-4829
Joan Rivers Worldwide 226 W 37th St *TF:* 800-337-4405	New York	NY	10018	212-751-2028	751-1967
Kirk's Folly 236 Chapman St *Web:* www.kirksfolly.com	Providence	RI	02905	401-941-4300	467-2360
Millard Wire 257 Industrial Dr *Web:* www.millardwire.com	Warwick	RI	02886	401-737-9330	737-9340
MJ Enterprises Inc 120 Railroad Ave *Web:* www.iopeners.com	Johnston	RI	02919	401-232-0200	232-7663
Museum Reproductions Inc 62 Harvard St *Web:* www.museumreproductions.com	Brookline	MA	02445	617-277-7707	277-3088
Plastic Craft Novelty Co Inc 12 Dunham St	Attleboro	MA	02703	508-222-1486	226-7295
Shira Accessories Ltd 30 W 36th St 5th Fl	New York	NY	10018	212-594-4455	594-4466
Speidel Corp 1425 Cranston St **Fax Area Code:* 800 ■ *Web:* www.speidel.com	Cranston	RI	02920	401-519-2000	928-2423*
Swank Inc 656 Joseph Warner Blvd	Taunton	MA	02780	508-822-2527	977-4428
Weingeroff Enterprises 1 Weingeroff Blvd	Cranston	RI	02910	401-467-2200	785-1320

412 JEWELRY - PRECIOUS METAL

	City	State	ZIP	Phone	Fax
American Achievement Corp 7211 Cir S Rd *TF:* 800-531-5131 ■ *Web:* www.artcarved.com	Austin	TX	78745	512-444-0571	444-0065
Armbrust International Ltd 735 Allens Ave *Web:* www.armbrustintl.com	Providence	RI	02905	401-781-3300	781-2590
Aurafin OroAmerica *Richline Group Inc* 6701 N Nob Hill Rd *TF:* 800-327-1808 ■ *Web:* www.richlinegroup.com/aurafin	Tamarac	FL	33321	954-718-3200	718-3208
BA Ballou & Co Inc 800 Waterman Ave *TF:* 800-729-3347 ■ *Web:* www.ballou.com	East Providence	RI	02914	401-438-7000	434-3336
Bijoux Terner LLC 6950 NW 77th Ct *Web:* www.bijouxterner.com	Miami	FL	33166	305-500-7500	262-9286
Brevard Designs 2304 Abbot Kinney Blvd PO Box 10999 *TF:* 866-669-7685 ■ *Web:* www.brevarddesign.com	Venice Beach	CA	90291	310-577-1888	306-7736
Colibri Group 100 Niantic Ave *TF Cust Svc:* 800-556-7354 ■ *Web:* www.colibri.com	Providence	RI	02907	401-943-2100	946-5276
Cordova Inc PO Box 521831 *TF Cust Svc:* 800-221-0744	Flushing	NY	11352	718-961-1020	353-5753
Creed Rosary Mfg Inc 15 Kenneth Miner Dr *TF Orders:* 800-255-7439 ■ *Web:* www.creedrosary.com	Wrentham	MA	02093	508-384-7600	384-2626
Danecraft Inc 1 Baker St *Web:* www.danecraft.com	Providence	RI	02905	401-941-7700	461-8715
David Friedman & Sons 10 E 38th St	New York	NY	10016	212-532-3253	481-3394
David Yurman Designs Inc 24 Vestry St *TF:* 800-593-1597 ■ *Web:* www.davidyurman.com	New York	NY	10013	212-896-1550	
Diablo Mfg Co Inc 900 Golden Gate Terr PO Box 1108 *TF Sales:* 800-551-2233 ■ *Web:* www.diablosilver.com	Grass Valley	CA	95945	530-272-2241	272-2243
Esposito Jewelry Inc 225 DuPont Dr	Providence	RI	02907	401-943-1900	943-1900
Excell Mfg Co 49 Pearl St *TF:* 800-343-8410 ■ *Web:* www.excellmfg.com	Attleboro	MA	02703	508-222-9234	222-6531
F Byard Brogan Inc 124 S Keswick Ave *TF:* 800-232-7642 ■ *Web:* www.bfbrogan.com	Glenside	PA	19038	215-885-3550	885-1366
Garden Jewelry Co Inc 36 47th St Suite 900 *TF:* 800-321-0259	New York	NY	10036	212-840-5500	421-7813
Gem East Corp 2124 2nd Ave *TF:* 800-426-0605 ■ *Web:* www.gemeast.com	Seattle	WA	98121	206-441-1700	448-1801
Gemveto Jewelry Co Inc 16 E 52nd St *TF:* 800-221-4438	New York	NY	10022	212-755-2522	755-2027
George H Fuller & Son Co 151 Exchange St *TF:* 800-237-0043 ■ *Web:* www.fullerfindings.com	Pawtucket	RI	02860	401-722-6530	723-1720
Gordon Erickson Co 13555 Grove Dr *TF:* 800-488-8443	Maple Grove	MN	55311	763-416-3771	416-3771
Hallmark Sweet 49 Pearl St *TF:* 800-225-2706 ■ *Web:* www.hallmarksweet.com	Attleboro	MA	02703	508-222-9234	222-6531
Hammerman Bros Inc 40 W 57th St Suite 400 *TF:* 800-223-6436	New York	NY	10019	212-956-2800	956-2769
Harry Winston Inc 718 5th Ave *TF:* 800-988-4110 ■ *Web:* www.harrywinston.com	New York	NY	10019	212-245-2000	489-0016
Herff Jones Inc 4501 W 62nd St **Fax:* Hum Res ■ *Web:* www.herffjones.com	Indianapolis	IN	46268	317-297-3740	329-3308*
Ira Green Inc 177 Georgia Ave *TF:* 800-663-7487 ■ *Web:* www.iragreen.com	Providence	RI	02905	401-467-4770	467-5557
J Jenkins Sons Co Inc 1801 Whitehead Rd *TF:* 800-296-3468 ■ *Web:* www.jjenkinssons.com	Baltimore	MD	21207	410-265-5200	298-4809
Jabel Inc 280 Sheffield St **Fax Area Code:* 908 ■ *TF:* 800-526-4597 ■ *Web:* www.jabel.com	Mountainside	NJ	07092	973-374-6000	654-4613*
Jacmel Jewelry Inc 30-30 47th Ave *Web:* www.jacmel.com	Long Island City	NY	11101	718-349-4300	349-4472
James Avery Craftsman Inc 145 Avery Rd N *TF:* 800-283-1770 ■ *Web:* www.jamesavery.com	Kerrville	TX	78029	830-895-1122	895-6623
Jewel America Inc 119 W 40th St *TF:* 800-328-7173	New York	NY	10018	212-220-4222	220-7227
Jostens Inc 3601 Minnesota Ave Suite 400 **Fax:* Hum Res ■ *TF:* 800-235-4774 ■ *Web:* www.jostens.com	Minneapolis	MN	55435	952-830-3300	830-3309*
Kinsley & Sons Inc 24 S Church St **Fax Area Code:* 800 ■ *TF:* 800-468-4428 ■ *Web:* www.gothic-jewelry.com	Union	MO	60384	636-583-9966	841-1228*
Klitzner Industries Inc 44 Warren St *TF:* 800-556-6860 ■ *Web:* www.klitzner.com	Providence	RI	02907	401-751-7500	273-7474
LG Balfour Co 7211 Cir S Rd *TF:* 888-225-3687 ■ *Web:* www.balfour.com	Austin	TX	78745	512-444-0571	
Loren Industries Inc 14051 NW 14th St *TF:* 800-772-8085 ■ *Web:* www.loren.com	Sunrise	FL	33023	954-835-0012	846-8819
Marfo Co 799 N Hague Ave	Columbus	OH	43204	614-276-3352	276-2279
Maui Divers of Hawaii 1520 Liona St *TF:* 800-462-4454 ■ *Web:* www.mauidivers.com	Honolulu	HI	96814	808-946-7979	946-0406
Michael Anthony Jewelers Inc 115 S Mac Questen Pkwy *TF:* 800-966-8800 ■ *Web:* www.michaelanthony.com	Mount Vernon	NY	10550	914-699-0000	699-2335
Michael Bondanza Inc 10 E 38th St *TF:* 800-835-0041 ■ *Web:* www.michaelbondanza.com	New York	NY	10016	212-869-0043	921-2565
Mtm Recognition Corp 3201 SE 29th St *TF:* 877-686-7464 ■ *Web:* www.mtmrecognition.com	Oklahoma City	OK	73115	405-670-4545	672-0964
Novell Design Studio 129 Chestnut St *Web:* www.novelldesignstudio.com	Roselle	NJ	07203	908-245-0700	245-5090
OC Tanner Co 1930 S State St *TF:* 800-453-7490 ■ *Web:* www.octanner.com	Salt Lake City	UT	84115	801-486-2430	483-8301
Oro-Cal Mfg Co Inc 1720 Bird St *TF:* 800-367-6225 ■ *Web:* www.orocal.com	Oroville	CA	95965	530-533-5085	533-5067
Ostbye & Anderson Inc 10055 51st Ave N **Fax Area Code:* 877 ■ *TF:* 800-328-4368 ■ *Web:* www.ostbye.com	Minneapolis	MN	55442	763-553-1515	553-1515*

Phone *Fax*

Paris 1624 Knowlton St. . . . . Cincinnati OH 45223 513-541-1888 542-8329
Web: www.paristiaras.com
Plainville Stock Co Inc
104 S St PO Box 1628 . . . . Plainville MA 02762 508-699-4434 695-0836
TF: 800-343-2112 ■ *Web:* www.plainvillestock.com
Relios Inc 6815 Academy Pkwy W Ne . . . . Albuquerque NM 87109 505-345-5304
TF: 800-827-6543 ■ *Web:* www.carolynpollack.com
Robert S Fisher & Co Inc
280 Sheffield St . . . . Mountainside NJ 07092 908-928-0002 928-0092
TF: 800-526-8052 ■ *Web:* www.rsfisher.com
Stamper Black Hills Gold Jewelry
7201 S Hwy 16. . . . . Rapid City SD 57702 605-342-0751 343-9783
TF Cust Svc: 800-523-7515 ■ *Web:* www.stamperbhg.com
Stanley Creations Inc 1414 Willow Ave . . . . Melrose Park PA 19027 215-635-6200 635-2708
TF: 800-220-1414 ■ *Web:* www.stanleycreations.com
Stern-Leach Co 49 Pearl St. . . . . Attleboro MA 02703 508-222-7400 699-4030
Web: www.sternleach.com
Sunshine Minting Inc
7600 Mineral Dr Suite 700. . . . . Coeur d""Alene ID 83815 208-772-9592 772-9739
TF: 800-274-5837 ■ *Web:* www.sunshinemint.com
Tache USA Inc 44-40 11th St . . . . Long Island City NY 11101 718-706-8989 392-0774
TF: 800-458-4300
Terryberry Co 2033 Oak Industrial Dr NE. . . . . Grand Rapids MI 49505 616-458-1391 458-5292
TF: 800-253-0882 ■ *Web:* www.terryberry.com
Tiffany & Co 727 5th Ave. . . . . New York NY 10022 212-755-8000 605-4465
NYSE: TIF ■ *TF Orders:* 800-526-0649 ■ *Web:* www.tiffany.com
Trebor Enterprises Ltd PO Box 88. . . . . Freeport IL 61032 815-235-1700 235-3900
Tru-Kay Mfg Co 2 Carol Dr . . . . Lincoln RI 02865 401-333-2105 334-0142
TF: 800-795-2105 ■ *Web:* www.richlinegroup.com
Uncas Mfg Co 150 Niantic Ave . . . . Providence RI 02907 401-944-4700 943-2951
Wheeler Mfg Co Inc 107 Main Ave PO Box 629 . . . . Lemmon SD 57638 605-374-3848 374-3655
TF: 800-843-1937 ■ *Web:* www.wheelerjewelry.com
Wright & Lato 800 Springdale Ave . . . . East Orange NJ 07017 973-674-8700 674-6964
TF: 800-724-1855 ■ *Web:* www.wrightandlato.com

413 JEWELRY STORES

Phone *Fax*

Albert S Smyth Co Inc 2020 York Rd. . . . . Timonium MD 21093 410-252-6666 252-2355
TF: 800-638-3333 ■ *Web:* www.smythjewelers.com
Argo & Lehne Jewelers Inc 3100 Tremont Rd . . . . Columbus OH 43221 614-457-6261 457-6716
Ashford.com 14001 NW 4th St. . . . . Sunrise FL 33325 954-453-2874 835-2236
TF: 888-342-6663 ■ *Web:* www.ashford.com
Ben Bridge Jeweler Inc PO Box 1908. . . . . Seattle WA 98111 206-239-6811 448-7456
TF Cust Svc: 888-917-9171 ■ *Web:* www.benbridge.com
Ben Moss Jewellers 300-201 Portage Ave . . . . Winnipeg MB R3B3K6 204-947-6682 988-0148
TF: 888-236-6677 ■ *Web:* www.benmoss.com
Blue Nile Inc 705 5th Ave S Suite 900. . . . . Seattle WA 98104 206-336-6700 336-7950
NASDAQ: NILE ■ *TF:* 800-242-2728 ■ *Web:* www.bluenile.com
Borsheim's Inc 120 Regency Pkwy . . . . Omaha NE 68114 402-391-0400 391-6694
TF: 800-642-4438 ■ *Web:* www.shop.borsheims.com
Brodkey Bros Inc 12165 W Ctr Rd Suite 73 . . . . Omaha NE 68144 402-330-9800 697-0603
Web: www.brodkeys.com
Bromberg & Co Inc 123 N 20th St . . . . Birmingham AL 35203 205-252-0221 458-0458
TF: 800-633-4616 ■ *Web:* www.brombergs.com
Carl Greve Jeweler Inc 640 SW Broadway . . . . Portland OR 97205 503-223-7121 223-9754
TF: 800-284-2044 ■ *Web:* www.carlgreve.com
Cartier Inc 2 E 52nd St. . . . . New York NY 10022 212-753-0111
TF Sales: 800-227-8437 ■ *Web:* www.cartier.com
Coleman E Adler & Sons Inc 722 Canal St. . . . . New Orleans LA 70130 504-523-5292 568-0610
TF: 800-925-7912 ■ *Web:* www.adlersjewelry.com
Corbo Jewelers Inc 58 Pk Ave . . . . Rutherford NJ 07070 201-438-4454 438-3108
Web: www.corbojewelers.com
De Von's Jewelers Inc 1910 29th St . . . . Sacramento CA 95816 916-451-6583 456-2514
Web: www.devonsjewelers.com
DGSE Cos Inc 11311 Reeder Rd. . . . . Dallas TX 75229 972-484-3662 241-0646
NASDAQ: DGSE ■ *TF:* 800-527-5307 ■ *Web:* www.dgse.com
Elegant Illusions Inc
542 Lighthouse Ave Suite 5 . . . . Pacific Grove CA 93950 831-649-1814 649-1001
TF: 800-551-5045 ■ *Web:* www.elegantillusions.com
Fantasy Diamond Corp 1550 W Carrol Ave . . . . Chicago IL 60607 312-583-3200 421-4444
TF: 800-621-4445 ■ *Web:* www.fantasydiamond.com
Finks Jewelry Inc 3545 Electric Rd . . . . Roanoke VA 24018 540-342-2991 342-5916
TF: 800-699-7464 ■ *Web:* www.finks.com
Firestone & Parson Inc 8 Newbury St. . . . . Boston MA 02116 617-266-1858
Freeman Jewelers Inc 76 Merchants Row. . . . . Rutland VT 05701 802-773-2792 773-1685
TF: 800-949-2792 ■ *Web:* www.freeman-jewelers.com
H Stern Jewelers Inc 645 5th Ave . . . . New York NY 10022 212-688-0300 888-5137
TF: 800-747-8376 ■ *Web:* www.hstern.net
H. E. Murdock Co Inc 88 Main St . . . . Waterville ME 04901 207-873-7036 859-9729
Web: www.daysjewelers.com
Haltoms Jewelers 317 Main St. . . . . Fort Worth TX 76102 817-336-4051 336-0064
TF: 800-850-2303 ■ *Web:* www.haltoms.com
Harry Ritchie's Jewelers Inc
956 Willamette St . . . . Eugene OR 97401 541-686-1787 485-8841
TF Cust Svc: 800-935-2850 ■ *Web:* www.harryritchies.com
Harry Winston Inc 718 5th Ave. . . . . New York NY 10019 212-245-2000 489-0016
TF: 800-988-4110 ■ *Web:* www.harrywinston.com
Helzberg Diamonds 1825 Swift Ave . . . . North Kansas City MO 64116 816-842-7780 221-5002*
**Fax: Sales* ■ *TF:* 800-669-7780 ■ *Web:* www.helzberg.com
JewelryWeb.com Inc 98 Cuttermill Rd # 464 . . . . Great Neck NY 11021 516-482-3982 955-2520*
**Fax Area Code: 800* ■ *TF:* 800-955-9245 ■ *Web:* www.jewelryweb.com
Karten's Jewelers 901 W Walnut Hill Ln . . . . Irving TX 75038 972-580-4000
TF: 800-333-6739
Kay Jewelers 375 Ghent Rd. . . . . Akron OH 44333 330-668-5000 668-5184
TF: 800-681-8796 ■ *Web:* www.kay.com
Levy Jewelers Inc 101 E Broughton St. . . . . Savannah GA 31401 912-233-1163 238-2110
TF: 800-237-5389 ■ *Web:* www.levyjewelers.com
Lux Bond & Green Inc 46 Lasalle Rd . . . . West Hartford CT 06107 860-521-3015 521-8693
TF: 800-524-7336 ■ *Web:* www.lbgreen.com
Mayor's Jewelers Inc
14051 NW 14th St Suite 200 . . . . Sunrise FL 33323 954-846-8000 846-2787
TF: 800-223-6964 ■ *Web:* www.mayors.com

Phone *Fax*

Morgan & Co 1131 Glendon Ave . . . . Los Angeles CA 90024 310-208-3377 208-6920
Web: www.morganjewellers.com
Odimo Inc 14001 NW 4th St. . . . . Sunrise FL 33325 954-993-4703 835-2236
NASDAQ: ODMO ■ *TF:* 888-342-6663
Osterman Jewelers 375 Ghent Rd . . . . Akron OH 44333 330-668-5000 668-5184
TF: 800-681-8796
Reeds Jewelers Inc 2525 S 17th St. . . . . Wilmington NC 28401 910-350-3100 350-3353
TF Orders: 877-406-3266 ■ *Web:* www.reeds.com
Ross Simons Jewelers Inc 9 Ross Simons Dr . . . . Cranston RI 02920 401-463-3100 463-8599
TF: 800-835-0919 ■ *Web:* www.ross-simons.com
Samuels Jewelers Inc
2914 Montopolis Dr Suite 200 . . . . Austin TX 78741 512-369-1400 369-1500
TF: 877-726-8357 ■ *Web:* www.samuelsjewelers.com
Sherwood Management Co Inc PO Box 3750 . . . . . . Culver City CA 90231 310-665-2100 665-2101
Web: www.danielsjewelers.com
Sultan Co 3049 Ualena St 14th Fl. . . . . Honolulu HI 96819 808-833-7772 837-1358
TF: 800-260-3912
Tiffany & Co 727 5th Ave. . . . . New York NY 10022 212-755-8000 605-4465
NYSE: TIF ■ *TF Orders:* 800-526-0649 ■ *Web:* www.tiffany.com
Trabert & Hoeffer Inc 111 E Oak St. . . . . Chicago IL 60611 312-787-1654 787-1446
Van Cleef & Arpels Inc 744 5th Ave . . . . New York NY 10019 212-644-9500 355-5697
TF: 877-826-2533 ■ *Web:* www.vancleef-arpels.com
Zale Corp 901 W Walnut Hill Ln. . . . . Irving TX 75038 972-580-4000 580-5907*
NYSE: ZLC ■ **Fax: Mail Rm* ■ *TF Cust Svc:* 800-866-9700 ■ *Web:* www.zalecorp.com
Zale Corp Bailey Banks & Biddle Div
901 W Walnut Hill Ln . . . . Irving TX 75038 972-580-4000 580-5907*
**Fax: Mail Rm* ■ *TF Cust Svc:* 800-651-4222 ■ *Web:* www.zalecorp.com
Zale Corp Gordon's Jewelers Div
901 W Walnut Hill Ln . . . . Irving TX 75038 972-580-4000 580-5523
TF Cust Svc: 888-467-3661 ■ *Web:* www.zalecorp.com
Zale Corp Zales Jewelers Div
901 W Walnut Hill Ln . . . . Irving TX 75038 972-580-4000 580-5907
TF Cust Svc: 800-866-9700 ■ *Web:* www.zales.com

414 JEWELRY, WATCHES, GEMS - WHOL

Phone *Fax*

Antwerp Diamond Distributors
6 E 45th St Suite 302 . . . . New York NY 10017 212-319-3300 207-8168
TF: 800-223-0444
Charles & Colvard Ltd
300 Perimiter Pk Dr Suite A . . . . Morrisville NC 27560 919-468-0399 468-0486
NASDAQ: CTHR ■ *TF:* 800-210-4367 ■ *Web:* www.moissanite.com
Charles Wolf Couture 579 5th Ave Suite 910 . . . . New York NY 10017 212-371-6130
Web: www.charleswolf.com
Citra Trading Corp 590 5th Ave 14th Fl . . . . New York NY 10036 212-354-1000 382-2024
TF Orders: 800-223-6515 ■ *Web:* www.citra.com
Continental Coin Corp 5627 Sepulveda Blvd. . . . . Van Nuys CA 91411 818-781-4232 779-6320
TF: 888-367-9456
Empire Diamond Corp 350 5th Ave Suite 7619 . . . . New York NY 10118 212-564-4777 564-4960
TF: 800-728-3425 ■ *Web:* www.empirediamond.com
Genender International Imports Inc
44 Century Dr. . . . . Wheeling IL 60090 847-541-3333 541-4444
TF: 800-547-3333
Gerson Co 1450 S Lone Elm St. . . . . Olathe KS 66061 913-262-7400 262-3568
TF: 800-999-7401 ■ *Web:* www.gersoncompany.com
Harry Winston Diamond Corp PO Box 4569. . . . . Toronto ON M5W4T9 416-362-2237 362-2230
Web: www.investor.harrywinston.com
Henri Stern Watch Agency Inc The
1 Rockefeller Plaza Suite 930 . . . . New York NY 10020 212-218-1240 218-1255
Web: www.patek.com
HS Strygler & Co Inc 37 W 20th St Suite 1210 . . . . New York NY 10011 212-758-4100 727-3700
Joseph Blank Inc 62 W 47th St Suite 808 . . . . New York NY 10036 212-575-9050 302-8521
TF: 800-223-7666 ■ *Web:* www.josephblank.com
Leo Wolleman Inc 45 W 45th St 10th Fl. . . . . New York NY 10036 212-840-1881 869-4216
TF: 800-223-5667 ■ *Web:* www.leowolleman.com
Lyles-De Grazier Co 2050 N Stemmons Fwy . . . . Dallas TX 75207 214-747-3558 741-3513
TF: 800-442-7125
Metal Marketplace International (MMI)
718 Sansom St . . . . Philadelphia PA 19106 215-592-8777 592-8195
TF: 800-523-9191 ■ *Web:* www.metalmarketplace.com
Paramount Sales Co Inc 10140 Gallows Pt Dr . . . . Knoxville TN 37931 865-470-9977 470-9801
TF Cust Svc: 800-251-9183 ■ *Web:* www.paramountjewelry.com
Roman Co 1201 Hanley Industrial Ct . . . . Saint Louis MO 63144 314-962-9750 968-5483
TF: 888-666-7744 ■ *Web:* www.romancompany.com
SKL Co Inc 545 Island Rd. . . . . Ramsey NJ 07446 201-825-6633 825-8009
STS Jewels Inc 30-30 47th Ave 5th Fl. . . . . Long Island City NY 11101 718-306-1700 306-1728
Web: www.stsjewels.com
Thunderbird Supply Co 1907 W Historic Rt 66 . . . . Gallup NM 87301 505-722-4323 722-6736
Web: www.thunderbirdsupply.com
Webster Watch Co Assoc 44 E 32nd St 7th Fl . . . . New York NY 10016 212-889-3560 213-2649*
**Fax: Sales* ■ *TF Orders:* 800-289-8963
World Minerals Inc 130 Castilian Dr . . . . Santa Barbara CA 93117 805-562-0200 562-0298
TF: 800-893-4445 ■ *Web:* www.worldminerals.com

415 JUVENILE DETENTION FACILITIES

SEE ALSO Correctional & Detention Management (Privatized) p. 1764; Correctional Facilities - Federal p. 1764; Correctional Facilities - State p. 1764
Listings Are Organized Alphabetically By States.

LABELS - FABRIC

SEE Narrow Fabric Mills p. 2710

Bethel Youth Facility
950 State Hwy PO Box 1989. . . . . Bethel AK 99559 907-543-5200 543-2710
TF: 800-478-9559
Fairbanks Youth Facility 1502 Wilbur St . . . . Fairbanks AK 99701 907-451-2150 451-5152
Johnson Youth Ctr 3252 Hospital Dr . . . . Juneau AK 99801 907-586-9433 463-4933
TF: 800-478-9433
McLaughlin Youth Ctr 2600 Providence Dr. . . . . Anchorage AK 99508 907-261-4399 261-4308

				Phone	Fax
Nome Youth Facility 804 E 4th St	Nome	AK	99762	907-443-5434	443-7295
Arkansas Juvenile Access & Treatment Ctr 1501 Woody Dr	Alexander	AR	72002	501-682-9800	682-9801
Web: www.arkansas.gov					
Colt Juvenile Treatment Ctr 1388 SFC 118	Colt	AR	72326	870-633-6467	633-6732
Jack Jones Jefferson County Juvenile Detention Ctr 301 E 2nd Ave	Pine Bluff	AR	71601	870-541-8502	541-8504
Web: www.jeffcoso.com					
Northwest Arkansas Regional Juvenile Program PO Box 487	Mansfield	AR	72944	479-928-0166	928-2060
El Paso de Robles Youth Correctional Facility 4545 Airport Rd PO Box 7008	Paso Robles	CA	93447	805-238-4040	227-2569
Web: www.cdcr.ca.gov					
OH Close Youth Correctional Facility 7650 S Newcastle Rd PO Box 213001	Stockton	CA	95213	209-944-6301	944-5612
Preston Youth Correctional Facility 201 Waterman Rd	Ione	CA	95640	209-274-8000	274-0276
Ventura Youth Correctional Facility 3100 Wright Rd	Camarillo	CA	93010	805-485-7951	485-2801
Web: www.cdcr.ca.gov					
Adams Youth Services Ctr 1933 E Bridge St	Brighton	CO	80601	303-659-4450	637-0471
Gilliam Youth Services Ctr 2844 Downing St	Denver	CO	80205	303-291-8951	291-8990
Grand Mesa Youth Services Ctr 360 28th Rd	Grand Junction	CO	81501	970-242-1521	242-8127
Web: www.colorado.gov					
Lookout Mountain Youth Services Ctr 2901 Ford St	Golden	CO	80401	303-273-2600	273-2622
Marvin W Foote Youth Services Ctr 13500 E Fremont Pl	Englewood	CO	80112	303-768-7520	768-7516
Web: www.colorado.gov					
Mount View Youth Services Ctr 7862 W Mansfield Pkwy	Denver	CO	80235	303-987-4525	987-4538
Platte Valley Youth Services Ctr 2200 'O' St	Greeley	CO	80631	970-304-6220	304-6228
Pueblo Youth Services Ctr 1406 W 17th St	Pueblo	CO	81003	719-546-4915	546-4923
Spring Creek Youth Services Ctr 3190 E Las Vegas St	Colorado Springs	CO	80906	719-390-2788	390-2792
Zebulon Pike Youth Services Ctr 1427 W Rio Grande St	Colorado Springs	CO	80906	719-329-6924	635-2549
Connecticut Juvenile Training School 1225 Silver St	Middletown	CT	06457	860-638-2400	638-2410
Manson Youth Institution 42 Jarvis St	Cheshire	CT	06410	203-806-2500	699-1845
Ferris School 959 Centre Rd	Wilmington	DE	19805	302-993-3800	993-3820
New Castle County Detention Ctr 963 Centre Rd	Wilmington	DE	19805	302-633-3100	995-8393
Stevenson House Detention Ctr 750 N Dupont Hwy	Milford	DE	19963	302-422-1407	422-1535
Bay Regional Juvenile Detention Ctr 450 E 11th St	Panama City	FL	32401	850-872-4706	873-7099
Web: www.djj.state.fl.us					
Brevard Regional Juvenile Detention Ctr 5225 DeWitt Ave	Cocoa	FL	32927	321-690-3400	504-0907
Duval Regional Juvenile Detention Ctr 1241 E 8th St	Jacksonville	FL	32206	904-798-4820	798-4825
Escambia Regional Juvenile Detention Ctr 1800 W St Mary Ave	Pensacola	FL	32501	850-595-8820	595-8410
Hillsborough Regional Juvenile Detention Center West 3948 ML King Jr Blvd	Tampa	FL	33614	813-871-7650	673-4459
Leon Regional Juvenile Detention Ctr 2303 Ronellis Dr	Tallahassee	FL	32310	850-488-7672	922-2842
Manatee Regional Juvenile Detention Ctr 1803 5th St W	Bradenton	FL	34205	941-741-3023	741-3061
Marion Regional Juvenile Detention Ctr 3040 NW 10th St	Ocala	FL	34475	352-732-1450	732-1457
Okaloosa Regional Juvenile Detention Ctr 4448 Straight Line Rd	Crestview	FL	32439	850-689-7800	689-0999
Orange Regional Juvenile Detention Ctr 2800 S Bumby Ave	Orlando	FL	32806	407-897-2800	893-3623*
Pasco Regional Juvenile Detention Ctr 28534 SR 52	San Antonio	FL	33576	352-588-5900	588-5909
Polk Regional Juvenile Detention Ctr 2155 Bob Phillips Rd	Bartow	FL	33830	863-534-7090	534-7024
Saint Lucie Regional Juvenile Detention Ctr 1301 Bell Ave	Fort Pierce	FL	34982	772-468-3940	468-4005
Seminole Regional Juvenile Detention Ctr 200 Bush Blvd	Sanford	FL	32773	407-330-6750	328-3947
Hawaii Youth Correctional Facility 42-477 Kalanianaole Hwy	Kailua	HI	96734	808-266-9500	266-9506
Juvenile Corrections Center-Nampa 1650 11th Ave N	Nampa	ID	83687	208-465-8443	465-8484
Juvenile Corrections Center-Saint Anthony 2220 E 600 N PO Box 40	Saint Anthony	ID	83445	208-624-3462	624-0973
Illinois Youth Center Chicago 136 N Western Ave	Chicago	IL	60612	312-633-5219	633-5229
Illinois Youth Center Harrisburg 1201 W Poplar St	Harrisburg	IL	62946	618-252-8681	252-2519
Illinois Youth Center Joliet 2848 W McDonough St	Joliet	IL	60436	815-725-1206	725-9819
Illinois Youth Center Saint Charles 3825 Campton Hills Rd	Saint Charles	IL	60175	630-584-0506	584-1014
Illinois Youth Center Warrenville 30 W 200 Ferry Rd	Warrenville	IL	60555	630-983-6231	983-6231
Camp Summit Boot Camp 2407 N 500 W	La Porte	IN	46350	219-326-1188	326-9218
Logansport Juvenile Correctional Facility 1118 S St Rd 25	Logansport	IN	46947	574-753-7571	732-0729
Web: www.in.gov/idoc					
Plainfield Re-Entry Educational Facility 501 W Main St	Plainfield	IN	46168	317-839-7751	838-7548
Web: www.in.gov/indcorrection/reentry/center					
South Bend Juvenile Correctional Facility 4650 Old Cleveland Rd	South Bend	IN	46628	574-232-8808	232-9270
Iowa Juvenile Home 701 S Church St	Toledo	IA	52342	641-484-2560	484-2816
State Training School 3211 Edgington Ave	Eldora	IA	50627	641-858-5402	858-2416
Atchison Juvenile Correctional Facility 1900 N 2nd St	Atchison	KS	66002	913-367-6590	367-2221
Beloit Juvenile Correctional Facility 1720 N Hersey St PO Box 427	Beloit	KS	67420	785-738-5735	738-3314
Larned Juvenile Correctional Facility 1301 Kansas Hwy 264	Larned	KS	67550	620-285-0300	285-0301
Topeka Juvenile Correctional Complex 1430 NW 25th St	Topeka	KS	66618	785-354-9800	354-9878
Mountainview Youth Development Ctr 1182 Dover Rd	Charleston	ME	04422	207-285-0880	285-0836
Web: www.maine.gov/corrections/juvenile/mvydc.htm					
MCF-Togo 62741 County Rd 551	Togo	MN	55723	218-376-4411	376-4489
Web: www.thistledewprograms.com					
Pine Hills Youth Correctional Facility 4 N Haynes Ave	Miles City	MT	59301	406-232-1377	232-7432
Web: www.cor.mt.gov					
Riverside Youth Correctional Facility 2 Riverside Rd PO Box 88	Boulder	MT	59632	406-225-4500	225-4511
Youth Transition Ctr 4212 3rd Ave S	Great Falls	MT	59405	406-452-1792	452-8745
Garden State Youth Correctional Facility PO Box 11401	Yardville	NJ	08620	609-298-6300	324-0677
Mountainview Youth Correctional Facility 31 Petticoat Ln	Annandale	NJ	08801	908-638-6191	638-4423
Carlsbad Community Residential Facility 106 N Mesquite St	Carlsbad	NM	88220	505-827-7629	885-8683
La Placita Reintegration Ctr 3102 N Florida PO Box 1966	Alamogordo	NM	88310	505-434-0515	439-0321
Web: www.nmjustice.net					
New Mexico Boys' School 201 Hwy 468	Springer	NM	87747	505-483-2475	483-5030
Crossroads Juvenile Ctr 17 Bristol St	Brooklyn	NY	11212	718-495-8160	495-8254
Horizon Juvenile Ctr 560 Brook Ave	Bronx	NY	10455	718-292-0065	401-8109
Bladen Correctional Ctr 5853 US 701 N	Elizabethtown	NC	28337	910-862-3107	862-8563
Web: www.doc.state.nc.us					
Foothills Correctional Institution 5150 Western Ave	Morganton	NC	28655	828-438-5585	438-5598
Morrison Youth Institution PO Box 169	Hoffman	NC	28347	910-281-3161	281-0116
Western Youth Institution 5155 Western Ave	Morganton	NC	28655	828-438-6037	438-6076
Cuyahoga Hills Juvenile Correctional Facility 4321 Green Rd	Highland Hills	OH	44128	216-464-8200	464-3540
Web: www.dys.ohio.gov/dysweb/CHBSfacility.aspx					
Indian River Juvenile Correctional Facility 2775 Indian River Rd SW	Massillon	OH	44648	330-837-4211	837-4740
Web: www.dys.ohio.gov					
Ohio Dept of Youth Services 51 N High St	Columbus	OH	43215	614-466-4314	
Web: www.dys.ohio.gov					
Ohio River Juvenile Correctional Facility 4696 Gallia Pike	Franklin Furnace	OH	45629	740-354-7000	354-7022
Scioto Juvenile Correctional Facility 5993 Home Rd	Delaware	OH	43015	740-881-3250	881-5944
Web: www.dys.ohio.gov/dysweb/SJJCfacility.aspx					
Central Oklahoma Detention Juvenile Ctr 700 S 9th St	Tecumseh	OK	74873	405-598-2135	598-8713
Web: www.ok.gov					
Southwest Oklahoma Juvenile Ctr 300 S Broadway	Manitou	OK	73555	580-397-3511	397-3491
Camp Florence 04859 S Jetty Rd	Florence	OR	97439	541-997-2076	997-4217
Camp Tillamook 6820 Barracks Cir	Tillamook	OR	97141	503-842-4243	842-1476
Eastern Oregon Youth Correctional Facility 1800 W Monroe St	Burns	OR	97720	541-573-3133	573-3665
Hillcrest Youth Correctional Facility 2450 Strong Rd SE	Salem	OR	97302	503-986-0400	986-0406
MacLaren Youth Correctional Facility 2630 N Pacific Hwy	Woodburn	OR	97071	503-981-9531	982-4439
Oregon Youth Authority Riverbend (OYA) 58231 Oregon Hwy 244	La Grande	OR	97850	541-663-8801	663-9181
Web: www.oregon.gov/OYA/FACLTY/riverbend.shtml					
Rogue Valley Youth Correctional Facility 2001 NE 'F' St	Grants Pass	OR	97526	541-471-2862	471-2861
Tillamook Youth Correctional Facility 6700 Officer Row	Tillamook	OR	97141	503-842-2565	842-4918
Web: www.oya.state.or.us/tycf.html					
Cresson Secure Treatment Unit 251 Corrections Rd PO Box 269	Cresson	PA	16630	814-886-6903	886-6296
Loysville Secure Treatment Unit 10 Opportunity Dr	Loysville	PA	17047	717-789-4449	789-5538
Loysville Youth Development Ctr 10 Opportunity Dr	Loysville	PA	17047	717-789-3841	789-5538
New Castle Youth Development Ctr 1745 Frew Mill Rd	New Castle	PA	16101	724-656-7300	656-0999
North Central Secure Treatment Unit 13 Kirk Bride Dr	Danville	PA	17821	570-271-4700	271-4749
TF: 877-264-9782					
South Mountain Secure Treatment Unit 10056 S Mountain Rd	South Mountain	PA	17261	717-749-7904	749-7905
Birchwood Institution 5000 Broad River Rd	Columbia	SC	29212	803-896-9104	896-6157
Web: www.scdjj.net					
STAR Academy 12279 Brady Dr	Custer	SD	57730	605-673-2521	673-5489
Web: www.doc.sd.gov					
Mountain View Youth Development Ctr 809 Peal Ln	Dandridge	TN	37725	865-397-0174	397-0738
Woodland Hills Youth Development Ctr 3965 Stewarts Ln	Nashville	TN	37218	615-532-2000	532-8402
Corsicana Residential Treatment Ctr 4000 W 2nd Ave	Corsicana	TX	75110	903-875-3200	872-6667
Web: www.tyc.state.tx.us					
Crockett State School 1701 SW Loop 304	Crockett	TX	75835	936-852-5000	544-2543
Evins Regional Juvenile Ctr 3801 E Monte Cristo Rd	Edinburg	TX	78541	956-289-5500	289-5577

Phone | Fax

Gainesville State School 1379 FM 678 Gainesville TX 76240 940-665-0701 665-0469
Web: www.tyc.state.tx.us

Giddings State School PO Box 600 Giddings TX 78942 979-542-3686 542-0177
Web: www.tyc.state.tx.us

Woodside Juvenile Rehabilitation Ctr
26 Woodside Dr E Colchester VT 05446 802-655-4990 655-3095
Web: www.jrsa.org

Beaumont Juvenile Correctional Ctr
3500 Beaumont Rd Beaumont VA 23014 804-556-3316 556-7288

Bon Air Juvenile Correctional Ctr
1900 Chatsworth Ave Bon Air VA 23235 804-323-2550 323-2440

Culpeper Juvenile Correctional Ctr
12240 Coffeewood Dr Mitchells VA 22729 540-727-3333 727-7117

Hanover Juvenile Correctional Ctr
7093 Broadneck Rd Hanover VA 23069 804-537-5316 537-5907

Oak Ridge Juvenile Correctional Ctr
1801 Old Bon Air Rd Richmond VA 23235 804-323-2335 323-2310

Davis Juvenile Correctional Ctr
Blackwater Falls Rd Davis WV 26260 304-259-5241 259-4851
Web: www.wvdjs.state.wv.us

Ethan Allen School PO Box 900 Wales WI 53183 262-646-3341 646-3761
Web: www.wi-doc.com

Lincoln Hills School W4380 Copper Lake Rd Irma WI 54442 715-536-8386 536-8236

Prairie du Chien Correctional Institution
500 E Parrish St Prairie du Chien WI 53821 608-326-7828 326-5960
Web: www.wi-doc.com

Racine Youthful Offender Correctional Facility
PO Box 2500 Racine WI 53404 262-638-1999 638-1777

Southern Oaks Girls School
21425-B Spring St Union Grove WI 53182 262-878-6500 878-6520

Regional Juvenile Detention Center Inc
201 N David St 3rd Fl Casper WY 82601 307-234-0057 268-8562

416 LABELS - OTHER THAN FABRIC

Phone | Fax

Accurate Dial & Nameplate Inc
329 Mira Loma Ave Glendale CA 91204 323-245-9181 243-6793*
**Fax Area Code:* 818 ■ *TF:* 800-400-4455 ■ *Web:* www.accuratedial.com

Acro Labels Inc 2530 Wyandotte Rd Willow Grove PA 19090 215-657-5366 657-3325
TF: 800-355-2235 ■ *Web:* www.acrolabels.com

Alcop Adhesive Label Co 826 Perkins Ln Beverly NJ 08010 609-871-4400 871-3017

AME Label Corp 25159 Ave Stanford Valencia CA 91355 661-257-2200 257-7981
Web: www.amelabel.com

American Law Label Inc 4135 S Pulaski Rd Chicago IL 60632 773-523-2222 523-3332
TF: 800-529-5223 ■ *Web:* www.americanlawlabel.com

Arch Crown Tags Inc 177 Main St West Orange NJ 07052 973-731-6300 731-2228
TF: 800-526-8353 ■ *Web:* www.archcrown.com

Art Style Printing Inc Dataware Div
7570 Renwick Dr Houston TX 77081 713-432-1023 432-1385
TF: 800-426-4844 ■ *Web:* www.datawarelabels.com

Avery Dennison Automotive Products Div
15939 Industrial Pkwy Cleveland OH 44135 216-267-8700
Web: www.iapna.averydennison.com

Avery Dennison Business Media Div
685 Howard St Buffalo NY 14206 716-852-2155 852-2175
TF: 800-777-2879 ■ *Web:* www.businessmedia.averydennison.com

Avery Dennison Corp 150 N Orange Grove Blvd Pasadena CA 91103 626-304-2000 304-2192
NYSE: AVY ■ *TF Cust Svc:* 800-252-8379 ■ *Web:* www.averydennison.com

Avery Dennison Industrial Products Div
17700 Foltz Industrial Pkwy Strongsville OH 44149 440-878-7000 878-7103
TF: 888-283-7998 ■ *Web:* www.iapna.averydennison.com

Best Label Co 2900 Faber St Union City CA 94587 510-489-5400 489-2914
TF: 800-637-5333 ■ *Web:* www.bestlabel.com

Blue Ribbon Tag & Label Corp
4035 N 29th Ave Hollywood FL 33020 954-922-9292 922-9977
TF: 800-433-4974 ■ *Web:* www.blueribbonlabel.com

Brady Corp 6555 W Good Hope Rd Milwaukee WI 53223 414-358-6600 292-2289*
NYSE: BRC ■ **Fax Area Code:* 800 ■ **Fax:* Cust Svc ■ *TF Cust Svc:* 800-537-8791 ■ *Web:* www.bradycorp.com

Brady Identification Solutions
6555 W Good Hope Rd Milwaukee WI 53223 414-358-6600 292-2289*
**Fax Area Code:* 800 ■ **Fax:* Cust Svc ■ *TF Cust Svc:* 800-537-8791 ■ *Web:* www.bradyid.com

CCL Label Inc 161 Worcester Rd Suite 502 Framingham MA 01701 508-872-4511 872-7671
Web: www.cclind.com

Cellotape Inc 47623 Fremont Blvd Fremont CA 94538 510-651-5551 651-8091
TF: 800-231-0608 ■ *Web:* www.cellotape.com

Chase Corp 26 Summer St Bridgewater MA 02324 508-279-1789 697-6419
AMEX: CCF ■ *Web:* www.chasecorp.com

Clamp Swing Pricing Co Inc 8386 Capwell Dr Oakland CA 94621 510-567-1600 567-1600
TF: 800-227-7615

Continental Identification Products Inc
PO Box 98 Sparta MI 49345 616-887-7341 887-0154
TF: 800-247-2499 ■ *Web:* www.continentalid.com

Cortegra 6 Commerce Rd Fairfield NJ 07004 973-808-8000 808-8010
Web: www.cortegra.com

Data Label Inc 1000 Spruce St Terre Haute IN 47807 812-232-0408 238-1847
TF: 800-457-0676

DeskTop Labels 7277 Boone Ave N Minneapolis MN 55428 763-531-5800 531-5764
TF: 800-241-9730 ■ *Web:* www.desktoplabels.com

Discount Labels Inc 4115 Profit Ct New Albany IN 47150 812-945-2617 995-9600*
**Fax Area Code:* 800 ■ *TF:* 800-995-9500 ■ *Web:* www.discountlabels.com

East-West Label Co Inc 1000 E Hector St Conshohocken PA 19428 610-825-0410 825-6077
TF: 800-441-7333 ■ *Web:* www.ewlabel.com

Ennis Tag & Label 118 W Main St Wolfe City TX 75496 903-496-2244 453-2674*
**Fax Area Code:* 800 ■ *TF:* 800-527-1008 ■ *Web:* www.ennistagandlabel.com

General Data Co Inc 4354 Ferguson Dr Cincinnati OH 45245 513-752-7978 752-6947*
**Fax:* Sales ■ *TF:* 800-733-5252 ■ *Web:* www.general-data.com

Phone | Fax

Gilbreth Packaging Systems 3001 State Rd Croydon PA 19021 215-785-3350 785-4077
TF: 800-630-2413 ■ *Web:* www.gilbrethusa.com

Grand Rapids Label Co
2351 Oak Industrial Dr NE Grand Rapids MI 49505 616-459-8134 459-4543
TF: 800-552-5215 ■ *Web:* www.grlabel.com

Graphic Technology Inc 301 Gardner Dr New Century KS 66031 913-829-8000 829-1462
TF: 800-767-9930 ■ *Web:* www.graphic-tech.com

Green Bay Packaging Inc 1700 Webster Ct Green Bay WI 54302 920-433-5111
TF: 800-558-4008 ■ *Web:* www.gbp.com

Harris Industries Inc
5181 Argosy Ave Huntington Beach CA 92649 714-898-8048 898-7108
TF: 800-222-6866 ■ *Web:* www.harrisind.com

Hooven-Dayton Corp 8060 Technology Blvd Dayton OH 45424 937-233-4473 233-9382
TF: 800-621-9291 ■ *Web:* www.hoovendaytonlabels.com

Impact Label Corp 3434 S Burdick St Kalamazoo MI 49001 269-381-4280 381-1055
TF: 800-820-0362 ■ *Web:* www.impactlabel.com

International Label & Printing Co Inc
2550 United Ln Elk Grove Village IL 60007 630-595-1442 595-1747
TF: 800-244-1442 ■ *Web:* www.internationallabel.com

Label Art 1 Riverside Way Wilton NH 03086 603-654-6131 733-7800*
**Fax Area Code:* 800 ■ **Fax:* Cust Svc ■ *TF:* 800-258-1050 ■ *Web:* www.labelart.com

Label Craft Corp 5140 Firestone Pl South Gate CA 90280 323-564-5956 564-8510

Label Graphics Co Inc
1225 Carnegie St Suite 104B Rolling Meadows IL 60008 847-454-1005 454-1008

Labelmaster Co 5724 N Pulaski Rd Chicago IL 60646 773-478-0900 478-6054
TF: 800-621-5808 ■ *Web:* www.labelmaster.com

Labeltape Inc 4489 E Paris Ave SE Grand Rapids MI 49512 616-698-1830 698-7831
TF: 800-928-4537 ■ *Web:* www.labeltape-inc.com

Lancer Label 301 S 74th St Omaha NE 68114 402-390-9119 390-9459
TF Cust Svc: 800-228-7074 ■ *Web:* www.lancerlabel.com

LGInternational 6700 SW Bradbury Ct Portland OR 97224 503-620-0520 620-3296
TF: 800-345-0534 ■ *Web:* www.lgintl.com

McCourt Label Co 20 Egbert Ln Lewis Run PA 16738 814-362-3851 362-4156
TF: 800-458-2390 ■ *Web:* www.mccourtlabel.com

Mepco Label Systems 29 N Aurora St Stockton CA 95202 209-946-0201 946-0164
TF: 800-975-2235 ■ *Web:* www.mepcolabel.com

Morgan Fabrics Corp 4265 Exchange Ave Los Angeles CA 90058 323-583-9981 923-2352
Web: www.morganfabrics.com

MPI Label Systems Inc 450 Courtney Rd Sebring OH 44672 330-938-2134 938-9878
TF: 800-837-2134 ■ *Web:* www.mpilabels.com

Multi-Color Corp 4053 Clough Woods Dr Batavia OH 45103 513-381-1480 381-2240
NASDAQ: LABL ■ *Web:* www.multicolorcorp.com

Nashua Corp Label Products Div 3838 S 108th St Omaha NE 68144 402-397-3600 392-6080
TF: 800-533-8806 ■ *Web:* www.nashua.com/units/label/label.html

National Label Co Inc 2025 Joshua Rd Lafayette Hill PA 19444 610-825-3250 834-8854
TF: 800-872-5223 ■ *Web:* www.nationallabel.com

National Printing Converters Inc
18 S Murphy Ave Brazil IN 47834 812-448-2555 669-0329*
**Fax Area Code:* 800 ■ *TF:* 800-877-6724 ■ *Web:* www.npclabels.com

Northeast Data Services 1316 College Ave Elmira NY 14901 607-733-5541 735-4540
TF Cust Svc: 800-845-3720 ■ *Web:* www.artisticlabels.com

Pamco Printed Tape & Label Co
2200 S Wolf Rd Des Plaines IL 60018 847-803-2200 803-2209
Web: www.pamcolabel.com

Paxar Corp 105 Corporate Pk Dr White Plains NY 10604 914-697-6800 697-6894
TF: 888-447-2927 ■ *Web:* www.paxar.com

Paxar Corp Systems Group 1 Wilcox St Sayre PA 18840 570-888-6641 888-4080
TF: 800-947-2927

Phifer Inc 4400 Kauloosa Ave PO Box 1700 Tuscaloosa AL 35401 205-345-2120 759-4450
Web: www.phifer.com

Precision Printing & Packaging Inc
801 Alfred Thun Rd Clarksville TN 37040 931-920-9000 920-9001

Print-O-Tape Inc 755 Tower Rd Mundelein IL 60060 847-362-1476 949-7449
TF: 800-346-6311 ■ *Web:* www.printotape.com

Printed Systems 1271 Gillingham Rd Neenah WI 54956 920-886-2000 886-2036*
**Fax:* Sales ■ *TF Sales:* 800-352-2332 ■ *Web:* www.psdtag.com

Quikstik Label Mfg Co 210 Broadway Everett MA 02149 617-389-7570 381-9280
TF: 800-225-3496 ■ *Web:* www.qsxlabels.com

Reidler Decal Corp
1 Reidler Rd St Clair Industrial Pk Saint Clair PA 17970 570-429-1812 429-1528
TF: 800-628-7770 ■ *Web:* www.reidlerdecal.com

Shamrock Scientific Specialty Systems Inc
34 Davis Dr Bellwood IL 60104 708-547-9005 248-1907*
**Fax Area Code:* 800 ■ *TF:* 800-323-0249 ■ *Web:* www.shamrocklabels.com

Smyth Cos Inc 1085 Snelling Ave N Saint Paul MN 55180 651-646-4544 646-8949
TF: 800-642-4544 ■ *Web:* www.smythco.com

Sohn Mfg Inc 544 Sohn Dr Elkhart Lake WI 53020 920-876-3361 876-2952
Web: www.sohnmanufacturing.com

Spear Inc 48 Powers St Milford NH 03055 603-673-6353 672-8107
TF: 800-627-7327 ■ *Web:* www.spearinc.com

Spec Print Inc 1710 N Mt Juliet Rd Mount Juliet TN 37122 615-758-5913 758-5103
TF: 800-989-3325 ■ *Web:* www.specprintinc.com

Spectrum Label Corp 30803 San Clemente St Hayward CA 94544 510-477-0707 477-0787
TF: 800-545-2235 ■ *Web:* www.spectrumlabel.com

Spinnaker Coating Inc 518 E Water St Troy OH 45373 937-332-6500 335-2843
TF: 800-543-9452 ■ *Web:* www.spinnakercoating.com

Strutz International Inc
440 Mars-Valencia Rd PO Box 509 Mars PA 16046 724-625-1501 625-3570
Web: www.strutz.com

Tag-It Pacific Inc
21900 Burbank Blvd Suite 270 Woodland Hills CA 91367 818-444-4100 444-4105
AMEX: TAG ■ *TF:* 800-335-4443 ■ *Web:* www.talonzippers.com

Tape & Label Converters Inc
8231 Allport Ave Santa Fe Springs CA 90670 562-945-3486 696-8198
TF: 888-285-2462 ■ *Web:* www.stickybiz.com

Tapecon Inc 10 Latta Rd Rochester NY 14612 585-621-8400 621-1677
TF: 800-333-2408 ■ *Web:* www.tapecon.com

TAPEMARK Co 1685 Marthaler Ln West Saint Paul MN 55118 651-455-1611 450-8403
TF: 800-535-1998 ■ *Web:* www.tapemark.com

Valmark Industries Inc 7900 National Dr Livermore CA 94550 925-960-9900 960-0900
TF: 800-770-7074 ■ *Web:* www.valmark.com

Company	City	State	ZIP	Phone	Fax
Vitachrome Graphics Group Inc 11517 Los Nietos Rd *TF:* 800-742-5507 ■ *Web:* www.vitachrome.com	Santa Fe Springs	CA	90670	562-692-9200	692-9055
Weber Marking Systems Inc 711 W Algonquin Rd *TF Sales:* 800-225-0883 ■ *Web:* www.webermarking.com	Arlington Heights	IL	60005	847-364-8500	364-8575
West Coast Tag & Label Co PO Box 4099 *TF Cust Svc:* 800-742-8247 ■ *Web:* www.tags-labels.com	West Hills	CA	91308	818-710-8484	710-7645
Whitlam Label Co Inc 24800 Sherwood Ave *TF:* 800-755-2235 ■ *Web:* www.whitlam.com	Center Line	MI	48015	586-757-5100	757-1243
Wise Tag & Label Co Inc 1077 Thomas Busch Memorial Hwy *TF:* 800-222-1327 ■ *Web:* www.wisetaglabel.com	Pennsauken	NJ	08110	856-663-2400	663-8610
Wright of Thomasville Corp 5115 Prospect St *TF:* 800-678-9019 ■ *Web:* www.wrightlabels.com	Thomasville	NC	27360	336-472-4200	476-8554
WS Packaging Group Inc 1102 Jefferson St *TF:* 800-236-3424 ■ *Web:* www.wspackaging.com	Algoma	WI	54201	920-487-3424	487-5644
YORK Label 405 Willow Springs Ln *TF Cust Svc:* 888-800-9675 ■ *Web:* www.yorklabel.com	York	PA	17402	717-266-9675	266-9835
Z International Inc 110 E 16th Ave *TF:* 800-528-4190 ■ *Web:* www.zintl.com	North Kansas City	MO	64116	816-474-8400	842-9179

417 LABOR UNIONS

Organization	City	State	ZIP	Phone	Fax
Actors' Equity Assn 1560 Broadway *Web:* www.actorsequity.org	New York	NY	10036	212-869-8530	719-9815
AFT Healthcare 555 New Jersey Ave NW *TF:* 800-238-1133 ■ *Web:* www.aft.org	Washington	DC	20001	202-879-4491	393-5672
Air Line Pilots Assn 535 Herndon Pkwy *TF:* 800-359-2572 ■ *Web:* www.alpa.org	Herndon	VA	20170	703-689-2270	689-4177
Amalgamated Transit Union (ATU) 5025 Wisconsin Ave NW 3rd Fl *TF:* 888-240-1196 ■ *Web:* www.atu.org	Washington	DC	20016	202-537-1645	244-7824
American Federation of Government Employees 80 F St NW *Web:* www.afge.org	Washington	DC	20001	202-737-8700	639-6441
American Federation of Labor & Congress of Industrial Organizations (AFL-CIO) 815 16th St NW *Web:* www.aflcio.org	Washington	DC	20006	202-637-5000	637-5058
American Federation of Musicians of the US & Canada (AFM) 1501 Broadway Suite 600 *TF:* 800-762-3444 ■ *Web:* www.afm.org	New York	NY	10036	212-869-1330	764-6134
American Federation of State County & Municipal Employees 1625 L St NW *Web:* www.afscme.org	Washington	DC	20036	202-429-1000	429-1293
American Federation of Teachers (AFT) 555 New Jersey Ave NW **Fax:* PR ■ *TF:* 800-238-1133 ■ *Web:* www.aft.org	Washington	DC	20001	202-879-4400	879-4556*
American Federation of Television & Radio Artists (AFTRA) 260 Madison Ave 7th Fl *Web:* www.aftra.com	New York	NY	10016	212-532-0800	532-2242
American Postal Workers Union 1300 L St NW *Web:* www.apwu.org	Washington	DC	20005	202-842-4200	842-8500
American Train Dispatchers Assn 4239 West 150th St *Web:* atdd.homestead.com	Cleveland	OH	44135	216-251-7984	
Assn of Civilian Technicians (ACT) 12620 Lake Ridge Dr *Web:* www.actnat.com	Woodbridge	VA	22192	703-494-4845	494-0961
Assn of Flight Attendants 501 3rd St NW *Web:* www.afanet.org	Washington	DC	20001	202-434-1300	434-1319
Assn of Professional Flight Attendants 1004 W Euless Blvd *TF:* 800-395-2732 ■ *Web:* www.apfa.org	Euless	TX	76040	817-540-0108	540-2077
Assn of Western Pulp & Paper Workers 1430 SW Clay St *Web:* www.awppw.org	Portland	OR	97208	503-228-7486	228-1346
Bakery Confectionery Tobacco Workers & Grain Millers International Union 10401 Connecticut Ave *Web:* www.bctgm.org	Kensington	MD	20895	301-933-8600	946-8452
Brotherhood of Locomotive Engineers & Trainmen (BLET) 1370 Ontario St Mezzanine Level *Web:* www.ble-t.org	Cleveland	OH	44113	216-241-2630	241-6516
Brotherhood of Maintenance of Way Employees (BMWED) 2300 Civic Ctr Dr Suite 320 *Web:* www.bmwed.org	Southfield	MI	48076	248-948-1010	948-7150
Brotherhood of Railroad Signalmen 917 Shenandoah Shores Rd *Web:* www.brs.org	Front Royal	VA	22630	540-622-6522	622-6532
Brotherhood Railway Carmen c/o Transportation Communications International Union 3 Research Pl *Web:* www.tcunion.org	Rockville	MD	20850	301-948-4910	948-1369
Canada Labour Congress 2841 Riverside Dr *Web:* www.clc-ctc.ca	Ottawa	ON	K1V8X7	613-521-3400	521-4655
Chicago Teachers Union 222 Merchandise Mart Plaza Suite 400 *Web:* www.ctunet.com	Chicago	IL	60654	312-329-9100	329-6200
Communications Workers of America (CWA) 501 3rd St NW **Fax:* Hum Res ■ *Web:* www.cwa-union.org	Washington	DC	20001	202-434-1100	434-1436*
Directors Guild of America 7920 W Sunset Blvd *TF:* 800-421-4173 ■ *Web:* www.dga.org	Los Angeles	CA	90046	310-289-2000	289-2029
Federal Education Assn 1201 16th St NW Suite 117 *Web:* www.feaonline.org	Washington	DC	20036	202-822-7850	822-7816
Florida Education Assn 213 S Adams St *TF:* 888-807-8007 ■ *Web:* www.feaweb.org	Tallahassee	FL	32301	850-201-2800	222-1840
Glass Molders Pottery Plastics & Allied Workers International Union 608 E Baltimore Pike *Web:* www.gmpiu.org	Media	PA	19063	610-565-5051	565-0983
Graphic Artists Guild Inc 32 Broadway Suite 1114 *Web:* www.graphicartistsguild.org	New York	NY	10004	212-791-3400	791-0333
Graphic Communications International Union 1900 L St NW 9th Fl *Web:* www.gciu.org	Washington	DC	20036	202-462-1400	721-0600
Inlandboatmen's Union of the Pacific (IBU) 1711 W Nickerson St Suite D *Web:* www.ibu.org	Seattle	WA	98119	206-284-6001	284-5043
International Alliance of Theatrical Stage Employees Moving Picture Technicians (IATSE) 1430 Broadway 20th Fl *TF:* 800-223-6872 ■ *Web:* www.iatse-intl.org	New York	NY	10018	212-730-1770	921-7699
International Assn of Bridge Structural Ornamental & Reinforcing Iron Workers 1750 New York Ave NW Suite 400 *TF:* 800-368-0105 ■ *Web:* www.ironworkers.org	Washington	DC	20006	202-383-4800	638-4856
International Assn of Fire Fighters (IAFF) 1750 New York Ave NW 3rd Fl *Web:* www.iaff.org	Washington	DC	20006	202-737-8484	737-8418
International Assn of Heat & Frost Insulators & Asbestos Workers 9602 ML King Jr Hwy *Web:* www.insulators.org	Lanham	MD	20706	301-731-9101	731-5058
International Assn of Machinists & Aerospace Workers 9000 Machinists Pl *Web:* www.goiam.org	Upper Marlboro	MD	20772	301-967-4500	967-4588
International Brotherhood of Boilermakers Iron Shipbuilders Blacksmiths Forgers & Helpers 753 State Ave Suite 570 *Web:* www.boilermakers.org	Kansas City	KS	66101	913-371-2640	281-8101
International Brotherhood of Correctional Officers (IBCO) 159 Burgin Pkwy *Web:* www.ibco.org	Quincy	MA	02169	617-376-0220	376-0285
International Brotherhood of Electrical Workers 900 7th St NW *Web:* www.ibew.org	Washington	DC	20001	202-833-7000	467-6316
International Brotherhood of Police Officers (IBPO) 159 Burgin Pkwy **Fax:* Legal Dept ■ *Web:* www.ibpo.org	Quincy	MA	02169	617-376-0220	376-0285*
International Brotherhood of Teamsters 25 Louisiana Ave NW **Fax:* PR ■ *Web:* www.teamster.org	Washington	DC	20001	202-624-6800	624-6918*
International Chemical Workers Union Council 1799 Akron Peninsula Rd *Web:* www.icwuc.org	Akron	OH	44313	330-926-1444	926-0816
International Federation of Professional & Technical Engineers 8630 Fenton St Suite 400 *Web:* www.ifpte.org	Silver Spring	MD	20910	301-565-9016	565-0018
International Longshore & Warehouse Union 1188 Franklin St 4th Fl *Web:* www.ilwu.org	San Francisco	CA	94109	415-775-0533	775-1302
International Longshoremen's Assn 17 Battery Pl Rm 930 *Web:* www.ila2000.org	New York	NY	10004	212-425-1200	425-2928
International Organization of Masters Mates & Pilots 700 Maritime Blvd *TF:* 877-667-5522 ■ *Web:* www.bridgedeck.org	Linthicum Heights	MD	21090	410-850-8700	850-0973
International Union of Bricklayers & Allied Craftworkers (BAC) 1776 'I' St NW *TF:* 888-880-8222 ■ *Web:* www.bacweb.org	Washington	DC	20006	202-783-3788	393-0219
International Union of Elevator Constructors (IUEC) 7154 Columbia Gateway Dr *Web:* www.iuec.org	Columbia	MD	21046	410-953-6150	953-6169
International Union of Operating Engineers 1125 17th St NW *Web:* www.iuoe.org	Washington	DC	20036	202-429-9100	778-2616
International Union of Painters & Allied Trades 1750 New York Ave NW 8th Fl *Web:* www.ibpat.org	Washington	DC	20006	202-637-0700	637-0771
International Union of Petroleum & Industrial Workers 8131 E Rosecrans Ave *TF:* 800-624-5842	Paramount	CA	90723	562-630-6232	408-1073
International Union of Police Associations 1549 Ringling Blvd Suite 600 *TF:* 800-247-4872 ■ *Web:* www.iupa.org	Sarasota	FL	34236	941-487-2560	487-2570
International Union Security Police & Fire Professionals of America (SPFPA) 25510 Kelly Rd *TF:* 800-228-7492 ■ *Web:* www.spfpa.org	Roseville	MI	48066	586-772-7250	772-9644
International Union United Automobile Aerospace & Agricultural Implement Workers of America 8000 E Jefferson Ave *Web:* www.uaw.org	Detroit	MI	48214	313-926-5000	823-6016
Laborers' International Union of North America 905 16th St NW *Web:* www.liuna.org	Washington	DC	20006	202-737-8320	737-2754
Marine Engineers' Beneficial Assn (MEBA) 444 N Capitol St NW Suite 800 *Web:* www.d1meba.org	Washington	DC	20001	202-638-5355	638-5369
NA of Broadcast Employees & Technicians-Communications Workers of America (NABET-CWA) 501 3rd St NW *Web:* www.nabetcwa.org	Washington	DC	20001	202-434-1254	434-1426
NA of Government Employees (NAGE) 159 Thomas Burgin Pkwy *Web:* www.nage.org	Quincy	MA	02169	617-376-0220	376-0285
NA of Letter Carriers 100 Indiana Ave NW *Web:* www.nalc.org	Washington	DC	20001	202-393-4695	737-1540
National Air Traffic Controllers Assn (NATCA) 1325 Massachusetts Ave NW *TF:* 800-266-0895 ■ *Web:* www.natca.org	Washington	DC	20005	202-628-5451	628-5767
National Alliance of Postal & Federal Employees 1628 11th St NW *Web:* www.napfe.com	Washington	DC	20001	202-939-6325	939-6389
National Basketball Players Assn (NBPA) 310 Malcolm X Blvd *Web:* www.nbpa.com	New York	NY	10027	212-655-0880	655-0881
National Conference of Firemen & Oilers 1023 15th St NW 10th Fl *Web:* www.ncfo.org	Washington	DC	20005	202-962-0981	872-1222
National Federation of Federal Employees 805-15th St NW Suite 500 *Web:* www.nffe.org	Washington	DC	20036	202-216-4420	862-4432

Phone *Fax*

National League of Postmasters of the US
5904 Richmond Hwy Suite 500 .... Alexandria VA 22303 703-329-4550 329-0466
Web: www.postmasters.org

National Organization of Industrial Trade Unions
148-06 Hillside Ave .... Jamaica NY 11435 718-291-3434 526-2920

National Rural Letter Carriers' Assn
1630 Duke St 4th Fl .... Alexandria VA 22314 703-684-5545 548-8735
Web: www.nrlca.org

National Treasury Employees Union
1750 H St NW 10th Fl. .... Washington DC 20006 202-572-5500 572-5643
Web: www.nteu.org

National Writers Union (NWU)
256 W 38th St Suite 703. .... New York NY 10018 212-254-0279 254-0673
Web: www.nwu.org

News Media Guild 424 W 33rd St Suite 260. .... New York NY 10001 212-869-9290 840-0687
Web: www.newsmediaguild.org

Newspaper Guild-Communications Workers of America The
501 3rd St NW 6th Fl .... Washington DC 20001 202-434-7177 434-1472
TF: 800-585-5864 ■ *Web:* www.newsguild.org

Office & Professional Employees International Union
265 W 14th St Suite 610. .... New York NY 10011 212-675-3210 727-3466
TF: 800-346-7348 ■ *Web:* www.opeiu.org

Professional Security Officers Union
2201 Broadway Suite 101. .... Oakland CA 94612 510-625-9913 625-0998
TF: 800-772-3326 ■ *Web:* www.seiu247.org

Retail Wholesale & Dept Store Union
30 E 29th St .... New York NY 10016 212-684-5300 779-2809
Web: www.rwdsu.org

Screen Actors Guild (SAG)
5757 Wilshire Blvd. .... Los Angeles CA 90036 323-954-1600 549-6775
TF: 800-724-0767 ■ *Web:* www.sag.org

Seafarers International Union
5201 Auth Way. .... Camp Springs MD 20746 301-899-0675 899-7355
TF: 800-252-4674 ■ *Web:* www.seafarers.org

Service Employees International Union
1800 Massachusetts Ave NW .... Washington DC 20036 202-730-7000 429-5660
TF: 800-424-8592 ■ *Web:* www.seiu.org

Sheet Metal Workers International Assn (SMWIA)
1750 New York Ave NW 6th Fl .... Washington DC 20006 202-783-5880 662-0894
TF: 800-457-7694 ■ *Web:* www.smwia.org

Transportation Communications International Union
3 Research Pl .... Rockville MD 20850 301-948-4910 948-1369
Web: www.goiam.org

UFCW International Union Distillery Wine & Allied Workers Div
219 Paterson Ave .... Little Falls NJ 07424 973-237-1241 890-1956

UFCW Textile & Garment Council
4207 Lebanon Pike Suite 200. .... Hermitage TN 37076 615-889-9221 885-3102
TF: 888-462-4892 ■ *Web:* www.ufcw.org

Union of American Physicians & Dentists
180 Grand Ave Suite 1380 .... Oakland CA 94612 510-839-0193 763-8756
TF: 800-622-0909 ■ *Web:* www.uapd.com

UNITE HERE 1710 Broadway. .... New York NY 10019 212-265-7000 265-3415
TF: 800-238-6483 ■ *Web:* www.unitehere.org

United Assn 901 Massachusetts Ave NW. .... Washington DC 20001 202-628-5823 628-5024
Web: www.ua.org

United Brotherhood of Carpenters & Joiners of America
101 Constitution Ave NW .... Washington DC 20001 202-546-6206 543-5724
Web: www.carpenters.org

United Electrical Radio & Machine Workers of America
1 Gateway Ctr Suite 1400. .... Pittsburgh PA 15222 412-471-8919 471-8999
Web: www.ueunion.org/index.html

United Farm Workers of America
29700 Woodford Techachpi Rd PO Box 62. .... Keene CA 93531 661-823-6151 823-6174
Web: www.ufw.org

United Food & Commercial Workers International Union (UFCW)
1775 K St NW. .... Washington DC 20006 202-223-3111 466-1562
TF: 800-551-4010 ■ *Web:* www.ufcw.org

United Scenic Artists 29 W 38th St 15th Fl. .... New York NY 10018 212-581-0300 977-2011
Web: www.usa829.org

United Steel Workers (USW)
3340 Perimeter Hill Dr .... Nashville TN 37211 615-834-8590 834-7741
Web: www.usw.org

United Steelworkers of America
5 Gateway Ctr Rm 701 .... Pittsburgh PA 15222 412-562-2575 562-2445
Web: www.usw.org

United Steelworkers of America Rubber/Plastics Industry Conference
5 Gateway Ctr 7th Fl. .... Pittsburgh PA 15222 412-562-6971 562-6963

United Transportation Union
14600 Detroit Ave. .... Lakewood OH 44107 216-228-9400 228-5755
TF: 800-558-8842 ■ *Web:* www.utu.org

Utility Workers Union of America
888 16th St NW # 550 .... Washington DC 20006 202-974-8200 974-8201
Web: www.uwua.org

Writers Guild of America East (WGAE)
250 Hudson St .... New York NY 10013 212-767-7800 582-1909
Web: www.wgaeast.org

Writers Guild of America West (WGAw)
7000 W 3rd St .... Los Angeles CA 90048 323-951-4000 782-4800
TF: 800-548-4532 ■ *Web:* www.wga.org

418 LABORATORIES - DENTAL

SEE ALSO Laboratories - Medical p. 2141

Phone *Fax*

Americus Dental Labs Inc 150-15 Hillside Ave .... Jamaica NY 11432 718-658-6655 523-1479
TF: 800-222-8980 ■ *Web:* www.dentalservices.net

Boos Dental Laboratories 801 12th Ave N .... Minneapolis MN 55411 612-529-9655 529-6918
TF: 800-333-2667 ■ *Web:* www.dentalservices.net

Dental Technologies Inc (DTI) 5601 Arnold Rd .... Dublin CA 94568 925-829-3611 828-0153
TF: 800-229-0936 ■ *Web:* www.dtidental.com

National Dentex Corp (NDX) 2 Vision Dr .... Natick MA 01760 508-907-7800 907-6050
NASDAQ: NADX ■ *Web:* www.nationaldentex.com

Posca Bros Dental Laboratory Inc
641 W Willow St. .... Long Beach CA 90806 562-427-1811 595-5821
TF: 800-338-1811 ■ *Web:* www.poscabrothers.com

Roe Dental Laboratory Inc
9565 Midwest Ave .... Garfield Heights OH 44125 216-663-2233 663-2237
TF: 800-228-6663 ■ *Web:* www.roedentallab.com

419 LABORATORIES - DRUG-TESTING

SEE ALSO Laboratories - Medical p. 2141

Phone *Fax*

Bio-Reference Laboratories Inc
481 Edward H Ross Dr .... Elmwood Park NJ 07407 201-791-2600 791-1941
NASDAQ: BRLI ■ *TF:* 800-229-5227 ■ *Web:* www.bioreference.com

Drug Detection Laboratories Inc
9700 Business Pk Dr Suite 407 .... Sacramento CA 95827 916-366-3113 366-3917
Web: www.drugdetection.net

ElSohly Laboratories Inc 5 Industrial Pk Dr .... Oxford MS 38655 662-236-2609 234-0253
Web: www.elsohly.com

Industrial Laboratories Co Inc The
4046 Youngfield St. .... Wheat Ridge CO 80033 303-287-9691 287-0964
Web: www.industriallabs.net

LabOne Inc 10101 Renner Blvd .... Lenexa KS 66219 913-888-1770 888-6374*
**Fax:* Sales ■ *TF:* 800-646-7788 ■ *Web:* www.labone.com

MEDTOX Scientific Inc 402 W County Rd D .... Saint Paul MN 55112 651-636-7466 636-5351
NASDAQ: MTOX ■ *TF:* 800-832-3244 ■ *Web:* www.medtox.com

SED Medical Laboratories
5601 Office Blvd. .... Albuquerque NM 87109 505-727-6300 727-6244
TF: 800-999-5227 ■ *Web:* www.sedlabs.com

US Drug Testing Laboratories
1700 S Mt Prospect Rd. .... Des Plaines IL 60018 847-375-0770 375-0775
TF: 800-235-2367 ■ *Web:* www.usdtl.com

420 LABORATORIES - GENETIC TESTING

SEE ALSO Laboratories - Medical p. 2141

Phone *Fax*

American Red Cross Pacific NorthWest Blood Service
3131 N Vancouver Ave .... Portland OR 97227 503-284-1234
Web: www.redcrossblood.org

Blood Systems Laboratories 2424 W Erie Dr .... Tempe AZ 85282 602-343-7000 343-7025
TF: 866-342-4275 ■ *Web:* www.bloodsystemslaboratories.org

BRT Laboratories Inc 400 W Franklin St .... Baltimore MD 21201 410-225-9595 383-0938
TF: 800-765-5170 ■ *Web:* www.brtlabs.com

Center for Genetic Testing at Saint Francis
6465 S Yale Ave # 1010 .... Tulsa OK 74136 918-502-1720 502-1723
TF: 800-299-7919 ■ *Web:* www.sfh-lab.com

Clinical Testing & Research Inc
20 Wilsey Sq .... Ridgewood NJ 07450 201-652-2088 652-2775
TF: 888-837-5267 ■ *Web:* www.clinicaltesting.com

Commonwealth Biotechnologies Inc
601 Biotech Dr. .... Richmond VA 23235 804-648-3820 648-2641
PINK: CBTEQ ■ *TF:* 800-735-9224 ■ *Web:* www.cbi-biotech.com

DNA Diagnostics Ctr 1 DDC Way. .... Fairfield OH 45014 513-881-7800 881-7803
TF: 800-362-2368 ■ *Web:* www.dnacenter.com

DNA Paternity Lab of Utah
2749 E Parleys Way Suite 100 .... Salt Lake City UT 84109 801-582-4200 582-8460
TF: 800-362-5559

Eurofins Scientific Inc
2200 Rittenhouse St Suite 150. .... Des Moines IA 50321 515-265-1461 266-5453
Web: www.eurofinsus.com

Genecare Medical Genetics Ctr
201 Sage Rd Suite 300. .... Chapel Hill NC 27514 919-942-0021 967-9519
TF: 800-277-4363 ■ *Web:* www.genecare.com

Genelex Corp 3000 1st Ave Suite 1 .... Seattle WA 98121 206-382-9591 219-4000
TF: 800-523-3080 ■ *Web:* www.healthanddna.com

Genetic Profiles Corp
10675 Treena St Suite 103 .... San Diego CA 92131 858-623-0840 348-0048
TF: 800-551-7763 ■ *Web:* www.geneticprofiles.com

Genetica DNA Laboratories Inc
8740 Montgomery Rd. .... Cincinnati OH 45236 513-985-9777 985-9983
TF: 800-433-6848 ■ *Web:* www.genetica.com

GenQuest DNA Analysis Laboratory
Univ of Nevada - Reno 1664 N Virginia St .... Reno NV 89557 775-784-4494 358-0657
TF: 877-362-5227 ■ *Web:* www.genquestdnalab.com

Genzyme Genetics 3400 Computer Dr .... Westborough MA 01581 508-898-9001 389-5548
TF: 800-326-7002 ■ *Web:* www.genzymegenetics.com

Hawaii medical center East 2230 Liliha St .... Honolulu HI 96817 808-547-6536 547-6149

Identigene Inc 5615 Kirby Dr Suite 800 .... Houston TX 77005 713-798-9510 798-9515
TF: 800-362-8973 ■ *Web:* www.identigene.com

Identity Genetics Inc 801 32nd Ave .... Brookings SD 57006 605-697-5300 697-5306
TF: 800-861-1054 ■ *Web:* www.identitygenetics.com

Laboratories at Bonfils 717 Yosemite St 2nd Fl .... Denver CO 80230 303-365-9000 343-6666
TF: 800-321-6088 ■ *Web:* www.labsatbonfils.com

Laboratory Corp of America Holdings
358 S Main St. .... Burlington NC 27215 336-229-1127 513-4510
NYSE: LH ■ *TF:* 800-334-5161 ■ *Web:* www.labcorp.com

Phone Fax

Maxxam Analytics Inc 335 Laird Rd Unit 2 .... Guelph ON N1H6J3 519-836-2400 836-4218
TF: 877-706-7678 ■ *Web:* www.thednalab.com

Medical Genetics Consultants
819 DeSoto St .... Ocean Springs MS 39564 228-872-3680 872-1893
TF: 800-362-4363 ■ *Web:* www.legalgenetics.com

Memorial Blood Centers (MBC) 737 Pelham Blvd .... Saint Paul MN 55114 651-332-7000 332-7001
TF Cust Svc: 888-448-3253 ■ *Web:* www.mbc.org

Molecular Pathology Laboratory Network Inc
250 E Broadway .... Maryville TN 37804 865-380-9746 380-9191
TF: 800-932-2943 ■ *Web:* www.mplnet.com

NMS Labs 3701 Welsh Rd .... Willow Grove PA 19090 215-657-4900 657-2972
TF: 800-522-6671 ■ *Web:* www.nmslab.com

Orchid Cellmark Forensic DNA Testing
13988 Diplomat Dr Suite 100 .... Farmers Branch TX 75234 214-271-8400 271-8322
TF: 800-752-2774 ■ *Web:* www.orchid.com

Orchid Cellmark Inc 4390 US Rt 1 .... Princeton NJ 08540 609-750-2200 750-6400
NASDAQ: ORCH ■ *TF:* 888-398-9352 ■ *Web:* www.orchid.com

Paternity Testing Corp (PTC) 300 Portland St .... Columbia MO 65201 573-442-9948 442-9870
TF: 888-837-8323 ■ *Web:* www.ptclabs.com

Rhode Island Blood Ctr 405 Promenade St .... Providence RI 02908 401-453-8360 453-8557
TF: 800-283-8385 ■ *Web:* www.ribc.org

Rj Lee Group Inc 350 Hochberg Rd .... Monroeville PA 15146 724-325-1776 733-1799
Web: www.rjlg.com

South Texas Blood & Tissue Ctr
6211 IH-10 W .... San Antonio TX 78201 210-731-5555 731-5501
TF: 800-292-5534 ■ *Web:* www.bloodntissue.org

State University of New York Upstate Medical University Tissue Typing Laboratory
750 E Adams St .... Syracuse NY 13210 315-464-4775 464-9557
Web: www.upstate.edu

Tuev America Inc 10 Centennial Dr Fl 2A .... Peabody MA 01960 978-573-2500 977-0157
Web: www.tuvam.com

University of North Texas Health Science Ctr
3500 Camp Bowie Blvd .... Fort Worth TX 76107 817-735-5015 735-5016
TF: 800-687-5301 ■ *Web:* www.hsc.unt.edu

421 LABORATORIES - MEDICAL

SEE ALSO Blood Centers p. 1529; Laboratories - Dental p. 2140; Laboratories - Drug-Testing p. 2140; Laboratories - Genetic Testing p. 2140; Organ & Tissue Banks p. 2330

Phone Fax

ANI Pharmaceuticals Inc 210 Main St W .... Gulfport MS 56623 218-634-3500 634-3540
Web: www.anipharmaceuticals.com

Applied Laboratories Inc
3240 N Indianapolis Rd PO Box 2127 .... Columbus IN 47202 812-372-2607 372-2631
Web: www.appliedlabs.com

Atherotech Inc 201 London Pkwy .... Birmingham AL 35211 205-871-8344 871-8392
TF: 800-719-9807 ■ *Web:* www.atherotech.com

Bio-Reference Laboratories Inc
481 Edward H Ross Dr .... Elmwood Park NJ 07407 201-791-2600 791-1941
NASDAQ: BRLI ■ *TF:* 800-229-5227 ■ *Web:* www.bioreference.com

Calvert Laboratories Inc
100 Discovery Dr Scott Technology Pk .... Olyphant PA 18447 570-586-2411 586-3450
TF: 800-300-8114 ■ *Web:* www.calvertlabs.com

Canadian Medical Laboratories Ltd
6560 Kennedy Rd .... Mississauga ON L5T2X4 905-565-0433 565-6704
TF: 800-263-0801 ■ *Web:* www.canmedlab.com

Cell Signaling Technology Inc 3 Trask Ln .... Danvers MA 01923 978-867-2300 867-2400
TF: 877-678-8324 ■ *Web:* www.cellsignal.com

Clinical Pathology Institute Co-op Inc
1526 Peach St .... Erie PA 16501 814-461-2400
TF: 800-937-8028 ■ *Web:* www.associatedclinicallabs.com

DIANON Systems Inc 200 Watson Blvd .... Stratford CT 06615 203-381-4000 381-4079
TF: 800-328-2666 ■ *Web:* www.dianon.com

Genova Diagnostics 63 Zillicoa St .... Asheville NC 28801 828-253-0621 252-9303*
**Fax:* Cust Svc ■ *TF:* 800-522-4762 ■ *Web:* www.gdx.net

Health Network Laboratory 2024 Lehigh St .... Allentown PA 18103 610-402-8170 402-5592
TF: 877-402-4221 ■ *Web:* www.healthnetworklabs.com

LabOne Inc 10101 Renner Blvd .... Lenexa KS 66219 913-888-1770 888-6374*
**Fax:* Sales ■ *TF:* 800-646-7788 ■ *Web:* www.labone.com

Laboratory Corp of America Holdings
358 S Main St .... Burlington NC 27215 336-229-1127 513-4510
NYSE: LH ■ *TF:* 800-334-5161 ■ *Web:* www.labcorp.com

Midwest Clinical Laboratories
11020 W Plank Ct Suite 100 .... Wauwatosa WI 53226 414-476-3400 256-5566
TF: 800-256-1522 ■ *Web:* www.midwestclinicallabs.com

National Genetics Institute
2440 S Blvd Suite 235 .... Los Angeles CA 90064 310-996-0036
TF: 800-352-7788 ■ *Web:* www.ngi.com

NMS Labs 3701 Welsh Rd .... Willow Grove PA 19090 215-657-4900 657-2972
TF: 800-522-6671 ■ *Web:* www.nmslab.com

Pathology Ctr 8303 Dodge St .... Omaha NE 68114 402-354-4540 354-4535
TF: 888-432-8980 ■ *Web:* www.thepathologycenter.org

Physician's Automated Laboratory Inc
PO Box 1500 .... Bakersfield CA 93302 661-325-0744
TF: 800-675-2271 ■ *Web:* www.pallab.org

Quest Diagnostics at Nichols Institute
33608 Ortega Hwy .... San Juan Capistrano CA 92675 949-728-4000 728-4985*
**Fax:* Hum Res ■ *TF:* 800-642-4657

Quest Diagnostics Inc 3 Giralda Farms .... Madison NJ 07940 201-393-5000 462-4169*
NYSE: DGX ■ **Fax:* Cust Svc ■ *TF:* 800-222-0446 ■ *Web:* www.questdiagnostics.com

Scientific Molding Corp Ltd 330 SMC Dr .... Somerset WI 54025 715-247-3500 247-3611
Web: www.smcltd.com

SED Medical Laboratories
5601 Office Blvd .... Albuquerque NM 87109 505-727-6300 727-6244
TF: 800-999-5227 ■ *Web:* www.sedlabs.com

Phone Fax

South Bend Medical Foundation
530 N Lafayette Blvd .... South Bend IN 46601 574-234-4176 288-2262
TF: 800-950-7263 ■ *Web:* www.sbmflab.org

Specialty Laboratories Inc 27027 Tourney Rd .... Valencia CA 91355 661-799-6543 799-6634
TF Sales: 800-421-7110 ■ *Web:* www.specialtylabs.com

Sunrise Medical Laboratories Inc
250 Miller Pl .... Hicksville NY 11801 631-435-1515
TF Cust Svc: 800-782-0282 ■ *Web:* www.sunriselab.com

VCA Antech Inc 12401 W Olympic Blvd .... Los Angeles CA 90064 310-571-6500 571-6700
NASDAQ: WOOF ■ *TF:* 800-966-1822 ■ *Web:* www.vcaantech.com

422 LABORATORY ANALYTICAL INSTRUMENTS

SEE ALSO Glassware - Laboratory & Scientific p. 1906; Laboratory Apparatus & Furniture p. 2142

Phone Fax

Abaxis Inc 3240 Whipple Rd .... Union City CA 94587 510-675-6500 441-6150
NASDAQ: ABAX ■ *TF:* 800-822-2947 ■ *Web:* www.abaxis.com

Advanced Measurement Technology
801 S Illinois Ave .... Oak Ridge TN 37831 865-482-4411 483-0396
TF: 800-251-9750 ■ *Web:* www.ametek-online.com

Agilent Technologies Inc
5301 Stevens Creek Blvd .... Santa Clara CA 95051 877-424-4536 345-8474*
NYSE: A ■ **Fax Area Code:* 408 ■ *TF:* 877-424-4536 ■ *Web:* www.home.agilent.com

Airpax Corp 550 Highland St .... Frederick MD 21701 301-663-5141 698-0624
Web: www.airpax.net

Alden Research Laboratory Inc
30 Shrewsbury St .... Holden MA 01520 508-829-6000 829-5939
Web: www.aldenlab.com

Alltech Assoc Inc 2051 Waukegan Rd .... Deerfield IL 60015 847-948-8600 948-1078
TF Cust Svc: 800-255-8324 ■ *Web:* www.alltechweb.com

American Biologics 1180 Walnut Ave .... Chula Vista CA 91911 619-429-8200 429-8004
TF: 800-227-4473 ■ *Web:* www.americanbiologics.com

Analytical Sensors & Instruments Ltd
12800 Pk One Dr .... Sugar Land TX 77478 281-565-8818 565-8811
Web: www.asi-sensors.com

Arcturus Engineering Inc 400 Logue Ave .... Mountain View CA 94043 650-962-3020 962-3039
TF: 888-446-7911 ■ *Web:* www.arctur.com

BBI Source Scientific Inc 2144 Michelson Dr .... Irvine CA 92612 714-898-9001

BD Biosciences 2350 Qume Dr .... San Jose CA 95131 408-432-9475 954-2347
TF: 800-223-8226 ■ *Web:* www.bdbiosciences.com

Bio/Data Corp PO Box 347 .... Horsham PA 19044 215-441-4000 443-8820
TF: 800-257-3282 ■ *Web:* www.biodatacorp.com

Bioanalytical Systems Inc
2701 Kent Ave .... West Lafayette IN 47906 765-463-4527 497-1102
NASDAQ: BASI ■ *TF:* 800-845-4246 ■ *Web:* www.basinc.com

BioTek Instruments Inc
100 Tigan St PO Box 998 .... Winooski VT 05404 802-655-4740 655-7941
TF: 888-451-5171 ■ *Web:* www.biotek.com

Brinkmann Instruments Inc
1 Cantiague Rd PO Box 1019 .... Westbury NY 11590 516-334-7500 334-7506
TF: 800-645-3050 ■ *Web:* www.brinkmann.com

Bruker Daltonics Inc 40 Manning Rd .... Billerica MA 01821 978-663-3660 667-5993
NASDAQ: BRKR ■ *Web:* www.bdal.de

Buehler Ltd 41 Waukegan Rd .... Lake Bluff IL 60044 847-295-6500 295-7979
TF Sales: 800-283-4537 ■ *Web:* www.mybuehler.com

California Analytical Instruments Inc
1312 W Grove Ave .... Orange CA 92865 714-974-5560 282-6280
Web: www.gasanalyzers.com

Caliper Life Sciences Inc 68 Elm St .... Hopkinton MA 01748 508-435-9500 435-3439
NASDAQ: CALP ■ *Web:* www.caliperls.com

Cao Group Inc 4628 Skyhawk Dr .... West Jordan UT 84084 801-256-9282 256-9287
TF: 877-877-9778 ■ *Web:* www.caogroup.com

Cargille-Sacher Laboratories Inc
55 Commerce Rd .... Cedar Grove NJ 07009 973-239-6633 239-6096
Web: www.cargille.com

CDS Analytical Inc 465 Limestone Rd PO Box 277 .... Oxford PA 19363 610-932-3636 932-4158
TF: 800-541-6593 ■ *Web:* www.cdsanalytical.com

Cellomics Inc 100 Technology Dr .... Pittsburgh PA 15219 412-770-2200 770-2201
Web: www.cellomics.com

CEM Corp 3100 Smith Farm Rd .... Matthews NC 28104 704-821-7015 821-7894
TF: 800-726-3331 ■ *Web:* www.cem.com

Cepheid 904 E Caribbean Dr .... Sunnyvale CA 94089 408-541-4191 541-4192
NASDAQ: CPHD ■ *TF:* 888-838-3222 ■ *Web:* www.cepheid.com

Cetac Technologies Inc 14306 Industrial Rd .... Omaha NE 68144 402-733-2829 733-5292
TF: 800-369-2822 ■ *Web:* www.cetac.com

Chemetrics Inc 4295 Catlett Rd .... Calverton VA 20138 540-788-9026 788-4856
Web: www.chemetrics.com

CMI Inc 316 E 9th St .... Owensboro KY 42303 270-685-6545 685-6678
TF: 866-835-0690 ■ *Web:* www.alcoholtest.com

CompuMed Inc
5777 W Century Blvd Suite 1285 .... Los Angeles CA 90045 310-258-5000 645-5880
TF: 800-421-3395 ■ *Web:* www.compumed.net

Corning Inc Life Sciences Div 45 Nagog Pk .... Acton MA 01720 978-635-2200 635-2476
TF: 800-492-1110 ■ *Web:* www.corning.com/lifesciences

Datacolor 5 Princess Rd .... Lawrenceville NJ 08648 609-924-2189 895-7414
TF: 800-433-1885 ■ *Web:* www.datacolor.com

Daxor Corp 350 5th Ave Suite 7120 .... New York NY 10118 212-244-0555 244-0806
AMEX: DXR ■ *Web:* www.daxor.com

DiaSys Corp 405 Lexington Ave 26th Fl .... New York NY 10174 212-541-2458 368-8005*
**Fax Area Code:* 917 ■ *TF:* 800-360-2003 ■ *Web:* www.diasys.com

EDAX Inc 91 McKee Dr .... Mahwah NJ 07430 201-529-4880 529-3156
Web: www.edax.com

Exergen Corp 400 Pleasant St .... Watertown MA 02472 617-923-9900 923-9911
Web: www.exergen.com

FEI Co 5350 NE Dawson Creek Dr .... Hillsboro OR 97124 503-640-7500 726-2570*
NASDAQ: FEIC ■ **Fax:* Sales ■ *TF Cust Svc:* 866-693-3426 ■ *Web:* www.fei.com

Fryer Co Inc 11177 Dundee Rd .... Huntley IL 60142 847-669-2000 669-2056

Gambro BCT 10811 W Collins Ave .... Lakewood CO 80215 303-231-4357 231-4357
TF: 877-339-4228 ■ *Web:* www.caridianbct.com

	City	State	Zip	Phone	Fax
Gatan Inc 5794 W Las Positas Blvd	Pleasanton	CA	94588	925-463-0200	463-0204
Web: www.gatan.com					
Hach Co PO Box 389	Loveland	CO	80539	970-669-3050	669-2932
TF: 800-227-4224 ■ *Web:* www.hach.com					
Harvard Bioscience Inc 84 October Hill Rd	Holliston	MA	01746	508-893-8999	429-5732
NASDAQ: HBIO ■ *TF:* 800-272-2775 ■ *Web:* www.harvardbioscience.com					
Helena Laboratories Inc 1530 Lindbergh Dr	Beaumont	TX	77704	409-842-3714	842-3094
TF: 800-231-5663 ■ *Web:* www.helena.com					
Hitachi High Technologies America Inc					
10 N Martingale Rd Suite 500	Schaumburg	IL	60173	847-273-4141	273-4407
Web: www.hii-hitachi.com					
Horiba Instruments Inc 17671 Armstrong Ave	Irvine	CA	92614	949-250-4811	250-0924
TF: 800-446-7422 ■ *Web:* www.horiba.com					
i-STAT Corp 104 Windsor Ctr Dr	East Windsor	NJ	08520	609-443-9300	443-9310
TF: 800-827-7828 ■ *Web:* www.i-stat.com					
Illumina Inc 9885 Towne Centre Dr	San Diego	CA	92121	858-202-4500	202-4545
NASDAQ: ILMN ■ *TF:* 800-809-4566 ■ *Web:* www.illumina.com					
Infolab Inc 17400 Hwy 61 N	Clarksdale	MS	38614	662-627-2283	627-1913
TF: 800-647-8222 ■ *Web:* www.infolabinc.com					
Instrumentation Laboratory Inc					
180 Hartwell Rd	Bedford	MA	01730	781-861-0710	861-1908
TF Sales: 800-955-9525 ■ *Web:* www.instrumentationlaboratory.com					
IRIS International Inc 9172 Eton Ave	Chatsworth	CA	91311	818-709-1244	700-9661
NASDAQ: IRIS ■ *TF:* 800-776-4747 ■ *Web:* www.proiris.com					
Isco Inc 4700 Superior St PO Box 82531	Lincoln	NE	68501	402-464-0231	465-3022*
**Fax:* Cust Svc ■ *TF:* 800-228-4250 ■ *Web:* www.isco.com					
JEOL USA Inc 11 Dearborn Rd	Peabody	MA	01960	978-535-5900	536-2205
Web: www.jeol.com					
Labcon North America Inc 3700 Lkeville Hwy	Petaluma	CA	94954	707-766-2100	766-2199
TF: 800-227-1466 ■ *Web:* www.labcon.com					
LaMotte Co 802 Washington Ave	Chestertown	MD	21620	410-778-3100	778-6394
TF: 800-344-3100 ■ *Web:* www.lamotte.com					
Leco Corp 3000 Lakeview Ave	Saint Joseph	MI	49085	269-985-5496	982-8977*
**Fax:* Sales ■ *TF:* 800-292-6141 ■ *Web:* www.leco.com					
Li Cor Inc PO Box 4425	Lincoln	NE	68504	402-467-3576	467-2819
TF: 800-447-3576 ■ *Web:* www.licor.com					
Luminex Corp 12212 Technology Blvd	Austin	TX	78727	512-219-8020	219-5195
NASDAQ: LMNX ■ *TF:* 888-219-8020 ■ *Web:* www.luminexcorp.com					
M. Braun Inc 14 Marin Way	Stratham	NH	03885	603-773-9333	773-0008
Web: www.mbraun.com					
Mandel Scientific Co Inc 2 Admiral Pl	Guelph	ON	N1G4N4	519-763-9292	763-2005
TF: 888-883-3636 ■ *Web:* www.mandel.ca					
Micromeritics Instrument Corp					
1 Micromeritics Dr	Norcross	GA	30093	770-662-3620	662-3696
Web: www.micromeritics.com					
Molecular Devices Inc (MDI)					
1311 Orleans Dr Suite 408	Sunnyvale	CA	94089	408-747-1700	747-3601
TF: 800-635-5577 ■ *Web:* www.moleculardevices.com					
Monogram Biosciences Inc					
345 Oyster Pt Blvd	South San Francisco	CA	94080	650-635-1100	624-4490
TF: 800-257-7121 ■ *Web:* www.monogrambio.com					
MPD Inc 316 E 9th St	Owensboro	KY	42303	270-685-6200	685-6494
TF: 866-225-5673 ■ *Web:* www.mpdinc.com					
Noran Instruments Inc 5225 Verona Rd	Madison	WI	53711	608-276-6100	273-5045
Nova Biomedical Corp 200 Prospect St	Waltham	MA	02454	781-894-0800	894-5915
TF Sales: 800-458-5813 ■ *Web:* www.novabiomedical.com					
OI Corp 151 Graham Rd PO Box 9010	College Station	TX	77842	979-690-1711	690-0440
TF: 800-653-1711 ■ *Web:* www.oico.com					
Olis Inc 130 Conway Dr Suites A, B & C	Bogart	GA	30622	706-353-6547	353-1972
TF: 800-852-3504 ■ *Web:* www.olisweb.com					
ONIX Systems Inc 9303 W Sam Houston Pkwy S	Houston	TX	77099	713-272-0404	272-2273
TF: 877-290-7422					
Pall Life Sciences 600 S Wagner Rd	Ann Arbor	MI	48103	734-665-0651	913-6495
TF: 800-521-1520 ■ *Web:* www.pall.com					
Particle Measuring Systems Inc					
5475 Airport Blvd	Boulder	CO	80301	303-443-7100	449-6870
TF Cust Svc: 800-238-1801 ■ *Web:* www.pmeasuring.com					
PerkinElmer Inc 45 William St	Wellesley	MA	02481	781-237-5100	237-9386
NYSE: PKI ■ *Web:* www.perkinelmer.com					
Phenomenex Inc 411 Madrid Ave	Torrance	CA	90501	310-212-0555	328-7768
Web: www.phenomenex.com					
Photo Research Inc 9731 Topanga Canyon Pl	Chatsworth	CA	91311	818-341-5151	725-9770
TF: 877-424-6423 ■ *Web:* www.photoresearch.com					
Physical Electronics Inc 18725 Lake Dr E	Chanhassen	MN	55317	952-828-6100	828-6322
TF: 800-328-7515 ■ *Web:* www.phi.com					
Real-Time Laboratories LLC					
990 S Rogers Cir Suite 5	Boca Raton	FL	33487	561-988-8826	988-6997
Web: www.real-timelabs.com					
Response Biomedical Corp 1781 75th Ave W	Vancouver	BC	V6P6P2	604-456-6010	456-6066
TF: 888-591-5577 ■ *Web:* www.responsebio.com					
Sakura Finetek USA Inc 1750 W 214th St	Torrance	CA	90501	310-972-7800	972-7888
Web: www.sakura-americas.com					
Sentry Equipment Corp 856 E Armour Rd	Oconomowoc	WI	53066	262-567-7256	567-4523
Web: www.sentry-equip.com					
Shimadzu Scientific Instruments Inc					
7102 Riverwood Dr	Columbia	MD	21046	410-381-1227	381-1222
TF: 800-477-1227 ■ *Web:* www.ssi.shimadzu.com					
Spectrum Laboratories Inc					
18617 Broadwick St	Rancho Dominguez	CA	90220	310-885-4600	885-4666
TF: 800-634-3300 ■ *Web:* www.spectrumlabs.com					
Spectrum Systems Inc 3410 W Nine-Mile Rd	Pensacola	FL	32526	850-944-3392	944-1011
TF: 877-837-6644 ■ *Web:* www.specsys.com					
StatSpin Inc 85 Morse St	Norwood	MA	02062	781-551-0100	551-0036
TF: 800-782-8774 ■ *Web:* www.statspin.com					
Supelco Inc 595 N Harrison Rd	Bellefonte	PA	16823	814-359-3441	325-5052*
**Fax Area Code:* 800 ■ *TF:* 800-247-6628 ■ *Web:* www.sigmaaldrich.com					
Temptronic Corp 41 Hampden Rd	Mansfield	MA	02048	781-688-2300	688-2301*
**Fax:* Sales ■ *TF Tech Support:* 800-558-5080 ■ *Web:* www.temptronic.com					
Thermo Fisher Scientific					
81 Wyman St PO Box 9046	Waltham	MA	02454	781-622-1000	622-1207
NYSE: TMO ■ *TF:* 800-678-5599 ■ *Web:* www.thermofisher.com					
Transgenomic Inc 12325 Emmet St	Omaha	NE	68164	402-452-5400	452-5401
NASDAQ: TBIO ■ *TF:* 888-233-9283 ■ *Web:* www.transgenomic.com					
Waters Corp 34 Maple St	Milford	MA	01757	508-478-2000	872-1990
NYSE: WAT ■ *TF:* 800-252-4752 ■ *Web:* www.waters.com					
Westover Scientific Inc					
18421 Bothell-Everett Hwy Suite 110	Bothell	WA	98012	425-398-1298	398-0717
TF: 800-304-3202 ■ *Web:* www.westoverfiber.com					

423 LABORATORY APPARATUS & FURNITURE

SEE ALSO Glassware - Laboratory & Scientific p. 1906; Laboratory Analytical Instruments p. 2141; Scales & Balances p. 2633

	City	State	Zip	Phone	Fax
Baker Co Inc 161 Gatehouse Rd PO Drawer E	Sanford	ME	04073	207-324-8773	324-3869
TF: 800-992-2537 ■ *Web:* www.bakerco.com					
Barnstead/Thermolyne Corp 2555 Kerper Blvd	Dubuque	IA	52001	563-556-2241	589-0516
TF: 800-446-6060 ■ *Web:* www.barnsteadthermolyne.com					
Bel-Art Products Inc 6 Industrial Rd	Pequannock	NJ	07440	973-694-0500	694-7199
TF: 800-423-5278 ■ *Web:* www.bel-art.com					
Boekel Scientific 855 Pennsylvania Blvd	Feasterville	PA	19053	215-396-8200	396-8264
TF: 800-336-6929 ■ *Web:* www.boekelsci.com					
Caliper Life Sciences Inc 68 Elm St	Hopkinton	MA	01748	508-435-9500	435-3439
NASDAQ: CALP ■ *Web:* www.caliperls.com					
Cole-Parmer Instrument Co					
625 E Bunker Ct	Vernon Hills	IL	60061	847-549-7600	247-2929
TF: 800-323-4340 ■ *Web:* www.coleparmer.com					
Comet Technologies Inc 3400 Gilchrist Rd	Akron	OH	44260	330-798-4800	784-9854
Web: www.yxlon.com					
Corning Inc Life Sciences Div 45 Nagog Pk	Acton	MA	01720	978-635-2200	635-2476
TF: 800-492-1110 ■ *Web:* www.corning.com/lifesciences					
Durcon Co 8464 Ronda Dr	Canton	MI	48187	734-455-4520	455-5506
Web: www.durcon.com					
Edstrom Industries Inc 819 Bakke Ave	Waterford	WI	53185	262-534-5181	534-5184
TF: 800-558-5913 ■ *Web:* www.edstrom.com					
Ets-Lindgren LP 1301 Arrow Pt Dr	Cedar Park	TX	78613	512-531-6400	531-6500
Web: www.ets-lindgren.com					
Ika-Works Inc 2635 Northchase Pkwy SE	Wilmington	NC	28405	910-452-7059	452-7693
TF: 800-733-3037 ■ *Web:* www.ika.net					
Infolab Inc 17400 Hwy 61 N	Clarksdale	MS	38614	662-627-2283	627-1913
TF: 800-647-8222 ■ *Web:* www.infolabinc.com					
Kalamazoo Technical Furniture					
6450 Valley Industrial Dr	Kalamazoo	MI	49009	269-372-6000	
TF: 800-832-5227 ■ *Web:* www.teclab.com					
Kewaunee Scientific Corp					
2700 W Front St PO Box 1842	Statesville	NC	28687	704-873-7202	873-5160*
NASDAQ: KEQU ■ **Fax:* Sales ■ *TF:* 800-824-6626 ■ *Web:* www.kewaunee.com					
Knf Neuberger Inc 2 Black Forest Rd	Trenton	NJ	08691	609-890-8889	890-2838
Web: www.knf.com					
Koch Modular Process Systems LLC					
45 Eisenhower Dr	Paramus	NJ	07652	201-368-2929	368-8989
Web: www.modular-process.com					
Lab Fabricators Co 1802 E 47th St	Cleveland	OH	44103	216-431-5444	431-5447
TF: 888-431-5444 ■ *Web:* www.labfabricators.com					
Labconco Corp 8811 Prospect Ave	Kansas City	MO	64132	816-333-8811	363-0130
TF Cust Svc: 800-821-5525 ■ *Web:* www.labconco.com					
Millipore Corp 290 Concord Rd	Billerica	MA	01821	781-533-6000	645-5439*
**Fax Area Code:* 800 ■ *TF:* 800-645-5476 ■ *Web:* www.millipore.com					
Nalge Nunc International					
75 Panorama Creek Dr	Rochester	NY	14625	585-586-8800	899-7045
TF: 800-625-4327 ■ *Web:* www.nalgenunc.com					
New Brunswick Scientific Co Inc					
44 Talmadge Rd PO Box 4005	Edison	NJ	08818	732-287-1200	287-4222
TF Cust Svc: 800-631-5417 ■ *Web:* www.nbsc.com					
Omnicell Inc 1201 Charleston Rd	Mountain View	CA	94043	650-251-6100	251-6266
NASDAQ: OMCL ■ *TF:* 800-850-6664 ■ *Web:* www.omnicell.com					
Pacific Combustion Engineering Co					
2107 Border Ave	Torrance	CA	90501	310-212-6300	212-5333
TF: 800-342-4442 ■ *Web:* www.pacificcombustion.com					
Parr Instrument Co 211 53rd St	Moline	IL	61265	309-762-7716	762-9453
TF: 800-872-7720 ■ *Web:* www.parrinst.com					
Parter Medical Products Inc					
17015 Kingsview Ave	Carson	CA	90746	310-327-4417	327-8601
TF: 800-666-8282 ■ *Web:* www.partermedical.com					
Percival Scientific Inc 505 Research Dr	Perry	IA	50220	515-465-9363	465-9464
TF: 800-695-2743 ■ *Web:* www.percival-scientific.com					
Preston Industries Inc 6600 W Touhy Ave	Niles	IL	60714	847-647-0611	647-1155
Web: www.prestonpub.com					
Samco Scientific Corp 1050 Arroyo Ave	San Fernando	CA	91340	818-838-2400	838-2488
TF: 800-522-3359 ■ *Web:* www.samcosci.com					
Sargent-Welch 60 Pearce Ave	Tonawanda	NY	15150	716-874-4093	676-2540*
**Fax Area Code:* 800 ■ *TF:* 800-727-4368 ■ *Web:* www.sargentwelch.com					
Skc Inc 863 Valley View Rd	Eighty Four	PA	15330	724-941-9701	941-1369
Web: www.skcinc.com					
Thermal Product Solutions					
2821 Old Rt 15 PO Box 150	New Columbia	PA	17856	570-538-7200	538-7380
TF: 800-586-2473 ■ *Web:* www.thermalproductsolutions.com					
Thermo Fisher Scientific					
81 Wyman St PO Box 9046	Waltham	MA	02454	781-622-1000	622-1207
NYSE: TMO ■ *TF:* 800-678-5599 ■ *Web:* www.thermofisher.com					
ThermoGenesis Corp 2711 Citrus Rd	Rancho Cordova	CA	95742	916-858-5100	858-5199
NASDAQ: KOOL ■ *TF:* 800-783-8357 ■ *Web:* www.thermogenesis.com					
Thomas Scientific 1654 Highville Rd	Swedesboro	NJ	08085	856-467-2000	467-3087
TF: 800-345-2100 ■ *Web:* www.thomassci.com					
Valley City Mfg Co Ltd 64 Hatt St	Dundas	ON	L9H2G3	905-628-2255	628-4470
TF: 800-828-7628 ■ *Web:* www.valleycity.com					
Westfalia Separator Inc 100 Fairway Ct	Northvale	NJ	07647	201-767-3900	767-3416
TF: 800-722-6622 ■ *Web:* www.wsus.com					

424 LADDERS

Company	City	State	Zip	Phone	Fax
ALACO Ladder Co 5167 G St *TF:* 888-310-7040 ■ *Web:* www.alacoladder.com	Chino	CA	91710	909-591-7561	591-7565
Ballymore Co 220 Garfield Ave *TF:* 800-762-8327 ■ *Web:* www.ballymore.com	West Chester	PA	19380	610-696-3250	696-1217
Cotterman Co 130 Seltzer Rd *TF:* 800-552-3337 ■ *Web:* www.cotterman.com	Croswell	MI	48422	810-679-4400	679-4510
Duo-Safety Ladder Corp 513 W 9th Ave *Web:* www.duosafety.com	Oshkosh	WI	54902	920-231-2740	231-2460
Green Bull Inc 11225 Bluegrass Pkwy *TF:* 800-558-2855 ■ *Web:* www.greenbullladder.com	Louisville	KY	40299	502-267-5577	267-6611
Lynn Ladder & Scaffolding Co Inc PO Box 346 *TF:* 800-596-6717 ■ *Web:* www.lynnladder.com	Lynn	MA	01905	781-598-6010	593-7666
Putnam Rolling Ladder Inc 32 Howard St *Web:* www.putnamrollingladder.com	New York	NY	10013	212-226-5147	941-1836
Werner Co 93 Werner Rd *TF:* 888-523-3371 ■ *Web:* www.wernerladder.com	Greenville	PA	16125	888-523-3371	456-8459
Wing Enterprises Inc 1198 N Spring Creek *TF:* 800-453-1192	Springville	UT	84663	801-489-3684	489-3685

425 LANDSCAPE DESIGN & RELATED SERVICES

Company	City	State	Zip	Phone	Fax
Annco Services Inc 8892 152nd Pl S *Web:* www.anncoservices.com	Delray Beach	FL	33446	561-638-2540	638-3993
Artistic Maintenance Inc 23676 Birtcher Dr *TF:* 800-698-9834 ■ *Web:* www.artisticmaintenance.com	Lake Forest	CA	92630	949-581-9817	581-0436
Brickman Group Ltd 375 S Flowers Mill Rd *TF:* 800-451-7272 ■ *Web:* www.brickmangroup.com	Langhorne	PA	19047	215-757-9400	891-1259
Cagwin & Dorward Inc 1565 S Novato Blvd Suite B *TF:* 800-891-7710 ■ *Web:* www.cagwin.com	Novato	CA	94947	415-892-7710	892-7864
Chapel Valley Landscape Co 3275 Jennings Chapel Rd PO Box 159 *Web:* www.chapelvalley.com	Woodbine	MD	21797	301-924-5400	854-6390
Creative Environments Inc 8920 S Party Drve *Web:* www.creativeenvironments.com	Tempe	AZ	84281	480-777-9305	777-9296
D Schumacher Landscaping Inc 635 Manley St *Web:* www.dschumacher.com	West Bridgewater	MA	02379	508-427-7707	427-7714
Davids Clarence & Co 22901 S Ridgeland Ave *Web:* www.clarencedavids.com	Matteson	IL	60443	708-720-4100	720-4200
Environmental Earthscapes Inc 5075 S Swan Rd *TF:* 800-571-1575 ■ *Web:* www.groundskeeper.com	Tucson	AZ	85706	520-571-1575	750-7480
Golden Bear International Inc 11780 US Hwy 1 *Web:* www.nicklaus.com	North Palm Beach	FL	33408	561-626-3900	227-0302
Hindsdale Nurseries Inc 7200 S Madison Rd *Web:* www.hinsdalenurseries.com	Willowbrook	IL	60527	630-323-1411	323-0918
Horizon Distributors Inc 261 N Roosevelt Ave *Web:* www.horizononline.com	Chandler	AZ	85226	480-337-9700	337-6701
Jensen Corp 10950 N Blaney Ave *Web:* www.jensencorp.com	Cupertino	CA	95014	408-446-1118	446-4881
Landscape Concepts Inc 31711 N Alleghany Rd *TF:* 866-655-3800 ■ *Web:* www.landscapeconcepts.com	Grayslake	IL	60030	847-223-3800	223-0169
Landscape Development Inc 28447 Witherspoon Pkwy *Web:* www.landscapedevelopment.com	Valencia	CA	91355	661-295-1970	295-1969
Lied's Landscape Design & Construction N63 W22039 Hwy 74 *Web:* www.lieds.com/design	Sussex	WI	53089	262-246-6901	246-3569
Lipinski Landscape & Irrigation Contractors Inc 100 Sharp Rd *Web:* www.lipinskiland.com	Marlton	NJ	08053	856-797-8000	983-0500
LMI Landscapes Inc 1437 Halsey Way *Web:* www.lmilandscapes.com	Carrollton	TX	75007	972-446-0020	446-0028
Lykes Bros Inc 106 SW CR 721 *Web:* www.lykesranch.com	Okeechobee	FL	34974	863-763-3401	763-3401
Mariani Enterprises Inc 300 Rockland Rd *Web:* www.marianilandscape.com	Lake Bluff	IL	60044	847-234-2172	234-2754
Mariposa Horticultural Enterprises Inc 15529 Arrow Hwy *TF:* 800-794-9458 ■ *Web:* www.mariposahorticultural.com	Irwindale	CA	91706	626-960-0196	960-8477
Metroplex Garden Design Landscaping LP 4347 W NW Highwy Suite 210 *Web:* www.gardendesignlandscaping.com	Dallas	TX	75220	214-366-2021	366-7994
Mission Landscape Services Inc 536 E Dyer Rd *TF:* 800-545-9963 ■ *Web:* www.missionlandscape.com	Santa Ana	CA	92707	714-545-9962	668-0119
Nicklaus Design 11780 US Hwy 1 Suite 500 *Web:* nicklaus.com/design	North Palm Beach	FL	33408	561-227-0300	227-0548
Park West Cos Inc 22421 Gilberto Suite A *Web:* www.parkwestlandscape.com	Rancho Santa Margarita	CA	92688	949-546-8300	546-8301
Peoria Landscaping Co Inc 2700 W Cedar Hills Dr *Web:* www.greenview.com	Dunlap	IL	61525	309-243-7761	243-9235
Schrickel Rollins & Assoc Inc 1161 Corporate Dr W Suite 200 *Web:* www.sradesign.com	Arlington	TX	76006	817-640-8212	649-7645
Spectrum Care Landscape 27181 Burbank *Web:* www.spectrumcarelandscape.com	Foothill Ranch	CA	92610	949-454-6900	454-6910
Summit Landscape Services Inc 12452 Cutten Rd *Web:* www.summitls.com	Houston	TX	77066	281-583-7900	583-7994
Sun City Landscapes 4270 W Patrick Ln *Web:* www.suncityls.com	Las Vegas	NV	89118	702-260-6309	260-6310
SWA Group 2200 Bridgeway Blvd *Web:* www.swagroup.com	Sausalito	CA	94965	415-332-5100	332-0719
Teufel Nursery Inc 100 SW Miller Rd *TF:* 800-483-8335 ■ *Web:* www.teufellandscape.com	Portland	OR	97225	503-646-1111	646-1112
TruGreen LandCare 860 Ridge Lake Blvd *TF:* 800-242-0442 ■ *Web:* www.trugreen.com	Memphis	TN	38120	901-681-1800	681-1906
Turf Management Systems Inc 2399 Royal Windsor Dr *Web:* www.weedmancanada.com	Mississauga	ON	L5J1K9	905-823-8550	823-4594
Underwood Bros 3747 E Southern Ave *Web:* www.aaalandscape.com	Phoenix	AZ	85040	602-437-2690	437-2970
US Lawns 4407 Vineland Rd Suite D-15 **Fax Area Code: 407* ■ *TF:* 800-875-2967 ■ *Web:* www.uslawns.com	Orlando	FL	32811	800-875-2967	246-1623*
ValleyCrest Cos 24151 Ventura Blvd *Web:* www.valleycrest.com	Calabasas	CA	91302	818-223-8500	223-8142
Vila & Son Landscaping Corp 20451 SW 216th St *Web:* www.vila-n-son.com	Miami	FL	33170	305-255-9206	255-9207

426 LANGUAGE SCHOOLS

SEE ALSO Translation Services p. 2726

Company	City	State	Zip	Phone	Fax
Access International Business Institute 609 E Liberty St *Web:* www.accessesl.org	Ann Arbor	MI	48104	734-994-1456	994-7341
AF International English School PO Box 6223 *Web:* www.afint.com	Westlake Village	CA	91362	805-496-6694	496-9622
Agape English Language Institute (AELI) 610 Pickens St PO Box 12504 *TF:* 877-476-2354 ■ *Web:* www.aeliusa.com	Columbia	SC	29201	803-799-3452	252-5500
American Academy of English 530 Golden Gate Ave *Web:* www.aae.edu	San Francisco	CA	94102	415-567-0189	567-1475
American Language Communication Ctr 15 Penn Plaza *Web:* www.learnenglish.com	New York	NY	10001	212-736-2373	947-6403
AmeriSpan Unlimited 1334 Walnut St # 6 *TF:* 800-879-6640 ■ *Web:* www.amerispan.com	Philadelphia	PA	19107	215-751-1100	751-1986
Berkeley English Academy 2161 Shattuck Ave Suite 313 *Web:* www.berkeleyenglishacademy.com	Berkeley	CA	94704	510-549-9054	549-3357
Berlitz Languages Inc 400 Alexander Pk *TF:* 800-257-9449 ■ *Web:* www.berlitz.com	Princeton	NJ	08540	609-514-9650	514-9648
Boston Academy of English 59 Temple Pl 2nd Fl *Web:* www.bostonacademyofenglish.com	Boston	MA	02111	617-338-6243	695-9349
Boston School of English 814 S St *Web:* www.bsml.com	Boston	MA	02131	617-325-2760	325-2763
Bouchereau Lingua International Inc (BLI) 407 St Laurent Blvd Suite 410 *Web:* www.bli.ca	Montreal	QC	H2Y2Y5	514-842-3847	842-3840
Brandon College 944 Market St # 200 *Web:* www.brandoncollege.com	San Francisco	CA	94102	415-391-5711	391-3918
Centre Linguista 500 Rene-Levesque Blvd W Suite 802 *Web:* www.centrelinguista.com	Montreal	QC	H2Z1W7	514-397-1736	397-9007
Colorado School of English 331 14th St Suite 300 *Web:* www.englishamerica.com	Denver	CO	80202	720-932-8900	932-0315
Converse International School of Languages 636 Broadway Suite 210 *Web:* www.cisl.org	San Diego	CA	92101	619-239-3363	239-3778
Cultural Center for Language Studies 3191 Coral Way Suite 114 *TF:* 800-704-8181 ■ *Web:* www.cclscorp.com	Miami	FL	33145	305-529-2257	443-8538
Diplomatic Language Services LLC 1901 N Fort Myer Dr 6th Fl *TF:* 800-642-7974 ■ *Web:* www.dlsdc.com	Arlington	VA	22209	703-243-4855	243-7003
EC Boston 729 Boylston St *Web:* www.olincenter.com	Boston	MA	02116	617-247-3033	247-2959
Educere International College 910 7th Ave SW Suite 1500	Calgary	AB	T2P3N8	403-232-8551	233-0239
ELS Language Centers 400 Alexander Pk *TF:* 800-468-8978 ■ *Web:* www.els.edu	Princeton	NJ	08540	609-750-3500	750-3599
Embassy CES 328 7th Ave 2nd Fl *Web:* www.embassyces.com	New York	NY	10001	212-497-0050	497-0045
English Connection Inc 77 Railroad Pl *Web:* www.englishconnection.com	Saratoga Springs	NY	12866	518-581-1478	581-1479
English Language Ctr (ELC) 20 Pk Plaza Suite 1201 *Web:* www.elc.edu	Boston	MA	02116	617-536-9788	536-5789
ESL Instruction & Consulting Inc 42 Broad St NW *TF:* 877-342-4785 ■ *Web:* www.eslinstruction.com	Atlanta	GA	30303	404-577-2366	577-2360
Global Village English Centres 888 Cambie St *Web:* www.gvenglish.com	Vancouver	BC	V6B2P6	604-684-1118	684-1117
HablEspana 59 Temple Pl 2nd Fl *Web:* www.hablespana.com	Boston	MA	02111	617-426-4868	695-9349
Human International Academy 123 Camino de la Reina Suite W-200 *TF:* 866-486-2687	San Diego	CA	92108	619-501-8091	501-9027
inlingua International 551 5th Ave 7th Fl *Web:* www.inlinguametrony.com	New York	NY	10176	212-682-8585	599-0977
Intercultural Communications College 1601 Kapiolani Blvd Suite 1000 *Web:* www.icchawaii.edu	Honolulu	HI	96814	808-946-2445	946-2231

	City	State	ZIP	Phone	Fax
International Center for Language Studies Inc					
1133 15th St NW Suite 600	Washington	DC	20005	202-639-8800	783-6587
Web: www.icls.com					
International English Institute					
2755 E Shaw Ave Suite 101	Fresno	CA	93710	559-294-1401	292-6231
Web: www.ieifresno.com					
International House Vancouver					
1215 W Broadway Suite 200	Vancouver	BC	V6H1G7	604-739-9836	739-9839
Web: www.ihvancouver.com					
International Language Institute					
7071 Bayers Rd	Halifax	NS	B3L2C2	902-429-3636	429-2900
Web: www.ili.ca					
International Language Institute					
1137 Connecticut Ave NW 4th Fl	Washington	DC	20005	202-362-2505	686-5603
Web: www.transemantics.com					
Internexus 455 E 400 S Suite 202	Salt Lake City	UT	84111	801-487-2499	487-2198
Web: www.internexus.to					
Intrax International Institute					
600 California St 10th Fl	San Francisco	CA	94108	415-434-1221	434-5404
Web: www.intraxusa.com					
Lado International College					
2233 Wisconsin Ave NW	Washington	DC	20007	202-223-0023	337-1118
Web: www.lado.com					
Language Academy					
300 NE 3rd Ave Suite 100	Fort Lauderdale	FL	33301	954-462-8373	462-3738
Web: www.languageacademy.com					
Language Co 189 W 15th St	Edmond	OK	73013	405-715-9996	715-1116
Web: www.thelanguagecompany.com					
Language Door LLC					
11870 Santa Monica Blvd Suite 202	Los Angeles	CA	90025	310-826-4140	
Web: www.languagedoor.com					
Language Exchange International					
500 NE Spanish River Blvd Suite 19	Boca Raton	FL	33431	561-368-3913	368-9380
TF: 800-223-5836 ■ *Web:* www.languageexchange.com					
Language Pacifica 585 Glenwood Ave	Menlo Park	CA	94025	650-321-1840	321-2510
Web: www.languagepacifica.com					
Language Plus Inc 4110 Rio Bravo Suite 202	El Paso	TX	79902	915-544-8600	544-8640
Web: www.languageplus.com					
Language Studies Canada					
124 Eglinton Ave W Suite 400	Toronto	ON	M4R2G8	416-488-2200	488-2225
Web: www.lsc-canada.com					
Language Studies International					
1706 5th Ave 3rd Fl	San Diego	CA	92101	619-234-2881	234-2883
Web: www.lsi.edu					
Lingua School Inc 4188 S University Dr	Davie	FL	33328	954-577-9955	577-9977
Web: www.linguaschool.com					
Michigan Language Ctr 309 S State St	Ann Arbor	MI	48107	734-663-9415	663-9623
Web: www.englishclasses.com					
New England School of English					
36 John F Kennedy St	Cambridge	MA	02138	617-864-7170	864-7282
Web: www.nese.com					
Nomen Global Language Centers 384 W Ctr St	Provo	UT	84601	801-377-3223	377-3993
Web: www.nomenglobal.com					
Pacific Language Institute					
755 Burrard St Suite 300	Vancouver	BC	V6Z1X6	604-688-8330	688-0638
Web: www.pli.ca					
POLY Languages Institute Inc					
4201 Wilshire Blvd	Los Angeles	CA	90010	323-933-9399	933-9361
Web: www.polylanguages.com					
Rennert Bilingual 216 E 45th St	New York	NY	10017	212-867-8700	867-7666
Web: www.rennert.com					
Rosemead College of English					
8705 E Valley Blvd	Rosemead	CA	91770	626-285-9668	285-1351
Web: www.rosemeadcollege.com					
Saint Giles International San Francisco					
785 Market St Suite 300	San Francisco	CA	94103	415-788-3552	788-1923
Web: www.stgiles-international.com					
Tamwood International College					
300-909 Burrard St	Vancouver	BC	V6Z2N2	604-899-4480	899-4481
Web: www.tamwood.com					
University Language Institute					
2448 E 81st St Suite 1400	Tulsa	OK	74137	918-493-8088	493-8084
Web: www.uli.net					
Wisconsin English as a Second Language Institute					
19 N Pinckney St	Madison	WI	53703	608-257-4300	257-4346
Web: www.wesli.com					
Zoni Language Centers 22W W 34th St	New York	NY	10001	212-736-9000	947-8030
Web: www.zoni.com					

427 LASER EQUIPMENT & SYSTEMS - MEDICAL

SEE ALSO Medical Instruments & Apparatus - Mfr p. 2227

	City	State	ZIP	Phone	Fax
BioLase Technology Inc					
981 Calle Amanecer	San Clemente	CA	92673	949-361-1200	361-0204
NASDAQ: BLTI ■ *TF:* 800-699-9462 ■ *Web:* www.biolase.com					
Candela Corp 530 Boston Post Rd	Wayland	MA	01778	508-358-7400	358-5602
NASDAQ: CLZR ■ *TF:* 800-733-8550 ■ *Web:* www.candelalaser.com					
CardioGenesis Corp					
26632 Towne Centre Dr Suite 320	Foothill Ranch	CA	92610	714-649-5000	649-5100
TF: 800-238-2205 ■ *Web:* www.cardiogenesis.com					
Convergent Laser Technologies 1660 S Loop Rd	Alameda	CA	94502	510-832-2130	832-1600
TF: 800-848-8200 ■ *Web:* www.convergentlaser.com					
Cynosure Inc 5 Carlisle Rd	Westford	MA	01886	978-256-4200	256-6556
NASDAQ: CYNO ■ *TF:* 800-886-2966 ■ *Web:* www.cynosure.com					
Iridex Corp 1212 Terra Bella Ave	Mountain View	CA	94043	650-940-4700	940-4710
NASDAQ: IRIX ■ *TF Cust Svc:* 800-388-4747 ■ *Web:* www.iridex.com					
Laserscope 3070 Orchard Dr	San Jose	CA	95134	408-943-0636	943-1051*
NASDAQ: LSCP ■ **Fax:* Sales ■ *TF:* 800-356-7600					
LaserSight Technologies Inc					
931 S Semoran Blvd Suite 204	Winter Park	FL	32792	407-678-9900	678-9981
TF: 888-527-3235 ■ *Web:* www.lase.com					
Lumenis Ltd 2400 Condensa St	Santa Clara	CA	95051	408-764-3000	764-3999
TF: 800-227-1914 ■ *Web:* www.lumenis.com					
Palomar Medical Technologies Inc					
15 Network Dr	Burlington	MA	01803	781-993-2300	993-2330
NASDAQ: PMTI ■ *TF:* 800-725-6627 ■ *Web:* www.palmed.com					
PhotoMedex Inc 147 Keystone Dr	Montgomeryville	PA	18936	215-619-3600	619-3208
NASDAQ: PHMD ■ *TF:* 800-366-4758 ■ *Web:* www.photomedex.com					
PLC Medical Systems Inc 10 Forge Pk	Franklin	MA	02038	508-541-8800	541-7944*
**Fax:* Sales ■ *TF:* 800-232-8422 ■ *Web:* www.plcmed.com					
Spectranetics Corp 96 Talamine Ct	Colorado Springs	CO	80907	719-447-2000	447-2022
NASDAQ: SPNC ■ *TF:* 800-231-0978 ■ *Web:* www.spectranetics.com					
Trimedyne Inc 15091 Bake Pkwy	Irvine	CA	92618	949-559-5300	855-8206
TF: 800-733-5273 ■ *Web:* www.trimedyne.com					

428 LASERS - INDUSTRIAL

	City	State	ZIP	Phone	Fax
Aegis Corp 614 Dartmouth Terr Ct	Wildwood	MO	63011	636-273-1011	273-1015
Web: www.goaegis.com					
AGL Corp 2202 N Redmond Rd	Jacksonville	AR	72076	501-982-4433	982-0880
TF: 800-643-9696 ■ *Web:* www.agl-lasers.com					
Baublys Control Laser Corp					
2419 Lake Orange Dr	Orlando	FL	32837	407-926-3500	926-3590
Web: www.controllaser.com					
Coherent Inc 5100 Patrick Henry Dr	Santa Clara	CA	95054	408-764-4000	764-4000
NASDAQ: COHR ■ *TF Sales:* 800-527-3786 ■ *Web:* www.cohr.com					
Continuum 3150 Central Expy	Santa Clara	CA	95051	408-727-3240	727-3550
TF: 800-956-7757 ■ *Web:* www.continuumlasers.com					
Cymer Inc 17075 Thornmint Ct	San Diego	CA	92127	858-385-7300	385-7100
NASDAQ: CYMI ■ *Web:* www.cymer.com					
Electro Scientific Industries Inc					
13900 NW Science Pk Dr	Portland	OR	97229	503-641-4141	671-5544*
NASDAQ: ESIO ■ **Fax:* Claims ■ *TF Cust Svc:* 800-547-5746 ■ *Web:* www.elcsci.com					
Excel Technology Inc 41 Research Way	East Setauket	NY	11733	631-784-6175	784-6195
Web: www.exceltechinc.com					
GSI Group Inc 39 Manning Rd	Billerica	MA	01821	978-439-5511	663-0131*
NASDAQ: GSIG ■ **Fax:* Sales ■ *TF:* 800-342-3757 ■ *Web:* www.gsilumonics.com					
Ionatron Inc 3590 E Columbia St	Tucson	AZ	85714	520-628-7415	622-3835
NASDAQ: IOTN ■ *Web:* www.appliedenergetics.com					
Ipg Photonics Corp 50 Old Webster Rd	Oxford	MA	01540	508-373-1100	373-1103
NASDAQ: IPGP ■ *TF:* 877-980-1550 ■ *Web:* www.ipgphotonics.com					
Isomet Corp 5263 Port Royal Rd	Springfield	VA	22151	703-321-8301	321-8546
Web: www.isomet.com					
Jodon Inc 62 Enterprise Dr	Ann Arbor	MI	48103	734-761-4044	761-3322
TF: 800-989-5636 ■ *Web:* www.jodon.com					
Kigre Inc 100 Marshland Rd	Hilton Head Island	SC	29926	843-681-5800	681-4559
Web: www.kigre.com					
Laser Excel N6323 Berlin Rd PO Box 279	Green Lake	WI	54941	920-294-6544	294-6588
TF: 800-285-6544 ■ *Web:* www.laserexcel.com					
Leica Geosystems Inc 3498 Kraft Ave SE	Grand Rapids	MI	49512	616-977-4189	942-4627
TF Sales: 800-367-9453 ■ *Web:* www.leica-geosystems.com					
OSI Laserscan 3259 Progress Dr	Orlando	FL	32826	407-381-8117	381-2779
Web: www.seo.com					
PRIMA North America Inc 711 E Main St	Chicopee	MA	01020	413-598-5200	589-5201
TF Cust Svc: 800-722-1133 ■ *Web:* www.prima-na.com					
PTR-Precision Technologies Inc 120 Post Rd	Enfield	CT	06082	860-741-2281	745-7932
TF: 888-478-7832 ■ *Web:* www.ptreb.com					
Robinson Laser LLC 4303 Kennedy Ave	East Chicago	IN	46312	219-398-4600	398-7735
TF: 800-367-3528 ■ *Web:* www.robinsonsteel.com					
Rofin-Sinar Inc 40984 Concept Dr	Plymouth	MI	48170	734-455-5400	455-5587
NASDAQ: RSTI ■ *Web:* www.rofin.com					
STI Optronics Inc 2755 Northup Way	Bellevue	WA	98004	425-827-0460	828-3517
Web: www.stioptronics.com					
Synrad Inc 4600 Campus Pl	Mukilteo	WA	98275	425-349-3500	349-3667
TF: 800-796-7231 ■ *Web:* www.synrad.com					
TRUMPF Group 111 Hyde Rd	Farmington	CT	06032	860-255-6000	255-6424*
**Fax:* Mktg ■ *Web:* www.trumpf.com					

429 LAUNDRY & DRYCLEANING SERVICES

SEE ALSO Linen & Uniform Supply p. 2180

	City	State	ZIP	Phone	Fax
1-800-DryClean LLC 3948 Ranchero Dr	Ann Arbor	MI	48108	866-822-6115	822-6888*
**Fax Area Code:* 734 ■ *TF:* 800-379-2532 ■ *Web:* www.1-800-dryclean.com					
ACW Management Corp					
2019 Eastchester Dr PO Box 6535	High Point	NC	27265	336-841-4188	841-4117
Web: www.acleanerworld.com					
Admiral Inc 10 Taylor Ave	Annapolis	MD	21401	410-267-8381	263-4225
TF: 800-864-4429 ■ *Web:* www.admiralcleaners.com					
Al Phillips the Cleaner					
3250 W Ali Baba Ln Suite C-F	Las Vegas	NV	89118	702-798-7333	798-1731
Web: www.alphillips-thecleaner.com					
AW Zengeler Cleaners 550 Dundee Rd	Northbrook	IL	60062	847-272-6550	272-5465
Web: www.zengelercleaners.com					
Coinmach Service Corp					
303 Sunnyside Blvd Suite 70	Plainview	NY	11803	516-349-8555	349-9125
TF: 877-264-6622 ■ *Web:* www.coinmachservicecorp.com					
Comet Cleaners 406 W Division St	Arlington	TX	76011	817-461-3555	861-4779
Web: www.cometcleaners.com					
Div Laundry & Cleaners Inc					
6649 Old Hwy 90 W	San Antonio	TX	78227	210-674-5110	673-8510
Dryclean USA Inc 290 NE 68th St	Miami	FL	33138	305-754-9966	754-8010
AMEX: EVI ■ *Web:* www.drycleanusa.com					
Laundromax 411 Theodore Fremd Ave S Lobby	Rye	NY	10580	914-921-8240	

	City	State	Zip	Phone	Fax
Martinizing Dry Cleaning 422 Wards Corner Rd *TF:* 800-827-0207 ■ *Web:* www.martinizing.com	Loveland	OH	45140	513-351-6211	731-0818
Nu-Yale Cleaners 6300 Hwy 62 *TF:* 888-644-7400 ■ *Web:* www.nuyale.com	Jeffersonville	IN	47130	812-285-7400	285-7421
Pressed4Time Inc 8 Clock Tower Pl Suite 110 *TF:* 800-423-8711 ■ *Web:* www.pressed4time.com	Maynard	MA	01754	978-823-8300	823-8301
Salem Laundry Co 1 Lafayette St	Salem	MA	01970	978-744-1340	744-4216
Sloan's Dry Cleaning Inc 3001 N Main St	Los Angeles	CA	90031	323-225-1303	223-5358
Spic & Span Inc 4301 N Richards St *Web:* www.spicandspan.com	Milwaukee	WI	53212	414-964-5050	964-5042
Swan Super Cleaners Inc 1535 Bethel Rd *Web:* www.swancleaners.com	Columbus	OH	43220	614-442-5000	442-5007
Walker's Inc 4919 Underwood Ave *Web:* www.maxiwalker.com	Omaha	NE	68132	402-558-3677	558-1957
Westco Inc 3418 Americana Terr	Boise	ID	83706	208-342-3631	344-6423

LAUNDRY EQUIPMENT - HOUSEHOLD

SEE Appliance & Home Electronics Stores p. 1396; Appliances - Major - Mfr p. 1397; Appliances - Whol p. 1398

430 LAUNDRY EQUIPMENT & SUPPLIES - COMMERCIAL & INDUSTRIAL

	City	State	Zip	Phone	Fax
Alliance Laundry Systems LLC PO Box 990 *Web:* www.comlaundry.com	Ripon	WI	54971	920-748-3121	748-4429
American Dryer Corp 88 Currant Rd *Web:* www.amdry.com	Fall River	MA	02720	508-678-9000	678-9447
American Textile Processing LLC 422 Wards Corner Rd	Loveland	OH	45140	513-699-4280	699-4221
Chicago Dryer Co 2200 N Pulaski Rd *Web:* www.chidry.com	Chicago	IL	60639	773-235-4430	235-4439
Coinmach Service Corp 303 Sunnyside Blvd Suite 70 *TF:* 877-264-6622 ■ *Web:* www.coinmachservicecorp.com	Plainview	NY	11803	516-349-8555	349-9125
Colmac Industries Inc PO Box 72 *TF:* 800-926-5622 ■ *Web:* www.colmacind.com	Colville	WA	99114	509-684-4506	684-4500
Dexter Co 2211 W Grimes Ave *Web:* www.dexter.com	Fairfield	IA	52556	641-472-5131	472-5131
Edro Corp 37 Commerce St *TF Sales:* 800-628-6434 ■ *Web:* www.edrodynawash.com	East Berlin	CT	06023	860-828-0311	828-5984
Ellis Corp 1400 W Bryn Mawr Ave *TF:* 800-611-6806 ■ *Web:* www.elliscorp.com	Itasca	IL	60143	630-250-9222	250-9241
Forenta LP 2300 W Andrew Johnson Hwy # A *Web:* www.forentausa.com	Morristown	TN	37814	423-586-5370	586-3470
GA Braun Inc 461 E Brighton Ave *TF:* 800-432-7286 ■ *Web:* www.gabraun.com	Syracuse	NY	13212	315-475-3123	475-4130
Hoyt Corp 251 Forge Rd *TF:* 800-343-9411	Westport	MA	02790	508-636-8811	636-2088
Kemco Systems Inc 11500 47th St N *TF:* 800-633-7055 ■ *Web:* www.kemcosystems.com	Clearwater	FL	33762	727-573-2323	573-2346
Marvel Petrol Dry 5922 San Pedro Ave	San Antonio	TX	78212	210-344-8551	344-3004
Minnesota Chemical Co 2285 Hampden Ave *TF:* 800-328-5689 ■ *Web:* www.minnesotachemical.com	Saint Paul	MN	55114	651-646-7521	649-1101
Pellerin Milnor Corp 700 Jackson St *Web:* www.milnor.com	Kenner	LA	70062	504-467-9591	712-3783
Rema Dri-Vac Corp 45 Ruby St *Web:* www.remadrivac.com	Norwalk	CT	06850	203-847-2464	847-3609
Thermal Engineering of Arizona Inc 2250 W Wetmore Rd *TF:* 866-832-7278 ■ *Web:* www.teatucson.com	Tucson	AZ	85705	520-888-4000	888-4457
Washex Inc 5000 Central Fwy N *TF Sales:* 800-433-0933	Wichita Falls	TX	76306	940-855-7200	855-9349

431 LAW FIRMS

SEE ALSO Arbitration Services - Legal p. 1401; Legal Professionals Associations p. 1458; Bar Associations - State p. 1515; Litigation Support Services p. 2181

	City	State	Zip	Phone	Fax
Akerman Senterfitt 1 SE 3rd Ave 25th Fl *Web:* www.akerman.com	Miami	FL	33131	305-374-5600	374-5095
Akin Gump Strauss Hauer & Feld LLP 1333 New Hampshire Ave NW *Web:* www.akingump.com	Washington	DC	20036	202-887-4000	887-4288
Alston & Bird LLP 1201 W Peachtree St *Web:* www.alston.com	Atlanta	GA	30309	404-881-7000	881-7777
Andrews Kurth LLP 600 Travis St Chase Towers Suite 4200 *Web:* www.andrewskurth.com	Houston	TX	77002	713-220-4200	220-4285
Arnold & Porter LLP 555 12th St NW *Web:* www.arnoldporter.com	Washington	DC	20004	202-942-5000	942-5999
Atkinson Andelson Loya Ruud & Romo A Professional Law Corp 17871 Pk Plaza Dr *Web:* www.aalrr.com	Cerritos	CA	90703	562-653-3200	
Baker & McKenzie LLP 130 E Randolph St Suite 3900 *Web:* www.bakermckenzie.com	Chicago	IL	60601	312-861-8800	861-2899
Baker Botts LLP 910 Louisiana St 1 Shell Plaza *Web:* www.bakerbotts.com	Houston	TX	77002	713-229-1234	229-1522
Baker Donelson Bearman Caldwell & Berkowitz PC 165 Madison Ave 1st Tennessee Bldg Suite 2000 *Web:* www.bakerdonelson.com	Memphis	TN	38103	901-526-2000	577-2303
Baker Hostetler LLP 1900 E 9th St National City Ctr Suite 3200 *Web:* www.bakerlaw.com	Cleveland	OH	44114	216-621-0200	696-0740
Ballard Spahr Andrews & Ingersoll LLP 1735 Market St 51st Fl *Web:* www.ballardspahr.com	Philadelphia	PA	19103	215-665-8500	864-8999
Barnes & Thornburg 11 S Meridian St *TF:* 800-753-5139 ■ *Web:* www.btlaw.com	Indianapolis	IN	46204	317-236-1313	231-7433
Best & Flanagan LLP 225 S 6th St Suite 4000 *Web:* www.bestlaw.com	Minneapolis	MN	55402	612-339-7121	339-5897
Bingham McCutchen LLP 1 Federal St *Web:* www.bingham.com	Boston	MA	02110	617-951-8000	951-8736
Black Srebnick Kornspan & Stumpf PA 201 S Biscayne Blvd Suite 1300 *Web:* www.royblack.com	Miami	FL	33131	305-371-6421	
Blank Rome LLP 1 Logan Sq 130 N 18th St *Web:* www.blankrome.com	Philadelphia	PA	19103	215-569-5500	569-5555
Boies Schiller & Flexner LLP 5301 Wisconsin Ave NW *Web:* www.boies-schiller&flexner.com	Washington	DC	20015	202-237-2727	237-6131
Bose McKinney & Evans LLP 111 Monument Cir Suite 2700 *Web:* www.boselaw.com	Indianapolis	IN	46204	317-684-5000	684-5173
Bracewell & Giuliani LLP 711 Louisiana St Suite 2300 *Web:* www.bracewellgiuliani.com	Houston	TX	77002	713-223-2300	221-1212
Bradford & Barthel LLP 2233 Watt Ave Suite 350 *Web:* www.bradfordbarthel.com	Sacramento	CA	95825	916-569-0790	569-0799
Bryan Cave LLP 1 Metropolitan Sq 211 N Broadway Suite 3800 *Web:* www.bryancave.com	Saint Louis	MO	63102	314-259-2000	259-2020
Buchalter Nemer Pc 1000 Wilshire Blvd *TF:* 877-783-8686 ■ *Web:* www.buchalter.com	Los Angeles	CA	90017	213-891-0700	896-0400
Buchanan Ingersoll & Rooney PC 301 Grant St 1 Oxford Ctr 20th Fl *TF:* 800-444-6738 ■ *Web:* www.buchananingersoll.com	Pittsburgh	PA	15219	412-562-8800	562-1041
Budd Larner P C 150 John F Kennedy Pkwy *Web:* www.buddlarner.com	Short Hills	NJ	07078	973-379-4800	379-7734
Burch Porter & Johnson Pllc 130 N Ct Ave *Web:* www.bpjlaw.com	Memphis	TN	38103	901-524-5000	524-5024
Cadwalader Wickersham & Taft LLP 1 World Financial Ctr *TF:* 800-489-8682 ■ *Web:* www.cadwalader.com	New York	NY	10281	212-504-6000	504-6666
Carlile Patchen & Murphy LLP 366 E Broad St *Web:* www.cpmlaw.com	Columbus	OH	43215	614-228-6135	221-0216
Carlsmith Ball LLP 1001 Bishop St Suite 2200 *Web:* www.carlsmith.com	Honolulu	HI	96813	808-523-2500	523-0842
Carroll Burdick & Mc Donough 44 Montgomery St # 400 *Web:* www.cbmlaw.com	San Francisco	CA	94104	415-989-5900	989-0932
Carter Ledyard & Milburn LLP 2 Wall St FL 13 *Web:* www.clm.com	New York	NY	10005	212-732-3200	732-3232
Cavanagh Law Firm The 1850 N Central Ave *TF:* 888-824-3476 ■ *Web:* www.cavanaghlaw.com	Phoenix	AZ	85004	602-322-4000	322-4100
Chadbourne & Parke LLP 30 Rockefeller Plaza *Web:* www.chadbourne.com	New York	NY	10112	212-408-5100	541-5369
Christensen Glaser Fink Jacobs Weil & Shapiro LLP 10250 Constellation Blvd 19th Fl *Web:* www.chrisglase.com	Los Angeles	CA	90067	310-553-3000	556-2920
Clifford Chance LLP 31 W 52nd St *Web:* www.cliffordchance.com	New York	NY	10019	212-878-8000	878-8375
Cobb & Cole 150 Magnolia Ave *Web:* www.cobbcole.com	Daytona Beach	FL	32114	386-255-8171	258-5066
Cochran Firm LLC 163 W Main St *TF:* 800-526-2472 ■ *Web:* www.cochranfirm.com	Dothan	AL	36301	334-793-1555	793-8280
Cohen & Grigsby Pc 625 Liberty Ave *Web:* www.cohenlaw.com	Pittsburgh	PA	15222	412-297-4900	209-0672
Cooley Godward Kronish LLP 3000 El Camino Real *Web:* www.cooley.com	Palo Alto	CA	94306	650-843-5000	849-7400
Covington & Burling LLP 1201 Pennsylvania Ave NW *Web:* www.cov.com	Washington	DC	20004	202-662-6000	662-6291
Cowles & Thompson A Professional Corp 901 Main St Suite 3900 *Web:* www.cowlesthompson.com	Dallas	TX	75202	214-672-2000	672-2020
Cozen O'Connor 1900 Market St *TF:* 800-523-2900 ■ *Web:* www.cozen.com	Philadelphia	PA	19103	215-665-2000	665-2013
Cranfill Sumner & Hartzog LLP PO Box 27808 *Web:* www.cshlaw.com	Raleigh	NC	27611	919-828-5100	828-2277
Cravath Swaine & Moore LLP 825 8th Ave Worldwide Plaza *Web:* www.cravath.com	New York	NY	10019	212-474-1000	474-3700
Davis Graham & Stubbs LLP 1550 17th St Suite 500 *Web:* www.dgslaw.com	Denver	CO	80202	303-892-9400	893-1379
Davis Polk & Wardwell 450 Lexington Ave *Web:* www.davispolk.com	New York	NY	10017	212-450-4000	701-5800
Davis Wright Tremaine LLP 1201 Third Ave #2200 *Web:* www.dwt.com	Seattle	WA	98101	206-622-3150	628-7699

				Phone	Fax
Day Pitney LLP 242 Trumbull St *Web:* www.daypitney.com	Hartford	CT	06103	860-275-0100	275-0343
De Cotiis Fitzpatrick Cole & Wisler LLP 500 Frank W Burr Blvd *Web:* www.decotiislaw.com	Teaneck	NJ	07666	201-928-1100	
Debevoise & Plimpton LLP 919 3rd Ave *Web:* www.debevoise.com	New York	NY	10022	212-909-6000	909-6836
Dechert LLP 2929 Arch St Cira Ctr *Web:* www.dechert.com	Philadelphia	PA	19104	215-994-4000	994-2222
Dickstein Shapiro LLP 1825 Eye St NW *Web:* www.dicksteinshapiro.com	Washington	DC	20006	202-420-2200	420-2201
DLA Piper 203 N LaSalle St Suite 1900 *Web:* www.dlapiper.com	Chicago	IL	60601	312-368-4000	236-7516
Dorsey & Whitney LLP 50 S 6th St Suite 1500 *TF:* 800-759-4929 ■ *Web:* www.dorsey.com	Minneapolis	MN	55402	612-340-2600	340-2868
Drinker Biddle & Reath LLP 1 Logan Sq # 2000 *Web:* www.drinkerbiddle.com	Philadelphia	PA	19103	215-988-2700	988-2757
Duane Morris LLP 30 S 17th St United Plaza *Web:* www.duanemorris.com	Philadelphia	PA	19103	215-979-1000	979-1020
Edwards Angell Palmer & Dodge LLP 111 Huntington Ave *Web:* www.eapdlaw.com	Boston	MA	02199	617-239-0100	227-4420
Epstein Becker & Green PC 250 Pk Ave *Web:* www.ebglaw.com	New York	NY	10177	212-351-4500	661-0989
Faegre & Benson LLP 90 S 7th St 2200 Wells Fargo Bldg *TF:* 800-328-4393 ■ *Web:* www.faegre.com	Minneapolis	MN	55402	612-766-7000	766-1600
Fieger Fieger Kenney & Giroux PC 19390 W 10-Mile Rd *Web:* www.fiegerlaw.com	Southfield	MI	48075	248-355-5555	355-5148
Fish & Richardson PC 225 Franklin St 31st Fl *TF:* 800-818-5070 ■ *Web:* www.fr.com	Boston	MA	02110	617-542-5070	542-8906
Fitzpatrick Cella Harper & Scinto 1290 Avenue of the Americas *Web:* www.fitzpatrickcella.com	New York	NY	10104	212-218-2100	218-2200
Foley & Lardner LLP 777 E Wisconsin Ave *TF:* 800-558-1548 ■ *Web:* www.foley.com	Milwaukee	WI	53202	414-271-2400	297-4900
Foster Pepper Pllc 1111 3rd Ave Suite 3400 *TF:* 800-995-5902 ■ *Web:* www.foster.com	Seattle	WA	98101	206-447-4400	447-9700
Fox Rothschild LLP 2000 Market St 10th Fl *Web:* www.foxrothschild.com	Philadelphia	PA	19103	215-299-2000	299-2150
Frankfurt Kurnit Klein & Selz Pc 488 Madison Ave FL 9 *Web:* www.fgks.com	New York	NY	10022	212-980-0120	593-9175
Freeborn & Peters 311 S Wacker Dr Suite 3000 *Web:* www.freebornpeters.com	Chicago	IL	60606	312-360-6000	360-6520
Freeman Freeman & Smiley LLP 3415 S Sepulveda Blvd *Web:* www.ffslaw.com	Los Angeles	CA	90034	310-255-6100	391-4042
Fried Frank Harris Shriver & Jacobson LLP (FFHSJ) 1 New York Plaza *Web:* www.friedfrank.com	New York	NY	10004	212-859-8000	859-4000
Frost Brown Todd LLC 201 E 5th St 2200 PNC Ctr *Web:* www.frostbrowntodd.com	Cincinnati	OH	45202	513-651-6800	651-6981
Fulbright & Jaworski LLP 1301 McKinney St Suite 5100 *TF:* 866-385-2744 ■ *Web:* www.fulbright.com	Houston	TX	77010	713-651-5151	651-5246
Garden City Group Inc The 105 Maxess Rd Suite 320 *TF:* 888-539-6030 ■ *Web:* www.gardencitygroup.com	Melville	NY	11747	631-470-5000	470-5100
Gary Williams Parenti Finney Lewis McManus Watson & Sperando PL 221 E Osceola St *TF:* 800-329-4279 ■ *Web:* www.garylawgroup.com	Stuart	FL	34994	772-283-8260	283-8260
Geragos & Geragos PC 644 S Figueroa St *Web:* www.geragos.com	Los Angeles	CA	90017	213-625-3900	625-1600
Gibbons PC 1 Gateway Ctr *Web:* www.gibbonslaw.com	Newark	NJ	07102	973-596-4500	596-0545
Gibson Dunn & Crutcher LLP 333 S Grand Ave Suite 4600 *TF:* 800-822-7152 ■ *Web:* www.gibsondunn.com	Los Angeles	CA	90071	213-229-7000	229-7520
Gipson Hoffman & Pancione 1901 Avenue of The Stars 11th Fl *Web:* www.ghplaw.com	Los Angeles	CA	90067	310-556-4660	356-8945
Goodell Devries Leech & Dann LLP 1 S St Suite 2000 *TF:* 888-229-4354 ■ *Web:* www.gdldlaw.com	Baltimore	MD	21202	410-783-4000	783-4040
Goodwin Procter LLP 53 Exchange St *Web:* www.goodwinprocter.com	Boston	MA	02109	617-570-1000	523-1231
Gordon Feinblatt Rothman Hoffberger & Hollander LLC 233 E Redwood St *Web:* www.gfrlaw.com	Baltimore	MD	21202	410-576-4156	576-4246
Gordon Thomas Honeywell LLP 1201 Pacific Ave Suite 2100 *Web:* www.gth-law.com	Tacoma	WA	98402	253-620-6500	620-6565
Graham & Dunn Pc 2801 Alaskan Way Suite 300 *Web:* www.grahamdunn.com	Seattle	WA	98121	206-624-8300	340-9599
Greenberg Glusker Fields Claman & Machtinger LLP 1900 Avenue of the Stars 21st Fl *Web:* www.greenbergglusker.com	Los Angeles	CA	90067	310-553-3610	553-0687
Gunster Yoakley & Stewart Pa 777 S Flagler Dr Suite 500 E *TF:* 800-749-1980 ■ *Web:* www.gunster.com	West Palm Beach	FL	33401	561-655-1980	655-5677
Haight Brown & Bonesteel LLP 6080 Ctr Dr Suite 800 *Web:* www.hbblaw.com	Los Angeles	CA	90045	310-215-7100	215-7300
Hall & Evans 1125 17th St Suite 600 *Web:* www.hallevans.com	Denver	CO	80202	303-628-3313	293-3232
Hall Render Killian Heath & Lyman Pc 1 American Sq Suite 2000 PO Box 82064 *Web:* www.hallrender.com	Indianapolis	IN	46282	317-633-4884	633-4878
Harter Secrest & Emery LLP (HSE) 1600 Bausch & Lomb Pl *Web:* www.hselaw.com	Rochester	NY	14604	585-232-6500	232-2152
Haynes & Boone LLP 2323 Victory Ave #700 *Web:* www.haynesboone.com	Dallas	TX	75219	214-651-5000	651-5940
Heyl Royster Voelker & Allen Pc 124 SW Adams St Suite 600 *Web:* www.hrva.com	Peoria	IL	61602	309-676-0400	
Hinckley Allen & Snyder LLP 28 State St *Web:* www.haslaw.com	Boston	MA	02109	617-345-9000	345-9020
Hinshaw & Culbertson LLP 222 N LaSalle St Suite 300 *TF:* 800-300-6812 ■ *Web:* www.hinshawlaw.com	Chicago	IL	60601	312-704-3000	704-3001
Hopkins & Carley A Law Corp PO Box 1469 *TF:* 800-998-3660 ■ *Web:* www.hopkinscarley.com	San Jose	CA	95109	408-286-9800	998-4790
Howard & Howard Attorneys Pc 39400 Woodward Ave Suite 101 *Web:* www.h2law.com	Bloomfield Hills	MI	48304	248-645-1483	645-1568
Howard Rice Nemerovski Canady Falk & Rabkin Pc 3 Embarcadero Ctr 7th Fl *Web:* www.hrice.com	San Francisco	CA	94111	415-434-1600	677-6262
Howrey LLP 1299 Pennsylvania Ave NW *TF:* 800-727-1730 ■ *Web:* www.howrey.com	Washington	DC	20004	202-783-0800	383-6610
Hughes Hubbard & Reed LLP 1 Battery Pk Plaza *Web:* www.hugheshubbard.com	New York	NY	10004	212-837-6000	422-4726
Hunton & Williams LLP 951 E Byrd St Riverfront Plaza E Tower *Web:* www.hunton.com	Richmond	VA	23219	804-788-8200	788-8218
Hurley Rogner Miller Cox 1560 Orange Ave # 500 *Web:* www.hrmcw.com	Winter Park	FL	32789	407-422-1455	422-1371
Hyman Phelps & Mcnamara Pc 700 13th St NW Suite 1200 *Web:* www.hpm.com	Washington	DC	20005	202-737-5600	737-9329
Irell & Manella LLP 1800 Avenue of the Stars Suite 900 *Web:* www.irell.com	Los Angeles	CA	90067	310-277-1010	203-7199
Jacob Medinger & Finnegan LLP (JMF) 1270 Avenue of the Americas *Web:* www.jmfnylaw.com	New York	NY	10020	212-332-7700	332-7777
Jenner & Block LLP 353 N Clark St *Web:* www.jenner.com	Chicago	IL	60654	312-222-9350	527-0484
Johnson & Bell Ltd 33 W Monroe St Suite 2700 *Web:* www.johnsonandbell.com	Chicago	IL	60603	312-372-0770	372-9818
Jones Day 51 Louisiana Ave NW *Web:* www.jonesday.com	Washington	DC	20001	202-879-3939	626-1700
Katten Muchin Rosenman LLP 525 W Monroe St Suite 1300 *TF:* 800-346-7400 ■ *Web:* www.kattenlaw.com	Chicago	IL	60661	312-902-5200	902-1061
Kaye Scholer LLP 425 Pk Ave *Web:* www.kayescholer.com	New York	NY	10022	212-836-8000	836-8689
Keating Muething & Klekamp Pll 1 E 4th St Suite 1400 *Web:* www.kmklaw.com	Cincinnati	OH	45202	513-579-6400	579-6457
Keesal Young & Logan 400 Oceangate PO Box 1730 *Web:* www.kyl.com	Long Beach	CA	90801	562-436-2000	436-7416
Keller & Heckman LLP 1001 G St NW Suite 500w *Web:* www.khlaw.com	Washington	DC	20001	202-434-4100	434-4646
Kelley Drye & Warren LLP 101 Pk Ave *Web:* www.kelleydrye.com	New York	NY	10178	212-808-7800	808-7897
Kemp & Smith LLP 221 N Kansas PO Box 2800 *Web:* www.kempsmith.com	El Paso	TX	79901	915-533-4424	546-5360
Kilpatrick Stockton LLP 1100 Peachtree St Suite 2800 *Web:* www.kilpatrickstockton.com	Atlanta	GA	30309	404-815-6500	815-6555
King & Spalding 1180 Peachtree St NE *Web:* www.kslaw.com	Atlanta	GA	30309	404-572-4600	572-5100
Kirkland & Ellis LLP 200 E Randolph Dr *TF:* 800-334-3133 ■ *Web:* www.kirkland.com	Chicago	IL	60601	312-861-2000	861-2200
Kirkpatrick & Lockhart Preston Gates Ellis LLP 210 Sixth Ave *Web:* www.klgates.com	Pittsburgh	PA	15222	412-355-6500	355-6501
Kitch Drutchas Wagner Valitutti & Sherbrook Pc 1 Woodward Ave Suite 2400 *Web:* www.kitch.com	Detroit	MI	48226	313-965-7900	

Firm / Address	City	State	ZIP	Phone	Fax
Kominiarek Bressler Harvick & Gudmundson LLC 33 N Dearborn St Suite 700 *Web:* www.kbhglaw.com	Chicago	IL	60602	312-322-1111	782-1432
Krieg DeVault Alexander & Capehart 1 Indiana Sq Suite 2800 *Web:* www.kriegdevault.com	Indianapolis	IN	46204	317-636-4341	636-1507
Kronick Moskovitz Tiedemann & Girard 400 Capitol Mall FL 27 *Web:* www.kmtg.com	Sacramento	CA	95814	916-321-4500	321-4555
Kutak Rock LLP 1650 Farnam St *Web:* www.kutakrock.com	Omaha	NE	68102	402-346-6000	346-1148
Ladas & Parry LLP 1040 Avenue of the Americas *Web:* www.ladas.com	New York	NY	10018	212-708-1800	246-8959
Lane & Waterman LLP 220 N Main St Suite 600 *Web:* www.l-wlaw.com	Davenport	IA	52801	563-324-3246	324-1616
Larson King LLP 2800 Wells Fargo Pl 30 E 7th St *Web:* www.larsonking.com	Saint Paul	MN	55101	651-312-6500	312-6618
Latham & Watkins LLP 885 3rd Ave *Web:* www.lw.com	New York	NY	10022	212-906-1200	751-4864
Lavin O'Neil Ricci Cedrone & Disipio 190 N Independence Mall W *Web:* www.lavin-law.com	Philadelphia	PA	19106	215-627-0303	627-2551
Law Weathers & Richardson Pc 333 Bridge St NW Suite 800 *Web:* www.lawweathers.com	Grand Rapids	MI	49504	616-459-1171	732-1740
Lemle & Kelleher LLP 601 Poydras St Fl 21 *Web:* www.lemle.com	New Orleans	LA	70130	504-586-1241	584-9142
Lewis Brisbois Bisgaard & Smith LLP 221 N Figueroa St Suite 1200 *Web:* www.lbbslaw.com	Los Angeles	CA	90012	213-250-1800	250-7900
Linowes & Blocher LLP 7200 Wisconsin Ave Suite 800 *Web:* www.linowes-law.com	Bethesda	MD	20814	301-654-0504	654-2801
Littler Mendelson PC 650 California St 20th Fl *TF:* 888-548-8537 ■ *Web:* www.littler.com	San Francisco	CA	94108	415-433-1940	399-8490
Locke Lord Bissell & Liddell LLP (LLBL) 2200 Ross Ave Suite 2200 *Web:* www.lockelord.com	Dallas	TX	75201	214-740-8000	740-8000
Mariscal Weeks Mcintyre & Friedlander Pa 2901 N Central Ave *Web:* www.mwmf.com	Phoenix	AZ	85012	602-285-5000	285-5100
Marshall Dennehey Warner Coleman & Goggin 1845 Walnut St 16th Fl *Web:* www.marshalldennehey.com	Philadelphia	PA	19103	215-575-2600	575-0856
Mc Connaughhay Duffy Coonrad Pope & Weaver Pa Drawer 229 *Web:* www.mcconnaughhay.com	Tallahassee	FL	32302	850-222-8121	
Mc Elroy Deutsch & Mulvaney LLP PO Box 2075 *Web:* www.mdmc-law.com	Morristown	NJ	07962	973-993-8100	292-1551
McAndrews Held & Malloy 500 W Madison St 34th Fl *Web:* www.mhmlaw.com	Chicago	IL	60661	312-775-8000	775-8100
McCarter & English LLP 4 Gateway Ctr 100 Mulberry St *Web:* www.mccarter.com	Newark	NJ	07102	973-622-4444	624-7070
McDermott Will & Emery 227 W Monroe St Suite 4700 *Web:* www.mwe.com	Chicago	IL	60606	312-372-2000	984-7700
Mcdowell Rice Smith & Buchanan Pc 605 W 47th St Suite 350 *Web:* www.mcdowellrice.com	Kansas City	MO	64112	816-753-5400	753-9996
Mcginnis Lochridge & Kilgore LLP 600 Congress Ave *Web:* www.mcginnislaw.com	Austin	TX	78701	512-495-6000	495-6093
McGuireWoods LLP 901 E Cary St 1 James Ctr *Web:* www.mcguirewoods.com	Richmond	VA	23219	804-775-1000	775-1061
McKenna Long & Aldridge LLP 303 Peachtree St Suite 5300 *Web:* www.mckennalong.com	Atlanta	GA	30308	404-527-4000	527-4198
McNees Wallace & Nurick LLC 1 S Church St Renaissance Ctr Suite 302 *Fax Area Code: 570 ■ *Web:* www.mwn.com	Hazleton	PA	18201	717-232-8000	455-8390*
Messerli & Kramer PA 1400 5th St Towers 100 S 5th St *Web:* www.messerlikramer.com	Minneapolis	MN	55402	612-672-3600	672-3777
Meyer Unkovic & Scott LLP 535 Smithfield St Suite 1300 *Web:* www.muslaw.com	Pittsburgh	PA	15222	412-456-2800	456-2864
Milbank Tweed Hadley & McCloy LLP 1 Chase Manhattan Plaza *Web:* www.milbank.com	New York	NY	10005	212-530-5000	530-5219
Miller & Chevalier Chartered 655 15th St NW Suite 900 *Web:* www.millerchevalier.com	Washington	DC	20005	202-626-5800	626-5801
Miller Canfield Paddock & Stone PLC 150 W Jefferson Ave Suite 2500 *Web:* www.millercanfield.com	Detroit	MI	48226	313-963-6420	496-7500
Miller Johnson Snell & Cummiskey Plc 250 Monroe Ave NW Suite 800 PO Box 306 *Web:* www.millerjohnson.com	Grand Rapids	MI	49503	616-831-1700	831-1701
Mintz Levin Cohn Ferris Glovsky & Popeo PC 1 Financial Ctr *Web:* www.mintz.com	Boston	MA	02111	617-542-6000	542-2241
Mitchell Williams Selig Gates & Woodyard Pllc 425 W Capitol Ave Suite 1800 *Web:* www.mitchellwilliamslaw.com	Little Rock	AR	72201	501-688-8800	688-8807
Modrall Sperling Roehl Harris & Sisk P.a PO Box 2168 *Web:* www.modrall.com	Albuquerque	NM	87103	505-848-1800	
Moisture Control Technologies Inc 27764 Volo Village Rd Suite A *Web:* www.moistcontech.com	Round Lake	IL	60073	815-385-0041	385-0106
Montgomery Little & Soran PC 5445 Dtc Pkwy Suite 800 *Web:* www.montgomerylittle.com	Greenwood Village	CO	80111	303-773-8100	220-0412
Morgan Lewis & Bockius LLP 1701 Market St *Web:* www.morganlewis.com	Philadelphia	PA	19103	215-963-5000	963-5001
Morris Polich & Purdy 1055 W 7th St Suite 2400 *Web:* www.mpplaw.com	Los Angeles	CA	90017	213-891-9100	488-1178
Morrison & Foerster LLP 425 Market St *TF:* 800-669-5996 ■ *Web:* www.mofo.com	San Francisco	CA	94105	415-268-7000	268-7522
Morrison Mahoney LLP 250 Summer St FL 1 Web: www.morrisonmahoney.com	Boston	MA	02210	617-439-7500	439-7590
Munsch Hardt Kopf Harr Pc 500 N Akard St *Web:* www.munsch.com	Dallas	TX	75201	214-855-7500	855-7584
Nelson Mullins Riley & Scarborough LLP 1320 Main St 17th Fl *TF:* 800-237-2000 ■ *Web:* www.nelsonmullins.com	Columbia	SC	29201	803-799-2000	256-7500
Niles Barton & Wilmer 111 S Calvert St Suite 1400 *Web:* www.nilesbarton.com	Baltimore	MD	21202	410-783-6300	783-6363
Nisen & Elliott LLC 200 W Adams St Suite 2500 *Web:* www.nisen.com	Chicago	IL	60606	312-346-7800	
Nysarc Inc 393 Delaware Ave *Web:* www.nysarc.org	Delmar	NY	12054	518-439-8311	439-1893
O'Melveny & Myers LLP 400 S Hope St 10th Fl *Web:* www.omm.com	Los Angeles	CA	90071	213-430-6000	430-6407
Orrick Herrington & Sutcliffe LLP 666 5th Ave *Web:* www.orrick.com	New York	NY	10103	212-506-5000	506-5151
Otten Johnson Robinson Neff & Ragonetti PC 950 17th St Suite 1600 *Web:* www.ojrnr.com	Denver	CO	80202	303-825-8400	825-6525
Pachulski Stang Ziehl Young & Jones Professional Corp 10100 Santa Monica Blvd *Web:* www.pszjlaw.com	Los Angeles	CA	90067	310-277-6910	
Patton Boggs LLP 2550 M St NW *Web:* www.pattonboggs.com	Washington	DC	20037	202-457-6000	457-6315
Paul Hastings Janofsky & Walker LLP 515 S Flower St 25th Fl *TF:* 888-745-9557 ■ *Web:* www.paulhastings.com	Los Angeles	CA	90071	213-683-6000	627-0705
Paul Weiss Rifkind Wharton & Garrison LLP 1285 Avenue of the Americas *Web:* www.paulweiss.com	New York	NY	10019	212-373-3000	757-3990
Peabody & Arnold LLP 600 Atlantic Ave *Web:* www.peabodyarnold.com	Boston	MA	02110	617-951-2100	951-2125
Pellettieri Rabstein & Altman 100 Nassau Pk Blvd *TF:* 800-432-5297 ■ *Web:* www.pralaw.com	Princeton	NJ	08540	609-520-0900	452-8796
Pepper Hamilton LLP 3000 Two Logan Sq 18th & Arch St *Web:* www.pepperlaw.com	Philadelphia	PA	19103	215-981-4000	981-4750
Perkins Coie LLP 1201 Third Ave # 4800 *TF:* 800-829-1177 ■ *Web:* www.perkinscoie.com	Seattle	WA	98101	206-359-8000	359-9000
Pillsbury Winthrop Shaw Pittman LLP 50 Fremont St *TF:* 800-477-0770 ■ *Web:* www.pillsburylaw.com	San Francisco	CA	94105	415-983-1000	983-1200
Polsinelli Shalton Flanigan Suelthaus PC 700 W 47th St Suite 1000 *Web:* www.polsinelli.com	Kansas City	MO	64112	816-753-1000	753-1536
Preffered Choice Management Systems Inc 1 Penn Plaza 46th Fl *TF:* 800-235-7267 ■ *Web:* www.magnacare.com	New York	NY	10119	516-282-8000	
Procopio Cory Hargreaves & Savitch LLP 525 B St Suite 2200 *Web:* www.procopio.com	San Diego	CA	92101	619-238-1900	235-0398
Proskauer Rose LLP 1585 Broadway *Web:* www.proskauer.com	New York	NY	10036	212-969-3000	969-2900
Quarles & Brady LLP 411 E Wisconsin Ave Suite 2040 *TF:* 800-446-7545 ■ *Web:* www.quarles.com	Milwaukee	WI	53202	414-277-5000	271-3552
Recordtrak Inc 651 Allendale Rd PO Box 61591 *TF:* 800-355-7400 ■ *Web:* www.recordtrak.com	King of Prussi	PA	19406	610-992-5000	354-8946
Reed Smith 435 6th Ave *Web:* www.reedsmith.com	Pittsburgh	PA	15219	412-288-3131	288-3063
Reminger & Reminger Co LPa 101 W Prospect Ave *TF:* 800-486-1311 ■ *Web:* www.reminger.com	Cleveland	OH	44115	216-687-1311	687-1841
Rhoades McKee PC 161 Ottawa Ave NW Suite 600 *Web:* www.rhoadesmckee.com	Grand Rapids	MI	49503	616-235-3500	459-5102

				Phone	Fax
Richards Layton & Finger PO Box 551	Wilmington	DE	19899	302-651-7700	651-7701
Web: www.rlf.com					
Riggs Abney Neal Orbison & Lewis Inc					
502 W 6TH St Frisco Bldg	Tulsa	OK	74119	918-587-3161	
Web: www.riggsabney.com					
Robinson Bradshaw & Hinson Pa					
101 N Tryon St Suite 1900	Charlotte	NC	28246	704-377-2536	378-4000
Web: www.rbh.com					
Rodey Dickason Sloan Akin & Robb P A					
201 3rd St NW Suite 2200	Albuquerque	NM	87102	505-765-5900	768-7395
Web: www.rodey.com					
Ropes & Gray LLP 1 International Pl	Boston	MA	02110	617-951-7000	951-7050
Web: www.ropesgray.com					
Rose Law Firm A Professional Assn					
120 E 4th St	Little Rock	AR	72201	501-375-9131	375-1309
Web: www.roselawfirm.com					
Rush Moore LLP 737 BISHOP St # 2400	Honolulu	HI	96813	808-521-0400	521-0497
Web: www.rmhawaii.com					
Rutan & Tucker LLP PO Box 1950	Costa Mesa	CA	92628	714-641-5100	546-9035
Web: www.rutan.com					
Ryley Carlock & Applewhite Pa					
1 N Central Ave Suite 1200	Phoenix	AZ	85004	602-258-7701	257-9582
Web: www.rcalaw.com					
Schiff Hardin LLP					
233 S Wacker Dr 6600 Sears Tower	Chicago	IL	60606	312-258-5500	258-5700
TF: 800-258-7799 ■ *Web:* www.schiffhardin.com					
Schulte Roth & Zabel LLP 919 3rd Ave	New York	NY	10022	212-758-0404	593-5955
TF: 800-346-9644 ■ *Web:* www.srz.com					
Sedgwick Detert Moran & Arnold LLP					
1 Market Plaza Steuart Tower 8th Fl	San Francisco	CA	94105	415-781-7900	781-2635
TF: 800-826-3262 ■ *Web:* www.sdma.com					
Selman Breitman LLP 11766 Wilshire Blvd	Los Angeles	CA	90025	310-445-0800	473-2525
Web: www.selmanbreitman.com.xohost.com					
Seward & Kissel 1 Battery Pk Plaza FL 21	New York	NY	10004	212-574-1200	480-8421
Web: www.sewkis.com					
Seyfarth Shaw LLP					
131 S Dearborn St Suite 2400	Chicago	IL	60603	312-460-5000	460-7000
TF: 866-460-3476 ■ *Web:* www.seyfarth.com					
Shartsis Friese & Ginsburg LLP					
1 Maritime Plaza 18th Fl	San Francisco	CA	94111	415-421-6500	421-2922
Web: www.sflaw.com					
Shearman & Sterling LLP 599 Lexington Ave	New York	NY	10022	212-848-4000	848-7179
TF: 800-521-2918 ■ *Web:* www.shearman.com					
Shefsky & Froelich 111 E Wacker Dr Suite 2800	Chicago	IL	60601	312-527-4000	527-4011
Web: www.shefskylaw.com					
Sheppard Mullin Richter & Hampton LLP					
333 S Hope St 48th Fl	Los Angeles	CA	90071	213-620-1780	620-1398
Web: www.sheppardmullin.com					
Sherman Richichi & Hickey LLC 27 5th St	Stamford	CT	06905	203-324-2296	348-7313
Web: www.srh-law.com					
Shook Hardy & Bacon LLP 2555 Grand Blvd	Kansas City	MO	64108	816-474-6550	421-5547
TF: 800-821-7962 ■ *Web:* www.shb.com					
Shumaker Loop & Kendrick LLP 1000 Jackson St	Toledo	OH	43624	419-241-9000	241-6894
Web: www.slk-law.com					
Sidley Austin LLP 1 S Dearborn St	Chicago	IL	60603	312-853-7000	853-7036
Web: www.sidley.com					
Simpson Thacher & Bartlett LLP					
425 Lexington Ave	New York	NY	10017	212-455-2000	455-2502
Web: www.stblaw.com					
Sirote & Permutt Pc					
2311 Highland Ave S PO Box 55727	Birmingham	AL	35205	205-930-5100	930-5101
Web: www.sirote.com					
Skadden Arps Slate Meagher & Flom LLP					
4 Times Sq	New York	NY	10036	212-735-3000	735-2000
Web: www.skadden.com					
Smith Hulsey & Busey					
225 Water St Suite 1800	Jacksonville	FL	32202	904-359-7700	359-7708
Web: www.smithhulsey.com					
Snell & Wilmer LLP 1 Arizona Ctr # 1000	Phoenix	AZ	85004	602-382-6000	382-6070
TF: 800-322-0430 ■ *Web:* www.swlaw.com					
Snow Christensen & Martineau					
10 Exchange Pl	Salt Lake City	UT	84111	801-521-9000	
Web: www.scmlaw.com					
Sommers Schwartz 2000 Town Ctr Suite 900	Southfield	MI	48075	248-266-2536	746-4001
TF: 800-967-1234 ■ *Web:* www.sommerspc.com					
Spence Law Firm LLC 15 S Jackson St	Jackson	WY	83001	307-733-7290	733-5248
TF: 800-967-2117 ■ *Web:* www.spencelawyers.com					
Spencer Fane Britt & Browne LLP					
1000 Walnut St Suite 1400	Kansas City	MO	64106	816-474-8100	474-3216
Web: www.spencerfane.com					
Squire Sanders & Dempsey LLP					
127 Public Sq 4900 Key Tower	Cleveland	OH	44114	216-479-8500	479-8780
TF: 800-743-2773 ■ *Web:* www.ssd.com					
Stark & Stark 993 Lenox Dr Bldg Two	Lawrenceville	NJ	08648	609-896-9060	896-0629
TF: 800-535-3425 ■ *Web:* www.stark-stark.com					
Stearns Weaver Miller Weissler Alhadeff & Sitterson Pa					
150 W Flagler St Lbby	Miami	FL	33130	305-789-3200	789-3395
Web: www.swmwas.com					
Steptoe & Johnson LLP					
1330 Connecticut Ave NW	Washington	DC	20036	202-429-3000	429-3902
Web: www.steptoe.com					
Stolar Partnership LLP The					
911 Wshington Ave Suite 700	Saint Louis	MO	63101	314-231-2800	436-8400
Web: www.stolarlaw.com					
Strauss & Troy 150 E 4th St	CINCINNATI	OH	45202	513-621-2120	241-8259
Web: www.strausstroy.com					
Sullivan & Cromwell LLP 125 Broad St	New York	NY	10004	212-558-4000	558-3588
Web: www.sullcrom.com					
Sutherland Asbill & Brennan LLP					
999 Peachtree St NE	Atlanta	GA	30309	404-853-8000	853-8806
Web: www.sutherland.com					
Thelen Reid Brown Raysman & Steiner LLP					
101 2nd St Suite 1800	San Francisco	CA	94105	415-371-1200	371-1211
Web: www.thelenreid.com					
Thompson & Knight LLP					
1700 Pacific Ave Suite 3300	Dallas	TX	75201	214-969-1700	969-1751
Web: www.tklaw.com					
Thompson Coe Cousins & irons					
700 N Pearl St 25th FL	Dallas	TX	75201	214-871-8200	871-8209
Web: www.thompsoncoe.com					
Thompson Hine LLP					
127 Public Sq 3900 Key Ctr	Cleveland	OH	44114	216-566-5500	566-5800
TF: 877-628-5500 ■ *Web:* www.thompsonhine.com					
Thorp Reed & Armstrong LLP					
301 Grant St Suite 14	Pittsburgh	PA	15219	412-394-7711	
TF: 800-221-7029 ■ *Web:* www.thorpreed.com					
Tompkins Mc Guire Wachenfeld & Barry					
100 Mulberry St	Newark	NJ	07102	973-622-3000	623-7780
Web: www.tompkinsmcguire.com					
Troutman Sanders LLP					
600 Peachtree St NE Suite 5200	Atlanta	GA	30308	404-885-3000	885-3900
TF: 800-255-8752 ■ *Web:* www.troutmansanders.com					
Tucker Arensberg Inc 1500 1 PPG Pl	Pittsburgh	PA	15222	412-594-5521	594-5619
Web: www.tuckerlaw.com					
Tucker Ellis & West LLP 925 Euclid Ave	Cleveland	OH	44115	216-592-5000	592-5009
Web: www.tuckerellis.com					
Updike Kelly & Spellacy Pc PO Box 231277	Hartford	CT	06123	860-548-2600	
Web: www.uks.com					
Venable LLP 575 7th St NW	Washington	DC	20004	202-344-4000	344-8300
Web: www.venable.com					
Verrill Dana LLP PO BOX 586	PORTLAND	ME	04112	207-774-4000	774-7499
Web: www.verrilldana.com					
Vinson & Elkins LLP					
1001 Fannin St First City Tower Suite 2500	Houston	TX	77002	713-758-2222	758-2346
Web: www.velaw.com					
Vorys Sater Seymour & Pease LLP (VSSP)					
52 E Gay St PO Box 1008	Columbus	OH	43216	614-464-6400	464-6350
Web: www.vorys.com					
Weber Gallagher Simpson Stapleton Fires & Newby LLP					
2000 Market St Suite 1300	Philadelphia	PA	19103	215-972-7900	
Web: www.wglaw.com					
Weil Gotshal & Manges LLP 767 5th Ave	New York	NY	10153	212-310-8000	310-8007
Web: www.weil.com					
Whitfield & Eddy Plc					
317 6th Ave Suite 1200	Des Moines	IA	50309	515-288-6041	246-1474
Web: www.whitfieldlaw.com					
Williams & Anderson PLC					
111 Ctr St 22nd Fl	Little Rock	AR	72201	501-372-0800	372-6453
Web: www.williamsanderson.com					
Williams & Connolly LLP 725 12th St NW	Washington	DC	20005	202-434-5000	434-5029
Web: www.wc.com					
Willkie Farr & Gallagher LLP					
787 7th Ave 2nd Fl	New York	NY	10019	212-728-8000	728-8111
Web: www.willkie.com					
Wilmer Cutler Pickering Hale & Dorr LLP					
1875 Pennsylvania Ave	Washington	DC	20006	202-663-6000	663-6363
Web: www.wilmerhale.com					
Wilson Elser Moskowitz Edelman & Dicker LLP					
150 E 42nd St	New York	NY	10017	212-490-3000	490-3038
Web: www.wilsonelser.com					
Wilson Sonsini Goodrich & Rosati					
650 Page Mill Rd	Palo Alto	CA	94304	650-493-9300	493-6811
Web: www.wsgr.com					
Windels Marx Ln Mittendorf LLP					
156 W 56th St	New York	NY	10019	212-237-1000	262-1215
Web: www.windelsmarx.com					
Womble Carlyle Sandridge & Rice PLLC					
1 W 4th St	Winston-Salem	NC	27101	336-721-3600	721-3660
Web: www.wcsr.com					
Woodcock Washburn LLP					
2929 Arch St FL 12	Philadelphia	PA	19104	215-568-3100	568-3439
Web: www.woodcock.com					
Wright Lindsey & Jennings LLP					
200 W Capitol Ave Suite 2300	Little Rock	AR	72201	501-371-0808	376-9442
Web: www.wlj.com					
Youth Advocate Programs Inc 2007 N 3rd St	Harrisburg	PA	17102	717-232-7580	
Web: www.yapinc.org					

432 LAWN & GARDEN EQUIPMENT

SEE ALSO Farm Machinery & Equipment - Mfr p. 1838

				Phone	Fax
American Biophysics Corp					
140 Frenchtown Rd	North Kingstown	RI	02852	401-884-3500	884-6688
TF: 877-699-8727 ■ *Web:* www.mosquitomagnet.com					

Phone | Fax

American Lawn Mower Co 2100 N Grandville Ave .... Muncie IN 47303 765-288-6624 284-5263
Web: www.reelin.com

Ames True Temper Inc 465 Railroad Ave .... Camp Hill PA 17011 717-737-1500 730-2550
TF: 800-393-1846 ■ Web: www.ames.com

Ariens Co 655 W Ryan St .... Brillion WI 54110 920-756-2141 756-2407
Web: www.ariens.com

Armatron International Inc 15 Highland Ave .... Malden MA 02148 781-321-2300 321-2309
TF: 800-343-3280 ■ Web: www.slowtron.com

Barker Implement & Motor Co Inc
412 W Van Buren .... Lenox IA 50851 641-333-2288 333-4481
Web: www.ebarkers.com

Blount Inc Oregon Cutting Systems Div
4909 SE International Way ....Portland OR 97222 503-653-8881 653-4201
TF: 800-223-5168 ■ Web: www.oregonchain.com

Blount Outdoor Products Group
4909 SE International Way ....Portland OR 97222 503-653-8881 653-4201
TF: 800-223-5168 ■ Web: www.blount.com/Cutsytm.html

Bluemkes Inc 101 W Division St PO Box 149..........Rosendale WI 54974 920-872-2131 872-2134
TF: 800-236-2133 ■ Web: www.bluemkes.com

Brinly-Hardy Co 3230 Industrial Pkwy..............Jeffersonville IN 47130 812-218-6080 218-6085
TF: 800-626-5329 ■ Web: www.brinly.com

California Flexrake Corp 9620 Gidley St .... Temple City CA 91780 626-443-4026 443-6887
TF: 800-266-4200 ■ Web: www.flexrake.com

CMD Products 1410 Flightline Dr Suite D............... Lincoln CA 95648 916-434-0228 434-0214
TF: 800-210-9949 ■ Web: www.cmdproducts.com

Commerce Corp 7603 Energy Pkwy ....Baltimore MD 21226 410-255-3500 255-3500*
*Fax: Cust Svc ■ TF: 800-289-0982 ■ Web: www.commercecorp.com

Corona Clipper Inc 22440 Tomasco Canyon Rd.......... Corona CA 92883 951-737-6515 737-6515
TF: 800-234-2547 ■ Web: www.coronatoolsusa.com

Cub Cadet Corp 1620 Welch St.................... Brownsville TN 38012 731-772-5600 779-5256
TF: 888-986-2288 ■ Web: www.cubcadet.com

Dixon Industries Inc
2612 Hwy 169 N PO Box 1569.....................Coffeyville KS 67337 877-288-6673 251-4117*
*Fax Area Code: 620 ■ TF: 877-288-6673 ■ Web: www.dixon-ztr.com

EarthWay Products Inc 1009 Maple St................. Bristol IN 46507 574-848-7491 848-4249
TF: 800-678-0671 ■ Web: www.earthway.com

Echo Inc 400 Oakwood Rd .... Lake Zurich IL 60047 847-540-8400 540-9741
TF: 800-673-1558 ■ Web: www.echo-usa.com

Frederick Mfg Corp 4840 E 12th St.................Kansas City MO 64127 816-231-5007 541-2152*
*Fax Area Code: 800 ■ TF: 800-743-3150

Gilmour Mfg Group 492 Drum Ave Industrial Pk.........Somerset PA 15501 814-443-4802 445-6605
TF Cust Svc: 800-458-0107 ■ Web: www.gilmour.com

Grasshopper Co 105 Old US Hwy 81................Moundridge KS 67107 620-345-8621 345-2301
Web: www.grasshoppermower.com

Grassland Equipment & Irrigation Corp
250 Lake Ave PO Box 2060 ....Blasdell NY 14219 716-822-2020 822-8836
Web: www.grasslandcorp.com

Great States Corp 2100 Grandville Ave .... Muncie IN 47303 765-288-6624 284-5263

Harnack Co 6016 Nordic Dr....................... Cedar Falls IA 50613 319-277-0660 277-2275
TF Cust Svc: 800-772-2022 ■ Web: www.harnack.net

Hoffco/Comet Industries Inc 358 NW 'F' St.......... Richmond IN 47374 765-966-8161 935-2346
TF: 800-999-8161 ■ Web: www.hoffcocomet.com

HoffcoComet Industries Inc 358 NW 'F' St .... Richmond IN 47374 765-966-8161 935-2346
Web: www.hoffcocomet.com

Holt Equipment Co LLC PO Box 436317 ....Louisville KY 40253 502-254-0758 254-0784
Web: www.holtequipment.net

Honda Power Equipment Mfg Inc
3721 Hwy 119 PO Box 37.......................Swepsonville NC 27359 336-578-5300 229-0768

Hound Dog Products Inc 465 Railroad Ave .... Camp Hill PA 17011 800-694-6863 567-1904
TF: 800-694-6863 ■ Web: www.hound-dog.com

Howard Price Turf Equipment Inc
18155 Edison Ave.............................Chesterfield MO 63005 636-532-7000 532-0201
Web: www.howardpriceturf.com

Husqvarna Turf Care Co 401 N Commerce St.......... Beatrice NE 68310 402-223-2391 223-1053
TF: 877-368-8873 ■ Web: www.yazookees.com

Jacobsen 11108 Quality Dr .... Charlotte NC 28273 704-504-6600 504-6661
TF: 866-522-6273 ■ Web: www.jacobsen.com

Janiak Mfg Inc 11 Machine Shop Hill Rd.........South Windham CT 06266 860-423-7741 423-2654

Kenney Corp 8420 Zionsville Rd ....Indianapolis IN 46268 317-872-4793 879-2331
TF: 800-878-8676 ■ Web: www.kmcturf.com

Lawn & Golf Supply Co Inc
647 Nutt Rd PO Box 447.........................Phoenixville PA 19460 610-933-5801 933-8890
TF: 800-362-5650 ■ Web: www.lawn-golf.com

Lawn-Boy Inc 8111 S Lyndale Ave................ Bloomington MN 55420 952-888-8801 887-8258
TF: 800-526-6937 ■ Web: www.lawn-boy.com

LR Nelson Corp 1 Sprinkler Ln .... Peoria IL 61615 309-690-2200 692-5847
TF Sales: 800-635-7668 ■ Web: www.lrnelson.com

MacKissic Inc PO Box 111 .... Parker Ford PA 19457 610-495-7181 495-5951
TF: 800-348-1117 ■ Web: www.mackissic.com

Magic Circle Corp 6302 E County Rd 100 N ....Coatesville IN 46121 765-246-6845 246-6146
Web: www.dixiechopper.com

Master Mark Plastic Products Inc
1 Master Mark Dr PO Box 662 ....Albany MN 56307 320-845-2111 845-7093
TF Cust Svc: 800-535-4838 ■ Web: www.mastermark.com

Maxim Mfg Corp PO Box 110................... Sebastopol MS 39359 601-625-7471 625-8227
TF: 800-621-2789 ■ Web: www.maximmfg.com

McLane Mfg Inc 7110 E Rosecrans Ave ....Paramount CA 90723 562-633-8158 602-0651
TF: 877-633-8158

Melnor Inc 260 W Brooke Rd..................... Winchester VA 22603 540-722-5600 411-2500*
*Fax Area Code: 888 ■ TF: 877-283-0697 ■ Web: www.melnor.com

Mid West Products Inc PO Box 301 ....Phillipsburg OH 45354 847-214-6261 756-3831
Web: www.lambertmfg.com

Modern Line Products Co
801 Industrial Pk Rd PO Box 110....................Indianola MS 38751 662-887-4151 887-5200

MTD Products Inc 5965 Grafton Rd ....Valley City OH 44280 330-225-2600 273-4617
TF: 800-800-7310 ■ Web: www.mtdproducts.com

National Mower Co 700 Raymond Ave............... Saint Paul MN 55114 651-646-4079 646-2887
Web: www.nationalmower.com

Precision Products Inc 316 Limit St.................. Lincoln IL 62656 217-735-1590 735-2435
TF Cust Svc: 800-225-5891 ■ Web: www.precisionprodinc.com

Phone | Fax

Rio Delmar Enterprises
8338 Elliott Rd PO Box 1409 ....Easton MD 21601 410-822-8866 822-9263
TF: 800-638-4402

Roeder Implement Co Inc
2804 Pembroke Rd........................... Hopkinsville KY 42240 270-886-3994 886-8752
TF: 800-844-3994 ■ Web: www.jddealer.deere.com

Rotary Corp PO Box 747 .... Glennville GA 30427 912-654-3433 654-3945
TF: 800-841-3989 ■ Web: www.rotarycorp.com

Rugg Mfg Co Inc 105 Newton St.................... Greenfield MA 01302 413-773-5471 774-4354
TF: 800-633-8772 ■ Web: www.rugg.com

Simplicity Mfg Inc PO Box 702 ....Milwaukee WI 53201 262-284-8669 377-8202
Web: www.simplicitymfg.com

Stens Corp 2424 Cathy Ln .... Jasper IN 47546 812-482-2526 482-1275
TF: 800-457-7444 ■ Web: www.stens.com

Stihl Inc 536 Viking Dr.......................Virginia Beach VA 23452 757-486-9100 784-8576*
*Fax Area Code: 888 ■ TF Cust Svc: 888-784-8575 ■ Web: www.stihlusa.com

Swisher Mower & Machine Co Inc
1602 Corporate Dr .... Warrensburg MO 64093 660-747-8183 747-8650
TF: 800-222-8183 ■ Web: www.swisherinc.com

Telsco Industries Inc Weathermatic
3301 W Kingsley Rd............................ Garland TX 75041 972-278-6131 271-5710
TF: 888-484-3776 ■ Web: www.weathermatic.com

Toro Co 8111 Lyndale Ave........................ Bloomington MN 55420 888-384-9939 887-8258*
NYSE: TTC ■ *Fax Area Code: 952 ■ TF: 800-595-6841 ■ Web: www.toro.com

Toro Co Commercial Products Div
8111 Lyndale Ave .... Bloomington MN 55420 952-888-8801 887-8258
TF Cust Svc: 800-348-2424 ■ Web: www.toro.com

Tuff Torq Corp 5943 Commerce Blvd................ Morristown TN 37814 423-585-2000 585-2003
Web: www.tufftorq.com

Z&m Ag & Turf 1756 Lindquist Dr.................... Falconer NY 14733 716-665-3110 665-4216
Web: www.zahmandmatson.com

433 LEATHER GOODS - PERSONAL

SEE ALSO Clothing & Accessories - Mfr p. 1607; Footwear p. 1876; Handbags, Totes, Backpacks p. 2003; Leather Goods (Misc) p. 2149; Luggage, Bags, Cases p. 2189

Phone | Fax

AD Sutton & Sons Inc 20 W 33rd St 2nd Fl ....New York NY 10001 212-695-7070 947-6253
Web: www.adsutton.com

Berman Leather Co
2 Old New Milford Rd Suite 3-F .... Brookfield CT 06804 203-312-1300 312-1067
TF: 800-992-3762 ■ Web: www.bermanleather.com

Bosca Hugo Co Inc 1905 W Jefferson St ....Springfield OH 45506 937-323-5523 323-7063
TF: 800-732-6722 ■ Web: www.bosca.com

Bottega Veneta Inc 699 5th Ave ....New York NY 10022 212-371-5511 371-4361
TF: 877-362-1715 ■ Web: www.bottegaveneta.com

Buxton Co 45 Plainfield St PO Box 1650 ....Chicopee MA 01013 413-734-5900 785-1367
TF: 800-426-3638 ■ Web: www.buxtonaccessories.com

California Optical Corp 2992 Alvarado St.......... San Leandro CA 94577 510-352-4774 352-3714
TF: 800-523-5567 ■ Web: www.californiaoptical.com

Carroll Cos Inc 1640 Old Hwy 421 S.................... Boone NC 28607 828-264-2521 264-2633
TF: 800-884-2521 ■ Web: www.clgco.com

Coach Inc 516 W 34th St ....New York NY 10001 212-594-1850 594-1682
NYSE: COH ■ TF: 800-444-3611 ■ Web: www.coach.com

Dooney & Bourke Inc 1 Regent St .... East Norwalk CT 06855 203-853-7515 838-7754
TF Cust Svc: 800-347-5000 ■ Web: www.dooney.com

Enger Kress Co 6510 Aurora Rd Suite C...............West Bend WI 53090 262-629-1553 629-1553
TF Cust Svc: 800-367-7547 ■ Web: www.buyimporter.com

International Accessories 717 School St............ Pawtucket RI 02860 401-725-4502 724-5180

Jaclyn Inc 197 W Spring Valley Ave...................Maywood NJ 07607 201-909-6000
AMEX: JLN ■ Web: www.jaclyninc.com

Sharif Designs Ltd 34-12 36th Ave............ Long Island City NY 11106 718-472-1100 937-2561

Stone Mountain Accessories (SMA)
10 W 33rd St Suite 728 ....New York NY 10001 212-563-2500 564-2879
TF Cust Svc: 866-865-0786 ■ Web: www.stonemountainhandbags.com

Westport Corp 331 Changdridge Rd .... Pinebrook NJ 07058 973-565-0110 575-8197
Web: www.mundiwestport.com

434 LEATHER GOODS (MISC)

Phone | Fax

Action Co 1425 N Tennessee St..................... McKinney TX 75069 972-542-8700 562-7300
TF Sales: 800-937-3700 ■ Web: www.actioncompany.com

Auburn Leather Co 125 N Caldwell St .... Auburn KY 42206 270-542-4116 542-7107
TF: 800-635-0617 ■ Web: www.auburnleather.com

Capitol Saddlery 8910 Research Blvd.................. Austin TX 78757 512-478-9309 474-2209
Web: www.capitolsaddlery.com

Carroll Cos Inc 1640 Old Hwy 421 S.................... Boone NC 28607 828-264-2521 264-2633
TF: 800-884-2521 ■ Web: www.clgco.com

Circle Y of Yoakum Inc 201 W Morris St .... Yoakum TX 77995 361-293-5251 293-7192
TF: 800-531-3600 ■ Web: www.circley.com

Colorado Saddlery Co 5295 Vivian St ....Arvada CO 80002 303-572-8350 692-7433*
*Fax Area Code: 800 ■ TF Cust Svc: 800-521-2465 ■ Web: www.coloradosaddlery.com

Garlin-Neumann Leathers Co Inc 66-D River Rd......... Hudson NH 03051 603-595-6319 881-9431

Gould & Goodrich Leather Inc
709 E McNeil St .... Lillington NC 27546 910-893-2071 893-4742
TF: 800-277-0732 ■ Web: www.gouldusa.com

Hunter Co Inc 3300 W 71st Ave..................Westminster CO 80030 303-427-4626 428-3980
TF: 800-676-4868 ■ Web: www.huntercompany.com

Strong Group Inc 39 Grove St......................Gloucester MA 01930 978-281-3300 281-6321
TF Orders: 800-225-0724

Tex Shoemaker & Son Inc 714 W Cienega Ave........San Dimas CA 91773 909-592-2071 592-2378
TF: 800-345-9959 ■ Web: www.texshoemaker.com

Tex Tan Western Leather Co 601 Hickey St .... Yoakum TX 77995 361-293-2314 293-2369
TF: 800-531-3608 ■ Web: www.textan.com

435 LEATHER TANNING & FINISHING

Name / Address	City	State	Zip	Phone	Fax
Carville National Leather Corp 10 Knox Ave PO Box 40 *Web:* www.carvillenational.com	Johnstown	NY	12095	518-762-1634	762-8973
Cromwell Leather Co Inc 147 Palmer Ave. *Web:* www.cromwellgroup.com	Mamaroneck	NY	10543	914-381-0100	381-0046
Eagle Ottawa Leather Co LLC 2930 W Auburn Rd *Web:* www.eagleottawa.com	Rochester Hills	MI	48309	248-853-3122	853-6135
GST AutoLeather Inc 20 Oak Hollow Dr Suite 300 *Web:* www.gstautoleather.com	Southfield	MI	48034	248-436-2300	436-2390
Gutmann Leather Co Inc 1511 W Webster Ave	Chicago	IL	60614	773-348-5300	348-7766
Hermann Oak Leather Co 4050 N 1st St *TF:* 800-325-7950 ■ *Web:* www.hermannoakleather.com	Saint Louis	MO	63147	314-421-1173	421-6152
Horween Leather Co 2015 N Elston Ave *Web:* www.horween.com	Chicago	IL	60614	773-772-2026	772-9235
Irving Tanning Co Inc 9 Main St PO Box 400 *Fax: Cust Svc ■ *Web:* www.irvingtanning.com	Hartland	ME	04943	207-938-4491	938-2977*
Leatherock International Inc 5285 Lovelock St *Web:* www.leatherock.com	San Diego	CA	92110	619-299-7625	299-7629
North American Tanning Corp 224 W 35th St Suite 506 *Web:* www.natanning.com	New York	NY	10001	212-643-1702	967-0068
Robus Leather Corp 1100 W Hutchinson Ln *Web:* www.robus.com	Madison	IN	47250	317-704-7021	872-8502
Seidel Tanning Corp 1306 E Meinecke Ave *Web:* www.seideltanning.com	Milwaukee	WI	53212	414-562-4030	562-4445
Simco Leather Corp 99 Pleasant Ave	Johnstown	NY	12095	518-762-7100	736-1514
Stahl USA 13 Corwin St *Web:* www.stahl.com	Peabody	MA	01961	978-531-0371	532-9062
WB Place LLC 368 W Sumner St *TF:* 800-826-4433 ■ *Web:* www.wbplace.com	Hartford	WI	53027	262-673-3130	673-6233
Wood & Hyde Leather Co Inc 68 Wood St *Web:* www.woodandhyde.com	Gloversville	NY	12078	518-725-7105	725-5158

436 LEGISLATION HOTLINES

Name / Address	City	State	Zip	Phone	Fax
Legislative Information 106 Legislative Bldg *TF:* 800-562-6000 ■ *Web:* www.leg.wa.gov	Olympia	WA	98504	360-786-7573	
Alabama Bill Status-House State House 11 S Union St *Web:* www.legislature.state.al.us	Montgomery	AL	36130	334-242-7600	242-2489
Alabama Bill Status-Senate State House 11 S Union St Rm 716 *TF:* 800-499-3051 ■ *Web:* www.alisdb.legislature.state.al.us	Montgomery	AL	36130	334-242-7826	242-8819
Alaska Bill Status State Capitol MS 3100 *Web:* www.legis.state.ak.us/basis	Juneau	AK	99811	907-465-4930	465-2864
Arizona Bill Status Capitol Complex 1700 W Washington St *TF:* 800-352-8404 ■ *Web:* www.azleg.state.az.us/legtext/bills.htm	Phoenix	AZ	85007	602-926-3559	926-3429
Arkansas Bill Status-House State Capitol Rm 350 *Web:* www.arkleg.state.ar.us	Little Rock	AR	72201	501-682-7771	
Arkansas Bill Status-Senate State Capitol Rm 320 *Web:* www.arkleg.state.ar.us	Little Rock	AR	72201	501-682-5951	
California Bill Status-Assembly State Capitol Rm 3196 *Web:* www.leginfo.ca.gov/bilinfo.html	Sacramento	CA	95814	916-445-2323	
California Bill Status-Senate State Capitol Rm 3044 *Web:* www.leginfo.ca.gov/bilinfo.html	Sacramento	CA	95814	916-445-4251	445-4450
Colorado Bill Status 200 E Colfax Ave *Web:* www.leg.state.co.us	Denver	CO	80203	303-866-3055	866-4543
Connecticut Bill Status Legislative Office Bldg	Hartford	CT	06106	860-240-0555	
Delaware Bill Status Legislative Hall PO Box 1401 *Web:* www.legis.delaware.gov/billtracking	Dover	DE	19903	302-744-4162	739-6890
District of Columbia Bill Status 1350 Pennsylvania Ave NW Suite 10 *Web:* www.dccouncil.washington.dc.us/lims/default.asp	Washington	DC	20004	202-724-8050	
Florida Bill Status 111 W Madison St Rm 704 *TF:* 800-342-1827 ■ *Web:* www.leg.state.fl.us	Tallahassee	FL	32399	850-488-4371	922-1534
Georgia Bill Status-House State Capitol Rm 309 *Web:* www.legis.state.ga.us	Atlanta	GA	30334	404-656-5015	
Georgia Bill Status-Senate State Capitol Rm 353 *Web:* www.legis.state.ga.us	Atlanta	GA	30334	404-656-5040	656-5043
Hawaii Bill Status 415 S Beretania St Rm 401 *Web:* www.capitol.hawaii.gov	Honolulu	HI	96813	808-587-0478	587-0793
Idaho Bill Status PO Box 83720 *Web:* www3.state.id.us/legislat/legtrack.html	Boise	ID	83720	208-334-2475	334-2125
Illinois Bill Status 705 Stratton Bldg *Web:* www.ilga.gov/legislation	Springfield	IL	62706	217-782-3944	524-6059
Indiana Bill Status State House 200 W Washington St Suite 301 *Web:* www.in.gov/apps/lsa/session/billwatch	Indianapolis	IN	46204	317-232-9856	
Iowa Bill Status State Capitol Bldg Rm 16 *Web:* www.legis.state.ia.us/Bills.html	Des Moines	IA	50319	515-281-3371	
Kansas Bill Status 300 SW 10th Ave State Capitol Bldg Rm 343N *Web:* www.kslegislature.org	Topeka	KS	66612	785-296-3296	296-6650
Kentucky Bill Status State Capitol Bldg 700 Capitol Ave Rm 300 *Web:* www.lrc.state.ky.us/legislat/legislat.htm	Frankfort	KY	40601	502-564-8100	564-6543
Louisiana Bill Status State Capitol 900 N 3rd St 13th Fl *TF:* 800-256-3793 ■ *Web:* www.legis.state.la.us	Baton Rouge	LA	70804	225-342-2456	
Maine Bill Status State House 100 State House Stn *Web:* www.mainelegislature.org/legis/bills	Augusta	ME	04333	207-287-1692	287-1580
Maryland Dept of Legislative Services 90 State Cir. *TF:* 800-492-7122 ■ *Web:* www.mlis.state.md.us	Annapolis	MD	21401	410-946-5400	946-5405
Massachusetts Bill Status 1 Ashburton Pl Rm 1611 *TF:* 800-392-6090 ■ *Web:* www.mass.gov/legis/ltsform.htm	Boston	MA	02108	617-727-7030	742-4528
Michigan Bill Status PO Box 30036 *Web:* www.legislature.mi.gov	Lansing	MI	48909	517-373-0630	
Minnesota Bill Status-House 75 ML King Jr Blvd Rm 211 *Web:* www.leg.state.mn.us/leg/legis.asp	Saint Paul	MN	55155	651-296-6646	
Minnesota Bill Status-Senate 75 ML King Jr Blvd Rm 231 *Web:* www.leg.state.mn.us/leg/legis.asp	Saint Paul	MN	55155	651-296-2887	
Mississippi Bill Status PO Box 1018 *Web:* billstatus.ls.state.ms.us	Jackson	MS	39215	601-359-3719	
Missouri Bill Status 117A State Capitol *Web:* www.house.state.mo.us	Jefferson City	MO	65101	573-751-4633	751-0130
Montana Legislative Services PO Box 201706 *Web:* www.leg.state.mt.us	Helena	MT	59620	406-444-4800	444-3036
Nebraska Bill Status 2018 State Capitol Bldg	Lincoln	NE	68509	402-471-2709	
Nevada Bill Status 401 S Carson St *TF:* 800-992-6761 ■ *Web:* www.leg.state.nv.us	Carson City	NV	89701	775-684-3360	
New Hampshire Bill Status 107 N Main St *Web:* gencourt.state.nh.us	Concord	NH	03301	603-271-3661	
New Jersey Bill Status State House Annex PO Box 068 *TF:* 800-792-8630 ■ *Web:* www.njleg.state.nj.us	Trenton	NJ	08625	609-292-4840	777-2440
New Mexico Legislative Council Services 490 Old Santa Fe Trail Rm 411 *Web:* www.legis.state.nm.us	Santa Fe	NM	87501	505-986-4600	986-4680
New York Bill Status 55 Elk St *TF:* 800-342-9860 ■ *Web:* www.assembly.state.ny.us	Albany	NY	12210	518-455-7545	455-7681
North Carolina Bill Status 16 W Jones St Rm 2226 *Web:* www.ncleg.net	Raleigh	NC	27601	919-733-7778	
North Dakota Legislative Council Services State Capitol Bldg 600 E Blvd Ave *Web:* www.state.nd.us/lr	Bismarck	ND	58505	701-328-2916	328-3615
Ohio Legislative Information Office 77 S High St *TF:* 800-282-0253 ■ *Web:* www.legislature.state.oh.us	Columbus	OH	43215	614-466-8842	644-1721
Oklahoma Legislation Service Bureau 2300 N Lincoln Blvd Rm B30 *Web:* www.lsb.state.ok.us	Oklahoma City	OK	73105	405-521-4081	521-5507
Oregon Publication & Distribution Services 900 Ct St NE Rm 49 *Web:* www.leg.state.or.us	Salem	OR	97310	503-986-1180	373-1527
Pennsylvania Bill Status Main Capitol Bldg Rm 648 *Web:* www.legis.state.pa.us	Harrisburg	PA	17120	717-787-2342	
Rhode Island Bill Status State House Rm 1 *Web:* www.rilin.state.ri.us	Providence	RI	02903	401-222-3580	
South Carolina Bill Status PO Box 142 *Web:* www.scstatehouse.gov	Columbia	SC	29201	803-212-6200	
South Dakota Bill Status 500 E Capitol *Web:* www.legis.state.sd.us	Pierre	SD	57501	605-773-3251	
Tennessee Bill Status 320 6th Ave N 1st Fl *Web:* www.legislature.state.tn.us	Nashville	TN	37243	615-741-3511	
Texas Bill Status State Capitol 1100 Congress Ave Rm 2N-3 *TF:* 877-824-7038 ■ *Web:* www.capitol.state.tx.us	Austin	TX	78711	512-463-2182	475-4626
Utah Bill Status 350 N State St *Web:* le.utah.gov/Documents/bills.htm	Salt Lake City	UT	84114	801-538-1588	538-1728
Vermont Bill Status 115 State St State House *Web:* www.leg.state.vt.us	Montpelier	VT	05633	802-828-2231	828-2424
Washington Bill Status PO Box 40600 *TF:* 800-562-6000 ■ *Web:* www.leg.wa.gov	Olympia	WA	98504	360-786-7573	
West Virginia Bill Status State Capitol Rm MB27 *TF:* 877-565-3447 ■ *Web:* www.legis.state.wv.us	Charleston	WV	25305	304-347-4831	347-4901
Wisconsin Bill Status 1 E Main St *TF:* 800-362-9472 ■ *Web:* www.legis.state.wi.us	Madison	WI	53708	608-266-9960	
Wyoming Legislative Service Office State Capitol Bldg Rm 213 *TF:* 800-342-9570 ■ *Web:* www.legisweb.state.wy.us	Cheyenne	WY	82002	307-777-7881	777-5466

437 LIBRARIES

SEE ALSO Library Systems - Regional - Canadian p. 2176

437-1 Medical Libraries

Phone *Fax*

Alfred Taubman Medical Library
University of Michigan 1135 E Catherine St
PO Box 0726 Ann Arbor MI 48109 734-764-1210 763-1473
Web: www.lib.umich.edu/taubman

Allen Memorial Medical Library
Case Western Reserve University
11000 Euclid Ave Cleveland OH 44106 216-368-3643 368-6396
Web: www.case.edu/chsl/allen.htm

Allyn & Betty Taylor Library
University of Western Ontario
Natural Sciences Centre London ON N6A5B7 519-661-3168 661-3435
Web: www.lib.uwo.ca/taylor

Augustus C Long Health Sciences Library
Columbia University Medical Ctr
701 W 168th St New York NY 10032 212-305-3605
Web: library.cumc.columbia.edu

Bernard Becker Medical Library
Washington University School of Medicine
660 S Euclid Ave CB 8132 Saint Louis MO 63110 314-362-7080 454-6606
Web: www.becker.wustl.edu

Boston University School of Medicine Alumni Medical Library
80 E Concord St Boston MA 02118 617-638-4232 638-4233
Web: www.med-libwww.bu.edu

Bracken Health Sciences Library
Queen's University Kingston Botterell Hall Kingston ON K7L3N6 613-533-2510 533-6892
Web: www.library.queensu.ca/webmed

Brown University Sciences Library
201 Thayer St PO Box 'I' Providence RI 02912 401-863-3333 863-2753
Web: www.brown.edu

C Everett Koop Community Health Information Ctr
College of Physicians of Philadelphia
19 S 22nd St Philadelphia PA 19103 215-563-3737 569-6477*
**Fax Area Code: 205* ■ *Web:* www.collphyphil.org/chic.html

Chandler Medical Center Library
University of Kentucky 800 Rose St Lexington KY 40536 859-323-5727 323-1040
Web: www.mc.uky.edu/medlibrary

Cleveland Health Sciences Library (CHSL)
Case Western Reserve University Robbins Bldg
2109 Adelbert Rd Cleveland OH 44106 216-368-4540 368-3008
Web: www.case.edu/chsl/library/index.html

Coy C Carpenter Library
Wake Forest University School of Medicine
Medical Ctr Blvd Winston-Salem NC 27157 336-716-2011 716-2186
Web: www.wakehealth.edu/library

Creighton University Health Sciences Library
2500 California Plaza Omaha NE 68178 402-280-5108 280-5134
Web: www.creighton.edu

D Samuel Gottesman Library
1300 Morris Pk Ave # 132 Bronx NY 10461 718-430-3108 430-8795
Web: www.library.aecom.yu.edu

Dahlgren Memorial Library
Georgetown University Medical Ctr 3900 Reservoir Rd NW
PO Box 571420 Washington DC 20057 202-687-1448 687-1862
Web: dml.georgetown.edu

Dana Biomedical Library Dartmouth College Hanover NH 03755 603-650-1658 650-1354
Web: www.dartmouth.edu

Del E Webb Memorial Library
Loma Linda University 11072 Anderson St Loma Linda CA 92350 909-558-4550 558-4188
Web: www.llu.edu/llu/library

Denison Memorial Library
University of Colorado Health Sciences Ctr
4200 E 9th Ave PO Box A-003 Denver CO 80262 303-315-7469 315-0294

Duke University Medical Center Library
103 Seeley Mudd Bldg DUMC 3702 Durham NC 27710 919-660-1150 681-7599
Web: www.mclibrary.duke.edu

Dykes Library
University of Kansas Medical Ctr
2100 W 39th Ave MS 1050 Kansas City KS 66160 913-588-7166 588-7304
Web: www.library.kumc.edu

Edward G Miner Library
Univ of Rochester School of Medicine & Dentistry
601 Elmwood Ave Rochester NY 14642 585-275-3361 756-7762
Web: www.urmc.rochester.edu/hslt/miner

Edwin A Mirand Library
Roswell Pk Cancer Institute
Elm & Carlton Sts Buffalo NY 14263 716-845-8825 845-8699

Fordham Health Sciences Library
Wright State University
3640 Colonel Glenn Hwy Dayton OH 45435 937-775-2003 775-2232
Web: www.libraries.wright.edu/about/lochours/#fhsl

Francis A Countway Library of Medicine The
10 Shattuck St Boston MA 02115 617-432-2136 432-4739
Web: www.countway.harvard.edu

Frederick L Ehrman Medical Library
New York University Medical Ctr School of Medicine
550 1st Ave Medical Science Bldg Elevator B New York NY 10016 212-263-5395 263-6534
Web: www.hsl.med.nyu.edu/ehrman

Galter Health Sciences Library
Northwestern University
303 E Chicago Ave Rm 2-212 Chicago IL 60611 312-503-8126
Web: www.galter.northwestern.edu

George F Smith Library of the Health Sciences
Univ of Medicine & Dentistry of New Jersey
30 12th Ave Office C-932 Newark NJ 07103 973-972-8538 972-3870
Web: www.umdnj.edu/librweb/newarklib/library

George T Harrell Health Sciences Library
Pennsylvania State University College of Medicine
500 University Dr Milton S Hershey Medical Hershey PA 17033 717-531-8626 531-8635
Web: www.hmc.psu.edu/library

Gerstein Science Information Centre
University of Toronto 9 King's College Cir Toronto ON M5S1A5 416-978-2280 971-2848
Web: www.library.utoronto.ca/gerstein

Gibson D Lewis Library
University of N Texas Health Science Ctr
3500 Camp Bowie Blvd Fort Worth TX 76107 817-735-2380 735-5158
Web: www.library.hsc.unt.edu

Gustave L & Janet W Levy Library
Mt Sinai Medical Ctr 1 Gustave L Levy Pl
PO Box 1102 New York NY 10029 212-241-7791
Web: www.mssm.edu/about-us/services-and-resources/levy-library

Hardin Library for the Health Sciences
University of Iowa 100 Hardin Library Iowa City IA 52242 319-335-9871 353-3752
Web: www.lib.uiowa.edu/hardin

Harvey Cushing/John Hay Whitney Medical Library
333 Cedar St PO Box 208014 New Haven CT 06520 203-785-5352 785-5636
Web: www.med.yale.edu

Health Sciences Center Medical Library Shreveport
Louisiana State University Shreveport
1501 Kings Hwy Shreveport LA 71130 318-675-5445 675-5442
Web: www.lib.sh.lsuhsc.edu

Himmelfarb Health Sciences Library
George Washington University Medical Ctr
2300 Eye St NW Washington DC 20037 202-994-2850 994-4343
Web: www.gwumc.edu/library

Houston Academy of Medicine - Texas Medical Center Library
1133 John Freeman Blvd Houston TX 77030 713-795-4200 790-7052
Web: www.library.tmc.edu

John A Prior Health Sciences Library
Ohio State University 376 W 10th Ave Columbus OH 43210 614-292-4861 292-1920
Web: www.hsl.osu.edu

John W Scott Health Sciences Library
University of Alberta
2K3.28 Walter Mackenzie Ctr Edmonton AB T6G2R7 780-492-3899 492-6960
Web: www.library.ualberta.ca/aboutus/health

Kornhauser Health Sciences Library
University of Louisville 500 S Preston St Louisville KY 40292 502-852-5771 852-1631
Web: www.louisville.edu

Lamar Soutter Library 55 N Lake Ave Worcester MA 01655 508-856-6099 856-5899
Web: www.library.umassmed.edu

Lane Medical Library
Stanford University Medical Ctr
300 Pasteur Dr Rm L-109 Stanford CA 94305 650-723-6831 725-7471
Web: www.lane.stanford.edu

Leon S McGoogan Library of Medicine
University of Nebraska Medical Ctr
986705 Nebraska Medical Ctr Omaha NE 68198 402-559-6221 559-5498
TF: 866-800-5209 ■ *Web:* www.unmc.edu/library

Library of Rush University
Rush University Medical Ctr
600 S Paulina St Suite 571 Chicago IL 60612 312-942-5950 942-3143
Web: www.lib.rush.edu/library

Louis Calder Memorial Library
University of Miami School of Medicine R-950
PO Box 016950 Miami FL 33101 305-243-6648 325-9670
Web: www.calder.med.miami.edu

Louise M Darling Biomedical Library
UCLA 12-077 Ctr for the Health Sciences
PO Box 951798 Los Angeles CA 90095 310-825-4904 825-0465
Web: www.library.ucla.edu/libraries/biomed

Loyola University Health Sciences Library
2160 S 1st Ave Maywood IL 60153 708-216-5301 216-6772
Web: www.library.luhs.org

Matthews-Fuller Health Sciences Library
Dartmouth College 1 Medical Ctr Dr MS 7300 Lebanon NH 03756 603-650-7658 650-4372
Web: www.dartmouth.edu/~biomed

Mayo Foundation Mayo Medical Center Libraries
200 1st St SW Rochester MN 55905 507-284-2061 284-1038
Web: www.mayo.edu/medlib

McGill University Life Sciences Library & Osler Library of the History of Medicine
3655 Sir William Osler Montreal QC H3G1Y6 514-398-4475 398-3890
Web: www.mcgill.ca

McMaster University Health Sciences Library
1200 Main St W Hamilton ON L8N3Z5 905-525-9140 528-3733
Web: hsl.mcmaster.ca

Medical University of South Carolina Library
171 Ashley Ave Suite 300 PO Box 250403 Charleston SC 29425 843-792-2372 792-4900
Web: www.library.musc.edu

Meharry Medical College Library
1005 DB Todd Blvd Nashville TN 37208 615-327-6318 327-6448
Web: www.library.mmc.edu

Memorial University of Newfoundland Health Sciences Library
300 Prince Philip Dr Health Science Ctr Saint John's NL A1B3V6 709-777-6672 777-6866
Web: www.library.mun.ca/hsl

Moody Medical Library 301 University Blvd Galveston TX 77555 409-772-2371 762-9782
Web: www.ar.utmb.edu
Library 10 Ctr Dr MSC 1150 Bldg 10 Bethesda MD 20892 301-496-5612 402-0254
Web: www.nihlibrary.nih.gov
National Library of Medicine
8600 Rockville Pike Bldg 38 Bethesda MD 20894 301-594-5983 402-1384
TF: 888-346-3656 ■ *Web:* www.nlm.nih.gov

Neil John Maclean Health Sciences Library
University of Manitoba 770 Bannatyne Ave Winnipeg MB R3E0W3 204-789-3342 789-3922
Web: www.umanitoba.ca/libraries/health

New York Academy of Medicine Library
1216 5th Ave New York NY 10029 212-822-7315 423-0266
Web: www.nyam.org/library

New York Medical College Medical Sciences Library
95 Grasslands Rd Basic Science Bldg Valhalla NY 10595 914-594-4200 594-3171
Web: www.library.nymc.edu

	City	State	Zip	Phone	Fax
Norris Medical Library					
University of Southern California					
2003 Zonal Ave.	Los Angeles	CA	90089	323-442-1111	221-1235
Web: www.usc.edu/hsc/nml					
Northeastern Ohio Universities College of Medicine Ocasek Library					
4209 SR 44 PO Box 95	Rootstown	OH	44272	330-325-2511	325-6522
Web: www.neoucom.edu/audience/library					
Oregon Health & Science University					
Library 3181 SW Sam Jackson Pk Rd	Portland	OR	97239	503-494-3460	494-3322
Web: www.ohsu.edu/xd/education/library					
Queen's Medical Ctr The Hawaii Medical Library					
1221 Punchbowl St	Honolulu	HI	96813	808-547-4300	547-4019
Web: hml.org					
Raymon H Mulford Library					
Medical College of Ohio Toledo					
3000 Arlington Ave	Toledo	OH	43614	419-383-4225	
Web: www.utoledo.edu/library/mulford/index.html					
Robert B Greenblatt MD Library					
Medical College of Georgia					
1459 Laney Walker Blvd	Augusta	GA	30912	706-721-3444	721-2018
Web: www.mcg.edu/library					
Robert M Bird Health Sciences Library					
OUHSC 1000 Stanton L Young Blvd					
PO Box 26901	Oklahoma City	OK	73190	405-271-2285	271-3297
Web: library.ouhsc.edu					
Rosalind Franklin University of Medicine & Science Learning Resource Ctr					
3333 Green Bay Rd	North Chicago	IL	60064	847-578-3242	578-3401
Web: www.rosalindfranklin.edu/lrc					
Rowland Medical Library					
University of Mississippi 2500 N State St.	Jackson	MS	39216	601-984-1231	984-1251
Web: www.library.umc.edu					
Library of Science & Medicine					
165 Bevier Rd	Piscataway	NJ	08854	732-445-3854	445-5703
Web: www.libraries.rutgers.edu					
Ruth Lilly Medical Library					
975 W Walnut St IB 100	Indianapolis	IN	46202	317-274-7182	278-2349
Web: www.library.medicine.iu.edu					
Health Sciences Center Library					
1402 S Grand Blvd.	Saint Louis	MO	63104	314-977-8800	977-5573
Web: www.slu.edu/libraries/hsc					
Schaffer Library of the Health Sciences					
Albany Medical College 47 New Scotland Ave	Albany	NY	12208	518-262-5586	262-5820
Web: www.amc.edu/Academic/Schaffer					
Scott Memorial Library					
1020 Walnut St # 310	Philadelphia	PA	19107	215-503-8848	923-3203
Web: www.jeffline.jefferson.edu					
Southern Illinois University School of Medicine Medical Library (SIU)					
801 N Rutledge St PO Box 19625	Springfield	IL	62794	217-545-2122	545-0988
Web: www.siumed.edu/lib					
Spencer S Eccles Health Sciences Library					
University of Utah Health Sciences Ctr					
10 N 1900 E Bldg 589	Salt Lake City	UT	84112	801-581-8771	581-3632
TF: 866-581-5534 ■ *Web:* www.medlib.med.utah.edu					
State University of New York at Buffalo (HSL)					
Health Sciences Library					
3435 Main St Abbott Hall Rm 102	Buffalo	NY	14214	716-829-3900	829-2211
Web: library.buffalo.edu/hsl					
State University of New York Upstate Medical University Health Sciences Library					
766 Irving Ave	Syracuse	NY	13210	315-464-7087	464-7199
Web: library.upstate.edu					
Stony Brook University Health Sciences Library					
8034 Suny HSC Level 3 Rm 136	Stony Brook	NY	11794	631-444-2512	444-6649
Web: www.hsclib.sunysb.edu					
SUNY Downstate Medical Ctr					
The Medical Research Library of Brooklyn					
450 Clarkson Ave PO Box 14	Brooklyn	NY	11203	718-270-7633	270-7471
Web: www.downstate.edu					
Temple University Health Sciences Center Library					
3440 N Broad St 2nd Fl Kresge Hall	Philadelphia	PA	19140	215-707-4032	707-4135
Web: www.temple.edu/schools/libraries.html					
Medical Sciences Library MS 4462	College Station	TX	77843	979-845-7428	845-7493
Texas Tech University Health Sciences Ctr					
Preston Smith Library of the Health Sciences					
3601 4th St MS 7781	Lubbock	TX	79430	806-743-2200	743-2218
Web: www.ttuhsc.edu/libraries/Guides/LubbockGuide.aspx#welcome					
Tompkins-McCaw Library 509 N 12th St	Richmond	VA	23298	804-828-0636	828-6089
Web: www.library.vcu.edu					
Tufts University Hirsh Health Sciences Library					
145 Harrison Ave	Boston	MA	02111	617-636-6705	636-4039
Web: www.library.tufts.edu/hsl					
Uniformed Services University of the Health Sciences Learning Resource Ctr					
4301 Jones Bridge Rd	Bethesda	MD	20814	301-295-3350	295-3795
Web: www.lrc.usuhs.mil					
Universite de Montreal Bibliotheque de la Sante					
2900 Rue Edouard-Montpetit Rm L623	Montreal	QC	H3C3J7	514-343-6826	343-2350
Web: www.bib.umontreal.ca/SA					
Universite de Montreal Bibliotheque Paramedicale					
2375 ch de la Cote Ste-Catherine					
PO Box 6128 Stn Centre-ville	Montreal	QC	H3C3J7	514-343-6180	343-6457
Web: www.bib.umontreal.ca					
Universite Laval					
Bibliotheque Scientifique					
Pavillon Alexandre-Vachon 1045 ave.	Quebec	QC	G1V0A6	418-656-3967	656-7699
Web: www.bibl.ulaval.ca					
University of Arizona Arizona Health Sciences Library					
1501 N Campbell Ave PO Box 245079	Tucson	AZ	85724	520-626-6125	626-2922
Web: www.ahsl.arizona.edu					
University of Calgary Health Sciences Library					
3330 Hospital Dr NW	Calgary	AB	T2N4N1	403-220-6855	210-9847
Web: www.library.ucalgary.ca/branches/hsl					
University of California San Diego					
Biomedical Library 9500 Gilman Dr	La Jolla	CA	92093	858-534-3253	534-6609
Web: www.libraries.ucsd.edu					
University of California San Diego Medical Ctr Library					
200 W Arbor Dr	San Diego	CA	92103	619-543-6222	543-3289
Web: health.ucsd.edu/index.aspx					
University of Cincinnati					
231 Albert Sabin Way PO Box 670574	Cincinnati	OH	45267	513-558-4553	558-2910
Web: www.health.uc.edu					
University of Florida Health Science Center Libraries					
1600 SW Archer Rd PO Box 100206	Gainesville	FL	32610	352-273-8400	392-2565
Web: www.library.health.ufl.edu					
University of Maryland Baltimore (HSHSL)					
Health Sciences & Human Services Library					
601 W Lombard St	Baltimore	MD	21201	410-706-7928	706-8403
Web: www.hshsl.umaryland.edu					
University of Nebraska Medical Ctr McGoogan Library of Medicine					
986705 Nebraska Medical Ctr	Omaha	NE	68198	402-559-4006	559-5498
Web: www.unmc.edu/library					
University of Ottawa Health Sciences Library					
451 Smyth Rd Rm 1020	Ottawa	ON	K1H8M5	613-562-5407	562-5401
Web: www.biblio.uottawa.ca/health					
Biomedical Library					
3610 Hamilton Walk Johnson Pavilion	Philadelphia	PA	19104	215-898-5815	573-4143
Web: www.library.upenn.edu/biomed					
University of Tennessee Health Science Ctr					
Health Sciences Library & Biocommunications Ctr					
877 Madison Ave.	Memphis	TN	38163	901-448-5634	448-7235
TF: 877-747-0004 ■ *Web:* www.library.uthsc.edu					
University of Texas Health Science Center San Antonio					
Libraries 7703 Floyd Curl Dr MSC 7940	San Antonio	TX	78229	210-567-2400	567-2490
Web: www.library.uthscsa.edu					
University of Texas Southwestern Medical Center at Dallas Library The					
5323 Harry Hines Blvd	Dallas	TX	75390	214-648-2001	648-2826
Web: www4.utsouthwestern.edu					
University of Washington Health Sciences Libraries & Information Ctr					
1959 NE Pacific St PO Box 357155	Seattle	WA	98195	206-543-3390	543-8066
Web: healthlinks.washington.edu/hsl					
Ebling Library 750 Highland Ave.	Madison	WI	53705	608-262-2020	262-4732
Web: www.ebling.library.wisc.edu					
Weill Cornell Medical Library					
Weill Medical College of Cornell University					
1300 York Ave.	New York	NY	10065	212-746-6050	746-6494
Web: www.library.med.cornell.edu					
Health Sciences Ctr Library					
1 Medical Ctr Dr PO Box 9801	Morgantown	WV	26506	304-293-2113	293-5995
Web: www.hsc.wvu.edu/library					
William E Laupus Health Sciences Library					
East Carolina University					
600 Moye Blvd Health Sciences Bldg	Greenville	NC	27834	252-744-2230	744-3512
Web: www.ecu.edu/cs-dhs/laupuslibrary					
William H Welch Medical Library					
Johns Hopkins University					
1900 E Monument St	Baltimore	MD	21205	410-955-3411	614-9555
Web: www.welch.jhu.edu					
WK Kellogg Health Sciences Library					
5850 College St					
Sir Charles Tupper Medical Bldg	Halifax	NS	B3H1X5	902-494-2458	494-3798
Web: www.library.dal.ca/kellogg					
Woodruff Health Sciences Center Library					
Emory University 1462 Clifton Rd NE	Atlanta	GA	30322	404-727-8727	727-9821
Web: www.health.library.emory.edu					
Woodward Biomedical Library					
2198 Health Sciences Mall	Vancouver	BC	V6T1Z3	604-822-2883	822-5596
Web: www.library.ubc.ca/woodward					

437-2 Presidential Libraries

	City	State	Zip	Phone	Fax
Abraham Lincoln Presidential Library & Museum					
112 N 6th St	Springfield	IL	62701	217-524-7216	785-6250
TF: 800-610-2094 ■ *Web:* www.alincoln-library.com					
Dwight D Eisenhower Presidential Library & Museum					
200 SE 4th St	Abilene	KS	67410	785-263-6700	263-6715
TF: 877-746-4453 ■ *Web:* www.eisenhower.utexas.edu					
Franklin D Roosevelt Presidential Library & Museum					
4079 Albany Post Rd	Hyde Park	NY	12538	845-486-7770	486-1147
TF: 800-337-8474 ■ *Web:* www.fdrlibrary.marist.edu					
George Bush Library & Museum					
1000 George Bush Dr W.	College Station	TX	77845	979-691-4000	691-4050
Web: www.bushlibrary.tamu.edu					
Gerald R Ford Library 1000 Beal Ave.	Ann Arbor	MI	48109	734-205-0555	205-0571
Web: www.fordlibrarymuseum.gov					
Harry S Truman Presidential Library & Museum					
500 W Hwy 24	Independence	MO	64050	816-268-8200	268-8295
TF: 800-833-1225 ■ *Web:* www.trumanlibrary.org					
Herbert Hoover Presidential Library & Museum					
210 Parkside Dr	West Branch	IA	52358	319-643-5301	643-6045
Web: www.hoover.archives.gov					
Jimmy Carter Library & Museum					
441 Freedom Pkwy	Atlanta	GA	30307	404-865-7100	865-7102
Web: www.jimmycarterlibrary.org					
John F Kennedy Presidential Library & Museum					
Columbia Pt	Boston	MA	02125	617-514-1600	514-1652
TF: 866-535-1960 ■ *Web:* www.jfklibrary.org					
LBJ Library & Museum 2313 Red River St.	Austin	TX	78705	512-721-0216	721-0170
Web: www.lbjlib.utexas.edu					
Richard Nixon Foundation The					
18001 Yorba Linda Blvd	Yorba Linda	CA	92886	714-993-5075	528-0544
Web: www.nixonfoundation.org					
Ronald Reagan Presidential Library & Museum					
40 Presidential Dr.	Simi Valley	CA	93065	805-577-4000	577-4074
TF: 800-410-8354 ■ *Web:* www.reagan.utexas.edu					
Rutherford B Hayes Presidential Ctr					
Spiegel Grove	Fremont	OH	43420	419-332-2081	332-4952
TF: 800-998-7737 ■ *Web:* www.rbhayes.org					
William J Clinton Presidential Ctr					
1200 President Clinton Ave	Little Rock	AR	72201	501-370-8000	375-0512
Web: www.clintonpresidentialcenter.org					

				Phone	Fax
Woodrow Wilson Presidential Library 18-24 N Coalter St PO Box 24 *Web:* www.woodrowwilson.org	Staunton	VA	24402	540-885-0897	886-9874

437-3 Public Libraries

Listings For Public Libraries Are Alphabetized By City Name Within Each State Grouping.

ALABAMA

				Phone	Fax
Aliceville Public Library (APL) 416 3rd Ave NE *Web:* www.home.nctv.com/apl	Aliceville	AL	35442	205-373-6691	373-3731
Public Library of Anniston-Calhoun County 108 E 10th St *Web:* www.anniston.lib.al.us	Anniston	AL	36201	256-237-8501	238-0474
Escambia County Library System 700 E Church St	Atmore	AL	36502	251-368-4130	
Auburn Public Library 749 E Thach Ave *Web:* www.auburnalabama.org	Auburn	AL	36830	334-501-3190	
Bay Minette Public Library 205 W 2nd St *Web:* www.bayminettepubliclibrary.org	Bay Minette	AL	36507	251-580-1648	937-0339
Bessemer Public Library 400 19th St *Web:* www.bessemerlibrary.org	Bessemer	AL	35020	205-428-7882	428-7885
Birmingham Public Library 2100 Pk Pl *Web:* www.bham.lib.al.us	Birmingham	AL	35203	205-226-3600	226-3731
Choctaw County Public Library 124 N Academy Ave *Web:* www.pinebelt.net	Butler	AL	36904	205-459-2542	459-4122
Harrison Regional Library 50 Lester St *Web:* www.shelbycounty-al.org	Columbiana	AL	35051	205-669-3910	669-3940
Cullman County Public Library System 200 Clark St NE *Web:* www.ccpls.com	Cullman	AL	35055	256-734-1068	734-6902
Horseshoe Bend Regional Library 207 N W St *Web:* www.mindspring.com/~hbrl/hbrl.html	Dadeville	AL	36853	256-825-9232	825-4314
Wheeler Basin Regional Library PO Box 1766	Decatur	AL	35602	256-353-2993	350-6736
Florence-Lauderdale Public Library 350 N Wood Ave *Web:* www.flpl.lib.al.us	Florence	AL	35630	256-764-6564	764-6629
Gadsden Public Library 2829 W Meighan Blvd *Web:* www.library.gadsden.com	Gadsden	AL	35904	256-549-4699	549-4766
Guntersville Public Library 1240 O'Brig Ave *Web:* www.guntersvillelibrary.org	Guntersville	AL	35976	256-571-7595	571-7596
Cheaha Regional Library 935 Coleman St *Web:* www.cheaharegionallibrary.org	Heflin	AL	36264	256-463-7125	463-7128
Hoover Public Library (HPL) 200 Municipal Dr *Web:* www.hooverlibrary.org	Hoover	AL	35216	205-444-7800	444-7878
Hueytown Public Library 1372 Hueytown Rd *Web:* www.hueytown.com	Hueytown	AL	35023	205-491-1443	491-6319
Huntsville-Madison County Public Library 915 Monroe St	Huntsville	AL	35801	256-532-5940	532-5997
Carl Elliott Regional Library 98 E 18th St	Jasper	AL	35501	205-221-2568	221-2584
Mobile Public Library 701 Government St *Web:* www.mplonline.org	Mobile	AL	36602	251-208-7076	208-7137
Montgomery City-County Public Library 245 High St *Web:* www.mccpl.lib.al.us	Montgomery	AL	36104	334-240-4999	240-4980
Lawrence County Public Library 401 College St *Web:* www.lawrencecountypublic.org	Moulton	AL	35650	256-974-0883	974-0890
Baldwin County Library Co-op (BCLC) 22743 Milwaukee St PO Box 399 *Web:* www.gulftel.com/bclc	Robertsdale	AL	36567	251-947-7632	947-2651
Troy Public Library 300 N Three Notch St	Troy	AL	36081	334-566-1314	566-4392
Tuscaloosa Public Library 1801 Jack Warner Pkwy *Web:* www.tuscaloosa-library.org	Tuscaloosa	AL	35401	205-345-5820	758-1735
Bradshaw-Chambers County Public Library 3419 20th Ave *Web:* www.chamberscountylibrary.org	Valley	AL	36854	334-768-2161	768-7272

ALASKA

				Phone	Fax
ZJ Loussac Public Library 3600 Denali St *Web:* www.muni.org	Anchorage	AK	99503	907-343-2975	343-2930
Big Lake Public Library PO Box 520829 *Web:* www.matsulibraries.org/biglake	Big Lake	AK	99652	907-892-6475	892-6546
Fairbanks North Star Borough Public Library 1215 Cowles St **Fax:* Admin ■ *Web:* library.fnsb.lib.ak.us	Fairbanks	AK	99701	907-459-1020	459-1024*
Homer Public Library 500 Hazel Ave *Web:* www.cityofhomer-ak.gov/library	Homer	AK	99603	907-235-3180	235-3136
Juneau Public Libraries 292 Marine Way *Web:* www.juneau.org	Juneau	AK	99801	907-586-5324	586-3419

ARIZONA

				Phone	Fax
Apache Junction Public Library 1177 N Idaho Rd *Web:* www.ajpl.org	Apache Junction	AZ	85119	480-983-0204	983-4540
Cochise County Library District 100 Quality Hill Rd *Web:* www.cochise.lib.az.us	Bisbee	AZ	85603	520-432-8930	432-7339
Chandler Public Library 22 S Delaware St *Web:* www.chandlerlibrary.org	Chandler	AZ	85225	480-782-2800	782-2823
Cottonwood Public Library 100 S 6th St	Cottonwood	AZ	86326	928-634-7559	634-0253
Flagstaff City-Coconino County Public Library System 300 W Aspen Ave *Web:* www.flagstaffpubliclibrary.org	Flagstaff	AZ	86001	928-779-7670	774-9573
Pinal County Library District (PCLD) 92 W Butte Ave *Web:* www.pinalcountyaz.gov/departments/Library	Florence	AZ	85132	520-866-6457	866-6533
Southeast Regional Library 775 N Greenfield Rd	Gilbert	AZ	85234	480-539-5100	539-5159
Glendale Public Library 5959 W Brown St *Web:* www.glendaleaz.com	Glendale	AZ	85302	623-930-3530	842-4209
Mesa Public Library 64 E 1st St *Web:* www.mesalibrary.org	Mesa	AZ	85201	480-644-2207	644-3490
Nogales City/Santa Cruz County Public Library 518 N Grand Ave	Nogales	AZ	85621	520-287-3343	287-4823
Page Public Library 479 Lake Powell Blvd *Web:* www.pagepubliclibrary.org	Page	AZ	86040	928-645-4270	645-5804
Peoria Public Library 8463 W Monroe St *Web:* www.peoriaaz.com	Peoria	AZ	85345	623-773-7555	773-7567
Maricopa County Library District 2700 N Central Ave Suite 700 *Web:* www.mcldaz.org	Phoenix	AZ	85004	602-652-3000	
Phoenix Public Library 1221 N Central Ave *Web:* www.phoenixpubliclibrary.org	Phoenix	AZ	85004	602-534-2468	261-8836
Safford City - Graham County Library 808 7th Ave *Web:* www.saffordlibrary.org	Safford	AZ	85546	928-428-1531	348-3209
Scottsdale Public Library System 3839 N Drinkwater Blvd *Web:* library.ci.scottsdale.az.us	Scottsdale	AZ	85251	480-312-2474	312-7993
Pima County Public Library 101 N Stone Ave *Web:* www.library.pima.gov	Tucson	AZ	85701	520-594-5600	594-5621

ARKANSAS

				Phone	Fax
Arkansas River Valley Regional Library 501 N Front St *Web:* www.arvrls.com	Dardanelle	AR	72834	479-229-4418	229-2595
Barton Library 200 E 5th St	El Dorado	AR	71730	870-863-5447	862-3944
Washington County Library System 1080 W Clydesdale Dr *Web:* www.wcls.lib.ar.us	Fayetteville	AR	72701	479-442-6253	442-6812
Fort Smith Public Library 3201 Rogers Ave *Web:* www.fspl.lib.ar.us	Fort Smith	AR	72903	479-783-0229	783-5129
Southwest Arkansas Regional Library 500 S Elm St	Hope	AR	71801	870-777-2957	777-2957
Crowley Ridge Regional Library 315 W Oak St *Web:* www.libraryinjonesboro.org	Jonesboro	AR	72401	870-935-5133	935-7987
Central Arkansas Library System *The Butler Ctr* 100 Rock St *Web:* www.cals.lib.ar.us	Little Rock	AR	72201	501-320-5700	537-4559
William F. Laman Public Library System 2801 Orange St *Web:* www.lamanlibrary.org	North Little Rock	AR	72114	501-758-1720	758-3539
Pope County Library System 116 E 3rd St	Russellville	AR	72801	479-968-4368	968-3222
White County Public Library 113 E Pleasure St	Searcy	AR	72143	501-268-2449	268-5682
West Memphis Public Library 213 N Avalon St	West Memphis	AR	72301	870-732-7590	732-7636

CALIFORNIA

				Phone	Fax
Alameda Free Library 1550 Oak St *Web:* www.cityofalamedaca.gov/library	Alameda	CA	94501	510-747-7777	337-1471
Alhambra Civic Center Library 101 S First St *Web:* www.alhambralibrary.org	Alhambra	CA	91801	626-570-5008	457-1104
Anaheim Public Library 500 W Broadway *Web:* www.anaheim.net/library	Anaheim	CA	92805	714-765-1880	765-1730
Placer County Library 350 Nevada St *Web:* www.placer.ca.gov	Auburn	CA	95603	530-886-4500	886-4555
Azusa City Library 729 N Dalton Ave *Web:* www.ci.azusa.ca.us	Azusa	CA	91702	626-812-5232	334-4868
Beale Memorial Library 701 Truxtun Ave *Web:* www.kerncountylibrary.org	Bakersfield	CA	93301	661-868-0701	868-0799
Beaumont Library District 125 E 8th St *Web:* www.bld.lib.ca.us	Beaumont	CA	92223	951-845-1357	845-6217
Benicia Public Library 150 E 'L' St *Web:* www.ci.benicia.ca.us	Benicia	CA	94510	707-746-4343	747-8122
Berkeley Public Library 2090 Kittredge St *Web:* www.berkeleypubliclibrary.org	Berkeley	CA	94704	510-981-6100	981-6111
Beverly Hills Public Library 444 N Rexford Dr *Web:* www.beverlyhills.org	Beverly Hills	CA	90210	310-288-2220	278-3387
Burbank Central Library 110 N Glenoaks Blvd *Web:* www.burbank.lib.ca.us	Burbank	CA	91502	818-238-5600	238-5553
Carlsbad City Library 1250 Carlsbad Village Dr	Carlsbad	CA	92008	760-434-2870	434-9975
Cerritos Civic Ctr 18025 Bloomfield Ave *Web:* www.cerritos.us	Cerritos	CA	90703	562-916-1350	916-1375
Chula Vista Public Library 365 F St *Web:* www.chulavistalibrary.com	Chula Vista	CA	91910	619-691-5069	427-4246
Colton Public Library 656 N 9th St	Colton	CA	92324	909-370-5083	422-0873
Corona Public Library 650 S Main St *Web:* www.coronapubliclibrary.org	Corona	CA	92882	951-736-2382	736-2499
Coronado Public Library 640 Orange Ave *Web:* www.coronado.lib.ca.us	Coronado	CA	92118	619-522-7390	522-0326
Covina Public Library 234 N 2nd Ave	Covina	CA	91723	626-967-3935	384-5315
Daly City Public Library 40 Wembley Dr *Web:* www.dalycity.org	Daly City	CA	94015	650-991-8025	991-8225

Library	City	State	ZIP	Phone	Fax
Dixon Public Library 230 N 1st St	Dixon	CA	95620	707-678-5447	678-3515
Web: www.dixonlibrary.com					
Downey City Library (DCL) 11121 Brookshire Ave.	Downey	CA	90241	562-904-7360	923-3763
Web: www.downeyca.org					
Los Angeles County Public Library 7400 E Imperial Hwy.	Downey	CA	90242	562-940-8462	803-3032
Web: www.colapublib.org					
El Centro Public Library 539 State St	El Centro	CA	92243	760-337-4565	352-1384
Web: www.cityofelcentro.org/library					
Imperial County Free Library 1125 W Main St	El Centro	CA	92243	760-482-4791	482-4792
Web: www.imperialcounty.net					
Escondido Public Library 239 S Kalmia St	Escondido	CA	92025	760-839-4601	741-4255
Web: www.library.escondido.org					
Humboldt County Library 1313 3rd St.	Eureka	CA	95501	707-269-1900	269-1999
Web: www.co.humboldt.ca.us/library					
Alameda County Library 2450 Stevenson Blvd	Fremont	CA	94538	510-745-1500	793-2987
Web: aclibrary.org					
Fremont Main Library 2400 Stevenson Blvd	Fremont	CA	94538	510-745-1400	797-6557
Web: www.aclibrary.org/siteindex.asp					
Fresno County Public Library 2420 Mariposa St.	Fresno	CA	93721	559-600-7323	488-1971
Web: www.fresnolibrary.org					
Fullerton Public Library 353 W Commonwealth Ave.	Fullerton	CA	92832	714-738-6333	447-3280
Web: www.ci.fullerton.ca.us					
Garden Grove Regional Library 11200 Stanford Ave	Garden Grove	CA	92840	714-530-0711	
Web: www.ocsd.org/ocgov/OCPublicLibraries/LibraryLocator/GardenGroveRegional					
Glendale Public Library 222 E Harvard St.	Glendale	CA	91205	818-548-2030	548-7225
Web: www.glendalepubliclibrary.org					
Glendora Public Library & Cultural Ctr 140 S Glendora Ave	Glendora	CA	91741	626-852-4891	852-4899
Web: www.ci.glendora.ca.us					
Kings County Library 401 N Douty St	Hanford	CA	93230	559-582-0261	583-6163
Web: www.kingscountylibrary.org					
Hayward Public Library 835 C St	Hayward	CA	94541	510-293-8685	733-6669
Web: www.library.ci.hayward.ca.us					
Hemet Public Library 300 E Latham Ave	Hemet	CA	92543	951-765-2440	765-2446
San Benito County Free Library 470 5th St.	Hollister	CA	95023	831-636-4107	636-4099
Web: www.sanbenitofl.org					
Huntington Beach Public Library (HBPL) 7111 Talbert Ave.	Huntington Beach	CA	92648	714-842-4481	375-5180
Web: www.huntingtonbeachca.gov/government/departments/library					
Inglewood Public Library 101 W Manchester Blvd	Inglewood	CA	90301	310-412-5397	412-8848
Amador County Library 530 Sutter St	Jackson	CA	95642	209-223-6400	223-6303
Web: www.co.amador.ca.us					
Lake County Library 1425 N High St	Lakeport	CA	95453	707-263-8816	263-6796
Livermore Public Library 1188 S Livermore Ave.	Livermore	CA	94550	925-373-5500	373-5503
Web: www.livermore.lib.ca.us					
Lodi Public Library 201 W Locust St	Lodi	CA	95240	209-333-5566	367-5944
Web: www.lodi.gov					
Lompoc Public Library 501 E N Ave	Lompoc	CA	93436	805-736-3477	
Web: www.cityoflompoc.com					
Long Beach Public Library 101 Pacific Ave	Long Beach	CA	90822	562-570-7500	570-7408
Web: www.lbpl.org					
Braille Institute of America Library Services (BILS) 741 N Vermont Ave.	Los Angeles	CA	90029	323-660-3880	663-0867
TF: 800-808-2555 ■ *Web:* www.braillelibrary.org					
Los Angeles Public Library 630 W 5th St.	Los Angeles	CA	90071	213-228-7000	228-7369
Web: www.lapl.org					
Los Gatos Public Library (LGPL) 110 E Main St.	Los Gatos	CA	95030	408-354-8600	354-0578
Web: www.losgatosca.gov/index.aspx?NID=42					
Santa Clara County Library 14600 Winchester Blvd.	Los Gatos	CA	95032	408-293-2326	364-0161
TF: 800-286-1991 ■ *Web:* www.sccl.org					
Madera County Library 121 N 'G' St	Madera	CA	93637	559-675-7871	675-7998
Web: www.madera-county.com					
Yuba County Library 303 2nd St	Marysville	CA	95901	530-749-7380	741-3098
Web: www.co.yuba.ca.us					
Menlo Park Public Library 800 Alma St.	Menlo Park	CA	94025	650-330-2501	327-7030
Web: www.menloparklibrary.org					
Merced County Library 2100 O St.	Merced	CA	95340	209-385-7643	726-7912
Web: www.co.merced.ca.us					
Mill Valley Public Library 375 Throckmorton Ave	Mill Valley	CA	94941	415-389-4292	388-8929
Web: www.millvalleylibrary.org					
Stanislaus County 3647 Cornucopia Way	Modesto	CA	95358	209-558-7800	529-4779
Web: www.stanislauslibrary.org					
Monrovia Public Library 321 S Myrtle Ave	Monrovia	CA	91016	626-256-8274	256-8255
Web: www.monroviapubliclibrary.org					
Monterey Public Library 625 Pacific St	Monterey	CA	93940	831-646-3932	646-5618
Web: www.monterey.org					
Bruggemeyer Memorial Library 318 S Ramona Ave	Monterey Park	CA	91754	626-307-1418	288-4251
Mountain View Public Library 585 Franklin St.	Mountain View	CA	94041	650-903-6335	962-0438
Web: www.library.ci.mtnview.ca.us					
Napa City-County Library 580 Coombs St	Napa	CA	94559	707-253-4241	253-4615
Web: www.co.napa.ca.us/library					
National City Public Library 1401 National City Blvd	National City	CA	91950	619-470-5800	470-5880
Web: www.ci.national-city.ca.us					
Nevada County Library 980 Helling Way	Nevada City	CA	95959	530-265-7050	265-9863
Web: www.mynevadacounty.com/library					
Newport Beach Public Library 1000 Avocado Ave	Newport Beach	CA	92660	949-717-3800	640-5648
Web: www.city.newport-beach.ca.us					
Oakland Public Library 125 14th St	Oakland	CA	94612	510-238-3144	238-2232
Web: www.oaklandlibrary.org					
Oceanside Public Library 330 N Coast Hwy	Oceanside	CA	92054	760-435-5600	435-5567
Web: www.library.ci.oceanside.ca.us					
Ontario City Library 215 E C St	Ontario	CA	91764	909-395-2004	395-2043
Web: www.ci.ontario.ca.us/library					
Orange Public Library 407 E Chapmen Ave.	Orange	CA	92866	714-288-2400	771-6126
Web: www.cityoforange.org/library					
Butte County Library 1820 Mitchell Ave	Oroville	CA	95966	530-538-7641	538-7235
Web: www.buttecounty.net/bclibrary					
Oxnard Public Library (OPL) 251 S 'A' St	Oxnard	CA	93030	805-385-7532	385-7526
Web: www.oxnardlibrary.net					
Palm Springs Public Library 300 S Sunrise Way	Palm Springs	CA	92262	760-322-7323	320-9834
Web: www.palmspringsca.gov					
Palmdale City Library 700 E Palmdale Blvd	Palmdale	CA	93550	661-267-5600	267-5606
Web: www.palmdalelibrary.org					
Palo Alto City Library 1213 Newell Rd	Palo Alto	CA	94303	650-329-2436	327-2033
Web: www.cityofpaloalto.org//library					
Metropolitan Co-op Library System 3675 E Huntington Dr Suite 100.	Pasadena	CA	91107	626-683-8244	683-8097
Pasadena Public Library 285 E Walnut St	Pasadena	CA	91101	626-744-4052	585-8396
Web: www.cityofpasadena.net					
El Dorado County Library 345 Fair Ln.	Placerville	CA	95667	530-621-5540	622-3911
Web: www.eldoradolibrary.org					
Contra Costa County Library 1750 Oak Pk Blvd	Pleasant Hill	CA	94523	925-646-6423	646-6461
TF: 800-984-4636 ■ *Web:* www.ccclib.org					
Pomona Public Library 625 S Garey Ave.	Pomona	CA	91766	909-620-2043	620-3713
Web: www.youseemore.com					
Porterville Public Library 41 W Thurman Ave	Porterville	CA	93257	559-784-0177	781-4396
Rancho Cucamonga Public Library 7368 Archibald Ave.	Rancho Cucamonga	CA	91730	909-477-2720	477-2721
Web: www.rcpl.lib.ca.us					
Tehama County Library 645 Madison St	Red Bluff	CA	96080	530-527-0604	527-1562
Shasta Public Library 1100 Parkview Ave	Redding	CA	96001	530-245-7250	
Web: www.shastalibraries.org					
AK Smiley Public Library 125 W Vine St.	Redlands	CA	92373	909-798-7565	798-7566
Web: www.akspl.org					
Redondo Beach Public Library 303 N Pacific Coast Hwy	Redondo Beach	CA	90277	310-318-0675	318-3809
Redwood City Public Library 1044 Middlefield Rd	Redwood City	CA	94063	650-780-7047	780-7008
Web: www.redwoodcity.org/library/index.html					
Richmond Public Library 325 Civic Ctr Plaza	Richmond	CA	94804	510-620-6555	620-6850
Web: www.ci.richmond.ca.us					
Riverside City Public Library 3581 Mission Inn Ave.	Riverside	CA	92501	951-826-5201	826-5407
Web: www.riversideca.gov/library					
Roseville Public Library 225 Taylor St	Roseville	CA	95678	916-774-5221	773-5594
Sacramento Public Library 828 'I' St	Sacramento	CA	95814	916-264-2770	264-2755
Web: www.saclibrary.org					
John Steinbeck Library 350 Lincoln Ave.	Salinas	CA	93901	831-758-7311	758-7336
Web: www.salinaspubliclibrary.org					
Calaveras County Library 891 Mountain Ranch Rd	San Andreas	CA	95249	209-754-6510	754-6512
Web: www.co.calaveras.ca.us					
Norman F Feldheym Central Library 555 W 6th St.	San Bernardino	CA	92410	909-381-8235	381-8229
San Bernardino County Library 104 W 4th St.	San Bernardino	CA	92415	909-387-5723	387-5724
Web: www.sbcounty.gov/library					
San Bruno Public Library 701 Angus Ave W	San Bruno	CA	94066	650-616-7078	876-0848
Web: www.sanbruno.ca.gov					
San Diego County Library System 5560 Overland Ave Suite 110	San Diego	CA	92123	858-694-2415	495-5981
Web: www.sdcl.org					
San Diego Public Library 820 E St	San Diego	CA	92101	619-236-5800	236-5878
Web: www.sandiego.gov/public-library					
San Francisco Public Library 100 Larkin St	San Francisco	CA	94102	415-557-4400	557-4239
Web: www.sfpl.org					
San Jose Public Library 150 E San Fernando St	San Jose	CA	95113	408-808-2000	
Web: www.sjpl.org					
San Leandro Public Library 300 Estudillo Ave	San Leandro	CA	94577	510-577-3980	577-3967
San Luis Obispo City-County Library 995 Palm St	San Luis Obispo	CA	93401	805-781-5991	781-1166
Web: www.slolibrary.org					
Peninsula Library System 2471 Flores St.	San Mateo	CA	94403	650-349-5538	349-5089
Web: www.plsinfo.org					
San Mateo County Library 25 Tower Rd	San Mateo	CA	94402	650-312-5258	312-5382
Web: www.smcl.org					
Civic Center Library 3501 Civic Ctr Dr Administration Bldg	San Rafael	CA	94903	415-499-6057	499-3726
Web: www.co.marin.ca.us/depts/LB/main/civic					
Marin County Free Library 3501 Civic Ctr Dr Suite 414	San Rafael	CA	94903	415-499-3220	499-3726
Web: www.co.marin.ca.us/depts/LB/main					
San Rafael Public Library 1100 E St	San Rafael	CA	94901	415-485-3323	485-3112
Web: www.cityofsanrafael.org					
Orange County Public Library 1501 E St Andrew Pl.	Santa Ana	CA	92705	714-566-3000	566-3042
Santa Ana Public Library 26 Civic Ctr Dr	Santa Ana	CA	92701	714-647-5250	647-5356
Web: www.ci.santa-ana.ca.us/library					
Santa Barbara Public Library 40 E Anapamu St	Santa Barbara	CA	93101	805-962-7653	564-5660
Web: www.sbplibrary.org					
Santa Clara City Library 2635 Homestead Rd	Santa Clara	CA	95051	408-615-2900	
Web: www.library.santaclaraca.gov					
Garfield Park Library 705 Woodrow Ave	Santa Cruz	CA	95060	831-420-6344	420-6345
Web: www.santacruzpl.org/branches/gp/index.shtml					

Library	City	State	Zip	Phone	Fax
Santa Maria Public Library 420 S Broadway *Web:* www.ci.santa-maria.ca.us/210.html	Santa Maria	CA	93454	805-925-0994	928-7432
Santa Monica Public Library 1343 6th St *Web:* www.smpl.org	Santa Monica	CA	90401	310-458-8608	394-8951
Sonoma County Library 3rd & E Sts *Web:* www.sonoma.lib.ca.us	Santa Rosa	CA	95404	707-545-0831	575-0437
Tuolumne County Free Library 480 Greenley Rd *Web:* www.tuolcolib.org	Sonora	CA	95370	209-533-5507	533-0936
South San Francisco Public Library 840 W Orange Ave	South San Francisco	CA	94080	650-829-3876	829-3866
Stockton-San Joaquin County Public Library (SSJCPL) 605 N El Dorado St *TF:* 866-805-7323 ■ *Web:* www.stockton.lib.ca.us	Stockton	CA	95202	209-937-8416	937-8683
Sunnyvale Public Library (SPL) 665 W Olive Ave *Web:* www.sunnyvale.ca.gov/Departments/SunnyvalePublicLibrary.aspx	Sunnyvale	CA	94088	408-730-7300	735-8767
Thousand Oaks Library 1401 E Janss Rd *Web:* www.tol.lib.ca.us	Thousand Oaks	CA	91362	805-449-2660	373-6858
Belvedere-Tiburon Public Library 1501 Tiburon Blvd *Web:* www.bel-tib-lib.org	Tiburon	CA	94920	415-789-2665	789-2650
Torrance Public Library 3301 Torrance Blvd *Web:* www.torranceca.gov	Torrance	CA	90503	310-618-5959	618-5952
Tulare Public Library 113 N 'F' St *Web:* www.sjvls.org/tularepub	Tulare	CA	93274	559-685-2341	685-2345
Mendocino County Library 105 N Main St *Web:* www.co.mendocino.ca.us	Ukiah	CA	95482	707-463-4491	463-5472
Upland Public Library 450 N Euclid Ave *Web:* www.uplandpl.lib.ca.us	Upland	CA	91786	909-931-4200	931-4209
EP Foster Library 651 E Main St *Web:* www.vencolibrary.org	Ventura	CA	93001	805-648-2716	648-3696
Ventura County Libraries 646 County Sq Dr Suite 150 *Web:* www.vencolibrary.org	Ventura	CA	93003	805-477-7331	477-7340
Tulare County Library System 200 W Oak Ave *Web:* www.tularecountylibrary.org	Visalia	CA	93291	559-733-6954	737-4586
Watsonville Public Library 275 Main St Suite 100 *Web:* www.watsonville.lib.ca.us	Watsonville	CA	95076	831-768-3400	763-4015
Whittier Public Library 7344 S Washington Ave *Web:* www.cityofwhittier.org	Whittier	CA	90602	562-464-3450	464-3569
Woodland Public Library 250 1st St *Web:* www.cityofwoodland.org/library	Woodland	CA	95695	530-661-5980	666-5408
Yolo County Library 226 Buckeye St *Web:* www.yolocounty.org	Woodland	CA	95695	530-666-8005	666-8006
Yorba Linda Public Library 18181 Imperial Hwy *Web:* www.ylpl.lib.ca.us	Yorba Linda	CA	92886	714-777-2873	777-0640
Siskiyou County Library 719 4th St *Web:* www.snowcrest.net/siskiyoulibrary	Yreka	CA	96097	530-842-8175	842-7001
Sutter County Library 750 Forbes Ave	Yuba City	CA	95991	530-822-7137	671-6539

COLORADO

Library	City	State	Zip	Phone	Fax
Aurora Public Library 14949 E Alameda Pkwy *Web:* www.odyssey.aurora.lib.co.us	Aurora	CO	80012	303-739-6600	739-6638
Basalt Regional Library 99 Midland Ave	Basalt	CO	81621	970-927-4311	927-1351
Boulder Public Library 1000 Canyon Blvd *Web:* www.boulder.lib.co.us	Boulder	CO	80302	303-441-3100	442-1808
Mamie Doud Eisenhower Public Library 3 Community Pk Rd *Web:* www.ci.broomfield.co.us	Broomfield	CO	80020	720-887-2300	887-1384
Arapahoe Library District *Koebel Public Library* 5955 S Holly St	Centennial	CO	80121	303-220-7704	220-1651
Pikes Peak Library District PO Box 1579 *Web:* www.ppld.org	Colorado Springs	CO	80901	719-531-6333	528-2810
Denver Public Library 10 W 14th Ave Pkwy *Web:* www.denverlibrary.org	Denver	CO	80204	720-865-1111	865-2085
Englewood Public Library 1000 Englewood Pkwy Englewood Civic Ctr First Fl *Web:* www.englewoodgov.org	Englewood	CO	80110	303-762-2560	783-6890
Poudre River Public Library 201 Peterson St *Web:* www.poudrelibraries.org	Fort Collins	CO	80524	970-221-6740	221-6398
Farr Regional Library 1939 61st Ave *Web:* www.mylibrary.us	Greeley	CO	80634	970-506-8550	506-8551
Bemis Public Library 6014 S Datura St *Web:* www.littletongov.org	Littleton	CO	80120	303-795-3961	795-3996
Longmont Public Library 409 4th Ave *Web:* www.ci.longmont.co.us/library/index.htm	Longmont	CO	80501	303-651-8470	651-8911
Pueblo Library District 100 E Abriendo Ave *Web:* www.pueblolibrary.org	Pueblo	CO	81004	719-562-5600	562-5610
Rangeview Library District 5877 E 120th Ave *Web:* www.anythinklibraries.org	Thornton	CO	80602	303-288-2001	451-0190
Westminster Public Library 7392 Irving St *Web:* www.ci.westminster.co.us	Westminster	CO	80030	303-430-2400	

CONNECTICUT

Library	City	State	Zip	Phone	Fax
Avon Free Public Library 281 Country Club Rd *Web:* www.avonctlibrary.info	Avon	CT	06001	860-673-9712	675-6364
Bridgeport Public Library 925 Broad St *Web:* www.bportlibrary.org	Bridgeport	CT	06604	203-576-7403	576-8255
Bristol Public Library 5 High St	Bristol	CT	06010	860-584-7787	584-7696
Cheshire Public Library 104 Main St *Web:* www.cheshirelibrary.org	Cheshire	CT	06410	203-272-2245	272-7714
Danbury Public Library 170 Main St *Web:* www.danburylibrary.org	Danbury	CT	06810	203-797-4505	796-1677
East Hartford Public Library 840 Main St *Web:* www.ehtfdlib.info	East Hartford	CT	06108	860-289-6429	291-9166
Enfield Public Library 104 Middle Rd *Web:* www.enfield-ct.gov	Enfield	CT	06082	860-763-7510	763-7514
Fairfield Public Library 1080 Old Post Rd *Web:* www.fairfieldpubliclibrary.org	Fairfield	CT	06824	203-256-3155	256-3162
Welles-Turner Memorial Library 2407 Main St *Web:* www.wtmlib.com	Glastonbury	CT	06033	860-652-7719	652-7721
Groton Public Library 52 Newtown Rd Rt 117	Groton	CT	06340	860-441-6750	448-0363
Hamden Library 2901 Dixwell Ave *Web:* www.hamdenlibrary.org	Hamden	CT	06518	203-287-2686	287-2685
Hartford Public Library 500 Main St *Web:* www.hplct.org	Hartford	CT	06103	860-695-6300	722-6900
Manchester Public Library 586 Main St *Web:* www.library.ci.manchester.ct.us	Manchester	CT	06040	860-643-2471	643-9453
Meriden Public Library 105 Miller St	Meriden	CT	06450	203-238-2344	238-3647
Milford Public Library 57 New Haven Ave	Milford	CT	06460	203-783-3290	877-1072
New Canaan Library 151 Main St *Web:* www.newcanaanlibrary.org	New Canaan	CT	06840	203-594-5000	594-5026
New Fairfield Free Public Library 2 Brush Hill Rd PO Box F *Web:* www.newfairfieldlibrary.org	New Fairfield	CT	06812	203-312-5679	312-5685
New Haven Free Public Library 133 Elm St *Web:* www.cityofnewhaven.com/library	New Haven	CT	06510	203-946-8130	946-8140
Lucy Robbins Welles Library 95 Cedar St *Web:* www.newingtonct.gov	Newington	CT	06111	860-665-8700	667-1255
Norwalk Public Library 1 Belden Ave *Web:* www.norwalklib.org	Norwalk	CT	06850	203-899-2780	866-7982
Plumb Memorial Library 65 Wooster St *Web:* www.plumblibrary.org	Shelton	CT	06484	203-924-1580	924-8422
Simsbury Public Library 725 Hopmeadow St *Web:* www.simsburylibrary.info	Simsbury	CT	06070	860-658-7663	658-6732
Southington Public Library 255 Main St *Web:* www.southingtonlibrary.org	Southington	CT	06489	860-628-0947	628-0488
Ferguson Library 1 Public Library Plaza *Web:* www.fergusonlibrary.org	Stamford	CT	06904	203-964-1000	357-9098
Willoughby Wallace Memorial Library (WWML) 146 Thimble Islands Rd *Web:* www.wwml.org	Stony Creek	CT	06405	203-488-8702	315-3347
Trumbull Library 33 Quality St *Web:* www.trumbullct-library.org	Trumbull	CT	06611	203-452-5197	452-5125
Silas Bronson Library (SBL) 267 Grand St *Web:* www.bronsonlibrary.org	Waterbury	CT	06702	203-574-8222	574-8055
West Hartford Public Library 20 S Main St *Web:* www.westhartfordlibrary.org	West Hartford	CT	06107	860-561-6950	561-6990
Windsor Public Library 323 Broad St *Web:* www.windsorlibrary.com	Windsor	CT	06095	860-285-1910	285-1889

DELAWARE

Library	City	State	Zip	Phone	Fax
Kent County Library 2319 S Dupont Hwy *Web:* www.co.kent.de.us/Departments/CommunitySvcs/Library	Dover	DE	19901	302-698-6440	698-6441
Hockessin Library 1023 Valley Rd *Web:* www.nccde.org	Hockessin	DE	19707	302-239-5160	239-1519
New Castle Public Library 424 Delaware St *Web:* www2.nccde.org	New Castle	DE	19720	302-328-1995	328-4412
Newark Free Library 750 Library Ave	Newark	DE	19711	302-731-7550	731-4019
Rehoboth Beach Public Library 226 Rehoboth Ave *Web:* www.rehobothlibrary.org	Rehoboth Beach	DE	19971	302-227-8044	227-0597
Kirkwood Library 6000 Kirkwood Hwy *Web:* www.nccde.org	Wilmington	DE	19808	302-995-7663	995-7687
Wilmington Public Library 10 E 10th St *Web:* www.wilmlib.org	Wilmington	DE	19801	302-571-7400	654-9132

DISTRICT OF COLUMBIA

Library	City	State	Zip	Phone	Fax
Library of Congress (LOC) 101 Independence Ave SE *Web:* www.loc.gov	Washington	DC	20540	202-707-5000	
Martin Luther King Jr Memorial Library (MLK) 901 G St NW *Web:* www.dclibrary.org	Washington	DC	20001	202-727-0321	
National Library of Education 400 Maryland Ave SW *TF:* 800-424-1616 ■ *Web:* www.ies.ed.gov/ncee/projects/nat_ed_library.asp	Washington	DC	20202	202-205-5015	260-7364

FLORIDA

Library	City	State	Zip	Phone	Fax
DeSoto County Library 125 N Hillsboro Ave *Web:* www.myhlc.org	Arcadia	FL	34266	863-993-4851	491-4095
Citrus County Library System 425 W Roosevelt Blvd *Web:* www.cclib.org	Beverly Hills	FL	34465	352-746-9077	746-9493
Boca Raton Public Library 200 NW Boca Raton Blvd *Web:* www.bocalibrary.org	Boca Raton	FL	33432	561-393-7852	393-7823

Library	City	State	ZIP	Phone	Fax
Boynton Beach City Library 208 S Seacrest Blvd *Web:* www.coala.org	Boynton Beach	FL	33435	561-742-6390	742-6381
Manatee County Public Library System 1301 Barcarrota Blvd W *Web:* www.mymanatee.org	Bradenton	FL	34205	941-748-5555	749-7191
Hernando County Public Library System 238 Howell Ave *Web:* www.hcpl.lib.fl.us	Brooksville	FL	34601	352-754-4043	754-4044
Seminole County Public Library 215 N Oxford Rd *Web:* www.seminolecountyfl.gov/lls/library	Casselberry	FL	32707	407-339-4000	339-7931
Clearwater Public Library 100 N Osceola Ave *Web:* www.myclearwater.com/cpl	Clearwater	FL	33755	727-562-4970	562-4977
Clewiston Public Library System 120 W Osceola Ave *Web:* www.hendrylibraries.org	Clewiston	FL	33440	863-983-1493	983-9194
Central Brevard Library 308 Forest Ave *Web:* www.brev.org	Cocoa	FL	32922	321-633-1792	633-1806
Volusia County Public Library 105 E Magnolia Ave *Web:* www.volusialibrary.org	Daytona Beach	FL	32114	386-257-6036	257-6026
Walton-De Funiak Library 3 Cir Dr	De Funiak Springs	FL	32435	850-892-3624	892-4438
Delray Beach Library 100 W Atlantic Ave *Web:* www.delraylibrary.org	Delray Beach	FL	33444	561-266-0194	266-9757
Broward County Library 100 S Andrews Ave *Web:* www.browardlibrary.org	Fort Lauderdale	FL	33301	954-357-7444	
Lee County Library 2050 Central Ave *Web:* www.lee-county.com/library	Fort Myers	FL	33901	239-338-3155	479-4634
Saint Lucie County Library System 101 Melody Ln *Web:* www.st-lucie.lib.fl.us	Fort Pierce	FL	34950	772-462-1615	462-2750
Alachua County Library District 401 E University Ave *Web:* www.acld.lib.fl.us	Gainesville	FL	32601	352-334-3900	334-3918
Gulfport Public Library 5501 28th Ave S *Web:* www.tblc.org	Gulfport	FL	33707	727-893-1074	893-1072
John F Kennedy Library (JFKL) 190 W 49th St *Web:* www.hialeahfl.gov/dep/library	Hialeah	FL	33012	305-821-2700	818-9144
Pasco County Library System 8012 Library Rd *Web:* www.pascolibraries.org	Hudson	FL	34667	727-861-3020	861-3025
Monroe County Public Library System 700 Fleming St	Key West	FL	33040	305-292-3595	295-3626
Columbia County Public Library 308 NW Columbia Ave PO Box 1529 *Web:* www.columbiacountyfla.com/default.asp	Lake City	FL	32055	386-758-2101	758-2135
Lake Worth Public Library 15 N 'M' St *Web:* www.lakeworth.org	Lake Worth	FL	33460	561-533-7354	586-1651
Lakeland Public Library 100 Lake Morton Dr *Web:* www.lakelandgov.net/library/home.html	Lakeland	FL	33801	863-834-4270	834-4293
Leesburg Public Library 100 E Main St *Web:* www.leesburgflorida.gov	Leesburg	FL	34748	352-728-9790	728-9794
Miami-Dade Public Library 101 W Flagler St *Web:* www.mdpls.org	Miami	FL	33130	305-375-2665	375-3048
Collier County Public Library (CCPL) 2385 Orange Blossom Dr *Web:* www.colliergov.net/index.aspx?page=108	Naples	FL	34109	239-593-0177	
North Miami Public Library 835 NE 132nd St	North Miami	FL	33161	305-891-5535	892-0843
North Miami Beach Public Library 1601 NE 164th St	North Miami Beach	FL	33162	305-948-2970	787-6007
Ocala Public Library 2720 E Silver Springs Blvd *Web:* www.marioncountyfl.org/library/li_home.htm	Ocala	FL	34470	352-671-8551	368-4545
Orange County Library System 101 E Central Blvd *Web:* www.ocls.lib.fl.us	Orlando	FL	32801	407-835-7323	835-7650
Putnam County Library System 601 College Rd *TF:* 800-231-4045 ■ *Web:* www.putnam-fl.com	Palatka	FL	32177	386-329-0126	329-1240
Flagler County Public Library (FCPL) 2500 Palm Coast Pkwy NW *Web:* www.flaglercounty.org	Palm Coast	FL	32137	386-446-6763	446-6773
Bay County Public Library 25 W Government St PO Box 59625 *Web:* www.nwrls.lib.fl.us	Panama City	FL	32412	850-872-7500	872-7507
Northwest Regional Library System 25 W Government St *Web:* www.nwrls.com	Panama City	FL	32401	850-872-7500	872-7507
West Florida Regional Library 200 W Gregory St *Web:* www.cityofpensacola.com	Pensacola	FL	32501	850-436-5060	436-5039
Helen B Hoffman Plantation Library 501 N Fig Tree Ln	Plantation	FL	33317	954-797-2140	797-2767
Gadsden County Public Library 341 E Jefferson St	Quincy	FL	32351	850-627-7106	627-7775
Riviera Beach Public Library 600 W Blue Heron Blvd	Riviera Beach	FL	33404	561-845-4195	881-7308
Saint Johns County Public Library 1960 N Ponce de Leon Blvd *Web:* www.sjcpls.org	Saint Augustine	FL	32084	904-827-6940	827-6945
Saint Petersburg Public Library 3745 9th Ave N *Web:* www.splibraries.org	Saint Petersburg	FL	33713	727-893-7724	892-5432
Seminole County Public Library - North Branch 150 N Palmetto Ave *Web:* www.seminolecountyfl.gov/lls/library	Sanford	FL	32771	407-330-3737	330-3120
North Sarasota Library 2801 Newtown Blvd *Web:* www.suncat.co.sarasota.fl.us	Sarasota	FL	34234	941-861-1360	
Selby Public Library 1331 1st St *Web:* www.suncat.co.sarasota.fl.us/libraries/selby.aspx	Sarasota	FL	34236	941-861-1100	316-1188
Heartland Library Co-op 319 W Ctr Ave *Web:* www.myhlc.org	Sebring	FL	33870	863-402-6716	402-6743
Martin County Public Library 2401 SE Monterey Rd *Web:* www.martin.fl.us	Stuart	FL	34996	772-288-5702	219-4959
Leon County Public Library System 200 W Pk Ave *Web:* www.leoncountylibrary.org	Tallahassee	FL	32301	850-487-2665	487-1793
Tampa-Hillsborough County Public Library 900 N Ashley Dr *Web:* www.hcplc.org	Tampa	FL	33602	813-273-3652	272-5640
Indian River County Library (IRCL) 1600 21st St *Web:* www.irclibrary.org	Vero Beach	FL	32960	772-770-5060	770-5066
Palm Beach County Public Library System 3650 Summit Blvd *Web:* www.pbclibrary.org	West Palm Beach	FL	33406	561-233-2600	233-2622
West Palm Beach Public Library 411 Clematis St *Web:* www.wpbpl.com	West Palm Beach	FL	33401	561-868-7700	835-7020

GEORGIA

Library	City	State	ZIP	Phone	Fax
Dougherty County Public Library 300 N Pine Ave *Web:* www.docolib.org	Albany	GA	31701	229-420-3200	
Athens/Clarke County Library 2025 Baxter St *Web:* www.clarke.public.lib.ga.us	Athens	GA	30606	706-613-3650	613-3660
Atlanta-Fulton Public Library 1 Margaret Mitchell Sq *Web:* www.af.public.lib.ga.us	Atlanta	GA	30303	404-730-1700	730-1990
Augusta-Richmond County Library 823 Telfair St *Web:* www.ecgrl.public.lib.ga.us	Augusta	GA	30901	706-821-2600	724-6762
Brunswick-Glynn County Regional Library 208 Gloucester St	Brunswick	GA	31520	912-267-1212	267-9597
West Georgia Regional Library 710 Rome St *Web:* www.wgrl.net	Carrollton	GA	30117	770-836-6711	836-4787
Bartow County Public Library 429 W Main St *Web:* www.bartowlibraryonline.org	Cartersville	GA	30120	770-382-4203	386-3056
Columbus Public Library 3000 Macon Rd	Columbus	GA	31906	706-243-2669	
Northwest Georgia Regional Library 310 Cappes St *Web:* www.ngrl.org	Dalton	GA	30720	706-876-1360	272-2977
DeKalb County Public Library 215 Sycamore St *Web:* www.dekalblibrary.org	Decatur	GA	30030	404-370-3070	370-8469
Flint River Regional Library 800 Memorial Dr	Griffin	GA	30223	770-412-4770	412-4771
Clayton County Library System 865 Battle Creek Rd *Web:* www.clayton.public.lib.ga.us	Jonesboro	GA	30236	770-473-3850	473-3858
LaFayette-Walker County Library 305 S Duke St *Web:* www.chrl.org	La Fayette	GA	30728	706-638-2992	638-4028
Gwinnett County Public Library 1001 Lawrenceville Hwy *Web:* www.gwinnettpl.org	Lawrenceville	GA	30046	770-822-4522	822-5379
Middle Georgia Regional Library System 1180 Washington Ave *Web:* www.co.bibb.ga.us	Macon	GA	31201	478-744-0800	744-0840
Cobb County Public Library System 266 Roswell St *Web:* www.cobbcat.org	Marietta	GA	30060	770-528-2320	528-2349
Henry County Public Library System 1001 Florence McGarity Blvd *Web:* www.henry.public.lib.ga.us	McDonough	GA	30252	770-954-2806	954-2808
Sara Hightower Regional Library 205 Riverside Pkwy NE *Web:* www.romelibrary.org	Rome	GA	30161	706-236-4600	236-4631
Live Oak Public Libraries 2002 Bull St *Web:* www.liveoakpl.org	Savannah	GA	31401	912-652-3600	652-3638
South Georgia Regional Library 300 Woodrow Wilson Dr *Web:* www.sgrl.org	Valdosta	GA	31602	229-333-0086	333-7669

IDAHO

Library	City	State	ZIP	Phone	Fax
Boise Public Library 715 S Capitol Blvd *Web:* www.boisepubliclibrary.org	Boise	ID	83702	208-384-4076	384-4025
Coeur d'Alene Public Library 702 E Front *Web:* www.cdalibrary.org	Coeur d'Alene	ID	83814	208-769-2315	769-2381
Idaho Falls Public Library 457 W Broadway *Web:* www.ifpl.org	Idaho Falls	ID	83402	208-612-8460	612-8467
Lewiston City Library 428 Thain Rd *Web:* www.cityoflewiston.org	Lewiston	ID	83501	208-743-6519	798-4446
Nampa Public Library (NPL) 101 11th Ave S *Web:* www.nampalibrary.org	Nampa	ID	83651	208-468-5800	465-2277
Marshall Public Library 113 S Garfield St *Web:* www.marshallpl.org	Pocatello	ID	83204	208-232-1263	232-9266
Twin Falls Public Library 201 4th Ave E *Web:* www.twinfallspubliclibrary.org	Twin Falls	ID	83301	208-733-2964	733-2965

ILLINOIS

Library	City	State	ZIP	Phone	Fax
Addison Public Library 4 Friendship Plaza *Web:* www.addisonlibrary.org	Addison	IL	60101	630-543-3617	543-7275
Arlington Heights Memorial Library 500 N Dunton Ave *Web:* www.ahml.info	Arlington Heights	IL	60004	847-392-0100	506-2650
Aurora Public Library 1 E Benton St *Web:* www.aurora.lib.il.us	Aurora	IL	60505	630-264-4100	896-3209
Belleville Public Library 121 E Washington St	Belleville	IL	62220	618-234-0441	234-9474
Bensenville Community Public Library 200 S Church Rd *Web:* www.bensenville.lib.il.us	Bensenville	IL	60106	630-766-4642	766-0788
Berwyn Public Library 2701 Harlem Ave *Web:* www.berwynlibrary.net	Berwyn	IL	60402	708-795-8000	795-8102
Bloomington Public Library 205 E Olive St PO Box 3308 *Web:* www.bloomingtonlibrary.org	Bloomington	IL	61702	309-828-6091	828-7312
Fountaindale Public Library					

				Phone	Fax
300 W Briarcliff Rd	Bolingbrook	IL	60440	630-759-2102	759-9519
Web: www.fountaindale.lib.il.us					
Calumet City Public Library					
660 Manistee Ave	Calumet City	IL	60409	708-862-6220	862-0872
Carbondale Public Library 405 W Main St	Carbondale	IL	62901	618-457-0354	457-0353
Web: www.carbondale.lib.il.us					
Carol Stream Public Library					
616 Hiawatha Dr	Carol Stream	IL	60188	630-653-0755	653-6809
Web: www.cslibrary.org					
Lincoln Trail Libraries System					
1704 W IH- Dr	Champaign	IL	61822	217-352-0047	352-7153
Web: www.lincolntrail.info					
Chicago Public Library 400 S State St	Chicago	IL	60605	312-747-4999	747-4968
Web: www.chipublib.org					
Gerber/Hart Library & Archives					
1127 W Granville Ave	Chicago	IL	60660	773-381-8030	381-8030
Web: www.gerberhart.org					
Cicero Public Library 5225 W Cermak Rd	Cicero	IL	60804	708-652-8084	652-1668
Crystal Lake Public Library					
126 W Paddock St	Crystal Lake	IL	60014	815-459-1687	459-5845
Web: www.crystallakelibrary.org					
Danville Public Library 319 N Vermilion St	Danville	IL	61832	217-477-5220	477-5230
Web: www.danville.lib.il.us					
Decatur Public Library 130 N Franklin St	Decatur	IL	62523	217-424-2900	233-4071
Web: www.decatur.lib.il.us					
DeKalb Public Library 309 Oak St	DeKalb	IL	60115	815-756-9568	756-7837
Web: www.dkpl.org					
Des Plaines Public Library					
1501 Ellinwood Ave	Des Plaines	IL	60016	847-827-5551	827-7974
Web: www.dppl.org					
Downers Grove Public Library					
1050 Curtiss St	Downers Grove	IL	60515	630-960-1200	960-9374
Web: www.downersgrovelibrary.org					
Alliance Library System					
600 High Pt Ln Suite 1	Eask Peoria	IL	61611	309-694-9200	694-9230
TF: 800-700-4857 ■ *Web:* www.alliancelibrarysystem.com					
East Saint Louis Public Library					
5300 State St	East Saint Louis	IL	62203	618-397-0991	397-1260
Web: www.esllibrary.org					
Elk Grove Village Public Library					
1001 Wellington Ave	Elk Grove Village	IL	60007	847-439-0447	439-0475
Web: www.egvpl.org					
Elmhurst Public Library 125 S Prospect Ave	Elmhurst	IL	60126	630-279-8696	279-0636
Web: www.elmhurstpubliclibrary.org					
Evanston Public Library 1703 Orrington Ave	Evanston	IL	60201	847-866-0300	866-0313
Web: www.eto.com					
Freeport Public Library 100 E Douglas St	Freeport	IL	61032	815-233-3000	297-8236
Web: www.freeportpubliclibrary.org					
Galesburg Public Library 40 E Simmons St	Galesburg	IL	61401	309-343-6118	343-4877
Web: www.galesburglibrary.org					
DuPage Library System 127 S 1st St	Geneva	IL	60134	630-232-8457	232-0699
Web: www.dupagels.lib.il.us					
Glenview Public Library 1930 Glenview Rd	Glenview	IL	60025	847-729-7500	729-7558
Web: www.glenviewpl.org					
Grande Prairie Public Library					
3479 W 183rd St	Hazel Crest	IL	60429	708-798-5563	798-5874
Web: www.grandeprairie.org					
Highland Park Public Library					
494 Laurel Ave	Highland Park	IL	60035	847-432-0216	432-9139
Web: www.hplibrary.org					
Joliet Public Library 150 N Ottawa St	Joliet	IL	60432	815-740-2660	740-6161
Web: www.joliet.lib.il.us					
Kankakee Public Library 200 E Ct St	Kankakee	IL	60901	815-939-4564	939-9057
Web: www.lions-online.org					
Ela Area Public Library District					
275 Mohawk Trail	Lake Zurich	IL	60047	847-438-3433	438-9290
Web: www.eapl.org					
Lewis O Flom Lansing Public Library					
2750 Indiana Ave	Lansing	IL	60438	708-474-2447	474-9466
Web: www.lansing.lib.il.us					
Helen M Plum Memorial Library 110 W Maple St	Lombard	IL	60148	630-627-0316	627-0336
Web: www.plum.lib.il.us					
Maywood Public Library 121 S 5th Ave	Maywood	IL	60153	708-343-1847	343-2115
Web: www.maywood.org					
Morton Grove Public Library					
6140 Lincoln Ave	Morton Grove	IL	60053	847-965-4220	965-7903
Web: www.webrary.org					
Mount Prospect Public Library					
10 S Emerson St	Mount Prospect	IL	60056	847-253-5675	253-5677
Web: www.mppl.org					
Naperville Public Libraries					
200 W Jefferson Ave	Naperville	IL	60540	630-961-4100	637-4870
Web: www.naperville-lib.org					
Normal Public Library 206 W College	Normal	IL	61761	309-452-1757	452-5312
Web: www.normalpl.org					
North Chicago Public Library					
2100 Argonne Dr	North Chicago	IL	60064	847-689-0125	689-9117
Web: www.northchicagopubliclibrary.org					
Northbrook Public Library 1201 Cedar Ln	Northbrook	IL	60062	847-272-6224	498-0440
Oak Lawn Public Library 9427 Raymond Ave	Oak Lawn	IL	60453	708-422-4990	442-5061
Web: www.lib.oak-lawn.il.us					
Oak Park Public Library 834 Lake St	Oak Park	IL	60301	708-383-8200	383-6384
Web: www.oppl.org					
Orland Park Public Library					
14921 Ravinia Ave	Orland Park	IL	60462	708-349-8138	349-8196
Web: www.orlandparklibrary.org					
Park Forest Public Library					
400 Lakewood Blvd	Park Forest	IL	60466	708-748-3731	748-8829
Web: www.pfpl.org					
Park Ridge Public Library					
20 S Prospect Ave	Park Ridge	IL	60068	847-825-3123	825-0001
Web: www.parkridgelibrary.org					
Pekin Public Library 301 S 4th St	Pekin	IL	61554	309-347-7111	347-6587
Web: www.pekin.net					
Peoria Public Library 107 NE Monroe St	Peoria	IL	61602	309-672-8835	674-0116
Web: www.peoriapubliclibrary.org					
Quincy Public Library 526 Jersey St	Quincy	IL	62301	217-223-1309	222-3052
Web: www.quincylibrary.org					
Rock Island Public Library 401 19th St	Rock Island	IL	61201	309-732-7323	732-7342
Web: www.rockislandlibrary.org					
Rockford Public Library 215 N Wyman St	Rockford	IL	61101	815-965-6731	965-6735
Web: www.rockfordpubliclibrary.org					
Schaumburg Township District Library (STDL)					
130 S Roselle Rd	Schaumburg	IL	60193	847-985-4000	923-3335
Web: www.schaumburglibrary.org					
Shorewood-Troy Public Library District					
650 Deerwood Dr	Shorewood	IL	60404	815-725-1715	725-1722
Web: www.shorewood.lib.il.us					
Skokie Public Library 5215 Oakton St	Skokie	IL	60077	847-673-7774	673-7797
Web: www.skokielibrary.org					
Lincoln Library 326 S 7th St	Springfield	IL	62701	217-753-4900	753-5329
Web: www.lincolnlibrary.info					
Tinley Park Public Library					
7851 Timber Dr	Tinley Park	IL	60477	708-532-0160	532-2981
Web: www.tplibrary.org					
Urbana Free Library 210 W Green St	Urbana	IL	61801	217-367-4057	367-4061
Web: www.urbanafreelibrary.org					
Waukegan Public Library 128 N County St	Waukegan	IL	60085	847-623-2041	623-2092
Web: www.waukeganpl.org					
Wheaton Public Library 225 N Cross St	Wheaton	IL	60187	630-668-1374	668-8950
Web: www.wheaton.lib.il.us					
North Suburban Library System					
200 W Dundee Rd	Wheeling	IL	60090	847-459-1300	459-0380
TF: 800-374-7134 ■ *Web:* www.nsls.info					
Woodridge Public Library 3 Plaza Dr	Woodridge	IL	60517	630-964-7899	964-0175
Web: www.woodridgelibrary.org					

INDIANA

				Phone	Fax
Anderson Public Library 111 E 12th St	Anderson	IN	46016	765-641-2456	641-2197
Web: www.and.lib.in.us					
Batesville Memorial Public Library (BMPL)					
131 N Walnut St	Batesville	IN	47006	812-934-4706	934-6288
Web: www.ebatesville.com/library					
Bedford Public Library 1323 K St	Bedford	IN	47421	812-275-4471	277-1145
Web: www.bedlib.org					
Monroe County Public Library					
303 E Kirkwood Ave	Bloomington	IN	47408	812-349-3050	349-3051
Web: www.monroe.lib.in.us					
Wells County Public Library					
200 W Washington St	Bluffton	IN	46714	260-824-1612	824-3129
Web: www.wellscolibrary.org					
Carmel Clay Public Library 55 4th Ave SE	Carmel	IN	46032	317-844-3361	571-4285
Web: www.carmel.lib.in.us					
Charlestown Clark County Public Library					
51 Clark Rd	Charlestown	IN	47111	812-256-3337	256-3890
Web: www.clarkco.lib.in.us					
Bartholomew County Public Library					
536 5th St	Columbus	IN	47201	812-379-1255	379-1275
Web: www.barth.lib.in.us					
Fayette County Public Library					
828 N Grand Ave	Connersville	IN	47331	765-827-0883	825-4592
Web: www.fcplibrary.lib.in.us					
East Chicago Public Library (ECPL)					
2401 E Columbus Dr	East Chicago	IN	46312	219-397-2453	397-6715
Web: www.ecpl.org					
Evansville Vanderburgh Public Library					
200 SE ML King Jr Blvd	Evansville	IN	47713	812-428-8200	428-8397
Web: www.evpl.org					
Allen County Public Library					
900 Library Plaza	Fort Wayne	IN	46802	260-421-1200	421-1386
Web: www.acpl.lib.in.us					
Frankfort Community Public Library (FCPL)					
208 W Clinton St	Frankfort	IN	46041	765-654-8746	654-8747
Web: www.fcpl.accs.net					
Johnson County Public Library					
401 S State St	Franklin	IN	46131	317-738-2833	738-9635
Web: www.jcplin.org					
Gary Public Library 220 W 5th Ave	Gary	IN	46402	219-886-2484	886-6829
Web: www.garypubliclibrary.org					
Putnam County Public Library					
103 E Poplar St PO Box 116	Greencastle	IN	46135	765-653-2755	653-2756
Web: www.putnam.lib.in.us					
Hammond Public Library 564 State St	Hammond	IN	46320	219-931-5100	931-3474
Web: www.hammond.lib.in.us					
Indianapolis-Marion County Public Library (IMCPL)					
PO Box 211	Indianapolis	IN	46206	317-275-4100	269-1768
Web: www.imcpl.org					

Library	City	State	ZIP	Phone	Fax
Jasper-Dubois County Public Library 1116 Main St	Jasper	IN	47546	812-482-2712	482-7123
Kokomo-Howard County Public Library 220 N Union St. *Web:* www.kokomo.lib.in.us	Kokomo	IN	46901	765-457-3242	457-3683
La Porte County Public Library 904 Indiana Ave *Web:* www.laportelibrary.org	La Porte	IN	46350	219-362-6156	362-6158
Tippecanoe County Public Library 627 S St. *Web:* www.tcpl.lib.in.us	Lafayette	IN	47901	765-429-0100	429-0150
LaGrange County Public Library 203 W Spring St *Web:* www.lagrange.lib.in.us	LaGrange	IN	46761	260-463-2841	
Logansport-Cass County Public Library 616 E Broadway *Web:* www.logan.lib.in.us	Logansport	IN	46947	574-753-6383	722-5889
Madison-Jefferson County Public Library 420 W Main St *Web:* www.madison-jeffco.lib.in.us	Madison	IN	47250	812-265-2744	265-2217
Marion Public Library 600 S Washington St. *Web:* www.marion.lib.in.us	Marion	IN	46953	765-668-2900	668-2911
Morgan County Public Library 110 S Jefferson St *Web:* www.morg.lib.in.us	Martinsville	IN	46151	765-342-3451	342-9992
Lake County Public Library 1919 W 81st Ave. *Web:* www.lakeco.lib.in.us	Merrillville	IN	46410	219-769-3541	769-0690
Mooresville Public Library 220 W Harrison St *Web:* www.mooresvillelib.org	Mooresville	IN	46158	317-831-7323	831-7383
New Albany-Floyd County Public Library 180 W Spring St. *Web:* www.nafclibrary.org	New Albany	IN	47150	812-944-8464	949-3734
New Castle-Henry County Public Library 376 S 15th St PO Box J *Web:* www.nchcpl.lib.in.us	New Castle	IN	47362	765-529-0362	521-3581
Morrisson-Reeves Public Library 80 N 6th St. *Web:* www.mrl.lib.in.us	Richmond	IN	47374	765-966-8291	962-1318
Jackson County Public Library (JCPL) 303 W 2nd St *Web:* www.myjclibrary.org	Seymour	IN	47274	812-522-3412	522-5456
Shelbyville-Shelby County Public Library 57 W Broadway *Web:* www.sscpl.lib.in.us	Shelbyville	IN	46176	317-398-7121	398-4430
Saint Joseph County Public Library 304 S Main St. *Web:* www.sjcpl.lib.in.us	South Bend	IN	46601	574-282-4630	
Vigo County Public Library 1 Library Sq *Web:* www.vigo.lib.in.us	Terre Haute	IN	47807	812-232-1113	232-3208
Valparaiso Public Library 103 Jefferson St *Web:* www.pcpls.lib.in.us	Valparaiso	IN	46383	219-462-0524	477-4867
Knox County Public Library 502 N 7th St. *Web:* www.kcpl.lib.in.us	Vincennes	IN	47591	812-886-4380	886-0342
West Lafayette Public Library 200 Northwestern Ave. *Web:* www.wlaf.lib.in.us	West Lafayette	IN	47906	765-743-2261	743-0540

IOWA

Library	City	State	ZIP	Phone	Fax
Ames Public Library 515 Douglas Ave. *Web:* www.amespubliclibrary.org	Ames	IA	50010	515-239-5630	232-4571
Kirkendall Public Library 1210 NW Prairie Ridge Dr *Web:* www.ankenyiowa.gov	Ankeny	IA	50023	515-965-6460	289-9122
Bettendorf Public Library 2950 Learning Campus Dr *Web:* www.bettendorflibrary.com	Bettendorf	IA	52722	563-344-4175	344-4185
Burlington Public Library 210 Ct St *Web:* www.burlington.lib.ia.us	Burlington	IA	52601	319-753-1647	229-0406
Cedar Falls Public Library 524 Main St *Web:* www.cedarfallspubliclibrary.org	Cedar Falls	IA	50613	319-273-8643	273-8648
Cedar Rapids Public Library 2600 Edgewood Rd SW # 330 *Web:* www.crlibrary.org	Cedar Rapids	IA	52404	319-398-5123	398-0476
East Central Regional Library 222 3rd St SE Suite 402	Cedar Rapids	IA	52401	319-365-0521	365-0194
Clinton Public Library 306 8th Ave S	Clinton	IA	52732	563-242-8441	242-8162
Council Bluffs Public Library 400 Willow Ave. *Web:* www.cbpl.lib.ia.us	Council Bluffs	IA	51503	712-323-7553	323-1269
Davenport Public Library 321 Main St *Web:* www.davenportlibrary.com	Davenport	IA	52801	563-326-7832	326-7809
Des Moines Public Library 1000 Grand Ave. *Web:* www.desmoineslibrary.com	Des Moines	IA	50309	515-283-4152	237-1654
Carnegie-Stout Public Library 360 W 11th St *Web:* www.dubuque.lib.ia.us	Dubuque	IA	52001	563-589-4225	589-4217
Scott County Library 200 N 6th Ave.	Eldridge	IA	52748	563-285-4794	285-4743
Fayette Community Library 104 W State St *Web:* www.fayetteia.com	Fayette	IA	52142	563-425-3344	425-3344
Fort Dodge Public Library 424 Central Ave. *Web:* www.fortdodgeiowa.org	Fort Dodge	IA	50501	515-573-8167	573-5422
Iowa City Public Library 123 S Linn St. *Web:* www.icpl.org	Iowa City	IA	52240	319-356-5200	356-5494
Marion Public Library 1095 6th Ave *Web:* www.cityofmarion.org/library	Marion	IA	52302	319-377-3412	377-0113
Marshalltown Public Library 105 W Boone St *Web:* www.marshalltownlibrary.org	Marshalltown	IA	50158	641-754-5738	754-5708
Mason City Public Library 225 2nd St SE *Web:* www.mcpl.org	Mason City	IA	50401	641-421-3668	423-2615
Musser Public Library 304 Iowa Ave. *Web:* www.musserpubliclibrary.org	Muscatine	IA	52761	563-263-3472	264-1033
Newton Public Library (NPL) 100 N 3rd Ave W PO Box 746	Newton	IA	50208	641-792-4108	791-0729
Ottumwa Public Library 102 W 4th St.	Ottumwa	IA	52501	641-682-7563	682-4970
Sioux City Public Library 529 Pierce St *Web:* www.siouxcitylibrary.org	Sioux City	IA	51101	712-255-2933	279-6432
Urbandale Public Library 3520 86th St. *Web:* www.urbandalelibrary.org	Urbandale	IA	50322	515-278-3945	278-3918
West Des Moines Public Library 4000 Mills Civic Pkwy *Web:* www.wdmlibrary.org	West Des Moines	IA	50265	515-222-3400	222-3401

KANSAS

Library	City	State	ZIP	Phone	Fax
Belleville Public Library 1327 19th St *Web:* www.bellevillepl.blogspot.com	Belleville	KS	66935	785-527-5305	527-5305
Emporia Public Library 110 E 6th Ave. *Web:* www.skyways.lib.ks.us	Emporia	KS	66801	620-342-6524	340-6444
Finney County Public Library Garden City 605 E Walnut St	Garden City	KS	67846	620-272-3680	272-3682
Hutchinson Public Library 901 N Main St *Web:* www.hutchpl.org	Hutchinson	KS	67501	620-663-5441	663-9506
Dorothy Bramlage Public Library Junction City 230 W 7th St. *Web:* www.jclib.org	Junction City	KS	66441	785-238-4311	238-7873
Kansas City Kansas Public Library 625 Minnesota Ave *Web:* www.kckpl.lib.ks.us	Kansas City	KS	66101	913-551-3280	279-2032
Lawrence Public Library 707 Vermont St. *Web:* www.lawrence.lib.ks.us	Lawrence	KS	66044	785-843-3833	843-3368
Leavenworth Public Library 417 Spruce St *Web:* www.skyways.lib.ks.us	Leavenworth	KS	66048	913-682-5666	682-1248
Manhattan Public Library 629 Poyntz Ave *TF:* 800-432-2796 ■ *Web:* www.manhattan.lib.ks.us	Manhattan	KS	66502	785-776-4741	776-1545
Salina Public Library 301 W Elm St. *Web:* www.salpublib.org	Salina	KS	67401	785-825-4624	823-0706
Johnson County Library PO Box 2933. *TF:* 800-386-8501 ■ *Web:* www.jocolibrary.org	Shawnee Mission	KS	66201	913-826-4600	826-4453
Topeka & Shawnee County Public Library 1515 SW 10th Ave *Web:* www.tscpl.org	Topeka	KS	66604	785-580-4400	580-4496
Wichita Public Library 223 S Main St. *Web:* www.wichita.lib.ks.us	Wichita	KS	67202	316-261-8500	262-4540

KENTUCKY

Library	City	State	ZIP	Phone	Fax
Boyd County Public Library 1740 Central Ave *Web:* www.thebookplace.org	Ashland	KY	41101	606-329-0518	329-0578
Kenton County Public Library 502 Scott Blvd *Web:* www.kenton.lib.ky.us	Covington	KY	41011	859-962-4060	962-4096
Boyle County Public Library 307 W Broadway	Danville	KY	40422	859-236-8466	236-7692
Hardin County Public Library 100 Jim Owen Dr *Web:* www.hcpl.info	Elizabethtown	KY	42701	270-769-6337	769-0437
Paul Sawyier Public Library 319 Wapping St. *Web:* www.pspl.org	Frankfort	KY	40601	502-352-2665	227-2250
Lexington Public Library 140 E Main St *Web:* www.lexpublib.org	Lexington	KY	40507	859-231-5504	231-5598
Louisville Free Public Library 301 York St. *Web:* www.lfpl.org	Louisville	KY	40203	502-574-1600	574-1666
Daviess County Public Library 2020 Frederica St *Web:* www.dcplibrary.org	Owensboro	KY	42301	270-684-0211	684-0218
McCracken County Public Library 555 Washington St. *Web:* www.mclib.net	Paducah	KY	42003	270-442-2510	
Pulaski County Public Library 304 S Main St *Web:* www.pulaskipubliclibrary.org	Somerset	KY	42501	606-679-8401	679-1779

LOUISIANA

Library	City	State	ZIP	Phone	Fax
Vermilion Parish Library 405 E St Victor	Abbeville	LA	70510	337-893-2655	898-0526
Rapides Parish Library 411 Washington St. *Web:* www.rpl.org	Alexandria	LA	71301	318-445-2411	445-6478
Tangipahoa Parish Library 739 W Oak St. *Web:* www.tangilibrary.com	Amite	LA	70422	985-748-7151	748-5476
Morehouse Parish Library 524 E Madesson Ave PO BOX 232 *Web:* www.youseemore.com/morehouse	Bastrop	LA	71221	318-281-3683	
East Baton Rouge Parish Library (EBRPL) 7711 Goodwood Blvd *Web:* www.ebrpl.com	Baton Rouge	LA	70806	225-231-3750	231-3759
Bossier Parish Library (BPL) 2206 Beckett St. *Web:* www.bossierlibrary.org	Bossier City	LA	71111	318-746-1693	746-7768
Plaquemines Parish Library 35572 Hwy 11 S	Buras	LA	70041	504-657-7121	657-6175
Saint Bernard Parish Library 1125 E St Bernard Hwy	Chalmette	LA	70043	504-279-0448	277-3645
Saint Tammany Parish Library 310 W 21st Ave.	Covington	LA	70433	985-893-6282	893-6283

Library	City	State	Zip	Phone	Fax
Acadia Parish Library 1125 N Parkerson Ave *Web:* www.acadia.lib.la.us	Crowley	LA	70526	337-788-1880	788-3759
Beauregard Parish Library 205 S Washington Ave *Web:* www.library.beau.org	DeRidder	LA	70634	337-463-6217	462-5434
Saint Mary Parish Library 206 Iberia St *TF:* 800-732-8698	Franklin	LA	70538	337-828-1624	828-2329
Washington Parish Library System 825 Free St *Web:* www.washington.lib.la.us	Franklinton	LA	70438	985-839-7806	839-7808
Terrebonne Parish Library 424 Roussell St *Web:* www.terrebonne.lib.la.us	Houma	LA	70360	985-876-5861	876-5864
Jefferson Davis Parish Library 118 W Plaquemine St *Web:* www.jefferson-davis.lib.la.us	Jennings	LA	70546	337-824-1210	824-5444
Lafayette Parish Public Library 301 W Congress St	Lafayette	LA	70501	337-261-5775	261-5782
Calcasieu Parish Public Library System 301 W Claude St *Web:* www.calcasieulibrary.org	Lake Charles	LA	70605	337-475-8798	475-8806
Saint John the Baptist Parish Library 2920 Hwy 51 *Web:* www.stjohn.lib.la.us	LaPlace	LA	70068	985-651-6733	652-2144
Vernon Parish Library 1401 Nolan Trace *TF:* 800-737-2231 ■ *Web:* www.youseemore.com	Leesville	LA	71446	337-239-2027	238-0666
Livingston Parish Library 13986 Florida Blvd PO Box 397 *Web:* www.main.mylpl.info	Livingston	LA	70754	225-686-2436	686-3888
DeSoto Parish Library 109 Crosby St	Mansfield	LA	71052	318-872-6100	872-6120
Avoyelles Parish Library 104 N Washington St *Web:* www.avoyelles.lib.la.us	Marksville	LA	71351	318-253-7559	253-6361
Jefferson Parish Library 4747 W Napoleon Ave *Web:* www.jefferson.lib.la.us	Metairie	LA	70001	504-838-1100	838-1117
Webster Parish Library 521 E & W Sts *Web:* www.webster.lib.la.us	Minden	LA	71055	318-371-3080	371-3081
Ouachita Parish Public Library 1800 Stubbs Ave *Web:* www.oplib.org	Monroe	LA	71201	318-327-1490	327-1373
Natchitoches Parish Library 450 2nd St *Web:* www.youseemore.com	Natchitoches	LA	71457	318-357-3280	357-7073
Iberia Parish Library 445 E Main St *Web:* www.iberia.lib.la.us	New Iberia	LA	70560	337-373-0075	373-0086
Opelousas-Eunice Public Libraries 212 E Grolee St	Opelousas	LA	70570	337-948-3693	948-5200
Iberville Parish Library 24605 J Gerald Berret Blvd *Web:* www.iberville.lib.la.us	Plaquemine	LA	70765	225-687-2520	687-9719
Lincoln Parish Library 910 N Trenton St *Web:* www.mylpl.org	Ruston	LA	71270	318-251-5030	251-5045
Saint Martin Parish Library 201 Porter St *Web:* www.stmartin.lib.la.us	Saint Martinville	LA	70582	337-394-2207	394-2248
Shreve Memorial Library 424 Texas St *Web:* www.shreve-lib.org	Shreveport	LA	71101	318-226-5897	226-4780
Lafourche Parish Library 303 W 5th St *Web:* www.lafourche.org/newsite	Thibodaux	LA	70301	985-446-1163	446-3848
Evangeline Parish Library 242 W Main St *Web:* www.evangeline.lib.la.us	Ville Platte	LA	70586	337-363-1369	363-2353

MAINE

Library	City	State	Zip	Phone	Fax
Auburn Public Library 49 Spring St *Web:* www.auburn.lib.me.us	Auburn	ME	04210	207-333-6640	333-6644
Lithgow Public Library 45 Winthrop St *Web:* www.lithgow.lib.me.us	Augusta	ME	04330	207-626-2415	626-2419
Bangor Public Library 145 Harlow St *TF:* 800-727-2120 ■ *Web:* www.bpl.lib.me.us	Bangor	ME	04401	303-863-1800	863-7767
Jessup Memorial Library 34 Mt Desert St	Bar Harbor	ME	04609	207-288-4245	288-9067
Camden Public Library (CPL) 55 Main St *Web:* www.librarycamden.org	Camden	ME	04843	207-236-3440	236-6673
Lewiston Public Library 200 Lisbon St *Web:* www.lplonline.org	Lewiston	ME	04240	207-784-0135	784-3011
Portland Public Library 5 Monument Sq *Web:* www.portlandlibrary.com	Portland	ME	04101	207-871-1700	871-1715

MARYLAND

Library	City	State	Zip	Phone	Fax
Anne Arundel County Public Library 5 Harry S Truman Pkwy *Web:* web.aacpl.lib.md.us	Annapolis	MD	21401	410-222-7371	222-7188
Enoch Pratt Free Library 400 Cathedral St *Web:* www.prattlibrary.org	Baltimore	MD	21201	410-396-5283	396-8134
Harford County Public Library 1221-A Brass Mill Rd Riverside Business Pk *Web:* www.hcplonline.org	Belcamp	MD	21017	410-575-6761	273-5606
Dorchester County Public Library 303 Gay St *Web:* www.dorchesterlibrary.org	Cambridge	MD	21613	410-228-7331	228-6313
Queen Anne's County Free Library 121 S Commerce St *Web:* www.quan.lib.md.us	Centreville	MD	21617	410-758-0980	758-0614
Howard County Central Library 10375 Little Patuxent Pkwy *Web:* www.hclibrary.org	Columbia	MD	21044	410-313-7800	313-7864
Allegany County Public Library System 31 Washington St *Web:* www.alleganycountylibrary.info	Cumberland	MD	21502	301-777-1200	777-7299
Caroline County Public Library 100 Market St *Web:* www.carolib.org	Denton	MD	21629	410-479-1343	479-1443
Talbot County Free Library 28712 Glebe Rd *Web:* www.tcfl.org/library	Easton	MD	21601	410-822-1626	820-8217
Cecil County Public Library (CCPL) 301 Newark Ave *Web:* www.cecil.ebranch.info	Elkton	MD	21921	410-996-1055	996-5604
Frederick County Public Libraries (FCPL) 110 E Patrick St *Web:* www.fcpl.org	Frederick	MD	21701	301-694-1630	631-3789
Washington County Free Library 101 pandy Dr *Web:* www.washcolibrary.org	Hagerstown	MD	21740	301-739-3250	739-7603
Prince George's County Memorial Library 6532 Adelphi Rd *Web:* www.prge.lib.md.us	Hyattsville	MD	20782	301-699-3500	699-0122
Charles County Public Library 2 Garrett Ave *Web:* www.somd.lib.md.us	La Plata	MD	20646	301-934-9001	934-2297
Laurel Library 507 7th St	Laurel	MD	20707	301-776-6790	
Saint Mary's County Memorial Library 23250 Hollywood Rd *Web:* www.stmalib.org	Leonardtown	MD	20650	301-475-2846	884-4415
Ruth Enlow Library 6 N 2nd St *Web:* www.relib.net	Oakland	MD	21550	301-334-3996	334-4152
Calvert County Public Library 850 Costley Way *Web:* www.calvert.lib.md.us	Prince Frederick	MD	20678	410-535-0291	535-3022
Wicomico County Free Library 122 S Division St *Web:* www.wicomicolibrary.org	Salisbury	MD	21801	410-749-3612	548-2968
Worcester County Library 307 N Washington St *Web:* www.worc.lib.md.us	Snow Hill	MD	21863	410-632-2600	632-1159
Baltimore County Public Library 320 York Rd *Web:* www.bcpl.info	Towson	MD	21204	410-887-6100	887-6103
Carroll County Public Library 115 Airport Dr 1100 green valley Rd new *Web:* www.library.carr.org	Westminster	MD	21776	410-386-4500	386-4509

MASSACHUSETTS

Library	City	State	Zip	Phone	Fax
Agawam Public Library 750 Cooper St *Web:* www.agawamlibrary.org	Agawam	MA	01001	413-789-1550	789-1552
Jones Library Inc 43 Amity St *Web:* www.joneslibrary.org	Amherst	MA	01002	413-256-4090	256-4096
Memorial Hall Library 2 N Main St *Web:* www.mhl.org	Andover	MA	01810	978-623-8400	623-8407
Robbins Library 700 Massachusetts Ave	Arlington	MA	02476	781-316-3200	
Attleboro Public Library 74 N Main St *Web:* www.sailsinc.org	Attleboro	MA	02703	508-222-0157	226-3326
Sturgis Library 3090 Main St *Web:* www.sturgislibrary.org	Barnstable	MA	02630	508-362-6636	362-5467
Bellingham Public Library 100 Blackstone St *Web:* www.bellinghamma.org/Library	Bellingham	MA	02019	508-966-1660	966-3189
Beverly Public Library 32 Essex St *Web:* www.noblenet.org	Beverly	MA	01915	978-921-6062	922-8329
Billerica Public Library 15 Concord Rd *Web:* www.billericalibrary.org	Billerica	MA	01821	978-671-0948	667-4242
Boston Public Library 700 Boylston St Copley Sq *Web:* www.bpl.org	Boston	MA	02116	617-536-5400	236-4306
Thayer Public Library 798 Washington St *Web:* www.thayerpubliclibrary.org	Braintree	MA	02184	781-848-0405	356-5447
Brockton Public Library 304 Main St *Web:* www.brocktonpubliclibrary.org	Brockton	MA	02301	508-580-7890	580-7898
Brookline Public Library 361 Washington St *Web:* www.brooklinelibrary.com	Brookline	MA	02445	617-730-2360	730-2160
Burlington Public Library 22 Sears St *Web:* www.burlingtonpubliclibrary.org	Burlington	MA	01803	781-270-1690	229-0406
Cambridge Public Library 449 Broadway *Web:* www.ci.cambridge.ma.us/~CPL	Cambridge	MA	02138	617-349-4036	349-4428
Centerville Public Library 585 Main St *Web:* www.centervillelibrary.org	Centerville	MA	02632	508-790-6220	790-6218
Chelmsford Public Library 25 Boston Rd *Web:* www.chelmsfordlibrary.org	Chelmsford	MA	01824	978-256-5521	256-8511
Chicopee Public Library 449 Front St *Web:* www.chicopeepubliclibrary.org	Chicopee	MA	01013	413-594-1800	594-1819
Dartmouth Public Libraries 732 Dartmouth St *Web:* www.dartmouthpubliclibraries.org	Dartmouth	MA	02748	508-999-0726	992-9914
Moses Greeley Parker Memorial Library 28 Arlington St *Web:* www.dracutlibrary.org	Dracut	MA	01826	978-454-5474	454-9120
Parlin Memorial Library 410 Broadway *Web:* www.noblenet.org/everett	Everett	MA	02149	617-394-2300	389-1230
Millicent Library 45 Ctr St *Web:* www.millicentlibrary.org	Fairhaven	MA	02719	508-992-5342	993-7288
Fall River Public Library 104 N Main St *Web:* www.sailsinc.org	Fall River	MA	02720	508-324-2700	324-2707
Falmouth Public Library 123 Katharine Lee Bates Rd *Web:* www.falmouthpubliclibrary.org	Falmouth	MA	02540	508-457-2555	457-2559
Fitchburg Public Library 610 Main St	Fitchburg	MA	01420	978-345-9635	345-9631
Sawyer Free Library 2 Dale Ave *Web:* www.sawyerfreelibrary.org	Gloucester	MA	01930	978-281-9763	281-9770

Library	City	State	ZIP	Phone	Fax
Holmes Public Library 470 Plymouth St	Halifax	MA	02338	781-293-2271	294-8518
Web: www.sailsinc.org/halifax					
Haverhill Public Library 99 Main St	Haverhill	MA	01830	978-373-1586	373-8466
Web: www.haverhillpl.org					
Holyoke Public Library 335 Maple St	Holyoke	MA	01040	413-322-5640	532-4230
Web: www.holyokelibrary.org					
Hyannis Public Library (HPL) 401 Main St	Hyannis	MA	02601	508-775-2280	790-0087
Web: www.hyannislibrary.org					
Leominster Public Library 30 W St	Leominster	MA	01453	978-534-7522	
Web: www.leominsterlibrary.org					
Cary Memorial Library 1874 Massachusetts Ave	Lexington	MA	02420	781-862-6288	862-7355
Web: www.carylibrary.org					
Pollard Memorial Library 401 Merrimack St	Lowell	MA	01852	978-970-4120	
Web: www.pollardml.org					
Lynn Public Library 5 N Common St	Lynn	MA	01902	781-595-0567	592-5050
Web: www.noblenet.org/lynn					
Malden Public Library 36 Salem St	Malden	MA	02148	781-324-0218	324-4467
Web: www.maldenpubliclibrary.org					
Marlborough Public Library 35 W Main St	Marlborough	MA	01752	508-624-6900	485-1494
Web: www.marlborough-ma.gov					
Ventress Memorial Library 15 Library Plaza	Marshfield	MA	02050	781-834-5535	837-8362
Web: www.ventresslibrary.org					
Marstons Mills Public Library 2160 Main St	Marstons Mills	MA	02648	508-428-5175	420-5194
Web: www.mmpl.org					
Medford Public Library 111 High St	Medford	MA	02155	781-395-7950	391-2261
Web: www.medfordlibrary.org					
Melrose Public Library 69 W Emerson St	Melrose	MA	02176	781-665-2313	662-4229
Web: www.melrosepubliclibrary.org					
Milford Town Library 80 Spruce St	Milford	MA	01757	508-473-2145	473-8651
Web: www.milfordtownlibrary.org					
Milton Public Library 476 Canton Ave	Milton	MA	02186	617-698-5757	698-0441
Web: www.miltonlibrary.org					
Morse Institute Library 14 E Central St	Natick	MA	01760	508-647-6520	647-6527
Web: www.morseinstitute.org					
Needham Free Public Library 1139 Highland Ave	Needham	MA	02494	781-455-7559	455-7591
Web: www.town.needham.ma.us					
New Bedford Free Public Library (NBFPL) 613 Pleasant St	New Bedford	MA	02740	508-991-6275	991-6368
Web: www.newbedford-ma.gov/Library					
Newton Free Library 330 Homer St	Newton Center	MA	02459	617-796-1360	965-8457
Web: www.ci.newton.ma.us/Library					
Norfolk Public Library The 139 Main St	Norfolk	MA	02056	508-528-3380	528-6417
Web: www.library.virtualnorfolk.org					
Richards Memorial Library 118 N Washington St	North Attleboro	MA	02760	508-699-0122	699-0122
Forbes Library 20 W St	NorthHampton	MA	01060	413-584-8550	587-1015
Web: www.forbeslibrary.org					
Northborough Free Library 34 Main St	Northborough	MA	01532	508-393-5025	393-5027
Web: www.northboroughlibrary.com					
Morrill Memorial Library 33 Walpole St PO Box 220	Norwood	MA	02062	781-769-0200	
Web: www.norwoodlibrary.org					
Osterville Free Library 43 Wianno Ave	Osterville	MA	02655	508-428-5757	428-5557
Web: www.ostervillefreelibrary.org					
Peabody Institute Library 82 Main St	Peabody	MA	01960	978-531-0100	532-1797
Web: www.peabodylibrary.org					
Berkshire Athenaeum 1 Wendell Ave	Pittsfield	MA	01201	413-499-9480	499-9489
Web: www.berkshire.net					
Plymouth Public Library 132 S St	Plymouth	MA	02360	508-830-4250	830-4258
Web: www.plymouthpubliclibrary.org					
Provincetown Public Library 366 Commercial St	Provincetown	MA	02657	508-487-7094	487-7096
Web: www.provincetonlibrary.org					
Thomas Crane Public Library 40 Washington St	Quincy	MA	02169	617-376-1300	376-1308
Web: www.thomascranelibrary.org					
Turner Free Library 2 N Main St	Randolph	MA	02368	781-961-0932	961-0933
Reading Public Library 64 Middlesex Ave	Reading	MA	01867	781-944-0840	942-9106
Web: www.readingpl.org					
Revere Public Library 179 Beach St	Revere	MA	02151	781-286-8380	286-8382
Salem Public Library 370 Essex St	Salem	MA	01970	978-744-0860	745-8616
Saugus Free Public Library 295 Central St	Saugus	MA	01906	781-231-4168	231-4169
Web: www.noblenet.org					
Sharon Public Library 11 N Main St	Sharon	MA	02067	781-784-1578	784-4728
Web: www.townofsharon.net					
Central Massachusetts Regional Library System 8 Flagg Rd	Shrewsbury	MA	01545	508-757-4110	757-4370
TF: 800-922-8326 ■ *Web:* www.cmrls.org					
Somerville Public Library (SPL) 79 Highland Ave	Somerville	MA	02143	617-623-5000	628-4052
Web: www.somervillepubliclibrary.org					
Bacon Free Library 58 Eliot St	South Natick	MA	01760	508-653-6730	651-7013
Springfield City Library 220 State St	Springfield	MA	01103	413-263-6828	263-6817
Web: www.springfieldlibrary.org					
Stoughton Public Library 84 Pk St	Stoughton	MA	02072	781-344-2711	344-7340
Taunton Public Library 12 Pleasant St	Taunton	MA	02780	508-821-1411	821-1414
Web: www.tauntonlibrary.org					
Tewksbury Public Library 300 Chandler St	Tewksbury	MA	01876	978-640-4490	
Web: www.tewksburypl.org					
Upton Town Library 2 Main St	Upton	MA	01568	508-529-6272	529-2453
Web: www.uptonlibrary.blogspot.com					
Lucius Beebe Memorial Library 345 Main St	Wakefield	MA	01880	781-246-6334	246-6385
Web: www.wakefieldlibrary.org					
Walpole Public Library 65 Common St	Walpole	MA	02081	508-660-7340	660-2714
Web: www.walpole.ma.us/library.htm					
Metrowest Massachusetts Regional Library System 135 Beaver St	Waltham	MA	02452	781-398-1819	398-1821
Waltham Public Library 735 Main St	Waltham	MA	02451	781-314-3425	647-5873
Web: www.waltham.lib.ma.us					
Watertown Free Public Library 123 Main St	Watertown	MA	02472	617-972-6431	926-4375
Web: www.watertownlib.org					
Wayland Free Public Library 5 Concord Rd	Wayland	MA	01778	508-358-2311	358-5249
Web: www.wayland.ma.us					
Wellesley Free Library 530 Washington St	Wellesley	MA	02482	781-235-1610	237-4875
Web: www.ci.wellesley.ma.us					
Whelden Memorial Library PO Box 147	West Barnstable	MA	02668	508-362-2262	362-1344
Web: www.home.comcast.net/~whelden					
West Falmouth Library Inc PO Box 1209	West Falmouth	MA	02574	508-548-4709	457-9534
West Springfield Public Library 200 Pk St	West Springfield	MA	01089	413-736-4561	736-6469
Web: www.wspl.org					
Westfield Athenaeum 6 Elm St	Westfield	MA	01085	413-568-7833	568-0988
Web: www.westath.org					
Tufts Library 46 Broad St	Weymouth	MA	02188	781-337-1402	682-6123
Milne Public Library 1095 Main St	Williamstown	MA	01267	413-458-5369	458-3085
Web: www.milnelibrary.org					
Woburn Public Library 45 Pleasant St	Woburn	MA	01801	781-933-0148	938-7860
Web: www.woburnpubliclibrary.org					
Woods Hole Public Library 581 Woods Hole Rd PO Box 185	Woods Hole	MA	02543	508-548-8961	540-1969

MICHIGAN

Library	City	State	ZIP	Phone	Fax
Lenawee County Library 4459 W US 223	Adrian	MI	49221	517-263-1011	
Web: www.lenawee.lib.mi.us					
Alpena County George N Fletcher Public Library 211 N 1st Ave	Alpena	MI	49707	989-356-6188	356-2765
Web: www.alpenalib.org					
Ann Arbor District Library (AADL) 343 S 5th Ave	Ann Arbor	MI	48104	734-327-4200	327-8309
Web: www.aadl.org					
Bay County Library System 500 Ctr Ave	Bay City	MI	48708	989-894-2837	894-2021
Web: www.baycountylibrary.org					
Baldwin Public Library 300 W Merrill St	Birmingham	MI	48009	248-647-1700	644-7297
Web: www.baldwinlib.org					
Bloomfield Township Public Library 1099 Lone Pine Rd	Bloomfield Hills	MI	48302	248-642-5800	642-4175
Web: www.btpl.org					
Cadillac-Wexford County Public Library 411 S Lake St	Cadillac	MI	49601	231-775-6541	775-1749
Web: www.cadillaclibrary.org					
Canton Public Library 1200 S Canton Ctr Rd	Canton	MI	48188	734-397-0999	397-1130
Web: www.cantonpl.org					
Macomb County reference & research centre 16480 Hall Rd	Clinton Township	MI	48038	586-286-6660	286-8951
Web: www.macombreference.org					
Kent District Library 814 W River Ctr Dr NE	Comstock Park	MI	49321	616-784-2007	647-3908
Web: www.kdl.org					
Henry Ford Centennial Library 16301 Michigan Ave	Dearborn	MI	48126	313-943-2330	943-3063
Detroit Public Library 5201 Woodward Ave	Detroit	MI	48202	313-833-1000	832-0877
Web: www.detroitpubliclibrary.org					
East Lansing Public Library 950 Abbott Rd	East Lansing	MI	48823	517-351-2420	351-9536
Web: www.elpl.org					
Eastpointe Memorial Library 15875 Oak St	Eastpointe	MI	48021	586-445-5096	775-0150
Web: www.cityofeastpointe.net/library.htm					
Escanaba Public Library 400 Ludington St	Escanaba	MI	49829	906-786-4463	786-0942
Web: www.uproc.lib.mi.us					
Ferndale Public Library 222 E Nine-Mile Rd	Ferndale	MI	48220	248-546-2504	545-5840
Web: www.ferndale.lib.mi.us					
Flint Public Library 1026 E Kearsley St	Flint	MI	48502	810-232-7111	249-2635
Web: www.flint.lib.mi.us					
Genesee District Library G-4195 W Pasadena Ave	Flint	MI	48504	810-732-0110	732-3146
Web: www.thegdl.org					
Garden City Public Library 31735 Maplewood St	Garden City	MI	48135	734-793-1830	793-1831
Web: www.garden-city.lib.mi.us					
Loutit District Library 407 Columbus St	Grand Haven	MI	49417	616-842-5560	847-0570
Web: www.loutitlibrary.org					
Grand Rapids Public Library 111 Library St NE	Grand Rapids	MI	49503	616-988-5400	988-5429
Web: www.grapids.lib.mi.us					
Dickinson County Library 401 Iron Mountain St	Iron Mountain	MI	49801	906-774-1218	774-4079
Web: www.dcl-lib.org					
Jackson District Library 244 W Michigan Ave	Jackson	MI	49201	517-788-4087	782-8635
Web: www.jackson.lib.mi.us					
Georgetown Township Library 1525 Baldwin St	Jenison	MI	49428	616-457-9620	457-3666
Web: www.gtwp.com					
Kalamazoo Public Library 315 S Rose St	Kalamazoo	MI	49007	269-342-9837	553-7921
Web: www.kpl.gov					
Orion Township Public Library 825 Joslyn Rd	Lake Orion	MI	48362	248-693-3000	693-3009
Web: www.orionlibrary.org					
Capital Area District Library 401 S Capitol Ave	Lansing	MI	48933	517-367-6339	374-1068
Web: www.cadl.org					
Lapeer District Library 201 Village W Dr S	Lapeer	MI	48446	810-664-9521	664-8527
Web: www.library.lapeer.org					
Livonia Public Library 32777 Five Mile Rd	Livonia	MI	48154	734-466-2491	458-6011
Web: www.livonia.lib.mi.us					
Madison Heights Public Library 240 W Thirteen Mile Rd	Madison Heights	MI	48071	248-588-2029	588-2470
Peter White Public Library 217 N Front St	Marquette	MI	49855	906-228-9510	226-1783
Web: www.uproc.lib.mi.us					

Library	City	State	ZIP	Phone	Fax
Grace A Dow Memorial Library 1710 W St Andrews Rd *Web:* www.midland-mi.org	Midland	MI	48640	989-837-3430	837-3468
Monroe County Library System 3700 S Custer Rd *TF:* 800-462-2050 ■ *Web:* www.monroe.lib.mi.us	Monroe	MI	48161	734-241-5277	241-4722
Veterans Memorial Library 301 S University Ave	Mount Pleasant	MI	48858	989-773-3242	772-3280
Muskegon Area District Library 4845 Airline Rd *Web:* www.madl.org	Muskegon	MI	49444	231-737-6248	737-6307
Niles District Library 620 E Main St *Web:* www.nileslibrary.com	Niles	MI	49120	269-683-8545	683-0075
Novi Public Library 45245 W 10 Mile Rd *Web:* www.novilibrary.org	Novi	MI	48375	248-349-0720	349-6520
Owosso Public Library 502 W Main St	Owosso	MI	48867	989-725-5134	723-5444
Pontiac Public Library 60 E Pike St *Web:* www.pontiac.lib.mi.us	Pontiac	MI	48342	248-758-3942	758-3990
Saint Clair County Library System 210 McMorran Blvd *TF:* 877-987-7323 ■ *Web:* www.sccl.lib.mi.us	Port Huron	MI	48060	810-987-7323	987-7874
Portage District Library 300 Library Ln *Web:* www.portagelibrary.info	Portage	MI	49002	269-329-4544	324-9222
Rochester Hills Public Library 500 Olde Towne Rd *Web:* www.rhpl.org	Rochester	MI	48307	248-656-2900	650-7131
Roseville Public Library 29777 Gratiot Ave *Web:* www.libcoop.net	Roseville	MI	48066	586-445-5407	445-5499
Royal Oak Public Library 222 E Eleven Mile Rd	Royal Oak	MI	48067	248-246-3700	545-6220
Public Libraries of Saginaw 505 Janes St *Web:* www.saginawlibrary.org	Saginaw	MI	48607	989-755-0904	755-9829
Saint Clair Shores Public Library 22500 11-Mile Rd *Web:* www.libcoop.net/stclairshores	Saint Clair Shores	MI	48081	586-771-9020	771-8935
Shelby Township Library 51680 Van Dyke Hwy *Web:* www.libcoop.net	Shelby Township	MI	48316	586-739-7414	726-0535
Southfield Public Library 26300 Evergreen Rd *Web:* www.sfldlib.org	Southfield	MI	48076	248-796-4200	354-5319
Sterling Heights Public Library 40255 Dodge Pk Rd *Web:* www.shpl.net	Sterling Heights	MI	48313	586-446-2665	276-4067
Troy Public Library 510 W Big Beaver Rd *Web:* www.libcoop.net	Troy	MI	48084	248-524-3538	524-0112
Warren Public Library 5460 Arden *Web:* www.libcoop.net/warren	Warren	MI	48092	586-751-5377	264-2811
Waterford Township Public Library 5168 Civic Ctr Dr *Web:* www.waterford.lib.mi.us	Waterford	MI	48329	248-674-4831	674-1910
West Bloomfield Township Public Library 4600 Walnut Lake Rd *Web:* www.wblib.org	West Bloomfield	MI	48323	248-682-2120	232-2333

MINNESOTA

Library	City	State	ZIP	Phone	Fax
Albert Lea Public Library 211 E Clark St *Web:* www.city.albertlea.org	Albert Lea	MN	56007	507-377-4350	377-4339
Douglas County Library 720 Fillmore St *Web:* www.douglascountylibrary.org	Alexandria	MN	56308	320-762-3014	762-3036
Anoka County Library 711 County Rd 10 *Web:* www.anoka.lib.mn.us	Blaine	MN	55434	763-717-3267	717-3259
East Central Regional Library 244 S Birch St *Web:* www.ecrl.lib.mn.us	Cambridge	MN	55008	763-689-7390	689-7389
Carver County Library 4 City Hall Plaza *Web:* www.carverlib.org	Chaska	MN	55318	952-448-9395	448-9392
Duluth Public Library 520 W Superior St *Web:* www.duluth.lib.mn.us	Duluth	MN	55802	218-730-4200	723-3822
Buckham Memorial Library 11 Division St E *Web:* www.ci.faribault.mn.us	Faribault	MN	55021	507-334-2089	
Minneapolis Public Library 300 Nicollet Mall *Web:* www.mplib.org	Minneapolis	MN	55401	612-630-6000	630-6210
Hennepin County Library (HCL) 12601 Ridgedale Dr *Web:* www.hclib.org	Minnetonka	MN	55305	952-847-8500	847-8600
Lake Agassiz Regional Library 118 5th St S *Web:* www.larl.org	Moorhead	MN	56560	218-233-3757	233-7556
Owatonna Public Library 105 N Elm St *Web:* www.owatonna.lib.mn.us	Owatonna	MN	55060	507-444-2460	444-2465
Rochester Public Library 101 2nd St SE *Web:* www.rochesterpubliclibrary.org	Rochester	MN	55904	507-285-8000	
Great River Regional Library 1300 W St Germain St *Web:* www.griver.org	Saint Cloud	MN	56301	320-650-2500	650-2501
Saint Paul Public Library 90 W 4th St *Web:* www.sppl.org	Saint Paul	MN	55102	651-266-7000	266-7060
Scott County Library System 13090 Alabama Ave S *Web:* www.scott.lib.mn.us	Savage	MN	55378	952-707-1770	707-1775
Ramsey County Public Library 4570 N Victoria St *Web:* www.ramsey.lib.mn.us	Shoreview	MN	55126	651-486-2200	486-2220
Pioneerland Library System 410 SW 5th St *Web:* www.pioneerland.lib.mn.us	Willmar	MN	56201	320-235-6106	214-0187
Winona Public Library 151 W 5th St PO Box 1247 *Web:* www.selco.lib.mn.us	Winona	MN	55987	507-452-4582	452-5842
Washington County Library 8595 Central Pk Pl *Web:* www.co.washington.mn.us	Woodbury	MN	55125	651-275-8500	275-8509
Nobles County Library 407 12th St	Worthington	MN	56187	507-372-2981	372-2982

MISSISSIPPI

Library	City	State	ZIP	Phone	Fax
Hancock County Library 312 Hwy 90 *Web:* www.hancock.lib.ms.us	Bay Saint Louis	MS	39520	228-467-5282	467-5503
Bolivar County Library 104 S Leflore Ave *TF:* 888-268-8076 ■ *Web:* www.bolivar.lib.ms.us	Cleveland	MS	38732	662-843-2774	843-4701
Columbus-Lowndes County Library 314 N 7th St *Web:* www.lowndes.lib.ms.us	Columbus	MS	39701	662-329-5300	329-5156
Greenwood-Leflore Public Library 405 W Washington St	Greenwood	MS	38930	662-453-3634	453-0683
Harrison County Library System 2600 24th Ave Suite 6 *Web:* www.harrison.lib.ms.us	Gulfport	MS	39501	228-868-1383	
Library of Hattiesburg Petal & Forrest County 329 Hardy St *Web:* www.hpfc.lib.ms.us	Hattiesburg	MS	39401	601-582-4461	582-5338
First Regional Library 370 W Commerce St	Hernando	MS	38632	662-429-4439	429-8853
Marshall County Library 109 E Gholson Ave *Web:* www.marshall.lib.ms.us	Holly Springs	MS	38635	662-252-3823	252-3066
Sunflower County Library 201 Cypress Dr	Indianola	MS	38751	662-887-2298	887-1618
Eudora Welty Library The 300 N State St *TF:* 800-968-5803 ■ *Web:* www.jhlibrary.com	Jackson	MS	39201	601-968-5811	968-5817
Laurel-Jones County Library 530 Commerce St *Web:* www.laurel.lib.ms.us	Laurel	MS	39440	601-428-4313	428-4314
Meridian-Lauderdale County Public Library 2517 7th St *Web:* www.meridian.lib.ms.us	Meridian	MS	39301	601-693-6771	486-2260
Jackson-George Regional Library System 3214 S Pascagoula St *Web:* www.jgrls.org	Pascagoula	MS	39567	228-769-3060	769-3113
Pearl River County Library System 900 Goodyear Blvd *Web:* www.pearlriver.lib.ms.us	Picayune	MS	39466	601-798-5081	798-5082
Starkville Public Library 326 University Dr *Web:* www.starkville.lib.ms.us	Starkville	MS	39759	662-323-2766	323-9140
Lee County Library 219 N Madison St	Tupelo	MS	38804	662-841-9027	840-7615
Warren County-Vicksburg Public Library 700 Veto St *Web:* www.warren.lib.ms.us	Vicksburg	MS	39180	601-636-6411	634-4809

MISSOURI

Library	City	State	ZIP	Phone	Fax
Bowling Green Public Library 201 W Locust St *Web:* www.bgmopl.org	Bowling Green	MO	63334	573-324-5030	324-6367
Taneyhills Community Library 200 S 4th St *Web:* WWW.dransoncommunitylibrary.org	Branson	MO	65616	417-334-1418	334-1629
Camden County Library District 89 Rodeo Rd PO Box 1320 *Web:* www.ccld.us	Camdenton	MO	65020	573-346-5954	346-1263
Cape Girardeau Public Library 711 N Clark St *Web:* www.capelibrary.org	Cape Girardeau	MO	63701	573-334-5279	334-8334
Daniel Boone Regional Library 100 W Broadway *TF:* 800-324-4806 ■ *Web:* www.dbrl.org	Columbia	MO	65203	573-443-3161	443-3281
Cass County Public Library 400 E Mechanic St *Web:* www.casscolibrary.org	Harrisonville	MO	64701	816-884-6223	884-2301
Mid-Continent Public Library 15616 E 24 Hwy *Web:* www.mymcpl.org	Independence	MO	64050	816-836-5200	521-7253
Missouri River Regional Library 214 Adams St *Web:* www.mrrl.org	Jefferson City	MO	65101	573-634-2464	634-7028
Joplin Public Library 300 S Main St *Web:* www.joplinpubliclibrary.org	Joplin	MO	64801	417-623-7953	624-5217
Kansas City Public Library The (KCPL) 14 W 10th St *Web:* www.kclibrary.org	Kansas City	MO	64105	816-701-3400	701-3401
Linda Hall Library 5109 Cherry St *TF:* 800-662-1545 ■ *Web:* www.lindahall.org	Kansas City	MO	64110	816-363-4600	926-8790
Dunklin County Library 209 N Main St	Kennett	MO	63857	573-888-3561	888-6393
Kirkwood Public Library 140 E Jefferson Ave *Web:* kpl.lib.mo.us	Kirkwood	MO	63122	314-821-5770	822-3755
Christian County Library 1005 N 4th Ave *Web:* www.christiancounty.lib.mo.us	Ozark	MO	65721	417-581-2432	581-8855
Saint Louis County Library (SLCL) 1640 S Lindbergh Blvd *Web:* www.slcl.org	Saint Louis	MO	63131	314-994-3300	997-7602
Saint Louis Public Library (SLPL) 1301 Olive St *Web:* www.slpl.org/index.asp	Saint Louis	MO	63103	314-241-2288	539-0393
Saint Charles City County Library District 77 Boone Hill Dr PO Box 529 *Web:* www.win.org	Saint Peters	MO	63376	636-441-2300	441-3132

Library	City	State	ZIP	Phone	Fax
Springfield-Greene County Library 4653 S Campbell; *Web:* www.thelibrary.springfield.missouri.org	Springfield	MO	65810	417-883-5366	889-2547
University City Public Library 6701 Delmar Blvd; *Web:* www.ucpl.lib.mo.us	University City	MO	63130	314-727-3150	727-6005

MONTANA

Library	City	State	ZIP	Phone	Fax
Parmly Billings Library 510 N Broadway; *Web:* www.ci.billings.mt.us	Billings	MT	59101	406-657-8258	657-8293
Bozeman Public Library 626 E Main St; *Web:* www.bozemanlibrary.org	Bozeman	MT	59715	406-582-2400	582-2424
Butte-Silver Bow Public Library 226 W Broadway	Butte	MT	59701	406-723-3361	782-1825
Great Falls Public Library 301 2nd Ave N; *Web:* www.greatfallslibrary.org	Great Falls	MT	59401	406-453-0349	453-0181
Lewis & Clark Library 120 S Last Chance Gulch; *Web:* www.lewisandclarklibrary.org	Helena	MT	59601	406-447-1690	447-1687
Flathead County Library 247 1st Ave E; *Web:* www.flatheadcountylibrary.org	Kalispell	MT	59901	406-758-5819	758-5868
Missoula Public Library 301 E Main St; *Web:* www.missoula.lib.mt.us	Missoula	MT	59802	406-721-2665	728-5900

NEBRASKA

Library	City	State	ZIP	Phone	Fax
Bellevue Public Library 1003 Lincoln Rd	Bellevue	NE	68005	402-293-3157	293-3163
Columbus Public Library 2504 14th St; *Web:* www.columbuslibrary.info	Columbus	NE	68601	402-564-7116	563-3378
Edith Abbott Memorial Library 211 N Washington St; *Web:* www.grand-island.com	Grand Island	NE	68801	308-385-5333	385-5339
Hastings Public Library 517 W 4th St; *Web:* www.hastings.lib.ne.us	Hastings	NE	68901	402-461-2346	461-2359
Kearney Public Library & Information Ctr 2020 1st Ave; *Web:* www.cityofkearney.org	Kearney	NE	68847	308-233-3282	233-3291
Lincoln City Libraries 136 S 14th St; *Web:* www.lincolnlibraries.org	Lincoln	NE	68508	402-441-8500	441-8586
North Platte Public Library 120 W 4th St	North Platte	NE	69101	308-535-8036	535-8296
Omaha Public Library 215 S 15th St; *Web:* www.omaha.lib.ne.us	Omaha	NE	68102	402-444-4800	444-4504

NEVADA

Library	City	State	ZIP	Phone	Fax
Carson City Library 900 N Roop St	Carson City	NV	89701	775-887-2247	887-2273
Las Vegas-Clark County Library District 1401 E Flamingo Rd; *Web:* www.lvccld.org	Las Vegas	NV	89119	702-734-7323	507-3598
Douglas County Library 1625 Library Ln	Minden	NV	89423	775-782-9841	782-5754
North Las Vegas Public Library 2300 Civic Ctr Dr	North Las Vegas	NV	89030	702-633-1070	649-2576
Washoe County Library (WCL) 301 S Ctr St; *Web:* www.washoecounty.us/library	Reno	NV	89501	775-327-8300	327-8341

NEW HAMPSHIRE

Library	City	State	ZIP	Phone	Fax
Amherst Town Library 14 Main St; *Web:* www.amherst.lib.nh.us	Amherst	NH	03031	603-673-2288	672-6063
Concord Public Library 45 Green St; *Web:* www.ci.concord.nh.us	Concord	NH	03301	603-225-8670	230-3693
Derry Public Library 64 E Broadway; *Web:* www.derry.lib.nh.us	Derry	NH	03038	603-432-6140	432-6128
Dover Public Library 73 Locust St; *Web:* www.dover.lib.nh.us	Dover	NH	03820	603-516-6050	516-6053
Howe Library 13 S St; *Web:* www.thehowe.org	Hanover	NH	03755	603-643-4120	643-0725
Hollis Social Library 2 Monument Sq; *Web:* www.hollis.nh.us/library	Hollis	NH	03049	603-465-7721	465-3507
Manchester City Library 405 Pine St; *Web:* www.manchesternh.gov	Manchester	NH	03104	603-624-6550	624-6559
Nashua Public Library 2 Ct St; *Web:* www.nashualibrary.org	Nashua	NH	03060	603-589-4600	594-3457
Rochester Public Library 65 S Main St; *Web:* www.rpl.lib.nh.us	Rochester	NH	03867	603-332-1428	335-7582
Kelley Library 234 Main St; *Web:* www.kelleylibrary.org	Salem	NH	03079	603-898-7064	898-8583

NEW JERSEY

Library	City	State	ZIP	Phone	Fax
Atlantic City Free Public Library 1 N Tennessee Ave; *Web:* www.acfpl.org	Atlantic City	NJ	08401	609-345-2269	345-5570
Bayonne Free Public Library 697 Ave C; *Web:* www.bayonnenj.org	Bayonne	NJ	07002	201-858-6970	437-6928
Belleville Public Library 221 Washington Ave; *Web:* www.bellepl.org	Belleville	NJ	07109	973-450-3434	759-6731
Warren County Library 199 Hardwick St; *Web:* www.youseemore.com/warrencl	Belvidere	NJ	07823	908-475-6322	475-6359
Bloomfield Public Library 90 Broad St	Bloomfield	NJ	07003	973-566-6200	566-6217
Cumberland County Library 800 E Commerce St; *Web:* www.clueslibs.org	Bridgeton	NJ	08302	856-453-2210	451-1940
Somerset County Library 1 Vogt Dr; *Web:* www.somerset.lib.nj.us	Bridgewater	NJ	08807	908-526-4016	526-5221
Camden Free Public Library 418 Federal St	Camden	NJ	08101	856-757-7640	757-7631
Cape May County Library (CMCL) 30 Mechanic St; *Web:* www.cmclibrary.org	Cape May Court House	NJ	08210	609-463-6350	465-3895
Clark Public Library 303 Westfield Ave; *Web:* www.clarklibrary.org	Clark	NJ	07066	732-388-5999	388-7866
Clifton Public Library 292 Piaget Ave; *Web:* www.cliftonpl.org	Clifton	NJ	07011	973-772-5500	772-2926
East Brunswick Public Library 2 Jean Walling Civic Ctr; *Web:* www.ebpl.org	East Brunswick	NJ	08816	732-390-6950	390-6869
East Orange Public Library 21 S Arlington Ave; *Web:* www.eopl.org	East Orange	NJ	07018	973-266-5600	674-1991
Edison Township Free Public Library 340 Plainfield Ave; *Web:* www.lmxac.org/edisonlib	Edison	NJ	08817	732-287-2298	819-9134
Elizabeth Public Library 11 S Broad St; *Web:* www.elizpl.org	Elizabeth	NJ	07202	908-354-6060	354-5845
Englewood Public Library 31 Engle St; *Web:* www.englewoodlibrary.org	Englewood	NJ	07631	201-568-2215	568-6895
Maurice M Pine Free Public Library 10-01 Fair Lawn Ave; *Web:* www.bccls.org/fairlawn	Fair Lawn	NJ	07410	201-796-3400	794-6344
Hunterdon County Library 314 SR 12; *Web:* www.hclibrary.us	Flemington	NJ	08822	908-788-1444	806-4862
Fort Lee Free Public Library 320 Main St; *Web:* www.bccls.org	Fort Lee	NJ	07024	201-592-3614	585-0375
Garfield Free Public Library 500 Midland Ave; *Web:* www.bccls.org	Garfield	NJ	07026	973-478-3800	478-7162
Johnson Public Library 274 Main St; *Web:* www.bccls.org	Hackensack	NJ	07601	201-343-4169	343-1395
Hoboken Public Library 500 Pk Ave	Hoboken	NJ	07030	201-420-2346	420-2299
Irvington Public Library 5 Civic Sq; *Web:* www.irvingtonpubliclibrary.org	Irvington	NJ	07111	973-372-6400	372-6860
Jersey City Public Library 472 Jersey Ave	Jersey City	NJ	07302	201-547-4500	547-4584
Kearny Public Library 318 Kearny Ave; *Web:* www.kearnylibrary.org	Kearny	NJ	07032	201-998-2666	998-1141
Mercer County Library (MCL) 2751 Brunswick Pike; *Web:* www.webserver.mcl.org	Lawrenceville	NJ	08648	609-989-6917	538-1208
Linden Public Library 31 E Henry St; *Web:* www2.youseemore.com/lindenfreepl/Default.asp	Linden	NJ	07036	908-298-3830	486-2636
Livingston Public Library 10 Robert H Harp Dr; *Web:* www.livingston.bccls.org	Livingston	NJ	07039	973-992-4600	994-2346
Long Branch Free Public Library 328 Broadway; *Web:* www.lmxac.org/longbranch	Long Branch	NJ	07740	732-222-3900	222-3799
Monmouth County Library (MCL) 125 Symmes Rd; *Web:* www.monmouthcountylib.org	Manalapan	NJ	07726	732-431-7220	409-2556
Atlantic County Library-Mays Landing 40 Farragut Ave; *Web:* www.atlanticlibrary.org	Mays Landing	NJ	08330	609-646-8699	625-8143
Middletown Township Library 55 New Monmouth Rd; *Web:* www.mtpl.org	Middletown	NJ	07748	732-671-3700	671-5839
South Brunswick Public Library 110 County Rd 681; *Web:* www.lmxac.org	Monmouth Junction	NJ	08852	732-329-4000	329-0573
Mount Arlington Public Library (MAPL) 300 Howard Blvd; *Web:* www.gti.net/mountarlington	Mount Arlington	NJ	07856	973-398-1516	398-0171
Mount Laurel Library 100 Walt Whitman Ave; *Web:* www.mtlaurel.lib.nj.us	Mount Laurel	NJ	08054	856-234-7319	234-6916
Gloucester County Library System 389 Wolfert Stn Rd; *Web:* www.gcls.org	Mullica Hill	NJ	08062	856-223-6000	223-6039
Neptune Public Library 25 Neptune Blvd; *Web:* www.neptunepubliclibrary.org	Neptune	NJ	07753	732-775-8241	774-1132
New Brunswick Free Public Library 60 Livingston Ave; *Web:* www.lmxac.org	New Brunswick	NJ	08901	732-745-5108	846-0226
Newark Public Library 5 Washington St; *Web:* www.npl.org	Newark	NJ	07101	973-733-7784	733-5919
Sussex County Library 125 Morris Tpke; *Web:* www.sussexcountylibrary.org	Newton	NJ	07860	973-948-3660	948-2071
North Bergen Free Public Library 8411 Bergenline Ave	North Bergen	NJ	07047	201-869-4715	868-0968
North Brunswick Public Library 880 Hermann Rd; *Web:* www.lmxac.org/northbrunswick	North Brunswick	NJ	08902	732-246-3545	246-1341
Nutley Free Public Library 93 Booth Dr; *Web:* www.bccls.org	Nutley	NJ	07110	973-667-0405	667-0408
Ocean City Public Library 1735 Simpson Ave Suite 4; *Web:* www.home.oceancitylibrary.org	Ocean City	NJ	08226	609-399-2434	398-8944
Old Bridge Public Library 1 Old Bridge Plaza	Old Bridge	NJ	08857	732-607-7921	607-4816
Orange Public Library 348 Main St; *Web:* www.orangepl.org	Orange	NJ	07050	973-673-0153	673-1847
Sayreville Free Public Library 1050 Washington Rd; *Web:* www.lmxac.org	Parlin	NJ	08859	732-727-0212	553-0776
Parsippany-Troy Hills Public Library 449 Halsey Rd; *Web:* www.parsippanylibrary.org	Parsippany	NJ	07054	973-887-8907	887-5150

Library	City	State	ZIP	Phone	Fax
Passaic Public Library 195 Gregory Ave. *Web:* www.bccls.org	Passaic	NJ	07055	973-779-0474	779-0889
Paterson Free Public Library 250 Broadway *Web:* www.patersonpl.org	Paterson	NJ	07501	973-321-1223	321-1205
Pennsauken Free Public Library 5605 N Crescent Blvd *Web:* www.pennsaukenlibrary.org	Pennsauken	NJ	08110	856-665-5959	486-0142
Perth Amboy Public Library 196 Jefferson St	Perth Amboy	NJ	08861	732-826-2600	324-8079
John F Kennedy Library 500 Hoes Ln *Web:* www.piscatawaylibrary.org/kennedy.html	Piscataway	NJ	08854	732-463-1633	463-9022
Plainfield Public Library 8th St & Park Ave *Web:* www.plainfield.lib.il.us	Plainfield	NJ	07060	908-757-1111	754-2305
Rahway Public Library 2 City Hall Plaza *Web:* www.lmxac.org	Rahway	NJ	07065	732-340-1551	340-0393
Margaret E Heggan Public Library 606 Delsea Dr *Web:* www.hegganlibrary.org	Sewell	NJ	08080	856-589-3334	582-2042
Franklin Township Public Library 485 DeMott Ln *Web:* www.franklintwp.org	Somerset	NJ	08873	732-873-8700	873-0746
Teaneck Public Library 840 Teaneck Rd *Web:* www.teaneck.org	Teaneck	NJ	07666	201-837-4171	837-0410
Ocean County Library 101 Washington St *Web:* www.oceancountylibrary.org	Toms River	NJ	08753	732-349-6200	473-1356
Trenton Public Library 120 Academy St *Web:* www.trentonlib.org	Trenton	NJ	08608	609-392-7188	396-8631
Union Township Public Library 1980 Morris Ave. *Web:* www.uplnj.org	Union	NJ	07083	908-851-5450	851-4671
Union City Public Library 324 43rd St	Union City	NJ	07087	201-866-7500	866-0962
Vineland Public Library 1058 E Landis Ave *Web:* www.vineland.lib.nj.us	Vineland	NJ	08360	856-794-4244	691-0366
Camden County Library 203 Laurel Rd *Web:* www.camden.lib.nj.us	Voorhees	NJ	08043	856-772-1636	772-6105
Wayne Public Library 461 Valley Rd *Web:* www.waynepubliclibrary.org	Wayne	NJ	07470	973-694-4272	692-0637
West Milford Township Library 1490 SR 513 *Web:* www.wmtl.org	West Milford	NJ	07480	973-728-2820	728-2106
West New York Public Library 425 60th St	West New York	NJ	07093	201-295-5135	662-1473
West Orange Public Library 46 Mt Pleasant Ave *Web:* www.wopl.lib.nj.us	West Orange	NJ	07052	973-736-0198	736-1655
Burlington County Library 5 Pioneer Blvd *Web:* www.bcls.lib.nj.us	Westampton	NJ	08060	609-267-9660	267-4091
Westfield Memorial Library 550 E Broad St *Web:* www.wmlnj.org	Westfield	NJ	07090	908-789-4090	789-0921
Morris County Library (MCL) 30 E Hanover Ave *Web:* www.gti.net/mocolib1	Whippany	NJ	07981	973-285-6930	285-6973
Monroe Township Free Public Library 713 Marsha Ave *Web:* www.monroetownshiplibrary.org	Williamstown	NJ	08094	856-629-1212	875-0191
Willingboro Public Library 220 Willingboro Pkwy *Web:* www.willingboro.org	Willingboro	NJ	08046	609-877-6668	835-1699
Woodbridge Public Library George Frederick Plaza *Web:* www.woodbridge.lib.nj.us	Woodbridge	NJ	07095	732-634-4450	634-1569

NEW MEXICO

Library	City	State	ZIP	Phone	Fax
Alamogordo Public Library 920 Oregon Ave www.ci.alamogordo.nm.us/coa/communityservices/library.htm	Alamogordo	NM	88310	505-439-4140	439-4108
Rio Grande Valley Library System 501 Copper Ave NW *Web:* www.cabq.gov/library	Albuquerque	NM	87102	505-768-5141	768-5191
Artesia Public Library The 306 W Richardson Ave *Web:* www.pvtnetworks.net/~apublib	Artesia	NM	88210	505-746-4252	746-3075
Carlsbad Public Library 101 S Halagueno *Web:* www.carlsbadpubliclibrary.org	Carlsbad	NM	88220	505-885-6776	885-8809
Clovis-Carver Public Library 701 Main St *Web:* www.library.cityofclovis.org	Clovis	NM	88101	505-769-7840	769-7842
Marshall Memorial Library 110 S Diamond St.	Deming	NM	88030	505-546-9202	546-9649
Espanola Public Library 314-A N Paseo de Onate *Web:* www.youseemore.com	Espanola	NM	87532	505-747-6087	753-5543
Farmington Public Library 2101 Farmington Ave	Farmington	NM	87401	505-599-1270	599-1257
Hobbs Public Library 509 N Shipp St *Web:* www.hobbspubliclibrary.org	Hobbs	NM	88240	505-397-9328	397-1508
Thomas Branigan Memorial Library 200 E Picacho Ave *Web:* www.library.las-cruces.org	Las Cruces	NM	88001	575-528-4000	528-4030
Roswell Public Library 301 N Pennsylvania Ave *Web:* www.roswellpubliclibrary.org	Roswell	NM	88201	505-622-7101	622-7107
Santa Fe Public Library 145 Washington Ave *Web:* www.santafelibrary.org	Santa Fe	NM	87501	505-955-6780	955-6676
Socorro Public Library 401 Pk St *Web:* www.adobelibrary.org	Socorro	NM	87801	505-835-1114	835-1182

NEW YORK

Library	City	State	ZIP	Phone	Fax
Albany Public Library (APL) 161 Washington Ave *Web:* www.albanypubliclibrary.org	Albany	NY	12210	518-427-4300	449-3386
Amherst Public Library 350 John James Audubon Pkwy	Amherst	NY	14228	716-689-4922	689-6116
Baldwinsville Public Library 33 E Genesee St *Web:* www.bville.lib.ny.us	Baldwinsville	NY	13027	315-635-5631	635-6760
Suffolk Co-op Library System 627 N Sunrise Service Rd PO Box 9000 *Web:* www.scls.suffolk.lib.ny.us	Bellport	NY	11713	631-286-1600	286-1647
Broome County Public Library 185 Ct St *Web:* www.bclibrary.info	Binghamton	NY	13901	607-778-6451	778-6429
Brentwood Public Library (BPL) 34 2nd Ave *Web:* www.brentwood.suffolk.lib.ny.us	Brentwood	NY	11717	631-273-7883	273-7896
Bronx Library Ctr 310 E Kings Bridge Rd	Bronx	NY	10458	718-579-4244	579-4264
Brooklyn Public Library (BPL) 496 Franklin Ave *Web:* www.brooklynpubliclibrary.org	Brooklyn	NY	11238	718-623-0012	230-2097
Buffalo & Erie County Public Library 1 Lafayette Sq *Web:* www.buffalolib.org	Buffalo	NY	14203	716-858-8900	858-6211
Reinstein Public Library 2580 Harlem Rd.	Cheektowaga	NY	14225	716-892-8089	
East Rochester Public Library 111 W Elm St *Web:* www.mcls.rochester.lib.ny.us	East Rochester	NY	14445	585-586-8302	
Steele Memorial Library 101 E Church St *Web:* www.steele.lib.ny.us	Elmira	NY	14901	607-733-9173	733-9176
Hamburg Public Library 102 Buffalo St.	Hamburg	NY	14075	716-649-4415	649-4160
Hempstead Public Library 115 Nichols Ct *Web:* www.nassaulibrary.org	Hempstead	NY	11550	516-481-6990	481-6719
Finger Lakes Library System 119 E Green St. *TF:* 800-909-3557 ■ *Web:* www.flls.org	Ithaca	NY	14850	607-273-4074	273-3618
Tompkins County Public Library 101 E Green St. *Web:* www.tcpl.org	Ithaca	NY	14850	607-272-4557	272-8111
Queens Borough Public Library 89-11 Merrick Blvd. *Fax: Hum Res ■ *Web:* www.queenslibrary.org	Jamaica	NY	11432	718-990-0700	658-2919*
Chautauqua-Cattaraugus Library System 106 W 5th St. *Web:* www.cclslib.org	Jamestown	NY	14701	716-484-7135	483-6880
Town of Tonawanda Public Library Kenmore Branch 160 Delaware Rd. *Web:* www.buffalolib.org	Kenmore	NY	14217	716-873-2842	873-8416
Lancaster Public Library 5466 Broadway	Lancaster	NY	14086	716-683-1120	686-0749
William K Sanford Town Library 629 Albany Shaker Rd *Web:* www.colonie.org	Loudonville	NY	12211	518-458-9274	438-0988
Ramapo Catskill Library System 619 Rt 17-M *TF:* 800-327-7343 ■ *Web:* www.rcls.org	Middletown	NY	10940	845-343-1131	342-1205
Mount Vernon Public Library 28 S 1st Ave *Web:* www.mountvernonpubliclibrary.org	Mount Vernon	NY	10550	914-668-1840	668-1018
New York Public Library 5th Ave & 42nd St *Web:* www.nypl.org	New York	NY	10018	212-930-0800	930-0572
Niagara Falls Public Library 1425 Main St *Web:* www.niagarafallspubliclib.org	Niagara Falls	NY	14305	716-286-4894	286-4885
Penfield Public Library 1985 Baird Rd *Web:* www.libraryweb.org	Penfield	NY	14526	585-383-0500	340-8748
Clinton-Essex-Franklin Library System 33 Oak St *Web:* www.cefls.org	Plattsburgh	NY	12901	518-563-5190	563-0421
Mid-Hudson Library System 103 Market St *Web:* www.midhudson.org	Poughkeepsie	NY	12601	845-471-6060	454-5940
Brighton Memorial Library 2300 Elmwood Ave *Web:* www.brightonlibrary.org	Rochester	NY	14618	585-784-5300	784-5333
Central Library of Rochester & Monroe County 115 S Ave *Web:* www.rochester.lib.ny.us/central	Rochester	NY	14604	585-428-8100	428-8353
Chili Public Library 3333 Chili Ave *Web:* www.libraryweb.org/chili	Rochester	NY	14624	585-889-2200	889-5819
Gates Public Library 1605 Buffalo Rd *Web:* www.gateslibrary.org	Rochester	NY	14624	585-247-6446	426-5733
Greece Public Library 2 Vince Tofany Blvd *Web:* www.rochester.lib.ny.us	Rochester	NY	14616	585-225-8951	225-2777
Henrietta Public Library 455 Calkins Rd *Web:* www.hpl.org	Rochester	NY	14623	585-359-7093	334-6369
Irondequoit Public Library 45 Cooper Rd. *Web:* www.libraryweb.org/irondequoit	Rochester	NY	14617	585-336-6062	336-6066
Schenectady County Public Library System 99 Clinton St *Web:* www.scpl.org	Schenectady	NY	12305	518-388-4500	386-2241
John C Hart Memorial Library 1130 E Main St	Shrub Oak	NY	10588	914-245-5262	245-5936
Saint George Library Ctr 5 Central Ave	Staten Island	NY	10301	718-442-8560	447-2703
Onondaga County Public Library 447 S Salina St *Web:* www.ocpl.lib.ny.us	Syracuse	NY	13202	315-435-1800	435-8533
Nassau Library System 900 Jerusalem Ave *Web:* www.nassaulibrary.org	Uniondale	NY	11553	516-292-8920	481-4777
Mid-York Library System 1600 Lincoln Ave *Web:* www.midyork.org	Utica	NY	13502	315-735-8328	735-0943
Henry Waldinger Memorial Library 60 Verona Pl *Web:* www.nassaulibrary.org	Valley Stream	NY	11582	516-825-6422	825-6551
Four County Library System 304 Clubhouse Rd. *Web:* www.4cls.org	Vestal	NY	13850	607-723-8236	723-1722
Vestal Public Library 320 Vestal Pkwy E *Web:* www.4cls.org	Vestal	NY	13850	607-754-4243	754-7936
North Country Library System 22072 CR 190 *Web:* www.northcountrylibraries.org	Watertown	NY	13601	315-782-5540	782-6883
Roswell P Flower Memorial Library 229 Washington St *Web:* www.flowermemoriallibrary.org	Watertown	NY	13601	315-788-2352	788-2584

Library	City	State	ZIP	Phone	Fax
Webster Public Library 980 Ridge Rd ; Webster Plaza *Web:* www.websterlibrary.org	Webster	NY	14580	585-872-7075	872-7073
West Islip Public Library 3 Higbie Ln *Web:* www.wipublib.org	West Islip	NY	11795	631-661-7080	661-7137
West Seneca Public Library 1300 Union Rd	West Seneca	NY	14224	716-674-2928	
White Plains Public Library 100 Martine Ave *Web:* www.whiteplainslibrary.org	White Plains	NY	10601	914-422-1400	422-1462
Yonkers Public Library 1 Larkin Ctr *Web:* www.ypl.org	Yonkers	NY	10701	914-337-1500	376-3676

NORTH CAROLINA

Library	City	State	ZIP	Phone	Fax
Stanly County Public Library 133 E Main St *Web:* www.stanlycountylibrary.org	Albemarle	NC	28001	704-986-3759	983-6713
Randolph Public Library 201 Worth St *Web:* www.randolphlibrary.org	Asheboro	NC	27203	336-318-6800	318-6823
Asheville-Buncombe Library System 67 Haywood St *Web:* www.buncombecounty.org/governing/depts/Library	Asheville	NC	28801	828-250-4746	255-5213
Transylvania County Library 212 S Gaston St *Web:* www.transylvania.lib.nc.us	Brevard	NC	28712	828-884-3151	877-4230
Pender County Public Library 103 S Cowan St PO Box 879 *Web:* www.youseemore.com/PenderPL/default.asp	Burgaw	NC	28425	910-259-1234	259-0656
May Memorial Library 342 S Spring St *Web:* www.cncrl.com	Burlington	NC	27215	336-229-3588	229-3592
Chapel Hill Public Library 100 Library Dr *Web:* www.townhall.townofchapelhill.org/library	Chapel Hill	NC	27514	919-968-2780	968-2838
Charlotte Mecklenburg Library 310 N Tryon St *Web:* www.plcmc.org	Charlotte	NC	28202	704-416-0100	336-2002
Sampson-Clinton Public Library 217 Graham St	Clinton	NC	28328	910-592-4153	590-3504
Durham County Library 300 N Roxboro St *Web:* www.durhamcountylibrary.org	Durham	NC	27701	919-560-0100	560-0106
Rockingham County Public Library 527 Boone Rd *Web:* www.rcpl.org	Eden	NC	27288	336-627-1106	623-1258
Northwestern Regional Library 111 N Front St *Web:* www.nwrl.org	Elkin	NC	28621	336-835-4894	526-2270
Cumberland County Public Library 300 Maiden Ln *Web:* www.cumberland.lib.nc.us	Fayetteville	NC	28301	910-483-1580	486-5372
Gaston County Public Library 1555 E Garrison Blvd *Web:* www.glrl.lib.nc.us	Gastonia	NC	28054	704-868-2164	853-0609
Greensboro Public Library 219 N Church St *Web:* www.greensboro-nc.gov	Greensboro	NC	27401	336-373-2471	333-6781
Halifax County Library System PO Box 97	Halifax	NC	27839	252-583-3631	583-8661
Leslie H Perry Memorial Library 134 Rose Ave	Henderson	NC	27536	252-438-3316	438-3744
Henderson County Public Library 301 N Washington St *Web:* www.henderson.lib.nc.us	Hendersonville	NC	28739	828-697-4725	692-8449
High Point Public Library (HPPL) 901 N Main St *Web:* www.highpointpubliclibrary.com	High Point	NC	27262	336-883-3660	883-3636
Onslow County Public Library 58 Doris Ave E *Web:* www.onslowcountync.gov/Library	Jacksonville	NC	28540	910-455-7350	455-1661
Duplin County Library 107 Bowdens Rd	Kenansville	NC	28349	910-296-2117	296-2172
Caldwell County Public Library 120 Hospital Ave *Web:* www.ccpl.us	Lenoir	NC	28645	828-757-1288	757-1413
Davidson County Public Library System (DCPLS) 602 S Main St *Web:* www.ils.unc.edu	Lexington	NC	27292	336-242-2064	249-8161
Harnett County Public Library PO Box 1149 *Web:* www.harnett.org/library	Lillington	NC	27546	910-893-3446	893-3001
Franklin County Library 906 N Main St	Louisburg	NC	27549	919-496-2111	496-1339
Robeson County Public Library 101 N Chestnut	Lumberton	NC	28359	910-738-4859	739-8321
McDowell County Public Library 90 W Ct St *Web:* www.main.nc.us	Marion	NC	28752	828-652-3858	652-2098
Davie County Public Library 371 N Main St *Web:* www.co.davie.nc.us	Mocksville	NC	27028	336-751-2023	751-1370
Union County Public Library 316 E Windsor St *Web:* www.union.lib.nc.us	Monroe	NC	28112	704-283-8184	282-0657
Burke County Public Library 204 S King St *Web:* www.bcpls.org	Morganton	NC	28655	828-437-5638	433-1914
New Bern-Craven County Public Library 400 Johnson St *Web:* www.newbern.cpclib.org	New Bern	NC	28560	252-638-7800	638-7817
Catawba County Library 115 W C St *Web:* www.catawbacountync.gov/library	Newton	NC	28658	828-465-8664	465-8293
Richard H Thornton Public Library 210 Main St *Web:* www.granville.lib.nc.us	Oxford	NC	27565	919-693-1121	693-2244
Wake County Public Library System 4020 Carya Dr *Web:* www.wakegov.com	Raleigh	NC	27610	919-250-1200	250-1209
Rowan Public Library PO Box 4039 *Web:* www.rowancountync.gov	Salisbury	NC	28145	704-216-8243	638-3002
Brunswick County Library 109 W Moore St *Web:* www.library.brunsco.net	Southport	NC	28461	910-457-6237	457-6977
Rutherford County Library 255 Callahan Koon Rd	Spindale	NC	28160	828-287-6117	287-6119
Iredell County Library PO Box 1810 *Web:* www.iredell.lib.nc.us	Statesville	NC	28687	704-878-3090	878-5449
Edgecombe County Memorial Library 909 N Main St *Web:* www.edgecombelibrary.org	Tarboro	NC	27886	252-823-1141	823-7699
Alexander County Library 77 1st Ave SW *Web:* www.alexanderlibrary.org	Taylorsville	NC	28681	828-632-4058	632-1094
Haywood County Public Library 678 S Haywood St *Web:* www.haywoodlibrary.org	Waynesville	NC	28786	828-452-5169	452-6746
New Hanover County Public Library 201 Chestnut St *Web:* www.nhcgov.com/LIB/LIBmain.asp	Wilmington	NC	28401	910-798-6320	798-6312
Wilson County Public Library 249 W Nash St *Web:* www.wilson-co.com	Wilson	NC	27893	252-237-5355	243-4311
Forsyth County Public Library 660 W 5th St *Web:* www.forsyth.cc	Winston-Salem	NC	27101	336-703-2665	727-2549
Gunn Memorial Public Library 161 Main St E	Yanceyville	NC	27379	336-694-9673	694-9846

NORTH DAKOTA

Library	City	State	ZIP	Phone	Fax
Bismarck Veterans Memorial Public Library 515 N 5th St *Web:* www.bismarck.org	Bismarck	ND	58501	701-355-1480	221-3729
Fargo Public Library 408 Robert St *Web:* www.cityoffargo.com/library	Fargo	ND	58102	701-241-1491	241-8581
Carnegie Regional Library 49 W 7th St *TF:* 800-568-5964	Grafton	ND	58237	701-352-2754	352-2757
Grand Forks Public Library 2110 Library Cir *Web:* www.grandforksgov.com/library	Grand Forks	ND	58201	701-772-8116	772-1379
Minot Public Library 516 2nd Ave SW *Web:* www.minotlibrary.org	Minot	ND	58701	701-852-1045	852-2595

OHIO

Library	City	State	ZIP	Phone	Fax
Akron-Summit County Public Library 60 S High St *Web:* www.ascpl.lib.oh.us	Akron	OH	44326	330-643-9000	643-9033
Rodman Public Library 215 E Broadway St *Web:* www.rodmanlibrary.com	Alliance	OH	44601	330-821-2665	821-5053
Ashtabula County District Library 335 W 44th St *Web:* www.ashtabula.lib.oh.us	Ashtabula	OH	44004	440-997-9341	992-7714
Clermont County Public Library System 326 Broadway St *Web:* www.clermonlibrary.org	Batavia	OH	45103	513-732-2736	732-3177
Logan County District Library 220 N Main St *Web:* www.logancountylibraries.org	Bellefontaine	OH	43311	937-599-4189	599-5503
Bexley Public Library 2411 E Main St *Web:* www.bexlib.org	Bexley	OH	43209	614-231-9709	231-0794
Wood County District Public Library 251 N Main St *Web:* www.wcdpl.lib.oh.us	Bowling Green	OH	43402	419-352-5104	354-0405
Guernsey County District Public Library 800 Steubenville Ave *Web:* www.gcdpl.lib.oh.us	Cambridge	OH	43725	740-432-5946	432-7142
Stark County District Library 715 Market Ave N *Web:* www.starklibrary.org	Canton	OH	44702	330-452-0665	452-0403
Carroll County District Library 70 2nd St NE *Web:* www.carroll.lib.oh.us	Carrollton	OH	44615	330-627-2613	627-2523
Geauga County Public Library 12701 Ravenwood Dr *Web:* www.geauga.lib.oh.us	Chardon	OH	44024	440-286-6811	286-7419
Chillicothe & Ross County Public Library 140 S Paint St *Web:* www.chillicothe.lib.oh.us	Chillicothe	OH	45601	740-702-4145	702-4156
Public Library of Cincinnati & Hamilton County 800 Vine St *Web:* www.cincinnatilibrary.org	Cincinnati	OH	45202	513-369-6900	369-3123
Pickaway County District Public Library 1160 N Ct St *TF:* 888-268-3756 ■ *Web:* www.pickawaylib.org	Circleville	OH	43113	740-477-1644	474-2855
Cleveland Public Library 325 Superior Ave *Web:* www.cpl.org	Cleveland	OH	44114	216-623-2800	623-7015
Cleveland Heights-University Heights Public Library 2345 Lee Rd *Web:* www.heightslibrary.org	Cleveland Heights	OH	44118	216-932-3600	932-0932
Columbus Metropolitan Library 96 S Grant Ave *Web:* www.columbuslibrary.org	Columbus	OH	43215	614-645-2275	645-2050
Dayton Metro Library 215 E 3rd St *Web:* www.daytonmetrolibrary.org	Dayton	OH	45402	937-227-9500	
Defiance Public Library 320 Fort St *Web:* www.defiance.lib.oh.us	Defiance	OH	43512	419-782-1456	782-6235
Delaware County District Library 84 E Winter St *Web:* www.delawarelibrary.org	Delaware	OH	43015	740-362-3861	369-0196
Brooke-Gould Memorial Library 450 S Barron St *TF:* 800-559-0254 ■ *Web:* www.pcdl.lib.oh.us/locations/eaton.html	Eaton	OH	45320	937-456-4331	456-4774
Findlay Hancock County District Public Library 206 Broadway *Web:* www.findlaylibrary.org	Findlay	OH	45840	419-422-1712	422-0638

				Phone	Fax
Birchard Public Library of Sandusky County 423 Croghan St	Fremont	OH	43420	419-334-7101	334-4788
Web: www.birchard.lib.oh.us					
Dr Samuel L Bossard Memorial Library 7 Spruce St	Gallipolis	OH	45631	740-446-7323	446-1701
Web: www.bossard.lib.oh.us					
Portage County District Library 10482 S St	Garrettsville	OH	44231	330-527-4378	527-4370
TF: 800-500-5179 ■ *Web:* www.portagecounty.lib.oh.us					
Lane Public Library 300 N 3rd St	Hamilton	OH	45011	513-894-7156	894-2718
Web: www.lanepl.org					
Highland County District Library 10 Willettsville Pike	Hillsboro	OH	45133	937-393-3114	393-2985
Briggs Lawrence County Public Library 321 S 4th St	Ironton	OH	45638	740-532-1124	532-4948
Web: www.briggslibrary.com					
Lakewood Public Library 15425 Detroit Ave	Lakewood	OH	44107	216-226-8275	521-4327
Web: www.lkwdpl.org					
Fairfield County District Library 219 N Broad St	Lancaster	OH	43130	740-653-2745	653-4199
Web: www.fairfield.lib.oh.us					
Lebanon Public Library 101 S Broadway	Lebanon	OH	45036	513-932-2665	932-7323
Lima Public Library 650 W Market St	Lima	OH	45801	419-228-5113	228-0955
Web: www.limalibrary.com					
Logan-Hocking County District Library 230 E Main St	Logan	OH	43138	740-385-2348	385-9093
Web: www.hocking.lib.oh.us					
Lorain Public Library System 351 W 6th St	Lorain	OH	44052	440-244-1192	244-4888
TF: 800-322-7323 ■ *Web:* www.lorain.lib.oh.us					
Mansfield-Richland County Public Library 43 W 3rd St	Mansfield	OH	44902	419-521-3100	525-4750
Web: www.mrcpl.org					
Washington County Public Library 615 5th St	Marietta	OH	45750	740-373-1057	373-2860
Web: www.wcplib.lib.oh.us					
Medina County District Library 210 S Broadway	Medina	OH	44256	330-725-0588	725-2053
Web: www.mcdl.info					
Middletown Public Library 125 S Broad St	Middletown	OH	45044	513-424-1251	424-6585
Web: www.middletownlibrary.org					
Holmes County District Public Library (HCDPL) 3102 Glen Dr	Millersburg	OH	44654	330-674-5972	674-1938
Web: www.holmeslibrary.org					
Mount Vernon & Knox County Public Library 201 N Mulberry St	Mount Vernon	OH	43050	740-392-2665	397-3866
Perry County District Library 117 S Jackson St	New Lexington	OH	43764	740-342-4195	342-4204
Web: www.pcdl.org					
Tuscarawas County Public Library 121 Fair Ave NW	New Philadelphia	OH	44663	330-364-4474	364-8217
Web: www.tusclibrary.org					
Newark Public Library 101 W Main St	Newark	OH	43055	740-349-5500	349-5575
Web: www.newarklibrary.info					
Putnam County District Library 136 Putnam Pkwy PO Box 230	Ottawa	OH	45875	419-523-3747	523-6477
Web: www.mypcdl.org					
Morely Library 184 Phelps St	Painesville	OH	44077	440-352-3383	352-9079
Web: www.morleylibrary.org					
Cuyahoga County Public Library 2111 Snow Rd	Parma	OH	44134	216-398-1800	749-9479
TF: 800-749-5560 ■ *Web:* www.cuyahogalibrary.org					
Paulding County Carnegie Library 205 S Main St	Paulding	OH	45879	419-399-2032	399-2114
Web: www.pauldingcountylibrary.org					
Portsmouth Public Library 1220 Gallia St	Portsmouth	OH	45662	740-354-5688	353-3483
Web: www.portsmouth.lib.oh.us					
Clark County Public Library 201 S Fountain Ave	Springfield	OH	45501	937-328-6903	328-6908
Web: www.ccpl.lib.oh.us					
Public Library of Steubenville & Jefferson County 407 S 4th St	Steubenville	OH	43952	740-282-9782	282-2919
Web: www.steubenville.lib.oh.us					
Tiffin-Seneca Public Library 77 Jefferson St	Tiffin	OH	44883	419-447-3751	447-3045
Web: www.tiffinsen.lib.oh.us					
Toledo-Lucas County Public Library 325 N Michigan St	Toledo	OH	43604	419-259-5207	255-1334
Web: www.toledolibrary.org					
Troy-Miami County Public Library 419 W Main St	Troy	OH	45373	937-339-0502	335-4880
Web: www.troypubliclibrary.org					
Upper Arlington Public Library 2800 Tremont Rd	Upper Arlington	OH	43221	614-486-9621	486-4530
Web: www.ualibrary.org					
Brumback Library 215 W Main St	Van Wert	OH	45891	419-238-2168	238-3180
Web: www.brumbacklib.com					
Warren-Trumbull County Public Library 444 Mahoning Ave NW	Warren	OH	44483	330-399-8807	395-3988
Web: www.wtcpl.lib.oh.us					
Carnegie Public Library 127 S N St	Washington Courthouse	OH	38614	740-335-2540	335-2928
Web: www.cplwcho.org					
Garnet A Wilson Public Library of Pike County 207 N Market St	Waverly	OH	45690	740-947-4921	947-2918
Web: www.pike.lib.oh.us					
Westerville Public Library 126 S State St	Westerville	OH	43081	614-882-7277	882-4160
TF: 800-816-0662 ■ *Web:* www.wpl.lib.oh.us					
Greene County Public Library 76 E Market St	Xenia	OH	45385	937-376-2996	372-4673
Web: www.greenelibray.info					
Public Library of Youngstown & Mahoning County 305 Wick Ave	Youngstown	OH	44503	330-744-8636	744-2258
Web: www.ymc.lib.oh.us					
Muskingum County Library System 220 N 5th St	Zanesville	OH	43701	740-453-0391	455-6357
Web: www.muskingumlibrary.org					

OKLAHOMA

				Phone	Fax
Bartlesville Public Library 600 S Johnstone Ave	Bartlesville	OK	74003	918-337-5353	337-5338
Web: www.bartlesville.lib.ok.us					
Lawton Public Library 110 SW 4th St	Lawton	OK	73501	580-581-3450	248-0243
Web: www.cityof.lawton.ok.us					
Southeastern Public Library System of Oklahoma (SEPLSO) 401 N 2nd St	McAlester	OK	74501	918-426-0456	426-0543
TF: 800-562-9520 ■ *Web:* www.oklibrary.net					
Eastern Oklahoma District Library System 814 W Okmulgee St	Muskogee	OK	74401	918-683-2846	683-0436
Web: www.eodls.lib.ok.us					
Pioneer Library System 225 N Webster Ave	Norman	OK	73069	405-321-1481	701-2608
Web: www.pioneer.lib.ok.us					
Ponca City Library 515 E Grand Ave	Ponca City	OK	74601	580-767-0345	767-0377
Stillwater Public Library 1107 S Duck St	Stillwater	OK	74074	405-372-3633	624-0552
Web: www.library.stillwater.org					
Tulsa City-County Library (TCCL) 400 Civic Ctr	Tulsa	OK	74103	918-549-7323	596-7990
Web: www.tulsalibrary.org					

ONTARIO

				Phone	Fax
Waterloo Public Library 35 Albert St	Waterloo	ON	N2L5E2	519-886-1310	886-7936
Web: www.wpl.ca					

OREGON

				Phone	Fax
Beaverton City Library 12375 SW 5th St	Beaverton	OR	97005	503-644-2197	526-2636
Web: www.beavertonlibrary.org					
Deschutes Public Library 507 NW Wall St	Bend	OR	97701	541-312-1020	389-2982
Web: www.deschuteslibrary.org					
Coos Bay Public Library 525 W Anderson Ave	Coos Bay	OR	97420	541-269-1101	269-7567
Web: bay.cooslibraries.org					
Corvallis-Benton County Library 645 NW Monroe Ave	Corvallis	OR	97330	541-766-6928	766-6915
Web: www.library.ci.corvallis.or.us					
Eugene Public Library 100 W 10th Ave	Eugene	OR	97401	541-682-5450	682-5898
Josephine County Library System 200 NW 'C' St PO Box 1684	Grants Pass	OR	97526	541-476-0571	660-6531
Web: www.josephinelibrary.org					
Hillsboro Public Library 2850 NE Brookwood Pkwy	Hillsboro	OR	97124	503-615-6500	615-6501
Web: www.ci.hillsboro.or.us					
Klamath County Library 126 S 3rd St	Klamath Falls	OR	97601	541-882-8894	882-6166
Lake Oswego Public Library 706 4th St	Lake Oswego	OR	97034	503-636-7628	635-4171
Web: www.ci.oswego.or.us					
McMinnville Public Library 225 NE Adams St	McMinnville	OR	97128	503-435-5555	435-5560
Web: www.maclibrary.org					
Jackson County Library System 205 S Central Ave	Medford	OR	97501	541-774-6427	774-6748
Web: www.jcls.org					
Ledding Library 10660 SE 21st Ave	Milwaukie	OR	97222	503-786-7580	659-9497
Web: www.ci.milwaukie.or.us					
Clackamas County Library 16201 SE McLoughlin Blvd	Oak Grove	OR	97267	503-655-8543	
Web: www.library.co.clackamas.or.us					
Oregon City Public Library 606 John Adams	Oregon City	OR	97045	503-657-8269	657-3702
Web: www.oregoncity.lib.or.us					
Multnomah County Library 801 SW 10th Ave	Portland	OR	97205	503-988-5123	988-5226
Web: www.multcolib.org					
Douglas County Library System 1409 NE Diamond Lake Blvd	Roseburg	OR	97470	541-440-4311	440-4315
Web: www.dclibrary.us					
Salem Public Library 585 Liberty St SE	Salem	OR	97301	503-588-6071	588-6055
Web: www.cityofsalem.net/departments/library					
Springfield Public Library 225 N 5th St	Springfield	OR	97477	541-726-3766	726-3747
Web: www.library.ci.springfield.or.us					
Tigard Public Library 13500 SW Hall Blvd	Tigard	OR	97223	503-684-6537	598-7515
Web: www.ci.tigard.or.us/library					

PENNSYLVANIA

				Phone	Fax
Allentown Public Library 1210 Hamilton St	Allentown	PA	18102	610-820-2400	820-0640
Web: www.allentownpl.org					
Altoona Area Public Library 1600 5th Ave	Altoona	PA	16602	814-946-0417	946-3230
Web: www.altoonalibrary.org					
Bethlehem Area Public Library 11 W Church St	Bethlehem	PA	18018	610-867-3761	867-2767
Web: www.bapl.org					
Bucks County Free Library 150 S Pine St	Doylestown	PA	18901	215-348-9081	348-4760
Web: www.buckslib.org					
Erie County Library System 160 E Front St	Erie	PA	16507	814-451-6900	451-6969
Web: www.erielibrary.org					
Raymond M Blasco MD Memorial Library 160 E Front St	Erie	PA	16507	814-451-6900	451-6969
Web: www.erielibrary.org					
Chester County Library 450 Exton Sq Pkwy	Exton	PA	19341	610-280-2600	280-2694
Web: www.ccls.org					
Adams County Public Library 140 Baltimore St	Gettysburg	PA	17325	717-334-5716	334-7992
Web: www.adamslibrary.org					

Library	City	State	ZIP	Phone	Fax
Dauphin County Library System 101 Walnut St. Web: www.dcls.org	Harrisburg	PA	17101	717-234-4961	234-7479
Cambria County Library System 248 Main St. Web: www.cclsys.org	Johnstown	PA	15901	814-536-5131	536-6905
Lancaster Public Library 125 N Duke St. Web: www.lancaster.lib.pa.us	Lancaster	PA	17602	717-394-2651	394-3083
Lebanon Community Library 125 N 7th St. Web: www.lebanoncountylibraries.org	Lebanon	PA	17046	717-273-7624	273-2719
Monessen Public Library & District Ctr Eastgate 11. Web: www.monpldc.org	Monessen	PA	15062	724-684-4750	684-7077
Montgomery County-Norristown Public Library 1001 Powell St. Web: www.mc-npl.org	Norristown	PA	19401	610-278-5100	277-0344
Oil Creek District Library Ctr 2 Central Ave. TF: 888-645-2489 ■ Web: www.oilcitylibrary.org	Oil City	PA	16301	814-678-3054	676-0359
Osceola Mills Public Library 600 Lingle St	Osceola Mills	PA	16666	814-339-7229	339-7719
Free Library of Philadelphia 1901 Vine St. Web: www.libwww.freelibrary.org	Philadelphia	PA	19103	215-686-5322	563-3628
Carnegie Library of Pittsburgh 4400 Forbes Ave. Web: www.carnegielibrary.org	Pittsburgh	PA	15213	412-622-3131	622-6278
Pottsville Free Public Library 215 W Market St. Web: www.pottsvillelibrary.org	Pottsville	PA	17901	570-622-8880	622-2157
Reading Public Library 100 S 5th St. Web: www.reading.lib.pa.us	Reading	PA	19602	610-655-6355	655-6609
Albright Memorial Library 500 Vine St. Web: www.lclshome.org	Scranton	PA	18509	570-348-3000	348-3020
Osterhout Free Library 71 S Franklin St. Web: www.osterhout.lib.pa.us	Wilkes-Barre	PA	18701	570-823-0156	
James V Brown Library of Williamsport & Lycoming County 19 E 4th St. Web: www.jvbrown.edu	Williamsport	PA	17701	570-326-0536	326-1671
Martin Memorial Library 159 E Market St. Web: www.yorklibraries.org	York	PA	17401	717-846-5300	848-2330

RHODE ISLAND

Library	City	State	ZIP	Phone	Fax
Coventry Public Library 1672 Flat River Rd. Web: www.coventrylibrary.org	Coventry	RI	02816	401-822-9100	822-9133
Cranston Public Library 140 Sockanosset Cross Rd. Web: www.cranstonlibrary.org	Cranston	RI	02920	401-943-9080	946-5079
Cumberland Public Library 1464 Diamond Hill Rd. Web: www.cumberlandlibrary.org	Cumberland	RI	02864	401-333-2552	334-0578
East Providence Public Library 41 Grove Ave. Web: www.eastprovidencelibrary.com	East Providence	RI	02914	401-434-2453	434-3324
Marion J Mohr Memorial Library 1 Memorial Ave.	Johnston	RI	02919	401-231-4980	231-4984
Newport Public Library 300 Spring St. Web: www.newportlibraryri.org	Newport	RI	02840	401-847-8720	842-0841
Pawtucket Public Library 13 Summer St. Web: www.PawtucketLibrary.com	Pawtucket	RI	02860	401-725-3714	728-2170
Providence Public Library 150 Empire St. Web: www.provlib.org	Providence	RI	02903	401-455-8000	455-8080
Warwick Public Library (WPL) 600 Sandy Ln. Web: www.warwicklibrary.org/wpl	Warwick	RI	02886	401-739-5440	732-2055
West Warwick Public Library System 1043 Main St. Web: www.wwlibrary.org	West Warwick	RI	02893	401-828-3750	828-8493
Westerly Public Library 44 Broad St. Web: www.westerlylibrary.org	Westerly	RI	02891	401-596-2877	596-5600
Woonsocket Harris Public Library 303 Clinton St. Web: www.woonsocketlibrary.org	Woonsocket	RI	02895	401-769-9044	767-4140

SOUTH CAROLINA

Library	City	State	ZIP	Phone	Fax
Aiken-Bamberg-Barnwell-Edgefield Regional Library System 314 Chesterfield St. Web: www.abbe-lib.org	Aiken	SC	29801	803-642-7575	642-7597
Anderson County Library 300 S McDuffie St. Web: www.andersonlibrary.org	Anderson	SC	29621	864-260-4500	260-4510
Marlboro County Library 203 Fayetteville Ave. Web: www.marlborocountylibrary.org	Bennettsville	SC	29512	843-479-5630	479-5645
Charleston County Public Library 68 Calhoun St. Web: www.ccpl.org	Charleston	SC	29401	843-805-6930	727-3741
Chester County Library 100 Ctr St. Web: www.chesterlibsc.org	Chester	SC	29706	803-377-8145	377-8146
Chesterfield County Library 119 Main St.	Chesterfield	SC	29709	843-623-7489	623-3295
Richland County Public Library (RCPL) 1431 Assembly St. Web: www.richland.lib.sc.us	Columbia	SC	29201	803-799-9084	
Darlington County Library 204 N Main St. Web: www.darlington-lib.org	Darlington	SC	29532	843-398-4940	398-4942
Dillon County Library 600 E Main St.	Dillon	SC	29536	843-774-0330	774-0733
Pickens County Library 304 Biltmore Rd.	Easley	SC	29640	864-850-7077	850-7088
Florence County Library 509 S Dargan St. Web: www.florencelibrary.org	Florence	SC	29506	843-662-8424	661-7544
Cherokee County Public Library 300 E Rutledge Ave.	Gaffney	SC	29340	864-487-2711	487-2752
Greenville County Library 25 Heritage Green Pl. Web: www.greenvillelibrary.org	Greenville	SC	29601	864-242-5000	235-8375
Greenwood-Abbeville Regional Library 106 N Main St	Greenwood	SC	29646	864-941-4650	941-4651
Hilton Head Library 11 Beach City Rd	Hilton Head Island	SC	29926	843-255-6500	342-9220
Williamsburg County Library 215 N Jackson St. Web: www.mywcl.org	Kingstree	SC	29556	843-355-9486	355-9991
Lancaster County Library 313 S White St. Web: www.lanclib.org	Lancaster	SC	29720	803-285-1502	285-6004
Laurens County Library 1017 W Main St. Web: www.lcpl.org	Laurens	SC	29360	864-681-7323	681-0598
Harvin Clarendon County Library 215 N Brooks St. Web: www.hccl.lib.sc.gov	Manning	SC	29102	803-435-8633	435-8101
Marion County Library (MCL) 101 E Ct St. Web: www.marioncountylibrary.org	Marion	SC	29571	843-423-8300	423-8302
Berkeley County Library 1003 Hwy 52. Web: www.berkeley.lib.sc.us	Moncks Corner	SC	29461	843-719-4223	719-4732
Chapin Memorial Library 400 14th Ave N. Web: www.cityofmyrtlebeach.com	Myrtle Beach	SC	29577	843-918-1275	918-1288
Orangeburg County Library 510 State Rd S-38-1062. Web: www.orangeburgcounty.org	Orangeburg	SC	29115	803-531-4636	533-5860
York County Library 138 E Black St. Web: www.yclibrary.org	Rock Hill	SC	29730	803-981-5858	328-9290
Dorchester County Library 506 N Parler Ave. Web: www.dcl.lib.sc.us	Saint George	SC	29477	843-563-9189	563-7823
Spartanburg County Public Library 151 S Church St. Web: www.infodepot.org	Spartanburg	SC	29306	864-596-3507	596-3518
Sumter County Library 111 N Harvin St. Web: www.midnet.sc.edu/sumtercls	Sumter	SC	29150	803-773-7273	773-4875
Union County Carnegie Library 300 E S St. Web: www.unionlibrary.org	Union	SC	29379	864-427-7140	427-5155
Oconee County Library 501 W S Broad St. Web: www.ocplibrary.org	Walhalla	SC	29691	864-638-4133	638-4132
Colleton County Memorial Library 600 Hampton St. Web: www.colletonlibrary.org	Walterboro	SC	29488	843-549-5621	549-5122

SOUTH DAKOTA

Library	City	State	ZIP	Phone	Fax
Brookings Public Library 515 3rd St. Web: www.brookingslibrary.org	Brookings	SD	57006	605-692-9407	692-9386
RE Rawlins Municipal Library 1000 E Church St. Web: www.rpllib.sdln.net	Pierre	SD	57501	605-773-7421	773-7423
Rapid City Public Library (RCPL) 610 Quincy St. Web: www.rcgov.org/Library	Rapid City	SD	57701	605-394-4171	394-4064
Siouxland Libraries 200 N Dakota Ave PO Box 7403. Web: www.siouxlandlib.org	Sioux Falls	SD	57117	605-367-8720	367-4312

TENNESSEE

Library	City	State	ZIP	Phone	Fax
Cheatham County Public Library 188 County Services Dr Suite 200	Ashland City	TN	37015	615-792-4828	792-2054
EG Fisher Public Library 1289 Ingleside Ave	Athens	TN	37303	423-745-7782	745-1763
Sullivan County Public Library 1655 Blountville Blvd PO 510. Web: www.wrlibrary.org/sullivan	Blountville	TN	37617	423-279-2714	279-2836
Chattanooga-Hamilton County Bicentennial Library 1001 Broad St. Web: www.lib.chattanooga.gov	Chattanooga	TN	37402	423-757-5310	757-4994
Clarksville Montgomery County Public Library 350 Pageant Ln Suite 501. Web: www.cmc-websvr.clarksville.org/default.htm	Clarksville	TN	37040	931-648-8826	648-8831
Cleveland Public Library 795 N Church St. Web: www.clevelandlibrary.org	Cleveland	TN	37311	423-472-2163	339-9791
Clinton Public Library 118 S Hicks St.	Clinton	TN	37716	865-457-0519	457-4233
Blue Grass Regional Library 104 E 6th St	Columbia	TN	38401	931-388-9282	388-1762
Putnam County Library 50 E Broad St. Web: www.pclibrary.org	Cookeville	TN	38501	931-526-2416	372-8517
Tipton County Public Library 300 W Church Ave	Covington	TN	38019	901-476-8289	476-0008
Art Circle Public Library 3 E St. Web: www.artcirclelibrary.info	Crossville	TN	38555	931-484-6790	484-2350
Dickson County Public Library 206 Henslee Dr. Web: www2.youseemore.com	Dickson	TN	37055	615-446-8293	446-9130
McIver's Grant Public Library 204 N Mill Ave	Dyersburg	TN	38024	731-285-5032	285-9332
Elizabethton-Carter County Public Library 201 N Sycamore St. Web: www.eccpl.org	Elizabethton	TN	37643	423-547-6360	
Fayetteville-Lincoln County Public Library 400 Rocky Knob Ln	Fayetteville	TN	37334	931-433-3286	433-0063
Williamson County Public Library 1314 Columbia Ave. Web: www.lib.williamson-tn.org	Franklin	TN	37064	615-794-3105	595-1245
EW Carmack-Sumner County Public Library 658 Hartsville Pike	Gallatin	TN	37066	615-452-1722	451-3319

Library	City	State	ZIP	Phone	Fax
Greeneville-Greene County Public Library 210 N Main St	Greeneville	TN	37745	423-638-5034	638-3841
Web: www.ggcpl.org					
Martin Curtis-Hendersonville Public Library 116 Dunn St PO Box 1099	Hendersonville	TN	37077	615-824-0656	824-3112
Jacksboro Public Library 585 Main St Suite 201	Jacksboro	TN	37757	423-562-3675	562-9587
Web: www.jacksboropubliclibrary.org					
Jackson-Madison County Library 433 E Lafayette St	Jackson	TN	38301	731-425-8600	425-8609
Web: www.jmcl.tn.org					
Johnson City Public Library 100 W Millard St	Johnson City	TN	37604	423-434-4450	434-4469
Web: www.jcpl.net					
Washington County-Jonesborough Library 200 E Sabine Dr	Jonesborough	TN	37659	423-753-1800	753-1802
Web: www.wrlibrary.org					
Kingsport Public Library 400 Broad St	Kingsport	TN	37660	423-224-2559	224-2558
Web: www.kingsportlibrary.org					
Knox County Public Library System 500 W Church Ave	Knoxville	TN	37902	865-215-8700	
Web: www.knoxcounty.org/library					
Lawrence County Public Library 519 E Gaines St	Lawrenceburg	TN	38464	931-762-4627	766-1597
Lebanon-Wilson County Public Library 108 S Hatton Ave	Lebanon	TN	37087	615-444-0632	444-0535
Web: www2.youseemore.com/lebanon-wilson/Default.asp					
Lenoir City Public Library 100 W Broadway St # 103	Lenoir City	TN	37771	865-986-3210	
Reelfoot Regional Library Ctr PO Box 168	Martin	TN	38237	731-587-2347	587-0027
Blount County Public Library 508 N Cusick St	Maryville	TN	37804	865-982-0981	977-1142
Web: www.blountlibrary.org					
Memphis/Shelby County Public Library 3030 Poplar Ave	Memphis	TN	38111	901-415-2700	323-7107
Web: www.memphislibrary.lib.tn.us					
Morristown-Hamblen Public Library 417 W Main St	Morristown	TN	37814	423-586-6410	587-6226
Nolichucky Regional Library Ctr 315 McCrary Dr	Morristown	TN	37814	423-586-6251	586-7741
Web: www.state.tn.us					
Highland Rim Regional Library Ctr 2118 E Main St	Murfreesboro	TN	37130	615-893-3380	895-6727
TF: 800-257-7323					
Linebaugh Public Library 105 W Vine St	Murfreesboro	TN	37130	615-893-4131	848-5038
Web: www.linebaugh.org					
Nashville Public Library 615 Church St	Nashville	TN	37219	615-862-5800	880-2119
Web: www.library.nashville.org					
Stokely Memorial Library 383 E Broadway	Newport	TN	37821	423-623-3832	623-3832
Oak Ridge Public Library 1401 Oak Ridge Tpke	Oak Ridge	TN	37830	865-425-3455	425-3429
Web: www.ci.oak-ridge.tn.us/lib-html/orlib.htm					
WG Rhea Library 400 W Washington St	Paris	TN	38242	731-642-1702	642-1777
Giles County Public Library 122 S 2nd St	Pulaski	TN	38478	931-363-2720	424-7032
Web: www.gilescountylibrary.org					
Hawkins County Public Library 407 E Main St	Rogersville	TN	37857	423-272-8710	272-9261
Sevier County Public Library 321 Ct Ave	Sevierville	TN	37862	865-453-3532	365-1667
Web: www.sevierlibrary.org					
Argie Cooper Public Library 100 S Main St	Shelbyville	TN	37160	931-684-7323	685-4848
Web: www.acolibrary.com					
Somerville-Fayette County Library 216 W Market St	Somerville	TN	38068	901-465-5248	465-5271
Gorham MacBane Public Library 405 White St	Springfield	TN	37172	615-384-5123	384-0106
Barbara Reynolds Carr Memorial Library 1304 Old Knoxville Rd	Tazewell	TN	37879	423-626-5414	626-9481
Obion County Public Library 1221 E Reelfoot Ave	Union City	TN	38261	731-885-7000	885-9638
Web: www.oclibrary.org					
Franklin County Library 105 S Porter St	Winchester	TN	37398	931-967-3706	962-1477

TEXAS

Library	City	State	ZIP	Phone	Fax
Abilene Public Library 202 Cedar St	Abilene	TX	79601	325-677-2474	738-8082
Web: www.abilenetx.com					
Alice Public Library 401 E 3rd St	Alice	TX	78332	361-664-9506	668-3248
Amarillo Public Library 413 SE 4th Ave	Amarillo	TX	79101	806-378-3054	
Web: www.amarillolibrary.org					
Brazoria County Library System 131 E Live Oak St	Angleton	TX	77515	979-864-1505	864-1298
Web: www.bcls.lib.tx.us					
Arlington Public Library 101 E Abram St	Arlington	TX	76010	817-459-6900	459-6902
Web: www.arlingtonlibrary.org					
Henderson County CW Murchison Memorial Library 121 S Prairieville St	Athens	TX	75751	903-677-7295	677-7275
Austin Public Library 800 Guadalupe St	Austin	TX	78701	512-974-7400	499-7403
Web: www.ci.austin.tx.us/library					
Sterling Municipal Library Mary Elizabeth Wilbanks Ave	Baytown	TX	77520	281-427-7331	420-5347
Web: www.baytownlibrary.org					
Beaumont Public Library System 801 Pearl St	Beaumont	TX	77701	409-838-6606	838-6838
Bedford Public Library 1805 L Don Dodson Dr	Bedford	TX	76021	817-952-2335	952-2396
Web: www.bedfordlibrary.org					
Howard County Library 500 S Main St	Big Spring	TX	79720	432-264-2260	264-2263
Nancy Carol Roberts Memorial Library 100 Martin Luther King Junior Pkwy	Brenham	TX	77833	979-337-7201	
Web: www.ci.brenham.tx.us					
Brownsville Public Library 4320 Southmost Rd	Brownsville	TX	78521	956-548-1055	548-0684
Web: www.bpl.us					
Brownwood Public Library 600 Carnegie Blvd	Brownwood	TX	76801	325-646-0155	646-6503
Web: www.brownwoodpubliclibrary.com					
Bryan Public Library 201 E 26th St	Bryan	TX	77803	979-209-5600	209-5610
Web: www.bcslibrary.org					
Van Zandt County Library 317 1st Monday Ln	Canton	TX	75103	903-567-4276	567-6981
Carrollton Public Library 4220 N Josey Ln	Carrollton	TX	75010	972-466-4800	466-4722
Web: www.cityofcarrollton.com/library					
Montgomery County Library 104 I-45 N	Conroe	TX	77301	936-788-8360	788-8398
Web: www.countylibrary.org					
Corpus Christi Public Libraries 805 Comanche St	Corpus Christi	TX	78401	361-880-7070	880-7046
Web: www.cclibraries.com					
Corsicana Public Library 100 N 12th St	Corsicana	TX	75110	903-654-4810	654-4814
Web: www.ci.corsicana.tx.us					
J Erik Jonsson Central Library 1515 Young St	Dallas	TX	75201	214-670-1400	670-1684
Web: www.dallaslibrary2.org/central/index.php					
Deer Park Public Library 3009 Ctr St	Deer Park	TX	77536	281-478-7208	478-7212
Val Verde County Library 300 Spring St	Del Rio	TX	78840	830-774-7595	774-7607
Web: www.vvcl.org					
Denison Public Library 300 W Gandy St	Denison	TX	75020	903-465-1797	465-1130
Web: www.barr.org					
Denton Public Library 502 Oakland St	Denton	TX	76201	940-349-8565	349-8260
Web: www.cityofdenton.com/pages/library.cfm					
DeSoto Public Library 211 E Pleasant Run Rd Suite C	DeSoto	TX	75115	972-230-9656	230-5797
Web: www.desotolibrary.info					
Duncanville Public Library 201 James Collins Blvd	Duncanville	TX	75116	972-780-5050	780-4958
Web: www.youseemore.com/duncanville					
Eagle Pass Public Library 589 E Main St	Eagle Pass	TX	78852	830-773-2516	773-4204
Web: www.eaglepass.lib.tx.us					
Edinburg Public Library 401 E Cano St	Edinburg	TX	78539	956-383-6246	292-2026
Web: www.edinburg.lib.tx.us					
Euless Public Library 201 N Ector Dr	Euless	TX	76039	817-685-1679	267-1979
Fort Worth Public Library 500 W 3rd St	Fort Worth	TX	76102	817-871-7323	871-7734
Web: www.fortworthgov.org					
Friendswood Public Library 416 S Friendswood Dr	Friendswood	TX	77546	281-482-7135	482-2685
Web: www.friendswood.lib.tx.us					
Rosenberg Library 2310 Sealy Ave	Galveston	TX	77550	409-763-8854	763-1064
Web: www.rosenberg-library.org					
Nicholson Memorial Library System 625 Austin St	Garland	TX	75040	972-205-2543	205-2523
Web: www.nmls.lib.tx.us					
Upshur County Library 702 W Tyler St	Gilmer	TX	75644	903-843-5001	843-3995
Hood County Library 222 N Travis St	Granbury	TX	76048	817-573-3569	573-3969
Grapevine Public Library 1201 Municipal Way	Grapevine	TX	76051	817-410-3400	410-3080
Web: www.ci.grapevine.tx.us/IndividualDepartments/Library/tabid/101/Default.aspx					
W Walworth Harrison Public Library 1 Lou Finney Ln	Greenville	TX	75401	903-457-2992	457-2961
Web: www.youseemore.com/harrison					
Haltom City Public Library 4809 Haltom Rd	Haltom City	TX	76117	817-222-7786	834-1446
Web: www.haltomcitytx.com					
Harlingen Public Library 410 76th Dr	Harlingen	TX	78550	956-430-6650	430-6654
Rusk County Library (RCL) 106 E Main St	Henderson	TX	75652	903-657-8557	657-7637
Web: www.rclib.org					
Harris County Public Library System 8080 El Rio St	Houston	TX	77054	713-749-9000	749-9090
Web: www.hcpl.net					
Houston Public Library 500 McKinney St	Houston	TX	77002	713-236-1313	393-1324*
**Fax Area Code: 832* ■ *Web:* www.houstonlibrary.org					
Hurst Public Library 901 Precinct Line Rd	Hurst	TX	76053	817-788-7300	590-9515
Web: www.ci.hurst.tx.us/lib/index.htm					
Irving Public Library 801 W Irving Blvd	Irving	TX	75060	972-721-2606	721-2463
Web: www.catalog.cityofirving.org					
Butt-Holdsworth Memorial Library 505 Water St	Kerrville	TX	78028	830-257-8422	792-5552
Web: www.kerrville.org					
Robert J Kleberg Public Library 220 N 4th St	Kingsville	TX	78363	361-592-6381	
Web: www.youseemore.com/rjkleberg/default.asp					
Laredo Public Library 1120 E Calton Rd	Laredo	TX	78041	956-795-2400	795-2403
Web: www.laredolibrary.org					
Helen Hall Library (HHL) 100 W Walker St	League City	TX	77573	281-554-1111	
Web: www.leaguecity.com					
Lewisville Public Library 1197 W Main St	Lewisville	TX	75067	972-219-3571	219-5094
Web: www.library.cityoflewisville.com					
Longview Public Library 222 W Cotton St	Longview	TX	75601	903-237-1351	237-1327
Web: www.longviewlibrary.com					
Lubbock Public Library 1306 9th St	Lubbock	TX	79401	806-775-2835	775-2827
Web: www.lubbocklibrary.com					
Marshall Public Library 300 S Alamo St	Marshall	TX	75670	903-935-4465	935-4463
McAllen Memorial Library 601 N Main St	McAllen	TX	78501	956-688-3300	
Web: www.mcallenlibrary.net					
Mesquite Public Library 300 W Grubb Dr	Mesquite	TX	75149	972-216-6220	216-6740
Web: www.cityofmesquite.com					
Midland County Public Library 301 W Missouri Ave	Midland	TX	79701	432-688-4320	688-4939
Web: www.co.midland.tx.us					
Speer Memorial Library 801 E 12th St	Mission	TX	78572	956-580-8750	580-8756
Web: www.mission.lib.tx.us					
Nacogdoches Public Library 1112 N St	Nacogdoches	TX	75961	936-559-2970	569-8282
Web: www.npl.sfasu.edu					
New Braunfels Public Library 700 E Common St	New Braunfels	TX	78130	830-221-4300	608-2151
Web: www.nbtexas.org					

				Phone	Fax
North Richland Hills Public Library 9015 grand Ave.	North Richland Hills	TX	76180	817-427-6800	427-6808
Web: www.library.nrhtx.com					
Ector County Library 321 W 5th St	Odessa	TX	79761	432-337-2501	332-4211
Web: www.ector.lib.tx.us					
Palestine Public Library 2000 S Loop 256 #42	Palestine	TX	75801	903-729-4121	729-4062
Web: www.youseemore.com					
Pasadena Public Library 1201 Jeff Ginn Memorial Dr	Pasadena	TX	77506	713-477-0276	473-9640
Web: www.ci.pasadena.tx.us					
Pharr Memorial Library 121 E Cherokee St.	Pharr	TX	78577	956-787-3966	787-3345
Unger Memorial Library 825 N Austin St	Plainview	TX	79072	806-296-1148	291-1245
Web: www.texasonline.net					
Plano Public Library System 5024 Custer Rd	Plano	TX	75023	972-769-4200	769-4210
Web: www.plano.gov/Departments/Libraries					
Port Arthur Public Library 4615 9th Ave.	Port Arthur	TX	77642	409-985-8838	985-5969
Web: www.pap.lib.tx.us					
Richardson Public Library 900 Civic Ctr Dr	Richardson	TX	75080	972-744-4350	744-5806
Web: www.cor.net					
George Memorial Library 1001 Golfview Dr	Richmond	TX	77469	281-342-4455	341-2689
Web: www.fortbend.lib.tx.us					
Starr County Public Library 700 E Canales St	Rio Grande City	TX	78582	956-487-4389	487-7390
Web: www.rgclibrary.org					
Round Rock Public Library 216 E Main St	Round Rock	TX	78664	512-218-7001	218-7061
Web: www.ci.round-rock.tx.us					
Tom Green County Library System 33 W Beauregard Ave	San Angelo	TX	76903	325-655-7321	659-4027
Web: www.tgclibrary.com					
Daughters of the Republic of Texas Library PO Box 1401	San Antonio	TX	78295	210-225-1071	212-8514
Web: www.drtl.org					
San Antonio Public Library 600 Soledad St	San Antonio	TX	78205	210-207-2500	207-2603
Web: www.sanantonio.gov/library					
San Benito Public Library 101 W Rose St	San Benito	TX	78586	956-361-3860	361-3867
Web: www.cityofsanbenito.com					
San Marcos Public Library 625 E Hopkins St	San Marcos	TX	78666	512-393-8200	754-8131
Web: www.ci.san-marcos.tx.us					
Sherman Public Library 421 N Travis St	Sherman	TX	75090	903-892-7240	892-7101
Web: www.barr.org					
Taylor Public Library 400 Porter St	Taylor	TX	76574	512-352-3434	352-8080
Web: www.ci.taylor.tx.us					
Temple Public Library 100 W Adams Ave	Temple	TX	76501	254-298-5555	298-5328
Terrell Public Library 301 N Rockwell Ave	Terrell	TX	75160	972-551-6663	551-6662
Texarkana Public Library 600 W 3rd St	Texarkana	TX	75501	903-794-2149	794-2139
Moore Memorial Public Library 1701 9th Ave N	Texas City	TX	77590	409-643-5979	948-1106
Web: www.texascity-library.org					
Colony Public Library The 6800 Main St	The Colony	TX	75056	972-625-1900	624-2245
Web: www.ci.the-colony.tx.us					
Tyler Public Library 201 S College Ave	Tyler	TX	75702	903-593-7323	531-1329
Web: www.tylerlibrary.com					
Waco-McLennan County Library 1717 Austin Ave	Waco	TX	76701	254-750-5941	750-5940
Web: www.waco-texas.com					
Watauga Public Library 7109 Whitley Rd	Watauga	TX	76148	817-514-5855	581-3910
Web: www.cowtx.org					
Weatherford Public Library 1014 Charles St	Weatherford	TX	76086	817-598-4150	598-4161
Weslaco Public Library 525 S Kansas Ave	Weslaco	TX	78596	956-968-4533	969-4069
Web: www.weslaco.lib.tx.us					
Wharton County Library 1920 N Fulton St	Wharton	TX	77488	979-532-8080	532-2792
Web: www.whartonco.lib.tx.us					
Wichita Falls Public Library 600 11th St.	Wichita Falls	TX	76301	940-767-0868	720-6672
Web: www.wfpl.net					

UTAH

				Phone	Fax
Davis County Library 38 S 100 E PO Box 115	Farmington	UT	84025	801-451-2322	451-9561
Web: www.co.davis.ut.us					
Logan Library 255 N Main St.	Logan	UT	84321	435-716-9123	716-9145
Web: www.library.loganutah.org					
Murray Public Library 166 E 5300 S	Murray	UT	84107	801-264-2574	264-2586
Web: www.murray.lib.ut.us					
Weber County Library 2464 Jefferson Ave.	Ogden	UT	84401	801-337-2632	337-2615
Web: www.weberpl.lib.ut.us					
Orem Public Library 58 N State St	Orem	UT	84057	801-229-7050	229-7130
Web: www.lib.orem.org					
Provo City Library 550 N University Ave.	Provo	UT	84601	801-852-6650	852-6688
Web: www.provolibrary.com					
Washington County Public Library 88 W 100 S.	Saint George	UT	84770	435-634-5737	634-5798
Web: www.library.washco.utah.gov					
Salt Lake City Public Library 210 E 400 S	Salt Lake City	UT	84111	801-524-8200	322-8196
Web: www.slcpl.lib.ut.us					
Salt Lake County Library System 2197 E Fort Union Blvd	Salt Lake City	UT	84121	801-943-4636	942-6323
Web: www.slcolibrary.org					

VERMONT

				Phone	Fax
Fletcher Free Public Library 235 College St	Burlington	VT	05401	802-863-3403	865-7227
Web: www.fletcherfree.org					
Kellogg-Hubbard Library 135 Main St	Montpelier	VT	05602	802-223-3338	223-3338
Web: www.kellogghubbard.org					

VIRGINIA

				Phone	Fax
Washington County Public Library 205 Oak Hill St	Abingdon	VA	24210	276-676-6222	676-6235
Web: www.wcpl.net					
Alexandria Library 717 Queen St	Alexandria	VA	22314	703-838-4555	838-5021
Web: www.alexandria.lib.va.us					
Amherst County Virgina 382 S Main St PO Box 370	Amherst	VA	24521	434-946-9388	946-9348
Web: www.countyofamherst.com					
Arlington County Central Library 1015 N Quincy St	Arlington	VA	22201	703-228-5990	228-7720
Web: www.arlingtonva.us					
Bristol Public Library 1400 Euclid Ave	Bristol	VA	24201	276-669-9444	669-5593
Web: www.wrlibrary.org/libraries/brpage.html					
Jefferson-Madison Regional Library 201 E Market St	Charlottesville	VA	22902	434-979-7151	971-7035
Web: www.jmrl.org					
Pittsylvania County Public Library 24 Military Dr	Chatham	VA	24531	434-432-3271	432-1405
Web: www.pcplib.org					
Chesapeake Public Library 298 Cedar Rd	Chesapeake	VA	23322	757-410-7100	410-7122
Web: www.chesapeake.lib.va.us					
Montgomery-Floyd Regional Library 125 Sheltman St	Christiansburg	VA	24073	540-382-6965	382-6964
Web: www.mfrl.org					
Culpeper County Library 271 Southgate Shopping Ctr	Culpeper	VA	22701	540-825-8691	825-7486
Web: www.tlc.library.net/culpeper					
Danville Public Library 511 Patton St	Danville	VA	24541	434-799-5195	972-5172
Web: www2.youseemore.com/danville/default.asp					
Shenandoah County Library 514 Stoney Creek Blvd	Edinburg	VA	22824	540-984-8200	984-8207
Web: www.shenandoah.co.lib.va.us					
Fairfax County Public Library 12000 Government Ctr Pkwy Suite 324	Fairfax	VA	22035	703-324-3100	222-3193
Web: www.fairfaxcounty.gov/library					
Augusta County Library 1759 Jefferson Hwy	Fishersville	VA	22939	540-949-6354	
Web: www.augustacountylibrary.org					
Samuels Public Library 330 e Criser Rd	Front Royal	VA	22630	540-635-3153	635-5653
Web: www.samuelslibrary.net					
Gloucester Library 6920 Main St	Gloucester	VA	23061	804-693-2998	693-1477
Buchanan County Public Library RR 2 PO Box 3	Grundy	VA	24614	276-935-6581	935-6292
Web: www.bcplnet.org					
Hampton Public Library 4207 Victoria Blvd	Hampton	VA	23669	757-727-1154	727-1152
Web: www.hamptonpubliclibrary.org					
Massanutten Regional Library 174 S Main St.	Harrisonburg	VA	22801	540-434-4475	434-4382
TF: 877-695-4272 ■ *Web:* www.mrlib.org					
Russell County Public Library 248 W Main St PO Box 247	Lebanon	VA	24266	276-889-8063	889-8045
Web: www.russell.lib.va.us					
Loudoun County Public Library Administration 380 Old Waterford Rd	Leesburg	VA	20175	703-777-0368	771-5620
Web: www.library.loudoun.gov					
Lynchburg Public Library 2315 Memorial Ave	Lynchburg	VA	24501	434-847-1577	845-1479
Web: www.lynchburgva.gov/publiclibrary					
Newport News Public Library 110 Main St	Newport News	VA	23601	757-591-4858	591-7425
Web: www.newportnewslib.org					
Newport News Public Library System 700 Town Ctr Dr Suite 300	Newport News	VA	23606	757-926-1350	926-1365
Web: www.nngov.com					
Norfolk Public Library 235 E Plume St	Norfolk	VA	23510	757-664-7323	664-7320
Web: www.npl.lib.va.us					
Petersburg Public Library 137 S Sycamore St	Petersburg	VA	23803	804-733-2387	733-7972
Web: www.ppls.org					
Portsmouth Public Library 601 Ct St	Portsmouth	VA	23704	757-393-8501	393-5107
Prince William Public Library System 13083 Chinn Pk Dr	Prince William	VA	22192	703-792-6100	792-4875
Pulaski County Library 60 3rd St NW	Pulaski	VA	24301	540-980-7770	980-7775
Web: www.pclibs.org					
Henrico County Public Library 1001 N Laburnum Ave	Richmond	VA	23223	804-290-9000	222-5566
Web: www.henricolibrary.org					
Richmond Public Library 101 E Franklin St	Richmond	VA	23219	804-646-4256	646-7685
Web: www.richmondpubliclibrary.org					
Roanoke City Public Libraries 706 S Jefferson St	Roanoke	VA	24016	540-853-2476	853-1781
Roanoke County Public Library 3131 Electric Rd	Roanoke	VA	24018	540-772-7507	989-3129
Web: www.roanokecountyva.gov					
Franklin County Public Library 355 Franklin St	Rocky Mount	VA	24151	540-483-3098	483-6652
Campbell County Public Library 684 Village Hwy PO Box 310	Rustburg	VA	24588	434-332-9560	332-9697
Web: www.campbellcountylibraries.org					
Tazewell County Public Library 310 E Main St.	Tazewell	VA	24651	276-988-3639	988-5980
Virginia Beach Public Library 4100 Virginia Beach Blvd	Virginia Beach	VA	23452	757-385-0150	
Web: www.vbgov.com/dept/library					
Williamsburg Regional Library 7770 Croaker Rd.	Williamsburg	VA	23188	757-259-4071	259-4077
Web: www.wrl.org					
Lonesome Pine Regional Library 124 Library Rd	Wise	VA	24293	276-328-8325	328-1739
York County Public Library 8500 George Washington Memorial Hwy	Yorktown	VA	23692	757-890-3377	890-2956
Web: www.yorkcounty.gov/library					

WASHINGTON

Library	City	State	ZIP	Phone	Fax
Anacortes Public Library 1220 10th St *Web:* www.library.cityofanacortes.org	Anacortes	WA	98221	360-293-1910	293-1929
Bellingham Public Library 210 Central Ave *Web:* www.bellinghampubliclibrary.org	Bellingham	WA	98225	360-676-6860	676-7795
Kitsap Regional Library 1301 Sylvan Way *TF:* 877-883-9900 ■ *Web:* www.krl.org	Bremerton	WA	98310	360-405-9110	405-9156
Everett Public Library 2702 Hoyt Ave *Web:* www.epls.org	Everett	WA	98201	425-257-8010	257-8016
King County Library System 960 Newport Way NW *Web:* www.kcls.org	Issaquah	WA	98027	425-369-3224	369-3214
Longview Public Library 1600 Louisiana St *Web:* www.longviewlibrary.org	Longview	WA	98632	360-442-5300	442-5954
Puyallup Public Library 324 S Meridian *Web:* www.cityofpuyallup.org	Puyallup	WA	98371	253-841-5454	841-5483
Richland Public Library 955 Northgate Dr *Web:* www.richland.lib.wa.us	Richland	WA	99352	509-942-7450	942-7447
Seattle Public Library 1000 4th Ave *Web:* www.spl.org	Seattle	WA	98104	206-386-4100	386-4119
Spokane Public Library 906 W Main Ave *Web:* www.spokanelibrary.org	Spokane	WA	99201	509-444-5300	444-5365
Pierce County Library System 3005 112th St E *Web:* www.piercecountylibrary.org	Tacoma	WA	98446	253-536-6500	537-4600
Tacoma Public Library 1102 Tacoma Ave S *Web:* www.tpl.lib.wa.us	Tacoma	WA	98402	253-591-5666	591-5470
Timberland Regional Library 415 Tumwater Blvd SW *Web:* www.timberland.lib.wa.us	Tumwater	WA	98501	360-943-5001	586-6838
Fort Vancouver Regional Library 1007 E Mill Plain Blvd *Web:* www.fvrl.org	Vancouver	WA	98663	360-695-1561	693-2681
Walla Walla Public Library 238 E Alder St *Web:* www.walnet.walla-walla.wa.us/walpub/Default.html	Walla Walla	WA	99362	509-527-4550	527-3748
North Central Regional Library 238 Olds Stn Rd *Web:* www.ncrl.org	Wenatchee	WA	98801	509-663-1117	662-8060
Yakima Valley Regional Library 102 N 3rd St *Web:* www.yvrl.org	Yakima	WA	98901	509-452-8541	575-2093

WEST VIRGINIA

Library	City	State	ZIP	Phone	Fax
Raleigh County Public Library 221 N Kanawha St	Beckley	WV	25801	304-255-0511	255-9161
Craft Memorial Library 600 Commerce St	Bluefield	WV	24701	304-325-3943	325-3702
Cabell County Public Library 455 9th St Plaza *Web:* www.cabell.lib.wv.us	Huntington	WV	25701	304-528-5700	528-5701
Ceredo-Kenova Public Library 1200 Oak St *Web:* www.wcpl.lib.wv.us	Kenova	WV	25530	304-453-2462	453-2462
Martinsburg-Berkeley County Public Library 101 W King St *Web:* www.youseemore.com	Martinsburg	WV	25401	304-267-8933	267-9720
Morgantown Public Library 373 Spruce St *Web:* www.morgantown.lib.wv.us	Morgantown	WV	26505	304-291-7425	291-7437
Miracle Valley Regional Library System *moundscill - marshall county public library* 700 5th St *Web:* moundscill.lib.wv.us	Moundsville	WV	26041	304-845-6911	845-6912
Fayette County Public Library 531 Summit St *Web:* www.fayette.lib.wv.us	Oak Hill	WV	25901	304-465-0121	465-5306
Parkersburg & Wood County Public Library 3100 Emerson Ave	Parkersburg	WV	26104	304-420-4587	420-4589
Mason County Public Library 508 Viand St	Point Pleasant	WV	25550	304-675-0894	675-0895
Jackson County Public Library 208 Church St N *Web:* www.jackson.park.lib.wv.us	Ripley	WV	25271	304-372-5343	372-7935
Mary H Weirton Public Library 3442 Main St *Web:* www.weirton.lib.wv.us	Weirton	WV	26062	304-797-8510	797-8526
McDowell Public Library 90 Howard St	Welch	WV	24801	304-436-3070	436-8079
Ohio County Public Library 52 16th St *Web:* wheeling.weirton.lib.wv.us	Wheeling	WV	26003	304-232-0244	232-6848

WISCONSIN

Library	City	State	ZIP	Phone	Fax
Northern Waters Library Service 3200 E Lakeshore Dr *TF:* 800-228-5684 ■ *Web:* www.nwls.lib.wi.us	Ashland	WI	54806	715-682-2365	685-2704
Beloit Public Library 605 Eclipse Blvd *Web:* www.als.lib.wi.us	Beloit	WI	53511	608-364-2905	364-2907
Brookfield Public Library 1900 N Calhoun Rd *Web:* www.ci.brookfield.wi.us/index.aspx?NID=38	Brookfield	WI	53005	262-782-4140	796-6670
Chippewa Falls Public Library 105 W Central St *Web:* www.chippewafallslibrary.org	Chippewa Falls	WI	54729	715-723-1146	720-6922
Indianhead Federated Library System 1538 Truax Blvd *Web:* www.ifls.lib.wi.us	Eau Claire	WI	54703	715-839-5082	839-5151
LE Phillips Memorial Public Library 400 Eau Claire St *Web:* www.ecpubliclibrary.info	Eau Claire	WI	54701	715-839-1648	839-3822
Southwest Wisconsin Library System 1775 4th St *Web:* www.swls.org	Fennimore	WI	53809	608-822-3393	822-6251
Fond du Lac Public Library 32 Sheboygan St *Web:* www.fdlpl.org	Fond du Lac	WI	54935	920-929-7080	929-7082
Germantown Community Library N112 W16957 Mequon Rd	Germantown	WI	53022	262-253-7760	253-7763
Grafton Public Library 1620 11th Ave *Web:* www.grafton.lib.wi.us	Grafton	WI	53024	262-375-5315	375-5317
Brown County Library 515 Pine St *Web:* www.co.brown.wi.us	Green Bay	WI	54301	920-448-4400	448-4388
Greenfield Public Library 5310 W Layton Ave *Web:* www.greenfieldlibrary.org	Greenfield	WI	53220	414-321-9595	321-8595
La Crosse County Library 103 State St *Web:* www.lacrossecountylibrary.com	Holmen	WI	54636	608-526-9600	526-3299
Arrowhead Library System 210 Dodge St *Web:* www.als.lib.wi.us	Janesville	WI	53548	608-758-6690	758-6689
Hedberg Public Library (HPL) 316 S Main St *Web:* www.hedbergpubliclibrary.org	Janesville	WI	53545	608-758-6600	758-6583
Kenosha Public Library 7979 38th Ave *Web:* www.kenosha.lib.wi.us	Kenosha	WI	53142	262-564-6100	564-6370
La Crosse Public Library 800 Main St *Web:* www.lacrosselibrary.org	La Crosse	WI	54601	608-789-7100	789-7106
Madison Public Library 201 W Mifflin St *Web:* www.madisonpubliclibrary.org	Madison	WI	53703	608-266-6300	266-4338
Manitowoc-Calumet Library System 707 Quay St *Web:* www.manitowoclibrary.org	Manitowoc	WI	54220	920-683-4863	683-4873
Marinette County Consolidated Public Library 1700 Hall Ave	Marinette	WI	54143	715-732-7570	732-7575
Marshfield Public Library 211 E 2nd St *Web:* www.marshfieldlibrary.org	Marshfield	WI	54449	715-387-8494	387-6909
Menasha Public Library 440 1st St *Web:* www.menashalibrary.org	Menasha	WI	54952	920-967-5166	967-5159
Menomonee Falls Public Library W156 N8436 Pilgrim Rd *Web:* www.mf.lib.wi.us	Menomonee Falls	WI	53051	262-532-8900	532-8939
Menomonie Public Library 600 Wolske Bay Rd *Web:* www.menomonielibrary.org	Menomonie	WI	54751	715-232-2164	232-2324
Middleton Public Library 7425 Hubbard Ave *Web:* www.midlibrary.org	Middleton	WI	53562	608-831-5564	836-5724
Milwaukee Public Library 814 W Wisconsin Ave *Web:* www.mpl.org	Milwaukee	WI	53233	414-286-3000	286-2798
Neenah Public Library 240 E Wisconsin Ave PO Box 569 *Web:* www.neenahlibrary.org	Neenah	WI	54956	920-886-6315	
New Berlin Public Library 15105 Library Ln *Web:* www.wcfls.lib.wi.us	New Berlin	WI	53151	262-785-4980	785-4984
Oshkosh Public Library 106 Washington Ave *Web:* www.oshkoshpubliclibrary.org	Oshkosh	WI	54901	920-236-5200	236-5227
Winnefox Library System 106 Washington Ave *Web:* www.winnefox.org	Oshkosh	WI	54901	920-236-5220	236-5228
Oxford Public Library 129 S Franklin Ave *Web:* www.oxfordlibrary.org	Oxford	WI	53952	608-586-4458	586-4559
Racine Public Library 75 7th St *Web:* www.racinelib.lib.wi.us	Racine	WI	53403	262-636-9170	636-9260
Mead Public Library 710 N 8th St *Web:* www.sheboygan.lib.wi.us	Sheboygan	WI	53081	920-459-3400	459-4336
Portage County Public Library 1001 Main St *Web:* www.library.uwsp.edu	Stevens Point	WI	54481	715-346-1544	346-1239
Door County Library (DCL) 107 S 4th Ave *Web:* www.doorcountylibrary.org	Sturgeon Bay	WI	54235	920-743-6578	743-6697
Superior Public Library 1530 Tower Ave *Web:* www.ci.superior.wi.us	Superior	WI	54880	715-394-8860	394-8870
Lakeshores Library System 106 W Main St *Web:* www.lakeshores.lib.wi.us	Waterford	WI	53185	262-514-4500	514-4544
Watertown Public Library 100 S Water St *Web:* www.watertownpubliclibrary.org	Watertown	WI	53094	920-262-4090	261-8943
Waukesha Public Library 321 Wisconsin Ave *Web:* www.waukesha.lib.wi.us	Waukesha	WI	53186	262-524-3680	650-2502
Marathon County Public Library 300 N 1st St *Web:* www.mcpl.lib.wi.us	Wausau	WI	54403	715-261-7200	261-7219
Wauwatosa Public Library 7635 W N Ave *Web:* www.wauwatosalibrary.org	Wauwatosa	WI	53213	414-471-8484	479-8984
West Allis Public Library 7421 W National Ave *Web:* www.ci.west-allis.wi.us	West Allis	WI	53214	414-302-8500	302-8545
West Bend Community Memorial Library 630 Poplar St *Web:* www.west-bendlibrary.org	West Bend	WI	53095	262-335-5151	335-5150
McMillan Memorial Library 490 E Grand Ave *Web:* www.mcmillanlibrary.org	Wisconsin Rapids	WI	54494	715-423-1040	423-2665

WYOMING

Library	City	State	ZIP	Phone	Fax
Natrona County Public Library 307 E 2nd St *Web:* www.natronacountylibrary.org	Casper	WY	82601	307-237-4935	266-3734
Laramie County Public Library 2200 Pioneer Ave *Web:* www.lclsonline.org	Cheyenne	WY	82001	307-634-3561	634-2082
Campbell County Public Library 2101 S 4-J Rd *Web:* www.ccpls.org	Gillette	WY	82718	307-682-3223	686-4009
Sweetwater County Library System 300 N 1st E St *Web:* www.sweetwaterlibraries.com	Green River	WY	82935	307-875-3615	872-3203
Teton County Public Library 125 Virginian Ln *Web:* www.tclib.org	Jackson	WY	83001	307-733-2164	733-4568
Fremont County Library System 451 N 2nd St	Lander	WY	82520	307-332-5194	332-3909
Albany County Public Library 310 S 8th St *Web:* www.albanycountylibrary.org	Laramie	WY	82070	307-721-2580	721-2584

437-4 Special Collections Libraries

Phone Fax

Academy of Motion Picture Arts & Sciences Herrick Library
333 S La Cienega Blvd ... Beverly Hills CA 90211 310-247-3020 657-5193
Web: www.oscars.org

Academy of Natural Sciences
Stewart Library
1900 Benjamin Franklin Pkwy ... Philadelphia PA 19103 215-299-1040
Web: www.ansp.org

Adirondack Museum
Library PO Box 99 ... Blue Mountain Lake NY 12812 518-352-7311 352-7653
Web: www.adkmuseum.org

AIDS Library 1233 Locust St 2nd Fl ... Philadelphia PA 19107 215-985-4851 985-4492
Web: www.aidslibrary.org

American Craft Council Library 72 Spring St ... New York NY 10012 212-274-0630 274-0650
Web: www.craftcouncil.org

American Film Institute Mayer Library
2021 N Western Ave ... Los Angeles CA 90027 323-856-7654 467-4578
Web: www.afi.com

American Kennel Club Library
260 Madison Ave 4th Fl ... New York NY 10016 212-696-8245 696-8281
Web: www.akc.org

American Library Assn Library 50 E Huron St ... Chicago IL 60611 312-944-6780 280-3255
TF: 800-545-2433 ■ *Web:* www.ala.org/ala/alalibrary

American Museum of Natural History
Library Central Pk W at 79th St ... New York NY 10024 212-769-5400 769-5009
Web: library.amnh.org

American Numismatic Society Library
75 Varick St 11th Fl ... New York NY 10013 212-571-4470 571-4479
Web: www.numismatics.org/library

American Philatelic Research Library (APRL)
100 Match Factory Pl ... Bellefonte PA 16823 814-237-3803 237-6128
Web: www.stamps.org/TheLibrary/lib_AbouttheAPRL.htm

Assn for Research & Enlightenment Library
215 67th St ... Virginia Beach VA 23451 757-428-3588
TF: 800-333-4499 ■ *Web:* www.edgarcayce.org/visit_are/are_library.htm

Athenaeum of Philadelphia 219 S 6th St ... Philadelphia PA 19106 215-925-2688 925-3755
Web: www.philaathenaeum.org

Basketball Hall of Fame
Hickox Library 1000 W Columbus Ave ... Springfield MA 01105 413-231-5523 781-1939
Web: www.hoophall.com

Bentley Historical Library 1150 Beal Ave ... Ann Arbor MI 48109 734-764-3482 936-1333
Web: www.bentley.umich.edu

Boston Athenaeum 10 1/2 Beacon St ... Boston MA 02108 617-227-0270 227-5266
Web: www.bostonathenaeum.org

Brookings Institution Library
1775 Massachusetts Ave NW ... Washington DC 20036 202-797-6240 797-2970
Web: www.brookings.edu

Center for Migration Studies of New York Inc
Library & Archives 209 Flagg Pl ... Staten Island NY 10304 718-351-8800 667-4598
Web: www.cmsny.library.net

Ernie Pyle Library 900 Girard Blvd SE ... Albuquerque NM 87106 505-256-2065

Folger Shakespeare Library
201 E Capitol St SE ... Washington DC 20003 202-544-4600 544-4623
Web: www.folger.edu

Frank Lloyd Wright Preservation Trust
Special Collections 931 Chicago Ave ... Oak Park IL 60302 312-994-4000 848-1248*
**Fax Area Code: 708* ■ *Web:* www.gowright.org

George E Brown Jr Library of the National Academies
500 5th St NW Keck Bldg Suite 304 ... Washington DC 20001 202-334-2125 334-1651
Web: www7.nationalacademies.org/nrclibrary

George Eastman House
Menschel Library 900 E Ave ... Rochester NY 14607 585-271-3361 271-3970
Web: www.eastmanhouse.org/inc/visit/research.php

George Peabody Library 17 E Mt Vernon Pl ... Baltimore MD 21202 410-659-8179 659-8137
Web: www.library.jhu.edu/collections

Gettysburg National Military Park Library & Research Ctr
97 Taneytown Rd ... Gettysburg PA 17325 717-334-1124 334-1997
Web: www.nps.gov/gett/library/libmain.htm

International Game Fish Assn
Harry Library of Fishes
300 Gulf Stream Way ... Dania Beach FL 33004 954-927-2628 924-4299
Web: www.igfa.org/lib.asp

Juilliard School The
Wallace Library 60 Lincoln Ctr Plaza ... New York NY 10023 212-799-5000 769-6421
Web: www.juilliard.edu

Library Co of Philadelphia
1314 Locust St ... Philadelphia PA 19107 215-546-3181 546-5167
Web: www.librarycompany.org

Lincoln Memorial Shrine 125 W Vine St ... Redlands CA 92373 909-798-7632 798-7566
Web: www.lincolnshrine.org

NA for the Advancement of Colored People Moon Library & Civil Rights Archives
4805 Mt Hope Dr ... Baltimore MD 21215 410-358-8900
TF: 877-622-2798 ■ *Web:* www.naacp.org

National Baseball Hall of Fame & Museum Library
25 Main St ... Cooperstown NY 13326 607-547-0330 547-4094
Web: www.baseballhall.org

Portsmouth Athenaeum 9 Market Sq ... Portsmouth NH 03801 603-431-2538 431-7180
Web: www.portsmouthathenaeum.org

Redwood Library & Athenaeum 50 Bellevue Ave ... Newport RI 02840 401-847-0292 841-5680
Web: www.redwoodlibrary.org

Salem Athenaeum The 337 Essex St ... Salem MA 01970 978-744-2540 744-7536
Web: www.salemathenaeum.net

Schomburg Center for Research in Black Culture
515 Malcolm X Blvd ... New York NY 10037 212-491-2200
Web: www.nypl.org/research/sc/sc.html

Phone Fax

Smithsonian Institution Cullman Library
Smithsonian Institution NHB CE-G15 MRC 154
PO Box 37012 ... Washington DC 20013 202-633-1184 633-0219
Web: www.sil.si.edu/libraries/cullman

Smithsonian Institution Dibner Library of the History of Science & Technology
Smithsonian Institution NMAH 1041 MRC 672
PO Box 37012 ... Washington DC 20013 202-633-3872 633-9102
Web: www.sil.si.edu/libraries/dibner

US Holocaust Memorial Museum Library
100 Raoul Wallenburg Pl SW ... Washington DC 20024 202-488-0400 488-2613
Web: www.ushmm.org/research/library

Vietnam Archive The
Texas Tech University PO Box 1041 ... Lubbock TX 79409 806-742-9010 742-0496
Web: www.vietnam.ttu.edu

Walter Reed Army Institute of Research Gorgas Memorial Library
503 Robert Grant Ave Rm 1W60 ... Washington DC 20307 301-319-9555 319-9402
Web: wrair-www.army.mil/Resources.asp

Yale University Beinecke Rare Book & Manuscript Library
121 Wall St ... New Haven CT 06511 203-432-2977 432-4047
Web: www.library.yale.edu

African American Museum & Library in Oakland
659 14th St ... Oakland CA 94612 510-637-0200 637-0204
Web: www.oaklandlibrary.org/AAMLO

Harriet Beecher Stowe House & Library
77 Forest St ... Hartford CT 06105 860-525-9258 522-9259
Web: www.harrietbeecherstowecenter.org

Karpeles Manuscript Library 453 Porter Ave ... Buffalo NY 14201 716-885-4139
Web: www.rain.org/~karpeles

Rosenbach Museum & Library
2008-2010 Delancey St ... Philadelphia PA 19103 215-732-1600 545-7529
Web: www.rosenbach.org

Providence Athenaeum 251 Benefit St ... Providence RI 02903 401-421-6970 421-2860
Web: www.providenceathenaeum.org

437-5 State Libraries

Phone Fax

Alabama Public Library Service
6030 Monticello Dr ... Montgomery AL 36130 334-213-3900 213-3993
Web: www.apls.state.al.us

Alaska State Library PO Box 110571 ... Juneau AK 99811 907-465-2921 465-2665
Web: www.library.state.ak.us

Arizona State Library
1700 W Washington St Rm 200 ... Phoenix AZ 85007 602-542-4035 542-4972
Web: www.lib.az.us

Arkansas State Library
900 W Capitol Suite 100 ... Little Rock AR 72201 501-682-2053 682-1529
Web: www.library.arkansas.gov

California State Library 900 N St ... Sacramento CA 95814 916-654-0261 654-0241
Web: www.library.ca.gov

Colorado State Library 201 E Colfax Ave Rm 309 ... Denver CO 80203 303-866-6900 866-6940
Web: www.cde.state.co.us

Connecticut State Library 231 Capitol Ave ... Hartford CT 06106 860-757-6510 757-6503
Web: www.cslib.org

Delaware Div of Libraries 43 S DuPont Hwy ... Dover DE 19901 302-739-4748 739-6787
Web: www.lib.de.us

Hawaii State Public Library System (HSPLS)
478 S King St ... Honolulu HI 96813 808-586-3500
Web: www.librarieshawaii.org

Idaho Commission for Libraries (ICFL)
325 W State St ... Boise ID 83702 208-334-2150 334-4016
TF: 800-458-3271 ■ *Web:* www.libraries.idaho.gov

Illinois State Library 300 S 2nd St ... Springfield IL 62701 217-782-2994 785-4326
Web: www.cyberdriveillinois.com/departments/library/home.html

Indiana State Library (ISL)
140 N Senate Ave ... Indianapolis IN 46204 317-232-3694 232-3728
Web: www.in.gov/library

Iowa State Library 112 E Grand Ave ... Des Moines IA 50319 515-281-4105 281-6191
Web: www.statelibraryofiowa.org

Kansas State Library
300 SW 10th Ave Capitol Bldg Rm 169 W ... Topeka KS 66612 785-296-3296 296-6650
Web: www.skyways.lib.ks.us

Kentucky Dept for Libraries & Archives
300 Coffee Tree Rd ... Frankfort KY 40602 502-564-8300 564-5773
Web: www.kdla.ky.gov

Library of Michigan The
702 W Kalamazoo St PO Box 30007 ... Lansing MI 48909 517-373-1580 373-4480
Web: www.michigan.gov/mde/0,1607,7-140-54504---,00.html

Library of Virginia 800 E Broad St ... Richmond VA 23219 804-692-3500 692-3594
Web: www.lva.lib.va.us

Louisiana State Library 701 N 4th St ... Baton Rouge LA 70821 225-342-4915 219-4725
Web: www.state.lib.la.us

Maine State Library 64 State House Stn ... Augusta ME 04333 207-287-5600 287-5615
Web: www.state.me.us

Massachusetts Board of Library Commissioners
98 N Washington St ... Boston MA 02114 617-725-1860 725-0140
TF: 800-952-7403 ■ *Web:* mblc.state.ma.us

Missouri State Library
600 W Main St PO Box 387 ... Jefferson City MO 65102 573-751-3615 526-1142
Web: www.sos.mo.gov/library

Montana State Library (MSL)
1515 E 6th Ave PO Box 201800 ... Helena MT 59620 406-444-3115 444-0266
Web: www.msl.mt.gov

Nebraska Library Commission
1200 N St Suite 120 ... Lincoln NE 68508 402-471-2045 471-2083
TF: 800-307-2665 ■ *Web:* www.nlc.state.ne.us

Nevada State Library & Archives (NSLA)
100 N Stewart St ... Carson City NV 89701 775-684-3360 684-3311
TF: 800-922-2880 ■ *Web:* www.nsla.nevadaculture.org

Library	City	State	ZIP	Phone	Fax
New Hampshire State Library 20 Pk St	Concord	NH	03301	603-271-2144	271-2205
Web: www.nh.gov					
New Jersey State Library 185 N State St PO Box 520	Trenton	NJ	08625	609-292-6200	292-2746
Web: www.state.nj.us/statelibrary/njlib.htm					
New York State Library Empire State Plaza	Albany	NY	12230	518-474-5355	474-5786
Web: www.nysl.nysed.gov					
North Dakota State Library (NDSL) 604 E Blvd Ave Dept 250	Bismarck	ND	58505	701-328-4622	328-2040
TF: 800-472-2104 ■ *Web:* www.library.nd.gov					
Oklahoma Dept of Libraries 200 NE 18th St	Oklahoma City	OK	73105	405-521-2502	525-7804
TF: 800-522-8116 ■ *Web:* www.odl.state.ok.us					
Oregon State Library 250 Winter NE State Library Bldg	Salem	OR	97301	503-378-4243	588-7119
Web: www.oregon.gov/OSL					
Pennsylvania Commonwealth Libraries 333 Market St	Harrisburg	PA	17126	717-787-2646	772-3265
Web: pa.gov/portal/server.pt/community/commonwealth_libraries/7225					
Rhode Island Office of Library & Information Services 1 Capitol Hill 4th Fl	Providence	RI	02908	401-222-2726	222-4195
South Carolina State Library 1430 Senate St	Columbia	SC	29201	803-734-8666	734-8676
Web: www.state.sc.us					
South Dakota State Library 800 Governors Dr	Pierre	SD	57501	605-773-3131	773-4950
TF: 800-423-6665 ■ *Web:* www.library.sd.gov					
State Library of Ohio 274 E 1st Ave	Columbus	OH	43201	614-644-6950	466-3584
TF: 800-686-1532					
Tennessee State Library & Archives 403 7th Ave N	Nashville	TN	37243	615-741-2764	741-6471
Web: www.state.tn.us/tsla					
Texas State Library & Archives Commission PO Box 12927	Austin	TX	78711	512-463-5455	
Web: www.tsl.state.tx.us					
Utah State Library 250 N 1950 W Suite A	Salt Lake City	UT	84116	801-715-6777	715-6767
Web: www.library.utah.gov					
Vermont Dept of Libraries 109 State St	Montpelier	VT	05609	802-828-3261	828-2199
Web: www.dol.state.vt.us					
Washington State Library PO Box 40220	Olympia	WA	98504	360-902-4151	586-7575
Web: www.sos.wa.gov					
West Virginia Library Commission 1900 Kanawha Blvd E	Charleston	WV	25305	304-558-2041	558-2044
Web: www.librarycommission.lib.wv.us					
Wisconsin Dept of Public Instruction Library Services Div 125 S Webster St PO Box 7841	Madison	WI	53707	608-266-3390	267-1052
TF: 800-441-4563 ■ *Web:* www.dpi.state.wi.us					
Wyoming State Library 2800 Central Ave	Cheyenne	WY	82001	307-777-6333	777-6289
Web: www-wsl.state.wy.us					

437-6 University Libraries

Listings For University Libraries Are Arranged By States.

Library	City	State	ZIP	Phone	Fax
Alabama Agricultural & Mechanical University J F Drake Memorial Learning Resources Ctr PO Box 489	Normal	AL	35762	256-372-4725	372-5768
Web: www.aamu.edu					
Tuskegee University Ford Motor Co Library/Learning Resource Ctr Hollis Burke Frissell Library Bldg	Tuskegee	AL	36088	334-727-8894	727-9282
Web: www.tuskegee.edu					
UAA/APU Consortium Library 3211 Providence Dr	Anchorage	AK	99508	907-786-1848	
Web: www.consortiumlibrary.org					
Northern Arizona University Cline Library PO Box 6022	Flagstaff	AZ	86011	928-523-6802	523-3770
TF: 800-247-3380 ■ *Web:* www.library.nau.edu					
University of Arizona Library 1510 E University Blvd	Tucson	AZ	85721	520-621-3430	621-9733*
**Fax:* Admin ■ *Web:* www.library.arizona.edu					
University of Central Arkansas Torreyson Library 201 Donaghey Ave	Conway	AR	72035	501-450-5000	450-5208
Web: www.uca.edu/library					
California Institute of Technology Library 1200 E California Blvd MC I-32	Pasadena	CA	91125	626-395-6405	792-7540
Web: www.library.caltech.edu					
California Lutheran University Pearson Library 60 W Olsen Rd	Thousand Oaks	CA	91360	805-493-3250	493-3842
Web: www.callutheran.edu					
California Polytechnic State University Kennedy Library 1 Grand Ave Bldg 35	San Luis Obispo	CA	93407	805-756-2029	756-2346
Web: www.lib.calpoly.edu					
California State Polytechnic University *Library* 3801 W Temple Ave	Pomona	CA	91768	909-869-3074	869-6922
Web: www.csupomona.edu/~library					
California State University Bakersfield *Stiern Library* 9001 Stockdale Hwy	Bakersfield	CA	93311	661-664-3172	654-3238
Web: www.csub.edu					
California State University Chico *Meriam Library* 400 W 1st St	Chico	CA	95929	530-898-6502	898-4443
Web: www.csuchico.edu/library					
California State University Dominguez Hills *Library* 1000 E Victoria St	Carson	CA	90747	310-243-3696	516-4219
Web: library.csudh.edu					
California State University Long Beach *University Library* 1250 Bellflower Blvd	Long Beach	CA	90840	562-985-4047	985-1703
Web: www.csulb.edu/library					
California State University Los Angeles *Kennedy Memorial Library* 5151 State University Dr	Los Angeles	CA	90032	323-343-3988	343-6401
Web: www.calstatela.edu/library					
California State University Northridge *Oviatt Library* 18111 Nordhoff St	Northridge	CA	91330	818-677-2285	677-2676
Web: library.csun.edu					
California State University Sacramento *Library* 2000 State University Dr E	Sacramento	CA	95819	916-278-6708	278-4160
Web: www.library.csus.edu					
California State University San Bernardino *Pfau Library* 5500 University Pkwy	San Bernardino	CA	92407	909-537-5000	537-7079
Web: www.lib.csusb.edu					
California State University San Marcos *Library* 333 S Twin Oaks Valley Rd	San Marcos	CA	92096	760-750-4340	
Web: www.biblio.csusm.edu					
California State University Stanislaus *Library* 801 W Monte Vista Ave	Turlock	CA	95382	209-667-3234	667-3164
Web: www.library.csustan.edu					
Humboldt State University Library 1 Harpst St	Arcata	CA	95521	707-826-3431	826-3440
Web: www.library.humboldt.edu					
John F Kennedy University Fisher Library 100 Ellinwood Way	Pleasant Hill	CA	94523	925-969-3100	969-3101
Web: library.jfku.edu					
Occidental College Clapp Library 1600 Campus Rd	Los Angeles	CA	90041	323-259-2640	341-4991
Web: www.departments.oxy.edu/library					
Pepperdine University Payson Library 24255 Pacific Coast Hwy	Malibu	CA	90263	310-506-4252	506-4117
Web: www.library.pepperdine.edu					
San Francisco State University Leonard Library 1630 Holloway Ave	San Francisco	CA	94132	415-338-1854	338-1504
Web: www.library.sfsu.edu					
Sonoma State University University Library 1801 E Cotati Ave	Rohnert Park	CA	94928	707-664-2397	664-2090
Web: library.sonoma.edu					
Stanford University Green Library 557 Escondido Mall	Stanford	CA	94305	650-723-9108	725-6874
Web: www.library.stanford.edu/depts/green					
University of California Davis *Shields Library* 100 NW Quad	Davis	CA	95616	530-752-6561	752-7815
Web: www.lib.ucdavis.edu					
University of California Irvine *Library* PO Box 19557	Irvine	CA	92623	949-824-6836	824-3644
Web: www.lib.uci.edu					
University of California Los Angeles *Library System* Charles E Young Research Library PO Box 951575	Los Angeles	CA	90095	310-825-4732	
Web: www.library.ucla.edu					
University of California Riverside *Libraries* PO Box 5900	Riverside	CA	92517	951-827-3220	827-3281
Web: www.library.ucr.edu					
University of California San Francisco *Kalmanovitz Library* 530 Parnassus Ave	San Francisco	CA	94143	415-476-8293	476-4653
Web: www.library.ucsf.edu					
University of California Santa Cruz *McHenry Library* 1156 High St	Santa Cruz	CA	95064	831-459-2076	459-8206
Web: www.library.ucsc.edu					
University of San Francisco Gleeson Library 2130 Fulton St	San Francisco	CA	94117	415-422-2660	422-2233
Web: www.usfca.edu/library					
University of Southern California Doheny Memorial Library 3550 Trousdale Pkwy University Pk Campus	Los Angeles	CA	90089	213-740-4039	
Web: www.usc.edu/isd/libraries					
University of Colorado at Boulder *Libraries* 1720 Pleasant St 184 UCB	Boulder	CO	80309	303-492-8705	492-9035*
**Fax:* library ■ *Web:* www.ucblibraries.colorado.edu					
University of Colorado at Colorado Springs *Kraemer Family Library* 1420 Austin Bluffs Pkwy PO Box 7150	Colorado Springs	CO	80918	719-262-3286	528-5227
Web: www.uccs.edu/~library					
University of Denver Westminster Law Library 2255 E Evans Ave	Denver	CO	80208	303-871-6190	871-6999
Web: www.law.du.edu/library					
University of Northern Colorado Michener Library 501 20th St	Greeley	CO	80639	970-351-2601	351-2963
Web: www.unco.edu					
Central Connecticut State University Burritt Library 1615 Stanley St	New Britain	CT	06050	860-832-2055	832-3409
Web: www.library.ccsu.edu/lib					
Connecticut College Shain Library 270 Mohegan Ave	New London	CT	06320	860-439-2655	439-2871
Web: www.conncoll.edu/is/info-resources					
Eastern Connecticut State University Smith Library 83 Windham St	Willimantic	CT	06226	860-465-4506	465-5522
Web: www.easternct.edu					
Southern Connecticut State University Buley Library 501 Crescent St	New Haven	CT	06515	203-392-5750	392-5775
Web: www.library.scsu.ctstateu.edu					
Trinity College Raether Library 300 Summit St	Hartford	CT	06106	860-297-2268	297-2251
Web: www.trincoll.edu/depts/library					
Wesleyan University Olin Library 252 Church St	Middletown	CT	06459	860-685-2660	685-2661
Web: www.wesleyan.edu					
Western Connecticut State University Haas Library 181 White St	Danbury	CT	06810	203-837-9100	837-9108
Web: www.library.wcsu.edu					
Yale University Sterling Memorial Library 120 High St	New Haven	CT	06511	203-432-1775	432-1294
Web: www.library.yale.edu					
University of Delaware Library 181 S College Ave	Newark	DE	19717	302-831-2965	831-1046
Web: www.lib.udel.edu					

Library	City	State	Zip	Phone	Fax
American University Bender Library 4400 Massachusetts Ave NW *Web:* www.library.american.edu	Washington	DC	20016	202-885-3200	885-3226
Catholic University of America The *Mullen Library* 620 Michigan Ave NE Rm308 *Web:* www.libraries.cua.edu	Washington	DC	20064	202-319-5060	319-4735
Gallaudet University Library 800 Florida Ave NE *Web:* www.gallaudet.edu/library.html	Washington	DC	20002	202-651-5217	651-5213
Georgetown University Lauinger Library 3700 'O' St NW PO Box 57174 *Web:* www.library.georgetown.edu	Washington	DC	20057	202-687-7452	687-1215
Coleman Memorial Library 1500 S Martin Luther King Blvd *Web:* www.famu.edu/library	Tallahassee	FL	32307	850-599-3370	561-2293
Wimberly Library 777 Glades Rd *Web:* www.fau.edu/library	Boca Raton	FL	33431	561-297-3760	297-2189
Florida International University Green Library 11200 SW 8th St *Web:* www.library.fiu.edu	Miami	FL	33199	305-348-2461	348-3408
Florida State University Strozier Library Rm 314 **Fax:* Admin ■ *Web:* www.lib.fsu.edu	Tallahassee	FL	32306	850-644-5211	644-5016*
Stetson University DuPont-Ball Library 421 N Woodland Blvd Unit 8418 *Web:* www.stetson.edu/departments/library	DeLand	FL	32720	386-822-7183	822-7199
University of Central Florida Library PO Box 162666 *Web:* www.library.ucf.edu	Orlando	FL	32816	407-823-2564	823-2529
University of Florida Libraries PO Box 117001 *Web:* www.uflib.ufl.edu	Gainesville	FL	32611	352-392-0342	392-7251
University of Miami Richter Library PO Box 248214 **Fax:* Admin ■ *Web:* www.library.miami.edu	Coral Gables	FL	33124	305-284-3551	284-4027*
University of North Florida Carpenter Library 4567 St Johns Bluff Rd S Bldg 12 *Web:* www.unf.edu/library	Jacksonville	FL	32224	904-620-2616	620-2719
Emory University Woodruff Library 540 Asbury Cir **Fax:* Admin ■ *Web:* www.emory.edu/libraries.cfm	Atlanta	GA	30322	404-727-6861	727-0805*
Georgia Institute of Technology Library 225 N Ave NW *Web:* www.library.gatech.edu	Atlanta	GA	30332	404-894-4500	894-0399
Georgia Southern University Henderson Library PO Box 8074 *Web:* www.library.georgiasouthern.edu	Statesboro	GA	30460	912-681-5115	681-0093
University of Georgia Library 320 S Jackson St **Fax:* Admin ■ *Web:* www.libs.uga.edu	Athens	GA	30602	706-542-0621	542-4144*
Valdosta State University Odum Library 1500 N Patterson St *Web:* www.valdosta.edu	Valdosta	GA	31698	229-333-5869	219-1362
University of Hawaii at Hilo *Edwin H. Mookini Library* 200 W Kawili St *Web:* hilo.hawaii.edu	Hilo	HI	96720	808-974-7344	974-4106
University of Hawaii at Manoa *Hamilton Library* 2550 McCarthy Mall *Web:* www.libweb.hawaii.edu	Honolulu	HI	96822	808-956-7214	956-7109
Boise State University Albertsons Library 1910 University Dr *Web:* library.boisestate.edu	Boise	ID	83725	208-426-1204	426-1885
Idaho State University Oboler Library 850 S 9th Ave Bldg 50 CB 8089 *Web:* www.isu.edu/library	Pocatello	ID	83209	208-282-2958	282-5847
Bradley University Cullom-Davis Library 1501 W Bradley Ave *Web:* library.bradley.edu	Peoria	IL	61625	309-677-2850	677-2558
DePaul University Loop Campus Library 1 E Jackson Blvd 10th Fl *Web:* www.lib.depaul.edu	Chicago	IL	60605	312-362-8433	362-6186
Illinois State University Milner Library 201 N School St **Fax:* Admin ■ *Web:* www.illinoisstate.edu	Normal	IL	61790	309-438-3451	438-3676*
Knox College Seymour Library 2 E S St *Web:* www.knox.edu	Galesburg	IL	61401	309-341-7246	341-7799
Northeastern Illinois University Williams Library 5500 N St Louis Ave *Web:* www.neiu.edu	Chicago	IL	60625	773-442-4470	442-4531
Northern Illinois University University Libraries 1425 W Lincoln Hwy *Web:* www.niu.edu	DeKalb	IL	60115	815-753-1094	753-9803
Northwestern University Library 1970 Campus Dr *Web:* www.library.northwestern.edu	Evanston	IL	60208	847-491-7658	491-8306
Quincy University Brenner Library 1800 College Ave *Web:* www.quincy.edu/library	Quincy	IL	62301	217-228-5345	228-5354
Southern Illinois University Carbondale Morris Library 605 Agriculture Dr MC 6632 *Web:* www.lib.siu.edu	Carbondale	IL	62901	618-453-2522	453-3440
University of Chicago Library 1100 E 57th St *Web:* www.lib.uchicago.edu	Chicago	IL	60637	773-702-8740	702-6623
University of Illinois Chicago *Daley Library* 801 S Morgan St Rm 1-280 *Web:* www.uic.edu/depts/lib	Chicago	IL	60607	312-996-2716	413-0424
University of Illinois Springfield *Brookens Library* 1 University Plaza *Web:* library.uis.edu	Springfield	IL	62703	217-206-6633	206-6208
University of Illinois Urbana-Champaign *Library* 1408 W Gregory Dr MC-522 *Web:* www.library.uiuc.edu	Urbana	IL	61801	217-333-2290	333-2214
Ball State University Bracken Library 2000 University Ave *Web:* www.cms.bsu.edu	Muncie	IN	47306	765-285-5143	285-2644
Butler University Irwin Library 4600 Sunset Ave *Web:* www.butler.edu/library	Indianapolis	IN	46208	317-940-9227	940-9711
DePauw University West Library 11 E Larabee St *Web:* www.depauw.edu/library	Greencastle	IN	46135	765-658-4420	658-4445
Indiana State University Cunningham Memorial Library 650 Sycamore St **Fax:* Admin ■ *TF reference:* 800-851-4279 ■ *Web:* www.odin.indstate.edu	Terre Haute	IN	47809	812-237-2580	237-2567*
Indiana University Bloomington *Libraries* 1320 E 10th St *Web:* www.libraries.iub.edu	Bloomington	IN	47405	812-855-8028	855-2576
Indiana University Northwest *Library* 3400 Broadway *Web:* www.iun.edu/lib	Gary	IN	46408	219-980-6580	980-6558
Indiana University South Bend *Schurz Library* 1700 Mishawaka Ave PO Box 7111 *Web:* www.iusb.edu/libg	South Bend	IN	46634	574-527-4440	520-4472
Indiana University-Purdue University Fort Wayne *Helmke Library* 2101 E Coliseum Blvd *Web:* www.lib.ipfw.edu	Fort Wayne	IN	46805	260-481-6514	481-6509
Indiana University-Purdue University Indianapolis *Library* 755 W Michigan St *Web:* www.ulib.iupui.edu	Indianapolis	IN	46202	317-274-0462	278-2300
University of Notre Dame Hesburgh Library 221 Hesburgh Library *Web:* www.library.nd.edu	Notre Dame	IN	46556	574-631-5252	631-6772
Drake University Cowles Library 2507 University Ave *Web:* www.library.drake.edu	Des Moines	IA	50311	515-271-2111	271-3933
Grinnell College Burling Library 6th Ave High St *Web:* www.grinnell.edu	Grinnell	IA	50112	641-269-3371	269-4283
Iowa State University Parks Library Osborn Dr & Morrill Rd *Web:* www.lib.iastate.edu	Ames	IA	50011	515-294-3642	294-5525
Saint Ambrose University O'Keefe Library 518 W Locust St *TF:* 888-272-8542 ■ *Web:* www.library.sau.edu	Davenport	IA	52803	563-333-6245	333-6248
University of Iowa Libraries 100 Main Library **Fax:* library ■ *Web:* www.lib.uiowa.edu	Iowa City	IA	52242	319-335-5299	335-5900*
Kansas State University Hale Library 137 Hale Library Mid-Campus Dr **Fax:* Admin ■ *Web:* www.lib.ksu.edu	Manhattan	KS	66506	785-532-3014	532-7415*
MidAmerica Nazarene University Mabee Library 2030 E College Way *Web:* www.mnu.edu/academics/mabee	Olathe	KS	66062	913-791-3485	791-3285
Pittsburg State University Axe Library 1701 S Broadway *Web:* www.library.pittstate.edu	Pittsburg	KS	66762	620-235-4882	235-4090
University of Kansas Watson Library 1425 Jayhawk Blvd **Fax:* Admin ■ *Web:* www.lib.ku.edu	Lawrence	KS	66045	785-864-3956	864-8986*
Wichita State University Ablah Library (WSU) 1845 Fairmount St PO Box 68 *Web:* www.library.wichita.edu	Wichita	KS	67260	316-978-3481	978-3048
Berea College Hutchins Library 100 Campus Dr *Web:* www.berea.edu/hutchinslibrary	Berea	KY	40404	859-985-3364	985-3912
Kentucky State University Blazer Library 400 E Main St *Web:* www.kysu.edu	Frankfort	KY	40601	502-597-6852	597-5068
University of Kentucky Young Library 500 S Limestone St *Web:* www.uky.edu/Libraries/wty.html	Lexington	KY	40506	859-257-0500	257-0505
University of Louisville Ekstrom Library 2301 S 3rd St *Web:* www.louisville.edu	Louisville	KY	40292	502-852-6747	852-7394
Western Kentucky University Libraries 1906 College Heights Blvd Suite 11067 *Web:* www.wku.edu/Library	Bowling Green	KY	42101	270-745-2904	745-6422
Grambling State University Lewis Memorial Library 100 Johnson St *Web:* www.gram.edu/library	Grambling	LA	71245	318-274-2568	274-3268
Louisiana Tech University Prescott Memorial Library PO Box 10408 *Web:* www.latech.edu/library	Ruston	LA	71272	318-257-3555	257-2447
McNeese State University Frazar Memorial Library PO Box 91445 *TF:* 800-622-3352 ■ *Web:* www.libguides.mcneese.edu	Lake Charles	LA	70609	337-475-5725	475-5727
Nicholls State University Ellender Memorial Library 906 E 1st St *Web:* www.nicholls.edu/library	Thibodaux	LA	70301	985-448-4646	448-4925
Northwestern State University Watson Memorial Library 913 University Pkwy *TF:* 888-540-9657 ■ *Web:* library.nsula.edu	Natchitoches	LA	71497	318-357-4477	357-4470
Southeastern Louisiana University Sims Memorial Library SLU 10896 *Web:* www.selu.edu/library	Hammond	LA	70402	985-549-3860	549-3995
Tulane University Howard-Tilton Memorial Library 7001 Freret St *Web:* www.library.tulane.edu	New Orleans	LA	70118	504-865-5131	865-6773

Library	City	State	ZIP	Phone	Fax
University of Louisiana at Lafayette *Dupre Library* 302 E St Mary Blvd *Web:* www.library.louisiana.edu	Lafayette	LA	70504	337-482-6025	482-5841
University of New Orleans Long Library 2000 Lakeshore Dr *Web:* www.library.uno.edu	New Orleans	LA	70148	504-280-6556	280-7277
Xavier University of Louisiana Library 1 Drexel Dr *Web:* www.xula.edu/library	New Orleans	LA	70125	504-520-7304	520-7917
Bates College Ladd Library 48 Campus Ave *Web:* www.abacus.bates.edu/library	Lewiston	ME	04240	207-786-6263	786-6055
Bowdoin College Hawthorne-Longfellow Library 3000 College Stn *Web:* www.library.bowdoin.edu	Brunswick	ME	04011	207-725-3280	725-3083
Colby College Miller Library 5100 Mayflower Hill *Web:* www.colby.edu/academics_cs/library	Waterville	ME	04901	207-859-5147	859-5105
Bowie State University Marshall Library 14000 Jericho Pk Rd *Web:* www.bowiestate.edu/research/libraries	Bowie	MD	20715	301-860-3850	860-3848
Frostburg State University Ort Library 1 Stadium Dr *Web:* www.frostburg.edu/dept/library	Frostburg	MD	21532	301-687-4395	687-7069
Johns Hopkins University Sheridan Libraries 3400 N Charles St *Web:* www.library.jhu.edu	Baltimore	MD	21218	410-516-8325	516-5080
Salisbury University Blackwell Library 1101 Camden Ave *Web:* www.salisbury.edu/library	Salisbury	MD	21801	410-543-6130	543-6203
Towson University Cook Library 8000 York Rd *Web:* cooklibrary.towson.edu	Towson	MD	21252	410-704-2461	704-3292
University of Baltimore Langsdale Library 1420 Maryland Ave *Web:* www.langsdale.ubalt.edu	Baltimore	MD	21201	410-837-4260	837-4248
University of Maryland Baltimore county *Kuhn Library* 1000 Hilltop Cir *Web:* www.umbc.edu/aok	Baltimore	MD	21250	410-455-2232	
Amherst College Frost Library PO Box 5000 *Web:* www.amherst.edu/library	Amherst	MA	01002	413-542-2373	542-2662
Boston College Libraries 140 Commonwealth Ave *Web:* www.bc.edu/libraries	Chestnut Hill	MA	02467	617-552-4472	552-0599
Boston University Mugar Memorial Library 771 Commonwealth Ave *Web:* www.bu.edu/library	Boston	MA	02215	617-353-3710	353-2084
Brandeis University Library PO Box 549110 *Web:* www.lts.brandeis.edu	Waltham	MA	02454	781-736-4700	736-4719
Bridgewater State College Maxwell Library 10 Shaw Rd *Web:* www.bridgew.edu/library	Bridgewater	MA	02325	508-531-1392	531-1349
College of the Holy Cross Dinand Library 1 College St *Web:* www.holycross.edu	Worcester	MA	01610	508-793-2642	793-2372
Harvard University Widener Library Hardvar yard Rm 110 *Web:* www.hul.harvard.edu	Cambridge	MA	02138	617-495-3650	496-8740
Massachusetts Institute of Technology Libraries 77 Massachusetts Ave *Web:* libraries.mit.edu	Cambridge	MA	02139	617-253-5651	253-8894
Mount Holyoke College Williston Memorial Library 50 College St *Web:* www.mtholyoke.edu/lits/library	South Hadley	MA	01075	413-538-2230	538-2370
Northeastern University Snell Library 360 Huntington Ave *Web:* www.lib.neu.edu	Boston	MA	02115	617-373-2350	373-5409
Simmons College Beatley Library 300 The Fenway *Web:* www.my.simmons.edu/library	Boston	MA	02115	617-521-2780	521-3093
Suffolk University Sawyer Library 8 Ashburton Pl *Web:* www.suffolk.edu/sawlib	Boston	MA	02108	617-573-8535	573-8756
Tufts University Tisch Library 35 Professors Row *Web:* www.library.tufts.edu/tisch	Medford	MA	02155	617-627-3345	627-3002
University of Massachusetts Amherst *Du Bois Library* 154 Hicks Way *Web:* www.library.umass.edu	Amherst	MA	01003	413-545-0284	545-6873
University of Massachusetts Boston *Healey Library* 100 Morrissey Blvd *Web:* www.lib.umb.edu	Boston	MA	02125	617-287-5900	287-5955
University of Massachusetts Dartmouth *Library* 285 Old Westport Rd *Web:* www.lib.umassd.edu	North Dartmouth	MA	02747	508-999-8675	999-9142
University of Massachusetts Lowell *Lydon Library* 84 University Ave *Web:* www.library.uml.edu	Lowell	MA	01854	978-934-3205	934-3014
Andrews University James White Library 4190 Administration Dr *TF:* 800-253-2874 ■ *Web:* www.andrews.edu/library	Berrien Springs	MI	49104	269-471-3264	471-6166
Calvin College Hekman Library 3201 Burton St SE *Web:* www.calvin.edu	Grand Rapids	MI	49546	616-957-7197	526-6470
Central Michigan University Clarke Historical Library 300 E Preston St *Web:* www.clarke.cmich.edu	Mount Pleasant	MI	48859	989-774-3352	774-2160
Eastern Michigan University Halle Library 955 W Cir Dr *Web:* www.emich.edu/halle	Ypsilanti	MI	48197	734-487-0020	487-8861
Grand Valley State University Zumberge Library 1 Campus Dr *TF:* 800-879-0581 ■ *Web:* www.gvsu.edu/library	Allendale	MI	49401	616-331-3252	
Hope College Van Wylen Library 53 Graves Pl *TF:* 800-968-7850 ■ *Web:* www.hope.edu	Holland	MI	49423	616-395-7790	395-7965
Kalamazoo College Upjohn Library 1200 Academy St *Web:* www.kzoo.edu/is/library	Kalamazoo	MI	49006	269-337-7153	337-7143
Lake Superior State University Shouldice Library 650 W Easterday Ave *Web:* www.lssu.edu/library	Sault Sainte Marie	MI	49783	906-632-6841	635-2111
Michigan State University Library 100 Library *TF:* 800-500-1554 ■ *Web:* www.lib.msu.edu	East Lansing	MI	48824	517-353-8700	432-1191
Michigan Technological University J R Van Pelt Library 1400 Townsend Dr *Web:* www.mtu.edu/library	Houghton	MI	49931	906-487-2507	487-2357
Saginaw Valley State University Zahnow Library 7400 Bay Rd *TF:* 800-968-9500 ■ *Web:* www.svsu.edu/library	University Center	MI	48710	989-964-4240	964-4383
University of Michigan Dearborn *Mardigian Library* 4901 Evergreen Rd *Web:* www.umd.umich.edu	Dearborn	MI	48128	313-593-5445	593-5561
Wayne State University Libraries 5150 Anthony Wayne Dr Suite 1210 *Web:* www.lib.wayne.edu	Detroit	MI	48202	313-577-4023	577-5265
Western Michigan University Waldo Library 1903 W Michigan Ave MS 5353 *Web:* www.wmich.edu	Kalamazoo	MI	49008	269-387-5202	387-5077
Bemidji State University Clark Library 1500 Birchmont Dr NE *Web:* www.bemidjistate.edu/library	Bemidji	MN	56601	218-755-3345	
Bethel University Library 3900 Bethel Dr *Web:* www.library.bethel.edu	Saint Paul	MN	55112	651-638-6222	635-1971
Carleton College Gould Library 1 N College St *Web:* www.apps.carleton.edu	Northfield	MN	55057	507-646-4260	646-4087
College of Saint Benedict Clemens Library 37 S College Ave *Web:* www.csbsju.edu/library	Saint Joseph	MN	56374	320-363-5611	363-5197
Hamline University Bush Memorial Library 1536 Hewitt Ave *Web:* www.hamline.edu	Saint Paul	MN	55104	651-523-2375	523-2199
Macalester College Wallace Library 1600 Grand Ave *Web:* www.macalester.edu/library	Saint Paul	MN	55105	651-696-6346	696-6617
Minnesota State University Mankato *Memorial Library* PO Box 8419 *Web:* www.lib.mnsu.edu	Mankato	MN	56002	507-389-5952	389-5155
Minnesota State University Moorhead *Lord Library* 1104 7th Ave S *Web:* www.mnstate.edu/library	Moorhead	MN	56563	218-477-2922	477-5924
Saint Cloud State University Library 720 4th Ave S *Web:* www.lrts.stcloudstate.edu/library	Saint Cloud	MN	56301	320-308-2022	308-4778
Saint Olaf College Libraries 1510 St Olaf Ave *Web:* www.stolaf.edu/library	Northfield	MN	55057	507-646-3224	646-3734
University of Minnesota Crookston *UMC Library* 2900 University Ave *Web:* www1.crk.umn.edu	Crookston	MN	56716	218-281-8399	281-8080
University of Minnesota Duluth *UMD Library* 416 Library Dr *Web:* www.d.umn.edu/lib	Duluth	MN	55812	218-726-8102	726-8019
University of Minnesota Morris *Briggs Library* 600 E 4th St *Web:* www.morris.umn.edu	Morris	MN	56267	320-589-6176	589-6168
University of Minnesota Twin Cities *Wilson Library* 309 19th Ave S *Web:* www.wilson.lib.umn.edu	Minneapolis	MN	55455	612-624-0303	626-9353
University of Saint Thomas O'Shaughnessy-Frey Library 2115 Summit Ave MS 5004 *Web:* www.stthomas.edu/libraries	Saint Paul	MN	55105	651-962-5494	962-5406
Winona State University Krueger Library PO Box 5838 *Web:* www.winona.edu/library	Winona	MN	55987	507-457-5140	457-5594
Mississippi State University Library PO Box 5408 *Web:* www.library.msstate.edu	Mississippi State	MS	39762	662-325-7667	325-0011
University of Central Missouri Kirkpatrick Library 601 S Missouri *Web:* www.library.ucmo.edu	Warrensburg	MO	64093	660-543-4565	543-8001
University of Missouri Columbia *Ellis Library* 104 Ellis Library **Fax:* library ■ *Web:* www.mulibraries.missouri.edu	Columbia	MO	65201	573-882-4701	882-8044*
University of Missouri Kansas City *Nichols Library* 800 E 51st St *Web:* www.umkc.edu	Kansas City	MO	64110	816-235-1534	333-5584
University of Missouri Saint Louis *Jefferson Library* 1 University Blvd *Web:* www.umsl.edu/services/tjl	Saint Louis	MO	63121	314-516-5060	516-5853
Washington University in Saint Louis Olin Library 1 Brookings Dr PO Box 1061 *Web:* library.wustl.edu	Saint Louis	MO	63130	314-935-5400	935-4045
University of Montana Missoula *Mansfield Library* 32 Campus Dr *Web:* www.lib.umt.edu	Missoula	MT	59812	406-243-6860	243-4067
University of Montana Western *Carson Library* 710 S Atlantic St *Web:* www.umwestern.edu/library	Dillon	MT	59725	406-683-7541	683-7493

	City	State	ZIP	Phone	Fax
Peru State College Library 600 Hoyt St PO Box 10 *Web:* www.peru.edu	Peru	NE	68421	402-872-2218	872-2311
University of Nebraska Lincoln *Love Memorial Library* 318 Love Library PO Box 884100 *Web:* www.libraries.unl.edu	Lincoln	NE	68588	402-472-2848	472-5131
University of Nebraska Omaha *University Library* 6001 Dodge St *Web:* library.unomaha.edu	Omaha	NE	68182	402-554-2800	554-3215
University of Nevada Las Vegas *Lied Library* 4505 S Maryland Pkwy *Web:* library.nevada.edu	Las Vegas	NV	89154	702-895-3011	895-2287
University of Nevada Reno *Getchell Library* 1664 N Virginia St *Web:* www.unr.edu/around-campus/facilities/getchell	Reno	NV	89557	775-784-1110	784-4529
Dartmouth College Baker-Berry Library HB 6025 **Fax:* Admin ■ *Web:* www.library.dartmouth.edu	Hanover	NH	03755	603-646-2236	646-3702*
Keene State College Mason Library 229 Main St *TF:* 800-573-1909 ■ *Web:* www.keene.edu	Keene	NH	03435	603-358-2711	
Plymouth State University Lamson Library Highland Ave *Web:* www.plymouth.edu/library	Plymouth	NH	03264	603-535-2258	535-2445
Princeton University Library 1 Washington Rd **Fax:* library ■ *Web:* www.library.princeton.edu	Princeton	NJ	08544	609-258-4820	258-0441*
Rider University Moore Library 2083 Lawrenceville Rd *Web:* www.rider.edu	Lawrenceville	NJ	08648	609-896-5111	896-8029
William Paterson University Cheng Library 300 Pompton Rd *Web:* www.wpunj.edu/library	Wayne	NJ	07470	973-720-2541	720-2585
Eastern New Mexico University Golden Library (ENMU) 1500 S Ave K *TF:* 800-367-3668 ■ *Web:* www.enmu.edu/academics/library	Portales	NM	88130	505-562-2624	562-2647
New Mexico Institute of Mining & Technology Skeen Library 801 Leroy Pl *Web:* www.nmt.edu	Socorro	NM	87801	505-835-5434	835-6666
Library 2911 McFie Cir Dept 3475 PO Box 30006 *Web:* www.lib.nmsu.edu	Las Cruces	NM	88003	575-646-6928	646-7477
University of New Mexico The *Zimmerman Library* 1 University of New Mexico MSC 05 3020 *Web:* www.elibrary.unm.edu	Albuquerque	NM	87131	505-277-9100	
Bard College Stevenson Library PO Box 5000 *Web:* www.bard.edu/library	Annandale-on-Hudson	NY	12504	845-758-6822	758-5801
Baruch College The William & Anita Newman Library 151 E 25th St *Web:* www.newman.baruch.cuny.edu	New York	NY	10010	646-312-1600	
Brooklyn College Library 2900 Bedford Ave *Web:* library.brooklyn.cuny.edu	Brooklyn	NY	11210	718-951-5335	951-4540
Buffalo State College EH Butler Library 1300 Elmwood Ave *Web:* www.buffalostate.edu/library	Buffalo	NY	14222	716-878-6314	878-4316
City College of New York Cohen Library NAC Bldg *Web:* www.ccny.cuny.edu/library	New York	NY	10031	212-650-7155	650-7604
Colgate University Case Library 13 Oak Dr *Web:* www.colgate.edu	Hamilton	NY	13346	315-228-7300	228-7934
Columbia University Butler Library 535 W 114th St *Web:* www.columbia.edu/cu/lweb	New York	NY	10027	212-854-2271	854-9099
Cornell University Olin Library Olin & Uris Libraries *Web:* www.olinuris.library.cornell.edu	Ithaca	NY	14853	607-255-4144	255-6788
Hamilton College Burke Library 198 College Hill Rd *Web:* www.hamilton.edu/library	Clinton	NY	13323	315-859-4475	859-4578
Hofstra University Axinn Library 123 Hofstra University *Web:* www.hofstra.edu	Hempstead	NY	11549	516-463-5940	463-6387
Hunter College Library 695 Pk Ave *Web:* www.library.hunter.cuny.edu	New York	NY	10021	212-772-4179	772-4142
Ithaca College Library 1201 Gannett Ctr *Web:* www.ithaca.edu/library	Ithaca	NY	14850	607-274-3206	274-1539
Jewish Theological Seminary Library 3080 Broadway *Web:* www.jtsa.edu/library	New York	NY	10027	212-678-8075	678-8891
Lehman College Library 250 Bedford Pk Blvd W *Web:* www.lehman.edu/provost/library	Bronx	NY	10468	718-960-8577	960-8952
New York University Bobst Library 70 Washington Sq S *Web:* www.library.nyu.edu	New York	NY	10012	212-998-2500	995-4829
Niagara University Library Lewison Rd *Web:* www.niagara.edu/library	Niagara University	NY	14109	716-286-8020	286-8030
Rensselaer Polytechnic Institute Folsom Library 110 8th St *Web:* library.rpi.edu	Troy	NY	12180	518-276-6000	276-8559
Rochester Institute of Technology Wallace Library 90 Lomb Memorial Dr *Web:* www.library.rit.edu	Rochester	NY	14623	585-475-2562	475-7007
Rockefeller University *Library* 1230 York Ave PO Box 263 *Web:* www.rockefeller.edu/library	New York	NY	10021	212-327-8915	327-7840
State University of New York College at Cortland *Memorial Library* PO Box 2000 *Web:* www2.cortland.edu	Cortland	NY	13045	607-753-2590	753-5669
State University of New York College at Geneseo *Milne Library* 1 College Cir *Web:* www.geneseo.edu	Geneseo	NY	14454	585-245-5594	245-5769
Syracuse University Bird Library 222 Waverly Ave **Fax:* Admin ■ *Web:* www.library.syr.edu	Syracuse	NY	13244	315-443-2093	443-9510*
University at Albany University Libraries 1400 Washington Ave *Web:* library.albany.edu	Albany	NY	12222	518-442-3600	442-3567
University at Buffalo *University Libraries* Capen Hall Rm 432 *Web:* www.ublib.buffalo.edu/libraries	Buffalo	NY	14260	716-645-2965	645-3844
University of Rochester River Campus Libraries 755 Library Rd PO Box 270055 *Web:* www.library.rochester.edu	Rochester	NY	14627	585-275-5804	273-5309
Vassar College Library 124 Raymond Ave PO Box 20 *Web:* www.library.vassar.edu	Poughkeepsie	NY	12604	845-437-5760	437-5864
Wells College Long Library Main St *Web:* www.wells.edu/LIBRARY/welcome.htm	Aurora	NY	13026	315-364-3351	364-3412
Appalachian State University *Belk Library* 218 College St PO Box 32026 **Fax:* Administration ■ *Web:* www.library.appstate.edu	Boone	NC	28608	828-262-2300	262-3001*
Duke University Perkins Library PO Box 90193 *Web:* www.library.duke.edu	Durham	NC	27708	919-660-5800	660-5923
East Carolina University Joyner Library E 5th St *Web:* www.ecu.edu/cs-lib	Greenville	NC	27858	252-328-6518	328-4834
North Carolina State University Libraries CB 7111 **Fax:* Admin ■ *Web:* www.lib.ncsu.edu	Raleigh	NC	27695	919-515-2843	515-3628*
University of North Carolina Chapel Hill *Davis Library* cb3900 *Web:* www.lib.unc.edu	Chapel Hill	NC	27514	919-962-1356	843-8936
University of North Carolina Charlotte *Atkins Library* 9201 University City Blvd *Web:* www.library.uncc.edu	Charlotte	NC	28223	704-687-2030	687-3050
University of North Carolina Greensboro *Jackson Library* PO Box 26170 *Web:* www.library.uncg.edu	Greensboro	NC	27402	336-334-5880	334-5399
University of North Carolina Wilmington *Randall Library* 601 S College Rd *Web:* www.library.uncwil.edu	Wilmington	NC	28403	910-962-3272	962-3078
Wake Forest University Reynolds Library PO Box 7777 *Web:* www.zsr.wfu.edu	Winston-Salem	NC	27109	336-758-4931	758-5605
North Dakota State University Library NDSU Dept 2080 PO Box 6050 *Web:* www.library.ndsu.edu	Fargo	ND	58108	701-231-8888	231-7138
University of North Dakota Chester Fritz Library 3051 university Ave Sp 9000 **Fax:* library ■ *Web:* www.library.und.edu	Grand Forks	ND	58202	701-777-2189	777-3319*
Ashland University Library 509 College Ave *Web:* www.ashland.edu	Ashland	OH	44805	419-289-5400	289-5422
Bowling Green State University Jerome Library 1001 E Wooster St *Web:* www.bgsu.edu/colleges/library	Bowling Green	OH	43403	419-372-2051	372-0475
Case Western Reserve University kelvin Smith Library 11055 Euclid Ave *Web:* www.library.case.edu/ksl	Cleveland	OH	44106	216-368-3506	368-3669
Cedarville University Centennial Library 251 N Main St *TF:* 800-233-2784 ■ *Web:* www.cedarville.edu/academics/library	Cedarville	OH	45314	937-766-7700	766-2337
Cleveland State University University Library 2121 Euclid Ave Rhodes Tower *Web:* www.ulib.csuohio.edu	Cleveland	OH	44115	216-687-5300	687-5098
Denison University Doane Library 400 W Loop PO Box L *Web:* www.denison.edu/library	Granville	OH	43023	740-587-6235	587-6285
Libraries PO Box 5190 **Fax:* Admin ■ *Web:* www.library.kent.edu	Kent	OH	44242	330-672-2962	672-4811*
Oberlin College Library 148 W College St *Web:* www.oberlin.edu	Oberlin	OH	44074	440-775-8285	775-8739
Ohio Northern University Heterick Memorial Library 525 S Main St *Web:* www.onu.edu/library	Ada	OH	45810	419-772-2181	772-1927
Shawnee State University Clark Memorial Library 940 2nd St *Web:* www.shawnee.edu/off/cml	Portsmouth	OH	45662	740-351-3267	351-3432
University of Akron Bierce Library 315 Buchtel Common Rm 161 *Web:* www.uakron.edu/libraries	Akron	OH	44325	330-972-7497	972-5106
University of Cincinnati Langsam Library PO Box 210033 **Fax:* Admin ■ *Web:* www.libraries.uc.edu	Cincinnati	OH	45221	513-556-1515	556-0325*
University of Toledo Carlson Library 2801 W Bancroft St MS 509 *Web:* www.utoledo.edu/library	Toledo	OH	43606	419-530-2324	530-2726
Wittenberg University Thomas Library 807 Woodlawn Ave PO Box 7207 *TF:* 800-677-7558 ■ *Web:* www6.wittenberg.edu/lib	Springfield	OH	45504	937-327-7511	327-6139
Wright State University Dunbar Library 3640 Colonel Glenn Hwy Rm 126 *Web:* www.libraries.wright.edu	Dayton	OH	45435	937-775-4125	775-2356
Xavier University McDonald Memorial Library 3800 Victory Pkwy *Web:* www.xavier.edu/library	Cincinnati	OH	45207	513-745-3884	745-1932

				Phone	Fax
Youngstown State University Maag Library					
1 University Plaza	Youngstown	OH	44555	330-941-3675	941-3734
Web: www.maag.ysu.edu					
East Central University Linscheid Library					
1100 E 14th St	Ada	OK	74820	580-310-5376	436-3242
Web: www.ecok.edu					
Oral Roberts University Library					
7777 S Lewis Ave	Tulsa	OK	74171	918-495-6723	495-6893
Web: www.oru.edu/university/library					
University of Oklahoma Bizzell Memorial Library					
401 W Brooks St	Norman	OK	73019	405-325-4142	325-7550*
**Fax:* Admin ■ *Web:* www.libraries.ou.edu					
University of Tulsa McFarlin Library					
2933 E 6th St	Tulsa	OK	74104	918-631-2352	631-3791
Web: www.lib.utulsa.edu					
Eastern Oregon University Pierce Library					
1 University Blvd	La Grande	OR	97850	541-962-3864	962-3335
Web: pierce.eou.edu/home					
Lewis & Clark College Watzek Library					
0615 Palatine Hill Rd	Portland	OR	97219	503-768-7270	768-7282
Web: library.lclark.edu					
Oregon State University Valley Library					
121 Valley Library	Corvallis	OR	97331	541-737-3411	737-3453*
**Fax:* Admin ■ *Web:* www.osulibrary.oregonstate.edu					
Pacific University Library					
2043 College Way	Forest Grove	OR	97116	503-352-1400	352-1416
Web: www.pacificu.edu/library					
Portland State University Millar Library					
1875 SW Pk Ave	Portland	OR	97201	503-725-4424	
Web: www.pdx.edu/library					
Reed College Library 3203 SE Woodstock Blvd	Portland	OR	97202	503-777-7702	777-7786
Web: library.reed.edu					
Southern Oregon University Hannon Library					
1250 Siskiyou Blvd	Ashland	OR	97520	541-552-6441	552-6429
Web: www.sou.edu/library					
University of Oregon Knight Library					
1299 University of Oregon	Eugene	OR	97403	541-346-3053	346-3485*
**Fax:* library ■ *Web:* www.libweb.uoregon.edu					
Western Oregon University Hamersly Library					
345 N Monmouth Ave	Monmouth	OR	97361	503-838-8418	838-8645
Web: www.wou.edu/provost/library					
Willamette University Hatfield Library					
900 State St	Salem	OR	97301	503-370-6312	370-6141
Web: library.willamette.edu					
Bloomsburg University Harvey A. Andruss Library					
400 E 2nd St	Bloomsburg	PA	17815	570-389-4000	389-3895
Web: www.guides.library.bloomu.edu					
Bucknell University Bertrand Library					
69 Coleman Hall Rd	Lewisburg	PA	17837	570-577-1557	577-3313
Web: www.bucknell.edu/isr					
California University of Pennsylvania Louis L Manderino Library					
250 University Ave	California	PA	15419	724-938-4091	938-5901
Web: www.library.calu.edu					
Carnegie Mellon University Libraries					
4909 Frew St	Pittsburgh	PA	15213	412-268-2446	268-2793
Web: www.search.library.cmu.edu					
Dickinson College Waidner-Spahr Library					
PO Box 1773	Carlisle	PA	17013	717-245-1397	245-1439
Web: lis.dickinson.edu					
Drexel University Hagerty Library					
33rd St & Market St	Philadelphia	PA	19104	215-895-2767	895-2070
TF: 888-278-8825 ■ *Web:* www.library.drexel.edu					
Duquesne University Gumberg Library					
600 Forbes Ave	Pittsburgh	PA	15282	412-396-6130	396-1658
Web: www.duq.edu/library					
East Stroudsburg University Kemp Library					
200 Prospect St	East Stroudsburg	PA	18301	570-422-3465	422-3151
Web: www.esu.edu/library					
Edinboro University of Pennsylvania Baron-Forness Library					
200 Tartan Rd	Edinboro	PA	16444	814-732-2273	732-2883
Web: www.edinboro.edu/cwis/Library/Menu.html					
Franklin & Marshall College Shadek-Fackenthal Library					
450 College Ave	Lancaster	PA	17604	717-291-4223	291-4160
Web: www.fandm.edu					
Haverford College Magill Library					
370 Lancaster Ave	Haverford	PA	19041	610-896-1163	896-1102
Web: www.haverford.edu/library					
Indiana University of Pennsylvania Stapleton Library					
431 S 11th St	Indiana	PA	15705	724-357-2330	357-4891
Web: www.lib.iup.edu/library					
Kutztown University Rohrbach Library					
15200 Kutztown Rd Bldg 5	Kutztown	PA	19530	610-683-4480	683-4483
Web: www.kutztown.edu/library					
La Salle University Connelly Library					
1900 W Olney Ave	Philadelphia	PA	19141	215-951-1287	951-1595
Web: www.lasalle.edu/library					
Lafayette College Skillman Library					
710 Sullivan Rd	Easton	PA	18042	610-330-5151	252-0370
Web: www.library.lafayette.edu					
Lehigh University EW Fairchild-Martindale Library					
8A E Packer Ave Asa Packer Campus	Bethlehem	PA	18015	610-758-3025	758-3004
Web: www4.lehigh.edu/default.aspx					
Mansfield University North Hall Library					
1 Mansfield University of Pennsylvania	Mansfield	PA	16933	570-662-4000	662-4993
Web: www.lib.mansfield.edu					
Libraries 510 Paterno Library	University Park	PA	16802	814-865-0401	865-3665
Web: www.libraries.psu.edu					
Swarthmore College McCabe Library					
500 College Ave	Swarthmore	PA	19081	610-328-8477	328-7329
Web: www.swarthmore.edu					
Temple University Paley Library					
1210 W Berks St MS 017-00	Philadelphia	PA	19122	215-204-8231	204-5201
Web: www.library.temple.edu					
University of Pennsylvania Van Pelt Library					
3420 Walnut St	Philadelphia	PA	19104	215-898-7091	898-0559
Web: www.library.upenn.edu/vanpelt					
Hillman Library 3960 Forbes Ave	Pittsburgh	PA	15260	412-648-7710	648-7887
Web: www.library.pitt.edu					
Villanova University Falvey Memorial Library					
800 Lancaster Ave	Villanova	PA	19085	610-519-4270	519-5018
Web: www.library.villanova.edu					
West Chester University Green Library					
29 W Rosedale Ave	West Chester	PA	19383	610-436-2747	738-0555
Web: www.wcupa.edu/library.fhg					
Brown University Rockefeller Library					
10 Prospect St	Providence	RI	02912	401-863-2162	863-1272
Web: www.brown.edu					
Bryant University Krupp Library					
1150 Douglas Pike	Smithfield	RI	02917	401-232-6125	232-6126
Web: www.bryant.edu/bryant/library.jsp					
Salve Regina University McKillop Library					
100 Ochre Pt Ave	Newport	RI	02840	401-341-2291	341-2951
Web: www.library.salve.edu					
Clemson University Library					
413 Cooper Library PO Box 343001	Clemson	SC	29634	864-656-5186	656-3025
Web: www.clemson.edu					
Francis Marion University Rogers Library					
PO Box 100547	Florence	SC	29501	843-661-1310	661-1309
Web: www.fmarion.edu/academics/library					
Dakota State University Mundt Library					
820 N Washington Ave	Madison	SD	57042	605-256-5203	256-5208
Web: www.departments.dsu.edu/library					
South Dakota State University Briggs Library					
N Campus Dr PO Box 2115	Brookings	SD	57007	605-688-5106	688-6133
TF: 800-786-2038 ■ *Web:* www.sdstate.edu					
University of South Dakota Weeks Library					
414 E Clark St	Vermillion	SD	57069	605-677-5371	677-5488
Web: www.usd.edu					
Austin Peay State University Woodward Library					
PO Box 4595	Clarksville	TN	37044	931-648-7346	221-7296
Web: www.library.apsu.edu					
Middle Tennessee State University Walker Library					
PO Box 13	Murfreesboro	TN	37132	615-898-2772	904-8505
Web: www.mtsu.edu/library					
Rhodes College Barret Library 2000 N Pkwy	Memphis	TN	38112	901-843-3900	843-3404
Web: www.rhodes.edu					
University of Memphis McWherter Library					
126 Ned R McWherter Library	Memphis	TN	38152	901-678-2201	678-8218
Web: www.memphis.edu					
University of Tennessee Chattanooga					
Lupton Library					
University of Tennessee at Chattanooga					
700 Vine St	Chattanooga	TN	37403	423-425-4501	425-4775
Web: www.lib.utc.edu					
University of Tennessee Knoxville					
Hodges Library 1015 Volunteer Blvd	Knoxville	TN	37996	865-974-4351	974-0555
Web: www.lib.utk.edu					
University of Tennessee Martin					
Meek Library 10 Wayne Fisher Dr	Martin	TN	38238	731-881-7061	881-7074
Web: www.utm.edu/library.php					
Vanderbilt University Heard Library					
419 21st Ave S	Nashville	TN	37240	615-322-7100	343-8279
Web: www.library.vanderbilt.edu					
Abilene Christian University Brown Library					
PO Box ACU29208	Abilene	TX	79699	325-674-2000	674-2202
TF: 800-460-6228 ■ *Web:* www.acu.edu/academics/library					
Angelo State University Henderson Library					
2025 S Johnson St	San Angelo	TX	76909	325-942-2051	942-2198
Web: www.angelo.edu					
Baylor University Moody Memorial Library & Jones Library					
PO Box 97148	Waco	TX	76798	254-710-2112	752-5332
Web: www.baylor.edu/lib					
Hardin-Simmons University Richardson Library					
2200 Hickory PO Box 16195	Abilene	TX	79698	325-670-1236	677-8351
Web: www.rupert.alc.org					
Lamar University Gray Library					
211 Redbird Ln	Beaumont	TX	77705	409-880-8118	880-2318
Web: www.biblos.lamar.edu					
McMurry University Jay-Rollins Library					
PO Box 218	Abilene	TX	79697	325-793-4692	793-4930
Web: www.mcm.edu/newsite/web/library					
Rice University Fondren Library					
6100 Main St MS 44	Houston	TX	77005	713-348-4022	348-5258
Web: www.rice.edu/fondren					
Sam Houston State University Gresham Library					
1830 Bobby K Marks Dr	Huntsville	TX	77340	936-294-1614	294-3615
TF: 866-645-4636 ■ *Web:* www.library.shsu.edu					
Sixth Floor Museum					
411 Elm St Suite 120 Dealey Plaza	Dallas	TX	75202	214-747-6660	747-6662
TF: 888-485-4854 ■ *Web:* www.jfk.org					
Southern Methodist University Central University Libraries					
6414 Hilltop Ln PO Box 750135	Dallas	TX	75205	214-768-2401	768-3815
Web: www.smu.edu/libraries					

Name / Address	City	State	Zip	Phone	Fax
Stephen F Austin State University Steen Library 1936 N St PO Box 13055	Nacogdoches	TX	75962	936-468-4101	468-7610
Web: www.libweb.sfasu.edu					
Texas Christian University Mary Couts Burnett Library 2800 S University Dr	Fort Worth	TX	76129	817-257-7000	257-7282
Web: www.tcu.edu					
Texas State University San Marcos *Alkek Library* 601 University Dr	San Marcos	TX	78666	512-245-2133	245-3002
Web: www.library.txstate.edu					
Texas Tech University Libraries 18th & Boston Ave PO Box 40002	Lubbock	TX	79409	806-742-2261	742-0737*
*Fax: Admin ■ *Web:* www.library.ttu.edu/ul					
Texas Woman's University Blagg-Huey Library 1301 Frame St	Denton	TX	76209	940-898-2665	898-3764
Web: www.twu.edu					
Trinity University Coates Library 1 Trinity Pl	San Antonio	TX	78212	210-999-8127	999-8021
Web: www.lib.trinity.edu					
University of North Texas Libraries 1155 union Cir PO Box 305190	Denton	TX	76203	940-565-2413	565-4949*
*Fax: circulation desk ■ *TF:* 877-872-0264 ■ *Web:* www.library.unt.edu					
University of Utah Marriott Library Marriott Library 295 S 1500 E	Salt Lake City	UT	84112	801-581-8558	585-3464*
*Fax: Admin ■ *Web:* www.lib.utah.edu					
Utah State University Merrill-Cazier Library 3000 Old Main Hill	Logan	UT	84322	435-797-2631	797-2880*
*Fax: Admin ■ *Web:* www.library.usu.edu					
Middlebury College Library 110 Storrs Ave	Middlebury	VT	05753	802-443-5494	443-5698
Web: www.middlebury.edu/academics/lis/lib					
University of Vermont Bailey/Howe Library 538 Main St	Burlington	VT	05405	802-656-2023	656-4038
Web: library.uvm.edu					
Christopher Newport University Smith Library 1 University Pl	Newport News	VA	23606	757-594-7133	594-7776
Web: library.cnu.edu					
College of William & Mary Swem Library PO Box 8794	Williamsburg	VA	23187	757-221-3067	221-2635
Web: www.swem.wm.edu					
Emory & Henry College Kelly Library 30480 Armbrister Dr PO Box 948	Emory	VA	24327	276-944-6208	944-4592
Web: www.library.ehc.edu					
James Madison University Carrier Library MSC 1704	Harrisonburg	VA	22807	540-568-6150	568-6339
Web: www.lib.jmu.edu/carrier					
Radford University McConnell Library PO Box 6881	Radford	VA	24142	540-831-5471	831-6138
Web: www.lib.radford.edu					
Regent University *Library* 1000 Regent University Dr	Virginia Beach	VA	23464	757-226-4150	226-4167
Web: www.regent.edu/general/library					
Sweet Briar College Cochran Library 134 Chapel Rd	Sweet Briar	VA	24595	434-381-6138	381-6173
Web: www.library.sbc.edu					
University of Virginia Clemons Library PO Box 400710	Charlottesville	VA	22904	434-924-3684	924-1431
Web: www.lib.virginia.edu/clemons					
Virginia Commonwealth University Cabell Library 901 Pk Ave PO Box 842033	Richmond	VA	23284	804-828-1105	828-0151
Web: www.library.vcu.edu/jbc					
Virginia Polytechnic Institute & State University Libraries PO Box 90001	Blacksburg	VA	24062	540-231-5593	231-7808*
*Fax: Admin ■ *Web:* www.lib.vt.edu					
Central Washington University Brooks Library 400 E University Way	Ellensburg	WA	98926	509-963-3682	963-3684
Web: www.lib.cwu.edu					
Evergreen State College Evans Library 2700 Evergreen Pkwy NW	Olympia	WA	98505	360-867-6250	866-6790
Web: www.evergreen.edu/library					
Gonzaga University Foley Library 502 E Boone Ave	Spokane	WA	99258	509-323-5931	323-5904
TF: 800-498-5941 ■ *Web:* www.gonzaga.edu/Campus+Resources					
Pacific Lutheran University Mortvedt Library 12180 Pk Ave S	Tacoma	WA	98447	253-535-7500	535-7315
Web: www.plu.edu/~libr					
Seattle University Lemieux Library 900 Broadway	Seattle	WA	98122	206-296-6233	296-2572
Web: www.seattleu.edu/lemlib					
University of Washington Libraries PO Box 352900	Seattle	WA	98195	206-543-0242	
Web: www.lib.washington.edu					
Marshall University Drinko Library 400 Hal Greer Blvd	Huntington	WV	25755	304-696-2321	696-5858
Web: www.marshall.edu/library					
Lawrence University Mudd Library PO Box 599	Appleton	WI	54911	920-832-6750	832-6967
Web: www.lawrence.edu/library					
Marquette University Raynor Memorial Library 1355 W Wisconsin Ave	Milwaukee	WI	53233	414-288-7556	288-5324
Web: www.marquette.edu/library					
University of Wisconsin Eau Claire *McIntyre Library* 105 Garfield Ave	Eau Claire	WI	54702	715-836-3715	836-2949
TF: 877-267-1384 ■ *Web:* www.uwec.edu					
University of Wisconsin Green Bay *Cofrin Library* 2420 Nicolet Dr	Green Bay	WI	54311	920-465-2333	465-2388
Web: www.uwgb.edu/library					
University of Wisconsin La Crosse *Murphy Library* 1631 Pine St	La Crosse	WI	54601	608-785-8505	785-8639
Web: www.uwlax.edu/murphylibrary					
University of Wisconsin Milwaukee (UWM) *Golda Meir Library* 2311 E Hartford Ave PO Box 604	Milwaukee	WI	53211	414-229-4785	
Web: www4.uwm.edu					
University of Wisconsin Oshkosh *Polk Library* 800 Algoma Blvd	Oshkosh	WI	54901	920-424-3334	424-7338
Web: www.uwosh.edu/library					
University of Wisconsin Parkside *Library* 900 Wood Rd	Kenosha	WI	53141	262-595-2360	595-2545
Web: www.uwp.edu					
University of Wisconsin River Falls *Davee Library* 410 S 3rd St	River Falls	WI	54022	715-425-3321	425-3590
Web: www.uwrf.edu					
University of Wisconsin Stevens Point *University Library* 900 Reserve St	Stevens Point	WI	54481	715-346-2540	346-2367
Web: www.library.uwsp.edu					
University of Wisconsin Stout *Library* 315 10th Ave E University of Wisconsin-Stout	Menomonie	WI	54751	715-232-1215	232-1783
TF: 800-787-8688 ■ *Web:* www.uwstout.edu/lib/index.cfm					
University of Wisconsin Superior *Jim Dan Hill Library* PO Box 2000	Superior	WI	54880	715-394-8343	394-8462
TF: 877-232-1727 ■ *Web:* www.uwsuper.edu/library/index.cfm					
University of Wisconsin Whitewater *Andersen Library* 800 W Main St PO Box 900	Whitewater	WI	53190	262-472-5511	472-5727
Web: www.library.uww.edu					
University of Wyoming Libraries PO Box 3334	Laramie	WY	82071	307-766-3190	766-2510*
*Fax: Admin ■ *Web:* www-lib.uwyo.edu					

438 LIBRARY ASSOCIATIONS - STATE & PROVINCE

Name / Address	City	State	Zip	Phone	Fax
Alabama Library Assn (ALLA) 9154 Eastchase Pkwy Suite 418	Montgomery	AL	36104	334-414-0113	265-1281
TF: 877-563-5146 ■ *Web:* www.allanet.org					
Arizona Library Assn (AzLA) 2302 N 3rd St Suite F	Phoenix	AZ	85004	602-712-9822	252-5265
Web: www.azla.org					
Illinois Library Assn (ILA) 33 W Grand Ave Suite 301	Chicago	IL	60610	312-644-1896	644-1899
Web: www.ila.org					
Indiana Library Federation (ILF) 941 E 86th St Suite 260	Indianapolis	IN	46240	317-257-2040	257-1389
Web: www.ilfonline.org					
Iowa Library Assn (ILA) 3636 Westown Pkwy Suite 202	West Des Moines	IA	50266	515-273-5322	273-5323
TF: 800-452-5507 ■ *Web:* www.iowalibraryassociation.org					
Maine Library Assn (MLA) 331 State St	Augusta	ME	04330	207-623-8428	626-5947
Web: www.mainelibraries.org					
Maryland Library Assn (MLA) 1401 Hollins St	Baltimore	MD	21223	410-947-5090	947-5089
Web: www.mdlib.org					
Michigan Library Assn (MLA) 1407 Rensen St Suite 2	Lansing	MI	48910	517-394-2774	394-2675
Web: www.mla.lib.mi.us					
Minnesota Library Assn (MLA) 1821 University Ave W Suite S256	Saint Paul	MN	55104	651-999-5343	917-1835
TF: 877-867-0982 ■ *Web:* www.mnlibraryassociation.org					
New Jersey Library Assn (NJLA) PO Box 1534	Trenton	NJ	08607	609-394-8032	394-8164
Web: www.njla.org					
New York Library Assn (NYLA) 252 Hudson Ave	Albany	NY	12210	518-432-6952	427-1697
TF: 800-252-6952 ■ *Web:* www.nyla.org					
North Carolina Library Assn (NCLA) 1811 Capital Blvd	Raleigh	NC	27604	919-839-6252	839-6253
Web: www.nclaonline.org					
Pennsylvania Library Assn (PaLA) 220 Cumberland Pkwy Suite 10	Mechanicsburg	PA	17055	717-766-7663	766-5440
Web: www.palibraries.org					
South Carolina Library Assn (SCLA) PO Box 1763	Columbia	SC	29202	803-252-1087	252-0589
Web: www.scla.org					
Tennessee Library Assn (TLA) PO Box 241074	Memphis	TN	38124	901-485-6952	
Web: www.tnla.org					
Wisconsin Library Assn (WLA) 4610 S Biltmore Ln # 100	Madison	WI	53718	608-245-3640	245-3646
Web: www.wla.lib.wi.us					

439 LIBRARY SYSTEMS - REGIONAL - CANADIAN

Name / Address	City	Prov	Postal Code	Phone	Fax
Bibliotheque Regionale Du Haut-Saint-Jean 540 Principale St	Saint-Basile	NB	E7C1J5	506-263-3423	263-3425
Cape Breton Regional Library 50 Falmouth St	Sydney	NS	B1P6X9	902-562-3279	564-0765
Centre Regional de Services Aux Bibliotheques Publiques de L'Estrie Inc 4155 Rue Brodeur	Sherbrooke	QC	J1L1K4	819-565-9744	565-9157
Web: www.reseaubiblioduquebec.qc.ca					
Centre Regional de Services Aux Bibliotheques Publiques de L'Outaouais Inc 2295 Rue St Louis	Gatineau	QC	J8T5L8	819-561-6008	561-6767
Centre Regional de Services Aux Bibliotheques Publiques de la Cote-Nord Inc 59 Rue Napoleon	Sept-Iles	QC	G4R5C5	418-962-1020	962-5124
Web: www.reseaubiblioduquebec.qc.ca					
Centre Regional de Services Aux Bibliotheques Publiques de la Monteregie Inc 275 Rue Conrad-Pelletier	La Prairie	QC	J5R4V1	450-444-5433	659-3364
Web: www.reseaubiblioduquebec.qc.ca					

Phone | Fax

Centre Regional de Services Aux Bibliotheques Publiques des Laurentides Inc
29 Rue Brissette .... Sainte-Agathe-des-Monts QC J8C3L1 819-326-6440 326-0885
Web: www.reseaubiblioduquebec.qc.ca

Centre Regional de Services Aux Bibliotheques Publiques du Bas-Saint-Laurent Inc
465 Rue St Pierre .... Riviere-du-Loup QC G5R4T6 418-867-1682 867-3434

Chaleur Regional Library
113-A Roseberry St .... Campbellton NB E3N2G7 506-789-6599 789-7318

Evergreen Regional Library 65 1st Ave .... Gimli MB R0C1B0 204-642-7912 642-8319

Lakeland Regional Library 318 Williams Ave.......... Killarney MB R0K1G0 204-523-4949 523-7460
Web: www.lakelandregionallibrary.ca

Ontario Library Service North - Sudbury
334 Regent St.................................. Sudbury ON P3C4E2 705-675-6467 675-2285

Palliser Regional Library 366 Coteau St W .... Moose Jaw SK S6H5C9 306-693-3669 692-5657
Web: www.palliserlibrary.ca

Provincial Information & Library Resources Board
Eastern Div Arts & Culture Ctr.................... Saint John's NL A1B3A3 709-737-3508 737-3571
Web: www.nlpl.ca
West Newfoundl and-Labrador Div
5 Union St .... Corner Brook NL A2H5M7 709-634-7333 634-7313
Web: www.nlpl.ca

Public Library InterLINK 7252 Kings Way.............. Burnaby BC V5E1G3 604-517-8441 517-8410
Web: www.interlinklibraries.ca

Saint John Regional Library 1 Market Sq............ Saint John NB E2L4Z6 506-643-7220 643-7225

South Shore Regional Library 547 King St .... Bridgewater NS B4V1B3 902-543-9222

Southeast Regional Library 49 Bison Ave .... Weyburn SK S4H0H9 306-848-3100 842-2665
Web: www.southeast.lib.sk.ca

Southwestern Manitoba Regional Library
149 Main St PO Box 670 .... Melita MB R0M1L0 204-522-3923 522-3923
Web: www.wix.com

Wapiti Regional Library 145 12th St E .... Prince Albert SK S6V1B7 306-764-0712 922-1516
Web: www.panet.pa.sk.ca

Western Manitoba Regional Library
710 Rosser Ave Unit 1 .... Brandon MB R7A3S4 204-727-6648 727-4447
Web: www.wmrl.ca

York Regional Library 4 Carleton St .... Fredericton NB E3B5P4 506-453-5380 457-4878

440 LIGHT BULBS & TUBES

Phone | Fax

Advanced Lighting Technologies Inc
32000 Aurora Rd .... Solon OH 44139 440-248-3510 836-7030
TF: 800-338-6161 ■ *Web:* www.adlt.com

AETEK UV Systems 1229 W Lakeview Ct .... Romeoville IL 60446 630-226-4200 226-4215
TF: 800-333-2304 ■ *Web:* www.fusionuv.com

Amglo Kemlight Laboratories Inc
215 Gateway Rd .... Bensenville IL 60106 630-350-9470 350-9474
Web: www.amglo.com

Bayco Products Inc 640 Sanden Blvd .... Wylie TX 75098 469-326-9400 326-9401
TF: 800-233-2155 ■ *Web:* www.baycoproducts.com

Carley Lamps Inc 1502 W 228th St .... Torrance CA 90501 310-325-8474 534-2912
Web: www.carleylamps.com

Empire Wire & Supply 270 Rex Blvd .... Auburn Hills MI 48326 248-853-6363 853-6667
TF: 800-826-1265 ■ *Web:* www.empirewc.com

Eye Lighting International NA
9150 Hendricks Rd................................ Mentor OH 44060 440-350-7000 350-7001
TF Cust Svc: 888-665-2677 ■ *Web:* www.eyelighting.com

General Electric Canada Inc
2300 Meadowvale Blvd......................... Mississauga ON L5N5P9 905-858-5100
Web: www.ge.com/canada

Hanovia Corp 825 Lehigh Ave .... Union NJ 07083 908-688-0050 686-8404
TF: 800-229-3666 ■ *Web:* www.hanovia-uv.com

Interlectric Corp 1401 Lexington Ave.................... Warren PA 16365 814-723-6061 723-1074
TF: 800-722-2184 ■ *Web:* www.interlectric.com

K & H Industries Inc 8656 Delamater Rd .... Angola NY 14006 716-549-0135 549-2725
Web: www.khindustries.com

LCD Lighting Inc 37 Robinson Blvd .... Orange CT 06477 203-795-1520 795-2874
TF: 800-826-9465 ■ *Web:* www.light-sources.com

Ledtronics Inc 23105 Kashiwa Ct..................... Torrance CA 90505 310-534-1505 534-1424
TF: 800-579-4875 ■ *Web:* www.led.net

Light Sources Inc 37 Connair Rd .... Orange CT 06477 203-799-7877 795-5267
TF: 800-245-4458 ■ *Web:* www.light-sources.com

Litetronics International Inc 4101 W 123rd St .... Alsip IL 60803 708-389-8000 371-0627
TF: 800-860-3392 ■ *Web:* www.litetronics.com

OSRAM Sylvania Glass Technologies
131 Portsmouth Ave.............................. Exeter NH 03833 603-772-4331 778-0674
TF: 800-258-8290 ■ *Web:* www.sylvania.com/pmc/glass

OSRAM Sylvania Inc 100 Endicott St .... Danvers MA 01923 978-777-1900 750-2152
Web: www.sylvania.com

PerkinElmer Inc 45 William St .... Wellesley MA 02481 781-237-5100 237-9386
NYSE: PKI ■ *Web:* www.perkinelmer.com

Philips Lighting Co 200 Franklin Sq Dr .... Somerset NJ 08875 732-563-3000 563-3641
TF: 800-555-0050 ■ *Web:* www.usa.lighting.philips.com/index.wpd

Rogers Corp Durel Div 2225 W Chandler Blvd.......... Chandler AZ 85224 480-917-6000 917-6049
Web: www.rogerscorp.com

Sun Ergoline Inc 1 Walter Kratz Dr .... Jonesboro AR 72401 870-935-1130 935-3618
TF: 800-643-0086 ■ *Web:* www.sundash.com

Technical Consumer Products Inc 300 Lena Dr......... Aurora OH 44202 330-995-6111 995-6188
TF: 800-324-1496 ■ *Web:* www.tcpi.com

Trojan Inc 198 Trojan St PO Box 850............. Mount Sterling KY 40353 859-498-0526 498-0528
TF: 800-264-0526 ■ *Web:* www.trojaninc.com

Ushio America Inc 5440 Cerritos Ave.................. Cypress CA 90630 714-236-8600 776-3641*
**Fax Area Code:* 800 ■ **Fax:* Mktg ■ *TF:* 800-326-1960 ■ *Web:* www.ushio.com

UVP Inc 2066 W 11th St............................ Upland CA 91786 909-946-3197 946-3597
TF Cust Svc: 800-452-6788 ■ *Web:* www.uvp.com

Venture Lighting International Inc
32000 Aurora Rd .... Solon OH 44139 440-248-3510 836-7030
TF: 800-338-6161 ■ *Web:* www.venturelighting.com

Phone | Fax

Welch Allyn Inc Lighting Products Div
4619 Jordan Rd .... Skaneateles Falls NY 13153 315-685-4347 685-2854

Westinghouse Lighting Corp
12401 McNulty Rd .... Philadelphia PA 19154 215-671-2000 464-4115
TF Orders: 800-999-2226 ■ *Web:* www.westinghouselighting.com

441 LIGHTING EQUIPMENT - VEHICULAR

Phone | Fax

Able 2 Products Co Inc PO Box 543 .... Cassville MO 65625 417-847-4791 847-2222
TF: 800-641-4098 ■ *Web:* www.able2products.com

Astronics Corp 130 Commerce Way .... East Aurora NY 14052 716-805-1599 655-0309
NASDAQ: ATRO ■ *Web:* www.astronics.com

ATC Lighting & Plastics Inc 107 N Eagle St............ Geneva OH 44041 440-466-7670 466-0186
Web: www.atc-lighting-plastics.com

Aurora Cord & Cable Co 325 S Union St................ Aurora IL 60505 630-851-1616 851-1626
Web: www.auroracord.com

Avtec Inc 6 Industrial Pk .... Cahokia IL 62206 618-337-7800 337-7976
TF: 800-552-8832 ■ *Web:* www.avteclighting.com

Bruce Industries Inc 101 Evans Ave .... Dayton NV 89403 775-246-0101 246-0451
Web: www.bruceind.com

Delphi Safety & Interior Systems 1401 Crooks Rd......... Troy MI 48084 248-813-2000 813-2108

Federal Signal Corp Emergency Products Div
2645 Federal Signal Dr....................... University Park IL 60466 708-534-3400 534-9050
Web: www.fedsig.com

Grakon LLC 1911 S 218th St PO Box 98984 .... Seattle WA 98198 206-824-6000 824-6098
Web: www.grakon.com

JW Speaker Corp
N 120 W 19434 Freistadt Rd PO Box 1011.......... Germantown WI 53022 262-251-6660 251-2918
TF: 800-558-7288 ■ *Web:* www.jwspeaker.com

Kc Hilites Inc PO Box 155.......................... Williams AZ 86046 928-635-2607 635-2486
Web: www.kchilites.com

Luminator 900 Klein Rd .... Plano TX 75074 972-424-6511 423-1540
TF: 800-388-8205 ■ *Web:* www.luminatormasstransit.com

North American Lighting Inc 227 S Main................ Paris IL 61944 217-465-6600 465-6606
Web: www.nal.com

Nova Electronics Inc 36 Doctor Foote Rd .... Colchester CT 06415 860-537-3471 537-0656
Web: www.strobe.com

Peterson Mfg Co 4200 E 135th St .... Grandview MO 64030 816-765-2000 761-6693
TF: 800-821-3490 ■ *Web:* www.pmlights.com

Soderberg Mfg Co Inc 20821 Currier Rd................ Walnut CA 91789 909-595-1291
Web: www.soderberg.aero

Teledyne Lighting & Display Products
12964 Panama St............................. Los Angeles CA 90066 310-574-2001 574-2070
Web: www.teledynelighting.com

Trans-Lite Inc 120 Wampus Ln...................... Milford CT 06460 203-878-8567 877-2630
Web: www.trans-liteinc.com

Truck-Lite Co Inc 310 E Elmwood Ave .... Falconer NY 14733 716-665-6214 665-6403
TF Cust Svc: 800-562-5012 ■ *Web:* www.truck-lite.com

Unity Mfg Co 1260 N Clybourn Ave.................... Chicago IL 60610 312-943-5200 943-5681
Web: www.unityusa.com

Valeo Sylvania 1231 A Ave .... North Seymour IN 47274 812-523-5200 524-5316
Web: www.valeosylvania.com

Vehicle Safety Mfg LLC 408 Central Ave............... Newark NJ 07107 973-643-3000 643-2167
TF: 800-832-7233 ■ *Web:* www.vehiclesafetymfg.com

Whelen Engineering Co Inc
51 Winthrop Rd & Rt 145 .... Chester CT 06412 860-526-9504 526-4078
Web: www.whelen.com

442 LIGHTING FIXTURES & EQUIPMENT

Phone | Fax

Altman Lighting Inc 57 Alexander St.................. Yonkers NY 10701 914-476-7987 966-1980
TF: 800-367-2586 ■ *Web:* www.altmanltg.com

American Fluorescent Corp
2345 Ernie Krueger Cir........................... Waukegan IL 60087 847-249-5970 249-2618
TF: 800-873-2326 ■ *Web:* www.americanfluorescent.com

American Louver Co 7700 N Austin Ave .... Skokie IL 60077 847-470-3300 966-8074
TF: 800-772-0355 ■ *Web:* www.americanlouver.com

Amerillum Corp 2835 La Mirada Dr..................... Vista CA 92083 760-727-7675 727-7695
Web: www.amerillum.com

Antique Street Lamps Inc 2011-B W Rundberg Ln........ Austin TX 78758 512-977-8444 832-1869
Web: www.antiquestreetlamps.com

Ashley Lighting Inc 405 Industrial Dr................. Trumann AR 72472 870-483-6181 483-7140
TF: 800-343-5267 ■ *Web:* www.ashley-lighting.com

Automatic Power Inc 213 Hutchinson St.............. Houston TX 77003 713-228-5208 228-3717
Web: www.automaticpower.com

Bieber Lighting Corp 626 S Isis Ave .... Inglewood CA 90301 310-645-6789 216-0333
TF: 800-243-2375 ■ *Web:* www.bieberlighting.com

Big Beam Emergency Systems Inc
290 E Prairie St PO Box 518..................... Crystal Lake IL 60039 815-459-6100 459-6126
Web: www.bigbeam.com

Boyd Corp 6325 San Pedro Ave .... San Antonio TX 78216 210-344-9222 349-2693
Web: www.boydlightingsa.com

Boyd Lighting Co 944 Folsom St .... San Francisco CA 94107 415-778-4300 778-4319
Web: www.boydlighting.com

Brinkmann Corp 4215 McEwen Rd .... Dallas TX 75244 972-387-4939 770-8515
TF: 800-527-0717 ■ *Web:* www.brinkmann.net

Bronzelite Commercial Landscape Lighting
100 Craftway.................................. Littlestown PA 17340 717-359-7131 359-3545
TF: 800-273-1569 ■ *Web:* www.bronzelite.com

California Lighting Sales Inc (CLS)
4900 Rivergrade Rd Suite D110.................. Baldwin Park CA 91706 626-775-6000 775-6001
Web: www.californialightingsales.com

Canlyte Inc 3015 Louis Amos .... Lachine QC H8T1C4 514-636-0670 636-0460
TF: 800-565-5486 ■ *Web:* www.canlyte.com

				Phone	Fax
Carlisle & Finch Co 4562 W Mitchell Ave *Web:* www.carlislefinch.com	Cincinnati	OH	45232	513-681-6080	681-6226
Catalina & Tensor Lighting 18191 NW 68th Ave *TF:* 800-872-5267 ■ *Web:* www.catalinaltg.com	Miami	FL	33015	305-558-4777	558-3024
Chapman Mfg Co Inc PO Box 359 *Web:* www.chapmanco.com	Avon	MA	02322	508-588-3200	587-7592
Chloride Systems 126 Chloride Rd **Fax Area Code:* 800 ■ *Web:* www.chloridesys.com	Burgaw	NC	28425	910-259-1000	258-8803*
Commercial Lighting Industries 30643 Front St *TF:* 800-755-0155 ■ *Web:* www.commercial-lighting.net	Thousand Palms	CA	92276	760-343-2704	262-3041
Con-Tech Lighting 2783 Shermer Rd *TF:* 800-728-0312 ■ *Web:* www.con-techlighting.com	Northbrook	IL	60062	847-559-5500	559-5505
Cooper Industries 600 Travis St Suite 5800 *NYSE: CBE* ■ *TF:* 866-853-4293 ■ *Web:* www.cooperindustries.com	Houston	TX	77002	713-209-8400	209-8995
Cooper Lighting Inc 1121 Hwy 74 S *Web:* www.cooperindustries.com	Peachtree City	GA	30269	770-486-4800	486-4801
Corbett Lighting Inc 14625 E Clark Ave **Fax Area Code:* 800 ■ *TF:* 800-533-8769 ■ *Web:* www.corbettlighting.com	City of Industry	CA	91745	626-336-4511	544-8769*
Coronet Lighting 16210 S Avalon Blvd *TF:* 800-421-2748 ■ *Web:* www.coronetlighting.com	Gardena	CA	90248	310-327-6700	532-8092
Crownlite Mfg Corp 1546 Ocean Ave	Bohemia	NY	11716	631-589-9100	589-4584
CW Cole & Co Inc 2560 Rosemead Blvd *Web:* www.colelighting.com	South El Monte	CA	91733	626-443-2473	443-9253
Dazor Mfg Corp 2079 Congressional *TF:* 800-345-9103 ■ *Web:* www.dazor.com	St. Louis	MO	63146	314-652-2400	652-2069
Deaver Industries Inc 3120 Morgan Rd *Web:* www.deaverind.com	Bessemer	AL	35022	205-426-4309	426-4364
Dual-Lite Inc 701 Millennium Blvd *Web:* www.dual-lite.com	Greenville	SC	29607	864-678-1000	678-1415
Duray Fluorescent Mfg Co 2050 W Balmoral Ave *Web:* www.durayinc.com	Chicago	IL	60625	773-271-2800	271-4410
Edison Price Lighting Inc (EPL) 41-50 22nd St *TF:* 800-275-8548 ■ *Web:* www.epl.com	Long Island City	NY	11101	718-685-0700	786-8530
El Products 55 County Rd 285 *Web:* www.limelite.com	Maxwell	TX	78656	512-357-2776	357-2786
Electrix Inc 45 Spring St *Web:* www.electrix.com	New Haven	CT	06519	203-776-5577	624-7545
Energy Focus Inc 32000 Aurora Rd *NASDAQ: EFOI* ■ *TF:* 800-327-7877 ■ *Web:* www.energyfocusinc.com	Solon	OH	44139	440-715-1300	715-1314
Entourage LA 100 Wilshire Blvd Suite 800 *Web:* www.entouragela.com	Santa Monica	CA	90401	310-656-0499	656-0269
ExceLine 2345 Vauxhall Rd *TF:* 800-334-2212 ■ *Web:* www.exceline.com	Union	NJ	07083	908-964-7000	964-0968
Ez Electric Inc 1250 Birchwood Dr *Web:* www.ez-electric.com	Sunnyvale	CA	94089	408-734-4282	734-0798
Finelite Inc 30500 Whipple Rd *Web:* www.finelite.com	Union City	CA	94587	510-441-1100	441-1510
Forecast 1600 Fleetwood Dr *TF:* 800-234-0416 ■ *Web:* www.forecastltg.com	Elgin	IL	60123	847-622-0416	622-2542
Frederick Cooper Lamp LLC 5750 W Bloomingdale Ave	Chicago	IL	60639	773-384-0800	384-7526
Fulton Industries Inc 135 E Linfoot St PO Box 377 *TF:* 800-537-5012 ■ *Web:* www.fultonindoh.com	Wauseon	OH	43567	419-335-3015	335-3215
Gardco Lighting 1611 Clovis Barker Rd *TF:* 800-227-0758 ■ *Web:* www.sitelighting.com	San Marcos	TX	78666	512-753-1000	
GE Lighting Systems Inc 3010 Spartanburg Hwy *TF:* 877-798-6702 ■ *Web:* www.gelightingsolutions.com	East Flat Rock	NC	28726	828-693-2000	693-2112
Good Earth Lighting Inc 5260 Capitol Dr *Web:* www.goodearthlighting.com	Wheeling	IL	60090	847-808-1133	808-0838
Guth Lighting 1324 Washington Ave Suite 200 PO Box 7079 *Web:* www.guth.com	Saint Louis	MO	63177	314-533-3200	533-9127
Hanover Lantern Inc 350 Kindig Ln *TF:* 800-233-7196 ■ *Web:* www.hanoverlantern.com	Hanover	PA	17331	717-632-6464	632-5039
HE Williams Inc 831 W Fairview Ave *TF:* 800-358-4064 ■ *Web:* www.hewilliams.com	Carthage	MO	64836	417-358-4065	358-6015
High End Systems Inc 2105 Gracy Farms Ln *TF:* 800-890-8989 ■ *Web:* www.highend.com	Austin	TX	78758	512-836-2242	837-5290
High Q Lighting Inc 11439 E Lakewood Blvd *Web:* www.hql.net	Holland	MI	49424	616-396-3591	396-8863
Hinkley Lighting 12600 Berea Rd *TF:* 800-446-5539 ■ *Web:* www.hinkleylighting.com	Cleveland	OH	44111	216-671-3300	671-4537
Holophane 214 Oakwood Ave PO Box 3004 *TF:* 866-465-6742 ■ *Web:* www.holophane.com	Newark	OH	43058	740-345-9631	349-4426
Honeywell Airport Systems 2121 Union Pl *TF:* 800-581-5591 ■ *Web:* www.honeywell.com	Simi Valley	CA	93065	805-581-5591	
Hubbell Lighting Inc 701 Millennium Blvd *TF:* 800-328-7480 ■ *Web:* www.hubbelllighting.com	Greenville	SC	29607	864-678-1000	678-1065
Hydrel 12881 Bradley Ave *TF:* 800-750-9773 ■ *Web:* www.hydrel.com	Sylmar	CA	91342	818-362-9465	362-6548
International Lighting 1825 N 19th St *TF:* 800-325-7050 ■ *Web:* www.internationalltg.com	Saint Louis	MO	63106	314-621-0600	621-6944
Jimco Lamp & Mfg Co 11759 Hwy 63 N PO Box 490 *TF:* 800-643-0092 ■ *Web:* www.jimcolamp.com	Bono	AR	72416	870-935-6820	935-6822
Justice Design Group Inc (JDG) 261 S Figueroa St Suite 450 *TF Cust Svc:* 800-533-4799 ■ *Web:* www.jdg.com	Los Angeles	CA	90012	213-437-0102	437-0860
Kenall Mfg 1020 Lakeside Dr *TF:* 800-453-6255 ■ *Web:* www.kenall.com	Gurnee	IL	60031	847-360-8200	360-1781
Kichler Lighting 7711 E Pleasant Valley Rd PO Box 318010 **Fax Area Code:* 888 ■ **Fax:* Cust Svc ■ *TF:* 888-659-8809 ■ *Web:* www.kichler.com	Cleveland	OH	44131	216-573-1000	659-8808*
Kim Lighting Inc 16555 E Gale Ave PO Box 60080 *Web:* www.kimlighting.com	City of Industry	CA	91745	626-968-5666	968-5716
Kirlin Co 3401 E Jefferson Ave *Web:* www.kirlinlighting.com	Detroit	MI	48207	313-259-6400	259-3121
Koehler-Bright Star Inc 380 Stewart Rd *TF Cust Svc:* 800-631-3814 ■ *Web:* www.flashlight.com	Hanover Township	PA	18706	570-825-1900	825-7108
Kurt Versen Co 10 Charles St *Web:* www.kurtversen.com	Westwood	NJ	07675	201-664-8200	664-4801
Kurtzon Lighting Inc 1420 S Talman Ave *TF:* 800-837-8937 ■ *Web:* www.kurtzon.com	Chicago	IL	60608	773-277-2121	277-9164
Lamplight Farms Inc W140 N4900 Lilly Rd *TF Cust Svc:* 888-473-1088 ■ *Web:* www.lamplight.com	Menomonee Falls	WI	53051	262-781-9590	781-6774
LC Doane Co 110 Pond Meadow Rd PO Box 700 *TF:* 800-447-5006 ■ *Web:* www.lcdoane.com	Ivoryton	CT	06442	860-767-8295	767-1397
Ledalite Architectural Products 19750-92A Ave *TF:* 800-665-5332 ■ *Web:* www.ledalite.com	Langley	BC	V1M3B2	604-888-6811	888-2003
Legion Lighting Co Inc 221 Glenmore Ave *TF:* 800-453-4466 ■ *Web:* www.legionlighting.com	Brooklyn	NY	11207	718-498-1770	498-0128
Lightguard 272 W Stag Pk Service Rd **Fax Area Code:* 800 ■ *Web:* www.lightguard.com	Burgaw	NC	28425	910-259-1131	403-6927*
Lighting Alliance Inc The 2700 Esters Blvd Suite 100 PO Box 613079 *Web:* www.thelightingalliance.com	Dallas	TX	75261	972-456-9800	456-9801
Lights of America 611 Reyes Dr *TF Cust Svc:* 800-321-8100 ■ *Web:* www.lightsofamerica.com	Walnut	CA	91789	909-594-7883	594-6758
Lite Energy 780 Salaberry *Web:* www.liteenergy.com	Laval	QC	H7S1H3	450-668-9620	668-9625
Litecontrol 100 Hawks Ave *Web:* www.litecontrol.com	Hanson	MA	02341	781-294-0100	293-2849
Lithonia Lighting 1 Lithonia Way *TF:* 800-858-7763 ■ *Web:* www.lithonia.com	Conyers	GA	30012	770-922-9000	483-2635
Louis Baldinger & Sons Inc 19-02 Steinway St *Web:* www.baldinger.com	Astoria	NY	11105	718-204-5700	721-4986
LSI Industries Inc 10000 Alliance Rd *NASDAQ: LYTS* ■ *TF:* 800-765-3454 ■ *Web:* www.lsi-industries.com	Cincinnati	OH	45242	513-793-3200	984-1335
Lumax Industries Inc 201 Chestnut Ave *Web:* www.lumaxlighting.com	Altoona	PA	16601	814-944-2537	944-6413
Lumec Inc 640 Blvd Curé-Boivin *Web:* www.lumec.com	Boisbriand	QC	J7G2A7	450-430-7040	430-1453
Luxo Corp Five Westchester Plaza **Fax:* Sales ■ *TF:* 800-222-5896 ■ *Web:* www.luxous.com	Elmsford	NY	10523	914-345-0067	345-0068*
Mag Instrument Inc 2001 S Hillman Ave **Fax Area Code:* 775 ■ *TF:* 800-289-6241 ■ *Web:* www.maglite.com	Ontario	CA	91761	909-947-1006	719-4586*
Manning Lighting 1810 N Ave PO Box 1063 *Web:* www.manningltg.com	Sheboygan	WI	53083	920-458-2184	458-2491
Mario Industries of Virginia Inc 2490 Patterson Ave SW PO Box 3190 *TF:* 800-458-1244 ■ *Web:* www.marioindustries.com	Roanoke	VA	24016	540-342-1111	345-4813
Mark Architectural Lighting 3 Kilmer Rd *TF:* 800-526-6280 ■ *Web:* www.marklighting.com	Edison	NJ	08817	732-985-2600	985-8441
Mercury Lighting Products Co Inc 20 Audrey Pl *TF:* 800-637-2879 ■ *Web:* www.mercltg.com	Fairfield	NJ	07004	973-244-9444	244-2584
Minka Group 1151 W Bradford Ct *TF:* 800-221-7977 ■ *Web:* www.minkagroup.net	Corona	CA	92882	951-735-9220	735-9758
Mole-Richardson Co Inc 937 N Sycamore Ave *Web:* www.mole.com	Hollywood	CA	90038	323-851-0111	851-5593
Mule Lighting Inc 46 Baker St *TF:* 800-556-7690 ■ *Web:* www.mulelighting.com	Providence	RI	02905	401-941-4446	941-2929
Multi-Electric Mfg Inc 4223 W Lake St *Web:* www.multielectric.com	Chicago	IL	60624	773-722-1900	722-5694
Musco Sports Lighting LLC 100 1st Ave W PO Box 808 *TF:* 800-825-6020 ■ *Web:* www.musco.com	Oskaloosa	IA	52577	641-673-0411	673-4852
National Lighting Co Inc 522 Cortlandt St *Web:* www.natltg.com	Belleville	NJ	07109	973-751-1600	751-4931
Nightscaping 1705 E Colton Ave *TF:* 800-544-4840 ■ *Web:* www.nightscaping.com	Redlands	CA	92374	909-794-2121	389-9088
North Star Lighting Inc 2150 Parkes Dr *TF:* 800-229-4330 ■ *Web:* www.northstarlightingsite.com	Broadview	IL	60155	708-681-4330	681-4006
Norwell Mfg Inc 82 Stevens St *TF:* 800-822-2831 ■ *Web:* www.norwellinc.com	East Taunton	MA	02718	508-822-5854	823-9431
Nulco Lighting 30 Beecher St PO Box 1328 *TF:* 800-668-5269 ■ *Web:* www.nulcolighting.com	Pawtucket	RI	02862	401-728-5200	728-8210
Omniglow LLC 91 Pinevale St *TF Cust Svc:* 866-783-3799 ■ *Web:* www.omniglow.com	Indian Orchard	MA	01151	413-241-6010	543-5470
OSRAM Sylvania Inc 100 Endicott St *Web:* www.sylvania.com	Danvers	MA	01923	978-777-1900	750-2152
Pacific Coast Lighting Inc 20310 Plummer St *TF:* 800-709-9004 ■ *Web:* www.pacificcoastlighting.com	Chatsworth	CA	91311	818-886-9751	886-5751
Paraflex Industries 2006 Inc 222 New Rd *Web:* www.paraflex.com	Parsippany	NJ	07054	973-340-6040	340-6043
Paramount Industries Inc 304 N Howard St *TF:* 800-521-5405 ■ *Web:* www.paramount-lighting.com	Croswell	MI	48422	810-679-2551	679-4045
Paul C Buff Inc 2725 Bransford Ave *TF:* 800-443-5542 ■ *Web:* www.paulcbuff.com	Nashville	TN	37204	615-383-3982	383-0676
Peerless Lighting Corp 2246 5th St *Web:* www.peerless-lighting.com	Berkeley	CA	94710	510-845-2760	845-2776
Philips Burton 21100 Lassen St *TF Cust Svc:* 800-444-9909 ■ *Web:* www.burtonmedical.com	Chatsworth	CA	91311	818-701-8700	701-8725
Philips Day-Brite 776 S Green St **Fax Area Code:* 662 ■ **Fax:* Hum Res ■ *TF:* 800-234-1890 ■ *Web:* www.daybrite.com/day-brite	Tupelo	MS	38804	800-234-1890	841-5501*
Pieri Creations LLC 100 W Oxford St *Web:* www.piericreations.net	Philadelphia	PA	19122	215-634-0700	634-5525
Prescolite Inc 701 Millennium Blvd *Web:* www.prescolite.com	Greenville	SC	29607	864-678-1000	678-1415
Progress Lighting Co PO Box 6701 *Web:* www.progresslighting.com	Greenville	SC	29303	864-678-1000	678-1415

				Phone	Fax
Prudential Ltd 1737 E 22nd St	Los Angeles	CA	90058	213-746-0360	741-8590
Web: www.prulite.com					
PSI Inc 10630 Marina Dr	Olive Branch	MS	38654	662-895-8777	895-8796
TF: 866-638-7926					
Quality Lighting 2930 S Fairview St	Santa Ana	CA	92704	714-371-2394	668-1107
TF: 800-545-1326 ■ *Web:* www.qualitylighting.com					
Quoizel Inc 6 Corporate Pkwy	Goose Creek	SC	29445	843-553-6700	553-1002
Web: www.quoizelonline.com					
RAB Lighting 170 Ludlow Ave	Northvale	NJ	07647	201-784-8600	784-0077
TF: 800-938-1010 ■ *Web:* www.rabweb.com					
Rangaire Co 501 S Wilhite St	Cleburne	TX	76031	817-556-6500	556-6549
Rejuvenation Inc 2550 NW Nicolai St	Portland	OR	97210	503-231-1900	526-7329*
**Fax Area Code:* 800 ■ *TF:* 888-401-1900 ■ *Web:* www.rejuvenation.com					
Renova Lighting Systems Inc 300 High Pt Ave	Portsmouth	RI	02871	401-682-1850	682-1860
TF: 800-635-6682 ■ *Web:* www.renova.com					
Schonbek Worldwide Lighting Inc 61 Industrial Blvd	Plattsburgh	NY	12901	518-563-7500	563-4228
TF: 800-836-1892 ■ *Web:* www.schonbek.com					
Sea Gull Lighting Products LLC A Generations Brands Co 301 W Washington St	Riverside	NJ	08075	856-764-0500	764-6308
TF: 800-347-5483 ■ *Web:* www.seagulllighting.com					
Sentry Electric 185 Buffalo Ave	Freeport	NY	11520	516-379-4660	378-0624
Web: www.sentrylighting.com					
Sesco Lighting Inc 1133 W Morse Blvd Suite 100	Winter Park	FL	32789	407-629-6100	629-6168
Web: www.sescolighting.com					
SIMKAR Corp 700 Ramona Ave	Philadelphia	PA	19120	215-831-7700	831-7703*
**Fax:* Cust Svc ■ *TF:* 800-523-3602 ■ *Web:* www.simkar.com					
Specialty Lighting 639 Washburn Switch Rd PO Box 1680	Shelby	NC	28151	704-482-3416	484-0818
Web: www.specialtylighting.com					
Spectrolab Inc 12500 Gladstone Ave	Sylmar	CA	91342	818-365-4611	898-7534
TF: 800-936-4888 ■ *Web:* www.spectrolab.com					
Spectrum Brands Inc 601 Rayovac Dr PO Box 44960	Madison	WI	53711	608-275-3340	275-4577
NYSE: SPC ■ *TF:* 800-237-7000 ■ *Web:* www.spectrumbrands.com					
Spring City Electrical Mfg Co PO Box 19	Spring City	PA	19475	610-948-4000	948-5577
Web: www.springcity.com					
Stonco Lighting 2345 Vauxhall Rd	Union	NJ	07083	908-964-7000	964-0968
TF: 800-334-2212 ■ *Web:* www.stoncolighting.com					
Strand Lighting Inc 6603 Darin Way	Cypress	CA	90630	714-230-8200	899-0042
TF: 800-733-0564 ■ *Web:* www.strandlight.com					
Streamlight Inc 30 Eagleville Rd	Eagleville	PA	19403	610-631-0600	631-0712
TF: 800-523-7488 ■ *Web:* www.streamlight.com					
Stylecraft Lamps Inc 4325 Executive Dr Suite 100	Southaven	MS	38672	662-429-5279	662-5279*
**Fax Area Code:* 601					
Super Sky Products Inc 10301 N Enterprise Dr	Mequon	WI	53092	262-242-2000	242-7409
TF: 800-558-0467 ■ *Web:* www.supersky.com					
Swivelier Co Inc 600 Bradley Hill Rd	Blauvelt	NY	10913	845-353-1455	353-1512
Web: www.swivelier.com					
Sylvan R. Shemitz Designs Inc 114 Boston Post Rd	West Haven	CT	06516	203-931-4455	934-2240
TF: 800-847-6067 ■ *Web:* www.elliptipar.com					
Tech Lighting LLC 7400 Linda Ave	Skokie	IL	60076	847-410-4400	410-4500
TF: 800-522-5315 ■ *Web:* www.techlighting.com					
Thomas Lighting Canada *Day-Brite Canada* 189 Bullock Dr	Markham	ON	L3P1W4	905-294-9570	268-0003*
**Fax Area Code:* 800 ■ *TF:* 800-463-5456 ■ *Web:* www.day-britecanada.com					
Translite Sonoma 22678 Broadway Suite 1	Sonoma	CA	95476	707-996-6906	996-6926
TF: 888-999-4540 ■ *Web:* www.translite.com					
Tri-Lite Inc 1642 N Besly Ct	Chicago	IL	60642	773-384-7765	384-5115
TF: 800-322-5250 ■ *Web:* www.triliteinc.com					
Troy-CSL Lighting Inc 14625 E Clark Ave	City of Industry	CA	91745	626-336-4511	330-4266
TF: 800-533-8769 ■ *Web:* www.troy-lighting.com					
Uspar Enterprises Inc 13404 S Monte Vista Ave	Chino	CA	91710	909-591-7506	590-3220
TF: 800-251-4612 ■ *Web:* www.uspar.com					
Western Reflections 261 Commerce Way	Gallatin	TN	37066	615-451-9700	452-0283
TF Cust Svc: 800-507-8302 ■ *Web:* www.western-reflections.com					
Westinghouse Lighting Corp 12401 McNulty Rd	Philadelphia	PA	19154	215-671-2000	464-4115
TF Orders: 800-999-2226 ■ *Web:* www.westinghouselighting.com					
Wide-Lite Corp 1611 Clovis Barker Rd PO Box 606	San Marcos	TX	78667	512-392-5821	753-1122
TF: 800-235-2314 ■ *Web:* www.wide-lite.com					
Wildwood Lamps & Accents 516 Paul St PO Box 672	Rocky Mount	NC	27803	252-446-3266	977-6669
Web: www.wildwoodlamps.com					
Wilshire Mfg Co 645 Myles Standish Blvd	Taunton	MA	02780	508-824-1970	822-7046
TF: 800-443-4695 ■ *Web:* www.wilshiremfg.com					
Winona Lighting Inc 3760 W 4th St	Winona	MN	55987	507-454-5113	452-8528
Web: www.winonalighting.com					

443 LIME

				Phone	Fax
Carmeuse North America 11 Stanwix St 11th Fl	Pittsburgh	PA	15222	412-995-5500	995-5570
TF: 800-445-3930 ■ *Web:* www.carmeusena.com					
Cemex Puerto Rico Inc RT 165 KM 2.7 Industrial Amelia Pk	Bucahna Guaynabo	PR	00968	787-783-3000	781-8850
Web: www.cemex.com					
Cheney Lime & Cement 478 Graystone Rd PO Box 160	Allgood	AL	35013	205-625-3031	625-3032
TF: 800-752-8282 ■ *Web:* www.cheneylime.com					
Graymont Inc 10991 Shellbridge Way Suite 200	Richmond	BC	V6X3C6	604-276-9331	276-9337
Web: www.graymont.com					
Martin Limestone Inc PO Box 550	Blue Ball	PA	17506	717-354-1300	766-0202*
**Fax Area Code:* 814 ■ *Web:* www.martinlimestone.com					
Martin Marietta Materials Inc 2710 Wycliff Rd	Raleigh	NC	27607	919-781-4550	
NYSE: MLM ■ *Web:* www.martinmarietta.com					
Mercer Lime & Stone Co 50 Abele Rd Suite 1006	Bridgeville	PA	15017	412-220-0316	220-0347
Web: www.mercerlime.com					
Schildberg Construction Co PO Box 358	Greenfield	IA	50849	641-743-2131	
Texas Industries Inc 1341 W Mockingbird Ln Suite 700W	Dallas	TX	75247	972-647-6700	647-3878
NYSE: TXI ■ *Web:* www.txi.com					
Texas Lime Co PO Box 851	Cleburne	TX	76033	817-641-4433	556-0905
TF Orders: 800-772-8000					
US Lime & Minerals Inc 5429 LBJ Fwy Suite 230	Dallas	TX	75240	972-991-8400	385-1340
NASDAQ: USLM ■ *TF:* 800-991-5463 ■ *Web:* www.uslm.com					
Western Lime Corp PO Box 57	West Bend	WI	53095	262-334-3005	334-2874
TF Cust Svc: 800-433-0036 ■ *Web:* www.westernlime.com					

444 LIMOUSINE SERVICES

				Phone	Fax
1st Corporate Limousine 245 University Ave	Atlanta	GA	30315	770-933-9000	933-9937
TF: 800-241-3943 ■ *Web:* www.careyatlanta.com					
A Family Limousine 6311 Stirling Rd	Davie	FL	33314	954-522-7455	522-7403
TF: 877-599-5466 ■ *Web:* www.afamilylimo.com					
A1 Worldwide Limousine Inc 69 Yorkville Ave Suite 205	Toronto	ON	M5R1B8	416-922-5466	922-4748
TF: 877-537-5466 ■ *Web:* www.a1worldwidelimo.com					
Advantage Limousine Services Inc 8310 Castleford St Suite 200	Houston	TX	77040	713-983-9991	983-9959
TF: 888-983-9991 ■ *Web:* www.advantagelimos.com					
Air Brook Limousine Inc 18 Overlook Ave PO Box 123	Rochelle Park	NJ	07662	201-843-6100	845-4480
TF: 800-800-1990 ■ *Web:* www.airbrook.com					
Alliance Limousine Inc 14553 Delano St Unit 210	Van Nuys	CA	91411	323-465-9406	786-8810*
**Fax Area Code:* 818 ■ *TF:* 800-954-5466 ■ *Web:* www.alliancelimo.net					
Ambassador Limousine 4676 Wynn Rd	Las Vegas	NV	89103	702-362-6200	889-0080
TF: 888-519-5466 ■ *Web:* www.ambassadorlasvegas.com					
American Coach Limousine 1550 W Fullerton Suite 1	Addison	IL	60101	630-629-0001	629-0002
TF: 888-709-5466 ■ *Web:* www.americancoachlimousine.com					
AnyPointLimo.com PO Box 242	Drexel Hill	PA	19026	610-626-9091	628-0782
Web: www.anypointlimo.com					
Arizona Limousines Inc 8900 N Central Ave Suite 101	Phoenix	AZ	85020	602-267-7097	870-3388
TF: 800-678-0033 ■ *Web:* www.arizonalimos.com					
Bayview Limousine Service 15701 Nelson Pl S	Seattle	WA	98188	206-824-6200	277-5895*
**Fax Area Code:* 425 ■ *TF:* 800-606-7880 ■ *Web:* www.bayviewlimo.com					
Bethany Limousine & Bus 2120 W Virginia Ave NE	Washington	DC	20002	202-857-0440	857-7826
TF: 800-424-2971					
Burgundy Global 336 W Passaic St	Rochelle Park	NJ	07662	201-291-4290	
Carey International Inc 4530 Wisconsin Ave NW 5th Fl	Washington	DC	20016	202-895-1200	895-1201
TF: 800-336-4646 ■ *Web:* www.carey.com					
Classic Transportation Group 1600 Locust Ave	Bohemia	NY	11716	631-567-5100	244-9006
TF: 800-666-4949 ■ *Web:* www.classictrans.com					
Connecticut Limousine LLC 230 Old Gate Ln	Milford	CT	06460	203-878-6867	783-6997
TF: 800-472-5466 ■ *Web:* www.ctlimo.com					
Cosmopolitan Limousine 1601 S Preston St	Louisville	KY	40217	502-634-5466	214-7409
TF: 800-603-6594 ■ *Web:* www.cosmolimoky.com					
Dav El Chauffeured Transportation Network 200 2nd St	Chelsea	MA	02150	617-887-0900	887-0902
TF: 800-922-0343 ■ *Web:* www.davel.com					
Elite Limousine Service Inc 1059 12th Ave Suite E	Honolulu	HI	96816	808-735-2431	735-5159
TF: 800-776-2098 ■ *Web:* www.elitelimohawaii.com					
Executive Transportation Brokers Inc PO Box 652	New York	NY	10040	212-927-7152	591-8290*
**Fax Area Code:* 917 ■ *TF:* 877-800-6500 ■ *Web:* www.airportspickup.com					
Executive Transportation Service Inc 7108 DeSoto Ave Suite 204	Canoga Park	CA	91303	818-716-7727	347-4633
TF: 800-348-4010 ■ *Web:* www.execlimoservice.com					
Four Seasons Limousine Co 2432 W Peoria Ave	Phoenix	AZ	85029	602-443-2200	443-2202
TF: 877-379-2200 ■ *Web:* www.fourseasonslimocompany.com					
Gateway Limousines 1550 Gilbreth Rd	Burlingame	CA	94010	650-345-7077	697-7739
TF: 800-486-7077 ■ *Web:* www.gatewaylimousine.com					
International Chauffeured Service Worldwide 53 E 34th St 4th Fl	New York	NY	10016	212-213-0302	266-5254*
**Fax Area Code:* 877 ■ *TF:* 800-266-5254 ■ *Web:* www.bookalimo.com					
Leros First Class 6 Skyline Dr	Hawthorne	NY	10532	914-747-2300	747-2917
TF: 800-825-3767 ■ *Web:* www.leroslimo.com					
Marriton Limousine 13900 N IH-35 Suite J	Austin	TX	78728	512-329-7007	989-7217
TF: 800-940-7007 ■ *Web:* www.marritonlimo.com					
Mears Transportation Group 324 W Gore St	Orlando	FL	32806	407-422-4561	422-6923
TF: 800-759-5219					
Olympic Airporter 5005 Rts 33 & 34 PO Box 708	Farmingdale	NJ	07727	732-938-6666	938-4015
TF: 800-822-9797 ■ *Web:* www.olympic-limo.com					
Omni Limousine Inc 1401 Helm Dr	Las Vegas	NV	89119	702-367-1000	871-6496
TF: 800-325-8003 ■ *Web:* www.omnilimo.com					
Park Cities Limousine 7129 Harry Hines Blvd	Dallas	TX	75235	214-824-0011	827-0136
TF: 888-559-0708 ■ *Web:* www.limodfw.com					

Name / Address	City	State	Zip	Phone	Fax
PHL Limousine Inc PO Box 210 TF: 866-264-5466 ■ Web: www.phl-limo.com	Riverton	NJ	08077	856-786-7151	786-7165
Pioneer Limousine Service 15643 Sherman Way Suite 410 TF: 800-640-0700 ■ Web: www.pioneerlimos.com	Van Nuys	CA	91406	818-609-1566	780-8310
Pontarelli Limousine Service 2225 W Hubbard St TF: 800-322-5466 ■ Web: www.pontarelliischicago.com	Chicago	IL	60612	312-226-5466	226-1300
Regency Limousine International 23-57 83rd St TF: 866-302-2201 ■ Web: www.rlilimo.com	East Elmhurst	NY	11370	718-507-4000	507-8283
Royal Coachman Worldwide 88 Ford Rd Suite 26 TF: 800-472-7433 ■ Web: www.royalcoachman.com	Denville	NJ	07834	973-400-3200	675-4365
Seattle Limousine Service 1237 S Director St TF: 800-274-3339 ■ Web: www.seattlelimo.com	Seattle	WA	98108	206-762-3339	762-3394
Starlite Limousines LLC 15111 N Hayden Rd Suite 300 TF: 877-474-4847 ■ Web: www.starlitelimos.com	Scottsdale	AZ	85260	480-905-1234	422-4396
SuperShuttle International Inc 14500 N Northsight Blvd Suite 329 Web: www.supershuttle.com	Scottsdale	AZ	85260	480-609-3000	607-9317
US Coachways Inc 87 Ellis St Suite 4 TF: 800-359-5991 ■ Web: www.uscoachways.com	Staten Island	NY	10307	718-477-4242	477-9009
VIPride.com 15111 N Hayden Rd Suite 300 TF: 877-474-4847 ■ Web: www.vipride.com	Scottsdale	AZ	85260	480-905-1234	422-4396

445 LINEN & UNIFORM SUPPLY

Name / Address	City	State	Zip	Phone	Fax
A & P Coat Apron & Linen Supply 161 S Macquesten Pkwy TF: 800-627-3682 ■ Web: www.rent-a-uniform.com	Mount Vernon	NY	10550	914-840-3200	662-4511
Ace ImageWear 4120 Truman Rd TF: 800-366-0564 ■ Web: www.aaauniform.com	Kansas City	MO	64127	816-231-5737	231-3550
Ace-Tex Enterprises 7601 Central St TF: 800-444-3800 ■ Web: www.ace-tex.com	Detroit	MI	48210	313-834-4000	834-0260
Admiral Linen Service Inc 2030 Kipling St TF: 800-321-1948 ■ Web: www.admiralservices.com	Houston	TX	77098	713-529-2608	529-3061
AmeriPride Services Inc 10801 Wayzata Blvd TF Cust Svc: 800-595-3913 ■ Web: www.ameripride.com	Minnetonka	MN	55305	952-738-4200	738-4252
Angelica Corp Ten Peachtree Pl NE NYSE: AGL ■ TF: 800-235-8410 ■ Web: www.aglresources.com	Atlanta	GA	30309	404-584-4000	584-3945
Apparelmaster 123 Harrison Ave TF: 877-543-1678 ■ Web: www.apparelmaster.net	Harrison	OH	45030	513-202-1600	202-1660
Arrow Uniform Rental Inc 6400 Monroe Blvd TF: 800-552-7769 ■ Web: www.arrowuniform.com	Taylor	MI	48180	313-299-5000	299-5093
Capitol Uniform & Linen Service PO Box 1414 TF: 800-323-1511	Dover	DE	19903	302-674-1511	674-1558
Cintas Corp PO Box 625737 NASDAQ: CTAS ■ TF: 800-786-4367 ■ Web: www.cintas.com	Cincinnati	OH	45262	513-459-1200	
Clean Textile Systems Inc PO Box 40330 TF: 800-222-7600 ■ Web: www.clncare.com	Pittsburgh	PA	15201	412-687-7900	687-5490
Continental Linen Services 4200 Manchester Rd TF: 800-875-4636 ■ Web: www.clsimage.com	Kalamazoo	MI	49001	269-343-2551	343-7246
Coyne Textile Services Inc 140 Cortland Ave TF: 800-672-6963 ■ Web: www.coynetextileservices.com	Syracuse	NY	13202	315-475-1626	475-2140
Domestic Linen Supply & Laundry Inc 3800 18th St TF: 800-430-0871 ■ Web: www.domesticuniform.com	Detroit	MI	48208	313-831-6700	831-2617
G & K Services fInc 324 Taylor St TF: 800-255-8391 ■ Web: www.gkservices.com	Manchester	NH	03103	603-625-9722	625-5413
G & K Services Inc 5995 Opus Pkwy Suite 500 Web: www.gkservices.com	Minnetonka	MN	55343	952-912-5500	912-5999
Healthcare Services Group Inc (HCSG) 3220 Tillman Dr Suite 300 NASDAQ: HCSG ■ TF: 800-363-4274 ■ Web: www.hcsgcorp.com	Bensalem	PA	19020	215-639-4274	639-2152
Hospital Laundry Services Inc (HLS) 45 W Hintz Rd Web: www.hlschicago.com	Wheeling	IL	60090	847-229-0900	537-9198
Industrial Towel & Uniform Inc 2700 S 160th St TF: 800-767-2487 ■ Web: www.itu-at.com	New Berlin	WI	53151	262-782-1950	782-1802
Iron City Uniform Rental 6640 Frankstown Ave TF: 800-532-2010 ■ Web: www.ironcityuniform.com	Pittsburgh	PA	15206	412-661-2001	661-9356
Linens of the Week 713 Lamont St NW TF: 800-355-8874 ■ Web: www.linensoftheweek.com	Washington	DC	20010	202-291-9200	291-6485
Mickey's Linen & Towel Supply 4601 W Addison St	Chicago	IL	60641	773-545-7211	545-9111
Mission Linen Supply 635 E Montecito St TF: 800-944-5539 ■ Web: www.missionlinen.com	Santa Barbara	CA	93103	805-963-1841	730-3718
Model Coverall Service Inc 100 28th St SE TF: 800-968-6491 ■ Web: www.modelcoverall.com	Grand Rapids	MI	49548	616-241-6491	241-0677
Morgan Services Inc 323 N Michigan Ave TF: 888-966-7426 ■ Web: www.morganservices.com	Chicago	IL	60601	312-346-3181	346-0144
Overall Laundry Service Inc 7200 Hardeson Rd TF: 800-683-7255	Everett	WA	98203	425-353-0800	290-6519
Prudential Overall Supply PO Box 11210 TF: 800-767-5536 ■ Web: www.pos-clean.com	Santa Ana	CA	92711	949-250-4855	261-1947
Roscoe Co 3535 W Harrison St TF Cust Svc: 888-476-7263 ■ Web: www.eroscoe.com	Chicago	IL	60624	773-722-5000	722-0827
S & R Uniforms Inc 1833 14th St W TF: 800-553-4065 ■ Web: www.sruniforms.com	Bradenton	FL	34205	941-748-1245	747-4699
Sitex Corp 1300 Commonwealth Dr TF: 800-278-3537 ■ Web: www.sitex-corp.com	Henderson	KY	42420	270-827-3537	826-5567
Superior Linen Service 1012 S Ctr St	Tacoma	WA	98409	253-383-2636	383-1061
Textile Care Services Inc 225 Wood Lake Dr SE TF: 800-422-0945 ■ Web: www.textilecs.com	Rochester	MN	55904	507-288-1861	252-7550
UniFirst Corp 68 Jonspin Rd NYSE: UNF ■ TF: 800-347-7888 ■ Web: www.unifirst.com	Wilmington	MA	01887	978-658-8888	657-5663
Unitech Services Group 295 Parker St TF: 800-344-3824 ■ Web: www.unitechus.com	Springfield	MA	01151	413-543-6911	543-6989
Valiant Products Corp 2727 5th Ave W TF Cust Svc: 800-347-2727 ■ Web: www.valiantproducts.com	Denver	CO	80204	303-892-1234	892-5535
Western Uniform & Towel Service Inc 1707 N Mosley St TF: 800-214-2342 ■ Web: www.westernuniform.com	Wichita	KS	67214	316-264-2342	264-9042
WH Christian & Sons Inc 22 Franklin St # 28 Web: www.whchristian.com	Brooklyn	NY	11222	718-389-7000	389-9644

446 LIQUOR STORES

Name / Address	City	State	Zip	Phone	Fax
21st Amendment Inc 1158 W 86th St Web: www.21stamendment.com	Indianapolis	IN	46260	317-846-1678	846-5687
ABC Fine Wines & Spirits 8989 S Orange Ave TF: 800-854-7283 ■ Web: www.abcfinewineandspirits.com	Orlando	FL	32824	407-851-0000	857-5500
Berbiglia Inc 1114 W 103 St Web: www.berbiglia.com	Kansas City	MO	64114	816-942-0070	942-1777
Bevmax Wines & Liquors 835 E Main St Web: www.bevmax.com	Stamford	CT	06902	203-357-9151	359-9967
BevMo! 1470 Enea Cir Suite 1600 Web: www.bevmo.com	Concord	CA	94520	925-609-6000	
BK Miller Co Inc 4501 Auth Pl TF: 800-801-7632 ■ Web: www.bkmiller.com	Suitland	MD	20746	301-423-6200	423-0251
Country Vintner The 12305 N Lakeridge Pkwy PO Box 217 Web: www.countryvintner.com	Oilville	VA	23129	804-752-3670	752-3685
Crown Liquors of Fort Lauderdale 910 NW 10th Pl TF: 888-563-9463 ■ Web: www.crownwineandspirits.com	Fort Lauderdale	FL	33311	954-763-6831	462-0125
Don's & Ben's Inc 10903 Industry Dr	San Antonio	TX	78217	210-646-9992	646-6145
Fine Wine Brokers Inc 4621 N Lincoln Ave Web: www.fwbchicago.com	Chicago	IL	60625	773-989-8166	989-8166
Flanigan's Enterprises Inc 5059 NE 18th Ave AMEX: BDL ■ Web: www.flanigans.net	Fort Lauderdale	FL	33334	954-377-1961	377-1980
Gold Standard Enterprises Inc 5100 W Dempster St TF: 888-942-9463 ■ Web: www.binnys.com	Skokie	IL	60077	847-674-4200	568-9905
Goody-Goody Liquors Inc 10301 Harry Hines Blvd Web: www.goodygoody.com	Dallas	TX	75229	214-350-5806	350-4258
Kings Liquor Inc 2810 W Berry St Web: www.kingsliquor.com	Fort Worth	TX	76109	817-923-3737	927-0021
Maggiore Cos 2927 Harrisburg Rd NE	Canton	OH	44705	330-454-7913	454-7978
MGM Liquor Stores Inc 1124 Larpenteur Ave W	Saint Paul	MN	55113	651-487-1006	487-9401
Mozingo Liquors Inc 120 S 6th St	Hartsville	SC	29550	843-332-6554	332-6921
Pearlstine Distributors Inc (PDI) 1600 Christon Rgonal Pkwy TF: 800-922-1048 ■ Web: www.pearlstine.net	Charleston	SC	29492	843-388-6800	388-6799
Pinkie's Inc 1426 E 8th St Web: www.pinkiesonline.com	Odessa	TX	79761	432-580-0439	580-0918
Richard's Liquors & Fine Wines 1701 Brun St Suite 200 Web: www.richardsliquors.com	Houston	TX	77219	713-529-6266	529-3884
Sherry-Lehmann Wine & Spirits 505 Pk Ave Web: www.sherry-lehmann.com	New York	NY	10022	212-838-7500	838-9285
Shop 'N Save Liquors 20 Independence Ave	Quincy	MA	02169	617-773-2060	786-9797
Sigel's Beverages LP 2960 Anode Ln Web: www.sigels.com	Dallas	TX	75220	214-350-1271	357-3490
Spec's Wines Spirits & Finer Foods 2410 Smith St TF: 888-526-8787 ■ Web: www.specsonline.com	Houston	TX	77006	713-526-8787	526-6129
Touring & Tasting 125 S Quarantina St TF: 800-850-4370 ■ Web: www.touringandtasting.com	Santa Barbara	CA	93103	805-965-2813	965-2873
Wine Club The 2110 E McFadden Ave Suite E TF: 800-966-5432 ■ Web: www.thewineclub.com	Santa Ana	CA	92705	714-835-6485	835-5062
Wine.com Inc 114 Sansome St 6th Fl *Fax Area Code: 415 ■ TF: 877-289-6886 ■ Web: www.wine.com	San Francisco	CA	94104	877-289-6886	291-9599*
Zachys Wine & Liquor Inc 16 E Pkwy TF: 800-723-0241 ■ Web: www.zachys.com	Scarsdale	NY	10583	914-723-0241	723-1033

447 LITERARY AGENTS

Name / Address	City	State	Zip	Phone	Fax
Aaron M Priest Literary Agency 708 3rd Ave 23rd FL	New York	NY	10017	212-818-0344	573-9417
Browne & Miller Literary Assoc LLC 410 S Michigan Ave Suite 460 Web: www.browneandmiller.com	Chicago	IL	60605	312-922-3063	922-1905
Carol Mann Agency 55 5th Ave Web: www.carolmannagency.wordpress.com	New York	NY	10003	212-206-5635	675-4809
David Black Literary Agency 156 5th Ave Suite 608	New York	NY	10010	212-242-5080	924-6609
Dominick Abel Literary Agency Inc 146 W 82nd St Suite 1B	New York	NY	10024	212-877-0710	595-3133
Don Congdon Assoc Inc 156 5th Ave Suite 625	New York	NY	10010	212-645-1229	727-2688
Donadio & Olsen Inc 121 W 27th St Suite 704	New York	NY	10001	212-691-8077	633-2837
Dystel & Goderich Literary Management 1 Union Sq W Suite 904 Web: www.dystel.com	New York	NY	10003	212-627-9100	627-9313

	City	State	Zip	Phone	Fax
Elaine Markson Literary Agency 44 Greenwich Ave	New York	NY	10011	212-243-8480	691-9014
Fifi Oscard Agency 110 W 40th St 16th Fl	New York	NY	10018	212-764-1100	840-5019
Web: www.fifioscard.com					
Frances Collin Literary Agent PO Box 33	Wayne	PA	19087	610-254-0555	254-5029
Web: www.francescollin.com					
George Borchardt Inc 136 E 57th St	New York	NY	10022	212-753-5785	838-6518
Harold Ober Assoc Inc 425 Madison Ave 10th Fl	New York	NY	10017	212-759-8600	759-9428
Web: www.haroldober.com					
Harvey Klinger Inc 300 W 55th St	New York	NY	10019	212-581-7068	315-3823
Web: www.harveyklinger.com					
IMG Literary 767 5th Ave	New York	NY	10153	646-558-8357	558-8399
Web: www.imgworld.com					
InkWell Management 521 5th Ave Suite 2600	New York	NY	10175	212-922-3500	922-0535
Web: www.inkwellmanagement.com					
Jane Rotrosen Agency 318 E 51st St	New York	NY	10022	212-593-4330	935-6985
Jean V Naggar Literary Agency Inc 216 E 75th St Suite 1E	New York	NY	10021	212-794-1082	794-3605
Web: www.jvnla.com					
John Hawkins & Assoc Inc 71 W 23rd St Suite 1600	New York	NY	10010	212-807-7040	807-9555
Web: www.jhalit.com					
Joy Harris Literary Agency 156 5th Ave Suite 617	New York	NY	10010	212-924-6269	924-6609
Larsen Pomada Literary Agents 1029 Jones St	San Francisco	CA	94109	415-673-0939	
Web: www.larsenpomada.com					
Loretta Barrett Books Inc 220 E 23rd St # 11	New York	NY	10010	212-242-3420	807-9579
Web: www.lorettabarrettbooks.com					
Lowenstein-Yost Assoc Inc 121 W 27th St Suite 601	New York	NY	10001	212-206-1630	727-0280
Web: www.lowensteinyost.com					
Manus & Assoc Literary Agency Inc 425 Sherman Ave Suite 200	Palo Alto	CA	94306	650-470-5151	470-5159
Web: www.manuslit.com					
New England Publishing Assoc Inc 59 Parker Hill Rd	Higganum	CT	06441	860-345-7323	345-3660
Web: www.nepa.com					
Nolan/Lehr Group Betsy Nolan Literary Agency Div 214 W 29th St Suite 1002	New York	NY	10001	212-967-8200	967-7292
Richard Curtis Assoc Inc 171 E 74th St 2nd Fl	New York	NY	10021	212-772-7363	772-7393
Web: www.curtisagency.com					
Sanford J Greenburger Assoc Inc 55 5th Ave 15th Fl	New York	NY	10003	212-206-5600	463-8718
Web: www.greenburger.com					
Sarah Jane Freymann Literary Agency 59 W 71st St Suite 9B	New York	NY	10023	212-362-9277	501-8240
Web: www.sarahjanefreymann.com					
Trident Media Group LLC 41 Madison Ave 36th Fl	New York	NY	10010	212-262-4810	262-4849
Web: www.tridentmediagroup.com					
Wallace Literary Agency 301 E 79th St Suite 14-J	New York	NY	10021	212-570-9090	772-8979
William Morris Agency 1325 Avenue of the Americas	New York	NY	10019	212-586-5100	246-3583
Web: www.wma.com					
William Morris Agency 1 William Morris Pl	Beverly Hills	CA	90212	310-859-4000	859-4462
Web: www.wma.com					
Writers House 21 W 26th St	New York	NY	10010	212-685-2400	685-1781
Web: www.writershouse.com					

448 LITIGATION SUPPORT SERVICES

	City	State	Zip	Phone	Fax
Al Betz & Assoc 12 Ridge View Dr	Westminster	MD	21157	410-752-1733	875-2857
Web: www.albetzreporting.com					
Alderson Reporting Co 1155 Connecticut Ave NW # 200	Washington	DC	20036	202-289-2260	289-2221
TF: 800-367-3376 ■ *Web:* www.aldersonreporting.com					
Allied Court Reporters Inc 115 Phenix Ave	Cranston	RI	02920	401-946-5500	946-9228
TF: 888-443-3767 ■ *Web:* www.alliedcourtreporters.com					
Atkinson-Baker Inc (ABI) 500 N Brand Blvd 3rd Fl	Glendale	CA	91203	818-551-7300	925-5910*
**Fax Area Code:* 800 ■ *TF:* 800-288-3376 ■ *Web:* www.depo.com/abtabi.htm					
Compex Legal Services Inc 325 S Maple Ave	Torrance	CA	90503	310-782-1801	479-3365*
**Fax Area Code:* 800 ■ *TF Cust Svc:* 800-426-6739 ■ *Web:* www.cpxlegal.com					
Courtroom Sciences Inc 4950 N O'Connor Rd Corporate Plaza 1 1st Fl	Irving	TX	75062	972-717-1773	717-3985
Web: www.courtroomsciences.com					
DecisionQuest 21535 Hawthorne Blvd Suite 310	Torrance	CA	90503	310-618-9600	618-1122
TF: 800-327-2449 ■ *Web:* www.decisionquest.com					
Depobook Reporting Services 1600 G St Suite 101	Modesto	CA	95354	209-544-6466	544-6566
TF: 800-830-8885 ■ *Web:* www.depobook.com					
DepoNet 25 A Vreeland Rd Suite 200	Florham Park	NJ	07932	800-337-6638	288-2473*
**Fax Area Code:* 723 ■ *TF:* 800-337-6638 ■ *Web:* www.deponet.com					
DOAR Litigation Consulting 170 Earle Ave	Lynbrook	NY	11563	516-823-4000	823-4400
Web: www.doar.com					
FTI Consulting Inc 900 Bestgate Rd	Annapolis	MD	21401	410-224-8770	224-8378
NYSE: FCN ■ *TF:* 800-334-5701					
Hahn & Bowersock Corp 151 Kalmus Dr Suite L1	Costa Mesa	CA	92626	714-549-3700	549-3641
TF: 800-660-3187 ■ *Web:* www.hahnbowersock.com					
Hutchings Court Reporters LLC 6055 E Washington Blvd 8th Fl	Los Angeles	CA	90040	323-888-6300	888-6333
TF Cust Svc: 800-697-3210 ■ *Web:* www.hutchings.com					
Jane Rose Reporting 74 5th Ave	New York	NY	10011	715-472-4631	825-9055*
**Fax Area Code:* 800 ■ *TF:* 800-825-3341 ■ *Web:* www.janerose.net					
Jury Research Institute 2617 Danville Blvd PO Box 100	Alamo	CA	94507	925-932-5663	932-8409
TF: 800-233-5879 ■ *Web:* www.jri-inc.com					
LegaLink 101 Arch St 3rd Fl	Boston	MA	02110	617-542-0039	542-2119
TF: 800-662-1466 ■ *Web:* www.legalink.com					
National Forensic Ctr PO Box 270529	San Diego	CA	92198	858-487-0300	487-7747
Professional Shorthand Reporters Inc 601 Poydras St Suite 1615	New Orleans	LA	70130	504-529-5255	529-5257
TF: 800-536-5255 ■ *Web:* www.psrdepo.com					
Ralph Rosenberg Court Reporters Inc 1001 Bishop St Suite 2460	Honolulu	HI	96813	808-524-2090	524-2596
TF: 888-524-5888 ■ *Web:* www.hawaiicourtreporters.com					
Starr Litigation Services Inc 1201 Grand Ave	West Des Moines	IA	50265	515-224-1616	224-4863
TF: 800-627-8277 ■ *Web:* www.starrlit.com					
Trial Behavior Consulting Inc 505 Sansome St Suite 1701	San Francisco	CA	94111	415-781-5879	362-8775
Web: www.trialbehavior.com					
US Legal Support Inc 363 N Sam Houston Pkwy E Suite 900	Houston	TX	77060	713-653-7100	653-7171
TF: 800-567-8757 ■ *Web:* www.uslegalsupport.com					
Verdict Systems LLC 1400 E Southern Ave Suite 710	Tempe	AZ	85282	480-627-2430	627-2431
Web: www.verdictsystems.com					
Veritext LLC 25 B Vreeland Rd Suite 301	Florham Park	NJ	07932	973-410-4040	410-1313
Web: www.veritextllc.com					
Z-Axis Corp 5445 DTC Pkwy Suite 450	Greenwood Village	CO	80111	303-713-0200	713-0299
TF: 800-827-2947 ■ *Web:* www.zaxis.com					

449 LIVESTOCK - WHOL

SEE ALSO Cattle Ranches, Farms, Feedlots (Beef Cattle) p. 1376; Hog Farms p. 1378

	City	State	Zip	Phone	Fax
Alabama Livestock Auction Inc 700 Hwy 80 E	Uniontown	AL	36786	334-628-2371	628-6268
Bales Continental Commission Co 39763 US Hwy 14 PO Box 1337	Huron	SD	57350	605-352-8682	352-9374
Web: www.balesccc.com					
Blackfoot Livestock Auction 93 Rich Ln PO Box 830	Blackfoot	ID	83221	208-785-0500	785-0503
Web: www.blackfootlivestockauction.com					
Blue Grass Stockyard 375 Lisle Industrial Ave PO Box 1023	Lexington	KY	40588	859-255-7701	255-5495
TF: 800-621-3972 ■ *Web:* www.bgstockyards.com					
Capital Land & Livestock Co PO Box 1	Schwertner	TX	76573	254-527-3342	527-4400
Web: www.cllnet.com					
Central Livestock Assn 310 Market Ln PO Box 419	South Saint Paul	MN	55075	651-451-1844	451-1774
TF: 800-733-1844 ■ *Web:* www.cri.crinet.com					
D & S Cattle Co 2167 SR 66 PO Box 172	Zolfo Springs	FL	33890	863-735-1112	735-1282
TF: 800-522-0534					
Delta Sales Yard 700 W 5th St	Delta	CO	81416	970-874-4612	874-3087
Empire Livestock Marketing LLC 5001 Brittonfield Pkwy	East Syracuse	NY	13035	315-433-9129	431-1328
TF: 800-462-8802 ■ *Web:* www.empirelivestock.com					
Equity Co-op Livestock Sales Assn 401 Commerce Ave	Baraboo	WI	53913	608-356-8311	356-0117
TF: 800-362-3989 ■ *Web:* www.equitycoop.com					
Farmers Livestock Auction Inc 1581 E Emma Ave	Springdale	AR	72764	479-751-5727	751-5896
Farmers Livestock Marketing Assn 840 IL Rt 127 PO Box 435	Greenville	IL	62246	618-664-1432	664-2868
TF: 800-743-9110 ■ *Web:* www.farmerslivestock.com					
Finger Lakes Livestock Exchange Inc 3865 SR 5 & 20	Canandaigua	NY	14424	585-394-1515	394-9151
Web: www.fingerlakeslivestockex.com					
Four States Livestock Sales 501 E 1st St	Hagerstown	MD	21741	301-733-8120	733-7318
High Plains Livestock Exchange LLC 28601 US Hwy 34	Brush	CO	80723	970-842-5115	842-5088
TF: 866-842-5115 ■ *Web:* www.hplivestock.com					
Jamestown Livestock Auction 3443 82nd Ave SE	Jamestown	ND	58401	701-252-2111	252-1520
TF: 800-718-2111 ■ *Web:* www.jamestownlivestock.com					
Kidron Auction Inc 4885 Kidron Rd	Kidron	OH	44636	330-857-2641	857-2507
TF: 800-589-9749					
Lewiston Sales Inc 21241 Dutchmans Crossing Rd	Lewiston	MN	55952	507-523-2112	523-2400
TF: 800-732-6334					
Lynch Livestock Co 331 3rd St NW	Waucoma	IA	52171	563-776-3311	
Web: www.lynchlivestock.com					
Midwest Land & Cattle Co Inc PO Box 816	Olathe	KS	66051	913-782-6677	782-7883
Miller Livestock Markets Inc 100 Sale Barn Rd	Dequincy	LA	70633	337-786-2995	786-3270
Mo-Kan Livestock Markets Inc RR 2 PO Box 152	Butler	MO	64730	660-679-6535	679-6540
TF: 800-887-8156 ■ *Web:* www.mokanlivestock.com					
O & S Cattle Co 100 Stockyards Rd Suite 106	South Saint Paul	MN	55075	651-455-1102	455-8394
TF: 800-328-0124					
Pipestone Livestock Auction Market 1500 7th St SE	Pipestone	MN	56164	507-825-3306	825-3308
Web: www.pipestonelivestock.com					
Prairie Livestock LLC 2139 Barton Ferry Rd	West Point	MS	39773	662-494-5651	494-2672
TF: 800-647-6350 ■ *Web:* www.prairielivestock.net					
Producers Livestock Auction Co 1131 N Bell St	San Angelo	TX	76903	325-653-3371	653-3370
Web: www.producersandcargile.com					
Producers Livestock Marketing Assn 4809 S 114th St	Omaha	NE	68137	402-597-9189	597-9505
TF: 800-257-4046 ■ *Web:* www.plmcoop.com					

Company	City	State	ZIP	Phone	Fax
Robert Winner Sons Inc 8544 St Rt 705 PO Box 39	Osgood	OH	45351	419-582-4321	582-3013
Web: www.arenspub.com					
Roswell Livestock Auction Sales Inc 900 N Garden PO Box 2041	Roswell	NM	88202	575-622-5580	623-5680*
*Fax Area Code: 505 ■ *Web:* www.roswelllivestockauction.com					
Sennett Sales Inc 3180 Tpke Rd	Sennett	NY	13021	315-253-3579	253-3579
Sheridan Livestock Auction Co Inc PO Box 378	Rushville	NE	69360	308-327-2406	327-2383
Stockmen's Livestock Market Inc E Hwy 50 PO Box 280	Yankton	SD	57078	605-665-9641	665-9644
TF: 800-532-0952 ■ *Web:* www.livestock-marketing.com					
Thomas Cattle Buying Services 14451 NE 20th St	Williston	FL	32696	352-528-4518	528-2510
TF: 800-654-1871					
Topeka Auction & Marketing Inc 601 E Lake St	Topeka	IN	46571	260-593-2522	593-2258
Turner County Stockyard 1315 US Hwy 41 S	Ashburn	GA	31714	229-567-3371	
United Producers Inc 5909 Cleveland Ave	Columbus	OH	43229	614-890-6666	890-4776
TF: 800-456-3276 ■ *Web:* www.uproducers.com					
Wayland Hopkins Livestock 3634 10th St	Wayland	MI	49348	269-792-2296	792-8055
Wiechman Pig Co Inc 725 Schneider	Fremont	NE	68025	402-721-5115	727-1919
TF: 800-727-5153					
Winner Livestock Auction Co 31690 Livestock Barn Rd	Winner	SD	57580	605-842-0451	842-3562
TF: 800-201-0451 ■ *Web:* www.winnerlivestock.com					
Winter Livestock Inc 11802 W Owen K Garriott Rd PO Box 909	Enid	OK	73703	580-237-4600	237-4604
Web: www.winterlivestock.com					
Wisconsin Livestock Brokers Inc PO Box 13125	Green Bay	WI	54307	920-865-7404	865-4001

450 LIVESTOCK & POULTRY FEEDS - PREPARED

Company	City	State	ZIP	Phone	Fax
Acco Feeds Inc 1025 China St	Abilene	TX	79602	325-672-3271	672-1704
TF: 800-592-4476 ■ *Web:* www.accofeeds.com					
ADM Alliance Nutrition Inc 1000 N 30th St	Quincy	IL	62301	217-222-7100	222-4069
TF: 800-292-3333 ■ *Web:* www.admani.com					
AG Partners Inc 512 S 8th St PO Box 467	Lake City	MN	55041	651-345-3328	345-2212
TF: 800-772-2990					
Ag Processing Inc 12700 W Dodge Rd PO Box 2047	Omaha	NE	68103	402-496-7809	498-5548
TF: 800-247-1345 ■ *Web:* www.agp.com					
Agri-King Inc 18246 Waller Rd	Fulton	IL	61252	815-589-2525	589-4700
TF: 800-435-9560 ■ *Web:* www.agriking.com					
Ahrberg Milling Co 200 S Depot St PO Box 968	Cushing	OK	74023	918-225-0267	225-0275
TF: 800-324-0267 ■ *Web:* www.ahrbergmilling.com					
AL Gilbert Co 304 N Yosemite Ave	Oakdale	CA	95361	209-847-1721	847-3542
TF: 800-847-1721					
Alabama Farmers Co-op Inc PO Box 2227	Decatur	AL	35601	256-353-6843	350-1770
TF: 800-737-6843 ■ *Web:* www.alafarm.com					
Alaska Garden & Pet Supply Inc PO Box 101246	Anchorage	AK	99510	907-279-4519	276-7416
Web: www.alaskamillandfeed.com					
Albion Laboratories Inc 101 N Main St	Clearfield	UT	84015	801-773-4631	773-4633
TF: 800-453-2406 ■ *Web:* www.albion-an.com					
Alderman Cave Feeds 158 N Main St PO Box 217	Winters	TX	79567	325-754-4546	754-4549
TF: 800-588-3333					
American Proteins Inc 4705 Leland Dr	Cumming	GA	30041	770-886-2250	886-2296
TF: 800-346-7476 ■ *Web:* www.americanproteins.com					
Bagdad Roller Mills Inc 5740 Elmburg Rd PO Box 7	Bagdad	KY	40003	502-747-8968	747-8960
TF: 800-928-3333 ■ *Web:* www.bagdadrollermills.com					
Belstra Milling Co Inc 424 15th St PO Box 460	Demotte	IN	46310	219-987-4343	987-5227
TF: 800-276-2789 ■ *Web:* www.belstramilling.com					
BioZyme Inc 6010 Stockyards Expy	Saint Joseph	MO	64504	816-238-3326	238-7549
TF: 800-821-3070 ■ *Web:* www.biozymeinc.com					
Blue Seal Feeds Inc 15 Buttrick Rd	Londonderry	NH	03053	603-437-3400	437-3403
TF Cust Svc: 800-367-2730 ■ *Web:* www.blueseal.com					
Buckeye Nutrition 330 E Schultz Ave PO Box 505	Dalton	OH	44618	330-828-2251	828-2309
TF: 800-417-6460 ■ *Web:* www.buckeyenutrition.com					
Cargill Inc North America 15407 McGinty Rd	Wayzata	MN	55391	952-742-7575	
TF: 800-227-4455					
Central AG Services 209 N Bridge St PO Box 98	Clarissa	MN	56440	218-756-2112	756-2451
TF: 800-432-6340 ■ *Web:* www.centralagserv.com					
Circle S Ranch Inc 1604 Cir S Ranch Rd	Monroe	NC	28112	704-764-7414	764-7646
Cumberland Valley Co-op Assn 908 Mt Rock Rd	Shippensburg	PA	17257	717-532-2191	532-4353
TF: 800-488-2197					
Cutler-Dickerson Co Inc 507 College Ave	Adrian	MI	49221	517-265-5191	263-4213
TF: 800-968-5191					
D & D Commodities Ltd PO Box 359	Stephen	MN	56757	218-478-3308	478-3533
TF: 800-543-3308 ■ *Web:* www.ddcommodities.com					
Dairymen's Feed & Supply Co-op 323 E Washington St	Petaluma	CA	94952	707-763-1585	763-5239
TF Cust Svc: 800-862-4699					
Darling International Inc 251 O'Connor Ridge Blvd Suite 300	Irving	TX	75038	972-717-0300	717-1588
AMEX: DAR ■ *TF:* 800-800-4841 ■ *Web:* www.darlingii.com					
DeKalb Feeds Inc 105 Dixon Ave	Rock Falls	IL	61071	815-625-4546	
Diamond V Mills Inc PO Box 74570	Cedar Rapids	IA	52407	319-366-0745	366-6333
TF: 800-373-7234 ■ *Web:* www.diamondv.com					
Eagle Roller Mill Co 1101 Airport Rd	Shelby	NC	28150	704-487-5061	482-1263
TF: 800-223-9108 ■ *Web:* www.eaglerollermill.com					
Effingham Equity Inc 201 W Roadway Ave	Effingham	IL	62401	217-342-4101	347-7601
TF: 800-223-1337 ■ *Web:* www.effinghamequity.com					
Elenbaas Co 411 W Front St	Sumas	WA	98295	360-988-5811	988-0411
TF: 800-808-6954 ■ *Web:* www.elenbaasco.com					
Farm Service Elevator Co 3939 County Rd 5 SW PO Box 933	Willmar	MN	56201	320-235-8870	235-8879
TF: 800-328-8847					
Farmers Co-op Elevator Co 177 W Main St PO Box 108	Cottonwood	MN	56229	507-423-5412	423-5551
Farmers Co-op Elevator Co 109 Isabella St	Radcliffe	IA	50230	515-899-2101	899-2105
Web: www.radcliffecoop.com					
Farmers Ranchers Co-op Assn Of Ainsworth 224 S Main St	Ainsworth	NE	69210	402-387-2811	387-0189
TF: 800-233-6627 ■ *Web:* www.farmersrancherscoop.com					
Farmers Union Co-op 14610 240th St E	Hastings	MN	55033	651-437-8333	
Feed Products Inc 1000 W 47th Ave	Denver	CO	80211	303-455-3646	477-6206
TF: 800-332-8285					
First Co-op Assn 113 N Lewis Ave	Cleghorn	IA	51014	712-436-2224	436-2655
TF: 800-594-9424 ■ *Web:* www.firstcoop.com					
FL Emmert Co Inc 2007 Dunlap St	Cincinnati	OH	45214	513-721-5808	721-6087
TF: 800-441-3343 ■ *Web:* www.emmert.com					
Flint River Mills Inc 1100 Dothan Rd PO Box 280	Bainbridge	GA	39818	229-246-2232	243-7376*
*Fax: Cust Svc ■ *TF Cust Svc:* 800-841-8502					
FM Brown's Sons Inc 127 S Furnace St PO Box 67	Birdsboro	PA	19508	610-582-2741	
TF: 800-362-6455 ■ *Web:* www.fmbrown.com					
Form-A-Feed Inc 740 Bowman St	Stewart	MN	55385	320-562-2413	562-2125
TF: 800-422-3649 ■ *Web:* www.formafeed.com					
Franklin Feed & Supply Co 1977 Philadelphia Ave	Chambersburg	PA	17201	717-264-6148	264-7865
TF: 800-722-2074					
Friona Industries LP 500 S Taylor St Suite 601 PO Box 15568	Amarillo	TX	79105	806-374-1811	374-1324
TF: 800-658-6014 ■ *Web:* www.frionaind.com					
Furst-McNess Co 120 E Clark St	Freeport	IL	61032	815-235-6151	232-9724
TF: 800-435-5131 ■ *Web:* www.mcness.com					
Goldsboro Milling Co 938 Millers Chapel Rd	Goldsboro	NC	27534	919-778-3130	778-8111
TF: 800-768-7823					
Grange Co-op 89 Alder St PO Box 3637	Central Point	OR	97502	541-664-1261	664-1246
TF: 800-888-6317 ■ *Web:* www.grangecoop.com					
Griffin Industries 4221 Alexandria Pike	Cold Spring	KY	41076	859-781-2010	572-2575
TF: 800-743-7413 ■ *Web:* www.griffinind.com					
H Rockwell & Son 164 Troy St	Canton	PA	17724	570-673-5148	673-5150
TF: 888-654-6626					
Harvest Land Co-op 711 Front St PO Box 278	Morgan	MN	56266	507-249-3196	641-2179
TF: 800-245-5819 ■ *Web:* www.harvestland.com					
Hogslat Midwest Inc 200 N & Meridian Rd	Camden	IN	46917	574-967-4145	967-4742
TF: 800-735-4135					
Hubbard Feeds Inc 424 N Riverfront Dr PO Box 8500	Mankato	MN	56001	507-388-9400	388-9453
TF: 800-869-7219 ■ *Web:* www.hubbardfeeds.com					
Hunt & Behrens Inc 30 Lakeville St	Petaluma	CA	94952	707-762-4594	762-9164
International Ingredient Corp 150 Larkin Williams Industrial Ct PO Box 26377	Fenton	MO	63026	636-343-4111	349-4845
Web: www.iicag.com					
J & H Milling Co Inc 101 W Mills St	Walstonburg	NC	27888	252-753-4290	753-4290
JBS United Inc 4310 W SR 38 PO Box 108	Sheridan	IN	46069	317-758-4495	758-9016
Web: www.jbsunited.com					
JD Heiskell & Co 116 W Cedar St	Tulare	CA	93274	559-685-6100	686-8697
TF: 800-366-1886 ■ *Web:* www.heiskell.com					
John A Van Den Bosch Co 4511 Holland Ave	Holland	MI	49424	616-848-2000	848-2100
TF Cust Svc: 800-968-6477 ■ *Web:* www.vbosch.com					
Kay Dee Feed Co Inc 1919 Grand Ave	Sioux City	IA	51106	712-277-2011	279-1946
TF Cust Svc: 800-831-4815 ■ *Web:* www.kay-flow.com					
Keith Smith Co Inc 130 K-Tech Ln PO Box 3800	Hot Springs	AR	71914	501-760-0100	760-9199
Web: www.keith-smith.com					
Kemin Industries Inc 2100 Maury St	Des Moines	IA	50317	515-266-2111	559-5223
TF: 800-777-8307 ■ *Web:* www.kemin.com					
Kent Feeds Inc 1600 Oregon St	Muscatine	IA	52761	563-264-4211	264-4318*
*Fax: Hum Res ■ *TF:* 800-552-9620					
Lakeland Animal Nutrition 2725 S Combee Rd	Lakeland	FL	33803	863-682-4995	686-9427
TF: 800-682-6144					
Land O'Lakes Farmland Feed LLC 4001 Lexington Ave N	Arden Hills	MN	55126	651-481-2222	
TF: 800-328-9680 ■ *Web:* www.landolakesinc.com					
Land O'Lakes Inc Western Feed Div 4001 Lexington Ave N	Arden Hills	MN	55126	800-328-9680	
TF: 800-328-9680 ■ *Web:* www.landolakesinc.com					
Lucta USA Inc Pine Meadow Corporate Ctr 950 Technology Way Suite 110	Libertyville	IL	60048	847-996-3400	996-3401
TF: 800-323-5341 ■ *Web:* www.lucta.com					
Madison County Co-op 323 W Fulton St	Canton	MS	39046	601-859-1271	859-1272
Manna Pro Corp 707 Spirit 40 Pk Dr Suite 150	Chesterfield	MO	63005	636-681-1700	681-1799
TF: 800-690-9908 ■ *Web:* www.mannapro.com					
Mark Hershey Farms Inc 479 Horseshoe Pike	Lebanon	PA	17042	717-867-4624	867-4313
TF: 888-801-3301 ■ *Web:* www.markhersheyfarms.com					
Merrick's Inc 2415 Parview Rd PO Box 620307	Middleton	WI	53562	608-831-3440	836-8943
TF: 800-637-7425 ■ *Web:* www.merricks.com					
MFA Inc 201 Ray Young Dr	Columbia	MO	65201	573-874-5111	876-5430
Web: www.mfaincorporated.com					
Milk Specialties Co 260 S Washington St	Carpentersville	IL	60110	847-426-3411	426-4121
TF: 800-323-4274 ■ *Web:* www.milkspecialties.com					
Moroni Feed Co 15 E 1900 S PO Box 368	Moroni	UT	84646	435-436-8221	436-8101
Mountaire Corp PO Box 1320	Millsboro	DE	19966	302-934-1100	
TF: 877-887-1490 ■ *Web:* www.mountaire.com					
Mountaire Farms of North Carolina 203 Morris Farm Rd	Candor	NC	27229	910-974-3232	974-3165
TF: 800-284-4528					
Moyer & Son Inc 113 E Reliance Rd	Souderton	PA	18964	215-723-6000	721-2814
TF: 800-345-0419 ■ *Web:* www.emoyer.com					
Novus International Inc 530 Maryville Ctr Dr Suite 100	Saint Louis	MO	63141	314-576-8886	576-2148
TF: 888-906-6887 ■ *Web:* www.novusint.com					

	City	State	ZIP	Phone	Fax
Nrv Inc N8155 American St	Ixonia	WI	53036	920-261-7000	261-1685
TF: 800-558-0002 ■ *Web:* www.calfmax1.com					
Oberbeck Grain Co 700 Walnut St	Highland	IL	62249	618-654-2387	654-5862
TF: 800-632-2012					
OMCO Inc 214 E Mill St	Odon	IN	47562	812-636-7362	636-4777
TF: 800-274-0203					
Pennfield Corp 711 Rohrerstown Rd	Lancaster	PA	17604	717-299-2561	295-8783
TF: 800-732-0467 ■ *Web:* www.dairyfeed.com					
Pied Piper Mills Inc 423 E Lake Dr	Hamlin	TX	79520	325-576-3684	576-3460
TF: 800-338-4610 ■ *Web:* www.piedpiperpetfood.net					
Preble Feed & Grain Inc Werling Dr PO Box 52	Preble	IN	46782	260-547-4452	
TF: 800-566-4452					
Prince Agri Products Inc 229 Radio Rd	Quincy	IL	62306	217-222-8854	222-5098
Web: www.princeagri.com					
Prince Mfg Co 229 Radio Rd	Quincy	IL	62305	646-747-4200	228-0466*
**Fax Area Code:* 217 ■ *Web:* www.princemfg.com					
Producers Co-op Assoc					
300 E Buffalo St PO Box 323	Girard	KS	66743	620-724-8241	724-8243
Web: www.girardcoop.com					
Provimi North America Inc					
10 Collective Way	Brookville	OH	45309	937-770-2400	770-2494
TF: 888-522-2420 ■ *Web:* www.nanutrition.com					
Quali Tech Inc 318 Lake Hazeltine Dr	Chaska	MN	55318	952-448-5151	448-3603
Web: www.qualitechco.com					
Ragland Mills Inc 14079 Hammer Rd	Neosho	MO	64850	417-451-2510	451-7499
Web: www.raglandmills.com					
Ralco Nutrition Inc 1600 Hahn Rd	Marshall	MN	56258	507-532-5748	532-5740
TF: 800-533-5306 ■ *Web:* www.ralconutrition.com					
Rangen Inc 115 13th Ave S	Buhl	ID	83316	208-543-6421	543-6090
TF Cust Svc: 800-657-6446 ■ *Web:* www.rangen.com					
Rivard's Quality Seeds Inc					
103 Main St PO Box 303	Argyle	MN	56713	218-437-6638	437-6392
TF: 888-543-6638 ■ *Web:* www.rivards.com					
Seminole Feed 335 NE Watula Ave PO Box 940	Ocala	FL	34470	352-732-4143	732-5968
TF: 800-683-1881 ■ *Web:* www.seminolefeed.com					
Star Milling Co 24067 Water St	Perris	CA	92570	951-657-3143	657-3114
TF: 800-733-6455 ■ *Web:* www.starmilling.com					
Stillwater Milling Co 512 E 6th St	Stillwater	OK	74074	405-372-3445	743-3730
TF: 800-364-6804 ■ *Web:* www.stillwatermill.com					
Triple Crown Nutrition Inc					
319 Barry Ave S Suite 303	Wayzata	MN	55391	952-473-6330	473-6571
TF: 800-451-9916 ■ *Web:* www.triplecrownfeed.com					
Trouw Nutrition 115 Executive Dr	Highland	IL	62249	618-654-2070	654-7012
TF: 800-365-1357 ■ *Web:* www.trouw-nutritionusa.com					
United Co-op Farmers Inc 22 Kimball Pl	Fitchburg	MA	01420	978-345-4103	345-7187
TF: 800-545-6655					
Ursa Farmers Co-op Inc 202 W Maple Ave PO Box 8	Ursa	IL	62376	217-964-2111	964-2260
Web: www.ursacoop.com					
Valley Proteins Inc 151 Valpro Dr	Winchester	VA	22603	540-877-2590	877-3215
Web: www.valleyproteins.com					
Vita Plus Corp 2514 Fish Hatchery Rd	Madison	WI	53713	608-256-1988	283-7990
TF: 800-362-8334 ■ *Web:* www.vitaplus.com					
Zeigler Bros Inc					
400 Gardner Stn Rd PO Box 95	Gardners	PA	17324	717-677-6181	677-6826
TF: 800-841-6800 ■ *Web:* www.zeiglerfeed.com					

451 LOGGING

	City	State	ZIP	Phone	Fax
B & S Logging Inc 4411 NW Elliott Ln	Prineville	OR	97754	541-447-3175	447-7141
Bowater Inc Forest Products Div					
5020 Hwy 11 S	Calhoun	TN	37309	423-336-2211	336-7330
Web: www.bowater.com/en/divisionsCanadianProducts.shtml					
Canal Wood LLC 2430 Main St	Conway	SC	29526	843-488-9663	488-3515
TF: 866-587-1460 ■ *Web:* www.canalwood.com					
Crane Mills Inc 22938 S Ave	Corning	CA	96021	530-824-5427	824-3157
Croman Corp 801 Ave C	White City	OR	97503	541-826-4455	826-7430
Freres Lumber Co Inc PO Box 276	Lyons	OR	97358	503-859-2121	859-2112
Greif Inc 425 Winter Rd	Delaware	OH	43015	740-549-6000	549-6100
NYSE: GEF ■ *TF:* 800-354-7343 ■ *Web:* www.greif.com					
Hopkes Logging Co Inc 2235 Hadley Rd N	Tillamook	OR	97141	503-842-2491	842-9858
Huffman & Wright Logging Inc					
801 SE 3rd St PO Box 910	Canyonville	OR	97417	541-839-4251	839-6463
Web: www.huffman-wright.com					
Klukwan Inc 425 Sawmill Rd	Haines	AK	99827	907-766-2211	766-2973
TF: 800-558-5926 ■ *Web:* www.klukwan.com					
Midwest Walnut Co 1914 Postevin St	Council Bluffs	IA	51503	712-325-9191	325-0156
TF: 800-592-5688 ■ *Web:* www.midwestwalnut.com					
Plum Creek Timber Co Inc					
999 3rd Ave Suite 4300	Seattle	WA	98104	206-467-3600	467-3795
NYSE: PCL ■ *TF:* 800-858-5347 ■ *Web:* www.plumcreek.com					
Roseburg Forest Products Co PO Box 1088	Roseburg	OR	97470	541-679-3311	
TF: 800-548-5275 ■ *Web:* www.rfpco.com					
Sealaska Corp 1 Sealaska Plaza Suite 400	Juneau	AK	99801	907-586-1512	586-2304
Web: www.sealaska.com					
Sierra Pacific Industries					
19794 Riverside Ave	Anderson	CA	96007	530-378-8000	378-8109
Web: www.sierrapacificind.com					
Western Forest Products Inc (WFP)					
435 Trunk Rd 3rd Fl	Duncan	BC	V9L2P9	250-748-3711	748-6045
TSE: WEF ■ *Web:* www.westernforest.com					
Yeomans Wood & Timber Inc					
714 Empire Expy PO Box 658	Swainsboro	GA	30401	478-237-9940	237-5098

452 LOGISTICS SERVICES (TRANSPORTATION & WAREHOUSING)

SEE ALSO Freight Forwarders p. 1888; Marine Services p. 2218; Rail Transport Services p. 2516; Trucking Companies p. 2736; Commercial Warehousing p. 2770

	City	State	ZIP	Phone	Fax
A Duie Pyle Inc					
650 Westtown Rd PO Box 564	West Chester	PA	19381	610-696-5800	696-3768
TF: 800-523-5020					
A&r Transport Inc 8440 Stabler Rd	Morris	IL	60450	815-941-5200	729-2325
TF: 800-542-8058 ■ *Web:* www.artransport.com					
A. C. Freight Systems Inc PO Box 611030	San Jose	CA	95161	408-392-8900	
Access Business Group 7575 Fulton St E	Ada	MI	49355	616-787-5358	
TF Cust Svc: 800-253-6500 ■ *Web:* www.accessbusinessgroup.com					
Accomack County School District					
23296 Courthouse Ave PO Box 330	Accomac	VA	23301	757-787-5754	787-2951
Web: www.sbo.accomack.k12.va.us/public					
ADS Tactical Inc					
Lynnwood Plaza, 621 Lynnhaven Pkwy					
Suite 400	Virginia Beach	VA	23452	757-481-7758	
TF: 800-948-9433 ■ *Web:* www.adsinc.com					
American Cargo Express Inc PO Box 483	Elizabeth	NJ	07207	908-351-3400	289-2490
Web: www.americancargoexpress.com					
AN Deringer Inc 64 N Main St	Saint Albans	VT	05478	802-524-8110	524-5970
TF: 800-448-8108 ■ *Web:* www.anderinger.com					
APL Logistics Inc					
16220 N Scottsdale Rd Suite 300	Scottsdale	AZ	85254	866-896-2005	586-4861*
**Fax Area Code:* 602 ■ *TF:* 866-896-2005 ■ *Web:* www.apllogistics.com					
Associated Global Systems Inc					
3333 New Hyde Pk Rd	New Hyde Park	NY	11042	516-627-8910	627-8851
TF Cust Svc: 800-645-8300 ■ *Web:* www.agsystems.com					
Atlantic Bulk Carrier Corp PO Box 112	Providence For	VA	23140	804-966-5459	966-5081
TF: 800-966-0030 ■ *Web:* www.atlanticbulk.com					
AutoInfo Inc 6413 Congress Ave Suite 260	Boca Raton	FL	33487	561-988-9456	994-8033
OTC: AUTO ■ *TF:* 800-759-7910 ■ *Web:* www.suntecktransport.com					
B-H Transfer Co 750 Sparta Rd PO Box 151	Sandersville	GA	31082	478-552-5119	552-0384
TF: 888-786-3664 ■ *Web:* www.b-htransfer.com					
BAX Global Inc 440 Exchange	Irvine	CA	92602	714-442-4500	442-2850
TF: 800-225-5229 ■ *Web:* www.baxglobal.com					
BDP International Inc 510 Walnut St	Philadelphia	PA	19106	215-629-8900	629-8940
TF: 888-999-2379 ■ *Web:* www.bdpinternational.com					
Bekins Co 330 S Mannheim Rd	Hillside	IL	60162	708-547-2000	
Web: www.bekins.com					
Bender Group 345 Parr Cir	Reno	NV	89512	775-788-8800	788-8811
TF: 800-621-9402 ■ *Web:* www.bendergroup.com					
Bestway Systems Inc					
5755 Granger Rd Suite 400	Independence	OH	44131	216-398-6090	398-0674
Web: www.bestwaysystems.com					
BFS Global 3101 Towercreek Pkwy Suite 570	Atlanta	GA	30339	770-956-1990	560-7077*
**Fax Area Code:* 678 ■ *TF:* 800-847-3865					
Bulldog Hiway Express 3390 Buffalo Ave	Charleston	SC	29418	843-744-1651	529-3345
TF: 800-331-9515 ■ *Web:* www.bulldoghiway.com					
Cardinal Logistics Management Corp					
5333 Davidson Hwy	Concord	NC	28027	704-786-6125	788-6618
TF: 800-800-8293 ■ *Web:* www.cardlog.com					
Cargo Solution Express Inc 14589 Valley Blvd	Fontana	CA	92335	909-350-1644	350-4349
Web: www.cargosolutionexpress.com					
CaseStack Inc					
2850 Ocean Pk Blvd Suite 100	Santa Monica	CA	90405	310-473-8885	943-4137
TF: 866-828-7120 ■ *Web:* www.ww2.casestack.com					
Caterpillar Logistics Services Inc					
500 N Morton Ave	Morton	IL	61550	309-266-3591	
TF: 800-447-6434 ■ *Web:* www.catlogistics.com					
Cdo Technologies Inc					
5200 Sprngfeld St Suite 320	Dayton	OH	45431	937-258-0022	258-1614
TF: 866-307-6616 ■ *Web:* www.cdotech.com					
Central Transportation Systems Inc					
4105 Rio Bravo Suite 100	El Paso	TX	79902	800-283-3106	
TF: 800-283-3106 ■ *Web:* www.centralsystems.com					
CH Robinson Worldwide Inc					
14701 Charlson Rd	Eden Prairie	MN	55347	952-683-3950	
NASDAQ: CHRW ■ *TF Cust Svc:* 855-229-6128 ■ *Web:* www.chrobinson.com					
Classical Academy 975 Stout Rd	Colorado Springs	CO	80921	719-484-0091	282-3226
Web: www.tcad20.org					
Clean Air Technology Inc 41105 Capital Dr	Canton	MI	48187	734-459-6320	459-9437
TF: 800-459-6320 ■ *Web:* www.cleanairtechnology.com					
Clipper Exxpress Inc					
9014 Heritage Pkwy Suite 300	Woodridge	IL	60517	630-739-0700	739-1817
TF: 800-678-2547 ■ *Web:* www.clippergroup.com					
Coleman American Cos Inc PO Box 960	Midland City	AL	36350	334-983-6505	983-5532
TF: 877-693-7060 ■ *Web:* www.colemanamerican.com					
Conley Transport Ii Inc 2104 Eastline Rd	Searcy	AR	72143	501-268-4672	268-6810
TF: 800-338-8700 ■ *Web:* www.conleytransport.com					
Cord Moving & Storage 4101 Rider Trail N	St. Louis	MO	63045	314-291-7440	291-6127
Web: www.cordmoving.com					
Coyote Logistics LLC 191 E Deerpath Rd	Lake Forest	IL	60045	847-295-2424	295-2828
TF: 877-626-9683 ■ *Web:* www.coyotelogistics.com					
Crowley Logistics Inc					
9487 Regency Sq Blvd	Jacksonville	FL	32225	904-727-2200	727-4062
TF: 800-874-6769 ■ *Web:* www.crowley.com					
CSX Intermodal Inc 301 W Bay St	Jacksonville	FL	32202	904-633-1000	633-1102
TF: 800-542-2754 ■ *Web:* www.csxi.com					
Daniel F Young Inc 1235 Westlakes Dr Suite 255	Berwyn	PA	19312	610-725-4000	725-0570
Web: www.dfyoung.com					
Danny Herman Trucking Inc PO Box 55	Mountain City	TN	37683	423-727-9061	727-5675
TF: 800-251-7500 ■ *Web:* www.dannyherman.com					
Davidson Oil Co PO Box 30308	Amarillo	TX	79120	806-374-6022	379-8704
Web: www.davidsonoil.com					

Company	City	State	ZIP	Phone	Fax
Daws Inc 758 280th Unit 10 *Web:* www.daws.com	Milford	NE	68405	402-761-2186	761-3711
Dennis K Burke Inc 284 Eastern Ave PO Box 6069 *TF:* 800-289-2875 ■ *Web:* www.burkeoil.com	Chelsea	MA	02150	617-884-7800	884-7638
Dependable Highway Express Inc 2440 S 48th Ave *TF:* 800-472-2037 ■ *Web:* www.godependable.com	Phoenix	AZ	85043	602-278-4401	278-4473
Distribution & Marking Services Inc (DMSI) 10708 Granite St Suite J *Web:* www.dmsi.net	Charlotte	NC	28273	704-749-7290	587-3693
Dixie Warehouse Services 6001 National Tpke PO Box 36158	Louisville	KY	40233	502-368-6564	368-6564
Dohrn Transfer Co 625 3rd Ave *TF:* 888-364-7621 ■ *Web:* www.dohrn.com	Rock Island	IL	61201	309-794-0723	794-1693
DSC Logistics 1750 S Wolf Rd *TF:* 800-372-1960 ■ *Web:* www.dsclogistics.com	Des Plaines	IL	60018	847-390-6800	390-7276
Dti Assoc Inc 2920 S Glebe Rd *Web:* www.dtiassociates.com	Arlington	VA	22206	703-299-1600	706-0474
Eagle Support Services Corp 2705 Artie St Bldg 400 Suite 30 *Web:* www.eaglesupport.com	Huntsville	AL	35805	256-534-2274	534-0606
Elston-Richards Inc 3701 Patterson Ave SE *Web:* www.elstonrichards.com	Grand Rapids	MI	49512	616-698-2698	698-8090
EMBASSY Products & Logistics PO Box 8066 *Web:* www.embassy-usa.com	Falls Church	VA	22041	703-845-0800	820-9385
Exel 570 Polaris Pkwy *TF:* 800-272-1052 ■ *Web:* www.exel.com	Westerville	OH	43082	614-865-8500	865-8877
Expeditors International of Washington Inc 1015 3rd Ave 12th Fl *NASDAQ: EXPD* ■ *TF:* 800-284-7474 ■ *Web:* www.expeditors.com	Seattle	WA	98104	206-674-3400	682-9777
Express-1 Expedited Solutions Inc 429 Post Rd PO Box 210 *AMEX: XPO* ■ *TF:* 800-800-5161 ■ *Web:* www.express-1.com	Buchanan	MI	49107	269-695-2700	695-7458
FedEx Supply Chain Services Inc 5455 Darrow Rd **Fax: Hum Res* ■ *TF:* 800-588-3020 ■ *Web:* www.fedex.com	Hudson	OH	44236	330-342-3000	342-8037*
FedEx Trade Networks 850 SW 7th St Suite 100 *Web:* www.ftn.fedex.com	Renton	WA	98057	425-793-1900	793-8600
Fremont Contract Carriers Inc (FCC) 865 S Bud Blvd *TF:* 800-228-9842 ■ *Web:* www.fcc-inc.com	Fremont	NE	68025	402-721-3020	727-8712
Frontier Logistic Services 1700 N Alameda St *Web:* www.frontier-logistics.com	Compton	CA	90222	310-604-8208	604-8135
Global Logistics 330 Madison Ave 6th Fl *AMEX: GLA* ■ *Web:* www.glacteam.com	New York	NY	08638	646-495-5155	495-5164
Global Transportation Services Inc 1930 6th Ave S Suite 400 *TF:* 800-580-6779 ■ *Web:* www.globalcontainerline.com	Seattle	WA	98134	206-624-4354	624-2116
Governor Wentworth Regional School District Sau 49 140 Pine Hill Rd PO Box 190 *Web:* www.govwentworth.k12.nh.us	Wolfeboro Fall	NH	03896	603-569-1658	569-6983
Griffin Transport Services Inc PO Box 11245 *TF:* 800-361-5028 ■ *Web:* www.griffintransport.com	Reno	NV	99510	775-331-8010	331-6745
Groton-Dunstable Regional School District PO Box 729 *Web:* www.gdrsd.org	Groton	MA	01450	978-448-5505	448-9402
Gypsum Express Ltd 8280 Sixty Rd PO Box 268 *TF:* 800-621-7901 ■ *Web:* www.gypsumexpress.com	Baldwinsville	NY	13027	315-638-2201	638-2453
H E Whitlock Inc 4808 Dillon Dr **Fax Area Code:* 719 ■ *Web:* www.hewhitlock.com	Pueblo	CO	81008	866-933-0709	544-1832*
H P Cummings Construction Co Inc PO Box 24 *Web:* www.hpcummings.com	Ware	MA	01082	413-967-6251	967-9896
Hankyu Hanshin Express (USA) Inc 909 W Irving Pk Rd **Fax Area Code:* 630 ■ *Web:* www.hankyu-usa.com	Itasca	IL	60143	638-285-7100	773-1498*
Hanson Logistics 2900 S State St Suite 4 E *TF:* 888-772-1197 ■ *Web:* www.hansonlogisticsgroup.com	Saint Joseph	MI	49085	269-982-1390	982-1506
Highway Transport Inc 1500 Amherst Rd *Web:* www.hytt.com	Knoxville	TN	37909	865-584-8631	584-2851
Horizon Air Freight Inc 152-15 Rockaway Blvd *TF:* 800-221-6028 ■ *Web:* www.haf.com	Jamaica	NY	11434	718-528-3800	949-0655
Hub Group Inc 3050 Highland Pkwy Suite 100 *NASDAQ: HUBG* ■ *TF:* 800-964-2515 ■ *Web:* www.hubgroup.com	Downers Grove	IL	60515	630-271-3600	964-6475
J A Moss Inc 1682 49 S Hwy *Web:* www.jamossconstruction.com	Florence	MS	39073	601-939-4141	931-4142
J Coleman Alvin & Son Inc 9 New Hampshire Rt 113 *TF:* 800-845-6707 ■ *Web:* www.ajcoleman.com	Conway	NH	03818	603-447-5936	447-5839
James Group International 4335 W Fort St *Web:* www.jamesgroupintl.com	Detroit	MI	48209	313-841-0070	841-5074
JB Hunt Transport Services Inc 615 JB Hunt Corporate Dr *NASDAQ: JBHT* ■ **Fax: Hum Res* ■ *TF:* 800-643-3622 ■ *Web:* www.jbhunt.com	Lowell	AR	72745	479-820-0000	820-8249*
Kenco Group Inc 2001 Riverside Dr *TF:* 800-758-3289 ■ *Web:* www.kencogroup.com	Chattanooga	TN	37406	423-756-5552	756-1529
Kintetsu World Express USA Inc 1 Jericho Plaza # 100 *TF:* 800-275-4045 ■ *Web:* www.kweusa.com	Jericho	NY	11753	516-933-7100	933-7731
Kom International 300 St-Sacrement Suite 307 *Web:* www.komintl.com	Montreal	QC	H2Y1X4	514-849-4000	849-8888
Kuehne & Nagel Inc 10 Exchange Pl *Web:* www.kn-portal.com	Jersey City	NJ	07302	201-413-5500	413-5777
L & L Oil Gas Services 3421 N Cswy Blvd Suite 502 *TF:* 800-445-6482	Metairie	LA	70002	504-832-8600	832-8620
L&B Transport LLC 708 Hwy 190 W *TF:* 800-545-9401 ■ *Web:* www.landbtransport.com	Port Allen	LA	70767	225-387-0894	387-0126
L-3 Communications Vertex Aerospace LLC 555 Industrial Dr S *Web:* www.l-3vertex.com	Madison	MS	39110	601-856-2274	856-8006
Landstar Logistics Inc 13410 Sutton Pk Dr S **Fax Area Code:* 800 ■ *TF:* 800-872-9400 ■ *Web:* www.landstar.com	Jacksonville	FL	32224	904-399-8909	872-8574*
Leicht Transfer & Storage Co 1401 State St PO Box 2447 *TF:* 800-338-5665	Green Bay	WI	54306	920-432-8632	432-4130
LeSaint Logistics 868 W Crossroads Pkwy *TF:* 877-566-9375 ■ *Web:* www.lesaint.com	Romeoville	IL	60446	630-243-5950	
Loggins Logistics Inc 5706 Commerce Sq *Web:* www.logginslogistics.com	Jonesboro	AR	72401	870-932-9231	802-2190
LogisticareInc 1275 Peachtree St NE 6th Fl **Fax Area Code:* 404 ■ *TF:* 800-486-7647 ■ *Web:* www.logisticare.com	Atlanta	GA	30309	770-907-7596	888-5999*
Lucas County Educational Service Ctr 2275 Collingwood Blvd *Web:* www.lucas.k12.oh.us	Toledo	OH	43602	419-245-4150	245-4186
M & J Transportation 3536 Nicholson Ave *TF:* 866-298-3858 ■ *Web:* www.mjtransportationkc.com	Kansas City	MO	64120	816-231-6733	231-7645
Matson Integrated Logistics Inc 1815 S Meyers Rd Suite 700 *TF:* 866-640-6050 ■ *Web:* www.matson.com	Villa Park	IL	60181	630-203-3500	916-4931
McElroy Truck Lines Inc 111 80 Spur PO Box 104 *TF:* 800-992-7863 ■ *Web:* www.mcelroytrucklines.com	Cuba	AL	36907	205-392-5579	392-7992
McLean Cargo Specialists Inc 1310 Rankin Rd	Houston	TX	77073	281-443-2777	443-3777
Menlo Worldwide Inc *Con-Way Inc* 2855 Campus Dr Suite 300 *TF:* 800-227-1981 ■ *Web:* www.con-way.com	San Mateo	CA	94403	650-378-5200	357-9160
Meridian IQ 10990 Roe Ave *TF:* 877-246-4909 ■ *Web:* www.meridianiq.com	Overland Park	KS	66211	913-906-6800	906-6996
Meteor Express Inc PO Box 248 *Web:* www.meteorx.com	Scottsboro	AL	35768	256-218-3000	259-3990
Metropolitan Trucking Inc (MRTK) 299 Market St Suite 300 **Fax Area Code:* 201 ■ *TF:* 800-967-3278 ■ *Web:* www.mtrk.com	Saddle Brook	NJ	07663	800-967-3278	843-6179*
Midwest Specialized Transportation Inc PO Box 6418 *Web:* www.midspec.com	Rochester	MN	55903	507-288-5649	288-6859
Millard Refrigerated Services Inc 4715 S 132nd St *Web:* www.millardref.com	Omaha	NE	68137	402-896-6600	896-6700
Miller Bros Express LC 560 W 400 N *TF:* 800-366-6239 ■ *Web:* www.mbexlc.com	Hyrum	UT	84319	435-245-6025	245-4853
Mitsui & Co (USA) Inc 200 Pk Ave 36th Fl *Web:* www.mitsui.com/us	New York	NY	10166	212-878-4000	878-4800
Modern Transportation Service Inc 2605 Nicholson Rd Suite 110 *Web:* www.moderntrans.com	Sewickley	PA	15143	412-489-4800	200-5050
Mount Vernon City School Dist 80 2710 N St *Web:* www.mtv80.org	Mount Vernon	IL	62864	618-244-8080	244-8082
Muscle Shoals City School District 3200 Wilson Dam Hwy *Web:* www.cft.mscs.k12.al.us	Muscle Shoals	AL	35661	256-389-2600	389-2662
National Distributors Inc 1517 Avco Blvd PO Box 255 *TF:* 800-334-9677 ■ *Web:* www.ndsin.com	Sellersburg	IN	47172	812-246-6306	246-9568
National Freight Inc (NFI) 71 W Pk Ave *TF:* 877-634-3777 ■ *Web:* www.natlfreight.com	Vineland	NJ	08360	856-691-7000	
Navis Logistics Network 5675 DTC Blvd Suite 280 *TF:* 800-525-6309 ■ *Web:* www.gonavis.com	Greenwood Village	CO	80111	303-741-6626	741-6653
New Breed Logistics 4043 Piedmont Pkwy *TF:* 800-781-0548 ■ *Web:* www.newbreed.com	High Point	NC	27265	800-781-0548	
New Century Transportation Inc 45 E Pk Dr *TF:* 877-870-4031 ■ *Web:* www.nctrans.com	Westampton	NJ	08060	609-265-1110	
Oakley Transport Inc 101 ABC Rd PO Box 4170 *TF:* 800-969-8265 ■ *Web:* www.oakleytransport.com	Lake Wales	FL	33859	863-638-1435	638-1927
ODW Logistics Inc 1580 Williams Rd *TF:* 800-743-7062 ■ *Web:* www.odwlogistics.com	Columbus	OH	43207	614-497-1660	497-1426
Odyssey Logistics & Technology Corp 39 Old Ridgebury Rd - N1 *Web:* www.odysseylogistics.com	Danbury	CT	06810	203-448-3900	
Pacer Global Logistics 6805 Perimeter Dr *TF:* 800-837-7584 ■ *Web:* www.pacerglobal.com	Dublin	OH	43016	614-923-1400	923-1410
Panalpina 1776 On-the-Green 67 E Pk Pl *TF:* 866-202-0377 ■ *Web:* www.panalpina.com	Morristown	NJ	07960	973-683-9000	254-5799
Park-Ohio Holdings Corp (PKOH) 6065 Parkland Blvd *NASDAQ: PKOH* ■ *Web:* www.pkoh.com	Cleveland	OH	44124	440-947-2000	947-2099
Pegasus Logistics Group Inc 615 Freeport Pkwy Suite 100 *TF:* 800-997-7226 ■ *Web:* www.pegasuslogistics.com	Coppell	TX	75019	469-671-0300	671-0317
Penske Logistics Rt 10 Green Hills **Fax Area Code:* 610 ■ *TF:* 800-529-6531 ■ *Web:* www.penskelogistics.com	Reading	PA	19603	800-529-6531	775-2449*
Pierce Distribution Services Co 2028 E Riverside Blvd PO Box 15600 *TF:* 800-466-7397 ■ *Web:* www.piercedistribution.com	Loves Park	IL	61132	815-636-5650	636-5660
Pilot Air Freight Corp 314 N Middletown Rd *TF Cust Svc:* 800-447-4568 ■ *Web:* www.pilotair.com	Lima	PA	19037	610-891-8100	565-4267
R.C. Dolner LLC 15 17 E 16th St FL 2 *Web:* www.rcdolner.com	New York	NY	10003	212-645-2190	633-1108
Red Rock Distributing Co PO Box 18755 *TF:* 800-323-7109 ■ *Web:* www.redrockdist.com	Oklahoma City	OK	73154	405-677-3373	557-7795

Phone Fax

Red Star Oil 802 Purser Dr. Raleigh NC 27603 919-772-1944 779-8871
TF: 800-774-6033 ■ *Web:* www.redstaroil.com

Reliant Transportation Inc
770 N Cotner Blvd Suite 410 PO Box 5158 Lincoln NE 68505 402-464-7771 464-8124
Web: www.reliant-transportation.com

Ridgewood High School 7500 W Montrose Ave Norridge IL 60706 708-456-4242 456-0342
Web: www.ridgenet.org

Rim Logistics Ltd 200 N Gary Ave Suite B Roselle IL 60172 630-595-0610 595-0614
TF: 888-275-0937 ■ *Web:* www.rimlogistics.com

Rinchem Co Inc 6133 Edith Blvd NE Albuquerque NM 87107 505-998-4143
TF: 888-375-2436 ■ *Web:* www.rinchem.com

ROACO Logistics Services
500 Country Club Dr Bensenville IL 60106 630-379-0069 993-2355
TF: 866-947-6227 ■ *Web:* www.roaco.com

Ryder System Inc 11690 NW 105th St Miami FL 33178 305-500-3726 500-4599
NYSE: R ■ *TF:* 800-327-3399 ■ *Web:* www.ryder.com

S & H Express Inc 400 Mulberry St PO Box 20219 York PA 17402 717-848-5015 852-7341
TF: 800-637-9782 ■ *Web:* www.sandhexpress.com

Saddle Creek Corp 3010 Saddle Creek Rd Lakeland FL 33801 863-665-0966 667-1813
Web: www.saddlecrk.com

Schirm USA Inc 2801 Oak Grove Rd Ennis TX 75119 972-878-4400 875-9859
Web: www.schirm.com

Schneider National Inc
3101 S Packerland Dr PO Box 2545 Green Bay WI 54306 920-592-2000 592-2517
TF: 800-558-6767 ■ *Web:* www.schneider.com

School District of Hartford
675 E Rossman St Hartford WI 53027 262-673-3155 673-3548
Web: www.hartfordjt1.k12.wi.us

Scully Oil Co & Svc Station
150 E Flint St PO BOX 398 Lyndon Station WI 53944 608-666-2662 666-2239
Web: www.scullyoil.com

Seko Worldwide Inc
1100 Arlington Heights Rd Suite 600 Itasca IL 60143 630-919-4800 773-9179
TF: 800-228-2711 ■ *Web:* www.sekologistics.com

Shaker Group Inc The 862 Albany Shaker Rd Latham NY 12110 518-786-9286 782-7226
Web: www.theshakergroup.com

Slay Industries Inc 1441 Hampton Ave Saint Louis MO 63139 314-647-7529 647-5240
TF: 800-852-7529 ■ *Web:* www.slay.com

Solid Systems Engineering Inc
6560 Odell Pl Suite A Boulder CO 80301 303-530-2985 530-3208

South Euclid-Lyndhurst Board of Education
5044 Mayfield Rd Lyndhurst OH 44124 216-691-2000 691-2033
Web: www.sel.k12.oh.us

Southeast Delco School District
1560 Delmar Dr Folcroft PA 19032 610-522-4300
Web: www.sedelco.org

Speegle Construction Inc
210 Government Ave PO Box 1325 Niceville FL 32588 850-729-2484 729-1993
Web: www.speegleconstruction.com

Star Line Trucking Corp
18480 W Lincoln Ave New Berlin WI 53146 262-786-8280 786-0071
Web: www.starlinetrucking.com

Store Opening Solutions (SOS)
800 Middle Tennessee Blvd Murfreesboro TN 37129 615-867-0858 867-4740
TF: 877-388-9262 ■ *Web:* www.store-solutions.com

Tbb Global Logistics Inc
802 Far Hills Dr New Freedom PA 17349 717-227-5000 227-5500
TF: 800-937-8224 ■ *Web:* www.tbbgl.com

Technical Transportation Inc
2850 Market Loop Southlake TX 76092 817-421-0470 488-0306
TF: 800-852-8726 ■ *Web:* www.techtrans.com

Thoroughbred Direct Intermodal Services
5165 Campus Dr Suite 400 Plymouth Meeting PA 19462 610-567-3360 567-3370
TF: 877-250-2902 ■ *Web:* www.ns-direct.com

Titan Global Distribution
1100 Corporate Sq Suite 150 Saint Louis MO 63132 314-817-0051 817-0070
TF: 800-325-4074 ■ *Web:* www.titanglobal.com

TNT Logistics North America
10751 Deerwood Pk Blvd Suite 200 Jacksonville FL 32256 904-928-1400 928-1410

TRANSFLO Corp
6735 Southpoint Dr S MC J975 Jacksonville FL 32216 904-279-6310 245-2136
Web: www.transflo.net

TransMontaigne Inc
1670 Broadway Suite 3100 PO Box 5660 Denver CO 80202 303-626-8200 626-8228
Web: www.transmontaigne.com

Transplace 3010 Gaylord Pkwy Suite 200 Frisco TX 75034 866-413-9266 770-7844*
**Fax Area Code: 479* ■ *TF:* 866-413-9266 ■ *Web:* www.transplace.com

TRANSPORTATION INSIGHT LLC 328 1st Ave NW Hickory NC 28601 828-485-5000
Web: www.t-insight.com

Transportation Solutions Inc
1900 Brannan Rd McDonough GA 30253 770-474-1555 954-0055
Web: www.tsilogistics.com

Trimar Construction Inc 1720 W Cass St Tampa FL 33606 813-258-5524 258-4743
Web: www.trimarconstruction.com

United Nations International School
24-50 Fdr Dr. New York NY 10010 212-684-7400
Web: www.unis.org

Unitrans International Corp
709 S Hindry Ave Inglewood CA 90301 310-410-7676 410-1719
Web: www.unitrans-us.com

University City School Dst
8346 Delcrest Dr. Saint Louis MO 63124 314-290-4000
Web: www.ucityschools.org

UPS Supply Chain Solutions
12380 Morris Rd Alpharetta GA 30005 678-746-4100 994-3125*
**Fax Area Code: 770* ■ *TF:* 800-982-9170 ■ *Web:* www.ups-scs.com

UTi Worldwide Inc 100 Oceangate Suite 1500 Long Beach CA 90802 562-552-9400
NASDAQ: UTIW ■ *Web:* www.go2uti.com

Phone Fax

Vimich Traffic Logistics
12201 Tecumseh Rd E Tecumseh ON N8N1M3 519-735-6933 735-4309
TF: 800-284-1045 ■ *Web:* www.vimich.com

Vitran Express West Inc 850 Bergin Way Sparks NV 89431 775-355-9595 355-0361

W M Schlosser Co Inc 2400 51st Pl Hyattsville MD 20781 301-773-1300 773-9263
Web: www.wmschlosser.com

Wadsworth City School District
360 College St Wadsworth OH 44281 330-336-3571
Web: www.wadsworth.k12.oh.us

Weber Logistics 13530 Rosecrans Ave. Santa Fe Springs CA 90670 562-802-8802 802-9792
Web: www.weberlogistics.com

Wiley Sanders Truck Lines Inc PO Box 707 Troy AL 36081 334-566-5184 566-3257
TF: 800-633-8740 ■ *Web:* www.wsanders.com

Wilheit Packaging LLC 1527 May Dr Gainesville GA 30507 770-532-4421 532-8956
TF: 800-727-4421 ■ *Web:* www.wilheit.com

453 LONG - TERM CARE FACILITIES

SEE ALSO Long-Term Care Facilities Operators p. 2188; Retirement Communities p. 2623; Veterans Nursing Homes - State p. 2760

Free-Standing Facilities Accredited By The Joint Commission On Accreditation Of Healthcare Organizations. Listings In This Category Are Organized Alphabetically By States.

Phone Fax

Canterbury Health Facility
1720 Knowles Rd Phenix City AL 36869 334-291-0485 297-4712

Mercy Medical 101 Villa Dr PO Box 1090 Daphne AL 36526 251-621-4200 621-4463
Web: www.mercymedical.com

Northside Health Care 700 Hutchins Ave Gadsden AL 35901 256-543-7101 543-2367

Catalina Care Ctr 2611 N Warren Ave Tucson AZ 85719 520-795-9574 321-4983

Coronado Care Ctr 11411 N 19th Ave Phoenix AZ 85029 602-256-7500 943-7697
Web: www.coronadocare.com

East Mesa Care Ctr 51 S 48th St Mesa AZ 85206 480-832-8333 830-2466

La Mesa Rehabilitation & Care Ctr
2470 S Arizona Ave. Yuma AZ 85364 928-344-8541 344-0823

Osborn Health & Rehabilitation
3333 N Civic Ctr Plaza Scottsdale AZ 85251 480-994-1333 990-3895

Casa Colina Center for Rehabilitation
255 E Bonita Ave. Pomona CA 91769 909-596-7733 596-7845
TF: 800-926-5462 ■ *Web:* www.casacolina.org

Clear View Sanitarium & Convalescent Ctr
15823 S Western Ave Gardena CA 90247 310-538-2323 538-3509

Driftwood Health Care Ctr 4109 Emerald St. Torrance CA 90503 310-371-4628 214-1882

English Oaks Nursing & Rehabilitation Ctr
2633 W Rumble Rd. Modesto CA 95350 209-577-1001 577-0366

Ensign Group Inc The
27101 Puerta Real Suite 450 Mission Viejo CA 92691 949-487-9500
NASDAQ: ENSG ■ *Web:* www.ensigngroup.net

Evergreen Rehabilitation & Care Ctr
2030 Evergreen Ave Modesto CA 95350 209-577-1055 550-3615
Web: www.evergreencare.com

Extended Care Hospital Westminster
206 Hospital Cir Westminster CA 92683 714-891-2769 893-1014

Fairfield Nursing & Rehabilitation Ctr
1255 Travis Blvd Fairfield CA 94533 707-425-0623 425-0704

French Park Care Ctr 600 E Washington Ave Santa Ana CA 92701 714-973-1656 836-4349
Web: www.frenchparkcenter.com

Front Porch Communities & Services
303 N Glenoaks Blvd Burbank CA 91502 818-729-8100
TF: 800-233-3709 ■ *Web:* www.frontporch.net

Gladstone Care & Rehabilitation Ctr
435 E Gladstone St Glendora CA 91740 626-963-5955 963-8683
Web: www.gladstonecare.com

Grand Terrace Healthcare Ctr
12000 Mt Vernon Ave Grand Terrace CA 92313 909-825-5221 783-4811

Hanford Nursing & Rehabilitation Hospital
1007 W Lacey Blvd Hanford CA 93230 559-582-2871 582-5853

Heritage Rehabilitation Ctr
21414 S Vermont Ave Torrance CA 90502 310-320-8714 320-1809

Horizon West Inc 4020 Sierra College Blvd Rocklin CA 95677 916-624-6230 624-6249
TF: 800-660-6230 ■ *Web:* www.horizonwest.com

Huntington Valley Health Care Ctr
8382 Newman Ave Huntington Beach CA 92647 714-842-5551 848-5359

Kisco Senior Living LLC
5790 Fleet St Suite 300 Carlsbad CA 92008 760-804-5900 804-5909
Web: www.kiscosl.com

La Jolla Nursing & Rehabilitation Ctr
2552 Torrey Pines Rd La Jolla CA 92037 858-453-5810 452-4301

La Mariposa Care & Rehabilitation
1244 Travis Blvd Fairfield CA 94533 707-422-7750 422-7818

New Orange Hills 5017 E Chapman Ave Orange CA 92869 714-997-7090 997-4631
Web: www.neworangehills.com

Orinda Convalescent Hospital 11 Altarinda Rd Orinda CA 94563 925-254-6500 254-9063

Pacific Coast Manor 1935 Wharf Rd Capitola CA 95010 831-476-0770 476-0737

Pacifica Nursing & Rehabilitation Ctr
385 Esplanade Ave Pacifica CA 94044 650-993-5576 359-9388

Park Anaheim HealthCare Ctr 3435 W Ball Rd Anaheim CA 92804 714-827-5880 827-5880

Park Regency Care Ctr 1770 W La Habra Blvd La Habra CA 90631 562-691-8810 697-8478
Web: www.parkregencycare.com

Seton Medical Center Coastside
600 Marine Blvd. Moss Beach CA 94038 650-563-7100 728-5314
Web: www.dochs.org

Subacute Saratoga Children's Hospital
13425 Sousa Ln Saratoga CA 95070 408-378-8875 378-7419
Web: www.subacutesaratoga.com

Facility	City	State	ZIP	Phone	Fax
Tulare Nursing & Rehabilitation 680 E Merritt Ave	Tulare	CA	93274	559-686-8581	686-5393
Tunnell Center for Rehabilitation & Healthcare 1359 Pine St *Web:* www.tunnellrehab.com	San Francisco	CA	94109	415-673-8405	563-2174
Villa Maria Care Ctr 425 E Barcellus Ave	Santa Maria	CA	93454	805-922-3558	922-5548
Village Square Nursing & Rehabilitation Ctr 1586 W San Marcos Blvd *Web:* www.villagesquarerehab.com	San Marcos	CA	92078	760-471-2986	471-5176
Windsor Rehabilitation Care Ctr 3806 Clayton Rd *Web:* www.windsorcares.com	Concord	CA	94521	925-689-2266	689-0509
Avon Health Center Inc 652 W Avon Rd	Avon	CT	06001	860-673-2521	675-1101
Branford Hills Health Care Ctr 189 Alps Rd *Web:* www.bhhcc.com	Branford	CT	06405	203-481-6221	483-1893
Brook Hollow Health Care Ctr 55 Kondracki Ln	Wallingford	CT	06492	203-265-6771	284-3883
Connecticut Health of Southport 930 Mill Hill Terr. *Web:* www.cthealthfacilities.com	Southport	CT	06890	203-259-7894	254-3720
Danbury Health Care Ctr 107 Osborne St	Danbury	CT	06810	203-792-8102	791-1441*
Elim Park Baptist Home Inc 140 Cook Hill Rd *TF:* 800-994-1776 ■ *Web:* www.elimpark.org	Cheshire	CT	06410	203-272-7550	271-7794
Golden Hill Health Care Ctr 2028 Bridgeport Ave	Milford	CT	06460	203-877-0371	877-6185
Harborside Healthcare - Glen Hill 1 Glen Hill Rd	Danbury	CT	06811	203-744-2840	792-1521
Haven Health Center of Sound View 1 Care Ln *Web:* www.havenhealthcare.com	West Haven	CT	06516	203-934-7955	934-1038
Haven Health Center of Windham 595 Valley St *Web:* www.havenhealthcare.com	Willimantic	CT	06226	860-423-2597	450-7070
Hebrew Health Care Inc 1 Abrahms Blvd *Web:* www.hebrewhealthcare.org	West Hartford	CT	06117	860-523-3800	523-3949
Highlands Health Care Ctr 745 Highland Ave	Cheshire	CT	06410	203-272-7285	250-6068*
Jewish Home for the Elderly of Fairfield County 175 Jefferson St *Web:* www.jhe.org	Fairfield	CT	06825	203-365-6400	374-8082
Kent Ltd 46 Maple St *TF General:* 800-353-5368 ■ *Web:* www.apple-rehab.com	Kent	CT	06757	860-927-5368	927-1594
Manchester Manor Health Care Ctr 385 W Ctr St *Web:* www.manchestermanorct.com	Manchester	CT	06040	860-646-0129	645-0313
Masonic Healthcare Ctr 22 Masonic Ave *Web:* www.masonicare.org	Wallingford	CT	06492	203-679-5900	679-6459
Miller Memorial Community 360 Broad St *Web:* www.emmci.org	Meriden	CT	06450	203-237-8815	630-3714
Montowese Health & Rehabilitation Center Inc 163 Quinnipiac Ave *Web:* www.montowesehealth.com	North Haven	CT	06473	203-624-3303	787-9243
Noble Horizons 17 Cobble Rd *Web:* www.noblehorizons.org	Salisbury	CT	06068	860-435-9851	435-0636
Pendleton Health & Rehabilitation Ctr 44 Maritime Dr	Mystic	CT	06355	860-572-1700	572-7830
River Glen Health Care Ctr 162 S Britain Rd	Southbury	CT	06488	203-264-9600	264-9603
Sharon Health Care Ctr 27 Hospital Hill Rd	Sharon	CT	06069	860-364-1002	364-0237
Subacute Center of Bristol 23 Fair St	Forestville	CT	06010	860-589-2923	589-3148
Summit at Plantsville 261 Summit St	Plantsville	CT	06479	860-628-0364	628-9166
Valerie Manor Inc 1360 Torringford St	Torrington	CT	06790	860-489-1008	496-9252
Village Green of Waterbury 128 Cedar Ave *Web:* www.reverawaterbury.com	Waterbury	CT	06705	203-757-9271	757-2988
Watrous Nursing Ctr 9 Neck Rd	Madison	CT	06443	203-245-9483	245-4668
Waveny Care Ctr 3 Farm Rd *Web:* www.waveny.org	New Canaan	CT	06840	203-594-5200	594-5327
West Hartford Health & Rehabilitation Ctr 130 Loomis Dr *Web:* www.westhartfordhealth.com	West Hartford	CT	06107	860-521-8700	521-7452
West River Health Care Ctr 245 Orange Ave	Milford	CT	06460	203-876-5123	876-5129
Westport Health Care Ctr 1 Burr Rd	Westport	CT	06880	203-226-4201	221-4766
Wethersfield Health Care Ctr 341 Jordan Ln	Wethersfield	CT	06109	860-563-0101	257-6107
Armed Forces Retirement Home - Washington 3700 N Capitol St NW *TF Admissions:* 800-422-9988 ■ *Web:* www.afrh.gov/afrh	Washington	DC	20011	202-730-3011	541-7519
Area Agency On Aging 9887 4th St N Suite 100 *TF:* 800-963-5337 ■ *Web:* www.agingcarefl.org	St. Petersburg	FL	33702	727-570-9696	893-7288
Bay Pointe Nursing Pavilion 4201 31st St S	Saint Petersburg	FL	33712	727-867-1104	867-9837
Bayside Rehabilitation & Health Ctr 811 Jackson St N	Saint Petersburg	FL	33705	727-896-3651	821-2453
Boca Raton Rehabilitation Ctr 755 Meadows Rd	Boca Raton	FL	33486	561-391-5200	391-0685
Consulate Health Care at Lake Parker 2020 W Lake Parker Dr *Web:* www.consulatemgt.com	Lakeland	FL	33805	863-682-7580	683-9564
Consulate Health Care of Brandon 701 Victoria St	Brandon	FL	33510	813-681-4220	689-5685
Consulate Health Care of Tallahassee 1650 Phillips Rd	Tallahassee	FL	32308	850-942-9868	942-1074
Harmony Health Center at Greenbriar 9820 N Kendall Dr	Miami	FL	33176	305-271-6311	274-5880
Heartland Health Care & Rehabilitation Ctr 5401 Sawyer Rd	Sarasota	FL	34233	941-925-3427	925-8469
Heartland Health Care Center Boynton Beach 3600 Old Boynton Rd *Web:* www.hcrmc-online.hcr-maorcare.com	Boynton Beach	FL	33436	561-736-9992	364-9527
Heartland South Jacksonville 3648 University Blvd S	Jacksonville	FL	32216	904-733-7440	448-9425
Leesburg Health & Rehabiltation LLC 715 E Dixie Ave	Leesburg	FL	34748	352-728-3020	728-6071
ManorCare Health Services - Carrollwood 3030 W Bearss Ave *Web:* www.hcr-manorcare.com	Tampa	FL	33618	813-968-8777	961-5189
Moody Manor Inc 7150 Holatee Trail	Southwest Ranches	FL	33330	954-434-2016	434-0561
River Garden Hebrew Home for the Aged 11401 Old St Augustine Rd *Web:* www.rivergarden.org	Jacksonville	FL	32258	904-260-1818	260-9733
Southern Pines Nursing Ctr 6140 Congress St	New Port Richey	FL	34653	727-842-8402	841-8060
Tandem Health Care of Orange Park 1215 Kingsley Ave **Fax Area Code:* 904	Orange Park	FL	32073	850-269-8922	269-1346*
Woods of Manatee Springs 5627 9th St E	Bradenton	FL	34203	941-753-8941	753-7576
Briarcliff Haven Healthcare & Rehabilitation Ctr 1000 Briarcliff Rd NE	Atlanta	GA	30306	404-875-6456	874-4606
Family Life Enrichment Centers Inc PO Box 10 *Web:* www.familylifecare.org	High Shoals	GA	30645	706-769-7738	769-5944
Magnolia Manor Inc 2001 S Lee St *Web:* www.magnoliamanor.com	Americus	GA	31709	229-924-9352	
Uhs Pruitt Corp 1626 Jeurgens Ct **Fax Area Code:* 706 ■ *Web:* www.uhs-pruitt.com	Norcross	GA	30093	770-279-6200	886-0542*
Kula Hospital 100 Keokea Pl *Web:* www.hhsc.org	Kula	HI	96790	808-878-1221	878-1791
Apostolic Christian Restmor Inc 935 E Jefferson St	Morton	IL	61550	309-266-7141	266-7877
Ballard Healthcare Residence 9300 W Ballard Rd *Web:* www.ballardhealthcare.com	Des Plaines	IL	60016	847-294-2300	299-4012
Barton W Stone Christian Home 873 Grove St	Jacksonville	IL	62650	217-479-3400	243-8553
Bethany Terrace Nursing Centre 8425 N Waukegan Rd *Web:* www.bethanyterrace.org	Morton Grove	IL	60053	847-965-8100	965-0114
Brentwood North Nursing & Rehabilitation Ctr 3705 Deerfield Rd *Web:* www.boulevardhealthcare.com	Riverwoods	IL	60015	847-459-1200	947-9005
Brentwood Subacute Rehabilitation Ctr 5400 W 87th St	Burbank	IL	60459	708-423-1200	423-8405
Community Nursing & Rehabilitation Ctr 1136 N Mill St *Web:* www.cnrcllc.com	Naperville	IL	60563	630-355-3300	355-1417
Evenglow Lodge Inc 215 E Washington St *Web:* www.evenglowlodge.org	Pontiac	IL	61764	815-844-6131	842-3558
Fairview Baptist Home 250 Village Dr	Downers Grove	IL	60516	630-769-6200	769-6226
Heritage Enterprises Inc 115 W Jefferson St *Web:* www.heritageofcare.com	Bloomington	IL	61702	309-823-7165	827-4293
John C Proctor Endowment 2724 W Reservoir Blvd *Web:* www.proctorendowment.org	Peoria	IL	61615	309-685-6580	566-4292
Lieberman Geriatric Health Centre 9700 Gross Pt Rd	Skokie	IL	60076	847-674-7210	674-6366
ManorCare Health Services - Arlington Heights 715 W Central Rd	Arlington Heights	IL	60005	847-392-2020	392-0174
ManorCare Health Services - Homewood 940 Maple Ave *TF:* 800-427-4012	Homewood	IL	60430	708-799-0244	799-1505
ManorCare Health Services - Oak Lawn East 9401 S Kostner Ave *TF:* 800-427-1902	Oak Lawn	IL	60453	708-423-7882	423-7947
Norridge Health Care & Rehabilitation Centre 7001 W Cullom Ave *Web:* www.norridgecare.com	Norridge	IL	60706	708-457-0700	457-8852
North Adams Home Inc 2259 E 1100th St *Web:* www.northadamshome.org	Mendon	IL	62351	217-936-2137	936-2818
Oakton Pavilion Healthcare Facility Inc 1660 Oakton Pl	Des Plaines	IL	60018	847-299-5588	493-6525
OSF Saint Clare Home 5533 N Galena Rd *Web:* www.osfhealthcare.org	Peoria Heights	IL	61616	309-682-5428	682-8478
Pinecrest Manor 414 S Wesley Ave	Mount Morris	IL	61054	815-734-4103	734-7318
Plymouth Place Inc 315 N LaGrange Rd *Web:* www.plymouthplace.org	La Grange Park	IL	60526	708-354-0340	482-6847
Regency Nursing Centre 6631 N Milwaukee Ave *Web:* www.regencyrehabcenter.com	Niles	IL	60714	847-647-7444	647-6403
Sherman West Court 1950 Larkin Ave	Elgin	IL	60123	847-742-7070	742-7248
Sherwin Manor Nursing Ctr 7350 N Sheridan Rd *Web:* www.sherwinmanor.com	Chicago	IL	60626	773-274-1000	274-2353
Cambridge Manor 8530 Township Line Rd	Indianapolis	IN	46260	317-876-9955	876-6016
Heritage Ctr 1201 W Buena Vista Rd *TF:* 800-704-0700 ■ *Web:* www.holidayhealthcare.com	Evansville	IN	47710	812-429-0700	429-1849
Miller's Merry Manor 612 E 11th St	Rushville	IN	46173	765-932-4127	932-3054
Miller's Merry Manor 1500 Grant St *Web:* www.millersmerrymanor.com	Huntington	IN	46750	260-356-5713	356-8671
Miller's Merry Manor 200 26th St PO Box 480 *Web:* www.millersmerrymanor.com	Logansport	IN	46947	574-722-4006	753-8753
Northwest Manor Health Care Ctr 6440 W 34th St	Indianapolis	IN	46224	317-293-4930	291-1543

Facility / Address	City	State	ZIP	Phone	Fax
Saint Vincent Pediatric Rehabilitation Ctr 1707 W 86th St *TF:* 866-338-2345 ■ *Web:* www.stvincent.org	Indianapolis	IN	46260	317-415-5500	415-5595
Waters of Covington 1600 E Liberty St *Web:* www.thewaters.net	Covington	IN	47932	765-793-4818	793-5047
Abcm Corp 1320 4th St NE PO Box 436 *Web:* www.abcmcorp.com	Hampton	IA	50441	641-456-5636	456-2320
Edgewood Convalescent Home PO Box 39	Edgewood	IA	52042	563-928-6461	928-6462
Monticello Nursing & Rehabilitation Ctr 500 Pinehaven Dr	Monticello	IA	52310	319-465-5415	465-3205
New Hampton Nursing & Rehabilitation Ctr 703 S 4th Ave	New Hampton	IA	50659	641-394-4153	394-5483
New London Nursing & Rehabilitation Ctr 100 Care Cir PO Box 136 *Web:* www.careinipiatives.com	New London	IA	52645	319-367-5753	367-2003
Saint Luke's Living Center East 1220 5th Ave SE *Web:* www.crlivingcenters.com	Cedar Rapids	IA	52403	319-366-8701	366-8702
State Center Nursing & Rehabilitation Ctr 702 3rd St	State Center	IA	50247	641-483-2812	483-2675
Wheatland Manor Inc PO Box 369	Wheatland	IA	52777	563-374-1295	374-1107
Christopher East Health Care Ctr 4200 Brown's Ln	Louisville	KY	40220	502-459-8900	459-5026
Signature Health Care LLC 12201 Bluegrass Pkwy **Fax Area Code: 561* ■ *Web:* www.signaturehealthcarellc.com	Louisville	KY	40299	502-568-7800	273-6178*
Winchester Centre for Health & Rehabilitation 200 Glenway Rd *Web:* www.kindred.com	Winchester	KY	40391	859-744-1800	744-0285
Fox Chase Rehabilitation & Nursing Ctr 2015 E W Hwy *Web:* www.foxchaserehabilitationandnursingcenter.com	Silver Spring	MD	20910	301-587-2400	587-2404
FutureCare Canton Harbor 1300 S Ellwood Ave *Web:* www.futurecarehealth.com	Baltimore	MD	21224	410-342-6644	327-3949
Keswick Multi-Care Ctr 700 W 40th St *Web:* www.keswick-multicare.org	Baltimore	MD	21211	410-235-8860	235-7425
Levindale Hebrew Geriatric Center & Hospital 2434 W Belvedere Ave *Web:* www.lifebridgehealth.org/Levindale	Baltimore	MD	21215	410-601-2400	601-2890
ManorCare Health Services - Rossville 6600 Ridge Rd	Baltimore	MD	21237	410-574-4950	391-4386
ManorCare Health Services - Ruxton 7001 N Charles St	Towson	MD	21204	410-821-9600	337-8313
Woodside Ctr 9101 2nd Ave	Silver Spring	MD	20910	301-588-5544	588-5547
Brookline Health Care Ctr 99 Pk St	Brookline	MA	02446	617-731-1050	731-6516
Cedar Hill Health Care Ctr 49 Thomas Patten Dr *Web:* www.healthbridgemanagement.com/cedar-hill	Randolph	MA	02368	781-961-1160	963-8610
Central Boston Elder Services Inc 2315 Washington St *Web:* www.centralboston.org	Boston	MA	02119	617-277-7416	277-2005
Colonial Nursing & Rehabilitation Inc 125 Broad St	Weymouth	MA	02188	781-337-3121	337-9831
Eastpointe Rehabilitation & Skilled Care Ctr 255 Central Ave	Chelsea	MA	02150	617-884-5700	884-7005
Essex Park Nursing & Rehabilitation Ctr 265 Essex St	Beverly	MA	01915	978-927-3260	922-8347
Fairview Commons Nursing & Rehabilitation Ctr 151 Christian Hill Rd *Web:* www.fairviewcommons.org	Great Barrington	MA	01230	413-528-4560	528-5767
Harrington House Nursing & Rehabilitation Ctr 160 Main St	Walpole	MA	02081	508-660-3080	660-1634
Holyoke Rehabilitation Ctr 260 Easthampton Rd *TF:* 800-394-9733	Holyoke	MA	01040	413-538-9733	538-9919
Jewish Nursing Home of Western Massachusetts Inc 770 Converse St **Fax: Admitting* ■ *Web:* www.jewishgeriatriacservices.org	Longmeadow	MA	01106	413-567-6211	567-2477*
JML Care Ctr 184 Ter Heun Dr *Web:* www.capecodhealthcare.org	Falmouth	MA	02540	508-457-4621	457-1218
Lowell Health Care Ctr 19 Varnum St *TF:* 800-966-5644	Lowell	MA	01850	978-454-5644	459-6520
Marlborough Hills Healthcare Ctr 121 Northboro Rd E	Marlborough	MA	01752	508-485-4040	481-5585
Meadow Green Nursing & Rehabilitation Ctr 45 Woburn St *Web:* www.meadowgreen.org	Waltham	MA	02454	781-899-8600	899-3124
Methuen Health & Rehabilitation Ctr 480 Jackson St	Methuen	MA	01844	978-686-3906	687-6007
Middleboro Skilled Care Ctr 23 Isaac St	Middleboro	MA	02346	508-947-9295	947-7974
Newton Health Care Ctr 2101 Washington St *Web:* www.newtonhealthcarecenter.com	Newton	MA	02462	617-969-4660	964-4622
North Adams Common Nursing Home 175 Franklin St *Web:* www.northadamscommons.org	North Adams	MA	01247	413-664-4041	664-8447
Peabody Glen Health Care Ctr 199 Andover St *Web:* www.healthbridgemanagement.com	Peabody	MA	01960	978-531-0772	531-7809
Port Health Care 113 Low St	Newburyport	MA	01950	978-462-7373	462-6510
Radius Healthcare Center at Danvers 56 Liberty St	Danvers	MA	01923	978-777-2700	774-4463
Sacred Heart Nursing Home 359 Summer St	New Bedford	MA	02740	508-996-6751	996-5189
Sherrill House Inc (SH) 135 S Huntington Ave *Web:* www.sherrillhouse.org	Jamaica Plain	MA	02130	617-731-2400	731-8671
Vinfen Corp 950 Cambridge St *Web:* www.vinfen.org	Cambridge	MA	02141	617-441-1800	441-1858
Williamstown Commons Nursing & Rehabilitation Ctr 25 Adams Rd *TF:* 800-869-6675	Williamstown	MA	01267	413-458-2111	458-3156
Wilmington Health Care Ctr 750 Woburn St	Wilmington	MA	01887	978-988-0888	658-6470
Worcester Skilled Care Ctr 59 Acton St *Web:* www.wingatehealthcare.com	Worcester	MA	01604	508-791-3147	753-6267
Bay County Medical Care Facility 564 W Hampton Rd *Web:* www.baycountymcf.com	Essexville	MI	48732	989-892-3591	892-6991
Clarkston Specialty Healthcare Ctr 4800 Clintonville Rd	Clarkston	MI	48346	248-674-0903	674-3431
Crestmont Health Care Ctr 111 Trealout Dr	Fenton	MI	48430	810-629-4105	629-7538
Farmington HealthCare Ctr 34225 Grand River Ave *Web:* www.farmingtonhealthcarecenter.com	Farmington	MI	48335	248-477-7373	477-2888
Golden Oaks Medical Care Facility 1200 N Telegraph Rd Bldg 32E	Pontiac	MI	48341	248-858-1415	858-4026
Grand Blanc Rehabilitation & Nursing Ctr 11941 Belsay Rd	Grand Blanc	MI	48439	810-694-1970	694-4081
Heartland Health Care Center Georgian Bloomfield 2975 N Adams Rd *TF:* 800-427-1902	Bloomfield Hills	MI	48304	248-645-2900	433-1415
Heartland Health Care Center University 28550 Five Mile Rd *Web:* www.hcr-manorcare.com/heartlandnursing/university	Livonia	MI	48154	734-427-8270	427-2135
Hope Network 3075 Orchard Vista Dr SE *TF:* 800-695-7273 ■ *Web:* www.hopenetwork.org	Grand Rapids	MI	49546	616-301-8000	301-8010
Howell Care Ctr 3003 W Grand River Ave *Web:* www.howellcarecenter.com	Howell	MI	48843	517-546-4210	546-9495
Isabella County Medical Care Facility 1222 N Dr	Mount Pleasant	MI	48858	989-772-2957	772-3669
Martha T Berry Memorial Medical Care Facility 43533 Elizabeth Rd *Web:* www.macombcountymi.gov	Mount Clemens	MI	48043	586-469-5265	466-7418
Sanctuary at Bellbrook 873 W Avon Rd *Web:* www.trinityseniorsanctuary.org/communities/sanctuary-bellbrook	Rochester Hills	MI	48307	248-656-6300	656-8160
Shore Haven A Mercy Living Ctr 900 S Beacon Blvd *Web:* www.mercyshorehaven.org	Grand Haven	MI	49417	616-846-1850	846-0971
Tendercare Clare 600 SE 4th St *Web:* www.tendercare.net	Clare	MI	48617	989-386-7723	386-4100
Big Bend Woods Health Care Ctr 110 Highland Ave	Valley Park	MO	63088	636-225-5144	225-8427
Sunset Hills Health & Rehabilitation Ctr 10954 Kennerly Rd	Saint Louis	MO	63128	314-843-4242	843-4031
Village North Health Ctr 11160 Village N Dr *Web:* www.bjc.org	Saint Louis	MO	63136	314-355-8010	653-4880
Good Shepherd Rehabilitation & Nursing Ctr 20 Plantation Dr	Jaffrey	NH	03452	603-532-8762	593-0006
Kindred Transitional Care & Rehabilitation - Greenbriar 55 Harris Rd *Web:* www.greenbriarterrace.com	Nashua	NH	03062	603-888-1573	888-5089
Pleasant Valley Nursing Ctr 8 Peabody Rd	Derry	NH	03038	603-434-1566	434-2299
Saint Ann Healthcare Ctr 195 Dover Pt Rd	Dover	NH	03820	603-742-2612	743-3055
Camden County Health Services Ctr 20 N Woodbury Turnersville Rd *Web:* www.cchsc.com	Blackwood	NJ	08012	856-374-6600	
Daughters of Miriam Center/Gallen Institute 155 Passaic County 702 *Web:* www.daughtersofmiriamcenter.org	Clifton	NJ	07011	973-772-3700	253-5389
Dunroven Health Care Ctr 221 County Rd *Web:* www.care-one.com	Cresskill	NJ	07626	201-567-9310	541-9224
Linwood Convalescent Ctr 201 New Rd & Central Ave *Web:* www.brandycare.com	Linwood	NJ	08221	609-927-6131	927-5899
ManorCare Health Services - Mountainside 1180 Rt 22 W *Web:* www.hcr-manorcare.com	Mountainside	NJ	07092	908-654-0020	654-8661
Morris View Nursing Home PO Box 437	Morris Plains	NJ	07950	973-285-2820	285-6062
Somerset Valley Rehabilitation & Nursing Ctr 1621 Rt 22 W	Bound Brook	NJ	08805	732-469-2000	469-8917
South Jersey Health Care Ctr 2 Cooper Plaza	Camden	NJ	08103	856-342-7600	968-0250
Valley Health Care Ctr 300 Old Hook Rd *Web:* www.care-one.com	Westwood	NJ	07675	201-664-8888	263-0545
Voorhees Pediatric Facility 1304 Laurel Oak Rd *TF:* 888-873-5437 ■ *Web:* www.forkidcare.com	Voorhees	NJ	08043	856-346-3300	346-3462
Willow Creek Rehabilitation & Care Ctr 1165 Easton Ave	Somerset	NJ	08873	732-246-4100	246-3926
Clove Lakes Health Care & Rehabilitation Ctr 25 Fanning St *Web:* www.clovelakes.com	Staten Island	NY	10314	718-289-7900	761-8701
Comprehensive Care Management Corp (CCM) 1250 Waters Pl Tower 1 Suite 602 *TF:* 877-226-8500 ■ *Web:* www.ccmny.org	Bronx	NY	10461	877-226-8500	
Dumont Masonic Home 676 Pelham Rd *Web:* www.dumontmasonichome.org	New Rochelle	NY	10805	914-632-9600	632-4766
Golden Gate Rehabilitation & Health Care Ctr 191 Bradley Ave	Staten Island	NY	10314	718-698-8800	698-5536
Grace Plaza of Great Neck Inc 15 St Paul's Pl *Web:* www.graceplaza.com	Great Neck	NY	11021	516-466-3001	466-7624
Haven Manor Health Care Ctr 1441 Gateway Blvd	Far Rockaway	NY	11691	718-471-1500	471-9606
Jewish Home Lifecare 120 W 106TH St *TF:* 800-544-0304 ■ *Web:* www.jewishhome.org	New York	NY	10025	212-870-5000	870-4715

Facility	City	State	ZIP	Phone	Fax
Lutheran Social Services 715 Falconer St *Web:* www.lutheran-jamestown.org	Jamestown	NY	14701	716-665-4905	665-8055
Margaret Tietz Center for Nursing Care 164-11 Chapin Pkwy *Web:* www.margarettietz.org	Jamaica	NY	11432	718-298-7800	262-8839
Mosholu Parkway Nursing & Rehabilitation Ctr 3356 Perry Ave	Bronx	NY	10467	718-655-3568	547-8295
Northwoods at Hilltop 1805 Providence Ave *TF:* 800-697-5374 ■ *Web:* www.northwoodshealth.net	Niskayuna	NY	12309	518-374-2212	381-1688
Northwoods at Rosewood Gardens 284 Troy Rd *Web:* www.northwoodshealth.net/rosewood_gardens.asp	Rensselaer	NY	12144	518-286-1621	286-1691
Northwoods at Troy 100 New Tpke Rd *TF:* 800-697-5374 ■ *Web:* www.northwoodshealth.net/troy.asp	Troy	NY	12182	518-235-1410	235-1632
Northwoods of Cortland 28 Kellogg Rd *Web:* www.northwoodshealth.net	Cortland	NY	13045	607-753-9631	756-2968
Palm Gardens Center for Nursing & Rehabilitation 615 Ave C	Brooklyn	NY	11218	718-633-3300	853-8680
Promenade Rehabilitation & Health Care Ctr 140 Beach 114th St	Rockaway Park	NY	11694	718-945-4600	634-8237
Providence Rest 3304 Waterbury Ave *Web:* www.providencerest.org	Bronx	NY	10465	718-931-3000	863-0185
Robinson Terrace 28652 New York 23 *Web:* www.robinsonterrace.com	Stamford	NY	12167	607-652-7521	652-3362
Saint Mary's Hospital for Children Inc 29-01 216th St *Web:* www.stmaryskids.org	Bayside	NY	11360	718-281-8800	281-8523
Sea View Hospital Rehabilitation Center & Home 460 Brielle Ave *Web:* www.nyc.gov/html/hhc/seaview	Staten Island	NY	10314	718-317-3221	351-7898
Victory Lake Nursing Ctr 419 N Quaker Ln	Hyde Park	NY	12538	845-229-9177	229-9819
Wesley Group Inc 3 Upton Pk	Rochester	NY	14607	585-241-2100	241-2180
Cypress Pointe Rehabilitation & HealthCare Ctr 2006 S 16th St	Wilmington	NC	28401	910-763-6271	251-9803
Erwin Garden Rehabilitation 3100 Erwin Rd	Durham	NC	27705	919-383-1546	383-0862
Kindred Hospital Greensboro 2401 Southside Blvd *TF:* 877-836-2671 ■ *Web:* www.kindredhospitalgreensboro.com	Greensboro	NC	27406	336-271-2800	271-2734
Long Leaf Medical Treatment Ctr 4761 Ward Blvd *Web:* www.ost.state.inc.us/jobs	Wilson	NC	27893	252-399-2112	399-2138
Valley Nursing Ctr 581 NC Hwy 16 S	Taylorsville	NC	28681	828-632-8146	635-0300
Arbors at Delaware 2270 Warrensburg Rd	Delaware	OH	43015	740-369-9614	
Arbors at Marietta 400 7th St	Marietta	OH	45750	740-373-3597	373-3915
Arbors at Toledo Subacute & Rehabilitation Ctr 2920 Cherry St	Toledo	OH	43608	419-242-7458	242-6514
Arbors East Subacute Nursing & Rehabilitation Ctr 5500 E Broad St	Columbus	OH	43213	614-575-9003	575-9101
Area Agency On Aging 10b Inc 1550 Corporate Woods Pkwy *TF:* 800-421-7277 ■ *Web:* www.services4aging.org	Uniontown	OH	44685	330-896-9172	896-6644
Cedarwood Plaza 12504 Cedar Rd	Cleveland Heights	OH	44106	216-371-3600	371-6766
Columbus Rehabilitation & Subacute Institute 44 S Souder Ave	Columbus	OH	43222	614-228-5900	228-3989
Community Multicare Ctr 908 Symmes Rd	Fairfield	OH	45014	513-868-6500	868-7150
Deaconess Long Term Care Inc (DLTC) 440 Lafayette Ave PO Box 198027 *Web:* www.deaconesslongtermcare.com	Cincinnati	OH	45220	513-487-3600	
Gateway Health Care Ctr 3 Gateway Dr *Web:* www.gatewaypathways.com	Euclid	OH	44119	216-486-4949	481-5155
Heartland of Beavercreek 1974 N Fairfield Rd	Dayton	OH	45432	937-429-1106	429-0902
Heartland of Centerburg 212 Fairview Ave	Centerburg	OH	43011	740-625-5774	625-7426
Heartland of Marysville 755 S Plum St	Marysville	OH	43040	937-644-8836	644-1811
Hennis Care Centre 1720 Cross St *Web:* www.henniscarecentre.com	Dover	OH	44622	330-364-8849	364-2128
ManorCare Health Services - North Olmsted 23225 Lorain Rd *Web:* www.hcr-manorcare.com	North Olmsted	OH	44070	440-779-6900	779-8091
Middlebury Manor 974 E Market St	Akron	OH	44305	330-762-9066	762-4004
Newark Healthcare Centre 75 McMillen Dr	Newark	OH	43055	740-344-0357	344-0452
Saint Augustine Manor 7801 Detroit Ave	Cleveland	OH	44102	216-634-7400	939-7577*
University Hospitals Health System Heather Hill 12340 Bass Lake Rd	Chardon	OH	44024	440-285-4040	285-7743
Villa Angela Nursing Rehabilitation Ctr 5700 Karl Rd	Columbus	OH	43229	614-846-5420	854-7830
Village of Westerville 1060 Eastwind Dr	Westerville	OH	43081	614-895-1038	895-1094
Walton Manor Health Care Ctr 19859 Alexander Rd	Walton Hills	OH	44146	440-439-4433	439-0691
Waterford Commons Nursing Ctr 955 Garden Lake Pkwy	Toledo	OH	43614	419-382-2200	381-0188
Oklahoma Veterans Center Norman 1776 E Robinson St PO Box 1668 *Web:* www.ok.gov/ODVA/Veterans_Centers/Norman.html	Norman	OK	73070	405-360-5600	364-8432
Beverly Healthcare Western Reserve 1521 W 54th St *TF:* 877-823-8375	Erie	PA	16509	814-864-0671	866-5681
Golden Living Ctr 350 Old Gilkeson Rd	Pittsburgh	PA	15228	412-257-4444	257-8226
Greenery of Canonsburg 2200 Hill Church-Houston Rd	Canonsburg	PA	15317	724-745-8000	746-8780
Jefferson Manor Health Ctr 417 Rt 28 *Web:* www.jeffersonmanor.com	Brookville	PA	15825	814-849-8026	849-3889
Kindred Hospital Philadelphia 6129 Palmetto St *Web:* www.kindredphila.com	Philadelphia	PA	19111	215-722-8555	725-8998
Kindred Hospital Pittsburgh 7777 Steubenville Pike *TF:* 800-654-5988 ■ *Web:* www.kindredhospitalpittsburgh.com	Oakdale	PA	15071	412-494-5500	494-5511
Laurel Ctr 125 Holly Rd	Hamburg	PA	19526	610-562-2284	562-0775
Liberty Nursing & Rehabilitation Ctr 535 N 17th St	Allentown	PA	18104	610-432-4351	435-4470
Presbyterian SeniorCare-Southminster Place 835 S Main St *Web:* www.srcare.org	Washington	PA	15301	724-222-4300	250-4998
Presbyterian SeniorCare-Westminster Place 1215 Hulton Rd *TF:* 877-772-6500 ■ *Web:* www.srcare.org	Oakmont	PA	15139	412-828-5600	826-6059
Quincy United Methodist Home & Village 6596 Orphanage Rd PO Box 217	Quincy	PA	17247	717-749-3151	749-2013
Redstone Highlands Health Care Ctr 6 Garden Ctr Dr *Web:* www.redstonehighlands.org	Greensburg	PA	15601	724-832-8400	836-3710
Rest Haven-York 1050 S George St *Web:* www.resthavenyork.com	York	PA	17403	717-843-9866	846-5894
South Mountain Restoration Ctr 10058 S Mountain Rd *TF:* 877-765-0331	South Mountain	PA	17261	717-749-3121	749-3946
Twinbrook Medical Ctr 3805 Field St *TF:* 800-427-9149	Erie	PA	16511	814-898-5600	899-9829
Woodhaven Care Ctr 2400 McGinley Rd	Monroeville	PA	15146	412-856-4770	856-6856
Oak Hill Nursing & Rehabilitation Ctr 544 Pleasant St *Fax: Admitting ■ *Web:* www.oakhillrehab.com	Pawtucket	RI	02860	401-725-8888	727-6731*
Saint Elizabeth Home 1 St Elizabeth Way *Web:* www.stelizabethcommunity.com	East Greenwich	RI	02818	401-471-6060	471-6072
CM Tucker Jr Nursing Care Ctr 2200 Harden St	Columbia	SC	29203	803-737-5300	737-5342
Driftwood Rehabilitation & Nursing Ctr 2375 Baker Hospital Blvd	North Charleston	SC	29405	843-744-2750	747-0406
Heartland Health Care Center Charleston 1800 Eagle Landing Blvd	Hanahan	SC	29406	843-553-0656	553-9773
Allen Morgan Health Ctr 177 N Highland Ave	Memphis	TN	38111	901-325-4003	325-4011
Briarcliff Health Care Ctr 100 Elmhurst Dr	Oak Ridge	TN	37830	865-481-3367	482-5961
Manor House of Dover 537 Spring St	Dover	TN	37058	931-232-6902	232-4256
Hearthstone of Round Rock 401 Oakwood Blvd *Web:* www.hearthstonehealth.com	Round Rock	TX	78681	512-388-7494	388-2166
Heartland Health Care Center Bedford 2001 Forest Ridge Dr	Bedford	TX	76021	817-571-6804	267-4176
Heartland of San Antonio 1 Heartland Dr	San Antonio	TX	78247	210-653-1219	653-8977
Kindred Hospital Fort Worth 815 8th Ave	Fort Worth	TX	76104	817-332-4812	332-8843
Plum Creek Healthcare Ctr 5601 Plum Creek Dr *Web:* www.plumcreekspecialtyhospital.com	Amarillo	TX	79124	806-351-1000	351-8117
Treemont Nursing & Rehabilitation Ctr 5550 Harvest Hill Rd Suite 500	Dallas	TX	75230	972-661-1862	980-6731
South Davis Community Hospital 401 S 400 E *TF:* 877-913-2847 ■ *Web:* www.sdch.com	Bountiful	UT	84010	801-295-2361	295-1398
Sunshine Terrace Foundation Inc 248 W 300 N *Web:* www.sunshineterrace.com	Logan	UT	84321	435-752-0411	752-1318
Berkshire Health Care Ctr 705 Clearview Dr	Vinton	VA	24179	540-982-6691	985-4899
James River Convalescent Ctr 540 Aberthaw Ave	Newport News	VA	23601	757-595-2273	595-2271
Laurels of University Park The 2420 Pemberton Rd	Richmond	VA	23233	804-747-9200	747-1574
Lucy Corr Village 6800 Lucy Corr Blvd *Web:* www.lucycorrvillage.com	Chesterfield	VA	23832	804-748-1511	706-5572
Lynchburg Health & Rehabilitation Ctr 5615 Seminole Ave	Lynchburg	VA	24502	434-239-2657	239-4062
ManorCare Health Services - Arlington 550 S Carlin Springs Rd *Web:* www.hcr-manorcare.com	Arlington	VA	22204	703-379-7200	578-5524
ManorCare Health Services - Fair Oaks 12475 Lee Jackson Memorial Hwy	Fairfax	VA	22033	703-352-7172	352-1455
Riverside Regional Convalescent Ctr 1000 Old Denbigh Blvd	Newport News	VA	23602	757-875-2000	875-2036
Ballard Care & Rehabilitation 820 NW 95th St	Seattle	WA	98117	206-782-0100	781-1448
Kitsap Mental Health Services 5455 Almira Dr Ne *Web:* www.kitsapmentalhealth.org	Bremerton	WA	98311	360-405-4010	
Seattle Medical & Rehabilitation Ctr 555 16th Ave	Seattle	WA	98122	206-324-8200	324-0780
Glenwood Park Retirement Village 1924 Glenwood Pk Rd *Fax: Admitting ■ *Web:* www.gwpinc.org	Princeton	WV	24740	304-425-8128	425-9711*
Brewster Village 3300 W Brewster St *Web:* www.co.outagamie.wi.us	Appleton	WI	54914	920-832-5400	832-4922
Clement Manor 3939 S 92nd St *Web:* www.clementmanor.com	Greenfield	WI	53228	414-321-1800	546-7357
Franciscan Villa 3601 S Chicago Ave *Web:* www.franciscanvilla.org	South Milwaukee	WI	53172	414-764-4100	764-0706
Middleton Village Nursing & Rehabilitation Ctr 6201 Elmwood Ave	Middleton	WI	53562	608-831-8300	831-4253

454 LONG-TERM CARE FACILITIES OPERATORS

Operator	City	State	ZIP	Phone	Fax
Active Services Corp 400 Redland Ct Suite 114 *TF:* 866-724-9599	Owings Mills	MD	21117	443-548-2200	548-2280
Advocat Inc 1621 Galleria Blvd *Web:* www.diversicaremanagement.com	Brentwood	TN	37027	615-771-7575	

Phone Fax

Aegis Assisted Living 17602 NE Union Hill Rd .... Redmond WA 98052 425-861-9993 861-7278
TF: 888-252-3447 ■ *Web:* www.aegisliving.com

American Religious Town Hall Inc
745 N Buckner Blvd .... Dallas TX 75218 214-328-9828 328-3042
TF: 800-783-9828 ■ *Web:* www.americanreligious.org

Americare Systems Inc 214 N Scott St .... Sikeston MO 63801 573-471-1113 471-8235
Web: www.americareusa.net

Atria Senior Living Group
401 S 4th St Suite 1900 .... Louisville KY 40202 502-779-4700
Web: www.atriaseniorliving.com

Autumn Corp 451 N Winstead Ave .... Rocky Mount NC 27804 252-443-6265 443-2703
Web: www.autumncorp.com

CabelTel International Corp
1755 Wittington Pl Suite 340 .... Dallas TX 75234 972-407-8400 407-8436
AMEX: GBR ■ *TF:* 888-407-8400 ■ *Web:* www.newconceptenergy.com

Cardinal Ritter Senior Services
7601 Watson Rd .... Saint Louis MO 63119 314-961-8000 961-1934
Web: www.ccstl.org

Comprehensive Systems Inc 1700 Clark St .... Charles City IA 50616 641-228-4842 228-4675

ElderWood Senior Care 7 Limestone Dr .... Williamsville NY 14221 716-633-3900 633-1153
TF: 888-826-9663 ■ *Web:* www.elderwood.com

Emeritus Corp 3131 Elliott Ave Suite 500 .... Seattle WA 98121 206-298-2909 301-4500
AMEX: ESC ■ *TF:* 800-429-4828 ■ *Web:* www.emeritus.com

Extendicare Inc 3000 Steeles Ave E .... Markham ON L3R9W2 905-470-4000 470-5588
Web: www.extendicare.com

Five Star Quality Care Inc 400 Centre St .... Newton MA 02458 617-796-8387 796-8385
AMEX: FVE ■ *TF:* 866-230-1286 ■ *Web:* www.fivestarqualitycare.com

Genesis HealthCare Corp
101 E State St .... Kennett Square PA 19348 610-444-6350 925-4000
TF: 800-944-7776 ■ *Web:* www.genesishcc.com

Golden Ventures 1000 Fianna Way .... Fort Smith AR 72919 479-201-2000 201-1101
TF: 877-823-8375 ■ *Web:* www.goldenven.com

HCF Inc 1100 Shawnee Rd .... Lima OH 45805 419-999-2010 999-6284
TF: 800-999-2110 ■ *Web:* www.hcfinc.com

HCR Manor Care 333 N Summit St PO Box 10086 .... Toledo OH 43699 419-252-5500 252-6404*
NYSE: HCR ■ **Fax:* Hum Res ■ *TF:* 800-422-2098 ■ *Web:* www.hcr-manorcare.com

Kindred Healthcare Inc 680 S 4th Ave .... Louisville KY 40202 502-596-7300 596-4052
NYSE: KND ■ *TF:* 800-545-0749 ■ *Web:* www.kindredhealthcare.com

Life Care Centers of America Inc
3570 Keith St NW PO Box 3480 .... Cleveland TN 37320 423-472-9585 339-8332
Web: www.lifecarecenters.com

Mid-America Health Centers Inc
200 W Douglas Suite 600 .... Wichita KS 67202 316-262-4206 262-1358

National HealthCare Corp
100 E Vine St PO Box 1398 .... Murfreesboro TN 37133 615-890-2020 890-0123
AMEX: NHC ■ *Web:* www.nhccare.com

Odyssey HealthCare Inc
717 N Harwood St Suite 1500 .... Dallas TX 75201 214-922-9711 922-9752
NASDAQ: ODSY ■ *TF:* 888-922-9711 ■ *Web:* www.odyssey-healthcare.com

Royal Management Corp 665 W N Ave .... Lombard IL 60148 630-458-4700 458-4797
Web: www.lexingtonhealth.com

Salem Senior Housing
1105 Brooktown Ave .... Winston-Salem NC 27101 336-724-1000 724-9955
TF: 800-721-8182

Skilled Healthcare LLC
27442 Portola Pkwy Suite 200 .... Foothill Ranch CA 90610 949-282-5800 282-5870
Web: www.skilledhealthcare.com

Sun Health Corp 13180 N 103rd Dr PO Box 1278 .... Sun City AZ 85351 623-876-5350 876-5498
Web: www.sunhealth.org

Sun Healthcare Group Inc
18831 Von Karman Suite 400 .... Irvine CA 92612 949-255-7100
NASDAQ: SUNH ■ *TF:* 800-729-6600 ■ *Web:* www.sunh.client.shareholder.com

Sun Healthcare Group Inc Inpatient Services
18831 Von Karman Suite 400 .... Irvine CA 92612 949-255-7100 468-4458*
**Fax Area Code:* 505 ■ *TF:* 800-729-6600 ■ *Web:* www.sunh.com

SunBridge Healthcare Corp
18831 Von Karman Suite 400 .... Irvine CA 92612 949-255-7100 468-4458*
**Fax Area Code:* 505 ■ *TF:* 800-729-6600 ■ *Web:* www.sunh.com

Sunrise Senior Living Inc
7902 Westpark Dr Suite T-900 .... McLean VA 22102 703-273-7500 744-1601
NYSE: SRZ ■ *TF:* 800-929-4124 ■ *Web:* www.sunriseseniorliving.com

455 LOTTERIES, GAMES, SWEEPSTAKES

SEE ALSO Games & Gaming p. 1901

Phone Fax

Arizona Lottery 4740 E University Dr .... Phoenix AZ 85034 480-921-4400 921-5512
Web: www.arizonalottery.com

Atlantic Lottery Corp 922 Main St .... Moncton NB E1C8W6 506-867-5800 867-5555
TF: 800-561-3942 ■ *Web:* www.alc.ca

British Columbia Lottery Corp (BCLC)
74 W Seymour St .... Kamloops BC V2C1E2 250-828-5500 828-5631
Web: www.bclc.com

California State Lottery Commission
600 N 10th St .... Sacramento CA 95814 916-323-7095 323-7087
Web: www.calottery.com

Colorado Lottery 212 W 3rd St Suite 210 .... Pueblo CO 81003 719-546-2400 546-5208
TF: 800-999-2959 ■ *Web:* www.coloradolottery.com

Delaware State Lottery 1575 McKee Rd Suite 102 .... Dover DE 19904 302-739-5291 739-7586
Web: lottery.state.de.us

District of Columbia Lottery & Charitable Games Control Board
2101 ML King Jr Ave SE .... Washington DC 20020 202-645-8000 645-8077
Web: www.dclottery.com

Florida Lottery Dept 250 Marriott Dr .... Tallahassee FL 32301 850-487-7777 487-7796*
**Fax:* Hum Res ■ *Web:* www.flalottery.com

Gamesville Inc 100 5th Ave .... Waltham MA 02451 781-370-2700 370-2600
Web: www.gamesville.com

Phone Fax

Georgia Lottery Corp
250 Williams St NW Suite 3000 .... Atlanta GA 30303 404-215-5000 215-8871
Web: www.galottery.com

Idaho Lottery 1199 Shoreline Ln Suite 100 .... Boise ID 83702 208-334-2600 334-2610
TF: 800-432-5688

Illinois Lottery 101 W Jefferson St .... Springfield IL 62702 217-524-5155 558-2468
TF: 800-252-1775 ■ *Web:* www.illinoislottery.com

Indiana Lottery
201 S Capitol Ave Suite 1100 .... Indianapolis IN 46225 317-264-4800 264-4933
TF: 800-955-6886 ■ *Web:* www.in.gov

Iowa Lottery 2323 Grand Ave .... Des Moines IA 50312 515-281-7900 281-7882*
**Fax:* Hum Res ■ *Web:* www.ialottery.com

iWin.com Inc 10940 Wilshire Blvd .... Los Angeles CA 90024 310-264-4300 264-4399
Web: www.iwin.com

iWon Inc 555 12th St Suite 500 .... Oakland CA 94607 510-985-7400 985-7410
Web: www.iwon.com

Jackpot.com
c/o Vendare Media
2141 Rosecrans Ave Suite 2000 .... El Segundo CA 90245 310-647-6000 647-6001
Web: www.jackpot.com

Kansas Lottery 128 N Kansas Ave .... Topeka KS 66603 785-296-5700 296-5712
TF: 800-544-9467

Kentucky Lottery Corp 1011 W Main St .... Louisville KY 40202 502-560-1500 560-1532
TF: 800-937-8946 ■ *Web:* www.kylottery.com

Loto-Quebec 500 Sherbrooke St W .... Montreal QC H3A3G6 514-282-8000 873-8999
Web: www.loto-quebec.com

Louisiana Lottery Corp 555 Laurel St .... Baton Rouge LA 70801 225-297-2000 297-2005
Web: www.louisianalottery.com

Maryland State Lottery
1800 Washington Blvd Suite 330 .... Baltimore MD 21230 410-230-8790 230-8728
Web: www.mdlottery.com

Massachusetts State Lottery Commission
60 Columbian St .... Braintree MA 02184 781-849-5555 849-5546
Web: www.masslottery.com

Michigan State Lottery
101 E Hillsdale St PO Box 30023 .... Lansing MI 48909 517-335-5600 335-5644
Web: www.michigan.gov/lottery

Minnesota State Lottery 2645 Long Lake Rd .... Roseville MN 55113 651-297-7456
Web: www.mnlottery.com

Missouri Lottery
1823 Southridge Dr PO Box 1603 .... Jefferson City MO 65109 573-751-4050 751-5188
Web: www.molottery.com

Montana Lottery 2525 N Montana Ave .... Helena MT 59601 406-444-5825 444-5830
Web: www.montanalottery.com

Multi-State Lottery Assn
4400 NW Urbandale Dr .... Urbandale IA 50322 515-453-1400 453-1420
Web: www.musl.com

Nebraska Lottery 1800 "O" St PO Box 98901 .... Lincoln NE 68509 402-471-6100 471-6108
TF: 800-587-5200 ■ *Web:* www.nelottery.com

New Hampshire Lottery Commission
14 Integra Dr .... Concord NH 03301 603-271-3391 271-1160
TF: 800-852-3324 ■ *Web:* www.nhlottery.org

New Jersey Lottery PO Box 041 .... Trenton NJ 08625 609-599-5800 599-5935
Web: www.state.nj.us

New Mexico Lottery
Lottery 4511 Osuna Rd NE PO Box 93190 .... Albuquerque NM 87199 505-342-7600 342-7511
Web: www.nmlottery.com

North Dakota Lottery 600 E Blvd Ave Dept 125 .... Bismark ND 58505 701-328-1574 328-1580
Web: www.ndlottery.org

Ohio Lottery Commission 615 W Superior Ave .... Cleveland OH 44113 216-787-3200 787-3313
TF: 800-686-4208 ■ *Web:* www.ohiolottery.com

Oregon Lottery 500 Airport Rd SE .... Salem OR 97301 503-540-1000 540-1001
Web: www.oregonlottery.org

pogo.com
c/o Electronic Arts Inc
209 Redwood Shores Pkwy .... Redwood City CA 94065 650-628-1500 628-1414
TF: 800-804-0836 ■ *Web:* www.pogo.com

Rhode Island Lottery 1425 Pontiac Ave .... Cranston RI 02920 401-463-6500 463-5008
Web: www.rilot.com

South Carolina Education Lottery
1333 Main St 4th Fl .... Columbia SC 29201 803-737-2002 737-2005
Web: www.sceducationlottery.com

Tennessee Lottery 200 Athens Way Suite 200 .... Nashville TN 37228 615-324-6500 324-8013*
**Fax:* Hum Res ■ *Web:* www.tnlottery.com

Texas Lottery Commission PO Box 16630 .... Austin TX 78761 512-344-5000 344-5240*
**Fax:* Hum Res ■ *TF:* 800-375-6886 ■ *Web:* www.txlottery.org

Vermont Lottery Commission
1311 US Rt 302 Suite 100 .... Barre VT 05641 802-479-5686 479-4294
TF: 800-322-8800 ■ *Web:* www.vtlottery.com

Virginia Lottery 900 E Main St .... Richmond VA 23219 804-692-7777 692-7775
Web: www.valottery.com

Washington State Lottery PO Box 43000 .... Olympia WA 98504 360-664-4720 664-2630
TF: 800-732-5101 ■ *Web:* www.walottery.com

West Virginia Lottery PO Box 2067 .... Charleston WV 25327 304-558-0500 558-0129
TF: 800-982-4946 ■ *Web:* www.wvlottery.com

Western Canada Lottery Corp
125 Garry St 10th Fl .... Winnipeg MB R3C4J1 204-942-8217 946-1442
Web: www.wclc.com

Wisconsin Lottery PO Box 8941 .... Madison WI 53708 608-261-4916 264-6644
Web: www.wilottery.com

456 LUGGAGE, BAGS, CASES

SEE ALSO Handbags, Totes, Backpacks p. 2003; Leather Goods - Personal p. 2149

Phone Fax

Ace Products Group 11 5th St Suite 106 .... Petaluma CA 94952 707-765-1500 762-1899
TF: 800-950-1095 ■ *Web:* www.aceproducts.com

Company	City	State	ZIP	Phone	Fax
AJ Siris Corp Inc 59 Lewis St *TF:* 800-526-5300 ■ *Web:* www.ajsiris.com	Paterson	NJ	07501	973-684-7700	684-3251
Anvil Cases 15730 Salt Lake Ave *TF:* 800-359-2684 ■ *Web:* www.anvilcase.com	City of Industry	CA	91745	626-968-4100	968-1703
Award Winner Group 202 W 3rd St *Web:* www.awardwinnergroup.com	Mount Vernon	NY	10550	914-664-7134	668-2858
Bergman Luggage Co 401 NE Northgate Way Suite 937 *Web:* www.bergmanluggage.com	Seattle	WA	98125	206-365-5775	
Brewer-Cantelmo Co Inc 350 7th Ave 4th Fl *Web:* www.brewer-cantelmo.com	New York	NY	10001	212-244-4600	244-1640
Calzone Case Co 225 Black Rock Ave *TF Cust Svc:* 800-243-5152 ■ *Web:* www.calzonecase.com	Bridgeport	CT	06605	203-367-5766	336-4406
CH Ellis Co Inc 2432 Southeastern Ave *TF Sales:* 800-466-3351 ■ *Web:* www.chellis.com	Indianapolis	IN	46201	317-636-3351	635-5140
Coach Inc 516 W 34th St *NYSE: COH* ■ *TF:* 800-444-3611 ■ *Web:* www.coach.com	New York	NY	10001	212-594-1850	594-1682
Delsey Luggage 6735 Business Pkwy Suite A *TF:* 800-558-3344 ■ *Web:* www.delsey.com	Elkridge	MD	21075	410-796-5655	796-4192
Fendi NA Inc 720 5th Ave 5th Fl *TF:* 800-336-3469 ■ *Web:* www.fendi.com	New York	NY	10019	212-920-8100	767-0545
Forward Industries Inc 1801 Green Rd Suite E *NASDAQ: FORD* ■ *TF:* 800-872-3935 ■ *Web:* www.forwardindustries.com	Pompano Beach	FL	33064	954-419-9544	419-9735
Hartmann Luggage 1301 Hartmann Dr *TF:* 800-331-0613 ■ *Web:* www.hartmann.com	Lebanon	TN	37087	615-444-5000	443-4619
High Sierra Sport Co 880 Corporate Woods Pkwy *TF:* 800-323-9590 ■ *Web:* www.hssc.com	Vernon Hills	IL	60061	847-913-1100	913-1145
Johnston Mfg 753 Arrow Grand Cir *TF:* 877-891-8899	Covina	CA	91722	626-967-1511	331-9725
LC Industries 401 N Western Ave **Fax Area Code:* 800 ■ *TF:* 800-539-6255	Chicago	IL	60612	312-455-0500	265-6569*
Leather Specialty Co 1088 Business Ln *TF:* 888-771-0200 ■ *Web:* www.leatherspecialty.com	Naples	FL	34110	239-333-1000	333-1004
LeSportsac Inc 350 5th Ave # 402 *TF:* 800-486-2247 ■ *Web:* www.lesportsac.com	New York	NY	10118	212-736-6262	643-8009
Mercury Luggage Mfg Co 4843 Victor St *TF:* 800-874-1885 ■ *Web:* www.mercuryluggage.com	Jacksonville	FL	32207	904-733-9595	733-9671
Pedro Cos 106 E 10th St *TF:* 800-328-9284 ■ *Web:* www.pedrocompanies.com	Saint Paul	MN	55101	651-224-9491	224-8674
Platt Luggage Inc 4051 W 51st St *TF:* 800-222-1555 ■ *Web:* www.plattcases.com/default.asp	Chicago	IL	60632	773-838-2000	838-2010
RJ Singer International Inc 4801 W Jefferson Blvd *Web:* www.rjsinger.com	Los Angeles	CA	90016	323-735-1717	735-3753
Royal Case Co Inc 315 S Montgomery St *Web:* www.royalcase.com	Sherman	TX	75090	903-868-0288	893-7984
Samsonite Corp 11200 E 45th Ave *TF:* 800-223-7267	Denver	CO	80239	303-373-2000	373-2000
SKB Corp 434 W Levers Pl *TF Sales:* 800-410-2024 ■ *Web:* www.skbcases.com	Orange	CA	92867	714-637-1252	637-0491
Skyway Luggage Co Inc 30 Wall St *Web:* www.skywayluggage.com	Seattle	WA	98121	206-256-1601	441-5306
Targus Inc 1211 N Miller St *TF:* 800-950-5122 ■ *Web:* www.targus.com	Anaheim	CA	92806	714-765-5555	765-5599
Travelpro USA 700 Banyan Trail *TF:* 888-741-7471 ■ *Web:* www.travelpro.com	Boca Raton	FL	33431	561-998-2824	998-8487
Zero Mfg Inc 500 W 200 N *TF:* 800-545-1030 ■ *Web:* www.zerocases.com	North Salt Lake	UT	84054	801-298-5900	292-9450

457 MACHINE SHOPS

SEE ALSO Precision Machined Products p. 2443

Company	City	State	ZIP	Phone	Fax
Acme Industries Inc 1325 Pratt Blvd *Web:* www.acmeind.com	Elk Grove Village	IL	60007	847-296-3346	296-8622
Acro Industries Inc 554 Colfax St *Web:* www.acroind.com	Rochester	NY	14606	585-254-3661	254-0415
Acutec Precision Machining Inc 16891 State Hwy 198 *Web:* www.acutecprecision.com	Saegertown	PA	16433	814-763-3214	763-3817
Advance Mfg Co Inc 8 Tpke Industrial Rd PO Box 726 *Web:* www.advancemfg.com	Westfield	MA	01085	413-568-2411	568-6011
Advanced Integration Technologies 3206 Scott Blvd *Web:* www.aitint.com	Santa Clara	CA	95054	408-454-5450	986-8873
Ajl Mfg Corp 100 Holleder Pkwy *Web:* www.ajlmfg.com	Rochester	NY	14615	585-254-1128	458-6400
AJR Industries Inc 117 Gordon St *Web:* www.ajrindustries.com	Elk Grove Village	IL	60007	847-439-0380	439-0230
Alken-Ziegler Inc 406 S Pk Dr *Web:* www.alken-ziegler.com	Kalkaska	MI	49646	231-258-4906	258-8062
Allied Engineering & Production Corp 2421 Blanding Ave *Web:* www.alliedeng.com	Alameda	CA	94501	510-522-1500	522-2868
American Grinding & Machine Co 2000 N Mango Ave *TF:* 877-988-4343 ■ *Web:* www.americangrinding.com	Chicago	IL	60639	773-889-4343	889-3781
Anderson Tool & Engineering Co Inc 1735 W 53 St PO Box 1158 *Web:* www.ateinc.com	Anderson	IN	46015	765-643-6691	643-5022
Bley LLC 700 Chase Ave *Web:* www.bley.com	Elk Grove Village	IL	60007	847-437-0022	437-0592
Bob Inc 8740 49th Ave N *Web:* www.bobinc.com	North Minneapolis	MN	55428	763-533-2261	533-1735

Company	City	State	ZIP	Phone	Fax
Chalmers & Kubeck Inc 150 Commerce Dr *TF:* 800-242-5637 ■ *Web:* www.candk.com	Aston	PA	19014	610-494-4300	485-1484
Chapel Steel Co 590 N Bethlehem Pike PO Box 1000 *TF:* 800-570-7674 ■ *Web:* www.chapelsteel.com	Spring House	PA	19002	215-793-0899	793-0919
Component Engineers Inc 108 N Plains Industrial Rd *Web:* www.componenteng.com	Wallingford	CT	06492	203-269-0557	269-1357
Craft Machine Works Inc 2102 48th St *TF:* 888-350-6006 ■ *Web:* www.craftmachine.com	Hampton	VA	23661	757-380-8615	380-9120
Daman Industrial Services Inc 754 Kittanning Hollow Rd PO Box 486 *Web:* www.damanindustrial.com	East Brady	PA	16028	724-526-5714	526-5277
Dechert Dynamics Corp 713 W Main St *Web:* www.decherts.com	Palmyra	PA	17078	717-838-1326	838-1525
Downey Grinding Co 12323 Bellflower Blvd *Web:* www.downeygrinding.com	Downey	CA	90242	562-803-5556	803-3237
Ebtec Corp 120 Shoemaker Ln *Web:* www.ebteccorp.com	Agawam	MA	01001	413-786-0393	789-2851
Electro-Tech Machining 2000 W Gaylord St *Web:* www.etmgraphite.com	Long Beach	CA	90813	562-436-9281	436-9281
Express Mfg Inc 3519 W Warner Ave *Web:* www.eminc.com	Santa Ana	CA	92704	714-979-2228	556-0575
Femco Machine Co 754 S Main St Ext *TF:* 800-458-3445 ■ *Web:* www.femcomachine.com	Punxsutawney	PA	15767	814-938-9763	938-9763
FM Industries Inc 221 Warren Ave *Web:* www.fmindustries.com	Fremont	CA	94539	510-668-1900	668-1920
Forged Components Inc 14527 Smith Rd *Web:* www.forgedcomponents.com	Humble	TX	77396	281-441-4088	441-8899
Framingham Welding & Engineering Corp 120 Leland St PO Box 112 *Web:* www.framinghamwelding.com	Framingham	MA	01702	508-875-3563	626-4234
Fraser Mfg Corp 7235 Boyington St	Lexington	MI	48450	810-359-5338	359-8731
Furmanite America 101 Old Underwood Rd Unit E *TF:* 800-444-5572 ■ *Web:* www.furmanite.com	La Porte	TX	77571	281-842-5100	842-5111
Grand Valley Mfg Co (GVM) 701 E Spring St Bldg 52 PO Box 8 *Web:* www.gvmco.com	Titusville	PA	16354	814-827-2707	827-4349
Granite State Mfg Co 124 Joliette St *Web:* www.gsmai.com	Manchester	NH	03102	603-668-1900	668-1906
GT Sales & Mfg Inc 2202 SW St PO Box 9408 *Web:* www.gtsales.com	Wichita	KS	67277	316-943-2171	943-4800
H.m. Dunn Co 3301 House Anderson Rd *Web:* www.hmdunn.com	Euless	TX	76040	817-283-3722	283-8402
Haas Automation Inc 2800 Sturgis Rd *TF:* 800-331-6746 ■ *Web:* www.haascnc.com	Oxnard	CA	93030	805-278-1800	278-2255
Hfw Industries Inc 196 Philadelphia St PO Box 8 *Web:* www.hfwindustries.com	Buffalo	NY	14207	716-875-3380	875-3385
Highway Machine Co Inc (HMC) 3010 S Old US Hwy 41 *TF:* 866-990-9462 ■ *Web:* www.hmcgears.com	Princeton	IN	47670	812-385-3639	385-8186
Hitachi High Technologies America Inc 10 N Martingale Rd Suite 500 *Web:* www.hii-hitachi.com	Schaumburg	IL	60173	847-273-4141	273-4407
Howard Engineering Co Inc 687 Wooster St PO Box 1315 *Web:* www.howardengineering.com	Naugatuck	CT	06770	203-729-5213	729-3843
Hughes Supply Co of Thomasville Inc 175 Kanoy Rd PO Box 1003 *TF:* 800-747-8141 ■ *Web:* www.hughessupplyco.com	Thomasville	NC	27360	336-475-8146	472-0404
Illinois Machine & Tool Works 1961 Edgewater Dr *Web:* www.illmachtool.com	North Pekin	IL	61554	309-382-3045	382-2644
Indiana Technology & Mfg Cos 6100 Michigan Rd PO Box 399 *Web:* www.itamco.com	Plymouth	IN	46563	574-936-2112	936-7224
Industrial Tool Inc 9210 52nd Ave N *TF Sales:* 800-776-4455 ■ *Web:* www.industrial-tool.com	Minneapolis	MN	55428	763-533-7244	533-1712
JF Fredericks Tool Co Inc 25 Spring Ln *Web:* www.jfftool.com	Farmington	CT	06032	860-677-2646	674-8679
Johnson Technology Corp 2034 Latimer Dr	Muskegon	MI	49442	231-777-2685	773-1397
JV Industrial Cos Ltd 4040 Red Bluff **Fax Area Code:* 713 ■ *Web:* www.jvic.com	Pasadena	TX	77503	281-842-9353	473-6156*
K & M Machine-Fabricating Inc 20745 Michigan 60 *Web:* www.k-mm.com	Cassopolis	MI	49031	269-445-2495	445-3002
Kay Mfg Co 602 State St *Web:* www.kaymfg.com	Calumet City	IL	60409	708-862-6800	862-8122
Kewaunee Fabrications LLC 520 N Main St *Web:* www.kewauneefabrications.com	Kewaunee	WI	54216	920-388-2000	388-0263
Keystone Honing Co PO Box 187 *TF:* 800-458-3847	Titusville	PA	16354	814-827-9641	827-6678
Kurt Mfg Co 5280 Main St NE **Fax:* Sales ■ *TF:* 800-458-7855 ■ *Web:* www.kurt.com	Minneapolis	MN	55421	763-572-1500	571-8466*
Laser Excel N6323 Berlin Rd PO Box 279 *TF:* 800-285-6544 ■ *Web:* www.laserexcel.com	Green Lake	WI	54941	920-294-6544	294-6588
LaVezzi Precision Inc 999 Regency Dr *TF:* 800-323-1772 ■ *Web:* www.lavezzi.com	Glendale Heights	IL	60139	630-582-1230	582-1238
Lb Steel LLC 15700 Lathrop Ave *Web:* www.lbsteel.com	Harvey	IL	60426	708-331-2600	331-8500
Leiss Tool & Die Co 801 N Pleasant Ave *Web:* www.leiss.com	Somerset	PA	15501	814-444-1444	445-3456
Lemco Tool Corp 1850 Metzger Ave *TF:* 800-233-8713 ■ *Web:* www.lemco-tool.com	Cogan Station	PA	17728	570-494-0620	494-0860

Company	City	State	Zip	Phone	Fax
Lindquist Machine Corp 610 Baeten Rd *TF:* 888-499-0831 ■ *Web:* www.lmc-corp.com	Green Bay	WI	54306	920-713-4100	499-8482
Lith-O-Roll Corp 9521 Telstar Ave **Fax Area Code:* 800 ■ *TF:* 800-423-4176 ■ *Web:* www.lithoroll.com	El Monte	CA	91731	626-579-0340	548-4676*
Logan Machine Co 1405 Home Ave *Web:* www.loganmachine.com	Akron	OH	44310	330-633-6163	633-6362
Mac Machine Co Inc 7209 Rutherford Rd *Web:* www.macmachine.com	Baltimore	MD	21244	410-944-6171	265-7582
Machinists Inc 7600 5th Ave S PO Box 80505 *TF:* 800-244-4130 ■ *Web:* www.machinistsinc.com	Seattle	WA	98108	206-736-0990	763-8709
Magna Machine & Tool Co Inc 3722 N Messick Rd *Web:* www.magnamachine.com	New Castle	IN	47362	765-766-5388	766-5300
Major Tool & Machine Inc 1458 E 19th St *Web:* www.majortool.com	Indianapolis	IN	46218	317-636-6433	634-9420
Manor Tool & Mfg Co 9200 Ivanhoe St *Web:* www.manortool.com	Schiller Park	IL	60176	847-678-2020	678-6937
Marine Exhaust Systems of Alabama Inc 757 Nichols Ave *Web:* www.mesamarine.com	Fairhope	AL	36532	251-928-1234	928-1234
Matrix Inc 1 Catamore Blvd Suite 3 *Web:* www.matrixincorporated.com	East Providence	RI	02914	401-434-3040	434-3822
McBride & Shoff Inc 723 N Weidman St PO Box 650 *Web:* www.mcbrideandshoff.com	Metamora	IL	61548	309-367-2368	367-2946
Merit Gage Inc 3954 Meadowbrook Rd *Web:* www.meritgage.com	Saint Louis Park	MN	55426	952-935-0113	935-2641
Metalex Mfg Inc 5750 Cornell Rd *Web:* www.metalexmfg.com	Cincinnati	OH	45242	513-489-0507	489-1020
Meyer Tool Inc 3055 Colerain Ave *Web:* www.meyertool.com	Cincinnati	OH	45225	513-853-4400	853-4439
Michigan Production Machining Inc 16700 23 Mile Rd *Web:* www.michpro.com	Macomb	MI	48044	586-228-9700	228-7347
Micro Instrument Corp (MIC) 1199 Emerson St PO Box 60619 *TF:* 800-200-3150 ■ *Web:* www.microinst.com	Rochester	NY	14606	585-458-3150	254-0922
Micro-Tronics Inc 2905 S Potter Dr *Web:* www.micro-tronics.com	Tempe	AZ	85282	602-437-8995	431-9480
Myrmo & Sons Inc 3600 Franklin Blvd *TF:* 800-683-7040 ■ *Web:* www.myrmo.com	Eugene	OR	97403	541-747-4565	747-6832
Nassau Tool Works Inc 34 Lamar St	West Babylon	NY	11704	631-643-5000	643-5062
NC Dynamics Inc (NCDI) 3401 E 69th St *Web:* www.ncdynamics.com	Long Beach	CA	90805	562-634-7392	634-6220
Norotos Inc 201 E Alton Ave *Web:* www.norotos.com	Santa Ana	CA	92707	714-662-3113	662-7950
Numerical Precision Inc 2204 S Foster Ave *Web:* www.numericalprecision.com	Wheeling	IL	60090	847-394-3610	394-3962
O & F Machine Products Co Inc 3020 W 20th St PO Box 1363 *Web:* www.ofmachine.com/index.html	Joplin	MO	64802	417-623-7476	623-4736
Ohio Fabricators Co 111 N 14th St *Web:* www.ohfab.com	Coshocton	OH	43812	740-622-5922	622-3307
Onamac Industries Inc 11504 Airport Rd Bldg G *TF:* 877-742-2718 ■ *Web:* www.onamac.com	Everett	WA	98204	425-743-6676	742-2718
OP Schuman & Sons Inc 2001 County Line Rd *Web:* www.ameripak-ops.com	Warrington	PA	18976	215-343-1530	343-1633
Owens Industries Inc 7815 S 6th St *Web:* www.owensind.com	Oak Creek	WI	53154	414-764-1212	764-6030
Parsons Co Inc 1386 SR- 117 *Web:* www.parsonscompany.com	Roanoke	IL	61561	309-467-9100	
PCI Energy Services 1 Energy Dr *TF:* 800-345-6108 ■ *Web:* www.pci-energy.com	Lake Bluff	IL	60044	847-680-8100	680-7140
Peko Precision Products Inc 1400 Emerson St *Web:* www.pekoprecision.com	Rochester	NY	14606	585-647-3010	647-1366
PEMCO-Naval Engineering Works Inc 3614 Frederic St *Web:* www.pemco-inc.com	Pascagoula	MS	39567	228-769-7081	769-6520
Perfekta Inc 480 E 21st St N *Web:* www.perfekta-inc.com	Wichita	KS	67214	316-263-2056	263-0106
Peterson Tool Co Inc 739 Fesslers Ln PO Box 100830 *Web:* www.petersontool.com	Nashville	TN	37224	615-242-7341	242-7362
Pioneer Products Inc 1917 S Memorial Dr PO Box 1348 *Web:* www.pioneerproducts.com	Racine	WI	53401	262-633-6304	633-0465
Poly Cycle Inc 5501 Campbells Run Rd *Web:* www.polycycle.com	Pittsburgh	PA	15205	412-747-1101	747-0749
Prattville Machine & Tool Co Inc 240 Jubilee Dr 2nd Fl *Web:* www.prattvillemachine.com	Peabody	MA	01960	978-538-5229	538-5238
Precision Gears Inc N 13 W 24705 Bluemound Rd *Web:* www.precisiongears.com	Pewaukee	WI	53072	262-542-4261	542-1592
Precision Metal Products Inc 307 Pepe's Farm Rd *Web:* www.pmpinc.biz	Milford	CT	06460	203-877-4258	878-8353
Precision Roll Grinders Inc 6356 Chapmans Rd *Web:* www.precisionrollgrinders.com	Allentown	PA	18106	610-395-6966	481-9130
Precision Screw Thread Corp S 82 W 19275 Apollo Dr *TF:* 800-828-3431 ■ *Web:* www.precisionscrewthread.com	Muskego	WI	53150	262-679-9000	679-9004
Process Equipment Co 6555 S SR-202 *TF:* 800-424-0325 ■ *Web:* www.peco-us.com	Tipp City	OH	45371	937-667-4451	667-9322
Process Fab Inc 15644 Clanton Cir *Web:* www.processfab.com	Santa Fe Springs	CA	90670	562-921-1979	921-3145
Process Industries 3860 N River Rd *TF:* 800-860-1631 ■ *Web:* www.processgear.com	Schiller Park	IL	60176	847-671-1631	671-6840
Prototype & Plastic Mold Co 35 Industrial Pk Pl *Web:* www.proppm.com	Middletown	CT	06457	860-632-2800	632-2249
Prototype Machine Co 818 Prototype Rd PO Box 249	Flatonia	TX	78941	361-865-3579	865-3235
Quality Engineering & Tool Co Inc 380 S Wheatfield St *Web:* www.qualityengineeringandtool.com	York	PA	17403	717-854-3875	843-0297
Quality Mfg Co Inc (QMI) PO Box 616 *TF:* 866-460-6459 ■ *Web:* www.qmiky.com	Winchester	KY	40392	859-744-0420	744-0696
Ridge Engineering Inc 3987 Hampstead Mexico Rd *Web:* www.ridgeeng.com	Hampstead	MD	21074	410-239-7716	239-8710
RM Kerner Co 2208 E 33rd St *Web:* www.rmkco.com	Erie	PA	16510	814-898-2000	
RS Hughes Co Inc Saunders Div 975 N Todd Ave *TF Sales:* 888-932-8836 ■ *Web:* www.saunderscorp.com	Azusa	CA	91702	626-691-1111	691-0116
Saegertown Mfg Corp 1 Crawford St *Web:* www.smcmfg.com	Saegertown	PA	16433	814-763-2655	763-2069
Santinelli International Inc 325 Oser Ave *TF:* 800-644-3343 ■ *Web:* www.santinelli.com	Hauppauge	NY	11788	631-435-3343	435-9200
Schaffer Grinding Co 848 S Maple Ave *Web:* www.schaffergrinding.com	Montebello	CA	90640	323-724-4476	724-2635
Scheirer Machine Co Inc 3200 Industrial Blvd *TF:* 800-448-4590 ■ *Web:* www.scheirer.com	Bethel Park	PA	15102	412-833-6500	833-8110
Scheu & Kniss Inc PO Box 2947 *TF:* 800-635-6303 ■ *Web:* www.scheu-kniss.com	Louisville	KY	40201	502-635-6303	635-7850
Schmiede Corp 1865 Riley Creek Rd PO Box 1630 *TF:* 800-535-1851 ■ *Web:* www.schmiedecorp.com	Tullahoma	TN	37388	931-455-4801	455-1703
Schobers Machine & Engineering 705 S Electric Ave	Alhambra	CA	91803	626-576-0685	576-8895
Schwartz Industries Inc 6909 E 11-Mile Rd *Web:* www.schwartzind.com	Warren	MI	48092	586-759-1777	759-0808
Scicon Technologies Corp 27525 Newhall Ranch Rd *Web:* www.scicontech.com	Valencia	CA	91355	661-295-8630	295-6611
Service Guide Inc 3605 Warren Meadville Rd *Web:* www.serviceguideinc.com	Cortland	OH	44410	330-637-6060	638-6229
SMF Inc 1550 Industrial Pk PO Box 157 *Web:* www.smf-inc.com	Minonk	IL	61760	309-432-2586	432-2390
Smith West Inc 404 W Guadalupe Rd	Tempe	AZ	85283	480-839-0501	838-2054
Solid Concepts Inc 28309 Ave Crocker *TF:* 888-311-1017 ■ *Web:* www.solidconcepts.com	Valencia	CA	91355	661-295-4400	257-9311
Sonfarrel Inc 3000-3010 E La Jolla St *Web:* www.sonfarrel.com	Anaheim	CA	92806	714-630-7280	632-7239
South Side Machine Works Inc 3761 Eiler St *Web:* www.southsidemachine.net	Saint Louis	MO	63116	314-481-7171	481-9271
Specialty Bar Products Co 200 Martha St PO Box 127 *Web:* www.specialty-bar.com	Blairsville	PA	15717	724-459-7500	459-0944
St George Steel Fabrication Inc 1301 E 700 N *Web:* www.stgeorgesteel.com	Saint George	UT	84770	435-673-4856	628-4139
Standard Locknut Inc 1045 E 169th St *TF:* 800-783-6887 ■ *Web:* www.stdlocknut.com	Westfield	IN	46074	317-867-0100	867-4231
Sterling Engineering Corp 236 Newhartford Rd *Web:* www.sterlingeng.com	Barkhamsted	CT	06063	860-379-3366	379-3278
Steward Machine Co Inc 3911 13th Ave N *TF:* 800-394-6461 ■ *Web:* www.stewardmachine.com	Birmingham	AL	35234	205-841-6461	849-8029
Sussek Machine Corp 805 Pierce St PO Box 98 *Web:* www.sussek.com	Waterloo	WI	53594	920-478-2126	478-3452
Tell Tool Inc PO Box 1278 *Web:* www.telltool.com	Westfield	MA	01086	413-568-1671	562-7237
Tibor Machine Products Inc 7400 W 100th Pl *Web:* www.tibormachine.com	Bridgeview	IL	60455	708-499-3700	499-6803
Tree City Tool & Engineering Co Inc 1954 N Montgomery Rd *Web:* www.treecitytool.com	Greensburg	IN	47240	812-663-4196	663-4220
True Position Technologies Inc 24900 Ave Standford *Web:* www.truepositiontech.com	Valencia	CA	91355	661-294-0030	294-1240
True-Tech Corp 4050 Technology Pl *Web:* www.true-tech.com	Fremont	CA	94538	510-353-1000	353-9000
Tss Technologies Inc 8800 Global Way *Web:* www.tss.com	West Chester	OH	45069	513-772-7000	772-2938
TurboCare Chicopee 2140 Westover Rd *TF:* 800-887-2622 ■ *Web:* www.turbocare.com	Chicopee	MA	01022	413-593-0500	593-3424
Twin City EDM 7940 Rancher Rd NE *Web:* www.twincityedm.com	Fridley	MN	55432	763-783-7808	783-7842
UMC Inc 500 Chelsea Rd *Web:* www.ultramc.com	Monticello	MN	55362	763-271-5200	271-5249
Unisource Mfg Inc 8040 NE 33rd Dr *TF:* 800-234-2566 ■ *Web:* www.unisource-mfg.com	Portland	OR	97211	503-281-4673	281-5845
Urban Mfg Inc 1288 Hickory St *Web:* www.urban-mfg.com	Pewaukee	WI	53072	262-691-2455	691-8938
Vaga Industries Inc 2505 Loma Ave *Web:* www.vaga.com	South El Monte	CA	91733	626-442-7436	442-4330
Van Dusen & Meyer Inc 50 Parrott Dr *TF:* 800-760-6242 ■ *Web:* www.naiad.com	Shelton	CT	06484	203-929-6355	929-3594

				Phone	Fax
Vermont Aerospace Mfg Inc 966 Industrial Pwy PO Box 1148 *Web:* www.vtaerospace.com	Lyndonville	VT	05851	802-748-8705	748-8437
Vescio Threading Co 14002 Anson Ave. *TF:* 800-361-4218 ■ *Web:* www.vesciothreading.com	Santa Fe Springs	CA	90670	562-802-1868	802-2073
Vickers Engineering Inc 3604 Glendora Rd PO Box 346 *Web:* www.vickerseng.com	New Troy	MI	49119	269-426-8545	426-8494
Wahlco Inc 2722 S Fairview St *Web:* www.wahlco.com	Santa Ana	CA	92704	714-979-7300	979-0603
Walco Tool & Engineering Co 18954 Airport Rd *TF:* 800-808-9365 ■ *Web:* www.walcotool.com	Lockport	IL	60441	815-834-0225	838-6046
Warren Fabricating & Machining 3240 Mahoning Ave PO Box 1032 *TF:* 800-827-0596 ■ *Web:* www.warfab.com	Warren	OH	44482	330-847-0596	847-7774
Washington Tool & Machine Co 1 S Baird Ave PO Box 873 *Web:* www.washtool.com	Washington	PA	15301	724-225-7470	225-7484
Wayne Metals LLC 400 E Logan St. *Web:* www.waynemetal.com	Markle	IN	46770	260-758-3121	758-2521
Weaver Industries Inc 425 S 4th St PO Box 326 *TF:* 800-292-7670 ■ *Web:* www.weaverind.com	Denver	PA	17517	717-336-7507	336-4182
Weldmac Mfg Co 1451 N Johnson Ave. *TF:* 800-252-1533 ■ *Web:* www.weldmac.com	El Cajon	CA	92020	619-440-2300	440-8723
Wesel Mfg Co 710 Layton Rd	Clark Summit	PA	18411	570-586-8978	585-2976
West Engineering Co Inc 10106 Louistown Rd. *Web:* www.west-engineering.net	Ashland	VA	23005	804-798-3966	798-8590
Whitworth Tool Inc 114 Industrial Pk Dr PO Box 759 *Web:* www.whittool.com	Hardinsburg	KY	40143	270-756-0098	756-0095
Wilco Machine & Fab Inc 1326 S Broadway PO Box 48 *Web:* www.wilcofab.com	Marlow	OK	73055	580-658-6993	658-6767
Will-Burt Co 169 S Main St *Web:* www.willburt.com	Orrville	OH	44667	330-682-7015	684-1190
Windings Inc PO Box 566 *TF:* 800-795-8533 ■ *Web:* www.windings.com	New Ulm	MN	56073	507-359-2034	354-5383
Wise Plastics Technologies Inc 3810 Stern Ave *Web:* www.wise-hamlin.com	Saint Charles	IL	60174	847-697-2840	697-0103
Wright Plastic Products LLC 201 E Condensery Rd *Web:* www.wrightplasticproducts.com	Sheridan	MI	48884	989-291-3211	291-5321
WSI Industries Inc 213 Chelsea Rd *NASDAQ: WSCI* ■ *Web:* www.wsiindustries.com	Monticello	MN	55362	763-295-9202	295-9212
Xtek Inc 11451 Reading Rd *TF:* 888-332-9835 ■ *Web:* www.xtek.com	Cincinnati	OH	45241	513-733-7800	733-7939
Youngers & Sons Mfg Co Inc 19223 W K 42 Hwy *TF:* 800-664-5551 ■ *Web:* www.youngersmfg.com	Viola	KS	67149	620-545-7133	545-7204

458 MACHINE TOOLS - METAL CUTTING TYPES

SEE ALSO Machine Tools - Metal Forming Types p. 2193; Metalworking Devices & Accessories p. 2244

				Phone	Fax
Abbco Inc 2401 American Ln *TF:* 866-986-6546 ■ *Web:* www.abbcoinc.net	Elkgrove Vlg	IL	60007	630-595-7115	595-6431
Accurate Boring Co 17420 Malyn Blvd *Web:* www.accurateboring.com	Fraser	MI	48026	586-294-7555	294-2530
Acme Mfg Co 4240 N Atlantic Blvd *TF:* 888-340-2263 ■ *Web:* www.acmemfg.com	Auburn Hills	MI	48326	248-393-7300	393-4060
Airtronics Gage & Machine Co 516 Slade Ave *Web:* www.airtronicsgage.com	Elgin	IL	60120	847-695-0911	695-8745
Allied Tool Products 9334 N 107th St *TF:* 800-558-5147 ■ *Web:* www.atptools.com	Milwaukee	WI	53224	414-355-8280	355-8297
Amada Cutting Technologies Inc 14921 Northam St *TF:* 800-877-4729 ■ *Web:* www.amadabandsaw.com	La Mirada	CA	90638	714-670-1704	670-2017
American GFM Corp 1200 Cavalier Blvd *Web:* www.agfm.com	Chesapeake	VA	23323	757-487-2442	487-5274
American Heller Corp 15285 Leone Dr *TF:* 800-950-2487 ■ *Web:* www.americanheller.com	Macomb	MI	48042	586-677-2300	677-2292
Automatic Tooling Corp 521 St Jean St	Detroit	MI	48214	313-822-9250	822-0192
Automation Assoc Inc 416 Campus Dr *TF:* 800-927-7348 ■ *Web:* www.autoinc.com	Arlington Heights	IL	60004	847-255-4500	255-9648
Babin Machine Works Inc 2510 N 9th St PO Box 2007 *TF:* 800-269-1274	Beaumont	TX	77704	409-892-1231	892-1236
Bardons & Oliver Inc 5800 Harper Rd *Web:* www.bardonsoliver.com	Solon	OH	44139	440-498-5800	498-2001
Barnes International Inc 814 Chestnut St PO Box 1203 *TF:* 800-435-4877 ■ *Web:* www.barnesintl.com	Rockford	IL	61105	815-964-8661	964-5074
Bourn & Koch Inc 2500 Kishwaukee St. *TF:* 800-248-8120 ■ *Web:* www.bourn-koch.com	Rockford	IL	61104	815-965-4013	965-0019
Bryant Grinder 65 Pearl St *Web:* www.bryantgrinder.com	Springfield	VT	05156	802-885-5161	885-9444
Burr Oak Tool & Gauge Co Inc PO Box 338 *Web:* www.burroak.com	Sturgis	MI	49091	269-651-9393	651-4324
C & G Systems Inc 1401 Glenlake Ave *Web:* www.cgsystems.com	Itasca	IL	60143	630-467-0600	467-0606
Carlson Tool & Machine Co 2300 Gary Ln. *Web:* www.carlson-tool.com	Geneva	IL	60134	630-232-2460	232-2016
Chas G Allen Co Inc 25 Williamsville Rd *Web:* www.chasgallen.com	Barre	MA	01005	978-355-2911	355-2917
Continental Machines Inc 5505 W 123rd St	Savage	MN	55378	952-890-3300	895-6450
Crafts Technologies 91 Joey Dr. *TF:* 800-323-6802 ■ *Web:* www.craftstech.net	Elk Grove Village	IL	60007	847-758-3100	758-0162
Cross Huller 13900 Lakeside Cir *TF:* 800-521-0166 ■ *Web:* www.crosshuller.com	Sterling Heights	MI	48313	586-566-2400	586-3726
Darex 210 E Hersey St PO Box 730 *TF:* 800-547-0222 ■ *Web:* www.darex.com	Ashland	OR	97520	541-488-2224	488-2229
Davenport Machine Inc 167 Ames St *TF:* 800-344-5748 ■ *Web:* www.davenportmachine.com	Rochester	NY	14611	585-235-4545	235-7997
Davis & Thompson Co N 58 W 14630 Shawn Cir *Web:* entrusttool.com/davisandthompson.htm	Menomonee Falls	WI	53051	262-252-3686	252-4075
Dayton Machine Tool Co 1314 Webster St *Web:* www.dmtnet.com	Dayton	OH	45404	937-222-6444	222-6444
Detroit Broach Co 2750 Paldan Dr *TF:* 800-383-6978 ■ *Web:* www.dbcbroach.com	Auburn Hills	MI	48326	248-370-0600	370-0600
DoALL Co 1480 S Wolf Rd *Web:* www.doall.com	Wheeling	IL	60090	847-495-6800	484-2045
DS Technology Inc 7861 Palace Dr. *TF:* 800-531-0135 ■ *Web:* www.ds-technologie.de	Cincinnati	OH	45249	513-247-2590	247-2599
Eagle Tool Co 101 Woodward Ave	Iron Mountain	MI	49801	906-774-0284	774-0342
EH Wachs Co 600 Knightsbridge Pkwy **Fax:* Sales ■ *TF:* 800-323-8185 ■ *Web:* www.ehwachs.com	Lincolnshire	IL	60069	847-537-8800	520-1147*
Entrust Tool & Design Co Inc N 58 W 14630 Shawn Cir *Web:* www.entrusttool.com	Menomonee Falls	WI	53051	262-252-3802	252-4075
Everite Machine Products Co 501 E Erie Ave. *Web:* www.everite.net	Philadelphia	PA	19134	215-425-3750	426-7768
Ex-Cell-O Machine Tools 13900 Lakeside Cir. *TF:* 800-837-6277	Sterling Heights	MI	48313	586-566-2400	566-2400
Extrude Hone Corp 235 Industry Blvd. *TF:* 800-367-1109 ■ *Web:* www.extrudehone.com	Irwin	PA	15642	724-863-5900	863-8759
Flow International Corp 23500 64th Ave S. *NASDAQ: FLOW* ■ *TF:* 800-446-3569 ■ *Web:* www.flowcorp.com	Kent	WA	98032	253-850-3500	813-9377
GF AgieCharmilles 560 Bond St. *TF:* 800-282-1336 ■ *Web:* www.us.gfac.com	Lincolnshire	IL	60069	847-913-5300	913-5340
Giddings & Lewis LLC 142 Doty St PO Box 590 **Fax:* Sales ■ *TF:* 800-343-2847 ■ *Web:* www.giddings.com	Fond du Lac	WI	54936	920-921-9400	906-2075*
Giddings & Lewis Machine Tools 142 Doty St PO Box 590 *Web:* www.glmachinetools.com	Fond du Lac	WI	54936	920-921-9400	906-2522
Gleason Corp 1000 University Ave. *TF:* 800-280-0825 ■ *Web:* www.gleason.com	Rochester	NY	14607	585-473-1000	264-9765
Grob Inc 1731 10th Ave *TF:* 800-225-6481 ■ *Web:* www.grobinc.com	Grafton	WI	53024	262-377-1400	377-2106
Hammond Roto-Finish 1600 Douglas Ave *TF:* 800-253-9896 ■ *Web:* www.hammondmach.com	Kalamazoo	MI	49007	269-345-7151	345-1710
Hanchett Mfg Inc 906 N State St *TF:* 800-454-7463 ■ *Web:* www.hanchett.com	Big Rapids	MI	49307	231-796-7678	796-4851
Hardinge Inc 1 Hardinge Dr. *NASDAQ: HDNG* ■ *TF:* 800-843-8801 ■ *Web:* www.hardinge.com	Elmira	NY	14905	607-734-2281	732-4925
Harrington Tool Co 105 N Rath Ave *Web:* www.harringtontool.com	Ludington	MI	49431	231-843-3445	845-7477
Hause Machines 809 S Pleasant St *TF:* 800-932-8665 ■ *Web:* www.hausemachines.com	Montpelier	OH	43543	419-485-3158	485-3146
Hausermann Abrading Process Co 300 W Laura Dr *Web:* www.hausermann.net	Addison	IL	60101	630-543-6688	543-6689
Hetran Inc 70 Pinedale Industrial Rd *Web:* www.hetraninc.com	Orwigsburg	PA	17961	570-366-1411	366-1829
Huffman Corp 1050 Huffman Way *TF:* 888-483-3626 ■ *Web:* www.huffmancorp.com	Clover	SC	29710	803-222-4561	222-7599
Hurco Cos Inc 1 Technology Way *NASDAQ: HURC* ■ *TF Sales:* 800-634-2416 ■ *Web:* www.hurco.com	Indianapolis	IN	46268	317-293-5309	298-2621
Hydromat Inc 11600 Adie Rd. **Fax:* Sales ■ *TF:* 888-432-0070 ■ *Web:* www.hydromat.com	Saint Louis	MO	63043	314-432-4644	432-7552*
Hypertherm Inc 21 Great Hollow Rd PO Box 5010 *TF:* 800-643-0030 ■ *Web:* www.hypertherm.com	Hanover	NH	03755	603-643-3441	643-5352
Hypneumat Inc 5900 W Franklin Dr *Web:* www.hypneumat.com	Franklin	WI	53132	414-423-7400	423-7414
Industrial Metal Products Corp (IMPCO) 3417 W St Joseph St **Fax:* Sales ■ *Web:* www.impco.com	Lansing	MI	48917	517-484-9411	484-0502*
Industrial Steel & Machine Sales Inc 2712 Lackland Dr *Web:* www.is-ms.net	Waterloo	IA	50702	319-296-1816	296-3630
ITW Heartland 3600 W Lake Ave. *TF:* 800-724-6166 ■ *Web:* www.itwinc.com	Glenview	IL	60026	847-724-7500	657-4572
Jasco Cutting Tools 1390 Mt Read Blvd *TF:* 800-868-1074 ■ *Web:* www.jascotools.com	Rochester	NY	14606	585-546-1254	254-2655
John J Adams Die Corp 10 Nebraska St. *TF:* 800-356-0110	Worcester	MA	01604	508-757-3894	753-8016
Kaufman Mfg Co 547 S 29th St PO Box 1056 *Web:* www.kaufmanmfg.com	Manitowoc	WI	54221	920-684-6641	686-4103
Kennametal Inc 1600 Technology Way PO Box 231 *NYSE: KMT* ■ *TF Cust Svc:* 800-446-7738 ■ *Web:* www.kennametal.com	Latrobe	PA	15650	724-539-5000	539-8787
Kingsbury Corp 80 Laurel St. *Web:* www.kingsburycorp.com	Keene	NH	03431	603-352-5212	352-8789
Kitamura Machinery of USA Inc 78 Century Dr. *Web:* www.kitamura-machinery.com	Wheeling	IL	60090	847-520-7755	520-7763
Klingelhofer Corp 165 Mill Ln *TF:* 800-879-5546 ■ *Web:* www.klingelhofer.com	Mountainside	NJ	07092	908-232-7200	232-1841
Koike Aronson Inc 635 W Main St PO Box 307 *TF:* 800-252-5232 ■ *Web:* www.koike.com	Arcade	NY	14009	585-492-2400	457-3517
Komatsu America Corp Cutting Technologies Div 92 Cummings Pk *TF:* 800-707-2767 ■ *Web:* www.fineplasma.com	Woburn	MA	01801	781-782-0505	782-0506

Company / Address	City	State	ZIP	Phone	Fax
Kyocera Tycom Corp 17862 Fitch Ave	Irvine	CA	92614	800-537-0294	955-0874*
*Fax Area Code: 949 ■ TF: 800-537-0294 ■ Web: www.kyoceratycom.com					
Lucas Precision LP 13020 St Clair Ave	Cleveland	OH	44108	216-451-5588	451-5174
Web: www.lucasprecision.com					
Makino 7680 Innovation Way	Mason	OH	45040	513-573-7200	573-7360
TF: 888-625-4661 ■ Web: www.makino.com					
McLean Inc 3409 E Miraloma Ave	Anaheim	CA	92806	714-996-5451	996-5453
TF Cust Svc: 800-451-2424 ■ Web: www.mcleanlathe.com					
Metal Cutting Corp 89 Commerce Rd	Cedar Grove	NJ	07009	973-239-1100	239-6651
Web: www.metalcutting.com					
Metl-Saw Systems Inc 2950 Bay Vista Ct	Benicia	CA	94510	707-746-6200	746-5085
Web: www.metlsaw.com					
MG Systems & Welding Inc					
W 141 N 9427 Fountain Blvd	Menomonee Falls	WI	53051	262-255-5520	255-5170
Web: www.mg-systems-welding.com					
Monarch Lathes LP 615 N Oaks Ave PO Box 4609	Sidney	OH	45365	937-492-4111	492-7958
Morgood Tools Inc 940 Millstead Way	Rochester	NY	14624	585-436-8828	436-2426
Web: www.morgood.com					
Nachi Machining Technology Co					
17500 23-Mile Rd	Macomb	MI	48044	586-263-8347	263-4571
NNT Corp 1320 Norwood Ave	Itasca	IL	60143	630-875-9600	875-8899
TF: 800-556-9999 ■ Web: www.nntcorp.com					
Normac Inc 10 Loop Rd PO Box 69	Arden	NC	28704	828-684-1002	209-9001
Web: www.normac.com					
North American Products Corp 1180 Wernsing Rd	Jasper	IN	47546	812-482-2000	457-7458*
*Fax Area Code: 800 ■ TF Cust Svc: 800-457-7468 ■ Web: www.napgladu.com					
Ohio Broach & Machine Co					
35264 Topps Industrial Pkwy	Willoughby	OH	44094	440-946-1040	946-0725*
*Fax: Sales ■ Web: www.ohiobroach.com					
Okuma America Corp 11900 W Hall Dr	Charlotte	NC	28278	704-588-7000	588-6503
Web: www.okuma.com					
Oliver of Adrian Inc					
1111 E Beecher St PO Box 189	Adrian	MI	49221	517-263-2132	265-8698
TF: 877-668-0885 ■ Web: www.oliverinstrument.com					
P & R Industries Inc 1524 Clinton Ave N	Rochester	NY	14621	585-266-6725	266-0075
Parker Majestic Inc 300 N Pike Rd	Sarver	PA	16055	724-352-1551	353-1196
TF: 866-572-7537 ■ Web: www.pennunited.com					
Peddinghaus Corp 300 N Washington Ave	Bradley	IL	60915	815-937-3800	937-4003
TF: 800-786-2448 ■ Web: www.peddinghaus.com					
Pilz Automation Safety LP 7150 Commerce Blvd	Canton	MI	48187	734-354-0272	354-3355
TF: 877-745-9872 ■ Web: www.pilzusa.com					
Pioneer Broach Co 6434 Telegraph Rd	Los Angeles	CA	90040	323-728-1263	722-1699
TF: 800-621-1945 ■ Web: www.pioneerbroach.com					
PMC Industries Inc 29100 Lakeland Blvd	Wickliffe	OH	44092	440-943-3300	944-1974
Web: www.pmc-colinet.com/default.asp?id=50					
Reno Machine Co Inc 170 Pane Rd	Newington	CT	06111	860-666-5641	667-4496
Web: www.reno-machine.com					
Republic-Lagun Machine Tool Co					
1000 E Carson St	Carson	CA	90745	310-518-1100	830-0923
TF: 800-421-2105 ■ Web: www.lagun.com					
Rex-Buckeye Co Inc 1230-A W 58th St	Cleveland	OH	44102	216-939-9000	939-3300
TF: 800-932-0011 ■ Web: www.rexbuckeye.com					
RF Cook Mfg Co 4585 Allen Rd	Stow	OH	44224	330-923-9797	923-8641
Web: www.rfcook.com					
Rothenberger USA 4455 Boeing Dr	Rockford	IL	61109	815-397-7617	451-2632*
*Fax Area Code: 800 ■ TF: 800-435-0786 ■ Web: www.rothenberger-usa.com					
Rottler Mfg 8029 S 200th St	Kent	WA	98032	253-872-7050	395-0230
TF: 800-452-0534 ■ Web: www.rottlermfg.com					
Royal Master Grinders Inc 143 Bauer Dr	Oakland	NJ	07436	201-337-8500	337-2324
Web: www.royalmaster.com					
RP Machine Enterprises Inc					
820 Cochran St	Statesville	NC	28677	704-872-8888	872-5777
Web: www.rpmachine.com					
S & M Machine Service Inc					
109 E Highland Dr	Oconto Falls	WI	54154	920-846-8130	846-4803
TF: 800-323-1579 ■ Web: www.snmmachine.com					
S & S Machinery Co 140 53rd St	Brooklyn	NY	11232	718-492-7400	439-3930
TF: 800-540-9723 ■ Web: www.sandsmachinery.com					
Saginaw Machine Systems Inc					
800 N Hamilton St	Saginaw	MI	48602	989-753-8465	758-5575
Web: www.saginawmachine.com					
Sandvik Coromant Co 1702 Nevins Rd	Fair Lawn	NJ	07410	201-794-5000	794-5165
TF Cust Svc: 800-726-3845 ■ Web: www.sandvik.com					
Savage Saws 100 Indel Ave PO Box 156	Rancocas	NJ	08073	609-267-8501	267-1366
TF: 877-779-8763 ■ Web: www.savagesaws.com					
Seneca Falls Technology Group					
314 Fall St	Seneca Falls	NY	13148	315-568-5804	568-5800
Web: www.sftg.com					
Servo Products Co 34940 Lakeland Blvd	East Lake	OH	44095	440-942-9999	942-9100
TF: 800-521-7359 ■ Web: www.servoproductsco.com					
Setco Sales Co 5880 Hillside Ave	Cincinnati	OH	45233	513-941-5110	941-6913
TF: 800-543-0470 ■ Web: www.setco.com					
SGS Tool Co 55 S Main St	Munroe Falls	OH	44262	330-688-6667	686-2128*
*Fax: Hum Res ■ Web: www.sgstool.com					
Simmons Machine Tool Corp 1700 N Broadway	Albany	NY	12204	518-462-5431	462-0371
Web: www.simmons-albany.com					
Snk America Inc 1800 Howard St	Elk Grove Village	IL	60007	847-364-0801	364-4363
TF: 888-765-6224 ■ Web: www.snkamerica.com					
Southwestern Industries Inc					
2615 Homestead Pl	Rancho Dominguez	CA	90220	310-608-4422	764-2668
TF: 800-421-6875 ■ Web: www.southwesternindustries.com					
Stephen Bader Co Inc					
10 Charles St PO Box 297	Valley Falls	NY	12185	518-753-4456	753-4962
Web: www.stephenbader.com					
Sunnen Products Co 7910 Manchester Ave	Saint Louis	MO	63143	314-781-2100	781-2268*
*Fax: Cust Svc ■ TF: 800-325-3670 ■ Web: www.sunnen.com					
Technidrill Systems Inc 429 Portage Blvd	Kent	OH	44240	330-678-9980	678-9981
TF: 800-914-5863 ■ Web: www.technidrillsystems.com					
Thermal Dynamics Corp 82 Benning St	West Lebanon	NH	03784	603-298-5711	298-0558
TF: 800-752-7621 ■ Web: www.thermadyne.com					
Thurston Mfg Co Inc 14 Thurber Blvd	Smithfield	RI	02917	401-232-9100	232-9101
Web: www.thurstonmfg.com					
Tool-Flo Mfg Inc 7803 Hansen Rd	Houston	TX	77061	713-941-1080	941-8099
TF: 800-780-7234 ■ Web: www.toolflo.com					
Tornos Technologies US Corp					
840 Parkview Blvd	Lombard	IL	60148	630-812-2040	812-2039
TF: 800-243-5027 ■ Web: www.tornos.ch					
Toyoda Machinery USA Inc					
316 W University Dr	Arlington Heights	IL	60004	847-253-0340	577-4680
TF: 800-257-2985 ■ Web: www.toyodausa.com					
TRI-CAM Inc 2730 Eastrock Dr PO Box 5046	Rockford	IL	61109	815-226-9200	226-0661
TRU TECH Systems Inc					
24550 N River Rd PO Box 46965	Mount Clemens	MI	48046	586-469-2700	469-1344
TF: 877-878-8324 ■ Web: www.harigproducts.com					
Turmatic Systems Inc 11600 Adie Rd	Saint Louis	MO	63043	314-993-0600	993-0676
TF: 888-432-0070					
US Tool Grinding Inc 701 S Desloge Dr	Desloge	MO	63601	573-431-3856	431-6655
TF: 800-775-8665 ■ Web: www.ustg.net					
Vernon Tool Co Ltd 503 Jones Rd	Oceanside	CA	92054	760-433-5860	757-2233
TF: 800-452-1542 ■ Web: www.vernontool.com					
WF Meyers Co 1017 14th St PO Box 426	Bedford	IN	47421	812-275-4485	275-4488
TF: 800-457-4055 ■ Web: www.wfmeyers.com					
WF Wells Inc 16645 Heimbach Rd	Three Rivers	MI	49093	269-279-5123	279-6337
Web: www.wfwells.com					
Whitney Tool Co Inc 906 R St PO Box 545	Bedford	IN	47421	812-275-4491	275-6458
TF: 800-536-1971 ■ Web: www.whitney-tool.com					
Wisconsin Machine Tool Corp					
3225 Gateway Rd Suite 100	Brookfield	WI	53045	262-317-3048	317-3079
TF: 800-243-3078 ■ Web: www.machine-tool.com					

459 MACHINE TOOLS - METAL FORMING TYPES

SEE ALSO Machine Tools - Metal Cutting Types p. 2192; Metalworking Devices & Accessories p. 2244; Rolling Mill Machinery p. 2628; Tool & Die Shops p. 2717

Company / Address	City	State	ZIP	Phone	Fax
Advanced Hydraulics Inc 13568 Vintage Pl	Chino	CA	91710	909-590-7644	590-7049
TF: 888-581-8079					
Ajax Technologies 1441 Chardon Rd	Cleveland	OH	44117	216-531-1010	481-6369
Alva Allen Industries Inc 1015 N 3rd St	Clinton	MO	64735	660-885-3331	885-3333
TF: 800-343-5657 ■ Web: www.alvaallenind.com					
Amada America Inc 7025 Firestone Blvd	Buena Park	CA	90621	714-739-2111	739-4099
TF: 800-626-6612 ■ Web: www.amada.com					
American Actuator Corp 89 Selleck St	Stamford	CT	06902	203-324-6334	324-4471
Web: www.americanactuator.com					
Anderson Cook Inc 17650 15-Mile Rd	Fraser	MI	48026	586-293-0800	293-0833
Web: www.andersoncook.com					
Atlas Technologies Inc 3100 Cotter Ave	Fenton	MI	48430	810-629-6663	629-8145
TF: 800-536-3162 ■ Web: www.atlastechnologies.com					
Badge A Minit Ltd 345 N Lewis Ave	Oglesby	IL	61348	815-883-8822	883-9696
TF: 800-223-4103 ■ Web: www.badgeaminit.com					
Beatty Machine & Mfg Co Inc 940 150th St	Hammond	IN	46327	219-931-3000	937-1662
Bedco Inc 4600 Bree Rd	East China	MI	48054	810-329-2292	329-4017
Web: www.bedcoinc.com					
Bliss Clearing Niagara (BCN) 1004 E State St	Hastings	MI	49058	269-948-3300	948-3313
TF: 800-642-5477 ■ Web: www.bcntechserv.com					
Bradbury Co Inc 1200 E Cole	Moundridge	KS	67107	620-345-6394	345-6381
TF: 800-397-6394 ■ Web: www.bradburygroup.net					
Bruderer Inc 1200 Hendricks Cswy	Ridgefield	NJ	07657	201-941-2121	886-2010
Web: www.bruderer.com					
CA Lawton Co Inc 1950 Enterprise Way	De Pere	WI	54115	920-337-2470	337-2477
TF: 800-842-6888 ■ Web: www.calawton.com					
California Aircraft Tool Co 821 W Olive St	Inglewood	CA	90301	323-670-2536	670-6862*
*Fax Area Code: 310					
Chicago Dreis & Krump Mfg Co					
7400 S Loomis Blvd	Chicago	IL	60636	773-874-1200	874-2622
Web: www.dreis-krump.com					
Cincinnati Inc 7420 Kilby Rd	Harrison	OH	45030	513-367-7100	367-7552
Web: www.e-ci.com					
CJ Winter Machine Technologies Inc					
167 Ames St	Rochester	NY	14611	585-429-5000	429-5095
TF: 800-288-7655 ■ Web: www.cjwinter.com					
Cyril Bath Co 1610 Airport Rd	Monroe	NC	28110	704-289-8531	289-3932
TF: 800-801-1418 ■ Web: www.cyrilbath.com					
DR Sperry & Co 623 Rathbone Ave	North Aurora	IL	60506	630-892-4361	892-1664
TF: 888-997-9297 ■ Web: www.drsperry.com					
Edwards Mfg Co 1107 Sykes St PO Box 166	Albert Lea	MN	56007	507-373-8206	373-9433
TF: 800-373-8206 ■ Web: www.edwardsironworkers.com					
Eitel Presses Inc					
97 Pinedale Industrial Rd	Orwigsburg	PA	17961	570-366-0585	366-2536
TF: 800-458-2218 ■ Web: www.eitelpresses.com					
Emery Corp PO Box 1104	Morganton	NC	28680	828-433-1536	433-6809
Web: www.emerycorp.com					
Erie Press Systems 1253 W 12th St PO Box 4061	Erie	PA	16512	814-455-3941	456-4819
TF: 800-222-3608 ■ Web: www.eriepress.com					
Feintool Cincinnati 11280 Cornell Pk Dr	Cincinnati	OH	45242	513-247-0110	247-0060
Web: www.feintool.com					
FH Peterson Machine Corp 143 S St	Stoughton	MA	02072	781-341-4930	341-6022
Web: www.fhpetersonmachine.com					
GEMCOR Corp 1750 Union Rd	West Seneca	NY	14224	716-674-9300	674-3171
Web: www.gemcor.com					
General Broach Co Spline Rolling Div					
307 Salisbury St	Morenci	MI	49256	517-458-7555	458-6821
Web: www.generalbroach.com					
Grant Assembly Technologies					
90 Silliman Ave	Bridgeport	CT	06605	203-366-4557	366-0370
TF: 800-227-2150 ■ Web: www.grantriveters.com					
Greenerd Press & Machine Co Inc 41 Crown St	Nashua	NH	03060	603-889-4101	889-7601
TF: 800-877-9110 ■ Web: www.greenerd.com					
H & H Tooling Inc 30505 Clemens Rd	Westlake	OH	44145	440-250-3204	250-3205
TF: 800-808-6840 ■ Web: www.hhtooling.com					
Heim LP 6360 W 73rd St	Chicago	IL	60638	708-496-7450	496-7428
Web: www.theheimgroup.com					
Hudson Machinery Worldwide PO Box 831	Haverhill	MA	01831	978-374-0303	373-7295
TF: 800-343-0772					
JF Helmold & Bros Inc					
901 Morse Ave	Elk Grove Village	IL	60007	847-437-7085	437-6033
TF: 800-323-8898 ■ Web: www.helmold.com					
Kinefac Corp 156 Goddard Memorial Dr	Worcester	MA	01603	508-754-6891	756-5342
TF: 800-458-5941 ■ Web: www.kinefac.com					
Koppy Corp 199 Kay Industrial Dr	Orion	MI	48359	248-373-5200	373-5201
L & F Industries Corp Div of Erie Press Systems					
1253 W 12th St PO Box 4061	Erie	PA	16512	814-455-3941	456-4819
TF: 800-222-3608 ■ Web: www.eriepress.com					
Lockformer Co 5480 6th St SW	Cedar Rapids	IA	52404	630-964-8000	364-3436*
*Fax Area Code: 319 ■ Web: www.lockformer.com					
Manor Industries Inc					
24400 Maplehurst	Clinton Township	MI	48036	586-463-4604	463-3905
TF: 800-921-1007 ■ Web: www.manorindustries.com					
Mate Precision Tooling Inc 1295 Lund Blvd	Anoka	MN	55303	763-421-0230	421-0285
TF: 800-328-4492 ■ Web: www.matept.com					
Mega Mfg Inc PO Box 457	Hutchinson	KS	67504	620-663-1127	664-9658
Web: www.megamfg.com					
Minster Machine Co 240 W 5th St PO Box 120	Minster	OH	45865	419-628-2331	628-3517
Web: www.minster.com					

Company	City	State	Zip	Phone	Fax
Murata Machinery USA Inc 2120 Queen City Dr TF: 800-428-8469 ■ Web: www.muratec-usa.com	Charlotte	NC	28208	704-394-8331	392-6541
National Diecasting Machinery & Kard Trim Presses 33 Plan Way Bldg 7 Web: www.nationalkard.com	Warwick	RI	02886	401-737-3005	739-2528
National Machinery LLC 161 Greenfield St Web: www.nationalmachinery.com	Tiffin	OH	44883	419-447-5211	443-2379
NFM Welding Engineers 577 Oberlin Rd SW Web: www.nfm.net	Massillon	OH	44647	330-837-3868	837-2230
Oak Products Inc 504 Wade St Web: www.oakpresses.com	Sturgis	MI	49091	269-651-8513	651-8513
Pacific Press Technologies 714 Walnut St TF: 800-851-3586 ■ Web: www.pacific-press.com	Mount Carmel	IL	62863	618-262-8666	262-7000
Pacific Roller Die Co 1321 W Winton Ave TF: 800-253-6463 ■ Web: www.prdcompany.com	Hayward	CA	94545	510-782-7242	887-5639
PCC Specialty Products Inc Reed-Rico Div 28 Sword St TF Cust Svc: 800-343-6068 ■ Web: www.reedrico.com	Auburn	MA	01501	508-753-6530	753-0127
PHI Inc 14955 E Salt Lake Ave Web: www.phi-tulip.com	City of Industry	CA	91746	626-968-9680	333-3610
Presses Inc 6360 W 73rd St Web: www.theheimgroup.com	Chicago	IL	60638	708-496-7400	496-7428
QPI Multipress Inc 2222 S 3rd St Web: www.multipress.com	Columbus	OH	43207	614-228-0185	228-2358
Reno Machine Co Inc 170 Pane Rd Web: www.reno-machine.com	Newington	CT	06111	860-666-5641	667-4496
Rimrock Corp 1700 Jetway Blvd Web: www.rimrockcorp.com	Columbus	OH	43219	614-471-5926	471-7388
Roper Whitney of Rockford Inc 2833 Huffman Blvd *Fax: Sales ■ Web: www.roperwhitney.com	Rockford	IL	61103	815-962-3011	962-2227*
Royle Systems Group 1000 Cannonball Rd Web: www.roylesystems.com	Pompton Lakes	NJ	07442	973-839-8118	839-7327
Schleuniger Inc 87 Colin Dr TF: 800-321-2211 ■ Web: www.schleuniger.com	Manchester	NH	03103	603-668-8117	668-8119
Strippit Inc/LVD 12975 Clarence Ctr Rd TF: 800-828-1527 ■ Web: www.lvdgroup.com	Akron	NY	14001	716-542-4511	542-5957
Taylors Industrial Services LLC HPM Div 820 W Marion Rd Web: www.taylorsind.com	Mount Gilead	OH	43338	419-946-0222	946-2473
Tetrahedron Assoc Inc PO Box 710157 TF: 800-958-3872 ■ Web: www.tetrahedronassociates.com	San Diego	CA	92171	619-661-0552	661-0559
Tools for Bending Inc 194 W Dakota Ave TF Cust Svc: 800-873-3305 ■ Web: www.toolsforbending.com	Denver	CO	80223	303-777-7170	777-4749
US Baird Corp 1700 Stratford Ave PO Box 9706 Web: www.usbaird.com	Stratford	CT	06615	203-375-3361	378-6006
US Machine Tools Corp 70 Horizon Dr TF: 800-664-0013	Bristol	CT	06010	860-953-8306	953-0364
Vamco International 555 Epsilon Dr Web: www.vamcointernational.com	Pittsburgh	PA	15238	412-963-7100	963-7160
WA Whitney Co 650 Race St PO Box 1206 Web: www.wawhitney.com	Rockford	IL	61105	815-964-6771	964-3175
Wabash MPI 1569 Morris St PO Box 298 Web: www.wabashmpi.com	Wabash	IN	46992	260-563-1184	563-1396
Williams White & Co 600 River Dr TF: 877-797-7650 ■ Web: www.williamswhite.com	Moline	IL	61265	309-797-7650	797-7677
Wysong & Miles Co Inc 4820 US 29 N TF: 800-299-7664 ■ Web: www.wysongmiles.com	Greensboro	NC	27405	336-621-3960	375-6187

460 MAGAZINES & JOURNALS

SEE ALSO Periodicals Publishers p. 2470

460-1 Agriculture & Farming Magazines

Company	City	State	Zip	Phone	Fax
Alfa News 2108 E S Blvd	Montgomery	AL	36116	334-288-3900	284-3957
American Agriculturist 5227-B Baltimore Pike Web: www.americanagriculturist.com	Littlestown	PA	17340	717-359-0150	359-0250
Beef Magazine 7900 International Dr Suite 300 TF Cust Svc: 800-722-5334 ■ Web: www.preview.beefmagazine.com	Minneapolis	MN	55425	952-851-9329	851-4601
Beef Today Magazine 555 SW Peak Rd Web: www.agweb.com/beeftoday.asp	Polo	MO	64671	816-586-5555	
Co-op Farmer Magazine PO Box 26234	Richmond	VA	23260	804-281-1369	281-1119
Dairy Herd Management 10901 W 84th Terr TF: 800-255-5113 ■ Web: www.dairyherd.com	Lenexa	KS	66214	913-438-8700	438-0695
Dairy Today Magazine 261 E Broadway PO Box 1167 Web: www.agweb.com/dairytoday.asp	Monticello	MN	55362	763-271-3363	271-3360
Farm & Ranch Living Magazine 5400 S 60th St TF: 800-344-6913 ■ Web: www.farmandranchliving.com	Greendale	WI	53129	414-423-0100	423-8463
Farm Bureau News 600 Maryland Ave SW Suite 1000-W Web: www.fb.org	Washington	DC	20024	202-484-3600	406-3606
Farm Bureau Press 10720 Kanis Rd Web: www.arfb.com	Little Rock	AR	72211	501-228-1300	
Farm Industry News 7900 International Dr Suite 300 TF Cust Svc: 800-722-5334 ■ Web: www.farmindustrynews.com	Minneapolis	MN	55425	952-851-9329	851-4601
Farm Journal 1818 Market St 31st Fl TF: 800-523-1538 ■ Web: www.agweb.com/farmjournal.asp	Philadelphia	PA	19103	215-557-8900	568-5012
Farm Show Magazine 20088 Kenwood Trial TF: 800-834-9665 ■ Web: www.farmshow.com	Lakeville	MN	55044	952-469-5572	469-5575
Floridagriculture Magazine PO Box 147030 Web: www.floridagriculture.org	Gainesville	FL	32614	352-374-1521	374-1530
Georgia Farm Bureau News 1620 Bass Rd TF: 800-342-1192 ■ Web: www.gfb.org	Macon	GA	31210	478-474-8411	474-8750
Hoard's Dairyman Magazine 28 Milwaukee Ave W PO Box 801 Web: www.hoards.com	Fort Atkinson	WI	53538	920-563-5551	563-7298
Iowa Farm Bureau Spokesman Magazine 5400 University Ave TF: 800-442-3276	West Des Moines	IA	50266	515-225-5413	225-5419
Kansas Living Magazine 2627 KFB Plaza TF: 800-406-3053 ■ Web: www.kfb.org	Manhattan	KS	66503	785-587-6000	587-6914
Neighbors Magazine 2108 E S Blvd Web: www.alfafarmers.org/neighbors/index.phtml	Montgomery	AL	36116	334-288-3900	284-3957
Pork Report PO Box 9114 TF: 800-456-7675 ■ Web: www.pork.org	Des Moines	IA	50306	515-223-2600	223-2646
Progressive Farmer Magazine 2204 Lakeshore Dr Suite 415 TF: 800-406-8992 ■ Web: www.about.dtnpf.com/ag	Birmingham	AL	35209	205-414-4700	
Soybean Digest 7900 International Dr Suite 300 TF Cust Svc: 800-722-5334 ■ Web: www.cornandsoybeandigest.com	Minneapolis	MN	55425	952-851-4667	851-4601
Successful Farming Magazine 1716 Locust St TF Cust Svc: 800-374-3276 ■ Web: www.agriculture.com/sfonline/index.html	Des Moines	IA	50309	515-284-3000	284-3127
Tennessee Farm Bureau News 147 Bear Creek Pike Web: www.tnfarmbureau.org	Columbia	TN	38401	931-388-7872	388-5818
Texas Agriculture Magazine 7420 Fish Pond Rd PO Box 2689 TF: 800-772-6535 ■ Web: www.txfb.org	Waco	TX	76710	254-772-3030	772-1766
Texas Farm Bureau 7420 Fish Pond Rd PO Box 2689 Web: www.txfb.org	Waco	TX	76710	254-772-3030	772-1766
Top Producer Magazine 1818 Market St 31st Fl TF: 800-523-1538	Philadelphia	PA	19103	215-557-8964	568-3989

460-2 Art & Architecture Magazines

Company	City	State	Zip	Phone	Fax
American Artist Magazine 770 Broadway Web: www.artistdaily.com	New York	NY	10003	646-654-5000	654-5514
AmericanStyle Magazine 3000 Chestnut Ave Suite 304 Web: www.americanstyle.com	Baltimore	MD	21211	410-889-3093	243-7089
Architectural Digest 6300 Wilshire Blvd 11th Fl Web: www.architecturaldigest.com	Los Angeles	CA	90048	323-965-3700	965-4978
Architectural Record Magazine 2 Penn Plaza 9th Fl Web: archrecord.construction.com	New York	NY	10121	212-904-2594	904-4256
Architectural West Magazine 546 Ct St Web: www.architecturalwest.com	Reno	NV	89501	775-333-1080	333-1081
Art & Antiques Magazine 29160 Heathercliff Rd Suite 200 *Fax Area Code: 310 ■ Web: www.artandantiquesmag.com	Malibu	CA	90265	770-955-5656	589-7701*
Art Calendar 1500 Pk Ctr Dr TF: 800-347-6969 ■ Web: www.artcalendar.com	Orlando	FL	32835	407-563-7000	563-7099
Art in America Magazine 575 Broadway *Fax: Cust Svc ■ TF Cust Svc: 800-925-8059 ■ Web: www.artinamericamagazine.com	New York	NY	10012	212-941-2800	941-2819*
Artforum International Magazine 350 7th Ave 19th Fl TF: 800-966-2783 ■ Web: www.artforum.com	New York	NY	10001	212-475-4000	529-1257
Artist's Magazine The 4700 E Galbraith Rd TF: 800-283-0963 ■ Web: www.artistsmagazine.com	Cincinnati	OH	45236	513-531-2222	531-2686
ARTnews Magazine 48 W 38th St 9th Fl TF: 800-284-4625 ■ Web: www.artnews.com	New York	NY	10018	212-398-1690	819-0394
Bomb Magazine 80 Hanson Pl Suite 703 TF: 866-354-0334 ■ Web: www.bombsite.com	Brooklyn	NY	11217	718-636-9100	636-9200
Design Journal 1431 7th St Suite 205 Web: www.designjournalmag.com	Santa Monica	CA	90401	310-394-4394	394-0966
Design/Build Business Magazine 3030 Salt Creek Ln Suite 200 TF: 800-547-7377 ■ Web: www.rdbmagazine.com	Arlington Heights	IL	60005	847-454-2714	454-2759
HOW Design Magazine 4700 E Galbraith Rd TF Cust Svc: 800-333-1115 ■ Web: www.howdesign.com	Cincinnati	OH	45236	513-531-2690	891-7153
Inland Architect Magazine 3525 W Peterson Ave # 103 TF: 888-641-3169 ■ Web: www.inlandarchitectmag.com	Chicago	IL	60659	773-866-9900	866-9881
Landscape Architecture Magazine 636 'I' St NW Web: www.asla.org/nonmembers/lam.cfm	Washington	DC	20001	202-898-2444	898-1185
Metropolis Magazine 61 W 23rd St 4th Fl TF: 800-344-3046 ■ Web: www.metropolismag.com	New York	NY	10010	212-627-9977	627-9988
Modernism Magazine 199 George St Web: www.modernismmagazine.com	Lambertville	NJ	08530	609-397-4104	397-4409
Pastel Journal 4700 E Galbraith Rd TF: 800-283-0963 ■ Web: www.artistsnetwork.com	Cincinnati	OH	45236	513-531-2222	531-2686
Preservation Magazine 1785 Massachusetts Ave NW TF: 800-944-6847 ■ Web: www.nationaltrust.org/Magazine	Washington	DC	20036	202-588-6388	588-6266
Solo Impression 601 W 26th St Web: www.soloimpression.com	New York	NY	10001	212-229-9292	
Southwest Art Magazine 921 Walnut St Suite 250 TF: 877-212-1938 ■ Web: www.southwestart.com	Boulder	CO	80302	303-449-4599	449-4635
Step Inside Design Magazine 6000 N Forest Pk Dr TF: 800-255-8800	Peoria	IL	61614	309-688-8800	688-8515
Studio Photography & Design Magazine 1233 Janesville Ave *Fax Area Code: 800 ■ Web: www.imaginginfo.com	Fort Atkinson	WI	53538	631-963-6200	547-7377*
Sunshine Artist Magazine 4075 LB McLeod Rd Suite E Web: www.sunshineartist.com	Orlando	FL	32811	407-648-7479	648-7454
Wildlife Art Magazine 611 Main St PO Box 219 TF: 800-221-6547 ■ Web: www.wildlifeartmag.com	Ramona	CA	92065	760-788-9453	788-9454

460-3 Automotive Magazines

Company	City	State	Zip	Phone	Fax
American Iron Magazine 1010 Summer St TF Cust Svc: 877-693-3572 ■ Web: www.aimag.com	Stamford	CT	06905	203-425-8777	425-8775
Automobile Magazine 120 E Liberty St Web: www.automobilemag.com	Ann Arbor	MI	48104	734-994-3500	994-1153
AutoWeek Magazine 1155 Gratiot Ave TF Circ: 888-288-6954 ■ Web: www.autoweek.com	Detroit	MI	48207	313-446-6000	446-0347
Backroads Magazine 160 County Rd 521	Newton	NJ	07860	973-948-4176	948-0823

				Phone	Fax
Web: www.backroadsusa.com					
Canadian Biker 735 Market St	Victoria	BC	V8T2E2	250-384-0333	384-1832
TF: 800-667-5667 ■ *Web:* www.canadianbiker.com					
Car & Driver Magazine 1585 Eisenhower Pl	Ann Arbor	MI	48108	734-971-3600	971-9188
TF: 800-666-9485 ■ *Web:* www.caranddriver.com					
Car Craft Magazine 6420 Wilshire Blvd	Los Angeles	CA	90048	323-782-2000	782-2263
TF: 800-436-6520 ■ *Web:* www.carcraft.com					
Classic Trucks Magazine					
1733 Alton Pkwy PO Box 420235	Irvine	CA	92606	800-777-6394	978-6390*
**Fax Area Code:* 714 ■ *TF:* 800-777-6394 ■ *Web:* www.classictrucks.com					
Cycle World Magazine 1499 Monrovia Ave	Newport Beach	CA	92663	949-720-5300	631-0651
TF: 800-876-8316 ■ *Web:* www.cycleworld.com					
Dirt Wheels Magazine 25233 Anza Dr	Valencia	CA	91355	661-295-1910	295-1278
Web: www.dirtwheelsmag.com					
Easyriders Magazine 28210 Dorothy Dr	Agoura Hills	CA	91301	818-889-8740	889-1252
Web: www.easyriders.com					
Friction Zone Magazine					
60166 Hop Patch Spring Rd	Mountain Center	CA	92561	951-659-9500	659-8182
TF: 877-713-9500 ■ *Web:* www.friction-zone.com					
Grassroots Motorsports Magazine					
915 Ridgewood Ave	Holly Hill	FL	32117	386-239-0523	239-0573
TF: 800-520-8292 ■ *Web:* www.grassrootsmotorsports.com					
Hemmings Motor News 222 Main St	Bennington	VT	05201	802-442-3101	447-9631
TF: 800-227-4373 ■ *Web:* www.hemmings.com					
Hot Rod Magazine 6420 Wilshire Blvd	Los Angeles	CA	90048	323-782-2000	782-2223
TF Orders: 800-800-4681 ■ *Web:* www.hotrod.com					
Lowrider Magazine 2400 E Katella Ave 11th Fl	Anaheim	CA	92806	714-939-2400	978-6390
Web: www.lowridermagazine.com					
Motor Age Magazine					
24950 Country Club Blvd Suite 200	North Olmsted	OH	44070	440-243-8100	756-5206
TF: 800-225-4569 ■ *Web:* www.motorage.com/motorage					
Motor Trend Magazine					
6420 Wilshire Blvd 7th Fl	Los Angeles	CA	90048	323-782-2000	782-2355
TF: 800-800-6848 ■ *Web:* www.motortrend.com					
Motorcycle Consumer News Magazine 3 Burroughs	Irvine	CA	92618	949-855-8822	855-0654
TF: 800-546-7730 ■ *Web:* www.mcnews.com/mcnews					
Motorcyclist Magazine PO Box 420235	Palm Coast	FL	32142	310-531-9857	
Web: www.motorcyclistonline.com					
National Speed Sport News Magazine					
PO Box 1210	Harrisburg	NC	28075	704-455-2531	455-2605
TF: 866-455-2531 ■ *Web:* www.nationalspeedsportnews.com					
Off-Road Magazine					
2400 E Katella Ave Suite 1100	Anaheim	CA	92806	714-939-2400	978-6390
Web: www.off-roadweb.com					
Popular Hot Rodding Magazine					
774 S Placentia Ave	Placentia	CA	92870	714-939-2400	572-1864
Web: www.popularhotrodding.com					
Road & Track Magazine					
1499 Monrovia Ave	Newport Beach	CA	92663	949-720-5300	631-2757
TF: 800-876-8316 ■ *Web:* www.roadandtrack.com					
Road King Magazine					
28 White Bridge Rd Suite 209	Nashville	TN	37205	615-627-2200	627-2197
TF: 877-280-1425 ■ *Web:* www.roadking.com					
Sound & Vision Magazine 2 Pk Ave 10th fl	New York	NY	10016	212-779-5000	779-5200
Web: www.soundandvisionmag.com					
Sport Rider Magazine 6420 Wilshire Blvd	Los Angeles	CA	90048	323-782-2584	782-2372
Web: www.sportrider.com					
Sports Car Magazine					
16842 Von Karman Ave Suite 125	Irvine	CA	92606	949-417-6700	417-6116
TF: 800-722-7140 ■ *Web:* www.sportscarmag.com					
Stock Car Racing Magazine PO Box 420235	Palm Coast	FL	32142	800-333-2633	
TF: 800-333-2633 ■ *Web:* www.stockcarracing.com					
Street & Smith's Sports Group Inc					
120 W Morehead St Suite 320	Charlotte	NC	28202	704-973-1300	973-1303
TF: 800-883-7323 ■ *Web:* www.scenedaily.com					
Super Chevy Magazine					
774 S Placentia Ave 2nd Fl	Placentia	CA	92870	714-939-2559	572-1864
Web: www.superchevy.com					
Truck Trend Magazine 6420 Wilshire Blvd	Los Angeles	CA	90048	323-782-2000	782-2313
Web: www.trucktrend.com					
Vette Magazine 774 S Placentia Ave 2nd Fl	Placentia	CA	92870	714-939-2559	572-1864
Web: www.vetteweb.com					

460-4 Boating Magazines

				Phone	Fax
48 Degrees North 6327 Seaview Ave NW	Seattle	WA	98107	206-789-7350	789-6392
Web: www.48north.com					
Blue Water Sailing Magazine					
747 Aquidneck Ave Suite 201 PO Box 268	Middletown	RI	02842	401-847-7612	845-8580
TF: 888-800-7245 ■ *Web:* www.bwsailing.com					
Boating Life Magazine					
460 N Orlando Ave Suite 200	Winter Park	FL	32789	407-628-4802	628-7061
Web: www.boatingmag.com					
Boating Magazine 1633 Broadway 41st Fl	New York	NY	10019	212-767-6041	767-4831
Web: www.boatingmag.com					
Boating World Magazine					
2100 Powers Ferry Rd Suite 300	Atlanta	GA	30339	770-955-5656	952-0669
Web: www.boatingworld.com					
Cruising World Magazine					
55 Hammerlund Way # A	Middletown	RI	02842	401-845-5100	845-5180
Web: www.cruisingworld.com					
Go Boating Magazine 17782 Cowan St Suite A	Irvine	CA	92614	949-660-6150	660-6172
Web: www.goboatingmag.com					
Good Old Boat Magazine 1501 8th Ave NW	Jamestown	MN	58401	701-952-9433	952-9434
Web: www.goodoldboat.com					
Lakeland Boating 727 S Dearborn St Suite 812	Chicago	IL	60605	312-276-0610	276-0619
TF: 800-331-0132 ■ *Web:* www.lakelandboating.com					
Motor Boating Magazine					
460 Orlando Ave Suite 200	Winter Park	FL	32789	407-628-4802	628-7061
TF: 800-888-9123 ■ *Web:* www.motorboating.com					
PassageMaker Magazine					
105 Eastern Ave Suite 203	Annapolis	MD	21403	410-990-9086	990-9094
TF: 888-487-2953 ■ *Web:* www.passagemaker.com					
Power & Motoryacht Magazine					
260 Madison Ave 4th Fl	New York	NY	10016	917-256-2277	
TF: 800-284-8036 ■ *Web:* www.powerandmotoryacht.com					
SAIL Magazine 98 N Washington St 2nd Fl	Boston	MA	02114	617-720-8600	723-0911
TF: 800-745-7245 ■ *Web:* www.sailmag.com					
Sailing World Magazine 55 Hammarlund Way	Middletown	RI	02842	401-845-5100	845-5180
TF Cust Svc: 866-436-2460 ■ *Web:* www.sailingworld.com					
Sea Magazine 17782 Cowan St Suite A	Irvine	CA	92614	949-660-6150	660-6172
TF: 800-873-7327 ■ *Web:* www.seamagazine.com					

460-5 Business & Finance Magazines

				Phone	Fax
ABA Banking Journal 345 Hudson St	New York	NY	10014	212-620-7200	633-1165
Web: www.ababj.com					
Accounting Today Magazine					
1 State St Plaza 27th Fl	New York	NY	10004	212-803-8855	292-5216
TF Cust Svc: 800-221-1809 ■ *Web:* www.accountingtoday.com					
Active Trader Magazine PO Box 487	Lake Zurich	IL	60047	312-719-9008	
Web: www.activetradermag.com					
Advisor Today 2901 Telestar Ct	Falls Church	VA	22042	800-247-4074	770-8212*
**Fax Area Code:* 703 ■ *TF:* 800-247-4074 ■ *Web:* www.advisortoday.com					
Adweek Magazine 770 Broadway	New York	NY	10003	646-654-5000	654-5835
TF: 800-722-6658 ■ *Web:* www.adweek.com					
Alaska Business Monthly					
501 W Northern Lights Blvd Suite 100	Anchorage	AK	99503	907-276-4373	279-2900
TF: 800-770-4373 ■ *Web:* www.akbizmag.com					
American Banker Magazine					
1 State St Plaza 27th Fl	New York	NY	10004	212-803-8200	843-9600
TF: 800-221-1809 ■ *Web:* www.americanbanker.com					
American Journalism Review					
University of Maryland					
1117 Journalism Bldg Rm 2116	College Park	MD	20742	301-405-8803	405-8323
TF: 800-827-0771 ■ *Web:* www.ajr.org					
American Statistician 732 N Washington St	Alexandria	VA	22314	703-684-1221	684-2037*
**Fax:* Cust Svc ■ *TF:* 888-231-3473 ■ *Web:* www.amstat.org/publications/tas					
Appraisal Journal 303 E Wacker Dr # 311	Chicago	IL	60601	312-335-4100	335-4400
Web: www.appraisalinstitute.org					
Area Development Magazine					
400 Post Ave Suite 304	Westbury	NY	11590	516-338-0900	338-0100
TF: 800-735-2732 ■ *Web:* www.area-development.com					
Arkansas Business LP 122 E 2nd St	Little Rock	AR	72201	501-372-1443	375-7933
TF: 888-322-6397 ■ *Web:* www.arkansasbusiness.com					
ASID Professional Designer Magazine					
608 Massachusetts Ave NE	Washington	DC	20002	202-546-3480	546-3240
Assn Management Magazine 1575 'I' St NW	Washington	DC	20005	202-371-0940	371-8825
Web: www.asaecenter.org					
Atlanta Business Chronicle					
3423 Piedmont Rd Suite 400	Atlanta	GA	30305	404-249-1000	249-1048
Web: www.bizjournals.com					
Austin Business Journal					
111 Congress Ave Suite 750	Austin	TX	78701	512-494-2500	494-2525*
**Fax:* Edit ■ *TF:* 888-819-4126 ■ *Web:* www.bizjournals.com					
Baltimore Business Journal					
111 Market Pl Suite 720	Baltimore	MD	21202	410-576-1161	752-3112
Web: www.bizjournals.com					
Banking Strategies Magazine					
115 S LaSalle St Suite 3300	Chicago	IL	60603	312-553-4600	683-2415
TF: 888-224-0037 ■ *Web:* www.bai.org/bankingstrategies/about.asp					

Entry	City	State	ZIP	Phone	Fax
Barron's The Dow Jones Business & Financial Weekly Magazine 1211 Avenue of the Americas *TF:* 800-544-0422 ■ *Web:* online.barrons.com	New York	NY	10036	212-416-2000	416-2829
Baton Rouge Business Report 445 N Blvd Suite 210 *Web:* www.businessreport.com	Baton Rouge	LA	70802	225-928-1700	926-1329
Best's Review Ambest Rd *Web:* www.ambest.com/review	Oldwick	NJ	08858	908-439-2200	439-3363
Birmingham Business Journal 2140 11th Ave S Suite 205 *Web:* www.bizjournals.com	Birmingham	AL	35205	205-322-0000	322-0040
BIV Publications Ltd (BIV) 102 E 4th Ave *TF:* 800-208-2011 ■ *Web:* www.biv.com	Vancouver	BC	V5T1G2	604-688-2398	688-1963
Black Enterprise Magazine 130 5th Ave *TF Cust Svc:* 800-727-7777 ■ *Web:* www.blackenterprise.com	New York	NY	10011	212-242-8000	886-9610
Bloomberg Magazine PO Box 840 *Web:* www.bloomberg.com	Princeton	NJ	08542	609-279-3000	897-8394
Boston Business Journal 160 Federal St 12th Fl *Web:* www.bizjournals.com	Boston	MA	02110	617-330-1000	330-1016
Boulder County Business Report 3180 Sterling Cir Suite 201 *Web:* www.bcbr.com	Boulder	CO	80301	303-440-4950	440-8954
Brandweek Magazine 770 Broadway 7th Fl *Web:* www.brandweek.com	New York	NY	10003	646-654-5000	654-5375
Broadcasting & Cable Magazine 360 Pk Ave S *TF:* 800-554-5729 ■ *Web:* www.broadcastingcable.com	New York	NY	10010	646-746-6965	746-7028
Business 2.0 Magazine 2 Embarcadero Ctr Suite 1900 *Web:* www.money.cnn.com	San Francisco	CA	94111	415-293-4800	293-5900
Business Credit Magazine 8840 Columbia 100 Pkwy *TF:* 800-955-8815 ■ *Web:* www.nacmo.org	Columbia	MD	21045	410-740-5560	740-5574
Business Facilities Magazine 44 Apple St Suite 3 *TF:* 800-524-0337 ■ *Web:* www.businessfacilities.com	Tinton Falls	NJ	07724	732-842-7433	758-6634
Business First 465 Main St *Web:* www.bizjournals.com	Buffalo	NY	14203	716-854-5822	854-3394
Business First 455 S 4th St Suite 278 *TF:* 800-704-3757 ■ *Web:* www.bizjournals.com	Louisville	KY	40202	502-583-1731	587-1703
Business Insurance Magazine 711 3rd Ave **Fax Area Code:* 312 ■ *TF:* 888-288-5900 ■ *Web:* www.businessinsurance.com	New York	NY	10017	212-210-0100	280-3174*
Business Journal of Milwaukee 825 N Jefferson St Suite 200 *Web:* www.bizjournals.com/milwaukee	Milwaukee	WI	53202	414-278-7788	278-7028
Business Journal of Phoenix 101 N 1st Ave Suite 2300 *Web:* www.bizjournals.com	Phoenix	AZ	85003	602-230-8400	230-0955
Business Journal of Portland 851 SW 6th Ave Suite 500 *Web:* www.bizjournals.com	Portland	OR	97204	503-274-8733	219-3450
Business Journal of San Jose 96 N 3rd St Suite 100 *Web:* www.bizjournals.com	San Jose	CA	95112	408-295-3800	295-5028
Business Journal of Tampa Bay 4890 W Kennedy Blvd Suite 850 *Web:* www.bizjournals.com/tampabay	Tampa	FL	33609	813-873-8225	876-1827
Business Journal The 25 E Boardman St *TF:* 800-837-6397 ■ *Web:* www.business-journal.com	Youngstown	OH	44501	330-744-5023	744-5838
Business Opportunities Journal 2185 Faraday Ave Suite 110 *TF:* 800-854-6570 ■ *Web:* www.boj.com	Carlsbad	CA	92008	760-930-1033	930-4037
Business Press 3509 Hulen St Suite 201 *Web:* www.fwbusinesspress.com	Fort Worth	TX	76107	817-336-8300	332-3038
Business Standards Magazine 12110 Sunset Hills Rd Suite 200 *TF:* 800-862-4977 ■ *Web:* www.businessstandards.com	Reston	VA	20190	703-437-9000	437-9001
BusinessWeek Magazine 1221 Avenue of the Americas *TF Cust Svc:* 800-635-1200 ■ *Web:* www.businessweek.com	New York	NY	10020	212-512-2511	
California Real Estate Magazine 525 S Virgil Ave *Web:* www.car.org	Los Angeles	CA	90020	213-739-8200	480-7724
Canadian Business Magazine 1 Mt Pleasant Rd 11th Fl *TF:* 800-465-0700 ■ *Web:* www.canadianbusiness.com	Toronto	ON	M4Y2Y5	416-764-1200	764-1255
Central New York Business Journal The 269 W Jefferson St *TF:* 800-836-3539 ■ *Web:* www.cnybj.com	Syracuse	NY	13202	315-579-3919	472-3644
CFO Magazine 253 Summer St *TF:* 800-877-5416 ■ *Web:* www.cfo.com	Boston	MA	02210	617-345-9700	951-4090
Charlotte Business Journal 1100 S Tryon St Suite 100 **Fax:* Edit ■ *TF:* 800-948-5323 ■ *Web:* www.bizjournals.com	Charlotte	NC	28203	704-973-1100	973-1101*
Chief Executive Magazine 110 Summit Ave *Web:* www.chiefexecutive.net	Montvale	NJ	07645	201-930-5959	930-5956
Cincinnati Business Courier 101 W 7th St *Web:* www.bizjournals.com	Cincinnati	OH	45202	513-621-6665	621-2462
CIO Magazine 492 Old Connecticut Path PO Box 9208 *TF:* 800-788-4605 ■ *Web:* www.cio.com	Framingham	MA	01701	508-872-0080	879-7784
Columbia Journalism Review Columbia University 2950 Broadway Journalism Bldg *Web:* www.cjr.org	New York	NY	10027	212-854-1881	854-8580
Columbus Business First 303 Dublin Ave *Web:* www.bizjournals.com	Columbus	OH	43215	614-461-4040	365-2980
Communications News 2500 N Tamiami Trail *TF:* 800-226-6113 ■ *Web:* www.comnews.com	Nokomis	FL	34275	941-966-9521	966-2590
Contract Design Magazine 770 Broadway *TF:* 800-950-1314 ■ *Web:* www.contractdesign.com	New York	NY	10003	646-654-5000	654-5000
CPA Journal 3 Pk Ave 18th Fl *TF:* 800-633-6320 ■ *Web:* www.cpaj.com	New York	NY	10016	212-719-8300	719-4755
Crain's Chicago Business Magazine 360 N Michigan Ave *TF:* 800-678-9595 ■ *Web:* www.chicagobusiness.com	Chicago	IL	60601	312-649-5200	
Crain's Cleveland Business Magazine 700 W St Clair Ave Suite 310 *TF:* 888-909-9111 ■ *Web:* www.crainscleveland.com	Cleveland	OH	44113	216-522-1383	694-4264
Crain's Detroit Business Magazine 1155 Gratiot Ave *TF:* 888-909-9111 ■ *Web:* www.crainsdetroit.com	Detroit	MI	48207	313-446-6000	446-1687
Crain's New York Business Magazine 711 3rd Ave 3rd Fl **Fax:* Edit ■ *TF:* 888-909-9111 ■ *Web:* www.newyorkbusiness.com	New York	NY	10017	212-210-0100	210-0799*
Daily Business Review 1 SE 3rd Ave Suite 900 **Fax:* Edit ■ *TF:* 800-777-7300 ■ *Web:* www.dailybusinessreview.com	Miami	FL	33131	305-377-3721	347-6626*
Dallas Business Journal 12801 N Central Expy Suite 800 **Fax:* Edit ■ *Web:* www.bizjournals.com	Dallas	TX	75243	214-696-5959	361-4045*
Denver Business Journal 1700 Broadway Suite 515 *Web:* www.bizjournals.com/denver	Denver	CO	80290	303-837-3500	837-3535
Des Moines Business Record 100 4th St *Web:* www.businessrecord.com	Des Moines	IA	50309	515-288-3336	288-0309
Drug Topics Magazine 24950 Country Club Blvd Suite 200 *TF Cust Svc:* 877-922-2022 ■ *Web:* www.drugtopics.modernmedicine.com	North Olmsted	OH	44070	440-891-2792	891-2735
E-Commerce Times (ECT) 17555 Ventura Blvd Suite 200 *TF:* 877-328-5500 ■ *Web:* www.ectnews.com	Encino	CA	91316	818-461-9700	461-9710
Eastern Pennsylvania Business Journal LLC (EPBJ) 65 E Elizabeth Ave Suite 700 *TF:* 800-328-1026 ■ *Web:* www.epbj.com	Bethlehem	PA	18018	610-807-9619	807-9612
Editor & Publisher Magazine 770 Broadway *TF:* 800-783-4903 ■ *Web:* www.editorandpublisher.com	New York	NY	10003	646-654-5000	654-5370
Electronic Business Magazine 225 Wyman St *TF Cust Svc:* 800-446-6551 ■ *Web:* www.reed-electronics.com	Waltham	MA	02451	781-734-8000	734-8076
Employee Benefit News 1325 G St NW Suite 900 *TF:* 800-221-1809 ■ *Web:* www.benefitnews.com	Washington	DC	20005	202-504-1122	772-1448
Enterprise Magazine 136 S Main St Suite 721 *Web:* www.slenterprise.com	Salt Lake City	UT	84101	801-533-0556	533-0684
Entrepreneur Magazine 2445 McCabe Way Suite 400 *TF:* 800-274-6229 ■ *Web:* www.entrepreneur.com	Irvine	CA	92614	949-261-2325	261-7729
Expansion Management Magazine 1300 E 9th St *TF:* 866-505-7173 ■ *Web:* www.industryweek.com	Cleveland	OH	44114	216-696-7000	
Fast Co Magazine 7 World Trade Ctr *TF:* 800-542-6029 ■ *Web:* www.fastcompany.com	New York	NY	10007	212-389-5300	389-5496
Finance & Commerce 730 2nd Ave S US Trust Bldg Suite 100 *TF:* 800-397-4348 ■ *Web:* www.finance-commerce.com	Minneapolis	MN	55402	612-333-4244	333-3243
Financial Planning Magazine 1 State St Plaza 27th Fl *TF:* 888-280-4820 ■ *Web:* www.financial-planning.com	New York	NY	10004	212-803-8200	843-9608
Fleet Owner Magazine 11 Riverbend Dr S PO Box 4211 *TF:* 800-776-1246 ■ *Web:* www.fleetowner.com	Stamford	CT	06907	203-358-9900	358-5819
Forbes Magazine 60 5th Ave *TF:* 800-295-0893 ■ *Web:* www.forbes.com	New York	NY	10011	212-366-8900	
Fortune Magazine Rockefeller Ctr Time & Life Bldg *TF:* 800-621-8000 ■ *Web:* money.cnn.com/magazines/fortune	New York	NY	10020	212-522-1212	467-0579
Fortune Small Business Magazine (FSB) 1271 Avenue of the Americas 4th Fl *Web:* www.money.cnn.com/magazines/fsb	New York	NY	10020	212-522-1212	522-8717
Foundation News & Commentary Magazine 1828 L St NW Suite 300 *Web:* www.foundationnews.org	Washington	DC	20036	202-467-0439	785-3926
Franchising World Magazine 1501 K St NW Suite 350 *TF:* 800-543-1038 ■ *Web:* www.franchise.org	Washington	DC	20005	202-628-8000	628-0812
Futures Magazine 222 S Riverside Plaza Suite 620 *TF:* 800-972-9316 ■ *Web:* www.futuresmag.com	Chicago	IL	60606	312-846-4600	846-4638
Global Finance Magazine 7E 20th St 2nd Fl *Web:* www.gfmag.com	New York	NY	10016	212-447-7900	777-2692
Grand Rapids Business Journal (GRBJ) 549 Ottawa Ave NW Suite 201 *Web:* www.grbj.com/GRBJ/Homepage.htm	Grand Rapids	MI	49503	616-459-4545	459-4800
Graphic Arts Blue Book (GABB) 2000 Clearwater Dr **Fax Area Code:* 678 ■ *TF:* 800-323-4958 ■ *Web:* www.gammag.com	Oak Brook	IL	60523	630-288-8333	680-1667*
Greater Lansing Business Monthly 120 N Washington Sq Suite 800 *Web:* www.lansingbusinessmonthly.com	Lansing	MI	48933	517-487-1714	487-9597
Greenville Business Magazine 303 Haywood Rd *Web:* www.greenvillemagazine.com	Greenville	SC	29607	864-271-1105	271-1165

Name / Address	City	State	Zip	Phone	Fax
Harvard Business Review 60 Harvard Way	Boston	MA	02163	617-783-7500	783-7555*
**Fax:* Cust Svc ■ *TF:* 800-274-3214 ■ *Web:* www.hbr.org					
Health Facilities Management Magazine 155 N Wacker Dr Suite 400	Chicago	IL	60606	312-893-6800	422-4500
TF: 800-621-6902 ■ *Web:* www.hfmmagazine.com					
Health Supplement Retailer Magazine 3300 N Central Ave Suite 300	Phoenix	AZ	85012	480-990-1101	567-6852*
**Fax Area Code:* 602 ■ *Web:* www.naturalproductsmarketplace.com					
Healthcare Informatics Magazine PO Box 2059	Skokie	IL	60076	847-763-9291	763-9287
TF Cust Svc: 800-215-8546 ■ *Web:* www.healthcare-informatics.com					
Hispanic Business Magazine 425 Pine Ave	Santa Barbara	CA	93117	805-964-4554	964-6139
TF Sales: 888-447-7287 ■ *Web:* www.hispanicbusiness.com					
Hospitals & Health Networks Magazine 155 N Wacker Suite 400	Chicago	IL	60606	312-893-6800	422-4500
TF: 800-621-6902 ■ *Web:* www.healthforum.com					
Hotels Magazine 2000 Clearwater Dr	Oak Brook	IL	60523	630-288-8000	288-8265
Web: www.hotelsmag.com					
Houston Business Journal 1233 W Loop S Suite 1300	Houston	TX	77027	713-688-8811	963-0482*
**Fax:* Edit ■ *Web:* www.bizjournals.com					
HRMagazine 1800 Duke St	Alexandria	VA	22314	703-548-3440	836-0367
TF: 800-283-7476 ■ *Web:* www.shrm.org/hrmagazine					
Human Resource Executive Magazine 747 Dresher Rd Suite 500	Horsham	PA	19044	215-784-0910	784-0275
Web: www.hreonline.com					
In Business Magazine 200 River Pl Suite 250	Madison	WI	53716	608-204-9655	204-9656
Web: www.ibmadison.com					
Inc Magazine 7 World Trade Ctr	New York	NY	10007	212-389-5377	389-5398
TF: 800-234-0999 ■ *Web:* www.inc.com					
Independent Agent Magazine 127 S Peyton St	Alexandria	VA	22314	703-706-5388	665-2756*
**Fax Area Code:* 866 ■ *Web:* www.iamagazine.com					
Indianapolis Business Journal 41 E Washington St Suite 200	Indianapolis	IN	46204	317-634-6200	263-5406*
**Fax:* Edit ■ *TF:* 800-968-1225 ■ *Web:* www.ibj.com					
Inside Collin County Business 2222 W Spring Creek Pkwy Suite 114	Plano	TX	75023	972-612-2425	612-9329
Web: www.insidetxbiz.com					
Internal Auditor Magazine 247 Maitland Ave	Altamonte Springs	FL	32701	407-937-1100	937-1101
Web: www.theiia.org/iia/index.cfm?doc_id=540					
Jacksonville Business Journal 1200 River Pl Blvd Suite 201	Jacksonville	FL	32207	904-396-3502	396-5706
Web: www.bizjournals.com					
Journal of Accountancy 220 Leigh Farm Rd	Durham	NC	27707	919-402-4500	
TF: 800-237-9851 ■ *Web:* www.aicpa.org/pubs/jofa/joahome.htm					
Journal of Business 429 E 3rd Ave	Spokane	WA	99202	509-456-5257	456-0624
Web: www.spokanejournal.com					
Journal of Financial Planning 4100 E Mississippi Ave Suite 400	Denver	CO	80246	303-759-4900	759-0749
TF: 800-322-4237 ■ *Web:* www.fpanet.org/journal					
Journal of Housing & Community Development 630 'I' St NW	Washington	DC	20001	202-289-3500	289-8181
TF: 877-866-2476 ■ *Web:* www.nahro.org					
Journal of Property Management 430 N Michigan Ave 7th Fl	Chicago	IL	60611	312-329-6000	661-0217
TF: 800-837-0706 ■ *Web:* www.irem.org/sechome.cfm?sec=jpm					
Kansas City Business Journal 1100 Main St Suite 210	Kansas City	MO	64105	816-421-5900	472-4010
Web: www.bizjournals.com					
Las Vegas Business Press 1385 Pama Ln Suite 111	Las Vegas	NV	89119	702-871-6780	220-5481
Web: www.lvbusinesspress.com					
Law Enforcement Technology Magazine 1233 Janesville Ave	Fort Atkinson	WI	53538	920-563-6388	563-1704
TF: 800-547-7377 ■ *Web:* www.officer.com					
Leadership Journal 465 Gundersen Dr	Carol Stream	IL	60188	630-260-6200	260-0114
TF: 800-777-3136 ■ *Web:* www.christianitytoday.com/leaders					
Life Insurance Selling Magazine 1801 Pk 270 Dr Suite 550	Saint Louis	MO	63146	314-824-5500	824-5640
TF: 888-772-8926 ■ *Web:* www.lifeinsuranceselling.com					
Lodging Magazine 385 Oxford Valley Rd Suite 420	Yardley	PA	19067	215-321-9662	321-5124
TF: 800-394-5157 ■ *Web:* www.lodgingmagazine.com					
Los Angeles Business Journal 5700 Wilshire Blvd Suite 170	Los Angeles	CA	90036	323-549-5225	549-5255
Web: www.labusinessjournal.com					
Management Accounting Quarterly 10 Paragon Dr Suite 1	Montvale	NJ	07645	201-573-9000	474-1603
TF Cust Svc: 800-638-4427 ■ *Web:* www.imanet.org/ima					
Marketing News 311 S Wacker Dr Suite 5800	Chicago	IL	60606	312-542-9000	922-3763
TF: 800-262-1150 ■ *Web:* www.marketingpower.com					
Meetings & Conventions Magazine 100 Lighting Way	Secaucus	NJ	07094	201-902-2000	902-1916
TF: 800-446-6551 ■ *Web:* www.meetings-conventions.com					
Memphis Business Journal 80 Monroe Ave Suite 600	Memphis	TN	38103	901-523-1000	526-5240
Web: www.bizjournals.com					
Mergers & Acquisitions Magazine 1 State St Plaza	New York	NY	10004	212-803-6051	
TF Cust Svc: 888-807-8667 ■ *Web:* www.themiddlemarket.com					
Midlands Business Journal 1324 S 119th St	Omaha	NE	68144	402-330-1760	758-9315
Web: www.mbj.com					
Minneapolis-Saint Paul Business Journal 333 S 7th St Suite 350	Minneapolis	MN	55402	612-288-2100	288-2121
TF: 800-704-3757 ■ *Web:* www.bizjournals.com/twincities					
Minority Business Entrepreneur Magazine 3528 Torrance Blvd Suite 101	Torrance	CA	90503	310-540-9398	792-8263
Web: www.mbemag.com					
Mississippi Business Journal 200 N Congress St	Jackson	MS	39201	601-364-1000	364-1007
TF: 800-283-4625 ■ *Web:* www.msbusiness.com					
Modern Healthcare Magazine 360 N Michigan Ave	Chicago	IL	60601	312-649-5200	280-3189
TF: 800-678-2724 ■ *Web:* www.modernhealthcare.com					
Nashville Business Journal 1800 Church St Suite 300	Nashville	TN	37203	615-248-2222	248-6246
Web: www.nashville.bizjournals.com/nashville					
National Notary Magazine 9350 DeSoto Ave	Chatsworth	CA	91311	818-739-4000	700-1942
TF Cust Svc: 800-876-6827 ■ *Web:* www.nationalnotary.org					
National Real Estate Investor Magazine 6151 Powers Ferry Rd NW Suite 200	Atlanta	GA	30339	770-955-2500	618-0348
Web: www.nreionline.com					
New Accountant Magazine 3550 W Peterson Ave Suite 403	Chicago	IL	60659	773-866-9900	866-9981
Web: www.newaccountantusa.com					
New Jersey Business Magazine 310 Passaic Ave	Fairfield	NJ	07004	973-882-5004	882-4648
Web: www.njbmagazine.com					
New Orleans City Business 111 Veterans Memorial Blvd Suite 1440	Metairie	LA	70005	504-834-9292	832-3550
Web: www.neworleanscitybusiness.com					
Northern Colorado Business Report 141 S College Ave	Fort Collins	CO	80524	970-221-5400	221-5432
TF: 800-440-3506 ■ *Web:* www.ncbr.com					
Office Solutions Magazine 252 N Main St Suite 200 PO Box 1028	Mount Airy	NC	27030	336-783-0000	783-0045
Orange County Business Journal (OCBJ) 18500 Von Karman Ave Suite 150	Irvine	CA	92612	949-833-8373	833-8751
Web: www.ocbj.com					
Orlando Business Journal (OBJ) 255 S Orange Ave Suite 700	Orlando	FL	32801	407-649-8470	420-1625
Web: www.bizjournals.com					
Ottawa Business Journal 5300 Canotek Rd Unit 30	Ottawa	ON	K1J1A4	613-744-4800	744-8232
Web: www.obj.ca					
Palm Beach Daily Business Review 324 Datura St Suite 140	West Palm Beach	FL	33401	561-820-2060	820-2077
TF: 800-777-7300 ■ *Web:* www.dailybusinessreview.com					
PCBE Inc PO Box 1575	Tacoma	WA	98401	253-404-0891	404-0892
TF: 800-540-8322 ■ *Web:* www.businessexaminer.com					
Pensions & Investments Magazine 711 3rd Ave	New York	NY	10017	212-210-0115	210-0117
TF Cust Svc: 888-446-1422 ■ *Web:* www.pionline.com					
Pharmaceutical Representative Magazine 641 Lexington Ave 8th Fl	New York	NY	10022	212-951-6600	951-6604
TF: 800-451-7838 ■ *Web:* www.pharmrep.com					
Philadelphia Business Journal 400 Market St Suite 1200	Philadelphia	PA	19106	215-238-1450	238-9489
TF: 800-220-3202 ■ *Web:* www.bizjournals.com/philadelphia					
Pittsburgh Business Times 424 S 27th St Suite 211	Pittsburgh	PA	15203	412-481-6397	481-9956
Web: www.bizjournals.com/pittsburgh					
Print Magazine 38 E 29th St 3rd Fl	New York	NY	10016	212-447-1400	447-5231
TF: 877-860-9145 ■ *Web:* www.printmag.com					
Providence Business News 220 W Exchange St Suite 210	Providence	RI	02903	401-273-2201	274-6580*
**Fax:* Hum Res ■ *Web:* www.pbn.com					
Purchasing Magazine 225 Wyman St	Waltham	MA	02451	781-734-8203	734-8076
TF: 800-446-6551					
Realtor Magazine 430 N Michigan Ave 9th Fl	Chicago	IL	60611	312-329-8458	329-5978
TF: 800-874-6500 ■ *Web:* www.realtor.org/rmodaily.nsf					
Red Herring Magazine 1900 Alameda de las Pulgas Suite 112	San Mateo	CA	94403	650-428-2900	428-2901
Web: www.redherring.com					
Registered Representative Magazine 249 W 17th St	New York	NY	10011	913-967-1710	206-3622*
**Fax Area Code:* 212 ■ **Fax:* Edit ■ *TF:* 866-505-7173 ■ *Web:* www.registeredrep.com					
Restaurant Business Magazine 90 Broad St Suite 402	New York	NY	10004	646-708-7300	708-7399
Web: www.restaurantbiz.com					
Risk Management Magazine 1065 Avenue of the Americas 13th Fl	New York	NY	10018	212-286-9292	986-9716
Web: www.rmmag.com					
Rochester Business Journal 45 E Ave Suite 500	Rochester	NY	14604	585-546-8303	546-3398
Web: www.rbj.net					
Rough Notes Co Inc The 11690 Technology Dr	Carmel	IN	46032	317-582-1600	816-1000
TF: 800-428-4384 ■ *Web:* www.roughnotes.com					
Sacramento Business Journal 1400 X St	Sacramento	CA	95818	916-447-7661	444-7779
Web: www.bizjournals.com/sacramento					
Sales & Marketing Management Magazine 770 Broadway	New York	NY	10003	646-654-5000	654-7616
Web: www.salesandmarketing.com					
San Antonio Business Journal 8200 IH 10 W Suite 820	San Antonio	TX	78230	210-341-3202	341-3031
Web: www.bizjournals.com/sanantonio					
San Diego Business Journal 4909 Murphy Canyon Rd Suite 200	San Diego	CA	92123	858-277-6359	277-2149
TF: 888-425-7325 ■ *Web:* www.sdbj.com					
Self-Employed America Magazine PO Box 241	Annapolis Junction	MD	20701	800-649-6273	
TF: 800-649-6273 ■ *Web:* www.nase.org					
Selling Power Magazine 1140 International Pkwy	Fredericksburg	VA	22406	540-752-7000	752-7001
TF: 800-752-7355 ■ *Web:* www.sellingpower.com					

Name / Address	City	State	ZIP	Phone	Fax
Signal Magazine 4400 Fair Lakes Ct. TF: 800-336-4583 ■ Web: www.afcea.org/signal	Fairfax	VA	22033	703-631-6100	631-6188
Sloan Management Review 77 Massachusetts Ave E60-100 TF: 800-876-5764 ■ Web: www.sloanreview.mit.edu	Cambridge	MA	02139	617-253-7170	258-9739
Small Business Opportunities Magazine 1115 Broadway 8th Fl Web: www.sbomag.com	New York	NY	10010	212-807-7100	924-8416
South Florida Business Journal 6400 N Andrews Ave Suite 200 Web: www.bizjournals.com	Fort Lauderdale	FL	33309	954-949-7600	949-7591
Springfield Business Journal 313 Pk Central W Web: www.sbj.net	Springfield	MO	65806	417-831-3238	831-5478
Staffdigest Magazine 7474 S Kirkwood Suite 108 TF: 800-444-0674 ■ Web: www.staffdigest.com	Houston	TX	77072	281-498-2913	530-7082
Strategic Finance Magazine 10 Paragon Dr Suite 1 TF: 800-638-4427 ■ Web: www.imanet.org/publications_sfm.asp	Montvale	NJ	07645	201-573-9000	474-1603
Successful Meetings Magazine 770 Broadway	New York	NY	10003	646-654-4400	
Toledo Business Journal 5301 Southwyck Blvd # 104 Web: www.toledobiz.com	Toledo	OH	43614	419-865-0972	865-2429
Training & Development Magazine 1640 King St. Web: www.astd.org/astd/publications/td_magazine	Alexandria	VA	22313	703-683-8100	683-8103
Training Magazine 770 Broadway Web: www.trainingmag.com	New York	NY	10003	646-654-4500	
Tri Cities Business Journal 2203 McKinley Rd Suite 133 Web: www.bjournal.com	Johnson City	TN	37604	423-854-0140	854-0171
Triangle Business Journal 3600 Glenwood Ave Suite 100 Web: www.bizjournals.com	Raleigh	NC	27612	919-878-0010	954-4898
Utah Business Magazine 859 W S Jordan Pkwy Suite 101 TF: 800-823-0038 ■ Web: www.utahbusiness.com	South Jordan	UT	84095	801-568-0114	568-0812
Vancouver Business Journal 1251 Officers Row Web: www.vbjusa.com	Vancouver	WA	98661	360-695-2442	695-3056
Virginia Business Magazine 333 E Franklin St Web: www.virginiabusiness.com	Richmond	VA	23219	804-649-6999	649-6311
Washington Business Journal 1555 Wilson Blvd Suite 400 Web: www.bizjournals.com	Arlington	VA	22209	703-258-0800	258-0802
Wichita Business Journal 121 N Mead St Suite 100 Web: www.bizjournals.com	Wichita	KS	67202	316-267-6406	267-8570
Women in Business Magazine 11050 Roe Ave Suite 200 *Fax Area Code: 816	Kansas City	MO	66211	913-732-5100	361-4991*
Your Church Magazine 465 Gundersen Dr Web: www.christianitytoday.com	Carol Stream	IL	60188	630-260-6200	260-0114

460-6 Children's & Youth Magazines

Name / Address	City	State	ZIP	Phone	Fax
American Girl LLC 8400 Fairway Pl PO Box 620497 TF: 800-360-1861 ■ Web: www.americangirl.com	Middleton	WI	53562	608-836-4848	
AppleSeeds Magazine 30 Grove St Suite C TF: 800-821-0115 ■ Web: www.cobblestonepub.com/magazine/APP	Peterborough	NH	03458	603-924-7209	924-7380
Archie Comics Magazine 325 Fayette Ave Web: www.archiecomics.com	Mamaroneck	NY	10543	914-381-5155	381-2335
Ask Magazine 30 Grove St Suite C TF: 800-821-0115 ■ Web: www.cobblestonepub.com/magazine/ASK	Peterborough	NH	03458	603-924-7209	924-7380
Babybug Magazine 30 Grove St Suite C TF: 800-821-0115 ■ Web: www.cobblestonepub.com/magazine/BBB	Peterborough	NH	03458	603-924-7209	924-7380
Boys' Life Magazine 1325 W Walnut Hill Ln Web: www.boyslife.org	Irving	TX	75038	972-580-2000	580-2502
Calliope Magazine 30 Grove St Suite C TF: 800-821-0115 ■ Web: www.cobblestonepub.com/magazine/CAL	Peterborough	NH	03458	603-924-7209	924-7380
Children's Digest 1100 Waterway Blvd TF: 800-558-2376	Indianapolis	IN	46202	317-634-1100	684-8094
Cicada Magazine 30 Grove St Suite C TF: 800-821-0115 ■ Web: www.cobblestonepub.com/magazine/CIC	Peterborough	NH	03458	603-924-7209	924-7380
Click Magazine 30 Grove St Suite C TF: 800-821-0115 ■ Web: www.cobblestonepub.com/magazine/CLK	Peterborough	NH	03458	603-924-7209	924-7380
Cobblestone Magazine 30 Grove St Suite C TF: 800-821-0115 ■ Web: www.cobblestonepub.com/magazine/COB	Peterborough	NH	03458	603-924-7209	924-7380
CosmoGIRL! Magazine 224 W 57th St Suite 1 TF: 800-827-3221	New York	NY	10019	212-649-3852	
Creative Kids Magazine PO Box 8813 TF: 800-998-2208 ■ Web: www.prufrock.com	Waco	TX	76714	254-756-3337	756-3339
Cricket Magazine 30 Grove St Suite C TF: 800-821-0115 ■ Web: www.cobblestonepub.com/magazine/CKT	Peterborough	NH	03458	603-924-7209	924-7380
DECA Dimensions Magazine 1908 Assn Dr Web: www.deca.org	Reston	VA	20191	703-860-5000	860-4013
Dig Magazine 30 Grove St Suite C TF: 800-821-0115 ■ Web: www.cobblestonepub.com/magazine/DIG	Peterborough	NH	03458	603-924-7209	924-7380
Faces Magazine About People 30 Grove St Suite C TF: 800-821-0115 ■ Web: www.cobblestonepub.com/magazine/FAC	Peterborough	NH	03458	603-924-7209	924-7380
FamilyFun Magazine 114 5th Ave *Fax: Hum Res ■ TF: 800-289-4849 ■ Web: family.go.com	New York	NY	10011	212-633-3620	633-5929*
Girls' Life Acqusition Co 4529 Hartford Rd TF: 888-999-3222 ■ Web: www.girlslife.com	Baltimore	MD	21214	410-426-9600	254-0991
Highlights for Children Magazine 1800 Watermark Dr PO Box 269 TF Cust Svc: 800-255-9517 ■ Web: www.highlights.com	Columbus	OH	43216	614-486-0631	
Ladybug Magazine 30 Grove St Suite C TF: 800-821-0115 ■ Web: www.cobblestonepub.com/magazine/LYB	Peterborough	NH	03458	603-924-7209	924-7380
Muse Magazine 30 Grove St Suite C TF: 800-821-0115 ■ Web: www.cobblestonepub.com/magazine/MUS	Peterborough	NH	03458	603-924-7209	924-7380
National Geographic Kids Magazine 1145 17th St NW TF: 800-647-5463 ■ Web: www.kids.nationalgeographic.com/kids	Washington	DC	20036	202-857-7000	775-6141
New Expression Magazine 619 S Wabash Ave Rm 207 Web: www.youthcommunicationchicago.org	Chicago	IL	60605	312-922-7150	922-7151
New Moon Magazine PO Box 161287 TF: 800-381-4743 ■ Web: www.newmoon.org	Duluth	MN	55816	218-728-5507	728-0314
New Youth Connections Magazine 224 W 29th St 2nd Fl	New York	NY	10001	212-279-0708	279-8856
Nickelodeon Magazine 1633 Broadway 7th Fl TF: 800-947-7052 ■ Web: www.nick.com/all_nick/nick_mag/index.jhtml	New York	NY	10019	212-654-7707	654-4870
Odyssey Magazine 30 Grove St Suite C TF: 800-821-0115 ■ Web: www.odysseymagazine.com	Peterborough	NH	03458	603-924-7209	924-7380
Owl Magazine 10 Lower Spadina Ave Suite 400 TF: 800-551-6957 ■ Web: www.owlkids.com	Toronto	ON	M5V2Z2	416-340-2700	340-9769
Ranger Rick Magazine 11100 Wildlife Ctr Dr TF: 800-822-9919 ■ Web: www.nwf.org/gowild	Reston	VA	20190	800-822-9919	
Seventeen Magazine 300 W 57th St 17th Fl TF: 800-388-1749 ■ Web: www.seventeen.com	New York	NY	10019	800-388-1749	
Spider Magazine 30 Grove St Suite C TF: 800-821-0115 ■ Web: www.cobblestonepub.com/magazine/SDR	Peterborough	NH	03458	603-924-7209	924-7380
Sports Illustrated for Kids Magazine 135 W 50th St TF Cust Svc: 800-992-0196 ■ Web: www.sikids.com	New York	NY	10020	212-522-1212	522-0120
Stone Soup Magazine 765 Cedar St # 201 TF: 800-447-4569 ■ Web: www.stonesoup.com	Santa Cruz	CA	95060	831-426-5557	426-1161
Teen Magazine 3000 Ocean Pk Blvd Suite 2010	Santa Maria	CA	90405	310-664-2950	664-2959
Teen People Magazine 1271 6th Ave Suite 3540 *Fax: Edit ■ TF: 800-284-0200 ■ Web: www.teenpeople.com	New York	NY	10020	212-522-2292	522-0601*
Teen Voices Magazine 80 Summer St Suite 300 Web: www.teenvoices.com	Boston	MA	02110	617-426-5505	426-5577
TeenVogue Magazine 4 Times Sq TF: 800-274-0084 ■ Web: www.teenvogue.com/magazine	New York	NY	10036	212-286-2860	286-8169
Turtle Magazine 1100 Waterway Blvd TF: 800-558-2376 ■ Web: www.uskidsmags.com/turtle-home	Indianapolis	IN	46202	317-634-1100	684-8094
Wild Animal Baby Magazine 11100 Wildlife Ctr Dr TF: 800-822-9919 ■ Web: www.nwf.org/wildanimalbaby	Reston	VA	20190	800-822-9919	
Your Big Backyard Magazine 11100 Wildlife Ctr Dr *Fax Area Code: 703 ■ TF: 800-822-9919 ■ Web: www.nwf.org/yourbigbackyard	Reston	VA	20190	800-822-9919	442-7332*
Your Prom Magazine 750 3rd Ave 4th Fl Web: www.yourprom.com	New York	NY	10017	212-630-4000	630-5890

460-7 Computer & Internet Magazines

Name / Address	City	State	ZIP	Phone	Fax
2600 Magazine PO Box 752 Web: www.2600.com	Middle Island	NY	11953	631-751-2600	474-2677
Computer Magazine 10662 Los Vaqueros Cir TF Orders: 800-272-6657 ■ Web: www.computer.org	Los Alamitos	CA	90720	714-821-8380	821-4010
Computers in Libraries Magazine 143 Old Marlton Pike TF: 800-300-9868 ■ Web: www.infotoday.com/cilmag	Medford	NJ	08055	609-654-6266	654-4309
Computerworld Magazine 1 Speen St *Fax: Mktg ■ TF: 800-343-6474 ■ Web: www.computerworld.com	Framingham	MA	01701	508-879-0700	875-3701*
Dr Dobb's Journal PO Box 1126 TF: 888-847-6188 ■ Web: www.drdobbs.com	Skokie	IL	60076	847-763-9581	763-9581
eContent Magazine 48 S Main St Suite 3 TF: 800-248-8466 ■ Web: www.econtentmag.com	Newtown	CT	06470	203-761-1466	304-9300
eWEEK Magazine 28 E 28th St 8th Fl TF: 888-663-8438 ■ Web: www.eweek.com	New York	NY	10016	212-503-3500	503-5317
Federal Computer Week Magazine 3141 Fairview Pk Dr Suite 777 Web: www.fcw.com	Falls Church	VA	22042	703-876-5100	876-5100
IEEE Computer Graphics & Applications Magazine 10662 Los Vaqueros Cir PO Box 3014 TF: 800-272-6657 ■ Web: www.computer.org/cga	Los Alamitos	CA	90720	714-816-2165	821-4010
IEEE Micro Magazine 10662 Los Vaqueros Cir PO Box 3014 TF: 800-272-6657 ■ Web: www.computer.org/micro	Los Alamitos	CA	90720	714-816-2165	821-4010
Information Today Magazine 143 Old Marlton Pike TF: 800-300-9868 ■ Web: www.infotoday.com	Medford	NJ	08055	609-654-6266	654-4309
InformationWeek Magazine 600 Community Dr TF: 800-645-6278 ■ Web: www.informationweek.com	Manhasset	NY	11030	516-562-5000	562-5036
InfoWorld Magazine 501 2nd St Suite 120 TF: 800-227-8365 ■ Web: www.infoworld.com	San Francisco	CA	94107	415-243-4344	978-3120
IT Architect 600 Harrison St	San Francisco	CA	94107	415-905-2200	905-2587
Law Technology News 120 Broadway 5th Fl TF Cust Svc: 800-888-8300	New York	NY	10271	212-457-9400	696-1848
MacHome 200 Folsom St Suite 150 TF: 800-800-6542	San Francisco	CA	94105	415-957-1911	882-9502
Macworld Magazine 501 2nd St Suite 120 TF Cust Svc: 800-873-4941 ■ Web: www.macworld.com	San Francisco	CA	94107	415-243-4141	442-3543

				Phone	Fax
Manufacturing Business Technology Magazine 2000 Clearwater Dr. *TF:* 800-662-7776 ■ *Web:* www.mbtmag.com	Oak Brook	IL	60523	630-288-8000	288-8764
Maximum PC Magazine 4000 Shoreline Ct Suite 400 *Web:* www.maximumpc.com	South San Francisco	CA	94080	650-872-1642	872-2207
MultiMedia Schools Magazine 143 Old Marlton Pike *TF:* 800-300-9868 ■ *Web:* www.infotoday.com/MMSchools	Medford	NJ	08055	609-654-6266	654-4309
Network Computing Magazine 600 Community Dr *Web:* www.networkcomputing.com	Manhasset	NY	11030	516-562-5000	562-5036
Network World Magazine 492 Old Connecticut Path Suite 200 PO Box 9208 **Fax Area Code:* 508 ■ *TF:* 800-622-1108 ■ *Web:* www.networkworld.com	Framingham	MA	01701	875-766-1101	490-6417*
Online Magazine 143 Old Marlton Pike *TF:* 800-300-9868 ■ *Web:* www.onlinemag.net	Medford	NJ	08055	609-654-6266	654-4309
Oracle Magazine 500 Oracle Pkwy MS OPL3 **Fax:* Cust Svc ■ *Web:* www.oracle.com/oramag/index.html	Redwood Shores	CA	94065	650-506-2835	633-2424*
PC Magazine 28 E 28th St *TF:* 800-289-0429 ■ *Web:* www.pcmag.com	New York	NY	10016	212-503-3500	503-5799
PC World Magazine 501 2nd St Suite 600 *TF:* 800-234-3498 ■ *Web:* www.pcworld.com	San Francisco	CA	94107	415-243-0500	442-1891
Publish.com c/o Ziff Davis Media Inc 462 Boston St *Web:* www.publish.com	Topsfield	MA	01983	978-887-2246	887-6117
Scientific Computing & Instrumentation Magazine 100 Enterprise Dr Suite 600 *TF:* 800-222-0289 ■ *Web:* www.scientificcomputing.com	Rockaway	NJ	07866	973-920-7000	920-7551
Searcher: The Magazine for Database Professionals 143 Old Marlton Pike *TF:* 800-300-9868 ■ *Web:* www.infotoday.com/searcher	Medford	NJ	08055	609-654-6266	654-4309
Software Magazine 233 Needham St Suite 300 *Web:* www.softwaremag.com	Newton	MA	02464	508-668-9928	

460-8 Education Magazines & Journals

				Phone	Fax
Academe Magazine 1133 19th St NW Suite 200 *TF:* 800-424-2973 ■ *Web:* www.aaup.org	Washington	DC	20036	202-737-5900	737-5526
Advocate Magazine 100 E Edwards St *TF:* 800-252-8076	Springfield	IL	62704	217-544-0706	544-6423
AEA Advocate Magazine 345 E Palm Ln *TF:* 800-352-5411 ■ *Web:* www.arizonaea.org	Phoenix	AZ	85004	602-264-1774	240-6887
Alabama School Journal 422 Dexter Ave *TF:* 800-392-5839 ■ *Web:* www.myaea.org	Montgomery	AL	36104	334-834-9790	262-8377
American Educator Magazine 555 New Jersey Ave NW *TF:* 800-238-1133 ■ *Web:* www.aft.org	Washington	DC	20001	202-879-4400	879-4534
American Libraries Magazine 50 E Huron St *TF:* 800-545-2433 ■ *Web:* www.ala.org/alonline	Chicago	IL	60611	312-944-6780	440-0901
American Teacher Magazine 555 New Jersey Ave NW *TF:* 800-238-1133 ■ *Web:* www.aft.org/publications/american_teacher	Washington	DC	20001	202-879-4400	783-2014
Arkansas Educator Magazine 1500 W 4th St	Little Rock	AR	72201	501-375-4611	375-4620
Cable in the Classroom 214 Lincoln St Suite 112 *Web:* www.ciconline.org	Allston	MA	02134	617-254-9481	254-9776
California Educator Magazine 1705 Murchison Dr *Web:* www.cta.org	Burlingame	CA	94010	650-697-1400	552-5002
Chronicle of Higher Education 1255 23rd St NW Suite 700 *TF Sales:* 800-728-2803 ■ *Web:* www.chronicle.com	Washington	DC	20037	202-466-1000	452-1033
Colorado School Journal 1500 Grant St *TF:* 800-332-5939 ■ *Web:* www.coloradoeas.org	Denver	CO	80203	303-837-1500	864-1685
Dance Teacher Magazine 110 William St 23rd Fl **Fax Area Code:* 646 ■ *TF:* 800-362-6765 ■ *Web:* www.dance-teacher.com	New York	NY	10038	800-362-6765	459-4900*
Education Center Inc 3515 W Market St Suite 200 *TF:* 800-714-7991 ■ *Web:* www.theeducationcenter.com	Greensboro	NC	27403	336-854-0309	547-1587
Education Digest 832 Phoenix Dr PO Box 8623 *TF:* 800-530-9673 ■ *Web:* www.eddigest.com	Ann Arbor	MI	48107	734-975-2800	975-2787
Education Week Magazine 6935 Arlington Rd *TF:* 800-346-1834 ■ *Web:* www.edweek.org	Bethesda	MD	20814	301-280-3100	280-3250
Educational Leadership Magazine 1703 N Beauregard St *TF:* 800-933-2723 ■ *Web:* www.ascd.org	Alexandria	VA	22311	703-578-9600	575-5400
FOCUS 1529 18th St NW *TF:* 800-741-9415 ■ *Web:* www.maa.org/pubs/focus.html	Washington	DC	20036	202-387-5200	265-2384
Harvard Educational Review 8 Story St 1st Fl *TF:* 800-513-0763 ■ *Web:* www.gse.harvard.edu	Cambridge	MA	02138	617-495-3432	496-3584
IEA Reporter Magazine PO Box 2638 *Web:* www.idahoea.org	Boise	ID	83701	208-344-1341	336-6967
ISTA Advocate Magazine 150 W Market St Suite 900 *TF:* 800-382-4037	Indianapolis	IN	46204	317-263-3400	655-3700
Journal of Physical Education Recreation & Dance (JOPERD) 1900 Assn Dr *Web:* www.aahperd.org	Reston	VA	20191	703-476-3477	476-9527
KEA News 401 Capital Ave *TF:* 800-231-4532 ■ *Web:* www.kea.org	Frankfort	KY	40601	502-875-2889	227-8062
LAE News 8322 One Kalais Ave *TF:* 800-256-4523 ■ *Web:* www.lae.org	Baton Rouge	LA	70809	225-343-9243	343-9272
Library Journal 360 Pk Ave S *Web:* www.libraryjournal.com	New York	NY	10010	646-746-6400	746-6734
Mailbox Bookbag Magazine 3515 W Market St Suite 200 *TF:* 800-714-7991 ■ *Web:* www.theeducationcenter.com	Greensboro	NC	27403	336-854-0309	547-1587
Mailbox Teacher Magazine 3515 W Market St Suite 200 *Web:* www.theeducationcenter.com	Greensboro	NC	27403	336-854-0309	547-1590
Maine Educator Magazine 35 Community Dr *TF:* 800-452-8709	Augusta	ME	04330	207-622-5866	623-2129
MEA Voice Magazine 1216 Kendale Blvd PO Box 2573 *TF:* 800-292-1934 ■ *Web:* www.mea.org	East Lansing	MI	48826	517-332-6551	337-5414
Minnesota Educator Magazine 41 Sherburne Ave *TF:* 800-652-9073	Saint Paul	MN	55103	651-227-9541	292-4802
Mississippi Educator Magazine 775 N State St *TF:* 800-530-7998	Jackson	MS	39202	601-354-4463	352-7054
Missouri State Teachers Assn PO Box 458 *TF:* 800-392-0532 ■ *Web:* www.msti.org	Columbia	MO	65205	573-442-3127	443-5079
MTA Today Magazine 20 Ashburton Pl *TF:* 800-392-6175	Boston	MA	02108	617-742-7950	742-7046
NCAE News Bulletin PO Box 27347 *TF:* 800-662-7924 ■ *Web:* www.ncae.org	Raleigh	NC	27611	919-832-3000	829-1626
NCTM News Bulletin 1906 Assn Dr *Web:* www.nctm.org/news	Reston	VA	20191	703-620-9840	476-2970
NEA Today Magazine 1201 16th St NW *TF:* 800-229-4200 ■ *Web:* www.nea.org/neatoday	Washington	DC	20036	202-822-7207	822-7206
New Hampshire Educator Magazine 9 S Spring St *Web:* www.neanh.org	Concord	NH	03301	603-224-7751	224-2648
New York Teacher Magazine 800 Troy-Schenectady Rd *Web:* www.nysut.org	Latham	NY	12110	518-213-6000	213-6415
NJEA Review 180 W State St *Web:* www.njea.org	Trenton	NJ	08607	609-599-4561	392-6321
NSEA Voice Magazine 605 S 14th St Suite 200 *TF:* 800-742-0047 ■ *Web:* www.nsea.org	Lincoln	NE	68508	402-475-7611	475-2630
OEA Focus Magazine PO Box 18485 *TF:* 800-522-8091	Oklahoma City	OK	73154	405-528-7785	524-0350
Ohio Schools Magazine 225 E Broad St PO Box 2550	Columbus	OH	43216	614-228-4526	228-8771
On Campus Magazine 555 New Jersey Ave NW *TF:* 800-238-1133 ■ *Web:* www.aft.org/publications/on_campus	Washington	DC	20001	202-879-4400	783-2014
Oregon Education Magazine (OEA) 6900 SW Atlanta St Bldg 1 *TF:* 800-858-5505 ■ *Web:* www.oregoned.org	Portland	OR	97223	503-684-3300	684-8063
Reading Teacher The PO Box 8139 *Web:* www.reading.org/publications/rt	Newark	DE	19711	302-731-1600	731-1057
Scholastic Coach & Athletic Director Magazine 557 Broadway *TF:* 800-724-6527 ■ *Web:* www.scholastic.com/coach	New York	NY	10012	212-343-6100	343-6930
School Library Journal 360 Pk Ave S *Web:* www.schoollibraryjournal.com	New York	NY	10010	646-746-6400	746-6689
Teacher Magazine 6935 Arlington Rd Suite 100 *TF:* 800-346-1834 ■ *Web:* www.edweek.org/tm	Bethesda	MD	20814	301-280-3100	280-3150
Teaching Exceptional Children Magazine 2900 Crystal Dr Suite 1000 *TF:* 888-232-7733	Arlington	VA	22201	703-620-3660	264-9494
Teaching Tolerance Magazine 400 Washington Ave *Web:* www.tolerance.org/teach/magazine/index.jsp	Montgomery	AL	36104	334-956-8200	956-8486
TSTA Advocate Magazine 316 W 12th St *TF:* 800-324-5355 ■ *Web:* www.tsta.org	Austin	TX	78701	512-476-5355	486-7049
Vermont NEA Today Magazine 10 Wheelock St *TF:* 800-649-6375 ■ *Web:* www.vtnea.org	Montpelier	VT	05602	802-223-6375	223-1253
Virginia Journal of Education 116 S 3rd St *TF:* 800-552-9554 ■ *Web:* www.veanea.org	Richmond	VA	23219	804-648-5801	775-8379
Voice Magazine 400 N 3rd St PO Box 1724 *TF:* 800-944-7732	Harrisburg	PA	17105	717-255-7000	255-7124
WEA News 115 E 22nd St Suite 1 *TF:* 800-442-2395 ■ *Web:* westfield.massteacher.org/newspg.html	Cheyenne	WY	82001	307-634-7991	778-8161
West Virginia School Journal 1558 Quarrier St *TF:* 800-642-8261 ■ *Web:* www.wvea.org	Charleston	WV	25311	304-346-5315	346-4325
Young Children Magazine 1313 L St NW Suite 500 PO Box 97156 *TF:* 800-424-2460 ■ *Web:* www.naeyc.org	Washington	DC	20005	202-232-8777	328-1846

460-9 Entertainment & Music Magazines

				Phone	Fax
American Cinematographer Magazine 1782 N Orange Dr *TF:* 800-448-0145 ■ *Web:* www.theasc.com	Hollywood	CA	90028	323-969-4333	876-4973
American Songwriter Magazine 1303 16th Ave S 2nd Fl *Web:* www.americansongwriter.com	Nashville	TN	37212	615-321-6096	321-6097
Back Stage Magazine 770 Broadway *Web:* www.backstage.com	New York	NY	10003	212-493-4420	
Bass Player Magazine 1111 Bayhill Dr *TF Cust Svc:* 800-234-1831 ■ *Web:* www.bassplayer.com	San Bruno	CA	94066	650-238-0300	238-0261
Broadcast Engineering Magazine 9800 Metcalf Ave *Web:* www.broadcastengineering.com	Overland Park	KS	66212	913-967-1737	967-1905
Cadence Magazine Cadence Bldg *Web:* www.cadencebuilding.com	Redwood	NY	13679	315-287-2852	287-2860
Canadian Musician Magazine 23 Hanover Dr **Fax Area Code:* 888 ■ *TF:* 877-746-4692 ■ *Web:* www.canadianmusician.com	Saint Catharines	ON	L2W1A3	905-641-3471	665-1307*
Casino Player Magazine 8025 Black Horse Pike Suite 470 *TF:* 800-969-0711 ■ *Web:* www.casinoplayer.com	West Atlantic City	NJ	08232	609-484-8866	645-1661

Phone | Fax

Country Weekly Magazine
118 16th Ave S Suite 230 .... Nashville TN 37203 615-259-1111 255-1110
Web: www.countryweekly.com
Creative Screenwriting Magazine
6404 Hollywood Blvd Suite 415 .... Los Angeles CA 90028 323-957-1405 957-1406
TF: 888-556-6274 ■ *Web:* www.creativescreenwriting.com
Dance Magazine 333 7th Ave 11th Fl .... New York NY 10001 212-979-4814 674-0102*
**Fax Area Code:* 646 ■ *TF:* 800-331-1750 ■ *Web:* www.dancemagazine.com
Down Beat Magazine 102 N Haven Rd PO Box 906 ..... Elmhurst IL 60126 651-251-9682 941-3210*
**Fax Area Code:* 630 ■ *TF:* 800-554-7470 ■ *Web:* www.downbeat.com
Dramatics Magazine 2343 Auburn Ave .... Cincinnati OH 45219 513-421-3900 421-3900
Web: www.schooltheatre.org
Emmy Magazine 5220 Lankershim Blvd .... North Hollywood CA 91601 818-754-2800
Web: www.emmys.tv
Entertainment Weekly Magazine
1675 Broadway 29th Fl .... New York NY 10019 212-522-5600 522-0074
TF: 800-828-6882 ■ *Web:* www.ew.com
Film Comment Magazine 165 W 65th St .... New York NY 10023 212-875-5610 875-5636
TF: 888-313-6085 ■ *Web:* www.filmlinc.com
GamePro Magazine 555 12th St Suite 1100 .... Oakland CA 94607 510-768-2700 768-2701
TF: 800-678-9097 ■ *Web:* www.gamepro.com
Grammy Magazine 3030 Olympic Blvd .... Santa Monica CA 90404 310-392-3777 392-9262
TF: 800-423-2017 ■ *Web:* www.grammy.com
Guitar Player Magazine 28 E 28th St 12th Fl .... New York NY 10016 212-378-0400 281-4704*
**Fax Area Code:* 917 ■ *TF Cust Svc:* 800-289-9839 ■ *Web:* www.guitarplayer.com
Hit Parader Magazine 210 Rt 4 E Suite 211 .... Paramus NJ 07652 201-843-4004 843-8636
Web: www.hitparader.com
Hollywood Reporter
5055 Wilshire Blvd Suite 600 .... Los Angeles CA 90036 323-525-2000 525-2377*
**Fax:* Edit ■ *TF:* 866-525-2150 ■ *Web:* www.hollywoodreporter.com
Hollywood Scriptwriter Magazine PO Box 3761 .... Cerritos CA 90703 310-283-1630 926-2060*
**Fax Area Code:* 562 ■ *Web:* www.hollywoodscriptwriter.com
International Musician 221 Walton St .... Syracuse NY 13202 315-422-4488 422-3837
Jazziz Magazine
2650 N Military Trail
Suite 140 Fountain Sq II Bldg .... Boca Raton FL 33431 561-893-6868 893-6867
TF: 800-742-3252 ■ *Web:* www.jazziz.com
JazzTimes Magazine 85 Quincy Ave Suite 2 .... Quincy MA 02169 617-706-9110 536-0102
Web: www.jazztimes.com
Keyboard Magazine 2800 Campus Dr .... San Mateo CA 94403 650-513-4300 513-4661
TF Cust Svc: 800-289-9919 ■ *Web:* www.keyboardmag.com
Las Vegas Magazine
2360 Corporate Cir Dr 3rd Fl .... Henderson NV 89074 702-383-7185 383-1089
TF: 800-746-9484 ■ *Web:* www.lasvegasmagazine.com
Live Design 249 W 17th St .... New York NY 10011 212-204-4272 204-4291
TF Sales: 800-505-7173 ■ *Web:* www.livedesignonline.com
Metal Edge Magazine 333 7th Ave Suite 1100 .... New York NY 10001 212-780-3500 979-4825
TF: 800-741-1289 ■ *Web:* www.zenbumedia.com/printDigital.html
Multichannel News 28 E 28th St 12th Fl .... New York NY 10016 917-281-4700 281-4704
TF Cust Svc: 888-343-5563 ■ *Web:* www.multichannel.com
Opera News Magazine
70 Lincoln Ctr Plaza 6th Fl .... New York NY 10023 212-769-7070 769-7007
Web: www.metoperafamily.org/operanews
Playbill Magazine 525 Fashion Ave # 1801 .... New York NY 10018 212-557-5757 682-2932
TF: 800-533-4330 ■ *Web:* www.playbill.com
Pollstar 4697 W Jacquelyn Ave .... Fresno CA 93722 559-271-7900 271-7979*
**Fax:* Edit ■ *TF:* 800-344-7383 ■ *Web:* www.pollstar.com
Premiere Magazine 1633 Broadway .... New York NY 10019 212-767-6000 767-5450
TF: 800-274-4027 ■ *Web:* www.premieremag.com
Rolling Stone Magazine
1290 Avenue of the Americas 2nd Fl .... New York NY 10104 212-484-1616 767-8203
TF: 800-568-7655 ■ *Web:* www.rollingstone.com
Satellite Direct Magazine PO Box 5763 .... Harlan IA 50513 800-285-5454
TF: 800-285-5454 ■ *Web:* www.directmagazine.com
Singing News Magazine
330 University Hall Dr PO Box 2810 .... Boone NC 28607 828-264-3700 264-4621
TF: 800-527-5226 ■ *Web:* www.singingnews.com
Soap Opera Digest 261 Madison Ave .... New York NY 10016 212-915-4249 915-4260
TF: 800-829-9095 ■ *Web:* www.soapoperadigest.com
Soap Opera Weekly Magazine
261 Madison Ave 9th Fl .... New York NY 10016 212-716-8400 661-1825
TF: 800-829-9096 ■ *Web:* www.soapoperadigest.com
Source Magazine The 11 Broadway Suite 315 .... New York NY 10004 212-253-3700 253-9344
Web: www.thesource.com
Spin Magazine 205 Lexington Ave 3rd Fl .... New York NY 10016 212-231-7400 231-7300
TF Cust Svc: 800-274-7597 ■ *Web:* www.spin.com
TV Guide 100 Matsonford Rd 4 Radnor Corp Ctr .... Radnor PA 19088 610-293-8500 293-4849
TF Cust Svc: 800-866-1400 ■ *Web:* www.tvguide.com
TV Hebdo Magazine 7 ch Bates Rd .... Montreal QC H2V4V7 514-848-7000 848-7070
Web: www.tvhebdo.com
Variety 5700 Wilshire Blvd Suite 120 .... Los Angeles CA 90036 323-857-6600 857-0494
TF: 800-552-3632 ■ *Web:* www.variety.com
Vibe Magazine 120 Wall St .... New York NY 10005 212-448-7300 448-7400
TF: 800-477-3974 ■ *Web:* www.vibe.com
Video Age International Magazine
216 E 75th St Suite PW .... New York NY 10021 212-288-3933 734-9033
Web: www.videoageinternational.com
Videomaker Magazine 1350 E 9th St PO Box 4591 .... Chico CA 95927 530-891-8410 891-8443
TF: 800-284-3226 ■ *Web:* www.videomaker.com

460-10 Fraternal & Special Interest Magazines

Phone | Fax

AARP the Magazine 601 E St NW .... Washington DC 20049 202-434-3525 434-6883
TF: 888-687-2277 ■ *Web:* www.aarp.org
AAUW Outlook Magazine 1111 16th St NW .... Washington DC 20036 202-785-7700 872-1425
TF: 800-326-2289 ■ *Web:* www.aauw.org
Adoptive Families Magazine
39 W 37th St 15th Fl .... New York NY 10018 646-366-0830 366-0842
TF: 800-372-3300 ■ *Web:* www.adoptivefamilies.com
American Legion Auxiliary National News
8945 N Meridian St 2nd Fl .... Indianapolis IN 46260 317-569-4500 569-4502
Web: www.legion-aux.org
American Legion Magazine
700 N Pennsylvania St .... Indianapolis IN 46204 317-630-1200 630-1280
Web: www.legion.org
American Scholar Magazine
1606 New Hampshire Ave NW .... Washington DC 20009 202-265-3808 986-1601
TF: 800-821-4567 ■ *Web:* www.pbk.org
American Spirit 1776 D St NW .... Washington DC 20006 202-628-1776 879-8283
Web: www.dar.org/natsociety/magazine.cfm
Civitan Magazine
1 Civitan Pl PO Box 130744 .... Birmingham AL 35213 205-591-8910 592-6307
TF: 800-248-4826 ■ *Web:* www.civitan.org
Columbia Magazine 1 Columbus Plaza .... New Haven CT 06510 203-752-4000 752-4000
TF: 800-380-9995 ■ *Web:* www.kofc.org
Commentary Magazine 165 E 56th St .... New York NY 10022 212-891-1400 891-6700
TF: 800-829-6270 ■ *Web:* www.commentarymagazine.com
Disabled American Veterans Magazine
3725 Alexandria Pike .... Cold Spring KY 41076 859-441-7300 441-1416
TF: 877-426-2838 ■ *Web:* www.dav.org/magazine/index.html
Eagle Magazine 1623 Gateway Cir S .... Grove City OH 43123 614-883-2200 883-2201
Web: www.foe.com/magazine
Elks Magazine 425 W Diversey Pkwy .... Chicago IL 60614 773-755-4700 755-4745
Web: www.elks.org/elksmag
Gettysburg Review 300 N Washington St .... Gettysburg PA 17325 717-337-6000 337-6775
TF: 800-431-0803 ■ *Web:* www.gettysburg.edu/academics/gettysburg_review
Hispanic Magazine 6355 NW 36th St .... Miami FL 33166 305-774-3550 774-3578
Web: www.hispaniconline.com
Kiwanis Magazine 3636 Woodview Trace .... Indianapolis IN 46268 317-875-8755 879-0204
TF: 800-549-2647 ■ *Web:* www.kiwanis.org/magazine
Lion Magazine 300 W 22nd St .... Oak Brook IL 60523 630-571-5466 571-8890
TF Circ: 800-710-7822 ■ *Web:* www.lionsclubs.org
Mensa Bulletin 1229 Corporate Dr W .... Arlington TX 76006 817-607-0060 649-5232
TF: 800-294-8035
Moose Magazine 155 S International Dr .... Mooseheart IL 60539 630-859-2000 859-6620
Web: www.mooseintl.org/public/moose_Magazine.aspx
Only Child Magazine
137 N Larchmont Blvd Suite 556 .... Los Angeles CA 90004 323-937-6815
Web: www.onlychild.com
Optimist Magazine 4494 Lindell Blvd .... Saint Louis MO 63108 314-371-6000 371-6006
TF: 800-500-8130
Phi Delta Kappan Magazine 408 N Union St .... Bloomington IN 47405 812-339-1156 339-0018
TF: 800-766-1156 ■ *Web:* www.pdkintl.org
Plus Magazine 654 Osos St .... San Luis Obispo CA 93401 805-544-8711 546-8827
Web: www.plus.maths.org
Poets & Writers Magazine
90 Broad St Suite 2100 .... New York NY 10004 212-226-3586 226-3963
Web: www.pw.org
Police Times Magazine 6350 Horizon Dr .... Titusville FL 32780 321-264-0911 264-0033
Web: www.aphf.org
Quill & Scroll Magazine
University of Iowa
E346 Adler Journalism Bldg .... Iowa City IA 52242 319-335-3457 335-3989
Web: www.uiowa.edu/quill-sc
Rotarian Magazine
1560 Sherman Ave
Rotary International Headquarters .... Evanston IL 60201 847-866-3000 328-8554
Web: www.rotary.org/newsroom/rotarian/index.shtml
Royal Neighbor Magazine 230 16th St .... Rock Island IL 61201 309-788-4561 788-9234
TF: 800-627-4762 ■ *Web:* www.royalneighbors.org
Scouting Magazine
1325 W Walnut Hill Ln PO Box 152079 .... Irving TX 75015 972-580-2000 580-2079
Web: www.scoutingmagazine.org
Tikkun Magazine 2342 Shattuck Ave Suite 1200 .... Berkeley CA 94704 510-644-1200 644-1255
Web: www.tikkun.org
United Commercial Travellers
1801 Watermark Dr Suite 100 .... Columbus OH 43215 614-228-3276 487-9675
TF: 800-848-0123 ■ *Web:* www.uct.org
VFW Auxiliary Magazine 406 W 34th St .... Kansas City MO 64111 816-561-8655 931-4753
Web: www.ladiesauxvfw.org
VFW Magazine 406 W 34th St .... Kansas City MO 64111 816-756-3390 968-1169
Web: www.vfw.org/index.cfm?fa=news.mag&did=578
WOODMEN Magazine 1700 Farnam St .... Omaha NE 68102 402-342-1890 271-7269
TF: 800-225-3108 ■ *Web:* www.woodmen.com/about/woodmag.cfm

460-11 General Interest Magazines

Phone | Fax

Alfred Hitchcock Mystery Magazine
475 Pk Ave S 11th Fl .... New York NY 10016 212-686-7188 686-7414
TF: 800-333-3311 ■ *Web:* www.themysteryplace.com
Allure Magazine 4 Times Sq .... New York NY 10036 212-286-2860 286-2690
TF: 800-223-0780 ■ *Web:* www.allure.com
American Baby Magazine 375 Lexington Ave .... New York NY 10017 212-499-2000 499-1590*
**Fax:* Edit ■ *TF:* 800-678-1208 ■ *Web:* www.americanbaby.com
American Profile Magazine
341 Cool Springs Blvd Suite 400 .... Franklin TN 37067 615-468-6000 468-6100
TF: 800-720-6323 ■ *Web:* www.americanprofile.com
Asimov's Science Fiction Magazine
475 Pk Ave S 11th Fl .... New York NY 10016 212-686-7188 686-7414
Web: www.asimovs.com
Atlantic Monthly Magazine
600 New Hampshire Ave NW .... Washington DC 20037 202-266-7231 266-6332
TF Cust Svc: 800-234-2411 ■ *Web:* www.theatlantic.com
Avenue Magazine 79 Madison Ave 16th Fl .... New York NY 10016 212-268-8600 268-0503
Web: www.avenuemagazine.com
BabyTalk Magazine 135 W 50th St .... New York NY 10020 212-522-1212 522-3611*
**Fax:* Sales ■ *TF:* 800-234-0847 ■
Web: www.parenting.com/parenting/babytalk/index.html

	City	State	ZIP	Phone	Fax
Better Homes & Gardens Magazine 1716 Locust St	Des Moines	IA	50309	515-284-3000	284-3763
TF: 800-374-4244 ■ Web: www.bhg.com					
Better Investing Magazine PO Box 220	Royal Oak	MI	48068	248-583-6242	583-4880
TF: 877-275-6242 ■ Web: www.betterinvesting.org					
Black Collegian Magazine 140 Carondelet St	New Orleans	LA	70130	504-523-0154	523-0271
Web: www.black-collegian.com					
Black Enterprise Magazine 130 5th Ave	New York	NY	10011	212-242-8000	886-9610
TF Cust Svc: 800-727-7777 ■ Web: www.blackenterprise.com					
Bon Appetit Magazine 4 Times Sq	New York	NY	10036	212-286-2860	630-5883
TF: 800-765-9419 ■ Web: www.epicurious.com/bonappetit					
Booklist Magazine PO Box 607	Mount Morris	IL	61054	888-350-0949	
TF: 888-350-0949 ■ Web: www.ala.org/ala/booklist/booklist.htm					
Brain Child Magazine 101 Henry St # A	Lexington	VA	24450	540-463-4817	441-4827*
*Fax Area Code: 928 ■ TF: 888-304-6667 ■ Web: www.brainchildmag.com					
Bridal Guide Magazine 330 7th Ave 10th Fl	New York	NY	10001	212-838-7733	308-7165
TF: 800-472-7744 ■ Web: www.bridalguide.com					
Bride's Magazine 750 3rd Ave 4th Fl	New York	NY	10017	212-630-5883	630-5889
TF: 800-777-5786 ■ Web: www.brides.com					
BusinessWeek Magazine 1221 Avenue of the Americas	New York	NY	10020	212-512-2511	
TF Cust Svc: 800-635-1200 ■ Web: www.businessweek.com					
Campus Life Magazine 465 Gundersen Dr	Carol Stream	IL	60188	630-260-6200	260-0114
TF Cust Svc: 800-678-6083 ■ Web: www.christianitytoday.com/teens					
Canadian Living Magazine 25 Sheppard Ave W Suite 100	Toronto	ON	M2N6S7	416-733-7600	733-3398
TF: 800-387-6332 ■ Web: www.canadianliving.com					
Chetelaine Magazine 1 Mt Pleasant Rd 8th Fl	Toronto	ON	M4Y2Y5	416-764-1888	764-2891
TF: 800-268-9119 ■ Web: www.chatelaine.com					
Chocolatier Magazine 45 W 34th St Suite 600	New York	NY	10001	212-239-0855	967-4184
Web: www.bakingshop.com/magazine/chocolatier.htm					
College Outlook & Career Opportunities Magazine 20 E Gregory Blvd	Kansas City	MO	64114	816-361-0616	361-6164
TF: 800-274-8867 ■ Web: www.collegeoutlook.net					
Consumer Reports Magazine 101 Truman Ave	Yonkers	NY	10703	914-378-2000	
TF Orders: 800-288-7898 ■ Web: www.consumerreports.org					
Consumers Digest 520 Lake Cook Rd Suite 500	Deerfield	IL	60015	847-607-3000	607-3009
Web: www.consumersdigest.com					
Cook's Illustrated Magazine 17 St Stn	Brookline	MA	02445	617-232-1000	
TF Circ: 800-526-8442 ■ Web: www.cooksillustrated.com					
Cosmopolitan Magazine 300 W 57th St	New York	NY	10019	212-649-2000	
TF: 800-888-2676 ■ Web: www.cosmomag.com					
Country Home Magazine 1716 Locust St	Des Moines	IA	50309	515-284-3000	284-2552
TF Cust Svc: 800-374-9431 ■ Web: www.countryhome.com					
Country Living Magazine 300 W 57th St	New York	NY	10019	212-649-2000	649-2000
TF: 800-888-0128 ■ Web: www.countryliving.com					
Country Magazine 5400 S 60th St	Greendale	WI	53129	414-423-0100	423-1143
TF: 800-344-6913 ■ Web: www.country-magazine.com					
Coup de Pouce Magazine 2001 Ave University Suite 900	Montreal	QC	H3A2A6	514-499-0561	499-1844
TF: 800-528-3836 ■ Web: www.coupdepouce.com					
Cuisine Magazine 2200 Grand Ave	Des Moines	IA	50312	800-311-3995	283-2003*
*Fax Area Code: 515 ■ TF: 800-311-3995 ■ Web: www.cuisineathome.com					
Delicious Living Magazine 1401 Pearl St Suite 200	Boulder	CO	80302	303-939-8440	998-9020
TF: 800-431-1255 ■ Web: www.deliciouslivingmag.com					
Details Magazine 4 Times Sq 23rd Fl	New York	NY	10036	212-381-7057	381-7233
Web: www.details.com					
Ebony Magazine 820 S Michigan Ave	Chicago	IL	60605	312-322-9200	
TF: 800-999-5954 ■ Web: www.ebony.com					
Elegant Bride Magazine 750 3rd Ave 4th Fl	New York	NY	10017	212-630-4000	630-5890
TF: 888-797-9893 ■ Web: www.brides.com					
Elle Decor Magazine 1633 Broadway 41st Fl	New York	NY	10019	212-767-6000	489-4216
TF: 800-274-4687 ■ Web: www.elledecor.com					
Elle Magazine 1633 Broadway 44th Fl	New York	NY	10019	212-767-5800	489-4216
TF: 800-876-8775 ■ Web: www.elle.com					
Ellery Queen Mystery Magazine 475 Pk Ave S 11th Fl	New York	NY	10016	212-686-7188	686-7414
Web: www.themysteryplace.com/eqmm/index.shtml					
Entrepreneur Magazine 2445 McCabe Way Suite 400	Irvine	CA	92614	949-261-2325	261-7729
TF: 800-274-6229 ■ Web: www.entrepreneur.com					
Esquire Magazine 300 W 57th St 21st Fl	New York	NY	10019	212-649-2000	649-2000
TF: 800-888-5400 ■ Web: www.esquire.com					
Essence Magazine 135 W 50th St 4th Fl	New York	NY	10020	800-274-9398	274-9398
TF: 800-274-9398 ■ Web: www.essence.com					
Family Circle Magazine 375 Lexington Ave 9th Fl	New York	NY	10017	212-499-2000	499-1987
TF: 800-627-4444 ■ Web: www.familycircle.com					
First For Women Magazine 270 Sylvan Ave	Englewood Cliffs	NJ	07632	201-569-6699	510-3297
TF: 800-938-8312 ■ Web: www.bauerpublishing.com					
Food & Wine Magazine 1120 Avenue of the Americas	New York	NY	10036	813-979-6625	
TF: 800-333-6569 ■ Web: www.foodandwine.com					
For the Bride Magazine 222 W 37th St	New York	NY	10018	212-967-0751	473-0927*
*Fax Area Code: 646 ■ Web: www.demetriosbride.com					
Franchise Handbook 1020 N Broadway Suite 111	Milwaukee	WI	53202	414-272-9977	272-9973
TF: 800-272-0246 ■ Web: www.franchise1.com					
Futurist Magazine 7910 Woodmont Ave Suite 450	Bethesda	MD	20814	301-656-8274	951-0394
TF: 800-989-8274 ■ Web: www.wfs.org					
Globe Magazine 1000 American Media Way	Boca Raton	FL	33464	561-997-7733	989-1275
TF: 800-749-7733					
Good Housekeeping Magazine 300 W 57 St	New York	NY	10019	212-649-2000	
TF: 800-888-7788 ■ Web: www.goodhousekeeping.com					
Gourmet Magazine 4 Times Sq	New York	NY	10036	212-286-2860	286-2672
TF: 800-365-2454 ■ Web: www.epicurious.com/gourmet					
GQ: Gentlemen's Quarterly Magazine 4 Times Sq	New York	NY	10036	212-286-2860	286-2860
TF: 800-289-9330 ■ Web: www.gq.com					
Harper's Bazaar Magazine 300 W 57th St	New York	NY	10019	212-903-5000	262-7101*
*Fax: Edit ■ TF: 800-888-3045 ■ Web: www.harpersbazaar.com					
Harper's Magazine 666 Broadway 11th Fl	New York	NY	10012	212-420-5720	228-5889
TF: 800-444-4653 ■ Web: www.harpers.org					
Hispanic Business Magazine 425 Pine Ave	Santa Barbara	CA	93117	805-964-4554	964-6139
TF Sales: 888-447-7287 ■ Web: www.hispanicbusiness.com					
House Beautiful Magazine 300 W 57th St 24th Fl	New York	NY	10019	212-221-9595	
TF: 800-444-6873 ■ Web: www.housebeautiful.com					
In Touch Weekly Magazine 270 Sylvan Ave	Englewood Cliffs	NJ	07632	201-569-6699	569-2510
TF: 800-938-8312 ■ Web: www.intouchweekly.com					
InStyle Magazine Rockefeller Ctr Time & Life Bldg	New York	NY	10020	212-522-1212	522-0325
TF: 800-274-6200 ■ Web: www.instyle.com					
Interview Magazine 575 Broadway 5th Fl	New York	NY	10012	212-941-2900	941-2819
TF: 800-925-9574 ■ Web: www.interviewmagazine.com					
Ladies' Home Journal 125 Pk Ave 20th Fl	New York	NY	10017	212-557-6600	455-1010
TF: 800-374-4545 ■ Web: www.lhj.com					
Latina Media Ventures LLC 625 Madison Ave 3rd Fl	New York	NY	10022	212-642-0200	575-3088
Web: www.latina.com					
Lucky Magazine 4 Times Sq	New York	NY	10036	212-286-2860	286-3816
TF: 800-223-0780 ■ Web: www.luckymag.com					
Mad Magazine 1700 Broadway	New York	NY	10019	212-506-4850	506-4848
TF: 800-462-3624 ■ Web: www.dccomics.com					
Marie Claire Magazine 300 W 57th St 34th Fl	New York	NY	10019	212-841-8400	280-1089*
*Fax Area Code: 646 ■ TF: 800-777-3287 ■ Web: www.marieclaire.com					
Martha Stewart Living Magazine 11 W 42nd St 25th Fl	New York	NY	10036	212-827-8000	827-8149
TF: 800-999-6518 ■ Web: www.marthastewart.com					
Maxim Magazine 1040 Avenue of the Americas	New York	NY	10018	212-302-2626	302-2635
TF: 800-829-5572 ■ Web: www.maximonline.com					
Men's Journal LLC 1290 Avenue of the Americas 2nd Fl	New York	NY	10104	212-484-1616	484-3435
TF: 800-677-6367 ■ Web: www.mensjournal.com					
Modern Bride Magazine 750 3rd Ave 4th Fl	New York	NY	10017	212-630-5883	630-5889
TF Cust Svc: 800-777-5786 ■ Web: www.brides.com					
Money Magazine Rockefeller Ctr Time & Life Bldg	New York	NY	10020	212-522-1212	522-0189
TF: 800-633-9970 ■ Web: money.cnn.com/magazines/moneymag					
More Magazine 1716 Locust St	DesMoines	IA	50309	515-284-3000	284-2083
TF: 888-699-4036 ■ Web: www.more.com					
Ms Magazine 1600 Wilson Blvd Suite 801	Arlington	VA	22209	703-522-4201	522-2219
TF: 866-672-6363 ■ Web: www.msmagazine.com					
National Geographic Adventure Magazine 1145 17th St NW	Washington	DC	20036	202-857-7000	775-6141
TF: 800-647-5463 ■ Web: www.nationalgeographic.com/adventure					
National Geographic Magazine 1145 17th St NW	Washington	DC	20036	202-857-7000	775-6141
TF: 800-647-5463 ■ Web: www.ngm.nationalgeographic.com/archives					
New York Review of Books 435 Hudson St 3rd Fl	New York	NY	10014	212-757-8070	333-5374
TF: 800-354-0050 ■ Web: www.nybooks.com					
New Yorker Magazine 4 Times Sq	New York	NY	10036	212-286-5400	286-5735*
*Fax: Edit ■ TF: 800-825-2510 ■ Web: www.newyorker.com					
Nylon Magazine 110 Greene St Suite 607	New York	NY	10012	212-226-6454	226-7738
TF: 866-639-8133 ■ Web: www.nylonmag.com					
O the Oprah Magazine 5700 Wilshire Blvd Suite 120	Los Angeles	CA	90036	323-602-5500	
TF: 888-446-4438 ■ Web: www.oprah.com/omagazine					
Parade Magazine 711 3rd Ave	New York	NY	10017	212-450-7000	450-7284
Web: www.parade.com					
Parents Magazine 1716 Locust St	DesMoines	IA	50309	515-284-3000	284-2083
TF: 800-727-3682 ■ Web: www.parents.com					
Penthouse Magazine 2 Penn Plaza 11th Fl	New York	NY	10121	212-702-6000	702-6262
TF: 800-289-7368 ■ Web: www.penthouse.com					
People Magazine Rockefeller Ctr Time & Life Bldg	New York	NY	10020	212-522-1212	522-0331
TF: 800-541-9000 ■ Web: www.people.com/people					
Playboy Magazine 680 N Lake Shore Dr	Chicago	IL	60611	312-751-8000	751-2818
TF: 800-999-4438 ■ Web: www.playboy.com					
Playgirl Magazine 801 2nd Ave 9th Fl	New York	NY	10017	212-661-7878	697-6343
TF: 800-877-6139 ■ Web: www.playgirl.com					
Psychology Today Magazine 115 E 23 St 9th Fl	New York	NY	10010	212-260-7210	260-7445*
*Fax: Edit ■ TF: 800-234-8361 ■ Web: www.psychologytoday.com					
Publishers Weekly Magazine 360 Pk Ave S	New York	NY	10010	646-746-6758	746-6631
TF: 800-278-2991 ■ Web: www.publishersweekly.com					
Reader's Digest Magazine Reader's Digest Rd	Pleasantville	NY	10570	914-238-1000	244-7620
TF Cust Svc: 800-234-9000 ■ Web: www.rd.com					
Real Simple Magazine Rockefeller Ctr Time & Life Bldg	New York	NY	10020	212-522-1212	522-0601
Web: www.realsimple.com					
Reminisce Magazine 5400 S 60th St	Greendale	WI	53129	414-423-0100	423-8463
TF: 800-344-6913 ■ Web: www.reminisce.com					
Saturday Evening Post The 1100 Waterway Blvd	Indianapolis	IN	46202	317-634-1100	637-0126
TF: 800-829-5576 ■ Web: www.saturdayeveningpost.com					
Saveur Magazine 15 E 32nd St 12th Fl	New York	NY	10016	212-219-7400	
Web: www.saveur.com					
Self Magazine 4 Times Sq	New York	NY	10036	212-286-2860	630-5883
TF: 800-274-6111 ■ Web: www.self.com					
Simple & Delicious 5400 S 60th St	Greendale	WI	53129	414-423-0100	423-1143
TF: 800-344-6913 ■ Web: www.tasteofhome.com					
SmartMoney Magazine 1755 Broadway 2nd Fl	New York	NY	10019	212-649-2000	
TF: 800-444-4204 ■ Web: www.smartmoney.com					
Smithsonian Magazine 750 9th St NW Suite 7100	Washington	DC	20001	202-633-6090	275-1972
TF: 800-766-2149 ■ Web: www.smithsonianmag.si.edu					

				Phone	Fax
Sun Magazine 1000 American Media Way *TF:* 800-749-7733	Boca Raton	FL	33464	561-997-7733	998-0798
Sunset Magazine 80 Willow Rd *TF:* 800-777-0117 ■ *Web:* www.sunset.com/sunset	Menlo Park	CA	94025	650-321-3600	327-7537
Surface Magazine 360 Pk Ave S 17th Fl *Web:* www.surfacemag.com	New York	NY	10010	646-805-0254	
Taste of Home Magazine 5400 S 60th St *TF:* 800-344-6913 ■ *Web:* www.tasteofhome.com	Greendale	WI	53129	414-423-0100	423-8463
Television Week Magazine 6500 Wilshire Blvd Suite 2300 **Fax:* Edit ■ *Web:* www.tvweek.com	Los Angeles	CA	90048	323-370-2400	653-4425*
This Old House Magazine 135 W 50th St 10th Fl *Web:* www.thisoldhouse.com/toh/magazines	New York	NY	10020	212-522-9465	522-9435
Town & Country Magazine 300 W 57th St **Fax:* Edit ■ *TF:* 800-289-8696 ■ *Web:* www.townandcountrymag.com	New York	NY	10019	212-649-2047	262-7107*
Traditional Home Magazine 1716 Locust St **Fax:* Edit ■ *TF Circ:* 800-374-8791 ■ *Web:* www.traditionalhome.com	Des Moines	IA	50309	515-284-3000	284-2083*
True Confessions Magazine 200 Madison Ave Suite 200 *TF:* 800-666-8783	New York	NY	10016	212-725-8811	
True Romance Magazine 200 Madison Ave Suite 2000 *TF:* 800-666-8783	New York	NY	10016	212-725-8811	979-4825
Upscale Magazine 2141 Powers Ferry Rd Suite 300 *Web:* www.upscalemagazine.com	Marietta	GA	30067	770-988-0015	
Us Weekly Magazine 1290 Avenue of the Americas *TF Cust Svc:* 800-283-3956 ■ *Web:* www.usmagazine.com	New York	NY	10104	212-484-1616	651-7890
USA Weekend Magazine 535 Madison Ave 21st Fl *TF Edit:* 800-487-2956 ■ *Web:* www.usaweekend.com	New York	NY	10022	212-715-2100	935-5576
Utne Reader Magazine 12 N 12th St Suite 400 *TF Cust Svc:* 800-736-8863 ■ *Web:* www.utne.com	Minneapolis	MN	55403	612-338-5040	338-6043
Vanity Fair Magazine 4 Times Sq **Fax:* Edit ■ *TF:* 800-690-6115 ■ *Web:* www.vanityfair.com	New York	NY	10036	212-286-2860	286-6707*
Vogue Magazine 4 Times Sq **Fax:* Edit ■ *TF:* 800-690-6115 ■ *Web:* www.style.com/vogue	New York	NY	10036	212-286-2860	286-8169*
W Magazine 750 3rd Ave 7th Fl *TF:* 800-289-0390 ■ *Web:* www.wmagazine.com	New York	NY	10017	212-630-4000	630-4919
Western Living Magazine 2608 Granville St Suite 560 *TF:* 800-363-3272 ■ *Web:* www.westernlivingmagazine.com	Vancouver	BC	V6H3V3	604-877-7732	877-4848
Wilson Quarterly Magazine 1300 Pennsylvania Ave NW 1 Woodrow Wilson Plaza *TF Orders:* 800-829-5108 ■ *Web:* www.wilsoncenter.org	Washington	DC	20004	202-691-4000	691-4036
Woman's Day Magazine 1633 Broadway 43rd Fl *TF:* 800-234-2960 ■ *Web:* www.womansday.com	New York	NY	10019	212-767-6000	767-5610
Woman's World Magazine 270 Sylvan Ave *TF:* 800-216-6981 ■ *Web:* www.bauerpublishing.com	Englewood Cliffs	NJ	07632	201-569-0006	510-3297
Women's Wear Daily Magazine 750 3rd Ave 5th Fl *TF:* 800-289-0273 ■ *Web:* www.wwd.com	New York	NY	10017	212-630-4600	630-4580
Working Mother Magazine 60 E 42nd St 27th Fl *TF:* 800-627-0690 ■ *Web:* www.workingmother.com	New York	NY	10165	212-351-6400	351-6487
Worth Magazine 58 W 40th St *TF:* 800-777-1851 ■ *Web:* www.worth.com	New York	NY	10018	212-665-6100	

460-12 Government & Military Magazines

				Phone	Fax
Air Force Magazine 1501 Lee Hwy *TF:* 800-727-3337 ■ *Web:* www.afa.org/magazine/aboutmag.asp	Arlington	VA	22209	703-247-5800	247-5853
Air Force Times Magazine 6883 Commercial Dr *TF:* 800-368-5718 ■ *Web:* www.airforcetimes.com	Springfield	VA	22159	703-750-7400	750-8601
Airman Magazine 203 Norton St *Web:* www.af.mil/news/airman/indxflas.html	San Antonio	TX	78226	210-925-7757	925-7219
ARMY Magazine 2425 Wilson Blvd *TF:* 800-336-4570 ■ *Web:* www.ausa.org	Arlington	VA	22201	703-841-4300	525-9039
FRA Today 125 N W St *TF:* 800-372-1924 ■ *Web:* www.fra.org	Alexandria	VA	22314	703-683-1400	549-6610
Governing Magazine 1100 Connecticut Ave NW Suite 1300 *TF:* 800-944-0922 ■ *Web:* www.governing.com	Washington	DC	20036	202-862-8802	862-0032
Government Executive Magazine 600 New Hampshire Ave NW Suite 400 *TF:* 800-207-8001 ■ *Web:* www.govexec.com	Washington	DC	20037	202-266-7000	266-7350
Government Product News Magazine 249 W 17th St *Web:* subscribe.penton.com/gpn	New York	NY	10011	216-696-7000	696-1752
Military & Aerospace Electronics Magazine 98 Spit Brook Rd *TF:* 800-225-0556 ■ *Web:* www.militaryaerospace.com	Nashua	NH	03062	603-891-9137	891-0574
Military Engineer Magazine 607 Prince St *TF Cust Svc:* 800-336-3097 ■ *Web:* www.fame.org	Alexandria	VA	22314	703-549-3800	548-6153
Military Officer Magazine 201 N Washington St *TF:* 800-234-6622 ■ *Web:* www.moaa.org/Magazine	Alexandria	VA	22314	703-549-2311	838-8179
Navy Times Magazine 6883 Commercial Dr *TF Cust Svc:* 800-368-5718 ■ *Web:* www.navytimes.com	Springfield	VA	22159	703-750-7400	750-8767
Public Employee Magazine 1625 L St NW *Web:* www.afscme.org	Washington	DC	20036	202-429-1130	429-1120
Soldier of Fortune Magazine 2135 11th St *TF:* 800-999-9718 ■ *Web:* www.sofmag.com	Boulder	CO	80302	303-449-3750	444-5617

460-13 Health & Fitness Magazines

				Phone	Fax
American Fitness Magazine 15250 Ventura Blvd Suite 200 *TF:* 800-446-2322 ■ *Web:* www.afaa.com	Sherman Oaks	CA	91403	818-905-0040	990-1139
Arthritis Today Magazine 1330 W Peachtree St Suite 100 *TF:* 800-283-7800 ■ *Web:* www.arthritis.org/resources/arthritistoday	Atlanta	GA	30309	404-872-7100	965-7575
Cooking Light Magazine 2100 Lakeshore Dr *TF:* 800-366-4712 ■ *Web:* www.cookinglight.com	Birmingham	AL	35209	205-445-6000	445-6600
Diabetes Forecast Magazine 1701 N Beauregard St *TF:* 800-676-4065 ■ *Web:* www.diabetes.org	Alexandria	VA	22311	703-549-1500	549-6995
Fitness Magazine 375 Lexington Ave *TF:* 800-888-1181 ■ *Web:* www.fitnessmagazine.com	New York	NY	10012	212-499-2000	499-1697
Fitness Rx for Men Magazine 690 Rt 25A Suite 8 PO Box 834 *Web:* www.fitnessrxformen.com	Setauket	NY	11733	631-751-9696	751-9699
Fitness Rx for Women Magazine 690 Rt 25A Suite 8	Setauket	NY	11733	631-751-9696	
FitPregnancy Magazine 21100 Erwin St *Web:* www.fitpregnancy.com	Woodland Hills	CA	91367	818-884-6800	992-6895
Flex Magazine 21100 Erwin St *TF:* 800-423-5590 ■ *Web:* www.flexonline.com	Woodland Hills	CA	91367	818-884-6800	884-6733
Health & You Magazine 780 Township Line Rd	Yardley	PA	19067	267-685-2800	685-2995
Heart & Soul Magazine 2514 Maryland Ave **Fax Area Code:* 410 ■ *TF:* 800-834-8813 ■ *Web:* www.heartandsoul.com	Baltimore	MD	21218	800-834-8813	576-8298*
Ironman Magazine 1701 Ives Ave *TF:* 800-447-0008 ■ *Web:* www.ironmanmagazine.com	Oxnard	CA	93033	805-385-3500	385-3515
Men's Fitness Magazine 1 Pk Ave 3rd Fl *Web:* www.mensfitness.com	New York	NY	10016	212-545-4800	
Men's Health Magazine 400 S 10th St *TF:* 800-666-2303 ■ *Web:* www.menshealth.com	Emmaus	PA	18098	610-967-5171	967-7725
Ms Fitness Magazine PO Box 2490 *Web:* www.msfitness.com	White City	OR	97503	541-830-0400	830-0410
Muscle & Fitness Hers Magazine 21100 Erwin St *Web:* www.muscleandfitnesshers.com	Woodland Hills	CA	91367	818-884-6800	226-0148
Muscle & Fitness Magazine 21100 Erwin St *TF Orders:* 800-423-5590 ■ *Web:* www.muscleandfitness.com	Woodland Hills	CA	91367	818-884-6800	595-0463
Natural Health Magazine 1 Pk Ave 3rd Fl *Web:* www.naturalhealthmag.com	New York	NY	10016	212-545-4800	
Prevention Magazine 400 S 10th St *TF:* 800-813-8070 ■ *Web:* www.prev.com	Emmaus	PA	18098	610-967-5171	967-7654
Runner's World Magazine 400 S 10th St *TF Cust Svc:* 800-666-2828 ■ *Web:* www.runnersworld.com	Emmaus	PA	18098	610-967-5171	967-7948
Shape Magazine 4 New York Pl *Web:* www.shape.com	New York	NY	10004	212-545-4800	679-2091
Vegetarian Times 300 N Continental Blvd Suite 650 *TF:* 800-423-4880 ■ *Web:* www.vegetariantimes.com	El Segundo	CA	90245	310-356-4100	356-4110
Vibrant Life Magazine 55 W Oak Ridge Dr *Web:* www.vibrantlife.com	Hagerstown	MD	21740	301-393-3000	393-4055
Vim & Vigor Magazine 1010 E Missouri Ave *TF:* 800-282-5850 ■ *Web:* www.mcmurry.com	Phoenix	AZ	85014	602-395-5850	395-5853
Yoga Journal Magazine 475 Sansome St Suite 850 *Web:* www.yogajournal.com	San Francisco	CA	94111	415-591-0555	591-0733

460-14 Hobby & Personal Interests Magazines

				Phone	Fax
Air Classics Magazine 9509 Vassar Ave Suite A *TF Cust Svc:* 800-562-9182	Chatsworth	CA	91311	818-700-6868	700-6282
American History Illustrated Magazine 19300 Promenade Dr *TF:* 800-829-3340 ■ *Web:* www.historynet.com/ah	Leesburg	VA	20176	703-771-9400	779-8345
American Photo Magazine 1633 Broadway 43rd Fl *TF:* 800-274-4514 ■ *Web:* www.popphoto.com	New York	NY	10019	212-767-6000	333-2439
American Square Dance Magazine 34 E Main St *TF:* 888-588-2362 ■ *Web:* www.americansquaredance.com	Apopka	FL	32703	407-886-7151	886-8464
Antique Trader 700 E State St *TF:* 800-258-0929 ■ *Web:* www.antiquetrader.com	Iola	WI	54990	715-445-2214	445-4087
Antiques Magazine 575 Broadway 5th Fl *TF Cust Svc:* 800-925-9271 ■ *Web:* www.themagazineantiques.com	New York	NY	10012	212-941-2800	941-2897
AOPA Pilot Magazine 421 Aviation Way *TF:* 800-872-2672 ■ *Web:* www.aopa.org	Frederick	MD	21701	301-695-2000	695-2375
Aquarium Fish Magazine 3 Burroughs *Web:* www.fishchannel.com	Irvine	CA	92618	949-855-8822	855-3045
Arabian Horse World Magazine 1316 Tamson Dr Suite 101 *TF:* 800-955-9423	Cambria	CA	94328	805-771-2300	927-6522
Astronomy Magazine 21027 Crossroads Cir **Fax:* Cust Svc ■ *TF Cust Svc:* 800-553-6644 ■ *Web:* www.astronomy.com/content/static/magazine	Waukesha	WI	53186	262-796-8776	796-1615*
Backpacker Magazine 2520 55th St Suite 210 *Web:* www.backpacker.com	Boulder	CO	80301	303-625-1600	413-1602
Bead & Button Magazine 21027 Crossroads Cir **Fax:* Cust Svc ■ *TF Cust Svc:* 800-533-6644 ■ *Web:* www.beadandbutton.com	Waukesha	WI	53186	262-796-8776	796-1615*
BeadStyle Magazine 21027 Crossroads Cir **Fax:* Cust Svc ■ *TF Cust Svc:* 800-533-6644 ■ *Web:* www.beadstylemag.com	Waukesha	WI	53186	262-796-8776	796-1615*
Beadwork Magazine PO Box 469105 *TF Cust Svc:* 800-849-8753 ■ *Web:* www.interweave.com/bead/default.asp	Escondido	CO	92046	760-291-1531	291-1567

Phone | Fax

Better Homes & Gardens WOOD Magazine
1716 Locust St Des Moines IA 50309 515-284-3000 284-2115*
*Fax: Edit ■ TF: 800-374-9663 ■ Web: www.woodmagazine.com

Bicycling Magazine 400 S Tenth St Emmaus PA 18098 800-666-2806
TF: 800-666-2806 ■ Web: www.bicycling.com

Bike Magazine
236 Avenida Fabricante Suite 201 San Clemente CA 92672 949-325-6200 325-6196
TF: 800-765-5501 ■ Web: www.bikemag.com

Bird Talk Magazine 3 Burroughs Irvine CA 92618 949-855-8822 855-3045
TF Cust Svc: 800-546-7730 ■ Web: www.animalnetwork.com/birdtalk

Birds & Blooms Magazine 5400 S 60th St Greendale WI 53129 414-423-0100 423-8463*
*Fax: Edit ■ TF: 800-344-6913 ■ Web: www.birdsandblooms.com

BirdWatching Magazine
21027 Crossroads Cir PO Box 1612 Waukesha WI 53186 262-796-8776 796-1615
TF: 800-533-6644 ■ Web: www.birdwatchingdaily.com

Blood-Horse Magazine PO Box 911088 Lexington KY 40591 859-278-2361 276-4450
TF: 800-866-2361 ■ Web: www.bloodhorse.com

British Heritage Magazine 19300 Promenade Dr Leesburg VA 20176 703-771-9400 779-8345
TF: 800-829-3340 ■ Web: www.historynet.com/bh

Camcorder & ComputerVideo Magazine
290 Maple Ct Suite 232 Ventura CA 93003 805-644-3824 644-3875
Web: www.candcv.com

Cat Fancy Magazine 3 Burroughs Irvine CA 92618 949-855-8822 855-3045
TF Cust Svc: 800-546-7730 ■ Web: www.catchannel.com

Ceramics Monthly
600 N Cleveland Ave Suite 210 Westerville OH 43082 614-794-5867 891-8960
TF: 800-342-3594 ■ Web: www.ceramicartsdaily.org

Chess Life Magazine PO Box 3967 Crossville TN 38557 931-787-1234 787-1200
TF Sales: 800-903-8723 ■ Web: www.uschess.org

Classic Trains Magazine
21027 Crossroads Cir PO Box 1612 Waukesha WI 53186 262-796-8776 796-1615
TF: 800-533-6644 ■ Web: ctr.trains.com

Coin Prices Magazine 700 E State St Iola WI 54990 715-445-2214 445-4087
TF: 800-258-0929 ■ Web: www.krausebooks.com

Coin World Magazine 911 S Vandemark Rd Sidney OH 45365 937-498-0800 498-0812
TF: 866-222-3621 ■ Web: www.coinworld.com

COINage Magazine 290 Maple Ct Suite 232 Ventura CA 93003 805-644-3824 644-3875
Web: coinagemag.com

Country Sampler Magazine 707 Kautz Rd Saint Charles IL 60174 630-377-8000 377-8194
Web: www.sampler.com

Country Woman Magazine 5400 S 60th St Greendale WI 53129 414-423-0100 423-8463*
*Fax: Edit ■ TF: 800-344-6913 ■ Web: www.countrywomanmagazine.com

Crafts 'n Things Magazine PO Box 926 Sidney OH 45365 866-222-3621 498-0876*
*Fax Area Code: 937 ■ TF: 800-444-0441 ■ Web: www.craftsnthings.com

Creating Keepsakes Magazine
14850 Pony Express Rd Bluffdale UT 84065 801-816-8300 816-8301
TF: 888-247-5282 ■ Web: www.creatingkeepsakes.com

Crochet World Magazine 306 E Parr Rd Berne IN 46711 260-589-4000 589-8093
Web: www.crochet-world.com

Daily Racing Form 100 Broadway 7th Fl New York NY 10005 212-366-7600 366-7738
TF Cust Svc: 800-306-3676 ■ Web: www.drf.com

Digital Photographer Magazine
12121 Wilshire Blvd 12th Fl Los Angeles CA 90025 310-820-1500 826-5008
TF: 800-537-4619 ■ Web: www.dpmag.com

Dog Fancy Magazine 3 Burroughs Irvine CA 92618 949-855-8822 855-3045
TF Cust Svc: 800-546-7730 ■ Web: www.dogchannel.com

Dog World Magazine 3 Burroughs Irvine CA 92618 949-855-8822 855-3045
TF: 800-546-7730 ■ Web: www.dogchannel.com

Dollhouse Miniatures Magazine 68132 250th Ave Casson MN 55944 507-634-3143 634-7691
TF Cust Svc: 866-606-6587 ■ Web: www.hobbyworld.tv

Equus Magazine
656 Quince Orchard Rd Suite 600 Gaithersburg MD 20878 301-977-3900 990-9015
TF Cust Svc: 800-829-5910 ■ Web: www.equisearch.com/magazines/Equus

Family Handyman Magazine
2915 Commers Dr Suite 700 Eagan MN 55121 651-454-9200 994-2250
TF: 800-285-4961 ■ Web: www.rd.com/familyhandyman

Family Tree Magazine 4700 E Galbraith Rd Cincinnati OH 45236 513-531-2690 891-7153
TF: 800-289-0963 ■ Web: www.familytreemagazine.com

Fine Cooking Magazine
63 S Main St PO Box 5506 Newtown CT 06470 203-426-8171 426-3434
TF: 800-283-7252 ■ Web: www.taunton.com/finecooking

Fine Woodworking Magazine
63 S Main St PO Box 5506 Newtown CT 06470 203-426-8171 270-6753
TF: 800-283-7252 ■ Web: www.taunton.com/finewoodworking

FineScale Modeler Magazine
21027 Crossroads Cir PO Box 1612 Waukesha WI 53187 262-796-8776 796-1615*
*Fax: Cust Svc ■ TF Cust Svc: 800-533-6644 ■ Web: www.finescale.com/fsm

Flying Magazine 1633 Broadway 43rd Fl New York NY 10019 212-767-6000 767-5600
TF Cust Svc: 800-274-6793 ■ Web: www.flyingmag.com

Garden Railways Magazine
21027 Crossroads Cir PO Box 1612 Waukesha WI 53186 262-796-8776 796-1615
TF: 800-533-6644 ■ Web: trc.trains.com

General Aviation News 7504 86th St SW # 150 Lakewood WA 98498 253-471-9888 471-9911
TF: 800-426-8538 ■ Web: www.generalaviationnews.com

Growing Edge Magazine PO Box 1027 Corvallis OR 97339 541-757-8477 757-0028
TF: 800-888-6785 ■ Web: www.growingedge.com/magazine

Horse Illustrated Magazine 3 Burroughs Irvine CA 92618 949-855-8822 855-3045
TF: 800-546-7730 ■ Web: www.horsechannel.com

Horticulture Magazine 4700 E Galbraith Rd Cincinnati OH 45236 513-531-2690 891-7153
Web: www.hortmag.com

McCall Patterns Magazine 120 Broadway New York NY 10271 212-465-6800
Web: www.mccall.com

McCall's Quilting Magazine
741 Corporate Cir Suite A Golden CO 80401 800-944-0736 277-0370*
*Fax Area Code: 303 ■ TF: 800-944-0736 ■ Web: www.mccallsquilting.com

Memory Makers Magazine
4700 E Galbraith Rd Cincinnati OH 45236 513-531-2690 891-7196
TF: 800-289-0963 ■ Web: www.memorymakersmagazine.com

Model Airplane News 20 Westport Rd Wilton CT 06897 203-431-9000 761-8744
TF: 800-877-5160 ■ Web: www.modelairplanenews.com

Model Railroader Magazine
21027 Crossroads Cir Waukesha WI 53186 262-796-8776 796-1615*
*Fax: Cust Svc ■ TF Cust Svc: 800-533-6644

Mountain Bike Magazine 400 S Tenth St Emmaus PA 18098 800-666-2806
TF: 800-666-2806 ■ Web: www.mountainbike.com

Nuts & Volts Magazine 430 Princeland Ct Corona CA 92879 951-371-8497 371-3052
TF Orders: 800-783-4624 ■ Web: www.nutsvolts.com

Organic Gardening Magazine 400 S 10th St Emmaus PA 18098 610-967-5171 967-7722
TF Circ: 800-666-2206 ■ Web: www.organicgardening.com

Outdoor Life Magazine 2 Pk Ave New York NY 10016 212-779-5004 779-5468
TF: 800-227-2224 ■ Web: www.outdoorlife.com

Outdoor Photographer Magazine
12121 Wilshire Blvd 12th Fl Los Angeles CA 90025 310-820-1500 826-5008
TF Cust Svc: 800-283-4410 ■ Web: www.outdoorphotographer.com

Outside Magazine 400 Market St Santa Fe NM 87501 505-989-7100 989-4700
TF: 800-688-7433 ■ Web: www.outsideonline.com

Paper Crafts Magazine
14850 Pony Express Rd Bluffdale UT 84065 801-816-8300 816-8301
TF: 800-727-2387 ■ Web: www.papercraftsmag.com

PC Gamer Magazine
4000 Shoreline Ct Suite 400 South San Francisco CA 94080 650-872-1642 872-2207
TF: 800-898-7159 ■ Web: www.pcgamer.com

Plane & Pilot Magazine
12121 Wilshire Blvd 12th Fl Los Angeles CA 90025 310-820-1500 826-5008
TF: 800-283-4330 ■ Web: www.planeandpilotmag.com

Popular Mechanics Magazine 300 W 57th St New York NY 10019 212-649-2000 280-1081*
*Fax Area Code: 646 ■ TF: 800-333-4948 ■ Web: www.popularmechanics.com

Popular Photography Magazine
460 N Orlando Ave Suite 200 Winter Park FL 32789 212-767-6000 767-5602
TF: 800-876-6636 ■ Web: www.popphoto.com

Popular Woodworking Magazine
4700 E Galbraith Rd Cincinnati OH 45236 513-531-2690 891-7196
TF Cust Svc: 877-860-9140 ■ Web: www.popularwoodworking.com

Practical Horseman Magazine
656 Quince Orchard Rd Suite 600 Gaithersburg MD 20878 301-977-3900 990-9015
Web: www.equisearch.com

QST Magazine 225 Main St Newington CT 06111 860-594-0200 594-0259
Web: www.arrl.org/qst

Quilter Magazine 7 Waterloo Rd Stanhope NJ 07874 973-347-6900 347-6909
TF: 800-940-6593 ■ Web: www.thequiltermag.com

Quilter's Newsletter Magazine
741 Corporate Cir Suite A Golden CO 80401 303-215-5600 277-0370
TF: 800-477-6089 ■ Web: www.quiltersnewsletter.com

Quiltmaker Magazine 741 Corporate Cir Suite A Golden CO 80401 800-388-7023 277-0370*
*Fax Area Code: 303 ■ TF: 800-388-7023 ■ Web: www.quiltmaker.com

Radio Control Boat Modeler 20 Westport Rd Wilton CT 06897 203-431-9000 761-8744
TF: 800-877-5160 ■ Web: www.rcboatmodeler.com

Reptiles Magazine 3 Burroughs Irvine CA 92618 949-855-8822 855-3045
TF: 800-546-7730 ■ Web: www.animalnetwork.com/reptiles

Rock & Gem Magazine 290 Maple Ct Suite 232 Ventura CA 93003 805-644-3824 644-3875
Web: www.rockngem.com

Rug Hooking Magazine 5067 Ritter Rd Mechanicsburg PA 17055 717-796-0411 796-0412
TF: 800-732-3669 ■ Web: www.rughookingonline.com

Scale Auto Magazine 21027 Crossroads Cir Waukesha WI 53186 262-796-8776 796-1615*
*Fax: Cust Svc ■ TF Cust Svc: 800-533-6644 ■ Web: www.scaleautomag.com

Sew Beautiful Magazine
149 Old Big Cove Rd Brownsboro AL 35741 256-533-9586 534-5486
TF: 888-825-5823 ■ Web: www.sewbeautiful.com

Shutterbug Magazine
1419 Chaffee Dr Suite 1 Titusville FL 32780 321-269-3212 225-3149
TF: 800-829-3340 ■ Web: www.shutterbug.net

Smoke Magazine 26 Broadway Suite 9-M New York NY 10004 212-391-2060 827-0945
Web: www.smokemag.com

Threads Magazine 63 S Main St PO Box 5506 Newtown CT 06470 203-426-8171 270-6753
TF: 800-283-7252 ■ Web: www.taunton.com/threads/index.asp

Western Horseman Magazine
2112 Montgomery St Fort Worth TX 76107 817-737-6397 737-9266
Web: www.westernhorseman.com

Wine Spectator Magazine 387 Pk Ave S 8th Fl New York NY 10016 212-684-4224 481-1540
TF Orders: 800-752-7799 ■ Web: www.winespectator.com

Woodshop News 10 Bokum Rd Essex CT 06426 860-767-8227 767-0645
TF: 800-444-7686 ■ Web: www.woodshopnews.com

Woodsmith Magazine 2200 Grand Ave Des Moines IA 50312 515-282-7000 282-6741
TF Cust Svc: 800-333-5075 ■ Web: www.woodsmith.com

Workbench Magazine 2200 Grand Ave Des Moines IA 50312 515-282-7000 282-6741
TF Cust Svc: 800-311-3991 ■ Web: www.workbenchmagazine.com

@Law Magazine 8159 E 41st St Tulsa OK 74145 918-582-5188 582-5907
Web: www.nals.org

460-15 Law Magazines & Journals

Phone | Fax

Advocate Magazine PO Box 895 Boise ID 83701 208-334-4500 334-4515

Alabama Lawyer Magazine 415 Dexter Ave Montgomery AL 36104 334-269-1515 261-6310
TF: 800-354-6154 ■ Web: www.alabar.org

Alaska Bar Rag Magazine PO Box 100279 Anchorage AK 99510 907-272-7469 279-1037

American Lawyer Magazine 120 Broadway 5th Fl New York NY 10271 212-457-9400 822-5146*
*Fax Area Code: 646 ■ TF: 800-888-8300 ■ Web: www.americanlawyer.com

				Phone	Fax
Arizona Attorney Magazine 4201 N 24th St Suite 200 *Web:* www.myazbar.org/AZAttorney	Phoenix	AZ	85016	602-252-4804	271-4930
Arkansas Lawyer Magazine 2224 Cottondale Ln *TF:* 800-609-5668 ■ *Web:* www.arkbar.com	Little Rock	AR	72202	501-375-4606	375-4901
Banking Law Journal 807 Las Cimas Pkwy Suite 300 *TF Cust Svc:* 800-456-2340 ■ *Web:* www.sheshunoff.com/store/819.html	Austin	TX	78746	512-472-2244	305-6541
Bench & Bar of Minnesota Magazine 600 Nicollet Mall Suite 380 *Web:* www2.mnbar.org/benchandbar	Minneapolis	MN	55402	612-333-1183	333-4927
California Bar Journal 180 Howard St. *Web:* www.calbar.ca.gov/state/calbar	San Francisco	CA	94105	415-538-2504	538-2247
California Lawyer Magazine 44 Montgomery St Suite 250 *Web:* www.dailyjournal.com	San Francisco	CA	94104	415-296-2400	296-2400
Colorado Lawyer Magazine 1900 Grant St Suite 900 *Web:* www.cobar.org/tcl/index.cfm	Denver	CO	80203	303-860-1115	830-3990
Connecticut Lawyer Magazine 30 Bank St PO Box 350 *Web:* www.ctbar.org	New Britain	CT	06050	860-223-4400	223-4488
Family Advocate Magazine 321 N Clark St *Web:* www.americanbar.org	Chicago	IL	60654	312-988-5638	932-8638
Florida Bar Journal 651 E Jefferson St. *TF:* 800-342-8060 ■ *Web:* www.floridabar.org	Tallahassee	FL	32399	850-561-5600	681-3859
Georgia Bar Journal 104 Marietta St NW Suite 100 *Web:* www.gabar.org/communications/georgia_bar_journal	Atlanta	GA	30303	404-527-8700	527-8717
Harvard Law Review 1511 Massachusetts Ave Gannett House *Web:* www.harvardlawreview.org	Cambridge	MA	02138	617-495-4650	495-2748
Hawaii Bar Journal 1100 Alakea St Suite 1000 *Web:* www.hsba.org/hawaii_bar_journal.aspx	Honolulu	HI	96813	808-537-1868	521-7936
In Re: Magazine 301 N Market St	Wilmington	DE	19801	302-658-5279	658-5212
InsideCounsel 222 S Riverside Plaza Suite 620 *Web:* www.insidecounsel.com	Chicago	IL	60606	312-654-3500	654-3525
Journal of the Kansas Bar Assn 1200 SW Harrison St *Web:* www.ksbar.org	Topeka	KS	66612	785-234-5696	234-3813
Journal of the Missouri Bar 326 Monroe St PO Box 119 *Web:* www.mobar.org/7b2e21b5-eb97-4f01-91da-1ff2beb5bb45.aspx	Jefferson City	MO	65102	573-635-4128	635-2811
Kentucky Bench & Bar Magazine 514 W Main St	Frankfort	KY	40601	502-564-3795	564-3225
Lawyers Journal 20 W St *Web:* www.massbar.org	Boston	MA	02111	617-338-0500	338-0650
Legal Management: Journal of the Assn of Legal Administrators (ALA) 75 Tri State International Suite 222 *Web:* www.alanet.org	Lincolnshire	IL	60069	847-267-1252	267-1329
Los Angeles Lawyer Magazine 261 S Figueroa St Suite 300 *Web:* www.lacba.org/showpage.cfm?pageid=40	Los Angeles	CA	90012	213-896-6503	613-1972
Louisiana Bar Journal 601 St Charles Ave *Web:* www.lsba.org/Benefits/louisiana_bar_journal.html	New Orleans	LA	70130	504-566-1600	566-0930
Maine Bar Journal 124 State St PO Box 788 *TF:* 800-475-7523 ■ *Web:* www.mainebar.org	Augusta	ME	04332	207-622-7523	623-0083
Maryland Bar Journal 520 W Fayette St *TF:* 800-492-1964 ■ *Web:* www.msba.org/departments	Baltimore	MD	21201	410-685-7878	685-1016
Michigan Bar Journal 306 Townsend St *Web:* www.michbar.org/journal	Lansing	MI	48933	517-346-6300	482-6248
Mississippi Lawyer Magazine 643 N State St *Web:* www.msbar.org	Jackson	MS	39202	601-948-4471	355-8635
Montana Lawyer Magazine 7 W 6th Ave Suite 2B *Web:* www.montanabar.org	Helena	MT	59601	406-442-7660	442-7763
National Jurist Magazine PO Box 939039 *TF:* 800-465-3462 ■ *Web:* www.nationaljurist.com	San Diego	CA	92193	858-503-7572	503-7588
National Law Journal The 120 Broadway 5th Fl *Fax Area Code: 646 ■ *TF:* 800-888-8300 ■ *Web:* www.law.com/jsp/nlj/index.jsp	New York	NY	10271	800-888-8300	822-5146*
Nevada Lawyer Magazine 600 E Charleston Blvd *Web:* www.nvbar.org/Publications/Publications.htm	Las Vegas	NV	89104	702-382-2200	385-2878
New Hampshire Bar News 2 Pillsbury St Suite 300 *Web:* www.nhbar.org	Concord	NH	03301	603-224-6942	224-2910
New Jersey Lawyer Magazine 1 Cragwood Rd. *Web:* www.njsba.com/magazine	South Plainfield	NJ	07080	908-226-0052	226-0139
New York Law Journal 120 Broadway 5th Fl *Fax Area Code: 646 ■ *TF:* 800-888-8300 ■ *Web:* www.law.com/jsp/nylj/index.jsp	New York	NY	10271	800-888-8300	822-5146*
New York State Bar News 1 Elk St *Web:* www.nysba.org	Albany	NY	12207	518-463-3200	463-4276
Oklahoma Bar Journal 1901 Lincoln Blvd *Web:* www.okbar.org/obj	Oklahoma City	OK	73105	405-524-2365	416-7001
Oregon State Bar Bulletin 16037 SW Upper Boones Ferry Rd PO Box 231935 *TF:* 800-452-8260 ■ *Web:* www.osbar.org/publications/bulletin/bulletin.html	Tigard	OR	97281	503-620-0222	684-1366
Pennsylvania Bar News 100 S St *TF:* 800-932-0311 ■ *Web:* www.pabar.org/public/membership/barnews.asp	Harrisburg	PA	17101	717-238-6715	238-7182
Rhode Island Bar Journal 115 Cedar St *Web:* www.ribar.com/About%20the%20Bar%20Association/BarJournal.aspx	Providence	RI	02903	401-421-5740	421-2703
South Carolina Lawyer Magazine 950 Taylor St.	Columbia	SC	29201	803-799-6653	799-4118
Student Lawyer Magazine 321 N Clark St *Web:* www.americanbar.org	Chicago	IL	60654	312-988-5638	932-8638
Tennessee Bar Journal 221 4th Ave N Suite 400 *Web:* www.tba.org/Journal_Current/tbj-200404.html	Nashville	TN	37219	615-383-7421	297-8058
Texas Bar Journal 1414 Colorado St Suite 312 *Web:* www.texasbar.com	Austin	TX	78701	512-463-1463	427-4107
Washington Lawyer Magazine 1101 K St NW Suite 200 *Web:* www.dcbar.org	Washington	DC	20005	202-737-4700	626-3471
Washington State Bar News 1325 4th Ave Suite 600 *TF:* 800-945-9722 ■ *Web:* www.wsba.org	Seattle	WA	98101	206-727-8215	727-8320
West Virginia Lawyer Magazine 2006 Kanawha Blvd E *Web:* www.wvbar.org/barinfo/lawyer/magtext.htm	Charleston	WV	25311	304-558-2456	558-2467
Wisconsin Lawyer Magazine 5302 Eastpark Blvd *TF:* 800-728-7788 ■ *Web:* www.wisbar.org/wislawmag	Madison	WI	53718	608-250-6127	257-5502
Wyoming Lawyer Magazine 4124 Laramie St.	Cheyenne	WY	82001	307-632-9061	632-3737
Yale Law Journal PO Box 208215 *Web:* www.yale.edu/yalelj	New Haven	CT	06520	203-432-1666	432-7482

460-16 Medical Magazines & Journals

				Phone	Fax
Academic Physician & Scientist Magazine 333 7th Ave.	New York	NY	10001	646-674-6536	674-6500
Access Magazine 444 N Michigan Ave Suite 3400 *TF:* 800-243-2342 ■ *Web:* www.adha.org/publications/index.html	Chicago	IL	60611	312-440-8900	467-1702
Alabama MD 19 S Jackson St *TF:* 800-239-6272	Montgomery	AL	36104	334-263-6441	269-5200
Alaska Medicine Magazine 4107 Laurel St	Anchorage	AK	99508	907-562-0304	561-2063
American Dental Assn News 211 E Chicago Ave *TF:* 800-621-1099 ■ *Web:* www.ada.org/prof/resources/pubs/adanews/index.asp	Chicago	IL	60611	312-440-2500	440-7494
American Family Physician Magazine (AAFP) 11400 Tomahawk Creek Pkwy. *TF:* 800-274-2237 ■ *Web:* www.aafp.org/afp.xml	Leawood	KS	66211	913-906-6000	906-6075
American Journal of Psychiatry 1000 Wilson Blvd Suite 1825 *TF:* 800-368-5777 ■ *Web:* www.ajp.psychiatryonline.org	Arlington	VA	22209	703-907-7300	907-1085
American Medical News 515 N State St *Web:* www.ama-assn.org/amednews	Chicago	IL	60654	312-464-4429	464-4445
American Nurse Magazine 8515 Georgia Ave Suite 400 *TF:* 800-274-4262 ■ *Web:* www.nursingworld.org	Silver Spring	MD	20910	301-628-5000	628-5001
American Psychologist Magazine 750 1st St NE *TF:* 800-374-2721 ■ *Web:* www.apa.org/journals/amp.html	Washington	DC	20002	202-336-5500	336-6091
Annals of Internal Medicine Magazine 190 N Independence Mall W. *TF:* 800-523-1546 ■ *Web:* www.annals.org	Philadelphia	PA	19106	215-351-2400	351-2644
Arizona Medicine Assn 810 W Bethany Home Rd *TF:* 800-482-3480 ■ *Web:* www.azmedassn.org	Phoenix	AZ	85013	602-246-8901	242-6283
CA-A Cancer Journal for Clinicians 250 William St Suite 600 *Web:* caonline.amcancersoc.org	Atlanta	GA	30303	404-320-3333	551-5605
Connecticut Medicine Magazine 160 St Ronan St *TF:* 800-635-7740 ■ *Web:* www.csms.org	New Haven	CT	06511	203-865-0587	865-4997
Contemporary Esthetics & Restorative Practice 103 College Rd E *Web:* www.dentallearning.com	Princeton	NJ	08540	609-524-9500	524-9658
Delaware Medical Journal 131 Continental Dr Suite 405 *Fax Area Code: 800 ■ *Web:* www.medicalsocietyofdelaware.org	Newark	DE	19713	302-658-7596	348-6800*
Dental Economics Magazine 1421 S Sheridan Rd *TF:* 800-633-1681 ■ *Web:* www.dentaleconomics.com	Tulsa	OK	74112	918-835-3161	835-3161
Diabetes Advisor Magazine 1701 N Beauregard St. *TF:* 800-342-2383 ■ *Web:* forecast.diabetes.org/magazine/features/diabetes-advisor	Alexandria	VA	22311	703-549-1500	549-6995
Emergency Medicine Magazine 7 Century Dr Suite 302 *TF:* 800-976-4040 ■ *Web:* www.emedmag.com	Parsippany	NJ	07054	973-206-3434	206-9378
EyeNet Magazine 655 Beach St *TF:* 866-561-8558 ■ *Web:* www.aao.org/news/eyenet	San Francisco	CA	94109	415-561-8500	561-8533
Family Practice Management 11400 Tomahawk Creek Pkwy. *TF:* 800-274-2237 ■ *Web:* www.aafp.org/fpm.xml	Leawood	KS	66211	913-906-6000	906-6075
Female Patient Magazine 7 Century Dr Suite 302	Parsippany	NJ	07054	973-206-3434	206-9378
Hospital Physician Magazine 125 Strafford Ave Suite 220	Wayne	PA	19087	610-975-4541	975-4564
Infection Control Today Magazine 3300 N Central Ave Suite 300 *Web:* www.infectioncontroltoday.com	Phoenix	AZ	85012	480-990-1101	990-0819
Internal Medicine News 5635 Fishers Ln Suite 6000 *TF:* 877-524-9336 ■ *Web:* www.internalmedicinenews.com	Rockville	MD	20852	240-221-4500	221-4400
Iowa Medicine Magazine 1001 Grand Ave *TF:* 800-747-3070 ■ *Web:* www.iowamedical.org	West Des Moines	IA	50265	515-223-1401	223-0590

	City	State	ZIP	Phone	Fax
Journal of Kentucky Medical Assn 4965 US Hwy 42 KMA Bldg Suite 2000 *Web:* www.kyma.org	Louisville	KY	40222	502-426-6200	426-6877
Journal of Oklahoma State Medical Assn 601 NW Grand Blvd *TF:* 800-522-9452 ■ *Web:* www.okmed.org	Oklahoma City	OK	73118	405-843-9571	842-1834
Journal of Practical Nursing (JPN) 1940 Duke St Suite 200 *Web:* www.napnes.org	Alexandria	VA	22314	703-933-1003	940-4089
Journal of the American Dental Assn 211 E Chicago Ave *TF:* 800-621-8099 ■ *Web:* www.ada.org/prof/pubs/jada	Chicago	IL	60611	312-440-2740	440-2550
Journal of the American Dietetic Assn 1600 John F Kennedy Blvd *Web:* www.adajournal.org	Philadelphia	PA	19103	215-239-3733	239-3734
Journal of the American Medical Assn (JAMA) 515 N State St *TF:* 800-262-2350 ■ *Web:* www.jama.ama-assn.org	Chicago	IL	60654	312-464-5000	464-4184
Journal of the American Pharmacists Assn 2215 Constitution Ave N W *TF:* 800-237-2742 ■ *Web:* www.pharmacist.com	Washington	DC	20037	202-628-4410	783-2351
Journal of the American Veterinary Medical Assn 1931 N Meacham Rd Suite 100 *TF All:* 800-248-2862	Schaumburg	IL	60173	847-925-8070	925-1329
Journal of the Arkansas Medical Society PO Box 55088 *TF:* 800-542-1058	Little Rock	AR	72215	501-224-8967	224-6489
Journal of the Florida Medical Assn 123 S Adams St *TF:* 800-762-0233	Tallahassee	FL	32301	850-224-6496	224-6627
Journal of the Louisiana State Medical Society 6767 Perkins Rd Suite 100 *TF:* 800-375-9508 ■ *Web:* www.lsms.org	Baton Rouge	LA	70808	225-763-8500	763-2332
Journal of the Medical Assn of Georgia 1849 The Exchange Suite 200 *TF:* 800-282-0224	Atlanta	GA	30339	678-303-9262	303-3932
Journal of the Mississippi State Medical Assn PO Box 2548 *Web:* www.msmaonline.com	Ridgeland	MS	39158	601-853-6733	853-6746
Mayo Clinic Proceedings Magazine 200 1st St SW Siebens Bldg 770 *TF:* 800-707-7040 ■ *Web:* www.mayoclinicproceedings.com	Rochester	MN	55905	507-284-2094	284-0252
Medicine & Health/Rhode Island Magazine 235 Promenade St Suite 500 PO Box 20 *Web:* www.rimed.org	Providence	RI	02908	401-331-3207	751-8050
Michigan Medicine Magazine 120 W Saginaw St *Web:* www.ms.org	East Lansing	MI	48823	517-337-1351	337-2490
Minnesota Medicine Magazine 1300 Godward St N E Suite 2500 *TF:* 800-342-5662 ■ *Web:* www.minnesotamedicine.com	Minneapolis	MN	55413	612-378-1875	378-3875
Missouri Medicine Magazine PO Box 1028 *Web:* www.msma.org	Jefferson City	MO	65102	573-636-5151	636-8552
Monitor on Psychology 750 1st Ave NE *Web:* www.apa.org/monitor	Washington	DC	20002	202-336-5500	336-6103
NASW News 750 1st St NE Suite 700 *TF:* 800-638-8799 ■ *Web:* www.naswpress.org	Washington	DC	20002	202-408-8600	336-8312
NCMS Bulletin 222 N Person St *TF:* 800-722-1350	Raleigh	NC	27601	919-833-3836	833-2023
New England Journal of Medicine 10 Shattuck St *TF:* 800-843-6356 ■ *Web:* www.nejm.org	Boston	MA	02115	617-734-9800	739-9864
News of New York Magazine 420 Lakeville Rd PO Box 5404 *Web:* www.mssny.org	Lake Success	NY	11042	516-488-6100	328-1982
Nurseweek Magazine 6860 Santa Teresa Blvd. *TF:* 800-859-2091	San Jose	CA	95119	408-574-1200	249-3756
Nursing 2011 Magazine 323 Norristown Rd Suite 200 *TF:* 800-346-7844 ■ *Web:* www.journals.lww.com	Ambler	PA	19002	215-646-8700	653-0826
Nursing Spectrum Greater New York/New Jersey Metro Magazine 900 Merchants Concourse	Westbury	NY	11590	516-222-0909	222-0131
Ohio Medicine Magazine 3401 Mill Run Dr *TF:* 800-766-6762	Hilliard	OH	43026	614-527-6762	527-6763
Pharmacy Today Magazine 2215 Constitution Ave NW *TF:* 800-327-2742 ■ *Web:* www.pharmacy-today.co.nz	Washington	DC	20037	202-429-7557	628-5425
Physician & Sportsmedicine Magazine 1235 Westlakes Dr Suite 220 *Web:* www.physsportsmed.com	Berwyn	PA	19312	610-889-3737	889-3731
Postgraduate Medicine Magazine 1235 Westlake Dr Suite 220 *Web:* www.postgradmed.com	Berwyn	PA	19312	610-889-3733	889-3731
Psychotherapy Networker 5135 MacArthur Blvd NW *TF:* 888-883-3782 ■ *Web:* www.psychotherapynetworker.org	Washington	DC	20016	202-537-8950	537-6869
Social Work Magazine 750 1st St NE Suite 700 *TF:* 800-638-8799 ■ *Web:* www.naswpress.org	Washington	DC	20002	202-408-8600	336-8312
South Dakota State Medical Assn (SDSMA) 2600 W 49th St Suite 200 PO Box 7406 *Web:* www.sdsma.org	Sioux Falls	SD	57117	605-336-1965	274-3274
Southern Medical Journal 35 Lakeshore Dr PO Box 190088 *TF:* 800-423-4992 ■ *Web:* journals.lww.com/smajournalonline/pages/default.aspx	Birmingham	AL	35209	205-945-1840	945-1548
Tennessee Medicine Magazine PO Box 120909	Nashville	TN	37212	615-385-2100	312-1908
Texas Medicine Magazine 401 W 15th St *TF:* 800-880-1300 ■ *Web:* www.texmed.org/ata/nrm/tme/texmed_mag.asp	Austin	TX	78701	512-370-1300	370-1693
US Pharmacist Magazine 100 Avenue of the Americas 9th Fl *TF:* 877-529-1746 ■ *Web:* www.uspharmacist.com	New York	NY	10013	212-274-7000	219-7835
Virginia Medical News 2924 Emerywood Pkwy Suite 300 *TF:* 800-746-6768	Richmond	VA	23294	804-353-2721	355-6189
West Virginia Medical Journal PO Box 4106 *Web:* www.wvsma.com	Charleston	WV	25364	304-925-0342	925-0345

460-17 Political & Current Events Magazines

	City	State	ZIP	Phone	Fax
American Prospect 1710 Rhode Island Ave NW 12th Fl *Web:* www.prospect.org	Washington	DC	20036	202-776-0730	776-0740
American Spectator Magazine 1611 N Kent St Suite 901 *TF:* 800-524-3469 ■ *Web:* www.spectator.org	Arlington	VA	22209	703-807-2011	807-2013
Assn on American Indian Affairs (AAIA) 966 Hungerford Dr Suite 12-B *Web:* www.indian-affairs.org	Rockville	MD	20850	240-314-7155	314-7159
Commonweal Magazine 475 Riverside Dr Suite 405 *TF:* 888-495-6755 ■ *Web:* www.commonwealmagazine.org	New York	NY	10115	212-662-4200	662-4183
Criminal Politics Magazine PO Box 37432 **Fax Area Code:* 859 ■ *TF:* 800-543-0486 ■ *Web:* www.criminalpolitics.com	Cincinnati	OH	45222	800-543-0486	341-1202*
Foreign Affairs Magazine 58 E 68th St. **Fax Area Code:* 212 ■ **Fax:* Edit ■ *TF Cust Svc:* 800-829-5539 ■ *Web:* www.foreignaffairs.com	New York	NY	10065	800-829-5539	861-1849*
Foreign Policy Magazine 1779 Massachusetts Ave NW *Web:* www.foreignpolicy.com	Washington	DC	20036	202-939-2230	483-4430
Freeman The 30 S Broadway *TF Sales:* 800-960-4333 ■ *Web:* www.fee.org/publications/the-freeman	Irvington-on-Hudson	NY	10533	914-591-7230	591-8910
Human Events Magazine 1 Massachusetts Ave NW Suite 600 *TF Cust Svc:* 800-787-7557 ■ *Web:* www.humanevents.com/contact.php	Washington	DC	20001	202-216-0600	216-0611
Maclean's Magazine 1 Mt Pleasant Rd 11th Fl *TF:* 800-268-9119 ■ *Web:* www2.macleans.ca	Toronto	ON	M4Y2Y5	416-764-1300	764-1332
Mother Jones Magazine 222 Sutter St Suite 600 *TF:* 800-438-6656 ■ *Web:* www.motherjones.com	San Francisco	CA	94108	415-321-1700	321-1701
Moving Ideas Network 2000 L St NW Suite 717 *Web:* www.movingideas.org	Washington	DC	20036	202-776-0730	
Nation Magazine 33 Irving Pl 8th Fl *TF Cust Svc:* 800-333-8536 ■ *Web:* www.thenation.com	New York	NY	10003	212-209-5400	982-9000
National Journal 600 New Hampshire Ave NW *TF:* 800-613-6701 ■ *Web:* www.nationaljournal.com	Washington	DC	20037	202-739-8400	833-8069
National Review 215 Lexington Ave 11th Fl *Web:* www.nationalreview.com	New York	NY	10016	212-679-7330	849-2835
National Voter Magazine 1730 'M' St NW Suite 1000 *Web:* www.lwv.org/elibrary/national_voter.html	Washington	DC	20036	202-429-1965	429-0854
New Republic The 1331 H St NW Suite 700 *TF:* 800-827-1289 ■ *Web:* www.tnr.com	Washington	DC	20005	202-508-4444	628-9383
Newsweek Magazine 555 W 18th St **Fax:* Edit ■ *TF Cust Svc:* 800-631-1040 ■ *Web:* www.newsweek.com	New York	NY	10011	212-445-4600	445-4425*
Reason Magazine 3415 S Sepulveda Blvd Suite 400 *TF Cust Svc:* 888-732-7668 ■ *Web:* www.reason.com	Los Angeles	CA	90034	310-391-2245	391-4395
Slate Magazine 95 Morton St 4th Fl *Web:* slate.com	New York	NY	10014	212-445-5330	445-5318
Slate Magazine 1350 Connecticut Ave NW *Web:* www.slate.com	Washington	DC	20036	202-261-1310	261-1310
US News & World Report 1050 Thomas Jefferson St NW *TF:* 800-436-6520 ■ *Web:* www.usnews.com	Washington	DC	20007	202-955-2000	
Weekly Standard Magazine 1150 17th St NW Suite 505 *TF Cust Svc:* 800-274-7293 ■ *Web:* www.weeklystandard.com	Washington	DC	20036	202-293-4900	293-4901
World Press Review 735 Mulberry Pl *Web:* www.worldpress.org	North Woodmere	NY	11581	516-791-6788	791-1007

460-18 Religious & Spiritual Magazines

	City	State	ZIP	Phone	Fax
B'Nai B'Rith Magazine 2020 K St NW 7th Fl *TF:* 888-388-4224 ■ *Web:* www.bnaibrith.org	Washington	DC	20006	202-857-6600	
Biblical Archaeology Review 4710 41st St NW *TF:* 800-221-4644 ■ *Web:* www.bib-arch.org	Washington	DC	20016	202-364-3300	364-2636
Body & Soul 42 Pleasant St *TF:* 800-755-1178 ■ *Web:* www.marthastewart.com	Watertown	MA	02472	617-926-0200	926-5021
Catholic Digest PO Box 6015 *TF:* 800-678-2836 ■ *Web:* www.catholicdigest.org	New London	CT	06320	860-437-3012	437-3013

Name / Address	City	State	ZIP	Phone	Fax
Charisma Magazine 600 Rinehart Rd	Lake Mary	FL	32746	407-333-0600	333-7100
TF: 800-829-3346 ■ *Web:* www.charismamag.com					
Christianity Today Magazine 465 Gundersen Dr	Carol Stream	IL	60188	630-260-6200	260-0114
TF: 800-999-1704 ■ *Web:* www.christianitytoday.com/ctmag					
Episcopal Life Magazine 815 2nd Ave Episcopal Church Ctr	New York	NY	10017	212-716-6000	716-6000
TF: 800-334-7626 ■ *Web:* www.episcopalchurch.org					
Gospel Today Magazine PO Box 800	Fairburn	GA	30213	770-719-4825	716-2660
Web: www.mygospeltoday.com					
Guideposts Magazine 39 Seminary Hill Rd	Carmel	NY	10512	845-225-3681	684-0679*
**Fax Area Code:* 212 ■ *TF:* 800-431-2344 ■ *Web:* www.guideposts.com					
Hadassah Magazine 50 W 58th St	New York	NY	10019	212-451-6289	451-6257
Kashrus Magazine PO Box 204	Brooklyn	NY	11204	718-336-8544	336-8550
Web: www.kashrusmagazine.com					
Lutheran Magazine 8765 W Higgins Rd	Chicago	IL	60631	773-380-2540	380-2751
TF: 800-638-3522 ■ *Web:* www.thelutheran.org					
Marriage Partnership Magazine 465 Gundersen Dr	Carol Stream	IL	60188	630-260-6200	260-0114
Web: www.christianitytoday.com/marriage					
Ministries Today Magazine 600 Rinehart Rd	Lake Mary	FL	32746	407-333-0600	333-7100
Web: www.ministriestoday.com					
Moment Magazine 4115 Wisconsin Ave NW Suite 102	Washington	DC	20016	202-363-6422	362-2514
Web: www.momentmag.com					
New Man Magazine 600 Rinehart Rd	Lake Mary	FL	32746	407-333-0600	333-7100
TF: 800-829-3346 ■ *Web:* www.newmanmag.com					
Presbyterians Today Magazine 100 Witherspoon St	Louisville	KY	40202	502-569-5637	569-8632
TF: 800-728-7228 ■ *Web:* www.tcusa.org/today					
Reform Judaism Magazine 633 3rd Ave	New York	NY	10017	212-650-4240	212-4249
Web: reformjudaismmag.org					
Saint Anthony Messenger Magazine 28 W Liberty St	Cincinnati	OH	45202	513-241-5616	241-1197
TF: 800-488-0488 ■ *Web:* www.americancatholic.org/messenger					
Spiritled Woman - Charisma Magazine 600 Rinehart Rd	Lake Mary	FL	32746	407-333-0600	333-7100
Web: www.charismamag.com/index.php/spiritled-woman					
Today's Christian Woman Magazine 465 Gundersen Dr	Carol Stream	IL	60188	630-260-6200	260-0114
TF Orders: 800-365-9484 ■ *Web:* www.christianitytoday.com/women					
Todays Christian Magazine 465 Gundersen Dr	Carol Stream	IL	60188	630-260-6200	260-0114
TF Cust Svc: 800-223-3161 ■ *Web:* www.christianitytoday.com/spiritual					
US Catholic Magazine 205 W Monroe	Chicago	IL	60606	312-236-7782	236-8207
TF Cust Svc: 800-328-6515 ■ *Web:* uscatholic.org					

460-19 Science & Nature Magazines

Name / Address	City	State	ZIP	Phone	Fax
American Forests Magazine 734 15th St NW Suite 800	Washington	DC	20005	202-737-1944	737-2457
TF: 800-368-5748 ■ *Web:* www.americanforests.org					
American Laboratory Magazine 30 Controls Dr	Shelton	CT	06484	203-926-9300	926-9310*
**Fax:* Edit ■ *Web:* www.iscpubs.com					
American Scientist Magazine 3106 E NC Hwy 54 PO Box 13975	Research Triangle Park	NC	27709	919-549-4691	549-0090
TF: 800-243-6534 ■ *Web:* www.americanscientist.org					
Annals of Improbable Research (AIR) PO Box 380853	Cambridge	MA	02238	617-491-4437	661-0927
Web: www.improbable.com					
Archaeology Magazine 36-36 33rd St	Long Island City	NY	11106	718-472-3050	472-3051
Web: www.archaeology.org					
Audubon Magazine 225 Varick St 7th Fl	New York	NY	10014	212-979-3000	477-9069
TF Cust Svc: 800-274-4201 ■ *Web:* www.magazine.audubon.org					
Aviation Week & Space Technology Magazine 1200 G St NW Suite 922	Washington	DC	20005	202-383-2314	383-2346*
**Fax:* Edit ■ *TF:* 800-525-5003 ■ *Web:* www.aviationweek.com					
BioScience 1444 'I' St NW Suite 200	Washington	DC	20005	202-628-1500	628-1509
TF: 800-992-2427 ■ *Web:* www.aibs.org/bioscience					
BioTechniques 52 Vanderbilt Ave 7th Fl	New York	NY	10017	212-520-7777	661-5052
Web: www.biotechniques.com					
California Wild Magazine California Academy of Sciences 55 Music Concourse Dr	San Francisco	CA	94118	415-379-5484	
Web: www.calacademy.org/calwild					
Defenders Magazine 1130 17th St NW	Washington	DC	20036	202-682-9400	682-1331
TF: 800-385-9712 ■ *Web:* www.defenders.org/defendersmag					
Discover Magazine 275 7th Ave	New York	NY	10001	212-624-4800	246-1020*
**Fax Area Code:* 515 ■ *TF:* 800-829-9132 ■ *Web:* www.discovermagazine.com					
E/The Environmental Magazine 28 Knight St PO Box 5098	Norwalk	CT	06851	203-854-5559	866-0602
TF: 800-967-6572 ■ *Web:* www.emagazine.com					
Earth Island Journal 300 Broadway Suite 28	San Francisco	CA	94133	415-788-3666	788-7324
Web: www.earthisland.org/eijournal					
Friends of the Earth Magazine 1100 15th St NW	Washington	DC	20005	202-783-7400	783-0444
TF: 877-843-8687 ■ *Web:* www.foe.org					
Garden Compass 1450 Front St	San Diego	CA	92101	619-239-2202	239-4621
TF: 800-566-3622 ■ *Web:* www.gardencompass.com					
International Laboratory 30 Controls Dr PO Box 870	Shelton	CT	06484	203-926-9300	926-9310
Web: www.internationallaboratory.com					
NASA Tech Briefs 1466 Broadway Suite 910	New York	NY	10036	212-490-3999	986-7864
TF: 800-944-6272 ■ *Web:* www.techbriefs.com					
National Parks Magazine 1300 19th St NW Suite 300	Washington	DC	20036	202-223-6722	659-0650
TF: 800-628-7275 ■ *Web:* www.npca.org/magazine					
National Wildlife Magazine 11100 Wildlife Ctr Dr	Reston	VA	22190	703-438-6000	438-6040
TF Cust Svc: 800-822-9919 ■ *Web:* www.nwf.org/nationalwildlife					
Natural History Magazine 105 W Hwy 54 Suite 265	Durham	NC	27713	646-356-6500	933-1867*
**Fax Area Code:* 919 ■ *Web:* www.naturalhistorymag.com					
Nature National Press Bldg 529 14th St NW Suite 968	Washington	DC	20045	202-737-2355	628-1609
TF: 800-524-0384 ■ *Web:* www.nature.com					
Orion Magazine 187 Main St	Great Barrington	MA	01230	413-528-4422	528-0676
TF: 888-909-6568 ■ *Web:* www.orionmagazine.org					
Physics Today Magazine 1 Physics Ellipse	College Park	MD	20740	301-209-3040	209-0842
TF: 800-344-6902 ■ *Web:* www.aip.org/pt					
Popular Science Magazine 2 Pk Ave	New York	NY	10016	212-779-5000	779-5108
TF Cust Svc: 800-289-9399 ■ *Web:* www.popsci.com					
R & D Magazine 100 Enterprise Dr Suite 600 Suite 600	Rockaway	NJ	07866	973-920-7000	920-7542
TF: 800-222-0289 ■ *Web:* www.rdmag.com					
Science Magazine 1200 New York Ave NW	Washington	DC	20005	202-326-6500	842-1065
TF: 800-731-4939 ■ *Web:* www.sciencemag.org					
Science News 1719 N St NW	Washington	DC	20036	202-785-2255	659-0365
TF Cust Svc: 800-552-4412 ■ *Web:* www.sciencenews.org					
Scientist The 400 Market St Suite 1250	Philadelphia	PA	19106	215-351-1660	351-1146
Web: www.the-scientist.com					
Sierra Magazine 85 2nd St 2nd Fl	San Francisco	CA	94105	415-977-5500	977-5794
Web: www.sierraclub.org/sierra					
Sky & Telescope Magazine 90 Sherman St	Cambridge	MA	02140	617-864-7360	864-6117
TF: 800-253-0245 ■ *Web:* www.skyandtelescope.com					
Smithsonian Air & Space Magazine PO Box 37012	Washington	DC	20013	202-633-6070	633-6085
TF Cust Svc: 800-766-2149 ■ *Web:* www.airspacemag.com					
Technology Review Magazine 1 Main St 7th Fl	Cambridge	MA	02142	617-475-8000	475-8042
Web: www.techreview.com					

460-20 Sports Magazines

Name / Address	City	State	ZIP	Phone	Fax
American Rifleman Magazine 11250 Waples Mill Rd	Fairfax	VA	22030	703-267-1379	267-3971
TF: 800-672-3888					
Baseball America Magazine 4319 S Alston Ave Suite 103	Durham	NC	27713	919-682-9635	682-2880
Web: www.baseballamerica.com/today					
Bassmaster Magazine 1170 Celebration Blvd Suite 200	Celebration	FL	34747	877-227-7872	
TF: 877-227-7872 ■ *Web:* www.bassmaster.com/topics/Bassmaster%20Magazine					
Beckett Baseball Card Monthly 4635 McEwen Rd	Dallas	TX	75244	972-991-6657	991-8930
Web: www.beckett.com					
Beckett Football Card Monthly 15850 Dallas Pkwy	Dallas	TX	75248	972-991-6657	991-8930
Web: www.beckett.com					
Bowhunting World Magazine 5959 Baker Rd Suite 300	Minnetonka	MN	55345	952-405-2280	405-2281
TF: 800-766-0039 ■ *Web:* www.bowhuntingworld.com					
Climbing Magazine 1260 Yellow Pine Ave	Boulder	CO	80304	303-225-4628	417-1371
TF: 800-829-5895 ■ *Web:* www.climbing.com					
Competitor Magazine 9477 Waples St Suite 150	San Diego	CA	92121	800-311-1255	768-6801*
**Fax Area Code:* 858 ■ *TF:* 800-311-1255 ■ *Web:* www.competitor.com					
Discovery YMCA Magazine 101 N Wacker Dr	Chicago	IL	60606	312-977-0031	977-4809
TF: 800-872-9622 ■ *Web:* www.ymca.net					
Ducks Unlimited Magazine 1 Waterfowl Way	Memphis	TN	38120	901-758-3825	758-3850
TF: 800-453-8257 ■ *Web:* www.ducks.org					
ESPN Magazine 19 E 34th St	New York	NY	10016	212-515-1000	515-1285
TF Cust Svc: 888-267-3684 ■ *Web:* www.espn.go.com/magazine					
Field & Stream Magazine 2 Pk Ave	New York	NY	10016	212-779-5000	725-3836
TF Cust Svc: 800-999-0869 ■ *Web:* www.fieldandstream.com					
Florida Sportsman Magazine 2700 S Kanner Hwy	Stuart	FL	34994	772-219-7400	219-6900
Web: www.flsportsman.com					
Game & Fish Magazine 2250 New Market Pkwy Suite 110	Marietta	GA	30067	770-953-9222	933-9510
Web: www.gameandfishmag.com					
Golf Digest 20 Westport Rd PO Box 850	Wilton	CT	06897	203-761-5100	761-5129
TF: 800-962-5513 ■ *Web:* www.golfdigest.com					
Golf Magazine 1271 Avenue of the Americas 32nd Fl	New York	NY	10020	212-522-1212	
TF: 800-541-1000 ■ *Web:* www.golf.com/golf					
Golf Tips Magazine 12121 Wilshire Blvd Suite 1200	Los Angeles	CA	90025	310-820-1500	826-5008
TF: 800-283-4330 ■ *Web:* www.golftipsmag.com					
Golf World Magazine 20 Westport Rd PO Box 850	Wilton	CT	06897	203-761-5100	761-5131
TF: 800-962-5513 ■ *Web:* www.golfdigest.com/newsandtour					
Gun World Magazine 265 S Anita Dr Suite 120	Orange	CA	92868	714-939-9991	939-9909
Web: www.gunworld.com					

Phone Fax

Hockey News Magazine 100-25 Sheppard Ave W........ Toronto ON M2N6S7 416-733-7600 733-3566
TF: 888-361-9768 ■ *Web:* www.thehockeynews.com

In-Fisherman Magazine 7819 Highland Scenic Rd........ Baxter MN 56425 218-829-1648 829-3091
TF: 800-441-1740 ■ *Web:* www.in-fisherman.com

Journal of the Philosophy of Sport
1607 N Market St.............................. Champaign IL 61820 217-351-5076 351-1549
TF: 800-747-4457 ■ *Web:* www.humankinetics.com

Links Magazine 10 Executive Pk Rd........... Hilton Head Island SC 29928 843-842-6200 842-6233
Web: www.linksmagazine.com

North American Fisherman Magazine
12301 Whitewater Dr........................... Minnetonka MN 55343 952-936-9333 936-9755
TF: 800-843-6232

North American Hunter Magazine
12301 Whitewater Dr........................... Minnetonka MN 55343 952-936-9333 936-9755
TF: 800-922-4868

Powder The Skier's Magazine
27500 Riverview Ctr Blvd...................... Bonita Springs CA 92629 239-949-4450 949-7689
Web: www.powdermag.com

Salt Water Sportsman Magazine
460 N Orlando Ave Suite 200..................... Winter Park FL 32789 407-628-4802 628-7061
TF: 800-759-2127 ■ *Web:* www.saltwatersportsman.com

Ski Magazine 5720 Flatiron Pkwy..................... Boulder CO 80301 303-253-6300
TF: 800-227-2224 ■ *Web:* www.skimag.com

Skiing Magazine 5720 Flatiron Pkwy.................. Boulder CO 80301 303-253-6300
TF: 800-227-2224 ■ *Web:* www.skiingmag.com/skiing

Snow Goer Magazine
6420 Sycamore Ln Suite 100.................... Maple Grove MN 55369 763-383-4400 383-4499
TF Cust Svc: 800-848-6247 ■ *Web:* www.snowgoer.com

Sport Aviation Magazine 3000 Poberezny Rd.......... Oshkosh WI 54902 920-426-4800 426-4828
Web: www.eaa.org/benefits/sportaviation

Sport Fishing Magazine
460 N Orlando Ave Suite 200........................ Orlando FL 32789 407-628-4802 628-7061
Web: www.sportfishingmag.com

Sporting Classics Magazine PO Box 23707........... Columbia SC 29224 803-736-2424 736-3404
TF: 800-849-1004 ■ *Web:* www.sportingclassics.com

Sporting News PO Box 420235.................... Palm Coast FL 32142 800-777-6785 485-6364*
**Fax Area Code:* 314 ■ *TF:* 800-443-1886 ■ *Web:* www.aol.sportingnews.com

Sports Afield Magazine
15621 Chemical Ln....................... Huntington Beach CA 92649 714-373-4910 894-4949
TF: 800-451-4788 ■ *Web:* www.sportsafield.com

Sports Business Daily
120 W Morehead St Suite 310...................... Charlotte NC 28202 704-973-1410 973-1401
TF: 800-829-9839 ■ *Web:* www.sportsbusinessdaily.com

Sports Illustrated Magazine
1271 Avenue of the Americas...................... New York NY 10020 212-522-1212
TF: 800-541-1000 ■ *Web:* sportsillustrated.cnn.com

Sports Spectrum Magazine
105 Corporate Blvd # 1.......................... Indian Trail NC 28079 704-821-2971 875-2669*
**Fax Area Code:* 866 ■ *TF:* 866-821-2971 ■ *Web:* www.sportsspectrum.com

Surfing Magazine
950 Calle Amanecer Suite C.................... San Clemente CA 92673 949-492-7873 498-6485
Web: www.surfingmagazine.com

Tennis Magazine 79 Madison Ave 8th Fl.............. New York NY 10016 212-636-2700 636-2720
Web: www.tennis.com

TransWorld SNOWboarding Magazine
353 Airport Rd.................................. Oceanside CA 92054 760-722-7777 722-0653
TF: 800-788-7072 ■ *Web:* www.snowboarding.transworld.net

TransWorld Surf Magazine
2052 Corte del Nogal Suite 100..................... Carlsbad CA 92011 760-722-7777 722-0653
Web: surf.transworld.net

Travel + Leisure Magazine
1120 Avenue of the Americas 10th Fl................. New York NY 10036 212-382-5600 382-5670
TF: 800-947-7961 ■ *Web:* www.travelandleisure.com

VeloNews Magazine 1830 N 55th St.................. Boulder CO 80301 303-440-0601 444-6788
Web: www.velonews.com

460-21 Trade & Industry Magazines

Phone Fax

AAPG Explorer Magazine 1444 S Boulder Ave............ Tulsa OK 74119 918-584-2555 560-2636
TF: 800-364-2274 ■ *Web:* www.aapg.org

Aerospace America Magazine
1801 Alexander Bell Dr Suite 500...................... Reston VA 20191 703-264-7500 264-7551
TF: 800-639-2422 ■ *Web:* www.aiaa.org

Air Conditioning Heating & Refrigeration News
2401 W Big Beaver Rd Suite 700........................ Troy MI 48084 248-362-3700 362-0317
TF: 800-837-8337 ■ *Web:* www.achrnews.com

Air Transport World Magazine
8380 Colesville Rd Suite 700.................... Silver Spring MD 20910 301-755-0200 514-3909*
**Fax Area Code:* 913 ■ *Web:* www.atwonline.com

American Salon Magazine 757 3rd Ave 5th Fl.......... New York NY 10017 212-895-8200 895-8210
TF: 800-342-8244 ■ *Web:* www.americansalonmag.com

American Society of Civil Engineers (ASCE)
1801 Alexander Bell Dr............................. Reston VA 20191 703-295-6200 295-6211
TF: 800-548-2723 ■ *Web:* www.asce.org

Automotive Executive Magazine
8400 Westpark Dr................................. McLean VA 22102 703-821-7150 821-7234
TF: 800-252-6232

Automotive News Magazine 1155 Gratiot Ave........... Detroit MI 48207 313-446-0450 446-0383
TF: 877-812-1584 ■ *Web:* www.autonews.com

Bartender Magazine PO Box 158................ Liberty Corner NJ 07938 908-766-6006 766-6607*
**Fax:* Edit ■ *TF Sales:* 800-463-7465 ■ *Web:* www.bartender.com

Phone Fax

Boating Industry Magazine
6420 Sycamore Ln Suite 100.................... Maple Grove MN 55369 763-383-4400 383-4499
TF: 800-848-6247 ■ *Web:* www.boating-industry.com

Builder Magazine 1 Thomas Cir NW Suite 600....... Washington DC 20005 202-452-0800 785-1974
TF: 800-636-0336 ■ *Web:* www.builderonline.com

Building Design & Construction Magazine
3030 W Salt Creek Ln Suite 201.............. Arlington Heights IL 60005 847-391-1000 390-0408
Web: www.bdcnetwork.com

Business & Commercial Aviation Magazine
54 Danbury Rd.................................. Ridgefield CT 06817 203-826-7134
TF Cust Svc: 800-525-5003 ■ *Web:* www.awgnet.com/bca

Chem.Info Magazine
100 Enterprise Dr PO Box 912...................... Rockaway NJ 07866 973-920-7000 920-7531
Web: www.chem.info

Chemical & Engineering News
1155 16th St NW.............................. Washington DC 20036 800-227-5558 964-8071*
**Fax Area Code:* 610 ■ *TF:* 800-227-5558 ■ *Web:* www.pubs.acs.org

Chemical Engineering Magazine
110 William St 11th Fl........................... New York NY 10038 212-621-4900 621-4800
Web: www.che.com

Chemical Processing Magazine
555 W Pierce Rd Suite 301............................ Itasca IL 60143 630-467-1300 467-1109
TF: 800-984-7644 ■ *Web:* www.chemicalprocessing.com

Chemical Week Magazine PO Box 749.............. Mount Morris IL 61054 815-734-5806 734-1223
TF Cust Svc: 800-774-5733 ■ *Web:* www.chemweek.com

Civil Engineering Magazine
1801 Alexander Bell Dr.............................. Reston VA 20191 703-295-6300 295-6300*
**Fax:* Edit ■ *TF:* 800-548-2723 ■ *Web:* www.apps.asce.org

Contract Employment Weekly
11711 N Creek Pkwy S # 112.......................... Bothell WA 98011 425-806-5200 806-5585
Web: www.ceweekly.com

Control Engineering Magazine
2000 Clearwater Dr............................. Oak Brook IL 60523 630-288-8000 288-8580
Web: www.controleng.com

Controller Magazine 120 W Harvest Dr................ Lincoln NE 68521 402-479-2143 479-2135
TF: 800-247-4890 ■ *Web:* www.controller.com

Convenience Store News 770 Broadway 6th Fl......... New York NY 10003 646-654-7658 654-4400
TF: 866-879-9144 ■ *Web:* www.csnews.com

DaySpa Magazine 7628 Densmore Ave............... Van Nuys CA 91406 818-782-7328 782-7450
TF: 800-442-5667 ■ *Web:* www.dayspamagazine.com

Design News 225 Wyman St........................ Waltham MA 02451 781-734-8000
TF: 800-446-6551 ■ *Web:* www.designnews.com

Designfax Magazine 2500 Tamiami Trail N............ Nokomis FL 34275 941-966-9521 966-2590
Web: www.manufacturingcenter.com/dfx

Digital Content Producer
9800 Metcalf Ave............................ Overland Park KS 66212 913-341-1300 967-1905
TF: 800-814-9511 ■ *Web:* digitalcontentproducer.com

EC & M Magazine 9800 Metcalf Ave............. Overland Park KS 66212 913-967-1782 514-6782
TF Acctg: 800-814-9511 ■ *Web:* www.ecmweb.com

EDN Magazine 225 Wyman St........................ Waltham MA 02451 781-734-8000
TF Orders: 800-446-6551 ■ *Web:* www.reed-electronics.com

EE Times Magazine 600 Community Dr............. Manhasset NY 11030 516-562-5000 562-5951
TF: 800-645-6278 ■ *Web:* www.eetimes.com

Electronic Component News
100 Enterprise Dr Suite 600....................... Rockaway NJ 07866 973-920-7000 920-7542
TF: 800-222-0289 ■ *Web:* www.ecnmag.com

Engineering News-Record (ENR)
2 Penn Plaza 9th Fl.............................. New York NY 10121 212-904-3507 904-2820
TF: 877-876-8208 ■ *Web:* enr.construction.com

EPRI Journal 3420 Hillview Ave...................... Palo Alto CA 94304 650-855-2121 855-2121
TF: 800-313-3774 ■ *Web:* www.epri.com/journal

Equipment Today Magazine
1233 Janesville Ave........................... Fort Atkinson WI 53538 920-563-1677

Fine Homebuilding Magazine
63 S Main St PO Box 5506......................... Newtown CT 06470 203-426-8171 270-6753
TF: 800-283-7252 ■ *Web:* www.taunton.com/finehomebuilding

Food Management Magazine 1300 E 9th St......... Cleveland OH 44114 216-696-7000 514-6738*
**Fax Area Code:* 913 ■ *Web:* www.penton.com

Food Processing Magazine
555 W Pierce Rd Suite 301............................ Itasca IL 60143 630-467-1300 467-1179
TF: 800-984-7644 ■ *Web:* www.foodprocessing.com

Furniture/Today Magazine
7025 Albert Pick Rd Suite 200.................... Greensboro NC 27409 336-605-0121 605-1143
Web: www.furnituretoday.com

Giftware News 20 W Kinzie St 12th Fl................. Chicago IL 60654 312-849-2220 849-2174
TF: 800-229-1967 ■ *Web:* www.talcott.com

Glass Magazine 8200 Greensboro Dr Suite 302.......... McLean VA 22102 703-442-4890 442-0630
Web: www.glass.org/magazine/index.htm

Graphicommunicator Magazine 1900 L St NW...... Washington DC 20041 202-462-1400 721-0641

Healthcare Foodservice Magazine
PO Box 470067.................................. Celebration FL 34747 407-566-1700
TF: 800-525-2015 ■ *Web:* www.healthcarefoodservice.ws/magazine.asp

Home Media Retailing
201 E Sandpointe Ave Suite 500.................... Santa Ana CA 92707 714-338-6751 338-6710*
**Fax:* Sales ■ *TF:* 800-371-6897 ■ *Web:* www.homemediamagazine.com

IEEE Spectrum Magazine 3 Pk Ave 17th Fl........... New York NY 10016 212-419-7555 419-7589
Web: www.spectrum.ieee.org

Industrial Equipment News
5 Penn Plaza 8th Fl.............................. New York NY 10001 212-695-0500 629-1585
Web: www.thomaspublishing.com

Industrial Maintenance & Plant Operation Magazine (IMPO)
100 Enterprise Dr Suite 600 PO Box 912............ Rockaway NJ 07866 973-920-7000 920-7542
TF: 800-222-0289 ■ *Web:* www.impomag.com

				Phone	Fax
IndustryWeek Magazine 1300 E 9th St *Web:* www.industryweek.com	Cleveland	OH	44114	216-696-7000	696-7670
Inside Self Storage Magazine 3300 N Central Ave Suite 3000 *Web:* www.insideselfstorage.com	Phoenix	AZ	85012	480-990-1101	990-0819
JEMS Communications Inc 525 B St Suite 1900 *TF Cust Svc:* 800-266-5367 ■ *Web:* www.jems.com	San Diego	CA	92101	619-687-3272	699-6396
Job Shop Technology Magazine 16 Waterbury Rd *TF:* 800-317-0474 ■ *Web:* www.jobshoptechnology.com	Prospect	CT	06712	203-758-4474	758-4475
Journal of Petroleum Technology 222 Palisades Creek Dr *TF:* 800-456-6863 ■ *Web:* www.spe.org	Richardson	TX	75080	972-952-9393	952-9435
Journal of Protective Coatings & Linings 2100 Wharton St Suite 310 *TF:* 800-837-8303 ■ *Web:* www.paintsquare.com	Pittsburgh	PA	15203	412-431-8300	431-5428
Laboratory Equipment Magazine 100 Enterprise Dr Suite 600 *TF:* 800-222-0289 ■ *Web:* www.laboratoryequipment.com	Rockaway	NJ	07866	973-920-7000	920-7542
Land Line Magazine 1 NW Oodia Dr *TF:* 800-444-5791 ■ *Web:* www.landlinemag.com	Grain Valley	MO	64029	816-229-5791	443-2227
Logistics Today Magazine 1300 E 9th St *Web:* mhlnews.com	Cleveland	OH	44114	216-696-7000	696-2737
Looking Fit Magazine 3300 N Central Ave Suite 3000 *Web:* www.lookingfit.com	Phoenix	AZ	85012	480-990-1101	990-0819
Machine Design Magazine 1300 E 9th St *Web:* machinedesign.com/?p=1	Cleveland	OH	44114	216-931-9403	621-8469
Make-Up Artist Magazine 4018 NE 112 Ave Suite D-8 *TF:* 800-805-6648 ■ *Web:* www.makeupmag.com	Vancouver	WA	98682	360-882-3488	885-1836
Manufacturing Engineering Magazine 1 SME Dr PO Box 930 *TF Cust Svc:* 800-733-4763 ■ *Web:* www.sme.org/cgi-bin/find-issues.pl?&&ME&SME	Dearborn	MI	48121	313-425-3000	425-3400
Material Handling & Logistics 1300 E 9th St *Web:* mhlnews.com	Cleveland	OH	44114	216-931-9709	696-2737
Modern Car Care Magazine 3300 N Central Ave Suite 3000 *Web:* www.moderncarcare.com	Phoenix	AZ	85012	480-990-1101	990-0819
Modern Machine Shop Magazine 6915 Valley Ave *TF:* 800-950-8020 ■ *Web:* www.mmsonline.com	Cincinnati	OH	45244	513-527-8800	527-8801
Modern Materials Handling Magazine 111 Speen St Suite 200 *TF:* 800-446-6551 ■ *Web:* www.mmh.com	Framingham	MA	01701	781-734-8000	
Modern Salon Magazine 400 Knightsbridge Pkwy *TF:* 800-621-2845 ■ *Web:* www.modernsalon.com	Lincolnshire	IL	60069	847-634-2600	634-4379
Motor Magazine 50 Charles Lindbergh Blvd Suite 100 *Web:* www.motor.com	Uniondale	NY	11553	516-227-1300	227-1901
Motorcycle Industry Magazine 1521 Church St *TF:* 800-576-4624	Gardnerville	NV	89410	775-782-0222	782-0266
MRO Today Magazine 730 Madison Ave *TF:* 800-932-7732	Fort Atkinson	WI	53538	920-563-5225	563-4269
Nailpro Magazine 7628 Densmore Ave *TF:* 800-442-5667 ■ *Web:* www.nailpro.com	Van Nuys	CA	91406	818-782-7328	782-7450
Nails Magazine 3520 Challenger St *Web:* www.nailsmag.com	Torrance	CA	90503	310-533-2400	533-2507
Nation's Restaurant News 425 Pk Ave 6th Fl **Fax:* Mktg ■ *TF:* 800-944-4676 ■ *Web:* www.nrn.com	New York	NY	10022	212-756-5000	756-5215*
National Clothesline Magazine 801 Easton Rd Suite 2 *Web:* www.natclo.com	Willow Grove	PA	19090	215-830-8467	830-8490
National Fisherman Magazine 121 Free St *TF:* 800-959-5073 ■ *Web:* www.nationalfisherman.com	Portland	ME	04101	207-842-5600	842-5603
National Fitness Trade Journal PO Box 2490 *Web:* www.msfitness.com/NationalFitness/TradeJournal/nftj.html	White City	OR	97503	541-830-0400	830-0410
National Jeweler Magazine 770 Broadway **Fax:* Sales ■ *TF Sales:* 800-250-2430 ■ *Web:* www.nationaljeweler.com	New York	NY	10003	646-654-5000	654-4949*
Natural Products Insider Magazine 3300 N Central Ave Suite 3000 *Web:* www.naturalproductsinsider.com	Phoenix	AZ	85012	480-990-1101	990-0819
New Equipment Digest 1300 E 9th St *Web:* www.pentonmsc.com	Cleveland	OH	44114	216-931-9269	
Oil & Gas Journal 1421 S Sheridan Rd *TF:* 800-331-4463 ■ *Web:* www.ogj.com/index.cfm	Tulsa	OK	74112	918-835-3161	831-9497
Overdrive Magazine 3200 Rice Mine Rd NE *TF:* 800-633-5953 ■ *Web:* www.etrucker.com	Tuscaloosa	AL	35406	205-349-2990	349-6359
Packaging Digest 2000 Clearwater Dr *Web:* www.packagingdigest.com	Oak Brook	IL	60523	630-288-8000	288-8750
Phoenix: Voice of the Scrap Recycling Industries Magazine 1615 L St NW Suite 6000 *Web:* www.isri.org	Washington	DC	20036	202-662-8500	626-0900
Phone+ International Magazine 3300 N Central Ave Suite 3000 *Web:* www.channelpartnersonline.com	Phoenix	AZ	85012	480-990-1101	990-0819
PHONE+ Magazine 3300 N Central Ave Suite 3000 *Web:* www.channelpartnersonline.com	Phoenix	AZ	85012	480-990-1101	990-0819
Plant Engineering Magazine 2000 Clearwater Dr *Web:* www.plantengineering.com	Oak Brook	IL	60523	630-288-8000	288-8781
Plant Services Magazine 555 W Pierce Rd Suite 301 *TF:* 800-984-7644 ■ *Web:* www.plantservices.com	Itasca	IL	60143	630-467-1300	467-1120
Plastics Technology Magazine 6915 Valley Ave *Web:* www.ptonline.com	Cincinnati	OH	45244	513-527-8800	527-8801
Pro Lights & Staging News Magazine 6000 S Eastern Suite 14-J *TF:* 866-776-2003 ■ *Web:* www.plsn.com	Las Vegas	NV	89119	702-932-5585	932-5584
Proceedings of the IEEE Magazine 445 Hoes Ln *Web:* www.ieee.org	Piscataway	NJ	08855	732-562-5478	562-5456
Processing Magazine 5724 Hwy 280 E PO Box 698 **Fax Area Code:* 205 ■ *Web:* www.processingmagazine.com	Birmingham	AL	35242	888-431-2877	408-3798*
Product Design & Development Magazine 100 Enterprise Dr Suite 600 *TF:* 800-222-0289	Rockaway	NJ	07866	973-920-7000	920-7542
Professional Surveyor Magazine 20 W 3rd St *Web:* www.profsurv.com	Frederick	MD	21701	301-682-6101	682-6105
Progressive Grocer Magazine 770 Broadway 5th Fl *Web:* www.progressivegrocer.com	New York	NY	10003	646-654-5000	654-7463
Publishers Weekly Magazine 360 Pk Ave S *TF:* 800-278-2991 ■ *Web:* www.publishersweekly.com	New York	NY	10010	646-746-6758	746-6631
Qualified Remodeler Magazine 1233 Janesville Ave *TF:* 800-547-7377 ■ *Web:* www.qualifiedremodeler.com	Fort Atkinson	WI	53538	920-563-6388	563-1707
Quality Progress Magazine PO Box 3005 *TF Cust Svc:* 800-248-1946 ■ *Web:* www.asq.org/pub/qualityprogress	Milwaukee	WI	53201	414-272-8575	272-1734
Remodeling Magazine 1 Thomas Cir NW Suite 600 *TF:* 888-269-8410 ■ *Web:* www.remodeling.hw.net	Washington	DC	20005	202-452-0800	785-1974
Retail Traffic 249 W 17th St **Fax Area Code:* 914 ■ *Web:* retailtrafficmag.com	New York	NY	10011	212-204-4200	514-9050*
Street & Smith's SportsBusiness Journal 120 W Morehead St Suite 310 *Web:* www.sportsbusinessjournal.com	Charlotte	NC	28202	704-973-1410	973-1401
Sun Wellness Magazine 3300 N Central Ave Suite 3000 *Web:* www.sun-wellness.com	Phoenix	AZ	85012	480-990-1101	990-0819
Supermarket News PO Box 155548 **Fax Area Code:* 818 ■ *TF:* 800-424-8698 ■ *Web:* www.supermarketnews.com	North Hollywood	CA	91615	800-424-8698	487-4550*
Telephony Magazine 330 N Wabash Ave Suite 2300 *TF:* 800-458-0479	Chicago	IL	60611	312-595-1080	595-0295
Travel Weekly Crossroads Magazine 100 Lighting Way *TF:* 877-705-8889 ■ *Web:* www.travelweekly.com	Secaucus	NJ	07094	201-902-2000	902-1916
Trucker's Connection Magazine 5960 Crooked Creek Rd Suite 15 *Web:* www.truckersconnection.com	Norcross	GA	30092	770-416-0927	416-1734
United Mine Workers Journal 8315 Lee Hwy	Fairfax	VA	22031	703-208-7200	208-7227
Urban Call Magazine 4265 Brownsboro Rd Suite 225 *Web:* www.urbancall.com	Winston-Salem	NC	27106	336-759-7477	759-7212
VARBusiness Magazine 600 Community Dr **Fax:* Edit ■ *Web:* www.ubm.com	Manhasset	NY	11030	516-562-5000	562-7850*
Videography Magazine 28 E 28th St 12th Fl *Web:* www.nbmedia.com	New York	NY	10016	212-378-0400	378-0470
Women's Wear Daily Magazine 750 3rd Ave 5th Fl *TF:* 800-289-0273 ■ *Web:* www.wwd.com	New York	NY	10017	212-630-4600	630-4580
Writer's Digest 4700 E Galbraith Rd *TF Cust Svc:* 800-283-0963 ■ *Web:* www.writersdigest.com	Cincinnati	OH	45236	513-531-2690	531-4744
X-Change Magazine 3300 N Central Ave Suite 3000 *Web:* www.vision2mobile.com	Phoenix	AZ	85012	480-990-1101	990-0819

460-22 Travel & Regional Interest Magazines

				Phone	Fax
AAA Motorist Magazine 5700 Brecksville Rd *Web:* www.aaa.com	Independence	OH	44131	216-606-6700	606-6710
Alaska Airlines Magazine 2701 1st Ave Suite 250 *Web:* www.alaskaairlinesmagazine.com	Seattle	WA	98121	206-441-5871	448-6939
Alaska Magazine 301 Arctic Slope Ave Suite 300 *TF:* 800-458-4010 ■ *Web:* www.alaskamagazine.com	Anchorage	AK	99518	907-275-2101	275-2117
American Way Magazine 4255 Amon Carter Blvd *Web:* www.americanwaymag.com	Fort Worth	TX	76155	817-967-1804	967-1571
Arizona Highways Magazine 2039 W Lewis Ave *TF:* 800-543-5432 ■ *Web:* www.arizonahighways.com	Phoenix	AZ	85009	602-712-2000	254-4505
Atlanta Magazine 260 Peachtree St Suite 300 *Web:* www.atlantamagazine.com	Atlanta	GA	30303	404-527-5500	527-5575
Baltimore Magazine 1000 Lancaster St Suite 400 *TF Cust Svc:* 800-935-0838 ■ *Web:* www.baltimoremagazine.net	Baltimore	MD	21202	410-752-4200	625-0280

	City	State	ZIP	Phone	Fax
Beverly Hills 213 1041 N Ogden Dr Suite 5 *Web:* www.beverlyhills213.com	West Hollywood	CA	90046	323-654-4450	
Boston Magazine 300 Massachusetts Ave *TF:* 800-333-2003 ■ *Web:* www.bostonmagazine.com	Boston	MA	02115	617-262-9700	262-4925
Boston Magazine 300 Massachusetts Ave Suite 506 *TF:* 800-233-1339 ■ *Web:* www.wheremagazine.com	Boston	MA	02115	617-262-9700	262-4925
Buffalo Spree Magazine 100 Corporate Pkwy Suite 220 *Web:* www.buffalospree.com	Buffalo	NY	14226	716-783-9119	783-9983
Business Travel News 770 Broadway **Fax Area Code:* 847 ■ *TF:* 800-950-1314 ■ *Web:* www.btnmag.com	New York	NY	10003	646-654-4500	763-9037*
Cape Cod Life Magazine 60 N St *TF:* 800-698-1717 ■ *Web:* www.capecodlife.com	Hyannis	MA	02601	508-775-9800	775-9801
Caribbean Travel & Life Magazine 460 N Orlando Ave Suite 200 *TF Sales:* 800-588-1689 ■ *Web:* www.bonniercorp.com	Winter Park	FL	32789	407-628-4802	628-7061
Carnegie Magazine 4400 Forbes Ave. *Web:* www.carnegiemuseums.org/cmag	Pittsburgh	PA	15213	412-622-3131	622-6258
Chesapeake Bay Magazine 1819 Bay Ridge Ave Suite 180 *TF:* 800-584-5066 ■ *Web:* www.chesapeakeboating.net	Annapolis	MD	21403	410-263-2662	267-6924
Chicago Life Magazine 1300 W Belmont Ave # 225 *Web:* www.chicagolife.net	Chicago	IL	60657	773-528-2737	
Chicago Magazine 435 N Michigan Ave Suite 1100 **Fax:* Edit ■ *TF:* 800-999-0879 ■ *Web:* www.chicagomag.com	Chicago	IL	60611	312-222-8999	222-0699*
Cincinnati Magazine 441 Vine St Suite 200 *Web:* www.cincinnatimagazine.com	Cincinnati	OH	45202	513-421-4300	562-2746
Cleveland Magazine 1422 Euclid Ave Suite 730 *TF:* 800-210-7293 ■ *Web:* www.clevelandmagazine.com	Cleveland	OH	44115	216-771-2833	781-6318
Coastal Living Magazine 2100 Lakeshore Dr *TF Cust Svc:* 888-252-3529 ■ *Web:* www.coastalliving.com	Birmingham	AL	35209	205-445-6000	445-6990
Columbus Monthly Magazine 5255 Sinclair Rd PO Box 29913 *TF:* 800-354-6031 ■ *Web:* www.columbusmonthly.com	Columbus	OH	43229	614-888-4567	848-3838
Conde Nast Traveler Magazine 4 Times Sq *TF:* 800-223-0780 ■ *Web:* www.concierge.com/cntraveler	New York	NY	10036	212-286-2860	286-2190
Connecticut Magazine 35 Nutmeg Dr *TF:* 800-974-2001 ■ *Web:* www.connecticutmag.com	Trumbull	CT	06611	203-380-6600	380-6610
Cruise Travel Magazine 990 Grove St Suite 400 *Web:* cruisetravelmag.com	Evanston	IL	60201	847-491-6440	491-0459
Departures Magazine 1120 Avenue of the Americas 11th Fl *TF:* 800-333-7483 ■ *Web:* www.departures.com	New York	NY	10036	212-827-6437	827-6413
Down East: The Magazine of Maine 680 Commercial St. *TF:* 800-766-1670	Rockport	ME	04856	207-594-9544	594-9544
Family Motor Coaching Magazine 8291 Clough Pike *TF:* 800-543-3622 ■ *Web:* www.fmca.com	Cincinnati	OH	45244	513-474-3622	474-2332
Going Places Magazine 1515 N Westshore Blvd *TF:* 800-222-7366 ■ *Web:* www.aaagoingplaces.com	Tampa	FL	33607	813-289-5000	288-7935
Gotham Magazine 100 Church St 7th Fl **Fax Area Code:* 212 ■ *TF:* 800-566-3622 ■ *Web:* www.gotham-magazine.com	New York	NY	10007	646-835-5200	760-0003*
Guest Informant Magazine 21200 Erwin St *TF:* 800-275-5885 ■ *Web:* www.morrisvisitorpublications.com/livepages/61.shtml	Woodland Hills	CA	91367	818-716-7484	716-7583
Hamptons Magazine 67 Hampton Rd Suite 5 *Web:* www.hamptons-magazine.com	SouthHampton	NY	11968	631-283-7125	283-7854
Hana Hou Magazine (Hawaiian Airlines) 1144 10th Ave Suite 401 *TF:* 888-733-3336 ■ *Web:* www.hanahou.com	Honolulu	HI	96816	808-733-3333	733-3340
Hemispheres Magazine 1301 Carolina St *Web:* www.hemispheresmagazine.com	Greensboro	NC	27401	336-378-6065	275-2864
Home & Away Magazine 10703 J St Suite 100 *TF:* 800-842-7294 ■ *Web:* www.homeandawaymagazine.com	Omaha	NE	68127	402-592-5000	331-5194
Honolulu Magazine 1000 Bishop St Suite 405 *TF:* 800-788-4230 ■ *Web:* www.honolulumagazine.com	Honolulu	HI	96813	808-534-7546	
Houston LifeStyle Magazine 10707 Corporate Dr Suite 170 *Web:* www.houstonlifestyles.com	Stafford	TX	77477	281-240-2445	240-5079
Hudson Valley Magazine 2678 S Rd 2nd Fl *TF:* 800-274-7844 ■ *Web:* www.hvmag.com	Poughkeepsie	NY	12601	845-463-0542	463-1544
Indianapolis Monthly Magazine 40 Monument Cir Suite 100 *TF Circ:* 888-403-9005 ■ *Web:* www.indianapolismonthly.com	Indianapolis	IN	46204	317-237-9288	684-2080
Inland Empire Magazine 3769 Tibbetts St Suite A *TF:* 877-357-2005 ■ *Web:* www.inlandempiremagazine.com	Riverside	CA	92506	951-682-3026	682-0246
InsideFlyer Magazine 1930 Frequent Flyer Pt *TF:* 800-767-8896 ■ *Web:* www.insideflyer.com	Colorado Springs	CO	80915	719-597-8889	597-6855
Islands Magazine 460 N Orlando Ave Suite 200 *TF:* 800-250-2153 ■ *Web:* www.islands.com	Winter Park	FL	32789	407-628-4802	628-7061
Jacksonville Magazine 1261 King St *TF:* 800-962-0214 ■ *Web:* www.jacksonvillemag.com	Jacksonville	FL	32204	904-389-3622	389-3628
Key Magazine PO Box 111266 *Web:* www.keymemphis.com	Memphis	TN	38111	901-458-3912	458-5723
Key: This Week in Chicago Magazine 226 E Ontario St Suite 300 *Web:* www.keymagazinechicago.com	Chicago	IL	60611	312-943-0838	664-6113
Los Angeles Confidential Magazine 1875 Century Pk E Suite 1130 *TF:* 800-566-3622 ■ *Web:* www.la-confidential-magazine.com	Los Angeles	CA	90067	310-289-7300	289-0444
Los Angeles Magazine 5900 Wilshire Blvd 10th Fl **Fax:* Edit ■ *TF Cust Svc:* 800-876-5222 ■ *Web:* www.lamag.com	Los Angeles	CA	90036	323-801-0100	801-0105*
Louisville Magazine 137 W Muhammad Ali Blvd Suite 102 *Web:* www.louisville.com	Louisville	KY	40202	502-625-0100	625-0109
Manhattan Bride Magazine 330 W 56th St *Web:* www.manhattanbride.com	New York	NY	10019	212-265-7970	265-8052
Memphis Magazine 460 Tennessee St Suite 200 *Web:* www.memphismagazine.com	Memphis	TN	38103	901-521-9000	521-0129
Michigan Out-of-Doors Magazine (MOOD) 2101 Wood St PO Box 30235 *TF:* 800-777-6720 ■ *Web:* www.mucc.org	Lansing	MI	48912	517-371-1041	371-1505
Midwest Living Magazine 1716 Locust St *TF:* 800-678-8093 ■ *Web:* www.midwestliving.com	Des Moines	IA	50309	515-284-3000	284-3836
Midwest Traveler Magazine 12901 N 40th Dr *TF:* 800-222-7623 ■ *Web:* www.aaa.com	Saint Louis	MO	63141	314-523-7350	523-6982
Milwaukee Magazine 417 E Chicago St *TF:* 800-662-4818 ■ *Web:* www.milwaukeemagazine.com	Milwaukee	WI	53202	414-273-1101	273-0016
Minneapolis-Saint Paul Magazine 220 S 6th St Suite 500 *TF:* 800-999-5589 ■ *Web:* www.mspmag.com	Minneapolis	MN	55402	612-339-7571	339-5806
Mississippi Magazine 5 Lakeland Cir PO Box 16445 *TF:* 800-844-8418 ■ *Web:* www.mississippimagazine.com	Jackson	MS	39236	601-982-8418	982-8447
MotorHome Magazine 2575 Vista Del Mar Dr *TF Cust Svc:* 800-678-1201 ■ *Web:* www.motorhomemagazine.com	Ventura	CA	93001	805-667-4100	667-4484
National Geographic Traveler Magazine 1145 17th St NW *TF:* 800-647-5463 ■ *Web:* www.travel.nationalgeographic.com/travel/traveler-magazine	Washington	DC	20036	202-857-7000	
Nevada Magazine 401 N Carson St *TF:* 800-495-3281 ■ *Web:* www.nevadamagazine.com	Carson City	NV	89701	775-687-5416	687-6159
New Jersey Monthly Magazine 55 Pk Pl PO Box 920 *TF:* 888-419-0419 ■ *Web:* www.njmonthly.com	Morristown	NJ	07963	973-539-8230	538-2953
New Mexico Magazine PO Box 12002 *TF:* 800-898-6639 ■ *Web:* www.nmmagazine.com	Santa Fe	NM	87504	505-476-0202	827-6496
New Orleans Magazine 110 Veterans Blvd Suite 123 *TF Edit:* 877-221-3512 ■ *Web:* www.myneworleans.com/New-Orleans-Magazine	Metairie	LA	70005	504-828-1380	828-1385
New York Magazine 75 Varick St *TF:* 800-678-0900 ■ *Web:* www.nymag.com	New York	NY	10013	212-508-0700	
Newport Beach 714 Magazine 1901 Westcliff Dr Suite 11	Newport Beach	CA	92660	949-722-1286	722-6632
Nob Hill Gazette 5 3rd St Suite 222 *Web:* www.nobhillgazette.com	San Francisco	CA	94103	415-227-0190	974-5103
Ohio Magazine 1422 Euclid Ave Suite 730 *TF:* 800-210-7293 ■ *Web:* www.ohiomagazine.com	Cleveland	OH	44115	216-771-2833	781-6318
Orange Coast Magazine 3701 Birch St Suite 100 *TF:* 800-397-8179 ■ *Web:* www.orangecoast.com	Newport Beach	CA	92660	949-862-1133	862-0133
Oregon Coast Magazine 4969 Hwy 101 Suite 2 *TF:* 800-348-8401 ■ *Web:* www.northwestmagazines.com	Florence	OR	97439	541-997-8401	997-1124
Orlando Magazine 801 N Magnolia Ave Suite 201 *Web:* www.orlandomagazine.com	Orlando	FL	32803	407-423-0618	237-6258
Palm Beach Illustrated Magazine 1000 N Dixie Hwy Suite C *TF:* 800-308-7346 ■ *Web:* www.palmbeachillustrated.com	West Palm Beach	FL	33401	561-659-0210	659-1736
Palm Springs Life Magazine 303 N Indian Canyon *Web:* www.palmspringslife.com	Palm Springs	CA	92262	760-325-2333	325-7008
Philadelphia Magazine 1818 Market St 36th Fl *TF:* 800-777-1003 ■ *Web:* www.phillymag.com	Philadelphia	PA	19103	215-564-7700	656-3500
Phoenix Magazine 15169 N Scottsdale Suite C10 *TF:* 866-481-6970 ■ *Web:* www.phoenixmag.com	Scottsdale	AZ	85254	480-664-3960	664-3962
Porthole Cruise Magazine 4517 NW 31st Ave *TF:* 888-774-4768 ■ *Web:* www.porthole.com	Fort Lauderdale	FL	33309	954-377-7777	377-7000
Saint Louis Bride Magazine 1006 Olive St Suite 202 *Web:* www.saintlouisbridemagazine.com	Saint Louis	MO	63101	314-588-8313	
San Francisco Magazine 243 Vallejo St *TF:* 866-736-2499 ■ *Web:* www.sanfran.com	San Francisco	CA	94111	415-398-2800	398-6777
Savannah Magazine PO Box 1088 *Web:* www.savannahmagazine.com	Savannah	GA	31402	912-652-0423	525-0611
Southern Accents Magazine 2100 Lakeshore Dr *TF:* 800-366-4712 ■ *Web:* www.southernaccents.com	Birmingham	AL	35209	205-445-6000	445-5936
Southern Living Magazine 2100 Lakeshore Dr *TF:* 800-366-4712 ■ *Web:* www.southernliving.com	Birmingham	AL	35209	205-445-6000	445-6700
Southwest Airlines Spirit Magazine 2811 McKinney Ave Suite 360 *Web:* www.spiritmag.com	Dallas	TX	75204	214-580-8070	580-2491
Sun Life Magazine PO Box 10187	Glendale	AZ	85318	623-878-2210	
Texas Monthly Magazine 701 Brazos St PO Box 1569 *TF:* 800-759-2000 ■ *Web:* www.texasmonthly.com	Austin	TX	78767	512-320-6900	476-9007
Today's Chicago Woman Magazine 150 E Huron St Suite 1001 *Web:* www.tcwmag.com	Chicago	IL	60613	312-951-7600	951-9083
Toronto Life Magazine 111 Queen St E Suite 320 *Web:* www.torontolife.com	Toronto	ON	M5C1S2	416-364-3333	861-1169
Trailer Life Magazine 2575 Vista Del Mar Dr *TF:* 800-765-1912 ■ *Web:* www.trailerlife.com	Ventura	CA	93001	805-667-4100	667-4484

	City	State	Zip	Phone	Fax
Travel Agent Magazine 757 3rd Ave 5th Fl *TF:* 800-895-8210 ■ *Web:* www.travelagentcentral.com	New York	NY	10017	212-895-8200	895-8210
TravelAge West Magazine 11400 W Olympic Blvd Suite 325 *Web:* www.travelagewest.com	Los Angeles	CA	90064	310-954-2510	954-2525
Travelhost Magazine 10701 N Stemmons Fwy *TF:* 800-527-1782 ■ *Web:* www.travelhost.com	Dallas	TX	75220	972-556-0541	432-8729
Tucson Lifestyle Magazine 7000 E Tanque Verde Rd Suite 11 *Web:* www.tucsonlifestyle.com	Tucson	AZ	85715	520-721-2929	721-8665
US Airways Magazine 1301 Carolina St *Web:* www.usairwaysmag.com	Greensboro	NC	27401	336-378-6065	275-2864
US Airways Magazine c/o Pace Communications Inc 1301 Carolina St *Web:* www.usairwaysmag.com	Greensboro	NC	27401	336-378-6065	
Vermont Life Magazine 1 National Life Dr *TF:* 800-284-3243 ■ *Web:* www.vtlife.com	Montpelier	VT	05620	802-828-3241	455-3399
VIA Magazine 150 Van Ness Ave *Web:* www.viamagazine.com	San Francisco	CA	94102	415-565-2451	863-4726
Washingtonian Magazine 1828 L St NW Suite 200 **Fax:* Edit ■ *TF:* 877-532-6083 ■ *Web:* www.washingtonian.com	Washington	DC	20036	202-296-3600	785-1822*
Waterway Guide Magazine 326 1st St Suite 400 *TF:* 800-233-3359 ■ *Web:* www.waterwayguide.com	Annapolis	MD	21403	443-482-9377	482-9422
Western Outdoors Magazine 185 Avenida La Plata *TF Cust Svc:* 800-290-2929	San Clemente	CA	92673	949-366-0030	366-0309
Westways Magazine 3333 Fairview Rd	Costa Mesa	CA	92626	714-885-2376	
Where Baltimore Magazine 575 S Charles St Suite 503 *Web:* www.wheretraveler.com	Baltimore	MD	21201	410-783-7520	783-1763
Where Chicago Magazine 1165 N Clark St Suite 302 *Web:* www.wheretraveler.com	Chicago	IL	60610	312-642-1896	642-5467
Where Los Angeles Magazine 3679 Motor Ave Suite 300 *Web:* www.wherela.com	Los Angeles	CA	90034	310-280-2880	280-2890
Where New Orleans Magazine 528 Wilkinson Row *Web:* www.wheretraveler.com	New Orleans	LA	70130	504-522-6468	522-0018
Where Phoenix Magazine 3295 N Drinkwater Blvd Suite 5	Scottsdale	AZ	85251	480-481-9981	481-9979
Where San Francisco Magazine 555 Montgomery St Suite 803 *Web:* www.wheretraveler.com	San Francisco	CA	94111	415-901-6260	901-6261
Where Washington Magazine 1720 Eye St NW Suite 600 *Web:* www.wheretraveler.com	Washington	DC	20006	202-463-4550	463-4553
Wisconsin Trails Magazine 333 W State St **Fax Area Code:* 414 ■ *TF:* 800-236-8088 ■ *Web:* www.wistrails.com	Milwaukee	WI	53201	800-877-5280	647-4723*
Yankee Magazine 1121 Main St PO Box 520 *TF:* 800-288-4284 ■ *Web:* www.yankeemagazine.com	Dublin	NH	03444	603-563-8111	563-8252

461 MAGNETS - PERMANENT

	City	State	Zip	Phone	Fax
Bangor Electronics Co 100 Industrial Pk Dr *Web:* www.bangorelectronics.com	Bangor	MI	49013	269-427-7944	
Bruker Energy & Supercon Technologies Inc 15 Fortune Dr *Web:* www.bruker-est.com	Billerica	MA	01821	978-901-7550	901-7551
Dexter Magnetic Technologies Inc 1050 Morse Ave *Web:* www.dextermag.com	Elk Grove Village	IL	60007	847-956-1140	956-8205
Electron Energy Corp 924 Links Ave *TF:* 800-824-2735 ■ *Web:* www.electronenergy.com	Landisville	PA	17538	717-898-2294	898-0660
Eneflux Armtek Magnetics Inc 700 Hicksville Rd Suite 110 *Web:* www.eamagnetics.com	Bethpage	NY	11714	516-349-0022	
Flexmag Industries Inc 107 Industry Rd *TF:* 800-543-4426 ■ *Web:* www.arnoldmagnetics.com	Marietta	OH	45750	740-374-8024	374-5068
Hitachi Magnetics Corp 7800 Neff Rd *TF:* 800-955-9321	Edmore	MI	48829	989-427-5151	427-5571
Jobmaster Corp 1505 Serpentine Rd *TF Cust Svc:* 800-642-1400	Baltimore	MD	21209	410-655-1400	521-5461
Magnaworks Technology Inc 36 Carlough Rd *Web:* www.magnaworkstechnology.com	Bohemia	NY	11716	631-218-3431	218-3432
Magnet Applications Inc 375 Horsham Rd Suite 200 *Web:* www.magnetapplications.com	Horsham	PA	19044	215-441-7704	441-7734
Magnet Technology Inc 1599 Kingsview Dr *Web:* www.magtech.cc	Lebanon	OH	45036	513-932-4416	932-4502
Magnetic Component Engineering Inc 2830 Lomita Blvd **Fax Area Code:* 310 ■ *TF:* 800-989-5656 ■ *Web:* www.mceproducts.com	Torrance	CA	90505	800-989-5656	784-3192*
Magnum Magnetics Corp 801 Masonic Pk Rd *TF:* 800-258-0991 ■ *Web:* www.magnummagnetics.com	Marietta	OH	45750	740-373-7770	373-2880
National Magnetics Group Inc 1210 Win Dr *Web:* www.magneticsgroup.com	Bethlehem	PA	18017	610-867-7600	867-0200
Permanent Magnet Co Inc 4437 Bragdon St *TF:* 800-547-1336	Indianapolis	IN	46226	317-547-1336	549-9259
Shin-etsu Magnetics Inc 2372 Qume Dr Suite B *Web:* www.shinetsumagnetics.com	San Jose	CA	95131	408-383-9240	383-9245
Thomas & Skinner Inc 1120 E 23rd St *Web:* www.thomas-skinner.com	Indianapolis	IN	46205	317-923-2501	923-5919

462 MAIL ORDER HOUSES

SEE ALSO Art Supply Stores p. 1403; Book, Music, Video Clubs p. 1534; Checks - Personal & Business p. 1598; Computer Stores p. 1694; Seed Companies p. 2650

	City	State	Zip	Phone	Fax
Advanced Image Direct 1415 S Acacia Ave *TF:* 800-540-3848 ■ *Web:* www.advancedimagedirect.com	Fullerton	CA	92831	714-502-3900	502-3901
Aerobic Life Industries Inc 2800 E Chambers St Suite 700 *TF Orders:* 800-798-0707 ■ *Web:* www.aerobiclife.com	Phoenix	AZ	85040	602-283-0755	283-0760
Allied Marketing Group Inc 1555 Regal Row *TF:* 800-762-3302 ■ *Web:* www.alliedmarketinggroup.com	Dallas	TX	75247	214-915-7000	915-7458
America's Hobby Ctr Inc 8300 Tonnelle Ave *TF:* 800-242-1931 ■ *Web:* www.ahc1931.com	North Bergen	NJ	07047	201-662-0777	662-1450
American Blind & Wallpaper Factory 909 N Sheldon Rd *TF Cust Svc:* 800-575-9019	Plymouth	MI	48170	734-207-5800	207-0947
Appleseed's Inc 30 Tozer Rd *TF Cust Svc:* 888-430-5711 ■ *Web:* www.appleseeds.com	Beverly	MA	01915	978-922-2040	922-7001
Backcountry.com 2607 S 3200 W Suite A *TF Orders:* 800-409-4502 ■ *Web:* www.backcountry.com	West Valley City	UT	84119	801-973-4553	746-7581
Bedford Fair Lifestyles 421 Landmark Dr **Fax Area Code:* 520 ■ *TF:* 800-964-9030 ■ *Web:* www.bedfordfair.com	Wilmington	NC	28410	800-964-9030	750-6767*
Boston Proper 6500 Park of Commerce Blvd *Web:* www.bostonproper.com	Boca Raton	FL	33487	561-241-1700	241-1055
Brokers Worldwide 701 Ashland Ave, Bldg 24 Suite 3 *TF:* 800-624-5287 ■ *Web:* www.brokersworldwide.com	Folcroft	PA	19032	610-461-3661	461-4239
Chadwick's of Boston 35 United Dr *TF Sales:* 800-525-6650 ■ *Web:* www.chadwicks.com	West Bridgewater	MA	02379	508-583-8110	587-8327
Childcraft Education Corp 1156 Four Star Dr **Fax Area Code:* 888 ■ *TF:* 800-631-5652	Mount Joy	PA	17552	717-653-7500	532-4453*
Cinmar LP 5566 W Chester Rd *TF:* 800-436-2100 ■ *Web:* www.frontgate.com	West Chester	OH	45069	513-603-1000	603-1270
Country Home Products Inc PO Box 25 *TF:* 800-376-9637 ■ *Web:* www.countryhomeproducts.com	Vergennes	VT	05491	802-877-1201	877-1212
Crutchfield Corp 1 Crutchfield Pk *TF Sales:* 800-955-3000 ■ *Web:* www.crutchfield.com	Charlottesville	VA	22911	434-817-1000	817-1010
Current USA Inc 1005 E Woodmen Rd *TF Cust Svc:* 800-525-7170 ■ *Web:* www.currentcatalog.com	Colorado Springs	CO	80920	719-594-4100	531-2820
Daniel Smith Artist Materials PO Box 84268 *TF:* 800-426-6740 ■ *Web:* www.danielsmith.com	Seattle	WA	98124	206-223-9599	224-3567
dELiA*s Inc 435 Hudson St *NASDAQ:* DLIA ■ *TF:* 800-335-4269 ■ *Web:* www.store.delias.com	New York	NY	10014	212-590-0000	
Design Toscano Inc 1400 Morse Ave *TF:* 800-525-5141 ■ *Web:* www.designtoscano.com	Elk Grove Village	IL	60007	847-357-1625	
Digi-Key Corp 701 Brooks Ave S *TF:* 800-344-4539 ■ *Web:* www.digikey.com	Thief River Falls	MN	56701	218-681-6674	681-3380
ET Wright & Co Inc 1356 Williams St	Chippewa Falls	WI	54729	715-720-4321	720-4247
Everglades Direct 720 International Pkwy *TF:* 800-999-9111 ■ *Web:* www.evergladesdirect.com	Sunrise	FL	33325	954-846-8899	846-0777
Fingerhut Cos Inc 6509 Flying Cloud Dr *Web:* www.fingerhut.com	Eden Prairie	MN	55344	952-656-4037	
Forestry Suppliers Inc 205 W Rankin St *TF Cust Svc:* 800-752-8460 ■ *Web:* www.forestry-suppliers.com	Jackson	MS	39201	601-354-3565	292-0165
Franklin Mint Corp 105 Commerce Dr *TF:* 800-523-7622 ■ *Web:* www.franklinmint.com	Aston	PA	19014	610-459-6000	459-6880
Gaiam Inc 833 W S Boulder Rd PO Box 3095 *NASDAQ:* GAIA ■ *TF:* 877-989-6321 ■ *Web:* www.gaiam.com	Boulder	CO	80307	303-464-3600	222-3700
Gardens Alive Inc 5100 Schenley Pl **Fax Area Code:* 513 ■ *Web:* www.gardensalive.com	Lawrenceburg	IN	47025	812-537-8665	354-1484*
Gooseberry Patch Co 2500 Farmers Dr 110 *TF:* 877-854-7403 ■ *Web:* www.gooseberrypatch.com	Columbus	OH	43235	740-369-1554	363-7225
Hammacher Schlemmer & Co 9307 N Milwaukee Ave *TF:* 800-233-4800 ■ *Web:* www.hammacher.com	Niles	IL	60714	847-581-8600	581-8616
Hanna Andersson Corp 1010 NW Flanders St *TF Cust Svc:* 800-222-0544 ■ *Web:* www.hannaandersson.com	Portland	OR	97209	503-242-0920	222-0544
Hanover Direct Inc 1500 Harbor Blvd *Web:* www.hanoverdirect.com	Weehawken	NJ	07086	201-863-7300	272-3280
Harry & David Holdings Inc 2500 S Pacific Hwy **Fax Area Code:* 877 ■ *TF Cust Svc:* 800-345-5655 ■ *Web:* www.harryanddavid.com	Medford	OR	97501	541-776-2121	233-2300*
Hello Direct Inc 77 Northeastern Blvd **Fax:* Sales ■ *TF:* 800-435-5634 ■ *Web:* www.hellodirect.com	Nashua	NH	03061	800-435-5634	456-2566*
Helm Inc 14310 Hamilton Ave *TF:* 800-448-8631 ■ *Web:* www.helminc.com	Highland Park	MI	48203	313-865-5000	865-2457
Houston Numismatic Exchange Inc 2486 Times Blvd *TF:* 800-231-3650 ■ *Web:* www.hnex.com	Houston	TX	77005	713-528-2135	528-7618
J Crew Group Inc 770 Broadway *TF:* 800-932-0043 ■ *Web:* www.jcrew.com	New York	NY	10003	212-209-2500	209-2666
Jackson & Perkins 2 Floral Ave *TF Cust Svc:* 800-872-7673 ■ *Web:* www.jacksonandperkins.com	Hodges	SC	29653	800-292-4769	
JC Whitney 761 Progress Pkwy **Fax Area Code:* 800 ■ *TF:* 800-529-4486 ■ *Web:* www.jcwhitney.com	La Salle	IL	61301	815-667-4486	537-2700*
JDR Microdevices Inc 1330 Kifer Rd **Fax Area Code:* 800 ■ *TF Sales:* 800-538-5000 ■ *Web:* www.jdr.com	Sunnyvale	CA	94086	408-736-1450	538-5005*
Lands' End Inc 1 Lands' End Ln *TF Orders:* 800-345-3696 ■ *Web:* www.landsend.com	Dodgeville	WI	53595	608-935-9341	935-4260
Levenger 420 S Congress Ave *TF Cust Svc:* 800-544-0880 ■ *Web:* www.levenger.com	Delray Beach	FL	33445	561-276-2436	243-3629
Lillian Vernon Corp 2600 International Pkwy *TF:* 800-505-2250 ■ *Web:* www.lillianvernon.com	Virginia Beach	VA	23452	757-427-7700	427-7819

	City	State	Zip	Phone	Fax
LL Bean Inc 1 Casco St *TF:* 800-341-4341 ■ *Web:* www.llbean.com	Freeport	ME	04033	207-865-4761	552-2802
Mary Maxim Inc 2001 Holland Ave PO Box 5019 *TF:* 800-962-9504 ■ *Web:* www.marymaxim.com	Port Huron	MI	48061	810-987-2000	987-5056
MBI Inc 47 Richards Ave **Fax:* Cust Svc ■ *TF:* 800-243-5160 ■ *Web:* www.mbi-inc.com	Norwalk	CT	06857	203-853-2000	866-1716*
McMaster-Carr Supply Co 600 County Line Rd *Web:* www.mcmaster.com	Elmhurst	IL	60126	630-834-9600	834-9427
MediaBay Inc 2 Ridgedale Ave *NASDAQ: MBAY* ■ *TF:* 800-688-8780	Cedar Knolls	NJ	07927	973-539-9528	539-1273
Miles Kimball Co 250 City Ctr Bldg *TF:* 800-546-2255 ■ *Web:* www.mileskimball.com	Oshkosh	WI	54906	920-231-3800	231-4804
Movies Unlimited Inc 3015 Darnell Rd *TF:* 800-668-4344 ■ *Web:* www.moviesunlimited.com	Philadelphia	PA	19154	215-637-4444	637-2429
Mystic Stamp Co 9700 Mill St *TF:* 866-660-7147 ■ *Web:* www.mysticstamp.com	Camden	NY	13316	315-245-2690	245-0036
NASCO International Inc 901 Janesville Ave *TF Orders:* 800-558-9595 ■ *Web:* www.enasco.com	Fort Atkinson	WI	53538	920-563-2446	563-8296
National Wholesale Co Inc 400 National Blvd *TF:* 800-433-0580 ■ *Web:* www.shopnational.com	Lexington	NC	27292	336-248-5904	249-9326
Newport News Inc 711 3rd Ave 4th Fl *TF Sales:* 800-894-9639 ■ *Web:* www.newport-news.com	New York	NY	10017	212-986-2585	916-8281
Norm Thompson Outfitters Inc 3188 NW Aloclek Dr *TF:* 800-547-1160 ■ *Web:* www.normthompson.com	Hillsboro	OR	97124	503-614-4600	614-4601
Northeast Data Services 1316 College Ave *TF Cust Svc:* 800-845-3720 ■ *Web:* www.artisticlabels.com	Elmira	NY	14901	607-733-5541	735-4540
Now Courier Inc PO Box 6066 **Fax Area Code:* 317 ■ *Web:* www.nowcourier.com	Indianapolis	IN	46206	800-543-6066	638-5750*
NRC Sports Inc 603 Pleasant St *TF:* 800-243-5033 ■ *Web:* www.nrcsports.com	Paxton	MA	01612	508-852-8206	852-8206
Oriental Trading Co Inc 5455 S 90th St *TF:* 800-225-6440 ■ *Web:* www.orientaltrading.com	Omaha	NE	68127	402-596-1200	596-2322
Patagonia Inc 259 W Santa Clara St PO Box 150 *TF Cust Svc:* 800-638-6464 ■ *Web:* www.patagonia.com	Ventura	CA	93001	805-643-8616	653-6355
PETsMART Direct 1989 Transit Way *TF:* 800-785-0504 ■ *Web:* www.petsmart.com	Brockport	NY	14420	585-637-7508	637-7625
Popular Club 20 Commerce Way *TF:* 800-767-2582 ■ *Web:* www.popularclub.com	Totowa	NJ	07512	973-470-3800	200-7033
Positive Promotions Inc PO Box 18021 *TF:* 800-635-2666 ■ *Web:* www.positivepromotions.com	Hauppauge	NY	11788	631-648-1200	
Publishers Clearing House 382 Ch Dr *TF:* 800-682-3124 ■ *Web:* www.pch.com	Port Washington	NY	11050	516-883-5432	944-5601
Real Goods Trading Corp 360 Interlocken Blvd Suite 300 *TF:* 800-762-7325 ■ *Web:* www.realgoods.com	Broomfield	CO	80021	303-222-3600	222-3700
Redcats USA 463 7th Ave *Web:* www.redcatsusa.com	New York	NY	10018	212-613-9500	613-9590
Roaman's 2300 Southeastern Ave *TF:* 800-677-0229 ■ *Web:* www.roamans.com	Indianapolis	IN	46283	800-677-0229	268-2657
S & S Worldwide Inc 75 Mill St *TF Orders:* 800-243-9232 ■ *Web:* www.ssww.com	Colchester	CT	06415	860-537-3451	537-2563
ShopNBC 6740 Shady Oak Rd **Fax:* Hum Res ■ *TF:* 800-676-5523 ■ *Web:* www.shopnbc.com	Eden Prairie	MN	55344	952-943-6000	943-6711*
SkyMall Inc 1520 E Pima St *TF:* 800-759-6255 ■ *Web:* www.skymall.com	Phoenix	AZ	85034	602-254-9777	254-6075
Specialty Catalog Corp 400 Manley St *TF:* 800-472-4017 ■ *Web:* www.scdirect.com	West Bridgewater	MA	02379	508-238-0199	894-0181
Spiegel Inc 1 Spiegel Ave **Fax Area Code:* 757 ■ *TF:* 800-345-4500	Hampton	VA	23630	800-345-4500	334-3994*
Sunnyland Farms Inc 2314 Willson Rd *TF:* 800-999-2488 ■ *Web:* www.sunnylandfarms.com	Albany	GA	31705	229-436-5654	888-8332
Super Duper Inc PO Box 24997 *Web:* www.superduperinc.com	Greenville	SC	29616	864-288-3426	288-3380
Swiss Colony Inc 1112 7th Ave *Web:* www.swisscolony.com	Monroe	WI	53566	608-328-8400	328-8457
Tog Shop Inc 30 Tozer Rd **Fax Area Code:* 800 ■ *TF Cust Svc:* 800-262-8888 ■ *Web:* www.togshop.com	Beverly	MA	01915	978-922-2040	755-7557*
TravelSmith Outfitters Inc 60 Leveroni Ct **Fax Area Code:* 800 ■ *TF:* 800-950-1600 ■ *Web:* www.travelsmith.com	Novato	CA	94949	415-382-1855	950-1656*
Unicover Corp 1 Unicover Ctr *TF Cust Svc:* 800-443-4225 ■ *Web:* www.unicover.com	Cheyenne	WY	82008	307-771-3000	771-3134
Unistar-Sparco Computers Inc 7089 Ryburn Dr *TF:* 800-840-8400 ■ *Web:* www.sparco.com	Millington	TN	38053	901-872-2272	872-8482
Van Dyke Supply Co 39771 Sd Hwy 34 *TF:* 800-843-3320 ■ *Web:* www.vandykes.com	Woonsocket	SD	57385	605-796-4425	796-4085
Victorian Trading Co 15600 W 99th St **Fax Area Code:* 800 ■ *TF Cust Svc:* 800-700-2035 ■ *Web:* www.victoriantradingco.com	Lenexa	KS	66219	913-438-3995	724-7697*
Williams-Sonoma Inc 3250 Van Ness Ave *NYSE: WSM* ■ *TF:* 800-541-1262 ■ *Web:* www.williams-sonomainc.com	San Francisco	CA	94109	415-421-7900	616-8359
Willow Ridge 421 Landmark Dr **Fax Area Code:* 910 ■ *TF:* 800-388-2012 ■ *Web:* www.willowridgecatalog.com	Wilmington	NC	28410	800-388-2012	798-2000*
Wintersilks Inc 212 E Washington Ave 4th Fl *TF:* 800-648-7455 ■ *Web:* www.wintersilks.com	Madison	WI	53703	608-280-9000	280-9448
Women's International Pharmacy Inc PO Box 6468 *TF:* 800-279-5708 ■ *Web:* www.womensinternational.com	Madison	WI	53716	608-221-7800	221-7819
Woodcraft Supply LLC 1177 Rosemar Rd PO Box 1686 **Fax Area Code:* 304 ■ *TF:* 800-535-4482 ■ *Web:* www.woodcraft.com	Parkersburg	WV	26105	800-535-4482	428-8271*
Zappos.com 271 Omega Pkwy Suite 104 *TF:* 800-927-7671 ■ *Web:* www.zappos.com	Shepherdsville	KY	40165	502-543-7200	543-5223

463 MALLS - SHOPPING

	City	State	Zip	Phone	Fax
Ala Moana Shopping Ctr 1450 Ala Moana Blvd *Web:* www.alamoanacenter.com	Honolulu	HI	96814	808-955-9517	955-2193
Allen Premium Outlets 820 W Stacy Rd *Web:* www.premiumoutlets.com	Allen	TX	75013	972-678-7000	678-7011
Altamonte Mall 451 E Altamonte Dr Suite 2165 *Web:* www.altamontemall.com	Altamonte Springs	FL	32701	407-830-4422	215-5125
Arizona Mills 5000 Arizona Mills Cir *Web:* www.arizonamills.com	Tempe	AZ	85282	480-491-7300	491-7400
Arrowhead Towne Ctr 7700 W Arrowhead Towne Ctr *Web:* www.arrowheadtownecenter.com	Glendale	AZ	85308	623-979-7777	979-4447
Arsenal Mall 485 Arsenal St *Web:* www.simon.com	Watertown	MA	02472	617-923-4700	924-0741
Aspen Grove Lifestyle Ctr 7301 S Santa Fe Dr *Web:* www.shopaspengrove.com	Littleton	CO	80120	303-794-0640	798-0238
Augusta Mall 3450 Wrightsboro Rd *Web:* www.augustamall.com	Augusta	GA	30909	706-733-1001	733-7980
Aventura Mall 19501 Biscayne Blvd *Web:* aventuramall.com	Aventura	FL	33180	305-935-1110	935-9360
Avenues Mall 10300 Southside Blvd *Web:* www.simon.com	Jacksonville	FL	32256	904-363-3054	363-3058
Barton Creek Square Mall 2901 S Capital of Texas Hwy *Web:* www.simon.com	Austin	TX	78746	512-327-7040	328-0923
Battlefield Mall 2825 S Glenstone Ave *Web:* www.simon.com	Springfield	MO	65804	417-883-7777	883-2641
Bel Air Mall 3299 Bel Air Mall *Web:* www.shopatbelairmall.com	Mobile	AL	36606	251-478-1893	476-5722
Block at Orange 20 City Blvd W *Web:* www.simon.com	Orange	CA	92868	714-769-4001	769-4010
Boulevard Mall 3528 S Maryland Pkwy *Web:* www.boulevardmall.com	Las Vegas	NV	89169	702-735-8949	732-9197
Boulevard Mall 730 Alberta Dr *Web:* www.boulevard-mall.com	Amherst	NY	14226	716-834-8600	836-6127
Boynton Beach Mall 801 N Congress Ave *Web:* www.simon.com	Boynton Beach	FL	33426	561-736-7902	736-7907
Brea Mall 1065 Brea Mall *Web:* www.simon.com	Brea	CA	92821	714-990-2732	990-5048
Buena Park Downtown 8308 On The Mall *Web:* www.buenaparkdowntown.com	Buena Park	CA	90620	714-503-5000	761-0748
Burbank Town Ctr 201 E Magnolia Blvd *Web:* www.burbanktowncenter.com	Burbank	CA	91502	818-566-8556	566-7936
Burlington Mall 75 Middlesex Tpke *Web:* www.simon.com/mall/?id=146	Burlington	MA	01803	781-272-8667	229-0420
Burnsville Center 1178 Burnsville Ctr *Web:* www.burnsvillecenter.com	Burnsville	MN	55306	952-435-8182	892-5073
Camarillo Premium Outlets 740 E Ventura Blvd *Web:* www.premiumoutlets.com	Camarillo	CA	93010	805-445-8520	445-8522
Carlsbad Premium Outlets 5620 Paseo del Norte *Web:* www.premiumoutlets.com	Carlsbad	CA	92008	760-804-9000	804-9044
Carolina Place Mall 11025 Carolina Pl Pkwy *Web:* www.shopcarolinaplace.com	Pineville	NC	28134	704-543-9300	543-6355
Carousel Ctr 9090 Carousel Ctr Dr *Web:* www.carouselcenter.com	Syracuse	NY	13290	315-466-7000	466-5808
Carousel Mall 295 Carousel Mall	San Bernardino	CA	92401	909-884-0106	885-6893
Cary Towne Ctr 1105 Walnut St *Web:* www.shopcarytownecentermall.com	Cary	NC	27511	919-460-1053	467-5509
Casino Factory Shoppes LLC 13118 Hwy 61 N # 110B *Web:* www.casinofactoryshoppes.com	Tunica Resorts	MS	38664	662-363-1940	363-1941
Castleton Square Mall 6020 E 82nd St *Web:* www.simon.com	Indianapolis	IN	46250	317-849-9993	849-4689
Centre at Salisbury 2300 N Salisbury Blvd *Web:* www.centreatsalisbury.com	Salisbury	MD	21801	410-548-1600	749-4256
Century III Mall 3075 Clairton Rd *Web:* www.simon.com	West Mifflin	PA	15123	412-653-1220	655-0202
Chapel Hills Mall 1710 Briargate Blvd *Web:* www.chapelhillsmall.com	Colorado Springs	CO	80920	719-594-0111	594-6439
Cherry Creek Shopping Ctr 3000 E 1st Ave *Web:* www.shopcherrycreek.com	Denver	CO	80206	303-388-3900	388-8203
Chicago Premium Outlets 1650 Premium Outlets Blvd *Web:* www.premiumoutlets.com	Aurora	IL	60502	630-585-2200	236-0036
Christiana Mall 132 Christiana Mal *Web:* www.shopchristianamall.com	Newark	DE	19702	302-731-9815	731-9950
Christown Spectrum Mall 1703 W Bethany Home Rd *Web:* www.christownspectrum.com	Phoenix	AZ	85015	602-249-0670	246-8690
Cielo Vista Mall 8401 Gateway Blvd W *Web:* www.simon.com	El Paso	TX	79925	915-779-7070	772-4926
Cincinnati Mills 600 Cincinnati Mills Dr *Web:* www.cincinnatimills.com	Cincinnati	OH	45240	513-671-2929	671-7502
Citadel Mall 2070 Sam Rittenberg Blvd Suite 200 *Web:* www.citadelmall.net	Charleston	SC	29407	843-766-8321	763-8534
Citadel Mall The 750 Citadel Dr E Suite 3114 *Web:* www.shopthecitadel.com	Colorado Springs	CO	80909	719-591-2900	597-4839
City Centre 1420 5th Ave	Seattle	WA	98101	206-624-8800	624-8884
Clackamas Town Ctr 12000 SE 82nd Ave *Web:* www.clackamastowncenter.com	Happy Valley	OR	97086	503-653-6913	496-0981
Collin Creek Mall 811 N Central Expy *Web:* www.collincreekmall.com	Plano	TX	75075	972-422-1070	881-1642
Colonie Ctr 1417 Central Ave *Web:* www.shopatcoloniecenter.com	Albany	NY	12205	518-459-9020	438-4835
Columbia Gorge Premium Outlets 450 NW 257th Way Suite 400 *Web:* www.premiumoutlets.com	Troutdale	OR	97060	503-669-8060	666-3062
Columbia Place 7201 Two Notch Rd *TF:* 800-699-2857 ■ *Web:* www.shopcolumbiaplace.com/shop/columbia.nsf/index	Columbia	SC	29223	803-788-4678	736-9168
Columbus City Ctr 111 S 3rd St *TF:* 800-882-4900	Columbus	OH	43215	614-221-4900	469-5093

Name / Address	City	State	Zip	Phone	Fax
Commons at Federal Way 1928 S Commons *Web:* www.tcafw.com	Federal Way	WA	98003	253-839-6151	839-7884
Complexe Les Ailes 677 Sainte-Catherine St W *Web:* www.complexelesailes.com	Montreal	QC	H3B5K3	514-288-3759	288-3779
Concord Mills 8111 Concord Mills Blvd *TF:* 877-626-4557 ■ *Web:* www.concordmillsmall.com	Concord	NC	28027	704-979-3000	979-5050
CoolSprings Galleria 1800 Galleria Blvd Suite 2075 *Web:* www.coolspringsgalleria.com	Franklin	TN	37067	615-771-2050	771-2127
Coral Ridge Mall 1451 Coral Ridge Ave *Web:* www.coralridgemall.com	Coralville	IA	52241	319-625-5500	625-5501
Coronado Ctr 6600 Menaul Blvd NE Suite 1 *Web:* www.coronadocenter.com	Albuquerque	NM	87110	505-881-2700	
Crabtree Valley Mall 4325 Glenwood Ave *Web:* www.crabtree-valley-mall.com	Raleigh	NC	27612	919-787-2506	787-7108
Crestwood Plaza 109 Crestwood Plaza Suite 100	Saint Louis	MO	63126	314-962-2395	962-2384
Cross County Shopping Ctr 8000 Mall Walk *Web:* www.crosscountycenter.com	Yonkers	NY	10704	914-968-9570	423-7760
Crossgates Mall 120 Washington Ave Ext # 250 *TF:* 800-439-2011 ■ *Web:* www.shopcrossgates.com	Albany	NY	12203	518-869-9565	869-9683
Crossroads Mall 7000 Crossroads Blvd *Web:* www.shopcrossroadsmall.com	Oklahoma City	OK	73149	405-631-4421	634-1503
Cumberland Mall 1000 Cumberland Mall *Web:* www.cumberlandmall.com	Atlanta	GA	30339	770-435-2206	435-0432
Cupertino Square 10123 N Wolfe Rd *Web:* www.cupertinosquare.com	Cupertino	CA	95014	408-777-3081	725-0370
Dallas Galleria 13350 N Dallas Pkwy *Web:* www.galleriadallas.com	Dallas	TX	75240	972-702-7100	702-7130
Dayton Mall 2700 Miamisburg Centerville Rd *Web:* www.daytonmall.com	Dayton	OH	45459	937-433-9833	433-5289
Deerbrook Mall 20131 Hwy 59 N *Web:* www.shopdeerbrookmall.com	Humble	TX	77338	281-446-5300	446-1921
Del Amo Fashion Ctr 3525 Carson St *Web:* www.simon.com	Torrance	CA	90503	310-542-8525	793-9235
Design Center of the Americas (DCOTA) 1855 Griffin Rd *TF:* 800-573-2682 ■ *Web:* www.dcota.com	Dania Beach	FL	33004	954-920-7997	920-8066
Dixie Outlet Mall 1250 S Service Rd *Web:* www.dixieoutletmall.shopping.ca	Mississauga	ON	L5E1V4	905-278-3494	278-4283
Dolphin Mall 11401 NW 12 St *Web:* www.shopdolphinmall.com	Miami	FL	33172	305-365-7446	436-9000
Domain The 11410 Century Oaks Terr *Web:* www.simon.com	Austin	TX	78758	512-795-4230	833-5173
East Towne Mall 89 E Towne Mall *Web:* www.shopeasttowne-mall.com	Madison	WI	53704	608-244-1501	244-8306
Eastern Shore Centre 30500 State Hwy 181 *Web:* www.easternshorecentre.com	Spanish Fort	AL	36527	251-625-0060	625-0039
Eastfield Mall 1655 Boston Rd *Web:* www.eastfieldmall.com	Springfield	MA	01129	413-543-8000	543-4221
Eastland Mall 800 N Green River Rd *Web:* www.simon.com	Evansville	IN	47715	812-477-4848	474-1691
Eastmont Town Ctr 7200 Bancroft Ave Suite 1	Oakland	CA	94605	510-632-1131	636-1727
Eastridge Mall 2200 Eastridge Loop Suite 2062 *Web:* www.eastridgecenter.com	San Jose	CA	95122	408-238-3600	274-9684
Eastwood Mall 5555 Youngstown-Warren Rd *Web:* www.eastwoodmall.net	Niles	OH	44446	330-652-6980	544-5929
Eastwood Towne Ctr 3003 Preyde Blvd *Web:* www.shopeastwoodtownecenter.com	Lansing	MI	48912	517-316-9209	316-9214
Edmonton City Centre 2000 10025-102A Ave	Edmonton	AB	T5J2Z2	780-426-8444	441-4700
El Con Mall 3601 E Broadway Blvd Suite 5B *Web:* www.shopelcon.com	Tucson	AZ	85716	520-795-9958	
Emerald Square Mall 999 S Washington St *Web:* www.simon.com/mall/?id=335	North Attleboro	MA	02760	508-699-7979	695-6684
Empire Mall The 5000 Empire Mall *Web:* www.theempiremall.com	Sioux Falls	SD	57106	605-361-0586	362-0283
Essex Shoppes & Cinema 21 Essex Way Suite 107 *Web:* www.essexshoppes.com	Essex	VT	05451	802-878-4200	879-5080
Factory Stores at North Bend *North Bend Premium Outlets* 461 S Fork Ave SW Suite E-1 *Web:* www.premiumoutlets.com	North Bend	WA	98045	425-888-4505	888-4514
Factory Stores of America 12101 S Factory Outlet Dr	Draper	UT	84020	801-571-2933	
Fair Oaks Mall 11750 Lee Jackson Hwy *Web:* www.shopfairoaksmall.com	Fairfax	VA	22030	703-359-8300	273-0547
Fairlane Town Ctr 18900 Michigan Ave *TF:* 800-992-9500 ■ *Web:* www.shopfairlane.com	Dearborn	MI	48126	313-593-3330	593-0572
Fallbrook Ctr 6633 Fallbrook Ave *Web:* www.ggp.com	West Hills	CA	91307	818-885-9700	885-0029
Fashion Island Shopping Ctr 401 Newport Ctr Dr *Web:* www.shopfashionisland.com	Newport Beach	CA	92660	949-721-2000	720-3350
Fashion Place 6191 S State St *Web:* www.fashionplace.com	Murray	UT	84107	801-262-9447	261-0660
Fashion Valley Mall 7007 Friars Rd *Web:* www.simon.com	San Diego	CA	92108	619-688-9113	294-8291
Fayette Mall 3401 Nicholasville Rd Suite 303 *Web:* www.shopfayette-mall.com	Lexington	KY	40503	859-272-3493	273-6376
Festival Bay Mall at International Drive 5250 International Dr Suite 650 *TF:* 800-481-1944 ■ *Web:* www.shopfestivalbaymall.com	Orlando	FL	32819	407-351-7718	351-7734
Fiesta Mall 1445 W Southern Ave Suite 2104 *Web:* www.shopfiesta.com	Mesa	AZ	85202	480-833-4121	844-8132
First Colony Mall 16535 SW Fwy Suite 1 *Web:* www.firstcolonymall.com	Sugar Land	TX	77479	281-265-6123	265-6124
Florida Mall 8001 S Orange Blossom Trail *Web:* www.simon.com	Orlando	FL	32809	407-851-6255	855-1827
Foothill Village 1300 S Foothill Dr *Web:* www.foothillvillage.com	Salt Lake City	UT	84108	801-487-6670	487-6671
Four Seasons Town Centre 410 Four Seasons Town Centre *Web:* www.shopfourseasons.com	Greensboro	NC	27427	336-292-0171	
Fox River Mall 4301 W Wisconsin Ave *TF:* 800-876-6255 ■ *Web:* www.foxrivermall.com	Appleton	WI	54913	920-739-4100	739-8210
Franklin Mills 1455 Franklin Mills Cir *TF:* 800-336-6255 ■ *Web:* www.franklinmills.com	Philadelphia	PA	19154	215-632-1500	632-7888
Freehold Raceway Mall 3710 Rt 9 *Web:* www.freeholdracewaymall.com	Freehold	NJ	07728	732-577-1300	577-6809
Galleria at Fort Lauderdale 2414 E Sunrise Blvd *Web:* www.galleriamall-fl.com	Fort Lauderdale	FL	33304	954-564-1015	566-9976
Galleria at Pittsburgh Mills 590 Pittsburgh Mills Cir *Web:* www.pittsburghmills.com	Tarentum	PA	15084	724-904-9010	904-9020
Galleria at Sunset 1300 W Sunset Rd Suite 1400 *Web:* www.galleriaatsunset.com	Henderson	NV	89014	702-434-2409	434-0259
Galleria at Tyler 1299 Galleria at Tyler St *Web:* www.galleriatyler.com	Riverside	CA	92503	951-351-3112	351-3139
Galleria at White Plains 100 Main St *Web:* www.galleriaatwhiteplains.com	White Plains	NY	10601	914-682-0111	682-1609
Galleria The 5085 Westheimer Rd Suite 4850 *Web:* www.simon.com	Houston	TX	77056	713-621-1907	966-3596
Gallery at Market East The 9th & Market Sts *Web:* galleryatmarketeast.com	Philadelphia	PA	19107	215-625-4962	440-0116
Garden State Plaza 1 Garden State Plaza *Web:* www.westfield.com	Paramus	NJ	07652	201-843-2404	843-1716
Gardens Mall The 3101 PGA Blvd *Web:* www.thegardensmall.com	Palm Beach Gardens	FL	33410	561-622-2115	694-9380
Genesee Valley Ctr 3341 S Linden Rd *Web:* www.geneseemall.com	Flint	MI	48507	810-732-4000	732-4343
Glenbrook Square 4201 Coldwater Rd *Web:* www.glenbrooksquare.com	Fort Wayne	IN	46805	260-483-2121	483-7756
Glendale Galleria 100 W Broadway *Web:* www.glendalegalleria.com	Glendale	CA	91210	818-240-9481	240-0587
Golf Mill Shopping Ctr 239 Golf Mill Ctr *Web:* www.golfmill.com	Niles	IL	60714	847-699-1070	699-1593
Governor's Square 1500 Apalachee Pkwy *Web:* www.governorssquare.com	Tallahassee	FL	32301	850-877-8106	942-0136
Grapevine Mills 3000 Grapevine Mills Pkwy *Web:* www.grapevinemills.com	Grapevine	TX	76051	972-724-4900	724-4920
Great Lakes Mall 7850 Mentor Ave *Web:* www.simon.com	Mentor	OH	44060	440-255-6900	255-0509
Great Mall 447 Great Mall Dr *Web:* www.simon.com	Milpitas	CA	95035	408-945-4022	945-4027
Great Mall of the Great Plains 20700 W 151st St *TF:* 888-386-6255 ■ *Web:* www.greatmallgreatplains.com	Olathe	KS	66061	913-829-3509	829-6748
Green Acres Mall 2034 Green Acres Mall *Web:* www.greenacresmallonline.com	Valley Stream	NY	11581	516-561-7360	561-3870
Greenspoint Mall 12300 IH-45 N Fwy *Web:* www.greenspointmall.com	Houston	TX	77060	281-875-6255	873-7144
Greenwood Park Mall 1251 US Hwy 31 N *Web:* www.simon.com/Mall/?id=165	Greenwood	IN	46142	317-881-6758	887-8606
Grove The 189 The Grove Dr *TF:* 888-315-8883 ■ *Web:* www.thegrovela.com	Los Angeles	CA	90036	323-900-8000	900-8001
Gurnee Mills 6170 W Grand Ave *TF:* 800-937-7467 ■ *Web:* www.gurneemills.com	Gurnee	IL	60031	847-263-7500	263-2423
Gwinnett Place Mall 2100 Pleasant Hill Rd *Web:* www.simon.com	Duluth	GA	30096	770-476-5160	476-9355
Halifax Shopping Centre 7001 Mumford Rd *Web:* www.halifaxshoppingcentre.com	Halifax	NS	B3L4N9	902-453-1752	454-6908
Hamilton Mall 4403 Black Horse Pike *Web:* www.shophamilton.com	Mays Landing	NJ	08330	609-646-6392	645-7837
Hamilton Place 2100 Hamilton Pl Blvd *Web:* www.hamiltonplace.com	Chattanooga	TN	37421	423-894-7177	892-0765
Hanes Mall 3320 Silas Creek Pkwy Suite 264 *Web:* www.shophanesmall.com	Winston-Salem	NC	27103	336-765-8323	765-3738
Haywood Mall 700 Haywood Rd *Web:* www.simon.com	Greenville	SC	29607	864-288-0511	297-6018
Hickory Hollow Mall 5252 Hickory Hollow Pkwy *Web:* www.hickoryhollowmall.com	Antioch	TN	37013	615-731-3500	731-1034
Highland Mall 6001 Airport Blvd Suite 1199 *Web:* www.highlandmall.com	Austin	TX	78752	512-454-9656	452-1463
Hillsdale Shopping Ctr 60 31st Ave *Web:* www.shophillsdale.com	San Mateo	CA	94403	650-345-8222	573-5457
Hilltop Mall 2200 Hilltop Mall Rd *Web:* www.shophilltop.com	Richmond	CA	94806	510-223-6900	223-1453
Holyoke Mall at Ingleside 50 Holyoke St *Web:* www.holyokemall.com	Holyoke	MA	01040	413-536-1441	536-5740
Independence Center 2035 Independence Center Dr *Web:* www.simon.com	Independence	MO	64057	816-795-8600	795-7836
Independence Mall 3500 Oleander Dr *Web:* www.shopindependencemall.com	Wilmington	NC	28403	910-392-1776	392-3417
Ingram Park Mall 6301 NW Loop 410 *Web:* www.simon.com	San Antonio	TX	78238	210-684-9570	681-4614
Irving Mall 3880 Irving Mall *Web:* www.simon.com	Irving	TX	75062	972-255-0571	570-7310
Jefferson Mall 4801 Outerloop Rd *Web:* www.shopjefferson-mall.com	Louisville	KY	40219	502-968-4101	969-0882
Jefferson Valley Mall 650 Lee Blvd *Web:* www.simon.com	Yorktown Heights	NY	10598	914-245-4200	245-3479
Jersey Gardens 651 Kapkowski Rd *Web:* www.jerseygardens.com	Elizabeth	NJ	07201	908-354-5900	436-3010

Name	City	State	ZIP	Phone	Fax
Katy Mills 5000 Katy Mills Cir	Katy	TX	77494	281-644-5000	644-5001
Web: www.simon.com					
Kenwood Towne Centre 7875 Montgomery Rd	Cincinnati	OH	45236	513-745-9100	745-9974
Web: www.kenwoodtownecentre.com					
King of Prussia Mall 160 N Gulph Rd	King of Prussia	PA	19406	610-265-5727	265-1640
Web: www.kingofprussiamall.com					
La Gran Plaza 4200 S Fwy Suite 2500	Fort Worth	TX	76115	817-922-8888	927-1833
Web: www.lagranplazamall.com					
Lafayette Square Mall 3919 Lafayette Rd	Indianapolis	IN	46254	317-329-4083	329-1860
Lakeland Station 3536 Canada Rd	Lakeland	TN	38002	901-386-3180	388-5707
Lakeline Mall 11200 Lakeline Mall Dr	Cedar Park	TX	78613	512-257-7467	257-0522
Web: www.simon.com					
Lakeside Mall 14600 Lakeside Cir	Sterling Heights	MI	48313	586-247-4131	247-0762
TF: 800-334-5573 ■ Web: www.shop-lakesidemall.com					
Lakewood Center Mall 500 Lakewood Ctr	Lakewood	CA	90712	562-633-0437	633-1452
Web: www.shoplakewoodcenter.com					
Las Vegas Premium Outlets 875 S Grand Central Pkwy	Las Vegas	NV	89106	702-474-7500	676-1184
Web: www.premiumoutlets.com					
Lehigh Valley Mall 250 Lehigh Valley Mall	Whitehall	PA	18052	610-264-5511	264-5957
Web: www.lehighvalleymall.com					
Lenox Square Mall 3393 Peachtree Rd NE	Atlanta	GA	30326	404-233-6767	233-7868
Web: www.simon.com					
Liberty Tree Mall 100 Independence Way	Danvers	MA	01923	978-777-0794	777-9857
Web: www.simon.com					
Lincoln Mall 208 Lincoln Mall Dr	Matteson	IL	60443	708-747-5600	747-5629
Web: www.lincoln-mall.com					
Lloyd Ctr 2201 Lloyd Ctr	Portland	OR	97232	503-282-2511	280-9407
Web: www.lloydcenter.com					
Los Cerritos Ctr 239 Los Cerritos Ctr	Cerritos	CA	90703	562-860-0341	860-5289
Web: www.shoploscerritos.com					
Lynnhaven Mall 701 Lynnhaven Pkwy Suite 1068	Virginia Beach	VA	23452	757-340-9340	463-8150
Web: www.lynnhavenmall.com					
Macon Mall 3661 Eisenhower Pkwy	Macon	GA	31206	478-477-8840	474-5238
Web: www.shopmaconmall.com					
Maine Mall 364 Maine Mall Rd	South Portland	ME	04106	207-774-0303	774-6813
Web: www.mainemall.com					
Mall at Cortana 9401 Cortana Pl	Baton Rouge	LA	70815	225-923-1412	928-7920
Web: www.cortanamall.com					
Mall at Fairfield Commons 2727 Fairfield Commons	Beavercreek	OH	45431	937-427-4300	427-3668
Web: www.mallatfairfieldcommons.com					
Mall at Greece Ridge The 271 Greece Ridge Center Dr	Rochester	NY	14626	585-225-0430	227-2525
Web: www.themallatgreeceridge.com					
Mall at Millenia 4200 Conroy Rd	Orlando	FL	32839	407-363-3555	363-6877
Web: www.mallatmillenia.com					
Mall at Robinson 100 Robinson Centre Dr	Pittsburgh	PA	15205	412-788-0816	788-1156
Web: www.shoprobinsonmall.com					
Mall at Short Hills 1200 Morris Tpke	Short Hills	NJ	07078	973-376-7350	376-2976
Web: www.shopshorthills.com					
Mall del Norte 5300 San Dario Suite 206C	Laredo	TX	78041	956-724-8191	724-9583
Web: www.malldelnorte.com					
Mall of America 60 E Broadway	Bloomington	MN	55425	952-883-8810	883-8866
Web: www.mallofamerica.com					
Mall of Louisiana 6401 Bluebonnet Blvd	Baton Rouge	LA	70836	225-761-7228	761-7225
Web: www.mallofluisiana.com					
Mall Saint Matthews 5000 Shelbyville Rd	Louisville	KY	40207	502-893-0311	897-5849
Web: www.mallstmatthews.com					
Marketplace Mall 1 Miracle Mile Dr	Rochester	NY	14623	585-424-6220	427-2745
Web: www.themarketplacemall.com					
Memorial City Mall 303 Memorial City	Houston	TX	77024	713-464-8640	464-7845
Web: www.memorialcitymall.com					
Merle Hay Mall 3800 Merle Hay Rd	Des Moines	IA	50310	515-276-8551	276-9227
Web: www.merlehaymall.com					
Metro North Mall 400 NW Barry Rd	Kansas City	MO	64155	816-436-7800	436-9952
Web: www.metronorthmallkc.com					
Metrocenter Mall 3645 Hwy 80 W	Jackson	MS	39209	601-969-7633	969-6820
Web: www.shopmetrocentermall.com					
Metrocenter Mall 9617 N Metro Pkwy W Suite 1001	Phoenix	AZ	85051	602-997-2641	870-9983
Web: www.metrocentermall.com					
Mic Mac Mall 21 MicMac Blvd	Dartmouth	NS	B3A4N3	902-463-5891	469-5268
Web: www.micmacmall.shopping.ca					
Mid Rivers Mall 1600 Mid Rivers Mall	Saint Peters	MO	63376	636-970-2610	970-2950
Web: www.shopmidriversmall.com					
Midway Mall 3343 Midway Mall	Elyria	OH	44035	440-324-5749	324-7276
Web: www.midwaymallshopping.com					
Mill Creek Mall 5800 Peach St # 654	Erie	PA	16565	814-868-9000	864-1193
Web: www.millcreekmall.net					
Monroeville Mall 200 Mall Blvd	Monroeville	PA	15146	412-243-8511	372-0205
Web: www.monroevillemall.com					
Montclair Plaza 5060 Montclair Plaza Ln	Montclair	CA	91763	909-626-2442	626-7032
Web: www.montclairplaza.com					
Montebello Town Ctr 2134 Montebello Town Ctr Dr	Montebello	CA	90640	323-722-1776	722-1268
Web: www.montebellotowncenter.com					
Moreno Valley Mall 22500 Town Cir Suite 1206	Moreno Valley	CA	92553	951-653-1177	653-1171
Web: www.morenovalleymall.com					
Natick Mall 1245 Worcester St	Natick	MA	01760	508-655-4800	650-9945
Web: www.natickmall.com					
Newpark Mall 2086 Newpark Mall	Newark	CA	94560	510-794-5523	796-7968
Web: www.newparkmall.com					
North East Mall 1101 Melbourne St Suite 1000	Hurst	TX	76053	817-284-3427	595-4471
Web: www.simon.com					
North Idaho Outlets 4300 W Riverbend Ave	Post Falls	ID	83854	208-773-4556	773-4556
North Star Mall 7400 San Pedro Ave Suite 2000	San Antonio	TX	78216	210-342-2325	342-7023
Web: www.northstarmall.com					
North Town Mall 4750 N Division St	Spokane	WA	99207	509-482-0209	483-0360
Web: www.northtownmall.com					
Northbrook Court 2171 Northbrook Ct	Northbrook	IL	60062	847-498-1770	498-5194
Web: www.northbrookcourt.com					
Northgate Mall 9501 Colerain Ave	Cincinnati	OH	45251	513-385-5600	385-5603
Web: www.mynorthgatemall.com					
Northgate Mall 401 NE Northgate Way Suite 210	Seattle	WA	98125	206-362-4777	361-8760
Web: www.simon.com					
NorthPark Ctr 8687 N Central Expy	Dallas	TX	75225	214-363-7441	363-0195
Web: www.northparkcenter.com					
Northpoint Mall 1000 N Pt Cir	Alpharetta	GA	30022	770-740-9273	442-8396
Web: www.northpointmall.com					
Northridge Fashion Ctr 9301 Tampa Ave	Northridge	CA	91324	818-885-9700	885-0029
Web: www.northridgefashioncenter.com					
Northridge Mall 796 Northridge Mall	Salinas	CA	93906	831-449-7226	449-6756
Web: www.shop-northridge-mall.com					
Northshore Mall 210 Andover St	Peabody	MA	01960	978-531-3440	532-9115
Web: www.simon.com					
Northwoods Mall 2150 Northwoods Blvd Unit 60	North Charleston	SC	29406	843-797-3060	797-8363
Web: www.shopnorthwoods-mall.com					
Oak Park Mall 11149 W 95th St	Overland Park	KS	66214	913-888-4400	599-5839
Web: www.thenewoakparkmall.com					
Oakbrook Shopping Ctr 100 Oakbrook Ctr	Oak Brook	IL	60523	630-573-0700	573-0710
Web: www.oakbrookcenter.com					
Oaks The 350 W Hillcrest Dr	Thousand Oaks	CA	91360	805-495-4628	495-9656
Web: www.shoptheoaksmall.com					
Oakwood Ctr 197 Westbank Expy	Gretna	LA	70056	504-361-1550	
Web: www.oakwoodcenter.com					
Ohio Valley Mall 67800 Mall Rd	Saint Clairsville	OH	43950	740-695-4526	695-4451
Web: www.ohiovalleymall.net					
Old Orchard Ctr 4999 Old Orchard Ctr Suite 66	Skokie	IL	60077	847-674-7070	674-7083
Web: www.westfield.com					
Ontario Mills 1 Mills Cir Suite 1	Ontario	CA	91764	909-484-8300	476-0241
TF: 888-526-4557 ■ Web: www.simon.com					
Orland Square 288 Orland Sq	Orland Park	IL	60462	708-349-1646	349-8419
Web: www.simon.com/mall/?id=189					
Orlando Fashion Square East Colonial Dr & Maguire	Orlando	FL	32803	407-896-1131	894-8381
Web: www.orlandofashionsquare.com					
Orlando Premium Outlets 8200 Vineland Ave	Orlando	FL	32821	407-238-7787	238-7649
Web: www.premiumoutlets.com					
Outlets at Loveland 5661 McWhinney Blvd	Loveland	CO	80538	970-663-1916	663-2421
Web: www.outletsatloveland.com					
Oxford Valley Mall 2300 E Lincoln Hwy	Langhorne	PA	19047	215-752-0222	750-0469
Web: www.oxfordvalleymall.com					
Paradise Valley Mall 4568 E Cactus Rd	Phoenix	AZ	85032	602-996-8846	494-1991
Web: www.theparadisevalleymall.com					
Park City Ctr 142 Pk City Ctr	Lancaster	PA	17601	717-393-3851	392-8577
Web: www.parkcitycenter.com					
Park Meadows Retail Resort 8401 Pk Meadows Ctr Dr	Littleton	CO	80124	303-792-2533	792-3360
Web: www.parkmeadows.com					
Park Meadows Town Ctr 8401 Pk Meadows Ctr Dr	Lone Tree	CO	80124	303-792-2533	792-3360
Web: www.parkmeadows.com					
Park Place 5870 E Broadway Blvd	Tucson	AZ	85711	520-747-7575	547-1038
Web: www.parkplacemall.com					
Parks at Arlington 3811 S Cooper St Suite 2206	Arlington	TX	76015	817-467-0200	468-5356
Web: www.theparksatarlington.com					
Parkway Place Mall 2801 Memorial Pkwy SW	Huntsville	AL	35801	256-533-0700	533-5637
Web: www.parkwayplacemall.com					
Parmatown Mall 7899 W Ridgewood Dr	Parma	OH	44129	440-885-5506	884-9330
Web: www.parmatown.com					
Pearlridge Ctr 98-1005 Moana Lua Rd Suite 231	Aiea	HI	96701	808-488-0981	488-9456
Web: www.pearlridgeonline.com					
Pembroke Lakes Mall 11401 Pines Blvd Suite 546	Pembroke Pines	FL	33026	954-436-3520	436-7992
Web: www.pembrokelakesmall.com					
Peninsula Town Ctr 4410 East Claiborne Sq Suite 212	Hampton	VA	23666	757-838-1505	827-9166
Web: www.peninsulatowncenter.com					
Penn Square Mall 1901 NW Expy	Oklahoma City	OK	73118	405-842-4424	842-4676
Web: www.simon.com					
Perimeter Mall 4400 Ashford-Dunwoody Rd Suite 1360	Atlanta	GA	30346	770-394-4270	396-4732
Web: www.perimetermall.com					
Place de la Cite 2600 Laurier Blvd	Quebec	QC	J0H1S0	418-657-6920	657-6924
Web: www.placedelacite.com					
Plaza The 9500 S Western Ave	Evergreen Park	IL	60805	708-422-5454	422-9780
Web: www.theplazamall.org					
Polaris Fashion Place 1500 Polaris Pkwy	Columbus	OH	43240	614-846-1500	846-4617
Web: www.polarisfashionplace.com					
Potomac Mills 2700 Potomac Mills Cir Suite 307	Woodbridge	VA	22192	703-496-9301	643-1054
Web: www.simon.com					
Prime Outlets at Birch Run 12240 S Beyer Rd	Birch Run	MI	48415	989-624-6226	624-6125
TF: 877-466-8853 ■ Web: www.primeoutlets.com					
Prime Outlets at Lebanon 1 Outlet Village Blvd	Lebanon	TN	37090	615-444-0433	444-6933
TF: 800-617-2588 ■ Web: www.primeoutlets.com					
Prime Outlets Ellenton 5461 Factory Shops Blvd	Ellenton	FL	34222	941-723-1150	723-9437
TF: 888-260-7608 ■ Web: www.primeoutlets.com					
Prime Outlets International Orlando 4951 International Dr	Orlando	FL	32819	407-352-9600	351-3873
Web: www.primeoutlets.com					
Prime Outlets Saint Augustine 500 Prime Outlet Blvd	Saint Augustine	FL	32084	904-826-1311	826-4470
Web: www.primeoutlets.com					
Prime Outlets San Marcos 3939 S IH-35	San Marcos	TX	78666	512-396-2200	396-2232
TF: 800-628-9465 ■ Web: www.primeoutlets.com					

Name / Address	City	State	Zip	Phone	Fax
Provo Towne Centre 1200 Towne Centre Blvd *Web:* www.provotownecentre.com	Provo	UT	84601	801-852-2400	852-2405
Puente Hills Mall 1600 Azusa Ave *Web:* www.puentehills-mall.com	City of Industry	CA	91748	626-912-8777	913-2719
Quail Springs Mall 2501 W Memorial Rd *Web:* www.quailspringsmall.com	Oklahoma City	OK	73134	405-755-6530	751-8344
Quaker Bridge Mall 150 Quaker Bridge Mall *Web:* www.quakerbridgemall.com	Lawrenceville	NJ	08648	609-799-8132	275-6523
Randhurst Shopping Ctr 999 N Elmhurst Rd *Web:* www.randhurstmall.com	Mount Prospect	IL	60056	847-259-0500	259-0228
Redmond Town Ctr 7525 166th Ave NE Suite D-210 *Web:* www.redmondtowncenter.com	Redmond	WA	98052	425-867-0808	867-1577
Regency Mall 5538 Durand Ave *Web:* www.shopregency-mall.com	Racine	WI	53406	262-554-7979	554-7477
Regency Square Mall 9501 Arlington Expy Suite 100 *Web:* www.regencysquaremall.com	Jacksonville	FL	32225	904-725-3830	724-7109
Ridgedale Ctr 12401 Wayzata Blvd *Web:* www.ridgedalecenter.com	Minnetonka	MN	55305	952-541-4864	540-0154
Ridgmar Mall 1888 Green Oaks Rd *Web:* www.ridgmar.com	Fort Worth	TX	76116	817-731-0856	763-5146
River Oaks Center 96 River Oaks Center Dr *Web:* www.simon.com/mall/?id=190	Calumet City	IL	60409	708-868-0600	868-1402
Riverchase Galleria 3000 Riverchase Galleria Suite 1000 *Web:* www.riverchasegalleria.com	Birmingham	AL	35244	205-985-3039	985-3040
Rivergate Mall 1000 Rivergate Pkwy Suite 1 *Web:* www.rivergate-mall.com	Goodlettsville	TN	37072	615-859-3456	851-9656
RiverTown Crossings 3700 Rivertown Pkwy *Web:* www.rivertowncrossings.com	Grandville	MI	49418	616-257-5000	257-0507
Rockaway Townsquare Mall 301 Mt Hope Ave *Web:* www.simon.com	Rockaway	NJ	07866	973-361-4070	361-1561
Rolling Oaks Mall 6909 N Loop 1604 E *Web:* www.simon.com	San Antonio	TX	78247	210-651-5513	651-6326
Roosevelt Field Mall 630 Old Country Rd *Web:* www.simon.com	Garden City	NY	11530	516-742-8001	742-8004
Rosedale Ctr 10 Rosedale Ctr *Web:* www.myrosedale.com	Roseville	MN	55113	651-638-3553	638-3599
Ross Park Mall 1000 Ross Pk Mall Dr *Web:* www.simon.com	Pittsburgh	PA	15237	412-369-4400	369-4408
Saint Clair Square 134 St Clair Sq *Web:* www.stclairsquare.com	Fairview Heights	IL	62208	618-632-7567	632-4452
Saint Louis Mills 5555 St Louis Mills Blvd *Web:* www.simon.com	Hazelwood	MO	63042	314-227-5900	227-5901
San Jacinto Mall 1496 San Jacinto Mall *Web:* www.sanjacintomall.com	Baytown	TX	77521	281-421-4533	421-7377
Sawgrass Mills 12801 W Sunrise Blvd *Web:* www.simon.com	Sunrise	FL	33323	954-846-2300	846-2312
Seattle Premium Outlets 10600 Quil Ceda Blvd Suite 750 *Web:* www.premiumoutlets.com	Tulalip	WA	98271	360-654-3000	654-3901
Security Square Mall 6901 Security Blvd *Web:* www.securitysquare.com	Baltimore	MD	21244	410-265-6000	281-1473
Seminole Towne Ctr 200 Towne Ctr Cir *Web:* www.simon.com	Sanford	FL	32771	407-323-2262	323-2464
Sharpstown Mall 7500 Bellaire Blvd Suite 201 *Web:* www.sharpstowncenter.net	Houston	TX	77036	713-777-1111	777-7924
Shops at Briargate 1885 Briargate Pkwy	Colorado Springs	CO	80920	719-265-6264	268-0738
Shops at La Cantera 15900 La Cantera Pkwy Suite 6698 *Web:* www.theshopsatlacantera.com	San Antonio	TX	78256	210-582-6255	582-6699
Shops at Riverwoods 4801 N University Ave *Web:* www.shopsatriverwoods.com	Provo	UT	84604	801-802-8430	802-8431
Shops at Tanforan The 1150 El Camino Real *Web:* www.theshopsattanforan.com	San Bruno	CA	94066	650-873-2000	873-4210
Shops at Willow Bend 6121 W Pk Blvd Suite 1000 *Web:* www.shopwillowbend.com	Plano	TX	75093	972-202-7115	202-7122
Shops at Woodlake 725 Woodlake Rd Suite Q *Web:* www.destinationkohler.com	Kohler	WI	53044	920-459-1713	208-2363
Solomon Pond Mall 601 Donald Lynch Blvd *Web:* www.simon.com/mall/?id=339	Marlborough	MA	01752	508-303-6255	303-0206
South Bay Galleria 1815 Hawthorne Blvd Suite 201 *Web:* www.southbaygalleria.com	Redondo Beach	CA	90278	310-371-7546	371-0103
South Coast Plaza 3333 Bristol St *TF:* 800-782-8888 ■ *Web:* www.southcoastplaza.com	Costa Mesa	CA	92626	714-435-2000	540-7334
South County Ctr 18 S County Centerway *Web:* www.shopsouthcountycenter.com	Saint Louis	MO	63129	314-892-5203	892-0006
South Mall 3300 Lehigh St *Web:* www.shopsouthmall.com	Allentown	PA	18103	610-791-0606	797-4065
South Park Mall 2310 SW Military Dr *Web:* www.visitsouthpark.com	San Antonio	TX	78224	210-921-0534	921-0628
South Plains Mall 6002 Slide Rd *Web:* www.southplainsmall.com	Lubbock	TX	79414	806-792-4653	799-2331
South Shore Plaza 250 Granite St *Web:* www.simon.com	Braintree	MA	02184	781-843-8200	843-4708
Southcenter Mall 2800 Southcenter Mall *Web:* www.westfield.com	Seattle	WA	98188	206-246-7400	244-8607
Southdale Ctr 10 Southdale Ctr *Web:* www.simon.com/Mall/?id=1249	Edina	MN	55435	952-925-7874	925-7856
Southern Park Mall 7401 Market St *Web:* www.simon.com	Youngstown	OH	44512	330-758-4511	726-2719
Southlake Mall 1000 Southlake Mall *Web:* www.southlakemall.com	Morrow	GA	30260	770-961-1050	961-1113
Southland Mall 1 Southland Mall Dr *Web:* www.southlandmall.com	Hayward	CA	94545	510-782-5050	887-9619
Southland Mall 20505 S Dixie Hwy *Web:* www.mysouthlandmall.com	Miami	FL	33189	305-235-8562	235-7956
SouthPark Mall 4400 Sharon Rd *TF:* 888-364-4411 ■ *Web:* www.simon.com	Charlotte	NC	28211	704-364-4411	364-4913
SouthPointe Pavilions 2910 Pine Lake Rd Suite Q *Web:* www.southpointeshopping.com	Lincoln	NE	68516	402-421-2114	421-2191
Southridge Mall 5300 S 76th St *Web:* www.simon.com	Greendale	WI	53129	414-421-1102	421-0492
Southridge Mall 1111 E Army Post Rd *Web:* www.shopsouthridgemall.com	Des Moines	IA	50315	515-287-3880	287-0983
Southwest Center Mall 3662 W Camp Wisdom Rd	Dallas	TX	75237	972-296-1491	861-5798
Southwest Plaza Mall 8501 W Bowles Ave Suite 2A-483 *Web:* www.southwestplaza.com	Littleton	CO	80123	303-973-5300	972-9516
Spring Hill Mall 1072 Spring Hill Mall *Web:* www.springhillmall.com	West Dundee	IL	60118	847-428-2200	428-2219
Springfield Mall 6500 Springfield Mall *Web:* www.springfieldmall.com	Springfield	VA	22150	703-971-3600	922-5018
Square One Mall 1201 Broadway *Web:* www.simon.com/mall/?id=340	Saugus	MA	01906	781-233-8787	231-9787
Stanford Shopping Ctr 680 Stanford Shopping Ctr *Web:* www.simon.com	Palo Alto	CA	94304	650-617-8200	617-8227
Staten Island Mall 2655 Richmond Ave *Web:* www.statenisland-mall.com	Staten Island	NY	10314	718-761-6800	494-6766
Stonebriar Centre 2601 Preston Rd *Web:* www.shopstonebriar.com	Frisco	TX	75034	972-668-6255	668-4902
Stoneridge Shopping Ctr 1 Stoneridge Mall *Web:* www.shopstoneridge.com	Pleasanton	CA	94588	925-463-2778	463-1467
Stratford Square Mall 152 Stratford Sq *Web:* stratfordmall.com	Bloomingdale	IL	60108	630-539-1000	351-9769
Summit Sierra 13925 S Virginia St Suite 212 *Web:* www.thesummitonline.com	Reno	NV	89511	775-853-7800	
Sunrise Mall 6041 Sunrise Mall *Web:* www.sunrisemallonline.com	Citrus Heights	CA	95610	916-961-7150	961-7326
Sunvalley Mall 1 Sunvalley Mall *Web:* www.shopsunvalley.com	Concord	CA	94520	925-825-0400	825-1392
SuperMall of the Great Northwest 1101 SuperMall Way *TF:* 800-729-8258 ■ *Web:* www.supermall.com	Auburn	WA	98001	253-833-9500	833-9006
Tacoma Mall 4502 S Steele St Suite 1177 *Web:* www.simon.com/mall/?id=238	Tacoma	WA	98409	253-475-4565	472-3413
Tallahassee Mall 2415 N Monroe St *Web:* www.shoptallahasseemall.com	Tallahassee	FL	32303	850-385-7145	385-6203
Tanger Outlet Center San Marcos 4015 S IH-35 Suite 319 *TF:* 800-408-8424 ■ *Web:* www.tangeroutlet.com	San Marcos	TX	78666	512-396-7446	396-7449
Town Center at Boca Raton 6000 Glades Rd Suite 100 *Web:* www.simon.com	Boca Raton	FL	33431	561-368-6000	338-0891
Town Center at Cobb 400 Ernest Barrett Pkwy NW Suite 100 *Web:* www.simon.com	Kennesaw	GA	30144	770-424-9486	424-7917
Town East Mall 2063 Town E Mall *Web:* www.towneastmall.com	Mesquite	TX	75150	972-270-4431	686-8974
Tri-County Mall 11700 Princeton Pike *Web:* www.tri-countymall.com	Cincinnati	OH	45246	513-671-0120	671-2931
Tucson Mall 4500 N Oracle Rd *Web:* www.tucsonmall.com	Tucson	AZ	85705	520-293-7330	293-0543
Tulsa Promenade 4107 S Yale Ave *Web:* www.tulsapromenade.com	Tulsa	OK	74135	918-627-9282	663-9385
Tyrone Square Mall 6901 Tyrone Sq *Web:* www.simon.com/mall/?id=135	Saint Petersburg	FL	33710	727-345-0126	345-5699
Tysons Corner Ctr 1961 Chain Bridge Rd *TF:* 888-289-7667 ■ *Web:* www.shoptysons.com	McLean	VA	22102	703-847-7300	847-3089
University Mall 2200 E Fowler Ave *Web:* www.universitymalltampa.com	Tampa	FL	33612	813-971-3465	971-0923
University Park Mall 6501 N Grape Rd *Web:* www.simon.com	Mishawaka	IN	46545	574-277-2223	272-5924
Valley Plaza Mall 2701 Ming Ave *Web:* www.valleyplazamall.com	Bakersfield	CA	93304	661-832-2436	832-8576
Valley View Antique Mall 7281 Sharon-Warren Rd *Web:* www.valleyviewinc.com	Brookfield	OH	44403	330-448-6866	448-2570
Valley View Center Mall 13331 Preston Rd *Web:* www.shopvalleyviewcenter.com	Dallas	TX	75240	972-661-2939	239-1344
Valley View Mall 4802 Valley View Blvd *Web:* www.valleyviewmall.com	Roanoke	VA	24012	540-563-4400	366-8742
Vaughan Mills 1 Bass Pro Mills Dr *Web:* www.vaughanmills.com	Vaughan	ON	L4K5W4	905-879-2110	879-1888
Viejas Outlet Ctr 5005 Willows *Web:* www.shopviejas.com	Alpine	CA	91901	619-659-2070	659-2077
Vintage Faire Mall 3401 Dale Rd Suite 483 *Web:* www.shopvintagefairemall.com	Modesto	CA	95356	209-527-3401	527-3428
Virginia Center Commons 10101 Brook Rd Suite 765 *Web:* www.simon.com	Glen Allen	VA	23059	804-266-9000	266-9148
Vista Ridge Mall 2401 S Stemmons Fwy *Web:* www.vistaridgemall.com	Lewisville	TX	75067	972-315-3641	315-3725
Volusia Mall 1700 W International Speedway Blvd *Web:* www.volusiamall.net	Daytona Beach	FL	32114	386-253-6783	254-8256
Voorhees Town Ctr 2120 Voorhees Town Ctr *Web:* www.voorheestowncenter.com	Voorhees	NJ	08043	856-772-1950	772-2831
Waccamaw Factory Shoppes 3071 Waccamaw Blvd	Myrtle Beach	SC	29579	843-236-8200	236-8748
Walden Galleria 1 Walden Galleria *Web:* www.waldengalleria.com	Buffalo	NY	14225	716-681-7600	681-1773
Warwick Mall 400 Bald Hill Rd Suite 100 *Web:* www.warwickmall.com	Warwick	RI	02886	401-739-7500	732-6052

	City	State	Zip	Phone	Fax
Washington Square Mall 10202 E Washington St	Indianapolis	IN	46229	317-899-4567	897-9428
Web: www.simon.com					
Washington Square Shopping Center 9585 SW Washington Sq Rd	Portland	OR	97223	503-639-8860	620-6602
Web: www.shopwashingtonsquare.com					
West Oaks Mall 2600 Hwy 6 S	Houston	TX	77082	281-531-1332	531-1579
Web: www.shopwestoaksmall.com					
West Oaks Mall 9401 W Colonial Dr Suite 728	Ocoee	FL	34761	407-294-6033	294-6051
Web: www.westoaksmall.com					
West Ridge Mall 1801 SW Wanamaker Rd	Topeka	KS	66604	785-272-5119	272-1483
Web: www.simon.com					
West Shore Plaza 250 W Shore Blvd	Tampa	FL	33609	813-286-0790	282-2126
Web: www.westshoreplaza.com					
West Town Mall 7600 Kingston Pike	Knoxville	TN	37919	865-693-0292	531-0503
Web: www.simon.com					
West Towne Mall 66 W Towne Mall	Madison	WI	53719	608-833-1544	833-5878
TF: 800-833-6330 ■ *Web:* www.shopwesttowne-mall.com					
Westchester The 125 Westchester Ave Suite 925	White Plains	NY	10601	914-421-1333	421-1475
Web: www.simon.com					
Westfarms Mall 1500 New Britian Ave	West Hartford	CT	06110	860-561-3420	521-8682
Web: www.shopwestfarms.com					
Westfield Broward Mall 8000 W Broward Blvd	Plantation	FL	33388	954-473-8100	472-4302
Web: www.westfield.com					
Westfield Citrus Park 8021 Citrus Pk Dr	Tampa	FL	33625	813-926-4644	926-4601
Web: www.westfield.com					
Westfield Countryside 27001 US 19 N Suite 2096	Clearwater	FL	33761	727-796-1070	791-8470
Web: www.westfield.com/countryside					
Westfield Fashion Square 14006 Riverside Dr	Sherman Oaks	CA	91423	818-783-0550	783-5955
Web: www.westfield.com					
Westfield Franklin Park 5001 Monroe St Suite 700	Toledo	OH	43623	419-473-3317	473-0199
Web: www.westfield.com					
Westfield Hawthorn R 122 Hawthorn Ctr	Vernon Hills	IL	60061	847-362-2600	362-2689
Web: www.westfield.com					
Westfield MainPlace 2800 N Main St	Santa Ana	CA	92705	714-547-7800	547-2643
Web: westfield.com/mainplace					
Westfield Mission Valley 1640 Camino del Rio N Suite 351	San Diego	CA	92108	619-296-6375	692-0555
Web: www.westfield.com					
Westfield Montgomery 7101 Democracy Blvd	Bethesda	MD	20817	301-469-6000	469-7612
Web: www.westfield.com/montgomery					
Westfield North Bridge 520 N Michigan Ave	Chicago	IL	60611	312-327-2300	222-1757
Web: www.theshopsatnorthbridge.com					
Westfield Parkway 415 Parkway Plaza	El Cajon	CA	92020	619-579-9932	579-1280
Web: www.westfield.com/parkway					
Westfield San Francisco Centre 865 Market St PO Box A	San Francisco	CA	94103	415-512-6776	512-6770
Web: www.westfield.com					
Westfield Santa Anita 400 S Baldwin Ave Suite 231	Arcadia	CA	91007	626-445-6255	446-9320
Web: www.westfield.com/santaanita					
Westfield Sarasota Square 8201 S Tamiami Tr	Sarasota	FL	34238	941-922-9609	921-2632
Web: www.westfield.com					
Westfield Shoppingtown Annapolis 2002 Annapolis Mall	Annapolis	MD	21401	410-266-5432	266-3572
Web: www.westfield.com					
Westfield Shoppingtown UTC 4545 La Jolla Village Dr	San Diego	CA	92122	858-546-8858	552-9065
Web: www.westfield.com					
Westfield Southgate 3501 S Tamiami Trail	Sarasota	FL	34239	941-955-0900	954-3087
Web: www.westfield.com					
Westfield SouthPark 500 Southpark Ctr	Strongsville	OH	44136	440-238-9000	846-8323
Web: www.westfield.com					
Westfield Topanga 6600 Topanga Canyon Blvd	Canoga Park	CA	91303	818-594-8740	999-0878
Web: www.westfield.com					
Westfield Trumbull Town Shopping Mall 5065 Main St	Trumbull	CT	06611	203-372-4500	372-0197
Web: www.westfield.com					
Westfield Valley Fair 2855 Stevens Creek Blvd Suite 2178	Santa Clara	CA	95050	408-248-4451	248-8614
Web: www.westfield.com					
Westfield West County Ctr 80 W County Ctr	Des Peres	MO	63131	314-288-2020	288-2030
Web: www.shopwestcountycenter.com					
Westfield West Covina 112 Plaza Dr	West Covina	CA	91790	626-960-1881	337-3337
Web: www.westfield.com					
WestGate Mall 205 W Blackstock Rd Suite 1	Spartanburg	SC	29301	864-574-0263	587-8363
Web: www.westgate-mall.com					
Westlake Ctr 400 Pine St	Seattle	WA	98101	206-467-1600	467-1603
Web: www.westlakecenter.com					
Westland Shopping Ctr 35000 W Warren Rd	Westland	MI	48185	734-425-5001	425-9205
Web: www.westlandcenter.com					
Westminster Mall 1025 Westminster Mall	Westminster	CA	92683	714-898-2558	892-8824
Web: www.simon.com					
Westminster Mall 5433 W 88th Ave	Westminster	CO	80031	303-428-5634	657-1604
Web: www.shopwestminstermall.com					
Westmoreland Mall 5256 Rt 30 E	Greensburg	PA	15601	724-836-5025	836-4825
Web: www.westmorelandmall.com					
White Marsh Mall 8200 Perry Hall Blvd	Baltimore	MD	21236	410-931-7100	931-7120
Web: www.whitemarshmall.com					
Willowbrook Mall 1400 Willowbrook Mall	Wayne	NJ	07470	973-785-1616	785-8632
Web: www.willowbrook-mall.com					
Willowbrook Mall 2000 Willowbrook Mall	Houston	TX	77070	281-890-8000	890-3109
Web: www.shopwillowbrookmall.com					
Wolfchase Galleria 2760 N Germantown Pkwy	Memphis	TN	38133	901-381-2769	388-5542
Web: www.simon.com					
Woodbridge Center 250 Woodbridge Ctr Dr	Woodbridge	NJ	07095	732-636-4777	636-0417
Web: www.woodbridgecenter.com					
Woodburn Co Stores 1001 N Arney Rd	Woodburn	OR	97071	503-981-1900	982-7434
TF: 888-664-7467 ■ *Web:* www.woodburncompanystores.com					
Woodfield Mall 5 Woodfield Mall	Schaumburg	IL	60173	847-330-1537	330-0251
Web: www.shopwoodfield.com					
Woodland Hills Mall 7021 S Memorial Dr Suite 225B	Tulsa	OK	74133	918-250-1449	250-9084
Web: www.simon.com					
Woodland Mall 3195 28th St SE	Grand Rapids	MI	49512	616-949-0012	949-7348
Web: www.shopwoodlandmall.com					
Worthington Square 150 W Wilson Bridge Rd	Worthington	OH	43085	614-841-1110	841-1109
Yorktown Shopping Ctr 203 Yorktown Ctr	Lombard	IL	60148	630-629-7330	629-7334
Web: www.yorktowncenter.com					

464 MALTING PRODUCTS

SEE ALSO Breweries p. 1544

	City	State	Zip	Phone	Fax
Briess Malting Co 625 S Irish Rd	Chilton	WI	53014	920-849-7711	849-4277
Web: www.briess.com					
Cargill Malt - Specialty Products Group 704 S 15th St	Sheboygan	WI	53081	920-459-4148	458-9034
TF Sales: 800-669-6258 ■ *Web:* www.specialtymalts.com					
Gambrinus Malting Corp 1101 Industrial Dr	Armstrong	BC	V0E1B6	250-546-8911	546-8798
LE Cooke Co 26333 Rd 140	Visalia	CA	93292	559-732-9146	732-3702
Premier Malt Products Inc 25760 Groesbeck Hwy Suite 103	Warren	MI	48089	586-443-3355	443-4580
TF Cust Svc: 800-521-1057 ■ *Web:* www.premiermalt.com					
Schoenmann Produce Co Inc 6950 Neuhaus St	Houston	TX	77061	713-923-2728	923-5897
Web: www.schoenmannproduce.com					
Texasweet Citrus Marketing Inc 901 Business Pk Dr	Mission	TX	78572	956-580-8004	580-1843
Web: www.texasweet.com					
United Canadian Malt Ltd 843 Pk St S	Peterborough	ON	K9J3V1	705-876-9110	876-9118
TF: 800-461-6400					

465 MANAGED CARE - BEHAVIORAL HEALTH

	City	State	Zip	Phone	Fax
Allen Group 2965 W State Rd 434 Suite 100	Longwood	FL	32779	407-788-8822	862-1477
TF: 800-272-7252 ■ *Web:* www.theallengroup.com					
American Behavioral Benefits Managers 550 Montgomery Hwy Suite 300	Birmingham	AL	35216	205-871-7814	868-9600
TF: 800-677-4544 ■ *Web:* www.americanbehavioral.com					
American Psych Systems 8403 Colesville Rd Suite 1600	Silver Spring	MD	20910	301-571-0633	493-0776
TF: 800-305-3720 ■ *Web:* www.apscare.com					
APC Hegeman 50 Dietz St Suite K	Oneonta	NY	13820	607-432-9039	432-7029
TF: 800-327-0085					
APS Healthcare Inc 8403 Colesville Rd	Silver Spring	MD	20910	301-563-5633	563-7348
TF: 800-305-3720 ■ *Web:* www.apshealthcare.com					
Associated Behavioral Health Care Inc 4700 42nd Ave SW Suite 480	Seattle	WA	98116	206-935-1282	937-1380
TF: 800-858-6702 ■ *Web:* www.abhc.com					
Baxter Assistance Services Inc 2800 E Broadway Suite C-416	Pearland	TX	77581	866-443-0005	910-1600
TF: 866-443-0005 ■ *Web:* www.bas-employeeassistance.com					
Bensinger DuPont & Assoc (BDA) 134 N LaSalle St Suite 2200	Chicago	IL	60602	312-726-8620	726-1061
TF: 800-227-8620 ■ *Web:* www.bensingerdupont.com					
CIGNA Behavioral Health Inc 11095 Viking Dr Suite 350	Eden Prairie	MN	55344	952-996-2000	
TF: 800-433-5768 ■ *Web:* www.cignabehavioral.com					
Comprehensive Behavioral Care Inc 204 S Hoover Blvd Suite 200	Tampa	FL	33609	813-288-4808	288-4844
TF: 800-435-5348 ■ *Web:* www.comprehensivecare.com					
Comprehensive EAP 5 Militia Dr	Lexington	MA	02421	781-863-8283	860-9839
TF: 800-344-1011 ■ *Web:* www.compeap.com					
ComPsych Corp 455 N City Front Plaza Dr NBC Tower 13th Fl	Chicago	IL	60611	312-595-4000	595-4029
TF: 800-272-7255 ■ *Web:* www.compsych.com					
Contact Behavioral Health Services 1400 E Southern Ave Suite 800	Tempe	AZ	85282	480-730-3023	730-5528
TF: 800-888-1477 ■ *Web:* www.contactbhs.com					
COPE Inc 1120 G St NW Suite 550	Washington	DC	20005	202-628-5100	628-5111
TF: 800-247-3054 ■ *Web:* www.cope-inc.com					
CorpCare Assoc Inc 7000 Peachtree Dunwoody Rd Bldg 4 Suite 300	Atlanta	GA	30328	770-396-5253	396-9522
TF: 800-728-9444 ■ *Web:* www.corpcareeap.com					
CorpHealth Inc 1300 Summit Ave Suite 600	Fort Worth	TX	76102	817-332-2519	335-9100
TF: 800-240-8388 ■ *Web:* www.corphealth.com					
Corporate Care Works 8665 Baypine Rd Suite 100	Jacksonville	FL	32256	904-296-9436	296-1511
TF: 800-327-9757 ■ *Web:* www.corporatecareworks.com					
EAP Consultants Inc 3901 Roswell Rd Suite 340	Marietta	GA	30062	770-951-8021	953-3174
TF: 800-869-0276 ■ *Web:* www.eapconsultants.com					
EAP Systems 500 W Cummings Pk Suite 6000	Woburn	MA	01801	781-935-8850	935-2594
TF: 800-327-6721 ■ *Web:* www.eapsystems.com					
FEI Behavioral Health 11700 W Lake Pk Dr	Milwaukee	WI	53224	414-359-1055	359-1973
TF: 800-782-1948 ■ *Web:* www.feinet.com					
FHC Health Systems 240 Corporate Blvd	Norfolk	VA	23502	757-459-5100	459-5219
TF: 800-451-3581 ■ *Web:* www.fhchealthsystems.com					
Frontier Health 1167 Spratlin Pk Dr PO Box 9054	Johnson City	TN	37615	423-467-3600	467-3710
Web: www.frontierhealth.org					
Gilsbar Inc PO Box 998	Covington	LA	70434	985-892-3520	898-1500
TF: 800-445-7227 ■ *Web:* www.gilsbar.com					

				Phone	Fax
Holman Group 21050 Vanowen St	Canoga Park	CA	91303	818-704-1444	704-9339
TF: 800-321-2843 ■ *Web:* www.holmangroup.com					
Horizon EAP 9370 Sky Pk Ct Suite 140	San Diego	CA	92123	858-571-1698	571-1868
TF: 800-372-4472 ■ *Web:* www.integratedinsights.com					
Horizon Health Corp 2941 S Lk Vista Dr	Lewisville	TX	75067	972-420-8300	420-8252
TF: 800-931-4646 ■ *Web:* www.hmhm.com					
Human Management Services Inc					
1463 Dunwoody Dr	Westchester	PA	19380	610-644-6000	644-1134
TF: 800-343-2186 ■ *Web:* www.hmsincorp.com					
Hurst Place 555 Sanatorium Rd	Hamilton	ON	L8N3Z5	905-521-8300	521-8166
TF: 888-521-8300 ■ *Web:* www.hurstplace.com					
Interface EAP Inc (IEAP)					
10370 Richmond Ave Suite 1100 PO Box 421879	Houston	TX	77042	713-781-3364	784-0425
TF: 800-324-4327 ■ *Web:* www.ieap.com					
Interpersonal Dynamics Inc					
2265 Teton Plaza	Idaho Falls	ID	83404	208-529-1737	529-1757
TF: 800-658-3837 ■ *Web:* www.idynamic.com					
Lexington Group 1200 Boston Post Rd	Guilford	CT	06437	800-571-0197	606-9800*
**Fax Area Code:* 860 ■ *TF:* 800-571-0197 ■ *Web:* www.the-lexington-group.com					
Magellan Health Services Inc 55 Nod Rd	Avon	CT	06001	860-507-1900	507-1990
NASDAQ: MGLN ■ *TF:* 800-458-2740 ■ *Web:* www.magellanhealth.com					
Managed Health Network Inc					
1600 Los Gamos Dr Suite 300	San Rafael	CA	94903	818-676-6775	
TF: 800-327-2133 ■ *Web:* www.mhn.com					
MHNet Behavioral Health					
9606 N MoPac Exwy Suite 600	Austin	TX	78759	888-646-6889	
Web: www.mhnet.com					
Midwest EAP Solutions Inc					
1015 W St Germain St # 440	Saint Cloud	MN	56301	320-253-1909	240-1501
TF: 800-383-1908 ■ *Web:* www.midwesteap.com					
National Employee Assistance Services Inc					
N 17 W 24100 Riverwood Dr Suite 300	Waukesha	WI	53188	262-574-2500	798-3928
TF: 800-634-6433 ■ *Web:* www.neas.com					
National MENTOR Inc 313 Congress St	Boston	MA	02210	617-790-4800	790-4848
TF: 800-388-5150 ■ *Web:* www.mentormpn.com					
New Directions Behavioral Health LLC					
PO Box 6729	Leawood	KS	66206	913-982-8200	982-8401
TF: 800-528-5763 ■ *Web:* www.ndbh.com					
PacifiCare Behavioral Health Inc					
3120 Lake Ctr Dr	Santa Ana	CA	92704	714-445-0300	513-6602
TF: 800-357-5850 ■ *Web:* www.pbhi.com					
Perspectives Ltd 20 N Clark St Suite 2650	Chicago	IL	60602	312-558-1560	558-1570
TF: 800-866-7556 ■ *Web:* www.perspectivesltd.com					
Preferred Mental Health Management Inc					
401 E Douglas Ave Suite 300	Wichita	KS	67202	316-262-0444	262-0003
TF: 800-776-4357 ■ *Web:* www.pmhm.com					
Providence Service Corp 64 E Broadway	Tucson	AZ	85701	520-748-7108	747-9787
NASDAQ: PRSC ■ *TF:* 800-747-6950 ■ *Web:* www.provcorp.com					
Stuecker & Assoc Inc					
1169 Eastern Pkwy Suite 2243	Louisville	KY	40217	502-452-9227	452-1529
TF: 800-799-9327 ■ *Web:* www.stueckerandassoc.com					
United Behavioral Health Inc					
425 Market St 27th Fl	San Francisco	CA	94105	415-547-5000	547-6200
TF: 800-888-2998 ■ *Web:* www.unitedbehavioralhealth.com					
ValueOptions Inc					
12369 Sunrise Valley Dr Suite C	Reston	VA	20191	703-390-6800	390-6810
TF: 866-221-0644 ■ *Web:* www.valueoptions.com					
Wellpoint Behavioral Health/Blue Cross					
9655 Granite Ridge Dr 6th Fl	San Diego	CA	92123	858-571-8300	278-7822
TF: 800-999-7222 ■ *Web:* www.wellpoint.com					
(i)Structure Inc					
11800 Ridge Pkwy Suite 200	Broomfield	CO	80021	888-757-7501	965-5866*
**Fax Area Code:* 402 ■ *TF:* 888-757-7501 ■ *Web:* www.i-structure.com					

466 MANAGEMENT SERVICES

SEE ALSO Association Management Companies p. 1404; Educational Institution Operators & Managers p. 1791; Facilities Management Services p. 1837; Hotels & Hotel Companies p. 2081; Incentive Program Management Services p. 2104; Investment Advice & Management p. 2129; Pharmacy Benefits Management Services p. 2418

				Phone	Fax
2 Places At 1 Time Inc					
739 Travert Ave Suite E	Atlanta	GA	30318	404-815-9980	572-2246
TF: 877-275-2237 ■ *Web:* www.2placesat1time.com					
Access Systems Inc					
11710 Plaza America Dr Suite 900	Reston	VA	20190	703-464-6900	464-6990
Web: www.accsys-inc.com					
Afognak Native Corp 215 Mission Rd Suite 212	Kodiak	AK	99615	907-486-6014	486-2514
TF: 800-770-6014 ■ *Web:* www.afognak.com					
Alan B Lancz & Assoc Inc 2400 N Reynolds Rd	Toledo	OH	43615	419-536-5200	536-5401
Web: www.ablonline.com					
Alliance of Professionals & Consultants Inc					
8200 Brownleigh Dr	Raleigh	NC	27617	919-510-9696	510-9668
Web: www.apc-services.com					
American Dental Partners Inc					
401 Edgewater Pl Suite 430	Wakefield	MA	01880	781-224-0880	224-4216
NASDAQ: ADPI ■ *TF:* 800-838-6563 ■ *Web:* www.amdpi.com					
AmeriPath Inc					
7111 Fairway Dr Suite 400	Palm Beach Gardens	FL	33418	561-627-8931	845-0129
TF: 800-330-6565 ■ *Web:* www.ameripath.com					
Amfm Inc 240 Capitol St Suite 500	Charleston	WV	25301	304-344-1623	
TF: 800-348-1623 ■ *Web:* www.amfmwv.com					
Archway Marketing Services Inc					
19850 S Diamond Lake Rd	Rogers	MN	55374	763-428-3300	428-3302
TF: 866-791-4826 ■ *Web:* www.archway.com					
Ares Management LLC					
2000 Avenue of the Stars 12th Fl	Los Angeles	CA	90067	310-201-4100	201-4170
Web: www.aresmgmt.com					
ATCO Properties & Management Inc					
555 5th Ave 16Fl	New York	NY	10017	212-687-5154	682-7599
Web: www.atco555.com					
Atrilogy Solutions Group Inc					
15375 Barranca Pkwy Suite 201 Bldg B	Irvine	CA	92618	949-754-0500	203-8766
Web: www.atrilogy.com					
AWC Inc 6655 Exchequer Dr	Baton Rouge	LA	70809	225-752-1100	751-9029
Web: www.awc-inc.com					
Birner Dental Management Services Inc					
1777 S Harrison St Suite 1400	Denver	CO	80210	303-691-0680	691-0889
NASDAQ: BDMS ■ *TF:* 877-898-1083 ■ *Web:* www.bdms-perfectteeth.com					
Blackhawk Management Corp 1335 Regents Pk Dr	Houston	TX	77058	281-286-5751	286-5752
Web: www.blackhawkmgmt.com					
Brock Enterprises Inc					
10343 Sam Houston Pk Dr Suite 200	Houston	TX	77064	281-807-8200	
Web: www.brockgroup.com					
Capgemini US LLC 623 5th Ave # 33	New York	NY	10022	917-934-8000	934-8001
Web: www.us.capgemini.com					
Cardon & Assoc Inc 2749 E Covenanter Dr	Bloomington	IN	47401	812-332-2265	
Web: www.cardon.us					
Catapult Technology Ltd					
7500 Old Georgetown Rd 11th Fl	Bethesda	MD	20814	240-482-2100	986-8688*
**Fax Area Code:* 301 ■ *Web:* www.catapulttechnology.com					
Central Management Co Inc 9258 Hwy 84	Winnfield	LA	71483	318-628-4116	628-1141
Web: www.centralmanagement.com					
Ceridian 3311 E Old Shakopee Rd	Minneapolis	MN	55425	952-853-8100	614-4600*
**Fax Area Code:* 248 ■ *Web:* www.ceridian.com/myceridian					
Ceridian Canada Ltd 675 Cochrane Dr	Markham	ON	L3R0B8	905-947-7200	947-7004
Web: www.ceridian.ca					
Coast Dental Services Inc					
4010 W Boy Scout Blvd Suite 1100	Tampa	FL	33607	813-288-1999	289-4500
TF: 800-983-3848 ■ *Web:* www.coastdental.com					
Combustion Components Assoc Inc 884 MN St	Monroe	CT	06468	203-268-3139	261-7697
Web: www.cca-inc.net					
Commodity Sourcing Group 19730 Ralston St	Detroit	MI	48203	313-366-0660	366-0110
Community Eldercare Services LLC PO Box 3667	Tupelo	MS	38803	662-680-3148	680-5703
TF: 877-461-1062 ■ *Web:* www.cesltc.com					
Compmanagement Inc PO Box 884	Dublin	OH	43017	614-766-5223	766-6888
TF: 800-825-6755 ■ *Web:* www.compmgt.com					
Comprehensive Care Corp					
3405 W Martin Luther King Hwy Suite 101	Tampa	FL	33609	813-288-4808	288-4844
Web: www.compcare.com					
Computer Sciences Corp Healthcare Group					
1160 Swedesford Rd # 200	Berwyn	PA	19312	610-251-0660	647-4912
Web: www.csc.com					
Concentra Inc 5080 Spectrum Dr Suite 1200 W	Addison	TX	75001	972-364-8000	387-0019
TF: 800-232-3550 ■ *Web:* www.concentra.com					
Connell Purchasing Services					
55 Shuman Blvd Suite 500	Naperville	IL	60563	630-210-7450	579-9123
Web: www.connellpurchasing.com					
Correctional Medical Services Inc (CMS)					
12647 Olive Blvd	Saint Louis	MO	63141	800-325-4809	
TF: 800-325-4809 ■ *Web:* www.cmsstl.com					
CorVel Corp 2010 Main St Suite 600	Irvine	CA	92614	949-851-1473	851-1469
NASDAQ: CRVL ■ *Web:* www.corvel.com					
CRAssoc Inc 8580 Cinderbed Rd Suite 2400	Newington	VA	22122	703-550-8145	249-3596*
**Fax Area Code:* 830 ■ *TF:* 877-272-8960 ■ *Web:* www.crassoc.com					
Critigen LLC 6161 S Syracuse Way	Greenwood Village	CO	80111	303-706-0990	706-1861
TF: 888-728-1551 ■ *Web:* www.critigen.com					
Cross Country Group LLC 1 Cabot Rd # 4	Medford	MA	02155	781-396-3700	391-7504
Web: www.ccgroup.com					
Data Processing Sciences Corp					
10810 Kenwood Rd	Cincinnati	OH	45242	513-791-7100	791-2371
Web: www.dpsciences.com					
De Maximis Inc 450 Montbrook Ln	Knoxville	TN	37919	865-691-5052	691-6485
Web: www.demaximis.com					
Dental Care Alliance Inc					
1 S School Ave Suite 1000	Sarasota	FL	34237	941-955-3150	330-0765
Development Alternatives Inc (DAI)					
7600 Wisconsin Ave Suite 200	Bethesda	MD	20814	301-771-7600	771-7777
Web: www.dai.com					
Discover Reinsurance Co Inc					
5 Batterson Pk	Farmington	CT	06032	860-674-2660	674-2671
Web: www.discover-re.com					
Dodge County Board of Education PO Box 1029	Eastman	GA	31023	478-374-3783	374-6697
Web: www.dodge.k12.ga.us					
DTE Energy Services 414 S Main St Suite 600	Ann Arbor	MI	48104	734-302-4800	
Web: www.dtees.com					
eLoyalty Corp 150 Field Dr Suite 250	Lake Forest	IL	60045	847-582-7000	582-7001
NASDAQ: ELOY ■ *TF:* 877-235-6925 ■ *Web:* www.eloyalty.com					
EmCare 1717 Main St Suite 5200	Dallas	TX	75201	214-712-2000	712-2444
TF: 800-527-2145 ■ *Web:* www.emcare.com					
Enernoc Inc 101 Federal St Suite 1100	Boston	MA	02110	617-224-9900	224-9910
NASDAQ: ENOC ■ *Web:* www.enernoc.com					
Engineering Management Concepts Inc					
5051 Verdugo Way Suite 200	Camarillo	CA	93012	805-484-9082	484-4607
Web: www.emc-inc.com					
Epic Energy Resources Inc					
1450 Lake Robbins Dr Suite 160	The Woodlands	TX	77380	281-419-3742	419-1114
PINK: EPCCQ ■ *Web:* www.1epic.com					
Executive Business Media Inc					
825 Old Country Rd	Westbury	NY	11590	516-334-3030	334-3059
Web: www.ebmpubs.com					
Fieldman Rolapp & Assoc 19900 Macarthur Blvd	Irvine	CA	92612	949-660-8500	474-8773
Web: www.fieldman.com					
File Keepers LLC 6277 E Slauson Ave	Los Angeles	CA	90040	323-728-3133	728-0867
TF: 800-332-3453 ■ *Web:* www.filekeepers.com					

				Phone	Fax
First Health Group Corp *Coventry* 3200 Highland Ave	Downers Grove	IL	60515	630-737-7900	719-0076
TF: 800-342-5888 ■ *Web:* www.firsthealth.com					
Focus Healthcare Management Inc 720 Cool Springs Blvd	Franklin	TN	37067	615-778-4000	778-0801
Fortune Practice Management 9888 Carroll Centre Rd Suite 100	San Diego	CA	92126	858-535-6287	535-6387
TF: 800-628-1052 ■ *Web:* www.fortunepractice.com					
Franchise Co The (TFC) 5397 Eglinton Ave W Suite 108	Etobicoke	ON	M9C5K6	416-620-4700	620-9955
Web: www.thefranchisecompany.com					
Genscape Inc 445 E Main St Suite 200	Louisville	KY	40202	502-583-3435	583-3464
Web: www.genscape.com					
Group Management Services Inc 3296 Columbia Rd Suite 101	Richfield	OH	44286	330-659-0100	659-0150
TF: 800-456-2885 ■ *Web:* www.groupmgmt.com					
Harold C Brown & Co Inc (HCB) 1 Hsbc Ctr Suite 3800	Buffalo	NY	14203	716-854-2500	847-6142
TF: 800-825-7498 ■ *Web:* www.hcb.com					
Hawthorne Corp 3955 Faber Pl Dr Suite 301	Neorth Charleston	SC	29405	843-553-2203	
Web: www.hawthornecorp.com					
HealthAxis Inc 7301 N State Hwy 161 Suite 300	Irving	TX	75039	972-443-5296	
PINK: HAXS ■ *TF:* 800-519-0679 ■ *Web:* www.healthaxis.com					
Healthrisk Group Inc 505 City Pkwy W Suite 100	Orange	CA	92868	714-704-0100	704-0111
TF: 800-955-9600 ■ *Web:* www.hrgi-online.com					
Hill Physicians Medical Group Inc 2409 Camino Ramon PO Box 5080	San Ramon	CA	94583	925-820-8300	820-8252
TF: 800-445-5747 ■ *Web:* www.hillphysicians.com					
Hospitality Ventures Management LLC 5 Concourse Pkwy Suite 2828	Atlanta	GA	30326	404-467-9299	467-1962
Web: www.hospitalityventures.com					
Hotchkis & Wiley Capital Management LLC 725 S Figueroa St Fl 39	Los Angeles	CA	90017	213-430-1000	430-1001
Web: www.hwcm.com					
Icon International Inc 4 Stamford Plaza 15th Fl 107 Elm St	Stamford	CT	06902	203-328-2300	328-2333
Web: www.icon-intl.com					
Ingenix Inc 12125 Technology Dr	Eden Prairie	MN	55344	952-833-7100	833-7201
TF: 888-445-8745 ■ *Web:* www.ingenix.com					
IntegraMed America Inc 2 Manhattanville Rd	Purchase	NY	10577	914-253-8000	253-8008
NASDAQ: INMD ■ *Web:* www.integramed.com					
Integreo Inc 400 Perimeter Ctr Terr Suite 249	Atlanta	GA	30346	770-225-9000	
InterDent Inc 222 N Sepulveda Blvd Suite 740	El Segundo	CA	90245	310-765-2400	765-2456
Web: www.interdent.com					
J. Calnan & Assoc Inc 1250 Hancock St Suite 302n	Quincy	MA	02169	617-801-0200	801-0201
Web: www.jcalnan.com					
Jdk Management Co Inc 1388 SR- 487	Bloomsburg	PA	17815	570-784-0111	784-3376
Web: www.jdkmgt.com					
JHT Inc 2710 Discovery Dr Suite 100	Orlando	FL	32826	407-381-7797	381-0017
TF: 888-657-2727 ■ *Web:* www.jht.com					
Juniper Group Inc 60 Cutter Mill Suite 611	Great Neck	NY	11021	516-829-4670	829-4691
Web: www.junipergroup.com					
Keiro Services 325 S Boyle Ave	Los Angeles	CA	90033	323-263-1007	
TF: 800-336-2722 ■ *Web:* www.keiro.org					
Linchris Hotel Corp 269 Hanover St Suite 2	Hanover	MA	02339	781-826-8824	826-2411
Web: www.linchris.com					
Magellan Medicaid Administration Inc 4300 Cox Rd	Glen Allen	VA	23060	804-965-7400	527-6849
TF: 800-884-2822 ■ *Web:* www.fhsc.com					
Management & Engineering Technologies International Inc (METI) 8600 Boeing Dr	El Paso	TX	79925	915-772-4975	772-2253
Web: www.meticorp.com					
Mci Products Group Inc 80 Skyline Dr	Plainview	NY	11803	516-822-1561	822-1584
Web: www.mciproducts.com					
Medcor Inc 4805 W Prime Pkwy	McHenry	IL	60050	815-363-9500	363-9696
Web: www.medcor.com					
Metropolitan Health Networks Inc 777 Yamato Rd Suite 510	Boca Raton	FL	33431	561-805-8500	805-8501
AMEX: MDF ■ *TF:* 888-663-8227 ■ *Web:* www.metcare.com					
MHM Services Inc 1593 Spring Hill Rd Suite 600	Vienna	VA	22182	703-749-4600	749-4604
TF: 800-416-3649 ■ *Web:* www.mhm-services.com					
Midwest Hospitality Group Inc 1220 Brookville Way	Indianapolis	IN	46239	317-356-4000	
Web: www.midwesthospitality.com					
Modis Inc 1 Independent Dr Suite 215	Jacksonville	FL	32202	904-360-2000	360-2110
TF: 800-372-2788 ■ *Web:* www.modis.com					
National Health Management Inc 4415 5th Ave Suite B	Pittsburgh	PA	15213	412-578-7800	681-8254
Web: www.independencecourt.com					
Netcracker Technology Corp 95 Sawyer Rd University Office Pk III	Waltham	MA	02453	781-419-3300	419-3301
TF: 800-477-5785 ■ *Web:* www.netcracker.com					
Ohm Systems Inc 10250 Chester Rd	Cincinnati	OH	45215	513-771-0008	771-0101
Web: www.ohmworld.com					
Patricia Seybold Group 210 Commercial St	Boston	MA	02109	617-742-5200	742-1028
TF: 800-826-2424 ■ *Web:* www.psgroup.com					
Pediatrix Medical Group Inc 1301 Concord Terr	Sunrise	FL	33323	954-384-0175	838-9961
TF: 800-243-3839 ■ *Web:* www.pediatrix.com					
PFSweb Inc 500 N Central Expwy Suite 500	Plano	TX	75074	972-881-2900	426-8616
NASDAQ: PFSW ■ *TF:* 888-330-5504 ■ *Web:* www.pfsweb.com					
Pitney Bowes Management Services 90 Pk Ave 11th Fl	New York	NY	10016	212-808-3800	
TF: 800-669-0800 ■ *Web:* www.pb.com					
Porter Medical Center Inc 115 Porter Dr	Middlebury	VT	05753	802-388-4701	
TF: 800-994-6610 ■ *Web:* www.portermedical.org					
Prospect Medical Holdings Inc 10780 Santa Monica Blvd Suite 400	Los Angeles	CA	90025	310-338-8677	943-4501
AMEX: PZZ ■ *TF:* 800-708-3230 ■ *Web:* www.prospectmedical.com					
Provell Inc 11100 Mayzata Blvd Suite 680	Minnetonka	MN	55305	952-258-2000	258-2100*
**Fax:* Hum Res ■ *Web:* www.provell.com					
Radiation Management Consultants 3019 Darnell Rd	Philadelphia	PA	19154	215-824-1300	824-1371
TF: 800-793-1304 ■ *Web:* www.rmcmedical.com					
Rector-Dunan & Assoc 314 E Highland Mall Blvd	Austin	TX	78752	512-454-5262	451-9599
Web: www.rector-duncan.com					
Restaurant Partners Inc 112 E Concord St	Orlando	FL	32801	407-839-5070	839-3388
Web: www.restaurantpartnersinc.com					
Rha Health Services Inc 17 Church St	Asheville	NC	28801	828-232-6844	665-1921
TF: 866-742-2428 ■ *Web:* www.rhahealthservices.org					
Select Medical Corp 4714 Gettysburg Rd	Mechanicsburg	PA	17055	717-972-1100	972-1042
TF: 888-735-6332 ■ *Web:* www.selectmedicalcorp.com					
Sentry Hospitality Ltd 136 E 57th St Suite 1003	New York	NY	10022	212-753-5347	688-2772
Web: www.sentryhospitality.com					
Sheridan Healthcare Inc 1613 NW 136th Ave # 200	Sunrise	FL	33323	954-838-2371	851-1715
TF: 800-437-2672 ■ *Web:* www.sheridanhealthcare.com					
SHPS Inc 11405 Bluegrass Pkwy	Louisville	KY	40299	502-267-4900	263-5610
TF: 888-421-7477 ■ *Web:* www.shps.com					
SpawGlass Construction Corp 13800 W Rd	Houston	TX	77041	281-970-5300	970-5305
Web: www.spawglass.com					
Specialized Services Inc 23077 Greenfield Rd Suite 470	Southfield	MI	48075	248-557-1030	557-0755
TF: 866-774-2004 ■ *Web:* www.ssi-inc.com					
Spectrum Healthcare Resources Inc 12647 Olive Blvd Suite 600	Saint Louis	MO	63141	314-744-4100	744-4180*
**Fax:* Hum Res ■ *TF:* 800-325-3982 ■ *Web:* www.spectrumhealth.com					
Staples Construction Co Inc 1501 Eastman Ave	Ventura	CA	93003	805-658-8786	658-8785
TF: 800-881-4650 ■ *Web:* www.staplesconstruction.com					
StarTek Inc 44 Cook St Suite 400	Denver	CO	80206	303-262-4500	
NYSE: SRT ■ *TF:* 800-541-1130 ■ *Web:* www.startek.com					
Sterling Healthcare 1000 Pk Forty Plaza Suite 500	Durham	NC	27713	919-383-0355	806-5180
TF: 800-476-4587 ■ *Web:* www.sterling-healthcare.com					
Stream International Inc 2220 Campbell Creek Blvd Suite 100	Richardson	TX	75080	469-624-5000	
TF: 888-284-5834 ■ *Web:* www.stream.com					
Sudler Property Management 875 N Michigan Ave Suite 2600	Chicago	IL	60611	312-751-0900	751-8052
Web: www.sudlerathome.com					
Summit Energy Services Inc 10350 Ormsby Pk Pl Suite 400	Louisville	KY	40223	502-429-3800	753-2248
TF: 866-907-8664 ■ *Web:* www.summitenergy.com					
Technology On Demand Inc 4 E Washington Ave	Athens	TN	37303	423-744-7071	744-3012
TF: 800-766-9404 ■ *Web:* www.hypersoft.net					
Tecolote Research Inc 420 S Fairview Ave Suite 201	Goleta	CA	93117	805-571-6366	571-6377
Web: www.tecolote.com					
Three Rivers Planning & Development District Inc 75 S Main St PO Box 690	Pontotoc	MS	38863	662-489-2415	489-6815
Web: www.trpdd.com					
TMC AmerInd Inc 3060 Williams Dr Suite 600	Fairfax	VA	22031	703-752-8380	560-1396
Transcend Services Inc 1Glenlake Pkwy Suite 1325	Atlanta	GA	30328	800-205-7047	
NASDAQ: TRCR ■ *TF:* 800-555-8727 ■ *Web:* www.transcendservices.com					
UCI Medical Affiliates Inc 1818 Henderson St	Columbia	SC	29206	803-782-4278	782-3445*
**Fax:* executive fax ■ *Web:* www.doctorscare.com					
United Temps Inc 1550 S Indiana Ave Suite 300	Chicago	IL	60605	312-922-8558	
Web: unitedhq.com/services/united-temps.html					
US Oncology Inc 16825 Northchase Dr Suite 1300	Houston	TX	77060	832-601-8766	
TF: 800-381-2637 ■ *Web:* www.usoncology.com					
Vanir Construction Management Inc 4540 Duckhorn Dr Suite 300	Sacramento	CA	95834	916-444-3700	575-8887
TF: 888-912-1201 ■ *Web:* www.vanir.com					
vCustomer Corp 4040 Lake Washington Blvd NE	Kirkland	WA	98033	206-802-0200	802-0201
Web: www.vcustomer.com					
Verisk Analytics 545 Washington Blvd	Jersey City	NJ	07310	201-469-3000	748-1472
NASDAQ: VRSK ■ *Web:* www.verisk.com					
Vetter Health Services Inc 5020 S 118th St	Omaha	NE	68137	402-895-3932	895-8165
Web: www.vetterhealthservices.com					
VHA Inc 220 Las Colinas Blvd E PO Box 140909	Irving	TX	75039	972-830-0626	830-0012
TF: 800-842-5146 ■ *Web:* www.vha.com					
VisionQuest National Ltd 600 N Swan Rd PO Box 12906	Tucson	AZ	85711	520-881-3950	881-3269
Web: www.vq.com					
Volt VIEWtech Inc 5109 E La Palma Suite D	Anaheim	CA	92807	714-695-3300	701-9893
TF: 800-998-8658 ■ *Web:* www.voltviewtech.com					
Warren Distribution Inc 727 S 13th St	Omaha	NE	68102	402-341-9397	977-5754
Web: www.wd-wpp.com					
Westin Engineering Inc 3100 Zinfandel Dr Suite 300	Rancho Cordova	CA	95670	916-889-8600	852-2311
Web: www.we-inc.com					
Xand Corp 11 Skyline Dr	Hawthorne	NY	10532	914-592-8282	592-3482
TF: 800-522-2823 ■ *Web:* www.xand.com					
Zerochaos LLC 420 S Orange Ave Suite 600	Orlando	FL	32801	407-770-6161	888-9376*
**Fax Area Code:* 877 ■ *Web:* www.zerochaos.com					

467 MANNEQUINS & DISPLAY FORMS

				Phone	Fax
Barnhart Display Inc 1170 Charming St	Maitland	FL	32751	407-637-2060	637-2053
Web: www.barnhartdisplay.com					
Goldsmith New York at Studio 350 601 W 26th St Suite 350	New York	NY	10001	212-366-9040	
Web: www.goldsmith-inc.com					
Ronis Bros 39 Harriet Pl	Lynbrook	NY	11563	516-887-5266	887-5288
Web: www.ronis.com					
Siegel & Stockman USA 126 W 25th St	New York	NY	10001	212-633-0138	366-0575
TF: 888-515-8949 ■ *Web:* www.siegel-stockman.com					
Silvestri Studio Inc 8125 Beach St	Los Angeles	CA	90001	323-277-4420	585-0861
TF: 800-647-8874 ■ *Web:* www.silvestricalifornia.com					

468 MARINE SERVICES

SEE ALSO Freight Transport - Deep Sea (Domestic Ports) p. 1889; Freight Transport - Deep Sea (Foreign Ports) p. 1889; Freight Transport - Inland Waterways p. 1890; Logistics Services (Transportation & Warehousing) p. 2183

Phone	Fax

Company	City	State	Zip	Phone	Fax
AEP River Operations 16150 Main Cir Dr Suite 400 *TF:* 800-207-8011 ■ *Web:* www.aepriverops.com	St. Louis	MO	63017	636-530-2100	530-4100
Allied Towing Corp 500 E Indian River Rd *TF:* 800-446-8241	Norfolk	VA	23523	757-545-7301	545-5692
American Port Service Inc 2901 Childs St *Web:* www.amports.com	Baltimore	MD	21226	410-350-0400	354-8812
Andrie Inc 561 E Western Ave PO Box 1548 *Web:* www.andrie.com	Muskegon	MI	49442	231-728-2226	726-6747
Bay Houston Towing Co 2243 Milford St *TF:* 800-324-3755 ■ *Web:* www.bayhouston.com	Houston	TX	77098	713-529-3755	529-2591
Bisso Towboat Co Inc 8237 Oak St *Web:* www.bissotowing.com	New Orleans	LA	70178	504-861-1411	861-9298
Boston Towing & Transportation Co LP 36 New St *TF:* 800-836-8847	East Boston	MA	02128	617-567-9100	567-2583
Bunkers International Corp 110 Timberlachen Cir Suite 1012 *Web:* www.bunkersinternational.com	Lake Mary	FL	32746	407-328-7757	328-0045
Cargo Express Inc 1790 Yardley-Langhorne Rd Suite 202 *Web:* www.cargoexpressinc.com	Yardley	PA	19067	215-493-2662	493-4430
Cenac Towing Co Inc PO Box 2617 *TF:* 800-942-5476	Houma	LA	70361	985-872-2413	851-1761
Ceres Terminals Inc 2 Tower Ctr Blvd *Web:* www.ceresglobal.com	East Brunswick	NJ	08816	201-974-3800	974-3850
Cooper/T Smith Stevedoring Co 118 N Royal St Commerce Bldg Suite 1100 *TF:* 800-239-8484 ■ *Web:* www.coopertsmith.com	Mobile	AL	36602	251-431-6100	431-6150
Crowley Maritime Corp 555 12th St Suite 2130 *TF:* 800-276-9539 ■ *Web:* www.crowley.com	Oakland	CA	94607	510-251-7500	251-7510
Dix Industries Inc 5500 RL Ostos Rd *Web:* www.dixshipping.com	Brownsville	TX	78521	956-831-4228	831-2559
Donjon Marine Co Inc 100 Central Ave *Web:* www.donjon.com	Hillside	NJ	07205	908-964-8812	964-7426
Eagle Marine Industries Inc 1 Riverview Ave	Sauget	IL	62201	618-875-1153	875-1505
Edison Chouest Offshore 16201 E Main St *TF:* 800-417-7144 ■ *Web:* www.chouest.com	Cut Off	LA	70354	985-601-4444	601-4237
Eller-ITO Stevedoring Co LLC 1007 N America Way *Web:* www.ellerito.com	Miami	FL	33132	305-379-3700	371-9969
Foss Maritime Co 660 W Ewing St *TF:* 800-426-2885 ■ *Web:* www.foss.com	Seattle	WA	98119	206-281-3800	281-4702
G & H Towing Co Inc PO Drawer 2270 *Web:* www.gandhtowing.com	Galveston	TX	77553	409-744-6311	740-2575
General Steamship Agencies Inc 575 Redwood Hwy Suite 200 *Web:* www.gensteam.com	Mill Valley	CA	94941	415-389-5200	389-9020
Golden Stevedoring Co Inc PO Box 869	Mobile	AL	36601	251-433-3726	433-3338
Great Lakes Towing Co 4500 Division Ave *TF:* 800-321-3663 ■ *Web:* www.thegreatlakesgroup.com	Cleveland	OH	44102	216-621-4854	621-7616
Hawaii Stevedores Inc PO Box 2160	Honolulu	HI	96805	808-527-3400	527-3448
Hawaiian Tug & Barge PO Box 3288 *TF:* 800-572-2743 ■ *Web:* www.htbyb.com	Honolulu	HI	96801	808-543-9311	543-9477
Higman Marine Services 1980 Post Oak Blvd Suite 1101	Houston	TX	77056	713-552-1101	552-0732
Hopkins-Carter Co Inc 3300 NW 21st St *TF:* 800-595-9656 ■ *Web:* www.hopkins-carter.com	Miami	FL	33142	305-635-7377	633-1310
Hornbeck Offshore Services Inc 103 Northpark Blvd Suite 300 *NYSE: HOS* ■ *TF:* 800-535-5843 ■ *Web:* www.hornbeckoffshore.com	Covington	LA	70433	985-727-2000	727-2006
Houston Pilots 8150 S Loop E Suite 118 *Web:* www.houston-pilots.com	Houston	TX	77017	713-645-9620	649-3513
International Marine Terminals Partnership 18559 Hwy 23	Port Sulphur	LA	70083	504-656-7341	656-2626
International Transportation Service Inc 1281 Pier J Way *Web:* www.itslb.com	Long Beach	CA	90802	562-435-7781	491-1935
J. F. Brennan Co Inc 820 Bainbridge PO Box 2557 *Web:* www.jfbrennan.com	La Crosse	WI	54602	608-784-7173	785-2090
James Marine Inc (JMI) PO Box 2305 *Web:* www.jamesmarine.com	Paducah	KY	42002	270-898-7392	448-0015
Kinder Morgan 5807 Navigation	Houston	TX	77011	713-923-6678	923-3128
Kinder Morgan Bulk Terminals Inc 7116 Hwy 22 *TF:* 800-535-8170 ■ *Web:* www.kindermorgan.com	Sorrento	LA	70778	225-675-5387	675-5923
Lambert's Point Docks PO Box 89	Norfolk	VA	23501	757-446-1212	446-1245
Leboeuf Bros Towing Co Inc PO Box 9036 *TF:* 800-256-5088	Houma	LA	70361	985-594-6692	594-5253
Luis A Ayala Colon Sucrs Inc 3091 Ave Santiago De Los *Web:* www.ayacol.com	Ponce	PR	00716	787-848-9000	848-0070
Marquette transportation 5135 Storey St *TF:* 800-735-5845	Harahan	LA	70123	504-733-5845	733-7637
McAllister Towing & Transportation Co Inc 17 Battery Pl Suite 1200 *Web:* www.mcallistertowing.com	New York	NY	10004	212-269-3200	509-1147

Company	City	State	Zip	Phone	Fax
McCabe Hamilton & Renny Co Ltd (MHR) 1130 N Nimitz Hwy Rm A265 *Web:* www.mhrhawaii.com	Honolulu	HI	96817	808-524-3255	545-3101
Murphy Marine Services Inc 11 Gist Rd 1st Fl	Port of Wilmington	DE	19801	302-571-4700	571-4702
Nassau Terminals LLC 501 N 3rd St	Fernandina Beach	FL	32034	904-261-0048	261-4407
New Haven Terminal Inc 100 Waterfront St	New Haven	CT	06512	203-468-0805	469-6374
New York State Canal Corp 200 Southern Blvd PO Box 189 *TF:* 800-422-6254 ■ *Web:* www.canals.ny.gov	Albany	NY	12201	518-436-2700	
Nicholson Terminal & Dock Co 380 E Great Lakes St *Web:* www.nicholson-terminal.com	River Rouge	MI	48218	313-842-4300	843-1091
North Star Terminal & Stevedore Co LLC 790 Ocean Dock Rd *Web:* www.northstarak.com	Anchorage	AK	99501	907-272-7537	272-8927
Odyssey Marine Exploration Inc 5215 W Laurel St *AMEX: OMR* ■ *Web:* www.shipwreck.net	Tampa	FL	33607	813-876-1776	876-1777
Otto Candies Inc 17271 Hwy 90 *TF:* 800-535-4563 ■ *Web:* www.ottocandies.com	Des Allemands	LA	70030	504-469-7700	469-7740
P & O Ports North America Inc 99 Wood Ave S Level 8 Suite 804 *Web:* www.portsamerica.com	Iselin	NJ	08830	732-635-3899	635-3874
Parker Towing Co Inc PO Box 20908 *TF:* 800-329-1677 ■ *Web:* www.parkertowing.com	Tuscaloosa	AL	35402	205-349-1677	758-0061
Pelicans Perch Marina & Boatyard 40 Audusson Ave *Web:* www.brownmarine.com	Pensacola	FL	32507	850-453-3471	457-1662
Port of Miami Terminal Operating Co LC 1007 N America Way Suite 400 *Web:* www.pomtoc.com	Miami	FL	33132	305-416-7600	374-6724
RMS Titanic Inc 3340 Peachtree Rd NE Suite 2250 *Web:* www.rmstitanic.net	Atlanta	GA	30326	404-842-2600	842-2626
Rukert Terminals Corp 2021 S Clinton St *Web:* www.rukert.com	Baltimore	MD	21224	410-276-1013	522-1031
Sause Bros 3710 NW Front Ave *TF:* 800-488-4167 ■ *Web:* www.sause.com	Portland	OR	97210	503-222-1811	222-2010
Sea Tow Services International Inc 1560 Youngs Ave PO Box 1178 *TF:* 800-473-2869 ■ *Web:* www.seatow.com	Southold	NY	11971	631-765-3660	765-5208
SSA Marine 1131 SW Klickitat Way *TF:* 800-422-3505 ■ *Web:* www.ssamarine.com	Seattle	WA	98134	206-623-0304	623-0179
Teco Barge Line 100 Scott St *TF:* 800-455-5731 ■ *Web:* www.tecobargeline.com	Metropolis	IL	62960	618-524-3100	524-8680
Tidewater Inc 601 Poydras St Suite 1900 *NYSE: TDW* ■ *TF:* 800-678-8433 ■ *Web:* www.tdw.com	New Orleans	LA	70130	504-568-1010	566-4580
Trans Pacific Container Service Corp 920 W Harry Bridges Blvd *Web:* www.trapac.com	Wilmington	CA	90744	310-830-2000	513-7400
Trimodal Inc 8009 34th Ave S	Minneapolis	MN	55425	952-253-6900	
Virginia International Terminals Inc 7737 Hampton Blvd # D224 *TF:* 800-541-2431 ■ *Web:* www.vit.org	Norfolk	VA	23505	757-440-7000	440-7221
Waxler Towing Co Inc PO Box 253 *Web:* www.waxler.com	Memphis	TN	38101	901-946-1607	947-1230
Western Towboat Co Inc 617 NW 40th St *TF:* 800-932-9651 ■ *Web:* www.westerntowboat.com	Seattle	WA	98107	206-789-9000	789-9755

469 MARKET RESEARCH FIRMS

Company	City	State	Zip	Phone	Fax
Abt Assoc Inc 55 Wheeler St *Web:* www.abtassociates.com	Cambridge	MA	02138	617-492-7100	492-5219
ACNielsen Corp 770 Broadway *Web:* www.acnielsen.com	New York	NY	10003	646-654-5000	654-5002
Amphenol Optimize Mfg Co 180 N Freeport Dr Bldg W *Web:* www.amphenol-optimize.com	Nogales	AZ	85621	520-397-7015	397-7014
Arbitron Inc 9705 Patuxent Woods Dr *NYSE: ARB* ■ **Fax:* Hum Res ■ *TF:* 800-272-4876 ■ *Web:* www.arbitron.com	Columbia	MD	21046	410-312-8000	312-8607*
Bensussen Deutsch & Assoc Inc (BDA) 15525 Woodinville-Redmond Rd NE *TF:* 800-451-4764 ■ *Web:* www.bdainc.com	Woodinville	WA	98072	425-492-6111	492-7222
Beverage Marketing USA Inc 222 Bloomingdale Rd Suite 400	White Plains	NY	10605	914-644-9200	644-9300
BRS Group 901 E St Suite 300 *TF:* 800-552-0810 ■ *Web:* www.brsgroup.com	San Rafael	CA	94901	415-526-2040	526-2075
Burke Inc 500 W 7th St *Web:* www.burke.com	Cincinnati	OH	45203	513-241-5663	684-7500
C & R Research Services Inc 500 N Michigan Ave Suite 1200 *TF:* 800-621-5022 ■ *Web:* www.cr-research.com	Chicago	IL	60611	312-828-9200	527-3113
CA Walker Research Solutions Inc 100 W Broadway Suite 1170 *Web:* www.cawalker.com	Glendale	CA	91210	626-584-8180	584-8199
Cheskin Research 255 Shoreline Dr Suite 350 *TF:* 888-969-3284 ■ *Web:* www.cheskin.com	Redwood City	CA	94065	650-802-2100	593-1125
comScore Inc 11950 Democracy Dr # 600 *Web:* www.comscore.com	Reston	VA	20190	703-438-2000	438-2051
Directions Research Inc 401 E Ct St Suite 200 *Web:* www.directionsrsch.com	Cincinnati	OH	45202	513-651-2990	651-2998
Firefly 274 Riverside Ave 4th Fl *TF:* 888-816-9901 ■ *Web:* www.fireflymb.com	Westport	CT	06880	203-221-0411	221-0791
Forrester Research Inc 400 Technology Sq *NASDAQ: FORR* ■ *TF:* 866-367-7378 ■ *Web:* www.forrester.com	Cambridge	MA	02139	617-497-7090	613-5000

Name / Address	City	State	Zip	Phone	Fax
Futures Co The 400 Meadowmont Village Cir Suite 431 *Web:* www.yankelovich.com	Chapel Hill	NC	27517	919-932-8858	932-8829
Gallup Organization 901 F St NW *TF:* 877-242-5587 ■ *Web:* www.gallup.com	Washington	DC	20004	202-715-3030	715-3041
Gartner Inc 56 Top Gallant Rd *NYSE: IT* ■ *TF:* 800-328-2776 ■ *Web:* www.gartner.com	Stamford	CT	06904	203-316-1111	316-6300
GFK Custom Research Inc 8401 Golden Valley Rd PO Box 27900 *TF:* 800-328-6784	Minneapolis	MN	55427	763-542-0800	542-0864
Graham & Assoc 3000 Riverchase Galleria Suite 310 *TF:* 800-360-9831 ■ *Web:* www.grahammktres.com	Birmingham	AL	35244	205-443-5399	443-5389
Harris Interactive Inc 60 Corporate Woods *NASDAQ: HPOL* ■ *TF:* 800-866-7655 ■ *Web:* www.harrisinteractive.com	Rochester	NY	14623	585-272-8400	272-7258
Ideas International Inc 800 Westchester Ave Suite N-337 *TF:* 800-253-1799 ■ *Web:* www.ideasinternational.com	Rye Brook	NY	10573	914-937-4302	937-2485
IMS Health Inc 901 Main Ave Suite 612 *Web:* www.imshealth.com	Norwalk	CT	06851	203-845-5200	845-5299
In-Stat 225 Wyman St *TF:* 800-283-3666 ■ *Web:* www.instat.com	Waltham	MA	02451	781-734-8000	
Information Resources Inc 150 N Clinton St *TF:* 866-262-5973 ■ *Web:* www.symphonyiri.com	Chicago	IL	60661	312-726-1221	
International Communications Research 53 W Baltimore Pike *TF Cust Svc:* 800-633-1986 ■ *Web:* www.icrsurvey.com	Media	PA	19063	484-840-4300	840-4599
International Data Corp (IDC) 5 Speen St *TF:* 800-343-4935 ■ *Web:* www.idcresearch.com	Framingham	MA	01701	508-872-8200	935-4015
Invoke Solutions Inc 375 Totten Pond Rd Suite 400 *Web:* www.invoke.com	Waltham	MA	02451	781-810-2700	810-2750
Ipsos-ASI Inc 301 Merritt 7 Corporate Pk *Web:* www.ipsos-asi.com	Norwalk	CT	06851	203-840-3400	840-3450
JD Power & Assoc 2625 Townsgate Rd Suite 100 *TF:* 800-274-5372 ■ *Web:* www.jdpower.com	West Lake Village	CA	91361	805-418-8000	418-8900
Kantar Group 501 Kings Hwy E 4th Fl	Fairfield	CT	06825	203-330-5200	330-5201
Knowledge Networks 1350 Willow Rd Suite 102 *Web:* www.knowledgenetworks.com	Menlo Park	CA	94025	650-289-2000	289-2001
Lieberman Research 98 Cutter Mill Rd *Web:* www.liebermanresearch.com	Great Neck	NY	11021	516-829-8880	829-8880
M/A/R/C Group 1660 Westridge Cir *TF:* 800-527-2680 ■ *Web:* www.marcresearch.com	Irving	TX	75038	972-983-0400	983-0404
Macro International Inc 11785 Beltsville Dr Suite 300 *Web:* www.macrointernational.com	Calverton	MD	20705	301-572-0200	572-0999
Maritz Inc 1375 N Hwy Dr **Fax:* Hum Res ■ *Web:* www.maritz.com	Fenton	MO	63099	636-827-4000	827-4336*
Maritz Research Inc 1355 N Hwy Dr *Web:* www.maritzresearch.com	Fenton	MO	63099	636-827-4000	827-2487
Market Decisions LLC 75 Washington Ave Suite 206 *TF:* 800-293-1538 ■ *Web:* www.marketdecisions.com	Portland	ME	04101	207-767-6440	767-8158
Market Strategies Inc 17430 College Pkwy *Web:* www.marketstrategies.com	Livonia	MI	48152	734-542-7600	542-7620
Marketing & Planning Systems 850 Winter St *TF:* 800-696-6605 ■ *Web:* www.mapsnet.com	Waltham	MA	02451	781-642-6277	642-9508
Marketing Analysts Inc (MAI) 7300 Carmel Executive Pk Suite 330 *TF:* 877-819-0948 ■ *Web:* www.mairesearch.com	Charleston	SC	28226	704-405-2150	405-2151
Marketing Research Services Inc 720 E Pete Rose Way Suite 200 *TF:* 800-729-6774 ■ *Web:* www.mrsi.com	Cincinnati	OH	45202	513-579-1555	562-8819
Marketing Workshop Inc The 3725 Da Vinci Ct Suite 200 *TF:* 800-284-7707 ■ *Web:* www.mwshop.com	Norcross	GA	30092	770-449-6767	449-6739
MarketVision Research Inc 10300 Alliance Rd Suite 200 *TF:* 800-232-4250 ■ *Web:* www.marketvisionresearch.com	Cincinnati	OH	45242	513-791-3100	794-3500
Millward Brown Group 4950 Yonge St Suite 600 *Web:* www.millwardbrown.com	North York	ON	M2N6K1	416-221-9200	221-7681
Millward Brown IntelliQuest 1250 Capital of Texas Hwy Bldg 1 Suite 600 *TF:* 800-283-9608 ■ *Web:* www.millwardbrown.com	Austin	TX	78746	512-329-0808	329-0888
MORPACE International Inc 31700 Middlebelt Rd Suite 200 *TF:* 800-878-7223 ■ *Web:* www.morpace.com	Farmington Hills	MI	48334	248-737-5300	737-5326
Mosaic Sales Solutions US Operating Co 6051 State Hwy 161 *Web:* www.mosaic.com	Irving	TX	75038	972-870-4800	870-4845
National Research Corp 1245 Q St *NASDAQ: NRCI* ■ *TF:* 800-388-4264 ■ *Web:* www.nationalresearch.com	Lincoln	NE	68508	402-475-2525	475-9061
Nicholson Kovac Inc 600 Broadway 5th Fl *Web:* www.nicholsonkovac.com	Kansas City	MO	64105	816-842-8881	842-6340
NPD Group Inc 900 W Shore Rd *TF:* 866-444-1411 ■ *Web:* www.npd.com	Port Washington	NY	11050	516-625-0700	625-2444
Opinion Research Corp (ORC) 902 Carnegie Ctr Suite 220 PO Box 183 *NASDAQ: ORCI* ■ *TF:* 800-444-4672 ■ *Web:* www.opinionresearch.com	Princeton	NJ	08540	609-452-5400	419-1892
Point Group The 5949 Sherry Ln Suite 1800 *Web:* www.thepointgroup.com	Dallas	TX	75225	214-378-7970	378-7967
PreTesting Group 38 Franklin St *Web:* www.pretesting.com	Tenafly	NJ	07670	201-569-4800	569-0611
Quick Test Inc 1061 E Indiantown Rd *TF:* 800-523-1288 ■ *Web:* www.quicktest.com	Jupiter	FL	33477	561-748-0931	748-3601
RDA Group 450 Enterprise Ct *TF:* 800-669-7324 ■ *Web:* www.rdagroup.com	Bloomfield Hills	MI	48302	248-332-5000	332-4168
Reis Inc 530 5th Ave 5th Fl *TF:* 800-366-7347 ■ *Web:* www.reis.com	New York	NY	10036	212-921-1122	921-2533
Research Director Inc 914 Bay Ridge Rd Suite 215 *Web:* www.researchdirectorinc.com	Annapolis	MD	21403	410-295-6619	268-1915
Rincon Research Corp 101 N Wilmot Rd Suite 101 *Web:* www.rincon.com	Tucson	AZ	85711	520-519-4600	519-4747
Savitz Research Solutions 13747 Montfort Dr Suite 330 *Web:* www.savitzresearch.com	Dallas	TX	75240	972-386-4050	661-3198
Schulman Ronca & Bucuvalas Inc 275 7th Ave Suite 2700 *Web:* www.srbi.com	New York	NY	10001	212-779-7700	779-7785
Strategic Analysis Inc 4075 Wilson Blvd Suite 200 *Web:* www.sainc.com	Arlington	VA	22203	703-527-5410	527-5445
Synovate Inc 222 S Riverside Plaza *TF:* 800-745-4267 ■ *Web:* www.synovate.com	Chicago	IL	60606	312-526-4000	526-4099
TeleSight Inc 820 N Franklin St *TF:* 800-608-3651 ■ *Web:* www.telesight.com	Chicago	IL	60610	312-640-2500	944-7872
Walker Information Inc 301 Pennsylvania Pkwy *TF:* 800-334-3939 ■ *Web:* www.walkerinfo.com	Indianapolis	IN	46280	317-843-3939	843-8904
Westat Inc 1600 Research Blvd *TF:* 800-937-8281 ■ *Web:* www.westat.com	Rockville	MD	20850	301-251-1500	294-2040

470 MARKING DEVICES

Name / Address	City	State	Zip	Phone	Fax
American Marking Systems Inc 1015 Paulison Ave PO Box 1677 *TF:* 800-782-6766 ■ *Web:* www.ams-stamps.com	Clifton	NJ	07011	973-478-5600	478-0039
Automark Marking Systems 13475 Lakefront Dr *TF:* 888-777-2303 ■ *Web:* www.automark.com	Earth City	MO	63045	314-739-0430	739-1483
Cable Markers Co Inc 22600 Lambert St # 1204F *TF:* 800-746-7655 ■ *Web:* www.cablemarkers.com	Lake Forest	CA	92630	949-699-1636	699-1642
Carco Inc 10333 Shoemaker PO Box 13859 *Web:* www.carcousa.com	Detroit	MI	48213	313-925-9000	925-9602
CH Hanson Co 2000 N Aurora Rd *TF:* 800-827-3398 ■ *Web:* www.chhanson.com	Naperville	IL	60563	630-848-2000	848-2515
Cosco Industries Inc 7220 W Wilson Ave *TF:* 800-323-0253 ■ *Web:* www.coscoindustries.com	Harwood Heights	IL	60706	800-323-0253	323-0253
DM Stamps & Specialties Inc 1101 N Riverfront Dr **Fax Area Code:* 800 ■ *Web:* www.dmpolystamps.com	Mankato	MN	56001	507-387-4444	658-7171*
Excelsior Marking Products 888 W Waterloo Rd *TF:* 800-433-3615 ■ *Web:* www.excelsiormarking.com	Akron	OH	44314	330-745-2300	745-2333
GB Products International Corp 5650 Imhoff Dr Suite B *TF:* 800-650-0341 ■ *Web:* www.gbproductsintl.com	Concord	CA	94520	925-825-3040	798-1468
Hampton Technologies LLC 19 Industrial Blvd *TF:* 800-229-1019 ■ *Web:* www.hamptontech.net	Medford	NY	11763	631-924-1335	924-1669
Hitt Marking Devices Inc 3231 W MacArthur Blvd *TF:* 800-969-6699 ■ *Web:* www.hittmarking.com	Santa Ana	CA	92704	714-979-1405	979-1407
Huntington Park Rubber Stamp 2761 E Slauson Ave *TF:* 800-882-0129 ■ *Web:* www.hprubberstamp.com	Huntington Park	CA	90255	323-582-6461	582-8046
Industrial Marking Products 1415 Grovenburg Rd *Web:* www.industrialmarking.com	Holt	MI	48842	517-699-2160	699-1505
Infosight Corp PO Box 5000 *TF:* 800-401-0716 ■ *Web:* www.infosight.com	Chillicothe	OH	45601	740-642-3600	642-5001
Jackson Marking Products Co 9105 N Rainbow Ln *TF:* 800-782-6722 ■ *Web:* www.rubber-stamp.com	Mount Vernon	IL	62864	618-242-1334	242-7732
JP Nissen Co 2544 Fairhill Ave PO Box 339 *Web:* www.nissenmarkers.com	Glenside	PA	19038	215-886-2025	886-0707
La-Co/Markal Co 1201 Pratt Blvd **Fax Area Code:* 800 ■ *TF:* 800-621-4025 ■ *Web:* www.laco.com	Elk Grove Village	IL	60007	847-956-7600	448-5436*
M & R Marking Systems Inc 100 Springfield Ave *TF:* 800-272-8550 ■ *Web:* www.mrmarking.com	Piscataway	NJ	08855	732-562-9500	562-9515
Mark Master Inc 11111 N 46th St *TF:* 800-441-6275 ■ *Web:* www.mmstamp.com	Tampa	FL	33617	813-988-6000	985-6860
Matthews International Corp Marking Products Div 6515 Penn Ave *TF:* 800-775-7775 ■ *Web:* www.matthewsmarking.com	Pittsburgh	PA	15206	412-665-2500	665-2550
Menke Marking Devices 13253 Alondra Blvd PO Box 2986 *TF:* 800-231-6023 ■ *Web:* www.menkemarking.com	Santa Fe Springs	CA	90670	562-921-1380	921-1184
New Method Steel Stamps Inc 31313 Kendall Ave **Fax Area Code:* 888 ■ *TF:* 888-318-6677 ■ *Web:* www.newmethod.com	Fraser	MI	48026	586-293-0200	908-6677*
Norwood Marking Systems 2538 Wisconsin Ave *TF:* 800-626-3464 ■ *Web:* www.itw-norwood.com	Downers Grove	IL	60515	630-968-0646	968-7672
Saint Paul Stamp Works Inc 87 Empire Dr *Web:* www.stpaulstamp.com	Saint Paul	MN	55103	651-222-2100	228-1314
Samoss Group Ltd 213 W 35th St 13th Fl	New York	NY	10001	212-239-6677	239-0041
Schwaab Inc 11415 W Burleigh St *TF:* 800-935-9877 ■ *Web:* www.schwaab.com	Milwaukee	WI	53222	414-771-4150	771-7165
Schwerdtle Stamp Co 166 Elm St *TF:* 800-535-0004 ■ *Web:* www.schwerdtle.com	Bridgeport	CT	06604	203-330-2750	330-2760
Signet Marking Devices 3121 Red Hill Ave *TF:* 800-421-5150 ■ *Web:* www.signetmarking.com	Costa Mesa	CA	92626	714-549-0341	549-0972
Stamp-Rite Inc 154 S Larch St *TF:* 800-328-1988 ■ *Web:* www.stamprite.com	Lansing	MI	48912	517-487-5071	487-6211
Tacoma Rubber Stamp & Sign 919 Market St *TF:* 800-544-7281 ■ *Web:* www.tacomarubberstamp.com	Tacoma	WA	98402	253-383-5433	383-0649
Telesis Technologies Inc 740 Welch Rd *TF Sales:* 800-654-5696 ■ *Web:* www.telesis.com	Commerce Township	MI	48390	248-624-4249	624-4431

Phone *Fax*

Volk Corp 23936 Industrial Pk Dr . . . Farmington Hills MI 48335 248-477-6700 478-6884
TF Cust Svc: 800-521-6799 ■ *Web:* www.volkcorp.com

Wendell's Inc
6601 Bunker Lake Blvd NW PO Box 458 . . . Ramsey MN 55303 763-576-8200 576-0995
TF: 800-936-3355 ■ *Web:* www.wendellsinc.com

471 MASS TRANSPORTATION (LOCAL & SUBURBAN)

SEE ALSO Bus Services - Intercity & Rural p. 1547

Phone *Fax*

Alameda-Contra Costa Transit District
1600 Franklin St 10th Fl . . . Oakland CA 94612 510-891-4777 891-4705*
**Fax:* Cust Svc ■ *Web:* www.actransit.org

Alaska Marine Highway System
6858 Glacier Hwy PO Box 112505 . . . Juneau AK 99801 907-465-3941 465-2476
TF: 800-642-0066 ■ *Web:* www.dot.state.ak.us/amhs

Altamont Commuter Express (ACE) 949 E Ch St . . . Stockton CA 95202 800-411-7245 944-6273*
**Fax Area Code:* 209 ■ *TF:* 800-411-7245 ■ *Web:* www.acerail.com

Ann Arbor Transportation Authority
2700 S Industrial Hwy . . . Ann Arbor MI 48104 734-973-6500 973-6338
Web: www.theride.org

Bay Area Rapid Transit District
300 Lakeside Dr . . . Oakland CA 94612 510-464-6000 464-7175*
**Fax:* Mktg ■ *Web:* www.bart.gov

BC Transit 520 Gorge Rd E . . . Victoria BC V8W2P3 250-385-2551 995-5639
Web: www.bctransit.com

Bi-State Development Agency 707 N 1st St . . . Saint Louis MO 63102 314-982-1400 923-3019*
**Fax:* Cust Svc ■ *Web:* www.metrostlouis.org

Bonneville Transloaders Inc (BTI)
642 S Federal Blvd . . . Riverton WY 82501 307-856-7480 856-4623
Web: www.bonntran.com

Caledonia Haulers LLC
420 W Lincoln St PO Box 31 . . . Caledonia MN 55921 507-725-9000 725-9015
TF: 800-325-4728 ■ *Web:* www.caledoniahaulers.com

Cape Cod Regional Transit Authority (CCRTA)
215 Iyannough Rd PO Box 1988 . . . Hyannis MA 02601 508-775-8504 775-8513
TF: 800-352-7155 ■ *Web:* www.capecodtransit.org

Capital District Transportation Authority (CDTA)
110 Watervliet Ave . . . Albany NY 12206 518-482-8822 437-8318
Web: www.cdta.org

Capital Metropolitan Transportation Authority
13701 Lyndhurst St . . . Austin TX 78729 512-389-7400 389-1283
Web: www.capmetro.org

Catalina Express Berth 95 . . . San Pedro CA 90731 310-519-7971 548-8425
TF: 800-481-3470 ■ *Web:* www.catalinaexpress.com

Central Florida Regional Transportation Authority (Inc)
455 N Garland Ave . . . Orlando FL 32801 407-841-2279
Web: www.golynx.com

Central New York Regional Transportation Authority
200 Cortland Ave . . . Syracuse NY 13205 315-442-3400 442-3337
Web: www.centro.org

Central Ohio Transit Authority (COTA)
33 N High St . . . Columbus OH 43215 614-228-1776 275-5933
Web: www.cota.com

Central Puget Sound Regional Transit Authority
401 S Jackson St . . . Seattle WA 98104 206-398-5000 689-3360*
**Fax:* Hum Res ■ *TF:* 800-201-4900 ■ *Web:* www.soundtransit.org

Champaign-Urbana Mass Transit District
1101 E University Ave . . . Urbana IL 61802 217-384-8188 384-8215
Web: www.cumtd.com

Charleston Area Regional Transportation Authority (CARTA)
36 John St . . . Charleston SC 29403 843-724-7420 720-1985
Web: www.ridecarta.com

Chicago Transit Authority (CTA) 567 W Lake St . . . Chicago IL 60661 312-664-7200 432-7185*
**Fax:* Cust Svc ■ *Web:* www.transitchicago.com

Cliff Viessman Inc 215 1st Ave PO Box 175 . . . Gary SD 57237 605-272-5241 272-5546
TF: 800-328-2408 ■ *Web:* www.viessmantrucking.com

Connecticut Transit 100 Leibert Rd . . . Hartford CT 06141 860-522-8101 247-1810
Web: www.cttransit.com

Dallas Area Rapid Transit Authority (DART)
1401 Pacific Ave PO Box 660163 . . . Dallas TX 75202 214-749-3278 749-3661
TF: 888-557-6669 ■ *Web:* www.dart.org

Delaware Transit Corp
119 Lower Beach St Suite 100 . . . Wilmington DE 19805 302-576-6000 577-6066
TF: 800-652-3278 ■ *Web:* www.dartfirststate.com

Erie Metropolitan Transit Authority (EMTA)
127 E 14th St . . . Erie PA 16503 814-452-3515
Web: www.emtaerie.com

Escambia County Area Transit (ECAT)
1515 W Fairfield Dr . . . Pensacola FL 32501 850-595-3228 595-3222
Web: www.goecat.com

Fort Wayne Public Transportation Corp
801 Leesburg Rd . . . Fort Wayne IN 46808 260-432-4546 436-7729
Web: www.fwcitilink.com

Fresno Area Express 2223 G St . . . Fresno CA 93706 559-621-7433 488-1065
Web: www.fresno.gov

GO Transit 20 Bay St Suite 600 . . . Toronto ON M5J2W3 416-869-3200 869-3525
Web: www.gotransit.com

Gold Coast Transit (GCT) 301 E 3rd St . . . Oxnard CA 93030 805-487-4222 487-0925
Web: www.goldcoasttransit.org

Golden Empire Transit District
1830 Golden State Ave . . . Bakersfield CA 93301 661-324-9874 869-6394
Web: www.getbus.org

Greater Cleveland Regional Transit Authority (RTA)
1240 W 6th St . . . Cleveland OH 44113 216-566-5285 781-4483
Web: www.riderta.com

Greater Peoria Mass Transit District
2105 NE Jefferson St . . . Peoria IL 61603 309-676-4040 676-8373
Web: www.mycitylink.info

Phone *Fax*

Greater Portland Transit District
114 Valley St . . . Portland ME 04102 207-774-0351 774-6241
Web: www.gpmetrobus.com

Greater Vancouver Transportation Authority
4720 Kingsway Suite 1600 . . . Burnaby BC V5H4N2 604-453-4500 453-4626
Web: www.translink.ca

GRTC Transit System 301 E Belt Blvd . . . Richmond VA 23224 804-358-3871 342-1933
Web: www.ridegrtc.com

Heniff Transportation Systems Inc
7416 S County Line Rd . . . Burr Ridge IL 60527 630-230-2100 230-2111
Web: www.heniff.com

Honolulu Dept of Transportation Services
650 S King St 3rd Fl . . . Honolulu HI 96813 808-768-8303 768-4954
Web: www1.honolulu.gov

Horizon Freight System Inc
6600 Bessemer Ave . . . Cleveland OH 44127 216-341-7410 429-3523
TF: 800-480-6829 ■ *Web:* www.horizonfreightsystem.com

Idaho Milk Transport Inc PO Box 1185 . . . Burley ID 83318 208-878-5000 878-5001
Web: www.idahomilktransport.com

Inter-Urban Transit Partnership
300 Ellsworth St SW . . . Grand Rapids MI 49503 616-776-1100 456-1941
Web: www.ridetherapid.org

Intermodal Cartage Co Inc 5707 E Holmes Rd . . . Memphis TN 38141 901-363-0050 362-7035
Web: www.imcg.com

Karl's Transport Inc PO Box 333 . . . Antigo WI 54409 715-623-2033 623-2791
TF: 800-586-9356 ■ *Web:* www.karlstransport.com

King County Dept of Transportation
201 S Jackson St . . . Seattle WA 98104 206-684-1481 684-1224
Web: www.kingcounty.gov

Los Angeles County Metropolitan Transportation Authority
1 Gateway Plaza . . . Los Angeles CA 90012 213-922-6000 922-2704
TF: 800-621-7828 ■ *Web:* www.metro.net

Mass Transit Administration of Maryland (MTA)
6 St Paul St . . . Baltimore MD 21202 410-539-5000 333-3279
Web: www.mta.maryland.gov

Massachusetts Bay Transportation Authority (MBTA)
10 Pk Plaza . . . Boston MA 02116 617-222-5000 222-3340*
**Fax:* Mktg ■ *Web:* www.mbta.com

Matthews Buses Inc 2900 State Rte 9 . . . Ballston Spa NY 12020 518-584-2400 584-1941
TF: 800-288-6287 ■ *Web:* www.matthewsbuses.com

Memphis Area Transit Authority (MATA)
1370 Levee Rd . . . Memphis TN 38108 901-722-7100 722-7123
Web: www.matatransit.com

Metro Transit 560 6th Ave N . . . Minneapolis MN 55411 612-349-7332 349-7675*
**Fax:* Mktg ■ *Web:* www.metrotransit.org

Metro Transit 300 SW 7th St . . . Oklahoma City OK 73109 405-235-7433 297-2111
Web: www.okladot.state.ok.us

Metro Transit 200 Ilsley Ave . . . Dartmouth NS B3B1V1 902-490-4000 490-6688
Web: www.halifax.ca/metrotransit

Metropolitan Atlanta Rapid Transit Authority (MARTA)
2424 Piedmont Rd NE . . . Atlanta GA 30324 404-848-5000
Web: www.itsmarta.com

Metropolitan Transit Authority of Harris County
1900 Maine . . . Houston TX 77002 713-739-4000 739-3769
Web: www.hou-metro.harris.tx.us

Metropolitan Transit Commission
560 6th Ave N . . . Minneapolis MN 55411 612-349-7400 349-7675
Web: www.metrotransit.org

Metropolitan Transportation Authority
347 Madison Ave . . . New York NY 10017 212-878-7000 878-0150*
**Fax:* Mktg ■ *Web:* www.mta.nyc.ny.us

Miami-Dade Transit (MDTA) 701 NW 1st Ct . . . Miami FL 33136 305-375-5675 469-5580*
**Fax Area Code:* 786 ■ *Web:* www.co.miami-dade.fl.us

Milwaukee County Transit System
1942 N 17th St . . . Milwaukee WI 53205 414-343-1700 343-1787*
**Fax:* Hum Res ■ *Web:* www.ridemcts.com

Mission Petroleum Carriers Inc 8450 Mosley . . . Houston TX 77075 713-943-8250 944-6080
TF: 800-737-9911 ■ *Web:* www.mipe.com

Monterey-Salinas Transit (MST) 1 Ryan Ranch Rd . . . Monterey CA 93940 831-899-2555
Web: www.mst.org

MV Transportation Inc 4620 W America Dr . . . Fairfield CA 94534 707-863-8980 863-8944
Web: www.mvtransit.com

New Jersey Transit Corp 1 Penn Plaza E . . . Newark NJ 07105 973-491-7000 491-7567*
**Fax:* Cust Svc ■ *TF Cust Svc:* 800-772-3606 ■ *Web:* www.njtransit.com

New York City Transit Authority 370 Jay St . . . Brooklyn NY 11201 718-330-1234 243-3283
Web: www.mta.nyc.ny.us/nyct

Niagara Frontier Transit Metro System Inc
181 Ellicott St Suite 1 . . . Buffalo NY 14202 716-855-7211 855-7657
Web: www.nfta.com/metro

Norfolk Southern Corp
3 Commercial Pl PO Box 227 . . . Norfolk VA 23510 757-823-5567 629-2361*
NYSE: NSC ■ **Fax:* Mktg ■ *TF Cust Svc:* 800-635-5768 ■ *Web:* www.nscorp.com

North County Transit District (NCTD)
810 Mission Rd . . . Oceanside CA 92054 760-966-6500 967-2001
Web: www.gonctd.com

Northeast Illinois Regional Commuter Railroad Corp
547 W Jackson Blvd . . . Chicago IL 60661 312-322-6777 322-6747*
**Fax:* Mktg ■ *Web:* www.metrarail.com

Northern Indiana Commuter Transportation District
33 E US Hwy 12 . . . Chesterton IN 46304 219-926-5744 929-4438
TF: 800-356-2079 ■ *Web:* www.nictd.com

Norwalk Transit District (NTD) 275 Wilson Ave . . . Norwalk CT 06854 203-852-0000 853-6761
Web: www.norwalktransit.com

Oahu Transit Services 811 Middle St . . . Honolulu HI 96819 808-848-4500 848-4419
Web: www.thebus.org

OC Transpo 1500 St Laurent Blvd . . . Ottawa ON K1G0Z8 613-842-3600 230-6543
Web: www.octranspo1.com

Office Movers Inc 6500 Kane Way . . . Elkridge MD 21075 410-799-7704 799-5992
TF: 800-331-4025 ■ *Web:* www.officemovers.com

Orange County Transportation Authority
550 S Main St PO Box 14184 . . . Orange CA 92863 714-560-6282 560-5899
Web: www.octa.net

Name / Address	City	State	ZIP	Phone	Fax
Pace Suburban Bus 550 W Algonquin Rd	Arlington Heights	IL	60005	847-364-8130	364-7236*
*Fax: Cust Svc ■ *Web:* www.pacebus.com					
Packard Transport Inc 24021 S Municipal Dr PO Box 380	Channahon	IL	60410	815-467-9260	467-6939
TF: 800-467-9260 ■ *Web:* www.packardtransport.com					
Pierce Transit 3701 96th St SW PO Box 99070	Lakewood	WA	98496	253-581-8000	581-8075
TF: 800-562-8109 ■ *Web:* www.piercetransit.org					
Port Authority of Allegheny County 345 6th Ave 3rd Fl	Pittsburgh	PA	15222	412-566-5500	566-5406*
*Fax: Cust Svc ■ *Web:* www.portauthority.org					
Pro Transportation Inc PO Box 190666	Little Rock	AR	72219	501-490-0700	490-0750
Regional Transit Authority (RTA) 2817 Canal St	New Orleans	LA	70118	504-827-8300	248-3637
Web: www.norta.com					
Regional Transit Service Inc 1372 E Main St	Rochester	NY	14609	585-654-0200	654-0293
Web: www.rgrta.org					
Regional Transit System (RTS) 100 SE 10th Ave	Gainesville	FL	32601	352-334-2600	334-2607
Web: www.go-rts.com					
Regional Transportation Authority 175 W Jackson Blvd Suite 1550	Chicago	IL	60604	312-913-3200	913-3118
Web: www.rtachicago.com					
Regional Transportation Commission of Southern Nevada (RTC) 600 S Grand Central Pkwy Suite 350	Las Vegas	NV	89106	702-676-1500	676-1518
TF: 800-228-3911 ■ *Web:* www.rtcsouthernnevada.com					
Regional Transportation District (RTD) 1600 Blake St	Denver	CO	80202	303-628-9000	299-2015
TF: 800-877-7433 ■ *Web:* www.rtd-denver.com					
Reliable Carriers Inc 41555 Koppernick Rd	Canton	MI	48187	734-453-9950	453-8609
TF: 800-521-6393 ■ *Web:* www.reliable-carriers.com					
Reliable Transportation Specialists Inc 139 Venturi Dr	Chesterton	IN	46304	219-926-8850	926-5174
Web: www.reliabletrans.com					
Rhode Island Public Transit Authority 265 Melrose St	Providence	RI	02907	401-781-9400	784-9595
Web: www.ripta.com					
Riverside Transit Agency (RTA) 1825 3rd St PO Box 59968	Riverside	CA	92517	951-565-5000	684-1007
TF: 800-800-7821 ■ *Web:* www.riversidetransit.com					
Sacramento Regional Transit District 1400 29th St	Sacramento	CA	95816	916-321-2800	444-2156
Web: www.sacrt.com					
San Diego Metropolitan Transit Development Board 1255 Imperial Ave Suite 1000	San Diego	CA	92101	619-231-1466	234-3407
Web: www.sdcommute.com					
San Diego Transit Corp 100 16th St	San Diego	CA	92101	619-238-0100	696-8159
Web: www.sdcommute.com					
San Francisco Municipal Railway 401 Van Ness Ave Suite 308	San Francisco	CA	94102	415-554-4103	554-4174
Web: www.sfmta.com					
San Joaquin Regional Transit District 1533 E Lindsay St	Stockton	CA	95205	209-948-5566	525-6507
Web: www.sanjoaquinrtd.com					
San Mateo County Transit District 1250 San Carlos Ave PO Box 3006	San Carlos	CA	94070	650-508-6200	508-6443
TF: 800-660-4287 ■ *Web:* www.smctd.com					
Santa Barbara Metropolitan Transit District 550 Olive St	Santa Barbara	CA	93101	805-963-3364	962-4794
Web: www.sbmtd.gov					
Santa Clara Valley Transportation Authority (VTA) 3331 N 1st St	San Jose	CA	95134	408-321-5555	955-0893*
*Fax: PR ■ *TF:* 800-894-9908 ■ *Web:* www.vta.org					
Societe de Transport de Montreal (STM) 800 Rue Gauchetiere O CP 2000	Montreal	QC	H5A1K6	514-288-6287	280-6126
Web: www.stcum.qc.ca					
Sonoma County Transit 355 W Robles Ave	Santa Rosa	CA	95407	707-585-7516	585-7713
TF: 800-345-7433 ■ *Web:* www.sctransit.com					
Southeastern Pennsylvania Transportation Authority (SEPTA) 1234 Market St	Philadelphia	PA	19107	215-580-7800	
Web: www.septa.org					
Southern California Regional Rail Authority 700 S Flower St Suite 2600	Los Angeles	CA	90017	213-452-0200	452-0429
TF: 800-371-5465 ■ *Web:* www.metrolinktrains.com					
Steamship Authority PO Box 284	Woods Hole	MA	02543	508-548-5011	548-8410
Web: www.steamshipauthority.com					
Suburban Mobility Authority for Regional Transportation (SMART) 660 Woodward Ave First National Bldg	Detroit	MI	48226	866-962-5515	223-2370*
*Fax Area Code: 313 ■ *Fax: Hum Res ■ *TF:* 866-962-5515 ■ *Web:* www.smartbus.org					
TLD Distribution Co LLC 505 S 7th Ave	City of Industry	CA	91746	310-324-5111	516-3960
Web: www.triple-l.com					
Toronto Transit Commission (TTC) 1900 Yonge St	Toronto	ON	M4S1Z2	416-393-4000	338-0128*
*Fax: PR ■ *Web:* www.ttc.ca					
Transcare Corp 1 Metrotech Ctr	Brooklyn	NY	11234	718-763-8888	209-1381
Web: www.transcare.com					
Transit Authority of River City (TARC) 1000 W Broadway	Louisville	KY	40203	502-585-1234	213-3243*
*Fax: Cust Svc ■ *Web:* www.ridetarc.com					
Tri-County Commuter Rail Authority 800 NW 33rd St Suite 100	Pompano Beach	FL	33064	954-942-7245	788-7878
Web: www.tri-rail.com					
Tri-County Metropolitan Transportation District of Oregon 4012 SE 17th Ave	Portland	OR	97202	503-962-5806	962-6469*
*Fax: Mktg ■ *Web:* www.trimet.org					
Triangle Transit Authority PO Box 13787	Research Triangle Park	NC	27709	919-549-9999	485-7441
Web: www.triangletransit.org					
Utah Transit Authority 3600 S 700 W PO Box 30810	Salt Lake City	UT	84130	801-262-5626	
TF: 800-743-3882 ■ *Web:* www.rideuta.com					
VIA Metropolitan Transit 800 W Myrtle St	San Antonio	TX	78212	210-362-2000	362-2563*
*Fax: Cust Svc ■ *TF:* 866-362-4200 ■ *Web:* www.viainfo.net					
Virginia Railway Express (VRE) 1500 King St Suite 202	Alexandria	VA	22314	703-684-1001	684-1313
TF: 800-743-3873 ■ *Web:* www.vre.org					
VPSI Inc 1220 Rankin St	Troy	MI	48083	248-597-3500	597-3501
TF: 800-826-7433 ■ *Web:* www.vpsiinc.com					
Washington Metropolitan Area Transit Authority 600 5th St NW	Washington	DC	20001	202-637-7000	962-1420
Web: www.wmata.com					
Westchester County Dept of Transportation 100 E 1st St	Mount Vernon	NY	10550	914-813-7777	813-7735
Web: www.co.westchester.ny.us/transportation					
Worcester Regional Transit Authority 287 Grove St	Worcester	MA	01605	508-791-9782	752-3153*
*Fax: Cust Svc ■ *Web:* www.therta.com					
York County Transportation Authority 1230 Roosevelt Ave	York	PA	17404	717-846-5562	848-4853
TF: 800-632-9063 ■ *Web:* www.rabbittransit.org					

472 MATCHES & MATCHBOOKS

Name / Address	City	State	ZIP	Phone	Fax
DD Bean & Sons Co 207 Peterborough St	Jaffrey	NH	03452	603-532-8311	532-6001*
*Fax: Sales ■ *TF:* 800-326-8311 ■ *Web:* www.ddbean.com					
Diamond Brands Div Jarden Home Brands 14611 W Commerce Rd PO Box 529	Daleville	IN	47334	800-392-2575	557-3250*
*Fax Area Code: 765 ■ *TF Cust Svc:* 800-392-2575 ■ *Web:* www.diamondbrands.com					
Maryland Match Corp 605 Alluvion St	Baltimore	MD	21230	410-752-8164	752-3441
TF: 800-423-0013 ■ *Web:* www.marylandmatch.com					
Universal Creative Concepts Corp 10143 Royalton Rd Suite E	North Royalton	OH	44133	440-230-1366	230-1919
Web: www.uccadv.com					

473 MATERIAL HANDLING EQUIPMENT

SEE ALSO Conveyors & Conveying Equipment p. 1762

Name / Address	City	State	ZIP	Phone	Fax
4Front Engineered Solutions Inc 1612 Hutton Dr Suite 140	Carrollton	TX	75006	972-466-0707	323-2661
TF: 877-778-3625 ■ *Web:* www.4frontes.com					
Abell-Howe Crane Inc 10321 Werch Dr Suite 100	Woodridge	IL	60517	800-366-0068	972-0897*
*Fax Area Code: 630 ■ *TF:* 800-366-0068 ■ *Web:* www.abellhowe.com					
Advance Lifts Inc 701 Kirk Rd	Saint Charles	IL	60174	630-584-9881	584-9405
TF: 800-843-3625 ■ *Web:* www.advancelifts.com					
Air Technical Industries 7501 Clover Ave	Mentor	OH	44060	440-951-5191	953-9237
TF: 800-321-9680 ■ *Web:* www.airtechnical.com					
American Crane & Equipment Corp 531 Old Swede Rd	Douglassville	PA	19518	610-385-6061	385-3191*
*Fax: Sales ■ *TF:* 877-877-6778 ■ *Web:* www.americancrane.com					
American Lifts 532 E Baili Ct	Greensburg	IN	47240	812-663-4085	663-4173
TF: 800-426-9772 ■ *Web:* www.americanlifts.com					
American Power Pull Corp 550 W Linfoot St PO Box 109	Wauseon	OH	43567	419-335-7050	335-7070
TF: 800-808-5922 ■ *Web:* www.americanpowerpull.com					
Atap Inc PO Box 98	Eastaboga	AL	36260	256-362-2221	362-2221
TF: 800-362-2827 ■ *Web:* www.atap.com					
Autoquip Corp 1058 W Industrial Rd	Guthrie	OK	73044	405-282-5200	282-8105
TF: 888-811-9876 ■ *Web:* www.autoquip.com					
Barloworld Handling LLC 440 E Westinghouse Blvd	Charlotte	NC	28273	704-587-1003	588-9313
Web: www.handling.barloworld.com					
Bayhead Products Corp 173 Crosby Rd	Dover	NH	03820	603-742-3000	743-4701
TF: 800-603-0053 ■ *Web:* www.bayheadproducts.com					
Berns Co 1250 W 17th St	Long Beach	CA	90813	562-437-0471	436-1074
TF: 800-421-3773 ■ *Web:* www.thebernsco.com					
BGK Finishing Systems 4131 Pheasant Ridge Dr NE	Minneapolis	MN	55449	763-784-0466	784-1362
TF: 800-663-5498 ■ *Web:* www.bgk.com					
Breeze-Eastern Corp 700 Liberty Ave	Union	NJ	07083	908-686-4000	686-9292
TF Sales: 800-929-1919 ■ *Web:* www.breeze-eastern.com					
Busse/SJI Corp 124 N Columbus St	Randolph	WI	53956	920-326-3131	326-3134
TF: 800-882-4995 ■ *Web:* www.arrowheadsystems.com					
Cannon Equipment Co 15100 Business Pkwy	Rosemount	MN	55068	651-322-6300	322-1583
TF: 800-825-8501 ■ *Web:* www.cannonequipment.com					
Cascade Corp 2201 NE 201st Ave	Fairview	OR	97024	503-669-6300	669-6716
NYSE: CASC ■ *TF:* 800-227-2233 ■ *Web:* www.cascorp.com					
Clark Material Handling Co 700 Enterprise Dr	Lexington	KY	40510	859-422-6400	
TF: 866-252-5275 ■ *Web:* www.clarkmhc.com					
Clyde Machines Inc 1150 State Hwy 55 N PO Box 194	Glenwood	MN	56334	320-634-4503	634-4506
Web: www.clydemachines.com					
Columbus McKinnon Corp 140 John James Audubon Pkwy	Amherst	NY	14228	716-689-5400	639-4250
NASDAQ: CMCO ■ *TF:* 800-888-0985 ■ *Web:* www.cmworks.com					
Cozzini Inc 4300 W Bryn Mawr Ave	Chicago	IL	60646	773-478-9700	478-8689
TF: 800-227-4447 ■ *Web:* www.cozzini.com					
Crane Tech Solutions LLC 2030 Ponderosa St	Portsmouth	VA	23701	757-405-0311	405-0313
TF: 800-996-6355 ■ *Web:* www.cranetechsolutions.com					
Craneveyor Corp 1524 Potrero Ave	South El Monte	CA	91733	626-442-1524	442-7308
TF: 800-423-4180					
Crosby McKissick 2801 Dawson Rd	Tulsa	OK	74110	918-834-4611	832-0940
TF: 800-772-1500 ■ *Web:* www.thecrosbygroup.com					
Crown Equipment Corp 44 S Washington St	New Bremen	OH	45869	419-629-2311	629-2900
Web: www.crown.com					

Company / Address	City	State	Zip	Phone	Fax
Crysteel Mfg Inc 52182 Ember Rd	Lake Crystal	MN	56055	507-726-2728	726-2442
TF Orders: 800-533-0494 ■ *Web:* www.crysteel.com					
Dematic 507 Plymouth Ave NE	Grand Rapids	MI	49505	616-913-6200	913-7701
TF Cust Svc: 800-530-9153 ■ *Web:* www.dematic.us					
Detroit Hoist Co 6650 Sterling Dr N	Sterling Heights	MI	48312	586-268-2600	268-0044
TF: 800-521-9126 ■ *Web:* www.detroithoist.com					
Downs Crane & Hoist Co Inc					
8827 Juniper St	Los Angeles	CA	90002	323-589-6061	589-6066
TF: 800-748-5994 ■ *Web:* www.downscrane.com					
Drake-Scruggs Equipment Inc					
2000 S Dirksen Pkwy	Springfield	IL	62703	217-753-3871	753-2760
Web: www.drake-scruggs.com					
Dynacon Inc 831 Industrial Blvd	Bryan	TX	77803	979-823-2690	823-0947
Web: www.dynacon.com					
Ederer LLC 3701 S Norfolk St Suite 301	Seattle	WA	98124	206-622-4421	623-8583
Web: www.par.com/our_companies_ederer.php					
Escalera Inc 708 S Industrial Dr	Yuba City	CA	95993	530-673-6318	673-6376
TF: 800-622-1359 ■ *Web:* www.escalera.com					
Excalibur Equipment LLC					
Gregory Industrial Trucks 285 Eldridge Rd	Fairfield	NJ	07004	973-808-8399	808-8398
Web: www.exforklifts.com					
Excellon Automation Inc					
20001 S Rancho Way	Rancho Dominguez	CA	90220	310-668-7700	668-7800
TF: 800-392-3556 ■ *Web:* www.excellon.com					
FL Smidth Inc 2040 Ave C	Bethlehem	PA	18017	610-264-6011	264-6701
TF: 800-523-9482 ■ *Web:* www.flsmidth.com					
Flexible Material Handling 9501 Granger Rd	Cleveland	OH	44125	216-587-1500	587-2833
TF: 800-669-1501					
Gaffey Inc 9655 Alawhe Dr	Claremore	OK	74019	918-343-1191	343-1199
TF: 800-331-3916					
Genie Industries Inc 18340 NE 76th St	Redmond	WA	98052	425-881-1800	883-3475
TF: 800-536-1800 ■ *Web:* www.genielift.com					
Goldco Industries Inc 5605 Goldco Dr	Loveland	CO	80538	970-663-4770	663-7212
TF: 800-527-0494 ■ *Web:* www.fgwa.com					
Gunnebo-Johnson Corp 1240 N Harvard Ave	Tulsa	OK	74115	918-832-8933	834-0984*
**Fax:* Cust Svc ■ *TF Sales:* 800-331-5460 ■ *Web:* www.gunnebojohnson.com					
Harlan Materials Handling Corp					
27 Stanley Rd	Kansas City	KS	66115	913-342-5650	321-5802
TF: 800-255-4262 ■ *Web:* www.harlan-corp.com					
Harlo Corp 4210 Ferry St SW	Grandville	MI	49418	616-538-0550	538-0554
TF: 800-391-4151 ■ *Web:* www.harlo.com					
Harper Trucks Inc PO Box 12330	Wichita	KS	67277	316-942-1381	942-8508
TF: 800-835-4099 ■ *Web:* www.harpertrucks.com					
Heyl & Patterson Inc					
2000 Cliff Mine Rd PO Box 36	Pittsburgh	PA	15230	412-788-9810	788-9822
Web: www.heylpatterson.com					
Hilman Inc 12 Timber Ln	Marlboro	NJ	07746	732-462-6277	462-6355
TF Cust Svc: 888-276-5548 ■ *Web:* www.hilmanrollers.com					
Hoist Equipment Co 26161 Cannon Rd	Bedford Heights	OH	44146	440-232-0300	232-3366
Web: www.hoistequipment.com					
Indusco Group 1200 W Hamburg St	Baltimore	MD	21230	410-727-0665	727-2538
TF: 800-727-0665 ■ *Web:* www.induscowirerope.com					
Industrial Vehicles International Inc (IVI)					
6737 E 12th St	Tulsa	OK	74112	918-836-6516	838-9529
Web: www.indvehicles.com					
Iowa Mold Tooling Co Inc (IMT) 500 W US Hwy 18	Garner	IA	50438	641-923-3711	923-2424
TF: 800-247-5958 ■ *Web:* www.imt.com					
James Walker Co 7109 Milford Industrial Rd	Baltimore	MD	21208	410-486-3950	486-5176
Jervis B Webb Co 34375 W 12-Mile Rd	Farmington Hills	MI	48331	248-553-1220	553-1200
TF: 800-526-9322 ■ *Web:* www.jervisbwebb.com					
Kelly Systems Inc 422 N Western Ave	Chicago	IL	60612	312-733-3224	733-6971
Web: www.kellytubesystems.com					
Key Handling Systems Inc					
137 W Commercial Ave	Moonachie	NJ	07074	201-933-9333	933-5732
Web: www.keyhandling.com					
Konecranes America 7300 Chippewa Blvd	Houston	TX	77086	281-445-2225	445-9355
TF: 800-231-0241 ■ *Web:* www.konecranesamericas.com					
Kornylak Corp 400 Heaton St	Hamilton	OH	45011	513-863-1277	863-7644
TF: 800-837-5676 ■ *Web:* www.kornylak.com					
KWD Mfg Co 2230 W Southcross Blvd	San Antonio	TX	78211	210-924-5999	924-6799
Landoll Corp 1900 N St	Marysville	KS	66508	785-562-5381	562-4891*
**Fax:* Sales ■ *TF Cust Svc:* 800-446-5175 ■ *Web:* www.landoll.com					
Leebaw Mfg Co Inc 3 Industrial Pk Dr	Canfield	OH	44406	330-533-3368	533-3917
TF: 800-841-8083 ■ *Web:* www.leebaw.com					
Lift-All Co Inc 1909 McFarland Dr	Landisville	PA	17538	717-898-6615	898-1215*
**Fax:* Cust Svc ■ *TF:* 800-909-1964 ■ *Web:* www.lift-all.com					
Liftex Inc 1230 Old York Rd Suite 101	Warminster	PA	18974	215-957-0810	957-9180
TF: 800-448-3079 ■ *Web:* www.liftex.com					
Linde Hydraulics Corp					
5089 W Western Reserve Rd PO Box 82	Canfield	OH	44406	330-533-6801	533-6893
Web: www.lindeamerica.com					
Lodi Metal Tech Inc 213 S Kelly St	Lodi	CA	95240	209-334-2500	334-1259
Web: www.lodirack.com					
Lovegreen Industrial Services Inc					
2280 Sibley Ct	Eagan	MN	55122	651-890-1166	890-8370
Web: www.lovegreen.com					
Luker Inc 514 National Ave	Augusta	GA	30901	706-724-0244	724-1050
TF: 800-982-9534 ■ *Web:* www.lukerinc.com					
MacCabe Electric Conductors Inc					
426 Stump Rd PO Box 590	Montgomeryville	PA	18936	215-368-9420	368-9220
Web: www.maccabeelectric.com					
Magline Inc 503 S Mercer St	Pinconning	MI	48650	989-879-2411	879-5399
TF: 800-624-5463 ■ *Web:* www.magliner.com					
Manitex Inc 3000 S Austin Ave	Georgetown	TX	78626	512-942-3000	869-7550
TF: 877-314-3390 ■ *Web:* www.manitex.com					
Manitou North America 6401 Imperial Dr	Waco	TX	76712	254-799-0232	799-0232
TF Cust Svc: 800-433-3304 ■ *Web:* www.us.manitou.com					
Matot Inc 2501 Van Buren St	Bellwood	IL	60104	708-547-1888	547-1608
TF: 800-369-1070 ■ *Web:* www.matot.com					
Maxon Industries Inc					
11921 Slauson Ave	Santa Fe Springs	CA	90670	562-464-0099	771-7713*
**Fax Area Code:* 888 ■ *TF:* 800-227-4116 ■ *Web:* www.maxonlift.com					
Mazzella Lifting Technologies					
21000 Aerospace Pkwy	Cleveland	OH	44142	440-239-7000	239-7010
TF: 800-362-4601 ■ *Web:* www.mazzellalifting.com					
McGuire					
W194 N11481 McCormick Dr PO Box 309	Germantown	WI	53022	518-828-7652	255-9399*
**Fax Area Code:* 262 ■ *TF:* 800-624-8473 ■ *Web:* www.wbmcguire.com					
Mertz Mfg LLC 1701 N Waverly St	Ponca City	OK	74601	580-762-5646	767-8411
TF: 800-654-6433 ■ *Web:* www.mertzok.com					
Mitsubishi Caterpillar Forklift America Inc					
2121 W Sam Houston Pkwy N	Houston	TX	77043	713-365-1000	365-1441
Web: www.mcfa.com					
Morris Material Handling Inc					
315 W Forest Hill Ave	Oak Creek	WI	53154	414-764-6200	570-2779
Web: www.morriscranes.com					
NACCO Materials Handling Group Inc					
650 NE Holladay St Suite 1600	Portland	OR	97232	503-721-6000	721-1352
Web: www.nmhg.com					
Nestaway Wire Fabricators 9501 Granger Rd	Cleveland	OH	44125	216-587-1500	587-2774
TF: 888-587-9473 ■ *Web:* www.nestawaywire.com					
Nissan Forklift Corp North America (NFC)					
240 N Prospect St	Marengo	IL	60152	815-568-0061	568-8340
TF: 800-871-5438 ■ *Web:* www.nissanforklift.com					
NMC-Wollard Inc 2021 Truax Blvd	Eau Claire	WI	54703	715-835-3151	835-6625
TF: 800-656-6867 ■ *Web:* www.nmc-wollard.com					
North American Industries Inc 80 Holton St	Woburn	MA	01801	781-897-4100	729-3343
TF: 800-847-8470 ■ *Web:* www.naicranes.com					
Nutting 450 Pheasant Ridge Dr	Watertown	SD	57201	605-882-3000	882-4226
TF: 800-533-0337 ■ *Web:* www.acconutting.com					
Ohio Magnetics Inc 5400 Dunham Rd	Maple Heights	OH	44137	216-662-8484	662-2911
TF: 800-486-6446 ■ *Web:* www.ohiomagnetics.com/ohio.htm					
Oki Systems Ltd 10685 Medallion Dr	Cincinnati	OH	45241	513-874-2600	874-8755
Web: www.okisys.com					
P & H Mining Equipment 4400 W National Ave	Milwaukee	WI	53214	414-671-4400	671-7604
Web: www.phmining.com					
Paceco Corp 25503 Whitesell St	Hayward	CA	94545	510-264-9288	264-9280
Web: www.pacecocorp.com					
Paragon Technologies Inc 600 Kuebler Rd	Easton	PA	18040	610-252-3205	252-3102
AMEX: PTG					
Pettibone Michigan LLC 1100 Superior Ave	Baraga	MI	49908	906-353-6611	353-6325
TF: 800-467-3884 ■ *Web:* www.pettibone-mi.com					
Phillips Mine & Mill Inc PO Box 409	Irwin	PA	15642	724-864-8900	864-8909
Web: www.phillipsmineandmill.com					
Positech Corp 191 N Rush Lake Rd	Laurens	IA	50554	712-841-4548	841-4765
TF: 800-831-6026 ■ *Web:* www.positech-solutions.com					
Powell Systems Inc					
162 Churchill-Hubbard Rd	Youngstown	OH	44505	330-759-9220	759-9434
Web: www.powellsystems.com					
Process Equipment Inc					
2770 Welborn St PO Box 1607	Pelham	AL	35124	205-663-5330	663-6037
TF: 888-663-2028 ■ *Web:* www.processbarron.com					
Production Equipment Co 401 Liberty St	Meriden	CT	06450	203-235-5795	237-5391
TF: 800-758-5697					
Proserv Anchor Crane Group					
455 Aldine Bender PO Box 670965	Houston	TX	77060	281-405-9048	448-7508
TF: 800-835-2223 ■ *Web:* www.proservanchor.com					
PTR Baler & Compactor Co					
2207 E Ontario St	Philadelphia	PA	19134	215-533-5100	537-8536
TF: 800-523-3654 ■ *Web:* www.ptrco.com					
Pucel Enterprises Inc 1440 E 36th St	Cleveland	OH	44114	216-881-4604	881-6731
TF: 800-336-4986 ■ *Web:* www.pucelenterprises.com					
Raymond Corp 8-20 S Canal St	Greene	NY	13778	607-656-2311	656-9005
TF: 800-235-7200 ■ *Web:* www.raymondcorp.com					
RKI Inc 2301 Central Pkwy	Houston	TX	77092	713-688-4414	688-5776
Web: www.rki-us.com					
Royal Tractor Co Inc 109 Overland Pk Pl	New Century	KS	66031	913-782-2598	782-4588
Web: www.royaltractor.com					
Scott Industrial Systems Inc					
4433 Interpoint Blvd PO Box 1387	Dayton	OH	45401	937-233-8146	416-6023*
**Fax Area Code:* 800 ■ *Web:* www.scottindustrialsystems.com					
Shepard Niles 220 N Genesee St	Montour Falls	NY	14865	607-535-7111	535-7323
TF: 800-481-2260 ■ *Web:* www.shepard-niles.com					
Sherman & Reilly Inc PO Box 11267	Chattanooga	TN	37401	423-756-5300	756-2948
TF Sales: 800-251-7780 ■ *Web:* www.sherman-reilly.com					
Solazyme Inc 225 Gateway Blvd	South San Francisco	CA	94080	650-780-4777	989-6700
Web: www.solazyme.com					
Southeast Industrial Equipment Inc					
12200 Steele Creek Rd PO Box 39110	Charlotte	NC	28273	704-399-9700	393-1714
TF: 800-752-6368 ■ *Web:* www.sielift.com					
Southworth Products Corp PO Box 1380	Portland	ME	04104	207-878-0700	797-4734
TF: 800-743-1000 ■ *Web:* www.southworthproducts.com					
Steel King Industries Inc					
2700 Chamber St	Stevens Point	WI	54481	715-341-3120	341-8792
TF: 800-826-0203 ■ *Web:* www.steelking.com					
Stock Fairfield Corp					
16490 Chillicothe Rd	chagrinfalls	OH	44023	740-387-3327	387-4869
TF: 800-827-3364 ■ *Web:* www.fairfieldengineering.com					
Streator Dependable Mfg Co					
1705 N Shabbona St	Streator	IL	61364	815-672-0551	672-7631
TF: 800-795-0551 ■ *Web:* www.streatordependable.com					
Sunston Equipment Inc 14133 Fwy Dr	Santa Fe Springs	CA	90670	562-802-9778	802-7157
TF: 888-802-9778 ■ *Web:* www.sunston.com					
Taylor-Dunn Mfg Co 2114 W Ball Rd	Anaheim	CA	92804	714-956-4040	956-3130
TF: 800-688-8680 ■ *Web:* www.taylor-dunn.com					
TC/American Monorail Inc					
12070 43rd St NE	Saint Michael	MN	55376	763-497-7000	497-7001
Web: www.tcamerican.com					
Terex Corp 200 Nyala Farm Rd	Westport	CT	06880	203-222-7170	222-7976
NYSE: TEX ■ *Web:* www.terex.com					
Terex Corp Crane Div 202 Raleigh St	Wilmington	NC	28412	910-395-8500	395-8551*
**Fax:* Hum Res ■ *TF:* 800-250-2726 ■ *Web:* www.terex.com					
Terex-Telelect Inc					
500 Oakwood Rd PO Box 1150	Watertown	SD	57201	605-882-4000	882-1842
TF: 800-982-8975 ■ *Web:* www.terexutilities.com					

Company	City	State	Zip	Phone	Fax
Thern Inc 5712 Industrial Pk Rd PO Box 347 *TF:* 800-843-7648 ■ *Web:* www.thern.com	Winona	MN	55987	507-454-2996	454-5282
Tomra Pacific Inc 150 Klug Cir *Web:* www.tomra.com	Corona	CA	92880	951-520-1700	520-1701
Trambeam Corp 206 Lee St *Web:* www.trambeam.com	Attalla	AL	35954	256-538-9983	538-8818
TransTechnology Corp 700 Liberty Ave	Union	NJ	07083	908-903-1600	903-1616
Triple/S Dynamics Inc 1031 S Haskell Ave PO Box 151027 *TF:* 800-527-2116 ■ *Web:* www.sssdynamics.com	Dallas	TX	75315	214-828-8600	828-8688
United Central Industrial Supply Co LLC 1241 Volunteer Pkwy Suite 1000 *Web:* www.unitedcentral.net	Bristol	VA	37620	423-573-7300	573-7392
UpRight Inc 2686 S Maple Ave *TF Cust Svc:* 800-926-5438 ■ *Web:* www.upright.com	Fresno	CA	93725	559-443-6600	268-2433
Valley Craft 2001 S Hwy 61 *TF:* 800-328-1480 ■ *Web:* www.valleycraft.com	Lake City	MN	55041	651-345-3386	345-3606
Vertical Storage Systems LLC 12633 Memorial Suite 3 *Web:* www.verticalstoragesystems.com	Houston	TX	77024	713-569-6362	784-4036
Vibra Screw Inc 755 Union Blvd *Web:* www.vibrascrewinc.com	Totowa	NJ	07512	973-256-7410	256-7567
WA Charnstrom Co 5391 12th Ave E **Fax Area Code:* 800 ■ *TF Cust Svc:* 800-328-2962 ■ *Web:* www.charnstrom.com	Shakopee	MN	55379	952-403-0303	916-3215*
Waldon Mfg LLC 201 W Oklahoma Ave *TF:* 866-283-2165 ■ *Web:* www.waldonequipment.com	Fiarview	OK	73737	580-227-3711	
Wayne Engineering Corp 701 Performance Dr *Web:* www.wayneusa.com	Cedar Falls	IA	50613	319-266-1721	266-8207
Wesco Industrial Products Inc PO Box 47 **Fax Area Code:* 800 ■ *Web:* www.wescomfg.com	Lansdale	PA	19446	215-699-7031	346-5511*
Western Hoist Inc 1839 Cleveland Ave *TF:* 888-994-6478 ■ *Web:* www.westernhoist.com	National City	CA	91950	619-474-3361	474-8261
Whiting Corp 26000 Whiting Way **Fax Area Code:* 708 ■ *TF:* 800-861-5744 ■ *Web:* www.whitingcorp.com	Monee	IL	60449	800-861-5744	587-2001*
Wiggins Lift Co Inc 2571 Cortez St *TF:* 800-350-7821 ■ *Web:* www.wigginslift.com	Oxnard	CA	93031	805-485-7821	485-5230
WinûHolt Equipment Group 141 Eileen Way *TF:* 800-444-3595 ■ *Web:* www.winholt.com	Syosset	NY	11791	516-222-0335	921-0538
Yale Materials Handling Corp 1400 Sullivan Dr Caller 12011 *Web:* northamerica.yale.com	Greenville	NC	27834	252-931-5100	931-7873
Zenar Corp 7301 S 6th St PO Box 107 *Web:* www.zenarcrane.com	Oak Creek	WI	53154	414-764-1800	764-1267

474 MATTRESSES & ADJUSTABLE BEDS

SEE ALSO Household Furniture p. 1896

Company	City	State	Zip	Phone	Fax
Aero Products International Inc 1834 Walden Office Sq 3rd Fl *TF Cust Svc:* 888-462-4468 ■ *Web:* www.thinkaero.com	Schaumburg	IL	60173	847-485-3200	485-3290
Ark-Ell Springs Div Leggett & Platt Inc 101 Industrial Rd PO Box 308	Houlka	MS	38850	662-568-3393	568-3325
Bechik Products Inc 1140 Homer St *TF:* 800-328-6569 ■ *Web:* www.bechik.com	Saint Paul	MN	55116	651-698-0364	698-1009
Bowles Mattress Co Inc 1220 Watt St *TF:* 800-223-7509 ■ *Web:* www.bowlesmattress.com	Jeffersonville	IN	47130	812-288-8614	288-8650
Classic Sleep Products Inc 8214 Wellmoor Ct **Fax Area Code:* 301 ■ *TF:* 877-707-7533 ■ *Web:* www.classicmattress.com	Jessup	MD	20794	410-904-0006	498-6149*
Comfortex Inc 1680 Wilkie Dr PO Box 850 *TF:* 800-445-4007 ■ *Web:* www.comfortexinc.com	Winona	MN	55987	507-454-6579	454-6581
Continental Silverline Products Inc 710 N Drennan St *TF:* 800-392-9205 ■ *Web:* www.restonic.com	Houston	TX	77003	713-222-7394	222-1934
Corsicana Bedding Inc PO Box 1050 **Fax Area Code:* 800 ■ *TF:* 800-323-4349 ■ *Web:* www.corsicanabedding.com	Corsicana	TX	75151	903-872-2591	983-2663*
Cotton Belt Inc 401 E Sater St *TF:* 800-849-4192 ■ *Web:* www.edgecombe.com	Pinetops	NC	27864	252-827-4192	827-5683
Craftmatic Organization Inc 2500 Interplex Dr *TF Cust Svc:* 800-677-8200 ■ *Web:* www.craftmatic.com	Trevose	PA	19053	215-639-1310	639-9941
Diamond Mattress Co Inc 3112 Las Hermanas St E **Fax Area Code:* 310 ■ *Web:* www.diamondmattress.com	Compton	CA	90221	323-774-6840	638-2005*
Dreamline Mfg Inc 1514 S 2nd St PO Box 1250 *TF:* 800-888-3585 ■ *Web:* www.dreamlinebedding.com	Cabot	AR	72023	501-843-3585	843-2990
Fraenkel Co Inc PO Box 15385 *TF:* 800-847-2580 ■ *Web:* www.fraenkel.com	Baton Rouge	LA	70895	225-275-4242	272-7319
Home-Style Industries Inc 1323 11th Ave N PO Box 1500 *Web:* www.home-style.com	Nampa	ID	83653	208-466-8481	467-9942
Imperial Bedding Co 720 11th St PO Box 5347 *TF:* 800-529-3321 ■ *Web:* www.imperialbedding.com	Huntington	WV	25703	304-529-3321	525-5317
International Bedding Corp 1000ßNW 65 St Suite 103 *TF:* 800-776-1166 ■ *Web:* www.ibcgroup.com	Fort Lauderdale	FL	33309	954-491-1002	974-7070
Jackson Mattress Co Inc 3154 Camden Rd PO Box 64609 *TF:* 800-763-7378	Fayetteville	NC	28306	910-425-0131	425-1602
Jamison Bedding Inc 238 Bedford Way *TF:* 800-255-1883 ■ *Web:* www.jamisonbedding.com	Franklin	TN	37064	615-794-1883	794-2254
King Koil Licensing Co Inc 7501 quincy *TF:* 800-525-8331 ■ *Web:* www.kingkoil.com	Willowbrook	IL	60527	630-230-9744	655-3928
Kingsdown Inc 126 W Holt St PO Box 388 **Fax:* Cust Svc ■ *TF Cust Svc:* 800-354-5464 ■ *Web:* www.kingsdown.com	Mebane	NC	27302	919-563-3531	563-6730*
Kolcraft Enterprises Inc 10832 NC Hwy 211 E *TF Cust Svc:* 800-453-7673 ■ *Web:* www.kolcraft.com	Aberdeen	NC	28315	910-944-9345	
Leggett & Platt Inc Number 1 Leggett Rd PO Box 757 *NYSE: LEG* ■ *TF:* 800-888-4569 ■ *Web:* www.leggett.com	Carthage	MO	64836	417-358-8131	358-6996
Lemoyne Sleeper Co Inc 57 S 3rd St PO Box 227 *TF:* 800-382-1217 ■ *Web:* www.lemoynesleeper.com	Lemoyne	PA	17043	717-763-1630	763-1634
Meridian Mattress Factory Inc 200 Rubush Rd PO Box 5127 *TF:* 800-844-3875	Meridian	MS	39302	601-693-3875	693-5462
National Bedding Co 61 Leona Dr *TF:* 800-343-1006 ■ *Web:* www.sertanational.com	Middleboro	MA	02346	508-946-4700	946-5217
Northwest Bedding Co 6102 S Hayford Rd *TF:* 800-456-7686	Spokane	WA	99224	509-244-3000	244-9905
Omaha Bedding Co 4011 S 60th St PO Box 27396 *TF:* 800-279-9018	Omaha	NE	68127	402-733-8600	733-0586
Paramount Industrial Cos Inc 1112 Kingwood Ave *TF:* 800-777-5337 ■ *Web:* www.paramountsleep.com	Norfolk	VA	23502	757-855-3321	855-2029
Restonic Mattress Corp 1540 E Dundee Rd Suite 102 *TF:* 800-898-6075 ■ *Web:* www.restonic.com	Palatine	IL	60074	847-241-1130	241-1136
Riverside Mattress Co Inc 225 Dunn Rd *TF:* 888-288-5195	Fayetteville	NC	28312	910-483-0461	484-2334
Sanitary Mattress Co Inc 5808 Berry Brook Dr *TF:* 800-603-3375	Houston	TX	77017	713-227-0121	227-8159
Sealy Corp 1 Office Pkwy at Sealy Dr *NYSE: ZZ* ■ *TF Cust Svc:* 800-697-3259 ■ *Web:* www.sealy.com	Trinity	NC	27370	336-861-3500	861-3501
Serta International Inc 5401 Trillium Blvd *TF:* 888-557-3782 ■ *Web:* www.serta.com	Hoffman Estates	IL	60192	847-645-0200	645-0205
Serta Mattress/AW Inc 8415 Ardmore Rd *TF:* 800-638-0520 ■ *Web:* www.serta.com	Landover	MD	20785	301-322-1000	341-4639
Simmons Co 1 Concourse Pkwy Suite 800 *Web:* www.simmons.com	Atlanta	GA	30328	770-512-7700	392-2560
Sleep Train Inc 4350 Warehouse Ct Suite 100 **Fax Area Code:* 866 ■ *TF:* 800-919-2337 ■ *Web:* www.sleeptrain.com	North Highlands	CA	95660	916-735-1300	293-5719*
Southerland Inc 1973 Southerland Dr *TF:* 888-226-9009 ■ *Web:* www.southerlandsleep.com	Nashville	TN	37207	615-226-9650	650-2653
Spring Air Co 1111 Nicholas Blvd	Elk Grove Village	IL	60007	847-439-4399	439-4322
Standard Mattress Co Inc 261 Weston St *TF:* 800-873-8498 ■ *Web:* www.goldbondmattress.com	Hartford	CT	06120	860-549-2000	527-3101
Stearns & Foster 1 Office Pkwy at Sealy Dr *TF:* 800-867-3259 ■ *Web:* www.sealy.com	Trinity	NC	27370	336-861-3500	861-3506
Symbol Mattress Co 4901 Fitzhugh Ave *TF Cust Svc:* 800-446-2791 ■ *Web:* www.symbolmattress.com	Richmond	VA	23230	804-353-8965	353-8762
Tempur-Pedic International Inc 1713 Jaggie Fox Way *NYSE: TPX* ■ *Web:* www.tempurpedic.com	Lexington	KY	40511	859-259-0754	259-9843
Therapedic Inc 103 College Rd E *TF:* 800-322-1054 ■ *Web:* www.therapedic.com	Princeton	NJ	08540	609-720-0700	720-0797
White Dove Ltd 3201 Harvard Ave *TF:* 800-218-3951 ■ *Web:* www.whitedoveusa.com	Cleveland	OH	44105	216-341-0200	341-3399
Winston-Salem Industries for the Blind 7730 N Pt Dr *Web:* www.wsifb.com	Winston-Salem	NC	27106	336-759-0551	759-0990
World Sleep Products Inc 12 Esquire Rd *TF:* 800-370-8700	North Billerica	MA	01862	978-667-6648	667-6683

475 MEASURING, TESTING, CONTROLLING INSTRUMENTS

SEE ALSO Electrical Signals Measuring & Testing Instruments p. 1808

Company	City	State	Zip	Phone	Fax
AAI Corp 404 Industrial Rd Suite 1 *Web:* www.aaicorp.com	Choctaw	MS	39350	601-389-5300	389-5336
ABB Inc 501 Merritt 7 *TF Prod Info:* 800-626-4999 ■ *Web:* www.abb.us	Norwalk	CT	06851	203-750-2200	435-7365
Adcole Corp 669 Forest St *TF:* 800-858-5802 ■ *Web:* www.adcole.com	Marlborough	MA	01752	508-485-9100	481-6142
Advanced Protection Technologies Inc 14550 58th St N *TF:* 800-237-4567 ■ *Web:* www.apttvss.com	Clearwater	FL	33760	727-535-6339	539-8955
AGR International Inc 615 Whitestown Rd *Web:* www.agrintl.com	Butler	PA	16001	724-482-2163	482-2767
Air Gage Co 12170 Globe Rd *Web:* www.airgage.com	Livonia	MI	48150	734-853-9220	853-2454
All Weather Inc 1165 National Dr *TF:* 800-824-5873 ■ *Web:* www.allweatherinc.com	Sacramento	CA	95834	916-928-1000	928-1165
AMETEK Aerospace 50 Fordham Rd **Fax:* Cust Svc ■ *Web:* www.ametek.com/aerospace	Wilmington	MA	01887	978-988-4101	988-4944*
AMETEK Inc Test & Calibration Instruments Div 8600 Somerset Dr *TF:* 800-527-9999 ■ *Web:* www.ametekcalibration.com	Largo	FL	33773	727-536-7831	539-6882
AMETEK US Gauge 820 Pennsylvania Blvd *TF:* 888-625-5895 ■ *Web:* www.ametekusg.com	Feasterville	PA	19053	215-355-6900	354-1802
AMETEK US Gauge PMT Products Div 820 Pennsylvania Blvd *TF:* 888-625-5895 ■ *Web:* www.ametekusg.com	Feasterville	PA	19053	215-355-6900	354-1800
Beta LaserMike Inc 8001 Technology Blvd *TF:* 800-886-9935 ■ *Web:* www.betalasermike.com	Dayton	OH	45424	937-233-9935	233-7284
Bruel & Kjaer Instruments Inc 2815 Colonnades Ct # A *TF:* 800-241-9188 ■ *Web:* www.bkhome.com	Norcross	GA	30071	770-209-6907	448-3246
Cambridge Technology Inc 25 Hartwell Ave *Web:* www.camtech.com	Lexington	MA	02421	781-541-1600	541-1601
Canberra Industries Inc 800 Research Pkwy *TF Sales:* 800-243-3955 ■ *Web:* www.canberra.com	Meriden	CT	06450	203-238-2351	235-1347

Company	State	ZIP	Phone	Fax
Century Equipment Inc 5959 Angola Rd PO Box 352889 . . . Toledo *Web:* www.centuryequip.com	OH	43615	419-865-7400	865-8215
Clayton Industries 17477 Hurley St . . . City of Industry *TF:* 800-423-4585 ■ *Web:* www.claytonindustries.com	CA	91744	626-435-1200	435-0180
Control Screening LLC 2 Gardner Rd . . . Fairfield *TF:* 800-231-6414 ■ *Web:* www.controlscreening.com	NJ	07004	973-276-6161	276-6162
Copley Controls Corp 20 Dan Rd . . . Canton *Web:* www.copleycontrols.com	MA	02021	781-828-8090	828-6547
Crane Nuclear Inc 2825 Cobb International Blvd . . . Kennesaw *TF:* 800-795-8013 ■ *Web:* www.cranenuclear.com	GA	30152	770-424-6343	429-4750
Cubic Transportation Systems Inc 5650 Kearny Mesa Rd . . . San Diego *Web:* www.cubic.com	CA	92111	858-268-3100	292-9987
Danaher Corp 2200 Pennsylvania Ave NW Suite 800 . . . Washington *NYSE: DHR* ■ *TF:* 866-873-5600 ■ *Web:* www.danaher.com	DC	20037	202-828-0850	828-0860
Davis Instrument Corp 3465 Diablo Ave . . . Hayward *TF:* 800-678-3669 ■ *Web:* www.davisnet.com	CA	94545	510-732-9229	670-0589
Delta Cooling Towers Inc PO Box 315 . . . Rockaway *Web:* www.deltacooling.com	NJ	07866	973-586-2201	586-2243
Dresser Inc 15455 Dallas Pkwy Suite 1100 . . . Addison *Web:* www.dresser.com	TX	75001	972-361-9800	361-9903
Dynisco LLC 38 Forge Pkwy . . . Franklin *TF:* 800-332-2215 ■ *Web:* www.dynisco.com	MA	02038	508-541-9400	541-6206
Emerson Process Management CSI 835 Innovation Dr . . . Knoxville *TF:* 800-675-4726 ■ *Web:* www.compsys.com	TN	37932	865-675-2110	218-1401
Endevco Corp 30700 Rancho Viejo Rd . . . San Juan Capistrano *TF:* 800-982-6732 ■ *Web:* www.endevco.com	CA	92675	949-493-8181	661-7231
Enidine Inc 7 Centre Dr . . . Orchard Park *TF:* 800-852-8508 ■ *Web:* www.enidine.com	NY	14127	716-662-1900	662-1909
Fairfield Industries Inc 1111 Gillingham Ln . . . Sugar Land *TF:* 800-231-9809 ■ *Web:* www.fairfieldnodal.com	TX	77478	281-275-7500	275-7500
FARO Technologies Inc 125 Technology Pk Dr . . . Lake Mary *NASDAQ: FARO* ■ *TF:* 800-736-0234 ■ *Web:* www.faro.com	FL	32746	407-333-9911	333-4181
Fiber Instruments Sales Inc 161 Clear Rd . . . Oriskany *TF Sales:* 800-500-0347 ■ *Web:* www.fiberinstrumentsales.com	NY	13424	315-736-2206	736-2285
Fisher Research Laboratory Inc 1465H Henry Brennan Suite H . . . El Paso *Web:* www.fisherlab.com	TX	79936	915-225-0333	225-0336
Flowline Inc 10500 Humbolt St . . . Los Alamitos *Web:* www.flowline.com	CA	90720	562-598-3015	431-8507
Garrett Metal Detectors 1881 W State St . . . Garland *TF:* 800-234-6151 ■ *Web:* www.garrett.com	TX	75042	972-494-6151	494-1881
GE Infrastructure Security 205 Lowell St . . . Wilmington **Fax Area Code: 866* ■ *TF:* 800-433-5346 ■ *Web:* www.gesecurity.com	MA	01887	978-658-3767	249-9105*
General Monitors Inc 26776 Simpatica Cir . . . Lake Forest *TF:* 866-686-0741 ■ *Web:* www.generalmonitors.com	CA	92630	949-581-4464	581-1151
Geokon Inc 48 Spencer St . . . Lebanon *Web:* www.geokon.com	NH	03766	603-448-1562	448-3216
Geometrics Inc 2190 Fortune Dr . . . San Jose *Web:* www.geometrics.com	CA	95131	408-954-0522	954-0902
George Risk Industries Inc 802 S Elm St . . . Kimball *TF Sales:* 800-523-1227 ■ *Web:* www.grisk.com	NE	69145	308-235-4645	235-2609
GFI Genfare 751 Pratt Blvd . . . Elk Grove Village *Web:* www.gfigenfare.com	IL	60007	847-593-8855	593-1824
Gleason M & M Precision Systems Corp 300 Progress Rd . . . Dayton *Web:* www.gleason.com	OH	45449	937-859-8273	859-4452
Goodrich Corp 2730 W Tyvola Rd 4 Coliseum Ctr . . . Charlotte *NYSE: GR* ■ *TF:* 800-784-7009 ■ *Web:* www.goodrich.com	NC	28217	704-423-7000	423-7002
Goodrich Corp Fuel & Utility Systems Div 100 Patton Rd . . . Vergennes *Web:* www.goodrich.com	VT	05491	802-877-4000	877-4111
Hamilton Sundstrand Sensor Systems 2771 N Garey Ave . . . Pomona *Web:* www.hssensorsystems.com	CA	91767	909-593-3581	392-3205
Herman H Sticht Co Inc 45 Main St Suite 701 . . . Brooklyn *TF:* 800-221-3203 ■ *Web:* www.stichtco.com	NY	11201	718-852-7602	852-7915
Hexagon Metrology Inc 660 S Military Rd PO Box 1658 . . . Fond du Lac *TF Cust Svc:* 800-535-1236 ■ *Web:* www.sheffieldmeasurement.com	WI	54936	920-906-7700	906-7701
Howell Instruments Inc 8945 S Fwy . . . Fort Worth *Web:* www.howellinst.com	TX	76140	817-336-7411	336-7874
Industrial Dynamics Co Ltd 3100 Fujita St . . . Torrance *TF:* 888-434-5832 ■ *Web:* www.filtec.com	CA	90505	310-325-5633	530-1000
Instron Corp 825 University Ave . . . Norwood *Web:* www.instron.com	MA	02062	781-828-2500	575-5750
Instron Corp Wilson Instruments Div 825 University Ave . . . Norwood *TF:* 800-695-4273 ■ *Web:* www.instron.us	MA	02062	781-575-6000	575-5770
Interface Inc 7401 E Butherus Dr . . . Scottsdale *TF:* 800-947-5598 ■ *Web:* www.interfaceforce.com	AZ	85260	480-948-5555	948-1924
Isra Surface Vision Inc 4470 Peachtree Lakes Dr . . . Duluth *Web:* www.lasorsystronics.com	GA	30096	770-449-7776	449-0399
Kahn & Co Inc 885 Wells Rd . . . Wethersfield *Web:* www.kahn.com	CT	06109	860-529-8643	529-1895
Kavlico Corp 14401 Princeton Ave . . . Moorpark *Web:* www.kavlico.com	CA	93021	805-523-2000	523-7125
Kinemetrics Inc 222 Vista Ave . . . Pasadena *Web:* www.kinemetrics.com	CA	91107	626-795-2220	795-0868
Kistler Instrument Corp 75 John Glenn Dr . . . Amherst *TF:* 888-547-8537 ■ *Web:* www.kistler.com	NY	14228	716-691-5100	691-5226
Konica Minolta Sensing Americas Inc 101 Williams Dr . . . Ramsey **Fax: Sales* ■ *TF:* 888-473-2656 ■ *Web:* www.konicaminolta.com	NJ	07446	201-825-4000	785-2480*
Ktech Corp 1300 Eubank Blvd SE . . . Albuquerque *TF:* 877-998-5830 ■ *Web:* www.ktech.com	NM	87123	505-998-5830	998-5848

Company	State	ZIP	Phone	Fax
L-3 Avionics Systems 5353 52nd St SE . . . Grand Rapids **Fax: Hum Res* ■ *TF:* 800-253-9525 ■ *Web:* www.as.l-3com.com	MI	49512	616-949-6600	285-4457*
Leica Geosystems Inc 3498 Kraft Ave SE . . . Grand Rapids *TF Sales:* 800-367-9453 ■ *Web:* www.leica-geosystems.com	MI	49512	616-977-4189	942-4627
Link Engineering Co Inc 43855 Plymouth Oaks Blvd . . . Plymouth *Web:* www.linkeng.com	MI	48170	734-453-0800	453-0802
Lockheed Martin Sippican 7 Barnabas Rd . . . Marion *Web:* www.sippican.com	MA	02738	508-748-1160	748-3626
Logis Tech Inc 9450 Innovation Dr Suite 1 . . . Manassas *Web:* www.logis-tech.com	VA	20110	703-393-0122	
Ludlum Measurements Inc 501 Oak St . . . Sweetwater *TF:* 800-622-0828 ■ *Web:* www.ludlums.com	TX	79556	325-235-5494	235-4672
Magnetic Analysis Corp 535 S 4th Ave . . . Mount Vernon *TF:* 800-463-8622 ■ *Web:* www.mac-ndt.com	NY	10550	914-699-9450	699-9837
Marposs Corp 3300 Cross Creek Pkwy . . . Auburn Hills *TF:* 800-627-7677 ■ *Web:* www.marposs.com	MI	48326	248-370-0404	370-0991
Mason Industries Inc 350 Rabro Dr . . . Hauppauge *Web:* www.mason-ind.com	NY	11788	631-348-0282	348-0279
Measurement Innovations Corp 34 Dutch Mill Rd . . . Ithaca *TF:* 800-353-3569 ■ *Web:* www.transonic.com	NY	14850	607-257-5300	257-7256
Metrix Instrument Co 8824 Fallbrook Dr . . . Houston *TF:* 800-638-7494 ■ *Web:* www.metrixvibration.com	TX	77064	713-461-2131	559-9417
Metrosonics 1060 Corporate Ctr Dr . . . Oconomowoc *TF:* 800-245-0779 ■ *Web:* www.metrosonics.com	WI	53066	262-567-9157	567-4047
Metrotech Corp 3251 Olcott St . . . Santa Clara *TF:* 800-446-3392 ■ *Web:* www.metrotech.com	CA	95054	408-734-1400	734-1415
Morcom International Inc 3656 Centerview Dr Unit 1 . . . Chantilly *Web:* www.morcom.com	VA	20151	703-263-9305	263-9308
MTS Systems Corp 14000 Technology Dr . . . Eden Prairie *NASDAQ: MTSC* ■ *TF Cust Svc:* 800-328-2255 ■ *Web:* www.mts.com	MN	55344	952-937-4000	937-4515
Mustang Dynamometer 2300 Pinnacle Pkwy . . . Twinsburg *TF:* 888-468-7826 ■ *Web:* www.mustangdyne.com	OH	44087	330-963-5400	425-3310
Nanometrics Inc 1550 Buckeye Dr . . . Milpitas *NASDAQ: NANO* ■ *TF:* 800-955-6266 ■ *Web:* www.nanometrics.com	CA	95035	408-435-9600	232-5910
Nextest Systems Corp 875 Embedded Way . . . San Jose *Web:* www.nextest.com	CA	95138	408-960-2400	960-7660
Novatron Corp 6000 Rinke Ave . . . Warren *Web:* www.novatroncorp.com	MI	48091	586-755-1300	755-9085
Ohmart/VEGA Corp 4241 Allendorf Dr . . . Cincinnati *TF:* 800-543-8668 ■ *Web:* www.ohmartvega.com	OH	45209	513-272-0131	272-0133
Olympus NDT NW 421 N Quay St . . . Kennewick **Fax: Sales* ■ *Web:* www.olympusndt.com	WA	99336	509-736-2751	735-4672*
On-Site Analysis Inc 7108 Fairway Dr Suite 130 . . . Palm Beach Gardens *TF:* 800-285-7708 ■ *Web:* www.on-siteanalysis.com	FL	33418	561-775-5756	691-5220
Oxford Instruments Measurement Systems 300 Bake Ave Suite 150 . . . Concord **Fax Area Code: 978* ■ *TF:* 800-447-4717 ■ *Web:* www.oxford-instruments.com	MA	01742	800-447-4717	369-8287*
OYO Geospace Corp 7007 Pinemont Dr . . . Houston *NASDAQ: OYOG* ■ *Web:* www.oyogeospace.com	TX	77040	713-986-4444	986-4445
Perceptron Inc 47827 Halyard Dr . . . Plymouth *NASDAQ: PRCP* ■ *TF:* 800-333-7753 ■ *Web:* www.perceptron.com	MI	48170	734-414-6100	414-4700
Preco Electronics Inc 415 N Maple Grove Rd . . . Boise *TF:* 866-977-7326 ■ *Web:* www.preco.com	ID	83704	208-323-1000	323-1034
Princeton Gamma-Tech Instruments Inc 303-C College Rd E . . . Princeton *TF:* 800-229-7484 ■ *Web:* www.pgt.com	NJ	08540	609-924-7310	924-1729
Promess Inc PO Box 748 . . . Brighton *Web:* www.promessinc.com	MI	48116	810-229-9334	229-8125
Radiation Monitoring Devices Inc (RMDINC) 44 Hunt St Suite 2 . . . Watertown *TF:* 800-532-3763 ■ *Web:* www.rmdinc.com	MA	02472	617-668-6800	926-9980
Rochester Gauges Inc of Texas 11616 Harry Hines Blvd . . . Dallas *TF:* 800-821-1829 ■ *Web:* www.rochestergauges.com	TX	75229	972-241-2161	620-1403
Rudolph Technologies Inc One Rudolph Rd PO Box 1000 . . . Flanders *NASDAQ: RTEC* ■ *TF:* 877-467-8365 ■ *Web:* www.rudolphtech.com	NJ	07836	973-691-1300	691-4863
Schenck Pegasus Corp 2890 John R Rd . . . Troy *TF:* 800-899-5119 ■ *Web:* www.schenckpegasuscorp.com	MI	48083	248-689-9000	689-8578
Schmitt Industries Inc 2765 NW Nicolai St . . . Portland *NASDAQ: SMIT* ■ *Web:* www.schmitt-ind.com	OR	97210	503-227-7908	223-1258
Schneeberger Inc 11 Deangelo Dr . . . Bedford *Web:* www.schneeberger.com	MA	01730	781-271-0140	275-4749
Sensor Systems LLC 2800 Anvil St N . . . Saint Petersburg *TF:* 800-688-2181 ■ *Web:* www.vsensors.com	FL	33710	727-347-2181	347-7520
Sercel Inc 17200 Pk Row . . . Houston *Web:* www.sercel.com	TX	77084	281-492-6688	579-6555
Setra Systems Inc 159 Swanson Rd . . . Boxborough *TF:* 800-257-3872 ■ *Web:* www.setra.com	MA	01719	978-263-1400	264-0292
Sierra Monitor Corp 1991 Tarob Ct . . . Milpitas *OTC: SRMC* ■ *Web:* www.sierramonitor.com	CA	95035	408-262-6611	262-9042
Smiths Detection 2202 Lakeside Blvd . . . Edgewood *Web:* www.smithsdetection.com	MD	21040	410-510-9100	510-9490
Sorrento Electronics Inc 4949 Greencraig Ln . . . San Diego *TF:* 800-252-1180 ■ *Web:* www.ga-esi.com	CA	92123	858-522-8300	522-8300
SuperFlow Technologies Group 4747 Centennial Blvd . . . Colorado Springs *TF:* 800-471-7701 ■ *Web:* www.superflow.com	CO	80919	719-471-1746	471-1490
Taber Industries 455 Bryant St . . . North Tonawanda *Web:* www.taberindustries.com	NY	14120	716-694-4000	694-1450
Taylor Hobson Inc 1725 Western Dr . . . West Chicago *TF:* 800-872-7265 ■ *Web:* www.taylor-hobson.com	IL	60185	630-621-3099	231-1739
Tel-Instrument Electronics Corp 728 Garden St . . . Carlstadt *AMEX: TIK* ■ *Web:* www.telinstrument.com	NJ	07072	201-933-1600	933-7340
Testing Machines Inc 2 Fleetwood Ct . . . Ronkonkoma *TF:* 800-678-3221 ■ *Web:* www.testingmachines.com	NY	11749	631-439-5400	439-5420
Thermo Fisher Scientific 81 Wyman St PO Box 9046 . . . Waltham *NYSE: TMO* ■ *TF:* 800-678-5599 ■ *Web:* www.thermofisher.com	MA	02454	781-622-1000	622-1207
Thermo Fisher Scientific Inc 10010 Mesa Rim Rd . . . San Diego *TF:* 800-488-4399 ■ *Web:* www.thermofisher.com	CA	92121	858-450-9811	546-1734
Tinius Olsen Testing Machine Co Inc 1065 Easton Rd PO Box 1009 . . . Horsham *Web:* www.tiniusolsen.com	PA	19044	215-675-7100	441-0899
Topcon Positioning Systems Inc 7400 National Dr . . . Livermore *Web:* www.topconpositioning.com	CA	94551	925-245-8300	245-8599

	City	State	ZIP	Phone	Fax
Ues Inc 4401 Dayton Xenia Rd	Dayton	OH	45432	937-426-6900	429-5433
Web: www.ues.com					
Unilux Inc 59 N 5th St	Saddle Brook	NJ	07663	201-712-1266	712-1366
TF: 800-522-0801 ■ *Web:* www.unilux.com					
Uster Technologies Inc 456 Troy Cir PO Box 51270	Knoxville	TN	37919	865-588-9716	588-0914
Web: www.uster.com					
Vaisala Inc 10-D Gill St	Woburn	MA	01801	781-933-4500	933-8029
TF: 888-824-7252 ■ *Web:* www.vaisala.com					
Vaisala-GAI 2705 E Medina Rd	Tucson	AZ	85706	520-741-2838	741-2848
TF: 800-294-3520 ■ *Web:* www.thunderstorm.vaisala.com					
Verity Instruments Inc 2901 Eisenhower St	Carrollton	TX	75007	972-446-9990	446-9586
Web: www.verityinst.com					
Vishay Americas 1 Greenwich Pl	Shelton	CT	06484	402-563-6866	563-6296
Web: www.vishay.com					
White's Electronics Inc 1011 Pleasant Valley Rd	Sweet Home	OR	97386	541-367-6121	367-6629
TF Sales: 800-547-6911 ■ *Web:* www.whitesdetectors.com					
Yamas Environmental Sytems Inc 5030 Hillsdale Cir Suite 102	El Dorado Hills	CA	95762	916-933-7750	933-7751
Web: www.yamasenvsystems.com					

476 MEAT PACKING PLANTS

SEE ALSO Poultry Processing p. 2441

	City	State	ZIP	Phone	Fax
Abbott's Meat Inc 3623 Blackington Ave	Flint	MI	48532	810-232-7128	232-7960
Abbyland Foods Inc 502 E Linden St PO Box 69	Abbotsford	WI	54405	715-223-6386	223-6388
TF: 800-732-5483 ■ *Web:* www.abbyland.com					
Academy Packing Co Inc 2881 Wyoming St	Dearborn	MI	48120	313-841-4900	841-9760
Allen Bros Inc 3737 S Halsted St	Chicago	IL	60609	773-890-5100	890-9377
TF: 800-548-7777 ■ *Web:* www.allenbrothers.com					
Alpine Packing Co 9900 Lower Sacramento Rd	Stockton	CA	95210	209-477-2691	477-1994
TF: 800-399-6328 ■ *Web:* www.alpinemeats.com					
American Foods Group Inc 544 Acme St	Green Bay	WI	54302	920-437-6330	436-6510
TF: 800-345-0293 ■ *Web:* www.americanfoodsgroup.com					
Atlantic Veal & Lamb Inc 275 Morgan Ave	Brooklyn	NY	11211	718-599-6400	599-6404
Bicara Ltd 4215 Exchange Ave	Los Angeles	CA	90058	323-582-7401	582-1813
Birchwood Foods 6009 Goshen Springs Rd	Norcross	GA	30071	770-448-9101	447-0459
Web: www.bwfoods.com					
Brown Packing Co Inc 1 Dutch Valley Dr	South Holland	IL	60473	708-849-7990	849-8094
TF: 800-832-8325					
Burnett & Son Meat Co Inc 1420 S Myrtle Ave	Monrovia	CA	91016	626-357-2165	357-7115
Web: www.burnettandson.com					
Cargill Meat Solutions 151 N Main PO Box 2519	Wichita	KS	67201	316-291-2500	291-2547*
Carolina Packers Inc 2999 Brightless Blvd PO Box 1109	Smithfield	NC	27577	919-934-2181	989-6794
TF: 800-682-7675 ■ *Web:* www.carolinapackers.com					
Central Beef Industry LLC 571 W Kings Hwy PO Box 399	Center Hill	FL	33514	352-793-3671	793-2227
Central Nebraska Packing Inc 2800 E 8th St	North Platte	NE	69103	308-532-1250	532-2744
TF Cust Svc: 800-445-2881 ■ *Web:* www.nebraskabrand.com					
Charles G Buchy Packing Co 1050 Progress St	Greenville	OH	45331	937-548-2128	548-6880
TF: 800-762-1060 ■ *Web:* www.buchyfoods.com					
Cherry Meat Packers Inc 4750 S California Ave	Chicago	IL	60632	773-927-1200	927-1520
Chiappetti Wholesale Meat Inc 3900 S Emerald Ave	Chicago	IL	60609	773-847-1556	847-3837
Chip Steak & Provision Co 232 Dewey St	Mankato	MN	56001	507-388-6277	388-6279
TF: 888-244-7783					
Chisesi Bros Meat Packing Co 5221 Jefferson Hwy	Harahan	LA	70123	504-822-3550	822-3916
TF: 800-966-3550					
Cimpl Meats Inc 1000 Cattle Dr PO Box 80	Yankton	SD	57078	605-665-1665	665-8908
Clougherty Packing Co 3049 E Vernon Ave	Los Angeles	CA	90058	323-583-4621	584-1699
TF Sales: 800-432-7637 ■ *Web:* www.farmerjohn.com					
Comer Packing 1000 Poplar St PO Box 33	Aberdeen	MS	39730	662-369-9325	369-9375
TF: 800-748-8916					
ConAgra Foods Retail Products Co Deli Foods Group 215 W Field Rd	Naperville	IL	60563	630-857-1000	512-1124
TF: 800-325-7424					
Cougle Commission Co 345 N Aberdeen St	Chicago	IL	60607	312-666-7861	666-6434
Web: www.couglecommission.com					
Cudahy Patrick Inc 1 Sweet Apple-Wood Ln	Cudahy	WI	53110	414-744-2000	744-2000
TF: 800-486-6900 ■ *Web:* www.patrickcudahy.com					
Curtis Packing Co 2416 Randolph Ave	Greensboro	NC	27406	336-275-7684	275-1901
TF: 800-852-7890 ■ *Web:* www.curtispackingcompany.com					
Dallas City Packing Inc 3049 Morrell St	Dallas	TX	75203	214-948-3901	942-2039
TF: 800-876-6328					
Demakes Enterprises Inc 37 Waterhill St	Lynn	MA	01905	781-595-1557	595-7523
TF: 800-628-3529					
DL Lee & Sons Inc 927 Hwy 32 E	Alma	GA	31510	912-632-4406	632-8298
TF Cust Svc: 800-673-9339					
EA Miller Inc 410 N 200 W	Hyrum	UT	84319	435-245-6456	245-6634
TF: 800-873-0939 ■ *Web:* www.eamiller.com					
Eddy Packing Co Inc 404 Airport Dr	Yoakum	TX	77995	361-293-2361	293-2254
TF: 800-292-2361 ■ *Web:* www.eddypacking.com					
EE Mucke & Sons Inc 2326 Main St	Hartford	CT	06120	860-246-5609	
Esskay Inc 8422 Bellona Ln Suite 200	Baltimore	MD	21204	410-823-2100	823-2100
TF: 800-638-7350 ■ *Web:* www.esskaymeat.com					
Fair Oaks Farms Inc 7600 95th St	Pleasant Prairie	WI	53158	262-947-0320	947-0340
TF: 800-528-8615 ■ *Web:* www.fairoaksfarms.com					
Farm Boy Meats PO Box 996	Evansville	IN	47706	812-425-5231	425-5231
TF: 800-852-3976 ■ *Web:* www.farmboyfoodservice.com					
Fort Pitt Brand Meat Co PO Box F	Evans City	PA	16033	724-538-3160	538-3262
Web: www.isalys.com					
Freirich Foods Inc 815 W Kerr St PO Box 1529	Salisbury	NC	28145	704-636-2621	636-4650
TF: 800-554-4788 ■ *Web:* www.freirich.com					
Fresh Mark Inc 1888 Southway St SE	Massillon	OH	44646	330-832-7491	830-3174
TF: 800-860-6777 ■ *Web:* www.freshmark.com					
Golden State Foods 18301 Von Karman Ave Suite 1100	Irvine	CA	92612	949-252-2000	252-2080
Web: www.goldenstatefoods.com					
Greater Omaha Packing Co Inc 3001 L St PO Box 7566	Omaha	NE	68107	402-731-3480	731-7542
TF: 800-747-5400 ■ *Web:* www.greateromaha.com					
Gwaltney of Smithfield Ltd 601 N Church St	Smithfield	VA	23430	757-357-3131	
TF: 800-888-7521 ■ *Web:* www.gwaltneyfoods.com					
Hansel 'n Gretel Brand Inc 79-36 Cooper Ave	Glendale	NY	11385	718-326-0041	326-2069
TF: 800-635-3354					
Harris Ranch Beef Co 16277 S McCall Ave PO Box 220	Selma	CA	93662	559-896-3081	896-3095
TF: 800-742-1955 ■ *Web:* www.harrisranchbeef.com					
Hatfield Quality Meats Inc 2700 Clemens Rd	Hatfield	PA	19440	215-368-2500	
TF: 800-523-5291 ■ *Web:* www.hatfieldqualitymeats.com					
Herman Falter Packing Co Inc 384 Greenlawn Ave	Columbus	OH	43223	614-444-1141	445-3915
TF: 800-325-6328					
Hill Meat Co PO Box 1066	Pendleton	OR	97801	541-276-7621	276-9253
Web: www.hillmeat.com					
JF O'Neill Packing Co Inc 3120 G St	Omaha	NE	68107	402-733-1200	733-1724
JH Routh Packing Co Inc 4413 W Bogart Rd	Sandusky	OH	44870	419-626-2251	625-4782
TF: 800-446-6759					
John Morrell & Co 805 E Kemper Rd	Cincinnati	OH	45246	513-346-3540	346-7552*
**Fax:* Cust Svc ■ *TF:* 800-445-2013 ■ *Web:* www.johnmorrell.com					
King Meat Co Inc 4215 Exchange Ave	Los Angeles	CA	90058	323-582-7401	582-1813
L & H Packing Co PO Box 831368	San Antonio	TX	78283	210-532-3241	532-9819
TF: 800-999-3241 ■ *Web:* www.lhpacking.com					
L Frankel Packing Co Inc 230 N Peoria St	Chicago	IL	60607	312-421-3200	421-6049
Land O'Frost Inc 16850 Chicago Ave	Lansing	IL	60438	708-474-7100	474-9329
TF: 800-323-3308 ■ *Web:* www.landofrost.com					
Long Prairie Packing Co 10 Riverside Dr	Long Prairie	MN	56347	320-732-2171	732-2914
Morrilton Packing Co Inc 51 Blue Diamond Dr	Morrilton	AR	72110	501-354-2474	354-2283
TF: 800-264-2475					
National Beef Packing Co LLC 12200 Ambassador Dr	Kansas City	MO	64163	816-713-8500	
TF: 800-449-2333 ■ *Web:* www.nationalbeef.com					
New City Packing & Provision 2600 Church Rd	Aurora	IL	60504	630-851-8800	898-3030
TF: 800-621-0397 ■ *Web:* www.newcitypacking.com					
Ohio Packing Co 1306 Harmon Ave	Columbus	OH	43223	614-239-1600	237-0885
TF: 800-282-6403 ■ *Web:* www.ohiopacking.com					
Olymel LP 2200 Pratte Ave Pratte	Saint-Hyacinthe	QC	J2S4B6	450-771-0400	771-0519
Web: www.olymel.com					
OSI Industries LLC 1225 Corporate Blvd	Aurora	IL	60504	630-851-6600	851-8223
Web: www.osigroup.com					
Pearl Meat Packing Co Inc 227 York Ave	Randolph	MA	02368	781-228-5100	228-5123
TF: 800-462-3022 ■ *Web:* www.pearlmeat.com					
Plumrose USA Inc 7 Lexington Ave	East Brunswick	NJ	08816	732-257-6600	257-6644
TF: 800-526-4909 ■ *Web:* www.plumroseusa.com					
Premium Standard Farms Inc Hwy 65 N PO Box 194	Princeton	MO	64673	660-748-4647	748-7341
Web: www.psfarms.com					
Quality Meats & Seafoods 700 Ctr St	West Fargo	ND	58078	701-282-0202	282-0583
TF: 800-959-4250 ■ *Web:* www.qualitymeats.com					
Quality Porks International Inc 10404 F Plaza	Omaha	NE	68127	402-339-1911	339-8383
Web: www.qpii.com					
Quincy Street Inc 13350 Quincy St	Holland	MI	49424	616-399-3330	399-0952
TF: 800-784-6290 ■ *Web:* www.quincystreetinc.com					
Rineharts Meat Processing Inc 133 Bell Rd PO Box 6880	Branson	MO	65615	417-334-2070	334-2059
RL Ziegler Co Inc 730 Energy Blvd Suite 1403	Northport	AL	35407	205-758-3621	758-0185
TF: 800-392-6328 ■ *Web:* www.zmeats.com					
Rochelle Foods Inc 1001 S Main St Po Box 45	Rochelle	IL	61068	815-562-4141	562-4149
Rose Packing Co Inc 65 S Barrington Rd	South Barrington	IL	60010	847-381-5700	381-9436*
**Fax:* Cust Svc ■ *TF:* 800-323-7363 ■ *Web:* www.rosepacking.com					
Sam Hausman Meat Packer Inc 4261 Beacon St PO Box 2422	Corpus Christi	TX	78403	361-883-5521	883-1003
TF: 800-364-5521 ■ *Web:* www.samhausman.com					
Sam Kane Beef Processors Inc 9001 Leopard St	Corpus Christi	TX	78409	361-241-5000	242-2999
TF: 800-242-4142 ■ *Web:* www.samkanebeef.com					
Schenk Packing Co Inc 8204 288th St NW	Stanwood	WA	98292	360-629-3939	629-4451
Web: www.schenkpacking.com					
Sioux-Preme Packing Co 4241 US 75th Ave PO Box 255	Sioux Center	IA	51250	712-722-2555	722-2666
TF: 800-735-7675 ■ *Web:* www.siouxpreme.com					
Smithfield Foods Inc 200 Commerce St	Smithfield	VA	23430	757-365-3000	365-3017
NYSE: SFD ■ *TF:* 800-276-6158 ■ *Web:* www.smithfieldfoods.com					
Smithfield Packing Co Inc 501 N Church St	Smithfield	VA	23430	757-357-4321	357-1366*
**Fax:* Hum Res ■ *TF:* 800-444-9180 ■ *Web:* www.smithfieldfoods.com					
Square-H Brands Inc 2731 S Soto St	Los Angeles	CA	90058	323-267-4600	261-7350
TF: 800-424-6339 ■ *Web:* www.squarehbrands.com					

	City	State	Zip	Phone	Fax
Superior Farms 1480 Drew Ave Suite 100 *TF:* 800-228-5262 ■ *Web:* www.superiorfarms.com	Davis	CA	95618	530-758-3091	758-3152
Thompson Packers Inc 550 Carnation St *TF:* 800-989-6328 ■ *Web:* www.thompack.com	Slidell	LA	70460	985-641-6640	645-2112
Travis Meats Inc 7210 Clinton Hwy PO Box 670 *TF:* 800-247-7606 ■ *Web:* www.travismeats.com	Powell	TN	37849	865-938-9051	938-9211
Tyson Fresh Meats Inc 800 Stevens Port Dr *TF:* 800-416-2272 ■ *Web:* www.tyson.com	Dakota Dunes	SD	57049	605-235-2061	235-2068
Washington Beef LLC 201 Elmwood Rd PO Box 832 *TF:* 800-289-2333	Toppenish	WA	98948	509-865-2121	865-2827
Wolverine Packing Co Inc 2535 Rivard St *TF:* 800-521-1390 ■ *Web:* www.wolverinepacking.com	Detroit	MI	48207	313-259-7500	568-1909

477 MEDICAL ASSOCIATIONS - STATE

SEE ALSO Health & Medical Professionals Associations p. 1452

	City	State	Zip	Phone	Fax
Alabama Medical Assn 19 S Jackson St *TF:* 800-239-6272 ■ *Web:* www.masalink.org	Montgomery	AL	36104	334-263-6441	269-5200
Alaska State Medical Assn 4107 Laurel St *Web:* www.aksma.org	Anchorage	AK	99508	907-562-0304	561-2063
Arizona Medical Assn 810 W Bethany Home Rd *TF:* 800-482-3480 ■ *Web:* www.armadoc.com	Phoenix	AZ	85013	602-246-8901	242-6283
Arkansas Medical Society PO Box 55088 *TF:* 800-542-1058 ■ *Web:* www.arkmed.org	Little Rock	AR	72215	501-224-8967	224-6489
California Medical Assn 1201 J St Suite 200 *Web:* www.cmanet.org	Sacramento	CA	95814	415-882-5100	882-3349
Colorado Medical Society 7351 Lowry Blvd *TF:* 800-654-5653 ■ *Web:* www.cms.org	Denver	CO	80230	720-859-1001	859-7509
Connecticut State Medical Society 160 St Ronan St *TF:* 800-635-7740 ■ *Web:* www.csms.org	New Haven	CT	06511	203-865-0587	865-4997
Delmarva Foundation For Medical Care Inc (DFMC) 9240 Centreville Rd *TF:* 800-999-3362 ■ *Web:* www.delmarvafoundation.org	Easton	MD	21601	410-822-0697	822-7971
Florida Medical Assn 1430 Piedmont Dr E *TF:* 800-762-0233 ■ *Web:* www.fmaonline.org	Tallahassee	FL	32308	850-224-6496	224-6627
Hawaii Medical Assn 1360 S Beretania St Suite 200 *TF:* 866-536-8666 ■ *Web:* www.hmaonline.net	Honolulu	HI	96814	808-536-7702	528-2376
Idaho Medical Assn 305 W Jefferson St *Web:* www.idmed.org	Boise	ID	83702	208-344-7888	344-7903
Illinois State Medical Society 20 N Michigan Ave Suite 700 *Web:* www.isms.org	Chicago	IL	60602	312-782-1654	782-2023
Indiana State Medical Assn 322 Canal Walk *TF:* 800-257-4762 ■ *Web:* www.ismanet.org	Indianapolis	IN	46202	317-261-2060	261-2076
Iowa Medical Society 1001 Grand Ave *TF:* 800-747-3070 ■ *Web:* www.iowamedicalsociety.org	West Des Moines	IA	50265	515-223-1401	223-0590
Kansas Medical Society 623 SW 10th Ave *TF:* 800-332-0156 ■ *Web:* kmsonline.org	Topeka	KS	66612	785-235-2383	235-5114
Kentucky Medical Assn 4965 US Hwy 42 KMA Bldg Suite 2000 *TF:* 800-686-9923 ■ *Web:* www.kyma.org	Louisville	KY	40222	502-426-6200	426-6877
Louisiana State Medical Society 6767 Perkins Rd Suite 100 *TF:* 800-375-9508 ■ *Web:* www.lsms.org	Baton Rouge	LA	70808	225-763-8500	763-6122
Maine Medical Assn 30 Assn Dr *TF:* 800-772-0815 ■ *Web:* www.mainemed.com	Manchester	ME	04351	207-622-3374	622-3332
Maryland State Medical Society 1211 Cathedral St *TF:* 800-492-1056 ■ *Web:* www.medchi.org	Baltimore	MD	21201	410-539-0872	547-0915
Massachusetts Medical Society (MMS) 860 Winter St *TF:* 800-322-2303 ■ *Web:* www.massmed.org	Waltham	MA	02451	781-893-4610	893-8009
Medical Assn of Georgia (MAG) 1849 The Exchange Suite 200 *TF:* 800-282-0224 ■ *Web:* www.mag.org	Atlanta	GA	30309	678-303-9290	303-3732
Medical Society of the District of Columbia 1115 30th St NW Suite 1002 *Web:* www.msdc.org	Washington	DC	20007	202-466-1800	452-1542
Michigan State Medical Society 120 W Saginaw St *Web:* www.msms.org	East Lansing	MI	48823	517-337-1351	337-2490
Minnesota Medical Assn 1300 Godward St NE Suite 2500 *TF:* 800-342-5662 ■ *Web:* www.mnmed.org	Minneapolis	MN	55413	612-378-1875	378-3875
Mississippi State Medical Assn 408 W PkwyPl *TF:* 800-898-0251	Ridgeland	MS	39157	601-853-6733	853-6746
Missouri State Medical Assn 113 Madison St *TF:* 800-869-6762 ■ *Web:* www.msma.org	Jefferson City	MO	65101	573-636-5151	636-8552
Montana Medical Assn 2021 11th Ave Suite 1 *TF:* 877-443-4000 ■ *Web:* www.mmaoffice.com	Helena	MT	59601	406-443-4000	443-4042
Nebraska Medical Assn 233 S 13th St Suite 1200 *Web:* www.nebmed.org	Lincoln	NE	68508	402-474-4472	474-2198
Nevada State Medical Assn (NSMA) 3660 Baker Ln Suite 101 *Web:* www.nsmadocs.org	Reno	NV	89509	775-825-6788	825-3202
New Hampshire Medical Society 7 N State St *TF:* 800-564-1909 ■ *Web:* www.nhms.org	Concord	NH	03301	603-224-1909	226-2432
New Jersey Medical Society 2 Princess Rd *TF:* 800-322-6765 ■ *Web:* www.msnj.org	Lawrenceville	NJ	08648	609-896-1766	896-1368
New Mexico Medical Society 7770 Jefferson NE Suite 400 *TF:* 800-748-1596 ■ *Web:* www.swcp.com	Albuquerque	NM	87109	505-828-0237	828-0336
New York State Medical Society 420 Lakeville Rd PO Box 5404 *TF:* 800-523-4405 ■ *Web:* www.mssny.org	Lake Success	NY	11042	516-488-6100	488-1267
North Carolina Medical Society 222 N Person St *TF:* 800-722-1350 ■ *Web:* www.ncmedsoc.org	Raleigh	NC	27601	919-833-3836	833-2023
North Dakota Medical Assn 1622 E I- Ave *Web:* www.ndmed.com	Bismarck	ND	58503	701-223-9475	223-9476
Ohio State Medical Assn 3401 Mill Run Dr *TF:* 800-766-6762 ■ *Web:* www.osma.org	Hilliard	OH	43026	614-527-6762	527-6763
Oklahoma State Medical Assn 601 NW Grand Blvd *TF:* 800-522-9452 ■ *Web:* www.osmaonline.org	Oklahoma City	OK	73118	405-843-9571	842-1834
Oregon Medical Assn (OMA) 11740 SW 68th Pkwy Suite 100 *Web:* www.theoma.org	Portland	OR	97223	503-619-8000	619-0609
Pennsylvania Medical Society 777 E Pk Dr *Web:* www.pamedsoc.org	Harrisburg	PA	17111	717-558-7750	558-7840
Rhode Island Medical Society 235 Promenade St Suite 500 *Web:* www.rimed.org	Providence	RI	02908	401-331-3207	751-8050
South Carolina Medical Assn 132 W Pk Blvd *TF:* 800-327-1021 ■ *Web:* www.scmanet.org	Columbia	SC	29210	803-798-6207	772-6783
Tennessee Medical Assn 2301 21st Ave A *TF:* 800-659-1862 ■ *Web:* www.medwire.org	Nashville	TN	37212	615-385-2100	383-5918
Texas Medical Assn 401 W 15th St *TF:* 800-880-1300 ■ *Web:* www.texmed.org	Austin	TX	78701	512-370-1300	370-1693
Utah Medical Assn 540 E 500 S *Web:* www.utahmed.org	Salt Lake City	UT	84102	801-355-7477	532-1550
Vermont Medical Society 134 Main St *TF:* 800-640-8767 ■ *Web:* www.vtmd.org	Montpelier	VT	05601	802-223-7898	223-1201
Virginia Medical Society 4205 Dover Rd *TF:* 800-746-6768 ■ *Web:* www.msv.org	Richmond	VA	23221	804-353-2721	355-6189
Washington State Medical Assn 2033 6th Ave Suite 1100 *TF:* 800-552-0612 ■ *Web:* www.wsma.org	Seattle	WA	98121	206-441-9762	441-5863
West Virginia State Medical Assn 4307 MacCorkle Ave SE PO Box 4106 *TF:* 800-257-4747 ■ *Web:* www.wvsma.com	Charleston	WV	25364	304-925-0342	925-0345
Wisconsin State Medical Society 330 E Lakeside St *TF:* 866-442-3800 ■ *Web:* www.wisconsinmedicalsociety.org	Madison	WI	53701	608-257-6781	442-3802
Wyoming Medical Society 1920 Evans Ave *Web:* www.wyomed.org	Cheyenne	WY	82001	307-635-2424	632-1973

478 MEDICAL & DENTAL EQUIPMENT & SUPPLIES - WHOL

	City	State	Zip	Phone	Fax
A Plus International Inc 5138 Eucalyptus Ave *TF:* 800-762-1123 ■ *Web:* www.aplusgroup.net	Chino	CA	91710	909-591-5168	591-0359
Ace Medical Inc 94-910 Moloalo St *TF:* 866-678-3601 ■ *Web:* www.acemedicalinc.com	Waipahu	HI	96797	808-678-3600	678-3604
Alpha Imaging Inc 4455 Glenbrook Rd *TF:* 800-331-7327 ■ *Web:* www.alpha-imaging.com	Willoughby	OH	44094	440-953-3800	953-1455
Ampronix Inc 15 Whatney *TF:* 800-400-7972 ■ *Web:* www.ampronix.com	Irvine	CA	92618	949-273-8000	
Buffalo Hospital Supply Co Inc 4039 Genesee St *TF:* 800-724-0530 ■ *Web:* www.buffalohospital.com	Buffalo	NY	14225	716-626-9400	626-4307
Burkhart Dental Supply Co 2502 S 78th St *TF Cust Svc:* 800-828-2089 ■ *Web:* www.burkhartdental.com	Tacoma	WA	98409	253-474-7761	472-4773
Butler Animal Health Supply LLC 400 Metro Pl N *TF PR:* 888-691-2724 ■ *Web:* www.accessbutler.com	Dublin	OH	43017	614-761-9095	761-9095
Byram Healthcare Centers Inc 120 Bloomingdale Rd *TF:* 800-354-4054 ■ *Web:* www.byramhealthcare.com	White Plains	NY	10605	914-286-2000	
Care Line Industries Inc 2210 Lake Rd *TF:* 800-251-1157 ■ *Web:* www.carelineinc.com	Greenbrier	TN	37073	615-643-4797	643-5904
China Yongxin Pharmaceuticals Inc 927 Canada Ct *PINK:* CYXN ■ *Web:* www.yongxinchina.com	City Of Industry	CA	91748	626-581-9098	581-9038
Crest Services 735 Plaza Blvd Suite 210 *TF:* 888-467-1536 ■ *Web:* www.crestservices.com	Coppell	TX	75019	214-488-9301	488-9299
Dedicated Distribution Inc 640 Miami Ave *TF:* 800-325-8367 ■ *Web:* www.dedicateddistribution.com	Kansas City	KS	66105	913-371-2200	
Derma Sciences Inc 214 Carnegie Ctr Suite 100 *TF:* 800-825-4325 ■ *Web:* www.dermasciences.com	Princeton	NJ	08540	609-514-4744	514-8554
Dr Fresh Inc 6645 Caballero Blvd *Web:* www.drfreshdental.com	Buena Park	CA	90620	714-690-1573	
Evans-Sherratt Co 13050 Northend Ave *TF:* 800-248-3826 ■ *Web:* www.evans-sherratt.com	Oak Park	MI	48237	248-584-5500	584-5510
Griswold Machine & Engineering Inc PO Box 98 *TF:* 800-248-2054 ■ *Web:* www.gme-shields.com	Union City	MI	49094	517-741-4471	
Grogans Health Care Supply Inc 1016 S Broadway St *TF:* 800-365-1020 ■ *Web:* www.grogans.com	Lexington	KY	40504	859-254-6661	254-6666
Henry Schein Inc 135 Duryea Rd *NASDAQ:* HSIC ■ *TF:* 800-582-2702 ■ *Web:* www.henryschein.com	Melville	NY	11747	631-843-5500	843-5652
Iowa Veterinary Supply Co (IVESCO) 124 Country Club Rd *TF:* 800-457-0118 ■ *Web:* www.ivescollc.com	Iowa Falls	IA	50126	641-648-2529	648-5994
Jorgensen Laboratories Inc 1450 Van Buren Ave *TF:* 800-525-5614 ■ *Web:* www.jorvet.com	Loveland	CO	80538	970-669-2500	663-5042

Phone | Fax

Karl Storz Endoscopy-america Inc
600 Corporate Pointe FL 5 .... Culver City CA 90230 310-338-8100 218-8525
TF: 800-321-1304 ■ Web: www.karlstorz.com

Kentec Medical Inc 17871 Fitch .... Irvine CA 92614 949-863-0810 724-8923
TF: 800-825-5996 ■ Web: www.kentecmedical.com

Laboratory Supply Co 250 Ottawa Ave .... Louisville KY 40209 502-363-1891 364-1609*
*Fax: Acctg ■ TF Cust Svc: 800-888-5227 ■ Web: www.labsco.com

Leeches USA Ltd 300 Shames Dr .... Westbury NY 11590 516-333-2570 997-4948
TF: 800-645-3569 ■ Web: www.leechesusa.com

Les Wilkins & Assoc Inc 6850 35th Ave Ne .... Seattle WA 98115 206-522-0908 522-5292
Web: www.leswilkins.com

Liberty Medical Supply Inc
10045 SE Federal Hwy .... Port Saint Lucie FL 34952 772-398-5800 762-0826*
*Fax Area Code: 800 ■ TF: 800-633-2001 ■ Web: www.libertymedical.com

Lynn Medical Instrument Co PO Box 930459 .... Wixom MI 48393 248-560-4500 338-6242
TF: 888-596-6633 ■ Web: www.lynnmed.com

Mabis Healthcare Inc 1931 Norman Dr. .... Waukegan IL 60085 800-526-4753 479-7968
TF: 800-728-6811 ■ Web: www.mabisdmi.com

Mada Medical Products Inc
625 Washington Ave .... Carlstadt NJ 07072 201-460-0454 460-3509
TF: 800-526-6370 ■ Web: www.madamedical.com

Marketlab Inc 6850 Southbelt Dr SE .... Caledonia MI 49316 616-656-2484 656-2475
Web: www.marketlabinc.com

McKesson Medical Group Extended Care
8121 10th Ave N .... Golden Valley MN 55427 763-595-6000 595-6677
TF: 800-328-8111 ■ Web: www.mckesson.com/ext_care.html

McKesson Medical-Surgical 8741 Landmark Rd .... Richmond VA 23228 804-264-7500 264-7679
TF: 800-446-3008 ■ Web: www.mckgenmed.com

Mesa Laboratories Inc 12100 W 6th Ave .... Lakewood CO 80228 303-987-8000 987-8989
NASDAQ: MLAB ■ TF Sales: 800-992-6372 ■ Web: www.mesalabs.com

Micro Bio-Medics Inc 846 Pelham Pkwy .... Pelham Manor NY 10803 914-738-8400 738-8999
TF: 800-431-2743

Midland Hospital Supply Inc
2011 Great Northern Dr .... Fargo ND 58102 701-235-4451 235-7920
TF: 800-747-4450

Midwest Veterinary Supply Inc
11965 Larc Industrial Blvd .... Burnsville MN 55337 952-894-4350 894-5407
TF: 800-328-2975 ■ Web: www.midwestveterinarysupply.com

Moore Medical Corp 389 John Downey Dr .... New Britain CT 06050 860-826-3600 223-2382
TF Sales: 800-234-1464 ■ Web: www.mooremedical.com

Mycone Dental Supply Co Inc
616 Hollywood Ave .... Cherry Hill NJ 08002 856-663-4700 663-0381
TF: 800-333-3131 ■ Web: www.keystoneind.com

Nihon Kohden America Inc 90 Icon .... Foothill Ranch CA 92610 949-580-1555 580-1550
TF: 800-325-0283 ■ Web: www.nkusa.com

Oakworks Inc 923 E Wellspring Rd .... New Freedom PA 17349 717-235-6807 235-6798
TF: 800-558-8850 ■ Web: www.oakworks.com

Omron Healthcare Inc 1200 Lakeside Dr .... Bannockburn IL 60015 847-680-6200 637-6763*
*Fax Area Code: 800 ■ *Fax: Cust Svc ■ TF: 800-323-1482 ■ Web: www.omronhealthcare.com

Otto Bock Healthcare North America Inc
2 Carlson Pkwy N Suite 100 .... Minneapolis MN 55447 763-553-9464
TF: 800-328-4058 ■ Web: www.ottobockus.com

Owens & Minor Inc 9120 Lockwood Blvd .... Mechanicsville VA 23116 804-723-7000 723-7100
NYSE: OMI ■ Web: www.owens-minor.com

Patterson Cos Inc 1031 Mendota Heights Rd .... Saint Paul MN 55120 651-686-1600 686-9331
NASDAQ: PDCO ■ TF: 800-328-5536 ■ Web: www.pattersondental.com

Pearson Dental Supplies Inc 13161 Telfair Ave .... Sylmar CA 91342 818-362-2600 835-3100
TF: 800-535-4535 ■ Web: www.pearsondental.com

Permobil Inc 6961 Eastgate Blvd .... Lebanon TN 37090 615-547-1889 231-3256*
*Fax Area Code: 800 ■ TF: 800-285-3114 ■ Web: www.permobil.com

PracticeWares Dental Supply
11291 Sunrise Pk Dr .... Rancho Cordova CA 95742 916-638-8020 344-6710*
*Fax Area Code: 800 ■ TF: 800-800-4939

Prima Tech USA PO Box 336 .... Kenansville NC 28349 910-296-6116 296-6263
TF: 888-833-7099 ■ Web: www.primatechusa.com

PSS World Medical Inc
4345 Southpoint Blvd .... Jacksonville FL 32216 904-332-3000 332-3395
NASDAQ: PSSI ■ Web: www.pssworldmedical.com

Radiometer America Inc 810 Sharon Dr .... Westlake OH 44145 440-871-8900 871-8117
TF: 800-736-0600 ■ Web: www.radiometer.com

Rgh Enterprises Inc
1810 Summit Commerce Pk .... Twinsburg OH 44087 330-963-6998 963-6839
TF: 800-307-5930 ■ Web: www.edgepark.com

Somagen Diagnostics Inc 9220 25th Ave .... Edmonton AB T6N1E1 780-702-9500 438-6595
TF: 800-661-9993 ■ Web: www.somagen.com

Southern Prosthetic Supply Co
6025 Shiloh Rd Suite A .... Alpharetta GA 30005 678-455-8888 869-7776*
*Fax Area Code: 800 ■ TF Cust Svc: 800-767-7776 ■ Web: www.spsco.com

Sullivan-Schein Dental
10920 W Lincoln Ave .... West Allis WI 53227 414-321-8881 321-8865
TF Cust Svc: 800-648-6684 ■ Web: www.henryschein.com

Sysmex America Inc 1 Nelson C White Pkwy .... Mundelein IL 60060 847-996-4500 996-4397
TF: 800-379-7639 ■ Web: www.sysmex.com

Talyst Inc 11100 NE 8th St 6 .... Bellevue WA 98004 425-289-5400 289-5401
Web: www.talyst.com

Tetra Medical Supply Corp 6364 W Gross Pt Rd .... Niles IL 60714 847-647-0590 647-9034
TF Cust Svc: 800-621-4041 ■ Web: www.tetramed.com

Trans Med USA Inc 31 Progress Ave .... Tyngsboro MA 01879 978-649-1970 649-1971
TF: 800-649-1200 ■ Web: www.transmed-usa.com

VWR International
100 Matsonford Rd Bldg 1 Suite 200 .... Radnorpa PA 19087 610-431-1700 431-9174
TF: 800-932-5000 ■ Web: www.vwrsp.com

William V MacGill & Co 1000 N Lombard Rd .... Lombard IL 60148 630-889-0500 727-3433*
*Fax Area Code: 800 ■ TF: 800-323-2841 ■ Web: www.macgill.com

Wise El Santo Co Inc 11000 Linpage Pl .... Saint Louis MO 63132 314-428-3100 428-7017
TF: 800-727-8541 ■ Web: www.wiseelsanto.com

Zee Medical Inc 22 Corporate Pk .... Irvine CA 92606 949-252-9500 252-9649
TF: 800-841-8417 ■ Web: www.zeemedical.com

MEDICAL FACILITIES

SEE Developmental Centers p. 1783; Health Care Providers - Ancillary p. 2005; Hospices p. 2028; Hospitals p. 2037; Imaging Services - Diagnostic p. 2104; Substance Abuse Treatment Centers p. 2679

479 MEDICAL INSTRUMENTS & APPARATUS - MFR

SEE ALSO Imaging Equipment & Systems - Medical p. 2103; Medical Supplies - Mfr p. 2229

Phone | Fax

Abbott Laboratories 100 Abbott Pk Rd .... Abbott Park IL 60064 847-937-6100
NYSE: ABT ■ TF: 800-323-9100 ■ Web: www.abbott.com

Accurate Surgical & Scientific Instruments Corp
300 Shames Dr .... Westbury NY 11590 516-333-2570 997-4948
TF: 800-645-3569 ■ Web: www.accuratesurgical.com

Accuray Inc 1310 Chesapeake Terr .... Sunnyvale CA 94089 408-716-4600 716-4601
NASDAQ: ARAY ■ TF: 888-522-3740 ■ Web: www.accuray.com

Acme United Corp 60 Round Hill Rd .... Fairfield CT 06824 203-254-6060 254-6019
AMEX: ACU ■ TF: 800-835-2263 ■ Web: www.acmeunited.com

Ad-tech Medical Instrument Inc
1901 William St .... Racine WI 53404 262-634-1555 634-5668
TF: 800-776-1555 ■ Web: www.adtechmedical.com

AESCULAP Inc 3773 Corporate Pkwy .... Center Valley PA 18034 800-282-9000 791-6886*
*Fax Area Code: 610 ■ TF: 800-282-9000 ■ Web: www.aesculapusa.com

Aksys Ltd 2 Marriott Dr .... Lincolnshire IL 60069 847-229-2020 229-2080
NASDAQ: AKSY ■ TF: 877-229-5700 ■ Web: www.aksys.com

Allied Healthcare Products Inc
1720 Sublette Ave .... Saint Louis MO 63110 314-771-2400 477-7701*
NASDAQ: AHPI ■ *Fax Area Code: 800 ■ *Fax: Cust Svc ■ TF: 800-444-3954 ■ Web: www.alliedhpi.com

Andover Healthcare Inc 9 Fanaras Dr .... Salisbury MA 01952 978-465-0044 462-0003
Web: www.andovercoated.com

Antares Pharma Inc
13755 1st Ave N Suite 100 .... Minneapolis MN 55441 763-475-7700 476-1009
AMEX: AIS ■ TF: 800-328-3077 ■ Web: www.antarespharma.com

Aradigm Corp 3929 Pt Eden Way .... Hayward CA 94545 510-265-9000 265-0277
NASDAQ: ARDM ■ Web: www.aradigm.com

Aspen Medical Products 6481 Oak Cyn .... Irvine CA 92618 949-681-0200 681-0222
TF: 800-295-2776 ■ Web: www.aspenmp.com

ATEK Medical Mfg 620 Watson St SW .... Grand Rapids MI 49504 616-643-5200 643-1482
TF: 800-690-2365 ■ Web: www.atekmedical.com

Atrion Corp 1 Allentown Pkwy .... Allen TX 75002 972-390-9800 396-7581
NASDAQ: ATRI ■ TF: 800-627-0226 ■ Web: www.atrioncorp.com

Atrium Medical Corp 5 Wentworth Dr .... Hudson NH 03051 603-880-1433 880-6718
Web: www.atriummed.com

B Braun Medical Inc 824 12th Ave .... Bethlehem PA 18018 610-691-5400 691-2202
TF: 800-523-9676 ■ Web: www.bbraunusa.com

Bard Access Systems Inc 605 N 5600 W .... Salt Lake City UT 84116 801-522-5000 522-4298
TF: 800-443-5505 ■ Web: www.bardaccess.com

Baxter Healthcare Corp 1 Baxter Pkwy .... Deerfield IL 60015 847-948-2000 948-3948
Web: www.baxter.com

Baxter International Inc 1 Baxter Pkwy .... Deerfield IL 60015 847-948-2000 948-3948
NYSE: BAX ■ Web: www.baxter.com

BD Medical 9450 S State St .... Sandy UT 84070 801-565-2300 565-2740
TF: 888-237-2762 ■ Web: www.bd.com

Becton Dickinson & Co 1 Becton Dr .... Franklin Lakes NJ 07417 201-847-6800 847-4882*
NYSE: BDX ■ *Fax: Cust Svc ■ TF Cust Svc: 888-237-2762 ■ Web: www.bd.com

Becton Dickinson Pharmaceutical Systems
1 Becton Dr MC407 .... Franklin Lakes NJ 07417 201-847-4017 847-4847
TF: 800-225-3310 ■ Web: www.bd.com/pharmaceuticals

Best Vascular
4350 International Blvd Suite E .... Norcross GA 30093 770-717-0904 717-1283
TF: 800-668-6783 ■ Web: www.bestvascular.com

BG Sulzle Inc 1 Needle Ln .... North Syracuse NY 13212 315-454-9879 454-9879
Web: www.bgsulzle.com

Biodex Medical Systems Inc 20 Ramsay Rd .... Shirley NY 11967 631-924-9000 924-8355
TF: 800-224-6339 ■ Web: www.biodex.com

Bioject Medical Technologies Inc
20245 SW 95 Ave .... Tualatin OR 97062 503-692-8001 692-6698
NASDAQ: BJCT ■ TF: 800-683-7221 ■ Web: www.bioject.com

BioMerieux Inc 595 Anglum Rd .... Hazelwood MO 63042 314-731-8500 325-1598*
*Fax Area Code: 800 ■ TF: 800-638-4835 ■ Web: www.biomerieux.com

Biomet Microfixation Inc
1520 Tradeport Dr .... Jacksonville FL 32218 904-741-4400 741-4500
TF: 800-874-7711 ■ Web: www.biometmicrofixation.com

Bionix Development Corp PO Box 935 .... Toledo OH 43697 419-727-8421 727-8426
TF: 800-551-7096 ■ Web: www.bionix.com

Biosense Webster Inc
3333 S Diamond Canyon Rd .... Diamond Bar CA 91765 909-839-8500 468-3841
TF: 800-729-9010 ■ Web: www.biosensewebster.com

Blackburn's Physicians Pharmacy Inc
301 Corbet St .... Tarentum PA 15084 724-224-9100 224-9124
TF: 800-472-2440 ■ Web: www.blackburnsmed.com

Boston Scientific Corp 1 Boston Scientific Pl .... Natick MA 01760 508-650-8000 272-9444*
NYSE: BSX ■ *Fax Area Code: 888 ■ *Fax: Cust Svc ■ TF: 800-272-3737 ■ Web: www.bostonscientific.com

Braemar Inc 1285 Corporate Ctr Dr .... Eagan MN 55121 651-286-8620 286-8630
TF: 800-328-2719 ■ Web: www.braemarinc.com

Cadwell Laboratories Inc 909 N Kellogg St .... Kennewick WA 99336 509-735-6481 783-6503
TF: 800-245-3001 ■ Web: www.cadwell.com

Cambridge Heart Inc
100 Ames Pond Dr Suite 100 .... Tewksbury MA 01876 978-654-7600 654-4501
TF: 888-226-9283 ■ Web: www.cambridgeheart.com

Cantel Medical Corp 150 Clove Rd 9th Fl .... Little Falls NJ 07424 973-890-7220 890-7270
NYSE: CMN ■ Web: www.cantelmedical.com

Cardica Inc 900 Saginaw Dr .... Redwood City CA 94063 650-364-9975 364-3134
NASDAQ: CRDC ■ Web: www.cardica.com

Cardinal Health Automation & Information Services
3750 Torrey View Ct .... San Diego CA 92130 858-480-6000 480-6329
TF: 800-367-9947 ■ Web: www.cardinal.com/content/businesses

CareFusion Corp 3750 Torrey View Ct .... San Diego CA 92130 858-617-2000 617-2900
NYSE: CFN ■ TF: 888-876-4287 ■ Web: www.carefusion.com

CAS Medical Systems Inc 44 E Industrial Rd .... Branford CT 06405 203-488-6056 488-9438
NASDAQ: CASM ■ TF: 800-227-4414 ■ Web: www.casmed.com

Celsion Corp 10220-L Old Columbia Rd .... Columbia MD 21046 410-290-5390 290-5394
NASDAQ: CLSN ■ TF: 800-262-0394 ■ Web: www.celsion.com

	City	State	Zip	Phone	Fax
Chad Therapeutics Inc 2975 Horseshoe Dr S Suite 600 — *PINK: CHADQ* ■ *TF:* 800-423-8870 ■ *Web:* www.chadtherapeutics.com	Naples	FL	34104	239-687-1285	687-1280
Conceptus Inc 331 E Evelyn — *NASDAQ: CPTS* ■ *TF:* 800-434-7240 ■ *Web:* www.conceptus.com	Mountain View	CA	94041	650-962-4000	962-5200
Conmed Corp 525 French Rd — *NASDAQ: CNMD* ■ **Fax Area Code:* 800 ■ **Fax:* Cust Svc ■ *TF:* 800-448-6506 ■ *Web:* www.conmed.com	Utica	NY	13502	315-797-8375	438-3051*
CONMED Endoscopic Technologies 129 Concord Rd Bldg 3 — *TF:* 800-225-1332 ■ *Web:* www.conmed.com	Billerica	MA	01821	978-663-8989	262-4802
CONMED Linvatec 11311 Concept Blvd — **Fax:* Cust Svc ■ *TF:* 800-325-5900 ■ *Web:* www.conmed.com	Largo	FL	33773	727-392-6464	399-5256*
Cook Critical Care 750 Daniels Way PO Box 489 — **Fax Area Code:* 800 ■ *TF:* 800-457-4500 ■ *Web:* www.cookmedical.com	Bloomington	IN	47404	812-339-2235	554-8335*
Cook Endoscopy 4900 Bethania Stn Rd — *TF:* 800-245-4717 ■ *Web:* www.cookmedical.com	Winston-Salem	NC	27115	336-744-0157	744-1147
Cook Inc PO Box 4195 — *TF:* 800-457-4500 ■ *Web:* www.cookmedical.com	Bloomington	IN	47402	812-339-2235	339-2235
Cook Medical Inc PO Box 4195 — **Fax Area Code:* 800 ■ *TF:* 800-457-4500 ■ *Web:* www.cookmedical.com	Bloomington	IN	47402	812-339-2235	554-8335*
Cook Urological Inc 1100 W Morgan St PO Box 227 — *TF:* 800-457-4500 ■ *Web:* www.cookmedical.com	Spencer	IN	47460	812-829-4891	829-1801
Cook Vascular Inc 1186 Montgomery Ln — *TF:* 800-245-4715 ■ *Web:* www.cookvascular.com	Vandergrift	PA	15690	724-845-8621	845-2848
Cooper Cos Inc 6140 Stoneridge Mall Rd Suite 590 — *NYSE: COO* ■ *TF:* 888-822-2660 ■ *Web:* www.coopercos.com	Pleasanton	CA	94588	925-460-3600	460-3649
CooperSurgical Inc 95 Corporate Dr — **Fax Area Code:* 800 ■ **Fax:* Cust Svc ■ *TF:* 800-645-3760 ■ *Web:* www.coopersurgical.com	Trumbull	CT	06611	203-929-6321	262-0105*
Cordis Corp 14201 NW 60th Ave — **Fax:* Mail Rm ■ *TF:* 800-327-2490 ■ *Web:* www.cordis.com	Miami Lakes	FL	33014	786-313-2000	313-2080*
Corpak Medsystems Inc 100 Chaddick Dr — *TF:* 800-323-6305 ■ *Web:* www.corpakmedsystems.com	Wheeling	IL	60090	847-537-4601	541-9526
CR Bard Inc 730 Central Ave — *NYSE: BCR* ■ *Web:* www.crbard.com	Murray Hill	NJ	07974	908-277-8000	
CR Bard Inc Medical Div 8195 Industrial Blvd — **Fax Area Code:* 800 ■ **Fax:* Cust Svc ■ *TF:* 800-526-4455 ■ *Web:* www.bardmedical.com	Covington	GA	30014	770-784-6100	852-1339*
CR Bard Inc Peripheral Vascular Div PO Box 1740 — **Fax Area Code:* 800 ■ **Fax:* Cust Svc ■ *TF:* 800-321-4254	Tempe	AZ	85281	480-894-9515	440-5316*
CR Bard Inc Urological Div 8195 Industrial Blvd — *TF:* 800-526-4455 ■ *Web:* www.bardurological.com	Covington	GA	30014	770-784-6100	
Criticare Systems Inc N7W22025 Johnson Dr — *TF:* 800-458-4615 ■ *Web:* www.csiusa.com	Waukesha	WI	53186	262-798-8282	798-8290
Cutera Inc 3240 Bayshore Blvd — *NASDAQ: CUTR* ■ *TF:* 888-428-8372 ■ *Web:* www.cutera.com	Brisbane	CA	94005	415-657-5500	330-2444
Dale Medical Products Inc PO Box 1556 — **Fax Area Code:* 508 ■ *TF:* 800-343-3980 ■ *Web:* www.dalemed.com	Plainville	MA	02762	800-343-3980	695-6587*
Davol Inc 100 Sockanossett Crossroad PO Box 8500 — **Fax:* Cust Svc ■ *TF:* 800-556-6756 ■ *Web:* www.davol.com	Cranston	RI	02920	401-463-7000	463-3142*
Electro-Optical Sciences Inc 50 S Buckhout St Suite 1 — *NASDAQ: MELA* ■ *Web:* www.melasciences.com	Irvington	NY	10533	914-591-3783	591-3785
Empi Inc 599 Cardigan Rd — **Fax Area Code:* 800 ■ *TF:* 800-328-2536 ■ *Web:* www.empi.com	Saint Paul	MN	55126	651-415-9000	450-3593*
Encision Inc 6797 Winchester Cir — *PINK: ECIA* ■ *TF:* 800-998-0986 ■ *Web:* www.encision.com	Boulder	CO	80301	303-444-2600	444-2693
Endologix Inc 11 Studebaker — *NASDAQ: ELGX* ■ **Fax Area Code:* 877 ■ *TF:* 800-983-2284 ■ *Web:* www.endologix.com	Irvine	CA	92618	949-457-9546	843-1500*
Escalon Medical Corp 435 Devon Pk Dr Bldg 100 — *NASDAQ: ESMC* ■ *Web:* www.escalonmed.com	Wayne	PA	19087	610-688-6830	688-3641
Ethicon Endo-Surgery Inc 4545 Creek Rd — *TF:* 800-556-8451 ■ *Web:* www.ethiconendosurgery.com	Cincinnati	OH	45242	513-337-7000	
ev3 Inc 3033 Campus Dr — *TF:* 800-716-6700 ■ *Web:* www.ev3.net	Plymouth	MN	55441	763-398-7000	398-7200
G & G Instrument Corp 466 Saw Mill River Rd — *TF:* 800-882-2288 ■ *Web:* www.datacut.com	Ardsley	NY	10502	914-693-6000	693-6738
Gaymar Industries Inc 10 Centre Dr — **Fax Area Code:* 800 ■ **Fax:* Cust Svc ■ *TF:* 800-828-7341 ■ *Web:* www.gaymar.com	Orchard Park	NY	14127	716-662-2551	993-7890*
Gettig Technologies Inc 1 Streamside Pl E — *Web:* www.gettig.com	Spring Mills	PA	16875	814-422-8892	422-8011
GF Health Products Inc 2935 NE Pkwy — **Fax Area Code:* 800 ■ *TF:* 800-235-4661 ■ *Web:* www.grahamfield.com	Atlanta	GA	30360	770-447-1609	726-0601*
Gyrus Medical Inc 6655 Wedgwood Rd Suite 160 — *TF:* 800-852-9361 ■ *Web:* www.gyrusgroup.com/medical	Maple Grove	MN	55311	763-416-3000	416-3070
Haemonetics Corp 400 Wood Rd — *NYSE: HAE* ■ **Fax Area Code:* 800 ■ *TF:* 800-225-5242 ■ *Web:* www.haemonetics.com	Braintree	MA	02184	781-848-7100	860-1512*
Harmac Medical Products Inc 2201 Bailey Ave — *Web:* www.harmac.com	Buffalo	NY	14211	716-897-4500	897-0016
Hill-Rom Services Inc 1069 SR 46 E — **Fax:* Hum Res ■ *Web:* www.hill-rom.com	Batesville	IN	47006	812-934-7777	931-3592*
Hoggan Health Industries Inc 8020 S 1300 W — *TF:* 800-678-7888 ■ *Web:* www.hogganhealth.com	West Jordan	UT	84088	801-572-6500	572-6514
Hospira Inc 275 N Field Dr — *NYSE: HSP* ■ *TF:* 877-946-7747 ■ *Web:* www.hospira.com	Lake Forest	IL	60045	224-212-2000	
Hypertension Diagnostics Inc 2915 Waters Rd Suite 108 — *TF:* 888-785-7392 ■ *Web:* www.hdi-pulsewave.com	Eagan	MN	55121	651-687-9999	687-0485
Implant Sciences Corp 600 Research Dr — *PINK: IMSC* ■ *TF:* 877-732-7333 ■ *Web:* www.implantsciences.com	Wilmington	MA	01887	978-752-1700	752-1711
Innovative Specialty Silicone Acquisition Corp 3034 Propeller Dr — *TF:* 800-394-4284 ■ *Web:* www.ssfab.com	Paso Robles	CA	93446	805-239-4284	239-0523
Integra LifeSciences Holdings Corp 311 Enterprise Dr — *NASDAQ: IART* ■ *TF:* 800-654-2873 ■ *Web:* www.integra-ls.com	Plainsboro	NJ	08536	609-275-0500	799-3297
Intuitive Surgical Inc 1266 Kifer Rd Bldg 101 — *NASDAQ: ISRG* ■ *TF:* 888-868-4647 ■ *Web:* www.intuitivesurgical.com	Sunnyvale	CA	94086	408-523-2100	523-1390
Jenckes Machine Co PO Box 364 — *TF Cust Svc:* 866-941-1455	Warren	RI	02885	401-247-1999	247-4575
Johnson Matthey Medical Products 1401 King Rd — *TF:* 800-442-1405 ■ *Web:* www.jmmedical.com	West Chester	PA	19380	610-648-8000	648-8111
Katecho Inc 4020 Gannett Ave — *Web:* www.katecho.com	Des Moines	IA	50321	515-244-1212	244-4912
Kensey Nash Corp 735 Pennsylvania Dr — *NASDAQ: KNSY* ■ *TF:* 800-524-1984 ■ *Web:* www.kenseynash.com	Exton	PA	19341	484-713-2100	713-2900
Kimberly-Clark/Ballard Medical Products 1175 Northmeadow Pkwy — **Fax Area Code:* 801 ■ *TF:* 800-528-5591 ■ *Web:* www.kchealthcare.com	Roswell	GA	30076	800-524-3577	572-6999*
Knit Rite Inc 120 Osage Ave — *TF:* 800-821-3094 ■ *Web:* www.knitrite.com	Kansas City	KS	66105	913-281-4600	281-5455
Lake Region Mfg Co Inc 340 Lake Hazeltine Dr — *Web:* www.lakeregionmedical.com	Chaska	MN	55318	952-448-5111	448-3441
Laserage Technology Corp 3021 N Delany Rd — *Web:* www.laserage.com	Waukegan	IL	60087	847-249-5900	336-1103
Life-tech Inc PO Box 1849 — *TF:* 800-231-9841 ■ *Web:* www.life-tech.com	Stafford	TX	77497	281-491-6600	491-6646
MAQUET Cardiac Assist 15 Law Dr — **Fax Area Code:* 201 ■ *TF:* 800-777-4222 ■ *Web:* www.ca.maquet.com	Fairfield	NJ	07004	973-244-6100	307-5400*
McKinley Medical LLP 4080 Youngfield St — *TF:* 800-578-0555 ■ *Web:* www.mckinleymed.com	Wheat Ridge	CO	80033	303-420-9569	420-4545
Medovations Inc 102 E Keefe Ave — *Web:* www.medovations.com	Milwaukee	WI	53212	414-265-7620	265-7628
Medrad Inc 1 Medrad Dr — **Fax:* Cust Svc ■ *TF Cust Svc:* 800-633-7237 ■ *Web:* www.medrad.com	Indianola	PA	15051	412-767-2400	767-4120*
Medtronic Inc 710 Medtronic Pkwy NE — *NYSE: MDT* ■ *TF Cust Svc:* 800-328-2518 ■ *Web:* www.medtronic.com	Minneapolis	MN	55432	763-514-4000	514-4879
Medtronic Neurosurgery 125 Cremona Dr — *TF Cust Svc:* 800-468-9710	Goleta	CA	93117	805-968-1546	968-5038
Medtronic Perfusion Systems 7611 Northland Dr — *TF:* 800-328-3320 ■ *Web:* www.medtronic.com	Brooklyn Park	MN	55428	763-391-9000	391-9100
Medtronic Vascular 3576 Unocal Pl — *TF:* 800-308-7868 ■ *Web:* www.medtronic.com/vascular	Santa Rosa	CA	95403	707-525-0111	525-0114
Megadyne Medical Products Inc 11506 S State St — *TF:* 800-747-6110 ■ *Web:* www.megadyne.com	Draper	UT	84020	801-576-9669	576-9698
Mercury Medical 11300 49th St N — *TF:* 800-237-6418 ■ *Web:* www.mercurymed.com	Clearwater	FL	33762	727-573-0088	571-3922
Meridian Medical Technologies Inc 6350 Stevens Forest Rd Suite 301 — *TF:* 800-638-8093 ■ *Web:* www.meridianmeds.com	Columbia	MD	21046	443-259-7800	259-7801
Merit Medical Systems Inc 1600 W Merit Pkwy — *NASDAQ: MMSI* ■ *TF:* 800-356-3748 ■ *Web:* www.merit.com	South Jordan	UT	84095	801-253-1600	253-1652
Micro-Tube Fabricators Inc 250 Lackland Dr	Middlesex	NJ	08846	732-469-7420	469-4314
MicroAire Surgical Instruments Inc 1641 Edlich Dr — *TF:* 800-538-5561 ■ *Web:* www.microaire.com	Charlottesville	VA	22911	434-975-8000	975-4144
Minntech Corp 14605 28th Ave N — *TF:* 800-328-3345 ■ *Web:* www.minntech.com	Minneapolis	MN	55447	763-553-3300	551-2688
Nephros Inc 41 Grand Ave — *OTC: NEPH* ■ *Web:* www.nephros.com	River Edge	NJ	07661	201-343-5202	343-5207
Novosci 2021 Airport Rd — *TF:* 800-854-0567 ■ *Web:* www.novosci.us	Conroe	TX	77301	281-363-4950	363-7080
Nspire Health Inc 1830 Lefthand Cir — *TF:* 800-574-7374 ■ *Web:* www.nspirehealth.com	Longmont	CO	80501	303-666-5555	666-5588
NuVasive Inc 7475 Lusk Blvd — *NASDAQ: NUVA* ■ *TF:* 800-475-9131 ■ *Web:* www.nuvasive.com	San Diego	CA	92121	858-909-1800	909-2000
NxStage Medical Inc 439 S Union St 5th Fl — *NASDAQ: NXTM* ■ *TF:* 866-697-8243 ■ *Web:* www.nxstage.com	Lawrence	MA	01843	978-687-4700	687-4809
Ortho-Clinical Diagnostics Inc 1001 US Rt 202 N PO Box 350 — **Fax Area Code:* 585 ■ **Fax:* Cust Svc ■ *TF:* 800-828-6316 ■ *Web:* www.orthoclinical.com	Raritan	NJ	08869	908-218-1300	453-3660*
Osteomed Corp 3885 Arapaho Rd — *TF Cust Svc:* 800-456-7779 ■ *Web:* www.osteomedcorp.com	Addison	TX	75001	972-677-4600	677-4601
Osteometer MediTech Inc 12525 Chadron Ave — *TF:* 866-421-7762 ■ *Web:* www.osteometer.com	Hawthorne	CA	90250	310-978-3073	676-0948
Pacific Bioscience Laboratories Inc 13222 SE 30th St Suite A1 — *TF:* 888-525-2747 ■ *Web:* www.clarisonic.com	Bellevue	WA	98005	425-283-5700	
Paramit Corp 18735 Madrone Pkwy — *Web:* www.paramit.com	Morgan Hill	CA	95037	408-782-5600	782-9991
PerkinElmer Inc 45 William St — *NYSE: PKI* ■ *Web:* www.perkinelmer.com	Wellesley	MA	02481	781-237-5100	237-9386
Pilling Surgical 2917 Weck Dr — *TF Cust Svc:* 866-246-6990 ■ *Web:* www.teleflex.com/en/emea/brands/pilling/index.html	Research Triangle Park	NC	27709	919-544-8000	361-3914
Precision Edge Surgical Products Co 415 W 12th Ave — *Web:* www.precisionedge.com	Sault Sainte Marie	MI	49783	906-632-4800	632-5620
PreMD Inc 4211 Yonge St Suite 615 — *PINK: PREMF*	Toronto	ON	M2P2A9	416-222-3449	222-4533
Propper Mfg Co Inc 36-04 Skillman Ave — *TF Cust Svc:* 800-832-4300 ■ *Web:* www.proppermfg.com	Long Island City	NY	11101	718-392-6650	482-8909
Ranfac Corp PO Box 635 — *Web:* www.ranfac.com	Avon	MA	02322	508-588-4400	584-8588
ResMed Inc 9001 Spectrum Ctr Blvd — *NYSE: RMD* ■ *TF:* 800-424-0737 ■ *Web:* www.resmed.com	San Diego	CA	92123	858-836-5000	836-5501
Rochester Medical Corp 1 Rochester Medical Dr — *NASDAQ: ROCM* ■ *TF:* 800-243-3315 ■ *Web:* www.rocm.com	Stewartville	MN	55976	507-533-9600	533-4232
Roho Group The 100 N Florida Ave — *Web:* www.rohoinc.com	Belleville	IL	62221	618-277-9173	277-9561

Company / Address	City	State	Zip	Phone	Fax
Safety Syringes Inc 2875 Loker Ave E	Carlsbad	CA	92010	760-918-9908	918-0565
Web: www.safetysyringes.com					
Saint Jude Medical 14901 DeVeau Pl	Minnetonka	MN	55345	952-933-4700	933-0307
NYSE: STJ ■ *TF:* 800-328-3873 ■ *Web:* www.sjm.com					
Salter Labs 100 Sycamore Rd	Arvin	CA	93203	661-854-3166	854-3850
TF: 800-421-0024 ■ *Web:* www.salterlabs.com					
Seabrook International LLC 15 Woodworkers Way	Seabrook	NH	03874	603-474-1919	474-1833
Web: www.seabrookinternational.com					
Sechrist Industries Inc 4225 E La Palma Ave	Anaheim	CA	92807	714-579-8400	579-0814
TF: 800-732-4747 ■ *Web:* www.sechristusa.com					
Seneca Medical Inc 85 Shaffer Pk Dr PO Box 399	Tiffin	OH	44883	419-447-0222	447-7201
TF: 800-447-0225 ■ *Web:* www.senecamedical.com					
Siemens Medical Solutions Inc 51 Valley Stream Pkwy	Malvern	PA	19355	610-448-6300	219-3124
TF: 866-872-9745 ■ *Web:* www.medical.siemens.com					
Smith & Nephew Inc Endoscopy Div 150 Minuteman Rd	Andover	MA	01810	978-749-1000	749-1599
TF: 800-343-8386 ■ *Web:* www.smith-nephew.com/what/endoscopy.jsp					
Smiths Medical MD Inc 1265 Grey Fox Rd	Saint Paul	MN	55112	651-633-2556	628-7459
TF: 800-258-5361 ■ *Web:* www.smiths-medical.com					
Sorin Group USA Inc 14401 W 65th Way	Arvada	CO	80004	303-425-5508	425-5508
TF: 800-289-5759 ■ *Web:* www.sorin.com					
SpectruMedix Corp 2124 Old Gatesburg Rd	State College	PA	16803	814-867-8600	867-4513
Web: www.spectrumedix.com					
SS White Medical Products Inc 151 Old New Brunswick Rd	Piscataway	NJ	08854	732-752-8300	752-8315
TF Cust Svc: 888-779-4483 ■ *Web:* www.sswhitemedical.com					
STERIS Corp 5960 Heisley Rd	Mentor	OH	44060	440-354-2600	639-4450*
NYSE: STE ■ **Fax:* Cust Svc ■ *TF:* 800-548-4873 ■ *Web:* www.steris.com					
Stryker Corp 2825 Airview Blvd	Kalamazoo	MI	49002	269-385-2600	385-1062
NYSE: SYK ■ *TF:* 800-726-2725 ■ *Web:* www.stryker.com					
Stryker Instruments 4100 E Milham Ave	Kalamazoo	MI	49001	269-323-7700	324-5367
TF Cust Svc: 800-253-3210 ■ *Web:* www.stryker.com/instruments					
Sunrise Medical Continuing Care Group 5001 Joerns Dr	Stevens Point	WI	54481	715-341-3600	341-3962
TF: 800-972-7581					
Synergetics USA Inc 3845 Corporate Ctr Dr	O"Fallon	MO	63368	636-939-5100	939-6885
NASDAQ: SURG ■ *TF:* 800-600-0565 ■ *Web:* www.synergeticsusa.com					
Techno-Aide Inc 7117 Centennial Blvd	Nashville	TN	37209	615-350-7030	350-7879
TF: 800-251-2629 ■ *Web:* www.techno-aide.com					
Teleflex Medical Group 2917 Weck Dr PO Box 12600	Research Triangle Park	NC	27709	919-544-8000	361-3914
TF: 866-246-6990 ■ *Web:* www.teleflex.com					
Terumo Cardiovascular Systems Corp 6200 Jackson Rd	Ann Arbor	MI	48103	734-663-4145	292-6551*
**Fax Area Code:* 800 ■ **Fax:* Cust Svc ■ *TF:* 800-262-3304 ■ *Web:* www.terumo-us.com					
Terumo Medical Corp 2101 Cottontail Ln	Somerset	NJ	08873	732-302-4900	302-3083
TF: 800-283-7866 ■ *Web:* www.terumomedical.com					
TFX Medical Inc 50 Plantation Dr	Jaffrey	NH	03452	603-532-7706	532-8211
TF: 800-548-6600 ■ *Web:* www.teleflexmedicaloem.com					
Topcon Medical Systems Inc 111 Bauer Dr	Oakland	NJ	07436	201-599-5100	599-5250
TF: 800-223-1130 ■ *Web:* www.topconmedical.com					
Trans1 Inc 301 Government Ctr Dr	Wilmington	NC	28403	910-332-1700	332-1701
NASDAQ: TSON ■ *TF:* 866-256-1206 ■ *Web:* www.trans1.com					
United States Endoscopy Group Inc 5976 Heisley Rd	Mentor	OH	44060	440-639-4494	639-4494
TF: 800-769-8226 ■ *Web:* www.usendoscopy.com					
Urologix Inc 14405 21st Ave N	Minneapolis	MN	55447	763-475-1400	475-1443
NASDAQ: ULGX ■ *TF:* 800-475-1403 ■ *Web:* www.urologix.com					
Uroplasty Inc 5420 Feltl Rd	Minnetonka	MN	55413	952-426-6140	426-6199
AMEX: UPI ■ *Web:* www.uroplasty.com					
US Surgical Corp 150 Glover Ave	Norwalk	CT	06856	203-845-1000	544-8772*
**Fax Area Code:* 800 ■ **Fax:* Cust Svc ■ *TF:* 800-722-8772					
Utah Medical Products Inc 7043 S 300 W	Midvale	UT	84047	801-566-1200	566-2062
NASDAQ: UTMD ■ *TF:* 800-533-4984 ■ *Web:* www.utahmed.com					
vasamed 7615 Golden Triangle Dr Suite C	Eden Prairie	MN	55344	952-944-5857	944-6022
TF: 800-695-2737 ■ *Web:* www.vasamed.com					
Vascular Solutions Inc 6464 Sycamore Ct	Minneapolis	MN	55369	763-656-4300	656-4251
NASDAQ: VASC ■ *TF:* 888-240-6001 ■ *Web:* www.vascularsolutions.com					
Ventana Medical Systems Inc 1910 Innovation Pk Dr	Tucson	AZ	85755	520-887-2155	887-2558
NASDAQ: VMSI ■ *TF:* 800-227-2155 ■ *Web:* www.ventanamed.com					
VirtualScopics Inc 350 Linden Oaks	Rochester	NY	14625	585-249-6231	218-7350
NASDAQ: VSCP ■ *Web:* www.virtualscopics.com					
Vital Signs Inc 20 Campus Rd	Totowa	NJ	07512	973-790-1330	790-3307
TF: 800-932-0760 ■ *Web:* www.vital-signs.com					
VNUS Medical Technologies Inc 5799 Fontanoso Way	San Jose	CA	95138	408-360-7200	365-8480
TF: 888-797-8346 ■ *Web:* www.vnus.com					
Walco International Inc 7 Village Cir Suite 200	Westlake	TX	76262	817-859-3000	859-3099
TF: 877-289-9252 ■ *Web:* www.walcoinc.com					
Wescor Inc 370 W 1700 S	Logan	UT	84321	435-752-6011	752-4127
TF: 800-453-2725 ■ *Web:* www.wescor.com					

480 MEDICAL SUPPLIES - MFR

SEE ALSO Personal Protective Equipment & Clothing p. 2409

Company / Address	City	State	Zip	Phone	Fax
3M Health Care Solutions 3M Ctr	Saint Paul	MN	55144	651-733-1110	733-9973
TF Prod Info: 888-364-3577 ■ *Web:* solutions.3m.com/wps/portal/3M/en_US/Products/ProdServ/Dir/HealthCare					
Abbott Vascular 400 Saginaw Dr	Redwood City	CA	94063	650-474-3000	474-3010
TF: 800-587-7965 ■ *Web:* www.abbottvascular.com					
Adhesives Research Inc 400 Seaks Run Rd PO Box 100	Glen Rock	PA	17327	717-235-7979	235-8320
TF: 800-445-6240 ■ *Web:* www.adhesivesresearch.com					
Adroit Medical Systems Inc 1146 Carding Machine Rd	Loudon	TN	37774	800-267-6077	267-6077
TF: 800-267-6077 ■ *Web:* www.adroitmedical.com					
Advanced Sterilization Products (ASP) 33 Technology Dr	Irvine	CA	92618	888-783-7723	450-6800*
**Fax Area Code:* 949 ■ **Fax:* Sales ■ *TF:* 800-595-0200 ■ *Web:* www.aspjj.com					
AESCULAP Inc 3773 Corporate Pkwy	Center Valley	PA	18034	800-282-9000	791-6886*
**Fax Area Code:* 610 ■ *TF:* 800-282-9000 ■ *Web:* www.aesculapusa.com					
Allergan 2525 Dupont Dr PO Box 19534	Irvine	CA	92612	714-246-4500	246-6987
TF: 800-347-4500 ■ *Web:* www.allergan.com					
Allied Healthcare Products Inc 1720 Sublette Ave	Saint Louis	MO	63110	314-771-2400	477-7701*
NASDAQ: AHPI ■ **Fax Area Code:* 800 ■ **Fax:* Cust Svc ■ *TF:* 800-444-3954 ■ *Web:* www.alliedhpi.com					
American Medical Systems Holdings Inc 10700 Bren Rd W	Minnetonka	MN	55343	952-930-6000	930-6373
NASDAQ: AMMD ■ *TF:* 800-328-3881 ■ *Web:* www.americanmedicalsystems.com					
Animas Corp 200 Lawrence Dr	West Chester	PA	19380	610-644-8990	644-8717
TF: 877-937-7867 ■ *Web:* www.animas.com					
Arizant Inc 10393 W 70th St	Eden Prairie	MN	55344	952-947-1200	947-1400
TF: 800-733-7775 ■ *Web:* www.arizant.com					
Armstrong Medical Industries Inc 575 Knightsbridge Pkwy	Lincolnshire	IL	60069	847-913-0101	913-0138
TF Cust Svc: 800-323-4220 ■ *Web:* www.armstrongmedical.com					
Arthrex Inc 1370 Creekside Blvd	Naples	FL	34108	239-643-5553	591-6980
TF: 800-934-4404 ■ *Web:* www.arthrex.com					
Aso LLC 300 Sarasota Ctr Blvd	Sarasota	FL	34240	941-379-0300	378-9040
Web: www.asocorp.com					
Aspen Surgical 6945 Southbelt Dr SE	Caledonia	MI	49316	616-698-7100	698-0525
TF: 888-364-7004 ■ *Web:* www.aspensurgical.com					
Avery Dennison Corp 150 N Orange Grove Blvd	Pasadena	CA	91103	626-304-2000	304-2192
NYSE: AVY ■ *TF Cust Svc:* 800-252-8379 ■ *Web:* www.averydennison.com					
Avitar Inc 65 Dan Rd	Canton	MA	02021	781-821-2440	821-4458
PINK: AVTI ■ *TF:* 800-255-0511					
Baxter International Inc 1 Baxter Pkwy	Deerfield	IL	60015	847-948-2000	948-3948
NYSE: BAX ■ *Web:* www.baxter.com					
Becton Dickinson & Co 1 Becton Dr	Franklin Lakes	NJ	07417	201-847-6800	847-4882*
NYSE: BDX ■ **Fax:* Cust Svc ■ *TF Cust Svc:* 888-237-2762 ■ *Web:* www.bd.com					
Becton Dickinson Consumer Healthcare 1 Becton Dr	Franklin Lakes	NJ	07417	201-847-6800	
TF: 888-237-2762 ■ *Web:* www.bd.com/consumer					
Beiersdorf North America 187 Danbury Rd	Wilton	CT	06897	203-563-5800	854-8112*
**Fax:* Hum Res ■ *TF:* 800-233-2340 ■ *Web:* www.beiersdorf.com					
Beltone Electronics Corp 2601 Patriot Blvd	Glenview	IL	60026	847-832-3300	832-3201
TF: 800-235-8663 ■ *Web:* www.beltone.com					
BioHorizons Inc 2300 Riverchase Ctr	Birmingham	AL	35244	205-967-7880	870-0304
TF: 888-246-8338 ■ *Web:* www.biohorizons.com					
Biomet Inc 56 E Bell Dr PO Box 587	Warsaw	IN	46582	574-267-6639	267-8137
TF: 800-348-9500 ■ *Web:* www.biomet.com					
Bristol-Myers Squibb Co 345 Pk Ave	New York	NY	10154	212-546-4000	546-4020
NYSE: BMY ■ *Web:* www.bms.com					
BSN Medical Inc 5825 Carnegie Blvd	Charlotte	NC	28209	704-331-0600	331-8785
TF: 800-552-1157 ■ *Web:* www.bsnmedical.com					
Burke Mobility Products Inc 1800 Merriam Ln	Kansas City	KS	66106	913-722-5658	722-2614
TF Sales: 800-255-4147					
Centurion Medical Products 100 Centurion Way	Williamston	MI	48895	517-546-5400	546-9388
TF: 800-248-4058 ■ *Web:* www.tshsc.com					
Chattanooga Group 4717 Adams Rd	Hixson	TN	37343	423-870-2281	870-7402
TF: 800-592-7329 ■ *Web:* www.chattgroup.com					
CMS Industries Ltd 1320 Alberta Ave	Saskatoon	SK	S7K1R5	306-955-8821	955-3090
TF: 800-668-8821 ■ *Web:* www.redimedic1.com					
Codman & Shurtleff Inc 325 Paramount Dr	Raynham	MA	02767	508-880-8100	880-8122
TF: 800-225-0460 ■ *Web:* www.depuy.com/about-depuy/depuy-divisions/about-codman					
Community Surgical Supply Inc 1390 Rt 37 W	Toms River	NJ	08757	732-349-2990	244-7588
TF: 800-349-2990 ■ *Web:* www.communitysurgical.com					
Connecticut Hypodermics Inc 519 Main St	Yalesville	CT	06492	203-265-4881	284-1520
Web: www.connhypo.com					
Covidien 15 Hampshire St	Mansfield	MA	02048	508-261-8000	
NYSE: COV ■ *Web:* www.covidien.com					
CR Bard Inc 730 Central Ave	Murray Hill	NJ	07974	908-277-8000	
NYSE: BCR ■ *Web:* www.crbard.com					
Cramer Products Inc 153 W Warren St	Gardner	KS	66030	913-856-7511	884-5626
TF: 800-345-2231 ■ *Web:* www.cramersportsmed.com					
Cyberonics Inc 100 Cyberonics Blvd The Cyberonics Bldg	Houston	TX	77058	281-228-7262	218-9332
NASDAQ: CYBX ■ *TF:* 800-332-1375 ■ *Web:* www.cyberonics.com					
DePuy Inc 700 225 E	Warsaw	IN	46582	574-267-8143	371-4847
TF: 800-473-3789 ■ *Web:* www.depuy.com					
DeRoyal Industries Inc 200 DeBusk Ln	Powell	TN	37849	865-938-7828	362-1245*
**Fax:* Hum Res ■ *TF:* 800-251-9864 ■ *Web:* www.deroyal.com					
DJ Orthopedics Inc 1430 Decision St	Vista	CA	92081	760-727-1280	936-6569*
NYSE: DJO ■ **Fax Area Code:* 800 ■ *TF:* 800-321-9549 ■ *Web:* www.djoglobal.com					
Ehob Inc 250 N Belmont Ave	Indianapolis	IN	46222	317-972-4600	972-4601
TF: 800-899-5553 ■ *Web:* www.ehob.com					
Electric Mobility Corp 1 Mobility Plaza	Sewell	NJ	08080	856-468-0270	468-3426
TF Cust Svc: 800-257-7955 ■ *Web:* www.electricmobility.com					
Environmental Tectonics Corp 125 James Way	SouthHampton	PA	18966	215-355-9100	357-4000
OTC: ETCC ■ *Web:* www.etcusa.com					
Ergodyne Corp 1410 Energy Pk Dr Suite 1	Saint Paul	MN	55108	651-642-9889	642-1882
TF: 800-225-8238 ■ *Web:* www.ergodyne.com					
Ethicon Inc US Hwy 22 W PO Box 151	Somerville	NJ	08876	908-218-0707	
Web: www.ethiconinc.com					
Exactech Inc 2320 NW 66th Ct	Gainesville	FL	32653	352-377-1140	378-2617
NASDAQ: EXAC ■ *TF:* 800-392-2832 ■ *Web:* www.exac.com					
Female Health Co 515 N State St Suite 2225	Chicago	IL	60610	312-595-9123	595-9122
TF: 800-635-0844 ■ *Web:* www.femalehealth.com					
Ferno-Washington Inc 70 Weil Way	Wilmington	OH	45177	937-382-1451	382-1191
TF: 800-733-3766 ■ *Web:* www.ferno.com					

Phone Fax

Fillauer Inc PO Box 5189 . . . Chattanooga TN 37406 423-624-0946 629-7936
TF: 800-251-6398 ■ *Web:* www.fillauer.com

Freeman Mfg Co 900 W Chicago Rd PO Box J . . . Sturgis MI 49091 269-651-2371 651-8248
TF: 800-253-2091 ■ *Web:* www.freemanmfg.com

GF Health Products Inc 2935 NE Pkwy . . . Atlanta GA 30360 770-447-1609 726-0601*
**Fax Area Code:* 800 ■ *TF:* 800-235-4661 ■ *Web:* www.grahamfield.com

GN ReSound Corp 8001 Bloomington Fwy . . . Bloomington MN 55420 952-769-8000 469-8001
TF: 800-248-4327 ■ *Web:* www.gnresound-group.com

Gyrus Medical Inc ENT Div 2925 Appling Rd . . . Bartlett TN 38133 901-373-0200 373-0237
TF: 800-262-3540 ■ *Web:* www.gyrus-ent.com

Hanger Orthopedic Group Inc
10910 Domain Dr Suite 300 . . . Austin TX 78758 301-986-0701 986-0702
NYSE: HGR ■ *TF:* 877-442-6437 ■ *Web:* www.hanger.com

Hanger Prosthetics & Orthopedics Inc
10910 Domain Dr Suite 300 . . . Austin TX 78758 877-442-6437
TF: 877-442-6437 ■ *Web:* www.hanger.com

Helix Medical LLC 1110 Mark Ave . . . Carpinteria CA 93013 805-684-3304 566-5395
TF: 800-266-4421 ■ *Web:* www.helixmed.com

Helvoet Pharma Inc 9012 Pennsauken Hwy . . . Pennsauken NJ 08110 856-663-2202 663-2636
TF: 800-874-3586 ■ *Web:* www.helvoetpharma.com

Hightech American Industrial Laboratories Inc (HAI)
320 Massachusetts Ave . . . Lexington MA 02420 781-862-9884 860-7722
Web: www.hailabs.com

Hollister Inc 2000 Hollister Dr . . . Libertyville IL 60048 847-680-1000 918-3446*
**Fax:* Hum Res ■ *TF:* 800-323-4060 ■ *Web:* www.hollister.com

Hosmer-Dorrance Corp 561 Division St . . . Campbell CA 95008 408-379-5151 379-5263
Web: www.hosmer.com

Hospira Inc 275 N Field Dr . . . Lake Forest IL 60045 224-212-2000
NYSE: HSP ■ *TF:* 877-946-7747 ■ *Web:* www.hospira.com

Hoveround Corp
2151 Whitfield Industrial Way . . . Sarasota FL 34243 941-739-6200 727-8686
TF: 800-701-3021 ■ *Web:* www.hoveround.com

Howard Leight Industries
7828 Waterville Rd . . . San Diego CA 92154 619-661-8383 232-3110*
**Fax Area Code:* 401 ■ *Web:* www.howardleight.com

Hy-Tape International Inc
70 Jon Barrett Rd . . . Patterson NY 12563 845-878-4848 878-4104
TF: 800-248-0101 ■ *Web:* www.hytape.com

I-Flow Corp 20202 Windrow Dr . . . Lake Forest CA 92663 949-206-2700 206-2600
TF: 800-448-3569 ■ *Web:* www.iflo.com

ICU Medical Inc 951 Calle Amanecer . . . San Clemente CA 92673 949-366-2183 366-8368
NASDAQ: ICUI ■ *TF:* 800-824-7890 ■ *Web:* www.icumed.com

Ideal Tape Co 1400 Middlesex St . . . Lowell MA 01851 978-458-6833 458-0302
TF: 800-284-3325 ■ *Web:* www.idealtape.com

Independence Technology LLC 45 Technology Dr . . . Warren NJ 07059 908-412-2200 412-2205
TF: 888-463-3000 ■ *Web:* www.independencenow.com

International Technidyne Corp 8 Olsen Ave . . . Edison NJ 08820 732-548-5700 548-2419
TF: 800-631-5945 ■ *Web:* www.itcmed.com

Invacare Corp 1 Invacare Way . . . Elyria OH 44036 440-329-6000 619-7996*
NYSE: IVC ■ **Fax Area Code:* 877 ■ *TF:* 800-333-6900 ■ *Web:* www.invacare.com

Iowa Veterinary Supply Co (IVESCO)
124 Country Club Rd . . . Iowa Falls IA 50126 641-648-2529 648-5994
TF: 800-457-0118 ■ *Web:* www.ivescollc.com

Johnson & Johnson Consumer Products Co
199 Grandview Rd . . . Skillman NJ 08558 908-874-1000
TF: 800-526-3967 ■ *Web:* www.johnsonsbaby.com

Johnson & Johnson Inc 7101 Notre-Dame E . . . Montreal QC H1N2G4 514-251-5100 251-6233
TF: 800-361-8990 ■ *Web:* www.jnjcanada.com

K-Tube Technologies 13400 Kirkham Way . . . Poway CA 92064 858-513-9229 513-9459
TF: 800-394-0058 ■ *Web:* www.k-tube.com

Kimberly-Clark (KCWW) PO Box 619100 . . . Dallas TX 75261 972-281-1200 281-1435
NYSE: KMB ■ *TF:* 800-321-1435 ■ *Web:* www.kimberly-clark.com

Kimberly-Clark Corp Professional Health Care Business
1400 Holcomb Bridge Rd . . . Roswell GA 30076 770-587-8000 587-7718
Web: www.kchealthcare.com

Kimberly-Clark/Ballard Medical Products
1175 Northmeadow Pkwy . . . Roswell GA 30076 800-524-3577 572-6999*
**Fax Area Code:* 801 ■ *TF:* 800-528-5591 ■ *Web:* www.kchealthcare.com

Kinetic Concepts Inc (KCI)
8023 Vantage Dr PO Box 659508 . . . San Antonio TX 78230 210-524-9000 255-6992*
NYSE: KCI ■ **Fax:* Hum Res ■ *TF Cust Svc:* 800-275-4524 ■ *Web:* www.kci1.com

Kloehn Inc 10000 Banburry Cross Dr . . . Las Vegas NV 89144 702-243-7727 243-6036
TF: 800-358-4342 ■ *Web:* www.kloehn.com

Kyphon Inc 1221 Crossman Ave . . . Sunnyvale CA 94089 408-548-6500 548-6501
TF: 877-459-7466 ■ *Web:* www.kyphon.com

Langer Inc 450 Commack Rd . . . Deer Park NY 11729 631-667-1200 667-1203
NASDAQ: GAIT ■ *TF:* 800-645-5520 ■ *Web:* www.langerbiomechanics.com

Leisure Lift 1800 Merriam Ln . . . Kansas City KS 66106 913-722-5658 722-2614
TF: 800-255-0285 ■ *Web:* www.pacesaver.com

LPS Industries Inc 10 Caesar Pl . . . Moonachie NJ 07074 201-438-3515 438-0040
TF Sales: 800-275-4577 ■ *Web:* www.lpsind.com

M & C Specialties Co 90 James Way . . . SouthHampton PA 18966 215-322-1600 322-1620
TF Cust Svc: 800-441-6996 ■ *Web:* www.mcspecialties.com

Martech Medical Products Inc
1500 Delp Dr . . . Harleysville PA 19438 215-256-8833 256-8837
Web: www.martechmedical.com

Medaire Inc 1250 W Washington St Suite 442 . . . Tempe AZ 85281 480-333-3700 333-3592
Web: www.medaire.com

Medical Action Industries Inc
500 Expy Dr S . . . Brentwood NY 11717 631-231-4600 231-3075
NASDAQ: MDCI ■ *TF:* 800-645-7042 ■ *Web:* www.medical-action.com

Medrad Inc 1 Medrad Dr . . . Indianola PA 15051 412-767-2400 767-4120*
**Fax:* Cust Svc ■ *TF Cust Svc:* 800-633-7237 ■ *Web:* www.medrad.com

Medtronic Inc 710 Medtronic Pkwy NE . . . Minneapolis MN 55432 763-514-4000 514-4879
NYSE: MDT ■ *TF Cust Svc:* 800-328-2518 ■ *Web:* www.medtronic.com

Medtronic Inc Heart Valve Div
1851 E Deere Ave . . . Santa Ana CA 92705 949-474-3943 474-3953
TF: 800-326-3330 ■ *Web:* www.medtronic.com

Medtronic MiniMed Inc 18000 Devonshire St . . . Northridge CA 91325 818-362-5958
TF: 800-933-3322 ■ *Web:* www.minimed.com

Medtronic Powered Surgical Solutions
4620 N Beach St . . . Fort Worth TX 76137 817-788-6400 788-6401*
**Fax:* Orders ■ *TF:* 800-643-2773 ■
Web: www.medtronic.com/for-healthcare-professionals/business-unit-landing-Page

Medtronic Xomed Inc
6743 Southpoint Dr N . . . Jacksonville FL 32216 904-296-9600 279-7593*
**Fax:* Hum Res ■ *TF:* 800-874-5797 ■ *Web:* www.xomed.com

Mentor Corp 201 Mentor Dr . . . Santa Barbara CA 93111 805-879-6000
NYSE: MNT ■ *TF:* 800-525-0245 ■ *Web:* www.mentorwwllc.com

Microtek Medical Holdings Inc
13000 Deerfield Pkwy Suite 300 . . . Alpharetta GA 30004 678-896-4400 896-4297
TF: 800-777-7977 ■ *Web:* www.microtekmed.com

Microtek Medical Inc 512 N Lehmberg Rd . . . Columbus MS 39702 662-327-1863 327-5921
TF: 800-824-3027 ■ *Web:* www.microtekmed.com

MicroVention Inc 1311 Valencia Ave . . . Tustin CA 92780 714-247-8000
TF: 800-990-8368 ■ *Web:* www.microvention.com

Micrus Endovascular 821 Fox Ln . . . San Jose CA 95131 408-433-1400 433-1401
TF Cust Svc: 888-550-4120 ■ *Web:* www.micruscorp.com

Milestone Scientific Inc 220 S Orange Ave . . . Livingston NJ 07039 973-535-2717 535-2829
TF: 800-862-1125 ■ *Web:* www.milestonescientific.com

Miracle-Ear Inc 5000 Cheshire Ln N Suite 1 . . . Plymouth MN 55446 763-268-4000 268-4365
TF: 800-234-7714 ■ *Web:* www.miracle-ear.com

MP Biomedicals LLC
3 Hutton Ctr Dr Suite 100 . . . Santa Ana CA 92707 949-833-2500 421-2539
TF: 800-633-1352 ■ *Web:* www.mpbio.com

National Fab 9561 Satellite Blvd Suite 350 . . . Orlando FL 32837 407-852-6170 852-6171
TF: 877-265-1491

NELCO Inc 800 W Cummings Pk Suite 3950 . . . Woburn MA 01801 781-933-1940 933-4763
TF: 800-635-2613 ■ *Web:* www.nelco-usa.com

Nice-Pak Products Inc 2 Nice-Pak Pk . . . Orangeburg NY 10962 845-365-1700 365-1717
TF: 800-999-6423 ■ *Web:* www.nicepak.com

Nonin Medical Inc 13700 1st Ave N Suite A . . . Plymouth MN 55441 763-553-9968 577-5500
Web: www.nonin.com

NorMed 4310 S 131 Pl . . . Seattle WA 98168 800-288-8200 242-3315*
**Fax Area Code:* 206 ■ *TF:* 800-288-8200 ■ *Web:* www.normed.com

Ortho Development Corp 12187 S Business Pk Dr . . . Draper UT 84020 801-553-9991 553-9993
TF: 800-429-8339 ■ *Web:* www.odev.com

Orthofix Inc 1720 Bray Central Dr . . . McKinney TX 75069 469-742-2500 742-2556
TF: 800-527-0404 ■ *Web:* www.orthofix.com

OrthoLogic Corp 1275 W Washington St Suite 101 . . . Tempe AZ 85281 602-286-5520 926-2616
NASDAQ: OLGC ■ *TF:* 800-937-5520 ■ *Web:* www.capstonethx.com

Orthovita Inc 77 Great Valley Pkwy . . . Malvern PA 19355 610-640-1775 640-2603
NASDAQ: VITA ■ *TF:* 800-676-8482 ■ *Web:* www.orthovita.com

Osteomed Corp 3885 Arapaho Rd . . . Addison TX 75001 972-677-4600 677-4601
TF Cust Svc: 800-456-7779 ■ *Web:* www.osteomedcorp.com

Pacific Medical Inc 1700 N Chrisman Rd . . . Tracy CA 95304 800-726-9180 861-5950
Web: www.pacmedical.com

Perma-Type Co Inc 83 NW Dr . . . Plainville CT 06062 860-747-9999 747-1986
TF: 800-243-4234 ■ *Web:* www.perma-type.com

Phonic Ear Inc 2080 Lakeville Hwy . . . Petaluma CA 94954 707-769-1110 781-9415
TF: 800-227-0735 ■ *Web:* www.phonicear.com

Posey Co 5635 Peck Rd . . . Arcadia CA 91006 626-443-3143 767-3933*
**Fax Area Code:* 800 ■ *TF:* 800-447-6739 ■ *Web:* www.posey.com

Precision Dynamics Corp
13880 Del Sur St . . . San Fernando CA 91340 818-897-1111 899-4045
TF: 800-847-0670 ■ *Web:* www.pdcorp.com

Precision Technology Inc 50 Maple St . . . Norwood NJ 07648 201-767-1600 767-6739
Web: www.ptiplastics.com

Pride Mobility Products Corp
182 Susquehanna Ave . . . Exeter PA 18643 800-800-8586 800-1636
TF: 800-800-8586 ■ *Web:* www.pridemobility.com

Rehab Plus Therapeutics Products Inc
105 Industrial Dr . . . Wolfforth TX 79382 806-791-2288 791-2288
TF: 800-288-8059

Retractable Technologies Inc 511 Lobo Ln . . . Little Elm TX 75068 972-294-1010 294-4400
AMEX: RVP ■ *TF:* 888-806-2626 ■ *Web:* www.vanishpoint.com

Rockford Medical & Safety Co
2420 Harrison Ave . . . Rockford IL 61108 815-394-4809 394-0320
TF: 800-541-2528 ■ *Web:* www.firensafety.com

Rusch Inc
2917 Weck Dr PO Box 12600 . . . Research Triangle Park NC 27009 919-544-8000 361-3914
TF: 866-246-6990 ■ *Web:* www.teleflex.com/en/usa/prod_rusch.php

Saint Jude Medical Inc 1 Lillehei Plaza . . . Saint Paul MN 55117 651-483-2000 756-3301
NYSE: STJ ■ *TF:* 800-328-9634 ■ *Web:* www.sjm.com

Sas Safety Corp 3031 Gardenia Ave . . . Long Beach CA 90807 562-427-2775 427-4646
TF: 800-262-0200 ■ *Web:* www.sassafety.com

SCOOTER Store Inc 1650 Independence Dr . . . New Braunfels TX 78132 830-626-5600 620-4598
TF: 800-723-4535 ■ *Web:* www.thescooterstore.com

Seattle Systems Inc 26296 Twelve Trees Ln NW . . . Poulsbo WA 98370 360-697-5656 697-5879
TF: 800-248-6463

Siemens Hearing Instruments Inc
10 Constitution Ave PO Box 1397 . . . Piscataway NJ 08855 800-766-4500 562-6696*
**Fax Area Code:* 732 ■ *TF:* 800-766-4500 ■ *Web:* www.medical.siemens.com

Smith & Nephew Inc 1450 E Brooks Rd . . . Memphis TN 38116 901-396-2121 396-9929
TF Cust Svc: 800-238-7538 ■ *Web:* www.smith-nephew.com

Smith & Nephew Inc Orthopaedic Div
1450 Brooks Rd . . . Memphis TN 38116 901-396-2121 621-6924*
**Fax Area Code:* 800 ■ *TF:* 800-821-5700 ■ *Web:* www.smith-nephew.com

Smith & Nephew Inc Wound Management Div
11775 Starkey Rd . . . Largo FL 33773 727-392-1261 392-6914
TF Cust Svc: 800-876-1261 ■ *Web:* www.smith-nephew.com/what/wound.jsp

Smiths Medical ASD Inc 160 Weymouth St . . . Rockland MA 02370 781-878-8011 878-8201
TF: 800-553-8352 ■ *Web:* www.smiths-medical.com

Smiths Medical MD Inc 1265 Grey Fox Rd . . . Saint Paul MN 55112 651-633-2556 628-7459
TF: 800-258-5361 ■ *Web:* www.smiths-medical.com

Smiths Medical Respiratory Support Products
9255 Custom House Plaza Suite N . . . San Diego CA 92154 619-710-1000
TF: 800-258-5361

Sonic Innovations Inc
4246 Riverboat Rd Suite 300 . . . Salt Lake City UT 84123 801-365-2800 365-3000
NASDAQ: SNCI ■ *TF:* 888-678-4327 ■ *Web:* www.sonicinnovations.com

Span-America Medical Systems Inc
70 Commerce Ctr . . . Greenville SC 29615 864-288-8877 288-8692
NASDAQ: SPAN ■ *TF:* 800-888-6752 ■ *Web:* www.spanamerica.com

	City	State	ZIP	Phone	Fax
SpectRx Inc 5835 Peachtree cr E Suite D *OTC: GTHP* ■ *Web:* www.guidedinc.com	Norcross	GA	30092	770-242-8723	242-8639
Spenco Medical Corp PO Box 2501 *TF:* 800-877-3626 ■ *Web:* www.spenco.com	Waco	TX	76702	254-772-6000	
SRI/Surgical Express Inc 12425 Race Track Rd *NASDAQ: STRC*	Tampa	FL	33626	813-891-9550	726-8959
SSL Americas Inc 3585 Engineering Dr Suite 200 *TF:* 888-387-3927 ■ *Web:* www.ssl-international.com	Norcross	GA	30092	770-582-2222	582-2233
Standard Textile Co Inc 1 Knollcrest Dr *TF:* 800-888-5000 ■ *Web:* www.standardtextile.com	Cincinnati	OH	45237	513-761-9255	761-0467
Starkey Laboratories Inc 6700 Washington Ave S *TF:* 800-328-8602 ■ *Web:* www.starkey.com	Eden Prairie	MN	55344	952-941-6401	828-6972
STERIS Corp 5960 Heisley Rd *NYSE: STE* ■ **Fax:* Cust Svc ■ *TF:* 800-548-4873 ■ *Web:* www.steris.com	Mentor	OH	44060	440-354-2600	639-4450*
Sunrise Medical Inc 2842 Business Pk Ave *TF:* 800-333-4000 ■ *Web:* www.sunrisemedical.com	Fresno	CA	93727	800-333-4000	
Surgical Appliance Industries Inc 3960 Rosslyn Dr **Fax Area Code:* 800 ■ *TF:* 800-888-0458 ■ *Web:* www.surgicalappliance.com	Cincinnati	OH	45209	513-271-4594	309-9055*
Symmetry Medical Inc 3724 N State Rd 15 *NYSE: SMA* ■ *Web:* www.symmetrymedical.com	Warsaw	IN	46582	574-268-2252	267-4551
Synovis Life Technologies Inc 2575 University Ave *NASDAQ: SYNO* ■ *TF:* 800-255-4018 ■ *Web:* www.synovislife.com	Saint Paul	MN	55114	651-796-7300	642-9018
Synthes USA 1302 Wrights Ln E	West Chester	PA	19380	610-719-5000	251-5046*
TIDI Products LLC 570 Enterprise Dr *TF:* 800-215-5464 ■ *Web:* www.tidiproducts.com	Neenah	WI	54956	800-521-1314	837-7770
Tillotson Healthcare Corp 8-10 Glenshaw St *TF:* 800-445-6830 ■ *Web:* www.thcnet.com	Orangeburg	NY	10962	845-365-8200	365-8201
Utah Medical Products Inc 7043 S 300 W *NASDAQ: UTMD* ■ *TF:* 800-533-4984 ■ *Web:* www.utahmed.com	Midvale	UT	84047	801-566-1200	566-2062
Venture Tape Corp 30 Commerce Rd *TF:* 800-343-1076 ■ *Web:* www.venturetape.com	Rockland	MA	02370	781-331-5900	871-0065
Vital Signs Inc 20 Campus Rd *TF:* 800-932-0760 ■ *Web:* www.vital-signs.com	Totowa	NJ	07512	973-790-1330	790-3307
Volcano Corp 3661 Valley Centre Dr Suite 200 **Fax Area Code:* 916 ■ *TF:* 800-228-4728 ■ *Web:* www.volcanocorp.com	San Diego	CA	92130	800-228-4728	638-8812*
West Pharmaceutical Services Inc 101 Gordon Dr *NYSE: WST* ■ *TF:* 800-345-9800 ■ *Web:* www.westpharma.com	Lionville	PA	19341	610-594-2900	594-3000
Wright & Filippis Inc 2845 Crooks Rd *TF:* 888-255-5585 ■ *Web:* www.firsttoserve.com	Rochester Hills	MI	48309	248-829-8200	853-1830
Wright Medical Group Inc 5677 Airline Rd *NASDAQ: WMGI* ■ *TF:* 800-238-7188 ■ *Web:* www.wmt.com	Arlington	TN	38002	901-867-9971	867-9534
Wright Medical Technology Inc 5677 Airline Rd **Fax:* Cust Svc ■ *TF:* 800-238-7188 ■ *Web:* www.wmt.com	Arlington	TN	38002	901-867-9971	867-9534*
Young Innovations Inc 13705 Shoreline Ct E *NASDAQ: YDNT* ■ *TF:* 800-325-1881 ■ *Web:* www.yiinc.com	Earth City	MO	63045	314-344-0010	344-0021
Zimmer Inc 1800 W Ctr St PO Box 708 *NYSE: ZMH* ■ *TF:* 800-613-6131 ■ *Web:* www.zimmer.com	Warsaw	IN	46580	574-267-6131	372-4988

481 MEDICAL TRANSCRIPTION SERVICES

Companies Listed Here Have A National Or Regional Clientele Base.

	City	State	ZIP	Phone	Fax
Acusis LLC 4 Smithfield St *Web:* www.acusis.com	Pittsburgh	PA	15222	412-209-1300	209-1299
MediGrafix Inc 11205 Wright Cir Suite 120 *TF:* 877-284-5147 ■ *Web:* www.medigrafix.com	Omaha	NE	68144	402-333-3323	333-1939
Rapid Transcript Inc 4311 Wilshire Blvd Suite 209 *Web:* www.rapidtranscript.com	Los Angeles	CA	90010	323-964-0400	964-0412
Thomas Transcription Services Inc 550 Balmoral Cir Suite 201 *TF:* 888-878-2889 ■ *Web:* www.thomastx.com	Jacksonville	FL	32218	904-751-5058	751-5240
Webmedx Inc 564 Alpha Dr *TF:* 888-932-6339 ■ *Web:* www.webmedx.com	Pittsburgh	PA	15238	412-968-9244	968-9144

482 MEDICINAL CHEMICALS & BOTANICAL PRODUCTS

SEE ALSO Biotechnology Companies p. 1525; Diagnostic Products p. 1784; Pharmaceutical Companies p. 2414; Pharmaceutical Companies - Generic Drugs p. 2416; Vitamins & Nutritional Supplements p. 2762

Companies Listed Here Manufacture Medicinal Chemicals And Botanical Products In Bulk For Sale To Pharmaceutical, Vitamin, And Nutritional Product Companies.

	City	State	ZIP	Phone	Fax
Acic Fine Chemicals Inc 81 St Claire Blvd *TF:* 800-265-6727 ■ *Web:* www.acic.com	Brantford	ON	N3S7X6	519-751-3668	751-1378
Advitech Inc 1150, Rue de Claire-Fontaine 7e étage *Web:* www.advitech.com	Quebec	QC	G1R5G4	418-948-4084	686-2446
AF-Zeta Inc 163 Madison Ave *Web:* www.afzeta.en.chemnet.com	Morristown	NJ	07960	973-267-2205	267-2208
AM Todd Co 1717 Douglas Ave *TF:* 800-968-2603 ■ *Web:* www.amtodd.com	Kalamazoo	MI	49007	269-343-2603	343-3399
American Laboratories Inc (ALI) 4410 S 102nd St *TF Cust Svc:* 800-445-5989 ■ *Web:* www.americanlaboratories.com	Omaha	NE	68127	402-339-2494	339-0801
Anika Therapeutics Inc 32 Wiggins Ave *NASDAQ: ANIK* ■ *Web:* www.anikatherapeutics.com	Bedford	MA	01730	781-457-9000	305-9720
Apotex Pharmachem Inc 34 Spalding Dr *Web:* www.apotexpharmachem.com	Brantford	ON	N3T6B8	519-756-8942	753-3051
Array BioPharma Inc 3200 Walnut St *NASDAQ: ARRY* ■ *TF:* 877-633-2436 ■ *Web:* www.arraybiopharma.com	Boulder	CO	80301	303-381-6600	449-5376
Avanti Polar Lipids Inc 700 Industrial Pk Dr *TF:* 800-227-0651 ■ *Web:* www.avantilipids.com	Alabaster	AL	35007	205-663-2494	663-0756
Bachem Bioscience Inc 3700 Horizon Dr *TF:* 800-634-3183 ■ *Web:* www.bachem.com	King of Prussia	PA	19406	610-239-0300	239-0800
Balchem Corp 52 Sunrise Pk Rd PO Box 600 *NASDAQ: BCPC* ■ *Web:* www.balchem.com	New Hampton	NY	10958	845-355-5600	326-5742
BCN Chemicals Inc 1320 Rt 9 PO Box 1290 *TF:* 800-661-1226	Champlain	NY	12919	514-630-1044	697-0201
Bedford Laboratories Inc 300 Northfield Rd *TF:* 800-562-4797 ■ *Web:* www.bedfordlabs.com	Bedford	OH	44146	440-232-3320	232-2772
Ben Venue Laboratories Inc 300 Northfield Rd *TF:* 800-562-4797 ■ *Web:* www.benvenue.com	Bedford	OH	44146	440-232-3320	232-2772
Betachem Inc 58 Ware Rd	Upper Saddle River	NJ	07458	201-327-4100	327-9366
BI Nutraceuticals 2550 El Presidio St *Web:* www.botanicals.com	Long Beach	CA	90810	310-669-2100	637-3644
Biddle Sawyer Corp 360 W 31st St 21 Penn Plaza Suite 1102 *TF:* 800-654-7001 ■ *Web:* www.biddlesawyer.com	New York	NY	10001	212-736-1580	239-1089
Bio-Botanica Inc 75 Commerce Dr *TF:* 800-645-5720 ■ *Web:* www.bio-botanica.com	Hauppauge	NY	11788	631-231-5522	231-7332
Blessed Herbs Inc 109 Barre Plains Rd **Fax Area Code:* 508 ■ *TF:* 800-489-4372 ■ *Web:* www.blessedherbs.com	Oakham	MA	01068	774-298-0966	882-3755*
Cambrex Charles City Inc 1205 11th St *TF:* 800-247-1833 ■ *Web:* www.cambrex.com	Charles City	IA	50616	641-257-1000	228-4152
Cambrex Corp 1 Meadowlands Plaza 15th Fl *NYSE: CBM* ■ *TF:* 800-638-8174 ■ *Web:* www.cambrex.com	East Rutherford	NJ	07073	201-804-3000	804-9852
Cedarburg Hauser Pharmaceuticals Inc 870 Badger Cir *Web:* www.cedarburghauser.com	Grafton	WI	53024	262-376-1467	376-1068
Charm Sciences Inc 659 Andover St *TF:* 800-343-2170 ■ *Web:* www.charm.com	Lawrence	MA	01843	978-687-9200	687-9216
Chemical Co The 19 Narragansett Ave *Web:* www.thechemco.com	Jamestown	RI	02835	401-423-3100	423-3102
ChemWerth Inc 1764 Litchfield Tpke *Web:* www.chemwerth.com	Woodbridge	CT	06525	203-387-7794	387-8132
Contract Pharmacal Corp 135 Adams Ave *Web:* www.cpc.com	Hauppauge	NY	11788	631-231-4610	231-4610
Cyanotech Corp 73-4460 Queen Kaahumanu Hwy Suite 102 *NASDAQ: CYAN* ■ *TF Sales:* 800-453-1187 ■ *Web:* www.cyanotech.com	Kailua-Kona	HI	96740	808-326-1353	329-4533
DSM Pharmaceuticals Inc 5900 Martin Luther King Jr Hwy *Web:* www.dsm.com	Greenville	NC	27834	252-758-3436	707-7050
Elge Inc 1000 Cole Ave *Web:* www.elgeinc.com	Rosenberg	TX	77471	281-342-8228	232-0476
Flavine North America Inc 10 Reuten Dr *Web:* www.flavine.com	Closter	NJ	07624	201-768-4190	768-2854
Garden State Nutritionals 8 Henderson Dr *TF:* 800-526-9095 ■ *Web:* www.gardenstatenutritionals.com	West Caldwell	NJ	07006	973-575-9200	575-6782
Gemini Pharmaceuticals Inc 87 Modular Ave *Web:* www.geminipharm.com	Commack	NY	11725	631-543-3334	543-3335
George Uhe Co Inc 219 River Dr *TF:* 800-850-4075 ■ *Web:* www.uhe.com	Garfield	NJ	07026	201-843-4000	843-7517
Greer Laboratories Inc 639 Nuway Cir NE PO Box 800 *TF Cust Svc:* 800-378-3906 ■ *Web:* www.greerlabs.com	Lenoir	NC	28645	828-754-5327	754-5320
GYMA Laboratories of America Inc 135 Cantiague Rock Rd *Web:* www.gyma.com	Westbury	NY	11590	516-933-0900	933-1075
Heel Inc 10421 Research Rd SE *TF:* 800-621-7644 ■ *Web:* www.heelusa.com	Albuquerque	NM	87123	505-293-3843	275-1672
ICC Industries Inc 460 Pk Ave *TF:* 800-422-1720 ■ *Web:* www.iccchem.com	New York	NY	10022	212-521-1700	521-1794
Interchem Corp 120 Rt 17 N *Web:* www.interchem.com	Paramus	NJ	07652	201-261-7333	261-7339
Johnson Matthey Inc Pharmaceutical Materials Div 2003 Nolte Dr *TF:* 800-444-8544 ■ *Web:* www.jmpharma.com	West Deptford	NJ	08066	856-853-8000	384-7186
Johnson Matthey Pharma Services 25 Patton Rd *Web:* www.jmpharmaservices.com	Devens	MA	01434	978-784-5000	784-5500
Lannett Co Inc (LCI) 13200 Townsend Rd *AMEX: LCI* ■ *TF:* 800-325-9994 ■ *Web:* www.lannett.com	Philadelphia	PA	19154	215-333-9000	333-9004
Libby Laboratories Inc 1700 6th St *Web:* www.libbylabs.com	Berkeley	CA	94710	510-527-5400	527-8687
LycoRed Corp 377 Crane St *TF:* 800-631-3424 ■ *Web:* www.lycored.com	Orange	NJ	07051	973-882-0322	882-0323
Mallinckrodt Baker Inc 222 Red School Ln **Fax:* Cust Svc ■ *TF:* 800-582-2537 ■ *Web:* www.mallbaker.com	Phillipsburg	NJ	08865	908-859-2151	859-6905*
Naturex Inc 375 Huyler St *Web:* www.naturex.com	South Hackensack	NJ	07606	201-440-5000	342-8000
NHK Laboratories Inc 12230 E Florience Ave *TF:* 877-645-5227 ■ *Web:* www.nhklabs.com	Santa Fe Springs	CA	90670	562-944-5400	944-0266
Nutraceutix Inc 9609 153rd Ave NE *TF:* 800-548-3222 ■ *Web:* www.nutraceutix.com	Redmond	WA	98052	425-883-9518	869-1020
NutriScience Innovations LLC 2450 Reservoir Ave *Web:* www.nutriscienceusa.com	Trumbull	CT	06611	203-372-8877	372-9977
Nutrition 21 Inc 4 Manhattanville Rd *NASDAQ: NXXI* ■ *TF:* 800-699-3533 ■ *Web:* www.nutrition21.com	Purchase	NY	10577	914-701-4500	696-0860
One Lambda Inc 21001 Kittridge St *TF:* 800-822-8824 ■ *Web:* www.onelambda.com	Canoga Park	CA	91303	818-702-0042	702-6904

Company / Address	City	State	ZIP	Phone	Fax
Paddock Laboratories Inc					
3940 Quebec Ave N	Minneapolis	MN	55427	763-546-4676	546-4842
TF Orders: 800-328-5113 ■ *Web:* www.paddocklabs.com					
Patheon Inc 2100 Syntex Ct	Mississauga	ON	L5N7K9	905-821-4001	812-6709
TF: 888-728-4366 ■ *Web:* www.patheon.com					
PendoPharm Inc					
5950 ch e la Cote-de-Liesse	Mont Royal	QC	H4T1E2	514-340-5045	733-9684
TF: 866-926-7653 ■ *Web:* www.pendopharm.com					
Pharma Tech Industries Inc 1310 Stylemaster Dr	Union	MO	63084	636-583-8664	583-5373
Web: www.pharma-tech.net					
Rainbow Light Nutritional Sys inc					
125 McPherson St	Santa Cruz	CA	95060	831-429-9089	429-0189
TF: 800-635-1233 ■ *Web:* www.rainbowlight.com					
Sabinsa Corp 20 Lake Dr	East Windsor	NJ	08520	732-777-1111	777-1443
Web: www.sabinsa.com					
Savient Pharmaceuticals Inc					
1 Tower Ctr Blvd 14th Fl	East Brunswick	NJ	08816	732-418-9300	418-9235
NASDAQ: SVNT ■ *TF:* 800-284-2480 ■ *Web:* www.savientpharma.com					
Scientific Protein Laboratories Inc					
700 E Main St PO Box 158	Waunakee	WI	53597	608-849-5944	849-4053
TF: 800-334-4775 ■ *Web:* www.spl-pharma.com					
Siegfried USA Inc 33 Industrial Pk Rd	Pennsville	NJ	08070	856-678-3601	678-8201
TF Cust Svc: 877-763-8630					
Sigma-Aldrich Corp 3050 Spruce St	Saint Louis	MO	63103	314-771-5765	325-5052*
NASDAQ: SIAL ■ **Fax Area Code:* 800 ■ *TF:* 800-325-3010 ■ *Web:* www.sigmaaldrich.com					
Spectrum Laboratory Products Inc					
14422 S San Pedro St PO Box 290	Gardena	CA	90248	310-516-8000	516-7512*
**Fax:* Cust Svc ■ *TF:* 800-342-6615 ■ *Web:* www.spectrumchemical.com					
SPI Pharma 321 Cherry Ln	New Castle	DE	19720	302-576-8554	576-8569
TF: 800-789-9755 ■ *Web:* www.spipharma.com					
SST Corp 635 Brighton Rd	Clifton	NJ	07012	973-473-4300	473-4326
TF: 800-222-0921 ■ *Web:* www.sst-corp.com					
Starwest Botanicals Inc					
11253 Trade Ctr Dr	Rancho Cordova	CA	95742	916-638-8100	638-8293
TF: 800-800-4372 ■ *Web:* www.starwestherb.com					
Terry Laboratories Inc 7005 Technology Dr	Melbourne	FL	32904	321-259-1630	242-0625
TF: 800-367-2563 ■ *Web:* www.terrylabs.com					
Tri-K Industries Inc 151 Veterans Dr	Northvale	NJ	07647	201-750-1055	750-9785
TF: 800-526-0372 ■ *Web:* www.tri-k.com					
Truett Laboratories Inc 798 N Coney Ave	Azusa	CA	91702	626-334-4438	969-3026
TSI Health Sciences Inc					
305 S 4th St East Suite 101	Missoula	MT	59808	406-549-9123	549-6139
TF: 877-549-9123 ■ *Web:* www.tsiinc.com					
United-Guardian Inc (UGI)					
230 Marcus Blvd PO Box 18050	Hauppauge	NY	11788	631-273-0900	273-0858
AMEX: UG ■ *TF:* 800-645-5566 ■ *Web:* www.u-g.com					
Vinchem Inc 301 Main St	Chatham	NJ	07928	973-635-4841	635-1459
Web: www.vinchem.com					
Wilcox Emporium Warehouse 161 Howard St	Boone	NC	28607	828-262-1221	264-1408
Web: www.wilcoxemporium.com					

483 METAL - STRUCTURAL (FABRICATED)

Company / Address	City	State	ZIP	Phone	Fax
Aerospace America Inc					
900 Harry Truman Pkwy PO Box 189	Bay City	MI	48706	989-684-2121	684-4486
TF: 800-237-6414 ■ *Web:* www.aerospaceamerica.com					
Afco Mfg Corp 428 Cogshall St PO Box 230	Holly	MI	48442	248-634-4415	634-6301
TF: 800-743-4415 ■ *Web:* www.afcomfg.com					
Afco Steel Inc 1423 E 6th St	Little Rock	AR	72202	501-340-6200	340-6333
Web: www.afcosteel.com					
Amerimax Bldg Products Inc					
5208 Tennyson Pkwy Suite 100	Plano	TX	75024	469-366-3200	366-3260
TF: 800-258-6295 ■ *Web:* www.amerimaxbp.com					
Amerimax Home Products Inc					
450 Richardson Dr	Lancaster	PA	17603	717-299-3711	299-3014
TF: 800-347-2586 ■ *Web:* www.amerimax.com					
APi Group Inc Fabrication & Mfg Group					
1100 Old Hwy 8 NW	New Brighton	MN	55112	651-636-4320	636-0312
TF: 800-223-4922 ■ *Web:* www.apigroupinc.com/ind_spec_profiles.php					
Artimex Iron Co Inc 315 Cypress Ln	El Cajon	CA	92020	619-444-3155	444-3902
Web: www.artimexiron.com					
Banker Steel Co LLC PO Box 10875	Lynchburg	VA	24506	434-847-4575	847-4533
Web: www.bankersteel.com					
Barker Steel Co Inc 55 Sumner St	Milford	MA	01757	508-473-8484	473-8512
TF: 800-370-0132 ■ *Web:* www.barker.com					
Berlin Steel Construction Co					
76 Depot Rd PO Box 428	Kensington	CT	06037	860-828-3531	828-5253
Web: www.berlinsteel.com					
Bohn & Dawson Inc					
3500 Tree Ct Industrial Blvd	Saint Louis	MO	63122	636-225-5011	825-6111
Web: www.bohnanddawson.com					
Braden Mfg LLC 5199 N Mingo Rd	Tulsa	OK	74117	918-272-5371	272-7414
TF: 800-272-3360 ■ *Web:* www.braden.com					
Brilex Industries Inc PO Box 749	Youngstown	OH	44501	330-744-1114	747-1565
Web: www.brilex.com					
BW Fabricators LP 1206 Halton Rd	Wichita Falls	TX	76302	940-855-2710	855-2833
TF: 800-508-2710 ■ *Web:* www.bwfabricators.com					
Canam Steel Corp 4010 Clay St	Point of Rocks	MD	21777	301-874-5141	874-5626
TF: 800-638-4293 ■ *Web:* www.canamsteel.com					
Carolina Steel Corp 1451 S Elm Eugene St	Greensboro	NC	27406	336-275-9711	691-5772
TF: 800-632-0286 ■ *Web:* www.carolinasteel.com					
Central Texas Iron Works Inc					
1000 Winchell St PO Box 2555	Waco	TX	76702	254-776-8000	776-8844
Web: www.ctiw.com					
CENTRIA 1005 Beaver Grade Rd	Moon Township	PA	15108	412-299-8000	299-8051*
**Fax:* Hum Res ■ *TF:* 800-759-7474 ■ *Web:* www.centria.com					
Cives Steel Co 210 Cives Ln	Winchester	VA	22603	540-667-3480	662-2680
Web: www.cives.com					
Clermont Steel Fabricators LLC					
2565 Old SR 32	Batavia	OH	45103	513-732-6033	732-5344
Web: www.clermontsteel.com					
CMC Alamo Steel Co 2784 Old Dallas Rd	Waco	TX	76705	254-799-2471	799-6227
TF: 800-810-3166 ■ *Web:* www.cmcalamosteel.com					
CMC Capitol City Steel 14501 I-35	Buda	TX	78610	512-282-8820	295-2500
TF: 800-333-8820 ■ *Web:* www.cmc.com					
CMC Rebar Carolinas 2528 N Chester St	Gastonia	NC	28052	704-865-8571	865-2713
TF: 800-476-6975 ■ *Web:* www.cmc.com					
CMC Rebar Georgia 251 Hosea Rd	Lawrenceville	GA	30045	770-963-6251	339-6623
Web: www.cmc.com					
CMC South Carolina Steel 114 E Warehouse Ct	Taylors	SC	29687	864-244-2860	244-8776
Web: www.cmc.com/cmcstructural/Default.aspx					
Contract Steel Sales Inc PO Box 3305	Greensboro	NC	27402	336-273-9704	273-4336
Web: www.contractsteelsales.com					
Eastern Bridge LLC 386 River Rd	Claremont	NH	03743	603-542-5202	542-5317
Enco Materials Inc 110 N 1st St	Nashville	TN	37213	615-256-3199	259-3589
TF: 800-876-3626 ■ *Web:* www.encomaterials.com					
Euramax International Inc					
5445 Triangle Pkwy Suite 350	Norcross	GA	30092	770-449-7066	
Web: www.euramax.com					
Fabral Inc 3449 Hempland Rd	Lancaster	PA	17601	717-397-2741	397-1040
TF: 800-477-2741 ■ *Web:* www.fabral.com					
Florig R & J Industrial Co Inc					
910 Brook Rd	Conshohocken	PA	19428	610-825-6655	825-7424
Web: www.rjflorig.com					
General Steel Fabricators					
927 S Schifferdecker Ave	Joplin	MO	64801	417-623-2224	623-2204
TF: 800-820-8644 ■ *Web:* www.generalsteelfabricators.com					
Glenco Steel Corp 8657 Live Oak Ave	Fontana	CA	92335	909-854-9000	854-9008
Web: www.glencometalbuildings.com					
Grain Belt Supply Co Inc PO Box 615	Salina	KS	67402	785-827-4491	827-4494
TF: 800-447-0522 ■ *Web:* www.grainbeltsupply.com					
Hirschfeld Steel Co Inc 112 W 29th St	San Angelo	TX	76903	325-486-4201	486-4380
TF: 800-375-3216 ■ *Web:* www.hirschfeld.com					
Hogan Mfg Inc 1704 1st St	Escalon	CA	95320	209-838-7323	838-8648
Web: www.hoganmfg.com					
Hyspan Precision Products Inc					
1685 Brandywine Ave	Chula Vista	CA	91911	619-421-1355	421-1702
Web: www.hyspan.com					
InterLock Industries Inc					
545 S 3rd St # 310	Louisville	KY	40202	502-569-2007	569-2016
Web: www.interlockindustries.com					
J. C. Macelroy Co Inc PO Box 850	Piscataway	NJ	08855	732-572-7100	572-7112
TF: 800-622-3576 ■ *Web:* www.macelroy.com					
Jesse Engineering Co 1840 Marine View Dr	Tacoma	WA	98422	253-922-7433	593-3742
Web: www.jesseengineering.com					
JH Industries Inc 1981 E Aurora Rd	Twinsburg	OH	44087	330-963-4105	963-4111
TF: 800-321-4968 ■ *Web:* www.copperloy.com					
Johnson Bros Metal Forming Co					
5520 McDermott Dr	Berkeley	IL	60163	708-449-7050	449-0042
Web: www.johnsonrollforming.com					
LeJeune Steel Co 118 W 60th St	Minneapolis	MN	55419	612-861-3321	861-2724
Web: www.lejeunesteel.com					
Lichtenwald-Johnston Iron Works Corp					
7840 Lehigh St PO Box 1328	Morton Grove	IL	60053	847-966-1100	966-1159
LSI Metal Fabrication Inc					
3871 Turkeyfoot Rd	Erlanger	KY	41018	859-342-9944	342-2275
TF: 800-546-1513					
M & J Materials Inc					
7561 Gadsden Hwy PO Box 428	Trussville	AL	35173	205-655-7451	655-4100
Magnolia Steel Co Inc PO Box 5007	Meridian	MS	39302	601-693-4301	693-3101
Web: www.magnoliasteel.com					
Mark Steel Corp					
1230 W 200 S PO Box 16006	Salt Lake City	UT	84104	801-521-0670	303-2040
Web: www.marksteel.net					
McElroy Metal Inc 1500 Hamilton Rd	Bossier City	LA	71111	318-747-8097	747-8657
TF: 800-562-3576 ■ *Web:* www.mcelroymetal.com					
Met-Con Inc 465 Canaveral Groves Blvd	Cocoa	FL	32926	321-632-4880	639-0158
Web: www.metconinc.com					
Midwest Metal Products Co					
800 66th Ave SW	Cedar Rapids	IA	52404	319-366-6264	366-6710
Web: www.mwestmp.com					
Miller Metal Fabricators Inc					
345 National Ave PO Box 3165	Staunton	VA	24402	540-886-5575	
Mound Technologies Inc 25 Mound Pk Dr	Springboro	OH	45066	937-748-2937	748-9763
Norlen Inc 900 Grossman Dr	Schofield	WI	54476	715-359-0506	359-0901
TF: 800-648-6594 ■ *Web:* www.norlen.com					
Nucor Corp 1915 Rexford Rd	Charlotte	NC	28211	704-366-7000	362-4208
NYSE: NUE ■ *Web:* www.nucor.com					
Nucor Corp Vulcraft Div					
1501 W Darlington St	Florence	SC	29501	843-662-0381	662-3132
Web: www.vulcraft.com					
Ornamental Metal Works Inc					
2100 N Woodford St	Decatur	IL	62526	217-428-3446	424-2326
Owen Industries Inc 501 Ave H	Carter Lake	IA	51510	712-347-5500	347-6166
TF: 800-831-9252 ■ *Web:* www.owenind.com					
Owen Steel Co 727 Mauney Dr	Columbia	SC	29201	803-251-7680	251-7613
TF: 800-922-5134 ■ *Web:* www.owensteel.com					
Owens Corning Fabricating Solutions					
426 N Main St	Elkhart	IN	46516	574-522-8473	632-2935*
**Fax Area Code:* 877 ■ *TF:* 877-632-2935					
Paxton & Vierling Steel Co 501 Ave H	Carter Lake	IA	51510	712-347-5500	347-6166
TF: 800-831-9252 ■					
Web: www.owenind.com/divisions/pvs-structural-fabrication					
PDM Bridge Corp 211 Comfort Rd	Palatka	FL	32177	386-328-4683	328-2804
Web: www.pdmbridge.com					
PSP Industries 300 Montague Expy Suite 200	Milpitas	CA	95035	408-942-1155	262-5388
Web: www.pspindustries.com					
Qualico Steel Co Inc PO Box 149	Webb	AL	36376	334-793-1290	794-0996
Web: www.qualicosteel.com					
Quality Machine & Welding Co Inc					
PO Box 27345	Knoxville	TN	37927	865-524-2162	524-1830
Web: www.qmwkx.com					

	City	State	Zip	Phone	Fax
Quincy Joist Co 520 S Virginia St *Web:* www.quincyjoist.com	Quincy	FL	32351	850-875-1075	875-1277
Ranor Inc 1 Bella Dr *TF:* 800-225-9552 ■ *Web:* www.ranor.com	Westminster	MA	01473	978-874-0591	874-2748
Rodney Hunt Co 46 Mill St *TF:* 800-448-8860 ■ *Web:* www.rodneyhunt.com	Orange	MA	01364	978-544-2511	544-7204
Roscoe Steel 1501 S 30th St W *Web:* www.roscoesteel.com	Billings	MT	59102	406-656-2253	656-8576
Schuff Steel Inc 1920 Ledo Rd *TF:* 800-528-0513 ■ *Web:* www.schuff.com	Albany	GA	31707	229-883-4506	438-8316
Shape Corp 1900 Hayes St *Web:* www.shapecorp.com	Grand Haven	MI	49417	616-846-8700	846-3464
Southeastern Steel Co 211 N Koppers Rd *TF:* 800-476-7372 ■ *Web:* www.sesteel.com	Florence	SC	29506	843-662-5236	662-6261
Standard Iron Inc 2516 Vance Ave *Web:* www.standardiron.com	Chattanooga	TN	37404	423-756-0940	756-0944
Steel Fabricators LLC 721 NE 44th St **Fax:* Sales ■ *Web:* www.sfab.com	Fort Lauderdale	FL	33334	954-772-0440	938-7527*
Structural Steel Services 6215 St Louis St S Industrial Pk	Meridian	MS	39307	601-482-8181	482-1520
Stupp Bros Inc 3800 Weber Rd *TF:* 800-899-1856 ■ *Web:* www.stupp.com	Saint Louis	MO	63125	314-638-5000	638-5439
T. Bruce Sales Inc PO Box 607 *Web:* www.tbrucesales.com	West Middlesex	PA	16159	724-528-9961	528-2050
Trinity Structural Towers Inc 2525 N Stemmons Fwy *TF:* 800-631-8501 ■ *Web:* www.trinitytowers.com	Dallas	TX	75207	214-631-4420	589-8640
TSF Structures Inc PO Box 2051 *Web:* www.tsf-structures.com	Cedar Rapids	IA	52406	319-365-7133	365-2410
Union Metal Corp 1432 Maple Ave NE *Web:* www.unionmetal.com	Canton	OH	44705	330-456-7653	456-0196
Unistrut Corp 4205 Elizabeth St *TF Cust Svc:* 800-521-7730 ■ *Web:* www.unistrut.com	Wayne	MI	48184	734-721-4040	721-4106
W & W Steel Co 1730 W Reno Ave *Web:* www.wwsteel.com	Oklahoma City	OK	73106	405-235-3621	236-4842
Wahlcometroflex Inc 29 Lexington St *TF:* 800-272-6652 ■ *Web:* www.wahlcometroflex.com	Lewiston	ME	04240	207-784-2338	753-3045
West Coast Wire & Steel Inc 1027 Palmyrita Ave *Web:* www.wcws.org	Riverside	CA	92507	951-683-7252	
Wisconsin Structural Steel Co Hwy 63 N	Barronett	WI	54813	715-822-2647	822-2906

484 METAL COATING, PLATING, ENGRAVING

	City	State	Zip	Phone	Fax
Alcoa Inc 201 Isabella St *NYSE:* AA ■ *Web:* www.alcoa.com	Pittsburgh	PA	15212	412-553-4545	553-4498
All Metals Processing of Orange County Inc 8401 Standustrial St *TF:* 800-894-4489 ■ *Web:* www.allmetalsprocessing.com	Stanton	CA	90680	714-828-8238	828-4552
Aluminum Coil Anodizing Corp 501 E Lake St *Web:* www.acacorp.com	Streamwood	IL	60107	630-837-4000	837-0814
American Nickeloid Co 2900 Main St *TF:* 800-645-5643 ■ *Web:* www.nickeloid.com	Peru	IL	61354	815-223-0373	223-5344
Archer Wire International Corp 7300 S Narragansett Ave *Web:* www.archerwire.com	Bedford Park	IL	60638	708-563-1700	563-1740
ATI Precision Finishing 499 Delaware Ave *Web:* www.atiromemetals.com	Rochester	PA	15074	724-775-1664	775-1668
Bredero Shaw A ShawCor Co 3838 N Sam Houston Pkwy E Suite 500 *Web:* www.brederoshaw.com	Houston	TX	77032	281-886-2350	886-2353
Certified Enameling Inc 3342 Emery St *Web:* www.certifiedenameling.com	Los Angeles	CA	90023	323-264-4403	264-9599
Chemart Co 15 New England Way *TF:* 800-521-5001 ■ *Web:* www.chemart.com	Lincoln	RI	02865	401-333-9200	333-1634
Chicago Metallic Corp 4849 S Austin Ave *TF:* 800-323-7164 ■ *Web:* www.chicago-metallic.com	Chicago	IL	60638	800-323-7164	222-3744
Crest Coating Inc 1361 S Allec St *Web:* www.crestcoating.com	Anaheim	CA	92805	714-635-7090	758-8752
Decorated Products Inc 1 Arch Rd *TF:* 800-639-4909 ■ *Web:* www.decorated.com	Westfield	MA	01086	413-568-0944	568-1875
Deposition Sciences Inc 3300 Coffey Ln *TF:* 866-433-7724 ■ *Web:* www.depsci.com	Santa Rosa	CA	95403	707-573-6700	579-0731
Donham Craft Inc 15 E Waterbury Rd *TF:* 800-739-1919 ■ *Web:* www.donhamcraft.com	Naugatuck	CT	06770	203-729-8244	729-8487
DS Mfg Co 67 5th St NE	Pine Island	MN	55963	507-356-8322	356-8436
Electric Coating Technologies (ECT) 8687 S 77th Ave *TF:* 800-752-9957	Bridgeview	IL	60455	708-598-5100	598-6990
Erler Industries Inc 418 Stockwell St PO Box 219 *Web:* www.erler.com	North Vernon	IN	47265	812-346-4421	346-1892
Galvan Industries Inc PO Box 369 *TF:* 800-277-5678 ■ *Web:* www.galvanizersonline.com	Harrisburg	NC	28075	704-455-5102	455-5215
General Extrusions Inc 4040 Lake Pk Rd *Web:* www.genext.com	Youngstown	OH	44512	330-783-0270	788-1250
General Metal Finishing Co Inc (GMF) 42 Frank Mossberg Dr *Web:* www.genmetal.com	Attleboro	MA	02703	508-226-5606	226-5656
GM Nameplate Inc 2040 15th Ave W *TF:* 800-366-7668 ■ *Web:* www.gmnameplate.com	Seattle	WA	98119	206-284-2200	284-3705
Interplex Engineered Products 231 Ferris Ave **Fax Area Code:* 508 ■ *Web:* www.interplex.com	East Providence	RI	02916	401-434-6543	399-7655*
IonBond LLC 200 Roundhill Dr *Web:* www.ionbond.com	Rockaway	NJ	07866	973-586-4700	586-4729
KNS Cos Inc 475 Randy Rd *Web:* www.knscompanies.com	Carol Stream	IL	60188	630-665-9010	665-1819
LB Foster Co 415 Holiday Dr *NASDAQ:* FSTR ■ **Fax:* Sales ■ *TF:* 800-255-4500 ■ *Web:* www.lbfoster.com	Pittsburgh	PA	15220	412-928-3431	928-7891*
Lorin Industries 1960 S Roberts St *TF:* 800-654-1159 ■ *Web:* www.lorin.com	Muskegon	MI	49443	231-722-1631	728-3139
Magnetic Metals Corp 1900 Hayes Ave *TF:* 800-257-8174 ■ *Web:* www.magmet.com	Camden	NJ	08105	856-964-7842	963-8569
Markland Industries Inc 1111 E McFadden Ave *Web:* www.marklandindustries.com	Santa Ana	CA	92705	714-245-2850	245-2853
Master Finish Co 2020 Nelson SE PO Box 7505 **Fax Area Code:* 616 ■ *TF:* 877-590-5819 ■ *Web:* www.masterfinishco.com	Grand Rapids	MI	49510	877-590-5819	245-0039*
Material Sciences Corp (MSC) 2200 E Pratt Blvd *NASDAQ:* MASC ■ *TF:* 800-877-9078 ■ *Web:* www.matsci.com	Elk Grove Village	IL	60007	847-439-2210	439-0737
Metal Cladding Inc 230 S Niagara St *TF:* 800-432-5513 ■ *Web:* www.metalcladding.com	Lockport	NY	14094	716-434-5513	439-4010
MetoKote Corp 1340 Neubrecht Rd *Web:* www.metokote.com	Lima	OH	45801	419-227-1100	996-7801
Microcast Technologies Corp (MTC) 1611 W Elizabeth Ave *Web:* www.mtcnj.com	Linden	NJ	07036	908-523-9503	523-0910
Midwest Products Finishing Co Inc 6194 Section Rd *Web:* www.midwestecoat.com	Ottawa Lake	MI	49267	734-856-5200	856-7267
Mills Cos Inc 5201 Gershwin Ave N *TF:* 800-367-9045	Saint Paul	MN	55128	651-770-6660	770-0224
National Coatings Inc 3520 Rennie School Rd *TF:* 888-947-2557 ■ *Web:* www.nationalcoatings.biz	Traverse City	MI	49685	231-943-2557	943-4262
Nd Industries Inc 1000 N Crooks Rd *TF:* 800-471-5000 ■ *Web:* www.ndindustries.com	Clawson	MI	48017	248-655-2520	288-0022
Nof Metal Coatings NA 275 Industrial Pkwy *Web:* www.metal-coatings.com	Chardon	OH	44024	440-285-2231	285-5009
Nor-Ell Inc 851 Hubbard Ave *Web:* www.nor-ell.com	Saint Paul	MN	55104	651-487-1441	488-1626
Northern Engraving Corp 803 S Black River St PO Box 377 *Web:* www.norcorp.com	Sparta	WI	54656	608-269-6911	269-6735
O E C Graphics Inc 555 W Waukau Ave PO Box 2443 *TF:* 800-388-7770 ■ *Web:* www.oecgraphics.com	Oshkosh	WI	54902	920-235-7770	235-2252
Passaic Engraving Co Inc 41 Brook Ave *Web:* www.passaicengraving.com	Passaic	NJ	07055	973-777-0621	777-7791
Pioneer Metal Finishing LLC 486 Globe Ave **Fax Area Code:* 920 ■ *TF:* 800-944-7634 ■ *Web:* www.pioneermetal.com	Green Bay	WI	54304	800-944-7634	884-1790*
Plasma Technology Inc 1754 Crenshaw Blvd *Web:* www.ptise.com	Torrance	CA	90501	310-320-3373	533-1677
Porcelen Ltd 333 Welton St *TF:* 800-243-6256 ■ *Web:* www.porcelen.com	Hamden	CT	06517	203-248-6346	248-8489
Porter Process Co 1600 Industry Rd *TF:* 800-618-4701 ■ *Web:* www.porterprocess.com	Hatfield	PA	19440	215-855-9916	855-3570
Precision Coating Co Inc 58 McDonald St *Web:* www.precisioncoating.com	Dedham	MA	02026	781-329-1420	329-3618
Precision Graphics Inc 21 County Line Rd *Web:* www.precisiongraphics.us	Somerville	NJ	08876	908-707-8880	707-8884
Premier Die Casting Co 1177 Rahway Ave *TF:* 800-394-3006 ■ *Web:* www.diecasting.com	Avenel	NJ	07001	732-634-3000	634-0590
Providence Metallizing Co Inc 51 Fairlawn Ave *Web:* www.provmet.com	Pawtucket	RI	02860	401-722-5300	724-3410
Quick Tanks Inc PO Box 338 *Web:* www.quicktanks.com	Kendallville	IN	46755	260-347-3850	347-3853
Rimex Metals (USA) Inc 2850 Woodbridge Ave *Web:* www.rimexmetals.com	Edison	NJ	08837	732-549-3800	549-6435
Roehlen Engraving 5901 Lewis Rd *Web:* www.roehlenengraving.com	Sandston	VA	23150	804-222-2821	226-3462
Roesch Inc 100 N 24th St *TF:* 800-423-6243 ■ *Web:* www.roeschinc.com	Belleville	IL	62222	618-233-2760	233-1186
Roll Coater Inc 8440 Woodfield Crossing Bldg 2 Suite 500 *Web:* www.rollcoater.com	Indianapolis	IN	46240	317-462-7761	467-7323
Sapa Inc 7933 NE 21st Ave *TF:* 800-547-0790 ■ *Web:* www.sapagroup.com	Portland	OR	97211	503-972-1404	802-3060
Savon Plating & Powder Coating Inc 15523 Illinois Ave	Paramount	CA	90723	562-634-6189	602-0690
Sequa Corp Precoat Metals Div 1310 Papin St 3rd Fl *Web:* www.precoatmetals.com	Saint Louis	MO	63103	314-436-7010	436-7050
Southwest Metal Finishing Inc 2445 S Calhoun Rd *Web:* www.swmetalfinishing.com	New Berlin	WI	53151	262-784-1919	641-7086
Standex International Corp Engraving Group 5901 Lewis Rd *Web:* www.standexengraving.com	Sandston	VA	23150	804-222-2821	226-3462
State Plating 450 N 9th St *TF:* 800-428-6340	Elwood	IN	46036	765-552-5047	552-6980
Sumco Inc 1351 S Girls School Rd	Indianapolis	IN	46231	317-241-7600	248-2352
Summit Corp of America 1430 Waterbury Rd *TF:* 800-854-0176 ■ *Web:* www.scact.com	Thomaston	CT	06787	860-283-4391	283-4010
Techno-Coat Inc 861 E 40th St *Web:* www.technocoat.com	Holland	MI	49423	616-396-6446	396-8211
Towne Technologies Inc 6-10 Bell Ave PO Box 460 *Web:* www.townetech.com	Somerville	NJ	08876	908-722-9500	722-8394
Unicote Corp 33165 Groesbeck Hwy *Web:* www.unicotecorporation.com	Fraser	MI	48026	586-296-0700	296-3155
US Chrome Corp 175 Garfield Ave *TF:* 800-637-9019 ■ *Web:* www.uschrome.com	Stratford	CT	06615	203-378-9622	386-0067
Vapor Technologies Inc 6400 Dry Creek Pkwy *TF:* 800-582-8388 ■ *Web:* www.vaportech.com	Longmont	CO	80503	303-652-8500	652-8600

				Phone	Fax
Whitford Corp PO Box 80 *Web:* www.whitfordww.com	Elverson	PA	19520	610-296-3200	286-3510
Womble Co Inc 12821 Industrial Rd *Web:* www.wombleco.com	Houston	TX	77015	713-635-8300	635-5209

485 METAL FABRICATING - CUSTOM

				Phone	Fax
Afco Industries Inc 3400 Roy Ave *TF:* 800-551-6576 ■ *Web:* www.afco-ind.com	Alexandria	LA	71302	318-448-1651	443-5158
Aldine Metal Products Corp 566 Danbury Rd Unit 1 *TF:* 877-775-2551 ■ *Web:* www.aldinemetal.com	New Milford	CT	06776	860-350-2552	350-1061
Alpha Sintered Metals Inc 95 Mason Run Rd *Web:* www.alphasintered.com	Ridgway	PA	15853	814-773-3191	776-1009
American Aluminum Co 230 Sheffield St *TF:* 800-315-3977 ■ *Web:* www.amalco.com	Mountainside	NJ	07092	908-233-3500	233-3241
Angell & Giroux Inc 2727 Alcazar St *Web:* www.angellandgiroux.com	Los Angeles	CA	90033	323-269-8596	269-0454
Applied Engineering Inc 2008 E Hwy 50 *Web:* www.appliedeng.com	Yankton	SD	57078	605-665-4425	665-1479
Aquarius Metal Products Corp 2475 Millennium Dr *Web:* www.aquariusmetal.com	Elgin	IL	60123	847-841-1400	841-8424
Arlington Metals Corp 11355 Franklin Ave *Web:* www.arlingtonmetals.com	Franklin Park	IL	60131	847-451-9100	451-9676
Ascension Industries 1254 Erie Ave *Web:* www.asmfab.com	North Tonawanda	NY	14120	716-695-2040	693-9882
Associated Steel Workers Ltd PO Box 488	Aiea	HI	96701	808-682-5588	682-7392
Autoswage Products Inc 726 River Rd *Web:* www.autoswage.com	Shelton	CT	06484	203-929-1401	929-6187
Brakewell Steel Fabricator Inc 55 Leone Ln *TF:* 888-914-9131 ■ *Web:* www.brakewell.com	Chester	NY	10918	845-469-9131	469-7618
Cerro Fabricated Products Inc 300 Triangle Dr *Web:* www.cerrofabricated.com	Weyers Cave	VA	24486	540-234-9252	234-8416
Chandler Industries Inc 1654 N 9th St *Web:* www.chandlerindustries.com	Montevideo	MN	56265	320-269-8893	269-5827
Chicago Metal Fabricators Inc 3724 S Rockwell St *Web:* www.chicagometal.com	Chicago	IL	60632	773-523-5755	523-8680
CMW Inc 70 S Gray St *Web:* www.cmwinc.com	Indianapolis	IN	46201	317-634-8884	630-2159
Compax Inc 1210 N Blue Gum St *Web:* www.compaxinc.com	Anaheim	CA	92806	714-630-3670	632-1344
Cross Bros Inc 5255 Sheila St *TF:* 866-939-1057 ■ *Web:* www.crossbrothersinc.com	Los Angeles	CA	90040	323-266-2000	266-2106
CSM Metal Fabricating & Engineering Inc 1800 S San Pedro St *TF:* 800-272-4806 ■ *Web:* www.csmworks.com	Los Angeles	CA	90015	213-748-7321	749-5106
D & S Mfg Inc 301 E Main St *Web:* www.dsmfg.com	Black River Falls	WI	54615	715-284-5376	284-4084
Daniel Tanney Co Inc 3268 Clive Ave	Bensalem	PA	19020	215-639-3131	638-3333
Demsey Mfg Co 78 New Wood Rd *TF:* 800-533-6739 ■ *Web:* www.demseymfg.com	Watertown	CT	06795	860-274-6209	274-6209
Diez Group 8111 Tireman Ave *Web:* www.diezgroup.com	Dearborn	MI	48126	313-491-1200	491-6210
Dynamic Materials Corp 5405 Spine Rd *NASDAQ: BOOM* ■ *TF:* 800-821-2666 ■ *Web:* www.dynamicmaterials.com	Boulder	CO	80301	303-665-5700	604-1893
Fabricated Components Inc PO Box 431 *TF:* 800-233-8163 ■ *Web:* www.fabricatedcomponents.com	Stroudsburg	PA	18360	570-421-4110	421-2553
Harford Systems Inc 2225 Pulaski Hwy PO Box 700 *TF:* 800-664-7620 ■ *Web:* www.harfordsystems.com	Aberdeen	MD	21001	410-272-3400	273-7892
Harris Mfg Inc 4775 E Vine Ave *Web:* www.harrismfg.com	Fresno	CA	93725	559-268-7422	268-2846
International Extrusions Inc 5800 Venoy Rd *TF:* 800-242-8876 ■ *Web:* www.extrusion.net	Garden City	MI	48135	734-427-8700	427-9319
Johnson Matthey Noble Metals 1397 King Rd *TF:* 800-441-8159 ■ *Web:* www.noble.matthey.com	West Chester	PA	19380	610-648-8067	648-8105
Lafayette Quality Products PO Box 5827	Lafayette	IN	47903	765-447-3106	448-6788
Liquidmetal Technologies Inc (LQMT) 30452 Esperanza *OTC: LQMT* ■ *Web:* www.liquidmetal.com	Rancho Santa Margarita	CA	92688	949-635-2100	635-2188
Ltc Roll & Engineering Co 23500 John Gorsuch Dr *Web:* www.ltcroll.com	Clinton Township	MI	48036	586-465-1023	465-0554
Lucasey Mfg Corp PO Box 14023 *TF:* 800-582-2739 ■ *Web:* www.lucasey.com	Oakland	CA	94614	510-534-1435	534-6828
Manufacturers Industrial Group LLC 659 Natchez Trace Dr *Web:* www.migllc.com	Lexington	TN	38351	731-967-0001	968-3320
MarathonNorco Aerospace Inc 8301 Imperial Dr *Web:* www.mnaerospace.com	Waco	TX	76712	254-776-0650	776-6558
Master Metal Products Co 495 Emory St *Web:* www.mastermetalproducts.com	San Jose	CA	95110	408-275-1210	275-0523
Matthews Industries 23 2nd St SW *Web:* www.matthewsindustries.com	Decatur	AL	35601	256-353-0271	353-3850
Metal Fabricating Corp 10408 Berea Rd *Web:* www.metalfabricatingcorp.com	Cleveland	OH	44102	216-631-2480	631-2453
MP Metal Products Inc W1250 Elmwood Ave *Web:* www.mpmetals.com	Ixonia	WI	53036	920-261-9650	261-9652
National Sintered Alloys Inc Heritage Pk, Rt 145 PO Box 332 *Web:* www.nationalsintered.com	Clinton	CT	06413	860-669-8653	669-5428
Newbrook Machines Inc PO Box 231	Silver Creek	NY	14136	716-934-2651	934-0453
Nor-Cal Metal Fabricators 1121 3rd St *Web:* www.nc-mf.com	Oakland	CA	94607	510-836-1451	208-2838
Progressive Tool & Mfg Co 290 5th St NE *Web:* www.ptmmn.com	Pine Island	MN	55963	507-356-8345	356-4557
Pulley-Kellam Co Inc 245 Erie St	Huntington	IN	46750	260-356-6326	356-1928
Quaker City Plating (QCP) PO Box 2406 *Web:* www.quakercityplating.com	Whittier	CA	90610	562-945-3721	945-9932
Right Mfg 7949 Stromesa Ct Suite G *Web:* www.rightmfg.com	San Diego	CA	92126	858-566-7002	566-7623
Rose Metal Products Inc 1955 E Division St *Web:* www.rosemetalproducts.com	Springfield	MO	65803	417-865-1676	865-7673
S & G Mfg Group LLC 4830 NW Pkwy *TF:* 888-529-1992 ■ *Web:* www.sgmgroup.com	Hilliard	OH	43026	614-334-3600	334-3631
Sioux Mfg Corp 1115 Dakotah Dr *Web:* www.siouxmanufacturing.com	Fort Totten	ND	58335	701-766-4211	766-4359
Sommer Metalcraft Corp 315 Poston Dr *TF:* 800-654-3124 ■ *Web:* www.sommermetalcraft.com	Crawfordsville	IN	47933	765-362-6200	359-4202
Sorini Mfg Co 2524 S Blue Island Ave	Chicago	IL	60608	773-247-5858	247-7186
Southwire Co Machinery Div 401 Fertilla St *TF:* 800-444-1700 ■ *Web:* www.southwire.com	Carrollton	GA	30117	770-832-4242	832-5228
Tomax Fabricating Inc 5449 Peck Rd	Arcadia	CA	91006	626-443-1796	443-1798
TPI Powder Metallurgy Inc 12030 Beaver Rd *Web:* www.tpipm.com	Saint Charles	MI	48655	989-865-9921	865-9924
Uni-Form Components Co 16969 Old Beaumont Hwy 90 *TF:* 800-231-3272 ■ *Web:* www.uniformcomponents.com	Houston	TX	77049	281-456-9310	456-0245
Unifab Corp 3030 Kersten Ct *TF:* 800-648-9569 ■ *Web:* www.unifabcorp.com	Kalamazoo	MI	49048	269-382-2803	382-2825
Unique Aluminum Extrusion LLC 333 Cedar Ave *TF:* 800-218-6004 ■ *Web:* www.americanmodernmetals.com	Middlesex	NJ	08846	732-271-1160	271-8327
Weldments Inc 10720 N 2nd St	Rockford	IL	61115	815-633-3393	633-2524
White River Distributors Inc 720 Ramsey *TF:* 800-548-7219 ■ *Web:* www.lpgbobtails.com	Batesville	AR	72501	870-793-2374	793-8230
Wire Products Mfg Corp PO Box 407	Merrill	WI	54452	715-536-7144	536-1476

486 METAL FORGINGS

				Phone	Fax
Alcoa Wheel Products International 1600 Harvard Ave *TF:* 800-242-9898 ■ *Web:* www.alcoawheels.com	Cleveland	OH	44105	216-641-3600	641-4032
Aluminum Precision Products Inc 3333 W Warner St *TF:* 800-411-8983 ■ *Web:* www.aluminumprecision.com	Santa Ana	CA	92704	714-546-8125	540-8862
Ameri-Forge Group Inc 13770 Industrial Rd *Web:* www.ameriforge.com	Houston	TX	77015	713-393-4200	455-8366
AMSTED Industries Inc 180 N Stetson St Suite 1800 **Fax:* Hum Res ■ *Web:* www.amsted.com	Chicago	IL	60601	312-645-1700	819-8504*
Anchor-Harvey Components Inc 600 W Lamm Rd *TF:* 888-367-4464 ■ *Web:* www.forgings.com	Freeport	IL	61032	815-235-4400	235-3587
ATI Ladish Co Inc 5481 S Packard Ave PO Box 8902 *Web:* www.ladish.com	Cudahy	WI	53110	414-747-2611	747-3540
Ball Chain Mfg Co Inc 741 S Fulton Ave *Web:* www.ballchain.com	Mount Vernon	NY	10550	914-664-7500	664-7460
Berkeley Forge & Tool Inc 1331 E Shore Hwy *Web:* www.berkforge.com	Berkeley	CA	94710	510-526-5034	525-9014
Bharat Forge America 2807 S ML King Jr Blvd *TF:* 800-968-2932 ■ *Web:* www.bharatforgeamerica.com	Lansing	MI	48910	517-393-5300	393-6256
Buchanan Metal Forming Inc 103 W Smith St *TF:* 800-253-0585 ■ *Web:* www.bmfcorp.com	Buchanan	MI	49107	269-695-3836	695-3830
Canton Drop Forge Inc 4575 Southway St SW *Web:* www.cantondropforge.com	Canton	OH	44706	330-477-4511	477-2046
Carlton Forge Works Inc 7743 E Adams St	Paramount	CA	90723	562-633-1131	531-8896
Clifford-Jacobs Forging Co 2410 N 5th St PO Box 830 *Web:* www.clifford-jacobs.com	Champaign	IL	61822	217-352-5172	352-4629
Consolidated Industries Inc 677 Mixville Rd *Web:* www.forgemetal.com	Cheshire	CT	06410	203-272-5371	272-5672
Cornell Forge Co 6666 W 66th St *TF:* 800-356-0204 ■ *Web:* www.cornellforge.com	Chicago	IL	60638	708-458-1582	728-9883
Corry Forge Co 441 E Main St	Corry	PA	16407	814-664-9664	664-9452
Coulter Forge Technology Inc 1494 67th St PO Box 8008 *TF:* 800-648-4884 ■ *Web:* www.coulter-forge.com	Emeryville	CA	94662	510-420-3500	420-3555
DeKalb Forge Co 1832 Pleasant St *Web:* www.dekalbforge.com	DeKalb	IL	60115	815-756-3538	756-6958
Doncasters Storms Forge Div 160 Cottage St	Springfield	MA	01104	413-785-1801	785-5680
Ellwood City Forge 800 Commercial Ave PO Box 31 *TF:* 800-843-0166 ■ *Web:* www.ellwoodgroup.com	Ellwood City	PA	16117	724-752-0055	752-3449
Enterprise Automotive Systems Inc 21445 Hoover Rd	Warren	MI	48089	586-755-3180	759-3540
Erie Forge & Steel Inc 1341 W 16th St *Web:* www.erieforge.com	Erie	PA	16502	814-452-2300	459-9170
Federal Flange 4014 Pinemont St *TF:* 800-231-0150 ■ *Web:* www.federalflange.com	Houston	TX	77018	713-681-0606	681-3005
Forged Components Inc 14527 Smith Rd *Web:* www.forgedcomponents.com	Humble	TX	77396	281-441-4088	441-8899
Forged Products Inc (FPI) 6505 N Houston Rosslyn Rd *TF:* 800-876-3416 ■ *Web:* www.fpitx.com	Houston	TX	77091	713-462-3416	460-9404
Forged Vessel Connections Inc 2525 DeSoto St *TF Cust Svc:* 800-231-2701 ■ *Web:* www.forgedvesselconn.com	Houston	TX	77091	713-688-9705	688-7954
Green Bay Drop Forge 1341 State St *TF:* 800-824-4896 ■ *Web:* www.greenbaydropforge.com	Green Bay	WI	54304	920-432-6401	432-0859

Company	City	State	Zip	Phone	Fax
H & L Tooth Co Inc 10055 E 56 St N *TF:* 800-458-6684 ■ *Web:* www.hltooth.com	Tulsa	OK	74117	918-272-0951	272-0163
Hammond & Irving Inc 254 N St *Web:* www.hammond-irving.com	Auburn	NY	13021	315-253-6265	253-3136
Hardware & Forging Co 3270 E 79th St *TF:* 800-321-1874 ■ *Web:* www.clevelandhardware.com	Cleveland	OH	44104	216-641-5200	641-0829
Hirschvogel Inc 2230 S 3rd St *TF:* 866-367-4464	Columbus	OH	43207	614-445-6060	445-7335
Impact Forge Group Inc 2805 Norcross Dr PO Box 1847 *TF:* 800-367-1433 ■ *Web:* www.impactforge.com	Columbus	IN	47201	812-342-4437	342-4553
Independent Forge Co 692 N Batavia St *Web:* www.independentforge.com	Orange	CA	92868	714-997-7337	997-7546
Jernberg Industries Inc 328 W 40th Pl *Web:* www.jernberg.com	Chicago	IL	60609	773-268-3004	268-3220
Kerkau Mfg Co 1321 S Valley Ctr Dr *TF:* 800-248-5060 ■ *Web:* www.kerkau.com	Bay City	MI	48706	989-686-0350	686-0399
Keystone Forging Co 215 Duke St PO Boxs 269 *Web:* www.keystoneforging.com	Northumberland	PA	17857	570-473-3524	473-7273
KomTeK Technologies 40 Rockdale St *TF:* 800-756-6835 ■ *Web:* www.komtektech.com	Worcester	MA	01606	508-853-4500	853-2753
Kropp Forge 5301 W Roosevelt Rd **Fax:* Sales ■ *Web:* www.kroppforge.com	Cicero	IL	60804	708-652-6691	652-9144*
Lakeview Forge Co 1725 Pittsburgh Ave *Web:* www.lakeviewforge.com	Erie	PA	16505	814-454-4518	455-5875
Lefere Forge & Machine Co 665 Hupp Ave *Web:* www.lefereforge.com	Jackson	MI	49203	517-784-7109	784-0929
Lehigh Heavy Forge Corp 1275 Daly Ave *Web:* www.lhforge.com	Bethlehem	PA	18015	610-332-8100	332-8101
Lenape Forged Products Corp 1334 Lenape Rd *Web:* www.lenapeforge.com	West Chester	PA	19382	610-793-5090	793-3070
Liberty Forge Inc 1507 Fort Worth St PO Drawer 1210 *TF:* 800-231-2377 ■ *Web:* www.libertyforgeinc.com	Liberty	TX	77575	936-336-5785	336-2740
Machine Specialty & Mfg Inc 215 Rousseau Rd *TF:* 800-256-1292 ■ *Web:* www.machine-specialty.com	Youngsville	LA	70592	337-837-0020	837-0062
McKees Rocks Forgings 75 Nichol Ave *TF:* 800-223-2818 ■ *Web:* www.mckeesrocksforgings.com	McKees Rocks	PA	15136	412-778-2020	778-2025
McKenzie Valve & Machining Co 145 Airport Rd *Web:* www.mckenzievalve.com	McKenzie	TN	38201	731-352-5027	352-3029
McWilliams Forge Co Inc 387 Franklin Ave *Web:* www.mcwilliamsforge.com	Rockaway	NJ	07866	973-627-0200	625-9316
Meadville Forging Co 15309 Baldwin St PO Box 459 *Web:* www.meadforge.com	Meadville	PA	16335	814-332-8200	333-4657
Mercer Forge Corp 200 Brown St PO Box 272 *TF:* 800-686-6677 ■ *Web:* www.mercerforge.com	Mercer	PA	16137	724-662-2750	662-5642
Metal Forming & Coining Corp (MFC) 1007 Illinois Ave *Web:* www.mfccorp.com	Maumee	OH	43537	419-893-8748	893-6828
Metalist International Inc 1159 S Pennsylvania Ave *Web:* www.metalist.com	Lansing	MI	48912	517-371-2940	371-3027
Mid-West Forge Corp 17301 St Clair Ave *Web:* www.mid-westforge.com	Cleveland	OH	44110	216-481-3030	481-7288
Millennium Forge Inc 990 W Ormsby Ave *Web:* www.millenniumforge.com	Louisville	KY	40210	502-635-3350	635-3028
Mmd Equipment 121 High Hill Rd *TF:* 800-433-1382 ■ *Web:* www.mmdequipment.com	Swedesboro	NJ	08085	856-467-3200	467-5235
Modern Drop Forge Co 13810 S Western Ave *Web:* www.modernforge.com	Blue Island	IL	60406	708-388-1806	597-3633
Modern Forge/Tennessee Inc 501 Rock Ln *Web:* www.modernforge.com	Piney Flats	TN	37686	423-538-8185	538-8110
Moline Forge Inc 4101 4th Ave *Web:* www.molineforge.com	Moline	IL	61265	309-762-5506	762-5508
National Flame & Forge Inc 330 W 25th St *Web:* www.nationalflame.com	Houston	TX	77008	713-869-5724	869-7737
National Flange & Fitting Co 4420 Creekmont St *TF:* 800-231-1424	Houston	TX	77091	713-688-2515	688-0205
Nonferrous Products Inc 401 Arvin Rd PO Box 349 *TF:* 800-423-5612 ■ *Web:* www.nonferrousproducts.com	Franklin	IN	46131	317-738-2558	738-2685
Norforge & Machining Inc 195 N Dean St *TF:* 800-457-7699 ■ *Web:* www.norforge.com	Bushnell	IL	61422	309-772-3124	772-9206
Ohio Star Forge Co (OSF) 4000 Mahoning Ave NW PO Box 430 *Web:* www.ohiostar.com	Warren	OH	44483	330-847-6360	847-6368
Pacific Forge Inc 10641 Etiwanda Ave *Web:* www.pacificforge.com	Fontana	CA	92337	909-390-0701	390-0708
Parish International Inc PO Box 468 *TF:* 877-496-8378 ■ *Web:* www.parishforge.com	Hempstead	TX	77445	979-826-8222	826-8224
Phoenix Forging Co Inc 800 Front St *TF:* 800-444-3674 ■ *Web:* www.phoenixforge.com	Catasauqua	PA	18032	610-264-2861	266-0530
Portland Forge 250 E Lafayette St *Web:* www.portlandforge.com	Portland	IN	47371	260-726-8121	726-8021
Powers & Sons LLC Pioneer Forge Div 1 Industrial Ave PO Box 598 *Web:* www.powersandsonsllc.com	Pioneer	OH	43554	419-737-2373	737-2978
Precision Metal Products Inc 850 W Bradley Ave *Web:* www.pmp-elcajon.com	El Cajon	CA	92020	619-448-2711	448-2005
Presrite Corp 3665 E 78th St *Web:* www.presrite.com	Cleveland	OH	44105	216-441-5990	441-2644
Randall Bearings Inc 1046 Greenlawn Ave PO Box 1258 *Web:* www.randallbearings.com	Lima	OH	45802	419-223-1075	228-0200
Saint Croix Forge Inc 5195 Scandia Trail *TF:* 800-966-3668 ■ *Web:* www.stcroixforge.com	Forest Lake	MN	55025	651-464-8967	464-8213

Company	City	State	Zip	Phone	Fax
Scot Forge Co 8001 Winn Rd PO Box 8 *TF:* 800-435-6621 ■ *Web:* www.scotforge.com	Spring Grove	IL	60081	847-587-1000	587-2000
Standard Steel LLC 500 N Walnut St *Web:* www.standardsteel.com	Burnham	PA	17009	717-248-4911	248-8050
Steel Industries Inc (SII) 12600 Beech-Daly Rd *TF:* 877-783-3599 ■ *Web:* www.steelindustriesinc.com	Redford Township	MI	48239	313-535-8505	534-2165
T & W Forge Inc 930 W Ely St *Web:* www.twforge.com	Alliance	OH	44601	330-821-5740	821-7309
Texas Metal Works Inc 13770 Industrial Rd *Web:* texmet.com	Houston	TX	77015	713-393-4200	455-8366
TFO Tech Co Ltd 221 State St	Jeffersonville	OH	43128	740-426-6381	426-6511
Thermal Structures Inc (TSI) 2362 Railroad St *TF:* 888-800-5811 ■ *Web:* www.thermalstructures.com	Corona	CA	92880	951-736-9911	736-1064
Thoro'Bred Inc 5020 E La Palma Ave *TF:* 800-854-6059 ■ *Web:* www.horseshoes.com	Anaheim	CA	92807	714-779-2581	779-1582
ThyssenKrupp Crankshaft Co LLC 1000 Lynch Rd *Web:* www.thyssenkruppgerlach.com	Danville	IL	61834	217-431-0060	431-8934
Trenton Forging Co 5523 Hoover St *Web:* www.trentonforging.com	Trenton	MI	48183	734-675-1620	675-4839
Trinity Forge Inc 947 Trinity Dr *Web:* www.trinityforge.com	Mansfield	TX	76063	817-473-1515	473-6743
Turbine Engine Components Technologies Corp (TECT) 1211 Old Albany Rd *TF:* 800-298-0333 ■ *Web:* www.tectcorp.com	Thomasville	GA	31792	229-228-2600	228-8949
Unit Drop Forge Co Inc 1903 S 62nd St PO Box 340350 *Web:* www.unitforgings.com	West Allis	WI	53234	414-545-3000	545-6318
United Brass Manufacturers Inc 35030 Goddard Rd PO Box 74095	Romulus	MI	48174	734-941-0700	941-0640
W Pat Crow Forgings Inc 200 Luxton St PO Box 1720 *Web:* www.wpatcrow.com	Fort Worth	TX	76104	817-536-2861	536-2861
Walker Forge Inc 222 E Erie St Suite 300 *Web:* www.walkerforge.com	Milwaukee	WI	53202	414-223-2000	223-2019
Webb Forging Co Inc 34375 W 12 Mile Rd *TF:* 800-526-9322 ■ *Web:* www.jervisbwebb.com	Farmington Hills	MI	48331	248-553-1000	553-1228
Weber Metals Inc 16706 Garfield Ave PO Box 318 *Web:* www.webermetals.com	Paramount	CA	90723	562-602-0260	602-0468
Western Forge & Flange Co 687 County Rd 2201 *TF:* 800-352-6433 ■ *Web:* www.western-forge.com	Cleveland	TX	77327	281-727-7000	727-7060
Wilton Precision Steel Co 320 W 1st St *Web:* www.wps01.com	Wilton	IA	52778	563-732-3363	732-3365
Wozniak Industries Inc 2 Mid America Plaza Suite 706 *Web:* www.wozniakindustries.com	Oakbrook Terrace	IL	60181	630-954-3400	954-3605
Wozniak Industries Inc Commercial Forged Products Div 5757 W 65th St *TF:* 800-637-2695 ■ *Web:* www.commercialforged.com	Bedford Park	IL	60638	708-458-1220	458-9346
Wyman-Gordon Co 10825 Telge Rd PO Box 40456 **Fax Area Code:* 508 ■ *TF:* 800-343-6070 ■ *Web:* www.wyman-gordon.com	Houston	TX	01536	281-856-9900	839-7500*

487 METAL HEAT TREATING

Company	City	State	Zip	Phone	Fax
Aerocraft Heat Treating Co Inc 15701 Minnesota Ave *Web:* www.aerocraft-ht.com	Paramount	CA	90723	562-634-3311	633-0364
Ajax Metal Processing Inc 4651 Bellevue St *Web:* www.ajaxmetal.com	Detroit	MI	48207	313-267-2100	267-2110
Alfred Heller Heat Treating Co 5 Wellington St	Clifton	NJ	07015	973-772-4200	772-0433
Bluewater Thermal Solutions 201 Brookfield Pwy Suite 102 *Web:* www.bluewaterthermal.com	Greenville	SC	29607	864-990-0050	990-0056
Chem-plate Industries Inc 1800 Touhy Ave *Web:* www.chemplateindustries.com	Elk Grove Village	IL	60007	847-640-1600	640-1699
Commercial Steel Treating Corp 31440 Stephenson Hwy *Web:* www.commercialsteel.com	Madison Heights	MI	48071	248-588-3300	588-3534
Curtiss-Wright Corp 10 Waterview Blvd 2nd Fl *NYSE: CW* ■ *Web:* www.curtisswright.com	Parsippany	NJ	07054	973-541-3700	541-3699
Dayton Forging & Heat Treating Co 215 N Findlay St *Web:* www.daytonforging.com	Dayton	OH	45403	937-253-4126	253-0409
Fisher-Barton Inc 201 Fredrick St	Watertown	WI	53094	920-261-0131	261-4549
Flame Metals Processing Corp 7317 W Lake St	Minneapolis	MN	55426	952-929-7815	925-0572
FPM LLC 1501 S Lively Blvd *TF:* 800-875-3316 ■ *Web:* www.fpmht.com	Elk Grove Village	IL	60007	847-228-2525	228-5912
Gibraltar Industries Inc 3556 Lakeshore Rd *NASDAQ: ROCK* ■ **Fax:* Sales ■ *TF:* 800-777-0675 ■ *Web:* www.gibraltar1.com	Buffalo	NY	14219	716-826-6500	826-1589*
Heat Treat Corp of America 1120 W 119th St	Chicago	IL	60643	773-264-1234	264-4321
Heat Treating Services Corp Of America PO Box 430269 *Web:* www.htsmi.com	Pontiac	MI	48343	248-858-2230	858-2242
HI TecMetal Group Inc 1101 E 55th St *TF:* 877-484-2867 ■ *Web:* www.htg.cc	Cleveland	OH	44103	216-881-8100	881-6811
Industrial Steel Treating Inc 613 Carroll St *Web:* www.indstl.com	Jackson	MI	49204	517-787-6312	787-5441
Maxco Inc 1005 Charlevoix Dr Suite 100 *Web:* www.maxc.com	Grand Ledge	MI	48837	517-627-1734	627-4951
Metal Improvement Co LLC 80 Rt 4 E Suite 310 *Web:* www.metalimprovement.com	Paramus	NJ	07652	201-843-7800	843-3460

Company	City	State	ZIP	Phone	Fax
Milastar Corp 7317 W Lake St *TF:* 877-888-8874	Minneapolis	MN	55426	952-929-7815	925-0572
Miller Consolidated Industries Inc 2221 Arbor Blvd *TF:* 800-589-4133	Dayton	OH	45439	937-294-2681	296-7986
Modern Industries Inc 613 W 11th St *Web:* www.mi-erie.com	Erie	PA	16501	814-455-8061	453-4382
Nitrex Metal Inc 3474 Poirier Blvd *Web:* www.nitrex.com	Saint-Laurent	QC	H4R2J5	514-335-7191	335-4160
Paulo Products Co 5620 W Pk Ave *Web:* www.paulo.com	Saint Louis	MO	63110	314-647-7500	647-7582
Rex Heat Treat 951 W 8th St PO Box 270 *TF:* 800-220-4739 ■ *Web:* www.rexht.com	Lansdale	PA	19446	215-855-1131	855-2028
Riverdale Plating & Heat Treating Inc 680 W 134th St *Web:* www.rpht.com	Riverdale	IL	60827	708-849-2050	849-6010
Robert Wooler Co 1755 Susquehanna Rd *Web:* www.robertwooler.com	Dresher	PA	19025	215-542-7600	542-0250
Specialty Steel Treating Inc 34501 Commerce Rd *Web:* www.specialtysteeltreating.com	Fraser	MI	48026	586-293-5355	293-5390
TC Industries Inc 3703 S Rt 31	Crystal Lake	IL	60012	815-459-2400	459-3303
ThyssenKrupp Stahl Co 11 E Pacific PO Box 6 *TF:* 888-395-1042 ■ *Web:* www.stahlspecialty.com	Kingsville	MO	64061	816-597-3322	597-3485
Tri-City Heat Treat Co 2020 5th St *Web:* www.tcht.com	Rock Island	IL	61201	309-786-2689	786-2691
Trutec Industries Inc 4700 Gateway Blvd *TF:* 800-933-8832 ■ *Web:* www.parkerionics.com	Springfield	OH	45502	937-323-8833	323-9192
Wall Colmonoy Corp 101 W Girard Ave *TF:* 800-521-2412 ■ *Web:* www.wallcolmonoy.com	Madison Heights	MI	48071	248-585-6400	585-7960
Ward Aluminum Casting Co 642 Growth Ave *TF:* 866-427-8700 ■ *Web:* www.wardcorp.com	Fort Wayne	IN	46808	260-426-8700	420-1919

488 METAL INDUSTRIES (MISC)

SEE ALSO Foundries - Investment p. 1881; Foundries - Iron & Steel p. 1881; Foundries - Nonferrous (Castings) p. 1883; Metal Heat Treating p. 2235; Metal Tube & Pipe p. 2240; Steel - Mfr p. 2676; Wire & Cable p. 2775

Company	City	State	ZIP	Phone	Fax
Alcoa Inc 201 Isabella St *NYSE: AA* ■ *Web:* www.alcoa.com	Pittsburgh	PA	15212	412-553-4545	553-4498
Alcoa Mill Products 4879 State St *TF:* 800-237-3254	Riverdale	IA	52722	563-459-3000	459-3021
Alcoa Primary Metals 900 S Gay St Riverview Tower Suite 1100 **Fax:* Sales ■ *TF:* 800-852-0238 ■ *Web:* www.alcoa.com	Knoxville	TN	37902	865-594-4700	594-4790*
Allegheny Technologies Inc 1000 Six PPG Pl *NYSE: ATI* ■ **Fax:* Hum Res ■ *TF Sales:* 800-258-3586 ■ *Web:* www.alleghenytechnologies.com	Pittsburgh	PA	15222	412-394-2800	394-3034*
Allvac Inc 2020 Ashcraft Ave PO Box 5030 **Fax:* Sales ■ *TF:* 800-841-5491 ■ *Web:* www.allvac.com	Monroe	NC	28110	704-289-4511	289-4018*
Altech LLC 242 America Pl *TF:* 800-264-8256	Jeffersonville	IN	47130	812-282-8256	280-6070
AMETEK Inc Specialty Metal Products Div 1085 Rt 519 PO Box 427 *Web:* www.ametekmetals.com	Eighty Four	PA	15330	724-225-8400	225-6622
AMETEK Specialty Metal Products 21 Toelles Rd *Web:* www.ametekmetals.com	Wallingford	CT	06492	203-265-6731	294-0196
Ampco Metal Inc 1117 E Algonquin Rd *TF:* 800-437-6100 ■ *Web:* www.ampcometal.com	Arlington Heights	IL	60005	847-437-6000	437-6008
Anaheim Extrusion Co Inc 1330 N Kraemer Blvd PO Box 6380 *TF:* 800-660-3318 ■ *Web:* www.anaheimextrude.com	Anaheim	CA	92806	714-630-3111	630-0443
Ansonia Copper & Brass Inc 75 Liberty St *TF Cust Svc:* 800-521-1703 ■ *Web:* www.ansoniacb.com	Ansonia	CT	06401	203-732-6600	735-3787
Arvinyl Metal Laminates Corp 233 N Sherman Ave *TF:* 800-278-4695 ■ *Web:* www.arvinyl.com	Corona	CA	92882	951-371-7800	371-7118
Audubon Metals LLC 3055 Ohio Dr *Web:* www.audubonmetals.com	Henderson	KY	42420	270-830-6622	830-9594
Big River Zinc Corp 2401 Mississippi Ave *TF:* 800-274-4002 ■ *Web:* www.bigriverzinc.com	Sauget	IL	62201	618-274-5000	274-4444
Bolton Metal Products Co 2022 Axemann Rd PO Box 388 **Fax:* Sales ■ *Web:* www.boltonmetals.com	Bellefonte	PA	16823	814-355-6330	355-6227*
Bonnell Aluminum 25 Bonnell St *Web:* www.bonlalum.com	Newnan	GA	30263	770-253-2020	254-7711
Broco Inc 10868 Bell Ct *TF:* 800-845-7259 ■ *Web:* www.broco-rankin.com	Rancho Cucamonga	CA	91730	909-483-3222	483-3233
Bunting Magnetics Co 500 S Spencer Ave *TF Cust Svc:* 800-835-2526 ■ *Web:* www.bunting-magnetics.com	Newton	KS	67114	316-284-2020	283-4975
Cabot Supermetals 1095 Windward Ridge Pkwy Suite 200 **Fax Area Code:* 678 ■ *TF:* 888-390-9430 ■ *Web:* www.cabot-corp.com	Alpharetta	GA	30005	610-367-1500	297-1498*
Cannon Muskegon Corp 2875 Lincoln St PO Box 506 *TF:* 800-253-0371 ■ *Web:* www.c-mgroup.com	Muskegon	MI	49441	231-755-1681	755-4975
Cardinal Aluminum Co 6910 Preston Hwy *TF Cust Svc:* 800-398-7833 ■ *Web:* www.1800extrude.com	Louisville	KY	40219	502-969-9302	968-4269
CCMA LLC 450 Corporate Pkwy Suite 100 *TF:* 800-828-6621 ■ *Web:* www.ccmetals.com	Amherst	NY	14226	716-446-8861	446-8897
Century Aluminum Co 2511 Garden Rd Suite 200 Bldg A *NASDAQ: CENX* ■ *TF:* 888-642-9300 ■ *Web:* www.centuryaluminum.com	Monterey	CA	93940	831-642-9300	657-1299
Century Aluminum of Kentucky 1627 SR 271 N PO Box 500	Hawesville	KY	42348	270-685-2493	852-2886
Certified Alloy Products Inc 3245 Cherry Ave *TF:* 800-421-3763	Long Beach	CA	90807	562-595-6621	427-8667
Chase Brass & Copper Co 14212 County Rd M 50 PO Box 152 **Fax:* Mail Rm ■ *TF:* 800-537-4291 ■ *Web:* www.chasebrass.com	Montpelier	OH	43543	419-485-3193	485-4850*
Chicago Extruded Metals Co (CXM) 1601 S 54th Ave *TF Cust Svc:* 800-323-8102 ■ *Web:* www.cxm.com	Cicero	IL	60804	708-656-7900	780-3479
Clarion Sintered Metals PO Box S	Ridgway	PA	15853	814-773-3124	776-5775
Colonial Metals Co 217 Linden St PO Box 311 *Web:* www.colonialmetalsco.com	Columbia	PA	17512	717-684-2311	684-9555
Columbia Falls Aluminum Co 2000 Alluminum Dr *Web:* www.cfaluminum.com	Columbia Falls	MT	59912	406-892-8400	892-8201
Cookson Electronics Assembly Materials 600 Rt 440 *TF:* 800-367-5450 ■ *Web:* www.alphametals.com	Jersey City	NJ	07304	201-434-6778	434-7508
Croft LLC 107 Oliver Emmerich Dr *TF:* 800-222-3195 ■ *Web:* www.croftllc.com	McComb	MS	39648	601-684-6121	684-5134
Curtis Steel Co LLC (CSC) 6504 Hurst St PO Box 7469 *TF:* 800-749-4621 ■ *Web:* www.curtissteelco.com	Houston	TX	77008	713-861-4621	861-9718
Custom Aluminum Products Inc 414 Division St *TF:* 800-745-6333 ■ *Web:* www.custom-aluminum.com	South Elgin	IL	60177	847-741-6333	741-2266
Danaher Motion 1500 Mittel Blvd *TF:* 866-993-2624 ■ *Web:* www.danahermotion.com	Wood Dale	IL	60191	630-860-7300	694-3305
Deringer-Ney Inc 616 Atrium Dr Suite 100 *Web:* www.deringerney.com	Vernon Hills	IL	60061	847-566-4100	367-6029
Doe Run Co 1801 Pk 270 Dr Suite 300 *TF:* 800-356-3786 ■ *Web:* www.doerun.com	Saint Louis	MO	63146	314-453-7110	453-7180
Dynamet Inc 195 Museum Rd *TF:* 800-237-9655 ■ *Web:* www.dynamet.com	Washington	PA	15301	724-228-1000	229-4195
Eastern Alloys Inc 11 Henry Henning Dr PO Box 317 *TF:* 800-456-1496 ■ *Web:* www.eazall.com	Maybrook	NY	12543	845-427-2151	427-5185
Elmet Technologies Inc 1560 Lisbon St *TF:* 800-343-8008 ■ *Web:* www.elmettechnologies.com	Lewiston	ME	04240	207-784-3591	786-8924
Empire Resources Inc 1 Parker Plaza *PINK: ERSO* ■ *Web:* www.empireresources.com	Fort Lee	NJ	07024	201-944-2200	944-2226
Erie Coke Corp 100 E Ave *Web:* www.eriecoke.com	Erie	PA	16507	814-454-0177	454-2331
Flat Rock Metal Inc (FRM) 26601 W Huron River Dr PO Box 1090 *Web:* www.frm.com	Flat Rock	MI	48134	734-782-4454	782-5640
Futura Industries Freeport Ctr Bldg H-11 PO Box 160350 **Fax:* Hum Res ■ *TF:* 800-824-2049 ■ *Web:* www.westlandfloral.com	Clearfield	UT	84016	801-773-6282	774-3271*
General Extrusions Inc 4040 Lake Pk Rd *Web:* www.genext.com	Youngstown	OH	44512	330-783-0270	788-1250
Glines & Rhodes Inc 189 E St PO Box 2285 *TF:* 800-343-1196 ■ *Web:* www.glinesandrhodes.com	Attleboro	MA	02703	508-226-2000	226-7136
Globe Metallurgical Corp 2401 Old Montgomery Hwy	Selma	AL	36703	334-872-3491	874-2098
H Kramer & Co 1345 W 21st St *TF:* 800-621-2305	Chicago	IL	60608	312-226-6600	226-4713
Handy & Harman 555 Theodore Fremd Ave *Web:* www.handyharman.com	Rye	NY	10580	914-921-5200	925-4496
Haynes International Inc 1020 W Pk Ave PO Box 9013 *TF:* 800-354-0806 ■ *Web:* www.haynesintl.com	Kokomo	IN	46904	765-456-6000	456-6905
HC Starck Inc 45 Industrial Pl *Web:* www.hcstarck.com	Newton	MA	02461	617-630-5800	630-4888
Hoeganaes Corp 1001 Taylors Ln **Fax:* Hum Res ■ *Web:* www.hoeganaes.com	Cinnaminson	NJ	08077	856-829-2220	303-2720*
Hoover & Strong Inc 10700 Trade Rd **Fax Area Code:* 800 ■ *TF Cust Svc:* 800-759-9997 ■ *Web:* www.hooverandstrong.com	Richmond	VA	23236	804-794-3700	616-9997*
Hoover Precision Products Inc 2200 Pendley Rd *Web:* www.hooverprecision.com	Cumming	GA	30041	770-889-9223	889-0828
Hussey Copper Ltd 100 Washington St *TF:* 800-733-8866 ■ *Web:* www.husseycopper.com	Leetsdale	PA	15056	724-251-4200	251-4243
Hydro Aluminum Rockledge Inc 100 Gus Hipp Blvd **Fax:* Sales ■ *Web:* www.hydro.com	Rockledge	FL	32955	321-636-8147	632-1486*
IMC Group 165 Township Line Rd 1 Pitcairn Pl Suite 1200 *TF:* 800-220-6800 ■ *Web:* www.imc-group.com	Jenkintown	PA	19046	215-517-6000	517-6050
Indalex Aluminum Solutions Group 75 Tri State International Dr *TF:* 877-276-1802 ■ *Web:* www.indalex.com	Lincolnshire	IL	60069	847-810-3000	295-3845
Industrial Tectonics Inc 7222 Huron River Dr *TF:* 800-482-2255 ■ *Web:* www.itiball.com	Dexter	MI	48130	734-426-4681	426-4701
Johnson Matthey Inc 435 Devon Pk Dr Suite 600 *Web:* www.matthey.com	Wayne	PA	19087	610-971-3000	971-3022
JW Aluminum 1100 Richmond St *Web:* www.jwaluminum.com	Jackson	TN	38301	731-424-2000	422-7805
JW Aluminum Co 435 Old Mt Holly Rd *TF:* 800-568-1100 ■ *Web:* www.jwaluminum.com	Mount Holly	SC	29445	843-572-1100	572-1049
Kaiser Aluminum Corp 27422 Portola Pkwy Suite 200 *TF Sales:* 800-873-2011 ■ *Web:* www.kaiseraluminum.com	Foothill Ranch	CA	92610	949-614-1740	614-1930
Keystone Powdered Metal Co 251 State St *Web:* www.keystonepm.com	Saint Marys	PA	15857	814-781-1591	781-7648
Light Metals Corp 2740 Prairie St SW *Web:* www.light-metals.com	Wyoming	MI	49509	616-538-3030	538-2713

	City	State	Zip	Phone	Fax
Linemaster Switch Corp 29 Plaine Hill Rd	Woodstock	CT	06281	860-974-1000	974-3668*
**Fax Area Code:* 800 ■ *Web:* www.linemaster.com					
Loxcreen Co Inc The 1630 Old Dunbar Rd PO Box 4004	West Columbia	SC	29172	803-822-8200	822-8547
TF: 800-394-8667 ■ *Web:* www.loxcreen.com					
Lucas-Milhaupt Inc 5656 S Pennsylvania Ave	Cudahy	WI	53110	414-769-6000	769-1093
TF: 800-558-3856 ■ *Web:* www.lucasmilhaupt.com					
Luvata Appleton LLC 553 Carter Ct	Kimberly	WI	54136	920-749-3820	749-3850
TF: 800-747-2912 ■ *Web:* www.luvata.com					
Luvata Buffalo Inc 70 Sayre St	Buffalo	NY	14207	716-879-6700	879-6892
TF Sales: 800-828-7426 ■ *Web:* www.luvata.com					
Luvata Ohio Inc 1376 Pittsburgh Dr	Delaware	OH	43015	740-363-1981	363-3847
Web: www.luvata.com					
Magnat-Fairview Inc 1102 Sheridan St	Chicopee	MA	01022	413-593-5742	593-9451
TF: 800-569-1286 ■ *Web:* www.magnatfairview.com					
Magnetech Industrial Services Inc 551 W Merrill St	Indianapolis	IN	46225	317-266-1659	637-5744
TF: 800-944-0141 ■ *Web:* www.magnetech.com					
Magnode Corp 400 E State St	Trenton	OH	45067	513-988-6351	988-6357
Web: www.magnode.com					
Magotteaux Inc 724 Cool Springs Blvd Suite 200	Franklin	TN	37067	615-385-3055	297-6743
Web: www.magotteaux.com					
Maurice Pincoffs Co Inc 1235 N Loop W Suite 510 PO Box 920919	Houston	TX	77292	713-681-5461	681-8521
TF: 888-268-0894 ■ *Web:* www.pincoffs.com					
Memry Corp 3 Berkshire Blvd	Bethel	CT	06801	203-739-1100	798-6606
TF: 866-466-3679 ■ *Web:* www.memry.com					
Metal Conversions Ltd Crawford Rd PO Box 787	Mansfield	OH	44901	419-525-0011	525-4961
Metallurgical Products Co 810 Lincoln Ave PO Box 598	West Chester	PA	19381	610-696-6770	430-8431
TF: 800-659-4672 ■ *Web:* www.metprodco.com					
Metglas Inc 440 Allied Dr	Conway	SC	29526	843-349-7319	349-6815
TF: 800-581-7654 ■ *Web:* www.metglas.com					
Micro Surface Engr Inc 1550 E Slauson Ave	Los Angeles	CA	90011	323-582-7348	582-0934
TF: 800-322-5832 ■ *Web:* www.precisionballs.com					
Midland Industries Inc 1424 N Halsted St	Chicago	IL	60622	312-664-7300	664-7371
TF: 800-662-8228 ■ *Web:* www.zincbig.com					
Miller Co 275 Pratt St	Meriden	CT	06450	203-235-4474	639-6924
Web: www.themillerco.com					
Mueller Brass Co 2199 Lapeer Ave	Port Huron	MI	48060	810-987-7770	987-9108
TF: 800-553-3336					
Mueller Industries Inc 8285 Tournament Dr Suite 150	Memphis	TN	38125	901-753-3200	753-3251
NYSE: MLI ■ *TF:* 800-348-8464 ■ *Web:* www.muellerindustries.com					
NetShape Technologies Inc 31005 Solon Rd	Solon	OH	44139	440-248-5456	248-5807
TF: 866-429-5724 ■ *Web:* www.netshapetech.com					
New England Miniature Ball Corp 163 Greenwood Rd W PO Box 585	Norfolk	CT	06058	860-542-5543	542-5058
Web: www.nemb.com					
Nichols Aluminum 1725 Rockingham Rd	Davenport	IA	52802	563-324-2121	324-7911
TF: 800-553-5508 ■ *Web:* www.nicholsal.com					
NN Inc 2000 Waters Edge Dr Bldg 3 Suite 12	Johnson City	TN	37604	423-743-9151	743-8870
NASDAQ: NNBR ■ *TF:* 800-733-9151 ■ *Web:* www.nnbr.com					
Noranda Aluminum Inc 801 Crescent Ctr Dr Suite 600	Franklin	TN	37067	615-771-5700	771-5701
TF: 800-344-7522					
Norandal USA Inc 400 Bill Brooks Dr	Huntingdon	TN	38344	731-986-5011	986-2739
Norandal USA Inc 1709 Jake Alexander Blvd S	Salisbury	NC	28146	704-633-6020	637-4582
Novelis North America 6060 Parkland Blvd	Cleveland	OH	44124	440-423-6600	423-6601
Web: www.novelis.com					
Nyrstar Clarksville 1800 Zinc Plant Rd PO Box 1104	Clarksville	TN	37041	931-552-4200	552-0471
Web: www.nyrstar.com					
Olin Corp Brass Div 427 N Shamrock St	East Alton	IL	62024	618-258-5665	258-5322
Web: www.olinbrass.com					
Ormet Corp 43840 State Rt 7 PO Box 176	Hannibal	OH	43931	740-483-1381	483-2622
TF: 800-282-9701 ■ *Web:* www.ormet.com					
Ormet Primary Aluminum Corp 43840 State Rd 7 PO Box 176	Hannibal	OH	43931	740-483-1381	483-2622
TF: 800-282-9701 ■ *Web:* www.ormet.com					
Pacal LLC 2500 W County Rd B	Roseville	MN	55113	651-631-1111	631-9268*
**Fax:* Sales ■ *TF:* 800-328-9836 ■ *Web:* www.pacal.com					
Patrick Industries Inc Patrick Metals Div 5020 Lincolnway E	Mishawaka	IN	46544	574-255-9692	256-6577
TF: 800-922-9692 ■ *Web:* www.patrickmetals.com					
Penn Aluminum International Inc 1117 N 2nd St PO Box 490	Murphysboro	IL	62966	618-684-2146	684-2463
TF: 800-445-7366 ■ *Web:* www.pennaluminum.com					
Phelps Dodge Refining Corp 897 Hawkins Blvd	El Paso	TX	79915	915-778-9881	782-7783
Piper Metal Forming Corp 795 Sam Barkley Dr	New Albany	MS	38652	662-534-5046	538-6561
Polymetallurgical Corp 262 Broad St	North Attleboro	MA	02760	508-695-7700	695-7700
Web: www.polymet.com					
Postle Aluminum Co 511 Pine Creek Ct	Elkhart	IN	46516	574-389-0800	389-0700
Web: www.postledistributors.com					
Profile Extrusion Co 100 Anderson Rd	Rome	GA	30161	706-234-7558	234-7649
Web: www.profile-extrusion.com					
Revere Copper Products Inc 1 Revere Pk	Rome	NY	13440	315-338-2022	338-2224*
**Fax:* Sales ■ *TF:* 800-448-1776 ■ *Web:* www.reverecopper.com					
RMI Titanium Co 1000 Warren Ave	Niles	OH	44446	330-652-9951	544-7796*
Ross Metals Corp 54 W 47th St	New York	NY	10036	212-869-4433	768-3018
TF: 800-654-7677 ■ *Web:* www.rossmetals.com					
RSR Corp 2777 Stemmons Fwy Suite 1800	Dallas	TX	75207	214-631-6070	631-6146
Sanders Lead Co 1 Sanders Rd PO Box 707	Troy	AL	36081	334-566-1563	566-0107
TF: 800-633-8744					
Sandvik Special Metals Corp 43507 S Piert Rd	Kennewick	WA	99337	509-586-4131	582-3552
Web: www.smt.sandvik.com					
Shieldalloy Metallurgical Corp 545 Beckett Rd Suite 201	Swedesboro	NJ	08085	856-692-4200	241-4655
TF: 800-762-2020 ■ *Web:* www.shieldalloy.com					
Simcala Inc 1940 Ohio Ferro Rd PO Box 68	Mount Meigs	AL	36057	334-215-7560	215-8969
TF: 800-321-9828					
Sipi Metals Corp 1720 N Elston Ave	Chicago	IL	60622	773-276-0070	276-7014
Web: www.sipimetals.com					
Southern Metals Co 301 Ashe St	Sheffield	AL	35660	256-383-3261	383-5204
TF: 800-843-2771 ■ *Web:* www.sometco.com					
Southwire Co 1 Southwire Dr	Carrollton	GA	30119	770-832-4242	838-6462
TF: 800-444-1700 ■ *Web:* www.southwire.com					
Special Metals Corp 4317 Middle Settlement Rd	New Hartford	NY	13413	315-798-2900	798-2016*
**Fax:* Sales ■ *TF:* 800-334-8351 ■ *Web:* www.specialmetals.com					
Spectro Alloys Corp 13220 Doyle Path	Rosemount	MN	55068	651-437-2815	438-3714
TF: 800-328-9321 ■ *Web:* www.spectroalloys.com					
Symmco Group Inc PO Box F	Sykesville	PA	15865	814-894-2461	894-5272
Web: www.symmco.com					
Taber Extrusions LP 915 S Elmira Ave	Russellville	AR	72802	479-968-1021	968-8645
TF: 800-563-6853 ■ *Web:* www.taberextrusions.com					
Titanium Metals Corp (TIMET) 5430 LBJ Fwy Suite 1700	Dallas	TX	75240	972-934-5300	934-5345
NYSE: TIE ■ *TF:* 800-753-1550 ■ *Web:* www.timet.com					
Tower Extrusions Ltd 1003 State Hwy 79 S	Olney	TX	76374	940-564-5681	564-5033
Web: www.towerextrusion.com					
Tree Island Industries 3933 Boundary Rd PO Box 50	New Westminster	BC	V3L4Y1	604-524-3744	524-2362
TF: 800-663-0955 ■ *Web:* www.treeisland.com					
US Bronze Powders Inc 408 Rt 202 N	Flemington	NJ	08822	908-782-5454	782-3489
TF: 800-544-0186 ■ *Web:* www.usbronzepowders.com					
US Magnesium LLC 238 N 2200 W	Salt Lake City	UT	84116	801-532-2043	534-1407
Web: www.usmagnesium.com					
Valimet Inc PO Box 31690	Stockton	CA	95213	209-982-4870	982-1365
Web: www.valimet.com					
Valmont Industries Inc 1 Valmont Plaza	Omaha	NE	68154	402-963-1000	963-1100
NYSE: VMI ■ *TF:* 800-825-6668 ■ *Web:* www.valmont.com					
Victory White Metal Co 6100 Roland Ave	Cleveland	OH	44127	216-271-1400	271-6430
TF: 800-635-5050 ■ *Web:* www.vwmc.com					
Wabash Alloys LLC 4525 W Old 24	Wabash	IN	46992	260-563-7461	563-5997
TF: 800-348-0571 ■ *Web:* www.wabashalloys.com					
Wah Chang 1600 Old Salem Rd NE	Albany	OR	97321	541-926-4211	812-7030
TF: 888-926-4211 ■ *Web:* www.wahchang.com					
Xyron Inc 8465 N 90th St Suite 6	Scottsdale	AZ	85258	480-443-9419	443-0118
TF: 800-793-3523 ■ *Web:* www.xyron.com					

489 METAL PRODUCTS - HOUSEHOLD

	City	State	Zip	Phone	Fax
Acme International Enterprises Inc 400 lyster Ave	saddleburk	NJ	07663	973-416-0400	416-0499
Web: www.acme-usa.com					
All-Clad Metalcrafters LLC 424 Morganza Rd	Canonsburg	PA	15317	724-745-8300	746-5035
TF Cust Svc: 800-255-2523 ■ *Web:* www.allclad.custhelp.com					
Calphalon Corp PO Box 583	Toledo	OH	43697	419-666-8700	666-2859*
**Fax:* Sales ■ *TF:* 800-809-7267 ■ *Web:* www.calphalon.com					
Chantal Cookware Corp 5425 N Sam Houston Pkwy W	Houston	TX	77086	281-587-7800	444-1253
TF: 800-365-4354 ■ *Web:* www.chantalcookware.com					
CM Packaging 800 Ela Rd	Lake Zurich	IL	60047	847-438-2171	438-0369
TF: 800-323-0422 ■ *Web:* www.cmpackaging.com					
G & S Metal Products Co Inc 3330 E 79th St	Cleveland	OH	44127	216-441-0700	441-0736
Web: www.gsmetal.com					
Kitchen-Quip Inc 405 E Marion St	Waterloo	IN	46793	260-837-8311	837-7919
Web: www.kqcasting.com					
Le Creuset of America Inc 114 Bob Gifford Blvd	Early Branch	SC	29916	803-943-4308	943-0241
TF: 800-827-1798 ■ *Web:* www.lecreuset.com					
Lifetime Brands Inc 1000 Steward Ave	Garden City	NY	11530	516-683-6000	683-6116
NASDAQ: LCUT ■ *TF:* 800-252-3390 ■ *Web:* www.lifetimebrands.com					
Lifetime Brands Inc Farberware Div 1000 Stewart Ave	Garden City	NY	11530	516-683-6000	683-6161
TF: 800-252-3390 ■ *Web:* www.farberware.com					
Lifetime Brands Inc Hoffritz Div 1000 Stewart Ave	Garden City	CA	11530	516-683-6000	555-0101
TF: 800-252-3390 ■ *Web:* www.lifetimebrands.com					
ME Heuck Co Inc 6386 Gano Rd	West Chester	OH	45069	513-573-9918	573-9919
TF Cust Svc: 866-634-3825 ■ *Web:* www.heuck.com					
Meyer Corp 525 Curtola Pkwy	Vallejo	CA	94590	707-551-2800	551-2953*
**Fax:* PR ■ *TF Cust Svc:* 800-888-3883 ■ *Web:* www.meyer.com					
Newell Rubbermaid Inc Home & Family Group 3 Glenlake Pkwy	Atlanta	GA	30328	770-418-7000	407-3970
Web: www.newellrubbermaid.com					
Nordic Products Inc 2215 Merrill Creek Pkwy	Everett	WA	98203	425-261-1000	261-1001
TF: 800-722-0202 ■ *Web:* www.norpro.com					
Northland Aluminum Products Inc 5005 Hwy 7	Minneapolis	MN	55416	952-920-2888	924-8561
TF: 800-328-4310 ■ *Web:* www.nordicware.com					
OXO International 75 9th Ave 5th Fl	New York	NY	10011	212-242-3333	242-3336
TF: 800-545-4411 ■ *Web:* www.oxo.com					
Regal Ware Inc 1675 Reigle Dr	Kewaskum	WI	53040	262-626-2121	626-8565
Web: www.regalware.com					
Rena Ware International Inc 15885 NE 28th St	Bellevue	WA	98008	425-881-6171	882-7500
Web: www.renaware.com					
Saladmaster Inc 230 Westway Pl Suite 101	Arlington	TX	76018	817-633-3555	633-5544
TF: 800-765-5795 ■ *Web:* www.saladmaster.com					
T-Fal Corp 1 Boland Dr Suite 101	West Orange	NJ	07052	973-736-0300	736-9078
TF: 800-395-8325 ■ *Web:* www.t-falusa.com					

Phone *Fax*

Whitesell Corp 2703 Avalon Ave ... Muscle Shoals AL 35661 256-248-8500 248-8585
TF: 800-826-3317 ■ *Web:* www.whitesellcorp.com

Wilton Armetale Co PO Box 600 ... Mount Joy PA 17552 717-653-4444 653-6573
TF: 800-553-2048 ■ *Web:* www.armetale.com

Wilton Industries Inc 2240 W 75th St ... Woodridge IL 60517 630-963-7100 963-7196*
**Fax:* Sales ■ *TF:* 800-794-5866 ■ *Web:* www.wilton.com

World Kitchen Inc 11911 Freedom Dr Suite 600 ... Reston VA 20190 703-456-4700 456-2020
TF Cust Svc: 800-999-3436 ■ *Web:* www.worldkitchen.com

Zyliss USA Corp 1 Post Suite 100 ... Irvine CA 92618 949-699-1884 699-1788
TF: 888-794-7623 ■ *Web:* www.zylissusa.com

490 METAL PRODUCTS (MISC)

Phone *Fax*

Accuride International Inc
12311 Shoemaker Ave ... Santa Fe Springs CA 90670 562-903-0200 903-0232
Web: www.accuride.com

Aerodyne Alloys LLC
350 Pleasant Valley Rd ... South Windsor CT 06074 860-289-6011 289-2841
TF: 800-243-4344 ■ *Web:* www.aerodynealloys.com

Alexandria Extrusion Co
401 County Rd 22 NW ... Alexandria MN 56308 320-763-6537 763-9250
TF: 800-568-6601 ■ *Web:* www.alexandriaextrusion.com

Aluchem Inc 1 Landy Ln ... Cincinnati OH 45215 513-733-8519 733-0608
TF: 800-336-8519 ■ *Web:* www.aluchem.com

Aluminum Ladder Co 1430 W Darlington St ... Florence SC 29501 843-662-2595 661-0972
TF: 800-752-2526 ■ *Web:* www.aluminumladder.com

Alwin Mfg Co Inc 2954 Holmgren Ave ... Green Bay WI 54304 920-499-1424 499-7254
Web: www.alwin.com

Amatom Electronic Hardware LLC
5 Pasco Hill Rd ... Cromwell CT 06416 860-828-0847 526-2057
TF: 800-243-6032 ■ *Web:* www.amatom.com

Arland Tool & Mfg Inc PO Box 207 ... Sturbridge MA 01566 508-347-3368 347-9397
Web: www.arland.com

Bead Industries Inc 11 Cascade Blvd ... Milford CT 06460 203-301-0270 301-0280
TF: 800-297-4851 ■ *Web:* www.beadindustries.com

Bobrick Washroom Equipment Inc
11611 Hart St ... North Hollywood CA 91605 818-764-1000 765-2700
Web: www.bobrick.com

Carolina Carports Inc PO Box 1263 ... Dobson NC 27017 336-367-6400 367-6410
TF: 800-670-4262 ■ *Web:* www.carolinacarportsinc.com

Ditto Sales Inc 2332 Cathy Ln ... Jasper IN 47546 812-482-3043 482-9318
Web: www.dittosales.com

Flinchbaugh Engineering Inc 4387 Run Way ... York PA 17406 717-755-1900 840-3217
TF: 866-967-5334 ■ *Web:* www.fei-york.com

Gonzalez Mfg Tech
29401 Stephenson Hwy ... Madison Heights MI 48071 916-955-4760
Web: www.gonzalezdesign.com

Iowa Laser Technology Inc
7100 Chancellor Dr ... Cedar Falls IA 50613 319-266-3561 383-3561*
**Fax Area Code:* 563 ■ *TF:* 800-254-7794 ■ *Web:* www.iowalaser.com

J.a. Reinhardt & Co Inc Spruce Cabin Rd ... Mountainhome PA 18342 570-595-7491 595-3551
Web: www.jareinhardt.com

Lechler Inc 445 Kautz Rd ... Saint Charles IL 60174 630-377-6611 444-7069*
**Fax Area Code:* 800 ■ *TF Cust Svc:* 800-777-2926 ■ *Web:* www.lechlerusa.com

Liberty Safe & Security Products Inc
1199 W Utah Ave ... Payson UT 84651 801-925-1000 465-2712
TF: 800-247-5625 ■ *Web:* www.libertysafe.com

Magnaplan Corp 1320 SR- 9 ... Champlain NY 12919 518-298-8404 298-2368
TF: 888-884-5444 ■ *Web:* www.visualplanning.com

Magnetic Instrumentation Inc
8431 Castlewood Dr ... Indianapolis IN 46250 317-842-7500 849-7600
Web: www.maginst.com

Metalworking Group Inc 9070 Pippin Rd ... Cincinnati OH 45251 513-521-4114 521-2816
TF: 800-476-9409 ■ *Web:* www.metalworkinggroup.com

Muza Metal Products Corp 606 E Murdock Ave ... Oshkosh WI 54901 920-236-3535 236-3520
Web: www.muzametal.com

Palmer International Inc PO Box 315 ... Skippack PA 19474 610-584-4241 584-4870
Web: www.palmerint.com

Polar Ware Co Inc PO Box 211 ... Sheboygan WI 53082 920-458-3561 458-2205
TF Cust Svc: 800-237-3655 ■ *Web:* www.polarware.com

Precision Valve Corp PO Box 309 ... Yonkers NY 10702 914-969-6500 966-4428
TF: 800-431-2697 ■ *Web:* www.precision-valve.com

Spirol International Corp 30 Rock Ave ... Danielson CT 06239 860-774-8571 774-2048
Web: www.spirol.com

Spraying Systems Co PO Box 7900 ... Wheaton IL 60189 630-665-5000 260-0842
TF: 800-957-7729 ■ *Web:* www.spray.com

Tooling & Equipment International Corp
12550 Tech Ctr Dr ... Livonia MI 48150 734-522-1422 522-1780
Web: www.teintl.net

Trailco Inc 900 E 14th St ... Chicago Heights IL 60411 708-757-4200 757-3933
Web: www.trialco.net

Trinity Industries Inc Head Div
11765 Hwy 6 S ... Navasota TX 77868 936-825-6581
Web: www.trinityheads.com

TST Inc 11601 Etiwanda Ave ... Fontana CA 92337 951-685-2155 685-7806
Web: www.tst-inc.com

Viking Materials Inc 3225 Como Ave SE ... Minneapolis MN 55414 612-617-5800 623-9070
TF: 800-682-3942 ■ *Web:* www.vikingmaterials.com

491 METAL STAMPINGS

SEE ALSO Closures - Metal or Plastics p. 1607; Electronic Enclosures p. 1815; Metal Stampings - Automotive p. 2240

Phone *Fax*

Accurate Perforating Co 3636 S Kedzie Ave ... Chicago IL 60632 773-254-3232 254-9453
TF: 800-621-0273 ■ *Web:* www.accurateperforating.com

Acme Metal Cap Inc Co 33-53 62nd St ... Woodside NY 11377 718-335-3000 335-3037
TF: 800-338-3581 ■ *Web:* www.acmepans.com

Admiral Craft Equipment Corp
940 S Oyster Bay Rd ... Hicksville NY 11801 516-433-3535 443-4453
TF: 800-223-7750 ■ *Web:* www.admiralcraft.com

AK Stamping Inc 1159 US Rt 22 ... Mountainside NJ 07092 908-232-7300 232-5202
TF Cust Svc: 800-227-3258 ■ *Web:* www.akstamping.com

Albest Metal Stamping Corp 1 Kent Ave ... Brooklyn NY 11211 718-388-6000 388-0404
Web: www.albest.com

Alcoa Inc 201 Isabella St ... Pittsburgh PA 15212 412-553-4545 553-4498
NYSE: AA ■ *Web:* www.alcoa.com

Alinabal Inc 28 Woodmont Rd ... Milford CT 06460 203-877-3241 874-5063
TF: 800-254-6763 ■ *Web:* www.alinabal.com

All New Stamping Co 10801 Lower Azusa Rd ... El Monte CA 91731 626-443-8813 877-8121*
**Fax Area Code:* 800 ■ *TF:* 800-877-7775 ■ *Web:* www.allnewstamping.com

American Metalcraft Inc 2074 George St ... Melrose Park IL 60160 708-345-1177 345-5758
TF: 800-333-9133 ■ *Web:* www.amnow.com

American Products LLC 597 Evergreen Rd ... Strafford MO 65757 417-736-2135 736-2662
Web: www.amprod.us

American Trim 1005 W Grand Ave ... Lima OH 45801 419-228-1145 996-4850
Web: www.amtrim.com

APG Cash Drawer LLC
5250 Industrial Blvd NE ... Minneapolis MN 55421 763-571-5000 571-5771
Web: www.apgcd.com

Aranda Tooling Inc
15301 Springdale St ... Huntington Beach CA 92649 714-379-6565 379-6570
Web: www.arandatooling.com

Argo Products Co 3500 Goodfellow Blvd ... Saint Louis MO 63120 314-385-1803 385-1808
Web: www.argoproducts.com

Arrow Tru-Line Inc 2211 S Defiance St ... Archbold OH 43502 419-446-2785 445-2068
TF: 877-285-7253 ■ *Web:* www.arrowtruline.com

Arvin Sango Inc 2905 Wilson Ave ... Madison IN 47250 812-265-2888 273-8339
Web: www.arvinsango.com

Assurance Mfg Co 9010 Evergreen Blvd ... Coon Rapids MN 55433 763-780-4252 780-8847
Web: www.assurancemfg.com

Ataco Steel Products Corp PO Box 270 ... Cedarburg WI 53012 262-377-3000 377-3452
TF: 800-536-4822 ■ *Web:* www.atacosteel.com

Atlantic Tool & Die Co (ATD)
19963 Progress Dr ... Strongsville OH 44149 440-238-6931 238-2210
Web: www.atlantictool.com

BAE Industries Inc 24400 Sherwood Ave ... Center Line MI 48015 586-754-3000 754-3007
Web: www.baeind.com

Banner Stamping Co 1308 Holly Ave ... Columbus OH 43212 614-291-3105 291-3125
Web: www.bannerstamping.com

Bazz Houston Co 12700 Western Ave ... Garden Grove CA 92841 714-898-2666 898-1389
TF: 800-385-9608 ■ *Web:* www.bazz-houston.com

Behrens Mfg Co 1250 E Sanborn St ... Winona MN 55987 507-454-4664 452-2106
Web: www.behrensmfg.com

Bermo Inc 4501 Ball Rd NE ... Circle Pines MN 55014 763-786-7676 785-2159
TF: 800-695-7676 ■ *Web:* www.bermo.com

Beta Shim Co 11 Progress Dr ... Shelton CT 06484 203-926-1150 929-5509
Web: www.betashim.com

Bettcher Amherst Metal Stamping
6801 S 33rd St Bldg M 2nd Fl Suite 9-19 ... McAllen TX 78503 713-856-6600
TF: 877-747-8267 ■ *Web:* www.bettcherllc.com

Bi-Link Ltd 391 S Glen Ellyn Rd ... Bloomingdale IL 60108 630-858-5900 858-5995
Web: www.bi-link.com

Bopp-Busch Mfg Co 545 E Huron Rd ... Au Gres MI 48703 989-876-7121 876-6555
Web: www.boppbusch.com

Btd Mfg Inc 1111 13th Ave SE ... Detroit Lakes MN 56501 218-847-4446 847-4448
TF: 866-562-3986 ■ *Web:* www.btdmfg.com

Burnside Industries LLC
6830 Grand Haven Rd ... Spring Lake MI 49456 231-798-3394 798-2316

Capitol Stampings Corp 2700 W N Ave ... Milwaukee WI 53208 414-372-3500 372-3535
Web: www.capitolstampings.com

Clairon Metals Corp 11194 Alcovy Rd ... Covington GA 30014 770-786-9681 786-4183
Web: www.clarionmetals.com

Clow Stamping Co 23103 County Rd 3 ... Merrifield MN 56465 218-765-3111 765-3904
Web: www.clowstamping.com

Cly-Del Mfg Co 151 Sharon Rd ... Waterbury CT 06705 203-574-2100 753-3326
Web: www.cly-del.com

Cooper Mfg Co 410 S 1st Ave ... Marshalltown IA 50158 641-752-6736 752-7476

Crest Mfg Co 5 Hood Dr PO Box 368 ... Lincoln RI 02865 401-333-1350 333-0821
TF: 800-652-7378 ■ *Web:* www.crestmfg.com

Custom Stamping & Mfg Inc 923 SE Madison St ... Portland OR 97214 503-238-3700 238-3742
Web: www.customstampingmfg.com

Danco Precision Inc
Wheatland & Mellon Sts ... Phoenixville PA 19460 610-933-8981 935-2011
Web: www.dancoprecision.com

Danville Metal Stamping Co Inc
20 Oakwood Ave ... Danville IL 61832 217-446-0647 446-0647
Web: www.danvillemetal.com

Dayton Rogers Mfg Co 8401 W 35 W Service Dr ... Blaine MN 55449 763-784-7714 784-7714
TF: 800-677-8881 ■ *Web:* www.daytonrogers.com

De Biasi Group 1555 Enterprise Rd ... Mississauga ON L4W4L4 905-670-1555 670-3415
Web: www.debiasi.com

Dee Zee Inc 2400 NE 46th Ave ... Des Moines IA 50317 515-265-7331 265-7926
TF: 800-779-2102 ■ *Web:* www.deezee.com

Defiance Metal Products 21 Seneca St ... Defiance OH 43512 419-784-5332 782-0148
Web: www.defiancemetal.com

Delta Consolidated Industries Inc
4800 Krueger Dr ... Jonesboro AR 72401 870-935-3711 935-4994
TF: 800-643-0084 ■ *Web:* www.deltastorage.com

Diamond Mfg Co 243 W 8th St ... Wyoming PA 18644 570-693-0300 693-3500
TF: 800-233-9601 ■ *Web:* www.diamondman.com

Diamond Perforated Metals Inc
7300 W Sunnyview Ave ... Visalia CA 93291 559-651-1889 651-1815
TF: 800-642-4334 ■ *Web:* www.diamondperf.com

Dixie Seal & Stamp Co 755 N Ave NE ... Atlanta GA 30306 404-875-8883 872-3504
Web: www.dixieseal.com

DORMA Architectural Hardware
1003 W Broadway PO Box 8 ... Steeleville IL 62288 618-965-3491 965-9022
Web: www.dorma-usa.com

Company	City	State	ZIP	Phone	Fax
Dove Die & Stamping Co 15665 Brookpark Rd *Web:* www.dovedie.com	Cleveland	OH	44142	216-267-3720	267-7250
Dubuque Stamping & Mfg Inc 3190 Jackson St *Web:* www.dbqstamp.com	Dubuque	IA	52001	563-583-5716	556-8729
Dudek & Bock Spring Mfg Co 5100 W Roosevelt Rd *Web:* www.dudek-bock.com	Chicago	IL	60644	773-379-4100	379-4715
DureX Inc 5 Stahuber Ave *Web:* www.durexinc.com	Union	NJ	07083	908-688-0800	688-0718
E S Investments LLC 14055 US Hwy 19 N *Web:* www.sunmicrostamping.com	Clearwater	FL	33764	727-536-8822	536-6667
East Moline Metal Products Co 1201 7th St *TF Sales:* 800-325-4151 ■ *Web:* www.emmetal.com	East Moline	IL	61244	309-752-1350	752-1380
Eclipse Mfg Co 1828 Oakland Ave *Web:* www.eclipsemfg.com	Sheboygan	WI	53081	920-457-2311	457-4935
Elmira Stamping & Mfg Corp 1704 Cedar St *Web:* www.elmirastamping.com	Elmira	NY	14904	607-734-2058	732-0573
Fraen Corp 80 Newcrossing Rd *TF:* 800-370-0078 ■ *Web:* www.fraen.com	Reading	MA	01867	781-205-5300	942-2426
Fuller Box Co 150 Chestnut St *Web:* www.fullerbox.com	North Attleboro	MA	02760	508-695-2525	695-2187
Fulton Industries Inc 135 E Linfoot St PO Box 377 *TF:* 800-537-5012 ■ *Web:* www.fultonindoh.com	Wauseon	OH	43567	419-335-3015	335-3215
Gasser & Sons Inc 440 Moreland Rd *Web:* www.gasser.com	Commack	NY	11725	631-543-6600	543-6649
General Press & Fabricating Co 1500 W St Paul Ave	Milwaukee	WI	53233	414-272-6000	272-1558
Genesee Group Inc 1470 Ave T *Web:* www.geneseegroup.com	Grand Prairie	TX	75050	972-623-2004	623-0404
Gilco Inc 16000 Common Rd *TF:* 800-424-4526 ■ *Web:* www.gilco.com	Roseville	MI	48066	586-779-5850	778-7190
GMP Metal Products Inc 3883 Delor St *TF:* 800-325-9808 ■ *Web:* www.gmpmetal.com	Saint Louis	MO	63116	314-481-0300	481-1379
Gr Spring & Stamping Inc 706 Bond Ave *Web:* www.grs-s.com	Grand Rapids	MI	49503	616-453-4491	453-4497
Griffiths Corp 2717 Niagara Ln N	Minneapolis	MN	55447	763-557-8935	559-5290
Guarantee Specialties Inc 9401 Carr Ave	Cleveland	OH	44108	216-451-9744	451-3332
Hamrock Inc 12521 Los Nietos Rd *Web:* www.hamrock.com	Santa Fe Springs	CA	90670	562-944-0255	944-5676
Hannibal Industries Inc 3851 S Santa Fe Ave *TF:* 800-513-1200 ■ *Web:* www.hannibalindustries.com	Los Angeles	CA	90058	323-588-4261	589-5640
Harvey Vogel Mfg Co 425 Weir Dr *Web:* www.harveyvogel.com	Woodbury	MN	55125	651-739-7373	739-8666
HEB Mfg Co Inc 67 Vermont Rt 110 PO Box 188 *TF:* 800-639-4187 ■ *Web:* www.hebmfg.com	Chelsea	VT	05038	802-685-4821	685-7755
Hendrick Mfg Co 1 7th Ave **Fax:* Sales ■ *TF Cust Svc:* 800-225-7373 ■ *Web:* www.hendrickmfg.com	Carbondale	PA	18407	570-282-1010	282-1506*
Heyco Products 1800 Industrial Way N *TF:* 800-526-4182 ■ *Web:* www.heyco.com	Toms River	NJ	08755	732-286-1800	244-8843
Hobson & Motzer Inc 30 Air Line Dr PO Box 427 *TF:* 800-476-5111 ■ *Web:* www.hobsonmotzer.com	Durham	CT	06422	860-349-1756	349-3602
HPL Stampings Inc 425 Enterprise Pkwy *TF:* 800-927-0397 ■ *Web:* www.hplstampings.com	Lake Zurich	IL	60047	847-540-1400	540-1422
Innovative Stamping Corp 2068 E Gladwick St *TF:* 800-400-0047 ■ *Web:* www.innovative-sys.com	Compton	CA	90220	310-537-6996	537-0312
Jagemann Stamping Co 5757 W Custer St PO Box 217 *TF:* 888-337-7853 ■ *Web:* www.jagemann.com	Manitowoc	WI	54221	920-682-4633	682-6002
Ken-Tron Mfg Inc PO Box 21250 *TF:* 800-872-9336 ■ *Web:* www.ken-tron.com	Owensboro	KY	42304	270-684-0431	684-0435
Kendale Industries Inc 7600 Hub Pkwy *TF:* 800-321-9308	Cleveland	OH	44125	216-524-5400	524-6750
Kennedy Mfg Co 1260 Industrial Dr *TF:* 800-413-8665 ■ *Web:* www.kennedymfg.com	Van Wert	OH	45891	419-238-2442	238-5644
Kerns Mfg Corp 3714 29th St *Web:* www.kernsmfg.com	Long Island City	NY	11101	718-784-4044	786-0534
Keystone Friction Hinge Co 520 Matthews Blvd	South Williamsport	PA	17702	570-323-9479	326-0217
Kickhaefer Mfg Co (KMC) 1221 S Pk St PO Box 348 *Web:* www.kmcstampings.com	Port Washington	WI	53074	262-377-5030	284-9774
Knaack Mfg Co 420 E Terra Cotta Ave *TF:* 800-456-7865 ■ *Web:* www.knaack.com	Crystal Lake	IL	60014	815-459-6020	459-9097
Kromet International Inc 200 Sheldon Dr *Web:* www.kromet.com	Cambridge	ON	N1R7K1	519-623-2511	624-9729
L H Carbide Corp 4420 Clubview Dr *Web:* www.lhcarbide.com	Fort Wayne	IN	46804	260-432-5563	432-2503
Lacey Mfg Co Inc 1146 Barnum Ave *Web:* www.laceymfg.com	Bridgeport	CT	06610	203-336-0121	336-1774
Larson Tool & Stamping Co 90 Olive St *Web:* www.larsontool.com	Attleboro	MA	02703	508-222-0897	226-7407
Macon Resources Inc 2121 Hubbard Ave *Web:* www.maconresources.org	Decatur	IL	62526	217-875-1910	875-8899
Mass Precision Sheetmetal Inc 2110 Oakland Rd *Web:* www.massprecision.com	San Jose	CA	95131	408-954-0200	954-0288
McAlpin Industries Inc 255 Hollenbeck St *Web:* www.mcalpin-ind.com	Rochester	NY	14621	585-266-3060	266-8091
Meriden Mfg Inc PO Box 694 *Web:* www.meridenmfg.com	Meriden	CT	06450	203-237-7481	235-3146
Merriam Mfg Co The 695 High St *TF:* 800-840-9243 ■ *Web:* www.americanmetalcraftersllc.com	Middletown	CT	06457	860-343-1960	343-1965
Metal Box International 11600 W King St *TF:* 800-622-2697 ■ *Web:* www.edsal.com	Franklin Park	IL	60131	847-455-8500	455-6030
Metal Components Inc 3281 Roger B Chaffee Memorial Blvd SE	Grand Rapids	MI	49548	616-252-1900	252-1970
Metal Flow Corp 11694 James St *Web:* www.metalflow.com	Holland	MI	49424	616-392-7976	392-5814
Micro Stamping Corp 140 Belmont Dr *Web:* www.microstamping.com	Somerset	NJ	08873	732-302-0800	302-0436
Midwest Wire Products LLC 649 S Lansing Ave PO Box 770 *TF:* 800-445-0225 ■ *Web:* www.wireforming.com	Sturgeon Bay	WI	54235	920-743-6591	743-3777
MJ Celco Inc 3900 Wesley Terr *Web:* www.mjcelco.com	Schiller Park	IL	60176	847-671-1900	671-1978
Morgal Machine Tool Co Inc 2100 S Yellow Springs St *Web:* www.morgal.com	Springfield	OH	45506	937-325-5561	325-1957
New Standard Corp 74 Commerce Way *Web:* www.newstandard.com	York	PA	17406	717-653-1811	757-2312
Niles Mfg & Finishing Inc 465 Walnut St *Web:* www.nilesmfg.com	Niles	OH	44446	330-544-0402	544-8018
Northern Stamping Corp 6600 Chapek Pkwy	Cuyahoga Heights	OH	44125	216-883-8888	883-8237
Oakland Tool & Mfg Co Inc 34700 Commerce Dr	Fraser	MI	48026	586-294-0100	294-6139
Okay Industries Inc 200 Ellis St *Web:* www.okayind.com	New Britain	CT	06051	860-225-8707	225-7047
P & G Steel Products Co Inc 54 Gruner Rd *TF:* 800-952-3696 ■ *Web:* www.pgsteel.com	Buffalo	NY	14227	716-896-7900	896-4129
Parkview Metal Products Inc 1275 Ensell Rd *Web:* www.parkviewmetal.com	Lake Zurich	IL	60047	847-540-2323	540-8648
Parkview South Dakota LLC 316 E Industrial Ave *Web:* www.parkviewmetal.com/south_dakota.html	Lennox	SD	57039	605-647-6000	647-6003
Pax Machine Works Inc PO Box 338 *Web:* www.paxmachine.com	Celina	OH	45822	419-586-2337	586-7123
Penn United Technology Inc 799 N Pike Rd *Web:* www.pennunited.com	Cabot	PA	16023	724-352-1507	352-4970
Perfection Spring & Stamping Corp 1449 E Algonquin Rd *Web:* www.pss-corp.com	Mount Prospect	IL	60056	847-437-3900	437-1322
Plainfield Cos 24035 Riverwalk Ct *Web:* www.plainfieldprecision.com	Plainfield	IL	60544	815-436-5671	439-2970
Precision Resource 25 Forest Pkwy *Web:* www.precisionresource.com	Shelton	CT	06484	203-925-0012	926-9010
Premium Allied Tool Inc 5680 Old Hwy 54	Philpot	KY	42366	270-729-4242	729-4332
Prestige Stamping Inc 23513 Groesbeck Hwy *Web:* www.prestigestamping.com	Warren	MI	48089	586-773-2700	773-2700
Punch Press Products Inc 2035 E 51st St *Web:* www.punch-press.com	Vernon	CA	90058	323-581-7151	581-0341
Quaker Mfg Corp PO Box 449 *Web:* www.quakermfg.com	Salem	OH	44460	330-337-6883	337-3571
Quality Perforating Inc 166 Dundaff St *TF:* 800-872-7373 ■ *Web:* www.qualityperf.com	Carbondale	PA	18407	570-282-4344	282-4627
Quality Tool & Stamping Co Inc 2642 Mcilwraith St *Web:* www.qtstamping.com	Muskegon	MI	49444	231-733-2538	733-0983
Ramcel Engineering Co 2926 MacArthur Blvd *Web:* www.ramcel.com	Northbrook	IL	60062	847-272-6980	272-7196
RES Mfg Co Inc 7801 N 73rd St *TF:* 800-334-8044 ■ *Web:* www.resmfg.com	Milwaukee	WI	53223	414-354-4530	354-9027
Rockford Toolcraft Inc 766 Research Pkwy *Web:* www.rockfordtoolcraft.com	Rockford	IL	61109	815-398-5507	398-0132
Saunders Mfg Co Inc 61 Nickerson Hill Rd *TF Cust Svc:* 800-341-4674 ■ *Web:* www.saunders-usa.com	Readfield	ME	04355	207-685-3385	685-9918
Slidematic Products Co 4520 W Addison St *Web:* www.slidematicproducts.com	Chicago	IL	60641	773-545-4213	545-0797
Small Parts Inc 600 Humphrey St PO Box 23 *Web:* www.smallpartsinc.com	Logansport	IN	46947	574-753-6323	753-6660
Sons Tool Inc 460 Thompson Rd *Web:* www.sonstool.com	Woodville	WI	54028	715-698-2471	698-2335
Spindustries LLC 1301 La Salle St *Web:* www.lgspin.com	Lake Geneva	WI	53147	262-248-6601	248-1277
Stack-On Products Co 1360 N Old Rand Rd *TF:* 800-323-9601 ■ *Web:* www.stack-on.com	Wauconda	IL	60084	847-526-1611	526-6599
Stamtex Metal Stampings 112 Erie St *Web:* www.stamtexmetalproducts.com	Niles	OH	44446	330-652-2558	652-7369
Stanco Metal Products Inc 2101 168th Ave *TF:* 800-530-9655 ■ *Web:* www.stancometal.com	Grand Haven	MI	49417	616-842-5000	842-9080
Stanley Spring & Stamping Corp 5050 W Foster Ave *Web:* www.stanleyspring.com	Chicago	IL	60630	773-777-2600	777-3894
Steel City Corp 190 N Meridian Rd *TF:* 800-321-0350 ■ *Web:* www.scity.com	Youngstown	OH	44501	330-792-7663	797-2947
Stewart EFI LLC 45 Old Waterbury Rd *TF:* 800-393-5387 ■ *Web:* www.stewartefi.com	Thomaston	CT	06787	860-283-8213	283-5610
T & D Metal Products Co 602 E Walnut St *TF:* 800-634-7267 ■ *Web:* www.tdmetal.com	Watseka	IL	60970	815-432-4938	432-6271
Taylor Metal Products Co 700 Springmill St *Web:* www.tmpind.com	Mansfield	OH	44903	419-522-0751	525-2948
Tech-Etch Inc 45 Aldrin Rd *Web:* www.tech-etch.com	Plymouth	MA	02360	508-747-0300	746-9639
Tempco Mfg Co Inc 2475 Hwy 55 *TF:* 800-263-8076 ■ *Web:* www.tempcomfg.com	St. Paul	MN	55120	651-452-1441	452-1125
Trans-Matic Mfg Co 300 E 48th St *Web:* www.transmatic.com	Holland	MI	49423	616-820-2500	820-2702
Triad Metal Products Co 12990 Snow Rd *Web:* www.triadmetal.com	Parma	OH	44130	216-676-6505	676-6510
Trident Precision Mfg Inc 734 Salt Rd *Web:* www.tridentprecision.com	Webster	NY	14580	585-265-2010	265-2386
Trine Products Corp 1421 Ferris Pl *TF:* 800-223-8075 ■ *Web:* www.trinecorp.com	Bronx	NY	10461	718-828-5200	828-4052
Triton Industries Inc 1020 N Kolmar Ave *Web:* www.tritonindustries.com	Chicago	IL	60651	773-384-3700	384-8748
Truelove & MacLean Inc 984 Waterville St	Waterbury	CT	06710	203-574-2240	753-1085
UMI Co Inc 1520 S 5th St	Hopkins	MN	55343	952-935-8431	935-6331
Waterloo Industries Inc 100 E 4th St *TF:* 800-833-8851 ■ *Web:* www.waterlooindustries.com	Waterloo	IA	50703	319-235-7131	232-3924

Company	City	State	ZIP	Phone	Fax
Wauconda Tool & Engineering					
821 W Algonquin Rd	Algonquin	IL	60102	847-658-4588	658-0788
Web: www.wauconda.com					
Weiss-Aug Co Inc 220 Merry Ln	East Hanover	NJ	07936	973-887-7600	887-8109
Web: www.weiss-aug.com					
Winzeler Stamping Co 910 E Main St	Montpelier	OH	43543	419-485-3147	485-5039
Web: www.winzelerstamping.com					
Wisconsin Tool & Stamping Co					
9521 Ainslie St	Schiller Park	IL	60176	847-678-7573	678-2950
Wls Stamping Co 3292 E 80th St	Cleveland	OH	44104	216-271-5100	341-3203
Web: www.wlsstamping.com					
Wolverine Metal Stamping Inc					
3600 Tennis Ct	Saint Joseph	MI	49085	269-429-6600	429-6657
Web: www.wms-inc.com					
Wozniak Industries Inc					
2 Mid America Plaza Suite 706	Oakbrook Terrace	IL	60181	630-954-3400	954-3605
Web: www.wozniakindustries.com					
Wrico Stamping Co 2727 Niagara Ln N	Minneapolis	MN	55447	763-559-2288	553-7976
Web: www.wrico-net.com					

492 METAL STAMPINGS - AUTOMOTIVE

SEE ALSO Automotive Parts & Supplies - Mfr p. 1497

Company	City	State	ZIP	Phone	Fax
Acemco Automotive 7297 Enterprise Dr	Spring Lake	MI	49456	231-799-8612	799-9904
Web: www.acemco.com					
Ada Metal Products Inc 3515 W Touhy Ave	Lincolnwood	IL	60712	847-673-1190	673-4860
Web: www.adametal.com					
Advance Engineering Co 12025 Dixie Ave	Redford	MI	48239	313-537-3500	537-7389
AJ Rose Mfg Co 38000 Chester Rd	Avon	OH	44011	440-934-7700	934-2802
Web: www.ajrose.com					
American Metal & Plastics Inc					
450 32nd St SW	Grand Rapids	MI	49548	616-452-6061	452-3835
Web: www.ampi-gr.com					
AMG Industries Inc 200 Commerce Dr	Mount Vernon	OH	43050	740-397-4044	397-3092*
**Fax:* Mail Rm ■ *Web:* www.amgindustries.com					
Automotive Engineered Products Inc					
7149 Mission Gorge Rd	San Diego	CA	92120	619-229-7797	599-6424*
**Fax Area Code:* 909 ■ *Web:* www.jbaheaders.com					
Benteler Automotive 1780 Pond Run	Auburn Hills	MI	48326	248-364-7190	364-7125
Web: www.benteler.de					
Brown Corp of America Inc 401 S Steele St	Ionia	MI	48846	616-527-4050	527-3385
TF: 800-530-9570 ■ *Web:* www.browncorp.com					
Burkland Inc 6520 S State Rd	Goodrich	MI	48438	810-636-2233	636-7525
C Cowles & Co Inc 83 Water St	New Haven	CT	06511	203-865-3117	773-1019
TF: 800-624-4483 ■ *Web:* www.ccowles.com					
Center Mfg Inc 990 84th St	Byron Center	MI	49315	616-878-3324	878-3477
Web: www.centermfg.com					
Checker Motors Corp 2016 N Pitcher St	Kalamazoo	MI	49007	269-343-6121	343-6823
Clark Metal Products Co 100 Serrell Dr	Blairsville	PA	15717	724-459-7550	459-0207
Web: www.clark-metal.com					
Concord Tool & Mfg Co Inc					
106 N Groesbeck Hwy	Mount Clemens	MI	48043	586-465-6537	465-2556
Web: www.concordtool.com					
Cooper-Standard Automotive Inc					
39550 Orchard Hill Pl Dr	Novi	MI	48375	248-596-5900	596-6540*
**Fax:* Hum Res ■ *Web:* www.cooperstandard.com					
Decoma International Inc					
magna exteriors & interiors 50 Casmir Ct	Concord	ON	L4K4J5	905-669-2888	669-4992
TF: 800-461-3967 ■ *Web:* www.magna.com					
Dixien LLC PO Box 337	Forest Park	GA	30298	404-366-7427	366-2403
Web: www.dixien.com					
Duffy Tool & Stamping LLC 3401 W 8th St	Muncie	IN	47302	765-288-1931	288-4784
Web: www.duffytool.com					
F & B Mfg Co Inc 4316 N 39th Ave	Phoenix	AZ	85019	602-272-3900	272-3326
Web: www.fbmfg.com					
Fisher Corp 1625 W Maple Rd	Troy	MI	48084	248-280-0808	280-0725
Web: www.fisherco.com					
Florida Production Engineering Co					
2 E Tower Cir	Ormond Beach	FL	32174	386-677-2566	673-1130
Web: www.fpe-inc.com					
Genco Stamping & Mfg Co 2001 Genco Dr	Cookeville	TN	38506	931-528-5574	528-8379
Gerstenslager Co 1425 E Bowman St PO Box 6011	Wooster	OH	44691	330-262-2015	262-4009*
**Fax:* Sales ■ *Web:* www.worthingtonindustries.com					
GHSP Co 1250 S Beechtree St	Grand Haven	MI	49417	616-842-5500	842-7230
Web: www.ghsp.com					
Grant Industries Inc 33415 Groesbeck Hwy	Fraser	MI	48026	586-293-9200	293-9346
Web: www.grantgrp.com					
Hamlin Newco LLC 2741 Wingate Ave	Akron	OH	44314	330-753-7791	753-5577
Web: www.hnmetalstamping.com					
Hatch Stamping Co 635 E Industrial Dr	Chelsea	MI	48118	734-475-8628	475-6255
Web: www.hatchstamping.com					
Industrial Components Inc					
IC Assemblies Inc 2250 NW 102nd Ave	Miami	FL	33172	305-477-0387	594-7332
Web: www.icassemblies.com					
ITW Drawform 500 Fairview Rd	Zeeland	MI	49464	616-772-1910	772-9572
Web: www.drawform.com					
ITW Highland 1240 Wolcott St PO Box 1858	Waterbury	CT	06722	203-574-3200	754-4019
Web: www.itwhighland.com					
Lake Air Metal Stamping 7709 Winpark Dr	Minneapolis	MN	55427	763-546-0994	546-4469
TF: 800-811-9362 ■ *Web:* www.lakeairmetals.com					
Lapeer Metal Stamping Co (LMS) 930 Saginaw St	Lapeer	MI	48446	810-664-8588	664-9810
Web: www.lapeermetal.com					
Lapeer Metal Stamping Cos Inc					
930 S Saginaw St	Lapeer	MI	48446	810-664-8588	664-9810
Web: www.lapeermetal.com					
Lenawee Stamping Corp 1200 E Chicago Blvd	Tecumseh	MI	49286	517-423-2400	423-3387
Web: www.lenaweestamping.com					
LMC Industries Inc 100 Manufacturers Dr	Arnold	MO	63010	636-282-8080	282-7114
Web: www.lmcindustries.com					
Logghe Stamping Co 16711 E 13-Mile Rd	Fraser	MI	48026	586-293-2250	293-7202
Luitink Mfg Co					
W140 N8700 Lilly Rd PO Box 366	Menomonee Falls	WI	53052	262-251-8800	251-8804
Web: www.luitink.com					
Manter Technology Corp					
7177 Marine City Airport	Marine City	MI	48039	810-765-8000	765-3373
Marquette Tool & Die Co					
3185 S Kingshighway Blvd	Saint Louis	MO	63139	314-771-8509	771-7964
Web: www.marquettetool.com					
McKechnie Vehicle Components					
5440 Corporate Dr Suite 100	Troy	MI	48098	586-491-2600	641-4731*
**Fax Area Code:* 248 ■ *Web:* www.mvcusa.com					
Means Industries Inc 1860 S Jefferson Ave	Saginaw	MI	48601	989-754-3300	754-3301
TF: 800-869-1433 ■ *Web:* www.meansindustries.com					
Midway Products Group Inc 1 Lyman E Hoyt Dr	Monroe	MI	48161	734-241-7242	241-7511*
**Fax:* Sales ■ *Web:* www.midwayproducts.com					
Modineer Co 2190 Industrial Dr PO Box 640	Niles	MI	49120	269-683-2550	683-7984
Web: www.modineer.com					
Moroso Performance Products Inc					
80 Carter Dr	Guilford	CT	06437	203-453-6571	453-6906*
**Fax:* Cust Svc ■ *Web:* www.moroso.com					
NAS Interplex Inc					
1434 110th St Suite 301	College Point	NY	11356	718-961-6212	886-0573
Noble Metal Processing Inc 28207 Van Dyke Ave	Warren	MI	48092	586-751-5300	751-5301
ODM Tool & Mfg Co 9550 Joliet Rd	McCook	IL	60525	708-485-6130	485-6540
Web: www.odmtool.com					
Ogihara America Corp 1480 W McPherson Pk Dr	Howell	MI	48843	517-548-4900	548-6036
Web: www.ogihara.com					
Pk USA Inc 600 W Northridge Dr	Shelbyville	IN	46176	317-398-5500	398-5501
Web: www.pkusa.com					
Pridgeon & Clay Inc					
50 Cottage Grove St SW	Grand Rapids	MI	49507	616-241-5675	281-1799
Web: www.pridgeonandclay.com					
Q3 Industries Inc 777 Manor Pk Dr	Columbus	OH	43228	800-770-0195	851-1494*
**Fax Area Code:* 614 ■ *TF:* 800-770-0195					
Radar Industries 27101 Grosbeck Hwy	Warren	MI	48089	586-779-0300	758-6445
TF: 800-779-0301 ■ *Web:* www.radarind.com					
Riviera Tool Co 5460 Executive Pkwy SE	Grand Rapids	MI	49512	616-698-2100	698-2470
Web: www.rivieratool.com					
S & Z Tool & Die Co Inc 3180 Berea Rd	Cleveland	OH	44111	216-252-4250	252-7270
Shiloh Industries Corp 5389 W 130th St	Cleveland	OH	44130	216-267-2600	265-4244
NASDAQ: SHLO ■ *Web:* www.shiloh.com					
Spartanburg Steel Products Inc					
1290 New Cut Rd PO Box 6428	Spartanburg	SC	29304	864-585-5211	583-5641
TF: 888-974-7500 ■ *Web:* www.ssprod.com					
Stamco Industries Inc 26650 Lakeland Blvd	Euclid	OH	44132	216-731-9333	731-9338
Stanco Metal Products Inc 2101 168th Ave	Grand Haven	MI	49417	616-842-5000	842-9080
TF: 800-530-9655 ■ *Web:* www.stancometal.com					
Steel Parts Corp 801 Berryman Pike	Tipton	IN	46072	765-675-2191	675-4232
Stewart EFI LLC 45 Old Waterbury Rd	Thomaston	CT	06787	860-283-8213	283-5610
TF: 800-393-5387 ■ *Web:* www.stewartefi.com					
Syracuse Stamping Co 1054 S Clinton St	Syracuse	NY	13202	315-476-5306	474-8876
TF: 800-581-5555 ■ *Web:* www.syraco.com					
Thiel Tool & Engineering Co Inc					
4622 Bulwer Ave PO Box 470007	Saint Louis	MO	63147	314-241-6121	241-7857
TF: 800-862-4145 ■ *Web:* www.thieltool.com					
Thomas Engineering Co					
7024 Northland Dr	Brooklyn Park	MN	55428	763-533-1501	533-8091
Web: www.thomasengineering.com					
ThyssenKrupp Budd Co					
3155 W Big Beaver Rd PO Box 2601	Troy	MI	48007	248-643-3500	643-3593
Web: www.buddcompany.com					
Triad Metal Products Co 12990 Snow Rd	Parma	OH	44130	216-676-6505	676-6510
Web: www.triadmetal.com					
Troy Design & Mfg Co (TDM) 12675 Berwyn	Redford	MI	48239	313-592-2300	537-8765
Web: www.troydm.com					
United Metal Products Corp 8101 Lyndon St	Detroit	MI	48238	313-933-8750	933-1001
Web: www.unitedmetalproducts.com					
Varbros LLC 16025 Brookpark Rd PO Box 42127	Cleveland	OH	44142	216-267-5200	267-5205
Web: www.varbroscorp.com					
Versatube Corp 4755 Rochester Rd	Troy	MI	48085	248-689-7373	689-8293
Web: www.versatubecorp.com					
Welarco Fabrications Inc 7400 W Plank Rd	Peoria	IL	61604	309-697-9400	697-2400
TF: 800-447-6464 ■ *Web:* www.philsystems.com					
Wellington Industries Inc					
39555 S I-94 Service Dr	Belleville	MI	48111	734-942-1060	942-9430
Web: www.wellingtonind.com					
Wisconsin Metal Products Co 1807 DeKovin Ave	Racine	WI	53403	262-633-6301	633-8962
Web: www.wmpco.com					
Wolverine Metal Specialties 1013 Thorrez Rd	Jackson	MI	49201	517-750-3414	750-1644

493 METAL TUBE & PIPE

Company	City	State	ZIP	Phone	Fax
AK Tube LLC 30400 E Broadway	Walbridge	OH	43465	419-661-4150	661-4380
TF: 800-955-8031 ■ *Web:* www.aktube.com					
American Cast Iron Pipe Co (ACIPCO)					
1501 31st Ave N	Birmingham	AL	35207	205-325-7701	307-2747
TF: 800-442-2347 ■ *Web:* www.acipco.com					
Atlas Tube 1855 122nd St	Chicago	IL	60633	773-646-4500	646-6128
TF: 800-733-5683 ■ *Web:* www.atlastube.com					
Atlas Tubular LP 1710 S Hwy 77	Robstown	TX	78380	361-387-7505	387-4613
Web: www.atlastubular.com					
Berg Steel Pipe Corp 5315 W 19th St	Panama City	FL	32401	850-769-2273	763-9683
TF: 800-874-0384 ■ *Web:* www.bergpipe.com					
Bristol Metals LLC					
390 Bristol Metals Rd PO Box 1589	Bristol	TN	37620	423-989-4700	989-4790
Web: www.brismet.com					
Bull Moose Tube Co					
1819 Clarkson Rd Suite 100	Chesterfield	MO	63017	636-537-2600	537-5848*
**Fax:* Sales ■ *TF:* 800-325-4467 ■ *Web:* www.bullmoosetube.com					

Company	City	State	Zip	Phone	Fax
California Steel & Tube 16049 Stephens St	City of Industry	CA	91745	626-968-5511	369-9660
TF: 800-338-8823					
Camdel Metals Corp 12244 Willow Grove Rd	Camden	DE	19934	302-697-9521	697-9620
Web: www.camdelmetals.com					
Cerro Flow Products Inc PO Box 66800	Saint Louis	MO	63166	618-337-6000	337-6958
TF: 888-237-7611 ■ *Web:* www.cerroflow.com					
Charlotte Pipe & Foundry Co 2109 Randolph Rd	Charlotte	NC	28207	704-372-5030	348-6450
TF: 800-432-6172 ■ *Web:* www.charlottepipe.com					
Clock Spring Co 14107 Interdrive W	Houston	TX	77032	281-590-8491	590-9528
Web: www.clockspring.com					
CMC Howell Metal Co 574 Depot Rd PO Box 218	New Market	VA	22844	540-740-4700	740-4778
TF: 800-247-2048 ■ *Web:* www.cmc.com					
CTP Corp 3750 Shelby St	Indianapolis	IN	46227	317-787-5747	782-9489
Web: www.tubeproc.com/ctp-corporation					
Dekoron Unitherm Inc 1531 Commerce Creek Blvd	Cape Coral	FL	33909	239-995-8111	995-8027
TF: 800-633-5015 ■ *Web:* www.unithermcc.com					
Dixie Pipe Sales Inc 2407 Broiller PO Box 300650	Houston	TX	77054	713-796-2021	799-8628
TF: 800-733-3494 ■ *Web:* www.dixiepipe.com					
Earle M Jorgensen Co 10650 S Alameda St	Lynwood	CA	90262	323-567-1122	563-5500
TF Sales: 800-336-5365 ■ *Web:* www.emjmetals.com					
Elano Corp 2455 Dayton-Xenia Rd	Dayton	OH	45434	937-426-0621	426-7181
Web: www.elanocorp.com					
Energy Alloys LLC 350 Glenborough Suite 300	Houston	TX	77067	832-601-5800	601-5801
TF: 800-899-3890 ■ *Web:* www.ealloys.com					
Felker Bros Corp 22 N Chestnut Ave	Marshfield	WI	54449	715-384-3121	387-6837
TF: 800-826-2304 ■ *Web:* www.felkerbrothers.com					
Friedman Industries Inc 4001 Homestead Rd PO Box 21147	Houston	TX	77026	800-527-8671	758-2265*
AMEX: FRD ■ *Fax Area Code:* 903 ■ *TF:* 800-527-8671 ■ *Web:* www.friedmanindustries.com					
Handy & Harman Tube Co Inc 12244 Willow Grove Rd	Camden	DE	19934	302-697-9521	697-7405
TF: 800-766-8823 ■ *Web:* www.handytube.com					
Hanna Steel Corp 3812 Commerce Ave PO Box 558	Fairfield	AL	35064	205-780-1111	783-8368
TF: 800-633-8252 ■ *Web:* www.hannasteel.com					
Hannibal Industries Inc 3851 S Santa Fe Ave	Los Angeles	CA	90058	323-588-4261	589-5640
TF: 800-513-1200 ■ *Web:* www.hannibalindustries.com					
Hofmann Industries Inc 3145 Shillington Rd	Sinking Spring	PA	19608	610-678-8051	670-2221
Web: www.hofmann.com					
Hydro Aluminum North America 801 International Dr Suite 200	Linthicum	MD	21090	410-487-4500	487-8053
TF: 888-935-5752 ■ *Web:* www.hydroaluminumna.com					
International Metal Hose Co 520 Goodrich Rd	Bellevue	OH	44811	419-483-7690	483-8225
TF: 800-458-6855 ■ *Web:* www.metalhose.com					
J D Rush C Inc 5900 E Lerdo Hwy	Shafter	CA	93263	661-392-1900	399-2728
TF: 800-537-6284 ■ *Web:* www.jdrush.com					
Jackson Tube Service Inc 8210 Industry Pk Dr	Piqua	OH	45356	937-773-8550	773-8806
TF: 800-543-8910 ■ *Web:* www.jackson-tube.com					
LeFiell Mfg Co 13700 Firestone Blvd	Santa Fe Springs	CA	90670	562-921-3411	921-5480
TF: 800-451-5971 ■ *Web:* www.lefiell.com					
Lock Joint Tube Inc 515 W Ireland Rd	South Bend	IN	46614	574-299-5326	299-3464*
*Fax: Sales ■ *TF:* 800-257-6859 ■ *Web:* www.ljtube.com					
Marcegaglia USA Inc 1001 E Waterfront Dr	Munhall	PA	15120	412-462-2185	462-6059*
*Fax: Sales ■ *Web:* www.gruppomarcegaglia.com					
Morris Coupling Co 2240 W 15th St	Erie	PA	16505	814-459-1741	453-5155
TF: 800-426-1579 ■ *Web:* www.morriscoupling.com					
National Metalwares Inc 900 N Russell Ave	Aurora	IL	60506	630-892-9000	892-2573
Web: www.nationalmetalwares.com					
Naylor Pipe Co 1230 E 92nd St	Chicago	IL	60619	773-721-9400	721-9494
Web: www.naylorpipe.com					
Northwest Pipe Co 12005 N Burgard	Portland	OR	97203	503-285-1400	978-2561
NASDAQ: NWPX ■ *TF:* 800-824-9824 ■ *Web:* www.nwpipe.com					
Oakley Industries Inc 3211 W Bear Creek Dr	Englewood	CO	80110	303-761-1835	781-7307
Web: www.oakleyindustries.com					
Outokumpu Stainless Pipe Inc 1101 N Main St	Wildwood	FL	34785	352-748-1313	416-7473*
Fax Area Code: 800 ■ *TF:* 800-731-7473 ■ *Web:* www.outokumpu.com					
Pipe Fabricating & Supply Co 1235 N Kraemer Blvd	Anaheim	CA	92806	714-630-5200	630-1277
Web: www.pipefab.com					
Plymouth Tube Co 29 W 150 Warrenville Rd	Warrenville	IL	60555	630-393-3550	393-3551
TF Mktg: 800-323-9506 ■ *Web:* www.plymouth.com					
PTC Alliance Copperleaf Corporate Ctr 6051 Wallace Rd Ext Suite 200	Wexford	PA	15090	412-299-7900	299-2619
TF: 888-299-8823 ■ *Web:* www.ptcalliance.com					
RathGibson LLC 475 Half Day Rd Suite 210	Lincolnshire	IL	60069	847-276-2100	276-2471
Web: www.rathgibson.com					
Salem Tube Inc 951 4th St	Greenville	PA	16125	724-646-4301	646-4311
Web: www.salemtube.com					
Sharon Tube Co 134 Mill St	Sharon	PA	16146	724-981-5200	983-1031
TF: 800-245-8115 ■ *Web:* www.sharontube.com					
Small Tube Products Co Inc PO Box 1017	Duncansville	PA	16635	814-695-4491	695-4304
TF: 800-458-3493 ■ *Web:* www.smalltubeproducts.com					
Southern Metals Co 301 Ashe St	Sheffield	AL	35660	256-383-3261	383-5204
TF: 800-843-2771 ■ *Web:* www.sometco.com					
Southland Tube Inc 3525 Richard Arrington Blvd N	Birmingham	AL	35234	205-251-1884	251-1553
TF: 800-543-9024 ■ *Web:* www.southlandtube.com					
Stupp Corp 12555 Ronaldson Rd	Baton Rouge	LA	70807	225-775-8800	775-7610
TF: 800-535-9999 ■ *Web:* www.stuppcorp.com					
Superior Tube Co 3900 Germantown Pike	Collegeville	PA	19426	610-489-5200	489-5252
TF: 800-658-8600 ■ *Web:* www.superiortube.com					
Swepco Tube Corp 1 Clifton Blvd	Clifton	NJ	07015	973-778-3000	778-9289
Web: www.swepcotube.com					
Synalloy Corp 2155 W Croft Cir PO Box 5627	Spartanburg	SC	29304	864-585-3605	596-1501
NASDAQ: SYNL ■ *TF Orders:* 800-763-1001 ■ *Web:* www.synalloy.com					
Tex-Tube Co 1503 N Post Oak Rd	Houston	TX	77055	713-686-4351	685-3222
TF: 800-839-7473 ■ *Web:* www.tex-tube.com					
Troxel Co 11495 Hwy 57	Moscow	TN	38057	901-877-6875	877-3439
Web: www.troxel.com					
Tube Methods Inc PO Box 460	Bridgeport	PA	19405	610-279-7700	277-2005
Web: www.tubemethods.com					
Tube Processing Corp 604 E Le Grande Ave	Indianapolis	IN	46203	317-787-1321	787-5384
TF: 800-776-4119 ■ *Web:* www.tubeproc.com					
United Industries Inc 1546 Henry Ave	Beloit	WI	53511	608-365-8891	365-1259
Web: www.unitedindustries.com					
UNR-Leavitt 1717 W 115th St	Chicago	IL	60643	773-239-7700	239-1023
TF: 800-532-8488 ■ *Web:* www.leavitt-tube.com					
Valmont Industries Inc 1 Valmont Plaza	Omaha	NE	68154	402-963-1000	963-1100
NYSE: VMI ■ *TF:* 800-825-6668 ■ *Web:* www.valmont.com					
Van Leeuwen Pipe & Tube Inc 2875 64th Ave	Edmonton	AB	T6P1R1	780-469-7410	466-5970
Web: www.vanleeuwen.com					
Webco Industries Inc 9101 W 21st St PO Box 100	Sand Springs	OK	74063	918-245-2211	245-0306
Web: www.webcoindustries.com					
Welded Tubes Inc 135 Penniman Rd	Orwell	OH	44076	440-437-5144	437-5180
Web: www.weldedtubes.com					
Western Mac Arthur Co Inc 2855 Mandela Pkwy # D	Oakland	CA	94608	510-251-2102	251-0308
TF: 800-992-7374 ■ *Web:* www.westernmacarthur.com					
Western Pneumatic Tube LLC 835 6th St S	Kirkland	WA	98033	425-822-8271	828-6669
Web: www.wptube.com					
Western Tube & Conduit Corp 2001 E Dominguez St	Long Beach	CA	90810	310-537-6300	604-9785
Web: www.westerntube.com					
Wheatland Tube Co 900 Haddon Ave Suite 500	Collingswood	NJ	08108	856-854-5400	854-0616
TF: 800-257-8182 ■ *Web:* www.wheatland.com					
Wieland Metals Inc 567 Northgate Pkwy	Wheeling	IL	60090	847-537-3990	537-4085
Web: www.wielandus.com					
Yarde Metals Inc 45 Newell St	Southington	CT	06489	860-406-6061	406-6040
TF: 800-444-9494 ■ *Web:* www.yarde.com					

494 METAL WORK - ARCHITECTURAL & ORNAMENTAL

Company	City	State	Zip	Phone	Fax
2nd Ave Design 737 W 2nd Ave	Mesa	AZ	85210	800-843-1602	826-2317
TF: 800-843-1602 ■ *Web:* www.2ndave.com					
Airflex Industrial Corp 937 Conklin St	Farmingdale	NY	11735	631-752-1234	752-1309
Web: www.airflexind.com					
Airolite Co LLC PO Box 410	Schofield	WI	54476	715-841-8757	841-8773
Web: www.airolite.com					
Alabama Metal Industries Corp (AMICO) 3245 Fayette Ave	Birmingham	AL	35208	205-787-2611	780-7838*
*Fax: Sales ■ *TF:* 800-366-2642 ■ *Web:* www.amico-online.com					
Aluma Systems 55 Costa Rd	Concord	ON	L4K1M8	905-669-5282	660-8045*
*Fax: safety ■ *TF:* 888-284-9897 ■ *Web:* www.aluma.com					
Alvarado Mfg Co Inc 12660 Colony St	Chino	CA	91710	909-591-8431	628-1403
TF: 800-423-4143 ■ *Web:* www.alvaradomfg.com					
American Stair Corp Inc 642 Forestwood Dr	Romeoville	IL	60446	815-886-9600	372-3684
TF: 800-872-7824 ■ *Web:* www.americanstair.com					
Ameristar Fence Products Inc 1555 N Mingo Rd	Tulsa	OK	74116	918-835-0898	
TF: 888-333-3422 ■ *Web:* www.ameristarfence.com					
ATAS International Inc 6612 Snowdrift Rd	Allentown	PA	18106	610-395-8445	395-9342
TF: 800-468-1441 ■ *Web:* www.atas.com					
Bil-Jax Inc 125 Taylor Pkwy	Archbold	OH	43502	419-445-8915	445-0367
TF: 800-537-0540 ■ *Web:* www.biljax.com					
Brand Energy & Infrastructure Services Inc 1325 Cobb International Dr Suite A-1	Kennesaw	GA	30152	678-285-1400	514-0285*
Fax Area Code: 770 ■ *TF:* 888-842-7263 ■ *Web:* www.beis.com					
Cherokee Metals Co Inc 4648 S Old Peachtree Rd	Norcross	GA	30071	770-449-1444	559-4933
TF: 877-656-1900					
Chicago Metallic Corp 4849 S Austin Ave	Chicago	IL	60638	800-323-7164	222-3744
TF: 800-323-7164 ■ *Web:* www.chicago-metallic.com					
Construction Specialties Inc 3 Werner Way	Lebanon	NJ	08833	908-236-0800	236-0801
TF: 800-972-7214					
Custom Enclosures Inc 500 Harvester Ct #4	Wheeling	IL	60090	847-520-5511	520-5588
Duvinage Corp 60 W Oak Ridge Dr	Hagerstown	MD	21740	301-733-8255	791-7240
TF: 800-541-2645 ■ *Web:* www.duvinage.com					
Fisher & Ludlow Tru-Weld Grating 2000 Corporate Dr Suite 400	Wexford	PA	15090	724-934-5320	934-5348
TF: 800-445-7093 ■ *Web:* www.fisherludlow.com					
Gadsden Scaffold Co Inc PO Box 1188	Gadsden	AL	35902	256-547-6918	549-5502
TF: 800-538-1780 ■ *Web:* www.gadsdenscaffold.com					
Goldline International Inc 1601 Cloverfield Blvd 100 S Tower	Santa Monica	CA	90404	310-587-1423	319-0265
TF: 877-376-2646 ■ *Web:* www.goldline.com					
Hafele America Co Inc 3901 Cheyenne Dr	Archdale	NC	27263	336-889-2322	325-6197*
Fax Area Code: 800 ■ *TF Cust Svc:* 800-423-3531 ■ *Web:* www.hafele.com					
Hapco Inc 26252 Hillman Hwy	Abingdon	VA	24210	276-628-7171	623-2594
TF: 800-368-7171 ■ *Web:* www.hapco.com					
Hart & Cooley Inc 500 E 8th St	Holland	MI	49423	616-392-7855	223-8461*
Fax Area Code: 800 ■ *TF:* 800-435-6341 ■ *Web:* www.hartandcooley.com					
IKG Industries 1514 S Sheldon Rd	Channelview	TX	77530	281-452-6637	378-3987*
Fax Area Code: 713 ■ *Web:* www.harscoikg.com					
Irvine Access Floors Inc 9425 Washington Blvd Suite Y-WW	Laurel	MD	20723	301-617-9333	617-9907
TF: 800-969-8870 ■ *Web:* www.intandem.com					
Jackburn Mfg Inc 438 Church St	Girard	PA	16417	814-774-3573	774-2854
Web: www.jackburn.com					
Jerith Mfg Co Inc 14400 McNulty Rd	Philadelphia	PA	19154	215-676-4068	676-9756
TF: 800-344-2242 ■ *Web:* www.jerith.com					

				Phone	Fax
King Architectural Metals Inc PO Box 271169 *TF:* 800-542-2379 ■ *Web:* www.kingmetals.com	Dallas	TX	75227	214-388-9834	388-1048
Lawrence Metal Products Inc 260 Spur Dr S PO Box 400 *Fax Area Code:* 631 ■ *TF:* 800-441-0019 ■ *Web:* www.lawrencemetal.com	Bay Shore	NY	11706	800-441-0019	666-0336*
Livers Bronze Co 4621 E 75th Terr *Web:* www.liversbronze.com	Kansas City	MO	64132	816-300-2828	300-0864
Marwas Steel Co 18 Mt Pleasant Rd *TF:* 800-426-1983 ■ *Web:* www.marwas.com	Scottdale	PA	15683	724-887-7720	887-9494
McGregor Industries Inc 46 Line St *TF:* 800-326-6786 ■ *Web:* www.mcgregorindustries.com	Dunmore	PA	18512	570-343-2436	343-4915
Milgo Industrial Inc 68 Lombardi St *Web:* www.milgo-bufkin.com	Brooklyn	NY	11222	718-388-4363	963-0614
Morton Mfg Co 700 Liberty Dr *Web:* www.mortonmfg.com	Libertyville	IL	60048	847-362-5400	362-5434
Moultrie Mfg Co 1403 Georgia Hwy 133 S PO Box 2948 *TF:* 800-841-8674 ■ *Web:* www.moultriemanufacturing.com	Moultrie	GA	31776	229-985-1312	890-7245
Overly Mfg Co 574 W Otterman St *TF:* 800-979-7300 ■ *Web:* www.overly.com	Greensburg	PA	15601	724-834-7300	830-2871
Perry Mfg Co Inc 1233 W 18th St *TF:* 800-428-7200	Indianapolis	IN	46202	317-231-9037	231-9161
Spider Staging Corp 365 Upland Dr *TF:* 800-428-7887 ■ *Web:* www.spiderstaging.com	Tukwila	WA	98188	206-575-6445	575-6240
Steel Ceilings Inc 451 E Coshocton St *TF:* 800-848-0496 ■ *Web:* www.steelceilings.com	Johnstown	OH	43031	740-967-1063	967-1478
Superior Aluminum Products Inc 555 E Main St PO Box 430 *TF:* 800-548-8656 ■ *Web:* www.superioraluminum.com	Russia	OH	45363	937-526-4065	526-3904
Swanton Welding & Machining Co 407 Broadway Ave *Web:* www.swantonweld.com	Swanton	OH	43558	419-826-4816	826-0489
Tate Access Floors Inc 7510 Montevideo Rd *TF:* 800-231-7788 ■ *Web:* www.tateaccessfloors.com	Jessup	MD	20794	410-799-4200	799-4207
Universal Builders Supply Inc (UBS) 27 Horton Ave *TF:* 800-582-0070 ■ *Web:* www.ubs1.com	New Rochelle	NY	10801	914-699-2400	699-2609
VELUX America Inc 450 Old Brickyard Rd *TF:* 800-688-3589 ■ *Web:* www.veluxusa.com	Greenwood	SC	29648	864-941-4700	941-4870
Vicwest Corp 1296 S Service Rd W *TF:* 800-265-6583 ■ *Web:* www.vicwest.com	Oakville	ON	L6L5T7	905-825-2252	825-2272
Waco Scaffolding & Equipment Co 4545 Spring Rd PO Box 318028 *TF:* 800-321-3150 ■ *Web:* www.wacoscaf.com	Cleveland	OH	44131	216-749-8900	741-8486
Wooster Products Inc 1000 Spruce St PO Box 6005 *TF:* 800-321-4936 ■ *Web:* www.wooster-products.com	Wooster	OH	44691	330-264-2844	262-4151

495 METALS SERVICE CENTERS

				Phone	Fax
A M Castle & Co 1420 Kensington Rd Suite 220 *TF:* 800-289-2785 ■ *Web:* www.castlemetals.com	Oak Brook	IL	60523	847-455-7111	455-0587
A-588 & A-572 Steel Co The 133 Sebago Lake Dr *Web:* www.a588a572steel.com	Sewickley	PA	15143	412-366-1980	366-3780
ABC Metals Inc 500 W Clinton St *TF:* 800-238-8470 ■ *Web:* www.abcmetals.com	Logansport	IN	46947	574-753-0471	753-6110
Accurate Alloys Inc 5455 Irwindale Ave *TF:* 800-842-2222 ■ *Web:* www.accuratealloys.com	Irwindale	CA	91706	626-338-4012	337-8393
Action Stainless & Alloys Inc 1505 Halsey Way *TF:* 800-749-2523 ■ *Web:* www.actionstainless.com	Carrollton	TX	75007	972-466-1500	466-0909
Aladdin Steel Inc PO Box 89 *TF:* 800-637-4455 ■ *Web:* www.aladdinsteel.com	Gillespie	IL	62033	217-839-2121	839-3823
Alaskan Copper & Brass Co 3223 6th Ave S *TF:* 800-552-7661 ■ *Web:* www.alascop.com	Seattle	WA	98134	206-623-5800	382-7335
Alcoa Inc 201 Isabella St *NYSE: AA* ■ *Web:* www.alcoa.com	Pittsburgh	PA	15212	412-553-4545	553-4498
All Foils Inc 16100 Imperial Pkwy *TF:* 800-521-0054 ■ *Web:* www.allfoils.com	Strongsville	OH	44149	440-572-3645	378-0161
All Metals Industries Inc PO Box 807 *TF:* 800-654-6043 ■ *Web:* www.allmetind.com	Belmont	NH	03220	603-267-7023	267-7025
Allied Metals Inc 2220 Canada Dry St *TF:* 800-947-9823 ■ *Web:* www.metalsinc.com	Houston	TX	77223	713-923-9491	923-5224
Alro Steel Corp 3100 E High St *TF:* 800-877-2576 ■ *Web:* www.alro.com	Jackson	MI	49203	517-787-5500	787-6390
Aluminum & Stainless Inc PO Box 3484 *TF:* 800-252-9074 ■ *Web:* www.aluminumandstainless.com	Lafayette	LA	70502	337-837-4381	837-5439
AM Castle & Co 1420 Kensington Rd Suite 220 *AMEX: CAS* ■ **Fax:* Sales ■ *TF:* 800-289-2785 ■ *Web:* www.amcastle.com	Oak Brook	IL	60523	847-455-7111	455-0587*
American Douglas Metals Inc 783 Thorpe Rd *TF:* 800-428-0023 ■ *Web:* www.americandouglasmetals.com	Orlando	FL	32824	407-855-6590	857-3290
American Strip Steel Inc 400 Metuchen Rd *TF:* 800-526-1216 ■ *Web:* www.americanstrip.com	South Plainfield	NJ	07080	908-757-9000	412-1442
AMI Metals Inc 1738 General George Patton Dr *TF:* 800-727-1903 ■ *Web:* www.amimetals.com	Brentwood	TN	37027	615-377-0400	377-0103
Amsco Steel Co PO Box 11037 *TF:* 800-772-2743 ■ *Web:* www.amscosteel.com	Fort Worth	TX	76110	817-926-3355	923-2860
Arbon Steel & Service Co Inc 2355 Bond St *Web:* www.arbonsteel.com	University Park	IL	60466	708-534-6800	534-6826
Art Iron Inc 860 Curtis St *TF:* 800-472-1113 ■ *Web:* www.artiron.com	Toledo	OH	43609	419-241-1261	242-9768
Atlas Steel Products Co 7990 Bavaria Rd *TF:* 800-444-1682 ■ *Web:* www.atlassteel.com	Twinsburg	OH	44087	330-425-1600	425-1611
Berg Steel Corp 4306 Normandy Ct *Web:* www.bergsteel.com	Royal Oak	MI	48073	248-549-6066	549-1374
Berlin Metals LLC 3200 Sheffield Ave *TF:* 800-754-8867 ■ *Web:* www.berlinmetals.com	Hammond	IN	46327	219-933-0111	933-0692
Bing Metals Group Steel Processing Div 1500 E Euclid St *TF:* 800-521-1564 ■ *Web:* www.binggroup.com	Detroit	MI	48211	313-875-2022	875-2328
Bmg Metals Inc 950 Masonic Ln *TF:* 800-552-1510 ■ *Web:* www.bmgmetals.com	Richmond	VA	23231	804-226-1024	222-3693
Bobco Metals Co 2000 S Alameda St **Fax Area Code:* 213 ■ *TF:* 800-262-2605 ■ *Web:* www.bobcomall.com	Los Angeles	CA	90058	800-262-2605	748-5824*
Bohler-Uddeholm North America 2505 Millenium Dr *TF:* 800-638-2520 ■ *Web:* www.bucorp.com	Elgin	IL	60124	630-883-3100	883-3101
Brown-Strauss Steel 2495 Uravan St *TF Sales:* 800-677-2778 ■ *Web:* www.brown-strauss.com	Aurora	CO	80011	303-371-2200	375-8122
Burgon Tool Steel Co Inc 20 Durham St *TF:* 800-258-7106 ■ *Web:* www.burgon.com	Portsmouth	NH	03801	603-430-9200	430-4004
Cambridge Street Metal Co Inc 82 Stevens St **Fax Area Code:* 508 ■ *TF:* 800-254-7580 ■ *Web:* www.csm.metal.net	Taunton	MA	02718	617-254-7580	822-4667*
Cambridge-Lee Industries Inc 1340 Soldiers Field Rd **Fax:* Sales ■ *TF:* 800-225-4378 ■ *Web:* www.camlee.com	Brighton	MA	02135	617-783-3100	746-1169*
Chatham Steel Corp 501 W Boundary St PO Box 2567 *TF:* 800-546-2650 ■ *Web:* www.chathamsteel.com	Savannah	GA	31402	912-233-4182	944-0238
Chicago Tube & Iron Co 1 Chicago Tube Dr *TF Cust Svc:* 800-972-0217 ■ *Web:* www.chicagotube.com	Romeoville	IL	60446	815-834-2500	588-3958
City Pipe & Supply Corp PO Box 2112 *TF:* 800-688-7473 ■ *Web:* www.citypipe.com	Odessa	TX	79760	432-332-1541	333-2300
Clayton Metals Inc 546 Clayton Ct **Fax Area Code:* 630 ■ *TF:* 800-323-7628 ■ *Web:* www.claytonmetals.com	Wood Dale	IL	60191	800-323-7628	860-1053*
CMC Rebar 4846 Singleton Blvd *Web:* www.cmc.com	Dallas	TX	75712	214-631-5250	637-1110
Coilplus Pennsylvania Inc 5135 Bleigh St *TF:* 800-355-5200 ■ *Web:* www.coilplus.com	Philadelphia	PA	19136	215-331-5200	331-9538
Columbia Pipe & Supply Co 1120 W Pershing Rd *TF:* 888-361-7700 ■ *Web:* www.columbiapipe.com	Chicago	IL	60609	773-927-6600	927-8415
Commercial Metals Co Dallas Trading Div 6565 N MacArthur Blvd Suite 800 *Web:* www.cmc.com	Irving	TX	75039	214-689-4300	689-5886
Conestoga Supply Corp 11011 Sheldon Rd **Fax Area Code:* 281 ■ *Web:* www.conestogasupply.com	Houston	TX	77044	832-391-9400	456-7574*
Consolidated Pipe & Supply Inc 1205 Hilltop Pkwy *TF Sales:* 800-467-7261 ■ *Web:* www.consolidatedpipe.com	Birmingham	AL	35204	205-323-7261	251-7838
Consolidated Steel Services Inc 632 Glendale Valley Blvd *TF:* 800-237-8783 ■ *Web:* www.csteel.com	Fallentimber	PA	16639	814-944-5890	943-8278
Consumers Pipe & Supply Co 5832 E 61st St *TF:* 800-338-7473 ■ *Web:* www.consumerspipe.com	Los Angeles	CA	90040	323-685-6870	724-3781
Contractors Steel Co 36555 Amrhein Rd **Fax:* Sales ■ *TF:* 800-521-3946 ■ *Web:* www.contractorssteel.com	Livonia	MI	48150	734-464-4000	452-3939*
Copper & Brass Sales 22355 W 11 Mile Rd *TF:* 800-926-2600 ■ *Web:* www.copperandbrass.com	Southfield	MI	48033	248-233-5600	233-5600
Coral Sales Co 9838 SE 17th Ave *TF:* 800-538-7245 ■ *Web:* www.coralsales.com	Milwaukie	OR	97222	503-655-6351	657-9649
Decker Steel & Supply Inc 4500 Train Ave *TF:* 800-321-6100 ■ *Web:* www.deckersteel.com	Cleveland	OH	44102	216-281-7900	281-1441
Delta Metals Co Inc 1388 N 7th St PO Box 70286 *Web:* www.delta-metals.com	Memphis	TN	38107	901-525-5000	575-3322
DenCol 4630 Washington St *Web:* www.dencol.com	Denver	CO	80216	303-295-1683	295-1689
Dubose National Energy Services Inc PO Box 499 *TF:* 800-590-2150 ■ *Web:* www.dubosenes.com	Clinton	NC	28329	910-590-2151	590-3444
Duhig & Co Inc 5071 Telegraph Rd *Web:* www.duhig.com	Los Angeles	CA	90022	323-263-7161	263-7161
East Coast Metal Distributors Inc 1313 S Briggs Ave *Web:* www.ecmdi.com	Durham	NC	27703	919-598-5030	598-1404
Eastern Metal Supply of North Carolina Inc 2925 Stewart Creek Blvd *TF:* 800-432-2204 ■ *Web:* www.easternmetal.com	Charlotte	NC	28216	704-391-2266	
Eaton Steel Corp 10221 Capital Ave *TF:* 800-527-3851 ■ *Web:* www.eatonsteel.com	Oak Park	MI	48237	248-398-3434	398-3434
Ed Fagan Inc 769 Susquehanna Ave *TF:* 800-335-6827 ■ *Web:* www.edfagan.com	Franklin Lakes	NJ	07417	201-891-4003	891-3207
Farwest Steel Corp 2000 Henderson Ave **Fax:* Hum Res ■ *TF:* 800-542-5091 ■ *Web:* www.farweststeel.com	Eugene	OR	97403	541-686-2000	681-7241*
Feralloy Corp 8755 W Higgins Rd Suite 970 *Web:* www.feralloy.com	Chicago	IL	60631	773-380-1500	380-1535
Frontier Steel Co Inc 4990 Grand Ave *Web:* www.frontiersteel.com	Pittsburgh	PA	15225	412-865-4444	865-0030
Future Metals Inc 10401 State St *TF:* 800-733-0960 ■ *Web:* www.futuremetals.com	Tamarac	FL	33321	954-724-1400	721-5050
General Steel Inc PO Box 1503 *TF:* 800-476-2794 ■ *Web:* www.steeldeal.com	Macon	GA	31202	478-746-2794	745-8136
Gerber Metal Supply Co 2 Boundary Rd *TF:* 800-836-4672 ■ *Web:* www.gerbermetal.com	Somerville	NJ	08876	908-823-9150	823-9160
Gibbs Wire & Steel Co Inc Metals Dr PO Box 520 *TF:* 800-800-4422 ■ *Web:* www.gibbswire.com	Southington	CT	06489	860-621-0121	628-7780
Hanna Steel Corp 3812 Commerce Ave PO Box 558 *TF:* 800-633-8252 ■ *Web:* www.hannasteel.com	Fairfield	AL	35064	205-780-1111	783-8368
Hickman Williams & Co 250 E 5th St Suite 300	Cincinnati	OH	45202	513-621-1946	621-0024
Horizon Steel Co 1808 Holste Rd *TF:* 800-575-9914 ■ *Web:* www.horizonsteel.com	Northbrook	IL	60062	847-291-0440	291-0460

Company	City	State	ZIP	Phone	Fax
Howard Precision Metals Inc PO Box 240127 TF: 800-444-0311 ■ Web: www.hpmi.com	Milwaukee	WI	53224	414-355-9611	355-2637
Hynes Industries 3760 Oakwood TF: 800-321-9257 ■ Web: www.hynesind.com	Youngstown	OH	44515	330-779-3221	779-9098
Independent Steel Co 615 Township Rd 232 Web: www.independentsteel.com	Valley City	OH	44280	330-225-7741	273-6265
Ken-Mac Metals Inc 17901 Englewood Dr TF: 800-831-9503 ■ Web: www.kenmacmetals.com	Cleveland	OH	44130	440-234-7500	234-4459
Kenwal Steel Corp 8223 W Warren Ave Web: www.kenwal.com	Dearborn	MI	48126	313-739-1000	739-1001
Kerry Steel Inc 31731 Northwestern Hwy Suite 200	Farmington Hills	MI	48334	248-352-0000	865-9064
Kivort Steel 380 Hudson River Rd TF: 800-462-2616 ■ Web: www.kivortsteel.com	Waterford	NY	12188	518-590-7233	235-2042
Klein Steel Service 105 Vanguarden Pkwy TF Cust Svc: 800-477-6789 ■ Web: www.kleinsteel.com	Rochester	NY	14606	585-328-4000	328-0470
Kreher Steel Co LLC 1550 N 25th Ave *Fax Area Code: 708 ■ TF: 800-323-0745 ■ Web: www.kreher.com	Melrose Park	IL	60160	800-323-0745	345-8293*
L Smith Cooper International Inc 2867 Vail Ave Web: www.smithcooper.com	Commerce	CA	90040	323-890-4455	890-4456
Landmann Wire Rope Products Inc 1818 Gilbreth Rd Suite 148 Web: www.landmannwire.com	Burlingame	CA	94010	650-777-4210	
Lane Steel Co Inc 4 River Rd Web: www.lanesteel.com	Mc Kees Rocks	PA	15136	412-777-1700	777-1709
Lapham-Hickey Steel Corp 5500 W 73rd St TF Cust Svc: 800-323-8443 ■ Web: www.lapham-hickey.com	Chicago	IL	60638	708-496-6111	496-8504
Latrobe Steel Distribution 1551 Vienna Pkwy TF: 800-321-6446	Vienna	OH	44473	330-609-5137	609-2054
Lexington Steel Corp 5443 W 70th Pl Web: www.lexsteel.com	Bedford Park	IL	60638	708-594-9200	594-5233
Lindquist Steels Inc 1050 Woodend Rd TF: 800-243-9637 ■ Web: www.lindquiststeels.com	Stratford	CT	06615	203-377-2828	386-0132
Livingston Pipe & Tube Inc 1612 Rt 4 N PO Box 300 TF: 800-548-7473 ■ Web: www.livingstonpipeandtube.com	Staunton	IL	62088	618-635-8700	635-8720
Loeffel Steel Products PO Box 2100 Web: www.loeffelsteel.com	Barrington	IL	60011	847-382-6770	382-2487
Loveman Steel Corp 5455 Perkins Rd *Fax Area Code: 440 ■ TF: 800-568-3626 ■ Web: www.lovemansteel.com	Cleveland	OH	44146	800-568-3626	232-0914*
Ludlow Steel Corp PO Box 28335 Web: www.ludlowsteel.com	Cleveland	OH	44128	216-475-4900	
M C Steel Inc 2 Braco International Blvd Web: www.mcsteel.com	Wilder	Ky	41076	859-781-8600	442-6040
Maas-Hansen Steel Corp 2435 E 37th St PO Box 58364 *Fax Area Code: 325 ■ TF: 800-647-8335 ■ Web: www.maashansen.com	Vernon	CA	90058	323-583-6321	586-0171*
Macsteel Service Centers USA 888 San Clemente Dr Suite 250 TF: 866-622-7833 ■ Web: www.macsteelusa.com	Newport Beach	CA	92660	949-219-9000	219-9000
Majestic Steel USA 5300 Majestic Pkwy TF: 800-321-5590 ■ Web: www.majesticsteel.com	Bedford Heights	OH	44146	440-786-2666	786-0576
Marmon/Keystone Corp PO Box 992 TF: 800-544-1748 ■ Web: www.marmonkeystone.com	Butler	PA	16003	724-283-3000	283-0558
Matenaer Corp 810 Schoenhaar Dr TF: 800-254-0873 ■ Web: www.matenaer.com	West Bend	WI	53090	262-338-0700	338-3491
Mazel & Co Inc 4300 W Ferdinand St TF: 800-525-4023 ■ Web: www.mazelandco.com	Chicago	IL	60624	773-533-1600	533-9490
McNichols Co 2502 N Rocky Pt Dr Suite 950 PO Box 30300 TF: 800-237-3828 ■ Web: www.mcnichols.com	Tampa	FL	33607	813-282-3828	287-1066
Merit USA 620 Clark Ave TF: 800-445-6374 ■ Web: www.meritsteel.com	Pittsburg	CA	94565	925-427-2500	427-6427
Metals USA Inc 1 Riverway Suite 1100 TF: 888-871-8701 ■ Web: www.metalsusa.com	Houston	TX	77056	713-965-0990	965-0067
Metalwest LLC 1229 S Fulton Ave TF: 800-336-3365 ■ Web: www.metalwest.com	Brighton	CO	80601	303-654-0300	654-0404
Metrolina Steel Inc 2601 Westinghouse Blvd TF: 800-849-7835 ■ Web: www.metrolinasteel.com	Charlotte	NC	28273	704-598-7007	598-9135
Metropolitan Alloys Corp 17385 Ryan Rd Web: www.metroalloys.com	Detroit	MI	48212	313-366-4443	366-9698
Miller Metals Service Corp 2400 Bond St Web: www.millermetals.com	University Park	IL	60484	708-534-7200	534-7211
Mitsubishi International Corp 655 3rd Ave Web: www.micusa.com	New York	NY	10017	212-605-2000	
Murphy & Nolan Inc 340 Peat St PO Box 6689 Web: www.murphynolan.com	Syracuse	NY	13217	315-474-8203	474-8208
N Merfish Plumbing Supply Co PO Box 15879 TF: 800-869-5731 ■ Web: www.merfish.com	Houston	TX	77220	713-869-5731	867-0738
Namasco Corp 500 Colonial Ctr Pkwy Suite 500 Web: www.namasco.com	Roswell	GA	30076	678-259-8800	259-8873
Napco Steel Inc 1800 Arthur Dr TF: 800-292-8010 ■ Web: www.napcosteel.com	West Chicago	IL	60185	630-293-1900	293-0881
National Electronic Alloys Inc 3 Fir Ct Web: www.nealloys.com	Oakland	NJ	07436	201-337-9400	337-9698
National Material LP 1965 Pratt Blvd Web: www.nmlp.com	Elk Grove Village	IL	60007	847-806-4700	806-7220
National Specialty Alloys LLC 18250 Keith Harrow Blvd TF: 800-847-5653 ■ Web: www.nationalspeciality.com	Houston	TX	77084	281-345-2115	345-1133
National Tube Supply Co 925 Central Ave TF: 877-534-2700 ■ Web: www.nationaltubesupply.com	University Park	IL	60484	708-534-2700	534-1825
New Process Steel Corp 5800 Westview Dr TF: 800-392-4989 ■ Web: www.nps.cc/?pgID=Home	Houston	TX	77055	713-686-9631	686-5358
Nippon Steel USA Inc 780 3rd Ave 34th Fl TF: 800-345-6477 ■ Web: www.nsc.co.jp	New York	NY	10017	212-486-7150	593-3049

Company	City	State	ZIP	Phone	Fax
North American Steel Co 18300 Miles Ave Web: www.northamerican-steel.com	Cleveland	OH	44128	216-475-7300	475-6143
North Shore Steel 1566 Miles St TF: 877-453-3533 ■ Web: www.nssco.com	Houston	TX	77015	713-453-3533	671-5500
North Star BlueScope Steel LLC 6767 County Rd Web: www.northstarbluescope.com	Delta	OH	43515	419-822-2200	822-2209
Northeast Air Solutions Inc 3 Lopez Rd Web: www.air-eng.com	Wilmington	MA	01887	978-988-2000	988-2200
O'Neal Steel Inc 744 41st St N *Fax: Sales ■ TF: 800-292-4090 ■ Web: www.onealsteel.com	Birmingham	AL	35222	205-599-8000	599-8211*
Olympic Steel Inc 5096 Richmond Rd NASDAQ: ZEUS ■ *Fax: Sales ■ TF: 800-321-6290 ■ Web: www.olysteel.com	Bedford Heights	OH	44146	216-292-3800	292-3974*
Overseas Development Corp 953 Washington Blvd Web: www.overseasdevelopment.com	Stamford	CT	06901	203-964-0111	964-4929
Owen Industries Inc 501 Ave H TF: 800-831-9252 ■ Web: www.owenind.com	Carter Lake	IA	51510	712-347-5500	347-6166
Pacesetter Steel Service Inc 3300 Town Pt Dr *Fax Area Code: 678 ■ TF: 800-749-6505 ■ Web: www.teampacesetter.com	Kennesaw	GA	30144	770-919-8000	581-8880*
Pacific Steel & Recycling 1401 3rd St NW TF: 800-889-6264 ■ Web: www.pacific-recycling.com	Great Falls	MT	59404	406-771-7222	453-4269
Paragon Steel Enterprises LLC 4211 County Rd 61 TF: 800-411-5677 ■ Web: www.pstparagonsteel.com	Butler	IN	46721	260-868-1100	868-1101
Parker Steel Co PO Box 2883 TF: 800-333-4140 ■ Web: www.metricmetal.com	Toledo	OH	43606	419-473-2481	471-2655
Peerless Steel Corp 2450 Austin TF: 866-678-3350 ■ Web: www.peerlesssteel.com	Troy	MI	48083	248-528-3200	528-9144
Peterson Steel Corp 61 W Mountain St TF: 800-325-3245 ■ Web: www.petersonsteel.com	Worcester	MA	01606	508-853-3630	853-7485
Petroleum Pipe & Supply Inc 516 Industry Way	Heidelberg	PA	15106	412-279-7710	279-9029
Phillips & Johnston Inc 21w179 Hill Ave TF: 877-411-8823 ■ Web: www.phillips-johnston.com	Glen Ellyn	IL	60137	630-469-8150	469-8048
Phoenix Electronic Enterprises Inc 131 Tillson Ave EXT Web: www.phoenixmfg.com	Highland	NY	12528	845-691-7700	691-7759
Phoenix Metals Co 4685 Buford Hwy TF: 800-241-2290 ■ Web: www.phoenixmetals.net	Norcross	GA	30071	770-447-4211	246-8166
Pierce Aluminum 34 Forge Pkwy Web: www.piercealuminum.com	Franklin	MA	02038	508-541-7007	541-6077
Pioneer Steel Corp 7447 Intervale St TF: 800-999-9440 ■ Web: www.pioneersteel-usa.com	Detroit	MI	48238	313-933-9400	933-8720
Posner Industries Inc 8641 Edgeworth Dr TF: 888-767-6377 ■ Web: www.posners.com	Capitol Heights	MD	20743	301-350-1000	350-1050
Precision Steel Warehouse Inc 3500 Wolf Rd TF: 800-323-0740 ■ Web: www.precisionsteel.com	Franklin Park	IL	60131	847-455-7000	455-1341
Rancocas Metals Corp 35 Indel Ave TF: 800-762-6382 ■ Web: www.rancocasmetals.com	Rancocas	NJ	08073	609-267-4120	267-5690
Reliance Steel & Aluminum Co 350 S Grand Ave Suite 5100 NYSE: RS ■ Web: www.rsac.com	Los Angeles	CA	90071	213-687-7700	687-8792
Remelt Sources Inc 27151 Tungsten Rd Web: www.remeltsources.com	Cleveland	OH	44132	216-289-4555	289-0939
Rolled Alloys Inc 125 W Sterns Rd TF: 800-521-0332 ■ Web: www.rolledalloys.com	Temperance	MI	48182	734-847-0561	847-6917
Rolled Steel Products Corp 2187 Garfield Ave TF: 800-400-7833 ■ Web: www.rolledsteel.com	Los Angeles	CA	90040	323-723-8836	888-9866
Russel Metals Inc 1900 Minnesota Ct Suite 210 TSX: RUS ■ TF: 800-268-0750 ■ Web: www.russelmetals.com	Mississauga	ON	L5N3C9	905-819-7777	819-7409
Russellville Steel Co Inc PO Box 1538 TF: 800-617-8335 ■ Web: www.rsvlsteel.com	Russellville	AR	72811	479-968-2211	968-3486
Ryerson Inc 455 85th Ave NW TF: 800-328-7800 ■ Web: www.ryerson.com	Minneapolis	MN	55433	763-717-9000	717-7168
Ryerson Inc 2621 W 15th Pl NYSE: RYI ■ *Fax: Hum Res ■ Web: www.ryerson.com	Chicago	IL	60608	773-762-2121	762-2194*
S & S Steel Services Inc 444 E 29th St Web: www.sssteelservices.com	Anderson	IN	46016	765-622-4545	622-4556
Sabel Steel Industries Inc 749 N Ct St TF: 800-392-5754 ■ Web: www.sabelsteel.com	Montgomery	AL	36104	334-265-6771	263-7949
Service Steel Inc 5555 N Ch Ave Bldg 2 Web: www.servicesteel.net	Portland	OR	97217	503-224-9500	
SGS Industrial Supplies Inc 2771 Robindale Rd Web: www.sgsindustrial.com	Brownsville	TX	78526	956-831-4291	831-9434
Shamrock Steel Sales Inc 238 W County Rd S TF: 800-299-2317 ■ Web: www.shamrocksteelsales.com	Odessa	TX	79763	432-337-2317	337-5049
Siskin Steel & Supply Co Inc 1901 Riverfront Pkwy TF: 800-756-3671 ■ Web: www.siskin.com	Chattanooga	TN	37408	423-756-3671	265-4758
SOS Metals Inc PO Box 8712 Web: www.sossteel.com	West Chester	OH	45071	513-896-2700	785-2350
Soudan Metals Co Inc 319 W 40th Pl Web: www.soudanmetals.com	Chicago	IL	60609	773-548-7600	548-4803
Southwestern Suppliers Inc 6815 E 14th Ave TF: 800-282-2867 ■ Web: www.sowes.com	Tampa	FL	33619	813-626-2193	628-0511
Specialty Pipe & Tube Inc PO Box 516 TF: 800-842-5839 ■ Web: www.specialtypipe.com	Mineral Ridge	OH	44440	330-505-8262	505-8260
State Pipe & Supply Inc 9615 S Norwalk Blvd TF: 800-733-6410 ■ Web: www.statepipe.com	Santa Fe Springs	CA	90670	562-695-5555	692-1054
Staub Metals Corp 7747 E Rosecrans Ave Web: www.staubmetals.com	Paramount	CA	90723	562-602-2200	633-1456
Steel & Pipe Supply Co 555 Poyntz Ave TF: 800-521-2345 ■ Web: www.spsci.com	Manhattan	KS	66502	785-537-2222	587-5176
Steel & Pipes Inc PO Box 5309 Web: www.steelandpipes.com	Caguas	PR	00726	787-747-9415	747-8986

				Phone	Fax
Steel Engineers Inc 716 W Mesquite Ave	Las Vegas	NV	89106	702-386-0023	386-6723
TF: 800-838-4043 ■ *Web:* www.steelengineers.com					
Steel Supply Co The 5101 Newport Dr	Rolling Meadows	IL	60008	800-323-7571	828-1553
Web: www.steelsupply.com					
Steel Warehouse Co Inc 2722 W Tucker Dr	South Bend	IN	46619	574-236-5100	236-5154
TF: 800-348-2529 ■ *Web:* www.steelwarehouse.com					
Steward Steel Inc					
1219 E US Hwy 62 PO Box 551	Sikeston	MO	63801	573-471-2121	471-2336
Web: www.stewardsteel.com					
Superior Steel Supply LLC PO Box 458	Spicer	MN	56288	320-796-4274	796-6819
Web: www.superiorsteelsupply.us					
Supra Alloys Inc 351 Cortez Cir	Camarillo	CA	93012	805-388-2138	388-2057
TF: 800-752-1786 ■ *Web:* www.supraalloys.com					
Sylvania Steel Corp 4169 Holland Sylvania Rd	Toledo	OH	43623	419-885-3838	882-7270
TF: 800-436-0986 ■ *Web:* www.sylvaniasteel.com					
Taco Metals Inc 50 NE 179th St	Miami	FL	33162	305-652-8566	653-1174
Web: www.tacometals.com					
TCI Aluminum/North Inc 2353 Davis Ave	Hayward	CA	94545	510-786-3750	786-3302
Web: www.tcialuminum.com					
Tenenbaum Recycling Group					
4500 W Bethany Rd	North Little Rock	AR	72117	501-945-0881	945-3865
Web: www.trg.net					
Texas Pipe & Supply Co Inc 2330 Holmes Rd	Houston	TX	77051	713-799-9235	799-8701
TF: 800-233-8736 ■ *Web:* www.texaspipe.com					
Thyssenkrupp Steel North America Inc					
1 Thyssen Pl	Detroit	MI	48210	313-899-6200	
Web: www.tksna.com					
Tioga Pipe Supply Co Inc					
2450 Wheatsheaf Ln	Philadelphia	PA	19137	215-831-0700	533-1645
TF: 800-523-3678 ■ *Web:* www.tiogapipe.com					
Titan Steel Corp 2500-B Broening Hwy	Baltimore	MD	21224	410-631-5200	631-5220
Web: www.titansteel.com					
Tomson Steel Co (inc) PO Box 940	Middletown	OH	45044	513-420-8600	420-8610
TF: 800-837-3001 ■ *Web:* www.tomsonsteel.com					
Totten Tubes Inc 500 Danlee St	Azusa	CA	91702	626-812-0220	812-0113
Web: www.tottentubes.com					
Toyota Tsusho America Inc					
805 3rd Ave 16th Fl	New York	NY	10022	212-355-3600	355-3670
TF: 800-883-0100 ■ *Web:* www.taiamerica.com					
Triple-S Steel Supply LLC PO Box 21119	Houston	TX	77226	713-697-7105	
TF: 800-231-1034 ■ *Web:* www.sss-steel.com					
Tubular Steel Inc 1031 Executive Pkwy Dr	Saint Louis	MO	63141	314-851-9200	851-9336
TF: 800-882-8527 ■ *Web:* www.tubularsteel.com					
Turret Steel Industries Inc 105 Pine St	Imperial	PA	15126	724-218-1014	218-1195
Web: www.turretsteel.com					
TW Metals Inc PO Box 644	Exton	PA	19341	610-458-1300	458-1399
Web: www.twmetals.com					
United States Brass & Copper Co Inc					
1418 Centre Cir Dr	Downers Grove	IL	60515	630-629-9340	629-9350
TF: 800-821-2854 ■ *Web:* www.usbrassandcopper.com					
Universal Steel Co 6600 Grant Ave	Cleveland	OH	44105	216-883-4972	341-0421
TF: 800-927-2659 ■ *Web:* www.univsteel.com					
Valiant Steel & Equipment Inc					
6455 Old Peachtree Rd	Norcross	GA	30071	770-417-1235	417-1669
Web: www.valiantsteel.com					
Victory Steel Products Corp PO Box 4370	Saint Louis	MO	63123	314-849-7272	849-4555
TF: 800-325-7902 ■ *Web:* www.vicsteel.com					
Viking Materials Inc 3225 Como Ave SE	Minneapolis	MN	55414	612-617-5800	623-9070
TF: 800-682-3942 ■ *Web:* www.vikingmaterials.com					
Vista Metals Inc 65 Ballou Blvd	Bristol	RI	02809	401-253-1772	
TF: 800-431-4113 ■ *Web:* www.vismet.com					
West Central Steel Inc					
110 19th St NW PO Box 1178	Willmar	MN	56201	320-235-4070	235-1816
TF: 800-992-8853 ■ *Web:* www.wcsteel.com					
Westfield Steel Inc 530 State Rd 32 W	Westfield	IN	46074	317-896-5587	896-5343
Web: www.westfieldsteel.com					
Willbanks Metals Inc 1155 NE 28th St	Fort Worth	TX	76106	817-625-6161	625-8487
TF: 800-772-2352 ■ *Web:* www.willbanksmetals.com					
Williams Metals & Welding Alloys Inc					
125 Strafford Ave Suite 108	Wayne	PA	19087	610-225-0105	
Web: www.wmwa.net					
Winchester Metals Inc 195 Ebert Rd	Winchester	VA	22603	540-667-9000	
TF: 800-535-2148 ■ *Web:* www.steelsupplier.com					
Wisconsin Steel & Tube Corp					
1555 N Mayfair Rd	Milwaukee	WI	53226	414-453-4441	453-0789
TF: 800-279-8335 ■ *Web:* www.wisteeltube.com					
Wrisco Industries Inc					
355 Hiatt Dr Suite B	Palm Beach Gardens	FL	33418	561-626-5700	627-3574
TF: 800-627-2646 ■ *Web:* www.wrisco.com					

496 METALWORKING DEVICES & ACCESSORIES

SEE ALSO Machine Tools - Metal Cutting Types p. 2192; Machine Tools - Metal Forming Types p. 2193; Tool & Die Shops p. 2717

				Phone	Fax
Acme Industrial Co 441 Maple Ave	Carpentersville	IL	60110	847-428-3911	428-1820
TF: 800-323-5582 ■ *Web:* www.acmeindustrial.com					
Advanced Machine & Engineering Co					
2500 Latham St	Rockford	IL	61103	815-962-6076	962-6483
TF: 800-255-2331 ■ *Web:* www.ame.com					
Ag Davis Gage & Engineering Co					
6533 Sims Dr	Sterling Heights	MI	48313	586-977-9000	977-9190
Web: www.agdavis-aagage.com					
Alcon Tool Co 568 E Crosier St	Akron	OH	44311	330-773-9171	773-8042
Web: www.alcontool.com					
Allied Machine & Engineering Corp 120 Deeds Dr	Dover	OH	44622	330-343-4283	343-4781
TF: 800-321-5537 ■ *Web:* www.alliedmachine.com					
American Broach & Machine Co					
4600 Jackson Rd	Ann Arbor	MI	48103	734-761-5021	761-7626
Web: www.americanbroach.com					
American Cutting Edge Inc 480 Congress Pk Dr	Dayton	OH	45459	937-438-2390	438-2398
TF: 888-252-3372 ■ *Web:* www.cbmfg.com					
American Drill Bushing Co					
7141 Paramount Blvd	Pico Rivera	CA	90660	323-725-1515	725-8740
TF: 800-423-4425 ■ *Web:* www.americandrillbushing.com					
Apex Broach & Machine Co 22862 Hoover Rd	Warren	MI	48089	586-758-2626	758-2627
Web: www.apexbroach.com					
ASKO Inc 501 W 7th Ave	Homestead	PA	15120	412-461-4110	461-5400
TF: 800-321-1310 ■ *Web:* www.askoinc.com					
ATI Metal Working Products 1 Teledyne Pl	La Vergne	TN	37086	615-641-4200	223-2219*
**Fax Area Code:* 800 ■ **Fax:* Sales ■ *TF:* 800-521-2375 ■ *Web:* www.metalworkingproducts.com					
Balax Inc PO Box 96	North Lake	WI	53064	262-966-2355	966-1028
Web: www.balax.com					
Besly Cutting Tools Inc					
16200 Woodmint Ln	South Beloit	IL	61080	815-389-2231	389-1339
TF: 800-435-2965 ■ *Web:* www.besly.com					
Big Kaiser Precision Tooling Inc					
641 Fargo Ave	Elk Grove Village	IL	60007	847-228-7660	228-0881
TF: 800-553-5113 ■ *Web:* www.bigkaiser.com					
Boley Tool & Machine Works Inc					
1044 Spring Bay Rd	East Peoria	IL	61611	309-694-2722	694-7879
Web: www.boleytool.com					
Brubaker Tool Corp 200 Front St	Millersburg	PA	17061	717-692-2113	692-4995
TF: 800-522-8665 ■ *Web:* www.brubakertool.com					
Buck Chuck Co 2155 Traversefield Dr	Traverse City	MI	49686	231-947-5755	947-4953
TF: 800-228-2825 ■ *Web:* www.buckchuckusa.com					
Carbro Corp 15724 Condon Ave PO Box 278	Lawndale	CA	90260	310-643-8400	643-9703
TF: 888-738-4400					
Carl Zeiss Industrial Metrology					
6250 Sycamore Ln N	Maple Grove	MN	55369	763-744-2400	533-0218
TF: 800-752-6181 ■ *Web:* www.zeiss.com					
Ceratizit USA Inc 5369 Rt 982 N PO Box 272	Latrobe	PA	15650	724-694-8100	694-8620
TF: 800-245-6880 ■ *Web:* www.ceratizit.com					
Cincinnati Gilbert Machine Tool Co LLC					
3366 Beekman St	Cincinnati	OH	45223	513-541-4815	541-4885
Web: www.cincinnatigilbert.com					
CJT Koolcarb Inc 494 Mission St	Carol Stream	IL	60188	630-690-5933	690-6355
TF: 800-323-2299 ■ *Web:* www.cjtkoolcarb.com					
Climax Portable Machine Tools Inc (CPMT)					
2712 E 2nd St	Newberg	OR	97132	503-537-3379	537-5282
TF: 800-333-8311 ■ *Web:* www.cpmt.com					
Cline Tool & Service Co PO Box 866	Newton	IA	50208	641-792-7081	792-0309
Web: www.clinetool.com					
Cogsdill Tool Products Inc PO Box 7007	Camden	SC	29020	803-438-4000	438-5263
Cole Carbide Industries Inc 24703 Ryan Rd	Warren	MI	48091	586-757-8700	758-6930
Web: www.colecarbide.com					
Deltronic Corp 3900 W Segerstrom Ave	Santa Ana	CA	92704	714-545-5800	545-9548
TF: 800-451-6922 ■ *Web:* www.deltronic.com					
Detroit Edge Tool Co 6570 E Nevada St	Detroit	MI	48234	313-366-4120	366-1661
TF: 800-404-2038 ■ *Web:* www.detroitedge.com					
Dundick Corp 4616 W 20th St	Cicero	IL	60804	708-656-6363	656-2359
TF: 800-322-4243 ■ *Web:* www.dundick.com					
Edmunds Gages 45 Spring Ln	Farmington	CT	06032	860-677-2813	677-4243
Web: www.edmundsgages.com					
Enmark Tool & Gage Co Inc 18100 Cross Ln	Fraser	MI	48026	586-293-2797	293-1037
Web: www.enmarktool.com					
Fastcut Tool Corp 200 Front St	Millersburg	PA	17061	717-692-8232	692-2707
TF: 800-682-8832 ■ *Web:* www.fastcut.com					
Fullerton Tool Co Inc 121 Perry St	Saginaw	MI	48602	989-799-4550	792-3335
TF: 800-248-8315 ■ *Web:* www.fullertontool.com					
Gaiser Tool Co 4544 McGrath St	Ventura	CA	93003	805-644-5583	644-2013
Web: www.gaisertool.com					
Garr Tool Co 7800 N Alger Rd	Alma	MI	48801	989-463-6171	463-3609
TF: 800-248-9003 ■ *Web:* www.garrtool.com					
General Broach Co 307 Salisbury St	Morenci	MI	49256	517-458-7555	458-6821
Web: www.generalbroach.com					
General Cutting Tool Inc					
6440 N Ridgeway Ave	Lincolnwood	IL	60712	847-677-8770	677-8786
Web: www.generalcuttingtools.com					
Giddings & Lewis Machine Tools					
142 Doty St PO Box 590	Fond du Lac	WI	54936	920-921-9400	906-2522
Web: www.glmachinetools.com					
Glassline Corp PO Box 147	Perrysburg	OH	43552	419-666-5942	666-1549
Web: www.glassline.com					
Glastonbury Southern Gage 46 Industrial Pk Rd	Erin	TN	37061	931-289-4243	242-7142*
**Fax Area Code:* 800 ■ *TF:* 800-251-4243 ■ *Web:* www.gsgage.com					
Gleason Cutting Tools Corp					
1351 Windsor Rd	Loves Park	IL	61111	815-877-8900	877-0264
Web: www.gleason.com					
Goss & DeLeeuw Machine Co 100 Harding St	Kensington	CT	06037	860-828-4121	828-8132
Guhring Inc 1445 Commerce Ave	Brookfield	WI	53045	262-784-6730	784-9096
TF: 800-776-6170 ■ *Web:* www.guhring.com					
Hanlo Gages & Engineering Co					
34403 Glendale St	Livonia	MI	48150	734-422-4224	422-2244
Web: www.hanlogages.com					
Hannibal Carbide Tool Inc					
5000 Paris Gravel Rd	Hannibal	MO	63401	573-221-2775	221-1147
TF: 800-451-9436 ■ *Web:* www.hannibalcarbide.com					
Hardinge Inc 1 Hardinge Dr	Elmira	NY	14905	607-734-2281	732-4925
NASDAQ: HDNG ■ *TF:* 800-843-8801 ■ *Web:* www.hardinge.com					
Hayden Twist Drill & Tool Co Inc					
22822 Globe St	Warren	MI	48089	586-754-7700	754-3312
TF: 800-521-1780 ■ *Web:* www.haydendrills.com					
Heidenhain Corp 333 E State Pkwy	Schaumburg	IL	60173	847-490-1191	490-3931
Web: www.heidenhain.com					
High Tech Tool Inc 7803 S Loop E	Houston	TX	77012	713-641-2303	641-6664
Web: www.hightechtool.com					
Hoppe Tool Inc 107 1st Ave	Chicopee	MA	01020	413-592-9213	592-4688
TF Sales: 800-742-6571 ■ *Web:* www.hoppetool.com					

Company	City	State	ZIP	Phone	Fax
Hougen Mfg Inc 3001 Hougen Dr *TF Orders:* 800-462-7818 ■ *Web:* www.hougen.com	Swartz Creek	MI	48473	810-635-7111	635-8277
Huron Machine Products Inc 228 SW 21st Terr **Fax:* Sales ■ *TF:* 800-327-8186 ■ *Web:* www.huronmachine.com	Fort Lauderdale	FL	33312	954-587-4541	583-2154*
Husqvarna Construction Products 17400 W 119th St *TF:* 800-288-5040 ■ *Web:* www.husqvarna.com	Olathe	KS	66061	800-288-5040	825-0028
Industrial Tools Inc (ITI) 1111 S Rose Ave *TF:* 800-266-5561 ■ *Web:* www.iti-abrasives.com	Oxnard	CA	93033	805-483-1111	483-6302
Iowa Precision Industries Inc 5480 6th St SW *Web:* www.iowaprecision.com	Cedar Rapids	IA	52404	319-364-9181	364-3436
ITW Workholding 2155 Traverse Field Dr *TF:* 800-544-3823 ■ *Web:* www.forkardt.us	Traverse City	MI	49686	231-947-5755	995-8361
Jasco Cutting Tools 1390 Mt Read Blvd *TF:* 800-868-1074 ■ *Web:* www.jascotools.com	Rochester	NY	14606	585-546-1254	254-2655
Jasco Tools Inc 1390 Mt Read Blvd PO Box 60497 *TF:* 800-724-5497 ■ *Web:* www.jascotools.com	Rochester	NY	14606	585-254-7000	254-2655
Jergens Inc 15700 S Waterloo Rd *TF:* 800-537-4367 ■ *Web:* www.jergensinc.com	Cleveland	OH	44110	216-486-2100	481-6193
Kennametal Inc 1600 Technology Way PO Box 231 *NYSE: KMT* ■ *TF Cust Svc:* 800-446-7738 ■ *Web:* www.kennametal.com	Latrobe	PA	15650	724-539-5000	539-8787
KEO Cutters Inc 25040 Easy St *TF:* 888-390-2050 ■ *Web:* www.keocutters.com	Warren	MI	48089	586-771-2050	771-2062
Lancaster Knives Inc 165 Ct St *TF:* 800-869-9666 ■ *Web:* www.lancasterknives.com	Lancaster	NY	14086	716-683-5050	683-5068
Lovejoy Tool Co Inc 133 Main St *TF:* 800-843-8376 ■ *Web:* www.lovejoytool.com	Springfield	VT	05156	802-885-2194	885-9511
Madison Cutting Tools Inc 485 Narragansett Pk Dr *Web:* www.madisontools.com	Pawtucket	RI	02861	401-333-0400	333-4011
Melin Tool Co 5565 Venture Dr Unit C **Fax Area Code:* 800 ■ *TF:* 800-521-1078 ■ *Web:* www.endmill.com	Cleveland	OH	44130	216-362-4230	521-1558*
Micro 100 Tool Corp 1410 E Pine Ave *TF:* 800-421-8065 ■ *Web:* www.micro100.com	Meridian	ID	83642	208-888-7310	888-2106
Micro-vu Corp 7909 Conde Ln *Web:* www.microvu.com	Windsor	CA	95492	707-838-6272	838-3985
NED Corp 18 Grafton St 2nd Fl *TF:* 800-343-6086 ■ *Web:* www.nedcorp.com	Worcester	MA	01604	508-798-8364	799-2796
Niagara Cutter Inc 200 John James Audubon Pkwy *TF:* 888-689-8400 ■ *Web:* www.niagaracutter.com	Amherst	NY	14228	716-689-8400	689-8485
North American Tool Corp 215 Elmwood Ave **Fax Area Code:* 800 ■ *TF:* 800-872-8277 ■ *Web:* www.natool.com	South Beloit	IL	61080	815-389-2300	872-3299*
Onsrud Cutter LP 800 Liberty Dr *TF:* 800-234-1560 ■ *Web:* www.onsrud.com	Libertyville	IL	60048	847-362-1560	362-5028
OSG Tap & Die Inc 676 E Fullerton Ave *TF:* 800-837-2223 ■ *Web:* www.osgtool.com	Glendale Heights	IL	60139	630-790-1400	790-1477
Phillips Corp 7390 Coca Cola Dr *TF:* 800-878-4242 ■ *Web:* www.phillipscorp.com	Hanover	MD	21076	410-564-2929	564-2949
Powers Fasteners Inc 2 Powers Ln *TF:* 800-524-3244 ■ *Web:* www.powers.com	Brewster	NY	10509	914-235-6300	576-6483
Precision Grinding & Mfg Corp 1305 Emerson St *Web:* www.pgmcorp.com	Rochester	NY	14606	585-458-4300	458-7281
Precitech Precision Inc 44 Blackbrook Rd *TF:* 800-295-2510 ■ *Web:* www.precitech.com	Keene	NH	03431	603-357-2511	358-6174
Products Engineering Corp 2645 Maricopa St *Web:* www.productsengineering.com	Torrance	CA	90503	310-787-4500	787-4501
Quinco Tool Products Co 21000 Hubbell Rd **Fax Area Code:* 800 ■ *TF:* 800-521-1910 ■ *Web:* www.quinco.com	Oak Park	MI	48237	248-968-5000	468-4730*
Regal-Beloit Corp 200 State St *NYSE: RBC* ■ *Web:* www.regalbeloit.com	Beloit	WI	53511	608-364-8800	364-8818
Reiff & Nestor Co 50 Reiff St PO Box 147 *TF:* 800-521-3422 ■ *Web:* www.rntap.com	Lykens	PA	17048	717-453-7113	453-7555
Royal Machine & Tool Corp 4 Willowbrook Dr *Web:* www.royalworkholding.com	Berlin	CT	06037	860-828-6555	828-1591
S-T Industries Inc 301 Armstrong Blvd N *TF:* 800-326-2039 ■ *Web:* www.stindustries.com	Saint James	MN	56081	507-375-3211	375-4503
Scotchman Industries Inc 180 E Hwy 14 *TF:* 800-843-8844 ■ *Web:* www.scotchman.com	Philip	SD	57567	605-859-2542	859-2499
Scully Jones Seibert Corp 1901 S Rockwell St *TF:* 800-752-8665 ■ *Web:* www.scullyjones.com	Chicago	IL	60608	773-247-5900	247-6088
Seco Tools 2805 Bellingham Dr **Fax:* Cust Svc ■ *Web:* www.secotools.com	Troy	MI	48083	248-528-5200	528-5600*
SKF Precision Technologies 1230 Cheyenne Ave *TF:* 800-445-6267 ■ *Web:* www.skfpt.com	Grafton	WI	53024	262-377-2434	377-9438
Somma Tool Co Inc 109 Scott Rd *Web:* www.sommatool.com	Waterbury	CT	06705	203-753-2114	756-5489
Spiralock Corp 25235 Dequindre Rd *TF:* 800-521-2688 ■ *Web:* www.spiralock.com	Madison Heights	MI	48071	248-543-7800	543-1403
Star Cutter Co 23461 Industrial Pk Dr *TF:* 800-968-2801 ■ *Web:* www.starcutter.com	Farmington	MI	48335	248-474-8200	474-9518
Starrett Webber Gage Div 24500 Detroit Rd *Web:* www.starrett-webber.com	Cleveland	OH	44145	440-835-0001	892-9555
Stilson Products 15935 Sturgeon St *TF:* 888-400-5978	Roseville	MI	48066	586-778-1100	778-4660
Strong Tool Co 1251 E 286th St *TF:* 800-362-0293 ■ *Web:* www.strongtool.com	Cleveland	OH	44132	216-289-2450	289-4562
Tapmatic Corp 802 S Clearwater Loop *TF:* 800-854-6019 ■ *Web:* www.tapmatic.com	Post Falls	ID	83854	208-773-8048	773-3021
Thread Check Inc 390 Oser Ave *TF:* 800-767-7633 ■ *Web:* www.threadcheck.com	Hauppauge	NY	11788	631-231-1515	231-1625
TM Smith Tool International Corp 360 Hubbard Ave PO Box 1065 *TF:* 800-521-4894 ■ *Web:* www.tmsmith-tool.com	Mount Clemens	MI	48046	586-468-1465	468-7190
Toolmasters LLC PO Box 1611 *Web:* www.toolmastersllc.com	Rockford	IL	61110	815-968-0961	968-0961
United Drill Bushing Corp 12200 Woodruff Ave **Fax Area Code:* 800 ■ *TF:* 800-486-3466 ■ *Web:* www.ucc-udb.com	Downey	CA	90241	562-803-1521	486-3465*
US Drill Head Co 5298 River Rd *Web:* www.usdrillhead.com	Cincinnati	OH	45233	513-941-0300	941-9110
Utica Enterprises Co 13231 23-Mile Rd	Shelby Township	MI	48315	586-726-4300	726-4316
Viking Drill & Tool Inc 355 State St *TF:* 800-328-4655 ■ *Web:* www.vikingdrill.com	Saint Paul	MN	55107	651-227-8911	227-1793
Vulcan Tool Co 730 Lorraine Ave *Web:* www.vulcancut.com	Dayton	OH	45401	937-253-6194	253-1062
Walker Magnetics Group Inc 20 Rockdale St *TF:* 800-962-4638 ■ *Web:* www.walkermagnet.com	Worcester	MA	01606	508-853-3232	852-8649
Walter USA Inc N22 W23855 Ridgeview Pkwy W *TF:* 800-945-5554 ■ *Web:* www.walter-tools.com	Waukesha	WI	53188	262-347-2401	347-2500
Wapakoneta Machine Co 300 N St PO Box 429 *TF:* 800-837-2131 ■ *Web:* www.wapakonetamachine.com	Wapakoneta	OH	45895	419-738-2131	738-5828
Weldon Tool Co 200 Front St *TF:* 800-622-7742 ■ *Web:* www.endmills.com	Millersburg	PA	17061	717-692-2113	692-5270
Westfield Gage Co Inc 34 Hudson Dr PO Box 1130 *Web:* www.westfieldgage.com	Southwick	MA	01077	413-569-9444	569-9449
Zagar Inc 24000 Lakeland Blvd *Web:* www.zagar.com	Cleveland	OH	44132	216-731-0500	731-8591
Zenith Cutter Co 5200 Zenith Pkwy *TF:* 800-223-5202 ■ *Web:* www.zenithcutter.com	Loves Park	IL	61111	815-282-5200	282-5232

497 METALWORKING MACHINERY

Company	City	State	ZIP	Phone	Fax
ADS Machinery Corp 1201 Vine Ave NE *Web:* www.adsmachinery.com	Warren	OH	44483	330-399-3601	399-1190
Armstrong Mfg Co 2700 SE Tacoma St *Web:* www.armstrongblue.com	Portland	OR	97202	503-228-8381	228-8384
Artos Engineering Co 21605 Gateway Ct *Web:* www.artosnet.com	Brookfield	WI	53045	262-252-4545	252-4544
ATD Engineering & Machine LLC 533 N Ct St *Web:* www.atdemllc.com	Au Gres	MI	48703	989-876-7161	876-7162
Bachi Co 1201 Ardmore Ave *Web:* www.bachiwinder.com	Itasca	IL	60143	630-773-5600	773-5610
Balance Technology Inc 7035 Jomar Dr *Web:* www.balancetechnology.com	Whitmore Lake	MI	48189	734-769-2100	769-2542
Bartell Machinery Systems LLC 6321 Elmer Hill Rd *Web:* www.bartellmachinery.com	Rome	NY	13440	315-336-7600	336-0947
Belvac Production Machinery Inc 237 Graves Mill Rd *TF:* 800-423-5822 ■ *Web:* www.belvac.com	Lynchburg	VA	24502	434-239-0358	239-1964
Delta Brands Inc (DBI) 2204 Century Ctr Blvd *Web:* www.dbimfg.com	Irving	TX	75062	972-438-7150	579-0100
Diversified Machine Inc 5353 Wilcox St *Web:* www.divmi.com	Montague	MI	49437	231-894-9051	894-4706
Eagle Technologies Group 9850 Red Arrow Hwy *Web:* www.eagletechnologies.com	Bridgman	MI	49106	269-465-6986	465-6952
Eubanks Engineering Co 3022 Inland Empire Blvd *Web:* www.eubanks.com	Ontario	CA	91764	909-483-2456	483-2498
FANTA Equipment Co 6521 Storer Ave *Web:* www.fantaequip.com	Cleveland	OH	44102	216-281-1515	281-7755
Finishing Equipment Inc 3640 Kennebec Dr	Saint Paul	MN	55122	651-452-1860	452-9851
Hogan Mfg Inc 1704 1st St *Web:* www.hoganmfg.com	Escalon	CA	95320	209-838-7323	838-8648
J.R. Automation Technologies LLC 13365 Tyler St *Web:* www.jrautomation.com	Holland	MI	49424	616-399-2168	399-5593
Jovil Mfg Co Inc 10 Precision Rd *Web:* www.jovil.com	Danbury	CT	06810	203-798-7255	790-8645
Merrill Tool & Machine Co Inc 21659 Gratiot Rd *Web:* www.merrilltool.com	Merrill	MI	48637	989-643-7981	643-7875
Pannier Corp 207 Sandusky St *TF:* 800-233-2009 ■ *Web:* www.pannier.com	Pittsburgh	PA	15212	412-323-4900	323-4962
Pines Mfg Inc 30505 Clemens Rd *TF:* 800-207-2840 ■ *Web:* www.pines-mfg.com	Westlake	OH	44145	440-835-5553	835-5556
Precision Strip Inc 86 S Ohio St PO Box 104 *Web:* www.precision-strip.com	Minster	OH	45865	270-535-3459	
Red Bud Industries 200 B & E Industrial Dr *TF Cust Svc:* 800-851-4612 ■ *Web:* www.redbudindustries.com	Red Bud	IL	62278	618-282-3801	282-6718
Rowe Machinery & Automation Inc 76 Hinckley Rd *TF:* 800-247-2645 ■ *Web:* www.runwithrowe.com	Clinton	ME	04927	207-426-2351	426-7453
Superior Machine Co of South Carolina Inc 692 N Cashua Rd *TF:* 800-736-9898	Florence	SC	29502	843-664-3001	664-3007
Sweed Machinery Inc 653 2nd Ave PO Box 228 *TF Sales:* 800-888-1352 ■ *Web:* www.sweed.com	Gold Hill	OR	97525	541-855-1512	855-1165
Tridan International Inc 130 N Jackson St PO Box 537 *TF:* 800-369-3544 ■ *Web:* www.tridan.com	Danville	IL	61834	217-443-3592	443-3894
US Baird Corp 1700 Stratford Ave PO Box 9706 *Web:* www.usbaird.com	Stratford	CT	06615	203-375-3361	378-6006
West Bond Inc 1551 S Harris Ct *Web:* www.westbond.com	Anaheim	CA	92806	714-978-1551	978-0431
Wright-K Technology Inc 2025 E Genesee Ave *TF:* 800-752-3103 ■ *Web:* www.wright-k.com	Saginaw	MI	48601	989-752-3103	752-0670

498 METERS & OTHER COUNTING DEVICES

Company	City	State	ZIP	Phone	Fax
AMETEK Inc Dixson Div 287 27 Rd *TF:* 888-302-0639 ■ *Web:* www.ametekdixson.com	Grand Junction	CO	81503	970-244-1241	245-6267
AMETEK Sensor Technology Drexelbrook Div 205 Keith Valley Rd *TF Cust Svc:* 800-553-9092 ■ *Web:* www.drexelbrook.com	Horsham	PA	19044	215-674-1234	674-2731
Auto Meter Products Inc 413 W Elm St *TF:* 866-248-6356 ■ *Web:* www.autometer.com	Sycamore	IL	60178	815-895-8141	895-3859
Badger Meter Inc 4545 W Brown Deer Rd *AMEX: BMI* ■ *TF:* 800-876-3837 ■ *Web:* www.badgermeter.com	Milwaukee	WI	53223	414-355-0400	
Beede Electrical Instrument Co 88 Village St *Web:* www.beede.com	Penacook	NH	03303	603-753-6362	753-6201

				Phone	Fax
Clark-Reliance Corp 16633 Foltz Pkwy *Web:* www.clark-reliance.com	Strongsville	OH	44149	440-572-1500	572-1500
Danaher Controls 1675 Delany Rd *TF:* 800-873-8731 ■ *Web:* www.dancon.com	Gurnee	IL	60031	847-662-2666	662-4150
Duncan Parking Technologies Inc 340 W Industrial Pk Rd *TF:* 800-338-6226 ■ *Web:* www.duncanindustries.com	Harrison	AR	72601	870-741-5481	741-6806
Electro-Sensors Inc 6111 Blue Cir Dr *NASDAQ: ELSE* ■ *TF:* 800-328-6170 ■ *Web:* www.electro-sensors.com	Minnetonka	MN	55343	952-930-0100	930-0130
Elster American Meter Co 2221 Industrial Rd *TF:* 888-295-7928 ■ *Web:* www.americanmeter.com	Nebraska City	NE	68410	402-873-8200	873-7616
Engineering Measurements Co (EMCO) 1831 Lefthand Cir Suite C *TF:* 800-356-9362 ■ *Web:* www.emcoflow.com	Longmont	CO	80501	303-651-0550	682-7069
Eugene Ernst Products Co Inc PO Box 925 **Fax Area Code: 888* ■ *TF:* 800-992-2843 ■ *Web:* www.ernstflow.com	Farmingdale	NJ	07727	732-938-2641	992-2843*
FMC Measurement Solutions 1602 Wagner Ave **Fax: Hum Res* ■ *TF:* 800-867-6484 ■ *Web:* www.fmctechnologies.com	Erie	PA	16510	814-898-5000	899-8249*
Greenwald Industries 212 Middlesex Ave *TF:* 800-221-0982 ■ *Web:* www.greenwaldindustries.com	Chester	CT	06412	860-526-0800	526-4205
Isspro Inc 2515 NE Riverside Way PO Box 11177 *TF:* 888-447-7776 ■ *Web:* www.issproinc.com	Portland	OR	97211	503-288-4488	249-2999
Laser Technology Inc 7070 S Tucson Way *TF:* 800-280-6113 ■ *Web:* www.lasertech.com	Englewood	CO	80112	303-649-1000	649-9710
Max Machinery Inc 1420 Healdsburg Ave *Web:* www.maxmachinery.com	Healdsburg	CA	95448	707-433-7281	433-0571
Maxima Technologies Stewart Warner 1811 Rohrerstown Rd *Web:* www.stewartwarner.com	Lancaster	PA	17601	717-581-1000	569-6372
McKesson Automated Prescription Systems 2800 S MacArthur Dr *TF:* 800-551-6578 ■ *Web:* www.mckesson.com	Alexandria	LA	71301	318-641-6448	767-2323
Metretek Inc 305 E Dr Suite A *TF:* 800-327-8559 ■ *Web:* www.metretekfl.com	Melbourne	FL	32904	321-259-9700	259-2900
PMP Corp 25 Security Dr *TF Cust Svc:* 800-243-6628 ■ *Web:* www.pmp-corp.com	Avon	CT	06001	860-677-9656	674-0196
POM Inc 200 S Elmira Ave PO Box 430 *TF:* 800-331-7275 ■ *Web:* www.pom.com	Russellville	AR	72802	479-968-2880	968-2840
Racine Federated Inc Hedland Div 8635 Washington Ave **Fax Area Code: 800* ■ **Fax: Sales* ■ *TF:* 800-433-5263 ■ *Web:* www.hedland.com	Racine	WI	53406	262-639-6770	245-3569*
Schlumberger Ltd 5599 San Felipe Suite 100 *NYSE: SLB* ■ *Web:* www.slb.com	Houston	TX	77056	713-513-2000	513-2006
Sparling Instruments Co Inc 4097 N Temple City Blvd *TF Sales:* 800-800-3569 ■ *Web:* www.sparlinginstruments.com	El Monte	CA	91731	626-444-0571	444-2314
Teleflex Morse Marine Products 640 N Lewis Rd *Web:* www.tfxmarine.com	Limerick	PA	19468	610-495-7011	495-7470
Thermo Polysonics 9303 W Sam Houston Pkwy S	Houston	TX	77099	713-272-0404	272-5388
Thomas G Faria Corp 385 Norwich-New London Tpke *TF:* 800-473-2742 ■ *Web:* www.faria-instruments.com	Uncasville	CT	06382	860-848-9271	848-2704

499 MICROGRAPHICS PRODUCTS & SERVICES

				Phone	Fax
Anacomp Inc 15378 Avenue of Science *Web:* www.anacomp.com	San Diego	CA	92128	858-716-3400	716-3775
BMI Imaging Systems 1115 E Arques Ave *TF:* 800-359-3456 ■ *Web:* www.bmiimaging.com	Sunnyvale	CA	94085	408-736-7444	736-4397
Comgraphics Inc 329 W 18th St 10th Fl *Web:* www.cgichicago.com	Chicago	IL	60616	312-226-0900	226-9411
Comstor Productivity Center Inc 2219 N Dickey Rd *TF:* 800-776-2451 ■ *Web:* www.comstorinc.com	Spokane	WA	99212	509-534-5080	536-0281
DPF Data Services Group Inc 1990 Swarthmore Ave *TF:* 800-431-4416 ■ *Web:* www.dpfdata.com	Lakewood	NJ	08701	732-370-8840	370-1751
DST Output 2534 Madison Ave *Web:* www.dstoutput.com	Kansas City	MO	64108	816-221-1234	843-6579
Eye Communication Systems Inc 455 E Industrial Dr *TF:* 800-558-2153 ■ *Web:* www.eyecom.com	Hartland	WI	53029	262-367-1360	367-1362
HF Group Inc 203 W Artesia Blvd *Web:* www.myhfi.com	Compton	CA	90220	310-605-0755	608-1556
Imaging Assoc 7297 P Lee Hwy *Web:* www.scanfilm.com	Falls Church	VA	22042	703-536-0101	536-0102
Indus International Inc 340 S Oak St PO Box 890 *TF:* 800-843-9377 ■ *Web:* www.indususa.com	West Salem	WI	54669	608-786-0300	786-0786
Micro Com Systems Ltd 27 E 7th Ave *Web:* www.microcomsys.com	Vancouver	BC	V5T1M5	604-872-6771	872-2533
microMEDIA Imaging Systems Inc 1979 Marcus Ave *Web:* www.imagingservices.com	Lake Success	NY	11042	516-355-0300	355-0316

500 MILITARY BASES

SEE ALSO Coast Guard Installations p. 1615

500-1 Air Force Bases

				Phone	Fax
Altus Air Force Base 209 E 6th St *Web:* www.altus.af.mil	Altus Afb	OK	73523	580-482-8100	481-5966
Andrews Air Force Base 1535 Command Dr Suite AB-209 *Web:* www.andrews.af.mil	Joint Base Andrews	MD	20762	301-981-4825	981-9039
Arnold Air Force Base 100 Kindel Dr Suite B-213 *Web:* www.arnold.af.mil	Arnold	TN	37389	931-454-3000	454-6086
Barksdale Air Force Base 2nd Bomb Wing Public Affairs *Web:* www.barksdale.af.mil	Barksdale AFB	LA	71110	318-456-3066	456-5986
Beale Air Force Base 17852 16th St Suite 125 *Web:* www.beale.af.mil	Beale AFB	CA	95903	530-634-3000	634-8895
Bolling Air Force Base 110 Luke Ave *Web:* www.bolling.af.mil	Washington	DC	20038	202-767-4011	404-6300
Brooks City-Base 3260 Sidney Brooks Bldg 537 **Fax Area Code: 240* ■ *Web:* www.brooks.af.mil	San Antonio	TX	78235	210-536-2444	536-2136*
Cannon Air Force Base 100 S DL Ingram Blvd Suite 1098 *Web:* www.cannon.af.mil	Cannon AFB	NM	88103	505-784-3311	784-2338
Charleston Air Force Base 102 E Hill Blvd *Web:* www.public.charleston.amc.af.mil	Charleston AFB	SC	29404	843-963-5608	963-5604
Columbus Air Force Base 555 7th St *Web:* www.columbus.af.mil	Columbus AFB	MS	39710	662-434-7068	434-7009
Davis-Monthan Air Force Base 5275 E Granite St *Web:* www.dm.af.mil	Davis-Monthan AFB	AZ	85707	520-228-3204	228-3328
Dover Air Force Base 201 Eagle Way *Web:* www.dover.af.mil	Dover AFB	DE	19902	302-677-3372	677-2901
Dyess Air Force Base Arnold Blvd & S 7th *Web:* www.dyess.af.mil	Dyess AFB	TX	79607	325-696-3113	696-2866
Edwards Air Force Base 305 E Popson Ave *Web:* www.edwards.af.mil	Edwards AFB	CA	93524	661-277-1110	277-2732
Eglin Air Force Base 403 N 7th St *Web:* www.eglin.af.mil	Eglin AFB	FL	32542	850-882-1113	882-6156
Eielson Air Force Base 354 Broadway St Unit 2B *Web:* www.eielson.af.mil	Eielson AFB	AK	99702	907-377-1110	377-1215
Ellsworth Air Force Base 1958 Scott Dr *Web:* www.ellsworth.af.mil	Ellsworth AFB	SD	57706	605-385-5056	385-4668
Elmendorf Air Force Base 8517 20th St Suite 111 *Web:* www.elmendorf.af.mil	Elmendorf AFB	AK	99506	907-552-8153	552-5111
Fairchild Air Force Base 100 W Ent St Suite 155 *Web:* www.fairchild.af.mil	Fairchild AFB	WA	99011	509-247-1212	247-5640
Goodfellow Air Force Base 351 Kearney Blvd *Web:* www.goodfellow.af.mil	Goodfellow AFB	TX	76908	325-654-3877	654-5414
Grand Forks Air Force Base 344 6th Ave Grand Forks AFB *Web:* public.grandforks.amc.af.mil	Grand Forks	ND	58205	701-747-3000	747-5022
Hanscom Air Force Base 81 Grenier St *Web:* www.hanscom.af.mil	Hanscom AFB	MA	01731	781-377-4441	377-5077
Hickam Air Force Base 800 Scott Cir *Web:* www.hickam.af.mil	Hickam AFB	HI	96853	808-449-2490	449-3017
Hill Air Force Base 7285 4th St Bldg 180 Suite 109 *Web:* www.hill.af.mil	Hill AFB	UT	84056	801-777-5201	777-4640
Holloman Air Force Base 596 4th St Bldg 224 Suite 105 *Web:* www.holloman.af.mil	Holloman AFB	NM	88330	505-572-7383	572-3650
Keesler Air Force Base 709 H St Bldg 902 Rm 201A *Web:* www.keesler.af.mil	Biloxi	MS	39534	228-377-1110	377-3940
Kirtland Air Force Base 2000 Wyoming Blvd SE Suite A-1 *TF:* 877-246-1453 ■ *Web:* www.kirtland.af.mil	Kirtland AFB	NM	87117	505-846-5991	
Lackland Air Force Base 1701 Kenly Ave Suite 102 *Web:* www.lackland.af.mil	Lackland AFB	TX	78236	210-671-1110	671-4592
Langley Air Force Base 49 Spruce St PCS Box 1000 **Fax: Library* ■ *Web:* www.langley.af.mil	Langley AFB	VA	23665	757-764-1110	764-3315*
Laughlin Air Force Base 561 Liberty Dr Suite 3 *Web:* www.laughlin.af.mil	Laughlin AFB	TX	78843	830-298-5988	298-5047
Little Rock Air Force Base 1250 Thomas Ave *Web:* www.littlerock.af.mil	Little Rock AFB	AR	72099	501-987-1110	987-6978
Los Angeles Air Force Base 483 N Aviation Blvd *Web:* www.losangeles.af.mil	El Segundo	CA	90245	310-653-1750	
Luke Air Force Base 14185 W Falcon St *Web:* www.luke.af.mil	Luke AFB	AZ	85309	623-856-5853	856-6013

				Phone	Fax
Malmstrom Air Force Base 7410 Flightline Dr Bldg 300 *Web:* www.malmstrom.af.mil	Malmstrom AFB	MT	59402	406-731-1110	731-4048
Maxwell Air Force Base 55 Le May Plaza S *Web:* www.maxwell.af.mil	Maxwell AFB	AL	36112	334-953-2014	953-3379
McChord Air Force Base 100 Col Joe Jackson Blvd Suite 3021 *Web:* www.62aw.af.mil	McChord AFB	WA	98438	253-982-2621	984-5825
McConnell Air Force Base 57837 Coffeyville St Suite 271 *Web:* www.mcconnell.af.mil	McConnell AFB	KS	67221	316-759-6100	759-3148
McGuire Air Force Base 2901 Falcon Ln Rm 235 *Web:* www.jointbasemdl.af.mil	McGuire AFB	NJ	08641	609-754-2104	754-6999
Minot Air Force Base 201 Summit Dr *Web:* www.minot.af.mil	Minot AFB	ND	58705	701-723-6212	723-6534
Moody Air Force Base 4343 George St Bldg 904 *Web:* www.moody.af.mil	Moody AFB	GA	31699	229-257-3395	257-4804
Mountain Home Air Force Base 366 Gunfighter Ave Suite 314 *Web:* www.mountainhome.af.mil	Mountain Home AFB	ID	83648	208-828-6800	828-4205
Nellis Air Force Base 4430 Grissom Ave Suite 107 *Web:* www.nellis.af.mil	Nellis AFB	NV	89191	702-652-2750	652-9838
Offutt Air Force Base 906 Sac Blvd Suite 1 *Web:* www.offutt.af.mil	Offutt AFB	NE	68113	402-294-1110	294-7172
Patrick Air Force Base 1201 Edward H White Suite C-129 *Web:* www.patrick.af.mil	Patrick AFB	FL	32925	321-494-5933	494-7302
Pope Air Force Base 5453 Reilly St *Web:* www.pope.af.mil	Pope AFB	NC	28308	910-394-1110	394-4266
Randolph Air Force Base 1 Washington Cir *Web:* www.randolph.af.mil	Randolph AFB	TX	78150	210-652-1110	652-5412
Robins Air Force Base 620 9th St Suite 230 Rm 215 *Web:* www.robins.af.mil	Robins AFB	GA	31098	478-926-1113	926-9597
Scott Air Force Base 101 Heritage Dr Suite 38 *Web:* www.scott.af.mil	Scott AFB	IL	62225	618-256-1110	
Seymour Johnson Air Force Base 1510 Wright Brothers Ave *Web:* www.seymourjohnson.af.mil	Seymour Johnson AFB	NC	27531	919-722-0027	722-0007
Shaw Air Force Base 517 Lance Ave Suite 106 *Web:* www.shaw.af.mil	Shaw AFB	SC	29152	803-895-2019	895-2028
Sheppard Air Force Base 419 G Ave Suite 3 *Web:* www.sheppard.af.mil	Sheppard AFB	TX	76311	940-676-2511	676-4245
Shriever Air Force Base 210 Falcon Pkwy Suite 2102 *Web:* www.schriever.af.mil	Colorado Springs	CO	80912	719-567-5040	567-5306
Tinker Air Force Base 3001 Staff Dr Suite 1AG85A *Web:* www.tinker.af.mil	Tinker AFB	OK	73145	405-739-2026	739-2882
Tyndall Air Force Base 445 Suwannee Rd 101 *Web:* www.tyndall.af.mil	Tyndall AFB	FL	32403	850-283-1110	283-3225
Vance Air Force Base 246 Brown Pkwy	Vance AFB	OK	73705	580-213-5000	213-6376
Vandenberg Air Force Base 706 Washington Ave Bldg 10122 *Web:* www.vandenberg.af.mil	Vandenberg	CA	93437	805-606-3595	606-8303
Warren Francis E Air Force Base 5305 Randall Ave *Web:* www.warren.af.mil	Warren AFB	WY	82005	307-773-1110	773-2074
Whiteman Air Force Base 1081 Arnold Ave Bldg 59 Suite 104 *Web:* www.whiteman.af.mil	Whiteman AFB	MO	65305	660-687-6123	687-7948
Wright-Patterson Air Force Base 1 Wright Patterson Afb *Web:* www.wpafb.af.mil	Dayton	OH	45433	937-257-1110	255-3370

500-2 Army Bases

				Phone	Fax
Fort AP Hill 18436 4th St *Web:* www.aphill.army.mil	Fort AP Hill	VA	22427	804-633-8120	633-8459
Fort Belvoir 5820 21st St Bldg 210 *Web:* www.belvoir.army.mil	Fort Belvoir	VA	22060	703-805-5454	805-5984
Fort Benning 6751 Constitution Loop 650 *Web:* www.army.mil/info/organization/benning	Fort Benning	GA	31905	706-545-5111	545-3329
Fort Bliss 1 Pershing Rd *Web:* www.bliss.army.mil	Fort Bliss	TX	79916	915-568-2121	568-2995
Fort Bragg Armistead & Macomb St Bldg 1-1333	Fort Bragg	NC	28310	910-396-3111	396-4568
Fort Buchanan 218 Brooke St *Web:* www.buchanan.army.mil	Fort Buchanan	PR	00934	787-707-5776	707-3323
Fort Campbell 2334 19th St *Web:* www.campbell.army.mil/Pages/CampHome.aspx	Fort Campbell	KY	42223	270-798-2151	798-6247
Fort Carson 1626 Ellis St Bldg 1118 Suite 200 *Web:* www.carson.army.mil	Fort Carson	CO	80913	719-526-4143	526-1021
Fort Detrick 810 Schreider St *Web:* www.detrick.army.mil	Frederick	MD	21702	301-619-7613	619-3207
Fort Dix 2270 Fort Dix Rd Bldg 5435 *Web:* www.dix.army.mil	Fort Dix	NJ	08640	609-562-1011	562-3337
Fort Drum 411 Tigris River Valley Rd *Web:* www.drum.army.mil	Fort Drum	NY	13602	315-772-6011	772-5165
Fort Eustis 300 Washington Blvd *Web:* www.eustis.army.mil	Fort Eustis	VA	23604	757-878-5251	878-1502
Fort Gillem 4705 N Wheeler Dr *Web:* www.mcpherson.army.mil	Forest Park	GA	30297	404-469-7326	464-3101
Fort Gordon 201 3rd Ave *Web:* www.gordon.army.mil	Fort Gordon	GA	30905	706-791-0110	791-2061
Fort Hamilton 113 Schum Ave Bldg 113 *Web:* www.hamilton.army.mil	Brooklyn	NY	11252	718-630-4101	630-4400
Fort Hood 761st Tank Battalion Ave Bldg 1001 Rm W105 *Web:* www.hood.army.mil	Fort Hood	TX	76544	254-287-1110	288-2750
Fort Huachuca Smith St Bldg 50010 *Web:* huachuca-www.army.mil	Fort Huachuca	AZ	85613	520-538-7111	533-5008
Fort Irwin PO Box 105067 *Web:* www.irwin.army.mil	Fort Irwin	CA	92310	760-380-3078	380-3075
Fort Jackson 5450 Strom Thurmond Blvd 1011 Columbia *Web:* www.jackson.army.mil	Fort Jackson	SC	29207	803-751-7511	751-3533
Fort Knox PO Box 995 *Web:* www.knox.army.mil	Fort Knox	KY	40121	502-624-4704	624-6074
Fort Leavenworth 881 Mcclellan Ave *Web:* www.leavenworth.army.mil	Fort Leavenworth	KS	66027	913-684-4021	684-3624
Fort Lee 500 Lee Ave *Web:* www.lee.army.mil	Fort Lee	VA	23801	804-765-3000	734-4659
Fort Leonard Wood Bldg 312 *Web:* www.wood.army.mil	Fort Leonard Wood	MO	65473	573-563-4013	563-4012
Fort McPherson 1777 Hardee Ave SW *Web:* www.mcpherson.army.mil	Fort McPherson	GA	30330	404-464-5668	464-5628
Fort Meade 4550 Parade Field Ln Rm 102 *Web:* www.ftmeade.army.mil	Fort Meade	MD	20755	301-677-1361	677-1305
Fort Monroe 66 Ingalls Rd Bldg 27 *Web:* www-tradoc.army.mil	Fort Monroe	VA	23651	757-788-2000	788-3358
Fort Polk 2030 14th St *Web:* www.jrtc-polk.army.mil	Fort Polk	LA	71459	337-531-2911	531-6014
Fort Richardson Richardson Dr Bldg 600 *TF:* 800-984-1517 ■ *Web:* www.usarak.army.mil/main	Fort Richardson	AK	99505	907-384-1110	384-2060
Fort Riley 1st Infantry Div Bldg 500 *Web:* www.riley.army.mil	Fort Riley	KS	66442	785-239-3032	239-2592
Fort Rucker Shamrock St 6th Ave Bldg 131 *Web:* www-rucker.army.mil	Fort Rucker	AL	36362	334-255-2252	255-1004
Fort Sam Houston 3630 Stanley Rd *Web:* www.cs.amedd.army.mil	Fort Sam Houston	TX	78234	210-221-8580	221-1198
Fort Shafter Bldg T100	Fort Shafter	HI	96858	808-438-9375	438-6354
Fort Sill 462 Hamilton Rd Suite 120 *Web:* sill-www.army.mil	Fort Sill	OK	73503	580-442-8111	355-6756
Fort Stewart 942 Dr Ben Hall Pl Suite 1087 *Web:* www.stewart.army.mil	Fort Stewart	GA	31314	912-435-9950	767-6673
Fort Story Shore Dr & Atlantic Ave *Web:* www.eustis.army.mil/Fort_story	Fort Story	VA	23459	757-422-7755	422-7750
Fort Wainwright 1047-1 Marks Rd Suite 5900 *Web:* www.wainwright.army.mil	Fort Wainwright	AK	99703	907-353-6701	353-6711
Joint Base Lewis-McChord (JBLM) PO Box 339500 *Web:* www.lewis.army.mil	Joint Base Lewis-McChord	WA	98433	253-967-0146	967-0612
Joint Base Myer 204 Lee Ave Bldg 59 *Web:* www.jbmhh.army.mil	Fort Myer	VA	22211	703-696-0584	696-2678

500-3 Marine Corps Bases

				Phone	Fax
Marine Corps Air Station Beaufort PO Box 55001 *Web:* www.beaufort.usmc.mil	Beaufort	SC	29904	843-228-7121	228-6005
Marine Corps Air Station Miramar PO Box 452001 *Web:* www.miramar.usmc.mil	San Diego	CA	92145	858-577-1245	577-4834
Marine Corps Air Station New River PSC PO Box 21002	Jacksonville	NC	28545	910-449-6623	449-6478
Marine Corps Air Station Yuma Shaw Ave Bldg 980 *Web:* www.yuma.usmc.mil	Yuma	AZ	85369	928-269-2252	269-3282
Marine Corps Base Camp Lejeune PSC PO Box 20004 *Web:* www.lejeune.usmc.mil	Camp Lejeune	NC	28542	910-451-1113	451-5882
Marine Corps Base Camp Pendleton PO Box 555010 *Web:* www.cpp.usmc.mil	Camp Pendleton	CA	92055	760-725-5012	725-5776
Marine Corps Base Hawaii PO Box 63002 *Web:* www.mcbh.usmc.mil	Kaneohe Bay	HI	96863	808-257-8840	257-2511
Marine Corps Base Quantico 3250 Catlin Ave *Web:* www.quantico.usmc.mil	Quantico	VA	22134	703-784-2741	784-0065
Marine Corps Logistics Base Albany 814 Radford Blvd Code 70000 *Web:* www.ala.usmc.mil	Albany	GA	31704	229-639-5215	639-5480
Marine Corps Recruit Depot Parris Island PO Box 19660 *Web:* www.mcrdpi.usmc.mil	Parris Island	SC	29905	843-228-2705	228-2122
Marine Corps Recruit Depot San Diego 1600 Henderson Ave *Web:* www.mcrdsd.usmc.mil	San Diego	CA	92145	619-524-8727	

500-4 Naval Installations

				Phone	Fax
Naval Air Station Corpus Christi 11101 D St *Web:* www.nascc.cnatra.navy.mil	Corpus Christi	TX	78419	361-961-2811	961-3402
Naval Air Station Fallon 4755 Pasture Rd *Web:* www.fallon.navy.mil	Fallon	NV	89496	775-426-2801	426-2848
Naval Air Station Jacksonville 6801 Roosevelt Blvd *TF:* 800-849-6024 ■ *Web:* www.cnic.navy.mil/Jacksonville/index.htm	Jacksonville	FL	32212	904-542-5588	

				Phone	Fax
Naval Air Station Joint Reserve Base Fort Worth 1303 Humphrey Dr *Web:* www.cnic.navy.mil/Fortworth/index.htm	Fort Worth	TX	76114	817-782-5000	782-7601
Naval Air Station Joint Reserve Base New Orleans 400 Russell Ave *Web:* www.airnav.com	New Orleans	LA	70143	504-678-3254	678-3244
Naval Air Station Joint Reserve Base Willow Grove PO Box 21 *Web:* www.cnic.navy.mil	Willow Grove	PA	19090	215-443-1000	443-6017
Naval Air Station Key West 1 Naval Air St PO Box 9001 *Web:* www.cnic.navy.mil/KeyWest/AboutCNIC/index.htm	Key West	FL	33040	305-293-4408	293-4415
Naval Air Station Kingsville 554 Mccain St *Web:* www.cnic.navy.mil/Kingsville/index.htm	Kingsville	TX	78363	361-516-6146	516-6875
Naval Air Station Lemoore 700 Avenger *Web:* www.cnic.navy.mil/Lemoore	Lemoore	CA	93246	559-998-3300	998-3395
Naval Air Station Meridian 255 Rosenbaum Ave *Web:* www.cnet.navy.mil/meridian	Meridian	MS	39309	601-679-2211	679-2447
Naval Air Station North Island PO Box 357033 *Web:* www.nasni.navy.mil	San Diego	CA	92135	619-545-8123	545-0182
Naval Air Station Oceana 1750 Tomcat Blvd *Web:* www.cnic.navy.mil/oceana/index.htm	Virginia Beach	VA	23460	757-433-3131	433-3156
Naval Air Station Patuxent River 2268 Cedar Pt Rd Bldg 408 Suite 204	Patuxent River	MD	20670	301-342-7710	342-7509
Naval Air Station Pensacola 190 Radford Blvd *Web:* www.naspensacola.navy.mil	Pensacola	FL	32508	850-452-0111	452-3939
Naval Air Station Whidbey Island 3730 N Charles Porter Ave *Web:* naswi.ahf.nmci.navy.mil	Oak Harbor	WA	98278	360-257-2286	
Naval Air Station Whiting Field 7550 USS Essex St **Fax:* PR ■ *Web:* wwwcfs.cnet.navy.mil	Milton	FL	32570	850-623-7341	623-7601*
Naval Air Systems Command Lakehurst Rt 547 *Web:* www.navair.navy.mil	Lakehurst	NJ	08733	732-323-2811	323-7676
Naval Base Kitsap 120 S Dewey St *Web:* www.nbk.navy.mil	Bremerton	WA	98314	360-476-2574	
Naval Base San Diego 3455 Senn Rd *Web:* www.navbasesd.navy.mil	San Diego	CA	92136	619-556-7359	556-2423
Naval Station Everett 2000 W Marine View Dr *Web:* www.everett.navy.mil	Everett	WA	98207	425-304-3000	304-3096
Naval Station Mayport PO Box 280048 *TF:* 800-872-7245 ■ *Web:* www.cnic.navy.mil/Mayport	Mayport	FL	32228	904-270-5401	270-5064
Naval Station Newport 690 Peary St *Web:* www.cnic.navy.mil/Newport	Newport	RI	02841	401-841-3456	841-2265
Naval Station Norfolk 1530 Gilbert St Suite 2000 *Web:* www.navstanorva.navy.mil	Norfolk	VA	23511	757-444-0000	444-0348
Naval Station Pearl Harbor 850 Ticonderoga St Suite 100 *Web:* www.pearlharbor.navy.mil	Pearl Harbor	HI	96860	808-473-2888	473-2876
Naval Submarine Base Kings Bay 1063 USS Tennessee Ave *Web:* www.cnic.navy.mil	Kings Bay	GA	31547	912-573-4714	573-4717
Naval Submarine Base New London PO Box 100 *Web:* www.subasenlon.navy.mil	Groton	CT	06349	860-694-3011	694-4699
Naval Support Activity 58 Bennion Rd *Web:* www.usna.edu	Annapolis	MD	21402	410-293-9320	293-3133
Naval Training Center Great Lakes 2601 Paul Jones St *Web:* www.nsgreatlakes.navy.mil	Great Lakes	IL	60088	847-688-3500	688-4235

501 MILITARY SERVICE ACADEMIES

				Phone	Fax
Royal Military College of Canada Stn Forces PO Box 17000 *Web:* www.rmc.ca	Kingston	ON	K7K7B4	613-541-6000	541-6599
US Air Force Academy (USAFA) 2304 Cadet Dr Suite 2300 *TF:* 800-443-9266 ■ *Web:* www.usafa.af.mil	Usaf Academy	CO	80840	719-333-1110	333-3012
US Naval Academy 121 Blake Rd **Fax:* Admissions ■ *TF Admissions:* 888-249-7707 ■ *Web:* www.usna.edu	Annapolis	MD	21402	410-293-1000	293-4348*
US Military Academy Admissions Bldg 606 3rd Fl *TF:* 800-822-8762 ■ *Web:* www.usma.edu	West Point	NY	10996	845-938-5746	938-8121

502 MILLWORK

SEE ALSO Lumber & Building Supplies p. 1733; Doors & Windows - Wood p. 1788; Home Improvement Centers p. 2024; Shutters - Window (All Types) p. 2656

				Phone	Fax
Accent' Windows Inc 12300 Pecos St *TF:* 888-284-3948 ■ *Web:* www.accentwindows.com	Westminster	CO	80234	303-420-2002	432-8674
All-Wood Components Inc 3205 Bay St PO Box 3068 *Web:* www.allwoodcomp.com	Union Gap	WA	98903	509-452-7494	452-7655
Allen Millwork Inc 6505 St Vincent Ave PO Box 6480 *TF:* 800-551-8737 ■ *Web:* www.allenmillwork.com	Shreveport	LA	71136	318-868-6541	865-6102
American Millwork Corp 4840 Beck Dr *Web:* www.americanmillwork.com	Elkhart	IN	46516	574-295-4158	293-5378
Anderson Wood Products Co 1381 Beech St *TF:* 800-825-5591 ■ *Web:* www.andersonwood.com	Louisville	KY	40211	502-778-5591	778-5599
Anlin Industries 1665 Tollhouse Rd *TF:* 800-287-7996 ■ *Web:* www.anlin.com	Clovis	CA	93611	559-322-1531	322-1532
Appalachian Wood Products Inc 171 Loop Rd *Web:* www.appwood.com	Clearfield	PA	16830	814-765-2003	762-8083
Black Millwork Co Inc 220 W Crescent Ave *TF:* 800-864-2356 ■ *Web:* www.blackmillwork.com	Allendale	NJ	07401	201-934-0100	934-8867
Bright Wood Corp 335 NW Hess St PO Drawer 828 *Web:* www.brightwood.com	Madras	OR	97741	541-475-2243	475-7086
Brockway-Smith Co (BWAY) 146 Dascomb Rd **Fax Area Code:* 800 ■ *TF:* 800-225-7912 ■ *Web:* www.brosco.com	Andover	MA	01810	978-475-7100	242-4533*
Carter-Lee Lumber Co Inc 1717 W Washington St **Fax:* Sales ■ *Web:* www.carterlee.com	Indianapolis	IN	46222	317-639-5431	639-6982*
Cascade Wood Products Inc PO Box 2429 *TF:* 800-423-3311 ■ *Web:* www.cascadewood.com	White City	OR	97503	541-826-2911	826-3985
Causeway Lumber Co 2627 S Andrews Ave *TF:* 800-375-5050 ■ *Web:* www.causewaylumber.com	Fort Lauderdale	FL	33316	954-763-1224	768-5921
Central Woodwork Inc 870 Keough Rd *TF:* 800-788-3775 ■ *Web:* www.centralwoodwork.com	Collierville	TN	38017	901-363-4141	363-4171
Columbia Woodworking Inc 935 Brentwood Rd NE	Washington	DC	20018	202-526-2387	526-5163
Commercial & Architectural Products Inc PO Box 250 *TF:* 800-377-1221 ■ *Web:* www.marlite.com	Dover	OH	44622	330-343-6621	343-7296
Contact Industries Inc 9200 SE Sunnybrook Blvd Suite 200 *TF:* 800-547-1038 ■ *Web:* www.contactind.com	Clackamas	OR	97015	503-228-7361	221-1340
Cox Interior Inc 1751 Old Columbia Rd *TF:* 800-733-1751 ■ *Web:* www.coxinterior.com	Campbellsville	KY	42718	270-789-3129	465-7977
CW Ohio Inc 1209 Maple Ave *TF:* 800-677-5801 ■ *Web:* www.cwohio.com	Conneaut	OH	44030	440-593-5800	593-4545
DeLeers Millwork Inc 1735 Sal St *Web:* www.deleersmillwork.com	Green Bay	WI	54302	920-465-6764	465-8835
Dubois Wood Products Inc 707 E 6th St PO Drawer 386 *Web:* www.duboiswood.com	Huntingburg	IN	47542	812-683-3613	683-3847
Eastern Millwork Co 3222 Oley Tpke Rd PO Box 4128 *TF:* 800-422-8545	Reading	PA	19606	610-779-3550	779-1241
Fetzers' Inc 6223 W Double Eagle Cir *Web:* www.fetzersinc.com	Salt Lake City	UT	84118	801-484-6103	484-6122
Giffin Interior & Fixture Inc 500 Scotti Dr	Bridgeville	PA	15017	412-221-1166	221-3745
Graves Lumber Co 1315 S Cleveland-Massillon Rd *TF:* 877-500-5515 ■ *Web:* www.graveslumber.com	Copley	OH	44321	330-666-1115	666-1377
Hb&g Inc PO Box 589 *TF:* 800-264-4424 ■ *Web:* www.hbgcolumns.com	Troy	AL	36081	334-566-5000	566-4629
Hoff Cos Inc 1840 N Lakes Ave	Meridian	ID	83642	208-884-2002	884-1115
Hollywood Woodwork Inc 2951 Pembroke Rd *Web:* www.hollywoodwoodwork.com	Hollywood	FL	33020	954-920-5009	920-6106
Homeshield Colonial Craft 2270 Woodale Dr *TF:* 800-727-5187 ■ *Web:* www.home-shield.com	Mounds View	MN	55112	763-231-4000	783-7218
Horner Millwork Corp 1255 Grand Army Hwy *TF:* 800-543-5403 ■ *Web:* www.hornermillwork.com	Somerset	MA	02726	508-679-6479	
Huttig Bldg Products Inc (HBP) 555 Maryville University Dr Suite 400 *NYSE:* HBP ■ *TF:* 800-325-4466 ■ *Web:* www.huttig.com	Saint Louis	MO	63141	314-216-2600	216-2601
Imperial Woodworking Co 310 N Woodwork Ln *Web:* www.imperialwoodworking.com	Palatine	IL	60067	847-358-6920	358-0905
Jeld-Wen Inc 401 Harbor Isles Blvd PO Box 1329 *TF:* 800-535-3462 ■ *Web:* www.jeld-wen.com	Klamath Falls	OR	97601	541-882-3451	850-2621
Lafayette Wood-Works Inc 3004 Cameron St *TF:* 800-960-3311 ■ *Web:* www.lafwoodworks.com	Lafayette	LA	70506	337-233-5250	233-1147
LJ Smith Co 35280 Scio-Bowerston Rd *Web:* www.ljsmith.net	Bowerston	OH	44695	740-269-2221	269-9047
Loudoun Stairs Inc 341 N Maple Ave *Web:* www.loudounstairs.com	Purcellville	VA	20132	540-338-7400	
Louisiana-Pacific Corp 414 Union St Suite 2000 *NYSE:* LPX ■ *TF:* 877-744-5600 ■ *Web:* www.lpcorp.com	Nashville	TN	37219	615-986-5600	986-5666
Mann & Parker Lumber Co Inc The 335 N Constitution Ave *TF:* 800-632-9098 ■ *Web:* www.m-pgoldbrand.com	New Freedom	PA	17349	717-235-4834	235-5547
Menzner Lumber & Supply Co PO Box 217 *TF:* 800-451-3986 ■ *Web:* www.menznerhardwoods.com	Marathon	WI	54448	715-443-2354	443-3798
Milliken Millwork Inc 6361 Sterling Dr N *TF:* 800-686-9218 ■ *Web:* www.millikenmillwork.com	Sterling Heights	MI	48312	586-264-0950	264-5430
Monarch Industries Inc 99 Main St **Fax:* Sales ■ *TF:* 800-669-9663 ■ *Web:* www.monarchinc.com	Warren	RI	02885	401-247-5200	247-5601*
MW Manufacturers Inc 433 N Main St **Fax Area Code:* 800 ■ *TF:* 888-999-8400 ■ *Web:* www.mwwindows.com	Rocky Mount	VA	24151	540-483-0211	950-3220*
New England Garage Door 15 Campanelli Cir *TF:* 800-969-5151 ■ *Web:* www.wayne-dalton.com	Canton	MA	02021	781-821-2737	821-8050
Norco Norwood Sash & Door 4953 Section Ave *Web:* www.norwoodsd.com	Cincinnati	OH	45212	513-531-5700	531-5706
Ohline Corp 1930 W 139th St *TF:* 800-585-3197 ■ *Web:* www.ohline.com	Gardena	CA	90249	310-327-4630	538-5742
Parenti & Raffaelli Ltd 215 Prospect Ave E *Web:* www.parentiwoodwork.com	Mount Prospect	IL	60056	847-253-5550	253-6055
PGM Products LLC 1 Commerce Dr Barrington Business Ctr Bldg 4	Barrington	NJ	08007	856-546-0704	546-0539

Phone | Fax

Randall Bros Inc 665 Marietta St NW ... Atlanta GA 30313 404-892-6666 875-6102
TF Cust Svc: 800-476-4539 ■ Web: www.randallbrothers.com

Raynor Garage Doors 1101 E River Rd ... Dixon IL 61021 815-288-1431 288-3720*
*Fax: Cust Svc ■ TF: 800-472-9667 ■ Web: www.raynor.com

ROW Window Co 612 Moen Ave ... Joliet IL 60434 815-725-5491 725-6926
TF: 800-966-3769

Ruffin & Payne Inc 4200 E Vawter Ave ... Richmond VA 23222 804-329-2691 321-4940

Scherer Bros Lumber Co 9 9th Ave NE ... Minneapolis MN 55413 612-379-9633 627-0679
Web: www.schererbros.com

Schuck Component Systems Inc
8205 N 67th Ave ... Glendale AZ 85302 623-931-3661 937-3435
TF Cust Svc: 866-991-3661 ■ Web: www.schuckaz.com

Shaw/Stewart Lumber Co 645 Johnson St NE ... Minneapolis MN 55413 651-488-2525 378-1484*
*Fax Area Code: 612 ■ *Fax: Sales ■ Web: www.shawstewartlumber.com

Shuster's Bldg Components 2920 Clay Pike ... Irwin PA 15642 724-446-7000 676-0640*
*Fax Area Code: 800 ■ TF: 800-366-6733 ■ Web: www.shusters.com

Sierra Pacific Industries
19794 Riverside Ave ... Anderson CA 96007 530-378-8000 378-8109
Web: www.sierrapacificind.com

Somerset Door & Column Co 174 Sagamore St ... Somerset PA 15501 814-444-9427 443-1658
TF: 800-242-7916

Southern Staircase Inc
6025 Shiloh Rd Suite E ... Alpharetta GA 30005 770-888-7333 888-7330
TF: 800-874-8408 ■ Web: www.southernstaircase.com

Standard Lumber Co 1912 Lehigh Ave ... Glenview IL 60026 847-729-7800 729-8500

Stephenson Millwork Co Inc 210 Harper St ... Wilson NC 27893 252-237-1141 237-4377
Web: www.smcinc.com

Superior Trim & Door Inc 2840 W Orange Ave ... Apopka FL 32703 407-598-1100 598-1102
TF: 800-255-2966 ■ Web: www.superiortrim.com

Swift Gailey 5 Concourse Pkwy Suite 2300 ... Atlanta GA 30328 770-901-6300 901-6309

Taney Corp 5130 Allendale Ln ... Taneytown MD 21787 410-756-6671 756-4103
Web: www.taneystair.com

Taylor Bros Inc
905 Graves Mill Rd PO Box 11198 ... Lynchburg VA 24506 434-237-8100 237-4227
TF: 800-288-6767

Tucker Door & Trim Corp 650 Hwy 83 ... Monroe GA 30655 770-267-4622 267-5997

Washington Woodworking Co Inc
2010 Beaver Rd ... Landover MD 20785 301-341-2500 341-2512
Web: www.washingtonwoodworking.com

Werzalit of America Inc
40 Holly Ave PO Box 373 ... Bradford PA 16701 814-362-3881 362-4237
TF: 800-999-3730 ■ Web: www.werzalit-usa.com

Western Millwork Inc 2940 W Willetta St ... Phoenix AZ 85009 602-233-1921 278-7101
Web: www.westernmillworkaz.com

Woodfold Mfg Inc
1811 18th Ave PO Box 346 ... Forest Grove OR 97116 503-357-7181 357-7185
Web: www.woodfold.com

Woodgrain Millworks Inc
300 NW 16th St PO Box 566 ... Fruitland ID 83619 208-452-3801 452-5474
TF: 800-452-3801 ■ Web: www.woodgrain.com

Woodharbor Doors & Cabinetry Inc
3277 9th St SW ... Mason City IA 50401 641-423-0444 423-0345
Web: www.woodharbor.com

Young Mfg Co Inc 521 S Main St PO Box 167 ... Beaver Dam KY 42320 270-274-3306 274-9522
TF: 800-545-6595

503 MINERAL PRODUCTS - NONMETALLIC

SEE ALSO Insulation & Acoustical Products p. 2110

Phone | Fax

3M Industrial Mineral Products Div
3M Ctr Bldg 0225-02-N-07 ... Saint Paul MN 55144 651-733-1812 736-8474
TF: 800-447-2914 ■
Web: www.3m.com/product/business-units/industrial-minerals.html

Asbury Graphite Mills Inc 405 Old Main St ... Asbury NJ 08802 908-537-2155 537-2908
Web: www.asburygraphite.com

Astro Met Inc 9974 Springfield Pike ... Cincinnati OH 45215 513-772-1242 772-9080
Web: www.astromet.com

Big River Industries Inc
12652 Airline Hwy ... Erwinville LA 70729 225-627-4242 627-5901
TF: 800-969-5634 ■ Web: www.bigriverind.com

Brubaker-Mann Inc 36011 Soap Mine Rd ... Barstow CA 92311 760-256-2520 256-0127

Buffalo Crushed Stone Co Inc 2544 Clinton St ... Buffalo NY 14224 716-826-7310 826-1342

Burgess Pigment Co Inc
525 Beck Blvd PO Box 349 ... Sandersville GA 31082 478-552-2544 552-4274
TF: 800-841-8999 ■ Web: www.burgesspigment.com

Ceradyne Inc 3169 Redhill Ave ... Costa Mesa CA 92626 714-549-0421 549-5787*
NASDAQ: CRDN ■ *Fax: Sales ■ TF: 800-839-2189 ■ Web: www.ceradyne.com

Christy Refractories Co 4641 McRee Ave ... Saint Louis MO 63110 314-773-7500 773-8371
Web: www.christyco.com

Consolidated Ceramic Products Inc
838 Cherry St ... Blanchester OH 45107 937-783-2476 783-2539
Web: www.ccpi-inc.com

Continental Mineral Processing Corp
11817 Mosteller Rd PO Box 62005 ... Cincinnati OH 45262 513-771-7190 771-9153
Web: www.continentalmineral.com

Crystex Composites LLC 125 Clifton Blvd ... Clifton NJ 07011 973-779-8866 779-2013
TF: 800-638-8235 ■ Web: www.crystexllc.com

Dri-Rite Co Inc
13116 S Western Ave PO Box 389 ... Blue Island IL 60406 708-385-7556 385-0622
Web: www.dririte.com

Eagle-Picher Minerals Inc PO Box 12130 ... Reno NV 89510 775-824-7600 824-7601
TF Cust Svc: 800-228-3865

Ferro Corp Electronic Materials Div
4150 E 56th St ... Cleveland OH 44105 216-641-8580 750-7339

GE Advanced Materials 1 Plastics Ave ... Pittsfield MA 01201 413-448-7110 448-5573
Web: www.GE.com

GE Quartz 4901 Campbell Rd ... Willoughby OH 44094 216-266-4121 266-2360
TF: 800-438-2100 ■ Web: www.gequartz.com

Phone | Fax

Graphel Corp
6115 Centre Pk Dr PO Box 369 ... West Chester OH 45071 513-779-6166 777-8959
TF: 800-255-1104 ■ Web: www.graphel.com

Graphite Metallizing Corp 1050 Nepperhan Ave ... Yonkers NY 10703 914-968-8400 968-8468
Web: www.graphalloy.com

Graphite Sales Inc 16710 W Pk Cir Dr ... Chagrin Falls OH 44023 440-543-8221 543-5183
TF: 800-321-4147 ■ Web: www.graphitesales.com

Grefco Minerals Inc 225 City Ave Suite 14 ... Bala Cynwyd PA 19004 610-660-8820 660-8817

Harborlite Corp 1950 W Ave E ... Vicksburg MI 49097 269-649-1352 649-3707
TF: 800-403-4869 ■ Web: www.worldminerals.com

Hill & Griffith Co 1085 Summer St ... Cincinnati OH 45204 513-921-1075 244-4199
TF: 800-543-0425 ■ Web: www.hillandgriffith.com

Hydraulic Press Brick Co
7225 Woodland Dr Suite 200 ... Indianapolis IN 46278 317-290-1140 290-1071

JS McCormick Co 503 Hegner Way ... Sewickley PA 15143 412-749-8222 749-2766

Kocour Co 4800 S St Louis Ave ... Chicago IL 60632 773-847-1111 847-3399
TF: 888-562-6871 ■ Web: www.kocour.net

La Habra Products Inc 240 S Loara St ... Anaheim CA 92802 714-778-2266 774-2079
TF: 800-649-8933 ■ Web: www.lahabrastucco.com

Merlex Stucco Co 2911 N Orange-Olive Rd ... Orange CA 92865 714-637-1700 637-4865
Web: www.merlex.com

Miller & Co LLC 9700 W Higgins Rd Suite 1000 ... Rosemont IL 60018 847-696-2400 696-2419
TF: 800-727-9847 ■ Web: www.millerandco.com

Miller Studios 734 Fair Ave NW ... New Philadelphia OH 44663 330-339-1100 339-4379
Web: www.miller-studios.com

Mission Stucco Co Inc 7751 70th St ... Paramount CA 90723 562-634-1400 634-4440

Multicoat Corp
23331 Antonio Pkwy ... Rancho Santa Margarita CA 92688 949-888-7100 888-2555
TF: 877-685-8426 ■ Web: www.multicoat.com

Norlite Corp 628 S Saratoga St PO Box 694 ... Cohoes NY 12047 518-235-0030 235-0233
Web: www.norliteagg.com

NYCO Minerals Inc 803 Mountain View Dr ... Willsboro NY 12996 518-963-4262 963-1110
Web: www.nycominerals.com

Oil-Dri Corp of America
410 N Michigan Ave Suite 400 ... Chicago IL 60611 312-321-1515 321-1271
NYSE: ODC ■ TF: 800-233-9802 ■ Web: www.oildri.com

Sacramento Stucco Co 1550 PkwyBlvd ... West Sacramento CA 95691 916-372-7442 372-4836
Web: www.sacstucco.com

San Jose Delta Assoc Inc 482 Sapena Ct ... Santa Clara CA 95054 408-727-1448 727-6019
Web: www.sanjosedelta.com

Schundler Co 150 Whitman Ave ... Edison NJ 08817 732-287-2244 287-4185
Web: www.schundler.com

Silbrico Corp 6300 River Rd ... Hodgkins IL 60525 708-354-3350 354-6698
TF: 800-323-4287 ■ Web: www.silbrico.com

Solite LLC 3900 Shannon St ... Chesapeake VA 23324 757-494-5200 545-3793

Squires-Belt Material Co 5467 Federal Blvd ... San Diego CA 92101 619-266-6100 266-6111
Web: www.squiresbelt.com

Tec Minerals Inc Hwy 787 ... Cleveland TX 77327 281-592-6428 592-7541
TF Cust Svc: 800-833-5442

US Diamond Wheel Co 101 Kendall Pt Dr ... Oswego IL 60543 630-898-9000 898-1796
TF: 800-223-0457

USG Corp 550 W Adams St ... Chicago IL 60661 312-436-4000 672-4093
NYSE: USG ■ TF: 800-621-9622 ■ Web: www.usg.com

Vesuvius USA 955 N 5th St ... Charleston IL 61920 217-345-7044 345-7124
Web: www.vesuvius.com

Von Roll Isola USA 1 W Campbell Rd ... Schenectady NY 12306 518-344-7100 344-7384*
*Fax: Cust Svc ■ TF: 800-654-7652

Winter Bros Material Co 13098 Gravois Rd ... Saint Louis MO 63127 314-843-1400 843-1403
TF: 800-722-5424 ■ Web: www.winterbrothersmaterial.com

Ziegler Chemical & Mineral Corp
366 N Broadway Suite 210 ... Jericho NY 11753 516-681-9600 681-9604
Web: www.zieglerchemical.com

Zircar Products Inc 100 N Main St ... Florida NY 10921 845-651-6600 651-0441
Web: www.zircar.com

504 MINING - COAL

Phone | Fax

Alliance Resource Partners LP
1717 S Boulder Ave Suite 400 ... Tulsa OK 74119 918-295-7600 295-7358
NASDAQ: ARLP ■ Web: www.arlp.com

Alpha Natural Resources Inc 1 Alpha Pl ... Abingdon VA 24212 276-619-4410 623-2853
NYSE: ANR ■ TF: 866-322-5742 ■ Web: www.alphanr.com

Amerikohl Mining Inc 202 Sunset Dr ... Butler PA 16001 724-282-2339 282-3226
Web: www.amerikohl.com

Arch Coal Inc One CityPlace Dr Suite 300 ... St. Louis MO 63141 314-994-2700 994-2878
NYSE: ACI ■ TF: 800-238-7398 ■ Web: www.archcoal.com

Black Beauty Coal Co
7100 Eagle Crest Blvd ... Evansville IN 47715 812-434-8500 428-0712
TF: 800-477-0514

Blue Mountain Energy Inc
10714 S Jordan Gtwy ... South Jordan UT 84095 801-619-6500 619-6599
Web: www.deseretpower.com

BNI Coal Ltd 1637 Burnt Boat Dr PO Box 897 ... Bismarck ND 58502 701-222-8828 222-1547
Web: www.bnicoal.com

C & K Coal Co 1062 E Main St PO Box 69 ... Clarion PA 16214 814-226-6911 226-9517

Coteau Properties Co 204 County Rd 15 ... Beulah ND 58523 701-873-2281 873-7226

DH Blattner & Sons Inc 400 CR 50 ... Avon MN 56310 320-356-7351 356-7392
TF: 800-877-2866 ■ Web: www.dhblattner.com

Drummond Co Inc PO Box 10246 ... Birmingham AL 35202 205-945-6500 945-6557*
*Fax: Hum Res ■ Web: www.drummondco.com

East Fairfield Coal Co
10900 S Ave PO Box 217 ... North Lima OH 44452 330-549-2165 549-0618
Web: www.eastfairfield.com

Emerald Intarnational Corp
6895 Burlington Pike ... Florence KY 41042 859-525-2522 525-4052
Web: www.emeraldcoal.com

Fording Canadian Coal Trust
205 9th Ave SE Suite 1000 ... Calgary AB T2G0R3 403-260-9800 264-7339
Web: www.fording.ca

Hepburnia Coal Co PO Box I ... Grampian PA 16838 814-236-0473 236-1624

	City	State	Zip	Phone	Fax
Holmes Limestone Co 4255 SR 39	Berlin	OH	44610	330-893-2721	893-2941
Humphreys Enterprises Inc 6999 Polk Rd	Norton	VA	24273	276-679-1400	679-4142
James River Coal Co 901 E Byrd St Suite 1600	Richmond	VA	23219	804-780-3000	780-0643
NASDAQ: JRCC ■ *TF:* 800-944-5190 ■ *Web:* www.jamesrivercoal.com					
Jewell Smokeless Coal Corp Rt 460 W PO Box 70	Vansant	VA	24656	276-935-8810	935-6019
Jim Walter Resources Inc					
16243 Hwy 216 PO Box 133	Brookwood	AL	35444	205-554-6150	481-6161
Web: www.walterenergy.com					
JM Huber Corp 499 Thornall St 8th Fl	Edison	NJ	08837	732-549-8600	549-2239*
**Fax:* Hum Res ■ *Web:* www.huber.com					
Lee Ranch Coal Co PO Box 757	Grants	NM	87020	505-285-4651	285-4650
Massey Energy Co 4 N 4th St	Richmond	VA	23219	804-788-1800	788-1801
NYSE: MEE ■ *Web:* www.masseyenergyco.com					
McIntire William Coal Co PO Box 171	Shelocta	PA	15774	724-354-2922	354-2102
Murray Energy Corp					
29325 Chagrin Blvd Suite 300	Pepper Pike	OH	44122	216-765-1240	
Web: www.murrayenergycorp.com					
Natural Resource Partners LP					
601 Jefferson St Suite 3600	Houston	TX	77002	713-751-7507	
NYSE: NRP ■ *TF:* 888-334-7102 ■ *Web:* www.nrplp.com					
North American Coal Corp					
14785 Preston Rd Suite 1100	Dallas	TX	75254	972-239-2625	448-5437
Web: www.nacoal.com					
Ohio River Collieries Co PO Box 128	Bannock	OH	43972	740-968-3504	968-3071
Ohio Valley Coal Co					
56854 Pleasant Ridge Rd	Alledonia	OH	43902	740-926-1351	926-9112
Peabody Coal Co 701 Market St	Saint Louis	MO	63101	314-342-3400	827-6166*
**Fax Area Code: 270* ■ *Web:* www.peabodyenergy.com					
Peabody Energy Corp					
701 Market St Suite 700	Saint Louis	MO	63101	314-342-3400	
NYSE: BTU ■ *Web:* www.peabodyenergy.com					
Pittsburg & Midway Coal Mining Co					
PO Box 6518	Englewood	CO	80155	303-930-3600	930-4204
RG Johnson Co Inc 25 S College St	Washington	PA	15301	724-222-6810	222-6815
Rio Tinto Energy America (RTEA)					
505 S Gillette Ave PO Box 3009	Gillette	WY	82717	307-687-6000	687-6015
TF: 800-305-1142 ■ *Web:* www.rtea.com					
Thunder Basin Coal Co PO Box 406	Wright	WY	82732	307-939-1300	464-2313
Web: www.archcoal.com					
Usibelli Coal Mine Inc 100 River Rd PO Box 1000	Healy	AK	99743	907-683-2226	683-2253
Web: www.usibelli.com					
Western Energy Co 138 Rosebud Ln PO Box 99	Colstrip	MT	59323	406-748-5100	748-5181
Westmoreland Coal Co					
2 N Cascade Ave 2nd Fl	Colorado Springs	CO	80903	719-442-2600	219-2594
AMEX: WLB ■ *Web:* www.westmoreland.com					
Westmoreland Resources Inc					
100 Sarpy Creek Rd PO Box 449	Hardin	MT	59034	406-342-5241	342-5401
Wilmore Coal Co 509 15th St	Windber	PA	15963	814-467-4519	467-4559
Wyodak Resources Development Corp					
3338 Garner Lake Rd	Gillette	WY	82716	307-682-3410	682-0208

505 MINING - METALS

	City	State	Zip	Phone	Fax
Agnico-Eagle Mines Ltd					
145 King St E Suite 500	Toronto	ON	M5C2Y7	416-947-1212	367-4681
TSE: AEM ■ *TF:* 888-822-6714 ■ *Web:* www.agnico-eagle.com					
Anooraq Resources Corp 1020-800 W Pender	Vancouver	BC	V6C2V6	604-684-6365	684-8092
AMEX: ANO ■ *TF:* 800-667-2114 ■ *Web:* www.anooraqresources.com					
Asarco Inc 1421 W Pima Mine Rd	Sahuarita	AZ	85629	520-625-7513	625-4756
Web: www.asarco.com					
AuRico Gold Inc 320 Bay St Suite 1520	Toronto	ON	M5H4A6	902-468-0614	468-0631
Web: www.auricogold.com					
Aurizon Mines Ltd					
Cathedral Pl 925 W Georgia St Suite 1120	Vancouver	BC	V6C3L2	604-687-6600	687-3932
TSE: ARZ ■ *Web:* www.aurizon.com					
B2 Gold Corp					
595 Burrard St Suite 3100 PO Box 49143	Vancouver	BC	V7X1J1	604-681-8371	681-6209
TF: 800-316-8855 ■ *Web:* www.b2gold.com					
Badger Mining Corp 409 S Church St PO Box 328	Berlin	WI	54923	920-361-2388	361-2826
TF: 800-932-7263 ■ *Web:* www.badgerminingcorp.com					
Barrick Gold Corp					
TD Canada Trust Tower 161 Bay St PO Box 212	Toronto	ON	M5J2S1	416-861-9911	861-2492
NYSE: ABX ■ *TF:* 800-720-7415 ■ *Web:* www.barrick.com					
Barrick Goldstrike Mines Inc PO Box 29	Elko	NV	89803	775-738-8043	738-6543
Web: www.barrick.com					
Black Hills Exploration & Production					
350 Indiana St Suite 400	Golden	CO	80401	720-210-1300	210-1301
Web: www.bhep.com					
Cameco Corp 2121 11th St W	Saskatoon	SK	S7M1J3	306-956-6200	956-6201
TSE: CCJ ■ *TF:* 866-789-8050 ■ *Web:* www.cameco.com					
Claude Resources Inc					
224 4th Ave S Suite 200	Saskatoon	SK	S7K5M5	306-668-7505	668-7500
AMEX: CGR ■ *Web:* www.clauderesources.com					
Cliffs Natural Resources					
200 Public Sq Suite 3300	Cleveland	OH	44114	216-694-5700	
Web: www.cliffsnaturalresources.com					
Climax Molybdenum Co PO Box 220	Fort Madison	IA	52627	319-463-7151	463-7640*
Coeur d'Alene Mines Corp (CDA)					
505 Front Ave PO Box I	Coeur d'Alene	ID	83816	208-667-3511	667-2213
NYSE: CDE ■ *TF:* 800-624-2824 ■ *Web:* www.coeur.com					
Corriente Resources Inc					
5811 Cooney Rd Unit S209	Richmond	BC	V6X3M1	604-282-7212	282-7568
TSX: CTQ ■ *Web:* www.corriente.com					
Crown Gold Corp 970 Caughlin Crossing Suite 100	Reno	NV	89519	775-284-7200	284-7202
Web: www.crowngoldcorp.com					
Crown Resources Corp					
4251 Kipling St Suite 390	Wheat Ridge	CO	80033	303-534-1030	534-1809
Web: www.crownresources.com					
Crystallex International Corp					
8 King St E Suite 1201	Toronto	ON	M5C1B5	416-203-2448	203-0099
TSE: KRY ■ *TF:* 800-738-1577 ■ *Web:* www.crystallex.com					

	City	State	Zip	Phone	Fax
Eldorado Gold Corp 550 Burrard St Suite 1188	Vanouver	BC	V6C2B5	604-687-4018	687-4026
TSE: ELD ■ *TF:* 888-353-8166 ■ *Web:* www.eldoradogold.com					
First Quantum Minerals Ltd					
543 Granville St 8th Fl	Vancouver	BC	V6C1X8	604-688-6577	688-3818
TSE: FM ■ *TF:* 888-688-6577 ■ *Web:* www.first-quantum.com					
Gold Reserve Inc 926 W Sprague Ave Suite 200	Spokane	WA	99201	509-623-1500	623-1634
AMEX: GRZ ■ *TF:* 800-625-9550 ■ *Web:* www.goldreserveinc.com					
Goldcorp Inc 666 Burrard St Suite 3400	Vancouver	BC	V6C2X8	604-696-3000	696-3001
NYSE: GG ■ *TF:* 800-567-6223 ■ *Web:* www.goldcorp.com					
Golden Star Resources Ltd					
10901 W Toller Dr Suite 300	Littleton	CO	80127	303-830-9000	830-9094
AMEX: GSS ■ *TF:* 800-553-8436 ■ *Web:* www.gsr.com					
Goldfield Corp 1684 W Hibiscus Blvd	Melbourne	FL	32901	321-724-1700	724-1163
AMEX: GV ■ *Web:* www.goldfieldcorp.com					
Great Basin Gold Ltd					
1108- 1030 W Georgia St	Vancouver	BC	V6E2Y3	604-633-9113	633-0190
AMEX: GBG ■ *TF:* 800-667-2114 ■ *Web:* www.greatbasingold.com					
Hecla Mining Co					
6500 N Mineral Dr Suite 200	Coeur d'Alene	ID	83815	208-769-4100	769-4107
NYSE: HL ■ *Web:* www.hecla-mining.com					
Hibbing Taconite Co PO Box 589	Hibbing	MN	55746	218-262-5950	262-6817
IAMGOLD Corp 401 Bay St Suite 3200 PO Box 153	Toronto	ON	M5H2Y4	416-360-4710	360-4750
NYSE: IAG ■ *TF:* 888-464-9999 ■ *Web:* www.iamgold.com					
Imperial Metals Corp					
580 Hornby St Suite 200	Vancouver	BC	V6C3B6	604-669-8959	687-4030
TSE: III ■ *Web:* www.imperialmetals.com					
International Minerals Corp					
7950 E Acoma Dr Suite 211	Scottsdale	AZ	85260	480-483-9932	483-9926
TSE: IMZ ■ *Web:* www.intlminerals.com					
Iron Gold Quebec Inc					
1111 St Charles St W E Tower Suite 750	Longueuil	QC	J4K5G4	450-677-0040	677-3382
Web: www.cambior.com					
Ivanhoe Mines Ltd 999 Canada Pl Suite 654	Vancouver	BC	V6C3T4	604-688-5755	682-2060
NYSE: IVN ■ *TF:* 888-273-9999 ■ *Web:* www.ivanhoemines.com					
Kennecott Uranium Co PO Box 1500	Rawlins	WY	82301	307-328-1476	324-4925
Kimber Resources Inc					
800 W Pender St Suite 215	Vancouver	BC	V6C2V6	604-669-2251	669-8577
AMEX: KBX ■ *TF:* 866-824-1100 ■ *Web:* www.kimberresources.com					
Kinross Gold Corp 25 York St 17th Fl	Toronto	ON	M5J2V5	416-365-5123	363-6622
TSE: K ■ *TF:* 866-561-3636 ■ *Web:* www.kinross.com					
Kinross Gold USA Inc 5370 Kietzke Ln	Reno	NV	89511	775-829-1000	829-1666
Materion Corp 6070 Parkland Blvd	Mayfield Heights	OH	44124	216-486-4200	383-4091
NYSE: MTRN ■ *TF:* 800-321-2076 ■ *Web:* www.materion.com					
Meridian Gold Co 9670 Gateway Dr Suite 200	Reno	NV	89521	775-850-3777	850-3733
TF: 800-557-4699					
Metallurg Inc					
1140 Avenue of the Americas Suite 1800	New York	NY	10017	212-835-0200	687-9621
Web: www.metallurg.com					
Mine Management Inc					
905 W Riverside Ave Suite 311	Spokane	WA	99201	509-838-6050	838-0486
AMEX: MGN ■ *Web:* www.minesmanagement.com					
MK Resources Co					
60 E S Temple St Suite 1225	Salt Lake City	UT	84111	801-297-6900	297-6950*
**Fax:* Hum Res ■ *TF:* 800-664-6528 ■ *Web:* www.mkgold.com					
Molycorp Inc 67750 Bailey Rd	Mountain Pass	CA	92366	760-856-6680	856-2253
Web: www.molycorp.com					
NA Degerstrom Inc 3303 N Sullivan Rd	Spokane	WA	99216	509-928-3333	927-2010
TF: 800-637-3773 ■ *Web:* www.nadinc.com					
New Gold Inc 666 Burrard St Suite 3110	Vancouver	BC	V6C2X8	604-696-4100	696-4110
AMEX: NGD ■ *Web:* www.newgoldinc.com					
Newmont Mining Corp					
889 Harbourside Dr Suite 300	North Vancouver	BC	V7P3S1	604-985-2572	980-0731
TF: 800-663-8780 ■ *Web:* www.newmont.com					
Newmont Mining Corp					
6363 S Fiddler's Green Cir					
Suite 800	Greenwood Village	CO	80111	303-863-7414	837-5837
NYSE: NEM ■ *Web:* www.newmont.com					
Nord Resources Corp 1 W Wetmore Rd Suite 107	Tucson	AZ	85705	520-292-0266	292-0268
TF: 800-543-2599 ■ *Web:* www.nordresources.com					
North American Palladium Ltd					
200 Bay Str Suite 2350	Toronto	ON	M5J2J2	416-360-7590	360-7709
AMEX: PAL ■ *Web:* www.napalladium.com					
Northgate Minerals Corp					
110 Yonge St Suite 1601	Toronto	ON	M5C1T4	416-363-1701	363-6392
AMEX: NXG ■ *Web:* www.northgateminerals.com					
NovaGold Resources Inc					
200 Grandville St Suite 2300 PO Box 24	Vancouver	BC	V6C1S4	604-669-6227	669-6272
TSE: NG ■ *TF:* 866-699-6227 ■ *Web:* www.novagold.com					
Optex Systems Holdings Inc					
1420 Presidential Dr	Richardson	TX	75081	972-644-0722	234-3544
OTC: OPXS ■ *Web:* www.optexsys.com					
Pacific Rim Mining Corp					
625 Howe St Suite 1050	Vancouver	BC	V6C2T6	604-689-1976	689-1978
TSE: PMU ■ *TF:* 888-775-7097 ■ *Web:* www.pacrim-mining.com					
Pan American Silver Corp					
625 Howe St Suite 1500	Vancouver	BC	V6C2T6	604-684-1175	684-0147
TSE: PAA ■ *Web:* www.panamericansilver.com					
QIT-Fer et Titane Inc					
1625 Marie-Victorin Rd	Sorel-Tracy	QC	J3R1M6	450-746-3000	746-4438
Web: www.qit.com					
Royal Gold Inc 1660 Wynkoop St Suite 1000	Denver	CO	80202	303-573-1660	595-9385
NASDAQ: RGLD ■ *Web:* www.royalgold.com					
Rubicon Minerals Corp					
800 W Pender St Suite 1540	Vancouver	BC	V6C2V6	604-623-3333	
AMEX: RBY ■ *TF:* 866-365-4706 ■ *Web:* www.rubiconminerals.com					
Seabridge Gold Inc 106 Front St E Suite 400	Toronto	ON	M5A1E1	416-367-9292	367-2711
AMEX: SA ■ *Web:* www.seabridgegold.net					
Sherritt International Corp 1133 Yonge St	Toronto	ON	M4T2Y7	416-924-4551	924-5015
TSE: S ■ *TF:* 800-704-6698 ■ *Web:* www.sherritt.com					
Silver Standard Resources Inc					
999 W Hastings St Suite 1180	Vancouver	BC	V6C2W2	604-689-3846	689-3847
NASDAQ: SSRI ■ *TF:* 888-338-0046 ■ *Web:* www.silverstandard.com					

				Phone	Fax
Southern Copper Corp 11811 N Tatum Blvd Suite 2500 NYSE: SCCO ■ Web: www.southernperu.com	Phoenix	AZ	85028	602-494-5328	494-5317
Southwestern Resources Corp 701 W Georgia St TSX: SWG	Vancouver	BC	V7Y1C6	604-669-2525	688-5175
Stillwater Mining Co 1321 Discovery Dr NYSE: SWC ■ Web: www.stillwatermining.com	Billings	MT	59102	406-322-8700	373-8701
Stratcor Inc 1180 Omega Dr # 1180 TF: 800-573-6052 ■ Web: www.stratcor.com	Pittsburgh	PA	15205	412-787-4500	787-5030
Teck Cominco American Inc 501 N Riverpoint Blvd Suite 300 Web: www.teck.com	Spokane	WA	99202	509-747-6111	747-6111
Umetco Minerals Corp PO Box 1029	Grand Junction	CO	81502	970-245-3700	245-7543
Uranium Resources Inc 405 State Hwy 121 Bypass A-110 NASDAQ: URRE ■ Web: www.uraniumresources.com	Lewisville	TX	75067	972-219-3330	219-3311
US Energy Corp 877 N 8th W NASDAQ: USEG ■ TF: 800-776-9271 ■ Web: www.usnrg.com	Riverton	WY	82501	307-856-9271	857-3050
Vale 200 Bay St Suite 1600 PO Box 70 Web: www.nickel.vale.com	Toronto	ON	M5J1E3	416-361-7511	361-7781
Vista Gold Corp 7961 Shaffer Pkwy Suite 5 AMEX: VGZ ■ TF: 866-981-1185 ■ Web: www.vistagold.com	Littleton	CO	80127	720-981-1185	981-1186
Western Copper Corp 1111 W Georgia St Suite 2050 AMEX: WTZ	Vancouver	BC	V6E4M3	604-684-9497	688-4670
Western Nuclear Inc 2801 Youngfield St Suite 340	Golden	CO	80401	303-274-1767	274-1762
Wharf Resources USA Inc 10928 Wharf Rd	Lead	SD	57754	605-584-1441	584-4188
Xstrata Canada Corp 100 King St W Suite 6900 PO Box 403 Web: www.xstrata.com	Toronto	ON	M5X1E3	416-775-1500	775-1744
Yamana Gold Inc 150 York St Suite 1102 TSE: YRI ■ TF: 888-809-0925 ■ Web: www.yamana.com	Toronto	ON	M5H3S5	416-815-0220	815-0021

506 MINING - MINERALS

506-1 Chemical & Fertilizer Minerals Mining

				Phone	Fax
American Borate Corp 5700 Cleveland St Suite 420 TF: 800-486-1072	Virginia Beach	VA	23462	757-490-2242	490-1548
Moab Salt LLC PO Box 1208	Moab	UT	84532	435-259-7171	259-7100
New Riverside Ochre Co Inc PO Box 460 TF Orders: 800-248-0176 ■ Web: www.nroonline.com	Cartersville	GA	30120	770-382-4568	387-1658
OCI Chemical Corp 5 Concourse Pkwy Suite 2500 *Fax Area Code: 770 ■ *Fax: Sales ■ TF: 800-865-1774 ■ Web: www.ocichemical.com	Atlanta	GA	30328	800-865-1774	375-2439*
Potash Corp 1101 Skokie Blvd TF: 800-645-2183 ■ Web: www.potashcorp.com	Northbrook	IL	60062	847-849-4200	849-4695
Searles Valley Minerals 9401 Indian Creek Pky Suite 1000 TF: 800-637-2775 ■ Web: www.svminerals.com	Overland Park	KS	66210	913-344-9500	344-9690
Solvay Minerals Inc 3333 Richmond Ave TF: 800-443-2785 ■ Web: www.solvaychemicals.us	Houston	TX	77098	713-525-6800	525-7805
United Salt Corp 4800 San Felipe St TF: 800-554-8658 ■ Web: www.unitedsalt.com	Houston	TX	77056	713-877-2600	877-2604

506-2 Clay, Ceramic, Refractory Minerals Mining

				Phone	Fax
AMCOL International Corp 2870 Forbs Ave NYSE: ACO ■ TF: 800-426-5564 ■ Web: www.amcol.com	Hoffman Estates	IL	60192	847-851-1500	851-1699
Black Hills Bentonite Co 55 Saltcreek Hwy TF Orders: 800-788-9443 ■ Web: www.bhbentonite.com	Casper	WY	82601	307-265-3740	235-8511
Dixie Clay Co 305 Dixie Clay Rd	Bath	SC	29816	803-593-2592	593-8761
HC Spinks Clay Co Inc 275 Carothers Loop PO Box 820 Web: www.spinksclay.com	Paris	TN	38242	731-642-5414	642-5493
Hecla Mining Co 6500 N Mineral Dr Suite 200 NYSE: HL ■ Web: www.hecla-mining.com	Coeur d'Alene	ID	83815	208-769-4100	769-4107
Holmes Limestone Co 4255 SR 39	Berlin	OH	44610	330-893-2721	893-2941
Imerys USA Inc 100 Mansell Ct E Suite 300 TF: 800-374-3224 ■ Web: www.imerys-paper.com	Roswell	GA	30076	770-594-0660	645-3384
Kyanite Mining Corp 30 Willis Mountain Ln Web: www.kyanite.com	Dillwyn	VA	23936	434-983-2085	983-5178
Milwhite Inc 5487 S Padre Island Hwy TF: 800-442-0082 ■ Web: www.milwhite.com	Brownsville	TX	78521	956-547-1970	547-1999
Riverside Clay Co Inc 201 Truss Ferry Rd TF: 800-226-4542 ■ Web: www.riversidefactories.com	Pell City	AL	35128	205-338-3366	338-7456
Riverside Refractories Inc 201 Truss Ferry Rd TF: 800-226-4542 ■ Web: www.riversiderefractories.com	Pell City	AL	35128	205-338-3366	338-7456
RT Vanderbilt Co Inc 30 Winfield St TF Cust Svc: 800-243-6064 ■ Web: www.rtvanderbilt.com	Norwalk	CT	06855	203-853-1400	853-1452
Southern Clay Products Inc 1212 Church St *Fax: Cust Svc ■ TF: 800-324-2891 ■ Web: www.scprod.com	Gonzales	TX	78629	830-672-2891	672-1903*
Texas Industries Inc 1341 W Mockingbird Ln Suite 700W NYSE: TXI ■ Web: www.txi.com	Dallas	TX	75247	972-647-6700	647-3878
Thiele Kaolin Co PO Box 1056 *Fax: Mail Rm ■ Web: www.thielekaolin.com	Sandersville	GA	31082	478-552-3951	552-4105*

				Phone	Fax
US Silica Co 106 Sand Mine Rd PO Box 187 TF: 800-243-7500 ■ Web: www.u-s-silica.com	Berkeley Springs	WV	25411	304-258-2500	258-8295
Wyo-Ben Inc 1345 Discovery Dr TF Cust Svc: 800-548-7055 ■ Web: www.wyoben.com	Billings	MT	59102	406-652-6351	656-0748

506-3 Minerals Mining (Misc)

				Phone	Fax
Gouverneur Talc Co Inc 1837 State Hwy 812 TF: 800-243-6064 ■ Web: www.rtvanderbilt.com/gouv.htm	Gouverneur	NY	13642	315-287-0100	287-0948
Harborlite Corp 130 Castilian Dr	Goleta	CA	93117	805-562-9905	
ILC Resources 10563 Justin Dr TF: 800-247-2133 ■ Web: www.ilcresources.com	Urbandale	IA	50322	515-243-8106	244-3200
Luzenac America Inc 8051 E Maplewood Ave TF: 800-325-0299 ■ Web: www.luzenac.com	Greenwood Village	CO	80111	303-643-0400	713-5769
Mountain Province Diamonds Inc 401 Bay St Suite 2700 AMEX: MDM ■ Web: www.mountainprovince.com	Toronto	ON	M5H2Y4	416-361-3562	603-8565
RT Vanderbilt Co Inc 30 Winfield St TF Cust Svc: 800-243-6064 ■ Web: www.rtvanderbilt.com	Norwalk	CT	06855	203-853-1400	853-1452
Stornoway Diamond Corp 980 W 1st St Unit 116 TSE: SWY ■ TF: 877-331-2232 ■ Web: www.stornowaydiamonds.com	N.Vancouver	BC	V7P3N4	604-983-7750	987-7107
Vanderbilt Minerals Corp 30 Winfield St TF: 800-243-6064 ■ Web: www.rtvanderbilt.com	Norwalk	CT	06855	203-853-1400	853-1452
WGI Heavy Minerals Inc 810 E Sherman Ave TF: 888-542-7638 ■ Web: www.wgiheavyminerals.com	Coeur d'Alene	ID	83814	208-666-6000	666-4000

506-4 Sand & Gravel Pits

				Phone	Fax
Best Sand Corp 11830 Ravenna Rd PO Box 87 TF: 800-237-4986 ■ Web: www.fairmountminerals.com	Chardon	OH	44024	440-285-3132	285-4109
Brox Industries Inc 1471 Methuen St Web: www.broxindustries.com	Dracut	MA	01826	978-454-9105	805-9720
Cadman Inc 7554 185th Ave NE Suite 100 PO Box 97038 TF: 888-322-6847 ■ Web: www.cadman.com	Redmond	WA	98052	425-868-1234	961-7390
Cemex Inc PO Box 3004 Web: www.cemexusa.com	Florida City	FL	33034	305-247-3011	248-9112
Edward C Levy Co 9300 Dix St *Fax: Sales ■ Web: www.edwclevy.com	Dearborn	MI	48120	313-843-7200	429-2448*
Elmer Larson LLC 21218 Airport Rd	Sycamore	IL	60178	815-895-4837	895-4437
ER Jahna Industries Inc 202 E Stuart Ave PO Drawer 840 Web: www.jahna.com	Lake Wales	FL	33859	863-676-9431	676-5137
Fisher Sand & Gravel Co 3020 Energy Dr PO Box 1034 TF: 800-932-8740	Dickinson	ND	58602	701-456-9184	456-9168
Hills Materials Co 3975 Sturgis Rd PO Box 2320 Web: www.hillsmaterials.com	Rapid City	SD	57709	605-394-3300	341-3446
Hilltop Basic Resources Inc 1 W 4th St Suite 1100 Web: www.hilltopbasicresources.com	Cincinnati	OH	45202	513-651-5000	684-8222
Janesville Sand & Lycon Co 1110 Harding St TF: 800-955-7702 ■ Web: www.jsandg.com	Janesville	WI	53547	608-754-7701	754-8555
Lafarge North America Inc 12950 Worldgate Dr Suite 600 Web: www.lafargenorthamerica.com	Herndon	VA	20170	703-480-3600	480-3899
LG Everist Inc 300 S Phillips Ave Suite 200 Web: www.lgeverist.com	Sioux Falls	SD	57117	605-334-5000	334-3656
Mark Sand & Gravel Co 525 Kennedy Pk Rd PO Box 458 TF: 800-427-8316	Fergus Falls	MN	56538	218-736-7523	736-2647
Martin Marietta Materials Inc 2710 Wycliff Rd NYSE: MLM ■ Web: www.martinmarietta.com	Raleigh	NC	27607	919-781-4550	
Miles Sand & Gravel Inc 400 PO Box 130	Auburn	WA	98071	253-833-3700	833-3746
Pete Lien & Sons Inc 3401 Universal Dr PO Box 440 Web: www.petelien.com	Rapid City	SD	57709	605-342-7224	342-6979
Pike Industries Inc 3 Eastgate Pk Rd TF: 800-283-7453 ■ Web: www.pikeindustries.com	Belmont	NH	03220	603-527-5100	527-5101
Pounding Mill Quarry Corp 171 St ClairÆs Crossing TF: 888-661-7625 ■ Web: www.pmqc.com	Bluefield	VA	24605	276-326-1145	322-1718
Rogers Group Inc 421 Great Cir Rd Web: www.rogersgroupinc.com	Nashville	TN	37228	615-242-0585	
Standard Sand & Silica Co 1850 Hwy 17-92 PO Box 1059 TF: 877-444-7263 ■ Web: www.standardsand.com	Davenport	FL	33836	863-422-7100	421-7349
Texas Industries Inc 1341 W Mockingbird Ln Suite 700W NYSE: TXI ■ Web: www.txi.com	Dallas	TX	75247	972-647-6700	647-3878
Thelen Sand & Gravel Inc 28955 W SR-173 TF: 800-537-2324 ■ Web: www.thelensg.com	Antioch	IL	60002	847-395-3313	395-3452
Tower Rock Stone Co 19829 Lower Frenchman Rd PO Box 111	Sainte Genevieve	MO	63670	573-883-7415	883-3067
Unimin Corp 258 Elm St TF: 800-223-2236 ■ Web: www.unimin.com	New Canaan	CT	06840	203-966-8880	966-1557
US Silica Co 106 Sand Mine Rd PO Box 187 TF: 800-243-7500 ■ Web: www.u-s-silica.com	Berkeley Springs	WV	25411	304-258-2500	258-8295

Company / Address	City	State	ZIP	Phone	Fax
Valco Cincinnati Inc 411 Cir Fwy Dr *Web:* www.valcomelton.com	Cincinnati	OH	45246	513-874-6550	874-3612
Wendling Quarries Inc 2647 225th St PO Box 230 *Web:* www.wendlingquarries.com	De Witt	IA	52742	563-659-9181	659-3393
Westroc Inc 670 W 220 S *Web:* www.westrocinc.com	Pleasant Grove	UT	84062	801-785-5600	785-7408
Whibco Inc 87 E Commerce St *TF:* 800-631-8010	Bridgeton	NJ	08302	856-455-9200	455-8884

506-5 Stone Quarries - Crushed & Broken Stone

Company / Address	City	State	ZIP	Phone	Fax
Aggregate Industries Management Inc 7529 Standish Pl Suite 200 *Web:* www.aggregate-us.com	Rockville	MD	20855	301-284-3600	284-3645
Anderson Columbia Co Inc 871 NW Guerdon St PO Box 1829 *Web:* www.andersoncolumbia.com	Lake City	FL	32056	386-752-7585	755-5430
Ararat Rock Products Co 525 Quarry Rd	Mount Airy	NC	27030	336-786-4693	786-2189
Berks Products Corp 965 Berkshire Blvd *TF:* 800-282-2375 ■ *Web:* www.berksproducts.com	Reading	PA	19610	610-374-5131	375-1469
Braen Stone Co 400 Central Ave PO Box 8310 *Web:* www.braenstone.com	Haledon	NJ	07538	973-595-6250	595-7087
Brox Industries Inc 1471 Methuen St *Web:* www.broxindustries.com	Dracut	MA	01826	978-454-9105	805-9720
Burroughs Materials Corp 51445 W 12-Mile Rd	Wixom	MI	48393	248-348-8511	349-9007
Cessford Construction Co 3808 Old Hwy 61 *TF:* 800-747-2297 ■ *Web:* www.cessfordconstruction.com	Burlington	IA	52601	319-753-2297	753-0926
Eastern Industries Inc 4401 Camp Meeting Rd Suite 200 *Web:* www.eastern-ind.com	Center Valley	PA	18034	610-866-0932	867-1886
Edward C Levy Co 9300 Dix St **Fax:* Sales ■ *Web:* www.edwclevy.com	Dearborn	MI	48120	313-843-7200	429-2448*
ER Jahna Industries Inc 202 E Stuart Ave PO Drawer 840 *Web:* www.jahna.com	Lake Wales	FL	33859	863-676-9431	676-5137
Hanson Aggregates North America 8505 Freeport Pkwy Suite 500 *TF:* 800-687-6549	Irving	TX	75063	972-621-0345	621-0506
Hanson Bldg Products North America 3500 Maple Ave *TF:* 800-527-2362 ■ *Web:* www.heidelbergcement.com	Dallas	TX	75219	214-525-5500	525-5563
Harney Rock & Paving Co 457 S Date Ave *TF:* 888-298-2681 ■ *Web:* www.harneyrock.com	Burns	OR	97720	541-573-7855	573-3532
HB Mellot Estate Inc 100 Mellott Dr Suite 100	Warfordsburg	PA	17267	301-678-2000	678-2012
Hills Materials Co 3975 Sturgis Rd PO Box 2320 *Web:* www.hillsmaterials.com	Rapid City	SD	57709	605-394-3300	341-3446
Hunt Midwest Enterprises Inc 8300 NE Underground Dr *TF:* 800-551-6877 ■ *Web:* www.huntmidwest.com	Kansas City	MO	64161	816-455-2500	
Hunt Midwest Mining Inc 8300 NE Underground Dr *Web:* www.huntmidwest.com	Kansas City	MO	64161	816-455-2500	455-4462
JF Shea Co Inc Redding Div 17400 Clear Creek Rd *Web:* www.jfshea.com	Redding	CA	96001	530-246-2200	246-0554
Lafarge North America Inc 12950 Worldgate Dr Suite 600 *Web:* www.lafargenorthamerica.com	Herndon	VA	20170	703-480-3600	480-3899
LG Everist Inc 300 S Phillips Ave Suite 200 *Web:* www.lgeverist.com	Sioux Falls	SD	57117	605-334-5000	334-3656
Martin Marietta Materials Inc 2710 Wycliff Rd *NYSE: MLM* ■ *Web:* www.martinmarietta.com	Raleigh	NC	27607	919-781-4550	
Meckley's Limestone Products Inc 1543 State Rt 225 *Web:* www.meckleys.com	Herndon	PA	17830	570-758-3011	758-2400
Meshberger Bros Stone Corp 6311 W St Rd 218 *Web:* www.meshbergerbros.com	Bluffton	IN	46714	260-334-5311	334-5353
Michigan Limestone Operations LP 1035 Calcite Rd *TF:* 800-221-3803 ■ *Web:* www.mlo.net	Rogers City	MI	49779	989-734-2131	734-4779
Midwest Minerals Inc 709 N Locust St PO Box 412 *Web:* www.midwestminerals.com	Pittsburg	KS	66762	620-231-8120	235-0840
Mulzer Crushed Stone Inc 534 Mozart St PO Box 249 *Web:* www.mulzer.com	Tell City	IN	47586	812-547-7921	547-6757
New Enterprise Stone & Lime Co Inc (NESL) 3912 Brumbaugh Rd PO Box 77 *Web:* www.nesl.com	New Enterprise	PA	16664	814-766-2211	766-4400
NR Hamm Quarry Inc 609 Perry Pl PO Box 17	Perry	KS	66073	785-597-5111	597-5117
Pennsy Supply Inc 1001 Paxton St *Web:* www.pennsysupply.com	Harrisburg	PA	17104	717-233-4511	238-7312
Pike Industries Inc 3 Eastgate Pk Rd *TF:* 800-283-7453 ■ *Web:* www.pikeindustries.com	Belmont	NH	03220	603-527-5100	527-5101
Piqua Materials Inc 1750 W Statler Rd *TF:* 800-338-2962	Piqua	OH	45356	937-773-4824	773-0791
Pounding Mill Quarry Corp 171 St ClairÆs Crossing *TF:* 888-661-7625 ■ *Web:* www.pmqc.com	Bluefield	VA	24605	276-326-1145	322-1718
Rogers Group Inc 421 Great Cir Rd *Web:* www.rogersgroupinc.com	Nashville	TN	37228	615-242-0585	
Staker Parson Cos Inc 2350 S 1900 W *TF:* 888-672-7766 ■ *Web:* www.westernrock.com	Ogden	UT	84409	801-731-1111	
Stoneco Inc 7555 Whiteford Rd	Ottawa Lake	MI	49267	734-856-2257	854-2607
Syar Industries Inc 2301 Napa Vallejo Hwy	Napa	CA	94558	707-252-8711	257-2630
Texas Crushed Stone Co 5300 S IH-35 *TF:* 800-772-8272	Georgetown	TX	78628	512-863-5511	244-6055
Texas Industries Inc 1341 W Mockingbird Ln Suite 700W *NYSE: TXI* ■ *Web:* www.txi.com	Dallas	TX	75247	972-647-6700	647-3878
Tilcon NY Inc 162 Old Mill Rd *TF:* 800-872-7762 ■ *Web:* www.tilconny.com	West Nyack	NY	10994	845-358-4500	480-3128
Tower Rock Stone Co 19829 Lower Frenchman Rd PO Box 111	Sainte Genevieve	MO	63670	573-883-7415	883-3067
Trap Rock Industries Inc 7 Laurel Ave *Web:* www.traprock.com	Kingston	NJ	08528	609-924-0300	
Valley Quarries Inc 297 Quarry Rd PO Box J *Web:* www.valleyquarries.com	Chambersburg	PA	17201	717-267-2244	267-2521
Vulcan Materials Co 1200 Urban Ctr Dr PO Box 385014 *NYSE: VMC* ■ *TF:* 800-615-4331 ■ *Web:* www.vulcanmaterials.com	Birmingham	AL	35238	205-298-3000	298-2942
Vulcan Materials Co Western Div 3200 San Fernando Rd *NYSE: VMC* ■ *TF:* 800-225-6280 ■ *Web:* www.vulcanmaterials.com	Los Angeles	CA	90065	323-258-2777	258-1583
Wendling Quarries Inc 2647 225th St PO Box 230 *Web:* www.wendlingquarries.com	De Witt	IA	52742	563-659-9181	659-3393
Wyroc Inc 2142 Industrial Ct PO Box 1239 *Web:* www.wyroc.com	Vista	CA	92085	760-727-0878	727-9238

506-6 Stone Quarries - Dimension Stone

Company / Address	City	State	ZIP	Phone	Fax
Cadman Inc 7554 185th Ave NE Suite 100 PO Box 97038 *TF:* 888-322-6847 ■ *Web:* www.cadman.com	Redmond	WA	98052	425-868-1234	961-7390
Eden Stone Co Inc W4520 Lime Rd *TF:* 800-472-2521 ■ *Web:* www.edenstone.net	Eden	WI	53019	920-477-2521	477-4700
Fletcher Granite Co Inc 534 Groton Rd *TF:* 800-253-8168 ■ *Web:* www.fletchergranite.com	Westford	MA	01886	978-251-4031	251-8773
Liter's Quarry Inc 5918 Haunz Ln *Web:* www.litersinc.com	Louisville	KY	40241	502-241-7637	241-9410
LW Rozzo Inc 17200 Pines Blvd	Pembroke Pines	FL	33029	954-435-8501	436-6243
Oldcastle Materials Inc 900 Ashwood Pkwy Suite 700 *TF:* 800-241-7074 ■ *Web:* www.apac.com	Atlanta	GA	30338	770-552-5600	522-5008
Pounding Mill Quarry Corp 171 St ClairÆs Crossing *TF:* 888-661-7625 ■ *Web:* www.pmqc.com	Bluefield	VA	24605	276-326-1145	322-1718
Swenson Granite Co LLC 369 N State St *Web:* www.swensongranite.com	Concord	NH	03301	603-225-2783	227-9541
Tower Rock Stone Co 19829 Lower Frenchman Rd PO Box 111	Sainte Genevieve	MO	63670	573-883-7415	883-3067
Wendling Quarries Inc 2647 225th St PO Box 230 *Web:* www.wendlingquarries.com	De Witt	IA	52742	563-659-9181	659-3393

507 MISSILES, SPACE VEHICLES, PARTS

SEE ALSO Weapons & Ordnance (Military) p. 2773

Company / Address	City	State	ZIP	Phone	Fax
Aerojet PO Box 13222 *Web:* www.aerojet.com	Sacramento	CA	95813	916-355-1000	351-8667
Aerojet Redmond Rocket Ctr 11411 139th Pl NE **Fax:* Mail Rm ■ *Web:* www.aerojet.com/about/redmond.php	Redmond	WA	98052	425-885-5000	882-5804*
Alliant Techsystems Inc (ATK) 7480 Flying Cloud Dr *NYSE: ATK* ■ *Web:* www.atk.com	Minneapolis	MN	55344	952-351-3000	351-3009
Applied Aerospace Structures Corp (AASC) 3437 S Airport Way PO Box 6189 *Web:* www.aascworld.com	Stockton	CA	95206	209-983-3224	983-3375
Astrotech Corp 401 Congress Ave Suite 1650 *NASDAQ: ASTC* ■ *Web:* www.astrotechcorp.com	Austin	TX	78701	512-485-9530	485-9531
Boeing Co Integrated Defense Systems PO Box 516 *Web:* www.boeing.com/ids	Saint Louis	MO	63166	314-232-0232	
Boeing Co The 100 N Riverside Plaza *NYSE: BA* ■ *Web:* www.boeing.com	Chicago	IL	60606	312-544-2000	544-2082
Coleman Aerospace Corp 7675 Municipal Dr *Web:* www.crc.com	Orlando	FL	32819	407-354-0047	354-1112
DRS Unmanned Technologies Inc 6300 Columbia St *Web:* www.drs.com	Mineral Wells	TX	76067	817-850-3860	850-3880
Esterline Mason 13955 Balboa Blvd **Fax:* Sales ■ *TF:* 800-232-7700 ■ *Web:* www.esterline.com	Sylmar	CA	91342	818-361-3366	365-6809*
Hamilton Sundstrand Corp 1 Hamilton Rd *Web:* www.hamiltonsundstrand.com	Windsor Locks	CT	06096	860-654-6000	654-4741
Herley Lancaster 3061 Industry Dr **Fax:* Sales ■ *Web:* www.herley.com	Lancaster	PA	17603	717-397-2777	735-8123*
Hi-Shear Technology Corp (HSTC) 24225 Garnier St *AMEX: HSR* ■ *TF Mktg:* 800-733-0321 ■ *Web:* www.hstc.com	Torrance	CA	90505	310-784-2100	325-5354
HITCO Carbon Composites Inc 1600 W 135th St *TF:* 800-421-5444 ■ *Web:* www.hitco.com	Gardena	CA	90249	310-527-0700	970-5468
Honeywell Space Systems 13350 US Hwy 19 N *Web:* www51.honeywell.com/aero/IndustryExpertise/Space.html	Clearwater	FL	33764	727-539-4000	
International Launch Services 1660 International Dr Suite 800 *Web:* www.ilslaunch.com	McLean	VA	22102	571-633-7400	633-7500
L'Garde Inc 15181 Woodlawn Ave *Web:* www.lgarde.com	Tustin	CA	92780	714-259-0771	259-7822
Lockheed Martin Corp 6801 Rockledge Dr *NYSE: LMT* ■ *TF:* 866-562-2363 ■ *Web:* www.lockheedmartin.com	Bethesda	MD	20817	301-897-6000	897-6083
Lockheed Martin Space Systems Co Michoud Operations 13800 Old Gentilly Rd *Web:* www.lockheedmartin.com/michoud	New Orleans	LA	70129	504-257-3311	257-4431
Orbital Sciences Corp 21839 Atlantic Blvd *NYSE: ORB* ■ *TF:* 877-672-4825 ■ *Web:* www.orbital.com	Dulles	VA	20166	703-406-5000	
Pratt & Whitney Government Engines & Space Propulsion Div PO Box 109600 **Fax:* Sales ■ *TF:* 800-327-3246	West Palm Beach	FL	33410	561-796-2000	796-5876*
Qualitor Inc 24800 Denso Dr Suite 255	Southfield	MI	48034	248-204-8600	204-8619

Phone Fax

Web: www.qualitorinc.com

Reinhold Industries Inc
12827 E Imperial Hwy ... Santa Fe Springs CA 90670 562-944-3281 944-7238
NASDAQ: RNHDA ■ *Web:* www.reinhold-ind.com

Rockwell Collins Electromechanical Systems
17000 Red Hill Ave ... Irvine CA 92614 949-250-1015 250-0497
TF: 800-866-5775 ■ *Web:* www.rockwellcollins.com

Sea Launch Co LLC 2700 Nimitz Rd ... Long Beach CA 90802 562-951-7000
Web: www.sea-launch.com

Space Vector Corp 9223 Deering Ave ... Chatsworth CA 91311 818-734-2600 886-4362
Web: www.spacevector.com

Westar Aerospace & Defense Group Inc
QinetiQ North America Inc
4 Research Pk Dr ... Saint Charles MO 63304 636-300-5000 300-5005
Web: www.qinetiq-na.com

508 MOBILE HOMES & BUILDINGS

Phone Fax

American Homestar Corp
2450 S Shore Blvd Suite 300 ... League City TX 77573 281-334-9700 334-6193*
**Fax:* Acctg ■ *TF:* 800-234-6269 ■ *Web:* www.americanhomestar.com

Buccaneer Homes of Alabama Inc
330 Buccaneer St PO Box 1418 ... Hamilton AL 35570 205-921-3135 921-7390
TF: 800-326-2822

Cavalier Homes Inc
32 Wilson Blvd Suite 100 PO Box 300 ... Addison AL 35540 256-747-1575 747-3044*
AMEX: CAV ■ **Fax:* Sales ■ *TF:* 877-747-9800 ■ *Web:* www.cavalierhomebuilders.com

Cavco Industries Inc
1001 N Central Ave 8th Fl ... Phoenix AZ 85004 602-256-6263 256-6189
NASDAQ: CVCO ■ *TF:* 800-790-9111 ■ *Web:* www.cavco.com

Champion Enterprises Inc
2701 Cambridge Dr Suite 300 ... Auburn Hills MI 48326 248-340-9090 340-9345
Web: www.championhomes.net

Chariot Eagle Inc 931 NW 37th Ave ... Ocala FL 34475 352-629-7007 629-6920
Web: www.charioteagle.com

Chief Custom Homes 111 Grant St PO Box 127 ... Aurora NE 68818 402-694-5250 694-5873
Web: www.bonnavillahomes.com

Commodore Corp 1423 Lincolnway E ... Goshen IN 46526 574-533-7100 534-2716
TF: 800-554-4285 ■ *Web:* www.commodorehomes.com

DHS Systems LLC 33 Kings Hwy ... Orangeburg NY 10962 845-359-6066 365-2114
Web: www.drash.com

Fairmont Homes Inc 502 S Oakland St ... Nappanee IN 46550 574-773-7941 773-2185
TF: 800-777-8787 ■ *Web:* www.fairmonthomes.com

Fleetwood Homes of Idaho Inc
2611 E Comstock Ave ... Nampa ID 83687 208-466-2438 467-1616*
**Fax:* Sales ■ *TF:* 800-334-8958

Fleetwood Homes of Northern California Inc
18 N Pioneer Ave ... Woodland CA 95776 916-448-1211 662-6425*
**Fax Area Code:* 530 ■ *TF:* 800-666-1210

Fleetwood Homes of Virginia Inc
90 Weaver St ... Rocky Mount VA 24151 540-483-5171 483-3517
Web: www.fleetwoodhomes.com

Fleetwood Homes of Washington Inc
211 5th St ... Woodland WA 98674 360-225-9461 225-5069
TF Sales: 800-275-6869 ■ *Web:* www.fleetwood.com

Fleetwood RV 3125 Myers St ... Riverside CA 92503 877-887-2921
NYSE: FLE ■ *TF:* 877-887-2921 ■ *Web:* www.fleetwood.com

Franklin Homes Inc 10655 Hwy 43 ... Russellville AL 35653 256-332-4510 331-2203
TF: 800-332-4511 ■ *Web:* www.franklinhomesusa.com

Fuqua Homes Inc 7100 S Cooper St ... Arlington TX 76001 817-465-3211 465-5125
TF: 800-336-0874 ■ *Web:* www.fuquahomes.com

Giles Industries Inc 405 S Broad St ... New Tazewell TN 37825 423-626-7243 626-6919
TF: 800-844-4537 ■ *Web:* www.gilesindustries.com

Homark Co Inc 100 3rd St PO Box 309 ... Red Lake Falls MN 56750 218-253-2777 253-2116
Web: www.detroiter.com

Homes of Merit Inc
Bartow Air Base Bldg 21 PO Box 1606 ... Bartow FL 33830 863-533-0593 533-0310
Web: www.homes-of-merit.com

Hometown America LLC
150 N Wacker Dr Suite 2800 ... Chicago IL 60606 312-604-7500 604-7501
TF: 888-735-4310 ■ *Web:* www.hometownamerica.com

Horton Homes Inc 101 Industrial Blvd ... Eatonton GA 31024 706-485-8506 485-4446
TF: 800-282-2680 ■ *Web:* www.hortonhomes.com

Jacobsen Homes
600 Packard Ct PO Box 368 ... Safety Harbor FL 34695 727-726-1138 726-7019
TF Sales: 800-843-1559 ■ *Web:* www.jachomes.com

Liberty Homes Inc 1101 Eisenhower Dr N ... Goshen IN 46526 574-533-0431 533-0438
TF: 800-733-0431 ■ *Web:* www.libertyhomesinc.com

Little Valley Homes Inc 45225 Grand River Ave ... Novi MI 48375 248-349-2500
Web: www.lvhomes.net

Manufactured Housing Enterprises Inc
09302 St Rt 6 Rt 6 ... Bryan OH 43506 419-636-4511 636-9144
TF: 800-821-0220 ■ *Web:* www.mheinc.com

Mark Line Industries Inc
51687 County Rd 133 PO Box 277 ... Bristol IN 46507 574-825-5851 825-9139
TF: 888-627-5563 ■ *Web:* www.marklineindustries.com

McGrath RentCorp 5700 Las Positas Rd ... Livermore CA 94551 925-606-9200 453-3200
NASDAQ: MGRC ■ *TF:* 800-352-2900 ■ *Web:* www.mgrc.com

Mobile/Modular Express Inc 1301 Trimble Rd ... Edgewood MD 21040 410-676-3700 676-7288*
**Fax:* Sales ■ *Web:* www.mobilemodular.com

Nashua Homes of Idaho Inc PO Box 170008 ... Boise ID 83717 208-345-0222 345-1144
Web: www.nashuahomesofidaho.com

Nobility Homes Inc 3741 SW 7th St ... Ocala FL 34474 352-732-5157 732-4203
NASDAQ: NOBH ■ *TF:* 800-476-6624 ■ *Web:* www.nobilityhomes.com

Norris Industries Inc
1160 Hwy 11 W PO Box 99 ... Bean Station TN 37708 865-993-3343 993-2832
TF: 800-550-1096

Oxford Homes Inc 7 Oxford Homes Ln PO Box 679 ... Oxford ME 04270 207-539-4412 539-4259
TF: 800-341-0436

Patriot Homes Inc 57420 County Rd 3 S ... Elkhart IN 46517 574-293-6507 522-2339*
**Fax:* Sales ■ *Web:* www.patriothomes.com

R-Anell Custom Homes Inc 235 Anthony Grave Rd ... Denver NC 28033 704-483-5511 483-5674
TF Cust Svc: 800-951-5511 ■ *Web:* www.r-anell.com

Ritz-Craft Corp of Pennsylvania Inc
15 Industrial Pk Rd ... Mifflinburg PA 17844 570-966-1053 966-9248
TF: 800-326-9827 ■ *Web:* www.ritz-craft.com

River Birch Homes Inc 400 River Birch Dr ... Hackleburg AL 35564 205-935-1997 935-3578
TF: 888-760-3314 ■ *Web:* www.riverbirchhomes.com

Satellite Industries Inc
2530 Xenium Ln N ... Minneapolis MN 55441 763-553-1900 551-7246
TF: 800-328-3332 ■ *Web:* www.satelliteindustries.com

Skyline Corp 2520 By-Pass Rd ... Elkhart IN 46514 574-294-6521 295-8601
NYSE: SKY ■ *TF:* 800-348-7469 ■ *Web:* www.skylinecorp.com

Sunshine Homes Inc 100 Sunshine Ave ... Red Bay AL 35582 256-356-4427 356-9694
TF: 800-462-7847 ■ *Web:* www.sunshinehomes-inc.com

Taylor Made Homes Inc PO Box 438 ... Anderson MO 64831 417-845-3311 845-6044
Web: www.taylormadehomes.com

VFP Inc 2840 Electric Rd Suite A-201 ... Roanoke VA 24018 540-977-0500 977-5555
Web: www.vfpinc.com

Virginia Homes Mfg Corp
142 Virginia Homes Ln PO Box 410 ... Boydton VA 23917 434-738-6107 738-6926
Web: www.virginiahomesmfg.com

Wick Bldg Systems Inc 405 Walter Rd ... Mazomanie WI 53560 608-795-4281 795-2294*
**Fax:* Sales ■ *TF:* 800-356-9682 ■ *Web:* www.wickbuildings.com

Williams Scotsman Inc 8211 Town Ctr Dr ... Baltimore MD 21236 410-931-6000 931-6000
TF: 800-782-1500 ■ *Web:* www.willscot.com

509 MODELING AGENCIES

SEE ALSO Modeling Schools p. 2253; Talent Agencies p. 2681

Phone Fax

Blitz Models & Talents
487 Adelaide St W Suite 305 ... Toronto ON M5V1T4 416-703-5799 703-6232

Boss Models USA 321 W 13th St ... New York NY 10011 212-242-2444 633-6127
Web: www.bossmodels.com

Click Model Management 129 W 27th St PH ... New York NY 10001 212-206-1616 206-6228*
**Fax:* Resv ■ *Web:* www.clickmodel.com

Dallas Model Group
12700 Hillcrest Rd Suite 180 ... Dallas TX 75230 972-980-7647 934-0941

DNA Model Management Inc 555 W 25th St ... New York NY 10001 212-226-0080 226-7711
Web: www.dnamodels.com

Elite Model Management Corp
404 Pk Ave S 9th Fl ... New York NY 10016 212-529-9700 475-0572
Web: www.elitemodel.com

Ford Models Inc 111 5th Ave 9th Fl ... New York NY 10003 212-219-6500 966-1531
Web: www.fordmodels.com

IMG Models 304 Pk Ave S PH N ... New York NY 10010 212-253-8884 253-8883
Web: www.imgmodels.com

Irene Marie Inc 728 Ocean Dr ... Miami Beach FL 33139 305-672-2929 674-1342
Web: www.irenemarie.com

LA Models 7700 Sunset Blvd ... Los Angeles CA 90046 323-436-7700 436-7755
Web: www.latalent.com

Marilyn Inc 32 Union Sq E PH ... New York NY 10003 212-260-6500 260-0821
Web: www.marilynagency.com

Next Model Management 15 Watts St 6th Fl ... New York NY 10013 212-925-5100 925-5931
Web: www.nextmodels.com

San Diego Model Management
438 Camino del Rio S Suite 116 ... San Diego CA 92108 619-296-1018 296-3422
Web: www.sdmodel.com

Wilhelmina Models Inc 300 Pk Ave S ... New York NY 10010 212-473-0700 473-3223
Web: www.wilhelmina.com

Women Management 199 Lafayette St 7th Fl ... New York NY 10012 212-334-7480 334-7492
Web: www.womenmanagement.com

510 MODELING SCHOOLS

Phone Fax

Ambiance Models & Talent Inc
1096 Dayton Blvd ... Chattanooga TN 37405 423-265-2121 265-2190
Web: www.ambiancemodels.com

Barbizon International LLC
311 N University Dr Suite 1002 ... Coral Springs FL 33065 954-345-4140 345-8055
Web: www.barbizonmodeling.com

John Robert Powers International
4311 Wilshire Blvd Suite 200 ... Los Angeles CA 90010 323-857-5300 857-5559

Mayo-Hill School of Modeling
7887 San Felipe St Suite 127 ... Houston TX 77063 713-789-7340 789-6163
Web: www.mayohill.com

Premiere School of Self-Improvement & Professional Modeling Inc
1918 Twin Cir Dr ... Mendota Heights MN 55118 952-920-0681 687-9096*
**Fax Area Code:* 651 ■ *Web:* www.premiere-modeling.com

511 MOPS, SPONGES, WIPING CLOTHS

SEE ALSO Brushes & Brooms p. 1544; Cleaning Products p. 1605

Company	City	State	Zip	Phone	Fax
A & B Wiper Supply Inc					
5601 Paschall Ave	Philadelphia	PA	19143	215-482-6100	482-6190
TF: 800-333-7247 ■ *Web:* www.bestrags.com					
Abco Cleaning Products 6800 NW 36th Ave	Miami	FL	33147	305-694-2226	694-0451
TF: 888-694-2226 ■ *Web:* www.abcoproducts.com					
Acme Sponge & Chamois Co Inc					
855 Pine St	Tarpon Springs	FL	34689	727-937-3222	942-3064
Web: www.acmesponge.com					
Acme Wiping Materials Co					
1327 Palmetto St	Los Angeles	CA	90013	213-624-8756	624-5185
Bro-Tex Inc 800 Hampden Ave	Saint Paul	MN	55114	651-645-5721	646-1876
TF: 800-328-2282 ■ *Web:* www.brotex.com					
Butler Home Products LLC					
237 Cedar Hill St	Marlborough	MA	01752	508-597-8000	597-8010
TF: 888-318-8521 ■ *Web:* www.cleanerhomeliving.com					
Cadie Products Corp 151 E 11th St	Paterson	NJ	07524	973-278-8300	278-0303
Web: www.cadie.com					
Colman Wolf Sanitary Supply Co					
15201 E 11-Mile Rd	Roseville	MI	48066	586-779-5500	779-5505
Web: www.theprofgroup.com					
Continental Mfg Co					
305 Rock Industrial Pk Dr	Bridgeton	MO	63044	314-656-4301	770-9938
TF: 800-325-1051 ■ *Web:* www.continental-mfg.com					
Disco Inc 1895 Brannan Rd	McDonough	GA	30253	770-474-7575	474-9464
TF: 800-548-5150 ■ *Web:* www.katyindustries.com					
Ettore Products Co 2100 N Loop Rd	Alameda	CA	94502	510-748-4130	748-4146
TF: 800-438-8673 ■ *Web:* www.ettore.com					
Golden Star Inc					
4770 N Belleview Ave Suite 209	Kansas City	MO	64116	816-842-0233	842-1129
TF: 800-821-2792 ■ *Web:* www.goldenstar.com					
Houston Wiper & Mill Supply Co 1234 Kress St	Houston	TX	77020	713-672-0571	673-7637
TF: 800-633-5968					
Kleen-Tex Industries Inc					
1516 Orchard Hill Rd	LaGrange	GA	30240	706-882-8134	882-0729
TF: 800-241-2323 ■ *Web:* www.kleen-tex.com					
L C Industries 1 Signature Dr	Hazlehurst	MS	39083	601-894-1771	894-2993
TF: 800-647-2468 ■ *Web:* www.buylci.com					
Magla Products LLC 159 S St	Morristown	NJ	07960	973-984-7998	984-2382
TF: 800-247-5281 ■ *Web:* www.magla.com					
O-Cedar/Vileda Inc 505 N Railroad Ave	North Lake	IL	60164	708-452-4100	452-9967
TF: 800-543-8105 ■ *Web:* www.ocedar.com					
Southern Wipers 100 Fairview Rd	Asheville	NC	28803	828-274-2100	274-0000
TF: 800-438-3893 ■ *Web:* www.slosman.com					
Tranzonic Cos					
26301 curtiss wright Pkwy Suite 200	clevland	OH	44143	440-449-6550	445-8366*
**Fax Area Code:* 800 ■ *TF:* 800-553-7979 ■ *Web:* www.tranzonic.com					
TxF Products					
2702 Mortris Shephard Dr PO Box 1118	Brownwood	TX	76801	325-646-1504	643-5943
TF: 800-441-7894					
United Textile Co Inc 751-143rd Ave	San Lorenzo	CA	94578	510-276-2288	278-1981
TF: 800-233-0077 ■ *Web:* www.unitedtextileinc.com					
Wipe-Tex International Corp 110 E 153rd St	Bronx	NY	10451	718-665-0013	665-0787
TF: 800-643-9607 ■ *Web:* www.wipe-tex.com					

512 MORTGAGE LENDERS & LOAN BROKERS

SEE ALSO Banks - Commercial & Savings p. 1506

Company	City	State	Zip	Phone	Fax
AAA Financial Corp 9600 W Sample Rd	Coral Springs	FL	33065	954-344-2530	344-0257
TF: 800-881-2530 ■ *Web:* www.aaafinancial.com					
Ace Mortgage Funding Inc					
7820 Innovation Blvd Suite 350	Indianapolis	IN	46278	317-246-5740	227-2864
TF: 888-223-9975 ■ *Web:* www.acerefi.com					
Advantage Mortgage Service Inc					
12111 Pacific St	Omaha	NE	68154	402-330-0770	330-7318
Ameritrust Mortgage Co LLC					
14045 Ballantyne Corp Pl	Charlotte	NC	28277	704-568-1020	926-8234
Web: www.ameritrust.com					
BRT Realty Trust					
60 Cutter Mill Rd Suite 303	Great Neck	NY	11021	516-466-3100	466-3132
NYSE: BRT ■ *TF:* 800-450-5816 ■ *Web:* www.brtrealty.com					
CapitalSource Inc					
4445 Willard Ave 12th Fl	Chevy Chase	MD	20815	800-370-9431	841-2340*
NYSE: CSE ■ **Fax Area Code:* 301 ■ *TF:* 866-876-8723 ■ *Web:* www.capitalsource.com					
Centerline Capital Group 625 Madison Ave	New York	NY	10022	212-317-5700	751-3550
NYSE: CHC ■ *TF:* 800-831-4826 ■ *Web:* www.chartermac.com					
CitiMortgage Inc 15851 Clayton Rd	Ballwin	MO	63011	800-283-7918	256-4337*
**Fax Area Code:* 636 ■ **Fax:* Cust Svc ■ *TF:* 800-283-7918 ■ *Web:* www.citimortgage.com					
Clarion Mortgage Capital					
6530 S Yosemite St	Englewood	CO	80111	303-843-0777	843-0999
Web: www.clarionmortgage.com					
Colony Mortgage Corp 22983 Lorraine Rd	Fairview Park	OH	44026	440-777-9999	777-9999
TF: 800-423-3085					
Community Preservation Corp The (CPC)					
28 E 28th St 9Fl	New York	NY	10016	212-869-5300	683-0694
Web: www.communityp.com					
Consumer Portfolio Services Inc					
16355 Laguna Canyon Rd PO Box 57071	Irvine	CA	92618	949-753-6800	753-6805
NASDAQ: CPSS ■ *TF:* 888-469-4520 ■ *Web:* www.consumerportfolio.com					
CreditMax 625 N Flagler Dr Suite 625	West Palm Beach	FL	33401	561-352-2200	352-2199
TF: 888-537-8123 ■ *Web:* www.creditmax.com					
CRIIMI MAE Inc 701 13th St NW Suite 1000	Washington	DC	20005	202-715-9500	
TF: 800-266-0535 ■ *Web:* www.cwcapital.com					
Dominion Capital Inc 120 Tredegar St	Richmond	VA	23219	804-819-2000	819-2227
Eastern Light Capital Inc					
100 Pine St Suite 560	San Francisco	CA	94111	415-693-9500	693-9501
AMEX: ELC ■ *Web:* www.caitreit.com					
EverHome Mortgage Co 8100 Nations Way	Jacksonville	FL	32256	800-669-9721	281-6380*
**Fax Area Code:* 904 ■ **Fax:* Cust Svc ■ *TF Cust Svc:* 800-669-9721					
Web: www.everhomemortgage.com					
Extraco Mortgage 7503 Bosque Blvd	Waco	TX	76712	254-772-0202	751-0702*
**Fax:* Cust Svc ■ *TF:* 800-227-4894 ■ *Web:* www.extracomortgage.com					
Family First Mortgage Corp					
33 Old Kings Rd N Suite 1	Palm Coast	FL	32137	386-246-6955	246-6953
Fannie Mae 3900 Wisconsin Ave NW	Washington	DC	20016	202-752-7000	752-5980
NYSE: FNM ■ *TF:* 800-732-6643 ■ *Web:* www.fanniemae.com					
Federal Agricultural Mortgage Corp					
1133 21st St NW Suite 600	Washington	DC	20036	202-872-7700	872-7713
NYSE: AGM ■ *TF:* 800-879-3276 ■ *Web:* www.farmermac.com					
Finance America 16802 Aston St	Irvine	CA	92606	949-440-1000	440-1054*
**Fax:* Mktg ■ *TF:* 800-690-8200					
Financial Fedcorp Inc 6305 Humphreys Blvd	Memphis	TN	38120	901-756-2848	747-4009
Web: www.finfedmem.com					
Financial Freedom Senior Funding Corp					
1 Banting	Irvine	CA	92618	949-341-9200	923-3801
TF: 800-500-5150 ■ *Web:* www.financialfreedom.com					
First Eastern Mortgage Corp					
100 Brickstone Sq	Andover	MA	01810	978-749-3100	749-3148
TF: 800-777-2240 ■ *Web:* www.firsteastern.com					
First Equity Mortgage Bankers Inc					
9130 S Dadeland Blvd Suite 1901	Miami	FL	33156	305-666-3333	666-3181
TF: 800-910-8499					
First Fidelity Mortgage Corp					
2 Ravinia Dr Suite 1600	Atlanta	GA	30346	678-287-3000	287-3001
Web: www.firstfidelitycompanies.com					
First Financial Services Inc (FFSI)					
6230 Fairview Rd Suite 450	Charlotte	NC	28210	704-365-3097	233-3129*
**Fax Area Code:* 980 ■ *Web:* www.ffsmortgages.com					
First Mortgage Corp 1131 W Sixth St	Ontario	CA	91762	909-595-1996	595-7430
PINK: FMOR ■ *Web:* www.firstmortgage.com					
First NLC Financial Services Inc					
700 W Hillsboro Blvd					
Bldg 1 Suite 204	Deerfield Beach	FL	33441	954-420-0060	964-8209*
**Fax Area Code:* 800 ■ *TF:* 800-950-3314 ■ *Web:* www.firstnlc.com					
Forest City Residential Management Inc					
50 Public Sq Terminal Tower Suite 1170	Cleveland	OH	44113	216-736-7646	
Web: www.forestcity.net/company/people/residential/Pages/default.aspx					
Freddie Mac 8200 Jones Branch Dr	McLean	VA	22102	703-903-2000	903-2447
NYSE: FRE ■ *TF:* 800-424-5401 ■ *Web:* www.freddiemac.com					
North Central Region					
333 W Wacker Dr Suite 2500	Chicago	IL	60606	312-407-7400	407-7398
TF: 800-373-3343 ■ *Web:* www.freddiemac.com					
Northeast Region 8200 Jones Branch Dr	McLean	VA	22102	703-903-2000	903-2447
TF: 800-373-3343 ■ *Web:* www.freddiemac.com					
Southeast/Southwest Region					
2300 Windy Ridge Pkwy Suite 200N	Atlanta	GA	30339	770-857-8800	857-8805
TF: 800-373-3343 ■ *Web:* www.freddiemac.com					
Western Region					
21700 Oxnard St Suite 1900	Woodland Hills	CA	91367	818-710-3000	710-3039
Web: www.freddiemac.com					
George Mason Mortgage Corp					
4100 Monu Crnr Dr Suite 100	Fairfax	VA	22030	703-273-2600	934-9122
TF: 800-867-6859 ■ *Web:* www.gmmllc.com					
GFI Capital Resources Group Inc 50 Broadway	New York	NY	10004	212-668-1444	668-1655
TF: 800-234-4358 ■ *Web:* www.gficap.com					
GMAC Mortgage Corp 100 Witmer Rd	Horsham	PA	19044	215-682-1000	682-3318*
**Fax:* Hum Res ■ *TF:* 800-627-0128 ■ *Web:* www.gmacmortgage.com					
Government National Mortgage Assn					
451 7th St SW Suite B-133	Washington	DC	20410	202-708-1535	708-0490
Web: www.ginniemae.gov					
Green Tree Servicing LLC					
345 St Peter St Suite 600	Saint Paul	MN	55102	651-293-3400	293-3622*
**Fax:* Hum Res ■ *TF:* 800-423-9527 ■ *Web:* www.gtservicing.com					
Guild Mortgage Co 5898 Copley Dr	San Diego	CA	92111	800-365-4441	
TF: 800-365-4441 ■ *Web:* www.guildmortgage.com					
Gulfstream Business Bank 2400 SE Monterey Rd	Stuart	FL	34996	772-426-8100	
TF: 800-768-5038 ■ *Web:* www.gsbb.com					
HomeSteps 500 Plano Pkwy	Carrollton	TX	75010	800-972-7555	702-2098*
**Fax Area Code:* 972 ■ *TF:* 800-972-7555 ■ *Web:* www.homesteps.com					
HSBC Mortgage Corp (USA) 2929 Walden Ave	Depew	NY	14043	800-338-4626	651-6945*
**Fax Area Code:* 716 ■ *TF:* 800-338-4626 ■ *Web:* www.us.hsbc.com					
Huntington Mortgage Co					
7575 Huntington Pk Dr	Columbus	OH	43235	614-480-6505	480-6880*
**Fax:* Cust Svc ■ *TF:* 800-323-4695					
Inland Mortgage Corp 2901 Butterfield Rd	Oak Brook	IL	60523	630-218-8000	218-4957
TF: 800-828-8999 ■ *Web:* www.inlandgroup.com/it/finance.htm					
Intervest Mortgage Investment Co					
2030 Franklin St 5th Fl	Oakland	CA	94612	510-622-8500	
Web: www.intervest-mortgage.com					
JI Kislak Inc 7900 Miami Lakes Dr W	Miami Lakes	FL	33016	305-364-4100	
Web: www.kislak.com					
Legg Mason Real Estate Investors Inc					
10880 Wilshire Blvd Suite 1750	Los Angeles	CA	90024	310-234-2100	234-2150
Web: www.lmrei.com					
Lender Processing Services Inc (LPS)					
601 Riverside Ave	Jacksonville	FL	32204	904-854-5100	854-4124
NYSE: LPS ■ *TF:* 800-991-1274 ■ *Web:* www.lpsvcs.com					
LendingTree Inc 11115 Rushmore Dr	Charlotte	NC	28277	704-541-5351	541-1824
TF: 877-510-2659 ■ *Web:* www.lendingtree.com					
Liberty Bank Fsb 6400 Westown Pkwy	West Des Moines	IA	50266	877-562-8938	224-5393*
**Fax Area Code:* 515 ■ *TF:* 877-562-8938 ■ *Web:* www.libertybankiowa.com					
Lion Inc 4700 42nd Ave SW Suite 430	Seattle	WA	98116	206-577-1440	577-1441
TF: 800-546-6463 ■ *Web:* www.lioninc.com					
Litton Loan Servicing LP					
4828 Loop Central Dr	Houston	TX	77081	713-960-9676	966-8830
Web: www.littonloan.com					
M & I Home Lending Solutions					
4121 NW Urbandale Dr	Urbandale	IA	50322	515-281-2807	277-2569*
**Fax Area Code:* 800 ■ *TF:* 800-827-2654 ■ *Web:* www.mihomelendingsolutions.com					

				Phone	Fax
Market Street Mortgage Corp 2650 McCormick Dr	Clearwater	FL	33759	727-724-7000	724-9191
TF: 800-669-3210					
Midland Mortgage Co PO Box 26648	Oklahoma City	OK	73126	800-654-4566	767-5500*
**Fax Area Code:* 405 ■ **Fax:* Cust Svc ■ *TF:* 800-654-4566 ■ *Web:* www.mymidlandmortgage.com					
Mortgage Investors Group 8320 E Walker Springs Ln	Knoxville	TN	37923	865-691-8910	691-7714
TF: 800-489-8910 ■ *Web:* www.migonline.com					
Mortgage Resources Inc 425 S Woods Mill Rd Suite 100	Chesterfield	MO	63017	314-576-5577	576-2703*
**Fax Area Code:* 413 ■ *TF:* 800-232-3717 ■ *Web:* www.mortgageresources.com					
MSN Lifestyle 1 Microsoft Way	Redmond	WA	98052	425-882-8080	936-7329
TF: 800-642-7676 ■ *Web:* www.lifestyle.msn.com					
Municipal Mortgage & Equity LLC (MuniMae) 621 E Pratt St Suite 600	Baltimore	MD	21202	443-263-2900	
PINK: MMAB ■ *TF:* 877-772-4308 ■ *Web:* www.munimae.com					
National Rural Utilities Co-op Finance Corp 2201 Co-op Way	Herndon	VA	20171	703-709-6700	709-6777
TF: 800-424-2954 ■ *Web:* www.nrucfc.coop					
Ncb Management Services Inc 1 Allied Dr	Trevose	PA	19053	215-244-4200	
Web: www.ncbi.com					
Nexstar Financial Corp 19 Missouri Research Pk Ct	Saint Charles	MO	63304	636-685-9100	
TF: 877-706-7382 ■ *Web:* www.nexstar.com					
Origen Financial Inc 27777 Franklin Rd Suite 1700	Southfield	MI	48034	248-746-7000	746-7094
NASDAQ: ORGN ■ *TF:* 866-467-4436 ■ *Web:* www.origenfinancial.com					
PHH Mortgage Corp 3000 Leadenhall Rd	Mount Laurel	NJ	08054	856-917-6000	917-8291*
**Fax:* Cust Svc ■ *TF:* 800-210-8849 ■ *Web:* www.phhmortgage.com					
Platinum Bank 802 W Lumsden Rd	Brandon	FL	33511	813-655-1234	
Web: www.platinumbank.com					
Plaza Home Mortgage Inc 5090 Shoreham Pl Suite 206	San Diego	CA	92122	858-346-1208	677-6741
TF: 866-260-2529 ■ *Web:* www.plazahomemortgage.com					
Prommis Solutions 400 Northridge Rd	Atlanta	GA	30350	877-685-3453	
TF: 877-685-3453 ■ *Web:* www.prommis.com					
Pulte Mortgage LLC 7475 S Joliet St	Englewood	CO	80112	303-740-8800	694-2082
TF: 800-488-0053 ■ *Web:* www.pulte.com/finance					
R-b Financial-mortgages Inc 44028 Mound Rd Suite 3	Sterling Heights	MI	48314	586-254-8435	254-8438
TF: 800-566-4663 ■ *Web:* www.rbfinancial.com					
RAIT Investment Trust 2929 Arch St Suite 1703	Philadelphia	PA	19104	215-701-9555	701-8282
NYSE: RAS ■ *TF:* 800-826-6096 ■ *Web:* www.raitinvestmenttrust.com					
Redwood Trust Inc 1 Belvedere Pl Suite 300	Mill Valley	CA	94941	415-389-7373	381-1773
NYSE: RWT ■ *TF:* 866-269-4976 ■ *Web:* www.redwoodtrust.com					
Regions Mortgage Inc 215 Forrest St	Hattiesburg	MS	39401	800-986-2462	
TF: 800-986-2462 ■ *Web:* www.regionsmortgage.com					
Residential Mortgage LLC 100 Calais Dr	Anchorage	AK	99503	907-222-8800	222-8801
TF: 888-357-2707 ■ *Web:* www.residentialmtg.com					
Ringler Assoc Inc 27422 Aliso Creek Rd Suite 200	Aliso Viejo	CA	92656	949-296-9000	
Web: www.ringlerassociates.com					
Safeguard Properties Inc 7887 Safeguard Cir	Valley View	OH	44125	216-739-2900	
TF: 800-852-8306 ■ *Web:* www.safeguardproperties.com					
Saxon Mortgage Inc 4840 Cox Rd	Glen Allen	VA	23060	804-967-7400	967-7408
TF: 800-538-8202 ■ *Web:* www.saxonmortgage.com					
Saxon Mortgage Services Inc PO Box 161489	Fort Worth	TX	76161	800-594-8422	360-7547*
**Fax Area Code:* 866 ■ *TF:* 800-594-8422 ■ *Web:* www.saxononline.com					
Security Savings Mortgage Corp 217 2nd St NW Suite 1000	Canton	OH	44702	330-455-5600	455-7726*
**Fax:* Cust Svc ■ *TF:* 800-421-8059					
Sovereign Bank Wholesale Lending Div 1022 E Lancaster Ave	Rosemont	PA	19010	610-525-1860	525-4637
TF: 888-696-8879 ■ *Web:* www.sovereignwholesale.com					
Sterling Centrecorp Inc 1 N Clematis St Suite 305	West Palm Beach	FL	33401	561-835-1810	
Web: www.sterlingorganization.com					
SunTrust Mortgage Inc 1001 Semmes Ave	Richmond	VA	23224	804-291-0740	291-0136*
**Fax:* Mktg ■ *TF:* 800-634-7928 ■ *Web:* www.suntrustmortgage.com					
Transnational Financial Network Inc 401 Taraval St 2nd Fl	San Francisco	CA	94116	415-242-7800	
AMEX: TFN ■ *TF:* 888-229-2344					
Truwest Credit Union PO Box 3489	Scottsdale	AZ	85271	480-441-5900	
TF: 855-878-9378 ■ *Web:* www.truwest.org					
Universal American Mortgage Co 15550 Lightwave Dr # 200	Clearwater	FL	33760	727-791-2111	791-2118
TF: 800-696-4619 ■ *Web:* www.uamc.com					
Universal Lending Corp (ULC) 6775 E Evans Ave	Denver	CO	80224	303-758-4969	756-2156
TF: 800-758-4063 ■ *Web:* www.ulc.com					
USA Lending Group 6925 Union Pk Dr Suite 600	Midvale	UT	84047	801-676-1200	676-1201
TF: 877-434-8042					
USA Mortgage Inc 12140 Woodcrest Executive Dr Suite 150	Saint Louis	MO	63141	314-628-2000	628-2036
TF: 877-434-4555 ■ *Web:* www.jgardner.usa-mortgage.com					
Valley Bank 36 Church Ave SW PO Box 2740	Roanoke	VA	24001	540-769-8577	342-4514
Web: www.myvalleybank.com					
Vanderbilt Mortgage & Finance Inc 500 Alcoa Trail	Maryville	TN	37804	800-970-7250	380-3418*
**Fax Area Code:* 865 ■ *TF:* 800-970-7250 ■ *Web:* www.vmf.com					
Vestin Group Inc 8880 W Sunset Rd # 200	Las Vegas	NV	89148	702-227-0965	227-5247
TF: 800-232-7613 ■ *Web:* www.vestinmortgage.com					
Wells Fargo Home Mortgage PO Box 10335	Des Moines	IA	50306	515-237-6000	278-1179*
**Fax Area Code:* 866 ■ *TF:* 800-288-3212 ■ *Web:* www.wellsfargo.com/mortgage					

513 MORTUARY, CREMATORY, CEMETERY PRODUCTS & SERVICES

				Phone	Fax
AJ Desmond & Sons Funeral Directors 2600 Crooks Rd	Troy	MI	48084	248-362-2500	362-0190
TF: 800-210-7135 ■ *Web:* www.desmondfuneralhome.com					
Baue Funeral Homes 620 Jefferson St	Saint Charles	MO	63301	636-724-0073	946-3084
TF: 888-724-0073 ■ *Web:* www.baue.com					
Bradford-O'Keefe Funeral Homes Inc 675 E Howard Ave	Biloxi	MS	39530	228-374-5650	435-3638
Web: www.bradfordokeefe.com					
Carriage Services Inc 3040 Post Oak Blvd Suite 300	Houston	TX	77056	713-332-8400	332-8401
NYSE: CSV ■ *TF:* 800-692-3092 ■ *Web:* www.carriageservices.com					
Church & Chapel Metal Arts Inc 2616 W Grand Ave	Chicago	IL	60612	773-489-3700	626-3299*
**Fax Area Code:* 800 ■ *TF:* 800-992-1234 ■ *Web:* www.church-chapel.com					
Dignity Memorial 1929 Allen Pkwy	Houston	TX	77019	713-522-5141	763-3801*
**Fax Area Code:* 818 ■ *TF:* 800-894-2024 ■ *Web:* www.dignitymemorial.com					
Forest Lawn Memorial-Parks & Mortuaries 1712 S Glendale Ave	Glendale	CA	91205	323-254-7251	551-5071*
**Fax:* Cust Svc ■ *TF:* 800-204-3131 ■ *Web:* www.forestlawn.com					
Neptune Society 4312 Woodman Ave 3rd Fl	Sherman Oaks	CA	91423	818-953-9995	953-9844
TF: 888-637-8863 ■ *Web:* www.neptunesociety.com					
Palm Mortuary Inc 1325 N Main St	Las Vegas	NV	89101	702-464-8300	464-8394
TF Cust Svc: 800-542-2902 ■ *Web:* www.palmmortuary.com					
Rabenhorst Funeral Home Inc PO Box 2666	Baton Rouge	LA	70821	225-383-6831	336-3374
Web: www.rabenhorst.com					
Service Corp International 1929 Allen Pkwy	Houston	TX	77019	713-522-5141	525-9056*
NYSE: SCI ■ **Fax:* Hum Res ■ *Web:* www.sci-corp.com					
Spring Grove Cemetery 4521 Spring Grove Ave	Cincinnati	OH	45232	513-681-6680	853-6802
TF: 888-853-2230 ■ *Web:* www.springgrove.org					
Stewart Enterprises Inc 1333 S Clearview Pkwy	Jefferson	LA	70121	504-729-1400	
NASDAQ: STEI ■ *TF:* 800-535-6017 ■ *Web:* www.stewartenterprises.com					
StoneMor Partners LP 311 Veterans Hwy	Levittown	PA	19056	215-826-2800	
NASDAQ: STON ■ *TF:* 877-857-8890 ■ *Web:* www.investors.stonemor.com					
Wilson Financial Group Inc 15915 Katy Fwy Suite 500	Houston	TX	77094	281-579-2760	579-9089

514 MOTION PICTURE DISTRIBUTION & RELATED SERVICES

				Phone	Fax
ABC News VideoSource 125 W End Ave 5th Fl	New York	NY	10023	212-456-5421	456-5428
TF: 800-789-1250 ■ *Web:* www.abcnewsvsource.com					
Alliance Entertainment Corp 4250 Coral Ridge Dr	Coral Springs	FL	33065	954-255-4000	255-4825
TF: 800-329-7664 ■ *Web:* www.aent.com					
Anchor Bay Entertainment Inc 1699 Stutz Dr	Troy	MI	48084	248-816-0909	816-3335
TF: 800-786-8777 ■ *Web:* www.anchorbayentertainment.com					
Baker & Taylor Inc 2550 W Tyvola Rd Suite 300	Charlotte	NC	28217	704-998-3100	998-3316
TF: 800-775-1800 ■ *Web:* www.btol.com					
Bridgestone Multimedia Group Inc 300 N McKemy Ave	Chandler	AZ	85226	480-940-5777	438-2702*
**Fax Area Code:* 602 ■ *TF Cust Svc:* 800-622-3070					
Buena Vista Home Entertainment Inc 500 S Buena Vista St MC 6570	Burbank	CA	91521	818-560-1000	
TF Cust Svc: 800-723-4763 ■ *Web:* www.bvhe.com					
Carsey-Werner LLC 16027 Ventura Blvd 6th Fl	Encino	CA	91436	818-299-9600	299-9650
Web: www.carseywerner.com/index.html					
Crown Media Holdings Inc 12700 Ventura Blvd Suite 200	Studio City	CA	91604	818-755-2400	755-2564
NASDAQ: CRWN ■ *TF:* 800-522-5131 ■ *Web:* www.hallmarkchannel.com					
Deluxe Media Services Inc 568 Atrium Dr	Vernon Hills	IL	60061	847-990-4100	549-8354
TF: 800-745-7265 ■ *Web:* www.bydeluxe.com					
Desert Island Films 11 Coggeshall Cir	Middletown	RI	02842	401-846-3453	846-0919
TF: 800-766-8550 ■ *Web:* www.desertislandfilms.com					
DG Fastchannel Inc 750 W John Carpenter Fwy Suite 700	Irving	TX	75039	972-581-2000	581-2001
NASDAQ: DGIT ■ *TF:* 800-324-5672 ■ *Web:* www.dgit.com					
Distribution Video & Audio Inc (DVA) 133 Candy Ln	Palm Harbor	FL	34683	727-447-4147	441-3069
TF: 800-683-4147 ■ *Web:* www.dva.com					
Facets Multimedia Inc 1517 W Fullerton Ave	Chicago	IL	60614	773-281-9075	929-5437
TF Cust Svc: 800-331-6197 ■ *Web:* www.facets.org					
First Run Features 630 9th Ave Suite 1213	New York	NY	10036	212-243-0600	989-7649
TF: 800-229-8575 ■ *Web:* www.firstrunfeatures.com					
Full Moon Features 1626 Wilcox Ave Suite 474	Hollywood	CA	90028	323-822-2100	468-0598
Web: www.fullmoonfeatures.com					
Image Entertainment Inc 20525 Nordhoff St Suite 200	Chatsworth	CA	91311	818-407-9100	407-9151
NASDAQ: DISK ■ *TF:* 800-473-3475 ■ *Web:* www.image-entertainment.com					
Ingram Entertainment Inc 2 Ingram Blvd	La Vergne	TN	37089	615-287-4000	287-4982
TF: 800-759-5000 ■ *Web:* www.ingramentertainment.com					
Insight Media 2162 Broadway	New York	NY	10024	212-721-6316	799-5309
TF: 800-233-9910 ■ *Web:* www.insight-media.com					
International Historic Films Inc 3533 S Archer Ave	Chicago	IL	60609	773-927-9091	927-9211
Web: www.ihffilm.com					
Kino International Corp 333 W 39th St Rm 503	New York	NY	10018	212-629-6880	714-0871
TF: 800-562-3330 ■ *Web:* www.kino.com					
Kultur International Films Ltd 195 Hwy 36	West Long Branch	NJ	07764	732-229-2343	229-0066
TF: 800-458-5887 ■ *Web:* www.kultur.com					
MGM/UA Home Entertainment 10250 Constellation Blvd	Los Angeles	CA	90067	310-449-3000	449-3100*
**Fax:* Mail Rm ■ *Web:* www.mgm.com					
MPI Media Group 16101 108th Ave	Orland Park	IL	60467	708-460-0555	460-0175
TF: 800-777-2223 ■ *Web:* www.mpimedia.com					

Company	City	State	ZIP	Phone	Fax
New Line Cinema Corp 888 7th Ave 19th Fl *Web:* www.newline.com	New York	NY	10106	212-649-4900	649-4966
Paramount Home Entertainment 5555 Melrose Ave *Web:* www.paramount.com/homevideo	Los Angeles	CA	90038	323-956-5000	
Paramount Pictures Corp 5555 Melrose Ave *Web:* www.paramount.com	Los Angeles	CA	90038	323-956-5000	862-4564
Questar Inc 680 N Lake Shore Dr Suite 900 *TF:* 800-544-8422 ■ *Web:* www.questarhomevideo.com	Chicago	IL	60611	312-266-9400	266-9523
Roadside Attractions LLC 421 S Beverly Dr 8th Fl *Web:* www.roadsideattractions.com	Beverly Hills	CA	90212	310-789-4710	789-4711
Sony Pictures Classics 550 Madison Ave 8th Fl *Web:* www.sonypictures.com/classics	New York	NY	10022	212-833-8833	833-8844
Sony Pictures Entertainment Inc 10202 W Washington Blvd *TF:* 800-326-9551 ■ *Web:* www.sonypictures.com	Culver City	CA	90232	310-244-4000	244-2626
Sony Pictures Home Entertainment 10202 W Washington Blvd *Web:* www.sonypictures.com/spe	Culver City	CA	90232	310-244-4000	244-2626
Terra Entertainment 11901 Santa Monica Blvd Suite 630 *TF:* 877-788-3772 ■ *Web:* www.terraentertainment.com	Los Angeles	CA	90025	310-268-1210	268-1240
Twentieth Century Fox Home Entertainment Inc 10201 W Pico Blvd *Web:* www.foxhome.com	Los Angeles	CA	90035	310-369-1000	
Twentieth Century Fox Licensing & Merchandising 10201 W Pico Blvd	Los Angeles	CA	90035	310-369-1000	
Universal Studios Home Entertainment 100 Universal City Plaza Bldg 1360 Fl 2 *Web:* www.universalstudiosentertainment.com	Universal City	CA	91608	818-777-2100	
Video Data Bank 112 S Michigan Ave *Web:* www.vdb.org	Chicago	IL	60603	312-345-3550	541-8073
Video Products Distributors 150 Parkshore Dr *TF:* 800-366-2111 ■ *Web:* www.vpdinc.com	Folsom	CA	95630	916-605-1500	605-1760
Warner Bros Domestic Television Distribution 4000 Warner Blvd	Burbank	CA	91522	818-954-6000	
Warner Bros Entertainment 4000 Warner Blvd *Web:* www.warnerbros.com	Burbank	CA	91522	818-954-6000	
WRS Motion Picture & Video Laboratory 213 Tech Rd *Web:* www.wrslabs.com	Pittsburgh	PA	15205	412-937-1200	922-1200

515 MOTION PICTURE PRE- & POST-PRODUCTION SERVICES

Company	City	State	ZIP	Phone	Fax
Aardvark Post 13400 Riverside Dr Suite 210 *Web:* www.aardvarkpost.com	Sherman Oaks	CA	91423	818-461-1630	461-1640
Alpha Cine Labs 9800 40th Ave S *Web:* www.alphacine.com	Seattle	WA	98118	206-682-8230	682-6649
American Media International LLC 2609 Tucker St *TF:* 800-849-3223 ■ *Web:* www.ami-media.com	Burlington	NC	27215	336-229-5554	228-1409
Ascent Media Group Inc 520 Broadway 5th Fl *Web:* www.ascentmedia.com	Santa Monica	CA	90401	310-434-7000	434-7001
Avenue Edit Inc 444 N Michigan Ave Suite 2500 *Web:* www.avenue-edit.com	Chicago	IL	60611	312-943-7100	943-9760
Beyond Pix Studios 950 Battery St 3rd Fl *Web:* www.beyondpix.com	San Francisco	CA	94111	415-434-1027	434-1032
Broadway Video Inc 1619 Broadway *Web:* www.broadwayvideo.com	New York	NY	10019	212-265-7600	713-1535
CafeFX 3130 Skyway Dr	Santa Maria	CA	93455	805-922-9479	922-3225
Cinema Libre Studio 8328 DeSoto Ave *Web:* www.cinemalibrestudio.com	Canoga Park	CA	91304	818-349-8822	349-9922
Colossalvision HDTV 26 Broadway 6th Fl *Web:* www.colossalvision.com	New York	NY	10004	212-269-6333	269-4334
Composite Image Systems LLC 1144 N Las Palmas Ave *Web:* www.cisvfxgroup.com	Hollywood	CA	90038	323-463-8811	962-1859
Crestdigital 3845 E Coronado St PO Box 68057 *TF:* 800-309-3472 ■ *Web:* www.crestnational.com	Anaheim	CA	92807	800-309-3472	
Crew Cuts 28 W 44th St 22nd Fl *Web:* www.crewcuts.com	New York	NY	10036	212-302-2828	302-9846
Crossman Post Production LLC 35 Lone Hollow *TF:* 888-553-1958 ■ *Web:* www.crossmanpost.com	Sandy	UT	84092	801-553-1958	553-0953
Downstream 1650 NW Naito Pkwy Suite 301 *Web:* www.downstream.com	Portland	OR	97209	503-226-1944	226-1283
Edit Bay 571 N Poplar Suite 'I' *Web:* www.theeditbay.com	Orange	CA	92868	714-978-7878	978-7858
Elastic Creative 550 Bryant St *Web:* www.elasticcreative.com	San Francisco	CA	94107	415-495-5595	543-8370
Elevation 905 Bernina Ave *TF:* 800-813-2214 ■ *Web:* www.elevate.tv	Atlanta	GA	30307	404-221-1705	221-0037
Encore Hollywood 6344 Fountain Ave *Web:* www.encorehollywood.com	Hollywood	CA	90028	323-466-7663	467-5539
Film Technology Co Inc 726 N Cole Ave *Web:* www.filmtech.com	Hollywood	CA	90038	323-464-3456	464-7439
Filmworks/Astro Lab 61 W Erie St *Web:* www.filmworkersastro.com	Chicago	IL	60610	312-280-5500	280-5510
FOX Studios 10201 W Pico Blvd *Web:* www.foxstudios.com	Los Angeles	CA	90035	310-369-1000	969-0468
Go Edit Inc 5614 Cahuenga Blvd *Web:* www.goedit.tv	North Hollywood	CA	90038	818-284-6260	985-6260
HDMG Corp 6573 City W Pkwy *Web:* www.hdmg.com	Eden Prairie	MN	55344	952-943-1711	943-1957
Henninger Media Services Inc 2601a Wilson Blvd *TF:* 888-243-3444 ■ *Web:* www.henninger.com	Arlington	VA	22201	703-243-3444	243-5697
LA Digital Post 11311 Camarillo St *Web:* www.ladigital.com	West Toluca Lake	CA	91602	818-487-5000	487-5015
LaserPacific Media Corp 809 N Cahuenga Blvd *Web:* www.laserpacific.com	Hollywood	CA	90038	323-462-6266	464-3233
Level 3 Post 2901 W Alameda Ave *Web:* www.level3post.com	Burbank	CA	91505	818-840-7200	840-7801
Mad House 240 Madison Ave 14th Fl *Web:* www.madhousenyc.com	New York	NY	10016	212-867-1515	697-7168
Mad River Post Inc 2415 Main St *Web:* www.madriverpost.com	Santa Monica	CA	90405	310-392-1577	392-3261
Match Frame *1080 inc* 8531 Fairhaven *TF:* 800-929-2790 ■ *Web:* www.1080.com	San Antonio	TX	78229	210-614-5678	616-0299
Method 1546 7th St *Web:* www.methodstudios.com	Santa Monica	CA	90401	310-899-6500	434-6501
Modern Videofilm Inc 4411 W Olive Ave *Web:* www.mvfinc.com	Burbank	CA	91505	818-840-1700	840-1745
Pacific Ocean Post 625 Arizona Ave *Web:* www.popstudios.com	Santa Monica	CA	90401	310-458-9192	587-1222
Pacific Title & Arts Studio Inc 6350 Santa Monica Blvd	Hollywood	CA	90038	323-464-0121	461-8325
Point.360 2777 Ontario St *NASDAQ: PTSX* ■ *Web:* www.point360.com	Burbank	CA	91504	818-565-1400	847-2503
Post Group Inc 6335 Homewood Ave *Web:* www.postgroup.com	Hollywood	CA	90028	323-462-2300	462-0836
Post Modern Co 2734 Walnut St *Web:* www.postmodernco.com	Denver	CO	80205	303-539-7001	539-7002
Post Modern Group LLC 2941 Alton Pkwy *Web:* www.postmoderngroup.com	Irvine	CA	92606	949-608-8700	608-8729
Postique 23475 Northwestern Hwy *TF:* 800-923-3322 ■ *Web:* www.gracewild.com	Southfield	MI	48075	248-352-2610	352-3708
Postworks New York 100 Avenue of the Americas 10th Fl *Web:* www.pwny.com	New York	NY	10013	212-894-4050	941-0439
Raleigh Studios Worldwide 5300 Melrose Ave **Fax Area Code:* 323 ■ *TF:* 888-960-3456 ■ *Web:* www.raleighstudios.com	Hollywood	CA	90038	888-960-3456	871-5600*
Rhythm & Hues Inc 5404 Jandy Pl *Web:* www.rhythm.com	Los Angeles	CA	90066	310-448-7500	448-7600
RPG Productions 632 S Glenwood Pl *Web:* www.rpgproductions.com	Burbank	CA	91506	818-848-0240	848-2257
Saul Zaentz Co 2600 10th St *TF:* 800-227-0466 ■ *Web:* www.zaentz.com	Berkeley	CA	94710	510-549-1528	486-2115
Skywalker Sound Div Lucasfilm Ltd 5858 Lucas Valley Rd *Web:* www.skysound.com	Nicosia	CA	94946	415-662-1300	
Sound One Corp 1619 Broadway 8th Fl *Web:* www.soundone.com	New York	NY	10019	212-765-4757	603-4363
Soundelux Entertainment Group 7080 Hollywood Blvd Suite 1100 *Web:* www.soundelux.com	Hollywood	CA	90028	323-603-3200	603-3233
Syndicate The 1207 4th St Suite 200	Santa Monica	CA	90401	310-260-2320	260-2420
Table Rock Productions 269 S Beverly Dr Suite 486 *Web:* www.tablerockers.com	Beverly Hillsq	CA	90212	805-451-1057	969-3925
Technicolor Complete Post Inc 6040 Sunset Blvd *Web:* www.technicolor.com	Hollywood	CA	90028	323-817-6600	461-2561
Technicolor USA Inc 10330 N Meridian St *Web:* www.technicolor.com	Indianapolis	IN	46290	317-587-3000	
Todd-AO 2901 W Alameda Ave *Web:* www.toddao.com	Burbank	CA	91505	818-840-7225	840-7871
Victory Studios 2247 15th Ave W *TF:* 888-282-1776 ■ *Web:* www.victorystudios.com	Seattle	WA	98119	206-282-1776	282-3535
Video Post & Transfer Inc 2727 Inwood Rd *Web:* www.videopost.com	Dallas	TX	75235	214-350-2676	352-1427
WRS Motion Picture & Video Laboratory 213 Tech Rd *Web:* www.wrslabs.com	Pittsburgh	PA	15205	412-937-1200	922-1200

516 MOTION PICTURE PRODUCTION - SPECIAL INTEREST

SEE ALSO Animation Companies p. 1396; Motion Picture & Television Production p. 2257

Company	City	State	ZIP	Phone	Fax
Active Parenting Publishers 1955 Vaughn Rd Suite 108 *TF:* 800-825-0060 ■ *Web:* www.activeparenting.com	Kennesaw	GA	30144	770-429-0565	429-0334
American Educational Products Inc 401 Hickory St PO Box 2121 *TF:* 800-289-9299 ■ *Web:* www.amep.com	Fort Collins	CO	80522	970-484-7445	484-1198
Automotive Services Training Network 4101 International Pkwy *TF:* 800-223-2786	Carrollton	TX	75007	972-309-4000	309-4619
Baby Einstein Co LLC 500 S Buena Vista St **Fax Area Code:* 818 ■ *TF:* 800-793-1454 ■ *Web:* www.babyeinstein.com	Burbank	CA	91521	800-793-1454	549-2060*
Broadview Media Inc 4455 W 77th St *Web:* www.broadviewmedia.com	Edina	MN	55435	952-835-4455	835-0971
Classic Worldwide Productions Inc 5001 E Royalton Rd *Web:* www.classicworldwide.com	Cleveland	OH	44147	440-838-5377	838-1240
Clock Wise Productions Inc 79 W 119 St Suite 3 **Fax Area Code:* 801 ■ *Web:* www.clockwiseproductions.com	New York	NY	10026	212-343-3099	843-7088*
Coastal Training Technologies Corp 500 Studio Dr *TF:* 888-776-8268 ■ *Web:* www.coastal.com	Virginia Beach	VA	23452	757-498-9014	498-3657
Comtel Pro Media LLC 2201 N Hollywood Way *TF:* 800-446-9612 ■ *Web:* www.comtelpm.com	Burbank	CA	91505	818-450-1100	

				Phone	Fax
Cookie Jar Co The 266 King St W 2nd Fl	Toronto	ON	M5V1H8	416-977-3238	977-4526
Web: www.thecookiejarcompany.com					
Critical Information Network					
4101 International Pkwy	Carrollton	TX	75007	972-309-4346	
TF: 800-624-2272 ■ *Web:* www.criticalinfonet.com					
CRM Learning 2218 Faraday Ave Suite 110	Carlsbad	CA	92008	760-431-9800	931-5792
TF: 800-421-0833 ■ *Web:* www.crmlearning.com					
Disney Educational Productions					
105 Terry Dr Suite 120	Newtown	PA	18940	800-295-5010	579-8589*
**Fax Area Code:* 215 ■ *TF:* 800-295-5010 ■ *Web:* www.dep.disney.go.com					
DSAT 30151 Tomas St	Rancho Santa Margarita	CA	92688	949-858-1953	267-1254
TF: 800-729-7234					
EDR Media LLC 23330 Commerce Pk Rd	Beachwood	OH	44122	216-292-7300	292-0545
Web: www.edr.com					
Fire & Emergency Training Network					
4101 International Pkwy	Carrollton	TX	75007	972-309-4000	309-5452
TF: 800-845-2443 ■ *Web:* www.trinityworkplacelearning.com					
Gail & Rice Productions Inc					
21301 Civic Ctr Dr	Southfield	MI	48076	248-799-5000	799-5001
TF: 800-860-1931 ■ *Web:* www.gail-rice.com					
Grace & Wild Inc					
23689 Industrial Pk Dr	Farmington Hills	MI	48335	248-471-6010	473-8330
TF: 800-451-6010 ■ *Web:* www.gracewild.com					
Hammond Communications Group Inc					
173 Trade St	Lexington	KY	40511	859-254-1878	254-4290
TF: 888-424-1878 ■ *Web:* www.hammondcg.com					
Hungry Man Inc 160 Varick St	New York	NY	10013	212-625-5600	625-5699
Web: www.hungryman.com					
Intaglio LLC					
5809 Cross Rds Commerce Pkwy Suite 200	Grand Rapids	MI	49519	616-243-3300	243-0923
TF: 800-632-9153 ■ *Web:* www.intaglioav.com					
Iris Films 2600 10th St Suite 413	Berkeley	CA	94710	510-845-5415	841-3336
Web: www.irisfilms.org					
Keystone Learning Systems LLC					
6030 Daybreak Cir Suite A150 116	Clarksville	MD	21029	410-800-4000	422-7015*
**Fax Area Code:* 866 ■ *TF:* 800-949-5590 ■ *Web:* www.keystonelearning.com					
Kultur International Films Ltd					
195 Hwy 36	West Long Branch	NJ	07764	732-229-2343	229-0066
TF: 800-458-5887 ■ *Web:* www.kultur.com					
Law Enforcement Training Network					
4101 International Pkwy	Carrollton	TX	75007	972-309-4000	
TF: 800-624-2272 ■ *Web:* www.letn.com					
Learning Communications LLC					
38 Discovery Suite 250	Irvine	CA	92618	949-788-9209	727-4323
TF: 800-622-3610 ■ *Web:* www.learncom.com					
Lingner Group Productions Inc					
1435 N Meridian St Suite 100	Indianapolis	IN	46202	317-631-2500	638-7184
Web: www.lgpinc.com					
Marcus Productions Inc					
1 Oakwood Blvd Suite 120	Hollywood	FL	33020	954-922-9166	
Web: www.marcusproductions.com					
Medcom Trainex 6060 Phyllis Dr	Cypress	CA	90630	714-891-1443	898-4852
TF Cust Svc: 800-877-1443 ■ *Web:* www.medcomrn.com					
National Film Board of Canada					
Stn Centre-Ville PO Box 6100	Montreal	QC	H3C3H5	514-283-9000	283-7564
Web: www.nfb.ca					
New Amsterdam Entertainment Inc					
1133 Avenue of the Americas #1621	New York	NY	10036	212-922-1930	922-0674
Web: www.newamsterdamnyc.com					
Nightingale-Conant Corp 6245 W Howard St	Niles	IL	60714	847-647-0300	647-5989
TF Cust Svc: 800-323-3938 ■ *Web:* www.nightingale.com					
NTN Buzztime Inc 5966 La Pl Ct Suite 100	Carlsbad	CA	92008	760-438-7400	438-3505
AMEX: NTN ■ *TF:* 888-752-9686 ■ *Web:* www.buzztime.com					
Onstream Media Corp 1291 SW 29th Ave	Pompano Beach	FL	33069	954-917-6655	917-6660
NASDAQ: ONSM ■ *TF:* 877-932-3400 ■ *Web:* www.onstreammedia.com					
PRN Corp 600 Harrison St 4th Fl	San Francisco	CA	94107	415-808-3500	808-3535
Web: www.prn.com					
Questar Inc 680 N Lake Shore Dr Suite 900	Chicago	IL	60611	312-266-9400	266-9523
TF: 800-544-8422 ■ *Web:* www.questarhomevideo.com					
Veritech Corp 168 Denslow Rd	East Longmeadow	MA	01028	413-525-3368	525-7449
TF: 800-525-5912 ■ *Web:* www.veritechmedia.com					
Wabash Valley Broadcasting					
4555 W 16th St	Indianapolis	IN	46222	317-492-8770	492-8746
Web: www.imsproductions.tv					
Weston Woods Studios 143 Main St	Norwalk	CT	06851	203-845-0197	845-0498
TF: 800-243-5020 ■ *Web:* www.westonwoods.scholastic.com					
Zelo Productions Inc 3 S Newton St	Denver	CO	80219	303-936-8995	936-8995
Web: www.zeloproductions.com					
@radical.media 435 Hudson St 6th Fl	New York	NY	10014	212-462-1500	462-1600
Web: www.radicalmedia.com					

517 MOTION PICTURE & TELEVISION PRODUCTION

SEE ALSO Animation Companies p. 1396; Motion Picture Production - Special Interest p. 2256

				Phone	Fax
40 Acres & A Mule Filmworks Inc					
124 DeKalb Ave	Brooklyn	NY	11217	718-624-3703	624-2008
Web: www.40acres.com					
4Kids Productions Inc 53 W 23rd St 11th Fl	New York	NY	10010	212-590-2100	727-8933
Web: www.4kidsentertainmentinc.com					
Adm Productions Inc 40 Seaview Blvd	Port Washington	NY	11050	516-484-6900	621-2531
TF: 800-236-3425 ■ *Web:* www.admpro.com					
American Zoetrope 916 Kearny St	San Francisco	CA	94133	415-788-7500	989-7910
Web: www.zoetrope.com					
Apostle Pictures 568 Broadway Suite 301	New York	NY	10012	212-541-4323	541-4330
Web: www.apostlenyc.com					
Associated Television International					
4401 Wilshire Blvd	Los Angeles	CA	90010	323-556-5600	556-5610
Web: www.associatedtelevision.com					
Atlantic Video Inc					
650 Massachusetts Ave NW	Washington	DC	20001	202-408-0900	408-8496
Audio General Inc (AGI)					
1680 Republic Rd	Huntingdon Valley	PA	19006	267-288-0300	288-0301
Web: www.audiogeneral.com					
Audio Video Systems Inc					
14120 Sullyfield Cir	Chantilly	VA	20151	703-263-1002	263-0722
TF: 877-AVS-1175 ■ *Web:* www.avsinc.net					
Avatar Studios Inc 2675 Scott Ave Suite G	Saint Louis	MO	63103	314-533-2242	533-3349
TF: 800-737-6065 ■ *Web:* www.avatar-studios.com					
Big Deahl Productions Inc 1450 N Dayton St	Chicago	IL	60622	312-573-0733	573-6036
Web: www.bigdeahl.com					
Big Foot Productions Inc					
3709 36th Ave	Long Island City	NY	11101	718-729-1900	729-8638
Web: www.bigfootnyc.com					
Big Idea Inc 230 Franklin Rd Bldg 2A	Franklin	TN	37064	615-224-2200	224-2250
Web: www.bigidea.com					
BRC Imagination Arts 2711 Winona Ave	Burbank	CA	91504	818-841-8084	841-4996
Web: www.brcweb.com					
Brillstein Grey Entertainment					
9150 Wilshire Blvd Suite 350	Beverly Hills	CA	90212	310-275-6135	275-6180
Brooksfilms Ltd 9336 W Washington Blvd	Culver City	CA	90232	310-202-3292	202-3225
Bunim/Murray Productions					
6007 Sepulveda Blvd	Van Nuys	CA	91411	818-756-5150	756-5140
Web: www.bunim-murray.com					
CBS News 524 W 57th St	New York	NY	10019	212-975-4114	975-1893*
**Fax:* News Rm ■ *Web:* www.cbsnews.com					
CBS Studio Ctr 4024 Radford Ave	Studio City	CA	91604	818-655-5000	655-5409*
**Fax:* Mail Rm ■ *Web:* www.cbssc.com					
CBS Television Distribution					
2401 Colorado Ave Suite 110	Santa Monica	CA	90404	310-264-3300	264-3301
Web: www.cbstvd.com					
Center City Film & Video 1503 Walnut St	Philadelphia	PA	19102	215-568-4134	568-6011
Web: www.ccfv.com					
Chambers Productions 2975 Chad Dr	Eugene	OR	97408	541-485-5614	342-1568
Web: www.cmc.net/~chambers					
Chelsea Pictures Inc 33 Bond St # 1	New York	NY	10012	212-431-3434	431-0199
Web: www.chelsea.com					
Cheyenne Enterprises 406 Wilshire Blvd	Santa Monica	CA	90401	310-455-5000	688-8000
Chicago Story 401 W Superior St	Chicago	IL	60610	312-642-3173	642-3149
TF: 800-642-3173 ■ *Web:* www.thestorycompanies.com					
Chuck Fries Productions					
1880 Century Pk E Suite 213	Los Angeles	CA	90067	310-203-9520	203-9519
CKX Inc 650 Madison Ave	New York	NY	10022	212-838-3100	872-1473
NASDAQ: CKXE ■ *Web:* www.ir.ckx.com					
Columbia TriStar Motion Picture Group					
10202 W Washington Blvd	Culver City	CA	90232	310-244-4000	244-2626*
**Fax:* Mail Rm ■ *Web:* www.sonypictures.com/movies					
Culver Studios 9336 W Washington Blvd	Culver City	CA	90232	310-202-1234	
Web: www.theculverstudios.com					
Cutters Productions Inc					
8349 Arrowridge Blvd Suite K	Charlotte	NC	28273	704-522-9900	522-9925
TF: 800-332-8427 ■ *Web:* www.foryourhome.com					
David Naylor & Assoc Inc					
6535 Santa Monica Blvd	Los Angeles	CA	90038	323-463-2826	463-2535
Web: www.dnala.com					
Dick Clark Productions Inc					
2900 Olympic Blvd	Santa Monica	CA	90404	310-225-4600	
Web: www.dickclarkproductions.com					
Dimension Films 345 Hudson St 13th Fl	New York	NY	10014	646-862-3400	368-7000*
**Fax Area Code:* 917 ■ *Web:* www.weinsteinco.com					
Dreamworks Animation LLC 1000 Flower St	Glendale	CA	91201	818-695-5000	695-7574
NYSE: DWA ■ *Web:* www.dreamworks.com					
DreamWorks LLC 1000 Flower St	Glendale	CA	91201	818-695-5000	
Web: www.dreamworks.com					
Edmonds Entertainment					
1635 N Cahuenga Blvd 5th Fl	Los Angeles	CA	90028	323-860-1550	860-1554
Web: www.edmondsent.com					
Edward R Pressman Film Corp					
1639 11th St Suite 251	Santa Monica	CA	90404	310-450-9692	450-9705
Web: www.pressman.com					
El Dorado Pictures Inc					
725 Arizona Ave Suite 404	Santa Monica	CA	90401	310-458-4800	458-4802
Web: www.alecbaldwin.com					
EUE/Screen Gems Studios 222 E 44th St	New York	NY	10017	212-450-1600	867-4503
Web: www.screengemsstudios.com					
F & F Productions LLC 14333 Myerlake Cir	Clearwater	FL	33760	727-535-6776	535-6547
Web: www.fandfhd.tv					
Family Communications Inc 4802 5th Ave	Pittsburgh	PA	15213	412-687-2990	687-1226
Web: www.fci.org					
First Look Studios Inc					
2000 Avenue of the Stars Suite 410	Century City	CA	90067	424-202-5000	
Web: www.firstlookstudios.com					
Focus Features 65 Bleeker St 3rd Fl	New York	NY	10012	212-539-4000	539-4099
Web: www.focusfeatures.com					
Fortis Films					
8581 Santa Monica Blvd Suite 1	West Hollywood	CA	90069	310-659-4533	659-4373
Web: www.sandra.com/fortis.html					
Forward Entertainment					
9255 Sunset Blvd Suite 805	Los Angeles	CA	90069	310-278-6700	278-6770
Fox Filmed Entertainment (FFE)					
10201 W Pico Blvd	Los Angeles	CA	90035	310-369-1000	969-0468
Web: www.foxmovies.com					
Fox Searchlight Pictures					
10201 W Pico Blvd Bldg 38	Los Angeles	CA	90035	310-369-1000	
Web: www.foxsearchlight.com					
Fox Television Studios 10201 W Pico Blvd	Los Angeles	CA	90035	310-369-7069	969-5660
Web: www.fox.com					
Fujisankei Communications International Inc					
150 E 52nd St 34th Fl	New York	NY	10022	212-753-8100	688-0392
Web: www.fci-ny.com					

Company / Address	City	State	ZIP	Phone	Fax
Furthur Films					
100 Universal City Plaza					
Bldg 1320 Suite 1-C	Universal City	CA	91608	818-777-6700	866-1278
Gold Circle Films					
233 Wilshire Blvd Suite 650	Santa Monica	CA	90401	310-278-4800	278-0885
Web: www.goldcirclefilms.com					
Gracie Films					
10202 W Washington Blvd					
Sidney Poitier Bldg Suite 2221	Culver City	CA	90232	310-244-4000	244-1681
Web: www.graciefilms.com					
Guthy-Renker Corp					
41550 Eclectic St Suite 200	Palm Desert	CA	92260	760-773-9022	773-9016
TF: 800-321-4730 ■ *Web:* www.guthy-renker.com					
Harpo Films Inc					
345 N Maple Dr Suite 315	Beverly Hills	CA	90210	310-278-5559	278-6110
Harpo Productions Inc 110 N Carpenter	Chicago	IL	60607	312-633-1000	633-1976
Web: www.oprah.com					
HBO Movies 1100 Avenue of the Americas	New York	NY	10036	212-512-1000	
Web: www.hbo.com/movies/index.html					
Hearst Entertainment & Syndication Group					
300 W 57th St	New York	NY	10019	212-969-7553	
Web: www.hearst.com/entertainment/index.php					
Hearst Entertainment Productions Inc					
20335 Ventura Blvd Suite 300	Woodland Hills	CA	91364	818-444-5010	444-5011
HKM Productions Inc 1641 N Ivar Ave	Hollywood	CA	90028	323-465-9494	465-4203
Web: www.helloandcompany.com					
Icon Productions					
808 Wilshire Blvd 4th Fl	Santa Monica	CA	90401	310-434-7300	434-7377
Web: www.iconmovies.us					
Imagine Entertainment Inc					
9465 Wilshire Blvd 7th Fl	Beverly Hills	CA	90212	310-858-2000	858-2020
Web: www.imagine-entertainment.com					
Jerry Bruckheimer Films 1631 10th St	Santa Monica	CA	90404	310-664-6260	664-6261
Web: www.jbfilms.com					
Jerry Weintraub Productions					
4000 Warner Blvd Bungalow 1	Burbank	CA	91522	818-954-2500	954-1399
Jim Henson Pictures 1416 N LaBrea Ave	Hollywood	CA	90028	323-802-1500	802-1825
Web: www.henson.com					
John Wells Productions					
4000 Warner Blvd Bldg 1	Burbank	CA	91522	818-954-1687	954-3657
Jon Voight Entertainment					
10203 Santa Monica Blvd Suite 5	Los Angeles	CA	90067	310-843-0223	553-9895
Web: www.crystalsky.com					
JTN Productions					
13743 Ventura Blvd Suite 200	Sherman Oaks	CA	91423	818-789-5891	789-5892
Web: www.jtnproductions.com					
Kartemquin Films Ltd 1901 W Wellington Ave	Chicago	IL	60657	773-472-4366	472-3348
Web: www.kartemquin.com					
Levinson/Fontana Co 185 Broome St	New York	NY	10002	212-206-3585	206-3581
Web: www.levinson.com/index_lf.htm					
Lightstorm Entertainment					
919 Santa Monica Blvd	Santa Monica	CA	90401	310-656-6100	656-6102
Lions Gate Entertainment					
2700 Colorado Ave Suite 200	Marina del Rey	CA	90404	310-449-9200	255-3970
Web: www.lionsgate.com					
Lions Gate Entertainment Corp					
2700 Colorado Ave Suite 200	Santa Monica	CA	90404	310-449-9200	255-3870
NYSE: LGF ■ *TF:* 877-848-3866 ■ *Web:* www.lionsgate.com					
Lions Gate Entertainment Corp Lions Gate Television Div					
2700 Colorado Ave Suite 200	Santa Monica	CA	90404	310-449-9200	255-3870
TF: 800-424-7070 ■ *Web:* www.lionsgate.com					
LivePlanet Inc 2644 30th St	Santa Monica	CA	90405	310-664-2400	664-2401
Lucasfilm Ltd PO Box 29901	San Francisco	CA	94129	415-448-2000	
Web: www.lucasfilm.com					
Lucasfilm Ltd Animation					
1110 Gorgas St PO Box 29901	San Francisco	CA	94129	415-662-1800	
Web: www.lucasfilm.com					
Lyon Video Inc 1201 Olentangy River Rd	Columbus	OH	43212	614-297-0001	297-0002
Web: www.lyonvideo.com					
M80 Films					
1040 Las Palmas Ave Upper Bldg 5	Los Angeles	CA	90038	310-899-9100	860-5181*
**Fax Area Code:* 323					
Mandalay Pictures					
4751 Wilshire Blvd 3rd Fl	Los Angeles	CA	90010	323-549-4300	549-9824
Web: www.mandalay.com					
Metro-Goldwyn-Mayer Pictures					
10250 Constellation Blvd	Los Angeles	CA	90067	310-449-3000	449-3092*
**Fax:* Mktg ■ *Web:* www.mgm.com					
Metro-Goldwyn-Mayer Studios Inc (MGM)					
10250 Constellation Blvd	Los Angeles	CA	90067	310-449-3000	449-3092*
**Fax:* Mktg ■ *Web:* www.mgm.com					
MGM Domestic Television Distribution					
10250 Constellation Blvd	Los Angeles	CA	90067	310-449-3000	449-3092
Web: www.mgm.com/television.do					
MGM Pictures 10250 Constellation Blvd	Los Angeles	CA	90067	310-449-3000	449-3092
Web: www.mgm.com					
Mirage Enterprises					
9220 Sunset Blvd Suite 106	West Hollywood	CA	90069	310-888-2830	888-2825
Web: www.mirageenterprises.com					
Miramax Films Corp					
161 Avenue of the Americas	New York	NY	10013	917-606-5500	
Web: www.miramax.com					
MPCA 1333 2nd St	Santa Monica	CA	90401	310-319-9500	319-9501
Web: www.mpcafilm.com					
Mr Mudd 5225 Wilshire Blvd Suite 604	Los Angeles	CA	90036	323-932-5656	932-5666
National Lampoon Inc 8228 Sunset Blvd	Los Angeles	CA	90046	310-474-5252	474-1219
PINK: NLMP ■ *Web:* www.nationallampoon.com					
NBA Entertainment 450 Harmon Meadow Blvd	Secaucus	NJ	07094	201-865-1500	865-2626*
New Line Cinema Corp 888 7th Ave 19th Fl	New York	NY	10106	212-649-4900	649-4966
Web: www.newline.com					
NTV International Corp 645 5th Ave Suite 303	New York	NY	10022	212-489-8390	660-6998
Web: www.ntvic.com					
Overbrook Entertainment					
450 N Roxbury Dr 4th Fl	Beverly Hills	CA	90210	310-432-2400	432-2401
Paramount Pictures Corp 5555 Melrose Ave	Los Angeles	CA	90038	323-956-5000	862-4564
Web: www.paramount.com					
Peace Arch Entertainment Group Inc					
1867 Young St Suite 650	Toronto	ON	M4S1Y5	416-783-8383	487-6141
PINK: PAEGF ■ *Web:* www.peacearch.com					
Phoenix Pictures					
10202 W Washington Blvd Frankovich Bldg	Culver City	CA	90232	310-244-6100	839-8915
Web: www.phoenixpictures.com					
Picturehouse 597 5th Ave 4th Fl	New York	NY	10017	212-303-1700	421-1163
Web: www.picturehouse.com					
Playboy Entertainment Group Inc					
2706 Media Ctr Dr	Los Angeles	CA	90065	323-276-4000	276-4500
Web: www.playboy.com					
Raleigh Studios 1600 Rosecrans Ave	Manhattan Beach	CA	90266	310-727-2700	727-2710
Web: www.raleighstudios.com					
Red Hour Films 629 N La Brea Ave	Los Angeles	CA	90036	323-602-5000	602-5001
Regency Enterprises					
10201 W Pico Blvd Bldg 12	Los Angeles	CA	90035	310-369-8300	969-0470
Web: www.newregency.com					
Revelations Entertainment					
1221 2nd St 4th Fl	Santa Monica	CA	90401	310-394-3131	394-3133
Web: www.revelationsent.com					
Revolution Studios 2900 W Olympic Blvd	Santa Monica	CA	90404	310-255-7000	255-7001
Web: www.revolutionstudios.com					
RHI Entertainment LLC					
1325 Avenue of the Americas	New York	NY	10019	212-977-9001	977-9049
Web: www.rhitv.com					
Rush Communications Inc					
512 Fashion Ave # 4300	New York	NY	10018	212-840-9399	840-9390
Samuel Goldwyn Films LLC					
9570 W Pico Blvd Suite 400	Los Angeles	CA	90035	310-860-3100	860-3195
Web: www.samuelgoldwynfilms.com					
Saturn Films					
9000 Sunset Blvd Suite 911	West Hollywood	CA	90069	310-887-0900	248-2965
Web: www.saturnfilms.com					
Sesame Workshop 1 Lincoln Plaza	New York	NY	10023	212-595-3456	875-7359
Web: www.sesameworkshop.org					
Sid & Marty Krofft Pictures					
CBS Studio Ctr 4024 Radford Ave					
Bldg 5 Suite 102	Studio City	CA	91604	818-655-5314	655-8235
Sikelia Productions 110 W 57th St 5th Fl	New York	NY	10019	212-906-8800	906-8891
Sony Pictures Entertainment Inc					
10202 W Washington Blvd	Culver City	CA	90232	310-244-4000	244-2626
TF: 800-326-9551 ■ *Web:* www.sonypictures.com					
Sony Pictures Television					
10202 W Washington Blvd	Culver City	CA	90232	310-244-4000	244-2626
TF: 888-476-6972 ■ *Web:* www.sonypictures.com					
Sony Wonder 550 Madison Ave	New York	NY	10022	212-833-8100	833-5414
Web: www.sonywonder.com					
Sony/BMG Music Entertainment Video					
550 Madison Ave	New York	NY	10022	212-833-8000	833-4818
Web: www.sonymusicvideo.com					
Spyglass Entertainment Group					
10900 Wilshire Blvd 10th Fl	Los Angeles	CA	90024	310-443-5800	443-5912
Web: www.spyglassent.com					
Studio Canal US					
9259 Wilshire Blvd Suite 210	Beverly Hills	CA	90210	310-247-0994	
Touchstone Pictures 500 S Buena Vista St	Burbank	CA	91521	818-560-1000	
Web: www.touchstone.movies.go.com					
Touchstone Television Production LLC					
500 S Buena Vista St	Burbank	CA	91521	818-560-1000	
Web: www.disneyworld.com					
Tribeca Productions 375 Greenwich St 8th Fl	New York	NY	10013	212-941-4040	941-3997
Web: www.tribecafilm.com					
True Blue Productions PO Box 27127	Los Angeles	CA	90027	323-661-9191	661-9190
Twentieth Century Fox Film Corp					
10201 W Pico Blvd	Los Angeles	CA	90064	310-369-1000	969-0144
Web: www.foxmovies.com					
Twentieth Television					
2121 Avenue of the Stars 21st Fl	Los Angeles	CA	90067	310-369-3293	
United Artists Corp					
10250 Constellation Blvd	Los Angeles	CA	90067	310-449-3000	449-8857
Web: www.unitedartists.com					
United Artists Pictures Inc					
10250 Constellation Blvd	Los Angeles	CA	90067	310-449-3000	449-3028
Web: www.unitedartists.com					
Universal Pictures					
100 Universal City Plaza	Universal City	CA	91608	818-777-1000	
Web: www.universalpictures.com					
Universal Studios Inc					
100 Universal City Plaza	Universal City	CA	91608	818-777-1000	866-9459
Web: www.universalstudios.com					
Viacom Entertainment Group					
4555 Melrose Ave	Hollywood	CA	90038	323-956-5000	
Web: www.viacom.com					
Walt Disney Pictures 500 S Buena Vista St	Burbank	CA	91521	818-560-1000	843-5346
Web: www.disney.go.com/disneypictures					
Walt Disney Studio Entertainment					
500 S Buena Vista St	Burbank	CA	91521	818-560-1000	560-1930
Web: www.disney.go.com/disneypictures					
Warner Bros Entertainment 4000 Warner Blvd	Burbank	CA	91522	818-954-6000	
Web: www.warnerbros.com					
Warner Bros Television Production Inc					
4000 Warner Blvd	Burbank	CA	91522	818-954-6000	
Web: www2.warnerbros.com					
Warner Home Video 4000 Warner Blvd Bldg 168	Burbank	CA	91522	818-954-6000	
Web: www.wbshop.com					
Weinstein Co LLC The 345 Hudson St 13th Fl	New York	NY	10014	646-862-3400	368-7000*
**Fax Area Code:* 917 ■ *Web:* www.weinsteinco.com					

	City	State	Zip	Phone	Fax
White Hawk Pictures Inc 567 Bishopgate Ln *Web:* www.whitehawkpictures.com	Jacksonville	FL	32204	904-634-0500	359-9455
Winkler Films 211 S Beverly Dr Suite 200	Beverly Hills	CA	90212	310-858-5780	858-5799
Working Title Films 9720 Wilshire Blvd 4th Fl *Web:* www.workingtitlefilms.com	Beverly Hills	CA	90212	310-777-3100	777-5243
Worldwide Pants Inc 1697 Broadway *Web:* www.cbs.com/latesho	New York	NY	10019	212-975-5300	975-4780

MOTION PICTURE THEATERS

SEE Theaters - Motion Picture p. 2712

518 MOTOR SPEEDWAYS

	City	State	Zip	Phone	Fax
Ace Speedway 3401 Altamahaw Race Track Rd *Web:* www.acespeedway.com	Altamahaw	NC	27244	336-585-1200	585-1209
Adams County Speedway 12th & John St *Web:* www.acspeedway.com	Corning	IA	50841	641-322-5285	
All Star Speedway 176 Exeter Rd Rt 27 **Fax Area Code:* 978	Epping	NH	03042	603-679-5306	927-3182*
Antioch Speedway 1201 W 10th St *Web:* www.antiochspeedway.com	Antioch	CA	94509	925-779-9220	779-9213
Atco Raceway 1000 Jackson Rd *Web:* www.atcorace.com	Atco	NJ	08004	856-768-2167	753-9604
Atlanta Dragway 500 E Ridgeway Rd *Web:* www.atlantadragway.com	Commerce	GA	30529	706-335-2301	335-7135
Atlanta Motor Speedway PO Box 500 *TF:* 877-926-7849 ■ *Web:* www.atlantamotorspeedway.com	Hampton	GA	30228	770-946-4211	946-3928
Bandimere Speedway 3051 S Rooney Rd *TF:* 800-664-8946 ■ *Web:* www.bandimere.com	Morrison	CO	80465	303-697-6001	697-0815
Big Country Speedway 4820 S Greeley Hwy *Web:* www.bigcountryspeedway.com	Cheyenne	WY	82007	307-632-2107	
Bloomington Speedway 5185 S Fairfax Rd *Web:* www.bloomingtonspeedway.com	Bloomington	IN	47401	812-824-8753	824-7400
Bolivar Speedway USA PO Box 683 *Web:* www.bolivarspeedwayusa.com	Bolivar	MO	65613	417-326-3966	
Brainerd International Raceway 5523 Birchdale Rd *TF:* 866-444-4455 ■ *Web:* www.brainerdraceway.com	Brainerd	MN	56401	218-824-7220	824-7240
Bristol Motor Speedway 151 Speedway Blvd PO Box 3966 *Web:* www.bristolmotorspeedway.com	Bristol	TN	37620	423-764-1161	764-1646
California Speedway 9300 Cherry Ave *TF:* 800-944-7223 ■ *Web:* www.californiaspeedway.com	Fontana	CA	92335	909-429-5000	429-5500
Carolina Dragway 302 Dragstrip Rd *Web:* www.carolinadragway.com	Jackson	SC	29803	803-471-2285	266-4651
Chicagoland Speedway 500 Speedway Blvd *Web:* www.chicagolandspeedway.com	Joliet	IL	60433	815-727-7223	727-7895
Colorado National Speedway 4281 Weld County Rd 10 *Web:* www.coloradospeedway.com	ErieDacono	CO	80514	303-828-0116	828-2403
Columbus Motor Speedway Inc 1841 Williams Rd *Web:* www.columbusspeedway.com	Columbus	OH	43207	614-491-1047	491-6010
Concord Motorsport Park 7940 US Hwy 601 *Web:* www.concordmotorsportpark.com	Concord	NC	28025	704-782-4221	782-4420
Corpus Christi Speedway 241 Flato Rd *Web:* www.ccspeedway.org	Corpus Christi	TX	78405	361-289-8847	
Darlington Raceway 1301 Harry Bird Hwy **Fax Area Code:* 843 ■ *TF:* 866-459-7223 ■ *Web:* www.darlingtonraceway.com	Darlington	SC	29532	866-459-7223	395-8920*
Daytona International Speedway 1801 W International Speedway Blvd *Web:* www.daytonainternationalspeedway.com	Daytona Beach	FL	32114	386-254-2700	257-0281
Dubuque Fairgrounds Speedway 14569 Old Highway Rd *Web:* www.dbqfair.com	Dubuque	IA	52068	563-588-1406	744-3598
Eagle Raceway 617 S 238th St *Web:* www.eagleraceway.com	Eagle	NE	68347	402-238-2595	238-3768
El Paso Speedway Park 14751 Marina Ave *TF:* 800-658-9650 ■ *Web:* www.epspeedwaypark.com	El Paso	TX	79938	915-791-8749	
Elko Speedway 26350 France Ave *TF:* 800-479-3630 ■ *Web:* www.goelkospeedway.com	Elko	MN	55020	952-461-7223	461-3397
Evergreen Speedway 14405 179th Ave SE Bldg 305 *Web:* www.evergreenspeedway.com	Monroe	WA	98272	360-805-6100	805-6110
Florence Motor Speedway 836 E Smith St *Web:* www.florencemotorspeedway.com	Timmonsville	SC	29161	843-346-7711	346-4637
Gainesville Raceway 11211 N County Rd 225 *Web:* www.gainesvilleraceway.com	Gainesville	FL	32609	352-377-0046	371-4212
Gateway International Raceway 700 Raceway Blvd PO Box 200 *TF:* 866-357-7333 ■ *Web:* www.gatewayraceway.com	Madison	IL	62060	618-482-2400	482-3919
Grandview Speedway 43 Passmore Rd *Web:* www.grandviewspeedway.com	Bechtelsville	PA	19505	610-754-7688	754-6303
Greenville-Pickens Speedway 3800 Calhoun Memorial Hwy *Web:* www.greenvillepickens.com	Greenville	SC	29611	864-269-0852	269-7683
Hamilton County Speedway 1200 Bluff St *Web:* www.hamiltoncospeedway.com	Webster City	IA	50595	515-832-1443	832-6972
Heart O' Texas Speedway 203 Trailwood Ave *Web:* www.heartotexspeedway.com	Waco	TX	76712	254-829-2294	776-1576
Heartland Park Topeka 7530 SW Topeka Blvd *TF:* 800-437-2237 ■ *Web:* www.hpt.com	Topeka	KS	66619	785-862-4781	862-2016
Hickory Motor Speedway 3130 Hwy 70 SE *Web:* www.hickorymotorspeedway.com	Newton	NC	28658	828-464-3655	465-5017
Holland NASCAR Motorsports Complex 11586 Holland Glenwood Rd *Web:* www.hollandspeedway.com	Holland	NY	14080	716-537-2272	537-9749
Homestead-Miami Speedway 1 Speedway Blvd *Web:* www.homesteadmiamispeedway.com	Homestead	FL	33035	305-230-5000	230-5140
Houston Motorsports Park 11620 N Lake Houston Pkwy *Web:* www.houstonmotorsportspark.com	Houston	TX	77044	281-458-1972	458-2836
Houston Raceway Park 2525 FM 565 S *Web:* www.houstonraceway.com	Baytown	TX	77523	281-383-2666	383-3777
Huntsville Dragway 502 Quarter Mountain Rd *Web:* www.huntsvilledragway.com	Harvest	AL	35749	256-859-0807	859-9261
Infineon Raceway Hwy S 37 & 121 *TF:* 800-870-7223 ■ *Web:* www.infineonraceway.com	Sonoma	CA	95476	707-938-8448	938-8430
International Speedway Corp One Daytona Blvd *NASDAQ: ISCA* ■ *Web:* www.internationalspeedwaycorporation.com	Daytona Beach	FL	32114	386-254-2700	257-0281
Jennerstown Speedway 224 Race St PO Box 230 *Web:* www.jennerstown.com	Jennerstown	PA	15547	814-629-6677	629-6171
Kalamazoo Speedway 7656 Ravine Rd *Web:* www.kalamazoospeedway.com	Kalamazoo	MI	49009	269-349-3978	692-2848
Kentucky Speedway 4760 Sparta Pike *Web:* www.kentuckyspeedway.com	Sparta	KY	41086	859-567-3400	567-3441
Kil-Kare Speedway 1166 Dayton-Xenia Rd *Web:* www.kilkare.com	Xenia	OH	45385	937-429-2961	426-5049
Lacrosse Fairgrounds Speedway N 4985 County Hwy M PO Box 853 *Web:* www.lacrossespeedway.com	West Salem	WI	54669	608-786-1525	786-1524
Lake Ozark Speedway 50 Twiggy Ln *Web:* www.capitalspeedway.com	Eldon	MO	65049	573-392-5452	
Langley Speedway 11 Dale Lemonds Dr *Web:* www.langley-speedway.com	Hampton	VA	23666	757-865-7223	865-1147
Lanier International Speedway 1 Raceway Dr *Web:* www.lanierspeedway.com	Braselton	GA	30517	770-967-8600	967-4411
Las Vegas Motor Speedway 7000 Las Vegas Blvd N *TF:* 800-644-4444 ■ *Web:* www.lvms.com	Las Vegas	NV	89115	702-644-4444	632-8021
Lime Rock Park 60 White Hollow Rd *TF:* 800-722-3577 ■ *Web:* www.limerock.com	Lakeville	CT	06039	860-435-5000	435-5010
Los Angeles County Fairplex 1101 W McKinley Ave *Web:* www.fairplex.com	Pomona	CA	91768	909-623-3111	865-3602
Lubbock Motor Speedway 114th & Martin Luther King Blvd *Web:* www.lubbockmotorspeedway.com	Lubbock	TX	79404	806-748-0750	863-2188
Magic Valley Speedway 3389 N 2800 E *Web:* www.magicvalleyspeedway.com	Twin Falls	ID	83301	208-734-3700	732-5559
Mansfield Motorsports Speedway 100 Crall Rd *Web:* www.mansfield-speedway.com	Mansfield	OH	44903	419-525-7223	524-0187
Maple Grove Raceway 30 Stauffer Pk Ln *Web:* www.maplegroveraceway.com	Mohnton	PA	19540	610-856-7812	856-1601
Marion County International Raceway 2303 Richwood-LaRue Rd *TF:* 800-422-6247 ■ *Web:* www.mcir.com	La Rue	OH	43332	740-499-3666	499-2185
Martinsville Speedway 340 Speedway Rd *Web:* www.martinsvillespeedway.com	Martinsville	VA	24112	276-956-3151	956-1298
Michigan International Speedway 12626 US 12 *TF:* 800-354-1010 ■ *Web:* www.mispeedway.com	Brooklyn	MI	49230	517-592-6666	592-3848
Mid-Ohio Sports Car Course 7721 Steam Corners Rd PO Box 3108 *TF:* 800-643-6446 ■ *Web:* www.midohio.com	Lexington	OH	44904	419-884-4000	884-0042
Midway Speedway 20377 Silver Dr *Web:* www.lebanonmidwayspeedway.com	Lebanon	MO	65536	417-588-4430	533-3203
Milwaukee Mile 640 S 84th St *Web:* www.milwaukeemile.com	West Allis	WI	53214	414-453-8277	266-7102
Monett Speedway 685 Chapel Dr *Web:* www.monettspeedway.com	Monett	MO	65708	417-732-2766	732-5979
Motordrome Speedway 164 Motordrome Rd *Web:* www.motordrome.com	Smithton	PA	15479	724-872-7555	872-7695
Myrtle Beach Speedway 455 Hospitality Ln *Web:* www.myrtlebeachspeedway.com	Myrtle Beach	SC	29579	843-236-0500	236-0525
New Hampshire International Speedway 1122 Rt 106N *Web:* www.nhmf.com	Loudon	NH	03307	603-783-4744	783-9691
New York International Raceway Park 2011 New Rd PO Box 296 *Web:* www.nyirp.com	Leicester	NY	14481	585-382-3030	382-9061
Ocean Speedway 4400 Auto Plaza Rd *Web:* www.oceanspeedway.com	Capitola	CA	95010	831-476-9466	464-2420
Oglethorpe Speedway Park 200 Jesup Rd PO Box 687 *Web:* www.ospracing.net	Pooler	GA	31322	912-964-8200	964-9501
Old Bridge Township Raceway Park 230 Pension Rd *Web:* www.etownraceway.com	Englishtown	NJ	07726	732-446-7800	446-1373
Old Dominion Speedway 10611 Dumfries Rd *Web:* www.olddominionspeedway.com	Manassas	VA	20112	703-361-7223	361-8796
Orange Show Speedway 689 S E St *Web:* www.orangeshowspeedway.net	San Bernardino	CA	92408	909-888-6788	889-7666
Oxford Plains Speedway 877 Main St PO Box 208 *Web:* www.oxfordplains.com	Oxford	ME	04270	207-539-8865	539-8860
Park Jefferson Speedway 48380 Co Rd 1b **Fax Area Code:* 402 ■ *Web:* www.parkjeffersonspeedway.com	Jefferson	SD	57038	605-966-5517	494-1893*
Peoria Speedway 3520 W Farmington Rd *Web:* www.peoriaspeedway.com	Peoria	IL	61604	309-357-3339	486-3620
Pocono Raceway Long Pond Rd PO Box 500 *TF:* 800-722-3929 ■ *Web:* www.poconoraceway.com	Long Pond	PA	18334	570-646-2300	646-2010
Proctor Speedway 800 N Boundary Ave *Web:* www.proctorspeedway.com	Proctor	MN	55810	218-624-0606	
Quincy Raceways 8000 Broadway St *Web:* www.quincyraceways.com	Quincy	IL	62305	217-224-3843	224-3859
Riverhead Raceway PO Box 148 *Web:* www.riverheadraceway.com	Lindenhurst	NY	11757	631-842-7223	789-1160

	City	State	ZIP	Phone	Fax
Road America N 7390 Hwy 67	Elkhart Lake	WI	53020	920-892-4576	892-4550
TF: 800-365-7223 ■ *Web:* www.roadamerica.com					
Road Atlanta Raceway 5300 Winder Hwy	Braselton	GA	30517	770-967-6143	967-2668
TF: 800-849-7223 ■ *Web:* www.roadatlanta.com					
Rockingham Dragway 2153 Hwy US 1 N PO Box 70	Rockingham	NC	28379	910-582-3400	582-8667
Web: www.rockinghamdragway.com					
San Antonio Speedway 14901 State Hwy 16 S	San Antonio	TX	78264	210-628-1499	628-6760
Sandusky Speedway 614 W Perkins Ave	Sandusky	OH	44870	419-625-4084	625-8110
Web: www.sanduskyspeedway.com					
Saugus Speedway 22500 Soledad Canyon Rd	Saugus	CA	91350	661-259-3886	259-8534
Web: www.saugusspeedway.com					
Sebring International Raceway 113 Midway Dr	Sebring	FL	33870	863-655-1442	655-1777
Web: www.sebringraceway.com					
South Boston Speedway 1188 James D Hagood Hwy PO Box 1066	South Boston	VA	24592	434-572-4947	575-8992
TF: 877-440-1540 ■ *Web:* www.southbostonspeedway.com					
South Sound Speedway 3730 183rd Ave SW	Rochester	WA	98579	360-273-6420	273-8113
Web: www.southsoundspeedway.com					
Southen New Mexico Speedway Inc 12100 Robert Larson Blvd	Las Cruces	NM	88007	575-524-7913	541-6398
TF: 800-658-9650 ■ *Web:* www.snmspeedway.com					
Stafford Motor Speedway 55 W St PO Box 105	Stafford Springs	CT	06076	860-684-2783	684-6236
Web: www.staffordspeedway.com					
Summit Motorsports Park 1300 Ohio 18	Norwalk	OH	44857	419-668-5555	663-0502
Web: www.summitmotorsportspark.com					
Superior Speedway 4700 Tower Ave	Superior	WI	54880	715-394-7848	394-7025
Web: www.superiorspeedway.com					
Texas Motorplex 7500 W Hwy 287	Ennis	TX	75119	972-878-2641	878-1848
TF: 800-668-6775 ■ *Web:* www.texasmotorplex.com					
Thompson Speedway 205 E Thompson Rd PO Box 278	Thompson	CT	06277	860-923-2280	923-2398
Web: www.thompsonspeedway.com					
Tucson Raceway Park 11955 S Harison Rd Pima County Fairgrounds	Tucson	AZ	85747	520-762-9200	762-5053
Web: www.tucsonracewaypark.com					
Viking Speedway 700 Cedar St # 231	Alexandria	MN	56308	320-762-1559	
Web: www.vikingspeedway.net					
Volusia Speedway Park 1500 E Hwy 40	De Leon Springs	FL	32130	386-985-4402	985-6258
Web: thevolusiaspeedway.com					
Watkins Glen International Inc 2790 CR 16	Watkins Glen	NY	14891	607-535-2486	535-8918
Web: www.theglen.com					
Wenatchee Valley Super Oval (WVSO) PO Box 2445	Wenatchee	WA	98807	509-884-8592	884-9712
Web: www.wvso.com					
West Liberty Raceway 101 N Clay St PO Box 261	West Liberty	IA	52776	319-627-2414	627-2299
Winchester Speedway 2656 W State Rd 32 PO Box 31	Winchester	IN	47394	765-584-9701	584-8111
Web: www.winchesterspeedway.com					

519 MOTOR VEHICLES - COMMERCIAL & SPECIAL PURPOSE

SEE ALSO All-Terrain Vehicles p. 1394; Automobiles - Mfr p. 1496; Campers, Travel Trailers, Motor Homes p. 1553; Motorcycles & Motorcycle Parts & Accessories p. 2263; Snowmobiles p. 2658; Weapons & Ordnance (Military) p. 2773

	City	State	ZIP	Phone	Fax
A.r.e. Inc PO Box 1100	Massillon	OH	44648	330-359-5450	730-4545
Web: www.4are.com					
Accubuilt Inc 2550 Central Pt Pkwy	Lima	OH	45804	419-222-1501	222-4450
Web: www.accubuilt.com					
Allianz Sweeper Co 1690 Eiffel St	Boucherville	QC	J4B7W1	450-616-8100	616-8103
TF: 800-862-3822 ■ *Web:* www.allianzsweeper.com					
Allied Body Works Inc 625 S 96th St	Seattle	WA	98108	206-763-7811	763-8836
TF: 800-733-7450 ■ *Web:* www.alliedbody.com					
Altec Industries Inc 210 Inverness Ctr Dr	Birmingham	AL	35242	205-991-7733	991-9993
Web: www.altec.com					
American LaFrance Aerials Inc 64 Cocalico Creek Rd	Ephrata	PA	17522	717-859-1176	859-2774
Web: www.americanlafrance.com/Products/Aerials					
American LaFrance Corp 1090 newtonway	summerville	SC	29456	843-486-7400	486-7400
TF Cust Svc: 888-253-8725 ■ *Web:* www.americanlafrance.com					
Arrow Truck Bodies & Equipment Inc 1639 S Campus St	Ontario	CA	91761	909-947-3991	947-4932
Art Moehn Chevrolet 2200 Seymour Rd	Jackson	MI	49201	517-879-4394	787-6137
Web: www.artmoehnchevy.com					
Auto Crane Co PO Box 580697	Tulsa	OK	74158	918-836-0463	834-5979
Web: www.autocrane.com					
Auto Truck Inc 1200 N Ellis St	Bensenville	IL	60106	630-860-5600	860-5631
TF: 877-284-4440 ■ *Web:* www.autotruck.com					
Benson International Inc Rt 14 S PO Box 970	Mineral Wells	WV	26150	304-489-9020	489-2828
TF: 877-489-9020 ■ *Web:* www.bensonintl.com					
Berrien Buggy Inc 10644 US Hwy 31	Berrien Springs	MI	49103	269-471-1411	
Web: www.berrienbuggy.com					
Bianchi Motors Inc 8430 Peach St PO Box 3086	Erie	PA	16508	814-868-9678	866-2921
TF: 866-979-8132 ■ *Web:* www.bianchi-motors.com					
Bill Jacobs Joliet 2101 LLC 2001 W Jefferson St	Joliet	IL	60435	815-725-7110	725-0801
TF: 866-301-2106 ■ *Web:* www.billjacobsjoliet.com					
Blue Bird Corp 402 Blue Bird Blvd	Fort Valley	GA	31030	478-825-2021	822-2457
TF: 800-486-7122 ■ *Web:* www.blue-bird.com					
Bob Ross Dealerships The 85 Loop Rd	Centerville	OH	45459	937-401-2037	428-4083
Web: www.bobrossauto.com					
Bobcat Co 250 E Beaton Dr	West Fargo	ND	58078	701-241-8700	241-8704
Web: www.bobcat.com					
BrandFX Body Co 2800 Golden Triangle Blvd	Fort Worth	TX	76177	817-431-1131	306-7649
TF: 866-431-1131 ■ *Web:* www.brandfxbody.com					
Bristol-Donald Co Inc 50 Roanoke Ave	Newark	NJ	07105	973-589-2640	589-2610
Web: www.bristoldonald.com					
Brumbaugh Body Co Inc RR 5 PO Box 579	Duncansville	PA	16635	814-696-9552	696-8640
Capacity of Texas Inc 401 Capacity Dr	Longview	TX	75604	903-759-0610	759-3209
TF: 800-323-0135 ■ *Web:* www.capacitytexas.com					
Carnegie Body Co 9500 Brookpark Rd	Cleveland	OH	44129	216-749-5000	749-5740
TF: 800-362-1989 ■ *Web:* www.carnegiebody.com					
Champion Bus Inc 331 Graham Rd	Imlay City	MI	48444	810-724-6474	724-1844*
**Fax:* Mktg ■ *TF:* 800-776-4943 ■ *Web:* www.championbus.com					
Chance Rides Mfg Inc 4200 W Walker St	Wichita	KS	67209	316-942-7411	942-7416
TF: 800-242-6231 ■ *Web:* www.rides.com					
Club Car Inc PO Box 204658	Augusta	GA	30917	706-863-3000	860-7231
TF: 800-227-0739 ■ *Web:* www.clubcar.com					
Coach & Equipment Mfg Corp 130 Horizon Pk Dr PO Box 36	Penn Yan	NY	14527	315-536-2321	
Web: www.coach-equipment.com					
Columbia ParCar Corp 1115 Commercial Ave	Reedsburg	WI	53959	608-524-8888	524-8380
TF: 800-222-4653 ■ *Web:* www.parcar.com					
Courtesy Chevrolet Ctr 750 Camino Del Rio N	San Diego	CA	92108	619-297-4321	297-3961
TF: 888-778-2877 ■ *Web:* www.courtesysandiego.com					
Crane Carrier Co 1925 N Sheridan Rd	Tulsa	OK	74115	918-836-1651	832-7348
Web: www.cranecarrier.com					
Curtis Tractor Cab Inc 111 Higgins St	Worcester	MA	01606	508-853-2200	854-3190
TF: 800-343-7676 ■ *Web:* www.curtisintl.com					
Dealers Truck Equipment Co 2460 Midway St	Shreveport	LA	71108	318-635-7567	635-3144
TF: 800-259-7569 ■ *Web:* www.dealerstruck.com					
Delphi Body Works Inc 313 S Washington St	Delphi	IN	46923	765-564-2212	564-4255
Web: www.delphibodyworks.com					
Delta-Waseca Inc 5200 Willson Rd Suite 307	Minneapolis	MN	55424	952-922-5569	922-1195
Web: www.deltawaseca.com					
Diamond Coach Corp 2300 W 4th St PO Box 489	Oswego	KS	67356	620-795-2191	795-2191
TF: 800-442-4645 ■ *Web:* www.diamondcoach.com					
Dick Gores Rv World 14590 Duval Pl W	Jacksonville	FL	32218	904-741-5100	741-6682
TF: 800-635-7008 ■ *Web:* www.dickgoresrvworld.com					
Douglass Truck Bodies Inc 231 21st St	Bakersfield	CA	93301	661-327-0258	327-3894
TF: 800-635-7641 ■ *Web:* www.douglasstruckbodies.com					
E-ONE Inc 1601 SW 37th Ave	Ocala	FL	34474	352-237-1122	237-1151
Web: www.e-one.com					
E-Z-GO 2421 Old Savannah Rd	Augusta	GA	30906	706-798-4311	771-4605
Web: www.ezgo.com					
Ebus Inc 9250 Washburn Rd	Downey	CA	90242	562-904-3474	904-3468
Web: www.ebus.com					
Electric Golf Car Co 1022 Douglas Blvd	Roseville	CA	95678	916-773-2244	773-6829
TF: 800-700-8857					
Elgin Sweeper Co 1300 W Bartlett Rd	Elgin	IL	60120	847-741-5370	742-3035
Web: www.elginsweeper.com					
Elliott Machine Works Inc 1351 Freese Works Pl	Galion	OH	44833	419-468-4709	468-4642
TF: 800-299-0412 ■ *Web:* www.elliottmachine.com					
Erie Vehicle Co 60 E 51st St	Chicago	IL	60615	773-536-6300	536-6300
TF: 888-550-3743					
Ewing Automotive Group 4464 W Plano Pkwy	Plano	TX	75093	972-964-7400	
TF: 866-973-3074 ■ *Web:* www.thinkewing.com					
Fisher Engineering 50 Gordon Dr PO Box 529	Rockland	ME	04841	207-701-4200	701-4313*
**Fax:* Hum Res ■ *Web:* www.fisherplows.com					
Fleet Engineers Inc 1800 E Keating Ave	Muskegon	MI	49442	231-777-2537	777-2720
TF Cust Svc: 800-333-7890 ■ *Web:* www.fleetengineers.com					
Fleet Equipment Corp 567 Commerce St	Franklin Lakes	NJ	07417	201-337-7332	337-3294
Web: www.fectrucks.com					
Florig Equipment Inc 904 W Ridge Pike	Conshohocken	PA	19428	610-825-0900	825-0909
Web: www.florig.com					
Fontaine Modification Co 9827 Mt Holly Rd	Charlotte	NC	28214	704-392-8502	391-1671
TF: 800-366-8246 ■ *Web:* www.fontainemod.com					
Fontaine Truck Equipment Co 2490 Pinson Valley Pkwy	Birmingham	AL	35217	205-841-8582	849-9615
TF: 800-824-3033 ■ *Web:* www.fontaine.com					
Ford of Ocala Inc 2816 NW Pine Ave	Ocala	FL	34475	352-732-4800	629-2666
TF: 888-255-1788 ■ *Web:* www.fordofocala.com					
Frank J Zamboni & Co Inc 15714 Colorado Ave	Paramount	CA	90723	562-633-0751	633-9365
Web: www.zamboni.com					
Frank Motors Hyundai 3150 National City Blvd	National City	CA	91950	619-245-4137	336-6159
Web: www.frankhyundai.com					
Gary Mathews Motors Inc 1100 Ashland City Rd	Clarksville	TN	37040	931-552-7100	572-3163
Web: www.garymathewsmotors.com					
Gehl Co 1 Gehl Way	West Bend	WI	53095	262-334-9461	338-7517
Web: www.gehl.com					
General Body Mfg Co 7110 Jensen Dr	Houston	TX	77093	713-692-5177	692-0700
TF: 800-395-8585 ■ *Web:* www.generalbody.com					
General Motors Corp (GMC) 100 Renaissance Ctr	Detroit	MI	48265	313-556-5000	696-7300*
NYSE: GM ■ **Fax Area Code:* 248 ■ *Web:* www.gm.com					
General Safety Equipment Corp 5181 260th St	Wyoming	MN	55092	651-462-1000	462-1700
George Heiser Body Co Inc 11210 Tukwila International Blvd	Seattle	WA	98168	206-622-7985	622-7135
Gillig Corp 25800 Clawiter Rd	Hayward	CA	94545	510-785-1500	785-6819
TF: 800-735-1500 ■ *Web:* www.gillig.com					
Gowans-Knight Co Inc 49 Knight St	Watertown	CT	06795	860-274-8801	274-7937
TF: 800-352-4871 ■ *Web:* www.gowansknight.com					
Graham Chevrolet Co Inc 1515 W Fourth St	Mansfield	OH	44906	419-529-1800	529-1859
Web: www.grahamautomall.com					
Hackney & Sons Inc 911 W 5th St	Washington	NC	27889	252-946-6521	975-8340
TF: 800-763-0700 ■ *Web:* www.hackneyandsons.com					

Company / Address	City	State	Zip	Phone	Fax
Heil Environmental Industries Ltd 5751 Cornelison Rd Bldg B *TF:* 800-824-4345 ■ *Web:* www.heil.com	Chattanooga	TN	37411	423-899-9100	855-3478
Hercules Mfg Co 800 Bob Posey St *TF:* 800-633-3031 ■ *Web:* www.herculesvanbodies.com	Henderson	KY	42420	270-826-9501	826-0439
Hi-Lex America Inc 5200 Wayne Rd *Web:* www.hi-lex.com	Battle Creek	MI	49037	269-968-0781	968-0885
HME Inc 1950 Byron Ctr Ave *Web:* www.hmetruck.com	Wyoming	MI	49519	616-534-1463	534-1967
Holiday Automotive 321 N Rolling Meadows Dr *Web:* www.holidayautomotive.com	Fond Du Lac	WI	54937	920-921-8898	923-8454
Honda of Tiffany Springs 9200 NW Prairie View Rd *Web:* www.hondaoftiffanysprings.com	Kansas City	MO	64153	816-452-7000	452-2651
IC Bus LLC 4201 Winfield Rd *TF:* 800-892-7761 ■ *Web:* www.icbus.com	Warrenville	IL	60555	800-892-7761	
International Truck & Engine Corp *Navistar Inc* 4201 Winfield Rd *TF:* 800-448-7825 ■ *Web:* www.navistar.com	Warrenville	IL	60555	630-753-5000	753-6888
Jackson Volvo 704 Ala Moana Blvd *Web:* www.jacksonautogroup.com	Honolulu	HI	96813	808-521-5151	440-1578
Jim Brown Chevrolet Inc 6877 Ctr St	Mentor	OH	44061	440-255-5511	255-5511
Johnson Refrigerated Truck Bodies 215 E Allen St *TF Sales:* 800-922-8360 ■ *Web:* www.johnsontruckbodies.com	Rice Lake	WI	54868	715-234-7071	234-4628
Joyce Koons Buick Gmc 10660 Automotive Dr *TF:* 866-207-1790 ■ *Web:* joycekoonsbuickgmc.com	Manassas	VA	20109	703-631-9500	366-1070
Kann Mfg Corp PO Box 400 *Web:* www.kannmfg.com	Guttenberg	IA	52052	563-252-2035	252-3069
Kassbohrer All Terrain Vehicles Inc 750a S Rock Blvd *Web:* www.katvpb.com	Reno	NV	89502	775-857-5000	857-5010
Kenworth Truck Co 10630 NE 38th Pl *Web:* www.kenworth.com	Kirkland	WA	98033	425-828-5000	828-5088
Kesler-Schaefer Auto Auction Inc 5333 W 46th St PO Box 53203 *Web:* www.ksaa1.com	Indianapolis	IN	46254	317-297-2300	297-6234
Keystone Chevrolet Inc 8700 Charles Page Blvd *Web:* www.keystonechevrolet.com	Sand Springs	OK	74063	918-245-2201	245-5820
Kidron Inc 13442 Emerson Rd *TF:* 800-321-5421 ■ *Web:* www.kidron.com	Kidron	OH	44636	330-857-3011	857-8451
KME Fire Apparatus 68 Sicker Rd *TF:* 800-394-5593 ■ *Web:* www.kovatch.com	Latham	NY	12110	518-785-0900	785-1794
Knapheide Mfg Co 1848 Westphalia Strasse PO Box 7140 *Web:* www.knapheide.com	Quincy	IL	62305	217-222-7131	222-5939
Labrie Environmental Group 175 du Pont *TF:* 800-463-6638 ■ *Web:* www.labriegroup.com	Saint-Nicolas	QC	G7A2T5	418-831-8250	831-5255
Laird Noller Ford Inc 2245 SW Topeka Blvd *Web:* www.nollerford.com	Topeka	KS	66611	785-235-9211	232-7766
Landers Toyota 10825 Colonel Glenn Rd *TF:* 888-364-4029 ■ *Web:* www.landerstoyota.com	Little Rock	AR	72204	501-570-0678	
Landmark Ford Inc 12000 SW 66th Ave PO Box 23970 *Web:* www.landmarkford.com	Tigard	OR	97223	503-639-1131	598-8350
Lang Chevrolet Co The 635 S Orchard Ln *Web:* www.langs.com	Beavercreek	OH	45434	937-372-3551	427-1655
Le Jeune Investment Inc 9393 Wayzata Blvd *Web:* www.liinc.net	Minneapolis	MN	55426	763-744-9100	744-9134
Leson Chevrolet Co Inc 1501 Westbank Express *Web:* www.lesonchevy.com	Harvey	LA	70058	504-366-4381	362-2135
Liberty Toyota Scion 4397 Rt 130 S *TF:* 888-809-7798 ■ *Web:* www.libertytoyota.com	Burlington	NJ	08016	609-386-6300	387-8385
Libertyville Chevrolet Inc 1001 S Milwaukee Ave *TF Sales:* 888-445-8801 ■ *Web:* www.libertyvillechevrolet.com	Libertyville	IL	60048	847-362-1400	
Lodal Inc 620 N Hooper St PO Box 2315 **Fax:* Orders ■ *TF:* 800-435-3500 ■ *Web:* www.lodal.com	Kingsford	MI	49802	906-779-1700	779-1160*
Loren Berg Chevrolet Inc 2700 Portland Rd *Web:* www.lorenberg.com	Newberg	OR	97132	503-476-3309	537-0747
Loren Hyundai Inc 1620 Waukegan Rd **Fax Area Code:* 847 ■ *Web:* www.lorenautogroup.com	Glenview	IL	60025	224-766-7189	724-8429*
Lumberton Honda Mitsubishi Inc 301 Wintergreen Dr *Web:* www.lumbertonhonda.com	Lumberton	NC	28358	910-739-9871	739-5214
Luther Brookdale Chevrolet 6701 Brooklyn Blvd *TF:* 800-716-1271 ■ *Web:* www.itenchev.com	Brooklyn Center	MN	55429	800-716-1271	
LZ Truck Equipment Co Inc 1881 Rice St *TF:* 800-247-1082 ■ *Web:* www.lztruckequipment.com	Roseville	MN	55113	651-488-2571	488-9857
M K Smith Chevrolet 12845 Central Ave PO Box 455 *Web:* www.mksmithchevrolet.com	Chino	CA	91710	909-239-4751	628-6637
M. H. Eby Inc PO Box 127 *TF:* 800-292-4752 ■ *Web:* www.mheby.com	Blue Ball	PA	17506	717-354-4971	355-2114
Mack Trucks Inc 2100 Mack Blvd **Fax:* Mail Rm ■ *TF:* 866-298-6586 ■ *Web:* www.macktrucks.com	Allentown	PA	18103	610-709-3011	709-2405*
Maple Shade Mazda 2921 Rt 73 S *Web:* www.msmazda.com	Maple Shade	NJ	08052	856-667-8004	667-8710
Marion Body Works Inc 211 W Ramsdell St PO Box 500 *Web:* www.marionbody.com	Marion	WI	54950	715-754-5261	754-5776
Martin Chevrolet 23505 Hawthorne Blvd *Web:* www.martinchevrolet.com	Torrance	CA	90505	310-378-0211	378-2011
Martin Chevrolet Sales Inc 8800 Gratiot Rd *Web:* www.martincars.com	Saginaw	MI	48609	989-781-4590	781-1722
Matt Castrucci Auto Mall of Dayton 3013 Mall Pk Dr *TF:* 877-321-5065 ■ *Web:* www.mattcastrucciautomall.com	Dayton	OH	45459	877-321-5065	
Matthews-Hargreaves Chevrolet Co 2000 E12 Mile Rd *Web:* www.mhchevy.com	Royal Oak	MI	48067	248-398-8800	548-4952
Mayflower Vehicle System 55 N Garfield St	Norwalk	OH	44857	419-668-8132	668-1096
Mc Clinton Chevrolet Co 712 Liberty St *Web:* www.mcclintonchevrolet.com	Parkersburg	WV	26101	304-699-2478	485-8197
Mc Dermott Auto Group 655 Main St *Web:* www.mcdermottauto.com	East Haven	CT	06512	203-466-1000	466-1999
Mc-Coy-Mills 700 W Commonwealth *TF Sales:* 888-640-9266 ■ *Web:* www.mccoymillsford.com	Fullerton	CA	92832	714-526-5501	992-5447
McCluskey Chevrolet Inc 9673 Kings Automall Dr *Web:* www.mccluskeychevrolet.com	Cincinnati	OH	45249	513-761-1111	679-9130
McDaniel Motor CO 1111 Mt Vernon Ave *Web:* www.mcdanielauto.com	Marion	OH	43302	740-389-2355	389-4207
McGuire Cadillac Inc 910 Rt 1-9 N *Web:* www.mcguirecadillac.com	Woodbridge	NJ	07095	732-326-0300	326-0385
McLaughlin Body Co 2430 River Dr *Web:* www.mclbody.com	Moline	IL	61265	309-762-7755	762-7807
McNamara Motors Inc 13 Labombard Rd *Web:* www.millerautogroup.com	West Lebanon	NH	03766	603-448-7002	443-9905
McNeilus Cos Inc 524 County Rd 34 E PO Box 70 *Web:* www.mcneiluscompanies.com	Dodge Center	MN	55927	507-374-6321	374-6394
Medical Coaches Inc 399 County Hwy 58 *TF:* 800-432-1339 ■ *Web:* www.medcoach.com	Oneonta	NY	13820	607-432-1333	432-8190
Mel Rapton Inc 3630 Fulton Ave *Web:* www.melraptonhonda.com	Sacramento	CA	95821	916-482-5400	488-8739
Mercedes-Benz Of Cincinnati 8727 Montgomery Rd *Web:* www.cincinnati.mercedescenter.com	Cincinnati	OH	45236	513-984-9000	984-9468
Mercedes-Benz USA LLC 11950 Bellevue Redmond Rd *Web:* www.bellevue.mercedesdealer.com	Bellevue	WA	98005	425-455-8535	637-5586
Metro Truck Body Inc 1201 W Jon St *Web:* www.metrotruckbody.com	Torrance	CA	90502	310-532-5570	532-0754
Meyer Truck Equipment Inc 196 State Rd 56 *TF:* 800-456-3451 ■ *Web:* www.meyertruckeq.com	Jasper	IN	47546	812-695-3451	695-3397
Mickey Truck Bodies Inc 1305 Trinity Ave PO Box 2044 *TF:* 800-334-9061 ■ *Web:* www.mickeybody.com	High Point	NC	27261	336-882-6806	882-6856
Mike Castrucci Ford Sales Inc 1020 SR- 28 *Web:* www.mikecastrucciford.com	Milford	OH	45150	513-831-7010	831-9620
Millennium Transit Services LLC 42 Earl Cummings Loop W *Web:* www.millenniumtransit.com	Roswell	NM	88201	505-347-7500	347-7504
Miller Industries Inc 8503 Hilltop Dr *NYSE: MLR* ■ *TF:* 800-292-0330 ■ *Web:* www.millerind.com	Ooltewah	TN	37363	423-238-4171	238-5371
Momentum Bmw Ltd 10002 SW Fwy **Fax Area Code:* 713 ■ *TF:* 800-731-8114 ■ *Web:* www.momentumbmw5.avxtrk.net	Houston	TX	77074	800-731-8114	596-3210*
Monroe Truck Equipment Inc 1051 W 7th St *TF:* 800-356-8134 ■ *Web:* www.monroetruck.com	Monroe	WI	53566	608-328-8127	328-4278
Morgan Corp 111 Morgan Way PO Box 588 *TF:* 800-666-7426 ■ *Web:* www.morgancorp.com	Morgantown	PA	19543	610-286-5025	286-2226
Morgan Olson Corp 1801 S Nottawa Rd *TF:* 800-624-9005 ■ *Web:* www.morganolson.com	Sturgis	MI	49091	800-233-4823	385-7039
Morse Operations Inc 3790 W Blue Herron Blvd *Web:* www.edmorsehonda.com	Riviera Beach	FL	33404	561-844-5700	
Motor Coach Industries International Co 1700 E Golf Rd Suite 300 *TF:* 800-743-3624 ■ *Web:* www.mcicoach.com	Schaumburg	IL	60173	847-285-2000	285-2066
Murrays Ford Inc 3007 Blinker Pkwy *TF:* 800-371-6601 ■ *Web:* murraysford.dealerconnection.com	Du Bois	PA	15801	814-371-6600	371-6776
Nacarato GMC Truck Inc 111 Polk Ave *Web:* www.nacaratotrucks.com	Nashville	TN	37120	615-259-9500	255-1473
Nash Chevrolet Co 630 Scenic Hwy **Fax Area Code:* 770 ■ *Web:* www.nashchevy.com	Lawrenceville	GA	30046	678-317-2797	822-6668*
Newby Buick Gmc Inc 1629 S Convention Ctr Dr *Web:* www.newbybuick.com	Saint George	UT	84790	435-673-1100	674-7550
Noble Ford Mercury Inc 2406 N Jefferson Way *Web:* www.nobleford.com	Indianola	IA	50125	515-961-8151	961-2413
North Florida Lincoln Mercury 4620 Southside Blvd *Web:* www.nflm.com	Jacksonville	FL	32216	888-579-9646	
O'Daniel Motor Sales Inc 5611 Illinois Rd *Web:* www.odanielauto.com	Fort Wayne	IN	46804	260-435-5300	435-5467
Obs Inc 1324 WTuscarawas St PO Box 6210 *Web:* www.obsinc.net	Canton	OH	44706	330-453-3725	580-2429
Olathe Toyota 685 N Rawhide *Web:* www.olathetoyota.com	Olathe	KS	66061	913-780-9919	780-9614
Omaha Standard Inc 3501 S 11th St Suite 1 *TF:* 800-279-2201 ■ *Web:* www.omahastd.com	Council Bluffs	IA	51501	712-328-7444	328-8383
Orlando Auto Auction Inc 4636 W Colonial Dr *Web:* www.orlandoautoauction.com	Orlando	FL	32808	407-299-3904	
Oshkosh Truck Corp 2307 Oregon St *NYSE: OSK* ■ *TF:* 800-392-9921 ■ *Web:* www.oshkoshdefense.com	Oshkosh	WI	54903	920-235-9150	233-9540
PACCAR Inc 777 106th Ave NE *NASDAQ: PCAR* ■ *Web:* www.paccar.com	Bellevue	WA	98004	425-468-7400	468-8216
PACCAR Inc International Div 777 106th Ave NE 12th Fl *Web:* www.paccar.com	Bellevue	WA	98004	425-468-7800	468-7850
Pak-Mor Ltd 2191 Rudeloff Rd *Web:* www.pakmor.com	Sequin	TX	78155	830-303-7256	303-3648
Papa's Dodge Inc 585 E Main St Suite 3 *Web:* www.papasdodge.com	New Britain	CT	06051	860-225-8751	826-4618
Parco-Hesse Corp 1060 Andre-Line St *TF:* 800-363-5975 ■ *Web:* www.grouphesse.com	Granby	QC	J2J1J9	450-378-4696	469-0341

Company	City	State	Zip	Phone	Fax
Parkhurst Mfg Co 18997 Hwy Y *TF:* 800-821-7380 ■ *Web:* www.parkhurstmfg.com	Sedalia	MO	65301	660-826-8685	826-8688
Parkway Chevrolet Inc 25500 Tomball Pkwy *Web:* www.parkwaychevrolet.com	Tomball	TX	77375	281-351-8211	357-3435
Patriot LP 4600 E Central Texas Expy *Web:* www.patriotcars.com	Killeen	TX	76543	254-247-3395	690-7701
Performance Chevrolet Inc 4811 Madison Ave *Web:* www.performancechevy.com	Sacramento	CA	95841	916-331-6777	332-9719
Peterbilt Motors Co 1700 Woodbrook St **Fax:* Hum Res ■ *Web:* www.peterbilt.com	Denton	TX	76205	940-591-4000	591-4259*
Peterbilt Utah Inc 2858 S 300 W PO Box 65616 *TF:* 800-633-7383 ■ *Web:* www.peterbiltofutah.com	Salt Lake City	UT	84115	801-486-8781	486-5907
Pierce Mfg Inc 2600 American Dr *TF Cust Svc:* 888-974-3723 ■ *Web:* www.piercemfg.com	Appleton	WI	54914	920-832-3000	832-3208
Pohanka of Salisbury 2007 N Salisbury Blvd *Web:* www.pohankaofsalisbury.com	Salisbury	MD	21801	410-749-2301	749-7704
Porter Truck Sales LP 135 McCarty St *Web:* www.portertrk.com	Houston	TX	77029	713-672-2400	672-7343
Powers-Swain Chevrolet Inc 4709 Bragg Blvd *Web:* www.pschevy.com	Fayetteville	NC	28303	910-864-9500	868-6159
Prevost Car Inc 35 boul Gagnon *Web:* www.prevostcar.com	Sainte-Claire	QC	G0R2V0	418-883-3391	883-4157
Progressive Chevrolet Co 8000 Hills and Dales Rd PO Box 997 *Web:* www.progressivechevrolet.com	Massillon	OH	44646	330-833-8564	833-2661
Quad-City Peterbilt Inc 8100 N Fairmount St **Fax Area Code:* 563 ■ *Web:* www.quadcitypeterbilt.com	Davenport	IA	52806	866-601-8607	391-0195*
R & B Car Co Inc 3811 S Michigan St *Web:* www.rbcarcompany.com	South Bend	IN	46614	574-299-4838	
R & S/Godwin Truck Body Co LLC 5168 S US Hwy 23 *TF:* 800-826-7413 ■ *Web:* www.rstruckbody.com	Ivel	KY	41642	606-874-2151	874-9136
R&H Motor Cars Ltd 9727 Reisterstown Rd *Web:* www.rhmotorcars.com	Owings Mills	MD	21117	410-363-3900	363-3987
Ramey Motors Inc PO Box 1755 *Web:* www.rameycars.com	Princeton	WV	24740	304-425-2134	425-5427
Rapid Chevrolet Co Inc 2090 Deadwood Ave PO Box 1765 *TF:* 800-456-2105 ■ *Web:* www.rapidchevrolet.com	Rapid City	SD	57702	605-343-1282	343-5458
Rdk Truck Sales Inc 3214 E Adamo Dr *Web:* www.rdk.com	Tampa	FL	33605	813-241-0711	241-0414
Reading Truck Body Inc Hancock Blvd & Gerry St *TF:* 800-458-2226 ■ *Web:* www.readingbody.com	Reading	PA	19611	610-775-3301	775-8683
Reed Lallier Chevrolet Inc 4500 Raeford Rd *Web:* www.reedlallier.com	Fayetteville	NC	28304	910-426-2000	
Ressler Motor Co 8474 Huffine Ln *Web:* www.resslermotors.com	Bozeman	MT	59771	406-587-5501	
RIHM Motor Co 2108 University Ave W *Web:* www.rihmkenworth.com	Saint Paul	MN	55114	651-646-7833	646-0630
RKI Inc 2301 Central Pkwy *Web:* www.rki-us.com	Houston	TX	77092	713-688-4414	688-5776
Road Rescue Inc 2914 Spartan Pl *TF:* 800-328-3804 ■ *Web:* www.roadrescue.com	Marion	SC	29571	843-676-2900	676-2998
Rochester Syracuse Auto Auction LP 1826 State Rt 414 PO Box 129 *Web:* www.rsautoauction.com	Waterloo	NY	13165	315-539-5006	539-9508
Rocket Supply Corp 404 N Hwy 115 *TF:* 800-252-6871 ■ *Web:* www.rocketsupply.com	Roberts	IL	60962	217-395-2278	395-2564
Rydell Chevrolet Inc 1325 E San Marnan Dr *Web:* www.rydellauto.com	Waterloo	IA	50702	319-234-4601	234-5660
Saf-T-Cab Inc 3241 S Pkwy Dr *TF:* 800-344-7491 ■ *Web:* www.saftcab.com	Fresno	CA	93725	559-268-5541	268-5822
Salvage Direct Inc 42336 Gilbert Dr *Web:* www.salvagedirect.com	Titusville	PA	16354	814-827-0300	827-9724
Sanborn Chevrolet Inc 1210 S Cherokee Ln *Web:* www.sanbornchevrolet.com	Lodi	CA	95240	209-642-4954	368-1849
Sanders Ford Inc 1135 Lejeune Blvd *TF:* 888-784-3673 ■ *Web:* www.sandersford.com	Jacksonville	NC	28540	910-455-1911	478-4277
Scania USA Inc 121 Interpark Blvd Suite 601 *TF:* 800-272-2642 ■ *Web:* www.scania.com	San Antonio	TX	78216	210-403-0007	403-0211
Scelzi Equipment Inc 1030 W Gladstone St *TF:* 866-972-3594 ■ *Web:* www.seinc.com	Azusa	CA	91702	626-334-0573	334-2753
Schetky Northwest Sales Inc 8430 NE Killingsworth St *TF:* 800-255-8341 ■ *Web:* www.schetkynw.com	Portland	OR	97220	503-287-4141	287-2931
Seagrave Fire Apparatus LLC 105 E 12th St *Web:* www.seagrave.com	Clintonville	WI	54929	715-823-2141	823-5768
Segway Inc 14 Technology Dr *TF:* 866-473-4929 ■ *Web:* www.segway.com	Bedford	NH	03110	603-222-6000	222-6001
Service Chevrolet Inc 4313 Cameron St **Fax Area Code:* 337 ■ *Web:* www.servicechevrolet.com	Lafayette	LA	70506	877-817-3720	264-9899*
Shealy's Truck Center Inc 1340 Bluff Rd *TF:* 800-951-8580 ■ *Web:* www.shealytruck.com	Columbia	SC	29201	803-771-0176	771-4879
Skaug Truck Body Works Inc 1404 1st St	San Fernando	CA	91340	818-365-9123	365-6634
Smith Chevrolet Co Inc 450 Keefer St *Web:* www.smithdeals.com	Idaho Falls	ID	83401	208-522-9800	529-3655
Smith-Cairns Ford 900 Central Pk Ave *Web:* www.smithcairns.com	Yonkers	NY	10704	914-377-8100	377-8118
Snethkamp Chrysler Jeep Inc 11600 Telegraph Rd *Web:* www.snethkamp.com	Redford	MI	48239	313-255-2700	532-4022
Snider Motor Cars Inc 9640 W Stockton Blvd	Elk Grove	CA	95757	916-405-8000	422-5721
Somerset Welding & Steel Inc 10558 Somerset Pike *TF:* 800-777-2671 ■ *Web:* www.jjbodies.com	Somerset	PA	15501	814-444-3400	443-2621
Southern Connecticut Freightliner 15 E Industrial Rd *Web:* www.netruck.com	Branford	CT	06405	203-481-0373	481-3780
Sovereign Motor Cars Ltd 1810 Shore Pkwy *Web:* www.benznow.com	Brooklyn	NY	11214	718-258-5100	859-3230
Spartan Motors Inc 1541 Reynolds Rd *NASDAQ: SPAR* ■ *TF:* 800-237-7806 ■ *Web:* www.spartanmotors.com	Charlotte	MI	48813	517-543-6400	543-9269
STAHL/A Scott Fetzer Co 3201 W Old Lincoln Way *TF:* 800-392-7251 ■ *Web:* www.stahl.cc	Wooster	OH	44691	330-264-7441	264-3319
Stanford Carr Development LLC 1100 Alakea St 27th Fl *Web:* www.stanfordcarr.com	Honolulu	HI	96813	808-537-5220	537-1801
Steelweld Equipment Co Inc 235 N Service Rd W *Web:* www.steelweld.net	Saint Clair	MO	63077	636-629-3704	629-3734
Sterling McCall Ford 6445 SW Fwy *Web:* www.sterlingmccallford.com	Houston	TX	77074	281-588-5000	588-5051
Sterling Truck Corp 12120 Telegraph Rd *TF Cust Svc:* 888-785-4357 ■ *Web:* www.sterlingtrucks.com	Redford Township	MI	48239	313-592-4200	592-4246
Steve Hopkins Inc 2499 Auto Mall Pkwy *TF:* 888-796-9999 ■ *Web:* www.hopkinsautogroup.com	Fairfield	CA	94533	707-427-1000	427-1286
Stewart Cadillac LP 2520 Main St *Web:* www.stewartcadillac.com	Houston	TX	77002	713-874-0900	874-0982
Sun Toyota Super Store 4023 US Hwy *Web:* www.suntoyota.com	New Port Riche	FL	34656	727-842-9735	845-8238
Sunbury Motor Co 943 N Fourth St *Web:* www.sunburymotors.com	Sunbury	PA	17801	570-286-7746	286-9389
Superior Auto Sales Inc 5201 Camp Rd *Web:* www.sascars.com	Hamburg	NY	14075	716-649-6695	
Superior Motors Inc 282 John C Calhoun Dr *Web:* www.superiormotors.com	Orangeburg	SC	29115	803-534-1123	533-7806
Superior Trailer Sales Co 501 Hwy 80 *Web:* www.stsco.com	Sunnyvale	TX	75182	972-226-3893	226-3899
Superstition Springs Enterprises Inc 6136 E Auto Loop Ave *Web:* www.earnhardttoyota.com	Mesa	AZ	85206	480-807-9700	807-3361
Supreme Corp 2581 E Kercher Rd PO Box 463 *TF:* 800-642-4889 ■ *Web:* www.supremeind.com	Goshen	IN	46528	574-642-4888	642-4540
Supreme Industries Inc 2581 E Kerchen Rd *AMEX: STS* ■ *TF:* 800-642-4889 ■ *Web:* www.supremeind.com	Goshen	IN	46528	574-642-3070	642-3208
Sutphen Corp PO Box 158 *TF:* 800-726-7030 ■ *Web:* www.sutphen.com	Amlin	OH	43002	614-889-1005	889-0874
Svi Inc 440 Mark Leany Dr *Web:* www.specialtyvehicles.com	Henderson	NV	89011	702-567-5256	567-3020
Sweeney Buick 7997 Market St *TF:* 877-360-4928 ■ *Web:* www.sweeneycars.com	Youngstown	OH	44512	877-360-4928	
Tafco Equipment Co Inc 1304 W 1st St *TF Sales:* 800-328-3189 ■ *Web:* www.tafcoequip.com	Blue Earth	MN	56013	507-526-3247	526-7346
Ten-8 Fire Equipment Inc 2904 59th Ave Dr E *Web:* www.ten8fire.com	Bradenton	FL	34203	941-756-7779	756-2598
Thiele Mfg LLC 309 Spruce St	Windber	PA	15963	814-467-4504	467-4172
Thomas Built Buses Inc 1408 Courtesy Rd *Web:* www.thomasbus.com	High Point	NC	27260	336-889-4871	881-6509
Thomson Motor Centre Inc 2158 Washington Rd NE *Web:* www.jeepcheap.com	Thomson	GA	30824	706-597-0062	597-8098
Thomson-Macconnell Cadillac Inc 2820 Gilbert Ave **Fax Area Code:* 513 ■ *Web:* www.thomsonmacconnell.com	Cincinnati	OH	45206	877-472-0738	221-5774*
Thor Industries Inc 419 W Pike St *NYSE: THO* ■ *Web:* www.thorindustries.com	Jackson Center	OH	45334	937-596-6849	596-7929
Tipton Motors Inc 3840 N Expy *Web:* www.tiptonmotors.com	Brownsville	TX	78526	956-350-5600	350-2489
Tom Nehl GMC Truck Co 417 S Edgewood Ave *Web:* www.tomnehl.com	Jacksonville	FL	32236	904-388-5443	384-2467
Tom Roush Inc 525 W David Brown Dr *Web:* www.tomroush.com	Westfield	IN	46074	317-896-5561	896-3591
Town & Country Chrysler Inc 27490 SW 95th Ave *Web:* www.cjdwilsonville.com	Wilsonville	OR	97070	503-659-0570	
Town East Ford II LP 18411 Lyndon B Jhnson Fwy *Web:* www.towneastford.com	Mesquite	TX	75150	972-270-6441	682-1245
Trailercraft Inc 1301 E 64th Ave *Web:* www.trailercraft.com	Anchorage	AK	99518	907-563-3238	561-4995
Truck Cab Manufacturers Inc PO Box 58400 *Web:* www.truckcab.com	Cincinnati	OH	45258	513-922-1300	922-8888
Truck Utilities Inc 2370 English St *TF:* 800-869-1075 ■ *Web:* www.truckutilities.com	Saint Paul	MN	55109	651-484-3305	484-0076
Trucks only 550 S Country Club Dr *Web:* www.trucksonlysales.com	Mesa	AZ	85210	480-844-7071	844-7488
Tymco Inc 225 E Industrial Blvd PO Box 2368 *TF:* 800-258-9626 ■ *Web:* www.tymco.com	Waco	TX	76703	254-799-5546	799-2722
Unicell Body Co 571 Howard St *TF Cust Svc:* 800-628-8914 ■ *Web:* www.unicell.com	Buffalo	NY	14206	716-853-8628	843-8638
United Ford Parts & Distribtion Center Inc 12007 E 61st St *Web:* www.unitedford.com	Tulsa	OK	74012	918-280-6000	280-6997
Universal Ford Sales Inc 10751 W Broad St *Web:* www.forduniversal.com	Glen Allen	VA	23060	804-273-9700	273-1591
Valley Chevrolet Inc 601 Kidder St *Web:* www.valleychevrolet.com	Wilkes Barre	PA	18702	570-821-2772	823-9639
Viking-Cives USA 14331 Mill St *Web:* www.vikingcives.com	Harrisville	NY	13648	315-543-2321	543-2366
Vista-pro Automotive LLC 15 Century Blvd Suite 600 *TF:* 888-250-2676 ■ *Web:* www.vistaproauto.com	Nashville	TN	37214	615-622-2200	622-2302
Volvo Construction Equipment of North America Inc 1 Volvo Dr *Web:* www.volvo.com/constructionequipment	Asheville	NC	28803	828-650-2000	650-2501
Volvo Group North America Inc 570 Lexington Ave 20th Fl *Web:* www.volvo.com	New York	NY	10022	212-418-7400	418-7436
Volvo Trucks North America Inc 7900 National Service Rd PO Box 26115 *Web:* www.volvo.com/trucks/na	Greensboro	NC	27402	336-393-2000	393-2362
Walnut Creek Assoc 1707 N Main St *TF:* 888-491-1668 ■ *Web:* www.walnutcreekhonda.com	Walnut Creek	CA	94596	925-934-0530	947-2945

				Phone	Fax
Walton Motors Inc 205 E Pawnee Dr *Web:* www.waltonmotorsinc.com	Savannah	MO	64485	816-324-3141	
Welch O C Ford Lincoln Mercury Inc 4920 Independence Blvd **Fax Area Code:* 843 ■ *Web:* www.goseeocford.com	Hardeeville	SC	29927	888-903-1516	288-0105*
Weld-Built Body Co Inc 276 Long Island Ave *Web:* www.weldbuilt.com	Wyandanch	NY	11798	631-643-9700	491-4728
Wendle Motors Inc 9000 N Division **Fax Area Code:* 509 ■ *Web:* www.wendle.com	Spokane	WA	99218	888-229-3929	484-7442*
Wentworth Chevytown 107 SE Grand Ave *Web:* www.wentworthchevrolet.com	Portland	OR	97214	503-200-2482	234-3370
West Texas Peterbilt 4515 Ave A *TF:* 888-987-2458 ■ *Web:* www.wtpeterbilt.com	Lubbock	TX	79404	806-747-2579	747-4171
Wheeled Coach Industries Inc 2737 Forsyth Rd *TF:* 800-342-0720 ■ *Web:* www.wheeledcoach.com	Winter Park	FL	32792	407-677-7777	679-1337
Wichita Kenworth Inc 5115 N Broadway *TF:* 800-825-5558 ■ *Web:* www.wichitakenworth.com	Wichita	KS	67219	316-838-0867	838-4845
Winrock Motors Inc 16100 Chenal Pkwy *Web:* www.riversideacura.com	Little Rock	AR	72211	501-376-3300	448-8008
Woburn Foreign Motors Inc 80-82 Olympia Ave *Web:* www.wfab.com	Woburn	MA	01801	781-935-3040	938-0225
World Wide Motors Inc 3900 E 96th St *Web:* www.wwmotors.mercedesdealer.com	Indianapolis	IN	46240	317-580-6800	
Worldwide Equipment Inc 1999 Kentucky Rt 1428 E PO Box 1370 *TF:* 800-307-4746 ■ *Web:* www.teamworldwide.com	Prestonsburg	KY	41653	606-874-2172	874-9079
Yamaha Golf Cars of California Inc 5605 S Front Rd *Web:* www.yamahagolfcarsofca.com	Livermore	CA	94551	925-371-5350	371-5311
Yark Automotive Group Inc 6019 W Central Ave *Web:* www.yarkauto.com	Toledo	OH	43615	419-841-7771	843-2986
Zangara Dodge Inc 8528 Lomas Blvd NE *Web:* www.zangara.com	Albuquerque	NM	87192	505-262-1111	262-5497

520 MOTORCYCLES & MOTORCYCLE PARTS & ACCESSORIES

				Phone	Fax
American Honda Motor Co Inc 1919 Torrance Blvd *TF:* 800-999-1009 ■ *Web:* www.honda.com	Torrance	CA	90501	310-783-2000	
American Ironhorse Motorcycle Co 4600 Blue Mound Rd *Web:* www.americanironhorse.com	Fort Worth	TX	76106	817-665-2000	
American Suzuki Motor Corp 3251 Imperial Hwy *Web:* www.suzuki.com	Brea	CA	92821	714-996-7040	524-2512
Andrews Products Inc 431 Kingston Ct *Web:* www.andrewsproducts.com	Mount Prospect	IL	60056	847-759-0190	759-0848
Big Dog Motorcycles 1520 E Douglas Ave *Web:* www.bigdogmotorcycles.com	Wichita	KS	67214	316-267-9121	267-2597
Corbin 2360 Technology Pkwy *TF:* 800-538-7035 ■ *Web:* www.corbin.com	Hollister	CA	95023	831-634-1100	634-1059
Cycle Shack Inc 1104 San Mateo Ave *Web:* www.cycle-shack.com	South San Francisco	CA	94080	650-583-7014	583-9154
CycoActive Inc 4021 Airport Way S *TF:* 800-491-2926 ■ *Web:* www.cycoactive.com	Seattle	WA	98108	206-323-2349	325-6016
Edelbrock Corp 2700 California St *TF:* 800-739-3737 ■ *Web:* www.edelbrock.com	Torrance	CA	90503	310-781-2222	320-1187
Fulmer Co 122 Gayoso Ave *TF:* 800-467-2400 ■ *Web:* www.fulmerhelmets.com	Memphis	TN	38103	901-525-5711	525-7993
Harley-Davidson Inc 3700 W Juneau Ave *NYSE: HOG* ■ **Fax:* Hum Res	Milwaukee	WI	53208	414-342-4680	343-4621*
Kawasaki Motors Corp USA PO Box 25252 *Web:* www.kawasaki.com	Santa Ana	CA	92799	949-770-0400	460-5600
Lehman Trikes Inc 125 Industrial Dr *CVE: LHT* ■ *TF:* 888-394-3357 ■ *Web:* www.lehmantrikes.com	Spearfish	SD	57783	605-642-2111	642-1184
Mag-Knight 18121 117th St SE *Web:* www.mag-knight.com	Snohomish	WA	98290	360-805-0100	805-0811
Motovan Corp 1391 Guy Lussac *Web:* www.motovan.com	Boucherville	QC	J4B7K1	450-449-3903	449-7773
National Cycle Inc 2200 Maywood Dr *TF:* 877-972-7336 ■ *Web:* www.nationalcycle.com	Maywood	IL	60153	708-343-0400	343-0625
Olympic Mountain & Marine Products Inc 8655 S 208th St *TF:* 800-937-2545 ■ *Web:* www.omplabs.com	Kent	WA	98031	253-850-2343	850-3545
Persons Majestic Mfg Co PO Box 370 *TF:* 800-772-2453 ■ *Web:* www.permaco.com	Huron	OH	44839	419-433-9057	433-0182
Polaris Industries Inc 2100 Hwy 55 *NYSE: PII* ■ *Web:* www.polarisindustries.com	Medina	MN	55340	763-542-0500	542-0599
Powroll Inc 4115 SW 19th St PO Box 920 *Web:* www.powroll.com	Redmond	OR	97756	541-923-1290	923-5637
Rivco Products Inc 440 S Pine St *TF:* 888-801-8222 ■ *Web:* www.rivcoproducts.com	Burlington	WI	53105	262-763-8222	763-8949
Yamaha Motor Corp USA 6555 Katella Ave *TF Cust Svc:* 800-962-7926 ■ *Web:* www.yamaha-motor.com	Cypress	CA	90630	714-761-7300	

MOTORS - FLUID POWER

SEE Pumps & Motors - Fluid Power p. 2474

521 MOTORS (ELECTRIC) & GENERATORS

SEE ALSO Automotive Parts & Supplies - Mfr p. 1497

				Phone	Fax
ADS/Transicoil 9 Iron Bridge Dr *TF:* 800-323-7115 ■ *Web:* www.adstcoil.com	Collegeville	PA	19426	484-902-1100	902-1150
Advanced Power & Controls LLC 605 E Alton Ave Suite A *Web:* www.advancedpowercontrols.com	Santa Ana	CA	92705	714-540-9010	540-5313
Aerotech Inc 101 Zeta Dr *Web:* www.aerotech.com	Pittsburgh	PA	15238	412-967-6440	967-6870
Alliance Winding Equipment Inc 3939 Vanguard Dr *Web:* www.alliance-winding.com	Fort Wayne	IN	46809	260-478-2200	
AMETEK Floorcare Specialty Motors 627 Lake St *Web:* www.ametekfsm.com	Kent	OH	44240	330-673-3451	673-8994
AMETEK Lamb Electric 627 Lake St *Web:* www.ametekfsm.com	Kent	OH	44240	330-673-3451	673-8994
AMK Drives & Controls Inc 5631 S Laburnum Ave *Web:* www.amkdrives.com	Richmond	VA	23231	804-222-0323	222-0339
AO Smith Corp 11270 W Pk Pl Suite 170 PO Box 245008 *NYSE: AOS* ■ *TF:* 800-359-4065 ■ *Web:* www.aosmith.com	Milwaukee	WI	53224	414-359-4000	359-4180
Arco Electric Products Corp 2325 E Michigan Rd *TF:* 800-428-4370 ■ *Web:* www.arco-electric.com	Shelbyville	IN	46176	317-398-9713	398-2655
Arkansas General Industries Inc 102 Miller St PO Box 260 *Web:* www.argenind.com	Bald Knob	AR	72010	501-724-3227	724-5915
Aura Systems Inc 1310 E Grand Ave *TF:* 800-909-2872 ■ *Web:* www.aurasystems.com	El Segundo	CA	90245	310-643-5300	643-7457
Autotrol Corp 365 E Prairie St PO Box 557 *TF:* 800-228-6207 ■ *Web:* www.autotrol.com	Crystal Lake	IL	60039	815-459-3080	459-3227
Axsys Technologies Motion Control Products 7603 St Andrew Ave Suite H *TF Cust Svc:* 800-777-3393 ■ *Web:* www.axsys.com	San Diego	CA	92154	619-671-5400	671-9292
Baldor Electric Co 5711 RS Boreham, Jr St PO Box 2400 **Fax:* Sales ■ *Web:* www.baldor.com	Fort Smith	AR	72901	479-646-4711	648-5792*
Baldor Linear Motion Products 5711 RS Boreham, Jr St PO Box 2400 *Web:* www.baldor.com	Fort Smith	AR	72901	479-646-4711	648-5792
Barta - Schoenewald Inc 3805 Calle Tecate *Web:* www.a-m-c.com	Camarillo	CA	93012	805-389-1935	389-1165
Berger Lahr Motion Technology Inc 44191 Plymouth Oaks Blvd *Web:* www.bergerlahrmotion.com	Plymouth	MI	48170	734-459-8300	459-8622
Bodine Electric Co 2500 W Bradley Pl *TF:* 800-726-3463 ■ *Web:* www.bodine-electric.com	Chicago	IL	60618	773-478-3515	478-3232
Bosch Rexroth Corp 5150 Prairie Stone Pkwy *TF:* 800-860-1055 ■ *Web:* www.boschrexroth-us.com	Hoffman Estates	IL	60192	847-645-3600	645-6201
Buehler Motor Inc 860 Aviation Pkwy Suite 300 *Web:* www.buehlermotor.com	Morrisville	NC	27560	919-380-3333	380-3256
CALEX Mfg Co 2401 Stanwell Dr *TF:* 800-542-3355 ■ *Web:* www.calex.com	Concord	CA	94520	925-687-4411	687-3333
Continental Electric Motors Inc 4 Timber Ln Bldg A *Web:* www.cecoinc.com	Marlboro	NJ	07746	732-863-0888	863-1886
Custom Sensors & Technologies 14501 Princeton Avew *Web:* www.cst.schneider-electric.com	Moorpark	CA	93021	805-552-3599	552-3577
D C Advanced Motors Inc 6268 E Molloy Rd *TF:* 800-417-3811 ■ *Web:* www.adcmotors.com	East Syracuse	NY	13057	315-434-9303	432-9290
Danaher Motion 1500 Mittel Blvd *TF:* 866-993-2624 ■ *Web:* www.danahermotion.com	Wood Dale	IL	60191	630-860-7300	694-3305
Data Electronic Devices Inc 32 Northwestern Dr *Web:* www.dataed.com	Salem	NH	03079	603-893-2047	893-2956
DRS Power Technology Inc 2 Fox Rd *Web:* www.drs.com	Hudson	MA	01749	978-562-2933	562-6830
Dumore Corp 1030 Veterans St **Fax Area Code:* 800 ■ *TF:* 888-467-8288 ■ *Web:* www.dumorecorp.com	Mauston	WI	53948	608-847-6420	338-6673*
EAD Motors Inc 1 Progress Dr *Web:* www.electrocraft.com	Dover	NH	03820	603-742-3330	742-3330
Electric Apparatus Co 409 Roosevelt St *Web:* www.elecapp.net	Howell	MI	48843	517-546-0520	546-0547
Electric Motor & Contracting Co Inc 3703 Cook Blvd *Web:* www.emc-co.com	Chesapeake	VA	23323	757-487-2121	487-5983
Electric Motors & Specialties Inc 701 W King St PO Box 180 *Web:* www.emsmotors.com	Garrett	IN	46738	260-357-4141	357-3888
Electrical Products Co 531 N 4th St *TF:* 800-543-9450 ■ *Web:* www.aosmith.com/compinfo/tippcity.htm	Tipp City	OH	45371	937-667-2431	669-5199
Electro Sales Inc 100 Fellsway W *TF:* 888-789-0500 ■ *Web:* www.electrosales.com	Somerville	MA	02145	617-666-0500	628-2800
Elwood Corp High Performance Motors Group 2701 N Green Bay Rd **Fax Area Code:* 414 ■ *TF:* 800-558-9489 ■ *Web:* www.elwood.com	Racine	WI	53404	262-637-6591	764-4298*
Emerson Electric Co 8000 W Florissant Ave *NYSE: EMR* ■ *Web:* www.emerson.com	Saint Louis	MO	63136	314-553-2000	553-2000
Emerson Motor Co 8000 W Florissant Ave PO Box 4100 *Web:* www.emerson.com	Saint Louis	MO	63136	314-553-2000	553-3712
Emoteq Corp 10002 E 43rd St S *TF Sales:* 800-221-7572 ■ *Web:* www.emoteq.com	Tulsa	OK	74146	918-627-1845	660-0207

Company	City	State	ZIP	Phone	Fax
Everson Tesla Inc 615 Daniel's Rd *Web:* www.eversontesla.com	Nazareth	PA	18064	610-746-1520	746-1520
Five Star Electric of Houston Inc 7007 Winding Walk Dr Suite 200 **Fax Area Code:* 888 ■ *Web:* www.fivestarelectric.com	Houston	TX	77095	210-492-7090	492-7080*
Franklin Electric Co Inc 400 E Spring St *NASDAQ: FELE* ■ *TF:* 800-269-0063 ■ *Web:* www.franklin-electric.com	Bluffton	IN	46714	260-824-2900	827-5800
Generac Power Systems Inc PO Box 8 *Web:* www.generac.com	Waukesha	WI	53187	262-544-4811	544-4851
Glentek Inc 208 Standard St *TF:* 800-232-4485 ■ *Web:* www.glentek.com	El Segundo	CA	90245	310-322-3026	322-7709
Hankscraft Inc 300 Wengel Dr *Web:* www.hankscraft-motors.com	Reedsburg	WI	53959	608-524-4341	524-4342
Hannon Co The 1605 Waynesburg Dr SE *Web:* www.hanco.com	Canton	OH	44707	330-456-4728	456-3323
Hansen Corp 901 S 1st St *Web:* www.hansen-motor.com	Princeton	IN	47670	812-385-3415	385-3013
Hansome Energy Systems Inc 365 Dalziel Rd	Linden	NJ	07036	908-862-9044	862-8195
Hurst Mfg 1551 E Broadway St **Fax:* Sales ■ *Web:* www.hurst-motors.com	Princeton	IN	47670	812-385-2564	386-7504*
Ideal Electric Co 330 E 1st St *Web:* www.idealelectricco.com	Mansfield	OH	44902	419-522-3611	522-9386
Imperial Electric Co 1503 Exeter Rd *Web:* www.imperialelectric.com	Akron	OH	44306	330-734-3600	734-3601
Johnson Electric North America Inc 10 Progress Dr *Web:* www.johnsonmotor.com	Shelton	CT	06484	203-447-5362	447-5383
Joliet Equipment Corp 1 Doris Ave PO Box 114 *TF:* 800-435-9350 ■ *Web:* www.joliet-equipment.com	Joliet	IL	60434	815-727-6606	727-6626
Kinetek Inc 1751 Lake Cook Rd ArborLake Ctr Suite 550 *Web:* www.kinetekinc.com	Deerfield	IL	60015	847-267-4473	945-9645
Kirkwood Industries Inc 1239 Rockside Rd *TF:* 800-262-2266 ■ *Web:* www.kirkwood-ind.com	Cleveland	OH	44134	216-267-6200	362-3878
Kollmorgen Corp 203A W Rock Rd *Web:* www.kollmorgen.com	Radford	VA	24141	540-633-3545	639-4162
Kraft Power Corp 199 Wildwood Ave *TF:* 800-969-6121 ■ *Web:* www.kraftpower.com	Woburn	MA	01801	781-938-9100	933-7812
Kurz Electric Solutions Inc 1325 McMahon Dr *TF:* 800-776-3629 ■ *Web:* www.kurz.com	Neenah	WI	54956	920-886-8200	886-8201
Leeson Electric Corp 2100 Washington St *Web:* www.leeson.com	Grafton	WI	53024	262-377-8810	
Letourneau Technologies Power System 6401 W Sam Houston Pkwy N *Web:* www.letourneau-inc.com	Houston	TX	77041	713-983-4700	983-4730
Lexel Corp PO Box 508	Franksville	WI	53126	262-886-2002	886-4639
Louis Allis Large Motor Corp 645 Lester Doss Rd *TF:* 866-568-4700	Warrior	AL	35180	205-590-2986	590-1571
Mabuchi Motor America Corp 3001 W Big Beaver Rd Suite 520 *Web:* www.mabuchi-motor.co.jp	Troy	MI	48084	248-816-3100	816-3242
Mamco Corp 8630 Industrial Dr *Web:* www.mamcomotors.com	Franksville	WI	53126	262-886-9069	886-4639
Marathon Electric Inc 100 E Randolf St PO Box 8003 *Web:* www.marathonelectric.com	Wausau	WI	54402	715-675-3311	675-8051
Martindale Electric Co 1375 Hird Ave *TF:* 800-344-9191 ■ *Web:* www.martindaleco.com	Lakewood	OH	44107	216-521-8567	521-9476
McMillan Electric Co 400 Best Rd *Web:* www.mcmillanelectric.com	Woodville	WI	54028	715-698-2488	698-2297
Merkle-Korff Industries Inc 25 NW Pt Blvd Suite 900 *Web:* www.merkle-korff.com	Elk Grove Village	IL	60007	847-439-3760	439-3963
Minarik Corp 905 E Thompson Ave *Web:* www.minarikcorp.com	Glendale	CA	91201	818-637-7500	637-7549
Molon Motor & Coil Corp 300 N Ridge Ave *TF:* 800-526-6867 ■ *Web:* www.molon.com	Arlington Heights	IL	60005	847-253-6000	259-5491
Morrill Motors Inc 229 S Main Ave *Web:* www.morrillmotors.com	Erwin	TN	37650	423-743-7000	743-5661
Motor Appliance Corp 555 Spirit of St Louis Blvd *TF:* 800-622-3406 ■ *Web:* www.macmc.com	Chesterfield	MO	63005	636-532-3406	532-4609
Motor Products Owosso Corp 201 S Delaney Rd *TF:* 800-248-3841 ■ *Web:* www.motorproducts.net	Owosso	MI	48867	989-725-5151	723-6035
Motor Specialty Inc PO Box 081278 *Web:* www.motorspecialty.com	Racine	WI	53408	262-632-2794	632-8899
MTU Onsite Energy Corp 100 Power Dr **Fax:* Sales ■ *TF:* 800-325-5450 ■ *Web:* www.mtuonsiteenergy.com	Mankato	MN	56001	507-625-7973	625-2968*
Nidec America Corp 100 River Ridge Dr Suite 300 *Web:* www.nidec.com	Norwood	MA	02062	781-769-0619	551-6825
Ohio Electric Motors Inc 30 Paint Fork Rd PO Box 168 *Web:* www.ohioelectricmotors.com	Barnardsville	NC	28709	828-626-2901	626-2155
PennEngineering & Mfg Corp 5190 Old Easton Rd *TF:* 800-237-4736 ■ *Web:* www.penn-eng.com	Danboro	PA	18916	215-766-8853	766-3680
Phytron Inc 600 Blair Pk Rd Suite 220 *Web:* www.phytron.com	Williston	VT	05495	802-872-1600	872-0311
Piller Inc 45 Turner Rd *TF:* 800-597-6937 ■ *Web:* www.piller.com	Middletown	NY	10941	845-695-5300	692-0295
Polyspede Electronics Co Inc 6770 Twin Hills Ave *TF:* 888-476-5944 ■ *Web:* www.polyspede.com	Dallas	TX	75231	214-363-7245	363-7245
ProVision Technologies Inc 69 Railroad Ave Suite A-7 *Web:* www.provisiontechnologies.com	Hilo	HI	96720	808-969-3281	934-7462
RAE Corp 4615 Prime Pkwy *TF:* 800-323-7049 ■ *Web:* www.raemotors.com	McHenry	IL	60050	815-385-3500	344-1580
Reagan Equipment Co Inc 2550 Belle Chasse Hwy *TF:* 800-494-6808 ■ *Web:* www.reaganpower.com	Gretna	LA	70053	504-368-9760	368-9768
Rudox Engine & Equipment Co 765 State Rt 17 *Web:* www.rudox.com	Carlstadt	NJ	07072	201-438-0111	438-3403
Sag Harbor Industries Inc 1668 Sag Harbor Tpke *TF:* 800-724-5952 ■ *Web:* www.sagharborind.com	Sag Harbor	NY	11963	631-725-0440	725-4234
Scott Fetzer Co Northland Div 968 Bradley St *Web:* www.northlandmotor.com	Watertown	NY	13601	315-782-2350	788-1180
Shinano Kenshi Corp 5737 Mesmer Ave *Web:* www.shinano.com	Culver City	CA	90230	818-889-5028	991-6439
Siemens Power Generation 4400 Alafaya Trail **Fax:* Hum Res ■ *Web:* www.energy.siemens.com	Orlando	FL	32826	407-736-4197	736-5009*
Skurka Aerospace Inc 4600 Calle Bolero PO Box 2869 *Web:* www.skurka-aero.com	Camarillo	CA	93011	805-484-8884	482-7771
SL-Montevideo Technology Inc 2002 Black Oak Ave *Web:* www.slmti.com	Montevideo	MN	56265	320-269-6562	269-7662
Specialty Motors Inc 25060 Ave Tibbitts *TF:* 800-232-2612 ■ *Web:* www.specialtymotors.com	Valencia	CA	91355	661-257-7388	257-7389
Sterling Electric Inc 7997 Allison Ave *TF Cust Svc:* 800-654-6220 ■ *Web:* www.sterlingelectric.com	Indianapolis	IN	46268	317-872-0471	872-0907
Stimple & Ward Co 3400 Babcock Blvd *TF:* 800-792-6457 ■ *Web:* www.swcoils.com	Pittsburgh	PA	15237	412-364-5200	364-5299
Swiger Coils Systems Inc 4677 Mfg Rd *TF:* 800-321-3310 ■ *Web:* www.swigercoil.com	Cleveland	OH	44135	216-362-7500	362-1496
Toledo Commutator 1101 S Chestnut St	Owosso	MI	48867	989-725-8192	725-5930
Toshiba International Corp 13131 W Little York Rd *TF:* 800-231-1412 ■ *Web:* www.toshiba.com	Houston	TX	77041	713-466-0277	896-5240
Unico Inc 3725 Nicholson Rd *TF:* 800-245-1859 ■ *Web:* www.unicous.com	Franksville	WI	53126	262-886-5678	504-7396
Unitron LP 10925 Miller Rd PO Box 38902 *TF:* 800-527-1279 ■ *Web:* www.unitronlp.com	Dallas	TX	75238	214-340-8600	341-2099
UQM Technologies Inc 4120 Specialty Pl *AMEX: UQM* ■ *Web:* www.uqm.com	Longmont	CO	80504	303-682-4900	682-4901
US Electrical Motors 8100 W Florissant Ave Bldg K *TF:* 888-637-7333 ■ *Web:* www.usmotors.com	Saint Louis	MO	63136	314-553-2000	553-1101
Vicor Corp 25 Frontage Rd *NASDAQ: VICR* ■ *TF:* 800-869-5300 ■ *Web:* www.vicorpower.com	Andover	MA	01810	978-470-2900	475-6715
Wabtec Railway Electronics 21200 Dorsey Mill Rd *TF:* 800-447-8573	Germantown	MD	20876	301-515-2000	515-2100
Ward Leonard Electric Co Inc 401 Watertown Rd *Web:* www.wardleonard.com	Thomaston	CT	06787	860-283-5801	283-5777
Welco Technologies 805 Lindbergh Ct Suite 200 *TF:* 800-715-6006 ■ *Web:* www.welco-tech.com	Hebron	KY	41048	859-334-5200	334-5201
Wenthe-Davidson Engineering Co 16300 W Rogers Dr PO Box 510286 *Web:* www.wenthe-davidson.com	New Berlin	WI	53151	262-782-1550	782-2020
Wolverine Power Systems Inc 3229 80th Ave *TF:* 800-485-8068 ■ *Web:* www.wolverinepower.com	Zeeland	MI	49464	616-879-0040	879-0045
Yamaha Motor Corp USA 6555 Katella Ave *TF Cust Svc:* 800-962-7926 ■ *Web:* www.yamaha-motor.com	Cypress	CA	90630	714-761-7300	
Yaskawa America Inc 2121 Norman Dr S **Fax:* Mktg ■ *TF:* 800-927-5292 ■ *Web:* www.yaskawa.com	Waukegan	IL	60085	847-887-7000	887-7310*

522 MOVING COMPANIES

SEE ALSO Trucking Companies p. 2736

Companies That Have The Moving Of Household Belongings As Their Primary Business.

Company	City	State	ZIP	Phone	Fax
A Colonial Moving & Storage Co 17 Mercer St *Web:* www.colonialmoving.com	Hackensack	NJ	07601	201-343-5777	343-1934
Ace World Wide Moving 1900 E College Ave *TF:* 800-223-6683 ■ *Web:* www.aceworldwide.com	Cudahy	WI	53110	414-764-1000	764-1650
Air Van Moving Group 10510 NE Northup Way Suite 110 *TF:* 800-877-1442 ■ *Web:* www.airvanmoving.com	Kirkland	WA	98033	425-629-4101	629-4120
Allied International NA Inc 700 Oakmont Ln *TF:* 800-323-1909 ■ *Web:* www.allied.com	Westmont	IL	60559	630-570-3500	570-3496
Allied Van Lines Inc 700 Oakmont Ln **Fax:* Sales ■ *TF Cust Svc:* 800-762-4689 ■ *Web:* www.alliedvan.com	Westmont	IL	60559	630-570-3000	570-3394*
American Red Ball International 9750 3rd Ave NE Suite 200 *TF:* 800-669-6424 ■ *Web:* www.americanredball.com	Seattle	WA	98115	206-526-1730	526-2967
American Red Ball Transit Co Inc 1335 Sadlier Cir E Dr **Fax:* Cust Svc ■ *TF:* 800-733-8077 ■ *Web:* www.americanredball.com	Indianapolis	IN	46239	317-353-8331	351-0652*
Amodio Van & Storage 1 Hartford Sq *TF:* 800-927-6683 ■ *Web:* www.amodiovan.com	New Britain	CT	06052	860-223-2725	223-0370
Andrews Van Lines Inc 310 S 7th St *TF Cust Svc:* 800-228-8146 ■ *Web:* www.andrewsvanlines.com	Norfolk	NE	68701	402-371-5440	371-1349
Arnoff Moving & Storage Inc 1282 Dutchess Tpke *TF:* 800-633-6683 ■ *Web:* www.arnoff.com	Poughkeepsie	NY	12603	845-471-1504	452-3606
Arpin Van Lines 99 James P Murphy Hwy *TF:* 800-343-3500 ■ *Web:* www.arpin.com	West Warwick	RI	02893	401-828-8111	821-5860
Atlantic Relocation Systems Inc 1314 Chattahoochee Ave NW *TF Cust Svc:* 800-241-1140 ■ *Web:* www.atlanticrelocation.com	Atlanta	GA	30318	404-351-5311	350-6530
Atlas Van Lines Inc 1212 St George Rd **Fax:* Cust Svc ■ *TF:* 800-638-9797 ■ *Web:* www.atlasvanlines.com	Evansville	IN	47711	812-424-2222	421-7129*

Name / Address	City	State	Zip	Phone	Fax
Barrett Moving & Storage Co 10230 W 70th St	Eden Prairie	MN	55344	952-944-6550	828-7110
TF: 800-879-1283 ■ Web: www.barrettmoving.com					
Bay State Moving Systems Inc 60 Haynes Cir	Chicopee	MA	01020	413-592-6381	594-3676
TF: 800-388-7411					
Bekins Co 330 S Mannheim Rd	Hillside	IL	60162	708-547-2000	
Web: www.bekins.com					
Bekins Van Lines LLC 330 S Mannheim Rd	Hillside	IL	60162	708-547-2000	547-2107
TF: 800-723-5467 ■ Web: www.bekins.com					
Berger Transfer & Storage Inc 2950 Long Lake Rd	Saint Paul	MN	55113	651-639-2260	639-2277
TF: 800-328-2459 ■ Web: www.berger-transfer.com					
Beverly Hills Transfer & Storage Co 221 S Beverly Dr	Beverly Hills	CA	90212	310-276-1121	538-0416
TF: 800-999-7114 ■ Web: www.beverlyhillstransfer.com					
Bohrens Moving & Storage Inc 3 Applegate Dr	Robbinsville	NJ	08691	609-208-1470	208-1471
TF: 800-326-4736 ■ Web: www.bohrensmoving.com					
Buehler Moving & Storage Co 3899 Jackson St	Denver	CO	80205	303-388-4000	388-0296
TF: 800-234-6683 ■ Web: www.movingservices.com					
Callan & Woodworth Moving & Storage 900 Hwy 212	Michigan City	IN	46360	219-874-3274	872-0776
TF: 877-678-0930 ■ Web: www.callanmoving.com					
Capital City Transfer Inc 1465 Johnson St NE	Salem	OR	97301	503-581-6683	581-6924
Cartwright Cos The 11901 Cartwright Ave	Grandview	MO	64030	816-763-2700	763-7863
TF: 800-821-2334 ■ Web: www.cartwrighttrans.com					
Castine Moving & Storage 1235 Chestnut St	Athol	MA	01331	978-249-9105	249-5337
TF: 800-225-8068 ■ Web: www.castinemovers.com					
Coast to Coast Moving & Storage Co 136 41st St	Brooklyn	NY	11232	718-443-5800	445-6435
TF: 800-872-6683 ■ Web: www.ctcvanlines.com					
Cook Moving Systems Inc 1845 Dale Rd	Buffalo	NY	14225	716-897-0700	893-0500
TF: 800-828-7144 ■ Web: www.movingsystems.com					
Corrigan Moving Systems 23923 Research Dr	Farmington Hills	MI	48335	248-471-4000	471-3746
TF: 800-267-7442 ■ Web: www.corriganmoving.com					
Davidson Transfer & Storage Co 6600 Frankford Ave	Baltimore	MD	21206	410-488-9200	488-7415
TF: 800-285-4387 ■ Web: www.davidsontransfer.com					
DeVries Moving Packing & Storage 3808 N Sullivan Rd Bldg 22	Spokane Valley	WA	99216	509-924-6000	924-6000
TF: 800-333-6352					
East Side Moving & Storage 4836 SE Powell Blvd	Portland	OR	97206	503-777-4181	775-8443
TF: 800-547-4600 ■ Web: www.move-northwest.com					
Graebel Van Lines Inc 16346 Airport Cir	Aurora	CO	80011	303-214-6683	214-2164
TF: 800-723-6683 ■ Web: www.graebel.com					
Hartford Despatch Moving & Storage Inc 225 Prospect St	East Hartford	CT	06108	860-528-2600	282-1224
TF: 866-502-8427 ■ Web: www.hartforddespatch.com					
Hilford Moving & Storage 1595 Arundell Ave	Ventura	CA	93003	805-642-0221	654-8402
TF: 800-739-6683 ■ Web: www.hilford.com					
Hollister Moving & Storage PO Box 1987	Hollister	CA	95024	831-637-6250	636-5029
I-Go Van & Storage 9820 S 142nd St	Omaha	NE	68138	402-891-1222	891-6762
TF: 800-228-9276 ■ Web: www.igovanandstorage.com					
Johnson Storage & Moving Co 221 Broadway	Denver	CO	80202	303-778-6683	698-0512
TF: 800-289-6683 ■ Web: www.johnsonstorage.com					
King Relocation Services 13535 Larwin Cir	Santa Fe Springs	CA	90670	800-854-3679	
TF: 800-854-3679 ■ Web: www.kingrelocation.com					
Lido Van & Storage Co Inc 2152 Alton Pkwy # N	Irvine	CA	92606	949-863-9000	474-7240
TF: 800-339-5436 ■ Web: www.lidomoving.com					
Mayflower Transit LLC 1 Mayflower Dr	Saint Louis	MO	63026	636-305-4000	326-1106
TF: 800-325-3924 ■ Web: www.mayflower.com/moving					
McCollister's Transportation Group Inc 1800 Rt 130 N PO Box 9	Burlington	NJ	08016	609-386-0600	386-5608
TF: 800-257-9595 ■ Web: www.mccollisters.com					
Nassau World Wide Movers Inc 63 Lamar St	West Babylon	NY	11704	631-491-3600	491-3600
TF: 800-327-9343 ■ Web: www.nwwm.net					
National Van Lines Inc 2800 W Roosevelt Rd	Broadview	IL	60155	708-450-2900	450-0069*
*Fax: Cust Svc ■ TF: 800-323-1962 ■ Web: www.nationalvanlines.com					
Nationwide Van Lines Inc 5450 S State Rd 7 Suite 39	Hollywood	FL	33314	954-585-3945	585-3970
TF: 800-310-0056 ■ Web: www.movingnationwide.com					
Nelson Westerberg Inc 1500 Arthur Ave Suite 200	Elk Grove Village	IL	60007	847-437-2080	437-2199
TF: 800-245-2080 ■ Web: www.nelsonwesterberg.com					
NorthStar Moving Corp 9120 Mason Ave	Chatsworth	CA	91311	818-727-0128	727-7527
TF: 800-275-7767 ■ Web: www.northstarmoving.com					
Palmer Moving & Storage 24660 Dequindre Rd	Warren	MI	48091	586-834-3400	834-3414
TF: 800-521-3954 ■ Web: www.palmermoving.com					
Paxton Van Lines Inc 5300 Port Royal Rd	Springfield	VA	22151	703-321-7600	321-7729
TF: 800-336-4536 ■ Web: www.paxton.com					
Pickens-Kane Moving Co 410 N Milwaukee Ave	Chicago	IL	60610	312-942-0330	243-3287
TF: 800-853-6462 ■ Web: www.pickenskane.com					
S & M Moving Systems Inc 12128 Burke St	Santa Fe Springs	CA	90670	562-567-2100	693-5690
TF: 800-336-5556 ■ Web: www.smmoving.com					
Security Storage Co 1701 Florida Ave NW	Washington	DC	20009	202-234-5600	234-3513
TF: 800-736-6825 ■ Web: www.sscw.com					
Smith Dray Line 320 Frontage Rd	Greenville	SC	29611	864-269-3696	269-3023
TF: 800-327-5673 ■ Web: www.smithdray.com					
Starving Students Moving & Storage Co 1850 Sawtelle Blvd Suite 300	Los Angeles	CA	90025	800-254-0375	825-1145
TF: 800-441-6683 ■ Web: www.ssmovers.com					
Stevens Worldwide Van Lines 527 Morley Dr	Saginaw	MI	48601	989-755-3000	755-0570
TF: 888-860-4566 ■ Web: www.stevensworldwide.com					
Suddath Cos 815 S Main St	Jacksonville	FL	32207	904-390-7100	390-7135*
*Fax: Hum Res ■ TF: 800-395-7100 ■ Web: www.suddath.com					
Truckin Movers Corp 1031 Harvest St	Durham	NC	27704	919-682-2300	688-2264
TF: 800-334-1651 ■ Web: www.truckinmovers.com					
Two Guys Relocation Systems Inc 3571 Pacific Hwy	San Diego	CA	92101	619-296-7995	296-7704
Two Men & A Truck International Inc 3400 Belle Chase Way	Lansing	MI	48911	517-394-7210	394-7432
TF: 800-345-1070 ■ Web: www.twomenandatruck.com					
UniGroup Inc 1 Premier Dr	Fenton	MO	63026	636-305-5000	349-8504*
*Fax: Mktg ■ TF: 800-325-3924 ■ Web: www.unigroupinc.com					
UniGroup Worldwide UTS 1 Worldwide Dr	Saint Louis	MO	63026	636-305-6000	305-6097
TF: 800-325-3924 ■ Web: www.unigroupworldwide.com					
United Van Lines Inc 1 United Dr	Saint Louis	MO	63026	636-326-3100	326-1106
TF: 800-325-3924 ■ Web: www.unitedvanlines.com					
Von Paris & Sons Inc 8691 Larkin Rd	Savage	MD	20763	410-888-8500	888-9062*
*Fax: Cust Svc ■ TF: 800-866-6355 ■ Web: www.vonparis.com					
Wald Relocation Services Ltd 8708 W Little York Rd Suite 190	Houston	TX	77040	713-512-4800	512-4881
TF: 800-527-1408 ■ Web: www.waldrelocation.com					
Werner-Donaldson Moving Services Inc 2901 E 10th Ave	Tampa	FL	33605	813-344-1756	
TF: 888-666-1834 ■ Web: www.wdmoving.com					
Wheaton Van Lines Inc 8010 Castleton Rd	Indianapolis	IN	46250	317-849-7900	570-4643*
*Fax: Cust Svc ■ TF: 800-932-7799 ■ Web: www.wheatonworldwide.com					

523 MUSEUMS

SEE ALSO Museums - Children's p. 2290; Museums & Halls of Fame - Sports p. 2292

Listings For Museums Are Organized Alphabetically Within State And Province Groupings. (Canadian Provinces Are Interfiled Among The Us States, In Alphabetical Order.)

ALABAMA

Name / Address	City	State	Zip	Phone	Fax
Alabama Constitution Village 109 Gates Ave	Huntsville	AL	35801	256-564-8100	564-8151
TF: 800-678-1819 ■ Web: www.earlyworks.com/village.html					
Alabama Dept of Archives & History 624 Washington Ave PO Box 300100	Montgomery	AL	36104	334-242-4435	240-3433
Web: www.archives.state.al.us					
Alabama Jazz Hall of Fame 1631 4th Ave	Birmingham	AL	35203	205-254-2731	254-2785
Web: www.jazzhall.com					
Alabama Museum of Natural History 427 6th Ave	Tuscaloosa	AL	35487	205-348-7550	348-9292
Web: www.amnh.ua.edu					
American Sport Art Museum & Archives 1 Academy Dr	Daphne	AL	36526	251-626-3303	621-2527
Web: www.asama.org					
Arlington Antebellum Home & Gardens 331 Cotton Ave SW	Birmingham	AL	35211	205-780-5656	788-0585
Web: www.informationbirmingham.com					
Barber Vintage Motorsports Museum 6030 Barber Motorsports Pkwy	Leeds	AL	35094	205-699-7275	702-8700
Web: www.barbermuseum.org					
Bessemer Hall of History 1905 Alabama Ave	Bessemer	AL	35020	205-426-1633	
Birmingham Civil Rights Institute 520 16th St N	Birmingham	AL	35203	205-328-9696	323-5219
TF: 866-328-9696 ■ Web: www.bcri.org					
Birmingham Museum of Art 2000 8th Ave N	Birmingham	AL	35203	205-254-2566	254-2714
Web: www.artsbma.org					
Bragg-Mitchell Mansion 1906 Springhill Ave	Mobile	AL	36607	251-471-6364	478-3800
TF: 866-471-6364 ■ Web: www.braggmitchellmansion.com					
Burritt on the Mountain 3101 Burritt Dr	Huntsville	AL	35801	256-536-2882	532-1784
Web: www.burrittonthemountain.com					
F Scott & Zelda Fitzgerald Museum 919 Felder Ave	Montgomery	AL	36106	334-264-4222	
Web: www.fitzgerald-museum.com					
First White House of the Confederacy 644 Washington Ave	Montgomery	AL	36104	334-242-1861	
Hank Williams Museum & Memorial 118 Commerce St	Montgomery	AL	36104	334-262-3600	262-3603
Web: www.thehankwilliamsmuseum.com					
Historic Huntsville Depot 320 Church St	Huntsville	AL	35801	256-564-8100	535-6018
TF: 800-678-1819 ■ Web: www.earlyworks.com/depot.html					
Huntsville Museum of Art 300 Church St SW	Huntsville	AL	35801	256-535-4350	532-1743
TF: 800-786-9095 ■ Web: www.hsvmuseum.org					
Jasmine Hill Gardens & Outdoor Museum 3001 Jasmine Hill Rd	Wetumpka	AL	36093	334-567-6463	
Web: www.jasminehill.org					
Kentuck Museum 503 Main Ave	Northport	AL	35476	205-758-1257	758-1258
Mann Wildlife Learning Museum 325 Vandiver Blvd Montgomery Zoo	Montgomery	AL	36110	334-240-4900	240-4916
Web: www.mannmuseum.com					
McWane Center Science Museum 200 19th St N	Birmingham	AL	35203	205-714-8300	714-8400
TF: 877-462-9263 ■ Web: www.mcwane.org					
Mobile Museum of Art 4850 Museum Dr	Mobile	AL	36608	251-208-5200	208-5201
Web: www.mobilemuseumofart.com					
Montgomery Museum of Fine Arts 1 Museum Dr PO Box 230819	Montgomery	AL	36117	334-240-4333	240-4384
Web: www.mmfa.org					
North Alabama Railroad Museum 694 Chase Rd	Huntsville	AL	35815	256-851-6276	
Web: www.northalabamarailroadmuseum.com					
Phoenix Fire Museum 203 S Claiborne St	Mobile	AL	36602	251-208-7554	
Richards-DAR House Museum 256 N Joachim St	Mobile	AL	36603	251-208-7320	
Web: www.richardsdarhouse.com					

				Phone	Fax
Rosa Parks Library & Museum 252 Montgomery St Troy University Montgomery *Web:* montgomery.troy.edu/rosaparks/museum	Montgomery	AL	36104	334-241-8661	241-9756
Sloss Furnaces National Historic Landmark 20 32nd St N *Web:* www.slossfurnaces.com	Birmingham	AL	35222	205-324-1911	324-6758
Southern Museum of Flight 4343 73rd St N *Web:* www.southernmuseumofflight.org	Birmingham	AL	35206	205-833-8226	836-2439
US Space & Rocket Ctr 1 Tranquility Base *TF:* 800-637-7223 ■ *Web:* www.spacecamp.com	Huntsville	AL	35805	256-837-3400	837-6137
Weeden House Museum 300 Gates Ave SE *Web:* www.weedenhousemuseum.com	Huntsville	AL	35801	256-536-7718	
Westervelt Warner Museum of American Art 8316 Mountbatten Rd NE *Web:* www.warnermuseum.org	Tuscaloosa	AL	35406	205-343-4543	345-1493

ALASKA

				Phone	Fax
Alaska Aviation Heritage Museum 4721 Aircraft Dr *Web:* www.alaskaairmuseum.com	Anchorage	AK	99502	907-248-5325	248-6391
Alaska Native Heritage Ctr 8800 Heritage Ctr Dr *TF:* 800-315-6608 ■ *Web:* www.alaskanative.net	Anchorage	AK	99504	907-330-8000	330-8030
Alaska State Museum 395 Whittier St *Web:* www.museums.state.ak.us	Juneau	AK	99801	907-465-2901	465-2976
Anchorage Museum of History & Art 121 W 7th Ave *Web:* www.anchoragemuseum.org	Anchorage	AK	99501	907-343-4326	343-6149
Baranov Museum The 101 Marine Way *Web:* www.baranov.us	Kodiak	AK	99615	907-486-5920	486-3166
Fraternal Order of Alaska State Troopers Museum 245 W 5th Ave *TF:* 800-770-5050 ■ *Web:* www.alaskatroopermuseum.com	Anchorage	AK	99501	907-279-5050	279-5054
Imaginarium Science Discovery Ctr 737 W 5th Ave Suite G *Web:* www.imaginarium.org	Anchorage	AK	99501	907-276-3179	258-4306
Juneau-Douglas City Museum 114 W 4th St *Web:* www.juneau.lib.ak.us	Juneau	AK	99801	907-586-3572	586-3203
Last Chance Mining Museum & Historic Park 1001 Basin Rd	Juneau	AK	99801	907-586-5338	586-5820
Oscar Anderson House Museum 420 M St Elderberry Pk	Anchorage	AK	99501	907-274-2336	
Pioneer Museum Airport Way & Peger Rd	Fairbanks	AK	99707	907-456-8579	
Sheldon Jackson Museum 104 College Dr *Web:* www.museums.state.ak.us	Sitka	AK	99835	907-747-8981	747-3004
Tongass Historical Museum 629 Dock St	Ketchikan	AK	99901	907-225-5600	225-5602
University of Alaska Museum of the North 907 Yukon Dr *Web:* www.uaf.edu/museum	Fairbanks	AK	99775	907-474-7505	474-5469

ALBERTA

				Phone	Fax
Aero Space Museum of Calgary 4629 McCall Way NE *Web:* www.asmac.ab.ca	Calgary	AB	T2E7H1	403-250-3752	250-8399
Alberta Aviation Museum 11410 Kingsway Ave *Web:* www.albertaaviationmuseum.com	Edmonton	AB	T5G0X4	780-451-1175	451-1607
Glenbow Museum 130-9 Ave SE *Web:* www.glenbow.org	Calgary	AB	T2G0P3	403-268-4100	265-9769
Naval Museum of Alberta 4520 Crowchild Trail SW	Calgary	AB	T2T5J4	403-242-8933	240-1966
Reynolds-Alberta Museum PO Box 6360 *TF:* 800-661-4726 ■ *Web:* www.culture.alberta.ca/museums	Wetaskiwin	AB	T9A2G1	780-361-1351	361-1239
Royal Alberta Museum 102nd Ave Suite 12845 *Web:* www.royalalbertamuseum.ca	Edmonton	AB	T5N0M6	780-453-9100	454-6629
Royal Tyrrell Museum of Palaeontology Hwy 838 Midland Provincial Pk *TF:* 888-440-4240 ■ *Web:* www.tyrrellmuseum.com	Drumheller	AB	T0J0Y0	403-823-7707	823-7131
TELUS World of Science 11211 142nd St *Web:* www.edmontonscience.com	Edmonton	AB	T5M4A1	780-451-3344	455-5882

ARIZONA

				Phone	Fax
390th Memorial Museum 6000 E Valencia Rd *Web:* www.390th.org	Tucson	AZ	85706	520-574-0287	574-3030
Arizona Doll & Toy Museum 602 E Adams St	Phoenix	AZ	85004	602-253-9337	
Arizona Historical Society Museum 1300 N College Ave *Web:* www.arizonahistoricalsociety.org	Tempe	AZ	85281	480-929-0292	967-5450
Arizona Historical Society Pioneer Museum 2340 N Fort Valley Rd *Web:* www.arizonahistoricalsociety.org	Flagstaff	AZ	86001	928-774-6272	774-1596
Arizona Museum for Youth 35 N Robson St *Web:* www.arizonamuseumforyouth.com	Mesa	AZ	85201	480-644-2468	644-2466
Arizona Science Ctr 600 E Washington St *Web:* www.azscience.org	Phoenix	AZ	85004	602-716-2000	716-2099
Arizona State Capitol Museum 1700 W Washington St *Web:* www.dlapr.lib.az.us	Phoenix	AZ	85007	602-542-4675	542-4690
Arizona State Museum 1013 E University Blvd University of Arizona *Web:* www.statemuseum.arizona.edu	Tucson	AZ	85721	520-621-6302	626-6761
Arizona State University Art Museum 10th St & Mill Ave Nelson Fine Arts Ctr Arizona State University *Web:* www.asuartmuseum.asu.edu	Tempe	AZ	85287	480-965-2787	965-5254
Arizona State University Museum of Anthropology Anthropology Bldg PO Box 872402 *Web:* www.shesc.asu.edu	Tempe	AZ	85287	480-965-6213	965-7671
Arizona Wing Commemorative Air Force Museum 2017 N Greenfield Rd Falcon Field *Web:* www.arizonawingcaf.org	Mesa	AZ	85215	480-924-1940	981-1954
Arizona-Sonora Desert Museum 2021 N Kinney Rd *Web:* www.desertmuseum.org	Tucson	AZ	85743	520-883-1380	883-2500
Center for Creative Photography 1030 N Olive Rd Bldg 103 University of Arizona *Web:* www.dizzy.library.arizona.edu	Tucson	AZ	85721	520-621-7968	621-9444
DeGrazia Gallery in the Sun 6300 N Swan Rd *TF:* 800-545-2185 ■ *Web:* www.degrazia.org	Tucson	AZ	85718	520-299-9191	299-1381
Flandrau Science Center & Planetarium University of Arizona 1601 E University Blvd *Web:* www.flandrau.org	Tucson	AZ	85721	520-621-4515	621-8451
Fort Lowell Museum 2900 N Craycroft Rd	Tucson	AZ	85712	520-885-3832	
Grand Canyon National Park Museum Collection Grand Canyon National Pk PO Box 129	Grand Canyon	AZ	86023	928-638-7769	638-7769
Hall of Flame Museum of Firefighting 6101 E Van Buren St *Web:* www.hallofflame.org	Phoenix	AZ	85008	602-275-3473	275-0896
Heard Museum 2301 N Central Ave *Web:* www.heard.org	Phoenix	AZ	85004	602-252-8840	252-9757
Huhugam Ki Museum 10005 E Osborn Rd Salt River Indian Reservation	Scottsdale	AZ	85256	480-362-6320	850-8961
International Wildlife Museum 4800 W Gates Pass Rd *Web:* www.thewildlifemuseum.org	Tucson	AZ	85745	520-629-0100	618-3561
Mesa Historical Museum 2345 N Horne St *Web:* www.mesaaz.org	Mesa	AZ	85203	480-835-7358	835-1442
Meteor Crater & Museum of Astrogeology Exit 233 off I-40 Meteor Crater Rd *TF:* 800-289-5898 ■ *Web:* www.meteorcrater.com	Winslow	AZ	86047	928-289-2362	289-2598
Museo Chicano 147 E Adams St	Phoenix	AZ	85004	602-257-5536	257-5539
Museum of Northern Arizona 3101 N Fort Valley Rd *TF:* 800-423-1069 ■ *Web:* www.musnaz.org	Flagstaff	AZ	86001	928-774-5211	774-1229
Old Pueblo Archaeology Ctr 2201 W 44th St *Web:* www.oldpueblo.org	Tucson	AZ	85713	520-798-1201	798-1966
Petersen House Museum 1414 W Southern Ave *Web:* www.tempe.gov/museum	Tempe	AZ	85282	480-350-5100	350-5150
Phoenix Art Museum 1625 N Central Ave *Web:* www.phxart.org	Phoenix	AZ	85004	602-257-1222	253-8662
Phoenix Police Museum 101 S Central Ave Suite 100 *Web:* www.phoenixpolicemuseum.com	Phoenix	AZ	85004	602-534-7278	495-2491
Pima Air & Space Museum 6000 E Valencia Rd *Web:* www.pimaair.org	Tucson	AZ	85706	520-574-0462	574-9238
Pioneer Arizona Living History Museum 3901 W Pioneer Rd *Web:* www.pioneeraz.org	Phoenix	AZ	85086	623-465-1052	465-0683
Pueblo Grande Museum & Archaeological Park 4619 E Washington St *TF:* 877-706-4408 ■ *Web:* www.phoenix.gov/email/svfdback.html	Phoenix	AZ	85034	602-495-0901	495-5645
Rosson House Historic Museum 7th & Washington Sts *Web:* www.rossonhousemuseum.org	Phoenix	AZ	85004	602-262-5029	
Scottsdale Historical Museum 7333 E Civic Ctr Mall PO Box 143 *Web:* www.scottsdalemuseum.com	Scottsdale	AZ	85251	480-945-4499	970-3251
Scottsdale Museum of Contemporary Art 7374 E 2nd St *Web:* www.scottsdalearts.org	Scottsdale	AZ	85251	480-874-4666	874-4699
Shemer Arts Center & Museum 5005 E Camelback Rd *Web:* phoenix.gov/PARKS/shemer.html	Phoenix	AZ	85018	602-262-4727	262-1605
Tempe Historical Museum 809 E Southern Ave *Web:* www.tempe.gov/museum	Tempe	AZ	85282	480-350-5100	350-5150
Tucson Museum of Art & Historic Block 140 N Main Ave *Web:* www.tucsonarts.com	Tucson	AZ	85701	520-624-2333	624-7202
University of Arizona Museum of Art Park Ave & Speedway Blvd University of Arizona *Web:* www.artmuseum.arizona.edu	Tucson	AZ	85721	520-621-7567	621-8770

ARKANSAS

				Phone	Fax
Aerospace Education Ctr 3301 E Roosevelt Rd *Web:* www.aerospaced.org	Little Rock	AR	72206	501-376-4232	372-4826
Arkansas Arts Ctr 501 E 9th St *TF:* 800-264-2787 ■ *Web:* www.arkarts.com	Little Rock	AR	72202	501-372-4000	375-8053
Arkansas Museum of Science & History *Museum of Discovery* 500 President Clinton Ave Suite 150 *TF:* 800-880-6475 ■ *Web:* www.amod.org	Little Rock	AR	72201	501-396-7050	396-7054
Arkansas State University Museum 110 Cooley Dr PO Box 490 *Web:* www.museum.astate.edu	State University	AR	72467	870-972-2074	972-2793
EMOBA -The Museum of Black Arkansans & Performing Arts Ctr 1208 Louisiana St *Web:* www.it1.ualr.edu	Little Rock	AR	72202	501-372-0018	661-1323
Fort Smith Art Ctr 701 Rogers Ave *Web:* www.fsram.org	Fort Smith	AR	72901	479-784-2787	784-9071
Fort Smith Museum of History 320 Rogers Ave	Fort Smith	AR	72901	479-783-7841	783-3244

	City	State	ZIP	Phone	Fax
Fort Smith Trolley Museum 100 S 4th St *Web:* www.fstm.org	Fort Smith	AR	72901	479-783-0205	782-0649
Historic Arkansas Museum 200 E 3rd St *Web:* www.arkansashistory.com	Little Rock	AR	72201	501-324-9351	324-9345
Josephine Tussaud Wax Museum 250 Central Ave *Web:* www.rideaduck.com	Hot Springs	AR	71901	501-623-5836	
MacArthur Museum of Arkansas Military History 503 E 9th St *Web:* www.arkmilitaryheritage.com	Little Rock	AR	72202	501-376-4602	376-4593
Mid-America Science Museum 500 Mid-America Blvd *TF:* 800-632-0583 ■ *Web:* www.direclynx.net	Hot Springs	AR	71913	501-767-3461	767-1170
Museum of Discovery 500 President Clinton Ave Suite 150 *TF:* 800-880-6475 ■ *Web:* www.amod.org	Little Rock	AR	72201	501-396-7050	396-7054
Old State House Museum 300 W Markham St *Web:* www.oldstatehouse.com	Little Rock	AR	72201	501-324-9685	324-9688
Terry House Community Gallery 501 East 9th St *Web:* www.arkarts.com	Little Rock	AR	72202	501-372-4000	375-8053
University of Arkansas Little Rock Gallery 2801 S University Ave *Web:* www.ualr.edu/artdept/gallery	Little Rock	AR	72204	501-569-3183	683-7022

BRITISH COLUMBIA

	City	Prov	Postal Code	Phone	Fax
Biblical Museum of Canada 3180 E 58th Ave Unit 70 *Web:* www.biblicalmuseum.com	Vancouver	BC	V5S3S8	604-432-6122	
Canadian Museum of Flight 5333 216th St Hangar 3 *Web:* www.canadianflight.org	Langley	BC	V2Y2N3	604-532-0035	532-0056
Canadian Museum of Rail Travel 57 Van Horne St S PO Box 400 *Web:* www.crowsnest.bc.ca/cmrt	Cranbrook	BC	V1C4H9	250-489-3918	489-5744
Comox Air Force Museum 19 Wing Comox PO Box 1000 Stn Forces *Web:* www.comoxairforcemuseum.ca	Lazo	BC	V0R2K0	250-339-8162	339-8162
Granville Island Model Ships Museum 1502 Duranleau St Granville Island *Web:* www.modelshipsmuseum.com	Vancouver	BC	V6H3S4	604-683-1939	683-7533
Granville Island Model Trains Museum 1502 Duranleau St Granville Island *Web:* www.modeltrainsmuseum.com	Vancouver	BC	V6H3S4	604-683-1939	683-7533
Museum of Vancouver 1100 Chestnut St Vanier Pk *Web:* www.museumofvancouver.ca	Vancouver	BC	V6J5E5	604-736-4431	736-5417
North Vancouver Museum & Archives 3203 Institute Rd *Web:* www.northvanmuseum.ca	North Vancouver	BC	V7K3E5	604-990-3700	987-5609
Royal British Columbia Museum (RBCM) 675 Belleville St *TF:* 888-447-7977 ■ *Web:* www.royalbcmuseum.bc.ca	Victoria	BC	V8W9W2	250-356-7226	387-5674
University of British Columbia Museum of Anthropology 6393 NW Marine Dr *Web:* www.moa.ubc.ca	Vancouver	BC	V6T1Z2	604-822-5087	822-2974

CALIFORNIA

	City	State	ZIP	Phone	Fax
African American Historical & Cultural Museum of San Joaquin Valley 1857 Fulton St	Fresno	CA	93721	559-268-7102	268-7171
African American Museum & Library in Oakland 659 14th St *Web:* www.oaklandlibrary.org/AAMLO	Oakland	CA	94612	510-637-0200	637-0204
Agua Caliente Cultural Museum 219 S Palm Canyon Dr *Web:* www.accmuseum.org	Palm Springs	CA	92262	760-323-0151	320-0350
Ainsley House 300 Grant St *Web:* www.campbellmuseums.org	Campbell	CA	95008	408-866-2119	866-2795
Albinger Archaeological Museum 113 E Main St	Ventura	CA	93001	805-648-5823	
Alice Arts Ctr 1428 Alice St	Oakland	CA	94612	510-238-7219	238-7225
Anaheim Museum 241 S Anaheim Blvd *Web:* www.anaheimmuseum.com	Anaheim	CA	92805	714-778-3301	778-6740
Ardenwood Historic Farm 34600 Ardenwood Blvd *TF:* 888-327-2757 ■ *Web:* www.ebparks.org	Fremont	CA	94555	510-544-2797	796-0231
Asian Art Museum 200 Larkin St Civic Ctr Plaza *Web:* www.asianart.org	San Francisco	CA	94102	415-581-3500	581-4700
Autry National Center Museum of the American West 4700 Western Heritage Way *Web:* www.theautry.com	Los Angeles	CA	90027	323-667-2000	660-5721
Bakersfield Museum of Art 1930 R St *Web:* www.bmoa.org	Bakersfield	CA	93301	661-323-7219	323-7266
Banning Museum The 401 E 'M' St *Web:* banningmuseum.org	Wilmington	CA	90744	310-548-7777	548-2644
Berkeley Art Museum & Pacific Film Archive 2626 Bancroft Way Suite 2250 *Web:* www.bampfa.berkeley.edu	Berkeley	CA	94720	510-642-0808	642-4889
Bonita Historical Museum 4355 Bonita Rd *Web:* www.bonitacalifornia.org	Bonita	CA	91902	619-267-5141	267-2143
Bowers Museum of Cultural Art 2002 N Main St *Web:* www.bowers.org	Santa Ana	CA	92706	714-567-3600	567-3603
Brand Library & Art Ctr 1601 W Mountain St *Web:* www.library.ci.glendale.ca.us	Glendale	CA	91201	818-548-2051	548-5079
Buena Vista Museum of Natural History 2018 Chester Ave *Web:* www.sharktoothhill.com	Bakersfield	CA	93301	661-324-6350	324-7522
Cabot's Pueblo Museum 67-616 E Desert View Ave *TF:* 866-941-7610 ■ *Web:* www.cabotsmuseum.org	Desert Hot Springs	CA	92240	760-329-7610	329-2738
California Academy of Sciences 55 Music Concourse Dr Golden Gate Pk *Web:* www.calacademy.org	San Francisco	CA	94103	415-321-8000	321-8610
California African American Museum 600 State Dr Exposition Pk *Web:* www.caamuseum.org	Los Angeles	CA	90037	213-744-7432	744-2050
California Living Museum (CALM) 10500 Alfred Harrell Hwy *Web:* www.calmzoo.org	Bakersfield	CA	93306	661-872-2256	872-2205
California Military Museum 1119 2nd St *Web:* www.militarymuseum.org	Sacramento	CA	95814	916-442-2883	442-7532
California Museum for History Women & the Arts 1020 'O' St *Web:* www.californiamuseum.org	Sacramento	CA	95814	916-653-7524	653-0314
California Museum of Photography 3824 Main St *Web:* www.cmp.ucr.edu	Riverside	CA	92501	951-784-3686	827-4797
California Science Ctr 700 State Dr *Web:* www.californiasciencecenter.org	Los Angeles	CA	90037	213-744-7400	744-2650
California State Archives 1020 'O' St *Web:* www.ss.ca.gov	Sacramento	CA	95814	916-653-7715	653-7134
California State Capitol Museum 10th & L Sts *TF:* 866-240-4655 ■ *Web:* www.capitolmuseum.ca.gov	Sacramento	CA	95814	916-324-0333	445-3628
California State Indian Museum c/o Capital District Office 101 J St *Web:* www.parks.ca.gov/default.asp?page_id=486	Sacramento	CA	95816	916-324-0971	322-5231
California State Railroad Museum c/o Capital District Office 111 'I' St *Web:* www.csrmf.org	Sacramento	CA	95814	916-323-9280	327-5655
Campbell Historical Museum 51 N Central Ave *Web:* www.campbellmuseums.org	Campbell	CA	95008	408-866-2757	866-2795
Carnegie Art Museum 424 S 'C' St *Web:* www.carnegieam.org	Oxnard	CA	93030	805-385-8158	483-3654
Cartoon Art Museum 655 Mission St *Web:* www.cartoonart.org	San Francisco	CA	94105	415-227-8666	243-8666
Center for Beethoven Studies & Museum 150 E San Fernando St Dr MLK Jr Library 5th Fl *Web:* www.sjsu.edu	San Jose	CA	95112	408-808-2058	808-2060
Chabot Space & Science Ctr 10000 Skyline Blvd *Web:* www.chabotspace.org	Oakland	CA	94619	510-336-7300	336-7491
Chula Vista Heritage Museum 360 3rd Ave *Web:* www.chulavistaca.gov	Chula Vista	CA	91910	619-427-8092	
Clarke Historical Museum 240 E St *Web:* www.clarkemuseum.org	Eureka	CA	95501	707-443-1947	443-0290
Coachella Valley History Museum 82-616 Miles Ave PO Box 595 *Web:* www.coachellavalleymuseum.org	Indio	CA	92201	760-342-6651	863-5232
Colton Hall Museum Pacific St Monterey City Hall *Web:* www.monterey.org/museum	Monterey	CA	93940	831-646-5640	646-3917
Contemporary Jewish Museum 121 Steuart St *Web:* www.jmsf.org	San Francisco	CA	94105	415-344-8800	344-8815
Crocker Art Museum 216 'O' St *Web:* www.crockerartmuseum.org	Sacramento	CA	95814	916-264-5423	264-7372
Crown Point Press 20 Hawthorne St *Web:* www.crownpoint.com	San Francisco	CA	94105	415-974-6273	495-4220
de Saisset Museum at Santa Clara University 500 El Camino Real *Web:* www.scu.edu/deSaisset	Santa Clara	CA	95053	408-554-4528	554-7840
Death Valley Museum Death Valley National Pk PO Box 579 *Web:* www.nps.gov/deva	Death Valley	CA	92328	760-786-2331	786-3283
Discovery Science Ctr 2500 N Main St *Web:* www.discoverycube.org	Santa Ana	CA	92705	714-542-2823	542-2828
Dr Willella Howe-Waffle House & Medical Museum 120 Civic Ctr Dr *Web:* www.santaanahistory.com	Santa Ana	CA	92701	714-547-9645	
Euphrat Museum of Art 21250 Stevens Creek Blvd De Anza College	San Jose	CA	95014	408-864-8836	
Exploratorium The 3601 Lyon St *Web:* www.exploratorium.edu	San Francisco	CA	94123	415-561-0360	561-0370
Firehouse Museum 1572 Columbia St	San Diego	CA	92101	619-232-3473	
Flying Leatherneck Aviation Museum Anderson Ave MCAS Miramar *Web:* www.flyingleathernecks.org	San Diego	CA	94018	858-693-1723	693-0037
Forest Lawn Museum 1712 S Glendale Ave *TF:* 800-204-3131 ■ *Web:* www.forestlawn.com	Glendale	CA	91205	800-204-3131	
Fort MacArthur Museum 3601 S Gaffey St *Web:* www.ftmac.org	San Pedro	CA	90731	310-548-2631	241-0847
Fresno Art Museum 2233 N 1st St *Web:* www.fresnoartmuseum.com	Fresno	CA	93703	559-441-4220	441-4227
Fresno Metropolitan Museum of Art History & Science 1555 Van Ness Ave *Web:* www.fresnomet.org	Fresno	CA	93721	559-441-1444	441-8607
George C Page Museum at La Brea Tar Pits 5801 Wilshire Blvd *Web:* www.tarpits.org	Los Angeles	CA	90036	323-857-6311	933-3974
Great Valley Museum of Natural History 1100 Stoddard Ave	Modesto	CA	95350	209-575-6196	549-7039
Grier-Musser Museum 403 S Bonnie Brae St	Los Angeles	CA	90057	213-413-1814	
Haggin Museum The 1201 N Pershing Ave *Web:* www.hagginmuseum.org	Stockton	CA	95203	209-940-6300	462-1404
Hellenic Heritage Museum 1650 Senter Rd *Web:* www.hellenicheritageinstitute.org	San Jose	CA	95112	408-247-4685	

Name / Address	City	State	ZIP	Phone	Fax
Heritage Museum of Orange County The 3101 W Harvard St *Web:* www.centennialmuseum.org	Santa Ana	CA	92704	714-540-0404	540-1932
Heritage of the Americas Museum 12110 Cuyamaca College Dr W *Web:* www.cuyamaca.net	El Cajon	CA	92019	619-670-5194	670-5198
Heritage Square Museum 3800 Homer St *Web:* www.heritagesquare.org	Los Angeles	CA	90031	323-225-2700	225-2725
Historical Glass Museum 1157 Orange St	Redlands	CA	92374	909-798-0868	
History San Jose - San Jose Historical Museum 1650 Senter Rd *Web:* www.historysanjose.org	San Jose	CA	95112	408-287-2290	287-2291
Hobby City Doll & Toy Museum 1238 S Beach Blvd	Anaheim	CA	92804	714-527-2323	236-9762
Hollywood Entertainment Museum 7021 Hollywood Blvd *Web:* www.hollywoodmuseum.com	Hollywood	CA	90028	323-465-7900	469-9576
Hollywood Museum 1660 N Highland Ave *Web:* www.thehollywoodmuseum.com	Hollywood	CA	90028	323-464-7776	464-3777
Hollywood Wax Museum 6767 Hollywood Blvd *Web:* www.hollywoodwaxmuseum.com	Hollywood	CA	90028	323-462-5991	462-3953
Intel Museum 2200 Mission College Blvd. *TF:* 800-628-8686 ■ *Web:* www.intel.com	Santa Clara	CA	95052	408-765-0503	765-1217
International Surfing Museum 411 Olive Ave *Web:* www.surfingmuseum.org	Huntington Beach	CA	92648	714-960-3483	960-1434
J Paul Getty Museum 1200 Getty Ctr Dr **Fax:* Hum Res ■ *Web:* www.getty.edu	Los Angeles	CA	90049	310-440-7300	440-7720*
Japanese American National Museum 369 E 1st St *TF:* 800-461-5266 ■ *Web:* www.janm.org	Los Angeles	CA	90012	213-625-0414	625-0414
Japanese-American Museum 535 N 5th St *Web:* www.jamsj.org	San Jose	CA	95112	408-294-3138	294-1657
Jensen-Alvarado Historic Ranch & Museum 4307 Briggs St	Riverside	CA	92509	951-369-6055	369-1153
Judah L Magnes Museum 2911 Russell St *Web:* www.magnes.org	Berkeley	CA	94705	510-549-6950	849-3673
Junipero Serra Museum 2727 Presidio Dr *Web:* www.sandiegohistory.org	San Diego	CA	92103	619-297-3258	297-3281
Kearney Mansion Museum 7160 W Kearney Blvd *Web:* www.valleyhistory.org	Fresno	CA	93706	559-441-0862	441-1372
Kern County Museum 3801 Chester Ave *Web:* www.kcmuseum.org	Bakersfield	CA	93301	661-852-5000	322-6415
Kern Valley Museum 49 Big Blue Rd PO Box 651	Kernville	CA	93238	760-376-6683	
Legion of Honor Museum 100 34th Ave Lincoln Pk. *Web:* www.legionofhonor.famsf.org	San Francisco	CA	94121	415-750-3600	
Legion of Valor Museum 2425 Fresno St Veterans Memorial Auditorium *Web:* www.legionofvalormuseum.org	Fresno	CA	93721	559-498-0510	498-3773
Long Beach Museum of Art 2300 E Ocean Blvd *Web:* www.lbma.org	Long Beach	CA	90803	562-439-2119	439-3587
Los Angeles County Museum of Art 5905 Wilshire Blvd *Web:* www.lacma.org	Los Angeles	CA	90036	323-857-6000	857-6212
March Field Air Museum 22550 Van Buren Blvd *Web:* www.marchfield.org	Riverside	CA	92518	951-902-5949	697-6605
Maritime Museum of San Diego 1492 N Harbor Dr *Web:* www.sdmaritime.org	San Diego	CA	92101	619-234-9153	234-8345
McClellan Aviation Museum 3200 Freedom Pk Dr. *Web:* www.mcclellanaviationmuseum.org	McClellan	CA	95652	916-643-3192	643-0389
McHenry Museum 1402 'I' St *Web:* www.mchenrymuseum.org	Modesto	CA	95354	209-577-5366	491-4407
Merritt Museum of Anthropology 12500 Campus Dr	Oakland	CA	94619	510-531-4911	436-2405
Meux Home Museum 1007 R St. *Web:* www.meux.mus.ca.us	Fresno	CA	93721	559-233-8007	233-2331
Mexican Museum Fort Mason Ctr Bldg D *Web:* www.mexicanmuseum.org	San Francisco	CA	94123	415-202-9700	441-7683
Mills College Art Museum 5000 MacArthur Blvd *Web:* www.mills.edu/campus_life/art_museum/index.php	Oakland	CA	94613	510-430-2164	430-3168
Mingei International Museum of Folk Art 1439 El Prado *Web:* www.mingei.org	San Diego	CA	92101	619-239-0003	239-0605
Minter Field Air Museum 401 Vultee St PO Box 445 *Web:* www.minterfieldairmuseum.com	Shafter	CA	93263	661-393-0291	393-3296
Mission Basilica San Diego de Alcala 10818 San Diego Mission Rd *Web:* www.missionsandiego.com	San Diego	CA	92108	619-283-7319	283-7762
Mission Inn Museum 3696 Main St *Web:* www.missioninnmuseum.com	Riverside	CA	92501	951-788-9556	341-6574
Monterey Maritime & History Museum 5 Custom House Plaza Stanton Ctr *Web:* www.montereyhistory.org	Monterey	CA	93940	831-373-2469	655-3054
Monterey Museum of Art 559 Pacific St *Web:* www.montereyart.org	Monterey	CA	93940	831-372-5477	372-5680
Museo Italo-Americano Fort Mason Ctr Bldg C *Web:* www.museoitaloamericano.org	San Francisco	CA	94123	415-673-2200	673-2292
Museum of Contemporary Art 250 S Grand Ave California Plaza *Web:* www.moca.org	Los Angeles	CA	90012	213-621-2766	620-8674
Museum of Craft & Folk Art 51 Yerba Buena Ln *Web:* www.mocfa.org	San Francisco	CA	94103	415-227-4888	227-4351
Museum of History & Art 1100 Orange Ave *Web:* www.coronadohistory.org	Coronado	CA	92118	619-435-7242	435-8504
Museum of Jurassic Technology 9341 Venice Blvd *Web:* www.mjt.org	Culver City	CA	90232	310-836-6131	287-2267
Museum of Latin American Art 628 Alamitos Ave *Web:* www.molaa.com	Long Beach	CA	90802	562-437-1689	437-7043
Museum of Local History 190 Anza St *Web:* www.museumoflocalhistory.org	Fremont	CA	94539	510-623-7907	
Museum of Making Music 5790 Armada Dr *Web:* www.museumofmakingmusic.org	Carlsbad	CA	92008	760-438-5996	438-8964
Museum of Neon Art 501 W Olympic Blvd Suite 101 *Web:* www.neonmona.org	Los Angeles	CA	90015	213-489-9918	489-9932
Museum of Photographic Arts 1649 El Prado *Web:* www.mopa.org	San Diego	CA	92101	619-238-7559	238-8777
Museum of San Diego History 1649 El Prado Balboa Pk *Web:* www.sandiegohistory.org	San Diego	CA	92101	619-232-6203	232-6297
Museum of Tolerance 9786 W Pico Blvd *TF:* 800-900-9036 ■ *Web:* www.wiesenthal.com	Los Angeles	CA	90035	310-553-8403	772-7655
National Steinbeck Ctr 1 Main St *Web:* www.steinbeck.org	Salinas	CA	93901	831-796-3833	796-3828
Natural History Museum of Los Angeles County 900 Exposition Blvd *Web:* www.nhm.org	Los Angeles	CA	90007	213-763-3466	746-2999
Newland House Museum 19820 Beach Blvd. *Web:* www.hbsurfcity.com/history/newland.htm	Huntington Beach	CA	92648	714-962-5777	
Niles Depot 3723 Darwin Dr *Web:* www.nilesdepot.railfan.net	Fremont	CA	94536	510-797-4449	
Norton Simon Museum 411 W Colorado Blvd *Web:* www.nortonsimon.org	Pasadena	CA	91105	626-449-6840	796-4978
Oakland Museum of California 1000 Oak St *TF:* 800-625-6873 ■ *Web:* www.museumca.org	Oakland	CA	94607	510-238-2200	238-2258
Orange County Museum of Art Newport Beach 850 San Clemente Dr *Web:* www.ocma.net	Newport Beach	CA	92660	949-759-1122	759-5623
Orange County Museum of Art South Coast Plaza 3333 Bear St 3rd Fl. *Web:* www.ocma.net	Costa Mesa	CA	92626	949-759-1122	759-5623
Pacific Asia Museum 46 N Los Robles Ave *Web:* www.pacificasiamuseum.org	Pasadena	CA	91101	626-449-2742	449-2754
Pacific Grove Museum of Natural History 165 Forest Ave *Web:* www.pgmuseum.org	Pacific Grove	CA	93950	831-648-5716	372-3256
Pacific Southwest Railway Museum 4695 Nebo Dr *Web:* www.psrm.org	La Mesa	CA	91941	619-465-7776	
Paley Center for Media The 465 N Beverly Dr *Web:* www.paleycenter.org	Beverly Hills	CA	90210	310-786-1000	786-1086
Palm Springs Air Museum 745 N Gene Autry Trail *Web:* palmspringsairmuseum.org	Palm Springs	CA	92262	760-778-6262	320-2548
Palm Springs Art Museum 101 Museum Dr *Web:* www.psmuseum.org	Palm Springs	CA	92262	760-322-4800	327-5069
Pardee Home Museum 672 11th St *Web:* www.pardeehome.org	Oakland	CA	94607	510-444-2187	444-7120
Petersen Automotive Museum 6060 Wilshire Blvd **Fax:* Admin ■ *Web:* www.petersen.org	Los Angeles	CA	90036	323-930-2277	930-6642*
Phoebe Apperson Hearst Museum of Anthropology 103 Kroeber Hall *Web:* www.hearstmuseum.berkeley.edu	Berkeley	CA	94720	510-642-3682	642-6271
Planes of Fame Air Museum 7000 Merrill Ave #17 *Web:* www.planesoffame.org	Chino	CA	91710	909-597-3722	597-4755
Port Hueneme Museum 220 N Market St	Port Hueneme	CA	93041	805-488-2023	488-6993
Queen Mary The 1126 Queens Hwy *TF:* 877-342-0738 ■ *Web:* www.queenmary.com	Long Beach	CA	90802	562-435-3511	437-4531
Rancho Los Alamitos Historic Ranch & Gardens 6400 E Bixby Hill Rd. *Web:* www.rancholosalamitos.com	Long Beach	CA	90815	562-431-3541	430-9694
Rancho Los Cerritos Historic Ranch 4600 Virginia Rd. *Web:* www.rancholoscerritos.org	Long Beach	CA	90807	562-570-1755	570-1893
Randall Museum 199 Museum Way *Web:* www.randallmuseum.org	San Francisco	CA	94114	415-554-9600	554-9609
Reuben H Fleet Science Center 1875 El Prado *Web:* www.rhfleet.org	San Diego	CA	92101	619-238-1233	685-5771
Richard Nixon Foundation The 18001 Yorba Linda Blvd *Web:* www.nixonfoundation.org	Yorba Linda	CA	92886	714-993-5075	528-0544
Ripley's Believe It or Not! Museum 7850 Beach Blvd	Buena Park	CA	90620	714-522-7045	
Ripley's Believe It or Not! Museum 6780 Hollywood Blvd *Web:* www.ripleys.com/hollywood	Hollywood	CA	90028	323-466-6335	466-6512
Riverside Art Museum 3425 Mission Inn Ave *Web:* www.riversideartmuseum.org	Riverside	CA	92501	951-684-7111	684-7332
Riverside Metropolitan Museum 3580 Mission Inn Ave *Web:* www.riversideca.gov/museum	Riverside	CA	92501	951-826-5273	369-4970
Robert V Fullerton Art Museum 5500 University Pkwy California State University *Web:* www.museum.csusb.edu	San Bernardino	CA	92407	909-537-7373	537-7068
Ronald Reagan Presidential Library & Museum 40 Presidential Dr *TF:* 800-410-8354 ■ *Web:* www.reagan.utexas.edu	Simi Valley	CA	93065	805-577-4000	577-4074

	City	State	Zip	Phone	Fax
Rosicrucian Egyptian Museum & Planetarium					
1342 Naglee Ave Rosicrucian Pk	San Jose	CA	95191	408-947-3636	947-3677
Web: www.rosicrucian.org					
San Bernardino County Museum					
2024 Orange Tree Ln.	Redlands	CA	92374	909-307-2669	307-0539
Web: www.co.san-bernardino.ca.us					
San Diego Air & Space Museum					
2001 Pan American Plaza Balboa Pk	San Diego	CA	92101	619-234-8291	233-4526
Web: www.aerospacemuseum.org					
San Diego Aircraft Carrier Museum					
910 N Harbor Dr Navy Pier	San Diego	CA	92101	619-544-9600	544-9188
Web: www.midway.org					
San Diego Archaeological Ctr					
16666 San Pasqual Valley Rd	Escondido	CA	92027	760-291-0370	291-0371
Web: www.sandiegoarchaeology.org					
San Diego Automotive Museum					
2080 Pan American Plaza Balboa Pk	San Diego	CA	92101	619-231-2886	231-9869
Web: www.sdautomuseum.org					
San Diego Hall of Champions Sports Museum					
2131 Pan American Plaza Balboa Pk	San Diego	CA	92101	619-234-2544	234-4543
Web: www.sdhoc.com					
San Diego Model Railroad Museum					
1649 El Prado Balboa Pk	San Diego	CA	92101	619-696-0199	696-0239
Web: www.sdmodelrailroadm.com					
San Diego Museum of Art					
1450 El Prado Balboa Pk PO Box 122107	San Diego	CA	92101	619-232-7931	232-9367
Web: www.sdmart.com					
San Diego Museum of Man					
1350 El Prado Balboa Pk	San Diego	CA	92101	619-239-2001	239-2749
Web: www.museumofman.org					
San Diego Natural History Museum					
1788 El Prado Po Box 121390	San Diego	CA	92101	619-232-3821	232-0248
Web: www.sdnhm.org					
San Francisco Fire Dept Museum					
655 Presidio Ave.	San Francisco	CA	94115	415-563-4630	
San Francisco Museum of Modern Art					
151 3rd St.	San Francisco	CA	94103	415-357-4000	357-4037
Web: www.sfmoma.org					
San Joaquin County Historical Society & Museum					
11793 N Micke Grove Rd	Lodi	CA	95240	209-331-2055	331-2057
Web: www.sanjoaquinhistory.org					
San Jose Museum of Art 110 S Market St.	San Jose	CA	95113	408-271-6840	294-2977
Web: www.sjmusart.org					
San Jose Museum of Quilts & Textiles					
520 S 1st St	San Jose	CA	95113	408-971-0323	971-7226
Web: www.sjquiltmuseum.org					
Santa Barbara Museum of Art					
1130 State St	Santa Barbara	CA	93101	805-963-4364	966-6840
Web: www.sbmuseart.org					
Santa Barbara Museum of Natural History					
2559 Puesta Del Sol Rd	Santa Barbara	CA	93105	805-682-4711	569-3170
Web: www.sbnature.org					
Santa Cruz Harley-Davidson Museum					
1148 Soquel Ave.	Santa Cruz	CA	95062	831-421-9600	427-9309
Web: www.santacruzharley.com					
Seabee Museum 1000 23rd Ave Bldg 99	Port Hueneme	CA	93043	805-982-5163	982-5595
Web: www.seabeehf.org					
Seymour Pioneer Museum					
Society of California Pioneers					
300 4th St.	San Francisco	CA	94107	415-957-1849	957-9858
Web: www.californiapioneers.org					
Sherman Indian Museum 9010 Magnolia Ave.	Riverside	CA	92503	951-276-6719	276-6336
Web: www.shermanindianmuseum.org					
Southwest Museum 234 Museum Dr.	Los Angeles	CA	90065	323-221-2164	224-8223
Stanley Ranch Museum					
12174 Euclid St PO Box 4297	Garden Grove	CA	92842	714-530-8871	534-2611
Tech Museum of Innovation 201 S Market St	San Jose	CA	95113	408-294-8324	279-7167
Web: www.thetech.org					
Timken Museum of Art					
1500 El Prado Balboa Pk	San Diego	CA	92101	619-239-5548	531-9640
Web: www.timkenmuseum.org					
Triton Museum of Art 1505 Warburton Ave	Santa Clara	CA	95050	408-247-3754	247-3796
Web: www.tritonmuseum.org					
Turtle Bay Exploration Park					
840 Auditorium Dr	Redding	CA	96001	530-243-8850	243-8898
TF: 800-887-8532 ■ *Web:* www.turtlebay.org					
UCLA Fowler Museum of Cultural History					
University of California					
308 Charles E Young Dr	Los Angeles	CA	90095	310-825-4361	206-7007
Web: www.fmch.ucla.edu					
UCLA Hammer Museum 10899 Wilshire Blvd	Los Angeles	CA	90024	310-443-7000	443-7099
Web: www.hammer.ucla.edu					
University Art Museum					
1250 N Bellflower Blvd	Long Beach	CA	90840	562-985-5761	985-7602
Web: www.csulb.edu					
USC Fisher Museum of Art					
823 Exposition Blvd University Pk	Los Angeles	CA	90089	213-740-4561	740-7676
Web: www.usc.edu					
USS Hornet Museum 707 W Hornet Ave Pier 3.	Alameda	CA	94501	510-521-8448	749-3699
Web: www.uss-hornet.org					
Ventura County Maritime Museum					
2731 S Victoria Ave	Oxnard	CA	93035	805-984-6260	984-5970
Ventura County Museum of History & Art					
100 E Main St.	Ventura	CA	93001	805-653-0323	653-5267
Web: www.venturamuseum.org					
Veterans Museum & Memorial Ctr					
2115 Pk Blvd	San Diego	CA	92101	619-239-2300	239-7445
Web: www.veteranmuseum.org					
Wax Museum at Fisherman's Wharf					
145 Jefferson St Suite 500	San Francisco	CA	94133	415-202-0402	771-9248
TF: 800-439-4305 ■ *Web:* www.waxmuseum.com					
Wells Fargo History Museum					
333 S Grand Ave.	Los Angeles	CA	90071	213-253-7166	680-2269
Web: www.wellsfargohistory.com					
Wells Fargo History Museum					
420 Montgomery St	San Francisco	CA	94163	415-396-2619	975-7430
Web: www.wellsfargohistory.com					
Wells Fargo History Museum					
400 Capitol Mall 7th Fl Wells Fargo Ctr	Sacramento	CA	95814	916-440-4161	492-2931
Web: www.wellsfargohistory.com					
Western Aerospace Museum					
Oakland International Airport N Field					
8260 Boeing St Bldg 621	Oakland	CA	94614	510-638-7100	638-6530
Web: www.westernaerospacemuseum.org					
Whaley House Museum 2476 San Diego Ave	San Diego	CA	92110	619-297-7511	291-3576
Web: www.whaleyhouse.org					
William S Hart Museum 24151 Newhall Ave	Newhall	CA	91321	661-254-4584	254-6499
Web: www.hartmuseum.org					
Wings of History Air Museum					
12777 Murphy Ave PO Box 495	San Martin	CA	95046	408-683-2290	683-2291
Web: www.wingsofhistory.org					
Yerba Buena Center for the Arts (YBCA)					
701 Mission St Fl 3	San Francisco	CA	94103	415-978-2787	978-9635
Web: www.ybca.org					

COLORADO

	City	State	Zip	Phone	Fax
American Numismatic Assn Money Museum					
818 N Cascade Ave.	Colorado Springs	CO	80903	719-632-2646	634-4085
TF: 800-367-9723 ■ *Web:* www.money.org/moneymus.html					
Aspen Art Museum 590 N Mill St.	Aspen	CO	81611	970-925-8050	925-8054
Web: www.aspenartmuseum.org					
Aurora History Museum 15051 E Alameda Pkwy.	Aurora	CO	80012	303-739-6660	739-6657
Web: www.auroramuseum.org					
Boulder History Museum 1206 Euclid Ave	Boulder	CO	80302	303-449-3464	938-8322
Web: www.boulderhistory.org					
Boulder Museum of Contemporary Art					
1750 13th St.	Boulder	CO	80302	303-443-2122	447-1633
Web: www.bmoca.org					
Buffalo Bill Memorial Museum					
987 1/2 Lookout Mountain Rd	Golden	CO	80401	303-526-0744	526-0197
Web: www.buffalobill.org					
Byers-Evans House Museum 1310 Bannock St	Denver	CO	80204	303-620-4933	620-4795
Web: www.coloradohistory.org					
Center of Southwest Studies 1000 Rim Dr	Durango	CO	81301	970-247-7456	247-7422
Web: www.swcenter.fortlewis.edu					
Colorado History Museum					
1560 Broadway Suite 400.	Denver	CO	80202	303-866-3682	866-5739
Web: www.historycolorado.org/adult-visitors/museums-and-historic-sites					
Colorado Railroad Museum 17155 W 44th Ave	Golden	CO	80402	303-279-4591	279-4229
TF: 800-365-6263 ■ *Web:* www.crrm.org					
Colorado Springs Fine Arts Ctr					
30 W Dale St.	Colorado Springs	CO	80903	719-634-5581	634-0570
Web: www.csfineartscenter.org					
Colorado Springs Pioneers Museum					
215 S Tejon St	Colorado Springs	CO	80903	719-385-5990	385-5645
Web: www.springsgov.com					
Comanche Crossing Museum					
56060 Colfax Ave Suite E	Strasburg	CO	80136	303-622-4322	
Denver Art Museum 100 W 14th Ave Pkwy	Denver	CO	80204	720-865-5000	913-0001
Web: www.denverartmuseum.org					
Denver Firefighters Museum 1326 Tremont Pl	Denver	CO	80204	303-892-1436	892-1436
TF: 888-623-7085 ■ *Web:* www.denverfirefightersmuseum.org					
Denver Museum of Miniatures Dolls & Toys					
1880 Gaylord St	Denver	CO	80206	303-322-1053	322-3704
Web: www.dmmdt.com					
Denver Museum of Nature & Science					
2001 Colorado Blvd	Denver	CO	80205	303-370-6357	331-6492
TF: 800-925-2250 ■ *Web:* www.dmnh.org					
Discovery Science Ctr 703 E Prospect Rd.	Fort Collins	CO	80525	970-472-3990	472-3997
Web: www.dcsm.org					
Forney Museum of Transportation					
4303 Brighton Blvd.	Denver	CO	80216	303-297-1113	297-3113
Web: www.forneymuseum.com					
Fort Collins Museum 200 Matthews St	Fort Collins	CO	80524	970-221-6738	416-2236
Web: www.ci.fort-collins.co.us					
Fort Collins Museum of Contemporary Art					
201 S College Ave	Fort Collins	CO	80524	970-482-2787	482-0804
Web: www.fcmoca.org					
Ghost Town Museum 400 S 21st St	Colorado Springs	CO	80904	719-634-0696	634-2435
Web: www.ghosttownmuseum.com					
Golden Pioneer Museum 923 10th St	Golden	CO	80401	303-278-7151	278-2755
Web: www.goldenhistorymuseums.org					
Leanin' Tree Museum of Western Art					
6055 Longbow Dr.	Boulder	CO	80301	303-530-1442	530-7283
TF: 800-777-8716 ■ *Web:* www.leanintree.com					
Manitou Cliff Dwellings Museum					
Hwy 24 W	Manitou Springs	CO	80829	719-685-5242	685-1562
TF: 800-354-9971 ■ *Web:* www.cliffdwellingsmuseum.com					
McAllister House Museum					
423 N Cascade Ave.	Colorado Springs	CO	80903	719-635-7925	
Web: www.mcallisterhouse.org					
Miramont Castle Museum					
9 Capitol Hill Ave	Manitou Springs	CO	80829	719-685-1011	685-1985
TF: 888-685-1011 ■ *Web:* www.miramontcastle.org					
Mizel Museum of Judaica 400 S Kearney St	Denver	CO	80224	303-394-9990	394-1119
Web: www.mizelmuseum.org					
Molly Brown House 1340 Pennsylvania St	Denver	CO	80203	303-832-4092	832-2340
Web: www.mollybrown.org					
Museo de las Americas 861 Santa Fe Dr	Denver	CO	80204	303-571-4401	607-9761
Web: www.museo.org					
Museum of Contemporary Art Denver					
1485 Delgany	Denver	CO	80202	303-298-7554	298-7553
Web: www.mcartdenver.org					

Museum	City	State	ZIP	Phone	Fax
Museum of Outdoor Arts 1000 Englewood Pkwy Suite 2-230 *Web:* www.artcom.com/museums/nv/mr/80111.htm	Englewood	CO	80110	303-806-0444	806-0504
Rocky Mountain Motorcycle Museum & Hall of Fame 5865 N Nevada Ave.	Colorado Springs	CO	80918	719-487-8005	487-8005
Rocky Mountain Quilt Museum 1111 Washington Ave. *Web:* www.rmqm.org	Golden	CO	80401	303-277-0377	215-1636
State Historical Society of Colorado 1560 Broadway Suite 400 *Web:* www.historycolorado.org	Denver	CO	80202	303-447-8679	866-5739
University of Colorado Museum of Natural History 1030 Broadway St. *Web:* www.cumuseum.colorado.edu	Boulder	CO	80309	303-492-6892	492-4195
Vance Kirkland Museum 1311 Pearl St *Web:* www.vancekirkland.org	Denver	CO	80203	303-832-8576	832-8404
Western Museum of Mining & Industry 225 N Gate Blvd *TF:* 800-752-6558 ■ *Web:* www.wmmi.org	Colorado Springs	CO	80921	719-488-0880	488-9261
Wings Over the Rockies Air & Space Museum 7711 E Academy Blvd. *Web:* www.wingsmuseum.org	Denver	CO	80230	303-360-5360	360-5328

CONNECTICUT

Museum	City	State	ZIP	Phone	Fax
American Clock & Watch Museum 100 Maple St. *Web:* www.clockmuseum.org	Bristol	CT	06010	860-583-6070	583-1862
Barnum Museum 820 Main St. *Web:* www.barnum-museum.org	Bridgeport	CT	06604	203-331-1104	331-0079
Bruce Museum of Arts & Science 1 Museum Dr *Web:* www.brucemuseum.org	Greenwich	CT	06830	203-869-0376	869-0963
Catherine Mitchell Museum 967 Academy Hill *Web:* www.stratfordhistoricalsociety.com	Stratford	CT	06615	203-378-0630	378-2562
Connecticut Audubon Society Birdcraft Museum & Sanctuary 314 Unquowa Rd *Web:* www.ctaudubon.org	Fairfield	CT	06824	203-259-0416	259-1344
Connecticut Historical Society Museum 1 Elizabeth St *Web:* www.chs.org	Hartford	CT	06105	860-236-5621	236-2664
Connecticut State Museum of Natural History 2019 Hillside Rd. *Web:* www.mnh.uconn.edu	Storrs	CT	06268	860-486-4460	486-0827
Dahesh Museum of Art 45 E Putnam Ave Suite 105 *Web:* www.daheshmuseum.org	Greenwich	CT	06830	212-759-0606	759-1235
Discovery Museum & Planetarium 4450 Pk Ave *Web:* www.discoverymuseum.org	Bridgeport	CT	06604	203-372-3521	374-1929
Eli Whitney Museum 915 Whitney Ave *Web:* www.eliwhitney.org	Hamden	CT	06517	203-777-1833	777-1229
Ethnic Heritage Ctr 270 Fitch St Southern Connecticut State University *Web:* www.southernct.edu	New Haven	CT	06515	203-392-6126	392-5140
Fairfield Museum & History Ctr 370 Beach Rd. *Web:* www.fairfieldhistoricalsociety.org	Fairfield	CT	06824	203-259-1598	255-2716
Henry Whitfield State Museum 248 Old Whitfield St *Web:* www.chc.state.ct.us	Guilford	CT	06437	203-453-2457	453-7544
Hill-Stead Museum 35 Mountain Rd *Web:* www.hillstead.org	Farmington	CT	06032	860-677-4787	677-0174
Housatonic Museum of Art Housatonic Community College 900 Lafayette Blvd *Web:* www.hcc.commnet.edu	Bridgeport	CT	06604	203-332-5000	332-5123
Institute for American Indian Studies The 38 Curtis Rd PO Box 1260 *Web:* www.birdstone.org	Washington Green	CT	06793	860-868-0518	868-1649
Knights of Columbus Museum 1 State St. *TF:* 800-524-3611 ■ *Web:* www.kofcmuseum.org/en/index.html	New Haven	CT	06511	203-865-0400	773-3000
Lock Museum of America 230 Main St Rt 6 PO Box 104. *Web:* www.lockmuseum.com	Terryville	CT	06786	860-589-6359	589-6359
Lockwood-Mathews Mansion Museum 295 W Ave *Web:* www.ohwy.com	Norwalk	CT	06850	203-838-9799	838-1434
Lyman Allyn Art Museum 625 Williams St *Web:* www.lymanallyn.org	New London	CT	06320	860-443-2545	443-1280
Mark Twain House & Museum 351 Farmington Ave *Web:* www.marktwainhouse.org	Hartford	CT	06105	860-247-0998	278-8148
Mattatuck Museum of the Mattatuck Historical Society 144 W Main St *Web:* www.mattatuckmuseum.org	Waterbury	CT	06702	203-753-0381	756-6283
Menczer Museum of Medicine & Dentistry 230 Scarborough St *Web:* library.uchc.edu/hms	Hartford	CT	06105	860-236-5613	236-8401
Mystic Seaport -- The Museum of America & the Sea 75 Greenmanville Ave PO Box 6000 *TF:* 888-973-2767 ■ *Web:* www.mysticseaport.org	Mystic	CT	06355	860-572-0711	572-5328
New Britain Museum of American Art 56 Lexington St *Web:* www.nbmaa.org	New Britain	CT	06052	860-229-0257	229-3445
Noah Webster House 227 S Main St *Web:* www.noahwebsterhouse.org	West Hartford	CT	06107	860-521-5362	521-4036
Raymond E Baldwin Museum of Connecticut History 231 Capitol Ave *Web:* www.cslib.org/museum.htm	Hartford	CT	06106	860-757-6500	757-6533
Shore Line Trolley Museum 17 River St *Web:* www.bera.org	East Haven	CT	06512	203-467-6927	467-7635
Slater Memorial Museum 108 Crescent St	Norwich	CT	06360	860-887-2506	885-0379
Stamford Historical Society Museum 1508 High Ridge Rd *Web:* www.stamfordhistory.org	Stamford	CT	06903	203-329-1183	322-1607
Stamford Museum & Nature Ctr 39 Scofieldtown Rd. *Web:* www.stamfordmuseum.org	Stamford	CT	06903	203-322-1646	322-0408
Wadsworth Atheneum Museum of Art 600 Main St *Web:* www.wadsworthatheneum.org	Hartford	CT	06103	860-278-2670	527-0803
Yale Center for British Art 1080 Chapel St PO Box 208280 *TF:* 877-274-8278 ■ *Web:* www.yale.edu/ycba	New Haven	CT	06510	203-432-2800	432-9695
Yale Peabody Museum of Natural History 170 Whitney Ave Yale University *Web:* www.peabody.yale.edu	New Haven	CT	06511	203-432-3759	432-9816
Yale University Art Gallery 1111 Chapel St *Web:* www.yale.edu	New Haven	CT	06520	203-432-0600	432-7159
Yale University Collection of Musical Instruments 15 Hillhouse Ave. *Web:* www.yale.edu	New Haven	CT	06511	203-432-0822	432-8342

DELAWARE

Museum	City	State	ZIP	Phone	Fax
Barratt's Chapel & Museum 6362 Bay Rd *Web:* www.barrattschapel.org	Frederica	DE	19946	302-335-5544	
Delaware Agricultural Museum & Village 866 N DuPont Hwy *Web:* www.agriculturalmuseum.org	Dover	DE	19901	302-734-1618	734-0457
Delaware Archaeology Museum 316 S Governor's Ave *Web:* www.destatemuseums.org	Dover	DE	19904	302-739-3260	
Delaware Art Museum 2301 Kentmere Pkwy. *Web:* www.delart.org	Wilmington	DE	19806	302-571-9590	571-0220
Delaware History Museum 504 N Market St. *Web:* www.hsd.org	Wilmington	DE	19801	302-656-0637	655-7844
Delaware Museum of Natural History 4840 Kennett Pike. *Web:* www.delmnh.org	Wilmington	DE	19807	302-658-9111	658-2610
Hagley Museum & Library 298 Buck Rd E *Web:* www.hagley.lib.de.us	Greenville	DE	19807	302-658-2400	658-0568
Harrington Museum 110 Fleming St	Harrington	DE	19952	302-398-3698	398-9589
Indian River Lifesaving Station Museum 130 Costal Hwy Indian River Inlet.	Rehoboth Beach	DE	19971	302-227-6991	227-6438
Johnson Victrola Museum Bank 375 S New St. *Web:* history.delaware.gov	Dover	DE	19901	302-744-5055	
Kalmar Nyckel Shipyard & Museum 1124 E 7th St *Web:* www.kalnyc.org	Wilmington	DE	19801	302-429-7447	429-0350
Lewes Historical Society 110 Shipcarpenter St *Web:* www.historiclewes.org	Lewes	DE	19958	302-645-7670	645-2375
Messick Agricultural Museum 325 Walt Messick Rd	Harrington	DE	19952	302-398-3729	398-4732
Mike's Famous Harley-Davidson Museum 2160 New Castle Ave *TF:* 800-326-6874 ■ *Web:* www.mikesfamous.com	New Castle	DE	19720	302-658-8800	656-9958
Museum of Small Town Life 375 S New St. *Web:* www.destatemuseums.org	Dover	DE	19904	302-739-4266	739-3943
Old Swedes Church & Hendrickson House Museum 606 Church St *Web:* www.oldswedes.org	Wilmington	DE	19801	302-652-5629	652-8615
Sewell C Biggs Museum of American Art 406 Federal St *Web:* www.biggsmuseum.org	Dover	DE	19901	302-674-2111	674-5133
Winterthur Museum & Country Estate 5105 Kennett Pike. *TF:* 800-448-3883 ■ *Web:* www.winterthur.org	Winterthur	DE	19735	302-888-4600	888-4880

DISTRICT OF COLUMBIA

Museum	City	State	ZIP	Phone	Fax
African-American Civil War Memorial & Museum 1200 U St NW. *Web:* www.afroamcivilwar.org	Washington	DC	20001	202-667-2667	667-6771
B'nai B'rith Klutznick National Jewish Museum 2020 K St NW. *Web:* www.bnaibrith.org	Washington	DC	20006	202-857-6583	857-6601
Cathedral Church of Saint Peter & Saint Paul 3101 Wisconsin Ave NW *TF:* 800-622-6304 ■ *Web:* www.cathedral.org/cathedral	Washington	DC	20016	202-537-6200	364-6600
Corcoran Gallery of Art 500 17th St NW. *Web:* www.corcoran.org	Washington	DC	20006	202-639-1700	639-1768
DAR Museum 1776 D St NW *Web:* www.dar.org/museum	Washington	DC	20006	202-879-3241	628-0820
Decatur House Museum 1610 H St NW *Web:* www.decaturhouse.org	Washington	DC	20006	202-218-4338	842-0030
Dumbarton Oaks 1703 32nd St NW *Web:* www.doaks.org	Washington	DC	20007	202-339-6400	339-6400
Frederick Douglass Museum & Hall of Fame for Caring Americans 320 A St NE *Web:* www.caringinstitute.org	Washington	DC	20002	202-544-6130	
Freer Gallery of Art (Smithsonian Institution) 1050 Independence Ave SW PO Box 37012 *Web:* www.asia.si.edu	Washington	DC	20013	202-633-1000	357-4911
Freer Gallery of Art / Arthur M. Sackler Gallery 1050 Independence Ave SW PO Box 37012 *Web:* www.asia.si.edu	Washington	DC	20013	202-633-1000	357-4911
Hillwood Estate Museum & Gardens 4155 Linnean Ave NW *TF:* 877-445-5966 ■ *Web:* www.hillwoodmuseum.org	Washington	DC	20008	202-686-8500	966-7846

Phone | Fax

Hirshhorn Museum & Sculpture Garden (Smithsonian Institution)
1100 Jefferson Dr . . . Washington DC 20560 202-633-4674 786-2682
Web: www.hirshhorn.si.edu

Historical Society of Washington DC
801 K St NW
Historical Society of Washington DC . . . Washington DC 20001 202-383-1800 383-1872
Web: www.historydc.org

International Spy Museum 800 F St NW . . . Washington DC 20004 202-393-7798 393-7797
TF: 866-779-6873 ■ *Web:* www.spymuseum.org

Kreeger Museum 2401 Foxhall Rd NW . . . Washington DC 20007 202-338-3552 337-3051
TF: 877-337-3050 ■ *Web:* www.kreegermuseum.com

Lillian & Albert Small Jewish Museum
701 3rd St NW . . . Washington DC 20001 202-789-0900 789-0485
Web: www.loc.gov/rr/main/religion/jhw.html

Marian Koshland Science Museum
6th & E Sts NW . . . Washington DC 20001 202-334-1201 334-1548
TF: 888-567-4526 ■ *Web:* www.koshland-science-museum.org

National Air & Space Museum (Smithsonian Institution)
Independence Ave & 6th St SW . . . Washington DC 20560 202-633-1000
Web: www.nasm.si.edu/museum/udvarhazy

National Bldg Museum 401 F St NW . . . Washington DC 20001 202-272-2448 272-2564
Web: www.nbm.org

National Gallery of Art
6th St & Constitution Ave NW . . . Washington DC 20565 202-737-4215 842-2356
Web: www.nga.gov

National Geographic Society Explorers Hall
1145 17th St NW . . . Washington DC 20036 202-857-7589 857-5530
TF: 800-647-5463 ■ *Web:* www.nationalgeographic.com

National Museum of African Art (Smithsonian Institution)
950 Independence Ave SW MRC 708 . . . Washington DC 20560 202-633-4600 357-4879
Web: www.africa.si.edu

National Museum of American History (Smithsonian Institution) (NMAH)
14th St & Constitution Ave NW . . . Washington DC 20560 202-633-1000 633-8053*
**Fax:* PR ■ *Web:* americanhistory.si.edu

National Museum of American Jewish Military History (JWV-NMI)
1811 R St NW . . . Washington DC 20009 202-265-6280 462-3192
Web: www.nmajmh.org

National Museum of Health & Medicine
6900 Georgia Ave NW . . . Washington DC 20306 202-782-2200 782-3573
Web: www.nmhm.washingtondc.museum

National Museum of Natural History (Smithsonian Institution)
10th St & Constitution Ave NW . . . Washington DC 20560 202-633-2664 357-4779
Web: www.mnh.si.edu

National Museum of the American Indian (Smithsonian Institution)
4th St & Independence Ave SW . . . Washington DC 20004 202-633-1000
Web: www.nmai.si.edu

National Museum of Women in the Arts
1250 New York Ave NW . . . Washington DC 20005 202-783-5000 393-3234
TF: 800-222-7270 ■ *Web:* www.nmwa.org

National Postal Museum (Smithsonian Institution)
2 Massachusetts Ave NE . . . Washington DC 20002 202-633-5555 633-9393
Web: www.postalmuseum.si.edu

Navy Museum
805 Kidder Breese St SE
Washington Navy Yard . . . Washington DC 20374 202-433-4882 433-8200
Web: www.history.navy.mil

Octagon Museum 1799 New York Ave NW . . . Washington DC 20006 202-638-3221 626-7420
Web: www.archfoundation.org

Phillips Collection 1600 21st St NW . . . Washington DC 20009 202-387-2151 387-2436
Web: www.phillipscollection.org

Pope John Paul II Cultural Ctr
3900 Harewood Rd NE . . . Washington DC 20017 202-635-5400 635-5411
Web: www.jp2cc.org

Renwick Gallery of the Smithsonian American Art Museum
1661 Pennsylvania Ave NW . . . Washington DC 20006 202-633-2850 786-2810
Web: americanart.si.edu/renwick

Smithsonian Institution
SI Bldg Rm 153 MRC 010 PO Box 37012 . . . Washington DC 20013 202-633-1000
Web: www.si.edu

Textile Museum The 2320 S St NW . . . Washington DC 20008 202-667-0441 483-0994
Web: www.textilemuseum.org

US Holocaust Memorial Museum
100 Raoul Wallenburg Pl SW . . . Washington DC 20024 202-488-0400 488-2613
Web: www.ushmm.org

Woodrow Wilson House Museum 2340 S St NW . . . Washington DC 20008 202-387-4062 483-1466
Web: www.woodrowwilsonhouse.org

FLORIDA

Phone | Fax

African American Museum of the Arts
325 S Clara Ave . . . DeLand FL 32721 386-736-4004 736-4088
Web: www.africanmuseumdeland.org

Amelia Island Museum of History
233 S 3rd St . . . Fernandina Beach FL 32034 904-261-7378 261-9701
Web: www.ameliamuseum.org

American Police Hall of Fame & Museum
6350 Horizon Dr . . . Titusville FL 32780 321-264-0911 264-0033
Web: www.aphf.org

Audubon House & Tropical Garden
250 Whitehead St . . . Key West FL 33040 305-294-2116 294-4513
Web: www.audubonhouse.com

Bailey Matthews Shell Museum
3075 Sanibel-Captiva Rd PO Box 1580 . . . Sanibel FL 33957 239-395-2233 395-6706
TF: 888-679-6450 ■ *Web:* www.shellmuseum.org

Bass Museum of Art 2121 Pk Ave . . . Miami Beach FL 33139 305-673-7530 673-7062
Web: www.bassmuseum.org

Black Archives Research Center & Museum
Florida A & M University Carnegie Ctr . . . Tallahassee FL 32307 850-599-3020 561-2604

Boca Raton Museum of Art
501 Plaza Real Mizner Pk . . . Boca Raton FL 33432 561-392-2500 391-6410
Web: www.bocamuseum.org

Phone | Fax

Bonnet House Museum & Garden
900 N Birch Rd . . . Fort Lauderdale FL 33304 954-563-5393 561-4174
Web: www.bonnethouse.org

Broward County Historical Commission
151 SW 2nd St . . . Fort Lauderdale FL 33301 954-765-4670 765-4437
Web: www.broward.org

Charles Hosmer Morse Museum of American Art
445 N Pk Ave . . . Winter Park FL 32789 407-645-5311 647-1284
Web: www.morsemuseum.org

Collier County Museum 3331 Tamiami Trail E . . . Naples FL 34112 239-774-8476 774-8580
Web: www.colliermuseums.com

Colonial Spanish Quarter Museum
29 St George St . . . Saint Augustine FL 32084 904-825-6830 825-6874

Cornell Fine Arts Museum 1000 Holt Ave . . . Winter Park FL 32789 407-646-2526 646-2524
Web: www.rollins.edu/cfam

Crowley Museum & Nature Ctr 16405 Myakka Rd . . . Sarasota FL 34240 941-322-1000 322-1000
Web: www.CrowleyMuseumNatureCtr.org

Cummer Museum of Art & Gardens
829 Riverside Ave . . . Jacksonville FL 32204 904-356-6857 353-4101
Web: www.cummer.org

East Martello Museum & Gallery
3501 S Roosevelt Blvd . . . Key West FL 33040 305-296-3913 296-6206
Web: www.kwahs.com

Florida Agricultural Museum
7900 Old Kings Rd . . . Palm Coast FL 32137 386-446-7630 446-7631

Florida Heritage Museum
167 San Marco Ave . . . Saint Augustine FL 33040 904-829-3800 829-6678
TF: 800-397-4071 ■ *Web:* www.amtrakvacations.com

Florida Holocaust Museum
55 5th St S . . . Saint Petersburg FL 33701 727-820-0100 821-8435
TF: 800-960-7448 ■ *Web:* www.flholocaustmuseum.org

Florida International Museum
244 2nd Ave N
St Petersburg College Downtown Ctr . . . Saint Petersburg FL 33701 727-341-7900 341-7908
Web: www.floridamuseum.org

Florida Museum of Natural History
Museum Rd & Newell Dr PO Box 117800 . . . Gainesville FL 32611 352-392-1721 392-8783
Web: www.flmnh.ufl.edu

Florida State University Museum of Fine Arts
W Tennessee & Copeland Sts
Fine Arts Bldg . . . Tallahassee FL 32306 850-644-6836 644-7229
Web: www.mofa.fsu.edu

Fort Lauderdale Antique Car Museum
1527 SW 1st Ave . . . Fort Lauderdale FL 33315 954-779-7300 779-2501
Web: www.antiquecarmuseum.org

Fort Lauderdale Historical Society
219 SW 2nd Ave . . . Fort Lauderdale FL 33301 954-463-4431 523-6228

Fort Lauderdale Museum of Art
1 E Las Olas Blvd . . . Fort Lauderdale FL 33301 954-525-5500 524-6011
Web: www.museumofart.org

Frost Art Museum at Florida International University
SW 8th St & 107th Ave University Pk PC110 . . . Miami FL 33199 305-348-2890 348-2762
Web: www.fiu.edu/~museum

Gillespie Museum of Minerals
421 N Woodland Blvd Unit 8403 . . . DeLand FL 32723 386-822-7330 822-7328
TF: 800-688-0101 ■ *Web:* www.stetson.edu

Gold Coast Railroad Museum 12450 SW 152nd St . . . Miami FL 33177 305-253-0063 233-4641
TF: 888-608-7246 ■ *Web:* www.goldcoast-railroad.org

Goodwood Museum & Gardens
1600 Miccosukee Rd . . . Tallahassee FL 32308 850-877-4202 877-3090
Web: www.goodwoodmuseum.org

Government House Museum 48 King St . . . Saint Augustine FL 32084 904-825-5033 825-5096
Web: www.saintaugustincityo.com

Gulf Beaches Historical Museum
115 10th Ave . . . Saint Pete Beach FL 33706 727-552-1610 363-6704

Gulf Coast Museum of Art 12211 Walsingham Rd . . . Largo FL 33778 727-518-6833 518-1852
Web: www.gulfcoastmuseum.org

Halifax Historical Museum
252 S Beach St . . . Daytona Beach FL 32114 386-255-6976 255-7605
Web: www.halifaxhistorical.org

Harry S Truman's Little White House Museum
111 Front St Truman Annex . . . Key West FL 33040 305-294-9911 294-9988
Web: www.trumanlittlewhitehouse.com

Henry B Plant Museum 401 W Kennedy Blvd . . . Tampa FL 33606 813-254-1891 258-7272
Web: www.plantmuseum.com

Henry Morrison Flagler Museum
1 Whitehall Way . . . Palm Beach FL 33480 561-655-2833 655-2826
Web: www.flaglermuseum.us

Heritage House Museum & Robert Frost Cottage
410 Caroline St . . . Key West FL 33040 305-296-3573 292-5723
Web: www.heritagehousemuseum.org

Historical Museum of Southern Florida
101 W Flagler St . . . Miami FL 33130 305-375-1492 375-1609
Web: www.historical-museum.org

Indian Temple Mound Museum
139 Miracle Strip Pkwy SE . . . Fort Walton Beach FL 32548 850-833-9595 833-9675
Web: www.fwb.org

Jacksonville Maritime Museum
1015 Museum Cir Unit 2 . . . Jacksonville FL 32207 904-398-9011 398-7248
Web: www.jaxmarmus.com

Jacksonville Museum of Modern Art
333 N Laura St . . . Jacksonville FL 32202 904-366-6911 366-6901
Web: www.jmoma.org

Jewish Museum of Florida
301 Washington Ave . . . Miami Beach FL 33139 305-672-5044 672-5933
Web: www.jewishmuseum.com

John & Mable Ringling Museum of Art
5401 Bay Shore Rd . . . Sarasota FL 34243 941-359-5700 358-3177
Web: www.ringling.org

John G Riley Center/Museum of African American History & Culture
419 E Jefferson St . . . Tallahassee FL 32301 850-681-7881 681-7000
Web: www.rileymuseum.org

Name / Address	City	State	ZIP	Phone	Fax
Karpeles Manuscript Library Museum 101 W 1st St *Web:* www.rain.org	Jacksonville	FL	32206	904-356-2992	356-4338
Key West Lighthouse & Keepers Quarters Museum 938 Whitehead St *Web:* www.kwahs.com/lighthouse.htm	Key West	FL	33040	305-294-0012	294-0012
Key West Museum of Art & History at the Custom House 281 Front St *Web:* www.kwahs.com	Key West	FL	33040	305-295-6616	295-6649
Key West Shipwreck Historeum Museum 1 Whitehead St *Web:* www.shipwreckhistoreum.com	Key West	FL	33040	305-292-8990	292-1617
Kingsley Plantation 11676 Palmetto Ave	Jacksonville	FL	32226	904-251-3537	251-3577
Knott House Museum 301 E Park Ave *Web:* www.flheritage.com/museum/sites/knotthouse	Tallahassee	FL	32301	850-922-2459	413-7261
Lightner Museum The 75 King St PO Box 334 *Web:* www.lightnermuseum.org	Saint Augustine	FL	32084	904-824-2874	824-2712
Lowe Art Museum University of Miami 1301 Stanford Dr *Web:* www.miami.edu/lowe	Coral Gables	FL	33124	305-284-3535	284-2024
Loxahatchee River Historical Museum 805 N US Hwy 1 Burt Reynolds Pk *Web:* www.lrhs.org	Jupiter	FL	33477	561-747-6639	575-3292
Mary Brogan Museum of Art & Science 350 S Duval St *Web:* www.thebrogan.org	Tallahassee	FL	32301	850-513-0700	513-0143
Mel Fisher Maritime Museum 200 Greene St *Web:* www.melfisher.org	Key West	FL	33040	305-294-2633	294-5671
Mennello Museum of American Folk Art 900 E Princeton St *Web:* www.mennellomuseum.com	Orlando	FL	32803	407-246-4278	246-4329
Miami Art Museum 101 W Flagler St *Web:* www.miamiartmuseum.org	Miami	FL	33130	305-375-3000	375-1725
Miami Museum of Science & Planetarium 3280 S Miami Ave *Web:* www.miamisci.org	Miami	FL	33129	305-646-4200	646-4300
Morikami Museum & Japanese Gardens 4000 Morikami Pk Rd *Web:* www.morikami.org	Delray Beach	FL	33446	561-495-0233	499-2557
Museum of Arts & Sciences 352 S Nova Rd *Web:* www.moas.org	Daytona Beach	FL	32114	386-255-0285	255-5040
Museum of Contemporary Art 770 NE 125th St Joan Lehman Bldg *Web:* www.mocanomi.org	North Miami	FL	33161	305-893-6211	891-1472
Museum of Discovery & Science 401 SW 2nd St *Web:* www.mods.org	Fort Lauderdale	FL	33312	954-467-6637	467-0046
Museum of Fine Arts 255 Beach Dr NE *Web:* www.fine-arts.org	Saint Petersburg	FL	33701	727-896-2667	894-4638
Museum of Florida History 500 S Bronough St RA Gray Bldg *Web:* www.dhr.dos.state.fl.us	Tallahassee	FL	32399	850-488-1484	245-6433
Museum of Science & History of Jacksonville 1025 Museum Cir *Web:* www.themosh.org	Jacksonville	FL	32207	904-396-6674	396-5799
Museum of Science & Industry 4801 E Fowler Ave *TF:* 800-995-6674 ■ *Web:* www.mosi.org	Tampa	FL	33617	813-987-6300	987-6310
Museum of Southern History 4304 Herschel St *Web:* www.scv-kirby-smith.org	Jacksonville	FL	32210	904-388-3574	
Museum of the Americas (MoA) 2500 NW 79th Ave Suite 104 *Web:* www.museumamericas.org	Doral	FL	33122	305-599-8089	
Museum of the Everglades 105 W Broadway PO Box 8	Everglades City	FL	34139	239-695-0008	695-0036
My Jewish Discovery Place Children's Museum 6501 W Sunrise Blvd *Web:* www.sorefjcc.org	Fort Lauderdale	FL	33313	954-792-6700	792-4839
Naples Museum of Art 5833 Pelican Bay Blvd *TF:* 800-597-1900 ■ *Web:* www.thephil.org	Naples	FL	34108	239-597-1111	597-8163
National Museum of Naval Aviation 1750 Radford Blvd Suite C *TF:* 800-327-5002 ■ *Web:* www.naval-air.org	Pensacola	FL	32508	850-452-3604	452-3296
Norton Museum of Art 1451 S Olive Ave *Web:* www.norton.org	West Palm Beach	FL	33401	561-832-5194	659-4689
Old Dillard Museum 1009 NW 4th St *Web:* www.flamuseums.org	Fort Lauderdale	FL	33311	754-322-8828	322-8824
Old Florida Museum 254-D San Marco Ave *TF:* 800-813-3208 ■ *Web:* www.oldfloridamuseum.com	Saint Augustine	FL	32084	904-824-8874	824-6848
Old Fort Lauderdale Village & Museum 231 SW 2nd Ave *Web:* www.oldfortlauderdale.org	Fort Lauderdale	FL	33301	954-463-4431	523-6228
Orange County Regional History Ctr 65 E Central Blvd *TF:* 800-965-2030 ■ *Web:* www.thehistorycenter.org	Orlando	FL	32801	407-836-8500	836-8550
Orlando Museum of Art 2416 N Mills Ave *Web:* www.omart.org	Orlando	FL	32803	407-896-4231	896-9920
Orlando Science Ctr 777 E Princeton St *TF:* 888-672-4386 ■ *Web:* www.osc.org	Orlando	FL	32803	407-514-2000	514-2277
Ormond Memorial Art Museum & Gardens 78 E Granada Blvd *Web:* www.ormondartmuseum.org	Ormond Beach	FL	32176	386-676-3347	676-3244
Palm Beach Photographic Centre 415 Clematis St *Web:* www.workshop.org	West Palm Beach	FL	33401	561-253-2600	
Pena-Peck House Museum 143 St George St	Saint Augustine	FL	32084	904-829-5064	829-6210
Pensacola Museum of Art 407 S Jefferson St *Web:* www.pensacolamuseumofart.org	Pensacola	FL	32502	850-432-6247	469-1532
Pinellas County Heritage Village 11909 125th St N *Web:* www.pinellascounty.org	Largo	FL	33774	727-582-2123	582-2455
Potter's Wax Museum 17 King St *TF:* 800-584-4781 ■ *Web:* www.potterswax.com	Saint Augustine	FL	32084	904-829-9056	824-3434
Ripley's Believe It or Not! Museum 19 San Marco Ave *Web:* www.ripleys.com	Saint Augustine	FL	32084	904-824-1606	829-1790
Ripley's Believe It or Not! Orlando Odditorium 8201 International Dr *Web:* www.ripleysorlando.com	Orlando	FL	32819	407-363-4418	345-0803
Ritz Theatre & La Villa Museum 829 N Davis St *Web:* www.ritzjacksonville.com	Jacksonville	FL	32202	904-632-5555	632-5553
Saint Augustine Lighthouse & Museum 81 Lighthouse Ave *Web:* www.staugustinelighthouse.com	Saint Augustine	FL	32080	904-829-0745	808-1248
Saint Petersburg Museum of History 335 2nd Ave NE *Web:* www.stpetemuseumofhistory.org	Saint Petersburg	FL	33701	727-894-1052	823-7276
Salvador Dali Museum 1 Dali Blvd *TF:* 800-442-3254 ■ *Web:* www.thedali.org	Saint Petersburg	FL	33701	727-823-3767	894-6068
Science Center of Pinellas County 7701 22nd Ave N *Web:* www.sciencecenterofpinellas.com	Saint Petersburg	FL	33710	727-384-0027	343-5729
South Florida Museum 201 10th St W *Web:* www.southfloridamuseum.org	Bradenton	FL	34205	941-746-4131	747-2556
South Florida Science Museum 4801 Dreher Trail N *Web:* www.sfsm.org	West Palm Beach	FL	33405	561-832-1988	833-0551
Southeast Museum of Photography 1200 W International Speedway Blvd Bldg 100 Daytona Beach Community College *Web:* www.smponline.org	Daytona Beach	FL	32114	386-506-4475	506-4487
Spanish Military Hospital Museum 3 Aviles St *TF:* 800-597-7177 ■ *Web:* www.ancientcitytours.net	Saint Augustine	FL	32084	904-827-0807	827-0590
Stranahan House 335 SE 6th Ave *Web:* www.stranahanhouse.com	Fort Lauderdale	FL	33301	954-524-4736	525-2838
Tallahassee Antique Car Museum 6800 Mahan Dr *Web:* www.tacm.com	Tallahassee	FL	32308	850-942-0137	576-8500
Tallahassee Museum of History & Natural Science 3945 Museum Dr *Web:* www.tallahasseemuseum.org	Tallahassee	FL	32310	850-576-1636	574-8243
Tampa Bay History Ctr 801 Old Water St *Web:* www.tampabayhistorycenter.org	Tampa	FL	33602	813-228-0097	223-7021
Tampa Museum of Art 120 W Gasparilla Plaza *Web:* www.tampagov.net	Tampa	FL	33602	813-274-8130	274-8732
University Gallery 400 SW 13th St Fine Arts Bldg B PO Box 115803 *Web:* www.arts.ufl.edu/galleries/default.aspx	Gainesville	FL	32611	352-273-3000	846-0266
University of South Florida Contemporary Art Museum 3821 Holly Dr *Web:* cam.arts.usf.edu	Tampa	FL	33620	813-974-4133	974-5130
Vizcaya Museum & Gardens 3251 S Miami Ave *Web:* www.vizcayamuseum.org	Miami	FL	33129	305-250-9133	285-2004
Wings Over Miami Aircraft Museum 14710 SW 128th St Tamiami Executive Airport *Web:* www.wingsovermiami.com	Miami	FL	33196	305-233-5197	232-4134
Wolfsonian Museum 1001 Washington Ave *Web:* www.wolfsonian.fiu.edu	Miami Beach	FL	33139	305-531-1001	531-2133
World Chess Hall of Fame & Museum 13755 SW 119th Ave **Fax Area Code: 305* ■ *Web:* www.chessmuseum.org	Miami	FL	33186	786-242-4255	477-9516*
Wrecker Museum 322 Duval St *Web:* www.oirf.org	Key West	FL	33040	305-294-9501	294-9501
Ximenez-Fatio House Museum 20 Aviles St *Web:* www.ximenezfatiohouse.org	Saint Augustine	FL	32084	904-829-3575	829-3445
Ybor City Museum State Park 1818 9th Ave *Web:* www.floridastateparks.org	Tampa	FL	33605	813-247-6323	

GEORGIA

Name / Address	City	State	ZIP	Phone	Fax
African-American Panoramic Experience Museum 135 Auburn Ave NE *Web:* www.apexmuseum.org	Atlanta	GA	30303	404-521-2739	523-3248
AT & T Telephone Museum 675 W Peachtree St NE *Web:* www.attpioneervolunteers.org	Atlanta	GA	30375	404-223-3661	
Atlanta History Ctr 130 W Paces Ferry Rd *Web:* www.atlantahistorycenter.com	Atlanta	GA	30305	404-814-4000	814-2041
Augusta Museum of History 560 Reynolds St *Web:* www.augustamuseum.org	Augusta	GA	30901	706-722-8454	724-5192
Beach Institute African American Cultural Ctr 502 E Harris St *Web:* www.kingtisdell.org/beachinst.html	Savannah	GA	31401	912-234-8000	234-8001
Cannonball House & Confederate Museum 856 Mulberry St *Web:* www.cannonballhouse.org	Macon	GA	31201	478-745-5982	745-5944
Challenger Learning Ctr 701 Front Ave Coca-Cola Space Science Ctr *Web:* www.ccssc.org/clc.htm	Columbus	GA	31901	706-649-1470	649-1478
Coca-Cola Space Science Ctr 701 Front Ave *Web:* www.ccssc.org	Columbus	GA	31901	706-649-1470	649-1478
Columbus Museum 1251 Wynnton Rd *Web:* www.columbusmuseum.com	Columbus	GA	31906	706-748-2562	748-2570

	City	State	Zip	Phone	Fax
Davenport House Museum 324 E State St Web: www.davenportsavga.com	Savannah	GA	31401	912-236-8097	233-7938
Fernbank Museum of Natural History 767 Clifton Rd NE Web: www.fernbank.edu	Atlanta	GA	30307	404-378-0127	370-8087
Fernbank Science Ctr 156 Heaton Pk Dr NE Web: www.fsc.fernbank.edu	Atlanta	GA	30307	678-874-7102	874-7110
Georgia Museum of Art 90 Carlton St University of Georgia Web: www.uga.edu	Athens	GA	30602	706-542-4662	542-1051
Georgia Music Hall of Fame 200 ML King Jr Blvd TF: 888-427-6257 ■ Web: www.gamusichall.com	Macon	GA	31202	478-751-3334	751-3100
Gertrude Herbert Institute of Art 506 Telfair St Web: www.ghia.org	Augusta	GA	30901	706-722-5495	722-3670
Goethe Institut Atlanta/German Cultural Ctr 1197 Peachtree St NE Web: www.goethe.de	Atlanta	GA	30361	404-892-2388	892-3832
High Museum of Art 1280 Peachtree St NE Web: www.high.org	Atlanta	GA	30309	404-733-4400	733-4502
Jimmy Carter Library & Museum 441 Freedom Pkwy Web: www.jimmycarterlibrary.org	Atlanta	GA	30307	404-865-7100	865-7102
King-Tisdell Cottage Foundation Inc 502 E Harris St Web: www.kingtisdell.org	Savannah	GA	31401	912-234-8000	234-8001
Lucy Craft Laney Museum 1116 Phillips St Web: www.lucycraftlaneymuseum.com	Augusta	GA	30901	706-724-3576	724-3576
Michael C Carlos Museum 571 S Kilgo St Web: www.carlos.emory.edu	Atlanta	GA	30322	404-727-4282	727-4292
Mighty Eighth Air Force Museum 175 Bourne Ave Web: www.mightyeighth.org	Pooler	GA	31322	912-748-8888	748-0209
Morris Museum of Art 1 10th St Web: www.themorris.org	Augusta	GA	30901	706-724-7501	724-7612
Museum of Arts & Sciences 4182 Forsyth Rd Web: www.masmacon.com	Macon	GA	31210	478-477-3232	477-3251
Museum of Design Atlanta 285 Peachtree Ctr Ave Web: www.museumofdesign.org	Atlanta	GA	30303	404-688-2467	521-9311
National Infantry Museum 1775 Legacy Way Web: www.nationalinfantrymuseum.com	Columbus	GA	31903	706-685-5800	545-5158
National Museum of Patriotism 1405 Spring St NW TF: 877-276-1692 ■ Web: www.museumofpatriotism.org	Atlanta	GA	30309	404-875-0691	875-0415
National Science Center Fort Discovery 1 7th St TF: 800-325-5445 ■ Web: www.nscdiscovery.org	Augusta	GA	30901	706-821-0200	821-0269
Oak Hill & Martha Berry Museum 2277 Martha Berry Hwy NW PO Box 490189 Web: www.berry.edu	Mount Berry	GA	30149	706-291-1883	802-0902
Oglethorpe University Museum of Art 4484 Peachtree Rd NE Web: www.museum.oglethorpe.edu	Atlanta	GA	30319	404-364-8555	364-8556
Port Columbus National Civil War Naval Museum 1002 Victory Dr Web: www.portcolumbus.org	Port Columbus	GA	31901	706-327-9798	324-7225
Ralph Mark Gilbert Civil Rights Museum 460 ML King Jr Blvd Web: www.sip.armstrong.edu	Savannah	GA	31401	912-231-8900	234-2577
Robert C Williams American Museum of Papermaking 500 10th St NW TF: 800-558-6611 ■ Web: www.ipst.gatech.edu	Atlanta	GA	30318	404-894-7840	894-4778
Savannah History Museum 303 ML King Jr Blvd Web: www.chsgeorgia.org	Savannah	GA	31401	912-238-1779	651-6827
Ships of the Sea Maritime Museum 41 Martin Luther King Junior Blvd Web: www.shipsofthesea.org	Savannah	GA	31401	912-232-1511	234-7363
Telfair Museum of Art 121 Barnard St Web: telfair.org	Savannah	GA	31401	912-790-8800	790-8803
Tubman African American Museum 340 Walnut St Web: www.tubmanmuseum.com	Macon	GA	31201	478-743-8544	743-9063
Tybee Island Lighthouse & Museum 30 Meddin Dr Web: www.tybeelighthouse.org	Tybee Island	GA	31328	912-786-5801	786-6538
Westville 1850's Village 1 ML King Blvd TF: 888-733-1850 ■ Web: www.westville.org	Lumpkin	GA	31815	229-838-6310	838-4000
William Breman Jewish Heritage Museum 1440 Spring St NW *Fax Area Code: 404 ■ Web: www.thebreman.org	Atlanta	GA	30309	678-222-3700	881-4009*
World of Coca-Cola Atlanta 121 Baker St NW TF: 800-676-2653 ■ Web: www.worldofcoca-cola.com	Atlanta	GA	30313	404-676-5151	676-5432
Wren's Nest House Museum 1050 Ralph David Abernathy Blvd SW	Atlanta	GA	30310	404-753-7735	753-8535

HAWAII

	City	State	Zip	Phone	Fax
Arizona Memorial Museum Assn 1 Arizona Memorial Pl TF: 888-485-1941 ■ Web: www.arizonamemorial.org	Honolulu	HI	96818	808-422-5664	483-8608
Bishop Museum 1525 Bernice St *Fax: Hum Res ■ Web: www.bishopmuseum.org	Honolulu	HI	96817	808-847-3511	848-4146*
Contemporary Museum 2411 Makiki Heights Dr Web: www.tcmhi.org	Honolulu	HI	96822	808-526-0232	536-5973
Hawaii's Plantation Village (HPV) 94-695 Waipahu St Web: www.hawaiiplantationvillage.org	Waipahu	HI	96797	808-677-0110	676-6727
Honolulu Academy of Arts 900 S Beretania St Web: www.honoluluacademy.org	Honolulu	HI	96814	808-532-8700	532-8787
Iolani Palace 1293 S King St Web: www.iolanipalace.org	Honolulu	HI	96813	808-522-0832	532-1051
Japanese Cultural Center of Hawaii 2454 S Beretania St Web: www.jcch.com	Honolulu	HI	96826	808-945-7633	944-1123
Judiciary History Ctr 417 S King St	Honolulu	HI	96813	808-539-4999	539-4996
Lyman Museum & Mission House 276 Haili St Web: www.lymanmuseum.org	Hilo	HI	96720	808-935-5021	969-7685
Mission Houses Museum 553 S King St Web: www.missionhouses.org	Honolulu	HI	96813	808-531-0481	545-2280
Polynesian Cultural Ctr 55-370 Kamehameha Hwy TF: 800-367-7060 ■ Web: www.polynesia.com	Laie	HI	96762	808-293-3000	293-3027
Tropic Lightning Museum Schofield Barracks Bldg 361 Waianae Ave Web: www.25idl.army.mil	Honolulu	HI	96857	808-655-0438	655-8301
US Army Museum of Hawaii 2161 Kalia Rd Web: www.hiarmymuseumsoc.org	Honolulu	HI	96830	808-438-2821	438-2819
USS Bowfin Submarine Museum & Park 11 Arizona Memorial Dr Web: www.bowfin.org	Honolulu	HI	96818	808-423-1341	422-5201

IDAHO

	City	State	Zip	Phone	Fax
Bannock County Historical Museum 3000 Alvord Loop	Pocatello	ID	83201	208-233-0434	
Basque Museum & Cultural Ctr 611 W Grove St Web: www.basquemuseum.com	Boise	ID	83702	208-343-2671	336-4801
Boise Art Museum 670 Julia Davis Dr Web: www.boiseartmuseum.org	Boise	ID	83702	208-345-8330	345-2247
Discovery Center of Idaho 131 Myrtle St Web: www.dcidaho.com	Boise	ID	83702	208-343-9895	343-0105
Idaho Black History Museum 508 Julia Davis Dr Web: www.ibhm.org	Boise	ID	83702	208-433-0017	433-0048
Idaho Historical Museum 610 E Julia Davis Dr TF: 877-653-4367 ■ Web: www.idahohistory.net	Boise	ID	83702	208-334-2120	334-4059
Idaho Military History Museum 4748 Lindbergh St Bldg 924 Web: www.inghro.state.id.us	Boise	ID	83705	208-272-4841	
Museum of North Idaho 115 NW Blvd PO Box 812 Web: www.museumni.org	Coeur d'Alene	ID	83816	208-664-3448	664-3448
Nez Perce County Historical Society & Museum 0306 3rd St	Lewiston	ID	83501	208-743-2535	
Warhawk Air Museum 201 Municipal Dr Web: www.warhawkairmuseum.org	Nampa	ID	83687	208-465-6446	465-6232

ILLINOIS

	City	State	Zip	Phone	Fax
Abraham Lincoln Presidential Library & Museum 112 N 6th St TF: 800-610-2094 ■ Web: www.alincoln-library.com	Springfield	IL	62701	217-524-7216	785-6250
African American Museum Hall of Fame 309 Du Sable St	Peoria	IL	61605	309-673-2206	495-0166
Art Institute of Chicago 111 S Michigan Ave Web: www.artic.edu	Chicago	IL	60603	312-443-3600	
Balzekas Museum of Lithuanian Culture 6500 S Pulaski Rd Web: www.balzekasmuseum.org	Chicago	IL	60629	773-582-6500	582-5133
Burpee Museum of Natural History 737 N Main St Web: www.burpee.org	Rockford	IL	61103	815-965-3433	965-2703
Chanute Air Museum 1011 Pacesetter Dr TF: 877-726-8685 ■ Web: www.aeromuseum.org	Rantoul	IL	61866	217-893-1613	892-5774
Chicago History Museum 1601 N Clark St Web: www.chicagohs.org	Chicago	IL	60614	312-642-4600	266-2077
Clarke House Museum 1827 S Indiana Ave Web: www.clarkehousemuseum.org	Chicago	IL	60616	312-745-0040	745-0077
Daughters of Union Veterans of the Civil War 503 S Walnut St PO Box 211 Web: www.duvcw.org	Springfield	IL	62704	217-544-0616	544-0606
David & Alfred Smart Museum of Art 5550 S Greenwood Ave Web: www.smartmuseum.uchicago.edu	Chicago	IL	60637	773-702-0200	702-3121
DuSable Museum of African American History 740 E 56th Pl Web: www.dusablemuseum.org	Chicago	IL	60637	773-947-0600	947-0716
Erlander Home Museum 404 S 3rd St Web: www.swedishhistorical.org	Rockford	IL	61104	815-963-5559	963-5559
Ernest Hemingway Museum 200 N Oak Pk Ave Web: www.ehfop.org	Oak Park	IL	60302	708-848-2222	386-2952
Ethnic Heritage Museum 1129 S Main St	Rockford	IL	61101	815-962-7402	962-7402
Field Museum The 1400 S Lake Shore Dr Web: www.fieldmuseum.org	Chicago	IL	60605	312-665-7600	665-7601
Frank Lloyd Wright Home & Studio 951 Chicago Ave Web: www.wrightplus.org	Oak Park	IL	60302	708-848-1976	848-1248
Glessner House Museum 1800 S Prairie Ave Web: www.glessnerhouse.org	Chicago	IL	60616	312-326-1480	326-1397
Grand Army of the Republic Memorial Museum 629 S 7th St Web: www.gar-museum.com	Springfield	IL	62703	217-522-4373	
Hellenic Museum & Cultural Ctr 333 S Halsted Ave Web: www.hellenicmuseum.org	Chicago	IL	60661	312-655-1234	655-1221
Illinois State Military Museum 1301 N MacArthur Blvd Bldg 30 Web: www.il.ngb.army.mil	Springfield	IL	62702	217-761-3910	761-3709
Illinois State Museum 502 S Spring St Web: www.museum.state.il.us	Springfield	IL	62706	217-782-7386	782-1254
International Museum of Surgical Science 1524 N Lake Shore Dr Web: www.imss.org	Chicago	IL	60610	312-642-6502	642-9516

Museum	City	State	Zip	Phone	Fax
ISM Dickson Mounds Museum 10956 N Dickson Mounds Rd *Web:* www.museum.state.il.us/ismsites/dickson	Lewistown	IL	61542	309-547-3721	547-3189
Krannert Art Museum 500 E Peabody Dr University of Illinois *Web:* www.art.uiuc.edu	Champaign	IL	61820	217-333-1860	333-0883
Lakeview Museum of Arts & Sciences 1125 W Lake St *Web:* www.lakeview-museum.org	Peoria	IL	61614	309-686-7000	686-0280
Lincoln's New Salem State Historic Site 15588 History Ln *Web:* www.lincolnsnewsalem.com	Petersburg	IL	62675	217-632-4000	632-4010
Lizzadro Museum of Lapidary Art 220 Cottage Hill Ave Wilder Pk *Web:* www.lizzadromuseum.org	Elmhurst	IL	60126	630-833-1616	833-1225
Midway Village Museum 6799 Guilford Rd *Web:* www.midwayvillage.com	Rockford	IL	61107	815-397-9112	397-9156
Museum of Contemporary Art 220 E Chicago Ave *TF:* 800-622-7858 ■ *Web:* www.mcachicago.org	Chicago	IL	60611	312-280-2660	397-4095
Museum of Contemporary Photography 600 S Michigan Ave Columbia College *Web:* www.mocp.org	Chicago	IL	60605	312-663-5554	344-8067
Museum of Funeral Customs 1440 Monument Ave *Web:* www.funeralmuseum.org	Springfield	IL	62702	217-544-3480	544-3484
Museum of Science & Industry 5700 S Lake Shore Dr *TF:* 800-468-6674 ■ *Web:* www.msichicago.org	Chicago	IL	60637	773-684-1414	684-7141
Museum of the Grand Prairie 600 N Lombard St PO Box 1040 *Web:* www.museumofthegrandprairie.org	Mahomet	IL	61853	217-586-3360	586-5724
National Museum of Mexican Art 1852 W 19th St *Web:* www.nationalmuseumofmexicanart.org	Chicago	IL	60608	312-738-1503	738-9740
National Museum of Surveying 521 E Washington St PO Box 522 *Web:* www.surveyhistory.org	Spriingfield	IL	62705	217-523-3130	
National Vietnam Veterans Art Museum 1801 S Indiana Ave *Web:* www.nvvam.org	Chicago	IL	60616	312-326-0270	326-9767
Oriental Institute Museum 1155 E 58th St University of Chicago *Web:* www.oi.uchicago.edu	Chicago	IL	60637	773-702-9514	702-9853
Peggy Notebaert Nature Museum 2430 N Cannon Dr *Web:* www.naturemuseum.org	Chicago	IL	60614	773-755-5100	755-5199
Polish Museum of America (PMA) 984 N Milwaukee Ave *Web:* www.pma.prcua.org	Chicago	IL	60642	773-384-3352	384-3799
Quincy Museum 1601 Maine St *Web:* www.thequincymuseum.com	Quincy	IL	62301	217-224-9323	224-9323
Rockford Art Museum 711 N Main St *Web:* www.rockfordartmuseum.org	Rockford	IL	61103	815-968-2787	316-2179
Ronald Reagan Museum 300 E College Ave *TF:* 888-438-7352 ■ *Web:* reagan.eureka.edu/lead_applied/museum.htm	Eureka	IL	61530	309-467-6407	467-6437
Sousa Archives & Center for American Music (SACAM) 1103 S 6th St 236 Harding Band Bldg *Web:* www.library.uiuc.edu	Champaign	IL	61820	217-244-9309	244-8695
Spertus Museum 610 S Michigan Ave *TF:* 888-322-1740 ■ *Web:* www.spertus.edu	Chicago	IL	60605	312-922-9012	922-6406
Spurlock Museum *University of Illinois at Urbana* 600 S Gregory St *Web:* www.spurlock.uiuc.edu	Urbana	IL	61801	217-333-2360	244-9419
Swedish American Museum 5211 N Clark St *Web:* www.samac.org	Chicago	IL	60640	773-728-8111	728-8870
Tinker Swiss Cottage Museum 411 Kent St *Web:* www.tinkercottage.com	Rockford	IL	61102	815-964-2424	964-2466
Ukrainian National Museum 2249 W Superior St *Web:* www.ukrainiannationalmuseum.org	Chicago	IL	60612	312-421-8020	
University Museum Southern Illinois University Faner Hall Rm 2469 *Web:* www.museum.siu.edu	Carbondale	IL	62901	618-453-5388	453-7409

INDIANA

Museum	City	State	Zip	Phone	Fax
Auburn Cord Duesenberg Museum 1600 S Wayne St *Web:* www.automobilemuseum.org	Auburn	IN	46706	260-925-1444	925-6266
Children's Museum of Indianapolis 3000 N Meridian St *TF:* 800-826-5431 ■ *Web:* www.childrensmuseum.org	Indianapolis	IN	46208	317-924-5431	920-2001
Conner Prairie Living History Museum 13400 Allisonville Rd *TF:* 800-966-1836 ■ *Web:* www.connerprairie.org	Fishers	IN	46038	317-776-6000	776-6014
Dan Quayle Ctr 815 Warren St PO Box 856 *Web:* www.quaylemuseum.org	Huntington	IN	46750	260-356-6356	356-1455
Eiteljorg Museum of American Indians & Western Art 500 W Washington St *Web:* www.eiteljorg.org	Indianapolis	IN	46204	317-636-9378	275-1400
Evansville Museum of Arts History & Science 411 SE Riverside Dr *Web:* www.emuseum.org	Evansville	IN	47713	812-425-2406	421-7509
Firefighters' Museum 226 W Washington Blvd	Fort Wayne	IN	46802	260-426-0051	
Fort Wayne Museum of Art 311 E Main St *Web:* www.fwmoa.org	Fort Wayne	IN	46802	260-422-6467	422-1374
Freetown Village Living History Museum PO Box 1041 *Web:* www.freetown.org	Indianapolis	IN	46206	317-631-1870	631-0224
History Ctr 302 E Berry St *Web:* www.fwhistorycenter.com	Fort Wayne	IN	46802	260-426-2882	424-4419
Indiana Medical History Museum 3045 W Vermont St *TF:* 866-910-7329 ■ *Web:* www.imhm.org	Indianapolis	IN	46222	317-635-7329	635-7349
Indiana State Museum 650 W Washington St *Web:* www.in.gov	Indianapolis	IN	46204	317-232-1637	
Indiana University Art Museum 1133 E 7th St *Web:* www.indiana.edu	Bloomington	IN	47405	812-855-5445	855-1023
Indianapolis Motor Speedway & Hall of Fame Museum 4790 W 16th St *Web:* www.indianapolismotorspeedway.com	Indianapolis	IN	46222	317-492-6747	492-6449
Indianapolis Museum of Art 4000 Michigan Rd *Web:* www.ima-art.org	Indianapolis	IN	46208	317-923-1331	931-1978
Indianapolis Museum of Contemporary Art 340 N Senate Ave *Web:* www.indymoca.org	Indianapolis	IN	46204	317-634-6622	634-1977
James Whitcomb Riley Museum Home 528 Lockerbie St *Web:* www.rileykids.org	Indianapolis	IN	46202	317-631-5885	
Macedonian Tribune Museum 124 W Wayne St Suite 204 *Web:* www.macedonian.org	Fort Wayne	IN	46802	260-422-5900	422-1348
Mathers Museum of World Cultures 416 N Indiana Ave *Web:* www.indiana.edu/mathers	Bloomington	IN	47408	812-855-6873	855-0205
Monroe County History Ctr 202 E 6th St	Bloomington	IN	47408	812-332-2517	355-5593
Northern Indiana Center for History 808 W Washington St *Web:* www.centerforhistory.org	South Bend	IN	46601	574-235-9664	235-9059
Reitz Home Museum 224 SE 1st St *Web:* www.reitzhome.evansville.net	Evansville	IN	47706	812-426-1871	426-2179
Science Central 1950 N Clinton St *TF:* 800-442-6376 ■ *Web:* www.sciencecentral.org	Fort Wayne	IN	46805	260-424-2400	422-2899
Snite Museum of Art University of Notre Dame *Web:* www.nd.edu/~sniteart	Notre Dame	IN	46556	574-631-5466	631-8501
South Bend Museum of Art (SBM) 120 S St Joseph St *Web:* www.southbendart.org	South Bend	IN	46601	574-235-9102	235-5782
Studebaker National Museum 201 Chapin St *TF:* 888-391-5600 ■ *Web:* www.studebakermuseum.org	South Bend	IN	46601	574-235-9714	235-5522
Swope Art Museum 25 S 7th St *Web:* www.swope.org	Terre Haute	IN	47807	812-238-1676	238-1677
Wylie House Museum 307 E 2nd St *Web:* www.indiana.edu	Bloomington	IN	47401	812-855-6224	

IOWA

Museum	City	State	Zip	Phone	Fax
African American Historical Museum & Cultural Center of Iowa 55 12th Ave SE *TF:* 877-526-1863 ■ *Web:* www.blackiowa.org	Cedar Rapids	IA	52406	319-862-2101	862-2105
Cedar Rapids Museum of Art 410 3rd Ave SE *Web:* www.crma.org	Cedar Rapids	IA	52401	319-366-7503	366-4111
Coe College Permanent Collection of Art 1220 1st Ave NE *Web:* www.public.coe.edu	Cedar Rapids	IA	52402	319-399-8500	399-8019
Des Moines Art Ctr 4700 Grand Ave *Web:* www.desmoinesartcenter.org	Des Moines	IA	50312	515-277-4405	271-0357
Dubuque Museum of Art 701 Locust St *Web:* www.dbqart.com	Dubuque	IA	52001	563-557-1851	557-7826
Duffy's Collectible Cars 250 Classic Car Ct *Web:* www.duffys.com	Cedar Rapids	IA	52404	319-364-7000	364-4036
Figge Art Museum 225 W 2nd St *Web:* www.figgeartmuseum.org	Davenport	IA	52801	563-326-7804	326-7876
Granger House Museum 970 10th St *Web:* www.community.marion.ia.us	Marion	IA	52302	319-377-6672	
Herbert Hoover Presidential Library & Museum 210 Parkside Dr *Web:* www.hoover.archives.gov	West Branch	IA	52358	319-643-5301	643-6045
Hoyt Sherman Place 1501 Woodland Ave *Web:* www.hoytsherman.org	Des Moines	IA	50309	515-244-0507	237-3582
Iowa Gold Star Military Museum 7105 NW 70th Ave *Web:* www.iowanationalguard.com	Johnston	IA	50131	515-252-4531	727-3107
Iowa Masonic Library & Museum 813 1st Ave SE *Web:* www.gl-iowa.org	Cedar Rapids	IA	52402	319-365-1438	365-1439
John Wayne Birthplace 216 S 2nd St *Web:* www.johnwaynebirthplace.org	Winterset	IA	50273	515-462-1044	462-3289
Living History Farms 2600 111th St *Web:* www.lhf.org	Urbandale	IA	50322	515-278-5286	278-9808
National Balloon Museum 1601 N Jefferson Way PO Box 149 *Web:* www.nationalballoonmuseum.com	Indianola	IA	50125	515-961-3714	
National Czech & Slovak Museum & Library 87 16th Ave SW *Web:* www.ncsml.org	Cedar Rapids	IA	52404	319-362-8500	363-2209
National Farm Toy Museum 1110 16th Ave SE *Web:* www.nftmonline.com	Dyersville	IA	52040	563-875-2727	875-8467
National Mississippi River Museum & Aquarium 350 E 3rd St *TF:* 800-226-3369 ■ *Web:* www.mississippirivermuseum.com	Dubuque	IA	52001	563-557-9545	583-1241
Pella Historical Village 507 Franklin St *Web:* www.pellatuliptime.com/historical-village	Pella	IA	50219	641-628-4311	628-9192
Science Center of Iowa 401 W Martin Luther King Jr Pkwy *Web:* www.sciowa.org	Des Moines	IA	50309	515-274-6868	274-3404

Name / Address	City	State	ZIP	Phone	Fax
Science Station & McLeod/Busse IMAX Dome Theatre 4444 1st St SE Suite 200 *Web:* www.sciencestation.org	Cedar Rapids	IA	52401	319-363-4629	366-4590
Sioux City Art Ctr 225 Nebraska St *Web:* www.siouxcityartcenter.org	Sioux City	IA	51101	712-279-6272	255-2921
Sioux City Public Museum 2901 Jackson St *Web:* www.sioux-city.org	Sioux City	IA	51104	712-279-6174	252-5615
State Historical Society of Iowa 600 E Locust St *Web:* www.iowahistory.org	Des Moines	IA	50319	515-281-5111	242-6498
University Museum 3219 Hudson Rd University of Northern Iowa *Web:* www.uni.edu/museum	Cedar Falls	IA	50614	319-273-2188	273-6924
University of Iowa Museum of Art 150 N Riverside Dr *Web:* www.uiowa.edu/uima	Iowa City	IA	52242	319-335-1727	335-3677

KANSAS

Name / Address	City	State	ZIP	Phone	Fax
Boot Hill Museum 500 W Wyatt Earp Blvd *Web:* www.boothill.org	Dodge City	KS	67801	620-227-8188	227-7673
Coleman Factory Outlet Store & Museum 235 N St Francis St *TF:* 800-835-3278 ■ *Web:* www.coleman.com	Wichita	KS	67202	316-264-0836	219-5287
Combat Air Museum 602 J St Forbes Field *Web:* www.combatairmuseum.org	Topeka	KS	66619	785-862-3303	862-3304
Dwight D Eisenhower Presidential Library & Museum 200 SE 4th St *TF:* 877-746-4453 ■ *Web:* www.eisenhower.utexas.edu	Abilene	KS	67410	785-263-6700	263-6715
Great Plains Transportation Museum 700 E Douglas St *Web:* www.gptm.us	Wichita	KS	67202	316-263-0944	
Indian Center Museum *Mid America All Indian Ctr* 650 N Seneca St *Web:* theindiancenter.org	Wichita	KS	67203	316-350-3340	262-4216
Kansas African American Museum 601 N Water St *Web:* www.tkaam.org	Wichita	KS	67203	316-262-7651	265-6953
Kansas Aviation Museum 3350 S George Washington Blvd *Web:* www.kansasaviationmuseum.org	Wichita	KS	67210	316-683-9242	683-0573
Kansas Museum of History 6425 SW 6th St *Web:* www.kshs.org	Topeka	KS	66615	785-272-8681	272-8682
Kansas National Guard Museum 6700 S Topeka Blvd Forbes Field Bldg 301	Topeka	KS	66619	785-862-1020	862-7204
Lowell D Holmes Museum of Anthropology 114 Neff Hall Wichita State University *Web:* webs.wichita.edu/anthropology	Wichita	KS	67260	316-978-3195	978-3351
Mulvane Art Museum 1700 SW Jewell Ave *Web:* www.washburn.edu	Topeka	KS	66621	785-670-1124	
Museum of World Treasures 835 E 1st St *Web:* www.worldtreasures.org	Wichita	KS	67202	316-263-1311	263-1495
National Agricultural Center & Hall of Fame 630 Hall of Fame Dr *Web:* www.aghalloffame.com	Bonner Springs	KS	66012	913-721-1075	721-1202
Old Cowtown Museum 1865 W Museum Blvd *Web:* www.oldcowtown.org	Wichita	KS	67203	316-219-1871	264-2937
Santa Fe Trail Ctr 1349 K-156 Hwy *Web:* www.santafetrailcenter.org	Larned	KS	67550	620-285-2054	285-7491
Spencer Museum of Art 1301 Mississippi St University of Kansas *Web:* www.spencerart.ku.edu	Lawrence	KS	66045	785-864-4710	864-3112
Strawberry Hill Museum & Cultural Ctr 720 N 4th St *Web:* www.strawberryhillmuseum.org	Kansas City	KS	66101	913-371-3264	
Ulrich Museum of Art 1845 Fairmount St Wichita State University *Web:* ulrich.wichita.edu	Wichita	KS	67260	316-978-3664	978-3898
Wichita Art Museum 1400 W Museum Blvd *Web:* www.wichitaartmuseum.org	Wichita	KS	67203	316-268-4921	268-4980
Wichita-Sedgwick County Historical Museum 204 S Main St *Web:* www.wichitahistory.org	Wichita	KS	67202	316-265-9314	265-9319
Wyandotte County Historical Society & Museum 631 N 126th St	Bonner Springs	KS	66012	913-721-1078	721-1394

KENTUCKY

Name / Address	City	State	ZIP	Phone	Fax
American Saddlebred Museum 4083 Iron Works Pkwy *TF:* 800-829-4438 ■ *Web:* www.american-saddlebred.com	Lexington	KY	40511	859-259-2746	255-4909
Aviation Museum of Kentucky 4316 Hanger Dr *Web:* www.aviationky.org	Lexington	KY	40510	859-231-1219	381-8739
Bluegrass Scenic Railroad & Museum 175 Beasley Rd Woodford County Pk *Web:* www.bgrm.org	Versailles	KY	40383	859-873-2476	873-0408
Conrad Caldwell House Museum The 1402 St James Ct *Web:* www.zexton.com	Louisville	KY	40208	502-636-5023	636-1264
Farmington Historic Plantation 3033 Bardstown Rd *Web:* www.farmingtonhistorichome.org	Louisville	KY	40205	502-452-9920	456-1976
Filson Historical Society Museum 1310 S 3rd St *Web:* www.filsonhistorical.org	Louisville	KY	40208	502-635-5083	635-5086
Frazier International History Museum 829 W Main St *TF:* 866-886-7103 ■ *Web:* www.frazierarmsmuseum.org	Louisville	KY	40202	502-412-2280	412-8148
Headley-Whitney Museum 4435 Old Frankfort Pike *TF:* 800-310-5085 ■ *Web:* www.headley-whitney.org	Lexington	KY	40510	859-255-6653	255-8375
International Museum of the Horse 4089 Iron Works Pkwy *TF:* 800-678-8813 ■ *Web:* www.imh.org/imh/imhmain.html	Lexington	KY	40511	859-259-4231	225-4613
John James Audubon Museum 3100 Hwy 41 N *Web:* www.go-henderson.com/audubon	Henderson	KY	42420	270-826-2247	826-2286
Kentucky Derby Museum 704 Central Ave *Web:* www.derbymuseum.org	Louisville	KY	40208	502-634-0676	636-5855
Kentucky Historical Society 100 W Broadway *Web:* history.ky.gov	Frankfort	KY	40601	502-564-1792	
Kentucky Military History Museum 125 E Main St *Web:* www.kyhistory.org	Frankfort	KY	40601	502-564-3265	564-4054
Kentucky Museum Western Kentucky University 1906 College Heights Blvd *Web:* www.web2.wku.edu	Bowling Green	KY	42101	270-745-2592	745-4878
Lexington History Museum 215 W Main St *Web:* www.lexingtonhistorymuseum.org	Lexington	KY	40507	859-254-0530	254-8372
Louisville Science Ctr 727 W Main St *TF:* 800-591-2203 ■ *Web:* www.louisvillescience.org	Louisville	KY	40202	502-561-6100	561-6145
Muhammad Ali Ctr 144 N 6th St *Web:* www.alicenter.org	Louisville	KY	40202	502-584-9254	589-4905
National Corvette Museum 350 Corvette Dr *TF:* 800-538-3883 ■ *Web:* www.corvettemuseum.com	Bowling Green	KY	42101	270-781-7973	781-5286
Old State Capitol Museum 300 W Broadway	Frankfort	KY	40601	502-564-2301	564-4701
Shaker Village of Pleasant Hill 3501 Lexington Rd *TF:* 800-734-7278 ■ *Web:* www.shakervillageky.org	Harrodsburg	KY	40330	859-734-5411	734-5411
Speed Art Museum The 2035 S 3rd St *Web:* www.speedmuseum.org	Louisville	KY	40208	502-634-2700	636-2899
Thomas Edison House 729-731 E Washington St *Web:* www.edisonhouse.org	Louisville	KY	40202	502-585-5247	585-5231
University of Kentucky Art Museum Rose St & Euclid Ave *Web:* www.uky.edu/ArtMuseum	Lexington	KY	40506	859-257-5716	323-1994
University of Kentucky Museum of Anthropology 211 Lafferty Hall *Web:* www.uky.edu/AS/Anthropology/Museum	Lexington	KY	40506	859-257-1944	323-1968

LOUISIANA

Name / Address	City	State	ZIP	Phone	Fax
Alexandre Mouton House/Lafayette Museum 1122 Lafayette St	Lafayette	LA	70501	337-234-2208	234-2208
American Italian Renaissance Foundation Museum 537 S Peters St *Web:* www.airf.org	New Orleans	LA	70130	504-522-7294	522-1657
Cathedral of Saint John the Evangelist Museum 515 Cathedral St *Web:* www.saintjohncathedral.org/Welcome.html	Lafayette	LA	70501	337-232-1322	232-1379
Confederate Museum 929 Camp St *Web:* www.confederatemuseum.com	New Orleans	LA	70130	504-523-4522	523-8595
Eighth Air Force Museum Barksdale Air Force Base 88 Shreveport Rd *Web:* www.eighthairforcemuseum.com	Bossier City	LA	71110	318-456-3067	456-5558
Enchanted Mansion Doll Museum 190 Lee Dr *Web:* www.enchantedmansion.org	Baton Rouge	LA	70808	225-769-0005	766-6822
Freeport McMoRan Science Complex 409 Williams Blvd Rivertown *Web:* www.kenner.la.us	Kenner	LA	70062	504-468-7231	471-2159
Gallier House Museum 1132 Royal St *Web:* www.hgghh.org	New Orleans	LA	70116	504-525-5661	568-9735
Grandmother's Buttons Museum 9814 Royal St *TF:* 800-580-6941 ■ *Web:* www.grandmothersbuttons.com	Saint Francisville	LA	70775	225-635-4107	635-6067
Heritage Museum & Cultural Ctr 1606 Main St PO Box 707 *Web:* www.bakerheritagemuseum.org	Baker	LA	70714	225-774-1776	775-5635
Historic New Orleans Collection 533 Royal St *Web:* www.hnoc.org	New Orleans	LA	70130	504-523-4662	598-7108
House of Broel's Historic Mansion & Dollhouse Museum 2220 St Charles Ave *TF:* 800-827-4325 ■ *Web:* www.houseofbroel.com	New Orleans	LA	70130	504-522-2220	524-6775
Imperial Calcasieu Museum 204 W Sallier St	Lake Charles	LA	70601	337-439-3797	439-6040
Lafayette Museum 1122 Lafayette St	Lafayette	LA	70501	337-234-2208	234-2208
Longue Vue House & Gardens 7 Bamboo Rd *Web:* www.longuevue.com	New Orleans	LA	70124	504-488-5488	486-7015
Louisiana Art & Science Museum 100 S River Rd *Web:* www.lasm.org	Baton Rouge	LA	70802	225-344-5272	344-9477
Louisiana Naval War Memorial 305 S River Rd *Web:* www.usskidd.com	Baton Rouge	LA	70802	225-342-1942	342-2039
Louisiana State Museum 751 Chartres St *TF:* 800-568-6968 ■ *Web:* www.lsm.crt.state.la.us	New Orleans	LA	70116	504-568-6968	568-4995
Louisiana State University Museum of Art 100 Lafayette St *Web:* www.lsumoa.com	Baton Rouge	LA	70801	225-389-7200	389-7219
Louisiana State University Museum of Natural Science 119 Foster Hall Louisiana State University *Web:* www.appl003.lsu.edu/natsci/lmns.nsf/index	Baton Rouge	LA	70803	225-578-2855	578-3075

			Phone	Fax
Louisiana State University Rural Life Museum & Windrush Gardens PO Box 80498 ... Baton Rouge	LA	70809	225-765-2437	765-2639
Web: www.appl027.lsu.edu/rlm/rurallifeweb.nsf/index				
Louisiana Toy Train Museum 519 Williams Blvd Rivertown ... Kenner	LA	70062	504-468-7231	471-2159
Magnolia Mound Plantation 2161 Nicholson Dr ... Baton Rouge	LA	70802	225-343-4955	343-6739
Meadows Museum of Art at Centenary College 2911 Centenary Blvd ... Shreveport	LA	71104	318-869-5169	869-5730
Web: www.centenary.edu/meadows				
Musee Conti-Wax Museum of Louisiana Legends 917 Rue Conti French Quarter ... New Orleans	LA	70112	504-525-2605	566-7636
TF: 800-233-5405 ■ *Web:* www.neworleanswaxmuseum.com				
New Orleans Museum of Art 1 Collins Diboll Cir ... New Orleans	LA	70124	504-658-4100	658-4199
Web: www.noma.org				
New Orleans Pharmacy Museum 514 Chartres St ... New Orleans	LA	70130	504-565-8027	565-8028
Web: www.pharmacymuseum.org				
Nottoway Plantation 31025 Louisiana Hwy 1 ... White Castle	LA	70788	225-545-2730	545-8632
TF: 866-428-4748 ■ *Web:* www.nottoway.com				
Ogden Museum of Southern Art 925 Camp St ... New Orleans	LA	70130	504-539-9600	539-9602
Web: www.ogdenmuseum.org				
Old Arsenal Museum PO Box 94125 ... Baton Rouge	LA	70804	225-342-0401	
Web: www.sos.louisiana.gov				
Pitot House Museum 1440 Moss St ... New Orleans	LA	70119	504-482-0312	482-0363
Web: www.pitothouse.org				
Plaquemine Lock Museum 57730 Main St ... Plaquemine	LA	70764	225-687-7158	687-8933
TF: 877-987-7158				
RW Norton Art Gallery 4747 Creswell Ave ... Shreveport	LA	71106	318-865-4201	869-0435
Web: www.rwnaf.org				
Saints Hall of Fame Museum 415 Williams Blvd Rivertown ... Kenner	LA	70062	504-468-7231	471-2159
Web: www.rivertownkenner.com/saints.html				
Sci-Port Discovery Ctr 820 Clyde Fant Pkwy ... Shreveport	LA	71101	318-424-3466	222-5592
TF: 877-724-7678 ■ *Web:* www.sciport.org				
Southern University Museum of Art Martin L Harvey Hall ... Baton Rouge	LA	70813	225-771-4513	771-4498
Web: www.sus.edu/PageDisplay.asp?p1=4371				
Southern University Museum of Art 610 Texas St Suite 110 ... Shreveport	LA	71101	318-678-4631	678-4607
TF: 800-458-1472				
Spring Street Historical Museum 525 Spring St ... Shreveport	LA	71101	318-424-0964	424-0964
Web: www.springstreetmuseum.com				
Stage of Stars Museum 705 Elvis Presley Blvd ... Shreveport	LA	71101	318-220-9434	220-7276
Web: www.stageofstars.com				
Touchstone Wildlife & Art Museum 3386 Hwy 80 E ... Haughton	LA	71037	318-949-2323	
University Art Museum 710 E St Mary Blvd PO Box 42571 ... Lafayette	LA	70503	337-482-5326	262-1268
Web: museum.louisiana.edu				
West Baton Rouge Museum 845 N Jefferson Ave ... Port Allen	LA	70767	225-336-2422	336-2448
Web: www.westbatonrougemuseum.com				
West Feliciana Historical Society Museum 11757 Ferdinand St ... Saint Francisville	LA	70775	225-635-6330	635-4626
TF: 800-789-4221				

MAINE

			Phone	Fax
Abbe Museum 26 Mt Desert St ... Bar Harbor	ME	04609	207-288-3519	288-8979
Web: www.abbemuseum.org				
Bangor Museum & History Ctr 159 Union St ... Bangor	ME	04401	207-942-5766	942-1910
Web: www.bangormuseum.org				
Bowdoin College Museum of Art 9400 College Stn ... Brunswick	ME	04011	207-725-3275	725-3762
Web: www.bowdoin.edu				
Brick Store Museum 117 Main St ... Kennebunk	ME	04043	207-985-4802	985-6887
Web: www.brickstoremuseum.org				
Colby College Museum of Art 5600 Mayflower Hill ... Waterville	ME	04901	207-859-5600	859-5606
Web: www.colby.edu				
Cole Land Transportation Museum 405 Perry Rd ... Bangor	ME	04401	207-990-3600	990-2653
Web: www.colemuseum.org				
Farnsworth Art Museum 16 Museum St ... Rockland	ME	04841	207-596-6457	596-0509
Web: www.farnsworthmuseum.org				
Hudson Museum 5746 Maine Ctr for the Arts ... Orono	ME	04469	207-581-1901	581-1950
Web: www.umaine.edu/hudsonmuseum				
Maine Forest & Logging Museum Inc PO Box 456 ... Orono	ME	04411	207-974-6278	581-9398
Web: www.leonardsmills.com				
Maine Historical Society 489 Congress St Maine Historical Society ... Portland	ME	04101	207-774-1822	775-4301
Web: www.mainehistory.com				
Maine Maritime Museum 243 Washington St ... Bath	ME	04530	207-443-1316	443-1665
Web: www.bathmaine.com				
Maine Narrow Gauge Railroad Museum 58 Fore St ... Portland	ME	04101	207-828-0814	879-6132
Web: www.mainenarrowgauge.org				
Maine State Museum 83 State House Stn State House Complex ... Augusta	ME	04333	207-287-2301	287-6633
Web: www.mainestatemuseum.org				
Museum at Portland Head Light 1000 Shore Rd ... Cape Elizabeth	ME	04107	207-799-2661	799-2800
Web: www.portlandheadlight.com/park.html				
Old Fort Western 16 Cony St ... Augusta	ME	04330	207-626-2385	626-2304
Web: www.oldfortwestern.org				
Old Town Museum 353 Main St ... Old Town	ME	04468	207-827-7256	
Web: www.old-town.org				
Penobscot Marine Museum 5 Church St ... Searsport	ME	04974	207-548-2529	548-2520
Web: www.acadia.net				
Portland Fire Museum 157 Spring St ... Portland	ME	04101	207-772-2040	
Web: www.portlandfiremuseum.com				
Portland Museum of Art 7 Congress Sq ... Portland	ME	04101	207-775-6148	773-7324
Web: www.portlandmuseum.org				
State House 1 State House Stn ... Augusta	ME	04333	207-287-3531	287-6548
Web: www.maine.gov				
Tate House Museum 1267 Westbrook St ... Portland	ME	04102	207-774-6177	774-6198
Web: www.tatehouse.org				
University of Maine Museum of Art 40 Harlow St Norumbega Hall ... Bangor	ME	04401	207-561-3350	561-3351
Web: www.umma.umaine.edu				

MANITOBA

			Phone	Fax
Ivan Franko Museum 200 McGregor St 595 Pritchard Ave ... Winnipeg	MB	R2W5L6	204-589-4397	589-3404
Web: www.museumsmanitoba.com/dir/winnipeg/17.html				
Living Prairie Museum 2795 Ness Ave ... Winnipeg	MB	R3J3S4	204-832-0167	986-4172
Web: www.livingprairie.ca/home.html?bg=2				
Manitoba Museum 190 Rupert Ave ... Winnipeg	MB	R3B0N2	204-956-2830	942-3679
Web: www.manitobamuseum.ca/main				
Royal Canadian Artillery Museum Horsham Rd Bldg N-118 ... Shilo	MB	R0K2A0	204-765-3000	765-5289
Web: www.rcamuseum.com				

MARYLAND

			Phone	Fax
Accokeek Foundation 3400 Bryan Pt Rd ... Accokeek	MD	20607	301-283-2113	283-2049
Web: www.accokeek.org				
American Visionary Art Museum 800 Key Hwy ... Baltimore	MD	21230	410-244-1900	244-5858
Web: www.avam.org				
Annapolis Maritime Museum 723 2nd St PO Box 3088 ... Annapolis	MD	21403	410-295-0104	295-3022
Web: www.amaritime.org				
B & O Railroad Museum 901 W Pratt St ... Baltimore	MD	21223	410-752-2490	752-2499
Web: www.borail.org				
Baltimore Museum of Art 10 Art Museum Dr ... Baltimore	MD	21218	443-573-1700	573-1582
Web: www.artbma.org				
Baltimore Museum of Industry 1415 Key Hwy ... Baltimore	MD	21230	410-727-4808	727-4869
Web: www.thebmi.org				
Baltimore Streetcar Museum 1901 Falls Rd ... Baltimore	MD	21211	410-547-0264	547-0264
Web: www.baltimoremd.com				
Banneker-Douglas Museum 84 Franklin St ... Annapolis	MD	21401	410-216-6180	974-2553
TF: 866-521-6173 ■ *Web:* www.bdmuseum.com				
Calvert Marine Museum 14200 Solomons Island Rd S ... Solomons	MD	20688	410-326-2042	326-6691
Web: www.calvertmarinemuseum.com				
Calvin B Taylor House Museum 208 N Main St ... Berlin	MD	21811	410-641-1019	
Web: www.taylorhousemuseum.org				
Chesapeake Bay Maritime Museum 213 N Talbot St ... Saint Michaels	MD	21663	410-745-2916	745-6088
Web: www.cbmm.org				
Contemporary Museum The 100 W Centre St ... Baltimore	MD	21201	410-783-5720	783-5722
Web: www.contemporary.org				
Edgar Allan Poe House 203 N Amity St ... Baltimore	MD	21223	410-396-7932	
Web: www.eapoe.org				
Fire Museum of Maryland 1301 York Rd ... Lutherville	MD	21093	410-321-7500	769-8433
Web: www.firemuseummd.org				
Fort McHenry National Monument & Historic Shrine 2400 E Fort Ave ... Baltimore	MD	21230	410-962-4290	962-2500
Web: www.nps.gov				
Hammond-Harwood House 19 Maryland Ave ... Annapolis	MD	21401	410-263-4683	267-6891
Web: www.hammondharwoodhouse.org				
Historic Annapolis Foundation Museum 77 Main St ... Annapolis	MD	21401	410-268-5576	
TF: 800-639-9153 ■ *Web:* www.annapolis.org				
Homewood Museum 3400 N Charles St Johns Hopkins University ... Baltimore	MD	21218	410-516-5589	516-7859
Web: www.jhu.edu/historichouses				
Jewish Museum of Maryland 15 Lloyd St ... Baltimore	MD	21202	410-732-6400	732-6451
TF: 877-376-7190 ■ *Web:* www.jhsm.org				
Lacrosse Hall of Fame & Museum 113 W University Pkwy ... Baltimore	MD	21210	410-235-6882	366-6735
Web: www.lacrosse.org				
Lovely Lane Museum 2200 St Paul St ... Baltimore	MD	21218	410-889-4458	889-1501
Web: www.lovelylanemuseum.com				
Maryland Historical Society Museum & Library 201 W Monument St ... Baltimore	MD	21201	410-685-3750	385-2105
Web: www.mdhs.org				
Maryland Science Ctr 601 Light St ... Baltimore	MD	21230	410-685-2370	545-5974
Web: www.mdsci.org				
Mount Clare Museum House 1500 Washington Blvd Carroll Pk ... Baltimore	MD	21230	410-837-3262	837-0251
Web: www.mountclare.org				
National Great Blacks in Wax Museum 1601-03 E North Ave ... Baltimore	MD	21213	410-563-3404	675-5040
Web: www.ngbiwm.com				
National Museum of Dentistry 31 S Greene St ... Baltimore	MD	21201	410-706-0600	706-8313
Web: www.dentalmuseum.org				
Ocean City Life-Saving Station Museum 813 S Atlantic Ave ... Ocean City	MD	21842	410-289-4991	289-4991
Web: www.ocmuseum.org				
Reginald F Lewis Museum of Maryland African American History & Culture 830 E Pratt St ... Baltimore	MD	21202	443-263-1800	333-1138*
**Fax Area Code: 410* ■ *Web:* www.africanamericanculture.org				

				Phone	Fax
Star-Spangled Banner Flag House The 844 E Pratt St *Web:* www.flaghouse.org	Baltimore	MD	21202	410-837-1793	837-1812
Top of the World Observation Level & Museum 401 E Pratt St World Trade Ctr 27th Fl *Web:* www.bop.org/topotheworld/topoftheworld.aspx	Baltimore	MD	21202	410-837-8439	837-0845
US Naval Academy Museum 118 Maryland Ave *Web:* www.usna.edu	Annapolis	MD	21402	410-293-2108	293-5220
Walters Art Museum 600 N Charles St *Web:* www.thewalters.org	Baltimore	MD	21201	410-547-9000	783-7969
Ward Museum of Wildfowl Art 909 S Schumaker Dr *Web:* www.wardmuseum.org	Salisbury	MD	21804	410-742-4988	742-3107
Washington County Museum of Fine Arts 401 Museum Dr PO Box 423 *Web:* www.wcmfa.org	Hagerstown	MD	21741	301-739-5727	745-3741
Wheels Of Yesterday Antique & Classic Cars Museum 12708 Ocean Gateway	Ocean City	MD	21842	410-213-7329	

MASSACHUSETTS

				Phone	Fax
American Jewish Historical Society 101 Newbury St *Web:* www.ajhs.org	Boston	MA	02116	617-226-1245	559-8881
American Textile History Museum 491 Dutton St *Web:* www.athm.org	Lowell	MA	01854	978-441-0400	441-1412
Berkshire County Historical Society 780 Holmes Rd	Pittsfield	MA	01201	413-442-1793	443-1449
Cape Cod Maritime Museum 135 S St *Web:* www.capecodmaritimemuseum.org	Hyannis	MA	02601	508-775-1723	775-1706
Cape Cod Museum of Natural History 869 Main St *Web:* www.ccmnh.org	Brewster	MA	02631	508-896-3867	896-8844
Connecticut Valley Historical Museum 220 State St *TF:* 800-625-7738 ■ *Web:* www.quadrangle.org	Springfield	MA	01103	413-263-6800	263-6875
Fogg Art Museum 32 Quincy St Harvard University *Web:* www.artmuseums.harvard.edu/fogg	Cambridge	MA	02138	617-495-9400	495-9936
Fuller Craft Museum 455 Oak St *Web:* www.fullermuseum.org	Brockton	MA	02301	508-588-6000	587-6191
Gibson House Museum 137 Beacon St *Web:* www.thegibsonhouse.org	Boston	MA	02116	617-267-6338	267-6338
Harvard Museum of Natural History 26 Oxford St Harvard University *Web:* www.mcz.harvard.edu	Cambridge	MA	02138	617-495-3045	496-8308
Higgins Armory Museum 100 Barber Ave *Web:* www.higgins.org	Worcester	MA	01606	508-853-6015	852-7697
Hinchman House Natural Science Museum 7 Milk St *Web:* www.mmo.org	Nantucket	MA	02554	508-228-0898	228-1031
Historic Deerfield PO Box 321 *Web:* www.historic-deerfield.org	Deerfield	MA	01342	413-774-5581	775-7220
Isabella Stewart Gardner Museum 280 Fenway *Web:* www.gardnermuseum.org	Boston	MA	02115	617-566-1401	278-5175
John F Kennedy Hyannis Museum 397 Main St *Web:* jfkhyannismuseum.org	Hyannis	MA	02601	508-790-3077	790-1970
John F Kennedy Presidential Library & Museum Columbia Pt *TF:* 866-535-1960 ■ *Web:* www.jfklibrary.org	Boston	MA	02125	617-514-1600	514-1652
Martha's Vineyard Historical Society Museum Cook & School Sts PO Box 1310 *Web:* www.marthasvineyardhistory.org	Edgartown	MA	02539	508-627-4441	627-4436
MIT Museum 265 Massachusetts Ave *Web:* www.web.mit.edu	Cambridge	MA	02139	617-253-4444	253-8994
Museum of African American History 46 Joy St *Web:* www.afroammuseum.org	Boston	MA	02114	617-725-0022	720-5225
Museum of Fine Arts Boston 465 Huntington Ave *Web:* www.mfa.org	Boston	MA	02115	617-267-9300	267-0280
Museum of Science Science Pk *TF:* 866-770-4363 ■ *Web:* www.mos.org	Boston	MA	02114	617-589-0100	589-0454
Museum of the National Center of Afro-American Artists 300 Walnut Ave *Web:* www.ncaaa.org/museum.html	Boston	MA	02119	617-442-8614	445-5525
National Heritage Museum 33 Marrett Rd *Web:* www.monh.org	Lexington	MA	02421	781-861-6559	861-9846
New Bedford Whaling Museum 18 Johnny Cake Hill *Web:* www.whalingmuseum.org	New Bedford	MA	02740	508-997-0046	994-4350
Nichols House Museum 55 Mt Vernon St *Web:* www.nicholshousemuseum.org	Boston	MA	02108	617-227-6993	723-8026
Old Sturbridge Village 1 Old Sturbridge Village Rd *Web:* www.osv.org	Sturbridge	MA	01566	508-347-3362	347-0375
Peabody Essex Museum 161 Essex St *Web:* www.pem.org	Salem	MA	01970	978-745-1876	744-6776
Peabody Museum of Archaeology & Ethnology 11 Divinity Ave *Web:* www.peabody.harvard.edu	Cambridge	MA	02138	617-496-1027	495-7535
Pilgrim Hall Museum 75 Court St *Web:* www.pilgrimhall.org	Plymouth	MA	02360	508-746-1620	747-4228
Revere Paul House 19 N Sq *Web:* www.paulreverehouse.org	Boston	MA	02113	617-523-2338	523-1775
Salem Witch Museum 19 1/2 Washington Sq N *TF:* 800-544-1692 ■ *Web:* www.salemwitchmuseum.com	Salem	MA	01970	978-744-1692	745-4414
Sandwich Glass Museum 129 Main St PO box 103 *Web:* www.sandwichglassmuseum.org	Sandwich	MA	02563	508-888-0251	888-4941
Springfield Museums 21 Edwards St *TF:* 800-625-7738 ■ *Web:* www.springfieldmuseums.org	Springfield	MA	01103	413-263-6800	263-6807
Sterling & Francine Clark Art Institute 225 S St **Fax:* PR ■ *Web:* www.clarkart.edu	Williamstown	MA	01267	413-458-9545	458-5902*
Storrowton Village Museum 1305 Memorial Ave Eastern States Exposition *Web:* www.thebige.com	West Springfield	MA	01089	413-205-5051	205-5054
Titanic Museum 208 Main St *Web:* www.titanic1.org	Indian Orchard	MA	01151	413-543-4770	583-3633
USS Constitution Museum PO Box 291812 *Web:* www.ussconstitutionmuseum.org	Boston	MA	02129	617-426-1812	242-0496
Whaling Museum 13 Broad St	Nantucket	MA	02554	508-228-1894	228-5618
Willard House & Clock Museum 11 Willard St *Web:* www.willardhouse.org	North Grafton	MA	01536	508-839-3500	
Worcester Art Museum 55 Salisbury St *Web:* www.worcesterart.org	Worcester	MA	01609	508-799-4406	798-5646
Worcester Historical Museum 30 Elm St *Web:* www.worcesterhistory.org	Worcester	MA	01609	508-753-8278	753-9070

MICHIGAN

				Phone	Fax
Alfred P Sloan Museum 1221 E Kearsley St *Web:* www.sloanmuseum.com	Flint	MI	48503	810-237-3450	237-3451
All Around the African World Museum & Resource Ctr 1136 Shepard St	Lansing	MI	48912	517-484-7480	318-0908
Ann Arbor Hands-On Museum 220 E Ann St *Web:* www.aahom.org	Ann Arbor	MI	48104	734-995-5439	995-1188
Automotive Hall of Fame 21400 Oakwood Blvd *Web:* www.automotivehalloffame.org	Dearborn	MI	48124	313-240-4000	240-8641
Charles H Wright Museum of African American History 315 E Warren Ave *Web:* www.chwmuseum.org	Detroit	MI	48201	313-494-5800	494-5855
Cranbrook Art Museum 39221 Woodward Ave *Web:* www.cranbrookart.edu/museum	Bloomfield Hills	MI	48303	248-645-3323	645-3324
Cranbrook Institute of Science 39221 Woodward Ave PO Box 801 *Web:* www.cranbrook.edu	Bloomfield Hills	MI	48303	248-645-3260	645-3050
Detroit Historical Museum 5401 Woodward Ave *Web:* www.detroithistorical.org	Detroit	MI	48202	313-833-1805	833-5342
Detroit Institute of Arts 5200 Woodward Ave *Web:* www.dia.org	Detroit	MI	48202	313-833-7900	
Detroit Science Ctr 5020 John R St *Web:* www.detroitsciencecenter.org	Detroit	MI	48202	313-577-8400	832-1623
Dossin Great Lakes Museum 100 Strand Dr Belle Isle *Web:* www.detroithistorical.org	Detroit	MI	48207	313-833-5538	833-5342
Exhibit Museum of Natural History 1109 Geddes Ave University of Michigan *Web:* www.lsa.umich.edu/exhibitmuseum	Ann Arbor	MI	48109	734-764-0478	647-2767
Flint Institute of Arts 1120 E Kearsley St *Web:* www.flintarts.org	Flint	MI	48503	810-234-1695	234-1692
Ford Henry Estate-University of Michigan 4901 Evergreen Rd *Web:* www.umd.umich.edu/fairlane	Dearborn	MI	48128	313-593-5590	593-5243
Gallerie 454 15105 Kercheval Ave *Web:* www.gallerie454.com	Grosse Pointe Park	MI	48230	313-822-4454	822-3768
Gerald R Ford Museum 303 Pearl St NW *Web:* www.ford.utexas.edu	Grand Rapids	MI	49504	616-254-0400	254-0386
Grand Rapids Art Museum 101 Monroe Ctr *Web:* www.gramonline.org	Grand Rapids	MI	49503	616-831-1000	831-1001
Greenfield Village 20900 Oakwood Blvd **Fax:* Cust Svc ■ *TF:* 800-835-5237 ■ *Web:* www.hfmgv.org/village	Dearborn	MI	48124	313-271-1620	982-6225*
Henry Ford Museum 20900 Oakwood Blvd *TF:* 800-835-5237 ■ *Web:* www.hfmgv.org	Dearborn	MI	48124	313-271-1620	982-6225
Historic Hack House Museum 775 County St	Milan	MI	48160	734-439-1664	
Holocaust Memorial Ctr 28123 Orchard Lake Rd *Web:* www.holocaustcenter.org	Farmington Hills	MI	48334	248-553-2400	553-2433
Impression 5 Science Ctr 200 Museum Dr *Web:* www.impression5.org	Lansing	MI	48933	517-485-8116	485-8125
International Gospel Music Hall of Fame & Museum 18031 W Mcnichols Rd **Fax Area Code:* 248 ■ *Web:* www.igmhf.org	Detroit	MI	48219	313-592-0017	552-0154*
International Institute of Metropolitan Detroit 111 E Kirby St *Web:* www.iimd.org	Detroit	MI	48202	313-871-8600	871-1651
Kelsey Museum of Archaeology 434 S State St University of Michigan *Web:* www.lsa.umich.edu/kelsey	Ann Arbor	MI	48109	734-763-3559	763-8976
Kempf House Museum 312 S Division St *Web:* www.kempfhousemuseum.org	Ann Arbor	MI	48104	734-994-4898	
Kingman Museum 175 Limit St *Web:* www.kingmanmuseum.org	Battle Creek	MI	49017	269-965-5117	965-3330
Kresge Art Museum Michigan State University *Web:* www.msu.edu/unit/kamuseum	East Lansing	MI	48824	517-353-9834	355-6577
Leslie Science & Nature Ctr 1831 Traver Rd	Ann Arbor	MI	48105	734-997-1553	997-1072
Manistee County Historical Museum 425 River St *Web:* www.manisteemuseum.org	Manistee	MI	49660	231-723-5531	
Michigan Historical Museum 702 W Kalamazoo St	Lansing	MI	48915	517-373-3559	241-3647
Michigan State University Museum W Cir Dr *Web:* www.museum.cl.msu.edu	East Lansing	MI	48824	517-355-2370	432-2846
Michigan Women's Historical Center & Hall of Fame 213 W Main St *Web:* www.michiganwomenshalloffame.org	Lansing	MI	48933	517-484-1880	372-0170
Midland Center for the Arts Inc 1801 W St Andrews Rd *Web:* www.mcfta.org	Midland	MI	48640	989-631-5930	631-7890

Museum / Address	City	State	Zip	Phone	Fax
Minibeast Zooseum & Education Ctr 6907 W Grand River Ave	Lansing	MI	48906	517-886-0630	886-0630
Monroe County Historical Museum 126 S Monroe St	Monroe	MI	48161	734-240-7780	240-7788
Montrose Historical & Telephone Pioneer Museum 144 E Hickory St	Montrose	MI	48457	810-639-6644	
Motown Museum 2648 W Grand Blvd *Web:* www.motownmuseum.com	Detroit	MI	48208	313-875-2264	875-2267
National Museum of the Tuskegee Airmen 6325 W Jefferson **Fax Area Code:* 800	Detroit	MI	48209	313-843-8849	595-6576*
Public Museum of Grand Rapids 272 Pearl St NW Van Andel Museum Ctr *Web:* www.grmuseum.org	Grand Rapids	MI	49504	616-456-3977	456-3873
RE Olds Transportation Museum 240 Museum Dr *Web:* www.reoldsmuseum.org	Lansing	MI	48933	517-372-0422	372-2901
University of Michigan Museum of Art 525 S State St *Web:* www.umma.umich.edu	Ann Arbor	MI	48109	734-764-0395	764-3731
Voigt House Victorian Museum 115 College Ave SE *Web:* www.grmuseum.org	Grand Rapids	MI	49503	616-456-4600	456-4603
Walter P Chrysler Museum 1 Chrysler Dr *TF:* 888-456-1924 ■ *Web:* www.chryslerheritage.com	Auburn Hills	MI	48326	248-944-0001	944-0460
Yankee Air Force Inc 47884 D St *Web:* www.yankeeairmuseum.org	Belleville	MI	48111	734-483-4030	483-5076
Ypsilanti Historical Museum 220 N Huron St *Web:* www.ypsilantihistoricalsociety.org	Ypsilanti	MI	48197	734-482-4990	483-7481

MINNESOTA

Museum / Address	City	State	Zip	Phone	Fax
American Swedish Institute The (ASI) 2600 Pk Ave *Web:* www.americanswedishinst.org	Minneapolis	MN	55407	612-871-4907	871-8682
Bakken The 3537 Zenith Ave S *Web:* www.thebakken.org	Minneapolis	MN	55416	612-927-6508	927-7265
Bell Museum of Natural History 10 Church St SE *Web:* www.bellmuseum.org	Minneapolis	MN	55455	612-624-7083	626-7704
Dakota County Historical Museum 130 3rd Ave N *Web:* www.dakotahistory.org	South Saint Paul	MN	55075	651-552-7548	552-7265
Depot The *Saint Louis County Heritage & Arts Ctr* 506 W Michigan St *Web:* www.duluthdepot.org	Duluth	MN	55802	218-727-8025	733-7506
Fitger's Brewery Museum 600 E Superior St *TF:* 888-348-4377 ■ *Web:* www.fitgers.com	Duluth	MN	55802	218-722-8826	722-8826
Gibbs Museum of Pioneer & Dakotah Life 2097 W Larpenteur Ave *Web:* www.rchs.com	Saint Paul	MN	55113	651-646-8629	659-0345
Hennepin History Museum 2303 3rd Ave S *Web:* www.hhmuseum.org	Minneapolis	MN	55404	612-870-1329	870-1320
Ironworld Discovery Ctr 801 SW Hwy 169 Suite 1 *TF:* 800-372-6437 ■ *Web:* www.ironworld.com	Chisholm	MN	55719	218-254-7959	254-7971
Karpeles Manuscript Library Museum 902 E 1st St *Web:* www.rain.org	Duluth	MN	55805	218-728-0630	
Lake Superior Maritime Visitors Ctr 600 Lake Ave S *Web:* www.lsmma.com	Duluth	MN	55802	218-727-2497	720-5270
Lake Superior Railroad Museum 506 W Michigan St *Web:* www.lsrm.org	Duluth	MN	55802	218-727-8025	733-7596
Mill City Museum 704 S 2nd St *Web:* www.millcitymuseum.org	Minneapolis	MN	55401	612-341-7555	341-7506
Minneapolis Institute of Arts 2400 3rd Ave S *TF:* 888-642-2787 ■ *Web:* www.artsmia.org	Minneapolis	MN	55404	612-870-3000	870-3004
Minnesota Historical Society History Center Museum 345 Kellogg Blvd W *TF:* 800-657-3773 ■ *Web:* www.mnhs.org	Saint Paul	MN	55102	651-259-3001	296-1004
Minnesota Museum of American Art Kellogg Blvd & Market St *Web:* www.mmaa.org	Saint Paul	MN	55102	651-266-1030	291-2947
Minnesota State University Moorhead Regional Science Ctr 1104 7th Ave S *TF:* 800-593-7246 ■ *Web:* www.mnstate.edu/regsci	Moorhead	MN	56563	218-477-2920	477-4372
Minnesota Transportation Museum 193 E Pennsylvania Ave *Web:* www.mtmuseum.org	Saint Paul	MN	55130	651-228-0263	293-0857
Minnesota Wing Commemorative Air Force Museum 310 Airport Rd Hanger 3 Fleming Field *Web:* www.cafmn.org	South Saint Paul	MN	55075	651-455-6942	455-2160
Museum of Russian Art 5500 Stevens Ave S *Web:* www.tmora.org	Minneapolis	MN	55419	612-821-9045	821-4392
Pavek Museum of Broadcasting 3517 Raleigh Ave *Web:* www.pavekmuseum.org	Saint Louis Park	MN	55416	952-926-8198	929-6105
Schubert Club Museum The 75 W 5th St 302 Landmark Ctr *Web:* www.schubert.org	Saint Paul	MN	55102	651-292-3267	292-4317
Science Museum of Minnesota 120 W Kellogg Blvd *Web:* www.smm.org	Saint Paul	MN	55102	651-221-9444	221-4777
Tweed Museum of Art 1201 Ordean Ct *Web:* www.d.umn.edu/tma	Duluth	MN	55812	218-726-8222	726-8503
Twin Cities Model Railroad Museum 1021 Bandana Blvd E Suite 222 *Web:* www.tcmrm.org	Saint Paul	MN	55108	651-647-9628	636-4140
Walker Art Ctr 1750 Hennepin Ave *Web:* www.walkerart.org	Minneapolis	MN	55403	612-375-7600	375-7618
Weisman Art Museum 333 E River Rd *Web:* www.weisman.umn.edu	Minneapolis	MN	55455	612-625-9494	625-9630

MISSISSIPPI

Museum / Address	City	State	Zip	Phone	Fax
African American Military History Museum 305 E 6th St *Web:* www.hattiesburg.org	Hattiesburg	MS	39401	601-268-3220	
Amory Regional Museum 801 3rd St S *Web:* www.amoryms.us	Amory	MS	38821	662-256-2761	
Armed Forces Museum Bldg 850 *Web:* www.armedforcesmuseum.us	Camp Shelby	MS	39407	601-558-2757	558-2377
Elvis Presley Birthplace & Museum 306 Elvis Presley Dr *Web:* www.elvispresleybirthplace.com	Tupelo	MS	38802	662-841-1245	690-6623
International Checker Hall of Fame 220 Lynn Ray Rd	Petal	MS	39465	601-582-7090	582-7090
International Museum of Muslim Cultures 201 E Pascagoula St Mississippi Arts Ctr *Web:* www.muslimmuseum.org	Jackson	MS	39209	601-960-0440	960-0316
Landrum's Homestead & Village 1356 Hwy 15 S *Web:* www.landrums.com	Laurel	MS	39443	601-649-2546	428-1663
Lauren Rogers Museum of Art 565 N 5th Ave *Web:* www.lrma.org	Laurel	MS	39440	601-649-6374	649-6379
Manship House Museum 420 E Fortification St PO Box 571 *Web:* www.mdah.state.ms.us/museum/manship.html	Jackson	MS	39202	601-961-4724	354-6043
Mississippi Agriculture & Forestry Museum/National Agricultural Aviation Museum 1150 Lakeland Dr *TF:* 800-844-8687 ■ *Web:* www.mdac.state.ms.us	Jackson	MS	39216	601-713-3365	982-4292
Mississippi Dept of Archives & History (MDAH) 200 N St *Web:* mdah.state.ms.us	Jackson	MS	39201	601-576-6876	576-6964
Mississippi Museum of Art 380 S Lamar St *Web:* www.msmuseumart.org	Jackson	MS	39201	601-960-1515	960-1505
Mississippi Museum of Natural Science 2148 Riverside Dr *Web:* www.mdwfp.state.ms.us	Jackson	MS	39202	601-354-7303	354-7227
Museum of the Southern Jewish Experience PO Box 16528 *Web:* www.msje.org	Jackson	MS	39236	601-362-6357	366-6293
Ohr-O'Keefe Museum of Art 1596 Glenn Swetman St *Web:* www.georgeohr.org	Biloxi	MS	39530	228-374-5547	436-3641
Old Capitol Museum 100 S State St *Web:* www.mdah.state.ms.us	Jackson	MS	39201	601-576-6920	576-6981
Oren Dunn City Museum 689 Rutherford Rd PO Box 2674 *Web:* www.orendunnmuseum.org	Tupelo	MS	38803	662-841-6438	841-6458
Smith Robertson Museum & Cultural Ctr 528 Bloom St	Jackson	MS	39202	601-960-1457	960-2070

MISSOURI

Museum / Address	City	State	Zip	Phone	Fax
Air & Military Museum 2305 E Kearney St *Web:* www.ammomuseum.org	Springfield	MO	65803	417-864-7997	866-2448
Airline History Museum 201 Lou Holland Dr Hangar 9 *TF:* 800-513-9484 ■ *Web:* www.airlinehistorymuseum.com	Kansas City	MO	64116	816-421-3401	421-3421
Alexander Majors Historic House & Museum 8201 State Line Rd	Kansas City	MO	64114	816-333-5556	
American Jazz Museum 1616 E 18th St *Web:* www.americanjazzmuseum.com	Kansas City	MO	64108	816-474-8463	474-0074
American Kennel Club Museum of the Dog 1721 S Mason Rd *Web:* www.akc.org	Saint Louis	MO	63131	314-821-3647	821-7381
American Presidential Museum 2849 Gretner Rd *TF:* 866-334-8683 ■ *Web:* www.americanpresidentialmuseum.com	Branson	MO	65616	417-334-8683	334-4927
American Royal Museum & Visitors Ctr 1701 American Royal Ct *TF:* 800-821-5857 ■ *Web:* www.americanroyal.com	Kansas City	MO	64102	816-221-9800	221-8189
Arabia Steamboat Museum 400 Grand Blvd *TF:* 800-471-1856 ■ *Web:* www.1856.com	Kansas City	MO	64106	816-471-1856	471-1616
Boone County Historical Society Museum 3801 Ponderosa St *Web:* boonehistory.org	Columbia	MO	65201	573-443-8936	875-5268
Chatillon-DeMenil Mansion & Museum 3352 DeMenil Pl *Web:* www.demenil.org	Saint Louis	MO	63118	314-771-5828	771-3475
City Museum 701 N 15th St PO Box 29 *Web:* www.citymuseum.org	Saint Louis	MO	63103	314-231-2489	231-1009
Cole County Historical Museum 109 Madison St *Web:* www.colecohistsoc.org	Jefferson City	MO	65101	573-635-1850	
Concordia Historical Institute 804 Seminary Pl *Web:* www.chi.lcms.org	Saint Louis	MO	63105	314-505-7900	505-7901
Contemporary Art Museum Saint Louis 3750 Washington Blvd *Web:* www.contemporarystl.org	Saint Louis	MO	63108	314-535-4660	535-1226
Dutton Family Theatre 3454 W 76 Country Blvd *TF:* 800-942-4626 ■ *Web:* www.theduttons.com	Branson	MO	65616	417-332-2772	334-2314
Eugene Field House & Saint Louis Toy Museum 634 S Broadway *Web:* www.eugenefieldhouse.org	Saint Louis	MO	63102	314-421-4689	588-9328

Museum	City	State	ZIP	Phone	Fax
Excelsior Springs Museum & Archives 101 E Broadway	Excelsior Springs	MO	64024	816-630-0101	
General Sweeny's Museum of Civil War History 5228 S State Hwy ZZ *Web:* www.civilwarmuseum.com	Republic	MO	65738	417-732-1224	
Harry S Truman Presidential Library & Museum 500 W Hwy 24 *TF:* 800-833-1225 ■ *Web:* www.trumanlibrary.org	Independence	MO	64050	816-268-8200	268-8295
Historic Aircraft Restoration Museum 3127 Creve Coeur Mill Rd *Web:* www.historicaircraftrestorationmuseum.org	Saint Louis	MO	63146	314-434-3368	878-6453
Historic Sappington House Museum 1015 S Sappington Rd	Crestwood	MO	63126	314-822-8171	
History Museum for Springfield/Greene County 830 Boonville Ave Historic City Hall 3rd Fl *Web:* www.springfieldhistorymuseum.org	Springfield	MO	65802	417-864-1976	864-2019
Hollywood Wax Museum 3030 W Hwy 76 *Web:* www.hollywoodwax.com	Branson	MO	65616	417-337-8277	334-8202
Holocaust Museum & Learning Ctr 12 Millstone Campus Dr *Web:* www.hmlc.org	Saint Louis	MO	63146	314-432-0020	432-1277
John Wornall House Museum 6115 Wornall Rd	Kansas City	MO	64113	816-444-1858	361-8165
Kansas City Museum 3218 Gladstone Blvd *Web:* www.unionstation.org	Kansas City	MO	64123	816-483-8300	483-6050
Kemper Museum of Contemporary Art 4420 Warwick Blvd *Web:* www.kemperart.org	Kansas City	MO	64111	816-753-5784	753-5806
Laumeier Sculpture Park & Museum 12580 Rott Rd *Web:* www.laumeier.com	Saint Louis	MO	63127	314-615-5278	615-5283
Laura Ingalls Wilder Museum & Home 3068 Hwy A *TF:* 877-924-7126 ■ *Web:* www.lauraingallswilderhome.com	Mansfield	MO	65704	417-924-3626	924-8580
Liberty Memorial Museum 100 W 26th St *Web:* www.theworldwar.org	Kansas City	MO	64108	816-784-1918	784-1929
Miniature Museum of Greater Saint Louis 4746 Gravois *Web:* www.miniaturemuseum.org	Saint Louis	MO	63116	314-832-7790	
Missouri History Museum 5700 Lindell Blvd PO Box 11940 *Web:* www.mohistory.org	Saint Louis	MO	63112	314-746-4599	454-3162
Missouri State Museum 201 W Capitol *Web:* mostateparks.com/park/missouri-state-museum	Jefferson City	MO	65101	573-751-2854	526-2927
Missouri Veterinary Medical Foundation Museum 2500 Country Club Dr *Web:* www.mvma.us	Jefferson City	MO	65109	573-636-8612	659-7175
Museum of Anthropology 104 Swallow Hall University of Missouri *Web:* www.coas.missouri.edu	Columbia	MO	65211	573-882-3573	884-3627
Museum of Art & Archaeology Pickard Hall University of Missouri *Web:* www.museum.research.missouri.edu	Columbia	MO	65211	573-882-3591	884-4039
Museum of Contemporary Religious Art 221 N Grand Blvd St Louis University Campus *Web:* mocra.slu.edu	Saint Louis	MO	63103	314-977-7170	977-2999
Museum of Missouri Military History 2007 Retention Dr *Web:* www.moguard.com	Jefferson City	MO	65101	573-638-9603	638-9848
Museums at 18th & Vine 1616 E 18th St *Web:* www.americanjazzmuseum.com	Kansas City	MO	64108	816-474-8463	474-0074
National World War I Museum 100 W 26th St *Web:* www.libertymemorialmuseum.org	Kansas City	MO	64108	816-784-1918	784-1929
Nelson-Atkins Museum of Art 4525 Oak St *Web:* www.nelson-atkins.org	Kansas City	MO	64111	816-561-4000	561-4011
Pony Express National Museum 914 Penn St *TF:* 800-530-5930 ■ *Web:* www.ponyexpress.org	Saint Joseph	MO	64503	816-279-5059	233-9370
Ralph Foster Museum College of the Ozarks PO Box 17 *Web:* www.rfostermuseum.com	Point Lookout	MO	65726	417-334-6411	335-2618
Ripley's Believe It or Not! Museum 3326 W Hwy 76 *TF:* 800-998-4418 ■ *Web:* www.ripleys.com	Branson	MO	65616	417-337-5300	337-5229
Roy Rogers-Dale Evans Museum 3950 Green Mountain Dr *Web:* www.royrogers.com	Branson	MO	65616	417-339-1900	
Saint Louis Art Museum 1 Fine Arts Dr *Web:* www.slam.org	Saint Louis	MO	63110	314-721-0072	721-6172
Saint Louis Science Ctr 5050 Oakland Ave *TF:* 800-456-7572 ■ *Web:* www.slsc.org	Saint Louis	MO	63110	314-289-4400	289-4420
Saint Louis University Museum of Art 3663 Lindell Blvd O"Donnell Hall *Web:* sluma.slu.edu	Saint Louis	MO	63103	314-977-3399	977-3581
Shoal Creek Living History Museum 7000 NE Barry Rd Hodge Pk *Web:* www.kcmo.org	Kansas City	MO	64156	816-792-2655	
Soldiers Memorial Military Museum 1315 Chestnut St	Saint Louis	MO	63103	314-622-4550	622-4237
Springfield Art Museum 1111 E Brookside Dr *Web:* www.springfieldmo.gov/art	Springfield	MO	65807	417-837-5700	837-5704
St Louis Museum of Transportation The 2967 Barrett Stn Rd *Web:* www.transportmuseumassociation.org	Saint Louis	MO	63122	314-965-6885	965-0242
State Historical Society of Missouri The 1020 Lowry St *TF:* 800-747-6366 ■ *Web:* shs.umsystem.edu/index.shtml	Columbia	MO	65201	573-882-7083	884-4950
Toy & Miniature Museum 5235 Oak St *Web:* www.umkc.edu/tmm	Kansas City	MO	64112	816-333-2055	333-2055

MONTANA

Museum	City	State	ZIP	Phone	Fax
Children's Museum of Montana 22 Railroad Sq *Web:* www.childrensmuseumofmt.org	Great Falls	MT	59401	406-452-6661	452-4462
CM Russell Museum 400 13th St N *Web:* www.cmrussell.org	Great Falls	MT	59401	406-727-8787	727-2402
Holter Museum of Art 12 E Lawrence St *Web:* www.holtermuseum.org	Helena	MT	59601	406-442-6400	442-2404
Malmstrom Air Force Base Museum & Air Park 21 77th St N Rm 144 *Web:* www.greatfallscvb.visitmt.com	Great Falls	MT	59402	406-731-2705	731-2769
Montana Historical Society Museum 225 N Roberts St *TF:* 800-243-9900 ■ *Web:* www.montanahistoricalsociety.org	Helena	MT	59620	406-444-2694	444-2696
Museum of the Plains Indians PO Box 410 *Web:* www.browningmontana.com	Browning	MT	59417	406-338-2230	338-7404
Museum of the Rockies 600 W Kagy Blvd Montana State University *Web:* www.museumoftherockies.org	Bozeman	MT	59717	406-994-3466	994-2682
Paris Gibson Square Museum of Art 1400 1st Ave N *Web:* www.the-square.org	Great Falls	MT	59401	406-727-8255	727-8256
Peter Yegen Jr Yellowstone County Museum 1950 Terminal Cir *Web:* www.pyjrycm.org	Billings	MT	59105	406-256-6811	254-6031
World Museum of Mining 155 Museum Way PO Box 33 *Web:* www.miningmuseum.org	Butte	MT	59703	406-723-7211	723-7211
Yellowstone Art Museum 401 N 27th St *Web:* www.yellowstone.artmuseum.org	Billings	MT	59101	406-256-6804	256-6817
Yellowstone Western Heritage Ctr 2822 Montana Ave *Web:* www.ywhc.org	Billings	MT	59101	406-256-6809	256-6850

NEBRASKA

Museum	City	State	ZIP	Phone	Fax
Bank of Florence Museum 8502 N 30th St	Omaha	NE	68112	402-496-9923	455-1424
Durham Museum 801 S 10th St *Web:* www.durhammuseum.org	Omaha	NE	68108	402-444-5071	444-5397
El Museo Latino 4701 S 25th St *Web:* www.elmuseolatino.org	Omaha	NE	68107	402-731-1137	733-7012
Great Plains Art Museum 1155 Q St	Lincoln	NE	68588	402-472-6220	472-0463
Hastings Museum 1330 N Burlington Ave *Web:* www.hastingsmuseum.org	Hastings	NE	68901	402-461-2399	461-2379
Joslyn Art Museum 2200 Dodge St *Web:* www.joslyn.org	Omaha	NE	68102	402-342-3300	342-2376
Lentz Center for Asian Culture 1155 Q St Hewit Pl *Web:* www.unl.edu	Lincoln	NE	68588	402-472-5841	472-0463
Museum of Nebraska History 131 Centennial Mall N *TF:* 800-833-6747 ■ *Web:* www.nebraskahistory.org/sites/mnh	Lincoln	NE	68508	402-471-4754	471-3314
National Museum of Roller Skating 4730 S St *Web:* www.rollerskatingmuseum.com	Lincoln	NE	68506	402-483-7551	483-1465
Nebraska Jewish Historical Museum 333 S 132nd St	Omaha	NE	68154	402-334-6441	334-6507
Sheldon Museum of Art PO Box 880300 *Web:* www.sheldonartmuseum.org	Lincoln	NE	68588	402-472-2461	472-4258
Strategic Air & Space Museum 28210 W Pk Hwy *TF:* 800-358-5029 ■ *Web:* www.strategicairandspace.com	Ashland	NE	68003	402-944-3100	944-3160
Stuhr Museum of the Prairie Pioneer 3133 W Hwy 34 *Web:* www.stuhrmuseum.org	Grand Island	NE	68801	308-385-5316	385-5028
University of Nebraska State Museum 14Th & U *Web:* www-museum.unl.edu	Lincoln	NE	68588	402-472-2642	472-8899

NEVADA

Museum	City	State	ZIP	Phone	Fax
Atomic Testing Museum 755 E Flamingo Rd *Web:* www.atomictestingmuseum.org	Las Vegas	NV	89119	702-794-5151	794-5155
Boulder City/Hoover Dam Museum 1305 Arizona St *Web:* www.bcmha.org	Boulder City	NV	89005	702-294-1988	294-4380
Carson Valley Museum & Cultural Ctr 1477 Hwy 395 N	Gardnerville	NV	89410	775-782-2555	783-8802
Churchill County Museum & Archives 1050 S Maine St *Web:* www.ccmuseum.org	Fallon	NV	89406	775-423-3677	423-3662
Clark County Museum 1830 S Boulder Hwy	Henderson	NV	89002	702-455-7955	455-7948
Guggenheim Hermitage Museum 3355 Las Vegas Blvd S Venetian Resort Hotel & Casino *Web:* www.guggenheimlasvegas.org	Las Vegas	NV	89109	702-414-2440	414-2442
Las Vegas Art Museum 3065 S Jones Blvd # 100 *Web:* www.lasvegasartmuseum.org	Las Vegas	NV	89146	702-360-8000	360-8080
Las Vegas Natural History Museum 900 Las Vegas Blvd N *Web:* www.lvnhm.org	Las Vegas	NV	89101	702-384-3466	
Liberace Museum 1775 E Tropicana Ave *Web:* www.flatwaremedia.com	Las Vegas	NV	89119	702-798-5595	798-7386
Lost City Museum of Archeology 721 S Moapa Valley Blvd *Web:* www.comnett.net	Overton	NV	89040	702-397-2193	397-8987
National Automobile Museum 10 S Lake St *Web:* www.automuseum.org	Reno	NV	89501	775-333-9300	333-9309

	City	State	Zip	Phone	Fax
Nevada Gambling Museum 50 S 'C' St	Virginia City	NV	89440	775-847-9022	847-9613
Nevada Museum of Art 160 W Liberty St *Web:* www.nevadaart.org	Reno	NV	89501	775-329-3333	329-1541
Nevada State Museum 600 N Carson St *Web:* www.museums.nevadaculture.org	Carson City	NV	89701	775-687-4810	687-4168
Nevada State Railroad Museum 2180 S Carson St *Web:* www.nsrm-friends.org	Carson City	NV	89701	775-687-6953	687-8294
Northeastern Nevada Museum 1515 Idaho St *Web:* www.museumelko.org	Elko	NV	89801	775-738-3418	778-9318
Roberts House Museum 1207 N Carson St	Carson City	NV	89701	775-887-2174	882-3559
Sparks Heritage Museum 820 Victorian Ave *Web:* www.sparksheritagemuseum.org	Sparks	NV	89431	775-355-1144	355-6788
University of Nevada Las Vegas Marjorie Barrick Museum of Natural History 4505 S Maryland Pkwy *Web:* www.hrcweb.lv-hrc.nevada.edu	Las Vegas	NV	89154	702-895-3381	895-5737
Warren Engine Co No 1 Fire Museum 777 S Stewart St	Carson City	NV	89701	775-887-2210	887-2209
Way It Was Museum 113 C St	Virginia City	NV	89440	775-847-0766	
Wilbur D May Museum 1595 N Sierra St *Web:* www.washoecounty.us	Reno	NV	89503	775-785-5961	785-4707

NEW BRUNSWICK

	City	Prov	Postal Code	Phone	Fax
Kings Landing Historical Settlement 5804 Rt 102 *TF:* 888-666-5547 ■ *Web:* www.kingslanding.nb.ca	Prince William	NB	E6K0A5	506-363-4999	363-4989
Musee Acadien 18 Ave Antonine-Maillet *Web:* www.umoncton.ca	Moncton	NB	E1A3E9	506-858-4088	858-4043
New Brunswick Museum 1 Market Sq *TF:* 888-268-9595 ■ *Web:* www.nbm-mnb.ca/index.php?option=com_content&view=article&id=121&Itemid=316	Saint John	NB	E2L4Z6	506-643-2300	643-6081

NEW HAMPSHIRE

	City	State	Zip	Phone	Fax
Canterbury Shaker Village 288 Shaker Rd *TF:* 866-783-9511 ■ *Web:* www.shakers.org	Canterbury	NH	03224	603-783-9511	783-9152
Currier Museum of Art 150 Ash St *Web:* www.currier.org	Manchester	NH	03104	603-669-6144	669-7194
Hood Museum of Art Dartmouth College *Web:* hoodmuseum.dartmouth.edu	Hanover	NH	03755	603-646-2808	646-1400
Lawrence L Lee Scouting Museum 40 Blondin Rd *Web:* www.scoutingmuseum.org	Manchester	NH	03105	603-669-8919	627-1492
Mount Kearsarge Indian Museum 18 Highlawn Rd *Web:* www.indianmuseum.com	Warner	NH	03278	603-456-2600	456-3092
Museum of New Hampshire History 6 Eagle Sq *Web:* www.nhhistory.org	Concord	NH	03301	603-226-3189	228-6308
New Hampshire Historical Society Museum 30 Pk St *Web:* www.nhhistory.org	Concord	NH	03301	603-225-3381	224-0463
New Hampshire Institute of Art 148 Concord St *TF:* 866-241-4918 ■ *Web:* www.nhia.edu	Manchester	NH	03104	603-623-0313	647-0658
SEE Science Ctr 200 Bedford St *Web:* www.see-sciencecenter.org	Manchester	NH	03101	603-669-0400	669-0400
Strawbery Banke Museum 14 Hancock St *Web:* www.strawberybanke.org	Portsmouth	NH	03801	603-433-1100	433-1129

NEW JERSEY

	City	State	Zip	Phone	Fax
Afro-American Historical Society Museum 1841 John F Kennedy Blvd	Jersey City	NJ	07305	201-547-5262	547-5392
Aljira Center for Contemporary Arts 591 Broad St *Web:* www.aljira.org	Newark	NJ	07102	973-622-1600	622-6526
American Labor Museum/Botto House National Landmark 83 Norwood St *Web:* www.geocities.com	Haledon	NJ	07508	973-595-7953	595-7291
Atlantic City Historical Museum PO Box 7273 *Web:* www.acmuseum.org	Atlantic City	NJ	08401	609-347-5839	
Atlantic County Historical Society Museum 907 Shore Rd *Web:* www.aclink.org	Somers Point	NJ	08244	609-927-5218	927-5218
Jersey City Museum 350 Montgomery St *Web:* www.jerseycitymuseum.org	Jersey City	NJ	07302	201-413-0303	413-9922
Liberty Science Ctr Liberty State Pk 222 Jersey City Blvd *Web:* www.lsc.org	Jersey City	NJ	07305	201-200-1000	
Marine Mammal Stranding Ctr 3625 Brigantine Blvd *Web:* www.mmsc.org	Brigantine	NJ	08203	609-266-0538	266-6300
Meredith Havens Fire Museum 244 Perry St	Trenton	NJ	08618	609-989-4038	989-4280
Montclair Art Museum 3 S Mountain Ave *Web:* www.montclair-art.com	Montclair	NJ	07042	973-746-5555	746-0536
Morris Museum 6 Normandy Heights Rd *Web:* www.morrismuseum.org	Morristown	NJ	07960	973-971-3700	538-0154
New Jersey Historical Society Museum 52 Pk Pl *Web:* www.jerseyhistory.org	Newark	NJ	07102	973-596-8500	596-6957
New Jersey State Museum 205 W State St *Web:* www.state.nj.us/state/museum	Trenton	NJ	08625	609-292-6300	292-7636
Newark Museum 49 Washington St *Web:* www.newarkmuseum.org	Newark	NJ	07102	973-596-6550	642-0459
Noyes Museum of Art 733 Lily Lake Rd *Web:* www.noyesmuseum.org	Oceanville	NJ	08231	609-652-8848	652-6166
Old Barracks Museum 101 Barrack St *TF:* 888-777-4042 ■ *Web:* www.barracks.org	Trenton	NJ	08608	609-396-1776	777-4000
Paterson Museum 2 Market St Thomas Rogers Bldg *Web:* www.thepatersonmuseum.com	Paterson	NJ	07501	973-321-1260	881-3435
Ripley's Believe It or Not! Museum 1441 Boardwalk *Web:* www.ripleys.com/bion/atlantic.html	Atlantic City	NJ	08401	609-347-2001	347-2009
Trenton City Museum at Ellarslie Mansion Cadawalader Pk *Web:* www.ellarslie.org	Trenton	NJ	08608	609-989-3632	989-3624

NEW MEXICO

	City	State	Zip	Phone	Fax
Albuquerque Museum 2000 Mountain Rd NW *Web:* www.cabq.gov	Albuquerque	NM	87104	505-243-7255	764-6546
American International Rattlesnake Museum 202 San Felipe NW Suite A *Web:* www.rattlesnakes.com	Albuquerque	NM	87104	505-242-6569	242-6569
Archaeology & Material Culture Museum 22 Calvary Rd *Web:* www.museumarch.org	Cedar Crest	NM	87008	505-281-2005	
Bataan Memorial Museum 1050 Old Pecos Trail	Santa Fe	NM	87505	505-474-1670	474-1670
Bradbury Science Museum 1350 Central PO Box 1663 *Web:* www.lanl.gov	Los Alamos	NM	87545	505-667-4444	665-6932
El Rancho de las Golondrinas Museum 334 Los Pinos Rd *Web:* www.golondrinas.org	Santa Fe	NM	87507	505-471-2261	471-5623
Explora 1701 Mountain Rd NW *Web:* www.explora.mus.nm.us	Albuquerque	NM	87104	505-224-8300	224-8325
Georgia O'Keeffe Museum 217 Johnson St *Web:* www.okeeffemuseum.org	Santa Fe	NM	87501	505-946-1000	
Historical Lawmen Museum 845 Motel Blvd *TF:* 800-332-2121	Las Cruces	NM	88007	575-525-1911	647-7800
Hubbard Museum of the American West 841 Hwy 70 W PO Box 40	Ruidoso Downs	NM	88346	575-378-4142	378-4166
Indian Pueblo Cultural Ctr 2401 12th St NW *TF:* 800-766-4405 ■ *Web:* www.indianpueblo.org	Albuquerque	NM	87104	505-843-7270	842-6959
Institute of American Indian Arts Museum 108 Cathedral Pl *TF:* 800-804-6423 ■ *Web:* www.iaia.edu	Santa Fe	NM	87501	505-983-8900	983-1222
Las Cruces Museum of Art 490 N Water St *Web:* www.las-cruces.org/public-services/museums/mfa.shtm	Las Cruces	NM	88001	575-541-2137	541-2173
Las Cruces Museum of Natural History 700 Telshor Blvd	Las Cruces	NM	88001	575-532-3372	532-3370
Log Cabin Museum 671 N Main St PO Box 20000 *Web:* www.newmexico.org/western/learn/log_cabin_museum.php	Las Cruces	NM	88001	575-541-2155	525-3645
Los Alamos Historical Museum 1921 Juniper St PO Box 43 *Web:* www.losalamos.com	Los Alamos	NM	87544	505-662-6272	662-6312
Maxwell Museum of Anthropology University of New Mexico *Web:* www.unm.edu	Albuquerque	NM	87131	505-277-4405	277-1547
Museum of Archaeology & Biblical History 10110 Constitution NE *Web:* www.mabh.org	Albuquerque	NM	87112	505-217-1330	217-1333
Museum of Indian Arts & Culture 710 Camino Lejo PO Box 2087 *Web:* www.miaclab.org	Santa Fe	NM	87501	505-476-1250	476-1330
Museum of International Folk Art 706 Camino Lejo *Web:* www.internationalfolkart.org	Santa Fe	NM	87505	505-476-1200	476-1300
Museum of Spanish Colonial Arts 750 Camino Lejo *Web:* www.spanishcolonial.org	Santa Fe	NM	87505	505-982-2226	982-4585
New Mexico Farm & Ranch Heritage Museum 4100 Dripping Springs Rd *Web:* www.nmfarmandranchmuseum.org	Las Cruces	NM	88011	575-522-4100	522-3085
New Mexico Holocaust & Intolerance Museum & Study Ctr 616 Central Ave SW *Web:* www.nmholocaustmuseum.org	Albuquerque	NM	87102	505-247-0606	323-3946
New Mexico Museum of Art 107 W Palace Ave *Web:* www.nmartmuseum.org	Santa Fe	NM	87501	505-476-5072	476-5076
New Mexico Museum of Natural History & Science 1801 Mountain Rd NW *Web:* www.nmnaturalhistory.org	Albuquerque	NM	87104	505-841-2800	841-2866
New Mexico Museum of Space History PO Box 5430 *TF:* 877-333-6589 ■ *Web:* www.spacefame.org	Alamogordo	NM	88311	505-437-2840	434-2245
New Mexico State University Museum University Ave & Solano Dr Kent Hall PO Box 30001 MSC 3564 *Web:* www.nmsu.edu/museum	Las Cruces	NM	88003	575-646-3739	646-1419
Roswell Museum & Art Ctr 100 W 11th St *Web:* www.roswellmuseum.org	Roswell	NM	88201	505-624-6744	624-6765
Space Murals Museum 12450 Hwy 70 E	Las Cruces	NM	88012	575-382-0977	382-7623
Telephone Pioneer Museum of New Mexico 110 4th St NW *Web:* www.museumsusa.org	Albuquerque	NM	87102	505-842-2937	
Tinkertown Museum 121 Sandia Crest Rd *Web:* www.tinkertown.com	Sandia Park	NM	87047	505-281-5233	286-9335
University of New Mexico Art Museum University of New Mexico Ctr for the Arts Rm 1017 *TF:* 800-225-5866 ■ *Web:* www.unmartmuseum.unm.edu	Albuquerque	NM	87131	505-277-4001	277-7315
University of New Mexico Museums 200 Yale Blvd NE University of New Mexico	Albuquerque	NM	87131	505-277-2747	277-3577

			Phone	Fax
Wheelwright Museum of the American Indian 704 Camino Lejo ... Santa Fe	NM	87505	505-982-4636	989-7386
TF: 800-607-4636 ■ *Web:* www.wheelwright.org				
White Sands Missile Range Museum & Missile Park US Hwy 70 ... White Sands	NM	88002	575-678-8824	678-2199
Web: www.wsmr-history.org				

NEW YORK

			Phone	Fax
Albany Institute of History & Art 125 Washington Ave. ... Albany	NY	12210	518-463-4478	462-1522
Web: www.albanyinstitute.org				
Albright-Knox Art Gallery 1285 Elmwood Ave ... Buffalo	NY	14222	716-882-8700	882-1958
Web: www.albrightknox.org				
Alice Austen House Museum & Garden 2 Hylan Blvd. ... Staten Island	NY	10305	718-816-4506	815-3959
Web: www.aliceausten.8m.com				
American Folk Art Museum 45 W 53rd St ... New York	NY	10019	212-265-1040	265-2350
Web: www.folkartmuseum.org				
American Numismatic Society 75 Varick St 11th Fl ... New York	NY	10013	212-571-4470	571-4479
Web: www.numismatics.org				
Amherst Museum 3755 Tonawanda Creek Rd. ... Amherst	NY	14228	716-689-1440	689-1409
Web: www.amherstmuseum.org				
Bartow-Pell Mansion Museum 895 Shore Rd Pelham Bay Pk. ... Bronx	NY	10464	718-885-1461	885-9164
Web: www.bartowpellmansionmuseum.org				
Bear Mountain Trailside Museums & Zoo Bear Mountain State Pk Rt 9 W ... Bear Mountain	NY	10911	845-786-2701	786-7157
Bronx County Historical Society 3309 Bainbridge Ave. ... Bronx	NY	10467	718-881-8900	881-4827
Web: www.bronxhistoricalsociety.org				
Bronx Museum of the Arts 1040 Grand Concourse ... Bronx	NY	10456	718-681-6000	681-6181
Web: www.bronxmuseum.org				
Brooklyn Museum of Art 200 Eastern Pkwy ... Brooklyn	NY	11238	718-638-5000	501-6136
Web: www.brooklynmuseum.org				
Buffalo & Erie County Historical Society 25 Nottingham Ct ... Buffalo	NY	14216	716-873-9644	873-8754
Web: www.intotem.buffnet.net				
Buffalo Fire Historical Museum 1850 William St ... Buffalo	NY	14206	716-892-8400	
Buffalo Museum of Science 1020 Humboldt Pkwy ... Buffalo	NY	14211	716-896-5200	897-6723
Web: www.sciencebuff.org				
Children's Museum of Science & Technology 250 Jordan Rd ... Troy	NY	12180	518-235-2120	235-6836
Web: www.cmost.org				
Cloisters Museum Fort Tryon Pk ... New York	NY	10040	212-923-3700	795-3640
Web: www.metmuseum.org				
Cooper-Hewitt National Design Museum (Smithsonian Institution) 2 E 91st St ... New York	NY	10128	212-849-8300	849-8401
Web: www.cooperhewitt.org				
Corning Museum of Glass 1 Museum Way ... Corning	NY	14830	607-937-5371	974-8470
TF Cust Svc: 800-732-6845 ■ *Web:* www.cmog.org				
Doyle New York 175 E 87th St. ... New York	NY	10128	212-427-2730	369-0892
TF: 800-808-0902 ■ *Web:* www.doylenewyork.com				
Dyckman Farmhouse Museum 4881 Broadway at 204th St ... New York	NY	10034	212-304-9422	304-0635
Web: www.dyckmanfarmhouse.org				
Ellis Island Immigration Museum Ellis Island ... New York	NY	10004	212-344-0996	344-0219
Web: www.ellisisland.com				
Empire State Aerosciences Museum 250 Rudy Chase Dr. ... Glenville	NY	12302	518-377-2191	377-1959
Web: www.esam.org				
Empire State Plaza Art Collection Empire State Plaza Curatorial & Services Corning Tower Rm 2978 ... Albany	NY	12242	518-473-7521	474-0984
Erie Canal Museum 318 Erie Blvd E ... Syracuse	NY	13202	315-471-0593	471-7220
Web: www.eriecanalmuseum.org				
Everson Museum of Art 401 Harrison St. ... Syracuse	NY	13202	315-474-6064	474-6943
Web: www.everson.org				
Franklin D Roosevelt Presidential Library & Museum 4079 Albany Post Rd ... Hyde Park	NY	12538	845-486-7770	486-1147
TF: 800-337-8474 ■ *Web:* www.fdrlibrary.marist.edu				
Frick Collection 1 E 70th St ... New York	NY	10021	212-288-0700	628-4417
Web: www.frick.org				
Genesee Country Village & Museum 1410 Flint Hill Rd ... Mumford	NY	14511	585-538-6822	538-6927
Web: www.gcv.org				
Harbor Defense Museum Fort Hamilton US Army Garrison 230 Sheridan Loop ... Brooklyn	NY	11252	718-630-4349	630-4888
Herbert F Johnson Museum of Art 114 Central Ave ... Ithaca	NY	14853	607-255-6464	255-9940
Web: www.museum.cornell.edu				
Hudson River Museum 511 Warburton Ave ... Yonkers	NY	10701	914-963-4550	963-8558
Web: www.hrm.org				
Hyde Collection 161 Warren St. ... Glens Falls	NY	12801	518-792-1761	792-9197
Web: www.hydecollection.org				
International Center of Photography 1133 Avenue of the Americas ... New York	NY	10036	212-857-0000	768-4688
Web: www.icp.org				
International Museum of Photography & Film at George Eastman House 900 E Ave ... Rochester	NY	14607	585-271-3361	271-3970
Web: www.eastmanhouse.org				
Intrepid Sea-Air-Space Museum W 46th St & 12th Ave Pier 86 ... New York	NY	10036	212-245-0072	
TF: 877-957-7447 ■ *Web:* www.intrepidmuseum.org				
Irish American Heritage Museum 2267 Rt 145 ... East Durham	NY	12423	518-634-7497	634-7497
Web: www.irishamericanheritagemuseum.org				
Iron Island Museum 998 E Lovejoy St ... Buffalo	NY	14206	716-892-3084	

			Phone	Fax
Iroquois Indian Museum 324 Caverns Rd PO Box 7 ... Howes Cave	NY	12092	518-296-8949	296-8955
Web: www.iroquoismuseum.org				
Jacques Marchais Museum of Tibetan Art 338 Lighthouse Ave ... Staten Island	NY	10306	718-987-3500	351-0402
Web: www.tibetanmuseum.com				
Jefferson County Historical Society 228 Washington St ... Watertown	NY	13601	315-782-3491	782-2913
Jewish Museum 1109 5th Ave ... New York	NY	10128	212-423-3200	423-3232
Web: www.thejewishmuseum.org				
Karpeles Manuscript Library 453 Porter Ave ... Buffalo	NY	14201	716-885-4139	
Web: www.rain.org/~karpeles				
Long Island Museum of American Art History & Carriages 1200 Rt 25A ... Stony Brook	NY	11790	631-751-0066	751-0353
Web: www.longislandmuseum.org				
Louis Armstrong House & Archives 65-30 Kissena Blvd ... Flushing	NY	11367	718-997-3670	997-3677
Web: www.satchmo.net				
Lower East Side Tenement Museum National Historic Site 108 Orchard St ... New York	NY	10002	212-431-0233	431-0402
Web: www.tenement.org				
Memorial Art Gallery of the University of Rochester 500 University Ave ... Rochester	NY	14607	585-276-8900	
Web: www.mag.rochester.edu				
Metropolitan Museum of Art 1000 5th Ave ... New York	NY	10028	212-879-5500	570-3879
TF: 800-468-7386 ■ *Web:* www.metmuseum.org				
Morris-Jumel Mansion 65 Jumel Terr at 160th St ... New York	NY	10032	212-923-8008	923-8947
Web: www.morrisjumel.org				
Mount Vernon Hotel Museum & Garden 421 E 61st St ... New York	NY	10065	212-838-6878	838-7390
Web: www.mvhm.org				
Munson-Williams-Proctor Arts Institute 310 Genesee St. ... Utica	NY	13502	315-797-0000	797-5608
Web: www.mwpai.org				
Museo del Barrio 1230 5th Ave ... New York	NY	10029	212-831-7272	831-7927
Web: www.elmuseo.org				
Museum for African Art 36-01 43rd Ave. ... Long Island City	NY	11101	718-784-7700	784-7718
Web: www.africanart.org				
Museum of American Financial History 48 Wall St ... New York	NY	10005	212-908-4110	908-4601
TF: 877-983-4626 ■ *Web:* www.financialhistory.org				
Museum of American Illustration 128 E 63rd St ... New York	NY	10065	212-838-2560	838-2561
TF: 800-746-8738 ■ *Web:* www.societyillustrators.org				
Museum of Arts & Design 2 Columbus Cir. ... New York	NY	10019	212-299-7777	459-0926
Web: www.americancraftmuseum.org				
Museum of Jewish Heritage 36 Battery Pl Battery Pk City ... New York	NY	10280	212-968-1800	437-4311
Web: www.mjhnyc.org				
Museum of Modern Art 11 W 53rd St ... New York	NY	10019	212-708-9400	
Web: www.moma.org				
Museum of Science & Technology 500 S Franklin St ... Syracuse	NY	13202	315-425-9068	425-9072
Web: www.most.org				
Museum of the City of New York 1220 5th Ave. ... New York	NY	10029	212-534-1672	423-0758
Web: www.mcny.org				
Museum of the Moving Image 3601 35th Ave ... Astoria	NY	11106	718-784-4520	784-4681
Web: www.ammi.org				
National Academy Museum of Art 1083 5th Ave ... New York	NY	10128	212-369-4880	360-6795
Web: www.nationalacademy.org				
National Museum of the American Indian (Smithsonian Institution) 1 Bowling Green ... New York	NY	10004	212-514-3700	
TF: 800-242-6624 ■ *Web:* www.nmai.si.edu				
National Women's Hall of Fame 76 Fall St PO Box 335 ... Seneca Falls	NY	13148	315-568-8060	568-2976
Web: www.greatwomen.org				
Neuberger Museum of Art 735 Anderson Hill Rd Purchase College SUNY ... Purchase	NY	10577	914-251-6100	251-6101
Web: www.neuberger.org				
New Museum of Contemporary Art 235 Bowery ... New York	NY	10002	212-219-1222	431-5328
Web: www.newmuseum.org				
New York City Fire Museum 278 Spring St ... New York	NY	10013	212-691-1303	924-0430
Web: www.nycfiremuseum.org				
New York City Police Museum 100 Old Slip ... New York	NY	10005	212-480-3100	480-9757
Web: www.nycpolicemuseum.org				
New York Hall of Science 47-01 111th St Flushing Meadows ... Queens	NY	11368	718-699-0005	699-1341
Web: www.nyhallsci.org				
New York Historical Society 170 Central Pk W ... New York	NY	10024	212-873-3400	874-8706
TF: 888-860-6947 ■ *Web:* www.nyhistory.org				
New York State Museum Rm 3023 Cultural Education Ctr Empire State Plaza ... Albany	NY	12230	518-474-5877	486-3696
Web: www.nysm.nysed.gov				
New York Transit Museum 130 Livingston St Fl 10 ... Brooklyn	NY	11201	718-694-1600	
Web: mta.info/mta/museum				
Pedaling History Bicycle Museum 3943 N Buffalo Rd ... Orchard Park	NY	14127	716-662-3853	662-4594
Web: www.pedalinghistory.com				
Pierpont Morgan Library 225 Madison Ave ... New York	NY	10016	212-685-0008	481-3484
TF Orders: 800-861-0001 ■ *Web:* www.themorgan.org				
Queens County Farm Museum 7350 Little Neck Pkwy Floral Pk ... Queens	NY	11004	718-347-3276	347-3243
Web: www.queensfarm.org				
Queens Museum of Art New York City Bldg Flushing Meadows Corona Pk ... Queens	NY	11368	718-592-9700	592-5778
Web: www.queensmuseum.org				

	City	State	Zip	Phone	Fax
Roberson Museum & Science Ctr 30 Front St *TF:* 888-269-5325 ■ *Web:* www.roberson.org	Binghamton	NY	13905	607-772-0660	771-8905
Rochester Museum & Science Ctr 657 E Ave. *Web:* www.rmsc.org	Rochester	NY	14607	585-271-4320	271-0492
Sainte Marie among the Iroquois Museum 6680 Onondaga Lake Pkwy *Web:* www.livinghistorymuseum.org	Liverpool	NY	13088	315-453-6767	453-6772
Schenectady Museum & Suits-Bueche Planetarium 15 Nott Terr Heights *Web:* www.schenectadymuseum.org	Schenectady	NY	12308	518-382-7890	382-7893
Solomon R Guggenheim Museum 1071 5th Ave *TF:* 800-329-6109 ■ *Web:* www.guggenheim.org	New York	NY	10128	212-423-3500	423-3640
South Street Seaport Museum 12 Fulton St *Web:* www.southstseaport.org	New York	NY	10038	212-748-8600	748-8610
Staten Island Institute of Arts & Sciences 75 Stuyvesant Pl *Web:* www.siiasmuseum.org	Staten Island	NY	10301	718-727-1135	273-5683
Steel Plant Museum 560 Ridge Rd Lackawanna Public Library *Web:* www.steelplantmuseum.org	Lackawanna	NY	14218	716-823-0630	827-1997
Strong - National Museum of Play 1 Manhattan Sq *Web:* www.strongmuseum.org	Rochester	NY	14607	585-263-2700	263-2493
Studio Museum in Harlem 144 W 125th St. *Web:* www.studiomuseuminharlem.org	New York	NY	10027	212-864-4500	864-4800
Suffolk County Historical Society 300 W Main St	Riverhead	NY	11901	631-727-2881	727-3467
Susan B Anthony House 17 Madison St *Web:* www.susanbanthonyhouse.org	Rochester	NY	14608	585-235-6124	235-6212
Ten Broeck Mansion 9 Ten Broeck Pl. *Web:* www.tenbroeck.org	Albany	NY	12210	518-436-9826	436-1489
Theodore Roosevelt Inaugural National Historic Site 641 Delaware Ave *Web:* www.nps.gov/thri/index.htm	Buffalo	NY	14202	716-884-0095	884-0330
Tinker Homestead & Farm Museum 1525 Calkins Rd	Henrietta	NY	14467	585-359-7042	
Toy Town Museum 636 Girard Ave PO Box 238 *Web:* www.toytownusa.com	East Aurora	NY	14052	716-687-5151	687-5098
Ukrainian Museum 222 E 6th St. *Web:* www.ukrainianmuseum.org	New York	NY	10003	212-228-0110	228-1947
University Art Museum 1400 Washington Ave SUNY Albany *Web:* www.albany.edu/museum	Albany	NY	12222	518-442-4035	442-5075
Victorian Doll Museum 4332 Buffalo Rd *Web:* www.victoriandollmuseum.com	North Chili	NY	14514	585-247-0130	
Whitney Museum of American Art 945 Madison Ave **Fax:* Library ■ *TF:* 800-944-8639 ■ *Web:* www.whitney.org	New York	NY	10021	212-570-3600	570-7729*
Yager Museum of Art & Culture The Hartwick College PO Box 4020 *Web:* www.hartwick.edu/academics/museum	Oneonta	NY	13820	607-431-4000	431-4468
Yeshiva University Museum 15 W 16th St *Web:* www.yu.edu	New York	NY	10011	212-294-8330	294-8335

NORTH CAROLINA

	City	State	Zip	Phone	Fax
Antique Car Museum/Grovewood Gallery 111 Grovewood Rd *TF:* 877-622-7238 ■ *Web:* www.grovewood.com	Asheville	NC	28804	828-253-7651	254-2489
Asheville Art Museum 2 S Pack Sq PO Box 1717 *Web:* www.ashevilleart.org	Asheville	NC	28801	828-253-3227	257-4503
Backing Up Classics Auto Museum 4545 Concord Pkwy S *Web:* www.backingupclassics.com	Concord	NC	28027	704-788-9500	788-9495
Biltmore House 1 Lodge St *TF:* 800-411-3812 ■ *Web:* www.biltmore.com	Asheville	NC	28803	828-225-1333	
Charlotte Hawkins Brown Museum 6136 Burlington Rd PO Box B *Web:* www.nchistoricsites.or	Sedalia	NC	27342	336-449-4846	449-0176
Charlotte Historic Trolley Museum 2104 S Blvd	Charlotte	NC	28203	704-375-0850	
Charlotte Museum of History & Hezekiah Alexander Homesite 3500 Shamrock Dr *Web:* www.charlottemuseum.org	Charlotte	NC	28215	704-568-1774	566-1817
Charlotte Nature Museum 1658 Sterling Rd. *TF:* 800-935-0553 ■ *Web:* www.discoveryplace.org/naturemuseum.asp	Charlotte	NC	28209	704-372-6261	333-8948
Colburn Earth Science Museum 2 S Pack Sq *Web:* www.colburnmuseum.org	Asheville	NC	28801	828-254-7162	257-4505
Contemporary Art Museum 409 W Martin St *Web:* www.camnc.org	Raleigh	NC	27603	919-513-0946	515-7330
Duke Homestead State Historic Site & Tobacco Museum 2828 Duke Homestead Rd *Web:* www.ibiblio.org/dukehome	Durham	NC	27705	919-477-5498	479-7092
EnergyExplorium 13339 Hagers Ferry Rd **Fax Area Code:* 704 ■ *TF:* 800-777-0003 ■ *Web:* www.duke-energy.com	Huntersville	NC	28078	980-875-5600	875-5602*
Estes-Winn Memorial Automobile Museum 111 Grovewood Rd *Web:* www.grovewood.com/about-us/estes-winn-antique-car-museum	Asheville	NC	28804	828-253-7651	254-2489
Fieldcrest Cannon Textile Museum *Cannon Village Visitor Ctr* 200 W Ave *Web:* www.cannonvillage.com/textilemuseum.htm	Kannapolis	NC	28081	704-938-3200	932-4188
Folk Art Ctr PO Box 9545 *Web:* www.southernhighlandguild.org	Asheville	NC	28815	828-298-7928	298-7962
Greensboro Historical Museum 130 Summit Ave *Web:* www.greensborohistory.org	Greensboro	NC	27401	336-373-2043	373-2204
Greenville Museum of Art 802 Evans St *Web:* www.gmoa.org	Greenville	NC	27834	252-758-1946	758-1946
International Civil Rights Center & Museum 134 S Elm St *TF:* 800-748-7116 ■ *Web:* www.sitinmovement.org	Greensboro	NC	27401	336-274-9199	274-6244
Joel Lane House Museum & Gardens 728 W Hargett St *Web:* www.joellane.org	Raleigh	NC	27603	919-833-3431	
Legends of Harley Drag Racing Museum 1126 S Saunders St *TF:* 800-394-2758 ■ *Web:* www.rayprice.com	Raleigh	NC	27603	919-832-2261	833-6846
Levine Museum of the New South 200 E 7th St *Web:* www.museumofthenewsouth.org	Charlotte	NC	28202	704-333-1887	333-1896
Marbles Kids Museum 201 E Hargett St *Web:* www.marbleskidsmuseum.org	Raleigh	NC	27601	919-834-4040	384-3516
Mattye Reed African Heritage Museum Dudley Bldg NC & A&T State University	Greensboro	NC	27411	336-334-3209	334-4378
Mint Museum of Art 2730 Randolph Rd. *Web:* www.mintmuseum.org	Charlotte	NC	28207	704-337-2000	337-2101
Museum of Anthropology Wake Forest University Wingate Rd PO Box 7267 *Web:* www.wfu.edu	Winston-Salem	NC	27109	336-758-5282	758-5116
Museum of Early Southern Decorative Arts (MESDA) 924 S Main St. *TF:* 800-441-5305 ■ *Web:* www.mesda.org	Winston-Salem	NC	27101	336-721-7360	721-7367
Museum of the Cherokee Indian Hwy 441 N PO Box 1599 *TF:* 888-665-7249 ■ *Web:* www.cherokeemuseum.org	Cherokee	NC	28719	828-497-3481	497-4985
Nasher Museum of Art at Duke University 2001 Campus Dr Duke University *Web:* www.duke.edu	Durham	NC	27701	919-684-5135	681-8624
Natural Science Center of Greensboro 4301 Lawndale Dr. *Web:* www.natsci.org	Greensboro	NC	27455	336-288-3769	288-2531
North Carolina Central University Art Museum 1801 Fayetteville St *Web:* www.ariel.acc.nccu.edu	Durham	NC	27707	919-530-6211	560-5649
North Carolina Museum of Art 2110 Blue Ridge Rd *Web:* www.ncartmuseum.org	Raleigh	NC	27607	919-839-6262	733-8034
North Carolina Museum of History 5 E Edenton St *Web:* www.ncmuseumofhistory.org	Raleigh	NC	27601	919-807-7900	733-8655
North Carolina Museum of Life & Science 433 Murray Ave *Web:* www.ncmls.org	Durham	NC	27704	919-220-5429	220-5575
North Carolina Museum of Natural Sciences 11 W Jones St *Web:* www.naturalsciences.org	Raleigh	NC	27601	919-733-7450	733-1573
North Carolina Railroad Museum PO Box 40 *Web:* www.nhvry.org	New Hill	NC	27562	919-362-5416	
Old Salem 600 S Main St *TF:* 800-441-5305 ■ *Web:* www.oldsalem.org	Winston-Salem	NC	27101	336-721-7300	721-7335
Raleigh City Museum 220 Fayetteville St Suite 100 *Web:* www.raleighcitymuseum.org	Raleigh	NC	27601	919-832-3775	832-3085
Reynolda House Museum of American Art 2250 Reynolda Rd *TF:* 888-663-1149 ■ *Web:* www.reynoldahouse.org	Winston-Salem	NC	27106	336-758-5150	758-5704
Richard Petty Museum 142 W Academy St. *Web:* www.pettyracing.com	Randleman	NC	27317	336-495-1143	495-1543
Schiele Museum of Natural History & James H Lynn Planetarium 1500 E Garrison Blvd *Web:* www.schielemuseum.org/planetarium.php	Gastonia	NC	28054	704-866-6908	866-6041
SciWorks Science Center & Environmental Park of Forsyth County 400 Hanes-Mill Rd *Web:* www.sciworks.org	Winston-Salem	NC	27105	336-767-6730	661-1777
Smith McDowell House Museum 283 Victoria Rd. *Web:* www.wnchistory.org	Asheville	NC	28803	828-253-9231	253-5518
Weatherspoon Art Museum 500 Tate St *Web:* www.uncg.edu	Greensboro	NC	27402	336-334-5770	334-5907

NORTH DAKOTA

	City	State	Zip	Phone	Fax
Bonanzaville USA 1351 Main Ave W. *TF:* 800-700-5317 ■ *Web:* www.bonanzaville.com	West Fargo	ND	58078	701-282-2822	282-7606
Fargo Air Museum 1609 19th Ave N. *Web:* www.fargoairmuseum.org	Fargo	ND	58102	701-293-8043	293-8103
Game & Fish Lobby Wildlife Museum 100 N Bismarck Expy	Bismarck	ND	58501	701-328-6300	328-6352
Myra Museum 2405 Belmont Rd *Web:* www.grandforkshistory.com	Grand Forks	ND	58201	701-775-2216	775-0317
North Dakota Museum of Art 261Centennial Dr S- 7305 *Web:* www.ndmoa.com	Grand Forks	ND	58202	701-777-4195	777-4425

NOVA SCOTIA

	City	State	Zip	Phone	Fax
Anne Murray Centre 36 Main St PO Box 610 *Web:* www.annemurraycentre.com	Springhill	NS	B0M1X0	902-597-8614	597-2001
Black Cultural Centre for Nova Scotia 1149 Main St *TF:* 800-465-0767 ■ *Web:* www.bccns.com	Dartmouth	NS	B2Z1A8	902-434-6223	434-2306
Fisheries Museum of the Atlantic 68 Bluenose Dr PO Box 1363 *TF:* 866-579-4909 ■ *Web:* museum.gov.ns.ca/fma/en/home/default.aspx	Lunenburg	NS	B0J2C0	902-634-4794	634-8990
Maritime Museum of the Atlantic 1675 Lower Water St. *Web:* museum.gov.ns.ca/mmanew/en/home/default.aspx	Halifax	NS	B3J1S3	902-424-7490	424-0612

	City	State	Postal Code	Phone	Fax
Nova Scotia Museum of Industry 147 N Foord St *Web:* museum.gov.ns.ca/moi/en/home/default.aspx	Stellarton	NS	B0K1S0	902-755-5425	755-7045
Nova Scotia Museum of Natural History 1747 Summer St *Web:* museum.gov.ns.ca/mnhnew/en/home/default.aspx	Halifax	NS	B3H3A6	902-424-7353	424-0560

OHIO

	City	State	ZIP	Phone	Fax
Akron Art Museum 1 S High St *Web:* www.akronartmuseum.org	Akron	OH	44308	330-376-9185	376-1180
American Classical Music Hall of Fame 1225 Elm St *Web:* www.americanclassicalmusic.org	Cincinnati	OH	45202	513-621-3263	621-9333
Arms Family Museum of Local History 648 Wick Ave *Web:* www.mahoninghistory.org	Youngstown	OH	44502	330-743-2589	743-7210
Blair Museum of Lithopanes Toledo Botanical Garden 5403 Elmer Dr *Web:* www.lithophanemuseum.org	Toledo	OH	43615	419-245-1356	
Boonshoft Museum of Discovery 2600 DeWeese Pkwy *Web:* www.boonshoftmuseum.org	Dayton	OH	45414	937-275-7431	275-5811
Butler Institute of American Art 524 Wick Ave *Web:* www.butlerart.com	Youngstown	OH	44502	330-743-1711	743-9567
Carillon Historical Park 100 Carillon Blvd *Web:* www.carillonpark.org	Dayton	OH	45409	937-293-2841	293-5798
Carriage Hills Farm Museum 7800 E Shull Rd *Web:* www.metroparks.org/Parks/CarriageHill	Dayton	OH	45424	937-278-2609	
Century Village 14653 E Pk St *Web:* www.geaugahistorical.org	Burton	OH	44021	440-834-1492	834-4012
Cincinnati Art Museum 953 Eden Pk Dr *TF:* 877-472-4226 ■ *Web:* www.cincinnatiartmuseum.com	Cincinnati	OH	45202	513-721-5204	721-0129
Cincinnati History Museum 1301 Western Ave Cincinnati Museum Ctr *TF:* 800-733-2077 ■ *Web:* www.cincymuseum.org	Cincinnati	OH	45203	513-287-7000	287-7029
Citizens Motorcar Co America's Packard Museum The 420 S Ludlow St *Web:* www.americaspackardmuseum.org	Dayton	OH	45402	937-226-1710	224-1918
Cleveland Museum of Art 11150 E Blvd *TF Sales:* 888-262-7175 ■ *Web:* www.clemusart.com	Cleveland	OH	44106	216-421-7340	229-5095
Cleveland Museum of Natural History 1 Wade Oval Dr University Cir *TF:* 800-317-9155 ■ *Web:* www.cmnh.org	Cleveland	OH	44106	216-231-4600	231-5919
Columbus Museum of Art 480 E Broad St *Web:* www.columbusmuseum.org	Columbus	OH	43215	614-221-6801	221-0226
COSI Columbus 333 W Broad St *TF:* 888-819-2674 ■ *Web:* www.cosi.org	Columbus	OH	43215	614-228-2674	228-6363
COSI Toledo 1 Discovery Way *Web:* www.cositoledo.org	Toledo	OH	43604	419-244-2674	255-2674
Crawford Auto-Aviation Museum 10825 E Blvd *Web:* www.wrhs.org/crawford	Cleveland	OH	44106	216-721-5722	721-0891
Dayton Art Institute 456 Belmonte Pk N *TF:* 800-296-4426 ■ *Web:* www.daytonartinstitute.org	Dayton	OH	45405	937-223-5277	223-3140
Dittrick Museum of Medical History 11000 Euclid Ave *Web:* www.cwru.edu	Cleveland	OH	44106	216-368-3648	368-0165
Dunham Tavern Museum 6709 Euclid Ave *Web:* www.dunhamtavern.org	Cleveland	OH	44103	216-431-1060	
Great Lakes Science Ctr 601 Erieside Ave *Web:* www.greatscience.com	Cleveland	OH	44114	216-694-2000	696-2140
Hale Farm & Village 2686 Oakhill Rd PO Box 296 *TF:* 800-589-9703 ■ *Web:* www.wrhs.org	Bath	OH	44210	330-666-3711	666-9497
Harriet Beecher Stowe House 2950 Gilbert Ave *Web:* www.ohiohistory.org	Cincinnati	OH	45206	513-751-0651	
Heritage Museum 530 E Town St	Columbus	OH	43215	614-228-6515	228-7809
Heritage Village Museum 11450 Lebanon Pike *Web:* www.heritagevillagecincinnati.org	Cincinnati	OH	45241	513-563-9484	563-0914
Hower House 60 Fir Hill University of Akron *Web:* www3.uakron.edu/howerhse	Akron	OH	44325	330-972-6909	384-2635
International Women's Air & Space Museum 1501 N Marginal Rd Burke Lakefront Airport *Web:* www.iwasm.org	Cleveland	OH	44114	216-623-1111	623-1113
Inventure Place 221 S Broadway *TF:* 800-968-4332 ■ *Web:* www.invent.org	Akron	OH	44308	330-762-4463	762-6313
Kelton House Museum 586 E Town St	Columbus	OH	43215	614-464-2022	464-3346
Kent State University Museum PO Box 5190 *Web:* dept.kent.edu/museum	Kent	OH	44242	330-672-3450	672-3218
Krohn Conservatory 1501 Eden Pk Dr	Cincinnati	OH	45202	513-421-5707	421-6007
Lake View Cemetery 12316 Euclid Ave	Cleveland	OH	44106	216-421-2665	421-2415
McDonough Museum of Art 525 Wick Ave *Web:* www.fpa.ysu.edu	Youngstown	OH	44502	330-941-1400	941-1492
Museum of Contemporary Art Cleveland 8501 Carnegie Ave *Web:* www.mocacleveland.org	Cleveland	OH	44106	216-421-8671	421-0737
Museum of Natural History & Science 1301 Western Ave Cincinnati Museum Ctr *TF:* 800-733-2077 ■ *Web:* www.cincymuseum.org	Cincinnati	OH	45203	513-287-7000	287-7029
National Afro-American Museum & Cultural Ctr 1350 Brush Row Rd PO Box 578 *TF:* 800-752-2603 ■ *Web:* www.ohiohistory.org	Wilberforce	OH	45384	937-376-4944	376-2007
National Cleveland-Style Polka Hall of Fame 605 E 222nd St *TF:* 866-667-6552 ■ *Web:* www.polkafame.com	Euclid	OH	44123	216-261-3263	261-4131
National Inventors Hall of Fame 221 S Broadway St Inventure Pl *TF:* 800-968-4332 ■ *Web:* www.invent.org	Akron	OH	44308	330-762-4463	762-6313
National Museum of the United States Air Force 1100 Spaatz St Wright-Patterson Air Force Base *Web:* www.nationalmuseum.af.mil	Dayton	OH	45433	937-255-3284	255-3286
National Underground Railroad Freedom Ctr 50 E Freedom Way *TF:* 877-648-4838 ■ *Web:* www.undergroundrailroad.com	Cincinnati	OH	45202	513-333-7500	
Ohio Craft Museum 1665 W 5th Ave *Web:* www.ohiocraft.org	Columbus	OH	43212	614-486-4402	486-7110
Ohio Historical Society 1982 Velma Ave *TF:* 800-686-6124 ■ *Web:* www.ohiohistory.org	Columbus	OH	43211	614-297-2300	
Patterson Homestead Historic House Museum Rental Facility 1815 Brown St *Web:* www.daytonhistory.org	Dayton	OH	45409	937-222-9724	222-0345
Police Museum 217 S High St Rm 402	Akron	OH	44308	330-375-2390	375-2412
Rock & Roll Hall of Fame & Museum 1100 Rock & Roll Blvd *Web:* www.rockhall.com	Cleveland	OH	44114	216-781-7625	515-1283
Roscoe Village 381 Hill St *TF:* 800-877-1830 ■ *Web:* www.roscoevillage.com	Coshocton	OH	43812	740-622-9310	623-6555
Sauder Village 22611 SR 2 PO Box 235 *TF:* 800-590-9755 ■ *Web:* www.saudervillage.org	Archbold	OH	43502	419-446-2541	445-5251
SS Willis B Boyer Maritime Museum Ship 26 Main St International Pk *Web:* www.willisbboyer.org	Toledo	OH	43605	419-936-3070	
Stan Hywet Hall & Gardens 714 N Portage Path *TF:* 888-836-5533 ■ *Web:* www.stanhywet.org	Akron	OH	44403	330-836-5533	836-2680
Steamship William G Mather Museum 305 Mather Way	Cleveland	OH	44114	216-574-9053	574-2536
Taft Museum of Art The 316 Pike St *Web:* www.taftmuseum.org	Cincinnati	OH	45202	513-241-0343	241-7762
Thurber House 77 Jefferson Ave *Web:* www.thurberhouse.org	Columbus	OH	43215	614-464-1032	280-3645
Toledo Firefighters Museum 918 W Sylvania Ave *Web:* www.toledofiremuseum.com	Toledo	OH	43612	419-478-3473	936-3293
Toledo Lake Erie & Western Railway & Museum 49 N 6th St PO Box 168 *Web:* www.tlew.org	Waterville	OH	43566	419-878-2177	
Toledo Museum of Art 2445 Monroe St *TF:* 800-644-6862 ■ *Web:* www.toledomuseum.org	Toledo	OH	43620	419-255-8000	255-5638
War Vet Museum 23 E Main St	Canfield	OH	44406	330-533-6311	533-6311
Western Reserve Historical Society Museum 10825 E Blvd **Fax:* Library ■ *Web:* www.wrhs.org	Cleveland	OH	44106	216-721-5722	721-5702*
Wexner Center for the Arts 1871 N High St Ohio State University *Web:* www.wexarts.org	Columbus	OH	43210	614-292-0330	292-3369
Wolcott House Museum 1031 River Rd *Web:* www.maumee.org/recreation/wolcott.htm	Maumee	OH	43537	419-893-9602	893-3108
Youngstown Historical Ctr 151 W Wood St *TF:* 800-262-6137 ■ *Web:* www.ohsweb.ohiohistory.org	Youngstown	OH	44503	330-743-5934	743-2999

OKLAHOMA

	City	State	ZIP	Phone	Fax
45th Infantry Div Museum 2145 NE 36th St *Web:* www.45thdivisionmuseum.com	Oklahoma City	OK	73111	405-424-5313	424-3748
Arkansas River Historical Society Museum 5350 Cimarron Rd *TF:* 888-512-7678 ■ *Web:* www.tulsaweb.com	Catoosa	OK	74015	918-266-2291	266-7678
Cherokee Heritage Center & National Museum 21192 S Keeler Dr *TF:* 888-999-6007 ■ *Web:* www.cherokeeheritage.org	Park Hill	OK	74451	918-456-6007	456-6165
Elsing Museum 777 S Lewis Ave Oral Roberts University *Web:* www.elsing.oru.edu	Tulsa	OK	74104	918-495-6262	
Five Civilized Tribes Museum 1101 Honor Heights Dr *Web:* www.fivetribes.org	Muskogee	OK	74401	918-683-1701	683-3070
Fred Jones Jr Museum of Art 555 Elm Ave University of Oklahoma *Web:* www.ou.edu	Norman	OK	73019	405-325-3272	325-7696
Gilcrease Museum 1400 N Gilcrease Museum Rd *TF:* 888-655-2278 ■ *Web:* www.gilcrease.org	Tulsa	OK	74127	918-596-2700	596-2770
Harn Homestead & 1889er Museum 1721 N Lincoln Blvd *Web:* www.harnhomestead.com	Oklahoma City	OK	73105	405-235-4058	235-4041
International Photography Hall of Fame & Museum 2100 NE 52nd St *Web:* www.iphf.org	Oklahoma City	OK	73111	405-424-4055	424-4058
JM Davis Arms & Historical Museum 333 N Lynn Riggs Blvd *Web:* www.thegunmuseum.com	Claremore	OK	74017	918-341-5707	341-5771
Lincoln County Historical Society Museum of Pioneer History 717 Manvel Ave *Web:* www.pioneermuseumok.org	Chandler	OK	74834	405-258-2425	258-2809
National Cowboy & Western Heritage Museum 1700 NE 63rd St *Web:* www.nationalcowboymuseum.org	Oklahoma City	OK	73111	405-478-2250	478-4714
Oklahoma City Museum of Art 415 Couch Dr *TF:* 800-579-9278 ■ *Web:* www.okcmoa.com	Oklahoma City	OK	73102	405-236-3100	236-3122
Oklahoma City National Memorial & Memorial Center Museum 620 N Harvey Ave *Web:* www.oklahomacitynationalmemorial.org	Oklahoma City	OK	73102	405-235-3313	235-3315
Oklahoma Jazz Hall of Fame 111 E 1st St Upper Level *TF:* 800-348-9336 ■ *Web:* www.okjazz.org	Tulsa	OK	74103	918-596-1001	596-1005
Oklahoma Museum of History 800 Nazih Zuhdi Dr *Web:* www.okhistorycenter.org	Oklahoma City	OK	73105	405-522-5248	522-5402

	City	State	Zip	Phone	Fax
Oklahoma Museum of Natural History 2401 Chautaugua Ave. *Web:* www.omnh.ou.edu	Norman	OK	73072	405-325-4712	325-7699
Oklahoma Territorial Museum 406 E Oklahoma Ave. *Web:* www.oklahomaterritorialmuseum.org	Guthrie	OK	73044	405-282-1889	282-7286
Philbrook Museum of Art & Gardens 2727 S Rockford Rd *TF:* 800-324-7941 ■ *Web:* www.philbrook.org	Tulsa	OK	74114	918-749-7941	743-4230
Science Museum Oklahoma 2100 NE 52nd St *TF:* 800-532-7652 ■ *Web:* www.omniplex.org	Oklahoma City	OK	73111	405-602-6664	602-3768
Sherwin Miller Museum of Jewish Art 2021 E 71st St *Web:* www.jewishmuseum.net	Tulsa	OK	74136	918-492-1818	492-1888
Tulsa Air & Space Museum 3624 N 74 E Ave. *Web:* www.tulsaairandspacemuseum.com	Tulsa	OK	74115	918-834-9900	834-6723
Will Rogers Memorial Museum 1720 W Will Rogers Blvd *TF:* 800-324-9455 ■ *Web:* www.willrogers.org/memorial.html	Claremore	OK	74017	918-341-0719	343-8119
Woolaroc Ranch Museum & Wildlife Preserve Hwy 123 S *TF:* 888-966-5276 ■ *Web:* www.woolaroc.org	Bartlesville	OK	74003	918-336-0307	336-0084
World Organization of China Painters Museum 2641 NW 10th St *Web:* www.theshop.net	Oklahoma City	OK	73107	405-521-1234	521-1265

ONTARIO

	City	Prov	Postal Code	Phone	Fax
Bytown Museum 1 Canal Ln PO Box 523 Stn B *Web:* www.bytownmuseum.com	Ottawa	ON	K1P5P6	613-234-4570	234-4846
Canada Agriculture Museum Prince of Wales Dr PO Box 9724 Sta T *TF:* 866-442-4416 ■ *Web:* www.agriculture.technomuses.ca	Ottawa	ON	K1G5A3	613-991-3044	993-7923
Canada Aviation Museum & Space Museum 11 Aviation Pkwy PO Box 9724 *TF:* 800-463-2038 ■ *Web:* aviation.technomuses.ca/mobile/index.html	Ottawa	ON	K1K4R3	613-993-2010	990-3655
Canada Science & Technology Museum 1867 St Laurent Blvd PO Box 9724 *TF:* 866-442-4416 ■ *Web:* www.sciencetech.technomuses.ca/english/index.cfm	Ottawa	ON	K1G5A3	613-991-3044	990-3654
Canadian Museum of Contemporary Photography 380 Sussex Dr PO Box 427 Sta A *TF:* 800-319-2787 ■ *Web:* www.gallery.ca	Ottawa	ON	K1N9N4	613-990-1985	993-4385
Canadian Museum of Nature 240 McLeod St **Fax:* Mktg ■ *TF:* 800-263-4433 ■ *Web:* www.nature.ca	Ottawa	ON	K1P6P4	613-566-4700	364-4021*
Currency Museum of the Bank of Canada 245 Sparks St *TF:* 800-303-1282 ■ *Web:* www.currencymuseum.ca	Ottawa	ON	K1A0G9	613-782-8914	782-7761
Fort Henry National Historic Site PO Box 213 *TF Cust Svc:* 800-437-2233 ■ *Web:* www.forthenry.com	Kingston	ON	K7L4V8	613-542-7388	542-3054
Gardiner Museum 111 Queen's Pk *Web:* www.gardinermuseum.on.ca	Toronto	ON	M5S2C7	416-586-8080	586-8085
Guinness World Records Museum 4943 Clifton Hill *Web:* www.guinnessniagarafalls.com	Niagara Falls	ON	L2G3N5	905-356-2299	356-8614
Lithuanian Museum/Archives of Canada 2185 Stavebank Rd	Mississauga	ON	L5C1T3	905-566-8755	
Mackenzie House Museum 82 Bond St *Web:* www.toronto.ca	Toronto	ON	M5B1X2	416-392-6915	392-0114
Movieland Wax Museum of the Stars 4848 Clifton Hill *Web:* www.cliftonhill.com/attractions/movieland-wax-museum-stars	Niagara Falls	ON	L2G3N4	905-358-3061	358-5738
Ontario Science Centre 770 Don Mills Rd *Web:* www.ontariosciencecentre.ca	Toronto	ON	M3C1T3	416-429-4100	696-3166
Presqu'ile Provincial Park Museum 328 Presqu'ile Pkwy	Brighton	ON	K0K1H0	613-475-4324	475-2209
Ripley's Believe It or Not! Museum 4960 Clifton Hill *Web:* ripleysniagara.com	Niagara Falls	ON	L2G3N4	905-356-2238	374-7345
Royal Canadian Military Institute 426 University Ave *TF:* 800-585-1072 ■ *Web:* www.rcmi.org	Toronto	ON	M5G1S9	416-597-0286	597-6919
Royal Ontario Museum 100 Queen's Pk. *Web:* www.rom.on.ca	Toronto	ON	M5S2C6	416-586-8000	586-5863
Scarborough Historical Museum 1007 Brimley Rd.	Toronto	ON	M1P3E8	416-338-8807	338-8805
Toronto Aerospace Museum 65 Carl Hall Rd PO Box 1 *TF:* 866-585-2227 ■ *Web:* www.casmuseum.org	Toronto	ON	M3K2E1	416-638-6078	638-5509
Toronto's First Post Office 260 Adelaide St E *Web:* www.townofyork.com	Toronto	ON	M5A1N1	416-865-1833	865-9414
York Museum 2694 Eglinton Ave W. *Web:* www.toronto.ca	Toronto	ON	M5M1V1	416-394-2759	394-2803

OREGON

	City	State	Zip	Phone	Fax
Antique Powerland Museum 3995 Brooklake Rd NE *Web:* www.antiquepowerland.com	Brooks	OR	97303	503-393-2424	393-2424
Bush House Museum 600 Mission St SE *Web:* www.oregonlink.com/bush_house	Salem	OR	97302	503-363-4714	
Columbia River Maritime Museum 1792 Marine Dr *Web:* www.crmm.org	Astoria	OR	97103	503-325-2323	325-2331
Hallie Ford Museum of Art 700 State St. *Web:* www.willamette.edu/museum_of_art	Salem	OR	97301	503-370-6855	375-5458
High Desert Museum 59800 S Hwy 97 *Web:* www.highdesertmuseum.org	Bend	OR	97702	541-382-4754	382-5256
Jensen Arctic Museum 590 W Church St *Web:* www.wou.edu/jensenmuseum	Monmouth	OR	97361	503-838-8468	838-8289
Jordan Schnitzer Museum of Art 1430 Johnson Ln *Web:* jsma.uoregon.edu	Eugene	OR	97403	541-346-3027	346-0976
Keizer Heritage Museum 980 Chemawa Rd NE *Web:* www.keizerheritage.org	Keizer	OR	97303	503-393-9660	393-0209
Klamath County Museum 1451 Main St	Klamath Falls	OR	97601	541-883-4208	883-5170
Lane County Historical Museum 740 W 13th Ave. *Web:* www.lchmuseum.org	Eugene	OR	97402	541-682-4242	682-7361
Marion County Historical Society Museum (MCHS) 260 12th St SE *Web:* www.marionhistory.org	Salem	OR	97301	503-364-2128	391-5356
Oregon Air & Space Museum 90377 Boeing Dr.	Eugene	OR	97402	541-461-1101	461-1101
Oregon Electric Railway Museum 3995 Brooklake Rd *Web:* www.trainweb.org	Brooks	OR	97303	503-888-4014	399-8051
Oregon Historical Society 1200 SW Pk Ave *Web:* www.ohs.org	Portland	OR	97205	503-222-1741	221-2035
Oregon Maritime Center & Museum 115 SW Ash St Suite 400-C *Web:* www.oregonmaritimemuseum.org	Portland	OR	97204	503-224-7724	224-7767
Oregon Museum of Science & Industry 1945 SE Water Ave *TF:* 800-955-6674 ■ *Web:* www.omsi.edu	Portland	OR	97214	503-797-4000	797-4500
Pittock Mansion 3229 NW Pittock Dr. *Web:* www.pittockmansion.com	Portland	OR	97210	503-823-3623	823-3619
Portland Art Museum 1219 SW Park Ave *Web:* www.portlandartmuseum.org	Portland	OR	97205	503-226-2811	226-4842
Springfield Museum 590 Main St. *Web:* www.springfieldmuseum.com	Springfield	OR	97477	541-726-2300	726-3688
Tillamook County Pioneer Museum 2106 2nd St *Web:* www.tcpm.org	Tillamook	OR	97141	503-842-4553	842-4553
University of Oregon Museum of Natural & Cultural History 1680 E 15th Ave *Web:* www.natural-history.uoregon.edu	Eugene	OR	97403	541-346-3024	346-5334

PENNSYLVANIA

	City	State	Zip	Phone	Fax
Academy of Natural Sciences Museum 1900 Benjamin Franklin Pkwy *Web:* www.acnatsci.org	Philadelphia	PA	19103	215-299-1000	299-1028
African-American Museum in Philadelphia 701 Arch St. *Web:* www.aampmuseum.org	Philadelphia	PA	19106	215-574-0380	574-3110
Allentown Art Museum 31 N 5th St. *Web:* www.allentownartmuseum.org	Allentown	PA	18101	610-432-4333	434-7409
American Civil War Museum 297 Steinwehr Ave *TF:* 800-877-7775 ■ *Web:* www.e-gettysburg.cc	Gettysburg	PA	17325	717-334-6245	334-9686
American Helicopter Museum & Education Ctr 1220 American Blvd W *Web:* www.helicoptermuseum.org	West Chester	PA	19380	610-436-9600	436-8642
American Swedish Historical Museum 1900 Pattison Ave. *Web:* www.americanswedish.org	Philadelphia	PA	19145	215-389-1776	389-7701
Andy Warhol Museum 117 Sandusky St *Web:* www.warhol.org	Pittsburgh	PA	15212	412-237-8300	237-8340
Atwater Kent Museum 15 S 7th St *Web:* www.philadelphiahistory.org	Philadelphia	PA	19106	215-685-4830	685-4837
Barnes Foundation 300 N Latch's Ln *Web:* www.barnesfoundation.org	Merion	PA	19066	610-667-0290	664-4026
Brandywine River Museum 1 Hoffman's Mill Rd PO Box 141 *Web:* www.brandywinemuseum.org	Chadds Ford	PA	19317	610-388-2700	388-1197
Carnegie Museum of Art 4400 Forbes Ave *Web:* www.web.cmoa.org	Pittsburgh	PA	15213	412-622-3131	622-3112
Carnegie Museum of Natural History 4400 Forbes Ave. *Web:* www.carnegiemnh.org	Pittsburgh	PA	15213	412-622-3131	622-6258
Carnegie Science Ctr 1 Allegheny Ave *TF:* 877-975-6787 ■ *Web:* www.carnegiesciencecenter.org	Pittsburgh	PA	15212	412-237-3400	237-3375
Da Vinci Discovery Center of Science & Technology 3145 Hamilton Blvd Bypass *Web:* www.davinci-center.org	Allentown	PA	18103	484-664-1002	
Electric City Trolley Station & Museum 300 Cliff St *Web:* www.ectma.org	Scranton	PA	18503	570-963-6590	963-6447
Elfreth's Alley Museum 126 Elfreth's Alley *Web:* www.elfrethsalley.org	Philadelphia	PA	19106	215-574-0560	922-7869
Erie Art Museum 411 State St. *Web:* www.erieartmuseum.org	Erie	PA	16501	814-459-5477	452-1744
Erie County History Ctr 419 State St Erie County Historical Society *Web:* www.eriecountyhistory.org	Erie	PA	16501	814-454-1813	454-6890
Everhart Museum 1901 Mulberry St. *Web:* everhart-museum.org	Scranton	PA	18510	570-346-7186	346-0652
Fabric Workshop & Museum 1214 Arch St *Web:* www.fabricworkshopandmuseum.org	Philadelphia	PA	19107	215-561-8888	561-8887
Fort Pitt Museum 101 Commonwealth Pl. *Web:* www.fortpittmuseum.com	Pittsburgh	PA	15222	412-281-9284	281-1417
Franklin Institute Science Museum 222 N 20th St *TF:* 800-285-0684 ■ *Web:* www.fi.edu	Philadelphia	PA	19103	215-448-1200	448-1235
Frick Art & Historical Ctr 7227 Reynolds St *Web:* www.frickart.org	Pittsburgh	PA	15208	412-371-0600	371-6140
Gettysburg Battle Theatre 571 Steinwehr Ave	Gettysburg	PA	17325	717-334-6100	334-6110

Name / Address	City	State	ZIP	Phone	Fax
Holocaust Museum & Resource Ctr 601 Jefferson Ave *Web:* www.jewishnepa.org	Scranton	PA	18510	570-961-2300	346-6147
Houdini Museum 1433 N Main Ave. *Web:* www.houdini.org	Scranton	PA	18508	570-342-5555	
Hugh Moore Historical Park & National Canal Museum 30 Centre Sq. *Web:* www.canals.org	Easton	PA	18042	610-559-6613	250-6686
Independence Seaport Museum 211 S Columbus Blvd. *Web:* www.phillyseaport.org	Philadelphia	PA	19106	215-925-5439	925-6713
Institute of Contemporary Art 118 S 36th St University of Pennsylvania *Web:* www.icaphila.org	Philadelphia	PA	19104	215-898-7108	898-5050
Kemerer Museum of Decorative Arts 427 N New St	Bethlehem	PA	18018	610-868-6868	866-0460
Lake Shore Railway Museum 31 Wall St Lake Shore Historical Society	North East	PA	16428	814-725-1911	725-1911
Lancaster Cultural History Museum 5 W King St *Web:* www.lancasterheritage.com	Lancaster	PA	17603	717-299-6440	299-6916
Lehigh County Museum 432 W Walnut St *Web:* www.lchs.museum	Allentown	PA	18102	610-435-4664	435-9812
Lincoln Train Museum 425 Steinwehr Ave. *Web:* www.gettysburgbattlefieldtours.com	Gettysburg	PA	17325	717-334-5678	334-6110
Mario Lanza Museum 712 Montrose St Columbia House *Web:* www.mario-lanza-institute.org	Philadelphia	PA	19147	215-238-9691	238-9694
Mummers Museum 1100 S 2nd St. *Web:* riverfrontmummers.com	Philadelphia	PA	19147	215-336-3050	389-5630
Museum of Indian Culture 2825 Fish Hatchery Rd *Web:* www.museumofindianculture.org	Allentown	PA	18103	610-797-2121	797-2801
National Constitution Ctr 525 Arch St Independence Mall *TF:* 866-917-1787 ■ *Web:* www.constitutioncenter.org	Philadelphia	PA	19106	215-409-6600	409-6650
National Liberty Museum 321 Chestnut St. *Web:* www.libertymuseum.org	Philadelphia	PA	19106	215-925-2800	925-3800
National Museum of American Jewish History 101 S Independence Mall E *Web:* www.nmajh.org	Philadelphia	PA	19106	215-923-3811	923-0763
National Toy Train Museum 300 Paradise Ln *Web:* www.traincollectors.org	Strasburg	PA	17579	717-687-8976	687-0742
National Watch & Clock Museum 514 Poplar St *Web:* www.nawcc.org	Columbia	PA	17512	717-684-8261	684-0878
North Museum of Natural History & Science 400 College Ave *Web:* www.northmuseum.org	Lancaster	PA	17603	717-291-3941	358-4504
Old Economy Village 270 16th St *Web:* www.oldeconomyvillage.org	Ambridge	PA	15003	724-266-4500	266-7506
Pennsylvania Academy of the Fine Arts Museum 118 N Broad St *Web:* www.pafa.org/splashFlash.jsp	Philadelphia	PA	19102	215-972-7600	569-0153
Pennsylvania Anthracite Heritage Museum RR1 Bald Mountain Rd *Web:* anthracitemuseum.org	Scranton	PA	18504	570-963-4804	963-4194
Philadelphia Museum of Art 26th & Benjamin Franklin Pkwy *Web:* www.philamuseum.org	Philadelphia	PA	19130	215-763-8100	236-4465
Photo Antiquities - Museum of Photographic History 531 E Ohio St *Web:* www.photoantiquities.com	Pittsburgh	PA	15212	412-231-7881	231-1217
Polish American Cultural Center Museum 308 Walnut St *Web:* www.polishamericancenter.org	Philadelphia	PA	19106	215-922-1700	922-1518
Reading Public Museum & Art Gallery 500 Museum Rd *Web:* readingpublicmuseum.org	Reading	PA	19611	610-371-5850	371-5632
Rodin Museum 22nd & Benjamin Franklin Pkwy PO Box 7646 *Web:* www.rodinmuseum.org	Philadelphia	PA	19101	215-568-6026	236-4465
Rosenbach Museum & Library 2008-2010 Delancey St *Web:* www.rosenbach.org	Philadelphia	PA	19103	215-732-1600	545-7529
Senator John Heinz Pittsburgh Regional History Ctr 1212 Smallman St *Web:* www.pghhistory.org	Pittsburgh	PA	15222	412-454-6000	454-6039
Shriver House Museum 309 Baltimore St *Web:* www.schriverhouse.com	Gettysburg	PA	17325	717-337-2800	
Soldier's National Museum 777 Baltimore St	Gettysburg	PA	17325	717-334-4890	
Soldiers & Sailors National Military Museum & Memorial 4141 5th Ave. *Web:* www.soldiersandsailorshall.org	Pittsburgh	PA	15213	412-621-4253	683-9339
State Museum of Pennsylvania The 300 N St *Web:* www.statemuseumpa.org	Harrisburg	PA	17120	717-787-4980	783-4558
Stenton Museum 4601 N 18th St *Web:* www.stenton.org	Philadelphia	PA	19140	215-329-7312	329-7312
Stephen Foster Memorial Museum University of Pittsburgh 4301 Forbes Ave. *Web:* www.pitt.edu/~amerimus/museum.htm	Pittsburgh	PA	15260	412-624-4100	624-7447
University of Pennsylvania Museum of Archaeology & Anthropology 3260 S St *Web:* www.penn.museum	Philadelphia	PA	19104	215-898-4000	898-0657
Wagner Free Institute of Science 1700 W Montgomery Ave *Web:* www.pacscl.org	Philadelphia	PA	19121	215-763-6529	763-1299
Woodmere Art Museum 9201 Germantown Ave *Web:* www.woodmereartmuseum.org	Philadelphia	PA	19118	215-247-0476	247-2387

PRINCE EDWARD ISLAND

Name / Address	City	Prov	Postal Code	Phone	Fax
Prince Edward Island Museum & Heritage Foundation 2 Kent St	Charlottetown	PE	C1A1M6	902-368-6600	368-6608

QUEBEC

Name / Address	City	Prov	Postal Code	Phone	Fax
Canadian Centre for Architecture 1920 Baile St *Web:* cca.qc.ca	Montreal	QC	H3H2S6	514-939-7000	939-7020
Canadian Museum of Civilization 100 Laurier St *TF:* 800-555-5621 ■ *Web:* www.civilization.ca	Gatineau	QC	K1A0M8	819-776-7000	776-8300
Canadian Postal Museum 100 Laurier St *Web:* www.civilization.ca/cpm/cpme.asp	Gatineau	QC	K1A0M8	819-776-7010	
Choco-Musee Erico 634 St Jean St *Web:* www.chocomusee.com	Quebec	QC	G1R1P8	418-524-2122	524-4558
Jules Saint-Michel Luthier - Economuseum of Violin-Making 57 Ontario St W *Web:* www.luthiersaintmichel.com	Montreal	QC	H2X1Y8	514-288-4343	288-9296
McCord Museum of Canadian History 690 Sherbrooke St W *Web:* www.mccord-museum.qc.ca/en	Montreal	QC	H3A1E9	514-398-7100	398-5045
Montreal Holocaust Memorial Centre 5151 Ch de la C(te-Sainte-Catherine *Web:* www.mhmc.ca	Montreal	QC	H3W1M6	514-345-2605	344-2651
Montreal Science Centre St Laurent Blvd & de la Commune St King-Edward Pier *TF:* 877-496-4724 ■ *Web:* www.montrealsciencecentre.com	Montreal	QC	H2Y2E2	514-496-4724	496-0067
Musee de la Civilisation 85 Dalhousie St PO Box 155 Stn B. *TF:* 866-710-8031 ■ *Web:* www.mcq.org/mcq/index.html	Quebec	QC	G1K7A6	418-643-2158	646-9705
Musee de la Moto (Harley-Davidson Museum) 2495 Hamel Blvd W *Web:* www.premont-harley.com	Quebec	QC	G1P2H9	418-683-1340	683-7597
Musee du Quebec Parc des Champs-de-Bataille *TF:* 866-220-2150 ■ *Web:* www.mdq.org	Quebec	QC	G1R5H3	418-643-2150	646-3330
Museum of French America 2 cote de la Fabrique *TF:* 866-710-8031 ■ *Web:* www.mcq.org/fr/maf/index.html	Quebec	QC	G1R3V6	418-692-2843	646-9705
Pointe-a-Calliere - The Montreal Museum of Archaeology & History 350 Royale Pl Angle Joint. *Web:* www.pacmusee.qc.ca	Old Montreal	QC	H2Y3Y5	514-872-9150	872-9151
Richard Robitaille Fourrures - Economusee de la Fourrure 329 St Paul St	Quebec	QC	G1K3W8	418-692-9699	692-3646
Saint-Laurent Art Museum 615 Ave Sainte-Croix.	Saint-Laurent	QC	H4L3X6	514-747-7367	747-8892

RHODE ISLAND

Name / Address	City	State	ZIP	Phone	Fax
Artillery Co of Newport Military Museum 23 Clark St *Web:* www.newportartillery.org	Newport	RI	02840	401-846-8488	846-1649
Culinary Arts Museum at Johnson & Wales University 315 Harborside Blvd. *Web:* www.culinary.org	Providence	RI	02905	401-598-2805	598-2807
Governor Henry Lippitt House Museum 199 Hope St	Providence	RI	02906	401-453-0688	453-8221
Haffenreffer Museum of Anthropology 300 Tower St. *Web:* www.brown.edu	Bristol	RI	02809	401-253-8388	253-1198
Heritage Harbor Museum 200 Allens Ave *Web:* www.heritageharbor.org	Providence	RI	02903	401-751-7979	751-8822
Museum of Natural History & Planetarium 1000 Elmwood Ave *Web:* www.osfn.org/museum	Providence	RI	02907	401-785-9450	461-5146
Museum of Newport History at the Brick Market 127 Thames St *Web:* newporthistorical.org	Newport	RI	02840	401-841-8770	846-1853
Museum of Yachting Fort Adams State Pk. *Web:* www.moy.org	Newport	RI	02840	401-847-1018	847-8320
National Museum of American Illustration 492 Bellevue Ave *Web:* www.americanillustration.org	Newport	RI	02842	401-851-8949	851-8974
Naval War College Museum 686 Cushing Rd. *Web:* www.usnwc.edu	Newport	RI	02841	401-841-4052	841-7074
Newport Art Museum 76 Bellevue Ave. *Web:* www.newportartmuseum.com	Newport	RI	02840	401-848-8200	848-8205
Newport Historical Society 82 Touro St. *Web:* www.newporthistorical.org	Newport	RI	02840	401-846-0813	846-1853
Providence Athenaeum 251 Benefit St *Web:* www.providenceathenaeum.org	Providence	RI	02903	401-421-6970	421-2860
Providence Jewelry Museum 4 Edward St. *Web:* www.providencejewelrymuseum.com	Providence	RI	02904	401-274-0999	861-2170
Rhode Island Historical Society 110 Benevolent St. *Web:* www.rihs.org	Providence	RI	02906	401-331-8575	351-0127
Rhode Island School of Design - Museum of Art 224 Benefit St *Web:* www.risdmuseum.org	Providence	RI	02903	401-454-6502	454-6556
Warwick Museum of Art 3259 Post Rd *Web:* www.warwickmuseum.org	Warwick	RI	02886	401-737-0010	737-1796

SASKATCHEWAN

Name / Address	City	Prov	Postal Code	Phone	Fax
Moose Jaw Museum & Art Gallery 461 Langdon Crescent Pk. *Web:* www.mjmag.ca	Moose Jaw	SK	S6H0X6	306-692-4471	694-8016

	City	State	Zip	Phone	Fax
Prince Albert Historical Museum 10 River St E *Web:* www.historypa.com	Prince Albert	SK	S6V8A9	306-764-2992	
RCMP Heritage Ctr 5907 Dewdney Ave *TF:* 866-567-7267 ■ *Web:* www.rcmpheritagecentre.com	Regina	SK	S4T0P4	306-522-7333	
Royal Saskatchewan Museum 2445 Albert St *Web:* www.royalsaskmuseum.ca	Regina	SK	S4P4W7	306-787-2815	787-2820
Western Development Museum 2610 Lorne Ave S *Web:* www.wdm.ca	Saskatoon	SK	S7J0S6	306-931-1910	934-0525

SOUTH CAROLINA

	City	State	Zip	Phone	Fax
Avery Research Center for African-American History & Culture 125 Bull St *Web:* www.cofc.edu	Charleston	SC	29424	843-953-7609	953-7607
Bob Jones University Museum & Gallery Bob Jones University 1700 Wade Hampton Blvd *Web:* www.bjumg.org	Greenville	SC	29614	864-770-1331	770-1306
Cayce Historical Museum 1800 12th St Ext *Web:* www.caycesc.net	Cayce	SC	29033	803-796-9020	796-9072
Challenger Learning Ctr 2600-A Barhamville Rd *Web:* www.richlandone.org	Columbia	SC	29204	803-929-3951	929-3959
Charleston Museum 360 Meeting St *Web:* www.charlestonmuseum.com	Charleston	SC	29403	843-722-2996	722-1784
Citadel Archives & Museum 171 Moultrie St The Citadel *Web:* www.citadel.edu	Charleston	SC	29409	843-953-6846	953-6956
Coastal Discovery Museum 100 William Hilton Pkwy *Web:* www.coastaldiscovery.org	Hilton Head Island	SC	29926	843-689-6767	689-6769
Columbia Museum of Art 1515 Main St *Web:* www.colmusart.org	Columbia	SC	29201	803-799-2810	343-2150
Fort Jackson Museum 2179 Sumter St	Fort Jackson	SC	29207	803-751-7419	751-4434
Franklin G Burroughs-Simeon B Chapin Art Museum 3100 S Ocean Blvd *Web:* www.myrtlebeachartmuseum.org	Myrtle Beach	SC	29577	843-238-2510	238-2910
Gibbes Museum of Art 135 Meeting St *Web:* www.gibbesmuseum.org	Charleston	SC	29401	843-722-2706	720-1682
Greenville County Museum of Art 420 College St *Web:* www.greenvillemuseum.org	Greenville	SC	29601	864-271-7570	271-7579
Horry County Museum 428 Main St *Web:* www.horrycountymuseum.org	Conway	SC	29526	843-915-5320	248-1854
Karpeles Manuscript Library Museum 68 Spring St *Web:* www.rain.org	Charleston	SC	29403	843-853-4651	853-4651
Patriots Point Naval & Maritime Museum 40 Patriots Pt Rd *TF:* 800-248-3508 ■ *Web:* www.state.sc.us	Mount Pleasant	SC	29464	843-884-2727	881-4232
Ripley's Believe It or Not! Museum 901 N Ocean Blvd *Web:* www.ripleys.com	Myrtle Beach	SC	29577	843-448-2331	626-2168
Roper Mountain Science Ctr 402 Roper Mountain Rd *Web:* www.ropermountain.org	Greenville	SC	29615	864-355-8900	355-8948
South Carolina Civil War Museum 4857 Hwy 17 Bypass S	Myrtle Beach	SC	29577	843-293-4344	
South Carolina Confederate Relic Room & Museum 301 Gervais St *Web:* www.state.sc.us/crr	Columbia	SC	29201	803-737-8095	737-8099
South Carolina Museum & Library of Confederate History 15 Boyce Ave *Web:* www.confederatemuseum.org	Greenville	SC	29601	864-421-9039	421-0938
South Carolina State Museum 301 Gervais St Loading Zone D *Web:* www.museum.state.sc.us	Columbia	SC	29201	803-898-4921	898-4969
University of South Carolina McKissick Museum University of South Carolina 816 Bull St *Web:* www.cas.sc.edu/mcks	Columbia	SC	29208	803-777-7251	777-2829

SOUTH DAKOTA

	City	State	Zip	Phone	Fax
1881 Custer County Courthouse Museum 411 Mt Rushmore Rd PO Box 826 *Web:* www.1881courthousemuseum.com	Custer	SD	57730	605-673-2443	673-2443
Adams Museum 54 Sherman St *Web:* www.adamsmuseumandhouse.org	Deadwood	SD	57732	605-578-1714	578-1194
Center for Western Studies 2101 S Summit Ave Augustana College *TF:* 800-727-2844 ■ *Web:* www.augie.edu	Sioux Falls	SD	57197	605-274-4007	274-4999
Delbridge Museum of Natural History 805 S Kiwanis Ave *Web:* www.gpzoo.org	Sioux Falls	SD	57104	605-367-7003	367-8340
Fort Meade Museum Sheridan St Bldg 55 PO Box 164 *Web:* www.fortmeademuseum.org	Fort Meade	SD	57741	605-347-9822	
Journey Museum 222 New York St *Web:* www.journeymuseum.org	Rapid City	SD	57701	605-394-6923	394-6940
Museum of Geology 501 E St Joseph St S Dakota School of Mines & Technology *TF:* 800-544-8162	Rapid City	SD	57701	605-394-2467	394-6131
Museum of South Dakota State Historical Society 900 Governors Dr Cultural Heritage Ctr *Web:* www.sdhistory.org	Pierre	SD	57501	605-773-3458	773-6041
National Museum of Woodcarving 12111 US Hwy 16 *Web:* www.blackhills.com	Custer	SD	57730	605-673-4404	673-3843
National Music Museum 414 E Clark St *Web:* www.usd.edu/smm	Vermillion	SD	57069	605-677-5306	677-6995
National Presidential Wax Museum 609 Hwy 16A *Web:* www.presidentialwaxmuseum.com	Keystone	SD	57751	605-666-4455	666-4560
Old Courthouse Museum 200 W 6th St	Sioux Falls	SD	57104	605-367-4210	367-6004
Pettigrew Home & Museum 131 N Duluth Ave	Sioux Falls	SD	57104	605-367-7097	331-0467
Sioux Empire Medical Museum 1305 W 18th St	Sioux Falls	SD	57117	605-333-6397	333-1577
South Dakota Air & Space Museum 2890 Davis Dr	Ellsworth AFB	SD	57706	605-385-5188	385-6295
South Dakota Discovery Center & Aquarium 805 W Sioux Ave *Web:* www.sd-discovery.com	Pierre	SD	57501	605-224-8295	224-2865
South Dakota National Guard Museum 301 E Dakota St	Pierre	SD	57501	605-224-9991	
Washington Pavilion of Arts & Science 301 S Main Ave PO Box 984 *TF:* 877-927-4728 ■ *Web:* www.boxoffice.washingtonpavilion.org	Sioux Falls	SD	57104	605-367-6000	367-7399
WH Over Museum 1110 Ratingen St	Vermillion	SD	57069	605-677-5228	

TENNESSEE

	City	State	Zip	Phone	Fax
Adventure Science Ctr 800 Fort Negley Blvd *Web:* www.adventuresci.com	Nashville	TN	37203	615-862-5160	862-5178
American Museum of Science & Energy 300 S Tulane Ave *Web:* www.amse.org	Oak Ridge	TN	37830	865-576-3200	576-6024
Art Museum of the University of Memphis 142 Communication & Fine Arts Bldgs The University of Memphis *Web:* www.memphis.edu	Memphis	TN	38152	901-678-2224	678-5118
B Carroll Reece Museum PO Box 70660 *Web:* www.etsu.edu/reece	Johnson City	TN	37614	423-439-4392	439-4283
Battles for Chattanooga Museum 1110 E Brow Rd *TF:* 800-854-0675 ■ *Web:* www.battlesforchattanooga.com	Lookout Mountain	TN	37350	423-821-2812	
Belle Meade Plantation 5025 Memphis-Bristol Hwy *TF:* 800-270-3991 ■ *Web:* www.bellemeadeplantation.com	Nashville	TN	37205	615-356-0501	356-2336
Bessie Smith Cultural Ctr 200 E Martin Luther King Blvd *Web:* www.bessiesmithcc.org	Chattanooga	TN	37403	423-266-8658	267-1076
Center for Southern Folklore 119 S Main St PO Box 226 *Web:* www.southernfolklore.com	Memphis	TN	38101	901-525-3655	544-9965
Chattanooga History Ctr 615 Lindsay St Suite 1000-W *Web:* www.chattanoogahistory.com	Chattanooga	TN	37403	423-265-3247	266-9280
Country Music Hall of Fame & Museum 222 5th Ave S *TF:* 800-852-6437 ■ *Web:* www.countrymusichalloffame.com	Nashville	TN	37203	615-416-2001	255-2245
Dixon Gallery & Gardens 4339 Pk Ave *Web:* www.dixon.org	Memphis	TN	38117	901-761-5250	682-0943
Doak House Museum 690 Erwin Hwy *TF:* 800-729-0256 ■ *Web:* www.doakhouse.tusculum.edu	Greeneville	TN	37743	423-636-8554	638-7166
East Tennessee Historical Society 601 S Gay St PO Box 1629 *Web:* www.easttnhistory.org	Knoxville	TN	37901	865-215-8824	215-8819
Farragut Folklife Museum 11408 Municipal Ctr Dr *Web:* www.townoffarragut.org	Farragut	TN	37934	865-966-7057	675-2096
Fire Museum of Memphis 118 Adams Ave *Web:* www.firemuseum.com	Memphis	TN	38103	901-320-5650	529-8422
Frank H McClung Museum 1327 Cir Pk Dr University of Tennessee *Web:* www.mcclungmuseum.utk.edu	Knoxville	TN	37996	865-974-2144	974-3827
Graceland (Elvis Presley Mansion) 3734 Elvis Presley Blvd *TF:* 800-238-2000 ■ *Web:* www.elvis.com/graceland	Memphis	TN	38186	901-332-3322	344-3131
Grand Ole Opry Museum 2802 Opryland Dr	Nashville	TN	37214	615-889-6611	871-5772
Harry V Steadman Mountain Heritage Farmstead Museum 853 Bays Mountain Pk Rd *Web:* www.baysmountain.com/exhibitdept/farm.html	Kingsport	TN	37660	423-229-9361	224-2589
Hartzler-Towner Multicultural Museum 1008 19th Ave S *Web:* www.scarrittbennett.org	Nashville	TN	37212	615-340-7500	340-7551
Hermitage The (Home of Andrew Jackson) 4580 Rachel's Ln *Web:* www.thehermitage.com	Hermitage	TN	37076	615-889-2941	889-9289
Historic Jonesborough Visitors Center & Museum 117 Boone St *TF:* 866-401-4223 ■ *Web:* www.historicjonesborough.com	Jonesborough	TN	37659	423-753-1010	753-1020
Houston Museum of Decorative Arts 201 High St *Web:* www.thehoustonmuseum.com	Chattanooga	TN	37403	423-267-7176	756-2156
Hunter Museum of American Art 10 Bluff View St *Web:* www.huntermuseum.org	Chattanooga	TN	37403	423-267-0968	267-9844
International Towing & Recovery Hall of Fame & Museum 3315 Broad St *Web:* www.internationaltowingmuseum.org	Chattanooga	TN	37408	423-267-3132	267-0867
James White's Fort 205 E Hill Ave *Web:* www.discoveret.org	Knoxville	TN	37915	865-525-6514	525-6514
Jonesborough-Washington County History Museum 117 Boone St	Jonesborough	TN	37659	423-753-1015	753-1020

	City	State	ZIP	Phone	Fax
Knoxville Museum of Art 1050 World Fair Park Dr *Web:* www.knoxart.org	Knoxville	TN	37916	865-525-6101	546-3635
Memphis Brooks Museum of Art 1934 Poplar Ave Overton Pk *Web:* www.brooksmuseum.org	Memphis	TN	38104	901-544-6200	725-4071
Memphis Pink Palace Museum 3050 Central Ave *Web:* www.memphismuseums.org	Memphis	TN	38111	901-320-6320	320-6391
Memphis Rock 'n' Soul Museum 191 Beale St *Web:* www.memphisrocknsoul.org	Memphis	TN	38103	901-205-2533	205-2534
Messianic Museum 1928 Hamill Rd *TF:* 888-876-8150	Hixson	TN	37343	423-876-8150	876-8156
Mississippi River Museum 101 Mud Island Dr *TF:* 800-507-6507 ■ *Web:* www.mudisland.com	Memphis	TN	38103	901-576-7241	576-6666
Museum of Appalachia 2819 Andersonville Hwy *Web:* www.museumofappalachia.com	Clinton	TN	37716	865-494-7680	494-8957
National Civil Rights Museum 450 Mulberry St *Web:* www.civilrightsmuseum.org	Memphis	TN	38103	901-521-9699	521-9740
National Medal of Honor Museum of Military History PO Box 11467 *Web:* www.mohm.org	Chattanooga	TN	37401	423-394-0710	
National Ornamental Metal Museum 374 Metal Museum Dr *Web:* www.metalmuseum.org	Memphis	TN	38106	901-774-6380	774-6382
Parthenon The 2600 W End Ave Centennial Pk PO Box 196340 *Web:* www.nashville.gov/parthenon	Nashville	TN	37203	615-862-8431	880-2265
Rocky Mount Museum 200 Hyder Hill Rd PO Box 160 *TF:* 888-538-1791 ■ *Web:* www.rockymountmuseum.com	Piney Flats	TN	37686	423-538-7396	538-1086
Slave Haven Underground Railroad Museum 826 N 2nd St *Web:* www.acropolisopa.com	Memphis	TN	38107	901-527-3427	527-8784
Soulsville USA - Stax Museum of American Soul Music 926 E McLemore Ave *Web:* www.soulsvilleusa.com	Memphis	TN	38106	901-946-2535	507-1463
Tennessee Agricultural Museum 440 Hogan Rd *Web:* www.picktnproducts.org	Nashville	TN	37204	615-837-5197	837-5224
Tennessee Sports Hall of Fame Museum 501 Broadway *Web:* www.tshf.net	Nashville	TN	37203	615-242-4750	242-4752
Tennessee State Museum 505 Deaderick St *TF:* 800-407-4324 ■ *Web:* www.tnmuseum.org	Nashville	TN	37243	615-741-2692	741-7231
Tennessee Valley Railroad Museum 4119 Cromwell Rd *Web:* www.tvrail.com	Chattanooga	TN	37421	423-894-8028	894-8029
Upper Room Chapel & Museum 1908 Grand Ave *TF:* 800-972-0433 ■ *Web:* www.upperroom.org	Nashville	TN	37212	615-340-7207	340-7293
Willie Nelson & Friends Showcase Museum 2613A McGavock Pike	Nashville	TN	37214	615-885-1515	885-1561

TEXAS

	City	State	ZIP	Phone	Fax
12th Armored Division Memorial Museum 1289 N 2nd St *Web:* www.12tharmoredmuseum.com	Abilene	TX	79601	325-677-6515	
African American Museum 3536 Grand Ave Fair Pk *Web:* www.aamdallas.org	Dallas	TX	75210	214-565-9026	421-8204
Alamo The 300 Alamo Plaza *Web:* www.thealamo.org	San Antonio	TX	78205	210-225-1391	229-1343
Amarillo Museum of Art 2200 S Van Buren St *Web:* www.amarilloart.org	Amarillo	TX	79109	806-371-5050	373-9235
American Airlines CR Smith Museum 4601 Hwy 360 at FAA Rd *TF:* 877-277-6484 ■ *Web:* www.crsmithmuseum.org	Fort Worth	TX	76155	817-967-1560	967-5737
American Quarter Horse Heritage Ctr & Museum 2601 E IH- 40 *TF:* 888-209-8322	Amarillo	TX	79104	806-376-5181	376-1005
American Wind Power Ctr 1701 Canyon Lake Dr *Web:* www.windmill.com	Lubbock	TX	79403	806-747-8734	740-0668
Amon Carter Museum 3501 Camp Bowie Blvd *TF:* 800-573-1933 ■ *Web:* www.cartermuseum.org	Fort Worth	TX	76107	817-738-1933	989-5099
Arlington Museum of Art 201 W Main St *Web:* www.arlingtonmuseum.org	Arlington	TX	76010	817-275-4600	860-4800
Asian Cultures Museum 1809 N Chaparral St *Web:* www.asianculturesmuseum.org	Corpus Christi	TX	78401	361-882-2641	882-5718
Austin Museum of Art Downtown 823 Congress Ave Suite 100 *Web:* www.amoa.org	Austin	TX	78701	512-495-9224	495-9029
Austin Museum of Art Laguna Gloria 3809 W 35th St *Web:* www.amoa.org	Austin	TX	78703	512-458-8191	458-1571
Ball-Edelman-McFarland House Museum 1110 Penn St *Web:* www.historicfortworth.org	Fort Worth	TX	76102	817-332-5875	336-2346
Battleship Texas SHS San Jacinto Battleground State Historic Site 3523 Independence Pkwy *Web:* www.tpwd.state.tx.us	La Porte	TX	77571	281-479-2431	479-5618
Bayou Bend Collection & Gardens 1 Westcott St *Web:* www.mfah.org/bayoubend	Houston	TX	77007	713-639-7750	639-7770
Blanton Museum of Art 1 University Stn D1303 University of Texas at Austin *Web:* blantonmuseum.org	Austin	TX	78712	512-471-7324	471-7023
Bob Bullock Texas State History Museum 1800 N Congress Ave *TF:* 866-369-7108 ■ *Web:* www.thestoryoftexas.com	Austin	TX	78701	512-936-8746	936-4699
Buckhorn Saloon & Museum 318 E Houston St *Web:* www.buckhornmuseum.com	San Antonio	TX	78205	210-247-4000	247-4020
Buddy Holly Ctr 1801 Crickets Ave *Web:* www.buddyhollycenter.org	Lubbock	TX	79401	806-767-2686	767-0732
Buffalo Gap Historic Village 133 William St PO Box 818 *Web:* www.tfhcc.com/buff/index.html	Buffalo Gap	TX	79508	325-572-3365	572-5449
Cattle Raisers Museum 1600 Gendy St PO Box 868 *TF:* 800-242-7420 ■ *Web:* www.cattleraisersmuseum.org	Fort Worth	TX	76107	817-332-8551	336-2470
Cavanaugh Flight Museum 4572 Claire Chennault Addison Airport *Web:* www.cavanaughflightmuseum.com	Addison	TX	75001	972-380-8800	248-0907
Center for Women & Their Work 1710 Lavaca St *Web:* www.womenandtheirwork.org	Austin	TX	78701	512-477-1064	477-1090
Charles D Tandy Archaeological Museum 2001 W Seminary Dr	Fort Worth	TX	76115	817-923-1921	921-8765
Confederate Air Force Museum *Rio Grande Valley Wing* 955 S Minnesota St Brownsville Airport *Web:* www.rgvwingcaf.com	Brownsville	TX	78521	956-541-8585	
Contemporary Arts Museum 5216 Montrose Blvd *Web:* www.camh.org	Houston	TX	77006	713-284-8250	284-8275
Corpus Christi Museum of Science & History 1900 N Chaparral St *Web:* www.ccmuseum.com	Corpus Christi	TX	78401	361-826-4667	
Dallas Firefighters Museum 3801 Parry Ave	Dallas	TX	75226	214-821-1500	821-1500
Dallas Heritage Village 1515 S Harwood *Web:* www.dallasheritagevillage.org	Dallas	TX	75215	214-421-5141	428-6351
Dallas Holocaust Museum 211 N Record St Suite 100 *TF:* 888-620-9933 ■ *Web:* www.dallasholocaustmuseum.org	Dallas	TX	75202	214-741-7500	747-2270
Dallas Museum of Art 1717 N Harwood St *TF:* 800-585-5770 ■ *Web:* www.dm-art.org	Dallas	TX	75201	214-922-1200	954-0174
El Paso Centennial Museum University & Wiggins University of Texas *Web:* www.utep.edu/museum	El Paso	TX	79968	915-747-5565	747-5411
El Paso Museum of Archaeology at Wilderness Park 4301 Woodrow Bean *Web:* www.epas.com	El Paso	TX	79924	915-755-4332	759-6824
El Paso Museum of Art 1 Art Festival Plaza *Web:* www.elpasoartmuseum.org	El Paso	TX	79901	915-532-1707	532-1010
El Paso Museum of History 510 Santa Fe St	El Paso	TX	79901	915-351-3588	
Elisabet Ney Museum 304 E 44th St *Web:* www.ci.austin.tx.us/elisabetney	Austin	TX	78751	512-458-2255	453-0638
Fielder House Museum 1616 W Abram St *Web:* www.fielderhouse.org	Arlington	TX	76013	817-460-4001	460-1315
Forbidden Gardens 23500 Franz Rd *Web:* www.forbidden-gardens.com	Katy	TX	77493	281-347-8000	347-8080
Fort Bend Museum 500 Houston St *Web:* www.fortbendmuseum.org	Richmond	TX	77469	281-342-6478	342-2439
Fort Sam Houston Museum & National Historic Landmark 2340 Stanley Rd Bldg 123	Fort Sam Houston	TX	78234	210-221-1886	221-1311
Fort Worth Museum of Science & History 1600 Gendy St *TF:* 888-255-9300 ■ *Web:* www.fortworthmuseum.org	Fort Worth	TX	76107	817-255-9300	732-7635
French Legation Museum 802 San Marcos St *Web:* www.frenchlegationmuseum.org	Austin	TX	78702	512-472-8180	472-9457
Frontiers of Flight Museum 6911 Lemon Ave *Web:* www.flightmuseum.com	Dallas	TX	75209	214-350-1651	351-0101
Garland Landmark Museum 200 Museum Plaza Dr *TF:* 888-879-0264	Garland	TX	75040	972-205-2749	205-3634
George Bush Library & Museum 1000 George Bush Dr W *Web:* www.bushlibrary.tamu.edu	College Station	TX	77845	979-691-4000	691-4050
George Ranch Historical Park 10215 FM 762 *Web:* www.georgeranch.org	Richmond	TX	77469	281-343-0218	343-9316
George Washington Carver Museum & Cultural Ctr 1165 Angelina St *Web:* www.ci.austin.tx.us/carver/default.htm	Austin	TX	78702	512-974-4926	974-3699
Grace Museum 102 Cypress St *Web:* www.thegracemuseum.org	Abilene	TX	79601	325-673-4587	675-5993
Guiness World Records Museum 329 Alamo Plaza *Web:* www.sa-guinness-haunted.com	San Antonio	TX	78205	210-226-2828	226-7462
Heard Natural Science Museum & Wildlife Sanctuary 1 Nature Pl *Web:* www.heardmuseum.org	McKinney	TX	75069	972-562-5566	548-9119
Heritage Farmstead Museum 1900 W 15th St *Web:* www.heritagefarmstead.org	Plano	TX	75075	972-881-0140	422-6481
Historic Brownsville Museum 641 E Madison St	Brownsville	TX	78520	956-548-1313	548-1391
Holocaust Museum Houston 5401 Caroline St *Web:* www.hmh.org	Houston	TX	77004	713-942-8000	942-7953
Houston Fire Museum 2403 Milam St *Web:* www.houstonfiremuseum.org	Houston	TX	77006	713-524-2526	520-7566
Houston Museum of Natural Science 5555 Hermann Park Dr *Web:* www.hmns.org	Houston	TX	77030	713-639-4629	639-4761
Insights Science Museum 505 N Santa Fe St *Web:* www.insightsmuseum.org	El Paso	TX	79901	915-542-2990	532-7416
Institute of Texan Cultures 801 E Durango Blvd *TF:* 800-776-7651 ■ *Web:* www.texancultures.utsa.edu	San Antonio	TX	78205	210-458-2300	458-2205
International Museum of Cultures 7500 W Camp Wisdom Rd *Web:* www.internationalmuseumofcultures.org	Dallas	TX	75236	972-708-7406	708-7341
Interurban Railway Museum 901 E 15th St *Web:* www.interurbanplano.org	Plano	TX	75074	972-941-2117	941-2656

Museum	City	State	ZIP	Phone	Fax
John E Conner Museum 905 W Santa Gertrudis Ave 700 University Blvd *Web:* www.tamuk.edu/artsci/museum	Kingsville	TX	78363	361-593-2810	593-2112
Kimbell Art Museum 3333 Camp Bowie Blvd *Web:* www.kimbellart.org	Fort Worth	TX	76107	817-332-8451	877-1264
Lawndale Art & Performance Ctr 4912 Main St *Web:* www.tsha.utexas.edu	Houston	TX	77002	713-528-5858	528-4140
LBJ Library & Museum 2313 Red River St *Web:* www.lbjlib.utexas.edu	Austin	TX	78705	512-721-0216	721-0170
Log Cabin Village 2100 Log Cabin Village Ln *Web:* www.logcabinvillage.org	Fort Worth	TX	76109	817-392-5881	
Lone Star Flight Museum 2002 Terminal Dr *Web:* www.lsfm.org	Galveston	TX	77554	409-740-7722	740-7612
Louis Tussaud's Plaza Wax Museum & Ripley's Believe It or Not! Museum 301 Alamo Plaza *Web:* www.plazawaxmuseum.com	San Antonio	TX	78205	210-224-9299	224-1516
Marion Koogler McNay Art Museum 6000 N New Braunfels Ave *Web:* www.mcnayart.org	San Antonio	TX	78209	210-824-5368	824-0218
Meadows Museum 5900 Bishop Blvd Southern Methodist University *Web:* www.smu.edu/meadowsmuseum	Dallas	TX	75205	214-768-2516	768-1688
Menil Collection 1515 Sul Ross St *Web:* www.menil.org	Houston	TX	77006	713-525-9400	525-9444
Mexic-Arte Museum 419 Congress Ave *Web:* www.main.org/mexic-arte	Austin	TX	78701	512-480-9373	480-8626
Modern Art Museum of Fort Worth 3200 Darnell St *Web:* www.mamfw.org	Fort Worth	TX	76107	817-738-9215	735-1161
Museum of Fine Arts 1001 Bissonnet St *TF:* 888-733-6324 ■ *Web:* www.mfah.org	Houston	TX	77005	713-639-7300	639-7784
Museum of Health & Medical Science 1515 Hermann Dr *Web:* www.mhms.org	Houston	TX	77004	713-521-1515	526-1434
Museum of Nature & Science 1318 S 2nd Ave *Web:* www.natureandscience.org	Dallas	TX	75210	214-421-3466	428-4356
Museum of Texas Tech University 3301 4th St *Web:* www.depts.ttu.edu/museumttu	Lubbock	TX	79409	806-742-2442	742-1136
Museum of the American Railroad 1105 Washington St Fair Pk *Web:* www.museumoftheamericanrailroad.org	Dallas	TX	75315	214-428-0101	426-1937
National Border Patrol Museum 4315 Woodrow Bean Transmountain Rd *TF:* 877-276-8738 ■ *Web:* www.borderpatrolmuseum.com	El Paso	TX	79924	915-759-6060	759-0992
National Center for Children's Illustrated Literature Museum 102 Cedar St *Web:* www.nccil.org	Abilene	TX	79601	325-673-4586	673-0085
National Cowgirl Museum & Hall of Fame 1720 Gendy St *TF:* 800-476-3263 ■ *Web:* www.cowgirl.net	Fort Worth	TX	76107	817-336-4475	336-2470
National Museum of Funeral History 415 Barren Springs Dr *Web:* www.nmfh.org	Houston	TX	77090	281-876-3063	876-4403
National Ranching Heritage Ctr 3121 4th St *Web:* www.depts.ttu.edu	Lubbock	TX	79409	806-742-0498	742-0616
National Scouting Museum 1329 W Walnut Hill Ln *TF:* 800-303-3047 ■ *Web:* www.bsamuseum.org	Irving	TX	75038	972-580-2100	580-2020
Nelson A Rockefeller Center for Latin American Art San Antonio Museum of Art 200 W Jones Ave *Web:* www.samuseum.org	San Antonio	TX	78215	210-978-8100	978-8134
O Henry Home & Museum 409 E 5th St *Web:* www.ci.austin.tx.us	Austin	TX	78701	512-472-1903	472-7102
Panhandle-Plains Historical Museum 2503 4th Ave *Web:* www.panhandleplains.org	Canyon	TX	79015	806-651-2244	651-2250
Plaza Wax Museum 301 Alamo Plaza *Web:* www.plazawaxmuseum.com	San Antonio	TX	78205	210-224-9299	224-1516
Ripley Entertainment Inc 601 E Palace Pkwy *Web:* www.palaceofwax.com	Grand Prairie	TX	75050	972-263-2391	263-5954
River Legacy Living Science Ctr 701 NW Green Oaks Blvd *Web:* www.riverlegacy.org	Arlington	TX	76006	817-860-6752	860-1595
San Antonio Museum of Art 200 W Jones Ave *Web:* www.samuseum.org	San Antonio	TX	78215	210-978-8100	978-8134
San Jacinto Museum of History 1 Monument Cir *Web:* www.sanjacinto-museum.org	La Porte	TX	77571	281-479-2421	479-2428
Science Spectrum Museum 2579 S Loop 289 *Web:* www.sciencespectrum.com	Lubbock	TX	79423	806-745-2525	745-1115
Sixth Floor Museum 411 Elm St Suite 120 Dealey Plaza *TF:* 888-485-4854 ■ *Web:* www.jfk.org	Dallas	TX	75202	214-747-6660	747-6662
South Texas Institute for the Arts 1902 N Shoreline Blvd *Web:* www.stia.org	Corpus Christi	TX	78401	361-825-3500	825-3520
Space Center Houston 1601 Nasa Rd 1 *Web:* www.spacecenter.org	Houston	TX	77058	281-244-2100	283-7724
Spanish Governor's Palace 105 Plaza de Armas	San Antonio	TX	78205	210-224-0601	223-5562
Steves Homestead Museum 509 King William St *Web:* www.saconservation.org/tours/steves.htm	San Antonio	TX	78204	210-225-5924	223-9014
Stillman House & Museum 1325 E Washington St *Web:* www.brownsvillehistory.org	Brownsville	TX	78520	956-542-3929	541-5524
Stockyards Museum 131 E Exchange Ave	Fort Worth	TX	76106	817-625-5087	625-5083
Texas Maritime Museum 1202 Navigation Cir *TF:* 866-729-2469 ■ *Web:* www.texasmaritimemuseum.org	Rockport	TX	78382	361-729-1271	729-9938
Texas Memorial Museum 2400 Trinity St *Web:* www.utexas.edu	Austin	TX	78705	512-471-1604	471-4794
Texas Military Forces Museum PO Box 5218 *Web:* www.texasmilitaryforcesmuseum.org	Austin	TX	78763	512-782-5659	782-6750
Texas Transportation Museum 11731 Wetmore Rd *Web:* www.txtransportationmuseum.org	San Antonio	TX	78247	210-490-3554	
Trail Drivers & Texas Rangers Museum 3805 Broadway	San Antonio	TX	78209	210-822-9011	
Umlauf Sculpture Garden & Museum 605 Robert E Lee Rd *Web:* www.umlaufsculpture.org	Austin	TX	78704	512-445-5582	445-5583
USS Lexington Museum on the Bay 2914 N Shoreline Blvd *TF:* 800-523-9539 ■ *Web:* www.usslexington.com	Corpus Christi	TX	78403	361-888-4873	883-8361
Vintage Flying Museum 505 NW 38th St Hanger 33 S Meacham Field *Web:* www.vintageflyingmuseum.org	Fort Worth	TX	76106	817-624-1935	485-4454
Witte Museum 3801 Broadway St *Web:* www.wittemuseum.org	San Antonio	TX	78209	210-357-1900	357-1882
Women's Museum 3800 Parry Ave *Web:* www.thewomensmuseum.org	Dallas	TX	75226	214-915-0860	915-0879

UTAH

Museum	City	State	ZIP	Phone	Fax
Brigham Young University Museum of Art 308 MOA N Campus Dr *TF:* 877-266-5053 ■ *Web:* www.moa.byu.edu	Provo	UT	84602	801-422-8214	422-0527
Brigham Young University Museum of Peoples & Cultures 700 N 100 E 105 Allen Hall *Web:* www.fhss.byu.edu	Provo	UT	84602	801-422-0020	422-0026
Chase Home Museum of Utah Folk Art 617 E S Temple *Web:* www.arts.utah.gov/things_to_do/exhibitions/galleries/chase.html	Salt Lake City	UT	84102	801-533-5760	533-4202
Crandall Historical Printing Museum 275 E Ctr St	Provo	UT	84606	801-377-7777	374-3333
Daughters of Utah Pioneers Museum 2148 Grant Ave	Ogden	UT	84401	801-393-4460	
Fort Douglas Military Museum 32 Potter St Fort Douglas *Web:* www.fortdouglas.org	Salt Lake City	UT	84113	801-581-1710	581-9846
Hill Aerospace Museum 7961 Wardleigh Rd Bldg 1955 *Web:* www.hill.af.mil/museum	Hill AFB	UT	84056	801-777-6818	775-3034
John Hutchings Museum of Natural History 55 N Ctr St *Web:* www.hutchingsmuseum.org	Lehi	UT	84043	801-768-7180	
John M Browning Firearms Museum 2501 Wall Ave Union Stn *Web:* theunionstation.org/index.php/museums-2/john-m-browning-firearms-museum	Ogden	UT	84401	801-393-9886	621-0230
Monte L Bean Life Science Museum Brigham Young University 645 E 1430 N *Web:* mlbean.byu.edu	Provo	UT	84602	801-422-5051	422-0093
Museum of Church History & Art 45 N W Temple St	Salt Lake City	UT	84150	801-240-3310	240-5342
Museum of Paleontology 1683 N Canyon Rd	Provo	UT	84602	801-422-3680	422-7919
Museum of Utah Art & History 125 S Main St *Web:* www.muahnet.org	Salt Lake City	UT	84111	801-355-5554	355-5222
Ogden Eccles Dinosaur Park 1544 E Park Blvd *Web:* www.dinosaurpark.org	Ogden	UT	84401	801-393-3466	399-0895
Pioneer Memorial Museum 300 N Main St *Web:* www.dupinternational.org	Salt Lake City	UT	84103	801-532-6479	532-4436
Roy Historical Museum 5550 S 1700 W	Roy	UT	84067	801-776-3626	
Salt Lake Art Ctr 20 S W Temple *Web:* www.slartcenter.org	Salt Lake City	UT	84101	801-328-4201	322-4323
Social Hall Heritage Museum 55 S State St	Salt Lake City	UT	84103	801-321-8745	
Springville Museum of Art 126 E 400 S *Web:* www.sma.nebo.edu	Springville	UT	84663	801-489-2727	489-2739
Union Station 2501 Wall Ave *Web:* www.ogden-ut.com/UnionStation.html	Ogden	UT	84401	801-393-9886	621-0230
Utah Museum of Fine Arts 410 Campus Center Dr University of Utah *Web:* www.umfa.utah.edu	Salt Lake City	UT	84112	801-581-7332	585-5198
Utah Museum of Natural History The 1390 E Presidents Cir University of Utah *Web:* umnh.utah.edu	Salt Lake City	UT	84112	801-581-4303	585-3684
Utah State Railroad Museum 2501 Wall Ave Union Stn *Web:* theunionstation.org/index.php/museums-2/utah-state-railroad-museum	Ogden	UT	84401	801-393-9886	621-0230
Wattis-Dumke Model Railroad Museum 2501 Wall Ave Union Stn *Web:* theunionstation.org/index.php/museums-2	Ogden	UT	84401	801-393-9886	621-0230
Wheeler Historic Farm 6351 S 900 E *Web:* www.wheelerfarm.com	Salt Lake City	UT	84121	801-264-2241	264-2213

VERMONT

Museum	City	State	ZIP	Phone	Fax
Bennington Museum 75 Main St *Web:* www.bennington.com	Bennington	VT	05201	802-447-1571	442-8305
ECHO at the Leahy Ctr 1 College St *TF:* 877-324-6386 ■ *Web:* www.echovermont.org	Burlington	VT	05401	802-864-1848	864-6832
Fairbanks Museum & Planetarium 1302 Main St *Web:* www.fairbanksmuseum.org	Saint Johnsbury	VT	05819	802-748-2372	748-1893

				Phone	Fax
Lake Champlain Maritime Museum 4472 Basin Harbor Rd *Web:* www.lcmm.org	Vergennes	VT	05491	802-475-2022	475-2953
National Museum of the Morgan Horse 122 Bostwick Rd PO Box 700 *Web:* www.morganmuseum.org	Shelburne	VT	05482	802-985-8665	985-5242
Robert Hull Fleming Museum 61 Colchester Ave University of Vermont *Web:* www.uvm.edu	Burlington	VT	05405	802-656-0750	656-8059
Rokeby Museum 4334 Rt 7 *Web:* www.rokeby.org	Ferrisburg	VT	05456	802-877-3406	877-3406
Shelburne Museum 5555 Shelburne Rd *Web:* www.shelburnemuseum.org	Shelburne	VT	05482	802-985-3346	985-2331

VIRGINIA

				Phone	Fax
Agecroft Hall 4305 Sulgrave Rd *Web:* www.agecrofthall.com	Richmond	VA	23221	804-353-4241	353-2151
Alexandria Archaeology Museum 105 N Union St Suite 327 *Web:* www.alexandriava.gov/historic/archaeology	Alexandria	VA	22314	703-838-4399	838-6491
Alexandria Black History Museum 902 Wythe St *Web:* www.alexandriava.gov/historic/blackhistory	Alexandria	VA	22314	703-838-4356	706-3999
Anderson Gallery 907 1/2 W Franklin St *Web:* www.vcu.edu	Richmond	VA	23284	804-828-1522	828-8585
Arlington Historical Museum 1805 S Arlington Ridge Rd *Web:* www.arlingtonhistoricalsociety.org	Arlington	VA	22202	703-892-4204	
Atlantic Wildfowl Heritage Museum 1113 Atlantic Ave *Web:* www.awhm.org	Virginia Beach	VA	23451	757-437-8432	437-9055
Beth Ahabah Museum & Archives 1109 W Franklin St *Web:* www.bethahabah.org	Richmond	VA	23220	804-353-2668	358-3451
Black History Museum & Cultural Center of Virginia 00 Clay St *Web:* www.blackhistorymuseum.org	Richmond	VA	23219	804-780-9093	780-9107
Carlyle House Historic Park 121 N Fairfax St *Web:* www.nvrpa.org	Alexandria	VA	22314	703-549-2997	549-5738
Chimborazo Medical Museum 3215 E Broad St	Richmond	VA	23223	804-226-1981	771-8522
Chrysler Museum of Art 245 W Olney Rd *Web:* www.chrysler.org	Norfolk	VA	23510	757-664-6200	664-6201
DeWitt Wallace Decorative Arts Museum 325 Francis St *TF:* 800-447-8679 ■ *Web:* www.colonialwilliamsburg.com	Williamsburg	VA	23185	757-220-7724	
Drug Enforcement Administration Museum & Visitors Ctr 700 Army Navy Dr *Web:* www.deamuseum.org	Arlington	VA	22202	202-307-3463	307-8956
Edgar Allan Poe Museum 1914 E Main St *TF:* 888-213-2763 ■ *Web:* www.poemuseum.org	Richmond	VA	23223	804-648-5523	648-8729
Endview Plantation 362 Yorktown Rd *Web:* www.endview.org	Newport News	VA	23603	757-887-1862	888-3369
Federal Reserve Money Museum 701 E Byrd St	Richmond	VA	23219	804-697-8135	
Fort Ward Museum & Historic Site 4301 W Braddock Rd *Web:* www.alexandriava.gov/FortWard	Alexandria	VA	22304	703-838-4848	671-7350
Gadsby's Tavern Museum Society 134 N Royal St *Web:* www.gadsbystavernmuseum.us	Alexandria	VA	22314	703-838-4242	838-4270
General Douglas MacArthur Memorial MacArthur Sq *Web:* www.sites.communitylink.org	Norfolk	VA	23510	757-441-2965	441-5389
Hampton Roads Naval Museum 1 Waterside Dr Suite 248 *Web:* www.hrnm.navy.mil	Norfolk	VA	23510	757-322-2987	445-1867
Harrison Museum of African-American Culture 10 S Jefferson St Suite 160 PO Box 12544 *Web:* www.harrisonmuseum.com	Roanoke	VA	24011	540-857-4395	224-1238
Henricus Historical Park Henricus Pk Rd *Web:* www.henricus.org	Richmond	VA	23832	804-706-1340	706-1356
Hermitage Foundation Museum 7637 N Shore Rd *Web:* www.hermitagefoundation.org	Norfolk	VA	23505	757-423-2052	423-1604
History Museum & Historical Society of Western Virginia 1 Market Sq Sq Bldg Suite 3 *Web:* www.history-museum.org	Roanoke	VA	24011	540-342-5770	224-1256
Hunter House Victorian Museum 240 W Freemason St *Web:* www.hunterhousemuseum.org	Norfolk	VA	23510	757-623-9814	623-0097
Lee-Fendall House Museum 614 Oronoco St *Web:* www.leefendallhouse.org	Alexandria	VA	22314	703-548-1789	548-0931
Lightship Museum Water St & London Slip *Web:* www.portsnavalmuseums.com	Portsmouth	VA	23704	757-393-8591	393-5224
Lyceum History Museum 201 S Washington St *Web:* www.alexandriava.gov/Lyceum	Alexandria	VA	22314	703-838-4994	838-4997
Magnolia Grange & Museum 10201 Iron Bridge Rd PO Box 40 *Web:* www.chesterfieldhistory.com	Chesterfield	VA	23832	804-796-7121	777-9643
Mariners' Museum 100 Museum Dr *TF:* 800-581-7245 ■ *Web:* www.marinersmuseum.org	Newport News	VA	23606	757-596-2222	591-7320
Maymont 2201 Shields Dr *Web:* www.maymont.org	Richmond	VA	23219	804-358-7166	358-9994
Moses Myers House 331 Bank St	Norfolk	VA	23510	757-333-1086	333-1089
Muscarelle Museum of Art PO Box 8795 *Web:* www.wm.edu/muscarelle	Williamsburg	VA	23187	757-221-2700	221-2711
Museum of the Confederacy 1201 E Clay St *Web:* www.moc.org	Richmond	VA	23219	804-649-1861	644-7150
National Firearms Museum 11250 Waples Mill Rd *Web:* www.nrahq.org/shooting/museum	Fairfax	VA	22030	703-267-1600	267-3913
National Museum of the Marine Corps 18900 Jefferson Davis Hwy *TF:* 877-635-1775 ■ *Web:* www.usmcmuseum.org	Triangle	VA	22172	703-221-1581	221-2988
NAUTICUS the National Maritime Ctr 1 Waterside Dr *TF:* 800-664-1080 ■ *Web:* www.nauticus.org	Norfolk	VA	23510	757-664-1000	623-1287
Newsome House Museum & Cultural Ctr 2803 Oak Ave *Web:* www.newsomehouse.org	Newport News	VA	23607	757-247-2360	926-6754
Old City Cemetery Museums & Arboretum 401 Taylor St *Web:* www.gravegarden.org	Lynchburg	VA	24501	434-847-1465	856-2004
Old Coast Guard Station 2401 Atlantic Ave *Web:* www.oldcoastguardstation.com	Virginia Beach	VA	23451	757-422-1587	491-8609
Old Guard Museum Sheridan Ave Fort Myer Bldg 249	Arlington	VA	22211	703-696-6670	696-4256
Portsmouth Naval Shipyard Museum 2 High St *Web:* www.portsnavalmuseums.com	Portsmouth	VA	23704	757-393-8591	393-5224
Richmond National Battlefield Park 3215 E Broad St *Web:* www.nps.gov	Richmond	VA	23223	804-226-1981	771-8522
Saint Dennis Chapel Museum 609 Brown Ave	Hopewell	VA	23860	804-458-4682	458-7900
Salem Museum 801 E Main St *Web:* www.salemmuseum.org	Salem	VA	24153	540-389-6760	389-6760
Science Museum of Western Virginia 1 Market Sq *Web:* www.smwv.org	Roanoke	VA	24011	540-342-5710	224-1240
Sherwood Forest Plantation 14501 John Tyler Memorial Hwy *Web:* www.sherwoodforest.org	Charles City	VA	23030	804-829-5377	829-2947
Stabler-Leadbeater Apothecary Museum 105-107 S Fairfax St *Web:* www.alexandriava.gov/Apothecary	Alexandria	VA	22314	703-838-3852	836-3713
Taubman Museum of Art 110 Salem Ave Se	Roanoke	VA	24011	540-342-5760	342-5798
US Army Transportation Museum 300 Washington Blvd *Web:* www.transchool.eustis.army.mil/Museum/Museum.html	Fort Eustis	VA	23604	757-878-1182	878-5656
US Patent & Trademark Museum 600 Dulany St Suite IC65 **Fax Area Code:* 703	Alexandria	VA	22314	571-272-0095	706-0484*
Valentine Richmond History Ctr 1015 E Clay St *Web:* www.richmondhistorycenter.com	Richmond	VA	23219	804-649-0711	643-3510
Virginia Aquarium & Marine Science Center 717 General Booth Blvd *Web:* www.virginiaaquarium.com/Pages/default.aspx	Virginia Beach	VA	23451	757-385-3474	
Virginia Aviation Museum 5701 Huntsman Rd *Web:* www.vam.smv.org	Richmond	VA	23250	804-236-3622	236-3623
Virginia Historical Society Museum of Virginia History 428 N Blvd *Web:* www.vahistorical.org	Richmond	VA	23220	804-358-4901	355-2399
Virginia Holocaust Museum 2000 E Cary St *Web:* www.va-holocaust.com	Richmond	VA	23223	804-257-5400	257-4314
Virginia Living Museum 524 J Clyde Morris Blvd *Web:* www.thevlm.org	Newport News	VA	23601	757-595-1900	599-4897
Virginia Museum of Fine Arts 200 N Blvd *Web:* www.vmfa.state.va.us	Richmond	VA	23220	804-340-1400	340-1548
Virginia Museum of Transportation 303 Norfolk Ave *Web:* www.vmt.org	Roanoke	VA	24016	540-342-5670	342-6898
Virginia War Museum 9285 Warwick Blvd *Web:* www.warmuseum.org	Newport News	VA	23607	757-247-8523	247-8627
Watermen's Museum 309 Water St *Web:* www.watermens.org	Yorktown	VA	23690	757-887-2641	888-2089
Wilton House Museum 215 S Wilton Rd *Web:* www.wiltonhousemuseum.org	Richmond	VA	23226	804-282-5936	288-9805

WASHINGTON

				Phone	Fax
Bellevue Arts Museum 510 Bellevue Way NE *Web:* www.bellevuearts.org	Bellevue	WA	98004	425-519-0770	637-1799
Bigelow House Museum 918 Glass Ave NE *Web:* www.bigelowhouse.org	Olympia	WA	98506	360-753-1215	
Burke Museum of Natural History & Culture University of Washington 17th Ave NE & NE 45th St *Web:* www.burkemuseum.org	Seattle	WA	98195	206-543-5590	685-3039
Center for Wooden Boats 1010 Valley St *Web:* www.cwb.org	Seattle	WA	98109	206-382-2628	382-2699
Clark County Historical Museum 1511 Main St	Vancouver	WA	98660	360-993-5679	993-5683
DuPont Historical Museum 207 Barksdale Ave *Web:* www.dupontmuseum.com	Dupont	WA	98327	253-964-2399	964-3554
Fireworks Fine Crafts Gallery 3307 Utah Ave S *TF:* 800-505-8882 ■ *Web:* www.fireworksgallery.net	Seattle	WA	98134	206-682-8707	467-6366
Fort Lewis Military Museum Fort Lewis Bldg 4320 *Web:* www.lewis.army.mil/DPTMS/POMFI/museum.htm	Fort Lewis	WA	98433	253-967-7207	966-3029
Foss Waterway Seaport 705 Dock St *Web:* www.fosswaterwayseaport.org	Tacoma	WA	98402	253-272-2750	273-3023
Frye Art Museum 704 Terry Ave *Web:* www.fryeart.org	Seattle	WA	98104	206-622-9250	223-1707
Henderson House Museum 602 Deschutes Way SW	Tumwater	WA	98501	360-754-4217	
Henry Art Gallery University of Washington 15th Ave NE & NE 41st St *Web:* www.henryart.org	Seattle	WA	98195	206-543-2281	685-3123

Museum	City	State	Zip	Phone	Fax
Jundt Art Museum 202 E Cataldo Ave *Web:* www.gonzaga.edu	Spokane	WA	99258	509-313-6611	313-5525
Karpeles Manuscript Library Museum 407 S 'G' St *Web:* www.rain.org	Tacoma	WA	98405	253-383-2575	572-6044
Lacey Museum 829 1/2 Lacey St SE	Lacey	WA	98503	360-438-0209	
Meeker Mansion 312 Spring St *Web:* www.meekermansion.org	Puyallup	WA	98372	253-848-1770	
Museum of Flight 9404 E Marginal Way S *Web:* www.museumofflight.org	Seattle	WA	98108	206-764-5700	764-5707
Museum of Glass 1801 Dock St *TF:* 866-468-7386 ■ *Web:* www.museumofglass.org	Tacoma	WA	98402	253-284-4750	369-1769
Museum of History & Industry 2700 24th Ave E *Web:* www.seattlehistory.org	Seattle	WA	98112	206-324-1125	324-1346
Nordic Heritage Museum 3014 NW 67th St *Web:* www.nordicmuseum.com	Seattle	WA	98117	206-789-5707	789-3271
Northwest Museum of Arts & Culture 2316 W 1st Ave *Web:* www.northwestmuseum.org	Spokane	WA	99204	509-456-3931	363-5303
Northwest Railway Museum 38625 SE King St PO Box 459 *Web:* www.trainmuseum.org	Snoqualmie	WA	98065	425-888-0373	888-9311
Odyssey Maritime Discovery Ctr 2205 Alaskan Way Pier 66 *Web:* www.ody.org	Seattle	WA	98121	206-374-4000	374-4002
Olympic Flight Museum 7637A Old Hwy 99 SE *Web:* www.olympicflightmuseum.com	Olympia	WA	98501	360-705-3925	
Pacific Science Ctr 200 2nd Ave N *Web:* www.pacsci.org	Seattle	WA	98109	206-443-2001	443-3631
Pearson Air Museum 1115 E 5th St	Vancouver	WA	98661	360-694-7026	694-0824
Port Townsend Marine Science Ctr 532 Battery Way *TF:* 800-566-3932 ■ *Web:* www.ptmsc.org	Port Townsend	WA	98368	360-385-5582	385-7248
Seattle Art Museum 1300 1st Ave *Web:* www.seattleartmuseum.org	Seattle	WA	98101	206-625-8900	654-3135
Seattle Asian Art Museum 1400 E Prospect St Volunteer Pk *Web:* www.seattleartmuseum.org	Seattle	WA	98112	206-654-3206	654-3191
Tacoma Art Museum 1701 Pacific Ave *Web:* www.tacomaartmuseum.org	Tacoma	WA	98402	253-272-4258	627-1898
Tenino Depot Museum 399 Pk Ave W	Tenino	WA	98589	360-264-4321	
Two Rivers Heritage Museum 001 Durgan St	Washougal	WA	98671	360-835-8742	
Washington State Capital Museum 211 21st Ave SW *Web:* www.wshs.org/scmoc	Olympia	WA	98501	360-753-2580	586-8322
Washington State History Museum 1911 Pacific Ave *TF:* 888-238-4373 ■ *Web:* www.wshs.org/wshm	Tacoma	WA	98402	253-272-3500	272-9518
Wing Luke Asian Museum 719 S King St *Web:* www.wingluke.org	Seattle	WA	98104	206-623-5124	623-4559
World Kite Museum & Hall of Fame 303 Sid Snyder Dr *Web:* www.worldkitemuseum.com	Long Beach	WA	98631	360-642-4020	642-4020

WEST VIRGINIA

Museum	City	State	Zip	Phone	Fax
Avampato Discovery Museum 1 Clay Sq *Web:* theclaycenter.org	Charleston	WV	25301	304-561-3547	561-3598
Challenger Learning Ctr 316 Washington Ave Wheeling Jesuit University *TF:* 800-624-6992 ■ *Web:* www.wju.edu/clc	Wheeling	WV	26003	304-243-4325	243-2497
Huntington Museum of Art Inc 2033 McCoy Rd *Web:* www.hmoa.org	Huntington	WV	25701	304-529-2701	529-7447
Kruger Street Toy & Train Museum 144 Kruger St *TF:* 877-242-8133 ■ *Web:* www.toyandtrain.com	Wheeling	WV	26003	304-242-8133	242-1925
Marks Toy Museum 915 2nd St *Web:* www.marxtoymuseum.com	Moundsville	WV	26041	304-845-6022	
Morgantown Glass Museum 1628 Mileground Rd *Web:* www.morgantownglassmuseum.com	Morgantown	WV	26505	304-291-2957	
Museums of Oglebay Institute 1330 National Rd *TF:* 800-624-6988 ■ *Web:* www.oionline.com	Wheeling	WV	26003	304-242-7272	
West Virginia State Museum 1900 Kanawha Blvd E The Cultural Ctr *Web:* www.wvculture.org/museum	Charleston	WV	25305	304-558-0220	558-2779

WISCONSIN

Museum	City	State	Zip	Phone	Fax
Charles Allis Art Museum 1801 N Prospect Ave *Web:* www.cavtmuseums.org	Milwaukee	WI	53202	414-278-8295	278-0335
Chazen Museum of Art 800 University Ave University of Wisconsin *Web:* www.chazen.wisc.edu	Madison	WI	53706	608-263-2246	263-8188
Circus World Museum 550 Water St *TF:* 866-693-1500 ■ *Web:* www.circusworldmuseum.com	Baraboo	WI	53913	608-356-8341	356-1800
Discovery World 500 N Harbor Dr *Web:* www.pierwisconsin.org	Milwaukee	WI	53202	414-765-9966	765-0311
EAA AirVenture Museum 3000 Poberezny Rd *Web:* www.airventuremuseum.org	Oshkosh	WI	54902	920-426-4800	426-6560
Fairlawn Museum 906 E 2nd St *Web:* www.superiorpublicmuseums.org	Superior	WI	54880	715-394-5712	394-2043
Greene Memorial Museum 3209 N Maryland Ave Lapham Hall UWM Campus *Web:* www.uwm.edu	Milwaukee	WI	53211	414-229-4561	229-5452
Hazelwood Historic Home Museum 1008 S Monroe Ave *Web:* www.browncohistoricalsoc.org	Green Bay	WI	54301	920-437-1840	455-4518
International Clown Hall of Fame Inc 640 S 84th St Suite 526 *Web:* www.theclownmuseum.org	West Allis	WI	53203	414-290-0105	290-0106
Kenosha Public Museum 5500 1st Ave *Web:* www.kenosha.org	Kenosha	WI	53140	262-653-4140	653-4437
Madison Geology Museum 1215 W Dayton St University of Wisconsin Weeks Hall *Web:* www.geologymuseum.org	Madison	WI	53706	608-262-2399	262-0693
Milwaukee Art Museum 700 N Art Museum Dr *Web:* www.mam.org	Milwaukee	WI	53202	414-224-3200	271-7588
Milwaukee Public Museum 800 W Wells St *Web:* www.mpm.edu	Milwaukee	WI	53233	414-278-2700	319-4656
Mitchell Gallery of Flight 5300 S Howell Ave General Mitchell International Airport *Web:* www.mitchellgallery.org	Milwaukee	WI	53207	414-747-5300	747-4525
National Railroad Museum 2285 S Broadway St *Web:* www.nationalrrmuseum.org	Green Bay	WI	54304	920-437-7623	437-1291
Neville Public Museum of Brown County 210 Museum Pl *Web:* www.nevillepublicmuseum.org	Green Bay	WI	54303	920-448-4460	448-4458
Old World Wisconsin W372 S9727 Hwy 67 PO Box 69 *Web:* www.wisconsinhistory.org/oww	Eagle	WI	53119	262-594-6301	594-6342
Oshkosh Public Museum 1331 Algoma Blvd *Web:* www.oshkoshmuseum.org	Oshkosh	WI	54901	920-236-5799	424-4738
Patrick & Beatrice Haggerty Museum of Art 13th & Clybourn Sts Marquette University *Web:* www.marquette.edu/haggerty	Milwaukee	WI	53223	414-288-7290	288-5415
Villa Terrace Decorative Arts Museum & Gardens 2220 N Terrace Ave *Web:* www.villaterracemuseum.org	Milwaukee	WI	53202	414-271-3656	271-3986
Wisconsin Black Historical Society Museum 2620 W Ctr St *Web:* www.wbhsm.org	Milwaukee	WI	53206	414-372-7677	372-4888
Wisconsin Historical Museum 30 N Carroll St *Web:* www.wisconsinhistory.org/museum	Madison	WI	53703	608-264-6555	264-6575
Wisconsin Maritime Museum 75 Maritime Dr *TF:* 866-724-2356 ■ *Web:* www.wisconsinmaritime.org	Manitowoc	WI	54220	920-684-0218	684-0219
Wisconsin Veterans Museum 30 W Mifflin St *Web:* museum.dva.state.wi.us	Madison	WI	53703	608-264-6086	264-7615

WYOMING

Museum	City	State	Zip	Phone	Fax
Buffalo Bill Historical Ctr 720 Sheridan Ave *Web:* www.bbhc.org	Cody	WY	82414	307-587-4771	587-5714
Cheyenne Depot Museum 121 W 15th St 1 Depot Sq *Web:* www.cheyennedepotmuseum.org	Cheyenne	WY	82001	307-632-3905	632-0614
Cheyenne Frontier Days Old West Museum 4610 N Carey Ave PO Box 2720 *Web:* www.oldwestmuseum.org	Cheyenne	WY	82001	307-778-7290	778-7288
FE Warren Heritage Museum 7405 Marne Loop Warren AFB Bldg 210 *Web:* www.pawnee.com	Fort Warren AFB	WY	82005	307-773-2980	773-2791
Fort Caspar Museum 4001 Fort Caspar Rd *Web:* www.casperwy.gov	Casper	WY	82604	307-235-8462	235-8464
Geological Museum 1000 E University Ave	Laramie	WY	82071	307-766-4227	766-6679
Jackson Hole Historical Society & Museum 105 Mercill *Web:* www.jacksonholehistory.org	Jackson	WY	83001	307-733-9605	739-9019
Laramie Plains Museum 603 E Ivinson St *Web:* www.laramiemuseum.org	Laramie	WY	82070	307-742-4448	
Museum of the Mountain Man 700 E Hennick St *TF:* 877-686-6266 ■ *Web:* www.pinedaleonline.com	Pinedale	WY	82941	307-367-4101	367-6768
National Museum of Wildlife Art 2820 Rungius Rd PO Box 6825 *TF:* 800-313-9553 ■ *Web:* www.wildlifeart.org	Jackson	WY	83002	307-733-5771	733-5787
Nelson Museum of the West 1714 Carey Ave *Web:* www.nelsonmuseum.com	Cheyenne	WY	82001	307-635-7670	778-3926
Nicolaysen Art Museum 400 E Collins Dr *Web:* www.thenic.org	Casper	WY	82601	307-235-5247	235-0923
Ripley's Believe It or Not! Museum 140 N Cache St *Web:* www.ripleyattractions.com	Jackson Hole	WY	83001	307-734-0000	734-0078
Sweetwater County Historical Museum 3 E Flaming Gorge Way *Web:* www.sweetwatermuseum.org	Green River	WY	82935	307-872-6435	872-3234
Werner Wildlife Museum 405 E 15th St	Casper	WY	82601	307-235-2108	
Wyoming Dinosaur Ctr 110 Carter Ranch Rd *TF:* 800-455-3466 ■ *Web:* www.wyodino.org	Thermopolis	WY	82443	307-864-2997	864-5762
Wyoming State Museum 2301 Central Ave *Web:* www.wyomuseum.state.wy.us	Cheyenne	WY	82002	307-777-7022	777-5375

YUKON

Museum	City	State	Zip	Phone	Fax
MacBride Museum 1124 1st Ave *Web:* www.macbridemuseum.com	Whitehorse	YT	Y1A1A4	867-667-2709	633-6607

524 MUSEUMS - CHILDREN'S

Children's Museums Are Organized Alphabetically By States.

Museum	City	State	Zip	Phone	Fax
Children's Hands-On Museum 2213 University Blvd *TF:* 877-349-4235 ■ *Web:* www.chomonline.org	Tuscaloosa	AL	35401	205-349-4235	349-4276

	City	State	Zip	Phone	Fax
EarlyWorks Children's Museum 404 Madison St *Web:* www.earlyworks.com/earlyworks.html	Huntsville	AL	35801	256-564-8100	564-8151
Gulf Coast Exploreum Science Ctr 65 Government St *TF:* 877-625-4386 ■ *Web:* www.exploreum.net	Mobile	AL	36602	251-208-6883	208-6889
Sci-Quest Hands on Science Ctr 102-D Wynn Dr *Web:* www.sci-quest.org	Huntsville	AL	35805	256-837-0606	837-4536
Tucson Children's Museum 200 S 6th Ave *Web:* www.tucsonchildrensmuseum.org	Tucson	AZ	85702	520-884-7511	792-0639
Bay Area Discovery Museum 557 McReynolds Rd *Web:* www.baykidsmuseum.org	Sausalito	CA	94965	415-339-3900	339-3905
Bowers Kidseum 1802 N Main St *Web:* www.bowers.org/kidseum.php/aboutus/directions	Santa Ana	CA	92706	714-480-1520	480-0053
Children's Discovery Museum of San Jose 180 Woz Way *Web:* www.cdm.org	San Jose	CA	95110	408-298-5437	298-6826
Children's Discovery Museum of the Desert 71701 Gerald Ford Dr *Web:* www.cdmod.org	Rancho Mirage	CA	92270	760-321-0602	321-1605
Children's Museum of Stockton 402 W Weber Ave *Web:* www.stocktongov.com	Stockton	CA	95202	209-465-4386	465-4394
Discovery Ctr 1944 N Winery Ave *Web:* www.thediscoverycenter.net	Fresno	CA	93703	559-251-5533	251-5531
Discovery Museum Science & Space Ctr 3615 Auburn Blvd *Web:* www.thediscovery.org	Sacramento	CA	95821	916-485-8836	575-3925
Gull Wings Children's Museum 418 W 4th St *Web:* www.gullwings.org	Oxnard	CA	93030	805-483-3005	483-3226
Lori Brock Children's Museum 3801 Chester Ave	Bakersfield	CA	93301	661-852-5000	322-6415
Museum of Children's Art 538 9th St Suite 210 *Web:* www.mocha.org	Oakland	CA	94607	510-465-8770	465-0772
My Museum 601 Wave St Suite 100 *Web:* www.mymuseum.org	Monterey	CA	93940	831-649-6444	649-1304
Sacramento History Museum 101 'I' St *Web:* www.historicoldsac.org/museum/default.asp	Sacramento	CA	95814	916-808-7059	264-5100
Youth Science Institute 296 Garden Hill Dr *Web:* www.ysi-ca.org	Los Gatos	CA	95032	408-356-4945	358-3683
Zeum 221 4th St *Web:* www.zeum.org	San Francisco	CA	94103	415-820-3320	820-3330
Children's Museum of Denver 2121 Children's Museum Dr *Web:* www.mychildsmuseum.org	Denver	CO	80211	303-433-7444	433-9520
Children's Museum of Durango 802 E 2nd Ave 2nd Fl *Web:* www.childsmuseum.org	Durango	CO	81301	970-259-9234	259-6320
Connecticut Children's Museum 22 Wall St *Web:* www.childrensbuilding.org	New Haven	CT	06511	203-562-5437	787-9414
Discovery Creek Children's Museum of Washington 2233 Wisconsin Ave NW Suite 410	Washington	DC	20007	202-488-0627	
Children's Museum 498 Crawford Blvd *Web:* www.cmboca.org	Boca Raton	FL	33432	561-368-6875	395-7764
Children's Science Explorium 300 S Military Trail	Boca Raton	FL	33486	561-347-3913	
G Wiz Hands on Science Museum 1001 Blvd of the Arts *Web:* www.gwiz.org	Sarasota	FL	34236	941-309-4949	906-7292
Great Explorations Children's Museum 1925 4th St N *Web:* www.greatexplorations.org	Saint Petersburg	FL	33704	727-821-8992	823-7287
Miami Children's Museum 980 MacArthur Cswy *Web:* www.miamichildrensmuseum.org	Miami	FL	33132	305-373-5437	373-5431
Young at Art Children's Museum 11584 W SR-84 *Web:* www.youngatartmuseum.org	Davie	FL	33325	954-424-0085	370-5057
Imagine It! Children's Museum of Atlanta 275 Centennial Olympic Pk Dr N W *Web:* www.childrensmuseumatlanta.org	Atlanta	GA	30313	404-223-5144	223-3675
Hawaii Children's Discovery Ctr 111 Ohe St *Web:* www.discoverycenterhawaii.org	Honolulu	HI	96813	808-524-5437	524-5400
Chicago Children's Museum 700 E Grand Ave *Web:* www.chichildrensmuseum.org	Chicago	IL	60611	312-527-1000	527-9082
Discovery Center Museum 711 N Main St *Web:* www.discoverycentermuseum.org	Rockford	IL	61103	815-963-6769	968-0164
Exploration Station-A Children's Museum 459 Kennedy Dr *Web:* www.exploration-station.org	Bourbonnais	IL	60914	815-933-9905	928-6054
Orpheum Children's Science Museum 346 N Neil St *Web:* www.orpheumkids.com	Champaign	IL	61820	217-352-5895	352-8610
Hannah Lindahl Children's Museum 1402 S Main St *Web:* www.hlcm.org	Mishawaka	IN	46544	574-254-4540	254-4585
HealthWorks! Kids' Museum 111 W Jefferson St Suite 200 *Web:* www.qualityoflife.org/healthworks	South Bend	IN	46601	574-287-5437	239-6459
Koch Family Children's Museum of Evansville 22 SE 5th St *Web:* www.cmoekids.org	Evansville	IN	47708	812-477-4929	477-4339
Muncie Children's Museum 515 S High St *Web:* www.munciechildrensmuseum.com	Muncie	IN	47305	765-286-1660	286-1662
Children's Museum of Kansas City 4601 State Ave *Web:* www.kidmuzm.org	Kansas City	KS	66102	913-287-8888	
Exploration Place 300 N McLean Blvd *TF:* 877-904-1444 ■ *Web:* www.exploration.org	Wichita	KS	67203	316-263-3373	263-4545
Kansas Cosmosphere & Space Ctr 1100 N Plum St *TF:* 800-397-0330 ■ *Web:* www.cosmo.org	Hutchinson	KS	67501	620-662-2305	662-3693
Explorium of Lexington 440 W Short St *Web:* www.explorium.com	Lexington	KY	40507	859-258-3253	258-3255
Children's Museum of Acadiana 201 E Congress St *Web:* www.childrensmuseumofacadiana.com/home	Lafayette	LA	70501	337-232-8500	232-8167
Children's Museum of Lake Charles 327 Broad St *Web:* www.swlakids.org	Lake Charles	LA	70601	337-433-9420	433-0144
Louisiana Children's Museum 420 Julia St *Web:* www.lcm.org	New Orleans	LA	70130	504-586-0725	529-3666
Children's Discovery Museum 265 Water St *Web:* www.childrensdiscoverymuseum.org	Augusta	ME	04330	207-622-2209	623-8389
Children's Museum of Maine 142 Free St PO Box 4041 *Web:* www.childrensmuseumofme.org	Portland	ME	04101	207-828-1234	828-5726
Chesapeake Children's Museum 25 Silopanna Rd *Web:* www.theccm.org	Annapolis	MD	21403	410-990-1993	990-1007
Port Discovery Children's Museum in Baltimore 35 Market Pl *Web:* www.portdiscovery.org	Baltimore	MD	21202	410-727-8120	727-3042
Boston Children's Museum 308 Congress St *Web:* www.bostonkids.org	Boston	MA	02210	617-426-6500	426-1944
Cape Cod Children's Museum 577 Great Neck Rd S *Web:* www.capecodchildrensmuseum.org	Mashpee	MA	02649	508-539-8788	539-3285
Cape Cod Discovery Museum 444 Main St	Dennisport	MA	02639	508-398-1600	
Children's Museum at Holyoke 444 Dwight St *Web:* www.childrensmuseumholyoke.org	Holyoke	MA	01040	413-536-7048	533-2999
EcoTarium 222 Harrington Way *Web:* www.ecotarium.org	Worcester	MA	01604	508-929-2700	929-2701
Flint Children's Museum 1602 W University Ave *Web:* www.flintchildrensmuseum.org	Flint	MI	48504	810-767-5437	767-4936
Grand Rapids Children's Museum 22 Sheldon Ave NE *Web:* www.grcm.org	Grand Rapids	MI	49503	616-235-4726	235-4728
Duluth Children's Museum 506 W Michigan St *Web:* www.duluthchildrensmuseum.org	Duluth	MN	55802	218-733-7543	733-7547
Minnesota Children's Museum 10 W 7th St *Web:* www.mcm.org	Saint Paul	MN	55102	651-225-6000	225-6006
Lynn Meadows Discovery Ctr 246 Dolan Ave *Web:* www.lmdc.org	Gulfport	MS	39507	228-897-6039	248-0071
Discovery Center of Springfield 438 E St Louis St *Web:* www.discoverycenter.org	Springfield	MO	65806	417-862-9910	862-6898
Kaleidoscope 2501 McGee St *Web:* www.hallmarkkaleidoscope.com	Kansas City	MO	64108	816-274-8301	274-3148
Magic House Saint Louis Children's Museum 516 S Kirkwood Rd *Web:* www.magichouse.org	Saint Louis	MO	63122	314-822-8900	822-8930
Worldways Children's Museum 15479 Clayton Rd *Web:* www.worldways.org	Ballwin	MO	63011	636-207-7405	207-7407
Lincoln Children's Museum 1420 P St *Web:* www.lincolnchildrensmuseum.org	Lincoln	NE	68508	402-477-0128	477-2004
Omaha Children's Museum 500 S 20th St *Web:* www.ocm.org	Omaha	NE	68102	402-342-6164	342-6165
Children's Museum of Northern Nevada 813 N Carson St *Web:* www.cmnn.org	Carson City	NV	89701	775-884-2226	884-2179
Lied Discovery Children's Museum 833 Las Vegas Blvd N *Web:* www.ldcm.org	Las Vegas	NV	89101	702-382-3445	382-0592
Children's Museum of New Hampshire 6 Washington St *Web:* www.childrens-museum.org	Dover	NH	03820	603-742-2002	834-6275
Santa Fe Children's Museum 1050 Old Pecos Trail *Web:* www.santafechildrensmuseum.org	Santa Fe	NM	87505	505-989-8359	989-7506
Brooklyn Children's Museum 145 Brooklyn Ave *Web:* www.bchildmus.org	Brooklyn	NY	11213	718-735-4400	604-7442
Children's Museum of History Natural History Science & Technology 311 Main St *Web:* www.museum4kids.net	Utica	NY	13501	315-724-6129	724-6120
Children's Museum of Manhattan 212 W 83rd St *Web:* www.cmom.org	New York	NY	10024	212-721-1223	721-1127
Children's Museum of the Arts 182 Lafayette St *Web:* www.cmany.org	New York	NY	10013	212-274-0986	274-1776
Discovery Center of the Southern Tier 60 Morgan Rd *Web:* www.thediscoverycenter.org	Binghamton	NY	13903	607-773-8661	773-8019
Explore & More-A Children's Museum 300 Gleed Ave *Web:* www.exploreandmore.org	East Aurora	NY	14052	716-655-5131	655-5466
Long Island Children's Museum 11 Davis Ave *Web:* www.licm.org	Garden City	NY	11530	516-224-5800	302-8188
Staten Island Children's Museum 1000 Richmond Terr at Snug Harbor *Web:* www.statenislandkids.org	Staten Island	NY	10301	718-273-2060	273-2836
Discovery Place 301 N Tryon St *TF:* 800-935-0553 ■ *Web:* www.discoveryplace.org	Charlotte	NC	28202	704-372-6261	337-2670
Greensboro Children's Museum 220 N Church St *Web:* www.gcmuseum.com	Greensboro	NC	27401	336-574-2898	574-3810
Rocky Mount Children's Museum 270 Gay St *Web:* www.ci.rocky-mount.nc.us	Rocky Mount	NC	27804	252-972-1167	972-1535
Yunker Farm Children's Museum 1201 28th Ave N *Web:* www.childrensmuseum-yunker.org	Fargo	ND	58102	701-232-6102	232-4605

Name / Address	City	State	ZIP	Phone	Fax
Children's Museum of Cleveland 10730 Euclid Ave *Web:* www.clevelandchildrensmuseum.org	Cleveland	OH	44106	216-791-7114	791-8838
Cincinnati Fire Museum 315 W Ct St *Web:* www.cincyfiremuseum.com	Cincinnati	OH	45202	513-621-5553	621-1456
Cinergy Children's Museum 1301 Western Ave Cincinnati Museum Ctr *TF:* 800-733-2077 ■ *Web:* www.cincymuseum.org	Cincinnati	OH	45203	513-287-7000	287-7079
AC Gilbert's Discovery Village 116 Marion St NE *Web:* www.acgilbert.org	Salem	OR	97301	503-371-3631	316-3485
Portland Children's Museum 4015 SW Canyon Rd *Web:* www.portlandcm.org	Portland	OR	97221	503-223-6500	223-6600
Science Factory Children's Museum & Planetarium 2300 Leo Harris Pkwy *Web:* www.sciencefactory.org	Eugene	OR	97401	541-682-7888	484-9027
Children's Museum of Pittsburgh 10 Children's Way *Web:* www.pittsburghkids.org	Pittsburgh	PA	15212	412-322-5059	322-4932
ExpERIEnce Children's Museum 420 French St *Web:* www.eriechildrensmuseum.org	Erie	PA	16507	814-453-3743	459-9735
Explore & More Hands-On Children's Museum 20 E High St *Web:* www.exploreandmore.com	Gettysburg	PA	17325	717-337-9151	
Hands-On House Children's Museum of Lancaster 721 Landis Valley Rd *Web:* www.handsonhouse.org	Lancaster	PA	17601	717-569-5437	581-9283
Please Touch Museum 210 N 21st St *Web:* www.pleasetouchmuseum.org	Philadelphia	PA	19103	215-963-0667	963-0424
Providence Children's Museum 100 S St *Web:* www.childrenmuseum.org	Providence	RI	02903	401-273-5437	273-1004
Children's Museum of South Carolina 2501 N Kings Hwy *Web:* www.cmsckids.org	Myrtle Beach	SC	29577	843-946-9469	946-7011
Children's Museum of the Lowcountry 25 Ann St *Web:* www.explorecml.org	Charleston	SC	29403	843-853-8962	853-1042
EdVenture Children's Museum 211 Gervais St *Web:* www.edventure.org	Columbia	SC	29201	803-779-3100	779-3144
Children's Museum of Memphis 2525 Central Ave *Web:* www.cmom.com	Memphis	TN	38104	901-458-2678	458-4033
Children's Museum of Oak Ridge 461 W Outer Dr *Web:* www.childrensmuseumofoakridge.org	Oak Ridge	TN	37830	865-482-1074	481-4889
Creative Discovery Museum 321 Chestnut St *Web:* www.cdmfun.org	Chattanooga	TN	37402	423-756-2738	267-9344
East Tennessee Discovery Ctr 516 N Beaman St Chilhowee Pk *Web:* www.etdiscovery.org	Knoxville	TN	37914	865-594-1494	594-1469
Hands On! Regional Museum 315 E Main St *Web:* www.handsonmuseum.org	Johnson City	TN	37601	423-434-4263	928-6915
Austin Children's Museum 201 Colorado St *Web:* www.austinkids.org	Austin	TX	78701	512-472-2499	472-2495
Children's Museum of Houston 1500 Binz St *Web:* www.cmhouston.org	Houston	TX	77004	713-522-1138	522-5747
Don Harrington Discovery Ctr 1200 Streit Dr *TF:* 800-784-9548 ■ *Web:* www.dhdc.org	Amarillo	TX	79106	806-355-9547	355-5703
Grace Museum 102 Cypress St *Web:* www.thegracemuseum.org	Abilene	TX	79601	325-673-4587	675-5993
Imaginarium of South Texas 5300 San Dario Ave Suite 505 *Web:* www.imaginariumstx.org	Laredo	TX	78040	956-728-0404	725-7776
Museum of Nature & Science 3535 Grand Ave Suite 308 *Web:* www.natureandscience.org	Dallas	TX	75210	214-428-5555	428-2003
San Antonio Children's Museum 305 E Houston St *Web:* www.sakids.org	San Antonio	TX	78205	210-212-4453	242-1313
Science Place The 1318 2nd Ave in Fair Pk *Web:* www.natureandscience.org	Dallas	TX	75210	214-428-5555	428-4356
Discovery Gateway 444 W 100 S *Web:* www.discoverygateway.org	Salt Lake City	UT	84101	801-456-5437	456-5440
Treehouse Museum 347 22nd St *Web:* www.treehousemuseum.org	Ogden	UT	84401	801-394-9663	528-5128
Children's Museum of Richmond 2626 W Broad St *TF:* 877-295-2667 ■ *Web:* www.c-mor.org	Richmond	VA	23220	804-474-7000	474-7099
Children's Museum of Virginia 221 High St *Web:* www.childrensmuseumva.com	Portsmouth	VA	23704	757-393-5258	393-8083
Virginia Discovery Museum 524 E Main St PO Box 1128 *Web:* www.vadm.org	Charlottesville	VA	22902	434-977-1025	977-9681
Children's Museum of Tacoma 936 Broadway *Web:* www.childrensmuseumoftacoma.org	Tacoma	WA	98402	253-627-6031	627-2436
Children's Museum Seattle 305 Harrison St *Web:* www.thechildrensmuseum.org	Seattle	WA	98109	206-441-1768	448-0910
Hands On Children's Museum 106 11th Ave SW *Web:* www.hocm.org	Olympia	WA	98501	360-956-0818	754-8626
Betty Brinn Children's Museum 929 E Wisconsin Ave *Web:* www.bbcmkids.org	Milwaukee	WI	53202	414-390-5437	291-0906
Madison Children's Museum 100 N Hamilton St *Web:* www.madisonchildrensmuseum.org	Madison	WI	53703	608-256-6445	256-3226

525 MUSEUMS & HALLS OF FAME - SPORTS

Name / Address	City	State	ZIP	Phone	Fax
1932 & 1980 Lake Placid Winter Olympic Museum Olympic Ctr 2634 Main St *TF:* 800-462-6236 ■ *Web:* www.orda.org	Lake Placid	NY	12946	518-523-1655	523-9275
Alabama Sports Hall of Fame 2150 Richard Arrington Junior Blvd *Web:* www.ashof.org	Birmingham	AL	35203	205-323-6665	252-2212
Alberta Sports Hall of Fame & Museum 4200 Hwy 2 Suite 102 *Web:* www.albertasportshalloffame.com	Red Deer	AB	T4N1E3	403-341-8614	341-8619
American Museum of Fly Fishing 4104 Main Rd *Web:* www.amff.com	Manchester	VT	05254	802-362-3300	362-3308
American Water Ski Hall of Fame & Museum 1251 Holy Cow Rd *TF:* 800-533-2972 ■ *Web:* www.waterskihalloffame.com	Polk City	FL	33868	863-324-2472	324-3996
Babe Ruth Birthplace Museum 216 Emory St *Web:* www.baberuthmuseum.com	Baltimore	MD	21230	410-727-1539	727-1652
Baseball Hall of Fame 910 S 3rd St *TF:* 888-375-9707 ■ *Web:* www.domeplus.com	Minneapolis	MN	55415	612-375-9707	
Baseball Reliquary PO Box 1850 *Web:* www.baseballreliquary.org	Monrovia	CA	91017	626-791-7647	
Bob Feller Museum 310 Mill St PO Box 95 *TF:* 866-996-2806 ■ *Web:* www.bobfellermuseum.org	Van Meter	IA	50261	515-996-2806	996-2952
Bobby Riggs Tennis Museum 875 Santa Fe Dr *Web:* www.bobbyriggstennis.com	Encinitas	CA	92024	760-753-4705	944-8474
British Columbia Sports Hall of Fame & Museum 999 Canada Pl Suite 200 *Web:* www.bcsportshalloffame.com	Vancouver	BC	V6C3C1	604-647-7414	647-7404
Canada Olympic Hall of Fame & Museum 88 Canada Olympic Rd SW *Web:* www.coda.ca	Calgary	AB	T3B5R5	403-247-5486	286-7213
Canada's Sports Hall of Fame 169 Canada Olympic Rd SW *Web:* www.sportshall.ca	Calgary	AB	T3B5R5	403-776-1040	
Canadian Baseball Hall of Fame & Museum 386 Church St PO Box 1838 *TF:* 877-250-2255 ■ *Web:* www.baseballhalloffame.ca	Saint Marys	ON	N4X1C2	519-284-1838	284-1234
Canadian Football Hall of Fame & Museum 58 Jackson St W *Web:* www.footballhof.com	Hamilton	ON	L8P1L4	905-528-7566	528-9781
Canadian Golf Hall of Fame & Museum Glen Abbey Golf Course 1333 Dorval Dr Suite 1 *TF:* 800-263-0009 ■ *Web:* www.cghf.org	Oakville	ON	L6M4X7	905-849-9700	845-7040
Catskill Fly Fishing Center & Museum 1031 Old Rt 17 PO Box 1295 *Web:* www.cffcm.net	Livingston Manor	NY	12758	845-439-4810	439-3387
College Football Hall of Fame 111 S St Joseph St *TF:* 800-440-3263 ■ *Web:* www.collegefootball.org	South Bend	IN	46601	574-235-9999	235-5720
Colorado Sports Hall of Fame 1701 Mile High Stadium # 500 **Fax Area Code:* 303 ■ *Web:* www.coloradosports.org	Denver	CO	80204	720-258-3888	244-1003*
Delaware Sports Museum & Hall of Fame 801 Shipyard Dr *Web:* www.desports.org	Wilmington	DE	19801	302-425-3263	425-3713
Don Garlits Museums 13700 SW 16th Ave *TF:* 877-271-3278 ■ *Web:* www.garlits.com	Ocala	FL	34473	352-245-8661	245-6895
Eastern Museum of Motor Racing PO Box 688 *Web:* www.emmr.org	Mechanics	PA	17055	717-528-8279	
Florida Air Museum at Sun 'n Fun 4175 Medulla Rd *Web:* www.sun-n-fun.org	Lakeland	FL	33811	863-644-0741	648-9264
Georgia Sports Hall of Fame 301 Cherry St PO Box 4644 *Web:* www.gshf.org	Macon	GA	31201	478-752-1585	752-1587
Green Bay Packers Hall of Fame 1265 Lombardi Ave *TF:* 888-442-7225 ■ *Web:* www.packers.com	Green Bay	WI	54304	920-569-7512	569-7122
Greyhound Hall of Fame 407 S Buckeye Ave *TF:* 800-932-7881 ■ *Web:* www.greyhoundhalloffame.com	Abilene	KS	67410	785-263-3000	263-2604
Harness Racing Museum & Hall of Fame 240 Main St PO Box 590 *Web:* www.harnessmuseum.com	Goshen	NY	10924	845-294-6330	294-3463
Hendrick Motorsports Museum 4400 Papa Joe Hendrick Blvd *TF:* 877-467-4890 ■ *Web:* www.hendrickmotorsports.com	Charlotte	NC	28262	704-455-3400	455-0346
Hockey Hall of Fame 30 Yonge St *Web:* www.hhof.com	Toronto	ON	M5E1X8	416-360-7735	360-1316
IGFA Fishing Hall of Fame & Museum 300 Gulf Stream Way *Web:* www.igfa.org	Dania Beach	FL	33004	954-922-4212	924-4220
Indiana Basketball Hall of Fame 408 Trojan Ln *Web:* www.hoopshall.com	New Castle	IN	47362	765-529-1891	529-0273
Indiana Football Hall of Fame 815 N A St	Richmond	IN	47374	765-966-2235	966-2235
International Bowling Museum & Hall of Fame 111 Stadium Plaza *TF:* 800-966-2695 ■ *Web:* www.bowlingmuseum.com	Saint Louis	MO	63102	314-231-6340	231-4054
International Boxing Hall of Fame Museum 1 Hall of Fame Dr *Web:* www.ibhof.com	Canastota	NY	13032	315-697-7095	697-5356
International Gymnastics Hall of Fame & Museum 2100 NE 52nd St *Web:* www.ighof.com	Oklahoma City	OK	73111	405-602-6664	602-3768
International Hockey Hall of Fame & Museum 277 York St PO Box 82 *Web:* www.ihhof.com	Kingston	ON	K7L4V6	613-544-2355	544-2844
International Jewish Sports Hall of Fame 7922 Turncrest Dr *Web:* www.jewishsports.net	Potomac	MD	20854	301-299-3300	765-9865

Name / Address	City	State	ZIP	Phone	Fax
International Motorsports Hall of Fame & Museum 3198 Speedway Blvd	Talladega	AL	35160	256-362-5002	
Web: www.motorsportshalloffame.com					
International Snowmobile Hall of Fame 25929 County Rd 59	Bovey	MN	55709	218-245-1725	
Web: www.ishof.com					
International Sports Hall of Fame & Olympic Museum PO Box 166	Depoe Bay	OR	97341	541-765-2923	
Web: www.olympicsource.org					
International Swimming Hall of Fame 1 Hall of Fame Dr	Fort Lauderdale	FL	33316	954-462-6536	525-4031
Web: www.ishof.org					
International Tennis Hall of Fame & Museum 194 Bellevue Ave	Newport	RI	02840	401-849-3990	849-8780
TF: 800-457-1144 ■ *Web:* www.tennisfame.com					
International Wrestling Institute & Museum 303 Jefferson St	Waterloo	IA	50701	319-233-0745	233-3477
Web: www.wrestlingmuseum.org					
Ivan Allen Jr Braves Museum & Hall of Fame 755 Hank Aaron Dr	Atlanta	GA	30315	404-614-2310	614-1423
Web: www.bravesmuseum.com					
Jack Nicklaus Museum 2355 Olentangy River Rd	Columbus	OH	43210	614-247-5959	247-5906
Web: www.nicklausmuseum.org					
Kansas Sports Hall of Fame 515 S Wichita	Wichita	KS	67202	316-262-2038	263-2539
Web: www.kshof.org					
Legends of the Game Baseball Museum 1000 Ballpark Way	Arlington	TX	76011	817-273-5023	273-5093
Web: museum.texasrangers.com					
Louisiana Sports Hall of Fame 500 Front St	Natchitoches	LA	71457	318-238-4255	238-4258
Web: www.lasportshall.com					
Louisville Slugger Museum 800 W Main St	Louisville	KY	40202	502-585-5226	585-1179
TF: 877-775-8443 ■ *Web:* www.sluggermuseum.org					
Lovelace Athletic Museum & Hall of Honor Auburn Univ Athletic Dept PO Box 351	Auburn	AL	36831	334-844-0764	844-0847
Web: www.lovelacemuseum.com					
Manitoba Sports Hall of Fame & Museum 145 Pacific Ave	Winnipeg	MB	R3B2Z6	204-925-5736	925-5916
Web: www.halloffame.mb.ca					
Mississippi Sports Hall of Fame & Museum 1152 Lakeland Dr	Jackson	MS	39216	601-982-8264	982-4702
TF: 800-280-3263 ■ *Web:* www.msfame.com					
Missouri Sports Hall of Fame 3861 E Stan Musial Dr	Springfield	MO	65809	417-889-3100	889-2761
TF: 800-498-5678 ■ *Web:* www.mosportshalloffame.com					
Motorcycle Hall of Fame Museum 13515 Yarmouth Dr	Pickerington	OH	43147	614-856-2222	856-2221
TF: 800-262-5646 ■ *Web:* www.ama-cycle.org					
Motorsports Hall of Fame of America 43700 Expo Ctr Dr	Novi	MI	48375	248-349-7223	349-2113
TF: 800-250-7223 ■ *Web:* www.mshf.com					
Muskegon Area Sports Hall of Fame LC Walker Arena 955 4th St	Muskegon	MI	49440	231-726-2939	726-4620
Naismith Memorial Basketball Hall of Fame 1000 W Columbus Ave	Springfield	MA	01105	413-781-6500	781-1939
TF: 877-446-6752 ■ *Web:* www.hoophall.com					
National Art Museum of Sport 850 W Michigan St	Indianapolis	IN	46202	317-274-3627	274-3878
Web: www.namos.iupui.edu					
National Baseball Hall of Fame & Museum 25 Main St	Cooperstown	NY	13326	607-547-7200	547-2044
TF: 888-425-5633 ■ *Web:* www.baseballhalloffame.org					
National Football Foundation & College Hall of Fame 111 S St Joseph St	South Bend	IN	46601	574-235-9999	235-5720
Web: www.collegefootball.org					
National Fresh Water Fishing Hall of Fame 10360 Hall of Fame Dr PO Box 690	Hayward	WI	54843	715-634-4440	634-4440
TF: 866-268-4333 ■ *Web:* www.freshwater-fishing.org					
National Italian American Sports Hall of Fame 1431 W Taylor St	Chicago	IL	60607	312-226-5566	226-5678
Web: www.niashf.org					
National Jousting Hall of Fame 94 Natural Chimneys Ln	Mount Solon	VA	22843	540-350-2510	350-2140
TF: 888-430-2267 ■ *Web:* www.nationaljousting.com					
National Museum of Polo & Hall of Fame 9011 Lake Worth Rd	Lake Worth	FL	33467	561-969-3210	964-8299
Web: www.polomuseum.com					
National Museum of Racing & Hall of Fame 191 Union Ave	Saratoga Springs	NY	12866	518-584-0400	584-4574
TF: 800-562-5394 ■ *Web:* www.racingmuseum.org					
National Polish-American Sports Hall of Fame 11727 Gallagher St	Hamtramck	MI	48212	313-407-3300	876-7724
Web: www.polishsportshof.com					
National Soaring Museum 51 Soaring Hill Dr	Elmira	NY	14903	607-734-3128	732-6745
Web: www.soaringmuseum.org					
National Soccer Hall of Fame 18 Stadium Cir	Oneonta	NY	13820	607-432-3351	432-8429
Web: www.soccerhall.org					
National Softball Hall of Fame & Museum 2801 NE 50th St	Oklahoma City	OK	73111	405-424-5266	424-3855
TF: 800-654-8337 ■ *Web:* www.softball.org/hall_of_fame					
National Sports Foundation PO Box 888886	Atlanta	GA	30356	678-417-0041	417-0043
Web: www.natlsportsfoundation.com					
National Sportscasters & Sportswriters Hall of Fame PO Box 1545	Salisbury	NC	28145	704-633-4275	633-2027
Web: www.nssahalloffame.com					
National Sprint Car Hall of Fame & Museum 1 Sprint Capital Pl	Knoxville	IA	50138	641-842-6176	842-6177
TF: 800-874-4488 ■ *Web:* www.sprintcarhof.com					
National Wrestling Hall of Fame 405 W Hall of Fame Ave	Stillwater	OK	74075	405-377-5243	377-5244
Web: www.wrestlinghalloffame.org					
NCAA Hall of Champions 1 NCAA Plaza 700 W Washington St	Indianapolis	IN	46204	317-917-6222	917-6596
TF: 800-735-6222 ■ *Web:* www.ncaahallofchampions.org					
Negro Leagues Baseball Museum 1616 E 18th St	Kansas City	MO	64108	816-221-1920	221-8424
TF: 888-221-6526 ■ *Web:* www.nlbm.com					
New Brunswick Sports Hall of Fame 503 Queen St PO Box 6000	Fredericton	NB	E3B1B8	506-453-3747	459-0481
Web: www.nbsportshalloffame.nb.ca/sports/default.aspx					
New England Sports Museum 100 Legends Way	Boston	MA	02114	617-624-1235	624-1818
Web: www.sportsmuseum.org					
Nolan Ryan Exhibit Ctr 2925 S Loop 35	Alvin	TX	77511	281-388-1134	388-1135
TF: 800-350-7926 ■ *Web:* www.nolanryanfoundation.org					
North Carolina Auto Racing Hall of Fame 119 Knob Hill Rd Lakeside Pk	Mooresville	NC	28117	704-663-5331	663-6949
Web: www.ncarhof.com					
North Carolina Sports Hall of Fame 5 E Edenton St NC Museum of History	Raleigh	NC	27601	919-807-7900	733-8655
Web: www.ncmuseumofhistory.org					
North Carolina Tennis Hall of Fame 2709 Henry St	Greensboro	NC	27405	336-852-8577	852-7334
Web: www.nctennis.com					
Northwestern Ontario Sports Hall of Fame 219 May St S	Thunder Bay	ON	P7E1B5	807-622-2852	622-2736
Web: www.nwosportshalloffame.com					
Oklahoma Sports Hall of Fame & Jim Thorpe Museum 4040 N Lincoln Blvd	Oklahoma City	OK	73105	405-427-1400	495-7602
Web: www.jimthorpeassoc.org					
Oregon Sports Hall of Fame & Museum 8500 SE McLoughlin Blvd Suite 101	Portland	OR	97222	503-227-7466	235-5688
Web: www.oregonsportshall.com					
Paul W Bryant Museum 300 Paul W Bryant Dr	Tuscaloosa	AL	35487	205-348-4668	348-8883
TF: 866-772-2327 ■ *Web:* www.bryantmuseum.ua.edu					
Peter J McGovern Little League Baseball Museum 539 US Rt 15 Hwy PO Box 3485	South Williamsport	PA	17701	570-326-1921	326-1074
Web: www.littleleague.org/museum					
Philadelphia Jewish Sports Hall of Fame & Adolph & Rose Levis Museum 401 S Broad St	Philadelphia	PA	19147	215-446-3045	790-1042
Web: www.phillyjewishsports.com					
Philadelphia Sports Hall of Fame Foundation 410 Waverly Rd	Wyncote	PA	19095	215-886-6657	
Web: www.phillyhof.org					
Pro Football Hall of Fame 2121 George Halas Dr NW	Canton	OH	44708	330-456-8207	456-8175
Web: www.profootballhof.com					
ProRodeo Hall of Fame & Museum of the American Cowboy 101 ProRodeo Dr	Colorado Springs	CO	80919	719-528-4764	548-4874
Web: www.prorodeo.org					
Roger Maris Museum 3902 13th Ave S PO Box 9978	Fargo	ND	58106	701-282-2222	282-2229
Web: www.rogermarismuseum.com					
Rose Bowl Hall of Fame 391 S Orange Grove Blvd	Pasadena	CA	91184	626-449-4100	449-9066
Web: www.tournamentofroses.com					
Saint Louis Cardinals Hall of Fame 111 Stadium Plaza Dr	Saint Louis	MO	63102	314-231-6340	231-4054
TF: 800-966-2695 ■ *Web:* www.stlouis.cardinals.mlb.com					
Saskatchewan Baseball Hall of Fame & Museum PO Box 1388	Battleford	SK	S0M0E0	306-446-1983	446-0509
Web: www.saskbaseball.ca					
Saskatchewan Sports Hall of Fame & Museum 2205 Victoria Ave	Regina	SK	S4P0S4	306-780-9232	780-9427
Web: www.sshfm.com					
Shanaman Sports Museum of Tacoma 2727 E 'D' St Tacoma Dome	Tacoma	WA	98421	253-272-3663	593-7620
Web: www.tacomasportsmuseum.com					
Skate Canada Hall of Fame 865 Shefford Rd	Ottowa	ON	K1J1H9	613-747-1007	748-5718
Web: www.skatecanada.ca					
Snowmobile Hall of Fame & Museum 8481 State Hwy 70 W	Saint Germain	WI	54558	715-542-4488	542-4477
Web: www.snowmobilehalloffame.com					
Sports Immortals Museum 6830 N Federal Hwy	Boca Raton	FL	33487	561-997-2575	997-6949
Web: www.sportsimmortals.com					
Sports Legends at Camden Yards 301 W Camden St	Baltimore	MD	21201	410-727-1539	727-1652
Web: www.baberuthmuseum.com					
Ted Williams Museum & Hitters Hall of Fame 2455 N Citrus Hills Blvd	Hernando	FL	34442	352-527-6566	527-4163
Web: www.twmuseum.com					
Texas Sports Hall of Fame 1108 S University Parks Dr	Waco	TX	76706	254-756-1633	756-2384
TF: 800-567-9561 ■ *Web:* www.tshof.org					
Trapshooting Hall of Fame & Museum 601 W National Rd	Vandalia	OH	45377	937-898-4638	898-5541
Web: www.traphof.org					
University of Iowa Athletics Hall of Fame KHF Bldg 446	Iowa City	IA	52242	319-384-1031	384-1032
TF: 866-469-2326 ■ *Web:* www.hawkeyesports.com					
US Golf Assn Museum 77 Liberty Corner Rd	Far Hills	NJ	07931	908-234-2300	234-9687
TF: 800-222-8742 ■ *Web:* www.usga.org					
US Hockey Hall of Fame PO Box 657	Eveleth	MN	55734	218-744-5167	744-2590
TF: 800-443-7825 ■ *Web:* www.ushockeyhall.com					
US National Ski Hall of Fame & Museum 610 Palms Ave	Ishpeming	MI	49849	906-485-6323	486-4570
Web: www.skihall.com					
US Olympic Hall of Fame 1750 E Boulder St	Colorado Springs	CO	80909	719-866-4500	866-4728
TF: 888-659-8687 ■ *Web:* www.usoc.org					
Virginia Sports Hall of Fame 206 High St	Portsmouth	VA	23704	757-393-8031	393-8288
Web: www.virginiasportshalloffame.com					
Volleyball Hall of Fame 444 Dwight St	Holyoke	MA	01040	413-536-0926	539-6673
Web: www.volleyhall.org					

				Phone	Fax
Women's Basketball Hall of Fame					
700 Hall of Fame Dr	Knoxville	TN	37915	865-633-9000	633-9294
Web: www.wbhof.com					
World Figure Skating Museum & Hall of Fame					
20 1st St	Colorado Springs	CO	80906	719-635-5200	635-9548
Web: www.worldskatingmuseum.org					
World Golf Hall of Fame					
1 World Golf Pl	Saint Augustine	FL	32092	904-940-4000	
Web: www.wgv.com					
World Sports Humanitarian Hall of Fame					
855 Broad St Lower Level	Boise	ID	83702	208-343-7224	343-0831
Web: www.sportshumanitarian.com					

526 MUSIC DISTRIBUTORS

				Phone	Fax
A-r Editions Inc					
8551 Research Way Suite 180	Middleton	WI	53562	608-836-9000	831-8200
TF: 800-736-0070 ■ *Web:* www.areditions.com					
Allegro Corp 20048 NE San Rafael St	Portland	OR	97230	503-491-8480	491-8488*
**Fax:* Orders ■ *TF:* 800-288-2007 ■ *Web:* www.allegro-music.com					
Alliance Entertainment Corp					
4250 Coral Ridge Dr	Coral Springs	FL	33065	954-255-4000	255-4825
TF: 800-329-7664 ■ *Web:* www.aent.com					
Alternative Distribution Alliance (ADA)					
72 Spring St 12th Fl	New York	NY	10012	212-343-2485	343-2504
TF: 800-239-3232 ■ *Web:* www.ada-music.com					
Baker & Taylor Inc					
2550 W Tyvola Rd Suite 300	Charlotte	NC	28217	704-998-3100	998-3316
TF: 800-775-1800 ■ *Web:* www.btol.com					
BMG Distribution Co 1540 Broadway	New York	NY	10036	212-930-4000	930-4512
Web: www.bmg.com					
Caroline Distribution 104 W 29th St 4th Fl	New York	NY	10001	212-886-7500	643-5563
TF: 800-275-2250 ■ *Web:* www.carolinedist.com					
EMI Christian Music Group 101 Winners Cir	Brentwood	TN	37024	615-371-6800	371-6980
TF: 800-669-8586 ■ *Web:* www.emicmg.com					
Gotham Distributing Corp 60 Portland Rd	Conshohocken	PA	19428	610-649-7650	649-0315
TF: 800-446-8426					
Inspired Corp 103 Eisenhower Pkwy	Roseland	NJ	07068	973-226-1234	226-6696
TF: 800-738-3747 ■ *Web:* www.inspired-studios.com/catalog					
Koch Entertainment Distribution					
22 Harbor Pk Dr	Port Washington	NY	11050	516-484-1000	484-4746
TF: 800-332-7553 ■ *Web:* www.kochdistribution.com					
Malaco Music Group Inc 3023 W Northside Dr	Jackson	MS	39213	601-982-4522	982-4528
TF Cust Svc: 800-272-7936 ■ *Web:* www.malaco.com					
Navarre Corp 7400 49th Ave N	New Hope	MN	55428	763-535-8333	533-2156
NASDAQ: NAVR ■ *TF:* 800-728-4000 ■ *Web:* www.navarre.com					
Orchard Enterprises Inc 100 Pk Ave 2nd Fl	New York	NY	10017	212-201-9280	201-9203
Web: www.theorchard.com					
Provident-Integrity Distribution					
741 Cool Springs Blvd	Franklin	TN	37067	615-261-6500	261-5909*
**Fax:* Hum Res ■ *TF Sales:* 800-333-9000 ■ *Web:* www.providentmusic.com					
RED Distribution 79 5th Ave 15th Fl	New York	NY	10003	212-404-0600	404-0619
TF: 800-733-1966 ■ *Web:* www.redmusic.com					
Select-O-Hits Inc 1981 Fletcher Creek Dr	Memphis	TN	38133	901-388-1190	388-3002
TF: 800-346-0723 ■ *Web:* www.selectohits.com					
Sony Music Distribution 550 Madison Ave	New York	NY	10022	212-833-8000	
Walt Disney Records 500 S Buena Vista St	Burbank	CA	91521	818-560-1000	
Web: www.disney.go.com/DisneyRecords					

527 MUSIC PROGRAMMING SERVICES

				Phone	Fax
DMX Music Inc 1703 W Fifth St Suite 600	Austin	TX	78703	512-380-8500	380-8500
TF: 800-345-5000 ■ *Web:* www.dmx.com					
Music Choice 110 Gibraltar Rd Suite 200	Horsham	PA	19044	215-784-5840	784-5869
Web: www.musicchoice.com					
Muzak LLC 3318 Lakemont Blvd	Fort Mill	SC	29708	803-396-3000	396-3136
TF: 800-331-3340 ■ *Web:* www.muzak.com					
PlayNetwork Inc 8727 148th Ave NE	Redmond	WA	98052	425-497-8100	497-8181
TF Sales: 888-567-7529 ■ *Web:* www.playnetwork.com					

528 MUSIC STORES

SEE ALSO Book, Music, Video Clubs p. 1534

				Phone	Fax
A & B Sound Ltd 3434 Cornett Rd	Vancouver	BC	V5M2H1	604-430-2999	430-5488
Web: www.absound.ca					
Amazon.com Inc 1200 12th Ave S Suite 1200	Seattle	WA	98144	206-266-1000	266-7601*
NASDAQ: AMZN ■ **Fax:* Hum Res ■ *TF Cust Svc:* 800-201-7575 ■ *Web:* www.amazon.com					
Archambault Group Inc					
500 Rue Sainte-Catherine E	Montreal	QC	H2L2C6	514-849-6206	849-0764
TF: 877-849-8589 ■ *Web:* www.archambault.ca					
Best Buy Co Inc 7601 Penn Ave S	Richfield	MN	55423	612-291-1000	238-3160*
NYSE: BBY ■ **Fax Area Code:* 952 ■ **Fax:* Cust Svc ■ *TF:* 888-237-8289 ■ *Web:* www.bestbuy.com					
CD Plus 70 Driver Rd	Brampton	ON	L6T5V2	905-624-7339	624-7310
Web: www.cdplus.com					
CD Universe 101 N Plains Industrial Rd	Wallingford	CT	06492	203-294-1648	294-0391
TF: 800-231-7937 ■ *Web:* www.cduniverse.com					
CD Warehouse 900 N Broadway	Oklahoma City	OK	73102	800-641-9394	949-2566*
**Fax Area Code:* 405 ■ *TF:* 800-641-9394 ■ *Web:* www.cdwarehouse.com					
Coconuts Music & Movies 38 Corporate Cir	Albany	NY	12203	518-452-1242	869-4819
TF: 800-540-1242 ■ *Web:* www.twec.com					
Djangos 2344 NW 21st Pl	Portland	OR	97210	503-241-6584	241-6436
eMusic.com Inc 244 5th Ave # 2070	New York	NY	10001	212-201-9240	201-9204
Web: www.emusic.com					
FirstCom Music 1325 Capital Pkwy Suite 109	Carrollton	TX	75006	972-446-8742	242-6526
TF Cust Svc: 800-858-8880 ■ *Web:* www.firstcom.com					
For Your Entertainment 38 Corporate Cir	Albany	NY	12203	518-452-1242	869-4819
TF: 800-540-1242 ■ *Web:* www.fye.com					
Global Electronic Music Marketplace					
PO Box 4062	Palm Springs	CA	92262	760-318-6250	318-6251
TF: 800-207-4366 ■ *Web:* gemm.com					
Half.com Inc PO Box 1469	Draper	UT	84020	800-545-9857	349-5782*
**Fax Area Code:* 877 ■ *TF:* 800-545-9857 ■ *Web:* www.half.ebay.com					
Hastings Entertainment Inc 3601 Plains Blvd	Amarillo	TX	79102	806-351-2300	351-2211
NASDAQ: HAST ■ *TF Cust Svc:* 877-427-8464 ■ *Web:* www.gohastings.com					
HMV Canada 5401 Eglinton Ave W Suite 110	Etobicoke	ON	M9C5K6	416-620-4470	620-5064
Web: www.hmv.com					
Inspired Distribution LLC					
103 Eisenhower Pkwy	Roseland	NJ	07068	973-226-1234	226-6696
TF: 800-272-4214 ■ *Web:* www.peterpan.com					
J & R Music World 23 Pk Row	New York	NY	10038	212-732-8600	238-9191
TF: 800-221-8180 ■ *Web:* www.jr.com					
Mississippi Music Inc 222 N Main St	Hattiesburg	MS	39401	601-544-5821	544-5841
TF: 800-844-5821 ■ *Web:* www.mississippimusic.com					
Musicnotes Inc 8020 Excelsior Dr Suite 201	Madison	WI	53717	608-662-1680	662-1688
TF: 800-944-4667 ■ *Web:* www.musicnotes.com					
Newbury Comics Inc 5 Guest St	Brighton	MA	02135	617-254-1666	254-2540
Web: www.newbury.com					
Record Exchange The 1105 W Idaho St	Boise	ID	83702	208-344-8010	336-2660
Web: www.therecordexchange.com					
SightSound Technologies Inc					
311 S Craig St Suite 205	Pittsburgh	PA	15213	412-621-6100	341-2442
Web: www.sightsound.com					
Trans World Entertainment Corp					
38 Corporate Cir	Albany	NY	12203	518-452-1242	452-7848
NASDAQ: TWMC ■ *TF:* 800-540-1242 ■ *Web:* www.twec.com					
Transcontinent Record Sales Inc 1762 Main St	Buffalo	NY	14208	716-883-9520	884-1432
TF: 800-836-0751 ■ *Web:* www.recordtheatre.com					
Virgin Megastores USA					
c/o SJ Communications 17012 Enadia Way	Lake Balboa	CA	91406	818-881-3889	332-4212
TF: 877-484-7446 ■ *Web:* www.virginmega.com					
Wherehouse Music 2330 Carson St	Carson	CA	90810	518-452-1242	516-9057*
**Fax Area Code:* 310 ■ *Web:* www.wherehouse.com					

529 MUSICAL INSTRUMENT STORES

				Phone	Fax
Alamo Music Ctr 425 N Main Ave	San Antonio	TX	78205	210-224-1010	226-8742
TF: 800-822-5010 ■ *Web:* www.alamomusic.com					
American Musical Supply 130 Lake Ave N	Spicer	MN	56288	320-796-2088	796-6036
TF: 800-458-4076 ■ *Web:* www.americanmusical.com					
Amro Music Stores 2918 Poplar Ave	Memphis	TN	38111	901-323-8888	325-6407
TF: 800-661-2676 ■ *Web:* www.amromusic.com					
Ardsley Musical Instrument Service Ltd					
219 Sprain Rd	Scarsdale	NY	10583	914-693-6639	693-6974
Web: www.ardsleymusic.com					
Bananas at Large 1504 4th St	San Rafael	CA	94901	415-457-7600	457-9148
Web: www.bananasmusic.com					
Bodine's Inc 6436 Penn Ave S	Richfield	MN	55423	612-866-2025	866-0463
TF: 800-535-6424					
Brook Mays Music Co 8605 John Carpenter Fwy	Dallas	TX	75247	214-631-0928	905-4964
TF Cust Svc: 800-637-8966 ■ *Web:* www.brookmays.com					
Buddy Rogers Music Inc 6891 Simpson Ave	Cincinnati	OH	45239	513-729-1950	728-6010
TF: 888-276-8742 ■ *Web:* www.buddyrogers.com					
Cascio Interstate Music					
13819 W National Ave	New Berlin	WI	53151	262-786-6210	786-6840
TF: 800-462-2263 ■ *Web:* www.interstatemusic.com					
Elderly Instruments 1100 N Washington Ave	Lansing	MI	48906	517-372-7890	372-5155
TF: 888-473-5810 ■ *Web:* www.elderly.com					
First Act Inc 745 Boylston St	Boston	MA	02116	617-226-7888	226-7890
TF: 888-551-1115 ■ *Web:* www.firstact.com					
Fletcher Music Centers Inc					
3966 Airway Cir	Clearwater	FL	33762	727-571-1088	572-4405
TF: 800-258-1088 ■ *Web:* www.fletchermusic.com					
Foxes Music Co 416 S Washington St	Falls Church	VA	22046	703-533-7393	536-2171
TF: 800-446-4414 ■ *Web:* www.foxesmusic.com					
Graves Piano & Organ Co Inc 5798 Karl Rd	Columbus	OH	43229	614-847-4322	847-0808
TF: 800-686-4322 ■ *Web:* www.gravespiano.com					
Gruhn Guitars 400 Broadway	Nashville	TN	37203	615-256-2033	255-2021
Web: www.gruhn.com					
Guitar Imports 334 N Marshall Way Suite 3	Layton	UT	84041	801-544-4060	991-4838
TF: 877-544-4060					
House of Guitars Corp 645 Titus Ave	Rochester	NY	14617	585-544-3500	544-8860
International Violin Co Ltd					
1421 Clarkview Rd	Baltimore	MD	21209	410-832-2525	832-2528
TF: 800-542-3538 ■ *Web:* www.internationalviolin.com					
JW Pepper & Son Inc 2480 Industrial Blvd	Paoli	PA	19301	610-648-0500	993-9716
TF: 800-345-6296 ■ *Web:* www.jwpepper.com					
Keyboard World Inc 23-25 E Main St	Frostburg	MD	21532	301-729-1817	689-2628
TF: 800-947-4266 ■ *Web:* www.keyboardworld.com					
Long & McQuade Musical Instruments					
722 Rosebank Rd	Pickering	ON	L1W4B2	905-837-9785	837-9786
Web: www.long-mcquade.com					
Lpd Music International Corp					
32575 Industrial Dr	Madison Heights	MI	48071	248-585-9630	585-7360
Web: www.lpdmusic.com					
M Steinert & Sons Co 162 Boylston St	Boston	MA	02116	617-426-1900	426-1905
Web: www.msteinert.com					
Music & Arts Centers Inc					
4626 Wedgewood Blvd	Frederick	MD	21703	301-620-4040	662-7753*
**Fax:* Mktg ■ *TF:* 800-237-7760 ■ *Web:* www.musicarts.com					
Music Go Round Inc					
605 Hwy 169 N Suite 400	Minneapolis	MN	55441	763-520-8419	520-8489
Web: www.musicgoround.com					
Musician's Friend Inc 931 Chevy Way	Medford	OR	97504	541-772-5173	776-1370
TF: 800-391-8762 ■ *Web:* www.musiciansfriend.com					

Company	City	State	Zip	Phone	Fax
Musiciansbuy.com Inc 11-7830 Byron Dr. *TF:* 877-778-7845 ■ *Web:* www.musiciansbuy.com	West Palm Beach	FL	33404	561-842-7451	840-9032
Paragon Music Center Inc 2119 W Hillsborough Ave. *Web:* www.paragon-music.com	Tampa	FL	33603	813-876-3459	876-0972
Sam Ash Music Corp PO Box 9047 *TF:* 888-615-5904 ■ *Web:* www.samashmusic.com	Hicksville	NY	11802	516-932-6400	931-3881
SameDayMusic 65 Greenwood Ave. **Fax Area Code:* 312 ■ *TF:* 866-744-7736 ■ *Web:* www.samedaymusic.com	Midland Park	NJ	07432	866-744-7736	276-0186*
Schmitt Music Co 2400 Fwy Blvd. *Web:* www.schmittmusic.com	Brooklyn Center	MN	55430	763-566-4560	
Stanton's Sheet Music 330 S 4th St *TF:* 800-426-8742 ■ *Web:* www.stantons.com	Columbus	OH	43215	614-224-4257	224-5929
Strait Music Co 2428 W Ben White Blvd. *TF:* 800-725-8877 ■ *Web:* www.straitmusic.com	Austin	TX	78704	512-476-6927	476-6968
Sweetwater Sound Inc 5501 US Hwy 30 W. *TF:* 800-222-4700 ■ *Web:* www.sweetwater.com	Fort Wayne	IN	46818	260-432-8176	432-1758
US Music Corp 444 E Courtland St **Fax Area Code:* 847 ■ *TF:* 800-877-6863 ■ *Web:* www.usmusiccorp.com	Mundelein	IL	60060	800-877-6863	949-8444*
Washington Music Ctr 11151 Veirs Mill Rd *Web:* www.wmcworld.com	Wheaton	MD	20902	301-946-8808	946-0487
West Music Inc 1212 5th St PO Box 5521 *TF:* 800-373-2000 ■ *Web:* www.westmusic.com	Coralville	IA	52241	319-351-2000	351-0479
Woodwind & Brasswind 4004 Technology Dr *TF:* 800-348-5003 ■ *Web:* www.wwbw.com	South Bend	IN	46628	574-251-3500	251-3501
zZounds Music 65 Greenwood Ave **Fax Area Code:* 312 ■ *TF:* 800-996-8637 ■ *Web:* www.zzounds.com	Midland Park	NJ	07432	800-996-8637	276-0186*

530 MUSICAL INSTRUMENTS

Company	City	State	Zip	Phone	Fax
Alembic Inc 3005 Wiljan Ct. *Web:* www.alembic.com	Santa Rosa	CA	95407	707-523-2611	523-2935
Allen Organ Co 150 Locust St PO Box 36 *Web:* www.allenorgan.com	Macungie	PA	18062	610-966-2202	965-3098
Austin Organs Inc 156 Woodland St. *Web:* www.austinorgans.com	Hartford	CT	06105	860-522-8293	524-9828
Avedis Zildjian Co 22 Longwater Dr *TF:* 800-229-8672 ■ *Web:* www.zildjian.com	Norwell	MA	02061	781-871-2200	871-3984
Bevin Bros 10 Bevin Rd PO Box 60 *Web:* www.bevinbells.com	East Hampton	CT	06424	860-267-4431	267-8557
Burkart-Phelan Inc 2 Shaker Rd Suite D-107 *Web:* www.burkart.com	Shirley	MA	01464	978-425-4500	425-9800
Carvin Corp 12340 World Trade Dr *TF:* 800-854-2235 ■ *Web:* www.carvin.com	San Diego	CA	92128	858-487-1600	487-8160
CF Martin & Co Inc 510 Sycamore St PO Box 329. *TF:* 888-433-9177 ■ *Web:* www.martinguitar.com	Nazareth	PA	18064	610-759-2837	759-5757
Chesbro Music Co Inc 327 Broadway PO Box 2009 *TF Cust Svc:* 800-243-7276 ■ *Web:* www.chesbromusic.com	Idaho Falls	ID	83403	208-522-8691	522-8712
Chime Master Systems PO Box 936 *TF:* 800-344-7464 ■ *Web:* www.chimemaster.com	Lancaster	OH	43130	740-746-8500	746-9566
Commercial Music Co Inc 1550 Edison St. *TF:* 800-442-7281	Dallas	TX	75207	214-741-6381	741-6381
Davitt & Hanser Music Co 3015 Kustom Dr **Fax Area Code:* 800 ■ *TF:* 800-999-5558 ■ *Web:* www.hansermusicgroup.com	Hebron	KY	41048	859-817-7100	451-4944*
Deering Banjo Co 3733 Kenora Dr *TF:* 800-845-7791 ■ *Web:* www.deeringbanjos.com	Spring Valley	CA	91977	619-464-8252	464-0833
E & O Mari Inc 256 Broadway *TF:* 800-750-3034 ■ *Web:* www.labella.com	Newburgh	NY	12550	845-562-4400	562-4491
Edwards Instrument Co 530 S Hwy H *TF:* 800-562-6838 ■ *Web:* www.edwards-instruments.com	Elkhorn	WI	53121	262-723-4221	723-4245
Emerson Flutes USA PO Box 310. *Web:* www.emersonflutes.com	Elkhart	IN	46515	574-522-1675	
Ernie Ball 151 Suburban Rd. *TF:* 866-823-2255 ■ *Web:* www.ernieball.com	San Luis Obispo	CA	93401	805-544-7726	544-3826
Fender Musical Instruments Corp 8860 E Chaparral Rd Suite 100. *TF Cust Svc:* 800-488-1818 ■ *Web:* www.fender.com	Scottsdale	AZ	85250	480-596-9690	596-1384
Fernandez Guitars International Inc 11044 Weddington St Suite 13. *Web:* www.fernandesguitars.com	North Hollywood	CA	91601	818-487-1940	760-0937
General Music Corp 1164 Tower Ln. *TF:* 800-323-0280 ■ *Web:* www.generalmusic.com	Bensenville	IL	60106	630-766-8230	766-8281
Getzen Co Inc 530 County Rd H *TF:* 800-366-5584 ■ *Web:* www.getzen.com	Elkhorn	WI	53121	262-723-4221	723-4245
GHS Corp 2813 Wilber Ave *TF:* 800-388-4447 ■ *Web:* www.ghsstrings.com	Battle Creek	MI	49037	269-968-3351	968-6913
Gibson Guitar Corp 309 Plus Pk Blvd. *TF:* 800-444-2766 ■ *Web:* www2.gibson.com	Nashville	TN	37217	615-871-4500	884-7256
Gibson Piano Ventures Inc 309 Plus Pk Blvd. *TF:* 800-444-2766 ■ *Web:* www.gibson.com	Nashville	TN	37217	615-871-4500	889-5509
Gretsch Co The PO Box 2468 *Web:* www.gretsch.com	Savannah	GA	31402	912-748-7070	748-6005
Hammond Suzuki USA Inc 733 Annoreno Dr. *TF:* 888-674-2623 ■ *Web:* www.hammondorganco.com	Addison	IL	60101	630-543-0277	543-0279
Hohner Inc 1000 Technology Pk Dr *TF:* 800-446-6010 ■ *Web:* www.hohnerusa.com	Glen Allen	VA	23059	804-515-1900	515-0347
Hoshino USA Inc 1726 Winchester Rd. *Web:* www.ibanez.com	Bensalem	PA	19020	215-638-8670	245-8583
J D'Addario & Co Inc 595 Smith St *TF:* 800-323-2746 ■ *Web:* www.daddario.com	Farmingdale	NY	11735	631-439-3300	439-3333
JD Calato Mfg Co Inc 4501 Hyde Pk Blvd *TF Cust Svc:* 800-358-4590 ■ *Web:* www.regaltip.com	Niagara Falls	NY	14305	716-285-3546	285-2710
Kawai America Corp PO Box 9045 *Web:* www.kawaius.com	Rancho Dominguez	CA	90224	310-631-1771	604-6913
Korg USA Inc 316 S Service Rd *Web:* www.korg.com	Melville	NY	11747	631-390-6800	390-8737
La Bella Strings 256 Broadway *TF:* 800-750-3034 ■ *Web:* www.labella.com	Newburgh	NY	12550	845-562-4400	562-4491
Latin Percussion Inc 160 Belmont Ave *Web:* www.lpmusic.com	Garfield	NJ	07026	973-478-6903	772-3568
Lowrey Organ Co 847 N Church Ct. *TF:* 800-451-5940 ■ *Web:* www.lowrey.com	Elmhurst	IL	60126	708-352-3467	
Ludwig Industries 2806 Mason St *Web:* www.ludwig-drums.com	Monroe	NC	28110	704-289-6459	289-8133
Lyon & Healy Harps Inc 168 N Ogden Ave. *TF:* 800-621-3881 ■ *Web:* www.lyonhealy.com	Chicago	IL	60607	312-786-1881	226-1502
Maas-Rowe Carillons Inc 2255 Meyers Ave. *TF:* 800-854-2023 ■ *Web:* www.maasrowe.com	Escondido	CA	92029	760-743-1311	747-2677
Manhasset Specialty Co 3505 Fruitvale Blvd *TF:* 800-795-0965 ■ *Web:* www.manhasset-specialty.com	Yakima	WA	98902	509-248-3810	248-3834
Mason & Hamlin Piano Co 35 Duncan St *Web:* www.masonhamlin.com	Haverhill	MA	01830	978-374-8888	374-8080
Morley Pedals 325 Cary Pt Dr. *TF:* 800-284-5172 ■ *Web:* www.morleypedals.com	Cary	IL	60013	847-639-4646	639-4723
Musicorp PO Box 63366 *TF:* 800-845-1922 ■ *Web:* www.musicorp.com	North Charleston	SC	29419	843-745-8501	745-8502
Noble & Cooley Co 42 Water St *Web:* www.noblecooley.com	Granville	MA	01034	413-357-6321	357-6314
Organ Supply Industries Inc 2320 W 50th St. *TF:* 800-458-0289 ■ *Web:* www.organsupply.com	Erie	PA	16506	814-835-2244	838-0349
OS Kelly Co 318 E N St.	Springfield	OH	45503	937-322-4921	322-1322
Ovation Guitars 37 Greenwoods Rd *TF Cust Svc:* 800-552-4681 ■ *Web:* www.ovationguitars.com	New Hartford	CT	06057	860-379-7575	379-8972
Paul Reed Smith Guitars (PRS) 380 Log Canoe Cir *Web:* www.prsguitars.com	Stevensville	MD	21666	410-643-9970	643-9980
PianoDisc 4111 N Fwy Blvd. *TF:* 800-566-3472 ■ *Web:* www.pianodisc.com	Sacramento	CA	95834	916-567-9999	567-1941
Prestini Musical Instruments Inc 2020 N Aurora Dr *TF:* 800-528-6569 ■ *Web:* www.prestiniusa.com	Nogales	AZ	85628	520-287-4931	287-4931
Remo Inc 28101 Industry Dr. *TF:* 800-525-5134 ■ *Web:* www.remo.com	Valencia	CA	91355	661-294-5600	294-5700
Reuter Organ Co 1220 Timberedge Rd *Web:* www.reuterorgan.com	Lawrence	KS	66049	785-843-2622	843-3302
Rodgers Instruments LLC 1300 NE 25th Ave *Web:* www.rodgersinstruments.com	Hillsboro	OR	97124	503-648-4181	681-0444
Roland Corp US 5100 S Eastern Ave *Web:* www.rolandus.com	Los Angeles	CA	90040	323-890-3700	890-3701
Saint Louis Music Inc 1400 Ferguson Ave *TF:* 800-727-4512 ■ *Web:* www.stlouismusic.com	Saint Louis	MO	63133	314-727-4512	727-8929
Schaff Piano Supply Co 451 Oakwood Rd. *TF:* 800-747-4266 ■ *Web:* www.schaffpiano.com	Lake Zurich	IL	60047	847-438-4556	438-4615
Schulmerich Carillons Inc 1 Carillon Hill *TF:* 800-772-3557 ■ *Web:* www.schulmerichbells.com	Sellersville	PA	18960	215-257-2771	257-1910
Steinway & Sons 1 Steinway Pl *TF:* 800-366-1853 ■ *Web:* www.steinway.com	Long Island City	NY	11105	718-721-2600	932-4332
Steinway Musical Instruments Inc 800 S St Suite 305 *NYSE:* LVB ■ *Web:* www.steinwaymusical.com	Waltham	MA	02453	781-894-9770	894-9803
Suzuki Musical Instrument Corp PO Box 261030 *TF Cust Svc:* 800-854-1594 ■ *Web:* www.suzukimusic.com	San Diego	CA	92196	619-873-2000	873-1997
Taylor-Listug Inc 1980 Gillespie Way *Web:* www.taylorguitars.com	El Cajon	CA	92020	619-258-1207	258-1623
Ultimate Support Systems Inc 5836 Wright Dr *TF:* 800-525-5628 ■ *Web:* www.ultimatesupport.com	Loveland	CO	80538	970-776-1920	776-1941
US Music Corp 444 E Courtland St **Fax Area Code:* 847 ■ *TF:* 800-877-6863 ■ *Web:* www.usmusiccorp.com	Mundelein	IL	60060	800-877-6863	949-8444*
Verne Q Powell Flutes Inc 1 Clock Tower Pl Suite 300. *Web:* www.powellflutes.com	Maynard	MA	01754	978-461-6111	461-6155
Wenger Corp 555 Pk Dr PO Box 448 *TF:* 800-493-6437 ■ *Web:* www.wengercorp.com	Owatonna	MN	55060	507-455-4100	455-4258
Wicks Pipe Organ Co 1100 5th St *TF Cust Svc:* 877-654-2191 ■ *Web:* www.organ.wicks.com	Highland	IL	62249	618-654-2191	654-3770
Wm S Haynes Co Inc 12 Piedmont St.	Boston	MA	02116	617-482-7456	482-1870
Yamaha Corp of America 6600 Orangethorpe Ave **Fax:* Hum Res ■ *Web:* www.yamaha.com	Buena Park	CA	90620	714-522-9011	522-9235*

531 MUTUAL FUNDS

Company	City	State	Zip	Phone	Fax
AARP Investment Funds PO Box 219735 *TF:* 800-253-2277	Kansas City	MO	64121	800-253-2277	
Alger Family of Funds PO Box 8480 *TF:* 800-992-3863 ■ *Web:* www.alger.com	Boston	MA	02266	800-992-3863	
Alger Fund PO Box 8480 *TF:* 800-992-3863 ■ *Web:* www.alger.com	Boston	MA	02266	800-992-3863	
American AAdvantage Funds 4151 Amon Carter Blvd MD 2450. *TF:* 800-388-3344 ■ *Web:* www.aafunds.com	Fort Worth	TX	76155	817-967-3509	967-0768
American Century Mutual Funds PO Box 419200 **Fax:* Cust Svc ■ *TF:* 800-345-2021 ■ *Web:* www.americancentury.com	Kansas City	MO	64141	816-531-5575	340-7962*
Aquila Group of Funds 380 Madison Ave Suite 2300 *TF:* 800-762-5955 ■ *Web:* www.aquilafunds.com	New York	NY	10017	212-697-6666	687-5373
Artisan Funds PO Box 8412 *TF Cust Svc:* 800-344-1770 ■ *Web:* www.artisanfunds.com	Boston	MA	02266	800-344-1770	
Aston Funds PO Box 9765. *Web:* www.astonfunds.com	Providence	RI	02940	312-268-1400	
Baron Funds 767 5th Ave 49th Fl. *TF:* 800-992-2766 ■ *Web:* www.baronfunds.com	New York	NY	10153	212-583-2000	583-2150

				Phone	Fax
BNY Hamilton Funds PO Box 182785	Columbus	OH	43218	800-426-9363	470-8720*
**Fax Area Code:* 614 ■ *TF:* 800-426-9363 ■ *Web:* www.bnyhamiltonfunds.com					
Brandywine Funds PO Box 701	Milwaukee	WI	53201	800-656-3017	773-6933*
**Fax Area Code:* 414 ■ *TF:* 800-656-3017 ■ *Web:* www.brandywinefunds.com					
Calvert Investments Inc 4550 Montgomery Ave Suite 1000N	Bethesda	MD	20814	301-951-4800	657-1982
TF: 800-368-2748 ■ *Web:* www.calvert.com					
CGM Funds 38 Newbury St # 8	Boston	MA	02116	617-859-7714	859-7295
TF: 800-345-4048 ■ *Web:* www.cgmfunds.com					
Clipper Fund 9601 Wilshire Blvd Suite 800	Beverly Hills	CA	90210	310-247-3940	273-0514
TF: 800-776-5033 ■ *Web:* www.clipperfund.com					
Davis Funds 2949 E Elvira Rd Suite 101	Tucson	AR	85756	800-279-0279	806-7601*
**Fax Area Code:* 520 ■ *TF:* 800-279-0279 ■ *Web:* www.davisfunds.com					
Dodge & Cox Funds 555 California St 40th Fl	San Francisco	CA	94104	415-981-1710	986-2924
TF: 800-621-3979 ■ *Web:* www.dodgeandcox.com					
Domini Social Investments PO Box 9785	Providence	RI	02940	800-582-6757	
TF: 800-582-6757 ■ *Web:* www.domini.com					
Dreyfus Family of Funds PO Box 55299	Boston	MA	02205	212-922-6000	922-7533
TF: 800-645-6561 ■ *Web:* public.dreyfus.com					
Eaton Vance Mutual Funds 255 State St	Boston	MA	02109	617-482-8260	482-4720*
**Fax:* Mktg ■ *TF:* 800-225-6265 ■ *Web:* www.eatonvance.com					
Federated Funds PO Box 8606	Boston	MA	02266	800-245-4770	681-3824*
**Fax Area Code:* 781 ■ *TF:* 800-245-4770 ■ *Web:* www.federatedinvestors.com					
Fidelity Advisor Funds PO Box 770002	Cincinnati	OH	45277	800-522-7297	321-7349*
**Fax Area Code:* 888 ■ **Fax:* Mktg ■ *TF:* 800-522-7297 ■ *Web:* www.advisor.fidelity.com					
Fidelity Investment Funds PO Box 770001	Cincinnati	OH	45277	800-343-3548	
TF: 800-343-3548 ■ *Web:* www.fidelity.com					
Fidelity Investments Institutional Operations Co Inc PO Box 770002	Cincinnati	OH	45277	877-208-0098	
TF: 877-208-0098 ■ *Web:* www.fidelity.com					
First American Funds PO Box 3011	Milwaukee	WI	53201	800-677-3863	666-6015*
**Fax Area Code:* 877 ■ *TF:* 800-677-3863 ■ *Web:* www.firstamericanfunds.com					
Firsthand Funds PO Box 8356	Boston	MA	02266	888-883-3863	
TF: 888-883-3863 ■ *Web:* www.firsthandfunds.com					
GAMCO Investors Inc 1 Corporate Ctr	Rye	NY	10580	914-921-5100	921-5118
TF: 800-422-3554 ■ *Web:* www.gabelli.com					
GE Elfun Funds 101 Savings St	Pawtucket	RI	02860	800-242-0134	
TF: 800-242-0134 ■ *Web:* www.gefunds.com/elfun					
GE Mutual Funds 101 Sabin St	Pawtucket	RI	02860	800-242-0134	
TF: 800-242-0134 ■ *Web:* www.gefunds.com					
Glenmede Funds 1650 Market St Suite 1200	Philadelphia	PA	19103	215-419-6000	419-6199
TF: 800-966-3200 ■ *Web:* www.glenmede.com					
GMO Trust Funds 40 Rowes Wharf	Boston	MA	02110	617-330-7500	261-0134
Web: www.gmo.com					
Goldman Sachs Funds PO Box 219711	Kansas City	MO	64121	312-655-4435	655-4489
TF: 800-526-7384 ■ *Web:* www2.goldmansachs.com					
Hartford Mutual Funds PO Box 9140	Minneapolis	MN	55480	888-843-7824	738-5534*
**Fax Area Code:* 651 ■ *TF:* 888-843-7824 ■ *Web:* www.hartfordinvestor.com					
Heartland Funds 789 N Water St Suite 500	Milwaukee	WI	53202	414-347-7777	347-1339
TF: 800-432-7856 ■ *Web:* www.heartlandfunds.com					
HighMark Funds PO Box 8416	Boston	MA	02266	800-433-6884	
TF: 800-433-6884 ■ *Web:* www.highmarkfunds.com					
Horace Mann Growth Fund 1 Horace Mann Plaza	Springfield	IL	62715	217-789-2500	788-5161
TF: 800-999-1030 ■ *Web:* www.horacemann.com					
ING Funds 7337 E Doubletree Ranch Rd	Scottsdale	AZ	85258	480-477-3000	477-2700
TF: 800-334-3444 ■ *Web:* www.ingfunds.com					
Invesco 11 Greenway Plaza Suite 100	Houston	TX	77046	713-626-1919	214-4109*
**Fax:* Mail Rm ■ *TF:* 800-347-1919 ■ *Web:* www.aimfunds.com					
Ivy Funds 6300 Lamar Ave	Overland Park	KS	66202	913-236-2000	236-2017
TF: 888-923-3355 ■ *Web:* www.ivyfunds.com					
Japan Fund PO Box 446	Portland	ME	04112	800-535-2726	821-6234
TF: 800-535-2726					
John Hancock Funds 101 Huntington Ave 10th Fl	Boston	MA	02199	617-375-1500	375-6250
TF: 800-338-8080 ■ *Web:* www.jhfunds.com					
Kopp Funds 7701 France Ave S Suite 500	Edina	MN	55435	952-841-0400	841-0411
TF: 888-533-5677 ■ *Web:* www.koppfunds.com					
Lazard Funds 30 Rockefeller Plaza 57th Fl	New York	NY	10112	800-823-6300	332-5613*
**Fax Area Code:* 212 ■ *TF:* 800-823-6300 ■ *Web:* www.lazardnet.com/lam/us/lazardfunds.shtml					
Legg Mason Family of Funds 100 Light St	Baltimore	MD	21202	410-539-0000	454-4174*
**Fax:* Mktg ■ *TF:* 800-368-2558 ■ *Web:* www.leggmason.com/funds					
Loomis Sayles Funds 1 Financial Ctr	Boston	MA	02111	617-482-2450	
TF: 800-633-3330 ■ *Web:* www.loomissayles.com					
Mairs & Power Funds 332 Minnesota St Suite W-1520	Saint Paul	MN	55101	651-222-8478	222-8470
TF: 800-304-7404 ■ *Web:* www.mairsandpower.com					
Manulife Mutual Funds 200 Bloor St E N Tower 3	Toronto	ON	M4W1E5	888-588-7999	
TF: 888-588-7999 ■ *Web:* www.manulife.ca					
Marshall Funds PO Box 1348	Milwaukee	WI	53201	800-236-3863	212-0922*
**Fax Area Code:* 414 ■ *TF:* 800-236-3863 ■ *Web:* www.marshallfunds.com					
Monetta Family of Mutual Funds 1776A S Naperville Rd Suite 100	Wheaton	IL	60189	630-462-9800	462-9332
TF: 800-666-3882 ■ *Web:* www.monetta.com					
Morgan Stanley Family of Funds 1585 Broadway	New York	NY	10036	212-761-4000	761-0086
TF: 800-223-2440 ■ *Web:* www.morganstanleyindividual.com					
Munder Funds 480 Pierce St	Birmingham	MI	48009	800-468-6337	
TF: 800-468-6337 ■ *Web:* www.munderfunds.com					
Mutual Benefit Group 409 Penn St PO Box 577	Huntingdon	PA	16652	814-643-3000	643-7210
TF: 800-283-3531 ■ *Web:* www.mutualbenefitgroup.com					
Neuberger Berman Funds PO Box 8403	Boston	MA	02266	212-476-8800	476-8848
TF: 800-877-9700 ■ *Web:* www.nb.com					
Nicholas Family of Funds 700 N Water St Suite 1010	Milwaukee	WI	53202	414-272-6133	
TF: 800-227-5987 ■ *Web:* www.nicholasfunds.com					
Northeast Investors Funds 100 High St	Boston	MA	02110	617-523-3588	523-5412
TF Cust Svc: 800-225-6704 ■ *Web:* www.northeastinvestors.com					
Northern Funds PO Box 75986	Chicago	IL	60675	312-557-2790	557-0411
TF: 800-595-9111 ■ *Web:* www.northernfunds.com					
Northern Institutional Funds 801 S Canal St C5S	Chicago	IL	60607	800-637-1380	557-0411*
**Fax Area Code:* 312 ■ *TF:* 800-637-1380 ■ *Web:* www.northerninstitutionalfunds.com					
Nuveen Mutual Funds 333 W Wacker Dr	Chicago	IL	60606	800-257-8787	917-8271*
**Fax Area Code:* 312 ■ *TF:* 800-257-8787 ■ *Web:* www.nuveen.com					
Oak Assoc Funds PO Box 8233	Denver	CO	80201	888-462-5386	
TF: 888-462-5386 ■ *Web:* www.oakfunds.com					
Oakmark Family of Funds 2 N La Salle St Suite 500	Chicago	IL	60602	312-621-0600	621-0372
TF: 800-625-6275 ■ *Web:* www.oakmark.com					
OppenheimerFunds Inc 2 World Financial Ctr 225 Liberty St	New York	NY	10281	212-323-0200	323-4070
TF: 800-525-7048 ■ *Web:* www.oppenheimerfunds.com					
Pax World Fund Family 30 Penhallow St # 400	Portsmouth	NH	03801	603-431-8022	
TF: 800-767-1729 ■ *Web:* www.paxworld.com					
PIMCO Funds 2187 Atlantic St	Stamford	CT	06902	800-628-1237	352-4962*
**Fax Area Code:* 203 ■ *TF:* 800-628-1237 ■ *Web:* www.allianzinvestors.com					
PIMCO Institutional Funds PO Box 219024	Kansas City	MO	64121	800-927-4648	421-2861*
**Fax Area Code:* 816 ■ *TF:* 800-927-4648 ■ *Web:* www.investments.pimco.com					
Pioneer Funds 60 State St	Boston	MA	02109	617-742-7825	422-4265*
**Fax:* Mail Rm ■ *TF:* 800-225-6292 ■ *Web:* www.us.pioneerinvestments.com					
Putnam Family of Funds PO Box 41203	Providence	RI	02940	800-225-1581	250-8411
TF: 800-225-1581 ■ *Web:* www.putnam.com					
Rainier Investment Management Mutual Funds 601 Union St Suite 2801	Seattle	WA	98101	206-464-0400	464-0616
TF: 800-248-6314 ■ *Web:* www.rainierfunds.com					
RidgeWorth Funds 50 Hurt Plaza Suite 1400	Atlanta	GA	30302	404-581-1589	575-2978
Web: www.ridgeworth.com					
Royce Funds 1414 Avenue of the Americas	New York	NY	10019	800-337-6923	
TF: 800-337-6923 ■ *Web:* www.roycefunds.com					
Rydex Funds 805 king farm Blvd Suite 600	Rockville	MD	20850	301-296-5100	296-5107
TF Cust Svc: 800-820-0888 ■ *Web:* www.rydexsgi.com					
Security Funds 1 Security Benefit Pl	Topeka	KS	66636	785-438-3000	438-5177
TF: 800-888-2461 ■ *Web:* www.securitybenefit.com					
SEI Global Funds Services 1 Freedom Valley Dr PO Box 1098	Oaks	PA	19456	610-676-1000	
TF: 800-342-5734 ■ *Web:* www.seiglobalfundservices.com					
Selected Funds PO Box 8243	Boston	MA	02266	800-243-1575	796-2955*
**Fax Area Code:* 781 ■ *TF:* 800-243-1575 ■ *Web:* www.selectedfunds.com					
Seligman Group of Funds 100 Pk Ave	New York	NY	10017	212-850-1864	922-5726
TF: 800-221-7844 ■ *Web:* www.seligman.com/individual/overview.htm					
Sequoia Fund Inc 767 5th Ave Suite 4701	New York	NY	10153	212-832-5280	832-5298
TF: 800-686-6884 ■ *Web:* www.sequoiafund.com					
Shay Assets Management Inc 230 W Monroe St Suite 2810	Chicago	IL	60606	312-214-7453	214-1424
TF: 800-982-1846 ■ *Web:* www.shayassets.com					
Sound Shore Fund 3435 Stelzer Rd	Columbus	OH	43219	800-754-8758	343-5884*
**Fax Area Code:* 866 ■ *TF:* 800-551-1980 ■ *Web:* www.soundshorefund.com					
SSgA funds 1 Lincoln St	Boston	MA	02111	617-664-6089	664-6011
TF: 800-997-7327 ■ *Web:* www.ssgafunds.com					
State Farm Mutual Funds PO Box 219548	Kansas City	MO	64121	800-447-4930	471-4832*
**Fax Area Code:* 816 ■ *TF:* 800-447-4930 ■ *Web:* www.statefarm.com/mutual/mutual.htm					
SunAmerica Mutual Funds 330 W 9th St PO Box 219186	Kansas City	MO	64105	800-858-8850	218-0519*
**Fax Area Code:* 816 ■ *TF:* 800-858-8850 ■ *Web:* www.sunamericafunds.com					
T Rowe Price Mutual Funds 100 E Pratt St	Baltimore	MD	21202	410-345-2000	539-4425
TF: 800-638-5660 ■ *Web:* www.troweprice.com					
TCW Group Inc 865 S Figueroa St Suite 1800	Los Angeles	CA	90017	213-244-0000	
TF: 800-386-3829 ■ *Web:* www.tcw.com					
Third Avenue Funds 622 3rd Ave 32nd Fl	New York	NY	10017	212-888-5222	
TF: 800-880-8442 ■ *Web:* www.thirdavenuefunds.com					
Thornburg Investment Management Funds 2300 N Ridgetop Rd	Santa Fe	NM	87506	505-984-0200	984-8973
TF: 800-533-9337 ■ *Web:* www.thornburginvestments.com					
TIAA-CREF Mutual Funds PO Box 8009	Boston	MA	02266	800-223-1200	
TF: 800-223-1200 ■ *Web:* www.tiaa-cref.org/mfs					
Torray Fund 7501 Wisconsin Ave Suite 1100	Bethesda	MD	20814	301-493-4600	530-0642
TF: 800-443-3036 ■ *Web:* www.torray.com					
Tweedy Browne Co LLC 350 Pk Ave 9th Fl	New York	NY	10022	212-916-0600	916-0649
TF: 800-432-4789 ■ *Web:* www.tweedy.com					
Unified Management Corp 429 N Pennsylvania St	Indianapolis	IN	46204	317-632-7805	266-8756
Web: www.ufsonline.com					
Vanguard Funds PO Box 1110	Valley Forge	PA	19482	800-871-3879	
TF: 800-871-3879 ■ *Web:* www.vanguard.com					
VantagePoint Funds 777 N Capitol St NW Suite 600	Washington	DC	20002	202-962-4600	962-4601
TF: 800-669-7400 ■ *Web:* www4.icmarc.org					
Victory Funds 127 Public Sq	Cleveland	OH	44114	800-539-3863	
TF: 800-539-3863 ■ *Web:* www.victoryconnect.com/vcn/home_victoryFunds.jsp					
Waddell & Reed Advisors Funds 6300 Lamar Ave	Shawnee Mission	KS	66202	913-236-2000	532-2749*
**Fax Area Code:* 800 ■ **Fax:* Cust Svc ■ *TF:* 800-366-5465 ■ *Web:* www1.waddell.com					
Waddell & Reed Inc 6300 Lamar Ave PO Box 29217	Shawnee Mission	KS	66201	913-236-1880	236-2017
TF: 800-532-2757 ■ *Web:* www1.waddell.com					
Weitz Funds 1125 S 103rd St Suite 600	Omaha	NE	68124	402-391-1980	391-2125
TF: 800-304-9745 ■ *Web:* www.weitzfunds.com					
Wilshire Target Funds Inc PO Box 9807	Providence	RI	02940	888-200-6796	
TF: 888-200-6796 ■ *Web:* www.wilfunds.com					

532 NAVIGATION & GUIDANCE INSTRUMENTS & SYSTEMS

				Phone	Fax
AAI Corp 124 Industry Ln PO Box 126	Hunt Valley	MD	21030	410-666-1400	628-3215
Web: www.aaicorp.com					

Phone Fax

Aero-Instruments Co LLC 14901 Emery Ave .... Cleveland OH 44135 216-671-3133 671-4177
Web: www.aero-inst.com
Aerosonic Corp 1212 N Hercules Ave .... Clearwater FL 33765 727-461-3000 447-5926
AMEX: AIM ■ *Web:* www.aerosonic.com
Alpine Electronics of America
19145 Gramercy Pl .... Torrance CA 90501 310-326-8000 212-0884*
**Fax:* Hum Res ■ *TF:* 800-257-4631 ■ *Web:* www.alpine-usa.com
American Reliance Inc (AMREL)
3445 Fletcher Ave .... El Monte CA 91731 626-443-6818 443-8600
Web: www.amrel.com
Astronautics Corp of America
4115 N Teutonia Ave PO Box 523 .... Milwaukee WI 53201 414-449-4000 447-8231
TF: 800-366-0666 ■ *Web:* www.astronautics.com
BAE Systems Inc 1601 Research Blvd .... Rockville MD 20850 301-838-6000
Web: www.baesystems.com/WorldwideLocations/UnitedStates
Ball Aerospace & Technologies Corp
1600 Commerce St .... Boulder CO 80301 303-939-4000 460-2315*
**Fax:* Mail Rm ■ *Web:* www.ballaerospace.com
Ball Aerospace & Technology Corp Aerospace Systems Div
1600 Commerce St .... Boulder CO 80301 303-939-4000 460-2315*
Boeing Co Integrated Defense Systems
PO Box 516 .... Saint Louis MO 63166 314-232-0232
Web: www.boeing.com/ids
Boeing Phantom Works
2201 Seal Beach Blvd PO Box 2515 .... Seal Beach CA 90740 562-797-2020
Web: www.boeing.com/phantom
Butler National Corp 19920 W 161st St .... Olathe KS 66062 913-780-9595 780-5088
Web: www.butlernational.com
CMI Inc 316 E 9th St .... Owensboro KY 42303 270-685-6545 685-6678
TF: 866-835-0690 ■ *Web:* www.alcoholtest.com
Computer Sciences Raytheon
1201 Edward H White II St
PO Box 4127 CSR 1500 .... Patrick AFB FL 32925 321-494-5272 494-6540
Web: www.computersciencesraytheon.com
Cubic Corp 9333 Balboa Ave PO Box 85587 .... San Diego CA 92186 858-277-6780 505-1523
NYSE: CUB ■ *Web:* www.cubic.com
Cubic Defense Systems 9333 Balboa Ave .... San Diego CA 92123 858-277-6780 505-1524
Web: www.cubic.com
Del Mar Avionics 1601 Alton Pkwy # C .... Irvine CA 92606 949-250-3200 261-0529
TF: 800-854-0481 ■ *Web:* www.dma.com
Deutsch Industrial Us 3850 Industrial Ave .... Hemet CA 92545 951-765-2250 765-2255
Web: www.deutsch.net
DRS C3 Systems LLC 400 Professional Dr .... Gaithersburg MD 20879 301-921-8100 921-8010
TF: 800-252-4734 ■ *Web:* www.drs.com
DRS Sensors & Targeting Systems - Infrared Technologies Div
13544 N Central Expy PO Box 740188 .... Dallas TX 75243 972-560-6000 560-6049
TF: 877-377-4783 ■ *Web:* www.drs.com
DRS Surveillance Support Systems Inc
6200 118th Ave .... Largo FL 33773 727-541-6681 544-4944
Web: www.drs.com
DRS Technologies Canada Co
115 Emily St .... Carlton Place ON K7C4J5 613-253-3020 253-3033
Web: www.drs.com
DRS Technologies Inc 5 Sylvan Way .... Parsippany NJ 07054 973-898-1500
TF: 800-694-5005 ■ *Web:* www.drs.com
DRS Training & Control Systems
645 Anchors St NW .... Fort Walton Beach FL 32548 850-302-3000 302-3371*
**Fax:* Hum Res ■ *TF:* 800-326-6724 ■ *Web:* www.drs.com
Dynalec Corp 87 W Main St .... Sodus NY 14551 315-483-6923 483-6656
Web: www.dynalec.com
Eaton Corp 1111 Superior Ave Eaton Ctr .... Cleveland OH 44114 216-523-5000 523-4787
NYSE: ETN ■ *Web:* www.eaton.com
Epsilon Systems Solutions Inc
1565 Hotel Cir S Suite 200 .... San Diego CA 92108 619-702-1700 702-1711
Web: www.epsilonsystems.com
Esterline Technologies Corp
500 108th Ave NE Suite 1500 .... Bellevue WA 98004 425-453-9400 453-2916
NYSE: ESL ■ *Web:* www.esterline.com
Flash Technology Corp 332 Nichol Mill Ln .... Franklin TN 37067 615-503-2000 261-2000
TF: 888-313-5274 ■ *Web:* www.flashtechnology.com
FLIR Systems Inc 27700-A SW Pkwy Ave .... Wilsonville OR 97070 503-498-3547 498-3904*
NASDAQ: FLIR ■ **Fax:* Sales ■ *TF:* 800-322-3731 ■ *Web:* www.flir.com
Frontier Electronic Systems Corp
4500 W 6th Ave .... Stillwater OK 74074 405-624-1769 624-7866*
**Fax:* Hum Res ■ *TF:* 800-677-1769 ■ *Web:* www.fescorp.com
Gables Engineering Inc 247 Greco Ave .... Coral Gables FL 33146 305-774-4400 774-4465
Web: www.gableseng.com
Garmin Ltd 1200 E 151st St .... Olathe KS 66062 913-397-8200 397-8282
NASDAQ: GRMN ■ *TF:* 888-442-7646 ■ *Web:* www.garmin.com
GE Aviation Systems Div
3290 Patterson Ave SE .... Grand Rapids MI 49512 616-241-7000 241-7533
Web: www.geaviationsystems.com
General Dynamics Advanced Information Systems
1421 Jefferson Davis Hwy Suite 600 .... Arlington VA 22202 703-271-7300 271-7302
Web: www.gd-ais.com
General Dynamics C4 Systems
400 John Quincy Adams Rd Bldg 80 .... Taunton MA 02780 508-880-4000 880-4800
TF: 888-483-2472 ■ *Web:* www.gdc4s.com
Goodrich Corp
2730 W Tyvola Rd 4 Coliseum Ctr .... Charlotte NC 28217 704-423-7000 423-7002
NYSE: GR ■ *TF:* 800-784-7009 ■ *Web:* www.goodrich.com
Honeywell Aerospace 1944 E Sky Harbor Cir .... Phoenix AZ 85034 800-601-3099 365-3343*
**Fax Area Code:* 602 ■ *TF:* 800-601-3099 ■ *Web:* www.honeywell.com
Honeywell Aerospace Electronic Systems
1944 E Sky Harbor Cir .... Phoenix AZ 85034 800-601-3099
TF: 800-601-3099
Honeywell Inc Commercial Aviation Systems
21111 N 19th Ave .... Phoenix AZ 85027 602-436-2311 822-7000
TF: 800-601-3099 ■ *Web:* www.honeywell.com
Honeywell Space Systems 13350 US Hwy 19 N .... Clearwater FL 33764 727-539-4000
Web: www51.honeywell.com/aero/IndustryExpertise/Space.html

Phone Fax

Innovative Solutions & Support Inc
720 Pennsylvania Dr .... Exton PA 19341 610-646-9800 646-0149
NASDAQ: ISSC ■ *Web:* www.innovative-ss.com
Interstate Electronics Corp
602 E Vermont Ave PO Box 3117 .... Anaheim CA 92803 714-758-0500 758-4148
TF: 800-854-6979 ■ *Web:* www.l-3com.com
ITT Defense 1650 Tysons Blvd Suite 1700 .... McLean VA 22102 703-790-6300 790-6360
Web: www.defense.itt.com
ITT Industries Inc 1133 Westchester Ave .... White Plains NY 10604 914-641-2000 696-2950
NYSE: ITT ■ *Web:* www.itt.com
Jewell Instruments LLC 850 Perimeter Rd .... Manchester NH 03103 603-669-6400 669-5962
TF: 800-227-5955 ■ *Web:* www.jewellinstruments.com
Kearfott Guidance & Navigation Corp
1150 McBride Ave .... Little Falls NJ 07424 973-785-6000 785-6025
Web: www.kearfott.com
Kelly Mfg Co 555 S Topeka St .... Wichita KS 67202 316-265-6868 265-6687
Web: www.kellymfg.com
Kollsman Inc 220 Daniel Webster Hwy .... Merrimack NH 03054 603-889-2500 889-7966
TF: 800-258-1350 ■ *Web:* www.kollsman.com
Kor Electronics 10855 Business Ctr Dr .... Cypress CA 90630 714-898-8200 895-7526
Web: www.korelectronics.com
KVH Industries Inc 50 Enterprise Ctr .... Middletown RI 02842 401-847-3327 849-0045
NASDAQ: KVHI ■ *Web:* www.kvh.com
L-3 Avionics Systems 5353 52nd St SE .... Grand Rapids MI 49512 616-949-6600 285-4457*
**Fax:* Hum Res ■ *TF:* 800-253-9525 ■ *Web:* www.as.l-3com.com
L-3 Communications Corp Aviation Recorders Div
6000 Fruitville Rd .... Sarasota FL 34232 941-371-0811 377-5598
Web: www.l-3ar.com
L-3 Communications Corp Communication Systems East Div
1 Federal St .... Camden NJ 08103 856-338-3000 338-6014
Web: www.l-3com.com/CS-East
L-3 Communications Corp Ocean Systems Div
15825 Roxford St .... Sylmar CA 91342 818-367-0111
TF: 800-654-8184
L-3 Communications Corp Randtron Antenna Systems Div
130 Constitution Dr .... Menlo Park CA 94025 650-326-9500 326-1033
TF Sales: 866-900-7270 ■ *Web:* www.l-3com.com/randtron
L-3 Communications Holdings Inc
640 N 2200 W PO Box 16850 .... Salt Lake City UT 84116 801-594-2000 594-3572
Web: www.l-3com.com/csw
Laitram LLC 200 Laitram Ln .... Harahan LA 70123 504-733-6000 733-2143
TF: 800-533-8253 ■ *Web:* www.laitram.com
Lockheed Martin Advanced Technology Laboratories
3 Executive Campus Suite 600 .... Cherry Hill NJ 08002 856-792-9815 792-9915
Web: www.atl.lmco.com
Lockheed Martin Canada 3001 Solandt Rd .... Kanata ON K2K2M8 613-599-3270 599-3282
Web: www.lockheedmartin.com/canada
Lockheed Martin Corp 6801 Rockledge Dr .... Bethesda MD 20817 301-897-6000 897-6083
NYSE: LMT ■ *TF:* 866-562-2363 ■ *Web:* www.lockheedmartin.com
Lockheed Martin MS2 199 Borton Landing Rd ...... Moorestown NJ 08057 856-722-4100
TF: 800-325-4019 ■ *Web:* www.lockheedmartin.com/manassas
Lockheed Martin Sippican 7 Barnabas Rd .... Marion MA 02738 508-748-1160 748-3626
Web: www.sippican.com
Lockheed Martin Systems Integration - Owego
1801 SR-17C .... Owego NY 13827 607-751-2000 751-3259*
Loral Space & Communications Ltd
600 3rd Ave .... New York NY 10016 212-697-1105 338-5660
NASDAQ: LORL ■ *Web:* www.loral.com
Lowrance Electronics Inc 12000 E Skelly Dr .... Tulsa OK 74128 918-437-6881 234-1705*
**Fax:* Hum Res ■ *TF:* 800-628-4487 ■ *Web:* www.lowrance.com
Mackay Communications Inc 3691 Trust Dr .... Raleigh NC 27616 919-850-3000 954-1707
Web: www.mackaycomm.com
NavCom Defense Electronics Inc
4323 Arden Dr .... El Monte CA 91731 626-442-0123 350-3191
TF: 800-729-8191
Navigation Solutions LLC
3314 N Central Expy Suite 210 .... Plano TX 75074 972-633-2301
Web: www.navigationsolutions.com
Northrop Grumman Corp 1840 Century Pk E .... Los Angeles CA 90067 310-553-6262 201-3023
NYSE: NOC ■ *Web:* www.northropgrumman.com
Northrop Grumman Electronic Systems
1580-A W Nursery Rd .... Linthicum MD 21090 410-765-4441
Web: www.es.northropgrumman.com/index.html
Orbit International Corp 80 Cabot Ct .... Hauppauge NY 11788 631-435-8300 435-8458
NASDAQ: ORBT ■ *TF:* 800-663-5366 ■ *Web:* www.orbitintl.com
Orbital Sciences Corp 21839 Atlantic Blvd .... Dulles VA 20166 703-406-5000
NYSE: ORB ■ *TF:* 877-672-4825 ■ *Web:* www.orbital.com
Parker Electronic Systems 300 Marcus Blvd .... Smithtown NY 11787 631-231-3737 434-8152
Web: www.parker.com
Professional Aircraft Accessories Inc
7035 Ctr Ln .... Titusville FL 32780 321-267-1040 269-0935
Web: www.gopaa.com
Radio Holland USA Inc 8943 Gulf Fwy .... Houston TX 77017 713-941-2290 378-2101
Web: www.radiohollandusa.com
Raymarine Inc 21 Manchester St .... Merrimack NH 03054 603-881-5200 864-4756
TF: 800-539-5539 ■ *Web:* www.raymarine.com
Raytheon Air Traffic Management Systems
870 Winter St .... Waltham MA 02451 781-522-3000 522-5200
Web: www.raytheon.com/products/cnsatm
Raytheon Canada Ltd 360 Albert St Suite 1640 .... Ottawa ON K1R7X7 613-233-4121 233-1099
Web: www.raytheon.ca
Raytheon Integrated Defense Systems
50 Apple Hill Dr .... Tewksbury MA 01876 978-858-5000
Web: www.raytheon.com/businesses/rids
Raytheon Intelligence & Information Systems
1200 S Jupiter Rd .... Garland TX 75042 972-205-5409 205-8988
TF: 800-752-6163 ■ *Web:* www.raytheon.com/businesses/riis
Raytheon Network Centric Systems
2501 W University .... McKinney TX 75071 972-952-2000
Rockwell Collins Inc 400 Collins Rd NE .... Cedar Rapids IA 52498 319-295-1000 295-9347*
NYSE: COL ■ **Fax:* PR ■ *TF:* 888-721-3094 ■ *Web:* www.rockwellcollins.com
Rodale Electronics Inc 20 Oser Ave .... Hauppauge NY 11788 631-231-0044 231-1345
Web: www.rodaleelectronics.com

	City	State	ZIP	Phone	Fax
Rostra Precision Controls Inc 2519 Dana Dr	Laurinburg	NC	28352	910-276-4853	276-1354
TF Cust Svc: 800-782-3379 ■ *Web:* www.rostra.com					
Safe Flight Instrument Corp 20 New King St	White Plains	NY	10604	914-946-9500	946-7882
Web: www.safeflight.com					
SELEX Inc 11300 W 89th St	Overland Park	KS	66214	913-495-2600	492-0870
TF: 800-765-0861 ■ *Web:* www.selex-si-us.com					
Sensis Corp 85 Collamer Crossing	East Syracuse	NY	13057	315-445-0550	446-2209
Web: www.sensis.com					
Sonatech Inc 879 Ward Dr	Santa Barbara	CA	93111	805-683-1431	690-5388
Web: www.sonatech.com					
Sperry Marine Northrop Grumman 1070 Seminole Trail	Charlottesville	VA	22901	434-974-2000	974-2259
TF Cust Svc: 800-368-2010 ■ *Web:* www.sperrymarine.northropgrumman.com					
Systron Donner Inertial 355 Lennon Ln	Walnut Creek	CA	94598	925-979-4400	979-9827
TF: 800-227-1625 ■ *Web:* www.systron.com					
Telair International 4175 Guardian St	Simi Valley	CA	93063	805-578-7301	578-7385
Web: www.telair.com					
Teledyne Benthos Inc 49 Edgerton Dr	North Falmouth	MA	02556	508-563-1000	563-6444
Web: www.benthos.com					
Textron Systems Corp 201 Lowell St	Wilmington	MA	01887	978-657-5111	657-1843
Web: www.systems.textron.com					
Thales ATM 23501 W 84th St	Shawnee	KS	66227	913-422-2600	422-2917
TF: 800-526-3433 ■ *Web:* www.thalesgroup.com					
Thales USA Inc 2733 S Crystal Dr Suite 1200	Arlington	VA	22202	703-838-9685	838-1688
Web: www.thalesgroup.com					
Tideland Signal Corp PO Box 52430	Houston	TX	77052	713-681-6101	682-4635
Web: www.tidelandsignal.com					
Transbotics Corp 3400 Latrobe Dr	Charlotte	NC	28211	704-362-1115	364-4039
Web: www.transbotics.com					
Trimble Navigation Ltd 935 Stewart Dr	Sunnyvale	CA	94085	408-481-8000	481-8585
NASDAQ: TRMB ■ *TF:* 800-827-8000 ■ *Web:* www.trimble.com					
Wellbore Navigation Inc 15032 Red Hill Ave Suite D	Tustin	CA	92780	714-259-7760	259-9257
Web: www.welnavinc.com					
Whistler Group Inc 13016 N Walton Blvd	Bentonville	AR	72712	479-273-6012	273-3188
TF Cust Svc: 800-531-0004 ■ *Web:* www.whistlergroup.com					
XATA Corp 965 Prairie Ctr Dr	Eden Prairie	MN	55344	952-707-5600	894-2463
NASDAQ: XATA ■ *TF:* 800-262-9282 ■ *Web:* www.xata.com					
Zonar Systems LLC 18200 Cascade Ave S	Seattle	WA	98188	206-878-2459	878-3082
TF: 877-843-3847 ■ *Web:* www.zonarsystems.com					

533 NEWS SYNDICATES, SERVICES, BUREAUS

	City	State	ZIP	Phone	Fax
AccuWeather Inc 385 Science Pk Rd	State College	PA	16803	814-235-8650	238-1339
TF Sales: 800-566-6606 ■ *Web:* www.accuweather.com					
Agence France-Presse (AFP) 1500 K St NW Suite 600	Washington	DC	20005	202-289-0700	414-0525
Web: www.afp.com					
AlterNet 77 Federal St 2nd Fl	San Francisco	CA	94107	415-284-1420	284-1414
Web: www.alternet.org					
American Baptist News Service PO Box 851	Valley Forge	PA	19482	610-768-2000	768-2320
TF: 800-222-3872 ■ *Web:* www.abc-usa.org/news					
American Stock Exchange Broadcast Services 86 Trinity Pl	New York	NY	10006	212-306-1000	306-1024
TF: 866-422-2639					
Andrews McMeel Universal 4520 Main St Suite 700	Kansas City	MO	64111	816-932-6700	932-6684
TF: 800-851-8923 ■ *Web:* www.amuniversal.com					
Associated Press (AP) 450 W 33rd St	New York	NY	10001	212-621-1500	621-1679
Web: www.ap.org					
Associated Press Information Services 450 W 33rd St	New York	NY	10001	212-621-1585	621-5488
TF: 800-272-2551 ■ *Web:* www.apnews.com					
Atlantic Syndication 1130 Walnut	Kansas City	MO	64106	816-581-7340	581-7346
Web: www.atlanticsyndication.com					
Bankrate Inc 1 N Wacker Dr Suite 4343	Villa Park	IL	60181	630-834-7555	834-7283
TF: 800-509-4636 ■ *Web:* www.bankrate.com					
Baptist Press 901 Commerce St	Nashville	TN	37203	615-244-2355	782-8736
Web: www.sbc.net					
Bloomberg LP 731 Lexington Ave	New York	NY	10022	212-318-2000	893-5000
Web: www.bloomberg.com					
Bloomberg News 731 Lexington Ave	New York	NY	10022	212-318-2000	369-5000*
**Fax Area Code:* 917 ■ *Web:* www.bloomberg.com					
Business Wire 44 Montgomery St 39th Fl	San Francisco	CA	94104	415-986-4422	788-5335
TF: 800-227-0845 ■ *Web:* www.businesswire.com					
California Newspaper Service Bureau 915 E 1st St	Los Angeles	CA	90012	213-229-5300	229-5481
TF: 800-788-7840					
Copley News Service 350 Camino De La Reina	San Diego	CA	92108	619-293-1818	
TF: 800-238-6196 ■ *Web:* www.copleynews.com					
Creators Syndicate Inc 5777 W Century Blvd Suite 700	Los Angeles	CA	90045	310-337-7003	337-7625
Web: www.creators.com					
Disaster News Network 9195-C Red Branch Rd	Columbia	MD	21045	410-884-7350	884-7353
TF: 888-384-3028 ■ *Web:* www.disasternews.net					
Dow Jones Newswires 800 Plaza 2 Harborside Financial Ctr	Jersey City	NJ	07311	201-938-5400	938-5600
Elias Sports Bureau Inc 500 5th Ave Suite 2140	New York	NY	10110	212-869-1530	354-0980
Web: www.esb.com					
Federal Network Inc (FedNet) 50 'F' St NW Suite 1C	Washington	DC	20001	202-393-7300	393-5965
Web: www.fednet.net					
Federal News Services 1000 Vermont Ave NW 5th Fl	Washington	DC	20005	202-347-1400	393-4733
Web: www.fednews.com					
Hearst News Service 700 12th St NW # 1000	Washington	DC	20005	202-263-6400	263-6441
Web: www.hearst.com					
Hispanic Link Inc 1420 N St NW	Washington	DC	20005	202-234-0280	234-4090
Web: www.hispaniclink.org					
ITAR-TASS Agency 780 3rd Ave 19th Fl	New York	NY	10017	212-245-4250	245-4258
Jewish Telegraphic Agency Inc 330 7th Ave 17th Fl	New York	NY	10001	212-643-1890	643-8498
Web: www.jta.org					
Kansas Press Assn Inc 5423 SW 7th St	Topeka	KS	66606	785-271-5304	271-7341
Web: www.kspress.com					
King Features Syndicate Inc 300 W 57th St 15th Fl	New York	NY	10019	212-969-7550	280-1550*
**Fax Area Code:* 646 ■ *TF:* 800-526-5464 ■ *Web:* www.kingfeatures.com					
Knight Ridder/Tribune Information Services 700 12th St NW Suite 1000	Washington	DC	20005	202-383-6080	393-2460
TF: 800-383-6181 ■ *Web:* www.mctdirect.com					
Los Angeles Times-Washington Post News Service Inc 1150 15th St NW	Washington	DC	20071	202-334-6000	334-5096
TF: 800-627-1150 ■ *Web:* www.washingtonpost.com					
Market Wire Inc 100 N Sepulveda Blvd # 300	El Segundo	CA	90245	310-765-3200	765-3297
TF: 800-774-9473 ■ *Web:* www.marketwire.com					
New York Times News Service Div 620 8th Ave 9th Fl	New York	NY	10018	212-556-1927	556-3535
TF: 888-346-9867 ■ *Web:* www.nytimes.com					
New York Times Syndicate Div 500 7th Ave 8th Fl	New York	NY	10018	212-499-3300	
Web: www.nytsyn.com					
New Yorker Magazine Cartoon Bank Div 28 Wells Ave Bldg 3 4th Fl	Yonkers	NY	10701	914-478-5527	478-5604
TF: 800-897-8666 ■ *Web:* www.cartoonbank.com					
Pacific News Service 275 9th St	San Francisco	CA	94103	415-503-4170	503-0970
Web: www.news.newamericamedia.org/news					
PR Newswire 810 7th Ave 35th Fl32nd Fl	New York	NY	10019	201-360-6000	596-1537*
**Fax Area Code:* 212 ■ *TF:* 800-832-5522 ■ *Web:* www.prnewswire.com					
Religion News Service (RNS) 529 14th St NW Suite 425	Washington	DC	20045	202-463-8777	463-0033
TF: 800-767-6781 ■ *Web:* www.religionnews.com					
Scripps Howard News Service (SHNS) 1090 Vermont Ave NW Suite 1000	Washington	DC	20005	202-408-1484	408-2062
Web: www.shns.com					
Sports Network 2200 Byberry Rd Suite 200	Hatboro	PA	19040	215-441-8444	441-9019
TF: 800-583-5499 ■ *Web:* www.sportsnetwork.com					
Stephens Media Group Washington News Bureau 666 11th St NW Rm 535	Washington	DC	20001	202-783-1760	783-1955
TF: 800-366-7390 ■ *Web:* www.stephensdc.com					
Talk Radio News Service 236 Massachusetts Ave NE Suite 306	Washington	DC	20002	202-337-5322	337-1174
Web: www.talkradionews.com					
Tribune Media Services Inc 435 N Michigan Ave Suite 1500	Chicago	IL	60611	312-222-4444	222-3459
TF: 800-245-6536 ■ *Web:* www.tribunemediaservices.com					
United Feature Syndicate Inc 200 Madison Ave 4th Fl	New York	NY	10016	212-293-8500	293-8717
TF: 800-888-3000 ■ *Web:* www.unitedfeatures.com					
United Media 200 Madison Ave 4th Fl	New York	NY	10016	212-293-8500	293-8717
TF: 800-221-4816 ■ *Web:* www.unitedfeatures.com					
United Methodist News Service 810 12th Ave S	Nashville	TN	37203	615-742-5470	742-5125
TF: 800-251-8140 ■ *Web:* www.umcom.org					
United Press International (UPI) 1133 19th St NW	Washington	DC	20036	202-898-8000	898-8057
TF: 800-783-4874 ■ *Web:* www.upi.com					
Universal Press Syndicate 4520 Main St Suite 700	Kansas City	MO	64111	816-932-6600	931-5018
TF: 800-255-6734 ■ *Web:* www.amuniversal.com/ups					
Washington Post Writers Group 1150 15th St NW	Washington	DC	20071	202-334-6375	334-5669
TF: 800-879-9794 ■ *Web:* www.postwritersgroup.com					
Wireless Flash News Service 827 W Washington St	San Diego	CA	92103	619-220-7191	220-8590
Web: www.flashnews.com					

534 NEWSLETTERS

534-1 Banking & Finance Newsletters

	City	State	ZIP	Phone	Fax
Banking Daily 1801 S Bell St	Arlington	VA	22202	800-372-1033	
TF: 800-372-1033 ■ *Web:* www.bna.com/banking-daily-p5439					
Bankruptcy Court Decisions 360 Hiatt Dr	Palm Beach Gardens	FL	33418	561-622-6520	622-2423
TF: 800-621-5463 ■ *Web:* www.lrp.com					
Best's Underwriting Newsletter Ambest Rd	Oldwick	NJ	08858	908-439-2200	439-3363
BestWeek Life/Health Newsletter Ambest Rd	Oldwick	NJ	08858	908-439-2200	439-3363
Web: www.ambest.com					
BestWeek Property/Casualty Newsletter Ambest Rd	Oldwick	NJ	08858	908-439-2200	439-3363
CEO Report 11300 Rockville Pike Suite 1100	Rockville	MD	20852	301-816-8950	816-8945
TF Cust Svc: 800-929-4824 ■ *Web:* www.cuceo.com					
Commercial Lending Litigation News 360 Hiatt Dr	Palm Beach Gardens	FL	33418	561-622-6520	622-2423
TF: 800-621-5463 ■ *Web:* www.lrp.com					
Consumer Bankruptcy News 360 Hiatt Dr	Palm Beach Gardens	FL	33418	561-622-6520	622-2423
TF: 800-621-5463 ■ *Web:* www.lrp.com					

				Phone	Fax

Consumer Credit & Truth-In-Lending Compliance Report
807 Las Cimas Pkwy Suite 300 .... Austin TX 78756 800-753-7577 305-6575*
*Fax Area Code: 512 ■ TF: 800-572-2797 ■ Web: www.sheshunoff.com/store/864.html

Controller's Report 3 Pk Ave 30th Fl .... New York NY 10016 212-244-0360 564-0465
TF: 800-401-5937 ■ Web: www.ioma.com

Corporate Financing Week PO Box 5018.......... Brentwood TN 37024 800-715-9195 377-0525*
*Fax Area Code: 615 ■ TF: 800-715-9195 ■ Web: www.corporatefinancingweek.com

Credit Union Directors Newsletter
5710 Mineral Pt Rd.......... Madison WI 53705 608-231-4000 231-1869*
*Fax: Cust Svc ■ TF: 800-356-9655 ■ Web: www.cuna.org

Credit Union Executive Newsletter
5710 Mineral Pt Rd.......... Madison WI 53705 608-231-4000 231-4370
TF Circ: 800-356-9655 ■ Web: www.cuna.org

Defined Contribution News 225 Pk Ave S .... New York NY 10003 212-224-3800 224-3491
TF: 800-543-4444 ■ Web: www.definedsavingsalert.com

Electronic Commerce & Law Report
1801 S Bell St.......... Arlington VA 22202 800-372-1033
TF: 800-372-1033 ■ Web: www.bna.com/electronic-commerce-law-p6796

Equipment Leasing Newsletter
1617 JFK Blvd Suite 1750 .... Philadelphia PA 19103 215-557-2310 557-2301
TF: 800-999-1916 ■ Web: www.lawjournalnewsletters.com

Forecaster Newsletter 19623 Ventura Blvd .... Tarzana CA 91356 818-345-4421 345-0468

Global Money Management 225 Pk Ave S .... New York NY 10003 212-224-3800 224-3491
TF: 800-715-9195 ■ Web: www.globalmoneymanagement.com

Internal Auditing Alert 395 Hudson St 5th Fl .... New York NY 10014 212-337-8444 337-8445
TF: 800-260-2793

International Business & Finance Daily
1801 S Bell St.......... Arlington VA 22202 800-372-1033
TF: 800-372-1033 ■
Web: www.bna.com/international-business-finance-p6707

International Tax Monitor 1801 S Bell St.......... Arlington VA 22202 800-372-1033
TF: 800-372-1033 ■ Web: www.bna.com/international-tax-monitor-p9111

Lender Liability Law Report
1901 Fort Myer Dr Suite 501 .... Arlington VA 22209 703-528-0145 528-1736
TF Cust Svc: 800-572-2797 ■ Web: www.sheshunoff.com

Louisiana Banker PO Box 2871 .... Baton Rouge LA 70821 225-387-3282 343-3159
Web: www.lba.org

Managing 401K Plans 30 Pk Ave 30th Fl.......... New York NY 10016 212-244-0360 564-0465
TF: 800-401-5937 ■ Web: www.ioma.com

Managing Accounts Payable 3 Pk Ave 30th Fl .... New York NY 10016 212-244-0360 564-0465
TF: 800-401-5937 ■ Web: www.ioma.com

Managing Benefits Plans 3 Pk Ave 30th Fl.......... New York NY 10016 212-244-0360 564-0465
TF: 800-401-5937 ■ Web: www.ioma.com

Managing Credit Receivables & Collections
3 Pk Ave 30th Fl .... New York NY 10016 212-244-0360 564-0465
TF: 800-401-5937 ■ Web: www.ioma.com

Money Management Letter 225 Pk Ave S 7th Fl .... New York NY 10003 212-224-3300 224-3171
Web: www.moneymanagementletter.com

New York Banker 99 Pk Ave 4th Fl.......... New York NY 10016 212-297-1600 297-1683*
*Fax: PR ■ Web: www.nyba.com

Price Perceptions
3030 NW Expy Suite 725 .... Oklahoma City OK 73112 405-604-8726 604-9696
TF: 800-231-0477 ■ Web: www.cis-okc.com/priceperceptions.asp

Regulatory Risk Monitor
11300 Rockville Pike Suite 1100 .... Rockville MD 20852 301-816-8950 816-8945
TF: 800-929-4824 ■ Web: www.rrmonitor.com/frcjsp

SEC Accounting Report 195 Broadway .... New York NY 10007 800-431-9025
TF: 800-431-9025 ■ Web: ria.thomsonreuters.com

Security Letter 166 E 96th St .... New York NY 10128 212-348-1553 534-2957

Specialty Finance 212 7th St NE .... Charlottesville VA 22902 434-977-1600 977-4466
Web: www.snl.com

VentureWire
800 Plaza 2 Harborside Financial Ctr .... Jersey City NJ 07311 866-291-1800 291-1300
TF: 800-326-3613 ■ Web: www.venturewire.com

534-2 Business & Professional Newsletters

				Phone	Fax

Accounting Dept Management & Administration Report
3 Pk Ave 30th Fl .... New York NY 10016 212-244-0360 564-0465
TF: 800-401-5937 ■ Web: www.ioma.com

Accounting Office Management & Administration Report
3 Pk Ave 30th Fl .... New York NY 10016 212-244-0360 564-0465
TF: 800-401-5937 ■ Web: www.ioma.com

AIArchitect Newsletter
1735 New York Ave NW .... Washington DC 20006 202-626-7465 626-7365
Web: info.aia.org/aiarchitect/2011/0218/newsletter

American Nurse
8515 Georgia Ave Suite 400.......... Silver Spring MD 20910 301-628-5000 628-5001
TF: 800-274-4262 ■ Web: www.nursingworld.org

American Speaker 2807 N Parham Rd Suite 200.......... Richmond VA 23294 804-762-9600 320-2079*
*Fax Area Code: 570 ■ TF: 800-722-9221 ■ Web: www.briefings.com

Antitrust & Trade Regulation Daily
1801 S Bell St.......... Arlington VA 22202 800-372-1033
TF: 800-372-1033 ■ Web: www.bna.com/antitrust-trade-daily-p5998

Authors Guild Bulletin 31 E 28th St 7th Fl.......... New York NY 10016 212-563-5904 564-5363
Web: www.authorsguild.org

Communication at Work
360 Hiatt Dr .... Palm Beach Gardens FL 33418 561-622-9914 622-2423
TF: 800-621-5463 ■ Web: www.lrp.com

Consulting Magazine
1 Phoenix Mill Ln 3rd FL.......... Peterborough NH 03458 603-924-1006 924-4460
TF: 800-531-0007 ■ Web: www.kennedyinfo.com/mc/cn.html

Corporate Counselor
1617 JFK Blvd Suite 1750 .... Philadelphia PA 19103 215-557-2310 557-2301
TF: 800-999-1916 ■ Web: www.lawjournalnewsletters.com

Corporate Writer & Editor
111 E Wacker Dr Suite 500.......... Chicago IL 60601 312-960-4140 861-3592
TF: 800-878-5331 ■ Web: www.ragan.com/Main/Home.aspx

Corrections Professional
360 Hiatt Dr .... Palm Beach Gardens FL 33418 561-622-6520 622-2423
TF: 800-621-5463 ■ Web: www.lrp.com

Customer Communicator The (TCC)
712 Main St Suite 187B .... Boonton NJ 07005 973-265-2300 402-6056
TF: 800-232-4317 ■
Web: www.customerservicegroup.com/the_customer_communicator.php

Customer Service Newsletter (CSN)
712 Main St Suite 187B .... Boonton NJ 07005 973-265-2300 402-6056
TF: 800-232-4317 ■
Web: www.customerservicegroup.com/customer_service_newsletter.php

Customers First 360 Hiatt Dr .... Palm Beach Gardens FL 33418 561-622-9914 622-2423
TF: 800-621-5463 ■ Web: www.lrp.com

Daily Report for Executives 1801 S Bell St .... Arlington VA 22202 800-372-1033
TF: 800-372-1033 ■ Web: www.bna.com/daily-report-executives-p6093

Daily Tax Report 1801 S Bell St .... Arlington VA 22202 800-372-1033
TF: 800-372-1033 ■ Web: www.bna.com/Daily-Tax-Report-p7889

Design Firm Management & Administration Report
3 Pk Ave 30th Fl .... New York NY 10016 212-244-0360 564-0465
Web: www.ioma.com

Distribution Center Management (DCM)
712 Main St Suite 187B .... Boonton NJ 07005 973-265-2300 402-6056
TF: 800-232-4317 ■
Web: www.distributiongroup.com/distribution_center_management.php

Downtown Idea Exchange (DIX)
712 Main St Suite 187B .... Boonton NJ 07005 973-265-2300 402-6056
TF: 800-232-4317 ■
Web: www.downtowndevelopment.com/downtown_idea_exchange.php

Economic Opportunity Report
222 Sedwick Dr Suite 101 .... Durham NC 27713 800-223-8720 508-2592
TF: 800-274-6737 ■ Web: www.bpinews.com

Effective Telephone Techniques
360 Hiatt Dr .... Palm Beach Gardens FL 33418 561-622-9914 622-2423
TF: 800-621-5463 ■ Web: www.lrp.com

Executive Excellence 1860 N 1120 W .... Provo UT 84604 801-375-4060 377-5960
TF: 800-304-9782 ■ Web: www.eep.com

Federal EEO Advisor 360 Hiatt Dr .... Palm Beach Gardens FL 33418 561-622-6520 622-2423
TF: 800-621-5462 ■ Web: www.lrp.com

Federal Human Resources Week
360 Hiatt Dr .... Palm Beach Gardens FL 33418 561-622-6520 622-2423
TF: 800-621-5463 ■ Web: www.lrp.com

First Line Supervisor
360 Hiatt Dr .... Palm Beach Gardens FL 33418 561-622-9914 622-9060
TF: 800-621-5463 ■ Web: www.lrp.com

First-Rate Customer Service
2807 N Parhan Rd Suite 200 .... Richmond VA 23294 804-762-9600 320-2079*
*Fax Area Code: 570 ■ TF: 800-722-9221 ■ Web: www.briefings.com

From 9 to 5 360 Hiatt Dr.......... Palm Beach Gardens FL 33418 561-622-9914 622-9060
TF: 800-621-5463 ■ Web: www.lrp.com

Getting Along 360 Hiatt Dr .... Palm Beach Gardens FL 33418 561-622-9914 622-9060
TF: 800-621-5463 ■ Web: www.lrp.com

Government Communicators Insider
111 E Wacker Dr Suite 500.......... Chicago IL 60601 312-960-4140 861-3592
TF: 800-878-5331 ■ Web: www.ragan.com/Main/Home.aspx

Government Employee Relations Report
1801 S Bell St.......... Arlington VA 22202 800-372-1033
TF: 800-372-1033 ■
Web: www.bna.com/government-employee-relations-p5468

Human Resources Dept Management Report
3 Pk Ave 30th Fl .... New York NY 10016 212-244-0360 564-0465
TF: 800-401-5937 ■ Web: www.ioma.com

Human Resources Report 1801 S Bell St .... Arlington VA 22202 800-372-1033
TF: 800-372-1033 ■ Web: www.bna.com/human-resources-report-p4458

International Trade Reporter
1801 S Bell St.......... Arlington VA 22202 800-372-1033
TF: 800-372-1033 ■ Web: www.bna.com/international-trade-reporter-p6101

Journal of Employee Communication Management
111 E Wacker Dr Suite 500.......... Chicago IL 60601 312-960-4100 861-3592
TF: 800-878-5331 ■ Web: www.ragan.com/Main/Home.aspx

Laboratory Industry Report (LNR)
3 Pk Ave 30th Fl .... New York NY 10016 212-244-0360 564-0465
TF: 800-401-5937

Law Firm Partnership & Benefits Report
1617 JFK Blvd Suite 1750 .... Philadelphia PA 19103 215-557-2310 557-2301
TF: 800-999-1916 ■ Web: www.lawjournalnewsletters.com

Law Office Management & Administration Report
3 Pk Ave 30th Fl .... New York NY 10016 212-244-0360 564-0465
TF: 800-401-5937 ■ Web: www.ioma.com

Law Officer's Bulletin 610 Opperman Dr.......... Eagan MN 55123 651-687-7000 562-1521*
*Fax Area Code: 301 ■ TF: 800-344-5008 ■ Web: www.west.thomson.com

Legislative Network for Nurses
222 Sedwick Dr Suite 101 .... Durham NC 27713 800-223-8720 508-2592
TF: 800-274-6737 ■ Web: www.bpinews.com

Mail Center Management Report
3 Pk Ave 30th Fl .... New York NY 10016 212-244-0360 564-0465
TF: 800-401-5937 ■ Web: www.ioma.com

Manager's Edge 2807 N Parham Rd Suite 200 .... Richmond VA 23294 804-762-9600 217-8999
TF: 800-791-8699 ■ Web: www.douglaspublications.com

Manager's Intelligence Report
111 E Wacker Dr Suite 500.......... Chicago IL 60601 312-960-4100 861-3592
TF: 800-878-5331 ■ Web: www.ragan.com/Main/Home.aspx

Managing Customer Service 3 Pk Ave 30th Fl.......... New York NY 10016 212-244-0360 564-0465
TF: 800-401-5937 ■ Web: www.ioma.com

Managing International Credit & Collections
3 Pk Ave 30th Fl .... New York NY 10016 212-244-0360 564-0465
TF: 800-401-5937 ■ Web: www.ioma.com

Managing Logistics 3 Pk Ave 30th Fl .... New York NY 10016 212-244-0360 564-0465
TF: 800-401-5937 ■ Web: www.ioma.com

Minorities in Business Insider
8204 Fenton St.......... Silver Spring MD 20910 301-588-6380 588-6385
TF: 800-666-6380 ■ Web: www.cdpublications.com/pubs

Motivational Manager
316 N Michigan Ave Suite 300.......... Chicago IL 60601 312-960-4100 960-4106
TF: 800-878-5331 ■ Web: www.motivateandinspire.com

Entry	City	State	ZIP	Phone	Fax
Pay for Performance 3 Pk Ave 30th Fl *TF:* 800-401-5937 ■ *Web:* www.ioma.com	New York	NY	10016	212-244-0360	564-0465
Payroll Manager's Report 3 Pk Ave 30th Fl *TF:* 800-401-5937 ■ *Web:* www.ioma.com	New York	NY	10016	212-244-0360	564-0465
Payroll Practitioner's Monthly 3 Bethesda Metro Ctr Suite 250 *TF:* 800-372-1033 ■ *Web:* ioma.bna.com/Newsletter.aspx?id=2147483666&libID=2147483666	Bethesda	MD	20814	800-372-1033	253-0332
Preventing Business Fraud 3 Pk Ave 30th Fl *TF:* 800-401-5937 ■ *Web:* www.ioma.com	New York	NY	10016	212-244-0360	564-0465
Professional Apartment Management 149 5th Ave 16th Fl **Fax Area Code:* 212 ■ *TF:* 800-643-8095 ■ *Web:* www.brownstone.com	New York	NY	10010	800-519-3692	473-8786*
Ragan Report 111 E Wacker Dr Suite 500 *TF Cust Svc:* 800-878-5331 ■ *Web:* www.ragan.com/Main/Home.aspx	Chicago	IL	60601	312-960-4100	861-3592
Report on Salary Surveys 3 Pk Ave 30th Fl *TF:* 800-401-5937 ■ *Web:* www.ioma.com	New York	NY	10016	212-244-0360	564-0465
Security Director's Report (SDR) 3 Pk Ave 30th Fl *TF:* 800-401-5937	New York	NY	10016	212-244-0360	564-0465
Small Tax Control 7910 Woodmont Ave Suite 1000 *TF:* 800-570-5744 ■ *Web:* www.imfpubs.com	Bethesda	MD	20814	301-951-1240	656-1709
Successful Supervisor 360 Hiatt Dr *TF:* 800-621-5463 ■ *Web:* www.lrp.com	Palm Beach Gardens	FL	33418	561-622-9914	622-2423
Supplier Selection & Management Report 3 Pk Ave 30th Fl *TF:* 800-401-5937 ■ *Web:* www.ioma.com	New York	NY	10016	212-244-0360	564-0465
Team Leader 360 Hiatt Dr *TF:* 800-621-5463 ■ *Web:* www.lrp.com	Palm Beach Gardens	FL	33418	561-622-9914	622-2423
Team Management Briefings *Briefings Media Group* 2807 N Parhan Rd Suite 200 **Fax Area Code:* 703 ■ *TF:* 800-791-8699 ■ *Web:* www.briefings.com	Richmond	VA	23294	804-762-9600	684-2136*
Teamwork Newsletter 2222 Sedwick Dr Suite 101 *TF:* 800-223-8720 ■ *Web:* www.dartnellcorp.com/teamwork.php	Durham	NC	27713	800-223-8720	508-2592
Trend Letter 2807 N Prhan Rd Suite 200 **Fax Area Code:* 703 ■ *TF:* 800-722-9221 ■ *Web:* www.briefings.com	Richmond	VA	23294	804-762-9600	684-2136*
Working Together 360 Hiatt Dr *TF:* 800-621-5463 ■ *Web:* www.lrp.com	Palm Beach Gardens	FL	33418	561-622-6520	622-2423

534-3 Computer & Internet Newsletters

Entry	City	State	ZIP	Phone	Fax
Biotechnology Software 140 Huguenot St 3rd Fl *TF:* 800-654-3237 ■ *Web:* www.liebertpub.com	New Rochelle	NY	10801	914-740-2100	740-2109
Business Intelligence Advisor 37 Broadway Suite 1 *TF:* 800-964-8702 ■ *Web:* www.cutter.com/bia	Arlington	MA	02474	781-648-8700	648-1950
CADCAMNet 8220 Stone Trail Dr *Web:* www.cadcamnet.com	Bethesda	MD	20817	301-365-9085	365-4586
Computer Economics Report The 2082 Business Ctr Dr Suite 240 *TF:* 800-326-8100 ■ *Web:* www.computereconomics.com	Irvine	CA	92612	949-831-8700	442-7688
Convergence & Voip Alert 118 Tpke Rd *TF:* 800-622-1108 ■ *Web:* www.networkworld.com/newsletters/converg/index.html	Southborough	MA	01772	508-460-3333	490-6438
Cutter Benchmark Review 37 Broadway Suite 1 *TF:* 800-964-8702 ■ *Web:* www.cutter.com	Arlington	MA	02474	781-648-8702	648-1950
Cutter IT Journal 37 Broadway Suite 1 *Web:* www.cutter.com/itjournal	Arlington	MA	02474	781-648-8700	648-1950
Electronic Information Report 60 Longridge Rd Suite 300 *Web:* www.simbanet.com	Stamford	CT	06902	203-325-8193	325-8915
eMarketer 75 Broad St 32nd Fl *TF:* 800-405-0844 ■ *Web:* www.emarketer.com	New York	NY	10004	212-763-6010	763-6020
Infoperceptives 123 7th Ave *Web:* www.tech-news.com	Brooklyn	NY	11215	718-369-7682	965-3039
Insider Weekly for AS/400 Managers 990 Washington St Suite 308 *TF:* 888-400-4768 ■ *Web:* www.the400group.com	Dedham	MA	02026	781-320-9460	320-9466
Internet Newsletter 1617 JFK Blvd Suite 1750 *TF Cust Svc:* 800-722-7670	Philadelphia	PA	19103	215-557-2300	557-2301
IT Best Practices Alert 118 Tpke Rd *TF:* 800-622-1108 ■ *Web:* www.networkworld.com/newsletters/techexec/index.html	Southborough	MA	01772	508-460-3333	490-6438
Legal Tech Newsletter 1617 JFK Blvd Suite 1750 *TF:* 800-999-1916 ■ *Web:* www.lawjournalnewsletters.com	Philadelphia	PA	19103	215-557-2310	557-2301
Linux Today 23 Old Kings Hwy S *Web:* www.linuxtoday.com	Darien	CT	06820	203-662-2800	655-4686
Microprocessor Report 298 S Sunnyvale Ave Suite 101 *TF:* 800-527-0288 ■ *Web:* www.mdronline.com	Sunnyvale	CA	94086	408-243-8838	737-2242
Security Identity Management Alert 118 Tpke Rd *TF:* 800-622-1108 ■ *Web:* www.networkworld.com/newsletters/dir/index.html	Southborough	MA	01772	508-460-3333	490-6438
Washington Internet Daily 2115 Ward Ct NW *TF:* 800-771-9202 ■ *Web:* www.warren-news.com	Washington	DC	20037	202-872-9200	293-3435
Web Content Report 111 E Wacker Dr Suite 500 **Fax:* Cust Svc ■ *TF:* 800-878-5331 ■ *Web:* www.ragan.com/Main/Home.aspx	Chicago	IL	60601	312-960-4100	861-3592*
Web Services Strategies 37 Broadway Suite 1 *TF:* 800-964-8702 ■ *Web:* www.cutter.com/webservices	Arlington	MA	02474	781-648-8700	648-1950
WebReference.com 23 Old Kings Hwy S *Web:* www.webreference.com	Darien	CT	06820	203-662-2800	655-4686

534-4 Education Newsletters

Entry	City	State	ZIP	Phone	Fax
Aid for Education Report 8204 Fenton St **Fax:* Edit ■ *TF:* 800-666-6380 ■ *Web:* www.cdpublications.com/pubs	Silver Spring	MD	20910	301-588-6380	588-6385*
California School Law Digest 747 Dresher Rd Suite 500 **Fax:* Mktg ■ *TF:* 800-341-7874 ■ *Web:* www.shoplrp.com	Horsham	PA	19044	215-784-0860	784-9639*
California Special Education Alert (CASEA) 360 Hiatt Dr *TF:* 800-621-5463 ■ *Web:* www.lrp.com	Palm Beach Gardens	FL	33418	561-622-6520	622-2423
Campus Crime 222 Sedwick Dr Suite 101 **Fax:* Edit ■ *TF:* 800-274-6737 ■ *Web:* www.bpinews.com	Durham	NC	27713	800-223-8720	508-2592*
Corporate Training & Development Advisor 60 Longridge Rd **Fax:* Sales ■ *Web:* www.simbanet.com	Stamford	CT	06902	203-325-8193	325-8915*
Early Childhood Report 360 Hiatt Dr *TF:* 800-621-5463 ■ *Web:* www.lrp.com	Palm Beach Gardens	FL	33418	561-622-6520	622-2423
Education Grants Alert 360 Hiatt Dr *TF:* 800-621-5463 ■ *Web:* www.lrp.com	Palm Beach Gardens	FL	33418	561-622-6520	622-2423
Education Technology News 222 Sedwick Dr Suite 101 **Fax:* Edit ■ *TF:* 800-274-6737 ■ *Web:* www.bpinews.com	Durham	NC	27713	800-223-8720	508-2592*
Education USA 747 Dresher Rd Suite 500 *TF Cust Svc:* 800-341-7874 ■ *Web:* www.lrp.com	Horsham	PA	19044	215-784-0860	784-9639
Educational Research Newsletter PO Box 2347 **Fax Area Code:* 815 ■ *Web:* www.ernweb.com	South Portland	ME	04116	207-632-1954	461-5647*
Electronic Education Report 60 Longridge Rd Suite 300 **Fax:* Sales ■ *Web:* www.simbanet.com	Stamford	CT	06902	203-325-8193	325-8915*
Library Hotline 360 Pk Ave S **Fax:* Mktg ■ *Web:* www.reedbusiness.com	New York	NY	10010	646-746-7059	746-6536*
Library of Congress Information Bulletin 101 Independence Ave SE *Web:* www.loc.gov/loc/lcib	Washington	DC	20540	202-707-2905	707-9199
New Jersey Law Journal PO Box 20081 *Web:* www.law.com	Newark	NJ	07101	973-642-0075	642-0920
New York Education Law Report 360 Hiatt Dr **Fax:* Edit ■ *TF:* 800-341-7874 ■ *Web:* www.lrp.com	Palm Beach	FL	33418	561-622-6520	622-1375*
Report on Literacy Programs 222 Sedwick Dr Suite 101 *TF:* 800-274-6737 ■ *Web:* www.bpinews.com	Durham	NC	27713	800-223-8720	508-2592
Report on Preschool Programs 222 Sedwick Dr Suite 101 *TF:* 800-274-6737 ■ *Web:* www.bpinews.com	Durham	NC	27713	800-223-8720	508-2592
Research Libraries Group News 1200 Villa St *TF:* 800-537-7546 ■ *Web:* www.rlg.org	Mountain View	CA	94041	650-962-9951	964-0943
School Law News 360 Hiatt Dr **Fax Area Code:* 561 ■ *TF:* 800-638-8437 ■ *Web:* www.lrp.com	Palm Beach Gardens	FL	33418	800-341-7874	622-2423*
School Superintendent's Insider 360 Hiatt Dr *TF:* 800-341-7874 ■ *Web:* www.shoplrp.com	Palm Beach Gardens	FL	33418	561-622-6520	622-0757
Special Education Report 360 Hiatt Dr *TF Sales:* 800-621-5463 ■ *Web:* www.lrp.com	Palm Beach Gardens	FL	33418	561-622-6520	622-2423
Student Aid News 360 Hiatt Dr **Fax Area Code:* 561 ■ *TF:* 800-638-8437 ■ *Web:* www.lrp.com	Palm Beach Gardens	FL	33418	800-341-7874	622-2423*
Teacher Education Reports 4401A Connecticut Ave NW Suite 212 *Web:* www.teach-now.org	Washington	DC	20008	202-822-8280	822-8284
Vocational Training News 360 Hiatt Dr **Fax Area Code:* 561 ■ *TF:* 800-638-8437 ■ *Web:* www.lrp.com	Palm Beach Gardens	FL	33418	800-341-7874	622-2423*
What Works in Teaching & Learning 360 Hiatt Dr *TF Sales:* 800-621-5463 ■ *Web:* www.lrp.com	Palm Beach Gardens	FL	33418	561-622-6520	622-2423

534-5 Energy & Environmental Newsletters

Entry	City	State	ZIP	Phone	Fax
AltFuels Advisor 40 Washington St Suite 110 **Fax Area Code:* 781 ■ *TF:* 866-285-7215 ■ *Web:* www.altfuels.com	Wellesley	MA	02481	866-285-7215	489-7308*
Asbestos & Lead Abatement Report 222 Sedwick Dr Suite 101 *TF:* 800-274-6737 ■ *Web:* www.bpinews.com	Durham	NC	27713	800-223-8720	508-2592
Chemical Regulation Reporter 1801 S Bell St *TF:* 800-372-1033 ■ *Web:* www.bna.com/chemical-regulation-reporter-p4750	Arlington	VA	22202	800-372-1033	
Clean Air Report 1919 S Eads St # 201 *Web:* www.insideepa.com	Arlington	VA	22202	703-416-8516	416-8543
Clean Water Report 222 Sedwick Dr Suite 101 *TF:* 800-274-6737 ■ *Web:* www.bpinews.com	Durham	NC	27713	800-223-8720	508-2592
Coal Outlook 1200 G St NW Suite 1100 **Fax Area Code:* 212 ■ *Web:* www.platts.com	Washington	DC	20005	202-383-2160	904-4209*
Daily Environment Report 1801 S Bell St *TF:* 800-372-1033 ■ *Web:* www.bna.com/daily-environment-report-p4751	Arlington	VA	22202	800-372-1033	
Electric Utility Week 2 Penn Plaza 25th Fl *TF:* 800-752-8878 ■ *Web:* www.platts.com	New York	NY	10121	212-904-3070	904-3738
Energy Compass 5 E 37th St 5th Fl *TF:* 888-427-7496 ■ *Web:* www.energyintel.com	New York	NY	10016	212-532-1112	532-4838
Environment Reporter 1801 S Bell St *TF:* 800-372-1033 ■ *Web:* www.bna.com/environment-reporter-p4885	Arlington	VA	22202	800-372-1033	
Environmental Compliance & Litigation Strategy 1617 JFK Blvd Suite 1750 **Fax Area Code:* 215 ■ *TF:* 800-999-1916 ■ *Web:* www.lawjournalnewsletters.com	Philadelphia	PA	19103	877-256-2472	557-2301*

Entry	City	State	ZIP	Phone	Fax
Environmental Compliance Bulletin					
1801 S Bell St.	Arlington	VA	22202	800-372-1033	
TF: 800-372-1033 ■					
Web: www.bna.com/environmental-compliance-bulletin-p4886					
Environmental Laboratory Washington Report					
360 Hiatt Dr	Palm Beach Gardens	FL	33418	561-622-6520	622-2423
TF: 800-621-5463 ■ *Web:* www.lrp.com					
Gas Daily 1200 G St NW Suite 1100	Washington	DC	20005	202-383-2000	904-4209*
**Fax Area Code:* 212 ■ *Web:* www.platts.com/Products/gasdaily					
Global Power Report 2 Penn Plaza 25th Fl	New York	NY	10121	800-752-8878	904-3738*
**Fax Area Code:* 212 ■ *TF:* 800-223-6180 ■ *Web:* www.platts.com					
HazMat Transportation News					
222 Sedwick Dr Suite 101	Durham	NC	27713	800-223-8720	508-2592
TF: 800-274-6737 ■ *Web:* www.bpinews.com					
Inside Energy 2 Penn Plaza 25th Fl	New York	NY	10121	800-752-8878	904-2723*
**Fax Area Code:* 212 ■ *TF:* 800-223-6180 ■ *Web:* www.platts.com					
Inside FERC 2 Penn Plaza 25th Fl	New York	NY	10121	800-752-8878	904-2723*
**Fax Area Code:* 212 ■ *TF:* 800-752-8878 ■ *Web:* www.platts.com					
Inside FERC's Gas Market Report					
2 Penn Plaza 25th Fl	New York	NY	10121	212-904-3070	904-3738
TF: 800-223-6180 ■ *Web:* www.platts.com					
Inside NRC 2 Penn Plaza 25th Fl	New York	NY	10121	800-752-8878	904-3738*
**Fax Area Code:* 212 ■ *TF:* 800-223-6180 ■ *Web:* www.platts.com					
Megawatt Daily 1200 G St NW Suite 1100	Washington	DC	20005	202-383-2000	904-4209*
**Fax Area Code:* 212 ■ *Web:* www.platts.com/Products/megawattdaily					
Natural Gas Week 5 E 37th St 5th Fl	New York	NY	10013	212-532-1112	532-4838
TF: 888-427-7496 ■ *Web:* www.energyintel.com					
Northeast Power Report 2 Penn Plaza 25th Fl	New York	NY	10121	800-752-8878	904-2723*
**Fax Area Code:* 212 ■ *TF:* 800-752-8878 ■ *Web:* www.platts.com					
Nuclear Waste News 222 Sedwick Dr Suite 101	Durham	NC	27713	800-223-8720	508-2592
TF: 800-274-6737 ■ *Web:* www.bpinews.com					
NuclearFuel 1200 G St NW Suite 1000	Washington	DC	20005	202-383-2000	383-2024
Web: www.platts.com/Products/nuclearfuel					
Nucleonics Week 1200 G St NW Suite 1100	Washington	DC	20005	202-383-2100	904-4209*
**Fax Area Code:* 212 ■ *TF:* 800-223-6180 ■ *Web:* www.platts.com/Products/nucleonicsweek					
Oil Daily 5 E 37th St 5th Fl	New York	NY	10016	212-532-1112	532-4938
TF: 888-427-7496 ■ *Web:* www.energyintel.com					
Oil Price Information Service					
3349 Hwy 138 Bldg D Suite D	Wall	NJ	07719	732-901-8800	901-5993
TF Cust Svc: 888-301-2645 ■ *Web:* www.opisnet.com					
OPIS 9737 Washingtonian Blvd Suite 100	Gaithersburg	MD	20878	301-287-2645	287-2820
TF: 888-301-2645 ■ *Web:* www.opisnet.com					
Petro-Chemical News 709 Turmeric Ln	Durham	NC	27713	919-544-1717	544-1999
Web: www.petrochemical-news.com					
Solid Waste Assn of North America (SWANA)					
1100 Wayne Ave Suite 700	Silver Spring	MD	20910	301-585-2898	589-7068
TF: 800-467-9262 ■ *Web:* swana.org					
Solid Waste Report 222 Sedwick Dr Suite 101	Durham	NC	27713	800-223-8720	508-2592
TF: 800-223-8720 ■ *Web:* www.bpinews.com					
State Environment Daily 1801 S Bell St	Arlington	VA	22202	800-372-1033	
TF: 800-372-1033 ■ *Web:* www.bna.com/state-environment-daily-p4905					
Toxics Law Reporter 1801 S Bell St	Arlington	VA	22202	800-372-1033	
TF: 800-372-1033 ■ *Web:* www.bna.com/toxics-law-reporter-p5947					
Toxics Law Reporter 1801 S Bell St	Washington	DC	20037	703-341-3500	253-0332*
**Fax Area Code:* 800 ■ *TF:* 800-372-1033 ■ *Web:* www.bna.com					
Utility Environment Report					
2 Penn Plaza 25th Fl	New York	NY	10121	800-752-8878	904-3738*
**Fax Area Code:* 212 ■ *TF:* 800-752-8878 ■ *Web:* www.platts.com					
Water Tech Online 19 British American Blvd W	Latham	NY	12110	518-783-1281	783-1386
Web: www.watertechonline.com					
World Gas Intelligence 5 E 37th St 5th Fl	New York	NY	10016	212-532-1112	532-4479
Web: www.energyintel.com					

534-6 General Interest Newsletters

Entry	City	State	ZIP	Phone	Fax
Bottom Line/Personal 281 Tresser Blvd 8th Fl	Stamford	CT	06901	203-973-5900	967-3621*
**Fax:* Edit ■ *TF Cust Svc:* 800-274-5611 ■ *Web:* www.boardroom.com					
Bottom Line/Tomorrow 281 Tresser Blvd	Stamford	CT	06901	203-973-5900	967-3621*
**Fax:* Edit ■ *TF Cust Svc:* 800-274-5611 ■ *Web:* www.boardroom.com					
CatWatch 800 Connecticut Ave 4-W	Norwalk	CT	06854	203-857-3100	857-3103
TF: 800-424-7887 ■ *Web:* www.belvoir.com					
DogWatch 800 Connecticut Ave 4-W	Norwalk	CT	06854	203-857-3100	857-3103
TF: 800-424-7887 ■ *Web:* www.belvoir.com					
FRM Weekly 54 Adams St	Garden City	NY	11530	516-746-6700	294-8141
Kiplinger California Letter 1729 H St NW	Washington	DC	20006	202-887-6400	778-8976
TF: 800-544-0155 ■ *Web:* www.kiplinger.com					
NRTA/AARP Bulletin 601 E St NW	Washington	DC	20049	202-434-2277	434-2809*
**Fax:* Hum Res ■ *TF:* 888-867-2277 ■ *Web:* www.aarp.org/nrta					
Older Americans Report					
222 Sedwick Dr Suite 101	Durham	NC	27713	800-223-8720	508-2592*
**Fax:* Edit ■ *TF:* 800-274-6737 ■ *Web:* www.bpinews.com					
Passport Newsletter 5315 N Clark St PMB 501	Chicago	IL	60640	773-769-6760	
TF: 800-542-6670 ■ *Web:* www.passportnewsletter.com					
Preferred Traveler 4501 Forbes Blvd	Lanham	MD	20706	301-459-8020	731-0525*
**Fax:* Edit ■ *Web:* www.preferredtraveller.com					
Sotheby's Newsletter 1334 York Ave	New York	NY	10021	212-606-7000	606-7107*
**Fax:* Hum Res ■ *Web:* www.sothebys.com					
Tax Hotline 281 Tresser Blvd	Stamford	CT	06901	203-973-5900	967-3621*
**Fax:* Edit ■ *TF Cust Svc:* 800-274-5611 ■ *Web:* www.boardroom.com					

534-7 Government & Law Newsletters

Entry	City	State	ZIP	Phone	Fax
AAJ Law Reporter 1050 31st St NW	Washington	DC	20007	202-965-3500	625-7084
TF: 800-424-2727 ■ *Web:* www.justice.org					
Alcoholic Beverage Control PO Box 7376	Alexandria	VA	22307	703-768-9600	768-9690
TF: 800-876-2545 ■ *Web:* statecapitals.com/alcoholbev.html					
Bankruptcy Law Letter 610 Opperman Dr	Eagan	MN	55123	651-687-7000	687-8722
TF: 800-937-8529 ■ *Web:* www.west.thomson.com					
BD Week					
9737 Washingtonian Blvd Suite 100	Gaithersburg	MD	20878	301-287-2389	287-2070
TF: 866-777-8567 ■ *Web:* www.bdweek.com					
Bioethics Legal Review					
1617 JFK Blvd Suite 1750	Philadelphia	PA	19103	215-557-2300	557-2301
TF: 800-722-7670 ■ *Web:* www.lawjournalnewsletters.com					
Civil Rights PO Box 7376	Alexandria	VA	22307	703-768-9600	768-9690
TF: 800-876-2545 ■ *Web:* statecapitals.com/civilrights.html					
Class Action Litigation Report					
1801 S Bell St	Arlington	VA	22202	800-372-1033	
TF: 800-372-1033 ■ *Web:* www.bna.com/class-action-litigation-p5442					
Community Development Digest					
8204 Fenton St	Silver Spring	MD	20910	301-588-6380	588-6385
TF: 800-666-6380 ■ *Web:* www.cdpublications.com					
Community Health Funding Week					
8204 Fenton St	Silver Spring	MD	20910	301-588-6380	588-0519
TF: 800-666-6380 ■ *Web:* www.cdpublications.com					
Computer Technology Law Report					
1801 S Bell St	Arlington	VA	22202	800-372-1033	
TF: 800-372-1033 ■ *Web:* www.bna.com/computer-technology-law-p6795					
Congress Daily					
600 New Hampshire Ave The Watergate	Washington	DC	20037	202-266-7000	296-6110
TF: 800-424-2921 ■ *Web:* nationaljournal.com					
Congressional Quarterly Budget Tracker					
1255 22nd St NW	Washington	DC	20037	202-419-8500	380-3810*
**Fax Area Code:* 800 ■ *TF:* 800-432-2250 ■					
Web: www.corporate.cqrollcall.com/wmspage.cfm?parm1=89					
Congressional Quarterly Green Sheets					
1255 22nd St NW Suite 700	Washington	DC	20037	202-419-8500	380-3810*
**Fax Area Code:* 800 ■ *TF:* 800-432-2250 ■ *Web:* www.cq.com					
Congressional Quarterly HealthBeat					
1255 22nd St NW	Washington	DC	20037	202-419-8500	380-3810*
**Fax Area Code:* 800 ■ *TF:* 800-432-2250 ■ *Web:* www.cq.com					
Congressional Quarterly Homeland Security					
1255 22nd St NW	Washington	DC	20037	202-419-8500	380-3810*
**Fax Area Code:* 800 ■ *TF:* 800-432-2250 ■					
Web: www.corporate.cqrollcall.com/wmspage.cfm?parm1=54					
Congressional Quarterly House Action Reports					
1255 22nd St NW	Washington	DC	20037	202-419-8500	380-3810*
**Fax Area Code:* 800 ■ *TF:* 800-432-2250 ■ *Web:* www.cq.com					
Congressional Quarterly Today					
1255 22nd St NW	Washington	DC	20037	202-419-8500	380-3810*
**Fax Area Code:* 800 ■ *TF Cust Svc:* 800-432-2250 ■ *Web:* www.cq.com					
Consumer Financial Services Law Report					
360 Hiatt Dr	Palm Beach Gardens	FL	33418	561-622-6520	622-2423
TF: 800-621-5463 ■ *Web:* www.lrp.com					
Corporate Compliance & Regulatory					
1617 JFK Blvd Suite 1750	Philadelphia	PA	19103	215-557-2300	557-2301
TF: 800-722-7670 ■ *Web:* www.lawjournalnewsletters.com					
Corporate Law Daily 1801 S Bell St	Arlington	VA	22202	800-372-1033	
TF: 800-372-1033 ■ *Web:* www.bna.com/corporate-law-daily-p6009					
Criminal Law Reporter 1801 S Bell St	Arlington	VA	22202	800-372-1033	
TF: 800-372-1033 ■ *Web:* www.bna.com/criminal-law-reporter-p5446					
Daily Labor Report 1801 S Bell St	Arlington	VA	22202	800-372-1033	
TF: 800-372-1033 ■ *Web:* www.bna.com/daily-labor-report-p5449					
Development Director's Letter					
8204 Fenton St	Silver Spring	MD	20910	301-588-6380	588-6385
TF: 800-666-6380 ■ *Web:* www.cdpublications.com/pubs					
Disability Law Compliance Report					
610 Opperman Dr	Eagan	MN	55123	651-687-7000	687-8722
TF Cust Svc: 800-328-4880 ■ *Web:* www.west.thomson.com					
DWI Journal Law & Science PO Box 224	Spencerville	MD	20868	301-384-1573	
Web: www.dwijournal.com					
e-Commerce Law & Strategy					
1617 JFK Blvd Suite 1750	Philadelphia	PA	19103	215-557-2300	557-2301
TF: 800-722-7670 ■ *Web:* www.lawjournalnewsletters.com					
e-Discovery Law & Strategy					
1617 JFK Blvd Suite 1750	Philadelphia	PA	19103	215-557-2300	557-2301
TF: 800-722-7670 ■ *Web:* www.lawjournalnewsletters.com					
Economic Development PO Box 7376	Alexandria	VA	22307	703-768-9600	768-9690
Web: statecapitals.com/ecodev.html					
Emergency Preparedness News					
222 Sedwick Dr Suite 101	Durham	NC	27713	800-223-8720	508-2592
TF: 800-223-8720 ■ *Web:* www.bpinews.com					
Employment Discrimination Report					
1801 S Bell St	Arlington	VA	22202	800-372-1033	
TF: 800-372-1033 ■					
Web: www.bna.com/employment-discrimination-report-p5458					
Expert Evidence Report 1801 S Bell St	Arlington	VA	22202	800-372-1033	
TF: 800-372-1033 ■ *Web:* www.bna.com/expert-evidence-report-p5463					
Family Law Reporter 1801 S Bell St	Arlington	VA	22202	800-372-1033	
TF: 800-372-1033 ■ *Web:* www.bna.com/family-law-reporter-p6014					
Federal Action Affecting the States					
PO Box 7376	Alexandria	VA	22307	703-768-9600	768-9600
Web: statecapitals.com/fedaction.html					
Federal Assistance Monitor					
8204 Fenton St	Silver Spring	MD	20910	301-588-6380	588-6385
TF: 800-666-6380 ■ *Web:* www.cdpublications.com					
Federal Contracts Report 1801 S Bell St	Arlington	VA	22202	800-372-1033	
TF: 800-372-1033 ■ *Web:* www.bna.com/federal-contracts-report-p6016					
Federal Discovery News					
360 Hiatt Dr	Palm Beach Gardens	FL	33418	561-622-6520	622-2423
TF: 800-621-5463 ■ *Web:* www.lrp.com					
Franchising Business & Law Alert					
1617 JFK Blvd Suite 1750	Philadelphia	PA	19103	215-557-2300	557-2301
TF: 800-722-7670 ■ *Web:* www.lawjournalnewsletters.com					
Government Contracts Update					
11300 Rockville Pike Suite 1100	Rockville	MD	20852	301-287-2700	816-8945
TF Cust Svc: 888-287-2223 ■ *Web:* www.ucg.com					
Health Care Fraud Report 1801 S Bell St	Arlington	VA	22202	800-372-1033	
TF: 800-372-1033 ■ *Web:* www.bna.com/health-care-fraud-p6025					

Phone Fax

Health Law Reporter 1801 S Bell St .... Arlington VA 22202 800-372-1033
TF: 800-372-1033 ■ *Web:* www.bna.com/health-law-reporter-p6785
Homeland Security Funding Week
8204 Fenton St.......................................Silver Spring MD 20910 301-588-6380 588-6385
TF: 800-666-6380 ■ *Web:* www.cdpublications.com
Hospital Litigation Reporter
590 Dutch Valley Rd NE ....Atlanta GA 30324 404-881-1141 881-0074
TF: 800-926-7926 ■ *Web:* www.straffordpub.com/products/hlr
Hospitality Law 360 Hiatt Dr................Palm Beach Gardens FL 33418 561-622-6520 622-2423
TF: 800-621-5463 ■ *Web:* www.lrp.com
Housing & Development Reporter 610 Opperman Dr..... Eagan MN 55123 651-687-7000 741-1414*
**Fax Area Code:* 800 ■ *TF General:* 800-937-8529 ■ *Web:* www.west.thomson.com
Insurance Coverage Law Bulletin The
1617 JFK Blvd Suite 1750 .... Philadelphia PA 19103 215-557-2300 557-2301
TF: 800-722-7670 ■ *Web:* www.lawjournalnewsletters.com
Insurance Regulation PO Box 7376 .... Alexandria VA 22307 703-768-9600 768-9690
Web: statecapitals.com
Intellectual Property Strategist
1617 JFK Blvd Suite 1750 .... Philadelphia PA 19103 215-557-2300 557-2301
TF: 800-722-7670 ■ *Web:* www.americanlawyer.com
Internet Law & Strategy
1617 JFK Blvd Suite 1750 .... Philadelphia PA 19103 215-557-2300 557-2301
TF: 800-722-7670 ■ *Web:* www.lawjournalnewsletters.com
IRS Practice Adviser 1801 S Bell St .... Arlington VA 22202 800-372-1033
TF: 800-372-1033 ■ *Web:* www.bna.com/IRS-Practice-Adviser-p7876
Kiplinger Tax Letter 1729 H St NW ....Washington DC 20006 202-887-6400 778-8976
TF: 800-544-0155 ■ *Web:* www.kiplinger.com
Kiplinger Washington Letter 1729 H St NW ....Washington DC 20006 202-887-6400 778-8976
TF: 800-544-0155
Landlord Law Report 8204 Fenton St............. Silver Spring MD 20910 301-588-6380 588-6385
TF: 800-666-6380 ■ *Web:* www.cdpublications.com/pubs/landlordlaw.php
Medical Research Law & Policy Report
1801 S Bell St.................................. Arlington VA 22202 800-372-1033
TF: 800-372-1033 ■ *Web:* www.bna.com/medical-research-law-p6788
Medicare Compliance Alert
11300 Rockville Pike Suite 1100 .... Rockville MD 20852 301-287-2700 816-8945
TF: 800-929-4824 ■ *Web:* www.compliancealert.net
Mergers & Acquisitions Law Report
1801 S Bell St.................................. Arlington VA 22202 800-372-1033
TF: 800-372-1033 ■ *Web:* www.bna.com/mergers-acquisitions-law-p5940
Money & Politics Report 1801 S Bell St............. Arlington VA 22202 800-372-1033
TF: 800-372-1033 ■ *Web:* www.bna.com/money-politics-report-p6103
Motor Vehicle Regulation PO Box 7376 .... Alexandria VA 22307 703-768-9600 768-9690
Web: statecapitals.com/motorreg.html
Municipal Litigation Reporter
590 Dutch Valley Rd NE ....Atlanta GA 30324 404-881-1141 881-0074
TF: 800-926-7926 ■ *Web:* www.straffordpub.com
Native American Report
222 Sedwick Dr Suite 101 ....Durham NC 27713 800-223-8720 508-2592
TF: 800-274-6737 ■ *Web:* www.bpinews.com
New York Real Estate Law Reporter
1617 JFK Blvd Suite 1750 .... Philadelphia PA 19103 215-557-2311
TF: 800-999-1916 ■ *Web:* www.lawcatalog.com
Non-Profit Legal & Tax Letter
PO Box 368 .... Lovettsville VA 20180 540-822-3928 822-3945
Web: www.taxexemptresources.com
Outlook from The State Capitals The
PO Box 7376 .... Alexandria VA 22307 703-768-9600 768-9690
Web: statecapitals.com/theoutlook.html
Patent Strategy & Management
1617 JFK Blvd Suite 1750 .... Philadelphia PA 19103 215-557-2300 557-2301
TF: 800-722-7670 ■ *Web:* www.lawjournalnewsletters.com
Patent Trademark & Copyright Law Daily
1801 S Bell St.................................. Arlington VA 22202 800-372-1033
TF: 800-372-1033 ■
Web: www.bna.com/patent-trademark-copyright-daily-p5943
Pharmaceutical Law & Industry Report
1801 S Bell St.................................. Arlington VA 22202 800-372-1033
TF: 800-372-1033 ■ *Web:* www.bna.com/pharmaceutical-law-industry-p6790
Postal World
11300 Rockville Pike Suite 1100 .... Rockville MD 20852 301-287-2700 816-8945
TF: 800-929-4824 ■ *Web:* www.ucg.com
Privacy & Security Law Report
1801 S Bell St.................................. Arlington VA 22202 800-372-1033
TF: 800-372-1033 ■ *Web:* www.bna.com/privacy-security-law-p6713
Private Security Case Law Reporter
590 Dutch Valley Rd NE ....Atlanta GA 30324 404-881-1141 881-0074
TF: 800-926-7926 ■ *Web:* www.straffordpub.com/products/psc
Product Safety & Liability Reporter
1801 S Bell St................................Washington DC 20037 703-341-3500 253-0332*
**Fax Area Code:* 800 ■ *TF:* 800-372-1033 ■ *Web:* www.bna.com
Property Taxes & School Funding
PO Box 7376 .... Alexandria VA 22307 703-768-9600 768-9690
Web: www.statecapitals.com/taxprop.html
Public Safety & Justice Policies
PO Box 7376 .... Alexandria VA 22307 703-768-9600 768-9690
TF: 800-876-2545 ■ *Web:* www.statecapitals.com/publicsafety.html
Real Estate Law Report 610 Opperman Dr.............. Eagan MN 55123 651-687-7000 741-1414*
**Fax Area Code:* 800 ■ **Fax:* Sales ■ *TF Cust Svc:* 800-328-4880 ■ *Web:* www.west.thomson.com
Roll Call 77 K St NE 8th Fl........................Washington DC 20002 202-650-6500 824-0475
TF: 800-432-2250 ■ *Web:* www.rollcall.com
Same Sex Partnership Law Report
1617 JFK Blvd Suite 1750 .... Philadelphia PA 19103 215-557-2300 557-2304
TF: 800-722-7670 ■ *Web:* www.lawjournalnewsletters.com
Securities Law Daily 1801 S Bell St .... Arlington VA 22202 800-372-1033
TF: 800-372-1033 ■ *Web:* www.bna.com/securities-law-daily-p5944
Securities Regulation & Law Report
1801 S Bell St.................................. Arlington VA 22202 800-372-1033
TF: 800-372-1033 ■ *Web:* www.bna.com/securities-regulation-law-p5945
Silica Legal News Report
1617 JFK Blvd Suite 1750 .... Philadelphia PA 19103 215-557-2300 557-2301
TF: 800-722-7670 ■ *Web:* www.lawjournalnewsletters.com

Phone Fax

Taxation & Revenue Policies PO Box 7376.......... Alexandria VA 22307 703-768-9600 768-9690
TF: 800-876-2545 ■ *Web:* www.statecapitals.com/taxandrev.html
Washington International Business Report
818 Connecticut Ave NW 12th Fl ....Washington DC 20006 202-872-8181 872-8696
Web: www.ibgc.com
Workplace Law Report 1801 S Bell St .... Arlington VA 22202 800-372-1033
TF: 800-372-1033 ■ *Web:* www.bna.com/workplace-law-report-p5953
World Securities Law Report 1801 S Bell St.......... Arlington VA 22202 800-372-1033
TF: 800-372-1033 ■ *Web:* www.bna.com

534-8 Health & Social Issues Newsletters

Phone Fax

Affordable Housing Update
8204 Fenton St...............................Silver Spring MD 20910 301-558-6385 588-6385
TF: 800-666-6380 ■ *Web:* www.cdpublications.com
Aging News Alert 8204 Fenton St................ Silver Spring MD 20910 301-588-6385 588-6385
TF: 800-666-6380 ■ *Web:* www.cdpublications.com/pubs
AICR Newsletter 1759 R St NW ....Washington DC 20009 202-328-7744 328-7226
TF: 800-843-8114 ■ *Web:* www.aicr.org
AIDS Policy & Law 360 Hiatt Dr .... Palm Beach Gardens FL 33418 561-622-6520 622-2423
TF: 800-621-5463 ■ *Web:* www.lrp.com
Alternatives 7811 Montrose Rd.................... Potomac MD 20854 301-340-2100 424-5059
TF: 800-861-5967 ■ *Web:* www.drdavidwilliams.com
American Parkinson's Disease Assn Newsletter
135 Parkinson Ave ....Staten Island NY 10305 718-981-8001 981-4399
TF: 800-223-2732 ■ *Web:* www.apdaparkinson.org
APCO Bulletin 351 N Williamson Blvd.............Daytona Beach FL 32114 386-322-2500 322-2501
TF: 888-272-6911 ■ *Web:* www.apcointl.org
Arthritis Advisor 800 Connecticut Ave 4 W ....Norwalk CT 06854 203-857-3100 857-3103
TF: 800-424-7887 ■ *Web:* www.arthritis-advisor.com
Bell The 2001 N Beauregard St 12th Fl................ Alexandria VA 22311 703-684-7722 684-5968
TF: 800-969-6642 ■ *Web:* www.nmha.org/newsroom/bell/index.cfm
Bottom Line/Health (BLH) PO Box 422318 .... Palm Coast FL 32142 800-289-0409 456-3787
TF Cust Svc: 800-289-0409 ■
Web: www.bottomlinesecrets.com/store/pubs/sub_blh.html
Cancer Letter 3821 Woodley Rd NW................Washington DC 20016 202-362-1809 318-4030
TF: 800-513-7042 ■ *Web:* www.cancerletter.com
Cancer Letter Business & Regulatory Report
PO Box 9905 ....Washington DC 20016 202-362-1809 318-4030
TF: 800-513-7042 ■ *Web:* www.cancerletter.com
Child Protection Law Report
222 Sedwick Dr Suite 101 ....Durham NC 27713 800-223-8720 508-2592*
**Fax:* Mktg ■ *TF:* 800-274-6737 ■ *Web:* www.bpinews.com
Children & Youth Funding Report
8204 Fenton St...............................Silver Spring MD 20910 301-588-6385 588-6385
TF: 800-666-6380 ■ *Web:* www.cdpublications.com/pubs
Congressional Quarterly HealthBeat
1255 22nd St NW.................................Washington DC 20037 202-419-8500 380-3810*
**Fax Area Code:* 800 ■ *TF:* 800-432-2250 ■ *Web:* www.cq.com
Consumer Reports On Health 101 Truman Ave .... Yonkers NY 10703 914-378-2000 378-2900
TF: 800-234-1645 ■ *Web:* www.consumerreports.org
CTD News 747 Dresher Rd Suite 500 .... Horsham PA 19044 215-784-0860 784-9639
TF: 800-341-7874 ■ *Web:* www.ctdnews.com
Dairy Council Digest
10255 W Higgins Rd Suite 900 .... Rosemont IL 60018 847-803-2000 803-2077
TF Cust Svc: 800-426-8271 ■ *Web:* www.nationaldairycouncil.org
Disability Funding Week 8204 Fenton St.......... Silver Spring MD 20910 301-588-6385 588-6385
TF: 800-666-6380 ■ *Web:* www.cdpublications.com/pubs
Drug Detection Report 222 Sedwick Dr Suite 101........ Durham NC 27713 800-223-8720 508-2592*
**Fax:* Mktg ■ *TF:* 800-274-6737 ■ *Web:* www.bpinews.com
Environment of Care Leader
9737 Washintonian Blvd Suite 100................ Gaithersburg MD 20878 301-287-2700 287-2039
TF Cust Svc: 800-929-4824 ■ *Web:* www.ucg.com
Family Relations Newsletter PO Box 7376 .... Alexandria VA 22307 703-768-9600 768-9690
Web: statecapitals.com/familyrelations.html
Focus on Healthy Aging
800 Connecticut Ave 4 W............................Norwalk CT 06854 203-857-3100 857-3103
TF: 800-424-7887 ■ *Web:* www.focusonhealthyaging.com
Food & Fitness Advisor 800 Connecticut Ave...........Norwalk CT 06854 203-857-3100 857-3103
TF: 800-424-7887 ■ *Web:* www.foodandfitnessadvisor.com
Harvard Heart Letter 1 Atlantic St Suite 604 .... Stamford CT 06901 203-975-8854 975-9901
Web: www.health.harvard.edu
Harvard Men's Health Watch
1 Atlantic St Suite 604 .... Stamford CT 06901 203-975-8854 975-9901
Web: www.health.harvard.edu
Harvard Mental Health Letter
1 Atlantic St Suite 604 .... Stamford CT 06901 203-975-8854 975-9901
Web: www.health.harvard.edu
Harvard Women's Health Watch
1 Atlantic St Suite 604 .... Stamford CT 06901 203-975-8854 975-9901
Web: www.health.harvard.edu
Health & Healing Newsletter 7811 Montrose Rd....... Potomac MD 20854 301-340-2100 424-5059
TF: 800-861-5967 ■ *Web:* www.drwhitaker.com
Health Care Daily Report 1801 S Bell St.............. Arlington VA 22202 800-372-1033
TF: 800-372-1033 ■ *Web:* www.bna.com/health-care-daily-p6781
Health Care Policy Report 1801 S Bell St .... Arlington VA 22202 800-372-1033
TF: 800-372-1033 ■ *Web:* www.bna.com/health-care-policy-p6782
Health Law Week 590 Dutch Valley Rd NE.................Atlanta GA 30324 404-881-1141 881-0074
TF: 800-926-7926 ■ *Web:* www.straffordpub.com
Health News 800 Connecticut Ave.......................Norwalk CT 06854 203-857-3100 857-3103
TF: 800-424-7887 ■ *Web:* www.belvoir.com
Health Plan & Provider Report
1801 S Bell St.................................. Arlington VA 22202 800-372-1033
TF: 800-372-1033 ■ *Web:* www.bnainfo.bna.com/current/mac/topc.htm
Healthcare Disparities Report
8204 Fenton St...............................Silver Spring MD 20910 301-588-6385 588-6380
TF: 800-666-6380 ■ *Web:* www.cdpublications.com
HealthFacts 239 Thompson St ....New York NY 10012 212-674-7105 674-7100
Web: www.medicalconsumers.org

Phone | Fax

Healthy Years 800 Connecticut Ave 4 W ... Norwalk CT 06854 203-857-3100 857-3103
TF: 800-424-7887 ■ *Web:* www.belvoir.com

Heart Advisor 800 Connecticut Ave 4-W ... Norwalk CT 06854 203-857-3100 857-3103
TF: 800-424-7887 ■ *Web:* www.heart-advisor.com

Heart Health & Nutrition 7811 Montrose Rd. ... Potomac MD 20854 301-340-2100 340-2561
TF: 800-861-5970 ■ *Web:* www.drsinatra.com

Home Health Line
11300 Rockville Pike Suite 1100 ... Rockville MD 20852 301-287-2700 816-8945
TF: 800-929-4824 ■ *Web:* www.ucg.com

International Medical Device Regulatory Monitor
300 N Washington St Suite 200 ... Falls Church VA 22046 703-538-7600 538-7676
TF: 888-838-5578 ■ *Web:* www.fdanews.com/newsletter?newsletterId=18

Johns Hopkins Medical Letter Health After 50
500 Fifth Ave Suite 1900 ... New York NY 10110 800-829-0422 695-2936*
**Fax Area Code:* 212 ■ *TF:* 800-829-0422 ■ *Web:* www.johnshopkinshealthalerts.com

Lark Letter 7811 Montrose Rd ... Potomac MD 20854 301-340-2100 424-5059
TF: 800-861-5967 ■ *Web:* www.drlark.com

Mayo Clinic Health Letter 200 1st St NW ... Rochester MN 55905 507-284-2094 284-0252
TF: 800-707-7040 ■ *Web:* www.bookstore.mayoclinic.com

Mayo Clinic Women's Healthsource
200 1st St SW ... Rochester MN 55905 507-284-2094 284-0252
TF: 800-707-7040 ■ *Web:* www.bookstore.mayoclinic.com

Medicare Compliance Alert
11300 Rockville Pike Suite 1100 ... Rockville MD 20852 301-287-2700 816-8945
TF: 800-929-4824 ■ *Web:* www.compliancealert.net

Men's Health Advisor 800 Connecticut Ave 4 W ... Norwalk CT 06854 203-857-3100 857-3103
TF: 800-424-7887 ■ *Web:* www.menshealthadvisor.com

Mental Health Law Reporter
222 Sedwick Dr Suite 101 ... Durham NC 27713 800-223-8720 508-2592
TF: 800-223-8720 ■ *Web:* www.bpinews.com

Mental Health Report 222 Sedwick Dr Suite 101 ... Durham NC 27713 800-223-8720 508-2592*
**Fax:* Mktg ■ *TF:* 800-274-6737 ■ *Web:* www.bpinews.com

Mind Mood & Memory 800 Connecticut Ave 4 W ... Norwalk CT 06854 203-857-3100 857-3103
TF: 800-424-7887 ■ *Web:* www.belvoir.com

Nutrition Action
1875 Connecticut Way NW Suite 300 ... Washington DC 20009 202-332-9110 265-4954
Web: www.cspinet.org

OSHA Up-to-Date Newsletter
1121 Spring Lake Dr ... Itasca IL 60143 630-285-1121 285-1315
TF Cust Svc: 800-621-7615 ■ *Web:* www.nsc.org

Physician Office Lab News
11300 Rockville Pike Suite 1100 ... Rockville MD 20852 301-287-2700 816-8945
TF: 800-929-4824 ■ *Web:* www.ucg.com

Public Assistance & Welfare Trends
PO Box 7376 ... Alexandria VA 22307 703-768-9600 768-9690
Web: statecapitals.com/publicassist.html

Public Health Newsletter PO Box 7376 ... Alexandria VA 22307 703-768-9600 768-9690
Web: statecapitals.com/publichealth.html

Report on Disability Programs
222 Sedwick Dr Suite 101 ... Durham NC 27713 800-223-8720 508-2592*
**Fax:* Mktg ■ *TF:* 800-274-6737 ■ *Web:* www.bpinews.com

StayWell Consumer Health Publishing
1 Atlantic St Suite 604 ... Stamford CT 06901 203-975-8854 975-9901
Web: www.swchp.com

Substance Abuse Funding Week
8204 Fenton St ... Silver Spring MD 20910 301-588-6385 588-6385
TF: 800-666-6380 ■ *Web:* www.cdpublications.com/pubs

UC Berkeley Wellness Letter
632 Broadway 11th Fl ... New York NY 10012 212-505-2255 505-5462
Web: www.berkeleywellness.com

United Communications Group
11300 Rockville Pike Suite 1100 ... Rockville MD 20852 301-287-2700 816-8945
TF: 800-929-4824

Women's Health Advisor
800 Connecticut Ave 4 W ... Norwalk CT 06854 203-857-3100 857-3103
TF: 800-424-7887 ■ *Web:* www.womens-health-advisor.com

534-9 Investment Newsletters

Phone | Fax

All-Star Fund Trader 60 5th Ave ... New York NY 10011 212-620-2200 206-5126
TF: 800-888-9896 ■ *Web:* www.newsletters.forbes.com

Bert Dohmen's Wellington Letter
1100 Glendon Ave Suite 1130 Westwood Ctr ... Los Angeles CA 90024 310-208-6622 208-1038
Web: dohmencapital.com

Blue Chip Economic Indicators
3663 Madison Ave ... Kansas City MO 64111 816-931-0131
TF Cust Svc: 800-234-1660 ■ *Web:* www.aspenpublishers.com

Blue Chip Financial Forecasts
3663 Madison Ave ... Kansas City MO 64111 816-931-0131
TF Cust Svc: 800-234-1660 ■ *Web:* www.aspenpublishers.com

Cabot Market Letter 176 N St PO Box 2049 ... Salem MA 01970 978-745-5532 745-1283
TF Orders: 800-777-2658 ■ *Web:* www.cabot.net

Chartist Newsletter
5122 Katella Ave Suite 200 ... Los Alamitos CA 90720 562-596-2385 596-1280
TF: 800-942-4278 ■ *Web:* www.thechartist.com

Dag Peter Portfolio Strategy & Management
65 Lake Front Dr ... Akron OH 44319 330-644-2782
Web: www.peterdag.com

Derivatives Week 225 Pk Ave S ... New York NY 10003 212-224-3800 224-3491
Web: www.derivativesintelligence.com

Dow Theory Forecasts 7412 Calumet Ave ... Hammond IN 46324 219-931-6480 931-6487
Web: www.dowtheory.com

Dow Theory Letters PO Box 1759 ... La Jolla CA 92038 858-454-0481 454-1265
Web: www.dowtheoryletters.com

DRIP Investor 7412 Calumet Ave ... Hammond IN 46324 219-931-6480 931-6487
Web: www.dripinvestor.com

Elliott Wave Theorist 200 Main St ... Gainesville GA 30501 770-536-0309 536-2514
TF: 800-336-1618 ■ *Web:* www.elliottwave.com

Phone | Fax

Fabian's Investment Resources
2100 Main St Suite 300 ... Huntington Beach CA 92648 800-950-8765 536-7066*
**Fax Area Code:* 714 ■ *TF:* 800-950-8765 ■ *Web:* www.fabian.com

Future Market Service
330 S Wells St Suite 612 ... Chicago IL 60606 312-554-8456 939-4135
TF: 800-621-5271 ■ *Web:* www.crbtrader.com

Global Market Perspective PO Box 1618 ... Gainesville GA 30503 770-536-0309 536-2514
TF: 800-336-1618 ■ *Web:* www.elliottwave.com/products/gmp

Gold Mining Stock Report PO Box 1217 ... Lafayette CA 94549 925-283-4848 284-1294

Gold Newsletter
2400 Jefferson Hwy Suite 600 ... Jefferson LA 70121 504-837-3033 837-4885
TF: 800-877-8847 ■ *Web:* www.goldnewsletter.com

Granville Market Letter
2510 Grand Blvd # 2201 ... Kansas City MO 64108 816-474-5353 421-3897
TF: 800-876-5388 ■ *Web:* www.granvilleletter.com

Growth Fund Guide PO Box 6600 ... Rapid City SD 57709 605-341-1971 341-7260
TF: 800-621-8322

Growth Stock Outlook
4405 East-West Hwy Suite 305 ... Bethesda MD 20814 301-654-5205 986-0722
TF: 800-742-5476

IA Week Newsletter
11300 Rockville Pike Suite 1100 ... Rockville MD 20852 301-287-2700 816-8945
Web: www.iaweek.com

Investment Quality Trends
7440 Girard Ave Suite 4 ... La Jolla CA 92037 858-459-3818 459-3819
Web: www.iqtrends.com

Investors Intelligence 30 Church St ... New Rochelle NY 10801 914-632-0422 632-0335
Web: www.investorsintelligence.com

Louis Rukeyser's Mutual Funds
7600A Leesburg Pike W Bldg, Suite 300 ... Falls Church VA 22043 703-394-4931 905-8100
TF: 800-832-2330 ■ *Web:* www.rukeyser.com

Mutual Fund Letter
5122 Katella Ave Suite 200 ... Los Alamitos CA 90720 562-596-2385 596-1280
TF: 800-942-4278 ■ *Web:* www.thechartist.com

Option Advisor 5151 Pfeiffer Rd Suite 250 ... Cincinnati OH 45242 513-589-3800 589-3810
TF: 800-448-2080 ■ *Web:* www.schaeffersresearch.com

Personal Finance Newsletter
7600A Leesburg Pike W Bldg, Suite 300 ... Falls Church VA 22043 703-394-4931 905-8100
TF: 800-832-2330 ■ *Web:* www.pfnewsletter.com

Profitable Investing 9420 Key W Ave ... Rockville MD 20850 301-279-4200
TF: 800-219-8592 ■ *Web:* www.profitableinvesting.investorplace.com

Prudent Speculator
32392 Coast Hwy Suite 260 ... Laguna Beach CA 92651 949-499-3215 499-3218
TF: 800-258-7786 ■ *Web:* www.theprudentspeculator.com

Richard Young's Intelligence Report
700 Indian Springs Dr ... Lancaster PA 17601 800-219-8592
TF: 800-219-8592 ■ *Web:* www.intelligencereport.com

Systems & Forecasts
150 Great Neck Rd Suite 301 ... Great Neck NY 11021 516-829-6444 466-4676
Web: www.systemsandforecasts.com

Timer Digest PO Box 1688 ... Greenwich CT 06836 203-629-3503 629-2175
TF: 800-356-2527 ■ *Web:* www.timerdigest.com

Utility Forecaster
7600A Leesburg Pike W Bldg, Suite 300 ... Falls Church VA 22043 703-394-4931 905-8100
TF: 800-832-2330 ■ *Web:* www.utilityforecaster.com

Value Line 600 220 E 42nd St 6th Fl ... New York NY 10017 212-907-1500 818-9670
Web: www.valueline.com

Value Line Convertibles Survey
220 E 42nd St 6th Fl ... New York NY 10017 212-907-1500 818-9670
Web: www.valueline.com

Value Line Investment Survey
220 E 42nd St 6th Fl ... New York NY 10017 212-907-1500 818-9670
Web: www.valueline.com

Value Line Mutual Funds Survey
220 E 42nd St 6th Fl ... New York NY 10017 212-907-1500 818-9670
Web: www.valueline.com

Value Line Options Survey
200 E 42nd St 6th Fl ... New York NY 10017 212-907-1500 818-9670
Web: www.valueline.com

Wall Street Digest
8830 S Tamiami Tr Suite 110 ... Sarasota FL 34238 941-954-5500 364-8447
TF: 800-785-5050 ■ *Web:* www.wallstreetdigest.com

Wall Street Letter 225 Pk Ave S 7th Fl ... New York NY 10003 212-224-3300 224-3491
Web: www.wallstreetletter.com

Wireless Telecom Investor
1 Lower Ragsdale Dr Bldg 1 Suite 130 ... Monterey CA 93940 831-624-1536 625-3225
TF: 800-307-2529 ■ *Web:* www.kagan.com

534-10 Marketing & Sales Newsletters

Phone | Fax

Book Marketing Update 135 E Plumstead Ave ... Lansdowne PA 19050 610-259-1070 284-3704
TF: 800-989-1400 ■ *Web:* www.bookmarket.com

Downtown Promotion Reporter (DPR)
712 Main St Suite 187B ... Boonton NJ 07005 973-265-2300 402-6056
TF: 800-232-4317 ■ *Web:* www.downtowndevelopment.com/dpr.php

Educational Marketer
11 Riverbend Dr S PO Box 4234 ... Stamford CT 06907 203-358-9900 358-5824
Web: www.simbanet.com/publications/news_em.htm

eMarketer 75 Broad St 32nd Fl ... New York NY 10004 212-763-6010 763-6020
TF: 800-405-0844 ■ *Web:* www.emarketer.com

Friday Report 224 7th St ... Garden City NY 11530 516-746-6700 294-8141
TF: 800-229-6700

Marketing Library Services
143 Old Marlton Pike ... Medford NJ 08055 609-654-6266 654-4309
TF: 800-300-9868 ■ *Web:* www.infotoday.com/mls

Sales Leader 2222 Sedwick Dr Suite 101 ... Durham NC 27713 800-223-8720 508-2592
TF: 800-223-8720 ■ *Web:* www.dartnellcorp.com

Selling to Seniors 8204 Fenton St ... Silver Spring MD 20910 301-588-6380 588-6385
TF: 800-666-6380 ■ *Web:* www.cdpublications.com/products.php

534-11 Media & Communications Newsletters

Name / Address	City	State	ZIP	Phone	Fax
Accuracy in Media Report 4455 Connecticut Ave NW Suite 330 *TF:* 800-787-4567 ■ *Web:* www.aim.org	Washington	DC	20008	202-364-4401	364-4098
Book Publishing Report 60 Long Ridge Rd Suite 300 *Web:* www.bookpublishingreport.com	Stamford	CT	06902	203-325-8193	325-8915
Broadband Adv 1 Lower Ragsdale Dr Bldg 1 Suite 130 *TF:* 800-307-2529 ■ *Web:* www.kagan.com	Monterey	CA	93940	831-624-1536	625-3225
Broadband Technology 1 Lower Ragsdale Dr Bldg 1 Suite 130 *TF:* 800-307-2529 ■ *Web:* www.kagan.com	Monterey	CA	93940	831-624-1536	625-3225
Broadcast Stats 1 Lower Ragsdale Dr Bldg 1 Suite 130 *TF:* 800-307-2529	Monterey	CA	93940	831-624-1536	625-3225
Broadcasters Letter 1400 Independence Ave SW Office of Communications Whitten Bldg Rm 402-A *Web:* www.usda.gov/agency/oc/bmtc/broad.htm	Washington	DC	20250	202-720-4623	720-5773
Capell's Circulation Report 104 W 40th St Suite 1700 *Web:* www.djgmarketing.com	New York	NY	10018	212-370-9700	370-9780
Children's Book Insider 901 Columbia Rd *TF:* 800-807-1916 ■ *Web:* www.write4kids.com	Fort Collins	CO	80525	970-495-0056	493-1810
Communication & Technology Insider 111 E Wacker Dr Suite 500 *TF:* 800-878-5331 ■ *Web:* www.ragan.com/Main/Home.aspx	Chicago	IL	60601	312-960-4140	861-3592
Communication Briefings 1101 King St Suite 110 *TF:* 800-888-2084 ■ *Web:* www.newentrepreneur.com	Alexandria	VA	22314	703-548-3800	684-2136
Communications Business Daily 2115 Ward Ct NW *TF:* 800-771-9202 ■ *Web:* www.warren-news.com	Washington	DC	20037	202-872-9200	293-3435
Communications Daily 2115 Ward Ct NW *TF:* 800-771-9202 ■ *Web:* www.warren-news.com	Washington	DC	20037	202-872-9200	293-3435
DBS Report 1 Lower Ragsdale Dr Bldg 1 Suite 130 *TF:* 800-307-2529 ■ *Web:* www.kagan.com	Monterey	CA	93940	831-624-1536	625-3225
Digital Television 1 Lower Ragsdale Dr Bldg 1 Suite 130 *TF:* 800-307-2529 ■ *Web:* www.kagan.com	Monterey	CA	93940	831-624-1536	625-3225
First Draft 111 E Wacker Dr Suite 500 *TF:* 800-878-5331 ■ *Web:* www.ragan.com/Main/Home.aspx	Chicago	IL	60601	312-960-4100	861-3592
Intellectual Property Strategist 1617 JFK Blvd Suite 1750 *TF:* 800-722-7670 ■ *Web:* www.americanlawyer.com	Philadelphia	PA	19103	215-557-2300	557-2301
Jack O'Dwyer's PR Newsletter 271 Madison Ave Suite 600 *Web:* www.odwyerpr.com	New York	NY	10016	212-679-2471	683-2750
Kagan Media Money 1 Lower Ragsdale Dr Bldg 1 Suite 130 *TF:* 800-307-2529 ■ *Web:* www.kagan.com	Monterey	CA	93940	831-624-1536	625-3225
Media Industry Newsletter (MIN) 110 William St 11th Fl *Web:* www.minonline.com	New York	NY	10038	212-621-4880	621-4879
Media Law Reporter 1801 S Bell St *TF:* 800-372-1033 ■ *Web:* www.bna.com/media-law-reporter-p5934	Arlington	VA	22202	800-372-1033	
Media Relations Report 111 E Wacker Dr Suite 500 *TF:* 800-878-5331 ■ *Web:* www.ragan.com/Main/Home.aspx	Chicago	IL	60601	312-960-4100	861-3592
Professional Publishing Report 60 Long Ridge Rd Suite 300 *Web:* www.simbanet.com	Stamford	CT	06902	203-325-8193	325-8915
Public Broadcasting Report 2115 Ward Ct NW *Web:* www.warren-news.com	Washington	DC	20037	202-872-9200	293-3435
Satellite Week 2115 Ward Ct NW *TF:* 800-771-9202 ■ *Web:* www.warren-news.com	Washington	DC	20037	202-872-9200	293-3435
Speechwriter's Newsletter 111 E Wacker Dr Suite 500 *TF:* 800-878-5331 ■ *Web:* www.ragan.com/Main/Home.aspx	Chicago	IL	60601	312-960-4100	861-3592
State Telephone Regulation Report 2115 Ward Ct NW *TF:* 800-771-9202 ■ *Web:* www.warren-news.com	Washington	DC	20037	202-872-9200	293-3435
Telecom AM 2115 Ward Ct NW *TF:* 800-771-9202 ■ *Web:* www.warren-news.com	Washington	DC	20037	202-872-9200	293-3435
Telecommunications Report 76 Ninth Ave 7th Fl *Web:* www.aspenpublishers.com	New York	NY	10011	212-771-0600	
TR's Last-Mile Telecom Report 1333 H St NW Suite 100 *Web:* www.tr.com/newsletters/lmtr	Washington	DC	20005	202-312-6060	312-6111
Voice Report 9737 Washingtonian Blvd Suite 1100 *TF:* 888-275-2264 ■ *Web:* www.thevoicereport.com	Gaithersburg	MD	20878	888-275-2264	
Wireless Broadband 1 Lower Ragsdale Dr Bldg 1 Suite 130 *TF:* 800-307-2529 ■ *Web:* www.kagan.com	Monterey	CA	93940	831-624-1536	625-3225
Wireless Market Stats 1 Lower Ragsdale Dr Bldg 1 Suite 130 *TF:* 800-307-2529 ■ *Web:* www.kagan.com	Monterey	CA	93940	831-624-1536	625-3225
Yellow Pages & Directory Report 60 Long Ridge Rd Suite 300 *Web:* www.simbanet.com	Stamford	CT	06902	203-325-8193	325-8915

534-12 Science & Technology Newsletters

Name / Address	City	State	ZIP	Phone	Fax
Flame Retardancy News 49 Walnut Pk Bldg 2 *TF:* 866-285-7215 ■ *Web:* www.bccresearch.com	Wellesley	MA	02481	781-489-7301	253-3933
Food Ingredient News 49 Walnut Pk Bldg 2 *TF:* 866-285-7215 ■ *Web:* www.bccresearch.com	Wellesley	MA	02481	781-489-7301	253-3933
Fuel Cell Technology News 70 New Canaan Ave *Web:* www.bccresearch.com	Norwalk	CT	06850	203-853-4266	229-0087
Genetic Engineering News 140 Huguenot St 3rd Fl *TF:* 800-799-9436 ■ *Web:* www.genengnews.com	New Rochelle	NY	10801	914-740-2100	740-2101
Genetic Technology News 7550 W I-10 Suite 400 **Fax Area Code:* 888 ■ *TF:* 877-463-7678 ■ *Web:* www.mindbranch.com	San Antonio	TX	78229	210-348-1000	690-3329*
Geophysical Research Letter 2000 Florida Ave NW *TF:* 800-966-2481 ■ *Web:* www.agu.org/journals/gl	Washington	DC	20009	202-462-6900	328-0566
High Tech Ceramics News 49 Walnut Pk Bldg 2 *TF:* 866-285-7215 ■ *Web:* www.bccresearch.com	Wellesley	MA	02481	781-489-7301	253-3933
High-Tech Materials Alert 7550 W I-10 Suite 400 **Fax Area Code:* 888 ■ *TF:* 877-463-7678 ■ *Web:* www.mindbranch.com	San Antonio	TX	77229	210-348-1000	690-3329*
In Vivo 383 Main Ave *Web:* www.windhoverinfo.com	Norwalk	CT	06851	203-838-4401	838-3214
Industrial Bioprocessing 7550 W I-10 Suite 400 **Fax Area Code:* 888 ■ *TF:* 877-463-7678 ■ *Web:* www.mindbranch.com	San Antonio	TX	78229	210-348-1000	690-3329*
International Pharmaceutical Regulatory Monitor 9700 Philadelphia Ct *TF:* 800-345-2611 ■ *Web:* www.pharmaceuticalmonitor.com/index.htm	Lanham	MD	20706	301-731-5200	731-5203
Medical Materials Update 49 Walnut Pk Bldg 2 *TF:* 866-285-7215 ■ *Web:* www.bccresearch.com	Wellesley	MA	02481	781-489-7301	253-3933
Membrane & Separation Technology News 70 New Canaan Ave *Web:* www.bccresearch.com	Norwalk	CT	06850	203-853-4266	229-0087
Microelectronics Technology Alert 7550 W 1-10 Suite 400 **Fax Area Code:* 888 ■ *TF:* 877-463-7678 ■ *Web:* www.mindbranch.com	San Antonio	TX	78229	210-348-1000	610-3329*
Nanoparticle News 70 New Canaan Ave. *Web:* www.bccresearch.com	Norwalk	CT	06850	203-853-4266	229-0087
Nanotech Alert 7550 W I-10 Suite 400 **Fax Area Code:* 888 ■ *TF:* 877-463-7678 ■ *Web:* www.mindbranch.com	San Antonio	TX	78229	210-348-1000	690-3329*
Physical Review Letters 1 Research Rd *Web:* www.prl.aps.org	Ridge	NY	11961	631-591-4000	591-4141
Sensor Technology 7550 W I-10 Suite 400 **Fax Area Code:* 888 ■ *TF:* 877-463-7678 ■ *Web:* www.mindbranch.com	San Antonio	TX	77229	210-348-1000	690-3329*
World Food Chemical News 1725 K St NW Suite 506 *TF:* 800-272-7737	Washington	DC	20006	202-887-6320	887-6339

534-13 Trade & Industry Newsletters

Name / Address	City	State	ZIP	Phone	Fax
Construction Claims Monthly 2222 Sedwick Dr Suite 101 *TF:* 800-223-8720 ■ *Web:* www.bpinews.com/spec_ccm.htm	Durham	NC	27713	800-223-8720	508-2592
Construction Labor Report 1801 S Bell St *TF:* 800-372-1033 ■ *Web:* www.bna.com/construction-labor-report-p6002	Arlington	VA	22202	800-372-1033	
Contractor's Business Management Report 3 Pk Ave 30th Fl *Web:* www.ioma.com/issues/CBMR	New York	NY	10016	212-244-0360	564-0465
Cotton's Week 1918 N Pkwy *TF:* 800-377-9030 ■ *Web:* www.cotton.org/news/cweek/index.cfm	Memphis	TN	38112	901-274-9030	725-0510
Cruise Industry News 441 Lexington Ave Suite 1209 *Web:* www.cruiseindustrynews.com	New York	NY	10017	212-986-1025	986-1033
DealersEdge PO Box 606 *TF:* 800-321-5312 ■ *Web:* www.dealersedge.com	Barnegat Light	NJ	08006	609-879-4456	
Death Care Business Advisor 360 Hiatt Dr *TF:* 800-621-5463 ■ *Web:* www.lrp.com	Palm Beach Gardens	FL	33418	561-622-6520	622-2423
Doane's Agricultural Report 77 Westport Plaza Suite 250 *TF:* 800-535-2342 ■ *Web:* www.doane.com	Saint Louis	MO	63146	314-569-2700	569-1083
Engineering Outlook 1308 W Green St 303 Engineering Hall *Web:* www.engr.uiuc.edu	Urbana	IL	61801	217-333-1510	244-7705
Food & Drink Weekly 6862 Elm St Suite 350 *Web:* www.sparksco.com	McLean	VA	22101	703-734-8787	556-7865
Food Chemical News 1725 K St NW Suite 506 *TF:* 888-272-7737 ■ *Web:* www.foodchemicalnews.com	Washington	DC	20006	202-887-6320	887-6335
Funeral Service Insider 3349 Hwy 138 Bldg D Suite D *TF:* 800-500-4585 ■ *Web:* www.kates-boylston.com/index.aspx?page=fsi	Wall	NJ	07719	800-500-4585	
Kane's Beverage Week 14305 Shoreham Dr. *TF:* 800-359-6049	Silver Spring	MD	20905	301-384-1573	879-8803
Kiplinger Agriculture Letter 1729 H St NW *TF:* 800-544-0155 ■ *Web:* www.kiplinger.com	Washington	DC	20006	202-887-6400	778-8976
Metals Week 55 Water St **Fax:* Edit ■ *TF:* 800-223-6180 ■ *Web:* www.platts.com	New York	NY	10041	212-438-2000	438-3079*
National Farmers Union News 11900 E Cornell Ave *TF:* 800-347-1961 ■ *Web:* www.nfu.org	Aurora	CO	80014	303-337-5500	368-1390
Office World News 275 Grove St Suite 2-130 *TF:* 800-542-6672 ■ *Web:* www.officeworldnews.com	Newton	MA	02466	617-219-8300	219-8310
PhotoLetter 1910 35th Ave Pine Lake Farm *TF:* 800-624-0266 ■ *Web:* www.photosource.com/cart/pl.php	Osceola	WI	54020	715-248-3800	248-7394
Pro Farmer 6612 Chancellor Dr Suite 300 *TF Cust Svc:* 800-772-0023 ■ *Web:* www.agweb.com	Cedar Falls	IA	50613	319-277-1278	277-7982
Service Dealers PO Box 241	Burtonsville	MD	20886	906-889-6336	

	City	State	Zip	Phone	Fax
Shopping Centers Today 1221 Avenue of the Americas **Fax Area Code:* 212 ■ *Web:* www.icsc.org	New York	NY	10020	646-728-3800	589-5555*
Uniform Commercial Code Law Letter PO Box 64526 **Fax Area Code:* 800 ■ *TF Cust Svc:* 800-328-4880 ■ *Web:* www.west.thomson.com	Saint Paul	MN	55164	651-687-7000	340-9378*
Union Labor Report 1801 S Bell St. *TF:* 800-372-1033 ■ *Web:* www.bna.com/union-labor-report-p6722	Arlington	VA	22202	800-372-1033	
Urban Transport News 65 E Wacker Pl Suite 400 *Web:* www.highbeam.com	Chicago	IL	60601	312-782-3900	782-3901
US Rail News 65 E Wacker Pl Suite 400 *Web:* www.highbeam.com	Chicago	IL	60601	312-782-3900	782-3901
Weekly of Business Aviation 1200 G St NW Suite 900 *TF:* 800-752-4959 ■ *Web:* www.aviationnow.com/avnow/news/channel_businessweekly.jsp	Washington	DC	20005	202-383-2350	383-2438

535 NEWSPAPERS

SEE ALSO Newspaper Publishers p. 2467

535-1 Daily Newspapers - Canada

	City	Prov	Postal Code	Phone	Fax
24 Heures 465 McGill St Fl 3 3rd Fl *Web:* www.24hmontreal.canoe.ca	Montreal	QC	H2Y4B4	514-393-1010	373-2400
24 Hours Vancouver 1070 SE Marine Dr *Web:* www.24hrs.ca	Vancouver	BC	V5X2V4	604-321-2231	322-3206
Brandon Sun 501 Rosser Ave *Web:* www.brandonsun.com	Brandon	MB	R7A0K4	204-727-2451	727-0385
Calgary Herald 215-16th St SE PO Box 2400 Stn M *TF:* 800-372-9219 ■ *Web:* www.calgaryherald.com	Calgary	AB	T2E7P5	403-235-7100	235-7379
Calgary Sun 2615 12th St NE **Fax:* Edit ■ *TF:* 877-624-1463 ■ *Web:* www.calgarysun.com	Calgary	AB	T2E7W9	403-410-1010	250-4176*
Cape Breton Post 255 George St PO Box 1500 *Web:* www.capebretonpost.com	Sydney	NS	B1P6K6	902-564-5451	564-6280
Chatham Daily News 138 King St W *Web:* www.chathamdailynews.ca	Chatham	ON	N7M1E3	519-354-2000	436-0949
Chronicle Herald The PO Box 610 *TF:* 800-563-1187 ■ *Web:* thechronicleherald.ca	Halifax	NS	B3J2T2	902-426-2811	426-1158
Chronicle-Journal The 75 S Cumberland St *Web:* www.chroniclejournal.com	Thunder Bay	ON	P7B1A3	807-343-6200	343-9409
Cornwall Standard Freeholder The 1150 Montreal Rd *Web:* www.standard-freeholder.com	Cornwall	ON	K6H1E2	613-933-3160	
Daily Courier 550 Doyle Ave *Web:* www.kelownadailycourier.ca	Kelowna	BC	V1Y7V1	250-762-4445	762-3866
Daily Gleaner 984 Prospect St W PO Box 3370 *Web:* dailygleaner.canadaeast.com	Fredericton	NB	E3B2T8	506-452-6671	457-6606
Edmonton Journal PO Box 2421 *TF:* 800-663-7810 ■ *Web:* www.canada.com	Edmonton	AB	T5J2S6	780-429-5100	429-5500
Edmonton Sun 4990 92nd Ave Suite 250 *TF:* 877-468-2401 ■ *Web:* www.edmontonsun.com	Edmonton	AB	T6B3A1	780-468-0100	468-0139
Expositor The 195 Henry St *Web:* www.brantfordexpositor.ca	Brantford	ON	N3T5S8	519-756-2020	756-4911
Gazette The 1010 Sainte-Catherine St W Suite 200 **Fax Area Code:* 866 ■ *TF:* 800-361-8478 ■ *Web:* www.canada.com	Montreal	QC	H3B5L1	514-987-2222	870-3386*
Globe & Mail Inc The 444 Front St W *Web:* www.theglobeandmail.com	Toronto	ON	M5V2S9	416-585-5000	585-5085
Guardian The 165 Prince St *Web:* www.theguardian.pe.ca	Charlottetown	PE	C1A4R7	902-629-6000	566-3808
Intelligencer The 45 Bridge St E *Web:* www.intelligencer.ca	Belleville	ON	K8N1L5	613-962-9171	962-9652
Journal Le Droit 47 Rue Clarence Suite 222 PO Box 8860 Stn T *Web:* www.cyberpresse.ca/le-droit	Ottawa	ON	K1G3J9	613-562-0111	562-7553
Kamloops Daily News 393 Seymour St *Web:* www.kamloopsnews.ca	Kamloops	BC	V2C6P6	250-372-2331	372-0823
Kenora Daily Miner & News 33 Main St S PO Box 1620 *Web:* www.kenoradailyminerandnews.com	Kenora	ON	P9N3X7	807-468-5555	468-4318
Kingston Whig-Standard The 6 Cataraqui St PO Box 2300 *Web:* www.thewhig.com/Default.aspx	Kingston	ON	K7L4Z7	613-544-5000	530-4122
L'Acadie-Nouvelle 476 Boul St-Pierre Ouest PO Box 5536 *TF:* 800-561-2255 ■ *Web:* www.capacadie.com	Caraquet	NB	E1W1B7	506-727-4444	727-7620
La Presse 7 St Jacques St *Web:* www.cyberpresse.ca/actualites/regional/montreal	Montreal	QC	H2Y1K9	514-285-7000	285-4816
La Tribune 1950 Rue Roy *Web:* www.cyberpresse.ca/la-tribune	Sherbrooke	QC	J1K2X8	819-564-5450	564-5480
La Voix de l'Est 76 Rue Dufferin *Web:* www.cyberpresse.ca/la-voix-de-lest	Granby	QC	J2G9L4	450-375-4555	777-7221
Le Devoir 2050 Bleury St 9th Fl *TF:* 800-463-7559 ■ *Web:* www.ledevoir.com	Montreal	QC	H3A3M9	514-985-3333	985-3360
Le Journal de Montreal 4545 Frontenac St *TF:* 800-521-4545 ■ *Web:* www.journalmtl.com	Montreal	QC	H2H2R7	514-521-4545	521-4416
Le Quotidien du Saguenay-Lac-Saint-Jean 1051 boul Talbot *Web:* www.cyberpresse.ca/le-quotidien	Chicoutimi	QC	G7H5C1	418-545-4474	690-8805
Le Soleil 410 Charest Blvd E PO Box 1547 *Web:* www.cyberpresse.ca/le-soleil	Quebec	QC	G1K7J6	418-686-3233	686-3374
Lethbridge Herald 7th St S Suite 504 PO Box 670 *Web:* www.lethbridgeherald.com	Lethbridge	AB	T1J2H1	403-328-4411	328-4536
London Free Press 369 York St PO Box 2280 *TF:* 866-541-6757 ■ *Web:* www.lfpress.com	London	ON	N6A4G1	519-679-1111	667-4528
National Post 1450 Don Mills Rd Suite 300 *TF:* 800-267-6568 ■ *Web:* www.nationalpost.com	Toronto	ON	M3B3R5	416-383-2300	383-2305
Niagara Falls Review 4801 Valley Way *Web:* www.niagarafallsreview.ca	Niagara Falls	ON	L2E6T6	905-358-5711	356-0785
Northern News 8 Duncan Ave PO Box 1030 *Web:* www.northernnews.ca	Kirkland Lake	ON	P2N3L4	705-567-5321	567-5377
Nugget The 259 Worthington St W *Web:* www.nugget.ca	North Bay	ON	P1B3B5	705-472-3200	472-1438
Observer The 140 S Front St *Web:* www.theobserver.ca	Sarnia	ON	N7T7M8	519-344-3641	332-2951
Ottawa Citizen 1101 Baxter Rd PO Box 5020 **Fax:* News Rm ■ *TF:* 800-267-6100 ■ *Web:* www.canada.com	Ottawa	ON	K2C3M4	613-829-9100	726-1198*
Ottawa Sun PO Box 9729 *TF:* 877-624-1463 ■ *Web:* www.ottawasun.com	Ottawa	ON	K1G5H7	613-739-7000	739-8041
Owen Sound Sun Times 290 9th St E *Web:* www.owensoundsuntimes.com	Owen Sound	ON	N4K5P2	519-376-2250	376-7190
Peterborough Examiner The 730 The King's Way	Peterborough	ON	K9J8L4	705-745-4641	743-4581
Prince George Citizen 150 Brunswick St PO Box 5700 *Web:* www.princegeorgecitizen.com	Prince George	BC	V2L2B3	250-562-2441	562-7453
Record The 160 King St E *TF:* 800-265-8261 ■ *Web:* www.therecord.com	Kitchener	ON	N2G4E5	519-894-2231	894-3829
Record The 1195 Galt St E *Web:* www.sherbrookerecord.com	Sherbrooke	QC	J1G1Y7	819-569-9525	821-3179
Red Deer Advocate 2950 Bremner Ave *Web:* www.albertalocalnews.com/reddeeradvocate	Red Deer	AB	T4R1M9	403-343-2400	341-6560
Regina Leader Post 1964 Pk St *Web:* www.leaderpost.com	Regina	SK	S4P3G4	306-781-5211	565-2588
Sault Star The 145 Old Garden River Rd *Web:* www.saultstar.com	Sault Sainte Marie	ON	P6A5M5	705-759-3030	942-8690
Spectator The 44 Frid St *TF:* 800-263-6902 ■ *Web:* www.thespec.com	Hamilton	ON	L8N3G3	905-526-3333	526-1395
Standard The 17 Queen St *Web:* www.stcatharinesstandard.ca	Saint Catharines	ON	L2R5G5	905-684-7251	684-6032
Star Phoenix The 204 5th Ave N *TF:* 800-667-2002 ■ *Web:* www.thestarphoenix.com	Saskatoon	SK	S7K2P1	306-657-6231	657-6437
StarPhoenix The 5th Ave N Suite 204 *TF:* 800-667-2002 ■ *Web:* www.thestarphoenix.com	Saskatoon	SK	S7K2P1	306-657-6231	657-6437
Sudbury Star The 33 MacKenzie St *Web:* www.thesudburystar.com	Sudbury	ON	P3C4Y1	705-674-5271	674-6834
Telegram The 430 Topsail Rd PO Box 86 *Web:* www.thetelegram.com	Saint John's	NL	A1E4N1	709-364-6300	364-3939
Telegraph-Journal 210 Crown St PO Box 2350 *Web:* telegraphjournal.canadaeast.com	Saint John	NB	E2L3V8	506-633-5599	645-3295
Thompson Citizen 141 Commercial Pl *Web:* www.thompsoncitizen.net	Thompson	MB	R8N1T1	204-677-4534	677-3681
Times Colonist 2621 Douglas St PO Box 300 *Web:* www.timescolonist.com	Victoria	BC	V8T4M2	250-380-5211	380-5353
Times-Transcript 939 Main St PO Box 1001 *Web:* timestranscript.canadaeast.com	Moncton	NB	E1C8P3	506-859-4905	859-4993
Toronto Star 1 Yonge St **Fax:* News Rm ■ *TF:* 800-268-9756 ■ *Web:* www.thestar.com	Toronto	ON	M5E1E6	416-869-4000	869-4328*
Toronto Sun 333 King St E *Web:* management.torontosun.com/home	Toronto	ON	M5A3X5	416-947-2222	947-2043
Tribune The 228 E Main St *Web:* www.wellandtribune.ca	Welland	ON	L3B5P5	905-732-2411	732-3660
Vancouver Province 200 Granville St Suite 1 *Web:* www.theprovince.com	Vancouver	BC	V6C3N3	604-605-2000	605-2720
Vancouver Sun 200 Granville St Suite 1 **Fax:* News Rm ■ *Web:* www.vancouversun.com	Vancouver	BC	V6C3N3	604-605-2000	605-2323*
Windsor Star The 167 Ferry St *TF:* 800-265-5647 ■ *Web:* www.windsorstar.com	Windsor	ON	N9A4M5	519-255-5711	255-5515
Winnipeg Free Press 1355 Mountain Ave **Fax:* News Rm ■ *TF:* 800-542-8900 ■ *Web:* www.winnipegfreepress.com	Winnipeg	MB	R2X3B6	204-697-7000	697-7412*
Winnipeg Sun 1700 Church Ave **Fax:* News Rm ■ *Web:* www.winnipegsun.com	Winnipeg	MB	R2X3A2	204-694-2022	697-0759*
World Journal 2288 Clark Dr	Vancouver	BC	V5N3G8	604-876-1338	876-9191

535-2 Daily Newspapers - US

Listings Here Are Organized By City Names Within State Groupings. Most Of The Fax Numbers Given Connect Directly To The Newsroom.

ALABAMA

	City	State	Zip	Phone	Fax
Anniston Star 4305 McClellan Blvd PO Box 189 *TF:* 888-649-1551 ■ *Web:* www.annistonstar.com	Anniston	AL	36202	256-236-1551	241-1991
Birmingham News 2201 4th Ave N *TF:* 800-283-4015 ■ *Web:* www.bhamnews.com	Birmingham	AL	35203	205-325-2222	325-3282
Decatur Daily 201 1st Ave SE *TF:* 888-353-4612 ■ *Web:* www.decaturdaily.com	Decatur	AL	35601	256-353-4612	340-2392
Dothan Eagle PO Box 1968 *TF:* 800-811-1771 ■ *Web:* www.dothaneagle.com	Dothan	AL	36302	334-792-3141	712-7979
Times Daily PO Box 797 *Web:* www.timesdaily.com	Florence	AL	35631	256-766-3434	740-4717
Gadsden Times 401 Locust St *TF:* 800-762-2464 ■ *Web:* www.gadsdentimes.com	Gadsden	AL	35901	256-549-2000	549-2105
Huntsville Times 2317 S Memorial Pkwy *TF:* 800-239-5271 ■ *Web:* www.htimes.com	Huntsville	AL	35801	256-532-4000	532-4420
Press-Register PO Box 2488 *Web:* www.mobileregister.com	Mobile	AL	36652	251-219-5343	
Montgomery Advertiser 425 Molton St *TF:* 800-488-3579 ■ *Web:* www.montgomeryadvertiser.com	Montgomery	AL	36104	334-262-1611	261-1521

	City	State	ZIP	Phone	Fax
Daily Sentinel 701 Veterans Dr *Web:* www.thedailysentinel.com	Scottsboro	AL	35768	256-259-1020	259-2709
Messenger The PO Box 727 *Web:* www.troymessenger.com	Troy	AL	36081	334-566-4270	566-4281
Tuscaloosa News 315 28th Ave *TF:* 800-888-8639 ■ *Web:* www.tuscaloosanews.com	Tuscaloosa	AL	35401	205-345-0505	722-0187

ALASKA

	City	State	ZIP	Phone	Fax
Anchorage Daily News 1001 Northway Dr **Fax:* Edit ■ *Web:* www.adn.com	Anchorage	AK	99508	907-257-4200	258-2157*
Fairbanks Daily News Miner 200 N Cushman St *Web:* www.news-miner.com	Fairbanks	AK	99707	907-456-6661	452-7917
Juneau Empire 3100 Ch Dr *Web:* www.juneauempire.com	Juneau	AK	99801	907-586-3740	586-9097

ARIZONA

	City	State	ZIP	Phone	Fax
Arizona Daily Sun 1751 S Thompson St *Web:* www.azdailysun.com	Flagstaff	AZ	86001	928-774-4545	774-4790
East Valley Tribune 120 W 1st Ave *TF:* 888-887-4286 ■ *Web:* www.eastvalleytribune.com	Mesa	AZ	85210	480-898-6500	898-6362
Arizona Republic 200 E Van Buren St **Fax:* News Rm ■ *TF:* 800-331-9303 ■ *Web:* www.azcentral.com/arizonarepublic	Phoenix	AZ	85004	602-444-8000	444-8044*
Daily Courier 1958 Commerce Ctr Cir *TF:* 888-349-3436 ■ *Web:* www.communitypapers.com	Prescott	AZ	86301	928-445-3333	445-2062
Scottsdale Tribune 6991 Camelback Rd Suite A110 *Web:* www.eastvalleytribune.com	Scottsdale	AZ	85251	480-970-2330	970-2360
Daily News-Sun 10102 Santa Fe Dr *Web:* www.dailynews-sun.com	Sun City	AZ	85351	623-977-8351	876-3698
Arizona Daily Star 4850 S Pk Ave *TF:* 800-695-4111 ■ *Web:* www.azstarnet.com	Tucson	AZ	85714	520-573-4220	573-4107
Tucson Citizen 4850 S Pk Ave *TF:* 800-695-4492 ■ *Web:* www.tucsoncitizen.com	Tucson	AZ	85714	520-573-4561	573-4569
Yuma Daily Sun 2055 Arizona Ave *TF:* 800-995-9862 ■ *Web:* www.yumasun.com	Yuma	AZ	85364	928-783-3333	539-6807

ARKANSAS

	City	State	ZIP	Phone	Fax
Jacksonville Patriot 903 S Pine St PO Box 1058 *Web:* www.jacksonvillepatriot.com	Cabot	AR	72023	501-982-6506	843-6447
Times Record 3600 Wheeler Ave *TF:* 888-274-4051 ■ *Web:* www.swtimes.com	Fort Smith	AR	72901	479-785-7700	784-0413
Sentinel-Record 300 Spring St *Web:* www.hotsr.com	Hot Springs National Park	AR	71901	501-623-7711	623-8465
Jonesboro Sun 518 Carson St *TF:* 800-237-5341 ■ *Web:* www.jonesborosun.com	Jonesboro	AR	72401	870-935-5525	935-5823
Arkansas Democrat-Gazette 121 E Capital St *TF Cust Svc:* 800-482-1121 ■ *Web:* www.arkansasonline.com	Little Rock	AR	72203	501-378-3400	372-4765
Newport Daily Independent 2408 Hwy 367 N *Web:* www.newportindependent.com	Newport	AR	72112	870-523-5855	523-6540
Pine Bluff Commercial 300 S Beech St *Web:* www.pbcommercial.com	Pine Bluff	AR	71601	870-534-3400	534-0113
Morning News of Northwest Arkansas 2560 N Lowell Rd *TF:* 888-692-1222 ■ *Web:* www.nwaonline.com	Springdale	AR	72764	479-751-6200	872-5055

CALIFORNIA

	City	State	ZIP	Phone	Fax
China Daily Press 2121 W Mission Rd *Web:* www.usqiatao.com	Alhambra	CA	91803	626-281-8500	281-7900
Record-Gazette 218 N Murray St *Web:* www.recordgazette.net	Banning	CA	92220	951-849-4586	849-2437
El Mexicano 4045 Bonita Rd Suite 209 *Web:* www.medicis.com	Bonita	CA	91902	619-267-6010	267-5965
Ventura County Star 550 Camarillo Ctr Dr *TF:* 800-221-7827 ■ *Web:* www.venturacountystar.com	Camarillo	CA	93010	805-437-0000	482-6167
Chico Enterprise Record 400 E Pk Ave PO Box 9 *TF:* 800-827-1421 ■ *Web:* www.chicoer.com	Chico	CA	95927	530-891-1234	342-3617
Diario San Diego 236 F St Suite A1	Chula Vista	CA	91910	619-409-1777	409-1771*
Daily Pilot 1375 Sunflower Ave *Web:* www.dailypilot.com	Costa Mesa	CA	92626	714-966-4600	966-4679
Los Angeles Times Orange County 1375 W Sunflower Ave *TF:* 800-528-4637	Costa Mesa	CA	92626	714-966-5600	966-7711
Sam Ramon Valley Times 524 Hartz Ave *Web:* www.contracostatimes	Danville	CA	94526	925-743-2202	837-4334
Davis Enterprise 315 G St *Web:* www.davisenterprise.com	Davis	CA	95616	530-756-0800	756-6707
Imperial Valley Press 205 N 8th St *Web:* www.ivpressonline.com	El Centro	CA	92243	760-337-3400	353-3003
North County Times 207 E Pennsylvania Ave *TF News Rm:* 800-200-0704 ■ *Web:* www.nctimes.com	Escondido	CA	92025	760-745-6611	745-3769
Times-Standard 930 6th St *Web:* www.times-standard.com	Eureka	CA	95501	707-442-1711	441-0501
Daily Republic 1250 Texas St *Web:* local.dailyrepublic.com	Fairfield	CA	94533	707-425-4646	425-5924
Fresno Bee 1626 E St *TF:* 800-877-7300 ■ *Web:* www.fresnobee.com	Fresno	CA	93786	559-441-6111	441-6436
Asbarez Armenian Daily 419 W Colorado St *Web:* www.asbarez.com	Glendale	CA	91204	818-500-9363	956-3230
Union The 464 Sutton Way *Web:* www.theunion.com	Grass Valley	CA	95945	530-273-9561	477-4292
Sentinel The 300 W 6th St *TF:* 800-582-0471 ■ *Web:* www.hanfordsentinel.com	Hanford	CA	93230	559-582-0471	587-1876
Daily Review 22533 Foothill Blvd *TF:* 800-595-9595 ■ *Web:* www.insidebayarea.com	Hayward	CA	94541	510-783-6111	293-2490
Lodi News-Sentinel 125 N Church St *Web:* www.lodinews.com	Lodi	CA	95240	209-369-2761	369-6706
Press-Telegram 300 Oceangate *Web:* www.presstelegram.com	Long Beach	CA	90844	562-435-1161	437-7892
Daily Commerce 915 E 1st St *TF:* 800-788-7840 ■ *Web:* www.dailyjournal.com	Los Angeles	CA	90012	213-229-5300	229-5481
Investor's Business Daily 12655 Beatrice St **Fax:* Cust Svc ■ *TF:* 800-831-2525 ■ *Web:* www.investors.com	Los Angeles	CA	90066	310-448-6000	577-7303*
La Opinion 700 S Flower St Suite 3000 *Web:* www.laopinion.com	Los Angeles	CA	90017	213-622-8332	896-2171
Los Angeles Times 202 W 1st St *TF:* 800-528-4637 ■ *Web:* www.latimes.com	Los Angeles	CA	90012	213-237-5000	237-4712
ViveloHoy 207 S Broadway 6th Fl *Web:* www.hoyinternet.com	Los Angeles	CA	90012	213-237-3001	237-4406
Appeal-Democrat 1530 Ellis Lake Dr PO Box 431 **Fax:* News Rm ■ *TF:* 800-831-2345 ■ *Web:* www.appeal-democrat.com	Marysville	CA	95901	530-741-2345	749-8390*
Merced Sun-Star 3033 N G St *Web:* www.mercedsun-star.com	Merced	CA	95340	209-722-1511	388-2460
Modesto Bee 1325 H St *TF:* 800-776-4233 ■ *Web:* www.modbee.com	Modesto	CA	95354	209-578-2000	578-2207
Monterey County Herald 8 Upper Ragsdale Dr *TF:* 888-646-4422 ■ *Web:* www.montereyherald.com	Monterey	CA	93940	831-372-3311	372-8401
Napa Valley Register 1615 Second St *TF:* 800-504-6397 ■ *Web:* www.napanews.com	Napa	CA	94559	707-226-3711	224-3963
Marin Independent Journal 150 Alameda Del Prado *TF:* 800-782-5277 ■ *Web:* www.marinij.com	Novato	CA	94948	415-883-8600	883-5458
Oakland Tribune 7677 Oakport St Suite 950 *Web:* www.insidebayarea.com	Oakland	CA	94621	510-208-6300	208-6477
Inland Valley Daily Bulletin 2041 E 4th St *Web:* www.dailybulletin.com	Ontario	CA	91764	909-987-6397	948-9038
Desert Sun 750 N Gene Autry Trail *TF:* 800-233-3741 ■ *Web:* www.thedesertsun.com	Palm Springs	CA	92263	760-322-8889	778-4654
Antelope Valley Press 37404 Sierra Hwy *TF:* 888-874-2527 ■ *Web:* www.avpress.com	Palmdale	CA	93550	661-273-2700	947-4870
Pasadena Star-News 911 E Colorado Blvd *TF:* 800-788-1200 ■ *Web:* www.pasadenastarnews.com	Pasadena	CA	91106	626-578-6300	432-5248
Tri-Valley Herald 127 Spring St *Web:* www.insidebayarea.com/trivalleyherald	Pleasanton	CA	94566	925-935-2525	
Valley Times PO Box 607	Pleasanton	CA	94566	925-462-4160	847-2189
Record Searchlight PO Box 492397 *TF:* 800-666-1331 ■ *Web:* www.redding.com	Redding	CA	96049	530-243-2424	225-8236
Journal The 4301 Lakeside Dr	Richmond	CA	94806	510-262-2724	262-2776
Press-Enterprise 3450 14th St *TF:* 800-933-1400 ■ *Web:* www.pe.com	Riverside	CA	92501	951-684-1200	368-9023
Sacramento Bee PO Box 15779 *TF Cust Svc:* 800-284-3233 ■ *Web:* www.sacbee.com	Sacramento	CA	95852	916-321-1000	321-1109
Californian The 123 W Alisal St *Web:* www.californianonline.com	Salinas	CA	93901	831-424-2221	754-4293
Sun The 4030 N Georgia Blvd *TF:* 800-922-0922 ■ *Web:* www.sbsun.com	San Bernardino	CA	92407	909-889-9666	885-8741
San Diego Daily Transcript 2131 3rd Ave **Fax:* Edit ■ *TF:* 800-697-6397 ■ *Web:* www.sddt.com	San Diego	CA	92101	619-232-4381	236-8126*
San Diego Union-Tribune 350 Camino De La Reina *TF:* 800-244-6397 ■ *Web:* www.signonsandiego.com	San Diego	CA	92108	619-299-3131	293-1896
Hokubei Mainichi 1710 Octavia St *Web:* www.hokubei.com	San Francisco	CA	94109	415-567-7330	567-1110
San Francisco Chronicle 901 Mission St *TF:* 866-732-4766 ■ *Web:* www.sfgate.com	San Francisco	CA	94103	415-777-1111	896-1107
San Francisco Examiner 71 Stevenson 2nd Fl *Web:* www.sfexaminer.com	San Francisco	CA	94105	415-359-2600	359-2766
Hemet News 474 W Esplanade Ave *Web:* www.pe.com	San Jacinto	CA	92583	951-763-3400	763-3450
San Jose Mercury News 750 Ridder Pk Dr *Web:* www.mercurynews.com	San Jose	CA	95190	408-920-5000	288-8060
Tribune The 3825 S Higuera St *TF:* 800-477-8799 ■ *Web:* www.sanluisobispo.com	San Luis Obispo	CA	93401	805-781-7800	781-7905
San Mateo County Times 477 Ninth Ave Suite 110 *TF:* 800-595-9595 ■ *Web:* www.mercurynews.com/san-mateo-county	San Mateo	CA	94402	650-348-4321	348-4446
Orange County Register 625 N Grand Ave *TF:* 877-469-7344 ■ *Web:* www.ocregister.com	Santa Ana	CA	92701	714-796-7000	796-5052
Santa Barbara News-Press 715 Anacapa St *TF:* 800-654-3292 ■ *Web:* www.newspress.com	Santa Barbara	CA	93101	805-564-5200	966-6258
Santa Maria Times PO Box 400 *Web:* www.santamariatimes.com	Santa Maria	CA	93456	805-925-2691	928-5657
Press Democrat 427 Mendocino Ave PO Box 569 *TF:* 800-675-5056 ■ *Web:* www.pressdemo.com	Santa Rosa	CA	95401	707-526-8570	521-5330
Tahoe Daily Tribune 3079 Harrison Ave *Web:* www.tahoedailytribune.com	South Lake Tahoe	CA	96150	530-541-3880	541-0373
Record The PO Box 900 *TF:* 800-606-9741 ■ *Web:* www.recordnet.com	Stockton	CA	95201	209-943-6397	547-8186
Daily Breeze 5215 Torrance Blvd **Fax:* Edit ■ *Web:* www.dailybreeze.com	Torrance	CA	90503	310-540-5511	540-6272*
Turlock Journal PO Box 800 *Web:* www.turlockjournal.com	Turlock	CA	95381	209-634-9141	632-8813
Reporter The 916 Cotting Ln PO Box 1509 *Web:* www.thereporter.com	Vacaville	CA	95688	707-448-6401	447-8411
Vallejo Times Herald 440 Curtola Pkwy *TF:* 800-600-1141 ■ *Web:* www.timesheraldonline.com	Vallejo	CA	94590	707-644-1141	643-0128

Phone Fax

Daily Press 13891 Pk Ave PO Box 1389 .... Victorville CA 92393 760-241-7744 241-1860
TF: 800-553-2006 ■ Web: www.vvdailypress.com
Visalia Times-Delta 330 N West St PO Box 31 .... Visalia CA 93279 559-735-3200 735-3399
Web: www.visaliatimesdelta.com
Contra Costa Times 2640 Shadelands Dr ....Walnut Creek CA 94598 925-935-2525 943-8362
Web: www.contracostatimes.com
San Gabriel Valley Tribune
1210 N Azusa Canyon Rd .... West Covina CA 91790 626-962-8811 338-9157
TF: 800-788-1200 ■ Web: www.sgvtribune.com
Nguoi Viet News 14771 Moran St. ....Westminster CA 92683 714-892-9414 894-1381
Web: www.nguoi-viet.com
Whittier Daily News 7612 Green Leaf Ave .... Whittier CA 90602 562-698-0955 698-0450
TF: 800-788-1200 ■ Web: www.whittierdailynews.com
Daily News of Los Angeles
21221 Oxnard St. .... Woodland Hills CA 91367 818-713-3000 713-0058
TF: 800-346-6397 ■ Web: www.dailynews.com

COLORADO

Phone Fax

Aspen Daily News 517 E Hopkins Ave .... Aspen CO 81611 970-925-2220 920-2118
TF: 800-889-9020 ■ Web: www.aspendailynews.com
Aspen Times 310 E Main St. .... Aspen CO 81611 970-925-3414 925-6240
Web: www.aspentimes.com
Boulder Daily Camera 1048 Pearl St .... Boulder CO 80302 303-442-1202 449-9358
TF: 800-783-1202 ■ Web: www.dailycamera.com
Colorado Daily 5450 Western Ave. .... Boulder CO 80301 303-473-1111 443-9357
Web: www.coloradodaily.com
Dirt 1048 Pearl St .... Boulder CO 80302 303-473-1170 473-1155
Web: www.boulderdirt.com
Gazette The 30 S Prospect St .... Colorado Springs CO 80903 719-632-5511 636-0266
TF News Rm: 800-800-4899 ■ Web: www.gazette.com
Denver Post 101 W Colfax Ave ....Denver CO 80202 303-820-1010 820-1369
TF: 800-336-7678 ■ Web: www.denverpost.com
Rocky Mountain News 101 W Colfax Ave ....Denver CO 80218 303-892-5000 892-2841
TF: 800-933-1990 ■ Web: www.rockymountainnews.com
Durango Herald 1275 Main Ave .... Durango CO 81301 970-247-3504 259-5011
TF: 800-530-8318 ■ Web: www.durangoherald.com
Coloradoan The 1300 Riverside Ave. ....Fort Collins CO 80524 970-493-6397 224-7899
TF: 800-872-0001 ■ Web: www.coloradoan.com
Daily Sentinel PO Box 668 .... Grand Junction CO 81502 970-242-5050 244-8578
TF: 800-332-5832 ■ Web: www.gjsentinel.com
Greeley Tribune 501 8th Ave. .... Greeley CO 80631 970-352-0211 356-5780
TF: 800-275-0321 ■ Web: www.greeleytrib.com
Gunnison Country Times 218 N Wisconsin St. ....Gunnison CO 81230 970-641-1414 641-6515
Web: www.gunnisontimes.com
Lamar Daily News 310 S 5th St PO Box 1217. .... Lamar CO 81052 719-336-2266 336-2526
Web: www.lamardaily.com
Daily Times-Call 350 Terry St .... Longmont CO 80501 303-776-2244 678-8615
TF: 800-796-8201 ■ Web: www.longmontfyi.com
Loveland Daily Reporter-Herald 201 E 5th St .... Loveland CO 80537 970-669-5050 667-1111
TF: 800-216-0680 ■ Web: www.lovelandfyi.com
Pueblo Chieftain 825 W 6th St PO Box 440. ....Pueblo CO 81003 719-544-3520
TF: 800-279-6397 ■ Web: www.chieftain.com

CONNECTICUT

Phone Fax

Connecticut Post 410 State St. ....Bridgeport CT 06604 203-333-0161 367-8158
TF Edit: 800-542-5620 ■ Web: www.connpost.com
News-Times 333 Main St. ....Danbury CT 06810 203-744-5100 792-8730
Web: www.newstimes.com
Hartford Courant 285 Broad St. ....Hartford CT 06115 860-241-6200 520-6941
TF: 800-524-4242 ■ Web: www.courant.com
Journal Inquirer
306 Progress Dr PO Box 510 ....Manchester CT 06045 860-646-0500 646-9867
TF: 800-237-3606 ■ Web: www.journalinquirer.com
Record-Journal 11 Crown St. ....Meriden CT 06450 203-235-1661 639-0210
Web: www.record-journal.com
Citizens News 71 Weid Dr. ....Naugatuck CT 06770 203-729-2228 729-9099
New Britain Herald The 1 Ct St 4th Fl .... New Britain CT 06051 860-225-4601 225-2611
Web: www.newbritainherald.com
New Haven Register 40 Sargent Dr .... New Haven CT 06511 203-789-5200 865-7894
TF: 800-925-2509 ■ Web: www.nhregister.com
Day The 47 Eugene O'Neil Dr PO Box 1231 .... New London CT 06320 860-442-2200 442-5599
TF: 800-542-3354 ■ Web: www.theday.com
Hour The 1 Selleck St ....Norwalk CT 06855 203-846-3281 840-1802
Web: www.thehour.com
Norwich Bulletin 66 Franklin St ....Norwich CT 06360 860-887-9211 887-9666
Web: www.norwichbulletin.com
Advocate The 75 Tresser Blvd. .... Stamford CT 06901 203-964-2200 964-2345*
*Fax: Edit ■ Web: www.stamfordadvocate.com
Republican-American 389 Meadow St .... Waterbury CT 06702 203-574-3636 596-9277
TF: 800-992-3232 ■ Web: www.rep-am.com

DELAWARE

Phone Fax

Delaware State News 110 Galaxy Dr PO Box 737 ....Dover DE 19903 302-674-3600 741-8252
TF: 800-282-8586 ■ Web: www.newszap.com
News Journal 950 W Basin Rd. .... New Castle DE 19720 302-324-2500 324-5509
TF: 800-235-9100 ■ Web: www.delawareonline.com

DISTRICT OF COLUMBIA

Phone Fax

Washington Examiner
1015 15th St NW Suite 500 ....Washington DC 20005 202-903-2000 459-4999*
*Fax: Edit ■ TF: 800-531-1223 ■ Web: www.examiner.com

Phone Fax

Washington Post 1150 15th St NW ....Washington DC 20071 202-334-6000
TF: 800-627-1150 ■ Web: www.washingtonpost.com
Washington Times The 3600 New York Ave NE. ......Washington DC 20002 202-636-3000 636-8906
Web: www.washingtontimes.com

FLORIDA

Phone Fax

Herald The 102 Manatee Ave W .... Bradenton FL 34205 941-748-0411 745-7097
Web: www.bradenton.com
Citrus County Chronicle
1624 N Meadowcrest Blvd .... Crystal River FL 34429 352-563-6363 563-3280
TF: 888-852-2340 ■ Web: www.chronicleonline.com
Daytona Beach News-Journal 901 6th St ....Daytona Beach FL 32117 386-252-1511 258-8465
Web: www.news-journalonline.com
Miami Herald Broward Edition
1520 E Sunrise Blvd ....Fort Lauderdale FL 33304 954-538-7001 538-7000
TF: 800-843-4372 ■ Web: www.miamiherald.com
South Florida Sun-Sentinel
200 E Las Olas Blvd ....Fort Lauderdale FL 33301 954-356-4000 356-4559
TF Cust Svc: 800-548-6397 ■ Web: www.sun-sentinel.com
News-Press 2442 Dr ML King Jr Blvd ....Fort Myers FL 33901 239-335-0200 334-0708
TF News Rm: 800-468-0350 ■ Web: www.news-press.com
Tribune 600 Edwards Rd. ....Fort Pierce FL 34982 772-461-2050 894-9851*
*Fax Area Code: 866 ■ TF: 800-444-8742 ■ Web: www.fptribune.com
Northwest Florida Daily News
PO Box 2949 ....Fort Walton Beach FL 32549 850-863-1111 863-7834
TF: 800-755-1185 ■ Web: www.nwfdailynews.com
Gainesville Sun 2700 SW 13th St. ....Gainesville FL 32614 352-378-1411 338-3128
TF Circ: 800-443-9493 ■ Web: www.sunone.com
Florida Times-Union 1 Riverside Ave. ....Jacksonville FL 32202 904-359-4111 359-4478
TF: 800-472-6397 ■ Web: www.jacksonville.com
Key West Citizen 3420 Northside Dr .... Key West FL 33040 305-294-6641 292-3008
Web: www.keysnews.com
Ledger The 300 W Lime St. .... Lakeland FL 33815 863-802-7000 802-7809
TF: 888-431-7323 ■ Web: www.theledger.com
Daily Commercial 212 E Main St .... Leesburg FL 34748 352-365-8200 365-1951
TF: 877-702-0600 ■ Web: www.dailycommercial.com
Diario Las Americas 2900 NW 39th St. .... Miami FL 33142 305-633-3341 635-7668
Web: www.diariolasamericas.com
El Nuevo Herald 1 Herald Plaza. .... Miami FL 33132 305-376-3535 376-2378
TF: 800-441-0444 ■ Web: www.elnuevoherald.com
Miami Herald 1 Herald Plaza .... Miami FL 33132 305-350-2111 376-5287
TF: 800-437-2535 ■ Web: www.miamiherald.com
Naples Daily News 1075 Central Ave ....Naples FL 34102 239-262-3161 263-4816
TF: 888-262-3161 ■ Web: www.naplesnews.com
Ocala Star-Banner PO Box 490 ....Ocala FL 34478 352-867-4010 867-4018
TF: 800-541-2172 ■ Web: www.starbanner.com
El Nuevo Dia 4780 N Orange Blossom Trail .... Orlando FL 32810 321-206-3000 206-3001
Web: www.endiorlando.com
Orlando Sentinel 633 N Orange Ave .... Orlando FL 32801 407-420-5000 420-5350
TF: 800-347-6868 ■ Web: www.orlandosentinel.com
News-Herald 501 W 11th St. .... Panama City FL 32401 850-747-5000 747-5097
TF: 800-345-8688 ■ Web: www.newsherald.com
Sun Herald 23170 Harborview Rd .... Port Charlotte FL 33980 941-206-1000 629-2085
TF: 877-818-6204 ■ Web: www.sun-herald.com
Port Saint Lucie News
760 NW Enterprise Dr. ....Port Saint Lucie FL 34986 772-408-5300 408-5369
Web: www.tcpalm.com
Florida Today 6650 US Hwy 1 .... Rockledge FL 32955 321-242-3500 242-6620
TF: 800-633-8449 ■ Web: www.flatoday.com
Saint Augustine Record 1 News Pl ....Saint Augustine FL 32086 904-829-6562 819-3558
Web: www.staugustine.com
Saint Petersburg Times
490 1st Ave S .... Saint Petersburg FL 33701 727-893-8111 893-8675
TF: 800-333-7505 ■ Web: www.tampabay.com
Seminole Herald PO Box 1667 .... Sanford FL 32772 407-322-2611 323-9408
Web: www.mysanfordherald.com
Sarasota Herald-Tribune 1741 Main St. .... Sarasota FL 34236 941-953-7755 361-4800
TF: 866-284-7102 ■ Web: www.heraldtribune.com
Highlands Today 315 US Hwy 27 N .... Sebring FL 33870 863-386-5800 382-2509
TF: 800-645-3423 ■ Web: www.highlandstoday.com
Stuart News PO Box 9009 ....Stuart FL 34995 772-287-1550 221-4246
TF: 800-381-6397 ■ Web: www.tcpalm.com
Tallahassee Democrat 277 N Magnolia Dr .... Tallahassee FL 32302 850-599-2100 599-2295
TF: 800-777-2154 ■ Web: www.tallahassee.com
Tampa Tribune 200 S Parker St. .... Tampa FL 33606 813-259-7600 259-7676
TF: 800-282-5588 ■ Web: www.tampatrib.com
Vero Beach Press-Journal PO Box 1268 .... Vero Beach FL 32961 772-562-2315 978-2364
TF: 866-894-9851 ■ Web: www.tcpalm.com
Palm Beach Post 2751 S Dixie Hwy. ....West Palm Beach FL 33405 561-820-4100 820-4407*
*Fax: News Rm ■ TF: 800-432-7595 ■ Web: www.palmbeachpost.com

GEORGIA

Phone Fax

Albany Herald 126 N Washington St. .... Albany GA 31701 229-888-9300 888-9357*
*Fax: Edit ■ TF: 800-685-4639 ■ Web: www.albanyherald.com
Athens Banner-Herald 1 Press Pl .... Athens GA 30601 706-549-0123 208-2246
TF: 800-533-4252 ■ Web: www.onlineathens.com
Atlanta Journal-Constitution
223 Perimeter Ctr Pkwy NE. ....Atlanta GA 30346 404-526-5151 526-5746
TF: 800-846-6672 ■ Web: www.ajc.com
Augusta Chronicle 725 Broad St .... Augusta GA 30901 706-724-0851 722-7403*
*Fax: News Rm ■ TF: 800-822-4077 ■ Web: www.chronicle.augusta.com
Brunswick News PO Box 1557 .... Brunswick GA 31521 912-265-8320 280-0926
Web: www.thebrunswicknews.com
Columbus Ledger-Enquirer 17 W 12th St .... Columbus GA 31902 706-324-5526 576-6290
TF: 800-282-7859 ■ Web: www.ledger-enquirer.com
Rockdale Citizen 969 S Main St NE .... Conyers GA 30012 770-483-7108 483-5797
Web: www.rockdalecitizen.com

				Phone	Fax
Gainesville Times 345 Green St NW *TF:* 800-395-5005 ■ *Web:* www.gainesvilletimes.com	Gainesville	GA	30501	770-532-1234	532-0457
Gwinnett Daily Post 725 Old Norcross Rd *Web:* www.gwinnettdailypost.com	Lawrenceville	GA	30045	770-963-9205	339-8081
Macon Telegraph 120 Broadway *TF:* 800-679-6397 ■ *Web:* www.macon.com	Macon	GA	31201	478-744-4200	744-4385
Marietta Daily Journal 580 Fairground St *Web:* www.mdjonline.com	Marietta	GA	30060	770-428-9411	428-7945
La Vision 2200 Norcross Pkwy Suite 210 *Web:* www.lavisionnewspaper.com	Norcross	GA	30071	770-963-7521	963-7218
Rome News-Tribune 305 E 6th Ave PO Box 1633 *Web:* www.romenews-tribune.com	Rome	GA	30161	706-290-5252	
Savannah Morning News 1375 Chatham Pkwy *Web:* www.savannahnow.com	Savannah	GA	31405	912-236-9511	525-0795
Valdosta Daily Times PO Box 968 *TF:* 800-600-4838 ■ *Web:* www.valdostadailytimes.com	Valdosta	GA	31603	229-244-1880	244-2560
Telegraph The 1553 Watson Blvd **Fax:* News Rm ■ *TF:* 800-679-6397	Warner Robins	GA	31093	478-923-6432	328-7682*

HAWAII

				Phone	Fax
Hawaii Tribune-Herald 355 Kinoole St *Web:* www.hawaiitribune-herald.com	Hilo	HI	96720	808-935-6621	961-3680
Honolulu Advertiser PO Box 3110 *TF:* 877-233-1133 ■ *Web:* www.honoluluadvertiser.com	Honolulu	HI	96801	808-525-8000	525-8037
Honolulu Star-Bulletin 500 Ala Moana Blvd Suite 7-500 *TF:* 800-417-3484 ■ *Web:* www.starbulletin.com	Honolulu	HI	96813	808-529-4700	529-4750
Maui News PO Box 550 **Fax:* Edit ■ *TF:* 800-827-0347 ■ *Web:* www.mauinews.com	Wailuku	HI	96793	808-244-3981	242-9087*

IDAHO

				Phone	Fax
Idaho Statesman PO Box 40 *TF:* 800-635-8934 ■ *Web:* www.idahostatesman.com	Boise	ID	83707	208-377-6400	377-6449
Coeur d'Alene Press 201 N 2nd St *Web:* www.cdapress.com	Coeur d'Alene	ID	83814	208-664-8176	664-0212
Post-Register PO Box 1800 *TF:* 800-574-6397 ■ *Web:* www.postregister.com	Idaho Falls	ID	83403	208-522-1800	529-9683
Lewiston Morning Tribune PO Box 957 *Web:* www.lmtribune.com	Lewiston	ID	83501	208-743-9411	746-1185
Idaho Press-Tribune 1618 N Midland Blvd *Web:* www.idahopress.com	Nampa	ID	83651	208-467-9251	467-9562
Idaho State Journal 305 S Arthur Ave *TF:* 800-275-0774 ■ *Web:* www.idahostatejournal.com	Pocatello	ID	83204	208-232-4161	233-8007
Times-News PO Box 548 *TF:* 800-658-3883 ■ *Web:* www.magicvalley.com	Twin Falls	ID	83303	208-733-0931	734-5538

ILLINOIS

				Phone	Fax
Telegraph The PO Box 278 **Fax:* Edit ■ *TF:* 800-477-1447 ■ *Web:* www.thetelegraph.com	Alton	IL	62002	618-463-2500	463-2578*
Daily Herald 155 E Algonquin Rd *Web:* www.dailyherald.com	Arlington Heights	IL	60005	847-427-4300	427-1301
Beacon News 101 S River St *TF:* 800-244-5844 ■ *Web:* www.suburbanchicagonews.com	Aurora	IL	60506	630-844-5800	844-1043
Belleville News-Democrat 120 S Illinois St *TF:* 877-338-7416 ■ *Web:* www.belleville.com	Belleville	IL	62220	618-234-1000	234-9597
Pantagraph PO Box 2907 *TF:* 800-747-7323 ■ *Web:* www.pantagraph.com	Bloomington	IL	61702	309-829-9000	829-7000
Southern Illinoisan 710 N Illinois Ave PO Box 2108 *TF:* 800-228-0429 ■ *Web:* www.thesouthern.com	Carbondale	IL	62902	618-529-5454	457-2935
Centralia Sentinel 232 E Broadway *TF:* 800-371-9892 ■ *Web:* www.morningsentinel.com	Centralia	IL	62801	618-532-5604	532-1212
News Gazette 15 Main St *Web:* www.news-gazette.com	Champaign	IL	61824	217-351-5252	351-5374
Chicago Defender 4445 S King Dr *Web:* www.chicagodefender.com	Chicago	IL	60653	312-225-2400	225-6954
Chicago Sun-Times 350 N Orleans St *Web:* www.suntimes.com	Chicago	IL	60654	312-321-3000	321-3084
Chicago Tribune 435 N Michigan Ave *TF:* 800-874-2863 ■ *Web:* www.chicagotribune.com	Chicago	IL	60611	312-222-3232	222-4760
Northwest Herald PO Box 250 **Fax:* News Rm ■ *TF:* 800-589-8910 ■ *Web:* www.nwherald.com	Crystal Lake	IL	60039	815-459-4122	459-5640*
Commercial-News 17 W N St **Fax:* News Rm ■ *TF:* 800-729-2922 ■ *Web:* www.commercial-news.com	Danville	IL	61832	217-446-1000	446-6648*
Herald & Review 601 E Williams St *TF:* 800-437-2533 ■ *Web:* www.herald-review.com	Decatur	IL	62523	217-429-5151	421-6913
Telegraph 113 S Peoria Ave *Web:* www.saukvalley.com	Dixon	IL	61021	815-284-2224	284-2078
Courier-News 300 Lake St PO Box 531 *TF:* 800-445-3538 ■ *Web:* www.suburbanchicagonews.com	Elgin	IL	60121	847-888-7800	888-7836
Journal-Standard 27 S State Ave *TF:* 800-325-6397 ■ *Web:* www.journalstandard.com	Freeport	IL	61032	815-232-1171	232-0105
Register-Mail 140 S Prairie St PO Box 310 *TF:* 800-747-7181 ■ *Web:* www.register-mail.com	Galesburg	IL	61401	309-343-7181	343-2382
Herald-News 300 Caterpillar Dr *TF:* 800-397-9397 ■ *Web:* www.suburbanchicagonews.com	Joliet	IL	60436	815-729-6161	729-6059
Daily Journal 8 Dearborn Sq *Web:* www.daily-journal.com	Kankakee	IL	60901	815-937-3300	937-3876
News-Tribune 426 2nd St *TF:* 800-892-6452 ■ *Web:* www.newstrib.com	La Salle	IL	61301	815-223-3200	224-6443
Macomb Journal 203 N Randolph St *TF:* 800-237-6858 ■ *Web:* www.macombjournal.com	Macomb	IL	61455	309-833-2114	833-2346
Dispatch The 1720 5th Ave *Web:* www.qconline.com	Moline	IL	61265	309-764-4344	797-0317
Daily Times 110 W Jefferson St *Web:* www.mywebtimes.com	Ottawa	IL	61350	815-433-2000	433-1639
Reporter 12247 S Harlem Ave *Web:* www.thereporteronline.net	Palos Heights	IL	60463	708-448-6161	448-4012
Pekin Daily Times PO Box 430 *Web:* www.pekintimes.com	Pekin	IL	61555	309-346-1111	346-9815
Peoria Journal Star 1 News Plaza **Fax:* News Rm ■ *TF:* 800-225-5757 ■ *Web:* www.pjstar.com	Peoria	IL	61643	309-686-3000	686-3296*
Quincy Herald-Whig PO Box 1049 *TF:* 800-373-9444 ■ *Web:* www.whig.com	Quincy	IL	62306	217-223-5100	221-3395
Rock Island Argus 1724 4th Ave *Web:* qconline.com	Rock Island	IL	61201	309-786-6441	786-7639
Rockford Register Star 99 E State St **Fax:* News Rm ■ *TF:* 800-383-7827 ■ *Web:* www.rrstar.com	Rockford	IL	61104	815-987-1200	987-1365*
Shelbyville Daily Union 100 W Main St *Web:* www.shelbyvilledailyunion.com	Shelbyville	IL	62565	217-774-2161	774-5732
State Journal-Register PO Box 219 *TF:* 800-397-6397 ■ *Web:* www.sj-r.com	Springfield	IL	62705	217-788-1300	788-1551
Southtown Star 6901 W 159th St *Web:* www.dailysouthtown.com	Tinley Park	IL	60477	708-633-6700	633-5999
News Sun 2383 N Delany Rd *Web:* www.suburbanchicagonews.com	Waukegan	IL	60087	847-336-7000	249-7202

INDIANA

				Phone	Fax
Herald Bulletin 1133 Jackson St *TF:* 800-750-5049 ■ *Web:* www.heraldbulletin.com	Anderson	IN	46015	765-622-1212	640-4815
Herald-Republican 45 S Public Sq *Web:* www.kpcnews.com	Angola	IN	46703	260-665-3117	665-2322
Times-Mail 813 16th St *Web:* www.tmnews.com	Bedford	IN	47421	812-275-3355	277-3472
Herald-Times 1900 S Walnut St *Web:* www.heraldtimesonline.com	Bloomington	IN	47401	812-332-4401	331-4383
Republic The 333 2nd St *TF:* 800-876-7811 ■ *Web:* www.therepublic.com	Columbus	IN	47201	812-372-7811	379-5711
Truth The PO Box 487 *TF:* 800-585-5416 ■ *Web:* www.etruth.com	Elkhart	IN	46515	574-294-1661	294-3895
Evansville Courier & Press 300 E Walnut St *TF:* 800-288-3200 ■ *Web:* www.courierpress.com	Evansville	IN	47713	812-424-7711	422-8196
Journal Gazette 600 W Main St *TF:* 800-444-3303 ■ *Web:* www.fortwayne.com/mld/journalgazette	Fort Wayne	IN	46802	260-461-8222	461-8648
News-Sentinel 600 W Main St *TF:* 800-444-3303 ■ *Web:* www.fortwayne.com/mld/newssentinel	Fort Wayne	IN	46802	260-461-8222	461-8817
Daily Journal 2575 N Morton St *TF:* 888-736-7101 ■ *Web:* www.thejournalnet.com	Franklin	IN	46131	317-736-7101	736-2766
Goshen News 114 S Main St PO Box 569 *TF:* 800-487-2151 ■ *Web:* www.goshennews.com	Goshen	IN	46527	574-533-2151	534-8830
Indianapolis Star 307 N Pennsylvania St *TF:* 800-669-7827 ■ *Web:* www.indystar.com	Indianapolis	IN	46204	317-444-4000	444-6600
Kokomo Tribune 300 N Union St *TF:* 800-382-0696 ■ *Web:* www.kokomotribune.com	Kokomo	IN	46901	765-459-3121	854-6733
Journal & Courier 217 N 6th St *TF News Rm:* 800-407-5813 ■ *Web:* www.jconline.com	Lafayette	IN	47901	765-423-5511	420-5246
Chronicle-Tribune 610 S Adams St *TF:* 800-955-7888 ■ *Web:* www.chronicle-tribune.com	Marion	IN	46953	765-664-5111	668-4256
Post-Tribune 1433 E 83rd Ave *TF:* 800-753-5533 ■ *Web:* www.posttrib.suntimes.com	Merrillville	IN	46410	219-648-3172	648-3232
Muncie Star-Press 345 S High St *TF:* 800-783-7827 ■ *Web:* www.thestarpress.com	Muncie	IN	47305	765-747-5700	213-5858
Times The 601 W 45th Ave *TF:* 800-837-3232 ■ *Web:* www.nwitimes.com	Munster	IN	46321	219-933-3200	933-3249
Palladium-Item 1175 N a St *Web:* www.pal-item.com	Richmond	IN	47374	765-962-1575	973-4570
South Bend Tribune 225 W Colfax Ave *TF:* 800-220-7378 ■ *Web:* www.southbendtribune.com	South Bend	IN	46626	574-235-6464	239-2642
Tribune-Star PO Box 149 *TF:* 800-783-8742 ■ *Web:* www.tribstar.com	Terre Haute	IN	47808	812-231-4200	231-4321

IOWA

				Phone	Fax
Hawk Eye The 800 S Main St PO Box 10 *TF:* 800-397-1708 ■ *Web:* www.thehawkeye.com	Burlington	IA	52601	319-754-8461	754-6824
Gazette The 500 3rd Ave SE *TF:* 800-397-8212 ■ *Web:* www.thegazette.com	Cedar Rapids	IA	52401	319-398-8313	398-5846
Daily Nonpareil 535 W Broadway Suite 300 *TF:* 800-283-1882 ■ *Web:* www.nonpareilonline.com	Council Bluffs	IA	51503	712-328-1811	325-5776
Quad-City Times 500 E 3rd St *TF:* 800-437-4641 ■ *Web:* www.qctimes.com	Davenport	IA	52801	563-383-2200	383-2370
Des Moines Register 715 Locust St *TF:* 800-247-5346 ■ *Web:* www.desmoinesregister.com	Des Moines	IA	50309	515-284-8000	286-2504
Telegraph Herald 801 Bluff St **Fax:* Edit ■ *TF:* 800-553-4801 ■ *Web:* www.thonline.com	Dubuque	IA	52001	563-588-5611	588-5745*
Messenger The 713 Central Ave *TF:* 800-622-6613 ■ *Web:* www.messengernews.net	Fort Dodge	IA	50501	515-573-2141	574-4529
Globe-Gazette 300 N Washington St PO Box 271 *TF:* 800-421-0546 ■ *Web:* www.globegazette.com	Mason City	IA	50402	641-421-0500	421-7108
Ottumwa Courier 213 E 2nd St **Fax:* News Rm ■ *TF:* 800-532-1504 ■ *Web:* www.ottumwacourier.com	Ottumwa	IA	52501	641-684-4611	684-7326*
Sioux City Journal 515 Pavonia St *TF:* 800-397-3530 ■ *Web:* www.siouxcityjournal.com	Sioux City	IA	51101	712-293-4300	279-5059
Pilot Tribune PO Box 1187 *TF:* 800-798-6397 ■ *Web:* www.stormlakepilottribune.com	Storm Lake	IA	50588	712-732-3130	732-3152

	City	State	Zip	Phone	Fax
Waterloo Cedar Falls Courier PO Box 540 *TF:* 800-798-1730 ■ *Web:* www.wcfcourier.com	Waterloo	IA	50701	319-291-1400	291-2069

KANSAS

	City	State	Zip	Phone	Fax
Goodland Star-News 1205 Main St *Web:* www.nwkansas.com	Goodland	KS	67735	785-899-2338	899-6186
Hiawatha World 607 Utah St *TF:* 800-803-3321	Hiawatha	KS	66434	785-742-2111	742-2276
Hutchinson News 300 W 2nd St *TF:* 800-766-3311 ■ *Web:* www.hutchnews.com	Hutchinson	KS	67504	620-694-5700	662-4186
Lawrence Journal-World 609 New Hampshire St **Fax:* Edit ■ *TF:* 800-578-8748 ■ *Web:* www.ljworld.com	Lawrence	KS	66044	785-843-1000	843-4512*
Norton Telegram 215 S Kansas St *Web:* www.nwkansas.com	Norton	KS	67654	785-877-3361	877-3732
Russell County News 958 Wichita Ave	Russell	KS	67665	785-483-2116	483-4012*
Salina Journal PO Box 740 *Web:* www.saljournal.com	Salina	KS	67402	785-823-6363	827-6363
Topeka Capital-Journal 616 SE Jefferson St *TF:* 800-777-7171 ■ *Web:* www.cjonline.com	Topeka	KS	66607	785-295-1111	295-1230
Wellington Daily News PO Box 368 *Web:* www.wgtndailynews.com	Wellington	KS	67152	620-326-3326	326-3290
Wichita Eagle The 825 E Douglas Ave *TF:* 800-200-8906 ■ *Web:* www.kansas.com/mld/eagle	Wichita	KS	67202	316-268-6000	268-6627
Winfield Daily Courier PO Box 543 *Web:* www.winfieldcourier.com	Winfield	KS	67156	620-221-1050	221-1101

KENTUCKY

	City	State	Zip	Phone	Fax
Daily Independent 226 17th St *TF:* 800-955-5860 ■ *Web:* www.dailyindependent.com	Ashland	KY	41101	606-326-2600	326-2678
Daily News 813 College St PO Box 90012 *TF:* 800-599-6397 ■ *Web:* www.bgdailynews.com	Bowling Green	KY	42102	270-781-1700	783-3237
Times-Tribune PO Box 516 **Fax:* News Rm ■ *Web:* www.corbintimes.com	Corbin	KY	40702	606-528-2464	528-9850*
News-Enterprise 408 W Dixie Ave *TF:* 800-653-6344 ■ *Web:* www.thenewsenterprise.com	Elizabethtown	KY	42701	270-769-1200	769-6965
Kentucky Enquirer 226 Grandview Dr *Web:* www.enquirer.com	Fort Mitchell	KY	41017	859-578-5555	578-5565
State Journal The 1216 Wilkinson Blvd *Web:* www.state-journal.com	Frankfort	KY	40601	502-227-4556	607-0123
Lexington Herald-Leader 100 Midland Ave *TF:* 800-274-7355 ■ *Web:* www.kentucky.com	Lexington	KY	40508	859-231-3100	231-3224
Courier-Journal 525 W Broadway PO Box 740031 *TF:* 800-765-4011 ■ *Web:* www.courier-journal.com	Louisville	KY	40201	502-582-4011	582-4200
Messenger-Inquirer 1401 Fredrica St *Web:* www.messenger-inquirer.com	Owensboro	KY	42301	270-926-0123	686-7868
Paducah Sun 408 Kentucky Ave *Web:* www.paducahsun.com	Paducah	KY	42003	270-575-8600	

LOUISIANA

	City	State	Zip	Phone	Fax
Alexandria Daily Town Talk PO Box 7558 *TF:* 800-523-8391 ■ *Web:* www.thetowntalk.com	Alexandria	LA	71306	318-487-6397	487-6488
Advocate The 7290 Blue Bonnet Blvd *TF:* 800-960-6397 ■ *Web:* www.2theadvocate.com	Baton Rouge	LA	70810	225-383-1111	388-0371
Courier The 3030 Barrow St *Web:* www.houmatoday.com	Houma	LA	70360	985-879-1557	857-2244
Daily Advertiser The 1100 Bertrand Dr PO Box 5310 **Fax:* Edit ■ *Web:* www.theadvertiser.com	Lafayette	LA	70506	337-289-6300	289-6443*
American Press 4900 Hwy 90 E *TF News Rm:* 800-531-4080 ■ *Web:* www.americanpress.com	Lake Charles	LA	70615	337-494-4080	494-4070
News-Star 411 N 4th St *TF:* 800-259-7788 ■ *Web:* www.thenewsstar.com	Monroe	LA	71201	318-322-5161	362-0273
Times-Picayune 3800 Howard Ave **Fax:* News Rm ■ *TF:* 800-925-0000 ■ *Web:* www.nola.com	New Orleans	LA	70125	504-826-3279	826-3007*
Times 222 Lake St *TF:* 800-551-8892 ■ *Web:* www.shreveporttimes.com	Shreveport	LA	71101	318-459-3200	459-3301

MAINE

	City	State	Zip	Phone	Fax
Kennebec Journal 274 Western Ave *TF:* 800-537-5508 ■ *Web:* www.kennebecjournal.mainetoday.com	Augusta	ME	04330	207-623-3811	623-2220
Bangor Daily News 491 Main St PO Box 1329 **Fax:* Edit ■ *TF:* 800-432-7964 ■ *Web:* www.bangordailynews.com	Bangor	ME	04402	207-990-8000	941-9476*
Sun-Journal PO Box 4400 *TF:* 800-482-0759 ■ *Web:* www.sunjournal.com	Lewiston	ME	04243	207-784-5411	777-3436
Morning Sentinel 31 Front St *TF:* 800-452-4666 ■ *Web:* morningsentinel.mainetoday.com	Waterville	ME	04901	207-873-3341	861-9191

MARYLAND

	City	State	Zip	Phone	Fax
Capital The 2000 Capital Dr *Web:* www.hometownannapolis.com	Annapolis	MD	21401	410-268-5000	268-4643
Baltimore Sun 501 N Calvert St *TF:* 800-829-8000 ■ *Web:* www.baltimoresun.com	Baltimore	MD	21278	410-332-6000	332-6455
Cumberland Times-News 19 Baltimore St *TF:* 800-742-8149 ■ *Web:* www.times-news.com	Cumberland	MD	21502	301-722-4600	722-5270
Star Democrat 29088 Airpark Dr PO Box 600 *Web:* www.stardem.com	Easton	MD	21601	410-822-1500	770-4019
Frederick News Post 200 E Patrick St *TF:* 800-486-1177 ■ *Web:* www.fredericknewspost.com	Frederick	MD	21701	301-662-1177	662-1615
Daily Times 115 E Carroll St *TF:* 877-335-6278 ■ *Web:* www.delmarvanow.com	Salisbury	MD	21801	410-749-7171	749-7290
Carroll County Times 201 Railroad Ave **Fax:* Edit ■ *Web:* www.carrollcountytimes.com	Westminster	MD	21157	410-848-4400	857-8749*

MASSACHUSETTS

	City	State	Zip	Phone	Fax
Sun Chronicle PO Box 600 *Web:* www.thesunchronicle.com	Attleboro	MA	02703	508-222-7000	236-0462
Salem Evening News 32 Dunham Rd *TF:* 800-745-5440 ■ *Web:* www.salemnews.com	Beverly	MA	01915	978-745-6969	927-4524
Boston Globe 135 Morrissey Blvd *Web:* www.boston.com	Boston	MA	02125	617-929-2000	929-3192
Boston Herald 300 Harrison Ave *TF:* 800-225-2040 ■ *Web:* www.bostonherald.com	Boston	MA	02118	617-426-3000	619-6450
Herald-News 207 Pocasset St *Web:* www.heraldnews.com	Fall River	MA	02722	508-676-8211	676-2566
Sentinel & Enterprise PO Box 730 *Web:* www.sentinelandenterprise.com	Fitchburg	MA	01420	978-343-6911	342-1158
MetroWest Daily News 33 New York Ave **Fax:* News Rm ■ *Web:* www.metrowestdailynews.com	Framingham	MA	01701	508-626-4412	626-4400*
Haverhill Gazette 181 Merrimack St *TF:* 800-370-0321 ■ *Web:* www.hgazette.com	Haverhill	MA	01831	978-374-0321	521-6790
Cape Cod Times 319 Main St **Fax:* Edit ■ *TF:* 800-451-7887 ■ *Web:* www.capecodonline.com	Hyannis	MA	02601	508-775-1200	771-3292*
Daily Item The 38 Exchange St PO Box 951 *Web:* www.itemlive.com	Lynn	MA	01903	781-593-7700	598-2891
Malden Evening News 277 Commercial St	Malden	MA	02148	781-321-8000	321-8008
Eagle-Tribune 100 Tpke St *Web:* www.eagletribune.com	North Andover	MA	01845	978-946-2000	687-6045
Daily Hampshire Gazette 115 Conz St *Web:* www.gazettenet.com	NorthHampton	MA	01060	413-584-5000	585-5299
Berkshire Eagle 75 S Church St PO Box 1171 *TF:* 800-234-7404 ■ *Web:* www.berkshireeagle.com	Pittsfield	MA	01202	413-447-7311	499-3419
Patriot Ledger 400 Crown Colony Dr PO 699159 *Web:* www.patriotledger.com	Quincy	MA	02269	617-786-7000	786-7025
Republican The 1860 Main St **Fax:* Edit ■ *TF:* 800-458-5877 ■ *Web:* www.masslive.com	Springfield	MA	01101	413-788-1000	788-1301*
Telegram & Gazette 20 Franklin St PO Box 15012 **Fax:* News Rm ■ *TF:* 800-678-6680 ■ *Web:* www.telegram.com	Worcester	MA	01615	508-793-9100	793-9281*

MICHIGAN

	City	State	Zip	Phone	Fax
Daily Telegram 133 N Winter St *TF:* 800-968-5111 ■ *Web:* www.lenconnect.com	Adrian	MI	49221	517-265-5111	263-4152
Ann Arbor News 340 E Huron St **Fax:* Edit ■ *TF:* 800-466-6989 ■ *Web:* www.mlive.com	Ann Arbor	MI	48104	734-994-6989	994-6879*
Huron Daily Tribune 211 N Heisterman St *Web:* www.michiganthumb.com	Bad Axe	MI	48413	989-269-6461	269-9435
Battle Creek Enquirer 155 W Van Buren St *TF:* 800-333-4139 ■ *Web:* www.battlecreekenquirer.com	Battle Creek	MI	49017	269-964-7161	964-8242
Bay City Times 311 5th St **Fax:* Edit ■ *Web:* www.mlive.com	Bay City	MI	48708	989-895-8551	893-0649*
Detroit Free Press 615 W Lafayette Blvd **Fax:* News Rm ■ *TF:* 800-678-6400 ■ *Web:* www.freep.com	Detroit	MI	48226	313-222-6400	222-5981*
Detroit News 615 W Lafayette Blvd **Fax:* News Rm ■ *TF:* 800-678-6400 ■ *Web:* www.detnews.com	Detroit	MI	48226	313-222-6400	222-2335*
Flint Journal 200 E 1st St **Fax:* Edit ■ *TF Circ:* 800-875-6200 ■ *Web:* www.flintjournal.com	Flint	MI	48502	810-766-6100	767-7518*
Grand Rapids Press 155 Michigan St NW *TF:* 800-878-1400 ■ *Web:* www.mlive.com	Grand Rapids	MI	49503	616-222-5400	222-5409
Holland Sentinel 54 W 8th St *TF:* 800-968-3495 ■ *Web:* www.hollandsentinel.com	Holland	MI	49423	616-392-2311	393-6710
Jackson Citizen Patriot 214 S Jackson St *TF:* 800-878-6397	Jackson	MI	49201	517-787-2300	787-9711
Kalamazoo Gazette 401 S Burdick St **Fax:* Edit ■ *TF:* 800-466-6397 ■ *Web:* www.mlive.com	Kalamazoo	MI	49007	269-345-3511	388-8447*
Lansing State Journal 120 E Lenawee St *TF:* 800-234-1719 ■ *Web:* www.lansingstatejournal.com	Lansing	MI	48919	517-377-1111	377-1298
Mining Journal PO Box 430 *Web:* www.miningjournal.net	Marquette	MI	49855	906-228-2500	228-2617
Midland Daily News 124 McDonald St *TF:* 800-835-6679 ■ *Web:* www.ourmidland.com	Midland	MI	48640	989-835-7171	835-6991
Monroe Evening News 20 W 1st St *Web:* www.monroenews.com	Monroe	MI	48161	734-242-1100	242-0937
Macomb Daily 100 Macomb Daily Dr **Fax:* Edit ■ *Web:* www.macombdaily.com	Mount Clemens	MI	48043	586-469-4510	469-2892*
Muskegon Chronicle 981 3rd St *TF:* 800-783-3161 ■ *Web:* www.mlive.com	Muskegon	MI	49440	231-722-3161	722-2552
Oakland Press PO Box 436009 **Fax:* News Rm ■ *Web:* www.theoaklandpress.com	Pontiac	MI	48343	248-332-8181	332-8885*
Times Herald 911 Military St **Fax:* Edit ■ *TF:* 800-462-4057 ■ *Web:* www.thetimesherald.com	Port Huron	MI	48060	810-985-7171	989-6294*
Daily Tribune 210 E 3rd St *TF:* 877-373-2387 ■ *Web:* www.dailytribune.com	Royal Oak	MI	48067	248-541-3000	541-7041
Saginaw News 203 S Washington Ave *TF:* 800-875-6397 ■ *Web:* www.mlive.com	Saginaw	MI	48607	989-752-7171	752-3115
Herald-Palladium 3450 Hollywood Rd PO Box 128 *TF:* 800-356-4262 ■ *Web:* www.heraldpalladium.com	Saint Joseph	MI	49085	269-429-2400	429-4398
Traverse City Record-Eagle PO Box 632 *Web:* www.record-eagle.com	Traverse City	MI	49685	231-946-2000	946-8632

MINNESOTA

	City	State	Zip	Phone	Fax
Duluth News-Tribune 424 W 1st St *TF Circ:* 800-456-8080 ■ *Web:* www.duluthsuperior.com	Duluth	MN	55802	218-723-5281	720-4120

				Phone	Fax
Free Press 418 S 2nd St *TF:* 800-657-4662 ■ *Web:* www.mankatofreepress.com	Mankato	MN	56001	507-625-4451	388-4355
Star Tribune 425 Portland Ave *TF:* 800-827-8742 ■ *Web:* www.startribune.com	Minneapolis	MN	55488	612-673-4000	673-4359
Post-Bulletin 18 1st Ave SE *TF:* 800-562-1758 ■ *Web:* www.postbulletin.com	Rochester	MN	55904	507-285-7600	285-7772
Saint Cloud Times PO Box 768 *Web:* www.sctimes.com	Saint Cloud	MN	56302	320-255-8700	255-8773
Saint Paul Pioneer Press 345 Cedar St *TF:* 800-950-9080 ■ *Web:* www.twincities.com	Saint Paul	MN	55101	651-228-5490	228-5500
West Central Tribune PO Box 839 *TF:* 800-450-1150 ■ *Web:* www.wctrib.com	Willmar	MN	56201	320-235-1150	235-6769

MISSISSIPPI

				Phone	Fax
Delta Democrat Times 988 N Broadway St *Web:* www.ddtonline.com	Greenville	MS	38701	662-335-1155	335-2860
Sun Herald 205 DeBuys Rd **Fax:* News Rm ■ *TF:* 800-346-5022 ■ *Web:* www.sunherald.com	Gulfport	MS	39507	228-896-2100	896-2104*
Hattiesburg American 825 N Main St **Fax:* News Rm ■ *TF:* 800-844-2637 ■ *Web:* www.hattiesburgamerican.com	Hattiesburg	MS	39401	601-582-4321	584-3130*
Clarion-Ledger 201 S Congress St *TF:* 800-367-3384 ■ *Web:* www.clarionledger.com	Jackson	MS	39201	601-961-7000	961-7211
Meridian Star The PO Box 1591 *TF:* 800-232-2525 ■ *Web:* www.meridianstar.com	Meridian	MS	39302	601-693-1551	485-1275
Mississippi Press PO Box 849 **Fax:* News Rm ■ *Web:* www.gulflive.com	Pascagoula	MS	39568	228-762-0033	934-1474*
Northeast Mississippi Daily Journal 1242 S Green St *TF:* 800-264-6397 ■ *Web:* www.djournal.com	Tupelo	MS	38804	662-842-2611	842-2233
Vicksburg Post 1601 N Frontage Rd # F *Web:* www.vicksburgpost.com	Vicksburg	MS	39180	601-636-4545	634-0897

MISSOURI

				Phone	Fax
Examiner The 500 NW Rd Mize Rd *Web:* www.examiner.net	Blue Springs	MO	64014	816-229-9161	229-6785
Branson Daily Independent 704 S Veterans Blvd	Branson	MO	65616	417-334-2285	334-4789
Linn County Leader 107 N Main St PO Box 40 *Web:* www.linncountyleader.com	Brookfield	MO	64628	660-258-7237	258-7238
Southeast Missourian 301 Broadway St *TF:* 800-879-1210 ■ *Web:* www.semissourian.com	Cape Girardeau	MO	63701	573-335-6611	334-7288
Columbia Daily Tribune 101 N 4th St *TF:* 800-333-6799 ■ *Web:* www.columbiatribune.com	Columbia	MO	65201	573-815-1700	815-1701
Columbia Missourian 221 S 8th St **Fax:* News Rm ■ *Web:* columbiamissourian.com	Columbia	MO	65201	573-882-5700	882-5702*
Excelsior Springs Standard 417 Thompson Ave *Web:* www.excelsiorspringsstandard.com	Excelsior Springs	MO	64024	816-637-6155	637-8411
Branson Daily News 200 Industrial Pk Dr *TF:* 800-490-8020 ■ *Web:* www.bransondailynews.com	Hollister	MO	65672	417-334-3161	335-3933
Examiner The PO Box 459 *Web:* www.examiner.net	Independence	MO	64051	816-254-8600	254-0211
Daily Capital News 210 Monroe St *TF:* 866-865-1690 ■ *Web:* www.newstribune.com	Jefferson City	MO	65101	573-636-3131	761-0235
Jefferson City Post-Tribune 210 Monroe St *TF:* 866-896-8088 ■ *Web:* www.newstribune.com	Jefferson City	MO	65101	573-636-3131	761-0235
Joplin Globe 117 E 4th St *TF:* 800-444-8514 ■ *Web:* www.joplinglobe.com	Joplin	MO	64801	417-623-3480	623-8598
Kansas City Star 1729 Grand Ave *TF:* 877-962-7827 ■ *Web:* www.kansascity.com	Kansas City	MO	64108	816-234-4141	234-4926
Daily Journal 1513 St Joe Dr PO Box A *Web:* www.mydjconnection.com	Park Hills	MO	63601	573-431-2010	431-7640
Daily American Republic 208 Poplar St PO Box 7 *TF:* 800-276-2242 ■ *Web:* www.info.darnews.com	Poplar Bluff	MO	63901	573-785-1414	785-2706
Saint Joseph News-Press PO Box 29 *TF:* 800-779-6397 ■ *Web:* www.stjoenews-press.com	Saint Joseph	MO	64502	816-271-8500	271-8692
Saint Louis Post-Dispatch 900 N Tucker Blvd *TF:* 800-365-0820 ■ *Web:* www.stltoday.com	Saint Louis	MO	63101	314-340-8000	340-3050
Springfield News Leader 651 N Boonville Ave *TF:* 800-695-2005 ■ *Web:* www.news-leader.com	Springfield	MO	65806	417-836-1100	837-1381

MONTANA

				Phone	Fax
Billings Gazette 401 N 28th St *TF:* 800-543-2505 ■ *Web:* www.billingsgazette.com	Billings	MT	59101	406-657-1200	657-1208
Montana Standard 25 W Granite St *TF:* 800-877-1074 ■ *Web:* www.mtstandard.com	Butte	MT	59701	406-496-5500	496-5551
Great Falls Tribune 205 River Dr S **Fax:* News Rm ■ *TF:* 800-438-6600 ■ *Web:* www.greatfallstribune.com	Great Falls	MT	59405	406-791-1444	791-1431*
Helena Independent Record 317 Cruse Ave PO Box 4249 *TF:* 800-523-2272 ■ *Web:* www.helenair.com	Helena	MT	59604	406-447-4000	447-4052
Independent-Record 317 Cruse Ave *TF:* 800-523-2272 ■ *Web:* www.helenair.com	Helena	MT	59601	406-447-4000	447-4052
Daily Inter Lake 727 E Idaho St *Web:* www.dailyinterlake.com	Kalispell	MT	59901	406-755-7000	752-6114
Missoulian PO Box 8029 *TF:* 800-366-7102 ■ *Web:* www.missoulian.com	Missoula	MT	59807	406-523-5200	523-5294

NEBRASKA

				Phone	Fax
Grand Island Independent 422 W 1st St *TF:* 800-658-3160 ■ *Web:* www.theindependent.com	Grand Island	NE	68801	308-382-1000	382-8129
Holdrege Daily Citizen 418 Garfield St PO Box 344	Holdrege	NE	68949	308-995-4441	995-5992
Lincoln Journal-Star 926 P St **Fax:* News Rm ■ *TF:* 800-742-7315 ■ *Web:* www.journalstar.com	Lincoln	NE	68508	402-475-4200	473-7291*
Norfolk Daily News PO Box 977 *TF:* 877-371-1020 ■ *Web:* www.norfolkdailynews.com	Norfolk	NE	68702	402-371-1020	371-5802
Omaha World-Herald 1314 Douglas St *TF:* 800-284-6397 ■ *Web:* www.omaha.com	Omaha	NE	68102	402-444-1000	345-0183
Star-Herald PO Box 1709 **Fax:* News Rm ■ *TF:* 800-846-6102 ■ *Web:* www.starherald.com	Scottsbluff	NE	69363	308-632-9000	632-9001*

NEVADA

				Phone	Fax
Nevada Appeal 580 Mallory Way *TF:* 800-221-8013 ■ *Web:* www.nevadaappeal.com	Carson City	NV	89701	775-882-2111	887-2420
Las Vegas Sun 2360 Corporate Cir *Web:* www.lasvegassun.com	Henderson	NV	89074	702-385-3111	383-7264
Las Vegas Review-Journal 1111 W Bonanza Rd PO Box 70 *Web:* www.lvrj.com	Las Vegas	NV	89106	702-383-0211	383-4676
Reno Gazette-Journal PO Box 22000 *TF:* 800-648-5048 ■ *Web:* www.rgj.com	Reno	NV	89520	775-788-6200	788-6458
Reno Gazette-Journal 955 Kuenzli St *Web:* www.rgj.com	Reno	NV	89502	775-788-6397	788-6458

NEW HAMPSHIRE

				Phone	Fax
Berlin Reporter 151 Main St PO Box 38 *Web:* www.breporter.com	Berlin	NH	03570	603-752-1200	752-2339
Concord Monitor 1 Monitor Dr PO Box 1177 *Web:* www.concordmonitor.com	Concord	NH	03302	603-224-5301	224-8120
Foster's Daily Democrat 150 Venture Dr *TF:* 800-660-8310 ■ *Web:* www.fosters.com	Dover	NH	03820	603-742-4455	749-7079
Union Leader 100 William Loeb Dr **Fax:* Edit ■ *TF:* 800-562-8218 ■ *Web:* www.theunionleader.com	Manchester	NH	03109	603-668-4321	668-0382*
Telegraph The PO Box 1008 *Web:* www.nashuatelegraph.com	Nashua	NH	03061	603-882-2741	882-2681
Portsmouth Herald 111 New Hampshire Ave *TF:* 800-439-0303 ■ *Web:* www.seacoastonline.com	Portsmouth	NH	03801	603-436-1800	433-5760
Valley News 24 Interchange Dr *TF:* 800-874-2226 ■ *Web:* www.vnews.com	West Lebanon	NH	03784	603-298-8711	298-0212

NEW JERSEY

				Phone	Fax
Millville/Bridgeton News 100 E Commerce St *Web:* www.nj.com	Bridgeton	NJ	08302	856-451-1000	455-3098
Courier-News 1201 Rt 22 W *Web:* www.c-n.com	Bridgewater	NJ	08807	908-722-8800	707-3252
Courier-Post 301 Cuthbert Blvd *TF:* 800-677-6289 ■ *Web:* www.courierpostonline.com	Cherry Hill	NJ	08002	856-663-6000	663-2831
Home News Tribune 35 Kennedy Blvd **Fax:* News Rm ■ *TF:* 800-627-4663 ■ *Web:* www.thnt.com	East Brunswick	NJ	08816	732-246-5500	565-7208*
Record The 150 River St *TF:* 888-473-2673	Hackensack	NJ	07601	201-646-4000	646-4135
Jersey Journal 30 Journal Sq **Fax:* News Rm ■ *Web:* www.thejerseyjournal.com	Jersey City	NJ	07306	201-653-1000	653-1414*
Asbury Park Press 3601 Hwy 66 PO Box 1550 **Fax:* News Rm ■ *Web:* www.app.com	Neptune	NJ	07750	732-922-6000	643-4014*
Star-Ledger The 1 Star Ledger Plaza *TF:* 800-501-2100 ■ *Web:* www.nj.com	Newark	NJ	07102	973-877-4141	392-5845
New Jersey Herald 2 Spring St *Web:* www.njherald.com	Newton	NJ	07860	973-383-1500	383-8477
Daily Record 800 Jefferson Rd PO Box 217 **Fax:* Edit ■ *TF:* 800-398-8991 ■ *Web:* www.dailyrecord.com	Parsippany	NJ	07054	973-428-6200	428-6666*
Press of Atlantic City 11 Devins Ln *Web:* www.pressofatlanticcity.com	Pleasantville	NJ	08232	609-272-1100	272-7224
Times of Trenton 500 Perry St *Web:* www.nj.com	Trenton	NJ	08618	609-396-3232	394-2819
Times The 500 Perry St *Web:* www.nj.com/times	Trenton	NJ	08618	609-989-5454	394-2819
Trentonian 600 Perry St *Web:* www.trentonian.com	Trenton	NJ	08618	609-989-7800	393-6072
Daily Journal 891 E Oak Rd *TF:* 800-222-0104 ■ *Web:* www.thedailyjournal.com	Vineland	NJ	08360	856-691-5000	563-5308
Herald News 1 Garret Mountain Plaza Suite 8 **Fax:* Edit ■ *Web:* www.northjersey.com	West Paterson	NJ	07424	973-569-7000	569-7129*
Burlington County Times 4284 Rt 130 *Web:* www.phillyburbs.com	Willingboro	NJ	08046	609-871-8000	871-0490
Gloucester County Times 309 S Broad St *Web:* www.nj.com	Woodbury	NJ	08096	856-845-3300	845-5480

NEW MEXICO

				Phone	Fax
Albuquerque Journal 7777 Jefferson St NE *TF:* 800-990-5765 ■ *Web:* www.abqjournal.com	Albuquerque	NM	87109	505-823-7777	823-3994
Albuquerque Tribune 7777 Jefferson St NE *TF:* 800-665-8742 ■ *Web:* www.abqtrib.com	Albuquerque	NM	87109	505-823-3653	823-3689

	City	State	ZIP	Phone	Fax
Carlsbad Current-Argus 620 S Main St PO Box 1629 — *Web:* www.currentargus.com	Carlsbad	NM	88221	505-887-5501	885-1066
Daily Times 201 N Allen Ave — *TF:* 800-395-6397 ■ *Web:* www.daily-times.com	Farmington	NM	87401	505-325-4545	564-4630
Gallup Independent 500 N 9th St — *TF:* 800-545-3817 ■ *Web:* www.gallupindependent.com	Gallup	NM	87305	505-863-6811	722-5750
Las Cruces Sun-News 256 W Las Cruces Ave — *TF:* 800-745-5851 ■ *Web:* www.lcsun-news.com	Las Cruces	NM	88005	575-541-5400	541-5498
Observer The 1594 Sara Rd SE Suite D — *Web:* www.rrobserver.com	Rio Rancho	NM	87124	505-892-8080	892-5719
Santa Fe New Mexican The 202 E Marcy St PO Box 2048 — **Fax:* News Rm ■ *Web:* www.santafenewmexican.com	Santa Fe	NM	87504	505-983-3303	986-9147*

NEW YORK

	City	State	ZIP	Phone	Fax
Times Union 645 Albany Shaker Rd PO Box 15000 — *TF:* 800-955-4388 ■ *Web:* www.timesunion.com	Albany	NY	12212	518-454-5420	454-5628
Daily News 2 Apollo Dr PO Box 870 — *TF:* 888-217-6397	Batavia	NY	14021	585-343-8000	343-2623
Daily Challenge 1195 Atlantic Ave — *Web:* www.challenge-group.com	Brooklyn	NY	11216	718-636-9500	857-9115
Buffalo News 1 News Plaza PO Box 100 — *TF:* 800-777-8680 ■ *Web:* www.home.buffalo.com	Buffalo	NY	14240	716-849-4627	849-6957
Evening Observer 8-10 E 2nd St PO Box 391 — *TF:* 800-836-0931 ■ *Web:* www.observertoday.com	Dunkirk	NY	14048	716-366-3000	366-3005
Star-Gazette 201 Baldwin St — *TF:* 800-836-8970 ■ *Web:* www.star-gazette.com	Elmira	NY	14902	607-734-5151	733-4408
Finger Lakes Times 218 Genesee St — *TF:* 800-388-6652 ■ *Web:* www.fltimes.com	Geneva	NY	14456	315-789-3333	789-4077
Post-Star 76 Lawrence St — *TF:* 800-724-2543 ■ *Web:* www.poststar.com	Glens Falls	NY	12801	518-792-3131	761-1255
Register-Star 364 Warren St — *Web:* www.registerstar.com	Hudson	NY	12534	518-828-1616	828-9437
Ithaca Journal 123 W State St — *Web:* www.theithacajournal.com	Ithaca	NY	14850	607-272-2321	272-4248
Post-Journal 15 W 2nd St — *TF:* 866-756-9600 ■ *Web:* www.post-journal.com	Jamestown	NY	14701	716-487-1111	664-5305
Daily Freeman 79 Hurley Ave — *Web:* www.dailyfreeman.com	Kingston	NY	12401	845-331-5000	331-3557
Newsday Inc 235 Pinelawn Rd — **Fax:* News Rm ■ *TF:* 800-639-7329 ■ *Web:* www.newsday.com	Melville	NY	11747	631-843-2020	843-2953*
Times Herald-Record 40 Mulberry St PO Box 2046 — *TF:* 800-295-2181 ■ *Web:* www.recordonline.com	Middletown	NY	10940	845-341-1100	343-2170
AM New York 330 W 34th St 17th Fl — *Web:* www.am-ny.com	New York	NY	10001	212-239-5555	239-2828
Financial Times 1330 Avenue of the Americas — *TF:* 800-628-8088 ■ *Web:* www.ft.com	New York	NY	10019	212-641-6500	641-6479
International Herald Tribune 229 W 43rd St 2nd Fl — *Web:* www.iht.com	New York	NY	10036	212-556-7714	556-7706
New York Daily News 450 W 33rd St 3rd Fl — *TF:* 800-692-6397 ■ *Web:* www.nydailynews.com	New York	NY	10001	212-210-2100	643-7831
New York Post 1211 Avenue of the Americas — *TF:* 800-552-7678 ■ *Web:* www.nypost.com	New York	NY	10036	212-930-8000	930-8540
New York Sun 105 Chambers St 2nd Fl — *TF:* 866-692-7861 ■ *Web:* www.nysun.com	New York	NY	10007	212-406-2000	571-9836
New York Times 620 8th Ave — *Web:* www.nytco.com	New York	NY	10018	212-556-1234	556-8828
Niagara Gazette 310 Niagara St PO Box 549 — *Web:* www.niagara-gazette.com	Niagara Falls	NY	14302	716-282-2311	286-3895
Olean Times-Herald 639 Norton Dr — **Fax:* News Rm ■ *TF:* 800-722-8812 ■ *Web:* www.oleantimesherald.com	Olean	NY	14760	716-372-3121	373-6397*
Daily Star 102 Chestnut St PO Box 250 — *TF:* 800-721-1000 ■ *Web:* www.thedailystar.com	Oneonta	NY	13820	607-432-1000	432-5707
Press-Republican 170 Margaret St PO Box 459 — *TF:* 800-288-7323 ■ *Web:* www.pressrepublican.com	Plattsburgh	NY	12901	518-561-2300	561-3362
Poughkeepsie Journal 85 Civic Ctr Plaza — *TF:* 800-765-1120 ■ *Web:* www.poughkeepsiejournal.com	Poughkeepsie	NY	12601	845-437-4800	437-4921
Daily Record 16 W Main St — *Web:* www.nydailyrecord.com	Rochester	NY	14614	585-232-6920	232-2740
Democrat & Chronicle 55 Exchange Blvd — **Fax:* News Rm ■ *TF:* 800-473-5274 ■ *Web:* www.democratandchronicle.com	Rochester	NY	14614	585-232-7100	258-2237*
Rome Sentinel PO Box 471 — *Web:* romesentinel.com	Rome	NY	13442	315-337-2480	339-6281
Daily Gazette 2345 Maxon Rd Ext — *TF:* 800-262-2211 ■ *Web:* www.dailygazette.com	Schenectady	NY	12301	518-374-4141	395-3089
Staten Island Advance 950 Fingerboard Rd — *Web:* www.silive.com	Staten Island	NY	10305	718-981-1234	981-5679
Post-Standard PO Box 4915 — *TF:* 800-765-4569 ■ *Web:* www.syracuse.com	Syracuse	NY	13221	315-470-0011	470-3081
Record The 501 Broadway — *Web:* www.troyrecord.com	Troy	NY	12180	518-270-1200	270-1202
Observer-Dispatch 221 Oriskany Plaza — *Web:* www.uticaod.com	Utica	NY	13501	315-792-5000	792-5033
Watertown Daily Times 260 Washington St — *TF:* 800-642-6222 ■ *Web:* www.watertowndailytimes.com	Watertown	NY	13601	315-782-1000	661-2523
Journal News 1 Gannett Dr — *TF:* 800-942-1010 ■ *Web:* www.thejournalnews.com	White Plains	NY	10604	914-694-9300	694-5018
Journal News The 1 Gannett Dr — *Web:* www.lohud.com	White Plains	NY	10604	914-694-9300	

NORTH CAROLINA

	City	State	ZIP	Phone	Fax
Courier-Tribune 500 Sunset Ave — *TF:* 800-967-1838 ■ *Web:* www.courier-tribune.com	Asheboro	NC	27203	336-625-2101	626-7074
Asheville Citizen Times 14 O'Henry Ave — *TF:* 800-800-4204 ■ *Web:* www.citizen-times.com	Asheville	NC	28801	828-252-5622	251-0585
Times-News PO Box 481 — *TF:* 800-488-0085 ■ *Web:* www.thetimesnews.com	Burlington	NC	27216	336-227-0131	229-2463
Charlotte Observer The 600 S Tryon St — *TF:* 800-332-0686 ■ *Web:* www.charlotteobserver.com	Charlotte	NC	28202	704-358-5000	358-5036
Herald-Sun 2828 Pickett Rd — *TF:* 800-672-0061 ■ *Web:* www.herald-sun.com	Durham	NC	27705	919-419-6500	419-6837
Bladen Daily Journal 228 W Broad St PO Box 70 — *Web:* www.bladenjournal.com	Elizabethtown	NC	28337	910-862-4163	862-6602
Fayetteville Observer 458 Whitfield St — *TF:* 800-345-9895 ■ *Web:* www.fayettevillenc.com	Fayetteville	NC	28306	910-323-4848	486-3545
Gaston Gazette 1893 Remount Rd — *TF:* 800-273-3315 ■ *Web:* www.gastongazette.com	Gastonia	NC	28054	704-869-1700	867-5751
Goldsboro News-Argus PO Box 10629 — **Fax:* News Rm ■ *Web:* www.newsargus.com	Goldsboro	NC	27532	919-778-2211	778-5408*
News & Record 200 E Market St — *TF:* 800-553-6880 ■ *Web:* www.news-record.com	Greensboro	NC	27401	336-373-7000	373-7382
Daily Reflector PO Box 1967 — *TF:* 800-849-6166 ■ *Web:* www.reflector.com	Greenville	NC	27835	252-329-9500	754-8140
Times-News PO Box 490 — *TF:* 800-849-8050 ■ *Web:* www.hendersonvillenews.com	Hendersonville	NC	28793	828-692-0505	693-5581
Hickory Daily Record 1100 Pk Pl — *TF:* 800-849-8586 ■ *Web:* www.hickoryrecord.com	Hickory	NC	28603	828-322-4510	324-8179
High Point Enterprise 210 Church Ave — *TF:* 800-933-5760 ■ *Web:* www.hpe.com	High Point	NC	27262	336-888-3500	841-5582
Daily News 724 Bell Fork Rd PO Box 196 — *TF:* 800-659-2873 ■ *Web:* www.jdnews.com	Jacksonville	NC	28541	910-353-1171	353-7316
Independent Tribune 924 Cloverleaf Plaza — **Fax:* News Rm ■ *Web:* www.independenttribune.com	Kannapolis	NC	28083	704-782-3155	786-0645*
Mount Airy News PO Box 808 — *TF:* 800-826-6397 ■ *Web:* www.mtairynews.com	Mount Airy	NC	27030	336-786-4141	789-2816
Sun Journal 3200 Wellons Blvd — *Web:* www.newbernsunjournal.com	New Bern	NC	28563	252-638-8101	638-4664
News & Observer 215 S McDowell St — *TF:* 800-365-3115 ■ *Web:* www.newsobserver.com	Raleigh	NC	27602	919-829-4500	829-4529
Salisbury Post 131 W Innes St — *TF:* 800-633-8957 ■ *Web:* www.salisburypost.com	Salisbury	NC	28144	704-633-8950	639-0003
Statesville Record & Landmark PO Box 1071 — *AMEX:* MEG ■ *Web:* www.statesville.com	Statesville	NC	28687	704-873-1451	872-3150
Star-News PO Box 840 — *TF:* 800-272-1277 ■ *Web:* www.starnewsonline.com	Wilmington	NC	28402	910-343-2000	343-2227
Wilson Daily Times PO Box 2447 — **Fax:* News Rm ■ *TF:* 800-849-8811 ■ *Web:* www.wilsondaily.com	Wilson	NC	27894	252-243-5151	243-7501*
Winston-Salem Journal 418 N Marshall St — *TF:* 800-642-0925 ■ *Web:* www.journalnow.com	Winston-Salem	NC	27101	336-727-7211	727-7315

NORTH DAKOTA

	City	State	ZIP	Phone	Fax
Bismarck Tribune 707 E Front Ave — **Fax:* Edit ■ *TF:* 866-476-5348 ■ *Web:* www.bismarcktribune.com	Bismarck	ND	58506	701-223-2500	223-2063*
Forum The 101 N 5th St — *TF:* 800-747-7311 ■ *Web:* www.in-forum.com	Fargo	ND	58102	701-235-7311	241-5487
Grand Forks Herald 375 2nd Ave N — *Web:* www.grandforks.com	Grand Forks	ND	58203	701-780-1100	780-1123
Minot Daily News 301 4th St SE — *TF:* 800-735-3119 ■ *Web:* www.minotdailynews.com	Minot	ND	58761	701-857-1900	857-1907

OHIO

	City	State	ZIP	Phone	Fax
Star Beacon PO Box 2100 — *TF:* 800-554-6768 ■ *Web:* www.starbeacon.com	Ashtabula	OH	44005	440-998-2323	998-7938
Repository 500 Market Ave S — **Fax:* News Rm ■ *TF:* 877-580-8300 ■ *Web:* www.cantonrep.com	Canton	OH	44702	330-580-8300	454-5745*
Chillicothe Gazette 50 W Main St PO Box 4400 — *Web:* www.chillicothegazette.com	Chillicothe	OH	45601	740-773-2111	772-9505
Cincinnati Enquirer 312 Elm St — *TF:* 800-876-4500 ■ *Web:* www.news.enquirer.com	Cincinnati	OH	45202	513-721-2700	768-8340
Kentucky Post 125 E Ct St Suite 500 — **Fax Area Code:* 513 ■ *TF:* 800-937-4954 ■ *Web:* www.kypost.com	Cincinnati	OH	45202	859-292-2600	621-3962*
Plain Dealer 1801 Superior Ave — *TF:* 800-688-4802 ■ *Web:* www.cleveland.com	Cleveland	OH	44114	216-999-5000	999-6366
Columbus Dispatch 34 S 3rd St — **Fax:* News Rm ■ *TF:* 800-848-1110 ■ *Web:* www.dispatch.com	Columbus	OH	43215	614-461-5000	461-7580*
Dayton Daily News 1611 S Main St — *Web:* www.daytondailynews.com	Dayton	OH	45409	937-225-2000	225-2489
Crescent-News 624 W 2nd St PO Box 249 — *TF:* 800-589-5441 ■ *Web:* www.crescent-news.com	Defiance	OH	43512	419-784-5441	784-1492
Chronicle-Telegram 225 E Ave — *TF:* 800-848-6397 ■ *Web:* www.chroniclet.com	Elyria	OH	44035	440-329-7000	329-7282
Courier The 701 W Sandusky St PO Box 609 — *Web:* www.thecourier.com	Findlay	OH	45839	419-422-5151	422-2937
Journal News 228 Ct St — *Web:* www.journal-news.com	Hamilton	OH	45011	513-863-8200	896-9489
Lancaster Eagle-Gazette 138 W Chestnut St — *TF:* 888-420-3883 ■ *Web:* www.lancastereaglegazette.com	Lancaster	OH	43130	740-681-4500	681-4505
Lima News 3515 Elida Rd — *TF:* 800-686-9924 ■ *Web:* www.limanews.com	Lima	OH	45807	419-223-1010	229-2926
Morning Journal 1657 Broadway Ave — *Web:* www.morningjournal.com	Lorain	OH	44052	440-245-6901	245-6912
News Journal 70 W 4th St — *TF:* 800-472-5547 ■ *Web:* www.mansfieldnewsjournal.com	Mansfield	OH	44902	419-522-3311	521-7415

Name / Address	City	State	ZIP	Phone	Fax
Star The Marion 150 Ct St *TF:* 800-626-1331 ■ *Web:* www.marionstar.com	Marion	OH	43302	740-387-0400	375-5188
Times Leader 200 S 4th St *TF:* 800-244-5671 ■ *Web:* www.timesleaderonline.com	Martins Ferry	OH	43935	740-633-1131	633-1122
Medina Gazette 885 W Liberty St *TF:* 800-633-4623 ■ *Web:* www.medina-gazette.com	Medina	OH	44256	330-725-4166	721-4016
Middletown Journal PO Box 490 *Web:* www.middletownjournal.com	Middletown	OH	45042	513-422-3611	423-6940
Times Reporter 629 Wabash Ave NW *TF:* 800-837-8666 ■ *Web:* www.timesreporter.com	New Philadelphia	OH	44663	330-364-5577	364-8416
Advocate The 22 N 1st St *TF:* 800-555-8350 ■ *Web:* www.newarkadvocate.com	Newark	OH	43055	740-345-4053	328-8581
Kroner Publications Inc 1123a W Pk Ave	Niles	OH	44446	330-544-5500	544-5511
Daily Sentinel 111 Ct St PO Box 729 *Web:* www.mydailysentinel.com	Pomeroy	OH	45769	740-992-2155	992-2157
Portsmouth Daily Times PO Box 581 *TF:* 800-298-5232 ■ *Web:* www.portsmouth-dailytimes.com	Portsmouth	OH	45662	740-353-3101	353-4676
Record-Courier 126 N Chestnut St PO Box 1201 *TF:* 800-560-9657 ■ *Web:* www.recordpub.com	Ravenna	OH	44266	330-296-9657	296-2698
Sandusky Register 314 W Market St *TF:* 800-466-1243 ■ *Web:* www.sanduskyregister.com	Sandusky	OH	44870	419-625-5500	625-3007
Daily Globe 37 W Main St *Web:* www.sdgnewsgroup.com	Shelby	OH	44875	419-342-3261	342-4246
Springfield News-Sun 202 N Limestone St *TF:* 888-890-7323 ■ *Web:* www.springfieldnewssun.com	Springfield	OH	45503	937-328-0300	328-0328
Blade 541 N Superior St *TF:* 888-252-3301 ■ *Web:* www.toledoblade.com	Toledo	OH	43660	419-724-6000	724-6439
Tribune Chronicle 240 Franklin St SE *TF:* 888-550-8742 ■ *Web:* www.tribune-chronicle.com	Warren	OH	44482	330-841-1600	841-1717
News-Herald 7085 Mentor Ave **Fax:* News Rm ■ *TF:* 800-947-2737 ■ *Web:* www.news-herald.com	Willoughby	OH	44094	440-951-0000	975-2293*
Daily Record 212 E Liberty St PO Box 918 *TF:* 888-323-1662 ■ *Web:* www.the-daily-record.com	Wooster	OH	44691	330-264-1125	264-3756
Vindicator The 107 Vindicator Sq PO Box 780 *TF:* 800-686-5199 ■ *Web:* www.vindy.com	Youngstown	OH	44501	330-747-1471	747-6712
Times Recorder 34 S 4th St **Fax:* News Rm ■ *TF:* 800-886-7326 ■ *Web:* www.zanesvilletimesrecorder.com	Zanesville	OH	43701	740-452-4561	450-6759*

OKLAHOMA

Name / Address	City	State	ZIP	Phone	Fax
Edmond Sun PO Box 2470 *Web:* www.edmondsun.com	Edmond	OK	73083	405-341-2121	340-7363
Enid News & Eagle 227 W Broadway *Web:* www.enidnews.com	Enid	OK	73701	580-233-6600	233-7645
Lawton Constitution 102 SW 3rd St Po Box 2069 *TF:* 800-364-3636 ■ *Web:* www.swoknews.com	Lawton	OK	73502	580-353-0620	585-5140
Muskogee Daily Phoenix 214 Wall St *TF:* 800-730-3649 ■ *Web:* www.muskogeephoenix.com	Muskogee	OK	74401	918-684-2828	684-2865
Norman Transcript 215 E Comanche St PO Box 1058 *Web:* www.normantranscript.com	Norman	OK	73069	405-321-1800	366-3516
Journal Record Oklahoma City 101 N Robinson St Suite 101 *Web:* www.journalrecord.com	Oklahoma City	OK	73102	405-235-3100	278-2890
Oklahoman The 9000 N Broadway *TF:* 800-375-6397 ■ *Web:* www.newsok.com	Oklahoma City	OK	73114	405-475-3311	475-3970
Tulsa World 315 S Boulder Ave *TF:* 800-897-3557 ■ *Web:* www.tulsaworld.com	Tulsa	OK	74102	918-583-2161	581-8353
Wewoka Times 210 S Wewoka Ave *Web:* www.wewokatimes.com	Wewoka	OK	74884	405-257-3341	257-3342

OREGON

Name / Address	City	State	ZIP	Phone	Fax
Albany Democrat-Herald 600 Lyons St SW *TF:* 800-677-3993 ■ *Web:* www.democratherald.com	Albany	OR	97321	541-926-2211	926-4799
Bulletin The 1777 SW Chandler Ave *TF:* 800-503-3933 ■ *Web:* www.bendbulletin.com	Bend	OR	97702	541-382-1811	385-5804
Register-Guard 3500 Chad Dr *Web:* www.registerguard.com	Eugene	OR	97408	541-485-1234	683-7631
Daily Courier 409 SE 7th St *TF:* 800-228-0457 ■ *Web:* www.thedailycourier.com	Grants Pass	OR	97526	541-474-3700	474-3824
Herald & News PO Box 788 *TF:* 800-275-0982 ■ *Web:* www.heraldandnews.com	Klamath Falls	OR	97601	541-885-4410	885-4456
Medford Mail Tribune PO Box 1108 *TF:* 800-366-2527 ■ *Web:* www.mailtribune.com	Medford	OR	97501	541-776-4411	776-4390
Daily Journal of Commerce 921 SW Washington St Suite 210 **Fax:* News Rm ■ *Web:* www.djc-or.com	Portland	OR	97296	503-226-1311	802-7239*
Oregonian 1320 SW Broadway *TF News Rm:* 800-238-8195 ■ *Web:* www.oregonlive.com	Portland	OR	97201	503-221-8100	227-5306
News-Review 345 NE Winchester St **Fax:* Edit ■ *TF:* 800-683-3321 ■ *Web:* www.nrtoday.com	Roseburg	OR	97470	541-672-3321	957-4270*
Statesman Journal 280 Church St NE **Fax:* News Rm ■ *Web:* www.statesmanjournal.com	Salem	OR	97301	503-399-6611	399-6706*

PENNSYLVANIA

Name / Address	City	State	ZIP	Phone	Fax
Morning Call PO Box 1260 *TF:* 800-666-5492 ■ *Web:* www.mcall.com	Allentown	PA	18105	610-820-6500	820-6693
Altoona Mirror 301 Cayuga Ave *TF:* 800-222-1962 ■ *Web:* www.altoonamirror.com	Altoona	PA	16602	814-946-7411	946-7540
Beaver County Times 400 Fair Ave **Fax:* Edit ■ *Web:* www.timesonline.com	Beaver	PA	15009	724-775-3200	775-4180*
Dispatch The 116 E Market St *TF:* 888-636-1116 ■ *Web:* www.pittsburghlive.com	Blairsville	PA	15717	724-459-6100	459-7366
Press-Enterprise 3185 Lackawanna Ave *TF:* 800-228-3483 ■ *Web:* www.pressenterprise.net	Bloomsburg	PA	17815	570-784-2121	784-9226
Butler Eagle 114 W Diamond St *Web:* www.butlereagle.com	Butler	PA	16001	724-282-8000	282-4180
Sentinel The 457 E N St *TF:* 800-829-5570 ■ *Web:* www.cumberlink.com	Carlisle	PA	17013	717-243-2611	243-3121
Public Opinion 77 N 3rd St **Fax:* News Rm ■ *Web:* www.publicopiniononline.com	Chambersburg	PA	17201	717-264-6161	264-0377*
Intelligencer The 333 N Broad St *Web:* www.phillyburbs.com	Doylestown	PA	18901	215-345-3000	345-3150
Express-Times 30 N 4th St *TF:* 800-360-3601 ■ *Web:* www.penn.nj.com	Easton	PA	18042	610-258-7171	258-7130
Erie Times-News 205 W 12th St *TF:* 800-352-0043 ■ *Web:* www.goerie.com	Erie	PA	16534	814-870-1600	870-1808
Gettysburg Times The 1570 Fairfield Rd *Web:* www.gettysburgtimes.com	Gettysburg	PA	17325	717-334-1131	334-4243
Tribune-Review 622 Cabin Hill Dr *Web:* www.triblive.com	Greensburg	PA	15601	724-834-1151	838-5171
Evening Sun 135 Baltimore St PO Box 514 *TF:* 800-877-3786 ■ *Web:* www.eveningsun.com	Hanover	PA	17331	717-637-3736	637-7730
Patriot-News 812 Market St *TF:* 800-692-7207 ■ *Web:* www.pennlive.com	Harrisburg	PA	17101	717-255-8100	255-8456
Hazleton Standard Speaker 21 N Wyoming St *TF:* 800-843-6680 ■ *Web:* www.standardspeaker.com	Hazleton	PA	18201	570-455-3636	455-4244
Wayne Independent 220 8th St *Web:* www.wayneindependent.com	Honesdale	PA	18431	570-253-3055	253-5387
Indiana Gazette 899 Water St *Web:* online.indianagazette.com	Indiana	PA	15701	724-465-5555	465-8267
Tribune-Democrat 425 Locust St *TF:* 800-473-0998 ■ *Web:* www.tribune-democrat.com	Johnstown	PA	15907	814-532-5050	539-1409
Intelligencer Journal 8 W King St *TF:* 800-809-4666 ■ *Web:* www.lancasteronline.com	Lancaster	PA	17603	717-291-8622	399-6507
Lancaster New Era 8 W King St *TF:* 800-809-4666 ■ *Web:* www.lancasteronline.com	Lancaster	PA	17603	717-291-8733	399-6506
Reporter The 307 Derstine Ave *Web:* www.thereporteronline.com	Lansdale	PA	19446	215-855-8440	855-3432
Lebanon Daily News 718 Poplar St *Web:* www.ldnews.com	Lebanon	PA	17042	717-272-5611	274-1608
Bucks County Courier Times 8400 Rt 13 **Fax:* Edit ■ *Web:* www.phillyburbs.com/couriertimes	Levittown	PA	19057	215-949-4000	949-4177*
Meadville Tribune 947 Federal Ct *TF:* 800-879-0006 ■ *Web:* www.meadvilletribune.com	Meadville	PA	16335	814-724-6370	724-8755
Valley Independent Eastgate 19 *Web:* www.pittsburghlive.com/x/valleyindependent	Monessen	PA	15062	724-684-2600	684-2602
Valley Mirror 3910 Main St *Web:* www.valleymirror.com	Munhall	PA	15120	412-462-0626	462-1847
New Castle News PO Box 60 *Web:* www.ncnewsonline.com	New Castle	PA	16103	724-654-6651	654-5976
Times Herald PO Box 591 *Web:* www.timesherald.com	Norristown	PA	19404	610-272-2500	272-0660
Derrick The 1510 W 1st St PO Box 928 *TF:* 800-352-1002 ■ *Web:* www.thederrick.com	Oil City	PA	16301	814-676-7444	677-8347
Evening Bulletin 1518 Walnut St Suite 1010 *TF:* 866-261-8650	Philadelphia	PA	19102	215-735-3012	735-3019
Philadelphia Daily News PO Box 8263 *Web:* www.philly.com	Philadelphia	PA	19101	215-854-2000	854-5910
Philadelphia Inquirer PO Box 8263 *Web:* www.philly.com/mld/inquirer	Philadelphia	PA	19101	215-854-2000	854-5099
Pittsburgh Post-Gazette 34 Blvd of the Allies *Web:* www.post-gazette.com	Pittsburgh	PA	15222	412-263-1100	391-8452
Pittsburgh Tribune-Review 503 Martindale St 3rd Fl *TF:* 800-433-3045 ■ *Web:* www.pittsburghlive.com	Pittsburgh	PA	15212	412-321-6460	320-7963
Mercury The 24 N Hanover St *Web:* www.pottsmerc.com	Pottstown	PA	19464	610-323-3000	323-0682
Pottsville Republican 111 Mahantongo St *TF:* 800-622-1737 ■ *Web:* www.pottsville.com	Pottsville	PA	17901	570-622-3456	628-6068
Delaware County Daily Times 500 Mildred Ave *Web:* www.delcotimes.com	Primos	PA	19017	610-622-8800	622-8889
Scranton Times-Tribune 149 Penn Ave *TF:* 800-228-4637 ■ *Web:* www.scrantontimes.com	Scranton	PA	18503	570-348-9100	348-9135
Herald The 52 S Dock St *Web:* www.sharonherald.com	Sharon	PA	16146	724-981-6100	981-5116
Centre Daily Times 3400 E College Ave **Fax:* News Rm ■ *TF:* 800-327-5500 ■ *Web:* www.centredaily.com	State College	PA	16801	814-238-5000	238-1811*
Pocono Record 511 Lenox St **Fax:* News Rm ■ *TF:* 800-756-4237 ■ *Web:* www.poconorecord.com	Stroudsburg	PA	18360	570-421-3000	421-6284*
Valley News Dispatch 210 4th Ave *TF:* 877-698-2553 ■ *Web:* www.pittsburghlive.com	Tarentum	PA	15084	724-226-1006	226-4677
Herald-Standard 8 E Church St Suite 18 *TF:* 800-342-8254 ■ *Web:* www.heraldstandard.com	Uniontown	PA	15401	724-439-7500	439-7559
Observer-Reporter 122 S Main St **Fax:* News Rm ■ *TF:* 800-222-6397 ■ *Web:* www.observer-reporter.com	Washington	PA	15301	724-222-2200	225-2077*
Daily Local News 250 N Bradford Ave *TF:* 800-456-6397 ■ *Web:* www.dailylocal.com	West Chester	PA	19382	610-696-1775	430-1194
Citizens' Voice 75 N Washington St **Fax:* News Rm ■ *Web:* www.citizensvoice.com	Wilkes-Barre	PA	18711	570-821-2000	821-2247*
Times Leader The 15 N Main St **Fax:* News Rm ■ *TF:* 800-427-8645 ■ *Web:* www.timesleader.com	Wilkes-Barre	PA	18711	570-829-7101	829-5537*
Williamsport Sun-Gazette 252 W 4th St *TF:* 800-339-0289 ■ *Web:* www.sungazette.com	Williamsport	PA	17701	570-326-1551	326-0314
York Daily Record (YDR) 1891 Loucks Rd *Web:* www.ydr.com	York	PA	17408	717-771-2000	771-2009
York Dispatch 205 N George St *TF:* 800-483-5517 ■ *Web:* www.yorkdispatch.com	York	PA	17401	717-854-1575	843-2814

RHODE ISLAND

Name / Address	City	State	ZIP	Phone	Fax
Newport Daily News 101 Malbone Rd *Web:* www.newportdailynews.com	Newport	RI	02840	401-849-3300	849-3306

	City	State	ZIP	Phone	Fax
Times The 23 Exchange St *Web:* www.pawtuckettimes.com	Pawtucket	RI	02860	401-722-4000	727-9280
Providence Journal 75 Fountain St *TF:* 888-697-7656 ■ *Web:* www.projo.com	Providence	RI	02902	401-277-7000	277-7346
Evening Call Publishing Co The 75 Main St *Web:* www.woonsocketcall.com	Woonsocket	RI	02895	401-762-3000	765-2834

SOUTH CAROLINA

	City	State	ZIP	Phone	Fax
Anderson Independent-Mail PO Box 2507 *TF:* 800-859-6397 ■ *Web:* www.independentmail.com	Anderson	SC	29622	864-224-4321	260-1276
Island Packet 10 Buck Island Rd *TF:* 877-706-8100 ■ *Web:* www.islandpacket.com	Bluffton	SC	29910	843-706-8100	706-3070
Post & Courier 134 Columbus St **Fax:* News Rm ■ *Web:* www.postandcourier.com	Charleston	SC	29403	843-577-7111	937-5579*
State The 1401 Shop Rd *TF:* 800-888-5353 ■ *Web:* www.thestate.com	Columbia	SC	29201	803-771-6161	771-8430
Morning News 310 S Dargan St *Web:* www.morningnewsonline.com	Florence	SC	29501	843-317-6397	317-7292
Greenville News 305 S Main St *TF:* 800-800-5116 ■ *Web:* www.greenvilleonline.com	Greenville	SC	29601	864-298-4100	298-4395
Index Journal 610 Phoenix St *Web:* www.indexjournal.com	Greenwood	SC	29648	864-223-1411	223-7331
Sun News 914 Frontage Rd E *TF:* 800-568-1800 ■ *Web:* www.myrtlebeachonline.com	Myrtle Beach	SC	29578	843-626-8555	626-0356
Times & Democrat PO Box 1766 *TF:* 877-534-1060 ■ *Web:* www.thetandd.com	Orangeburg	SC	29115	803-533-5500	533-5595
Herald The 132 W Main St *TF:* 800-697-4111 ■ *Web:* www.heraldonline.com	Rock Hill	SC	29730	803-329-4000	329-4021
Spartanburg Herald-Journal 189 W Main St *TF:* 800-922-4158 ■ *Web:* www.goupstate.com	Spartanburg	SC	29306	864-582-4511	594-6350
Item The 20 N Magnolia St PO Box 1677 *Web:* www.theitem.com	Sumter	SC	29151	803-774-1200	774-1210

SOUTH DAKOTA

	City	State	ZIP	Phone	Fax
Aberdeen American News 124 S 2nd St *TF:* 800-925-4100 ■ *Web:* www.aberdeennews.com/mld/americannews	Aberdeen	SD	57402	605-225-4100	225-0421
Capital Journal 333 W Dakota Ave *TF:* 800-658-3063 ■ *Web:* www.capjournal.com	Pierre	SD	57501	605-224-7301	224-9210
Rapid City Journal 507 Main St *TF:* 800-843-2300 ■ *Web:* www.rapidcityjournal.com	Rapid City	SD	57701	605-394-8300	394-8463
Argus Leader 200 S Minnesota Ave **Fax:* Edit ■ *TF:* 800-530-6397 ■ *Web:* www.argusleader.com	Sioux Falls	SD	57104	605-331-2200	331-2294*
Black Hills Pioneer 315 Seaton Cir *TF:* 800-676-2761 ■ *Web:* www.zwire.com	Spearfish	SD	57783	605-642-2761	642-9060

TENNESSEE

	City	State	ZIP	Phone	Fax
Chattanooga Times Free Press 400 E 11th St *Web:* www.timesfreepress.com	Chattanooga	TN	37403	423-756-6900	757-6383
Leaf-Chronicle PO Box 31029 *Web:* www.theleafchronicle.com	Clarksville	TN	37040	931-552-1808	552-5859
Greeneville Sun 121 W Summer St *Web:* www.greene.xtn.net	Greeneville	TN	37743	423-638-4181	638-7348
Jackson Sun 245 W LaFayette St *TF:* 800-372-3922 ■ *Web:* www.jacksonsun.com	Jackson	TN	38301	731-427-3333	425-9639
Johnson City Press 204 W Main St *Web:* www.johnsoncitypress.com	Johnson City	TN	37604	423-929-3111	929-7484
Kingsport Times-News 701 Lynn Garden Dr *TF:* 800-251-0328 ■ *Web:* www.timesnews.net	Kingsport	TN	37660	423-246-8121	392-1385
Knoxville News-Sentinel 2332 News Sentinel Dr **Fax:* Edit ■ *TF:* 800-237-5821 ■ *Web:* www.knoxnews.com	Knoxville	TN	37921	865-521-8181	342-8635*
Daily Times 307 E Harper St *Web:* www.thedailytimes.com	Maryville	TN	37804	865-981-1100	981-1175
Commercial Appeal 495 Union Ave *TF:* 800-444-6397 ■ *Web:* www.commercialappeal.com	Memphis	TN	38103	901-529-2345	529-2522
Citizen Tribune 1609 W 1st N St PO Box 625 *TF:* 800-624-0281 ■ *Web:* www.citizentribune.com	Morristown	TN	37815	423-581-5630	581-8863
Daily News Journal 224 N Walnut St *Web:* www.dnj.com	Murfreesboro	TN	37130	615-893-5860	893-4186
City Paper The 3322 W End Ave *Web:* www.nashvillecitypaper.com	Nashville	TN	37203	615-298-9833	298-2780
Tennessean 1100 Broadway *TF:* 800-342-8237 ■ *Web:* www.tennessean.com	Nashville	TN	37203	615-259-8800	259-8093

TEXAS

	City	State	ZIP	Phone	Fax
Abilene Reporter-News 101 Cypress St **Fax:* Edit ■ *TF:* 800-588-6397 ■ *Web:* www.reporternews.com	Abilene	TX	79601	325-673-4271	670-5242*
Amarillo Globe News PO Box 2091 *Web:* www.amarillo.com	Amarillo	TX	79166	806-376-4488	373-0810
Austin American-Statesman 305 S Congress Ave *TF:* 800-627-2121 ■ *Web:* www.statesman.com	Austin	TX	78704	512-445-3500	445-3679
Bay City Tribune 2901 16th St *Web:* www.baycitytribune.com	Bay City	TX	77414	979-245-5555	244-5908
Beaumont Enterprise 380 Main St *Web:* www.beaumontenterprise.com	Beaumont	TX	77701	409-838-2888	880-0757
Banner-Press PO Box 585 *Web:* www.brenhambanner.com	Brenham	TX	77834	979-836-7956	830-8577
Brownsville Herald The 1135 E Van Buren St *TF:* 800-488-4301 ■ *Web:* www.brownsvilleherald.com	Brownsville	TX	78520	956-542-4301	542-0840
El Bravo 1144 Lincoln St	Brownsville	TX	78521	956-542-5800	542-6023
Bryan-College Station Eagle 1729 Briarcrest Dr *Web:* www.bcseagle.com	Bryan	TX	77802	979-776-4444	776-8923
Brazosport Facts 720 S Main St *TF:* 800-864-8340 ■ *Web:* www.thefacts.com	Clute	TX	77531	979-265-7411	265-9052
Caller-Times 820 N Lower Broadway **Fax:* Edit ■ *TF:* 800-827-2011 ■ *Web:* www.caller.com	Corpus Christi	TX	78401	361-884-2011	886-3732*
Dallas Morning News 508 Young St *TF:* 800-431-0010 ■ *Web:* www.dallasnews.com	Dallas	TX	75202	214-977-8222	977-8319
Focus Daily News 1337 Marilyn Ave *Web:* www.focus-news.com	De Soto	TX	75115	972-223-9175	223-9202
Herald Democrat 331 W Woodard *Web:* www.heralddemocrat.com	Denison	TX	75020	903-465-7171	465-7188
Denton Record-Chronicle 314 E Hickory St *TF:* 800-275-1722 ■ *Web:* www.dentonrc.com	Denton	TX	76201	940-387-3811	566-6888
El Paso Times 300 N Campbell St Times Plaza **Fax:* News Rm ■ *TF:* 800-351-6007 ■ *Web:* www.elpasotimes.com	El Paso	TX	79901	915-546-6100	546-6415*
Fort Worth Star-Telegram 685 John B Sias Memorial Pkwy *TF:* 800-776-7827 ■ *Web:* www.dfw.com	Fort Worth	TX	76134	817-390-7400	390-7789
Galveston County Daily News 8522 Teichman Rd *TF:* 800-561-3611 ■ *Web:* www.galvestondailynews.com	Galveston	TX	77554	409-683-5200	740-3421
Valley Morning Star PO Box 511 *TF:* 866-578-7827 ■ *Web:* www.valleystar.com	Harlingen	TX	78551	956-430-6200	430-6233
Houston Chronicle 801 Texas Ave *TF:* 800-735-3800 ■ *Web:* www.chron.com	Houston	TX	77002	713-362-7171	362-6806
Killeen Daily Herald 1809 Florence Rd PO Box 1300 *Web:* www.kdhnews.com	Killeen	TX	76540	254-634-2125	200-7640
Laredo Morning Times 111 Esperanza Dr **Fax:* Edit ■ *TF:* 800-728-3118 ■ *Web:* www.lmtonline.com	Laredo	TX	78041	956-728-2500	724-3036*
Longview News-Journal 320 E Methvin St **Fax:* News Rm ■ *TF:* 800-825-9799 ■ *Web:* www.news-journal.com	Longview	TX	75601	903-757-3311	757-3742*
Lubbock Avalanche-Journal 710 Ave J *TF:* 800-692-4021 ■ *Web:* www.lubbockonline.com	Lubbock	TX	79401	806-762-8844	744-9603
Lufkin Daily News 300 Ellis Ave *Web:* www.lufkindailynews.com	Lufkin	TX	75904	936-632-6631	632-6655
Monitor The 1400 E Nolana Loop *TF:* 800-366-4343 ■ *Web:* www.themonitor.com	McAllen	TX	78504	956-683-4000	683-4401
Midland Reporter-Telegram PO Box 1650 *TF:* 800-542-3952 ■ *Web:* www.mywesttexas.com	Midland	TX	79702	432-682-5311	570-7650
Odessa American PO Box 2952 *TF:* 888-375-6262 ■ *Web:* www.oaoa.com	Odessa	TX	79760	432-337-4661	333-7742
Pecos Enterprise PO Box 2057 *Web:* www.pecos.net	Pecos	TX	79772	432-445-5475	445-4321
Plano Star Courier 624 Crona Dr Suite 170 *Web:* www.planostar.com	Plano	TX	75074	972-398-4200	398-4270
Port Arthur News 3501 Turtle Creek Dr # 105 *Web:* www.panews.com	Port Arthur	TX	77642	409-729-6397	724-6854
Fort Bend Herald 1902 S 4th St *Web:* www.herald-coaster.com	Rosenberg	TX	77471	281-342-4474	342-3219
San Angelo Standard-Times 34 W Harris Ave *TF:* 800-588-1884 ■ *Web:* www.gosanangelo.com	San Angelo	TX	76903	325-659-8200	659-8173
Metrocom Herald 17400 Judson Rd *Web:* www.primetimenewspapers.com	San Antonio	TX	78247	210-453-3300	828-3787
San Antonio Express-News Ave E & 3rd St *TF:* 800-555-1551 ■ *Web:* www.mysanantonio.com	San Antonio	TX	78205	210-250-3000	250-3105
Herald Democrat 603 S Sam Rayburn Fwy *TF:* 800-827-7183 ■ *Web:* www.heralddemocrat.com	Sherman	TX	75090	903-893-8181	868-2106
Texarkana Gazette 315 Pine St *TF:* 800-955-8518 ■ *Web:* www.texarkanagazette.com	Texarkana	TX	75501	903-794-3311	794-3315
Tyler Morning Telegraph PO Box 2030 **Fax:* News Rm ■ *TF:* 800-333-8411 ■ *Web:* www.tylerpaper.com	Tyler	TX	75710	903-597-8111	595-0335*
Victoria Advocate PO Box 1518 **Fax:* News Rm ■ *TF:* 800-234-8108 ■ *Web:* www.thevictoriaadvocate.com	Victoria	TX	77902	361-575-1451	574-1220*
Waco Tribune-Herald 900 Franklin Ave *TF:* 800-678-8742 ■ *Web:* www.wacotrib.com	Waco	TX	76701	254-757-5757	757-0302
Times Record News PO Box 120 *TF:* 800-627-1646 ■ *Web:* www.timesrecordnews.com	Wichita Falls	TX	76307	940-767-8341	767-1741

UTAH

	City	State	ZIP	Phone	Fax
Herald Journal 75 W 300 North PO Box 487 *TF:* 800-275-0423 ■ *Web:* www.hjnews.com	Logan	UT	84323	435-752-2121	753-6642
Standard-Examiner 332 Standard Way *TF:* 800-234-5505 ■ *Web:* www.standard.net	Ogden	UT	84404	801-625-4200	625-4299
Daily Herald 1555 N Freedom Blvd *TF:* 800-880-8075 ■ *Web:* www.heraldextra.com	Provo	UT	84604	801-373-5050	344-2985
Spectrum The 275 E Saint George Blvd *Web:* www.thespectrum.com	Saint George	UT	84770	435-674-6200	674-6265
Deseret News 30 E 100 S # 400 *TF:* 888-337-6397 ■ *Web:* www.deseretnews.com	Salt Lake City	UT	84111	801-236-6000	237-2121
Salt Lake Tribune 90 S 400 W Suite 700 *Web:* www.sltrib.com	Salt Lake City	UT	84101	801-257-8742	257-8525

VERMONT

	City	State	ZIP	Phone	Fax
Burlington Free Press 191 College St *TF:* 800-427-3124 ■ *Web:* www.burlingtonfreepress.com	Burlington	VT	05401	802-863-3441	660-1802
Rutland Herald PO Box 668 *TF:* 800-776-5512 ■ *Web:* www.rutlandherald.com	Rutland	VT	05702	802-775-5511	747-6133

VIRGINIA

	City	State	ZIP	Phone	Fax
Bristol Herald-Courier 320 Bob Morrison Blvd *TF:* 888-228-2098 ■ *Web:* www.bristolnews.com	Bristol	VA	24201	276-669-2181	669-3696
Free Lance Star 616 Amelia St **Fax:* News Rm ■ *TF:* 800-877-0500 ■ *Web:* www.fredericksburg.com	Fredericksburg	VA	22401	540-374-5000	373-8455*

Name / Address	City	State	Zip	Phone	Fax
Daily News-Record 231 S Liberty St. Web: www.dnronline.com	Harrisonburg	VA	22801	540-574-6200	433-9112
News & Advance PO Box 10129. TF: 800-275-8831 ■ Web: www.newsadvance.com	Lynchburg	VA	24506	434-385-5555	385-5538
Martinsville Bulletin PO Box 3711. TF: 800-234-6575 ■ Web: www.martinsvillebulletin.com	Martinsville	VA	24115	276-638-8801	638-7409
Daily Press 7505 Warwick Blvd. Web: www.dailypress.com	Newport News	VA	23607	757-247-4600	245-8618
Virginian-Pilot 150 W Bramelton Ave. TF: 800-446-2004 ■ Web: www.hamptonroads.com	Norfolk	VA	23510	757-446-2000	446-2414
Progress-Index 15 Franklin St. Web: www.progress-index.com/site/news.asp?brd=2271	Petersburg	VA	23803	804-732-3456	732-8417
Roanoke Times 201 W Campbell Ave SW. TF: 800-346-1234 ■ Web: www.roanoke.com	Roanoke	VA	24011	540-981-3340	981-3346
News Leader 11 N Central Ave. TF: 800-793-2459 ■ Web: www.newsleader.com	Staunton	VA	24401	540-885-7281	885-1904
Winchester Star 2 N Kent St. TF: 800-296-8639 ■ Web: www.winchesterstar.com	Winchester	VA	22601	540-667-3200	667-1649
Potomac News 14010 Smoke Town Rd. Web: www.potomacnews.com	Woodbridge	VA	22192	703-878-8000	878-8099

WASHINGTON

Name / Address	City	State	Zip	Phone	Fax
Daily World 315 S Michigan St. TF: 800-829-7880 ■ Web: www.thedailyworld.com	Aberdeen	WA	98520	360-532-4000	533-6039
Bellingham Herald 1155 N State St. *Fax: News Rm ■ Web: www.bellinghamherald.com	Bellingham	WA	98225	360-676-2600	756-2826*
Kitsap Sun PO Box 259. TF: 888-377-3711 ■ Web: www.kitsapsun.com	Bremerton	WA	98337	360-377-3711	415-2681
Daily Herald 1213 California Ave. Web: www.heraldnet.com	Everett	WA	98201	425-339-3000	339-3049
Tri-City Herald 333 W Canal Dr. TF: 800-874-0445 ■ Web: www.tri-cityherald.com	Kennewick	WA	99336	509-582-1500	582-1510
Daily News 770 11th Ave PO Box 189. *Fax: News Rm ■ TF: 800-341-4745 ■ Web: www.tdn.com	Longview	WA	98632	360-577-2500	577-2538*
Skagit Valley Herald 1000 E College Way PO Box 578. *Fax: News Rm ■ TF: 800-683-3300 ■ Web: www.goskagit.com	Mount Vernon	WA	98273	360-424-3251	424-5300*
Olympian The PO Box 407. *Fax: News Rm ■ Web: www.theolympian.com	Olympia	WA	98507	360-754-5400	357-0202*
Peninsula Daily News 305 W 1st St PO Box 1330. TF: 800-826-7714 ■ Web: www.peninsuladailynews.com	Port Angeles	WA	98362	360-452-2345	417-3521
Seattle Daily Journal of Commerce PO Box 11050. Web: www.djc.com	Seattle	WA	98111	206-622-8272	622-8416
Seattle Post-Intelligencer 101 Elliott Ave W 2nd Fl. TF: 800-542-0820 ■ Web: www.seattlepi.nwsource.com	Seattle	WA	98119	206-448-8000	448-8166
Seattle Times 1120 John St. Web: www.seattletimes.nwsource.com	Seattle	WA	98109	206-464-2111	464-2261
News Tribune 1950 S State St. TF: 800-388-8742 ■ Web: www.thenewstribune.com	Tacoma	WA	98405	253-597-8686	597-8274
Columbian 701 W 8th St PO Box 180. TF: 800-743-3391 ■ Web: www.columbian.com	Vancouver	WA	98660	360-694-3391	699-6033
Wenatchee World 14 N Mission St. TF: 800-572-4433 ■ Web: www.wenworld.com	Wenatchee	WA	98801	509-663-5161	665-1183
Yakima Herald-Republic PO Box 9668. TF: 800-343-2799 ■ Web: www.yakima-herald.com	Yakima	WA	98909	509-248-1251	577-7767

WEST VIRGINIA

Name / Address	City	State	Zip	Phone	Fax
Register-Herald 801 N Kanawha St. TF: 800-950-0250 ■ Web: www.register-herald.com	Beckley	WV	25801	304-255-4400	255-4427
Charleston Daily Mail 1001 Virginia St E. TF: 800-982-6397 ■ Web: www.dailymail.com	Charleston	WV	25301	304-348-5140	348-4847
Charleston Gazette 1001 Virginia St E. TF: 800-982-6397 ■ Web: www.wvgazette.com	Charleston	WV	25301	304-348-5140	348-1233
Clarksburg Exponent Telegram 324 Hewes Ave. TF: 800-982-6034 ■ Web: www.cpubco.com	Clarksburg	WV	26301	304-626-1400	624-4188
Exponent Telegram 324 Hewes Ave. TF: 800-982-6034 ■ Web: www.cpubco.com	Clarksburg	WV	26301	304-624-6411	624-4188
Herald-Dispatch 946 5th Ave. TF: 800-444-2446 ■ Web: www.herald-dispatch.com	Huntington	WV	25720	304-526-4000	526-2857
Journal The 207 W King St. *Fax: PR ■ TF: 800-448-1895 ■ Web: www.journal-news.net	Martinsburg	WV	25401	304-263-8931	267-2903*
Daily Athenaeum 284 Prospect St. Web: www.thedaonline.com	Morgantown	WV	26505	304-293-4141	293-6857
Dominion Post 1251 Earl L Core Rd. TF: 800-654-4676 ■ Web: olive.dominionpost.com	Morgantown	WV	26505	304-292-6301	291-2326
Parkersburg News 519 Juliana St. Web: www.newsandsentinel.com	Parkersburg	WV	26101	304-485-1891	485-5122
Intelligencer The 1500 Main St. Web: www.theintelligencer.net	Wheeling	WV	26003	304-233-0100	232-1399
Wheeling News-Register 1500 Main St. *Fax: Edit ■ Web: www.news-register.net	Wheeling	WV	26003	304-233-0100	232-1399*

WISCONSIN

Name / Address	City	State	Zip	Phone	Fax
Beloit Daily News 149 State St. TF: 800-356-3411 ■ Web: www.beloitdailynews.com	Beloit	WI	53511	608-365-8811	365-1420
Leader-Telegram 701 S Farwell St. *Fax: Edit ■ TF: 800-236-8808 ■ Web: www.leadertelegram.com	Eau Claire	WI	54701	715-833-9200	858-7308*
Reporter The PO Box 630. TF: 800-261-7323 ■ Web: www.fdlreporter.com	Fond du Lac	WI	54936	920-922-4600	922-5388
Green Bay Press-Gazette PO Box 23430. TF: 800-289-8221 ■ Web: www.greenbaypressgazette.com	Green Bay	WI	54305	920-431-8400	431-8379
Janesville Gazette 1 S Parker Dr PO Box 5001. *Fax: Edit ■ TF: 800-362-6712 ■ Web: www.gazetteextra.com	Janesville	WI	53547	608-754-3311	755-8349*
Kenosha News 5800 7th Ave. TF: 800-292-2700 ■ Web: www.kenoshanews.com	Kenosha	WI	53140	262-657-1000	657-8455
La Crosse Tribune 401 N 3rd St. *Fax: Edit ■ TF: 800-262-0420 ■ Web: www.lacrossetribune.com	La Crosse	WI	54601	608-782-9710	782-9723*
Capital Times 1901 Fish Hatchery Rd. TF: 800-362-8333	Madison	WI	53713	608-252-6000	252-6082
Wisconsin State Journal 1901 Fish Hatchery Rd. TF: 800-362-8333 ■ Web: www.madison.com/wisconsinstatejournal	Madison	WI	53713	608-252-6200	252-6445
Herald Times Reporter 902 Franklin St. TF: 800-783-7323 ■ Web: www.htrnews.com	Manitowoc	WI	54221	920-684-4433	686-2103
Milwaukee Journal Sentinel 333 W State St. TF: 800-456-5943 ■ Web: www.jsonline.com	Milwaukee	WI	53201	414-224-2000	224-2047
Oshkosh Northwestern 224 State St. TF: 800-924-6168 ■ Web: www.thenorthwestern.com	Oshkosh	WI	54901	920-235-7700	426-6600
Journal Times 212 4th St. Web: www.journaltimes.com	Racine	WI	53403	262-634-3322	631-1780
Sheboygan Press PO Box 358. TF: 800-686-3900 ■ Web: www.sheboygan-press.com	Sheboygan	WI	53082	920-457-7711	457-3573
Waukesha County Freeman PO Box 7	Waukesha	WI	53187	262-542-2501	542-8259*
Wausau Daily Herald PO Box 1286. TF: 800-477-4838 ■ Web: www.wausaudailyherald.com	Wausau	WI	54402	715-842-2101	848-9361

WYOMING

Name / Address	City	State	Zip	Phone	Fax
Star-Tribune 170 Star Ln. Web: www.trib.com	Casper	WY	82604	307-266-0500	266-0568
Wyoming Tribune-Eagle 702 W Lincolnway. TF: 800-561-6268 ■ Web: www.wyomingnews.com	Cheyenne	WY	82001	307-634-3361	633-3189

535-3 National Newspapers

Name / Address	City	State	Zip	Phone	Fax
Christian Science Monitor 210 Massachusetts Ave. TF: 800-288-7090 ■ Web: www.csmonitor.com	Boston	MA	02115	617-450-2000	450-7575
USA Today 7950 Jones Branch Dr. *Fax: News Rm ■ TF Cust Svc: 800-872-0001 ■ Web: www.usatoday.com	McLean	VA	22108	703-854-3400	854-3053*
Wall Street Journal PO Box 300. Web: www.online.wsj.com	Princeton	NJ	08543	609-520-7023	520-7810
Wall Street Journal (Midwestern Edition) 1 S Wacker Dr Suite 2100	Chicago	IL	60606	312-750-4000	750-4153
Wall Street Journal The 1211 Avenue of the Americas. TF: 800-568-7625 ■ Web: online.wsj.com/home-page?mod=WSJ_footer	New York	NY	10036	212-416-2000	416-4155

535-4 Weekly Newspapers

Listings Here Are Organized By City Names Within State Groupings.

ALABAMA

Name / Address	City	State	Zip	Phone	Fax
Corner News PO Box 3240. Web: www.thecornernews.com	Auburn	AL	36831	334-821-7150	887-0037
Birmingham Times 115 3rd Ave W. Web: www.thebirminghamtimes.com	Birmingham	AL	35204	205-251-5158	323-2294
Over The Mountain Journal 2016 Columbiana Rd. Web: www.otmj.com	Birmingham	AL	35216	205-823-9646	824-1246
Shelby County Reporter 115 N Main St. Web: www.shelbycountyreporter.com	Columbiana	AL	35051	205-669-3131	669-4217
Courier Journal 1828 Darby Dr. Web: www.courierjournal.net	Florence	AL	35630	256-764-4268	760-9618
Greenville Advocate The PO Box 507. Web: www.greenvilleadvocate.com	Greenville	AL	36037	334-382-3111	382-7104
Hartselle Enquirer PO Box 929. Web: www.hartselleenquirer.com	Hartselle	AL	35640	256-773-6566	773-1953
Montgomery Independent 141 Market Pl. Web: www.al.com	Montgomery	AL	36117	334-265-7323	265-7320

ALASKA

Name / Address	City	State	Zip	Phone	Fax
Anchorage Press 540 E 5th Ave. Web: www.anchoragepress.com	Anchorage	AK	99501	907-561-7737	561-7777
Capital City Weekly 134 S Franklin St. Web: www.capitalcityweekly.com	Juneau	AK	99801	907-789-4144	789-0987

ARIZONA

Name / Address	City	State	Zip	Phone	Fax
Apache Junction Independent 850 S Ironwood Dr Suite 112. *Fax: News Rm ■ Web: www.newszap.com/apache	Apache Junction	AZ	85220	480-982-7799	671-0016*

	City	State	Zip	Phone	Fax
East Mesa Independent 850 S Ironwood Dr Suite 112 **Fax:* News Rm ■ *Web:* www.newszap.com/eastmesa	Apache Junction	AZ	85220	480-982-7799	671-0016*
West Valley View 200 W Wigwam Blvd *Web:* www.westvalleyview.com	Litchfield Park	AZ	85340	623-535-8439	935-2103
Ahwatukee Foothills News 10631 S 51st St Suite 1 **Fax:* News Rm ■ *Web:* www.ahwatukee.com	Phoenix	AZ	85044	480-898-7900	893-1684*
Paradise Valley Independent 11000 N Scottsdale Rd Suite 210 **Fax:* News Rm ■ *Web:* www.newszap.com	Scottsdale	AZ	85254	480-483-0977	948-0496*
Sun Cities Independent 17220 N Boswell Blvd # 101 *Web:* www.newszap.com	Sun City	AZ	85373	623-972-6101	974-6004

ARKANSAS

	City	State	Zip	Phone	Fax
East Arkansas News Leader PO Box 308	Wynne	AR	72396	870-238-2375	238-4655

CALIFORNIA

	City	State	Zip	Phone	Fax
Alameda Journal 1516 Oak St	Alameda	CA	94501	510-748-1666	748-1665
Bakersfield News Observer 1219 20th St	Bakersfield	CA	93301	661-324-9466	324-9472
Beverly Hills Courier 8840 W Olympic Blvd *Web:* www.thebeverlyhillscourier.com	Beverly Hills	CA	90211	310-278-1322	271-5118
Ceres Courier 2940 4th St *Web:* www.mantecabulletin.com	Ceres	CA	95307	209-537-5032	537-0543
Chino Champion PO Box 607 *Web:* www.championnewspapers.com	Chino	CA	91708	909-628-5501	590-1217
Chino Hills Champion PO Box 607 *Web:* www.championnewspapers.com	Chino	CA	91708	909-628-5501	590-1217
Star-News The 296 3rd Ave *Web:* www.thestarnews.com	Chula Vista	CA	91910	619-427-3000	426-6346
Huntington Beach Independent 1375 Sunflower Ave *Web:* www.hbindependent.com	Costa Mesa	CA	92626	714-966-4600	
Heroald Publications 312 E Imperial Ave *Web:* www.heraldpublications.com	El Segundo	CA	90245	310-322-1830	322-2787
Elk Grove Citizen 8970 Elk Grove Blvd *Web:* www.egcitizen.com	Elk Grove	CA	95624	916-685-3945	686-6675
Humboldt Beacon The 936 Main St *Web:* www.humboldtbeacon.com	Fortuna	CA	95540	707-725-6166	725-6837
Garden Grove Journal 12866 Main St Suite 203 *Web:* www.ggjournal.com	Garden Grove	CA	92840	714-539-6018	892-7052
Gardena Valley News 15005 S Vermont Ave *TF:* 800-329-6351	Gardena	CA	90247	310-329-6351	329-7501
Burbank Leader 111 W Wilson Ave *Web:* www.burbankleader.com	Glendale	CA	91203	818-637-3200	241-1975
Hesperia Resorter PO Box 400937 *Web:* www.valleywidenewspaper.com	Hesperia	CA	92340	760-244-0021	244-6609
Pinnacle The 350 6th St # 102 *Web:* www.pinnaclenews.com	Hollister	CA	95023	831-637-6300	637-8174
Kingsburg Recorder 1467 Marion St *Web:* www.kingsburgrecorder.com	Kingsburg	CA	93631	559-897-2993	897-4868
Independent The 2250 1st St *Web:* www.independentnews.com	Livermore	CA	94550	925-447-8700	447-0212
Los Altos Town Crier 138 Main St *Web:* www.latc.com	Los Altos	CA	94022	650-948-9000	948-6647
East Los Angeles/Brooklyn Belvedere Comet 111 S Ave 59 *Web:* www.egpnews.com	Los Angeles	CA	90042	323-341-7970	341-7976
Los Angeles Downtown News 1264 W 1st St *Web:* www.ladowntownnews.com	Los Angeles	CA	90026	213-481-1448	250-4617
Mammoth Times The PO Box 3929 *Web:* www.mammothtimes.com	Mammoth Lakes	CA	93546	760-934-3929	934-3951
Argonaut The PO Box 11209 *Web:* www.argonautnewspaper.com	Marina del Rey	CA	90295	310-822-1629	821-8029
Almanac The 3525 Alameda De Las Pulgas *Web:* www.almanacnews.com	Menlo Park	CA	94025	650-854-2626	854-0677
Milpitas Post 59 Maryland Dr *Web:* www.themilpitaspost.com	Milpitas	CA	95035	408-262-2454	263-9710
Bay Area Press 1520 Broadway *Web:* www.bayarearapidpress.com	Oakland	CA	94612	510-835-2731	839-0164
Paradise Post 5399 Clark Rd *TF:* 800-924-0908 ■ *Web:* www.paradisepost.com	Paradise	CA	95969	530-877-4413	877-1326
Paso Robles Press PO Box 427 *Web:* www.pasoroblespress.com	Paso Robles	CA	93447	805-237-6060	237-6066
Palos Verdes Peninsula News 500 Silver Spur Rd Suite 300 **Fax:* Edit ■ *Web:* www.pvnews.nminews.com	Rancho Palos Verdes	CA	90275	310-377-6877	544-4322*
Riverside County Record PO Box 3187 *Web:* www.riversidecountyrecord.com	Riverside	CA	92519	951-685-6191	685-2961
Community Voice PO Box 2038 *Web:* www.thecommunityvoice.com	Rohnert Park	CA	94927	707-584-2222	285-3226
Rialto Record PO Box 6247 *Web:* www.iecn.com	San Bernardino	CA	92412	909-381-9898	384-0406
Cupertino Courier 1095 The Alameda *Web:* www.cupertinocourier.com	San Jose	CA	95126	408-200-1000	200-1013
Sunnyvale Sun 1095 The Alameda *Web:* www.sunnyvalesun.com	San Jose	CA	95126	408-200-1000	200-1013
Willow Glen Resident 1095 The Alameda *Web:* www.wgresident.com	San Jose	CA	95126	408-200-1000	200-1013
Sonoma Index-Tribune PO Box C *Web:* www.sonomanews.com	Sonoma	CA	95476	707-938-2111	938-1600
Covina Highlander Press Courier 1210 N Azusa Canyon Rd *Web:* www.sgvtribune.com/highlanders/covina	West Covina	CA	91790	818-854-8700	854-8719
Glendora Highlander Press 1210 N Azusa Canyon Rd *Web:* www.sgvtribune.com/highlanders/glendora	West Covina	CA	91790	626-962-8811	854-8719

COLORADO

	City	State	Zip	Phone	Fax
Aurora Sentinel 14305 E Alameda Ave Suite 200 *Web:* www.aurorasentinel.com	Aurora	CO	80012	303-750-7555	750-7699
Eagle Valley Enterprise 108 W 2nd St *Web:* www.eaglevalleyenterprise.com	Eagle	CO	81631	970-328-6656	328-6393
Columbine Courier 9719 W Coal Mine Ave Unit N *Web:* www.columbinecourier.com	Littleton	CO	80123	303-933-2233	933-4449

CONNECTICUT

	City	State	Zip	Phone	Fax
Rivereast News Bulletin PO Box 373 *Web:* www.glcitizen.com	Glastonbury	CT	06033	860-633-4691	657-3258
Hartford News 563 Franklin Ave	Hartford	CT	06114	860-296-6128	296-3350
Milford Weekly PO Box 5339 *Web:* www.milfordweekly.com	Milford	CT	06460	203-876-6800	877-4772
Stratford Bard PO Box 5339 *Web:* www.zwire.com/site/news.cfm?brd=1637	Milford	CT	06460	203-876-6800	877-4772
Bridgeport News 1000 Bridgeport Ave *TF Advestisement:* 800-372-2790 ■ *Web:* www.acorn-online.com/joomla15/thebridgeportnews/news.html	Shelton	CT	06484	203-926-2080	926-2092
Milford Mirror 1000 Bridgeport Ave *TF Advestisement:* 800-372-2790 ■ *Web:* www.milfordmirror.com	Shelton	CT	06484	203-402-2315	926-2092
Stratford Star 1000 Bridgeport Ave *TF Advestisement:* 800-372-2790 ■ *Web:* www.stratfordstar.com	Shelton	CT	06484	203-402-2319	926-2091
Voices PO Box 383 *Web:* www.voicesnews.com	Southbury	CT	06488	203-262-6631	262-6665
Reminder The PO Box 210 *TF:* 888-456-2211 ■ *Web:* www.remindernet.com	Vernon	CT	06066	860-875-3366	872-4614
Westport Minuteman 1775 Post Rd E *Web:* www.westportminuteman.com	Westport	CT	06880	203-226-8877	221-7540

DELAWARE

	City	State	Zip	Phone	Fax
Dover Post 1196 S Little Creek Rd *TF:* 800-942-1616 ■ *Web:* www.doverpost.com	Dover	DE	19901	302-678-3616	678-8291
Sussex Post PO Box 737 *TF:* 800-282-8586 ■ *Web:* www.newszap.com	Dover	DE	19903	302-934-9261	645-2267
Cape Gazette PO Box 213 *Web:* capegazette.com	Lewes	DE	19958	302-645-7700	645-1664
Dialog The 1925 Delaware Ave PO Box 2208 *Web:* www.cdow.org	Wilmington	DE	19806	302-573-3109	573-6948

FLORIDA

	City	State	Zip	Phone	Fax
Bonita Banner PO Box 40 *Web:* www.bonitanews.com	Bonita Springs	FL	34133	239-765-0110	213-6088
Hernando Today 15299 Cortez Blvd *Web:* www.hernandotoday.com	Brooksville	FL	34613	352-544-5200	799-5246
Broward News & Senior News 11874 Wiles Rd *Web:* www.flabrowardseniornews.com	Coral Springs	FL	33076	954-344-5156	344-0107
Boca Times 1701 Green Rd Suite B *TF:* 800-275-8820 ■ *Web:* www.forumpublishing.com	Deerfield Beach	FL	33064	954-698-6397	429-1207
Delray Beach Times 1701 Green Rd Suite B *TF:* 800-275-8820	Deerfield Beach	FL	33064	954-698-6397	429-1207
Margate/Coconut Creek Forum 1701 Green Rd Suite B	Deerfield Beach	FL	33064	954-698-6397	421-9002
Observer The 201 N Federal Hwy Suite 103 *Web:* www.observernewspaperonline.com	Deerfield Beach	FL	33441	954-428-9045	428-9096
Tamarac/North Lauderdale Forum 1701 Green Rd *Web:* www.sun-sentinel.com/services/newspaper/fpg	Deerfield Beach	FL	33064	954-698-6397	698-6719
Osceola News-Gazette PO Box 422068 *TF:* 800-327-2166 ■ *Web:* www.oscnewsgazette.com	Kissimmee	FL	34742	407-846-7600	846-8516
Lake Worth Herald/Coastal Observer 130 S 'H' St *TF:* 888-544-0047	Lake Worth	FL	33460	561-585-9387	585-5434
Lehigh Acres News-Star PO Box 908 *Web:* www.lehighnewsstar.com	Lehigh Acres	FL	33970	239-369-2191	369-1396
Longboat Observer 5570 Gulf of Mexico Dr PO Box 8100 *Web:* www.longboatobserver.com	Longboat Key	FL	34228	941-383-5509	383-7193
Miami Today 710 Brickell Ave *Web:* www.miamitodaynews.com	Miami	FL	33131	305-358-2663	358-4811
Clay Today 1560 Kingsley Ave Suite 1 *TF:* 888-424-6220 ■ *Web:* www.claytoday.biz	Orange Park	FL	32073	904-264-3200	269-6958
Pelican Press 5011 Ocean Blvd Suite 206 *Web:* www.pelicanpress.org	Sarasota	FL	34242	941-349-4949	346-7118
News-Sun 2227 US 27 S *Web:* www.newssun.com	Sebring	FL	33870	863-385-6155	385-1954
Seminole Beacon 9911 Seminole Blvd *TF:* 866-224-9233 ■ *Web:* www.tbnweekly.com	Seminole	FL	33772	727-397-5563	397-5900
Kendall News Gazette 6796 SW 62nd Ave *Web:* www.communitynewspapers.com	South Miami	FL	33143	305-669-7355	661-0954
Carrollwood News 5625 W Waters Ave Suite G *Web:* carrollwood.tbo.com	Tampa	FL	33634	813-865-1500	249-5316
Town 'n Country News 5625 W Waters Ave Suite G *Web:* carrollwood.tbo.com	Tampa	FL	33634	813-865-1500	249-5316

Newspaper	City	State	ZIP	Phone	Fax
Daily Sun 1100 Main St *TF:* 800-726-6592 ■ *Web:* www.thevillagesdailysun.com	The Villages	FL	32159	352-753-1119	753-2380
Venice Gondolier Sun 200 E Venice Ave *TF:* 866-357-6204 ■ *Web:* www.venicegondolier.com	Venice	FL	34285	941-207-1000	485-3036
Town-Crier 12794 W Forest Hill Blvd Suite 31 *Web:* www.thecrier.com	Wellington	FL	33414	561-793-7606	793-6090

GEORGIA

Newspaper	City	State	ZIP	Phone	Fax
Revue & News The 319 N Main St *Web:* www.northfulton.com	Alpharetta	GA	30004	770-442-3278	475-1216
DeKalb Neighbor 3060 Mercer University Dr Suite 210 *Web:* www.neighbornewspapers.com	Atlanta	GA	30341	770-454-9388	454-9131
Northside Neighbor & Sandy Springs Neighbor 5290 Roswell Rd NW Suite M *Web:* www.neighbornewspapers.com	Atlanta	GA	30342	404-256-3100	256-3292
Metropolitan Spirit 700 Broad St *Web:* www.metspirit.com	Augusta	GA	30901	706-738-1142	733-6663
Paulding Neighbor 31 Courthouse Sq *Web:* www.neighbornewspapers.com	Dallas	GA	30132	770-445-9401	445-0565
Douglas Neighbor 8434 Price Ave *Web:* www.neighbornewspapers.com	Douglasville	GA	30134	770-942-1611	942-4348
Crier Newspapers LLC 5064 Nandina Ln Suite C *Web:* www.thecrier.net	Dunwoody	GA	30338	770-451-4147	451-4223
Columbia News Times 4272 Washington Rd Suite 3B *TF:* 888-464-9988 ■ *Web:* www.newstimes.augusta.com	Evans	GA	30809	706-863-6165	868-9824
Fayette Neighbor 635 N Glynn St Suite 1 *Web:* www.neighbornewspapers.com	Fayetteville	GA	30214	770-461-1136	461-1385
Clayton Neighbor 5300 Frontage Rd Suite B *Web:* www.neighbornewspapers.com	Forest Park	GA	30297	404-363-8484	363-0212
Henry Neighbor 5300 Frontage Rd Suite B *Web:* www.neighbornewspapers.com	Forest Park	GA	30297	404-363-8484	363-0212
South Fulton Neighbor 5300 Frontage Rd Suite B *Web:* www.neighbornewspapers.com	Forest Park	GA	30297	404-363-8484	363-0212
East Cobb Neighbor PO Box 449 *Web:* www.mdjonline.com	Marietta	GA	30061	770-428-9411	422-9533
Alpharetta-Roswell Neighbor 10930 Crabapple Rd Suite 9	Roswell	GA	30075	770-993-7400	518-6062
Barrow County News 189 W Athens St # 22 *Web:* www.barrowcountynews.com	Winder	GA	30680	770-867-7557	867-1034

HAWAII

Newspaper	City	State	ZIP	Phone	Fax
Midweek 45-525 Luluku Rd *Web:* www.midweek.com	Kaneohe	HI	96744	808-235-5881	247-7246

ILLINOIS

Newspaper	City	State	ZIP	Phone	Fax
Times Record 219 S College Ave *TF:* 800-582-4373 ■ *Web:* www.aledotimesrecord.com	Aledo	IL	61231	309-582-5112	582-5319
Herald/Country Market 500 Brown Blvd *Web:* www.bbherald.com	Bourbonnais	IL	60914	815-933-1131	933-3785
Bridgeport News 3252 S Halstead St *Web:* www.bridgeportnews.net	Chicago	IL	60608	312-842-5883	842-5097
Chicago's Northwest Side Press 4937 N Milwaukee Ave	Chicago	IL	60630	773-286-6100	286-8151
Inside Publications 4159 Northwestern Ave 2nd Fl *Web:* www.insideonline.com	Chicago	IL	60618	773-313-2000	313-2006
Granite City Journal 2 Executive Dr *TF:* 800-766-3278	Collinsville	IL	62234	618-877-7700	344-3831
Des Plaines Journal 622 Graceland Ave *Web:* www.journal-topics.com	Des Plaines	IL	60016	847-299-5511	298-8549
MySuburbanLife.com 1101 W 31st St Suite 100 *Web:* www.mysuburbanlife.com	Downers Grove	IL	60515	630-368-1100	368-1199
Galena Gazette 716 S Bench St *TF:* 800-373-6397 ■ *Web:* www.galenagazette.com	Galena	IL	61036	815-777-0019	777-3809
Lombardian 116 S Main St	Lombard	IL	60148	630-627-7010	627-7027
Rockford Journal 11512 N 2nd St	Machesney Park	IL	61115	815-877-4044	654-4857
Naperville Sun 1500 W Ogden Ave *Web:* www.suburbanchicagonews.com/sunpub/naper	Naperville	IL	60540	630-355-0063	416-5163
Suburban Life Citizen 709 Enterprise Dr	Oak Brook	IL	60523	630-368-1100	368-1199*
Regional News 12243 S Harlem Ave *Web:* www.theregionalnews.com	Palos Heights	IL	60463	708-448-4000	448-4012
Chicago Heights Star 6901 W 159th St *Web:* www.starnewspapers.com/index/s-ch-nws.html	Tinley Park	IL	60477	708-802-8800	802-8088
Chicago Ridge/Worth Star 6901 W 159th St *Web:* www.starnewspapers.com/index/s-wornws.html	Tinley Park	IL	60477	708-802-8800	802-8088
Homer Township Star 6901 W 159th St *Web:* www.starnewspapers.com/index/s-ho-nws.html	Tinley Park	IL	60477	708-802-8800	802-8088
Washington Courier 100 Ford Ln *Web:* www.courierpapers.com	Washington	IL	61571	309-444-3139	444-8505

INDIANA

Newspaper	City	State	ZIP	Phone	Fax
Hendricks County Flyer 8109 Kingston St Suite 500 *TF:* 800-359-3747 ■ *Web:* www.flyergroup.com	Avon	IN	46123	317-272-5800	272-5887
Topics 13095 Publishers Dr *Fax: News Rm ■ *Web:* www.topics.com	Fishers	IN	46038	317-444-5500	444-5550*
Westside Community News 608 S Vine St	Indianapolis	IN	46241	317-241-7363	240-6397*
Papers The PO Box 188 *TF:* 800-733-4111	Milford	IN	46542	574-658-4111	658-4701
Banner-Gazette 490 E State Rd 60 PO Box 38 *Web:* www.gbpnews.com	Pekin	IN	47165	812-967-3176	967-3194
Giveaway The 183 E McClain St *Web:* www.gbpnews.com	Scottsburg	IN	47170	812-752-3171	

KENTUCKY

Newspaper	City	State	ZIP	Phone	Fax
West Kentucky News PO Box 1135 *Web:* www.ky-news.com	Paducah	KY	42002	270-442-7380	442-5220

LOUISIANA

Newspaper	City	State	ZIP	Phone	Fax
Bossier Press Tribune 4250 Viking Dr *Web:* www.bossierpress.com	Bossier City	LA	71111	318-747-7900	747-5298
Times of Acadiana 1100 Bertrand Dr *TF:* 877-289-2216 ■ *Web:* www.theadvertiser.com	Lafayette	LA	70506	337-289-6300	289-6443
Avoyelles Journal 105 N Main St	Marksville	LA	71351	318-253-5413	253-7223
Ouachita Citizen 1400 N 7th St *Web:* www.ouachitacitizen.com	West Monroe	LA	71291	318-322-3161	325-2285

MAINE

Newspaper	City	State	ZIP	Phone	Fax
Bar Harbor Times PO Box 68 *Web:* www.mdi.villagesoup.com	Bar Harbor	ME	04609	207-288-3311	288-5813
Coastal Journal 832 Washington St # 3 *TF:* 800-649-6241 ■ *Web:* www.coastaljournal.com	Bath	ME	04530	207-443-6241	443-5605
Biddeford-Saco-OOB Courier 180 Main St *TF:* 800-617-3984 ■ *Web:* www.biddefordsacooobcourier.com	Biddeford	ME	04005	207-282-4337	282-4339
Forecaster The 5 Fundy Rd *Web:* www.theforecaster.net	Falmouth	ME	04105	207-781-3661	781-2060

MARYLAND

Newspaper	City	State	ZIP	Phone	Fax
Baltimore Times 2513 N Charles St *Web:* www.btimes.com	Baltimore	MD	21218	410-366-3900	243-1627
Aegis The 10 N Hays St *TF:* 888-879-1710 ■ *Web:* www.theaegis.com	Bel Air	MD	21014	410-838-4400	838-7867
Columbia Flier 10750 Little Patuxent Pkwy	Columbia	MD	21044	410-730-3620	997-0885
Howard County Times 10750 Little Patuxent Pkwy	Columbia	MD	21044	410-730-3990	997-4564
Dundalk Eagle PO Box 8936 *Web:* www.dundalkeagle.com	Dundalk	MD	21222	410-288-6060	288-6963
Gaithersburg Gazette 9030 Comprint Ct *Fax: Edit ■ *Web:* www.gazette.net/gaithersburg/news	Gaithersburg	MD	20877	301-670-2565	670-7183*
Maryland Gazette 306 Crain Hwy SW *Web:* www.hometownglenburnie.com	Glen Burnie	MD	21061	410-766-3700	766-7031
Maryland Beachcomber 12417 Ocean Gateway Suite A-7 *Web:* www.delmarvanow.com	Ocean City	MD	21842	410-213-9442	213-9458
Northeast Times Reporter 409 Washington Ave *TF:* 877-696-0660	Towson	MD	21204	410-337-2400	337-2490

MASSACHUSETTS

Newspaper	City	State	ZIP	Phone	Fax
Sunday Republican 1860 Main St *Web:* www.masslive.com	Springfield	MA	01101	413-788-1000	788-1301

MICHIGAN

Newspaper	City	State	ZIP	Phone	Fax
Camden Publications 331 E Bell St *TF:* 800-222-6336 ■ *Web:* www.farmersadvance.com	Camden	MI	49232	517-368-0365	368-5131
Cedar Springs Post 36 W Maple *Web:* www.cedarspringspost.com	Cedar Springs	MI	49319	616-696-3655	696-9010
Dearborn Times-Herald 13730 Michigan Ave	Dearborn	MI	48126	313-584-4000	584-1357
Grosse Pointe News 96 Kercheval Ave *Web:* www.grossepointenews.com	Grosse Pointe Farms	MI	48236	313-882-6900	882-1585
Ada/Cascade/Forest Hills Advance PO Box 9 *Web:* www.advancenewspapers.com	Jenison	MI	49429	616-669-2700	669-4848
Advance Newspaper PO Box 9 *Web:* www.advancenewspapers.com	Jenison	MI	49429	616-669-2700	669-4848
Grand Valley Advance PO Box 9 *Web:* www.advancenewspapers.com	Jenison	MI	49428	616-669-2700	669-4848
Northfield Advance PO Box 9	Jenison	MI	49429	616-669-2700	669-4848
Walker/Westside Advance PO Box 9 *Web:* www.advancenewspapers.com	Jenison	MI	49429	616-669-2700	669-4848
Wyoming Advance PO Box 9 *Web:* www.advancenewspapers.com	Jenison	MI	49429	616-669-2700	669-4848
County Press PO Box 220 *Web:* www.countypress.com	Lapeer	MI	48446	810-664-0811	664-5852
Observer & Eccentric The 36251 Schoolcraft Rd *Web:* www.observer-eccentric.com	Livonia	MI	48150	734-591-2300	591-7279
Manistee News Advocate PO Box 317	Manistee	MI	49660	231-723-3592	723-4733
Bay Voice PO Box 760 *Web:* www.voicenews.com	New Baltimore	MI	48047	586-716-8100	716-8918
Independent Advisor 1907 W M-21 *TF:* 877-723-1119	Owosso	MI	48867	989-723-1118	725-1834
News-Herald 1 Heritage Pl Suite 100 *Web:* www.thenewsherald.com	Southgate	MI	48195	734-246-0800	246-2727

				Phone	Fax
Spinal Column Newsweekly PO Box 14	Union Lake	MI	48387	248-360-6397	360-1220
Web: www.spinalcolumnonline.com					
Clinton-Fraser-Mount Clemens-Macomb-Harrison Advisor 48075 Van Dyke Ave.	Utica	MI	48317	586-731-1000	731-8172
Web: www.sourcenewspapers.com					
Sterling Heights/Utica/Shelby Source Newspaper 48075 Van Dyke Ave.	Utica	MI	48317	586-731-1000	731-8172
Web: www.sourcenewspapers.com					

MINNESOTA

				Phone	Fax
Morrison County Record 216 SE 1st St.	Little Falls	MN	56345	320-632-2345	632-2348
TF: 888-637-2345 ■ *Web:* www.mcrecord.com					
Downtown Journal 1115 Hennepin Ave S.	Minneapolis	MN	55403	612-825-9205	825-0929
Web: www.skywaynews.net					
Roseville Review 2515 E 7th Ave	North Saint Paul	MN	55109	651-777-8800	777-8288
Web: www.rosevillereview.com					
Shoreview/Arden Hills Bulletin 2515 E Seventh Ave	North Saint Paul	MN	55109	651-777-8800	777-8288
Web: bulletin-news.com					
South-West Review 2515 E 7th Ave	North Saint Paul	MN	55109	651-777-8800	777-8288
Web: www.southwestreviewnews.com					
Plainview News 409 W Broadway	Plainview	MN	55964	507-534-3121	534-3920
Proctor Journal 215 5th St	Proctor	MN	55810	218-624-3344	624-7037
Web: www.proctorjournal.com					
Brooklyn Park Brooklyn Center Sun Post 4080 W Broadway Ave Suite 113	Robbinsdale	MN	55422	763-536-7500	536-7519
Northern Watch PO Box 100	Thief River Falls	MN	56701	218-681-4450	681-4455
Web: www.nwatch.com					

MISSISSIPPI

				Phone	Fax
Times The 4 Willow Pointe PO Box 15	Hattiesburg	MS	39402	601-268-2331	268-2965*
**Fax:* News Rm ■ *Web:* www.thetimeswire.com					

MISSOURI

				Phone	Fax
Bethany Republican-Clipper 202 N 16 St PO Box 351	Bethany	MO	64424	660-425-6325	425-3441
Web: www.bethanyclipper.com					
Chesterfield Journal 14522 S Outer 40 Dr.	Chesterfield	MO	63017	314-821-1110	821-0843
News Democrat Journal 14522 S Outer 40 Rd	Chesterfield	MO	63017	636-296-1800	657-3342*
**Fax Area Code:* 314 ■ *Web:* www.stltoday.com					
Press Journal 14522 S Outer 40 Dr.	Chesterfield	MO	63017	314-821-1110	657-3342
TF: 866-440-4500 ■ *Web:* www.stltoday.com					
Webster-Kirkwood Journal 14522 S Outer 40 Dr.	Chesterfield	MO	63017	314-821-1110	821-0843
Farmington Press 218 N Washington St PO Box 70	Farmington	MO	63640	573-756-8927	756-9160
Web: www.mydjconnection.com					
Jefferson County Journal 1405 N Truman Blvd	Festus	MO	63028	636-937-9811	931-2638
Liberty Tribune 104 N Main St	Liberty	MO	64068	816-781-4941	781-0909
Web: www.libertytribune.com					
Big Nickel Advertiser 127 W Main St	Malden	MO	63863	573-276-5148	276-3687
Saint Louis American 4242 Lindell Blvd	Saint Louis	MO	63108	314-533-8000	533-0038
Web: www.stlamerican.com					
Washington Missourian 14 W Main St PO Box 336	Washington	MO	63090	636-239-7701	239-0915
TF: 888-239-7701 ■ *Web:* www.emissourian.com					

MONTANA

				Phone	Fax
Billings Times 2919 Montana Ave.	Billings	MT	59101	406-245-4994	245-5115

NEBRASKA

				Phone	Fax
Bellevue Leader 604 Fort Crook Rd N	Bellevue	NE	68005	402-733-7300	733-9116
Web: www.bellevueleader.com					
West Nebraska Register PO Box 608	Grand Island	NE	68802	308-382-4660	382-6569
Web: www.gidiocese.org					

NEVADA

				Phone	Fax
Ely Times 297 11th St E PO Box 150820	Ely	NV	89315	775-289-4491	289-4566
Web: www.elynews.com					

NEW HAMPSHIRE

				Phone	Fax
Messenger The PO Box 1190	Hillsboro	NH	03244	603-464-3388	464-4106
TF: 800-281-2859 ■ *Web:* www.themessengernh.com					
Broadcaster The 255 Main St.	Nashua	NH	03063	603-886-6075	886-8180
Web: www.nhbroadcaster.com					

NEW JERSEY

				Phone	Fax
Suburban News/Elizabeth City News 301 Central Ave	Clark	NJ	07066	732-396-4404	396-4770*
**Fax:* Edit ■ *TF:* 800-472-0102					
Suburbanite 210 Knickerbocker Rd 2nd Fl.	Cresskill	NJ	07626	201-894-6700	568-4360
Twin-Boro News 210 Knickerbocker Rd.	Cresskill	NJ	07626	201-894-6715	568-6209
Bergen Newspaper Group LLC 115 River Rd Pier 112	Edgewater	NJ	07020	855-855-6225	947-5055*
**Fax Area Code:* 201 ■ *Web:* www.bergennews.com					
Current The 3120 Fire Rd.	Egg Harbor Township	NJ	08234	609-383-8994	383-9072
Hunterdon County Democrat 8 Minneakoning Rd	Flemington	NJ	08822	908-782-4747	782-6572
Web: www.hcdemocrat.com					
Hunterdon Observer 18 Minneakoning Rd	Flemington	NJ	08822	908-782-4747	
Sentinel The PO Box 5001	Freehold	NJ	07728	732-358-5200	780-4192
Web: www.gmnews.com					
Hoboken Reporter 1400 Washington St	Hoboken	NJ	07030	201-798-7800	798-0018
Web: www.zwire.com/site/news.cfm?brd=1292					
Hudson Reporter 1400 Washington St	Hoboken	NJ	07030	201-798-7800	798-0018
Web: www.hudsonreporter.com					
Suburban Trends 300 Kakeout Rd	Kinnelon	NJ	07405	973-283-5600	283-5623
Central Record PO Box 1027	Medford	NJ	08055	609-654-5000	654-8237
Web: www.zwire.com/site/news.cfm?brd=2244					
Reminder Newspaper 2 W Vine St.	Millville	NJ	08332	856-825-8811	825-0011
Web: www.nreminder.com					
Independent Press 80 South St	New Providence	NJ	07974	908-464-4018	464-9085
Web: www.nj.com/independentpress					
Town Topics 305 Witherspoon St.	Princeton	NJ	08542	609-924-2200	924-8818
Web: www.towntopics.com					
Two River Times 46 Newman Springs Rd E Suite C	Red Bank	NJ	07701	732-219-5788	747-7213
Web: www.tworivertimes.net					
Cape May County Herald 1508 Rt 47	Rio Grande	NJ	08242	609-886-8600	886-1879
Web: www.capemaycountyherald.com					
Cape May County Gazette Leader 2087 S Shore Rd	Seaville	NJ	08230	609-624-8900	624-3470
Community Life 372 Kinderkamack Rd	Westwood	NJ	07675	201-664-2501	664-1332

NEW MEXICO

				Phone	Fax
Las Cruces Bulletin 840 N Telshor Blvd # E	Las Cruces	NM	88011	575-524-8061	526-4621
Web: www.lascrucesbulletin.com					

NEW YORK

				Phone	Fax
Queens Courier 38-15 Bell Blvd	Bayside	NY	11361	718-224-5863	224-5441
Web: www.queenscourier.com					
Brooklyn Heights Press & Cobble Hill News 30 Henry St.	Brooklyn	NY	11201	718-858-2300	858-3291
Web: www.brooklyneagle.com					
Queens Tribune 174-15 Horace Harding Expy	Fresh Meadows	NY	11365	718-357-7400	357-9417
Web: www.queenstribune.com					
Chronicle The 15 Ridge St.	Glens Falls	NY	12801	518-792-1126	793-1587
Web: www.readthechronicle.com					
Forum South 102-05 159th Ave	Howard Beach	NY	11414	718-845-3221	738-7645
New York Observer 915 Broadway 9th Fl	New York	NY	10010	212-755-2400	688-4889*
**Fax:* Edit ■ *Web:* www.observer.com					
People's Weekly World 235 W 23rd St	New York	NY	10011	212-924-2523	229-1713
Web: pww.org					
Villager The 145 6th Ave 1st Fl	New York	NY	10013	212-229-1890	229-2790
Web: www.thevillager.com					
Our Town 36 Ridge St	Pearl River	NY	10965	845-735-1342	620-9533
Times Newsweekly PO Box 860299	Ridgewood	NY	11386	718-821-7500	456-0120
Web: www.timesnewsweekly.com					
Suburban News 1776 Hilton Palmar Corners Rd	Spencerport	NY	14559	585-352-3411	352-4811
Web: www.westsidenewsonline.com					
Southern Duchess News 84 E Main St	Wappingers Falls	NY	12590	845-297-3723	297-6810

NORTH CAROLINA

				Phone	Fax
Mountain Times PO Box 1815	Boone	NC	28607	828-264-6397	262-0282
Web: www.mountaintimes.com					
Chapel Hill News 505 W Franklin St.	Chapel Hill	NC	27516	919-932-2000	968-4953
TF: 800-365-6115 ■ *Web:* www.chapelhillnews.com					
Journal-Patriot PO Box 70	North Wilkesboro	NC	28659	336-838-4117	838-9864
Pilot The PO Box 58	Southern Pines	NC	28388	910-692-7271	692-9382
Web: www.thepilot.com					

NORTH DAKOTA

				Phone	Fax
West Fargo Pioneer PO Box 457	West Fargo	ND	58078	701-282-2443	282-9248
Web: www.westfargopioneer.com					
Plains Reporter PO Box 1447	Williston	ND	58802	701-572-2165	572-9563
TF: 800-950-2165 ■ *Web:* www.willistonherald.com					

OHIO

				Phone	Fax
News Sun 32 Pk St	Berea	OH	44017	216-986-7550	986-7551
TF: 800-362-8008 ■ *Web:* www.sunnews.com					
Parma Sun Post 32 Pk St	Berea	OH	44017	216-986-7550	986-7551
Web: www.sunnews.com					
Boardman Town Crier 100 DeBartolo Pl Suite 210	Boardman	OH	44512	330-629-6200	629-6210
Web: www.towncrieronline.com					

Name / Address	City	State	Zip	Phone	Fax
Cincinnati Downtowner 600 Vine St Suite 106	Cincinnati	OH	45202	513-241-9906	241-7235
Hilltop News Press 5556 Cheviot Rd *Web:* news.communitypress.com	Cincinnati	OH	45247	513-923-3111	923-1806
Northwest Press 5556 Cheviot Rd *Web:* www.communitypress.com	Cincinnati	OH	45247	513-923-3111	923-1806
Western Hills Press 5556 Cheviot Rd *Web:* www.communitypress.com	Cincinnati	OH	45247	513-923-3111	923-1806
Sun Messenger 5510 Cloverleaf Pkwy *Web:* www.cleveland.com/sunmessenger	Cleveland	OH	44125	216-986-2600	
Sun Press 5510 Cloverleaf Pkwy *Web:* www.cleveland.com/sunpress	Cleveland	OH	44125	216-986-2600	
Rural-Urban Record PO Box 966 *Web:* www.rural-urbanrecord.com	Columbia Station	OH	44028	440-236-8982	236-9198
Dublin News 5257 Sinclair Rd PO Box 29912 **Fax:* Edit ■ *Web:* www.snponline.com	Columbus	OH	43229	614-785-1212	842-4760*
Eastside Messenger 3500 Sullivant Ave *Web:* www.columbusmessenger.com	Columbus	OH	43204	614-272-5422	272-0684
Northland News 5257 Sinclair Rd PO Box 29912 *Web:* www.snponline.com	Columbus	OH	43229	614-785-1212	842-4760
Southeast Messenger 3500 Sullivant Ave *Web:* www.columbusmessenger.com	Columbus	OH	43204	614-272-5422	272-0684
Southwest Messenger 3500 Sullivant Ave *Web:* www.columbusmessenger.com	Columbus	OH	43204	614-272-5422	272-0684
Upper Arlington News 5257 Sinclair Rd PO Box 29912 **Fax:* Edit ■ *Web:* www.snponline.com	Columbus	OH	43229	614-785-1212	842-4760*
Westerville News 5257 Sinclair Rd PO Box 29912 *Web:* www.snponline.com	Columbus	OH	43229	614-785-1212	842-4760
Westland News 5257 Sinclair Rd PO Box 29912 *Web:* www.snponline.com	Columbus	OH	43229	614-785-1212	842-4760
Westside Messenger 3500 Sullivant Ave *Web:* www.columbusmessenger.com	Columbus	OH	43204	614-272-5422	272-0684
Enon Messenger PO Box 335 *Web:* www.tcnewsnet.com	Enon	OH	45323	937-864-1136	845-3577
Early Bird The 5312 Sebring Warner Rd *TF:* 800-548-5312 ■ *Web:* www.earlybirdpaper.com	Greenville	OH	45331	937-548-3330	548-3376
Centerville-Bellbrook Times 3085 Woodman Dr Suite 170 *Web:* www.tcnewsnet.com	Kettering	OH	45420	937-294-7000	294-2981
Sunday Western Star 200 Harmon Ave *Web:* www.western-star.com	Lebanon	OH	45036	513-932-3010	932-6056
Delaware This Week 7801 N Central Dr *Web:* www.thisweeknews.com	Lewis Center	OH	43035	740-888-6100	888-6006
Dublin Villager 7801 N Central Dr. *Web:* www.thisweeknews.com	Lewis Center	OH	43035	740-888-6100	888-6006
Hilliard This Week 7801 N Central Dr *Web:* www.thisweeknews.com	Lewis Center	OH	43035	740-888-6100	888-6006
Reynoldsburg This Week 7801 N Central Dr. *Web:* www.thisweeknews.com	Lewis Center	OH	43035	740-888-6100	888-6006
Southside This Week 7801 N Central Dr *Web:* www.thisweeknews.com	Lewis Center	OH	43035	740-888-6100	888-6006
This Week in Upper Arlington 7801 N Central Dr. *Web:* www.thisweeknews.com	Lewis Center	OH	43035	740-888-6100	888-6006
Westerville This Week 7801 N Central Dr. *Web:* www.thisweeknews.com	Lewis Center	OH	43035	740-888-6100	888-6006
Worthington This Week 7801 N Central Dr. *Web:* www.thisweeknews.com	Lewis Center	OH	43035	740-888-6100	888-6006
Fairfield Echo 7320 Yankee Rd *Web:* www.fairfield-echo.com	Liberty Township	OH	45044	513-755-5060	483-5252
Pulse-Journal 7320 Yankee Rd *Web:* www.pulsejournal.com	Liberty Township	OH	45044	513-755-5060	483-5252
Forest Hills Journal 394 Wards Corner Rd Suite 170 *Web:* news.communitypress.com	Loveland	OH	45140	513-248-8600	248-1938
Loveland Herald 394 Wards Corner Rd Suite 170 *Web:* news.communitypress.com	Loveland	OH	45140	513-248-8600	248-1938
Suburban Press & Metro Press 1550 Woodville Rd *TF:* 800-300-6158 ■ *Web:* www.presspublications.com	Millbury	OH	43447	419-836-2221	836-1319
Sun Post-Herald 28895 Lorain Rd. *TF:* 800-466-7861 ■ *Web:* www.sunnews.com	North Olmsted	OH	44070	216-986-6070	986-6071
West Side Sun News 28895 Lorain Rd. *TF:* 800-466-7861 ■ *Web:* www.sunnews.com	North Olmsted	OH	44070	216-986-6070	986-6071
Beacon The 205 SE Catawba Rd Suite G *Web:* www.thebeacon.net	Port Clinton	OH	43452	419-732-2154	734-5382
Cuyahoga Falls News-Press PO Box 1549 *TF:* 800-966-6565 ■ *Web:* www.recordpub.com	Stow	OH	44224	330-688-0088	688-1588
Gateway News 1619 Commerce Dr. *TF:* 800-560-9657 ■ *Web:* www.recordpub.com	Stow	OH	44224	330-688-0088	688-1588
Budget The PO Box 249 *Web:* www.budgetnewspaper.com	Sugarcreek	OH	44681	330-852-4634	852-4421
West Life PO Box 45014 *Web:* www.westlifenews.com	Westlake	OH	44145	440-871-5797	871-3824
Star-Republican 47 S S St	Wilmington	OH	45177	937-382-7796	382-4392

OKLAHOMA

Name / Address	City	State	Zip	Phone	Fax
El Reno Tribune 201 N Rock Island Ave *Web:* www.elrenotribune.com	El Reno	OK	73036	405-262-5180	262-3541
Holdenville News PO Box 751	Holdenville	OK	74848	405-379-5411	379-5413

OREGON

Name / Address	City	State	Zip	Phone	Fax
Hillsboro Argus 150 SE 3rd Ave *Web:* www.hillsboroargus.com	Hillsboro	OR	97123	503-648-1131	648-9191
Woodburn Independent 650 N 1st St *Web:* www.woodburnindependent.com	Woodburn	OR	97071	503-981-3441	981-1253

PENNSYLVANIA

Name / Address	City	State	Zip	Phone	Fax
Lancaster Farming PO Box 609 *Web:* www.lancasterfarming.com	Ephrata	PA	17522	717-626-1164	733-6058
Progress of Montgomery County 390 Easton Rd	Horsham	PA	19044	215-675-8250	675-8251
Almanac The 395 Valley Brook Rd Suite 2 **Fax:* Edit ■ *Web:* www.thealmanac.net	McMurray	PA	15317	724-941-7725	941-8685*
Leader The 2385 W Cheltenham Ave Suite 182 *Web:* www.zwire.com/site/news.cfm?brd=1682	Philadelphia	PA	19150	215-885-4111	885-0226
Review The 6220 Ridge Ave. *Web:* www.zwire.com/site/news.cfm?brd=1680	Philadelphia	PA	19128	215-483-7300	483-2073
Northeast Times 2512 Metropolitan Dr. *Web:* www.northeasttimes.com	Trevose	PA	19053	215-355-9009	355-4812
Suburban Advertiser PO Box 409 *Web:* www.suburbanadvertiser.com	Wayne	PA	19087	610-688-3000	964-1346
Main Line Life 311 E Lancaster Ave *Web:* www.mainlinelife.com	Wynnewood	PA	19096	610-896-9555	896-9560
York Sunday News 1891 Loucks Rd PO Box 15122 *TF:* 800-483-5517 ■ *Web:* www.ydr.com	York	PA	17408	717-767-6397	771-2009

RHODE ISLAND

Name / Address	City	State	Zip	Phone	Fax
Newport Mercury 101 Malbone Rd. *Web:* www.newportmercury.com	Newport	RI	02840	401-380-2371	
Newport This Week 86 Broadway *Web:* www.newportchamber.com	Newport	RI	02840	401-847-7766	846-4974

SOUTH CAROLINA

Name / Address	City	State	Zip	Phone	Fax
Bluffton Today 52 Persimmon St *Web:* www.blufftontoday.com	Bluffton	SC	29910	843-815-0800	815-0898
Chronicle Independent 909 W Dekalb St *TF:* 800-698-3514 ■ *Web:* www.chronicle-independent.com	Camden	SC	29020	803-432-6157	432-7609
Georgetown Times 615 Front St.	Georgetown	SC	29440	843-546-4148	546-2395
Myrtle Beach Herald 4761 Hwy 501 # 4 *Web:* www.myrtlebeachherald.com	Myrtle Beach	SC	29579	843-626-3131	448-4860
Star The 106 E Buena Vista Ave *Web:* www.northaugustastar.com	North Augusta	SC	29841	803-279-2793	278-4070
Moultrie News PO Box 279 *Web:* www.islandpapers.com	Sullivans Island	SC	29482	843-849-1778	849-0214

SOUTH DAKOTA

Name / Address	City	State	Zip	Phone	Fax
Meade County Times-Tribune PO Box 69 *Web:* www.bhcn.com	Sturgis	SD	57785	605-347-2503	347-2321

TENNESSEE

Name / Address	City	State	Zip	Phone	Fax
Dickson Herald PO Box 587 *Web:* www.dicksonherald.com	Dickson	TN	37056	615-446-2811	446-5560
Farragutpress 11863 Kingston Pike *Web:* www.farragutpress.com	Knoxville	TN	37934	865-675-6397	675-1675
Monroe County Advocate & Democrat PO Box 389 *Web:* www.monroe.xtn.net	Sweetwater	TN	37874	423-337-7101	337-5932

TEXAS

Name / Address	City	State	Zip	Phone	Fax
Preston Hollow People 4311 Oaklawn Ave Suite 350 *Web:* www.peoplenewspapers.com	Dallas	TX	75219	214-739-2244	363-6948
Edinburg Review 215 E University Dr	Edinburg	TX	78540	956-383-2705	383-3172
Houston Forward Times PO Box 8346 *Web:* www.forwardtimes.com	Houston	TX	77288	713-526-4727	526-3170
Leader The PO Box 924487	Houston	TX	77292	713-686-8494	686-0970
Pearland Journal 650 FM 1959 *Web:* www.yourhoustonnews.com/pearland	Houston	TX	77034	281-674-1340	922-4499
Humble Observer 907 E Main St Suite B. *Web:* www.thehumbleobserver.com	Humble	TX	77338	281-446-4438	964-4423
Hardin County News PO Box 8240 *Web:* www.thehardincountynews.com	Lumberton	TX	77657	409-755-4912	755-7731
Valley Town Crier 1811 N 23rd St *TF:* 800-285-5667 ■ *Web:* www.valleytowncrier.com	McAllen	TX	78501	956-682-2423	630-6371
North San Antonio Times 17400 Judson Rd *Web:* www.clickitsa.com	San Antonio	TX	78247	210-453-3300	828-3787

UTAH

Name / Address	City	State	Zip	Phone	Fax
Millard County Chronicle Progress 40 N 300 W **Fax Area Code:* 775	Delta	UT	84624	435-864-2400	514-2931*

VERMONT

Name / Address	City	State	Zip	Phone	Fax
World The 403 US Rt 302-Berlin *TF:* 800-639-9753 ■ *Web:* www.vt-world.com	Barre	VT	05641	802-479-2582	479-7916

VIRGINIA

	City	State	Zip	Phone	Fax
Loudon Times Mirror 9 E Market St PO Box 359 *Web:* www.timespapers.com	Leesburg	VA	20178	703-777-1111	771-0036
Loudoun Times-Mirror PO Box 359 *Web:* www.timescommunity.com	Leesburg	VA	20178	703-777-1111	771-0036
Alexandria Gazette Packet 7913 W Pk Dr *Web:* www.connectionnewspapers.com	McLean	VA	22102	703-821-5050	917-0991
Arlington Connection 7913 W Pk Dr *Web:* www.connectionnewspapers.com	McLean	VA	22102	703-917-5050	917-0991
Delaware Beachcomber 7950 Jones Branch Dr *Web:* www.delmarvanow.com/debeachcomber	McLean	VA	22107	302-227-9466	227-9469
Delaware Coast Press 7950 Jones Branch Dr *Web:* www.delmarvanow.com/deweybeach	McLean	VA	22107	302-227-9466	227-9469
Mechanicsville Local 6400 Mechanicsville Tpke *TF:* 800-476-0197 ■ *Web:* www.mechlocal.com	Mechanicsville	VA	23111	804-746-1235	730-0476
Fairfax County Times 1760 Reston Pkwy Suite 411 *Web:* www.timescommunity.com	Reston	VA	20190	703-437-5400	437-6019
Fauquier Times-Democrat 39 Culpeper St *Web:* www.fauquier.com	Warrenton	VA	20186	540-347-4222	349-8676
Virginia Gazette 216 Ironbound Rd *TF:* 800-944-6908 ■ *Web:* www.vagazette.com	Williamsburg	VA	23188	757-220-1736	220-1665

WASHINGTON

	City	State	Zip	Phone	Fax
Reflector The PO Box 2020 *Web:* www.thereflector.com	Battle Ground	WA	98604	360-687-5151	687-5162
Bothell/Kenmore Reporter 18322 Bothell Way NE *Web:* reporternewspapers.com	Bothell	WA	98011	425-483-3732	453-4215
Dispatch The 133 Mashell Ave N. *Web:* www.dispatchnews.com	Eatonville	WA	98328	360-832-4411	832-4972
Journal of the San Juan Islands PO Box 519 *Web:* www.sanjuanjournal.com	Friday Harbor	WA	98250	360-378-4191	378-5128
Issaquah Press PO Box 1328 *Web:* www.issaquahpress.com	Issaquah	WA	98027	425-392-6434	391-1541
Weekly Herald 4303 198th St SW *TF:* 800-944-3630 ■ *Web:* www.enterprisenewspapers.com	Lynnwood	WA	98036	425-673-6500	774-8622
Port Orchard Independent PO Box 27 *Web:* www.portorchardindependent.com	Port Orchard	WA	98366	360-876-4414	876-4458
Puyallup Herald PO Box 517 *Web:* www.puyallup-herald.com	Puyallup	WA	98371	253-841-2481	840-8249
Capitol Hill Times 636 S Alaska St *Web:* www.pacificpublishingcompany.com	Seattle	WA	98108	206-461-1300	461-1285
Mach Pubishing PO Box 499 *Web:* www.snoho.com	Snohomish	WA	98291	360-568-4121	568-1484
Tribune Newspapers of Snohomish County 127 Ave C Suite B PO Box 499 *Web:* www.snoho.com	Snohomish	WA	98291	360-568-4121	568-1484

WEST VIRGINIA

	City	State	Zip	Phone	Fax
Coal Valley News 475 Main St *Web:* www.coalvalleynews.com	Madison	WV	25130	304-369-1165	369-1166

WISCONSIN

	City	State	Zip	Phone	Fax
Burlington Standard Press 700 N Pine St *Web:* www.standardpress.com	Burlington	WI	53105	262-763-3511	763-2238
Country Today 701 S Farwell St *TF:* 800-236-4004 ■ *Web:* www.thecountrytoday.com	Eau Claire	WI	54701	715-833-9270	858-7307
Foto News 807 E 1st St *Web:* www.merrillfotonews.com	Merrill	WI	54452	715-536-7121	539-3686
Milwaukee Courier 6310 N Port Washington Rd # 9 *Web:* www.milwaukeecourier.org	Milwaukee	WI	53217	414-449-4860	449-4872
Wisconsin State Farmer PO Box 152 *TF:* 800-236-3313 ■ *Web:* www.wisfarmer.com	Waupaca	WI	54981	715-258-5546	258-8162

WYOMING

	City	State	Zip	Phone	Fax
Jackson Hole News & Guide 1225 Maple Way *Web:* www.jhnewsandguide.com	Jackson	WY	83001	307-733-2047	733-2138

535-5 Weekly Newspapers - Alternative

	City	State	Zip	Phone	Fax
Ace Weekly 185 Jefferson *Web:* www.aceweekly.com	Lexington	KY	40508	859-225-4889	226-0569
Arkansas Times 201 East Markham Suite 200 *Web:* www.arktimes.com	Little Rock	AR	72201	501-375-2985	375-3623
ArtVoice 810 Main St *Web:* www.artvoice.com	Buffalo	NY	14202	716-881-6604	881-6682
Athens NEWS 14 N Ct St *Web:* www.athensnews.com	Athens	OH	45701	740-594-8219	592-5695
Austin Chronicle PO Box 49066 *Web:* www.austinchronicle.com	Austin	TX	78765	512-454-5766	458-6910
Baltimore City Paper 812 Park Ave *Web:* citypaper.com	Baltimore	MD	21201	410-523-2300	523-2222
Birmingham Weekly 2014 6th Ave N *Web:* www.bhamweekly.com	Birmingham	AL	35203	205-939-4030	212-1005
Black & White 2210 2nd Ave N 2nd Fl *Web:* www.bwcitypaper.com	Birmingham	AL	35203	205-933-0460	933-0467
Boise Weekly 523 Broad St *Web:* www.boiseweekly.com	Boise	ID	83702	208-344-2055	342-4733
Boston Phoenix The 126 Brookline Ave **Fax:* Advertising ■ *Web:* thephoenix.com	Boston	MA	02215	617-536-5390	536-1463*
Bostons Weekly Dig 242 E Berkeley St 5th Fl *Web:* www.weeklydig.com	Boston	MA	02118	617-426-8942	426-8942
Boulder Weekly 690 S Lashley Ln *Web:* www.boulderweekly.com	Boulder	CO	80305	303-494-5511	494-2585
C-Ville Weekly 106 E Main St *Web:* www.c-ville.com	Charlottesville	VA	22902	434-817-2749	817-2758
Charleston City Paper 1049 Morrison Dr # B *Web:* www.charlestoncitypaper.com	Charleston	SC	29403	843-577-5304	576-0380
Chicago Reader 11 E Illinois St *Web:* www.chicagoreader.com	Chicago	IL	60611	312-828-0350	828-9926
Chico News & Review 353 E 2nd St *TF:* 800-225-3369 ■ *Web:* www.newsreview.com	Chico	CA	95928	530-894-2300	894-0143
Cincinnati CityBeat 811 Race St 5th Fl *Web:* www.citybeat.com	Cincinnati	OH	45202	513-665-4700	665-4368
City Link 6501 Nob Hill Rd *Web:* www.southflorida.metromix.com	Tamarac	FL	33321	954-356-4943	356-4949
City Newspaper 250 N Goodman St *Web:* www.rochestercitynewspaper.com	Rochester	NY	14607	585-244-3329	244-1126
City Pages 300 3rd St *Web:* www.thecitypages.com	Wausau	WI	54403	715-845-5171	848-5887
Cityview 414 61st St *Web:* www.dmcityview.com	Des Moines	IA	50312	515-953-4822	953-1394
Coast The 5435 Portland Pl *Web:* www.thecoast.ca	Halifax	NS	B3K6R7	902-422-6278	425-0013
Colorado Springs Independent 235 S Nevada Ave *Web:* www.csindy.com	Colorado Springs	CO	80903	719-577-4545	577-4107
Columbus Alive 34 S 3rd St *Web:* www.columbusalive.com	Columbus	OH	43215	614-221-2449	461-8746
Creative Loafing Atlanta 384 Northyards Blvd Suite 600 *TF:* 800-950-5623 ■ *Web:* atlanta.creativeloafing.com	Atlanta	GA	30313	404-688-5623	522-1532
Creative Loafing Charlotte 820 Hamilton St Suite B-11 *Web:* www.charlotte.creativeloafing.com	Charlotte	NC	28206	704-333-0144	522-8088
Creative Loafing Tampa 1911 N 13th St Suite W200 *Web:* www.posting.cltampa.com	Tampa	FL	33605	813-739-4800	739-4801
Dallas Observer 2501 Oak Lawn Ave Suite 700 PO Box 190289 *Web:* www.dallasobserver.com	Dallas	TX	75219	214-757-9000	757-8590
Dayton City Paper 126 N Main St # 240 *Web:* www.daytoncitypaper.com	Dayton	OH	45402	937-222-8855	222-6113
East Bay Express 1335 Stanford Ave Suite 100 *Web:* www.eastbayexpress.com	Emeryville	CA	94608	510-879-3700	879-3794
Easy Reader 832 Hermosa Ave **Fax Area Code:* 424 ■ *Web:* www.easyreadernews.com	Hermosa Beach	CA	90254	310-372-4611	212-6782*
Eugene Weekly 1251 Lincoln St *Web:* www.eugeneweekly.com	Eugene	OR	97401	541-484-0519	484-4044
Fairfield County Weekly 350 Fairfield Ave Suite 605 *Web:* www.fairfieldweekly.com	Bridgeport	CT	06604	203-382-9666	382-9657
Flagpole PO Box 1027 *Web:* www.flagpole.com	Athens	GA	30603	706-549-9523	548-8981
Folio Weekly 9456 Philips Hwy Suite 11 *TF:* 800-940-9770 ■ *Web:* www.folioweekly.com	Jacksonville	FL	32256	904-260-9770	260-9773
Fort Worth Weekly 3311 Hamilton Ave *Web:* www.fwweekly.com	Fort Worth	TX	76107	817-321-9700	335-9575
Gambit Weekly 3923 Bienville St *Web:* www.bestofneworleans.com	New Orleans	LA	70119	504-486-5900	483-3116
Georgia Straight 1701 W Broadway *Web:* www.straight.com	Vancouver	BC	V6J1Y3	604-730-7000	730-7010
Hartford Advocate 121 Wawarme Ave 1st Fl' *Web:* www.hartfordadvocate.com	Hartford	CT	06114	860-548-9300	548-9335
Honolulu Weekly 1111 Ford St Mall Suite 214 *Web:* www.honoluluweekly.com	Honolulu	HI	96813	808-528-1475	528-3144
Hour Magazine 355 St Catherine St W 7th Fl *TF:* 877-631-8647 ■ *Web:* www.hour.ca	Montreal	QC	H3B1A5	514-848-0777	848-9004
Houston Press 1621 Milam St Suite 100 *Web:* www.houstonpress.com	Houston	TX	77002	713-280-2400	280-2444
Illinois Times 1320 S State St *Web:* www.illinoistimes.com	Springfield	IL	62704	217-753-2226	753-2281
Independent Weekly PO Box 2690 *TF:* 800-948-8699 ■ *Web:* www.indyweek.com	Durham	NC	27715	919-286-1972	286-4274
Isthmus Publishing Co Inc 101 King St *Web:* www.thedailypage.com	Madison	WI	53703	608-251-5627	251-2165
Ithaca Times 109 N Cayuga St *Web:* www.ithaca.com	Ithaca	NY	14850	607-277-7000	277-1012
Jackson Free Press PO Box 2047 *Web:* www.jacksonfreepress.com	Jackson	MS	39225	601-362-6121	510-9019
LA Weekly 6715 Sunset Blvd *Web:* www.laweekly.com	Los Angeles	CA	90028	323-465-4414	465-3220
Las Vegas Weekly 2290 Corporate Cir Suite 250 *Web:* www.lasvegasweekly.com	Henderson	NV	89074	702-990-2550	990-2424
Long Island Press 575 Underhill Blvd Suite 210 *Web:* www.longislandpress.com	Syosset	NY	11791	516-284-3300	284-3311
Louisville Eccentric Observer 640 S 4th St Suite 100 *Web:* www.leoweekly.com	Louisville	KY	40202	502-895-9770	895-9779

				Phone	Fax
Maui Time Weekly 33 N Market St Suite 201 Web: www.mauitime.com	Wailuku	HI	96793	808-244-0777	244-0446
Memphis Flyer 460 Tennessee St Web: www.memphisflyer.com	Memphis	TN	38103	901-521-9000	521-0129
Metro Pulse 602 S Gay St Mezzanine Ste Web: www.metropulse.com	Knoxville	TN	37902	865-522-5399	522-2955
Metro Santa Cruz 550 S 1st St Web: www.metroactive.com	San Jose	CA	95113	408-200-1300	
Metro Silicon Valley 550 S 1st St Web: www.metroactive.com	San Jose	CA	95113	408-298-8000	298-0602
Metro Times 733 St Antoine St Web: www.metrotimes.com	Detroit	MI	48226	313-961-4060	961-6598
Metroland 419 Madison Ave Web: www.metroland.net	Albany	NY	12210	518-463-2500	463-3712
Miami New Times 2800 Biscayne Blvd Web: www.miaminewtimes.com	Miami	FL	33137	305-576-8000	571-7677
Minneapolis/St. Paul City Pages 401 N 3rd St Suite 550 Web: www.citypages.com	Minneapolis	MN	55401	612-375-1015	372-3737
Missoula Independent 317 S Orange St Web: www.missoulanews.com	Missoula	MT	59801	406-543-6609	543-4367
Monday Magazine 818 Broughton St TF: 800-661-6335 ■ Web: www.mondaymag.com	Victoria	BC	V8W1E4	250-382-6188	381-2662
Monterey County Weekly 668 Williams Ave Web: www.montereycountyweekly.com	Seaside	CA	93955	831-394-5656	394-2909
Montreal Mirror 465 McGill St 3rd Fl Web: www.montrealmirror.com/wp	Montreal	QC	H2Y4B4	514-393-1010	393-3173
Mountain Xpress 2 Wall St # 211 Web: www.mountainx.com	Asheville	NC	28801	828-251-1333	251-1311
Nashville Scene 2120 8th Ave S Web: www.nashscene.com	Nashville	TN	37204	615-244-7989	254-4743
New Haven Advocate 900 Chapel St Suite 1100 Web: www.newhavenadvocate.com	New Haven	CT	06510	203-789-0010	787-1418
New Times Broward Palm Beach 16 NE 4th St Web: www.browardpalmbeach.com	Fort Lauderdale	FL	33301	954-233-1600	233-1521
New York Press 333 7th Ave 14th Fl Web: www.nypress.com	New York	NY	10001	212-244-2282	244-9864
Newcity 770 N Halsted St Suite 303 Web: newcity.com	Chicago	IL	60622	312-243-8786	243-8802
North Bay Bohemian 847 5th St Web: www.bohemian.com	Santa Rosa	CA	95404	707-527-1200	527-1288
NOW Magazine 189 Church St Web: www.nowtoronto.com	Toronto	ON	M5B1Y7	416-364-1300	364-1166
NUVO Newsweekly 3951 N Meridian St Suite 200 Web: www.nuvo.net	Indianapolis	IN	46208	317-254-2400	254-2405
OC Weekly 2975 Red Hill Ave Suite 150 Web: www.ocweekly.com	Costa Mesa	CA	92626	714-550-5900	550-5908
Oklahoma Gazette 3701 N Shartel Ave Web: www.okgazette.com	Oklahoma City	OK	73118	405-528-6000	528-4600
Orlando Weekly 1505 E Colonial Dr St #200 Web: www.orlandoweekly.com	Orlando	FL	32803	407-377-0400	377-0420
Other Paper The PO Box 29913 Web: www.theotherpaper.com	Columbus	OH	43229	614-847-3800	848-3838
Pacific Northwest Inlander 9 S Washington St Web: www.inlander.com	Spokane	WA	99201	509-325-0634	325-0638
Pacific Sun 835 4th St Suite B Web: www.pacificsun.com	San Rafael	CA	94901	415-485-6700	485-6226
Palo Alto Weekly 450 Cambridge Ave Web: www.paloaltoonline.com/weekly	Palo Alto	CA	94306	650-326-8210	326-3928
Pasadena Weekly 50 S Delacey Ave Suite 200 Web: www.pasadenaweekly.com	Pasadena	CA	91105	626-584-1500	795-0149
Philadelphia City Paper 123 Chestnut St 3rd Fl Web: www.citypaper.net	Philadelphia	PA	19106	215-735-8444	
Phoenix New Times 1201 E Jefferson Web: www.phoenixnewtimes.com	Phoenix	AZ	85034	602-271-0040	340-8806
Pitch The 1701 Main St Web: www.pitch.com	Kansas City	MO	64108	816-561-6061	756-0502
Pittsburgh City Paper 650 Smithfield St Suite 2200 Web: www.pittsburghcitypaper.ws	Pittsburgh	PA	15222	412-316-3342	316-3388
Portland Phoenix 16 York St Suite 102 Web: www.portlandphoenix.com	Portland	ME	04101	207-773-8900	773-8905
Providence Phoenix 150 Chestnut St	Providence	RI	02903	401-273-6397	273-0920
PW-Philadelphia Weekly 1500 Sansom St 3rd Fl Web: www.philadelphiaweekly.com	Philadelphia	PA	19102	215-563-7400	563-0620
Random Lengths News 1300 S Pacific Ave Web: www.randomlengthsnews.com	San Pedro	CA	90731	310-519-1442	832-1000
Reader The 5015 Underwood Ave Suite 101 Web: www.thereader.com	Omaha	NE	68132	402-341-7323	341-6967
Reno News & Review 708 N Ctr St Web: www.newsreview.com	Reno	NV	89501	775-324-4440	324-4572
Riverfront Times 6358 Delmar Blvd Suite 200 Web: www.riverfronttimes.com	Saint Louis	MO	63130	314-754-5966	754-5955
Sacramento News & Review 1124 Del Paso Blvd Web: www.newsreview.com	Sacramento	CA	95815	916-498-1234	498-7920
Salt Lake City Weekly 248 S Main St Web: www.slweekly.com	Salt Lake City	UT	84101	801-575-7003	575-6106
San Antonio Current 915 Dallas St Web: sacurrent.com	San Antonio	TX	78215	210-227-0044	227-6611
San Diego CityBeat 3550 Camino Del Rio N Suite 207 Web: www.sdcitybeat.com	San Diego	CA	92108	619-281-7526	281-5273
San Diego Reader PO Box 85803 Web: www.sandiegoreader.com	San Diego	CA	92186	619-235-3000	231-0489
San Francisco Bay Guardian 135 Mississippi St Web: www.sfbg.com	San Francisco	CA	94107	415-255-3100	255-8959
San Luis Obispo New Times 505 Higuera St TF: 800-215-0300 ■ Web: www.newtimesslo.com	San Luis Obispo	CA	93401	805-546-8208	546-8641
Santa Barbara Independent 122 W Figueroa St Web: www.independent.com	Santa Barbara	CA	93101	805-965-5205	965-5518
Santa Fe Reporter 132 E Marcy St Web: www.sfreporter.com/santafe	Santa Fe	NM	87501	505-988-5541	988-5348
Scene 1468 W 9th St Suite 805 Web: www.clevescene.com	Cleveland	OH	44113	216-241-7550	802-7212
Seattle Weekly 1008 Western Ave Suite 300 Web: www.seattleweekly.com	Seattle	WA	98104	206-623-0500	467-4377
Seven Days 255 S Champlain St Suite 5 PO Box 1164 Web: www.7dvt.com	Burlington	VT	05401	802-864-5684	865-1015
SF Weekly 185 Berry St Lobby 4 Suite 3800 Web: www.sfweekly.com	San Francisco	CA	94107	415-536-8100	777-1839
Shepherd Express 207 E Buffalo St Suite 410 Web: www.expressmilwaukee.com	Milwaukee	WI	53202	414-276-2222	276-3312
Stranger The 1535 11th Ave 3rd Fl Web: www.thestranger.com	Seattle	WA	98122	206-323-7101	323-7203
Style Weekly 1707 Summit Ave Suite 201 Web: www.styleweekly.com	Richmond	VA	23230	804-358-0825	358-9089
Syracuse New Times 1415 W Genesee St Web: www.syracusenewtimes.com	Syracuse	NY	13204	315-422-7011	422-1721
Tucson Weekly 3280 E Hemisphere Loop Suite 180 PO Box 27087 Web: www.tucsonweekly.com	Tucson	AZ	85706	520-294-1200	792-2096
Urban Tulsa PO Box 50499 Web: www.urbantulsa.com	Tulsa	OK	74150	918-592-5550	592-5970
Valley Advocate 116 Pleasant St Suite 3350 Web: www.valleyadvocate.com	EastHampton	MA	01027	413-529-2840	529-2844
Ventura County Reporter 700 E Main St Web: www.vcreporter.com	Ventura	CA	93001	805-648-2244	648-7801
Village Voice 36 Cooper Sq TF Cust Svc: 800-875-2997 ■ Web: www.villagevoice.com	New York	NY	10003	212-475-3300	475-8944
Washington City Paper 2390 Champlain St NW Web: www.washingtoncitypaper.com	Washington	DC	20009	202-332-2100	332-8500
Weekly Alibi 2118 Central Ave SE Suite 151 Web: www.alibi.com	Albuquerque	NM	87106	505-346-0660	256-9651
Westword 969 Broadway Web: www.westword.com	Denver	CO	80203	303-296-7744	296-5416
Willamette Week 2220 NW Quimby St Web: www.wweek.com	Portland	OR	97210	503-243-2122	243-1115

536 NURSES ASSOCIATIONS - STATE

SEE ALSO Health & Medical Professionals Associations p. 1452

				Phone	Fax
Alabama State Nurses Assn (ASNA) 360 N Hull St TF: 800-270-2762 ■ Web: www.alabamanurses.org	Montgomery	AL	36104	334-262-8321	262-8578
Alaska Nurses Assn (AaNA) 3701 E Tudor Rd Suite 208 Web: www.aknurse.org	Anchorage	AK	99507	907-274-0827	272-0292
American Nurses Assn California (ANA\C) 1121 L St Suite 409 Web: www.anacalifornia.org	Sacramento	CA	95814	916-447-0225	442-4394
Arizona Nurses Assn (AzNA) 1850 E Southern Ave Suite 1 Web: www.aznurse.org	Tempe	AZ	85282	480-831-0404	839-4780
Arkansas Nurses Assn (ARNA) 1123 S University Suite 1015 Web: www.arna.org	Little Rock	AR	72204	501-244-2363	244-9903
California Nurses Assn (CNA) 2000 Franklin St Web: www.calnurses.org	Oakland	CA	94612	510-273-2200	663-1625
Colorado Nurses Assn (CNA) 1221 S Clarkson St Suite 205 Web: www.nurses-co.org	Denver	CO	80210	303-757-7483	757-8833
Connecticut Nurses Assn (CNA) 377 Research Pkwy Suite 2D Web: www.ctnurses.org	Meriden	CT	06450	203-238-1207	238-3437
Delaware Nurses Assn (DNA) 2644 Capitol Trail Suite 330 TF: 800-381-0939 ■ Web: www.nursingworld.org	Newark	DE	19711	302-368-2333	366-1775
District of Columbia Nurses Assn (DCNA) 5100 Wisconsin Ave NW Suite 306 TF: 800-783-2705 ■ Web: www.dcna.org	Washington	DC	20016	202-244-2705	362-8285
Florida Nurses Assn (FNA) 1325 E Concord St PO Box 536985 Web: www.floridanurse.org	Orlando	FL	32853	407-896-3261	896-9042
Georgia Nurses Assn (GNA) 3032 Briarcliff Rd NE TF: 800-324-0462 ■ Web: www.georgianurses.org	Atlanta	GA	30329	404-325-5536	325-0407
Hawaii Nurses Assn (HNA) 677 Ala Moana Blvd Suite 301 TF: 800-486-8550 ■ Web: www.hawaiinurses.org	Honolulu	HI	96813	808-531-1628	524-2760
Idaho Nurses Assn (INA) 2417 Bank Dr Suite 111 Web: www.nursingworld.org	Boise	ID	83709	208-345-0500	345-1163
Illinois Nurses Assn (INA) 105 W Adams St Suite 2101 Web: www.illinoisnurses.com	Chicago	IL	60603	312-419-2900	419-2920
Indiana State Nurses Assn (ISNA) 2915 N High School Rd Web: www.indiananurses.org	Indianapolis	IN	46224	317-299-4575	297-3525

	City	State	Zip	Phone	Fax
Iowa Nurses Assn (INA) 1501 42nd St Suite 471 *Web:* www.iowanurses.org	West Des Moines	IA	50266	515-225-0495	225-2201
Kansas State Nurses Assn (KSNA) 1109 SW Topeka Blvd *Web:* www.nursingworld.org	Topeka	KS	66612	785-233-8638	233-5222
Kentucky Nurses Assn (KNA) 1400 S 1st St PO Box 2616 *TF:* 800-348-5411 ■ *Web:* www.kentucky-nurses.org	Louisville	KY	40201	502-637-2546	637-8236
Louisiana State Nurses Assn (LSNA) 5800 One Perkins Pl Suite 2B *TF:* 800-457-6378 ■ *Web:* www.lsna.org	Baton Rouge	LA	70808	225-201-0993	201-0971
Maine State Nurses Assn (MSNA) 160 Capitol St Suite 1 *Web:* www.mainenurse.org	Augusta	ME	04330	207-622-1057	623-4072
Maryland Nurses Assn (MNA) 21 Governor's Ct Suite 195 *Web:* www.nursingworld.org	Baltimore	MD	21244	410-944-5800	944-5802
Massachusetts Assn of Registered Nurses (MARN) PO Box 70668 *TF:* 866-627-6262 ■ *Web:* www.marnonline.org	Worcester	MA	01607	508-881-8812	
Massachusetts Nurses Assn (MNA) 340 Tpke St *TF:* 800-882-2056 ■ *Web:* www.massnurses.org	Canton	MA	02021	781-821-4625	821-4445
Michigan Nurses Assn (MNA) 2310 Jolly Oak Rd *TF:* 800-646-8773 ■ *Web:* www.minurses.org	Okemos	MI	48864	517-349-5640	349-5818
Minnesota Nurses Assn (MNA) 1625 Energy Pk Dr *TF:* 800-536-4662 ■ *Web:* www.mnnurses.org	Saint Paul	MN	55108	651-646-4807	647-5301
Mississippi Nurses Assn (MNA) 31 Woodgreen Pl *Web:* www.msnurses.org	Madison	MS	39110	601-898-0670	898-0190
Missouri Nurses Assn (MONA) 1904 Bubba Ln PO Box 105228 *TF:* 888-662-6662 ■ *Web:* www.missourinurses.org	Jefferson City	MO	65110	573-636-4623	636-9576
Montana Nurses Assn (MNA) 104 Broadway Suite G-2 *Web:* www.mtnurses.org	Helena	MT	59601	406-442-6710	442-1841
Nebraska Nurses Assn (NNA) 1320 Lincoln Mall Suite 9 *TF:* 800-201-3625 ■ *Web:* www.nursingworld.org	Lincoln	NE	68508	402-475-3859	475-3961
Nevada Nurses Assn (NNA) 1155 W 4th St Suite 224 PO Box 34660 *Web:* www.nvnurses.org	Reno	NV	89533	775-747-2333	329-3334
New Hampshire Nurses Assn (NHNA) 210 N State St # 1A *Web:* www.nhnurses.org	Concord	NH	03301	603-225-3783	228-6672
New Jersey State Nurses Assn (NJSNA) 1479 Pennington Rd *TF:* 888-876-5762 ■ *Web:* www.njsna.org	Trenton	NJ	08618	609-883-5335	883-5343
New Mexico Nurses Assn (NMNA) 3692 New Mexico 14 *Web:* www.nmna.org	Santa Fe	NM	87508	505-471-3324	471-3314
New York Professional Nurses Union (NYPNU) 1104 Lexington Ave Suite 2D *Web:* www.nypnu.org	New York	NY	10021	212-988-5565	
New York State Nurses Assn (NYSNA) 11 Cornell Rd *TF:* 800-724-6976 ■ *Web:* www.nysna.org	Latham	NY	12110	518-782-9400	782-9530
North Carolina Nurses Assn (NCNA) 103 Enterprise St PO Box 12025 *TF:* 800-626-2153 ■ *Web:* www.ncnurses.org	Raleigh	NC	27605	919-821-4250	829-5807
North Dakota Nurses Assn (NDNA) 531 Airport Rd Suite D *Web:* www.ndna.org	Bismarck	ND	58504	701-223-1385	223-0575
Ohio Nurses Assn (ONA) 4000 E Main St *Web:* www.ohnurses.org	Columbus	OH	43213	614-237-5414	237-6074
Oklahoma Nurses Assn (ONA) 6414 N Santa Fe Ave Suite A *Web:* www.oknurses.com	Oklahoma City	OK	73116	405-840-3476	840-3013
Oregon Nurses Assn (ONA) 18765 SW Boones Ferry Rd *TF:* 800-634-3552 ■ *Web:* www.oregonrn.org	Tualatin	OR	97062	503-293-0011	293-0013
Pennsylvania Assn of Staff Nurses & Allied Professionals (PASNAP) 1 Fayette St # 475 *TF:* 800-500-7850 ■ *Web:* www.pennanurses.org	Conshohocken	PA	19428	610-567-2907	567-2915
Pennsylvania State Nurses Assn (PSNA) 2578 IH- Dr Suite 101 *TF:* 888-707-7762 ■ *Web:* www.psna.org	Harrisburg	PA	17110	717-657-1222	657-3796
Rhode Island State Nurses Assn (RISNA) 550 S Water St Suite 540B *Web:* www.risnarn.org	Providence	RI	02903	401-421-9703	421-6793
South Carolina Nurses Assn (SCNA) 1821 Gadsden St *Web:* www.scnurses.org	Columbia	SC	29201	803-252-4781	779-3870
South Dakota Nurses Assn (SDNA) 105 S Euclid Ave *Web:* www.nursingworld.org	Pierre	SD	57501	605-945-4265	945-4266
Tennessee Nurses Assn (TNA) 545 Mainstream Dr Suite 405 *Web:* www.tnaonline.org	Nashville	TN	37228	615-254-0350	254-0303
Texas Nurses Assn (TNA) 7600 Burnet Rd Suite 440 *TF:* 800-862-2022 ■ *Web:* www.texasnurses.org	Austin	TX	78757	512-452-0645	452-0648
Utah Nurses Assn (UTA) 4505 S Wastch Blvd Suite 290 *TF:* 800-236-1617 ■ *Web:* www.utahnurses.org	Salt Lake City	UT	84124	801-272-4510	272-4322
Vermont State Nurses Assn (VSNA) 100 Dorset St Suite 13 *TF:* 800-540-9390 ■ *Web:* www.vsna-inc.org	South Burlington	VT	05403	802-651-8886	651-8998
Virginia Nurses Assn (VNA) 7113 Three Chopt Rd Suite 204 *TF:* 800-868-6877 ■ *Web:* www.virginianurses.com	Richmond	VA	23226	804-282-1808	282-4916
Visiting Nurse Assn of Staten Island Inc 400 Lake Ave *Web:* www.vnasi.org	Staten Island	NY	10303	718-816-3500	
Washington State Nurses Assn (WSNA) 575 Andover Pk W Suite 101 *TF:* 800-231-8482 ■ *Web:* www.wsna.org	Seattle	WA	98188	206-575-7979	575-1908
West Virginia Nurses Assn (WVNA) 405 Capitol St Suite 600 *TF:* 800-400-1226 ■ *Web:* www.wvnurses.org	Charleston	WV	25301	304-342-1169	346-1861
Wisconsin Nurses Assn (WNA) 6117 Monona Dr *Web:* www.wisconsinnurses.org	Madison	WI	53716	608-221-0383	221-2788

537 OFFICE & SCHOOL SUPPLIES

SEE ALSO Office Supply Stores p. 2322; Writing Paper p. 2335; Pens, Pencils, Parts p. 2391; Printing & Photocopying Supplies p. 2453

	City	State	Zip	Phone	Fax
3M Consumer & Office Div 3M Ctr *NYSE: MMM* ■ *TF:* 888-364-3577 ■ *Web:* www.3m.com	Saint Paul	MN	55144	651-733-1110	736-2133
A & W Products Co Inc 14 Gardner St *TF:* 800-223-5156 ■ *Web:* www.awproducts.com	Port Jervis	NY	12771	845-856-5156	856-9772
Aakron Rule Corp PO Box 418 *Web:* www.aakronline.com	Akron	NY	14001	716-542-5483	542-2205
Acroprint Time Recorder Co 5640 Departure Dr *TF:* 800-334-7190 ■ *Web:* www.acroprint.com	Raleigh	NC	27616	919-872-5800	850-0720
American Product Distributors Inc 8350 Arrowridge Blvd *TF:* 877-769-0752 ■ *Web:* www.americanproduct.com	Charlotte	NC	28273	704-522-9411	522-9413
American Solutions for Business 31 E Minnesota Ave PO Box 218 *TF:* 800-862-3690 ■ *Web:* www.abfweb01.americanbus.com	Glenwood	MN	56334	320-634-5471	634-5265
Arlington Industries Inc 1616 Lakeside Dr *TF:* 800-323-4147 ■ *Web:* www.arli.com	Waukegan	IL	60085	847-689-2754	689-1616
Arthur Brown & Brother Inc 2 W 45th St *TF:* 800-772-7367 ■ *Web:* www.artbrown.com	New York	NY	10036	212-575-5555	575-5825
Aurora Corp of America 3500 Challenger St *TF:* 800-327-8508 ■ *Web:* www.auroracorp.com	Torrance	CA	90503	310-793-5650	793-5658
Avery Dennison Corp 150 N Orange Grove Blvd *NYSE: AVY* ■ *TF Cust Svc:* 800-252-8379 ■ *Web:* www.averydennison.com	Pasadena	CA	91103	626-304-2000	304-2192
Avery Dennison Worldwide Office Products Div 50 Pointe Dr *TF:* 800-462-8379 ■ *Web:* www.avery.com	Brea	CA	92821	714-674-8500	674-6929
Bartizan Corp 217 Riverdale Ave *TF:* 800-431-2682 ■ *Web:* www.bartizan.com	Yonkers	NY	10705	914-965-7977	965-7746
Bassotech Inc 5034 N Hiatus Rd *Web:* www.bassotech.com	Fort Lauderdale	FL	33351	954-578-5005	578-0049
Baumgarten's 144 Ottley Dr *TF:* 800-247-5547 ■ *Web:* www.b3.net	Atlanta	GA	30324	404-874-7675	881-1442
Best Computer Supplies 895 E Patriot Blvd Suite 110 *TF:* 800-544-3472 ■ *Web:* www.theschoolsupplier.com	Reno	NV	89511	775-850-2600	850-2610
Brodart Co Contract Library Furniture Div 280 N Rd Clinton County Industrial Pk *TF:* 888-521-1884 ■ *Web:* www.shopbrodart.com	McElhattan	PA	17748	570-769-7412	769-7641
Business Stationery LLC 4944 Commerce Pkwy *TF:* 800-234-9954 ■ *Web:* www.bsiprint.com	Cleveland	OH	44128	216-514-1277	
C & S Sales Inc 12947 Chadron Ave *Web:* www.cssales.com	Hawthorne	CA	90250	310-538-1219	538-2814
C-Line Products Inc 1100 E Business Ctr Dr *TF:* 800-323-6084 ■ *Web:* www.c-lineproducts.com	Mount Prospect	IL	60056	847-827-6661	827-3329
Cardinal Brands Inc 643 Massachusetts St Suite 200 *TF:* 800-364-8713 ■ *Web:* www.cardinalbrands.com	Lawrence	KS	66044	785-344-1400	344-1200
Cardinal Office Systems Inc 576 E Main St *TF:* 800-589-5886	Frankfort	KY	40601	502-875-3300	875-3737
Case Logic Inc 6303 Dry Creek Pkwy *TF:* 800-447-4848 ■ *Web:* www.caselogic.com	Longmont	CO	80503	303-652-1000	652-1091
Champion Industries Inc 2450-90 First Ave PO Box 2968 *NASDAQ: CHMP* ■ *TF:* 800-624-3431 ■ *Web:* www.champion-industries.com	Huntington	WV	25728	304-528-2700	528-2765
Costas Custom Office Supply 575 San Mateo Ave	San Bruno	CA	94066	650-871-9410	588-7545
CPP International LLC 11707 Steele Creek Rd *TF:* 800-888-3190 ■ *Web:* www.carolinapad.com	Charlotte	NC	28273	704-588-3190	588-1123
Dahle North America Inc 49 Vose Farm Rd # 110 *TF:* 800-243-8145 ■ *Web:* www.dahle.com	Peterborough	NH	03458	603-924-0003	924-1616
Dart Mfg Co Inc 4012 Bronze Way **Fax Area Code:* 800 ■ *TF:* 800-345-3278 ■ *Web:* www.dartpromo.com	Dallas	TX	75237	214-333-4221	833-3278*
Datavision & Devices 2709 Brookmere Rd *TF Cust Svc:* 800-237-5658 ■ *Web:* www.datavisionergonomics.com	Charlottesville	VA	22901	800-237-5658	808-9254
Deflect-O Corp 7035 E 86th St *TF:* 800-428-4328 ■ *Web:* www.deflecto.com	Indianapolis	IN	46250	317-849-9555	915-4456
Douglas Stewart Co The 2402 Advance Rd *TF:* 800-279-2795 ■ *Web:* www.dstewart.com	Madison	WI	53718	608-221-1155	221-5217
Eaton Office Supply Co Inc 180 John Glenn Dr *TF:* 800-365-3237 ■ *Web:* www.eatonofficesupply.com	Amherst	NY	14228	716-691-6100	691-0074
GBS Corp 7233 Freedom Ave NW *TF:* 800-552-2427 ■ *Web:* www.gbscorp.com	North Canton	OH	44720	330-494-5330	494-8316
Great North American Cos 2828 Forest Ln Suite 2000 *TF:* 800-527-2782 ■ *Web:* www.gnamerican.com	Dallas	TX	75234	972-481-6100	481-6200
International Imaging Materials Inc 310 Commerce Dr *TF:* 888-464-4625 ■ *Web:* www.iimak.com	Amherst	NY	14228	716-691-6333	691-3395
Lakeshore Learning Materials 2695 E Dominguez St *TF:* 800-778-4456 ■ *Web:* www.lakeshorelearning.com	Carson	CA	90895	800-778-4456	537-5403
Lee Products Co 800 E 80th St *TF:* 800-989-3544 ■ *Web:* www.leeproducts.com	Bloomington	MN	55420	952-854-3544	854-7177

Company	City	State	ZIP	Phone	Fax
Magna Visual Inc 9400 Watson Rd TF: 800-843-3399 ■ Web: www.magnavisual.com	Saint Louis	MO	63126	314-843-9000	843-0000
McGill Inc 131 E Prairie St PO Box 177 TF: 800-982-9884 ■ Web: www.mcgillinc.com	Marengo	IL	60152	815-568-7244	568-6860
Millennium Marking Co 2600 Greenleaf Ave Web: www.millmarking.com	Elk Grove Village	IL	60007	847-806-1750	806-1751
Mod-Systems Inc 2172-B River Rd PO Box 585 TF: 800-637-2937	Greer	SC	29652	864-879-3850	879-3158
New England Newspaper Supply Co (NENSCO) 9 Railroad Ave PO Box 348 TF: 800-347-7377 ■ Web: www.nensco.com	Millbury	MA	01527	508-865-0800	865-0811
Nina Enterprises 1350 S Leavitt St TF: 800-886-8688 ■ Web: www.buddyproducts.com	Chicago	IL	60608	312-733-6400	733-8356
PBS Supply Co Inc 7013 So 216th St TF: 877-727-7515 ■ Web: www.pbssupply.com	Kent	WA	98032	253-395-5550	395-5575
PerfectData Corp 1323 Conshohocken Rd TF: 800-973-7332 ■ Web: www.perfectdata.com	Plymouth Meeting	PA	19462	610-277-1010	277-4390
PerkCom LLC 924 Chevy Way Web: www.perkcom.com	Medford	OR	97504	541-772-4224	734-9893
Promedia Computer Supplies Ltd Co 12806 Schabarum Ave Suite C TF: 800-583-5833	Baldwin Park	CA	91706	626-960-5778	960-5770
Reliable Corp 263 Shuman Blvd TF Cust Svc: 800-359-5000 ■ Web: www.reliable.com	Naperville	IL	60563	800-735-4000	326-3233
Staples Business Advantage 500 Staples Dr TF: 877-826-7755 ■ Web: www.staplesadvantage.com	Framingham	NJ	01702	508-253-5000	
TAB Products Co 605 4th St TF: 888-822-9777 ■ Web: www.tab.com	Mayville	WI	53050	920-387-3131	387-1805
United Stationers Inc 1 PkwyN Blvd Suite 100 NASDAQ: USTR ■ TF: 800-424-4003 ■ Web: www.unitedstationers.com	Deerfield	IL	60015	847-627-7000	627-7001
United Stationers Supply Co (USSCO) 1 Pkwy N Blvd Suite 100 PO Box 25665 Web: www.ussco.com	Deerfield	IL	60015	847-627-7000	627-7001
Van Ausdall & Farrar Inc 6430 E 75th St TF: 800-467-7474 ■ Web: www.vanausdall.com	Indianapolis	IN	46250	317-634-2913	638-1843
Weeks-Lerman Group 58-38 Page Pl TF: 800-544-5959 ■ Web: www.weekslerman.com	Maspeth	NY	11378	718-803-5000	821-1515

538 OFFICE SUPPLY STORES

Company	City	State	ZIP	Phone	Fax
Airline Stationery Co 284 Madison Ave Web: www.airlineinc.com	New York	NY	10017	212-532-6525	779-7257
AJ Stationers Inc 7601 Brandon Woods Blvd	Baltimore	MD	21226	410-360-4900	360-4291
Allied Office Products Inc 100 Delawanna Ave TF: 800-275-2554 ■ Web: www.askallied.com	Clifton	NJ	07014	973-594-3000	594-3600
Artlite Office Supply Co 1860 Chshire Bridge Rd Ne Web: www.artlite.net	Atlanta	GA	30324	404-875-7271	875-2623
Ashland Office Supply Co Inc 2100 29th St TF: 800-926-1267	Ashland	KY	41101	606-329-1400	329-2452
Burkett's Office Supplies Inc 8520 Younger Creek Dr Web: www.burkettsoffice.com	Sacramento	CA	95828	916-387-8900	381-3383
Church & Stagg Office Supply Co Inc 3421 6th Ave TF: 800-239-5336 ■ Web: www.churchandstagg.com	Birmingham	AL	35222	205-251-2951	324-6874
Corporate Express Inc 1 Environmental Way TF: 888-664-3945 ■ Web: www.corporate-express.com	Broomfield	CO	80021	303-664-2000	664-3474
D & D Office Supplies 1751 Lincoln Hwy Rt 30 TF: 877-829-1200 ■ Web: www.ddoffice.com	North Versailles	PA	15137	412-829-1200	829-1201
DBI Inc 912 E Michigan Ave TF: 800-968-1324 ■ Web: www.dbiyes.com	Lansing	MI	48912	517-485-3200	485-3202
Eakes Office Plus 617 W 3rd St TF: 800-652-9396 ■ Web: www.eakes.com	Grand Island	NE	68801	308-382-8026	382-7401
Econ-o-copy Inc 4437 Trenton St Suite A TF: 877-256-0310 ■ Web: www.econ-o-copy.com	Metairie	LA	70006	504-457-0032	457-0114
Egyptian Stationers Inc 107 W Main St TF: 800-642-3949 ■ Web: www.egyptian-stationers.com	Belleville	IL	62220	618-234-2323	234-0693
Fisher Hawaii 450 Cooke St Web: www.fisherhawaii.biz	Honolulu	HI	96813	808-524-8770	524-8785
Friend's Professional Stationery Inc 1535 Lewis Ave TF: 800-323-4394 ■ Web: www.friendsstationery.com	Zion	IL	60099	847-746-1248	746-4962
Gobin's Inc 615 N Santa Fe Ave TF: 800-425-2324 ■ Web: www.gobins.com	Pueblo	CO	81003	719-544-2324	544-2378
Great American Office LLC 513 Donald St Web: www.gaos.com	Bedford	NH	03110	603-472-5199	296-0791
Halsey & Griffith Inc 313 Datura St *Fax: Cust Svc ■ TF: 800-466-1921 ■ Web: www.halsey-griffith.com	West Palm Beach	FL	33401	561-820-8000	820-8026*
Hurst Group 257 E Short St TF: 800-926-4423 ■ Web: www.hurstgroup.net	Lexington	KY	40507	859-255-4422	255-4471
International Staple & Machine Co PO Box 629 TF: 800-378-3430	Butler	PA	16003	800-378-3430	827-4762
Iowa Office Supply Inc 731 Lake Ave TF: 800-373-9182 ■ Web: www.iowaofficesupply.com	Storm Lake	IA	50588	712-732-4801	732-4426
Kennedy Office Supply 4211-A Atlantic Ave TF: 800-733-9401 ■ Web: www.kennedyofficesupply.com	Raleigh	NC	27604	919-878-5400	790-9649
Koch Bros 325 Grand Ave TF: 800-944-5624 ■ Web: www.kochbros.com	Des Moines	IA	50309	515-283-2451	243-3147
Laser Tek Industries 4909 US Hwy 12 TF: 800-322-8137	Richmond	IL	60071	815-675-1199	675-6149
Latta's School Supply 1502 4th Ave TF: 800-624-3501 ■ Web: www.lattascatalog.com	Huntington	WV	25701	304-523-8400	525-5038
Louisiana Office Supply Co 7643 Florida Blvd TF: 866-342-0286 ■ Web: www.losco.com	Baton Rouge	LA	70806	225-927-1110	927-3085
Newport Stationers Inc 17681 Mitchell N Web: www.newportstationers.com	Irvine	CA	92614	949-863-1200	852-8970
Northern Business Products Inc PO Box 16127 TF: 800-647-8775 ■ Web: www.nbpoffice.com	Duluth	MN	55816	218-726-0167	726-1023
Novacopy Inc 5520 Shelby Oaks Dr TF: 800-264-0637 ■ Web: www.novacopy.net	Memphis	TN	38134	901-432-2679	432-2682
Office Depot Inc 2200 Old Germantown Rd NYSE: ODP ■ *Fax: Hum Res ■ TF: 800-937-3600 ■ Web: www.officedepot.com	Delray Beach	FL	33445	561-438-4800	438-4406*
Office Resources Inc 374 Congress St TF: 866-423-9100 ■ Web: www.ori.com	Boston	MA	02210	617-423-9100	423-5590
Office Suppliers Inc 13716 Crayton Blvd TF: 800-225-2723 ■ Web: www.osimd.com	Hagerstown	MD	21742	301-797-3120	797-1504
OfficeMax Inc 150 E Pierce Rd NYSE: OMX ■ *Fax: Sales ■ TF: 800-472-6473 ■ Web: www.officemax.com	Itasca	IL	60143	630-438-7800	773-6708*
Patrick & Co 560 Market St TF: 800-792-0755 ■ Web: www.patrickandco.com	San Francisco	CA	94104	415-392-2640	591-0773
Phillips Group 501 Fulling Mill Rd TF: 800-538-7500 ■ Web: www.buyphillips.com	Middletown	PA	17057	717-944-0400	948-5248
Printers & Stationers Inc 113 N Ct St TF: 800-624-5334 ■ Web: www.psi-online.net	Florence	AL	35630	256-764-8061	764-5024
Sav-On Office Supplies 6601 Will Rogers Blvd Suite B TF: 866-571-8177 ■ Web: www.sav-onofficesupplies.com	Fort Worth	TX	76140	817-568-5200	568-5204
Smith & Butterfield Co Inc 2800 Lynch Rd TF: 800-321-6543 ■ Web: www.smithbutterfield.com	Evansville	IN	47733	812-422-3261	429-0532
Stationers Inc 615 4th Ave TF: 800-862-7200 ■ Web: www.stationers-wv.com	Huntington	WV	25701	304-528-2780	528-2795
Supply Room Cos Inc 14140 N Washington Hwy TF: 800-849-7239 ■ Web: www.thesupplyroom.com	Ashland	VA	23005	804-412-1200	412-1313
Triplett Office Essentials Corp 3553 109th St TF: 800-437-5034 ■ Web: www.tripletts.com	Des Moines	IA	50322	515-270-9150	270-9683
Wist Office Products Co 107 W Julie Dr TF: 800-999-9478 ■ Web: www.wist.com	Tempe	AZ	85283	480-921-2900	921-2121
Xpedx Paper & Graphics 1376 Rankin Rd Web: www.xpedxstores.com/about.html	Troy	MI	48083	248-585-3980	585-0945
Xpedx Paper Store 3351 W Addison St TF: 800-866-6332 ■ Web: www.xpedxstores.com	Chicago	IL	60618	773-463-6423	442-6415

539 OIL & GAS EXTRACTION

Company	City	State	ZIP	Phone	Fax
Abraxas Petroleum Corp 18803 Meisner Dr AMEX: ABP ■ *Fax: Acctg ■ Web: www.abraxaspetroleum.com	San Antonio	TX	78258	210-490-4788	490-8816*
Adams Resources & Energy Inc 4400 Post Oak Pkwy AMEX: AE ■ Web: www.adamsresources.com	Houston	TX	77027	713-881-3600	881-3491
Aeropres Corp 1324 N Hearne Ave Suite 200 Web: www.aeropres.com	Shreveport	LA	71107	318-221-6282	213-1270
American Trading & Production Corp 10 E Baltimore St Suite 1600 Web: www.atapco.com	Baltimore	MD	21202	410-347-7150	347-7151
Anadarko Petroleum Corp 1201 Lake Robbins Dr NYSE: APC ■ TF: 800-800-1101 ■ Web: www.anadarko.com	The Woodlands	TX	77380	832-636-1000	636-8022
Anadarko Petroleum Corp Alaska Div 3201 C St Suite 603 Web: www.anadarko.com	Anchorage	AK	99503	907-273-6300	563-9479
Apache Corp 2000 Post Oak Blvd Suite 100 NYSE: APA ■ *Fax: Mail Rm ■ TF: 800-272-2434 ■ Web: www.apachecorp.com	Houston	TX	77056	713-296-6000	296-6488*
Apco Argentina Inc 1 William Ctr PO box 2400 MD 35-8 NASDAQ: APAGF ■ Web: www.apcooilandgas.com	Tulsa	OK	74172	918-573-1616	573-3082
Approach Resources Inc 1 Ridgmar Centre 6500 W Fwy Suite 800 NASDAQ: AREX ■ Web: www.approachresources.com	Fort Worth	TX	76116	817-989-9000	989-9001
Aramco Services Co 9009 W Loop S TF: 800-343-4272 ■ Web: www.aramcoservices.com	Houston	TX	77096	713-432-4000	432-8566
ATP Oil & Gas Corp 4600 Post Oak Pl Suite 200 NASDAQ: ATPG ■ Web: www.atpog.com	Houston	TX	77027	713-622-3311	622-5101
Aviva Petroleum Inc 8235 Douglas Ave Suite 400	Dallas	TX	75225	214-691-3464	691-6151
Barnwell Industries Inc 1100 Alakea St Suite 2900 AMEX: BRN ■ Web: www.brninc.com	Honolulu	HI	96813	808-531-8400	531-7181
Bayou State Oil Corp 1115 Hawn Ave	Shreveport	LA	71107	318-222-0737	222-0730
Berry Petroleum Co 1999 Broadway Suite 3700 NYSE: BRY ■ Web: www.bry.com	Denver	CO	80202	303-999-4400	999-4122
Bettis Boyle & Stovall Inc 505 5th St PO Box 1240	Graham	TX	76450	940-549-2060	549-7405
BHP Billiton Petroleum (Americas) Inc 1360 Post Oak Blvd Suite 150 Web: www.bhpbilliton.com	Houston	TX	77056	713-961-8500	961-8400
Blue Dolphin Energy Co 801 Travis St Suite 2100 NASDAQ: BDCO ■ Web: www.blue-dolphin.com	Houston	TX	77002	713-568-4725	227-7626
BP Canada Energy Co 240 4th Ave SW *Fax: Mail Rm ■ TF: 877-833-1359 ■ Web: www.bp.com	Calgary	AB	T2P2H8	403-233-1359	233-1476*
BP Plc 28100 Torch Pkwy NYSE: BP ■ *Fax Area Code: 281 ■ TF: 866-427-6947 ■ Web: www.bp.com	Warrenville	IL	60555	630-420-5111	298-0738*
Brigham Exploration Co 6300 Bridge Pt Pkwy Bldg 2 Suite 500 NASDAQ: BEXP ■ Web: www.bexp3d.com	Austin	TX	78730	512-427-3300	427-3400
Cabot Oil & Gas Corp 840 Gessner Rd Suite 1200 NYSE: COG ■ *Fax: Hum Res ■ TF: 800-434-3985 ■ Web: www.cabotog.com	Houston	TX	77024	281-848-2799	589-4910*
Callon Petroleum Co 200 N Canal St NYSE: CPE ■ TF: 800-541-1294 ■ Web: www.callon.com	Natchez	MS	39120	601-442-1601	446-1410
Calpine Energy Inc 717 Texas Ave Suite 1000 TF: 800-251-6165 ■ Web: www.calpine.com	Houston	TX	77002	713-830-2000	830-2001

Company	City	State	Zip	Phone	Fax
Canadian Natural Resources Ltd (CNRL) 855 2nd St SW Suite 2500 *TSE: CNQ* ■ *TF:* 888-878-3700 ■ *Web:* www.cnrl.com	Calgary	AB	T2P4J8	403-517-6700	517-7350
Cano Petroleum Inc 6500 N Belt Line Rd Suite 200 *AMEX: CFW* ■ *Web:* www.canopetro.com	Irving	TX	75063	214-687-0030	
Carrizo Oil & Gas Inc 1000 Louisiana Suite 1500 *NASDAQ: CRZO* ■ *Web:* www.crzo.net	Houston	TX	77002	713-328-1000	328-1035
Case Pomeroy & Co Inc 529 5th Ave Suite 1600	New York	NY	10017	212-867-2211	682-2353
Celtic Exploration Ltd 321 6th Ave SW Suite 600, W Tower *TSE: CLT* ■ *Web:* www.celticex.com	Calgary	AB	T2P3H3	403-201-9153	201-9163
CGAS Exploration Inc 300 Capitol St Suite 700 *TF:* 800-686-2427	Charleston	WV	25301	304-343-5505	343-5525
Challenger Minerals Inc 1311 Broadfield Blvd Suite 500 *Web:* www.challengerminerals.com	Houston	TX	77084	832-587-5400	587-5430
Chesapeake Energy Corp PO Box 18496 *NYSE: CHK* ■ *TF:* 877-845-1427 ■ *Web:* www.chk.com	Oklahoma City	OK	73154	405-935-8000	879-9563
Chevron Corp 6001 Bollinger Canyon Rd *NYSE: CVX* ■ **Fax Area Code:* 866 ■ *TF Cust Svc:* 800-243-8766 ■ *Web:* www.chevron.com	San Ramon	CA	94583	925-842-1000	420-0335*
Cimarex Energy Co 1700 Lincoln St Suite 1800 *NYSE: XEC* ■ *Web:* www.cimarex.com	Denver	CO	80203	303-295-3995	295-3494
Clayton Williams Energy Inc 6 Desta Dr Suite 3000 *NASDAQ: CWEI* ■ *Web:* www.claytonwilliams.com	Midland	TX	79705	432-682-6324	682-1452
Cobra Oil & Gas Corp 2201 Kell Blvd PO Box 8206 *Web:* www.cobraogc.com	Wichita Falls	TX	76308	940-716-5100	716-5190
Compton Petroleum Corp 850 - 2nd St SW Suite 500, Bankers Court *TSE: CMT* ■ *TF:* 888-480-6888 ■ *Web:* www.comptonpetroleum.com	Calgary	AB	T2P0R8	403-237-9400	237-9410
Comstock Resources Inc 5300 Town & Country Blvd Suite 500 *NYSE: CRK* ■ *TF:* 800-877-1322 ■ *Web:* www.comstockresources.com	Frisco	TX	75034	972-668-8800	668-8812
ConocoPhillips 600 N Dairy Ashford Rd *NYSE: COP* ■ *TF:* 800-527-5476 ■ *Web:* www.conocophillips.com	Houston	TX	77079	281-293-1000	
ConocoPhillips Canada 401 9th Ave SW PO Box 130 Stn M *Web:* www.conocophillips.ca	Calgary	AB	T2P2H7	403-233-4000	233-5143
Contango Oil & Gas Co 3700 Buffalo Speedway Suite 960 *AMEX: MCF* ■ *Web:* www.contango.com	Houston	TX	77098	713-960-1901	960-1065
Credo Petroleum Corp 1801 Broadway Suite 900 *NASDAQ: CRED* ■ *TF:* 800-297-2366 ■ *Web:* www.credopetroleum.com	Denver	CO	80202	303-297-2200	297-2204
Crown Central Petroleum Corp 1 N Charles St **Fax:* Hum Res ■ *Web:* www.crowncentral.com	Baltimore	MD	21201	410-539-7400	659-4875*
DCP Midstream Partners LP 370 17th St Suite 2775 *NYSE: DPM*	Denver	CO	80202	303-633-2900	605-2225
Denbury Resources Inc 5100 Tennyson Pkwy Suite 3000 *NYSE: DNR* ■ *TF:* 800-364-5482 ■ *Web:* www.denbury.com	Plano	TX	75024	972-673-2000	673-2001
Devon Energy Corp 20 N Broadway *NYSE: DVN* ■ *TF:* 800-361-3377 ■ *Web:* www.devonenergy.com	Oklahoma City	OK	73102	405-235-3611	552-4667
Dorchester Minerals LP 3838 Oak Lawn Ave Suite 300 *NASDAQ: DMLP*	Garland	TX	75219	214-559-0330	559-0301
Dugan Production Corp 709 E Murray Dr *TF:* 800-618-1821	Farmington	NM	87499	505-325-1821	327-4613
Duke Energy Inc 777 Walker St Suite 2300 *Web:* www.duneenergy.com	Houston	TX	77002	713-229-6300	229-6388
EnCana Corp 855 2nd St SW Suite 1800 *TSE: ECA* ■ *TF:* 888-568-6322 ■ *Web:* www.encana.com	Calgary	AB	T2P2S5	403-645-2000	645-3400
Eni Petroleum Co Inc 1201 Louisiana St Suite 3500	Houston	TX	77002	713-393-6100	393-6205
EQT Corp 625 Liberty Ave Suite 1700 *NYSE: EQT* ■ *TF:* 800-242-1776 ■ *Web:* www.eqt.com	Pittsburgh	PA	15222	412-553-5700	
Exxon Mobil Corp 5959 Las Colinas Blvd *NYSE: XOM* ■ *TF:* 800-252-1800 ■ *Web:* www.exxonmobil.com	Irving	TX	75039	972-444-1000	444-1348
ExxonMobil Canada 237 4th Ave SW *Web:* www.mobil.ca	Calgary	AB	T2P0H6	403-260-7910	237-2197
Fairborne Energy Ltd 3400-450 1st St SW Suite 3400 *TSE: FEL* ■ *Web:* www.fairborne-energy.com	Calgary	AB	T2P5H1	403-290-7750	290-7724
FieldPoint Petroleum Corp 1703 Edelweiss Dr Suite 301 *AMEX: FPP* ■ *Web:* www.fppcorp.com	Cedar Park	TX	78613	512-250-8692	335-1294
Flying J Inc 1104 Country Hill Dr *TF Sales:* 877-218-9290 ■ *Web:* www.flyingj.com	Ogden	UT	84403	801-624-1000	395-8005
Forest Oil Corp 707 17th St Suite 3600 *NYSE: FST* ■ *Web:* www.forestoil.com	Denver	CO	80202	303-812-1400	812-1602
Frontier Oil Co 151 S Whittier St # 2100	Wichita	KS	67207	316-263-1201	
Frontier Oil Corp 10000 Memorial Dr Suite 600 *NYSE: FTO* ■ *Web:* www.frontieroil.com	Houston	TX	77024	713-688-9600	688-0616
Gary-Williams Energy Corp 370 17th St Suite 5300 *Web:* www.gwec.com	Denver	CO	80202	303-628-3800	628-3834
Gasco Energy Inc 8 Inverness Dr E Suite 100 *AMEX: GSX* ■ *Web:* www.gascoenergy.com	Englewood	CO	80112	303-483-0044	483-0011
Gastar Exploration Ltd 1331 Lamar St Suite 1080 *AMEX: GST* ■ *Web:* www.gastar.com	Houston	TX	77010	713-739-1800	739-0458
GeoResources Inc 110 Cypress Stn Dr Suite 220 *NASDAQ: GEOI* ■ *TF:* 800-735-5984 ■ *Web:* www.georesourcesinc.com	Williston	ND	58802	281-537-9920	537-8324
GMX Resources Inc 9400 N Broadway 1 Benham Pl Suite 600 *NASDAQ: GMXR* ■ *TF:* 877-600-0711 ■ *Web:* www.gmxresources.com	Oklahoma City	OK	73114	405-600-0711	600-0600
Great Western Drilling Co Inc 700 W Louisiana St *Web:* www.gwdc.com	Midland	TX	79701	432-682-5241	684-3702
Gunnison Energy Corp 1801 Broadway Suite 1200 *Web:* www.oxbow.com	Denver	CO	80202	303-296-4222	296-4555
Harken Energy Corp 180 State St Suite 200 *AMEX: HKN* ■ *Web:* www.hkninc.com	Southlake	TX	76092	817-424-2424	488-4307
Harvest Natural Resources Inc 1177 Enclave Pkwy Suite 300 *NYSE: HNR* ■ *Web:* www.harvestnr.com	Houston	TX	77077	281-899-5700	899-5702
Headington Oil Co 2711 N Haskell Ave # 2800 *TF:* 800-245-5773 ■ *Web:* www.headington.com	Dallas	TX	75204	214-696-0606	696-7728
Hess Corp PO Box 224866 *NYSE: AHC* ■ *TF:* 800-437-7645 ■ *Web:* www.ahbelo.com	Dallas	TX	75222	214-977-8200	977-8201
Hunt Oil Co 1900 N Akard St *TF:* 800-435-7794 ■ *Web:* www.huntoil.com	Dallas	TX	75201	214-978-8000	978-8888
Husky Energy Inc 707 8th Ave SW PO Box 6525 *TSE: HSE* ■ *TF:* 877-262-2111 ■ *Web:* www.huskyenergy.com	Calgary	AB	T2P3G7	403-298-6111	298-7464
Hyperdynamics Corp 12012 Wickchester Ln Suite 175 *AMEX: HDY* ■ *Web:* www.hyperdynamics.com	Houston	TX	77079	713-353-9400	353-9421
Independent Propane Co 2591 Dallas Pkwy Suite 105 *TF:* 888-790-9022 ■ *Web:* www.independentpropane.com	Frisco	TX	75034	888-790-9022	
Jack Lawton LLC 1409 Kirkman St	Lake Charles	LA	70601	337-497-0137	497-9461
Jerry Scott Drilling Co Inc 11977 N Hwy 99 PO Box 1488	Seminole	OK	74818	405-382-2202	382-8334
JM Huber Corp 499 Thornall St 8th Fl **Fax:* Hum Res ■ *Web:* www.huber.com	Edison	NJ	08837	732-549-8600	549-2239*
Lario Oil & Gas Co 301 S Market St *TF:* 800-865-5611	Wichita	KS	67202	316-265-5611	265-5610
Lenape Resources Inc 9489 Alexander Rd *Web:* www.lenaperesources.com	Alexander	NY	14005	585-344-1200	344-3283
Mack Energy Co 1202 N 10th St *Web:* www.mackenergy.com	Duncan	OK	73533	580-252-5580	255-1471
Magellan Petroleum Corp 10 Columbus Blvd 10th Fl *NASDAQ: MPET* ■ **Fax Area Code:* 860 ■ *Web:* www.magpet.com	Hartford	CT	06106	207-619-8500	293-2349*
Maguire Oil Co 1201 Elm St Suite 4000 *TF:* 800-969-6248	Dallas	TX	75270	214-741-5137	658-8005
Marathon Oil Corp 5555 San Felipe St *Web:* www.marathonoil.com	Houston	TX	77056	713-629-6600	296-2952
Meridian Resource Corp 1401 Enclave Pkwy Suite 300 *NYSE: TMR*	Houston	TX	77077	281-597-7000	597-8880
Mexco Energy Corp 214 W Texas Ave Suite 1101 *AMEX: MXC* ■ *Web:* www.mexicoenergy.com	Midland	TX	79701	432-682-1119	682-1123
Mull Drilling Co Inc 221 N Main St Suite 300 *Web:* www.mulldrlg.com	Wichita	KS	67202	316-264-6366	264-6440
Murphy Oil Corp 200 Peach St *NYSE: MUR* ■ *TF:* 800-643-2364 ■ *Web:* www.murphyoilcorp.com	El Dorado	AR	71730	870-862-6411	864-6373
National Energy Group Inc (NEGI) 4925 Greenville Ave Suite 1352 *TF:* 800-733-9211	Dallas	TX	75206	214-692-9211	692-9310
Newfield Exploration Co 363 N Sam Houston Pkwy E Suite 100 *NYSE: NFX* ■ *TF:* 800-419-4789 ■ *Web:* www.newfld.com	Houston	TX	77060	281-847-6000	405-4242
Nexen Inc 801 7th Ave SW *TSE: NXY* ■ *Web:* www.nexeninc.com	Calgary	AB	T2P3P7	403-699-4000	699-5800
Nexen Petroleum USA Inc 5601 Granite Pkwy Suite 1400 *Web:* www.nexen.com	Plano	TX	75024	972-450-4600	450-4729
NGAS Hunter LLC 120 Prosperous Pl Suite 201 *TF:* 800-977-2363 ■ *Web:* www.magnumhunterresources.com	Lexington	KY	40509	859-263-3948	263-4228
Niko Resources Ltd 400 3rd Ave SW Suite 4600 *TSE: NKO* ■ *Web:* www.nikoresources.com	Calgary	AB	T2P4H2	403-262-1020	263-2686
Noble Energy Inc 100 Glenborough Dr Suite 100 *NYSE: NBL* ■ *TF:* 800-220-5824 ■ *Web:* www.nobleenergyinc.com	Houston	TX	77067	281-872-3100	872-3111
North Coast Energy Inc 1 GOJO Plaza Suite 325 *TF:* 800-645-6427 ■ *Web:* www.northcoastenergy.com	Akron	OH	44311	330-572-8500	252-0199
NW Natural 220 NW 2nd Ave PO Box 6017 **Fax:* Cust Svc ■ *TF:* 800-422-4012 ■ *Web:* www.nwnatural.com	Portland	OR	97209	503-226-4211	721-2517*
Occidental Oil & Gas Corp 5 Greenway Plaza Suite 110 *Web:* www.oxy.com	Houston	TX	77046	713-215-7000	215-7201
Occidental Petroleum Corp 10889 Wilshire Blvd *NYSE: OXY* ■ *TF:* 800-752-5151 ■ *Web:* www.oxy.com	Los Angeles	CA	90024	310-208-8800	443-6690
Ohio Gas Co PO Box 528 *TF:* 800-331-7396 ■ *Web:* www.ohiogas.com	Bryan	OH	43506	419-636-1117	636-9837
Oxbow Carbon & Minerals Inc 1601 Forum Pl Suite 1400 *Web:* www.oxbow.com	West Palm Beach	FL	33401	561-697-4300	640-8727

				Phone	Fax
Penn Virginia Corp 100 Matsonford Rd Suite 200	Radnor	PA	19087	610-687-8900	687-3688
NYSE: PVA ■ *Web:* www.pennvirginia.com					
Penn West Petroleum Ltd 9th Ave SW Suite 200	Calgary	AB	T2P1K3	403-777-2500	777-2699
TSE: PWT ■ *TF:* 866-693-2707 ■ *Web:* www.pennwest.com					
Petrobras USA 10350 Richmond Ave Suite 1400	Houston	TX	77042	713-808-2000	808-2017
Web: www.petrobras.com					
Petrohawk Energy Corp					
1100 Louisiana Suite 5600	Houston	TX	77002	832-204-2700	204-2800
NYSE: HK ■ *Web:* www.petrohawk.com					
Petroleum Development Corp 103 E Main St	Bridgeport	WV	26330	304-842-6256	842-0913
NASDAQ: PETD ■ *TF:* 800-624-3821 ■ *Web:* www.petd.com					
Petrominerals Corp 1221 Puerta Del Sol	San Clemente	CA	92673	949-366-3888	366-3889
Pioneer Natural Resources Co					
303 W Wall St Suite 101	Midland	TX	79701	432-683-4768	571-5063
NYSE: PXD ■ *TF:* 800-532-5291					
Plains Exploration & Production Co					
700 Milam St Suite 3100	Houston	TX	77002	713-579-6000	239-6500*
NYSE: PXP ■ **Fax Area Code:* 832 ■ *TF:* 800-934-6083 ■ *Web:* www.plainsxp.com					
PrimeEnergy Corp 1 Landmark Sq Suite 1100	Stamford	CT	06901	203-358-5700	358-5786
NASDAQ: PNRG ■ *Web:* www.primeenergy.com					
Range Resources Corp					
100 Throckmorton St Suite 1200	Fort Worth	TX	76102	817-870-2601	869-9100
NYSE: RRC ■ *Web:* www.rangeresources.com					
Read & Stevens Inc					
400 N Pennsylvania St Suite 1000	Roswell	NM	88201	505-622-3770	622-8643
RL Adkins Corp 301 Oak St	Sweetwater	TX	79556	325-235-4316	235-3460
Web: www.adkinssupply.com					
Saint Mary Land & Exploration Co (SM)					
1775 Sherman St Suite 1200	Denver	CO	80203	303-861-8140	861-0934
NYSE: SM ■ *TF:* 866-740-3117 ■ *Web:* www.sm-energy.com					
Samson Energy Co LP 2 W 2nd St Samson Plaza	Tulsa	OK	74103	918-583-1791	591-1796
TF: 800-283-1791					
Samson Investment Co 2 W 2nd St	Tulsa	OK	74103	918-583-1791	591-1796
TF: 800-283-1791 ■ *Web:* www.samson.com					
Seaboard Oil Co 3100 N A St Bldg B Suite 200	Midland	TX	79705	432-684-7005	684-7060
Seneca Resources Corp					
1201 Louisiana St Suite 400	Houston	TX	77002	713-654-2600	654-2654
TF: 800-622-6695 ■ *Web:* www.nationalfuelgas.com					
Shell Canada Ltd 400 4th Ave SW	Calgary	AB	T2P0J4	403-691-3111	269-8031
Web: www.shell.ca					
Shell Oil Co 910 Louisanna St	Houston	TX	77002	713-241-6161	241-4044
TF: 888-467-4355 ■ *Web:* www.shellus.com					
Slawson Cos Inc 727 N Waco St Suite 400	Wichita	KS	67203	316-263-3201	268-0702
Web: www.slawsoncompanies.com					
SONDE Resources Corp 4th Ave SW Suite 3300	Calgary	AB	T2P2V6	403-294-1411	216-8551
TSE: SOQ ■ *Web:* www.sonderesources.com					
Southern Bay Energy LLC					
110 Cypress Stn Dr Suite 220	Houston	TX	77090	281-537-9920	537-8324
TF General: 800-249-8178 ■ *Web:* www.georesourcesinc.com					
Southwestern Energy Co					
2350 N Sam Houston Pkwy E Suite 300	Houston	TX	77032	281-618-4700	618-4757
NYSE: SWN ■ *TF:* 866-322-0801 ■ *Web:* www.swn.com					
Stelbar Oil Corp Inc					
1625 N Waterfront Pkwy Suite 200	Wichita	KS	67206	316-264-8378	264-0592
Stone Energy Corp 625 E Kaliste Saloom Rd	Lafayette	LA	70508	337-237-0410	232-8061
NYSE: SGY ■ *TF:* 800-551-3340 ■ *Web:* www.stoneenergy.com					
Storm Cat Energy Corp 1125 17th St Suite 2310	Denver	CO	80202	303-991-5070	991-5070
AMEX: SCU					
SulphCo Inc					
4333 W.Sam Houston Pkwy N. Suite 190	Houston	TX	77043	713-896-9100	896-8803
AMEX: SUF ■ *Web:* www.sulphco.com					
Suncor Energy Inc 150 - 6 Ave SW PO Box 2844	Calgary	AB	T2P2V5	403-296-8000	296-3030
NYSE: SU ■ *TF:* 800-558-9071 ■ *Web:* www.suncor.com					
Sunoco Inc 1735 Market St Suite LL	Philadelphia	PA	19103	215-977-3000	977-3409
NYSE: SUN ■ *TF:* 800-786-6261 ■ *Web:* www.sunocoinc.com					
Superior Well Services Inc					
121 Airport Professional Bldg	Indiana	PA	15701	724-465-8904	465-8907
TF: 888-465-8904 ■ *Web:* www.superiorwells.com					
Swift Energy Co 16825 Northchase Dr Suite 400	Houston	TX	77060	281-874-2700	874-2162*
NYSE: SFY ■ **Fax:* Hum Res ■ *TF:* 800-777-2412 ■ *Web:* www.swiftenergy.com					
Syntroleum Corp 5416 S Yale Ave Suite 400	Tulsa	OK	74135	918-592-7900	592-7979
NASDAQ: SYNM ■ *Web:* www.syntroleum.com					
Talisman Energy Inc 888 3rd St SW Suite 2000	Calgary	AB	T2P5C5	403-237-1234	237-1902
TSE: TLM ■ *Web:* www.talisman-energy.com					
Tengasco Inc 11121 Kingston Pk Suite E	Knoxville	TN	37934	865-675-1554	675-1621
AMEX: TGC ■ *TF:* 800-351-1111 ■ *Web:* www.tengasco.com					
THUMS Long Beach Co					
111 W Ocean Blvd Suite 800	Long Beach	CA	90802	562-624-3400	624-3295
Web: www.oxy.com					
Tidelands Oil Production Co					
301 E Ocean Blvd Suite 300	Long Beach	CA	90802	562-436-9918	495-1950
Toreador Resources Corp					
4809 Cole Ave Suite 108	Dallas	TX	75205	214-559-3933	559-3945
NASDAQ: TRGL ■ *TF:* 800-966-2141 ■ *Web:* www.toreador.net					
Tri-Valley Corp					
4550 California Ave Suite 600	Bakersfield	CA	93309	661-864-0500	864-0600
AMEX: TIV ■ *TF:* 800-579-9314 ■ *Web:* www.tri-valleycorp.com					
True Cos 455 N Poplar St PO Drawer 2360	Casper	WY	82602	307-237-9301	266-0252
Web: www.truecos.com					
Ultra Petroleum Corp					
363 N Sam Houston Pkwy E Suite 1200	Houston	TX	77060	281-876-0120	876-2831
AMEX: UPL ■ *Web:* www.ultrapetroleum.com					
Unit Corp 7130 S Lewis Ave Suite 1000	Tulsa	OK	74136	918-493-7700	493-7711
NYSE: UNT ■ *TF:* 800-722-3612 ■ *Web:* www.unitcorp.com					
W & T Offshore Inc 9 Greenway Plaza Suite 300	Houston	TX	77046	713-626-8525	626-8527
Web: www.wtoffshore.com					
Wagner & Brown Ltd					
300 N Marienfeld St Suite 1100	Midland	TX	79701	432-682-7936	686-5928
TF: 800-777-7936					
Wagner Oil Co 500 Commerce St Suite 600	Fort Worth	TX	76102	817-335-2222	332-3876
TF: 800-457-5332 ■ *Web:* www.wagneroil.com					
Ward Petroleum Corp 502 S Fillmore PO Box 1187	Enid	OK	73702	580-234-3229	242-6850
Web: www.wardpetroleum.com					
Warren Resources Inc					
1114 Avenue of the Americas 34th Fl	New York	NY	10036	212-697-9660	697-9466
NASDAQ: WRES ■ *Web:* www.warrenresources.com					
Wexpro Co 180 E 100 S PO Box 45003	Salt Lake City	UT	84145	801-324-2534	324-2637
Web: www.questar.com					
Whiting Petroleum Corp					
1700 Broadway Suite 2300	Denver	CO	80290	303-837-1661	861-4023
NYSE: WLL ■ *Web:* www.whiting.com					
Wilshire Enterprises Inc					
100 Eagle Rock Ave Suite 100	East Hanover	NJ	07102	201-420-2796	420-6012
PINK: WOC ■ *TF:* 888-697-3962 ■ *Web:* www.wilshireenterprisesinc.com					
XTO Energy Inc 810 Houston St	Fort Worth	TX	76102	817-870-2800	870-1671
TF: 800-299-2800 ■ *Web:* www.xtoenergy.com					
Yates Petroleum Corp 105 S 4th St	Artesia	NM	88210	505-748-1471	748-4571*
**Fax:* Hum Res ■ *Web:* www.yatespetroleum.com					

540 OIL & GAS FIELD EQUIPMENT

				Phone	Fax
Alberta Oil Tool 9530 60th Ave	Edmonton	AB	T6E0C1	780-434-8566	436-4329
Web: www.albertaoiltool.com					
Baker Hughes Inc (BHI)					
2929 Allen Pkwy Suite 1200	Houston	TX	77019	713-439-8600	439-8699
NYSE: BHI ■ *TF:* 800-229-7447 ■ *Web:* www.bakerhughes.com					
Bolt Technology Corp 4 Duke Pl	Norwalk	CT	06854	203-853-0700	854-9601
AMEX: BTJ ■ *Web:* www.bolt-technology.com					
Carbo Ceramics Inc					
6565 N MacArthur Blvd Suite 1050	Irving	TX	75039	972-401-0090	401-0705
NYSE: CRR ■ *TF:* 800-551-3247 ■ *Web:* www.carboceramics.com					
Cooper Cameron Corp 1333 W Loop S Suite 1700	Houston	TX	77027	713-513-3300	513-3456
NYSE: CAM ■ *TF:* 800-654-3760 ■ *Web:* www.coopercameron.com					
Cuming Corp 225 Bodwell St	Avon	MA	02322	508-580-2660	580-0960
TF: 800-432-6464 ■ *Web:* www.cumingcorp.com					
Dril-Quip Inc 13550 Hempstead Hwy	Houston	TX	77040	713-939-7711	939-8063
NYSE: DRQ ■ *Web:* www.dril-quip.com					
Drillers Service Inc					
1792 Highland Ave NE PO Box 1407	Hickory	NC	28603	828-322-1100	322-7857
TF: 800-334-2308 ■ *Web:* www.dsidsi.com					
Driltech Mission LLC 13500 NW CR 235	Alachua	FL	32615	386-462-4100	462-4100
En-fab Inc 3905 Jensen Dr	Houston	TX	77026	713-225-4913	224-7937
Web: www.en-fabinc.com					
Flotek Industries Inc					
2930 W Sam Houston Pkwy N Suite 300	Houston	TX	77043	713-849-9911	896-4511
AMEX: FTK ■ *Web:* www.flotekind.com					
FMC Technologies Inc 1803 Gears Rd	Houston	TX	77067	281-591-4000	591-4102
NYSE: FTI ■ *TF:* 800-869-6999 ■ *Web:* www.fmctechnologies.com					
Gearench Inc 4450 S Hwy 6 PO Box 192	Clifton	TX	76634	254-675-8651	675-6100
TF: 800-221-1848 ■ *Web:* www.gearench.com					
George E Failing Co (GEFCO) 2215 S Van Buren St	Enid	OK	73701	580-234-4141	233-6807
TF: 800-759-7441 ■ *Web:* www.gefco.com					
Gulf Island Fabrication Inc					
567 Thompson Rd PO Box 310	Houma	LA	70361	985-872-2100	876-5414
NASDAQ: GIFI ■ *Web:* www.gulfisland.com					
Halliburton Energy Services					
10200 Bellaire Blvd	Houston	TX	77072	281-575-4400	575-5939
Web: www.halliburton.com					
Harbison-Fischer 901 N Crowley Rd	Crowley	TX	76039	817-297-2211	297-4248
TF: 800-364-7867 ■ *Web:* www.hfpumps.com					
IDM Equipment Ltd 11616 N Galayda St	Houston	TX	77086	281-447-2731	477-9077
Kimray Inc 52 NW 42nd St	Oklahoma City	OK	73118	405-525-6601	525-7520
Web: www.kimray.com					
LDI Industries Inc					
1864 Nage Ave PO Box 1810	Manitowoc	WI	54221	920-682-6877	684-7210
Web: www.ldi-industries.com					
Lufkin Industries Inc 601 S Raguet St	Lufkin	TX	75902	936-634-2211	637-5474
NASDAQ: LUFK ■ *Web:* www.lufkin.com					
M & M Supply Co 909 W Peach Ave PO Box 548	Duncan	OK	73534	580-252-7879	252-7708
TF: 800-404-7879 ■ *Web:* www.mmsupply.com					
Morris Industries Inc					
777 Rt 23 PO Box 278	Pompton Plains	NJ	07444	973-835-6600	835-7414
TF: 800-835-0777 ■ *Web:* www.morrispipe.com					
Morrison Bros Co 570 E 7th St	Dubuque	IA	52001	563-583-5701	583-5028
TF: 800-553-4840 ■ *Web:* www.morbros.com					
National Oilwell Varco Inc					
7909 Parkwood Cir Dr	Houston	TX	77036	713-375-3700	935-8233
NYSE: NOV ■ *TF:* 888-262-8645 ■ *Web:* www.nov.com					
Natural Gas Services Group Inc (NGSG)					
508 W Wall Suite 550	Midland	TX	79701	432-262-2700	262-2701
NYSE: NGS ■ *Web:* www.ngsgi.com					
Norriseal 11122 W Little York Rd	Houston	TX	77041	713-466-3552	896-7386*
**Fax:* Sales ■ *Web:* www.norriseal.com					
Omsco ShawCor 6418 Esperson St	Houston	TX	77011	713-844-3700	926-7103*
**Fax:* Sales ■ *TF:* 800-426-6726					

	City	State	Zip	Phone	Fax
Orbix Corp 4550 S Hwy 6	Clifton	TX	76634	254-675-8371	675-2747
Perry Equipment Corp 118 Washington Walters Industrial Pk	Mineral Wells	TX	76067	940-325-2575	325-4622
TF: 800-877-7326 ■ *Web:* www.pecousa.com					
Plant Process Equipment Inc 280 Reynolds Ave	League City	TX	77573	281-332-2589	332-6280
Web: www.plant-process.com					
Schramm Inc 800 E Virginia Ave	West Chester	PA	19380	610-696-2500	696-6950
Web: www.schramminc.com					
ShawCor Ltd 25 Bethridge Rd	Toronto	ON	M9W1M7	416-743-7111	743-7199
TSE: SCL.A ■ *TF:* 800-668-4842 ■ *Web:* www.shawcor.com					
Smeal Mfg Co 610 W 4th St	Snyder	NE	68664	402-568-2221	568-2223
Web: www.smealderricks.com					
Southern Co Inc 3101 Carrier St	Memphis	TN	38116	901-345-2531	345-3555
TF: 800-264-7626 ■ *Web:* www.socomemphis.com					
Southtex Treaters LP 13405 Hwy 191	Odessa	TX	79765	432-563-2766	563-1729
Web: www.southtex.com					
Stewart & Stevenson LLC 1000 Louisiana St	Houston	TX	77002	713-751-2600	751-2601
Web: www.ssss.com					
Stratco Inc 14821 N 73rd St	Scottsdale	AZ	85260	480-991-0450	991-0314
Web: www.stratco.com					
Tam International Inc 4620 Southerland Rd	Houston	TX	77092	713-462-7617	462-1536
TF: 800-462-7617 ■ *Web:* www.tamintl.com					
TD Williamson Inc (TDW) 6120 S Yale Suite 1700	Tulsa	OK	74136	918-447-5001	447-5050
TF: 888-839-6766 ■ *Web:* www.tdwilliamson.com					
Titan Specialties Inc 11785 Hwy 152 PO Box 2316	Pampa	TX	79066	806-665-3781	665-8882
TF Sales: 800-692-4486 ■ *Web:* www.titanspecialties.com					
TIW Corp 12300 S Main St PO Box 35729	Houston	TX	77035	713-729-2110	728-4767
Web: www.tiwtools.com					
Weatherford Artificial Lift Systems 918 Hodgkins St	Houston	TX	77032	281-449-1383	449-6235
Web: www.weatherford.com					
Weatherford International Inc 515 Post Oak Blvd Suite 600	Houston	TX	77027	713-693-4000	693-4313*
NYSE: WFT ■ **Fax:* Hum Res ■ *TF:* 800-257-3826 ■ *Web:* www.weatherford.com					
Winston F2S Corp 1604 Cherokee Trace	White Oak	TX	75693	903-757-7341	759-6986
TF: 800-527-8465 ■ *Web:* www.winstonf2s.com					

541 OIL & GAS FIELD EXPLORATION SERVICES

	City	State	Zip	Phone	Fax
Adams Resources Exploration Co 4400 Post Oak Pkwy Suite 2700	Houston	TX	77027	713-881-3600	881-3491
Anchor Gasoline 114 E 5th St	Tulsa	OK	74103	918-584-5291	583-6373
TF: 800-321-4086					
Arctic Slope Regional Corp 1230 Agvik St PO Box 129	Barrow	AK	99723	907-852-8633	852-5733
TF: 800-770-2772 ■ *Web:* www.asrc.com					
Arena Energy 4200 RES Forest Dr Suite 500	The Woodlands	TX	77381	281-681-9500	681-9503
Web: www.arenaenergy.com					
Atlas America Inc 1550 Coraopolis Heights Rd Suite 300	Moon Township	PA	15108	800-251-0171	262-7430*
NASDAQ: ATLS ■ **Fax Area Code:* 412 ■ *TF:* 800-251-0171 ■ *Web:* www.atlasamerica.com					
Baker Hughes Inc Baker Atlas Div 2001 Rankin Rd	Houston	TX	77073	713-625-4200	625-4525
Web: www.bakerhughes.com/bakeratlas					
Baker Hughes INTEQ 2001 Rankin Rd	Houston	TX	77073	713-625-4200	625-5200
Web: www.bakerhughes.com					
Bill Barrett Corp 1099 18th St Suite 2300	Denver	CO	80202	303-293-9100	291-0420
NYSE: BBG ■ *Web:* www.billbarrettcorp.com					
BP Prudhoe Bay Royalty Trust 101 Barclay St	New York	NY	10286	212-815-6908	815-2293
NYSE: BPT					
Breitburn Energy Partners LP 515 S Flower St Suite 4800	Los Angeles	CA	90071	213-225-5900	225-5916
NASDAQ: BBEP ■ *Web:* www.breitburn.com					
CAMAC Holdings Inc 1330 Post Oak Blvd Suite 2200	Houston	TX	77056	713-965-5100	965-5128
Web: www.camacholdings.com					
Central Resources Inc 1775 Sherman St Suite 2600	Denver	CO	80203	303-830-0100	830-9297
Web: www.centralresources.com					
Chaparral Energy Inc 701 Cedar Lake Blvd	Oklahoma City	OK	73114	405-478-8770	478-1947
TF: 800-314-0064 ■ *Web:* www.chaparralenergy.com					
Chevron Overseas Petroleum Co 6001 Bollinger Canyon Rd PO Box 6046	San Ramon	CA	94583	925-842-1000	842-1509
Concho Resources Inc 550 W Texas Ave Suite 100	Midland	TX	79701	432-683-7443	683-7441
NYSE: CXO ■ *Web:* www.conchoresources.com					
ConocoPhillips 600 N Dairy Ashford Rd	Houston	TX	77079	281-293-1000	
NYSE: COP ■ *TF:* 800-527-5476 ■ *Web:* www.conocophillips.com					
Danlin Industries Corp PO Box 307	Thomas	OK	73669	580-661-3248	661-3215
TF: 888-881-3248 ■ *Web:* www.danlin.us					
Dawson Geophysical Co 508 W Wall St Suite 800	Midland	TX	79701	432-684-3000	684-3030
NASDAQ: DWSN ■ *TF:* 800-332-9766 ■ *Web:* www.dawson3d.com					
Delta Petroleum Corp 370 17th St Suite 4300	Denver	CO	80202	303-293-9133	298-8251
NASDAQ: DPTR ■ *Web:* www.deltapetro.com					
Endeavour international corp 1001 Fannin Suite 1600	Houston	TX	77002	713-307-8700	
NYSE: END ■ *Web:* www.endeavourcorp.com					
Energy Partners Ltd 201 St Charles Ave Suite 3400	New Orleans	LA	70170	504-569-1875	569-1874
NYSE: EPL ■ *Web:* www.eplweb.com					

	City	State	Zip	Phone	Fax
EOG Resources Inc 1111 Bagby Sky Lobby 2	Houston	TX	77002	713-651-7000	651-6479
NYSE: EOG ■ *TF:* 877-363-3647 ■ *Web:* www.eogresources.com					
Equal Energy Ltd 500 4th Ave SW Suite 2700	Calgary	AB	T2P2V6	403-263-0262	294-1197
NYSE: ENT ■ *TF:* 877-263-0262 ■ *Web:* www.equalenergy.ca					
EXCO Resources Inc 12377 Merit Dr Suite 1700	Dallas	TX	75251	214-368-2084	368-2087
NYSE: XCO ■ *Web:* www.excoresources.com					
ExxonMobil Exploration Co 233 Benmar Dr Suite 10	Houston	TX	77060	713-656-3000	680-7436
Fidelity Exploration & Production Co 1700 Lincoln St Suite 2800	Denver	CO	80203	303-893-3133	893-1964
TF: 800-986-3133 ■ *Web:* www.fidelityepco.com					
GeoGlobal Resources Inc (GGR) 625 4th Ave SW Suite 200	Calgary	AB	T2P0K2	403-777-9250	777-9199
AMEX: GGR ■ *Web:* www.geoglobal.com					
Goodrich Petroleum Corp 333 Texas St Suite 1375	Shreveport	LA	71101	318-429-1375	429-2296
Web: www.goodrichpetroleum.com					
Great White Energy Services 14201 Caliber Dr Suite 300	Oklahoma City	OK	73134	405-285-5812	
Web: www.greatwhiteenergy.com					
GulfMark Energy Inc 4400 Post Oak Pkwy Suite 2700	Houston	TX	77027	713-881-3600	881-3491
Halliburton Energy Services 10200 Bellaire Blvd	Houston	TX	77072	281-575-4400	575-5939
Web: www.halliburton.com					
Hydro Aluminum Metal Products 999 Corporate Blvd Suite 100	Linthicum	MD	21090	410-487-4500	487-8053
Web: www.hydro.com					
Kennecott Exploration Co 224 N 2200 W	Salt Lake City	UT	84116	801-238-2400	238-2430
McMoRan Exploration Co 1615 Poydras St	New Orleans	LA	70112	504-582-4000	582-1847
NYSE: MMR ■ *TF:* 800-535-7094 ■ *Web:* www.mcmoran.com					
Mustang Fuel Corp 13439 Broadway Ext	Oklahoma City	OK	73114	405-748-9400	748-9200
TF: 800-332-9400 ■ *Web:* www.mustangfuel.com					
New Jersey Natural Gas Co 1415 Wyckoff Rd	Wall	NJ	07719	732-938-1480	938-3154
TF: 800-221-0051 ■ *Web:* www.njliving.com					
Northern Oil & Gas Inc 315 Manitoba Ave Suite 200	Wayzata	MN	55391	952-476-9800	476-9801
AMEX: NOG ■ *Web:* www.northernoil.com					
Occidental International Corp 1717 Pennsylvania Ave NW Suite 400	Washington	DC	20006	202-857-3000	857-3030
Web: www.oxy.com					
Occidental Petroleum Corp 10889 Wilshire Blvd	Los Angeles	CA	90024	310-208-8800	443-6690
NYSE: OXY ■ *TF:* 800-752-5151 ■ *Web:* www.oxy.com					
Panhandle Royalty Co 5400 N Grand Blvd Grand Centre Bldg, Suite 300	Oklahoma City	OK	73112	405-948-1560	948-2038
AMEX: PHX ■ *Web:* www.panhandleoilandgas.com					
Patterson-UTI Energy Inc 450 Gears Rd Suite 500	Houston	TX	77067	281-765-7100	765-7175
NASDAQ: PTEN ■ *TF:* 800-245-0167 ■ *Web:* www.patenergy.com					
Pearl Development Co 7110 W Jefferson Ave	Lakewood	CO	80235	303-984-8090	838-1630
Web: www.pearldc.com					
PetroQuest Energy Inc 400 E Kaliste Saloom Rd Suite 6000	Lafayette	LA	70508	337-232-7028	232-0044
NYSE: PQ ■ *TF:* 800-755-8381 ■ *Web:* www.petroquest.com					
Power Service Products Inc PO Box 1089	Weatherford	TX	76086	817-599-9486	599-4893
TF: 800-643-9089 ■ *Web:* www.powerservice.com					
Quicksilver Resources Inc 777 W Rosedale St Suite 300	Fort Worth	TX	76104	817-665-5000	665-5014
NYSE: KWK ■ *TF:* 877-665-8600 ■ *Web:* www.qrinc.com					
Rosetta Resources Inc 717 Texas Suite 2800	Houston	TX	77002	713-335-4000	335-4197
NASDAQ: ROSE ■ *TF:* 800-526-2112 ■ *Web:* www.rosettaresources.com					
Schlumberger Ltd 5599 San Felipe Suite 100	Houston	TX	77056	713-513-2000	513-2006
NYSE: SLB ■ *Web:* www.slb.com					
Seitel Inc 10811 S Westview Cir Dr Bldg C Suite 100	Houston	TX	77043	832-295-8300	295-8301
Web: www.seitel.com					
Slawson Cos Inc 727 N Waco St Suite 400	Wichita	KS	67203	316-263-3201	268-0702
Web: www.slawsoncompanies.com					
Statoil Marketing & Trading 120 Long Ridge Rd Suite 3E01	Stamford	CT	06902	203-978-6900	978-6952
Web: www.statoil.com					
Superior Energy Services Inc 601 Poydras St Suite 2400	New Orleans	LA	70130	504-587-7374	362-1818
NYSE: SPN ■ *TF:* 800-259-7774 ■ *Web:* www.superiorenergy.com					
TGC Industries Inc 101 E Pk Blvd Suite 955	Plano	TX	75074	972-881-1099	424-3943
AMEX: TGE ■ *TF:* 800-223-7470 ■ *Web:* www.tgcseismic.com					
Total E & P USA Inc 1201 Louisiana St Total Plaza Suite 1800	Houston	TX	77002	713-647-3000	647-3003
Web: www.total.com					
TransGlobe Energy Corp 250 5th St SW Suite 2300	Calgary	AB	T2P3H5	403-264-9888	770-8855
NASDAQ: TGA ■ *Web:* www.trans-globe.com					
VAALCO Energy Inc 4600 Post Oak Pl Suite 309	Houston	TX	77027	713-623-0801	623-0982
AMEX: EGY ■ *Web:* www.vaalco.com					
Veritas DGC Inc 10300 Townpark Dr	Houston	TX	77072	832-351-8300	351-8300
NYSE: VTS ■ *TF:* 800-344-4266					
Walter Oil & Gas Corp 1100 Louisiana St Suite 200	Houston	TX	77002	713-659-1221	756-1155
TF: 888-756-7880 ■ *Web:* www.walteroil.com					
WesternGeco 10001 Richmond Ave	Houston	TX	77042	713-789-9600	789-0172
Web: www.westerngeco.com					

	City	State	ZIP	Phone	Fax
Williams Energy Services 1 Williams Ctr PO Box 2400 *TF:* 800-945-5426 ■ *Web:* www.williams.com	Tulsa	OK	74102	918-573-2000	573-2296
Zion Oil & Gas Inc 6510 Abrams Rd Suite 300 *Web:* www.zionoil.com	Dallas	TX	75231	214-221-4610	221-6510

542 OIL & GAS FIELD SERVICES

SEE ALSO Oil & Gas Field Exploration Services p. 2325

	City	State	ZIP	Phone	Fax
Baker Hughes Inc (BHI) 2929 Allen Pkwy Suite 1200 *NYSE: BHI* ■ *TF:* 800-229-7447 ■ *Web:* www.bakerhughes.com	Houston	TX	77019	713-439-8600	439-8699
Baker Hughes Inc Baker Atlas Div 2001 Rankin Rd *Web:* www.bakerhughes.com/bakeratlas	Houston	TX	77073	713-625-4200	625-4525
Basic Energy Services Inc 500 W Illinois Suite 800 PO Box 10460 *NYSE: BAS* ■ *Web:* www.basicenergyservices.com	Midland	TX	79701	432-620-5500	570-0437
BJ Services Co 4601 W Way Pk Blvd PO Box 4442 *NYSE: BJS* ■ **Fax:* Hum Res ■ *TF:* 800-234-6487 ■ *Web:* www.bjservices.com	Houston	TX	77041	713-462-4239	895-5897*
Blarney Castle Oil Co 12218 W St Po Box 246 *Web:* www.blarneycastleoil.com	Bear Lake	MI	49614	231-864-3111	
Central Industries Inc 329 Westgate Rd PO Box 1380 *TF:* 800-326-3171	Lafayette	LA	70583	337-233-3171	234-4008
Colloid Environmental Technologies Co (CETCO) 1500 W Shure Dr *TF:* 800-527-9948 ■ *Web:* www.cetco.com	Arlington Heights	IL	60004	847-392-5800	577-6150
Core Laboratories 6316 Windfern Rd *NYSE: CLB* ■ *Web:* www.corelab.com	Houston	TX	77040	713-328-2673	328-2150
Crain Bros Inc 2715 Grand Chenier Hwy *TF:* 800-737-2767 ■ *Web:* www.crainbrothers.com	Grand Chenier	LA	70643	337-538-2411	538-2700
Danos & Curole Marine Contractors Inc 13083 Louisiana 308 *TF:* 800-487-5971 ■ *Web:* www.danos.com	Larose	LA	70373	985-693-3313	693-4698
Diamond Services Corp 503 S DeGravelle Rd *TF:* 800-879-1162 ■ *Web:* www.dscgom.com	Amelia	LA	70340	985-631-2187	631-2442
Evertson Well Service Inc PO Box 397 *Web:* www.evertson.com	Kimball	NE	69145	308-235-4871	235-4871
Fairweather LLC 9525 King St *TF:* 866-925-5161 ■ *Web:* www.fairweather.com	Anchorage	AK	99515	907-346-3247	349-1920
FESCO Ltd 1000 Fesco Ave *TF:* 800-375-3479 ■ *Web:* www.fescoinc.com	Alice	TX	78332	361-661-7000	661-7000
Gas Field Specialists Inc 2107 SR- 44 S *Web:* www.gfsinc.net	Shinglehouse	PA	16748	814-698-2122	698-2124
Global Industries Ltd 8000 Global Dr *NASDAQ: GLBL* ■ *TF:* 800-525-3483 ■ *Web:* www.globalind.com	Carlyss	LA	70665	337-583-5000	583-5100
Goodrich Petroleum Corp 801 Louisiana Suite 700 *NYSE: GDP* ■ *TF:* 800-256-2380 ■ *Web:* www.goodrichpetroleum.com	Houston	TX	77002	713-780-9494	780-9254
Gulfmark Offshore Inc 10111 Richmond Ave Suite 340 *NYSE: GLF* ■ **Fax Area Code:* 281 ■ *Web:* www.gulfmark.com	Houston	TX	77042	713-963-9522	664-5057*
Halliburton Energy Services 10200 Bellaire Blvd *Web:* www.halliburton.com	Houston	TX	77072	281-575-4400	575-5939
Hanover Inc 11000 Corporate Ctr Dr Suite 200 *TF:* 800-366-0980	Houston	TX	77041	281-854-3000	854-3195
Helix Energy Solutions Inc 400 N Sam Houston Pkwy E Suite 400 *NYSE: HELX* ■ *TF:* 888-345-2347 ■ *Web:* www.helixesg.com	Houston	TX	77060	281-618-0400	618-0500
Houma Industries PO Box 685 *TF:* 800-348-5340	Harvey	LA	70059	504-347-4585	348-4230
ICO Inc 1811 Bering Dr *TF:* 877-777-0877 ■ *Web:* www.icopolymers.com	Houston	TX	77057	713-351-4100	335-2201
Indel-Davis Inc 4401 S Jackson Ave *TF:* 800-331-6300 ■ *Web:* www.indel-davis.com	Tulsa	OK	74107	918-587-2151	446-1583
Key Energy Services Inc 6 Desta Dr Suite 4400 *Web:* www.keyenergy.com	Midland	TX	79705	432-620-0300	620-0307
Koch Specialty Plant Services 12221 E Sam Houston Pkwy N *TF:* 800-497-1789 ■ *Web:* www.kochservices.com	Houston	TX	77044	713-427-7700	427-7748
Matrix Service Co 5100 E Skelly Dr 74135 *NASDAQ: MTRX* ■ **Fax Area Code:* 918 ■ *TF:* 866-367-6879 ■ *Web:* www.matrixservice.com	Tulsa	OK	74135	866-367-6879	838-8810*
Milbar Hydro-Test Inc 651 Aero Dr *TF:* 800-259-8210 ■ *Web:* www.milbarhydro-test.com	Shreveport	LA	71107	318-227-8210	222-2558
Nabors Industries Ltd 515 W Greens Rd Suite 1200 *NYSE: NBR* ■ *TF:* 888-622-6777 ■ *Web:* www.nabors.com	Houston	TX	77067	281-874-0035	872-5205
Nabors Offshore Corp 515 W Greens Rd Suite 500 *Web:* www.nabors.com	Houston	TX	77067	281-874-0406	872-5205
Newcomb Oil Co LLC 1360 E John Rowan Blvd *Web:* www.newcomboil.com	Bardstown	KY	40004	502-348-3961	348-6346
Newpark Mats & Integrated Services LLC 2700 Research Forest Dr Suite 100 **Fax Area Code:* 337 ■ *TF:* 877-628-7623 ■ *Web:* www.newparkmats.com	The Woodlands	TX	77381	281-362-6800	984-4445*
Newpark Resources Inc 3850 N Cswy Blvd Suite 1770 *NYSE: NR* ■ *Web:* www.newpark.com	Metairie	LA	70002	504-838-8222	833-9506
Oceaneering International Inc 11911 FM 529 *NYSE: OII* ■ *TF:* 800-527-1865 ■ *Web:* www.oceaneering.com	Houston	TX	77041	713-329-4500	329-4951
Oil States International Inc 333 Clay St Three Allen Ctr Suite 4620 *NYSE: OIS* ■ *Web:* www.oilstatesintl.com	Houston	TX	77002	713-652-0582	652-0499
Oil Well Service Co 1241 E Burnett St	Signal Hill	CA	90755	562-595-4501	424-8026
Peak Oilfield Services Co 2525 C St Suite 201 *Web:* www.peakalaska.com	Anchorage	AK	99503	907-263-7000	263-7041
Petrochem Field Services Inc PO Box 60047 *TF:* 800-255-4737 ■ *Web:* www.pfs-us.com	Houston	TX	77205	281-441-2550	441-2022
Pinnergy Ltd 111 Congress Ave Suite 2020 **Fax Area Code:* 903 ■ *Web:* www.pinnergy.com	Austin	TX	78701	512-343-8880	693-5401*
Pool Co Texas Ltd 5208 N Lovington Hwy PO Box 2545 *TF:* 800-299-1388	Hobbs	NM	88240	505-392-6591	392-3100
Pride International Inc 5847 San Felipe St Suite 3300 *NYSE: PDE* ■ *TF:* 800-645-2067 ■ *Web:* www.prideinternational.com	Houston	TX	77057	713-789-1400	789-1430
Production Management Industries LLC 9761 Hwy 90 E *TF:* 800-229-3837 ■ *Web:* www.pmi.net	Morgan City	LA	70380	985-631-3837	631-0729
Reliable Production Service Inc 1090 Cinclare Dr	Port Allen	LA	70767	225-343-3900	343-3200
RPC Inc 2801 Buford Hwy Suite 520 *NYSE: RES* ■ *Web:* www.rpc.net	Atlanta	GA	30324	404-321-2140	321-5483
Schlumberger Technology Corp 300 Schlumberger Dr **Fax:* Hum Res ■ *Web:* www.slb.com	Sugar Land	TX	77478	281-285-8400	285-8548*
Schlumberger Wireline & Testing 210 Schlumberger Dr **Fax:* Hum Res ■ *Web:* www.slb.com	Sugar Land	TX	77478	281-285-8500	285-8970*
Stewart & Stevenson LLC 1000 Louisiana St *Web:* www.ssss.com	Houston	TX	77002	713-751-2600	751-2601
Supreme Oil Co 2109 W Monte Vista Rd **Fax Area Code:* 602 ■ *TF:* 800-752-7888 ■ *Web:* www.supremeoil.com	Phoenix	AZ	85009	800-752-7888	258-8801*
T-3 Energy Services Inc 140 Cypress Stn Dr Suite 225 *NASDAQ: TTES* ■ **Fax Area Code:* 281 ■ *Web:* www.t3energy.com	Houston	TX	77090	713-996-4110	943-2042*
Team Inc 200 Hermann Dr *AMEX: TISI* ■ *TF:* 800-662-8326 ■ *Web:* www.teamindustrialservices.com	Alvin	TX	77511	281-331-6154	331-4107
Tiorco Inc 2422 S Trenton Way Unit H *TF:* 800-525-0578 ■ *Web:* www.tiorco.com	Denver	CO	80231	303-935-0046	935-1514
TK Stanley Inc 6739 Hwy 184 PO Box 31 *TF:* 800-477-2855 ■ *Web:* www.tkstanley.com	Waynesboro	MS	39367	601-735-2855	735-2857
Trican Well Service Ltd 645 7th Ave SW Suite 2900 *TSE: TCW* ■ *TF:* 877-587-4226 ■ *Web:* www.trican.ca	Calgary	AB	T2P4G8	403-266-0202	237-7716
Weatherford Completion Systems 11420 W Hwy 80 E *TF:* 800-777-7957 ■ *Web:* www.weatherford.com	Midland	TX	79711	432-563-7957	563-7956
Williams Energy Services 1 Williams Ctr PO Box 2400 *TF:* 800-945-5426 ■ *Web:* www.williams.com	Tulsa	OK	74102	918-573-2000	573-2296

543 OIL & GAS WELL DRILLING

	City	State	ZIP	Phone	Fax
Allis-Chalmers Energy Inc 11125 Equity Dr Suite 200 *NYSE: ALY* ■ *Web:* www.alchenergy.com	Houston	TX	77041	713-856-4222	856-4246
Applied Drilling Technology Inc 15375 Memorial Dr Suite A-200 *TF Cust Svc:* 800-990-2384 ■ *Web:* www.rigcentral.com	Houston	TX	77079	281-925-7100	925-7167
Atlantic Maritime Services Inc 2800 Post Oak Blvd Suite 5450 *Web:* www.rowaencompanies.com	Houston	TX	77056	713-621-7800	960-7560
Atwood Oceanics Inc 15835 Pk Ten Pl Dr Suite 200 *NYSE: ATW* ■ *TF:* 800-231-5924 ■ *Web:* www.atwd.com	Houston	TX	77084	281-749-7800	492-0345
Berenergy Corp PO Box 5850	Denver	CO	80217	303-295-2323	297-3752
Callon Petroleum Co 200 N Canal St *NYSE: CPE* ■ *TF:* 800-541-1294 ■ *Web:* www.callon.com	Natchez	MS	39120	601-442-1601	446-1410
Chesley Pruet 315 E Oak St Rm 100	El Dorado	AR	71730	870-863-7196	863-0077
Cyclone Drilling Inc 5800 Mohan Rd *TF:* 800-318-3724 ■ *Web:* www.cyclonedrilling.com	Gillette	WY	82718	307-682-4161	682-3158
Diamond Offshore Drilling Inc 15415 Katy Fwy *NYSE: DO* ■ *TF:* 800-848-1980 ■ *Web:* www.diamondoffshore.com	Houston	TX	77094	281-492-5300	492-5316
Doyon Drilling Inc 3201 C St Suite 700 *TF:* 800-478-9675 ■ *Web:* www.doyondrilling.com	Anchorage	AK	99503	907-563-5530	
Ensco International Inc 500 N Akard St Suite 4300 *NYSE: ESV* ■ *TF:* 800-423-8006 ■ *Web:* www.enscous.com	Dallas	TX	75201	214-397-3000	397-3376
Ensign Energy Services Inc 400 5th Ave SW Suite 1000 *Web:* www.ensignenergy.com	Calgary	AB	T2P0L6	403-262-1361	262-8215
GEO Drilling Fluids Inc 1431 Union Ave *TF:* 800-438-7436 ■ *Web:* www.geodf.com	Bakersfield	CA	93305	661-325-5919	325-5648
Halliburton Energy Services 10200 Bellaire Blvd *Web:* www.halliburton.com	Houston	TX	77072	281-575-4400	575-5939
Helmerich & Payne Inc 1437 S Boulder Ave *NYSE: HP* ■ *TF:* 800-331-7250 ■ *Web:* www.hpinc.com	Tulsa	OK	74119	918-742-5531	742-0237
Hercules Offshore Inc 9 Greenway Plaza Suite 2200 *NASDAQ: HERO* ■ *Web:* www.herculesoffshore.com	Houston	TX	77046	713-350-5100	350-5105

Phone Fax

Justiss Oil Co Inc 1120 E Oak St . . . . Jena LA 71342 318-992-4111 992-7201
TF: 800-256-2501 ■ *Web:* www.justissoil.com

Nabors Alaska Drilling Inc
2525 C St Suite 200 . . . . Anchorage AK 99503 907-263-6000 563-3734
Web: www.nabors.com

Nabors Drilling International Ltd
515 W Greens Rd Suite 1000 . . . . Houston TX 77067 281-874-0035 872-5205
TF: 877-622-6777 ■ *Web:* www.nabors.com/international

Nabors Drilling USA Inc
515 W Greens Rd Suite 1000 . . . . Houston TX 77067 281-874-0035 872-5205
TF: 888-622-6777 ■ *Web:* www.nabors.com/us

Nabors Industries Ltd
515 W Greens Rd Suite 1200 . . . . Houston TX 77067 281-874-0035 872-5205
NYSE: NBR ■ *TF:* 888-622-6777 ■ *Web:* www.nabors.com

Noble Corp
13135 S Dairy Ashford Rd Suite 800 . . . . Sugar Land TX 77478 281-276-6100 491-2092
NYSE: NE ■ *TF:* 800-231-6326 ■ *Web:* www.noblecorp.com

ONEOK Inc 100 W 5th St. . . . . Tulsa OK 74103 918-588-7000 588-7331*
**Fax: Hum Res* ■ *Web:* www.oneok.com

Parker Drilling Co
1401 Enclave Pkwy Suite 600 . . . . Houston TX 77077 281-406-2000 406-2001
NYSE: PKD ■ *TF:* 800-545-3645 ■ *Web:* www.parkerdrilling.com

Patterson Drilling Co PO Box 1416 . . . . Snyder TX 79550 325-574-6300 574-6390
TF: 800-245-0167

Patterson-UTI Energy Inc
450 Gears Rd Suite 500 . . . . Houston TX 77067 281-765-7100 765-7175
NASDAQ: PTEN ■ *TF:* 800-245-0167 ■ *Web:* www.patenergy.com

Pioneer Drilling Co
1250 NE Loop 410 Suite 1000 . . . . San Antonio TX 78209 210-828-7689 447-6080
AMEX: PDC ■ *Web:* www.pioneerdrlg.com

Range Resources Corp
100 Throckmorton St Suite 1200 . . . . Fort Worth TX 76102 817-870-2601 869-9100
NYSE: RRC ■ *Web:* www.rangeresources.com

Reliance Well Service PO Box 787 . . . . Magnolia AR 71754 870-234-2700 234-4776
TF: 800-458-6451

Ringo Drilling I LP PO Box 368 . . . . Tye TX 79563 325-695-5600 695-5639
Web: www.ringodrilling.com

Rowan International Inc
2800 Post Oak Blvd Suite 5450 . . . . Houston TX 77056 713-621-7800 960-7560
Web: www.rowancompanies.com

Scientific Drilling Controls Inc
1100 Rankin Rd . . . . Houston TX 77073 281-443-3300 443-3311
Web: www.scientificdrilling.com

Sperry Sun Drilling Services Inc
2819864400 3000 N Sam Houston Pkwy E . . . . Houston TX 77032 281-871-4000 871-5565*

Sst Energy Corp 8901 W Yellowstone Hwy . . . . Casper WY 82604 307-235-3529 473-1650
Web: www.sstenergy.com

Total Energy Services Ltd
2550, 300-5th Ave SW . . . . Calgary AB T2P3C4 403-216-3939 234-8731
TSX: TOT ■ *TF:* 877-818-6825 ■ *Web:* www.totalenergy.ca

Transocean Inc 4 Greenway Plaza . . . . Houston TX 77046 713-232-7500 232-7027
NYSE: RIG ■ *TF:* 888-748-6334 ■ *Web:* www.deepwater.com

Tri-Valley Corp
4550 California Ave Suite 600 . . . . Bakersfield CA 93309 661-864-0500 864-0600
AMEX: TIV ■ *TF:* 800-579-9314 ■ *Web:* www.tri-valleycorp.com

True Drilling LLC 455 N Poplar PO Drawer 2360 . . . . Casper WY 82602 307-237-9301 266-0373
Web: www.truecos.com/Drilling

Union Drilling Inc
4055 International Plaza Suite 610 . . . . Fort Worth TX 76109 817-735-8793 546-4368
NASDAQ: UDRL ■ *TF:* 800-352-3839 ■ *Web:* www.uniondrilling.com

Unit Corp 7130 S Lewis Ave Suite 1000 . . . . Tulsa OK 74136 918-493-7700 493-7711
NYSE: UNT ■ *TF:* 800-722-3612 ■ *Web:* www.unitcorp.com

Vantage Drilling Co
777 Post Oak Blvd Suite 800 . . . . Houston TX 77056 281-404-4700 404-4749
AMEX: VTG ■ *Web:* www.vantagedrilling.com

Vermilion Energy Trust 3500, 520 3rd Ave SW . . . . Calgary AB T2P0R3 403-269-4884 476-8100
TSE: VET.UN ■ *TF:* 866-895-8101 ■ *Web:* www.vermilionenergy.com

544 OILS & GREASES - LUBRICATING

SEE ALSO Chemicals - Specialty p. 1600; Petroleum Refineries p. 2413

Phone Fax

American Grease Stick Co
2651 Hoyt St. . . . . Muskegon Heights MI 49444 231-733-2101 733-1784
TF: 800-253-0403 ■ *Web:* www.agscompany.com

American Lubricants Co
1227 Deeds Ave PO Box 696 . . . . Dayton OH 45401 937-222-2851 461-7729

Amsoil Inc 925 Tower Ave . . . . Superior WI 54880 715-392-7101 392-5225
TF Sales: 800-777-7094 ■ *Web:* www.amsoil.com

Anderol Inc 215 Merry Ln PO Box 518 . . . . East Hanover NJ 07936 973-887-7410 887-8404
TF: 888-263-3765 ■ *Web:* www.anderol.com

Battenfeld Grease & Oil Corp of New York
1174 Erie Ave PO Box 728 . . . . North Tonawanda NY 14120 716-695-2100 695-0367
Web: www.battenfeld-grease.com

Bel Ray Co Inc PO Box 526 . . . . Farmingdale NJ 07727 732-938-2421 938-4232
Web: www.belray.com

Benz Oil Inc 2724 W Hampton Ave . . . . Milwaukee WI 53209 414-442-2900 442-8388
TF: 800-991-2369 ■ *Web:* www.benzoil.com

BG Products Inc 740 S Wichita St PO Box 1282 . . . . Wichita KS 67213 316-265-2686 265-1082
TF: 800-961-6228 ■ *Web:* www.bgprod.com

Blachford Corp 401 Ctr Rd . . . . Frankfort IL 60423 815-464-2100 464-2112
TF: 800-435-5942 ■ *Web:* www.blachford.com

Phone Fax

Bolton Oil Co Ltd 1316 54th St PO Box 3176 . . . . Lubbock TX 79412 806-747-1629
Web: www.boltonoil.com

BP Lubricants USA Inc 1500 Valley Rd . . . . Wayne NJ 07470 973-633-2200 633-9867
TF: 800-633-6163 ■ *Web:* www.bp.com

Break-Free Inc 13386 International Pkwy . . . . Jacksonville FL 32218 904-741-5400 741-5404
TF: 800-347-1200 ■ *Web:* www.break-free.com

Castrol Industrial North America Inc
150 W Warrenville Rd . . . . Naperville IL 60563 877-641-1600 648-9801
TF: 877-641-1600 ■ *Web:* www.castrol.com

Cenex (CHS) 5500 Cenex Dr . . . . Inver Grove Heights MN 55077 651-355-6000
TF: 800-232-3639 ■ *Web:* www.cenex.com

Chem-Trend LP 1445 McPherson Pk Dr . . . . Howell MI 48843 517-546-4520
TF: 800-727-7730 ■ *Web:* www.chemtrend.com

Colorado Petroleum Products Co
4080 Globeville Rd . . . . Denver CO 80216 303-294-0302 294-9128
TF: 800-580-4080 ■ *Web:* www.colopetro.com

Condat Corp 250 S Industrial Dr . . . . Saline MI 48176 734-944-4994 944-4995
TF: 800-883-7876 ■ *Web:* www.condatcorp.com

CRC Industries Inc 885 Louis Dr . . . . Warminster PA 18974 215-674-4300 674-2196
TF Cust Svc: 800-556-5074 ■ *Web:* www.crcindustries.com

D-A Lubricant Co 1340 W 29th St . . . . Indianapolis IN 46208 317-923-5321 923-3884*
**Fax: Cust Svc* ■ *TF:* 800-645-5823 ■ *Web:* www.dalube.com

Delta Petroleum Co 10352 River Rd . . . . Saint Rose LA 70087 504-467-1399 467-1398
Web: www.deltacompanies.net

Elco Corp 1000 Belt Line St . . . . Cleveland OH 44109 216-749-2605 749-7462
TF: 800-321-0467 ■ *Web:* www.elcocorp.com

Ergon Inc Petroleum Specialties Marketing Div
2829 Jakeland Rd PO Box 1639 . . . . Jackson MS 39215 601-933-3000 933-3373*
**Fax: Hum Res* ■ *TF:* 800-824-2626

Fiske Bros Refining Co 129 Lockwood St . . . . Newark NJ 07105 973-589-9150 589-4432
TF: 800-733-4755 ■ *Web:* www.lubriplate.com

Fuchs Lubricants Canada Ltd Eastern Canada Div
405 Dobbie Dr PO Box 909 . . . . Cambridge ON N1R5X9 519-622-2040 622-2220
Web: www.fuchs.ca

Fuchs Lubricants Co 17050 Lathrop Ave . . . . Harvey IL 60426 708-333-8900 333-9180
TF: 800-323-7755 ■ *Web:* www.fuchs.com

Hangsterfer's Laboratories Inc 175 Ogden Rd . . . . Mantua NJ 08051 856-468-0216 468-0200
TF: 800-433-5823 ■ *Web:* www.hangsterfers.com

Hercules Chemical Co Inc 111 S St . . . . Passaic NJ 07055 973-778-5000 777-4115
TF: 800-221-9330 ■ *Web:* www.herchem.com

Houghton International Inc
945 Madison Ave PO Box 930 . . . . Valley Forge PA 19482 610-666-4000 666-0174
TF: 888-459-9844 ■ *Web:* www.houghtonintl.com

Hydrotex Inc 12920 Senlac D Suite 190 . . . . Farmers Branch TX 75234 972-389-8500 389-8526
TF: 800-527-9439 ■ *Web:* www.hydrotexlube.com

Jackson Oil & Solvents Inc
1970 Kentucky Ave . . . . Indianapolis IN 46221 317-636-4421 685-2403
TF: 800-221-4603 ■ *Web:* www.jacksonoilsolvents.com

JD Streett & Co Inc 144 Weldon Pkwy . . . . Maryland Heights MO 63043 314-432-6600 432-4248
TF: 800-678-6600 ■ *Web:* www.jdstreett.com

Jesco Resources Inc
1440 Erie St PO Box 12337 . . . . North Kansas City MO 64116 816-471-4590 471-2240
Web: www.jescolube.com

Jet-Lube Inc 4849 Homestead Rd Suite 232 . . . . Houston TX 77226 713-670-5700 678-4604
TF: 800-538-5823 ■ *Web:* www.jetlube.com

Kluber Lubrication North America LP
32 Industrial Dr . . . . Londonderry NH 03053 603-647-4104 647-4106
Web: www.klueber.com

Leadership Performance Sustainability Laboratories
4647 Hugh Howell Rd . . . . Tucker GA 30084 770-934-7800 243-8899
TF: 800-241-8334 ■ *Web:* www.lpslabs.com

Lubricating Specialties Co
8015 Paramount Blvd . . . . Pico Rivera CA 90660 562-776-4000 776-4004
Web: www.lsc-online.com

Lubrication Engineers Inc 300 Bailey Ave . . . . Fort Worth TX 76107 817-834-6321 228-1142*
**Fax Area Code: 800* ■ **Fax: Sales* ■ *TF:* 800-537-7683 ■ *Web:* www.le-inc.com

Lubrication Technologies Inc
900 Mendelssohn Ave N . . . . Golden Valley MN 55427 763-545-0707 545-9256
TF: 800-328-5573 ■ *Web:* www.lube-tech.com

Lubrizol Corp 29400 Lakeland Blvd . . . . Wickliffe OH 44092 440-943-4200 347-3583
NYSE: LZ ■ *TF:* 800-522-4125 ■ *Web:* www.lubrizol.com

Master Chemical Corp
501 W Boundry St PO Box 10001 . . . . Perrysburg OH 43551 419-874-7902 874-0684
TF Sales: 800-874-6329 ■ *Web:* www.masterchemical.com

Metalworking Lubricants Co
25 Silverdome Industrial Pk . . . . Pontiac MI 48342 248-332-3500 332-4959
TF: 800-394-5494 ■ *Web:* www.metalworkinglubricants.com

Northland Products Co PO Box 418 . . . . Waterloo IA 50704 319-234-5585 234-5580
TF: 800-772-1724

Nye Lubricants Inc 12 Howland Rd . . . . Fairhaven MA 02719 508-996-6721 997-5285
Web: www.nyelubricants.com

Oil Center Research LLC 106 Montrose Ave . . . . Lafayette LA 70503 337-993-3559 993-3149
TF: 800-256-8977 ■ *Web:* www.oilcenter.com

Oil Chem Inc 711 W 12th St . . . . Flint MI 48503 810-235-3040 238-5260
Web: www.oilcheminc.com

Orelube Corp The 20 Sawgrass Dr . . . . Bellport NY 11713 631-205-9700 205-9797
TF: 800-645-9124 ■ *Web:* www.orelube.com

Primrose Oil Co Inc
11444 Benton Dr PO Box 29665 . . . . Dallas TX 75229 972-241-1100 241-4188
TF: 800-275-2772 ■ *Web:* www.primrose.com

Richards-Apex Inc 4202-24 Main St . . . . Philadelphia PA 19127 215-487-1100 487-3090
Web: www.richardsapex.com

Schaeffer Mfg Co Inc 102 Barton St . . . . Saint Louis MO 63104 314-865-4100 865-4107
TF Cust Svc: 800-325-9962 ■ *Web:* www.schaefferoil.com

Phone | Fax

Sentinel Lubricants Corp
15755 NW 15th Ave PO Box 694240 .... Miami FL 33269 305-625-6400 625-6565
TF: 800-842-6400 ■ *Web:* www.sentinelsynthetic.com

Shell Lubricants
2 Houston Ctr Plaza Level 1 909 Fannin St. .... Houston TX 77010 713-767-5400
TF Cust Svc: 800-281-2824 ■ *Web:* www.shell.us

Smitty's Supply Inc
63399 Hwy 51 N PO Box 530 .... Roseland LA 70456 985-748-9687 748-3004
TF: 800-256-7575 ■ *Web:* www.smittysinc.net

Southwestern Petroleum Corp PO Box 961005 .... Fort Worth TX 76161 817-332-2336 877-4047
TF: 800-877-9372 ■ *Web:* www.swepcousa.com

STP Products Mfg Co 1221 Broadway .... Oakland CA 94612 510-271-7000 832-1463
TF: 888-464-7871 ■ *Web:* www.stp.com

Sun Drilling Products Corp
503 Main St PO Box 129 .... Belle Chasse LA 70037 504-393-2778 391-1383
TF: 800-962-6490 ■ *Web:* www.sundrilling.com

Texas Refinery Corp 840 N Main St .... Fort Worth TX 76106 817-332-1161 336-8441
TF: 800-827-0711 ■ *Web:* www.texasrefinery.com

Total Lubricants USA 5 N Stiles St .... Linden NJ 07036 908-862-9300 862-1647
TF: 800-344-2241

Valvoline Co 3499 Blazer Pkwy PO Box 14000 .... Lexington KY 40509 859-357-7777 357-7918
TF: 800-354-9061 ■ *Web:* www.valvoline.com

WD-40 Co 1061 Cudahy Pl .... San Diego CA 92110 619-275-1400 275-5823
NASDAQ: WDFC ■ *TF:* 800-448-9340 ■ *Web:* www.wd40company.com

Wynn's Oil Co 1050 W 5th St .... Azusa CA 91702 626-334-0231
TF: 800-989-8363 ■ *Web:* www.wynnsusa.com

545 OPHTHALMIC GOODS

SEE ALSO Personal Protective Equipment & Clothing p. 2409

Phone | Fax

AAI Foster Grant
500 George Washington Hwy .... Smithfield RI 02917 401-231-3800 231-4625
TF: 800-388-0258 ■ *Web:* www.fostergrant.com

Aearo Co 5457 W 79th St .... Indianapolis IN 46268 317-692-6666 692-6772
TF: 800-327-3431 ■ *Web:* www.aearo.com

Art Optical Contact Lens Inc
PO Box 1848 .... Grand Rapids MI 49501 616-453-1888 453-8702
Web: www.artoptical.com

Art-Craft Optical Co Inc 57 Goodway Dr S .... Rochester NY 14623 585-546-6640 546-5133
TF: 800-828-8288 ■ *Web:* www.artcraftoptical.com

Bausch & Lomb Inc 1 Bausch & Lomb Pl .... Rochester NY 14604 585-338-6000 338-6007
TF: 800-344-8815 ■ *Web:* www.bausch.com

Bausch & Lomb Inc Vision Care Div
1400 N Goodman St .... Rochester NY 14609 585-338-6000 338-6896
TF: 800-344-8815

Beitler-Mckee Optical Co 160 S 22nd St .... Pittsburgh PA 15203 412-481-4700
TF: 800-989-4700 ■ *Web:* www.beitlermckee.com

Bolle Inc 9200 Cody St .... Overland Park KS 66214 913-752-3400 752-3550
TF: 800-222-6553 ■ *Web:* www.bolle.com

Carl Zeiss Optical Inc 13005 N Kingston Ave .... Chester VA 23836 804-530-8300 561-2016*
**Fax Area Code:* 800 ■ *TF:* 800-338-2984 ■ *Web:* www.zeiss.com

Carskadden Optical Co 1525 Highpoint Ct .... Zanesville OH 43701 740-452-9306 452-6119

Charmant USA 400 American Rd .... Morris Plains NJ 07950 973-538-1511 248-1524*
**Fax Area Code:* 800 ■ *TF:* 800-645-2121 ■ *Web:* www.charmant.com

CIBA Vision Corp 11460 Johns Creek Pkwy .... Duluth GA 30097 770-476-3937 242-5214
TF: 800-227-1524 ■ *Web:* www.cibavision.com

Conforma Laboratories Inc 4705 Colley Ave .... Norfolk VA 23508 757-321-0200 321-0201
TF: 800-426-1700 ■ *Web:* www.conforma.com

Cooper Cos Inc
6140 Stoneridge Mall Rd Suite 590 .... Pleasanton CA 94588 925-460-3600 460-3649
NYSE: COO ■ *TF:* 888-822-2660 ■ *Web:* www.coopercos.com

CooperVision Inc 370 Woodcliff Dr Suite 200 .... Fairport NY 14450 858-385-6810
TF: 800-538-7850 ■ *Web:* www.coopercos.com

Costa Del Mar 123 N Orchard St Bldg 6 .... Ormond Beach FL 32174 386-677-3700 677-3737
TF: 800-447-3700 ■ *Web:* www.costadelmar.com

Cumberland Optical Laboratory
806 Olympic St .... Nashville TN 37203 615-254-5868 254-5868
TF: 800-888-8316

DAC Vision 3630 W Miller Suite 350 .... Garland TX 75041 972-677-2700 677-2800
TF: 800-800-1550 ■ *Web:* www.dacvision.com

Dakota Smith Signature Eyewear
498 N Oak St .... Inglewood CA 90302 310-330-2700 330-2748
TF: 800-765-3937 ■ *Web:* www.signatureeyewear.com

De'Vons Optics Inc 10823 Bell Ct .... Rancho Cucamonga CA 91730 909-466-4700 466-4703
TF: 888-333-8667

Dispensers Optical Service Corp
1815 Plantside Dr .... Louisville KY 40299 502-491-3440 491-3440
TF Cust Svc: 800-626-4545

Duffens Langley Optical Co 8140 Marshall Dr .... Lenexa KS 66214 913-492-5379 888-5375*
**Fax Area Code:* 800 ■ *TF:* 800-888-5379

Essilor of America Inc 13515 N Stemmons Fwy .... Dallas TX 75234 214-496-4000
TF: 800-366-6342 ■ *Web:* www.essilorusa.com

Eye-Kraft Optical Inc 8 McLeland Rd .... Saint Cloud MN 56303 320-251-0141 950-7070*
**Fax Area Code:* 800 ■ *TF:* 888-455-2022 ■ *Web:* www.eyekraft.com

Eyeglass Services Industries
469 Sunrise Hwy .... Lynbrook NY 11563 516-599-1135 599-4825

Eyetech 7016 6th St N .... Oakdale MN 55128 651-501-8114 501-8853
TF: 800-328-9060

Phone | Fax

Gargoyles Inc 500 George Washington Hwy .... Smithfield RI 02917 401-231-3800 232-7235
TF: 800-388-0258

Gentex Optics Inc 324 Main St .... Simpson PA 18407 570-282-3550 282-8555
TF: 800-343-6062 ■ *Web:* www.gentexcorp.com

Hilco USA 33 W Bacon St .... Plainville MA 02762 508-699-4406 995-2154*
**Fax Area Code:* 800 ■ *TF:* 800-955-6544 ■ *Web:* www.hilco.com

HL Bouton Co Inc 11 Kendrick Rd .... Wareham MA 02571 508-295-3300 295-3521
TF Cust Svc: 800-426-1881 ■ *Web:* www.hlbouton.com

Homer Optical Co Inc 2401 Linden Ln .... Silver Spring MD 20910 301-585-9060 585-5934
TF: 800-627-2710 ■ *Web:* www.homeroptical.com

Hoya Holdings Inc 3285 Scott Blvd .... San Jose CA 95054 408-654-2300 441-9400
Web: www.hoya.co.jp

Icare Industries Inc 4399 35th St N .... Saint Petersburg FL 33714 727-812-3000 522-1408
TF: 800-648-7463 ■ *Web:* www.icarelabs.com

IcareLabs 4399 35th St N .... Saint Petersburg FL 33714 727-812-3000 522-1408
TF: 800-648-7463 ■ *Web:* www.icarelabs.com

Johnson & Johnson Vision Care Inc (JNJVCI)
7500 Centurion Pkwy .... Jacksonville FL 32256 904-443-1000 443-1083
TF: 800-843-2020 ■ *Web:* www.jnjvisioncare.com

LBI Eyewear 20801 Nordhoff St .... Chatsworth CA 91311 818-407-1890 407-1895
TF Cust Svc: 800-423-5175 ■ *Web:* www.lbieyewear.com

Marchon Eyewear Inc 35 Hub Dr .... Melville NY 11747 631-755-2121 755-9157
TF: 800-645-1300 ■ *Web:* www.marchon.com

Maui Jim Inc 721 Wainee St .... Lahaina HI 96761 808-661-8841 661-0351
TF: 888-352-2001 ■ *Web:* www.mauijim.com

Oakley Inc 1 Icon .... Foothill Ranch CA 92610 949-951-0991 699-3519*
**Fax:* Cust Svc ■ *TF Cust Svc:* 800-431-1439 ■ *Web:* www.oakley.com

Omega Optical Co Inc 13515 N Stemmons Fwy .... Dallas TX 75234 972-241-4141 241-1162
TF: 800-366-6342

Orange 21 Inc 2070 Las Palmas Dr .... Carlsbad CA 92009 760-804-8420 804-8421
NASDAQ: ORNG ■ *TF:* 800-779-3937 ■ *Web:* www.orangetwentyone.com

Rosin Eyecare Ctr 6233 W Cermak Rd .... Berwyn IL 60402 708-749-2020 749-7944
Web: www.rosineyecare.com

Serengeti Eyewear Inc 9200 Cody St .... Overland Park KS 66214 913-752-3400 752-3550
TF Cust Svc: 800-423-3537 ■ *Web:* www.serengeti-eyewear.com

Signature Eyewear Inc 498 N Oak St .... Inglewood CA 90302 310-330-2700 330-2765
TF: 800-765-3937 ■ *Web:* www.signatureeyewear.com

Signet Armorlite Inc 130 N Bingham Dr .... San Marcos CA 92069 760-744-4000 471-6255
TF Cust Svc: 800-759-0075 ■ *Web:* www.signetarmorlite.com

SOLA Optical USA Inc 2277 Pine View Way .... Petaluma CA 94954 707-763-9911 765-1378

Southern Optical Co Inc 1909 N Church St .... Greensboro NC 27405 336-272-8146 273-6625
TF: 800-888-8842

STAAR Surgical Co 1911 Walker Ave .... Monrovia CA 91016 626-303-7902 303-2962*
NASDAQ: STAA ■ **Fax:* Mktg ■ *TF:* 800-292-7902 ■ *Web:* www.staar.com

Sun Rams Products Inc 8736 Lion St .... Rancho Cucamonga CA 91730 909-980-1160 941-0321

Transitions Optical Inc
9251 Belcher Rd .... Pinellas Park FL 33782 727-545-0400 546-3394
TF: 800-533-2081 ■ *Web:* www.en-us.transitions.com

US Vision Inc
1 Harmon Dr Glen Oaks Industrial Pk .... Glendora NJ 08012 856-228-1000 232-1848
TF: 800-524-0789 ■ *Web:* www.usvision.com

Vision-Ease Lens Inc 6975 Saukview Dr .... Saint Cloud MN 56303 320-251-8782 251-4312
TF Cust Svc: 800-367-2544 ■ *Web:* www.vision-ease.com

Viva International Group 3140 Rt 22 W .... Branchburg NJ 08876 908-595-6200 884-2329*
**Fax Area Code:* 800 ■ *TF:* 800-345-8482 ■ *Web:* www.vivagroup.com

Walman Optical Co Inc 801 12th Ave N .... Minneapolis MN 55411 612-520-6000 520-6069
TF: 800-873-9256 ■ *Web:* www.walman.com

X-Cel Optical Co Inc 806 S Benton Dr .... Sauk Rapids MN 56379 320-251-8404 251-0511
TF: 800-747-9235 ■ *Web:* www.x-celoptical.com

Younger Optics 2925 California St .... Torrance CA 90503 310-783-1533 783-6477
TF: 800-366-5367 ■ *Web:* www.youngeroptics.com

546 OPTICAL GOODS STORES

Phone | Fax

Bard Optical 7722 N Crestline Dr .... Peoria IL 61615 309-693-9540 693-9542
TF: 800-752-3295 ■ *Web:* www.bardoptical.com

Cliff Weil Inc 8043 Industrial Pk Rd .... Mechanicsville VA 23116 804-746-1321 746-2595
TF: 800-446-9345 ■ *Web:* www.cliffweil.com

Co/op Optical Vision Designs
2424 E Eight-Mile .... Detroit MI 48234 313-366-5100 366-7313
TF: 866-733-2667 ■ *Web:* www.coopoptical.com

Colonial Opticians 4942 St Elmo Ave .... Bethesda MD 20814 301-657-3332 657-4092

Consolidated Vision Group Inc
7255 N Crescent Blvd .... Pennsauken NJ 08110 856-486-4300 486-9615
TF: 800-896-7247 ■ *Web:* www.twopair.com

Crown Vision Ctr 211 E Broadway .... Alton IL 62002 314-741-8183
Web: www.crownvisioncenter.com

DOC Optics Corp 19800 W Eight-Mile Rd .... Southfield MI 48075 248-354-7100 353-1603
TF: 800-289-3937 ■ *Web:* www.docoptics.com

Doctors Vision Ctr 413 Mill St .... Rocky Mount NC 27804 252-442-0802 442-2820
Web: www.doctorsvisioncenter.com

Dr Bizer's Vision World
1030 Veterans Pkwy .... Clarksville IN 47129 812-282-2020 288-2807

Dr Tavel Optical Group
2839 Lafayette Rd .... Indianapolis IN 46222 317-924-1300 924-3741
Web: www.taveloptical.com

Phone | Fax

Emerging Vision Inc 520 Eighth Ave 23rd Fl .... New York NY 10018 646-737-1500
Web: www.emergingvision.com

Empire Vision Centers 2921 Erie Blvd E .... Syracuse NY 13224 315-446-5120
TF: 877-446-3145 ■ *Web:* www.empirevision.com

Europtics Inc 2960 E 2nd Ave Suite C.................. Denver CO 80206 303-322-7507 322-7591
TF: 888-322-4521 ■ *Web:* www.eoptics.com

Exact Eye Care 431 Pierce St .... Sioux City IA 51101 712-252-4691 252-5339
Web: www.exacteyecare.com

Eye Care Centers of America Inc
11103 W Ave .... San Antonio TX 78213 210-340-3531 524-6784
TF: 800-669-1183 ■ *Web:* www.ecca.com

Eye Glass World Inc 3801 S Congress Ave .... Lake Worth FL 33461 561-965-9110 969-7840*
**Fax:* Hum Res ■ *TF:* 800-529-4345 ■ *Web:* www.eyeglassworld.com

Eye To Eye Vision Ctr
2255 Sewell Mill Rd Suite 310....................... Marietta GA 30062 770-578-1900 578-6623
Web: www.eyetoeyevisioncenter.com

Eye-Mart Express Inc
2110 Hutton Dr Suite 100......................... Carrollton TX 75006 972-488-2002 488-8563
TF: 800-755-3936 ■ *Web:* www.eyemartexpress.com

Eye-Mate Inc 77 N Centre Ave................. Rockville Centre NY 11570 516-678-9613 678-0626
TF: 800-393-6283 ■ *Web:* www.eyemate.com

For Eyes/Insight Optical 285 W 74th Pl .... Hialeah FL 33014 305-557-9004 556-2575
TF: 800-367-3937 ■ *Web:* www.foreyes.com

General Vision Services LLC
520 8th Ave 9th Fl .... New York NY 10018 212-594-2580 967-4781
TF: 800-847-4661 ■ *Web:* www.generalvision.com

H Rubin Vision Centers
7539 Garners Sperry Rd .... Columbia SC 29209 803-779-9313 779-9551*
**Fax:* Cust Svc ■ *Web:* www.hrubinvision.com

Henry Ford OptimEyes
655 W 13-Mile Rd .... Madison Heights MI 48071 248-588-9300 588-3355
TF: 800-393-2273 ■ *Web:* www.henryfordoptimeyes.com

Horner-Rausch Optical 968 Main St .... Nashville TN 37206 615-226-0251 226-8527

JC Penney Optical Co 6501 Legacy Dr .... Plano TX 75024 972-431-1000 431-1362
NYSE: JCP ■ *Web:* www.jcpeyes.com

LensCrafters Inc 4000 Luxottica Pl..................... Mason OH 45040 513-765-4321
TF: 877-753-6727 ■ *Web:* www.lenscrafters.com

Lockport Optical 36 E Ave .... Lockport NY 14094 716-434-6900 434-8461

Magnifying Ctr 10086 W McNab Rd .... Tamarac FL 33321 954-722-1580 726-1757
TF: 800-364-1612 ■ *Web:* www.magnifyingcenter.com

Malbar Vision Ctr 409 N 78th St .... Omaha NE 68114 402-393-4500 393-7457
TF: 800-701-3937 ■ *Web:* www.malbar.com

National Vision Inc 296 Grayson Hwy .... Lawrenceville GA 30045 770-822-3600 822-3601
TF Cust Svc: 800-637-3597 ■ *Web:* www.nationalvision.com

OptiCare Health Systems Inc
87 Grandview Ave.............................. Waterbury CT 06708 203-574-2020 596-2230
TF: 800-225-5393 ■ *Web:* www.opticare.com

Palmetto Optical 5115 Forest Dr Suite B-160 .... Columbia SC 29206 803-799-8168 799-0854
TF: 800-845-2231

Pearle Vision Inc 4000 Luxottica Pl .... Mason OH 45040 877-486-6486 486-3596*
**Fax Area Code:* 330 ■ *TF:* 800-282-3931 ■ *Web:* www.pearlevision.com

ProCare Vision Centers Inc
1949 Newark-Granville Rd .... Granville OH 43023 740-587-3937 587-3589
TF: 800-837-5569

Raymond Opticians Inc 359 E Main St .... Mount Kisco NY 10549 914-666-4202 244-1542

Rite-Style Optical Co 12240 Emmet St .... Omaha NE 68164 402-492-8822 492-9414
TF: 800-373-3200

Rosin Eyecare Ctr 6233 W Cermak Rd................. Berwyn IL 60402 708-749-2020 749-7944
Web: www.rosineyecare.com

Rubold Management Co 3102 Millwood Ave .... Columbia SC 29205 803-251-3308 251-3303*
**Fax:* Cust Svc ■ *Web:* www.primecarevision.com

Rx Optical 1700 S Pk St......................... Kalamazoo MI 49001 269-342-0003 342-4284
TF: 800-792-2737 ■ *Web:* www.rxoptical.com

Saint Charles Vision 840 St Charles Ave........... New Orleans LA 70118 504-522-0826 866-8217
Web: www.stcharlesvision.com

ShopKo Optical Centers 1450 W Main Ave............. De Pere WI 54115 920-429-7200 429-7889
Web: www.shopko.com

Singer Specs 211 W Lincoln Hwy .... Exton PA 19341 610-524-8886 524-7333

Stein Optical Express 825 W Mooreland Blvd......... Waukesha WI 53188 262-542-9885 542-4740
TF: 800-349-5120 ■ *Web:* www.ecca.com

Sterling Optical 520 Eighth Ave 23rd Fl .... New York NY 10018 516-390-2117 390-2183
Web: www.sterlingoptical.com

Sunglass Hut International Inc
4000 Luxottica Pl .... Mason OH 45040 513-765-6000 786-4327*
**Fax Area Code:* 800 ■ *TF:* 800-786-4527 ■ *Web:* www.sunglasshut.com

SVS Vision 140 Macomb Pl .... Mount Clemens MI 48043 586-468-7370 468-7682
TF: 800-225-3095 ■ *Web:* www.svsvision.com

Today's Vision 6970 FM 1960 W Suite A .... Houston TX 77069 281-469-2020 469-7531
Web: www.todaysvision.com

Total Vision Care 854 Plaza Blvd .... Lancaster PA 17601 717-295-3111 295-7320

Union Eyecare Centers 4750 Beidler Rd .... Willoughby OH 44094 216-986-9700 986-1996
TF: 800-443-9699 ■ *Web:* www.unioneyecare.com

United Optical 2811 Lord Baltimore Dr................ Baltimore MD 21244 888-267-8422 265-6068*
**Fax Area Code:* 410 ■ *TF:* 888-267-8422 ■ *Web:* www.united-optical.com

US Vision Inc
1 Harmon Dr Glen Oaks Industrial Pk................. Glendora NJ 08012 856-228-1000 232-1848
TF: 800-524-0789 ■ *Web:* www.usvision.com

Vision World 481 Sunrise Hwy .... Lynbrook NY 11563 516-599-1135 599-4825

547 OPTICAL INSTRUMENTS & LENSES

SEE ALSO Laboratory Analytical Instruments p. 2141

Phone | Fax

Allergan Inc PO Box 19534 .... Irvine CA 92623 714-246-4500 246-6987*
NYSE: AGN ■ **Fax:* Mail Rm ■ *TF:* 800-347-4500 ■ *Web:* www.allergan.com

American Technology Network Corp
1341 San Mateo Ave.................... South San Francisco CA 94080 650-875-0130
TF: 800-910-2862 ■ *Web:* www.atncorp.com

Phone | Fax

Applied Fiber Inc 1300 W Oakridge Dr.................. Albany GA 31707 229-888-3212 888-3119
TF: 800-226-5394 ■ *Web:* www.appliedfiber.com

Awareness Technology Inc PO Box 1679............ Palm City FL 34991 772-283-6540 283-8020
Web: www.awaretech.com

Axsys Technologies Inc
175 Capital Blvd Suite 103......................... Rocky Hill CT 06067 860-257-0200 594-5750
Web: www.axsys.com

B E Meyers & Co Inc 14540 NE 91st St .... Redmond WA 98052 425-881-6648 867-1759
TF: 800-327-5648 ■ *Web:* www.bemeyers.com

Bond Optics LLC 76 Etna Rd PO Box 422 .... Lebanon NH 03766 603-448-2300 448-5489
Web: www.bondoptics.com

Burris Co Inc 331 E 8th St.......................... Greeley CO 80631 970-356-1670 356-8702
TF: 888-228-7747 ■ *Web:* www.burrisoptics.com

Bushnell Corp 9200 Cody St .... Overland Park KS 66214 913-752-3400 752-3550
TF: 800-423-3537 ■ *Web:* www.bushnell.com

Carl Zeiss Inc 1 Zeiss Dr .... Thornwood NY 10594 914-747-1800 682-8296
Web: www.zeiss.com

Carl Zeiss Optical Inc 13005 N Kingston Ave .... Chester VA 23836 804-530-8300 561-2016*
**Fax Area Code:* 800 ■ *TF:* 800-338-2984 ■ *Web:* www.zeiss.com

CST/Berger Corp 255 W Fleming St .... Watseka IL 60970 815-432-5237 913-0049*
**Fax Area Code:* 800 ■ *TF:* 800-435-1859 ■ *Web:* www.cstberger.us

Deltronic Corp 3900 W Segerstrom Ave .... Santa Ana CA 92704 714-545-5800 545-9548
TF: 800-451-6922 ■ *Web:* www.deltronic.com

Directed Energy Solutions
890 Elkton Dr Suite 101 .... Colorado Springs CO 80907 719-593-7848 593-7846
Web: www.denergysolutions.com

DRS Sensors & Targeting Systems - Optronics Div
2330 Commerce Pk Dr NE Suite 2 .... Palm Bay FL 32905 321-984-9030 984-8746
Web: www.drs.com

Edmund Optics Inc 101 E Gloucester Pike .... Barrington NJ 08007 856-547-3488 573-6295
TF: 800-363-1992 ■ *Web:* www.edmundoptics.com

Exotic Materials Inc 36570 Briggs Rd................. Murrieta CA 92563 951-926-2994 926-1984
Web: www.exotic-eo.com

Fosta-Tek Optics Inc 320 Hamilton St.............. Leominster MA 01453 978-534-6511 537-2168
Web: www.fosta-tek.com

Fraser-Volpe Corp
Warminster Industrial Pk 1025 Thomas Dr........... Warminster PA 18974 215-443-5240 443-0966
Web: www.fraser-volpe.com

Fujinon Inc 10 High Pt Dr .... Wayne NJ 07470 973-633-5600 633-8818
TF: 800-490-0661 ■ *Web:* www.fujifilm.com

G-S Supplies 408 St Paul St...................... Rochester NY 14605 585-295-0250 232-3866
TF: 800-295-3050 ■ *Web:* www.gssupplies.com

General Scientific Corp
1201 M St SE Suite 120.......................... Washington DC 20003 202-547-4299 547-7550
Web: www.genscicorp.com

Hitachi High Technologies America Inc
10 N Martingale Rd Suite 500.................... Schaumburg IL 60173 847-273-4141 273-4407
Web: www.hii-hitachi.com

II-VI Inc 375 Saxonburg Blvd .... Saxonburg PA 16056 724-352-4455 360-5848
NASDAQ: IIVI ■ *Web:* www.ii-vi.com

Intevac Inc 3560 Bassett St...................... Santa Clara CA 95054 408-986-9888 986-8636*
NASDAQ: IVAC ■ **Fax:* Hum Res ■ *TF:* 800-468-3822 ■ *Web:* www.intevac.com

ITT Night Vision & Imaging
7635 Plantation Rd............................... Roanoke VA 24019 540-563-0371 362-4979
TF: 800-448-8678 ■ *Web:* www.nightvision.com

Janos Technology LLC 55 Black Brook Rd............... Keene NH 03431 603-757-0070 365-4596*
**Fax Area Code:* 802 ■ *TF:* 888-300-5056 ■ *Web:* www.janostech.com

JML Optical Industries Inc 820 Linden Ave .... Rochester NY 14625 585-342-8900 342-6125
TF Sales: 800-456-5462 ■ *Web:* www.jmloptical.com

Kollmorgen Corp Electro-Optical Div
50 Prince St .... NorthHampton MA 01060 413-586-2330 586-1324*
**Fax:* Sales ■ *Web:* www.eo.kollmorgen.com

LightPath Technologies Inc
2603 Challenger Tech Ct Suite 100 .... Orlando FL 32826 407-382-4003 382-4007
NASDAQ: LPTH ■ *Web:* www.lightpath.com

Lincoln Laser Co 234 E Mohave St.................... Phoenix AZ 85004 602-257-0407 257-0728
Web: www.lincolnlaser.com

Meade Instruments Corp 27 Hubble.................... Irvine CA 92618 949-451-1450 451-1460
NASDAQ: MEAD ■ *TF:* 800-626-3233 ■ *Web:* www.meade.com

Microvision Inc 6222 185th Ave NE .... Redmond CA 98052 425-415-6847 415-6600
NASDAQ: MVIS ■ *TF:* 888-822-6847 ■ *Web:* www.microvision.com

Newport Corp 1791 Deere Ave.......................... Irvine CA 92606 949-863-3144 253-1680*
NASDAQ: NEWP ■ **Fax:* Sales ■ *TF Sales:* 800-222-6440 ■ *Web:* www.newport.com

Ocean Optics Inc 830 Douglas Ave .... Dunedin FL 34698 727-733-2447 733-3962
Web: www.oceanoptics.com

Optical Gaging Products Inc 850 Hudson Ave........ Rochester NY 14621 585-544-0450 544-4998
Web: www.ogpnet.com

Parker Hannifin Corp Daedal Div
1140 Sandy Hill Rd.................................. Irwin PA 15642 724-861-8200 861-3300
TF: 800-245-6903 ■ *Web:* www.parker.com/daedal

PerkinElmer Inc 45 William St .... Wellesley MA 02481 781-237-5100 237-9386
NYSE: PKI ■ *Web:* www.perkinelmer.com

ProPhotonix Inc 32 Hampshire Rd .... Salem NH 03079 603-893-8778 893-5604
PINK: STKR ■ *TF:* 800-843-8011 ■ *Web:* www.prophotonix.com

Raytheon Canada Ltd 360 Albert St Suite 1640........... Ottawa ON K1R7X7 613-233-4121 233-1099
Web: www.raytheon.ca

Raytheon Network Centric Systems
2501 W University .... McKinney TX 75071 972-952-2000

Recon/Optical Inc 550 W NW Hwy................. Barrington IL 60010 847-381-2400 381-4987

Research Electro-optics Inc
5505 Airport Blvd .... Boulder CO 80301 303-938-1960 245-4396
Web: www.reoinc.com

Ross Optical Industries Inc
1410 Gail Borden Pl Suite A-3 .... El Paso TX 79935 915-595-5417 595-5466
TF: 800-880-5417 ■ *Web:* www.rossoptical.com

Santur Corp 40931 Encyclopedia Cir .... Fremont CA 94538 510-933-4100 656-7563
Web: www.santurcorp.com

Schott North America Inc 555 Taxter Rd.............. Elmsford NY 10523 914-831-2200 831-2201
Web: www.us.schott.com

Science & Engineering Services
6992 Columbia Gateway Dr .... Columbia MD 21046 443-539-0139 539-1757
Web: www.sesi-md.com

	City	State	ZIP	Phone	Fax
Seiler Instrument & Mfg Co Inc 170 E Kirkham Ave *TF:* 800-489-2282 ■ *Web:* www.seilerinst.com	Saint Louis	MO	63119	314-968-2282	968-2637
Servo Corp of America 123 Frost St *Web:* www.servo.com	Westbury	NY	11590	516-938-9700	938-9644
Stevens Water Monitoring Systems 12067 NE Glenn Widing Dr Suite 106 *TF:* 800-452-5272 ■ *Web:* www.stevenswater.com	Portland	OR	97220	503-469-8000	469-8100
Veeco Instruments Inc 1 Terminal Dr *NASDAQ: VECO* ■ *TF:* 888-248-3326 ■ *Web:* www.veeco.com	Plainview	NY	11803	516-677-0200	714-1200
Western Ophthalmics Corp 19019 36th Ave W Suite G **Fax Area Code:* 800 ■ *TF:* 800-426-9938 ■ *Web:* www.west-op.com	Lynnwood	WA	98036	425-672-9332	423-4284*
Xenonics Holdings Inc 3186 Lionshead Ave *OTC: XNNH* ■ *Web:* www.xenonics.com	Carlsbad	CA	92010	760-477-8900	477-8897
Zygo Corp Laurel Brook Rd *NASDAQ: ZIGO* ■ *TF:* 800-994-6669 ■ *Web:* www.zygo.com	Middlefield	CT	06455	860-347-8506	347-3968

548 ORGAN & TISSUE BANKS

	City	State	ZIP	Phone	Fax
Alamo Tissue Service Ltd 4414 Centerview St Suite 167 *TF:* 800-226-9091	San Antonio	TX	78228	210-738-2663	732-4263
AlloSource 6278 S Troy Cir *TF:* 888-873-8330 ■ *Web:* www.allosource.org	Centennial	CO	80111	720-873-0213	873-0212
AppTec Laboratory Services 2540 Executive Dr *TF:* 888-794-0077 ■ *Web:* www.apptec-usa.com	Saint Paul	MN	55120	651-675-2000	675-2005
Bio-Tissue 7000 SW 97th Ave Suite 211 *TF:* 888-296-8858 ■ *Web:* www.biotissue.com	Miami	FL	33173	305-412-4430	412-4429
Blood & Tissue Center of Central Texas 4300 N Lamar Blvd *Web:* www.bloodandtissue.org	Austin	TX	78756	512-206-1266	458-3859
Bone Bank Allografts 4808 Research Dr *TF Sales:* 800-397-0088 ■ *Web:* www.bonebank.com	San Antonio	TX	78240	210-696-7616	696-7609
Caitlin Raymond International Registry University of Massachusetts Medical Ctr 55 Lake Ave N *TF:* 800-726-2824 ■ *Web:* www.crir.org	Worcester	MA	01655	508-334-8969	334-8969
California Cryobank Inc 11915 Jake Range Ave *TF:* 800-231-3373 ■ *Web:* www.cryobank.com	Los Angeles	CA	90025	310-443-5244	208-8477
California Cryobank Inc 950 Massachusetts Ave *TF:* 888-810-2796 ■ *Web:* www.cryobank.com	Cambridge	MA	02139	617-497-8646	497-6531
California Cryobank Inc 700 Welch Rd Suite 103 *Web:* www.cryobank.com	Palo Alto	CA	94304	650-324-1900	324-1946
Community Tissue Services 3425 N 1st St Suite 103 *TF:* 800-201-8477 ■ *Web:* www.communitytissue.org	Fresno	CA	93726	559-224-1168	229-7217
Community Tissue Services 3573 Bristol Pike Suite 201 *TF:* 800-456-5445 ■ *Web:* www.communitytissue.org	Bensalem	PA	19020	215-245-4506	937-9858
Comprehensive Tissue Ctr 11402 University Ave 7415 Aberhart Ctr 1 *TF:* 866-407-1970	Edmonton	AB	T6G2J3	780-407-7510	407-7509
Cryobiology Inc 4830D Knightsbridge Blvd *TF:* 800-359-4375 ■ *Web:* www.cryobio.com	Columbus	OH	43214	614-451-4375	451-5284
Cryogenic Laboratories Inc 1944 Lexington Ave N *TF:* 800-466-2796 ■ *Web:* www.cryolab.com	Roseville	MN	55113	651-489-8000	489-8989
Doheny Eye & Tissue Transplant Bank 1127 Wilshire Blvd Suite 602 *Web:* www.dettb.org	Los Angeles	CA	90017	213-482-9355	482-9343
Donor Alliance Inc 720 S Colorado Blvd Suite 800-N *TF:* 888-868-4747 ■ *Web:* www.donoralliance.org	Denver	CO	80246	303-329-4747	321-1183
Gift of Hope Organ & Tissue Donor Network 425 spring lake Dr *TF:* 800-545-4438 ■ *Web:* www.giftofhope.org	Itasca	IL	60143	630-758-2600	
Gift of Life Donor Program 401 N 3rd St *TF:* 800-543-6391 ■ *Web:* www.donors1.org	Philadelphia	PA	19123	215-557-8090	
Idant Laboratories 350 5th Ave Suite 7120 *Web:* www.idant.com	New York	NY	10118	212-330-8500	330-8536
Indiana Organ Procurement Organization 3760 Guion Rd *TF:* 888-275-4676 ■ *Web:* www.iopo.org	Indianapolis	IN	46222	317-685-0389	685-1687
Interpore Cross International 181 Technology Dr *TF:* 800-722-4489 ■ *Web:* www.interpore.com/home.html	Irvine	CA	92618	949-453-3200	453-3225
Kentucky Organ Donor Affiliates (KODA) 106 E Broadway *TF:* 800-525-3456 ■ *Web:* www.kyorgandonor.org	Louisville	KY	40202	502-581-9511	589-5157
Legacy of Life 4804 Research Dr *TF:* 800-397-3077	San Antonio	TX	78240	210-696-7677	691-1472
LifeBanc 20600 Chagrin Blvd Suite 350 *TF:* 888-552-5433 ■ *Web:* www.lifebanc.org	Cleveland	OH	44122	216-752-5433	751-4204
LifeCell Corp 1 Millennium Way **Fax Area Code:* 908 ■ *TF:* 800-367-5737 ■ *Web:* www.lifecell.com	Branchburg	NJ	08876	800-226-2714	947-1089*
Lifeline of Ohio 770 Kinnear Rd Suite 200 *TF:* 800-525-5667 ■ *Web:* www.lifelineofohio.org	Columbus	OH	43212	614-291-5667	291-0660
LifeLink Tissue Bank 8510 Sunstate St *TF:* 800-683-2400 ■ *Web:* www.lifelinkfound.org/bank.asp	Tampa	FL	33634	813-886-8111	888-9419
LifeNet 1864 Concert Dr *TF:* 800-847-7831 ■ *Web:* www.lifenet.org	Virginia Beach	VA	23453	757-464-4761	301-6582
LifeShare of the Carolinas 5000 D Airport Ctr Pkwy *TF:* 800-932-4483 ■ *Web:* www.lifesharecarolinas.org	Charlotte	NC	28208	704-697-3303	512-3056
LifeShare Transplant Donor Services of Oklahoma 7200 N Broadway *TF:* 888-580-5680 ■ *Web:* www.lifeshareoklahoma.org	Oklahoma City	OK	73116	405-840-5551	840-9748
Lifesharing Community Organ & Tissue Donation 3465 Camino del Rio S Suite 410 *Web:* www.lifesharing.org	San Diego	CA	92108	619-521-1983	521-2833
Louisiana Organ Procurement Agency 4441 N I-10 Service Rd *TF:* 800-521-4483 ■ *Web:* www.lopa.org	Metairie	LA	70006	504-837-3355	837-3587
Mid-America Transplant Services 1139 Olivette Executive Pkwy *TF:* 888-376-4854 ■ *Web:* www.mts-stl.org	Saint Louis	MO	63132	314-991-1661	993-5179
Musculoskeletal Transplant Foundation 125 May St Suite 300 *Web:* www.mtf.org	Edison	NJ	08837	732-661-0202	661-2298
Nevada Donor Network Inc 2085 E Sahara Ave *Web:* www.nvdonor.org	Las Vegas	NV	89104	702-796-9600	796-4225
New England Organ Bank 60 1st Ave *TF:* 800-446-6362 ■ *Web:* www.neob.org	Waltham	MA	02451	617-244-8000	244-8755
New York Cryo 900 Northern Blvd Suite 230 *Web:* www.newyorkcryo.com	Great Neck	NY	11021	516-487-2700	487-2007
Northern California Transplant Bank 7700 Edgewater Dr Suite 526	Oakland	CA	94621	510-957-9595	957-9594
Northwest Tissue Ctr 921 Terry Ave *TF:* 800-858-2282 ■ *Web:* www.nwts.org	Seattle	WA	98104	206-292-1879	292-1873
NuMed Technologies Inc 7225 S 85th E Ave Suite 200 *TF:* 800-640-3131	Tulsa	OK	74133	918-249-2697	461-0682
OneLegacy Transplant Donor Network 221 S Figueroa St Suite 500 *TF:* 800-786-4077 ■ *Web:* www.onelegacy.org	Los Angeles	CA	90012	213-229-5600	229-5601
Regional Tissue Bank QEII Health Sciences Centre 5788 University Ave Rm 431 McKenzie Bldg Ctr *TF:* 800-314-6515 ■ *Web:* www.cdha.nshealth.ca/tissuebank/tissueBank.html	Halifax	NS	B3H1V7	902-473-4171	473-2170
Rocky Mountain Tissue Bank 2993 S Peoria St Suite 390 *TF:* 800-424-5169 ■ *Web:* www.rmtb.org	Aurora	CO	80014	303-337-3330	337-9383
RTI Donor Services Northeast Div 1 Edgewater Plaza Suite 704 *Web:* rtidonorservices.com	Staten Island	NY	10305	718-273-5913	226-1035
Rubinoff Bone & Tissue Bank 600 University Ave Mt Sinai Hospital Rm 539 *Web:* www.allograsttechnologies.com	Toronto	ON	M5G1X5	416-586-8870	586-4458
ScienceCare Inc 21410 N 19th Ave Suite 126 *TF:* 800-417-3747 ■ *Web:* www.sciencecare.com	Phoenix	AZ	85027	602-331-3641	331-4344
Sierra Eye & Tissue Donor Services 1760 Creekside Oak Dr Suite 160 *TF:* 800-762-8819 ■ *Web:* www.dcids.org/sierra.htm	Sacramento	CA	95833	916-569-0200	569-0300
South Texas Blood & Tissue Ctr 6211 IH-10 W *TF:* 800-292-5534 ■ *Web:* www.bloodntissue.org	San Antonio	TX	78201	210-731-5555	731-5501
Southeast Tissue Alliance (SETA) 6241 NW 23rd St Suite 400 *TF:* 866-432-1164 ■ *Web:* www.donorcare.org	Gainesville	FL	32653	352-248-2114	384-9323
Tennessee/DCI Donor Services 1600 Hayes St *TF:* 888-234-4440 ■ *Web:* www.donatelifetn.org	Nashville	TN	37203	615-234-5251	234-5270
Tissue Banks International (TBI) 815 Pk Ave *TF:* 800-756-4824 ■ *Web:* www.tbionline.org	Baltimore	MD	21201	410-752-3800	783-0183
Transplant Services Center University of Texas 5323 Harry Hines Blvd MC 9074 *TF:* 800-433-6667	Dallas	TX	75390	214-648-2609	648-2086
University of California San Francisco Tissue Bank 3924 Williams Rd Suite 201 *TF:* 800-553-5536	San Jose	CA	95117	408-345-3515	345-3520
Wright Medical Technology Inc 5677 Airline Rd **Fax:* Cust Svc ■ *TF:* 800-238-7188 ■ *Web:* www.wmt.com	Arlington	TN	38002	901-867-9971	867-9534*

549 PACKAGE DELIVERY SERVICES

	City	State	ZIP	Phone	Fax
Air Courier Dispatch 1395 S Marietta Pkwy Bldg 200 Suite 222 *TF:* 800-257-7162	Marietta	GA	30067	770-933-9496	933-9598
Air T Inc 3524 Airport Rd *NASDAQ: AIRT* ■ *Web:* www.airt.net/mac	Maiden	NC	28650	828-464-8741	465-5281
AirNet Systems Inc 7250 Star Check Dr *AMEX: ANS* ■ **Fax Area Code:* 800 ■ **Fax:* Hum Res ■ *TF:* 800-477-6257 ■ *Web:* www.airnet.com	Columbus	OH	43217	614-409-4900	432-1580*
Careful Courier Service Inc 2444 Old Middlefield Way *Web:* www.carefulcourier.com	Mountain View	CA	94043	650-903-9393	903-9397
Central Delivery Service 6501 Virginia Manor Rd *TF:* 800-938-4151 ■ *Web:* www.centraldelivery.com	Beltsville	MD	20705	301-210-0100	210-1223
Columbia Fruit Packers Inc 2575 Euclid Ave PO Box 920 *Web:* www.columbiafruit.com	Wenatchee	WA	98801	509-662-7153	662-0933
Corporate Express Inc 1 Environmental Way *TF:* 888-664-3945 ■ *Web:* www.corporate-express.com	Broomfield	CO	80021	303-664-2000	664-3474
Crosscountry Courier Inc PO Box 4030 *Web:* www.crosscountrycourier.com	Bismarck	ND	58502	701-222-8498	223-5963
Deutsche Post Global Mail Ltd 196 Van Buren St Suite 200 *TF:* 800-426-7478 ■ *Web:* www.deutschepost-globalmail.com	Herndon	VA	20170	703-480-7610	450-7637
DHL Airways 1200 S Pine Island Rd *TF:* 800-225-5345 ■ *Web:* www.dhl.com	Plantation	FL	33324	800-225-5345	
Dynamex Inc 5429 LBJ Fwy Suite 1000 **Fax Area Code:* 972 ■ *TF Cust Svc:* 888-478-1660 ■ *Web:* www.dynamex.com	Dallas	TX	75240	214-560-9000	560-9349*

Phone Fax

Federal Express Corp 3610 Hacks Cross Rd .... Memphis TN 38125 901-369-3600
TF: 800-463-3339 ■ *Web:* www.fedex.com
FedEx Custom Critical Inc 1475 Boettler Rd. .... Uniontown OH 44685 234-310-4090
TF Cust Svc: 800-762-3787 ■ *Web:* customcritical.fedex.com
Financial Courier Service Inc
6099 Mt Moriah Ext Suite 13 .... Memphis TN 38115 901-761-4555 366-6165
Hot Shot Messenger Inc
747 N Shepherd Dr Suite 100. .... Houston TX 77007 713-869-5525 862-6354
Web: www.hotshot.to
Howard Ternes Packaging Co 12285 Dixie .... Redford MI 48239 313-531-5867 531-5868
Web: www.ternespackaging.com
International Bonded Couriers Inc
1403 4th Ave. .... New Hyde Park NY 11040 516-627-8200 627-8263
TF: 800-422-4124 ■ *Web:* www.ibcinc.com
Jersey Shore Courier Service Inc
101 Oakland St. .... Red Bank NJ 07701 732-747-0644
National Delivery Systems Inc
8700 Robert Fulton Dr .... Columbia MD 21046 410-312-4770
Web: www.national-delivery.com
Network Courier Service Corp
9010 Bellanca Ave .... Los Angeles CA 90045 310-410-7700 410-7716*
**Fax:* Cust Svc ■ *TF:* 800-938-1801
One Source Industries LLC
15215 Alton Pkwy Suite 100. .... Irvine CA 92618 949-784-7700 784-7701
Web: www.onesource-ind.com
Priority Express Courier Service
5 Chelsea Pkwy .... Boothwyn PA 19061 610-364-3300 364-3310
TF: 800-526-4646
Purolator Courier Ltd 5995 Avebury Rd. .... Mississauga ON L5R3T8 905-712-1251 712-6696
TF: 888-744-7123 ■ *Web:* www.purolator.com
Spotless Enterprises Inc 12-B Gerber Rd. .... Ashville NC 28803 828-274-7311 963-8521*
**Fax Area Code:* 800 ■ *TF:* 800-738-7396 ■ *Web:* www.spotless.com
Sterling Courier Systems Inc
570 Herndon Pkwy Suite 300 .... Herndon VA 20170 703-471-4488 471-4557
TF: 800-633-6666 ■ *Web:* www.sterlingcourier.com
TNT Express Worldwide Corp
68 S Service Rd Suite 340 .... Melville NY 11747 631-760-0700 760-0985*
**Fax:* Hum Res ■ *TF Cust Svc:* 800-558-5555 ■ *Web:* www.tnt.com
Tricor America Inc
717 Airport Blvd .... South San Francisco CA 94080 650-877-3650 583-3197
TF: 800-669-7631 ■ *Web:* www.tricor.com
Unishippers Assn Inc
746 E Winchester Suite 200 .... Salt Lake City UT 84107 801-487-0600 487-7468
TF: 800-999-8721 ■ *Web:* www.unishippers.com
United Parcel Service Inc (UPS)
55 Glenlake Pkwy NE .... Atlanta GA 30328 404-828-6000 828-6440
NYSE: UPS ■ *TF Cust Svc:* 800-742-5877 ■ *Web:* www.ups.com
United Shipping Solutions
6985 Union Pk Ctr Suite 565 .... Midvale UT 84047 801-352-0012 352-0339
TF: 866-744-7486 ■ *Web:* www.usshipit.com
Universal Express Inc
5295 Town Ctr Rd Suite 101 .... Boca Raton FL 33486 561-367-6177 367-6124
Web: www.usxp.com
Velocity Express Corp
11104 W Airport Blvd Suite 130 .... Stafford TX 77477 888-839-7669
PINK: VEXPQ ■ *TF:* 888-839-7669 ■ *Web:* www.velocityexp.com
Washington Express Service LLC
12240 Indian Creek Ct Suite 100 .... Beltsville MD 20705 301-210-0899 419-7075
TF: 800-939-5463 ■ *Web:* www.washingtonexpress.net
World Courier Inc 1313 4th Ave .... New Hyde Park NY 11040 516-354-2600 354-2637*
**Fax:* Cust Svc ■ *TF:* 800-221-6600 ■ *Web:* www.worldcourier.com
Worldwide Express 2828 Routh St Suite 400 .... Dallas TX 75201 214-720-2400 720-2446
TF: 800-758-7447 ■ *Web:* www.wwex.com
WPX Delivery Solutions
3320 W Valley Hwy N Suite 110 .... Auburn WA 98001 253-876-2760 876-2799
TF: 800-562-1091 ■ *Web:* www.wpx.com
Yamato Transport USA Inc 80 Seaview Dr .... Secaucus NJ 07094 201-583-9706 583-9703
Web: www.yamatoamerica.com

550 PACKAGING MACHINERY & EQUIPMENT

Phone Fax

A-B-C Packaging Machine Corp
811 Live Oak St .... Tarpon Springs FL 34689 727-937-5144 938-1239
TF: 800-237-5975 ■ *Web:* www.abcpackaging.com
ACMA USA Inc 501 Southlake Blvd .... Richmond VA 23236 804-794-9777 794-6187
TF: 800-525-2735 ■ *Web:* www.acmagd.com
Acraloc Corp 113 Flint Rd PO Box 4129 .... Oak Ridge TN 37831 865-483-1368 483-3500
Web: www.acraloc.com
Adolph Gottscho Inc 835 Lehigh Ave. .... Union NJ 07083 908-688-2400 687-9250
Web: www.gottscho.com
ARPAC Group 9511 W River St. .... Schiller Park IL 60176 847-678-9034 671-7006
Web: www.arpac.com
Automated Packaging Systems Inc
10175 Phillip Pkwy. .... Streetsboro OH 44241 330-528-2000 342-2400
TF Sales: 800-824-5282 ■ *Web:* www.autobag.com
B & H Mfg Co 3461 Roeding Rd. .... Ceres CA 95307 209-537-5785 537-6854
TF: 888-643-0444 ■ *Web:* www.bhlabeling.com
Barry-Wehmiller Cos Inc 8020 Forsyth Blvd. .... Clayton MO 63105 314-862-8000 862-2744*
**Fax:* Sales ■ *TF:* 800-862-8200 ■ *Web:* www.barry-wehmiller.com
Barry-Wehmiller Cos Inc Accraply Div
3580 Holly Ln N .... Plymouth MN 55447 763-557-1313 519-9656
TF: 800-328-3997 ■ *Web:* www.accraply.com
Belco Packaging Systems Inc
910 S Mountain Ave .... Monrovia CA 91016 626-357-9566 359-3440
TF: 800-833-1833 ■ *Web:* www.belcopackaging.com
Bell-Mark Corp 331 Changebridge Rd .... Pine Brook NJ 07058 973-882-0202 808-4616
Web: www.bell-mark.com
Brenton LLC 4750 County Rd 13 Ne. .... Alexandria MN 56308 320-852-7705 852-7621
TF: 800-535-2730 ■ *Web:* www.brentonengineering.com
Butler Automatic Inc 41 Leona Dr. .... Middleborough MA 02346 508-923-0544 923-0886
TF Cust Svc: 800-544-0070 ■ *Web:* www.butlerautomatic.com

Phone Fax

Campbell Wrapper Corp 1415 Fortune Ave .... De Pere WI 54115 920-983-7100 983-7300*
**Fax:* Sales ■ *TF:* 800-727-4210 ■ *Web:* www.campbellwrapper.com
Corrugated Gear & Services Inc
100 Anderson Rd .... Alpharetta GA 30004 770-475-8929 442-3371
Web: www.corrugatedgear.com
Data Technology Inc 260-J Fordham Rd .... Wilmington MA 01887 978-694-0055 694-0055
TF: 800-331-5797
Delkor Systems Inc 8700 Rendova St Ne .... Circle Pines MN 55014 763-783-0855 783-0875
TF: 800-328-5558 ■ *Web:* www.delkorsystems.com
Dynaric Inc 5740 Bayside Rd. .... Virginia Beach VA 23455 757-363-5850
TF: 800-526-0827 ■ *Web:* www.dynaric.com
E-pak Machinery Inc 1535 S State Rd 39 .... La Porte IN 46350 219-393-5541 324-2884
TF: 800-328-0466 ■ *Web:* www.epakmachinery.com
Elliott Mfg Co Inc
2664 Cherry Ave PO Box 11277 .... Fresno CA 93772 559-233-6235 233-6235
Web: www.elliott-mfg.com
Elmar Worldwide Inc 200 Gould Ave PO Box 245 .... Depew NY 14043 716-681-5650 681-5650
TF Cust Svc: 800-433-3562 ■ *Web:* www.elmarworldwide.com
Evergreen Packaging Equipment
2400 6th St SW .... Cedar Rapids IA 52406 319-399-3200 399-3543
Web: www.evergreenpackaging.com
Fischbein Co 151 Walker Rd .... Statesville NC 28625 704-871-1159 872-3303
Web: www.fischbein.com
Flexicon Corp 2400 Emrick Blvd .... Bethlehem PA 18020 610-814-2400 814-0600
TF: 888-353-9426 ■ *Web:* www.flexicon.com
Fowler Products Co
150 Collins Industrial Blvd .... Athens GA 30601 706-549-3300 548-1278
Web: www.fowlerproducts.com
Hartness International Inc
1200 Garlington Rd PO Box 26509 .... Greenville SC 29616 864-297-1200 288-5390
TF: 800-845-8791 ■ *Web:* www.hartness.com
Heat Seal LLC 4580 E 71st St .... Cleveland OH 44125 216-341-2022 341-2163
Web: www.heatsealco.com
Heisler Industries Inc 224 Passaic Ave .... Fairfield NJ 07004 973-227-6300 227-7627
Web: www.heislerind.com
ITW Angleboard 595 Telser Rd Suite 100 .... Lake Zurich IL 60047 800-457-5777 719-9201*
**Fax Area Code:* 847 ■ *TF:* 800-252-4777 ■ *Web:* www.itwangleboard.com
Kirk Rudy Inc 125 Lorraine Pkwy. .... Woodstock GA 30188 770-427-4203 427-4036
Web: www.kirkrudy.com
Kliklok-Woodman USA 5224 Snapfinger Woods Dr. ...... Decatur GA 30035 770-981-5200 987-7160
Web: www.kliklok.com
Kortec Inc 29 Old Right Rd .... Ipswich MA 01938 978-238-7100 238-7171
Web: www.kortec.com
Krones Inc 9600 S 58th St PO Box 321801 .... Franklin WI 53132 414-409-4000 409-4100*
**Fax:* Cust Svc ■ *TF:* 800-752-3787 ■ *Web:* www.kronesusa.com
Label-Aire Inc 550 Burning Tree Rd .... Fullerton CA 92833 714-449-5155 526-0300
Web: www.label-aire-inc.com
Lantech Inc 11000 Bluegrass Pkwy. .... Louisville KY 40299 502-267-4200 266-5031
TF: 800-866-0322 ■ *Web:* www.lantech.com
Loveshaw Corp 2206 Easton Tpke. .... South Canaan PA 18459 570-937-4921
TF Cust Svc: 800-747-1586 ■ *Web:* www.loveshaw.com
Matthews International Corp Graphics Systems Div
252 Pk W Dr .... Pittsburgh PA 15275 412-788-2111 788-2297
TF: 800-245-1129 ■ *Web:* www.matthewsgsd.com
Metro Machine & Engineering Corp
8001 Wallace Rd. .... Eden Prairie MN 55344 952-937-2800 937-2374
Web: www.metromachine.com
Mid-States Packaging Inc
119 S Boggs St PO Box 339 .... DeGraff OH 43318 937-585-5361 585-6819
Web: www.midstatespackaging.com
Moen Industries 12333 Los Nietos Rd .... Santa Fe Springs CA 90670 562-946-6381 946-3200
TF: 800-423-4747 ■ *Web:* www.moenindustries.com
Mooney General Paper Co
1451 Chestnut Ave PO Box 3800 .... Hillside NJ 07205 973-926-3800 926-0425
Web: www.mooneygeneral.com
MTS Medication Technologies Inc
2003 Gandy Blvd N. .... Saint Petersburg FL 33702 727-571-1616 579-8067
TF: 800-845-0053 ■ *Web:* www.mtsp.com
Muller Martini Mailroom Systems Inc
444 Innovation Way .... Allentown PA 18109 610-266-7000 231-3990
TF: 800-331-5674 ■ *Web:* www.mullermartini.com/ms
Nalbach Engineering Co Inc
621 E Plainfield Rd .... Countryside IL 60525 708-579-9100 579-0122
Web: www.nalbach.com
National Instrument LLC 4119 Fordleigh Rd. .... Baltimore MD 21215 410-764-0900 764-7719
TF: 866-258-1914 ■ *Web:* www.filamatic.com
New England Machinery Inc 2820 62nd Ave E. .... Bradenton FL 34203 941-755-5550 751-6281
Web: www.neminc.com
New Jersey Machine Inc 56 Etna Rd. .... Lebanon NH 03766 603-448-0300 448-4810*
**Fax:* Sales ■ *TF Sales:* 800-432-2990 ■ *Web:* www.njmcli.com
New Way Packaging Machinery Inc
210 Blettner Ave PO Box 467 .... Hanover PA 17331 717-637-2133 637-2966
Ossid Corp PO Drawer 1968 4000 College Rd .... Rocky Mount NC 27802 252-446-6177 442-7694
TF: 800-334-8369 ■ *Web:* www.ossid.com
OYSTAR Packaging Technologies
807 W Kimberly Rd. .... Davenport IA 52806 563-391-1100 391-4951
TF Sales: 800-257-5622 ■ *Web:* www.oystar-group.com
Package Machinery Co
380 Union St Suite 58 .... West Springfield MA 01089 413-732-4000 732-1163
Web: www.packagemachinery.com
Packaging Systems International Inc
4990 Acoma St .... Denver CO 80216 303-296-4445 298-1016
Web: www.pkgsys.com
PMC Industries 275 Hudson St. .... Hackensack NJ 07601 201-342-3684 342-3568
Web: www.pmc-industries.com
Pmi Cartoning Inc 850 Pratt Blvd. .... Elk Grove Village IL 60007 847-437-1427
Web: www.pmicartoning.com
Pneumatic Scale Angelus 4485 Allen Rd. .... Stow OH 44224 330-247-1800 928-7077
Web: www.angelusmachine.com
Prodo-Pak Corp 77 Commerce St. .... Garfield NJ 07026 973-777-7770 772-0471
Web: www.prodo-pak.com

Company / Address	City	State	Zip	Phone	Fax
Qed Systems Inc 4646 N Witchduck Rd	Virginia Beach	VA	23455	757-490-5000	490-5027
Web: www.qedsysinc.com					
RA Pearson Co 8120 W Sunset Hwy	Spokane	WA	99224	509-838-6226	747-8532
TF: 800-732-7766 ■ *Web:* www.pearsonpkg.com					
Raque Food Systems LLC PO Box 99594	Louisville	KY	40269	502-267-9641	267-2352
Web: www.raque.com					
Renco Machine Co 1421 Eastman Ave	Green Bay	WI	54302	920-448-8000	448-8008
TF: 888-320-8552 ■ *Web:* www.rencomachine.com					
Ro-An Industries Corp 64-20 Admiral Ave	Middle Village	NY	11379	718-821-1115	821-3838
TF: 800-255-7626 ■ *Web:* www.roan.com					
Robert Bosch Corp Packaging Technology Div 2440 Summer Blvd	Raleigh	NC	27616	919-877-2016	877-0976
TF: 800-292-6724 ■ *Web:* www.boschpackaging.com					
Rollstock Inc 1728 N Topping Ave	Kansas City	MO	64120	816-455-8055	455-8469
TF: 800-295-2949 ■ *Web:* www.rollstock.com					
Rutherford Engineering Inc 5469 Pine Ln PO Box 560	Roscoe	IL	61073	815-623-2141	623-7170
Satake USA Inc 10905 Cash Rd	Stafford	TX	77477	281-276-3600	494-1427
Web: www.satake-usa.com					
Scandia Packaging Machinery Co 15 Industrial Rd	Clifton	NJ	07004	973-473-6100	473-7226
Web: www.scandiapack.com					
Schneider Packaging Equipment Co Inc 5370 Guy Young Rd	Brewerton	NY	13029	315-676-3035	676-2875
Web: www.schneiderequip.com					
Shibuya Hoppmann Corp 13129 Airpark Dr Suite 120	Elkwood	VA	22718	540-829-2654	829-1726
TF Cust Svc: 800-368-3582 ■ *Web:* www.hoppmann.com					
Sidel Inc 5600 Sun Ct	Norcross	GA	30092	678-221-3087	447-0084*
**Fax Area Code:* 770 ■ *TF:* 800-453-7439 ■ *Web:* www.sidel.com					
Speedline Technologies Inc 16 Forge Pk	Franklin	MA	02038	508-520-0083	520-2288
Web: www.speedlinetech.com					
Standard Knapp Inc 63 Pickering St	Portland	CT	06480	860-342-1100	342-0782
TF Cust Svc: 800-628-9565 ■ *Web:* www.standard-knapp.com					
Stolle Machinery Co LLC 6949 S Potomac St	Centennial	CO	80112	303-708-9044	708-9045
TF: 800-228-4593 ■ *Web:* www.stollemachinery.com					
Summit Packaging Systems Inc 400 Gay St PO Box 5304	Manchester	NH	03108	603-669-5410	644-2594
SWF Cos 1949 E Manning Ave	Reedley	CA	93654	559-638-8484	638-7478
TF: 800-344-8951 ■ *Web:* www.swfcompanies.com					
Thiele Technologies Inc 315 27th Ave NE	Minneapolis	MN	55418	612-782-1200	782-1203
TF: 800-932-3647 ■ *Web:* www.thieletech.com					
Tri-Pak Machinery Inc 1102 N Commerce St	Harlingen	TX	78550	956-423-5140	423-9362
Web: www.tri-pakmachinery.com					
Triangle Package Machinery Co 6655 W Diversey Ave	Chicago	IL	60707	773-889-0200	889-4221
TF: 800-621-4170 ■ *Web:* www.trianglepackage.com					
U S Bottlers Machinery Co PO Box 7203	Charlotte	NC	28241	704-588-4750	588-3808
Web: www.usbottlers.com					
Us Digital Media Inc 1929 W Lone Cactus Dr	Phoenix	AZ	85027	623-587-4900	587-4920
TF: 877-992-3766 ■ *Web:* www.usdigitalmedia.com					
Weiler Engineering Inc 1395 Gateway Dr	Elgin	IL	60123	847-697-4900	697-4915
Web: www.weilerengineering.com					

551 PACKAGING MATERIALS & PRODUCTS - PAPER OR PLASTICS

SEE ALSO Bags - Paper p. 1504; Bags - Plastics p. 1505; Blister Packaging p. 1529; Coated & Laminated Paper p. 2335; Paper Converters p. 2336; Plastics Foam Products p. 2426

Company / Address	City	State	Zip	Phone	Fax
Acme Paper & Supply Co Inc 8229 Sandy Ct PO Box 422	Savage	MD	20763	410-792-2333	792-2177
TF: 800-462-5812 ■ *Web:* www.acmepaper.com					
Adhesive Packaging Specialties Inc PO Box 31	Peabody	MA	01960	978-531-3300	532-8901
TF: 800-222-1117 ■ *Web:* www.adhesivepackaging.com					
Admiral Packaging inc 10 Admiral St	Providence	RI	02908	401-274-7000	331-1910
TF: 800-556-6454 ■ *Web:* www.admiralpkg.com					
Advance Bag & Packaging Technologies 5720 Williams Lake Rd	Waterford	MI	48329	248-674-3126	674-2630
TF: 800-475-2247 ■ *Web:* www.advancepac.com					
Advanced Paper Forming 541 W Rincon St	Carona	CA	92880	951-738-1800	738-1234
Web: www.advancedpaper.com					
Aldelano Packaging Corp 2010 S Lynx Ave	Ontario	CA	91761	909-861-3970	861-6039
TF: 800-972-2599 ■ *Web:* www.aldelano.com					
Alliance Rubber Co 210 Carpenter Dam Rd	Hot Springs	AR	71901	501-262-2700	262-8192
TF: 800-626-5940 ■ *Web:* www.rubberband.com					
American Packaging Corp 777 Driving Pk Ave	Rochester	NY	14613	585-254-9500	254-5801
TF: 800-551-8801 ■ *Web:* www.ampkcorp.com					
American Packaging Corp Extrusion Div 777 Driving Pk Ave	Rochester	NY	14613	585-254-9500	254-5801
TF: 800-551-8801 ■ *Web:* www.ampkcorp.com					
American Paper & Plastics Inc (APP) 10511 Valley Blvd	El Monte	CA	91731	626-444-0000	444-1000
Web: www.appinc.com					
American Transparent Plastics Corp 180 National Rd	Edison	NJ	08817	732-287-3000	287-1421
TF Orders: 800-942-8725					
Automated Packaging Systems Inc 10175 Phillip Pkwy	Streetsboro	OH	44241	330-528-2000	342-2400
TF Sales: 800-824-5282 ■ *Web:* www.autobag.com					
BagcraftPapercon 3900 W 43rd St	Chicago	IL	60632	773-254-8000	254-8204
TF: 800-621-8468 ■ *Web:* www.bagcraft.com					
Beaver Mfg Co Inc 12 Ed Needham Dr	Mansfield	GA	30055	770-786-1622	
Web: www.beaverloc.com					
Beaverite Corp 128 Main St	Beaver Falls	NY	13305	315-346-6011	346-1575
TF Cust Svc: 800-424-6337 ■ *Web:* www.beaverite.com					
Bedford Industries Inc 1659 Rowe Ave	Worthington	MN	56187	507-376-4136	376-6742
TF Cust Svc: 800-533-5314 ■ *Web:* www.bedfordind.com					
Bemis Co Inc 1 Neenah Ctr 4th Fl PO Box 669	Neenah	WI	54957	920-727-4100	
NYSE: BMS ■ *Web:* www.bemis.com					
Bemis Co Inc Bemis Clysar Div 2451 Badger Ave	Oshkosh	WI	54904	920-303-7800	303-7820
TF: 800-425-9727 ■ *Web:* www.clysar.com					
Bemis Co Inc Milprint Div 3550 Moser St PO Box 2968	Oshkosh	WI	54903	920-527-2300	527-2310
Web: www.milprint.com					
Bemis Co Inc Paper Packaging Div 2445 Deer Pk Blvd	Omaha	NE	68105	800-541-4303	938-2609*
**Fax Area Code:* 402 ■ *TF:* 800-541-4303 ■ *Web:* www.bemispaper.com					
Bomarko Inc 1955 N Oak Rd PO Box 1510	Plymouth	IN	46563	574-936-9901	936-5314
Web: www.bomarko.com					
BPM Inc 200 W Front St	Peshtigo	WI	54157	715-582-4551	582-4853
TF: 800-826-0494 ■ *Web:* www.bpmpaper.com					
Bryce Corp 4505 Old Lamar Ave PO Box 18338	Memphis	TN	38118	901-369-4400	369-4419*
**Fax:* Sales ■ *TF:* 800-238-7277 ■ *Web:* www.brycecorp.com					
Burrows Paper Corp Packaging Group 1722 53rd St	Fort Madison	IA	52627	319-372-4241	372-2537
TF: 800-779-7779 ■ *Web:* www.burrowspaper.com					
Carton Service Inc First Quality Dr PO Box 702	Shelby	OH	44875	419-342-5010	342-4804
TF: 800-533-7744 ■ *Web:* www.cartonservice.com					
Catty Corp 6111 White Oaks Rd	Harvard	IL	60033	815-943-2288	943-4473
TF: 800-572-2766 ■ *Web:* www.cattycorp.com					
CCL Industries Inc 105 Gordon Baker Rd Suite 500	Toronto	ON	M2H3P8	416-756-8500	756-8555
TSE: CCL.B ■ *Web:* www.cclind.com					
Cello-Pack Corp 55 Innsbruck Dr	Cheektowaga	NY	14227	716-668-3111	668-3816
TF: 800-778-3111 ■ *Web:* www.cello-pack.com					
Charter Films Inc 1901 Winter St PO Box 277	Superior	WI	54880	715-395-8258	395-8259
TF: 877-411-3456 ■ *Web:* www.charterfilms.com					
Clear Lam Packaging Inc 1950 Pratt Blvd	Elk Grove Village	IL	60007	847-439-8570	439-8589
TF: 800-305-4409 ■ *Web:* www.clearlam.com					
Cleo Inc 4025 Viscount Ave	Memphis	TN	38118	901-369-6300	362-1099
TF: 800-289-2536 ■ *Web:* www.cleowrap.com					
Command Plastic Corp 124 W Ave	Tallmadge	OH	44278	330-434-3497	434-8316
TF: 800-321-8001 ■ *Web:* www.commandplastic.com					
Consolidated Container Co (CCC) 3101 Towercreek Pkwy Suite 300	Atlanta	GA	30339	678-742-4600	742-4750
TF Sales: 888-831-2184 ■ *Web:* www.cccllc.com					
Crawford Industries LLC 1414 Crawford Dr	Crawfordsville	IN	47933	800-428-0840	962-3343
TF: 800-428-0840 ■ *Web:* www.crawford-industries.com					
Crown Packaging Corp 17854 Chesterfld Airport Rd	Chesterfield	MO	63005	636-681-8000	681-9600
TF: 800-883-9400 ■ *Web:* www.crownpack.com					
Curwood Inc 2200 Badger Ave PO Box 2968	Oshkosh	WI	54903	920-303-7300	303-7309
TF: 800-544-4672 ■ *Web:* www.curwood.com					
Dade Paper & Bag Co 9601 NW 112th Ave	Miami	FL	33178	305-805-2600	889-3594
Web: www.dadepaper.com					
Dopaco Inc 100 Arrandale Blvd	Exton	PA	19341	610-269-1776	524-9188
Web: www.dopaco.com					
DuPont Packaging & Industrial Polymers Barley Mill Plaza 26-2122 PO Box 80026	Wilmington	DE	19880	302-996-1511	892-7390
TF: 800-438-7225 ■ *Web:* www2.dupont.com					
Exopack LLC 3070 Southport Rd PO Box 5687	Spartanburg	SC	29304	864-596-7140	596-7222
TF: 877-447-3539 ■ *Web:* www.exopack.com					
Fibercel Packaging LLC 46 Brooklyn St PO Box 610	Portville	NY	14770	716-933-8703	933-6948
TF: 800-545-8546 ■ *Web:* www.fibercel.com					
Fibre Converters Inc PO Box 130	Constantine	MI	49042	269-435-8431	
Web: www.fibreconverters.com					
Fisher Container Corp 1111 Busch Pkwy	Buffalo Grove	IL	60089	847-541-0000	541-0075
TF: 800-837-2247 ■ *Web:* www.fishercontainer.com					
Flextron Industries Inc 720 Mt Rd	Aston	PA	19014	610-459-4600	459-5379
TF: 800-633-2181 ■ *Web:* www.flextronindustries.com					
Flower City Tissue Mills Inc 700 Driving Pk Ave	Rochester	NY	14613	585-458-9200	458-3812
TF: 800-595-2030 ■ *Web:* www.flowercitytissue.com					
FPC Flexible Packaging Corp 1891 Eglinton Ave E	Toronto	ON	M1L2L7	416-288-3060	288-0808
TF: 888-288-7386 ■ *Web:* www.fpcflexible.com					
Gateway Packaging Co 20 Central Industrial Dr Northgate Industrial Pk	Granite City	IL	62040	618-451-0010	876-4856
Web: www.gatewaypackaging.com					
General Plastic Extrusions Inc 1238 Kasson Dr	Prescott	WI	54021	715-262-3806	262-3836
TF: 800-532-3888 ■ *Web:* www.generalplastic.com					
Genpak Corp 68 Warren St	Glens Falls	NY	12801	518-798-9511	798-3302
TF: 800-626-6695 ■ *Web:* www.genpak.com					
Gift Wrap Co 1 Industrial Dr	Midway	GA	31320	912-884-9727	884-9702
TF: 800-443-4429 ■ *Web:* www.giftwrapcompany.com					
Grayling Industries 1008 Branch Dr	Alpharetta	GA	30004	770-751-9095	751-3710
TF: 800-635-1551 ■ *Web:* www.graylingindustries.com					
Green Bay Packaging Inc 1700 Webster Ct	Green Bay	WI	54302	920-433-5111	
TF: 800-558-4008 ■ *Web:* www.gbp.com					
HCP Packaging USA Inc 370 Monument Rd	Hinsdale	NH	03451	603-256-3141	256-6979
Web: www.hcpackaging.com					
Highland Supply Corp 1111 6th St	Highland	IL	62249	618-654-2161	654-3411
TF: 800-472-3645 ■ *Web:* www.highlandsupply.com					
Honeywell Specialty Films 98 Westwood Rd	Pottsville	PA	17901	570-621-6000	621-6109
TF Cust Svc: 800-934-5679					
Huhtamaki Inc North America 9201 Packaging Dr	DeSoto	KS	66018	913-583-3025	583-8756*
**Fax:* Hum Res ■ *TF:* 800-255-4243 ■ *Web:* www2.huhtamaki.com					
Indiana Ribbon Inc 206 E Market St	Wolcott	IN	47995	219-279-2112	279-4747*
**Fax Area Code:* 800 ■ *TF:* 800-531-3100 ■ *Web:* www.giftwrapgifts.com					

	City	State	Zip	Phone	Fax
Innovative Enterprises Inc 25 Town & Country Dr	Washington	MO	63090	636-390-0300	390-4004
TF: 800-280-0300 ■ *Web:* www.innovative-1.com					
International Paper Co 6400 Poplar Ave.	Memphis	TN	38297	901-419-7000	
NYSE: IP ■ *TF Prod Info:* 800-223-1268 ■ *Web:* www.internationalpaper.com					
International Paper Co Kraft Paper Div 6400 Poplar Ave	Memphis	TN	38197	901-419-9000	
Web: www.internationalpaper.com					
ITW Hi-Cone 1140 W Bryn Mawr Ave	Itasca	IL	60143	630-438-5300	438-5315
Web: www.itwhicone.com					
Jim Pattison Group The 1067 W Cordova St Suite 1800	Vancouver	BC	V6C1C7	604-688-6764	687-2601
Web: www.jimpattison.com					
Joshen Paper & Packaging Co Inc 5808 Grant Ave	Cleveland	OH	44105	216-441-5600	441-7647
Web: www.joshen.com					
Kimberly-Clark Corp Technical Paper Div 1400 Holcomb Bridge Rd	Roswell	GA	30076	920-721-2000	721-4219
TF: 800-544-1847 ■ *Web:* www.kimberly-clark.com					
Komplete Packaging Inc (KPAK) 2020 Singleton Blvd	Dallas	TX	75212	214-252-8100	646-9922
TF: 800-811-6374 ■ *Web:* www.kpak.com					
L Gordon Packaging Inc 22 W Padonia Rd Suite 304A	Timonium	MD	21093	410-308-2202	308-2207
LallyPak Inc 1209 Central Ave	Hillside	NJ	07205	908-351-4141	351-4411
TF: 800-523-8484 ■ *Web:* www.lallypak.com					
Laminations 3010 E Venture Dr	Appleton	WI	54911	920-831-0596	831-0612
TF: 800-925-2626 ■ *Web:* www.laminations-net.com					
Lerman Container Co 10 Great Hill Rd	Naugatuck	CT	06770	203-723-6681	723-6687
TF: 800-453-7626 ■ *Web:* www.lermancontainer.com					
Letica Corp 52585 Dequindre Rd PO Box 5005	Rochester	MI	48307	248-652-0557	608-2153
Web: www.letica.com					
LPS Industries Inc 10 Caesar Pl	Moonachie	NJ	07074	201-438-3515	438-0040
TF Sales: 800-275-4577 ■ *Web:* www.lpsind.com					
Menominee Paper Co 144 1st St	Menominee	MI	49858	906-863-5595	864-3320
Multifilm Packaging Corp 1040 N McLean Blvd	Elgin	IL	60123	847-695-7600	695-7645
TF: 800-837-9727 ■ *Web:* www.multifilm.com					
Novacel 21 3rd St	Palmer	MA	01069	413-283-3468	283-3964
TF: 877-668-2235 ■ *Web:* www.novacelinc.com					
Oracle Packaging 220 E Polo Rd	Winston-Salem	NC	27105	336-777-5000	777-5440
Web: www.oraclepackaging.com					
Overwraps Packaging LP 3950 La Reunion Pkwy	Dallas	TX	75212	214-634-0427	634-9531
Web: www.overwraps.com					
Packaging Concepts Inc 9832 Evergreen Indus Dr	Saint Louis	MO	63123	314-329-9700	487-2666
Web: www.packagingconceptsinc.com					
Pactiv Corp 1900 W Field Ct	Lake Forest	IL	60045	847-482-2000	482-4738
NYSE: PTV ■ *TF:* 888-828-2850 ■ *Web:* www.pactiv.com					
Pak West Paper & Packaging 4042 W Garry Ave	Santa Ana	CA	92799	714-557-7420	557-9469
TF: 800-927-7299 ■ *Web:* www.pakwest.com					
Perfecseal Inc 3500 N Main St PO Box 2968	Oshkosh	WI	54903	920-303-7000	303-7002
TF: 800-568-7626 ■ *Web:* www.perfecseal.com					
Polyair Inter Pack Inc 330 Humberline Dr	Toronto	ON	M9W1R2	416-679-6600	679-6610
PINK: PPK ■ *TF:* 888-456-4348 ■ *Web:* www.polyair.com					
Pratt Industries USA 1800C Sarasota Pkwy	Conyers	GA	30013	770-918-5678	918-5679
Web: www.prattindustries.com					
Printpack Inc 2800 Overlook PkwyNE	Atlanta	GA	30339	404-691-5830	505-7407
TF: 800-241-9984 ■ *Web:* www.printpack.com					
Printpack Inc Film Products Div PO Box 110	New Castle	DE	19720	302-323-0900	323-1698
TF: 800-572-4345					
Rexam Inc 4201 Congress St Suite 340	Charlotte	NC	28209	704-551-1500	551-1571
TF: 800-289-2800 ■ *Web:* www.rexam.com					
Robert Family Holdings Inc (RFH) 12430 Tesson Ferry Rd Suite 313	Saint Louis	MO	63128	636-305-2830	729-7133*
**Fax Area Code:* 314 ■ *Web:* www.rf-holdings.com					
Robinson Industries Inc 3051 W Curtis Rd	Coleman	MI	48618	989-465-6111	465-1217
TF: 800-525-0391 ■ *Web:* www.robinsonind.com					
Rollprint Packaging Products Inc 320 S Stewart Ave	Addison	IL	60101	630-628-1700	628-8510
TF: 800-276-7629 ■ *Web:* www.rollprint.com					
Sabert Corp 2288 Main St	Sayreville	NJ	08872	732-721-5544	721-0622
TF: 800-722-3781 ■ *Web:* www.sabert.com					
Scholle Custom Packaging Inc 200 W N Ave	Northlake	IL	60164	708-562-7290	562-6569
Web: www.scholle.com					
Scott Fetzer Co Western Plastics Div 105 Western Dr	Portland	TN	37148	615-325-7331	325-4924
Web: www.wplastics.com					
Sealed Air Corp Cryovac Div 100 Rogers Bridge Rd Bldg A	Duncan	SC	29334	864-433-2000	433-2689
TF General: 800-845-7551 ■ *Web:* www.sealedair.com					
Sealed Air Corp Packaging Products Div 301 Mayhill St	Saddle Brook	NJ	07663	201-712-7000	712-7070
TF: 800-346-5855					
SI Jacobson Mfg Co 1414 Jacobson Dr	Waukegan	IL	60085	847-623-1414	623-2556
TF: 800-621-5492 ■ *Web:* www.sij.com					
Silgan Holdings Inc 4 Landmark Sq Suite 400	Stamford	CT	06901	203-975-7110	975-7902
NASDAQ: SLGN ■ *Web:* www.silganholdings.com					
Sonoco 1 N 2nd St	Hartsville	SC	29550	843-383-7000	383-7008*
NYSE: SON ■ **Fax:* PR ■ *TF:* 800-377-2692 ■ *Web:* www.sonoco.com					
Southern Container Corp 115 Engineers Rd	Hauppauge	NY	11788	631-231-0400	231-0174
Web: www.southern-container.com					
Southern Container Ltd 10410 Papalote St Suite 130	Houston	TX	77041	713-466-5661	466-4223
Web: www.southerncontainer.com					
Specialized Packaging International Inc 3190 Whitney Ave Bldg 7	Hamden	CT	06518	203-248-3370	230-8906
Web: www.spgroup-inc.com					
Technimark Inc 180 Commerce Pl	Asheboro	NC	27203	336-498-4171	498-5042
Web: www.technimark.com					
Technipaq Inc 975 Lutter Dr	Crystal Lake	IL	60014	815-477-1800	477-0777
Web: www.technipaq.com					
Tegrant Corp 850 4th Ave	New Brighton	PA	15066	724-843-8200	843-4845
TF: 800-289-9966 ■ *Web:* www.tegrant.com					
Trinity Packaging Corp 84 Business Pk Dr	Armonk	NY	10504	914-273-4111	273-4715
Web: www.trinitypackaging.com					
UFP Technologies Inc 172 E Main St	Georgetown	MA	01833	978-352-2200	352-7169
NASDAQ: UFPT ■ *TF:* 800-372-3172 ■ *Web:* www.ufpt.com					
Unger Co 12401 Berea Rd	Cleveland	OH	44111	216-252-1400	252-1427
TF: 800-321-1418 ■ *Web:* www.ungerco.com					
Unicorr 455 Sackett Pt Rd	North Haven	CT	06473	203-248-2161	248-0241
TF: 800-229-4269 ■ *Web:* www.unicorr.com					
Vision Plastics Inc 26000 SW Pkwy Ctr Dr	Wilsonville	OR	97070	503-685-9000	685-9254
Web: www.visionplastics.com					
Viskase Cos Inc 8205 S Cass Suite 115	Darien	IL	60561	630-874-0700	874-0178
TF: 800-323-8562 ■ *Web:* www.viskase.com					
Walter G. Anderson Inc 4535 Willow Dr	Hamel	MN	55340	763-478-2133	478-6572
Web: www.wgacarton.com					
Warp Bros Flex-O-Glass Inc 4647 W Augusta Blvd	Chicago	IL	60651	773-261-5200	261-5204
TF: 800-621-3345 ■ *Web:* www.warpbros.com					
Wausau Paper Corp 100 Paper Pl	Mosinee	WI	54455	715-693-4470	692-2083
NYSE: WPP ■ *Web:* www.wausaupaper.com					
Weyerhaeuser Co 33663 Weyerhaeuser Way S	Federal Way	WA	98003	253-924-2345	924-2685
NYSE: WY ■ *TF:* 800-525-5440 ■ *Web:* www.weyerhaeuser.com					
Winpak Ltd 100 Salteaux Crescent	Winnipeg	MB	R3J3T3	204-889-1015	888-7806
NYSE: WPK ■ *TF:* 800-841-2600 ■ *Web:* www.winpak.com					
WS Packaging Group Inc 1102 Jefferson St	Algoma	WI	54201	920-487-3424	487-5644
TF: 800-236-3424 ■ *Web:* www.wspackaging.com					
Wynalda Packaging 8221 Graphic Dr NE PO Box 370	Belmont	MI	49306	616-866-1561	866-4316
TF: 800-952-8668 ■ *Web:* www.wynalda.com					
Zimmer Custom-Made Packaging Inc 1450 E 20th St	Indianapolis	IN	46218	317-636-3333	263-3427
TF: 888-692-4299 ■ *Web:* www.zcmp.com					

552 PACKING & CRATING

	City	State	Zip	Phone	Fax
American Copak Corp 9175 Eton Ave	Chatsworth	CA	91311	818-576-1000	882-1637
Web: www.americancopak.com					
Bentley World Packaging Ltd 4080 N Port Washington Rd	Milwaukee	WI	53212	414-967-8000	967-8001
Web: www.bentleywp.com					
Cooke's Crating Inc 3124 E 11th St	Los Angeles	CA	90023	323-268-5101	262-2001
Web: www.cookescrating.com					
Craters & Freighters 331 Corporate Cir Suite J	Golden	CO	80401	800-736-3335	399-9964*
**Fax Area Code:* 303 ■ *TF:* 800-736-3335 ■ *Web:* www.cratersandfreighters.com					
Export Packaging Co 525 E 10th Ave	Moline	IL	61264	309-787-0440	787-0448
Web: www.xpac.com					
Fapco Inc 216 Post Rd	Buchanan	MI	49107	269-695-6889	695-5145
TF: 800-782-0167 ■ *Web:* www.fapcoinc.com					
Hydrosol Inc 8407 S 77th Ave	Bridgeview	IL	60455	708-598-7180	598-6572
Navis Logistics Network 5675 DTC Blvd Suite 280	Greenwood Village	CO	80111	303-741-6626	741-6653
TF: 800-525-6309 ■ *Web:* www.gonavis.com					
Navis Pack & Ship Centers 5675 DTC Blvd Suite 280	Greenwood Village	CO	80111	303-741-6626	741-6653
TF: 800-525-6309 ■ *Web:* www.gonavis.com					
Packaging Services of Maryland Inc 16461 Elliott Pkwy	Williamsport	MD	21795	301-223-6200	223-8247
TF: 800-223-6255 ■ *Web:* www.psimd.com					
Southern States Packaging Co PO Box 650	Spartanburg	SC	29304	800-621-2051	579-3932*
**Fax Area Code:* 864 ■ *TF:* 800-621-2051 ■ *Web:* www.sspc.biz					
Strive Group The 350 N Clark St Suite 300	Chicago	IL	60639	312-880-4620	
Web: www.strivegroup.com					
Tech Packaging Inc 11902 Central Pkwy	Jacksonville	FL	32224	904-564-9838	564-9839
TF: 866-453-8324 ■ *Web:* www.techpackaging.net					
Trans-Pak Inc 520 Marburg Way	San Jose	CA	95133	408-254-0500	254-0551
TF: 800-773-2811 ■ *Web:* www.transpak.com					
Trisept Solutions 777 W Glencoe Pl	Milwaukee	WI	53217	414-934-3900	934-3950
Web: www.triseptsolutions.com					
Unicep Packaging Inc 1702 Industrial Dr	Sandpoint	ID	83864	208-265-9696	265-4726
TF: 800-854-9396 ■ *Web:* www.unicep.com					
Venchurs Packaging 800 Liberty St	Adrian	MI	49221	517-263-8937	265-7468
Web: www.venchurs.com					
Warren Industries Inc 3100 Mt Pleasant St	Racine	WI	53404	262-639-7800	639-0920
Web: www.wrnind.com					

553 PAINTS, VARNISHES, RELATED PRODUCTS

	City	State	Zip	Phone	Fax
Aervoe Industries Inc PO Box 485	Gardnerville	NV	89410	775-783-3100	782-5687
TF: 800-227-0196 ■ *Web:* www.aervoe.com					
Aexcel Corp 7373 Production Dr	Mentor	OH	44060	440-974-3800	974-3808
Web: www.aexcelcorp.com					
Akron Paint & Varnish Inc 1390 Firestone Pkwy	Akron	OH	44301	330-773-8911	773-1028
TF: 800-772-3452 ■ *Web:* www.apv-eng-coatings.com					
AkzoNobel Wood Finishes & Adhesives 2031 Nelson Miller Pkwy	Louisville	KY	40223	502-254-0470	253-0573
Web: www.akzonobel.com					
American Safety Technologies Inc 565 Eagle Rock Ave	Roseland	NJ	07068	973-403-2600	403-0046
TF: 800-631-7841 ■ *Web:* www.astantislip.com					
AP Nonweiler Co 3321 County Rd A PO Box 1007	Oshkosh	WI	54903	920-231-0850	231-8085
Behr Process Corp 3400 W Segerstrom Ave	Santa Ana	CA	92704	714-545-7101	241-1002
TF: 800-854-0133 ■ *Web:* www.behr.com					
Benjamin Moore & Co 101 Paragon Dr	Montvale	NJ	07645	201-573-9600	949-6645
TF: 800-344-0400 ■ *Web:* www.benjaminmoore.com					
C. E. Bradley Laboratories Inc PO Box 8238	Brattleboro	VT	05304	802-257-7971	257-7070
Web: www.cebradley.com					

Company	City	State	ZIP	Phone	Fax
California Products Corp 150 Dascomb Rd *Fax Area Code: 800 ■ TF: 800-225-1141 ■ Web: www.californiapaints.com	Andover	MA	01810	978-623-9980	533-6788*
Carboline Co 350 Hanley Industrial Ct. TF: 800-848-4645 ■ Web: www.carboline.com	Saint Louis	MO	63144	314-644-1000	644-4617
Cintech Industrial Coatings 2217 Langdon Farm Rd	Cincinnati	OH	45237	513-631-4270	366-4444
Coating & Adhesive Corp (CAC) 1901 Popular St PO Box 1080 TF: 800-410-2999 ■ Web: www.cacoatings.com	Leland	NC	28451	910-371-3184	371-5580
Coatings Resource Corp 15541 Commerce Ln Web: www.coatingsresource.com	Huntington Beach	CA	92649	714-894-5252	893-2322
Color Putty Co Inc PO Box 738 Web: www.colorputty.com	Monroe	WI	53566	608-325-6033	325-6397
Color Wheel Paint Mfg Co Inc 2814 Silver Star Rd. Web: www.colorwheel.com	Orlando	FL	32808	407-293-6810	293-0945
Coronado Paint Co Inc 308 S Old County Rd *Fax Area Code: 800 ■ TF: 800-883-4193 ■ Web: www.coronadopaint.com	Edgewater	FL	32132	386-428-6461	394-9022*
DAP Inc 2400 Boston St Suite 200 *Fax: Cust Svc ■ TF Cust Svc: 800-584-3840 ■ Web: www.dap.com	Baltimore	MD	21224	410-675-2100	558-1068*
Davis Paint Co Inc 1311 Iron St PO Box 7589 TF: 800-821-2029 ■ Web: www.davispaint.com	North Kansas City	MO	64116	816-471-4447	471-1460
Day-Glo Color Corp 4515 St Clair Ave TF: 800-289-3294 ■ Web: www.dayglo.com	Cleveland	OH	44103	216-391-7070	391-7751
Deft Inc 17451 Von Karman Ave. Web: www.deftfinishes.com	Irvine	CA	92614	949-474-0400	474-7269
Delta Creative Inc 2690 Pellissier Pl TF: 800-423-4135 ■ Web: www.deltacreative.com	City of Industry	CA	90601	562-695-7969	695-4227
Diamond Vogel Paints 1110 Albany Pl SE PO Box 380 TF: 800-728-6435 ■ Web: www.vogelpaint.com	Orange City	IA	51041	712-737-8880	737-4998
Duckback Products 2644 Hegan Ln PO Box 980 TF: 800-825-5382 ■ Web: www.superdeck.com	Chico	CA	95927	530-343-3261	343-3283
Dunn-Edwards Corp 4885 E 52nd Pl TF: 800-537-4098 ■ Web: www.dunnedwards.com	Los Angeles	CA	90058	323-771-3330	771-4440
DuPont Automotive 950 Stephenson Hwy PO Box 7013 TF: 800-533-1313 ■ Web: www2.dupont.com	Troy	MI	48007	248-583-8000	
DuPont Performance Coatings 1007 Market St. TF: 800-441-7515 ■ Web: www.pc.dupont.com	Wilmington	DE	19898	302-774-1000	999-4399
Duron Inc 10406 Tucker St TF: 800-723-8766 ■ Web: www.duron.com	Beltsville	MD	20705	301-937-4700	
Farrell-Calhoun Inc 221 E Carolina Ave. Web: www.farrell-calhoun.com	Memphis	TN	38126	901-526-2211	774-4213
Ferro Corp 1000 Lakeside Ave NYSE: FOE ■ Web: www.ferro.com	Cleveland	OH	44114	216-641-8580	875-6195
Ferro Corp Liquid Coatings & Dispersions Div 1301 N Flora St TF: 800-882-1456	Plymouth	IN	46563	574-935-5131	935-4261
Ferro Corp Plastics Colorants Div 3 Railroad Ave. TF: 800-521-9094 ■ Web: www.ferro.com	Stryker	OH	43557	419-682-3311	682-4924
FinishMaster Inc 54 Monument Cir 8th Fl TF: 888-311-3678 ■ Web: www.finishmaster.com	Indianapolis	IN	46204	317-237-3678	237-2150
Flex Bon Paints 2131 Andrea Ln. TF: 800-353-9266 ■ Web: www.flexbon.com	Fort Myers	FL	33912	239-489-2332	433-0203
Gallagher-Kaiser Corp 13710 Mt Elliott St Web: www.gkcorp.com	Detroit	MI	48212	313-368-3100	368-3109
General Coatings Technology Inc 24 Woodward Ave. TF: 800-522-3664	Ridgewood	NY	11385	718-821-1232	381-6935
Hallman Lindsay Paints Inc 1717 N Bristol St Web: www.hallmanlindsay.com	Sun Prairie	WI	53590	608-834-8844	837-1064
Harrison Paint Co 1329 Harrison Ave SW TF: 800-321-0680 ■ Web: www.harrisonpaint.com	Canton	OH	44706	330-455-5125	454-1750
HB Fuller Co 1200 Willow Lake Blvd PO Box 64683 NYSE: FUL ■ TF: 888-423-8553 ■ Web: www.hbfuller.com	Saint Paul	MN	55164	651-236-5900	236-5898
Hentzen Coatings Inc 6937 W Mill Rd. Web: www.hentzen.com	Milwaukee	WI	53218	414-353-4200	353-0286
Hirshfield's Inc 725 2nd Ave N Web: www.hirshfields.com	Minneapolis	MN	55405	612-377-3910	436-3384
Insl-X Products Corp 101 Paragon Dr *Fax Area Code: 888 ■ TF Cust Svc: 800-225-5554 ■ Web: www.insl-x.com	Montvel	NY	10980	845-786-5000	248-2143*
Kelly-Moore Paint Co Inc 987 Commercial St. *Fax: Hum Res ■ TF: 800-874-4436 ■ Web: www.kellymoore.com	San Carlos	CA	94070	650-592-8337	508-8563*
Kenyon Plastering Inc 4001 W Indian School Rd. TF: 800-949-4319 ■ Web: www.kenyonweb.com	Phoenix	AZ	85019	602-233-1191	278-6801
KJ Quinn & Co Inc 34 Folly Mill Rd	Seabrook	NH	03874	603-474-5753	474-7122
Kop-Coat Inc 436 7th Ave Koppers Bldg Suite 1850 Web: www.kop-coat.com	Pittsburgh	PA	15219	412-227-2700	227-2618
Kwal Paint 3900 Joliet St. TF Cust Svc: 800-383-8406 ■ Web: www.kwalhowells.com	Denver	CO	80239	303-371-5600	373-5688
Lancaster Distributing Co 1310 Union St. TF: 800-845-8287 ■ Web: www.lancasterco.com	Spartanburg	SC	29302	864-583-3011	542-1315
Lansco Colors 305 W Grand Ave. TF: 800-526-2783 ■ Web: www.pigments.com	Montvale	NJ	07645	201-307-5995	307-5855
MAB Paints 600 Reed Rd. TF: 800-622-1899 ■ Web: www.mabpaints.com	Broomall	PA	19008	610-353-5100	353-8189
Magni Group Inc 390 Pk St Suite 300. Web: www.themagnigroup.com	Birmingham	MI	48009	248-647-4500	647-7506
Magni-Industries Inc 2771 Hammond St. Web: www.magniindustries.com	Detroit	MI	48209	313-843-7855	842-6730
Mantros-Haeuser & Co Inc 1175 Post Rd E TF: 800-344-4229 ■ Web: www.mbzgroup.com	Westport	CT	06880	203-454-1800	227-0558
Martin-Senour Paints 101 Prospect Ave NW. TF: 800-677-5270 ■ Web: www.martinsenour.com	Cleveland	OH	44115	216-566-2000	566-2947
Masterchem Industries LLC 3135 Old Hwy M TF: 800-325-3552 ■ Web: www.masterchem.com	Imperial	MO	63052	636-942-2510	942-3663
Michelman Inc 9080 Shell Rd. TF: 800-477-0498 ■ Web: www.michelman.com	Cincinnati	OH	45236	513-793-7766	793-2504
Miller Paint Co Inc 12812 NE Whitaker Way Web: www.millerpaint.com	Portland	OR	97230	503-255-0190	255-0192
Minwax Co 10 Mountainview Rd TF: 800-523-9299 ■ Web: www.minwax.com	Upper Saddle River	NJ	07458	201-818-7500	818-7605
Mobile Paint Mfg Co 4775 Hamilton Blvd TF: 800-621-6952 ■ Web: www.blpmobilepaint.com	Theodore	AL	36582	251-443-6110	408-0410
Mohawk Finishing Products 22 S Ctr St *Fax Area Code: 800 ■ TF: 800-545-0047 ■ Web: www.mohawk-finishing.com	Hickory	NC	28601	828-261-0325	721-1545*
Morwear Mfg Inc 620 Lamar St Web: www.morwear.com	Los Angeles	CA	90031	323-222-7000	227-7153
Muralo Co Inc 148 E 5th St TF: 800-631-3440 ■ Web: www.muralo.com	Bayonne	NJ	07002	201-437-0770	437-0664
Neogard Div Jones-blair Co 2728 Empire Central St. *Fax: Cust Svc ■ TF: 800-492-9400 ■ Web: www.jones-blair.com	Dallas	TX	75235	214-353-1600	325-6321*
Norton & Son Inc 148 E 5th St TF: 800-631-3440 ■ Web: www.muralo.com	Bayonne	NJ	07002	201-437-0770	437-0664
O'Leary Paint 300 E Oakland Ave TF: 800-477-2066 ■ Web: www.olearypaint.com	Lansing	MI	48906	517-487-2066	487-1680
Parker Paint Mfg Co Inc 3003 S Tacoma Way TF: 800-826-4308 ■ Web: www.parkerpaint.com	Tacoma	WA	98409	253-473-1122	473-0448
Penn Color Inc 400 Old Dublin Pike TF: 800-523-6032 ■ Web: www.penncolor.com	Doylestown	PA	18901	215-345-6550	345-0270
Pioneer Mfg 4529 Industrial Pkwy. TF: 800-877-1500 ■ Web: www.pioneerathletics.com	Cleveland	OH	44135	216-671-5500	671-5502
PPG Industries Inc 1 PPG Pl NYSE: PPG ■ *Fax: Hum Res ■ Web: www.ppg.com	Pittsburgh	PA	15272	412-434-3131	434-2011*
Red Spot Paint & Varnish Co Inc 1107 E Louisiana St TF: 800-457-3544 ■ Web: www.redspot.com	Evansville	IN	47711	812-428-9100	
Republic Powdered Metals Inc 2628 Pearl Rd TF: 800-551-7081 ■ Web: www.rpmrepublic.com	Medina	OH	44256	330-225-3192	273-5061
Rodda Paint Co 6107 N Marine Dr Web: www.roddapaint.com	Portland	OR	97203	503-521-4300	521-4400
Roymal Inc 3 Roymal Ln PO Box 658 Web: www.roymalinc.com	Newport	NH	03773	603-863-2410	863-9065
RPM International Inc 2628 Pearl Rd NYSE: RPM ■ TF: 800-776-4488 ■ Web: www.rpminc.com	Medina	OH	44256	330-273-5090	225-8743
Rust-Oleum Corp 11 E Hawthorn Pkwy TF: 800-323-3584 ■ Web: www.rustoleum.com	Vernon Hills	IL	60061	847-367-7700	816-2300
Samuel Cabot Inc 100 Hale St TF: 800-877-8246 ■ Web: www.cabotstain.com	Newburyport	MA	01950	978-465-1900	
Seymour Of Sycamore Inc 917 Crosby Ave. TF: 800-435-4482 ■ Web: www.seymourpaint.com	Sycamore	IL	60178	815-895-9101	895-8475
Sheboygan Paint Co Inc 1439 N 25th St PO Box 417 TF: 800-773-7801 ■ Web: www.shebpaint.com	Sheboygan	WI	53082	920-458-2157	458-5620
Sherwin-Williams Co Automotive Div 4440 Warrensville Ctr Rd	Warrensville Heights	OH	44128	216-332-8330	
Sherwin-Williams Co Coatings Div 101 Prospect Ave NW. Web: www.oem.sherwin-williams.com	Cleveland	OH	44115	216-566-2000	
Sterling-Clark-Lurton Corp PO Box 130 TF: 800-225-9872 ■ Web: www.sclsterling.com	Norwood	MA	02062	781-762-5400	762-1095
Talbot Industries Inc 5725 Howard Bush Dr TF: 800-749-6894	Neosho	MO	64850	417-451-7440	451-6244
TCI Powder Coatings Inc 734 Dixon Dr *Fax Area Code: 800 ■ TF: 800-533-9067 ■ Web: www.tcipowder.com	Ellaville	GA	31806	229-937-5411	265-0404*
Textured Coatings Of America 2422 E 15th St TF: 800-454-0340 ■ Web: www.texcote.com	Panama City	FL	32405	850-769-0347	769-8339
Tnemec Co Inc 6800 Corporate Dr TF: 800-483-3969 ■ Web: www.tnemec.com	Kansas City	MO	64120	816-483-3400	483-3969
Troy Corp 8 Vreeland Rd PO Box 955 Web: www.troycorp.com	Florham Park	NJ	07932	973-443-4200	443-0258
United Gilsonite Laboratories 1369 Jefferson Ave PO Box 70 TF: 800-845-5227 ■ Web: www.ugl.com	Scranton	PA	18501	570-344-1202	969-7634
Valspar Refinish Inc 210 Crosby St. TF Cust Svc: 800-556-1347 ■ Web: www.valsparrefinish.com	Picayune	MS	39466	601-798-4731	798-6147
Vista Paint Corp 2020 E Orangethorpe Ave Web: www.vistapaint.com	Fullerton	CA	92831	714-680-3810	459-4708
Whitmore Mfg Co PO Box 9300 TF: 800-699-6318 ■ Web: www.whitmores.com	Rockwall	TX	75087	972-771-1000	722-2108
Willamette Valley Co 1075 Arrowsmith St TF: 800-333-9826 ■ Web: www.wilvaco.com	Eugene	OR	97402	541-484-9621	345-7480
WM Barr & Co Inc 2105 Ch Ave *Fax Area Code: 800 ■ TF: 800-782-9928 ■ Web: www.wmbarr.com	Memphis	TN	38109	901-775-0100	621-9508*
Wolf Gordon Inc 33-00 47th Ave. TF: 800-347-0550 ■ Web: www.wolf-gordon.com	Long Island City	NY	11101	718-361-6611	361-1090
Yenkin-Majestic Paint Corp 1920 Leonard Ave. TF: 800-848-1898 ■ Web: www.yenkin-majestic.com	Columbus	OH	43219	614-253-8511	253-6327

554 PALLETS & SKIDS

Company	City	State	ZIP	Phone	Fax
Allied Container Corp 435 E Hedding St.	San Jose	CA	95112	408-293-3628	293-2014
American Fibertech Corp PO Box 220 Web: www.ind-pallet-corp.com	Remington	IN	47977	219-261-3586	261-2211
American Pallet Inc 1001 Knox Rd Web: www.americanpallet.com	Oakdale	CA	95361	209-847-6122	847-6154
Anderson Forest Products Inc 1267 Old Edmonton Rd PO Box 520. TF: 800-489-6778 ■ Web: www.afp-usa.com	Tompkinsville	KY	42167	270-487-6778	487-8953

Company	City	State	Zip	Phone	Fax
Brunswick Box Co Inc 852 Planters Rd PO Box 7 *TF:* 800-343-9913 ■ *Web:* www.brunswickbox.com	Lawrenceville	VA	23868	434-848-2222	848-3647
Clinch-Tite Corp 5264 Lake St PO Box 456 *TF:* 800-241-0900 ■ *Web:* www.clinchtite.com	Sandy Lake	PA	16145	724-376-7315	376-2785
Cutter Lumber Products 10 Rickenbacker Cir *Web:* www.cutterlumber.com	Livermore	CA	94551	925-443-5959	443-0648
Daniel Lumber Co Inc 309 Pierce St PO Box 340 *TF:* 800-251-0398	LaGrange	GA	30241	706-884-5686	883-8010
Day Lumber Corp 34 S Broad St PO Box 9 *Web:* www.daylumber.com	Westfield	MA	01086	413-568-3511	568-6668
Delisa Pallet Corp 91 Blanchard St *Web:* www.delisapallet.com	Newark	NJ	07105	973-344-8600	344-0689
Eastern Wood Products Inc 2020 Mill Ln PO Box 1056 *TF:* 800-445-5428	Williamsport	PA	17703	570-326-1946	327-1390
Edwards Wood Products Inc 2215 Old Lawyers Rd PO Box 219 *Web:* www.ewpi.com	Marshville	NC	28103	704-624-5098	624-6812
Hill Wood Products Inc 948 Ashawa Rd PO Box 398 *TF:* 800-788-9689 ■ *Web:* www.hillwoodproducts.com	Cook	MN	55723	218-666-5933	666-5726
Hinchcliff Products Co 13477 Prospect Rd *Web:* www.hinchcliffproducts.com	Strongsville	OH	44149	440-238-5200	238-5202
Hunter Woodworks Inc 21038 S Wilmington Ave PO Box 4937 *TF:* 800-966-4751 ■ *Web:* www.hunterpallets.com	Carson	CA	90749	323-775-2544	775-2540
Ifco Systems 6829 Flintlock Rd *TF:* 800-771-1148 ■ *Web:* www.ifcosystems.com	Houston	TX	77040	713-332-6145	332-6146
Litco International Inc 1 Litco Dr *Web:* www.litco.com	Vienna	OH	44473	330-539-5433	539-5388
Mountain Valley Farms & Lumber Inc 1240 Nawakwa Rd *Web:* www.mtvalleyfarms.com	Biglerville	PA	17307	717-677-6166	677-9283
Nelson Co 2116 Sparrows Pt Rd *Web:* www.nelsoncompany.com	Baltimore	MD	21219	410-477-3000	388-0246
Nepa Pallet & Container Co Inc 12027 Three Lakes Rd PO Box 399 *TF:* 800-562-3932	Snohomish	WA	98291	360-568-3185	568-9135
Packing Material Co 27280 Haggerty Rd Suite C-16 *TF:* 888-927-4797 ■ *Web:* www.packingmaterial.com	Farmington Hills	MI	48331	248-489-7000	489-7009
Pallet Consultants Corp PO Box 1692 *TF:* 888-782-2909 ■ *Web:* www.palletconsultants.com	Pompano Beach	FL	33061	954-946-2212	
Pallet Masters Inc 655 E Florence Ave *TF:* 800-675-2579 ■ *Web:* www.palletmasters.com	Los Angeles	CA	90001	323-758-6559	758-9600
PalletOne Inc 1470 US Hwy 17 S *TF:* 800-771-1148 ■ *Web:* www.palletone.com	Bartow	FL	33830	863-533-1147	533-3065
Potomac Supply Corp 1398 Kinsale Rd *TF Sales:* 800-365-3900 ■ *Web:* www.potomacsupply.com	Kinsale	VA	22488	804-472-2527	472-4300
Precision Wood Products Inc 16363 NE Sandy Blvd PO Box 529 *TF:* 877-743-9663	Vancouver	WA	98660	503-285-0393	252-6046
Remmey the Pallet Co 317 Davisville Rd PO Box 558 *TF:* 800-725-5385 ■ *Web:* www.remmey.com	Willow Grove	PA	19090	267-913-0002	913-0510
Savanna Pallets Co 106 E 1st Ave PO Box 308 *TF:* 800-348-5708 ■ *Web:* www.savannapallets.com	McGregor	MN	55760	218-768-2077	768-3112
Tasler Inc 1804 Tasler Dr PO Box 726 *TF:* 800-482-7537 ■ *Web:* www.tasler.com	Webster City	IA	50595	515-832-5200	832-2721
United Wholesale Lumber Co 8009 Doe Ave *TF:* 800-651-2037 ■ *Web:* www.uwlco.com	Visalia	CA	93291	559-651-2037	651-0742
Walczak Lumber Inc Rt 106 PO Box 340 *TF:* 800-445-1215	Clifford	PA	18413	570-222-9651	222-9650
Walters Bros Lumber Mfg Co Inc 10489 W Hwy 27/70	Radisson	WI	54867	715-945-2217	945-2878
Williamsburg Millwork Corp PO Box 427 *TF:* 888-699-8900	Bowling Green	VA	22427	804-994-2151	994-5371
WNC Pallet & Forest Products Co Inc 1414 Smokey Pk Hwy PO Box 38 *Web:* www.wncpallet.com	Candler	NC	28715	828-667-5426	665-4759
Wooden Pallets Gp LLC PO Box 555 *Web:* www.woodenpalletsltd.com	Silsbee	TX	77656	409-385-1234	385-6203
Yoder Lumber Co Inc 3799 County Rd 70 *Web:* www.yoderlumber.com	Sugarcreek	OH	44681	330-893-3131	893-3032

555 PAPER - MFR

SEE ALSO Packaging Materials & Products - Paper or Plastics p. 2332

555-1 Coated & Laminated Paper

Company	City	State	Zip	Phone	Fax
Appleton Papers Inc 825 E Wisconsin Ave PO Box 359 *TF:* 800-558-8390 ■ *Web:* www.appletonideas.com	Appleton	WI	54912	920-734-9841	
Arkwright Inc 538 Main St *TF Cust Svc:* 800-942-5900 ■ *Web:* www.arkwright-ri.com	Fiskeville	RI	02823	401-821-1000	826-3926
Avery Dennison Worldwide Graphics Div 250 Chester St Bldg 6 *TF:* 800-443-9380 ■ *Web:* www.averygraphics.com	Painesville	OH	44077	440-358-3700	358-3665
BPM Inc 200 W Front St *TF:* 800-826-0494 ■ *Web:* www.bpmpaper.com	Peshtigo	WI	54157	715-582-4551	582-4853
Cardinal Industries Inc 37 W 750 Rt 64 *TF:* 800-323-5018 ■ *Web:* www.cardind.com	Saint Charles	IL	60175	630-513-5400	513-5609
Diversified Labeling Solutions 1285 Hamilton Pkwy *TF:* 800-397-3013 ■ *Web:* www.teamdlsolutions.com	Itasca	IL	60143	630-625-1225	
Felix Schoeller North America Inc PO Box 250 *Web:* www.schoeller.com	Pulaski	NY	13142	315-298-5133	
Fortifiber Corp 1001 Tahoe Blvd *TF:* 800-443-4079 ■ *Web:* www.fortifiber.com	Incline Village	NV	89451	775-833-6161	833-6151
Fraser Papers Inc 2273 Congress St *TF:* 800-920-9988 ■ *Web:* www.fraserpapers.com	Portland	ME	04102	207-523-2350	523-2392
French Paper Co 100 French St *TF:* 800-253-5952 ■ *Web:* www.frenchpaper.com	Niles	MI	49120	269-683-1100	683-3025
Horizon Paper Co Inc 1010 Washington Blvd # 2-9 *TF:* 866-358-0855 ■ *Web:* www.horizonpaper.com	Stamford	CT	06901	203-358-0855	358-0828
InteliCoat Technologies 28 Gaylord St *TF:* 800-628-9285 ■ *Web:* www.intelicoat.com	South Hadley	MA	01075	413-536-7800	536-4414
Kimberly-Clark Corp Technical Paper Div 1400 Holcomb Bridge Rd *TF:* 800-544-1847 ■ *Web:* www.kimberly-clark.com	Roswell	GA	30076	920-721-2000	721-4219
Knowlton Specialty Papers Inc 213 Factory St *Web:* www.knowlton-co.com	Watertown	NY	13601	315-782-0600	782-7517
Lofton Label Inc 6290 Claude Way *TF:* 877-447-8118 ■ *Web:* www.loftonlabel.com	Inver Grove Heights	MN	55076	651-457-8118	457-3709
MeadWestvaco Specialty Paper 40 Willow St **Fax:* Mktg ■ *Web:* www.meadwestvaco.com/specialtypapers.nsf	South Lee	MA	01260	413-243-1231	243-4602*
Nashua Corp 11 Trafalgar Sq 2nd Fl *TF:* 800-258-1370 ■ *Web:* www.nashua.com	Nashua	NH	03063	603-880-2323	880-5671
National/AZON 1148 Rochester Rd **Fax Area Code:* 866 ■ *TF:* 800-325-5939 ■ *Web:* www.azon.com	Troy	MI	48083	248-307-9308	318-7323*
NewPage Corp 10 W 2nd St **Fax Area Code:* 937 ■ *TF:* 877-855-7243 ■ *Web:* www.newpagecorp.com	Dayton	OH	45402	877-855-7243	242-9327*
Sappi Fine Paper North America 255 State St **Fax:* Mail Rm ■ *Web:* www.na.sappi.com	Boston	MA	02109	617-423-7300	423-5494*
Shawsheen Rubber Co Inc PO Box 4296 *Web:* www.shawsheencc.com	Andover	MA	01810	978-475-1710	475-8603
Technicote Westfield Inc 222 Mound Ave *Web:* www.technicote.com	Miamisburg	OH	45342	937-859-4448	859-9096
TST/Impreso Inc 652 Southwestern Blvd **Fax Area Code:* 800 ■ **Fax:* Cust Svc ■ *TF:* 800-527-2878 ■ *Web:* www.tstimpreso.com	Coppell	TX	75019	972-462-0100	562-5359*
Wausau Paper Corp 100 Paper Pl *NYSE: WPP* ■ *Web:* www.wausaupaper.com	Mosinee	WI	54455	715-693-4470	692-2083
Wausau Paper Corp Specialty Paper Div 100 Paper Pl *NASDAQ: WPP* ■ *TF:* 800-723-0008 ■ *Web:* www.wausaupaper.com	Mosinee	WI	54455	715-693-4470	692-2082
Wcp Solutions 6703 S 234th St Suite 120 *Web:* www.wcpc.com	Kent	WA	98032	253-850-3560	852-9272

555-2 Writing Paper

Company	City	State	Zip	Phone	Fax
American Scholar Inc 335 Crooked Hill Rd	Brentwood	NY	11717	631-273-6550	273-6019
Anna Griffin Inc 99 Armour Dr *TF:* 888-817-8170 ■ *Web:* www.annagriffin.com	Atlanta	GA	30324	404-817-8170	817-0590
Crane & Co Inc 30 S St **Fax:* Orders ■ *TF Cust Svc:* 800-572-0024 ■ *Web:* www.crane.com	Dalton	MA	01226	413-684-2600	684-0726*
DiversaFile LLC 721 111th St	Arlington	TX	76011	817-640-0800	640-0800
Geographics LLC 93 N Ave **Fax Area Code:* 908 ■ *TF:* 800-526-4280 ■ *Web:* www.geographics.com	Garwood	NJ	07027	800-526-4280	789-9461*
Gordon Paper Co Inc PO Box 1806 *TF:* 800-457-7366 ■ *Web:* www.gordonpaper.com	Norfolk	VA	23501	757-464-3581	363-9355
Louisiana Assn For The Blind The 1750 Claiborne Ave *TF:* 877-913-6471 ■ *Web:* www.lablind.com	Shreveport	LA	71103	318-635-6471	635-8902
Mafcote Industries Inc 108 Main St *TF Cust Svc:* 800-221-3056 ■ *Web:* www.mafcote.com	Norwalk	CT	06851	203-847-8500	849-9177
MeadWestvaco Consumer & Office Products 4751 Hempstead Stn Dr *TF:* 800-648-6323 ■ *Web:* www.meadwestvaco.com/cop.nsf	Kettering	OH	45429	937-495-6323	
Mohawk Fine Papers Inc 465 Saratoga St *TF:* 800-843-6455 ■ *Web:* www.mohawkpaper.com	Cohoes	NY	12047	518-237-1740	237-7394
Neenah Paper Inc 3460 Preston Ridge Rd Suite 600 *NYSE: NP* ■ *Web:* www.neenah.com	Alpharetta	GA	30005	678-566-6500	
Paper Conversions Inc (PCI) 6761 Thompson Rd N *TF:* 800-729-2823 ■ *Web:* www.padmaker.com	Syracuse	NY	13211	315-437-1641	437-3634
Performance Office Papers 21673 Cedar Ave **Fax Area Code:* 800 ■ *TF:* 800-458-7189 ■ *Web:* www.perfpapers.com	Lakeville	MN	55044	952-469-1400	488-5058*
Rytex Co 100 N Pk Ave *TF:* 800-277-5458 ■ *Web:* www.rytex.com	Peru	IN	46970	800-277-5458	329-1669
Schurman Fine Papers 500 Chadbourne Rd PO Box 6030 *TF Sales:* 800-333-6724 ■ *Web:* www.papyrusonline.com	Fairfield	CA	94533	707-428-0200	428-0641
Southworth Co 265 Main St *TF:* 800-225-1839 ■ *Web:* www.southworth.com	Agawam	MA	01001	413-789-1200	786-1529
Specialty Loose Leaf Inc 1 Cabot St *TF:* 800-848-8020 ■ *Web:* www.specialtyll.com	Holyoke	MA	01040	413-532-0106	887-0195
Top Flight Inc 1300 Central Ave *TF:* 800-777-3740 ■ *Web:* www.topflightpaper.com	Chattanooga	TN	37408	423-266-8171	266-6857
Wausau Paper Corp 100 Paper Pl *NYSE: WPP* ■ *Web:* www.wausaupaper.com	Mosinee	WI	54455	715-693-4470	692-2083
Wausau Paper Corp Printing & Writing Paper Div 1 Clark's Island *NASDAQ: WPP* ■ *TF:* 800-723-0008 ■ *Web:* www.wausaupaper.com	Wausau	WI	54403	715-675-3361	675-8355
William Arthur Inc 7 Alewive Pk Rd *TF:* 800-985-6581 ■ *Web:* www.williamarthur.com	West Kennebunk	ME	04094	207-985-6581	985-0407

556 PAPER - WHOL

Company	City	State	Zip	Phone	Fax
America Chung Nam Inc 1163 Fairway Dr *Web:* www.acni.net	City of Industry	CA	91789	909-839-8383	869-6310

Company	City	State	ZIP	Phone	Fax
Anchor Paper Co Inc 480 Broadway St *TF:* 800-652-9755 ■ *Web:* www.anchorpaper.com	Saint Paul	MN	55101	651-298-1311	298-0060
AT Clayton & Co Inc 300 Atlantic St. *TF:* 800-282-5298 ■ *Web:* www.atclayton.com	Stamford	CT	06901	203-658-1200	658-1326
Atlantic Packaging Co 806 N 23rd St *TF:* 800-722-5841 ■ *Web:* www.atlanticpkg.com	Wilmington	NC	28405	910-343-0624	763-5421
Atlus USA Inc 199 Technology Dr *Web:* www.atlus.com	Irvine	CA	92618	949-788-0455	
Bradner Smith & Co 2300 Arthur Ave. *TF:* 800-678-1852 ■ *Web:* www.bradnersmith.com	Elk Grove Village	IL	60007	847-290-8485	290-8486
Central Lewmar Paper Co 60 McClellan St. *Web:* www.centrallewmar.com	Newark	NJ	07114	973-622-6377	623-4323
CJ Duffey Paper Co Inc 528 Washington Ave N *TF:* 800-752-8190 ■ *Web:* www.duffeypaper.com	Minneapolis	MN	55401	612-338-8701	338-1320
Clampitt Paper Co of Dallas 9207 Ambassador Row *Web:* www.clampitt.com	Dallas	TX	75247	214-638-3300	634-7837
Clifford Paper Inc 600 E Crescent Ave *Web:* www.cliffordpaper.com	Upper Saddle River	NJ	07458	201-934-5115	934-5188
Cole Papers Inc 1300 N 38th St *TF:* 800-800-8090 ■ *Web:* www.colepapers.com	Fargo	ND	58102	701-282-5311	282-5513
Dennis Paper Co 910 Acorn Dr *TF:* 800-441-5684 ■ *Web:* www.dennispaper.com	Nashville	TN	37210	615-883-9010	885-2969
Donco Paper Supply Co 737 N Michigan Ave Suite 1450 *Web:* www.doncosolutions.com	Chicago	IL	60611	312-337-7822	337-7822
Eastern Data Paper Inc PO Box 202 *TF:* 800-524-2528	Little Falls	NJ	07424	973-472-5252	472-5333
Elof Hansson Pulp Inc 565 Taxter Rd. *Web:* www.elofhansson.com	Elmsford	NY	10523	914-345-8380	345-8112
Field Paper Co 3950 D St *TF:* 800-969-3435 ■ *Web:* www.fieldpaper.com	Omaha	NE	68107	402-733-3600	731-7113
Gould Paper Corp 11 Madison Ave 14th Fl. *TF:* 800-275-4685 ■ *Web:* www.gouldpaper.com	New York	NY	10010	212-301-0000	481-0067
GPA Specialty Substrate Solutions 8740 W 50th St. *Fax Area Code: 800 ■ *TF:* 800-395-9000 ■ *Web:* www.askgpa.com	McCook	IL	60525	773-650-2020	395-3581*
GreenLine Paper Co Inc 631 S Pine St *TF:* 800-641-1117 ■ *Web:* www.greenlinepaper.com	York	PA	17403	717-845-8697	846-3806
Hearn Paper Co 556 N Meridian Rd *TF:* 800-225-2989 ■ *Web:* www.hearnpaper.com	Youngstown	OH	44509	330-792-6533	792-4762
Heinzel Imports-Exports Inc 220 E 42nd St Suite 3010 *Web:* www.heinzelsales.com	New York	NY	10017	212-953-3210	953-3211
Hudson Valley Paper Co 981 Broadway *TF:* 800-473-5525	Albany	NY	12207	518-471-5111	455-8803
Kelly Paper Co 288 Brea Canyon Rd *Fax Area Code: 909 ■ *TF:* 800-675-3559 ■ *Web:* www.kellypaper.com	City of Industry	CA	91789	800-675-3559	859-8903*
Lindenmeyr Book Publishing Papers 521 5th Ave 6th Fl *Web:* www.lindenmeyr.com	New York	NY	10175	212-551-3900	213-1457
Lindenmeyr Central 3 Manhattanville Rd *TF:* 800-221-3042 ■ *Web:* www.lindenmeyr.com	Purchase	NY	10577	914-696-9300	696-9333
Lindenmeyr Munroe Central Central National-Gottesman Inc 3 Manhattanville Rd *Web:* www.lindenmeyr.com	Purchase	NY	10577	914-696-9300	696-9333
Lindenmeyr Munroe Paper Corp 115 Moonachie Ave *TF:* 800-631-0193 ■ *Web:* www.lindenmeyr.com	Moonachie	NJ	07074	201-440-6491	440-6492
Mac Papers Inc 3300 Phillips Hwy PO Box 5369 *TF:* 800-622-2968 ■ *Web:* www.macpapers.com	Jacksonville	FL	32207	904-348-3300	348-3340
Marquardt & Co 161 6th Ave 2nd Fl *TF:* 800-813-7788	New York	NY	10013	212-645-7200	536-0282
Midland Paper 101 E Palatine Rd *TF:* 800-323-8522 ■ *Web:* www.midlandpaper.com	Wheeling	IL	60090	847-777-2700	777-2555
Millcraft Paper Co 6800 Grant Ave *TF:* 800-826-4444 ■ *Web:* www.millcraft.com	Cleveland	OH	44105	216-441-5500	441-4128
Morrisette Paper Co Inc 5925 Summit Ave PO Box 20768 *TF:* 800-822-8882 ■ *Web:* www.morrisettepaper.com	Greensboro	NC	27214	336-375-1515	621-0751
Murnane Paper Corp 345 Fischer Farm Rd *Web:* www.murnanepaper.com	Elmhurst	IL	60126	630-530-8222	530-8325
Newell Paper Co 1212 Grand Ave PO Box 631 *TF:* 800-844-8894 ■ *Web:* www.newellpaper.com	Meridian	MS	39301	601-693-1783	483-4900
PaperDirect Inc 1005 E Woodmen Rd *TF:* 800-272-7377 ■ *Web:* www.paperdirect.com	Colorado Springs	CO	80920	719-594-4100	534-1741
Paterson Card & Paper Co PO Box 2286 *Web:* www.patersonpapers.com	Paterson	NJ	07509	973-278-2410	278-0677
Perez Trading Co Inc 3490 NW 125th St *TF:* 800-999-7599 ■ *Web:* www.pereztrading.com	Miami	FL	33167	305-769-0761	681-7963
Quimby-Walstrom Paper Co 2944 Walkent Dr NW *TF Cust Svc:* 800-632-5930 ■ *Web:* www.quimby.com	Grand Rapids	MI	49544	616-784-4700	784-7813
Redd Paper Co 3851 Ctr Loop *TF:* 800-961-6656 ■ *Web:* www.reddpaper.com	Orlando	FL	32808	407-299-6656	299-8142
Roosevelt Paper Co 1 Roosevelt Dr *Fax: Sales ■ *TF:* 800-523-3470 ■ *Web:* www.rooseveltpaper.com	Mount Laurel	NJ	08054	856-303-4100	642-1949*
Spicers Paper Inc 12310 Slauson Ave *TF:* 800-774-2377 ■ *Web:* www.spicers.com	Santa Fe Springs	CA	90670	562-698-1199	945-2597
Streco Fibres Inc 168 Business Pk Dr Suite 200 *Web:* www.strecofibreskraftandtissuepaper.com	Virginia Beach	VA	23462	757-473-3720	473-3721
Unisource Worldwide Inc 6600 Governors Lake Pkwy *TF:* 800-282-7958 ■ *Web:* www.unisourcelink.com	Norcross	GA	30071	770-447-9000	209-6550
White Paper Co 9990 River Way *TF:* 888-840-7300 ■ *Web:* www.whitepaper.com	Delta	BC	V4G1M9	604-951-3900	951-3944
Wilcox Paper LLC 11100 Jefferson HWY N. *Web:* www.wilcoxpaper.com	Champlin	MN	55316	763-404-8400	

557 PAPER CONVERTERS

Company	City	State	ZIP	Phone	Fax
Ameri-Fax Corp 7709 W 20th Ave *TF:* 800-969-1601 ■ *Web:* www.faxpaper.com	Hialeah	FL	33014	305-828-1701	824-1606
Artistry in Motion Inc 15101 Keswick St. *Web:* www.artistryinmotion.com	Van Nuys	CA	91405	818-994-7388	994-7688
B & B Paper Converters Inc 12500 Elmwood Ave	Cleveland	OH	44111	216-941-8100	941-8174
BagcraftPapercon 3900 W 43rd St *TF:* 800-621-8468 ■ *Web:* www.bagcraft.com	Chicago	IL	60632	773-254-8000	254-8204
C-P Converters Inc 15 Grumbacher Rd *TF:* 800-815-0667 ■ *Web:* www.cpconverters.com	York	PA	17406	717-764-1193	764-2039
Caraustar Industries Inc 5000 Austell-Powder Sprngs Rd Suite 300 *TF:* 800-223-1373 ■ *Web:* www.caraustar.com	Austell	GA	30106	770-948-3100	
Case Paper Co Inc 500 Mamaroneck Ave 2nd Fl *TF:* 800-222-2922 ■ *Web:* www.casepaper.com	Harrison	NY	10528	914-899-3500	777-1028
Cindus Corp 515 Stn Ave *TF:* 800-543-4691 ■ *Web:* www.cindus.com	Cincinnati	OH	45215	513-948-9951	948-8805
Crocker Technical Papers 431 Westminster St.	Fitchburg	MA	01420	978-345-7771	342-4052
Crusader Paper Co Inc 350 Holt Rd. *Web:* www.crusaderpaper.com	North Andover	MA	01845	978-794-4900	794-1625
Damsky Paper Co 3501 1st Ave N *Web:* www.damskypaper.com	Birmingham	AL	35222	205-521-9840	521-9840
Delta Craft Paper Co 99 Bud Mil Dr *TF:* 800-735-5735 ■ *Web:* www.deltacraft.com	Buffalo	NY	14206	716-856-5135	856-5130
Extra Packaging Corp 736 Glouchester St. *TF:* 800-872-7548 ■ *Web:* www.extrapackaging.com	Boca Raton	FL	33487	561-416-2060	416-9545
Fabricon Products 1721 W Pleasant Ave *TF:* 800-676-9727 ■ *Web:* www.fabriconproducts.com	River Rouge	MI	48218	313-841-8200	841-4819
Graphic Converting LLC 877 N Larch Ave *TF:* 800-447-1935 ■ *Web:* www.graphicconverting.com	Elmhurst	IL	60126	630-758-4100	833-1058
Hampden Papers Inc PO Box 149 *TF:* 800-456-0200 ■ *Web:* www.hampdenpapers.com	Holyoke	MA	01041	413-536-1000	532-9161
Hazen Paper Co 240 S Water St PO Box 189 *Web:* www.hazen.com	Holyoke	MA	01041	413-538-8204	533-1420
International Converter Inc 17153 Industrial Hwy *TF:* 800-962-8572 ■ *Web:* www.ici-laminating.com	Caldwell	OH	43724	740-423-7525	423-5799
Interstate Paper Supply Co Inc (IPSCO) 103 Good St PO Box 670 *Web:* www.ipscoinc.com	Roscoe	PA	15477	724-938-2218	938-3415
Kanzaki Specialty Papers 1 Monarch Pl Suite 800 *TF:* 888-526-9254 ■ *Web:* www.kanzakiusa.com	Springfield	MA	01144	888-526-9254	
Label Art Southeast Div 100 Clover Green *Web:* www.labelart.com	Peachtree City	GA	30269	770-487-7575	487-3230
Lauterbach Group Inc W222 N5710 Miller Way *TF Sales:* 800-841-7301 ■ *Web:* www.lauterbachgroup.com	Sussex	WI	53089	262-820-8130	820-1806
Loyola Paper Co 951 W Lunt Ave	Elk Grove Village	IL	60007	847-956-7770	956-6897
Mac Paper Converters PO Box 5369 *TF:* 800-334-7026	Jacksonville	FL	32247	904-733-9660	733-9622
Mafcote Industries Inc 108 Main St. *TF Cust Svc:* 800-221-3056 ■ *Web:* www.mafcote.com	Norwalk	CT	06851	203-847-8500	849-9177
Newark Paperboard Products Inc 20 Jackson Dr. *TF:* 800-777-7890 ■ *Web:* www.newarkgroup.com	Cranford	NJ	07016	908-276-4000	276-2888
North Hill Paper Converters 278 19th St NE *Web:* www.northhill.net/converting/home.htm	Calgary	AB	T2E8P7	403-248-9993	248-1001
Northeastern PA Carton & Finishing Co Inc 4820 Birney Ave US Rt 11 *Web:* www.nepacartons.com	Moosic	PA	18507	570-457-7711	457-3801
PAC Paper Inc 6416 NW Whitney Rd. *TF:* 800-223-4981 ■ *Web:* www.pacpaperinc.com	Vancouver	WA	98665	360-695-7771	694-0943
Pacon Corp 2525 N Casaloma Dr. *TF:* 800-333-2545 ■ *Web:* www.pacon.com	Appleton	WI	54912	920-830-5050	830-5099
Paper Systems Inc 185 S Pioneer Blvd *TF:* 888-564-6774 ■ *Web:* www.papersystems.com	Springboro	OH	45066	937-746-6841	746-1089
PM Co 1500 Kemper Meadow Dr. *Fax Area Code: 800 ■ *TF:* 800-327-4359 ■ *Web:* www.pmcompany.com	Cincinnati	OH	45240	513-825-7626	626-2140*
Pride-Made Products Inc 740 Lloyd Rd	Matawan	NJ	07747	732-583-3030	583-7855
RiteMade Paper Converters 1015 Tyler St *TF Cust Svc:* 800-368-3485 ■ *Web:* www.ritemade.com	Fredericksburg	VA	22401	540-371-8626	371-4154
Solo Cup Co 1505 E Main St *Fax: Hum Res ■ *TF Cust Svc:* 800-367-2877 ■ *Web:* www.solocup.com	Urbana	IL	61802	217-384-1800	365-2318*
Spinnaker Coating Inc 518 E Water St *TF:* 800-543-9452 ■ *Web:* www.spinnakercoating.com	Troy	OH	45373	937-332-6500	335-2843
Texpack USA Inc 1001 Brickell Bay Dr Suite 2402 *Web:* www.texpack.com	Miami	FL	33131	305-358-9696	358-9797
TimeMed Labeling Systems Inc 144 Tower Dr *TF Cust Svc:* 800-323-4840 ■ *Web:* www.timemed.com	Burr Ridge	IL	60527	630-986-1800	986-0016
Tufco Technologies Inc PO Box 23500 *NASDAQ: TFCO* ■ *TF:* 800-558-8145	Green Bay	WI	54305	920-336-0054	336-9041
Wedlock Paper Converters Ltd 2327 Stanfield Rd *Web:* www.wedlockpaper.com	Mississauga	ON	L4Y1R6	905-277-9461	272-1108

558 PAPER FINISHERS (EMBOSSING, COATING, GILDING, STAMPING)

Company	City	State	ZIP	Phone	Fax
Colad Group 801 Exchange St *TF:* 800-950-1755 ■ *Web:* www.colad.com	Buffalo	NY	14210	716-961-1776	961-1753
Complemar Partners 500 Lee Rd Suite 200 *TF:* 866-742-5274 ■ *Web:* www.complemar.com	Rochester	NY	14606	585-647-5800	647-5800
Diecrafters Inc 1349 55th Ct *Web:* www.diecrafters.com	Cicero	IL	60804	708-656-3336	656-3386
Graphic Arts Finishers Inc 32 Cambridge St.	Charlestown	MA	02129	617-241-9292	241-7326

	City	State	ZIP	Phone	Fax
Jen-Coat Inc 132 N Elm St	Westfield	MA	01086	413-562-2315	568-6944*
**Fax:* Sales ■ *Web:* www.jencoat.com					
Loroco Industries Inc 5000 Creek Rd	Cincinnati	OH	45242	513-891-9544	891-9549
TF: 800-215-9474 ■ *Web:* www.loroco-industries.com					
Madison Cutting Die Inc 2547 Progress Rd	Madison	WI	53716	608-221-3422	223-6850
TF: 800-395-9405 ■ *Web:* www.mcd.net					
Malahide Design & Mfg Inc 1238 Melville St Suite 206	Vancouver	BC	V6E4N2	604-688-3400	000-0000
TF: 800-867-5077 ■ *Web:* www.hotstamping.com					
Markal Finishing Corp 400 Bostwick Ave	Bridgeport	CT	06605	203-384-8219	336-1231
McGraphics Inc 601 Hagan St	Nashville	TN	37203	615-242-8779	254-3031*
**Fax:* Orders ■ *TF:* 888-280-8200 ■ *Web:* www.mcgraphicsinc.com					
Unifoil Corp 12 Daniel Rd	Fairfield	NJ	07004	973-244-9900	244-5555
Web: www.unifoil.com					
Walton Press 402 Mayfield Dr	Monroe	GA	30655	770-267-2596	267-9463
TF: 800-354-0235 ■ *Web:* www.waltonpress.com					

559 PAPER INDUSTRIES MACHINERY

	City	State	ZIP	Phone	Fax
ASC Machine Tools Inc PO Box 11619	Spokane	WA	99211	509-534-6600	536-7658
Web: www.ascmt.com					
Baumfolder Corp 1660 Campbell Rd	Sidney	OH	45365	937-492-1281	492-7280
TF: 800-543-6107 ■ *Web:* www.baumfolder.com					
Black Clawson Converting Machinery Inc 46 N 1st St	Fulton	NY	13069	315-598-7121	593-0396
Web: www.bcconverting.com					
Cranston Machinery Co Inc 2251 SE Oak Grove Blvd	Oak Grove	OR	97267	503-654-7751	654-7751
TF: 800-547-1012 ■ *Web:* www.cranston-machinery.com					
Curt G Joa Inc 100 Crocker Ave PO Box 903	Sheboygan Falls	WI	53085	920-467-6136	467-2924
Web: www.joa.com					
Double E Co 319 Manley St	West Bridgewater	MA	02379	508-588-8099	580-2915
Web: www.doubleeusa.com					
Entwistle Co Dietzco Div 6 Bigelow St	Hudson	MA	01749	508-481-4000	481-4004
Web: www.entwistleco.com					
Faustel Inc W 194 N 11301 McCormick Dr PO Box 1000	Germantown	WI	53022	262-253-3333	253-3334
Web: www.faustel.com					
HG Weber & Co Inc 725 Fremont St	Kiel	WI	53042	920-894-2221	894-3786
Web: www.hgweber.com					
Holyoke Machine Co 514 Main St PO Box 988	Holyoke	MA	01040	413-534-5612	532-9244
Web: www.holyokemachine.com					
Kadant Black Clawson 7312 Central Pk Blvd	Mason	OH	45040	513-229-8100	424-1168
Web: www.blackclawson.com					
Kadant Inc One Technology Pk Dr	Westford	MA	01886	978-776-2000	635-1593
NYSE: KAI ■ *Web:* www.kadant.com					
Kempsmith Machine Co 1818 S 71st St	Milwaukee	WI	53214	414-256-8160	476-0564
Web: www.kempsmith-dl.com					
Magna Machine Co 11180 Southland Rd	Cincinnati	OH	45240	513-851-6900	851-6904
Web: www.magna-machine.com					
MarquipWardUnited 1300 N Airport Rd	Phillips	wi	54555	715-339-2191	339-4469
Web: www.marquipwardunited.com					
Maxson Automatic Machinery Co 70 Airport Rd PO Box 1517	Westerly	RI	02891	401-596-0162	596-1050
Web: www.maxsonautomatic.com					
Metso Paper USA Inc 25 Beloit St	Aiken	SC	29805	803-649-1541	649-1036
Web: www.metso.com					
Paco Winders Mfg Inc 2040 Bennett Rd	Philadelphia	PA	19116	215-673-6265	673-2027
Web: www.pacowinders.com					
Paper Machinery Corp 8900 W Bradley Rd PO Box 240100	Milwaukee	WI	53224	414-354-8050	354-8614
Web: www.papermc.com					
Pemco Inc 3333 Crocker Ave	Sheboygan	WI	53082	920-458-2500	458-1265
TF: 888-310-1898 ■ *Web:* www.pemco.kpl.net					
Sandusky International Inc 615 W Market St	Sandusky	OH	44870	419-626-5340	626-8674
Web: www.sanduskyintl.com					
Shreiner Co 1 Taylor Dr PO Box 347	Killbuck	OH	44637	330-276-6135	276-1605
TF: 800-722-9915 ■ *Web:* www.shreinerco.com					
Voith Paper Inc 2200 N Roemer Rd PO Box 2337	Appleton	WI	54912	920-731-7724	739-8081
Web: www.voithpaper.com					
Zerand Corp 15800 W Overland Dr	New Berlin	WI	53151	262-827-3800	827-3913
TF: 800-889-9984					

560 PAPER MILLS

SEE ALSO Paperboard Mills p. 2339; Pulp Mills p. 2474

	City	State	ZIP	Phone	Fax
AbitibiBowater Inc 1155 Metcalfe St Suite 800	Montreal	QC	H3B5H2	514-875-2160	875-6284
TF: 800-361-2888 ■ *Web:* www.abitibibowater.com					
Augusta News Print Co 2434 Doug Bernard Pkwy PO Box 1647	Augusta	GA	30913	706-798-3440	312-6473
Blue Heron Paper Co 427 Main St	Oregon City	OR	97045	503-650-4211	650-4595*
**Fax:* Sales ■ *TF:* 800-331-9991 ■ *Web:* www.blueheronpaper.com					
Boise Cascade LLC 1111 W Jefferson St Suite 300	Boise	ID	83702	208-384-6161	384-7189
Web: www.bc.com					
Boise Paper Solutions Corp 222 NE Pk Plaza Dr Suite 105	Vancouver	WA	98684	360-891-8787	
Web: www.bc.com					
Bowater Inc Newsprint & Directory Div 55 E Camper Down Way PO Box 1028	Greenville	SC	29602	864-271-7733	282-9496
TF: 800-845-6002 ■ *Web:* www.bowater.com/en/divisionsNewsprint.shtml					
BPM Inc 200 W Front St	Peshtigo	WI	54157	715-582-4551	582-4853
TF: 800-826-0494 ■ *Web:* www.bpmpaper.com					
Brant Allen Industries 80 Field Pt Rd 3rd Fl	Greenwich	CT	06830	203-661-3344	661-3349
Burrows Paper Corp 405 W Oak St	Little Falls	NY	13365	315-823-2300	823-0867
TF: 800-272-7122 ■ *Web:* www.burrowspaper.com					
Cascades Fine Papers Group Inc 2 Rolland Ave	Saint-Jerome	QC	J7Z5S1	450-569-3910	569-3947*
**Fax:* Mktg ■ *TF:* 800-567-9872 ■ *Web:* www.cascades.com					
Catalyst Paper Corp 3600 Lysander Ln 2nd Fl	Richmond	BC	V7B1C3	604-247-4400	247-0512
TSE: CTL ■ *Web:* www.catalystpaper.com					
Cauthorne Paper Co 205 Hull St	Richmond	VA	23224	804-232-6736	231-4779
TF: 800-552-3011 ■ *Web:* www.cauthornepaper.com					
Climax Mfg Co 7840 SR 26	Lowville	NY	13367	315-376-8000	376-2034
TF: 800-225-4629 ■ *Web:* www.climaxpkg.com					
Ecological Fibers Inc 40 Pioneer Dr	Lunenburg	MA	01462	978-537-0003	537-2238
Web: www.ecofibers.com					
FiberMark Inc Technical Specialities Div 161 Wellington Rd	Brattleboro	VT	05031	802-257-0365	257-5900
TF Cust Svc: 800-784-8558 ■ *Web:* www.fibermark.com					
Finch Pruyn & Co Inc 1 Glen St	Glens Falls	NY	12801	518-793-2541	793-7364
TF: 800-833-9981 ■ *Web:* www.finchpaper.com					
Gabriel Container Co 8844 S Millergrove Dr PO Box 3188	Santa Fe Sprin	CA	90670	562-699-1051	699-3284
Web: www.gabrielcontainer.com					
Glatfelter 96 S George St Suite 500	York	PA	17401	717-225-4711	846-7208
NYSE: GLT ■ *Web:* www.glatfelter.com					
Grays Harbor Paper LP 801 23rd St	Hoquiam	WA	98550	360-532-9600	538-5636
Web: www.ghpaper.com					
Hollingsworth & Vose Co 112 Washington St	East Walpole	MA	02032	508-668-0295	668-6526
Web: www.hollingsworth-vose.com					
Inland Empire Paper Co 3320 N Argonne	Millwood	WA	99212	509-924-1911	927-8461
Web: www.iepco.com					
International Paper Co 6400 Poplar Ave	Memphis	TN	38297	901-419-7000	
NYSE: IP ■ *TF Prod Info:* 800-223-1268 ■ *Web:* www.internationalpaper.com					
Interstate Resources Inc 1300 Wilson Blvd Suite 1075	Arlington	VA	22209	703-243-3355	243-4681
Web: www.interstateresources.com					
kapstone 5600 Virginia Ave PO Box 118005	Charleston	SC	29423	843-745-3000	745-3641
KapStone Paper & Packaging Corp 1101 Skokie Blvd Suite 300	Northbrook	IL	60062	847-239-8800	205-7551
NYSE: KS ■ *Web:* www.kapstonepaper.com					
Katahdin Paper Co 50 Main St	East Millinocket	ME	04430	207-723-5131	723-2200
Kimberly-Clark Corp 351 Phelps Dr	Irving	TX	75038	972-281-1200	281-1435
NYSE: KMB ■ *TF:* 800-544-1847 ■ *Web:* www.kimberly-clark.com					
Kruger Inc 3285 ch Bedford	Montreal	QC	H3S1G5	514-737-1131	343-3124
Web: www.kruger.com					
Longview Fibre Paper & Packaging Inc 300 Fibre Way PO Box 639	Longview	WA	98632	360-425-1550	230-5135
Web: www.longviewfibre.com					
Madison Paper Co 13101 S Pulaski Rd	Alsip	IL	60803	708-389-8520	389-8237
Madison Paper Industries Main St PO Box 129	Madison	ME	04950	207-696-3307	696-1104
Manistique Papers Inc 453 S Mackinac Ave	Manistique	MI	49854	906-341-2175	341-5635
TF: 800-743-2389 ■ *Web:* www.manistiquepapers.com					
Maryland Paper Co LP 16144 Elliott Pkwy	Williamsport	MD	21795	301-223-6550	223-7730
Web: www.marylandpaper.com					
Monadnock Paper Mills Inc 117 Antrim Rd	Bennington	NH	03442	603-588-3311	588-3158*
**Fax:* Sales ■ *TF Orders:* 800-221-2159 ■ *Web:* www.mpm.com					
Newbrook Paper Corp 215 14th St	Jersey City	NJ	07310	201-659-6700	659-6707
NewPage Corp 10 W 2nd St	Dayton	OH	45402	877-855-7243	242-9327*
**Fax Area Code:* 937 ■ *TF:* 877-855-7243 ■ *Web:* www.newpagecorp.com					
Norkol Inc & Converting 11650 W Grand Ave	Melrose Park	IL	60164	708-531-1000	531-0030
Web: www.norkol.com					
Potlatch Corp 601 W 1st Ave Suite 1600	Spokane	WA	99201	509-835-1500	835-1555
NASDAQ: PCH ■ *Web:* www.potlatchcorp.com					
Pratt Industries USA 1800C Sarasota Pkwy	Conyers	GA	30013	770-918-5678	918-5679
Web: www.prattindustries.com					
Sabin Robbins Paper Co 497 Cir Fwy Dr Suite 490	Cincinnati	OH	45246	513-874-5270	874-5785
TF: 800-424-5574 ■ *Web:* www.sabinrobbins.com					
Schweitzer-Mauduit International Inc 100 N Pt Ctr E Suite 600	Alpharetta	GA	30022	770-569-4272	569-4275
NYSE: SWM ■ *TF:* 800-514-0186 ■ *Web:* www.swmintl.com					
Seaman Paper Co of Massachusetts Inc 51 Main St	Otter River	MA	01436	978-939-5356	939-2359
Web: www.satinwrap.com					
SP Newsprint Co 709 Papermill Rd	Dublin	GA	31027	478-272-1600	275-6301
Web: www.spnewsprinteast.com					
Stora Enso North America Corp 201 Broad St 3rd Fl	Stamford	CT	06901	203-541-5100	353-1143
NYSE: SEO ■ *TF:* 888-807-8672 ■ *Web:* www.storaenso.com					
UPM-Kymmene Inc 999 Oakmont Plaza Dr Suite 200	Westmont	IL	60559	630-850-3310	850-3322
Web: www.upm.com					
Verso Paper Corp 6775 Lenox Ctr Ct Suite 400	Memphis	TN	38115	877-837-7606	369-4174*
NYSE: VRS ■ **Fax Area Code:* 901 ■ *Web:* www.versopaper.com					
West Carrollton Parchment Co 1 S Elm St	West Carrollton	OH	45449	937-859-3621	859-7610
West Linn Paper Co 4800 Mill St PO Box 68	West Linn	OR	97068	503-557-6500	557-6616
Web: www.wlinpco.com					
White Birch Paper Co Bear Island Div 10026 Old Ridge Rd	Ashland	VA	23005	804-227-3394	227-4014
Web: www.whitebirchpaper.com					
Xamax Industries Inc 63 Silvermine Rd	Seymour	CT	06483	203-888-7200	888-1002
Web: www.xamax.com					

561 PAPER PRODUCTS - SANITARY

Company	City	State	Zip	Phone	Fax
Arquest Inc 101 Interchange Plaza *Web:* www.arquest.com	Cranbury	NJ	08512	609-395-9500	395-9778
Aspen Products Inc 4231 Clary Blvd *Web:* www.aspenpro.com	Kansas City	MO	64130	816-921-0234	924-1488
Associated Hygienic Products LLC 3400 River Green Ct Suite 600 *TF:* 888-639-5863 ■ *Web:* www.ahp-dsg.com	Duluth	GA	30096	770-497-9800	623-8679
Atlas Paper Mills Ltd 3725 E 10th Ct *Web:* www.atlaspapermills.com	Hialeah	FL	33013	305-835-8046	691-6018
Bright of America Inc 300 Greenbrier Rd *TF:* 800-877-1925	Summersville	WV	26651	304-872-3000	872-3033
EMJA Co Inc PO Box 767189 *TF:* 800-992-3652 ■ *Web:* www.emja.com	Roswell	GA	30076	770-992-9464	
Erving Paper Mills 97 E Main St *TF:* 800-225-8014	Erving	MA	01344	413-422-2700	422-2710
Georgia-Pacific Corp 133 Peachtree St NE *Web:* www.gp.com	Atlanta	GA	30303	404-652-4000	230-5774
Hoffmaster 2920 N Main St *TF:* 800-558-9300 ■ *Web:* www.hoffmaster.com	Oshkosh	WI	54901	920-235-9330	235-1642
International Absorbents Inc 6960 Salashan Pkwy *TF:* 800-242-2287 ■ *Web:* www.absorbent.com	Ferndale	WA	98248	360-734-7415	671-1588
Kimberly-Clark Corp 351 Phelps Dr *NYSE: KMB* ■ *TF:* 800-544-1847 ■ *Web:* www.kimberly-clark.com	Irving	TX	75038	972-281-1200	281-1435
Kleen Test Products Inc 1611 Sunset Rd *TF:* 800-558-6842 ■ *Web:* www.kleentest.com	Port Washington	WI	53074	262-284-6600	284-6623
Nice-Pak Products Inc 2 Nice-Pak Pk *TF:* 800-999-6423 ■ *Web:* www.nicepak.com	Orangeburg	NY	10962	845-365-1700	365-1717
Orchids Paper Products Co 4826 Hunt St *AMEX: TIS* ■ *TF:* 800-832-4908 ■ *Web:* www.orchidspaper.com	Pryor	OK	74361	918-825-0616	825-0060
Personal Products Co 199 Grandview Rd *Web:* www.jnj.com/our_company/family_of_companies	Skillman	NJ	08558	908-874-1000	
Potlatch Corp 601 W 1st Ave Suite 1600 *NASDAQ: PCH* ■ *Web:* www.potlatchcorp.com	Spokane	WA	99201	509-835-1500	835-1555
Principle Business Enterprises Inc PO Box 129 *TF:* 800-467-3224 ■ *Web:* www.tranquilityproducts.com	Dunbridge	OH	43414	419-352-1551	352-8340
Proctor & Gamble Co - Tambrands 2879 Hotel Rd *Web:* www.tampax.com	Auburn	ME	04210	207-753-4000	753-5227
Roses Southwest Papers Inc 1701 2nd St SW *Web:* www.rosessouthwest.com	Albuquerque	NM	87102	505-842-0134	242-0342
SCA Americas 2929 Arch St Suite 2600 *TF Cust Svc:* 800-328-9043 ■ *Web:* www.scanorthamerica.com	Philadelphia	PA	19022	610-499-3700	499-3391
Tranzonic Cos 26301 curtiss wright Pkwy Suite 200 **Fax Area Code:* 800 ■ *TF:* 800-553-7979 ■ *Web:* www.tranzonic.com	clevland	OH	44143	440-449-6550	445-8366*
Wausau Paper Corp 100 Paper Pl *NYSE: WPP* ■ *Web:* www.wausaupaper.com	Mosinee	WI	54455	715-693-4470	692-2083

562 PAPER PRODUCTS - WHOL

Company	City	State	Zip	Phone	Fax
A & M Tape & Packaging 5201 Nob Hill Rd *TF:* 800-231-8806 ■ *Web:* www.mrboxonline.com	Sunrise	FL	33351	954-572-2500	572-8902
American Hotel Register Co 100 S Milwaukee Ave **Fax Area Code:* 800 ■ **Fax:* Sales ■ *TF:* 800-323-5686 ■ *Web:* www.americanhotel.com	Vernon Hills	IL	60061	847-743-3000	688-9108*
American Paper & Twine Co 7400 Cockrill Bend Blvd **Fax Area Code:* 877 ■ *TF:* 800-251-2437 ■ *Web:* www.aptcommerce.com	Nashville	TN	37209	615-350-9000	413-5055*
Atlantic Paper & Twine Co Inc 85 York Ave *TF:* 800-613-0950 ■ *Web:* www.atlanticpaper.com	Pawtucket	RI	02860	401-725-0950	724-7840
Bgr Inc 6392 Gano Rd *TF:* 800-628-9195 ■ *Web:* www.bgrinc.com	West Chester	OH	45069	513-755-7100	755-7855
Billhorn Board & Paper LLC 463 Industrial Pkwy *Web:* www.billhornconverters.com	West Monroe	LA	71291	318-397-9079	
Brame Specialty Co Inc 2021 S Briggs Ave *TF:* 800-672-0011 ■ *Web:* www.brameco.com	Durham	NC	27703	919-598-1500	596-9264
Bunzl Distribution USA Inc 701 Emerson Rd Suite 500 *TF:* 888-997-5959 ■ *Web:* www.bunzldistribution.com	Saint Louis	MO	63141	314-997-5959	997-1405
Butler-Dearden Paper Service Inc PO Box 1069 *TF:* 800-392-6089 ■ *Web:* www.butlerdearden.com	Boylston	MA	01505	508-869-9000	869-0211
Central Paper Products Co Inc 350 Gay St Brown Ave Industrial Pk *TF:* 800-339-4065 ■ *Web:* www.centralpaper.com	Manchester	NH	03103	603-624-4065	624-8795
Continental Paper & Plastic Converting Inc 5 Clark St *Web:* www.cont-paper.com	Orchard Park	NY	14127	716-662-6606	662-0829
D-k Trading Corp PO Box E *Web:* www.dk-t.com	Clarks Summit	PA	18411	570-586-9662	342-7511
Dacotah Paper Co 3940 15th Ave NW *TF:* 800-270-6352 ■ *Web:* www.dacotahpaper.com	Fargo	ND	58102	701-281-1734	281-9799
Ernest Paper Products 5777 Smithway St *TF:* 800-233-7788 ■ *Web:* www.ernestpaper.com	Commerce	CA	90040	323-583-6561	583-6561
First Choice Distribution 1770 NE 58th Ave *TF:* 800-369-8733	Des Moines	IA	50313	515-262-9776	261-3453
Fleetwood-Signode 2222 Windsor Ct *TF:* 800-862-7997 ■ *Web:* www.fleetsig.com	Addison	IL	60101	630-268-9999	268-9919
Garland C Norris Co 1101 Terry Rd PO Box 28 *TF:* 800-331-8920 ■ *Web:* www.gcnorris.com	Apex	NC	27502	919-387-1059	387-1325
Gem State Paper & Supply Co PO Box 469 *TF:* 800-727-2737 ■ *Web:* www.gemstatepaper.com	Twin Falls	ID	83303	208-733-6081	734-9870
George H Swatek Inc 1095 Edgewater Ave PO Box 356	Ridgefield	NJ	07657	201-941-2400	941-8681
H. T. Berry Co Inc PO Box B *TF:* 800-736-2206 ■ *Web:* www.htberry.com	Canton	MA	02021	781-828-6000	828-9788
Harder Paper & Packaging 5301 Verona Rd *TF:* 800-261-3400	Madison	WI	53711	608-271-5127	271-4677
Hathaway Inc PO Box 1618 *TF:* 800-323-2138 ■ *Web:* www.hathawaypaper.com	Waynesboro	VA	22980	540-949-8285	943-7619
Heartland Paper Co 808 W Cherokee St *TF Cust Svc:* 800-843-7922 ■ *Web:* www.heartland-paper.com	Sioux Falls	SD	57104	605-336-1190	332-8378
Johnston Paper Co 2 Eagle Dr *TF:* 800-800-7123 ■ *Web:* www.johnstonpaper.com	Auburn	NY	13021	315-253-8435	253-8744
Kent H Landsberg Co 1640 S Greenwood Ave **Fax:* Cust Svc ■ *Web:* www.landsberg.com	Montebello	CA	90640	323-726-7776	721-0190*
Leonard Paper Co 725 N Haven St *TF Cust Svc:* 800-327-5547 ■ *Web:* www.leonardpaper.com	Baltimore	MD	21205	410-563-0800	563-0249
M Conley Co 1312 4th St SE **Fax:* Cust Svc ■ *TF:* 800-362-6001 ■ *Web:* www.conleypackaging.com	Canton	OH	44707	330-456-8243	588-2572*
Main Paper & Party Inc 611 E Main St *Web:* www.mainpaperparty.com	League City	TX	77573	281-332-1119	332-7298
Max-Pak LLC 2808 New Tampa Hwy *TF:* 800-940-0243 ■ *Web:* www.maxpak.cc	Lakeland	FL	33815	863-682-0123	683-7895
Mayfield Paper Co 1115 S Hill St *TF:* 800-725-1441 ■ *Web:* www.mayfieldpaper.com	San Angelo	TX	76903	325-653-1444	653-7031
National Paper & Sanitary Supply 2511 S 156th Cir *TF:* 800-647-2737 ■ *Web:* www.npaper.com	Omaha	NE	68130	402-330-5507	330-4109
Nichols Paper & Supply Co Inc PO Box 291 *TF:* 800-442-0213 ■ *Web:* www.enichols.com	Muskegon	MI	49443	231-799-2120	777-8250
Northwest Arkansas Paper Co 2400 Cantrell Rd Suite 116 *TF:* 800-643-3068	Little Rock	AR	72202	501-374-5884	374-5129
Pacific Packaging Products Inc 24 Industrial Way *TF:* 800-777-0300 ■ *Web:* www.pacificpkg.com	Wilmington	MA	01887	978-657-9100	658-4933
Packaging Distribution Services Inc (PDS) 2308 Sunset Rd *TF:* 800-747-2699 ■ *Web:* www.pdspack.com	Des Moines	IA	50321	515-243-3156	243-1741
Paper Products Co Inc 36 Terminal Way *TF:* 800-837-2702 ■ *Web:* www.paperproducts-pgh.com	Pittsburgh	PA	15219	412-481-6200	481-4787
Paterson Pacific Parchment Co 625 Greg St *TF:* 800-678-8104 ■ *Web:* www.patersonpaper.com	Sparks	NV	89431	775-353-3000	353-3017
Perez Trading Co Inc 3490 NW 125th St *TF:* 800-999-7599 ■ *Web:* www.pereztrading.com	Miami	FL	33167	305-769-0761	681-7963
Phillips Distribution Inc 3000 E Houston St PO Box 200067 *TF:* 800-580-2397 ■ *Web:* www.phillipsdistribution.com	San Antonio	TX	78220	210-227-2397	222-0790
Pollock Paper & Packaging 1 Pollock Pl *TF Cust Svc:* 800-843-7320 ■ *Web:* www.pollockpaper.com	Grand Prairie	TX	75050	972-263-2126	262-4737
Qupaco Inc 300 N Sherman St *TF:* 800-533-2553 ■ *Web:* www.quakercitypaper.com	York	PA	17403	717-843-9061	843-7850
S. Freedman & Sons Inc 3322 Pennsy Dr *TF:* 800-545-7277 ■ *Web:* www.sfreedman.com	Landover	MD	20785	301-322-5000	772-7563
Saint Louis Paper & Box Co 3843 Garfield Ave *TF:* 800-779-7901 ■ *Web:* www.stlpaper.com	Saint Louis	MO	63113	314-531-7900	531-0968
Schwarz 8338 Austin Ave *TF:* 800-323-4903 ■ *Web:* www.schwarz.com	Morton Grove	IL	60053	847-966-2550	966-1271
Shorr Packaging Inc 800 N Commerce St *TF:* 888-978-1122 ■ *Web:* www.shorr.com	Aurora	IL	60504	630-978-1000	978-1300
Snyder Paper Corp 250 26th St Dr SE *TF:* 800-222-8562 ■ *Web:* www.snyderpaper.com	Hickory	NC	28602	828-328-2501	328-6972
Tricorbraun Inc 10330 Old Olive St Rd *TF:* 800-325-7782 ■ *Web:* www.tricorbraun.com	Saint Louis	MO	63141	314-569-3633	569-5087
TSN Inc 4001 Salazar Way PO Box 679 *TF:* 800-800-4131 ■ *Web:* www.tsndist.com	Frederick	CO	80530	303-530-0600	530-1919
Unisource Worldwide Inc 6600 Governors Lake Pkwy *TF:* 800-282-7958 ■ *Web:* www.unisourcelink.com	Norcross	GA	30071	770-447-9000	209-6550
Western Paper Distributors Inc PO Box 17425 *Web:* www.westernpaper.com	Denver	CO	80217	303-371-6000	371-6111
xpedx 6285 Tri-Ridge Blvd *Web:* www.xpedx.com	Loveland	OH	45140	513-965-2900	965-2849

563 PAPERBOARD & CARDBOARD - DIE-CUT

Company	City	State	Zip	Phone	Fax
Alvah Bushnell Co 519 E Chelten Ave *TF:* 800-255-7434 ■ *Web:* www.bushnellco.com	Philadelphia	PA	19144	215-842-9520	843-7725
Blanks/USA Inc 8625 Xylon Ct **Fax Area Code:* 800 ■ *TF:* 800-328-7311 ■ *Web:* www.laserblanks.com	Minneapolis	MN	55445	763-391-8001	328-7312*
Book Covers Inc 4501 W 16th St	Chicago	IL	60623	773-521-7800	521-2125*
Cardinal Brands Inc 643 Massachusetts St Suite 200 *TF:* 800-364-8713 ■ *Web:* www.cardinalbrands.com	Lawrence	KS	66044	785-344-1400	344-1200
Crescent Cardboard Co LLC 100 W Willow Rd *TF:* 800-323-1055 ■ *Web:* www.crescentcardboard.com	Wheeling	IL	60090	847-537-3400	537-7153
Demco Inc 4810 Forest Run Rd *TF Orders:* 800-356-1200 ■ *Web:* www.demco.com	Madison	WI	53704	608-241-1201	241-1799
Esselte Corp 225 Broadhollow Rd *TF:* 800-645-6051 ■ *Web:* www.esselte.com	Melville	NY	11747	631-675-5700	675-3456
GBS Filing Solutions 224 Morges Rd **Fax Area Code:* 800 ■ *TF:* 800-873-4427 ■ *Web:* www.gbscorp.com	Malvern	OH	44644	330-863-1828	444-9427*
MeadWestvaco Beauty & Personal Care 299 Pk Ave *Web:* www.meadwestvaco.com/BeautyandPersonalCare/index.htm	New York	NY	10171	212-318-5600	
Redweld 32-00 Skillman Ave *TF:* 800-221-3218 ■ *Web:* www.redweld.com	Long Island City	NY	11101	718-433-3800	433-3050

				Phone	Fax
Smead Mfg Co 600 Smead Blvd	Hastings	MN	55033	651-437-4111	437-9134
TF Cust Svc: 888-737-6323 ■ *Web:* www.smead.com					
Tap Packaging Solutions 2160 Superior Ave	Cleveland	OH	44114	216-781-6000	771-2572
TF: 800-827-5679 ■ *Web:* www.tappackagingsolutions.com					
Topps Co Inc 1 Whitehall St	New York	NY	10004	212-376-0300	376-0573
TF: 800-489-9149 ■ *Web:* www.topps.com					
University Products Inc PO Box 101	Holyoke	MA	01041	413-532-3372	532-9281*
**Fax Area Code:* 800 ■ **Fax:* Cust Svc ■ *TF Cust Svc:* 800-628-1912 ■ *Web:* www.universityproducts.com					
Warren Industries Inc 3100 Mt Pleasant St	Racine	WI	53404	262-639-7800	639-0920
Web: www.wrnind.com					
Westcott Displays Inc 450 Amsterdam St	Detroit	MI	48202	313-872-1200	875-3275
Web: www.westcottdisplays.com					
Xertrex International Inc 1530 W Glenlake Ave	Itasca	IL	60143	630-773-4020	773-4696
TF: 800-822-2437					
Xertrex International Inc Tabbies Div 1530 W Glenlake Ave	Itasca	IL	60143	630-773-4020	773-4696
TF: 800-822-2437 ■ *Web:* www.tabbies.com					

564 PAPERBOARD MILLS

				Phone	Fax
Cascades Boxboard Group Inc 772 Sherbrooke St W Suite 300	Montreal	QC	H3A1G1	514-284-9800	289-1773
TF: 800-465-9917 ■ *Web:* www.cascades.com					
Cascades Inc 404 Marie-Victorin Blvd	Kingsey Falls	QC	J0A1B0	819-363-5100	363-5155
TSX: CAS ■ *TF:* 800-361-4070 ■ *Web:* www.cascades.com					
FiberMark Inc 161 Wellington Rd	Brattleboro	VT	05301	802-257-0365	257-5907*
**Fax:* Sales ■ *Web:* www.fibermark.com					
FiberMark Inc Technical Specialities Div 161 Wellington Rd	Brattleboro	VT	05031	802-257-0365	257-5900
TF Cust Svc: 800-784-8558 ■ *Web:* www.fibermark.com					
Green Bay Packaging Inc Mill Div 1601 N Quincy St	Green Bay	WI	54302	920-433-5111	433-5105
TF: 800-558-4008 ■ *Web:* www.gbp.com					
International Paper Co 6400 Poplar Ave	Memphis	TN	38297	901-419-7000	
NYSE: IP ■ *TF Prod Info:* 800-223-1268 ■ *Web:* www.internationalpaper.com					
Longview Fibre Paper & Packaging Inc 300 Fibre Way PO Box 639	Longview	WA	98632	360-425-1550	230-5135
Web: www.longviewfibre.com					
Lydall Inc 1 Colonial Rd	Manchester	CT	06042	860-646-1233	646-4917
NYSE: LDL ■ *TF:* 800-365-9325 ■ *Web:* www.lydall.com					
Menominee Paper Co 144 1st St	Menominee	MI	49858	906-863-5595	864-3320
Newark Group 20 Jackson Dr	Cranford	NJ	07016	908-276-4000	276-2888
TF: 800-777-7890 ■ *Web:* www.newarkgroup.com					
Newman & Co Inc 6101 Tacony St	Philadelphia	PA	19135	215-333-8700	332-8586
TF: 800-523-3256					
Packaging Corp of America 1900 W Field Ct	Lake Forest	IL	60045	847-482-2000	615-6379
NYSE: PKG ■ *TF:* 888-828-2850 ■ *Web:* www.packagingcorp.com					
Pactiv Corp 1900 W Field Ct	Lake Forest	IL	60045	847-482-2000	482-4738
NYSE: PTV ■ *TF:* 888-828-2850 ■ *Web:* www.pactiv.com					
Potlatch Corp 601 W 1st Ave Suite 1600	Spokane	WA	99201	509-835-1500	835-1555
NASDAQ: PCH ■ *Web:* www.potlatchcorp.com					
Potlatch Corp Pulp & Paperboard Div 805 Mill Rd	Lewiston	ID	83501	208-799-1429	750-7809*
**Fax:* Hum Res ■ *Web:* www.potlatchcorp.com					
Simkins Industries Inc 317 Foxon Rd	East Haven	CT	06513	203-787-7171	787-7402
Web: www.simkinsindustries.com					
Sonoco 1 N 2nd St	Hartsville	SC	29550	843-383-7000	383-7008*
NYSE: SON ■ **Fax:* PR ■ *TF:* 800-377-2692 ■ *Web:* www.sonoco.com					

565 PARKING SERVICE

				Phone	Fax
Ace Parking Management Inc 645 Ash St	San Diego	CA	92101	619-233-6624	233-0741
TF: 800-925-7275 ■ *Web:* www.aceparking.com					
AMPCO System Parking 801 S Grand Ave	Los Angeles	CA	90017	213-624-6065	689-7992
Web: www.abm.com					
Baltimore County Revenue Authority 115 Towsontown Blvd E	Baltimore	MD	21286	410-887-3127	296-7459
TF: 888-246-5384 ■ *Web:* www.baltimoregolfing.com					
Central Parking System 2401 21st Ave S	Nashville	TN	37212	615-297-4255	297-6240
TF: 800-423-6613 ■ *Web:* www.parking.com					
Colonial Parking Inc 1050 Thomas Jefferson St NW Suite 100	Washington	DC	20007	202-295-8100	295-8111
Web: www.ecolonial.com					
Denison Parking 36 S Pennsylvania St Suite 200	Indianapolis	IN	46204	317-655-3100	655-3101
Web: www.denisonparking.com					
Diamond Parking Inc 605 1st Ave Suite 6000	Seattle	WA	98104	206-284-3100	285-5598
TF: 800-340-7275 ■ *Web:* www.diamondparking.com					
Edison Properties LLC 100 Washington St	Newark	NJ	07102	973-643-7700	643-2272
TF: 800-248-7275 ■ *Web:* www.parkfast.com					
Ft Lauderdale Transportation Inc 1330 SE 4th Ave Suite D	Fort Lauderdal	FL	33316	954-524-6500	524-3609
Web: www.usapark.com					
Imperial Parking Corp 601 W Cordova St Suite 300	Vancouver	BC	V6B1G1	604-681-7311	681-4098
Web: www.impark.com					
InterPark 200 N LaSalle St Suite 1400	Chicago	IL	60601	312-935-2900	935-2999
Web: www.interparkholdings.com					
Lanier Parking Systems 1355 Peachtree St NE	Atlanta	GA	30309	404-881-6076	881-1815
Web: www.lanierparking.com					
Park 'N Fly 2060 Mt Paran Rd Suite 207	Atlanta	GA	30327	404-264-1000	264-1114*
**Fax:* Hum Res ■ *TF Cust Svc:* 800-325-4863 ■ *Web:* www.pnf.com					
Park To Fly Inc 7800 Narcoossee Rd	Orlando	FL	32822	407-851-8044	851-8011
TF: 888-851-8875 ■ *Web:* www.parktofly.com					
Parking Co of America 11101 Lakewood Blvd	Downey	CA	90241	562-862-2118	862-4409
TF: 866-727-5728 ■ *Web:* www.parkpca.com					
Parking Co of America Airports 200 W Monroe Suite 1500	Chicago	IL	60606	312-453-1700	
Web: www.avistarparking.com					
Parking Management Inc 1725 Desales St NW Suite 300	Washington	DC	20036	202-785-9191	303-3672
Web: www.pmi-parking.com					
Republic Parking System 633 Chestnut St Suite 2000	Chattanooga	TN	37450	423-756-2771	265-5728
Web: www.republicparking.com					
Robbins Parking Service Ltd 1102 Fort St	Victoria	BC	V8V3K8	250-382-4411	380-7275
Web: www.robbinsparking.com					
Standard Parking Corp 900 N Michigan Ave Suite 1600	Chicago	IL	60611	312-274-2000	640-6169*
NASDAQ: STAN ■ **Fax:* Hum Res ■ *TF:* 888-700-7275 ■ *Web:* www.standardparking.com					
Valet Parking Service 1335 S Flower St	Los Angeles	CA	90015	213-342-3388	222-0981
TF: 800-794-7275 ■ *Web:* www.valetparkingservice.com					

PARKS - AMUSEMENT

SEE Amusement Park Companies p. 1394; Amusement Parks p. 1394

566 PARKS - NATIONAL - CANADA

				Phone	Fax
Parks Canada 25-7 N Eddy St	Gatineau	QC	K1A0M5	819-997-0055	953-9745
TF: 888-773-8888 ■ *Web:* www.pc.gc.ca/eng/index.aspx					
Aulavik National Park of Canada PO Box 29	Sachs Harbour	NT	X0E0Z0	867-690-3904	690-4808
Web: www.pc.gc.ca					
Auyuittuq National Park PO Box 353	Pangnirtung	NU	X0A0R0	867-473-2500	473-8612
Web: www.pc.gc.ca/pn-np/nu/auyuittuq/contact.aspx					
Banff National Park PO Box 900	Banff	AB	T1L1K2	403-762-1550	762-1551
TF: 877-737-3783 ■ *Web:* www.pc.gc.ca					
Bruce Peninsula National Park 7374 Hwy 6 PO Box 189	Tobermory	ON	N0H2R0	519-596-2233	596-2298
TF: 877-737-3783 ■ *Web:* www.pc.gc.ca					
Elk Island National Park Site 4 RR Suite 1	Fort Saskatchewan	AB	T8L2N7	780-992-2950	992-2951
Web: www.pc.gc.ca/pn-np/ab/elkisland/contact.aspx					
Fathom Five National Marine Park PO Box 189	Tobermory	ON	N0H2R0	519-596-2233	596-2298
Web: www.pc.gc.ca					
Forillon National Park 122 Gaspe Blvd	Gaspe	QC	G4X1A9	418-368-5505	368-6837
TF: 888-773-8888 ■ *Web:* www.pc.gc.ca/pn-np/qc/forillon/index.aspx					
Fundy National Park PO Box 1001	Alma	NB	E4H1B4	506-887-6000	887-6008
TF Campground Resv: 877-737-3783 ■ *Web:* www.pc.gc.ca/pn-np/nb/fundy/index.aspx					
Georgian Bay Islands National Park of Canada 901 Wye Valley Rd PO Box 9	Midland	ON	L4R4K6	705-526-9804	526-5939
Web: www.pc.gc.ca/pn-np/on/georg/index.aspx					
Glacier National Park PO Box 350	Revelstoke	BC	V0E2S0	250-837-7500	837-7536
Web: www.pc.gc.ca/pn-np/bc/glacier/index.aspx					
Grasslands National Park PO Box 150	Val Marie	SK	S0N2T0	306-298-2257	298-2042
Web: www.pc.gc.ca/pn-np/sk/grasslands/index.aspx					
Gros Morne National Park PO Box 130	Rocky Harbour	NL	A0K4N0	709-458-2417	458-2059
TF Campground Resv: 877-737-3783 ■ *Web:* www.pc.gc.ca/pn-np/nl/grosmorne/index.aspx					
Gwaii Haanas National Park Reserve/Haida Heritage Site PO Box 37	Queen Charlotte	BC	V0T1S0	250-559-8818	559-8366
Web: www.pc.gc.ca/eng/pn-np/bc/gwaiihaanas/visit/secur.aspx					
Ivvavik National Park Western Arctic Field Unit PO Box 1840	Inuvik	NT	X0E0T0	867-777-8800	777-8820
Web: www.pc.gc.ca/pn-np/yt/ivvavik/index.aspx					
Jasper National Park of Canada PO Box 10	Jasper	AB	T0E1E0	780-852-6176	852-6152
TF Campground Resv: 877-737-3783 ■ *Web:* www.pc.gc.ca/pn-np/ab/jasper/index.aspx					
Kejimkujik National Park PO Box 236	Maitland Bridge	NS	B0T1B0	902-682-2772	682-3367
TF Campground Resv: 877-737-3783 ■ *Web:* www.pc.gc.ca/pn-np/ns/kejimkujik/index.aspx					
Kluane National Park & Reserve of Canada PO Box 5495	Haines Junction	YT	Y0B1L0	867-634-7250	634-7208
Web: www.pc.gc.ca/pn-np/yt/kluane/index.aspx					
Kootenay National Park of Canada PO Box 220	Radium Hot Springs	BC	V0A1M0	250-347-9505	347-9980
TF Campground Resv: 877-737-3783 ■ *Web:* www.pc.gc.ca/pn-np/bc/kootenay/index.aspx					
Kouchibouguac National Park of Canada 186 Rt 117	Kouchibouguac	NB	E4X2P1	506-876-2443	876-4802
TF Campground Resv: 877-737-3783 ■ *Web:* www.pc.gc.ca/pn-np/nb/kouchibouguac/index.aspx					
La Mauricie National Park of Canada 702 5th St PO Box 160	Shawinigan	QC	G9N6T9	819-538-3232	536-3661
TF Campground Resv: 877-737-3783 ■ *Web:* www.pc.gc.ca/pn-np/qc/mauricie/index.aspx					
Mingan Archipelago National Park Reserve of Canada 1340 de la Digue St	Havre-Saint-Pierre	QC	G0G1P0	418-538-3331	538-3595
TF: 888-773-8888 ■ *Web:* www.pc.gc.ca/pn-np/qc/mingan/index.aspx					
Mount Revelstoke National Park of Canada PO Box 350	Revelstoke	BC	V0E2S0	250-837-7500	837-7536
Web: www.pc.gc.ca/pn-np/bc/revelstoke/index.aspx					
Nahanni National Park Reserve of Canada 10002 100 St PO Box 348	Fort Simpson	NT	X0E0N0	867-695-7750	695-2446
Web: www.pc.gc.ca/pn-np/nt/nahanni/index.aspx					
Pacific Rim National Park Reserve of Canada 2185 Ocean Terr Rd PO Box 280	Ucluelet	BC	V0R3A0	250-726-3500	726-3520
TF Campground Resv: 877-737-3783 ■ *Web:* www.pc.gc.ca/pn-np/bc/pacificrim/natcul/natcul9.aspx					
Point Pelee National Park of Canada 407 Monarch Ln RR 1	Leamington	ON	N8H3V4	519-322-2365	322-1277
TF: 888-773-8888 ■ *Web:* www.pc.gc.ca/pn-np/on/pelee/index.aspx					
Prince Albert National Park of Canada Northern Prairies Field Unit PO Box 100	Waskesiu Lake	SK	S0J2Y0	306-663-4522	663-5424
TF Campground Resv: 877-737-3783 ■ *Web:* www.pc.gc.ca/pn-np/sk/princealbert/index.aspx					

Phone | Fax

Prince Edward Island National Park of Canada
2 Palmers Ln .... Charlottetown PE C1A5V8 902-672-6350 672-6370
TF Campground Resv: 888-733-8888 ■
Web: www.pc.gc.ca/eng/pn-np/pe/pei-ipe/natcul/natcul3.aspx
Pukaskwa National Park of Canada
PO Box 212 .... Heron Bay ON P0T1R0 807-229-0801 229-2097
Web: www.pc.gc.ca/pn-np/on/pukaskwa/index.aspx
Quttinirpaaq National Park PO Box 278 .... Iqaluit NU X0A0H0 867-975-4673 975-4674
Web: www.pc.gc.ca/pn-np/nu/quttinirpaaq/contact.aspx
Saguenay-Saint Lawrence Marine Park
182 Rue de l'Eglise PO Box 220 .... Tadoussac QC G0T2A0 418-235-4703 235-4686
Web: www.pc.gc.ca/amnc-nmca/qc/saguenay
Saint Lawrence Islands National Park of Canada
2 County Rd 5 RR 3 .... Mallorytown ON K0E1R0 613-923-5261 923-1021
Web: www.pc.gc.ca/pn-np/on/lawren/index.aspx
Sirmilik National Park PO Box 300 .... Pond Inlet NU X0A0S0 867-899-8092 899-8104
Web: www.pc.gc.ca
Terra Nova National Park of Canada
General Delivery .... Glovertown NL A0G2L0 709-533-2801 533-2706
TF Campground Resv: 877-737-3783 ■ *Web:* www.pc.gc.ca/pn-np/nl/terranova/index.aspx
Tuktut Nogait National Park of Canada
PO Box 91 .... Paulatuk NT X0E1N0 867-580-3233 580-3234
Web: www.pc.gc.ca/pn-np/nt/tuktutnogait/index.aspx
Vuntut National Park of Canada PO Box 19 .... Old Crow YT Y0B1N0 867-667-3910 393-6701
Web: www.pc.gc.ca/pn-np/yt/vuntut/index.aspx
Wapusk National Park of Canada PO Box 127 .... Churchill MB R0B0E0 204-675-8863 675-2026
TF: 888-773-8888 ■ *Web:* www.pc.gc.ca/pn-np/mb/wapusk/index.aspx
Waterton Lakes National Park
PO Box 100 .... Waterton Park AB T0K2M0 403-859-2224 859-5152
Web: www.watertonpark.com
Wood Buffalo National Park of Canada
PO Box 750 .... Fort Smith NT X0E0P0 867-872-7900 872-3910
Web: www.pc.gc.ca/pn-np/nt/woodbuffalo/index.aspx
Yoho National Park of Canada PO Box 99 .... Field BC V0A1G0 250-343-6783 343-6012
Web: www.pc.gc.ca/pn-np/bc/yoho/index.aspx

567 PARKS - NATIONAL - US

SEE ALSO Nature Centers, Parks, Other Natural Areas p. 1482; Cemeteries - National p. 1561; Parks - State p. 2346

ALABAMA

Phone | Fax

Horseshoe Bend National Military Park
11288 Horseshoe Bend Rd .... Daviston AL 36256 256-234-7111 329-9905
Web: www.nps.gov
Little River Canyon National Preserve
2141 Gault Ave N .... Fort Payne AL 35967 256-845-9605 997-9129
Web: www.nps.gov
Russell Cave National Monument
3729 County Rd 98 .... Bridgeport AL 35740 256-495-2672 495-9220
Web: www.nps.gov/ruca
Tuskegee Airmen National Historic Site
1616 Chappie James Ave .... Tuskegee AL 36083 334-724-0922 724-0952
Web: www.nps.gov
Tuskegee Institute National Historic Site
1212 W Montgomery Rd .... Tuskegee Institute AL 36088 334-727-3200 727-1448
Web: www.nps.gov/tuin

ALASKA

Phone | Fax

Alagnak Wild River PO Box 245 .... King Salmon AK 99613 907-246-3305 246-2116
Web: www.nps.gov/alag
Aniakchak National Monument & Preserve
PO Box 245 .... King Salmon AK 99613 907-246-3305 246-2116
Web: www.nps.gov/ania
Bering Land Bridge National Preserve PO Box 220 .... Nome AK 99762 907-443-2522 443-6139
Web: www.nps.gov
Cape Krusenstern National Monument
PO Box 1029 .... Kotzebue AK 99752 907-442-3890 442-8316
Web: www.nps.gov/cakr/index.htm
Denali National Park & Preserve PO Box 9 .... Denali Park AK 99755 907-683-2294 683-9617
Web: www.nps.gov
Gates of the Arctic National Park & Preserve
4175 Geist Rd .... Fairbanks AK 99709 907-457-5752 455-0601
TF: 866-869-6887 ■ *Web:* www.nps.gov/gaar
Glacier Bay National Park & Preserve
1 Park Rd PO Box 140 .... Gustavus AK 99826 907-697-2230 697-2654
Web: www.nps.gov/glba
Katmai National Park & Preserve
#1 King Salmon Mall PO Box 7 .... King Salmon AK 99613 907-246-3305 246-2116
Web: www.nps.gov/katm
Kenai Fjords National Park PO Box 1727 .... Seward AK 99664 907-224-7500 224-7505
Web: www.nps.gov
Klondike Gold Rush National Historical Park
2nd St & Broadway PO Box 517 .... Skagway AK 99840 907-983-2921 983-9249
Web: www.nps.gov/klgo
Kobuk Valley National Park PO Box 1029 .... Kotzebue AK 99752 907-442-3890 442-8316
Web: www.nps.gov/kova
Lake Clark National Park & Preserve
240 W 5th Ave Suite 236 .... Anchorage AK 99501 907-644-3626 644-3810
Web: www.nps.gov
National Park Service Regional Offices
Alaska Region 240 W 5th Ave Suite 114 .... Anchorage AK 99501 907-644-3510 644-3816

Phone | Fax

Noatak National Preserve PO Box 1029 .... Kotzebue AK 99752 907-442-3890 442-8316
Web: www.nps.gov/noat
Sitka National Historical Park
106 Metlakatla St .... Sitka AK 99835 907-747-6281 747-5938
Web: www.nps.gov
Wrangell-Saint Elias National Park & Preserve
Mile 106.8 Richardson Hwy PO Box 439 .... Copper Center AK 99573 907-822-5234 822-7216
Web: www.nps.gov/wrst
Yukon-Charley Rivers National Preserve
4175 Geist Rd .... Fairbanks AK 99709 907-457-5752 455-0601
Web: www.nps.gov/yuch

AMERICAN SAMOA

Phone | Fax

National Park of American Samoa
PO Box 1147 .... Pago Pago AS 96799 684-633-7082 699-3986
Web: www.nps.gov/npsa

ARIZONA

Phone | Fax

Canyon de Chelly National Monument PO Box 588 ...... Chinle AZ 86503 928-674-5500 674-5507
Web: www.nps.gov
Casa Grande Ruins National Monument
1100 W Ruins Dr .... Coolidge AZ 85128 520-723-3172 723-7209
Web: www.nps.gov
Chiricahua National Monument
12856 E Rhyolite Creek Rd .... Wilcox AZ 85643 520-824-3560 824-3421
Web: www.nps.gov/chir
Coronado National Memorial
4101 E Montezuma Canyon Rd .... Hereford AZ 85615 520-366-5515 366-5705
Web: www.nps.gov/coro
Fort Bowie National Historic Site
3203 S Old Ft Bowie Rd .... Bowie AZ 85605 520-847-2500 847-2221
Web: www.nps.gov/fobo
Glen Canyon National Recreation Area
691 Scenic View Dr PO Box 1507 .... Page AZ 86040 928-608-6200 608-6259
Web: www.nps.gov/glca
Grand Canyon National Park PO Box 129 .... Grand Canyon AZ 86023 928-638-7888 638-7797*
**Fax:* Mail Rm ■ *Web:* www.nps.gov
Hohokam Pima National Monument
c/o Casa Grande Ruins National Monument
1100 W Ruins Dr .... Coolidge AZ 85228 520-723-3172 723-7209
Web: www.nps.gov/pima
Hubbell Trading Post National Historic Site
1/2 Mile W Hwy 191 on Hwy 264 PO Box 150 .... Ganado AZ 86505 928-755-3475 755-3405
Web: www.nps.gov
Montezuma Castle National Monument
527 S Main St .... Camp Verde AZ 86322 928-567-5276 567-3597
Web: www.nps.gov/moca
Navajo National Monument HC 71 PO Box 3 .... Tonalea AZ 86044 928-672-2700 672-2703
Web: www.nps.gov
Organ Pipe Cactus National Monument
10 Organ Pipe Dr .... Ajo AZ 85321 520-387-6849
Web: www.nps.gov
Petrified Forest National Park
PO Box 2217 .... Petrified Forest AZ 86028 928-524-6228 524-3567
Web: www.nps.gov
Pipe Spring National Monument
406 N Pipe Spring Rd HC 65 PO Box 5 .... Fredonia AZ 86022 928-643-7105 643-7583
Web: www.nps.gov/pisp
Rainbow Bridge National Monument
c/o Glen Canyon National Recreation Area
PO Box 1507 .... Page AZ 86040 928-608-6200 608-6259
Web: www.nps.gov/rabr
Saguaro National Park
3693 S Old Spanish Trail .... Tucson AZ 85730 520-733-5100 733-5183
Web: www.nps.gov
Sunset Crater Volcano National Monument
c/o Flagstaff Area National Monuments
6400 N Hwy 89 .... Flagstaff AZ 86004 928-526-0502 714-0565
Web: www.nps.gov/sucr
Tonto National Monument
26260 N Az Hwy 188 2 .... Roosevelt AZ 85545 928-467-2241 467-2225
Web: www.nps.gov/tont
Tumacacori National Historical Park
1891 E Frontage Rd PO Box 8067 .... Tumacacori AZ 85640 520-398-2341 398-9271
Web: www.nps.gov/tuma
Tuzigoot National Monument 527 S Main St .... Camp Verde AZ 86322 928-634-5564 567-3597
Web: www.nps.gov/tuzi
Walnut Canyon National Monument
c/o Flagstaff Area National Monuments
6400 N Hwy 89 .... Flagstaff AZ 86004 928-526-3367 527-0246
Web: www.nps.gov/waca
Wupatki National Monument
Flagstaff Area National Monuments
6400 N Hwy 89 .... Flagstaff AZ 86004 928-679-2365 679-2349
Web: www.nps.gov/wupa

ARKANSAS

Phone | Fax

Arkansas Post National Memorial
1741 Old Post Rd .... Gillett AR 72055 870-548-2207 548-2431
Web: www.nps.gov
Buffalo National River
402 N Walnut St Suite 136 .... Harrison AR 72601 870-741-5443 741-7286
Web: www.nps.gov

Name / Address	City	State	Zip	Phone	Fax
Fort Smith National Historic Site 301 Parker Ave *Web:* www.nps.gov	Fort Smith	AR	72901	479-783-3961	783-5307
Hot Springs National Park 101 Reserve St *Web:* www.nps.gov	Hot Springs	AR	71901	501-620-6715	620-6778
Little Rock Central High School National Historic Site 1500 Pk St *Web:* www.nps.gov	Little Rock	AR	72202	501-374-1957	376-4728
Pea Ridge National Military Park 15930 Hwy 62 E *Web:* www.nps.gov	Garfield	AR	72732	479-451-8122	451-0219

CALIFORNIA

Name / Address	City	State	Zip	Phone	Fax
Cabrillo National Monument 1800 Cabrillo Memorial Dr *Web:* www.nps.gov	San Diego	CA	92106	619-557-5450	226-6311
Channel Islands National Park 1901 Spinnaker Dr *Web:* www.nps.gov	Ventura	CA	93001	805-658-5730	658-5799
Death Valley National Park PO Box 579 *Web:* www.nps.gov/deva	Death Valley	CA	92328	760-786-3200	786-3283
Devils Postpile National Monument PO Box 3999 *Web:* www.nps.gov/depo	Mammoth Lakes	CA	93545	760-934-2289	934-2289
Eugene O'Neill National Historic Site 1000 Kuss Rd *Web:* www.nps.gov	Danville	CA	94526	925-838-0249	838-9471
Fort Point National Historic Site Fort Mason Bldg 201 *Web:* www.nps.gov/fopo	San Francisco	CA	94123	415-556-1693	561-4390
Golden Gate National Recreation Area Fort Mason Bldg 201 **Fax:* Hum Res ■ *Web:* www.nps.gov/goga	San Francisco	CA	94123	415-561-4700	561-4750*
John Muir National Historic Site 4202 Alhambra Ave. *Web:* www.nps.gov	Martinez	CA	94553	925-228-8860	228-8192
Joshua Tree National Park 74485 National Pk Dr *Web:* www.nps.gov	Twentynine Palms	CA	92277	760-367-5500	367-6392
Lassen Volcanic National Park 38050 Hwy 36 E PO Box 100 *Web:* www.nps.gov/lavo	Mineral	CA	96063	530-595-4480	595-3262
Lava Beds National Monument 1 Indian Well Headquarters *Web:* www.nps.gov/labe	Tulelake	CA	96134	530-260-0537	
Manzanar National Historic Site 5001 Hwy 395 PO Box 426 *Web:* www.nps.gov/manz	Independence	CA	93526	760-878-2194	878-2949
Mojave National Preserve 2701 Barstow Rd *Web:* www.nps.gov/moja	Barstow	CA	92311	760-252-6100	252-6174
Muir Woods National Monument 1 Muir Woods Rd *Web:* www.nps.gov/muwo/index.htm	Mill Valley	CA	94941	415-388-2596	389-6957
National Park Service Regional Offices Pacific West Region 1111 Jackson St Suite 700	Oakland	CA	94607	510-817-1304	817-1485
Pinnacles National Monument 5000 Hwy 146 *TF:* 877-444-6777 ■ *Web:* www.nps.gov/pinn	Paicines	CA	95043	831-389-4485	389-4489
Point Reyes National Seashore 1 Bear Valley Rd *Web:* www.nps.gov	Point Reyes Station	CA	94956	415-663-8522	663-8132
Redwood National & State Parks 1111 2nd St *Web:* www.nps.gov/redw	Crescent City	CA	95531	707-465-7335	464-1812
Rosie the Riveter/World War II Home Front National Historical Park 1401 S Marina Way *Web:* www.nps.gov	Richmond	CA	94804	510-232-5050	
San Francisco Maritime National Historical Park Lower Fort Mason Bldg E Rm 265 *Web:* www.nps.gov/safr	San Francisco	CA	94123	415-561-7000	556-1624
Santa Monica Mountains National Recreation Area 401 W Hillcrest Dr *Web:* www.nps.gov/samo	Thousand Oaks	CA	91360	805-370-2300	370-1851
Sequoia & Kings Canyon National Parks 47050 Generals Hwy. *Web:* www.nps.gov/seki	Three Rivers	CA	93271	559-565-3341	565-3730
Whiskeytown-Shasta-Trinity National Recreation Area PO Box 188 *Web:* www.nps.gov	Whiskeytown	CA	96095	530-242-3400	246-5154
Yosemite National Park 9039 Village Dr PO Box 577 *Web:* www.nps.gov/yose	Yosemite	CA	95389	209-372-0200	379-1800

COLORADO

Name / Address	City	State	Zip	Phone	Fax
Bent's Old Fort National Historic Site 35110 Hwy 194 E *Web:* www.nps.gov/beol	La Junta	CO	81050	719-383-5010	383-2129
Black Canyon of the Gunnison National Park 102 Elk Creek *Web:* www.nps.gov/blca	Gunnison	CO	81230	970-641-2337	641-3127
Colorado National Monument Monument Rd *Web:* www.nps.gov	Fruita	CO	81521	970-858-3617	858-0372
Curecanti National Recreation Area 102 Elk Creek *Web:* www.nps.gov/cure	Gunnison	CO	81230	970-641-2337	641-3127
Dinosaur National Monument 4545 E Hwy 40 *Web:* www.nps.gov/dino	Dinosaur	CO	81610	970-374-3000	374-3003
Florissant Fossil Beds National Monument PO Box 185 *Web:* www.nps.gov	Florissant	CO	80816	719-748-3253	748-3164
Great Sand Dunes National Park & Preserve 11500 Hwy 150 *Web:* www.nps.gov/grsa	Mosca	CO	81146	719-378-6300	378-6310
Hovenweep National Monument McElmo Rt. *Web:* www.nps.gov/hove	Cortez	CO	81321	970-562-4282	562-4283
Mesa Verde National Park PO Box 8 *Web:* www.nps.gov/meve	Mesa Verde	CO	81330	970-529-4465	529-4637
National Park Service Regional Offices Intermountain Region 12795 W Alameda Pkwy	Denver	CO	80225	303-969-2500	
Rocky Mountain National Park 1000 Hwy 36 *Web:* www.nps.gov	Estes Park	CO	80517	970-586-1206	586-1256
Yucca House National Monument c/o Mesa Verde National Pk PO Box 8 *Web:* www.nps.gov/yuho	Mesa Verde	CO	81330	970-529-4465	529-4637

CONNECTICUT

Name / Address	City	State	Zip	Phone	Fax
Weir Farm National Historic Site 735 Nod Hill Rd *Web:* www.nps.gov/wefa	Wilton	CT	06897	203-834-1896	834-2421

DISTRICT OF COLUMBIA

Name / Address	City	State	Zip	Phone	Fax
National Park Service (NPS) 1849 C St NW Rm 1013 *Web:* www.nps.gov	Washington	DC	20240	202-208-6843	219-0910
Constitution Gardens 900 Ohio Dr SW *Web:* www.nps.gov/coga	Washington	DC	20024	202-426-6841	724-0764
Ford's Theatre National Historic Site 511 10th St NW *Web:* www.nps.gov/foth	Washington	DC	20004	202-233-0701	233-0706
Franklin Delano Roosevelt Memorial c/o National Capital Parks Central 900 Ohio Dr SW *Web:* www.nps.gov/frde	Washington	DC	20024	202-426-6841	
Frederick Douglass National Historic Site 1900 Anacostia Dr SE *Web:* www.nps.gov/frdo	Washington	DC	20020	202-426-5961	426-0880
Korean War Veterans Memorial c/o National Capital Parks - Central 900 Ohio Dr SW *Web:* www.nps.gov/kowa	Washington	DC	20004	202-426-6841	
Lincoln Memorial c/o National Capitol Parks - Central 900 Ohio Dr SW *Web:* www.nps.gov/linc	Washington	DC	20024	202-426-6841	724-0764
Mary McLeod Bethune Council House National Historic Site 1318 Vermont Ave NW *Web:* www.nps.gov/mamc	Washington	DC	20005	202-673-2402	673-2414
National Mall c/o National Capitol Parks - Central 900 Ohio Dr SW *Web:* www.nps.gov/nama	Washington	DC	20024	202-426-6841	426-1835
National Park Service Regional Offices National Capital Region 1100 Ohio Dr SW *Web:* www.nps.gov/ncro	Washington	DC	20242	202-619-7000	619-7220
Pennsylvania Avenue National Historic Site c/o National Capitol Parks - Central 900 Ohio Dr SW *Web:* www.nps.gov/paav	Washington	DC	20024	202-606-8691	
President's Park (White House) c/o White House Visitor Ctr 1450 Pennsylvania Ave NW *Web:* www.nps.gov/whho	Washington	DC	20230	202-208-1631	208-1643
Rock Creek Park 5200 Glover Rd NW *Web:* www.nps.gov	Washington	DC	20015	202-895-6000	895-6015
Thomas Jefferson Memorial c/o National Capital Parks - Central 900 Ohio Dr SW *Web:* www.nps.gov/thje	Washington	DC	20024	202-426-6841	426-1835
Vietnam Veterans Memorial The c/o National Capitol Pk - Central 900 Ohio Dr SW *Web:* www.thewall-usa.com	Washington	DC	20242	202-426-6841	426-1844
Washington Monument c/o National Capitol Pk - Central 900 Ohio Dr SW *Web:* www.nps.gov/wamo	Washington	DC	20024	202-426-6841	

FLORIDA

Name / Address	City	State	Zip	Phone	Fax
Big Cypress National Preserve 33100 Tamiami Trail E *Web:* www.nps.gov	Ochopee	FL	34141	239-695-2000	695-3901
Biscayne National Park 9700 SW 328th St. *Web:* www.nps.gov/bisc	Homestead	FL	33033	305-230-1144	230-1190
Canaveral National Seashore 212 S Washington Ave *Web:* www.nps.gov/cana	Titusville	FL	32796	321-267-1110	264-2906
Castillo de San Marcos National Monument 1 S Castillo Dr *Web:* www.nps.gov/casa	Saint Augustine	FL	32084	904-829-6506	823-9388
De Soto National Memorial 8300 Desoto Memorial Hwy *Web:* www.nps.gov	Bradenton	FL	34209	941-792-0458	792-5094
Dry Tortugas National Park PO Box 6208 *Web:* www.nps.gov/drto	Key West	FL	33041	305-242-7700	242-7711

				Phone	Fax
Everglades National Park 40001 SR-9336 *Web:* www.nps.gov/ever	Homestead	FL	33034	305-242-7700	242-7728
Fort Caroline National Memorial 12713 Fort Caroline Rd *Web:* www.nps.gov/foca	Jacksonville	FL	32225	904-641-7155	641-3798
Fort Matanzas National Monument 8635 A1A S *Web:* www.nps.gov/foma	Saint Augustine	FL	32080	904-471-0116	471-7605
Gulf Islands National Seashore (Florida) 1801 Gulf Breeze Pkwy *Web:* www.nps.gov	Gulf Breeze	FL	32563	850-934-2600	932-9654
Timucuan Ecological & Historic Preserve c/o Fort Caroline National Memorial 12713 Fort Caroline Rd *Web:* www.nps.gov/timu	Jacksonville	FL	32225	904-641-7155	641-3798

GEORGIA

				Phone	Fax
Andersonville National Historic Site 496 Cemetery Rd *Web:* www.nps.gov/ande	Andersonville	GA	31711	229-924-0343	924-1086
Chattahoochee River National Recreation Area 1978 Island Ford Pkwy **Fax Area Code:* 770 ■ *Web:* www.nps.gov/chat	Atlanta	GA	30350	678-538-1200	399-8087*
Chickamauga & Chattanooga National Military Park 3370 Lafayette Rd PO Box 2128 **Fax Area Code:* 423 ■ *Web:* www.nps.gov/chch	Fort Oglethorpe	GA	30742	706-866-9241	752-5215*
Cumberland Island National Seashore 117 W St Mary's St PO Box 806 *TF:* 877-860-6787 ■ *Web:* www.nps.gov	Saint Marys	GA	31558	912-882-4335	673-7747
Fort Frederica National Monument 6515 Frederica Rd *Web:* www.nps.gov	Saint Simons Island	GA	31522	912-638-3639	634-5357
Fort Pulaski National Monument US Hwy 80 E *Web:* www.nps.gov	Savannah	GA	31410	912-786-5787	786-6023
Jimmy Carter National Historic Site 300 N Bond St *Web:* www.nps.gov/jica	Plains	GA	31780	229-824-4104	824-3441
Kennesaw Mountain National Battlefield Park 900 Kennesaw Mountain Dr *Web:* www.nps.gov	Kennesaw	GA	30152	770-427-4686	528-8398
Martin Luther King Jr National Historic Site 450 Auburn Ave NE *Web:* www.nps.gov/malu	Atlanta	GA	30312	404-331-5190	730-3112
Ocmulgee National Monument 1207 Emery Hwy *Web:* www.nps.gov/ocmu	Macon	GA	31217	478-752-8257	752-8259

HAWAII

				Phone	Fax
Haleakala National Park PO Box 369 *Web:* www.nps.gov	Makawao	HI	96768	808-572-4400	572-1304
Hawaii Volcanoes National Park PO Box 52 *Web:* www.nps.gov	Hawaii National Park	HI	96718	808-985-6000	985-6004
Kalaupapa National Historical Park PO Box 2222 *Web:* www.nps.gov	Kalaupapa	HI	96742	808-567-6802	567-6729
Kaloko-Honokohau National Historical Park 73-4786 Kanalani St Suite 14 *Web:* www.nps.gov	Kailua-Kona	HI	96740	808-329-6881	
Pu'uhonua O Honaunau National Historical Park PO Box 129 *Web:* www.nps.gov	Honaunau	HI	96726	808-328-2326	328-8251
Puukohola Heiau National Historic Site 62-3601 Kawaihae Rd *Web:* www.nps.gov	Kawaihae	HI	96743	808-882-7218	882-1215
USS Arizona Memorial 1 Arizona Memorial Pl *Web:* www.nps.gov/usar	Honolulu	HI	96818	808-422-0561	483-8608

IDAHO

				Phone	Fax
City of Rocks National Reserve PO Box 169 *Web:* www.nps.gov/ciro	Almo	ID	83312	208-824-5910	824-5563
Craters of the Moon National Monument & Preserve PO Box 29 *Web:* www.nps.gov/crmo	Arco	ID	83213	208-527-1335	527-3073
Hagerman Fossil Beds National Monument 221 N State St PO Box 570 *Web:* www.nps.gov	Hagerman	ID	83332	208-933-4100	837-4857
Minidoka National Historic Site PO Box 570 *Web:* www.nps.gov/miin	Hagerman	ID	83332	208-933-4127	837-4857
Nez Perce National Historical Park 39063 US Hwy 95 *Web:* www.nps.gov/nepe	Spalding	ID	83540	208-843-2261	843-2817

ILLINOIS

				Phone	Fax
Lincoln Home National Historic Site 413 S 8th St *Web:* www.nps.gov	Springfield	IL	62701	217-492-4241	492-4673

INDIANA

				Phone	Fax
George Rogers Clark National Historical Park 401 S 2nd St *Web:* www.nps.gov	Vincennes	IN	47591	812-882-1776	882-7270
Indiana Dunes National Lakeshore 1100 N Mineral Springs Rd *Web:* www.nps.gov/indu	Porter	IN	46304	219-395-1772	926-7561
Lincoln Boyhood National Memorial 2916 E S St PO Box 1816 *Web:* www.nps.gov/libo	Lincoln City	IN	47552	812-937-4541	937-9929

IOWA

				Phone	Fax
Effigy Mounds National Monument 151 Hwy 76 **Fax Area Code:* 800 ■ *Web:* www.nps.gov/efmo	Harpers Ferry	IA	52146	563-873-3491	322-1704*
Herbert Hoover National Historic Site 110 Parkside Dr PO Box 607 *Web:* www.nps.gov/heho	West Branch	IA	52358	319-643-2541	643-7864

KANSAS

				Phone	Fax
Brown Vs Board of Education National Historic Site 1515 SE Monroe St *Web:* www.nps.gov	Topeka	KS	66612	785-354-4273	354-7213
Fort Larned National Historic Site 1767 Kansas Hwy 156 *Web:* www.nps.gov	Larned	KS	67550	620-285-6911	285-3571
Fort Scott National Historic Site PO Box 918 *Web:* www.nps.gov	Fort Scott	KS	66701	620-223-0310	223-0188
Nicodemus National Historic Site 304 Washington Ave *Web:* www.nps.gov	Nicodemus	KS	67625	785-839-4233	839-4325
Tallgrass Prairie National Preserve 226 Broadway PO Box 585 *Web:* www.nps.gov	Cottonwood Falls	KS	66845	620-273-6034	273-6099

KENTUCKY

				Phone	Fax
Abraham Lincoln Birthplace National Historic Site 2995 Lincoln Farm Rd *Web:* www.nps.gov	Hodgenville	KY	42748	270-358-3137	358-3874
Cumberland Gap National Historical Park 91 Bartlett Park Rd PO Box 1848 *Web:* www.nps.gov/cuga	Middlesboro	KY	40965	606-248-2817	248-7276
Mammoth Cave National Park 1 Mammoth Cave Pkwy PO Box 7 *Web:* www.nps.gov/maca	Mammoth Cave	KY	42259	270-758-2180	758-2349

LOUISIANA

				Phone	Fax
Cane River Creole National Historical Park 400 Rapides Dr *Web:* www.nps.gov/cari	Natchitoches	LA	71457	318-356-8441	352-4549
Jean Lafitte National Historical Park & Preserve 419 Decatur St *Web:* www.nps.gov	New Orleans	LA	70130	504-589-3882	589-3851
New Orleans Jazz National Historical Park 419 Decatur St *TF:* 877-520-0677 ■ *Web:* www.nps.gov	New Orleans	LA	70130	504-589-4806	589-3865
Poverty Point National Monument c/o Poverty Pt State Historic Site PO Box 276 *TF:* 888-926-5492 ■ *Web:* www.nps.gov	Epps	LA	71237	318-926-5492	926-5366

MAINE

				Phone	Fax
Acadia National Park 109 Cottage St *Web:* www.nps.gov	Bar Harbor	ME	04609	207-288-3338	288-8813
Saint Croix Island International Historic Site PO Box 247 *Web:* www.nps.gov/sacr	Calais	ME	04619	207-454-3871	288-8813

MARYLAND

				Phone	Fax
Antietam National Battlefield 5831 Dunker Church Rd PO Box158 *Web:* www.nps.gov/anti	Sharpsburg	MD	21782	301-432-5124	432-4590
Assateague Island National Seashore 7206 National Seashore Ln PO Box 38 *Web:* www.nps.gov/asis	Berlin	MD	21811	410-641-1441	
Catoctin Mountain Park 6602 Foxville Rd *Web:* www.nps.gov	Thurmont	MD	21788	301-663-9330	
Chesapeake & Ohio Canal National Historical Park 1850 Dual Hwy Suite 100 *Web:* www.nps.gov/choh	Hagerstown	MD	21740	301-739-4200	739-5275
Clara Barton National Historic Site 5801 Oxford Rd *Web:* www.nps.gov/clba	Glen Echo	MD	20812	301-320-1410	
Fort McHenry National Monument & Historic Shrine 2400 E Fort Ave *Web:* www.nps.gov	Baltimore	MD	21230	410-962-4290	962-2500
Fort Washington Park 13551 Fort Washington Rd *Web:* www.nps.gov	Fort Washington	MD	20744	301-763-4600	763-1389

				Phone	Fax
Greenbelt Park 6565 Greenbelt Rd *Web:* www.nps.gov/gree	Greenbelt	MD	20770	301-344-3948	344-1012
Hampton National Historic Site 535 Hampton Ln *Web:* www.nps.gov	Towson	MD	21286	410-823-1309	823-8394
Monocacy National Battlefield 5201 Urbana Pike *Web:* www.nps.gov	Frederick	MD	21704	301-662-3515	662-3420
Piscataway Park c/o Fort Washington Pk 13551 Fort Washington Rd *Web:* www.nps.gov/pisc	Fort Washington	MD	20744	301-763-4600	763-1389
Thomas Stone National Historic Site 6655 Rose Hill Rd *Web:* www.nps.gov	Port Tobacco	MD	20677	301-392-1776	934-8793

MASSACHUSETTS

				Phone	Fax
Adams National Historical Park 135 Adams St *Web:* www.nps.gov	Quincy	MA	02169	617-773-1177	472-7562
Boston African-American National Historic Site 14 Beacon St Suite 401 *Web:* www.nps.gov	Boston	MA	02108	617-742-5415	720-0848
Boston Harbor Islands National Recreation Area 408 Atlantic Ave Suite 228 *Web:* www.nps.gov	Boston	MA	02110	617-223-8666	223-8671
Boston National Historical Park Charlestown Navy Yard *Web:* www.nps.gov/bost	Boston	MA	02129	617-242-5601	242-6006
Cape Cod National Seashore Marconi Site Rd *Web:* www.nps.gov	Wellfleet	MA	02667	508-349-3785	349-9052
Frederick Law Olmsted National Historic Site 99 Warren St *Web:* www.nps.gov/frla	Brookline	MA	02445	617-566-1689	232-4073
John F Kennedy National Historic Site 83 Beals St *Web:* www.nps.gov/jofi	Brookline	MA	02446	617-566-7937	730-9884
Longfellow National Historic Site 105 Brattle St *Web:* www.nps.gov/long	Cambridge	MA	02138	617-876-4491	497-8718
Lowell National Historical Park 67 Kirk St *Web:* www.nps.gov	Lowell	MA	01852	978-970-5000	970-5085
Minute Man National Historical Park 174 Liberty St *Web:* www.nps.gov	Concord	MA	01742	978-369-6993	318-7800
New Bedford Whaling National Historical Park 33 William St *Web:* www.nps.gov/nebe	New Bedford	MA	02740	508-996-4095	984-1250
Salem Maritime National Historic Site 160 Derby St *Web:* www.nps.gov/sama	Salem	MA	01970	978-740-1650	740-1654
Saugus Iron Works National Historic Site 244 Central St *Web:* www.nps.gov	Saugus	MA	01906	781-233-0050	231-7345
Springfield Armory National Historic Site 1 Armory Sq Suite 2 *Web:* www.nps.gov/spar	Springfield	MA	01105	413-734-8551	747-8062

MICHIGAN

				Phone	Fax
Isle Royale National Park 800 E Lakeshore Dr *Web:* www.nps.gov	Houghton	MI	49931	906-482-0984	482-8753
Keweenaw National Historical Park 25970 Red Jacket Rd PO Box 471 *Web:* www.nps.gov	Calumet	MI	49913	906-337-3168	337-3169
Pictured Rocks National Lakeshore N8391 Sandpoint Rd PO Box 40 *Web:* www.nps.gov	Munising	MI	49862	906-387-2607	387-4025
Sleeping Bear Dunes National Lakeshore 9922 Front St *Web:* www.nps.gov/slbe	Empire	MI	49630	231-326-5134	326-5382

MINNESOTA

				Phone	Fax
Grand Portage National Monument PO Box 668 *Web:* www.nps.gov	Grand Marais	MN	55604	218-387-2788	387-2790
Mississippi National River & Recreation Area 111 E Kellogg Blvd Suite 105 *Web:* www.nps.gov/miss	Saint Paul	MN	55101	651-290-4160	290-3214
Pipestone National Monument 36 Reservation Ave *Web:* www.nps.gov/pipe	Pipestone	MN	56164	507-825-5464	825-5466
Voyageurs National Park 360 Hwy 11 E *TF:* 888-381-2873 ■ *Web:* www.nps.gov/voya	International Falls	MN	56649	218-286-5258	285-7407

MISSISSIPPI

				Phone	Fax
Brice's Crossroads National Battlefield Site 2680 Natchez Trace Pkwy *TF:* 800-305-7417 ■ *Web:* www.nps.gov/brcr	Tupelo	MS	38804	662-680-4025	680-4033
Gulf Islands National Seashore (Mississippi) 3500 Park Rd *Web:* www.nps.gov/guis	Ocean Springs	MS	39564	228-875-0823	875-2358
Natchez National Historical Park 1 Melrose Montebello Pkwy *Web:* www.nps.gov/natc	Natchez	MS	39120	601-446-5790	442-9516
Natchez Trace National Scenic Trail 2680 Natchez Trace Pkwy *Web:* www.nps.gov/natt	Tupelo	MS	38804	662-680-4025	680-4036
Natchez Trace Parkway 2680 Natchez Trace Pkwy *TF:* 800-305-7417 ■ *Web:* www.nps.gov/natr	Tupelo	MS	38804	662-680-4025	680-4036
Tupelo National Battlefield c/o Natchez Trace Pkwy 2680 Natchez Trace Pkwy *TF:* 800-305-7417 ■ *Web:* www.nps.gov	Tupelo	MS	38804	662-680-4025	680-4033
Vicksburg National Military Park 3201 Clay St *Web:* www.nps.gov/vick	Vicksburg	MS	39183	601-636-0583	636-9497

MISSOURI

				Phone	Fax
George Washington Carver National Monument 5646 Carver Rd *Web:* www.nps.gov	Diamond	MO	64840	417-325-4151	325-4231
Harry S Truman National Historic Site 223 N Main St *Web:* www.nps.gov	Independence	MO	64050	816-254-9929	254-4491
Jefferson National Expansion Memorial 11 N 4th St *Web:* www.nps.gov/jeff	Saint Louis	MO	63102	314-655-1700	655-1641
Ozark National Scenic Riverways 404 Watercress Dr PO Box 490 *Web:* www.nps.gov/ozar	Van Buren	MO	63965	573-323-4236	323-4140
Ulysses S Grant National Historic Site 7400 Grant Rd *Web:* www.nps.gov/ulsg	Saint Louis	MO	63123	314-842-3298	842-1659
Wilson's Creek National Battlefield 6424 W Farm Rd 182 *Web:* www.nps.gov	Republic	MO	65738	417-732-2662	732-1167

MONTANA

				Phone	Fax
Big Hole National Battlefield 16425 Hwy 43 W *Web:* www.nps.gov	Wisdom	MT	59761	406-689-3155	689-3151
Bighorn Canyon National Recreation Area 5 Ave B PO Box 7458 *Web:* www.nps.gov/bica	Fort Smith	MT	59035	406-666-2412	666-2415
Glacier National Park PO Box 128 *Web:* www.nps.gov/glac	West Glacier	MT	59936	406-888-7800	888-7808
Grant-Kohrs Ranch National Historic Site 266 Warren Ln *Web:* www.nps.gov	Deer Lodge	MT	59722	406-846-2070	846-3962
Little Bighorn Battlefield National Monument PO Box 39 *Web:* www.nps.gov/libi	Crow Agency	MT	59022	406-638-3214	638-2623

NEBRASKA

				Phone	Fax
Agate Fossil Beds National Monument 301 River Rd *Web:* www.nps.gov	Harrison	NE	69346	308-668-2211	668-2318
Homestead National Monument of America 8523 W State Hwy 4 *Web:* www.nps.gov	Beatrice	NE	68310	402-223-3514	228-4231
National Park Service Regional Offices Midwest Region 601 Riverfront Dr	Omaha	NE	68102	402-661-1524	661-1984
Niobrara National Scenic River 146 S Hall St PO Box 319 *Web:* www.nps.gov/niob	Valentine	NE	69201	402-376-1901	376-1949
Scotts Bluff National Monument PO Box 27 *Web:* www.nps.gov	Gering	NE	69341	308-436-4340	436-7611

NEVADA

				Phone	Fax
Great Basin National Park 100 Great Basin National Pk *Web:* www.nps.gov/grba	Baker	NV	89311	775-234-7331	234-7269
Lake Mead National Recreation Area 601 Nevada Hwy *Web:* www.nps.gov	Boulder City	NV	89005	702-293-8990	293-8936

NEW HAMPSHIRE

				Phone	Fax
Saint-Gaudens National Historic Site 130 St Gaudens Rd *Web:* www.sgnhs.org	Cornish	NH	03745	603-675-2175	675-2701

NEW JERSEY

				Phone	Fax
Morristown National Historical Park 30 Washington Pl *Web:* www.nps.gov/morr	Morristown	NJ	07960	973-543-4030	451-9212
Thomas Edison National Historic Site 211 Main St *Web:* www.nps.gov/edis	West Orange	NJ	07052	973-736-0550	736-6567

NEW MEXICO

Name / Address	City	State	Zip	Phone	Fax
Aztec Ruins National Monument 84 Ruins Rd *Web:* www.nps.gov	Aztec	NM	87410	505-334-6174	334-6372
Bandelier National Monument 15 Entrance Rd *Web:* www.nps.gov	Los Alamos	NM	87544	505-672-0343	672-9607
Capulin Volcano National Monument PO Box 40 *Web:* www.nps.gov/cavo/index.htm	Capulin	NM	88414	505-278-2201	278-2211
Carlsbad Caverns National Park 3225 National Parks Hwy *Web:* www.nps.gov	Carlsbad	NM	88220	505-785-2232	785-2133
Chaco Culture National Historical Park PO Box 220 *Web:* www.nps.gov/chcu	Nageezi	NM	87037	505-786-7014	786-7061
El Malpais National Monument 123 E Roosevelt Ave *Web:* www.nps.gov	Grants	NM	87020	505-285-4641	285-5661
El Morro National Monument HC 61 PO Box 43 *Web:* www.nps.gov	Ramah	NM	87321	505-783-4226	783-4689
Fort Union National Monument PO Box 127 *Web:* www.nps.gov	Watrous	NM	87753	505-425-8025	454-1155
Gila Cliff Dwellings National Monument HC 68 PO Box 100 *Web:* www.nps.gov/gicl	Silver City	NM	88061	505-536-9461	536-9344
Pecos National Historical Park PO Box 418 *Web:* www.nps.gov/peco	Pecos	NM	87552	505-757-7200	757-7207
Petroglyph National Monument 6001 Unser Blvd NW *Web:* www.nps.gov	Albuquerque	NM	87120	505-899-0205	899-0207
Salinas Pueblo Missions National Monument PO Box 517 *Web:* www.nps.gov	Mountainair	NM	87036	505-847-2585	847-2441
White Sands National Monument PO Box 1086 *Web:* www.nps.gov/whsa	Holloman AFB	NM	88330	505-679-2599	

NEW YORK

Name / Address	City	State	Zip	Phone	Fax
African Burial Ground National Monument 290 Broadway *Web:* www.africanburialground.gov	New York	NY	10007	212-637-2019	
Castle Clinton National Monument 26 Wall St *Web:* www.nps.gov/cacl/index.htm	New York	NY	10005	212-825-6990	668-2899
Eleanor Roosevelt National Historic Site 4097 Albany Post Rd *Web:* www.nps.gov/elro	Hyde Park	NY	12538	845-229-9115	229-0739
Federal Hall National Memorial 26 Wall St *Web:* www.nps.gov/feha	New York	NY	10005	212-825-6888	825-6874
Fire Island National Seashore 120 Laurel St *Web:* www.nps.gov/fiis	Patchogue	NY	11772	631-687-4750	289-4898
Fort Stanwix National Monument 112 E Park St *Web:* www.nps.gov/fost	Rome	NY	13440	315-338-7730	334-5051
Gateway National Recreation Area 210 New York Ave *Web:* www.nps.gov/gate	Staten Island	NY	10305	718-354-4606	354-4605
General Grant National Memorial Riverside Dr & W 122nd St *Web:* www.nps.gov/gegr	New York	NY	10027	212-666-1640	932-9631
Governors Island National Monument 10 S St Slip #7 *Web:* www.governorsislandnationalmonument.org	New York	NY	10004	212-825-3045	825-3055
Hamilton Grange National Memorial 122 St @ Riverside Dr *Web:* www.nps.gov/hagr	New York	NY	10027	212-666-1640	
Home of Franklin D Roosevelt National Historic Site 4097 Albany Post Rd *Web:* www.nps.gov/hofr	Hyde Park	NY	12538	845-229-9115	229-0739
Martin Van Buren National Historic Site 1013 Old Post Rd *Web:* www.nps.gov	Kinderhook	NY	12106	518-758-9689	758-6986
Sagamore Hill National Historic Site 20 Sagamore Hill Rd *Web:* www.nps.gov/sahi	Oyster Bay	NY	11771	516-922-4788	922-4792
Saint Paul's Church National Historic Site 897 S Columbus Ave *Web:* www.nps.gov	Mount Vernon	NY	10550	914-667-4116	667-3024
Saratoga National Historical Park 648 Rt 32 *Web:* www.nps.gov/sara	Stillwater	NY	12170	518-664-9821	664-3349
Statue of Liberty National Monument & Ellis Island Liberty Island *Web:* www.nps.gov/stli	New York	NY	10004	212-363-3200	
Theodore Roosevelt Birthplace National Historic Site 28 E 20th St *Web:* www.nps.gov/thrb	New York	NY	10003	212-260-1212	
Vanderbilt Mansion National Historic Site 4097 Albany Post Rd *Web:* www.nps.gov/vama	Hyde Park	NY	12538	845-229-9115	229-0739
Women's Rights National Historical Park 136 Fall St *Web:* www.nps.gov/wori	Seneca Falls	NY	13148	315-568-2991	568-2141

NORTH CAROLINA

Name / Address	City	State	Zip	Phone	Fax
Blue Ridge Parkway 199 Hemphill Knob Rd *Web:* www.nps.gov	Asheville	NC	28803	828-271-4779	271-4313
Cape Hatteras National Seashore 1401 National Pk Dr *Web:* www.nps.gov/caha	Manteo	NC	27954	252-473-2111	473-2595
Cape Lookout National Seashore 131 Charles St *Web:* www.nps.gov	Harkers Island	NC	28531	252-728-2250	728-2160
Carl Sandburg Home National Historic Site 81 Carl Sadburg Ln *Web:* www.nps.gov	Flat Rock	NC	28731	828-693-4178	693-4179
Fort Raleigh National Historic Site 1401 National Pk Dr *Web:* www.nps.gov	Manteo	NC	27954	252-473-5772	473-2595
Guilford Courthouse National Military Park 2332 New Garden Rd *Web:* www.nps.gov/guco	Greensboro	NC	27410	336-288-1776	282-2296
Moores Creek National Battlefield 29044 Nc Hwy 210 *Web:* www.nps.gov	Currie	NC	28435	910-283-5591	283-5351
Wright Bros National Memorial 1401 National Pk Dr *Web:* www.nps.gov/wrbr	Manteo	NC	27954	252-473-2111	473-2595

NORTH DAKOTA

Name / Address	City	State	Zip	Phone	Fax
Fort Union Trading Post National Historic Site 15550 Hwy 1804 *Web:* www.nps.gov	Williston	ND	58801	701-572-9083	572-7321
Knife River Indian Villages National Historic Site 564 County Rd 37 PO Box 9 *Web:* www.nps.gov	Stanton	ND	58571	701-745-3300	745-3708
Theodore Roosevelt National Park 315 2nd Ave PO Box 7 *Web:* www.nps.gov/thro	Medora	ND	58645	701-623-4466	623-4840

OHIO

Name / Address	City	State	Zip	Phone	Fax
Cuyahoga Valley National Park 15610 Vaughn Rd **Fax Area Code:* 440 ■ *TF:* 800-445-9667 ■ *Web:* www.nps.gov	Brecksville	OH	44141	216-524-1497	546-5989*
Dayton Aviation Heritage National Historical Park 16 S Williams St *Web:* www.nps.gov	Dayton	OH	45402	937-225-7705	222-4512
First Ladies National Historic Site 205 Market Ave S *Web:* www.nps.gov	Canton	OH	44702	330-452-0876	456-3414
Hopewell Culture National Historical Park 16062 SR-104 *Web:* www.nps.gov/hocu	Chillicothe	OH	45601	740-774-1126	774-1140
James A Garfield National Historic Site 8095 Mentor Ave *Web:* www.nps.gov/jaga	Mentor	OH	44060	440-255-8722	255-8545
Perry's Victory & International Peace Memorial 93 Delaware Ave PO Box 549 *Web:* www.nps.gov/pevi	Put-in-Bay	OH	43456	419-285-2184	285-2516
William Howard Taft National Historic Site 2038 Auburn Ave *Web:* www.nps.gov/wiho	Cincinnati	OH	45219	513-684-3262	684-3627

OKLAHOMA

Name / Address	City	State	Zip	Phone	Fax
Chickasaw National Recreation Area 1008 W 2nd St *Web:* www.nps.gov	Sulphur	OK	73086	580-622-3165	622-6931
Washita Battlefield National Historic Site 426 E Broadway *Web:* www.nps.gov/waba	Cheyenne	OK	73628	580-497-2742	497-2712

OREGON

Name / Address	City	State	Zip	Phone	Fax
Crater Lake National Park PO Box 7 *Web:* www.nps.gov	Crater Lake	OR	97604	541-594-3000	594-3010
John Day Fossil Beds National Monument 32651 Hwy 19 *Web:* www.nps.gov/joda	Kimberly	OR	97848	541-987-2333	987-2336
Oregon Caves National Monument 19000 Caves Hwy *Web:* www.nps.gov/orca	Cave Junction	OR	97523	541-592-2100	592-3981

PENNSYLVANIA

Name / Address	City	State	Zip	Phone	Fax
Allegheny Portage Railroad National Historic Site 110 Federal Pk Rd *Web:* www.nps.gov	Gallitzin	PA	16641	814-886-6150	884-0206
Delaware National Scenic River Delaware Water Gap National Recreation Area 1 River Rd *Web:* www.nps.gov/dela	Bushkill	PA	18324	570-426-2435	588-2780
Delaware Water Gap National Recreation Area 1 River Rd *Web:* www.nps.gov/dewa	Bushkill	PA	18324	570-828-2253	426-2402
Edgar Allan Poe National Historic Site 532 N 7th St *Web:* www.nps.gov/edal	Philadelphia	PA	19123	215-597-8780	597-1901

				Phone	Fax
Eisenhower National Historic Site 250 Eisenhower Farm Ln *Web:* www.nps.gov	Gettysburg	PA	17325	717-338-9114	338-0821
Flight 93 National Memorial *National Park Service* 109 W Main St Suite 104 *Web:* www.nps.gov/flni/index.htm	Somerset	PA	15501	814-443-4557	443-2180
Fort Necessity National Battlefield 1 Washington Pkwy *Web:* www.nps.gov	Farmington	PA	15437	724-329-5512	329-8682
Friendship Hill National Historic Site 223 New Geneva Rd *Web:* www.nps.gov/frhi	Point Marion	PA	15474	724-725-9190	725-1999
Gettysburg National Military Park 97 Taneytown Rd *Web:* www.nps.gov/gett	Gettysburg	PA	17325	717-334-1124	334-1891
Great Egg Harbor National Wild & Scenic & Recreational River c/o National Pk Service 200 Chestnut St *Web:* www.nps.gov/greg	Philadelphia	PA	19106	215-597-5823	597-5747
Hopewell Furnace National Historic Site 2 Mark Bird Ln *Web:* www.nps.gov	Elverson	PA	19520	610-582-8773	582-2768
Independence National Historical Park 143 S 3rd St *Web:* www.nps.gov/inde	Philadelphia	PA	19106	215-597-8787	861-4950
Johnstown Flood National Memorial 733 Lake Rd *Web:* www.nps.gov/jofl	South Fork	PA	15956	814-495-4643	495-7463
National Park Service Regional Offices NortheastRegion 200 Chestnut St # 3 *Web:* www.nps.gov	Philadelphia	PA	19106	215-597-7013	597-0815
Steamtown National Historic Site 150 S Washington Ave *TF:* 888-693-9391 ■ *Web:* www.nps.gov	Scranton	PA	18503	570-340-5200	340-5328
Thaddeus Kosciuszko National Memorial c/o Independence National Historical Pk 143 S 3rd St *Web:* www.nps.gov/thko	Philadelphia	PA	19106	215-597-9618	861-4950
Upper Delaware Scenic & Recreation River 274 River Rd *Web:* www.nps.gov/upde	Beach Lake	PA	18405	570-729-7134	729-7148
Valley Forge National Historical Park 1400 N Outer Line Dr *Web:* www.nps.gov/vafo/index.htm	King of Prussia	PA	19406	610-783-1077	783-1060

PUERTO RICO

				Phone	Fax
San Juan National Historic Site 501 Norzagaray St *Web:* www.nps.gov/saju	San Juan	PR	00901	787-729-6960	289-7972

RHODE ISLAND

				Phone	Fax
Roger Williams National Memorial 282 N Main St *Web:* www.nps.gov/rowi	Providence	RI	02903	401-521-7266	521-7239

SOUTH CAROLINA

				Phone	Fax
Charles Pinckney National Historic Site 1214 Middle St *Web:* www.nps.gov/chpi	Sullivans Island	SC	29482	843-881-5516	881-7070
Congaree National Park 100 National Pk Rd *Web:* www.nps.gov	Hopkins	SC	29061	803-776-4396	783-4241
Cowpens National Battlefield 4001 Chesnee Hwy PO Box 308 *Web:* www.nps.gov/cowp	Gaffney	SC	29341	864-461-2828	461-7795
Fort Sumter National Monument 1214 Middle St *Web:* www.nps.gov/fosu	Sullivans Island	SC	29482	843-883-3123	883-3910
Kings Mountain National Military Park 2625 Pk Rd *Web:* www.nps.gov	Blacksburg	SC	29702	864-936-7921	936-9897
Ninety Six National Historic Site 1103 Hwy 248 PO Box 418 *Web:* www.nps.gov/nisi	Ninety Six	SC	29666	864-543-4068	543-2058

SOUTH DAKOTA

				Phone	Fax
Badlands National Park 25216 Ben Reifel Rd PO Box 6 *Web:* www.nps.gov/badl	Interior	SD	57750	605-433-5361	433-5404
Jewel Cave National Monument 11149 US Hwy 16 Bldg B-12 *Web:* www.nps.gov	Custer	SD	57730	605-673-2288	673-3294
Minuteman Missile National Historic Site 21280 SD Hwy 240 *Web:* www.nps.gov	Philip	SD	57567	605-433-5552	433-5558
Missouri National Recreational River 508 E 2nd St *Web:* www.nps.gov/mnrr	Yankton	SD	57078	605-665-0209	665-4183
Mount Rushmore National Memorial 13000 Hwy 244 Bldg 31 Suite 1 *Web:* www.nps.gov	Keystone	SD	57751	605-574-2523	574-2307
Wind Cave National Park 26611 US Hwy 385 *Web:* www.nps.gov	Hot Springs	SD	57747	605-745-4600	745-4207

TENNESSEE

				Phone	Fax
Andrew Johnson National Historic Site 121 Monument Ave *Web:* www.nps.gov	Greeneville	TN	37743	423-638-3551	638-9194
Big South Fork National River & Recreation Area 4564 Leatherwood Rd *Web:* www.nps.gov	Oneida	TN	37841	423-569-9778	569-5505
Fort Donelson National Battlefield PO Box 434 *Web:* www.nps.gov	Dover	TN	37058	931-232-5706	232-4085
Great Smoky Mountains National Park 107 Pk Headquarters Rd *Web:* www.nps.gov	Gatlinburg	TN	37738	865-436-1200	436-1220
Obed Wild & Scenic River 208 N Maiden St *Web:* www.nps.gov	Wartburg	TN	37887	423-346-6294	346-3362
Shiloh National Military Park 1055 Pittsburg Landing Rd *Web:* www.nps.gov/shil	Shiloh	TN	38376	731-689-5696	689-5450
Stones River National Battlefield 3501 Old Nashville Hwy *Web:* www.nps.gov	Murfreesboro	TN	37129	615-893-9501	893-9508

TEXAS

				Phone	Fax
Alibates Flint Quarries National Monument PO Box 1460 *Web:* www.nps.gov/alfl	Fritch	TX	79036	806-857-3151	857-2319
Amistad National Recreation Area 4121 Hwy 90 W *Web:* www.nps.gov	Del Rio	TX	78840	830-775-7491	778-9248
Big Bend National Park PO Box 129 *Web:* www.nps.gov/bibe	Big Bend National Park	TX	79834	432-477-2251	477-1175
Big Thicket National Preserve 6044 FM420 *Web:* www.nps.gov/bith	Kountze	TX	77625	409-951-6700	951-6714
Chamizal National Memorial 800 S San Marcial St *Web:* www.nps.gov	El Paso	TX	79905	915-532-7273	532-7240
Fort Davis National Historic Site PO Box 1379 *Web:* www.nps.gov/foda	Fort Davis	TX	79734	432-426-3224	426-3122
Guadalupe Mountains National Park 400 Pine Canyon Rd *Web:* www.nps.gov	Salt Flat	TX	79847	915-828-3251	828-3269
Lake Meredith National Recreation Area 419 E Broadway *Web:* www.nps.gov/lamr	Fritch	TX	79036	806-857-3151	857-2319
Lyndon B. Johnson National Historical Park 100 Lady Bird Ln *Web:* www.nps.gov/lyjo	Johnson City	TX	78636	830-868-7128	868-7863
Padre Island National Seashore PO Box 181300 *Web:* www.nps.gov/pais	Corpus Christi	TX	78480	361-949-8068	949-8023
Palo Alto Battlefield National Historic Site 1623 Central Blvd Suite 213 *Web:* www.nps.gov	Brownsville	TX	78520	956-541-2785	541-6356
Rio Grande Wild & Scenic River PO Box 129 *Web:* www.nps.gov/rigr	Big Bend National Park	TX	79834	432-477-2251	477-1175
San Antonio Missions National Historical Park 2202 Roosevelt Ave *Web:* www.nps.gov/saan	San Antonio	TX	78210	210-534-8833	534-1106

UTAH

				Phone	Fax
Arches National Park PO Box 907 *Web:* www.nps.gov	Moab	UT	84532	435-719-2299	719-2300
Bryce Canyon National Park PO Box 640201 *Web:* www.nps.gov	Bryce Canyon	UT	84764	435-834-5322	834-4102
Canyonlands National Park 2282 S W Resource Blvd *Web:* www.nps.gov/cany	Moab	UT	84532	435-719-2313	719-2300
Capitol Reef National Park 52 Scenic Dr *Web:* www.nps.gov	Torrey	UT	84775	435-425-3791	425-3026
Cedar Breaks National Monument 2390 W Hwy 56 Suite 11 *Web:* www.nps.gov	Cedar City	UT	84720	435-586-9451	586-3813
Golden Spike National Historic Site PO Box 897 *Web:* www.nps.gov/gosp	Brigham City	UT	84302	435-471-2209	471-2341
Natural Bridges National Monument HC 60 PO Box 1 *Web:* www.nps.gov/nabr	Lake Powell	UT	84533	435-692-1234	692-1111
Timpanogos Cave National Monument RR 3 PO Box 200 *Web:* www.nps.gov	American Fork	UT	84003	801-756-5239	756-5661
Zion National Park SR 9 *Web:* www.nps.gov/zion	Springdale	UT	84767	435-772-3256	772-3426

VERMONT

				Phone	Fax
Marsh-Billings-Rockefeller National Historical Park 54 Elm St *Web:* www.nps.gov	Woodstock	VT	05091	802-457-3368	457-3405

VIRGIN ISLANDS

				Phone	Fax
Buck Island Reef National Monument 2100 Church St Suite 100 *Web:* www.nps.gov/buis	Christiansted	VI	00820	340-773-1460	773-5995
Christiansted National Historic Site 2100 Church St Suite 100 Christiansted *Web:* www.nps.gov/chri	Saint Croix	VI	00820	340-773-1460	773-4995
Salt River Bay National Historical Park & Ecological Preserve c/o Christiansted National Historic Site 2100 Church St Suite 100 *Web:* www.nps.gov/sari	Christiansted	VI	00820	340-773-1460	773-5995
Virgin Islands Coral Reef National Monument 1300 Cruz Bay Creek *Web:* www.nps.gov/vicr/index.htm	Saint John	VI	00830	340-776-6201	776-6139
Virgin Islands National Park 1300 Cruz Bay Creek *Web:* www.nps.gov/viis	Saint John	VI	00830	340-776-6201	775-9592

VIRGINIA

				Phone	Fax
Appomattox Court House National Historical Park Hwy 24 PO Box 218 *Web:* www.nps.gov/apco	Appomattox	VA	24522	434-352-8987	352-8330
Arlington House-Robert E Lee Memorial George Washington Memorial Pkwy Turkey Run Pk *Web:* www.nps.gov/arho/index.htm	McLean	VA	22101	703-235-1530	235-1546
Booker T. Washington National Monument 12130 Booker T Washington Hwy *Web:* www.nps.gov/bowa	Hardy	VA	24101	540-721-2094	721-8311
Cedar Creek & Belle Grove National Historical Park 7718 1/2 Main St *Web:* www.nps.gov	Middletown	VA	22645	540-868-9176	869-4527
Colonial National Historical Park PO Box 210 *Web:* www.nps.gov/colo	Yorktown	VA	23690	757-898-3400	898-6346
Fredericksburg & Spotsylvania National Military Park 120 Chatham Ln *Web:* www.nps.gov/frsp	Fredericksburg	VA	22405	540-371-0802	371-1907
George Washington Birthplace National Monument 1732 Popes Creek Rd *Web:* www.nps.gov/gewa	Washington's Birthplace	VA	22443	804-224-1732	224-2142
George Washington Memorial Parkway Turkey Run Pk *Web:* www.nps.gov/gwmp	McLean	VA	22101	703-289-2500	289-2598
Lyndon Baines Johnson Memorial Grove on the Potomac Turkey Run Pk George Washington Memorial Pkwy *Web:* www.nps.gov/lyba	McLean	VA	22101	703-289-2500	289-2598
Maggie L Walker National Historic Site 3215 E Broad St *Web:* www.nps.gov/malw	Richmond	VA	23223	804-771-2017	771-2226
Manassas National Battlefield Park 12521 Lee Hwy *Web:* www.nps.gov	Manassas	VA	20109	703-361-1339	754-1107
Petersburg National Battlefield 1539 Hickory Hill Rd *Web:* www.nps.gov/pete	Petersburg	VA	23803	804-732-3531	732-0835
Prince William Forest Park 18100 Pk Headquarters Rd *Web:* www.nps.gov	Triangle	VA	22172	703-221-7181	221-3258
Richmond National Battlefield Park 3215 E Broad St *Web:* www.nps.gov	Richmond	VA	23223	804-226-1981	771-8522
Shenandoah National Park 3655 US Hwy 211E *TF:* 800-732-0911 ■ *Web:* www.nps.gov/shen	Luray	VA	22835	540-999-3500	999-3601
Theodore Roosevelt Island Park c/o Turkey Run Pk George Washington Memorial Pkwy *Web:* www.nps.gov/this	McLean	VA	22101	703-289-2500	289-2598
Wolf Trap National Park for the Performing Arts 1551 Trap Rd *Web:* www.nps.gov/wotr	Vienna	VA	22182	703-255-1800	255-1971

WASHINGTON

				Phone	Fax
Ebey's Landing National Historical Reserve 162 Cemetery Rd *Web:* www.nps.gov	Coupeville	WA	98239	360-678-6084	678-2246
Fort Vancouver National Historic Site 612 E Reserve St *TF:* 800-832-3599 ■ *Web:* www.nps.gov	Vancouver	WA	98661	360-816-6230	
Klondike Gold Rush National Historical Park - Seattle Unit 319 2nd Ave S *Web:* www.nps.gov	Seattle	WA	98104	206-220-4240	
Lake Chelan National Recreation Area c/o N Cascades National Pk 810 State Suite 20 *Web:* www.nps.gov/lach	Sedro-Woolle	WA	98284	360-854-7200	856-1934
Lake Roosevelt National Recreation Area 1008 Crest Dr *Web:* www.nps.gov	Coulee Dam	WA	99116	509-633-9441	633-9332
Mount Rainier National Park 55210 238th Ave E *Web:* www.nps.gov/mora	Ashford	WA	98304	360-569-2211	569-6519
North Cascades National Park 810 SR 20 *Web:* www.nps.gov/noca	Sedro Woolley	WA	98284	360-856-5700	856-1934
Olympic National Park 600 E Pk Ave *Web:* www.nps.gov	Port Angeles	WA	98362	360-565-3130	565-3015
Ross Lake National Recreation Area 810 SR- 20 *Web:* www.nps.gov/rola	Sedro Woolley	WA	98284	360-854-7200	856-1934
San Juan Island National Historical Park 4668 Cattle Point Rd PO Box 429 *Web:* www.nps.gov/sajh	Friday Harbor	WA	98250	360-378-2240	378-2615
Whitman Mission National Historic Site 328 Whitman Mission Rd *Web:* www.nps.gov	Walla Walla	WA	99362	509-522-6360	522-6355

WEST VIRGINIA

				Phone	Fax
Appalachian National Scenic Trail PO Box 807 *Web:* www.nps.gov/appa	Harpers Ferry	WV	25425	304-535-6331	535-2667
Bluestone National Scenic River 104 Main St PO Box 246 *Web:* www.nps.gov/blue	Glen Jean	WV	25846	304-465-0508	466-9194
Gauley River National Recreation Area 104 Main St PO Box 246 *Web:* www.nps.gov/gari	Glen Jean	WV	25846	304-465-0508	465-0591
Harpers Ferry National Historic Park PO Box 65 *Web:* www.nps.gov/hafe	Harpers Ferry	WV	25425	304-535-6029	535-6244
New River Gorge National River 104 Main St PO Box 246 *Web:* www.nps.gov/neri	Glen Jean	WV	25846	304-465-0508	465-0591
Potomac Heritage National Scenic Trail PO Box B *Web:* www.nps.gov/pohe	Harpers Ferry	WV	25425	304-535-4014	

WISCONSIN

				Phone	Fax
Apostle Islands National Lakeshore 415 Washington Ave *Web:* www.nps.gov	Bayfield	WI	54814	715-779-3397	779-3049
Saint Croix National Scenic Riverway 401 N Hamilton St *Web:* www.nps.gov	Saint Croix Falls	WI	54024	715-483-3284	483-3288

WYOMING

				Phone	Fax
Devils Tower National Monument Hwy 110 Bldg 170 PO Box 10 *Web:* www.nps.gov/deto	Devils Tower	WY	82714	307-467-5283	467-5350
Fort Laramie National Historic Site 965 Grey Rocks Rd *Web:* www.nps.gov/fola	Fort Laramie	WY	82212	307-837-2221	837-2120
Fossil Butte National Monument PO Box 592 *Web:* www.nps.gov	Kemmerer	WY	83101	307-877-4455	877-4457
Grand Teton National Park Teton Pk Rd PO Drawer 170 *Web:* www.nps.gov/grte	Moose	WY	83012	307-739-3300	739-3438
John D. Rockefeller Jr Memorial Parkway PO Box 170 *Web:* www.nps.gov/jodr	Moose	WY	83012	307-739-3300	739-3438
Yellowstone National Park PO Box 168 **Fax:* Mail Rm ■ *Web:* www.nps.gov	Yellowstone National Park	WY	82190	307-344-7381	344-2323*

568 PARKS - STATE

SEE ALSO Nature Centers, Parks, Other Natural Areas p. 1482; Parks - National - Canada p. 2339; Parks - National - US p. 2340

ALABAMA

				Phone	Fax
Bladon Springs State Park 3921 Bladon Rd *Web:* www.alapark.com/parks	Bladon Springs	AL	36919	251-754-9207	754-9207
Blue Springs State Park 2595 Alabama 10 *Web:* www.alapark.com	Clio	AL	36017	334-397-4875	397-4875
Buck's Pocket State Park 393 County Rd 174 *Web:* www.alapark.com	Grove Oak	AL	35975	256-659-2000	659-2000
Cathedral Caverns State Park 637 Cave Rd *Web:* www.alapark.com	Woodville	AL	35776	256-728-8193	728-8193
Cheaha Resort State Park 19644 Hwy 281 *TF:* 800-610-5801 ■ *Web:* www.alapark.com	Delta	AL	36258	256-488-5111	488-5885
Chewacla State Park 124 Shell Toomer Pkwy *Web:* www.alapark.com	Auburn	AL	36830	334-887-5621	821-2439
Chickasaw State Park 26955 US Hwy 43 *Web:* www.alapark.com	Gallion	AL	36742	334-295-8230	295-8230
DeSoto Resort State Park 13883 County Rd 89 *Web:* www.alapark.com	Fort Payne	AL	35967	256-845-0051	845-8286
Florala State Park 22738 Azalea Dr *Web:* www.alapark.com	Florala	AL	36442	334-858-6425	858-6425

				Phone	Fax
Frank Jackson State Park 100 Jerry Adams Dr ... Opp	AL	36467		334-493-6988	493-2478
Web: www.alapark.com					
Gulf State Park 20115 Alabama 135 ... Gulf Shores	AL	36542		251-948-7275	948-7726
Web: www.alapark.com					
Joe Wheeler Resort State Park 201 McLean Dr ... Rogersville	AL	35652		256-247-5466	247-1449
Web: www.alapark.com					
Lake Guntersville Resort State Park 7966 Alabama Hwy 227 ... Guntersville	AL	35976		256-571-5444	
Web: www.dcnr.state.al.us					
Lake Lurleen State Park 13226 Lake Lurleen Rd ... Coker	AL	35452		205-339-1558	339-8885
Web: www.alapark.com					
Lakepoint Resort State Park 104 Lakepoint Dr ... Eufaula	AL	36027		334-687-8011	687-3273
TF: 800-544-5253 ■ *Web:* www.alapark.com					
Meaher State Park 5200 Battleship Pkwy ... Spanish Fort	AL	36577		251-626-5529	626-5529
Web: www.alapark.com					
Monte Sano State Park 5105 Nolen Ave ... Huntsville	AL	35801		256-534-3757	539-7069
TF: 800-252-7275 ■ *Web:* www.alapark.com					
Oak Mountain State Park 200 Terr Dr PO Box 278 ... Pelham	AL	35124		205-620-2520	620-2531
Web: www.alapark.com					
Paul M. Grist State Park 1546 Grist Rd ... Selma	AL	36701		334-872-5846	872-5846
Web: www.alapark.com					
Rickwood Caverns State Park 370 Rickwood Pk Rd ... Warrior	AL	35180		205-647-9692	647-9692
Web: www.alapark.com					
Roland Cooper State Park 285 Deer Run Dr ... Camden	AL	36726		334-682-4838	682-4050
Web: www.alapark.com					
Wind Creek State Park 4325 Al Hwy 128 ... Alexander City	AL	35010		256-329-0845	234-4870
Web: www.alapark.com					

ALASKA

			Phone	Fax
Afognak Island State Park c/o Kodiak Area Office 1400 Abercrombie Dr ... Kodiak	AK	99615	907-486-6339	
Web: dnr.alaska.gov/parks/units/kodiak/afognak.htm				
Alaska Chilkat Bald Eagle Preserve c/o SE Area Office 400 Willoughby Ave 4th Fl PO Box 111071 ... Juneau	AK	99811	907-465-4563	
Web: www.dnr.state.ak.us/parks/units/eagleprv.htm				
Anchor River State Recreation Area c/o Kenai/PWS Area Office PO Box 1247 ... Soldotna	AK	99669	907-262-5581	
Web: dnr.alaska.gov/parks/units/anchoriv.htm				
Baranof Castle Hill State Historic Site c/o SE Area Office 400 Willoughby Ave 4th Fl PO Box 111071 ... Juneau	AK	99811	907-465-4563	
Web: www.dnr.alaska.gov/parks/aspunits/southeast/baranofcastle.htm				
Beecher Pass State Marine Park c/o SE Area Office 400 Willoughby Ave 4th Fl PO Box 111071 ... Juneau	AK	99811	907-465-4563	
Web: www.dnr.alaska.gov/parks/aspbro/charts/sewrang.htm				
Bettles Bay State Marine Park c/o Kenai/PWS Area Office PO Box 1247 ... Soldotna	AK	99669	907-262-5581	
Web: dnr.alaska.gov/parks/units/pwssmp/smpwhit2.htm				
Big Bear/Baby Bear State Marine Park c/o SE Area Office 400 Willoughby Ave 4th Fl PO Box 111071 ... Juneau	AK	99811	907-465-4563	
Web: www.dnr.alaska.gov/parks/aspunits/marinepark/bigbrbabybrsmp.htm				
Big Delta State Historical Park c/o Northern Area Office 3700 Airport Way ... Fairbanks	AK	99709	907-451-2695	
Web: www.dnr.alaska.gov/parks/units/deltajct/bigdelta.htm				
Birch Lake State Recreation Area c/o Northern Area Office 3700 Airport Way ... Fairbanks	AK	99709	907-451-2695	
Web: www.dnr.alaska.gov/parks/units/birch.htm				
Black Sands Beach State Marine Park c/o SE Area Office 400 Willoughby Ave 4th Fl PO Box 111071 ... Juneau	AK	99811	907-465-4563	
Web: www.dnr.alaska.gov/parks/aspunits/southeast/blacksand.htm				
Blair Lake State Recreation Site c/o Mat-Su/CB Area Office HC 32 PO Box 6706 ... Wasilla	AK	99654	907-745-3975	
Blueberry Lake State Recreation Site 23 Richardson Hwy ... Valdez	AK	99686	907-269-8400	
Web: dnr.alaska.gov/parks/aspunits/kenai/blueberrylksrs.htm				
Boswell Bay State Marine Park PO Box 1247 ... Soldotna	AK	99669	907-262-5581	
Web: dnr.alaska.gov/parks/units/pwssmp/smpcord.htm				
Buskin River State Recreation Site c/o Kodiak Area Office 1400 Abercrombie Dr ... Kodiak	AK	99615	907-486-6339	
Web: dnr.alaska.gov/parks/units/kodiak/buskin.htm				
Caines Head State Recreation Area c/o Kenai/PWS Area Office PO Box 1247 ... Soldotna	AK	99669	907-262-5581	
Web: dnr.alaska.gov/parks/units/caineshd.htm				
Canoe Passage State Marine Park c/o Kenai/PWS Area Office PO Box 1247 ... Soldotna	AK	99669	907-262-5581	
Web: dnr.alaska.gov/parks/units/pwssmp/smpcord.htm				
Captain Cook State Recreation Area c/o Kenai/PWS Area Office PO Box 1247 ... Soldotna	AK	99669	907-262-5581	
Web: dnr.alaska.gov/parks/units/captcook.htm				
Chena River State Recreation Area c/o Northern Area Office 3700 Airport Way ... Fairbanks	AK	99709	907-451-2695	
Web: www.dnr.alaska.gov/parks/units/chena				
Chena River State Recreation Site c/o Northern Area Office 3700 Airport Way ... Fairbanks	AK	99709	907-451-2695	
Web: www.dnr.alaska.gov/parks/units/chenasrs.htm				
Chilkat Islands State Marine Park c/o SE Area Office 400 Willoughby Ave 4th Fl PO Box 111071 ... Juneau	AK	99811	907-465-4563	
Web: www.dnr.alaska.gov/parks/units/haines.htm#cismp				
Chilkat State Park c/o SE Area Office 400 Willoughby Ave 4th Fl PO Box 111071 ... Juneau	AK	99811	907-465-4563	
Web: www.dnr.alaska.gov/parks/aspunits/southeast/chilkatsp.htm				
Chilkoot Lake State Recreation Site c/o SE Area Office 400 Willoughby Ave 4th Fl PO Box 111071 ... Juneau	AK	99811	907-465-4563	
Web: www.dnr.alaska.gov/parks/aspunits/southeast/chilkootlksrs.htm				
Chugach State Park c/o Chugach Area Office HC 52 PO Box 8999 ... Indian	AK	99540	907-345-5014	345-6982
Web: www.dnr.state.ak.us/parks/units/chugach				
Clam Gulch State Recreation Area c/o Kenai/PWS Area Office PO Box 1247 ... Soldotna	AK	99669	907-262-5581	
Web: dnr.alaska.gov/parks/units/clamglch.htm				
Clearwater State Recreation Site c/o Northern Area Office 3700 Airport Way ... Fairbanks	AK	99709	907-451-2695	
Web: www.dnr.alaska.gov/parks/units/deltajct/clearwtr.htm				
Crooked Creek State Recreation Site c/o Kenai/PWS Area Office PO Box 1247 ... Soldotna	AK	99669	907-262-5581	
Web: dnr.alaska.gov/parks/units/kasilof.htm				
Dall Bay State Marine Park c/o SE Area Office 400 Willoughby Ave 4th Fl PO Box 111071 ... Juneau	AK	99811	907-465-4563	
Web: www.dnr.alaska.gov/parks/aspunits/marinepark/dallbay.htm				
Decision Point State Marine Park c/o Kenai/PWS Area Office PO Box 1247 ... Soldotna	AK	99669	907-262-5581	
Web: dnr.alaska.gov/parks/units/pwssmp/smpwhit1.htm				
Deep Creek State Recreation Area c/o Kenai/PWS Area Office PO Box 1247 ... Soldotna	AK	99669	907-262-5581	
Web: dnr.alaska.gov/parks/units/deepck.htm				
Delta State Recreation Site c/o Northern Area Office 3700 Airport Way ... Fairbanks	AK	99709	907-451-2695	
Web: www.dnr.alaska.gov/parks/units/deltajct/deltasrs.htm				
Denali State Park c/o Mat-Su/CB Area Office HC 32 PO Box 6706 ... Wasilla	AK	99654	907-745-3975	745-0938
Web: dnr.alaska.gov/parks/units/denali1.htm				
Donnelly Creek State Recreation Site c/o Northern Area Office 3700 Airport Way ... Fairbanks	AK	99709	907-451-2695	
Web: www.dnr.alaska.gov/parks/units/deltajct/donnelly.htm				
Driftwood Bay State Marine Park c/o Kenai/PWS Area Office PO Box 1247 ... Soldotna	AK	99669	907-262-5581	
Web: dnr.alaska.gov/parks/units/pwssmp/smpsewd.htm				
Eagle Beach State Recreation Area c/o SE Area Office 400 Willoughby Ave 4th Fl PO Box 111071 ... Juneau	AK	99811	907-465-4563	
Web: www.dnr.alaska.gov/parks/aspunits/southeast/eaglebeachsra.htm				
Eagle Trail State Recreation Site c/o Northern Area Office 3700 Airport Way ... Fairbanks	AK	99709	907-883-3686	
Web: www.dnr.alaska.gov/parks/aspunits/northern/eagletrailsrs.htm				
Entry Cove State Marine Park c/o Kenai/PWS Area Office PO Box 1247 ... Soldotna	AK	99669	907-262-5581	
Web: dnr.alaska.gov/parks/units/pwssmp/smpwhit1.htm				
Ernest Gruening State Historical Park c/o SE Area Office 400 Willoughby Ave 4th Fl PO Box 111071 ... Juneau	AK	99811	907-465-4563	
Web: www.dnr.alaska.gov/parks/aspunits/southeast/ernestgrushp.htm				
Fielding Lake State Recreation Site c/o Northern Area Office 3700 Airport Way ... Fairbanks	AK	99709	907-451-2695	
Web: www.dnr.alaska.gov/parks/units/deltajct/fielding.htm				
Finger Lake State Recreation Area c/o Mat-Su/CB Area Office 7278 E Bogard Rd ... Wasilla	AK	99654	907-745-3975	
Web: dnr.alaska.gov/parks/aspunits/matsu/fingerlksrs.htm				
Fort Abercrombie State Historical Park 550 W 7th Ave Suite 1050 ... Anchorage	AK	99501	907-269-8915	
Web: dnr.alaska.gov/parks/units/kodiak/ftaber.htm				
Funter Bay State Marine Park c/o SE Area Office 400 Willoughby Ave 4th Fl PO Box 111071 ... Juneau	AK	99811	907-465-4563	
Web: www.dnr.alaska.gov/parks/aspbro/charts/sejuneau.htm				
Granite Bay State Marine Park c/o Kenai/PWS Area Office PO Box 1247 ... Soldotna	AK	99669	907-262-5581	
Web: dnr.alaska.gov/parks/units/pwssmp/smpwhit2.htm				
Grindall Island State Marine Park c/o SE Area Office 400 Willoughby Ave 4th Fl PO Box 111071 ... Juneau	AK	99811	907-465-4563	
Web: www.dnr.alaska.gov/parks/aspunits/southeast/grindallimp.htm				
Halibut Point State Recreation Site c/o SE Area Office 400 Willoughby Ave 4th Fl PO Box 111071 ... Juneau	AK	99811	907-465-4563	
Web: www.dnr.alaska.gov/parks/aspunits/southeast/halibutptsrs.htm				
Harding Lake State Recreation Area c/o Northern Area Office 3700 Airport Way ... Fairbanks	AK	99709	907-451-2695	
Web: www.dnr.alaska.gov/parks/units/harding.htm				
Horseshoe Bay State Marine Park c/o Kenai/PWS Area Office PO Box 1247 ... Soldotna	AK	99669	907-262-5581	
Web: dnr.alaska.gov/parks/units/pwssmp/smpwhit2.htm				
Independence Mine State Historical Park c/o Mat-Su/CB Area Office HC 32 PO Box 6706 ... Wasilla	AK	99654	907-745-3975	
Web: www.dnr.state.ak.us/parks/units/indmine.htm				
Jack Bay State Marine Park c/o Kenai/PWS Area Office PO Box 1247 ... Soldotna	AK	99669	907-262-5581	
Web: dnr.alaska.gov/parks/units/pwssmp/smpvald.htm				
Joe Mace Island State Marine Park c/o SE Area Office 400 Willoughby Ave 4th Fl PO Box 111071 ... Juneau	AK	99811	907-465-4563	
Web: www.dnr.alaska.gov/parks/aspbro/charts/sewrang.htm				
Johnson Creek State Recreation Site c/o SE Area Office 400 Willoughby Ave 4th Fl PO Box 111071 ... Juneau	AK	99811	907-465-4563	
Web: www.encyclopedia2.thefreedictionary.com/Johnson+Creek+State+Recreation+Site				
Johnson Lake State Recreation Area c/o Kenai/PWS Area Office PO Box 1247 ... Soldotna	AK	99669	907-262-5581	
Web: dnr.alaska.gov/parks/units/kasilof.htm				
Juneau Trail System c/o SE Area Office 400 Willoughby Ave 4th Fl PO Box 111071 ... Juneau	AK	99811	907-465-4563	
Web: www.dnr.alaska.gov/parks/aspbro/charts/sejuneau.htm				

Phone | Fax

Kachemak Bay State Park & State Wilderness Park
c/o Kenai/PWS Area Office PO Box 1247 ... Soldotna AK 99669 907-262-5581
Web: dnr.alaska.gov/parks/units/kbay/kbay.htm

Kasilof River State Recreation Site
c/o Kenai/PWS Area Office PO Box 1247 ... Soldotna AK 99669 907-262-5581
Web: dnr.alaska.gov/parks/units/kasilof.htm

Kayak Island State Marine Park
c/o Kenai/PWS Area Office PO Box 1247 ... Soldotna AK 99669 907-262-5581
Web: dnr.alaska.gov/parks/units/pwssmp/smpcord.htm

Kenai River Special Management Area
c/o Kenai/PWS Area Office PO Box 1247 ... Soldotna AK 99669 907-262-5581
Web: dnr.alaska.gov/parks/units/kenairiv.htm

Kepler-Bradley Lakes State Recreation Area
c/o Mat-Su/CB Area Office 7278 E Bogard Rd ... Wasilla AK 99654 907-745-3975
Web: dnr.alaska.gov/parks/aspunits/matsu/keplerbradlksra.htm

King Mountain State Recreation Site
c/o Mat-Su/CB Area Office 7278 E Bogard Rd ... Wasilla AK 99654 907-745-3975
Web: dnr.alaska.gov/parks/aspunits/matsu/kingmtnsrs.htm

Lake Louise State Recreation Area
c/o Mat-Su/CB Area Office 7278 E Bogard Rd ... Wasilla AK 99654 907-745-3975
Web: dnr.alaska.gov/parks/aspunits/matsu/lklouisesra.htm

Liberty Falls State Recreation Site
c/o Mat-Su/CB Area Office 7278 E Bogard Rd ... Wasilla AK 99654 907-745-3975
Web: dnr.alaska.gov/parks/aspunits/matsu/libertyflsrs.htm

Lower Chatanika River State Recreation Area
c/o Northern Area Office 3700 Airport Way ... Fairbanks AK 99709 907-269-8400
Web: www.dnr.alaska.gov/parks/aspunits/northern/lrchatrivsra.htm

Magoun Islands State Marine Park
c/o SE Area Office 400 Willoughby Ave 4th Fl
PO Box 111071 ... Juneau AK 99811 907-465-4563
Web: www.dnr.alaska.gov/parks/aspunits/marinepark/magounissmp.htm

Matanuska Glacier State Recreation Site
c/o Mat-Su/Copper Basin Area Office
7278 E Bogard Rd. ... Wasilla AK 99654 907-745-3975
Web: dnr.alaska.gov/parks/aspunits/matsu/matsuglsrs.htm

Moon Lake State Recreation Site
c/o Northern Area Office 3700 Airport Way ... Fairbanks AK 99709 907-883-3686
Web: www.dnr.alaska.gov/parks/aspunits/northern/moonlksrs.htm

Mosquito Lake State Recreation Site
c/o SE Area Office 400 Willoughby Ave 4th Fl
PO Box 111071 ... Juneau AK 99811 907-465-4563
Web: www.dnr.alaska.gov/parks/aspunits/southeast/mosqlksrs.htm

Nancy Lake State Recreation Area
c/o Mat-Su/CB Area Office HC 32 PO Box 6706 ... Wasilla AK 99654 907-745-3975
Web: dnr.alaska.gov/parks/units/nancylk/nancylk.htm

Ninilchik State Recreation Area
c/o Kenai/PWS Area Office PO Box 1247 ... Soldotna AK 99669 907-262-5581
Web: dnr.alaska.gov/parks/units/nilchik.htm

Old Sitka State Historic Site
c/o SE Area Office 400 Willoughby Ave 4th Fl
PO Box 111071 ... Juneau AK 99811 907-465-4563
Web: www.dnr.alaska.gov/parks/units/sitka.htm#oldsitka

Oliver Inlet State Marine Park
c/o SE Area Office ; 400 Willoughby Ave, 5th Fl
PO Box 111071 ... Juneau AK 99801 907-465-4563 586-3113
Web: www.dnr.alaska.gov/parks

Pasagshak River State Recreation Site
c/o Kodiak Area Office 1400 Abercrombie Dr ... Kodiak AK 99615 907-486-6339 486-3320
Web: dnr.alaska.gov/parks/units/kodiak/pasagshak.htm

Petroglyph Beach State Historic Site
c/o SE Area Office 400 Willoughby Ave 4th Fl
PO Box 111071 ... Juneau AK 99811 907-465-4563
Web: www.dnr.alaska.gov/parks/aspunits/southeast/wrangpetroshs.htm

Point Bridget State Park
c/o SE Area Office 400 Willoughby Ave 4th Fl
PO Box 111071 ... Juneau AK 99811 907-465-4563
Web: www.dnr.alaska.gov/parks/units/ptbridg1.htm

Porcupine Creek State Recreation Site
c/o Mat-Su/Copper Basin Area Office
7278 E Gogard Rd ... Wasilla AK 99654 907-745-3975 745-0938

Portage Cove State Recreation Site
c/o SE Area Office 400 Willoughby Ave 4th Fl
PO Box 111071 ... Juneau AK 99811 907-465-4563
Web: www.dnr.alaska.gov/parks/aspunits/southeast/portcovesrs.htm

Quartz Lake State Recreation Area
c/o Northern Area Office 3700 Airport Way ... Fairbanks AK 99709 907-451-2695
Web: www.dnr.alaska.gov/parks/units/deltajct/quartz.htm

Refuge Cove State Recreation Site
c/o SE Area Office 400 Willoughby Ave 4th Fl
PO Box 111071 ... Juneau AK 99811 907-465-4563
Web: www.dnr.alaska.gov/parks/aspunits/southeast/refugecvsrs.htm

Rocky Lake State Recreation Site
c/o Mat-Su/CB Area Office 7278 E Bogard Rd ... Wasilla AK 99654 907-745-3975

Safety Cove State Marine Park
c/o Kenai/PWS Area Office PO Box 1247 ... Soldotna AK 99669 907-262-5581
Web: dnr.alaska.gov/parks/units/pwssmp/smpsewd.htm

Saint James Bay State Marine Park
c/o SE Area Office 400 Willoughby Ave, 4th Fl ... Juneau AK 99801 907-465-4563 586-3113
Web: www.dnr.alaska.gov/park

Salcha River State Recreation Site
c/o Northern Area Office 3700 Airport Way ... Fairbanks AK 99709 907-451-2695
Web: www.dnr.alaska.gov/parks/units/salcha.htm

Sandspit Point State Marine Park
c/o Kenai/PWS Area Office PO Box 1247 ... Soldotna AK 99669 907-262-5581
Web: dnr.alaska.gov/parks/units/pwssmp/smpsewd.htm

Sawmill Bay State Marine Park
c/o Kenai/PWS Area Office PO Box 1247 ... Soldotna AK 99669 907-262-5581
Web: dnr.alaska.gov/parks/units/pwssmp/smpvald.htm

Sea Lion Cove State Marine Park
c/o SE Area Office 400 Willoughby Ave 4th Fl
PO Box 111071 ... Juneau AK 99811 907-465-4563
Web: www.dnr.alaska.gov/parks/aspunits/southeast/sealioncvsmp.htm

Phone | Fax

Security Bay State Marine Park
c/o SE Area Office 400 Willoughby Ave 4th Fl
PO Box 111071 ... Juneau AK 99811 907-465-4563
Web: www.dnr.alaska.gov/parks/units/sitka.htm#security

Settlers Cove State Recreation Site
c/o SE Area Office 400 Willoughby Ave, 4th Fl ... Juneau AK 99801 907-465-4563 586-3113

Shelter Island State Marine Park
c/o SE Area Office 400 Willoughby Ave 4th Fl
PO Box 111071 ... Juneau AK 99811 907-465-4563
Web: www.dnr.alaska.gov/parks/cabins/south.htm#sismp

Shoup Bay State Marine Park
c/o Kenai/PWS Area Office PO Box 1247 ... Soldotna AK 99669 907-262-5581
Web: dnr.alaska.gov/parks/units/pwssmp/smpvald.htm

Shuyak Island State Park
c/o Kodiak Area Office 1400 Abercrombie Dr ... Kodiak AK 99615 907-486-6339
Web: dnr.alaska.gov/parks/units/kodiak/shuyak.htm

South Esther Island State Marine Park
c/o Kenai/PWS Area Office PO Box 1247 ... Soldotna AK 99669 907-262-5581
Web: dnr.alaska.gov/parks/units/pwssmp/smpwhit2.htm

Sullivan Island State Marine Park
c/o SE Area Office 400 Willoughby Ave 4th Fl
PO Box 111071 ... Juneau AK 99811 907-465-4563
Web: www.dnr.alaska.gov/parks/units/haines.htm#sullivan

Summit Lake State Recreation Site
c/o Mat-Su/CB Area Office 7278 E Bogard Rd ... Wasilla AK 99654 907-745-3975
Web: dnr.alaska.gov/parks/units/summit.htm

Sunny Cove State Marine Park
c/o Kenai/PWS Area Office PO Box 1247 ... Soldotna AK 99669 907-262-5581
Web: dnr.alaska.gov/parks/units/pwssmp/smpsewd.htm

Surprise Cove State Marine Park
c/o Kenai/PWS Area Office PO Box 1247 ... Soldotna AK 99669 907-262-5581
Web: dnr.alaska.gov/parks/units/pwssmp/smpwhit1.htm

Taku Harbor State Marine Park
c/o SE Area Office 400 Willoughby Ave 4th Fl
PO Box 111071 ... Juneau AK 99811 907-465-4563
Web: www.dnr.alaska.gov/parks/aspunits/marinepark/takuharbrsmp.htm

Thom's Place State Marine Park
c/o SE Area Office 400 Willoughby Ave 4th Fl
PO Box 111071 ... Juneau AK 99811 907-465-4563
Web: www.dnr.alaska.gov/parks/aspbro/charts/sewrang.htm

Thumb Cove State Marine Park
c/o Kenai/PWS Area Office PO Box 1247 ... Soldotna AK 99669 907-262-5581
Web: dnr.alaska.gov/parks/units/pwssmp/smpsewd.htm

Tok River State Recreation Site
c/o Northern Area Office 3700 Airport Way ... Fairbanks AK 99709 907-883-3686
Web: www.dnr.alaska.gov/parks/aspunits/northern/tokrvsrs.htm

Tokositna River State Recreation Site
c/o Mat-Su/CB Area Office HC 32 PO Box 6706 ... Wasilla AK 99654 907-745-3975 745-0938

Totem Bight State Historical Park
c/o SE Area Office 400 Willoughby Ave 4th Fl
PO Box 111071 ... Juneau AK 99811 907-465-4563
Web: www.dnr.alaska.gov/parks/units/totembgh.htm

Upper Chatanika River State Recreation Site
c/o Northern Area Office 3700 Airport Way ... Fairbanks AK 99709 907-456-1104
Web: www.dnr.alaska.gov/parks/aspunits/northern/upchatrvsrs.htm

Wickersham State Historic Site
c/o SE Area Office 400 Willoughby Ave 4th Fl
PO Box 111071 ... Juneau AK 99811 907-465-4563
Web: www.dnr.alaska.gov/parks/units/wickrshm.htm

Willow Creek State Recreation Area
c/o Mat-Su/CB Area Office 7278 E Bogard Rd ... Wasilla AK 99654 907-745-3975
Web: dnr.alaska.gov/parks/aspunits/matsu/willowcksra.htm

Wood-Tikchik State Park
550 W 7th Ave Suite 1390 ... Anchorage AK 99510 907-269-8698
Web: www.dnr.state.ak.us

Worthington Glacier State Recreation Site
28.7 Richardson Hwy ... Soldotna AK 99669 907-262-5581
Web: dnr.alaska.gov/parks/aspunits/kenai/worthglsrs.htm

Ziegler Cove State Marine Park
c/o Kenai/PWS Area Office PO Box 1247 ... Soldotna AK 99669 907-262-5581
Web: dnr.alaska.gov/parks/units/pwssmp/smpwhit1.htm

ARIZONA

Phone | Fax

Alamo Lake State Park PO Box 38 ... Wenden AZ 85357 928-669-2088
Web: www.pr.state.az.us

Boyce Thompson Arboretum State Park
37615 US Hwy 60 ... Superior AZ 85273 520-689-2811 689-5858
Web: www.pr.state.az.us

Buckskin Mountain State Park 5476 Hwy 95 ... Parker AZ 85344 928-667-3231
Web: www.pr.state.az.us

Catalina State Park 11570 N Oracle Rd ... Tucson AZ 85737 520-628-5798 628-5797
Web: www.pr.state.az.us

Cattail Cove State Park PO Box 1990 ... Lake Havasu City AZ 86405 928-855-1223 855-1730
Web: www.pr.state.az.us/Parks/parkhtml/cattail.html

Dead Horse Ranch State Park
675 Dead Horse Ranch Rd ... Cottonwood AZ 86326 928-634-5283
Web: www.pr.state.az.us

Fool Hollow Lake Recreation Area
1500 N Fool Hollow Lake Rd ... Show Low AZ 85901 928-537-3680
Web: www.pr.state.az.us

Fort Verde State Historic Park PO Box 397 ... Camp Verde AZ 86322 928-567-3275 567-4036
Web: www.pr.state.az.us

Homolovi Ruins State Park 87 N Rd ... Winslow AZ 86047 928-289-4106 289-2021
Web: www.pr.state.az.us

Jerome State Historic Park PO Box D ... Jerome AZ 86331 928-634-5381
Web: www.pr.state.az.us

Kartchner Caverns State Park PO Box 1849 ... Benson AZ 85602 520-586-4100
Web: www.pr.state.az.us

	Phone	Fax

Lake Havasu State Park
699 London Bridge Rd ... Lake Havasu City AZ 86403 928-855-2784 453-9358
Web: www.pr.state.az.us

Lost Dutchman State Park
6109 N Apache Tr ... Apache Junction AZ 85219 480-982-4485
Web: www.pr.state.az.us

Lyman Lake State Park PO Box 1428 ... Saint Johns AZ 85936 928-337-4441
Web: www.pr.state.az.us

McFarland State Historic Park PO Box 109 ... Florence AZ 85232 520-868-5216
Web: www.pr.state.az.us

Oracle State Park 3820 Wildlife Dr ... Oracle AZ 85623 520-896-2425
Web: www.pr.state.az.us

Patagonia Lake State Park
400 Patagonia Lake Rd ... Patagonia AZ 85624 520-287-6965
Web: www.pr.state.az.us

Picacho Peak State Park PO Box 275 ... Picacho AZ 85241 520-466-3183
Web: www.pr.state.az.us

Red Rock State Park 4050 Red Rock Loop Rd ... Sedona AZ 86336 928-282-6907 282-5972
Web: www.pr.state.az.us

Riordan Mansion State Historic Park
409 W Riordan Rd ... Flagstaff AZ 86001 928-779-4395 556-0253
Web: www.pr.state.az.us

Roper Lake State Park 101 E Roper Lake Rd ... Safford AZ 85546 928-428-6760 428-7879
Web: www.pr.state.az.us

San Rafael Ranch State Park
2036 Duquesne Rd ... Patagonia AZ 85624 520-394-2447
Web: www.pr.state.az.us

Slide Rock State Park 6871 N Hwy 89A ... Sedona AZ 86336 928-282-3034
Web: www.pr.state.az.us

Tombstone Courthouse State Historic Park
223 E Toughnut St ... Tombstone AZ 85638 520-457-3311
Web: www.pr.state.az.us

Tonto Natural Bridge State Park PO Box 1245 ... Payson AZ 85547 928-476-4202 476-2264
Web: www.pr.state.az.us

Tubac Presidio State Historic Park
1 Burruel St ... Tubac AZ 85646 520-398-2252
Web: www.pr.state.az.us

Yuma Crossing State Historic Park 201 N 4th Ave ... Yuma AZ 85364 928-329-0471
Web: www.pr.state.az.us/Parks/parkhtml/yumacross.html

Yuma Territorial Prison State Historic Park
1 Prison Hill Rd PO Box 10792 ... Yuma AZ 85364 928-783-4771
Web: www.pr.state.az.us/Parks/parkhtml/yuma.html

ARKANSAS

	Phone	Fax

Arkansas Museum of Natural Resources
3853 Smackover Hwy ... Smackover AR 71762 870-725-2877 725-2161
Web: www.arkansasstateparks.com

Arkansas Post Museum 5530 Hwy 165 S ... Gillett AR 72055 870-548-2634
Web: www.arkansasstateparks.com

Bull Shoals-White River State Park
129 Bull Shoals Pk ... Bull Shoals AR 72642 870-431-5521
Web: www.arkansasstateparks.com

Cane Creek State Park 50 State Pk Rd ... Star City AR 71667 870-628-4714 628-3611
Web: www.arkansasstateparks.com

Conway Cemetery State Park
c/o Arkansas State Parks 1 Capitol Mall ... Little Rock AR 72201 888-287-2757
TF: 888-287-2757 ■ *Web:* www.arkansasstateparks.com/conwaycemetery

Cossatot River State Park-Natural Area
1980 Hwy 278 W ... Wickes AR 71973 870-385-2201 385-7858
Web: www.arkansasstateparks.com

Crater of Diamonds State Park
209 State Pk Rd ... Murfreesboro AR 71958 870-285-3113 285-4169
Web: www.craterofdiamondsstatepark.com

Crowley's Ridge State Park 2092 Hwy 168 N ... Paragould AR 72450 870-573-6751
Web: www.arkansasstateparks.com

Daisy State Park 103 E Pk ... Kirby AR 71950 870-398-4487
Web: www.arkansasstateparks.com

DeGray Lake Resort State Park
2027 State Pk Entrance Rd ... Bismarck AR 71929 501-865-2801
Web: www.degray.com

Delta Heritage Trail State Park
9871 Great River Rd ... Watson AR 71674 870-644-3474
Web: www.arkansasstateparks.com

Devil's Den State Park
11333 W Arkansas Hwy 74 ... West Fork AR 72774 479-761-3325 761-3676
Web: www.arkansasstateparks.com

Hampson Archeological Museum State Park
PO Box 156 ... Wilson AR 72395 870-655-8622 655-8061
Web: www.arkansasstateparks.com

Herman Davis State Park
Corner of Ark, 18 Baltimore St ... Manila AR 72442 888-287-2757
TF: 888-287-2757 ■ *Web:* www.arkansasstateparks.com/hermandavis

Hobbs State Park-Conservation Area
21392 E Hwy 12 ... Rogers AR 72756 479-789-2380
Web: www.arkansasstateparks.com

Jacksonport State Park 205 Ave St ... Newport AR 72112 870-523-2143 523-4620
Web: www.arkansasstateparks.com

Lake Catherine State Park
1200 Catherine Pk Rd ... Hot Springs AR 71913 501-844-4176 844-4244
Web: www.arkansasstateparks.com

Lake Charles State Park 3705 Hwy 25 ... Powhatan AR 72458 870-878-6595
Web: www.arkansasstateparks.com/parks/park.asp?id=14

Lake Chicot State Park 2542 Hwy 257 ... Lake Village AR 71653 870-265-5480
Web: www.arkansasstateparks.com

Lake Dardanelle State Park
100 State Pk Dr ... Russellville AR 72802 479-967-5516
Web: www.arkansasstateparks.com

Lake Fort Smith State Park PO Box 4 ... Mountainburg AR 72946 479-369-2469
Web: www.arkansasstateparks.com

Lake Frierson State Park 7900 Hwy 141 S ... Jonesboro AR 72401 870-932-2615
Web: www.arkansasstateparks.com

Lake Ouachita State Park
5451 Mountain Pine Rd ... Mountain Pine AR 71956 501-767-9366
Web: www.arkansasstateparks.com

Lake Poinsett State Park 5752 State Pk Ln ... Harrisburg AR 72432 870-578-2064
Web: www.arkansasstateparks.com

Logoly State Park PO Box 245 ... McNeil AR 71752 870-695-3561
Web: www.arkansasstateparks.com

Louisiana Purchase State Park AR Hwy 362 ... Brinkley AR 72049 888-287-2757
TF: 888-287-2757 ■ *Web:* www.arkansasstateparks.com/louisianapurchase

Lower White River Museum State Park
2009 Main St ... Des Arc AR 72040 870-256-3711 256-9202
Web: www.arkansasstateparks.com

Mammoth Spring State Park PO Box 36 ... Mammoth Spring AR 72554 870-625-7364 625-3255
Web: www.arkansasstateparks.com

Millwood State Park 1564 Hwy 32 E ... Ashdown AR 71822 870-898-2800 898-2632
Web: www.arkansasstateparks.com

Moro Bay State Park 6071 US Hwy 600 ... Jersey AR 71651 870-463-8555
Web: www.arkansasstateparks.com

Mount Magazine State Park 16878 Hwy 309 S ... Paris AR 72855 479-963-8502 963-1031
Web: www.arkansasstateparks.com

Mount Nebo State Park
16728 W State Hwy 155 ... Dardanelle AR 72834 479-229-3655
Web: www.arkansasstateparks.com

Old Davidsonville State Park
7953 Hwy 166 S ... Pocahontas AR 72455 870-892-4708
Web: www.arkansasstateparks.com

Old Washington Historic State Park
PO Box 129 ... Washington AR 71862 870-983-2684 983-2736
Web: www.historicwashingtonstatepark.com

Ozark Folk Center State Park
1032 Pk Ave ... Mountain View AR 72560 870-269-3851 269-2909
Web: www.ozarkfolkcenter.com

Parkin Archeological State Park PO Box 1110 ... Parkin AR 72373 870-755-2500 755-2676
Web: www.arkansasstateparks.com

Petit Jean State Park
1285 Petit Jean Mountain Rd ... Morrilton AR 72110 501-727-5441
Web: www.petitjeanstatepark.com

Pinnacle Mountain State Park
11901 Pinnacle Valley Rd ... Little Rock AR 72223 501-868-5806 868-5018
Web: www.arkansasstateparks.com

Plantation Agriculture Museum 4815 Hwy 161 S ... Scott AR 72142 501-961-1409
Web: www.arkansasstateparks.com

Powhatan Historic State Park PO Box 93 ... Powhatan AR 72458 870-878-6765
Web: www.arkansasstateparks.com/parks/park.asp?id=46

Prairie Grove Battlefield State Park
506 E Douglas St ... Prairie Grove AR 72753 479-846-2990
Web: www.arkansasstateparks.com

Queen Wilhelmina State Park 3877 Arkansas 88 ... Mena AR 71953 479-394-2863
Web: www.arkansasstateparks.com

South Arkansas Arboretum PO Box 7010 ... El Dorado AR 71731 888-287-2757
TF: 888-287-2757 ■
Web: www.arkansasstateparks.com/southarkansasarboretum

Toltec Mounds Archeological State Park
490 Toltec Mounds Rd ... Scott AR 72142 501-961-9442 961-9221
Web: www.arkansasstateparks.com

Village Creek State Park 201 County Rd 754 ... Wynne AR 72396 870-238-9406 238-9415
Web: www.arkansasstateparks.com

White Oak Lake State Park 563 Hwy 387 ... Bluff City AR 71722 870-685-2748
Web: www.arkansasstateparks.com

Withrow Springs State Park 33424 Spur 23 ... Huntsville AR 72740 479-559-2593
Web: www.arkansasstateparks.com

Woolly Hollow State Park
82 Woolly Hollow Rd ... Greenbrier AR 72058 501-679-2098
Web: www.arkansasstateparks.com

CALIFORNIA

	Phone	Fax

Admiral William Standley State Recreation Area
c/o N Coast Redwoods District Office
PO Box 2006 ... Eureka CA 95502 707-247-3318
Web: www.parks.ca.gov/default.asp?page_id=424

Ahjumawi Lava Springs State Park
c/o Northern Buttes District Office
400 Glen Dr ... Oroville CA 95966 530-538-2200
Web: www.parks.ca.gov/?page_id=464

Anderson Marsh State Historic Park
c/o Northern Buttes District Office
400 Glen Dr ... Oroville CA 95966 707-994-0688
Web: www.parks.ca.gov/default.asp?page_id=483

Andrew Molera State Park
c/o Monterey District Office 2211 Garden Rd ... Monterey CA 93940 831-667-2315
Web: www.parks.ca.gov/default.asp?page_id=582

Angel Island State Park 98 Main St Suite 236 ... Tiburon CA 94920 415-897-0715
Web: www.angelisland.com

Annadel State Park
c/o Diablo Vista District Office
845 Casa Grande Rd ... Petaluma CA 94954 707-938-1519
Web: www.parks.ca.gov/default.asp?page_id=480

Ano Nuevo State Reserve
c/o Santa Cruz District Office
303 Big Trees Pk Rd ... Felton CA 95018 650-879-2025
Web: www.parks.ca.gov/default.asp?page_id=523

Antelope Valley California Poppy Reserve
c/o Inland Empire District Office
17801 Lake Perris Dr ... Perris CA 92571 661-724-1180
Web: www.parks.ca.gov/default.asp?page_id=627

Antelope Valley Indian Museum State Historic Park
Antelope Valley Fwy Ave M ... Perris CA 92571 661-946-3055
Web: www.avim.parks.ca.gov

Phone Fax

Anza-Borrego Desert State Park
c/o Colorado Desert District Office
200 Palm Canyon Dr .... Borrego Springs CA 92004 760-767-4205 767-3427
Web: www.anzaborrego.statepark.org

Armstrong Redwoods State Reserve
17000 Armstrong Woods Rd........ Guerneville CA 95446 707-869-2015 869-5629
Web: www.parks.ca.gov/default.asp?page_id=450

Asilomar State Beach & Conference Grounds
c/o Monterey District Office 2211 Garden Rd .... Monterey CA 93940 831-646-6440
Web: www.parks.ca.gov/default.asp?page_id=566

Auburn State Recreation Area
c/o Gold Fields District Office
7806 Folsom-Auburn Rd .... Folsom CA 95630 530-885-4527
Web: www.parks.ca.gov/default.asp?page_id=502

Austin Creek State Recreation Area
17000 Armstrong Woods Rd........ Guerneville CA 95446 707-869-2015
Web: www.parks.ca.gov/default.asp?page_id=452

Azalea State Reserve
c/o N Coast Redwoods District Office
PO Box 2006 .... Eureka CA 95502 707-677-3132
Web: www.parks.ca.gov/default.asp?page_id=420

Bale Grist Mill State Historic Park
c/o Diablo Vista District Office
845 Casa Grande Rd........ Petaluma CA 94954 707-942-4575
Web: www.parks.ca.gov/default.asp?page_id=482

Bean Hollow State Beach
c/o Santa Cruz District Office
303 Big Trees Pk Rd .... Felton CA 95018 650-879-2170
Web: www.parks.ca.gov/default.asp?page_id=527

Benbow Lake State Recreation Area
c/o N Coast Redwoods District Office
PO Box 2006 .... Eureka CA 95502 707-923-3238
Web: www.parks.ca.gov/default.asp?page_id=426

Benicia Capitol State Historic Park
c/o Diablo Vista District Office
845 Casa Grande Rd........ Petaluma CA 94954 707-745-3385
Web: www.parks.ca.gov/default.asp?page_id=475

Benicia State Recreation Area
c/o Diablo Vista District Office
845 Casa Grande Rd........ Petaluma CA 94954 707-648-1911
Web: www.parks.ca.gov/default.asp?page_id=476

Bethany Reservoir State Recreation Area
c/o Central Valley District Office
22708 Broadway St........ Columbia CA 95310 209-874-2056
Web: www.parks.ca.gov/default.asp?page_id=562

Bidwell Mansion State Historic Park
c/o Northern Buttes District Office
400 Glen Dr .... Oroville CA 95966 530-895-6144
Web: www.parks.ca.gov/default.asp?page_id=460

Bidwell-Sacramento River State Park
c/o Northern Buttes District Office
400 Glen Dr .... Oroville CA 95966 530-342-5185
Web: www.parks.ca.gov/default.asp?page_id=463

Big Basin Redwoods State Park
21600 Big Basin Way .... Boulder Creek CA 95006 831-338-8860
Web: www.parks.ca.gov

Bodie State Historic Park PO Box 515........ Bridgeport CA 93517 760-647-6445
Web: www.parks.ca.gov

Bolsa Chica State Beach
c/o Orange Coast District Office
3030 Avenida del Presidente........ San Clemente CA 92672 949-492-0802 492-8412
Web: www.parks.ca.gov/?page_id=25215

Border Field State Park
c/o San Diego Coast District Office
4477 Pacific Hwy .... San Diego CA 92110 619-575-3613
Web: www.parks.ca.gov/default.asp?page_id=664

Bothe-Napa Valley State Park
c/o Diablo Vista District Office
845 Casa Grande Rd........ Petaluma CA 94954 707-942-4575
Web: www.parks.ca.gov/default.asp?page_id=477

Brannan Island State Recreation Area
c/o Gold Fields District Office
7806 Folsom-Auburn Rd .... Folsom CA 95630 916-777-7701
Web: www.parks.ca.gov/default.asp?page_id=487

Burleigh H. Murray Ranch
c/o Santa Cruz District Office
303 Big Trees Pk Rd .... Felton CA 95018 650-726-8819
Web: www.parks.ca.gov/default.asp?page_id=535

Burton Creek State Park
c/o Sierra District Office PO Box 266 .... Tahoma CA 96142 530-583-5475
Web: www.parks.ca.gov/default.asp?page_id=512

Butano State Park
c/o Santa Cruz District Office
303 Big Trees Pk Rd .... Felton CA 95018 650-879-2040
Web: www.parks.ca.gov/default.asp?page_id=536

Calaveras Big Trees State Park
c/o Central Valley District Office
22708 Broadway St........ Columbia CA 95310 209-795-2334
Web: www.parks.ca.gov/default.asp?page_id=551

California Citrus State Historic Park
c/o Inland Empire District Office
17801 Lake Perris Dr .... Perris CA 92571 951-780-6222
Web: www.parks.ca.gov/default.asp?page_id=649

California State Capitol Museum
c/o Capital District Office 101 J St .... Sacramento CA 95814 916-324-0333
Web: www.parks.ca.gov/parkindex/results.asp?ckAlpha3=on&searchtype=14

California State Indian Museum
c/o Capital District Office 101 J St .... Sacramento CA 95816 916-324-0971 322-5231
Web: www.parks.ca.gov/default.asp?page_id=486

California State Mining & Mineral Museum
PO Box 1192 .... Mariposa CA 95338 209-742-7625 966-3597
Web: www.parks.ca.gov/default.asp?page_id=588

California State Railroad Museum
c/o Capital District Office 111 'I' St........ Sacramento CA 95814 916-323-9280 327-5655
Web: www.csrmf.org

Candlestick Point State Recreation Area
c/o Diablo Vista District Office
845 Casa Grande Rd........ Petaluma CA 94954 415-671-0145
Web: www.parks.ca.gov/default.asp?page_id=519

Cardiff State Beach
c/o San Diego Coast District Office
4477 Pacific Hwy .... San Diego CA 92110 760-753-5091
Web: www.parks.ca.gov/default.asp?page_id=656

Carlsbad State Beach
c/o San Diego Coast District Office
4477 Pacific Hwy .... San Diego CA 92110 760-438-3143
Web: www.parks.ca.gov/default.asp?page_id=653

Carmel River State Beach
c/o Monterey District Office 2211 Garden Rd .... Monterey CA 93940 831-624-4909
Web: www.parks.ca.gov/default.asp?page_id=567

Carnegie State Vehicular Recreation Area
c/o Twin Cities District Office
13300 White Rock Rd........ Rancho Cordova CA 95742 925-447-9027
Web: www.parks.ca.gov

Carpinteria State Beach
c/o Ch Coast District Office
911 San Pedro St .... Ventura CA 93001 805-684-2811
Web: www.parks.ca.gov/default.asp?page_id=599

Caspar Headlands State Beach & State Reserve
c/o Mendocino District Office PO Box 440........ Mendocino CA 95460 707-937-5804
Web: www.parks.ca.gov/parkindex

Castaic Lake State Recreation Area
c/o Angeles District Office
1925 Las Virgenes .... Calabasas CA 91302 213-798-2961
Web: www.parks.ca.gov/default.asp?page_id=628

Castle Crags State Park
c/o Northern Buttes District Office
400 Glen Dr .... Oroville CA 95966 530-235-2684
Web: www.parks.ca.gov/default.asp?page_id=454

Castle Rock State Park
c/o Santa Cruz District Office
303 Big Trees Pk Rd .... Felton CA 95018 831-335-6318
Web: www.parks.ca.gov/default.asp?page_id=538

Caswell Memorial State Park
c/o Central Valley District Office
22708 Broadway St........ Columbia CA 95310 209-599-3810
Web: www.parks.ca.gov/default.asp?page_id=557

Cayucos State Beach
c/o San Luis Obispo Coast District Office
750 Hearst Castle Rd .... San Simeon CA 93452 805-549-3312
Web: www.parks.ca.gov/default.asp?page_id=596

China Camp State Park
101 Peacock Gap Trail .... San Rafael CA 94901 415-456-0766
Web: www.parks.ca.gov/default.asp?page_id=466

Chino Hills State Park
c/o Inland Empire District Office
17801 Lake Perris Dr .... Perris CA 92571 951-780-6222
Web: www.parks.ca.gov/default.asp?page_id=648

Chumash Painted Cave State Historic Park
c/o Ch Coast District Office
911 San Pedro St .... Ventura CA 93001 805-968-1033
Web: www.parks.ca.gov/default.asp?page_id=602

Clay Pit State Vehicular Recreation Area
400 Glen Dr .... Oroville CA 95966 530-538-2200
Web: www.parks.ca.gov

Clear Lake State Park
c/o Northern Buttes District Office
400 Glen Dr .... Oroville CA 95966 707-279-4293
Web: www.parks.ca.gov/default.asp?page_id=473

Colonel Allensworth State Historic Park
c/o Central Valley District Office
22708 Broadway St........ Columbia CA 95310 661-849-3433
Web: www.parks.ca.gov/default.asp?page_id=583

Columbia State Historic Park
11255 Jackson St........ Columbia CA 95310 209-588-9128
Web: www.parks.ca.gov

Colusa-Sacramento River State Recreation Area
c/o Northern Buttes District Office
400 Glen Dr .... Oroville CA 95966 530-458-4927
Web: www.parks.ca.gov/default.asp?page_id=461

Corona del Mar State Beach
c/o Orange Coast District Office
3030 Avenida del Presidente........ San Clemente CA 92672 949-492-0802
Web: www.parks.ca.gov/default.asp?page_id=652

Crystal Cove State Park
c/o Orange Coast District Office
3030 Avenida del Presidente........ San Clemente CA 92672 949-494-3539
Web: www.parks.ca.gov/default.asp?page_id=644

Cuyamaca Rancho State Park
c/o Colorado Desert District Office
200 Palm Canyon Dr .... Borrego Springs CA 92004 760-765-0755 765-3021
TF: 800-444-7275 ■ *Web:* www.parks.ca.gov/default.asp?page_id=667

Del Norte Coast Redwoods State Park
c/o N Coast Redwoods District Office
PO Box 2006 .... Eureka CA 95502 707-464-6101
Web: www.parks.ca.gov/default.asp?page_id=414

Delta Meadows
c/o Gold Fields District Office
7806 Folsom-Auburn Rd .... Folsom CA 95630 916-777-7701
Web: www.parks.ca.gov/default.asp?page_id=492

DL Bliss State Park
c/o Sierra District Office PO Box 266 .... Tahoma CA 96142 530-525-7277
Web: www.parks.ca.gov/?page_id=505

Phone | Fax

Dockweiler State Beach
c/o Los Angeles County Dept of Beaches & Harbors
13837 Fiji Way . . . . . Marina del Rey CA 90292 310-305-9503
Web: www.parks.ca.gov

Doheny State Beach
25300 Dana Pt Harbor Dr . . . . . Dana Point CA 92629 949-496-6172
Web: www.parks.ca.gov

Donner Memorial State Park
c/o Sierra District Office PO Box 266 . . . . . Tahoma CA 96142 530-582-7892
Web: www.parks.ca.gov/default.asp?page_id=503

Edward Z'Berg Sugar Pine Point State Park
c/o Sierra District Office PO Box 266 . . . . . Tahoma CA 96142 530-525-7232
Web: www.parks.ca.gov/default.asp?page_id=510

El Capitan State Beach
c/o Ch Coast District Office
911 San Pedro St . . . . . Ventura CA 93001 805-968-1033
Web: www.parks.ca.gov/default.asp?page_id=601

El Presidio de Santa Barbara State Historic Park
c/o Ch Coast District Office
911 San Pedro St . . . . . Ventura CA 93001 805-965-0093
Web: www.parks.ca.gov/default.asp?page_id=608

Emerald Bay State Park
c/o Sierra District Office PO Box 266 . . . . . Tahoma CA 96142 530-525-7277
Web: www.parks.ca.gov/default.asp?page_id=506

Emma Wood State Beach
c/o Ch Coast District Office
911 San Pedro St . . . . . Ventura CA 93001 805-968-1033
Web: www.parks.ca.gov/default.asp?page_id=604

Empire Mine State Historic Park
c/o Sierra District Office PO Box 266 . . . . . Tahoma CA 96142 530-273-8522
Web: www.parks.ca.gov/default.asp?page_id=499

Folsom Lake State Recreation Area
c/o Gold Fields District Office
7806 Folsom-Auburn Rd . . . . . Folsom CA 95630 916-988-0205
Web: www.parks.ca.gov/default.asp?page_id=500

Folsom Powerhouse State Historic Park
c/o Folsom Lake State Recreation Area
7806 Folsom-Auburn Rd . . . . . Folsom CA 95630 916-985-4843
Web: www.parks.ca.gov

Forest of Nisene Marks State Park
c/o Santa Cruz District Office
303 Big Trees Pk Rd . . . . . Felton CA 95018 831-763-7062
Web: www.parks.ca.gov/?page_id=666

Fort Humboldt State Historic Park
c/o N Coast Redwoods District Office
PO Box 2006 . . . . . Eureka CA 95502 707-445-6567
Web: www.parks.ca.gov/default.asp?page_id=665

Fort Ross State Historic Park
19005 Coast Hwy 1 . . . . . Jenner CA 95450 707-847-3286
Web: www.parks.ca.gov/default.asp?page_id=449

Fort Tejon State Historic Park
c/o Central Valley District Office
22708 Broadway St. . . . . . Columbia CA 95310 661-248-6692 248-8373
Web: www.parks.ca.gov/default.asp?page_id=585

Franks Tract State Recreation Area
c/o Gold Fields District Office
7806 Folsom-Auburn Rd . . . . . Folsom CA 95630 916-777-7701
Web: www.parks.ca.gov/default.asp?page_id=490

Fremont Peak State Park
c/o Monterey District Office 2211 Garden Rd . . . . . Monterey CA 93940 831-623-4255
Web: www.parks.ca.gov/default.asp?page_id=564

Garrapata State Park
c/o Monterey District Office 2211 Garden Rd . . . . . Monterey CA 93940 831-624-4909
Web: www.parks.ca.gov/default.asp?page_id=579

Gaviota State Park
c/o Ch Coast District Office
911 San Pedro St . . . . . Ventura CA 93001 805-968-1033
Web: www.parks.ca.gov/default.asp?page_id=606

George J. Hatfield State Recreation Area
c/o Central Valley District Office
22708 Broadway St. . . . . . Columbia CA 95310 209-632-1852
Web: www.parks.ca.gov/default.asp?page_id=556

Governor's Mansion State Historic Park
1526 H St . . . . . Sacramento CA 95814 916-323-3047
Web: www.parks.ca.gov

Gray Whale Cove State Beach
c/o Santa Cruz District Office
303 Big Trees Pk Rd . . . . . Felton CA 95018 650-726-8819
Web: www.parks.ca.gov/?page_id=528

Great Valley Grasslands State Park
c/o Central Valley District Office
22708 Broadway St. . . . . . Columbia CA 95310 209-826-1197
Web: www.parks.ca.gov/default.asp?page_id=559

Greenwood State Beach
c/o Mendocino District Office PO Box 440 . . . . . Mendocino CA 95460 707-937-5804
Web: www.parks.ca.gov/default.asp?page_id=447

Grizzly Creek Redwoods State Park
c/o N Coast Redwoods District Office
PO Box 2006 . . . . . Eureka CA 95502 707-777-3683
Web: www.parks.ca.gov/default.asp?page_id=421

Grover Hot Springs State Park
c/o Sierra District Office PO Box 266 . . . . . Tahoma CA 96142 530-694-2248
Web: www.parks.ca.gov/default.asp?page_id=508

Half Moon Bay State Beach
c/o San Mateo Coast Sector Office
95 Kelly Ave . . . . . Half Moon Bay CA 94019 650-726-8819 726-8816
Web: www.parks.ca.gov

Harry A. Merlo State Recreation Area
c/o N Coast Redwoods District Office
PO Box 2006 . . . . . Eureka CA 95502 707-677-3132
Web: www.parks.ca.gov/default.asp?page_id=431

Hearst San Simeon State Historical Monument
750 Hearst Castle Rd . . . . . San Simeon CA 93452 805-927-2020
TF: 800-444-4445 ■ *Web:* www.parks.ca.gov/default.asp?page_id=591

Heber Dunes State Vehicular Recreation Area
c/o Ocotillo Wells District Office
PO Box 356 . . . . . Borrego Springs CA 92004 760-768-9379
Web: www.parks.ca.gov

Hendy Woods State Park
c/o Mendocino District Office PO Box 440 . . . . . Mendocino CA 95460 707-895-3141
Web: www.parks.ca.gov/default.asp?page_id=438

Henry Cowell Redwoods State Park
c/o Santa Cruz District Office
303 Big Trees Pk Rd . . . . . Felton CA 95018 831-335-4598
Web: www.parks.ca.gov/default.asp?page_id=546

Henry W. Coe State Park
c/o Monterey District Office 2211 Garden Rd . . . . . Monterey CA 93940 408-779-2728
Web: www.parks.ca.gov/default.asp?page_id=561

Hollister Hills State Vehicular Recreation Area
c/o Hollister Hills District Office
7800 Cienega Rd . . . . . Hollister CA 95023 831-637-3874
Web: www.parks.ca.gov

Humboldt Lagoons State Park
c/o N Coast Redwoods District Office
PO Box 2006 . . . . . Eureka CA 95502 707-677-3132
Web: www.parks.ca.gov/default.asp?page_id=416

Humboldt Redwoods State Park
c/o N Coast Redwoods District Office
PO Box 2006 . . . . . Eureka CA 95502 707-946-2409
Web: www.parks.ca.gov/default.asp?page_id=425

Hungry Valley State Vehicular Recreation Area
46001 Orwin Way . . . . . Gorman CA 93243 661-248-7007
Web: www.parks.ca.gov

Huntington State Beach
c/o Orange Coast District Office
3030 Avenida del Presidente. . . . . . San Clemente CA 92672 714-846-3460
Web: www.parks.ca.gov/?page_id=643

Indio Hills Palms
c/o Colorado Desert District Office
200 Palm Canyon Dr . . . . . Borrego Springs CA 92004 619-393-3059
Web: www.parks.ca.gov/default.asp?page_id=640

Jack London State Historic Park
c/o Diablo Vista District Office
845 Casa Grande Rd. . . . . . Petaluma CA 94954 707-938-5216
Web: www.parks.ca.gov/default.asp?page_id=478

Jedediah Smith Redwoods State Park
c/o N Coast Redwoods District Office
PO Box 2006 . . . . . Eureka CA 95502 707-464-6101
Web: www.parks.ca.gov/default.asp?page_id=413

John Little State Reserve
c/o Monterey District Office 2211 Garden Rd . . . . . Monterey CA 93940 831-667-2315
Web: www.parks.ca.gov/default.asp?page_id=568

Jug Handle State Reserve
c/o Mendocino District Office PO Box 440 . . . . . Mendocino CA 95460 707-937-5804
Web: www.parks.ca.gov/default.asp?page_id=441

Julia Pfeiffer Burns State Park
c/o Monterey District Office 2211 Garden Rd . . . . . Monterey CA 93940 831-667-2315
Web: www.parks.ca.gov/default.asp?page_id=578

Kenneth Hahn State Recreation Area
c/o Angeles District Office
1925 Las Virgenes . . . . . Calabasas CA 91302 323-298-3660
Web: www.parks.ca.gov/default.asp?page_id=612

Kings Beach State Recreation Area
c/o Sierra District Office PO Box 266 . . . . . Tahoma CA 96142 530-546-4212
Web: www.parks.ca.gov/default.asp?page_id=511

Kruse Rhododendron State Reserve
c/o N Bay District Office PO Box 123 . . . . . Duncan Mills CA 95430 707-847-2391
Web: www.parks.ca.gov/default.asp?page_id=448

La Purisima Mission State Historic Park
c/o Ch Coast District Office
911 San Pedro St . . . . . Ventura CA 93001 805-733-3713
Web: www.parks.ca.gov/default.asp?page_id=598

Lake Del Valle State Recreation Area
c/o Diablo Vista District Office
845 Casa Grande Rd. . . . . . Petaluma CA 94954 510-635-0135
Web: www.parks.ca.gov/default.asp?page_id=537

Lake Oroville State Recreation Area
c/o Northern Buttes District Office
400 Glen Dr . . . . . Oroville CA 95966 530-538-2200
Web: www.parks.ca.gov/default.asp?page_id=462

Lake Perris State Recreation Area
17801 Lake Perris Dr . . . . . Perris CA 92571 951-657-0676
Web: www.parks.ca.gov

Lake Valley State Recreation Area
c/o Sierra District Office PO Box 266 . . . . . Tahoma CA 96142 530-577-0802
Web: www.parks.ca.gov/default.asp?page_id=515

Leland Stanford Mansion State Historic Park
800 N St . . . . . Sacramento CA 95814 916-324-0575 324-5885
Web: www.stanfordmansion.org

Leo Carillo State Park
c/o Angeles District Office
1925 Las Virgenes . . . . . Calabasas CA 91302 818-880-0350
Web: www.parks.ca.gov/default.asp?page_id=616

Leucadia State Beach
c/o San Diego Coast District Office
4477 Pacific Hwy . . . . . San Diego CA 92110 760-633-2740
Web: www.parks.ca.gov/default.asp?page_id=661

Lighthouse Field State Beach
c/o Santa Cruz District Office
303 Big Trees Pk Rd . . . . . Felton CA 95018 831-420-5270
Web: www.parks.ca.gov/default.asp?page_id=550

Phone | Fax

Limekiln State Park
c/o San Luis Obispo Coast District Office
750 Hearst Castle Rd .... San Simeon CA 93452 831-667-2403
Web: www.parks.ca.gov/default.asp?page_id=577

Little River State Beach
c/o N Coast Redwoods District Office
PO Box 2006 .... Eureka CA 95502 707-677-3132
Web: www.parks.ca.gov/default.asp?page_id=419

Los Encinos State Historic Park
c/o Angeles District Office
1925 Las Virgenes .... Calabasas CA 91302 818-784-4849
Web: www.parks.ca.gov/default.asp?page_id=619

Los Osos Oaks State Reserve
c/o San Luis Obispo Coast District
750 Hearst Castle Rd .... San Simeon CA 93452 805-772-7434
Web: www.parks.ca.gov/default.asp?page_id=597

MacKerricher State Park
c/o Mendocino District Office PO Box 440 .... Mendocino CA 95460 707-964-9112
Web: www.parks.ca.gov/default.asp?page_id=436

Maillard Redwoods State Reserve
c/o Mendocino District Office PO Box 440 .... Mendocino CA 95460 707-937-5804
Web: www.parks.ca.gov/default.asp?page_id=439

Malakoff Diggins State Historic Park
c/o Sierra District Office PO Box 266 .... Tahoma CA 96142 530-265-2740
Web: www.parks.ca.gov/default.asp?page_id=494

Malibu Creek State Park
c/o Angeles District Office
1925 Las Virgenes .... Calabasas CA 91302 818-880-0367
Web: www.parks.ca.gov/default.asp?page_id=614

Malibu Lagoon State Beach
c/o Angeles District Office
1925 Las Virgenes .... Calabasas CA 91302 818-880-0350
Web: www.parks.ca.gov/default.asp?page_id=835

Manchester State Park
c/o Mendocino District Office PO Box 440 .... Mendocino CA 95460 707-937-5804
Web: www.parks.ca.gov/default.asp?page_id=437

Mandalay State Beach
c/o Ch Coast District Office
911 San Pedro St .... Ventura CA 93001 805-968-1033
Web: www.parks.ca.gov/default.asp?page_id=609

Manresa State Beach
c/o Santa Cruz District Office
303 Big Trees Pk Rd .... Felton CA 95018 831-761-1795
Web: www.parks.ca.gov/default.asp?page_id=543

Marconi Conference Center State Historic Park
18500 California 1 .... Marshall CA 94940 415-663-9020
Web: www.parks.ca.gov

Marina State Beach
c/o Monterey District 2211 Garden Rd .... Monterey CA 93940 831-384-7695
Web: www.parks.ca.gov

Marshall Gold Discovery State Historic Park
c/o Gold Fields District Office
7806 Folsom-Auburn Rd .... Folsom CA 95630 530-622-3470
Web: www.parks.ca.gov/default.asp?page_id=484

McArthur-Burney Falls Memorial State Park
c/o Northern Buttes District Office
400 Glen Dr .... Oroville CA 95966 530-538-2200
Web: www.parks.ca.gov/?page_id=455

McConnell State Recreation Area
c/o Central Valley District Office
22708 Broadway St .... Columbia CA 95310 209-394-7755
Web: www.parks.ca.gov/default.asp?page_id=554

McGrath State Beach
c/o Ch Coast District Office
911 San Pedro St .... Ventura CA 93001 805-654-4744
Web: www.parks.ca.gov/default.asp?page_id=607

Mendocino Headlands State Park
c/o Mendocino District Office PO Box 440 .... Mendocino CA 95460 707-937-5804
Web: www.parks.ca.gov/default.asp?page_id=442

Mendocino Woodlands State Park
39350 Little Lake Rd .... Mendocino CA 95460 707-937-5755
Web: www.parks.ca.gov

Mono Lake Tufa State Reserve PO Box 99 .... Lee Vining CA 93541 760-647-6331
Web: www.parks.ca.gov

Monta±a de Oro State Park
c/o San Luis Obispo Coast District Office
750 Hearst Castle Rd .... San Simeon CA 93452 805-528-0513
Web: www.parks.ca.gov/default.asp?page_id=592

Montara State Beach
c/o Santa Cruz District Office
303 Big Trees Pk Rd .... Felton CA 94018 650-726-8819
Web: www.parks.ca.gov/?page_id=532

Monterey State Beach
c/o Monterey District Office 2211 Garden Rd .... Monterey CA 93940 831-384-7695
Web: www.parks.ca.gov/default.asp?page_id=576

Monterey State Historic Park
20 Custom House Plaza .... Monterey CA 93940 831-649-7118
Web: www.parks.ca.gov

Montgomery Woods State Reserve
c/o Mendocino District Office PO Box 440 .... Mendocino CA 95460 707-937-5804
Web: www.parks.ca.gov/default.asp?page_id=434

Moonlight State Beach
c/o San Diego Coast District Office
4477 Pacific Hwy .... San Diego CA 92110 858-642-4200
Web: www.parks.ca.gov/default.asp?page_id=659

Morro Bay State Park
c/o San Luis Obispo Coast District Office
Morro Bay State Pk Rd .... Morro Bay CA 93442 805-772-2560
Web: www.parks.ca.gov/?page_id=23793

Morro Strand State Beach
c/o San Luis Obispo Coast District Office
Morro Bay State Pk Rd .... Morro Bay CA 93442 805-772-2560
Web: www.parks.ca.gov/?page_id=23793

Moss Landing State Beach
c/o Monterey District Office 2211 Garden Rd .... Monterey CA 93940 831-384-7695
Web: www.parks.ca.gov/default.asp?page_id=574

Mount Diablo State Park
c/o Diablo Vista District Office
845 Casa Grande Rd .... Petaluma CA 94954 925-837-2525
Web: www.parks.ca.gov/default.asp?page_id=517

Mount San Jacinto State Park
c/o Inland Empire District Office
17801 Lake Perris Dr .... Perris CA 92571 951-659-2607
Web: www.parks.ca.gov/default.asp?page_id=636

Natural Bridges State Beach
c/o Santa Cruz District Office
303 Big Trees Pk Rd .... Felton CA 95018 831-423-4609
Web: www.parks.ca.gov/default.asp?page_id=541

Navarro River Redwoods State Park
c/o Mendocino District Office PO Box 440 .... Mendocino CA 95460 707-937-5804
Web: www.parks.ca.gov/default.asp?page_id=435

New Brighton State Beach
c/o Santa Cruz District Office
303 Big Trees Pk Rd .... Felton CA 95018 831-464-6330
Web: www.parks.ca.gov/default.asp?page_id=542

Oceano Dunes State Vehicular Recreation Area
1416 9th St .... Sacramento CA 95814 916-653-6995
Web: www.parks.ca.gov/default.asp?page_id=406

Ocotillo Wells State Vehicular Recreation Area
5172 Hwy 78 # 10 .... Borrego Springs CA 92004 760-767-5391
Web: www.parks.ca.gov

Old Sacramento State Historic Park
c/o Capital District Office 101 J St .... Sacramento CA 95814 916-442-7644
Web: www.parks.ca.gov

Old Town San Diego State Historic Park
4002 Wallace St .... San Diego CA 92110 619-220-5422 688-3229
TF: 800-777-0369 ■ *Web:* www.parks.ca.gov

Olompali State Historic Park PO Box 1016 .... Novato CA 94948 415-892-3383
Web: www.parks.ca.gov

Pacheco State Park
c/o Central Valley District Office
22708 Broadway St .... Columbia CA 95310 209-826-6283
Web: www.parks.ca.gov/default.asp?page_id=560

Pacifica State Beach
c/o Santa Cruz District Office
303 Big Trees Pk Rd .... Felton CA 95018 650-738-7381
Web: www.parks.ca.gov/default.asp?page_id=524

Palomar Mountain State Park
c/o Colorado Desert District Office
200 Palm Canyon Dr .... Borrego Springs CA 92004 760-742-3462
Web: www.parks.ca.gov/default.asp?page_id=637

Patrick's Point State Park
4150 Patrick's Pt Dr .... Trinidad CA 95570 707-677-3570
Web: www.parks.ca.gov

Pelican State Beach
c/o N Coast Redwoods District Office
PO Box 2006 .... Eureka CA 95502 707-464-6101
Web: www.parks.ca.gov/default.asp?page_id=412

Pescadero State Beach
c/o Santa Cruz District Office
303 Big Trees Pk Rd .... Felton CA 95018 650-879-2170
Web: www.parks.ca.gov/?page_id=522

Petaluma Adobe State Historic Park
3325 Old Adobe Rd .... Petaluma CA 94954 707-762-4871
Web: www.parks.ca.gov

Pfeiffer Big Sur State Park
c/o Monterey District Office 2211 Garden Rd .... Monterey CA 93940 831-667-2315
Web: www.parks.ca.gov/default.asp?page_id=570

Picacho State Recreation Area
c/o Colorado Desert District Office
200 Palm Canyon Dr .... Borrego Springs CA 92004 760-393-3052
Web: www.picacho.statepark.org

Pigeon Point Light Station State Historic Park
210 Pigeon Pt Rd .... Pescadero CA 94060 650-879-0633
Web: www.parks.ca.gov

Pio Pico State Historic Park
c/o Angeles District Office
1925 Las Virgenes .... Calabasas CA 91302 562-695-1217
Web: www.parks.ca.gov/default.asp?page_id=621

Pismo State Beach 555 Pier Ave .... Oceano CA 93445 805-489-1869
Web: www.parks.ca.gov/default.asp?page_id=595

Plumas-Eureka State Park 310 Johnsville Rd .... Blairsden CA 96103 530-836-2380
Web: www.parks.ca.gov

Point Dume State Beach
c/o Angeles District Office
1925 Las Virgenes .... Calabasas CA 91302 310-457-8143
Web: www.parks.ca.gov/default.asp?page_id=623

Point Lobos State Reserve
c/o Monterey District Office 2211 Garden Rd .... Monterey CA 93940 831-624-4909
Web: www.parks.ca.gov/default.asp?page_id=571

Point Montara Light Station
c/o Santa Cruz District Office
303 Big Trees Pk Rd .... Felton CA 95018 650-728-7177
Web: www.parks.ca.gov/default.asp?page_id=534

Point Mugu State Park
c/o Angeles District Office
1925 Las Virgenes .... Calabasas CA 91302 805-488-5223
Web: www.parks.ca.gov/default.asp?page_id=630

Point Sur State Historic Park
c/o Monterey District Office 2211 Garden Rd .... Monterey CA 93940 831-625-4419
Web: www.parks.ca.gov/default.asp?page_id=565

Name / Address	City	State	Zip	Phone	Fax
Pomponio State Beach c/o Santa Cruz District Office 303 Big Trees Pk Rd *Web:* www.parks.ca.gov/?page_id=521	Felton	CA	95018	650-879-2170	
Portola Redwoods State Park c/o Santa Cruz District Office 303 Big Trees Pk Rd *Web:* www.parks.ca.gov/default.asp?page_id=539	Felton	CA	95018	650-948-9098	
Prairie City State Vehicular Recreation Area 13300 White Rock Rd *Web:* www.parks.ca.gov	Rancho Cordova	CA	95742	916-985-7378	
Prairie Creek Redwoods State Park c/o N Coast Redwoods District Office PO Box 2006 *Web:* www.parks.ca.gov/default.asp?page_id=415	Eureka	CA	95502	707-464-6101	
Railtown 1897 State Historic Park c/o Capital District Office 101 J St *Web:* www.railtown1897.org	Sacramento	CA	95814	209-984-3953	
Refugio State Beach c/o Ch Coast District Office 911 San Pedro St *Web:* www.parks.ca.gov/default.asp?page_id=603	Ventura	CA	93001	805-968-1033	
Richardson Grove State Park c/o N Coast Redwoods District Office PO Box 2006 *Web:* www.parks.ca.gov/default.asp?page_id=422	Eureka	CA	95502	707-247-3318	
Robert H. Meyer Memorial State Beach c/o Angeles District Office 1925 Las Virgenes *Web:* www.parks.ca.gov/default.asp?page_id=633	Calabasas	CA	91302	310-457-8143	
Robert Louis Stevenson State Park c/o Diablo Vista District Office 845 Casa Grande Rd *Web:* www.parks.ca.gov/default.asp?page_id=472	Petaluma	CA	94954	707-942-4575	
Robert W. Crown Memorial State Beach c/o Diablo Vista District Office 845 Casa Grande Rd *Web:* www.parks.ca.gov/default.asp?page_id=526	Petaluma	CA	94954	510-562-7275	
Russian Gulch State Park c/o Mendocino District Office PO Box 440 *Web:* www.parks.ca.gov/default.asp?page_id=432	Mendocino	CA	95460	707-937-4296	
Salinas River State Beach c/o Monterey District Office 2211 Garden Rd *Web:* www.parks.ca.gov/default.asp?page_id=573	Monterey	CA	93940	831-384-7695	
Salt Point State Park 25050 Hwy 1 *Web:* www.parks.ca.gov/default.asp?page_id=453	Jenner	CA	95450	707-847-3221	
Salton Sea State Recreation Area c/o Colorado Desert District Office 200 Palm Canyon Dr *Web:* www.saltonsea.statepark.org	Borrego Springs	CA	92004	760-393-3052	
Samuel P. Taylor State Park PO Box 251 *Web:* www.parks.ca.gov	Lagunitas	CA	94938	415-488-9897	
San Buenaventura State Beach c/o Ch Coast District Office 911 San Pedro St *Web:* www.parks.ca.gov/default.asp?page_id=600	Ventura	CA	93001	805-648-3918	
San Clemente State Beach c/o Orange Coast District Office 3030 Avenida del Presidente *Web:* www.parks.ca.gov/default.asp?page_id=646	San Clemente	CA	92672	949-492-3156	
San Elijo State Beach c/o San Diego Coast District Office 4477 Pacific Hwy *TF:* 800-444-7275 ■ *Web:* www.parks.ca.gov/?page_id=662	San Diego	CA	92110	760-753-5091	
San Gregorio State Beach c/o Santa Cruz District Office 303 Big Trees Pk Rd *Web:* www.parks.ca.gov/?page_id=529	Felton	CA	95018	650-879-2170	
San Juan Bautista State Historic Park c/o Monterey District Office 2211 Garden Rd *Web:* www.parks.ca.gov/default.asp?page_id=563	Monterey	CA	93940	831-623-4881	
San Luis Reservoir State Recreation Area c/o Central Valley District Office 22708 Broadway St. *Web:* www.parks.ca.gov/default.asp?page_id=558	Columbia	CA	95310	209-826-1196	
San Onofre State Beach c/o Orange Coast District Office 3030 Avenida del Presidente *Web:* www.parks.ca.gov/default.asp?page_id=647	San Clemente	CA	92672	714-492-4872	
San Pasqual Battlefield State Historic Park 15808 San Pasqual Valley Rd *Web:* www.parks.ca.gov	Escondido	CA	92027	760-737-2201	
San Simeon State Park c/o San Luis Obispo Coast District Office San Simeon Creek Rd *Web:* www.parks.ca.gov/?page_id=23793	San Simeon	CA	93428	805-927-2020	
Santa Cruz Mission State Historic Park c/o Santa Cruz District Office 144 School St *Web:* www.parks.ca.gov/default.asp?page_id=548	Santa Cruz	CA	95060	831-425-5849	429-2870
Santa Monica State Beach c/o Angeles District Office 1925 Las Virgenes *Web:* www.parks.ca.gov/default.asp?page_id=624	Calabasas	CA	91302	310-458-8974	
Santa Susana Pass State Historic Park c/o Angeles District Office 1925 Las Virgenes *Web:* www.parks.ca.gov/default.asp?page_id=611	Calabasas	CA	91302	213-620-6152	
Schooner Gulch State Beach c/o Mendocino District Office PO Box 440 *Web:* www.parks.ca.gov/default.asp?page_id=446	Mendocino	CA	95460	707-937-5804	
Seacliff State Beach c/o Santa Cruz District Office 303 Big Trees Pk Rd *Web:* www.parks.ca.gov/default.asp?page_id=543	Felton	CA	95018	831-685-6500	
Shasta State Historic Park c/o Northern Buttes District Office 400 Glen Dr *Web:* www.parks.ca.gov/default.asp?page_id=456	Oroville	CA	95966	530-243-8194	
Silver Strand State Beach c/o San Diego Coast District Office 4477 Pacific Hwy *Web:* www.parks.ca.gov/default.asp?page_id=654	San Diego	CA	92110	619-435-5184	
Silverwood Lake State Recreation Area c/o Inland Empire District Office 17801 Lake Perris Dr *Web:* www.parks.ca.gov/default.asp?page_id=650	Perris	CA	92571	760-389-2281	
Sinkyone Wilderness State Park PO Box 245 *Web:* www.parks.ca.gov	Whitethorn	CA	95489	707-986-7711	
Smithe Redwoods State Reserve c/o N Coast Redwoods District Office PO Box 2006 *Web:* www.parks.ca.gov/default.asp?page_id=427	Eureka	CA	95502	707-247-3318	
Sonoma Coast State Beach 3095 Hwy 1 *Web:* www.parks.ca.gov/default.asp?page_id=451	Bodega Bay	CA	94923	707-875-3483	
Sonoma State Historic Park c/o Diablo Vista District Office 845 Casa Grande Rd *Web:* www.parks.ca.gov	Petalulma	CA	94954	707-938-9560	
South Carlsbad State Beach c/o San Diego Coast District 9609 Waples St, Suite 200 *Web:* www.parks.ca.gov	San Diego	CA	92121	760-438-3143	
South Yuba River State Park 17660 Pleasant Valley Rd *Web:* www.parks.ca.gov	Penn Valley	CA	95946	530-432-2546	
Standish-Hickey State Recreation Area c/o N Coast Redwoods District Office PO Box 206 *Web:* www.parks.ca.gov/default.asp?page_id=423	Eureka	CA	95502	707-925-6482	
Sugarloaf Ridge State Park c/o Diablo Vista District Office 845 Casa Grande Rd *Web:* www.parks.ca.gov/default.asp?page_id=481	Petaluma	CA	94954	707-833-5712	
Sunset State Beach c/o Santa Cruz District Office 303 Big Trees Pk Rd *Web:* www.parks.ca.gov/?page_id=544	Felton	CA	95018	831-763-7062	
Sutter's Fort State Historic Park 2701 L St *Web:* www.parks.ca.gov	Sacramento	CA	95816	916-445-4422	447-9318
Tahoe State Recreation Area c/o Sierra District Office PO Box 266 *Web:* www.parks.ca.gov/default.asp?page_id=504	Tahoma	CA	96142	530-583-3074	
Tolowa Dunes State Park 1375 Elk Valley Rd *Web:* www.parks.ca.gov	Crescent City	CA	95531	707-465-2145	
Tomales Bay State Park 1208 Pierce Pt Rd. *Web:* www.parks.ca.gov/default.asp?page_id=470	Inverness	CA	94937	415-669-1140	
Tomo-Kahni State Historic Park c/o Inland Empire District Office 17801 Lake Perris Dr *Web:* www.parks.ca.gov/default.asp?page_id=610	Perris	CA	92571	661-942-0662	
Topanga State Park c/o Angeles District Office 1925 Las Virgenes *Web:* www.parks.ca.gov/default.asp?page_id=629	Calabasas	CA	91302	310-455-2465	
Torrey Pines State Beach c/o San Diego Coast District 4477 Pacific Hwy *Web:* www.parks.ca.gov/default.asp?page_id=658	San Diego	CA	92110	858-755-2063	
Torrey Pines State Reserve c/o San Diego Coast District 4477 Pacific Hwy *Web:* www.parks.ca.gov/?page_id=657	San Diego	CA	92110	858-755-2063	
Trinidad State Beach c/o N Coast Redwoods District Office PO Box 2006 *Web:* www.parks.ca.gov/default.asp?page_id=418	Eureka	CA	95502	707-677-3132	
Tule Elk State Reserve c/o Central Valley District Office 22708 Broadway St. *Web:* www.parks.ca.gov/default.asp?page_id=584	Columbia	CA	95310	661-764-6881	
Turlock Lake State Recreation Area c/o Central Valley District Office 22708 Broadway St. *Web:* www.parks.ca.gov/default.asp?page_id=555	Columbia	CA	95310	209-874-2056	
Twin Lakes State Beach c/o Santa Cruz District Office 303 Big Trees Pk Rd *Web:* www.parks.ca.gov/default.asp?page_id=547	Felton	CA	95018	831-427-4868	
Van Damme State Park c/o Mendocino District Office PO Box 440 *Web:* www.parks.ca.gov/default.asp?page_id=433	Mendocino	CA	95460	707-937-5804	
Verdugo Mountains c/o Angeles District Office 1925 Las Virgenes *Web:* www.parks.ca.gov/default.asp?page_id=635	Calabasas	CA	91302	213-620-6152	
Washoe Meadows State Park c/o Sierra District Office Sawmill Rd at Lake Tahoe Blvd *Web:* www.parks.ca.gov/?page_id=516	South Lake Tahoe	CA	96150	530-525-7232	

				Phone	Fax
Watts Towers of Simon Rodia State Historic Park c/o Angeles District Office 1925 Las Virgenes *Web:* www.parks.ca.gov/default.asp?page_id=613	Calabasas	CA	91302	213-847-4646	
Weaverville Joss House State Historic Park c/o Northern Buttes District Office 400 Glen Dr *Web:* www.parks.ca.gov/default.asp?page_id=457	Oroville	CA	95966	530-623-5282	
Westport-Union Landing State Beach c/o Mendocino District Office PO Box 440 *Web:* www.parks.ca.gov/default.asp?page_id=440	Mendocino	CA	95460	707-937-5804	
Wilder Ranch State Park c/o Santa Cruz District Office 303 Big Trees Pk Rd *Web:* www.parks.ca.gov/default.asp?page_id=549	Felton	CA	95018	831-426-0505	
Will Rogers State Beach c/o Angeles District Office 1925 Las Virgenes *Web:* www.parks.ca.gov/default.asp?page_id=625	Calabasas	CA	91302	310-305-9503	
Will Rogers State Historic Park c/o Angeles District Office 1925 Las Virgenes *Web:* www.parks.ca.gov/default.asp?page_id=626	Calabasas	CA	91302	310-454-8212	
William B. Ide Adobe State Historic Park c/o Northern Buttes District Office 400 Glen Dr *Web:* www.parks.ca.gov/default.asp?page_id=458	Oroville	CA	95966	530-529-8599	
William Randolph Hearst Memorial State Beach c/o San Luis Obispo Coast District Office 750 Hearst Castle Rd *Web:* www.parks.ca.gov/?page_id=23793	San Simeon	CA	93452	805-927-2020	
Woodland Opera House State Historic Park c/o Capital District Office 101 J St *Web:* www.parks.ca.gov/default.asp?page_id=488	Sacramento	CA	95814	530-666-9617	
Woodson Bridge State Recreation Area c/o Northern Buttes District Office 400 Glen Dr *Web:* www.parks.ca.gov/default.asp?page_id=459	Oroville	CA	95966	530-839-2112	
Zmudowski State Beach c/o Monterey District Office 2211 Garden Rd *Web:* www.parks.ca.gov/default.asp?page_id=572	Monterey	CA	93940	831-384-7695	

COLORADO

				Phone	Fax
Arkansas Headwaters Recreation Area 307 W Sackett Ave *Web:* www.parks.state.co.us	Salida	CO	81201	719-539-7289	
Barr Lake State Park 13401 Picadilly Rd. *Web:* www.parks.state.co.us	Brighton	CO	80603	303-659-6005	
Bonny Lake State Park 30010 County Rd 3 *Web:* www.parks.state.co.us	Idalia	CO	80735	970-354-7306	
Boyd Lake State Park 3720 N County Rd 11-C *Web:* www.parks.state.co.us	Loveland	CO	80539	970-669-1739	
Castlewood Canyon State Park 2989 S Hwy 83 *Web:* www.parks.state.co.us	Franktown	CO	80116	303-688-5242	
Chatfield State Park 11500 N Roxborough Pk Rd *Web:* www.parks.state.co.us	Littleton	CO	80125	303-791-7275	
Cherry Creek State Park 4201 S Parker Rd *Web:* www.parks.state.co.us	Aurora	CO	80014	303-699-3860	699-3864
Cheyenne Mountain State Park 4255 Sinton Rd. *Web:* www.parks.state.co.us	Colorado Springs	CO	80907	719-227-5256	
Crawford State Park PO Box 147 *Web:* www.parks.state.co.us	Crawford	CO	81415	970-921-5721	
Crawford State Park 40468 Hwy 92 *Web:* www.parks.state.co.us/parks/crawford/Pages/CrawfordHome.aspx	Crawford	CO	81415	970-921-5721	
Eldorado Canyon State Park 9 Kneale Rd PO Box B *Web:* www.parks.state.co.us	Eldorado Springs	CO	80025	303-494-3943	499-2729
Eleven Mile State Park 4229 County Rd 92 *Web:* www.parks.state.co.us	Lake George	CO	80827	719-748-3401	
Golden Gate Canyon State Park 92 Crawford Gulch Rd *Web:* www.parks.state.co.us	Golden	CO	80403	303-582-3707	582-3712
Harvey Gap State Park c/o Rifle Gap State Pk 5775 Hwy 325 *Web:* www.parks.state.co.us	Rifle	CO	81650	970-625-1607	
Highline Lake State Park 1800 11.8 Rd *Web:* www.parks.state.co.us	Loma	CO	81524	970-858-7208	
Jackson Lake State Park 26363 County Rd 3 *Web:* www.parks.state.co.us	Orchard	CO	80649	970-645-2551	
James M. Robb - Colorado River State Park PO Box 700 *Web:* www.parks.state.co.us	Clifton	CO	81520	970-434-3388	
Lake Pueblo State Park 640 Pueblo Reservoir Rd *Web:* www.parks.state.co.us	Pueblo	CO	81005	719-561-9320	
Lathrop State Park 70 County Rd 502 *Web:* www.parks.state.co.us	Walsenburg	CO	81089	719-738-2376	
Lory State Park 708 Lodgepole Dr *Web:* www.parks.state.co.us	Bellvue	CO	80512	970-493-1623	
Mancos State Park 42545 County Rd N *Web:* www.parks.state.co.us	Mancos	CO	81328	970-533-7065	
Mueller State Park PO Box 39 *Web:* www.parks.state.co.us	Divide	CO	80814	719-687-2366	
Navajo State Park PO Box 1697 *Web:* www.parks.state.co.us	Arboles	CO	81121	970-883-2208	
North Sterling State Park 24005 County Rd 330 *Web:* www.parks.state.co.us	Sterling	CO	80751	970-522-3657	
Paonia State Park PO Box 147 *Web:* www.parks.state.co.us	Crawford	CO	81415	970-921-5721	
Pearl Lake State Park PO Box 750 *Web:* www.parks.state.co.us	Clark	CO	80428	970-879-3922	
Ridgway State Park 28555 Hwy 550 *Web:* www.parks.state.co.us	Ridgway	CO	81432	970-626-5822	
Rifle Falls State Park 5775 Hwy 325 *Web:* www.parks.state.co.us	Rifle	CO	81650	970-625-1607	
Rifle Gap State Park 5775 Hwy 325 *Web:* www.parks.state.co.us	Rifle	CO	81650	970-625-1607	
Roxborough State Park 4751 Roxborough Dr *Web:* www.parks.state.co.us	Littleton	CO	80125	303-973-3959	
Saint Vrain State Park 3525 State Hwy 119 *Web:* www.parks.state.co.us	Longmont	CO	80504	303-678-9402	
San Luis State Park & Wildlife Area 16399 Ln 6 N *Web:* www.parks.state.co.us	Mosca	CO	81146	719-378-2020	
Spinney Mountain State Park c/o Eleven Mile State Pk 4229 County Rd 92 *Web:* www.parks.state.co.us	Lake George	CO	80827	719-748-3401	
Stagecoach State Park 25500 County Rd 14 *Web:* www.parks.state.co.us	Oak Creek	CO	80467	970-736-2436	
State Forest State Park 56750 Hwy 14 *Web:* www.parks.state.co.us	Walden	CO	80480	970-723-8366	723-8325
Steamboat Lake State Park PO Box 750 *Web:* www.parks.state.co.us	Clark	CO	80428	970-879-3922	
Sweitzer Lake State Park 1735 E Rd PO Box 173 *Web:* www.parks.state.co.us	Delta	CO	81416	970-874-4258	
Sylvan Lake State Park 10200 Brush Creek Rd PO Box 1475 *Web:* www.parks.state.co.us	Eagle	CO	81631	970-328-2021	
Trinidad Lake State Park 32610 State Hwy 12 *Web:* www.parks.state.co.us	Trinidad	CO	81082	719-846-6951	
Vega State Park PO Box 186 *Web:* www.parks.state.co.us	Collbran	CO	81624	970-487-3407	
Yampa River State Park 6185 W US Hwy 40 *Web:* www.parks.state.co.us	Hayden	CO	81639	970-276-2061	

CONNECTICUT

				Phone	Fax
American Legion & Peoples State Forests PO Box 161 *Web:* www.dep.state.ct.us/stateparks/forests/amerlegion.htm	Pleasant Valley	CT	06063	860-379-2469	
Bigelow Hollow State Park & Nipmuck State Forest c/o Shenipsit State Forest 166 Chestnut Hill Rd *Web:* www.dep.state.ct.us	Stafford Springs	CT	06076	860-684-3430	
Black Rock State Park c/o Topsmead State Forest PO Box 1081 *Web:* www.dep.state.ct.us	Litchfield	CT	06759	860-567-5694	
Bluff Point State Park c/o Fort Trumbull State Pk 90 Walbach St. *Web:* www.dep.state.ct.us	New London	CT	06320	860-444-7591	
Burr Pond State Park 384 Burr Mountain Rd. *Web:* www.dep.state.ct.us	Torrington	CT	06790	860-482-1817	
Chatfield Hollow State Park 381 Rt 80 *Web:* www.dep.state.ct.us	Killingworth	CT	06419	860-663-2030	
Cockaponset State Forest c/o Chatfield Hollow State Pk 381 Rt 80 *Web:* www.dep.state.ct.us	Killingworth	CT	06419	860-663-2030	
Collis P. Huntington State Park c/o Putnam Memorial State Pk 492 Black Rd Tpke *Web:* www.dep.state.ct.us	Redding	CT	06896	203-938-2285	
Connecticut Valley Railroad State Park 1 Railroad Ave PO Box 452 *Web:* www.essexsteamtrain.com	Essex	CT	06426	860-767-0103	767-0104
Day Pond State Park c/o Eastern District HQ 209 Hebron Rd. *Web:* www.dep.state.ct.us	Marlborough	CT	06447	860-295-9523	
Dennis Hill State Park c/o Burr Pond State Pk 385 Burr Mountain Rd *Web:* www.dep.state.ct.us	Torrington	CT	06790	860-482-1817	
Devil's Hopyard State Park 366 Hopyard Rd *Web:* www.dep.state.ct.us/stateparks/parks/devilshopyard.htm	East Haddam	CT	06423	860-873-8566	
Dinosaur State Park 400 W St *Web:* www.dep.state.ct.us	Rocky Hill	CT	06067	860-529-5816	257-1405
Fort Griswold Battlefield State Park c/o Fort Trumbull State Pk 90 Walbach St. *Web:* www.dep.state.ct.us	New London	CT	06320	860-444-7591	
Fort Trumbull State Park 90 Walbach St. *Web:* www.ct.gov/dep/cwp/view.asp?A=2716&Q=325200	New London	CT	06320	860-444-7591	
Gay City State Park c/o Eastern District HQ 209 Hebron Rd. *Web:* www.dep.state.ct.us	Marlborough	CT	06447	203-295-9523	
Gillette Castle State Park 67 River Rd. *Web:* www.dep.state.ct.us	East Haddam	CT	06423	860-526-2336	
Haley Farm State Park c/o Fort Trumbull State Pk 90 Walbach St. *Web:* www.dep.state.ct.us	New London	CT	06320	860-444-7591	
Hammonasset Beach State Park 1288 Boston Post Rd PO Box 271 *Web:* www.dep.state.ct.us	Madison	CT	06443	203-245-2785	245-9201
Harkness Memorial State Park 275 Great Neck Rd *Web:* www.dep.state.ct.us/stateparks/parks/harkness.htm	Waterford	CT	06385	203-443-5725	

Name / Address	City	State	Zip	Phone	Fax
Haystack Mountain State Park c/o Burr Pond State Pk 385 Burr Mountain Rd *Web:* www.dep.state.ct.us	Torrington	CT	06790	860-482-1817	
Hopeville Pond State Park 193 Roode Rd *Web:* www.dep.state.ct.us	Jewett City	CT	06351	860-376-2920	
Housatonic Meadows State Park c/o Macedonia Brook State Pk 159 Macedonia Brook Rd *Web:* www.dep.state.ct.us	Kent	CT	06757	860-927-3238	
Hurd State Park c/o Gillette Castle State Pk 67 River Rd *Web:* www.dep.state.ct.us	East Haddam	CT	06423	860-526-2336	
Indian Well State Park c/o Osbornedale State Pk PO Box 113 *Web:* www.dep.state.ct.us	Derby	CT	06418	203-735-4311	
James L. Goodwin State Forest Goodwin Forest Conservation Education Ctr 23 Potter Rd *Web:* www.dep.state.ct.us	Hampton	CT	06226	860-455-9534	455-9857
John A. Minetto State Park c/o Burr Pond State Pk 385 Burr Mountain Rd *Web:* www.dep.state.ct.us	Torrington	CT	06790	860-482-1817	
Kent Falls State Park c/o Macedonia Brook State Pk 159 Macedonia Brook Rd *Web:* www.dep.state.ct.us	Kent	CT	06757	860-927-3238	
Kettletown State Park 1400 Georges Hill Rd *Web:* www.dep.state.ct.us	Southbury	CT	06488	203-264-5678	
Lake Waramaug State Park 30 Lake Waramaug Rd *Web:* www.dep.state.ct.us/stateparks/parks/lakewaramaug.htm	New Preston	CT	06777	860-868-2592	
Macedonia Brook State Park 159 Macedonia Brook Rd *Web:* www.dep.state.ct.us	Kent	CT	06757	860-927-3238	
Mansfield Hollow State Park c/o Mashamoquet Brook State Pk RFD 1 147 Wolf Den Rd *Web:* www.dep.state.ct.us	Pomfret Center	CT	06259	860-928-6121	
Mashamoquet Brook State Park 147 Wolf Den Dr *Web:* www.dep.state.ct.us	Pomfret Center	CT	06259	860-928-6121	
Mohawk State Forest 20 Mohawk Mountain Rd *Web:* www.dep.state.ct.us	Goshen	CT	06756	860-491-3620	
Mount Tom State Park c/o Lake Waramaug State Pk 30 Lake Waramaug Rd *Web:* www.dep.state.ct.us	New Preston	CT	06777	860-868-2592	
Natchaug State Forest c/o Mashamoquet Brook State Pk RFD #1 Wolf Den Rd *Web:* www.dep.state.ct.us	Pomfret Center	CT	06259	860-928-6121	
Osbornedale State Park 555 Roosevelt Dr *Web:* www.dep.state.ct.us/stateparks/parks/osbornedale.htm	Derby	CT	06418	203-735-4311	
Pachaug State Forest Rt 49 PO Box 5 *Web:* www.dep.state.ct.us	Voluntown	CT	06384	860-376-4075	
Penwood State Park 57 Gunn Mill Rd *Web:* www.dep.state.ct.us	Bloomfield	CT	06002	860-242-1158	
Putnam Memorial State Park 429 Black Rock Tpke *Web:* www.dep.state.ct.us	Redding	CT	06896	203-938-2285	
Quaddick State Park c/o Mashamoquet Brook State Pk 147 Wolf Den Dr *Web:* www.dep.state.ct.us	Pomfret Center	CT	06259	860-928-6121	
Rocky Neck State Park PO Box 676 *Web:* www.dep.state.ct.us	Niantic	CT	06357	860-739-5471	
Salmon River State Forest c/o Eastern District HQ 209 Hebron Rd *Web:* www.dep.state.ct.us	Marlborough	CT	06447	860-295-9523	
Selden Neck State Park c/o Gillette Castle State Pk 67 River Rd *Web:* www.dep.state.ct.us	East Haddam	CT	06423	860-526-2336	
Shenipsit State Forest 166 Chestnut Hill Rd Rt 190 *Web:* www.ct.gov/dep/cwp/view.asp?A=2716&Q=332506	Stafford Springs	CT	06076	860-684-3430	684-4130
Sherwood Island State Park PO Box 188 *Web:* www.dep.state.ct.us/stateparks/parks/sherwood.htm	Greens Farms	CT	06838	203-226-6983	
Silver Sands State Park c/o Osbornedale State Pk PO Box 113 *Web:* www.ct.gov/dep/cwp/view.asp?A=2716&Q=325262	Derby	CT	06418	203-735-4311	
Sleeping Giant State Park 200 Mt Carmel Ave *Web:* www.dep.state.ct.us	Hamden	CT	06518	203-789-7498	
Southford Falls State Park Quaker Farms Rd Rt 188 *Web:* www.dep.state.ct.us	Southbury	CT	06488	203-264-5169	
Squantz Pond State Park 178 Shortwoods Rd *Web:* www.dep.state.ct.us/stateparks/parks/squantz.htm	New Fairfield	CT	06810	203-797-4165	
Stratton Brook State Park 57 Gun Mill Rd *Web:* www.dep.state.ct.us/stateparks/parks/stratton.htm	Bloomfield	CT	06002	860-658-1388	
Talcott Mountain State Park c/o Penwood State Pk 57 Gunn Mill Rd *Web:* www.dep.state.ct.us	Bloomfield	CT	06002	860-242-1158	
Topsmead State Forest PO Box 1081 *Web:* www.dep.state.ct.us	Litchfield	CT	06759	860-567-5694	
Wadsworth Falls State Park c/o Chatfield Hollow State Pk 381 Rt 80 *Web:* www.dep.state.ct.us	Killingworth	CT	06419	860-663-2030	
West Rock Ridge State Park 200 Mt Carmel Ave c/o Sleeping Giant State Pk *Web:* www.dep.state.ct.us	Hamden	CT	06518	203-789-7498	
Wharton Brook State Park 200 Mt Carmel Ave c/o Sleeping Giant State Pk *Web:* www.dep.state.ct.us	Hamden	CT	06518	203-789-7498	

DELAWARE

Name / Address	City	State	Zip	Phone	Fax
Bellevue State Park 800 Carr Rd *Web:* www.destateparks.com	Wilmington	DE	19809	302-761-6963	761-6951
Brandywine Creek State Park PO Box 3782 *Web:* www.destateparks.com	Greenville	DE	19807	302-577-3534	
Cape Henlopen State Park 42 Cape Henlopen Dr *Web:* www.destateparks.com	Lewes	DE	19958	302-645-8983	
Delaware Seashore State Park 130 Coastal Hwy *Web:* www.destateparks.com/dssp/dssp.asp	Rehoboth Beach	DE	19971	302-227-2800	
Fenwick Island State Park c/o Delaware Seashore State Pk Inlet 850 *Web:* www.destateparks.com/park/fenwick-island/index.asp	Rehoboth Beach	DE	19971	302-227-2800	
Fort Delaware State Park PO Box 170 *Web:* www.destateparks.com	Delaware City	DE	19706	302-834-7941	836-2539
Fort DuPont State Park 45 Clinton St *Web:* www.destateparks.com	Delaware City	DE	19706	302-834-7941	
Fox Point State Park c/o Bellevue State Pk 800 Carr Rd *Web:* www.destateparks.com/foxpt/foxpt.htm	Wilmington	DE	19809	302-761-6963	
Holts Landing State Park PO Box 76 *Web:* www.destateparks.com	Millville	DE	19970	302-539-9060	
Killens Pond State Park 5025 Killens Pond Rd *Web:* www.destateparks.com	Felton	DE	19943	302-284-4526	284-4694
Lums Pond State Park 1068 Howell School Rd *Web:* www.destateparks.com	Bear	DE	19701	302-368-6989	
Trap Pond State Park 33587 Baldcypress Ln *Web:* www.destateparks.com	Laurel	DE	19956	302-875-5153	
White Clay Creek State Park 425 Wedgewood Rd *Web:* www.destateparks.com	Newark	DE	19711	302-368-6900	
Wilmington State Parks 1021 W 18th St *Web:* www.destateparks.com/wilmsp/wilmsp.htm	Wilmington	DE	19802	302-577-7020	577-7084

FLORIDA

Name / Address	City	State	Zip	Phone	Fax
Alafia River State Park 14326 S County Rd 39 *Web:* www.floridaparks.org	Lithia	FL	33547	813-672-5320	
Alfred B. Maclay Gardens State Park 14326 S County Rd 39 *Web:* www.floridaparks.org	Lithia	FL	33547	813-672-5320	
Amelia Island State Park 12157 Heckscher Dr *Web:* www.floridastateparks.org/ameliaisland	Jacksonville	FL	32226	904-251-2320	
Anastasia State Park 1340-A A1A S *TF:* 800-326-3521 ■ *Web:* www.floridastateparks.org	Saint Augustine	FL	32080	904-461-2033	461-2006
Anclote Key Preserve State Park 1 Cswy Blvd ; c/o Honeymoon Island State Pk *Web:* www.floridastateparks.org	Dunedin	FL	34698	727-469-5942	
Bahia Honda State Park 36850 Overseas Hwy *Web:* www.floridastateparks.org	Big Pine Key	FL	33043	305-872-2353	
Bald Point State Park 146 PO Box Cut *Web:* www.floridastateparks.org	Alligator Point	FL	32346	850-349-9146	
Barnacle Historic State Park The 3485 Main Hwy *Web:* www.floridastateparks.org	Coconut Grove	FL	33133	305-442-6866	442-6872
Big Lagoon State Park 12301 Gulf Beach Hwy *Web:* www.floridastateparks.org/biglagoon	Pensacola	FL	32507	850-492-1595	492-4380
Big Shoals State Park PO Drawer G *Web:* www.floridastateparks.org	White Springs	FL	32096	386-397-4331	
Big Talbot Island State Park 12157 Heckscher Dr *Web:* www.floridastateparks.org/bigtalbotisland	Jacksonville	FL	32226	904-251-2320	
Bill Baggs Cape Florida State Park 1200 S Crandon Blvd *Web:* www.floridastateparks.org	Key Biscayne	FL	33149	305-361-5811	365-0003
Blackwater River State Park 7720 Deaton Bridge Rd *Web:* www.floridastateparks.org	Holt	FL	32564	850-983-5363	983-5364
Blue Spring State Park 2100 W French Ave *Web:* www.floridastateparks.org	Orange City	FL	32763	386-775-3663	
Bulow Creek State Park 2099 N Beach St *Web:* www.floridastateparks.org/bulowcreek	Ormond Beach	FL	32174	386-676-4050	676-4060
Bulow Plantation Ruins Historic State Park PO Box 655 *Web:* www.floridastateparks.org	Bunnell	FL	32110	386-517-2084	
Caladesi Island State Park 1 Cswy Blvd *Web:* www.floridastateparks.org/caladesiisland	Dunedin	FL	34698	727-469-5918	298-2320
Camp Helen State Park 23937 Panama City Beach Pkwy *Web:* www.floridastateparks.org	Panama City Beach	FL	32413	850-233-5059	236-3204
Cayo Costa State Park 880 Belche Rd *Web:* www.floridastateparks.org/cayocosta	Boca Grande	FL	33921	941-964-0375	
Cedar Key Museum State Park 12231 SW 166 Ct *Web:* www.floridastateparks.org	Cedar Key	FL	32625	352-543-5350	
Cedar Key Scrub State Reserve 8312 SW 125th Ct *Web:* www.floridastateparks.org/cedarkeyscrub	Cedar Key	FL	32625	352-543-5567	
Collier-Seminole State Park 20200 E Tamiami Trail *Web:* www.floridastateparks.org/collier-seminole	Naples	FL	34114	239-394-3397	394-5113

Phone | Fax

Constitution Convention Museum State Park
200 Allen Memorial Way ... Port Saint Joe FL 32456 850-229-8029
Web: www.floridastateparks.org

Crystal River Archaeological State Park
3400 N Museum Pointe ... Crystal River FL 34428 352-795-3817
Web: www.floridastateparks.org/crystalriver

Dade Battlefield Historic State Park
7200 County Rd 603 S Battlefield Dr ... Bushnell FL 33513 352-793-4781
Web: www.floridastateparks.org

Dagny Johnson Key Largo Hammock Botanical State Park
905 County Rd ... Key Largo FL 33037 305-451-1202
Web: www.floridastateparks.org/keylargohammock

De Leon Springs State Park
601 Ponce De Leon Blvd ... De Leon Springs FL 32130 386-985-4212 985-2014
Web: www.floridastateparks.org

Deer Lake State Park 357 Main Pk Rd ... Santa Rosa Beach FL 32459 850-231-0337 231-1879
Web: www.floridastateparks.org/deerlake

Delnor-Wiggins Pass State Park
11135 Gulfshore Dr ... Naples FL 34108 239-597-6196 597-8223
Web: www.floridastateparks.org/delnorwiggins/default.cfm

Devil's Millhopper Geological State Park
4732 Millhopper Rd ... Gainesville FL 32653 352-955-2008
Web: www.floridastateparks.org/devilsmillhopper

Don Pedro Island State Park
880 Belche Rd ... Boca Grande FL 33921 941-964-0375
Web: www.floridastateparks.org/donpedroisland

Dr Julian G. Bruce Saint George Island State Park
1900 E Gulf Beach Dr ... Saint George Island FL 32328 850-927-2111
Web: www.floridastateparks.org

Dudley Farm Historic State Park
18730 W Newberry Rd ... Newberry FL 32669 352-472-1142
Web: www.floridastateparks.org

Dunn's Creek 320 Cisco Rd ... Pomona Park FL 32181 386-329-3721 329-3718
Web: www.floridastateparks.org

Econfina River State Park
4741 Econfina River Rd ... Lamont FL 32336 850-922-6007
Web: www.floridastateparks.org

Eden Gardens State Park PO Box 26 ... Point Washington FL 32454 850-231-4214
Web: www.floridastateparks.org

Edward Ball Wakulla Springs State Park
550 Wakulla Pk Dr ... Wakulla Springs FL 32327 850-224-5950 561-7251
Web: www.floridastateparks.org

Egmont Key State Park
4801 37th St S ... Saint Petersburg FL 33711 727-893-2627 893-2627
Web: www.floridastateparks.org

Fakahatchee Strand Preserve State Park
137 Coastland Dr ... Copeland FL 34137 239-695-4593
Web: www.floridastateparks.org

Falling Waters State Park 1130 State Pk Rd ... Chipley FL 32428 850-638-6130
Web: www.floridastateparks.org

Fanning Springs State Park
18020 NW Hwy 19 ... Fanning Springs FL 32693 352-463-3420 463-3420
Web: www.floridastateparks.org

Faver-Dykes State Park
1000 Faver Dykes Rd ... Saint Augustine FL 32086 904-794-0997 446-6781*
**Fax Area Code: 386* ■ *Web:* www.floridastateparks.org

Florida Caverns State Park 3345 Caverns Rd ... Marianna FL 32446 850-482-9598
Web: www.floridastateparks.org

Forest Capital Museum State Park
204 Forest Pk Dr ... Perry FL 32348 850-584-3227
Web: www.floridastateparks.org

Fort Clinch State Park
2601 Atlantic Ave ... Fernandina Beach FL 32034 904-277-7274 277-7225
Web: www.floridastateparks.org

Fort Cooper State Park
3100 S Old Floral City Rd ... Inverness FL 34450 352-726-0315
Web: www.floridastateparks.org

Fort George Island Cultural State Park
12157 Heckscher Dr ... Jacksonville FL 32226 904-251-2320
Web: www.floridastateparks.org/fortgeorgeisland

Fort Mose Historic State Park
15 Fort Mose Trail ... Saint Augustine FL 32084 904-823-2232
Web: www.floridastateparks.org/fortmose

Fort Pierce Inlet State Park
905 Shorewinds Dr ... Fort Pierce FL 34949 772-468-3985
Web: www.floridastateparks.org

Fort Zachary Taylor Historic State Park
PO Box 6560 ... Key West FL 33041 305-292-6713 292-6881
Web: www.floridastateparks.org

Fred Gannon Rocky Bayou State Park
4281 E Hwy 20 ... Niceville FL 32578 850-833-9144
Web: www.floridastateparks.org

Gainesville-Hawthorne State Trail
3400 SE 15th St ... Gainesville FL 32641 352-466-3397
Web: www.floridastateparks.org/gainesville-hawthorne

Gamble Plantation Historic State Park
3708 Patten Ave ... Ellenton FL 34222 941-723-4536
Web: www.floridastateparks.org

Gamble Rogers Memorial State Recreation Area at Flagler Beach
3100 S A1A ... Flagler Beach FL 32136 386-517-2086 517-2089
Web: www.floridastateparks.org

Gasparilla Island State Park
880 Belche Rd ... Boca Grande FL 33921 941-964-0375
Web: www.floridastateparks.org/gasparillaisland

Grayton Beach State Park
357 Main Pk Rd ... Santa Rosa Beach FL 32459 850-267-8300
Web: www.floridastateparks.org/graytonbeach

Henderson Beach State Park
17000 Emerald Coast Pkwy ... Destin FL 32541 850-837-7550
Web: www.floridastateparks.org

Highlands Hammock State Park 5931 Hammock Rd ... Sebring FL 33872 863-386-6094 386-6095
Web: www.floridastateparks.org/highlandshammock

Hillsborough River State Park
15402 US 301 N ... Thonotosassa FL 33592 813-987-6771
Web: www.floridastateparks.org

Homosassa Springs Wildlife State Park
4150 S Suncoast Blvd ... Homosassa FL 34446 352-628-5343 628-4243
Web: www.floridastateparks.org

Honeymoon Island State Park 1 Cswy Blvd ... Dunedin FL 34698 727-469-5942
Web: www.floridastateparks.org

Hontoon Island State Park 2309 River Ridge Rd ... DeLand FL 32720 386-736-5309
Web: www.floridastateparks.org

Hugh Taylor Birch State Park
3109 E Sunrise Blvd ... Fort Lauderdale FL 33304 954-564-4521 762-3737
Web: www.floridastateparks.org

Ichetucknee Springs State Park
12087 SW US Hwy 27 ... Fort White FL 32038 386-497-2511
Web: www.floridastateparks.org

Indian Key Historic State Park
US 1 Mile Marker 84 9 ... Islamorada FL 33036 305-664-2540
Web: www.floridastateparks.org/indiankey

John D. MacArthur Beach State Park
10900 SR 703 (A1A) ... North Palm Beach FL 33408 561-624-6950
Web: www.floridastateparks.org

John Gorrie Museum State Park
PO Box 267 ... Apalachicola FL 32329 850-653-9347
Web: www.floridastateparks.org

John Pennekamp Coral Reef State Park
US 1 Mile Marker 102 Hwy ... Key Largo FL 33037 305-451-1202
Web: www.floridastateparks.org/pennekamp

John U. Lloyd Beach State Park 6503 N Ocean Dr ... Dania FL 33004 954-923-2833
Web: www.floridastateparks.org

Jonathan Dickinson State Park
16450 SE Federal Hwy ... Hobe Sound FL 33455 772-546-2771
Web: www.floridastateparks.org

Kissimmee Prairie Preserve State Park
33104 NW 192 Ave ... Okeechobee FL 34972 239-462-5360
Web: www.floridastateparks.org

Koreshan State Historic Site
3800 Corkscrew Rd ... Estero FL 33928 239-992-0311 992-1607
Web: www.floridastateparks.org

Lake Griffin State Park
3089 US 441-27 ... Fruitland Park FL 34731 352-360-6760
Web: www.floridastateparks.org

Lake Jackson Mounds Archaeological State Park
3600 Indian Mounds Rd ... Tallahassee FL 32303 850-922-6007 488-0366
Web: floridastateparks.org/lakejackson/default.cfm

Lake June-in-Winter Scrub State Park
Daffodil Rd ... Sebring FL 33872 863-386-6099
Web: www.floridastateparks.org/lakejuneinwinter

Lake Kissimmee State Park
14248 Camp Mack Rd ... Lake Wales FL 33853 863-696-1112
Web: www.floridastateparks.org

Lake Louisa State Park 7305 US Hwy 27 ... Clermont FL 34714 352-394-3969
Web: www.floridastateparks.org

Lake Manatee State Park 20007 Hwy 64 E ... Bradenton FL 34202 941-741-3028
Web: www.floridastateparks.org

Lake Talquin State Park
1022 DeSoto Pk Dr ... Tallahassee FL 32301 850-922-6007
Web: www.floridastateparks.org

Lignumvitae Key Botanical State Park
Offshore Island ... Islamorada FL 33036 305-664-2540
Web: www.floridastateparks.org/lignumvitaekey

Little Manatee River State Park
215 Lightfoot Rd ... Wimauma FL 33598 813-671-5005
Web: www.floridastateparks.org

Little Talbot Island State Park
12157 Heckscher Dr ... Jacksonville FL 32226 904-251-2320 251-2325
Web: www.floridastateparks.org/littletalbotisland

Long Key State Park PO Box 776 ... Long Key FL 33001 305-664-4815
Web: www.floridastateparks.org

Lovers Key State Park
8700 Estero Blvd ... Fort Myers Beach FL 33931 239-463-4588 463-8851
Web: www.floridastateparks.org

Lower Wekiva River Preserve State Park
1800 Wekiwa Cir ... Apopka FL 32712 407-884-2008 884-2039
Web: www.floridastateparks.org

Manatee Springs State Park
11650 NW 115th St ... Chiefland FL 32626 352-493-6072
Web: www.floridastateparks.org

Marjorie Kinnan Rawlings Historic State Park
18700 S County Rd 325 ... Cross Creek FL 32640 352-466-3672
Web: www.floridastateparks.org

Mike Roess Gold Head Branch State Park
6239 SR 21 ... Keystone Heights FL 32656 352-473-4701
Web: www.floridastateparks.org

Myakka River State Park 13208 SR 72 ... Sarasota FL 34241 941-361-6511 361-6501
TF: 800-326-3521 ■ *Web:* www.floridastateparks.org

Natural Bridge Battlefield Historic State Park
7502 Natural Bridge Rd ... Tallahassee FL 32305 850-922-6007 488-0366
Web: www.floridastateparks.org/naturalbridge

O'Leno State Park 410 SE Oleno Pk Rd ... High Springs FL 32643 386-454-1853
Web: www.floridastateparks.org

Ochlockonee River State Park
429 State Pk Rd ... Sopchoppy FL 32358 850-962-2771
Web: www.floridastateparks.org

Oleta River State Park
3400 NE 163rd St ... North Miami Beach FL 33160 305-919-1846 919-1845
Web: www.floridastateparks.org

Olustee Battlefield Historic State Park
PO Box 40 ... Olustee FL 32072 386-758-0400
Web: www.floridastateparks.org

Oscar Scherer State Park 1843 S Tamiami Trail ... Osprey FL 34229 941-483-5956 480-3007
Web: www.floridastateparks.org

	City	State	Zip	Phone	Fax
Paynes Creek Historic State Park 888 Lake Branch Rd *Web:* www.floridastateparks.org	Bowling Green	FL	33834	863-375-4717	375-4510
Paynes Prairie Preserve State Park 100 Savannah Blvd *Web:* www.floridastateparks.org	Micanopy	FL	32667	352-466-3397	
Peacock Springs State Park Administration Office 18081 185th Rd *Web:* www.floridastateparks.org	Live Oak	FL	32060	386-776-2194	
Perdido Key State Park 15301 Perdido Key Dr *Web:* www.floridastateparks.org/perdidokey	Pensacola	FL	32507	850-492-1595	492-4380
Ponce de Leon Springs State Park 2860 Ponce de Leon Springs Rd *Web:* www.floridastateparks.org	Ponce de Leon	FL	32455	850-836-4281	
Rainbow Springs State Park 19158 SW 81st Pl Rd *Web:* www.floridastateparks.org	Dunnellon	FL	34432	352-465-8555	
Ravine Gardens State Park 1600 Twigg St *Web:* www.floridastateparks.org	Palatka	FL	32177	386-329-3721	329-3718
Rock Springs Run State Reserve 30601 CR 433 *Web:* www.floridastateparks.org/rockspringsrun	Sorrento	FL	32776	407-884-2008	884-2039
Saint Andrews State Park 4607 State Pk Ln *Web:* www.floridastateparks.org	Panama City	FL	32408	850-233-5140	
Saint Lucie Inlet Preserve State Park 4810 SE Cove Rd *Web:* www.floridastateparks.org	Stuart	FL	34997	772-219-1880	
San Felasco Hammock Preserve State Park 12720 NW 109 Ln *Web:* www.floridastateparks.org	Alachua	FL	32615	386-462-7905	
San Marcos de Apalache Historic State Park 148 Old Fort Rd *Web:* www.floridastateparks.org	Saint Marks	FL	31355	850-925-6216	
San Pedro Underwater Archaeological Preserve State Park US 1 *Web:* www.floridastateparks.org/sanpedro	Islamorada	FL	33036	305-664-2540	
Savannas Preserve State Park 9551 Gumbo Limbo Ln *Web:* www.floridastateparks.org	Jensen Beach	FL	34957	772-398-2779	
Sebastian Inlet State Park 9700 S A1A *Web:* www.floridastateparks.org	Melbourne Beach	FL	32951	321-984-4852	984-4854
Silver River State Park 1425 NE 58th Ave *Web:* www.floridastateparks.org	Ocala	FL	34470	352-236-7148	236-7150
Stephen Foster Folk Culture Center State Park 11016 Lillian Saunders Dr *Web:* www.floridastateparks.org	White Springs	FL	32096	386-397-2733	
Stump Pass Beach State Park Barrier Islands State Parks PO Box 1150 *Web:* www.floridastateparks.org	Boca Grande	FL	33921	941-964-0375	964-1154
Suwannee River State Park 3631 201st Path *Web:* www.floridastateparks.org	Live Oak	FL	32060	386-362-2746	
Tarkiln Bayou Preserve State Park c/o Big Lagoon State Pk *Web:* www.floridastateparks.org	Pensacola	FL	32507	850-492-1595	
TH Stone Memorial Saint Joseph Peninsula State Park 8899 Cape San Blas Rd *Web:* www.floridastateparks.org	Port Saint Joe	FL	32456	850-227-1327	227-1488
Three Rivers State Park 7908 Three Rivers Pk Rd *Web:* www.floridastateparks.org	Sneads	FL	32460	850-482-9006	
Tomoka State Park 2099 N Beach St *Web:* www.floridastateparks.org/tomoka	Ormond Beach	FL	32174	386-676-4050	676-4050
Topsail Hill Preserve State Park 7525 W Scenic Hwy 30A *Web:* www.floridastateparks.org	Santa Rosa Beach	FL	32459	850-267-0299	
Torreya State Park 2576 NW Torreya Pk Rd *Web:* www.floridastateparks.org	Bristol	FL	32321	850-643-2674	
Waccasassa Bay Preserve State Park 8312 SW 125th Ct *Web:* www.floridastateparks.org/waccasassabay	Cedar Key	FL	32625	352-543-5567	
Washington Oaks Gardens State Park 6400 N Oceanshore Blvd *Web:* www.floridastateparks.org	Palm Coast	FL	32173	386-446-6780	446-6781
Wekiwa Springs State Park 1800 Wekiwa Cir *Web:* www.floridastateparks.org/wekiwasprings	Apopka	FL	32712	407-884-2008	884-2039
Werner-Boyce Salt Springs State Park PO Box 490 *Web:* www.floridastateparks.org	Port Richey	FL	34673	727-816-1890	816-1888
William Beardall Tosohatchee State Reserve 3365 Taylor Creek Rd	Christmas	FL	32709	407-568-5893	568-1704
Windley Key Fossil Reef Geological State Park US 1 Mile Marker 84 9 *Web:* www.floridastateparks.org/windleykey	Islamorada	FL	33036	305-664-2540	
Ybor City Museum State Park 1818 9th Ave *Web:* www.floridastateparks.org	Tampa	FL	33605	813-247-6323	
Yulee Sugar Mill Ruins Historic State Park c/o Crystal River Archaeological State Pk 3400 N Museum Pointe *Web:* www.floridastateparks.org/yuleesugarmill	Crystal River	FL	34428	352-795-3817	

GEORGIA

	City	State	Zip	Phone	Fax
AH Stephens State Historic Park 456 Alexander St NW *Web:* www.gastateparks.org	Crawfordville	GA	30631	706-456-2602	
Amicalola Falls State Park & Lodge 418 Amicalola Falls State Pk Rd *Web:* www.gastateparks.org	Dawsonville	GA	30534	706-265-4703	
Black Rock Mountain State Park 3085 Black Rock Mountain Pkwy *Web:* www.gastateparks.org	Mountain City	GA	30562	706-746-2141	
Bobby Brown State Park 2509 Bobby Brown State Pk Rd *Web:* www.gastateparks.org/info/bobbybrown	Elberton	GA	30635	706-213-2046	
Chief Vann House State Historic Site 82 Hwy 225 N *Web:* www.gastateparks.org	Chatsworth	GA	30705	706-695-2598	
Cloudland Canyon State Park 122 Cloudland Canyon Pk *Web:* www.gastateparks.org	Rising Fawn	GA	30738	706-657-4050	
Crooked River State Park 6222 Charlie Smith Sr Hwy *Web:* www.gastateparks.org	Saint Mary's	GA	31558	912-882-5256	
Dahlonega Gold Museum State Historic Site 1 Public Sq *Web:* www.gastateparks.org	Dahlonega	GA	30533	706-864-2257	
Elijah Clark State Park 2959 McCormick Hwy *Web:* www.gastateparks.org	Lincolnton	GA	30817	706-359-3458	
Etowah Indian Mounds State Historic Site 813 Indian Mounds Rd SW *Web:* www.gastateparks.org	Cartersville	GA	30120	770-387-3747	
FD Roosevelt State Park 2970 GA Hwy 190 *TF:* 800-864-7275 ■ *Web:* www.gastateparks.org	Pine Mountain	GA	31822	706-663-4858	663-8906
Florence Marina State Park Rt 1 PO Box 36 *Web:* www.gastateparks.org	Omaha	GA	31821	229-838-4244	
Fort King George State Historic Site 1600 Wayne St *Web:* www.gastateparks.org	Darien	GA	31305	912-437-4770	
Fort McAllister State Historic Park 3894 Fort McAllister Rd *TF:* 800-864-7275 ■ *Web:* www.gastateparks.org	Richmond Hill	GA	31324	912-727-2339	727-3614
Fort Morris State Historic Site 2559 Fort Morris Rd *Web:* www.gastateparks.org	Midway	GA	31320	912-884-5999	
Fort Mountain State Park 181 Fort Mountain Pk Rd *Web:* www.gastateparks.org	Chatsworth	GA	30705	706-695-2621	
Fort Yargo State Park 210 S Broad St *Web:* www.gastateparks.org	Winder	GA	30680	770-867-3489	
General Coffee State Park 46 John Coffee Rd *Web:* www.gastateparks.org	Nicholls	GA	31554	912-384-7082	
George L. Smith State Park 371 Geo L Smith St Pk Rd *Web:* www.gastateparks.org	Twin City	GA	30471	478-763-2759	
George T. Bagby State Park & Lodge 330 Bagby Pkwy *Web:* www.gastateparks.org	Fort Gaines	GA	31751	229-768-2571	
Georgia Veterans State Park 2459 US 280 W *Web:* www.gastateparks.org	Cordele	GA	31015	229-276-2371	
Gordonia-Alatamaha State Park 322 Pk Ln US 280 W *Web:* www.gastateparks.org	Reidsville	GA	30453	912-557-7744	
Hamburg State Park 6071 Hamburg State Pk Rd *Web:* www.gastateparks.org	Mitchell	GA	30820	478-552-2393	
Hard Labor Creek State Park Knox Chapel Rd *Web:* www.gastateparks.org	Rutledge	GA	30663	706-557-3001	
Hart State Park 330 Hart Pk Rd *Web:* www.gastateparks.org	Hartwell	GA	30643	706-376-8756	
High Falls State Park 76 High Falls Pk Dr *Web:* www.gastateparks.org	Jackson	GA	30233	478-993-3053	
Hofwyl-Broadfield Plantation State Historic Site 5556 US Hwy 17 N *Web:* www.gastateparks.org	Brunswick	GA	31525	912-264-7333	
Indian Springs State Park 678 Lake Clark Rd *Web:* www.gastateparks.org	Flovilla	GA	30216	770-504-2277	
James H. Sloppy Floyd State Park 2800 Sloppy Floyd Lake Rd *Web:* www.gastateparks.org	Summerville	GA	30747	706-857-0826	
Jarrell Plantation State Historic Site 711 Jarrell Plantation Rd *Web:* www.gastateparks.org	Juliette	GA	31046	478-986-5172	
Jefferson Davis Memorial State Historic Site 338 Jeff Davis Pk Rd *Web:* www.gastateparks.org	Fitzgerald	GA	31750	229-831-2335	
John Tanner State Park 354 Tanner's Beach Rd *Web:* www.gastateparks.org	Carrollton	GA	30117	770-830-2222	
Kolomoki Mounds State Historic Park 205 Indian Mounds Rd *Web:* www.gastateparks.org	Blakely	GA	39823	229-724-2150	
Lapham-Patterson House State Historic Site 626 N Dawson St *Web:* www.gastateparks.org	Thomasville	GA	31792	229-225-4004	
Laura S. Walker State Park 5653 Laura Walker Rd *Web:* www.gastateparks.org	Waycross	GA	31503	912-287-4900	
Little Ocmulgee State Park & Lodge PO Drawer 149 *Web:* www.gastateparks.org	McRae	GA	31055	229-868-7474	
Little White House State Historic Site 401 Little White House Rd *Web:* gastateparks.org/info/littlewhite	Warm Springs	GA	31830	706-655-5870	655-5872
Magnolia Springs State Park 1053 Magnolia Springs Dr *Web:* www.gastateparks.org	Millen	GA	30442	478-982-1660	
Mistletoe State Park 3723 Mistletoe Rd *Web:* www.gastateparks.org	Appling	GA	30802	706-541-0321	
Moccasin Creek State Park 3655 Hwy 197 *Web:* www.gastateparks.org	Clarkesville	GA	30523	706-947-3194	

			Phone	Fax
New Echota State Historic Site 1211 Chatsworth Hwy NE.....Calhoun *Web:* www.gastateparks.org	GA	30701	706-624-1321	
Panola Mountain State Park 2600 Georgia 155.....Stockbridge *Web:* www.gastateparks.org	GA	30281	770-389-7801	
Pickett's Mill Battlefield State Historic Site 4432 Mt Tabor Church Rd.....Dallas *Web:* www.gastateparks.org	GA	30157	770-443-7850	
Providence Canyon State Park Rt 1 PO Box 158.....Lumpkin *Web:* www.gastateparks.org	GA	31815	229-838-6202	838-6735
Red Top Mountain State Park & Lodge 659 Red Top Mountain Rd SE.....Cartersville *Web:* www.gastateparks.org	GA	30121	770-975-0055	
Reed Bingham State Park 542 Reed Bingham Rd.....Adel *Web:* www.gastateparks.org	GA	31620	229-896-3551	
Richard B. Russell State Park 2650 Russell State Pk Rd.....Elberton *Web:* www.gastateparks.org	GA	30635	706-213-2045	
Robert Toombs House State Historic Site 216 E Robert Toombs Ave.....Washington *Web:* www.gastateparks.org	GA	30673	706-678-2226	
Seminole State Park 7870 State Pk Dr.....Donalsonville *Web:* www.gastateparks.org	GA	39845	229-861-3137	
Skidaway Island State Park 52 Diamond Cswy.....Savannah *Web:* www.gastateparks.org/info/skidaway	GA	31411	912-598-2300	598-2365
Smithgall Woods Conservation Area & Lodge 61 Tsalaki Trail.....Helen *Web:* www.gastateparks.org/info/smithgall	GA	30545	706-878-3087	
Sprewell Bluff State Park 740 Sprewell Bluff Rd.....Thomaston *Web:* www.gastateparks.org	GA	30286	706-646-6026	
Stephen C. Foster State Park 17515 Hwy 177.....Fargo *Web:* www.gastateparks.org	GA	31631	912-637-5274	
Sweetwater Creek State Park 1750 Mt Vernon Rd PO Box 816.....Lithia Springs *Web:* www.gastateparks.org/SweetwaterCreek	GA	30122	770-732-5871	
Tallulah Gorge State Park 338 Jane Hurt Yarn Dr.....Tallulah Falls *Web:* www.gastateparks.org	GA	30573	706-754-7970	
Traveler's Rest State Historic Site 4339 Riverdale Rd.....Toccoa *Web:* www.gastateparks.org	GA	30577	706-886-2256	
Tugaloo State Park 1763 Tugaloo State Pk Rd.....Lavonia *Web:* www.gastateparks.org	GA	30553	706-356-4362	
Unicoi State Park & Lodge 1788 Hwy 356 Rd.....Helen *TF:* 800-573-9659 ■ *Web:* www.gastateparks.org/info/unicoi	GA	30545	800-573-9659	
Victoria Bryant State Park 166 Bryant Pk Cir.....Royston *Web:* www.gastateparks.org	GA	30662	706-245-6270	
Vogel State Park 7485 Vogel State Pk Rd.....Blairsville *Web:* www.gastateparks.org	GA	30512	706-745-2628	
Watson Mill Bridge State Park 650 Watson Mill Rd.....Comer *Web:* www.gastateparks.org	GA	30629	706-783-5349	
Wormsloe State Historic Site 7601 Skidaway Rd.....Savannah *Web:* www.gastateparks.org/info/wormsloe	GA	31406	912-353-3023	692-4530

HAWAII

			Phone	Fax
Ahukini State Recreation Pier c/o Kauai District Office 3060 Eiwa St, Rm 306.....Lihue *Web:* www.hawaii.gov	HI	96766	808-274-3444	
Aiea Bay State Recreation Area c/o Oahu District Office PO Box 621.....Honolulu *Web:* www.hawaiistateparks.org/parks/oahu/index.cfm?park_id=14	HI	96809	808-587-0300	
Akaka Falls State Park c/o Hawaii District Office PO Box 936.....Hilo *Web:* www.hawaii.gov	HI	96721	808-974-6200	
Diamond Head State Monument c/o Oahu District Office PO Box 621.....Honolulu *Web:* www.hawaii.gov	HI	96809	808-587-0300	
Haena State Park c/o Kauai District Office 3060 Eiwa St, Rm 306.....Lihue *Web:* www.hawaii.gov	HI	96766	808-274-3444	
Halekii-Pihana Heiau State Monument c/o Maui District Office 54 S High St, Rm 101.....Wailuku *Web:* www.hawaii.gov	HI	96793	808-984-8109	
Hanauma Bay State Underwater Park c/o Oahu District Office PO Box 621.....Honolulu *Web:* www.hawaii.gov	HI	96809	808-587-0300	
Hapuna Beach State Recreation Area c/o Hawaii District Office PO Box 936.....Hilo *Web:* www.hawaii.gov	HI	96721	808-974-6200	
Heeia State Park c/o Oahu District Office PO Box 621.....Honolulu *Web:* www.hawaii.gov	HI	96809	808-587-0300	
Iao Valley State Monument c/o Maui District Office 54 S High St, Rm 101.....Wailuku *Web:* www.hawaii.gov	HI	96793	808-984-8109	
Iolani Palace State Monument c/o Oahu District Office PO Box 621.....Honolulu *Web:* www.hawaii.gov	HI	96809	808-587-0300	
Kaena Point State Park c/o Oahu District Office PO Box 621.....Honolulu *Web:* www.hawaii.gov	HI	96809	808-587-0300	
Kahana Valley State Park c/o Oahu District Office PO Box 621.....Honolulu *Web:* www.hawaii.gov	HI	96809	808-587-0300	
Kakaako Waterfront Park c/o Oahu District Office PO Box 621.....Honolulu *Web:* www.hawaii.gov	HI	96809	808-587-0300	
Kalopa State Recreation Area c/o Hawaii District Office PO Box 936.....Hilo *Web:* www.hawaii.gov	HI	96721	808-974-6200	
Kaumahina State Wayside c/o Maui District Office 54 S High St, Rm 101.....Wailuku *Web:* www.hawaii.gov	HI	96793	808-984-8109	
Keaiwa Heiau State Recreation Area c/o Oahu District Office PO Box 621.....Honolulu *Web:* www.hawaii.gov	HI	96809	808-587-0300	
Kealakekua Bay State Historical Park c/o Hawaii District Office PO Box 936.....Hilo *Web:* www.hawaii.gov	HI	96721	808-974-6200	
Kekaha Kai (Kona Coast) State Park c/o Hawaii District Office PO Box 936.....Hilo *Web:* www.hawaii.gov	HI	96721	808-974-6200	
Kohala Historical Sites State Monument c/o Hawaii District Office PO Box 936.....Hilo *Web:* www.hawaii.gov	HI	96721	808-974-6200	
Kokee State Park c/o Kauai District Office 3060 Eiwa St, Rm 306.....Lihue *Web:* www.hawaii.gov	HI	96766	808-274-3444	
Kukaniloko Birthstones State Monument c/o Oahu District Office PO Box 621.....Honolulu *Web:* www.hawaiistateparks.org/parks/oahu/index.cfm?park_id=24	HI	96809	808-587-0300	
Laie Point State Wayside c/o Oahu District Office PO Box 621.....Honolulu *Web:* www.hawaiistateparks.org/parks/oahu/index.cfm?park_id=25	HI	96809	808-587-0300	
Lapakahi State Historical Park c/o Hawaii District Office PO Box 936.....Hilo *Web:* www.hawaii.gov	HI	96721	808-974-6200	
Lava Tree State Monument c/o Hawaii District Office PO Box 936.....Hilo *Web:* www.hawaii.gov	HI	96721	808-974-6200	
MacKenzie State Recreation Area c/o Hawaii District Office PO Box 936.....Hilo *Web:* www.hawaii.gov	HI	96721	808-974-6200	
Makapuu Point State Wayside c/o Oahu District Office PO Box 621.....Honolulu *Web:* www.wildernet.com/pages/area.cfm?areaID=HISPMP&CU_ID=1	HI	96809	808-587-0300	
Malaekahana State Recreation Area c/o Oahu District Office PO Box 621.....Honolulu *Web:* www.hawaii.gov	HI	96809	808-587-0300	
Manuka State Wayside c/o Hawaii District Office PO Box 936.....Hilo *Web:* www.hawaiistateparks.org/parks/hawaii/index.cfm?park_id=53	HI	96721	808-974-6200	
Mauna Kea State Recreation Area c/o Hawaii District Office PO Box 936.....Hilo *Web:* www.hawaii.gov	HI	96721	808-974-6200	
Na Pali Coast State Park c/o Kauai District Office 3060 Eiwa St, Rm 306.....Lihue *Web:* www.state.hi.us	HI	96766	808-274-3444	
Nuuanu Pali State Wayside c/o Oahu District Office PO Box 621.....Honolulu *Web:* www.hawaii.gov	HI	96809	808-587-0300	
Old Kona Airport State Recreation Area c/o Hawaii District Office PO Box 936.....Hilo *Web:* www.hawaii.gov	HI	96721	808-974-6200	
Palaau State Park c/o Oahu District Office PO Box 621.....Honolulu *Web:* www.hawaii.gov	HI	96809	808-587-0300	
Polihale State Park c/o Kauai District Office 3060 Eiwa St, Rm 306.....Lihue *Web:* www.hawaii.gov	HI	96766	808-274-3444	
Polipoli Spring State Recreation Area c/o Maui District Office 54 S High St, Rm 101.....Wailuku *Web:* www.hawaii.gov	HI	96793	808-984-8109	
Puaa Kaa State Wayside c/o Maui District Office 54 S High St, Rm 101.....Wailuku *Web:* www.hawaii.gov	HI	96793	808-984-8109	
Puu o Mahuka Heiau State Monument c/o Oahu District Office PO Box 621.....Honolulu *Web:* www.hawaii.gov	HI	96809	808-587-0300	
Puu Ualakaa State Wayside c/o Oahu District Office PO Box 621.....Honolulu *Web:* www.hawaii.gov	HI	96809	808-587-0300	
Royal Mausoleum State Monument c/o Oahu District Office PO Box 621.....Honolulu *Web:* www.hawaii.gov	HI	96809	808-587-0300	
Russian Fort Elizabeth State Historical Park c/o Kauai District Office 3060 Eiwa St, Rm 306.....Honolulu *Web:* www.hawaii.gov	HI	96766	808-274-3444	
Sand Island State Recreation Area c/o Oahu District Office PO Box 621.....Honolulu *Web:* www.hawaii.gov	HI	96809	808-587-0300	
Ulupo Heiau State Monument c/o Oahu District Office PO Box 621.....Honolulu *Web:* www.hawaii.gov	HI	96809	808-587-0300	
Waahila Ridge State Recreation Area c/o Oahu District Office PO Box 621.....Honolulu *Web:* www.hawaii.gov	HI	96809	808-587-0300	
Wahiawa Freshwater State Recreation Area c/o Oahu District Office PO Box 621.....Honolulu *Web:* www.hawaii.gov	HI	96809	808-587-0300	

	Phone	Fax

Waianapanapa State Park
c/o Maui District Office
54 S High St, Rm 101 . . . Wailuku HI 96793 808-984-8109
Web: www.hawaii.gov

Wailoa River State Recreation Area
c/o Hawaii District Office PO Box 936 . . . Hilo HI 96721 808-964-6200
Web: www.hawaii.gov

Wailua River State Park
c/o Kauai District Office 3060 Eiwa St, Rm 306 . . . Lihue HI 96766 808-274-3444
Web: www.hawaii.gov

Wailua Valley State Wayside
c/o Maui District Office
54 S High St, Rm 101 . . . Wailuku HI 96793 808-984-8109
Web: www.hawaii.gov

Wailuku River State Park
c/o Hawaii District Office PO Box 936 . . . Hilo HI 96721 808-974-6200
Web: www.hawaii.gov

Waimea Canyon State Park
c/o Kauai District Office 3060 Eiwa St, Rm 306 . . . Lihue HI 96766 808-274-3444
Web: www.hawaii.gov

Waimea State Recreation Pier
c/o Kauai District Office 3060 Eiwa St, Rm 306 . . . Lihue HI 96766 808-274-3444

IDAHO

	Phone	Fax

Bear Lake State Park PO Box 297 . . . Paris ID 83261 208-847-1045 847-1056
TF: 866-634-3246 ■ *Web:* www.idahoparks.org/parks/bearlake.aspx

Bruneau Dunes State Park
27608 Sand Dunes Rd . . . Mountain Home ID 83647 208-366-7919 366-2844
Web: www.parksandrecreation.idaho.gov

Coeur d'Alene Parkway State Park
2885 Kathleen Ave Suite 1 . . . Coeur d'Alene ID 83815 208-699-2224
Web: www.parksandrecreation.idaho.gov

Dworshak State Park PO Box 115 . . . Ahsahka ID 83520 208-476-5994
Web: www.idahoparks.org/parks/dworshak.aspx

Eagle Island State Park 4000 W Hatchery Rd . . . Eagle ID 83616 208-939-0696 939-9708
Web: www.idahoparks.org

Farragut State Park 13550 E Hwy 54 . . . Athol ID 83801 208-683-2425 683-7416
Web: www.idahoparks.org

Harriman State Park 3489 Green Canyon Rd . . . Island Park ID 83429 208-558-7368 558-7045
TF: 866-634-3246 ■ *Web:* www.idahoparks.org

Hells Gate State Park 5100 Hells Gate Rd . . . Lewiston ID 83501 208-799-5015 799-5187
TF: 866-634-3246 ■ *Web:* www.idahoparks.org

Henrys Lake State Park 3917 E 5100 N . . . Island Park ID 83429 208-558-7532
TF: 866-634-3246 ■ *Web:* www.idahoparks.org/parks/henryslake.aspx

Heyburn State Park 1291 Chatcolet Rd . . . Plummer ID 83851 208-686-1308 686-3003
TF: 866-634-3246 ■ *Web:* www.idahoparks.org

Lake Cascade State Park PO Box 709 . . . Cascade ID 83611 208-382-6544 382-4071
TF: 866-634-3246 ■ *Web:* www.parksandrecreation.idaho.gov

Lake Walcott State Park 959 E Minidoka Dam . . . Rupert ID 83350 208-436-1258 436-1268
Web: www.parksandrecreation.idaho.gov

Land of the Yankee Fork State Park
PO Box 1086 . . . Challis ID 83226 208-879-5244 879-5243
Web: www.parksandrecreation.idaho.gov

Lucky Peak State Park 9725 E Hwy 21 . . . Boise ID 83716 208-334-2432
Web: www.idahoparks.org

Massacre Rocks State Park
3592 N Pk Ln . . . American Falls ID 83211 208-548-2672 548-2671
Web: www.idahoparks.org

McCroskey State Park 2750 Kathleen Ave . . . Coeur d'Alene ID 83815 208-666-6711
Web: www.idahoparks.org

Old Mission State Park PO Box 30 . . . Cataldo ID 83810 208-682-3814 682-4032
Web: www.idahoparks.org/parks/oldmission.aspx

Ponderosa State Park PO Box 89 . . . McCall ID 83638 208-634-2164 634-5370
Web: www.idahoparks.org

Priest Lake State Park
1314 Indian Creek Pk Rd . . . Coolin ID 83821 208-443-2200 443-3893
TF: 866-634-3246 ■ *Web:* www.idahoparks.org/parks/priestlake.aspx

Round Lake State Park PO Box 170 . . . Sagle ID 83860 208-263-3489
TF: 866-634-3246 ■ *Web:* www.idahoparks.org/parks/roundlake.aspx

Three Island Crossing State Park
PO Box 609 . . . Glenns Ferry ID 83623 208-366-2394 366-7913
TF: 866-634-3246 ■ *Web:* www.idahoparks.org

Winchester Lake State Park PO Box 186 . . . Winchester ID 83555 208-924-7563 924-5941
TF: 866-634-3246 ■ *Web:* www.idahoparks.org

ILLINOIS

	Phone	Fax

Anderson Lake Conservation Area
647 N State Hwy 100 . . . Astoria IL 61501 309-759-4484
Web: www.dnr.state.il.us

Apple River Canyon State Park
8763 E Canyon Rd . . . Apple River IL 61001 815-745-3302
Web: www.dnr.state.il.us

Argyle Lake State Park 640 Argyle Pk Rd . . . Colchester IL 62326 309-776-3422
Web: www.dnr.state.il.us

Banner Marsh State Fish & Wildlife Area
19721 N US 24 . . . Canton IL 61520 309-647-9184
Web: www.dnr.state.il.us/Lands/Landmgt/PARKS/R1/banner.htm

Beall Woods State Park
9285 Beall Woods Ave . . . Mount Carmel IL 62863 618-298-2442
Web: www.dnr.state.il.us

Beaver Dam State Park 14548 Beaver Dam Ln . . . Plainview IL 62685 217-854-8020
Web: www.dnr.state.il.us

Big Bend State Fish & Wildlife Area
PO Box 181 . . . Prophetstown IL 61277 815-537-2270
Web: www.dnr.state.il.us/lands/Landmgt/PARKS/R1/BIGBEND.HTM

Big River State Forest RR 1 PO Box 118 . . . Keithsburg IL 61442 309-374-2496
Web: www.dnr.state.il.us/Lands/Landmgt/PARKS/R1/BIGRIVER.HTM

	Phone	Fax

Buffalo Rock State Park & Effigy Tumuli
1300 N 27th Rd PO Box 2034 . . . Ottawa IL 61350 815-433-2220
Web: www.dnr.state.il.us

Cache River State Natural Area
930 Sunflower Ln . . . Belknap IL 62908 618-634-9678
Web: www.dnr.state.il.us

Cahokia Mounds State Historic Site
30 Ramey St . . . Collinsville IL 62234 618-346-5160 346-5162
Web: www.cahokiamounds.com

Carlyle Lake State Fish & Wildlife Area
RR 2 . . . Vandalia IL 62471 618-425-3533
Web: www.dnr.state.il.us

Castle Rock State Park 1365 W Castle Rd . . . Oregon IL 61061 815-732-7329
Web: www.dnr.state.il.us/Lands/Landmgt/PARKS/R1/CASTLE.HTM

Cave-In-Rock State Park
1 New State Pk Rd PO Box 338 . . . Cave-In-Rock IL 62919 618-289-4325
Web: www.dnr.state.il.us

Chain O'Lakes State Park 8916 Wilmot Rd . . . Spring Grove IL 60081 847-587-5512
Web: www.dnr.state.il.us

Channahon State Park 25302 W Story St . . . Channahon IL 60410 815-467-4271
Web: www.dnr.state.il.us

Clinton Lake State Recreation Area
RR 1 PO Box 4 . . . DeWitt IL 61735 217-935-8722
Web: www.dnr.state.il.us

Coffeen Lake State Fish & Wildlife Area
15084 N 4th Ave . . . Coffeen IL 62017 217-537-3351
Web: www.dnr.state.il.us

Crawford County State Fish & Wildlife Area
12609 E 1700th Ave . . . Hutsonville IL 62433 618-563-4405
Web: www.dnr.state.il.us

Delabar State Park RR 2 PO Box 27 . . . Oquawka IL 61469 309-374-2496
Web: www.dnr.state.il.us

Des Plaines State Fish & Wildlife Area
24621 N River Rd . . . Wilmington IL 60481 815-423-5326
Web: www.dnr.state.il.us

Dixon Springs State Park RR 2 PO Box 178 . . . Golconda IL 62938 618-949-3394
Web: www.dnr.state.il.us

Donnelley/DePue State Fish & Wildlife Areas
1001 W 4th St PO Box 52 . . . DePue IL 61322 815-447-2353
Web: www.dnr.state.il.us

Eagle Creek State Recreation Area PO Box 16 . . . Findlay IL 62534 217-756-8260
Web: www.dnr.state.il.us

Edward R. Madigan State Fish & Wildlife Area
1366 1010th Ave . . . Lincoln IL 62656 217-735-2424
Web: www.dnr.state.il.us

Eldon Hazlet State Recreation Area
20100 Hazlet Pk Rd . . . Carlyle IL 62231 618-594-3015
Web: www.dnr.state.il.us/Lands/Landmgt/PARKS/R4/ELDON.HTM

Ferne Clyffe State Park PO Box 10 . . . Goreville IL 62939 618-995-2411
Web: www.dnr.state.il.us

Fort Massac State Park 1308 E 5th St . . . Metropolis IL 62960 618-524-4712
Web: www.dnr.state.il.us

Fox Ridge State Park 18175 State Pk Rd . . . Charleston IL 61920 217-345-6416
Web: www.dnr.state.il.us

Frank Holten State Recreation Area
4500 Pocket Rd . . . East Saint Louis IL 62205 618-874-7920
Web: www.dnr.state.il.us

Franklin Creek State Natural Area
1872 Twist Rd . . . Franklin Grove IL 61031 815-456-2878
Web: www.dnr.state.il.us

Fults Hill Prairie & Kidd Lake State Natural Areas
c/o Randolph County State Recreation Area
4301 S Lake Dr . . . Chester IL 62233 618-826-2706
Web: dnr.state.il.us/Lands/Landmgt/PARKS/R4/fhp.htm

Gebhard Woods State Park
401 Ottawa St PO Box 272 . . . Morris IL 60450 815-942-0796
Web: www.dnr.state.il.us/Lands/Landmgt/PARKS/I&M/EAST/GEBHARD/Park.htm

Giant City State Park 235 Giant City Rd . . . Makanda IL 62958 618-457-4836
Web: www.dnr.state.il.us

Goose Lake Prairie State Natural Area
5010 N Jugtown Rd . . . Morris IL 60450 815-942-2899
Web: www.dnr.state.il.us/Lands/Landmgt/PARKS/I&M/EAST/GOOSE/HOME.HTM

Green River State Wildlife Area 375 Game Rd . . . Harmon IL 61042 815-379-2324
Web: www.dnr.state.il.us

Hamilton County State Fish & Wildlife Area
RR 4 PO Box 242 . . . McLeansboro IL 62859 618-773-4340
Web: www.dnr.state.il.us

Harry "Babe" Woodyard State Natural Area
19284 E 670 N . . . Georgetown IL 61846 217-442-4915
Web: www.dnr.state.il.us

Hazel & Bill Rutherford Wildlife Prairie State Park
3826 N Taylor Rd . . . Hanna City IL 61536 309-676-0998 676-7783
Web: www.wildlifeprairiestatepark.org

Heidecke Lake State Fish & Wildlife Area
5010 N Jugtown Rd . . . Morris IL 60450 815-942-6352
Web: www.dnr.state.il.us

Henderson County Conservation Area
PO Box 118 . . . Keithsburg IL 61442 309-374-2496
Web: www.dnr.state.il.us/lands/Landmgt/PARKS/R1/HENDERSO.HTM

Hennepin Canal Parkway State Park
16006 875 E St . . . Sheffield IL 61361 815-454-2328
Web: www.dnr.state.il.us/Lands/Landmgt/PARKS/R1/HENNPIN.HTM

Hidden Springs State Forest
RR 1 PO Box 200 . . . Strasburg IL 62465 217-644-3091
Web: www.dnr.state.il.us

Horseshoe Lake State Fish & Wildlife Area (Alexander County)
21204 Promised Land Rd . . . Miller City IL 62962 618-776-5689
Web: www.dnr.state.il.us

Horseshoe Lake State Park (Madison County)
3321 Hwy 111 . . . Granite City IL 62040 618-931-0270
Web: www.dnr.state.il.us

Illini State Park 2660 E 2350th Rd . . . Marseilles IL 61341 815-795-2448
Web: www.dnr.state.il.us/Lands/Landmgt/PARKS/I&M/EAST/ILLINI/PARK.HTM

Name / Address	City	State	ZIP	Phone	Fax
Illinois & Michigan Canal State Trail PO Box 272	Morris	IL	60450	815-942-0796	942-9690
Web: www.dnr.state.il.us/Lands/Landmgt/PARKS/I&M/Main.htm					
Illinois Beach State Park Lake Front	Zion	IL	60099	847-662-4811	662-6433
Web: www.dnr.state.il.us					
Illinois Caverns State Natural Area 10981 Conservation Rd	Baldwin	IL	62217	618-458-6699	
Web: www.dnr.state.il.us					
Iroquois County State Wildlife Area RR 1 2803 E 3300 N Rd	Beaverville	IL	60912	815-435-2218	
Web: www.dnr.state.il.us					
Jim Edgar Panther Creek State Fish & Wildlife Area (JEPC) 10149 County Hwy 11	Chandlerville	IL	62627	217-452-7741	
Web: www.dnr.state.il.us/Lands/Landmgt/PARKS/R4/jepc.htm					
Johnson-Sauk Trail State Park 28616 Sauk Trail Rd	Kewanee	IL	61443	309-853-5589	
Web: www.dnr.state.il.us					
Jubilee College State Park 13015 W Fussner Rd	Brimfield	IL	61517	309-446-3758	446-3183
Web: www.dnr.state.il.us					
Kankakee River State Park 5314 W Rt 102 PO Box 37	Bourbonnais	IL	60914	815-933-1383	
Web: www.dnr.state.il.us					
Kaskaskia River State Fish & Wildlife Area 10981 Conservation Rd	Baldwin	IL	62217	618-785-2555	
Web: www.dnr.state.il.us/Lands/Landmgt/PARKS/R4/kaskas.htm					
Kickapoo State Recreation Area 10906 Kickapoo Pk Rd	Oakwood	IL	61858	217-442-4915	
Web: www.dnr.state.il.us/Lands/Landmgt/PARKS/R3/KICKAPOO.HTM					
Kinkaid Lake State Fish & Wildlife Area 52 Cinder Hill Dr	Murphysboro	IL	62966	618-684-2867	
Web: www.dnr.state.il.us/lands/landmgt/PARKS/R5/Kinkaid.htm					
Lake Le-Aqua-Na State Recreation Area 8542 N Lake Rd	Lena	IL	61048	815-369-4282	
Web: www.dnr.state.il.us					
Lake Murphysboro State Park 52 Cinder Hill Dr	Murphysboro	IL	62966	618-684-2867	
Web: www.dnr.state.il.us/Lands/Landmgt/PARKS/R5/MURPHYSB.HTM					
LaSalle Lake State Fish & Wildlife Area 2660 E 2350th Rd	Marseilles	IL	61341	815-357-1608	
Web: www.dnr.state.il.us					
Lincoln Trail Homestead State Memorial c/o Spitler Woods State Natural Area 705 Spitler Pk Dr	Mount Zion	IL	62549	217-864-3121	
Web: www.dnr.state.il.us/lands/Landmgt/PARKS/R3/LINCTRL.HTM					
Lincoln Trail State Park 16985 E 1350th Rd	Marshall	IL	62441	217-826-2222	
Web: www.dnr.state.il.us					
Lowden State Park 1411 N River Rd	Oregon	IL	61061	815-732-6828	
Web: www.dnr.state.il.us/Lands/Landmgt/PARKS/R1/LOWDENSP.HTM					
Lowden-Miller State Forest 1365 W Castle Rock Rd	Oregon	IL	61061	815-732-7329	
Web: www.dnr.state.il.us/Lands/Landmgt/PARKS/R1/LOWDENMI.HTM					
Mackinaw River State Fish & Wildlife Area 15470 Nelson Rd	Mackinaw	IL	61755	309-963-4969	
Web: www.dnr.state.il.us					
Marshall State Fish & Wildlife Area 236 State Rt 26	Lacon	IL	61540	309-246-8351	
Web: www.dnr.state.il.us					
Matthiessen State Park PO Box 509	Utica	IL	61373	815-667-4868	
Web: www.dnr.state.il.us/Lands/Landmgt/PARKS/R1/mttindex.htm					
Mautino State Fish & Wildlife Area 16006-875 E St	Sheffield	IL	61361	815-454-2328	
Web: www.dnr.state.il.us/Lands/Landmgt/PARKS/R1/MAUTINO.HTM					
Mazonia-Braidwood State Fish & Wildlife Areas 7705 County Rd 5000 S	Braceville	IL	60407	815-237-0063	
Web: www.dnr.state.il.us					
Mermet Lake State Fish & Wildlife Area 1812 Grinnell Rd	Belknap	IL	62908	618-524-5577	
Web: www.dnr.state.il.us					
Middle Fork State Fish & Wildlife Area 10906 Kickapoo Pk Rd	Oakwood	IL	61858	217-442-4915	
Web: www.dnr.state.il.us/Lands/Landmgt/PARKS/R3/Middle.htm					
Mississippi Palisades State Park 16327A IL Rt 84	Savanna	IL	61074	815-273-2731	
Web: www.dnr.state.il.us					
Mississippi River State Fish & Wildlife Area 17836 State Hwy 100 N	Grafton	IL	62037	618-376-3303	
Web: www.dnr.state.il.us/Lands/Landmgt/PARKS/R4/MISS.HTM					
Moraine Hills State Park 1510 S River Rd	McHenry	IL	60051	815-385-1624	
Web: www.dnr.state.il.us					
Moraine View State Recreation Area 27374 Moraine View Pk Rd	LeRoy	IL	61752	309-724-8032	
Web: www.dnr.state.il.us					
Morrison-Rockwood State Park 18750 Lake Rd	Morrison	IL	61270	815-772-4708	
Web: www.dnr.state.il.us					
Nauvoo State Park PO Box 426	Nauvoo	IL	62354	217-453-2512	
Web: www.dnr.state.il.us					
Newton Lake State Fish & Wildlife Area 3490 E 500th Ave	Newton	IL	62448	618-783-3478	
Web: www.dnr.state.il.us					
Peabody River King State Fish & Wildlife Area 10981 Conservation Rd	Baldwin	IL	62217	618-475-9339	
Web: www.dnr.state.il.us/Lands/Landmgt/PARKS/R4/PEABODY.HTM					
Pere Marquette State Park Rt 100 PO Box 158	Grafton	IL	62037	618-786-3323	
Web: www.dnr.state.il.us/lands/Landmgt/PARKS/R4/Peremarq.htm					
Piney Creek Ravine State Natural Area 4301 N Lake Dr	Chester	IL	62233	618-826-2706	
Web: www.dnr.state.il.us					
Powerton Lake State Fish & Wildlife Area 7982 S Pk Rd	Manito	IL	61546	309-968-7135	
Web: www.dnr.state.il.us/lands/Landmgt/PARKS/R1/POWERTON.HTM					
Prophetstown State Recreation Area Riverside Dr PO Box 181	Prophetstown	IL	61277	815-537-2926	
Web: www.dnr.state.il.us/Lands/Landmgt/PARKS/R1/PROPHET.HTM					
Pyramid State Recreation Area 1562 Pyramid Pk Rd	Pinckneyville	IL	62274	618-357-2574	
Web: www.dnr.state.il.us					
Ramsey Lake State Recreation Area Ramsey Lake Rd PO Box 97	Ramsey	IL	62080	618-423-2215	
Web: www.dnr.state.il.us					
Randolph County State Recreation Area 4301 S Lake Dr	Chester	IL	62233	618-826-2706	
Web: www.dnr.state.il.us/Lands/Landmgt/PARKS/R4/RAND.HTM					
Ray Norbut State Fish & Wildlife Area 46816 290th Ave	Griggsville	IL	62340	217-833-2811	
Web: www.dnr.state.il.us					
Red Hills State Park RR 2 PO Box 252A	Sumner	IL	62466	618-936-2469	
Web: www.dnr.state.il.us					
Rend Lake State Fish & Wildlife Area 10885 E Jefferson Rd	Bonnie	IL	62816	618-279-3110	
Web: www.dnr.state.il.us					
Rice Lake State Fish & Wildlife Area 19721 N US Hwy 24	Canton	IL	61520	309-647-9184	
Web: www.dnr.state.il.us/Lands/Landmgt/PARKS/R1/Rice.htm					
Rock Cut State Park 7318 Harlem Rd	Loves Park	IL	61111	815-885-3311	
Web: www.dnr.state.il.us					
Rock Island Trail State Park 311 E Williams St PO Box 64	Wyoming	IL	61491	309-695-2228	
Web: www.dnr.state.il.us					
Saline County State Fish & Wildlife Area 85 Glen O Jones Rd	Equality	IL	62934	618-276-4405	
Web: www.dnr.state.il.us					
Sam Dale Lake State Conservation Area RR 1	Johnsonville	IL	62850	618-835-2292	
Web: www.dnr.state.il.us					
Sam Parr State Fish & Wildlife Area 13225 E State Hwy 33	Newton	IL	62448	618-783-2661	
Web: www.dnr.state.il.us					
Sand Ridge State Forest PO Box 111	Forest City	IL	61532	309-597-2212	
Web: www.dnr.state.il.us					
Sanganois State Fish & Wildlife Area 3594 County Rd 200 N	Chandlerville	IL	62627	309-546-2628	
Web: www.dnr.state.il.us/Lands/Landmgt/PARKS/R4/SANGILL.HTM					
Sangchris Lake State Park 9898 Cascade Rd	Rochester	IL	62563	217-498-9208	
Web: www.dnr.state.il.us					
Shabbona Lake State Park 4201 Shabbona Grove Rd	Shabbona	IL	60550	815-824-2106	
Web: www.dnr.state.il.us					
Shelbyville State Fish & Wildlife Area RR 1 PO Box 42A	Bethany	IL	61914	217-665-3112	
Web: www.dnr.state.il.us					
Siloam Springs State Park 938 E 3003rd Ln	Clayton	IL	62324	217-894-6205	
Web: www.dnr.state.il.us					
Silver Springs State Fish & Wildlife Area 13608 Fox Rd	Yorkville	IL	60560	630-553-6297	
Web: www.dnr.state.il.us					
Snakeden Hollow State Fish & Wildlife Area 1936 State Hwy 167	Victoria	IL	61485	309-879-2607	
Web: www.dnr.state.il.us					
South Shore State Park c/o Eldon Hazlet State Recreation Area 20100 Hazlet Pk Rd	Carlyle	IL	62231	618-594-3015	
Web: www.dnr.state.il.us/Lands/Landmgt/PARKS/R4/sts.htm					
Spitler Woods State Natural Area 705 Spitler Pk Dr	Mount Zion	IL	62549	217-864-3121	
Web: www.dnr.state.il.us/Lands/Landmgt/PARKS/R3/SPITLER.HTM					
Spring Lake State Fish & Wildlife Area 7982 S Pk Rd	Manito	IL	61546	309-968-7135	
Web: www.dnr.state.il.us/Lands/Landmgt/PARKS/R1/SPL.HTM					
Starved Rock State Park PO Box 509	Utica	IL	61373	815-667-4726	
Web: www.dnr.state.il.us/Lands/Landmgt/PARKS/I&M/EAST/STARVE/PARK.HTM					
Stephen A. Forbes State Park 6924 Omega Rd	Kinmundy	IL	62854	618-547-3381	
Web: www.dnr.state.il.us					
Ten Mile Creek State Fish & Wildlife Area RR 1 PO Box 179	McLeansboro	IL	62859	618-643-2862	
Web: www.dnr.state.il.us					
Trail of Tears State Forest 3240 State Forest Rd	Jonesboro	IL	62952	618-833-4910	
Web: www.dnr.state.il.us					
Tunnel Hill State Trail 302 E Vine St	Vienna	IL	62995	618-658-2168	
Web: www.dnr.state.il.us					
Turkey Bluffs State Fish & Wildlife Area 4301 S Lakeside Dr	Chester	IL	62233	618-826-2706	
Union County State Fish & Wildlife Area 2755 Refuge Rd	Jonesboro	IL	62952	618-833-5175	
Web: www.dnr.state.il.us					
Volo Bog State Natural Area 28478 W Brandenburg Rd	Ingleside	IL	60041	815-344-1294	
Web: www.dnr.state.il.us					
Walnut Point State Park 2331 E County Rd 370 N	Oakland	IL	61943	217-346-3336	
Web: www.dnr.state.il.us					
Washington County State Recreation Area 18500 Conservation Dr	Nashville	IL	62263	618-327-3137	
Web: www.dnr.state.il.us					
Wayne Fitzgerrell State Recreation Area 11094 Ranger Rd	Whittington	IL	62897	618-629-2320	
Web: www.dnr.state.il.us					
Weinberg-King State Park PO Box 203	Augusta	IL	62311	217-392-2345	
Web: www.dnr.state.il.us					
Weldon Springs State Park 1159 500 N RR 2 PO Box 87	Clinton	IL	61727	217-935-2644	
Web: www.dnr.state.il.us					

	City	State	ZIP	Phone	Fax
White Pines Forest State Park 6712 W Pines Rd *Web:* www.dnr.state.il.us	Mount Morris	IL	61054	815-946-3717	
William W. Powers State Recreation Area 12949 S Ave O *Web:* www.dnr.state.il.us	Chicago	IL	60633	773-646-3270	
Wolf Creek State Park RR 1 PO Box 99 *Web:* www.dnr.state.il.us	Windsor	IL	61957	217-459-2831	
Woodford State Fish & Wildlife Area 524 Conservation Ln *Web:* www.dnr.state.il.us	Low Point	IL	61545	309-822-8861	

INDIANA

	City	State	ZIP	Phone	Fax
Brookville Lake PO Box 100 *Web:* www.in.gov	Brookville	IN	47012	765-647-2657	
Brown County State Park 1405 State Rd 46 W PO Box 608 *Web:* www.in.gov	Nashville	IN	47448	812-988-6406	
Cagles Mill Lake 1317 W Lieber Rd Suite 1 *Web:* www.in.gov	Cloverdale	IN	46120	765-795-4576	
Cecil M. Harden Lake 1588 S Raccoon Pkwy *Web:* www.in.gov	Rockville	IN	47872	765-344-1412	
Chain O'Lakes State Park 2355 E 75 S *Web:* www.in.gov	Albion	IN	46701	260-636-2654	
Charlestown State Park 12500 Indiana 62 *Web:* www.in.gov	Charlestown	IN	47111	812-256-5600	
Clifty Falls State Park 1501 Green Rd *Web:* www.in.gov	Madison	IN	47250	812-273-8885	
Deam Lake State Recreation Area 1217 Deam Lake Rd *Web:* www.in.gov	Borden	IN	47106	812-246-5421	
Falls of the Ohio State Park 201 W Riverside Dr *Web:* www.in.gov	Clarksville	IN	47129	812-280-9970	280-7110
Fort Harrison State Park 5753 Glenn Rd *Web:* www.in.gov	Indianapolis	IN	46216	317-591-0904	
Hardy Lake 4171 E Harrod Rd *Web:* www.in.gov	Scottsburg	IN	47170	812-794-3800	
Harmonie State Park 3451 Harmonie State Pk Rd *Web:* www.in.gov	New Harmony	IN	47631	812-682-4821	
Indiana Dunes State Park 1600 N 25 E *Web:* www.in.gov	Chesterton	IN	46304	219-926-1952	
J. Edward Roush Lake 517 N Warren Rd *Web:* www.in.gov	Huntington	IN	46750	260-468-2165	
Lincoln State Park Hwy 162 PO Box 216 *Web:* www.in.gov	Lincoln City	IN	47552	812-937-4710	
McCormick's Creek State Park 250 McCormick's Creek Rd *Web:* www.in.gov	Spencer	IN	47460	812-829-2235	
Mississinewa Lake 4673 S 625 E *Web:* www.in.gov	Peru	IN	46970	765-473-6528	
Monroe Lake 4850 S State Rd 446 *Web:* www.in.gov	Bloomington	IN	47401	812-837-9546	
Mounds State Park 4306 Mounds Rd *Web:* www.in.gov	Anderson	IN	46017	765-642-6627	
O'Bannon Woods State Park 7234 Old Forest Rd SW *Web:* www.in.gov	Corydon	IN	47112	812-738-8232	
Ouabache State Park 4930 E State Rd 201 *Web:* www.in.gov	Bluffton	IN	46714	260-824-0926	
Patoka Lake 3084 N Dillard Rd *Web:* www.in.gov	Birdseye	IN	47513	812-685-2464	
Pokagon State Park 450 Ln 100 Lake James *Web:* www.in.gov/dnr/parklake/properties/park_pokagon.html	Angola	IN	46703	260-833-2012	
Potato Creek State Park 25601 State Rd 4 PO Box 908 *Web:* www.in.gov	North Liberty	IN	46554	574-656-8186	
Salamonie Lake 9214 Lost Bridge Rd W *Web:* www.in.gov	Andrews	IN	46702	260-468-2125	
Shades State Park Rt 1 PO Box 72 *Web:* www.in.gov	Waveland	IN	47989	765-435-2810	
Shakamak State Park 6265 W State Rd 48 *Web:* www.in.gov	Jasonville	IN	47438	812-665-2158	
Spring Mill State Park PO Box 376 *Web:* www.in.gov	Mitchell	IN	47446	812-849-4129	
Starve Hollow State Recreation Area 4345 S County Rd 275 W *Web:* www.in.gov	Vallonia	IN	47281	812-358-3464	
Summit Lake State Park 5993 N Messick Rd *Web:* www.in.gov	New Castle	IN	47362	765-766-5873	
Tippecanoe River State Park 4200 N US Hwy 35 *Web:* www.in.gov	Winamac	IN	46996	574-946-3213	
Turkey Run State Park 8121 Pk Rd *Web:* www.in.gov	Marshall	IN	47859	765-597-2635	
Versailles State Park US Hwy 50 PO Box 205 *Web:* www.in.gov	Versailles	IN	47042	812-689-6424	
White River State Park 801 W Washington St *TF:* 800-665-9056 ■ *Web:* www.in.gov	Indianapolis	IN	46204	317-233-2434	233-2367
Whitewater Memorial State Park 1418 S State Rd 101 *Web:* www.in.gov	Liberty	IN	47353	765-458-5565	
Wyandotte Caves State Recreation Area 7315 S Wyandotte Cave Rd *Web:* www.in.gov	Leavenworth	IN	47137	812-738-2782	

IOWA

	City	State	ZIP	Phone	Fax
Ambrose A. Call State Park Rt 1 PO Box 264 *Web:* www.iowadnr.com	Algona	IA	50511	515-295-3669	
Backbone State Park 1347 129th St *Web:* www.iowadnr.com	Dundee	IA	52038	563-924-2527	924-2827
Beed's Lake State Park 1422 165th St *Web:* www.iowadnr.com	Hampton	IA	50441	641-456-2047	
Bellevue State Park 24668 Hwy 52 *Web:* www.iowadnr.com	Bellevue	IA	52031	563-872-4019	872-4773
Big Creek State Park 12397 NW 89th Ct *Web:* www.iowadnr.com	Polk City	IA	50226	515-984-6473	984-9320
Black Hawk State Park 228 S Blossom *Web:* www.iowadnr.com	Lake View	IA	51450	712-657-8712	657-0999
Brushy Creek State Recreation Area 3175 290th St *Web:* www.iowadnr.com	Lehigh	IA	50557	515-543-8298	843-8395
Cedar Rock PO Box 250 *Web:* www.iowadnr.com	Quasqueton	IA	52326	319-934-3572	
Clear Lake State Park 2730 S Lakeview Dr *Web:* www.iowadnr.com	Clear Lake	IA	50428	641-357-4212	357-4242
Dolliver Memorial State Park 2757 Dolliver Pk Ave *Web:* www.iowadnr.com	Lehigh	IA	50557	515-359-2539	359-2542
Elinor Bedell State Park c/o Gull Pt State Pk 1500 Harpen St *Web:* www.iowabeautiful.com	Milford	IA	51351	712-337-3211	
Elk Rock State Park 811 146th Ave *Web:* www.iowadnr.com	Knoxville	IA	50138	641-842-6008	
Fairport State Recreation Area c/o Wildcat Den State Pk 1884 Wildcat Den Rd	Muscatine	IA	52761	563-263-4337	264-8329
Fort Atkinson State Preserve c/o Volga River State Recreation Area 10225 Ivy Rd *Web:* www.iowadnr.com/parks/state_park_list/fort_atkinson.html	Fayette	IA	52142	563-425-4161	
Fort Defiance State Park c/o Gull Pt State Pk 1500 Harpen St *Web:* www.iowadnr.gov	Milford	IA	51351	712-337-3211	
Geode State Park 3333 Racine Ave *Web:* www.iowadnr.com	Danville	IA	52623	319-392-4601	
George Wyth Memorial State Park 3659 Wyth Rd *Web:* www.iowadnr.com	Waterloo	IA	50703	319-232-5505	232-1508
Green Valley State Park 1480 130th St *Web:* www.iowadnr.com	Creston	IA	50801	641-782-5131	782-8330
Gull Point State Park 1500 Harpen St *Web:* www.iowadnr.com	Milford	IA	51351	712-337-3211	
Honey Creek State Park 12194 Honey Creek Pl *Web:* www.iowadnr.com	Moravia	IA	52571	641-724-3739	724-9846
Lacey-Keosauqua State Park 22895 Lacey Trial *Web:* www.iowadnr.com	Keosauqua	IA	52565	319-293-3502	293-3329
Lake Ahquabi State Park 1650 118th Ave *Web:* www.iowadnr.com	Indianola	IA	50125	515-961-7101	962-9424
Lake Anita State Park 55111 750th St *Web:* www.iowadnr.com	Anita	IA	50020	712-762-3564	762-4352
Lake Darling State Park 111 Lake Darling Rd *Web:* www.iowadnr.com	Brighton	IA	52540	319-694-2323	
Lake Keomah State Park 2720 Keomah Ln *Web:* www.iowadnr.com	Oskaloosa	IA	52577	641-673-6975	673-0647
Lake Macbride State Park 3525 Hwy 382 NE *Web:* www.iowadnr.com	Solon	IA	52333	319-624-2200	624-2188
Lake Manawa State Park 1100 S Shore Dr *Web:* www.iowadnr.com	Council Bluffs	IA	51501	712-366-0220	366-0474
Lake of Three Fires State Park 2303 Lake Rd *Web:* www.iowadnr.com	Bedford	IA	50833	712-523-2700	523-3104
Lake Wapello State Park 15248 Campground Rd *Web:* www.iowadnr.com	Drakesville	IA	52552	641-722-3371	722-3384
Ledges State Park 1519 250th St *Web:* www.iowadnr.com	Madrid	IA	50156	515-432-1852	432-0757
Lewis & Clark State Park 21914 Pk Loop *Web:* www.iowadnr.com	Onawa	IA	51040	712-423-2829	
Maquoketa Caves State Park 10970 98th St *Web:* www.iowadnr.com	Maquoketa	IA	52060	563-652-5833	652-0061
McIntosh Woods State Park 1200 E Lake St *Web:* www.iowadnr.com	Ventura	IA	50482	641-829-3847	829-3841
Mines of Spain State Recreation Area 8991 Bellevue Heights *Web:* www.iowadnr.com	Dubuque	IA	52003	563-556-0620	556-8474
Nine Eagles State Park RR 1 *Web:* www.iowadnr.com	Davis City	IA	50065	641-442-2855	442-2856
Palisades-Kepler State Park 700 Kepler Dr *Web:* www.iowadnr.com	Mount Vernon	IA	52314	319-895-6039	895-9660
Pikes Peak State Park 15316 Great River Rd *Web:* www.iowadnr.com	McGregor	IA	52157	563-873-2341	873-3167
Pilot Knob State Park 2148 340th St *Web:* www.iowadnr.com	Forest City	IA	50436	641-581-4835	
Pine Lake State Park 22620 County Hwy S56 *Web:* www.iowadnr.com	Eldora	IA	50627	641-858-5832	858-5641
Pleasant Creek State Recreation Area 4530 McClintock Rd *Web:* www.iowadnr.com	Palo	IA	52324	319-436-7716	436-7715
Prairie Rose State Park 680 Rd M47 *Web:* www.iowadnr.com	Harlan	IA	51537	712-773-2701	773-2702
Preparation Canyon State Park c/o Lewis & Clark State Pk 21914 Pk Loop *Web:* www.iowadnr.com	Onawa	IA	51040	712-423-2829	
Red Haw State Park 24550 US Hwy 34 *Web:* www.iowadnr.com	Chariton	IA	50049	641-774-5632	774-8821
Rock Creek State Park 5627 Rock Creek E *Web:* www.iowadnr.com	Kellogg	IA	50135	641-236-3722	236-5599

	City	State	Zip	Phone	Fax
Shimek State Forest 33653 Rt J56	Farmington	IA	52626	319-878-3811	
Web: www.iowadnr.com					
Springbrook State Park 2437 160th Rd	Guthrie Center	IA	50115	641-747-3591	747-8401
Web: www.iowadnr.com					
Stephens State Forest 1111 N 8th St	Chariton	IA	50049	641-774-4559	
Web: www.iowadnr.com					
Stone State Park 5001 Talbot Rd	Sioux City	IA	51103	712-255-4698	
Web: www.iowadnr.com					
Twin Lakes State Park					
c/o Black Hawk Lake State Pk					
228 S Blossom St	Lake View	IA	51450	712-657-8712	657-2289
Web: www.iowadnr.gov					
Union Grove State Park 1215 220th St	Gladbrook	IA	50635	641-473-2556	473-3059
Web: www.iowadnr.com					
Viking Lake State Park 2780 Viking Lake Rd	Stanton	IA	51573	712-829-2235	829-2842
Web: www.iowadnr.com					
Volga River State Recreation Area					
10225 Ivy Rd	Fayette	IA	52142	563-425-4161	425-3004
Web: www.iowadnr.com/parks/state_park_list/volga_river.html					
Walnut Woods State Park					
3155 Walnut Woods Dr	West Des Moines	IA	50265	515-285-4502	285-7476
Web: www.iowadnr.com					
Wapsipinicon State Park 21301 County Rd E34	Anamosa	IA	52205	319-462-2761	462-4878
Web: www.iowadnr.com					
Waubonsie State Park 2689 State Hwy 2	Hamburg	IA	51640	712-382-2786	382-9860
Web: www.iowadnr.com					
Wildcat Den State Park 1884 Wildcat Den Rd	Muscatine	IA	52761	563-263-4337	264-8329
Web: www.iowadnr.com/parks/state_park_list/wildcat_den.html					
Wilson Island State Recreation Area					
32801 Campground Ln	Missouri Valley	IA	51555	712-642-2069	642-4390
Web: www.iowadnr.com					
Yellow River State Forest					
729 State Forest Rd	Harpers Ferry	IA	52146	563-586-2254	
Web: www.iowadnr.com					

KANSAS

	City	State	Zip	Phone	Fax
Cedar Bluff State Park Rt 2 PO Box 76A	Ellis	KS	67637	785-726-3212	
Cheney State Park 16000 NE 50th St	Cheney	KS	67025	316-542-3664	542-9979
Web: www.kdwp.state.ks.us/news/state_parks/locations/cheney					
Clinton State Park 798 N 1415 Rd	Lawrence	KS	66049	785-842-8562	
Web: www.kdwp.state.ks.us/news/state_parks/locations/clinton					
Crawford State Park 1 Lake Rd	Farlington	KS	66734	620-362-3671	
Web: www.kdwp.state.ks.us/news/state_parks/locations/crawford					
Cross Timbers State Park 144 Hwy 105	Toronto	KS	66777	620-637-2213	
Web: www.kdwp.state.ks.us/news/state_parks/locations/cross_timbers					
Eisenhower State Park 29810 S Fairlawn Rd	Lyndon	KS	66523	785-528-4102	
Web: www.kdwp.state.ks.us					
El Dorado State Park 618 NE Bluestem Rd	El Dorado	KS	67042	316-321-7180	
Web: www.kdwp.state.ks.us					
Elk City State Park 4825 Squaw Creek Rd	Independence	KS	67301	620-331-6295	
Web: www.kdwp.state.ks.us/news/state_parks/locations/elk_city					
Glen Elder State Park 2131 180 Rd	Glen Elder	KS	67446	785-545-3345	
Web: www.kdwp.state.ks.us					
Hillsdale State Park 26001 W 255th St	Paola	KS	66071	913-783-4507	
Web: www.kdwp.state.ks.us					
Kanopolis State Park 200 Horsethief Rd	Marquette	KS	67464	785-546-2565	
Web: www.kdwp.state.ks.us					
Lovewell State Park 2446 250 Rd	Webber	KS	66970	785-753-4971	
Web: www.kdwp.state.ks.us					
Meade State Park 13051 V Rd	Meade	KS	67864	620-873-2572	
Web: www.kdwp.state.ks.us/news/state_parks/locations/meade					
Milford State Park 8811 State Pk Rd	Milford	KS	66514	785-238-3014	
Web: www.kdwp.state.ks.us					
Mushroom Rock State Park 200 Horsethief Rd	Marquette	KS	67464	785-546-2565	
Web: www.kdwp.state.ks.us					
Perry State Park 5441 Westlake Rd	Ozawkie	KS	66070	785-246-3449	246-0224
Web: www.kdwp.state.ks.us					
Pomona State Park 22900 S Hwy 368	Vassar	KS	66543	785-828-4933	
Web: www.kdwp.state.ks.us					
Prairie Dog State Park PO Box 431	Norton	KS	67654	785-877-2953	
Web: www.kdwp.state.ks.us/news/state_parks/locations/prairie_dog					
Prairie Spirit Trail State Park 419 S Oak St	Garnett	KS	66032	785-448-6767	
Sand Hills State Park 4207 E 56th	Hutchinson	KS	67502	316-542-3664	
TF: 800-496-9077					
Scott State Park 520 W Scott Lake Dr	Scott City	KS	67871	620-872-2061	
Web: www.kdwp.state.ks.us					
Tuttle Creek State Park					
5800-A River Pond Rd	Manhattan	KS	66502	785-539-7941	
Web: www.kdwp.state.ks.us					
Webster State Park 1210 Nine Rd	Stockton	KS	67669	785-425-6775	
Web: www.kdwp.state.ks.us					
Wilson State Park Rt 1 PO Box 181	Sylvan Grove	KS	67481	785-658-2465	
Web: www.kdwp.state.ks.us					

KENTUCKY

	City	State	Zip	Phone	Fax
Ben Hawes State Park 400 Boothfield Rd	Owensboro	KY	42301	270-684-9808	
Web: www.parks.ky.gov					
Big Bone Lick State Park 3380 Beaver Rd	Union	KY	41091	859-384-3522	
Web: www.parks.ky.gov					
Blue Licks Battlefield State Resort Park					
Hwy 68	Mount Olivet	KY	41064	800-443-7008	
TF: 800-443-7008 ■ *Web:* www.parks.ky.gov					
Boone Station State Historic Site					
240 Gentry Rd	Lexington	KY	40502	859-263-1073	
Web: www.parks.ky.gov					
Buckhorn Lake State Resort Park					
4441 Kentucky Hwy 1833	Buckhorn	KY	41721	800-325-0058	
TF: 800-325-0058 ■ *Web:* www.parks.ky.gov					
Carr Creek State Park Hwy 15	Sassafras	KY	41759	606-642-4050	
Web: www.parks.ky.gov					
Carter Caves State Resort Park					
344 Caveland Dr	Olive Hill	KY	41164	800-325-0059	
TF: 800-325-0059 ■ *Web:* www.parks.ky.gov/resortparks/cc					
Columbus-Belmont State Park 350 Pk Rd	Columbus	KY	42032	270-677-2327	
Web: www.parks.ky.gov					
Constitution Square State Historic Site					
134 S 2nd St	Danville	KY	40422	859-239-7089	
Web: www.parks.ky.gov					
Cumberland Falls State Resort Park					
7351 Hwy 90	Corbin	KY	40701	800-325-0063	
TF: 800-325-0063 ■ *Web:* www.parks.ky.gov					
Dale Hollow Lake State Resort Park					
6371 State Pk Rd	Burkesville	KY	42717	800-325-2282	
TF: 800-325-2282 ■ *Web:* www.parks.ky.gov					
Dr Thomas Walker State Historic Site					
4929 KY 459	Barbourville	KY	40906	606-546-4400	
Web: www.parks.ky.gov					
EP "Tom" Sawyer State Park					
3000 Freys Hill Rd	Louisville	KY	40241	502-426-8950	429-7273
Web: www.parks.ky.gov					
Fort Boonesborough State Park					
4375 Boonesborough Rd	Richmond	KY	40475	859-527-3131	
Web: www.parks.ky.gov					
General Burnside Island State Park					
8801 S Hwy 27	Burnside	KY	42519	606-561-4104	
Web: www.parks.ky.gov					
Grayson Lake State Park					
314 Grayson Lake Pk Rd	Olive Hill	KY	41164	606-474-9727	
Web: www.parks.ky.gov					
Green River Lake State Park					
179 Pk Office Rd	Campbellsville	KY	42718	270-465-8255	
Web: www.parks.ky.gov					
Greenbo Lake State Resort Park					
HC 60 PO Box 562	Greenup	KY	41144	800-325-0083	
TF: 800-325-0083 ■ *Web:* www.parks.ky.gov					
Isaac Shelby Cemetery State Historic Site					
6725 Kentucky Hwy 300	Stanford	KY	40484	859-239-7089	
Web: www.parks.ky.gov					
Jefferson Davis Monument State Historic Site					
Hwy 68 E	Fairview	KY	42221	270-886-1765	
Web: www.parks.ky.gov					
Jenny Wiley State Resort Park					
75 Theatre Ct	Prestonsburg	KY	41653	800-325-0142	
TF: 800-325-0142 ■ *Web:* www.parks.ky.gov					
John James Audubon State Park					
3100 US Hwy 41 N	Henderson	KY	42419	270-826-2247	
Web: www.parks.ky.gov					
Kenlake State Resort Park 542 Kenlake Rd	Hardin	KY	42048	270-474-2211	
TF: 800-325-0143 ■ *Web:* www.parks.ky.gov/findparks/resortparks/kl					
Kentucky Dam Village State Resort Park					
113 Administration Dr	Gilbertsville	KY	42044	270-362-4271	
TF: 800-325-0146 ■ *Web:* www.parks.ky.gov/findparks/resortparks/kd					
Kincaid Lake State Park 565 Kincaid Pk Rd	Falmouth	KY	41040	859-654-3531	
Web: www.parks.ky.gov					
Kingdom Come State Park 502 Pk Rd	Cumberland	KY	40823	606-589-2479	
Web: www.parks.ky.gov					
Lake Barkley State Resort Park					
3500 State Pk Rd	Cadiz	KY	42211	800-325-1708	
TF: 800-325-1708 ■ *Web:* parks.ky.gov/findparks/resortparks/lb					
Lake Malone State Park 331 State Rd 8001	Dunmor	KY	42339	270-657-2111	
Web: www.parks.ky.gov					
Levi Jackson State Park					
998 Levi Jackson Mill Rd	London	KY	40744	606-878-8000	
Web: www.parks.ky.gov					
Lincoln Homestead State Park					
5079 Lincoln Pk Rd	Springfield	KY	40069	859-336-7461	
Web: www.parks.ky.gov					
Mineral Mound State Park 48 Finch Ln	Eddyville	KY	42038	270-388-3673	
Web: www.parks.ky.gov					
My Old Kentucky Home State Park					
501 E Stephen Foster Ave	Bardstown	KY	40004	502-348-3502	
Web: www.parks.ky.gov					
Natural Bridge State Resort Park					
2135 Natural Bridge Rd	Slade	KY	40376	800-325-1710	
TF: 800-325-1710 ■ *Web:* www.parks.ky.gov					
Nolin Lake State Park PO Box 340	Bee Spring	KY	42207	270-286-4240	
Web: www.parks.ky.gov					
Old Fort Harrod State Park					
100 S College St	Harrodsburg	KY	40330	859-734-3314	
Web: www.parks.ky.gov					
Old Mulkey Meetinghouse State Historic Site					
1819 Old Mulkey Pk Rd	Tompkinsville	KY	42167	270-487-8481	
Web: www.parks.ky.gov					
Paintsville Lake State Park					
1551 KY Rt 2275	Staffordsville	KY	41256	606-297-8486	
Web: www.parks.ky.gov					
Pennyrile Forest State Resort Park					
20781 Pennyrile Lodge Rd	Dawson Springs	KY	42408	800-325-1711	
TF: 800-325-1711 ■ *Web:* www.parks.ky.gov					
Perryville Battlefield State Historic Site					
1825 Battlefield Rd	Perryville	KY	40468	606-332-8631	
Web: www.parks.ky.gov					
Pine Mountain State Resort Park					
1050 State Pk Rd	Pineville	KY	40977	800-325-1712	
TF: 800-325-1712 ■ *Web:* www.parks.ky.gov					
Rough River Dam State Resort Park					
450 Lodge Rd	Falls of Rough	KY	40119	800-325-1713	
TF: 800-325-1713 ■ *Web:* www.parks.ky.gov					

				Phone	Fax
Taylorsville Lake State Park 1320 Pk Rd. Taylorsville		KY	40071	502-477-8713	
Web: www.parks.ky.gov					
Waveland Museum State Historic Site 225 Waveland Museum Ln. Lexington		KY	40514	859-272-3611	
Web: www.parks.ky.gov					
White Hall State Historic Site 500 White Hall Shrine Rd. Richmond		KY	40475	859-623-9178	
Web: www.parks.ky.gov					
William Whitley House State Historic Site 625 William Whitley Rd. Stanford		KY	40484	606-355-2881	
Web: www.parks.ky.gov					
Yatesville Lake State Park PO Box 767. Louisa		KY	41230	606-673-1492	
Web: www.parks.ky.gov					

LOUISIANA

			Phone	Fax
Audubon State Historic Site 11788 Louisiana Hwy 965. Saint Francisville	LA	70775	225-635-3739	784-0578
TF: 888-677-2838 ■ *Web:* www.crt.state.la.us/parks/iaudubon.aspx				
Bayou Segnette State Park 7777 Westbank Expy. Westwego	LA	70094	504-736-7140	436-4788
TF: 888-677-2296 ■ *Web:* www.crt.state.la.us				
Centenary State Historic Site 3522 College St. Jackson	LA	70748	225-634-7925	
TF: 888-677-2364 ■ *Web:* www.crt.state.la.us				
Chemin-A-Haut State Park 14656 State Pk Rd. Bastrop	LA	71220	318-283-0812	
TF: 888-677-2436 ■ *Web:* www.crt.state.la.us				
Chicot State Park 3469 Chicot Pk Rd. Ville Platte	LA	70586	337-363-2403	
TF: 888-677-2442 ■ *Web:* www.crt.state.la.us				
Cypremort Point State Park 306 Beach Ln. Cypremort Point	LA	70538	337-867-4510	
TF: 888-867-4510 ■ *Web:* www.crt.state.la.us				
Fairview-Riverside State Park 119 Fairview Dr. Madisonville	LA	70447	985-845-3318	
TF: 888-677-3247 ■ *Web:* www.crt.state.la.us				
Fontainebleau State Park 67825 US Hwy 190. Mandeville	LA	70448	985-624-4443	
TF: 888-677-3668 ■ *Web:* www.crt.state.la.us				
Fort Jesup State Historic Site 32 Geoghagan Rd. Many	LA	71449	318-256-4117	
TF: 888-677-5378 ■ *Web:* www.crt.state.la.us				
Fort Pike State Historic Site 27100 Chef Menteur Hwy. New Orleans	LA	70129	504-662-5703	
TF: 888-662-5703 ■ *Web:* www.crt.state.la.us				
Fort Saint Jean Baptiste State Historic Site 155 Jefferson St. Natchitoches	LA	71457	318-357-3101	
TF: 888-677-7853 ■ *Web:* www.crt.state.la.us				
Grand Isle State Park 108 Admiral Craik Dr. Grand Isle	LA	70358	985-787-2559	
TF: 888-787-2559 ■ *Web:* www.crt.state.la.us				
Jimmie Davis State Park 1209 State Pk Rd. Chatham	LA	71226	318-249-2595	
TF: 888-677-2263 ■ *Web:* www.crt.state.la.us				
Lake Bistineau State Park 103 State Pk Rd. Doyline	LA	71023	318-745-3503	
TF: 888-677-2478 ■ *Web:* www.crt.state.la.us				
Lake Bruin State Park 201 State Pk Rd. Saint Joseph	LA	71366	318-766-3530	
TF: 888-677-2784 ■ *Web:* www.crt.state.la.us				
Lake Claiborne State Park 225 State Pk Rd. Homer	LA	71040	318-927-2976	
TF: 888-677-2524 ■ *Web:* www.crt.state.la.us				
Lake D'Arbonne State Park 3628 Evergreen Rd. Farmerville	LA	71241	318-368-2086	
TF: 888-677-5200 ■ *Web:* www.crt.state.la.us				
Lake Fausse Pointe State Park 5400 Levee Rd. Saint Martinville	LA	70582	318-229-4764	
TF: 888-677-7200 ■ *Web:* www.crt.state.la.us				
Locust Grove State Historic Site c/o Audubon State Historic Site PO Box 546. Saint Francisville	LA	70775	225-635-3789	
TF: 888-677-2838 ■ *Web:* www.crt.state.la.us/parks/ilocust.aspx				
Longfellow-Evangeline State Historic Site 1200 N Main St. Saint Martinville	LA	70582	337-394-3754	
TF: 888-677-2900 ■ *Web:* www.crt.state.la.us				
Los Adaes State Historic Site 6354 Hwy 485. Robeline	LA	71469	318-472-9449	
TF: 888-677-5378 ■ *Web:* www.crt.state.la.us				
Louisiana State Arboretum 4213 Chicot Pk Rd. Ville Platte	LA	70586	337-363-6289	
TF: 888-677-6100 ■ *Web:* www.crt.state.la.us				
Mansfield State Historic Site 15149 Hwy 175. Mansfield	LA	71052	318-872-1474	
TF: 888-677-6267 ■ *Web:* www.crt.state.la.us				
Marksville State Historic Site 837 ML King Dr. Marksville	LA	71351	318-253-8954	
TF: 888-253-8954 ■ *Web:* www.crt.state.la.us				
North Toledo Bend State Park 2907 N Toledo Pk Rd. Zwolle	LA	71486	318-645-4715	
TF: 888-677-6400 ■ *Web:* www.crt.state.la.us				
Palmetto Island State Park c/o Louisiana Office of State Parks PO Box 44426. Baton Rouge	LA	70804	225-342-8111	
TF: 888-677-1400 ■ *Web:* www.crt.state.la.us/parks/iconstruction.aspx				
Plaquemine Lock State Historic Site 57730 Main St. Plaquemine	LA	70764	225-687-7158	
TF: 877-987-7158 ■ *Web:* www.crt.state.la.us				
Port Hudson State Historic Site 236 Hwy 61. Jackson	LA	70748	225-654-3775	654-4413
TF: 888-677-3400 ■ *Web:* www.crt.state.la.us				
Poverty Point Reservoir State Park 1500 Poverty Pt Pkwy. Delhi	LA	71232	318-878-7536	
TF: 800-474-0392 ■ *Web:* www.crt.state.la.us				
Poverty Point State Historic Site 6859 Hwy 577. Pioneer	LA	71266	318-926-5492	
TF: 888-926-5492 ■ *Web:* www.crt.state.la.us				
Rebel State Historic Site 1260 Hwy 1221. Marthaville	LA	71450	318-472-6255	
TF: 888-677-3600 ■ *Web:* www.crt.state.la.us				
Saint Bernard State Park 501 St Bernard Pkwy. Braithwaite	LA	70040	504-682-2101	
TF: 888-677-7823 ■ *Web:* www.crt.state.la.us				
Sam Houston Jones State Park 107 Sutherland Rd. Lake Charles	LA	70611	337-855-2665	
TF: 888-677-7264 ■ *Web:* www.crt.state.la.us				
South Toledo Bend State Park 120 Bald Eaglel Rd. Anacoco	LA	71403	337-286-9075	
TF: 888-398-4770 ■ *Web:* www.crt.state.la.us				
Tickfaw State Park 27225 Patterson Rd. Springfield	LA	70462	225-294-5020	
TF: 888-981-2020 ■ *Web:* www.crt.state.la.us				
Winter Quarters State Historic Site 4929 Hwy 608. Newellton	LA	71357	318-467-9750	
TF: 888-677-9468 ■ *Web:* www.crt.state.la.us				

MAINE

			Phone	Fax
Allagash Wilderness Waterway 106 Hogan Rd # 7. Bangor	ME	04401	207-941-4014	
Web: www.maine.gov				
Aroostook State Park 87 State Pk Rd. Presque Isle	ME	04769	207-768-8341	
Web: www.maine.gov				
Baxter State Park 64 Balsam Dr. Millinocket	ME	04462	207-723-5140	
Web: www.baxterstateparkauthority.com				
Birch Point Beach State Park c/o Bureau of Parks & Lands 106 Hogan Rd. Bangor	ME	04401	207-941-4014	
Web: www.maine.gov/doc/nrimc/mgs/explore/bedrock/sites/jun09.htm				
Bradbury Mountain State Park 528 Hallowell Rd. Pownal	ME	04069	207-688-4712	
Web: www.maine.gov				
Camden Hills State Park 280 Belfast Rd. Camden	ME	04843	207-236-3109	
Web: www.maine.gov				
Cobscook Bay State Park RR 1 PO Box 127. Dennysville	ME	04628	207-726-4412	
Web: www.maine.gov				
Colonial Pemaquid State Historic Site PO Box 117. New Harbor	ME	04554	207-677-2423	
Web: www.maine.gov				
Crescent Beach State Park 66 Two Lights Rd. Cape Elizabeth	ME	04107	207-799-5871	
Web: www.maine.gov				
Damariscotta Lake State Park 8 State Pk Rd. Jefferson	ME	04348	207-549-7600	
Web: www.maine.gov				
Eagle Island State Historic Site PO Box 161. South Harpswell	ME	04079	207-624-6075	
Web: www.maine.gov				
Ferry Beach State Park 95 Bayview Rd. Saco	ME	04072	207-283-0067	
Web: www.maine.gov				
Fort Edgecomb State Historic Site 66 Fort Rd. Edgecomb	ME	04556	207-882-7777	
Web: www.maine.gov				
Fort Halifax State on the Kennebec c/o Bureau of Parks & Lands 106 Hogan Rd. Bangor	ME	04401	207-941-4014	
Web: www.maine.gov/doc/parks/history/forthalifax/index.htm				
Fort Kent State Historic Site c/o Bureau of Parks & Lands 106 Hogan Rd. Bangor	ME	04401	207-941-4014	
Web: www.maine.gov/cgi-bin/online/doc/parksearch/index.pl				
Fort Knox State Historic Site 711 Fort Knox Rd. Prospect	ME	04981	207-469-7719	
Web: www.maine.gov/doc/parks/programs/db_search				
Fort McClary State Historic Site Rte 103 near Kittery. Kittery Point	ME	03908	207-384-5160	
Web: www.maine.gov/doc/parks/programs/db_search				
Fort O'Brien State Historic Site c/o Bureau of Parks & Lands 106 Hogan Rd. Bangor	ME	04401	207-941-4014	
Web: www.maine.gov/cgi-bin/online/doc/parksearch/index.pl				
Fort Point State Park c/o Bureau of Parks & Lands 106 Hogan Rd. Bangor	ME	04401	207-941-4014	
Web: www.maine.gov/doc/parks/programs/history/fortpownall/history.htm				
Fort Popham State Historic Site 10 Perkins Farm Ln. Phippsburg	ME	04562	207-389-1335	
Web: www.maine.gov				
Grafton Notch State Park 1941 Bear River Rd. Newry	ME	04261	207-824-2912	
Web: www.maine.gov				
Holbrook Island Sanctuary PO Box 35. Brooksville	ME	04617	207-326-4012	
Web: www.maine.gov				
John Paul Jones State Historic Site c/o Bureau of Parks & Lands 106 State House Stn. Bangor	ME	04401	207-941-4014	941-4222
Web: www.maine.gov/doc/parks/volunteer/volunteer.html				
Katahdin Iron Works State Historic Site c/o Bureau of Parks & Lands 106 Hogan Rd. Bangor	ME	04401	207-941-4014	
Web: www.maine.gov/doc/nrimc/mgs/explore/mining/sites/sept03.htm				
Lake Saint George State Park 278 Belfast Augusta Rd. Liberty	ME	04949	207-589-4255	
Web: www.maine.gov				
Lamoine State Park 23 State Pk Rd. Ellsworth	ME	04605	207-667-4778	
Web: www.maine.gov				
Lily Bay State Park 13 Myrle's Way. Greenville	ME	04441	207-695-2700	
Web: www.maine.gov				
Moose Point State Park 310 W Main St. Searsport	ME	04974	207-548-2882	
Web: www.maine.gov				
Mount Blue State Park 299 Ctr Hill Rd. Weld	ME	04285	207-585-2347	
Web: www.maine.gov				
Peacock Beach State Park PO Box 2305. Richmond	ME	04357	207-582-2813	
Web: www.maine.gov				
Peaks-Kenny State Park 401 State Pk Rd. Dover-Foxcroft	ME	04426	207-564-2003	
Web: www.maine.gov				
Popham Beach State Park 10 Perkins Farm Ln. Phippsburg	ME	04562	207-389-1335	
Web: www.maine.gov				
Quoddy Head State Park 973 S Lubec Rd. Lubec	ME	04652	207-733-0911	
Web: www.maine.gov				

Name / Address	City	State	Zip	Phone	Fax
Range Ponds State Park PO Box 475 *Web:* www.maine.gov	Poland Spring	ME	04274	207-998-4104	
Rangeley Lake State Park HC 32 PO Box 5000 *Web:* www.maine.gov	Rangeley	ME	04970	207-864-3858	
Reid State Park 375 Seguinland Rd *Web:* www.maine.gov	Georgetown	ME	04548	207-371-2303	
Roque Bluffs State Park 145 Schoppee Pt Rd *Web:* www.maine.gov	Roque Bluffs	ME	04654	207-255-3475	
Sebago Lake State Park 11 Pk Access Rd *Web:* www.maine.gov	Casco	ME	04055	207-693-6613	
Shackford Head State Park c/o Bureau of Parks & Lands 106 Hogan Ave *Web:* www.maine.gov/cgi-bin/online/doc/parksearch/search_name.pl?state_park=68	Bangor	ME	04401	207-941-4014	
Swan Lake State Park 100 W Pk Ln *Web:* www.maine.gov	Swanville	ME	04915	207-525-4404	
Two Lights State Park 7 tower Dr *Web:* www.maine.gov	Cape Elizabeth	ME	04107	207-799-5871	
Vaughan Woods State Park 28 Oldfields Rd *Web:* www.maine.gov/cgi-bin/online/doc/parksearch/index.pl	South Berwick	ME	03908	207-490-4079	
Warren Island State Park PO Box 105 *Web:* www.maine.gov	Lincolnville	ME	04849	207-941-4014	
Whaleback Shell Midden State Historic Site c/o Damariscotta River Assn PO Box 333 *Web:* www.maine.gov	Damariscotta	ME	04543	207-563-1393	
Wolfe's Neck Woods State Park 426 Wolfe's Neck Rd *Web:* www.maine.gov	Freeport	ME	04032	207-865-4465	

MARYLAND

Name / Address	City	State	Zip	Phone	Fax
Assateague State Park 7307 Stephen Decatur Hwy *TF:* 888-432-2267 ■ *Web:* www.dnr.state.md.us	Berlin	MD	21811	410-641-2120	641-3615
Big Run State Park c/o New Germany State Pk 10368 Savage River Rd *Web:* www.dnr.state.md.us/publiclands/western/bigrun.asp	Swanton	MD	21561	301-895-5453	
Calvert Cliffs State Park c/o Smallwood State Pk 9500 H G Trueman Rd *Web:* www.dnr.state.md.us/publiclands/southern/calvertcliffs.asp	Lusby	MD	20657	301-743-7613	
Casselman River Bridge State Park c/o New Germany State Pk 349 Headquarters Ln *Web:* www.dnr.state.md.us/publiclands/western/casselman.html	Grantsville	MD	21536	301-895-5453	
Cedarville State Forest 10201 Bee Oak Rd *Web:* www.dnr.state.md.us	Brandywine	MD	20613	301-888-1410	
Choptank River Fishing Piers 29761 Bolingbroke Pt Dr *Web:* www.dnr.state.md.us	Trappe	MD	21673	410-820-1668	
Cunningham Falls State Park 14039 Catoctin Hollow Rd *Web:* www.dnr.state.md.us/publiclands/western/cunninghamfalls.html	Thurmont	MD	21788	301-271-7574	
Dans Mountain State Park c/o Rocky Gap State Pk 17410 Recreation Area Rd SW *Web:* www.dnr.state.md.us/publiclands/western/dansmountain.asp	Lonaconing	MD	21539	301-722-1480	
Deep Creek Lake State Park & Natural Resources Management Area 898 State Pk Rd *Web:* www.dnr.state.md.us/publiclands/western/deepcreeklake.html	Swanton	MD	21561	301-387-5563	387-4462
Elk Neck State Park 4395 Turkey Pt Rd *Web:* www.dnr.state.md.us	North East	MD	21901	410-287-5333	
Fair Hill Natural Resources Management Area 300 Tawes Dr *Web:* www.dnr.state.md.us	Elkton	MD	21921	410-398-1246	
Fort Frederick State Park 11100 Fort Frederick Rd *Web:* www.dnr.state.md.us/publiclands/western/fortfrederick.html	Big Pool	MD	21711	301-842-2155	
Gambrill State Park c/o Cunningham Falls State Pk 8602 Gambrill Pk Rd *TF:* 800-830-3974 ■ *Web:* www.dnr.state.md.us/publiclands/western/gambrill.asp	Frederick	MD	21702	301-271-7574	
Garrett State Forest 1431 Potomac Camp Rd *Web:* www.dnr.state.md.us/publiclands/western/garrett.html	Oakland	MD	21550	301-334-2038	
Gathland State Park c/o Greenbrier State Pk 900 Arnoldstown Rd *Web:* www.dnr.state.md.us/publiclands/western/gathland.asp	Burkittsville	MD	21718	301-791-4767	
Green Ridge State Forest 28700 Headquarters Dr NE *Web:* www.dnr.state.md.us/publiclands/western/greenridge.html	Flintstone	MD	21530	301-478-3124	
Greenbrier State Park 21843 National Pike *Web:* www.dnr.state.md.us	Boonsboro	MD	21713	301-791-4767	
Greenwell State Park 25450 Rosedale Manor Ln *Web:* www.dnr.state.md.us	Hollywood	MD	20636	301-373-9775	
Gunpowder Falls State Park 2813 Jerusalem Rd PO Box 480 *Web:* www.dnr.state.md.us	Kingsville	MD	21087	410-592-2897	
Hart-Miller Island State Park c/o Gunpowder Falls State Pk 2813 Jerusalem Rd PO Box 480 *Web:* www.dnr.state.md.us/publiclands/central/hartmiller.html	Kingsville	MD	21087	410-592-2897	
Herrington Manor State Park 222 Herrington Ln *Web:* www.dnr.state.md.us/publiclands/western/herringtonmanor.html	Oakland	MD	21550	301-334-9180	
Janes Island State Park 26280 Alfred Lawson Dr *Web:* www.dnr.state.md.us	Crisfield	MD	21817	410-968-1565	968-2515
Martinak State Park 137 Deep Shore Rd *Web:* www.dnr.state.md.us	Denton	MD	21629	410-820-1668	
Merkle Wildlife Sanctuary 11704 Fenno Rd *Web:* www.dnr.state.md.us/publiclands/southern/merkle.html	Upper Marlboro	MD	20772	301-888-1410	
Monocacy River Natural Resources Management Area c/o Seneca Creek State Pk 11950 Clopper Rd *Web:* www.dnr.state.md.us/publiclands/central/monocacy.html	Gaithersburg	MD	20878	301-924-2127	
Morgan Run Natural Environment Area c/o Patapsco Valley State Pk Benros Ln *TF:* 800-830-3974 ■ *Web:* www.dnr.state.md.us/publiclands/central/morganrun.asp	Westminster	MD	21157	410-461-5005	
New Germany State Park 349 Headquarters Ln *Web:* www.dnr.state.md.us/publiclands/western/newgermany.html	Grantsville	MD	21536	301-895-5453	
North Point State Park c/o Gunpowder Falls State Pk 2813 Jerusalem Rd PO Box 480 *Web:* www.dnr.state.md.us/publiclands/central/northpoint.html	Kingsville	MD	21087	410-592-2897	
Patapsco Valley State Park 8020 Baltimore National Pike *Web:* www.dnr.state.md.us	Ellicott City	MD	21043	410-461-5005	
Patuxent River State Park c/o Seneca Creek State Pk 11950 Clopper Rd *Web:* www.dnr.state.md.us/publiclands/central/patuxentriver.asp	Gaithersburg	MD	20878	301-924-2127	
Pocomoke River State Park 3461 Worcester Hwy *Web:* www.dnr.state.md.us	Snow Hill	MD	21863	410-632-2566	632-2914
Pocomoke State Forest 6572 Snow Hill Rd *Web:* www.dnr.state.md.us	Snow Hill	MD	21863	410-632-3732	
Point Lookout State Park 11175 Pt Lookout Rd *Web:* www.dnr.state.md.us	Scotland	MD	20687	301-872-5688	872-5084
Potomac State Forest 1431 Potomac Camp Rd *Web:* www.dnr.state.md.us/publiclands/western/potomacforest.html	Oakland	MD	21550	301-334-2038	
Rocks State Park 3318 Rocks Chrome Hill Rd *Web:* www.dnr.state.md.us/publiclands/central/rocks.html	Jarrettsville	MD	21084	410-557-7994	
Rocky Gap State Park 12500 Pleasant Valley Rd *Web:* www.dnr.state.md.us/publiclands/western/rockygap.html	Flintstone	MD	21530	301-722-1480	
Rosaryville State Park 8714 Rosaryville Rd *Web:* www.dnr.state.md.us/publiclands/southern/rosaryville.asp	Upper Marlboro	MD	20772	301-856-9656	
Saint Clement's Island State Park c/o Pt Lookout State Pk 11175 Pt Lookout Rd *TF:* 800-830-3974 ■ *Web:* www.dnr.state.md.us/publiclands/southern/stclements.asp	Scotland	MD	20687	301-872-5688	
Saint Mary's River State Park c/o Pt Lookout State Pk 11175 Pt Lookout Rd *TF:* 800-830-3974 ■ *Web:* www.dnr.state.md.us/publiclands/southern/stmarysriver.asp	Scotland	MD	20687	301-872-5688	
Sandy Point State Park 1100 E College Pkwy *Web:* www.dnr.state.md.us	Annapolis	MD	21409	410-974-2149	974-2647
Sassafras Natural Resources Management Area c/o Tuckahoe State Pk 13070 Crouse Mill Rd *Web:* www.dnr.state.md.us/publiclands/eastern/sassafras.asp	Queen Anne	MD	21657	410-820-1668	
Savage River State Forest 127 Headquarters Ln *Web:* www.dnr.state.md.us/publiclands/western/savageriver.html	Grantsville	MD	21536	301-895-5759	
Seneca Creek State Park 11950 Clopper Rd *Web:* www.dnr.state.md.us	Gaithersburg	MD	20878	301-924-2127	
Sideling Hill Exhibit Ctr c/o Fort Frederick State Pk 11100 Fort Frederick Rd *Web:* www.dnr.state.md.us/publiclands/western/sidelinghill.html	Big Pool	MD	21711	301-842-2155	
Smallwood State Park 2750 Sweden Pt Rd *Web:* www.dnr.state.md.us/publiclands/southern/smallwood.html	Marbury	MD	20658	301-743-7613	
Soldiers Delight Natural Environment Area c/o Patapsco Valley State Pk 5100 Deer Pk Rd *TF:* 800-830-3974 ■ *Web:* www.dnr.state.md.us/publiclands/central/soldiersdelight.asp	Owings Mills	MD	21117	410-461-5005	
Somers Cove Marina 715 Broadway PO Box 67 *TF:* 800-967-3474 ■ *Web:* www.dnr.state.md.us	Crisfield	MD	21817	410-968-0925	968-1408
South Mountain State Park c/o S Mountain Recreation Area 21843 National Pike *Web:* www.dnr.state.md.us/publiclands/western/southmountain.asp	Boonsboro	MD	21713	301-791-4767	
Susquehanna State Park c/o Rocks State Pk 3318 Rocks Chrome Hill Rd *Web:* www.dnr.state.md.us/publiclands/central/susquehanna.html	Jarrettsville	MD	21084	410-557-7994	
Swallow Falls State Park c/o Herrington Manor State Pk 222 Herrington Ln *Web:* www.dnr.state.md.us/publiclands/western/swallowfalls.asp	Oakland	MD	21550	301-387-6938	
Tuckahoe State Park 13070 Crouse Mill Rd *Web:* www.dnr.state.md.us	Queen Anne	MD	21657	410-820-1668	
Washington Monument State Park c/o Greenbrier State Pk 6620 Zittlestown Rd *Web:* www.dnr.state.md.us/publiclands/western/washington.asp	Middletown	MD	21769	301-791-4767	
Wye Island Natural Resources Management Area 632 Wye Island Rd *Web:* www.dnr.state.md.us	Queenstown	MD	21658	410-827-7577	

Name / Address	City	State	ZIP	Phone	Fax
Wye Oak State Park c/o Tuckahoe State Pk 13070 Crouse Mill Rd *Web:* www.dnr.state.md.us/publiclands/eastern/wyeoak.asp	Queen Anne	MD	21657	410-820-1668	
Youghiogheny River Natural Resources Management Area c/o Deep Creek Lake State Pk 898 State Pk Rd *Web:* www.dnr.state.md.us/publiclands/western/youghiogheny.html	Swanton	MD	21561	301-387-5563	387-4462

MASSACHUSETTS

Name / Address	City	State	ZIP	Phone	Fax
Ames Nowell State Park Linwood St *Web:* www.mass.gov	Abington	MA	02351	781-857-1336	
Ashland State Park c/o Hopkinton State Pk 71 Cedar St *Web:* www.mass.gov/dcr/parks/northeast/ashl.htm	Hopkinton	MA	01748	508-435-4303	
Bash Bish Falls State Park c/o Mt Washington State Forest RD 3 E St *Web:* www.mass.gov/dcr/parks/western/bash.htm	Mount Washington	MA	01258	413-528-0330	
Beartown State Forest 69 Blue Hill Rd PO Box 97 *Web:* www.mass.gov/dcr/parks/western/bear.htm	Monterey	MA	01245	413-528-0904	
Blackstone River & Canal Heritage State Park 287 Oak St *Web:* www.mass.gov	Uxbridge	MA	01569	508-278-7604	
Borderland State Park Massapoag Ave *Web:* www.mass.gov	North Easton	MA	02356	508-238-6566	
Bradley Palmer State Park Asbury St *Web:* www.mass.gov/dcr/parks/northeast/brad.htm	Topsfield	MA	01983	978-887-5931	
Brimfield State Forest 100 Dearth Hill Rd *Web:* www.mass.gov	Brimfield	MA	01010	413-267-9687	
Callahan State Park 93 Commonwealth Rd *Web:* www.mass.gov/dcr/parks/northeast/call.htm	Wayland	MA	01778	508-653-9641	
Cape Cod Rail Trail c/o Nickerson State Pk 3488 Main St *Web:* www.mass.gov/dcr/parks/southeast/ccrt.htm	Brewster	MA	02631	508-896-3491	
Chester-Blandford State Forest Rte 20 PO Box 105 *Web:* www.mass.gov/dcr/parks/western/chbl.htm	Chester	MA	01011	413-354-6347	
Chicopee Memorial State Park 570 Burnett Rd *Web:* www.mass.gov	Chicopee Falls	MA	01020	413-594-9416	
Clarksburg State Park 1199 Middle Rd *Web:* www.mass.gov	Clarksburg	MA	01247	413-664-8345	
CM Gardner State Park Rte 112 PO Box 105 *Web:* www.mass.gov/dcr/parks/western/gdsp.htm	Chester	MA	01011	413-354-6347	
Cochituate State Park 93 Commonwealth Rd *Web:* www.mass.gov/dcr/parks/northeast/coch.htm	Wayland	MA	01778	508-653-9641	
Connecticut River Greenway State Park 136 Damon Rd *Web:* www.mass.gov/dcr/parks/central/crgw.htm	NorthHampton	MA	01060	413-586-8706	
DAR State Forest 78 Cape St Rt 112 *Web:* www.mass.gov/dcr/parks/western/darf.htm	Goshen	MA	01032	413-268-7098	
Demarest Lloyd State Park Barney's Joy Rd *Web:* www.mass.gov	Dartmouth	MA	02748	508-636-8816	
Dighton Rock State Park c/o Freetown State Forest PO Box 171 *Web:* www.mass.gov	Assonet	MA	02702	508-822-7537	
Douglas State Forest 107 Wallum Lake Rd *Web:* www.mass.gov	Douglas	MA	01516	508-476-7872	
Dunn State Park Rt 101 *Web:* www.mass.gov/dcr/parks/central/dunn.htm	Gardner	MA	01440	978-632-7897	
Ellisville Harbor State Park Rt 3A *Web:* www.mass.gov	Plymouth	MA	02360	508-866-2580	
Erving State Forest 200 E Main St Rt 2A *Web:* www.mass.gov	Erving	MA	01344	978-544-3939	
F. Gilbert Hills State Forest 45 Mill St *Web:* www.mass.gov	Foxboro	MA	02035	508-543-5850	
Fall River Heritage State Park 200 Davol St *Web:* www.mass.gov	Fall River	MA	02720	508-675-5759	
Federated Women's Club State Forest West St *Web:* www.mass.gov/dcr/parks/central/fwsf.htm	Petersham	MA	01366	978-939-8962	
Fort Phoenix State Reservation Green St *Web:* www.mass.gov/dcr/parks/southeast/ftph.htm	Fairhaven	MA	02719	508-992-4524	
Freetown-Fall River State Forest 110 Slab Bridge Rd *Web:* www.mass.gov	Assonet	MA	02702	508-644-5522	
Gardner Heritage State Park (GHSP) 265 Ctr St *Web:* www.mass.gov/dcr/parks/central/ghsp.htm	Gardner	MA	01440	978-632-7897	
Georgetown-Rowley State Forest Rte97 *Web:* www.mass.gov/dcr/parks/northeast/grow.htm	Georgetown	MA	01833	978-887-5931	887-7292
Granville State Forest 323 W Hartland Rd *Web:* www.mass.gov	Granville	MA	01034	413-357-6611	
Great Brook Farm State Park 984 Lowell Rd PO Box 0829 *Web:* www.mass.gov	Carlisle	MA	01741	978-369-6312	
Halibut Point State Park 5 Gott Ave *Web:* www.mass.gov	Rockport	MA	01966	978-546-2997	
Hampton Ponds State Park 1048 N Rd *Web:* www.mass.gov	Westfield	MA	01085	413-532-3985	533-1837
Harold Parker State Forest 1951 Tpke St *Web:* www.mass.gov	North Andover	MA	01845	978-686-3391	
Holyoke Heritage State Park 221 Appleton St *Web:* www.mass.gov/dcr/parks/central/hhsp.htm	Holyoke	MA	01040	413-534-1723	534-0909
Hopkinton State Park 71 Cedar St *Web:* www.mass.gov	Hopkinton	MA	01748	508-435-4303	
Horseneck Beach State Reservation PO Box 328 *Web:* www.mass.gov	Westport	MA	02791	508-636-8816	
JA Skinner State Park PO Box 91 *Web:* www.mass.gov	Hadley	MA	01035	413-586-0350	
Jug End State Reservation & Wildlife Management Area c/o Mt Washington State Forest RD 3 E St *Web:* www.mass.gov/dcr/parks/western/juge.htm	Mount Washington	MA	01258	413-528-0330	
Kenneth Dubuque Memorial State Forest c/o Mohawk State Forest PO Box 7 *Web:* www.mass.gov/dcr/parks/western/dubq.htm	Charlemont	MA	01339	413-339-5504	
Lake Dennison Recreation Area Rt 202 *Web:* www.mass.gov	Winchendon	MA	01475	978-939-8962	
Lake Wyola State Park 94 Lake View Rd *Web:* www.mass.gov	Shutesbury	MA	01072	413-367-0317	
Lawrence Heritage State Park 1 Jackson St *Web:* www.mass.gov	Lawrence	MA	01840	978-794-1655	
Leominster State Forest 90 Fitchburg Rd Rt 31 *Web:* www.mass.gov	Westminster	MA	01473	978-874-2303	
Lowell Heritage State Park 160 Pawtucket Blvd *Web:* www.mass.gov/dcr/parks/northeast/llhp.htm	Lowell	MA	01854	978-458-8750	
Lowell-Dracut-Tyngsboro State Forest Trotting Pk Rd *Web:* www.mass.gov/dcr/parks/northeast/ldtf.htm	Lowell	MA	01854	978-369-6312	
Manuel F. Correllus State Forest PO Box 1612 *Web:* www.mass.gov	Vineyard Haven	MA	02568	508-693-2540	
Massasoit State Park 1361 Middleboro Ave *Web:* www.mass.gov	East Taunton	MA	02718	508-822-7405	
Maudslay State Park 74 Curzon Mill Rd *Web:* www.mass.gov	Newburyport	MA	01950	978-465-7223	
Mohawk Trail State Forest 175 Mohawk Trail/ Rt 2 PO Box 7 *Web:* www.mass.gov/dcr/parks/western/mhwk.htm	Charlemont	MA	01339	413-339-5504	
Monroe State Forest c/o Mohawk Trail State Forest PO Box 7 *Web:* www.mass.gov/dcr/parks/western/mnro.htm	Charlemont	MA	01339	413-339-5504	
Moore State Park Mill St *Web:* www.mass.gov	Paxton	MA	01612	508-792-3969	
Mount Everett State Reservation c/o Rd 3 E St *Web:* www.mass.gov/dcr/parks/western/meve.htm	Mount Washington	MA	01258	413-528-0330	
Mount Grace State Forest Winchester Rd *Web:* www.mass.gov	Warwick	MA	01378	978-544-3939	
Mount Greylock State Reservation 30 Rockwell Rd *Web:* www.mass.gov	Lanesborough	MA	01225	413-499-4262	
Mount Holyoke Range State Park Rt 116 *Web:* www.mass.gov	Amherst	MA	01059	413-586-0350	
Mount Sugarloaf State Reservation Rt 116 *Web:* www.mass.gov	South Deerfield	MA	01373	413-545-5993	
Mount Tom State Reservation 125 Reservation Rd *Web:* www.mass.gov/dcr/parks/central/mtom.htm	Holyoke	MA	01027	413-534-1186	
Mount Washington State Forest Rd 3 E St *Web:* www.mass.gov/dcr/parks/western/mwas.htm	Mount Washington	MA	01258	413-528-0330	
Myles Standish Monument State Reservation Crescent St Duxbury *Web:* www.mass.gov	Plymouth	MA	02332	508-747-5360	
Myles Standish State Forest PO Box 66 *Web:* www.mass.gov	South Carver	MA	02366	508-866-2526	
Nasketucket Bay State Reservation c/o Fort Phoenix State Reservation Green St *Web:* www.mass.gov/dcr/parks/southeast/nbsr.htm	Fairhaven	MA	02719	508-992-4524	
Natural Bridge State Park PO Box 1757 *Web:* www.mass.gov	North Adams	MA	01247	413-663-6392	
Nickerson State Park 3488 Main St Rte 6A *TF:* 877-422-6762 ■ *Web:* www.mass.gov/dcr/parks/southeast/nick.htm	Brewster	MA	02631	508-896-3491	
Norwottuck Rail Trail c/o Connecticut River Greenway State Pk 136 Damon Rd *Web:* www.mass.gov/dcr/parks/central/nwrt.htm	NorthHampton	MA	01060	413-586-8706	
October Mountain State Forest 317 Woodland Rd *Web:* www.mass.gov	Lee	MA	01238	413-243-1778	
Otter River State Forest 86 Winchendon Rd *Web:* www.mass.gov/dcr/parks/central/ottr.htm	Baldwinville	MA	01436	978-939-8962	
Pearl Hill State Park 595 Main St *Web:* www.mass.gov	Townsend	MA	01474	508-597-8802	
Pilgrim Memorial (Plymouth Rock) State Park Water St *Web:* www.mass.gov/dcr/parks/southeast/plgm.htm	Plymouth	MA	02360	508-866-2580	
Pittsfield State Forest 1041 Cascade St *Web:* www.mass.gov/dcr/parks/western/pitt.htm	Pittsfield	MA	01201	413-442-8992	
Purgatory Chasm State Reservation Purgatory Rd *Web:* www.mass.gov	Sutton	MA	01590	508-234-3733	
Quinsigamond State Park 10 Lake Ave N *Web:* www.mass.gov	Worcester	MA	01605	508-755-6880	755-5347
Robinson State Park 428 N St *Web:* www.mass.gov	Agawam	MA	01001	413-786-2877	
Rutland State Park Rt 122A *Web:* www.mass.gov	Rutland	MA	01543	508-886-6333	
Salisbury Beach State Reservation Beach Rd Rt 1A *Web:* www.mass.gov/dcr/parks/northeast/salb.htm	Salisbury	MA	01952	978-462-4481	

Phone Fax

Sandisfield State Forest PO Box 97 .... Monterey MA 01245 413-229-8212
Web: www.mass.gov/dcr/parks/western/sand.htm

Sandy Point State Reservation
Parker River Wildlife Refuge Rd .... Ipswich MA 01938 978-462-4481
Web: www.mass.gov/dcr/parks/northeast/sndp.htm

Savoy Mountain State Forest
260 Central Shaft Rd. .... Florida MA 01247 413-663-8469
Web: www.mass.gov

Scusset Beach State Reservation
140 Scusset Beach Rd .... Sagamore Beach MA 02562 508-888-0859
Web: www.mass.gov

Shawme-Crowell State Forest PO Box 621 .... Sandwich MA 02563 508-888-0351
Web: www.mass.gov

South Cape Beach State Park Great Neck Rd .... Mashpee MA 02649 508-457-0495
Web: www.mass.gov

Spencer State Forest Howe Pond Rd .... Spencer MA 01562 508-886-6333
Web: www.mass.gov

Streeter Point Recreation Area
6 Streeter Pt Ave .... Sturbridge MA 01566 508-347-9316
Web: www.mass.gov/dcr/parks/central/stpt.htm

Tolland State Forest
410 Tolland Rd PO Box 342 .... East Otis MA 01029 413-269-6002
Web: www.mass.gov

Upton State Forest 205 Westboro Rd. .... Upton MA 01568 508-278-6486
Web: www.mass.gov

Wachusett Mountain State Reservation
345 Mountain Rd .... Princeton MA 01541 978-464-2987
Web: www.mass.gov

Wahconah Falls State Park
c/o Pittsfield State Forest
1041 Cascade St. .... Pittsfield MA 01201 413-442-8992
Web: www.mass.gov/dcr/parks/western/wahf.htm

Walden Pond State Reservation 915 Walden St .... Concord MA 01742 978-369-3254
Web: www.mass.gov

Watson Pond State Park Bay Rd. .... Taunton MA 02783 508-884-8280
Web: www.mass.gov

Wells State Park 159 Walker Pond Rd .... Sturbridge MA 01566 508-347-9257
Web: www.mass.gov/dcr/parks/central/well.htm

Wendell State Forest Montague Rd. .... Wendell MA 01379 413-659-3797
Web: www.mass.gov

Western Gateway Heritage State Park
115 State St # 4 .... North Adams MA 01247 413-663-6312
Web: www.mass.gov

Whitehall State Park 71 Cedar St .... Hopkinton MA 01748 508-435-4303
Web: www.mass.gov/dcr/parks/northeast/whit.htm

Willard Brook State Forest 595 Main St .... Townsend MA 01474 978-597-8802
Web: www.mass.gov

Willowdale State Forest 383 Linebrook Rd .... Ipswich MA 01938 978-887-5931
Web: www.mass.gov/dcr/parks/northeast/wild.htm

Windsor State Forest 555 E St .... Williamsburg MA 01096 413-684-0948
Web: www.mass.gov/dcr/parks/western/wnds.htm

Wompatuck State Park 204 Union St .... Hingham MA 02043 781-749-7160
Web: www.mass.gov

MICHIGAN

Phone Fax

Albert E. Sleeper State Park
6573 State Pk Rd .... Caseville MI 48725 989-856-4411
Web: www.michigandnr.com/parksandtrails/ParksandTrailsInfo.aspx?id=494

Algonac State Park 8732 River Rd. .... Marine City MI 48039 810-765-5605
Web: www.michigandnr.com

Aloha State Park 4347 3rd St. .... Cheboygan MI 49721 231-625-2522
Web: www.michigandnr.com/parksandtrails/ParksandTrailsInfo.aspx?id=434

Bald Mountain Recreation Area
1330 E Greenshield Rd .... Lake Orion MI 48360 248-693-6767
Web: www.michigandnr.com

Baraga State Park 1300 US Hwy 41 S .... Baraga MI 49908 906-353-6558
Web: www.michigandnr.com

Bass River Recreation Area
c/o Hoffmaster State Pk 6585 Lake Harbor Rd .... Lamont MI 49430 231-798-3711
Web: www.michigandnr.com/ParksandTrails/ParksandTrailsInfo.aspx?id=436

Bay City Recreation Area 3582 State Pk Dr .... Bay City MI 48706 989-684-3020
Web: www.michigandnr.com

Bewabic State Park 720 Idlewild Rd .... Crystal Falls MI 49920 906-875-3324
Web: www.michigandnr.com

Brighton Recreation Area 6360 Chilson Rd .... Howell MI 48843 810-229-6566
Web: www.michigandnr.com

Brimley State Park 9200 W 6-Mile Rd. .... Brimley MI 49715 906-248-3422
Web: www.michigandnr.com

Burt Lake State Park 6635 State Pk Dr .... Indian River MI 49749 231-238-9392
Web: www.michigandnr.com

Cambridge Junction Historic State Park
13220 M-50 .... Brooklyn MI 49230 517-467-4414
Web: www.michigandnr.com

Charles Mears State Park 400 W Lowell St .... Pentwater MI 49449 231-869-2051
Web: www.michigandnr.com

Cheboygan State Park 4490 Beach Rd .... Cheboygan MI 49721 231-627-2811
Web: www.michigandnr.com

Clear Lake State Park 20500 M-33 N. .... Atlanta MI 49709 989-785-4388
Web: www.michigandnr.com

Coldwater Lake State Park Copeland Rd. .... Coldwater MI 49036 517-780-7866
Web: www.michigandnr.com

Colonial Michilimackinac State Park & Old Mackinac Point Lighthouse
c/o Mackinac State Historic Parks
PO Box 370 .... Mackinac Island MI 49757 906-847-3328 847-3815
Web: www.mackinacparks.com

Craig Lake State Park
851 County Rd AKE PO Box 88 .... Champion MI 49814 906-339-4461
Web: www.michigandnr.com/parksandtrails/ParksandTrailsInfo.aspx?id=415

Dodge #4 State Park 4250 Pkwy Dr. .... Waterford MI 48327 248-682-7323 682-5587
Web: www.michigandnr.com/parksandtrails/ParksandTrailsInfo.aspx?id=445

Phone Fax

Duck Lake State Park 3560 Memorial Dr .... North Muskegon MI 49445 231-744-3480
Web: www.michigandnr.com/parksandtrails/Details.aspx?type=SPRK&id=446

Fayette Historic State Park 13700 13.25 Ln. .... Garden MI 49835 906-644-2603
Web: www.michigandnr.com

Fisherman's Island State Park
Bells Bay Rd PO Box 456 .... Charlevoix MI 49720 231-547-6641
Web: www.michigandnr.com

FJ McLain State Park 18350 Hwy M-203 .... Hancock MI 49930 906-482-0278
Web: www.michigandnr.com

Fort Custer Recreation Area
5163 Fort Custer Dr .... Augusta MI 49012 269-731-4200
Web: www.michigandnr.com

Fort Wilkins State Park
15223 US Hwy 41 .... Copper Harbor MI 49918 906-289-4215
Web: www.michigandnr.com

Fred Meijer White Pine Trail State Park
6093 M-115 .... Cadillac MI 49601 231-775-7911
Web: www.michigandnr.com/parksandtrails/ParksandTrailsInfo.aspx?id=508

Grand Haven State Park 1001 S Harbor Dr. .... Grand Haven MI 49417 616-847-1309
Web: www.michigandnr.com

Grand Mere State Park
c/o Warren Dunes State Pk Thornton Dr. .... Stevensville MI 49127 269-426-4013

Harrisville State Park
248 State Pk Rd PO Box 326 .... Harrisville MI 48740 989-724-5126
Web: www.michigandnr.com/parksandtrails/ParksandTrailsInfo.aspx?id=451

Hart-Montague Trail State Park
c/o Silver Lake State Pk 9679 W State Pk Dr .... Mears MI 49436 231-873-3083
Web: www.michigandnr.com/parksandtrails/Details.aspx?id=452&type=SPRK

Hartwick Pines State Park 4216 Ranger Rd. .... Grayling MI 49738 989-348-7068
Web: www.michigandnr.com

Highland Recreation Area
5200 E Highland Rd .... White Lake MI 48383 248-889-3750
Web: www.michigandnr.com

Historic Mill Creek Discovery Park
c/o Mackinac State Historic Parks
PO Box 370 .... Mackinac Island MI 49757 231-436-4226 847-3815*
**Fax Area Code:* 906 ■ *Web:* www.mackinacparks.com/historic-mill-creek-discovery-park

Holland State Park 2215 Ottawa Beach Rd. .... Holland MI 49424 616-399-9390
Web: www.michigandnr.com

Holly Recreation Area 8100 Grange Hall Rd .... Holly MI 48442 248-634-8811
Web: www.michigandnr.com

Indian Lake State Park
8970W County Rd 442 .... Manistique MI 49854 906-341-2355
Web: www.michigandnr.com

Interlochen State Park M-137 .... Interlochen MI 49643 231-276-9511
Web: www.michigandnr.com

Ionia Recreation Area 2880 W David Hwy .... Ionia MI 48846 616-527-3750
Web: www.michigandnr.com

Island Lake Recreation Area
12950 E Grand River Rd .... Brighton MI 48116 810-229-7067
Web: www.michigandnr.com

JW Wells State Park N7670 Hwy M-35 .... Cedar River MI 49887 906-863-9747
Web: www.michigandnr.com

Kal-Haven Trail State Park
c/o Van Buren State Pk 23960 Ruggles Rd .... South Haven MI 49090 269-637-2788
Web: www.michigandnr.com/parksandtrails/ParksandTrailsInfo.aspx?id=463

Lake Gogebic State Park
N9995 State Hwy M-64 .... Marenisco MI 49947 906-842-3341
Web: www.michigandnr.com

Lake Hudson Recreation Area 5505 Morey Hwy .... Clayton MI 49235 517-445-2265
Web: www.michigandnr.com

Lakelands Trail State Park
8555 Silver Hill Rd 8555 Silver Hill Rt 1 .... Pinckney MI 48169 734-426-4913
Web: www.michigandnr.com/parksandtrails/ParksandTrailsInfo.aspx?id=465

Lakeport State Park 7605 Lakeshore Rd .... Lakeport MI 48059 810-327-6224
Web: www.michigandnr.com

Laughing Whitefish Falls Scenic Site
Dorsey Rd. .... Sundell MI 49885 906-341-2355
Web: www.michigan.gov/dnr/0,1607,7-153-30301_31154_31260-54016--,00.html

Leelanau State Park
15310 N Lighthouse Pt Rd .... Northport MI 49670 231-386-5422
Web: www.michigandnr.com

Ludington State Park PO Box 709 .... Ludington MI 49431 231-843-2423
Web: www.michigandnr.com

Mackinac Island State Park & Fort Mackinac
c/o Mackinac State Historic Parks
PO Box 370 .... Mackinac Island MI 49757 906-847-3328 847-3815
Web: www.mackinacparks.com/fort-mackinac

Maybury State Park 20145 Beck Rd .... Northville MI 48167 248-349-8390
Web: www.michigandnr.com

Meridian-Baseline State Park
c/o Waterloo Recreation Area
16345 McClure Rd .... Chelsea MI 48118 734-475-8307
Web: www.michigandnr.com/parksandtrails/details.aspx?type=SPRK&id=471

Metamora-Hadley Recreation Area
3871 Herd Rd .... Metamora MI 48455 810-797-4439
Web: www.michigandnr.com

Muskallonge Lake State Park
30042 County Rd 407 .... Newberry MI 49868 906-658-3338
Web: www.michigandnr.com

Muskegon State Park 3560 Memorial Dr .... North Muskegon MI 49445 231-744-3480
Web: www.michigandnr.com/parksandtrails/Details.aspx?type=SPRK&id=475

Negwegon State Park
c/o Harrisville State Pk PO Box 326 .... Harrisville MI 48740 989-724-5126
Web: www.michigandnr.com/parksandtrails/ParksandTrailsInfo.aspx?id=476

Newaygo State Park 2793 Beech St. .... Newaygo MI 49337 231-856-4452
Web: www.michigandnr.com

North Higgins Lake State Park
11747 N Higgins Lake Dr .... Roscommon MI 48653 989-821-6125
Web: www.michigandnr.com/parksandtrails/ParksandTrailsInfo.aspx?id=478

Onaway State Park 3622 N M 211 Rd .... Onaway MI 49765 989-733-8279
Web: www.michigandnr.com

Phone | Fax

Orchard Beach State Park
2064 N Lakeshore Rd ... Manistee MI 49660 231-723-7422
Web: www.michigandnr.com
Ortonville Recreation Area 5779 Hadley Rd ... Ortonville MI 48462 810-797-4439
Web: www.michigandnr.com
Otsego Lake State Park 7136 Old 27 S ... Gaylord MI 49735 989-732-5485
Palms Book State Park Rt 2 PO Box 2500 ... Manistique MI 49854 906-341-2355
Web: www.michigandnr.com/parksandtrails/Details.aspx?type=SPRK&id=425
Petoskey State Park 2475 M-119 Hwy ... Petoskey MI 49712 231-347-2311
Web: www.michigandnr.com
PH Hoeft State Park 5001 US Hwy 23 N ... Rogers City MI 49779 989-734-2543
Web: www.michigandnr.com
Pinckney Recreation Area 8555 Silver Hill ... Pinckney MI 48169 734-426-4913
Web: www.michigandnr.com/parksandtrails/ParksandTrailsInfo.aspx?id=484
PJ Hoffmaster State Park
6585 Lake Harbor Rd ... Muskegon MI 49441 231-798-3711
Web: www.michigandnr.com/parksandtrails/ParksandTrailsInfo.aspx?id=457
Pontiac Lake Recreation Area 7800 Gale Rd ... Waterford MI 48327 248-666-1020
Web: www.michigandnr.com/parksandtrails/ParksandTrailsInfo.aspx?id=485
Porcupine Mountains Wilderness State Park
33303 Headquarters Rd ... Ontonagon MI 49953 906-885-5275
Web: www.michigandnr.com
Port Crescent State Park
1775 Port Austin Rd ... Port Austin MI 48467 989-738-8663
Web: www.michigandnr.com
Proud Lake Recreation Area
3540 Wixom Rd ... Commerce Township MI 48382 248-685-2433
Web: www.michigandnr.com
Rifle River Recreation Area 2550 Rose City Rd ... Lupton MI 48635 989-473-2258
Web: www.michigandnr.com
Sanilac Petroglyphs Historic State Park
8251 Germania Rd ... Cass City MI 48726 989-856-4411
Web: www.michigan.gov/dnr/0,1607,7-153-54463_18595_18612---,00.html
Saugatuck Dunes State Park 6575 138th Ave ... Saugatuck MI 49453 269-637-2788
Web: www.michigandnr.com
Seven Lakes State Park 14390 Fish Lake Rd ... Holly MI 48442 248-634-7271
Web: www.michigandnr.com
Silver Lake State Park 9679 W State Pk Rd ... Mears MI 49436 231-873-3083
Web: www.michigandnr.com/parksandtrails/ParksandTrailsInfo.aspx?id=493
Sleepy Hollow State Park 7835 E Price Rd ... Laingsburg MI 48848 517-651-6217
Web: www.michigandnr.com
South Higgins Lake State Park
106 State Pk Dr ... Roscommon MI 48653 989-821-6374
Web: www.michigandnr.com
Sterling State Park 2800 State Pk Rd ... Monroe MI 48162 734-289-2715
Web: www.michigandnr.com
Straits State Park 720 Church St ... Saint Ignace MI 49781 906-643-8620
Web: www.michigandnr.com
Tahquamenon Falls State Park 41382 W M-123 ... Paradise MI 49768 906-492-3415
Web: www.michigandnr.com
Tawas Point State Park 686 Tawas Beach Rd ... East Tawas MI 48730 989-362-5041
Web: www.michigandnr.com
Thompson's Harbor State Park
c/o Cheboygan Field Office
120 A St PO Box 117 ... Cheboygan MI 49721 231-627-9011
Web: www.michigandnr.com/parksandtrails/ParksandTrailsInfo.aspx?id=500
Traverse City State Park 1132 US-31 N ... Traverse City MI 49686 231-922-5270
Web: www.michigandnr.com
Tri-Centennial State Park & Harbor
1900 Atwater St ... Detroit MI 48207 313-396-0217
Web: www.michigandnr.com
Twin Lakes State Park 6204 E Poyhonen Rd ... Toivola MI 49965 906-288-3321
Web: www.michigandnr.com
Van Buren State Park 23960 Ruggles Rd ... South Haven MI 49090 269-637-2788
Web: www.michigandnr.com/parksandtrails/ParksandTrailsInfo.aspx?id=502
Van Buren Trail State Park
23960 Ruggles Rd ... South Haven MI 49090 269-637-2788
Web: www.michigandnr.com
Van Riper State Park
851 County Rd AKE PO Box 88 ... Champion MI 49814 906-339-4461
Web: www.michigandnr.com/parksandtrails/ParksandTrailsInfo.aspx?id=430
Warren Dunes State Park 12032 Red Arrow Hwy ... Sawyer MI 49125 269-426-4013
Web: www.michigandnr.com
Warren Woods State Park
c/o Warren Dunes State Pk Elm Valley Rd ... Three Oaks MI 49128 269-426-4013
Waterloo Recreation Area 16345 McClure Rd ... Chelsea MI 48118 734-475-8307
Web: www.michigandnr.com/parksandtrails/ParksandTrailsInfo.aspx?id=506
WC Wetzel State Recreation Area
28681 Old N River Rd ... Harrison Township MI 48045 810-765-5605
Web: www.michigandnr.com
Wilderness State Park 903 Wilderness Pk Dr ... Carp Lake MI 49718 231-436-5381
Web: www.michigandnr.com
William Mitchell State Park 6093 E M-115 ... Cadillac MI 49601 231-775-7911
Web: www.michigandnr.com/parksandtrails/ParksandTrailsInfo.aspx?id=474
Wilson State Park 910 N 1st St PO Box 333 ... Harrison MI 48625 989-539-3021
Web: www.michigandnr.com
WJ Hayes State Park 1220 Wampler's Lake Rd ... Onsted MI 49265 517-467-7401
Web: www.michigandnr.com
Yankee Springs Recreation Area
2104 S Briggs Rd ... Middleville MI 49333 269-795-9081
Web: www.michigandnr.com
Young State Park 02280 Boyne City Rd ... Boyne City MI 49712 231-582-7523
Web: www.michigandnr.com

MINNESOTA

Phone | Fax

Afton State Park 6959 Peller Ave S ... Hastings MN 55033 651-436-5391 436-6912
Web: www.dnr.state.mn.us
Banning State Park
61101 Banning Pk Rd PO Box 643 ... Sandstone MN 55072 320-245-2668 245-0251
Web: www.dnr.state.mn.us
Bear Head Lake State Park
9301 Bear Head State Pk Rd ... Ely MN 55731 218-365-7229 365-7204
Web: www.dnr.state.mn.us
Beaver Creek Valley State Park
15954 County Rd 1 ... Caledonia MN 55921 507-724-2107 724-2107
Web: www.dnr.state.mn.us
Big Bog State Recreation Area
55716 Hwy 72 NE ... Waskish MN 56685 218-647-8592 647-8730
Web: www.dnr.state.mn.us
Big Stone Lake State Park
35889 Meadowbrook State Pk Rd ... Ortonville MN 56278 320-839-3663 839-3676
Web: www.dnr.state.mn.us
Blue Mounds State Park 1410 161st St ... Luverne MN 56156 507-283-1307 283-1306
Web: www.dnr.state.mn.us
Buffalo River State Park
155 S St Hwy 10 PO Box 352 ... Glyndon MN 56547 218-498-2124 498-2583
Web: www.dnr.state.mn.us
Camden State Park 1897 County Rd ... Lynd MN 56157 507-865-4530 865-4608
Web: www.dnr.state.mn.us
Carley State Park
c/o Whitewater State Pk 19041 Hwy 74 ... Altura MN 55910 507-932-3007
TF Resv: 866-857-2757 ■ *Web:* www.stateparks.com/carley.html
Cascade River State Park 3481 W Hwy 61 ... Lutsen MN 55612 218-387-3053 387-3054
Web: www.dnr.state.mn.us
Charles A. Lindbergh State Park
1615 Lindbergh Dr S PO Box 364 ... Little Falls MN 56345 320-616-2525 616-2526
Web: www.dnr.state.mn.us
Crow Wing State Park 3124 State Pk Rd ... Brainerd MN 56401 218-825-3075 825-3077
Web: www.dnr.state.mn.us
Cuyuna Country State Recreation Area
307 3rd St PO Box 404 ... Ironton MN 56455 218-546-5926 546-7369
Web: www.dnr.state.mn.us
Father Hennepin State Park
41294 Father Hennepin Pk Rd PO Box 397 ... Isle MN 56342 320-676-8763 676-3748
Web: www.dnr.state.mn.us
Flandrau State Park 1300 Summit Ave ... New Ulm MN 56073 507-233-9800 359-1544
Web: www.dnr.state.mn.us
Forestville/Mystery Cave State Park
21071 County 118 ... Preston MN 55965 507-352-5111 352-5113
Web: www.dnr.state.mn.us
Fort Ridgely State Park 72158 County Rd 30 ... Fairfax MN 55332 507-426-7840 426-7112
Web: www.dnr.state.mn.us
Fort Snelling State Park
101 Snelling Lake Rd ... Saint Paul MN 55111 612-725-2389 725-2391
Web: www.dnr.state.mn.us
Franz Jevne State Park
c/o Zippel State Pk 3684 54th Ave NW ... Williams MN 56686 218-783-6252 783-6253
Web: www.dnr.state.mn.us/state_parks/franz_jevne
Frontenac State Park 29223 County 28 Blvd ... Frontenac MN 55026 651-345-3401 345-3694
Web: www.dnr.state.mn.us
Garden Island State Recreation Area
c/o Zippel Bay State Pk 3684 54th Ave NW ... Williams MN 56686 218-783-6252 783-6253
Web: www.dnr.state.mn.us/state_parks/garden_island
George H. Crosby Manitou State Park
c/o Tettegouche State Pk 5702 Hwy 61 ... Silver Bay MN 55614 218-226-6365 226-6366
Web: www.dnr.state.mn.us/state_parks/george_crosby_manitou
Glacial Lakes State Park 25022 County Rd 41 ... Starbuck MN 56381 320-239-2860 239-4605
Web: www.dnr.state.mn.us
Glendalough State Park
25287 Whitetail Ln ... Battle Lake MN 56515 218-644-0110 864-0587
Web: www.dnr.state.mn.us/state_parks/glendalough/index.html
Gooseberry Falls State Park 3206 Hwy 61 ... Two Harbors MN 55616 218-834-3855 834-3787
Web: www.dnr.state.mn.us/state_parks/gooseberry_falls
Grand Portage State Park 9393 E Hwy 61 ... Grand Portage MN 55605 218-475-2360 475-2365
Web: www.dnr.state.mn.us
Great River Bluffs State Park 43605 Kipp Dr ... Winona MN 55987 507-643-6849 643-6849
Web: www.dnr.state.mn.us
Hayes Lake State Park 48990 County Rd 4 ... Roseau MN 56751 218-425-7504
Web: www.dnr.state.mn.us/state_parks/hayes_lake
Hill Annex Mine State Park PO Box 376 ... Calumet MN 55716 218-247-7215 247-7449
Web: www.dnr.state.mn.us/state_parks/hill_annex_mine
Interstate State Park
307 Milltown Rd PO Box 254 ... Taylors Falls MN 55084 651-465-5711 465-0517
Web: www.dnr.state.mn.us
Itasca State Park 36750 Main Pk Dr ... Park Rapids MN 56470 218-266-2100 266-3942
Web: www.dnr.state.mn.us
Jay Cooke State Park 780 Hwy 210 ... Carlton MN 55718 218-384-4610 384-4851
Web: www.dnr.state.mn.us
John A. Latsch State Park
c/o Whitewater State Pk 43605 Kipp Dr ... Winona MN 55987 507-643-6849
TF: 866-857-2757 ■ *Web:* www.stateparks.com/john_latsch.html
Judge CR Magney State Park
4051 E Hwy 61 ... Grand Marais MN 55604 218-387-3039 387-3051
Web: www.dnr.state.mn.us
Kilen Woods State Park
50200 860th St Rt 1 PO Box 122 ... Lakefield MN 56150 507-662-6258 662-5501
Web: www.dnr.state.mn.us
Lac Qui Parle State Park 14047 20th St NW ... Watson MN 56295 320-752-4450 734-4452
Web: www.dnr.state.mn.us
Lake Bemidji State Park 3401 State Pk Rd NE ... Bemidji MN 56601 218-755-3843 755-4073
Web: www.dnr.state.mn.us
Lake Bronson State Park PO Box 9 ... Lake Bronson MN 56734 218-754-2200 754-6141
Web: www.dnr.state.mn.us
Lake Carlos State Park 2601 County Rd 38 NE ... Carlos MN 56319 320-852-7200 852-7349
Web: www.dnr.state.mn.us
Lake Louise State Park
c/o Forestville/Mystery Cave State Pk
21071 County Rd 118 ... Preston MN 55965 507-352-5111 352-5113
Web: www.dnr.state.mn.us

Name / Address	City	State	ZIP	Phone	Fax
Lake Maria State Park 11411 Clementa Ave NW *Web:* www.dnr.state.mn.us	Monticello	MN	55362	763-878-2325	878-2620
Lake Shetek State Park 163 State Pk Rd *Web:* www.dnr.state.mn.us	Currie	MN	56123	507-763-3256	763-3330
Maplewood State Park 39721 Pk Entrance Rd *Web:* www.dnr.state.mn.us	Pelican Rapids	MN	56572	218-863-8383	863-8384
McCarthy Beach State Park 7622 McCarthy Beach Rd *Web:* www.dnr.state.mn.us	Side Lake	MN	55781	218-254-7979	254-7980
Mille Lacs Kathio State Park 15066 Kathio State Pk Rd *Web:* www.dnr.state.mn.us	Onamia	MN	56359	320-532-3523	532-3529
Minneopa State Park 54497 Gadwall Rd *Web:* www.dnr.state.mn.us	Mankato	MN	56001	507-389-5464	389-5174
Minnesota Valley State Recreation Area c/o Fort Snelling State Pk 101 Snelling Lake Rd *Web:* www.dnr.state.mn.us	Saint Paul	MN	55111	612-725-2389	
Monson Lake State Park 1690 15th St NE *Web:* www.dnr.state.mn.us	Sunburg	MN	56289	320-366-3797	366-3882
Moose Lake State Park 4252 County Rd 137 *Web:* www.dnr.state.mn.us	Moose Lake	MN	55767	218-485-5420	485-5422
Myre-Big Island State Park 19499 780th Ave *Web:* www.dnr.state.mn.us	Albert Lea	MN	56007	507-379-3403	379-3405
Nerstrand-Big Woods State Park 9700 170th St E *Web:* www.dnr.state.mn.us	Nerstrand	MN	55053	507-333-4840	333-4852
Old Mill State Park 33489 240th Ave NW Rt 1 PO Box 43 *Web:* www.dnr.state.mn.us	Argyle	MN	56713	218-437-8174	437-8104
Red River State Recreation Area 515 2nd St NW *Web:* www.dnr.state.mn.us	East Grand Forks	MN	56721	218-773-4950	773-4951
Rice Lake State Park 8485 Rose St *Web:* www.dnr.state.mn.us	Owatonna	MN	55060	507-455-5871	446-2326
Saint Croix State Park 30065 St Croix Pk Rd *Web:* www.dnr.state.mn.us	Hinckley	MN	55037	320-384-6591	384-7070
Sakatah Lake State Park 50499 Sakatah Lake State Pk Rd *Web:* www.dnr.state.mn.us	Waterville	MN	56096	507-362-4438	362-4558
Savanna Portage State Park 55626 Lake Pl *Web:* www.dnr.state.mn.us	McGregor	MN	55760	218-426-3271	426-4437
Scenic State Park 56956 Scenic Hwy 7 *Web:* www.dnr.state.mn.us	Bigfork	MN	56628	218-743-3362	743-1362
Sibley State Park 800 Sibley Pk Rd *Web:* www.dnr.state.mn.us	New London	MN	56273	320-354-2055	354-2372
Soudan Underground Mine State Park PO Box 335 *Web:* www.dnr.state.mn.us	Soudan	MN	55782	218-753-2245	753-2246
Split Rock Creek State Park 336 50th Ave *Web:* www.dnr.state.mn.us	Jasper	MN	56144	507-348-7908	348-8940
Split Rock Lighthouse State Park 3755 Split Rock Lighthouse Rd *Web:* www.dnr.state.mn.us/state_parks/split_rock_lighthouse	Two Harbors	MN	55616	218-226-6377	226-6378
Temperance River State Park 7620 W Hwy 61 PO Box 33 *Web:* www.dnr.state.mn.us	Schroeder	MN	55613	218-663-7476	663-7374
Tettegouche State Park 5702 Hwy 61 *Web:* www.dnr.state.mn.us/state_parks/tettegouche	Silver Bay	MN	55614	218-226-6365	226-6366
Upper Sioux Agency State Park 5908 Hwy 67 *Web:* www.dnr.state.mn.us	Granite Falls	MN	56241	320-564-4777	564-4838
Whitewater State Park 19041 Hwy 74 *Web:* www.dnr.state.mn.us	Altura	MN	55910	507-932-3007	932-5938
Wild River State Park 39797 Pk Trail *Web:* www.dnr.state.mn.us	Center City	MN	55012	651-583-2125	583-3101
William O'Brien State Park 16821 O'Brien Trail N *Web:* www.dnr.state.mn.us	Marine-on-Saint Croix	MN	55047	651-433-0500	433-0504
Zippel Bay State Park 3684 54th Ave NW *Web:* www.dnr.state.mn.us/state_parks/zippel_bay	Williams	MN	56686	218-783-6252	783-6253

MISSISSIPPI

Name / Address	City	State	ZIP	Phone	Fax
Buccaneer State Park 1150 S Beach Blvd *Web:* www.mdwfp.com	Waveland	MS	39576	228-467-3822	
Clarkco State Park 386 Clarkco Rd *Web:* www.mdwfp.com/parkView/parks.asp?ID=4842	Quitman	MS	39355	601-776-6651	776-5131
George Payne Cossar State Park 165 County Rd 170 *Web:* www.mdwfp.com/parkView/parks.asp?ID=2811	Oakland	MS	38948	662-623-7356	623-0113
Golden Memorial State Park 2104 Damascus Rd *Web:* www.mdwfp.com/parkView/parks.asp?ID=4843	Walnut Grove	MS	39189	601-253-2237	
Great River Road State Park PO Box 292 *Web:* www.mdwfp.com/parkView/parks.asp?ID=3823	Rosedale	MS	38769	662-759-6762	
Holmes County State Park 5369 State Pk Rd *Web:* www.mdwfp.com/parkView/parks.asp?ID=3824	Durant	MS	39063	662-653-3351	
Hugh White State Park PO Box 725 *Web:* www.mdwfp.com/parkView/parks.asp?ID=2812	Grenada	MS	38902	662-226-4934	
John W. Kyle State Park 4235 State Pk Rd *Web:* www.mdwfp.com	Sardis	MS	38666	662-487-1345	
JP Coleman State Park 613 County Rd 321 *Web:* www.mdwfp.com/parkView/parks.asp?ID=1814	Iuka	MS	38852	662-423-6515	
Lake Lincoln State Park 2573 Sunset Dr *Web:* www.home.mdwfp.com	Wesson	MS	39191	601-643-9044	
Lake Lowndes State Park 3319 Lake Lowndes Rd *Web:* www.mdwfp.com	Columbus	MS	39702	662-328-2110	
LeFleur's Bluff State Park 2140 Riverside Dr	Jackson	MS	39202	601-987-3923	354-6930
Legion State Park 635 Legion State Pk Rd *Web:* www.mdwfp.com	Louisville	MS	39339	662-773-8323	
Leroy Percy State Park PO Box 176 *Web:* www.mdwfp.com	Hollandale	MS	38748	662-827-5436	
Natchez State Park 230-B Wickcliff Rd *Web:* www.mdwfp.com	Natchez	MS	39120	601-442-2658	
Paul B. Johnson State Park 319 Geiger Lake Rd *TF:* 800-467-2757 ■ *Web:* www.ohwy.com	Hattiesburg	MS	39401	601-582-7721	545-5611
Percy Quin State Park 2036 Percy Quin Dr *Web:* www.mdwfp.com/parkView/parks.asp?ID=5847	McComb	MS	39648	601-684-3938	
Roosevelt State Park 2149 Hwy 13 S *Web:* www.mdwfp.com	Morton	MS	39117	601-732-6316	
Shepard State Park 1034 Graveline Rd *Web:* www.mdwfp.com	Gautier	MS	39553	228-497-2244	
Tishomingo State Park PO Box 880 *Web:* www.mdwfp.com/parkView/parks.asp?ID=1816	Tishomingo	MS	38873	662-438-6914	438-6755
Tombigbee State Park 264 Cabin Dr *TF:* 800-467-2757 ■ *Web:* www.mdwfp.com	Tupelo	MS	38804	662-842-7669	840-5594
Wall Doxey State Park 3946 Hwy 7 S *Web:* www.mdwfp.com	Holly Springs	MS	38635	662-252-4231	

MISSOURI

Name / Address	City	State	ZIP	Phone	Fax
Arrow Rock State Historic Site PO Box 1 *Web:* www.mostateparks.com	Arrow Rock	MO	65320	660-837-3330	
Battle of Athens State Historic Site Rt 1 PO Box 26 *Web:* www.mostateparks.com	Revere	MO	63465	660-877-3871	
Battle of Carthage State Park c/o Harry S Truman Birthplace State Historic Site 1009 Truman *Web:* mostateparks.com	Lamar	MO	64759	417-682-2279	
Battle of Lexington State Historic Site 1300 N John Shea Dr *Web:* www.mostateparks.com	Lexington	MO	64067	660-259-4654	
Bennett Spring State Park 26250 Hwy 64A *Web:* www.mostateparks.com	Lebanon	MO	65536	417-532-4338	
Big Lake State Park 204 Lake Shore Dr *Web:* www.mostateparks.com	Craig	MO	64437	660-442-3770	
Big Oak Tree State Park 13640 S Hwy 102 *Web:* www.mostateparks.com	East Prairie	MO	63845	573-649-3149	
Big Sugar Creek State Park c/o Roaring River State Pk 12716 Farm Rd 2239 *Web:* mostateparks.com	Cassville	MO	65625	417-847-2539	
Bollinger Mill State Historic Site 113 Bollinger Mill Rd *Web:* www.mostateparks.com	Burfordville	MO	63739	573-243-4591	
Boone's Lick State Historic Site Hwy 187 *Web:* www.mostateparks.com/booneslick.htm	Boonsboro	MO	21713	660-837-3330	
Bothwell Lodge State Historic Site 19349 Bothwell State Pk Rd *Web:* www.mostateparks.com	Sedalia	MO	65301	660-827-0510	
Castlewood State Park 1401 Kiefer Creek Rd *Web:* www.mostateparks.com	Ballwin	MO	63021	636-227-4433	
Confederate Memorial State Historic Site 211 W 1st St *Web:* www.mostateparks.com	Higginsville	MO	64037	660-584-2853	
Crowder State Park 76 Hwy 128 *Web:* www.mostateparks.com	Trenton	MO	64683	660-359-6473	
Cuivre River State Park 678 State Rt 147 *Web:* www.mostateparks.com	Troy	MO	63379	636-528-7247	
Deutschheim State Historic Site 107 W 2nd St *Web:* www.mostateparks.com	Hermann	MO	65041	573-486-2200	
Dillard Mill State Historic Site 142 Dillard Mill Rd *Web:* www.mostateparks.com	Davisville	MO	65456	573-244-3120	
Dr. Edmund A Babler Memorial State Park 800 Guy Pk Dr *Web:* www.mostateparks.com	Chesterfield	MO	63005	636-458-3813	
Elephant Rocks State Park 7406 Hwy 21 *Web:* www.mostateparks.com/elephantrock.htm	Belleview	MO	63623	573-546-3454	
Felix Valle House State Historic Site 198 Merchant St PO Box 89 *Web:* mostateparks.com/park/felix-valle-house-state-historic-site	Sainte Genevieve	MO	63670	573-883-7102	
Finger Lakes State Park 1505 E Peabody Rd *Web:* www.mostateparks.com	Columbia	MO	65202	573-443-5315	443-4999
First Missouri State Capitol State Historic Site 200-216 S Main St *Fax Area Code: 636 ■ *TF:* 800-334-6946 ■ *Web:* www.mostateparks.com	Saint Charles	MO	63301	800-334-6946	940-3324*
Fort Davidson State Historic Site 118 E Maple *Web:* www.mostateparks.com/ftdavidson.htm	Pilot Knob	MO	63663	573-546-3454	
General John J. Pershing Boyhood Home State Historic Site 1100 Pershing Dr *Web:* www.mostateparks.com	Laclede	MO	64651	660-963-2525	
Governor Daniel Dunklin's Grave State Historic Site c/o Southern Missouri Historic District 2901 Hwy 61 *Web:* www.mostateparks.com	Festus	MO	63028	636-937-3697	
Graham Cave State Park 217 Hwy TT *TF:* 800-334-6946 ■ *Web:* www.mostateparks.com/park/graham-cave-state-park	Montgomery City	MO	63361	573-564-3476	564-2534
Grand Gulf State Park Rt 3 PO Box 3554 *Web:* www.mostateparks.com	Thayer	MO	65791	417-264-7600	
Ha Ha Tonka State Park 1491 State Rd D *Web:* www.mostateparks.com	Camdenton	MO	65020	573-346-2986	

				Phone	Fax

Harry S Truman Birthplace State Historic Site
1009 Truman St .... Lamar MO 64759 417-682-2279
Web: www.mostateparks.com
Harry S Truman State Park 28761 State Pk Rd .... Warsaw MO 65355 660-438-7711
Web: www.mostateparks.com
Hawn State Park 12096 Pk Dr .... Sainte Genevieve MO 63670 573-883-3603
Web: www.mostateparks.com
Hunter-Dawson State Historic Site
PO Box 308 .... New Madrid MO 63869 573-748-5340
Web: www.mostateparks.com
Iliniwek Village State Historic Site
c/o Battle of Athens State Historic Site
Rt 1 PO Box 26 .... Revere MO 63465 660-877-3871
Web: www.mostateparks.com
Jefferson Landing State Historic Site & Missouri State Museum
Jefferson St & Capitol Ave .... Jefferson City MO 65101 573-751-2854
Web: www.mostateparks.com/jeffersonland.htm
Jewell Cemetery State Historic Site
c/o Rock Bridge Memorial State Pk
5901 S Hwy 163 .... Columbia MO 65203 573-449-7402
Web: www.mostateparks.com/jewellcem.htm
Johnson's Shut-Ins State Park
148 Taum Sauk Trail .... Middlebrook MO 63656 573-546-2450
Web: mostateparks.com/park/johnsons-shut-ins-state-park
Katy Trail State Park
Missouri Dept of Natural Resources
PO Box 196 .... Jefferson City MO 65102 573-449-7402 751-8656
TF: 800-334-6946 ■ *Web:* mostateparks.com/park/katy-trail-state-park
Knob Noster State Park 873 SE 10th .... Knob Noster MO 65336 660-563-2463
Web: www.mostateparks.com
Lake of the Ozarks State Park PO Box 170 .... Kaiser MO 65047 573-348-2694
Web: www.mostateparks.com
Lake Wappapello State Park
HC 2 PO Box 102 .... Williamsville MO 63967 573-297-3232
Web: www.mostateparks.com
Lewis & Clark State Park
801 Lake Crest Blvd .... Rushville MO 64484 816-579-5564
Web: www.mostateparks.com
Locust Creek Covered Bridge State Historic Site
16957 Dart Rd .... Laclede MO 64651 660-963-2525
Web: www.mostateparks.com/locustbridge.htm
Long Branch State Park 28615 Visitor Ctr Rd .... Macon MO 63552 660-773-5229
Web: www.mostateparks.com
Mark Twain Birthplace State Historic Site
37352 Shrine Rd .... Florida MO 65283 573-565-3449
Web: mostateparks.com/park/mark-twain-birthplace-state-historic-site
Mark Twain State Park 20057 State Pk Rd .... Stoutsville MO 65283 573-565-3440
Web: www.mostateparks.com
Mastodon State Historic Site
1050 Charles J Becker Dr .... Imperial MO 63052 636-464-2976
TF: 800-334-6946 ■ *Web:* www.mostateparks.com
Meramec State Park 115 Meramec Pk Dr .... Sullivan MO 63080 573-468-6072
Web: www.mostateparks.com
Missouri Mines State Historic Site
4000 Missouri 32 .... Park Hills MO 63601 573-431-6226
Web: www.mostateparks.com
Montauk State Park RR 5 PO Box 279 .... Salem MO 65560 573-548-2201
Web: www.mostateparks.com
Morris State Park HW WW .... Campbell MO 63933 573-748-5340
Web: www.mostateparks.com/morris.htm
Nathan Boone Homestead State Historic Site
7850 N State Hwy V .... Ash Grove MO 65604 417-751-3266
Web: www.mostateparks.com
Onondaga Cave State Park 7556 Hwy H .... Leasburg MO 65535 573-245-6576
Web: www.mostateparks.com
Osage Village State Historic Site
c/o Harry S Truman Birthplace State Historic Site
1009 Truman .... Lamar MO 64759 417-682-2279
Web: mostateparks.com
Pershing State Park 29277 Hwy 130 .... Laclede MO 64651 660-963-2299
Web: www.mostateparks.com
Pomme de Terre State Park HC 77 PO Box 890 .... Pittsburg MO 65724 417-852-4291
Web: www.mostateparks.com
Prairie State Park 128 NW 150th Ln .... Liberal MO 64769 417-843-6711
Web: www.mostateparks.com
Roaring River State Park
12716 Farm Rd 2239 .... Cassville MO 65625 417-847-2539
Web: mostateparks.com
Robertsville State Park PO Box 186 .... Robertsville MO 63072 636-257-3788
Web: www.mostateparks.com
Rock Bridge Memorial State Park
5901 S Hwy 163 .... Columbia MO 65203 573-449-7402 442-2249
TF: 800-334-6946 ■ *Web:* www.mostateparks.com
Route 66 State Park 97 N Outer Rd Suite 1 .... Eureka MO 63025 636-938-7198 938-7804
Web: www.mostateparks.com
Saint Francois State Park
8920 US Hwy 67 N .... Bonne Terre MO 63628 573-358-2173
Web: www.mostateparks.com
Saint Joe State Park 2800 Pimville Rd .... Park Hills MO 63601 573-431-1069
Web: www.mostateparks.com
Sam A. Baker State Park Rt 1 PO Box 113 .... Patterson MO 63956 573-856-4411
Web: www.mostateparks.com
Sandy Creek Covered Bridge State Historic Site
c/o Mastodon State Historic Site
1050 Museum Dr .... Imperial MO 63052 636-464-2976
Web: www.mostateparks.com
Sappington Cemetery State Historic Site
Rte AA c/o Arrow Rock State Historic Site .... Nelson MO 65320 660-837-3330
Web: www.mostateparks.com/sappingtoncem.htm
Scott Joplin House State Historic Site
2658 Delmar Blvd .... Saint Louis MO 63103 314-340-5790 340-5793
Web: www.mostateparks.com
Stockton State Park 19100 S Hwy 215 .... Dadeville MO 63635 417-276-4259
Web: www.mostateparks.com
Table Rock State Park 5272 State Hwy 165 .... Branson MO 65616 417-334-4704 334-4782
Web: www.mostateparks.com
Taum Sauk Mountain State Park
148 Taum Sauk Trail .... Middlebrook MO 63656 573-546-2450
Web: mostateparks.com/park/taum-sauk-mountain-state-park
Thomas Hart Benton Home & Studio State Historic Site
3616 Belleview .... Kansas City MO 64111 816-931-5722
Web: www.mostateparks.com
Thousand Hills State Park
20431 State Hwy 157 .... Kirksville MO 63501 660-665-6995
Web: www.mostateparks.com
Towosahgy State Historic Site
County Rd 502 .... East Prairie MO 63845 573-748-5340
Web: www.mostateparks.com/towosahgy.htm
Trail of Tears State Park
429 Moccasin Springs .... Jackson MO 63755 573-334-1711
Web: www.mostateparks.com
Union Covered Bridge State Historic Site
20700 Monroe County Rd 962 .... Paris MO 65275 573-565-3449
Web: mostateparks.com/park/union-covered-bridge-state-historic-site
Van Meter State Park Rt 1 PO Box 47 .... Miami MO 65344 660-886-7537
Web: www.mostateparks.com
Wakonda State Park 32836 State Pk Rd .... LaGrange MO 63448 573-655-2280
Web: www.mostateparks.com
Wallace State Park 10621 NE Hwy 121 .... Cameron MO 64429 816-632-3745
Web: www.mostateparks.com
Washington State Park 13041 State Hwy 104 .... DeSoto MO 63020 636-586-2995
Web: www.mostateparks.com
Watkins Woolen Mill State Park & State Historic Site
26600 Pk Rd N .... Lawson MO 64062 816-580-3387
Web: www.mostateparks.com
Weston Bend State Park 16600 Hwy 45 N .... Weston Bend MO 64098 816-640-5443
Web: www.mostateparks.com

MONTANA

				Phone	Fax

Ackley Lake State Park
4600 Giant Springs Rd .... Great Falls MT 59405 406-454-5840
Web: www.fwp.mt.gov
Anaconda Smoke Stack State Park
3201 Spurgin Rd FWP Region 2 Office .... Missoula MT 59804 406-542-5500
Web: fwp.mt.gov/parks/visit/anacondaSmokeStack
Bannack State Park 721 Bannack Rd # 2 .... Dillon MT 59725 406-834-3413
Web: www.fwp.mt.gov
Beaverhead Rock State Park
c/o Bannack State Pk 4200 Bannack Rd .... Dillon MT 59725 406-834-3413
Web: fwp.mt.gov/parks/visit/beaverheadRock
Beavertail Hill State Park
3201 Spurgin Rd FWP Region 2 Office .... Missoula MT 59804 406-542-5500
Web: fwp.mt.gov/parks/visit/beavertailHill
Big Arm State Park 490 N Meridian Rd .... Kalispell MT 59901 406-752-5501
Web: www.fwp.mt.gov
Black Sandy State Park
1420 E 6thAve PO Box 200701 .... Helena MT 59620 406-444-2535
Web: fwp.mt.gov/lands/site_281944.aspx
Chief Plenty Coups State Park PO Box 100 .... Pryor MT 59066 406-252-1289
Web: www.fwp.mt.gov
Clark's Lookout State Park
c/o Bannack State Pk 4200 Bannack Rd .... Dillon MT 59725 406-834-3413
Web: fwp.mt.gov/parks/visit/clarksLookout
Cooney State Park PO Box 254 .... Joliet MT 59041 406-445-2326
Web: www.fwp.mt.gov
Council Grove State Park
3201 Spurgin Rd FWP Region 2 Office .... Missoula MT 59804 406-542-5500
Web: fwp.mt.gov/parks/visit/councilGrove
Elkhorn State Park 1420 E 6thAve PO Box 200701 .... Helena MT 59620 406-444-2535
Web: fwp.mt.gov/lands/site_281892.aspx
Finley Point State Park 490 N Meridian Rd .... Kalispell MT 59901 406-887-2715
Web: www.fwp.mt.gov
First Peoples Buffalo Jump State Park
342 Ulm Vaughn Rd .... Ulm MT 59485 406-866-2217
Web: www.fwp.mt.gov
Fort Owen State Park PO Box 995 .... Lolo MT 59847 406-273-4253
Web: fwp.mt.gov/parks/visit/fortOwen
Frenchtown Pond State Park
3201 Spurgin Rd FWP Region 2 Office .... Missoula MT 59804 406-542-5500
Web: fwp.mt.gov/parks/visit/frenchtownPond
Giant Springs State Park
4600 Giant Springs Rd .... Great Falls MT 59405 406-454-5840 761-8477
Web: www.fwp.mt.gov
Granite Ghost Town State Park
3201 Spurgin Rd .... Missoula MT 59804 406-542-5500
Web: fwp.mt.gov/parks/visit/graniteGhostTown
Greycliff Prairie Dog Town State Park
2300 Lake Elmo Dr .... Billings MT 59105 406-247-2940
Web: fwp.mt.gov/parks/visit/greycliffPrairieDogTown
Hell Creek State Park PO Box 1630 .... Miles City MT 59301 406-557-2362
Web: www.fwp.mt.gov/parks/visit/hellCreek
Lake Elmo State Park 2300 Lake Elmo Dr .... Billings MT 59105 406-247-2955
Web: fwp.mt.gov/parks/visit/lakeElmo
Lake Mary Ronan State Park
490 N Meridian Rd .... Kalispell MT 59901 406-849-5082
Web: www.fwp.mt.gov
Lewis & Clark Caverns State Park
PO Box 489 .... Whitehall MT 59759 406-287-3541
Web: fwp.mt.gov/parks/visit/lewisAndClarkCaverns
Logan State Park 490 N Meridian Rd .... Kalispell MT 59901 406-293-7190
Web: www.fwp.mt.gov
Lone Pine State Park 490 N Meridian .... Kalispell MT 59901 406-752-5501
Web: www.fwp.mt.gov

Phone Fax

Lost Creek State Park 3201 Spurgin Rd Missoula MT 59804 406-542-5500
Web: fwp.mt.gov/parks/visit/lostCreek

Madison Buffalo Jump State Park
1400 S 19th St Bozeman MT 59715 406-994-4042
Web: www.fwp.mt.gov

Makoshika State Park PO Box 1242 Glendive MT 59330 406-377-6256
Web: www.fwp.mt.gov

Medicine Rocks State Park PO Box 1630 Miles City MT 59301 406-234-0926
Web: www.fwp.mt.gov/parks/visit/medicineRocks

Missouri Headwaters State Park
c/o Region 3 Office 1400 S 19th St. Bozeman MT 59715 406-994-4042
Web: fwp.mt.gov/lands/site_281910.aspx

Painted Rocks State Park 3201 Spurgin Rd. Missoula MT 59804 406-542-5500
Web: fwp.mt.gov/parks/visit/paintedRocks

Pictograph Cave State Park
c/o Region 5 Office 2300 Lake Elmo Dr Billings MT 59105 406-247-2955 248-5026
Web: www.fwp.mt.gov

Pirogue Island State Park PO Box 1630 Miles City MT 59301 406-234-0926
Web: www.fwp.mt.gov/parks/visit/pirogueIsland

Placid Lake State Park PO Box 136 Seeley Lake MT 59868 406-677-6804
Web: fwp.mt.gov/parks/visit/placidLake

Rosebud Battlefield State Park
PO Box 1630 Miles City MT 59301 406-757-2219
Web: www.fwp.mt.gov/parks/visit/rosebudBattlefield

Salmon Lake State Park PO Box 136 Seeley Lake MT 59868 406-677-6804
Web: fwp.mt.gov/parks/visit/salmonLake

Sluice Boxes State Park
4600 Giant Springs Rd Great Falls MT 59406 406-454-5840
Web: www.fwp.mt.gov

Smith River State Park
4600 Giant Springs Rd Great Falls MT 59405 406-454-5840
Web: www.fwp.mt.gov

Spring Meadow Lake State Park
1420 E 6thAve PO Box 200701 Helena MT 59620 406-444-2535
Web: fwp.mt.gov/lands/site_281949.aspx

Thompson Falls State Park
490 N Meridian Rd Kalispell MT 59901 406-752-5501
Web: www.fwp.mt.gov

Tongue River Reservoir State Park
PO Box 1630 Miles City MT 59301 406-757-2298
Web: www.fwp.mt.gov/parks/visit/tongueRiverReservoir

Travelers Rest State Park 6550 Mormon Creek Rd Lolo MT 59847 406-273-4253
Web: www.fwp.mt.gov

Wayfarers State Park 490 N Meridian Rd Kalispell MT 59901 406-752-5501
Web: www.fwp.mt.gov

West Shore State Park 490 N Meridian Rd Kalispell MT 59901 406-752-5501
Web: www.fwp.mt.gov

Whitefish Lake State Park
490 N Meridian Rd Kalispell MT 59901 406-862-3991
Web: www.fwp.mt.gov

Wild Horse Island State Park
490 N Meridian Rd Kalispell MT 59901 406-752-5501
Web: www.fwp.mt.gov

Yellow Bay State Park 490 N Meridian Rd Kalispell MT 59901 406-752-5501
Web: www.fwp.mt.gov

NEBRASKA

Phone Fax

Alexandria State Recreation Area
57426 710th Rd Fairbury NE 68352 402-729-5777
Web: www.ngpc.state.ne.us

Arbor Lodge State Historical Park
PO Box 15 Nebraska City NE 68410 402-873-7222
Web: www.ngpc.state.ne.us

Arnold State Recreation Area
HC 69 PO Box 117 Anselmo NE 68813 308-749-2235
Web: www.outdoornebraska.ne.gov/parks

Ash Hollow State Historical Park PO Box 70 Lewellen NE 69147 308-778-5651
Web: www.ngpc.state.ne.us/parks/guides/parksearch/findpark.asp

Ashfall Fossil Beds State Historical Park
86930 517th Ave. Royal NE 68773 402-893-2000
Web: www.ngpc.state.ne.us

Atkinson Lake State Recreation Area
PO Box 508 Bassett NE 68714 402-684-2921
Web: www.ngpc.state.ne.us/parks/guides/parksearch/findpark.asp

Blue River State Recreation Area
3019 Apple St. Lincoln NE 68503 402-471-0641
Web: www.ngpc.state.ne.us

Bowman Lake State Recreation Area
PO Box 117 Loup City NE 68853 308-745-0230
Web: www.ngpc.state.ne.us

Bowring Ranch State Historical Park
PO Box 38 Merriman NE 69218 308-684-3428
Web: www.ngpc.state.ne.us/parks/guides/parksearch/findpark.asp

Branched Oak State Recreation Area
12000 W Branched Oak Rd. Raymond NE 68428 402-783-3400
Web: www.ngpc.state.ne.us/parks/guides/parksearch/findpark.asp

Brownville State Recreation Area
c/o Indian Cave State Pk RR 1, PO Box 30 Shubert NE 68437 402-883-2575
Web: www.ngpc.state.ne.us

Buffalo Bill Ranch State Historical Park
2921 Scouts Rest Ranch Rd North Platte NE 69101 308-535-8035
Web: www.ngpc.state.ne.us

Calamus State Recreation Area
HC 79 PO Box 20L Burwell NE 68823 308-346-5666
Web: www.ngpc.state.ne.us/parks/guides/parksearch/findpark.asp

Chadron State Park 15951 Hwy 385 Chadron NE 69337 308-432-6167
Web: www.ngpc.state.ne.us

Champion Lake State Recreation Area
73122 338 Ave Enders NE 69027 308-394-5118
Web: www.ngpc.state.ne.us/parks/guides/parksearch/findpark.asp

Phone Fax

Champion Mill State Historical Park
73122 338 Ave Enders NE 69027 308-778-5651
Web: www.ngpc.state.ne.us/parks/guides/parksearch/findpark.asp

Cheyenne State Recreation Area
PO Box 944 Grand Island NE 68832 308-385-6210
Web: www.ngpc.state.ne.us

Conestoga State Recreation Area
RR 4 PO Box 41B Lincoln NE 68524 402-796-2362
Web: www.ngpc.state.ne.us

Cottonwood Lake State Recreation Area
PO Box 38 Merriman NE 69218 308-684-3428
Web: www.ngpc.state.ne.us/parks/guides/parksearch/findpark.asp

Crystal Lake State Recreation Area
7425 S US Hwy 281 Doniphan NE 68832 308-385-6210
Web: www.ngpc.state.ne.us

Dead Timber State Recreation Area
227 County Rd & 12 Blvd. Scribner NE 68057 402-664-3597
Web: www.ngpc.state.ne.us/parks/guides/parksearch/findpark.asp

DLD State Recreation Area 7425 S US Hwy 281 Doniphan NE 68832 308-385-6211
Web: www.ngpc.state.ne.us/parks/guides/parksearch/findpark.asp

Enders Reservoir State Recreation Area
73122 338th Ave. Enders NE 69027 308-394-5118
Web: www.ngpc.state.ne.us/parks/guides/parksearch/findpark.asp

Eugene T Mahoney State Park 28500 W Pk Hwy Ashland NE 68003 402-944-2523
Web: www.ngpc.state.ne.us

Fort Atkinson State Historical Park
PO Box 240 Fort Calhoun NE 68023 402-468-5611 468-5066
Web: www.ngpc.state.ne.us

Fort Hartsuff State Historical Park
RR 1 PO Box 37 Burwell NE 68823 308-346-4715
Web: www.ngpc.state.ne.us

Fort Kearny State Recreation Area
c/o Fort Kearny State Historical Pk
1020 'V' Rd Kearney NE 68847 308-865-5305
Web: www.ngpc.state.ne.us

Fort Robinson State Park PO Box 392 Crawford NE 69339 308-665-2900
Web: www.ngpc.state.ne.us

Fremont Lakes State Recreation Area
2351 County Rd 18. Ames NE 68621 402-727-3290
Web: www.ngpc.state.ne.us/parks/guides/parksearch/findpark.asp

Gallagher Canyon State Recreation Area
1 E Pk Dr 25A Elwood NE 68937 308-785-2685
Web: www.ngpc.state.ne.us

Indian Cave State Park 65296 720 Rd Shubert NE 68437 402-883-2575
Web: www.ngpc.state.ne.us/parks/guides/parksearch/findpark.asp

Johnson Lake State Recreation Area
1 E Pk Dr 25A Elwood NE 68937 308-785-2685
Web: www.ngpc.state.ne.us

Keller Park State Recreation Area PO Box 508 Bassett NE 68714 402-684-2921
Web: www.ngpc.state.ne.us/parks/guides/parksearch/findpark.asp

Lake McConaughy State Recreation Area
1450 Hwy 61N Ogallala NE 69153 308-284-8800
Web: www.ngpc.state.ne.us/parks/guides/parksearch/findpark.asp

Lake Minatare State Recreation Area
PO Box 188 Minatare NE 69356 308-783-2911
Web: www.ngpc.state.ne.us

Lake Ogallala State Recreation Area
1450 Hwy 61N Ogallala NE 69153 308-284-8800
Web: www.ngpc.state.ne.us

Lewis & Clark State Recreation Area
54731 897 Rd. Crofton NE 68730 402-388-4169
Web: www.ngpc.state.ne.us

Long Lake State Recreation Area
524 Panzer St PO Box 508 Bassett NE 68714 402-684-2921
Web: www.ngpc.state.ne.us/parks/guides/parksearch/findpark.asp

Long Pine State Recreation Area
524 Panzer St PO Box 508 Bassett NE 68714 402-684-2921
Web: www.ngpc.state.ne.us/parks/guides/parksearch/findpark.asp

Louisville State Recreation Area
15810 Hwy 50 Louisville NE 68037 402-234-6855
Web: www.ngpc.state.ne.us

Medicine Creek State Recreation Area
40611 Rd 728 Cambridge NE 69022 308-697-4667
Web: www.ngpc.state.ne.us

Merritt Reservoir State Recreation Area
420 E 1st St Valentine NE 69201 402-376-3320
Web: www.ngpc.state.ne.us

Mormon Island State Recreation Area
7425 S Hwy 281 Doniphan NE 68832 308-385-6211
Web: www.ngpc.state.ne.us

Niobrara State Park 89261 522 Ave Niobrara NE 68760 402-857-3373
Web: www.ngpc.state.ne.us

North Loup State Recreation Area
7425 S US Hwy 281 Doniphan NE 68832 308-385-6211
Web: www.ngpc.state.ne.us/parks/guides/parksearch/findpark.asp

Oliver Reservoir State Recreation Area
210615 Hwy 71 Gering NE 69341 308-436-3777
Web: www.ngpc.state.ne.us

Pawnee State Recreation Area RR 4 PO Box 41B Lincoln NE 68524 402-796-2362
Web: www.ngpc.state.ne.us

Pelican Point State Recreation Area
640 County Rd 19. Craig NE 68019 402-374-1727
Web: www.ngpc.state.ne.us

Pibel Lake State Recreation Area
HC 79 PO Box 20L Burwell NE 68823 308-346-5666
Web: www.ngpc.state.ne.us/parks/guides/parksearch/findpark.asp

Platte River State Park 14421 346th St Louisville NE 68037 402-234-2217
Web: www.ngpc.state.ne.us

Ponca State Park 88090 Spur 26 E PO Box 688 Ponca NE 68770 402-755-2284
Web: www.outdoornebraska.ne.gov/parks

Red Willow Reservoir State Recreation Area
RR 1 PO Box 145 McCook NE 69001 308-345-5899
Web: www.outdoornebraska.ne.gov/parks

Name / Address	City	State	ZIP	Phone	Fax
Riverview Marina State Recreation Area PO Box 15 *Web:* www.ngpc.state.ne.us	Nebraska City	NE	68410	402-873-7222	
Rock Creek Lake State Recreation Area 73122 338 Ave *Web:* www.ngpc.state.ne.us/parks/guides/parksearch/findpark.asp	Enders	NE	69027	308-394-5118	
Rock Creek Station State Historical Park 57426 710th Rd *Web:* www.ngpc.state.ne.us	Fairbury	NE	68352	402-729-5777	
Rock Creek Station State Recreation Area 57426 710th Rd *Web:* www.outdoornebraska.ne.gov/parks	Fairbury	NE	68352	402-729-5777	
Sandy Ch State Recreation Area 1020 'V' Rd *Web:* www.ngpc.state.ne.us/parks/guides/parksearch/findpark.asp	Kearney	NE	68847	308-865-5305	
Schramm Park State Recreation Area 15810 Hwy 50 *Web:* www.outdoornebraska.ne.gov/parks	Louisville	NE	68037	402-234-6855	
Sherman Reservoir State Recreation Area RR 2 PO Box 117 *Web:* www.ngpc.state.ne.us	Loup City	NE	68853	308-745-0230	
Smith Falls State Park HC 13 PO Box 25 *Web:* www.ngpc.state.ne.us	Valentine	NE	69201	402-376-1306	
Summit Lake State Recreation Area 640 County Rd 19 *Web:* www.ngpc.state.ne.us	Craig	NE	69019	402-374-1727	
Sutherland Reservoir State Recreation Area 301 E State Farm Rd *Web:* www.outdoornebraska.org	North Platte	NE	69101	308-535-8025	
Swanson Reservoir State Recreation Area RR 2 PO Box 20 *Web:* www.outdoornebraska.ne.gov/parks/guides/parksearch/showpark.asp?Area_No=172	Stratton	NE	69043	308-276-2671	
Two Rivers State Recreation Area 27702 'F' St *Web:* www.ngpc.state.ne.us	Waterloo	NE	68069	402-359-5165	
Verdon State Recreation Area c/o Indian Cave State Pk RR 1, PO Box 30 *Web:* www.ngpc.state.ne.us	Shubert	NE	68437	402-883-2575	
Wagon Train State Recreation Area 3019 Apple St *Web:* www.ngpc.state.ne.us/parks/guides/parksearch/findpark.asp	Lincoln	NE	68503	402-471-5566	
Walgren Lake State Recreation Area 15951 Hwy 385 *Web:* www.ngpc.state.ne.us/parks/guides/parksearch/findpark.asp	Chadron	NE	69337	308-432-6167	432-6102
War Axe State Recreation Area PO Box 427 *Web:* www.ngpc.state.ne.us/parks/guides/parksearch/findpark.asp	Gibbon	NE	68840	308-468-5700	
Wildcat Hills State Recreation Area 210615 Hwy 71 *Web:* www.ngpc.state.ne.us	Gering	NE	69341	308-436-3777	
Willow Creek State Recreation Area 54876 852 Rd *Web:* www.ngpc.state.ne.us	Pierce	NE	68767	402-329-4053	
Windmill State Recreation Area PO Box 427 *Web:* www.ngpc.state.ne.us/parks/guides/parksearch/findpark.asp	Gibbon	NE	68840	308-468-5700	

NEVADA

Name / Address	City	State	ZIP	Phone	Fax
Beaver Dam State Park PO Box 985 *Web:* www.parks.nv.gov	Caliente	NV	89008	775-728-4460	
Belmont Courthouse State Historic Site c/o Fallon Region Headquarters 16799 Lahontan Dam *Web:* www.parks.nv.gov/bc.htm	Fallon	NV	89406	775-867-3001	
Berlin-Ichthyosaur State Park HC 61 PO Box 61200 *Web:* www.parks.nv.gov	Austin	NV	89310	775-964-2440	964-2012
Big Bend of the Colorado State Recreation Area PO Box 32850 *Web:* www.parks.nv.gov	Laughlin	NV	89028	702-298-1859	
Cathedral Gorge State Park PO Box 176 *Web:* www.parks.nv.gov	Panaca	NV	89042	775-728-4460	
Cave Lake State Park PO Box 151761 *Web:* www.parks.nv.gov/cl.htm	Ely	NV	89315	775-867-3001	
Dayton State Park PO Box 1478 *Web:* www.parks.nv.gov	Dayton	NV	89403	775-687-5678	
Echo Canyon State Park HC 74 PO Box 295 *Web:* www.parks.nv.gov	Pioche	NV	89043	775-962-5103	
Fort Churchill State Historic Park 1000 Hwy 95A *Web:* www.parks.nv.gov	Silver Springs	NV	89429	775-577-2345	
Kershaw-Ryan State Park PO Box 985 *Web:* www.parks.nv.gov/kr.htm	Caliente	NV	89008	775-726-3564	726-3557
Lahontan State Recreation Area 16799 Lahontan Dam *Web:* www.parks.nv.gov	Fallon	NV	89406	775-577-2235	
Lake Tahoe Nevada State Park PO Box 8867 *Web:* www.parks.nv.gov	Incline Village	NV	89452	775-831-0494	831-2514
Mormon Station State Historic Park PO Box 302 *Web:* www.parks.nv.gov/ms.htm	Genoa	NV	89411	775-782-2590	
Old Las Vegas Mormon Fort State Historic Park 908 Las Vegas Blvd N *Web:* www.parks.nv.gov	Las Vegas	NV	89101	702-486-3511	486-3734
Rye Patch State Recreation Area 2505 Rye Patch Reservoir Rd *Web:* www.parks.nv.gov	Lovelock	NV	89419	775-538-7321	
South Fork State Recreation Area 353 Lower S Fork Unit 8 *Web:* www.parks.nv.gov	Spring Creek	NV	89815	775-744-4346	
Spring Mountain Ranch State Park PO Box 124 *Web:* www.parks.nv.gov	Blue Diamond	NV	89004	702-875-4141	
Spring Valley State Park HC 74 PO Box 201 *Web:* www.parks.nv.gov	Pioche	NV	89043	775-962-5102	
Valley of Fire State Park Valley Fire Rd PO Box 515 *Web:* www.parks.nv.gov	Overton	NV	89040	702-397-2088	397-2621
Walker Lake State Recreation Area c/o Fallon Region Headquarters 16799 Lahontan Dam *Web:* www.parks.nv.gov/walk.htm	Fallon	NV	89406	775-867-3001	
Ward Charcoal Ovens State Historic Park PO Box 151761 *Web:* www.parks.nv.gov/ww.htm	Ely	NV	89315	775-867-3001	
Washoe Lake State Park 4855 E Lake Blvd *Web:* www.parks.nv.gov	Carson City	NV	89704	775-687-4319	
Wild Horse State Recreation Area HC 31 PO Box 265 *Web:* www.parks.nv.gov	Elko	NV	89801	775-758-6493	

NEW HAMPSHIRE

Name / Address	City	State	ZIP	Phone	Fax
Ahern State Park Right Way Path *Web:* www.nhstateparks.org/explore/state-parks/ahern-state-park.aspx	Laconia	NH	03246	603-485-2034	
Androscoggin Wayside Park Rte 16 *Web:* www.nhstateparks.org/explore/state-parks/androscoggin-wayside-park.aspx	Errol	NH	03579	603-538-6707	
Annett Wayside Park Cathedral Rd *Web:* www.nhstateparks.org	Rindge	NH	03461	603-485-2034	
Bear Brook State Park 157 Deerfield Rd *Web:* www.nhstateparks.org	Allenstown	NH	03275	603-271-3556	271-3553
Beaver Brook Falls Wayside Park Rt 145 *Web:* www.nhstateparks.org/explore/state-parks/beaver-brook-falls-wayside.aspx	Colebrook	NH	03576	603-538-6707	
Bedell Bridge State Park Rts 10 & 25 *Web:* www.nhstateparks.org/explore/state-parks/bedell-bridge-state-historic-site.aspx	Haverhill	NH	03765	603-823-7722	
Cardigan State Park Rt 18 *Web:* www.nhstateparks.org/explore/state-parks/cardigan-state-park.aspx	Orange	NH	03741	603-485-2034	
Chesterfield Gorge Natural Area Rt 9 *Web:* www.nhstateparks.org	Chesterfield	NH	03443	603-363-8373	
Clough State Park 455 Clough Pk Rd *Web:* www.nhstateparks.org/explore/state-parks/clough-state-park.aspx	Weare	NH	03281	603-529-7112	
Coleman State Park 1155 Diamond Pond Rd *Web:* www.nhstateparks.org	Stewartstown	NH	03597	603-237-5382	
Crawford Notch State Park Rt 302 *Web:* www.nhstateparks.org	Harts Location	NH	03812	603-374-2272	
Daniel Webster Birthplace 131 N Rd *Web:* www.nhstateparks.org	Franklin	NH	03235	603-934-5057	
Deer Mountain Campground 5309 N Main St *Web:* www.nhstateparks.org/explore/state-parks/deer-mountain-campground.aspx	Pittsburg	NH	03592	603-538-6965	
Dixville Notch State Park Rt 26 *Web:* www.nhstateparks.org	Dixville	NH	03576	603-538-6707	
Echo Lake State Park 60 Echo Lake Rd *Web:* www.nhstateparks.org/explore/state-parks/echo-lake-state-park.aspx	Conway	NH	03818	603-356-2672	
Eisenhower Memorial Wayside Park Rt 302 *Web:* www.nhstateparks.org	Carroll	NH	03598	603-323-2087	
Ellacoya State Park 280 Scenic Dr *Web:* www.nhstateparks.org	Gilford	NH	03246	603-293-7821	
Endicott Rock Rt 3 *Web:* www.nhstateparks.org/explore/state-parks/endicott-rock.aspx	Laconia	NH	03246	603-271-3556	
Forest Lake State Park 397 Forest Lake Rd *Web:* www.nhstateparks.org/explore/state-parks/forest-lake-state-park.aspx	Dalton	NH	03598	603-466-3860	
Fort Constitution Historic Site 25 Wentworth Rd *Web:* www.nhstateparks.org/ParksPages/FortConstitution/FortConstitution.html	New Castle	NH	03854	603-436-1552	
Fort Stark Historic Site Wildrose Ln *Web:* www.nhstateparks.org	New Castle	NH	03854	603-436-1552	
Franconia Notch State Park Rt 93 *Web:* www.nhstateparks.org/explore/state-parks/franconia-notch-state-park.aspx	Franconia	NH	03580	603-745-8391	
Franklin Pierce Homestead Historic Site c/o Hillsborough Historical Society PO Box 896 *Web:* www.nhstateparks.org	Hillsboro	NH	03244	603-478-3165	
Gardner Memorial Wayside Park Rt 4A *Web:* www.nhstateparks.org/explore/state-parks/gardner-memorial-wayside-park.aspx	Springfield	NH	03284	603-485-2034	
Governor Wentworth Historic Site Rt 109 *Web:* www.nhstateparks.org	Wolfeboro	NH	03894	603-823-7722	
Greenfield State Park Rt 136 *Web:* www.nhstateparks.org	Greenfield	NH	03047	603-547-3497	
Hampton Beach State Park Rt 1A *Web:* www.nhstateparks.org	Hampton	NH	03842	603-926-3784	
Hannah Duston Memorial Exit 17 off I-93 *Web:* www.nhstateparks.org	Boscawen	NH	03303	603-271-3556	
Jenness State Beach Rt 1A *Web:* www.nhstateparks.org/explore/state-parks/jenness-state-beach.aspx	Rye	NH	03870	603-436-1552	
John Wingate Weeks Historic Site Rt 3 *Web:* www.nhstateparks.org/explore/state-parks/weeks-state-park.aspx	Lancaster	NH	03584	603-788-4004	
Kingston State Park 124 Main St *Web:* www.nhstateparks.org	Kingston	NH	03848	603-642-5471	
Lake Francis State Park 439 River Rd *Web:* www.nhstateparks.org/ParksPages/LakeFrancis/LakeFrancis.html	Pittsburg	NH	03592	603-538-6965	
Lake Tarleton State Park Rt 25C *Web:* www.nhstateparks.org	Piermont	NH	03779	603-823-7722	
Madison Boulder Natural Area Rt 113 *Web:* www.nhstateparks.org/explore/state-parks/madison-boulder-natural-area.aspx	Madison	NH	03849	603-485-2034	
Milan Hill State Park Rt 16 *Web:* www.nhstateparks.org/ParksPages/MilanHill/MilanHill.html	Milan	NH	03588	603-466-3860	
Miller State Park Rt 101E *Web:* www.nhstateparks.org	Peterborough	NH	03458	603-924-3672	
Mollidgewock State Park Rte 16 *Web:* www.nhstateparks.org/explore/state-parks/mollidgewock-state-park.aspx	Errol	NH	03579	603-482-3373	
Monadnock State Park 116 Poole Rd *Web:* www.nhstateparks.org	Jaffrey	NH	03452	603-532-8862	

Phone | Fax

Moose Brook State Park RFD 1 30 Jimtown Rd .... Gorham NH 03581 603-466-3860
Web: www.nhparks.state.nh.us

Mount Sunapee State Park 1460 Rt 103 .... Newbury NH 03255 603-763-5561
Web: www.nhstateparks.org/explore/state-parks/mount-sunapee-state-park.aspx

Mount Washington State Park
Rt 302 .... Sargent's Purchase NH 03581 603-466-3347
Web: www.nhstateparks.org

Nansen Wayside Park Rt 16 .... Milan NH 03588 603-823-7722
Web: www.nhstateparks.org/ParksPages/Nansen/Nansen.html

North Beach Rt 1A .... Hampton NH 03842 603-436-1552
Web: www.nhparks.state.nh.us/ParksPages/NorthBeach/NorthBeach.html

North Hampton State Beach Rt 1A .... Hampton NH 03862 603-436-1552
Web: www.nhstateparks.org/ParksPages/NHampton/NHampton.html

Northwood Meadows State Park NH Rt 4 .... Northwood NH 03261 603-485-2034
Web: www.nhstateparks.org/explore/state-parks/northwood-meadows-state-park.aspx

Odiorne Point State Park Rt 1A .... Rye NH 03870 603-436-7406
Web: www.nhstateparks.org/explore/state-parks/odiorne-point-state-park.aspx

Pawtuckaway State Park 128 Mountain Rd .... Nottingham NH 03290 603-895-3031
Web: www.nhstateparks.org

Pillsbury State Park Rt 31 .... Washington NH 03280 603-863-2860
Web: www.nhstateparks.org/explore/state-parks/pillsbury-state-park.aspx

Pisgah State Park PO Box 242 .... Winchester NH 03470 603-239-8153
Web: www.nhstateparks.org

Rhododendron State Park Rt 119W .... Fitzwilliam NH 03447 603-532-8862
Web: www.nhstateparks.org

Robert Frost Farm Historic Site
122 Rockingham Rd .... Derry NH 03038 603-432-3091
Web: www.nhstateparks.org

Rollins State Park 1066 Kearsarge Mountain Rd .... Warner NH 03278 603-456-3808
Web: www.nhstateparks.org

Rye Harbor State Park Rt 1A .... Rye NH 03870 603-436-1552
Web: www.nhstateparks.org/explore/state-parks/rye-harbor-state-park.aspx

Sculptured Rocks Natural Area Rts 3A & 118 .... Groton NH 03241 603-485-2034
Web: www.nhstateparks.org/explore/state-parks/sculptured-rocks-natural-area.aspx

Silver Lake State Park 138 Silver Lake Rd .... Hollis NH 03049 603-465-2342
Web: www.nhstateparks.org

Umbagog Lake State Park Rt 26 .... Cambridge NH 03579 603-482-7795
Web: www.nhstateparks.org

Wadleigh State Park Rt 114 .... Sutton NH 03260 603-927-4724
Web: www.nhstateparks.org

Wallis Sands State Beach 900 Ocean Blvd .... Rye NH 03870 603-436-9404
Web: www.nhstateparks.org/explore/state-parks/wallis-sands-state-beach.aspx

Wellington State Park 650 W Shore Rd .... Alexandria NH 03222 603-744-2197
Web: www.nhstateparks.org/explore/state-parks/wellington-state-park.aspx

Wentworth State Park
297 Governor Wentworth Hwy .... Wolfeboro NH 03894 603-569-3699
Web: www.nhstateparks.org

Wentworth-Coolidge Mansion Historic Site
375 Little Harbor Rd .... Portsmouth NH 03801 603-436-6607
Web: www.nhparks.state.nh.us

White Lake State Park Rt 16 .... Tamworth NH 03886 603-323-7350
Web: www.nhstateparks.org

Winslow State Park Kearsarge Mountain Rd .... Wilmot NH 03287 603-526-6168
Web: www.nhstateparks.org/explore/state-parks/winslow-state-park.aspx

NEW JERSEY

Phone | Fax

Abram S. Hewitt State Forest
c/o Wawayanda State Pk 885 Warwick Tpke .... Hewitt NJ 07421 973-853-4462
Web: www.njparksandforests.org/parks/abram.html

Allaire State Park PO Box 220 .... Farmingdale NJ 07727 732-938-2371
Web: www.njparksandforests.org

Allamuchy Mountain State Park
c/o Stephens State Pk
800 Willow Grove St .... Hackettstown NJ 07840 908-852-3790
Web: www.njparksandforests.org

Atsion Recreation Area
c/o Wharton State Forest 4110 Nesco Rd .... Hammonton NJ 08037 609-268-0444
Web: www.njparksandforests.org/parks/wharton.html

Barnegat Lighthouse State Park
208 Broadway .... Barnegat Light NJ 08006 609-494-2016
Web: www.njparksandforests.org

Bass River State Forest 762 Stage Rd .... Tuckerton NJ 08087 609-296-1114
Web: www.njparksandforests.org

Batsto Village State Historic Site Rd 9 .... Hammonton NJ 08037 609-561-0024
Web: www.njparksandforests.org/historic/index.html

Belleplain State Forest
County Rt 50 PO Box 450 .... Woodbine NJ 08270 609-861-2404
Web: www.njparksandforests.org/parks/belle.html

Boxwood Hall State Historic Site
1073 E Jersey St .... Elizabeth NJ 07201 908-282-7167
Web: www.njparksandforests.org

Brendan T. Byrne State Forest PO Box 215 .... New Lisbon NJ 08064 609-726-1191
Web: www.njparksandforests.org/parks/byrne.html

Bull's Island Recreation Area
2185 Daniel Bray Hwy .... Stockton NJ 08559 609-397-2949
Web: www.njparksandforests.org

Cape May Point State Park PO Box 107 .... Cape May Point NJ 08212 609-884-2159
Web: www.njparksandforests.org

Cheesequake State Park 300 Gordon Rd .... Matawan NJ 07747 732-566-2161
Web: www.njparksandforests.org

Corson's Inlet State Park
c/o Belleplain State Forest
County Rt 550, PO Box 450 .... Woodbine NJ 08270 609-861-2404
Web: www.njparksandforests.org/parks/corsons.html

Craig House State Historic Site
347 Freehold-Englishtown Rd .... Manalapan NJ 07726 732-462-9616
Web: www.njparksandforests.org/historic/index.html

Delaware & Raritan Canal State Park
145 Mapleton Rd .... Princeton NJ 08540 609-924-5705
Web: www.njparksandforests.org

Double Trouble State Park PO Box 175 .... Bayville NJ 08721 732-341-6662
Web: www.njparksandforests.org

Farny State Park
c/o Ringwood State Pk 1304 Sloatsburg Rd .... Ringwood NJ 07456 973-962-7031
Web: www.njparksandforests.org/parks/farny.html

Fort Mott State Park 454 Fort Mott Rd .... Pennsville NJ 08070 856-935-3218
Web: www.njparksandforests.org

Grover Cleveland Birthplace State Historic Site
207 Bloomfield Ave .... Caldwell NJ 07006 973-226-0001
Web: www.njparksandforests.org

Hacklebarney State Park
c/o Voorhees State Pk
119 Hacklebarney Rd .... Long Valley NJ 07853 908-638-6969
Web: www.njparksandforests.org

Hancock House State Historic Site
3 Front St .... Hancock's Bridge NJ 08038 856-935-4373
Web: www.njparksandforests.org

Hermitage State Historic Site The
335 N Franklin Tpke .... Ho-Ho-Kus NJ 07423 201-445-8311 445-0437
Web: www.thehermitage.org

High Point State Park 1480 Rt 23 .... Sussex NJ 07461 973-875-4800
Web: www.njparksandforests.org

Hopatcong State Park PO Box 8519 .... Landing NJ 07850 973-398-7010
Web: www.njparksandforests.org

Indian King Tavern State Historic Site
233 Kings Hwy .... Haddonfield NJ 08033 856-429-6792
Web: www.njparksandforests.org

Island Beach State Park PO Box 37 .... Seaside Park NJ 08752 732-793-0506
Web: www.njparksandforests.org

Jenny Jump State Forest 330 State Pk Rd .... Hope NJ 07844 908-459-4366
Web: www.njparksandforests.org

Kittatinny Valley State Park PO Box 621 .... Andover NJ 07821 973-786-6445
Web: www.njparksandforests.org

Liberty State Park 200Morris Pesin Dr .... Jersey City NJ 07305 201-915-3440 915-3408
Web: www.njparksandforests.org/parks/liberty.html

Long Pond Ironworks State Park
c/o Ringwood State Pk 1304 Sloatsburg Rd .... Ringwood NJ 07456 973-962-7031
Web: www.njparksandforests.org/parks/longpond.html

Monmouth Battlefield State Park
347 Freehold-Englishtown Rd .... Manalapan NJ 07726 732-462-9616
Web: www.njparksandforests.org/parks/monbat.html

Norvin Green State Forest
c/o Ringwood State Pk 1304 Sloatsburg Rd .... Ringwood NJ 07456 973-962-7031
Web: www.njparksandforests.org/parks/norvin.html

Parvin State Park 701 Almond Rd .... Pittsgrove NJ 08318 856-358-8616
Web: www.njparksandforests.org

Penn State Forest
c/o Bass River State Forest 762 Stage Rd .... Tuckerton NJ 08087 609-296-1114
Web: www.njparksandforests.org

Princeton Battlefield State Park
500 Mercer Rd .... Princeton NJ 08540 609-921-0074
Web: www.njparksandforests.org

Ramapo Mountain State Forest
c/o Ringwood State Pk 1304 Sloatsburg Rd .... Ringwood NJ 07456 973-962-7031
Web: www.njparksandforests.org/parks/ramapo.html

Rancocas State Park
c/o Brendan T Byrne State Forest
PO Box 215 .... New Lisbon NJ 08064 609-726-1191
Web: www.njparksandforests.org/parks/rancocas.html

Ringwood State Park 1304 Sloatsburg Rd .... Ringwood NJ 07456 973-962-7031
Web: www.njparksandforests.org

Rockingham State Historic Site
84 Laurel Ave .... Kingston NJ 08528 609-683-7132
Web: www.rockingham.net

Round Valley Recreation Area
1220 Lebanon-Stanton Rd .... Lebanon NJ 08833 908-236-6355
Web: www.njparksandforests.org

Somers Mansion State Historic Site
1000 Shore Rd .... Somers Point NJ 08244 609-927-2212
Web: www.njparksandforests.org

Spruce Run Recreation Area
68 Van Syckel's Rd .... Clinton NJ 08809 908-638-8572
Web: www.njparksandforests.org

Stephens State Park 800 Willow Grove St .... Hackettstown NJ 07840 908-852-3790
Web: www.njparksandforests.org

Steuben House State Historic Site
1209 Main St .... River Edge NJ 07661 201-487-1739
Web: www.njparksandforests.org

Stokes State Forest 1 Coursen Rd .... Branchville NJ 07826 973-948-3820
Web: www.njparksandforests.org

Swartswood State Park PO Box 123 .... Swartswood NJ 07877 973-383-5230
Web: www.njparksandforests.org

Trenton Battle Monument State Historic Site
348 N Warren St .... Trenton NJ 08638 609-737-0623
Web: www.njparksandforests.org/historic/Trentonbattlemonument/index.htm

Twin Lights State Historic Site
Lighthouse Rd .... Highlands NJ 07732 732-872-1886
Web: www.twin-lights.org

Voorhees State Park 251 County Rd 513 .... Glen Gardner NJ 08826 908-638-6969
Web: www.njparksandforests.org

Wallace House State Historic Site
71 Somerset St .... Somerville NJ 08876 908-725-1015
Web: www.njparksandforests.org

Walt Whitman House State Historic Site
330 Mickle Blvd .... Camden NJ 08103 609-964-5383
Web: www.njparksandforests.org

Washington Crossing State Park
355 Washington Crossing-Pennington Rd .... Titusville NJ 08560 609-737-0623
Web: www.njparksandforests.org

Washington Rock State Park
c/o Liberty State Pk Morris Pesin Dr .... Jersey City NJ 07305 201-915-3401
Web: www.njparksandforests.org/parks/washrock.html

Phone | Fax

Wawayanda State Park 885 Warwick Tpke — Hewitt NJ 07421 973-853-4462
Web: www.njparksandforests.org/parks/wawayanda.html
Wharton State Forest 4110 Nesco Rd — Hammonton NJ 08037 609-561-0024
Web: www.njparksandforests.org/parks/wharton.html
Worthington State Forest HC 62 PO Box 2 — Columbia NJ 07832 908-841-9575
Web: www.njparksandforests.org

NEW MEXICO

Phone | Fax

Bluewater Lake State Park New Mexico 412 — Prewitt NM 87045 505-876-2391
Web: www.emnrd.state.nm.us
Bottomless Lakes State Park
HC 12 PO Box 1200 — Roswell NM 88201 505-624-6058 624-6029
Web: www.emnrd.state.nm.us/PRD/bottomless.htm
Brantley Lake State Park PO Box 2288 — Carlsbad NM 88221 505-457-2384 457-2385
Web: www.emnrd.state.nm.us/PRD/ParksPages/Brantley.htm
Caballo Lake State Park PO Box 32 — Caballo NM 87931 505-743-3942
Web: www.emnrd.state.nm.us/PRD/caballo.htm
Cimarron Canyon State Park PO Box 185 — Eagle Nest NM 87718 505-377-6271
Web: www.emnrd.state.nm.us
City of Rocks State Park PO Box 50 — Faywood NM 88034 505-536-2800
Web: www.emnrd.state.nm.us/PRD/cityrocks.htm
Conchas Lake State Park PO Box 976 — Conchas Dam NM 88416 505-868-2270
Web: www.emnrd.state.nm.us/PRD/Conchas.htm
Coyote Creek State Park PO Box 477 — Guadalupita NM 87722 505-387-2328
Web: www.emnrd.state.nm.us/PRD/CoyoteCreek.htm
El Vado Lake State Park PO Box 367 — Tierra Amarilla NM 87575 505-588-7247
Web: www.emnrd.state.nm.us/PRD/elvado.htm
Elephant Butte Lake State Park
PO Box 13 — Elephant Butte NM 87935 505-744-5923
Web: www.emnrd.state.nm.us/PRD/elephant.htm
Fenton Lake State Park 455 Fenton Lake — Jemez Springs NM 87025 505-829-3630
Web: www.emnrd.state.nm.us/PRD/Fenton.htm
Heron Lake State Park PO Box 159 — Los Ojos NM 87551 505-588-7470
Web: www.emnrd.state.nm.us/PRD/heron.htm
Hyde Memorial State Park 740 Hyde Pk Rd — Santa Fe NM 87501 505-983-7175
Web: www.emnrd.state.nm.us/PRD/Hyde.htm
Leasburg Dam State Park PO Box 6 — Radium Springs NM 88054 575-524-4068 526-5420
Web: www.emnrd.state.nm.us
Living Desert Zoo & Gardens State Park
PO Box 100 — Carsbad NM 88221 505-887-5516 885-4478
Web: www.emnrd.state.nm.us/PRD/LivingDesert.htm
Manzano Mountains State Park
HC 66 PO Box 202 — Mountainair NM 87036 505-847-2820
Web: www.emnrd.state.nm.us
Navajo Lake State Park 1448 NM 511 #1 — Najavo Dam NM 87419 505-632-2278
Web: www.emnrd.state.nm.us
Oasis State Park 1891 Oasis Rd — Portales NM 88130 505-356-5331 356-5331
Web: www.emnrd.state.nm.us/PRD/Oasis.htm
Oliver Lee Memorial State Park
409 Dog Canyon Rd — Alamogordo NM 88310 505-437-8284 439-1290
Web: www.emnrd.state.nm.us/PRD/oliverlee.htm
Pancho Villa State Park PO Box 450 — Columbus NM 88029 505-531-2711
Web: www.emnrd.state.nm.us/PRD/PanchoVilla.htm
Percha Dam State Park PO Box 32 — Caballo NM 87931 505-743-3942
Web: www.emnrd.state.nm.us/PRD/Percha.htm
Rio Grande Nature Center State Park
2901 Candelaria Rd NW — Albuquerque NM 87107 505-344-7240 344-4505
Web: www.emnrd.state.nm.us
Santa Rosa Lake State Park PO Box 384 — Santa Rosa NM 88433 505-472-3110 472-5956
Web: www.emnrd.state.nm.us/PRD/santarosa.htm
Smokey Bear Historical State Park
118 Smokey Bear Blvd PO Box 591 — Capitan NM 88316 505-354-2748
Web: www.smokeybearpark.com
Storrie Lake State Park
HC 33 PO Box 109 #2 — Las Vegas NM 87701 505-425-7278
Web: www.emnrd.state.nm.us
Sugarite Canyon State Park HC 63 PO Box 386 — Raton NM 87740 505-445-5607
Web: www.emnrd.state.nm.us/PRD/Sugarite.htm
Sumner Lake State Park HC 64 PO Box 125 — Fort Sumner NM 88119 505-355-2541 355-2542
Web: www.emnrd.state.nm.us/PRD/SumnerLake.htm
Villanueva State Park PO Box 40 — Villanueva NM 87583 505-421-2957 421-3231
Web: www.emnrd.state.nm.us/PRD/Villanueva.htm

NEW YORK

Phone | Fax

Allan H. Treman State Marine Park
c/o Robert H Tremin State Pk
105 Enfield Falls Rd — Ithaca NY 14850 607-273-3440
Web: nysparks.state.ny.us
Allegany State Park 2373 ASP, Rt 1 Suite 3 — Salamanca NY 14779 716-354-9121
Web: www.nysparks.state.ny.us
Battle Island State Park 2150 State Rt 48 — Fulton NY 13069 315-593-3408
Web: www.nysparks.state.ny.us
Bayard Cutting Arboretum State Park
PO Box 466 — Oakdale NY 11769 631-581-1002 581-1031
Web: www.bayardcuttingarboretum.com
Bayswater Point State Park
c/o Gantry Plaza State Pk
50-50 2nd St — Long Island City NY 11101 718-471-2212
Web: www.nysparks.state.ny.us
Bear Mountain State Park
c/o Palisades IH- Pk Commission
Adminstration Bldg Rt 9 W — Bear Mountain NY 10911 845-786-2701
Web: www.nysparks.com/parks/13/details.aspx
Beaver Island State Park
2136 W Oakfield Rd — Grand Island NY 14072 716-773-3271
Web: www.nysparks.state.ny.us

Phone | Fax

Belmont Lake State Park PO Box 247 — Babylon NY 11702 631-667-5055
Web: www.nysparks.state.ny.us
Bennington Battlefield State Historic Site
c/o Grafton Lakes State Pk PO Box 163 — Grafton NY 12082 518-686-7109 279-1902
Web: www.nysparks.com/sites/info.asp?siteID=3
Bethpage State Park Bethpage Pkwy — Farmingdale NY 11735 516-249-0701
Web: www.nysparks.state.ny.us
Big Six Mile Creek Marina State Park
c/o Beaver Island State Pk
2136 W Oakfield Rd — Grand Island NY 14072 716-773-3271
Web: nysparks.state.ny.us/parks/50/details.aspx
Blauvelt State Park
c/o Palisades IH- Pk Commission
Adminstration Bldg Rt 9 W — Bear Mountain NY 10911 845-359-0544
Web: www.nysparks.com/parks/49/details.aspx
Bonavista State Park Golf Course
7194 County Rd 132 — Ovid NY 14521 607-869-5482
Web: www.nysparks.com/parks/160/details.aspx
Bowman Lake State Park 745 Bliven Sherman Rd — Oxford NY 13830 607-334-2718
Web: www.nysparks.state.ny.us
Buckhorn Island State Park
c/o Beaver Island State Pk
2136 W Oakfield Rd — Grand Island NY 14072 716-773-3271
Web: nysparks.state.ny.us/parks/174/details.aspx
Burnham Point State Park
340765 NYS Rt 12E — Cape Vincent NY 13618 315-654-2522
Web: www.nysparks.state.ny.us
Buttermilk Falls State Park
c/o Robert H Tremin State Pk
105 Enfield Falls Rd — Ithaca NY 14850 607-273-5761
Web: nysparks.state.ny.us
Caleb Smith State Park Preserve PO Box 963 — Smithtown NY 11787 631-265-1054
Web: www.nysparks.state.ny.us
Camp Hero State Park 50 S Fairview Ave — Montauk NY 11954 631-668-3781
Web: www.nysparks.state.ny.us
Canandaigua Lake State Marine Park
620 S Main St — Canandaigua NY 14424 315-789-2331
Web: www.nysparks.com/parks/3/details.aspx
Canoe-Picnic Point State Park
36661 Cedar Pt State Pk Dr — Clayton NY 13624 315-654-2522
Web: nysparks.state.ny.us/parks/64/details.aspx
Captree State Park PO Box 247 — Babylon NY 11702 631-669-0449
Web: nysparks.state.ny.us/parks/65/details.aspx
Caumsett State Historic Park
25 Lloyd Harbor Rd — Huntington NY 11743 631-423-1770 423-8645
Web: www.nysparks.com
Cayuga Lake State Park
2678 Lower Lake Rd — Seneca Falls NY 13148 315-568-5163
Web: www.nysparks.state.ny.us
Cedar Island State Park County Rt 93 — Hammond NY 13646 315-482-3331
Web: nysparks.state.ny.us/parks/25/details.aspx
Cedar Point State Park
36661 Cedar Pt State Pk Dr — Clayton NY 13624 315-654-2522
Web: www.nysparks.state.ny.us
Chenango Valley State Park
153 State Pk Rd — Chenango Forks NY 13746 607-648-5251
Web: www.nysparks.state.ny.us
Cherry Plain State Park
26 State Pk Rd PO Box 11 — Cherry Plain NY 12040 518-733-5400
Web: www.nysparks.state.ny.us
Chittenango Falls State Park
2300 Rathbun Rd — Cazenovia NY 13035 315-655-9620
Web: www.nysparks.state.ny.us
Clarence Fahnestock State Park 1498 Rt 301 — Carmel NY 10512 845-225-7207
Web: www.nysparks.state.ny.us
Clark Reservation State Park
6105 E Seneca Tpke — Jamesville NY 13078 315-492-1590
Web: www.nysparks.state.ny.us
Clay Pit Ponds State Park Preserve
83 Nielsen Ave — Staten Island NY 10309 718-967-1976
Web: www.nysparks.state.ny.us
Clermont State Historic Site
1 Clermont Ave — Germantown NY 12526 518-537-4240 537-6240
Web: www.nysparks.com
Clinton House State Historic Site
549 Main St PO Box 88 — Poughkeepsie NY 12602 845-471-1630 471-8777
Web: www.nysparks.state.ny.us
Cold Spring Harbor State Park
c/o Caumsett State Historic Pk
25 Lloyd Harbor Rd — Huntington NY 11743 631-423-1770
Web: www.nysparks.state.ny.us
Coles Creek State Park PO Box 442 — Waddington NY 13694 315-388-5636
Web: www.nysparks.state.ny.us
Connetquot River State Park Preserve
PO Box 505 — Oakdale NY 11769 631-581-1005
Web: nysparks.state.ny.us/parks/8/details.aspx
Crailo State Historic Site
9 1/2 Riverside Ave — Rensselaer NY 12144 518-463-8738
Web: www.nysparks.com
Crown Point State Historic Site
739 Bridge Rd — Crown Point NY 12928 518-597-4666 597-3666
Web: www.nysparks.com
Cumberland Bay State Park
152 Cumberland Head Rd — Plattsburg NY 12901 518-563-5240
Web: www.nysparks.state.ny.us
Darien Lakes State Park
10289 Harlow Rd — Darien Center NY 14040 585-547-9242
Web: www.nysparks.state.ny.us
Darwin Martin House State Historic Site
125 Jewett Pkwy — Buffalo NY 14214 716-856-3858 856-4009
Web: www.nysparks.state.ny.us/sites/info.asp?siteID=35

	City	State	Zip	Phone	Fax
Delta Lake State Park 8797 SR- 46 *Web:* www.nysparks.state.ny.us	Rome	NY	13440	315-337-4670	
Devil's Hole State Park c/o Niagara Frontier Region PO Box 1132 *Web:* nysparks.state.ny.us/parks/42/details.aspx	Niagara Falls	NY	14303	716-284-5778	
Dewolf Point State Park 45920 County Rt 191 *Web:* www.nysparks.state.ny.us	Fineview	NY	13640	315-482-2012	
Earl W. Brydges Artpark State Park 450 S 4th St *Web:* www.nysparks.state.ny.us	Lewiston	NY	14092	716-754-9000	
Eel Weir State Park Rd 3 *Web:* www.nysparks.state.ny.us	Ogdensburg	NY	13669	315-393-1138	
Empire-Fulton Ferry State Park 26 New Dock St *Web:* www.nysparks.state.ny.us	Brooklyn	NY	11201	718-858-4708	
Evangola State Park 10191 Old Lake Shore Rd *Web:* www.nysparks.state.ny.us	Irving	NY	14081	716-549-1802	
Fair Haven Beach State Park PO Box 16 ; Rt 104A *Web:* www.nysparks.state.ny.us	Fair Haven	NY	13064	315-947-5205	
Fillmore Glen State Park 1686 State Rt 38 *Web:* www.nysparks.state.ny.us	Moravia	NY	13118	315-497-0130	
Fort Montgomery State Historic Site c/o Bear Mountain State Pk *Web:* www.nysparks.com/sites/info.asp?siteID=36	Bear Mountain	NY	10911	845-786-2701	786-5367
Fort Niagara State Park Rt 18F *Web:* www.nysparks.com/parks/175/details.aspx	Youngstown	NY	14174	716-745-7273	
Fort Ontario State Historic Site 1 E 4th St *Web:* www.nysparks.com	Oswego	NY	13126	315-343-4711	343-1430
Four Mile Creek State Park 1055 Lake Rd *Web:* www.nysparks.com/parks/info.asp?parkId=110	Youngstown	NY	14174	716-745-3802	
Franklin D. Roosevelt State Park 2957 Crompond Rd *Web:* www.nysparks.com	Yorktown Heights	NY	10598	914-245-4434	
Ganondagan State Historic Site 1488 SR 444 *Web:* www.nysparks.com	Victor	NY	14564	585-924-5848	
Gantry Plaza State Park 4-74 48th Ave *Web:* www.nysparks.com	Long Island City	NY	11109	718-786-6385	
Gilbert Lake State Park 870 county Hwy 12 *Web:* www.nysparks.com	Laurens	NY	13796	607-432-2114	
Glimmerglass State Park 1527 County Hwy 31 *Web:* www.nysparks.com/parks/info.asp?parkId=22	Cooperstown	NY	13326	607-547-8662	
Golden Hill State Park 9691 Lower Lake Rd *Web:* www.nysparks.com	Barker	NY	14102	716-795-3885	
Goosepond Mountain State Park c/o Palisades IH- Pk Commission Adminstration Bldg Rt 9 W *Web:* www.nysparks.com/parks/55/details.aspx	Bear Mountain	NY	10911	845-786-2701	
Grafton Lakes State Park 61 N Long Pond Rd *Web:* www.nysparks.com/parks/info.asp?parkId=116	Grafton	NY	12082	518-279-1155	
Grant Cottage State Historic Site PO Box 2294 *Web:* www.nysparks.com	Wilton	NY	12831	518-587-8277	
Grass Point State Park 42247 Grassy Pt Rd *Web:* www.nysparks.state.ny.us	Alexandria Bay	NY	13607	315-686-4472	
Green Lakes State Park 7900 Green Lakes Rd *Web:* www.nysparks.com	Fayetteville	NY	13066	315-637-6111	
Hamlin Beach State Park 1 Camp Rd *TF:* 800-456-2267 ■ *Web:* www.nysparks.com/parks/info.asp?parkId=6	Hamlin	NY	14464	585-964-2462	964-7821
Harriet Hollister Spencer State Recreation Area 1082 Rt 36 S *Web:* www.nysparks.com/parks/164/details.aspx	Dansville	NY	14437	585-335-8111	
Harriman State Park c/o Palisades IH- Pk Commission Adminstration Bldg Rt 9 W *Web:* www.nysparks.com/parks/145/details.aspx	Bear Mountain	NY	10911	845-786-2701	
Heckscher State Park PO Box 160 *Web:* www.nysparks.com	East Islip	NY	11730	631-581-2100	
Hempstead Lake State Park 1 Hempstead Lake State Pk *Web:* nysparks.state.ny.us/parks/31/details.aspx	West Hempstead	NY	11552	516-766-1029	
Herkimer Home State Historic Site 200 SR- 169 *Web:* www.nysparks.com	Little Falls	NY	13365	315-823-0398	823-0587
High Tor State Park c/o Palisades IH- Pk Commission *Web:* www.nysparks.com/parks/info.asp?parkId=58	Bear Mountain	NY	10911	845-634-8074	
Highland Lakes State Park c/o Palisades IH- Pk Commission Adminstration Bldg Rt 9 W *Web:* www.nysparks.com/parks/5/details.aspx	Bear Mountain	NY	10911	845-786-2701	
Higley Flow State Park 442 Cold Brook Dr *Web:* www.nysparks.com	Colton	NY	13625	315-262-2880	
Hither Hills State Park 50 S Fairview Ave *Web:* www.nysparks.com	Montauk	NY	11754	631-668-2554	
Hudson Highlands State Park Rt 9D *Web:* www.nysparks.com	Beacon	NY	10512	845-225-7207	
Hudson River Islands State Park Schodack Island State Pk *Web:* www.nysparks.com	Schodack Landing	NY	12156	518-732-0187	732-0263
Hunt's Pond State Park c/o Bowman Lake State Pk 745 Bliven Sherman Rd *Web:* www.nysparks.com	Oxford	NY	13830	607-859-2249	
Hyde Hall State Historic Site PO Box 721 *Web:* www.nysparks.com/sites/info.asp?siteID=13	Cooperstown	NY	13326	607-547-5098	547-8462
Irondequoit Bay State Marine Park c/o Hamlin Beach State Pk 1 Camp Rd *Web:* www.nysparks.com/parks/info.asp?parkId=7	Hamlin	NY	14464	585-964-2462	
Jacques Cartier State Park PO Box 380 *Web:* www.nysparks.com	Morristown	NY	13664	315-375-6371	
James Baird State Park 280 Club House Rd # 1 *Web:* www.nysparks.com	Pleasant Valley	NY	12569	845-452-1489	
John Boyd Thacher State Park 1 Hailes Cave Rd *Web:* www.nysparks.com	Voorheesville	NY	12186	518-872-1237	872-9133
John Brown Farm State Historic Site 115 John Brown Rd *Web:* www.nysparks.com	Lake Placid	NY	12946	518-523-3900	
John Burroughs Memorial State Historic Site c/o Mine Kill State Pk PO Box 923, Rte 30 *Web:* www.nysparks.com/sites/info.asp?siteID=15	North Blenheim	NY	12131	518-827-6111	827-6782
John Jay Homestead State Historic Site PO Box 832 *Web:* www.nysparks.com	Katonah	NY	10536	914-232-5651	232-8085
Johnson Hall State Historic Site 139 Hall Ave *Web:* www.nysparks.com	Johnstown	NY	12095	518-762-8712	762-2330
Jones Beach State Park PO Box 1000 *Web:* www.nysparks.com	Wantagh	NY	11793	516-785-1600	
Joseph Davis State Park 4143 Lower River Rd *Web:* www.nysparks.com	Lewiston	NY	14092	716-754-4596	
Keewaydin State Park 46165 NYS Rt 12 PO Box 247 *Web:* www.nysparks.com	Alexandria Bay	NY	13607	315-482-3331	
Keuka Lake State Park 3370 Pepper Rd *Web:* www.nysparks.com	Bluff Point	NY	14478	315-536-3666	
Knox's Headquarters State Historic Site PO Box 207 *Web:* www.nysparks.com	Vails Gate	NY	12584	845-561-5498	
Kring Point State Park 25950 Kring Pt Rd *Web:* www.nysparks.com	Redwood	NY	13679	315-482-2444	
Lake Erie State Park 5905 Lake Rd *Web:* www.nysparks.com	Brockton	NY	14716	716-792-9214	
Lake Superior State Park c/o Sullivan County Dept of Public Works PO Box 5012 *Web:* www.nysparks.com	Monticello	NY	12701	845-794-3000	
Lake Taghkanic State Park 1528 Rt 82 *Web:* www.nysparks.com	Ancram	NY	12502	518-851-3631	851-3633
Lakeside Beach State Park Rt 18 *Web:* www.nysparks.com/parks/info.asp?parkId=8	Waterport	NY	14571	585-682-4888	
Letchworth State Park 1 Letchworth State Pk *Web:* www.nysparks.com	Castile	NY	14427	585-493-3600	
Lodi Point State Marine Park c/o Sampson State Pk 6096 Rt 96A *Web:* www.nysparks.com/parks/info.asp?parkId=38	Romulus	NY	14541	315-585-6392	
Long Point State Park - Finger Lakes 2063 Lake Rd *Web:* www.nysparks.com	Aurora	NY	13026	315-497-0130	
Long Point State Park - Thousand Islands 7495 State Pk Rd *Web:* www.nysparks.com	Three Mile Bay	NY	13693	315-649-5258	
Long Point State Park on Lake Chautauqua 4459 Rt 430 *Web:* www.nysparks.com	Bemus Point	NY	14712	716-386-2722	
Lorenzo State Historic Site 17 Rippleton Rd *Web:* www.nysparks.com	Cazenovia	NY	13035	315-655-3200	655-4304
Macomb Reservation State Park 201 Campsite Rd *Web:* www.nysparks.com	Schuyler Falls	NY	12985	518-643-9952	
Margaret Lewis Norrie State Park 9 Old Post Rd PO Box 308 *Web:* www.nysparks.state.ny.us/parks/info.asp?parkId=134	Staatsburg	NY	12580	845-889-4646	889-8321
Mark Twain State Park & Soaring Eagles Golf Course 201 Middle Rd *Web:* www.nysparks.com	Horseheads	NY	14845	607-739-0034	
Mary Island State Park c/o Cedar Pt State Pk 36661 Cedar Pt State Pk Dr *Web:* www.nysparks.com/parks/info.asp?parkId=150	Clayton	NY	13624	315-654-2522	
Max V. Shaul State Park Rt 30 PO Box 23 *Web:* www.nysparks.com	Fultonham	NY	12071	518-827-4711	
Mine Kill State Park PO Box 923 Rt 30 *Web:* www.nysparks.com/parks/info.asp?parkId=117	North Blenheim	NY	12131	518-827-6111	827-6782
Minnewaska State Park Preserve PO Box 893 *Web:* www.nysparks.com	New Paltz	NY	12561	845-256-0579	
Montauk Downs State Park 50 S Fairview Ave *Web:* www.nysparks.com/parks/info.asp?parkId=165	Montauk	NY	11954	631-668-3781	
Montauk Point State Park c/o Montauk Downs State Pk 50 S Fairview Ave *Web:* www.nysparks.com/parks/info.asp?parkId=136	Montauk	NY	11954	631-668-3781	
Moreau Lake State Park 605 Old Saratoga Rd *Web:* www.nysparks.com	Gansevoort	NY	12831	518-793-0511	761-6843
New Windsor Cantonment State Historic Site 374 Temple Hill Rd Rt 300 *Web:* www.nysparks.com	Vails Gate	NY	12584	845-561-1765	
Niagara Falls State Park PO Box 1132 *Web:* www.nysparks.com/parks/info.asp?parkId=113	Niagara Falls	NY	14303	716-278-1796	
Nissequogue River State Park St Johnland Rd PO Box 639 *Web:* www.nysparks.com/parks/info.asp?parkId=79	Kings Park	NY	11754	631-269-4927	
Nyack Beach State Park 698 N Broadway *Web:* www.nysparks.com/parks/info.asp?parkId=62	Upper Nyack	NY	10960	845-358-1316	
Oak Orchard State Marine Park c/o Lakeside Beach State Pk Rt 18 *Web:* www.nysparks.com/parks/131/details.aspx	Waterport	NY	14571	585-682-4888	

				Phone	Fax
Ogden Mills & Ruth Livingston Mills State Park Old Post Rd PO Box 893 *Web:* www.nysparks.com/parks/info.asp?parkId=133	Staatsburg	NY	12580	845-889-4646	
Olana State Historic Site 5720 State Rt 9G *Web:* www.olana.org	Hudson	NY	12534	518-828-0135	828-6742
Old Croton Aqueduct State Historic Park 15 Walnut St *Web:* www.nysparks.com	Dobbs Ferry	NY	10522	914-693-5259	674-8529
Old Erie Canal State Historic Park 8729 Andrus Rd *Web:* www.nysparks.state.ny.us	Kirkville	NY	13082	315-687-7821	
Old Fort Niagara State Historic Site 2 Scott Ave *Web:* www.nysparks.com	Youngstown	NY	14174	716-745-7611	745-9141
Oquaga Creek State Park 5995 County Rt 20 *Web:* www.nysparks.com	Bainbridge	NY	13733	607-467-4160	
Orient Beach State Park PO Box 117 *Web:* www.nysparks.com	Orient	NY	11957	631-323-2440	
Oriskany Battlefield State Historic Site 7801 State Rt 69 *Web:* www.nysparks.com/sites/info.asp?siteID=23	Oriskany	NY	13424	315-768-7224	377-3081
Peebles Island State Park PO Box 295 *Web:* www.nysparks.com/parks/111/details.aspx	Waterford	NY	12188	518-237-8643	
Philipse Manor Hall State Historic Site PO Box 496	Yonkers	NY	10702	914-965-4027	965-6485
Pinnacle State Park & Golf Course 1904 Pinnacle Rd *Web:* www.nysparks.state.ny.us	Addison	NY	14801	607-359-2767	
Pixley Falls State Park 11430 SR- 46 *Web:* www.nysparks.com	Boonville	NY	13309	315-942-4713	
Planting Fields Arboretum State Historic Park/Coe Hall Historic House Museum PO Box 58 *Web:* www.nysparks.com	Oyster Bay	NY	11771	516-922-9200	922-8610
Point Au Roche State Park 19 Camp Red Cloud Rd *Web:* www.nysparks.com	Plattsburg	NY	12901	518-563-0369	
Reservoir State Park c/o Niagara Frontier Region PO Box 1132 *Web:* www.nysparks.com/parks/info.asp?parkId=112	Niagara Falls	NY	14303	716-284-4691	
Riverbank State Park 679 Riverside Dr *Web:* www.nysparks.com	New York	NY	10031	212-694-3600	
Robert H. Treman State Park 105 Enfield Falls Rd *Web:* www.nysparks.com	Ithaca	NY	14850	607-273-3440	
Robert Moses State Park - Long Island c/o Long Island Regional Office PO Box 247 *Web:* www.nysparks.com/parks/info.asp?parkId=45	Babylon	NY	11702	631-669-0449	
Robert Moses State Park - Thousand Islands PO Box 548 *Web:* www.nysparks.com	Massena	NY	13662	315-769-8663	
Roberto Clemente State Park 1 W Tremont Ave *Web:* www.nysparks.state.ny.us	Bronx	NY	10453	718-299-8750	
Rockefeller State Park Preserve PO Box 338 *Web:* www.nysparks.com	Tarrytown	NY	10591	914-631-1470	
Rockland Lake State Park PO Box 217 *Web:* www.nysparks.state.ny.us/parks/info.asp?parkId=64	Congers	NY	10920	845-268-3020	
Sackets Harbor Battlefield State Historic Site 505 W Washington St PO Box 27 *Web:* www.nysparks.state.ny.us	Sackets Harbor	NY	13685	315-646-3634	646-1203
Saint Lawrence State Park Golf Course 4955 State Hwy 37 *Web:* www.nysparks.com	Ogdensburg	NY	13669	315-393-2286	
Sampson State Park 6096 Rt 96A *Web:* www.nysparks.com/parks/info.asp?parkId=100	Romulus	NY	14541	315-585-6392	
Saratoga Spa State Park 19 Roosevelt Dr *Web:* www.saratogaspastatepark.org	Saratoga Springs	NY	12866	518-584-2535	
Schodack Island State Park 1 Schodack Way PO Box 7 *Web:* www.nysparks.com/parks/info.asp?parkId=87	Schodack Landing	NY	12156	518-732-0187	
Schoharie Crossing State Historic Site 129 Schoharie St PO Box 140 *Web:* www.nysparks.com	Fort Hunter	NY	12069	518-829-7516	829-7491
Schuyler Mansion State Historic Site 32 Catherine St *Web:* www.nysparks.state.ny.us	Albany	NY	12202	518-434-0834	434-3821
Selkirk Shores State Park 7101 State Rt 3 *Web:* www.nysparks.com	Pulaski	NY	13142	315-298-5737	
Senate House State Historic Site 312 Fair St *Web:* www.nysparks.com	Kingston	NY	12401	845-338-2786	334-8173
Seneca Lake State Park 1 Lakefront Dr *Web:* www.nysparks.com	Geneva	NY	14456	315-789-2331	
Shadmoor State Park c/o Montauk Downs State Pk 50 S Fairview Ave *Web:* www.nysparks.com/parks/info.asp?parkId=83	Montauk	NY	11954	631-668-3781	
Silver Lake State Park c/o Letchworth State Pk *Web:* www.nysparks.com	Castile	NY	14427	585-493-3600	
Southwick Beach State Park 8119 Southwicks Pl *Web:* www.nysparks.com	Woodville	NY	13650	315-846-5338	
Staatsburgh State Historic Site 75 Mills Mansion Rd *Web:* www.nysparks.com	Staatsburg	NY	12580	845-889-8851	889-8321
Sterling Forest State Park 116 Old Forge Rd *Web:* www.nysparks.com	Tuxedo	NY	10987	845-351-5907	
Steuben Memorial State Historic Site c/o Oriskany Battlefield SHS 7801 State Rt 69 *Web:* www.nysparks.com/sites/info.asp?siteID=6	Oriskany	NY	13424	315-831-3737	337-3081
Stony Brook State Park 10820 Rt 36 S *Web:* www.nysparks.com/parks/118/details.aspx	Dansville	NY	14437	585-335-8111	
Stony Point Battlefield State Historic Site 44 Battlefield Rd *Web:* www.nysparks.state.ny.us	Stony Point	NY	10980	845-786-2521	
Storm King State Park c/o Palisades IH- Pk Commission Adminstration Bldg Rt 9 W *Web:* www.nysparks.com/parks/152/details.aspx	Bear Mountain	NY	10911	845-786-2701	
Sunken Meadow State Park Rte 25A *Web:* www.nysparks.com/parks/37/details.aspx	Kings Park	NY	11754	631-269-4333	
Taconic State Park - Copake Falls Area Rte 344 PO Box 100 *Web:* www.nysparks.com	Copake Falls	NY	12517	518-329-3993	
Taconic State Park - Rudd Pond Area 59 Rudd Pond Dr *Web:* www.nysparks.com	Millerton	NY	12546	518-789-3059	
Tallman Mountain State Park c/o Palisades IH- Pk Commission Adminstration Bldg Rt 9 W *Web:* www.nysparks.com/parks/119/details.aspx	Bear Mountain	NY	10911	845-359-0544	
Taughannock Falls State Park 2221 Taughannock Rd *Web:* www.nysparks.com	Trumansburg	NY	14886	607-387-6739	
Thompson's Lake State Park 68 Thompson's Lake Rd *Web:* www.nysparks.com	East Berne	NY	12059	518-872-1674	872-9133
Valley Stream State Park PO Box 670 *Web:* www.nysparks.com	Valley Stream	NY	11580	516-825-4128	
Verona Beach State Park PO Box 245 *Web:* www.nysparks.com	Verona Beach	NY	13162	315-762-4463	
Walt Whitman Birthplace State Historic Site 246 Old Walt Whitman Rd *Web:* www.nysparks.com	Huntington Station	NY	11746	631-427-5240	427-5247
Washington's Headquarters State Historic Site PO Box 1783 *Web:* www.nysparks.state.ny.us	Newburgh	NY	12551	845-562-1195	
Waterson Point State Park 44927 Cross Island Rd *Web:* nysparks.state.ny.us/parks/48/details.aspx	Fineview	NY	13640	315-482-2722	
Watkins Glen State Park PO Box 304 *Web:* www.nysparks.com	Watkins Glen	NY	14891	607-535-4511	
Wellesley Island State Park 44927 Cross Island Rd *Web:* www.nysparks.com	Fineview	NY	13640	315-482-2722	
Westcott Beach State Park PO Box 339 *Web:* www.nysparks.com	Sackets Harbor	NY	13685	315-646-2239	
Whetstone Gulf State Park Rd 2 PO Box 69 *Web:* www.nysparks.com	Lowville	NY	13367	315-376-6630	
Whirlpool State Park c/o Niagara Frontier Region PO Box 1132 *Web:* www.nysparks.com/parks/info.asp?parkId=29	Niagara Falls	NY	14303	716-284-4691	
Wildwood State Park N Wading River Rd PO Box 518 *Web:* www.nysparks.com	Wading River	NY	11792	631-929-4314	
Wilson-Tuscarora State Park 3371 Lake Rd *Web:* www.nysparks.com	Wilson	NY	14172	716-751-6361	
Woodlawn Beach State Park 3580 Lake Shore Rd *Web:* www.nysparks.com	Blasdell	NY	14219	716-826-1930	827-0293

NORTH CAROLINA

				Phone	Fax
Carolina Beach State Park PO Box 475 *Web:* ils.unc.edu/parkproject/visit/cabe/home.html	Carolina Beach	NC	28428	910-458-8206	458-6350
Cliffs of the Neuse State Park 345-A Pk Entrance Rd *Web:* www.ils.unc.edu	Seven Springs	NC	28578	919-778-6234	778-7447
Crowders Mountain State Park 522 Pk Office Ln *Web:* www.crowdersmountain.com	Kings Mountain	NC	28086	704-853-5375	853-5391
Eno River State Park 6101 Cole Mill Rd *Web:* www.ncparks.gov	Durham	NC	27705	919-383-1686	382-7378
Falls Lake State Recreation Area 13304 Creedmoor Rd *Web:* www.ils.unc.edu	Wake Forest	NC	27587	919-676-1027	676-2954
Fort Fisher State Recreation Area 1000 Loggerhead Rd *Web:* www.ils.unc.edu	Kure Beach	NC	28449	910-458-5798	458-5799
Fort Macon State Park PO Box 127 *Web:* ils.unc.edu	Atlantic Beach	NC	28512	252-726-3775	726-2497
Goose Creek State Park 2190 Camp Leach Rd *Web:* www.ils.unc.edu	Washington	NC	27889	252-923-2191	923-0052
Gorges State Park PO Box 100 *Web:* ils.unc.edu/parkproject/visit/gorg/home.html	Sapphire	NC	28774	828-966-9009	
Hammocks Beach State Park 1572 Hammock Beach Rd *Web:* www.ils.unc.edu	Swansboro	NC	28584	910-326-4881	326-2060
Hanging Rock State Park PO Box 278 *Web:* www.ils.unc.edu	Danbury	NC	27016	336-593-8480	593-9166
Jockey's Ridge State Park PO Box 592 *Web:* www.ils.unc.edu	Nags Head	NC	27959	252-441-7132	441-8416
Jones Lake State Park 4117 NC 242 Hwy *Web:* www.ncparks.gov	Elizabethtown	NC	28337	910-588-4550	
Jordan Lake State Recreation Area 280 State Pk Rd *Web:* www.ils.unc.edu	Apex	NC	27523	919-362-0586	362-1621

				Phone	Fax
Kerr Lake State Recreation Area 6254 Satterwhite Pt Rd *Web:* www.incparks.gov	Henderson	NC	27537	252-438-7791	438-7582
Lake James State Park PO Box 340 *Web:* www.ils.unc.edu	Nebo	NC	28761	828-652-5047	659-8911
Lake Norman State Park 159 Inland Sea Ln *Web:* ils.unc.edu/parkproject/visit/lano/home.html	Troutman	NC	28166	704-528-6350	528-5623
Lake Waccamaw State Park 1866 State Pk Dr. *Web:* www.ils.unc.edu	Lake Waccamaw	NC	28450	910-646-4748	646-4915
Lumber River State Park 2819 Princess Ann Rd. *Web:* ils.unc.edu/parkproject/visit/luri/home.html	Orrum	NC	28369	910-628-9844	628-8172
Medoc Mountain State Park 1541 Medoc State Pk Rd *Web:* www.ils.unc.edu	Hollister	NC	27844	252-586-6588	
Merchants Millpond State Park 71 US Hwy 158E. *Web:* www.ils.unc.edu	Gatesville	NC	27938	252-357-1191	357-0149
Morrow Mountain State Park 49104 Morrow Mountain Rd. *Web:* www.ils.unc.edu	Albemarle	NC	28001	704-982-4402	982-5323
Mount Jefferson State Natural Area PO Box 48 *Web:* www.ils.unc.edu	Jefferson	NC	28640	336-246-9653	246-3386
Mount Mitchell State Park 2388 State Hwy 128 *Web:* www.ils.unc.edu	Burnsville	NC	28714	828-675-4611	675-9655
New River State Park PO Box 48. *Web:* www.ils.unc.edu	Jefferson	NC	28640	336-982-2587	982-3943
Occoneechee Mountain State Natural Area c/o Eno River State Pk 6101 Cole Mill Rd. *Web:* www.ncparks.gov/Visit/parks/ocmo/main.php	Durham	NC	27705	919-383-1686	
Pettigrew State Park 2252 Lake Shore Rd *Web:* www.ils.unc.edu	Creswell	NC	27928	252-797-4475	797-7405
Pilot Mountain State Park 1792 Pilot Knob Pk Rd *Web:* www.ils.unc.edu	Pinnacle	NC	27043	336-325-2355	325-2751
Raven Rock State Park 3009 Raven Rock Rd *Web:* www.ils.unc.edu	Lillington	NC	27546	910-893-4888	814-2200
Singletary Lake State Park 6707 NC 53 Hwy E *Web:* www.ils.unc.edu	Kelly	NC	28448	910-669-2928	669-2034
South Mountains State Park 3001 S Mountains State Pk Ave *Web:* www.ils.unc.edu	Connelly Springs	NC	28612	828-433-4772	433-4778
Stone Mountain State Park 3042 Frank Pkwy *Web:* ils.unc.edu/parkproject/visit/stmo/home.html	Roaring Gap	NC	28668	336-957-8185	957-3985
Weymouth Woods Sandhills Nature Preserve 1024 Fort Bragg Rd *Web:* www.ils.unc.edu	Southern Pines	NC	28387	910-692-2167	692-8042
William B Umstead State Park 8801 Glenwood Ave *Web:* www.ils.unc.edu	Raleigh	NC	27617	919-571-4170	571-4161

NORTH DAKOTA

				Phone	Fax
Beaver Lake State Park 3850 70th St SE *Web:* www.ndparks.com	Wishek	ND	58495	701-452-2752	
Black Tiger Bay State Recreation Area 152 S Duncan Dr *Web:* www.ndparks.com	Devils Lake	ND	58301	701-766-4015	
Cross Ranch State Park c/o N Dakota Parks & Recreation Dept 1403 River Rd. *Web:* www.ndparks.com	Hensler	ND	58530	701-794-3731	
Cross Ranch State Park 1403 River Rd. *Web:* www.ndparks.com/Parks/CRSP.htm	Center	ND	58530	701-794-3731	794-3262
De Mores State Historic Site PO Box 106 *Web:* www.state.nd.us	Medora	ND	58645	701-623-4355	
Double Ditch State Historic Site c/o State Historical Society of N Dakota 612 E Blvd Ave *Web:* www.history.nd.gov/historicsites/doubleditch/index.html	Bismarck	ND	58505	701-328-2666	328-3710
Doyle Memorial State Park 5981 Walt Hjelle Pkwy *Web:* www.ndparks.com/parks/doyle-memorial-state-park	Wishek	ND	58495	701-452-2351	
Former Governors' Mansion State Historic Site 612 E Blvd Ave *Web:* www.state.nd.us	Bismarck	ND	58505	701-328-2666	328-3710
Fort Abercrombie State Historic Site PO Box 148 *Web:* www.state.nd.us	Abercrombie	ND	58001	701-553-8513	
Fort Abraham Lincoln State Park 4480 Fort Lincoln Rd *Web:* www.ndparks.com/Parks/FLSP.htm	Mandan	ND	58554	701-667-6340	667-6349
Fort Buford State Historic Site 15349 39th Ln NW *Web:* www.state.nd.us	Williston	ND	58801	701-572-9034	
Fort Clark Trading Post State Historic Site HC 2 PO Box 26 *Web:* www.state.nd.us	Center	ND	58530	701-794-8832	
Fort Ransom State Park 5981 Walt Hjelle Pkwy *Web:* www.ndparks.com	Fort Ransom	ND	58033	701-973-4331	973-4151
Fort Stevenson State Park 1252A 41st St NW *Web:* www.ndparks.com	Garrison	ND	58540	701-337-5576	337-5313
Fort Totten State Historic Site PO Box 224 *Web:* www.state.nd.us	Fort Totten	ND	58335	701-766-4441	
Gingras Trading Post State Historic Site RR 1 PO Box 55 *Web:* www.state.nd.us	Walhalla	ND	58202	701-549-2775	
Graham's Island State Park 152 S Duncan Dr *Web:* www.ndparks.com	Devils Lake	ND	58301	701-766-4015	
Gunlogson State Nature Preserve c/o N Dakota Parks & Recreation Dept 13571 Hwy 5 *Web:* www.ndparks.com	Cavalier	ND	58220	701-265-4561	
Head of the Mountain State Nature Preserve c/o N Dakota Parks & Recreation Dept 5981 Walt Hjelle Pkwy *Web:* www.ndparks.com	Fort Ransom	ND	58033	701-973-4331	
Homen State Forest c/o N Dakota Forest Service 307 1st St E *Web:* www.ndsu.nodak.edu/forestservice/stateforest/homen.htm	Bottineau	ND	58318	701-228-5422	228-5448
HR Morgan State Nature Preserve c/o N Dakota Parks & Recreation Dept 100 N Bismarck *Web:* www.ndparks.com	Bismarck	ND	58501	701-328-6300	
Icelandic State Park 13571 Hwy 5 *Web:* www.ndparks.com	Cavalier	ND	58220	701-265-4561	265-4443
Indian Hills State Recreation Area & Resort 7302 14th St NW *Web:* www.ndparks.com	Garrison	ND	58540	701-743-4122	
Lake Metigoshe State Park 2 Lake Metigoshe State Pk *Web:* www.ndparks.com	Bottineau	ND	58318	701-263-4651	263-4648
Lake Sakakawea State Park PO Box 732 *Web:* www.ndparks.com	Riverdale	ND	58565	701-487-3315	487-3305
Lewis & Clark State Park 4904 119th Rd NW *Web:* www.ndparks.com	Epping	ND	58843	701-859-3071	859-3001
Little Missouri State Park c/o Cross Ranch State Pk 1403 River Rd *Web:* www.ndparks.com/parks/little-missouri-state-park	Center	ND	58530	701-974-3731	
Mouse River State Forest 307 - 1st St E *Web:* www.ndsu.edu	Bottineau	ND	58318	701-228-5422	228-5448
Sentinel Butte State Nature Preserve c/o N Dakota Parks & Recreation Dept 1600 E Century Ave Suite 3 *Web:* www.ndparks.com	Bismarck	ND	58503	701-328-5357	
Sheyenne River State Forest c/o N Dakota Forest Service 307 1st St E *Web:* www.ndsu.nodak.edu/forestservice/stateforest/sheyenne_river.htm	Bottineau	ND	58318	701-228-5422	228-5448
Sully Creek State Recreation Area c/o Fort Abraham Lincoln State Pk 4480 Fort Lincoln Rd *Web:* www.ndparks.com	Mandan	ND	58554	701-663-9571	
Tetrault Woods State Forest c/o N Dakota Forest Service 307 1st St E *Web:* www.ndsu.nodak.edu/forestservice/stateforest/tetrault_woods.htm	Bottineau	ND	58318	701-228-5422	228-5448
Turtle Mountain State Forest c/o N Dakota Forest Service 307 1st St E *Web:* www.ndsu.nodak.edu/forestservice/stateforest/turtle_mtn.htm	Bottineau	ND	58318	701-228-5422	228-5448
Turtle River State Park 3084 Pk Ave. *Web:* www.ndparks.com	Arvilla	ND	58214	701-594-4445	594-2556
Whitestone Hill Battlefield State Historic Site RR 1 PO Box 125 *Web:* www.state.nd.us	Kulm	ND	58456	701-396-7731	

OHIO

				Phone	Fax
A W Marion State Park 7317 Warner Huffer Rd *Web:* www.ohiodnr.com/parks/awmarion/tabid/712/Default.aspx	Circleville	OH	43143	740-869-3124	
Adams Lake State Park c/o Shawnee State Pk 4404 State Rt 125 *Web:* www.ohiodnr.com	Portsmouth	OH	45663	740-858-6652	
Alum Creek State Park 3615 S Old State Rd. *Web:* www.ohiodnr.com/parks/parks/alum.htm	Delaware	OH	43015	740-548-4631	
Barkcamp State Park 65330 Barkcamp Rd *Web:* www.ohiodnr.com	Belmont	OH	43718	740-484-4064	
Beaver Creek State Park 12021 Echo Dell Rd *Web:* www.ohiodnr.com	East Liverpool	OH	43920	330-385-3091	
Blue Rock State Park c/o Dillon State Pk 5265 Dillon Hills Dr *Web:* www.ohiodnr.com/parks/parks/bluerock.htm	Nashport	OH	43830	740-453-4377	
Buck Creek State Park 1901 Buck Creek Ln. *Web:* www.ohiodnr.com	Springfield	OH	45502	937-322-5284	
Buckeye Lake State Park 2905 Liebs Island Rd *Web:* www.ohiodnr.com	Millersport	OH	43046	740-467-2690	
Burr Oak State Park 10220 Burr Oak Lodge Rd *Web:* www.ohiodnr.com	Glouster	OH	45732	740-767-3570	
Caesar Creek State Park 8570 E State Rt 73 *Web:* www.ohiodnr.com/parks/parks/caesarck.htm	Waynesville	OH	45068	513-897-3055	
Catawba Island State Park 4049 E Moores Dock Rd *Web:* www.ohiodnr.com	Port Clinton	OH	43452	419-797-4530	
Cleveland Lakefront State Park 8701 Lakeshore Blvd NE *Web:* www.ohiodnr.com/parks/parks/clevelkf.htm	Cleveland	OH	44108	216-881-8141	
Cowan Lake State Park 1750 Osborn Rd *Web:* www.ohiodnr.com	Wilmington	OH	45177	937-382-1096	
Crane Creek State Park 13531 W SR- 2 *Web:* www.ohiodnr.com	Oak Harbor	OH	43449	419-836-7758	
Deer Creek State Park 20635 Waterloo Rd *Web:* www.ohiodnr.com	Mount Sterling	OH	43143	740-869-3124	
Delaware State Park 5202 US Hwy 23 N. *Web:* www.ohiodnr.com/parks/parks/delaware.htm	Delaware	OH	43015	740-369-2761	

				Phone	Fax
Dillon State Park 5265 Dillon Hills Dr *Web:* www.ohiodnr.com	Nashport	OH	43830	740-453-4377	
East Fork State Park 3294 Elklick Rd *Web:* www.ohiodnr.com	Bethel	OH	45106	513-734-4323	
East Harbor State Park 1169 N Buck Rd *Web:* www.ohiodnr.com/parks/parks/eastharbor.htm	Lakeside-Marblehead	OH	43440	419-734-4424	
Findley State Park 25381 State Rt 58 *Web:* www.ohiodnr.com	Wellington	OH	44090	440-647-4490	
Forked Run State Park 63300 SR- 124 PO Box 127 *Web:* www.ohiodnr.com	Reedsville	OH	45772	740-378-6206	
Geneva State Park 4499 Pandanarum Rd PO Box 429 *Web:* www.ohiodnr.com	Geneva	OH	44041	440-466-8400	
Grand Lake Saint Marys State Park 834 Edgewater Dr *Web:* www.ohiodnr.com	Saint Marys	OH	45885	419-394-3611	
Great Seal State Park 635 Rocky Rd *Web:* www.ohiodnr.com	Chillicothe	OH	45601	740-663-2125	
Guilford Lake State Park 6835 E Lake Rd *Web:* www.ohiodnr.com	Lisbon	OH	44432	330-222-1712	
Harrison Lake State Park 26246 Harrison Lake Rd *Web:* www.ohiodnr.com	Fayette	OH	43521	419-237-2593	
Headlands Beach State Park c/o Cleveland Lakefront State Pk 8701 Lakeshore Blvd NE *Web:* www.ohiodnr.com/parks/parks/headlnds.htm	Cleveland	OH	44108	216-881-8141	
Hocking Hills State Park 19852 State Rt 664 S *Web:* www.ohiodnr.com/parks/parks/hocking.htm	Logan	OH	43138	740-385-6842	
Hueston Woods State Park 6301 Pk Office Rd *Web:* www.ohiodnr.com	College Corner	OH	45003	513-523-6347	
Independence Dam State Park 27722 SR- 424 *Web:* www.ohiodnr.com	Defiance	OH	43512	419-237-1503	
Indian Lake State Park 12774 State Rt 235 N *Web:* www.ohiodnr.com	Lakeview	OH	43331	937-843-2717	
Jackson Lake State Park 35 Tommy Been Rd PO Box 174 *Web:* www.ohiodnr.com	Oak Hill	OH	45656	740-596-5253	
Jefferson Lake State Park 501 Township Rd 261A *Web:* www.ohiodnr.com	Richmond	OH	43944	740-765-4459	
John Bryan State Park 3790 SR- 370 *Web:* www.ohiodnr.com	Yellow Springs	OH	45387	937-767-1274	
Kelleys Island State Park c/o Catawba Island State Pk 4049 E Moores Dock Rd *Web:* www.ohiodnr.com/parks/parks/lakeerie.htm	Port Clinton	OH	43452	419-797-4530	
Kiser Lake State Park 4889 N SR- 235 *Web:* www.ohiodnr.com	Saint Paris	OH	43072	937-362-3822	
Lake Alma State Park c/o Lake Hope State Pk 27331 State Rt 278 *Web:* www.ohiodnr.com/parks/parks/lakealma.htm	McArthur	OH	45651	740-384-4474	
Lake Hope State Park 27331 State Rt 278 *Web:* www.ohiodnr.com/parks/parks/lakehope.htm	McArthur	OH	45651	740-596-5253	
Lake Logan State Park 20160 State Rd 664 *Web:* www.ohiodnr.com/parks/parks/lklogan.htm	Logan	OH	43138	740-385-6842	
Lake Loramie State Park 4401 Fort Loramie Swanders Rd *Web:* www.ohiodnr.com	Minster	OH	45865	937-295-2011	
Lake Milton State Park 16801 Mahoning Ave *Web:* www.ohiodnr.com	Lake Milton	OH	44429	330-654-4989	
Lake White State Park 2767 SR- 551 *Web:* www.ohiodnr.com	Waverly	OH	45690	740-947-4059	
Little Miami Scenic State Park c/o Caesar Creek State Pk 8570 E State Rt 73 *Web:* www.ohiodnr.com/parks/parks/lilmiami.htm	Waynesville	OH	45068	513-897-3055	
Madison Lake State Park 4860 E Pk Dr *Web:* www.ohiodnr.com/parks/madison/tabid/761/Default.aspx	London	OH	43140	937-322-5284	
Malabar Farm State Park 4050 Bromfield Rd *Web:* www.ohiodnr.com	Lucas	OH	44843	419-892-2784	892-3988
Marblehead Lighthouse State Park c/o E Harbor State Pk 1169 N Buck Rd *Web:* www.dnr.state.oh.us/parks/parks/marblehead	Lakeside-Marblehead	OH	43440	419-734-4424	
Mary Jane Thurston State Park 1-466 State Rt 65 *Web:* www.ohiodnr.com/parks/parks/mjthrstn.htm	McClure	OH	43534	419-832-7662	
Maumee Bay State Park 1400 State Pk Rd *Web:* www.ohiodnr.com	Oregon	OH	43618	419-836-7758	836-8711
Middle Bass Island State Park c/o Catawba Island State Pk 4049 E Moores Dock Rd *Web:* www.ohiodnr.com/parks/parks/middlebass.htm	Port Clinton	OH	43452	419-797-4530	
Mohican State Park 3116 SR- 3 *Web:* www.ohiodnr.com	Loudonville	OH	44842	419-994-5125	
Mosquito Lake State Park 1439 Wilson Sharpsville Rd *Web:* www.ohiodnr.com	Cortland	OH	44410	330-637-2856	
Mount Gilead State Park 4119 State Rt 95 *Web:* www.ohiodnr.com	Mount Gilead	OH	43338	419-946-1961	
Muskingum River State Park 1390 Ellis Dam Rd *Web:* www.ohiodnr.com	Zanesville	OH	43701	740-453-4377	
Nelson-Kennedy Ledges State Park c/o Punderson State Pk PO Box 338 *Web:* www.ohiodnr.com	Newberry	OH	44065	440-564-2279	
Oak Point State Park c/o Catawba Island State Pk 4049 E Moores Dock Rd *Web:* www.ohiodnr.com/parks/parks/lakeerie.htm	Port Clinton	OH	43452	419-797-4530	
Paint Creek State Park 14265 US Hwy 50 *Web:* www.ohiodnr.com/parks/parks/paintcrk.htm	Bainbridge	OH	45612	937-365-1401	
Pike Lake State Park 1847 Pike Lake Rd *Web:* www.ohiodnr.com/parks/parks/pikelake.htm	Bainbridge	OH	45612	740-493-2212	
Portage Lakes State Park 5031 Manchester Rd *Web:* www.ohiodnr.com	Akron	OH	44319	330-644-2220	644-7550
Punderson State Park 11755 Kinsman Rd PO Box 338 *TF:* 800-282-5393 ■ *Web:* www.ohiodnr.com/parks/parks/punderson.htm	Newbury	OH	44065	440-564-2279	
Pymatuning State Park PO Box 1000 *Web:* www.ohiodnr.com	Andover	OH	44003	440-293-6030	
Quail Hollow State Park 13340 Congress Lake Ave *Web:* www.ohiodnr.com	Hartville	OH	44632	330-877-1528	
Rocky Fork State Park 9800 N Shore Dr *Web:* www.ohiodnr.com	Hillsboro	OH	45133	937-393-4284	
Salt Fork State Park 14755 Cadiz Rd *Web:* www.ohiodnr.com	Lore City	OH	43755	740-439-3521	432-1515
Scioto Trail State Park 144 Lake Rd *Web:* www.ohiodnr.com/parks/parks/sciototr.htm	Chillicothe	OH	45601	740-663-2125	
Shawnee State Park 4404 SR- 125 *Web:* www.ohiodnr.com	West Portsmouth	OH	45663	740-858-6652	
South Bass Island State Park c/o Catawba Island State Pk 4049 E Moores Dock Rd *Web:* www.ohiodnr.com/parks/parks/lakeerie.htm	Port Clinton	OH	43452	419-797-4530	
Stonelick State Park 2895 Lake Dr *Web:* www.ohiodnr.com	Pleasant Plain	OH	45162	513-734-4323	
Strouds Run State Park c/o Burr Oak State Pk 1022 Burr Oak Lodge Rd *Web:* www.ohiodnr.com	Glouster	OH	45732	740-592-2302	
Sycamore State Park c/o Hueston Woods State Pk 6301 Pk Office Rd *Web:* www.ohiodnr.com	College Corner	OH	45003	513-523-6347	
Tar Hollow State Park 16396 Tar Hollow Rd *Web:* www.ohiodnr.com	Laurelville	OH	43135	740-887-4818	
Tinkers Creek State Park c/o Punderson State Pk 11755 Kinsman Rd *Web:* www.ohiodnr.com/parks/parks/tinkers.htm	Newbury	OH	44065	440-564-2279	
Van Buren State Park c/o Mary Jane Thurston State Pk 1-466 State Rt 65 *Web:* www.dnr.state.oh.us/parks/parks/vanburen	McClure	OH	43534	419-832-7662	
West Branch State Park 5708 Esworthy Rd *Web:* www.ohiodnr.com	Ravenna	OH	44266	330-296-3239	
Wolf Run State Park 16170 Wolf Run Rd *Web:* www.ohiodnr.com	Caldwell	OH	43724	740-732-5035	

OKLAHOMA

				Phone	Fax
Adair State Park Hwy 51 & Hwy 59 *Web:* www.oklahomaparks.com	Stilwell	OK	74960	918-696-6613	696-2908
Alabaster Caverns State Park Hwy 50 & Hwy 50-A *Web:* www.oklahomaparks.com	Freedom	OK	73842	580-621-3381	621-3572
Arrowhead State Park HC 67 PO Box 57 *Web:* www.oklahomaparks.com	Canadian	OK	74425	918-339-2204	339-7236
Beaver Dunes State Park PO Box 1190 *Web:* www.oklahomaparks.com	Beaver	OK	73932	580-625-3373	625-3525
Beavers Bend Resort Park PO Box 10 *Web:* www.oklahomaparks.com	Broken Bow	OK	74728	580-494-6300	494-6689
Bernice State Park 901 State Pk Rd *Web:* www.oklahomaparks.com	Grove	OK	74344	918-786-9447	787-5634
Black Mesa State Park & Nature Preserve County Rd 325 *Web:* www.oklahomaparks.com	Kenton	OK	73946	580-426-2222	426-2405
Boggy Depot State Park 120 N Robinson Suite 600 *Web:* www.oklahomaparks.com/uploads/tx_okstateparksmaps/BoggyDepot.pdf	Oklahoma City	OK	73102	405-230-8440	
Boiling Springs State Park 207697 Boiling Springs Rd *Web:* www.oklahomaparks.com	Woodward	OK	73801	580-256-7664	256-4338
Brushy Lake State Park Rt 3 PO Box 36 *Web:* www.oklahomaparks.com	Sallisaw	OK	74955	918-775-6507	775-0970
Cherokee Landing State Park 28610 Pk 20 *Web:* www.oklahomaparks.com	Park Hill	OK	74451	918-457-5716	457-4871
Cherokee State Park 232 Cliff Heights *Web:* www.oklahomaparks.com	Disney	OK	74340	918-435-8066	435-4067
Clayton Lake State Park HC 60 PO Box 33-10 *Web:* www.oklahomaparks.com	Clayton	OK	74536	918-569-7981	569-7981
Crowder Lake University Park RR 1 PO Box 186 *Web:* www.swosu.edu	Colony	OK	73031	580-343-2443	774-7059
Disney/Little Blue State Park c/o Cherokee State Pk PO Box 220 *Web:* www.oklahomaparks.com	Disney	OK	74340	918-435-8066	
Dripping Springs State Park 16830 Dripping Springs Rd *Web:* www.travelok.com/listings/view.profile/id.2368	Okmulgee	OK	74447	918-756-5971	759-9933
Fort Cobb Lake State Park 27022 Copperhead Rd *Web:* www.oklahomaparks.com	Fort Cobb	OK	73038	405-643-2249	643-5167
Foss State Park HC 66 PO Box 111 *Web:* www.oklahomaparks.com	Foss	OK	73647	580-592-4433	592-4701

Phone | Fax

Great Plains State Park
Hwy 183 & County Rd .... Mountain Park OK 73552 580-569-2032 569-2375
Web: www.oklahomaparks.com

Great Salt Plains State Park Rt 1 PO Box 28 .... Jet OK 73749 580-626-4731 626-4730
Web: www.oklahomaparks.com

Greenleaf State Park Rt 1 PO Box 119 .... Braggs OK 74423 918-487-5196 487-5406
Web: www.oklahomaparks.com

Heavener Runestone State Park
18365 Runestone Rd .... Heavener OK 74937 918-653-2241 653-3435
Web: www.oklahomaparks.com

Hochatown State Park
c/o Beavers Bend State Pk PO Box 10 .... Broken Bow OK 94728 580-494-6452 494-6453

Honey Creek State Park 901 State Pk Rd .... Grove OK 74344 918-786-9447 787-5634
Web: www.oklahomaparks.com

Hugo Lake State Park PO Box 907 .... Hugo OK 74743 580-326-0303 326-0505

Keystone State Park 1926 S Hwy 151 .... Sand Springs OK 74063 918-865-4991 865-2083
TF: 800-654-8240 ■ *Web:* www.travelok.com/listings/view.profile/id.4163

Lake Eucha State Park Hwy 59 S PO Box 349 .... Jay OK 74346 918-253-8790
Web: www.oklahomaparks.com

Lake Eufaula State Park HC 60 PO Box 1340 .... Checotah OK 74426 918-689-5311 689-5039
Web: www.touroklahoma.com

Lake Murray State Park
18407 Scenic State Hwy 77 .... Ardmore OK 73401 580-223-4044 223-4052
Web: www.oklahomaparks.com

Lake Thunderbird State Park 13101 Alameda Dr. .... Norman OK 73026 405-360-3572 366-8150
Web: www.oklahomaparks.com

Lake Wister State Park 25567 US Hwy 270 .... Wister OK 74966 918-655-7212 655-7274
Web: www.oklahomaparks.com

Little Sahara State Park 101 Main St. .... Waynoka OK 73860 580-824-1471 824-1472
Web: www.oklahomaparks.com

McGee Creek State Park
576-A S McGee Creek Dam Rd. .... Atoka OK 74525 580-889-5822 889-7868
Web: www.oklahomaparks.com

Natural Falls State Park
Rt 4 PO Box 32 .... West Siloam Springs OK 74338 918-422-5802 422-0026
Web: www.oklahomaparks.com

Okmulgee State Park
16830 Dripping Springs Rd .... Okmulgee OK 74447 918-756-5971 759-9933
Web: www.travelok.com/listings/view.profile/id.5520

Osage Hills State Park Hwy 60 W .... Bartlesville OK 74006 918-336-4141 337-2176
Web: www.oklahomaparks.com

Quartz Mountain Resort 22469 Lodge Rd. .... Lone Wolf OK 73655 580-563-2424 563-2422
Web: www.quartzmountainresort.com

Raymond Gary State Park
HC 63 PO Box 1450 .... Fort Towson OK 74735 580-873-2307 326-2305
Web: www.oklahomaparks.com

Red Rock Canyon State Park PO Box 502 .... Hinton OK 73047 405-542-6344 542-6342
Web: www.oklahomaparks.com

Robbers Cave State Park PO Box 9 .... Wilburton OK 74578 918-465-2565 465-5763
Web: www.oklahomaparks.com

Roman Nose Resort Park Rt 1 PO Box 2-2 .... Watonga OK 73772 580-623-4215 623-2190
Web: www.oklahomaparks.com

Sequoyah Bay State Park 6237 E 100th St N .... Wagoner OK 74467 918-683-0878 687-6797
Web: www.oklahomaparks.com

Sequoyah State Park & Western Hills Guest Ranch
17131 Pk 10 .... Hulbert OK 74441 918-772-2545 772-2030
TF: 800-368-1486 ■ *Web:* www.oklahomaparks.com

Snowdale State Park PO Box 6 .... Salina OK 74365 918-434-2651 435-4067
Web: www.oklahomaparks.com

Spavinaw State Park Hwy 82 S .... Spavinaw OK 74366 918-589-2651 435-4067
Web: www.oklahomaparks.com

Talimena State Park 50884 US Hwy 271 .... Talihina OK 74571 918-567-2052 567-2052
Web: www.oklahomaparks.com

Tenkiller State Park HCR 68 PO Box 1095 .... Vian OK 74962 918-489-5643 489-2111
Web: www.oklahomaparks.com

Twin Bridges State Park 14801 Hwy 137 S .... Fairland OK 74343 918-540-2545 540-2545
Web: www.oklahomaparks.com

Wah-Sha-She State Park Hwy 10 W .... Copan OK 74022 918-336-4141 337-2176
Web: www.oklahomaparks.com

Walnut Creek State Park 209th W Ave .... Prue OK 74060 918-865-4991 865-2050
Web: www.travelok.com/listings/view.profile/id.8380

OREGON

Phone | Fax

Agate Beach State Recreation Site
c/o Beverly Beach Management Unit
198 NE 123rd St .... Newport OR 97365 800-551-6949
TF: 800-551-6949 ■ *Web:* www.oregonstateparks.org

Ainsworth State Park
c/o Columbia River Gorge Management Unit
PO Box 100 .... Corbett OR 97019 800-551-6949
TF: 800-551-6949 ■ *Web:* www.oregonstateparks.org

Alderwood State Wayside
c/o Southern Willamette Management Unit
PO Box 511 .... Lowell OR 97452 800-551-6949
TF: 800-551-6949 ■ *Web:* www.oregonstateparks.org

Alfred A. Loeb State Park
c/o Harris Beach Management Unit
1655 Hwy 101 N. .... Brookings OR 97415 541-469-2021
TF: 800-551-6949 ■ *Web:* www.oregonstateparks.org/park_72.php

Alsea Bay Historic Interpretive Ctr
c/o S Beach Management Unit 5580 S Coast Hwy .... Newport OR 97366 800-551-6949
TF: 800-551-6949 ■ *Web:* www.oregonstateparks.org

Arcadia Beach State Recreation Site
9500 Sandpiper Ln, c/o Nehalem Bay Management Unit
PO Box 366 .... Nehalem OR 97131 800-551-6949
TF: 800-551-6949 ■ *Web:* www.oregonstateparks.org

Phone | Fax

Bald Peak State Scenic Viewpoint
c/o Champoeg Management Unit
7679 Champoeg Rd NE .... Saint Paul OR 97137 800-551-6949
TF: 800-551-6949 ■ *Web:* www.oregonstateparks.org

Bandon State Natural Area
c/o Bullards Beach Management Unit PO Box 569 .... Bandon OR 97411 800-551-6949
TF: 800-551-6949 ■ *Web:* www.oregonstateparks.org

Battle Mountain Forest State Scenic Corridor
c/o Blue Mountain Management Unit PO Box 85 .... Meacham OR 97859 800-551-6949
TF: 800-551-6949 ■ *Web:* www.oregonstateparks.org

Beachside State Recreation Site
c/o S Beach Management Unit 5580 S Coast Hwy .... Newport OR 97366 800-551-6949
TF: 800-551-6949 ■ *Web:* www.oregonstateparks.org

Benson State Recreation Area
c/o Columbia River Gorge Management Unit
PO Box 100 .... Corbett OR 97019 800-551-6949
TF: 800-551-6949 ■ *Web:* www.oregonstateparks.org

Beverly Beach State Park 198 NE 123rd St .... Newport OR 97365 541-265-9278
Web: www.oregonstateparks.org

Blue Mountain Forest State Scenic Corridor
c/o Blue Mountain Management Unit PO Box 85 .... Meecham OR 97859 800-551-6949
TF: 800-551-6949 ■ *Web:* www.oregonstateparks.org

Bob Straub State Park
c/o Cape Lookout Management Unit
13000 Whiskey Creek Rd W .... Tillamook OR 97141 800-551-6949
TF: 800-551-6949 ■ *Web:* www.oregonstateparks.org

Boiler Bay State Scenic Viewpoint
c/o Beverly Beach Management Unit
198 NE 123rd St .... Newport OR 97365 800-551-6949
TF: 800-551-6949 ■ *Web:* www.oregonstateparks.org

Bolon Island Tideways State Scenic Corridor
c/o Honeyman Management Unit
84505 Hwy 101 S .... Florence OR 97439 800-551-6949
TF: 800-551-6949 ■ *Web:* www.oregonstateparks.org

Bonnie Lure State Recreation Area
c/o Tryon Creek Management Unit
11321 SW Terwilliger Blvd .... Portland OR 97219 800-551-6949
TF: 800-551-6949 ■ *Web:* www.oregonstateparks.org

Booth State Scenic Corridor
c/o LaPine Management Unit
15800 State Recreation Rd .... La Pine OR 97739 800-551-6949
TF: 800-551-6949 ■ *Web:* www.oregonstateparks.org

Bradley State Scenic Viewpoint
c/o Fort Stevens Management Unit
100 Peter Iredale Rd .... Hammond OR 97121 800-551-6949
TF: 800-551-6949 ■ *Web:* www.oregonstateparks.org

Bridal Veil Falls State Scenic Viewpoint
c/o Columbia River Gorge Management Unit
PO Box 100 .... Corbett OR 97019 800-551-6949
TF: 800-551-6949 ■ *Web:* www.oregonstateparks.org

Bullards Beach State Park PO Box 569 .... Bandon OR 97411 541-347-2209
Web: www.oregonstateparks.org/park_71.php

Cape Arago State Park
c/o Sunset Bay Management Unit
89814 Cape Arago Hwy .... Coos Bay OR 97420 541-888-3778
Web: www.oregonstateparks.org

Cape Blanco State Park 39745 S Hwy 101 .... Port Orford OR 97465 541-332-6774
Web: www.oregonstateparks.org

Cape Kiwanda State Natural Area
c/o Cape Lookout Management Unit
13000 Whiskey Creek Rd W .... Tillamook OR 97141 800-551-6949
TF: 800-551-6949 ■ *Web:* www.oregonstateparks.org

Cape Lookout State Park
13000 Whiskey Creek Rd W .... Tillamook OR 97141 503-842-4981
Web: www.oregonstateparks.org/park_186.php

Cape Meares State Scenic Viewpoint
c/o Cape Lookout Management Unit
13000 Whiskey Creek Rd W .... Tillamook OR 97141 800-551-6949
TF: 800-551-6949 ■ *Web:* www.oregonstateparks.org

Cape Sebastian State Scenic Corridor
c/o Harris Beach Management Unit
1655 Hwy 101 N .... Brookings OR 97415 800-551-6949
TF: 800-551-6949 ■ *Web:* www.oregonstateparks.org

Carl G. Washburne Memorial State Park
9311 Hwy 101 N .... Florence OR 97439 541-547-3416
Web: www.oregonstateparks.org

Cascadia State Park PO Box 736 .... Cascadia OR 97329 541-367-6021
Web: www.oregonstateparks.org

Casey State Recreation Site
c/o Joseph Stewart Management Unit
35251 Hwy 62 .... Trail OR 97541 541-560-3334 560-3855
Web: www.oregonstateparks.org

Catherine Creek State Park
c/o Blue Mountain Management Unit PO Box 85 .... Meacham OR 97859 800-551-6949
TF: 800-551-6949 ■ *Web:* www.oregonstateparks.org

Champoeg State Heritage Area
7679 Champoeg Rd NE .... Saint Paul OR 97137 503-678-1251
Web: www.oregonstateparks.org

Chandler State Wayside
c/o LaPine Management Unit
15800 State Recreation Rd .... La Pine OR 97739 800-551-6949
TF: 800-551-6949 ■ *Web:* www.oregonstateparks.org

Cline Falls State Scenic Viewpoint
c/o Tumalo Management Unit 62976 OB Riley Rd .... Bend OR 97701 800-551-6949
TF: 800-551-6949 ■ *Web:* www.oregonstateparks.org

Clyde Holliday State Recreation Site
PO Box 10 .... Mount Vernon OR 97865 541-932-4453
Web: www.oregonstateparks.org

Collier Memorial State Park 46000 Hwy 97 N. .... Chiloquin OR 97624 541-783-2471
Web: www.oregonstateparks.org

Coquille Myrtle Grove State Natural Site
c/o Bullards Beach Management Unit PO Box 569 .... Bandon OR 97411 800-551-6949
TF: 800-551-6949 ■ *Web:* www.oregonstateparks.org

Phone Fax

Cove Palisades State Park 7300 Jordan Rd. . . . . Culver OR 97734 541-546-3412
Web: www.oregonstateparks.org

Crissey Field State Recreation Site
c/o Harris Beach Management Unit
1655 Hwy 101 N. . . . . Brookings OR 97415 800-551-6949
TF: 800-551-6949 ■ *Web:* www.oregonstateparks.org

Crown Point State Scenic Corridor
c/o Columbia River Gorge Management Unit
PO Box 100 . . . . Corbett OR 97019 800-551-6949
TF: 800-551-6949 ■ *Web:* www.oregonstateparks.org

D River State Recreation Site
c/o Beverly Beach Management Unit
198 NE 123rd St. . . . . Newport OR 97365 800-551-6949
TF: 800-551-6949 ■ *Web:* www.oregonstateparks.org

Dabney State Recreation Area
c/o Columbia River Gorge Management Unit
PO Box 100 . . . . Corbett OR 97019 800-551-6949
TF: 800-551-6949 ■ *Web:* www.oregonstateparks.org

Darlingtonia State Natural Site
c/o Honeyman Management Unit
84505 Hwy 101 S. . . . . Florence OR 97439 800-551-6949
TF: 800-551-6949 ■ *Web:* www.oregonstateparks.org

Del Rey Beach State Recreation Site
c/o Fort Stevens Management Unit
100 Peter Iredale Rd. . . . . Hammond OR 97121 800-551-6949
TF: 800-551-6949 ■ *Web:* www.oregonstateparks.org

Deschutes River State Recreation Area
89600 Biggs-Rufus Hwy. . . . . Wasco OR 97065 541-739-2322
Web: www.oregonstateparks.org/park_37.php

Detroit Lake State Recreation Area
PO Box 549 . . . . Detroit OR 97342 503-854-3346
Web: www.oregonstateparks.org

Devil's Lake State Recreation Area
c/o Beverly Beach Management Unit
198 NE 123rd St. . . . . Newport OR 97365 800-551-6949
TF: 800-551-6949 ■ *Web:* www.oregonstateparks.org

Devil's Punchbowl State Natural Area
c/o Beverly Beach Management Unit
198 NE 123rd St. . . . . Newport OR 97365 800-551-6949
TF: 800-551-6949 ■ *Web:* www.oregonstateparks.org

Dexter State Recreation Site
c/o Southern Willamette Management Unit
PO Box 511 . . . . Lowell OR 97452 541-937-1173
Web: www.oregonstateparks.org

Driftwood Beach State Recreation Site
c/o S Beach Management Unit 5580 S Coast Hwy . . . . Newport OR 97366 800-551-6949
TF: 800-551-6949 ■ *Web:* www.oregonstateparks.org

Ecola State Park
c/o Nehalem State Pk PO Box 366 . . . . Nehalem OR 97131 503-436-2844
Web: www.oregonstateparks.org

Elijah Bristow State Park
c/o Southern Willamette Management Unit
PO Box 511 . . . . Lowell OR 97452 800-551-6949
TF: 800-551-6949 ■ *Web:* www.oregonstateparks.org

Ellmaker State Wayside
c/o Beverly Beach Management Unit
198 NE 123rd St. . . . . Newport OR 97365 800-551-6949
TF: 800-551-6949 ■ *Web:* www.oregonstateparks.org

Emigrant Springs State Heritage Area
c/o Blue Mountain Management Unit PO Box 85 . . . . Meacham OR 97859 800-551-6959
TF: 800-551-6959 ■ *Web:* www.oregonstateparks.org

Erratic Rock State Natural Site
c/o Willamette Mission Management Unit
10991 Wheatland Rd NE. . . . . Gervais OR 97026 800-551-6949
TF: 800-551-6949 ■ *Web:* www.oregonstateparks.org

Face Rock State Scenic Viewpoint
c/o Bullards Beach Management Unit PO Box 569. . . . . Bandon OR 97411 800-551-6949
TF: 800-551-6949 ■ *Web:* www.oregonstateparks.org

Fall Creek State Recreation Area
45 S Moss St PO Box 511 . . . . Lowell OR 97452 541-937-1173
Web: www.oregonstateparks.org/park_241.php

Farewell Bend State Recreation Area
23751 Old Hwy 30 . . . . Huntington OR 97907 541-869-2365
Web: www.oregonstateparks.org

Fogarty Creek State Recreation Area
c/o Beverly Beach Management Unit
198 NE 123rd St. . . . . Newport OR 97365 800-551-6949
TF: 800-551-6949 ■ *Web:* www.oregonstateparks.org

Fort Rock State Natural Area
c/o LaPine Management Unit
15800 State Recreation Rd . . . . La Pine OR 97739 800-551-6949
TF: 800-551-6949 ■ *Web:* www.oregonstateparks.org

Fort Stevens State Park 100 Peter Iredale Rd. . . . . Hammond OR 97121 503-861-1671
Web: www.oregonstateparks.org

Frenchglen Hotel State Heritage Site
c/o Clyde Holliday Management Unit
PO Box 10 . . . . Mount Vernon OR 97865 800-551-6949
TF: 800-551-6949 ■ *Web:* www.oregonstateparks.org

Geisel Monument State Heritage Site
c/o Cape Blanco Management Unit
PO Box 1345 . . . . Port Orford OR 97465 800-551-6949
TF: 800-551-6949 ■ *Web:* www.oregonstateparks.org

George W. Joseph State Natural Area
c/o Columbia River Gorge Management Unit
PO Box 100 . . . . Corbett OR 97019 800-551-6949
TF: 800-551-6949 ■ *Web:* www.oregonstateparks.org

Gleneden Beach State Recreation Site
c/o Beverly Beach Management Unit
198 NE 123rd St. . . . . Newport OR 97365 800-551-6949
TF: 800-551-6949 ■ *Web:* www.oregonstateparks.org

Golden & Silver Falls State Natural Area
c/o Sunset Bay Management Unit
89814 Cape Arago Hwy . . . . Coos Bay OR 97420 541-888-3778
Web: www.oregonstateparks.org

Goose Lake State Recreation Area
c/o LaPine Management Unit
15800 State Recreation Rd . . . . La Pine OR 97739 800-551-6949
TF: 800-551-6949 ■ *Web:* www.oregonstateparks.org

Government Island State Recreation Area
c/o Columbia River Gorge Management Unit
PO Box 100 . . . . Corbett OR 97019 800-551-6949
TF: 800-551-6949 ■ *Web:* www.oregonstateparks.org/park_250.php

Governor Patterson Memorial State Recreation Site
c/o S Beach Management Unit 5580 S Coast Hwy . . . . Newport OR 97439 800-551-6949
TF: 800-551-6949 ■ *Web:* www.oregonstateparks.org

Guy W. Talbot State Park
c/o Columbia River Gorge Management Unit
PO Box 100 . . . . Corbett OR 97019 800-551-6949
TF: 800-551-6949 ■ *Web:* www.oregonstateparks.org

H. B. Van Duzer Forest State Scenic Corridor
c/o Beverly Beach Management Unit
198 NE 123rd St. . . . . Newport OR 97365 800-551-6949
TF: 800-551-6949 ■ *Web:* www.oregonstateparks.org

Harris Beach State Park 1655 Hwy 101 N . . . . Brookings OR 97415 541-469-2021
Web: www.oregonstateparks.org/park_79.php

Hat Rock State Park
c/o Blue Mountain Management Unit PO Box 85 . . . . Meacham OR 97859 800-551-6959
TF: 800-551-6959 ■ *Web:* www.oregonstateparks.org

Heceta Head Lighthouse State Scenic Viewpoint
c/o Washburne Management Unit
93111 Hwy 101 N. . . . . Florence OR 97439 800-551-6949
TF: 800-551-6949 ■ *Web:* www.oregonstateparks.org

Hilgard Junction State Park
c/o Blue Mountain Management Unit PO Box 85 . . . . Meacham OR 97859 800-551-6949
TF: 800-551-6949 ■ *Web:* www.oregonstateparks.org

Historic Columbia River Highway State Trail
c/o Columbia River Gorge Management Unit
PO Box 100 . . . . Corbett OR 97019 800-551-6949
TF: 800-551-6949 ■ *Web:* www.oregonstateparks.org

Hoffman Memorial State Wayside
c/o Bullards Beach Management Unit PO Box 569. . . . . Bandon OR 97411 800-551-6949
TF: 800-551-6949 ■ *Web:* www.oregonstateparks.org

Holman State Wayside
c/o Willamette Mission Management Unit
10991 Wheatland Rd NE. . . . . Gervais OR 97026 800-551-6949
TF: 800-551-6949 ■ *Web:* www.oregonstateparks.org

Hug Point State Recreation Site
9500 Sandpiper Ln, c/o Nehalem Bay Management Unit
PO Box 366 . . . . Nehalem OR 97131 800-551-6949
TF: 800-551-6949 ■ *Web:* www.oregonstateparks.org

Humbug Mountain State Park
c/o Cape Blanco Management Unit
PO Box 1345 . . . . Port Orford OR 97465 541-332-6774
Web: www.oregonstateparks.org

Jackson F. Kimball State Recreation Site
c/o Collier Memorial Management Unit
46000 Hwy 97 N. . . . . Chiloquin OR 97624 800-551-6949
TF: 800-551-6949 ■ *Web:* www.oregonstateparks.org

Jasper State Recreation Site
c/o Southern Willamette Management Unit
PO Box 511 . . . . Lowell OR 97452 541-937-1173
Web: www.oregonstateparks.org

Jessie M. Honeyman Memorial State Park
c/o Honeyman Management Unit
84505 Hwy 101 S. . . . . Florence OR 97439 800-551-6949
TF: 800-551-6949 ■ *Web:* www.oregonstateparks.org

John B. Yeon State Scenic Corridor
c/o Columbia River Gorge Management Unit
PO Box 100 . . . . Corbett OR 97019 800-551-6949
TF: 800-551-6949 ■ *Web:* www.oregonstateparks.org

Joseph H. Stewart State Recreation Area
35251 Hwy 62 . . . . Trail OR 97541 541-560-3334
Web: www.oregonstateparks.org

Kam Wah Chung State Heritage Site (KWC)
c/o Clyde Holliday Management Unit
PO Box 10 . . . . Mount Vernon OR 97865 541-575-2800
TF: 800-551-6949 ■ *Web:* www.oregonstateparks.org/park_8.php

Koberg Beach State Recreation Site
c/o Columbia River Gorge Management Unit
PO Box 100 . . . . Corbett OR 97019 800-551-6949
TF: 800-551-6949 ■ *Web:* www.oregonstateparks.org/park_157.php

Lake Owyhee State Park
c/o Farewell Bend Management Unit
23751 Old Hwy 30 . . . . Huntington OR 97907 800-551-6949
TF: 800-551-6949 ■ *Web:* www.oregonstateparks.org/park_14.php

LaPine State Park 15800 State Recreation Rd . . . . La Pine OR 97739 800-551-6949
TF: 800-551-6949 ■ *Web:* www.oregonstateparks.org/park_41.php

Lewis & Clark State Recreation Site
c/o Columbia River Gorge Management Unit
PO Box 100 . . . . Corbett OR 97019 800-551-6949
TF: 800-551-6949 ■ *Web:* www.oregonstateparks.org/park_159.php

Lost Creek State Recreation Site
c/o S Beach Management Unit 5580 S Coast Hwy . . . . Newport OR 97366 800-551-6949
TF: 800-551-6949 ■ *Web:* www.oregonstateparks.org/park_205.php

Lowell State Recreation Site
c/o Southern Willamette Management Unit
PO Box 511 . . . . Lowell OR 97452 541-937-1173
TF: 800-551-6949 ■ *Web:* www.oregonstateparks.org/park_242.php

Manhattan Beach State Recreation Site
c/o Nehalem Bay Management Unit
9500 Sandpiper Ln - PO Box 366. Nehalem OR 97131 800-551-6949
TF: 800-551-6949 ■ *Web:* www.oregonstateparks.org/park_193.php

Phone Fax

Maud Williamson State Recreation Site
c/o Willamette Mission Management Unit
10991 Wheatland Rd NE. . . . . Gervais OR 97026 800-551-6949
TF: 800-551-6949 ■ *Web:* www.oregonstateparks.org/park_137.php

Mayer State Park
c/o Columbia River Gorge Management Unit
PO Box 100 . . . . Corbett OR 97019 800-551-6949
TF: 800-551-6949 ■ *Web:* www.oregonstateparks.org

McVay Rock State Recreation Site
c/o Harris Beach Management Unit
1655 Hwy 101 N. . . . . Brookings OR 97415 800-551-6949
TF: 800-551-6949 ■ *Web:* www.oregonstateparks.org

Memaloose State Park PO Box 472 . . . . Mosier OR 97040 541-478-3008
Web: www.oregonstateparks.org

Milo McIver State Park 24101 SE Entrance Rd. . . . . Estacada OR 97023 503-630-7150
Web: www.oregonstateparks.org

Minam State Recreation Area
72214 Marina Ln
c/o Wallowa Lake Management Unit. . . . . Joseph OR 97846 800-551-6949
TF: 800-551-6949 ■ *Web:* www.oregonstateparks.org

Molalla River State Park
c/o Willamette Mission Management Unit
7679 Champoeg Rd NE . . . . Saint Paul OR 97137 800-551-6949
TF: 800-551-6949 ■ *Web:* www.oregonstateparks.org

Munson Creek Falls State Natural Site
c/o Cape Lookout Management Unit
13000 Whiskey Creek Rd W . . . . Tillamook OR 97141 800-551-6949
TF: 800-551-6949 ■ *Web:* www.oregonstateparks.org

Muriel O. Ponsler Memorial State Scenic Viewpoint
c/o Washburne Management Unit
93111 Hwy 101 N. . . . . Florence OR 97439 800-551-6949
TF: 800-551-6949 ■ *Web:* www.oregonstateparks.org

Nehalem Bay State Park
9500 Sandpiper Ln PO Box 366 . . . . Nehalem OR 97131 503-368-5154
Web: www.oregonstateparks.org

Neptune State Scenic Viewpoint
c/o Washburne Management Unit
93111 Hwy 101 N. . . . . Florence OR 97439 800-551-6949
TF: 800-551-6949 ■ *Web:* www.oregonstateparks.org

Neskowin Beach State Recreation Site
c/o Beverly Beach Management Unit
198 NE 123rd St. . . . . Newport OR 97365 800-551-6949
TF: 800-551-6949 ■ *Web:* www.oregonstateparks.org

North Santiam State Recreation Area
c/o Detroit Management Unit PO Box 549 . . . . Detroit OR 97342 800-551-6949
TF: 800-551-6949 ■ *Web:* www.oregonstateparks.org

OC&E Woods Line State Trail
c/o Collier Memorial Management Unit
46000 Hwy 97 N. . . . . Chiloquin OR 97624 541-783-2471
TF: 800-551-6949 ■ *Web:* www.oregonstateparks.org/park_230.php

Oceanside Beach State Recreation Site
c/o Cape Lookout Management Unit
13000 Whiskey Creek Rd W . . . . Tillamook OR 97141 800-551-6949
TF: 800-551-6949 ■ *Web:* www.oregonstateparks.org

Ona Beach State Park
c/o S Beach Management Unit 5580 S Coast Hwy . . . . Newport OR 97366 800-551-6949
TF: 800-551-6949 ■ *Web:* www.oregonstateparks.org

Ontario State Recreation Site
c/o Farewell Bend Management Unit
23751 Old Hwy 30 . . . . Huntington OR 97907 800-551-6949
TF: 800-551-6949 ■ *Web:* www.oregonstateparks.org

Oswald West State Park
c/o Nehalem Bay State Pk PO Box 366. . . . . Nehalem OR 97131 503-368-5154
Web: www.oregonstateparks.org

Otter Crest State Scenic Viewpoint
c/o Beverly Beach Management Unit
198 NE 123rd St. . . . . Newport OR 97365 800-551-6949
TF: 800-551-6949 ■ *Web:* www.oregonstateparks.org

Otter Point State Recreation Site
c/o Cape Blanco Management Unit
PO Box 1345 . . . . Port Orford OR 97465 800-551-6949
TF: 800-551-6949 ■ *Web:* www.oregonstateparks.org

Paradise Point State Recreation Site
c/o Cape Blanco Management Unit
PO Box 1345 . . . . Port Orford OR 97465 800-551-6949
TF: 800-551-6949 ■ *Web:* www.oregonstateparks.org

Peter Skene Ogden State Scenic Viewpoint
c/o Cove Palisades Management Unit
7300 Jordan Rd . . . . Culver OR 97734 800-551-6949
TF: 800-551-6949 ■ *Web:* www.oregonstateparks.org/park_50.php

Pilot Butte State Scenic Viewpoint
c/o Tumalo Management Unit 62976 OB Riley Rd . . . . Bend OR 97701 800-551-6949
TF: 800-551-6949 ■ *Web:* www.oregonstateparks.org

Pistol River State Scenic Viewpoint
c/o Harris Beach Management Unit
1655 Hwy 101 N. . . . . Brookings OR 97415 800-551-6949
TF: 800-551-6949 ■ *Web:* www.oregonstateparks.org

Port Orford Heads State Park
c/o Cape Blanco Management Unit
PO Box 1345 . . . . Port Orford OR 97465 800-551-6949
TF: 800-551-6949 ■ *Web:* www.oregonstateparks.org

Portland Women's Forum State Scenic Viewpoint
c/o Columbia River Gorge Management Unit
PO Box 100 . . . . Corbett OR 97019 800-551-6949
TF: 800-551-6949 ■ *Web:* www.oregonstateparks.org

Prineville Reservoir State Park
19020 SE Parkland Dr . . . . Prineville OR 97754 541-447-4363
Web: www.oregonstateparks.org

Prospect State Scenic Viewpoint
c/o Joseph Stewart Management Unit
35251 Hwy 62 . . . . Trail OR 97541 800-551-6949
TF: 800-551-6949 ■ *Web:* www.oregonstateparks.org

Red Bridge State Wayside
c/o Blue Mountain Management Unit PO Box 85 . . . . Meacham OR 97859 800-551-6949
TF: 800-551-6949 ■ *Web:* www.oregonstateparks.org

Roads End State Recreation Site
c/o Beverly Beach Management Unit
198 NE 123rd St . . . . Newport OR 97365 800-551-6949
TF: 800-551-6949 ■ *Web:* www.oregonstateparks.org

Rooster Rock State Park PO Box 100. . . . . Corbett OR 97019 503-695-2261
Web: www.oregonstateparks.org

Saddle Mountain State Natural Area
9500 Sandpiper Ln, c/o Nehalem Bay Management Unit
PO Box 366 . . . . Nehalem OR 97131 800-551-6949
TF: 800-551-6949 ■ *Web:* www.oregonstateparks.org

Samuel H. Boardman State Scenic Corridor
c/o Harris Beach Management Unit
1655 Hwy 101 N. . . . . Brookings OR 97415 800-551-6949
TF: 800-551-6949 ■ *Web:* www.oregonstateparks.org

Sarah Helmick State Recreation Site
c/o Willamette Mission Management Unit
10991 Wheatland Rd NE. . . . . Gervais OR 97026 800-551-6949
TF: 800-551-6949 ■ *Web:* www.oregonstateparks.org

Seal Rock State Recreation Site
c/o S Beach Management Unit 5580 S Coast Hwy . . . . Newport OR 97366 800-551-6949
TF: 800-551-6949 ■ *Web:* www.oregonstateparks.org

Seneca Fouts Memorial State Natural Area
c/o Columbia River Gorge Management Unit
PO Box 100 . . . . Corbett OR 97019 800-551-6949
TF: 800-551-6949 ■ *Web:* www.oregonstateparks.org

Seven Devils State Recreation Site
c/o Bullards Beach Management Unit PO Box 569. . . . . Bandon OR 97411 800-551-6949
TF: 800-551-6949 ■ *Web:* www.oregonstateparks.org

Shepperd's Dell State Natural Area
c/o Columbia River Gorge Management Unit
PO Box 100 . . . . Corbett OR 97019 800-551-6949
TF: 800-551-6949 ■ *Web:* www.oregonstateparks.org

Shore Acres State Park
c/o Sunset Bay Management Unit
89814 Cape Arago Hwy . . . . Coos Bay OR 97420 541-888-3778
Web: www.oregonstateparks.org

Silver Falls State Park
20024 Silver Falls Hwy SE . . . . Sublimity OR 97385 503-873-8681 873-8925
Web: www.oregonstateparks.org

Smelt Sands State Recreation Site
c/o S Beach Management Unit 5580 S Coast Hwy . . . . Newport OR 97366 800-551-6949
TF: 800-551-6949 ■ *Web:* www.oregonstateparks.org

Smith Rock State Park
9241 NE Crooked River Dr . . . . Terrebonne OR 97760 541-548-7501
Web: www.oregonstateparks.org

South Beach State Park 5580 S Coast Hwy . . . . South Beach OR 97366 541-867-4715
TF: 800-452-5687 ■ *Web:* www.oregonstateparks.org/park_209.php

Starvation Creek State Park
c/o Columbia River Gorge Management Unit
PO Box 100 . . . . Corbett OR 97019 503-695-2261
Web: www.oregonstateparks.org

Stonefield Beach State Recreation Site
c/o Area 3 Field Office 84505 Hwy 101 S. . . . . Florence OR 97439 541-997-5755
Web: www.oregonstateparks.org

Succor Creek State Natural Area
c/o Farewell Bend Management Unit
23751 Old Hwy 30 . . . . Huntington OR 97907 800-551-6949
TF: 800-551-6949 ■ *Web:* www.oregonstateparks.org

Sumpter Valley Dredge State Heritage Area
c/o Clyde Holliday Management Unit
PO Box 10 . . . . Mount Vernon OR 97865 541-894-2486
TF: 800-551-6949 ■ *Web:* www.oregonstateparks.org/park_239.php

Sunset Bay State Park
c/o Sunset Bay Management Unit
89814 Cape Arago Hwy . . . . Coos Bay OR 97420 541-888-4902
Web: www.oregonstateparks.org

Tokatee Klootchman State Natural Site
c/o Washburne Management Unit
93111 Hwy 101 N. . . . . Florence OR 97439 800-551-6949
TF: 800-551-6949 ■ *Web:* www.oregonstateparks.org

Tolovana Beach State Recreation Site
9500 Sandpiper Ln, c/o Nehalem Bay Management Unit
PO Box 366 . . . . Nehalem OR 97131 800-551-6949
TF: 800-551-6949 ■ *Web:* www.oregonstateparks.org

Touvelle State Recreation Site
c/o Valley of the Rogue Management Unit
3792 N River Rd . . . . Gold Hill OR 97525 800-551-6949
TF: 800-551-6949 ■ *Web:* www.oregonstateparks.org

Tryon Creek State Natural Area
11321 SW Terwilliger Blvd . . . . Portland OR 97219 503-636-9886
Web: www.oregonstateparks.org

Tub Springs State Wayside
c/o Valley of the Rogue Management Unit
3792 N River Rd . . . . Gold Hill OR 97525 800-551-6949
TF: 800-551-6949 ■ *Web:* www.oregonstateparks.org

Tumalo State Park 62976 OB Riley Rd. . . . . Bend OR 97701 541-382-3586
Web: www.oregonstateparks.org

Ukiah-Dale Forest State Scenic Corridor
c/o Blue Mountain Management Unit PO Box 85 . . . . Meacham OR 97859 800-551-6949
TF: 800-551-6949 ■ *Web:* www.oregonstateparks.org

Umpqua Lighthouse State Park
c/o Honeyman Management Unit
84505 Hwy 101 S. . . . . Florence OR 97439 800-551-6949
TF: 800-551-6949 ■ *Web:* www.oregonstateparks.org

Phone | Fax

Unity Forest State Scenic Corridor
c/o Farewell Bend Management Unit
23751 Old Hwy 30 .... Huntington OR 97907 800-551-6949
TF: 800-551-6949 ■ *Web:* www.oregonstateparks.org

Unity Lake State Recreation Site
c/o Clyde Holliday Management Unit
PO Box 10 .... Mount Vernon OR 97865 800-551-6949
TF: 800-551-6949 ■ *Web:* www.oregonstateparks.org

Valley of the Rogue State Park
3792 N River Rd .... Gold Hill OR 97525 541-582-1118
Web: www.oregonstateparks.org/park_109.php

Viento State Park PO Box 472 .... Mosier OR 97040 541-374-8811
Web: www.oregonstateparks.org

Vinzenz Lausmann Memorial State Natural Area
c/o Columbia River Gorge Management Unit
PO Box 100 .... Corbett OR 97019 800-551-6949
TF: 800-551-6949 ■ *Web:* www.oregonstateparks.org

W.B. Nelson State Recreation Site
c/o S Beach Management Unit 5580 S Coast Hwy .... Newport OR 97366 800-551-6949
TF: 800-551-6949 ■ *Web:* www.oregonstateparks.org

Wallowa Lake Highway Forest State Scenic Corridor
c/o Wallowa Lake Management Unit
72214 Marina Ln .... Joseph OR 97846 541-432-4185
Web: www.oregonstateparks.org

Wallowa Lake State Park 72214 Marina Ln .... Joseph OR 97846 541-432-4185 432-4141
Web: www.oregonstateparks.org

Washburne State Wayside
c/o Southern Willamette Management Unit
PO Box 511 .... Lowell OR 97452 800-551-6949
TF: 800-551-6949 ■ *Web:* www.oregonstateparks.org

White River Falls State Park
c/o Deschutes River Management Unit
PO Box 2330 .... Wasco OR 97065 800-551-6949
TF: 800-551-6949 ■ *Web:* www.oregonstateparks.org

Willamette Mission State Park
10991 Wheatland Rd NE .... Gervais OR 97026 503-393-1172 393-8863
Web: www.oregonstateparks.org

Willamette Stone State Heritage Site
c/o Tryon Creek Management Unit
11321 SW Terwilliger Blvd .... Portland OR 97219 800-551-6949
TF: 800-551-6949 ■ *Web:* www.oregonstateparks.org

William M. Tugman State Park 72549 Hwy 101 .... Lakeside OR 97449 800-551-6949
TF: 800-551-6949 ■ *Web:* www.oregonstateparks.org/park_98.php

Winchuck State Recreation Site
c/o Harris Beach Management Unit
1655 Hwy 101 N .... Brookings OR 97415 800-551-6949
TF: 800-551-6949 ■ *Web:* www.oregonstateparks.org

Wolf Creek Inn State Heritage Site
PO Box 6 .... Wolf Creek OR 97497 541-866-2474 866-2692
Web: www.oregonstateparks.org

Wygant State Natural Area
c/o Columbia River Gorge Management Unit
PO Box 100 .... Corbett OR 97019 800-551-6949
TF: 800-551-6949 ■ *Web:* www.oregonstateparks.org

Yachats Ocean Road State Natural Site
c/o S Beach Management Unit 5580 S Coast Hwy .... Newport OR 97366 800-551-6949
TF: 800-551-6949 ■ *Web:* www.oregonstateparks.org

Yachats State Recreation Area
c/o S Beach Management Unit 5580 S Coast Hwy .... Newport OR 97366 800-551-6949
TF: 800-551-6949 ■ *Web:* www.oregonstateparks.org

Yaquina Bay State Recreation Site
c/o S Beach Management Unit 5580 S Coast Hwy .... Newport OR 97366 800-551-6949
TF: 800-551-6949 ■ *Web:* www.oregonstateparks.org

PENNSYLVANIA

Phone | Fax

Allegheny Islands State Park
c/o Region 2 Office .... Prospect PA 16052 724-865-2131
Web: www.dcnr.state.pa.us/stateparks/parks/alleghenyislands.aspx

Bald Eagle State Park 149 Main Pk Rd .... Howard PA 16841 814-625-2775
Web: www.dcnr.state.pa.us

Beltzville State Park 2950 Pohopoco Dr .... Lehighton PA 18235 610-377-0045
Web: www.dcnr.state.pa.us

Bendigo State Park 533 State Pk Rd .... Johnsonburg PA 15845 814-965-2646
Web: www.dcnr.state.pa.us

Benjamin Rush State Park
c/o Fort Washington State Pk .... Fort Washington PA 19034 215-591-5250
Web: www.dcnr.state.pa.us

Big Pocono State Park
c/o Tobyhanna State Pk PO Box 387 .... Tobyhanna PA 18466 570-894-8336
Web: www.dcnr.state.pa.us/stateparks/parks/bigpocono.aspx

Big Spring State Park
c/o Colonel Denning State Pk
1599 Doubling Gap Rd .... Newville PA 17241 717-776-5272
Web: www.dcnr.state.pa.us/stateparks/parks/bigspring.aspx

Black Moshannon State Park
4216 Beaver Rd .... Philipsburg PA 16866 814-342-5960
Web: www.dcnr.state.pa.us

Blue Knob State Park 124 Pk Rd .... Imler PA 16655 814-276-3576
Web: www.dcnr.state.pa.us

Boyd Big Tree Conservation Area
c/o Little Buffalo State Pk RR 2 PO Box 256A .... Newport PA 17074 717-567-9255
Web: www.dcnr.state.pa.us/stateparks/parks/boydbigtree.aspx

Buchanan's Birthplace State Park
c/o Cowans Gap State Pk 6235 Aughwick Rd .... Fort Loudon PA 17224 717-485-3948
Web: www.dcnr.state.pa.us/stateparks/parks/buchanansbirthplace.aspx

Bucktail State Park c/o Region 1 Office .... Emporium PA 15834 814-486-3365
Web: www.dcnr.state.pa.us

Caledonia State Park 101 Pine Grove Rd .... Fayetteville PA 17222 717-352-2161 352-7026
Web: www.dcnr.state.pa.us/stateparks/parks/caledonia.aspx

Canoe Creek State Park
205 Canoe Creek Rd .... Hollidaysburg PA 16648 814-695-6807
Web: www.dcnr.state.pa.us

Phone | Fax

Chapman State Park PO Box 1610 .... Clarendon PA 16313 814-723-0250
Web: www.dcnr.state.pa.us

Cherry Springs State Park
c/o Lyman Run State Pk 454 Lyman Run Rd .... Galeton PA 16922 814-435-5010
Web: www.dcnr.state.pa.us/stateparks/parks/cherrysprings.aspx

Clear Creek State Park
38 Clear Creek State Pk Rd .... Sigel PA 15860 814-752-2368
Web: www.dcnr.state.pa.us

Codorus State Park 2600 Smith Stn Rd .... Hanover PA 17331 717-637-2816 637-4720
Web: www.dcnr.state.pa.us

Colonel Denning State Park
1599 Doubling Gap Rd .... Newville PA 17241 717-776-5272
Web: www.dcnr.state.pa.us

Colton Point State Park
c/o Leonard Harrison State Pk 4797 Rt 660 .... Wellsboro PA 16901 570-724-3061
Web: www.dcnr.state.pa.us/stateparks/parks/coltonpoint.aspx

Cook Forest State Park PO Box 120 .... Cooksburg PA 16217 814-744-8407
Web: www.dcnr.state.pa.us

Cowans Gap State Park 6235 Aughwick Rd .... Fort Loudon PA 17224 717-485-3948
Web: www.dcnr.state.pa.us/stateparks/parks/cowansgap.aspx

Delaware Canal State Park
11 Lodi Hill Rd .... Upper Black Eddy PA 18972 610-982-5560
Web: www.dcnr.state.pa.us

Denton Hill State Park
c/o Lyman Run 454 Lyman Run Rd .... Galeton PA 16922 814-435-2115
Web: www.dcnr.state.pa.us/stateparks/parks/dentonhill.aspx

Elk State Park
c/o Bendigo State Pk 533 State Pk Rd .... Johnsonburg PA 15845 814-965-2646
Web: www.dcnr.state.pa.us/stateparks/parks/elk.aspx

Evansburg State Park 851 May Hall Rd .... Collegeville PA 19426 610-409-1150
Web: www.dcnr.state.pa.us

Fort Washington State Park
500 Bethlehem Pike .... Fort Washington PA 19034 215-591-5250
Web: www.dcnr.state.pa.us

Fowlers Hollow State Park
c/o Colonel Denning State Pk
1599 Doubling Gap Rd .... Newville PA 17241 717-776-5272
Web: www.dcnr.state.pa.us/stateparks/parks/fowlershollow.aspx

Frances Slocum State Park 565 Mt Olivet Rd .... Wyoming PA 18644 570-696-3525
Web: www.dcnr.state.pa.us/stateparks/parks/francesslocum.aspx

French Creek State Park 843 Pk Rd .... Elverson PA 19520 610-582-9680
Web: www.dcnr.state.pa.us

Gifford Pinchot State Park
2200 Rosstown Rd .... Lewisberry PA 17339 717-432-5011
Web: www.dcnr.state.pa.us

Gouldsboro State Park
c/o Tobyhanna State Pk PO Box 387 .... Tobyhanna PA 18466 570-894-8336
Web: www.dcnr.state.pa.us/stateparks/parks/gouldsboro.aspx

Greenwood Furnace State Park
15795 Greenwood Rd .... Huntingdon PA 16652 814-667-1800
Web: www.dcnr.state.pa.us

Hickory Run State Park PO Box 81 .... White Haven PA 18661 570-443-0400
Web: www.dcnr.state.pa.us/stateparks/parks/hickoryrun.aspx

Hills Creek State Park 111 Spillway Rd .... Wellsboro PA 16901 570-724-4246
Web: www.dcnr.state.pa.us

Hyner Run State Park 56 Hyner Pk Rd .... Hyner PA 17738 570-923-6000
Web: www.dcnr.state.pa.us/stateparks/parks/hynerrun.aspx

Hyner View State Park
c/o Hyner Run State Pk 56 Hyner Pk Rd .... Hyner PA 17738 570-923-6000
Web: www.dcnr.state.pa.us/stateparks/parks/hynerview.aspx

Jacobsburg Environmental Education Ctr
835 Jacobsburg Rd .... Wind Gap PA 18091 610-746-2801
Web: www.dcnr.state.pa.us

Jennings Environmental Education Ctr
2951 Prospect Rd .... Slippery Rock PA 16057 724-794-6011
Web: www.dcnr.state.pa.us

Joseph E. Ibberson Conservation Area
c/o Little Buffalo State Pk 1579 State Pk Rd .... Newport PA 17074 717-567-9255
Web: www.dcnr.state.pa.us/stateparks/parks/josepheibberson.aspx

Kettle Creek State Park 97 Kettle Creek Pk Ln .... Renovo PA 17764 570-923-6004
Web: www.dcnr.state.pa.us

Keystone State Park 1150 Keystone Pk Rd .... Derry PA 15627 724-668-2939
Web: www.dcnr.state.pa.us

Kings Gap Environmental Education & Training Ctr
500 Kings Gap Rd .... Carlisle PA 17015 717-486-5031
Web: www.dcnr.state.pa.us

Kinzua Bridge State Park
c/o Bendigo State Pk 533 State Pk Rd .... Johnsonburg PA 15845 814-965-2646
Web: www.dcnr.state.pa.us/stateparks/parks/kinzuabridge.aspx

Kooser State Park 943 Glades Pike .... Somerset PA 15501 814-445-8673
Web: www.dcnr.state.pa.us

Lackawanna State Park PO Box 230 .... Dalton PA 18414 570-945-3239
Web: www.dcnr.state.pa.us/stateparks/parks/lackawanna.aspx

Laurel Hill State Park
1454 Laurel Hill Pk Rd .... Somerset PA 15501 814-445-7725
Web: www.dcnr.state.pa.us

Laurel Mountain State Park
c/o Linn Run State Pk PO Box 50 .... Rector PA 15677 724-238-6623
Web: www.dcnr.state.pa.us/stateparks/parks/laurelmountain.aspx

Laurel Ridge State Park
1117 Jim Mountain Rd .... Rockwood PA 15557 724-455-3744
Web: www.dcnr.state.pa.us

Laurel Summit State Park
c/o Linn Run State Pk PO Box 50 .... Rector PA 15677 724-238-6623
Web: www.dcnr.state.pa.us/stateparks/parks/laurelsummit.aspx

Lehigh Gorge State Park RR 1 PO Box 81 .... White Haven PA 18661 570-443-0400
Web: www.dcnr.state.pa.us/stateparks/parks/lehighgorge.aspx

Leonard Harrison State Park 4797 Rt 660 .... Wellsboro PA 16901 570-724-3061
Web: www.dcnr.state.pa.us/stateparks/parks/leonardharrison.aspx

Linn Run State Park PO Box 50 .... Rector PA 15677 724-238-6623
Web: www.dcnr.state.pa.us

Name / Address	City	State	Zip	Phone	Fax
Little Buffalo State Park 1579 State Pk Rd *Web:* www.dcnr.state.pa.us	Newport	PA	17074	717-567-9255	
Little Pine State Park 4205 Little Pine Creek Rd *Web:* www.dcnr.state.pa.us/stateparks/parks/littlepine.aspx	Waterville	PA	17776	570-753-6000	
Locust Lake State Park 687 Tuscarora Pk Rd *Web:* www.dcnr.state.pa.us/stateparks/parks/locustlake.aspx	Barnesville	PA	18214	570-467-2404	
Lyman Run State Park 454 Lyman Run Rd *Web:* www.dcnr.state.pa.us/stateparks/parks/lymanrun.aspx	Galeton	PA	16922	814-435-5010	
Marsh Creek State Park 675 Pk Rd *Web:* www.dcnr.state.pa.us	Downingtown	PA	19335	610-458-5119	
Maurice K. Goddard State Park 684 Lake Wilhelm Rd *Web:* www.dcnr.state.pa.us	Sandy Lake	PA	16145	724-253-4833	
McCalls Dam State Park c/o R B Winter State Pk 17215 Buffalo Rd *Web:* www.dcnr.state.pa.us/stateparks/parks/mccallsdam.aspx	Mifflinburg	PA	17844	570-966-1455	
McConnells Mill State Park PO Box 16 ; RR 2 *Web:* www.dcnr.state.pa.us/stateparks/parks/mcconnellsmill.aspx	Portersville	PA	16051	724-368-8091	
Memorial Lake State Park 18 Boundary Rd *Web:* www.dcnr.state.pa.us/stateparks/parks/memoriallake.aspx	Grantville	PA	17028	717-865-6470	
Milton State Park c/o Shikellamy State Pk Bridge Ave *Web:* www.dcnr.state.pa.us/stateparks/parks/milton.aspx	Sunbury	PA	17801	570-988-5557	
Mont Alto State Park c/o Caledonia State Pk 101 Pine Grove Rd *Web:* www.dcnr.state.pa.us/stateparks/parks/montalto.aspx	Fayetteville	PA	17222	717-352-2161	352-7026
Moraine State Park 225 Pleasant Valley Rd *Web:* www.dcnr.state.pa.us/stateparks/parks/moraine.aspx	Portersville	PA	16051	724-368-8811	
Mount Pisgah State Park 28 Entrance Rd *Web:* www.dcnr.state.pa.us/stateparks/parks/mtpisgah.aspx	Troy	PA	16947	570-297-2734	
Nescopeck State Park c/o Hickory Run State Pk RR 1, PO Box 81 *Web:* www.dcnr.state.pa.us/stateparks/parks/nescopeck.aspx	White Haven	PA	18661	570-443-0400	
Neshaminy State Park 3401 State Rd *Web:* www.dcnr.state.pa.us	Bensalem	PA	19020	215-639-4538	
Nockamixon State Park 1542 Mountain View Dr *Web:* www.dcnr.state.pa.us	Quakertown	PA	18951	215-529-7300	
Nolde Forest Environmental Education Ctr 2910 New Holland Rd *Web:* www.dcnr.state.pa.us	Reading	PA	19607	610-796-3699	
Norristown Farm Park 2500 Upper Farm Rd *Web:* www.dcnr.state.pa.us	Norristown	PA	19403	610-270-0215	
Ohiopyle State Park 7 Sheridan St *Web:* www.dcnr.state.pa.us	Ohiopyle	PA	15470	724-329-8591	
Oil Creek State Park 305 State Pk Rd *Web:* www.dcnr.state.pa.us	Oil City	PA	16301	814-676-5915	
Ole Bull State Park 31 Valhella VW *Web:* www.dcnr.state.pa.us	Cross Fork	PA	17729	814-435-5000	
Parker Dam State Park 28 Fairview Rd *Web:* www.dcnr.state.pa.us/stateparks/parks/parkerdam.aspx	Penfield	PA	15849	814-765-0630	
Patterson State Park c/o Lyman Run State Pk 454 Lyman Run Rd *Web:* www.dcnr.state.pa.us/stateparks/parks/patterson.aspx	Galeton	PA	16922	814-435-5010	
Penn-Roosevelt State Park c/o Greenwood Furnace State Pk RR 2, PO Box 118 *Web:* www.dcnr.state.pa.us/stateparks/parks/pennroosevelt.aspx	Huntingdon	PA	16652	814-667-1800	
Pine Grove Furnace State Park 1100 Pine Grove Rd *TF:* 888-727-2757 ■ *Web:* www.dcnr.state.pa.us	Gardners	PA	17324	717-486-7174	486-4961
Poe Paddy State Park c/o Reeds Gap State Pk 1405 New Lancaster Valley Rd *Web:* www.dcnr.state.pa.us/stateparks/parks/poepaddy.aspx	Milroy	PA	17063	717-667-3622	
Poe Valley State Park c/o Reeds Gap State Pk 1405 New Lancaster Valley Rd *Web:* www.dcnr.state.pa.us/stateparks/parks/poevalley.aspx	Milroy	PA	17063	814-349-2460	
Point State Park 101 Commonwealth Pl *Web:* www.dcnr.state.pa.us	Pittsburgh	PA	15222	412-471-0235	
Presque Isle State Park 301 Peninsula Dr Suite 1 *Web:* www.dcnr.state.pa.us	Erie	PA	16505	814-833-7424	833-0266
Prince Gallitzin State Park 966 Marina Rd *Web:* www.dcnr.state.pa.us	Patton	PA	16668	814-674-1000	
Promised Land State Park PO Box 96 *Web:* www.dcnr.state.pa.us	Greentown	PA	18426	570-676-3428	
Prompton State Park c/o Lackawanna State Pk PO Box 230 *TF:* 888-727-2757 ■ *Web:* www.dcnr.state.pa.us/stateparks/parks/prompton.aspx	Dalton	PA	18414	570-945-3239	
Prouty Place State Park c/o Lyman Run State Pk 454 Lyman Run Rd *Web:* www.dcnr.state.pa.us/stateparks/parks/proutyplace.aspx	Galeton	PA	16922	814-435-5010	
Pymatuning State Park 2660 Williamsfield Rd *Web:* www.dcnr.state.pa.us	Jamestown	PA	16134	724-932-3141	
R. B. Winter State Park 17215 Buffalo Rd *Web:* www.dcnr.state.pa.us/stateparks/parks/rbwinter.aspx	Mifflinburg	PA	17844	570-966-1455	
Raccoon Creek State Park 3000 State Rt 18 *Web:* www.dcnr.state.pa.us/stateparks/parks/raccooncreek.aspx	Hookstown	PA	15050	724-899-2200	
Ralph Stover State Park c/o Delaware Canal State Pk 11 Lodi Hill Rd *Web:* www.dcnr.state.pa.us	Upper Black Eddy	PA	18972	610-982-5560	
Ravensburg State Park c/o R B Winter State Pk 17215 Buffalo Rd *Web:* www.dcnr.state.pa.us/stateparks/parks/ravensburg.aspx	Mifflinburg	PA	17844	570-966-1455	
Reeds Gap State Park 1405 New Lancaster Valley Rd *Web:* www.dcnr.state.pa.us	Milroy	PA	17063	717-667-3622	
Ricketts Glen State Park 695 State Rt 487 *Web:* www.dcnr.state.pa.us/stateparks/parks/rickettsglen.aspx	Benton	PA	17814	570-477-5675	
Ridley Creek State Park 1023 Sycamore Mills Rd *Web:* www.dcnr.state.pa.us	Media	PA	19063	610-892-3900	
Ryerson Station State Park 361 Bristoria Rd *Web:* www.dcnr.state.pa.us	Wind Ridge	PA	15380	724-428-4254	
S. B. Elliott State Park c/o Parker Dam State Pk 28 Fairview Rd *Web:* www.dcnr.state.pa.us/stateparks/parks/sbelliott.aspx	Penfield	PA	15849	814-765-0630	
Salt Springs State Park c/o Lackawanna State Pk PO Box 230 *TF:* 888-727-2757 ■ *Web:* www.dcnr.state.pa.us/stateparks/parks/saltsprings.aspx	Dalton	PA	18414	570-945-3239	
Samuel S. Lewis State Park c/o Gifford Pinchot State Pk 2200 Rosstown Rd *Web:* www.dcnr.state.pa.us	Lewisberry	PA	17339	717-432-5011	
Sand Bridge State Park c/o R B Winter State Pk RR 2, PO Box 314 *Web:* www.dcnr.state.pa.us/stateparks/parks/sandbridge.aspx	Mifflinburg	PA	17844	570-966-1455	
Shawnee State Park 132 State Pk Rd *Web:* www.dcnr.state.pa.us	Schellsburg	PA	15559	814-733-4218	
Shikellamy State Park Bridge Ave *Web:* www.dcnr.state.pa.us	Sunbury	PA	17801	570-988-5557	
Sinnemahoning State Park 8288 First Fork Rd *Web:* www.dcnr.state.pa.us	Austin	PA	16720	814-647-8401	
Sizerville State Park 199 E Cowley Run Rd *Web:* www.dcnr.state.pa.us	Emporium	PA	15834	814-486-5605	
Susquehanna State Park c/o Shikellamy State Pk Bridge Ave *Web:* www.dcnr.state.pa.us/stateparks/parks/susquehanna.aspx	Sunbury	PA	17801	570-988-5557	
Susquehannock State Park 1880 Pk Dr *Web:* www.dcnr.state.pa.us	Drumore	PA	17518	717-432-5011	
Tobyhanna State Park PO Box 387 *Web:* www.dcnr.state.pa.us	Tobyhanna	PA	18466	570-894-8336	
Trough Creek State Park PO Box 211 *Web:* www.dcnr.state.pa.us/stateparks/parks/troughcreek.aspx	James Creek	PA	16657	814-658-3847	
Tuscarora State Park 687 Tuscarora Pk Rd *Web:* www.dcnr.state.pa.us/stateparks/parks/tuscarora.aspx	Barnesville	PA	18214	570-467-2404	
Tyler State Park 101 Swamp Rd *Web:* www.dcnr.state.pa.us	Newtown	PA	18940	215-968-2021	
Upper Pine Bottom State Park c/o Little Pine State Pk 4205 Little Pine Creek Rd *Web:* www.dcnr.state.pa.us/stateparks/parks/upperpinebottom.aspx	Waterville	PA	17776	570-753-6000	
Warriors Path State Park c/o Trough Creek State Pk RR 1, PO Box 211 *Web:* www.dcnr.state.pa.us/stateparks/parks/warriorspath.aspx	James Creek	PA	16657	814-658-3847	
Whipple Dam State Park c/o Greenwood Furnace State Pk RR 2, PO Box 118 *Web:* www.dcnr.state.pa.us/stateparks/parks/whippledam.aspx	Huntingdon	PA	16652	814-667-1800	
White Clay Creek Preserve PO Box 172 *Web:* www.dcnr.state.pa.us	Landenberg	PA	19350	610-274-2900	
Worlds End State Park PO Box 62 *Web:* www.dcnr.state.pa.us/stateparks/parks/worldsend.aspx	Forksville	PA	18616	570-924-3287	
Yellow Creek State Park 170 Rt 259 Hwy *Web:* www.dcnr.state.pa.us	Penn Run	PA	15765	724-357-7913	

RHODE ISLAND

Name / Address	City	State	Zip	Phone	Fax
Arcadia Management Area 1037 Hartford Pike *Web:* www.riparks.com	North Scituate	RI	02857	401-789-3094	
Beavertail State Park c/o Goddard Memorial State Pk Beavertail Rd *Web:* www.riparks.com	Jamestown	RI	02835	401-423-9941	885-7720
Blackstone River Bikeway c/o Lincoln Woods State Pk 2 Manchester Print Works Rd *Web:* www.riparks.com/blacksto.htm	Lincoln	RI	02865	401-723-7892	
Brenton Point State Park c/o Fort Adams State Pk 84 Adams Dr *Web:* www.riparks.com/BRENTON.HTM	Newport	RI	02840	401-847-2400	841-9821
Burlingame State Park Santuary Rd *Web:* www.riparks.com/burlingastatepark.htm	Charlestown	RI	02813	401-322-8910	
Charlestown Breachway Charlestown Beach Rd *Web:* www.riparks.com/charlesbreach.htm	Charlestown	RI	02813	401-364-7000	322-3083
Colt State Park Hope St *Web:* www.riparks.com	Bristol	RI	02809	401-253-7482	253-6766
East Bay Bike Path c/o Colt State Pk Hope St *Web:* www.riparks.com/eastbay.htm	Bristol	RI	02809	401-253-7482	
East Beach 598 E Beach Rd *Web:* www.riparks.com	Charlestown	RI	02813	401-322-0450	322-3083
East Matunuck State Beach 950 Succotash Rd *Web:* www.riparks.com	South Kingstown	RI	02881	401-789-8585	
Fishermen's Memorial State Park 1011 Pt Judith Rd *Web:* www.riparks.com	Narragansett	RI	02882	401-789-8374	
Fort Adams State Park 84 Adams Dr *Web:* www.riparks.com/fortadams.htm	Newport	RI	02840	401-847-2400	841-9821

Name / Address	City	State	Zip	Phone	Fax
Fort Wetherill State Park c/o Goddard Memorial State Pk Ives Rd *Web:* www.riparks.com/fortweth.htm	Warwick	RI	02818	401-423-1771	
George Washington Management Area 2185 Putnam Pike	Gloucester	RI	02814	401-568-2013	
Goddard Memorial State Park 1095 Ives Rd *Web:* www.riparks.com/goddard.htm	Warwick	RI	02818	401-884-2010	885-7720
Haines Memorial State Park Rte 103 *Web:* www.riparks.com/haines.htm	East Providence	RI	00291	401-253-7482	253-6766
Lincoln Woods State Park 2 Manchester Print Works Rd *Web:* www.riparks.com	Lincoln	RI	02865	401-723-7892	724-7951
Misquamicut State Beach c/o Burlingame State Pk 1 Burlingame State Pk Rd *Web:* www.riparks.com/misquamicut.htm	Charlestown	RI	02813	401-596-9097	
Roger W. Wheeler State Beach 100 Sand Hill Cove Rd *Web:* www.riparks.com	Narragansett	RI	02882	401-789-3563	
Salty Brine State Beach 254 Great Rd *Web:* www.riparks.com/saltybrine.htm	Narragansett	RI	02882	401-789-3563	
Scarborough North State Beach 870 Ocean Rd *Web:* www.riparks.com/scarborough.htm	Narragansett	RI	02882	401-789-2324	
Snake Den State Park 2321 Hartford Ave *Web:* www.riparks.com	Johnston	RI	02919	401-222-2632	
World War II Memorial State Park c/o Lincoln Woods State Pk 2 Manchester Print Works Rd *Web:* www.riparks.com/worldwar.htm	Lincoln	RI	02865	401-762-9717	

SOUTH CAROLINA

Name / Address	City	State	Zip	Phone	Fax
Aiken State Natural Area 1145 State Pk Rd *Web:* www.southcarolinaparks.com	Windsor	SC	29856	803-649-2857	
Andrew Jackson State Park 196 Andrew Jackson Pk Rd *Web:* www.southcarolinaparks.com	Lancaster	SC	29720	803-285-3344	
Baker Creek State Park 863 Baker Creek Rd *Web:* www.southcarolinaparks.com/park-finder/state-park/1764.aspx	McCormick	SC	29835	864-443-2457	
Barnwell State Park 223 State Pk Rd *Web:* www.southcarolinaparks.com	Blackville	SC	29817	803-284-2212	
Caesars Head State Park 8155 Geer Hwy *Web:* www.southcarolinaparks.com	Cleveland	SC	29635	864-836-6115	836-3081
Calhoun Falls State Recreation Area 46 Maintenance Shop Rd *Web:* www.southcarolinaparks.com	Calhoun Falls	SC	29628	864-447-8267	447-8638
Charles Towne Landing State Historic Site 1500 Old Towne Rd *Web:* www.southcarolinaparks.com	Charleston	SC	29407	843-852-4200	852-4205
Cheraw State Park 100 State Pk Rd *Web:* www.southcarolinaparks.com	Cheraw	SC	29520	843-537-9656	
Chester State Park 759 State Pk Dr *Web:* www.southcarolinaparks.com	Chester	SC	29706	803-385-2680	
Colleton State Park 147 Wayside Ln *Web:* www.southcarolinaparks.com	Canadys	SC	29433	843-538-8206	
Colonial Dorchester State Historic Site 300 State Pk Rd *Web:* www.southcarolinaparks.com	Summerville	SC	29485	843-873-1740	
Croft State Natural Area 450 Croft State Pk Rd *Web:* www.southcarolinaparks.com	Spartanburg	SC	29302	864-585-1283	
Devils Fork State Park 161 Holcombe Cir *Web:* www.southcarolinaparks.com	Salem	SC	29676	864-944-2639	944-8777
Dreher Island State Recreation Area 3677 State Pk Rd *TF:* 866-345-7275 ■ *Web:* www.southcarolinaparks.com	Prosperity	SC	29127	803-364-4152	364-0756
Edisto Beach State Park 8377 State Cabin Rd *Web:* www.southcarolinaparks.com	Edisto Island	SC	29438	843-869-2756	869-4428
Givhans Ferry State Park 746 Givhans Ferry Rd *Web:* www.southcarolinaparks.com	Ridgeville	SC	29472	843-873-0692	
Goodale State Park 650 Pk Rd *Web:* www.southcarolinaparks.com	Camden	SC	29020	803-432-2772	
Hamilton Branch State Recreation Area 111 Campground Rd *Web:* www.southcarolinaparks.com	Plum Branch	SC	29845	864-333-2223	
Hampton Plantation State Historic Site 1950 Rutledge Rd *Web:* www.southcarolinaparks.com	McClellanville	SC	29458	843-546-9361	527-4995
Hickory Knob State Resort Park Rt 4 PO Box 199-B *Web:* www.southcarolinaparks.com/park-finder/state-park/1109.aspx	McCormick	SC	29835	864-391-2450	391-5390
Hunting Island State Park 2555 Sea Island Pkwy *Web:* www.southcarolinaparks.com	Hunting Island	SC	29920	843-838-2011	838-4263
Huntington Beach State Park 16148 Ocean Hwy *Web:* www.southcarolinaparks.com	Murrells Inlet	SC	29576	843-237-4440	237-3387
Jones Gap State Park 303 Jones Gap Rd *Web:* www.southcarolinaparks.com	Marietta	SC	29661	864-836-3647	
Keowee-Toxaway State Natural Area 108 Residence Dr *Web:* www.southcarolinaparks.com	Sunset	SC	29685	864-868-2605	
Kings Mountain State Park 1277 Pk Rd *Web:* www.southcarolinaparks.com	Blacksburg	SC	29702	803-222-3209	222-6948
Lake Greenwood State Recreation Area 302 State Pk Rd *Web:* www.southcarolinaparks.com	Ninety Six	SC	29666	864-543-3535	
Lake Hartwell State Recreation Area 19138 S Hwy 11 # A *Web:* www.southcarolinaparks.com	Fair Play	SC	29643	864-972-3352	
Lake Warren State Park 1079 Lake Warren Rd *Web:* www.southcarolinaparks.com	Hampton	SC	29924	803-943-5051	943-4736
Lake Wateree State Recreation Area 881 State Pk Rd *Web:* www.southcarolinaparks.com	Winnsboro	SC	29180	803-482-6401	482-6126
Landsford Canal State Park 2051 Pk Dr *Web:* www.southcarolinaparks.com	Catawba	SC	29704	803-789-5800	
Lee State Natural Area 487 Loop Rd *Web:* www.southcarolinaparks.com	Bishopville	SC	29010	803-428-5307	
Little Pee Dee State Park 2400 Pk Access Rd *Web:* www.southcarolinaparks.com	Dillon	SC	29536	843-774-8872	
Musgrove Mill State Historic Site 92 State Pk Rd *Web:* www.southcarolinaparks.com	Clinton	SC	29325	864-938-0100	
Myrtle Beach State Park 4401 S Kings Hwy *Web:* www.southcarolinaparks.com	Myrtle Beach	SC	29575	843-238-5325	
Oconee State Park 624 State Pk Rd *Web:* www.southcarolinaparks.com	Mountain Rest	SC	29664	864-638-5353	638-8776
Oconee Station State Historic Site 500 Oconee Stn Rd *Web:* www.southcarolinaparks.com	Walhalla	SC	29691	864-638-0079	
Paris Mountain State Park 2401 State Pk Rd *TF:* 866-345-7275 ■ *Web:* www.southcarolinaparks.com	Greenville	SC	29609	864-244-5565	
Poinsett State Park 6660 Poinsett Pk Rd *Web:* www.southcarolinaparks.com	Wedgefield	SC	29168	803-494-8177	
Redcliffe Plantation State Historic Site 181 Redcliffe Rd *Web:* www.southcarolinaparks.com	Beech Island	SC	29842	803-827-1473	
Rivers Bridge State Historic Site 325 State Pk Rd *Web:* www.southcarolinaparks.com	Ehrhardt	SC	29801	803-267-3675	
Rose Hill Plantation State Historic Site 2677 Sardis Rd *Web:* www.southcarolinaparks.com	Union	SC	29379	864-427-5966	
Sadlers Creek State Recreation Area 940 State Rd S-4-741 *Web:* www.southcarolinaparks.com	Anderson	SC	29626	864-226-8950	
Santee State Park 251 State Pk Rd *Web:* www.southcarolinaparks.com	Santee	SC	29142	803-854-2408	854-4834
Sesquicentennial State Park 9564 Two Notch Rd *Web:* www.southcarolinaparks.com	Columbia	SC	29223	803-788-2706	788-4414
Table Rock State Park 158 E Ellison Ln *Web:* www.southcarolinaparks.com	Pickens	SC	29671	864-878-9813	878-9077
Woods Bay State Natural Area 11020 Woods Bay Rd *Web:* www.southcarolinaparks.com	Olanta	SC	29114	843-659-4445	

SOUTH DAKOTA

Name / Address	City	State	Zip	Phone	Fax
Adams Homestead & Nature Preserve 272 Westshore Dr *Web:* www.sdgfp.info	McCook Lake	SD	57049	605-232-0873	
Angostura Recreation Area 13157 N Angostura Rd *Web:* www.sdgfp.info	Hot Springs	SD	57747	605-745-6996	
Bear Butte State Park E Hwy 79 PO Box 688 *Web:* www.sdgfp.info	Sturgis	SD	57785	605-347-5240	
Beaver Creek Nature Area c/o Palisades State Pk 25495 485th Ave *Web:* www.sdgfp.info	Garretson	SD	57030	605-594-3824	
Big Sioux Recreation Area c/o Palisades State Pk 25495 485th Ave *Web:* www.sdgfp.info	Garretson	SD	57030	605-594-3824	
Big Stone Island Nature Area c/o Hartford Beach State Pk RR 1 PO Box 50 *Web:* www.sdgfp.info	Corona	SD	57227	605-432-6374	
Burke Lake Recreation Area c/o Snake Creek Recreation Area 35316 SD Hwy 44 *Web:* www.sdgfp.info	Platte	SD	57369	605-337-2587	
Buryanek Recreation Area 27450 Buryanek Rd *Web:* www.gfp.sd.gov/state-parks/directory/buryanek	Burke	SD	57523	605-337-2587	
Chief White Crane Recreation Area 31323 Toe Rd *Web:* www.gfp.sd.gov/state-parks/directory/chief-white-crane	Yankton	SD	57078	605-668-2985	
Cow Creek Recreation Area 28229 Cow Creek Rd *Web:* www.gfp.sd.gov/state-parks/directory/cow-creek	Ft Pierre	SD	57532	605-223-7722	
Custer State Park 13329 US Hwy 16A *Web:* www.sdgfp.info	Custer	SD	57730	605-255-4515	255-4460
Farm Island Recreation Area 1301 Farm Island Rd *Web:* www.sdgfp.info	Pierre	SD	57501	605-773-2885	
Fisher Grove State Park c/o Lake Louise Recreation Area 35250 191st St *Web:* www.sdgfp.info	Miller	SD	57362	605-853-2533	
Fort Sisseton State Historical Park c/o Roy Lake State Pk 11545 434th Ave *Web:* www.sdgfp.info	Lake City	SD	57247	605-448-5474	
George S. Mickelson Trail c/o Black Hills Trails Office PO Box 604 *Web:* www.sdgfp.info	Lead	SD	57754	605-584-3896	
Hartford Beach State Park PO Box 50 *Web:* www.sdgfp.info	Corona	SD	57227	605-432-6374	

	City	State	Zip	Phone	Fax
Indian Creek Recreation Area 12905 288th Ave. *Web:* www.gfp.sd.gov/state-parks/directory/indian-creek	Mobridge	SD	57601	605-845-7112	
LaFramboise Island Nature Area c/o Farm Island Recreation Area 1301 Farm Island Rd *Web:* www.gfp.sd.gov/state-parks/directory/laframboise	Pierre	SD	57501	605-773-2885	
Lake Alvin Recreation Area c/o Newton Hills State Pk 28771 482nd Ave. *Web:* www.sdgfp.info	Canton	SD	57013	605-987-2263	
Lake Cochrane Recreation Area c/o Pelican Lake Recreation Area 400 W Kemp *Web:* www.sdgfp.info	Watertown	SD	57201	605-882-5200	
Lake Herman State Park 23409 State Pk Dr *Web:* www.sdgfp.info	Madison	SD	57042	605-256-5003	
Lake Hiddenwood Recreation Area c/o W Whitlock Recreation Area 16157A W Whitlock Rd. *Web:* www.sdgfp.info	Gettysburg	SD	57442	605-765-9410	
Lake Louise Recreation Area 35250 191st St *Web:* www.sdgfp.info	Miller	SD	57362	605-853-2533	
Lake Poinsett Recreation Area 46109 202nd St. *Web:* www.state.sd.us	Bruce	SD	57220	605-627-5441	
Lake Thompson Recreation Area 21176 Flood Club Rd *Web:* www.sdgfp.info	Lake Preston	SD	57249	605-847-4893	
Lake Vermillion Recreation Area 26140 451st Ave. *Web:* www.sdgfp.info/Parks/Regions/heartland/lakevermillion.htm	Canistota	SD	57012	605-296-3643	
Lewis & Clark Recreation Area 43349 SD Hwy 52 *Web:* www.sdgfp.info	Yankton	SD	57078	605-668-2985	
Little Moreau Recreation Area c/o Shadehill Recreation Area 19150 Summerville PO Box 63 *Web:* www.sdgfp.info	Shadehill	SD	57653	605-374-5114	
Llewellyn Johns Recreation Area c/o Shadehill Recreation Area 19150 Summerville PO Box 63 *Web:* www.sdgfp.info	Shadehill	SD	57653	605-374-5114	
Mina Lake Recreation Area c/o Richmond Lake Recreation Area 37908 Youth Camp Rd *Web:* www.sdgfp.info	Aberdeen	SD	57401	605-626-3488	
Newton Hills State Park 28767 482nd Ave *Web:* www.sdgfp.info	Canton	SD	57013	605-987-2263	
North Point Recreation Area 38180 297th St. *Web:* www.gfp.sd.gov/state-parks/directory/north-point	Lake Andes	SD	57356	605-487-7046	
North Wheeler Recreation Area 29084 N Wheeler Rd. *Web:* www.gfp.sd.gov/state-parks/directory/north-wheeler	Geddes	SD	57342	605-487-7046	
Oahe Downstream Recreation Area 20439 Marina Loop Rd. *Web:* www.gfp.sd.gov/state-parks/directory/oahe-downstream	Fort Pierre	SD	57532	605-223-7722	
Oakwood Lakes State Park 46109 202nd St *Web:* www.state.sd.us	Bruce	SD	57220	605-627-5441	
Okobojo Point Recreation Area 19425 Okobojo Pt Dr *Web:* www.gfp.sd.gov/state-parks/directory/okobojo-point	Fort Pierre	SD	57532	605-223-7722	
Pease Creek Recreation Area 37270 293rd St *Web:* www.gfp.sd.gov/state-parks/directory/pease-creek	Geddes	SD	57532	605-487-7046	
Pelican Lake Recreation Area 400 W Kemp *Web:* www.sdgfp.info/Parks/Regions/GlacialLakes/PelicanLake.htm	Watertown	SD	57201	605-882-5200	
Pickerel Lake Recreation Area 12980 446th Ave. *Web:* www.sdgfp.info/Parks/Regions/GlacialLakes/pickerellake.htm	Grenville	SD	57239	605-882-5200	
Pierson Ranch Recreation Area 31144 Toe Rd *Web:* www.gfp.sd.gov/state-parks/directory/pierson-ranch	Yankton	SD	57078	605-668-2985	
Platte Creek Recreation Area c/o Snake Creek Recreation Area 35316 SD Hwy 44 *Web:* www.sdgfp.info	Platte	SD	57369	605-337-2587	
Randall Creek Recreation Area 136 Randall Creek Rd *Web:* www.sdgfp.info/parks/regions/lewisclark/randallcreek.htm	Pickstown	SD	57367	605-487-7046	
Richmond Lake Recreation Area 37908 Youth Camp Rd *Web:* www.sdgfp.info	Aberdeen	SD	57401	605-626-3488	
Roy Lake State Park 11545 Northside Dr *Web:* www.sdgfp.info	Lake City	SD	57247	605-448-5701	
Sandy Shore Recreation Area c/o S Dakota Dept of Game Fish & Parks 400 W Kemp Ave *Web:* www.sdgfp.info	Watertown	SD	57201	605-882-5200	
Shadehill Recreation Area 19150 Summerville Rd PO Box 63 *Web:* www.sdgfp.info/parks/Regions/northernhills/shadehill.htm	Shadehill	SD	57653	605-374-5114	
Sica Hollow State Park c/o Roy Lake State Pk 11545 Northside Dr. *Web:* www.sdgfp.info	Lake City	SD	57247	605-448-5701	
Snake Creek Recreation Area 35316 SD Hwy 44 *Web:* www.sdgfp.info	Platte	SD	57369	605-337-2587	
Spirit Mound Historic Prairie 31148 SD Hwy 19. *Web:* www.gfp.sd.gov/state-parks/directory/spirit-mound	Vermillion	SD	57069	605-987-2263	
Spring Creek Recreation Area c/o Oahe Downstream Recreation Area 20439 Marina Loop Rd. *Web:* www.gfp.sd.gov/state-parks/directory/spring-creek	Fort Pierre	SD	57532	605-223-7722	
Springfield Recreation Area c/o Lewis & Clark Recreation Area 43349 SD Hwy 52 *Web:* www.sdgfp.info	Yankton	SD	57078	605-668-2985	
Swan Creek Recreation Area c/o W Whitlock Recreation Area 16157A W Whitlock Rd. *Web:* www.sdgfp.info	Gettysburg	SD	57442	605-765-9410	
Union Grove State Park c/o Newton Hills State Pk 28771 482nd Ave. *Web:* www.sdgfp.info	Canton	SD	57013	605-987-2263	
Walkers Point Recreation Area 23409 State Pk Dr. *Web:* www.sdgfp.info	Madison	SD	57042	605-256-5003	
West Bend Recreation Area c/o Farm Island Recreation Area 1301 Farm Island Rd *Web:* www.sdgfp.info	Pierre	SD	57501	605-773-2885	
West Pollock Recreation Area c/o Indian Creek Recreation Area 12905 288th Ave. *Web:* www.gfp.sd.gov/state-parks/directory/west-pollock	Mobridge	SD	57601	605-845-7112	
West Whitlock Recreation Area 16157A W Whitlock Rd. *Web:* www.sdgfp.info	Gettysburg	SD	57442	605-765-9410	

TENNESSEE

	City	State	Zip	Phone	Fax
Bicentennial Capitol Mall State Park 600 James Robertson Pkwy *Web:* www.state.tn.us	Nashville	TN	37243	615-741-5280	
Big Cypress Tree State Park 297 Big Cypress Rd *Web:* www.state.tn.us	Greenfield	TN	38230	731-235-2700	
Big Hill Pond State Park 1435 John Howell Rd *Web:* www.state.tn.us	Pocahontas	TN	38061	731-645-7967	
Big Ridge State Park 1015 Big Ridge Rd. *Web:* www.state.tn.us	Maynardville	TN	37807	865-992-5523	
Bledsoe Creek State Park 400 Zieglers Fort Rd. *Web:* www.state.tn.us	Gallatin	TN	37066	615-452-3706	
Booker T. Washington State Park 5801 Champion Rd. *Web:* www.state.tn.us	Chattanooga	TN	37416	423-894-4955	855-7879
Burgess Falls State Natural Area 4000 Burgess Falls Dr *Web:* www.state.tn.us	Sparta	TN	38583	931-432-5312	
Cedars of Lebanon State Park 328 Cedar Forest Rd. *Web:* www.state.tn.us	Lebanon	TN	37087	615-443-2769	443-2793
Chickasaw State Park 20 Cabin Ln. *Web:* www.state.tn.us	Henderson	TN	38340	731-989-5141	
Cordell Hull Birthplace State Park 1300 Cordell Hull Memorial Dr *Web:* www.state.tn.us	Byrdstown	TN	38549	931-864-3247	864-6389
Cove Lake State Park 110 Cove Lake Ln. *Web:* www.state.tn.us	Caryville	TN	37714	423-566-9701	566-9717
Cumberland Mountain State Park 24 Office Dr *Web:* www.state.tn.us	Crossville	TN	38555	931-484-6138	
David Crockett State Park 1400 W Gaines PO Box 398 *Web:* www.state.tn.us	Lawrenceburg	TN	38464	931-762-9408	766-0047
Davy Crockett Birthplace State Park 1245 Davy Crockett Pk Rd *Web:* www.state.tn.us	Limestone	TN	37681	423-257-2167	257-2430
Dunbar Cave State Natural Area 401 Dunbar Cave Rd. *Web:* www.state.tn.us	Clarksville	TN	37043	931-648-5526	
Edgar Evins State Park 1630 Edgar Evins State Pk Rd. *Web:* www.state.tn.us	Silver Point	TN	38582	931-858-2446	
Fall Creek Falls State Resort Park 2009 Village Camp Rd Rt 3 PO Box 300 *Web:* www.state.tn.us	Pikeville	TN	37367	423-881-5298	
Fort Loudoun State Historic Park 338 Fort Loudoun Rd *Web:* www.state.tn.us	Vonore	TN	37885	423-884-6217	
Fort Pillow State Historic Park 3122 Pk Rd *Web:* www.state.tn.us	Henning	TN	38041	731-738-5581	738-9117
Frozen Head State Natural Area 964 Flat Fork Rd *Web:* www.state.tn.us	Wartburg	TN	37887	423-346-3318	346-6629
Harpeth River State Park Hwy 70 *Web:* www.state.tn.us	Kingston Springs	TN	37887	615-797-6096	
Harrison Bay State Park 8411 Harrison Bay Rd. *Web:* www.state.tn.us	Harrison	TN	37341	423-344-6214	
Henry Horton State Resort Park 4358 Nashville Hwy *Web:* www.state.tn.us	Chapel Hill	TN	37034	931-364-2222	
Hiwassee/Ocoee Scenic River State Park PO Box 5 *Web:* www.state.tn.us	Delano	TN	37325	615-263-4133	
Indian Mountain State Park 143 State Pk Cir *Web:* www.state.tn.us	Jellico	TN	37762	423-784-7958	
Johnsonville State Historic Park Rt 1 PO Box 374 *Web:* www.state.tn.us	New Johnsonville	TN	37134	931-535-2789	535-3776

Name / Address	City	State	ZIP	Phone	Fax
Justin P. Wilson Cumberland Trail State Park 220 Pk Rd *Web:* www.state.tn.us	Caryville	TN	38555	423-566-2229	566-2290
Long Hunter State Park 2910 Hobson Pike *Web:* www.state.tn.us	Hermitage	TN	37076	615-855-2422	
Meeman-Shelby Forest State Park 910 Riddick Rd *TF:* 800-471-5293 ■ *Web:* www.state.tn.us	Millington	TN	38053	901-876-5215	876-3217
Montgomery Bell State Resort Park 1020 Jackson Hill Rd *Web:* www.state.tn.us	Burns	TN	37029	615-797-9052	
Mousetail Landing State Park 99 Campground Rd *Web:* www.state.tn.us	Linden	TN	37096	731-847-0841	
Natchez Trace State Park 24845 Natchez Trace Rd *Web:* www.state.tn.us	Wildersville	TN	38388	731-968-3742	
Nathan Bedford Forrest State Park 1825 Pilot Knob Rd *Web:* www.state.tn.us	Eva	TN	38333	731-584-6356	584-1841
Norris Dam State Resort Park 125 Village Green Cir *Web:* www.state.tn.us	Lake City	TN	37769	865-426-7461	
Old Stone Fort State Archaeological Park 732 Stone Fort Dr *Web:* www.state.tn.us	Manchester	TN	37355	931-723-5073	
Panther Creek State Park 2010 Panther Creek Pk Rd *Web:* www.state.tn.us	Morristown	TN	37814	423-587-7046	587-7047
Paris Landing State Park 16055 Hwy 79N *Web:* www.state.tn.us	Buchanan	TN	38222	731-641-4465	
Pickett State Park 4605 Pickett Pk Hwy *Web:* www.state.tn.us	Jamestown	TN	38556	931-879-5821	
Pickwick Landing State Resort Park PO Box 15 *Web:* www.state.tn.us	Pickwick Dam	TN	38365	731-689-3129	
Pinson Mounds State Archaeological Park 460 Ozier Rd *Web:* www.state.tn.us	Pinson	TN	38366	731-988-5614	
Port Royal State Historic Park 3300 Old Clarksville Hwy *Web:* www.state.tn.us	Adams	TN	37010	931-648-5526	
Radnor Lake State Park 1160 Otter Creek Rd *Web:* www.state.tn.us/environment/parks/RadnorLake	Nashville	TN	37220	615-373-3467	
Red Clay State Historic Park 1140 Red Clay Pk Rd *Web:* www.state.tn.us	Cleveland	TN	37311	423-478-0339	
Reelfoot Lake State Park 3120 SR 213 *Web:* www.state.tn.us	Tiptonville	TN	38079	731-253-7756	
Roan Mountain State Park 1015 Hwy 143 *Web:* www.state.tn.us	Roan Mountain	TN	37687	423-772-0190	
Rock Island State Park 82 Beach Rd *Web:* www.state.tn.us	Rock Island	TN	38581	931-686-2471	
Sergeant Alvin C. York State Historic Park General Delivery Hwy 127 *Web:* www.state.tn.us	Pall Mall	TN	38577	931-879-9406	
South Cumberland Recreation Area Rt 1 PO Box 2196 *Web:* www.state.tn.us	Monteagle	TN	37356	931-692-3887	
Standing Stone State Park 1674 Standing Stone Pk Hwy *Web:* www.state.tn.us	Hilham	TN	38568	931-823-6347	
Sycamore Shoals State Historic Park 1651 W Elk Ave *Web:* www.state.tn.us	Elizabethton	TN	37643	423-543-5808	543-0078
T. O. Fuller State Park 1500 Mitchell Rd *Web:* www.state.tn.us	Memphis	TN	38109	901-543-7581	785-8485
Tims Ford State Park 570 Tims Ford Dr *Web:* www.state.tn.us	Winchester	TN	37398	931-962-1183	
Warriors' Path State Park PO Box 5026 *Web:* www.state.tn.us	Kingsport	TN	37663	423-239-8531	239-4982

TEXAS

Name / Address	City	State	ZIP	Phone	Fax
Abilene State Park 150 Pk Rd 32 *Web:* www.tpwd.state.tx.us	Tuscola	TX	79562	325-572-3204	572-3008
Acton State Historic Site c/o Cleburne State Pk 5800 Pk Rd 21 *Web:* www.tpwd.state.tx.us/spdest/findadest/parks/acton	Cleburne	TX	76031	817-645-4215	
Admiral Nimitz State Historic Site 328 E Main St *Web:* www.thc.state.tx.us	Fredericksburg	TX	78624	830-997-4379	
Atlanta State Park 927 Pk Rd 42 *Web:* www.tpwd.state.tx.us	Atlanta	TX	75551	903-796-6476	
Balmorhea State Park PO Box 15 *Web:* www.tpwd.state.tx.us	Toyahvale	TX	79786	432-375-2370	
Barton Warnock Environmental Education Ctr HC 70 PO Box 375 *Web:* www.tpwd.state.tx.us	Terlingua	TX	79852	432-424-3327	
Bastrop State Park 3005 Hwy 21 E *Web:* www.tpwd.state.tx.us	Bastrop	TX	78602	512-321-2101	
Bentsen-Rio Grande Valley State Park 2800 S Bensen Palm Dr *Web:* www.worldbirdingcenter.org	Mission	TX	78572	956-585-1107	584-9126
Big Bend Ranch State Park PO Box 2319 *Web:* www.tpwd.state.tx.us/spdest/findadest/parks/big_bend_ranch	Presidio	TX	79845	432-229-3416	
Big Spring State Park 1 Scenic Dr *Web:* www.tpwd.state.tx.us	Big Spring	TX	79720	432-263-4931	
Blanco State Park PO Box 493 *Web:* www.tpwd.state.tx.us	Blanco	TX	78606	830-833-4333	
Bonham State Park 1363 State Pk 24 *Web:* www.tpwd.state.tx.us	Bonham	TX	75418	903-583-5022	
Brazos Bend State Park 21901 FM 762 *Web:* www.tpwd.state.tx.us	Needville	TX	77461	409-553-5101	
Buescher State Park PO Box 75 *Web:* www.tpwd.state.tx.us	Smithville	TX	78957	512-237-2241	
Caddo Lake State Park 245 Pk Rd 2 *Web:* www.tpwd.state.tx.us	Karnack	TX	75661	903-679-3351	
Caddoan Mounds State Historic Site 1649 Texas 21 *Web:* www.tpwd.state.tx.us	Alto	TX	75925	936-858-3218	
Caprock Canyons State Park & Trailway 850 Caprock Canyon Pk Rd *Web:* www.tpwd.state.tx.us	Quitaque	TX	79255	806-455-1492	
Casa Navarro State Historic Site 228 S Laredo St *Web:* www.tpwd.state.tx.us	San Antonio	TX	78207	210-226-4801	226-4801
Cedar Hill State Park 1570 W FM 1382 *Web:* www.tpwd.state.tx.us	Cedar Hill	TX	75104	972-291-3900	
Choke Canyon State Park PO Box 2 *Web:* www.tpwd.state.tx.us	Calliham	TX	78007	361-786-3868	
Cleburne State Park 5800 Pk Rd 21 *Web:* www.tpwd.state.tx.us/spdest/findadest/parks/cleburne	Cleburne	TX	76031	817-645-4215	
Colorado Bend State Park 6031 Colorado Pk Rd *Web:* www.tpwd.state.tx.us	Bend	TX	76824	325-628-3240	
Confederate Reunion Grounds State Historic Site c/o Fort Parker State Pk 194 Pk Rd 28 *Web:* www.tpwd.state.tx.us/spdest/findadest/parks/confederate_reunion_grounds	Mexia	TX	76667	254-562-5751	
Cooper Lake State Park 1664 Farm Rd 1529 S *Web:* www.tpwd.state.tx.us	Cooper	TX	75432	903-395-3100	
Copper Breaks State Park 777 Pk Rd 62 *Web:* www.tpwd.state.tx.us	Quanah	TX	79252	940-839-4331	
Daingerfield State Park 455 Pk Rd 17 *Web:* www.tpwd.state.tx.us	Daingerfield	TX	75638	903-645-2921	
Davis Mountains State Park PO Box 1458 *Web:* www.tpwd.state.tx.us	Fort Davis	TX	79734	432-426-3337	
Devil's Sinkhole State Natural Area 101 N Sweeten St *Web:* www.tpwd.state.tx.us	Rocksprings	TX	78880	830-683-3762	
Devils River State Natural Area HC 01 PO Box 513 *Web:* www.tpwd.state.tx.us	Del Rio	TX	78840	830-395-2133	
Dinosaur Valley State Park 205 Farm to Market 56 *Web:* www.tpwd.state.tx.us	Glen Rose	TX	76043	254-897-4588	
Eisenhower Birthplace State Historic Site 609 S Lamar Ave *Web:* www.tpwd.state.tx.us	Denison	TX	75021	903-465-8908	
Eisenhower State Park 50 Pk Rd 20 *Web:* www.tpwd.state.tx.us	Denison	TX	75020	903-465-1956	
Enchanted Rock State Natural Area 16710 Ranch Rd 965 *Web:* www.tpwd.state.tx.us	Fredericksburg	TX	78624	325-247-3903	
Fairfield Lake State Park 123 State Pk Rd 64 *Web:* www.tpwd.state.tx.us/spdest/findadest/parks/fairfield_lake	Fairfield	TX	75840	903-389-4514	
Falcon State Park PO Box 2 *Web:* www.tpwd.state.tx.us	Falcon Heights	TX	78545	956-848-5327	
Fannin Battleground State Historic Site c/o Goliad State Pk 108 Pk Rd 6 *Web:* www.tpwd.state.tx.us	Goliad	TX	77963	361-645-3405	
Fanthorp Inn State Historic Site 579 Main St *Web:* www.tpwd.state.tx.us	Anderson	TX	77830	936-873-2633	
Fort Griffin State Park & Historic Site 1701 N US Hwy 283 *Web:* www.tpwd.state.tx.us	Albany	TX	76430	325-762-3592	
Fort Lancaster State Historic Site PO Box 306 *Web:* www.tpwd.state.tx.us	Sheffield	TX	79781	432-836-4391	
Fort Leaton State Historic Site PO Box 2319 *Web:* www.tpwd.state.tx.us/spdest/findadest/parks/fort_leaton	Presidio	TX	79845	432-229-3413	
Fort McKavett State Historic Site 7066 FM 864 Rd *Web:* www.tpwd.state.tx.us	Fort McKavett	TX	76841	325-396-2358	
Fort Parker State Park 194 Pk Rd 28 *Web:* www.tpwd.state.tx.us/spdest/findadest/parks/fort_parker	Mexia	TX	76667	254-562-5751	
Fort Richardson State Park Historic Site & Lost Creek Reservoir State Trailway 228 State Pk Rd 61 *Web:* www.tpwd.state.tx.us	Jacksboro	TX	76458	817-567-3506	
Franklin Mountains State Park 1331 McKelligon Canyon Rd *Web:* www.tpwd.state.tx.us	El Paso	TX	79930	915-566-6441	
Fulton Mansion State Historic Site PO Box 1859 *Web:* www.tpwd.state.tx.us	Fulton	TX	78358	361-729-0386	
Galveston Island State Park 14901 Termini San Luis Pass Rd *Web:* www.tpwd.state.tx.us	Galveston	TX	77554	409-737-1222	
Garner State Park HCR 70 PO Box 599 *Web:* www.tpwd.state.tx.us	Concan	TX	78838	830-232-6132	
Goliad State Park 108 Pk Rd 6 *Web:* www.tpwd.state.tx.us	Goliad	TX	77963	361-645-3405	
Goose Island State Park 202 S Palmetto St *Web:* www.tpwd.state.tx.us	Rockport	TX	78382	361-729-2858	
Government Canyon State Natural Area 12861 Galm Rd *Web:* www.tpwd.state.tx.us	San Antonio	TX	78254	210-688-9055	
Guadalupe River State Park 3350 Pk Rd 31 *Web:* www.tpwd.state.tx.us	Spring Branch	TX	78070	830-438-2656	
Hill Country State Natural Area 10600 Bandera Creek Rd *Web:* www.tpwd.state.tx.us	Bandera	TX	78003	830-796-4413	

				Phone	Fax
Honey Creek State Natural Area c/o Guadalupe River State Pk 3350 Pk Rd 31 *Web:* www.tpwd.state.tx.us	Spring Branch	TX	78070	210-438-2656	
Hueco Tanks State Historic Site 6900 Hueco Tanks Rd No 1 *Web:* www.tpwd.state.tx.us	El Paso	TX	79938	915-857-1135	857-3628
Huntsville State Park PO Box 508 *Web:* www.tpwd.state.tx.us	Huntsville	TX	77342	936-295-5644	
Inks Lake State Park 3630 Pk Rd 4 *Web:* www.tpwd.state.tx.us	Burnet	TX	78611	512-793-2223	
Kickapoo Cavern State Park 23 Miles N Ranch Rd *Web:* www.tpwd.state.tx.us	Brackettville	TX	78832	830-563-2342	
Lake Arrowhead State Park 229 Pk Rd 63 *Web:* www.tpwd.state.tx.us/spdest/findadest/parks/lake_arrowhead	Wichita Falls	TX	76310	940-528-2211	
Lake Bob Sandlin State Park 341 State Pk Rd 2117 *Web:* www.tpwd.state.tx.us	Pittsburg	TX	75686	903-572-5531	
Lake Brownwood State Park 200 Hwy Pk Rd 15 *Web:* www.tpwd.state.tx.us	Lake Brownwood	TX	76801	325-784-5223	
Lake Casa Blanca International State Park 6101 Bob Bullock Loop *Web:* www.tpwd.state.tx.us	Laredo	TX	78041	956-725-3826	
Lake Colorado City State Park 4582 FM 2836 *Web:* www.tpwd.state.tx.us	Colorado City	TX	79512	325-728-3931	
Lake Corpus Christi State Park 23194 Pk Rd 25 *Web:* www.tpwd.state.tx.us	Mathis	TX	78368	361-547-2635	
Lake Livingston State Park 1024 State St *Web:* www.tpwd.state.tx.us	Livingston	TX	77351	936-365-2201	
Lake Mineral Wells State Park & Trailway 100 Pk Rd 71 *Web:* www.tpwd.state.tx.us	Mineral Wells	TX	76067	940-328-1171	
Lake Somerville State Park 14222 Pk Rd 57 *Web:* www.tpwd.state.tx.us	Somerville	TX	77879	979-535-7763	
Lake Tawakoni State Park 10822 Fm 2475 *Web:* www.tpwd.state.tx.us	Wills Point	TX	75169	903-560-7123	
Lake Texana State Park 46 Pk Rd 1 *Web:* www.tpwd.state.tx.us	Edna	TX	77957	361-782-5718	
Lake Whitney State Park PO Box 1175 *Web:* www.tpwd.state.tx.us	Whitney	TX	76692	254-694-3793	
Landmark Inn State Historic Site 402 E Florence St *Web:* www.tpwd.state.tx.us	Castroville	TX	78009	830-931-2133	
Lipantitlan State Historic Site c/o Lake Corpus Christi State Pk PO Box 1167 *Web:* www.tpwd.state.tx.us	Mathis	TX	78368	361-547-2635	
Lockhart State Park 4179 State Pk Rd *Web:* www.tpwd.state.tx.us	Lockhart	TX	78644	512-398-3479	
Longhorn Cavern State Park 6211 Pk Rd 4 S *Web:* www.tpwd.state.tx.us	Burnet	TX	78611	830-598-2283	
Lost Maples State Natural Area 37221 FM 187 *Web:* www.tpwd.state.tx.us	Vanderpool	TX	78885	830-966-3413	
Lyndon B. Johnson State Park & Historic Site PO Box 238 *Web:* www.tpwd.state.tx.us	Stonewall	TX	78671	830-644-2252	
Martin Creek Lake State Park 9515 CR 2181D *Web:* www.tpwd.state.tx.us	Tatum	TX	75691	903-836-4336	
Martin Dies Jr State Park 634 Private Rd 5025 *Web:* www.tpwd.state.tx.us	Jasper	TX	75951	409-384-5231	
Matagorda Island Wildlife Management Area 1700 7th St *Web:* www.tpwd.state.tx.us	Bay City	TX	77414	979-244-6824	
McKinney Falls State Park 5808 McKinney Falls Pkwy *Web:* www.tpwd.state.tx.us	Austin	TX	78744	512-243-1643	243-0536
Meridian State Park 173 Pk Rd 7 *Web:* www.tpwd.state.tx.us	Meridian	TX	76665	254-435-2536	
Mission Tejas State Park 120 State Pk Rd 44 *Web:* www.tpwd.state.tx.us	Grapeland	TX	75844	936-687-2394	
Monahans Sandhills State Park PO Box 1738 *Web:* www.tpwd.state.tx.us	Monahans	TX	79756	432-943-2092	
Monument Hill & Kreische Brewery State Historic Sites 414 State Loop 92 *Web:* www.tpwd.state.tx.us	La Grange	TX	78945	979-968-5658	
Mother Neff State Park 1680 Texas 236 Hwy *Web:* www.tpwd.state.tx.us	Moody	TX	76557	254-853-2389	
Mustang Island State Park 17047 State Hwy 361 *Web:* www.tpwd.state.tx.us	Port Aransas	TX	78373	361-749-5246	749-6455
Palmetto State Park 78 Pk Rd 11 S *Web:* www.tpwd.state.tx.us	Gonzales	TX	78629	830-672-3266	
Palo Duro Canyon State Park 11450 Pk Rd 5 *Web:* www.tpwd.state.tx.us	Canyon	TX	79015	806-488-2227	488-2729
Pedernales Falls State Park 2585 Pk Rd 6026 *Web:* www.tpwd.state.tx.us	Johnson City	TX	78636	830-868-7304	
Port Isabel Lighthouse State Historic Site 421 E Queen Isabella Blvd *Web:* www.tpwd.state.tx.us	Port Isabel	TX	78578	956-943-2262	
Possum Kingdom State Park PO Box 70 *Web:* www.tpwd.state.tx.us	Caddo	TX	76429	940-549-1803	
Purtis Creek State Park 14225 FM 316 *Web:* www.tpwd.state.tx.us	Eustace	TX	75124	903-425-2332	
Ray Roberts Lake State Park 100 PW 4137 *Web:* www.tpwd.state.tx.us	Pilot Point	TX	76258	940-686-2148	
Rusk/Palestine State Park 1 Hwy 84 W *Web:* www.tpwd.state.tx.us	Rusk	TX	75785	903-683-5126	
Sabine Pass Battleground State Park & Historic Site c/o Sea Rim State Pk PO Box 1066 *Web:* www.tpwd.state.tx.us/spdest/findadest/parks/sabine_pass_battleground	Sabine Pass	TX	77655	409-971-2559	
Sam Bell Maxey House State Historic Site 812 S Church St *Web:* www.tpwd.state.tx.us	Paris	TX	75460	903-785-5716	
San Angelo State Park 3900 Mercedes St # 2 *Web:* www.tpwd.state.tx.us	San Angelo	TX	76901	325-949-4757	
San Jacinto Battleground State Historic Site 3523 Battleground Rd *Web:* www.tpwd.state.tx.us/spdest/findadest/parks/san_jacinto_battleground	La Porte	TX	77571	281-479-2431	479-5618
Sea Rim State Park PO Box 356 *Web:* www.tpwd.state.tx.us/spdest/findadest/parks/sea_rim	Sabine Pass	TX	77655	409-971-2559	
Sebastopol State Historic Site PO Box 900 *Web:* www.tpwd.state.tx.us	Seguin	TX	78156	830-379-4833	
Seminole Canyon State Park & Historic Site PO Box 820 *Web:* www.tpwd.state.tx.us	Comstock	TX	78837	432-292-4464	
Sheldon Lake State Park & Environmental Learning Ctr 15315 Beaumont Hwy at Pk Rd 138 *Web:* www.tpwd.state.tx.us	Houston	TX	77049	281-456-2800	
South Llano River State Park HC 15 PO Box 224 *Web:* www.tpwd.state.tx.us	Junction	TX	76849	325-446-3994	
Starr Family State Historic Site 407 W Travis St *Web:* www.tpwd.state.tx.us	Marshall	TX	75670	903-935-3044	
Stephen F. Austin State Park & San Felipe State Historic Site 120 Main St *Web:* www.tpwd.state.tx.us	San Felipe	TX	77473	979-885-3613	
Texas State Railroad State Park PO Box 39 *Web:* www.tpwd.state.tx.us	Rusk	TX	75785	903-683-2561	
Tyler State Park 789 Pk Rd 16 *Web:* www.tpwd.state.tx.us	Tyler	TX	75706	903-597-5338	
Varner-Hogg Plantation State Historic Site 1702 N 13th St *Web:* www.tpwd.state.tx.us	West Columbia	TX	77486	979-345-4656	
Village Creek State Park 8854 Pk Rd 74 *Web:* www.tpwd.state.tx.us	Lumberton	TX	77657	409-755-7322	
Washington-on-the-Brazos State Historic Site 17700 Pickens Rd *Web:* www.tpwd.state.tx.us	Washington	TX	77880	936-878-2214	

UTAH

				Phone	Fax
Anasazi State Park Museum 460 N Hwy 12 *Web:* www.stateparks.utah.gov	Boulder	UT	84716	435-335-7308	
Antelope Island State Park 4528 W 1700 S *Web:* www.stateparks.utah.gov	Syracuse	UT	84075	801-652-2043	
Bear Lake State Park 1030 N Bear Lake Blvd *Web:* www.stateparks.utah.gov	Garden City	UT	84028	435-946-3343	
Camp Floyd/Stagecoach Inn State Park & Museum 18035 W 1540 N *Web:* www.stateparks.utah.gov	Fairfield	UT	84013	801-768-8932	
Coral Pink Sand Dunes State Park PO Box 95 *Web:* www.stateparks.utah.gov	Kanab	UT	84741	435-648-2800	
Dead Horse Point State Park PO Box 609 *Web:* www.stateparks.utah.gov	Moab	UT	84532	435-259-2614	
Deer Creek State Park PO Box 257 *Web:* www.stateparks.utah.gov	Midway	UT	84049	435-654-0171	
East Canyon State Park 5535 S Hwy 66 *Web:* www.stateparks.utah.gov	Morgan	UT	84050	801-829-6866	
Edge of the Cedars State Park Museum 660 W 400 N *Web:* stateparks.utah.gov	Blanding	UT	84511	435-678-2238	
Escalante State Park 710 N Reservoir Rd *Web:* www.stateparks.utah.gov	Escalante	UT	84726	435-826-4466	
Fremont Indian State Park & Museum 3820 W Clear Creek Canyon Rd *Web:* www.stateparks.utah.gov	Sevier	UT	84766	435-527-4631	
Goblin Valley State Park PO Box 637 *Web:* www.utah.com	Green River	UT	84525	435-275-4584	
Goosenecks State Park c/o Edge of Cedars State Pk 660 W 400 N *Web:* stateparks.utah.gov	Blanding	UT	84511	435-678-2238	
Great Salt Lake State Marina PO Box 16658 *Web:* www.stateparks.utah.gov	Salt Lake City	UT	84116	801-250-1898	
Green River State Park PO Box 637 *Web:* www.utah.com	Green River	UT	84525	435-564-3633	
Gunlock State Park 4405 W 3600 S *Web:* www.stateparks.utah.gov	Hurricane	UT	84737	435-680-0715	
Historic Union Pacific Rail Trail State Park PO Box 754 *Web:* www.stateparks.utah.gov	Park City	UT	84060	435-649-6839	
Huntington State Park PO Box 1343 *TF:* 800-322-3770 ■ *Web:* stateparks.utah.gov	Huntington	UT	84528	435-687-2491	
Hyrum State Park 405 300 S *Web:* www.stateparks.utah.gov	Hyrum	UT	84319	435-245-6866	
Iron Mission State Park 635 N Main St *Web:* www.stateparks.utah.gov	Cedar City	UT	84720	435-586-9290	
Jordanelle State Park SR 319 515 PO Box 4 *Web:* www.stateparks.utah.gov	Heber City	UT	84032	435-649-9540	
Kodachrome Basin State Park S Of Cannonville *Web:* www.stateparks.utah.gov	Cannonville	UT	84718	435-679-8562	
Millsite State Park c/o Huntington State Pk PO Box 1343 *TF:* 800-322-3770 ■ *Web:* stateparks.utah.gov	Huntington	UT	84528	435-384-2552	

				Phone	Fax
Otter Creek State Park PO Box 43 *Web:* www.stateparks.utah.gov	Antimony	UT	84712	435-624-3268	
Palisade State Park 2200 E Palisade Rd *Web:* www.stateparks.utah.gov	Sterling	UT	84665	435-835-7275	
Piute State Park c/o Otter Creek State Pk PO Box 43 *Web:* www.stateparks.utah.gov	Antimony	UT	84712	435-624-3268	
Quail Creek State Park PO Box 1943 *Web:* www.stateparks.utah.gov	Saint George	UT	84771	435-879-2378	
Red Fleet State Park 8750 N Hwy 191 *TF:* 800-322-3770 ■ *Web:* stateparks.utah.gov	Vernal	UT	84078	435-789-4432	
Rockport State Park 9040 N State Hwy 302 *Web:* www.stateparks.utah.gov	Peoa	UT	84061	801-336-2241	
Sand Hollow State Park 4405 W 3600 S *Web:* www.stateparks.utah.gov	Hurricane	UT	84737	435-680-0715	
Scofield State Park 1343 Huntington *Web:* www.stateparks.utah.gov	Price	UT	84528	435-448-9449	
Snow Canyon State Park 1002 Snow Canyon Dr *Web:* www.stateparks.utah.gov	Ivins	UT	84738	435-628-2255	
Starvation State Park PO Box 584 *Web:* www.stateparks.utah.gov	Duchesne	UT	84021	435-738-2326	
Steinaker State Park 4335 N Hwy 191 *TF:* 800-322-3770 ■ *Web:* stateparks.utah.gov	Vernal	UT	84078	435-789-4432	
Territorial Statehouse State Park 50 W Capitol Ave *Web:* www.stateparks.utah.gov	Fillmore	UT	84631	435-743-5316	
Utah Field House of Natural History State Park 496 E Main St *Web:* www.stateparks.utah.gov/park/index.php?id=UFSP	Vernal	UT	84078	435-789-3799	
Utah Lake State Park 4400 W Ctr St *Web:* www.stateparks.utah.gov	Provo	UT	84601	801-375-0731	373-4215
Wasatch Mountain State Park 1281 Warm Springs Rd *Web:* www.stateparks.utah.gov	Midway	UT	84049	435-654-1791	
Willard Bay State Park 900 W 650 N #A *TF:* 800-322-3770 ■ *Web:* www.stateparks.utah.gov	Willard	UT	84340	435-734-9494	734-2659
Yuba State Park 12225 S Yuba Dam Rd *Web:* www.stateparks.utah.gov	Levan	UT	84639	435-758-2611	

VERMONT

				Phone	Fax
Alburg Dunes State Park 151 Coon Pt Rd *Web:* www.vtstateparks.com	Alburg	VT	05440	802-796-4170	
Allis State Park 284 Allis State Pk Rd *Web:* www.vtstateparks.com	Randolph	VT	05060	802-276-3175	
Ascutney State Park 1826 Black Mountain Rd *Web:* www.vtstateparks.com	Windsor	VT	05089	802-674-2060	
Big Deer State Park 1467 Boulder Beach Rd *Web:* www.vtstateparks.com/htm/bigdeer.cfm	Groton	VT	05046	802-584-3822	
Bomoseen State Park 22 Cedar Mountain Rd *Web:* www.vtstateparks.com	Fair Haven	VT	05743	802-265-4242	
Boulder Beach State Park 44 Stillwater Rd *Web:* www.vtstateparks.com	Groton	VT	05046	802-584-3823	
Branbury State Park 3570 Lake Dunmore Rd Rt 53 *Web:* www.vtstateparks.com	Brandon	VT	05733	802-247-5925	
Brighton State Park 102 State Pk Rd *Web:* www.vtstateparks.com	Island Pond	VT	05846	802-723-4360	
Burton Island State Park PO Box 123 *Web:* www.vtstateparks.com/htm/burton.htm	Saint Albans Bay	VT	05481	802-524-6353	
Button Bay State Park 5 Button Bay State Pk Rd *Web:* www.vtstateparks.com	Vergennes	VT	05491	802-475-2377	
Camp Plymouth State Park 2008 Scout Camp Rd *Web:* www.vtstateparks.com	Ludlow	VT	05149	802-228-2025	
Coolidge State Park 855 Coolidge State Pk Rd *Web:* www.vtstateparks.com	Plymouth	VT	05056	802-672-3612	
Crystal Lake State Park 96 Bellwater Ave *Web:* www.vtstateparks.com	Barton	VT	05822	802-525-6205	
D.A.R. State Park 6750 VT Rt 17 W *Web:* www.vtstateparks.com	Addison	VT	05491	802-759-2354	
Elmore State Park 856 VT Rt 12 *Web:* www.vtstateparks.com	Lake Elmore	VT	05657	802-888-2982	
Emerald Lake State Park 65 Emerald Lake Ln *Web:* www.vtstateparks.com	East Dorset	VT	05253	802-362-1655	
Fort Dummer State Park 517 Old Guilford Rd *Web:* www.vtstateparks.com	Brattleboro	VT	05301	802-254-2610	
Gifford Woods State Park 34 Gifford Woods *Web:* www.vtstateparks.com	Killington	VT	05751	802-775-5354	
Grand Isle State Park 36 E Shore S *Web:* www.vtstateparks.com	Grand Isle	VT	05458	802-372-4300	
Green River Reservoir State Park 29 Sunset Dr Suite 1 *Web:* www.vtstateparks.com	Morrisville	VT	05661	802-888-1349	
Half Moon Pond State Park 1621 Black Pond Rd *Web:* www.vtstateparks.com/htm/halfmoon.cfm	Fair Haven	VT	05743	802-273-2848	
Jamaica State Park 48 Salmon Hole Ln *Web:* www.vtstateparks.com	Jamaica	VT	05343	802-874-4600	
Kettle Pond State Park 4239 VT Rd 232 *Web:* www.vtstateparks.com/htm/kettlepond.cfm	Marshfield	VT	05658	802-426-3042	
Kill Kare State Park c/o Burton Island State Pk PO Box 123 *Web:* www.vtstateparks.com/htm/killkare.htm	Saint Albans Bay	VT	05481	802-524-6021	
Kingsland Bay State Park 787 Kingsland Bay State Pk Rd *Web:* www.vtstateparks.com	Ferrisburgh	VT	05456	802-877-3445	
Knight Island State Park c/o Burton Island State Pk PO Box 123 *Web:* www.vtstateparks.com/htm/knightisland.htm	Saint Albans Bay	VT	05481	802-524-6353	
Knight Point State Park 31 Knights Pt Rd *Web:* www.vtstateparks.com	North Hero	VT	05474	802-372-8389	
Lake Carmi State Park 69 Stn Rd *Web:* www.vtstateparks.com	Enosburg Falls	VT	05450	802-933-8383	
Lake Saint Catherine State Park 3034 VT Rt 30 S *Web:* www.vtstateparks.com	Poultney	VT	05764	802-287-9158	
Lake Shaftsbury State Park 262 Shaftsbury State Pk Rd *Web:* www.vtstateparks.com	Shaftsbury	VT	05262	802-375-9978	
Little River State Park 3444 Little River Rd *Web:* www.vtstateparks.com	Waterbury	VT	05676	802-244-7103	
Lowell Lake State Park 1756 Little Pond Rd *Web:* www.vtstateparks.com	Londonderry	VT	05148	802-824-4035	
Maidstone State Park Rt 1 PO Box 388 *Web:* www.vtstateparks.com	Guildhall	VT	05905	802-676-3930	
Molly Stark State Park 705 Rt 9 E *Web:* www.vtstateparks.com	Wilmington	VT	05363	802-464-5460	
Mount Philo State Park 5425 Mt Philo Rd *Web:* www.vtstateparks.com	Charlotte	VT	05445	802-425-2390	
New Discovery State Park 4239 VT Rt 232 *Web:* www.vtstateparks.com/htm/newdiscovery.cfm	Marshfield	VT	05658	802-426-3042	
North Hero State Park 3803 Lakeview Dr *Web:* www.vtstateparks.com	North Hero	VT	05474	802-372-8727	
Quechee State Park 764 Dewey Mills Rd *Web:* www.vtstateparks.com	White River Junction	VT	05001	802-295-2990	
Ricker Pond State Park 18 Ricker Pond Camp Ground Rd *Web:* www.vtstateparks.com	Groton	VT	05046	802-584-3821	
Sand Bar State Park 1215 US Rt 2 *Web:* www.vtstateparks.com	Milton	VT	05468	802-893-2825	
Seyon Lodge State Park 2967 Seyon Pond Rd *Web:* www.vtstateparks.com/htm/seyon.htm	Groton	VT	05046	802-584-3829	
Silver Lake State Park 214 N Rd *Web:* www.vtstateparks.com	Bethel	VT	05032	802-234-9451	
Smugglers Notch State Park 6443 Mountain Rd *Web:* www.vtstateparks.com	Stowe	VT	05672	802-253-4014	
Stillwater State Park 445 Stillwater Rd *Web:* www.vtstateparks.com	Groton	VT	05046	802-584-3822	
Thetford Hill State Park 622 Academy Rd *Web:* www.vtstateparks.com	Thetford	VT	05074	802-785-2266	
Townshend State Park 2755 State Forest Rd *Web:* www.vtstateparks.com	Townshend	VT	05353	802-365-7500	
Underhill State Park PO Box 249 *Web:* www.vtstateparks.com	Underhill Center	VT	05490	802-899-3022	
Waterbury Center State Park 177 Reservoir Rd *Web:* www.vtstateparks.com	Waterbury Center	VT	05677	802-244-1226	
Wilgus State Park PO Box 196 *Web:* www.vtstateparks.com	Ascutney	VT	05030	802-674-5422	
Woodford State Park 142 State Pk Rd *Web:* www.vtstateparks.com	Bennington	VT	05201	802-447-7169	
Woods Island State Park c/o Burton Island State Pk PO Box 123 *Web:* www.vtstateparks.com/htm/woodsisland.htm	Saint Albans Bay	VT	05481	802-524-6353	

VIRGINIA

				Phone	Fax
Bear Creek Lake State Park 22 County Rd 666 *Web:* www.dcr.state.va.us	Cumberland	VA	23040	804-492-4410	
Belle Isle State Park 1632 Belle Isle Rd *Web:* www.dcr.state.va.us	Lancaster	VA	22503	804-462-5030	
Breaks Interstate Park PO Box 100 *TF:* 800-982-5122 ■ *Web:* www.parks.ky.gov	Breaks	VA	24607	800-982-5122	
Caledon Natural Area 11617 Caledon Rd *Web:* www.dcr.state.va.us	King George	VA	22485	540-663-3861	
Chippokes Plantation State Park 695 Chippokes Pk Rd *Web:* www.dcr.state.va.us	Surry	VA	23883	757-294-3625	
Claytor Lake State Park 6620 Ben H Boden Dr *Web:* www.dcr.state.va.us	Dublin	VA	24084	540-643-2500	
Clinch Mountain Wildlife Management Area 2387 Tumbling Creek Rd *Web:* www.dgif.state.va.us	Saltville	VA	24370	276-783-3422	
Douthat State Park 14239 Douthat State Pk Rd *Web:* www.dcr.state.va.us	Millboro	VA	24460	540-862-8100	
Fairy Stone State Park 967 Fairystone Lake Dr *Web:* www.dcr.state.va.us	Stuart	VA	24171	276-930-2424	
False Cape State Park 4001 Sandpiper Rd *TF:* 800-933-7275 ■ *Web:* www.dcr.state.va.us	Virginia Beach	VA	23456	757-426-7128	426-0055
First Landing State Park 2500 Shore Dr *Web:* www.dcr.state.va.us	Virginia Beach	VA	23451	757-412-2300	
George Washington's Grist Mill Historical State Park Mount Vernon Hwy Rte 235 *Web:* www.dcr.state.va.us/parks/georgewa.htm	Mount Vernon	VA	22121	703-780-3383	

Phone | Fax

Grayson Highlands State Park
829 Grayson Highland Ln ... Mouth of Wilson VA 24363 276-579-7092
Web: www.dcr.state.va.us

Holliday Lake State Park 2759 State Pk Rd ... Appomattox VA 24522 434-248-6308
Web: www.dcr.state.va.us

Hungry Mother State Park 2854 Pk Blvd ... Marion VA 24354 276-781-7400
Web: www.dcr.state.va.us

James River State Park 751 Pk Rd ... Gladstone VA 24553 434-933-4355
Web: www.dcr.state.va.us

Kiptopeke State Park 3540 Kiptopeke Dr ... Cape Charles VA 23310 757-331-2267
Web: www.dcr.state.va.us

Lake Anna State Park 6800 Lawyers Rd ... Spotsylvania VA 22553 540-854-5503
Web: www.dcr.state.va.us

Leesylvania State Park
2001 Daniel K Ludwig Dr ... Woodbridge VA 22191 703-730-8205
Web: www.dcr.state.va.us

Mason Neck State Park 7301 High Pt Rd ... Lorton VA 22079 703-550-0960
Web: www.dcr.state.va.us

Natural Tunnel State Park Rt 3 PO Box 250 ... Duffield VA 24244 276-940-2674
Web: www.dcr.state.va.us

New River Trail State Park
176 Orphanage Dr ... Foster Falls VA 24360 276-699-6778
Web: www.dcr.state.va.us

Occoneechee State Park
1192 Occoneechee Pk Rd ... Clarksville VA 23927 434-374-2210
Web: www.dcr.state.va.us

Pocahontas State Park 10301 State Pk Rd ... Chesterfield VA 23832 804-796-4255 796-4004
TF: 800-933-7275 ■ *Web:* www.dcr.state.va.us

Raymond R. "Andy" Guest Jr. Shenandoah River State Park
Daughter of Stars Dr PO Box 235 ... Bentonville VA 22610 540-622-6840 622-6841
Web: www.dcr.state.va.us

Sailor's Creek Battlefield State Park
6541 Saylers Creek Rd ... Rice VA 23966 804-561-7510
Web: www.dcr.virginia.gov

Shot Tower Historical State Park
Rt 1 PO Box 81X ... Austinville VA 24312 276-699-6778
Web: www.dcr.state.va.us

Sky Meadows State Park 11012 Edmonds Ln ... Delaplane VA 20144 540-592-3556
Web: www.dcr.state.va.us

Smith Mountain Lake State Park
1235 State Pk Rd ... Huddleston VA 24104 540-297-6066
Web: www.dcr.state.va.us

Southwest Virginia Museum Historical State Park
10 W 1st St ... Big Stone Gap VA 24219 276-523-1322
Web: www.dcr.state.va.us

Staunton River Battlefield State Park
1035 Fort Hill Tr ... Randolph VA 23962 434-454-4312
Web: www.dcr.state.va.us

Staunton River State Park
1170 Staunton Tr ... Scottsburg VA 24589 434-572-4623
Web: www.dcr.state.va.us

Twin Lakes State Park 788 Twin Lakes Rd ... Green Bay VA 23942 434-392-3435
TF: 800-933-7275 ■ *Web:* www.dcr.virginia.gov

Westmoreland State Park 1650 State Pk Rd ... Montross VA 22520 804-493-8821
Web: www.dcr.state.va.us

Wilderness Road State Park Rt 2 PO Box 115 ... Ewing VA 24248 276-445-3065
Web: www.dcr.state.va.us

York River State Park 5526 Riverview Rd ... Williamsburg VA 23188 757-566-3036
Web: www.dcr.state.va.us

WASHINGTON

Phone | Fax

Alta Lake State Park 40 Star Rt ... Pateros WA 98846 509-923-2473
Web: www.parks.wa.gov

Anderson Lake State Park PO Box 42650 ... Olympia WA 98504 360-385-1259
Web: www.parks.wa.gov/parkpage.asp?selectedpark=Anderson%20Lake

Battle Ground Lake State Park
18002 NE 249th St ... Battle Ground WA 98604 360-687-4621
TF: 888-226-7688 ■ *Web:* www.parks.wa.gov

Bay View State Park
10901 Bay View-Edison Rd ... Mount Vernon WA 98273 360-757-0227 757-1029
Web: www.parks.wa.gov

Beacon Rock State Park 34841 State Rd 14 ... Skamania WA 98648 509-427-8265 427-3242
Web: www.parks.wa.gov

Belfair State Park 410 NE Beck Rd ... Belfair WA 98528 360-275-0668 275-8734
Web: www.parks.wa.gov

Birch Bay State Park 5105 Helwig Rd ... Blaine WA 98230 360-371-2800 371-0455
Web: www.parks.wa.gov

Blake Island State Park PO Box 277 ... Manchester WA 98353 360-731-8330
Web: www.parks.wa.gov/parkpage.asp?selectedpark=Blake%20Island

Bogachiel State Park 185983 Hwy 101 ... Forks WA 98331 360-374-6356
Web: www.parks.wa.gov

Bridgeport State Park 191 Alta Lake Rd ... Pateros WA 98846 509-923-2473
Web: www.parks.wa.gov/parks/?selectedpark=Bridgeport

Bridle Trails State Park
c/o Lake Sammamish State Pk
20606 SE 56th St ... Issaquah WA 98027 425-455-7010
Web: www.parks.wa.gov

Brooks Memorial State Park 2465 Hwy 97 ... Goldendale WA 98620 509-773-4611
Web: www.parks.wa.gov

Camano Island State Park
2269 S Lowell Pt Rd ... Camano Island WA 98282 360-387-3031
Web: www.parks.wa.gov/parks/?selectedpark=Camano%20Island

Cape Disappointment State Park PO Box 488 ... Ilwaco WA 98624 360-642-3078
Web: www.parks.wa.gov/parkpage.asp?selectedpark=Cape%20Disappointment

Centennial Trail State Park
c/o Riverside State Pk
9711 W Charles Rd ... Nine Mile Falls WA 99206 509-465-5064
Web: www.parks.wa.gov/parks/?selectedpark=Centennial%20Trail

Columbia Hills State Park PO Box 426 ... Dallesport WA 98617 509-767-1159
Web: www.parks.wa.gov

Phone | Fax

Columbia Plateau Trail State Park
100 SW Main St ... Washtucna WA 99371 509-235-4696
Web: www.parks.wa.gov

Conconully State Park 119 W Broadway Ave ... Conconully WA 98819 509-826-7408
Web: www.parks.wa.gov

Curlew Lake State Park
974 Curlew Lake State Pk Rd ... Republic WA 99166 509-775-3592
Web: www.parks.wa.gov

Damon Point State Park
c/o Ocean City State Pk 148 State Rt 115 ... Hoquiam WA 98550 360-289-3553
Web: www.parks.wa.gov/parks/?selectedpark=Damon%20Point&subject=all

Daroga State Park 1 S Daroga Pk Rd ... Orondo WA 98843 509-664-6380
Web: www.parks.wa.gov

Dash Point State Park 5700 SW Dash Pt Rd ... Federal Way WA 98023 253-661-4955 661-4995
TF: 888-226-7688 ■ *Web:* www.parks.wa.gov

Deception Pass State Park
41229 Washington 20 ... Oak Harbor WA 98277 360-675-2417 675-8991
Web: www.parks.wa.gov

Dosewallips State Park PO Box K ... Brinnon WA 98320 888-226-7688
TF: 888-226-7688

Doug's Beach State Park
c/o Maryhill State Pk 50 Hwy 97 ... Goldendale WA 98620 509-773-5007
Web: www.parks.wa.gov/parkpage.asp?selectedpark=Doug%27s%20Beach

Fay Bainbridge State Park
15446 Sunrise Dr NE ... Bainbridge Island WA 98110 206-842-3931
Web: www.parks.wa.gov

Federation Forest State Park
49201 SE Enumclaw Chinook Pass ... Enumclaw WA 98022 360-663-2207
Web: www.parks.wa.gov

Fields Spring State Park 992 Pk Rd ... Anatone WA 99401 509-256-3332
Web: www.parks.wa.gov

Flaming Geyser State Park
23700 SE Flaming Geyser Rd ... Auburn WA 98092 253-931-3930
Web: www.parks.wa.gov

Fort Casey State Park 1280 S Engle Rd ... Coupeville WA 98239 360-678-4519
Web: www.parks.wa.gov

Fort Columbia State Park PO Box 488 ... Chinook WA 98614 360-642-3078
Web: www.parks.wa.gov

Fort Ebey State Park 400 Hill Valley Dr ... Coupeville WA 98239 360-678-4636
Web: www.parks.wa.gov

Fort Flagler State Park 10541 Flagler Rd ... Nordland WA 98358 360-385-1259
Web: www.parks.wa.gov

Fort Okanogan State Park
c/o Alta Lake State Pk 40 Star Rt ... Pateros WA 98846 509-923-2473
Web: www.parks.wa.gov/parkpage.asp?selectedpark=Fort%20Okanogan

Fort Simcoe State Park
5150 Fort Simcoe Rd ... White Swan WA 98952 509-874-2372
Web: www.parks.wa.gov

Fort Ward State Park
2241 Pleasant Beach ... Bainbridge Island WA 98110 206-842-3931
Web: www.parks.wa.gov/parks/?selectedpark=Fort%20Ward

Fort Worden State Park 200 Battery Way ... Port Townsend WA 98368 360-385-4730
Web: www.parks.wa.gov/fortworden

Ginkgo Petrified Forest State Park
4511 Huntzinger Rd ... Vantage WA 98950 509-856-2700
Web: www.parks.wa.gov

Goldendale Observatory State Park
1602 Observatory Dr ... Goldendale WA 98620 509-773-3141
Web: www.parks.wa.gov

Grayland Beach State Park
c/o Twin Harbors State Pk Hwy 105 ... Westport WA 98595 360-268-9717
Web: www.parks.wa.gov/parks/?selectedpark=Grayland%20Beach

Griffiths-Priday Ocean State Park
1111 Israel Rd SW ... Olympia WA 98504 360-902-8500
Web: www.parks.wa.gov/parks/?selectedpark=Griffiths-Priday

Hope Island State Park
c/o Jarrell Cove State Pk E 391 Wingert Rd ... Shelton WA 98584 360-426-9226
Web: www.parks.wa.gov

Ike Kinswa State Park 873 SR 122 ... Silver Creek WA 98585 360-983-3402
Web: www.parks.wa.gov

Illahee State Park 3540 NE Bahia Vista Dr ... Bremerton WA 98310 360-478-6460
Web: www.parks.wa.gov

Iron Horse State Park
c/o Ginkgo Petrified Forest State Pk
PO Box 1203 ... Vantage WA 98950 509-856-2700
Web: www.parks.wa.gov

Jarrell Cove State Park 391 E Wingert Rd ... Shelton WA 98584 360-426-9226
Web: www.parks.wa.gov

Joemma Beach State Park 20001 Bay Rd KPS ... Lakebay WA 98459 253-884-1944
Web: www.parks.wa.gov/parkpage.asp?selectedpark=Joemma%20Beach

Joseph Whidbey State Park 1111 Israel Rd SW ... Olympia WA 89504 360-902-8500
Web: www.parks.wa.gov/parks/?selectedpark=Joseph%20Whidbey

Kanaskat-Palmer State Park
32101 Kanaskat-Cumberland Rd ... Ravensdale WA 98051 360-886-0148
Web: www.parks.wa.gov

Kitsap Memorial State Park 202 NE Pk St ... Poulsbo WA 98370 360-779-3205
Web: www.parks.wa.gov

Kopachuck State Park 11101 56th St NW ... Gig Harbor WA 98335 253-265-3606
Web: www.parks.wa.gov

Lake Chelan State Park 7544 S Lakeshore Dr ... Chelan WA 98816 509-687-3710
Web: www.parks.wa.gov

Lake Easton State Park
150 Lake Easton State Pk Rd ... Easton WA 98925 509-656-2230
Web: www.parks.wa.gov

Lake Sammamish State Park 20606 SE 56th St ... Issaquah WA 98027 425-455-7010
Web: www.parks.wa.gov

Lake Sylvia State Park PO Box 701 ... Montesano WA 98563 360-249-3621
Web: www.parks.wa.gov

Lake Wenatchee State Park
21588 A Hwy 207 ... Leavenworth WA 98826 509-763-3101
Web: www.parks.wa.gov

Larrabee State Park 245 Chuckanut Dr ... Bellingham WA 98226 360-676-2093
Web: www.parks.wa.gov

Phone | Fax

Lewis & Clark State Park 4583 Jackson Hwy .... Winlock WA 98596 360-864-2643
Web: www.parks.wa.gov
Lewis & Clark Trail State Park 36149 Hwy 12 .... Dayton WA 99328 509-337-6457
Web: www.parks.wa.gov
Lime Kiln Point State Park
1567 Westside Rd .... Friday Harbor WA 98250 360-378-2044
Web: www.parks.wa.gov
Lincoln Rock State Park
13253 State Rt 2 .... East Wenatchee WA 98802 509-884-8702
Web: www.parks.wa.gov
Manchester State Park 7767 E Hilldale .... Port Orchard WA 98366 360-871-4065
Web: www.parks.wa.gov/parks/?selectedpark=Manchester
Maryhill State Park 50 Hwy 97 .... Goldendale WA 98620 509-773-5007
Web: www.parks.wa.gov/parkpage.asp?selectedpark=Maryhill
Millersylvania State Park 12245 Tilley Rd S .... Olympia WA 98512 360-753-1519 664-2180
Web: www.parks.wa.gov
Moran State Park 3572 Olga Rd .... Eastsound WA 98245 360-376-2326
Web: www.parks.wa.gov
Mount Pilchuck State Park
c/o Wenburg State Pk
15430 E Lake Goodwin Rd .... Stanwood WA 98292 360-652-7417
Web: www.parks.wa.gov/parks/?selectedpark=Mount%20Pilchuck&subject=all
Mount Spokane State Park
N 26107 Mt Spokane Pk Dr .... Mead WA 90021 509-238-4258 238-4078
Web: www.parks.wa.gov/parks/?selectedpark=Mount%20Spokane
Mystery Bay State Park 1111 Israel Rd SW .... Olympia WA 98504 360-902-8500
Web: www.parks.wa.gov/parks/?selectedpark=Mystery%20Bay
Nolte State Park 36921 Veazie Cumberland Rd .... Enumclaw WA 98022 360-825-4646
Web: www.parks.wa.gov
Ocean City State Park 148 State Rt 115 .... Hoquiam WA 98550 360-289-3553
Web: www.parks.wa.gov
Olallie State Park
c/o Lake Sammamish State Pk
20606 SE 56th St .... Issaquah WA 98027 360-455-7010
Web: www.parks.wa.gov/parks/?selectedpark=Olallie
Old Fort Townsend State Park
1370 Old Fort Townsend Rd .... Port Townsend WA 98368 360-385-3595
Web: www.parks.wa.gov
Olmstead Place State Park
921 N Ferguson Rd .... Ellensburg WA 98926 509-925-1943
Web: www.parks.wa.gov
Osoyoos Lake State Park 2207 Juniper .... Oroville WA 98844 509-476-3321
Web: www.parks.wa.gov
Pacific Pines State Park 25904 R St .... Ocean Park WA 98640 360-902-8844
Web: www.parks.wa.gov/parks/?selectedpark=Pacific%20Pines
Palouse Falls State Park 10152 SR 127 .... Pomeroy WA 99347 509-549-3551
Web: www.parks.wa.gov
Paradise Point State Park
33914 NW Paradise Pk Rd .... Ridgefield WA 98642 360-263-2350
Web: www.parks.wa.gov
Peace Arch State Park PO Box 87 .... Blaine WA 98230 360-332-8221
Web: www.parks.wa.gov
Pearrygin Lake State Park 561 Bear Creek Rd .... Winthrop WA 98862 509-996-2370
Web: www.parks.wa.gov
Penrose Point State Park 321 158th KPS .... Lakebay WA 98349 253-884-2514
Web: www.parks.wa.gov/parkpage.asp?selectedpark=Penrose%20Point
Peshastin Pinnacles State Park
c/o Wenatchee Confluence State Pk
333 Old Stn Rd .... Wenatchee WA 98801 509-664-6373
Web: www.parks.wa.gov/parks/?selectedpark=Peshastin%20Pinnacles
Potholes State Park 6762 Hwy 262 SE .... Othello WA 99344 509-346-2759
Web: www.parks.wa.gov
Potlatch State Park PO Box 1051 .... Hoodsport WA 98548 360-877-5361
Web: www.parks.wa.gov
Rainbow Falls State Park 4008 Washington 6 .... Chehalis WA 98532 360-291-3767 291-3377
Web: www.parks.wa.gov
Rasar State Park 38730 Cape Horn Rd .... Concrete WA 98237 360-826-3942
Web: www.parks.wa.gov
Riverside State Park 1111 Israel Rd SW .... Olympia WA 98504 360-902-8844
Web: www.parks.wa.gov/parks/?selectedpark=Riverside
Rockport State Park 51905 Washington 20 .... Rockport WA 98283 360-853-8461
Web: www.parks.wa.gov
Sacajawea State Park 2503 Sacajawea Pk Rd .... Pasco WA 99301 509-545-2361
Web: www.parks.wa.gov
Saint Edward State Park 14445 Juanita Dr NE .... Kenmore WA 98028 425-823-2992
Web: www.parks.wa.gov
Saltwater State Park 25205 8th Pl S .... Des Moines WA 98198 253-661-4956
Web: www.parks.wa.gov
Scenic Beach State Park PO Box 7 .... Seabeck WA 98380 360-830-5079
Web: www.parks.wa.gov
Schafer State Park W 1365 Schafer Pk Rd .... Elma WA 98541 360-482-3852
Web: www.parks.wa.gov
Seaquest State Park 3030 Spirit Lake Hwy .... Castle Rock WA 98611 360-274-8633
Web: www.parks.wa.gov
Sequim Bay State Park 269035 Hwy 101 .... Sequim WA 98382 360-683-4235
Web: www.parks.wa.gov
Shine Tidelands State Park 202 NE Pk St .... Poulsbo WA 98370 360-779-3205
Web: www.parks.wa.gov
South Whidbey Island State Park
4128 Smugglers Cove Rd .... Freeland WA 98249 360-331-4559
Web: www.parks.wa.gov
Spencer Spit State Park
521-A Bakerview Rd .... Lopez Island WA 98261 360-468-3176
Web: www.parks.wa.gov
Squilchuck State Park
c/o Wenatchee Confluence State Pk
333 Olds Stn Rd .... Wenatchee WA 98801 509-664-6373
Web: www.parks.wa.gov/parks/?selectedpark=Squilchuck
Steamboat Rock State Park
51052 Washington 155 .... Electric City WA 99123 509-633-1304
Web: www.parks.wa.gov

Steptoe Battlefield State Park
c/o Central Ferry State Pk
10152 State Hwy 127 .... Pomeroy WA 99347 509-549-3551
Web: www.parks.wa.gov/parks/?selectedpark=Steptoe%20Battlefield&subject=all
Steptoe Butte State Park
c/o Central Ferry State Pk
10152 State Hwy 127 .... Pomeroy WA 99347 509-549-3551
Web: www.parks.wa.gov/parks/?selectedpark=Steptoe%20Butte
Sun Lakes State Park 34875 Pk Ln Rd NE .... Coulee City WA 99115 509-632-5583
Web: www.parks.wa.gov
Tolmie State Park 7730 61st Ave NE .... Olympia WA 98506 360-456-6464 459-0104
Web: www.parks.wa.gov
Triton Cove State Park 1111 Israel Rd SW .... Olympia WA 98504 360-902-8844
Web: www.parks.wa.gov/parks/?selectedpark=Triton%20Cove
Twanoh State Park 12190 E Hwy 106 .... Union WA 98592 360-275-2222
Web: www.parks.wa.gov
Twenty-Five Mile Creek State Park
20530 S Lakeshore Rd .... Chelan WA 98816 509-687-3710 687-0350
Web: www.parks.wa.gov
Twin Harbors Beach State Park Hwy 105 .... Westport WA 98595 360-268-9717
Web: www.parks.wa.gov/parkpage.asp?selectedpark=Twin%20Harbors
Wallace Falls State Park
14503 Wallace Lake Rd .... Gold Bar WA 98251 360-793-0420
Web: www.parks.wa.gov
Wenatchee Confluence State Park
333 Olds Stn Rd .... Wenatchee WA 98801 509-664-6373
Web: www.parks.wa.gov
Wenberg State Park 15430 E Lake Goodwin Rd .... Stanwood WA 98292 360-652-7417
Web: www.parks.wa.gov/parkpage.asp?selectedpark=Wenberg
Westport Light State Park PO Box 42650 .... Olympia WA 98504 360-268-9717
Web: www.parks.wa.gov/parkpage.asp?selectedpark=Westport%20Light
Yakima Sportsman State Park 904 Keys Rd .... Yakima WA 98901 509-575-2774
Web: www.parks.wa.gov

WEST VIRGINIA

Phone | Fax

Audra State Park Rt 4 PO Box 564 .... Buckhannon WV 26201 304-457-1162
Web: www.audrastatepark.com
Babcock State Park HC 35 PO Box 150 .... Clifftop WV 25831 304-438-3004
Web: www.babcocksp.com
Beartown State Park HC 64 PO Box 189 .... Hillsboro WV 24946 304-653-4254
TF: 800-225-5982 ■ *Web:* www.beartownstatepark.com
Beech Fork State Park
5601 Long Branch Rd .... Barboursville WV 25504 304-528-5794
Web: www.beechforksp.com
Berkeley Springs State Park
121 S Washington St .... Berkeley Springs WV 25411 304-258-2711
Web: www.berkeleyspringssp.com
Blackwater Falls State Park PO Drawer 490 .... Davis WV 26260 304-259-5216
Web: www.blackwaterfalls.com
Blennerhassett Island Historical State Park
137 Juliana St .... Parkersburg WV 26101 304-420-4800
Web: www.blennerhassettislandstatepark.com
Bluestone State Park HC 78 PO Box 3 .... Hinton WV 25951 304-466-2805
Web: www.bluestonesp.com
Cabwaylingo State Forest Rt 1 PO Box 85 .... Dunlow WV 25511 304-385-4255
Web: www.cabwaylingo.com
Cacapon Resort State Park
818 Cacapon Lodge Dr .... Berkeley Springs WV 25411 304-258-1022
Web: www.cacaponresort.com
Calvin Price State Forest
c/o Watoga State Pk HC 82 PO Box 252 .... Marlinton WV 24954 304-799-4087
Web: www.wvforestry.com
Camp Creek State Forest
2390 Camp Creek Rd .... Camp Creek WV 25820 304-425-9481
Web: www.wvforestry.com
Camp Creek State Park PO Box 119 .... Camp Creek WV 25820 304-425-9481
Web: www.campcreekstatepark.com
Canaan Valley Resort State Park
230 Main Lodge Rd .... Davis WV 26260 304-866-4121 866-2172
TF: 800-622-4121 ■ *Web:* www.canaanresort.com
Carnifex Ferry Battlefield State Park
Rt 2 PO Box 435 .... Summersville WV 26651 304-872-0825
Web: www.carnifexferrybattlefieldstatepark.com
Cass Scenic Railroad State Park 242 Main St .... Cass WV 24927 304-456-4300
Web: www.cassrailroad.com
Cathedral State Park Rt 1 PO Box 370 .... Aurora WV 26705 304-735-3771
Web: www.cathedralstatepark.com
Cedar Creek State Park 2947 Cedar Creek Rd .... Glenville WV 26351 304-462-7158
Web: www.cedarcreeksp.com
Chief Logan State Park General Delivery .... Logan WV 25601 304-792-7125
Web: www.chiefloganstatepark.com
Coopers Rock State Forest
Rt 1 PO Box 270 .... Bruceton Mills WV 26525 304-594-1561 594-9024
Web: www.coopersrockstateforest.com
Droop Mountain Battlefield State Park
HC 64 PO Box 189 .... Hillsboro WV 24946 304-653-4254
Web: www.droopmountainbattlefield.com
Greenbrier River Trail
c/o Watoga State Pk HC 82 PO Box 252 .... Marlinton WV 24954 304-799-4087
Web: www.greenbrierrivertrail.com
Greenbrier State Forest HC 30 PO Box 154 .... Caldwell WV 24925 304-536-1944
Web: www.greenbriersf.com
Hawks Nest State Park PO Box 857 .... Ansted WV 25812 304-658-5212 658-4549
TF: 800-225-5982 ■ *Web:* www.hawksnestsp.com
Holly River State Park PO Box 70 .... Hacker Valley WV 26222 304-493-6353
Web: www.hollyriver.com
Kanawha State Forest Rt 2 PO Box 285 .... Charleston WV 25314 304-558-3500 558-3508
Web: www.kanawhastateforest.com
Kumbrabow State Forest PO Box 65 .... Huttonsville WV 26273 304-335-2219
Web: www.kumbrabow.com

Phone | Fax

Little Beaver State Park 1402 Grandview Rd — Beaver WV 25813 — 304-763-2494
Web: www.littlebeaverstatepark.com

Lost River State Park 321 Pk Dr — Mathias WV 26812 — 304-897-5372
Web: www.lostriversp.com

Moncove Lake State Park HC 83 PO Box 73A — Gap Mills WV 24941 — 304-772-3450
Web: www.moncovelakestatepark.com

North Bend Rail Trail
c/o N Bend State Pk Rt 1 PO Box 221 — Cairo WV 26337 — 304-643-2931
Web: www.wvparks.com

North Bend State Park Rt 1 PO Box 221 — Cairo WV 26337 — 304-643-2931
Web: www.northbendsp.com

Panther State Forest PO Box 287 — Panther WV 24872 — 304-938-2252
Web: www.pantherstateforest.com

Pinnacle Rock State Park PO Box 1 — Bramwell WV 24715 — 304-248-8565
Web: www.pinnaclerockstatepark.com

Pipestem Resort State Park PO Box 150 — Pipestem WV 25979 — *304-466-1800* — 466-2803
Web: www.pipestemresort.com

Pricketts Fort State Park Rt 3 PO Box 403 — Fairmont WV 26554 — 304-367-2731 — 363-3857
Web: www.prickettsfortstatepark.com

Seneca State Forest Rt 1 PO Box 140 — Dunmore WV 24934 — 304-799-6213
Web: www.senecastateforest.com

Tomlinson Run State Park PO Box 97 — New Manchester WV 26056 — 304-564-3651
Web: www.tomlinsonrunsp.com

Tu-Endie-Wei State Park PO Box 486 — Point Pleasant WV 25550 — 304-675-0869
Web: www.tu-endie-weistatepark.com

Twin Falls Resort State Park PO Box 1023 — Mullens WV 25882 — 304-294-4000
Web: www.twinfallsresort.com

Tygart Lake State Park Rt 1 PO Box 260 — Grafton WV 26354 — 304-265-6144
Web: www.tygartlake.com

Valley Falls State Park Rt 6 PO Box 244 — Fairmont WV 26554 — 304-367-2719 — 367-2763
Web: www.valleyfallsstatepark.com

Watoga State Park HC 82 PO Box 252 — Marlinton WV 24954 — 304-799-4087 — 653-4620
TF: 800-225-5982 ■ Web: www.watoga.com

Watters Smith Memorial State Park
PO Box 296 — Lost Creek WV 26385 — 304-745-3081
Web: www.watterssmithstatepark.com

WISCONSIN

Phone | Fax

Amnicon Falls State Park 6294 S State Rd 35 — Superior WI 54880 — 715-398-3000
Web: www.dnr.state.wi.us/ORG/land/parks/specific/amnicon

Aztalan State Park 1213 S Main St — Lake Mills WI 53551 — 920-648-8774 — 648-5166
Web: www.dnr.state.wi.us

Big Bay State Park PO Box 589 — Bayfield WI 54814 — 715-747-6425
Web: www.dnr.state.wi.us

Big Foot Beach State Park 1452 Wells St — Lake Geneva WI 53147 — 262-248-2528
Web: www.dnr.state.wi.us

Black River State Forest
910 Hwy 54 E — Black River Falls WI 54615 — 715-284-4103
Web: www.dnr.state.wi.us

Blue Mound State Park 4350 Mounds Pk Rd — Blue Mounds WI 53517 — 608-437-5711
Web: www.dnr.state.wi.us

Browntown-Cadiz Springs State Recreation Area
PO Box 805 — New Glarus WI 53574 — 608-966-3777
Web: www.dnr.state.wi.us/org/land/parks/specific/browntown

Brule River State Forest 6250 S Ranger Rd — Brule WI 54820 — 715-372-5678 — 372-4836
Web: www.dnr.state.wi.us

Brunet Island State Park 23125 255th St — Cornell WI 54732 — 715-239-6888
Web: www.dnr.state.wi.us

Buckhorn State Park W8450 Buckhorn Pk Ave — Necedah WI 54646 — 608-565-2789
Web: www.dnr.state.wi.us

Capital Springs Centennial State Recreation Area
3101 Lake Farm Rd — Madison WI 53711 — 608-224-3606
Web: www.dnr.state.wi.us

Chippewa Moraine Ice Age State Recreation Area
13394 County Hwy M — New Auburn WI 54757 — 715-967-2800 — 967-2801
Web: www.dnr.state.wi.us

Copper Culture State Park N10008 Paust Ln — Crivitz WI 54114 — 715-757-3979
Web: www.dnr.wi.gov

Copper Falls State Park 36764 Copper Falls Rd — Mellen WI 54546 — 715-274-5123
Web: www.dnr.state.wi.us

Council Grounds State Park
N1895 Council Grounds Dr — Merrill WI 54452 — 715-536-8773 — 536-6772

Devil's Lake State Park S5975 Pk Rd — Baraboo WI 53913 — 608-356-8301 — 356-4281
Web: www.dnr.state.wi.us

Flambeau River State Forest W1613 County Rd — Winter WI 54896 — 715-332-5271
Web: www.dnr.state.wi.us

Governor Dodge State Park 4175 Hwy 23 — Dodgeville WI 53533 — 608-935-2315
Web: www.dnr.state.wi.us

Governor Knowles State Forest 325 SR 70 — Grantsburg WI 54840 — 715-463-2897
Web: www.dnr.state.wi.us

Governor Nelson State Park
5140 County Hwy M — Waunakee WI 53597 — 608-831-3005 — 831-4071
Web: www.dnr.state.wi.us

Governor Thompson State Park
N 10008 Paust Ln — Crivitz WI 54115 — 715-757-3979 — 757-3779
Web: www.dnr.state.wi.us/org/land/parks/specific/govthompson

Harrington Beach State Park 531 County Rd D — Belgium WI 53004 — 262-285-3015
Web: www.dnr.state.wi.us

Hartman Creek State Park
N2480 Hartman Creek Rd — Waupaca WI 54981 — 715-258-2372
Web: www.dnr.state.wi.us

Havenwoods State Forest 6141 N Hopkins St — Milwaukee WI 53209 — 414-527-0232 — 527-0761
Web: www.dnr.state.wi.us/org/land/parks/specific/havenwoods

Heritage Hill State Historical Park
2640 S Webster Ave — Green Bay WI 54301 — 920-448-5150
Web: www.heritagehillgb.org

High Cliff State Park N7630 State Pk Rd — Sherwood WI 54169 — 920-989-1106
Web: www.dnr.state.wi.us

Hoffman Hills Recreation Area
921 Brickyard Rd — Menomonie WI 54751 — 715-232-1242
Web: www.dnr.state.wi.us

Interstate State Park PO Box 703 — Saint Croix Falls WI 54024 — 715-483-3747
Web: www.dnr.state.wi.us

Kettle Moraine State Forest - Lapham Peak Unit
W329 N846 County Hwy C — Delafield WI 53018 — 262-646-3025
Web: www.dnr.state.wi.us

Kettle Moraine State Forest - Loew Lake Unit
c/o Pike Lake Unit 3544 Kettle Moraine Rd — Hartford WI 53027 — 262-670-3400 — 670-3411

Kettle Moraine State Forest - Northern Unit
N1765 Hwy G — Campbellsport WI 53010 — 262-626-2116
Web: www.dnr.state.wi.us

Kettle Moraine State Forest - Pike Lake Unit
3344 Kettle Moraine Rd — Hartford WI 53027 — 262-670-3400
Web: www.dnr.state.wi.us

Kettle Moraine State Forest - Southern Unit
S91 W39091 Hwy 59 — Eagle WI 53119 — 262-594-6201
Web: www.dnr.state.wi.us

Kinnickinnic State Park W11983 820th Ave — River Falls WI 54022 — 715-425-1129 — 425-0010

Kohler-Andrae State Park 1020 Beach Pk Ln — Sheboygan WI 53081 — 920-451-4080
Web: www.dnr.state.wi.us

Lake Kegonsa State Park 2405 Door Creek Rd — Stoughton WI 53589 — 608-873-9695 — 873-0674
TF: 888-947-2757 ■ Web: www.dnr.state.wi.us

Lake Wissota State Park
18127 County Hwy 'O' — Chippewa Falls WI 54729 — 715-382-4574 — 382-5187
Web: www.dnr.state.wi.us

Lakeshore State Park
2300 N Martin Luther King Jr Dr — Milwaukee WI 53212 — 414-263-8570
Web: www.dnr.state.wi.us/org/land/parks/specific/lakeshore

Mill Bluff State Park PO Box 99 — Ontario WI 54651 — 608-427-6692

Mirror Lake State Park E10320 Fern Dell Rd — Baraboo WI 53913 — 608-254-2333

Nelson Dewey State Park PO Box 658 — Cassville WI 53806 — 608-725-5374

New Glarus Woods State Park
W5446 County Hwy NN — New Glarus WI 53574 — 608-527-2335
Web: www.dnr.state.wi.us/org/land/parks/specific/ngwoods

Newport State Park 475 County Rd NP — Ellison Bay WI 54210 — 920-854-2500 — 854-1914
Web: www.dnr.state.wi.us

Northern Highland - American Legion State Forest
4125 County Hwy M — Boulder Junction WI 54512 — 715-385-2727
Web: www.dnr.state.wi.us

Pattison State Park 6294 S State Rd 35 — Superior WI 54880 — 715-399-3111
Web: www.dnr.state.wi.us/org/land/parks/specific/pattison

Peninsula State Park 9462 Shore Rd — Fish Creek WI 54212 — 920-868-3258
Web: www.dnr.state.wi.us

Perrot State Park Rt 1 PO Box 407 — Trempealeau WI 54661 — 608-534-6409

Peshtigo River State Forest N 10008 Paust Ln — Crivitz WI 54114 — 715-757-3965
Web: www.dnr.state.wi.us/org/land/Forestry/StateForests/meet.htm#Peshtigo

Point Beach State Forest
9400 County Hwy 'O' — Two Rivers WI 54241 — 920-794-7480
Web: www.dnr.state.wi.us

Potawatomi State Park 3740 County PD — Sturgeon Bay WI 54235 — 920-746-2890
Web: www.dnr.state.wi.us/org/land/parks/specific/Potawatomi

Rib Mountain State Park 5301 Rib Mountain Dr — Wausau WI 54401 — 715-842-2522

Richard Bong State Recreation Area
26313 Burlington Rd — Kansasville WI 53139 — 262-878-5600 — 878-5615
Web: www.dnr.state.wi.us

Roche-A-Cri State Park 1767 Hwy 13 — Friendship WI 53934 — 608-339-6881
Web: www.dnr.state.wi.us

Rock Island State Park
Rt 1 PO Box 118A — Washington Island WI 54246 — 920-847-2235
Web: www.dnr.state.wi.us

Rocky Arbor State Park
c/o Mirror Lake State Pk E10320 Fern Dell Rd — Baraboo WI 53913 — 608-254-8001

Tower Hill State Park 5808 County Rd C — Spring Green WI 53588 — 608-588-2116

Whitefish Dunes State Park
3275 County Hwy WD — Sturgeon Bay WI 54235 — 920-823-2400
Web: www.dnr.state.wi.us/org/land/parks/specific/whitefish

Wildcat Mountain State Park
E13660 SR 33 PO Box 99 — Ontario WI 54651 — 608-337-4775
Web: www.dnr.state.wi.us

Willow River State Park 1034 County Hwy A — Hudson WI 54016 — 715-386-5931 — 386-0431
Web: www.dnr.state.wi.us

Wyalusing State Park 13081 State Pk Ln — Bagley WI 53801 — 608-996-2261 — 996-2410
Web: www.dnr.state.wi.us

Yellowstone Lake State Park
8495 Lake Rd — Blanchardville WI 53516 — 608-523-4427
Web: www.dnr.state.wi.us

WYOMING

Phone | Fax

Bear River State Park 601 Bear River Dr — Evanston WY 82930 — 307-789-6547
Web: www.wyoparks.state.wy.us

Boysen State Park 15 Ash St — Shoshoni WY 82649 — 307-876-2796
Web: www.wyoparks.state.wy.us

Buffalo Bill State Park 47 Lakeside Rd — Cody WY 82414 — 307-587-9227
Web: www.wyoparks.state.wy.us

Connor Battlefield State Historic Site
Hwy 14 — Ranchester WY 82842 — 307-684-7629
Web: wyoparks.state.wy.us/Site/SiteInfo.aspx?siteID=15

Curt Gowdy State Park 1319 Hynds Lodge Rd — Cheyenne WY 82009 — 307-632-7946 — 635-1056
Web: www.wyoparks.state.wy.us

Edness K. Wilkins State Park
8704 E US Hwy 20 26 — Evansville WY 82636 — 307-577-5150
Web: www.wyomingtourism.org/overview/Edness-K--Wilkins-State-Park/2983

Fort Bridger State Historic Site
PO Box 35 — Fort Bridger WY 82933 — 307-782-3842
Web: www.wyoparks.state.wy.us

Fort Fetterman State Historic Site
752 Hwy 93 — Douglas WY 82633 — 307-684-7629
Web: www.wyoparks.state.wy.us

	City	State	ZIP	Phone	Fax
Fort Fred Steele State Historic Site 80 Exit 228 *Web:* wyoparks.state.wy.us	Sinclair	WY	82334	307-320-3013	
Fort Phil Kearny State Historic Site PO Box 520 *Web:* wyoparks.state.wy.us	Story	WY	82842	307-684-7629	
Glendo State Park PO Box 398 *Web:* www.wyoparks.state.wy.us	Glendo	WY	82213	307-735-4433	
Guernsey State Park PO Box 429 *Web:* wyoparks.state.wy.us/Site/SiteInfo.aspx?siteID=7	Guernsey	WY	82214	307-836-2334	
Hawk Springs State Recreation Area 2301 Central Ave *Web:* wyoparks.state.wy.us/Permits/Index.aspx	Cheyenne	WY	82002	307-777-6323	
Historic Governors' Mansion 300 E 21st St	Cheyenne	WY	82009	307-777-7878	
Hot Springs State Park 220 Pk St *Web:* www.wyoparks.state.wy.us	Thermopolis	WY	82443	307-864-2176	
Independence Rock State Historic Site US Hwy 220 MM 63 *Web:* www.wyomingtourism.org/overview/Independence-Rock-State-Historic-Site/3337	Casper	WY	82601	307-577-5150	
Keyhole State Park 22 Marina Rd *Web:* www.wyoparks.state.wy.us	Moorcroft	WY	82721	307-756-3596	
Medicine Lodge State Archaeological Site PO Box 62 *Web:* www.wyoparks.state.wy.us	Hyattville	WY	82428	307-469-2234	
Seminoe State Park HCR 67 PO Box 30 *Web:* wyoparks.state.wy.us	Sinclair	WY	82334	307-320-3013	
Sinks Canyon State Park 3079 Sinks Canyon Rd *Web:* www.wyoparks.state.wy.us	Lander	WY	82520	307-332-3077	
South Pass City State Historic Site 125 S Pass Main *Web:* www.wyoparks.state.wy.us	South Pass City	WY	82520	307-332-3684	
Trail End State Historic Site 400 Clarendon Ave *Web:* www.trailend.org	Sheridan	WY	82801	307-674-4589	672-1720
Wyoming Territorial Prison State Historic Site 975 Snowy Range Rd *Web:* www.wyoprisonpark.org	Laramie	WY	82070	307-746-6161	

569 PARTY GOODS

	City	State	ZIP	Phone	Fax
Alin Party Supplies Co 14150 Artesia Blvd *Web:* www.alinpartysupply.com	Cerritos	CA	90703	562-282-0422	282-0432
Amscan Inc 80 Grasslands Rd *TF:* 800-284-4333 ■ *Web:* www.amscan.com	Elmsford	NY	10523	914-345-2020	345-3884
Balloons Everywhere Inc 16474 Greeno Rd *TF:* 800-239-2000 ■ *Web:* www.balloons.com	Fairhope	AL	36532	251-210-2100	210-2105
Beistle Co 1 Beistle Plaza *Web:* www.beistle.com	Shippensburg	PA	17257	717-532-2131	532-7789
Designware Inc 54 Fieldstone-Bashan Dr *Web:* www.designwareinc.com	East Haddam	CT	06423	860-873-8938	873-9993
iParty Corp 270 Bridge St Suite 301 *AMEX:* IPT ■ *TF:* 888-727-8970 ■ *Web:* www.iparty.com	Dedham	MA	02026	781-329-3952	326-7143
Paper Shack & Party Store Inc 2430 E Texas St *Web:* www.papershackpartystore.com	Bossier City	LA	71111	318-746-8636	747-6091
Paper Store Inc 20 Main St *Web:* www.thepaperstore.com	Acton	MA	01720	978-263-2198	263-2466
Party America 980 Atlantic Ave Suite 103 *Web:* www.partyamerica.com	Alameda	CA	94501	510-747-1800	747-1810
Party City Corp 25 Green Pond Rd Suite 1 *TF:* 800-727-8924 ■ *Web:* www.partycity.com	Rockaway	NJ	07866	925-965-7112	
Party Fair Inc 4345 US Hwy 9 *Web:* www.partyfair.com	Freehold	NJ	07728	732-780-1110	780-5174
Stumps Inc 1 Party Pl PO Box 305 *TF:* 800-348-5084 ■ *Web:* www.stumpsparty.com	South Whitley	IN	46787	260-723-5171	723-6979

570 PATTERNS - INDUSTRIAL

	City	State	ZIP	Phone	Fax
Allen Pattern of Michigan 202 McGrath Pl	Battle Creek	MI	49014	269-963-4131	963-4327
Anderson Global Inc 500 W Sherman Blvd *Web:* www.andersonglobal.com	Muskegon Heights	MI	49444	231-733-2164	733-1288
Central Pattern Co 8830 Pershall Rd *Web:* www.centralpattern.com	Hazelwood	MO	63042	314-524-3626	522-8399
Cunningham Pattern & Engineering Inc 4399 US 31 N *Web:* www.cpepattern.com	Columbus	IN	47201	812-379-9571	379-9574
D & F Corp 42455 Merrill Rd *TF:* 800-959-3456 ■ *Web:* www.d-f.com	Sterling Heights	MI	48314	586-254-5300	254-5610
Foley Pattern Co Inc 500 W 11th St PO Box 150	Auburn	IN	46706	260-925-4113	925-4115
Freeman Mfg & Supply Co 1101 Moore Rd *TF:* 800-321-8511 ■ *Web:* www.freemansupply.com	Avon	OH	44011	440-934-1902	934-7200
General Pattern Co Inc 3075 84th Ln NE *Web:* www.generalpattern.com	Blaine	MN	55449	763-780-3518	780-3770
Gopher Pattern Works Inc 422 Roosevelt St NE	Minneapolis	MN	55413	612-331-5512	331-6513
Hub Pattern Corp 2113 Salem Ave *TF:* 800-482-3505 ■ *Web:* www.hubcorp.net	Roanoke	VA	24016	540-342-3505	343-5337
Jacob Pattern Works Inc 449 Old Reading Pike	Pottstown	PA	19464	610-326-1100	326-7981
Kakivik Asset Management LLC 560 E 34th Ave Suite 200 *Web:* www.kakivik.com	Anchorage	AK	99503	907-770-9400	770-9450
Paragon Pattern & Mfg Co 2620 Pk St	Muskegon Heights	MI	49444	231-733-1582	739-1276
Production Pattern Co 560 Solon Rd *Web:* www.prodpatt.com	Bedford	OH	44146	440-439-3243	439-0918

	City	State	ZIP	Phone	Fax
United Industries Inc 1901 Revere Beach Pkwy *Web:* www.united-ind.com	Everett	MA	02149	617-387-9500	387-6331

571 PATTERNS - SEWING

	City	State	ZIP	Phone	Fax
Bonfit America Inc 8460 Higuera St *TF:* 800-526-6348 ■ *Web:* www.bonfit.com	Culver City	CA	90232	310-204-7880	204-7893
Kwik-Sew Pattern Co Inc 3000 Washington Ave N *TF:* 888-594-5739 ■ *Web:* www.kwiksew.com	Minneapolis	MN	55411	612-521-7651	521-1662
McCall Pattern Co 615 McCall Rd **Fax Area Code:* 785 ■ *TF:* 800-255-2762 ■ *Web:* www.mccall.com	Manhattan	KS	66502	800-255-2762	776-1471*
Simplicity Pattern Co Inc 2 Pk Ave 12th Fl *TF:* 888-588-2700 ■ *Web:* www.simplicity.com	New York	NY	10016	212-372-0500	372-0628
Stretch & Sew Inc 2035 S Elcamino Dr *TF:* 800-547-7717 ■ *Web:* www.stretch-and-sew.com	Tempe	AZ	85282	480-966-1462	966-1914

572 PAWN SHOPS

	City	State	ZIP	Phone	Fax
Camco Inc 4635 W Flamingo Rd *TF:* 800-511-2568 ■ *Web:* www.cashamerica.com	Las Vegas	NV	89103	702-252-7296	
Cash America International Inc 1600 W 7th St *NYSE:* CSH ■ **Fax:* Mktg ■ *TF:* 800-223-8738 ■ *Web:* www.cashamerica.com	Fort Worth	TX	76102	817-335-1100	570-1225*
EZCORP Inc 1901 Capital Pkwy *NASDAQ:* EZPW ■ *TF:* 800-873-7296 ■ *Web:* www.ezcorp.com	Austin	TX	78746	512-314-3400	314-3404
EZPAWN 1901 Capital Pkwy *TF:* 800-873-7296 ■ *Web:* www.ezpawn.com	Austin	TX	78746	512-314-3400	314-3404
First Cash Financial Services Inc 690 E Lamar Blvd Suite 400 *NASDAQ:* FCFS ■ *Web:* www.firstcash.com	Arlington	TX	76011	817-460-3947	461-7019
PawnMart Inc 6400 Atlantic Blvd Suite 190 *TF:* 800-729-6261 ■ *Web:* www.pawnmart.com	Norcross	GA	30071	678-720-0660	720-0671

573 PAYROLL SERVICES

SEE ALSO Data Processing & Related Services p. 1781; Professional Employer Organizations (PEOs) p. 2455

	City	State	ZIP	Phone	Fax
ADP ProBusiness Div 4125 Hopyard Rd *Web:* www.probusiness.com	Pleasanton	CA	94588	925-737-3500	225-9077
Advantage Payroll Services Inc 126 Merrow Rd PO Box 1330 *TF Cust Svc:* 800-876-0178 ■ *Web:* www.advantagepayroll.com	Auburn	ME	04211	207-784-0178	786-0490
Automatic Data Processing Inc (ADP) 1 ADP Blvd *NASDAQ:* ADP ■ *TF:* 800-225-5237 ■ *Web:* www.adp.com	Roseland	NJ	07068	973-994-5000	974-5390
Basic Pay LLC 231 W 29th St Suite 1207 *Web:* www.basicpay.biz	New York	NY	10001	212-684-8827	684-6036
Ceridian Corp 3311 E Old Shakopee Rd *TF:* 800-767-4969 ■ *Web:* www.ceridian.com	Minneapolis	MN	55425	952-853-8100	
CheckPoint HR 2035 Lincoln Hwy Suite 1080 *TF:* 800-385-0331 ■ *Web:* www.checkpointhr.com	Edison	NJ	08817	732-287-8270	287-2297
DSI Payroll Services 300 Atrium Dr *TF:* 800-254-0780 ■ *Web:* www.dsipayrollservices.com	Somerset	NJ	08873	732-748-1700	
Employers Resource Management Co 1301 S Vista Ave Suite 200 *TF:* 800-574-4668 ■ *Web:* www.employersresource.com	Boise	ID	83705	208-376-3000	363-7356
Media Services 500 S Sepulveda Blvd 4th Fl *TF:* 800-333-7518 ■ *Web:* www.media-services.com	Los Angeles	CA	90049	310-440-9600	472-9979
Paychex Inc 911 Panorama Trail S *NASDAQ:* PAYX ■ **Fax:* Hum Res ■ *TF:* 800-828-4411 ■ *Web:* www.paychex.com	Rochester	NY	14625	585-385-6666	383-3449*
Paychex Major Market Services 12647 Alcosta Blvd #200 *Web:* www.paychex.com	San Ramon	CA	94583	925-242-0700	790-0223
Payroll Management Inc 127 Miracle Strip Pkwy SW Suite N7 *Web:* www.pmipeo.com	Fort Walton Beach	FL	32548	850-243-5604	243-5640
Paywise Inc 122 E 42nd St Suite 520 *TF:* 800-975-8607	New York	NY	10168	212-953-1287	953-1287
SurePayroll 2350 Ravine Way Suite 100 *TF:* 877-954-7873 ■ *Web:* www.surepayroll.com	Glenview	IL	60025	847-676-8420	676-8150
TeamStaff Inc 1 Executive Dr Suite 130 *NASDAQ:* TSTF ■ *TF:* 866-352-5304 ■ *Web:* www.teamstaff.com	Somerset	NJ	08873	866-352-5304	

574 PENS, PENCILS, PARTS

SEE ALSO Art Materials & Supplies - Mfr p. 1402; Office & School Supplies p. 2321

	City	State	ZIP	Phone	Fax
Alvin & Co Inc 1335 Blue Hills Ave **Fax Area Code:* 800 ■ *TF:* 800-444-2584 ■ *Web:* www.alvinco.com	Bloomfield	CT	06002	860-243-8991	777-2896*
AT Cross Co 1 Albion Rd *AMEX:* ATX ■ **Fax Area Code:* 800 ■ **Fax:* Cust Svc ■ *TF:* 800-722-1719 ■ *Web:* www.cross.com	Lincoln	RI	02865	401-333-1200	722-1729*
Avery Dennison Corp 150 N Orange Grove Blvd *NYSE:* AVY ■ *TF Cust Svc:* 800-252-8379 ■ *Web:* www.averydennison.com	Pasadena	CA	91103	626-304-2000	304-2192
BIC Corp 1 BIC Way Suite 1 **Fax:* Hum Res ■ *TF:* 800-546-1111 ■ *Web:* www.bicworld.com	Shelton	CT	06484	203-783-2000	783-2660*
California Cedar Products Co 1340 N Washington St *Web:* www.calcedar.com	Stockton	CA	95203	209-944-5800	944-9072
Dixon Ticonderoga Co 195 International Pkwy **Fax Area Code:* 800 ■ **Fax:* Cust Svc ■ *TF:* 800-824-9430 ■ *Web:* www.dixonticonderoga.com	Heathrow	FL	32746	407-829-9000	232-9396*

				Phone	Fax
Dri Mark Products Inc 15 Harbor Pk Dr *TF:* 800-645-9118 ■ *Web:* www.drimark.com	Port Washington	NY	11050	516-484-6200	484-6279
Fisher Space Pen Co 711 Yucca St *TF:* 800-634-3494 ■ *Web:* www.spacepen.com	Boulder City	NV	89005	702-293-3011	293-6616
Garland Industries Inc 1 S Main St *Web:* www.garlandpen.com	Coventry	RI	02816	401-828-9582	823-7460
General Pencil Co Inc 3160 Bay Rd *Web:* www.generalpencil.com	Redwood City	CA	94063	650-369-4889	369-7169
Harcourt Pencil Co 7765 S 175 W *TF:* 800-215-4024 ■ *Web:* www.harcourtoutlines.com	Milroy	IN	46156	765-629-2244	629-2218
Hartley-Racon 280 N Midland Ave Bldg C-1 *Web:* www.hartleyraconusa.com	Saddle Brook	NJ	07663	201-703-0663	703-0733
HPC Global 14 Industrial Dr *TF:* 800-233-4463	Hanover	PA	17331	717-637-6681	637-9190
Jensen's Inc 715 W Jackson St	Shelbyville	TN	37160	931-684-5021	685-9229
Listo Pencil Corp 1925 Union St *TF:* 800-547-8648 ■ *Web:* www.listo.com	Alameda	CA	94501	510-522-2910	522-3798
Mercury Pen Co Inc 245 Eastline Rd *Web:* www.mercurypen.com	Ballston Lake	NY	12019	518-899-9653	899-9657
Moon Products Inc 1150 5th Ave N PO Box 1309 *TF:* 800-541-3758	Lewisburg	TN	37091	931-359-1501	359-8381
Musgrave Pencil Co Inc PO Box 290 *TF:* 800-736-2450 ■ *Web:* www.musgravepencil.com	Shelbyville	TN	37162	931-684-3611	685-1049
National Pen Corp 12121 Scripps Summit Dr # 200 *TF:* 800-854-1000 ■ *Web:* www.pens.com	San Diego	CA	92131	858-675-3000	675-0890
Newell Rubbermaid Inc Office Products Group 3 Glenlake Pkwy *Web:* www.newellrubbermaid.com/public/Our-Brands/Office-Products.aspx	Atlanta	GA	30328	770-418-7000	
Pencoa Mfg Corp 5620 1st A Ave **Fax Area Code:* 800 ■ *TF Cust Svc:* 800-989-7527 ■ *Web:* www.pencoa.com	Brooklyn	NY	11220	516-997-2330	989-7704*
Pentel of America Ltd 2715 Columbia St *TF:* 800-262-1127 ■ *Web:* www.pentel-usa.com	Torrance	CA	90503	310-320-3831	533-0697
Rotary Pen Corp 746 Colfax Ave	Kenilworth	NJ	07033	908-245-2437	245-1557
Sanford Brands Div Newell Rubbermaid Inc 2707 Butterfield Rd **Fax:* Cust Svc ■ *TF:* 800-323-0749 ■ *Web:* www.newellrubbermaid.com	Oak Brook	IL	60523	630-481-2200	481-2099*

575 PERFORMING ARTS FACILITIES

SEE ALSO Convention Centers p. 1749; Stadiums & Arenas p. 2671; Theaters - Broadway p. 2712; Theaters - Resident p. 2713

Most Of The Fax Numbers Provided For These Facilities Are For The Box Office.

ALABAMA

				Phone	Fax
Alabama Theatre 1817 3rd Ave N *Web:* www.alabamatheatre.com	Birmingham	AL	35203	205-252-2262	251-3155
Bama Theatre 600 Greensboro Ave *Web:* www.tuscarts.org	Tuscaloosa	AL	35401	205-758-5195	345-2787
Birmingham Festival Theater 1901 1/2 11th Ave S PO Box 55321 *Web:* www.bftonline.org	Birmingham	AL	35205	205-933-2383	
Davis Theatre for the Performing Arts 251 Montgomery St *Web:* www.montgomey.troy.edu/davistheartre	Montgomery	AL	36104	334-241-9567	241-9756
Library Theatre 200 Municipal Dr *Web:* www.thelibrarytheatre.com	Hoover	AL	35216	205-444-7888	444-7894
Playhouse in the Park 4851 Museum Dr PO Box 8145 *Web:* www.mobilepip.org	Mobile	AL	36608	251-344-1537	
Renaissance Theatre Inc 1214 Meridian St N # B *Web:* www.renaissancetheatre.net	Huntsville	AL	35801	256-536-3117	
Saenger Theatre 6 S Joachim St *Web:* www.mobilesaenger.com	Mobile	AL	36602	251-208-5600	208-5609
Tuscaloosa Fine Arts Centre 9500 Old Greensboro Rd	Tuscaloosa	AL	35405	205-391-2400	391-2329
Wynton M Blount Cultural Park 6055 Vaughn Rd *Web:* www.blountculturalpark.org	Montgomery	AL	36116	334-244-5700	273-9666
Birmingham-Jefferson Convention Complex 2100 Richard Arrington Jr Blvd N *TF:* 877-843-2522 ■ *Web:* www.bjcc.org	Birmingham	AL	35203	205-458-8400	458-8437
Von Braun Ctr 700 Monroe St *Web:* www.vonbrauncenter.com	Huntsville	AL	35801	256-533-1953	551-2203

ALASKA

				Phone	Fax
Alaska Center for the Performing Arts 621 W 6th Ave *Web:* www.myalaskacenter.com	Anchorage	AK	99501	907-263-2900	263-2927
Charles W Davis Concert Hall University of Alaska Fairbanks Music Dept PO Box 755660	Fairbanks	AK	99775	907-474-7555	474-6420

ARIZONA

				Phone	Fax
Arizona State University's Kerr Cultural Ctr 6110 N Scottsdale Rd *Web:* www.asukerr.com	Scottsdale	AZ	85253	480-596-2660	483-9646
Ashley Furniture HomeStore Pavilion 2121 N 83rd Ave	Phoenix	AZ	85035	602-254-7200	254-6060
Celebrity Theatre 440 N 32nd St *Web:* www.celebritytheatre.com	Phoenix	AZ	85008	602-267-1600	267-4882
Chandler Center for the Arts 250 N Arizona Ave *Web:* www.chandlercenter.org	Chandler	AZ	85225	480-782-2680	782-2684
Dodge Theatre 400 W Washington St	Phoenix	AZ	85003	602-379-2800	379-2002
Grady Gammage Memorial Auditorium 1200 S Forest Ave *Web:* www.asugammage.com	Tempe	AZ	85188	480-965-3434	965-3583
Herberger Theater Ctr 222 E Monroe St *Web:* www.herbergertheater.org	Phoenix	AZ	85004	602-254-7399	258-9521
Maricopa County Events Ctr 19403 N R H Johnson Blvd *Web:* www.maricopacountyeventscenter.com	Sun City West	AZ	85375	623-544-2888	544-4050
Orpheum Theatre 203 W Adams St *Web:* www.phoenix.gov	Phoenix	AZ	85003	602-534-5600	
Rialto The 318 E Congress St *Web:* www.rialtotheatre.com	Tucson	AZ	85701	520-740-0126	
Scottsdale Center for the Performing Arts 7380 E 2nd St *Web:* www.scottsdaleperformingarts.org	Scottsdale	AZ	85251	480-994-2787	874-4699
Tucson Convention Ctr 260 S Church Ave *Web:* www.tucsonaz.gov/tcc	Tucson	AZ	85701	520-791-4101	791-5572

ARKANSAS

				Phone	Fax
Robinson Ctr 426 W Markham St 7 Statehouse Plaza *TF:* 800-844-4781 ■ *Web:* www.littlerockmeetings.com	Little Rock	AR	72201	501-376-4781	374-2255
Fort Smith Convention Ctr 55 S 7th St *Web:* www.fortsmith.org	Fort Smith	AR	72901	479-788-8932	788-8930

BRITISH COLUMBIA

				Phone	Fax
Orpheum Theatre 865 Seymour St *Web:* www.vancouver.ca	Vancouver	BC	V6B5J3	604-665-3050	665-2149

CALIFORNIA

				Phone	Fax
Ahmanson Theatre *Music Center of Los Angeles County* 135 N Grand Ave *Web:* www.centertheatregroup.org	Los Angeles	CA	90012	213-628-2772	972-7224
Alex Theatre 216 N Brand Blvd *Web:* www.alextheatre.org	Glendale	CA	91203	818-243-7700	241-2089
Annenberg Theater 101 Museum Dr Palm Springs Art Museum *Web:* www.psmuseum.org	Palm Springs	CA	92262	760-325-4490	322-3246
B Street Theatre 2711 B St *Web:* www.bstreettheatre.org	Sacramento	CA	95816	916-443-5300	443-0874
Bayview Opera House 4705 3rd St *Web:* www.bayviewoperahouse.org	San Francisco	CA	94124	415-824-0386	824-7124
Bill Graham Civic Auditorium 99 Grove St	San Francisco	CA	94102	510-548-3010	
Bruce Ariss Wharf Theatre Fisherman's Wharf Wharf 1	Monterey	CA	93940	831-649-2332	373-7944
California Center for the Arts 340 N Escondido Blvd *TF:* 800-988-4253 ■ *Web:* www.artcenter.org	Escondido	CA	92025	760-839-4138	
California Theatre of Performing Arts 562 W 4th St *TF:* 800-511-6449 ■ *Web:* www.californiatheatre.net	San Bernardino	CA	92401	909-885-5152	885-8948
Center for the Performing Arts 255 Almaden Blvd *TF:* 800-726-5673 ■ *Web:* www.sanjose.org	San Jose	CA	95113	408-792-4111	277-3535
Cerritos Center for the Performing Arts 12700 Ctr Ct Dr *TF:* 800-300-4345 ■ *Web:* www.cerritoscenter.com	Cerritos	CA	90703	562-916-8501	916-8514
EXIT Theatre 156 Eddy St *Web:* www.theexit.org	San Francisco	CA	94102	415-931-1094	931-2699
Fox Theater 2001 H St *Web:* www.foxtheateronline.com	Bakersfield	CA	93301	661-324-1369	324-1854
Gary Soren Smith Center for the Fine & Performing Arts *Ohlone College* 43600 Mission Blvd *Web:* www.ohlone.edu/org/smithcenter	Fremont	CA	94539	510-659-6031	659-6188
Glendale Centre Theatre 324 N Orange St *Web:* www.glendalecentretheatre.com	Glendale	CA	91203	818-244-8481	244-5042
Greek Theatre The 2700 N Vermont Ave *Web:* www.greektheatrela.com	Los Angeles	CA	90027	323-665-5857	666-8202
Hollywood Bowl 2301 N Highland Ave *Web:* www.hollywoodbowl.com	Hollywood	CA	90068	323-850-2000	850-2155
Irvine Barclay Theatre 4242 Campus Dr *Web:* www.thebarclay.org	Irvine	CA	92612	949-854-4646	854-8490
John Anson Ford Theatres 2580 Cahuenga Blvd E *Web:* www.fordamphitheatre.org	Hollywood	CA	90068	323-461-3673	871-5904
Kodak Theatre 6801 Hollywood Blvd Suite 180 *Web:* www.kodaktheatre.com	Hollywood	CA	90028	323-308-6300	308-6381
Long Beach Playhouse 5021 E Anaheim St *Web:* www.lbplayhouse.org	Long Beach	CA	90804	562-494-1014	961-8616

Name / Address	City	State	Zip	Phone	Fax
Luckman Fine Arts Complex 5151 State University Dr *Web:* www.luckmanarts.org	Los Angeles	CA	90032	323-343-6611	343-6423
Marines Memorial Theatre 609 Sutter St *Web:* www.marineclub.com/theatre.php	San Francisco	CA	94102	415-771-6900	441-3649
McCallum Theatre 73000 Fred Waring Dr *Web:* www.mccallumtheatre.com	Palm Desert	CA	92260	760-340-2787	779-9445
Monterey Peninsula College Theatre 980 Fremont St *Web:* www.mpctheatreco.com	Monterey	CA	93940	831-646-4213	
Music Center of Los Angeles County 135 N Grand Ave *Web:* www.musiccenter.org	Los Angeles	CA	90012	213-972-7211	972-7323
New Conservatory Theatre Centre 25 Van Ness Ave *Web:* www.nctcsf.org	San Francisco	CA	94102	415-861-4914	861-6988
Old Globe 1363 Old Globe Way *Web:* www.oldglobe.org	San Diego	CA	92101	619-231-1941	231-5879
Orange County Performing Arts Ctr 600 Town Ctr Dr *Web:* www.scfta.org/home/default.aspx	Costa Mesa	CA	92626	714-556-2121	556-8984
Oxnard Performing Arts & Convention Ctr (PACC) 800 Hobson Way *Web:* www.oxnardpacc.com	Oxnard	CA	93030	805-486-2424	483-7303
Palace of Fine Arts Theatre 3301 Lyon St *Web:* www.palaceoffinearts.org	San Francisco	CA	94123	415-567-6642	567-4062
Palm Canyon Theatre 538 N Palm Canyon Dr *Web:* www.palmcanyontheatre.org	Palm Springs	CA	92262	760-323-5123	323-7365
Paramount Theatre 2025 Broadway *Web:* www.paramounttheatre.com	Oakland	CA	94612	510-465-6400	893-5098
Pasadena Ctr 300 E Green St *Web:* www.pasadenacal.com/faciliti.htm	Pasadena	CA	91101	626-793-2122	793-8014
Pentages Theatre 6233 Hollywood Blvd *Web:* www.pantages-theater.com	Hollywood	CA	90028	323-468-1770	
Plaza Theater 128 S Palm Canyon Dr *Web:* www.psfollies.com/plaza.html	Palm Springs	CA	92262	760-327-0225	322-3196
Redding Civic Auditorium 777 Auditorium Dr *TF:* 888-225-4130	Redding	CA	96001	530-225-4130	225-4118
Redlands Bowl 25 Grant St PO Box 466 *Web:* www.redlandsbowl.org	Redlands	CA	92373	909-793-7316	793-5086
Richard & Karen Carpenter Performing Arts Ctr (CPAC) 6200 Atherton St *Web:* www.carpenterarts.org	Long Beach	CA	90815	562-985-7000	985-7023
Robert & Margrit Mondavi Center for the Performing Arts 1 Shields Ave *TF:* 866-754-2787 ■ *Web:* www.mondaviarts.org	Davis	CA	95616	530-754-2787	754-5383
San Francisco War Memorial & Performing Arts Ctr (SFWMPAC) 401 Van Ness Ave Rm 110 *Web:* www.sfwmpac.org	San Francisco	CA	94102	415-621-6600	621-5091
San Jose Center for the Performing Arts 255 Almaden Blvd *Web:* www.sanjose.org	San Jose	CA	95113	408-792-4111	277-3535
San Manuel Amphitheater 2575 Glen Helen Pkwy *Web:* www.livenation.com	San Bernardino	CA	92407	909-880-6500	885-6563
Santa Cruz Civic Auditorium 307 Church St *Web:* www.cityofsantacruz.com	Santa Cruz	CA	95060	831-420-5240	420-5261
Second Space Theater 928 E Olive Ave	Fresno	CA	93728	559-266-0211	266-1342
Shoreline Amphitheatre 1 Amphitheatre Pkwy	Mountain View	CA	94043	650-967-3000	967-4994
Sleep Train Amphitheatre 2677 Forty Mile Rd	Wheatland	CA	95901	530-743-5200	634-0157
Sleep Train Pavilion at Concord 2000 Kirker Pass Rd *Web:* www.livenation.com	Concord	CA	94521	925-676-8742	676-7262
State Theatre 1307 J St PO Box 1492 *Web:* www.thestate.org	Modesto	CA	95354	209-527-4697	
Sturges Center for the Fine Arts 780 N E St *Web:* www.sturgescenter.org	San Bernardino	CA	92410	909-384-5415	384-5449
Thousand Oaks Civic Arts Plaza 2100 Thousand Oaks Blvd *Web:* www.toaks.org/theatre	Thousand Oaks	CA	91362	805-449-2787	
Tower Theatre for the Performing Arts 815 E Olive Ave *Web:* www.towertheatrefresno.org	Fresno	CA	93728	559-485-9050	
Walt Disney Concert Hall 111 S Grand Ave	Los Angeles	CA	90012	323-850-2000	
Warnors Center for the Performing Arts 1400 Fulton St *Web:* www.warnors.org	Fresno	CA	93721	559-264-2848	264-5643
Western Stage Theatre 411 Central Ave *Web:* www.westernstage.org	Salinas	CA	93901	831-755-6816	770-6105
Wiltern Theatre 3790 Wilshire Blvd *Web:* www.wilterntheatertickets.com	Los Angeles	CA	90010	213-388-1400	388-0242
Fresno Convention Ctr 848 M St *Web:* www.fresnoconventioncenter.com	Fresno	CA	93721	559-445-8100	445-8110
Bren Events Ctr 100 Bren Events Ctr *Web:* www.bren.uci.edu	Irvine	CA	92697	949-824-5050	824-5097
Shrine Auditorium & Exposition Ctr 665 W Jefferson Blvd *Web:* www.shrineauditorium.com	Los Angeles	CA	90007	213-748-5116	742-9922
San Jose Convention & Cultural Facilities (SJC) 150 W San Carlos St *TF:* 800-726-5673 ■ *Web:* www.sanjose.org/plan-a-meeting-event/venues/convention-center	San Jose	CA	95110	408-792-4194	277-3535

COLORADO

Name / Address	City	State	Zip	Phone	Fax
Arvada Center for the Arts & Humanities 6901 Wadsworth Blvd *Web:* www.arvadacenter.org	Arvada	CO	80003	720-898-7200	898-7204
Aurora Fox Arts Ctr 9900 E Colfax Ave *Web:* www.aurorafoxartscenter.org	Aurora	CO	80010	303-739-1970	739-1975
Denver Center for the Performing Arts 1101 13th St *TF:* 800-641-1222 ■ *Web:* www.denvercenter.org	Denver	CO	80204	303-893-4000	595-9634
Denver Performing Arts Complex 1245 Champa St 1St Fl *Web:* www.artscomplex.com	Denver	CO	80204	720-865-4220	865-4247
Macky Auditorium Concert Hall 285 UCB University Ave *Web:* www.colorado.edu	Boulder	CO	80309	303-492-8423	492-1651
Newman Center for the Performing Arts 2344 E Iliff Ave *Web:* www.du.edu/newmancenter	Denver	CO	80208	303-871-6200	871-6507
Paramount Theatre 1631 Glenarm Pl *Web:* www.paramountdenver.com	Denver	CO	80202	303-405-1100	
Pikes Peak Ctr 190 S Cascade Ave *Web:* www.pikespeakcenter.com	Colorado Springs	CO	80903	719-477-2100	477-2199
Red Rocks Amphitheater 18300 W Alameda Pkwy *Web:* www.redrocksonline.com	Morrison	CO	80465	720-865-2494	865-2467
Sangre de Cristo Arts & Conference Ctr 210 N Santa Fe Ave *Web:* www.sdc-arts.org	Pueblo	CO	81003	719-295-7200	295-7230
Wheeler Opera House 320 E Hyman St *TF:* 866-449-0464 ■ *Web:* www.wheeleroperahouse.com	Aspen	CO	81611	970-920-5770	920-5780

CONNECTICUT

Name / Address	City	State	Zip	Phone	Fax
Austin Arts Ctr 300 Summit St *Web:* www.austinarts.org	Hartford	CT	06106	860-297-2199	297-5380
Bushnell Center for the Performing Arts 166 Capitol Ave *TF:* 888-824-2874 ■ *Web:* www.bushnell.org	Hartford	CT	06106	860-987-6000	987-6070
Fairmount Theatre 33 Main St Annex	New Haven	CT	06512	203-467-3832	467-3832
Garde Arts Ctr 325 State St *Web:* www.gardearts.org	New London	CT	06320	860-444-7373	701-0189
John Lyman Center for the Performing Arts 501 Crescent St *Web:* tickets.southernct.edu	New Haven	CT	06515	203-392-6154	392-6158
Long Wharf Theatre 222 Sargent Dr *TF:* 800-782-8497 ■ *Web:* www.longwharf.org	New Haven	CT	06511	203-787-4282	776-2287
Meadows Music Theatre 61 Savitt Way	Hartford	CT	06102	860-548-7370	548-7386
Norwalk Concert Hall 125 E Ave *Web:* www.norwalkct.org	Norwalk	CT	06851	203-854-7900	854-7939
Oakdale Theatre 95 S Tpke Rd *Web:* www.oakdale.com	Wallingford	CT	06492	203-269-8721	284-1816
Palace Theater of the Arts 61 Atlantic St	Stamford	CT	06901	203-325-4466	358-2313
Playhouse on the Green 177 State St *Web:* www.playhouseonthegreen.org	Bridgeport	CT	06604	203-333-3666	696-0045
Quick Center for the Arts Fairfield University 1073 NBenson Rd *TF:* 877-278-7396 ■ *Web:* www.quickcenter.com	Fairfield	CT	06824	203-254-4010	254-4113
Sacred Heart University Edgerton Center for Performing Arts 5151 Pk Ave *Web:* www.edgertoncenter.org	Fairfield	CT	06825	203-371-7908	365-4858
Shubert Theater 247 College St *Web:* www.shubert.com	New Haven	CT	06510	203-624-1825	789-2286
Stamford Center for the Arts 61 Atlantic St *Web:* www.stamfordcenterforthearts.org	Stamford	CT	06901	203-358-2305	358-2313
Sterling Farms Theatre Complex 1349 Newfield Ave *Web:* www.curtaincallinc.com	Stamford	CT	06905	203-329-8207	322-3656
TheaterWorks 233 Pearl St *Web:* www.theaterworkshartford.org	Hartford	CT	06103	860-527-7838	525-0758
Westport Country Playhouse 25 Powers Ct *TF:* 888-927-7529 ■ *Web:* www.westportplayhouse.org	Westport	CT	06880	203-227-4177	221-7482
Yale University Theatre 222 York St *Web:* www.yalerep.org	New Haven	CT	06520	203-432-1234	432-6423

DELAWARE

Name / Address	City	State	Zip	Phone	Fax
Christina Cultural Arts Ctr 705 N Market St *Web:* www.ccac-de.org	Wilmington	DE	19801	302-652-0101	652-7480
DuPont Theatre 1007 N Market St *TF:* 800-338-0881 ■ *Web:* www.duponttheatre.com	Wilmington	DE	19801	302-656-4401	594-1437
Grand Opera House 818 N Market St *Web:* www.thegrandwilmington.org	Wilmington	DE	19801	302-658-7897	657-5692
Schwartz Center for the Arts 226 S State St *Web:* www.schwartzcenter.com	Dover	DE	19901	302-678-5152	678-1267

DISTRICT OF COLUMBIA

Name / Address	City	State	Zip	Phone	Fax
Arena Stage 1101 6th St SW *Web:* www.arenastage.org	Washington	DC	20024	202-554-9066	488-4056
Carter Barron Amphitheatre 4850 Colorado Ave NW *Web:* www.nps.gov/rocr/cbarron	Washington	DC	20008	202-426-0486	
DAR Constitution Hall 1776 D St NW *Web:* www.dar.org/conthall	Washington	DC	20006	202-628-1776	628-2570
Discovery Theater 1100 Jefferson Dr SW *Web:* www.discoverytheater.org	Washington	DC	20560	202-633-8700	343-1073
John F Kennedy Center for the Performing Arts 2700 F St NW *TF:* 800-444-1324 ■ *Web:* www.kennedy-center.org	Washington	DC	20566	202-416-8000	416-8205
National Theatre 1321 Pennsylvania Ave NW *TF:* 800-447-7400 ■ *Web:* www.nationaltheatre.org	Washington	DC	20004	202-628-6161	638-4830

Name / Address	City	State	ZIP	Phone	Fax
Warner Theatre 513 13th St *Web:* www.warnertheatre.com	Washington	DC	20004	202-783-4000	783-0204

FLORIDA

Name / Address	City	State	ZIP	Phone	Fax
Adrienne Arsht Center for the Performing Arts of Miami-Dade County Inc 1300 Biscayne Blvd *Web:* www.arshtcenter.org	Miami	FL	33132	786-468-2000	468-2001
American Stage 163 3rd St N *Web:* www.americanstage.org	Saint Petersburg	FL	33731	727-823-1600	821-2444
Bailey Hall 3501 SW Davie Rd *Web:* www.broward.edu/campuslife/culturalarts	Davie	FL	33314	954-201-6500	201-6959
Barbara B Mann Performing Arts Hall 8099 College Pkwy SW *TF:* 800-440-7469 ■ *Web:* www.bbmannpah.com	Fort Myers	FL	33919	239-489-3033	481-4620
Bob Carr Performing Arts Centre 401 W Livingston St *Web:* www.orlandovenues.net	Orlando	FL	32801	407-849-2000	849-2329
Broward Center for the Performing Arts 201 SW 5th Ave *TF:* 800-564-9539 ■ *Web:* www.browardcenter.org	Fort Lauderdale	FL	33312	954-462-0222	462-3541
Coral Springs Center for the Arts 2855 Coral Springs Dr *Web:* www.coralspringscenterforthearts.com	Coral Springs	FL	33065	954-344-5990	344-5980
Cruzan Amphitheatre 601 Sansburys Way # 7 *Web:* www.livenation.com	West Palm Beach	FL	33411	561-795-8883	795-6608
Curtis M Phillips Center for the Performing Arts 315 Hull Rd PO Box 112750 *Web:* www.performingarts.ufl.edu	Gainesville	FL	32611	352-392-1900	392-3775
David A. Straz Jr Center for The Performing Arts The 1010 N WC MacInnes Pl *TF:* 800-955-1045 ■ *Web:* www.strazcenter.org	Tampa	FL	33602	813-222-1000	222-1057
Florida Theatre 128 E Forsyth St Suite 300 *Web:* www.floridatheatre.com	Jacksonville	FL	32202	904-355-5661	358-1874
GableStage 1200 Anastasia Ave Biltmore Hotel *Web:* www.gablestage.org	Coral Gables	FL	33134	305-446-1116	445-8645
Gusman Center for the Performing Arts 174 E Flagler St *Web:* www.gusmancenter.org	Miami	FL	33131	305-374-2444	374-0303
Harbour event & conference centre 75 Taylor St. *Web:* www.charlotteharborecc.com	Punta Gorda	FL	33950	941-639-5833	833-5451
Jackie Gleason Theater of the Performing Arts 1700 Washington Ave. *Web:* www.gleasontheater.com	Miami Beach	FL	33139	305-673-7300	
James L Knight International Ctr 400 SE Second Ave. *Web:* www.jlkc.com	Miami	FL	33131	305-372-4634	350-7910
Limelight Theatre 11 Old Mission Ave. *Web:* www.limelight-theatre.org	Saint Augustine	FL	32084	904-825-1164	825-4662
Mahaffey Theater for the Performing Arts 400 1st St S *TF:* 800-874-9015 ■ *Web:* www.mahaffeytheater.com	Saint Petersburg	FL	33701	727-892-5798	892-5897
Marina Civic Ctr 8 Harrison Ave *Web:* www.marinaciviccenter.com	Panama City	FL	32401	850-769-1217	785-5165
Mary McLeod Bethune Performing Arts Ctr 698 W International Speedway Blvd *Web:* www.mmbcenter.com	Daytona Beach	FL	32114	386-481-2778	481-2927
Miami-Dade County Auditorium 2901 W Flagler St.	Miami	FL	33135	305-547-5414	541-7782
North Miami Beach/Julius Littman Performing Arts Theater 17011 NE 19th Ave. *Web:* www.littmantheater.com	North Miami Beach	FL	33162	305-787-6005	787-6040
Old School Square Cultural Arts Ctr 51 N Swinton Ave *Web:* www.oldschool.org	Delray Beach	FL	33444	561-243-7922	243-7018
Orlando Repertory Theatre 1001 E Princeton St *Web:* www.orlandorep.com	Orlando	FL	32803	407-896-7365	897-3284
Parker Playhouse 707 NE 8th St *Fax: Administration ■ *Web:* www.parkerplayhouse.com	Fort Lauderdale	FL	33304	954-764-1441	524-9952*
Peabody Auditorium 600 Auditorium Blvd. *TF:* 866-605-4276 ■ *Web:* www.peabodyauditorium.org	Daytona Beach	FL	32118	386-671-3460	239-6435
Pensacola Civic Ctr 201 E Gregory St *Web:* www.pensacolaciviccenter.com	Pensacola	FL	32502	850-432-0800	432-1707
Pensacola Cultural Ctr (PCC) 400 S Jefferson St *Web:* www.pensacolalittletheatre.com/PCC	Pensacola	FL	32502	850-434-0257	438-2787
Philharmonic Center for the Arts 5833 Pelican Bay Blvd *TF:* 800-597-1900 ■ *Web:* www.thephil.org	Naples	FL	34108	239-597-1111	597-8163
Plaza Theatre 425 N Bumby Ave *TF:* 888-243-8849 ■ *Web:* www.plazaliveorlando.com	Orlando	FL	32803	407-228-1220	228-4428
Pompano Beach Amphitheater 1801 NE 6th St	Pompano Beach	FL	33060	954-946-2402	
Raymond F Kravis Center for the Performing Arts 701 Okeechobee Blvd *Fax: Mktg ■ *TF:* 800-572-8471 ■ *Web:* www.kravis.org	West Palm Beach	FL	33401	561-832-7469	833-0691*
Red Barn Theatre 319 Duval St *Web:* redbarntheater.com	Key West	FL	33040	305-296-9911	293-3035
Ritz Theatre & La Villa Museum 829 N Davis St *Web:* www.ritzjacksonville.com	Jacksonville	FL	32202	904-632-5555	632-5553
Ruth Eckerd Hall 1111 McMullen Booth Rd *TF:* 800-875-8682 ■ *Web:* www.rutheckerdhall.com	Clearwater	FL	33759	727-791-7060	724-5976
Saenger Theatre 118 S Palafox Pl *Web:* www.pensacolasaenger.com	Pensacola	FL	32502	850-595-3880	595-3886
Schmdit Family Centre for The Arts at Mizner Park The 433 Plaza Real Suite 339 *Web:* www.centre4artsboca.com	Boca Raton	FL	33432	561-368-8445	961-2098
Sugden Community Theatre 701 5th Ave S *Web:* www.naplesplayers.org	Naples	FL	34102	239-263-7990	434-7772
Tallahassee Little Theatre The (TLT) 1861 Thomasville Rd *Web:* www.tallahasseelittletheatre.org	Tallahassee	FL	32303	850-224-4597	224-4464
Tampa Theater 711 N Franklin St *Web:* www.tampatheatre.org	Tampa	FL	33602	813-274-8286	274-8978
Tennessee Williams Theatre 5901 W College Rd. *Web:* www.tennesseewilliamstheatre.com	Key West	FL	33040	305-296-1520	292-3725
University of West Florida Center for Fine & Performing Arts 11000 University Pkwy Bldg 82 *Web:* uwf.edu/cfpa	Pensacola	FL	32514	850-474-2541	857-6176
Van Wezel Performing Arts Ctr 777 N Tamiami Trail *TF:* 800-826-9303 ■ *Web:* www.vanwezel.org	Sarasota	FL	34236	941-953-3368	951-1449
Waterfront Playhouse Mallory Sq 407 Wall St *Web:* www.waterfrontplayhouse.com	Key West	FL	33041	305-294-5015	294-0398
Ocean Ctr 101 N Atlantic Ave *TF:* 800-858-6444 ■ *Web:* www.oceancenter.com	Daytona Beach	FL	32118	386-254-4500	254-4512
Lakeland Ctr 701 W Lime St *Web:* www.thelakelandcenter.com	Lakeland	FL	33815	863-834-8100	834-8101
Tallahassee-Leon County Civic Ctr (TLCCC) 505 W Pensacola St PO Box 10604 *TF:* 800-322-3602 ■ *Web:* www.tlccc.org	Tallahassee	FL	32301	850-487-1691	222-6947

GEORGIA

Name / Address	City	State	ZIP	Phone	Fax
14th Street Playhouse 173 14th St	Atlanta	GA	30309	404-733-4750	733-5356
Academy Theatre 119 Ctr St *Web:* www.academytheatre.org	Avondale Estates	GA	30002	404-474-8332	806-7721
Boisfeuillet Jones Atlanta Civic Ctr 395 Piedmont Ave. *Web:* www.atlantaciviccenter.com	Atlanta	GA	30308	404-523-6275	525-4634
Douglass Theatre 355 ML King Jr Blvd *Web:* www.douglasstheatre.org	Macon	GA	31201	478-742-2000	742-0270
Fox Theatre 660 Peachtree St NE. *Web:* www.foxtheatre.org	Atlanta	GA	30308	404-881-2100	872-2972
Grand Opera House 651 Mulberry St *Web:* www.thegrandmacon.com	Macon	GA	31201	478-301-5460	301-5469
Imperial Theatre 749 Broad St *Web:* www.imperialtheatre.com	Augusta	GA	30901	706-722-8293	312-1202
Macon City Auditorium 415 1st St *TF:* 877-532-6144 ■ *Web:* www.maconcentreplex.com	Macon	GA	31201	478-751-9152	751-9154
Macon Little Theater 4220 Forsyth Rd *Web:* www.maconlittletheatre.org	Macon	GA	31210	478-477-3342	471-8711
Rialto Center for the Arts 80 Forsyth St NW PO Box 2627 *Web:* www.rialtocenter.org	Atlanta	GA	30303	404-413-9800	413-9801
Savannah Civic Ctr 301 W Oglethorp Ave *TF:* 800-351-7469 ■ *Web:* www.savannahcivic.com	Savannah	GA	31401	912-651-6550	651-6552
Spivey Hall Clayton College & State University 2000 Clayton State Blvd *Web:* www.spiveyhall.org	Morrow	GA	30260	678-466-4200	466-4494
Springer Opera House 103 10th St *Web:* www.springeroperahouse.org	Columbus	GA	31901	706-327-3688	324-4461
Townsend Center for the Performing Arts 1601 Maple St *Web:* www.westga.edu/tcpa	Carrollton	GA	30118	678-839-4722	839-4804
Woodruff Arts Ctr 1280 Peachtree St NE *Web:* www.woodruffcenter.org	Atlanta	GA	30309	404-733-4200	733-4281
Georgia Mountains Ctr 301 Main St SW PO Box 2496 *Web:* www.gainesville.org	Gainesville	GA	30503	770-534-8420	534-8425

IDAHO

Name / Address	City	State	ZIP	Phone	Fax
Idaho Falls Civic Auditorium 501 S Holmes Ave	Idaho Falls	ID	83401	208-612-8396	542-0476
Morrison Center for the Performing Arts 2201 Cesar Chavez Ln Boise State University *Web:* www.mc.boisestate.edu	Boise	ID	83725	208-426-1609	426-3021

ILLINOIS

Name / Address	City	State	ZIP	Phone	Fax
Apollo Fine Arts & Entertainment Centre 311 Main St	Peoria	IL	61602	309-673-4343	673-6052
Apollo Theater 2540 N Lincoln Ave *Web:* www.apollochicago.com	Chicago	IL	60614	773-935-6100	935-6214
Auditorium Theatre 50 E Congress Pkwy. *Web:* www.auditoriumtheatre.org	Chicago	IL	60605	312-922-4046	431-2360
Bailiwick Arts Ctr 1229 W Belmont Ave.	Chicago	IL	60657	773-883-1090	883-2017
Chicago Shakespeare Theater 800 E Grand Ave Navy Pier *Web:* www.chicagoshakes.com	Chicago	IL	60611	312-595-5600	595-5644
Civic Opera House 20 N Wacker Dr *Web:* www.lyricopera.org	Chicago	IL	60606	312-332-2244	332-8120
Coronado Theatre 314 N Main St. *Web:* www.coronadopac.org	Rockford	IL	61101	815-968-2722	968-1318
Ford Center for the Performing Arts/Oriental Theatre 24 W Randolph St. *Web:* www.broadwayinchicago.com	Chicago	IL	60601	312-977-1700	977-0519
Goodman Theatre 170 N Dearborn St. *Web:* www.goodmantheatre.org	Chicago	IL	60601	312-443-3811	443-3821

Facility	City	State	ZIP	Phone	Fax
Krannert Center for the Performing Arts 500 S Goodwin Ave *TF:* 800-527-2849 ■ *Web:* www.krannertcenter.com	Urbana	IL	61801	217-333-6700	244-0810
Lifeline Theatre 6912 N Glenwood Ave *Web:* www.lifelinetheatre.com	Chicago	IL	60626	773-761-4477	761-4582
Marriott Theatre in Lincolnshire 10 Marriott Dr *Web:* www.marriotttheatre.com	Lincolnshire	IL	60069	847-634-0200	850-7736
North Shore Center for the Performing Arts in Skokie 9501 N Skokie Blvd *Web:* www.northshorecenter.org	Skokie	IL	60077	847-673-6300	679-1879
Paramount Theatre 8 E Galena Blvd # 230 *Web:* www.paramountarts.com	Aurora	IL	60506	630-896-7676	892-1084
Parkland College Theatre 2400 W Bradley Ave *TF:* 800-346-8089 ■ *Web:* www.parkland.edu/theatre	Champaign	IL	61821	217-351-2528	373-3899
Peoria Civic Ctr 201 SW Jefferson St *Web:* www.peoriaciviccenter.com	Peoria	IL	61602	309-673-8900	673-9223
Rosemont Theatre 5400 N River Rd *Web:* www.rosemonttheatre.com	Rosemont	IL	60018	847-671-5100	671-6405
Royal George Theatre Ctr 1641 N Halsted St *Web:* www.theroyalgeorgetheatre.com	Chicago	IL	60614	312-988-9105	988-4027
Springfield Theatre Centre 420 S 6th St	Springfield	IL	62701	217-523-0878	523-4895
Station Theatre 223 N Broadway Ave *Web:* www.stationtheatre.com	Urbana	IL	61801	217-384-4000	
Steppenwolf Theatre 1650 N Halsted St *Web:* www.steppenwolf.org	Chicago	IL	60614	312-335-1650	335-0440
Symphony Ctr 220 S Michigan Ave **Fax:* Mktg ■ *TF Cust Svc:* 800-223-7114 ■ *Web:* www.cso.org	Chicago	IL	60604	312-294-3000	294-3035*
Virginia Theatre 203 W Pk Ave *Web:* www.thevirginia.org	Champaign	IL	61820	217-356-9053	356-5729

INDIANA

Facility	City	State	ZIP	Phone	Fax
American Cabaret Theatre 121 Monument Cir *Web:* www.thecabaret.org	Indianapolis	IN	46204	317-275-1169	
Christel DeHaan Fine Arts Ctr 1400 E Hanna Ave University of Indianapolis *TF:* 800-232-8634 ■ *Web:* www.uindy.edu/arts	Indianapolis	IN	46227	317-788-3566	788-3383
Embassy Theatre 125 W Jefferson Blvd *Web:* www.embassycentre.org	Fort Wayne	IN	46802	260-424-6287	424-4806
Evansville Civic Theatre 717 N Fulton St *Web:* www.civic.evansville.net	Evansville	IN	47710	812-425-2800	423-2636
Hilbert Circle Theatre 45 Monument Cir *Web:* www.hilbertcircletheatreindy.org	Indianapolis	IN	46204	317-262-1110	262-1159
Indiana University Auditorium 1211 E 7th St *Web:* www.iuauditorium.com	Bloomington	IN	47405	812-855-1103	855-4244
Indianapolis Artsgarden Above the intersection of Washington Illinois St *Web:* www.indyarts.org	Indianapolis	IN	46204	317-624-2563	624-2564
Madame Walker Theatre Ctr 617 Indiana Ave *Web:* www.walkertheatre.com	Indianapolis	IN	46202	317-236-2099	236-2097
Morris Performing Arts Ctr 211 N Michigan St *TF:* 800-537-6415 ■ *Web:* www.morriscenter.org	South Bend	IN	46601	574-235-9190	235-5945
Murat Centre 502 N New Jersey St *Web:* www.livenation.com/Murat-Theatre-at-Old-National-Centre-tickets-Indianapolis	Indianapolis	IN	46204	317-231-0000	231-9410
South Bend Civic Theatre 211 W Madison PO Box 1146 *Web:* www.sbct.org	South Bend	IN	46624	574-234-1112	288-3412
Warren Performing Arts Ctr 9500 E 16th St	Indianapolis	IN	46229	317-532-6280	532-6440
Evansville Auditorium & Convention Ctr 715 Locust St *Web:* www.smgevansville.com/centre/centre.html	Evansville	IN	47708	812-435-5770	435-5500

IOWA

Facility	City	State	ZIP	Phone	Fax
Civic Center of Greater Des Moines 221 Walnut St *Web:* www.civiccenter.org	Des Moines	IA	50309	515-246-2300	246-2305
Grand Opera House 135 W 8th St *Web:* www.thegrandoperahouse.com	Dubuque	IA	52001	563-588-1305	588-3497
Paramount Theatre 123 3rd Ave SE *Web:* www.uscellularcenter.com/theatre_info	Cedar Rapids	IA	52401	319-398-5211	362-2102
RiverCenter Adler Theatre 136 E 3rd St *Web:* www.riverctr.com	Davenport	IA	52801	563-326-8500	326-8505

KANSAS

Facility	City	State	ZIP	Phone	Fax
Helen Hocker Theater Center for the Performing Arts 700 SW Zoo Pkwy Gage Pk *Web:* www.topeka.org	Topeka	KS	66606	785-368-0191	228-6065
Orpheum Performing Arts Centre 200 N Broadway Suite 102 *Web:* www.wichitaorpheum.com	Wichita	KS	67202	316-263-0884	263-8641
Sandstone Amphitheater 633 N 130th St	Bonner Springs	KS	66012	913-721-3400	
Topeka Performing Arts Ctr 214 SE 8th Ave *Web:* www.tpactix.org	Topeka	KS	66603	785-234-2787	234-2307
Wichita Center for the Arts 9112 E Central Ave *Web:* www.wcfta.com	Wichita	KS	67206	316-634-2787	634-0593
Wichita Community Theatre 258 N Fountain *Web:* www.wichitacommunitytheatre.com	Wichita	KS	67208	316-686-1282	652-0531
Century II Performing Arts & Convention Ctr 225 W Douglas Ave *Web:* www.century2.org	Wichita	KS	67202	316-264-9121	303-8688

KENTUCKY

Facility	City	State	ZIP	Phone	Fax
Kentucky Center for The Performing Arts The 501 W Main St *Web:* www.kentuckycenter.org	Louisville	KY	40202	502-562-0100	562-0150
Kentucky Theater 214 E Main St *Web:* www.toysfortots.org	Lexington	KY	40507	859-231-7924	
Lexington Opera House 401 W Short St *Web:* www.lexingtonoperahouse.com	Lexington	KY	40507	859-233-4567	253-2718
Louisville Palace 625 S 4th St *Web:* www.louisvillepalace.com	Louisville	KY	40202	502-583-4555	583-9955

LOUISIANA

Facility	City	State	ZIP	Phone	Fax
Baton Rouge Little Theater 7155 Florida Blvd *Web:* www.brlt.org	Baton Rouge	LA	70806	225-924-6496	924-9972
Contemporary Arts Ctr 900 Camp St *Web:* www.cacno.org	New Orleans	LA	70130	504-528-3805	528-3828
East Bank Theatre 630 Barksdale Blvd *Web:* www.sites.bossierarts.org/main/east-bank-theatre	Bossier City	LA	71111	318-741-8310	741-8312
Heymann Performing Arts Ctr 1373 S College Rd *Web:* www.heymann-center.com	Lafayette	LA	70503	337-291-5540	291-5580
Lake Charles Civic Ctr 900 Lakeshore Dr *Web:* www.cityoflakecharles.com	Lake Charles	LA	70601	337-491-1256	491-1534
Preservation Hall 726 St Peter St *TF:* 888-946-5299 ■ *Web:* www.preservationhall.com	New Orleans	LA	70116	504-522-2841	558-9192
Shaver Theater Louisiana State Univ 217 Music & Dramatic Arts Bldg *Web:* www.theatre.lsu.edu/prod_venues/shaver.htm	Baton Rouge	LA	70803	225-578-4174	578-4135
Strand Theatre 619 Louisiana Ave *TF:* 800-313-6373 ■ *Web:* www.thestrandtheatre.com	Shreveport	LA	71101	318-226-1481	424-5434
Baton Rouge River Ctr 275 S River Rd *Web:* www.brrivercenter.com	Baton Rouge	LA	70802	225-389-3030	389-4954
Monroe Civic Ctr 401 Lea Joyner Expy	Monroe	LA	71201	318-329-2225	329-2548

MAINE

Facility	City	State	ZIP	Phone	Fax
Criterion Theatre & Arts Ctr The 35 Cottage St *Web:* www.criteriontheater.com	Bar Harbor	ME	04609	207-288-3441	
Cumberland County Civic Ctr 1 Civic Ctr Sq *Web:* www.theciviccenter.com	Portland	ME	04101	207-775-3481	828-8344
Maine Center for the Arts 5746 Maine Center for the Arts *Web:* www.ume.maine.edu/~mca	Orono	ME	04469	207-581-1755	581-1837
Merrill Auditorium 20 Myrtle St *Web:* www.portlandevents.com/Merrill.htm	Portland	ME	04101	207-874-8200	756-8434

MANITOBA

Facility	City	Province	Postal Code	Phone	Fax
Burton Cummings Theatre 364 Smith St *Web:* www.burtoncummingstheatre.com	Winnipeg	MB	R3B2H2	204-956-5656	956-2581
Lyric Theatre 55 Pavilion Crescent	Winnipeg	MB	R2P2N6	204-888-5466	889-8136

MARYLAND

Facility	City	State	ZIP	Phone	Fax
Annapolis Summer Garden Theatre 143 Compromise St *Web:* www.summergarden.com	Annapolis	MD	21401	410-268-9212	
Chesapeake Arts Ctr 194 Hammonds Ln *Web:* www.chesapeakearts.org	Brooklyn Park	MD	21225	410-636-6597	636-9653
Everyman Theatre 1727 N Charles St *Web:* www.everymantheatre.org	Baltimore	MD	21201	410-752-2208	752-5891
France-Merrick Performing Arts Ctr 12 N Eutaw St *Web:* www.france-merrickpac.com	Baltimore	MD	21201	410-837-7400	837-7410
Gordon Center for Performing Arts 3506 Gwynnbrook Ave *Web:* www.gordoncenter.com	Owings Mills	MD	21117	410-356-7469	356-7605
Joseph Meyerhoff Symphony Hall 1212 Cathedral St *TF:* 800-442-1198 ■ *Web:* www.music.org	Baltimore	MD	21201	410-783-8100	783-8077
Lyric Opera House 110 W Mt Royal Ave *Web:* www.lyricoperahouse.com	Baltimore	MD	21201	410-685-5086	332-8234
Maryland Hall for the Creative Arts 801 Chase St *TF:* 866-438-3808 ■ *Web:* www.mdhallarts.org	Annapolis	MD	21401	410-263-5544	263-5114
Maryland Theatre 21 S Potomac St *Web:* www.mdtheatre.org	Hagerstown	MD	21740	301-790-3500	791-6114
Merriweather Post Pavilion (MPP) 10475 Little Patuxent Pkwy *Web:* www.merriweathermusic.com	Columbia	MD	21044	410-715-5550	715-5560
Pumpkin Theatre 8415 Bellona Ln Ruxton Towers Suite 115 *Web:* www.pumpkintheatre.com	Baltimore	MD	21204	410-828-1645	828-1954

	City	State	Zip	Phone	Fax
Recher Theatre The 512 York Rd *Web:* www.rechertheatre.com	Towson	MD	21204	410-337-7178	321-8175

MASSACHUSETTS

	City	State	Zip	Phone	Fax
Bank of America Pavilion 290 Northern Ave	Boston	MA	02109	617-728-1600	737-2292
Berklee Performance Ctr 136 Massachusetts Ave *Web:* www.berkleebpc.com	Boston	MA	02115	617-747-2261	375-9228
Boston Center for the Arts 539 Tremont St *Web:* www.bcaonline.org	Boston	MA	02116	617-426-5000	426-5336
Boston Symphony Hall 301 Massachusetts Ave *TF:* 888-266-1200 ■ *Web:* www.bso.org/symphonyhallhome.jhtml	Boston	MA	02115	617-266-1492	638-9367
Charles Playhouse 74 Warrenton St *Web:* www.broadwayacrossamerica.com	Boston	MA	02116	617-426-6912	695-1230
Colonial Theatre 106 Boylston St *Web:* www.bostonscolonialtheatre.com	Boston	MA	02116	617-426-9366	880-2449
Comcast Ctr 885 S Main St	Mansfield	MA	02048	508-339-2331	339-0550
Cutler Majestic Theatre at Emerson College 219 Tremont St *Web:* www.emerson.edu	Boston	MA	02116	617-824-8000	824-3209
Mechanics Hall 321 Main St *Web:* www.mechanicshall.org	Worcester	MA	01608	508-752-5608	754-8442
Shubert Theatre 265 Tremont St	Boston	MA	02116	617-482-9393	451-1436
South Shore Music Circus 130 Sohier St *Web:* www.musiccircus.com	Cohasset	MA	02025	781-383-9850	383-9804
Stuart Street Playhouse 200 Stuart St *Web:* www.stuartstreetplayhouse.com	Boston	MA	02116	617-457-2618	
Wang Theatre 270 Tremont St	Boston	MA	02116	617-482-9393	451-1436
Wilbur Theatre 246 Tremont St *Web:* www.thewilburtheatre.com	Boston	MA	02116	617-248-9700	

MICHIGAN

	City	State	Zip	Phone	Fax
Ann Arbor Civic Theatre 322 W Ann St *Web:* www.a2ct.org	Ann Arbor	MI	48104	734-971-0605	971-2769
Buckham Alley Theatre 816 S Saginaw St *Web:* www.buckhamtheatre.com	Flint	MI	48502	810-964-0791	
Chenery Auditorium 714 S Westnedge Ave	Kalamazoo	MI	49007	269-337-0424	337-0490
Circle Theatre 161 Ottawa Ave NW *Web:* www.circletheatre.org	Grand Rapids	MI	49503	616-632-1980	456-8540
Detroit Opera House 1526 Broadway *Web:* www.michiganopera.org	Detroit	MI	48226	313-961-3500	237-3412
Detroit Symphony Orchestra Hall 3711 Woodward Ave *Web:* www.detroitsymphony.com	Detroit	MI	48201	313-576-5100	576-5101
Dow Event Ctr 303 Johnson St *Web:* www.doweventcenter.com	Saginaw	MI	48607	989-759-1320	759-1322
Fillmore Detroit The 2115 Woodward Ave	Detroit	MI	48201	313-961-5451	965-2808
Fisher Theatre 3011 W Grand Blvd *Web:* www.broadwayindetroit.com	Detroit	MI	48202	313-872-1000	872-0632
Fox Theatre 2211 Woodward Ave *Web:* www.olympiaentertainment.com	Detroit	MI	48201	313-983-6611	
Gem Theatre& Century Grille 333 Madison Ave *Web:* www.gemtheatre.com	Detroit	MI	48226	313-963-9800	963-0873
Grand Rapids Civic Theatre 30 N Division Ave *TF:* 866-455-4728 ■ *Web:* www.grct.org	Grand Rapids	MI	49503	616-222-6650	222-6660
Interlochen Center for the Arts 4000 Michigan 137 *Web:* www.interlochen.org	Interlochen	MI	49643	231-276-7200	276-7444
Kerrytown Concert House 415 N 4th Ave *Web:* www.kerrytownconcerthouse.com	Ann Arbor	MI	48104	734-769-2999	769-7791
Majestic Theatre 4120 Woodward Ave *Web:* www.majesticdetroit.com	Detroit	MI	48201	313-833-9700	833-1213
Masonic Temple Theatre 500 Temple St *Web:* www.themasonic.com	Detroit	MI	48201	313-832-7100	832-2922
Michigan Theater 603 E Liberty St *Web:* www.michtheater.org	Ann Arbor	MI	48104	734-668-8397	668-7136
Midland Center for the Arts Inc 1801 W St Andrews Rd *Web:* www.mcfta.org	Midland	MI	48640	989-631-5930	631-7890
Millennium Centre 15600 JL Hudson Dr	Southfield	MI	48075	248-796-5191	796-5199
Music Hall Center for the Performing Arts 350 Madison *Web:* www.musichall.org	Detroit	MI	48226	313-887-8500	887-8502
Riverside Arts Ctr 76 N Huron St *Web:* www.riversidearts.org	Ypsilanti	MI	48197	734-480-2787	
Riverwalk Theatre 228 Museum Dr *Web:* www.riverwalktheatre.com	Lansing	MI	48933	517-482-5700	482-9812
University of Michigan - Flint Theater 303 E Kearsley St *Web:* www.umflint.edu/theatredance	Flint	MI	48502	810-762-3230	766-6630
Wharton Center for the Performing Arts Michigan State University *TF:* 800-942-7866 ■ *Web:* www.whartoncenter.com	East Lansing	MI	48824	517-432-2000	353-5329
Whiting Auditorium 1241 E Kearsley St *TF:* 888-823-6837 ■ *Web:* www.thewhiting.com	Flint	MI	48503	810-237-7333	237-7335

MINNESOTA

	City	State	Zip	Phone	Fax
Duluth Playhouse 506 W Michigan St *Web:* www.duluthplayhouse.org	Duluth	MN	55802	218-733-7555	733-7554
Fitzgerald Theater 45 Exchange St E *Web:* www.fitzgeraldtheater.publicradio.org	Saint Paul	MN	55101	651-290-1200	290-1195
Great American History Theatre 30 E 10th St *Web:* www.historytheatre.com	Saint Paul	MN	55101	651-292-4323	292-4322
Guthrie Theater 818 S 2nd St *TF:* 877-447-8243 ■ *Web:* www.guthrietheater.org	Minneapolis	MN	55415	612-377-2224	225-6004
Historic Orpheum Theatre 910 Hennepin Ave *Web:* www.hennepintheatretrust.org	Minneapolis	MN	55403	612-339-0075	339-4146
Historic Pantages Theatre 710 Hennepin Ave *Web:* www.hennepintheatretrust.org	Minneapolis	MN	55403	612-339-7007	339-4146
Historic State Theatre 805 Hennepin Ave *Web:* www.hennepintheatretrust.org	Minneapolis	MN	55402	612-339-0075	339-4146
Jungle Theater 2951 Lindale Ave S *Web:* www.jungletheater.com	Minneapolis	MN	55408	612-822-4002	822-9408
MacPhail Center for the Arts 501 S 2nd St *Web:* www.macphail.org	Minneapolis	MN	55401	612-321-0100	321-9740
Music Box Theatre 1407 Nicollet Ave	Minneapolis	MN	55403	612-871-1414	874-8987
Orchestra Hall 1111 Nicollet Mall *TF:* 800-292-4141 ■ *Web:* www.minnesotaorchestra.org	Minneapolis	MN	55403	612-371-5600	371-0838
Ordway Center for the Performing Arts 345 Washington St *Web:* www.ordway.org	Saint Paul	MN	55102	651-282-3000	282-3160
Penumbra Theatre 270 Kent St *Web:* www.penumbratheatre.org	Saint Paul	MN	55102	651-224-3180	288-6789
Reif Ctr 720 NW Conifer Dr *Web:* www.reifcenter.org	Grand Rapids	MN	55744	218-327-5780	327-5798
Renegade Comedy Theatre 222 E Superior St *TF:* 888-722-6627 ■ *Web:* www.renegadecomedy.org	Duluth	MN	55802	218-722-6775	
Rochester Civic Theatre 20 Civic Ctr Dr SE *Web:* www.rochestercivictheatre.org	Rochester	MN	55904	507-282-8481	282-0608

MISSISSIPPI

	City	State	Zip	Phone	Fax
Thalia Mara Hall 255 E Pascagoula St *Web:* www.thaliamara.org	Jackson	MS	39201	601-960-1537	960-1583
Tupelo Community Theatre 201 N Broadway PO Box 1094 *Web:* www.tctwebstage.com/lyric.htm	Tupelo	MS	38802	662-844-1935	844-2990

MISSOURI

	City	State	Zip	Phone	Fax
American Heartland Theatre 2450 Grand Blvd Suite 314 *Web:* ahtkc.com	Kansas City	MO	64108	816-842-0202	842-1881
Andy Williams Moon River Theatre 2500 W Hwy 76 *TF:* 800-666-6094 ■ *Web:* www.andywilliams.com	Branson	MO	65616	417-334-4500	337-9627
Coterie Theatre The 2450 Grand Blvd Suite 144 *Web:* www.coterietheatre.org	Kansas City	MO	64108	816-474-6785	474-7112
Folly Theater 1020 Central Suite 200 PO Box 26505 *Web:* www.follytheater.com	Kansas City	MO	64105	816-474-4444	842-8709
Fox Theatre 527 N Grand Blvd Suite 300 *TF:* 800-293-5949 ■ *Web:* www.fabulousfox.com	Saint Louis	MO	63103	314-534-1678	534-1678
Gem Theater Cultural & Performing Arts Ctr 1615 E 18th St	Kansas City	MO	64108	816-474-6262	474-0074
Jim Stafford Theatre 3440 W 76 Country Blvd *TF:* 800-677-8533 ■ *Web:* www.jimstafford.com	Branson	MO	65616	417-335-8080	335-2643
Juanita K Hammons Hall for the Performing Arts 901 S National Ave *TF:* 888-476-7849 ■ *Web:* www.hammonshall.com	Springfield	MO	65897	417-836-6776	836-6891
Kansas City Music Hall 301 W 13th St *TF:* 800-821-7060 ■ *Web:* www.kcconvention.com	Kansas City	MO	64105	816-513-5000	513-5001
Legends Theater 1600 W Hwy 76 *Fax: Investor Rel ■ *TF:* 800-374-7469 ■ *Web:* www.legendsinconcert.com	Branson	MO	65616	417-339-3003	335-2768*
Maplewood Barn Community Theatre Nifong Blvd Nifong Pk *Web:* www.maplewoodbarn.com	Columbia	MO	65201	573-449-7517	
Midland by AMC The 1228 Main St *Web:* www.midlandkc.com	Kansas City	MO	64105	816-283-9900	
Missouri Theatre Center for the Arts 203 S 9th St *Web:* www.motheatre.org	Columbia	MO	65201	573-875-0600	449-4214
Muny Musical Theater Forest Pk *Web:* www.muny.com	Saint Louis	MO	63112	314-361-1900	361-0009
Powell Symphony Hall 718 N Grand Blvd *TF:* 800-232-1880 ■ *Web:* www.stlsymphony.org	Saint Louis	MO	63103	314-533-2500	286-4142
Quality Hill Playhouse 303 W 10th St *Web:* www.qualityhillplayhouse.com	Kansas City	MO	64105	816-421-1700	221-6556
Rhynsburger Theatre 129 Fine Arts Bldg University of Missouri-Columbia Campus	Columbia	MO	65211	573-882-7529	884-4034
Roberts Orpheum Theater 416 N 9th St *Web:* www.robertsorpheum.com	Saint Louis	MO	63101	314-588-0388	588-9828
Shepherd of the Hills Homestead & Outdoor Theatre 5586 W Hwy 76 *TF:* 800-653-6288 ■ *Web:* www.branson.com/branson/shepherd/shepherd.htm	Branson	MO	65616	417-334-4191	334-4617
Stained Glass Theatre 1996 W Evangel *Web:* www.sgtheatre.com	Ozark	MO	65721	417-581-9192	485-2282
Starlight Theatre 4600 Starlight Rd Swope Pk *Web:* www.kcstarlight.com	Kansas City	MO	64132	816-363-7827	361-6398
Unicorn Theatre 3828 Main St *Web:* www.unicorntheatre.org	Kansas City	MO	64111	816-531-7529	531-0421
Verizon Wireless Amphitheater 14141 Riverport Dr *Web:* www.livenation.com	Maryland Heights	MO	63043	314-298-9944	291-4719

MONTANA

				Phone	Fax
Alberta Bair Theater for the Performing Arts 2722 3rd Ave N Suite 200 PO Box 1556 *TF:* 877-321-2074 ■ *Web:* www.albertabairtheater.org	Billings	MT	59103	406-256-8915	256-5060
Billings Studio Theatre (BST) 1500 Rimrock Rd *Web:* www.billingsstudiotheatre.com	Billings	MT	59102	406-248-1141	248-1576
Grand Street Theater 325 N Pk Ave *Web:* www.grandstreettheatre.com	Helena	MT	59601	406-442-4270	447-1573
Helena Civic Ctr 340 Neill Ave *Web:* www.ci.helena.mt.us/index.php?id=279	Helena	MT	59601	406-447-8481	447-8480

NEBRASKA

				Phone	Fax
Blue Barn Theatre 614 S 11th St *Web:* www.bluebarn.org	Omaha	NE	68102	402-345-1576	
Lied Center for Performing Arts 301 N 12th St *TF:* 800-432-3231 ■ *Web:* www.unl.edu	Lincoln	NE	68588	402-472-4700	472-2725
Lincoln Community Playhouse 2500 S 56th St *Web:* www.lincolnplayhouse.com	Lincoln	NE	68506	402-489-7529	489-1035
Omaha Community Playhouse 6915 Cass St *TF:* 888-782-4338 ■ *Web:* www.omahaplayhouse.com	Omaha	NE	68132	402-553-0800	553-6288
Orpheum Theatre 409 S 16th St *Web:* www.omahaperformingarts.org	Omaha	NE	68102	402-345-0202	345-0222
Pershing Ctr 226 Centennial Mall S *Web:* www.pershingcenter.com	Lincoln	NE	68508	402-441-8744	441-7913

NEVADA

				Phone	Fax
Artemus W Ham Concert Hall 4505 Maryland Pkwy *Web:* www.unlvtickets.com	Las Vegas	NV	89154	702-895-2787	895-4714
Brewery Arts Ctr 449 W King St *Web:* www.breweryarts.org	Carson City	NV	89703	775-883-1976	883-1922
Reed Whipple Cultural Arts Ctr 821 Las Vegas Blvd N	Las Vegas	NV	89101	702-229-6211	382-5199
University of Nevada Las Vegas Performing Arts Ctr (UNLV) 4505 S Maryland Pkwy PO Box 450003 *Web:* www.unlvtickets.com	Las Vegas	NV	89154	702-895-3761	895-4714

NEW HAMPSHIRE

				Phone	Fax
Capitol Center for the Arts 44 S Main St *Web:* www.ccanh.com	Concord	NH	03301	603-225-1111	224-3408
Hopkins Center for the Arts 6041 Wilson Hall *Web:* www.hop.dartmouth.edu	Hanover	NH	03755	603-646-2422	646-1375
Palace Theatre 80 Hanover St *Web:* www.palacetheatre.org	Manchester	NH	03101	603-668-5588	668-5804

NEW JERSEY

				Phone	Fax
Count Basie Theatre 99 Monmouth St *Web:* www.countbasietheatre.org	Red Bank	NJ	07701	732-842-9000	842-9323
McCarter Theatre 91 University Pl *Web:* www.mccarter.org	Princeton	NJ	08540	609-258-6500	497-0369
New Jersey Performing Arts Ctr 1 Ctr St *TF:* 888-466-5722 ■ *Web:* www.njpac.org	Newark	NJ	07102	973-642-8989	648-6724
Newark Symphony Hall 1030 Broad St *Web:* www.newarksymphonyhall.org	Newark	NJ	07102	973-643-8009	
Patriots Theater Memorial Dr *Web:* www.state.nj.us	Trenton	NJ	08608	609-984-8484	777-0581
PNC Bank Art Ctr Exit 116 Garden State Pkwy *Web:* www.livenation.com/PNC-Bank-Arts-Center-tickets-Holmdel/venue/16839	Holmdel	NJ	07733	732-203-2500	335-8637
State Theatre 15 Livingston Ave *TF:* 877-782-8311 ■ *Web:* www.statetheatrenj.org	New Brunswick	NJ	08901	732-247-7200	247-4005
Stockton Performing Arts Ctr Richard Stockton College Jimmie Leeds Rd PO Box 195 *Web:* www.loki.stockton.edu/pac	Pomona	NJ	08240	609-652-9000	626-5523

NEW MEXICO

				Phone	Fax
Adobe Theater 9813 4th St NW *Web:* www.adobetheater.com	Albuquerque	NM	87107	505-898-9222	
Albuquerque Little Theatre 224 San Pasquale SW *Web:* www.albuquerquelittletheatre.org	Albuquerque	NM	87104	505-242-4750	843-9489
Armory of the Arts Theatre 1050 Old Pecos Trail *Web:* www.sfperformingarts.org	Santa Fe	NM	87502	505-982-7992	
Flickinger Center for Performing Arts 1110 New York Ave *Web:* www.flickingercenter.com	Alamogordo	NM	88310	575-437-2202	434-0067
Greer Garson Theatre Ctr 1600 St Michael's Dr College of Santa Fe *TF:* 800-456-2673 ■ *Web:* www.santafeuniversity.edu	Santa Fe	NM	87505	505-473-6011	473-6016
KiMo Theater 423 Central Ave NW *Web:* www.cabq.gov/kimo	Albuquerque	NM	87102	505-768-3522	768-3542
Las Cruces Community Theater 313 N Downtown Mall *Web:* www.lcctnm.org	Las Cruces	NM	88001	575-523-1200	525-0015
Lensic Performing Arts Ctr 211 W San Francisco St *Web:* www.lensic.com	Santa Fe	NM	87501	505-988-7050	988-4370
Popejoy Hall UNM Public Events 1 Univ of New Mexico MSC 04 2580 *Web:* www.popejoyhall.com	Albuquerque	NM	87131	505-277-3824	277-7353
Santa Fe Playhouse 142 E DeVargas St *Web:* www.santafeplayhouse.org	Santa Fe	NM	87501	505-988-4262	820-1922

NEW YORK

				Phone	Fax
Alleyway Theatre 1 Curtain Up Alley *Web:* www.alleyway.com/alleyway	Buffalo	NY	14202	716-852-2600	852-2266
Apollo Theatre 253 W 125th St *Web:* www.apollotheater.org	New York	NY	10027	212-531-5300	749-2743
Artpark 450 S 4th St *TF:* 800-659-7275 ■ *Web:* www.artpark.net	Lewiston	NY	14092	716-754-9000	754-2741
Auditorium Ctr 875 E Main St Suite 200 *Web:* www.auditoriumcenter.com	Rochester	NY	14605	585-423-0295	423-9539
Avery Fisher Hall W 65th St & Broadway *Web:* www.new.lincolncenter.org	New York	NY	10023	212-875-5030	875-5027
Brooklyn Academy of Music (BAM) 30 Lafayette Ave *Web:* www.bam.org	Brooklyn	NY	11217	718-636-4100	636-4179
Brooklyn Center for the Performing Arts 2900 Campus Rd PO Box 100163 *Web:* www.brooklyncenter.com	Brooklyn	NY	11210	718-951-4600	951-4343
Capitol Theatre 149 Westchester Ave *Web:* www.thecapitoltheatre.net	Port Chester	NY	10573	914-934-9362	
Carnegie Hall 881 7th Ave *Web:* www.carnegiehall.org	New York	NY	10019	212-247-7800	581-6539
Center for the Arts 103 Ctr for the Arts N Campus University at Buffalo *Web:* www.arts.buffalo.edu	Buffalo	NY	14260	716-645-2787	645-6973
Eastman Theatre 26 Gibbs St *Web:* www.rochester.edu/eastman	Rochester	NY	14604	585-274-1110	274-1067
Egg The Empire State Plaza Concourse Level Performing Arts Ctr *Web:* www.theegg.org	Albany	NY	12220	518-473-1845	473-1848
Emelin Theater 153 Library Ln *Web:* www.emelin.org	Mamaroneck	NY	10543	914-698-0098	698-1404
Geva Theatre Ctr 75 Woodbury Blvd *Web:* www.gevatheatre.org	Rochester	NY	14607	585-232-1366	232-4031
Kavinoky Theatre 320 Porter Ave *Web:* www.kavinokytheatre.com	Buffalo	NY	14201	716-881-7668	829-7790
Kleinhans Music Hall 370 Pennsylvania *Web:* www.kleinhansmusichall.org	Buffalo	NY	14201	716-883-3560	883-7430
Landmark Theatre 362 S Salina St *Web:* www.landmarktheatre.org	Syracuse	NY	13202	315-475-7980	475-7993
Lehman Center for the Performing Arts Inc 250 Bedford Pk Blvd W *Web:* www.lehmancenter.org	Bronx	NY	10468	718-960-8232	960-8233
Lincoln Center for the Performing Arts 70 Lincoln Ctr Plaza *Web:* www.new.lincolncenter.org/live	New York	NY	10023	212-875-5000	875-5242
Lucille Lortel Theatre 121 Christopher St *Web:* www.lortel.org	New York	NY	10014	212-924-2817	
Manhattan Center Studios 311 W 34th St *Web:* www.mcstudios.com	New York	NY	10001	212-279-7740	564-1072
Mid-Hudson Civic Ctr 14 Civic Ctr Plaza *Web:* www.midhudsoncivicenter.org	Poughkeepsie	NY	12601	845-454-5800	454-5877
New Phoenix Theatre The 95 Johnson Pk *Web:* www.newphoenixtheatre.com	Buffalo	NY	14201	716-853-1334	
New York City Ctr 130 W 56th St *Web:* www.nycitycenter.org	New York	NY	10019	212-247-0430	246-9778
New York State Theater 63rd St & Columbus Ave *Web:* www.nycballet.com/about/aboutnyst.html	New York	NY	10023	212-870-5570	870-5693
Palace Theatre 19 Clinton Ave *Web:* www.palacealbany.com	Albany	NY	12207	518-465-3334	427-0151
Paul Robeson Theatre *Theatre Alliance of Buffalo* 350 Masten Ave *Web:* www.theatreallianceofbuffalo.com	Buffalo	NY	14209	716-884-2013	885-2590
Performing Arts Center at Rockwell Hall 1300 Elmwood Ave Rockwell Hall Rm 210 *Web:* www.buffalostate.edu	Buffalo	NY	14222	716-878-3005	878-4234
Performing Arts Ctr 735 Anderson Hill Rd *Web:* www.artscenter.org	Purchase	NY	10577	914-251-6200	251-6171
Proctor's Theatre 432 State St *Web:* www.proctors.org	Schenectady	NY	12305	518-382-3884	346-2468
Public theater The 425 Lafayette St *Web:* www.publictheater.org	New York	NY	10003	212-539-8500	539-8505
Radio City Music Hall 1260 Avenue of the Americas *Web:* www.radiocity.com	New York	NY	10020	212-247-4777	
Rockefeller Ctr 45 Rockefeller Plaza *Web:* www.rockefellercenter.com	New York	NY	10111	212-332-6500	319-1745
Saratoga Performing Arts Ctr (SPAC) 108 Avenue of the Pines *Web:* www.spac.org	Saratoga Springs	NY	12866	518-584-9330	584-0809
Shea's Performing Arts Ctr 646 Main St *Web:* www.sheas.org	Buffalo	NY	14202	716-847-1410	847-1644
Snug Harbor Cultural Ctr 1000 Richmond Terr *Web:* www.snug-harbor.org	Staten Island	NY	10301	718-448-2500	442-8534
Stanley Center for the Arts 261 Genesee St *Web:* www.cnyarts.com	Utica	NY	13501	315-724-1113	732-8468
Tarrytown Music Hall 13 Main St PO Box 686 *TF:* 877-840-0457 ■ *Web:* www.tarrytownmusichall.org	Tarrytown	NY	10591	914-631-3390	

				Phone	Fax
TRIBECA Performing Arts Ctr 199 Chambers St *Web:* www.tribecapac.org	New York	NY	10007	212-220-1459	732-2482

NORTH CAROLINA

				Phone	Fax
Actor's Theatre of Charlotte 650 E Stonewall St *Web:* www.actorstheatrecharlotte.org	Charlotte	NC	28202	704-342-2251	342-1229
Asheville Community Theatre 35 E Walnut St *Web:* www.ashevilletheatre.org	Asheville	NC	28801	828-254-1320	252-4723
Broach Theatre 520 S Elm St *Web:* www.broachtheatre.org	Greensboro	NC	27406	336-378-9300	378-9301
Carolina Theatre 310 S Greene St *Web:* www.carolinatheatre.com	Greensboro	NC	27401	336-333-2600	333-2604
Carolina Theatre of Durham The 309 W Morgan St *Web:* www.carolinatheatre.org	Durham	NC	27701	919-560-3040	560-3065
Diana Wortham Theatre at Pack Place 2 S Pack Sq *Web:* www.dwtheatre.com	Asheville	NC	28801	828-257-4530	251-5652
Flat Rock Playhouse 2661 Greenville Hwy *Web:* www.flatrockplayhouse.org	Flat Rock	NC	28731	828-693-0731	693-6795
Neighborhood Theatre 511 E 36th St *Web:* www.neighborhoodtheatre.com	Charlotte	NC	28205	704-358-9298	373-0170
North Carolina Blumenthal Performing Arts Ctr PO Box 37322 *Web:* www.performingartsctr.org	Charlotte	NC	28227	704-372-1000	444-2127
Theatre in the Park 107 Pullen Rd *Web:* www.theatreinthepark.com	Raleigh	NC	27607	919-831-6936	831-9475
Time Warner Cable Music Pavilion at Walnut Creek 3801 Rock Quarry Rd *Web:* www.livenation.com/venue/getVenue/venueId/502	Raleigh	NC	27610	919-831-6400	831-6415
Greensboro Coliseum Complex 1921 W Lee St *Web:* www.greensborocoliseum.com	Greensboro	NC	27403	336-373-7400	373-2170

NORTH DAKOTA

				Phone	Fax
Chester Fritz Auditorium 3475 University Ave PO Box 9028 *TF:* 800-375-4068 ■ *Web:* www.cfa.und.edu	Grand Forks	ND	58202	701-777-3076	777-4710
Empire Arts Ctr 415 DeMers Ave *Web:* www.empireartscenter.com	Grand Forks	ND	58201	701-746-5500	746-0500
Fargo Theatre 314 Broadway N PO Box 2190 *Web:* www.fargotheatre.org	Fargo	ND	58102	701-239-8385	235-0893
Festival Concert Hall *North Dakota State University* PO Box 5691 *Web:* www.ndsu.nodak.edu/finearts	Fargo	ND	58105	701-231-9441	231-2085
Fire Hall Theatre 412 2nd Ave N	Grand Forks	ND	58203	701-746-0847	

OHIO

				Phone	Fax
Akron Civic Theatre 182 S Main St *Web:* www.akroncivic.com	Akron	OH	44308	330-535-3179	535-9828
Aronoff Center for the Arts 650 Walnut St *Web:* www.cincinnatiarts.org	Cincinnati	OH	45202	513-721-3344	977-4150
Benjamin & Marian Schuster Performing Arts Ctr 109 Main St *TF:* 888-228-3630 ■ *Web:* www.schustercenter.org	Dayton	OH	45402	937-228-3630	449-5068
Blossom Music Center Tickets 1145 W Steels Corners Rd *Web:* www.livenation.com/Blossom-Music-Center-tickets-Cuyahoga-Falls/venue/40964	Cuyahoga Falls	OH	44223	330-920-8040	920-0968
Cain Park Theatre Superior & Lee Rds Cain Pk *Web:* www.cainpark.com	Cleveland Heights	OH	44118	216-371-3000	
Canton Palace Theatre 605 Market Ave N *Web:* www.cantonpalacetheatre.org	Canton	OH	44702	330-454-8172	454-8171
Cincinnati Music Hall 650 Walnut St *Web:* www.cincinnatiarts.org	Cincinnati	OH	45202	513-744-3344	744-3345
Cincinnati Playhouse in the Park 962 Mt Adams Cir PO Box 6537 *TF:* 800-582-3208 ■ *Web:* www.cincyplay.com	Cincinnati	OH	45202	513-345-2242	345-2250
Coach House Theatre 732 W Exchange St *Web:* www.coachhousetheatre.org	Akron	OH	44302	330-434-7741	
Dobama Theater 2490 Lee Blvd Suite 325 *Web:* www.dobama.org	Cleveland Heights	OH	44118	216-932-6838	932-3259
Edward W Powers Auditorium 260 Federal Plaza W *Web:* www.youngstownsymphony.com/symphony_center.html	Youngstown	OH	44503	330-744-4269	744-1441
EJ Thomas Performing Arts Hall 198 Hill St University of Akron *Web:* www.destinationdowntownakron.com/ej	Akron	OH	44325	330-972-7570	972-2700
Fraze Pavilion 695 Lincoln Pk Blvd *Web:* www.fraze.com	Kettering	OH	45429	937-296-3300	296-3302
Ohio Theatre 55 E State St *Web:* www.capa.com/columbus/venues/ohio_about.php	Columbus	OH	43215	614-469-1045	461-0429
Palace Theatre 34 W Broad St	Columbus	OH	43215	614-469-1331	
Playhouse Square 1501 Euclid Ave Suite 200 *TF:* 866-546-1353 ■ *Web:* www.playhousesquare.com	Cleveland	OH	44115	216-771-4444	771-0217
Riverbend Music Ctr 6295 Kellogg Ave *Web:* www.riverbend.org	Cincinnati	OH	45230	513-232-6220	232-7577
Severance Hall 11001 Euclid Ave *TF:* 800-686-1411 ■ *Web:* www.clevelandorchestra.com	Cleveland	OH	44106	216-231-7300	231-0202
Stambaugh Auditorium 1000 5th Ave *Web:* www.stambaughauditorium.com	Youngstown	OH	44504	330-747-5175	747-1981
Stranahan Theater 4645 Heatherdowns Blvd *TF:* 866-381-7469 ■ *Web:* www.stranahantheater.org	Toledo	OH	43614	419-381-8851	381-9525
Taft Theatre The 317 E 5th St *Web:* www.tafttheatre.org	Cincinnati	OH	45202	513-232-6220	721-2864
Valentine Theatre The 410 Adams St *Web:* www.valentinetheatre.com	Toledo	OH	43604	419-242-3490	242-2791
Victoria Theatre 138 N Main St *TF:* 888-228-3630 ■ *Web:* www.victoriatheatre.com	Dayton	OH	45402	937-228-3630	449-5068
WD Packard Music Hall 1703 Mahoning Ave NW *Web:* www.packardmusichall.com	Warren	OH	44483	330-841-2619	393-5348
Weathervane Community Playhouse 1301 Weathervane Ln *Web:* www.weathervaneplayhouse.com	Akron	OH	44313	330-836-2626	873-2150
Youngstown Playhouse 600 Playhouse Ln PO Box 11108 *Web:* www.theyoungstownplayhouse.com	Youngstown	OH	44511	330-788-8739	788-1208
Veterans Memorial Civic & Convention Ctr 7 Town Sq *Web:* www.limaciviccenter.com	Lima	OH	45801	419-224-5222	224-6964

OKLAHOMA

				Phone	Fax
Civic Center Music Hall 201 N Walker St *Web:* www.okcciviccenter.org	Oklahoma City	OK	73102	405-297-2584	297-3890
Jewel Box Theatre 3700 N Walker Ave *Web:* www.jewelboxtheatre.org	Oklahoma City	OK	73118	405-521-1786	525-6562
Mabee Ctr 8100 S Lewis Ave *TF:* 800-678-1353 ■ *Web:* www.mabeecenter.com	Tulsa	OK	74171	918-495-6000	495-7438
Tulsa Performing Arts Ctr 110 E 2nd St *TF:* 800-364-7122 ■ *Web:* www.tulsapac.com	Tulsa	OK	74103	918-596-7122	596-7144

ONTARIO

				Phone	Fax
Centre in the Square 101 Queen St N *TF:* 800-265-8977 ■ *Web:* www.centre-square.com	Kitchener	ON	N2H6P7	519-578-1570	578-9230
Massey Hall 178 Victoria St *Web:* www.masseyhall.com	Toronto	ON	M5B1T7	416-593-4822	593-4224

OREGON

				Phone	Fax
Historic Elsinore Theatre (HET) 170 High St SE *Web:* www.elsinoretheatre.com	Salem	OR	97301	503-375-3574	375-0284
Hult Center for the Performing Arts 1 Eugene Ctr *Web:* www.hultcenter.org	Eugene	OR	97401	541-682-5087	682-5426
McDonald Theatre 1010 Willamette St *Web:* www.mcdonaldtheatre.com	Eugene	OR	97401	541-345-4442	762-8093
Pentacle Theater 324 52nd Ave NW *Web:* www.pentacletheatre.org	Salem	OR	97304	503-364-7121	362-6393
Portland Center for the Performing Arts 1111 SW Broadway *Web:* www.pcpa.com	Portland	OR	97205	503-248-4335	274-7490
Woodmen of the World Hall 291 W 8th Ave *Web:* www.wowhall.org	Eugene	OR	97401	541-687-2746	687-1664
Florence Events Ctr 715 Quince St *TF:* 888-968-4086 ■ *Web:* www.eventcenter.org	Florence	OR	97439	541-997-1994	902-0991

PENNSYLVANIA

				Phone	Fax
Academy of Music 204 S Broad St *Web:* www.kimmelcenter.org	Philadelphia	PA	19102	215-790-5800	
Annenberg Center for the Performing Arts 3680 Walnut St *Web:* www.annenbergcenter.org	Philadelphia	PA	19104	215-898-3900	573-9568
Benedum Center for the Performing Arts 719 Liberty Ave *Web:* www.pgharts.com	Pittsburgh	PA	15222	412-456-6666	391-7219
Carnegie Music Hall 4400 Forbes Ave	Pittsburgh	PA	15213	412-622-3360	688-8664
Civic Theatre of Allentown 527 N 19th St *Web:* www.civictheatre.com	Allentown	PA	18104	610-432-8943	432-7381
Eichelberger Performing Arts Ctr 195 Stock St Suite 203	Hanover	PA	17331	717-632-9356	637-4504
Erie Playhouse 13 W 10th St *Web:* www.erieplayhouse.org	Erie	PA	16501	814-454-2851	454-0601
Fulton Opera House Foundation 12 N Prince St PO Box 1865 *TF:* 888-480-1265 ■ *Web:* www.fultontheatre.org	Lancaster	PA	17603	717-397-7425	397-3780
Heinz Hall for the Performing Arts 600 Penn Ave *TF:* 800-743-8560 ■ *Web:* www.pittsburghsymphony.org	Pittsburgh	PA	15222	412-392-4800	392-4910
Kimmel Center for the Performing Arts 260 S Broad St Suite 901 *Web:* www.kimmelcenter.org	Philadelphia	PA	19102	215-790-5800	790-5801
Liacouras Ctr 1776 N Broad St *Web:* www.liacourascenter.com	Philadelphia	PA	19121	215-204-2400	204-2405
Mann Center for the Performing Arts 5201 Parkside Ave *Web:* www.manncenter.org	Philadelphia	PA	19131	215-546-7900	546-9524
Music Box Dinner Playhouse 196 Hughes St *Web:* www.musicbox.org	Swoyersville	PA	18704	570-283-2195	283-0751
Providence Playhouse 1256 Providence Rd	Scranton	PA	18508	570-342-9707	
Scranton Cultural Ctr 420 N Washington Ave *Web:* www.scrantonculturalcenter.org	Scranton	PA	18503	570-346-7369	346-7365
Society Hill Playhouse 507 S 8th St *Web:* www.societyhillplayhouse.com	Philadelphia	PA	19147	215-923-0210	923-1789

Facility	City	State	ZIP	Phone	Fax
Sovereign Performing Arts Ctr 136 N 6th St *Web:* www.sovereigncenter.com	Reading	PA	19601	610-898-7299	898-7297
Wachovia Arena at Casey Plaza 255 Highland Pk Blvd *Web:* www.wachoviaarena.com	Wilkes-Barre	PA	18702	570-970-7600	970-7601
Walnut Street Theatre 825 Walnut St *Web:* www.wstonline.org	Philadelphia	PA	19107	215-574-3550	574-3598
Warner Theatre 811 State St *Web:* www.erieevents.com	Erie	PA	16501	814-452-4857	455-9931
Wilma Theater 265 S Broad St *Web:* www.wilmatheater.org	Philadelphia	PA	19107	215-893-9456	893-0895

RHODE ISLAND

Facility	City	State	ZIP	Phone	Fax
AS220 115 Empire St *Web:* www.as220.org	Providence	RI	02903	401-831-9327	454-7445
Perishable Theatre Arts Ctr 95 Empire St *Web:* www.perishable.org	Providence	RI	02903	401-331-2695	331-7811
Providence Performing Arts Ctr 220 Weybosset St *Web:* www.ppacri.org	Providence	RI	02903	401-421-2997	351-7827
Veterans Memorial Auditorium 1 Avenue of the Arts	Providence	RI	02903	401-222-1467	222-1466

SOUTH CAROLINA

Facility	City	State	ZIP	Phone	Fax
Alabama Theatre 4750 Hwy 17 S *TF:* 800-342-2262 ■ *Web:* www.alabama-theatre.com	North Myrtle Beach	SC	29582	843-272-1111	272-7748
Arts Center of Coastal Carolina 14 Shelter Cove Ln *TF:* 888-860-2787 ■ *Web:* www.artshhi.com	Hilton Head Island	SC	29928	843-686-3945	842-7877
Carolina Opry 8901 Hwy 17 N Suite A *TF:* 800-843-6779 ■ *Web:* www.cgp.net	Myrtle Beach	SC	29572	843-238-8888	913-1442
Gaillard Municipal Auditorium 77 Calhoun St	Charleston	SC	29403	843-577-7400	724-7389
Greenville Little Theatre 444 College St *Web:* www.greenvillelittletheatre.org	Greenville	SC	29601	864-233-6238	233-6237
Ira & Nancy Koger Center for the Arts 1051 Greene St *Web:* www.koger.sc.edu	Columbia	SC	29201	803-777-7500	777-9774
Palace Theatre The 1420 Celebrity Cir Broadway at the Beach *TF:* 888-841-2787 ■ *Web:* www.palacetheatremyrtlebeach.com	Myrtle Beach	SC	29577	843-448-9224	626-9659
Peace Center for the Performing Arts 300 S Main St *Web:* www.peacecenter.org	Greenville	SC	29601	864-467-3000	467-3025
Town Theatre 1012 Sumter St *Web:* www.towntheatre.com	Columbia	SC	29201	803-799-4764	799-6463
Township Auditorium 1703 Taylor St *Web:* www.thetownship.org	Columbia	SC	29201	803-576-2350	576-2359
Trustus Theatre 520 Lady St *Web:* www.trustus.org	Columbia	SC	29201	803-254-9732	771-9153
Warehouse Theatre 37 Augusta St *Web:* www.warehousetheatre.com	Greenville	SC	29601	864-235-6948	
Workshop Theatre 1136 Bull St *Web:* www.workshoptheatre.com	Columbia	SC	29211	803-799-4876	799-0227

SOUTH DAKOTA

Facility	City	State	ZIP	Phone	Fax
Black Hills Community Theatre 1202 E St Francis St *Web:* www.bhct.org	Rapid City	SD	57701	605-394-1787	394-2679
Matthews Opera House 612 Main St *Web:* www.spearfishartscenter.org	Spearfish	SD	57783	605-642-7973	642-3477

TENNESSEE

Facility	City	State	ZIP	Phone	Fax
Bessie Smith Performance Hall 200 E ML King Blvd	Chattanooga	TN	37401	423-266-8658	267-1079
Chattanooga Theatre Centre 400 River St *Web:* www.theatrecentre.com	Chattanooga	TN	37405	423-267-8534	664-1211
Circuit Playhouse The 51 S Cooper St *Web:* www.playhouseonthesquare.org	Memphis	TN	38104	901-725-0776	726-5521
Clarence Brown Theatre *University of Tennessee* 206 McClung Tower *Web:* www.clarencebrowntheatre.com	Knoxville	TN	37996	865-974-5161	974-4867
Darkhorse Theater 4610 Charlotte Ave *Web:* www.web.mac.com	Nashville	TN	37209	615-297-7113	665-3336
Germantown Performing Arts Centre (GPAC) 1801 Exeter Rd *Web:* www.gpacweb.com	Germantown	TN	38138	901-751-7500	751-7514
Grand Ole Opry 2804 Opryland Dr *Web:* www.opry.com	Nashville	TN	37214	615-871-6779	871-6166
Knoxville Civic Auditorium/Coliseum 500 Howard Baker Jr Ave *Web:* www.knoxvillecoliseum.com	Knoxville	TN	37915	865-215-8900	215-8989
Laurel Theatre 1538 Laurel Ave *Web:* www.jubileearts.org	Knoxville	TN	37916	865-522-5851	522-5386
Nashville Municipal Auditorium 417 4th Ave N *Web:* www.nashville.gov	Nashville	TN	37201	615-862-6390	862-6394
Orpheum Theatre 203 S Main St *Web:* www.orpheum-memphis.com	Memphis	TN	38103	901-525-3000	526-5499
Playhouse on the Square 51 S Cooper St *Web:* www.playhouseonthesquare.org	Memphis	TN	38104	901-726-4656	272-7530
Ryman Auditorium 116 5th Ave N *Web:* www.ryman.com	Nashville	TN	37219	615-458-8700	458-8701
Soldiers & Sailors Memorial Auditorium 399 McCallie Ave *Web:* www.chattanooga.gov	Chattanooga	TN	37402	423-757-5156	757-5326
Tennessee Performing Arts Ctr 505 Deaderick St *Web:* www.tpac.org	Nashville	TN	37219	615-782-4000	782-4001
Texas Troubadour Theatre 2416 Music Valley Dr Suite 108	Nashville	TN	37214	615-889-2474	885-6949
Theatre Memphis 630 Perkins Ext *Web:* www.theatrememphis.org	Memphis	TN	38117	901-682-8323	763-4096
Tivoli Theatre 709 Broad St	Chattanooga	TN	37402	423-757-5050	757-5326
University of Tennessee Music Hall 1741 Volunteer Blvd *Web:* www.music.utk.edu	Knoxville	TN	37996	865-974-3241	974-1941
Memphis Cook Convention Ctr 3205 Elvis Presley Blvd *Web:* www.memphisconvention.com	Memphis	TN	38116	901-543-5333	

TEXAS

Facility	City	State	ZIP	Phone	Fax
Abilene Civic Ctr 1100 N 6th St *Web:* www.abilenetx.com	Abilene	TX	79601	325-676-6211	676-6343
Abilene Community Theatre 801 S Mockingbird Ln	Abilene	TX	79605	325-673-6271	
Alley Theatre 615 Texas Ave *Web:* www.alleytheatre.org	Houston	TX	77002	713-228-9341	222-6542
Arneson River Theatre 418 Villita St La Villita *Web:* www.lavillita.com/arneson/index.htm	San Antonio	TX	78205	210-207-8610	207-4390
Austin Music Hall 208 Nueces St *Web:* www.austinmusichall.com	Austin	TX	78701	512-263-4146	263-4194
Bass Performance Hall 4th & Calhoun Sts *Web:* www.basshall.com	Fort Worth	TX	76102	817-212-4200	810-9294
Camille Lightner Playhouse 1 Dean Porter Pk	Brownsville	TX	78520	956-542-8900	986-0639
Carpenter Performance Hall 3333 N MacArthur Blvd *Web:* www.irvingartscenter.com	Irving	TX	75062	972-252-2787	570-4962
Casa Manana Theatre 3101 W Lancaster Ave *Web:* www.casamanana.org	Fort Worth	TX	76107	817-332-2272	332-5711
Circle Theatre 230 W 4th St *Web:* www.circletheatre.com	Fort Worth	TX	76102	817-877-3040	877-3536
Creative Arts Theatre & School 1100 W Randol Mill Rd *Web:* www.creativearts.org	Arlington	TX	76012	817-861-2287	274-0793
Cynthia Woods Mitchell Pavilion 2005 Lake Robbins Dr *Web:* www.woodlandscenter.org	The Woodlands	TX	77380	281-363-3300	364-3011
Dupree Theater 3333 N MacArthur Blvd *Web:* www.irvingartscenter.com	Irving	TX	75062	972-252-2787	570-4962
Ensemble Theatre 3535 Main St *Web:* www.ensemblehouston.com	Houston	TX	77002	713-520-0055	520-1269
Grand 1894 Opera House 2020 Postoffice St *TF:* 800-821-1894 ■ *Web:* www.thegrand.com	Galveston	TX	77550	409-765-1894	763-1068
Harbor Playhouse 1 Bayfront Pk *Web:* www.harborplayhouse.com	Corpus Christi	TX	78401	361-882-5500	888-4779
Hobby Center for the Performing Arts 800 Bagby St Suite 300 *Web:* www.thehobbycenter.org	Houston	TX	77002	713-315-2400	315-2402
Irving Arts Ctr 3333 N MacArthur Blvd *Web:* www.irvingartscenter.com	Irving	TX	75062	972-252-7558	570-4962
Jesse H Jones Hall for the Performing Arts 615 Louisiana St Suite 101 *Web:* www.houstontx.gov	Houston	TX	77002	713-227-3974	315-4830
Jubilee Theatre 506 Main St *Web:* www.jubileetheatre.org	Fort Worth	TX	76102	817-338-4204	338-4206
Lila Cockrell Theatre 200 E Market St *TF:* 877-504-8895 ■ *Web:* www.sahpgcc.com	San Antonio	TX	78205	210-207-8500	223-1495
Majestic Theatre 1925 Elm St *Web:* www.liveatthemajestic.com	Dallas	TX	75201	214-880-0137	880-0097
Majestic Theatre 224 E Houston St *Web:* www.themajestic.com/theatre.htm	San Antonio	TX	78205	210-226-5700	226-3377
Miller Outdoor Theatre 6000 Hermann Pk Dr **Fax Area Code:* 713 ■ *Web:* www.milleroutdoortheatre.com	Houston	TX	77030	281-823-9103	942-0863*
Morton H Meyerson Symphony Ctr 2301 Flora St *Web:* www.dallasculture.org	Dallas	TX	75201	214-670-3600	670-4334
Music Hall at Fair Park 909 1st Ave *Web:* www.liveatthemusichall.com	Dallas	TX	75210	214-565-1116	565-0071
One World Theatre 7701 Bee Caves Rd *Web:* www.oneworldtheatre.org	Austin	TX	78746	512-330-9500	330-9600
Palace Arts Ctr 300 S Main St *Web:* www.grapevinetexasusa.com/Heritage/PalaceArtsCenter	Grapevine	TX	76099	817-410-3100	
Paramount Theatre 352 Cypress St *Web:* www.paramount-abilene.org	Abilene	TX	79601	325-676-9620	676-0642
Paramount Theatre The 713 Congress Ave *Web:* www.austintheatre.org	Austin	TX	78701	512-472-5470	472-5824
Patty Granville Performing Arts Ctr 300 N 5th St	Garland	TX	75040	972-205-2780	205-2775
Perot Theatre 219 Main St *Web:* www.trahc.org	Texarkana	TX	75501	903-792-4992	793-8511
Reliant Arena 1 Reliant Pk *Web:* www.reliantpark.com	Houston	TX	77054	832-667-1400	
Rockport Center for the Arts 902 Navigation Cir *Web:* www.rockportartcenter.com	Rockport	TX	78382	361-729-5519	729-3551
Ryan Little Theatre 1642 Sayles Blvd McMurry University Ryan Fine Arts Bldg	Abilene	TX	79697	325-793-3889	793-4662

	City	State	ZIP	Phone	Fax
Sammons Center for the Arts 3630 Harry Hines Blvd *Web:* www.sammonsartcenter.org	Dallas	TX	75219	214-520-7789	522-9174
San Antonio Municipal Auditorium 100 Auditorium Cir *TF:* 877-504-8895 ■ *Web:* www.sanantonio.gov/convfac	San Antonio	TX	78205	210-207-8511	207-4263
San Pedro Playhouse 800 W Ashby Pl PO Box 12356 *Web:* www.sanpedroplayhouse.com	San Antonio	TX	78212	210-733-7258	734-2651
Theatre Three 2800 Routh St Suite 168 *Web:* www.theatre3dallas.com	Dallas	TX	75201	214-871-3300	871-3139
University of Texas at Austin Performing Arts Ctr E 23rd St & E Robert Dedman Dr *TF:* 800-687-6010 ■ *Web:* www.texasperformingarts.org	Austin	TX	78705	512-471-1444	471-4783
Verizon Wireless Amphitheater 16765 Lookout Rd	Selma	TX	78154	210-657-8300	
Verizon Wireless Theater 520 Texas Ave	Houston	TX	77002	713-230-1600	230-1669
Vortex Theatre 2307 Manor Rd *Web:* www.vortexrep.org	Austin	TX	78722	512-478-5282	472-8644
Wichita Falls Memorial Auditorium 1300 7th St	Wichita Falls	TX	76301	940-716-5506	
Williams Performing Arts Ctr *Abilene Christian University* 1600 Campus Ct *TF:* 800-460-6228 ■ *Web:* www.acu.edu/aboutacu/map_acu/pac.html	Abilene	TX	79699	325-674-2370	674-2369
Zachary Scott Theatre Ctr 1510 Toomey Rd *Web:* www.zachtheatre.org	Austin	TX	78704	512-476-0541	476-0314
Amarillo Civic Ctr 401 S Buchanan St *Web:* www.civicamarillo.com	Amarillo	TX	79101	806-378-4297	378-4234
American Bank Ctr 1901 N Shoreline Blvd *Web:* www.americanbankcenter.com	Corpus Christi	TX	78401	361-826-4700	826-4905
El Paso Convention & Performing Arts Ctr 1 Civic Ctr Plaza *TF:* 800-351-6024 ■ *Web:* www.visitelpaso.com/cpac_index.sstg	El Paso	TX	79901	915-534-0600	534-0687

UTAH

	City	State	ZIP	Phone	Fax
Capitol Theatre 50 W 200 S *TF:* 888-451-2787 ■ *Web:* www.arttix.org	Salt Lake City	UT	84101	801-323-6800	538-2272
Hale Center Theater Orem 225 W 400 N *Web:* www.haletheater.com	Orem	UT	84057	801-226-8600	852-3189
Hale Centre Theater (HCT) 3333 S Decker Lake Dr *Web:* www.halecentretheatre.org	West Valley City	UT	84119	801-984-9000	984-9009
Maurice Abravanel Hall 123 W S Temple *TF:* 888-451-2787 ■ *Web:* www.utahsymphony.org	Salt Lake City	UT	84101	801-533-6683	869-9026
Off Broadway Theatre 272 S Main St *Web:* www.theobt.com	Salt Lake City	UT	84101	801-355-4628	355-4641
Salt Lake Community College Grand Theatre 1575 S State St *Web:* www.slcc.edu/the-grand	Salt Lake City	UT	84115	801-957-3322	957-3059
Salt Lake County Center for the Arts 50 W 200 S *TF:* 888-451-2787 ■ *Web:* www.arttix.org	Salt Lake City	UT	84101	801-323-6800	538-2272
Terrace Plaza Playhouse 99 W 4700 S *Web:* www.terraceplayhouse.com	Ogden	UT	84405	801-393-0070	
Tuacahn Amphitheatre & Center for the Arts 1100 Tuacahn Dr *Web:* www.tuacahn.org	Ivins	UT	84738	435-652-3200	652-3227
Valley Center Playhouse 780 N 200 E *Web:* www.valleycenterplayhouse.com	Lindon	UT	84042	801-785-1186	

VERMONT

	City	State	ZIP	Phone	Fax
Barre Opera House 6 N Main St PO Box 583 *Web:* www.barreoperahouse.org	Barre	VT	05641	802-476-8188	476-5648
Flynn Center for the Performing Arts 153 Main St *Web:* www.flynncenter.org	Burlington	VT	05401	802-863-5966	863-8788

VIRGINIA

	City	State	ZIP	Phone	Fax
Clark Street Playhouse 601 S Clark St *TF:* 800-494-7499 ■ *Web:* www.washingtonshakespeare.org	Arlington	VA	22202	703-418-4808	
Generic Theater 215 St Paul's Blvd *Web:* www.generictheater.org	Norfolk	VA	23510	757-441-2160	441-2729
George Mason University's Center for the Arts George Mason University 4400 University Dr MS 2F5 *Web:* www.gmu.edu/cfa	Fairfax	VA	22030	703-993-8888	993-8650
Harrison Opera House 160 E Virginia Beach Blvd *Web:* www.vaopera.org	Norfolk	VA	23510	757-623-1223	622-0058
Jefferson Ctr 541 Luck Ave Suite 221 *Web:* www.jeffcenter.org	Roanoke	VA	24016	540-343-2624	343-3744
Landmark Theater 6 N Laurel St *TF:* 877-297-5729	Richmond	VA	23220	804-646-4213	646-6101
Little Theatre of Alexandria 600 Wolfe St *Web:* www.thelittletheatre.com	Alexandria	VA	22314	703-683-5778	683-1378
Little Theatre of Norfolk 801 Claremont Ave *Web:* www.ltnonline.org	Norfolk	VA	23507	757-627-8551	
MetroStage 1201 N Royal St *Web:* www.metrostage.org	Alexandria	VA	22314	703-548-9044	548-9089
Mill Mountain Theatre 1 Market Sq 2nd Fl *TF:* 800-317-6455 ■ *Web:* www.millmountain.org	Roanoke	VA	24011	540-342-5740	857-4391
Peninsula Community Theatre 10251 Warwick Blvd PO Box 11056 *Web:* www.pctlive.org	Newport News	VA	23601	757-595-5728	596-7436
Roper Performing Arts Ctr 340 Granby St *Web:* www.tcc.edu/roper	Norfolk	VA	23510	757-822-1450	822-1451
Thomas Jefferson Theatre 125 S Old Glebe Rd	Arlington	VA	22204	703-228-5885	
Virginia Beach Convention Ctr 2101 Parks Ave Suite 500 *TF:* 800-700-7702 ■ *Web:* www.visitvirginiabeach.com	Virginia Beach	VA	23451	757-385-4700	437-4747
Willett Hall 3701 Willett Dr *Web:* www.willetthall.com	Portsmouth	VA	23707	757-393-5144	393-7324
Wolf Trap Foundation for the Performing Arts 1645 Trap Rd *Web:* www.wolf-trap.org	Vienna	VA	22182	703-255-1900	255-4077

WASHINGTON

	City	State	ZIP	Phone	Fax
A Contemporary Theatre (ACT) 700 Union St Kreielsheimer Pl *Web:* www.acttheatre.org	Seattle	WA	98101	206-292-7660	292-7670
Behnke Center for Contemporary Performance 100 W Roy St PO Box 19515 *Web:* www.ontheboards.org	Seattle	WA	98119	206-217-9886	217-9887
Broadway Center for the Performing Arts 901 Broadway *TF:* 800-291-7593 ■ *Web:* www.broadwaycenter.org	Tacoma	WA	98402	253-591-5890	591-2013
Metropolitan Performing Arts Ctr 901 W Sprague Ave *Web:* www.mettheater.com	Spokane	WA	99204	509-455-7811	227-7778
Olympia Little Theatre 1725 Miller Ave NE PO Box 7882 *Web:* www.olympialittletheater.org	Olympia	WA	98506	360-786-9484	
Pantages Theater 901 Broadway *TF:* 800-291-7593 ■ *Web:* www.broadwaycenter.org	Tacoma	WA	98402	253-591-5890	591-2013
Rialto Theater 310 S 9th St *TF:* 800-291-7593 ■ *Web:* www.broadwaycenter.org	Tacoma	WA	98402	253-591-5890	591-2013
Seattle Ctr 305 Harrison St *Web:* www.seattlecenter.com	Seattle	WA	98109	206-684-7200	684-7342
Spokane Civic Theatre 1020 N Howard St *Web:* www.spokanecivictheatre.com	Spokane	WA	99201	509-325-1413	325-9287
Tacoma Little Theatre 210 N 'I' St *Web:* www.tacomalittletheatre.com	Tacoma	WA	98403	253-272-2281	272-3972
Washington Center for the Performing Arts 512 Washington St SE *Web:* www.washingtoncenter.org	Olympia	WA	98501	360-753-8586	754-1177
Spokane Ctr 720 W Mallon Ave *Web:* www.spokanecenter.com	Spokane	WA	99201	509-279-7000	279-7050

WEST VIRGINIA

	City	State	ZIP	Phone	Fax
Capitol Music Hall 1015 Main St *TF:* 800-624-5456 ■ *Web:* www.jamboreeusa.com/capitol.htm	Wheeling	WV	26003	304-234-0050	233-0058
Clay Center for the Arts & Sciences 1 Clay Sq *Web:* www.theclaycenter.org	Charleston	WV	25301	304-561-3570	561-3598
Oglebay Institute's Towngate Theatre 2118 Market St *Web:* www.oionline.com	Wheeling	WV	26003	304-233-4257	
Victoria Vaudeville Theater 1228 Market St *TF:* 800-505-7464 ■ *Web:* www.victoria-theater.com	Wheeling	WV	26003	304-233-7464	
Charleston Civic Center & Coliseum 200 Civic Ctr Dr *Web:* www.charlestonwvciviccenter.com	Charleston	WV	25301	304-345-1500	345-3492

WISCONSIN

	City	State	ZIP	Phone	Fax
American Players Theater 5950 Golf Course Rd PO Box 819 *Web:* www.americanplayers.org	Spring Green	WI	53588	608-588-7401	588-7085
Barrymore Theatre 2090 Atwood Ave *Web:* www.barrymorelive.com	Madison	WI	53704	608-241-8633	241-8861
Broom Street Theatre 1119 Williamson St *Web:* www.broomstreet.org	Madison	WI	53703	608-244-8338	
Marcus Center for the Performing Arts 929 N Water St *TF:* 888-612-3500 ■ *Web:* www.marcuscenter.org	Milwaukee	WI	53202	414-273-7206	273-5480
Milwaukee Chamber Theatre 158 N Broadway Broadway Theatre Ctr *Web:* www.chamber-theatre.com	Milwaukee	WI	53202	414-276-8842	277-4477
Mitby Theatre 3550 Anderson St *Web:* www.matcmadison.edu	Madison	WI	53704	608-243-4000	243-4011
Overture Center for the Arts 201 State St *Web:* www.overturecenter.com	Madison	WI	53703	608-258-4177	258-4971
Pabst Theater 144 E Wells St *TF:* 800-511-1552 ■ *Web:* www.pabsttheater.org	Milwaukee	WI	53202	414-286-3665	286-2154
Rave The 2401 W Wisconsin Ave *Web:* www.therave.com	Milwaukee	WI	53233	414-342-7283	342-0359
Riverside Theatre 116 W Wisconsin Ave *Web:* www.pabsttheater.org	Milwaukee	WI	53203	414-286-3663	
Weidner Center for the Performing Arts 2420 Nicolet Dr University of Wisconsin at Green Bay *TF:* 800-328-8587 ■ *Web:* www.uwgb.edu/weidner	Green Bay	WI	54311	920-465-2726	465-2619
Wisconsin Union Theater 800 Langdon St *Web:* www.union.wisc.edu/theater	Madison	WI	53706	608-262-0234	265-5084

WYOMING

Organization	City	State	Zip	Phone	Fax
Cheyenne Civic Ctr 510 W 20th St *TF:* 877-691-2787 ■ *Web:* www.cheyennecity.org	Cheyenne	WY	82001	307-637-6364	637-6365
Cheyenne Little Theatre Players PO Box 20087 *Web:* www.cheyennelittletheatre.org	Cheyenne	WY	82003	307-638-6543	638-6430
Jackson Hole Playhouse 145 W Deloney Ave PO Box 2788 *Web:* www.jhplayhouse.com	Jackson	WY	83001	307-733-6994	739-0414
Stage III Community Theatre 904 N Ctr St	Casper	WY	82601	307-234-0946	

576 PERFORMING ARTS ORGANIZATIONS

SEE ALSO Arts & Artists Organizations p. 1411

576-1 Dance Companies

Organization	City	State	Zip	Phone	Fax
Abilene Ballet Theatre 1265 N 2nd St *Web:* www.abileneballettheatre.org	Abilene	TX	79601	325-675-0303	
Alabama Ballet 2726 1st Ave S *Web:* www.alabamaballet.org	Birmingham	AL	35233	205-322-4300	322-4444
Alabama Dance Theatre 1018 Madison Ave *Web:* www.alabamadancetheatre.com	Montgomery	AL	36104	334-241-2590	241-2504
Alonzo King's LINES Contemporary Ballet 26 7th St *Web:* www.linesballet.org	San Francisco	CA	94102	415-863-3040	863-1180
Alvin Ailey American Dance Theater 405 W 55th St *Web:* www.alvinailey.org	New York	NY	10019	212-405-9000	405-9001
American Ballet Theatre (ABT) 890 Broadway 3rd Fl *Web:* www.abt.org	New York	NY	10003	212-477-3030	254-5938
American Indian Dance Theatre 223 E 61st St	New York	NY	10021	212-308-9555	826-0724
American Repertory Ballet 7 Livingston Ave PO Box 250 *Web:* www.americanrepertoryballet.org	New Brunswick	NJ	08901	732-249-1254	249-8475
Ann Arbor Civic Ballet 525 E Liberty St	Ann Arbor	MI	48104	734-668-8066	428-7782
Aspen Santa Fe Ballet 0245 Sage Way *Web:* www.aspensantafeballet.com	Aspen	CO	81611	970-925-7175	925-1127
Atlanta Ballet 1695 Marietta Blvd NW *Web:* www.atlantaballet.com	Atlanta	GA	30318	404-873-5811	874-7905
Augusta Ballet Inc 1301 Greene St Suite 204 *Web:* www.augustaballet.org	Augusta	GA	30901	706-261-0555	261-0551
Axis Dance Co 1428 Alice St Suite 200 *Web:* www.axisdance.org	Oakland	CA	94612	510-625-0110	625-0321
Ballet Arizona 3645 E Indian School Rd *TF:* 888-322-5538 ■ *Web:* www.balletaz.org	Phoenix	AZ	85018	602-381-0184	381-0189
Ballet Arkansas 1521 Merrill Dr *Web:* www.balletarkansas.org	Little Rock	AR	72211	501-223-5150	
Ballet Austin 501 W 3rd St *Web:* www.balletaustin.org	Austin	TX	78705	512-476-9051	472-3073
Ballet British Columbia 677 Davie St 6th Fl *Web:* www.balletbc.com	Vancouver	BC	V6B2G6	604-732-5003	732-4417
Ballet Chicago 17 N State St ; #1900 *Web:* www.balletchicago.org	Chicago	IL	60602	312-251-8838	251-8840
Ballet Florida 500 Fern St	West Palm Beach	FL	33401	561-659-2000	
Ballet Hispanico of New York 167 W 89th St *Web:* www.ballethispanico.org	New York	NY	10024	212-362-6710	362-7809
Ballet Idaho 501 S 8th St Suite A *Web:* www.balletidaho.org	Boise	ID	83702	208-343-0556	424-3129
Ballet Lubbock 5702 Genoa Ave Suite A9 *Web:* www.balletlubbock.org	Lubbock	TX	79424	806-785-3090	785-3309
Ballet Magnificat 5406 I-55 N *Web:* www.balletmagnificat.com	Jackson	MS	39211	601-977-1001	977-8948
Ballet Memphis PO Box 3675 *Web:* www.balletmemphis.org	Cordova	TN	38088	901-737-7322	737-7037
Ballet Mississippi 201 E Pascagoula St Suite 106 PO Box 1787 *Web:* www.balletms.com	Jackson	MS	39215	601-960-1560	960-2135
Ballet Pacifica 1824 Kaiser Ave *Web:* www.balletpacifica.com	Irvine	CA	92614	949-851-9130	851-9974
Ballet Quad Cities 613 17th St *Web:* www.balletquadcities.com	Rock Island	IL	61201	309-786-3779	786-2677
Ballet Tech 890 Broadway 8th Fl *Web:* www.ballettech.org	New York	NY	10003	212-777-7710	353-0936
Ballet Tennessee 3202 Kelly's Ferry Rd *Web:* www.ballettennessee.org	Chattanooga	TN	37419	423-821-2055	821-2156
Ballet Theatre of Maryland 801 Chase St Maryland Hall for the Creative Arts *Web:* www.balletmaryland.org	Annapolis	MD	21401	410-263-8289	626-1835
Ballet Theatre of New Mexico 6913 Natalie NE *Web:* www.btnm.org	Albuquerque	NM	87110	505-888-1054	888-1054
Ballet Theatre of Scranton 310 Penn Ave *Web:* www.ballettheatre.com	Scranton	PA	18503	570-347-0208	347-8774
Ballet West 50 W 200 S *Web:* www.balletwest.org	Salt Lake City	UT	84101	801-323-6900	359-3504
Ballet Western Reserve 218 W Boardman St Morley Ctr for the Arts *Web:* www.balletwesternreserve.org	Youngstown	OH	44501	330-744-1934	744-2631
BalletMet Columbus 322 Mt Vernon Ave *Web:* www.balletmet.org	Columbus	OH	43215	614-229-4860	229-4858
Baton Rouge Ballet Theatre 275 S River Rd PO Box 82288 *Web:* www.batonrougeballet.org	Baton Rouge	LA	70884	225-766-8379	
Bill T Jones/Arnie Zane Dance Co 27 W 120th St Suite 1 *Web:* www.billtjones.org	New York	NY	10027	212-426-6655	426-5883
Boston Ballet 19 Clarendon St *Web:* www.bostonballet.org	Boston	MA	02116	617-695-6950	695-6995
Boulder Ballet 2590 Walnut St Suite 10 *Web:* www.boulderballet.org	Boulder	CO	80302	303-443-0028	441-5266
Buglisi Dance Theatre 229 W 42nd St Suite 502 *Web:* www.buglisi-foreman.org	New York	NY	10036	212-719-3301	719-3302
California Ballet Co (CBC) 4819 Ronson Ct *Web:* www.californiaballet.org	San Diego	CA	92111	858-560-5676	560-0072
Canyon Concert Ballet 4103 S Mason St # A *Web:* www.ccballet.org	Fort Collins	CO	80525	970-472-4156	472-4158
Carolina Ballet Inc 3401-131 Atlantic Ave *Web:* www.carolinaballet.com	Raleigh	NC	27604	919-719-0800	719-0910
Carolyn Dorfman Dance Co (CDDC) 2780 Morris Ave Suite 1-A *Web:* www.cddc.info	Union	NJ	07083	908-687-8855	686-5245
Cassandra Ballet of Toledo 3157 Sylvania Ave	Toledo	OH	43613	419-475-0458	
Central West Ballet Co 3125 McHenry Ave Suite D *Web:* www.centralwestballet.com	Modesto	CA	95350	209-576-8957	576-1308
Charleston Ballet 822 Virginia St E *Web:* www.thecharlestonballet.com	Charleston	WV	25301	304-342-6541	345-1134
Charleston Ballet Theatre 477 King St *Web:* www.charlestonballet.com	Charleston	SC	29403	843-723-7334	723-9099
Chitresh Das Dance Co 2325 3rd St # 320 *Web:* www.kathak.org	San Francisco	CA	94107	415-333-9000	333-9029
Cincinnati Ballet 1555 Central Pkwy *Web:* www.cballet.org	Cincinnati	OH	45214	513-621-5219	621-4844
Cleo Parker Robinson Dance 119 Pk Ave W *Web:* www.cleoparkerdance.org	Denver	CO	80205	303-295-1759	295-1328
Collage Dance Theatre 2934 1/2 Beverly Glen Cir Suite 25 *Web:* www.collagedancetheatre.org	Los Angeles	CA	90077	818-784-8669	981-4116
Colorado Ballet 1278 Lincoln St *Web:* www.coloradoballet.org	Denver	CO	80203	303-837-8888	861-7174
Columbia City Ballet 1545 Main St *TF:* 800-899-7408 ■ *Web:* www.columbiacityballet.com	Columbia	SC	29201	803-799-7605	799-7928
Configuration PO Box 48	West Chatham	MA	02633	508-945-4096	
Connecticut Ballet 20 Acosta St *Web:* www.connecticutballet.com	Stamford	CT	06902	203-964-1211	961-1928
Contemporary Dance Theatre 1805 Larch Ave *Web:* www.cdt-dance.org	Cincinnati	OH	45224	513-591-1222	
Corpus Christi Ballet 1621 N Mesquite St *Web:* www.corpuschristiballet.com	Corpus Christi	TX	78401	361-882-4588	881-9291
Dallas Black Dance Theatre 2700 Flora St *Web:* www.dbdt.com	Dallas	TX	75201	214-871-2376	871-2842
Dance Alloy 5530 Penn Ave *Web:* www.dancealloy.org	Pittsburgh	PA	15206	412-363-4321	363-4320
Dance Theatre of Harlem Inc 466 W 152nd St *Web:* www.dancetheatreofharlem.org	New York	NY	10031	212-690-2800	690-8736
David Taylor Dance Theatre 1760 Glen Moor Dr *Web:* www.dtdt.org	Lakewood	CO	80215	303-789-2030	789-2165
Dayton Ballet 140 N Main St *Web:* www.daytonballet.org	Dayton	OH	45402	937-449-5060	461-8353
Dayton Contemporary Dance Co 840 Germantown St *TF:* 800-788-3310 ■ *Web:* www.dcdc.org	Dayton	OH	45402	937-228-3232	223-6156
Doug Varone & Dancers 37 W 32nd St Suite 4A *Web:* www.dougvaroneanddancers.org	New York	NY	10001	212-279-3344	279-3344
Ethnic Dance Theatre 4000 Winnetka Ave N *Web:* www.ethnicdancetheatre.com	New Hope	MN	55427	763-545-1333	559-0840
Evansville Dance Theatre 333 N Plaza E Blvd Suite E *Web:* www.edtdance.org	Evansville	IN	47715	812-473-8937	473-0392
Festival Ballet of Providence 825 Hope St *Web:* www.festivalballet.com	Providence	RI	02906	401-353-1129	353-8853
First State Ballet Theatre 818 N Market St *Web:* www.firststateballet.com	Wilmington	DE	19801	302-658-7897	
Flamenco Vivo Carlota Santana 481 8th Ave Suite 744 *Web:* flamenco-vivo.org	New York	NY	10001	212-736-4499	736-1326
Fort Wayne Ballet Inc 324 Penn Ave *Web:* www.fortwayneballet.org	Fort Wayne	IN	46805	260-484-9646	484-9647
Fort Wayne Dance Collective 437 E Berry St *Web:* www.fwdc.org	Fort Wayne	IN	46802	260-424-6574	424-2789
Garth Fagan Dance 50 Chestnut St *Web:* www.garthfagandance.org	Rochester	NY	14604	585-454-3260	454-6191
Georgia Ballet 1255 Field Pkwy *Web:* www.georgiaballet.org	Marietta	GA	30066	770-528-0881	528-0891
Grand Rapids Ballet Co 341 Ellsworth Ave SW *Web:* www.grballet.com	Grand Rapids	MI	49503	616-454-4771	454-0672
Greater Lansing Ballet Co 2224 E Michigan Ave *Web:* www.greaterlansingballet.org	Lansing	MI	48912	517-372-9887	372-9887
Hawaii State Ballet 1418 Kapiolani Blvd *Web:* www.hawaiistateballet.com	Honolulu	HI	96814	808-947-2755	
Honolulu Dance Theatre 3041 Manoa Rd *Web:* www.honoluludancetheatre.com	Honolulu	HI	96822	808-988-3202	988-5199
Houston Ballet 601 Preston St *Web:* www.houstonballet.org	Houston	TX	77002	713-523-6300	523-4038
HT Chen & Dancers 70 Mulberry St 2nd Fl *Web:* www.chendancecenter.org	New York	NY	10013	212-349-0126	349-0494

	City	State	Zip	Phone	Fax
Hubbard Street Dance Chicago 1147 W Jackson Blvd *Web:* www.hubbardstreetdance.com	Chicago	IL	60607	312-850-9744	455-8240
Huntsville Ballet 800 Regal Dr SW *Web:* www.huntsvilleballet.org	Huntsville	AL	35801	256-539-0961	539-1837
Idaho Dance Theatre (IDT) 405 S 8th St Suite 363 PO Box 6635 *Web:* www.idahodancetheatre.org	Boise	ID	83702	208-331-9592	331-8205
Inland Pacific Ballet 5050 Arrow Hwy *Web:* www.ipballet.org	Montclair	CA	91763	909-482-1590	482-1589
Interweave Dance Theatre 2224 Bruce St Suite C **Fax:* Sales ■ *Web:* www.bcn.boulder.co.us/arts/idt/idt.html	Boulder	CO	80202	303-449-0399	492-7722*
James Sewell Ballet 528 Hennepin Ave Suite 205 *Web:* www.jsballet.org	Minneapolis	MN	55403	612-672-0480	
Joe Goode Performance Group (JGPG) 499 Alabama St Suite 150 *Web:* www.joegoode.org	San Francisco	CA	94110	415-561-6565	561-6562
Joffrey Ballet of Chicago 70 E Lake St Suite 1300 *Web:* www.joffrey.com	Chicago	IL	60601	312-739-0120	739-0119
John Jasperse Co 140 2nd Ave Suite 501 *Web:* www.johnjasperse.org	New York	NY	10003	212-375-0187	375-8283
Jose Matteo's Ballet Theatre 400 Harvard St *Web:* www.ballettheatre.org	Cambridge	MA	02138	617-354-7467	354-7856
Kansas City Ballet 1616 Broadway *Web:* www.kcballet.org	Kansas City	MO	64108	816-931-2232	931-1172
Lar Lubovitch Dance Co 229 W 42nd St 8th Fl *Web:* www.lubovitch.org	New York	NY	10036	212-221-7909	221-7938
Lexington Ballet Co (LBC) 161 N Mill St *Web:* www.lexingtonballet.org	Lexington	KY	40507	859-233-3925	
Limon Dance Co 307 W 38th St Suite 1105 *Web:* www.limon.org	New York	NY	10018	212-777-3353	777-4764
Liz Lerman Dance Exchange 7117 Maple Ave *Web:* www.danceexchange.org	Takoma Park	MD	20912	301-270-6700	270-2626
Louisville Ballet 315 E Main St *Web:* www.louisvilleballet.org	Louisville	KY	40202	502-583-3150	583-0006
Madison Ballet 2822 Index Rd *Web:* www.madisonballet.org	Madison	WI	53713	608-278-7990	278-7992
Maine State Ballet 348 US Rt 1 *Web:* www.mainestateballet.org	Falmouth	ME	04105	207-781-7672	781-3663
Mark Morris Dance Group 3 Lafayette Ave *Web:* www.markmorrisdancegroup.org	Brooklyn	NY	11217	718-624-8400	624-8900
Maximum Dance Co 9220 SW 158th Ln *Web:* www.maximumdancecompany.com	Miami	FL	33157	305-259-9775	259-3160
Merce Cunningham Dance Co 55 Bethune St *Web:* www.merce.org	New York	NY	10014	212-255-8240	633-2453
Miami City Ballet 2200 Liberty Ave *TF:* 877-929-7010 ■ *Web:* www.miamicityballet.org	Miami Beach	FL	33139	305-929-7000	929-7012
Milwaukee Ballet 504 W National Ave *Web:* www.milwaukeeballet.org	Milwaukee	WI	53204	414-643-7677	649-4066
Minnesota Ballet 301 W 1st St Suite 800 *Web:* www.minnesotaballet.org	Duluth	MN	55802	218-529-3742	529-3744
Minnesota Dance Theatre 528 Hennepin Ave 6th Fl *Web:* www.mndance.org	Minneapolis	MN	55403	612-338-0627	338-5160
Montgomery Ballet 6009 E Shirley Ln *Web:* www.montgomeryballet.com	Montgomery	AL	36117	334-409-0522	409-2311
Mordine & Co Dance Theatre 1016 N Dearborn Pkwy *Web:* www.mordine.org	Chicago	IL	60610	312-654-9540	654-9542
Nai-Ni Chen Dance Co PO Box 1121 **Fax Area Code:* 201 ■ *TF:* 800-650-0246 ■ *Web:* www.nainichen.org	Fort Lee	NJ	07024	800-650-0246	242-9807*
Nashville Ballet 3630 Redmon St *Web:* www.nashvilleballet.com	Nashville	TN	37209	615-297-2966	297-9972
National Ballet 15701 Alameda Dr *Web:* www.nationalballet.com	Bowie	MD	20716	301-218-9822	249-9296
National Ballet of Canada Walter Carsen Centre for the National Ballet of Canada 470 Queens Quay W *Web:* www.national.ballet.ca	Toronto	ON	M5V3K4	416-345-9686	345-8323
Nevada Ballet Theatre 1651 Inner Cir *Web:* www.nevadaballet.com	Las Vegas	NV	89134	702-243-2623	804-0365
New Haven Ballet 70 Audubon St *Web:* www.newhavenballet.org	New Haven	CT	06510	203-782-9038	
New Jersey Ballet Co 15 Microlab Rd *Web:* www.njballet.org	Livingston	NJ	07039	973-597-9600	597-9442
New York City Ballet Inc 20 Lincoln Ctr New York State Theatre *TF:* 800-580-8730 ■ *Web:* www.nycballet.com	New York	NY	10023	212-870-5656	870-7791
New York Theatre Ballet 30 E 31st St *Web:* www.nytb.org	New York	NY	10016	212-679-0401	679-8171
North Carolina Dance Theatre 800 N College St *Web:* www.ncdance.org	Charlotte	NC	28206	704-372-0101	375-0260
Northern Ballet Theatre 36 Arlington St *Web:* www.nbti.org	Nashua	NH	03060	603-889-8406	889-6621
Northwest Florida Ballet 310 Perry Ave SE *Web:* www.nfballet.org	Fort Walton Beach	FL	32548	850-664-7787	664-0130
Oakland Ballet Co 2201 Broadway Suite 206 *TF:* 866-711-6037 ■ *Web:* www.oaklandballet.org	Oakland	CA	94612	510-893-3132	
Ocheami Culture Club PO Box 31635 *Web:* www.home.earthlink.net/~ocheami	Seattle	WA	98103	206-329-8876	
ODC/San Francisco 3153 17th St *Web:* www.odcdance.org	San Francisco	CA	94110	415-863-6606	863-9833
Ohio Ballet 354 E Market St *Web:* www.ohioballet.org	Akron	OH	44325	330-972-7900	972-7902
Oklahoma City Ballet 7421 N Classen Blvd *Web:* www.okcballet.com	Oklahoma City	OK	73116	405-843-9898	843-9894
Oregon Ballet Theatre 818 SE 6th Ave *Web:* www.obt.org	Portland	OR	97214	503-227-0977	227-4186
Orlando Ballet 1111 N Orange Ave *Web:* www.orlandoballet.org	Orlando	FL	32804	407-426-1733	426-1734
Pacific Northwest Ballet 301 Mercer St *Web:* www.pnb.org	Seattle	WA	98109	206-441-9411	441-2440
Parsons Dance Co 229 W 42nd St Suite 800 *Web:* www.parsonsdance.org	New York	NY	10036	212-869-9275	944-7417
Paul Taylor Dance Co 551 Grand St *Web:* www.ptdc.org	New York	NY	10002	212-431-5562	966-5673
Peninsula Ballet Theatre 1880 S Grant St Suite 206 *Web:* www.peninsulaballet.org	San Mateo	CA	94401	650-342-3262	
Pennsylvania Ballet 1819 John F Kennedy Blvd *Web:* www.paballet.org	Philadelphia	PA	19103	215-551-7000	551-7224
Pennsylvania Youth Ballet (PYB) 556 Main St *Web:* www.bglv.org	Bethlehem	PA	18018	610-865-0353	865-2698
Peoria Ballet 809 W Detweiller Dr # C *Web:* www.peoriaballet.com	Peoria	IL	61615	309-690-7990	690-7991
Philadelphia Dance Co 9 N Preston St *Web:* www.philadanco.org	Philadelphia	PA	19104	215-387-8200	387-8203
Pittsburgh Ballet Theatre 2900 Liberty Ave *Web:* www.pbt.org	Pittsburgh	PA	15201	412-281-0360	281-9901
Randy James Dance Works PO Box 4452 *Web:* www.rjdw.org	Highland Park	NJ	08904	732-247-2653	247-5353
Repertory Dance Theatre 138 W 300 S *Web:* www.xmission.com/~rdt	Salt Lake City	UT	84101	801-534-1000	534-1110
Richmond Ballet 407 E Canal St 1st Fl *Web:* www.richmondballet.com	Richmond	VA	23219	804-344-0906	344-0901
Ririe-Woodbury Dance Co 138 W Broadway *Web:* www.ririewoodbury.com	Salt Lake City	UT	84101	801-297-4241	297-4235
Robinson Ballet 107 Union St *Web:* www.robinsonballet.org	Bangor	ME	04401	207-990-3140	
Rochester City Ballet 1326 University Ave *Web:* www.rochestercityballet.org	Rochester	NY	14607	585-461-5850	473-8847
Sacramento Ballet 1631 K St *Web:* www.sacballet.org	Sacramento	CA	95814	916-552-5800	552-5815
San Diego Ballet 5304 Metro St Suite B *Web:* www.sandiegoballet.org	San Diego	CA	92110	619-294-7378	294-7315
San Francisco Ballet 455 Franklin St *Web:* www.sfballet.org	San Francisco	CA	94102	415-861-5600	861-2684
Sarasota Ballet of Florida 5555 N Tamiami Trail *Web:* www.sarasotaballet.org	Sarasota	FL	34243	941-359-0099	358-1504
State Ballet of Rhode Island The 52 Sherman Ave PO Box 155 *Web:* www.stateballet.com	Lincoln	RI	02865	401-334-2560	334-0412
Stuart Pimsler Dance & Theater 1937 Glenwood Pkwy *Web:* www.stuartpimsler.com	Minneapolis	MN	55422	763-521-7738	
Tallahassee Ballet Co 218 E 3rd Ave *Web:* www.tallaballet.com	Tallahassee	FL	32303	850-224-6917	224-7681
Texas Ballet Theater 6841 Green Oaks Rd # B *Web:* www.texasballettheater.org	Fort Worth	TX	76116	817-763-0207	763-0624
Texas International Theatrical Arts Society (TITAS) 3625 N Hall St # 740 *Web:* www.titas.org	Dallas	TX	75204	214-528-6112	528-2617
Trisha Brown Dance Co 625 W 55th St 2nd Fl *Web:* www.trishabrowncompany.org	New York	NY	10019	212-977-5365	977-5347
Tulsa Ballet 1212 E 45th Pl *Web:* www.tulsaballet.org	Tulsa	OK	74105	918-749-6030	749-0532
Tupelo Ballet Co 775 Poplarville Dr *Web:* www.tupeloballet.com	Tupelo	MS	38801	662-844-1928	844-1951
Urban Bush Women 138 S Oxford St Suite 4B *Web:* www.urbanbushwomen.org	Brooklyn	NY	11217	718-398-4537	398-4783
Virginia Ballet Theatre 134 W Olney Rd	Norfolk	VA	23510	757-622-4822	622-7904
Washington Ballet 3515 Wisconsin Ave NW *Web:* www.washingtonballet.org	Washington	DC	20016	202-362-3606	362-1311
Zenon Dance Co & School 528 Hennepin Ave Suite 400 *Web:* www.zenondance.org	Minneapolis	MN	55403	612-338-1101	338-2479

576-2 Opera Companies

	City	State	Zip	Phone	Fax
Academy of Vocal Arts (AVA) 1920 Spruce St *Web:* www.avaopera.com	Philadelphia	PA	19103	215-735-1685	732-2189
Amarillo Opera 2223 S Van Buren St *Web:* www.amarilloopera.org	Amarillo	TX	79109	806-372-7464	372-7465
Anchorage Opera 1507 Spar Ave *Web:* www.anchorageopera.org	Anchorage	AK	99501	907-279-2557	279-7798
Annapolis Opera Inc 801 Chase St Suite 304 Maryland Hall for the Creative Arts *Web:* www.annapolisopera.org	Annapolis	MD	21401	410-267-8135	267-6440
Arizona Opera Co 3501 N Mountain Ave *Web:* www.azopera.org	Tucson	AZ	85719	520-293-4336	293-5097
Arizona Opera Co 4600 N 12th St *TF:* 877-473-1497 ■ *Web:* www.azopera.org	Phoenix	AZ	85014	602-266-7464	266-5806
Aspen Opera Theater 2 Music School Rd *Web:* www.aspenmusicfestival.com	Aspen	CO	81611	970-925-3254	925-3802
Atlanta Opera 728 W Peachtree St NW *TF:* 800-356-7372 ■ *Web:* www.atlantaopera.org	Atlanta	GA	30308	404-881-8801	881-1711
Augusta Opera PO Box 240 *Web:* www.theaugustaopera.com	Augusta	GA	30903	706-364-9114	

Organization	City	State	Zip	Phone	Fax
Austin Lyric Opera 901 Barton Springs Rd *Web:* www.austinlyricopera.org	Austin	TX	78704	512-472-5927	472-4143
Baltimore Opera Co 110 W Mt Royal Ave Suite 306 *Web:* www.baltimoreopera.com	Baltimore	MD	21201	410-625-1600	625-6474
Boston Lyric Opera 45 Franklin St 4th Fl *Web:* www.blo.org	Boston	MA	02110	617-542-4912	542-4913
Central City Opera 400 S Colorado Blvd Suite 530 *TF:* 800-851-8175 ■ *Web:* www.centralcityopera.org	Denver	CO	80246	303-292-6500	292-4958
Charleston Light Opera Guild 200 Civic Ctr Dr *Web:* www.charlestonlightoperaguild.org	Charleston	WV	25301	304-343-2287	
Chicago Opera Theater 70 E Lake St Suite 815 *Web:* www.chicagooperatheater.org	Chicago	IL	60601	312-704-8420	704-8421
Cincinnati Opera 1243 Elm St *Web:* www.cincinnatiopera.org	Cincinnati	OH	45202	513-768-5500	768-5553
Civic Light Opera 7400 Sand Pt Way NE Suite 101-N *Web:* www.seattlemusicaltheatre.org	Seattle	WA	98115	206-363-4807	363-0702
Civic Opera Theater of Kansas City 3614 Main St *Web:* www.kccivicopera.org	Kansas City	MO	64111	816-569-3226	
Connecticut Grand Opera & Orchestra 307 Atlantic St *Web:* www.ctgrandopera.org	Stamford	CT	06901	203-327-2867	327-1417
Connecticut Opera 226 Farmington Ave *Web:* www.connecticutopera.org	Hartford	CT	06105	860-527-0713	293-1715
Dallas Opera 8350 N Central Expy Suite 210 *Web:* www.dallasopera.org	Dallas	TX	75206	214-443-1043	443-1060
Dayton Opera 138 N Main St *Web:* www.daytonopera.org	Dayton	OH	45402	937-228-7591	228-9612
Des Moines Metro Opera 106 W Boston Ave *Web:* www.desmoinesmetroopera.org	Indianola	IA	50125	515-961-6221	961-6221
Eugene Opera PO Box 11200 *Web:* www.eugeneopera.com	Eugene	OR	97440	541-221-2934	683-3783
Fargo-Moorhead Opera Co 114 Broadway Suite S-1 *Web:* www.fmopera.org	Fargo	ND	58102	701-239-4558	476-1991
Florentine Opera Co 700 N Water St Suite 950 *TF:* 800-326-7372 ■ *Web:* www.florentineopera.org	Milwaukee	WI	53202	414-291-5700	291-5706
Florida Grand Opera 8390 NW 25th St *TF:* 800-741-1010 ■ *Web:* www.fgo.org	Miami	FL	33122	305-854-1643	856-1042
Fort Worth Opera 1300 Gendy St *TF:* 877-396-7372 ■ *Web:* www.fwopera.org	Fort Worth	TX	76107	817-731-0833	731-0835
Fresno Grand Opera 2405 Capitol St Suite 103 *Web:* www.fresnograndopera.org	Fresno	CA	93721	559-442-5699	442-5649
Fullerton Civic Light Opera 201 E Chapman Ave *Web:* www.fclo.com	Fullerton	CA	92832	714-526-3832	992-1193
Glimmerglass Festival 7300 State Hwy 80 PO Box 191 *Web:* www.glimmerglass.org	Cooperstown	NY	13326	607-547-0700	547-6030
Hawaii Opera Theatre 848 S Beretania St #301 *Web:* www.hawaiiopera.org	Honolulu	HI	96813	808-596-7372	596-0379
Houston Grand Opera 510 Preston St Suite 500 *TF:* 800-626-7372 ■ *Web:* www.houstongrandopera.org	Houston	TX	77002	713-546-0200	236-8121
Indianapolis Opera 250 E 38th St *Web:* www.indyopera.org	Indianapolis	IN	46205	317-283-3531	923-5611
John F Kennedy Center for The Performing Arts The 2700 F St NW Suite 301 *TF:* 800-444-1324 ■ *Web:* www.kennedy-center.org	Washington	DC	20566	202-467-4600	
Kentucky Opera Assn 323 W Broadway Suite 601 *TF:* 800-690-9236 ■ *Web:* www.kyopera.org	Louisville	KY	40202	502-584-4500	584-7484
Knoxville Opera Co 612 E Depot Ave *Web:* www.knoxvilleopera.com	Knoxville	TN	37917	865-524-0795	524-7384
Long Beach Opera 100 W Broadway Suite 110 *Web:* www.longbeachopera.org	Long Beach	CA	90802	562-439-2580	683-2109
Los Angeles Opera 135 N Grand Ave Suite 327 *Web:* www.losangelesopera.com	Los Angeles	CA	90012	213-972-7219	687-3490
Lyric Opera of Chicago 20 N Wacker Dr Civic Opera House Suite 860 *Web:* www.lyricopera.org	Chicago	IL	60606	312-332-2244	332-8120
Lyric Opera of Kansas City 1029 Central St *TF:* 877-673-7252 ■ *Web:* www.kcopera.org	Kansas City	MO	64105	816-471-4933	471-0602
Metropolitan Opera 65th St & Broadway *Web:* www.metoperafamily.org	New York	NY	10023	212-799-3100	870-7410
Michigan Opera Theatre 1526 Broadway *Web:* www.motopera.org	Detroit	MI	48226	313-961-3500	237-3412
Minnesota Opera 620 N 1st St *TF:* 800-676-6737 ■ *Web:* www.mnopera.org	Minneapolis	MN	55401	612-333-2700	333-0869
Mississippi Opera 201 E Pascagoula St # 105 *TF:* 877-676-7372 ■ *Web:* www.msopera.org	Jackson	MS	39201	601-960-1528	960-1526
Mobile Opera Inc 257 Dauphin St *Web:* www.mobileopera.org	Mobile	AL	36602	251-432-6772	431-7613
Musical Theatre Southwest 6427 Linn Ave *Web:* www.musicaltheatresw.com	Albuquerque	NM	87108	505-265-9119	262-9319
Nevada Opera Assn PO Box 3256 *Web:* www.nevadaopera.org	Reno	NV	89505	775-786-4046	786-4063
New Jersey State Opera 50 Pk Pl 9th Fl *Web:* www.njstateopera.org	Newark	NJ	07102	973-623-5757	623-5761
New Orleans Opera Assn 1010 Common St Suite 1820 *TF:* 800-881-4459 ■ *Web:* www.neworleansopera.org	New Orleans	LA	70112	504-529-3000	529-7668
New York City Opera 20 Lincoln Ctr Plaza New York State Theater *Web:* www.nycopera.com	New York	NY	10023	212-870-5600	724-1120
Ohio Light Opera The 1189 Beall Ave *Web:* www.ohiolightopera.org	Wooster	OH	44691	330-263-2345	263-2272
Opera Birmingham 3601 6th Ave S *Web:* www.operabirmingham.org	Birmingham	AL	35222	205-322-6737	322-6206
Opera Carolina 345 N College St Suite 409 *Web:* www.operacarolina.org	Charlotte	NC	28202	704-332-7177	332-6448
Opera Cleveland 4700 Lakeside *Web:* www.operacleveland.org	Cleveland	OH	44114	216-575-0903	575-0903
Opera Co of Brooklyn 33 Indian Rd Suite 1G *Web:* www.operabrooklyn.org	New York	NY	10034	212-567-3283	
Opera Co of North Carolina 612 Wade Ave Suite 100 *Web:* www.ncopera.org	Raleigh	NC	27605	919-792-3850	783-5638
Opera Co of Philadelphia 1420 Locust St Suite 210 *Web:* www.operaphila.org	Philadelphia	PA	19102	215-893-3600	893-7801
Opera Colorado 695 S Colorado Blvd Suite 20 *Web:* www.operacolorado.org	Denver	CO	80246	303-778-1500	778-6533
Opera Columbus 177 E Naghten St *Web:* www.operacolumbus.org	Columbus	OH	43215	614-461-8101	
Opera Idaho 501 S 8th St Suite B *Web:* www.operaidaho.org	Boise	ID	83702	208-345-3531	342-7566
Opera Illinois 416 Hamilton Blvd	Peoria	IL	61602	309-673-7253	673-7211
Opera Memphis 6745 Wolf River Pkwy *Web:* www.operamemphis.org	Memphis	TN	38120	901-257-3100	257-3109
Opera Omaha 1625 Farnam St Suite 100 *TF:* 877-346-7372 ■ *Web:* www.operaomaha.org	Omaha	NE	68102	402-346-4398	346-7323
Opera Roanoke 541 Luck Ave *Web:* www.operaroanoke.org	Roanoke	VA	24016	540-982-2742	982-3601
Opera San Jose 2149 Paragon Dr *Web:* www.operasj.org	San Jose	CA	95131	408-437-4450	437-4455
Opera Santa Barbara 1330 State St *Web:* www.operasb.com	Santa Barbara	CA	93101	805-898-3890	898-3892
Opera Theatre at Wildwood 20919 Denny Rd *TF:* 888-278-7727 ■ *Web:* www.wildwoodpark.org	Little Rock	AR	72223	501-821-7275	821-7280
Opera Theatre of Saint Louis PO Box 191910 *Web:* www.opera-stl.org	Saint Louis	MO	63119	314-961-0171	961-7463
OperaDelaware 4 S Poplar St *TF:* 800-374-7263 ■ *Web:* www.operade.org	Wilmington	DE	19801	302-658-8063	658-4991
Orlando Opera 1111 N Orange Ave *TF:* 800-336-7372	Orlando	FL	32804	407-426-1717	426-1705
Palm Beach Opera 415 S Olive Ave *TF:* 877-444-3030 ■ *Web:* www.pbopera.org	West Palm Beach	FL	33401	561-833-7888	833-8294
Pensacola Opera 75 S Tarragona St PO Box 1790 *Web:* www.pensacolaopera.com	Pensacola	FL	32501	850-433-6737	433-1082
Pittsburgh Civic Light Opera 719 Liberty Ave *Web:* www.pittsburghclo.org	Pittsburgh	PA	15222	412-281-3973	281-5339
Pittsburgh Opera 2425 Liberty Ave *Web:* www.pittsburghopera.org	Pittsburgh	PA	15222	412-281-0912	281-4324
Pocket Opera 469 Bryant St *Web:* www.pocketopera.org	San Francisco	CA	94107	415-972-8930	348-0931
Portland Opera 211 SE Caruthers St *Web:* www.portlandopera.org	Portland	OR	97214	503-241-1407	241-4212
Sacramento Opera Assn 3811 J St *Web:* www.sacopera.org	Sacramento	CA	95816	916-737-1000	737-1032
San Diego Civic Light Opera 2005 Pan American Plaza Starlight Bowl *Web:* www.starlighttheatre.org	San Diego	CA	92101	619-544-7827	544-7832
San Diego Opera 1200 3rd Ave Civic Ctr Plaza 18th Fl *Web:* www.sdopera.com	San Diego	CA	92101	619-232-7636	231-6915
San Francisco Opera 301 Van Ness Ave *Web:* www.sfopera.com	San Francisco	CA	94102	415-861-4008	
Santa Fe Opera The 301 Opera Dr *TF:* 800-280-4654 ■ *Web:* www.santafeopera.org	Santa Fe	NM	87506	505-986-5900	986-5999
Sarasota Opera 61 N Pineapple Ave *TF:* 888-673-7212 ■ *Web:* www.sarasotaopera.org	Sarasota	FL	34236	941-366-8450	955-5571
Seattle Opera PO Box 9248 *TF Sales:* 800-426-1619 ■ *Web:* www.seattleopera.org	Seattle	WA	98109	206-389-7600	389-7651
Shreveport Opera 212 Texas St Suite 101 *Web:* www.shreveopera.org	Shreveport	LA	71101	318-227-9503	227-9518
Skylight Opera Theatre 158 N Broadway *Web:* www.skylightopera.com	Milwaukee	WI	53202	414-291-7811	291-7815
Syracuse Opera 411 Montgomery St Suite 60 *Web:* www.syracuseopera.com	Syracuse	NY	13202	315-475-5915	475-6319
Tacoma Opera 1119 Pacific Ave *Web:* www.tacomaopera.com	Tacoma	WA	98405	253-627-7789	627-1620
Toledo Opera 425 Jefferson Ave Suite 601 *TF:* 866-860-9048 ■ *Web:* www.toledoopera.org	Toledo	OH	43604	419-255-7464	255-6344
Tri-Cities Opera 315 Clinton St *Web:* www.tricitiesopera.com	Binghamton	NY	13905	607-729-3444	797-6344
Tulsa Opera 1610 S Boulder Ave *TF:* 866-298-2530 ■ *Web:* www.tulsaopera.com	Tulsa	OK	74119	918-582-4035	592-0380
Utah Opera Co 123 W S Temple *Web:* www.utahopera.org	Salt Lake City	UT	84101	801-533-5626	869-9026
Virginia Opera 300 W Franklin St *Web:* www.vaopera.org	Richmond	VA	23220	804-644-8168	644-0415
Virginia Opera 160 E Virginia Beach Blvd *Web:* www.vaopera.org	Norfolk	VA	23510	757-627-9545	622-0058
Wichita Grand Opera 225 W Douglas Ave Century II Performing Arts Ctr *Web:* www.wichitagrandopera.org	Wichita	KS	67202	316-683-3444	263-2126

576-3 Orchestras

Organization	City	State	Zip	Phone	Fax
Abilene Philharmonic Orchestra 402 Cypress St Suite 130 *TF:* 800-460-0610 ■ *Web:* www.abilenephilharmonic.org	Abilene	TX	79601	325-677-6710	677-1299
Acadiana Symphony Orchestra 412 Travis St *Web:* www.acadianasymphony.org	Lafayette	LA	70503	337-232-4277	237-4712

Organization	City	State	ZIP	Phone	Fax
Akron Symphony Orchestra 17 N Broadway *Web:* www.akronsymphony.org	Akron	OH	44308	330-535-8131	535-7302
Alabama Symphony Orchestra 3621 6th Ave S *Web:* www.alabamasymphony.org	Birmingham	AL	35222	205-251-6929	251-6840
Albany Symphony Orchestra 19 Clinton Ave *Web:* www.albanysymphony.com	Albany	NY	12207	518-465-4755	465-3711
Albany Symphony Orchestra 308 Flint Ave PO Box 70065 *Web:* www.albanysymphony.org	Albany	GA	31708	229-430-8933	430-8934
Alexandria Symphony Orchestra 2121 Eisenhower Ave Suite 608 *Web:* www.alexsym.org	Alexandria	VA	22314	703-548-0885	548-0985
Allentown Symphony Orchestra 23 N 6th St *Web:* www.allentownsymphony.org	Allentown	PA	18101	610-432-6715	432-6735
Amarillo Symphony 1000 S Polk St *Web:* www.amarillosymphony.org	Amarillo	TX	79101	806-376-8782	376-7127
American Composers Orchestra 240 W 35th St Suite 405 *Web:* www.americancomposers.org	New York	NY	10001	212-977-8495	977-8995
American Symphony Orchestra 333 W 39th St Suite 1101 *Web:* www.americansymphony.org	New York	NY	10018	212-868-9276	868-9277
Anchorage Symphony Orchestra 400 D St Suite 230 *TF:* 866-364-8668 ■ *Web:* www.anchoragesymphony.org	Anchorage	AK	99501	907-274-8668	272-7916
Anderson Symphony Orchestra (ASO) 1124 Meridian Plaza PO Box 741 *TF:* 888-644-9490 ■ *Web:* www.andersonsymphony.org	Anderson	IN	46016	765-644-2111	644-7703
Ann Arbor Symphony Orchestra 220 E Huron St Suite 470 *Web:* www.a2so.com	Ann Arbor	MI	48104	734-994-4801	994-3949
Annapolis Symphony Orchestra 801 Chase St Maryland Hall *Web:* www.annapolissymphony.org	Annapolis	MD	21401	410-269-1132	263-0616
Arapahoe Philharmonic 2100 W Littleton Blvd Suite 250 *Web:* www.arapahoe-phil.org	Littleton	CO	80120	303-781-1892	781-4918
Arkansas Symphony Orchestra 2417 N Tyler St PO Box 7328 *Web:* www.arkansassymphony.org	Little Rock	AR	72217	501-666-1761	666-3193
Asheville Symphony Orchestra 87 Haywood St PO Box 2852 *TF:* 888-860-7378 ■ *Web:* www.ashevillesymphony.org	Asheville	NC	28802	828-254-7046	254-1761
Aspen Chamber Symphony 2 Music School Rd *Web:* www.aspenmusicfestival.com	Aspen	CO	81611	970-925-3254	920-1643
Atlanta Pops 1830 Briarcliff Cir NE *Web:* www.altieriandassociates.com	Atlanta	GA	30329	404-636-0020	636-0020
Atlanta Symphony Orchestra 1280 Peachtree St NE Suite 4074 *Web:* www.atlantasymphony.org	Atlanta	GA	30309	404-733-4900	733-4901
Augusta Symphony 1301 Greene St Suite 200 *Web:* www.augustasymphony.org	Augusta	GA	30901	706-826-4705	826-4735
Aurora Symphony Orchestra PO Box 441481 *Web:* www.aurorasymphony.org	Aurora	CO	80044	303-873-6622	
Austin Chamber Music Ctr 3814 Medical Pkwy *Web:* www.austinchambermusic.org	Austin	TX	78756	512-454-7562	454-0029
Austin Civic Orchestra PO Box 27132 *Web:* www.austincivicorchestra.org	Austin	TX	78755	512-301-7370	301-3373
Austin Symphony Orchestra 1101 Red River St *TF:* 888-462-3787 ■ *Web:* www.austinsymphony.org	Austin	TX	78701	512-476-6064	476-6242
Bakersfield Symphony Orchestra 1328 34th St Suite A *Web:* www.bakersfieldsymphony.org	Bakersfield	CA	93301	661-323-7928	323-7331
Baltimore Symphony Orchestra 1212 Cathedral St *Web:* www.bsomusic.org	Baltimore	MD	21201	410-783-8100	783-8004
Bangor Symphony Orchestra 891 Broadway *TF:* 800-639-3221 ■ *Web:* www.bangorsymphony.com	Bangor	ME	04401	207-942-5555	990-1272
Baton Rouge Symphony 7330 Highland Rd PO Box 14209 *TF:* 877-800-4099 ■ *Web:* www.brso.org	Baton Rouge	LA	70808	225-383-0500	346-1191
Berkeley Symphony Orchestra 1942 University Ave Suite 207 *Web:* www.berkeleysymphony.org	Berkeley	CA	94704	510-841-2800	841-5422
Billings Symphony 2721 2nd Ave N *Web:* www.billingssymphony.org	Billings	MT	59101	406-252-3610	252-3353
Bismarck-Mandan Symphony Orchestra 215 N 6th St *Web:* www.bismarckmandansymphony.org	Bismarck	ND	58501	701-258-8345	258-8345
Boise Philharmonic Assn Inc 516 S 9th St *Web:* www.boisephilharmonic.org	Boise	ID	83702	208-344-7849	336-9078
Boston Modern Orchestra Project 9 Birch St *Web:* www.bmop.org	Roslindale	MA	02131	617-363-0396	363-0395
Boston Philharmonic Orchestra 295 Huntington Ave Suite 210 *Web:* www.bostonphil.org	Boston	MA	02115	617-236-0999	236-8613
Boston Pops 301 Massachusetts Ave Symphony Hall *TF:* 888-266-1200 ■ *Web:* www.bso.org	Boston	MA	02115	617-266-1492	638-9493
Boston Symphony Orchestra 301 Massachusetts Ave Symphony Hall *TF:* 888-266-1200 ■ *Web:* www.bso.org	Boston	MA	02115	617-266-1492	638-9367
Boulder Philharmonic Orchestra 2590 Wallnut St Suite 100 *Web:* www.boulderphil.org	Boulder	CO	80302	303-449-1343	443-9203
Bozeman Symphony 1822 W Lincoln St Suite 3 *Web:* www.bozemansymphony.org	Bozeman	MT	59715	406-585-9774	585-0285

Organization	City	State	ZIP	Phone	Fax
Brockton Symphony Orchestra 156 W Elm St *Web:* www.brocktonsymphony.org	Brockton	MA	02301	508-588-3841	588-3818
Brooklyn Philharmonic (BKLN | PHIL) 55 Washington St Suite 656 *Web:* www.brooklynphilharmonic.org	Brooklyn	NY	11201	718-488-5700	488-5901
Buffalo Philharmonic Orchestra 499 Franklin St *Web:* www.bpo.org	Buffalo	NY	14202	716-885-0331	885-9372
Calgary Philharmonic Orchestra 205 8th Ave SE 2nd Fl *Web:* www.cpo-live.com	Calgary	AB	T2G0K9	403-571-0270	294-7424
California Philharmonic Orchestra 1120 Huntington Dr *Web:* www.calphil.org	San Marino	CA	91108	626-300-8200	300-8010
Camellia Symphony Orchestra 1545 River Pk Dr Suite 506 PO Box 19786 *Web:* www.camelliasymphony.org	Sacramento	CA	95815	916-929-6655	929-4292
Canton Symphony Orchestra 1001 Market Ave N *Web:* www.cantonsymphony.org	Canton	OH	44702	330-452-3434	452-4429
Cape Symphony Orchestra 712A Main St *Web:* www.capesymphony.org	Yarmouth Port	MA	02675	508-362-1111	362-7916
Carson City Symphony 191 Heidi Cir PO Box 2001 *Web:* www.ccsymphony.com	Carson City	NV	89702	775-883-4154	883-4371
Chamber Orchestra of Philadelphia 1520 Locust St Suite 500 *Web:* www.chamberorchestra.org	Philadelphia	PA	19102	215-545-5451	545-3868
Champaign-Urbana Symphony Orchestra (CUSO) 701 Devonshire Dr Suite C-24 *Web:* www.cusymphony.org	Champaign	IL	61820	217-351-9139	398-0413
Charleston Symphony Orchestra 145 King St Suite 311 *Web:* www.charlestonsymphony.com	Charleston	SC	29401	843-723-7528	722-3463
Charlotte Philharmonic Orchestra 8008 Corporate Ctr Dr Suite 206 PO Box 470987	Charlotte	NC	28247	704-543-5551	543-5542
Charlotte Symphony Orchestra 301 S Tryon St # 1700 *Web:* www.charlottesymphony.org	Charlotte	NC	28282	704-972-2003	972-2012
Chattanooga Symphony & Opera (CSO) 701 Broad St *Web:* www.chattanoogasymphony.org	Chattanooga	TN	37402	423-267-8583	265-6520
Cheyenne Symphony Orchestra (CSO) 1904 Thomes Ave *Web:* www.cheyennesymphony.org	Cheyenne	WY	82001	307-778-8561	634-7512
Chicago Chamber Orchestra 65 W Jackson Blvd *Web:* www.chicagochamberorchestra.org	Chicago	IL	60604	312-357-1551	
Chicago Sinfonietta 70 E Lake St Suite 226 *Web:* www.chicagosinfonietta.org	Chicago	IL	60601	312-236-3681	236-5429
Chicago Symphony Orchestra 220 S Michigan Ave *TF:* 800-223-7114 ■ *Web:* www.cso.org	Chicago	IL	60604	312-294-3000	294-3035
Cincinnati Chamber Orchestra 105 W 4th St Suite 810 *Web:* www.ccocincinnati.com	Cincinnati	OH	45202	513-723-1182	723-1057
Cincinnati Symphony Orchestra 1241 Elm St Music Hall *Web:* www.cincinnatisymphony.org	Cincinnati	OH	45202	513-621-1919	744-3535
Civic Orchestra of Tucson (COT) PO Box 42764 *Web:* www.cotmusic.org	Tucson	AZ	85733	520-730-3371	
Cleveland Chamber Symphony 2001 Euclid Ave Cleveland State University *Web:* www.clevelandchambersymphony.org	Cleveland	OH	44115	216-687-9243	687-9279
Cleveland Orchestra The 11001 Euclid Ave Severance Hall *TF:* 800-686-1141 ■ *Web:* www.clevelandorchestra.com	Cleveland	OH	44106	216-231-7300	231-0202
Cleveland Pops Orchestra 24000 Mercantile Rd Suite 11 *Web:* www.clevelandpops.com	Cleveland	OH	44122	216-765-7677	765-1931
Colorado Springs Philharmonic PO Box 60730 *Web:* www.csphilharmonic.org	Colorado Springs	CO	80960	719-884-2110	884-2111
Colorado Symphony Orchestra 1000 14th St Unit 15 *TF:* 877-292-7979 ■ *Web:* www.coloradosymphony.org	Denver	CO	80202	303-623-7876	293-2649
Columbus Symphony Orchestra 935 1st Ave PO Box 1499 *Web:* www.csoga.org	Columbus	GA	31904	706-323-5059	323-7051
Columbus Symphony Orchestra 55 E State St *Web:* www.columbussymphony.com	Columbus	OH	43215	614-228-9600	224-7273
Corpus Christi Symphony Orchestra 555 N Carancahua St Tower II Suite 410 PO Box 495 *TF:* 877-286-6683 ■ *Web:* www.ccsymphony.org	Corpus Christi	TX	78478	361-882-2717	882-4132
Da Camera of Houston 1427 Branard St *TF:* 800-233-2226 ■ *Web:* www.dacamera.com	Houston	TX	77006	713-524-7601	524-4148
Dallas Symphony Orchestra 2301 Flora St Suite 300 *Web:* www.dallassymphony.com	Dallas	TX	75201	214-692-0203	871-4049
Dayton Philharmonic Orchestra 109 N Main St Suite 200 *Web:* www.daytonphilharmonic.com	Dayton	OH	45402	937-224-3521	223-9189
Daytona Beach Symphony Society PO Box 2 *Web:* www.dbss.org	Daytona Beach	FL	32115	386-253-2901	253-5774
Dearborn Symphony Orchestra 23400 Michigan Ave PO Box 2063 *Web:* www.dearbornsymphony.org	Dearborn	MI	48123	313-565-2424	982-1978
DeKalb Symphony Orchestra (DSO) PO Box 1313 *Web:* www.dekalbsymphony.com	Tucker	GA	30085	678-891-3565	891-3575

Organization	City	State	ZIP	Phone	Fax
Delaware Symphony Orchestra 818 N Market St *Web:* www.desymphony.org	Wilmington	DE	19801	302-656-7442	656-7754
Des Moines Symphony 221 Walnut St *Web:* www.dmsymphony.org	Des Moines	IA	50309	515-280-4000	280-4005
Detroit Symphony Orchestra 3711 Woodward Ave *Web:* www.detroitsymphony.com	Detroit	MI	48201	313-576-5111	576-5109
Dubuque Symphony Orchestra 2728 Asbury Rd Suite 900 *TF:* 866-803-9280 ■ *Web:* www.dubuquesymphony.org	Dubuque	IA	52001	563-557-1677	557-9841
Duluth-Superior Symphony Orchestra 331 W Superior St Suite 100 *Web:* www.dsso.com	Duluth	MN	55802	218-733-7575	623-3789
Durham Symphony Orchestra 120 Morris St PO Box 1993 *Web:* www.durhamsymphony.org	Durham	NC	27702	919-560-2736	560-2752
Eastern Connecticut Symphony Orchestra 289 State St *Web:* www.ectsymphony.org	New London	CT	06320	860-443-2876	444-7601
Edmonton Symphony Orchestra 9720 102nd Ave *TF:* 800-563-5081 ■ *Web:* www.edmontonsymphony.com	Edmonton	AB	T5J4B2	780-428-1108	425-0167
El Paso Symphony Orchestra 1 Civic Ctr Plaza *Web:* www.epso.org	El Paso	TX	79901	915-532-3776	533-8162
Erie Philharmonic 1006 State St *Web:* www.eriephil.org	Erie	PA	16501	814-455-1375	455-1377
Eugene Symphony 115 W 8th Ave Suite 115 *Web:* www.eugenesymphony.org	Eugene	OR	97401	541-687-9487	687-0527
Evansville Philharmonic Orchestra 530 Main St *Web:* www.evansvillephilharmonic.org	Evansville	IN	47708	812-425-5050	426-7008
Fairbanks Symphony Orchestra 312 Tanana Loop *Web:* www.fairbankssymphony.org	Fairbanks	AK	99709	907-474-5733	474-5147
Fairfax Symphony Orchestra 3905 Railroad Ave Suite 202-N *Web:* www.fairfaxsymphony.org	Fairfax	VA	22030	703-563-1990	293-9349
Fargo-Moorhead Symphony 810 4th Ave S Suite 250	Moorhead	MN	56560	218-233-8397	236-1845
Flagstaff Symphony Orchestra 113 E Aspen Ave # A *TF:* 888-520-7214 ■ *Web:* www.flagstaffsymphony.org	Flagstaff	AZ	86001	928-774-5107	774-5109
Florida Orchestra 101 S Hoover Blvd Suite 100 *TF:* 800-662-7286 ■ *Web:* www.floridaorchestra.org	Tampa	FL	33609	813-286-1170	286-8227
Florida Symphony Youth Orchestra 812 E Rollins St Suite 300 *Web:* www.fsyo.org	Orlando	FL	32803	407-999-7800	896-5250
Fort Collins Symphony 214 S College Ave *Web:* www.fcsymphony.org	Fort Collins	CO	80524	970-482-4823	482-4858
Fort Smith Symphony Orchestra 511 Central Mall Suite 617 PO Box 3151	Fort Smith	AR	72913	479-452-7575	452-8985
Fort Worth Symphony Orchestra Assn 330 E 4th St Suite 200 *Web:* www.fwsymphony.org	Fort Worth	TX	76102	817-665-6500	665-6600
Fresno Philharmonic 2377 W Shaw Ave Suite 101 *Web:* www.fresnophil.org	Fresno	CA	93711	559-261-0600	261-0700
Glendale Symphony Orchestra 1157 N Brand Blvd *Web:* www.glendalesymphony.org	Glendale	CA	91202	818-500-8720	500-8721
Grand Rapids Symphony 300 Ottawa Ave NW Suite 100 *Web:* www.grsymphony.org	Grand Rapids	MI	49503	616-454-9451	454-7477
Grant Park Orchestra 205 E Randolph Dr *Web:* www.grantparkmusicfestival.com	Chicago	IL	60601	312-742-7638	742-7662
Greater Bridgeport Symphony (GBS) 446 University Ave *Web:* www.gbs.org	Bridgeport	CT	06604	203-576-0263	367-0064
Greater Trenton Symphony Orchestra 28 W State St Suite 202 *Web:* www.trentonsymphony.org	Trenton	NJ	08608	609-394-1338	394-1394
Green Bay Symphony Orchestra 1240 Main St Suite 2 *Web:* www.gbsymphony.org	Green Bay	WI	54302	920-435-3465	435-1427
Greensboro Symphony Orchestra 200 N Davie St Suite 301 *Web:* www.greensborosymphony.org	Greensboro	NC	27401	336-335-5456	335-5580
Greenville Symphony Orchestra 200 S Main St *Web:* www.greenvillesymphony.org	Greenville	SC	29601	864-232-0344	467-3113
Greenwich Symphony Orchestra PO Box 35 *Web:* www.greenwichsym.org	Greenwich	CT	06836	203-869-2664	
Handel & Haydn Society 300 Massachusetts Ave *Web:* www.handelandhaydn.org	Boston	MA	02115	617-262-1815	266-4217
Harrisburg Symphony Orchestra 800 Corporate Cir Suite 101 *Web:* www.harrisburgsymphony.org	Harrisburg	PA	17110	717-545-5527	545-6501
Hartford Symphony Orchestra 99 Pratt Ave Suite 500 *Web:* www.hartfordsymphony.org	Hartford	CT	06103	860-246-8742	247-5430
Houston Symphony Orchestra 615 Louisiana St Suite 102 *Web:* www.houstonsymphony.org	Houston	TX	77002	713-224-4240	222-7024
Huntsville Symphony Orchestra 700 Monroe St PO Box 2400 *Web:* www.hso.org	Huntsville	AL	35801	256-539-4818	539-4819
Idaho State Civic Symphony 921 S 8th Ave S- 8099 Idaho State University Fine Arts Dept *Web:* www.thesymphony.us	Pocatello	ID	83209	208-282-3636	282-4884
Illinois Symphony Orchestra 524 1/2 E Capitol Ave *TF:* 800-401-7222 ■ *Web:* www.ilsymphony.org	Springfield	IL	62701	217-522-2838	522-7374
Indianapolis Symphony Orchestra 45 Monument Cir *TF:* 800-366-8457 ■ *Web:* www.indianapolissymphony.org	Indianapolis	IN	46204	317-262-1100	262-1159
Jacksonville Symphony Orchestra (JSO) 300 W Water St Suite 200 *TF:* 877-662-6731 ■ *Web:* www.jaxsymphony.org	Jacksonville	FL	32202	904-354-5479	354-9238
Johnson City Symphony Orchestra 112 E Myrtle Ave # 503 *Web:* www.jcsymphony.com	Johnson City	TN	37601	423-926-8742	926-8979
Juneau Symphony Orchestra 522 W 10th St PO Box 21236 *Web:* www.juneausymphony.org	Juneau	AK	99802	907-586-4676	463-2555
Kalamazoo Symphony Orchestra 359 S Kalamazoo Mall Suite 100 *Web:* www.kalamazoosymphony.com	Kalamazoo	MI	49007	269-349-7759	349-9229
Kansas City Symphony 1020 Central St Suite 300 *Web:* www.kcsymphony.org	Kansas City	MO	64105	816-471-1100	471-0976
Kennedy Center Opera House Orchestra John F Kennedy Ctr for the Performing Arts 2700 F St NW *TF:* 800-444-1324 ■ *Web:* www.kennedy-center.org	Washington	DC	20566	202-416-8200	416-8205
Kentucky Symphony Orchestra 540 Linden Ave PO Box 72810 *Web:* www.kyso.org	Newport	KY	41072	859-431-6216	431-3097
Knoxville Symphony Orchestra 100 S Gay St Suite 302 *Web:* www.knoxvillesymphony.com	Knoxville	TN	37902	865-523-1178	546-3766
Lansing Symphony Orchestra (LSO) 501 S Capitol Ave Suite 400 *Web:* www.lansingsymphony.org	Lansing	MI	48933	517-487-5001	487-0210
Las Cruces Symphony Orchestra 1075 N Horseshoe Cir *Web:* www.lascrucessymphony.com	Las Cruces	NM	88003	575-646-3709	646-1086
Lexington Philharmonic 161 N Mill St *TF:* 888-494-4226 ■ *Web:* www.lexphil.org	Lexington	KY	40507	859-233-4226	233-7896
Lincoln Symphony Orchestra 233 S 13th St Suite B-102 *Web:* www.lincolnsymphony.com	Lincoln	NE	68508	402-476-2211	476-2236
Long Beach Symphony Orchestra 110 W Ocean Blvd Suite 22 *Web:* www.lbso.org	Long Beach	CA	90802	562-436-3203	491-3599
Long Island Baroque Ensemble PO Box 7 *Web:* www.longislandbaroqueensemble.com	Locust Valley	NY	11560	631-724-7386	
Long Island Philharmonic (LIP) 1 Huntington Quadrangle Suite 2C21 *Web:* www.liphilharmonic.com	Melville	NY	11747	631-293-2223	293-2655
Los Angeles Chamber Orchestra 707 Wilshire Blvd Suite 1850 *Web:* www.laco.org	Los Angeles	CA	90017	213-622-7001	955-2071
Los Angeles Philharmonic Assn 111 S Grand Ave **Fax Area Code:* 213 ■ *Web:* www.laphil.org	Los Angeles	CA	90012	323-850-2000	972-7560*
Louisiana Philharmonic Orchestra 1010 Common St Suite 2120 *Web:* www.lpomusic.com	New Orleans	LA	70112	504-523-6530	595-8468
Louisville Orchestra 323 W Broadway Suite 700 *Web:* www.louisvilleorchestra.org	Louisville	KY	40202	502-587-8681	589-7870
Macon Symphony Orchestra 400 Poplar St *Web:* www.maconsymphony.com	Macon	GA	31201	478-301-5300	301-5505
Madison Symphony Orchestra 201 State St *Web:* www.madisonsymphony.org	Madison	WI	53703	608-257-3734	280-6192
Manitoba Chamber Orchestra 393 Portage Ave Portage Pl Suite Y300 *Web:* www.manitobachamberorchestra.org	Winnipeg	MB	R3B3H6	204-783-7377	783-7383
Marin Symphony 4340 Redwood Hwy Suite 409C *Web:* www.marinsymphony.org	San Rafael	CA	94903	415-479-8100	479-8110
Maryland Symphony Orchestra The 30 W Washington St *Web:* www.marylandsymphony.org	Hagerstown	MD	21740	301-797-4000	797-2314
Massachusetts Symphony Orchestra 10 Tuckerman St Tuckerman Hall *Web:* www.tuckermanhall.org/pops.html	Worcester	MA	01609	508-754-1234	752-3671
Memphis Symphony Orchestra 585 S Mendenhall Rd *Web:* www.memphissymphony.org	Memphis	TN	38117	901-537-2525	537-2550
Mesa Symphony Orchestra 56 S Ctr St *Web:* www.mesasymphony.org	Mesa	AZ	85210	480-827-2143	827-2070
Miami Symphony Orchestra The (MISO) 10689 N Kendall Dr Suite 307 *Web:* www.miamisymphony.org	Miami	FL	33176	305-275-5666	275-4363
Milwaukee Symphony Orchestra 929 N Water St Suite 700 *TF:* 800-291-7605 ■ *Web:* www.milwaukeesymphony.org	Milwaukee	WI	53202	414-291-6010	291-7610
Minnesota Orchestra 1111 Nicollet Mall Orchestra Hall *TF:* 800-292-4141 ■ *Web:* www.minnesotaorchestra.org	Minneapolis	MN	55403	612-371-5600	371-0838
Mississippi Symphony Orchestra 201 E Pascagoula St *Web:* www.msorchestra.com	Jackson	MS	39201	601-960-1565	960-1564
Mobile Symphony PO Box 3127 *Web:* www.mobilesymphony.org	Mobile	AL	36652	251-432-2010	432-6618
Modesto Symphony Orchestra 911 13th St *Web:* www.modestosymphony.org	Modesto	CA	95354	209-523-4156	523-0201
Muncie Symphony Orchestra 2000 W University Ave # Ac112 *Web:* www.munciesymphony.org	Muncie	IN	47306	765-285-5531	285-9128
Music of the Baroque 111 N Wabash Ave Suite 810 *Web:* www.baroque.org	Chicago	IL	60602	312-551-1414	551-1444
Napa Valley Symphony 3379 Solano Ave Suite 1000 *Web:* www.napavalleysymphony.org	Napa	CA	94558	707-944-9900	944-9912

Organization / Address	City	State	Zip	Phone	Fax
Nashville Chamber Orchestra 1114 17th Ave S Suite 202 *Web:* www.nco.org	Nashville	TN	37212	615-256-6546	322-1228
Nashville Symphony 1 Symphony Pl *Web:* www.nashvillesymphony.org	Nashville	TN	37201	615-687-6500	687-6505
National Philharmonic 5301 Tuckerman Ln *Web:* www.nationalphilharmonic.org	North Bethesda	MD	20852	301-493-9283	493-9284
National Symphony Orchestra JFK Ctr for the Performing Arts 2700 F St NW *TF:* 800-444-1324 ■ *Web:* www.kennedy-center.org/nso	Washington	DC	20566	202-416-8000	416-8105
New Hampshire Music Festival Orchestra 52 Symphony Ln *Web:* www.nhmf.org	Center Harbor	NH	03226	603-279-3300	279-3484
New Haven Symphony Orchestra 105 Ct St # 302 *Web:* www.newhavensymphony.com	New Haven	CT	06510	203-865-0831	789-8907
New Jersey Symphony Orchestra 60 Pk Pl *Web:* www.njsymphony.org	Newark	NJ	07102	973-624-3713	624-2115
New West Symphony 2100 E Thousand Oaks Blvd Suite D *Web:* www.newwestsymphony.org	Thousand Oaks	CA	91362	805-497-5800	497-5839
New World Symphony 500 17th St *TF:* 800-597-3331 ■ *Web:* www.nws.edu	Miami Beach	FL	33139	305-673-3330	673-6749
New York Philharmonic 10 Lincoln Ctr Plaza Avery Fisher Hall **Fax:* Mktg ■ *Web:* www.nyphil.org	New York	NY	10023	212-875-5900	875-5717*
New York Pops 333 W 52nd St Suite 600 *Web:* www.newyorkpops.org	New York	NY	10019	212-765-7677	315-3199
North Arkansas Symphony 605 W Dixon St PO Box 1243 *Web:* www.nasymphony.org	Fayetteville	AR	72702	479-521-4166	695-1229
North Carolina Symphony 2 E S St Memorial Auditorium *Web:* www.ncsymphony.org	Raleigh	NC	27601	919-733-2750	733-9920
Northeastern Pennsylvania Philharmonic 4101 Birney Ave *TF:* 800-836-3413 ■ *Web:* www.nepaphil.org	Moosic	PA	18507	570-341-1568	941-0318
Oklahoma City Philharmonic 428 W California Ave Suite 210 *Web:* www.okcphilharmonic.org	Oklahoma City	OK	73102	405-232-7575	232-4353
Omaha Symphony 1605 Howard St *Web:* www.omahasymphony.org	Omaha	NE	68102	402-342-3836	342-3819
Opera Orchestra Of New York The 344 E 63rd St Suite B-1 *Web:* www.operaorchestrany.org	New York	NY	10065	212-906-9137	906-9021
Orange County's Pacific Symphony 3631 S Harbor Blvd Suite 100 *Web:* www.pacificsymphony.entericorp.com	Santa Ana	CA	92704	714-755-5788	755-5789
Orchestra Iowa 119 3rd Ave SE *TF:* 800-369-8863 ■ *Web:* www.orchestraiowa.org	Cedar Rapids	IA	52401	319-366-8206	366-5206
Orchestra New England 70 Audubon St *Web:* www.orchestranewengland.org	New Haven	CT	06510	203-777-4690	772-0578
Orchestra of Saint Luke's 330 W 42nd St 9th Fl *Web:* www.oslmusic.org	New York	NY	10036	212-594-6100	594-3291
Orchestre Metropolitain du Grand Montreal 486 St Catherine St W Suite 401 *Web:* www.orchestremetropolitain.com	Montreal	QC	H3B1A6	514-598-0870	840-9195
Orchestre Symphonique de Montreal 260 de Maisonneuve Blvd W 2nd Fl *TF:* 888-842-9951 ■ *Web:* www.osm.ca	Montreal	QC	H2X1Y9	514-842-9951	842-0728
Oregon Symphony Orchestra 921 SW Washington St Suite 200 *TF:* 800-228-7343 ■ *Web:* www.orsymphony.org	Portland	OR	97205	503-228-4294	228-4150
Orlando Philharmonic Orchestra 812 E Rollins St Suite 300 *TF:* 888-262-8122 ■ *Web:* www.orlandophil.org	Orlando	FL	32803	407-896-6700	896-5512
Orpheus Chamber Orchestra 490 Riverside Dr 11th Fl *Web:* www.orpheusnyc.com	New York	NY	10027	212-896-1700	896-1717
Ottawa Symphony Orchestra (OSO) 2 Daly Ave Suite 250 *Web:* www.ottawasymphony.com	Ottawa	ON	K1N6E2	613-231-7802	231-3610
Owensboro Symphony Orchestra 211 E 2nd St *Web:* www.owensborosymphony.org	Owensboro	KY	42303	270-684-0661	683-0740
Paducah Symphony Orchestra 2101 Broadway *TF:* 800-738-3727 ■ *Web:* www.paducahsymphony.com	Paducah	KY	42001	270-444-0065	444-0456
Pasadena Symphony 117 E Colorado Blvd *Web:* www.pasadenasymphony.org	Pasadena	CA	91105	626-793-7172	793-7180
Pensacola Symphony Orchestra 205 E Zaragossa St PO Box 1752 *Web:* www.pensacolasymphony.com	Pensacola	FL	32502	850-435-2533	444-9910
Peoria Symphony Orchestra 203 Harrison St *Web:* www.peoriasymphony.org	Peoria	IL	61602	309-637-2787	637-7388
Peter Nero & the Philly Pops 260 S Broad St 16th Fl *Web:* www.phillypops.com	Philadelphia	PA	19102	215-893-1900	893-1948
Philadelphia Orchestra 260 S Broad St Suite 1600 *TF:* 800-457-8354 ■ *Web:* www.philorch.org	Philadelphia	PA	19102	215-893-1900	893-1948
Philharmonia Baroque Orchestra 180 Redwood St Suite 200 *Web:* www.philharmonia.org	San Francisco	CA	94102	415-252-1288	252-1488
Philharmonic Center for The Arts The 5833 Pelican Bay Blvd *TF:* 800-597-1900 ■ *Web:* www.thephil.org	Naples	FL	34108	239-597-1900	597-8163
Philharmonic Orchestra of New Jersey 50 Mt Bethel Rd PO Box 4064	Warren	NJ	07059	908-226-7300	226-7337
Phoenix Symphony 455 N 3rd St Suite 390 *TF:* 800-776-9080 ■ *Web:* www.phoenixsymphony.org	Phoenix	AZ	85004	602-495-1117	253-1772
Pittsburgh Symphony Orchestra 600 Penn Ave Heinz Hall for the Performing Arts *TF:* 800-743-8560 ■ *Web:* www.pittsburghsymphony.org	Pittsburgh	PA	15222	412-392-4800	392-3311
Plano Symphony Orchestra 5236 Tennyson Pkwy Suite 200 *Web:* www.planosymphony.org	Plano	TX	75024	972-473-7262	473-4639
Plymouth Philharmonic Orchestra 16 Ct St PO Box 3174 *Web:* www.plymouthphilharmonic.com	Plymouth	MA	02361	508-746-8008	746-0115
Portland Baroque Orchestra 1020 SW Taylor St Suite 275 *TF:* 800-494-8497 ■ *Web:* www.pbo.org	Portland	OR	97205	503-222-6000	226-6635
Portland Symphony Orchestra 50 Monument Sq 2nd Fl PO Box 3573 *Web:* www.portlandsymphony.com	Portland	ME	04101	207-773-6128	773-6089
ProMusica Chamber Orchestra 243 N 5th St Suite 202 *Web:* www.promusicacolumbus.org	Columbus	OH	43215	614-464-0066	464-4141
Raleigh Symphony Orchestra 2414 White Cliff Rd PO Box 25878 *Web:* www.raleighsymphony.com	Raleigh	NC	27611	919-546-9755	546-0251
Redlands Symphony 1200 E Colton Ave. *Web:* www.redlandssymphony.com	Redlands	CA	92373	909-335-5202	335-5213
Reno Chamber Orchestra 925 Riverside Dr Suite 5 *Web:* www.renochamberorchestra.org	Reno	NV	89503	775-348-9413	348-0643
Reno Philharmonic Orchestra 925 Riverside Dr Suite 3 *Web:* www.renophilharmonic.com	Reno	NV	89503	775-323-6393	323-6711
Rhode Island Philharmonic Orchestra 667 Waterman Ave *Web:* www.ri-philharmonic.org	East Providence	RI	02914	401-831-3123	248-7071
Richmond Symphony 300 W Franklin St Suite 103E *Web:* www.richmondsymphony.com	Richmond	VA	23220	804-788-4717	788-1541
Richmond Symphony Orchestra 380 Hubelchison Pkwy PO Box 982 *Web:* www.richmondsymphony.org	Richmond	IN	47375	765-966-5181	962-8447
Ridgefield Symphony Orchestra 90 E Ridge PO Box 289 *Web:* www.ridgefieldsymphony.org	Ridgefield	CT	06877	203-438-3889	438-0222
River City Brass Band 500 Grant St Suite 2720 One Mellon Ctr *TF:* 800-292-7222 ■ *Web:* www.rcbb.com	Pittsburgh	PA	15219	412-434-7222	434-6436
Roanoke Symphony Orchestra 541 Luck Ave Suite 200 *TF:* 866-277-9127 ■ *Web:* www.rso.com	Roanoke	VA	24016	540-343-6221	343-0065
Rochester Orchestra & Chorale 400 S Broadway *TF:* 877-286-8742 ■ *Web:* www.rochestersymphony.org	Rochester	MN	55904	507-286-8742	280-4136
Rochester Philharmonic Orchestra 108 E Ave *Web:* www.rpo.org	Rochester	NY	14604	585-454-7311	325-4905
Rockford Symphony Orchestra 711 N Main St *Web:* www.rockfordsymphony.com	Rockford	IL	61103	815-965-0049	965-0642
Saint Louis Symphony Orchestra 718 N Grand Blvd *TF:* 800-232-1880 ■ *Web:* www.stlsymphony.org	Saint Louis	MO	63103	314-533-2500	286-4111
Saint Paul Chamber Orchestra 408 St Peter St 3rd Fl *Web:* www.thespco.org	Saint Paul	MN	55102	651-292-3248	292-3281
San Antonio Symphony 222 E Houston Suite 200 PO Box 658 *Web:* www.sasymphony.org	San Antonio	TX	78293	210-554-1000	554-1008
San Diego Symphony Orchestra 1245 7th Ave. *Web:* www.sandiegosymphony.com	San Diego	CA	92101	619-235-0804	231-8178
San Francisco Symphony 201 Van Ness Ave. *Web:* www.sfsymphony.org	San Francisco	CA	94102	415-552-8000	431-6857
Santa Barbara Symphony 1900 State St Suite G *Web:* www.thesymphony.org	Santa Barbara	CA	93101	805-898-9626	898-9326
Santa Cruz Symphony 307 Church St *Web:* www.santacruzsymphony.com	Santa Cruz	CA	95060	831-462-0553	426-1193
Santa Fe Symphony Orchestra & Chorus Inc 551 W Cordova Rd Suite D PO Box 9692 *TF:* 800-480-1319 ■ *Web:* www.santafesymphony.org	Santa Fe	NM	87504	505-983-3530	982-3888
Santa Rosa Symphony (SRS) 50 Santa Rosa Ave Suite 410 *Web:* www.santarosasymphony.com	Santa Rosa	CA	95404	707-546-8742	546-7284
Sarasota Orchestra 709 N Tamiami Trail *TF:* 866-508-0611 ■ *Web:* www.sarasotaorchestra.org	Sarasota	FL	34236	941-953-4252	953-3059
Scottsdale Symphony Orchestra 3127 N 81st Pl	Scottsdale	AZ	85251	480-945-8071	946-8770
Seattle Symphony 200 University St. *Web:* www.seattlesymphony.org	Seattle	WA	98101	206-215-4700	215-4701
Shreveport Symphony Orchestra 619 Louisiana Ave Suite 400 *Web:* www.shreveportsymphony.com	Shreveport	LA	71101	318-222-7496	222-7490
Sioux City Symphony Orchestra 520 Pierce St PO Box 754 *Web:* www.siouxcitysymphony.org	Sioux City	IA	51102	712-277-2111	252-0224
South Bend Symphony Orchestra (SBSO) 127 N Michigan St *TF:* 800-537-6415 ■ *Web:* www.southbendsymphony.com	South Bend	IN	46601	574-232-6343	232-6627
South Carolina Philharmonic 721 Lady St *Web:* www.scphilharmonic.com	Columbia	SC	29201	803-771-7937	771-0268
South Dakota Symphony Orchestra 315 S Main Ave 4th Fl *TF:* 866-681-7376 ■ *Web:* www.sdsymphony.org	Sioux Falls	SD	57104	605-335-7933	335-1958
South Florida Symphony 221 SW 3rd Ave Fort Lauderdale **Fax Area Code:* 954 ■ *TF:* 800-775-4086 ■ *Web:* www.southfloridasymphony.org	Key West	FL	33312	800-775-4086	522-8430*
Spokane Symphony PO Box 365 *Web:* www.spokanesymphony.org	Spokane	WA	99210	509-624-1200	252-2637

	City	State	Zip	Phone	Fax
Springfield Symphony Orchestra 1350 Main St *Web:* www.springfieldsymphony.org	Springfield	MA	01103	413-733-0636	781-4129
Springfield Symphony Orchestra 411 N Sherman Pkwy *Web:* www.springfieldmosymphony.org	Springfield	MO	65802	417-864-6683	864-8967
Symphony Nova Scotia 6101 University Ave Dalhousie Arts Ctr *TF:* 800-874-1669 ■ *Web:* www.symphonynovascotia.ca	Halifax	NS	B3H3J5	902-494-3820	494-2883
Symphony of the Mountains 1200 E Ctr St *Web:* www.symphonyofthemountains.org	Kingsport	TN	37660	423-392-8423	392-8428
Symphony Silicon Valley 345 S 1st St *Web:* www.symphonysiliconvalley.org	San Jose	CA	95113	408-286-2600	286-2600
Syracuse Symphony Orchestra 411 Montgomery St Suite 40 *TF:* 800-724-3810 ■ *Web:* www.syracusesymphony.org	Syracuse	NY	13202	315-424-8222	424-1131
Tacoma Symphony 901 Broadway # 600 *Web:* www.tacomasymphony.org	Tacoma	WA	98402	253-272-7264	274-8187
Tallahassee Symphony Orchestra 1345 Thomasville Rd *Web:* www.tsolive.org	Tallahassee	FL	32303	850-224-0461	222-9092
Thayer Symphony Orchestra 14 Monument Sq # 406 *Web:* www.thayersymphony.org	Leominster	MA	01453	978-466-1800	840-1000
Toledo Symphony 1838 Parkwood Ave *TF:* 800-348-1253 ■ *Web:* www.toledosymphony.com	Toledo	OH	43604	419-246-8000	321-6890
Topeka Symphony 2100 SE 29th St PO Box 2206 *Web:* www.topekasymphony.org	Topeka	KS	66601	785-232-2032	232-6204
Traverse Symphony Orchestra 300 E Front St # 230 *TF:* 866-947-7120 ■ *Web:* www.tso-online.org	Traverse City	MI	49684	231-947-7120	947-8118
Tucson Symphony Orchestra 2175 N 6th Ave *Web:* www.tucsonsymphony.org	Tucson	AZ	85705	520-792-9155	792-9314
Tupelo Symphony Orchestra 1800 W Main St PO Box 474 *Web:* www.tupelosymphony.com	Tupelo	MS	38801	662-842-8433	842-9565
Tuscaloosa Symphony Orchestra 600 Greensboro Ave *Web:* www.tsoonline.org	Tuscaloosa	AL	35401	205-752-5515	345-2787
US Air Force Strings 201 McChord St Bolling Air Force Base *Web:* www.usafband.af.mil	Washington	DC	20032	202-767-4225	767-0686
Utah Symphony & Opera 123 W S Temple *Web:* www.utahsymphony.org	Salt Lake City	UT	84101	801-533-5626	869-9026
Vermont Symphony Orchestra 2 Church St Suite 19 *TF:* 800-876-9293 ■ *Web:* www.vso.org	Burlington	VT	05401	802-864-5741	864-5109
Virginia Symphony Orchestra 861 Glenrock Rd Suite 200 *Web:* www.virginiasymphony.org	Norfolk	VA	23502	757-466-3060	466-3046
Wallingford Symphony Orchestra PO Box 6023 *Web:* www.wallingfordsymphony.org	Wallingford	CT	06492	203-697-2261	
Washington Metropolitan Philharmonic PO Box 120 *Web:* www.washingtonmetrophilharmonic.org	Mount Vernon	VA	22121	703-799-8229	360-7391
Washington Symphony Orchestra (WSO) PO Box 178 *Web:* www.washsym.org	Washington	PA	15301	724-223-9796	
Waterbury Symphony Orchestra 110 Bank St *Web:* www.waterburysymphony.org	Waterbury	CT	06702	203-574-4283	756-3507
Waterloo-Cedar Falls Symphony Orchestra Gallagher-Bluedorn Performing Arts Ctr Suite 17 *Web:* www.wcfsymphony.org	Cedar Falls	IA	50614	319-273-3373	
Westchester Philharmonic 123 Main St Lobby Level *Web:* www.westchesterphil.org	White Plains	NY	10601	914-682-3707	682-3716
Western Piedmont Symphony 243 3rd Ave NE Suite 1-N *Web:* www.wpsymphony.org	Hickory	NC	28601	828-324-8603	324-1301
Wheeling Symphony Orchestra 1025 Main St Suite 811 *TF:* 800-395-9241 ■ *Web:* www.wheelingsymphony.org	Wheeling	WV	26003	304-232-6191	232-6192
Wichita Symphony Orchestra 225 W Douglas St Suite 207 *Web:* www.wso.org	Wichita	KS	67202	316-267-5259	267-1937
Windsor Symphony Orchestra 487 Oullette Ave *Web:* www.windsorsymphony.com	Windsor	ON	N9A4J2	519-973-1238	973-0764
Winnipeg Symphony Orchestra 555 Main St Suite 1020 *Web:* www.wso.mb.ca	Winnipeg	MB	R3B1C3	204-949-3950	956-4271
Winston-Salem Symphony 680 W 4th St *Web:* www.wssymphony.org	Winston-Salem	NC	27101	336-725-1035	725-3924
Wyoming Symphony Orchestra 111 W 2nd St *Web:* www.wyomingsymphony.org	Casper	WY	82601	307-266-1478	266-4522
Youngstown Symphony Orchestra 260 Federal Plaza W *Web:* www.youngstownsymphony.com	Youngstown	OH	44503	330-744-4269	744-1441

576-4 Theater Companies

	City	State	Zip	Phone	Fax
Actors Theatre of Louisville 316 W Main St *TF:* 800-428-5849 ■ *Web:* www.actorstheatre.org	Louisville	KY	40202	502-584-1265	561-3300
Alabama Shakespeare Festival 1 Festival Dr *TF:* 800-841-4273 ■ *Web:* www.asf.net	Montgomery	AL	36117	334-271-5300	271-5348
Alaska Junior Theater 329 F St Suite 204 *Web:* www.akjt.org	Anchorage	AK	99501	907-272-7546	272-3035
Alliance Theatre Co 1280 Peachtree St NE Woodruff Arts Ctr *Web:* www.alliancetheatre.org	Atlanta	GA	30309	404-733-4650	733-4625
American Conservatory Theater (ACT) 30 Grant Ave 6th Fl *Web:* www.act-sf.org	San Francisco	CA	94108	415-834-3200	834-3360
Arden Theatre Co 40 N 2nd St *Web:* www.ardentheatre.org	Philadelphia	PA	19106	215-922-8900	922-7011
Arizona Theatre Co 343 S Scott Ave *TF:* 888-772-9449 ■ *Web:* www.arizonatheatre.org	Tucson	AZ	85701	520-884-8210	628-9129
Arkansas Repertory Theatre 601 Main St PO Box 110 *TF:* 866-684-3737 ■ *Web:* www.therep.org	Little Rock	AR	72201	501-378-0445	378-0012
Artists Repertory Theatre 1516 SW Alder St *Web:* www.artistsrep.org	Portland	OR	97205	503-241-9807	241-8268
Augusta Players The 1301 Greene St Suite 304 PO Box 2352 *Web:* www.augustaplayers.com	Augusta	GA	30901	706-826-4707	826-4709
Bakersfield Community Theater 2400 S Chester Ave *Web:* www.bakersfieldcommunitytheatre.com	Bakersfield	CA	93304	661-831-8114	
Barter Theatre 127 W Main St *Web:* www.bartertheatre.com	Abingdon	VA	24210	276-628-3991	619-3335
Berkshire Theatre Festival PO Box 797 *TF:* 866-811-4111 ■ *Web:* www.berkshiretheatre.org	Stockbridge	MA	01262	413-298-5576	298-3368
Biloxi Little Theatre 220 Lee St *Web:* www.4blt.org	Biloxi	MS	39530	228-432-8543	392-7639
BoarsHead Theater 425 S Grand Ave Center for the Arts *Web:* www.boarshead.org	Lansing	MI	48933	517-484-7805	484-2564
Caldwell Theatre Co 7873 N Federal Hwy *TF:* 877-245-7432 ■ *Web:* www.caldwelltheatre.com	Boca Raton	FL	33487	561-241-7380	997-6917
Capital Repertory Theatre 432 State St *Web:* www.capitalrep.org	Schenectady	NY	12305	518-462-4531	881-1823
Carpenter Square Theatre 1015 N Broadway Ave *Web:* www.carpentersquare.com	Oklahoma City	OK	73102	405-232-6500	270-4806
Center Stage 700 N Calvert St *Web:* www.centerstage.org	Baltimore	MD	21202	410-986-4000	539-3912
Center Theatre Group 601 W Temple St *Web:* www.centertheatregroup.org	Los Angeles	CA	90012	213-628-2772	972-7402
Charleston Stage Co 629 Johnny Dodds Blvd *TF:* 800-454-7093 ■ *Web:* www.charlestonstage.com	Mount Pleasant	SC	29404	843-577-5967	577-5422
Children's Musical Theater San Jose (CMTS) 1401 Parkmoor Ave Suite 100 *Web:* www.cmtsj.org	San Jose	CA	95126	408-288-5437	288-6241
City Lights Theatre 529 S 2nd St *Web:* www.cltc.org	San Jose	CA	95112	408-295-4200	295-8318
City Theatre Co 1300 Bingham St *Web:* www.citytheatrecompany.org	Pittsburgh	PA	15203	412-431-4400	431-5535
Cleveland Play House 8500 Euclid Ave *Web:* www.clevelandplayhouse.com	Cleveland	OH	44106	216-795-7000	795-7005
Cleveland Public Theatre 6415 Detroit Ave *Web:* www.cptonline.org	Cleveland	OH	44102	216-631-2727	631-2575
Community Theatre of Greensboro (CTG) 200 N Davie St Suite 9 *Web:* www.ctgso.org	Greensboro	NC	27401	336-333-7470	333-2607
Corn Stock Theatre 1700 Pk Rd *TF:* 800-220-1185 ■ *Web:* www.cornstocktheatre.com	Peoria	IL	61604	309-676-2196	676-9036
Court Theatre 5535 S Ellis Ave *Web:* www.courttheatre.org	Chicago	IL	60637	773-702-7005	834-1897
Dallas Theater Ctr 3636 Turtle Creek Blvd *Web:* www.dallastheatercenter.org	Dallas	TX	75219	214-526-8210	521-7666
Downtown Cabaret Theatre 263 Golden Hill St *Web:* www.dtcab.com	Bridgeport	CT	06604	203-576-1636	576-1444
Ensemble Theatre of Cincinnati 1127 Vine St *Web:* www.cincyetc.com	Cincinnati	OH	45202	513-421-3555	562-4104
Fairbanks Shakespeare Theatre PO Box 73447 *Web:* www.fstalaska.org	Fairbanks	AK	99707	907-457-7638	457-4511
Fargo-Moorhead Community Theatre 333 4th St S *TF:* 877-687-7469 ■ *Web:* www.fmct.org	Fargo	ND	58103	701-235-1901	235-2685
Florida Stage 262 S Ocean Blvd *TF:* 800-514-3837 ■ *Web:* www.floridastage.org	Manalapan	FL	33462	561-585-3404	588-4708
Ford's Theatre 511 10th St NW *TF:* 800-899-2367 ■ *Web:* www.fordstheatre.org	Washington	DC	20004	202-638-2941	347-6269
Fort Smith Little Theatre 401 N 6th St *Web:* www.fslt.org	Fort Smith	AR	72913	479-783-2966	
Fort Wayne Civic Theater 303 E Main St *Web:* www.fwcivic.org	Fort Wayne	IN	46802	260-422-8641	422-6699
Garland Civic Theatre 108 N 6th St *Web:* www.garlandcivictheatre.org	Garland	TX	75040	972-485-8884	487-2159
Geffen Playhouse 10886 Le Conte Ave *Web:* www.geffenplayhouse.com	Los Angeles	CA	90024	310-508-5454	208-8383
Georgia Shakespeare 4484 Peachtree Rd NE *Web:* www.gashakespeare.org	Atlanta	GA	30319	404-504-3400	504-3414
Goodspeed Musicals PO Box A *Web:* www.goodspeed.org	East Haddam	CT	06423	860-873-8664	873-2329
Great Lakes Theater Festival 1501 Euclid Ave Suite 300 *TF:* 800-766-6048 ■ *Web:* www.greatlakestheater.org	Cleveland	OH	44115	216-241-5490	241-6315
Huntington Beach Playhouse (HBPH) 7111 Talbert Ave *Web:* www.hbplayhouse.com	Huntington Beach	CA	92648	714-375-0696	847-0457
Huntington Theatre Co 264 Huntington Ave Boston University Theatre *Web:* www.huntingtontheatre.org	Boston	MA	02115	617-266-7900	353-8300
Indiana Repertory Theatre Inc 140 W Washington St *Web:* www.irtlive.com	Indianapolis	IN	46204	317-635-5277	236-0767

Organization	City	State	Zip	Phone	Fax
Indianapolis Civic Theatre Inc 3200 Cold Spring Rd *Web:* www.civictheatre.org	Indianapolis	IN	46222	317-923-4597	923-3548
International City Theatre 1 World Trade Ctr Suite 300 PO Box 32069 *Web:* www.ictlongbeach.com	Long Beach	CA	90832	562-495-4595	436-7895
Invisible Theatre 1400 N 1st Ave *Web:* www.invisibletheatre.com	Tucson	AZ	85719	520-882-9721	884-5410
Irish Classical Theatre 625 Main St *Web:* www.irishclassicaltheatre.com	Buffalo	NY	14203	716-853-4282	853-0592
La Jolla Playhouse PO Box 12039 *Web:* www.lajollaplayhouse.com	La Jolla	CA	92039	858-550-1070	550-1075
Laguna Playhouse The 606 Laguna Canyon Rd PO Box 1747 *Web:* www.lagunaplayhouse.com	Laguna Beach	CA	92651	949-497-2787	497-6948
Lincoln Center Theater 150 W 65th St *Web:* www.lct.org	New York	NY	10023	212-362-7600	873-0761
Lost Nation Theater 39 Main St *Web:* www.lostnationtheater.org	Montpelier	VT	05602	802-229-0492	223-9608
Lyric Theatre of Oklahoma 1727 NW 16th St *Web:* www.lyrictheatreokc.com	Oklahoma City	OK	73106	405-524-9312	524-9316
Maltz Jupiter Theatre 1001 E Indiantown Rd *TF:* 800-445-1666 ■ *Web:* www.jupitertheatre.org	Jupiter	FL	33477	561-743-2666	743-0107
Manhattan Theatre Club Inc 311 W 43rd St 8th Fl *Web:* www.manhattantheatreclub.com	New York	NY	10036	212-399-3000	399-4329
Merrimack Repertory Theatre 132 Warren St *Web:* www.merrimackrep.org	Lowell	MA	01852	978-654-7550	654-7575
Milwaukee Repertory Theater 108 E Wells St *Web:* www.milwaukeerep.com	Milwaukee	WI	53202	414-224-1761	224-9097
Music Theatre Louisville 321 W Broadway *Web:* www.musictheatrelouisville.com	Louisville	KY	40202	502-589-4060	589-0741
Music Theatre of Wichita 225 W Douglas Suite 202 *Web:* www.mtwichita.org	Wichita	KS	67202	316-265-3253	265-8708
National Theatre of the Deaf (NTD) 139 N Main St *Web:* www.ntd.org	West Hartford	CT	06107	860-236-4193	236-4163
Nebraska Repertory Theatre 12th & R Sts 215 Temple Bldg *TF:* 800-432-3231 ■ *Web:* www.unl.edu	Lincoln	NE	68588	402-472-2072	472-9055
New Stage Theatre 1100 Carlisle St *Web:* www.newstagetheatre.com	Jackson	MS	39202	601-948-3531	948-3538
North Carolina Theatre 1 E S St Memorial Auditorium *Web:* www.nctheatre.com	Raleigh	NC	27601	919-831-6941	831-6951
Northlight Theatre 9501 Skokie Blvd *Web:* www.northlight.org	Skokie	IL	60077	847-679-9501	679-1879
Old Globe Theatre 1363 Old Globe Way *Web:* www.oldglobe.org	San Diego	CA	92101	619-231-1941	231-5879
Pacific Repertory Theater PO Box 222035 *Web:* www.pacrep.org	Carmel	CA	93922	831-622-0700	622-0703
Paper Bag Players 225 W 99th St *TF:* 800-777-2247 ■ *Web:* www.paperbagplayers.org	New York	NY	10025	212-663-0390	663-1076
Park Playhouse Inc PO Box 525 *Web:* www.parkplayhouse.com	Albany	NY	12201	518-434-2035	434-1048
Pasadena Playhouse The 39 S El Molino Ave *Web:* www.pasadenaplayhouse.org	Pasadena	CA	91101	626-356-7529	204-7399
Penobscot Theatre Co 131 Main St *TF:* 877-782-8499 ■ *Web:* www.penobscottheatre.org	Bangor	ME	04401	207-942-3333	947-6678
Pensacola Little Theatre (PLT) 400 S Jefferson St Pensacola Cultural Ctr *Web:* www.pensacolalittletheatre.com	Pensacola	FL	32502	850-432-2042	438-2787
People's Light & Theatre Co 39 Conestoga Rd *Web:* www.peopleslight.org	Malvern	PA	19355	610-647-1900	640-9521
Perseverance Theatre 914 3rd St *Web:* www.perseverancetheatre.org	Douglas	AK	99824	907-364-2421	364-2603
Pittsburgh Public Theater 621 Penn Ave *Web:* www.ppt.org	Pittsburgh	PA	15222	412-316-8200	316-8219
PlayMakers Repertory Co 150 Country Club Rd **Fax Area Code:* 866 ■ *Web:* www.playmakersrep.org	Chapel Hill	NC	27599	919-962-7529	904-8396*
Portland Center Stage (PCS) 128 NW Eleventh Ave *Web:* www.pcs.org	Portland	OR	97205	503-445-3700	445-3701
Portland Stage Co PO Box 1458 *Web:* www.portlandstage.org	Portland	ME	04104	207-774-1043	774-0576
Prince Music Theater 1412 Chestnut St *Web:* www.princemusictheater.org	Philadelphia	PA	19102	215-569-9700	972-1020
Repertory Theatre of Saint Louis 130 Edgar Rd PO Box 191730 *Web:* www.repstl.org	Saint Louis	MO	63119	314-968-7340	968-9638
Rochester Repertory Theatre Co 314 1/2 S Broadway *Web:* www.rochesterrep.org	Rochester	MN	55904	507-289-1737	
Roundabout Theatre Co 231 W 39th St Suite 1200 *Web:* www.roundabouttheatre.org	New York	NY	10018	212-719-9393	869-8817
Sacramento Theatre Co 1419 H St *TF:* 888-478-2849 ■ *Web:* www.sactheatre.org	Sacramento	CA	95814	916-443-6722	446-4066
San Diego Repertory Theatre 79 Horton Plaza *Web:* www.sandiegorep.com	San Diego	CA	92101	619-231-3586	231-4304
San Jose Repertory Theatre 101 Paseo de San Antonio *Web:* www.sjrep.com	San Jose	CA	95113	408-367-7255	367-7236
San Jose Stage Co 490 S 1st St *Web:* www.sanjose-stage.com	San Jose	CA	95113	408-283-7142	283-7146
Sandra Feinstein-Gamm Theatre 172 Exchange St *Web:* www.gammtheatre.org	Pawtucket	RI	02860	401-723-4266	723-0440
Seattle Repertory Theatre (SRT) 155 Mercer St PO Box 900923 *TF:* 877-900-9285 ■ *Web:* www.seattlerep.org	Seattle	WA	98109	206-443-2210	443-2379
Second City Chicago 1608 N Wells St *TF:* 877-778-4707 ■ *Web:* www.secondcity.com	Chicago	IL	60614	312-664-4032	664-9837
Shakespeare Theatre 516 8th St SE *TF:* 877-487-8849 ■ *Web:* www.shakespearetheatre.org	Washington	DC	20003	202-547-3230	547-0226
Signature Theatre 4200 Campbell Ave *Web:* www.signature-theatre.org	Arlington	VA	22206	703-820-9771	820-7790
South Carolina Children's Theatre 153 Augusta St *Web:* www.scchildrenstheatre.org	Greenville	SC	29601	864-235-2885	235-0208
South Coast Repertory 655 Town Ctr Dr *Web:* www.scr.org	Costa Mesa	CA	92626	714-708-5500	708-5576
Springfield Little Theatre 311 E Walnut St *Web:* www.landerstheatre.org	Springfield	MO	65806	417-869-1334	869-4047
Stage Coach Theatre 5296 Overland Rd *Web:* www.stagecoachtheatre.com	Boise	ID	83705	208-342-2000	
Stages Repertory Theatre 3201 Allen Pkwy Suite 101 *Web:* www.stagestheatre.com	Houston	TX	77019	713-527-0220	527-8669
Stockton Civic Theatre (SCT) 2312 Rose Marie Ln *Web:* www.sctlivetheatre.com	Stockton	CA	95207	209-473-2400	473-1502
Studio Arena Theatre 710 Main St *TF:* 800-777-8243	Buffalo	NY	14202	716-856-8025	856-3415
Swine Palace Productions Tower Dr Louisiana State University *Web:* www.wix.com/swinepalace/sp-test	Baton Rouge	LA	70803	225-578-3527	578-4135
Syracuse Stage 820 E Genesee St *Web:* www.syracusestage.org	Syracuse	NY	13210	315-443-4008	443-9846
Tacoma Musical Playhouse 7116 6th Ave *Web:* www.tmp.org	Tacoma	WA	98406	253-565-6867	564-7863
Tempe Live! Theatre Inc PO Box 24718 *Web:* tempelivetheater.org	Tempe	AZ	85285	480-350-8388	
Tennessee Repertory Theatre 161 Rains Ave *Web:* www.tennesseerep.org	Nashville	TN	37203	615-244-4878	349-3222
Theater of the Stars 1100 Spring St Suite 301 *Web:* www.theaterofthestars.com	Atlanta	GA	30309	404-252-8960	252-1460
THEATERWORK 3201 Richards Ln # B *Web:* www.theaterwork.org	Santa Fe	NM	87507	505-471-1799	
Theatre Arlington 305 W Main St *Web:* www.theatrearlington.org	Arlington	TX	76010	817-275-7661	275-3370
Theatre Cedar Rapids 102 3rd St SE *Web:* www.theatrecr.org	Cedar Rapids	IA	52401	319-366-8592	366-8593
Theatre Charlotte 501 Queens Rd *Web:* www.theatrecharlotte.org	Charlotte	NC	28207	704-376-3777	347-5216
Theatre For A New Audience 154 Christopher St #3D *Web:* www.tfana.org	New York	NY	10014	212-229-2819	229-2911
Theatre Harrisburg 513 Hurlock St *Web:* www.theatreharrisburg.com	Harrisburg	PA	17110	717-232-5501	232-5912
Theatre IV 114 W Broad St *Web:* www.theatreiv.org	Richmond	VA	23220	804-344-8040	643-2671
Theatre of Youth (TOY) 203 Allen St *Web:* www.theatreofyouth.org	Buffalo	NY	14201	716-884-4400	819-9653
Theatre Tulsa 207 N Main St *Web:* www.theatretulsa.org	Tulsa	OK	74103	918-587-8402	587-8403
Theatre Tuscaloosa 9500 Old Greensboro Rd Suite 135 *Web:* www.theatretusc.com	Tuscaloosa	AL	35405	205-391-2277	391-2329
Theatre Under the Stars 800 Bagby St Suite 200 *Web:* www.tuts.com	Houston	TX	77002	713-558-2600	558-2650
TheatreWorks 1100 Hamilton Ct PO Box 50458 *Web:* www.theatreworks.org	Palo Alto	CA	94303	650-463-1950	463-1963
Tihati Productions Ltd 3615 Harding Ave Suite 507 *Web:* www.tihati.com	Honolulu	HI	96816	808-735-0292	735-9479
Toledo Repertoire Theatre 16 10th St *Web:* www.toledorep.org	Toledo	OH	43604	419-243-9277	
Trinity Repertory Co 201 Washington St *Web:* www.trinityrep.com	Providence	RI	02903	401-521-1100	751-5577
Tuscaloosa Children's Theatre 10889 Magnolia Ln *Web:* www.tuscaloosachildrenstheatre.com	Coaling	AL	35453	205-462-0100	
Virginia Stage Co 254 Granby St PO Box 3770 *Web:* www.vastage.com	Norfolk	VA	23510	757-627-6988	628-5958
West Virginia Public Theatre 111 High St *TF:* 877-999-9878 ■ *Web:* www.wvpublictheatre.org	Morgantown	WV	26505	304-291-4122	291-4125
Western Nevada Musical Theater Co *Western Nevada College* 2201 W College Pkwy Cedar Bldg 113 *Web:* www.wnc.edu	Carson City	NV	89703	775-445-4249	445-3154
Westport Community Theatre 110 Myrtle Ave *Web:* www.westportcommunitytheatre.com	Westport	CT	06880	203-226-1983	
Wild Swan Theater 416 W Huron St *Web:* www.wildswantheater.org	Ann Arbor	MI	48103	734-995-0530	668-7292
Wilmington Drama League 10 W Lea Blvd *Web:* www.wdl.org	Wilmington	DE	19802	302-764-1172	764-7904
Yale Repertory Theatre 1120 Chapel St PO Box 1257 *Web:* www.yale.edu/yalerep	New Haven	CT	06505	203-432-1234	432-6423
Birmingham Festival Theater 1901 1/2 11th Ave S PO Box 55321 *Web:* www.bftonline.org	Birmingham	AL	35205	205-933-2383	
Arena Stage 1101 6th St SW *Web:* www.arenastage.org	Washington	DC	20024	202-554-9066	488-4056
American Stage 163 3rd St N *Web:* www.americanstage.org	Saint Petersburg	FL	33731	727-823-1600	821-2444

Phone | Fax

GableStage
1200 Anastasia Ave Biltmore Hotel .... Coral Gables FL 33134 305-446-1116 445-8645
Web: www.gablestage.org
Academy Theatre 119 Ctr St .... Avondale Estates GA 30002 404-474-8332 806-7721
Web: www.academytheatre.org
Goodman Theatre 170 N Dearborn St .... Chicago IL 60601 312-443-3811 443-3821
Web: www.goodmantheatre.org
Evansville Civic Theatre 717 N Fulton St .... Evansville IN 47710 812-425-2800 423-2636
Web: www.civic.evansville.net
Baton Rouge Little Theater
7155 Florida Blvd .... Baton Rouge LA 70806 225-924-6496 924-9972
Web: www.brlt.org
Circle Theatre 161 Ottawa Ave NW .... Grand Rapids MI 49503 616-632-1980 456-8540
Web: www.circletheatre.org
Guthrie Theater 818 S 2nd St .... Minneapolis MN 55415 612-377-2224 225-6004
TF: 877-447-8243 ■ *Web:* www.guthrietheater.org
Unicorn Theatre 3828 Main St .... Kansas City MO 64111 816-531-7529 531-0421
Web: www.unicorntheatre.org
Omaha Community Playhouse 6915 Cass St .... Omaha NE 68132 402-553-0800 553-6288
TF: 888-782-4338 ■ *Web:* www.omahaplayhouse.com
McCarter Theatre 91 University Pl .... Princeton NJ 08540 609-258-6500 497-0369
Web: www.mccarter.org
Geva Theatre Ctr 75 Woodbury Blvd .... Rochester NY 14607 585-232-1366 232-4031
Web: www.gevatheatre.org
Public theater The 425 Lafayette St .... New York NY 10003 212-539-8500 539-8505
Web: www.publictheater.org
Erie Playhouse 13 W 10th St .... Erie PA 16501 814-454-2851 454-0601
Web: www.erieplayhouse.org
Wilma Theater 265 S Broad St .... Philadelphia PA 19107 215-893-9456 893-0895
Web: www.wilmatheater.org
Warehouse Theatre 37 Augusta St .... Greenville SC 29601 864-235-6948
Web: www.warehousetheatre.com
Clarence Brown Theatre
University of Tennessee 206 McClung Tower .... Knoxville TN 37996 865-974-5161 974-4867
Web: www.clarencebrowntheatre.com
Playhouse on the Square 51 S Cooper St .... Memphis TN 38104 901-726-4656 272-7530
Web: www.playhouseonthesquare.org
Alley Theatre 615 Texas Ave .... Houston TX 77002 713-228-9341 222-6542
Web: www.alleytheatre.org
Casa Manana Theatre 3101 W Lancaster Ave .... Fort Worth TX 76107 817-332-2272 332-5711
Web: www.casamanana.org
Jubilee Theatre 506 Main St .... Fort Worth TX 76102 817-338-4204 338-4206
Web: www.jubileetheatre.org
San Pedro Playhouse
800 W Ashby Pl PO Box 12356 .... San Antonio TX 78212 210-733-7258 734-2651
Web: www.sanpedroplayhouse.com
Generic Theater 215 St Paul's Blvd .... Norfolk VA 23510 757-441-2160 441-2729
Web: www.generictheater.org
Little Theatre of Alexandria 600 Wolfe St .... Alexandria VA 22314 703-683-5778 683-1378
Web: www.thelittletheatre.com
A Contemporary Theatre (ACT)
700 Union St Kreielsheimer Pl .... Seattle WA 98101 206-292-7660 292-7670
Web: www.acttheatre.org

577 PERFUMES

SEE ALSO Cosmetics, Skin Care, and Other Personal Care Products p. 1772

Phone | Fax

Alpine Aromatics International Inc
51 Ethel Rd W .... Piscataway NJ 08854 732-572-5600 572-0944
TF: 800-631-5389 ■ *Web:* www.alpinearomatics.com
Aramis Inc 5 Thornton Rd .... Oakland NJ 07436 973-492-3600 492-3690
Web: www.elcompanies.com
Avon Products Inc
1345 Avenue of the Americas .... New York NY 10105 212-282-5000 282-6825
NYSE: AVP ■ *TF Cust Svc:* 800-367-2866 ■ *Web:* www.avon.com
Bijan Boutique 420 N Rodeo Dr .... Beverly Hills CA 90210 310-273-6544 273-6535
Web: www.bijan.com
Chanel Inc 57th St Botique 44th Fl .... New York NY 10019 212-355-5050 752-1851
TF: 800-550-0005 ■ *Web:* www.chanel.com
Coty & Lancaster Inc 1 Pk Ave 4th Fl .... New York NY 10016 212-389-7000 532-7003
Web: www.coty.com
Crabtree & Evelyn Ltd 102 Peake Brook Rd .... Woodstock CT 06281 860-928-2761 928-0462
TF: 800-624-5211 ■ *Web:* www.crabtree-evelyn.com
Eagle Marketing Inc Perfume Originals Products Div
2412 Sequoia Pk .... Yukon OK 73099 405-354-1027 354-7882
TF: 800-233-7424 ■ *Web:* www.eimi.com
Elizabeth Arden Inc
2400 NE 145th Ave Suite 200 .... Miramar FL 33027 954-364-6900 364-6910
NASDAQ: RDEN ■ *TF:* 800-227-2445 ■ *Web:* www.elizabetharden.com
FragranceNet.com Inc 104 Pkwy Dr S .... Hauppauge NY 11788 631-582-5204 582-8433
TF: 800-727-3867 ■ *Web:* www.fragrancenet.com
Guerlain Inc 19 E 57th St .... New York NY 10022 212-931-2400 931-2445
Web: www.guerlain.com
Inter Parfums Inc 551 5th Ave Suite 1500 .... New York NY 10176 212-983-2640 983-4197
NASDAQ: IPAR ■ *Web:* www.interparfumsinc.com
Key West Fragrance & Cosmetics Factory Inc
419 Duval St .... Key West FL 33040 305-293-1885
TF: 800-445-2563 ■ *Web:* www.keywestaloe.com
Noville Inc 124 Case Dr .... South Plainfield NJ 07080 908-754-2222 754-0167
TF: 888-668-4553
Parfums de Coeur Ltd 85 Old Kings Hwy N .... Darien CT 06820 203-655-8807 656-2121
TF: 800-887-2738 ■ *Web:* www.parfumsdecoeur.com
Parfums Givenchy LLC 19 E 57th St .... New York NY 10022 212-931-2600 931-2630
TF: 800-479-6427 ■ *Web:* www.givenchybeauty.com
Parlux Fragrances Inc
5900 N Andrews Ave Suite 500 .... Fort Lauderdale FL 33312 954-316-9008 491-1187
NASDAQ: PARL ■ *Web:* www.parlux.com

Phone | Fax

Perfumania 251 International Pkwy .... Sunrise FL 33325 954-335-9100 335-9166
NASDAQ: ECMV ■ *TF:* 866-600-3600 ■ *Web:* www.perfumania.com
Perfumania Inc 251 International Pkwy .... Sunrise FL 33325 954-335-9100 335-9166
TF: 866-600-3600 ■ *Web:* www.perfumania.com
Ulta3 Inc 1135 Arbor Dr .... Romeoville IL 60446 630-226-0020 226-8210
TF: 866-304-3704 ■ *Web:* www.ulta.com

578 PERSONAL EMERGENCY RESPONSE SYSTEMS

Phone | Fax

AlertOne Services Inc 24 W 4th St .... Williamsport PA 17701 570-321-5433 321-9882
TF Cust Svc: 800-693-5433 ■ *Web:* www.alert-1.com
American Medical Alert Corp
3265 Lawson Blvd .... Oceanside NY 11572 516-536-5850 536-5276
NASDAQ: AMAC ■ *TF:* 800-645-3244 ■ *Web:* www.amacalert.com
Life Alert 16027 Ventura Blvd Suite 400 .... Encino CA 91436 818-700-7000 922-3367*
**Fax:* Acctg ■ *TF Cust Svc:* 800-700-7000 ■ *Web:* www.lifealert.com
LifeFone 16 Yellowstone Ave .... White Plains NY 10607 914-948-0282 686-0669
TF: 800-882-2280 ■ *Web:* www.lifefone.com
Lifeline Systems Inc
5791 Van Allen Way PO Box 6482 .... Carlsbad CA 92008 760-603-7200 602-6500
NASDAQ: LIFE ■ *TF:* 800-451-0525 ■ *Web:* www.lifetechnologies.com
Medic Aid Response Systems Ltd
167 Village Rd .... Herring Cove NS B3V1H2 902-477-6125 477-0749
TF: 800-565-9135 ■ *Web:* www.medicaid-canada.com

579 PERSONAL PROTECTIVE EQUIPMENT & CLOTHING

SEE ALSO Medical Supplies - Mfr p. 2229; Safety Equipment - Mfr p. 2630; Safety Equipment - Whol p. 2630; Sporting Goods p. 2664

Phone | Fax

3M Occupational Health & Environmental Safety Products Div
3M Ctr Bldg 0235-02-W-70 .... Saint Paul MN 55144 651-733-8029 542-9373*
**Fax Area Code:* 800 ■ **Fax:* Cust Svc ■ *TF Cust Svc:* 800-328-1667 ■
Web: solutions.3m.com/wps/portal/3M/en_US/Health/Safety
3M Security Systems Div
3M Ctr Bldg 0225-04-N-14 .... Saint Paul MN 55144 651-733-9557 736-2298
TF: 800-328-0067 ■
Web: www.3m.com/product/business-units/security-systems.html
Aearo Co 5457 W 79th St .... Indianapolis IN 46268 317-692-6666 692-6772
TF: 800-327-3431 ■ *Web:* www.aearo.com
AGO Industries Inc
500 Sovereign Rd PO Box 7132 .... London ON N6M1A6 519-452-3780 452-3053
Web: www.ago1.com
AHPC Holdings Inc 500 Pk Blvd Suite 1260 .... Itasca IL 60143 630-285-9191 285-9289
TF: 800-828-2964
Allen-Vanguard Corp 2400 St Laurent Blvd .... Ottawa ON K1G6C4 613-739-9646 739-4536
TF: 800-644-9078 ■ *Web:* www.allenvanguard.com
American Body Armor & Equipment Inc
13386 International Pkwy .... Jacksonville FL 32218 904-741-5400 741-5407
TF: 800-654-9943 ■ *Web:* www.americanbodyarmor.com
Ansell Healthcare Inc 200 Schulz Dr .... Red Bank NJ 07701 732-345-5400 219-5114
TF: 800-232-1309 ■ *Web:* www.ansell.com
Athletic Supporter Ltd
24601 Hallwood Ct .... Farmington Hills MI 48335 248-474-6000 474-4615
TF: 800-521-6500
Bell Sports Corp
6225 N State Hwy 161 Suite 300 .... Irving TX 75038 469-417-6600 492-1639*
**Fax Area Code:* 214 ■ *TF:* 866-525-2355 ■ *Web:* www.bellsports.com
Biomarine Inc 456 Creamery Way .... Exton PA 19341 610-524-8800 524-8807
TF: 800-378-2287 ■ *Web:* www.neutronicsinc.com
Bullard Co 1898 Safety Way .... Cynthiana KY 41031 859-234-6611 234-4352
TF: 800-227-0423 ■ *Web:* www.bullard.com
Carleton Technologies Inc 10 Cobham Dr .... Orchard Park NY 14127 716-662-0006 662-0747
TF: 800-395-4074 ■ *Web:* www.carltech.com
Choctaw-Kaul Distribution Co
3540 Vinewood Ave .... Detroit MI 48208 313-894-9494 894-7977
Web: www.choctawkaul.com
David Clark Co Inc 360 Franklin St .... Worcester MA 01615 508-751-5800 753-5827*
**Fax:* Sales ■ *TF Cust Svc:* 800-298-6235 ■ *Web:* www.davidclark.com
Desco Industries Inc 3651 Walnut Ave .... Chino CA 91710 909-627-8178 627-7449
Web: www.desco.com
DHB Industries Inc 2102 SW 2nd St .... Pompano Beach FL 33069 954-630-0900 630-9225
AMEX: DHB ■ *TF:* 800-413-5155 ■ *Web:* www.pointblanksolutionsinc.com
Encon Safety Products Co
6825 W Sam Houston Pkwy N PO Box 3826 .... Houston TX 77041 713-466-1449 466-1703
TF: 800-283-6266 ■ *Web:* www.enconsafety.com
Essex PB& R Corp 8007 Chivvis Dr .... Saint Louis MO 63123 314-351-6116 351-7181
Web: www.smokehoods.com
Fibre-Metal Products Co
Rt 1 at S Brinton Wake Rd PO Box 248 .... Concordville PA 19331 610-459-5300 358-9138
TF: 800-523-7048 ■ *Web:* www.fibre-metal.com
Fire-End & Croker Corp 7 Westchester Plaza .... Elmsford NY 10523 914-592-3640 592-3892
TF: 800-759-3473 ■ *Web:* www.fire-end.com
Galls Inc 2680 Palumbo Dr .... Lexington KY 40509 859-266-7227 269-4360
TF: 800-477-7766 ■ *Web:* www.galls.com
Gateway Safety Inc 4722 Spring Rd .... Cleveland OH 44131 216-889-2000 889-1200
TF: 800-822-5347 ■ *Web:* www.gatewaysafety.com
General Econopak Inc 1725 N 6th St .... Philadelphia PA 19122 215-763-8200 763-8118
TF: 888-871-8568 ■ *Web:* www.generaleconopak.com
Gexco 3460 Vine St PO Box 6514 .... Norco CA 92860 951-735-4951 479-5154
TF: 800-829-8222
Globe Mfg Co 37 Loudon Rd PO Box 128 .... Pittsfield NH 03263 603-435-8323 289-0836*
**Fax Area Code:* 888 ■ *TF:* 800-232-8323 ■ *Web:* www.globeturnoutgear.com
Handgards Inc 901 Hawkins Blvd .... El Paso TX 79915 915-779-6606 779-1312
TF: 800-351-8161 ■ *Web:* www.handgards.com

Company	City	State	Zip	Phone	Fax
HeatMax Inc 513 Hill Rd	Dalton	GA	30721	706-226-1800	226-2195
TF: 800-432-8629 ■ *Web:* www.heatmax.com					
Helmet House Inc 26855 Malibu Hill Rd	Calabasas Hills	CA	91301	818-880-0000	880-4550
TF: 800-421-7247 ■ *Web:* www.helmethouse.com					
HL Bouton Co Inc 11 Kendrick Rd	Wareham	MA	02571	508-295-3300	295-3521
TF Cust Svc: 800-426-1881 ■ *Web:* www.hlbouton.com					
ILC Dover Inc 1 Moonwalker Rd	Frederica	DE	19946	302-335-3911	335-0762
TF: 800-631-9567 ■ *Web:* www.ilcdover.com					
Indiana Mills & Mfg Inc 18881 US 31 N	Westfield	IN	46074	317-896-9531	896-2142
Web: www.imminet.com					
International Sew-Right Co 6190 Don Murie St	Niagara Falls	ON	L2E6X8	905-374-3600	374-6121
Web: www.safetyclothing.com					
Jackson Products Inc 801 Corporate Ctr Dr Suite 300	Saint Charles	MO	63304	636-300-2700	207-2805
TF: 800-253-7281 ■ *Web:* www.jpisafety.com					
Kappler Inc 115 Grimes Dr PO Box 490	Guntersville	AL	35976	256-505-4005	505-4151
TF: 800-600-4019 ■ *Web:* www.kappler.com					
Kimberly-Clark (KCWW) PO Box 619100	Dallas	TX	75261	972-281-1200	281-1435
NYSE: KMB ■ *TF:* 800-321-1435 ■ *Web:* www.kimberly-clark.com					
Lakeland Industries Inc 701-7 Koehler Ave	Ronkonkoma	NY	11779	631-981-9700	981-9751
NASDAQ: LAKE ■ *TF:* 800-645-9291 ■ *Web:* www.lakeland.com					
Landauer Inc 2 Science Rd	Glenwood	IL	60425	708-755-7000	755-7016
NYSE: LDR ■ *TF:* 800-323-8830 ■ *Web:* www.landauer.com					
Little Rapids Corp 2273 Larsen Rd	Green Bay	WI	54303	920-496-3040	494-5340
TF: 800-496-3040 ■ *Web:* www.littlerapids.com					
Little Rapids Corp Graham Professional Div 2273 Larsen Rd PO Box 19100	Green Bay	WI	54304	920-494-8701	494-7877*
**Fax Area Code:* 800 ■ **Fax:* Cust Svc ■ *TF Cust Svc:* 800-558-6765 ■ *Web:* www.littlerapids.com/graham					
Louis M Gerson Co Inc 15 Sproat St	Middleboro	MA	02346	508-947-4000	947-5442
TF: 800-225-8623 ■ *Web:* www.gersonco.com					
Magla Products LLC 159 S St	Morristown	NJ	07960	973-984-7998	984-2382
TF: 800-247-5281 ■ *Web:* www.magla.com					
MAPA Spontex Inc 100 Spontex Dr	Columbia	TN	38401	931-388-5632	388-8924
TF Cust Svc: 800-537-2897 ■ *Web:* www.mapaglove.com					
MCR Safety 5321 E Shelby Dr	Memphis	TN	38118	901-795-5810	999-3908*
**Fax Area Code:* 800 ■ **Fax:* Sales ■ *TF:* 800-955-6887 ■ *Web:* www.mcrsafety.com					
Medline Industries Inc 1 Medline Pl	Mundelein	IL	60060	847-949-5500	643-3126
TF Cust Svc: 800-351-1512 ■ *Web:* www.medline.com					
Miller Products Co Inc 2511 S Tricenter Blvd	Durham	NC	27713	919-313-2100	313-2101
TF: 800-782-7437 ■ *Web:* www.millerproducts.com					
Moldex Metric Inc 10111 W Jefferson Blvd	Culver City	CA	90232	310-837-6500	837-9563*
**Fax:* Sales ■ *TF:* 800-421-0668 ■ *Web:* www.moldex.com					
MTS Safety Products Inc 150 2nd St	Belmont	MS	38827	662-454-9245	454-9385
TF: 800-647-8168 ■ *Web:* www.mts-safety.com					
National Safety Apparel Inc (NSA) 3865 W 150th St	Cleveland	OH	44111	216-941-1111	941-1130
TF: 800-553-0672 ■ *Web:* www.nsamfg.com					
Newtex Industries Inc 8050 Victor Mendon Rd	Victor	NY	14564	585-924-9135	924-4645
TF: 800-836-1001 ■ *Web:* www.newtex.com					
Norcross Safety Products LLC 1136 2nd St	Rock Island	IL	61201	309-786-7741	786-8670
TF Cust Svc: 800-777-9021 ■ *Web:* www.nspusa.com					
North Safety Products 2000 Plainfield Pike	Cranston	RI	02921	401-943-4400	572-6346*
**Fax Area Code:* 800 ■ *TF Cust Svc:* 800-430-4110 ■ *Web:* www.northsafety.com					
Para-Flite Inc 5800 Magnolia Ave	Pennsauken	NJ	08109	856-663-1275	663-3028
Parmelee Industries Inc 8101 Lenexa Dr	Lenexa	KS	66214	913-599-5555	599-1703
TF: 800-821-5218 ■ *Web:* www.ussafety.com					
Parmelee Industries Inc US Safety Div 8101 Lenexa Dr	Lenexa	KS	66214	913-599-5555	599-1703
TF: 800-821-5218 ■ *Web:* www.ussafety.com					
Performance Designs Inc 1300 E International Speedway Blvd	DeLand	FL	32724	386-738-2224	734-8297
Web: www.performancedesigns.com					
Plastic Safety Systems Inc 2444 Baldwin Rd	Cleveland	OH	44104	800-662-6338	231-2702*
**Fax Area Code:* 216 ■ *TF:* 800-662-6338 ■ *Web:* www.plasticsafety.com					
PolyConversions Inc 505 Condit Dr	Rantoul	IL	61866	217-893-3330	893-3003
TF: 888-893-3330 ■ *Web:* www.polyconversions.com					
Precept Medical Products Inc 370 Airport Rd PO Box 2400	Arden	NC	28704	828-681-0209	681-8626
TF: 800-851-4431 ■ *Web:* www.preceptmed.com					
Protech Armored Products 13386 International Pkwy	Jacksonville	FL	32218	904-741-5400	741-5407
TF: 800-428-0588					
Right-Gard Corp 531 N 4th St PO Box 286	Denver	PA	17517	717-336-7594	484-2180
TF: 800-535-1122					
Sabee Products Inc 1843 W Reeve St	Appleton	WI	54914	920-830-2814	830-2878
Saf-T-Gard International Inc 205 Huehl Rd	Northbrook	IL	60062	847-291-1600	291-1610
TF: 800-548-4273 ■ *Web:* www.saftgard.com					
Safe-T-Gard Corp 12105 W Cedar Dr	Lakewood	CO	80228	303-763-8900	763-8071
TF Cust Svc: 800-356-9026 ■ *Web:* www.safetgard.com					
Schutt Sports 1200 E Union Ave PO Box 426	Litchfield	IL	62056	217-324-2712	324-2732
TF: 800-637-2047 ■ *Web:* www.schuttsports.com					
Scott Health & Safety 4320 Goldmine Rd PO Box 569	Monroe	NC	28110	704-291-8300	291-8340
TF: 800-247-7257 ■ *Web:* www.scotthealthsafety.com					
Seattle Mfg Corp 6930 Salashan Pkwy	Ferndale	WA	98248	360-366-5534	366-5723
TF: 800-426-6251 ■ *Web:* www.smcgear.net					
Sellstrom Mfg Co 1 Sellstrom Dr	Palatine	IL	60067	847-358-2000	358-2036
TF: 800-323-7402 ■ *Web:* www.sellstrom.com					
SSL Americas Inc 3585 Engineering Dr Suite 200	Norcross	GA	30092	770-582-2222	582-2233
TF: 888-387-3927 ■ *Web:* www.ssl-international.com					
Standard Textile Co Inc 1 Knollcrest Dr	Cincinnati	OH	45237	513-761-9255	761-0467
TF: 800-888-5000 ■ *Web:* www.standardtextile.com					
Steel Grip Inc 700 Garfield St	Danville	IL	61832	217-442-6240	442-9370
TF: 800-223-1595 ■ *Web:* www.steelgripinc.com					
Steele Inc 26112 Iowa Ave NE	Kingston	WA	98346	360-297-4555	297-2816
TF: 888-783-3538 ■ *Web:* www.steelevest.com					
Steiner Industries 5801 N Tripp Ave	Chicago	IL	60646	773-588-3444	588-3450
TF: 800-621-4515 ■ *Web:* www.steinerindustries.com					
Stemaco Products Inc 2211 Ogden Rd	Rock Hill	SC	29730	803-328-2191	328-2808
Strong Enterprises Inc 11236 Satellite Blvd	Orlando	FL	32837	407-859-9317	850-6978
TF: 800-344-6319 ■ *Web:* www.strongparachutes.com					
TASER International Inc 17800 N 85th St	Scottsdale	AZ	85255	480-905-2000	991-0791
NASDAQ: TASR ■ *TF:* 800-978-2737 ■ *Web:* www.taser.com					
Tillotson Corp 1 Cranberry Hill Suite 105	Lexington	MA	02421	781-402-1731	402-1737
Tingley Rubber Corp 1 Cragwood Rd PO Box 100	South Plainfield	NJ	07080	800-631-5498	757-9239*
**Fax Area Code:* 866 ■ *TF Cust Svc:* 800-631-5498 ■ *Web:* www.tingleyrubber.com					
TVI Corp 7100 Holladay Tyler Rd Suite 200	Glenn Dale	MD	20769	301-352-8800	352-8818
NASDAQ: TVIN ■ *TF:* 800-598-9711 ■ *Web:* www.imresponse.thomasnet-navigator.com					
United Knitting LP 310 Industrial Dr SW	Cleveland	TN	37311	423-476-9163	476-1163
Web: www.unitedknitting.com					
United Pioneer Co 2777 Summer St Suite 206	Stamford	CT	06905	800-466-9823	466-9828
TF: 800-466-9823 ■ *Web:* www.b340.com					
Uvex Safety Inc 10 Thurber Blvd	Smithfield	RI	02917	401-232-1200	231-4903
TF: 800-343-3411 ■ *Web:* www.uvex.com					
White Knight Engineered Products 10 National Ave	Fletcher	NC	28732	828-687-0940	687-6275
TF: 800-743-4700 ■ *Web:* www.wkep.com					
Wolf X-Ray Corp 100 W Industry Ct	Deer Park	NY	11729	631-242-9729	925-5003
TF Cust Svc: 800-356-9729 ■ *Web:* www.wolfxray.com					

580 PEST CONTROL SERVICES

Company	City	State	Zip	Phone	Fax
Arrow Exterminators Inc 8613 Roswell Rd	Atlanta	GA	30350	770-993-8705	640-0073
TF: 800-281-8978 ■ *Web:* www.arrowexterminators.com					
Cats USA Pest Control PO Box 151	North Hollywood	CA	91603	818-506-1000	506-4973
TF: 800-924-3626					
Copesan Services Inc W175 N5711 Technology Dr	Menomonee Falls	WI	53051	262-783-6261	783-6267
TF: 800-267-3726 ■ *Web:* www.copesan.com					
Dodson Bros Exterminating Co Inc 3712 Campbell Ave	Lynchburg	VA	24501	434-847-9051	847-2034
TF: 800-446-0977 ■ *Web:* www.dodsonbros.com					
Ecolab Inc 370 N Wabasha St	Saint Paul	MN	55102	651-293-2233	293-2069
NYSE: ECL ■ *TF:* 800-352-5326 ■ *Web:* www.ecolab.com					
Ecolab Pest Elimination Services 370 N Wabasha St	Saint Paul	MN	55102	651-293-2233	293-2092
TF: 800-352-5326 ■ *Web:* www.ecolab.com					
Fischer Environmental Service Inc PO Box 1319	Mandeville	LA	70471	985-626-7378	626-7490
TF: 800-391-2565 ■ *Web:* www.fischerenv.com					
Florida Pest Control & Chemical Co Inc 116 NW 16th Ave	Gainesville	FL	32601	352-376-2661	376-2791
Web: www.flapest.com					
Home Paramount Pest Control Cos Inc PO Box 850	Forest Hill	MD	21050	410-510-0700	
TF: 888-888-4663 ■ *Web:* www.homeparamount.com					
Horizon Termite & Pest Control Corp 45 Cross Ave	Midland Park	NJ	07432	201-447-2530	447-9541
TF: 888-612-2847 ■ *Web:* www.horizonpestcontrol.com					
JC Ehrlich Co Inc PO Box 13848	Reading	PA	19612	610-372-9700	378-9525
TF: 800-488-9495 ■ *Web:* www.jcehrlich.com					
Knockout Pest Control Inc 1009 Front St	Uniondale	NY	11553	516-489-7817	489-4348
TF: 800-244-7378 ■ *Web:* www.knockoutpest.com					
Lawn Doctor Inc 142 SR 34	Holmdel	NJ	07733	732-946-0029	946-9089
TF: 800-631-5660 ■ *Web:* www.lawndoctor.com					
Massey Services Inc 610 N Wymore Rd	Maitland	FL	32751	407-645-2500	645-0098*
**Fax:* Cust Svc ■ *TF:* 800-432-1820 ■ *Web:* www.masseyservices.com					
McCall Service Inc 2861 College St	Jacksonville	FL	32205	904-389-5561	389-3212
TF: 800-342-6948 ■ *Web:* www.mccallservice.com					
NaturaLawn of America Inc 1 E Church St	Frederick	MD	21701	301-694-5440	846-0320
TF: 800-989-5444 ■ *Web:* www.nl-amer.com					
Nutrilawn Inc 202-2077 Dundas St E Suite 202	Mississauga	ON	L4X1M2	416-620-7100	620-7771
Web: www.nutri-lawn.com					
Orkin Exterminating Co Inc 2170 Piedmont Rd NE	Atlanta	GA	30324	404-888-2000	633-2323*
**Fax:* Cust Svc ■ *TF:* 800-346-7546 ■ *Web:* www.orkin.com					
Presto-X Co 4521 Elavenworth St	Omaha	NE	68106	402-554-1942	554-1544
TF: 800-759-1942 ■ *Web:* www.prestox.com					
Rollins Inc 2170 Piedmont Rd NE	Atlanta	GA	30324	404-888-2000	888-2672*
NYSE: ROL ■ **Fax:* Hum Res ■ *Web:* www.rollins.com					
Schendel Pest Services 1035 SE Quincy St	Topeka	KS	66612	785-232-9357	232-4165
TF: 800-233-3956 ■ *Web:* www.schendelpest.com					
Scotts Lawn Service 14111 Scottslawn Rd	Marysville	OH	43040	937-644-0011	578-5444
NYSE: SMG ■ *TF Cust Svc:* 800-221-1760 ■ *Web:* www.scotts.com					
Smithereen Exterminators Inc 7400 N Melvina Ave	Niles	IL	60714	847-647-0010	647-0606
TF: 800-336-3500 ■ *Web:* www.smithereen.com					
Spring-Green Lawn Care Corp 11909 Spaulding School Dr	Plainfield	IL	60544	815-436-8777	436-9056
TF: 800-435-4051 ■ *Web:* www.spring-green.com					
Terminix International Co LP 860 Ridge Lake Blvd	Memphis	TN	38120	901-766-1333	766-1491*
**Fax:* Mktg ■ *TF:* 800-654-7848 ■ *Web:* www.terminix.com					
TruGreen ChemLawn 860 Ridge Lake Blvd	Memphis	TN	38120	901-681-1800	681-1900
TF: 800-878-4733 ■ *Web:* www.trugreen.com					
Truly Nolen of America Inc 3636 E Speedway Blvd	Tucson	AZ	85716	520-327-3447	322-4011
TF: 800-528-3442 ■ *Web:* www.trulynolen.com					
Turf Management Systems Inc 2399 Royal Windsor Dr	Mississauga	ON	L5J1K9	905-823-8550	823-4594
Web: www.weedmancanada.com					
Waltham Services Inc 817 Moody St	Waltham	MA	02453	781-893-1810	893-7921
TF: 866-974-7378 ■ *Web:* www.walthamservices.com					
WB McCloud & Co 2500 W Higgins Rd Suite 850	Hoffman Estates	IL	60169	847-585-0650	585-0655
TF Cust Svc: 800-332-7805 ■ *Web:* www.mccloudservices.com					
Weed Man 1645 Finfar Ct	Mississauga	ON	L5J4K1	905-823-8550	823-4594
Web: www.weedmancanada.com					

				Phone	Fax
Western Exterminator Co 305 N Crescent Way	Anaheim	CA	92801	714-517-9000	533-1199
TF: 800-698-2440 ■ Web: www.west-ext.com					
Young Pest Control Inc 2011 W Platt St	Tampa	FL	33606	813-251-1025	254-2686
TF: 800-330-6996					

PESTICIDES

SEE Fertilizers & Pesticides p. 1843

581 PET PRODUCTS

SEE ALSO Leather Goods - Personal p. 2149; Livestock & Poultry Feeds - Prepared p. 2182

				Phone	Fax
Absorption Corp 6960 Salashan Pkwy	Ferndale	WA	98248	360-734-7415	671-1588
TF: 800-242-2287 ■ Web: www.absorptioncorp.com					
American Leather Specialties Corp 87 34th St	Brooklyn	NY	11232	718-965-3900	499-2481
American Nutrition Inc 2813 Wall Ave	Ogden	UT	84401	801-394-3477	394-3674
TF: 800-257-4530 ■ Web: www.anibrands.com					
Applica Consumer Products Inc 3633 Flamingo Rd	Miramar	FL	33027	954-883-1000	883-1070
TF Cust Svc: 800-231-9786 ■ Web: www.applicainc.com					
Bailey Farms LLC 549 Karem Dr	Marshall	WI	53559	608-655-3439	655-4767
TF: 800-655-1705					
BioZyme Inc 6010 Stockyards Expy	Saint Joseph	MO	64504	816-238-3326	238-7549
TF: 800-821-3070 ■ Web: www.biozymeinc.com					
Blitz USA Inc 404 26th Ave NW	Miami	OK	74354	918-540-1515	542-1380
TF Cust Svc: 800-331-3795 ■ Web: www.blitzusa.com					
Church & Dwight Co Inc 469 N Harrison St	Princeton	NJ	08543	609-683-5900	
NYSE: CHD ■ Web: www.churchdwight.com					
Clorox Co 1221 Broadway	Oakland	CA	94612	510-271-7000	832-1463
NYSE: CLX ■ TF Cust Svc: 800-292-2808 ■ Web: www.thecloroxcompany.com					
Clorox Co The 1221 Broadway PO Box 24305	Oakland	CA	94612	510-271-7000	832-1463
Web: www.thecloroxcompany.com					
Colgate-Palmolive Co 300 Pk Ave	New York	NY	10022	212-310-2000	310-2595
NYSE: CL ■ Web: www.colgate.com					
Companion Pets Inc (CPI) 2001 N Black Canyon Hwy	Phoenix	AZ	85009	602-255-0166	255-0841
TF: 800-646-3611 ■ Web: www.cpipets.com					
Dad's Pet Care Inc 18746 Mill St	Meadville	PA	16335	814-724-7710	724-7710
TF: 800-458-1801					
Doctors Foster & Smith Inc 2253 Air Pk Rd PO Box 100	Rhinelander	WI	54501	715-369-3305	562-7169*
*Fax Area Code: 800 ■ *Fax: Cust Svc ■ TF: 800-826-7206 ■ Web: www.drsfostersmith.com					
Doskocil Mfg Co Inc 4209 Barnett Blvd	Arlington	TX	76017	817-467-5116	419-6886*
*Fax: Sales ■ TF: 800-433-5185 ■ Web: www.petmate.com					
Eagle Pack Pet Foods Inc 1011 W 11th St	Mishawaka	IN	46544	574-259-7834	259-0730
TF: 800-255-5959 ■ Web: www.eaglepack.com					
Ethical Products Inc 27 Federal Plaza	Bloomfield	NJ	07003	800-223-7768	707-0701*
*Fax Area Code: 973 ■ TF: 800-223-7768 ■ Web: www.ethicalpet.com					
FL Emmert Co Inc 2007 Dunlap St	Cincinnati	OH	45214	513-721-5808	721-6087
TF: 800-441-3343 ■ Web: www.emmert.com					
Golden Products 901 Chouteau Ave	Saint Louis	MO	63102	314-982-2400	982-3338
Hartz Mountain Corp The 400 Plaza Dr	Secaucus	NJ	07094	201-271-4800	271-0164
TF: 800-275-1414 ■ Web: www.hartz.com					
Heath Mfg Co 140 Mill St	Coopersville	MI	49404	616-997-8181	997-9491
TF: 800-678-8183 ■ Web: www.heathmfg.com					
Hi-Tek Rations Inc PO Box 1223	Dublin	GA	31040	478-272-8826	275-7510
Web: www.hitekrations.com					
Hill's Pet Nutrition Inc 400 SW 8th St PO Box 148	Topeka	KS	66601	785-354-8523	368-5509
TF: 800-255-0449 ■ Web: www.hillspet.com					
Iams Co 7250 Poe Ave	Dayton	OH	45414	937-898-7387	
TF Cust Svc: 800-675-3849 ■ Web: www.iams.com					
Jeffers Inc 310 W Saunders Rd PO Box 100	Dothan	AL	36301	334-793-6257	793-5179
TF: 800-533-3377 ■ Web: www.jefferspet.com					
John A Van Den Bosch Co 4511 Holland Ave	Holland	MI	49424	616-848-2000	848-2100
TF Cust Svc: 800-968-6477 ■ Web: www.vbosch.com					
Kasel Assoc Industries Inc 3315 Walnut St	Denver	CO	80205	303-296-4417	293-9825
TF: 800-218-4417 ■ Web: www.kasel.net					
Kaytee Products Inc 521 Clay St	Chilton	WI	53014	920-849-2321	849-4734
TF: 800-669-9580 ■ Web: www.kaytee.com					
Kennel-Aire LLC 801 E N St	Ottawa	KS	66067	785-242-8484	242-8383
TF: 800-346-0134 ■ Web: www.kennel-aire.com					
Manna Pro Corp 707 Spirit 40 Pk Dr Suite 150	Chesterfield	MO	63005	636-681-1700	681-1799
TF: 800-690-9908 ■ Web: www.mannapro.com					
Mark Hershey Farms Inc 479 Horseshoe Pike	Lebanon	PA	17042	717-867-4624	867-4313
TF: 888-801-3301 ■ Web: www.markhersheyfarms.com					
Mars Pet Care 315 Cool Springs Blvd	Franklin	TN	37067	615-373-7774	468-2686
TF: 800-789-4639 ■ Web: www.mars.com					
Mars Snack Food 800 High St	Hackettstown	NJ	07840	908-852-1000	850-2734
TF: 800-432-1093 ■ Web: www.mars.com					
Menu Foods Inc 9130 Griffith Morgan Ln	Pennsauken	NJ	08110	856-662-7412	662-4673
Merrick Pet Foods 101 SE 11th Ave Suite 200	Amarillo	TX	79101	806-322-2800	322-2854
TF: 800-664-7387 ■ Web: www.merrickpetcare.com					
MFM Industries Inc PO Box 68	Lowell	FL	32663	352-854-0070	854-1576
TF Cust Svc: 800-922-6369 ■ Web: www.cedarfreshscoop.com					
MIDWEST Homes for Pets 4211 E Jackson St	Muncie	IN	47303	765-289-3355	289-6524
TF: 800-428-8560 ■ Web: www.midwesthomes4pets.com					
Moyer & Son Inc 113 E Reliance Rd	Souderton	PA	18964	215-723-6000	721-2814
TF: 800-345-0419 ■ Web: www.emoyer.com					
Multipet International Inc 265 W Commercial Ave	Moonachie	NJ	07074	201-438-6600	438-2990
TF: 800-900-6738 ■ Web: www.multipet.com					
Natural Life Pet Products Inc 112 N Elon St Suite A	Pittsburg	KS	66762	620-230-0888	230-0403
TF: 800-367-2391 ■ Web: www.nlpp.com					
Nature House Inc Purple Martin Junction PO Box 390	Griggsville	IL	62340	217-833-2406	833-2512
TF: 877-833-2478 ■ Web: www.naturesociety.org					
Nestle Purina PetCare Co 901 Chouteau Ave	Saint Louis	MO	63102	314-982-1000	982-3327
TF: 800-778-7462 ■ Web: www.purina.com					
North States Industries Inc 1507 92nd Ln NE	Blaine	MN	55449	763-486-1756	486-1763
Web: www.northstatesind.com					
Novalek Inc 2242 Davis Ct	Hayward	CA	94545	510-782-4058	784-0945
TF: 800-877-7387 ■ Web: www.novalek.com					
Nutro Products Inc 445 Wilson Way	City of Industry	CA	91744	626-968-0532	968-3525
TF: 800-833-5330 ■ Web: www.nutro.com					
Orrco Inc 515 Collins Blvd PO Box 147	Orrville	OH	44667	330-683-5015	683-0738
TF: 800-321-3085 ■ Web: www.orrvillepet.com					
Penn-Plax Inc 35 Marcus Blvd	Hauppauge	NY	11788	631-273-3787	879-6075*
*Fax Area Code: 888 ■ TF: 800-645-6055 ■ Web: www.pennplax.com					
Pet Food Express 500 85th Ave	oakland	CA	94621	510-346-7777	346-7788
Web: www.petfoodexpress.com					
Pet Supermarket Inc 1100 International Pkwy	Sunrise	FL	33323	954-351-0834	351-0897
TF: 866-434-1990 ■ Web: www.petsupermarket.com					
Pet Supplies "Plus" Inc 22710 Haggerty Rd Suite 100	Farmington Hills	MI	48335	248-374-1900	374-7900
TF: 866-477-7747 ■ Web: www.petsuppliesplus.com					
Pet Valu Canada Inc 121 McPherson St	Markham	ON	L3R3L3	905-946-1200	305-6166
TF: 800-738-8258 ■ Web: www.petvalu.com					
PETCO Animal Supplies Inc 9125 Rehco Rd	San Diego	CA	92121	858-453-7845	638-2164
NASDAQ: PETC ■ TF: 877-738-6742 ■ Web: www.petco.com					
PetFoodDirect.com 189 Main St	Harleysville	PA	19438	215-513-1999	513-7286
TF Cust Svc: 800-865-1333 ■ Web: www.petfooddirect.com					
Petland Discounts Inc 355 Crooked Hill Rd	Brentwood	NY	11717	631-273-6363	273-6513
Web: www.petlanddiscounts.com					
Petland Inc 250 Riverside St	Chillicothe	OH	45601	740-775-2464	775-2574
TF: 800-221-5935 ■ Web: www.petland.com					
PetMed Express Inc 1441 SW 29th Ave	Pompano Beach	FL	33069	954-979-5995	971-0544
NASDAQ: PETS ■ TF: 800-738-6337 ■ Web: www.1800petmeds.com					
PETsMART Inc 19601 N 27th Ave	Phoenix	AZ	85027	623-580-6100	580-6502
NASDAQ: PETM ■ TF Cust Svc: 800-738-1385 ■ Web: www.petsmart.com					
Pied Piper Mills Inc 423 E Lake Dr	Hamlin	TX	79520	325-576-3684	576-3460
TF: 800-338-4610 ■ Web: www.piedpiperpetfood.net					
Prevue Pet Products Inc 224 N Maplewood Ave	Chicago	IL	60612	312-243-3624	243-3624
TF: 800-243-3624 ■ Web: www.prevuepet.com					
Prince Corp 8351 County Rd H	Marshfield	WI	54449	715-384-3105	387-6924
TF: 800-777-2486 ■ Web: www.prince-corp.com					
Pro-Pet LLC 1400 McKinley Rd	Saint Marys	OH	45885	419-394-3374	394-8024
TF: 800-245-4125 ■ Web: www.joypetfood.com					
Radio Systems Corp 10427 Electric Ave	Knoxville	TN	37932	865-777-5404	777-5419
TF Cust Svc: 800-732-2677 ■ Web: www.petsafe.net					
Ralco Nutrition Inc 1600 Hahn Rd	Marshall	MN	56258	507-532-5748	532-5740
TF: 800-533-5306 ■ Web: www.ralconutrition.com					
Rolf C. Hagen Corp 305 Forbes Blvd	Mansfield	MA	02048	508-339-9531	339-6973
TF Cust Svc: 800-724-2436 ■ Web: www.hagen.com					
Royal Canin USA Inc 500 Fountain Lakes Blvd Suite 100	Saint Charles	MO	63301	636-926-0003	552-7920*
*Fax Area Code: 800 ■ TF: 800-592-6687 ■ Web: www.royalcanin.us					
Sergeant's Pet Care Products 2625 S 158th Plaza	Omaha	NE	68130	402-938-7000	938-7091
TF: 800-224-7387 ■ Web: www.sergeants.com					
Simmons Allied Pet Foods Inc 601 N Hico	Siloan Springs	AR	72761	479-524-8151	215-2772
TF: 800-241-8504 ■ Web: www.simmonspetfood.com					
Star Milling Co 24067 Water St	Perris	CA	92570	951-657-3143	657-3114
TF: 800-733-6455 ■ Web: www.starmilling.com					
Sunshine Mills Inc 500 6th St SW	Red Bay	AL	35582	256-356-9541	356-8287*
*Fax: Sales ■ TF: 800-633-3349 ■ Web: www.sunshinemills.com					
Texas Farm Products Co 915 S Fredonia St	Nacogdoches	TX	75964	936-564-3711	560-8200
TF: 800-392-3110 ■ Web: www.texasfarm.com					
Triumph Pet Industries Inc 500 6th St SW	Red Bay	AL	35582	256-356-9541	331-5140*
*Fax Area Code: 800 ■ TF: 800-331-5144 ■ Web: www.triumphpet.com					
United Pacific Pet 12060 Cabernet Dr	Fontana	CA	92337	951-360-8550	360-8540
TF: 800-979-3333 ■ Web: www.uppet.com					
United Pharmacal Co of Missouri Inc 3705 Pear St	Saint Joseph	MO	64503	816-233-8800	233-9696
TF: 800-254-8726 ■ Web: www.upco.com					
Virbac Corp 3200 Meacham Blvd	Fort Worth	TX	76137	817-831-5030	831-8327
Web: www.virbac.com					
Wild Birds Unlimited Inc 11711 N College Ave Suite 146	Carmel	IN	46032	317-571-7100	571-7110
TF: 800-326-4928 ■ Web: www.wbu.com					

582 PETROLEUM & PETROLEUM PRODUCTS - WHOL

				Phone	Fax
A & W Oil Co Inc 1101 N Liberty St	Waynesboro	GA	30830	706-554-2121	554-7825
Web: www.awoil.com					
Abercrombie Oil Co Inc PO Box 1422	Danville	VA	24543	434-792-8022	793-0143
Web: www.abercrombieoil.com					
Ada Resources Inc 6603 Kirbyville St	Houston	TX	77033	713-644-2111	640-0141*
*Fax: Acctg ■ Web: www.adamsresources.com					
Advance Petroleum Distributing Co Inc 2451 Great SW Pkwy	Fort Worth	TX	76106	817-626-5458	624-3102
TF: 800-515-5458 ■ Web: www.advancefuel.com					
Allied Oil & Supply Inc 2209 S 24th St	Omaha	NE	68103	402-344-4343	344-4360
TF: 800-333-3717 ■ Web: www.allied-oil.com					
AmeriGas Propane Inc PO Box 965	Valley Forge	PA	19482	610-337-7000	768-7647*
*Fax: Mktg ■ Web: www.amerigas.com					
Apex Oil Co Inc 8235 Forsyth Blvd Suite 400	Clayton	MO	63105	314-889-9600	854-8539
Web: www.apexoil.com					
Arkansas Valley Petroleum Inc 8336 E 73rd St Suite 100	Tulsa	OK	74133	918-252-0508	250-4921
TF: 800-888-1389					

Company	City	State	ZIP	Phone	Fax
Atlas Oil Co 24501 Ecorse Rd	Taylor	MI	48180	313-292-5500	731-0264
TF: 800-878-2000 ■ Web: www.atlasoil.com					
Bagwell Oil Co Inc PO Box 136	Onancock	VA	23417	757-787-3580	
Web: www.bagwelloil.com					
Barrows Coal Co Inc 35 Main St	Brattleboro	VT	05301	802-254-4574	254-5353
Web: www.barrowsoil.com					
Beach Oil Co Inc					
631 US Hwy 76 PO Box 3010	Clarksville	TN	37041	931-358-9303	358-9331
Web: www.beachoil.com					
Bell Gas Inc PO Box 490	Roswell	NM	88202	505-622-4800	622-4710
Berry Oil 104 Leigh Ave	Tetonia	ID	83452	208-456-2271	456-2091
Web: www.berryoil.net					
Bluewave Energy 30 Oland Ct	Dartmouth	NS	B3B1V2	902-481-0515	481-9181
Web: www.bluewaveenergy.ca					
Boyett Petroleum 601 McHenry Ave	Modesto	CA	95350	209-577-6000	577-6040
TF: 800-545-9212 ■ Web: www.boyett.net					
BP Lubricants USA Inc 1500 Valley Rd	Wayne	NJ	07470	973-633-2200	633-9867
TF: 800-633-6163 ■ Web: www.bp.com					
Brewer Oil Co 2701 Candelaria NE	Albuquerque	NM	87107	505-884-2040	884-1978
Web: www.breweroil.com					
Campbell Oil Co Inc 611 Erie St S	Massillon	OH	44646	330-833-8555	833-1083
TF: 800-589-8555 ■ Web: www.cambhelloil.com					
Cargill Energy PO Box 9300	Minneapolis	MN	55440	952-742-7575	
TF: 800-227-4455 ■ Web: www.cargill.com					
Carson Oil Co Inc					
3125 NW 35th Ave PO Box 10948	Portland	OR	97296	503-224-8500	222-0186
TF: 800-998-7767 ■ Web: www.carsonoil.com					
Castle Oil Corp 500 Mamaroneck Ave	Harrison	NY	10528	914-381-6600	381-6601
Web: www.castleoil.com					
Castrol Canada Inc 3660 Lake Shore Blvd W	Toronto	ON	M8W1P2	416-252-5511	252-1774
Web: www.castrol.com					
Center Oil Co					
600 Mason Ridge Ctr Dr 2nd Fl	Saint Louis	MO	63141	314-682-3500	682-3599
Web: www.centeroil.com					
Chemoil Corp					
4 Embarcadero Ctr Suite 1100	San Francisco	CA	94111	415-268-2700	268-2701
Web: www.chemoil.com					
Colonial Group Inc 101 N Lathrop Ave	Savannah	GA	31415	912-236-1331	235-2938
Concord Energy LLC 7901 Schaffer Pkwy	Littleton	CO	80127	303-468-1900	468-1901
Web: www.concordenergy.com					
Condon Oil Co Inc 126 E Jackson St	Ripon	WI	54971	920-748-3186	748-3201
TF: 800-452-1212 ■ Web: www.condoncompanies.com					
Consolidated Energy Co 910 Main St PO Box 317	Jesup	IA	50648	319-827-1211	827-3154
TF: 800-338-3021 ■ Web: www.cecgas.com					
Crossroads Fuel Service Inc					
335 Centerville Tnpk S Suite G	Chesapeake	VA	23322	757-482-2179	482-7849
Web: www.crossroadsfuel.com					
Crown Oil & Gas Co 1 N Charles St	Baltimore	MD	21201	410-539-7400	659-4747
Web: www.crowncentral.com					
District Petroleum Products Inc					
1814 River Rd Suite 100	Huron	OH	44839	419-433-8373	433-9646
Dixie Oil Co Inc 1284 US Hwy 82	Tifton	GA	31794	229-382-2700	387-6905
Drake Petroleum Co Inc					
221 Quinebaug Rd	North Grosvenordale	CT	06255	860-935-5200	935-9396
Web: www.drakepetro.com					
Englefield Oil Co 1935 James Pkwy	Heath	OH	43056	740-928-8215	928-3844
TF: 800-282-1675 ■ Web: www.englefieldoil.com					
Fannon Petroleum Services Inc					
7755 Progress Ct	Gainesville	VA	20155	703-836-1133	836-4398
Web: www.fannonpetroleum.com					
Farm & Home Oil Co 3115 State Rd PO Box 389	Telford	PA	18969	215-257-0131	257-2088
TF: 800-473-1562 ■ Web: www.fhoil.com					
Fleet Card Fuels Inc PO Box 81685	Bakersfield	CA	93380	661-321-9961	321-9125
Web: www.fleetcardfuels.com					
Flint Hills Resources LP 4111 E 37th St N	Wichita	KS	67220	316-828-5500	828-4228
Web: www.fhr.com					
Flying J Inc 1104 Country Hill Dr	Ogden	UT	84403	801-624-1000	395-8005
TF Sales: 877-218-9290 ■ Web: www.flyingj.com					
Fraley & Co Inc 6723 Hwy 160-491	Cortez	CO	81321	970-565-8538	565-8743
Web: www.fraleyandcompany.com					
Gate Petroleum Co					
9540 San Jose Blvd PO Box 23627	Jacksonville	FL	32241	904-737-7220	732-7660
Web: www.gatepetro.com					
George E Warren Corp					
3001 Ocean Dr Suite 203	Vero Beach	FL	32963	772-778-7100	778-7171
Web: www.gewarren.com					
Global Partners LP 800 S St Suite 200	Waltham	MA	02454	781-894-8800	398-4160
NYSE: GLP ■ TF: 800-685-7222 ■ Web: www.globalp.com					
Gulf Oil LP 90 Everett Ave	Chelsea	MA	02150	617-889-9000	884-3325*
*Fax: Mktg ■ TF: 800-256-4853 ■ Web: www.gulfoil.com					
Gull Industries 3404 4th Ave S	Seattle	WA	98134	206-624-5900	624-5412
TF: 800-866-4855					
Harold E Dickey Co PO Box 809	Packwood	IA	52580	319-695-3601	695-3051
Herdrich Petroleum 210 E US 52	Rushville	IN	46173	765-932-3224	932-4622
Hicks Oil & Hicks Gas Inc 204 N Rt 54	Roberts	IL	60962	217-395-2281	395-2572
TF: 800-252-6871					
Highland Corp PO Box 190	Hohenwald	TN	38462	931-796-2274	796-5258
TF: 800-924-8514 ■ Web: www.highlandcorp.com					
Inergy LP 2 Brush Creek Blvd Suite 200	Kansas City	MO	64112	816-842-8181	842-1904
NASDAQ: NRGY ■ TF: 877-446-3749 ■ Web: www.inergypropane.com					
Inter City Oil Co Inc PO Box 3048	Duluth	MN	55803	218-728-3641	728-5140
TF All: 800-642-5542					
Intercontinental Fuels					
17617 Aldine Westfield Rd	Houston	TX	77073	281-821-2225	
Web: www.ifl-usa.com					
Isobunkers LLC					
C/O ISOindustries Inc					
5353 E Princess Anne Rd Suite F	Norfolk	VA	23502	757-855-0900	855-6200
Web: www.isoindustries.com					
Jackson-Jennings Farm Bureau Co-op Assn Inc					
PO Box 304	Seymour	IN	47274	812-522-4911	522-3242
TF: 800-742-9385 ■ Web: www.jacksonjennings.com					
JH Williams Oil Co Inc 1237 E Twiggs St	Tampa	FL	33602	813-228-7776	224-9413
TF: 800-683-0536 ■ Web: www.jhwoil.com					
Johnson Oil Co (JOC) 1113 E Sara DeWitt Dr	Gonzales	TX	78629	830-672-9574	672-6659
TF: 800-284-2432 ■ Web: www.johnsonoilcompany.com					
Lakeside Oil Co Inc					
555 W Brown Deer Rd Suite 200	Milwaukee	WI	53217	414-540-4000	540-4100
TF: 800-289-3835					
Lanman Oil Co Inc PO Box 108	Charleston	IL	61920	217-348-8020	348-8031
TF: 800-677-2819 ■ Web: www.lanmanoil.com					
Leffler Energy Inc 15 Mt Joy St	Mount Joy	PA	17552	717-653-1411	653-2728
TF: 800-984-1411 ■ Web: www.lefflerenergy.com					
Licking Valley Oil Inc PO Box 246	Butler	KY	41006	859-472-7111	472-7112
TF: 800-899-9449 ■ Web: www.lvoinc.com					
Lone Star Co Inc PO Box 2067	Jonesboro	AR	72402	870-932-6679	932-2925
Web: www.starcompanies.net					
Loos & Dilworth Inc 61 Green Ln	Bristol	PA	19007	215-785-3591	785-3597
TF: 800-229-5667 ■ Web: www.loosanddilworth.com					
Lucky Lady Oil Co 107 NW 28th St	Fort Worth	TX	76106	817-740-7400	740-0245
TF: 800-303-1412					
Lyden Oil Co Inc 3711 Lee Harps Rd	Youngstown	OH	44515	330-792-1100	792-1462
TF: 800-362-9410 ■ Web: www.lydenoilcompany.com					
M. O. Dion & Sons Inc 1543 W 16th St	Long Beach	CA	90813	562-432-3946	432-7969
TF: 888-424-3466 ■ Web: www.dionandsons.com					
Main-Care Energy PO Box 11029	Albany	NY	12211	518-438-4195	438-5991
TF: 800-542-5552 ■ Web: www.maincareenergy.com					
Maritime Energy Inc 234 Pk St PO Box 485	Rockland	ME	04841	207-594-4487	594-1648
TF: 800-333-4489 ■ Web: www.maritimeenergy.com					
Martin Midstream Partners LP 4200 Stone Rd	Kilgore	TX	75662	903-983-6200	983-6277
NASDAQ: MMLP ■ TF: 800-395-2368 ■ Web: www.vmartincompany.com					
Mid South Sales Inc 243 County Rd 414	Jonesboro	AR	72404	870-933-6457	933-0446
Web: www.mid-southsales.com					
Mid-Atlantic Petroleum Properties LLC (MAPP)					
12311 Middlebrook Rd	Germantown	MD	20874	301-972-4116	972-3137
Web: www.mappllc.com					
Miller Oil Co 1000 E City Hall Ave	Norfolk	VA	23504	757-623-6600	640-2175
TF: 800-333-4645 ■ Web: www.milleroil.com					
Mitsubishi International Corp 655 3rd Ave	New York	NY	10017	212-605-2000	
Web: www.micusa.com					
Montour Oil Service Co					
112 Broad St PO Box 128	Montoursville	PA	17754	570-368-8611	368-8618
TF: 800-332-8915					
National Oil & Gas Inc PO Box 476	Bluffton	IN	46714	260-824-2220	824-2223
TF: 800-322-8454					
Nisbet Oil Co PO Box 35367	Charlotte	NC	28235	704-332-7755	377-1607
Web: www.nisbetoil.com					
NOCO Energy Corp 2440 Sheridan Dr	Tonawanda	NY	14150	716-614-1000	832-6461
TF: 800-500-6626 ■ Web: www.noco.com					
Nuvera Fuel Cells 129 Concord Rd Bldg 1	Billerica	MA	01821	617-245-7500	245-7511
Web: www.nuvera.com					
O2Diesel Delaware 100 Commerce Dr Suite 301	Newark	DE	19713	302-266-6000	266-7076
Parker Oil Co Inc PO Box 120	South Hill	VA	23970	434-447-3146	447-2646
Web: www.parkeroilcompany.com					
Parker Oil Products Inc					
508 California Parker PO Box 775	Parker	AZ	85344	928-669-2617	669-2120
Web: www.parkeroilproducts.com					
Peerless Distributing Co					
21700 Northwestern Hwy Suite 1160	Southfield	MI	48075	248-559-1800	559-1861
Petro Lock Inc 45315 N Trevor Ave	Lancaster	CA	93534	661-948-6044	948-3792
Web: www.petrolock.com					
Petroleum Products Corp					
900 S Eisenhower Blvd	Middletown	PA	17057	717-939-0466	939-0294
PetroLiance LLC 739 N State St	Elgin	IL	60123	847-741-2577	741-2590
TF: 800-628-7231 ■ Web: www.petroliance.com					
Phoenix Fuel Co Inc 2502 N Black Canyon Hwy	Phoenix	AZ	85009	602-269-6500	278-7196
TF: 800-444-5823					
Piasa Motor Fuels Inc PO Box 484	Alton	IL	62002	618-254-7341	254-8281
Pioneer Oil LLC 1728 Lampman Dr Suite A	Billings	MT	59102	406-254-7071	254-2560
Web: www.pioneeroil-co.com					
Pro Petroleum Inc PO Box 10128	Lubbock	TX	79408	806-764-8785	795-6574
TF: 800-791-4939 ■ Web: www.propetroleum.com					
R K Allen Oil Inc					
36002 AL Hwy 21 PO Box 456	Talladega	AL	35161	256-362-4261	362-6792
Web: www.rkallenoil.com					
Ramos Oil Co Inc 1515 S River Rd	West Sacramento	CA	95691	916-371-2570	371-0635
TF Cust Svc: 800-477-7266 ■ Web: www.ramosoil.com					
Reeder Distributors Inc PO Box 8237	Fort Worth	TX	76124	817-429-5957	429-9052
TF: 800-722-3103 ■ Web: www.reederdistributors.com					
Rentech Inc 10877 Wilshire Blvd Suite 710	Los Angeles	CA	90024	310-571-9800	571-9799
AMEX: RTK ■ Web: www.rentechinc.com					
Retif Oil & Fuel Inc					
527 Destrehan Ave PO Box 52679	Harvey	LA	70059	504-349-9000	349-9009
TF: 800-349-9000 ■ Web: www.retif.com					
Rex Oil Co Inc					
814 & 1000 Lexington Ave PO Box 1050	Thomasville	NC	27360	336-472-3368	843-0572*
*Fax Area Code: 800 ■ Web: www.rexoil.com					
Rhodes 101 Stop 1620 N Kings Hwy	Cape Girardeau	MO	63701	573-334-7733	334-2578
Web: www.rhodes101.com					
Risser Oil Corp 2865 Executive Dr	Clearwater	FL	33762	727-573-4000	572-9075
TF: 800-572-0075 ■ Web: www.therissercompanies.com					
Rite Way Oil & Gas Co Inc PO Box 27049	Omaha	NE	68127	402-331-6400	331-7408
TF: 800-279-6401					
River City Petroleum Inc PO Box 235	West Sacramento	CA	95691	916-371-4960	371-7983
TF: 800-441-2108 ■ Web: www.rcpfuel.com					
Russell Petroleum Corp 3378 Tankview Ct	Montgomery	AL	36108	334-834-3750	834-3755
San Luis Butane Distributors Inc					
PO Box 3068	Paso Robles	CA	93447	805-239-0616	239-2607
Web: www.deltaliquidenergy.com					
Sierra Energy					
1020 Winding Creek Rd Suite 100	Roseville	CA	95678	916-218-1600	218-1680
TF: 800-576-2264 ■ Web: www.sierraenergy.net					
Silco Oil Co Inc 181 E 56th Ave Suite 600	Denver	CO	80216	303-292-0500	293-8069
TF: 800-707-4526					

				Phone	Fax
Silvas Oil Co Inc PO Box 1048 *Web:* www.silvasoil.com	Fresno	CA	93714	559-233-5171	233-8562
Sinclair Marketing 550 E S Temple St *TF:* 800-325-3265 ■ *Web:* www.sinclairoil.com	Salt Lake City	UT	84102	801-524-2700	524-2721
SMF Energy Corp 200 W Cypress Creek Rd Suite 400 *TF:* 800-423-6224 ■ *Web:* www.hwpetro.com	Ft. Lauderdale	FL	33309	954-308-4200	
South Central Oil Co Inc 2121 W Main St *Web:* www.southcentraloil.com	Albemarle	NC	28001	704-982-2173	982-6434
Southern Maryland Oil Co Inc (SMO) 109 N Maple Ave **Fax:* Cust Svc ■ *TF:* 800-492-3420 ■ *Web:* www.smoenergy.com	La Plata	MD	20646	301-932-3600	932-3718*
Spencer Cos Inc 120 Woodson St NW *TF:* 800-633-2910 ■ *Web:* www.spencercos.com	Huntsville	AL	35801	256-533-1150	535-2910
Sprague Energy 2 International Dr Suite 200 **Fax:* Hum Res ■ *TF:* 800-225-1560 ■ *Web:* www.spragueenergy.com	Portsmouth	NH	03801	603-431-1000	430-7299*
St Martin Oil & Gas Inc 2040 Terr Hwy *TF:* 800-984-6457 ■ *Web:* www.stmartinoil.com	Saint Martinville	LA	70582	337-394-3163	394-7365
Stern Oil Co Inc PO Box 218 *TF:* 800-477-2744 ■ *Web:* www.sternoil.com	Freeman	SD	57029	605-925-7999	925-4367
SulphCo Inc 4333 W.Sam Houston Pkwy N. Suite 190 *AMEX: SUF* ■ *Web:* www.sulphco.com	Houston	TX	77043	713-896-9100	896-8803
Sun Coast Resources Inc 6405 Cavalcade St *TF:* 800-677-3835 ■ *Web:* www.suncoastresources.com	Houston	TX	77026	713-844-9600	844-9696
Super-Lube Inc 1311 N Paul Russell Rd *Web:* www.superlube.com	Tallahassee	FL	32301	850-222-5823	222-5152
Tauber Oil Co 55 Waugh Dr # 700 *Web:* www.tauberoil.com	Houston	TX	77007	713-869-8700	869-8069
Taylor Enterprises Inc (TEI) 2586 Southport Rd *TF:* 800-922-3149 ■ *Web:* www.teifms.com	Spartanburg	SC	29302	864-573-9518	583-4150
Tesoro Refining & Marketing Co 3450 S 344th Way Suite 201 *TF:* 800-473-1123 ■ *Web:* www.tsocorp.com	Auburn	WA	98001	253-896-8700	896-8887
Tetco Inc 1100 NE Loop 410 Suite 900 *Web:* www.tetco.com	San Antonio	TX	78217	210-821-5900	826-3003
Time Oil Co 2737 W Commodore Way *TF:* 800-552-0748	Seattle	WA	98199	206-285-2400	286-4394
Titan Laboratories 1380 Zuni St PO Box 40567 *TF:* 800-848-4826 ■ *Web:* www.titanlab.com	Denver	CO	80204	303-893-5273	539-0158
Tower Sales Inc 936 E Grand Ave PO Box 36 *TF:* 800-832-3304 ■ *Web:* www.towersalesoil.com	Tower City	PA	17980	717-647-2137	647-2664
Trans-Mountain Oil Co 6080 Surety Dr	El Paso	TX	79995	915-779-3211	779-7971
Truman Arnold Cos 701 S Robison Rd *TF:* 800-235-5343 ■ *Web:* www.tacair.com	Texarkana	TX	75504	903-794-3835	832-7226
Tulco Oils Inc 5240 E Pine PO Box 582410 *TF:* 800-375-2347 ■ *Web:* www.tulco.com	Tulsa	OK	74158	918-838-3354	834-1263
Turner Gas Co Inc PO Box 26554 *TF:* 800-932-4277 ■ *Web:* www.turnergas.com	Salt Lake City	UT	84126	801-973-6886	973-6882
Ullman Oil Inc PO Box 23399 *TF:* 800-543-5195 ■ *Web:* www.ullmanoil.com	Chagrin Falls	OH	44023	440-543-5195	543-6549
Union Distributing Co of Tucson 4000 E Michigan St *Web:* www.uniondistributing.connekt2.com	Tucson	AZ	85714	520-571-7600	
US Oil Co Inc 425 S Washington St *TF:* 800-444-0202 ■ *Web:* www.usoil.com	Combined Locks	WI	54113	920-739-6101	788-5910
Vesco Oil Corp 16055 W 12-Mile Rd *TF:* 800-527-5358 ■ *Web:* www.vesco-oil.com	Southfield	MI	48076	248-557-1600	557-2236
Veterans Oil Inc 2070 Hwy 150 *TF:* 800-813-6753 ■ *Web:* www.veteransoil.com	Bessemer	AL	35022	205-424-4400	424-4448
Waguespack Oil Co Inc 1818 HWY 3185 PO Box 326 *Web:* www.wagoil.com	Thibodaux	LA	70302	985-447-3668	447-5730
Warren Oil Co Inc PO Box 1507 *TF:* 800-779-6456 ■ *Web:* www.warrenoil.com	Dunn	NC	28335	910-892-6456	892-4245
Webber Energy Fuels 700 Main St *TF:* 800-932-2371 ■ *Web:* www.wenergy.com	Bangor	ME	04401	207-942-5501	941-9597
Wesson Inc PO Box 2127 *Web:* www.wessonenergy.com	Waterbury	CT	06722	203-757-7950	754-6664
Western Petroleum Co 9531 W 78th St *TF:* 800-972-3835 ■ *Web:* www.westernpetro.com	Eden Prairie	MN	55344	952-941-9090	941-7470
Windward Petroleum Inc 1064 Goffs Falls Rd *Web:* www.windwardpetroleum.com	Manchester	NH	03103	603-222-2900	622-0834
World Fuel Services Corp 9800 NW 41st St Suite 400 *NYSE: INT* ■ *TF:* 800-345-3818 ■ *Web:* www.wfscorp.com	Miami	FL	33178	305-428-8000	392-5600
World Fuel Services Inc 9800 NW 41st St Suite 400 *TF:* 800-345-3818 ■ *Web:* www.wfscorp.com	Miami	FL	33178	305-428-8000	392-5600

583 PETROLEUM REFINERIES

				Phone	Fax
Alon USA Energy Inc 7616 LBJ Fwy Suite 300 *NYSE: ALJ* ■ *Web:* www.alonusa.com	Dallas	TX	75251	972-367-3600	367-3728
Bootheel Petroleum Co Inc 623 N SR- 25 PO Box 187 *Web:* www.bootheelpetroleum.com	Dexter	MO	63841	573-624-4160	624-2439
BP Plc 28100 Torch Pkwy *NYSE: BP* ■ **Fax Area Code:* 281 ■ *TF:* 866-427-6947 ■ *Web:* www.bp.com	Warrenville	IL	60555	630-420-5111	298-0738*
Calumet Lubricants Co 2780 Waterfront Pkwy Dr E Suite 200 *TF:* 800-437-3188 ■ *Web:* www.calumetlub.com	Indianapolis	IN	46214	317-328-5660	328-5668
Calumet Specialty Products Partners LP 2780 Waterfront Pkwy E Dr Suite 200 *NASDAQ: CLMT* ■ *Web:* www.calumetspecialty.com	Indianapolis	IN	46214	317-328-5660	328-5668
Chevron Canada Ltd 1200 - 1050 W Pender St *TF:* 800-663-1650 ■ *Web:* www.chevron.ca	Vancouver	BC	V6E3T4	604-668-5300	668-5559
Chevron Corp 6001 Bollinger Canyon Rd *NYSE: CVX* ■ **Fax Area Code:* 866 ■ *TF Cust Svc:* 800-243-8766 ■ *Web:* www.chevron.com	San Ramon	CA	94583	925-842-1000	420-0335*
CITGO Petroleum Corp 1293 Eldridge Pkwy *TF:* 800-424-9300 ■ *Web:* www.citgo.com	Houston	TX	77077	832-486-4700	
Coffeyville Resources LLC 10 E Cambridge Cir Dr *Web:* www.coffeyvillegroup.com	Kansas City	KS	66103	913-982-0500	981-0001
ConocoPhillips 600 N Dairy Ashford Rd *NYSE: COP* ■ *TF:* 800-527-5476 ■ *Web:* www.conocophillips.com	Houston	TX	77079	281-293-1000	
Cross Oil Refining & Marketing Inc 484 E 6th St *TF:* 800-725-3066 ■ *Web:* www.crossoil.com	Smackover	AR	71762	870-881-8700	864-8656
Crown Central Petroleum Corp 1 N Charles St **Fax:* Hum Res ■ *Web:* www.crowncentral.com	Baltimore	MD	21201	410-539-7400	659-4875*
Duke Energy Corp 5400 Westheimer Ct **Fax:* Hum Res ■ *Web:* www.duke-energy.com	Houston	TX	77056	713-627-5400	989-1503*
Ergon Refining 2611 Haining Rd *TF:* 877-888-9758 ■ *Web:* www.ergon.com	Vicksburg	MS	39183	601-933-3000	630-8311
Exxon Mobil Corp 5959 Las Colinas Blvd *NYSE: XOM* ■ *TF:* 800-252-1800 ■ *Web:* www.exxonmobil.com	Irving	TX	75039	972-444-1000	444-1348
Flint Hills Resources LP 4111 E 37th St N *Web:* www.fhr.com	Wichita	KS	67220	316-828-5500	828-4228
Flying J Inc 1104 Country Hill Dr *TF Sales:* 877-218-9290 ■ *Web:* www.flyingj.com	Ogden	UT	84403	801-624-1000	395-8005
Galaxie Corp 5170 Galaxie Dr	Jackson	MS	39206	601-366-8465	366-8466
Gary-Williams Energy Corp 370 17th St Suite 5300 *Web:* www.gwec.com	Denver	CO	80202	303-628-3800	628-3834
Hermes Consolidated Inc 1600 Broadway Suite 2300	Denver	CO	80202	303-894-9966	837-9089
Hess Corp PO Box 224866 *NYSE: AHC* ■ *TF:* 800-437-7645 ■ *Web:* www.ahbelo.com	Dallas	TX	75222	214-977-8200	977-8201
Holly Corp 100 Crescent Ct Suite 1600 *NYSE: HOC* ■ *Web:* www.hollycorp.com	Dallas	TX	75201	214-871-3555	871-3560
Hovensa LLC 1 Estate Hope-Christiansted *Web:* www.hovensa.com	Saint Croix	VI	00820	340-692-3000	692-3521
Hunt Oil Co 1900 N Akard St *TF:* 800-435-7794 ■ *Web:* www.huntoil.com	Dallas	TX	75201	214-978-8000	978-8888
Hunt Refining Co 100 Towncenter Blvd Suite 300 *Web:* www.huntrefining.com	Tuscaloosa	AL	35406	205-391-3300	752-6480
Imperial Oil Resources Ltd 237 4th Ave SW PO Box 2480 Stn M *TF:* 800-567-3776 ■ *Web:* www.imperialoil.ca	Calgary	AB	T2P3M9	403-237-3737	237-2072
International Group Inc 85 Old Eagle School Rd *TF:* 800-852-6537 ■ *Web:* www.igiwax.com	Wayne	PA	19087	610-687-9030	687-2792
La Gloria Oil & Gas Co 425 McMurrey Dr	Tyler	TX	75710	903-579-3400	596-0103
Lyondell-Citgo Refining Co 12000 Lyondell St	Houston	TX	77017	713-321-4111	
Montana Refining Co 1900 10th St NE	Great Falls	MT	59404	406-761-4100	761-0174
Motiva Enterprises LLC 700 Milam St *TF:* 888-467-4355 ■ *Web:* www.motivaenterprises.com	Houston	TX	77002	713-277-8000	277-9099
Murphy Oil Corp 200 Peach St *NYSE: MUR* ■ *TF:* 800-643-2364 ■ *Web:* www.murphyoilcorp.com	El Dorado	AR	71730	870-862-6411	864-6373
Murphy Oil USA Inc 200 Peach St *TF:* 800-643-2364 ■ *Web:* www.murphyoilcorp.com	El Dorado	AR	71730	870-862-6411	864-6373
National Co-op Refinery Assn 2000 S Main St *Web:* www.ncrarefinery.com	McPherson	KS	67460	620-241-2340	241-5531
Navajo Refining Co 501 E Main St	Artesia	NM	88210	505-748-3311	746-5458
Paramount Petroleum Corp 14700 Downey Ave **Fax:* Hum Res ■ *Web:* www.ppcla.com	Paramount	CA	90723	562-531-2060	630-3276*
Petro-Hunt LLC 1601 Elm St Thanksgiving Tower Suite 3400 *Web:* www.petro-hunt.com	Dallas	TX	75201	214-880-8400	880-7101
Placid Refining Co LLC 1940 Louisiana Hwy 1 N *Web:* www.placidrefining.com	Port Allen	LA	70767	225-387-0278	346-7403
Red Apple Group Inc 823 11th Ave	New York	NY	10019	212-956-5803	247-4509
San Joaquin Refining Co Inc 3129 Standard St *Web:* www.sjr.com	Bakersfield	CA	93308	661-327-4257	327-3236
Silver Eagle Refining 2355 S 1100 W *TF:* 800-927-9736	Woods Cross	UT	84087	801-298-3211	298-1112
Sinclair Oil Corp PO Box 30825 *TF:* 800-552-8695 ■ *Web:* www.sinclairoil.com	Salt Lake City	UT	84130	801-524-2700	524-2880
Somerset Oil Inc 600 Monticello St	Somerset	KY	42501	606-679-6301	677-2710
Southland Oil Co 5170 Galaxie Dr *TF:* 800-222-7630 ■ *Web:* www.southlandoilco.com	Jackson	MS	39206	601-981-4151	362-1967
Sunoco Inc 1735 Market St Suite LL *NYSE: SUN* ■ *TF:* 800-786-6261 ■ *Web:* www.sunocoinc.com	Philadelphia	PA	19103	215-977-3000	977-3409
Tesoro Corp 19100 Ridgewood Pkwy *NYSE: TSO* ■ *TF:* 800-299-0570 ■ *Web:* www.tsocorp.com	San Antonio	TX	78259	210-626-6000	745-4474
Texas Oil & Chemical Co 7752 FM 418 *TF:* 800-324-1123	Silsbee	TX	77656	409-385-1400	385-2453
Ultramar Ltd 2200 Ave McGill College *TF Cust Svc:* 800-363-6949 ■ *Web:* www.ultramar.ca	Montreal	QC	H3A3H8	514-499-6446	499-6320
United Refining Co Inc 15 Bradley St *TF:* 800-458-6097 ■ *Web:* www.urc.com	Warren	PA	16365	814-723-1500	726-4709
US Oil & Refining Co 3001 Marshall Ave *TF:* 800-424-2012 ■ *Web:* www.usor.com	Tacoma	WA	98421	253-383-1651	383-9970
Valero Energy Corp 1 Valero Way *NYSE: VLO* ■ *TF:* 800-531-7911 ■ *Web:* www.valero.com	San Antonio	TX	78249	210-370-2000	345-2646
Western Refining Inc 123 W Mills Ave *NYSE: WNR* ■ *Web:* www.wnr.com	El Paso	TX	79905	915-534-1400	881-0002
World Oil Co 9302 Garfield Ave *TF:* 800-266-6551	South Gate	CA	90280	562-928-0100	928-0391

584 PETROLEUM STORAGE TERMINALS

				Phone	Fax
C Steinweg Inc 1201 Wallace St *Web:* www.steinweg.com	Baltimore	MD	21230	410-752-8254	
Cary Oil Co Inc 110 Mackenan Dr PO Box 5189 *TF:* 800-227-9645 ■ *Web:* www.caryoil.com	Cary	NC	27511	919-462-1100	481-6862
Central Crude inc 4187 Hwy 3059 PO Box 1863 *TF:* 800-245-8408 ■ *Web:* www.centralcrude.com	Lake Charles	LA	70602	337-436-1000	436-9602
Diversified Information Technologies Inc 123 Wyoming Ave *TF:* 800-458-4710 ■ *Web:* www.divintech.com	Scranton	PA	18503	570-343-2300	342-4736
DuraTherm Inc PO Box 58466 *Web:* www.duratherm-intl.com	Houston	TX	77258	281-339-1352	339-1352
Fortress Corp The 1 Design Ctr Pl *Web:* www.thefortress.com	Boston	MA	02210	617-790-3070	790-3077
Greenway Co-op Service Co 3520 E River Rd PO Box 6878 *TF:* 888-254-0632 ■ *Web:* www.greenway.coop	Rochester	MN	55903	507-289-4086	289-7653
Houston Fuel Oil Terminal Co 16642 Jacintoport Blvd *Web:* www.hfotco.com	Houston	TX	77015	281-452-3390	452-6306
Kellerstrass Oil Co 1500 W 2550 S	Ogden	UT	84401	801-392-9516	392-9589
LBC Houston LP 11666 Port Rd *TF:* 888-922-4433 ■ *Web:* www.lbchouston.com	Seabrook	TX	77586	281-474-4433	291-3428
Magellan Midstream Partners LP 1 Williams Ctr *NYSE: MMP* ■ **Fax:* Mail Rm ■ *TF:* 800-574-6671 ■ *Web:* www.magellanlp.com	Tulsa	OK	74172	918-574-7000	573-6714*
NuStar Terminal Canada Partnership 4090 Port Malcolm Rd	Point Tupper	NS	B9A1Z5	902-625-1711	625-3098
Oiltanking Houston LP 15602 Jacinto Port Blvd *Web:* www.oiltanking.com	Houston	TX	77015	281-457-7900	457-7917
TransMontaigne Partners LP 1670 Broadway Suite 3100 *NYSE: TLP* ■ *Web:* www.transmontaignepartners.com	Denver	CO	80202	303-626-8200	626-8228
Vital Records Inc PO Box 688 *Web:* www.vitalrecords.com	Flagtown	NJ	08821	908-369-6900	369-7319

585 PHARMACEUTICAL COMPANIES

SEE ALSO Biotechnology Companies p. 1525; Diagnostic Products p. 1784; Medicinal Chemicals & Botanical Products p. 2231; Pharmaceutical Companies - Generic Drugs p. 2416; Pharmaceutical & Diagnostic Products - Veterinary p. 2417; Vitamins & Nutritional Supplements p. 2762

				Phone	Fax
aaiPharma Inc 1726 N 23rd St *TF:* 800-575-4224 ■ *Web:* www.aaipharma.com	Wilmington	NC	28405	910-254-7000	815-2300
Abbott Laboratories 100 Abbott Pk Rd *NYSE: ABT* ■ *TF:* 800-323-9100 ■ *Web:* www.abbott.com	Abbott Park	IL	60064	847-937-6100	
Abbott Laboratories Pharmaceutical Products Div 100 Research Dr Bioresearch Ctr *TF:* 800-255-5162 ■ *Web:* www.abbott.com	Worcester	MA	01605	508-849-2500	
Accentia BioPharmaceuticals Inc 324 S Hyde Pk Ave Suite 350 *NASDAQ: ABPI* ■ *TF:* 888-423-1046 ■ *Web:* www.accentia.net	Tampa	FL	33606	813-864-2554	258-6912
Accucaps Industries Ltd 2125 Ambassador Dr *TF:* 800-665-7210 ■ *Web:* www.accucaps.com	Windsor	ON	N9C3R5	519-969-5404	250-3321
Advanced Life Sciences Inc 1440 Davey Rd *OTC: ADLSE* ■ *Web:* www.advancedlifesciences.com	Woodridge	IL	60517	630-739-6744	739-6754
Advancis Pharmaceutical Corp 20425 Seneca Meadows Pkwy	Germantown	MD	20876	301-944-6600	944-6700
AkPharma Inc PO Box 111 *TF:* 800-994-4711 ■ *Web:* www.akpharma.com	Pleasantville	NJ	08232	609-645-5100	645-0767
Allergan Canada Inc 110 Cochrane Dr *TF:* 800-668-6424 ■ *Web:* www.allergan.com	Markham	ON	L3R9S1	905-940-1660	940-1902
Allergan Inc PO Box 19534 *NYSE: AGN* ■ **Fax:* Mail Rm ■ *TF:* 800-347-4500 ■ *Web:* www.allergan.com	Irvine	CA	92623	714-246-4500	246-6987*
Allion Healthcare Inc 1660 Walt Whitman Rd Suite 105 *Web:* www.allionhealthcare.com	Melville	NY	11747	631-547-6520	249-5863
Alpharma Inc 1 Executive Dr *NYSE: ALO* ■ **Fax:* Cust Svc ■ *TF:* 800-645-4216 ■ *Web:* www.alpharma.com	Fort Lee	NJ	07024	201-947-7774	947-3275*
Altana Inc Savage Laboratories Div 60 Baylis Rd *TF:* 800-231-0206 ■ *Web:* www.savagelabs.com	Melville	NY	11747	631-454-7677	454-0732
Alva-Amco Pharmacal Cos Inc 7711 Merrimac Ave *TF:* 800-792-2582 ■ *Web:* www.alva-amco.com	Niles	IL	60714	847-663-0700	663-1400
Amphastar Pharmaceuticals Inc 11570 6th St *TF:* 800-423-4136 ■ *Web:* www.amphastar.com	Rancho Cucamonga	CA	91730	909-980-9484	980-8296
Amylin Pharmaceuticals Inc 9360 Towne Ctr Dr *NASDAQ: AMLN* ■ *Web:* www.amylin.com	San Diego	CA	92121	858-552-2200	552-2212
Anadys Pharmaceuticals Inc 5871 Oberlin Dr Suite 200 *NASDAQ: ANDS* ■ *Web:* www.anadyspharma.com	San Diego	CA	92121	858-530-3600	527-1540
Angiotech Pharmaceuticals Inc 1618 Stn St *TSE: ANP* ■ *TF:* 877-991-1110 ■ *Web:* www.angiotech.com	Vancouver	BC	V6A1B6	604-221-7676	221-2330
AP Pharma Inc 123 Saginaw Dr *NASDAQ: APPA* ■ *Web:* www.appharma.com	Redwood City	CA	94063	650-366-2626	365-6490
Apotex Inc 150 Signet Dr *TF:* 800-268-4623 ■ *Web:* www.apotex.com	Toronto	ON	M9L1T9	416-749-9300	401-3835
Apothecus Pharmaceutical Corp 220 Townsend Sq *TF:* 800-227-2393 ■ *Web:* www.apothecus.com	Oyster Bay	NY	11771	516-624-8200	624-8201
Armstrong Pharmaceuticals Inc 423 Lagrange St *Web:* www.armstrong-pharma.com	West Roxbury	MA	02132	617-323-7404	323-6940
Astellas Pharma US Inc 3 Pkwy N *TF:* 800-888-7704 ■ *Web:* www.astellas.us	Deerfield	IL	60015	847-317-8800	317-7296
AstraZeneca Canada Inc 1004 Middlegate Rd *TF:* 800-565-5877 ■ *Web:* www.astrazeneca.ca	Mississauga	ON	L4Y1M4	905-277-7111	270-3248
AstraZeneca Pharmaceuticals LP 1800 Concord Pike PO Box 15437 *TF:* 800-456-3669 ■ *Web:* www.astrazeneca-us.com	Wilmington	DE	19850	302-886-3000	
AutoImmune Inc 1199 Madia St *Web:* www.autoimmuneinc.com	Pasadena	CA	91103	626-792-1235	792-1236
Auxilium Pharmaceuticals Inc 40 Valley Stream Pkwy *NASDAQ: AUXL* ■ *TF:* 877-663-0412 ■ *Web:* www.auxilium.com	Malvern	PA	19355	484-321-5900	321-5999
Axm Pharma Inc 20955 Pathfinder Rd Suite 100 *OTCPK: AXMP* ■ *Web:* www.axmpharma.com	Diamond Bar	CA	91765	909-843-6338	843-6350
Banner Pharmacaps Inc 4100 Mendenhall Oaks Pkwy *TF:* 800-447-1140 ■ *Web:* www.banpharm.com	High Point	NC	27265	336-812-3442	812-8777
Banner Pharmacaps Ltd 5807 47th Ave *TF Cust Svc:* 866-507-3484 ■ *Web:* www.banpharm.com	Olds	AB	T4H1S7	403-556-2531	556-8596
Bausch & Lomb Inc 1 Bausch & Lomb Pl *TF:* 800-344-8815 ■ *Web:* www.bausch.com	Rochester	NY	14604	585-338-6000	338-6007
Bausch & Lomb Pharmaceuticals Inc 8500 Hidden River Pkwy *TF Cust Svc:* 800-323-0000 ■ *Web:* www.bausch.com	Tampa	FL	33637	813-975-7700	975-7770
Baxter International Inc 1 Baxter Pkwy *NYSE: BAX* ■ *Web:* www.baxter.com	Deerfield	IL	60015	847-948-2000	948-3948
Bayer Corp 100 Bayer Rd *TF:* 800-422-9374 ■ *Web:* www.bayerus.com	Pittsburgh	PA	15205	412-777-2000	778-4430
Bayer Corp Consumer Care Div 36 Columbia Rd PO Box 1910 *Web:* www.bayerus.com	Morristown	NJ	07962	973-254-5000	408-8113
Bayer Inc 77 Belfield Rd **Fax:* Hum Res ■ *TF:* 800-622-2937 ■ *Web:* www.bayer.ca	Toronto	ON	M9W1G6	416-248-0771	248-1297*
Berlex Laboratories Inc 6 W Belt *TF:* 888-237-2394 ■ *Web:* www.berlex.com	Wayne	NJ	07470	973-694-4100	305-5475
BioSante Pharmaceuticals Inc 111 Barclay Blvd Suite 280 *NASDAQ: BPA* ■ *Web:* www.biosantepharma.com	Lincolnshire	IL	60069	847-478-0500	478-9152
BioSpecifics Technologies Corp 35 Wilbur St *Web:* www.biospecifics.com	Lynbrook	NY	11563	516-593-7000	593-7039
Blistex Inc 1800 Swift Dr *TF Cust Svc:* 800-837-1800 ■ *Web:* www.blistex.com	Oak Brook	IL	60523	630-571-2870	571-3437
Boehringer Ingelheim Ltd 5180 S Service Rd *TF:* 800-263-9107 ■ *Web:* www.boehringer-ingelheim.com	Burlington	ON	L7L5H4	905-639-0333	639-3769
Boehringer Ingelheim Pharmaceuticals Inc 900 Ridgebury Rd **Fax:* Cust Svc ■ *TF:* 800-243-0127 ■ *Web:* www.boehringer-ingelheim.com	Ridgefield	CT	06877	203-798-9988	798-4735*
Botanical Laboratories Inc 1441 W Smith Rd *TF:* 800-232-4005 ■ *Web:* www.botlab.com	Ferndale	WA	98248	360-384-5656	384-1140
Brioschi Inc 19-01 Pollitt Dr *TF:* 800-274-6724 ■ *Web:* www.brioschi-usa.com	Fair Lawn	NJ	07410	201-796-4226	796-0391
Bristol-Myers Squibb Canada Inc 2344 Alfred-Nobel Blvd Suite 300 *TF Cust Svc:* 800-267-0005 ■ *Web:* www.bmscanada.ca	Montreal	QC	H4S0A4	514-333-3200	335-4102
Bristol-Myers Squibb Co 345 Pk Ave *NYSE: BMY* ■ *Web:* www.bms.com	New York	NY	10154	212-546-4000	546-4020
Bristol-Myers Squibb Co Worldwide Medicines Group 311 Pennington Rocky Hill Rd	Princeton	NJ	08534	609-818-3000	
Caraco Pharmaceutical Laboratories Ltd 1150 Elijah McCoy Dr *AMEX: CPD* ■ *TF:* 800-818-4555 ■ *Web:* www.caraco.com	Detroit	MI	48202	313-871-8400	871-8314
Cardiovascular Consultants Pc 4330 Wornall Rd Suite 2000 *Web:* www.cc-pc.com	Kansas City	MO	64111	816-931-1883	
Care-Tech Laboratories Inc 3224 S Kingshighway Blvd *TF:* 800-325-9681 ■ *Web:* www.caretechlabs.com	Saint Louis	MO	63139	314-772-4610	772-4613
CB Fleet Inc 4615 Murray Pl PO Box 11349 **Fax:* Cust Svc ■ *TF:* 800-999-9711 ■ *Web:* www.cbfleet.com	Lynchburg	VA	24502	434-528-4000	528-4235*
Chattem Inc 1715 W 38th St PO Box 2219 *NASDAQ: CHTT* ■ *TF:* 800-366-6077 ■ *Web:* www.chattem.com	Chattanooga	TN	37409	423-821-4571	821-0395
Chembio Diagnostics Inc 3661 Horseblock Rd *PINK: CEMI* ■ *Web:* www.chembio.com	Medford	NY	11763	631-924-1135	924-6033
Cirrus Healthcare Products LLC 60 Main St PO Box 220 *TF:* 800-327-6151 ■ *Web:* www.cirrushealthcare.com	Cold Spring Harbor	NY	11724	631-692-7600	692-9844
Coating Place Inc 200 Paoli St *Web:* www.encap.com	Verona	WI	53593	608-845-9521	845-9526
Columbia Laboratories Inc 354 Eisenhower Pkwy Plaza 1 2nd Fl *NASDAQ: CBRX* ■ *TF:* 866-566-5636 ■ *Web:* www.columbialabs.com	Livingston	NJ	07039	973-994-3999	994-3001
Combe Inc 1101 Westchester Ave *TF:* 800-873-7400 ■ *Web:* www.combe.com	White Plains	NY	10604	914-694-5454	694-6233
Corium International Inc 4558 50th St SE *Web:* www.coriumgroup.com	Grand Rapids	MI	49512	616-656-4563	
Cortex Pharmaceuticals Inc 1050 17th St Suite 800 *AMEX: COR* ■ **Fax Area Code:* 303 ■ *TF:* 866-777-2673 ■ *Web:* www.coresite.com	Denver	CO	80265	866-777-2673	405-1011*
Daiichi Sankyo Inc 2 Hilton Ct *Web:* www.dsi.com	Parsippany	NJ	07054	973-359-2600	359-2645
Darby Group Cos Inc 300 Jericho Quad **Fax Area Code:* 800 ■ *TF:* 800-468-1001 ■ *Web:* www.darbygroup.com	Jericho	NY	11753	516-683-1800	957-7362*
Del Laboratories Inc 726 Reckson Plaza PO Box 9357 *TF:* 800-952-5080 ■ *Web:* www.dellabs.com	Uniondale	NY	11553	516-844-2020	
Delavau LLC 10101 Roosevelt Blvd *Web:* www.delavau.com	Philadelphia	PA	19154	215-671-1400	671-1401

Company	City	State	ZIP	Phone	Fax
Dey LP 2751 Napa Valley Corporate Dr	Napa	CA	94558	707-224-3200	224-9264
TF: 800-869-9005 ■ *Web:* www.dey.com					
Dickinson Brands Inc 31 E High St	East Hampton	CT	06424	860-267-2279	267-2279
TF: 888-860-2279					
DPT Laboratories Ltd 318 McCullough	San Antonio	TX	78215	210-476-8150	476-0794
TF: 866-225-5378 ■ *Web:* www.dptlabs.com					
Dr Reddy's Laboratories Inc					
200 Summerset Corporate Blvd	Bridgewater	NJ	08807	908-203-4900	203-4940
NYSE: RDY ■ *Web:* www.drreddys.com					
Dynavax Technologies Corp					
2929 7th St Suite 100	Berkeley	CA	94710	510-848-5100	848-1327
NASDAQ: DVAX ■ *TF:* 877-848-5100 ■ *Web:* www.dynavax.com					
Eco-Med Pharmaceuticals Inc					
7050B Bramalea Rd Unit 58	Mississauga	ON	L5S1S9	905-405-1050	405-0775
Web: www.eco-med.com					
Edwards Lifesciences Corp 1 Edwards Way	Irvine	CA	92614	949-250-2500	250-2525*
NYSE: EW ■ **Fax:* Cust Svc ■ *TF:* 800-424-3278 ■ *Web:* www.edwards.com					
Eisai Inc 100 Tice Blvd	Woodcliff Lake	NJ	07677	201-692-1100	746-3201
TF: 888-793-4724 ■ *Web:* www.eisai.com					
Eli Lilly & Co Lilly Corporate Ctr	Indianapolis	IN	46285	317-276-2000	535-4615*
NYSE: LLY ■ **Fax Area Code:* 800 ■ **Fax:* Cust Svc ■ *TF Prod Info:* 800-545-5979 ■ *Web:* www.lilly.com					
Eli Lilly Canada Inc 3650 Danforth Ave	Toronto	ON	M1N2E8	416-694-3221	699-7241*
**Fax:* Hum Res ■ *TF:* 888-545-5972 ■ *Web:* www.lilly.ca					
Elona Bio Technologies Inc					
1040 Sierra Dr Suite 1000	Greenwood	IN	46143	317-865-4770	865-4775
Web: www.elonabiotech.com					
Endo Pharmaceuticals Holdings Inc					
100 Endo Blvd	Chadds Ford	PA	19317	610-558-9800	558-8979
NASDAQ: ENDP ■ *TF Cust Svc:* 800-462-3636 ■ *Web:* www.endo.com					
Ferndale Laboratories Inc					
780 W Eight-Mile Rd	Ferndale	MI	48220	248-548-0900	548-8427
TF: 800-621-6003 ■ *Web:* www.ferndalelabs.com					
First Priority Inc 1590 Todd Farm Dr	Elgin	IL	60123	847-289-1600	
TF: 800-650-4899 ■ *Web:* www.prioritycare.com					
Forest Laboratories Inc 909 3rd Ave 23rd Fl	New York	NY	10022	212-421-7850	750-9152
NYSE: FRX ■ *TF:* 800-947-5227 ■ *Web:* www.frx.com					
Forest Pharmaceutical Inc					
13600 Shoreline Dr	Saint Louis	MO	63045	314-493-7000	493-7450
TF: 800-678-1605 ■ *Web:* www.frx.com					
G & W Laboratories Inc					
111 Coolidge St	South Plainfield	NJ	07080	908-753-2000	753-5174*
**Fax:* Sales ■ *TF:* 800-922-1038 ■ *Web:* www.gwlabs.com					
Galderma Laboratories Inc 14501 N Fwy	Fort Worth	TX	76177	817-961-5000	
TF: 800-582-8225 ■ *Web:* www.galderma.com					
Germiphene Corp					
1379 Colborne St E PO Box 1748	Brantford	ON	N3T5M1	519-759-7100	759-1625
TF: 800-265-9931 ■ *Web:* www.germiphene.com					
GlaxoSmithKline PO Box 13398	Research Triangle Park	NC	27709	919-483-2100	315-1053*
**Fax:* Hum Res ■ *TF:* 888-825-5249 ■ *Web:* www.us.gsk.com					
GlaxoSmithKline Inc					
7333 Mississauga Rd N	Mississauga	ON	L5N6L4	905-819-3000	819-3099
TF: 800-387-7374 ■ *Web:* www.gsk.ca					
Gmp Laboratories of America Inc					
2931 E La Jolla St	Anaheim	CA	92806	714-630-2467	237-1374
Web: www.gmplabs.com					
Goyescas Corp of Florida Inc PO Box 524207	Miami	FL	33152	305-591-1474	591-7446
Web: www.goyescasusa.com					
Halocarbon Products Corp PO Box 661	River Edge	NJ	07661	201-262-8899	262-0019
TF: 800-338-5803 ■ *Web:* www.halocarbon.com					
Halozyme Therapeutics Inc					
11588 Sorrento Valley Rd Suite 17	San Diego	CA	92121	858-794-8889	704-8311
NASDAQ: HALO ■ *Web:* www.halozyme.com					
Hi-Tech Pharmacal Co Inc 369 Bayview Ave	Amityville	NY	11701	631-789-8228	789-8429
NASDAQ: HITK ■ *TF:* 800-262-9010 ■ *Web:* www.hitechpharm.com					
Hoffmann-La Roche Ltd					
2455 Meadowpine Blvd	Mississauga	ON	L5N6L7	905-542-5555	542-7130
TF: 800-561-1759 ■ *Web:* www.rochecanada.com					
Hoffmann-LaRoche Inc 340 Kingsland St	Nutley	NJ	07110	973-235-5000	235-7605
TF: 800-526-6367 ■ *Web:* www.roche.com					
Hope Pharmaceuticals Inc					
8260 E Gelding Dr Suite 104	Scottsdale	AZ	85260	480-607-1970	607-1971
TF: 800-755-9595 ■ *Web:* www.hopepharm.com					
Hospira Inc 275 N Field Dr	Lake Forest	IL	60045	224-212-2000	
NYSE: HSP ■ *TF:* 877-946-7747 ■ *Web:* www.hospira.com					
Human Genome Sciences Inc					
14200 Shady Grove Rd	Rockville	MD	20850	301-309-8504	309-8512
NASDAQ: HGSI ■ *Web:* www.hgsi.com					
Humco Holding Group Inc 7400 Alumax Dr	Texarkana	TX	75501	903-334-6200	334-6300
TF: 800-662-3435 ■ *Web:* www.humco.com					
Hyland's Inc 210 W 131st St	Los Angeles	CA	90061	310-768-0700	516-8579
Web: www.hylands.com					
Hythiam Inc					
11150 Santa Monica Blvd Suite 1500	Los Angeles	CA	90025	310-268-0011	444-5300
NASDAQ: HYTM ■ *TF:* 866-321-6558 ■ *Web:* www.prometainfo.com					
Ikaria Inc 53 Frontage Rd 3rd Fl PO Box 9001	Hampton	NJ	08827	908-238-6600	238-6633
Web: www.ikaria.com					
Immtech Pharmaceuticals 1 N End Ave	New York	NY	10282	212-791-2911	791-2917
TF: 877-898-8038 ■ *Web:* www.immtechpharma.com					
Infinity Pharmaceuticals Inc					
780 Memorial Dr	Cambridge	MA	02139	617-453-1000	453-1001
NASDAQ: INFI ■ *Web:* www.infi.com					
Innovative Health Products Inc					
6950 Bryan Dairy Rd	Largo	FL	33777	727-544-8866	544-4386
TF: 800-654-2347 ■ *Web:* www.onlineihp.com					
InterMune Inc 3280 Bayshore Blvd	Brisbane	CA	94005	415-466-2200	466-2300
NASDAQ: ITMN ■ *TF:* 877-862-2292 ■ *Web:* www.intermune.com					
Interpharm Holdings Inc 75 Adams Ave	Hauppauge	NY	11788	631-952-0214	952-9587
PINK: IPAH					
Jaapharm Canada Inc					
510 Rowntree Dairy Rd Unit 4	Woodbridge	ON	L4L8H2	905-851-7885	856-5838
Web: www.jaapharm.com					
Janssen Healthcare Learning Ctr					
PO Box 200	Titusville	NJ	08560	800-526-7736	
TF: 800-775-5514 ■ *Web:* www.janssenpharmaceuticalsinc.com					
Janssen Pharmaceutica Inc					
1125 Trenton-Harbourton Rd PO Box 200	Titusville	NJ	08560	609-730-2000	730-2323
TF: 800-526-7736 ■ *Web:* www.janssen.com					
Janssen-Ortho Inc 19 Green Belt Dr	North York	ON	M3C1L9	416-449-9444	449-2658
TF: 800-387-8781 ■ *Web:* www.janssen-ortho.com					
Jazz Pharmaceuticals Inc 3180 Porter Dr	Palo Alto	CA	94304	650-496-3777	496-3781
NASDAQ: JAZZ ■ *TF:* 888-867-7426 ■ *Web:* www.jazzpharmaceuticals.com					
K P Pharmaceutical Technology Inc					
1212 W Rappel Ave	Bloomington	IN	47404	812-330-8121	330-8363
Web: www.kppt.com					
Keryx Biopharmaceuticals Inc					
750 Lexington Ave 20th Fl	New York	NY	10022	212-531-5965	531-5961
NASDAQ: KERX ■ *Web:* www.keryx.com					
King Bio Pharmaceuticals Inc 3 Westside Dr	Asheville	NC	28806	828-255-0201	255-0940
TF: 800-543-3245 ■ *Web:* www.kingbio.com					
Konsyl Pharmaceuticals Inc					
8050 Industrial Pk Rd	Easton	MD	21601	410-822-5192	820-7032
TF: 800-356-6795 ■ *Web:* www.konsyl.com					
Kramer Laboratories Inc 8778 SW 8th St	Miami	FL	33174	305-223-1287	223-5510
TF: 800-824-4894 ■ *Web:* www.kramerlabs.com					
Kyowa Hakko USA Inc					
212 Carnegie Ctr Suite 101	Princeton	NJ	08540	609-919-1100	919-1111
TF: 888-464-6574 ■ *Web:* www.kyowa-usa.com					
Leiner Health Products Inc 901 E 233rd St	Carson	CA	90745	310-835-8400	952-7760
TF: 800-421-1168					
Ligand Pharmaceuticals Inc					
11085 N Torrey Pines Rd Suite 300	La Jolla	CA	92037	858-550-7500	550-7506
NASDAQ: LGND ■ *Web:* www.ligand.com					
Major Pharmaceutical Co 31778 Enterprise Dr	Livonia	MI	48150	734-525-8700	525-8393
TF: 800-521-5098					
Manhattan Pharmaceuticals Inc					
48 Wall St Suite 1100	New York	NY	10005	212-582-3950	582-3957
OTC: MHAN ■ *Web:* www.manhattanpharma.com					
Map Pharmaceuticals Inc					
2400 Bayshore Pkwy Suite 200	Mountain View	CA	94043	650-386-3100	386-3101
NASDAQ: MAPP ■ *Web:* www.mappharma.com					
Matrixx Initiatives Inc PO Box 28486	Scottsdale	AZ	85255	602-385-8888	385-8850
Web: www.matrixxinc.com					
McNeil Consumer & Specialty Pharmaceuticals					
7050 Camp Hill Rd	Fort Washington	PA	19034	215-273-7000	273-4070*
**Fax:* Cust Svc ■ *TF:* 800-962-5357					
Medical Products Laboratories Inc					
9990 Global Rd PO Box 14366	Philadelphia	PA	19115	215-677-2700	677-7736
TF: 800-523-0191 ■ *Web:* www.medicalproductslaboratories.com					
Medicis Pharmaceutical Corp					
7720 N Dobson Rd	Scottsdale	AZ	85256	602-808-8800	808-0822
NYSE: MRX ■ *TF Cust Svc:* 800-550-5115 ■ *Web:* www.medicis.com					
Medivation Inc 201 Spear St 3rd Fl	San Francisco	CA	94105	415-543-3470	543-3411
NASDAQ: MDVN ■ *Web:* www.medivation.net					
MedPointe Pharmaceuticals					
265 Davidson Ave Suite 300	Somerset	NJ	08873	732-564-2200	564-2434
Web: www.medpointeinc.com					
Melaleuca Inc 3910 S Yellowstone Hwy	Idaho Falls	ID	83402	208-522-0700	528-2090*
**Fax Area Code:* 888 ■ *TF Sales:* 800-282-3000 ■ *Web:* www.melaleuca.com					
Mentholatum Co Inc 707 Sterling Dr	Orchard Park	NY	14127	716-677-2500	677-9528
TF: 800-688-7660 ■ *Web:* www.mentholatum.com					
Merck & Co Inc					
1 Merck Dr PO Box 100	Whitehouse Station	NJ	08889	908-423-1000	
NYSE: MRK ■ *TF Cust Svc:* 800-672-6372 ■ *Web:* www.merck.com					
Merck Frosst Canada Ltd					
16711 Trans Canada Hwy	Kirkland	QC	H9H3L1	514-428-8600	428-2670
TF: 800-587-2594 ■ *Web:* www.merckfrosst.ca					
Merz Pharmaceuticals Inc					
4215 Tudor Ln PO Box 18806	Greensboro	NC	27419	336-856-2003	856-0107
TF: 888-637-9872 ■ *Web:* www.merzusa.com					
Mikart Inc 1750 Chattahoochee Ave NW	Atlanta	GA	30318	404-351-4510	350-0432
TF: 888-464-5278 ■ *Web:* www.mikart.com					
Mission Pharmacal PO Box 786099	San Antonio	TX	78278	210-696-8400	696-6010
TF: 800-531-3333 ■ *Web:* www.missionpharmacal.com					
Mylan Pharmaceuticals Inc					
781 Chestnut Ridge Rd	Morgantown	WV	26505	800-796-9526	598-3232*
**Fax Area Code:* 304 ■ *TF:* 800-796-9526 ■ *Web:* www.mylanpharms.com					
Nature's Value Inc 468 Mill Rd	Coram	NY	11727	631-846-2500	846-2527
Web: www.naturesvalue.com					
Neos Therapeutics					
2940 N Hwy 360 Suite 100	Grand Prairie	TX	75050	972-408-1300	408-1143
Web: www.neostx.com					
NextPharma Technologies Inc					
5340 Eastgate Mall	San Diego	CA	92121	858-450-3123	450-0785
Web: www.nextpharma.com					
Noramco Inc 1440 Olympic Dr	Athens	GA	30601	706-353-4400	353-3205
Web: www.noramco.com					
NovaDel Pharma Inc					
1200 Rt 22 E Suite 2000	Bridgewater	NJ	08807	908-203-4640	203-4744
OTC: NVDL ■ *Web:* www.novadel.com					
Novartis Consumer Health PO Box 83288	Lincoln	NE	68501	402-464-6311	467-8889*
**Fax:* Hum Res ■ *TF:* 800-452-0051 ■ *Web:* www.novartis.com/consumerhealth					
Novartis Pharmaceuticals Canada Inc					
385 boul Bouchard	Dorval	QC	H9S1A9	514-631-6775	435-4423*
**Fax Area Code:* 800 ■ **Fax:* Cust Svc ■ *TF:* 800-465-2244 ■ *Web:* www.novartis.ca					
Novartis Pharmaceuticals Corp					
1 Health Plaza	East Hanover	NJ	07936	862-778-8300	781-8265*
**Fax Area Code:* 973 ■ *TF Cust Svc:* 888-669-6682 ■ *Web:* www.pharma.us.novartis.com					
Noven Pharmaceuticals Inc 11960 SW 144th St	Miami	FL	33186	305-253-5099	251-1887
Web: www.noven.com					
Novo Nordisk of North America Inc					
100 College Rd W	Princeton	NJ	08540	609-987-5800	987-5394
TF: 800-727-6500 ■ *Web:* www.novonordisk-us.com					

				Phone	Fax
Novo Nordisk Pharmaceuticals Inc 100 College Rd W *TF Cust Svc:* 800-727-6500 ■ *Web:* www.novonordisk-us.com	Princeton	NJ	08540	609-987-5800	987-5394
Numark Laboratories Inc 164 Northfield Ave *TF:* 800-338-8079 ■ *Web:* www.numarklabs.com	Edison	NJ	08837	732-417-1870	225-0066
Nutramax Laboratories Inc 2208 Lakeside Blvd *TF:* 800-925-5187 ■ *Web:* www.nutramaxlabs.com	Edgewood	MD	21040	410-776-4000	776-4009
Nutramax Products Inc Cough & Cold Div 170 Oak Hill Way *Web:* www.nutramax.com/cough_cold.html	Brockton	MA	02301	508-584-8100	584-8704
NutriCology Inc 2300 N Loop Rd *Web:* www.nutricology.com	Alameda	CA	94502	510-263-2000	263-2100
Odor Management Inc 18-6 E Dundee Rd Suite 101 *TF:* 800-662-6367 ■ *Web:* www.odormanagement.com	Barrington	IL	60010	847-304-9111	304-0989
Odyssey Pharmaceuticals Inc 72 Eagle Rock Ave *TF:* 877-427-9068	East Hanover	NJ	07936	877-427-9068	427-9069
Ono Pharma USA Inc 2000 Lenox Dr *Web:* www.ono.co.jp	Lawrenceville	NJ	08648	609-219-1010	219-9229
Optimer Pharmaceuticals Inc 10110 Sorrento Valley Rd Suite C *Web:* www.optimerpharma.com	San Diego	CA	92121	858-909-0736	909-0737
Pain Therapeutics Inc 7801 N Capital of Texas Hwy Suite 260 *NASDAQ: PTIE* ■ *Web:* www.paintrials.com	Austin	TX	78731	512-501-2444	614-0414
Particle Dynamics International LLC 2629 S Hanley Rd *TF:* 800-452-4682 ■ *Web:* www.particledynamics.com	Saint Louis	MO	63144	314-968-2376	781-3354
Pegasus Laboratories Inc 8809 Ely Rd *Web:* www.pegasuslabs.com	Pensacola	FL	32514	850-478-2770	478-5639
Pfizer Canada Inc 17300 TransCanada Hwy *TF:* 800-463-6001 ■ *Web:* www.pfizer.ca	Kirkland	QC	H9J2M5	514-695-0500	426-6831
Pfizer Inc 235 E 42nd St *NYSE: PFE* ■ *TF:* 800-733-4717 ■ *Web:* www.pfizer.com	New York	NY	10017	212-733-2323	573-7851
Pfizer Inc Pharmaceuticals Group 235 E 42nd St *Web:* www.pfizer.com	New York	NY	10017	212-573-2323	
PharmAthene Inc One Pk Pl Suite 450 *Web:* www.pharmathene.com	Annapolis	MD	21401	410-269-2600	269-2601
Pharmos Corp 99 Wood Ave S Suite 311 *NASDAQ: PARS* ■ *TF:* 888-308-5520 ■ *Web:* www.pharmoscorp.com	Iselin	NJ	08830	732-452-9556	452-9557
Procter & Gamble Pharmaceuticals Canada Inc PO Box 355 *TF:* 800-668-0150 ■ *Web:* www.pgpharma.com/canada_welcome.shtml	Toronto	ON	M5W1C5	416-730-6054	730-4415
Procter & Gamble Pharmaceuticals Inc One Proctor & Gamble Plaza *TF:* 800-331-3774	Cincinnati	OH	45202	513-983-1100	
Prometheus Laboratories Inc 9410 Carroll Pk Dr *TF:* 888-423-5227 ■ *Web:* www.prometheus-labs.com	San Diego	CA	92121	858-824-0895	824-0896
ProPhase Labs Inc 621 Shady Retreat Rd *NASDAQ: PRPH* ■ *TF:* 877-265-3339 ■ *Web:* www.quigleyco.com	Doylestown	PA	18091	215-345-0919	345-5920
Protide Pharmaceuticals Inc 505 Oakwood Rd Suite 200 *TF:* 800-552-3569 ■ *Web:* www.protidepharma.com	Lake Zurich	IL	60047	847-726-3100	726-3110
Purdue Pharma LP 1 Stamford Forum *TF Cust Svc:* 800-877-5666 ■ *Web:* www.purduepharma.com	Stamford	CT	06901	203-588-8000	588-8850
QLT USA Inc 2579 Midpoint Dr *Web:* www.qltinc.com	Fort Collins	CO	80525	970-482-5868	482-9735
Qualicaps Inc 6505 Franz Warner Pkwy *TF:* 800-227-7853 ■ *Web:* www.qualicaps.com	Whitsett	NC	27377	336-449-3900	449-3333
Qualitest Pharmaceuticals Inc 130 Vintage Dr Ne *Web:* www.qualitestrx.com	Huntsville	AL	35811	256-859-4011	859-4021
Quatrx Pharmaceuticals Co 777 E Eisenhower Pkwy Suite 100 *Web:* www.quatrx.com	Ann Arbor	MI	48108	734-913-9900	913-0743
Quintiles Canada Inc 100 Alexis-Nihon Suite 800 *TF:* 800-799-6166 ■ *Web:* www.quintiles.com	Saint Laurent	QC	H4M2P4	514-855-0888	
Quintiles Transnational Corp 4820 Emperor Blvd *TF:* 800-875-2888 ■ *Web:* www.quintiles.com	Durham	NC	27703	919-998-2000	998-9113
R X Systems Inc 121 Pt W Blvd *TF:* 800-922-9142 ■ *Web:* www.rxsystems.com	Saint Charles	MO	63301	636-925-0001	925-0041
Ratiopharm 6975 Creditview Rd Unit 5 *TF:* 800-266-2584 ■ *Web:* www.ratiopharm.ca	Mississauga	ON	L5N8E9	905-858-9612	858-9610
RegeneRx Biopharmaceuticals Inc 15245 Shady Grove Rd Suite 470 *OTC: RGRX* ■ *Web:* www.regenerx.com	Rockville	MD	20850	301-208-9191	208-9194
Regis Technologies Inc 8210 Austin Ave *TF:* 800-323-8144 ■ *Web:* www.registech.com	Morton Grove	IL	60053	847-967-6000	967-5876
Roxane Laboratories Inc 1809 Wilson Rd *TF Cust Svc:* 800-520-1631 ■ *Web:* www.roxane.com	Columbus	OH	43228	614-276-4000	274-0974
Rules-based Medicine Inc 3300 Duval Rd *TF:* 866-726-6277 ■ *Web:* www.rulesbasedmedicine.com	Austin	TX	78759	512-835-8026	835-4687
SAFC 3050 Spruce St *TF:* 800-244-1173 ■ *Web:* www.safcglobal.com	Saint Louis	MO	63103	314-534-4900	652-0000
Sagent Pharmaceuticals Inc 1901 N Roselle Rd *NASDAQ: SGNT* ■ *Web:* www.sagentpharma.com	Schaumburg	IL	60195	847-908-1600	908-1601
Salix Pharmaceuticals Inc 1700 Perimeter Pk Dr *NASDAQ: SLXP* ■ *TF:* 800-508-0024 ■ *Web:* www.salix.com	Morrisville	NC	27560	919-862-1000	862-1095
Sanofi-Aventis US LLC 55 Corp Dr *TF:* 800-981-2491 ■ *Web:* www.sanofi-aventis.us	Bridgewater	NJ	08807	908-231-4000	231-3614
Schering Canada Inc 3535 TransCanada Hwy *Web:* www.schering.ca	Pointe-Claire	QC	H9R1B4	514-426-7300	695-7641
Schering Corp 2000 Galloping Hill Rd *TF:* 800-222-7579 ■ *Web:* www.schering-plough.com	Kenilworth	NJ	07033	908-298-4000	595-3699
Schering-Plough Pharmaceuticals 2000 Galloping Hill Rd *TF:* 888-793-7253 ■ *Web:* www.schering-plough.com	Kenilworth	NJ	07033	908-298-4000	
SciClone Pharmaceuticals Inc 950 Tower Ln Suite 900 *NASDAQ: SCLN* ■ *TF:* 800-724-2566 ■ *Web:* www.sciclone.com	Foster City	CA	94404	650-358-3456	358-3469
Shire Pharmaceuticals Inc 725 Chesterbrook Blvd *Web:* www.shire.com	Wayne	PA	19087	484-595-8248	595-8200
Shire US Inc 725 Chesterbrook Blvd *Web:* www.shire.com	Wayne	PA	19087	484-595-8800	595-8200
Sigma-Tau Pharmaceutical Inc 9841 Washingtonian Blvd Suite 500 *TF:* 800-447-0169 ■ *Web:* www.sigmatau.com	Gaithersburg	MD	20878	301-948-1041	948-1862
Silipos Inc 7049 Williams Rd *TF:* 800-229-4404 ■ *Web:* www.silipos.com	Niagara Falls	NY	14304	716-283-0700	283-0600
Solvay America Inc 3333 Richmond Ave *TF:* 800-231-6313 ■ *Web:* www.solvay.com	Houston	TX	77098	713-525-6000	525-7887
Solvay Pharma Inc 60 Columbia Way Suite 207 *TF:* 800-268-4276	Markham	ON	L3R6H3	905-944-2480	944-2481
Somaxon Pharmaceuticals Inc 3570 Carmel Mountain Rd Suite 100 *NASDAQ: SOMX* ■ *Web:* www.somaxon.com	San Diego	CA	92130	858-876-6500	509-1761
Sovereign Pharmaceuticals Ltd 7590 Sand St *TF:* 877-248-0228 ■ *Web:* www.sovpharm.com	Fort Worth	TX	76118	817-284-0429	284-0531
SSS Co 71 University Ave PO Box 4447 *TF:* 800-237-3843 ■ *Web:* www.ssspharmaceuticals.com	Atlanta	GA	30302	404-521-0857	880-0383
Stiefel Laboratories Inc 255 Alhambra Cir Suite 1000 *TF:* 888-784-3335 ■ *Web:* www.stiefel.com	Coral Gables	FL	33134	305-443-3807	443-3467
Sucampo Pharmaceuticals Inc 4520 East-West Hwy Suite 300 3rd Fl *NASDAQ: SCMP* ■ *Web:* www.sucampo.com	Bethesda	MD	20814	301-961-3400	961-3440
Summa Laboratories Inc 2940 FM 3028 *Web:* www.summalabs.com	Mineral Wells	TX	76067	940-325-0771	325-0807
Synta Pharmaceuticals Corp 45 Hartwell Ave *NASDAQ: SNTA* ■ *Web:* www.syntapharma.com	Lexington	MA	02421	781-274-8200	274-8228
Taisho Pharmaceutical California Inc 3878 W Carson St # 216 *TF:* 877-531-4559	Torrance	CA	90503	310-543-2035	543-9636
Tamir Biotechnology Inc 11 Deer Pk Dr Suite 204 *NASDAQ: ACEL* ■ *Web:* www.alfacell.com	Monmouth Junction	NJ	08852	732-823-1003	652-4575
Targacept Inc 200 E 1st St Suite 300 *NASDAQ: TRGT* ■ *Web:* www.targacept.com	Winston-Salem	NC	27101	336-480-2100	480-2107
Taro Pharmaceuticals Inc 130 E Dr *TF:* 800-268-1975 ■ *Web:* www.taro.ca	Brampton	ON	L6T1C1	905-791-8276	791-4473
Tower Laboratories Ltd PO Box 306 *Web:* www.towerlabs.com	Centerbrook	CT	06409	860-767-2127	767-2129
Trident Enterprises International Inc 9735a Bethel Rd *TF:* 888-422-3337 ■ *Web:* www.deerbusters.com	Frederick	MD	21702	301-694-6072	694-9254
UCB Pharma Inc 1950 Lake Pk Dr **Fax:* Hum Res ■ *TF:* 800-477-7877 ■ *Web:* www.ucb.com	Smyrna	GA	30080	770-970-7500	970-8482*
Unipack Inc 3253 Old Frankstown Rd *Web:* www.unipackinc.com	Pittsburgh	PA	15239	724-733-7381	327-6265
Unipharm Inc 350 5th Ave Suite 6701 *Web:* www.unipharmus.com	New York	NY	10118	212-594-3260	594-3261
United Therapeutics Corp 1040 Spring St *NASDAQ: UTHR* ■ *TF:* 877-864-8437 ■ *Web:* www.unither.com	Silver Spring	MD	20910	301-608-9292	608-9291
Upsher-Smith Laboratories Inc 6701 Evenstad Dr *TF:* 800-328-3344 ■ *Web:* www.upsher-smith.com	Maple Grove	MN	55369	763-315-2000	476-4026
Vanda Pharmaceuticals Inc 9605 Medical Ctr Dr Suite 300 *NASDAQ: VNDA* ■ **Fax Area Code:* 301 ■ *Web:* www.vandapharmaceuticals.com	Rockville	MD	20850	240-599-4500	294-1900*
Vivus Inc 1172 Castro St *NASDAQ: VVUS* ■ *TF:* 888-367-6873 ■ *Web:* www.vivus.com	Mountain View	CA	94040	650-934-5200	934-5389
Watson Pharmaceuticals Inc Morris Corporate Ctr III 400 Interpace Pkwy *NYSE: WPI* ■ *TF:* 800-900-1644 ■ *Web:* www.watson.com	Parsippany	NJ	07054	862-261-7000	
WF Young Inc 302 Benton Dr PO Box 1990 *TF:* 800-628-9653 ■ *Web:* www.absorbine.com	East Longmeadow	MA	01028	413-526-9999	526-8990
Wright Group The 6428 Airport Rd **Fax Area Code:* 318 ■ *TF:* 800-201-3096 ■ *Web:* www.thewrightgroup.net	Crowley	LA	70526	337-783-3096	783-3802*
Zalicus Inc 245 1st St 3rd Fl *NASDAQ: ZLCS* ■ *Web:* www.zalicus.com	Cambridge	MA	02412	617-425-7000	425-7010
ZLB Behring LLC 1020 1st Ave PO Box 61501 *TF:* 800-683-1288 ■ *Web:* www.zlbbehring.com	King of Prussia	PA	19406	610-878-4000	878-4009
Zogenix Inc 12671 High Bluff Dr Suite 200 *Web:* www.zogenix.com	San Diego	CA	92130	858-259-1165	259-1166

586 PHARMACEUTICAL COMPANIES - GENERIC DRUGS

SEE ALSO Biotechnology Companies p. 1525; Diagnostic Products p. 1784; Medicinal Chemicals & Botanical Products p. 2231; Pharmaceutical Companies p. 2414; Pharmaceutical & Diagnostic Products - Veterinary p. 2417; Vitamins & Nutritional Supplements p. 2762

				Phone	Fax
Actavis North America 200 Elmora Ave *Web:* www.actavis.us	Elizabeth	NJ	07207	908-527-9100	527-0649

	City	State	Zip	Phone	Fax
Apotex Corp 2400 N Commerce Pkwy Suite 400	Weston	FL	33326	954-384-8007	706-5576*
**Fax Area Code:* 800 ■ *TF:* 800-706-5575 ■ *Web:* www.apotex.com					
APP Pharmaceuticals					
1501 E Woodfield Rd Suite 300 E	Schaumburg	IL	60173	847-969-2700	
TF: 888-391-6300 ■ *Web:* www.apppharma.com					
Capricorn Pharma Inc					
6900 English Muffin Way	Frederick	MD	21703	301-696-8520	696-1424
Web: www.capricornpharma.com					
E Fougera & Co 60 Baylis Rd	Melville	NY	11747	631-454-6996	454-6996
TF: 800-645-9833 ■ *Web:* www.fougera.com					
Ethex Corp 10888 Metro Ct	Saint Louis	MO	63043	314-646-3750	646-3751
TF: 800-321-1705 ■ *Web:* www.ethex.com					
Glenwood LLC 111 Cedar Ln	Englewood	NJ	07631	201-569-0050	569-0250
TF: 800-542-0772 ■ *Web:* www.glenwood-llc.com					
Healthpoint Ltd 3909 Hulen St	Fort Worth	TX	76107	817-900-4000	900-4100*
**Fax:* Cust Svc ■ *TF:* 800-441-8227 ■ *Web:* www.healthpoint.com					
Impax Laboratories Inc 3735 Castor Ave	Philadelphia	PA	19124	215-289-2220	289-2223
TF: 800-296-5227 ■ *Web:* www.impaxlabs.com					
Martec USA LLC 9229 Dart Pkwy	Kansas City	MO	64114	816-241-4144	483-5432
TF: 800-822-6782					
Merical Inc 233 E Bristol Ln	Orange	CA	92865	714-238-7225	238-7247
Web: www.merical.com					
Mericon Industries Inc 8819 N Pioneer Rd	Peoria	IL	61615	309-693-2150	693-2158
TF: 800-242-6464 ■ *Web:* www.mericon-industries.com					
Morton Grove Pharmaceuticals Inc					
6451 Main St	Morton Grove	IL	60053	847-967-5600	967-2211
TF: 800-346-6854 ■ *Web:* www.wockhardtusa.com					
Mylan Laboratories Inc					
1500 Corporate Dr Suite 400	Canonsburg	PA	15317	724-514-1800	514-1870
NYSE: MYL ■ *Web:* www.mylan.com					
Mylan Pharmaceuticals ULC 85 Advance Rd	Etobicoke	ON	M8Z2S6	416-236-2631	236-2940
TF: 877-540-7377 ■ *Web:* www.mylan.ca					
Neostem Inc 420 Lexington Ave Suite 450	New York	NY	10170	212-584-4180	514-7787*
AMEX: NBS ■ **Fax Area Code:* 646 ■ *Web:* www.neostem.com					
Nephron Pharmaceuticals Corp 4121 SW 34th St	Orlando	FL	32811	407-999-2225	872-1733
TF: 800-443-4313 ■ *Web:* www.nephronpharm.com					
Nexgen Pharma Inc 46 Corporate Pk Suite 100	Irvine	CA	92606	949-863-0340	261-2928
Web: www.nexgenpharma.com					
Par Pharmaceutical Cos Inc					
300 Tice Blvd	Woodcliff Lake	NJ	07677	201-802-4000	802-4600
NYSE: PRX ■ *TF:* 800-828-9393 ■ *Web:* www.parpharm.com					
Par Pharmaceutical Inc 1 Ram Ridge Rd	Spring Valley	NY	10977	201-802-4000	802-4600
TF: 800-828-9393 ■ *Web:* www.parpharm.com					
Payless Drug Stores Inc					
16100 SW 72nd Ave PO Box 230969	Portland	OR	97224	503-626-9436	372-1792
TF: 800-330-3665 ■ *Web:* www.paylessdrug.com					
Pedinol Pharmacal Inc 30 Banfi Plaza N	Farmingdale	NY	11735	631-293-9500	293-7359
TF: 800-733-4665 ■ *Web:* www.pedinol.com					
Perrigo Co 515 Eastern Ave	Allegan	MI	49010	269-673-8451	673-9128
NASDAQ: PRGO ■ *TF:* 800-253-3606 ■ *Web:* www.perrigo.com					
Pharmanet Development Group Inc					
504 Carnegie Ctr	Princeton	NJ	08540	609-951-6800	514-0390
Web: www.pharmanet.com					
Pharmics Inc 2702 3600 W	Salt Lake City	UT	84119	801-966-4138	966-4177
TF: 800-456-4138 ■ *Web:* www.pharmics.com					
Ranbaxy Pharmaceuticals Inc					
600 College Rd E Suite 2100	Princeton	NJ	08540	609-720-9200	720-1155
Web: www.ranbaxyusa.com					
Sandoz Inc 506 Carnegie Ctr Suite 400	Princeton	NJ	08540	609-627-8500	627-8659
Web: www.us.sandoz.com					
Skilled Care Pharmacy Inc 6175 Hl Tek Ct	Mason	OH	45040	513-459-7455	459-8278
TF: 800-334-1624 ■ *Web:* www.skilledcare.com					
Stratus Pharmaceuticals Inc 14377 SW 142nd St	Miami	FL	33186	305-254-6793	254-6875
TF: 800-442-7882 ■ *Web:* www.stratuspharmaceuticals.com					
Taro Pharmaceuticals USA Inc 3 Skyline Dr	Hawthorne	NY	10532	914-345-9001	345-8728
PINK: TARO ■ *TF:* 800-544-1449 ■ *Web:* www.tarousa.com					
Tercica Inc 2000 Sierra Pt Pkwy Suite 400	Brisbane	CA	94005	650-624-4900	243-5111
Web: www.tercica.com					
Teva Pharmaceutical USA 1090 Horsham Rd	North Wales	PA	19454	215-591-3000	591-8600
NASDAQ: TEVA ■ *TF:* 800-545-8800 ■ *Web:* www.tevapharmusa.com					
UDL Laboratories Inc 1718 Northrock Ct	Rockford	IL	61103	815-282-1201	282-9391
TF: 800-435-5272 ■ *Web:* www.udllabs.com					
USL Pharma 301 S Cherokee St	Denver	CO	80223	303-607-4500	607-4503
TF: 800-445-8091 ■ *Web:* www.upsher-smith.com					
Warner Chilcott					
100 Enterprise Dr Suite 280					
Rockaway 80 Corporate Ctr	Rockaway	NJ	07866	973-442-3200	442-3283
TF: 800-521-8813 ■ *Web:* www.wcrx.com					
West-Ward Pharmaceutical Corp					
465 Industrial Way W	Eatontown	NJ	07724	732-542-1191	542-0940
TF Cust Svc: 800-631-2174					
X-Gen Pharmaceuticals Inc					
300 Daniels Anchor Dr PO Box 445	Big Flats	NY	14814	607-732-4411	562-2760
TF: 866-390-4411 ■ *Web:* www.x-gen.us					
Xanodyne Pharmaceuticals Inc 1 Riverfront Pl	Newport	KY	41071	859-371-6383	371-6391
TF: 877-926-6396 ■ *Web:* www.xanodyne.com					

587 PHARMACEUTICAL & DIAGNOSTIC PRODUCTS - VETERINARY

	City	State	Zip	Phone	Fax
Abbott Laboratories Animal Health Div					
1401 Sheridan Rd	North Chicago	IL	60064	847-937-6100	938-0659
TF: 888-299-7416 ■ *Web:* www.abbottanimalhealth.com					
ABS Corp 7031 N 16th St	Omaha	NE	68112	402-453-6970	453-1052
Web: www.abs-corporation.com					
Addison Biological Laboratory Inc					
507 N Cleveland Ave	Fayette	MO	65248	660-248-2215	248-2554
TF: 800-331-2530 ■ *Web:* www.addisonlabs.com					
Alltech Inc 3031 Catnip Hill Pike	Nicholasville	KY	40356	859-885-9613	887-3256
TF: 800-289-8324 ■ *Web:* www.alltech.com					
Bell Pharmaceuticals PO Box 128	Belle Plaine	MN	56011	952-873-2288	873-2289
TF: 800-328-5890					
Bimeda Inc Oakbrook Terr Tower Suite 2250	Oakbrook	IL	60181	630-928-0361	928-0362
Web: www.bimeda.com					
Bimeda-MTC Animal Health Inc					
420 Beaverdale Rd	Cambridge	ON	N3C2W4	519-654-8000	654-8001
Web: www.bimeda.com/dotcom/canadaabout.htm					
Bio-Serv 1 8th St Suite 1	Frenchtown	NJ	08825	908-996-2155	996-4123
TF: 800-996-9908 ■ *Web:* www.bio-serv.com					
Biomune Co 8906 Rosehill Rd	Lenexa	KS	66215	913-894-0230	894-0236
TF: 800-846-0230 ■ *Web:* www.biomunecompany.com					
Bioniche Animal Health Canada Inc					
231 Dundas St E	Belleville	ON	K8N1E2	613-966-8058	966-4177
TSX: BNC ■ *TF:* 800-265-5464 ■ *Web:* www.bioniche.com					
Biovet Inc 4375 Ave Beaudry	Saint-Hyacinthe	QC	J2S8W2	450-771-7291	771-4158
TF: 888-824-6838 ■ *Web:* www.biovet-inc.com					
Biovet USA Inc 3055 Old Hwy 8 Suite 100	Saint Anthony	MN	55418	612-781-2952	781-2941
TF: 877-824-6838 ■ *Web:* www.biovet-inc.com					
Boehringer Ingelheim Vetmedica Inc					
2621 N Belt Hwy	Saint Joseph	MO	64506	816-233-2571	390-0605*
**Fax:* Hum Res ■ *TF:* 800-821-7467 ■ *Web:* www.bi-vetmedica.com					
Cut-Heal Animal Care Products Inc					
923 S Cedar Hill Rd	Cedar Hill	TX	75104	972-293-9700	293-8335
TF: 800-288-4325					
Dairy Assn Co Inc 91 Williams St	Lyndonville	VT	05851	802-626-3610	626-3433
TF: 800-232-3610 ■ *Web:* www.bagbalm.com					
Darby Group Cos Inc 300 Jericho Quad	Jericho	NY	11753	516-683-1800	957-7362*
**Fax Area Code:* 800 ■ *TF:* 800-468-1001 ■ *Web:* www.darbygroup.com					
Dawe's LLC					
3355 N Arlington Heights Rd	Arlington Heights	IL	60004	847-577-2020	577-1898
TF: 800-323-4317					
Delmont Laboratories Inc					
715 Harvard Ave PO Box 269	Swarthmore	PA	19081	610-543-3365	543-6298
TF: 800-562-5541 ■ *Web:* www.delmont.com					
DiagXotics Inc 3371 Rt 1 Suite 200	Lawrenceville	NJ	08648	405-809-1314	809-1944
TF: 866-358-9282					
DMS Laboratories Inc 2 Darts Mill Rd	Flemington	NJ	08822	908-782-3353	782-0832
TF: 800-567-4367 ■ *Web:* www.rapidvet.com					
Dominion Veterinary Laboratories Inc					
1199 Sanford St	Winnipeg	MB	R3E3A1	204-589-7361	943-9612
TF: 800-465-7122 ■ *Web:* www.domvet.com					
Elanco Animal Health 2001 W Main St	Greenfield	IN	46140	317-276-2000	276-9434
Web: www.elanco.com					
Farnam Cos Inc 301 W Osborn Rd	Phoenix	AZ	85013	602-285-1660	285-1803
TF: 800-234-2269 ■ *Web:* www.farnam.com					
Heska Corp 3760 Rocky Mountain Ave	Loveland	CO	80538	970-493-7272	619-3005
NASDAQ: HSKA ■ *TF:* 800-464-3752 ■ *Web:* www.heska.com					
IGI Inc 105 Lincoln Ave	Buena	NJ	08310	856-697-1441	697-2259
AMEX: IG ■ *Web:* www.igilabs.com					
IMMVAC Inc 6080 Bass Ln	Columbia	MO	65201	573-443-5363	874-7108
TF: 800-944-7563 ■ *Web:* www.immvac.com					
K & K Veterinary Supply Inc					
675 E Laura Ave PO Box 1090	Tontitown	AR	72770	479-361-1516	
Web: www.kkvet.com					
King Bio Pharmaceuticals Inc 3 Westside Dr	Asheville	NC	28806	828-255-0201	255-0940
TF: 800-543-3245 ■ *Web:* www.kingbio.com					
Lake Immunogenics Inc 348 Berg Rd	Ontario	NY	14519	585-265-1973	265-2306
TF: 800-648-9990 ■ *Web:* www.lakeimmunogenics.com					
Lextron Inc 620 'O' St PO Box 1240	Greeley	CO	80632	970-353-2600	356-4623
Web: www.lextron-inc.com					
Lloyd Inc 604 W Thomas Ave PO Box 130	Shenandoah	IA	51601	712-246-4000	246-5245
TF: 800-831-0004 ■ *Web:* www.lloydinc.com					
Luitpold Pharmaceuticals Inc					
1 Luitpold Dr PO Box 9001	Shirley	NY	11967	631-924-4000	924-1731
TF: 800-645-1706 ■ *Web:* www.luitpold.com					
Merial Ltd 3239 Satellite Blvd Bldg 500	Duluth	GA	30096	678-638-3000	
TF: 888-637-4251 ■ *Web:* www.merial.com					
MetaMorphix Inc					
4061 Powdermill Rd Suite 320 Ctr Park II	Calverton	MD	20705	301-575-2508	617-9075
Web: www.metamorphixinc.com					
MVP Laboratories Inc 4805 G St	Omaha	NE	68117	402-331-5106	331-8776
TF: 800-856-4648 ■ *Web:* www.mvplabs.com					
MWI Veterinary Supply Inc 3041 W Pasadena Dr	Boise	ID	83705	208-955-8930	955-8902
NASDAQ: MWIV ■ *Web:* www.mwivet.com					
Novartis Animal Health US Inc					
1447 140th St	Larchwood	IA	51241	712-477-2811	628-4673*
**Fax Area Code:* 866 ■ *TF:* 800-454-3424 ■ *Web:* www.livestock.novartis.com					
Nutra-Blend Inc 3200 2nd St	Neosho	MO	64850	417-451-6111	451-4515
TF: 800-657-5657 ■ *Web:* www.nutrablend.net					
Pfizer Inc Animal Health Group					
235 E 42nd St	New York	NY	10017	212-573-2323	
TF: 800-733-5500 ■ *Web:* www.pfizer.com/ah					
Polydex Pharmaceuticals Ltd 421 Comstock Rd	Toronto	ON	M1L2H5	416-755-2231	755-0334
PINK: POLXF ■ *Web:* www.polydex.com					
ProtaTek International Inc					
2635 University Ave W Suite 140	Saint Paul	MN	55114	651-644-5391	644-6831
Web: www.protatek.com					
Renco Corp 116 3rd Ave N	Minneapolis	MN	55401	612-338-6124	333-9026
TF: 800-359-8181 ■ *Web:* www.rencocorp.com					
Synbiotics Corp 11011 Via Frontera	San Diego	CA	92127	858-451-3771	613-1273
TF: 800-228-4305 ■ *Web:* www.synbiotics.com					
Texas Vet Lab Inc 1702 N Bell St	San Angelo	TX	76903	325-653-4505	
TF: 800-284-8403 ■ *Web:* www.texasvetlab.com					
Thomas Veterinary Drug 9165 W VanBuren St	Tolleson	AZ	85353	623-936-3363	936-4499
TF: 800-359-8387 ■ *Web:* www.thomasveterinarydrug.com					
TW Medical Veterinary Supply					
3610 Lohman Ford Rd	Lago Vista	TX	78645	512-267-8800	267-8860
TF: 888-787-4483 ■ *Web:* www.twmedical.com					
Veterinary Pharmacies of America Inc					
2854 Antoine Dr	Houston	TX	77092	877-838-7979	329-7979
TF: 877-838-7979 ■ *Web:* www.vetrxrx.com					

	City	State	Zip	Phone	Fax
Vetoquinol Canada Inc 2000 ch Georges *TF:* 800-363-1700 ■ *Web:* www.vetoquinol.ca	Lavaltrie	QC	J5T3S5	450-586-2252	586-4649
VetriCare 590 Main St Suite B *TF:* 800-238-5999	Templeton	CA	93465	805-434-5969	434-5967
Wildlife Pharmaceuticals Inc 1635 Blue Spruce Dr PO Box 2023 *TF:* 866-823-9314 ■ *Web:* www.wildpharm.com	Fort Collins	CO	80524	970-484-6267	484-4941
XF Enterprises Inc 211 Pedigo Dr *TF:* 800-783-5616	Pratt	KS	67124	620-672-5616	672-5564

588 PHARMACY ASSOCIATIONS - STATE

SEE ALSO Health & Medical Professionals Associations p. 1452

	City	State	Zip	Phone	Fax
Alabama Pharmacy Assn 1211 Carmichael Way *TF:* 800-529-7533 ■ *Web:* www.aparx.org	Montgomery	AL	36106	334-271-4222	271-5423
Alaska Pharmacist's Assn 4107 Laurel St Suite 101 *Web:* www.alaskapharmacy.org	Anchorage	AK	99508	907-563-8880	563-7880
Arizona Pharmacy Assn 1845 E Southern Ave *Web:* www.azpharmacy.org	Tempe	AZ	85282	480-838-3385	838-3557
Arkansas Pharmacists Assn 417 S Victory St *Web:* www.arpharmacists.org	Little Rock	AR	72201	501-372-5250	372-0546
California Pharmacists Assn (CPhA) 4030 Lennane Dr *TF:* 800-444-3851 ■ *Web:* www.cpha.com	Sacramento	CA	95834	916-779-1400	779-1401
Colorado Pharmacists Society 6825 E Tennessee Ave Suite 440 *Web:* www.copharm.org	Denver	CO	80224	303-756-3069	756-3649
Connecticut Pharmacists Assn 35 Cold Spring Rd Suite 121 *Web:* www.ctpharmacists.org	Rocky Hill	CT	06067	860-563-4619	257-8241
Delaware Pharmacists Society PO Box 454 *Web:* www.depharmacy.net	Smyrna	DE	19977	302-659-3088	659-3089
Florida Pharmacy Assn 610 N Adams St *Web:* www.pharmview.com	Tallahassee	FL	32301	850-222-2400	561-6758
Georgia Pharmacy Assn (GPhA) 50 Lenox Pointe NE *Web:* www.gpha.org	Atlanta	GA	30324	404-231-5074	237-8435
Idaho State Pharmacy Assn 702 W Idaho St Suite 1000 *Web:* www.idahopharmacy.org	Boise	ID	83702	208-947-7272	947-5910
Illinois Pharmacists Assn (IPhA) 204 W Cook St *Web:* www.ipha.org	Springfield	IL	62704	217-522-7300	522-7349
Indiana Pharmacists Alliance 729 N Pennsylvania St *Web:* www.indianapharmacists.org	Indianapolis	IN	46204	317-634-4968	632-1219
Iowa Pharmacy Assn 8515 Douglas Ave Suite 16 *Web:* www.iarx.org	Des Moines	IA	50322	515-270-0713	270-2979
Kansas Pharmacists Assn 1020 SW Fairlawn Rd *Web:* www.kansaspharmacy.org	Topeka	KS	66604	785-228-2327	228-9147
Kentucky Pharmacists Assn 1228 US 127 S	Frankfort	KY	40601	502-227-2303	227-2258
Louisiana Pharmacists Assn 450 Laurel St Suite 1400 *TF:* 800-611-8307 ■ *Web:* www.louisianapharmacists.com	Baton Rouge	LA	70801	225-346-6883	344-1132
Maine Pharmacy Assn 127 Pleasant Hill Rd **Fax Area Code:* 207 ■ *TF:* 800-639-1609 ■ *Web:* www.mparx.com	Scarborough	ME	04074	800-639-1609	396-5341*
Maryland Pharmacists Assn 650 W Lombard St *Web:* www.marylandpharmacist.org	Baltimore	MD	21201	410-727-0746	727-2253
Massachusetts Pharmacists Assn 500 W Cummings Pk Suite 3475 *Web:* www.masspharmacists.org	Woburn	MA	01801	781-933-1107	933-1109
Michigan Pharmacists Assn 815 N Washington Ave *Web:* www.michiganpharmacists.org	Lansing	MI	48906	517-484-1466	484-4893
Minnesota Pharmacists Assn (MPhA) 1935 W County Rd B2 *Web:* www.mpha.org	Roseville	MN	55113	651-697-1771	697-1776
Mississippi Pharmacists Assn 341 Edgewood Terr Dr *Web:* www.mspharm.org	Jackson	MS	39206	601-981-0416	981-0451
Missouri Pharmacy Assn 211 E Capitol Ave *Web:* www.morx.com	Jefferson City	MO	65101	573-636-7522	636-7485
Montana Pharmacy Assn 34 W 6th Ave Suite 2E *Web:* www.rxmt.org	Helena	MT	59601	406-449-3843	443-1592
Nebraska Pharmacists Assn 6221 S 58th St Suite A *Web:* www.npharm.org	Lincoln	NE	68516	402-420-1500	420-1406
New Hampshire Pharmacists Assn 105 N Main St *Web:* www.nhpharmacists.org	Concord	NH	03301	603-229-0292	224-7769
New Jersey Pharmacists Assn 760 Alexander Rd CN1 *Web:* www.njpharma.org	Princeton	NJ	08543	609-275-4246	275-4066
New Mexico Pharmacists Assn (NMPhA) 2716 San Pedro Dr NE # C *Web:* www.nm-pharmacy.com	Albuquerque	NM	87110	505-265-8729	255-8476
North Carolina Assn of Pharmacists 109 Church St *Web:* www.ncpharmacists.org	Chapel Hill	NC	27516	919-967-2237	968-9430
North Dakota Pharmacists Assn (NDPhA) 1641 Capitol Way *Web:* www.nodakpharmacy.net	Bismarck	ND	58501	701-258-4968	258-9312
Ohio Pharmacists Assn 2155 Riverside Dr *Web:* www.ohiopharmacists.org	Columbus	OH	43221	614-586-1497	586-1545
Oklahoma Pharmacists Assn 45 NE 52nd St *Web:* www.opha.com	Oklahoma City	OK	73105	405-528-3338	528-1417
Oregon State Pharmacy Assn 29702-B SW Town Ctr Loop W *Web:* www.oregonpharmacy.org	Wilsonville	OR	97070	503-582-9055	582-9046
Pennsylvania Pharmacists Assn 508 N 3rd St *Web:* www.papharmacists.com	Harrisburg	PA	17101	717-234-6151	236-1618
Pharmacists Society of the State of New York 210 Washington Ave Ext *Web:* www.pssny.org	Albany	NY	12203	518-869-6595	464-0618
Pharmacy Society of Wisconsin 701 Heartland Trail *Web:* www.pswi.org	Madison	WI	53717	608-827-9200	827-9292
Rhode Island Pharmacists Assn 1643 Warwick Ave PMB 113 *Web:* www.ripharmacists.org	Warwick	RI	02889	401-737-2600	737-0959
South Carolina Pharmacy Assn 1350 Browning Rd *Web:* www.scrx.org	Columbia	SC	29210	803-354-9977	354-9207
South Dakota Pharmacists Assn PO Box 518 *Web:* www.sdpha.org	Pierre	SD	57501	605-224-2338	224-1280
Tennessee Pharmacists Assn 500 Church St Suite 650 *Web:* www.tnpharm.org	Nashville	TN	37219	615-256-3023	255-3528
Texas Pharmacy Assn 1624 E Anderson Ln PO Box 14709 *Web:* www.txpharmacy.com	Austin	TX	78761	512-836-8350	836-0308
Virginia Pharmacists Assn 5501 Patterson Ave Suite 200 *Web:* www.vapharmacy.org	Richmond	VA	23226	804-285-4145	285-4227
Washington State Pharmacy Assn 411 Williams Ave S *Web:* www.wsparx.org	Renton	WA	98057	425-228-7171	277-3897
West Virginia Pharmacists Assn 2016 1/2 Kanawha Blvd E	Charleston	WV	25311	304-344-5302	344-5316
Wyoming Pharmacists Assn PO Box 366 *Web:* www.wpha.net	Cheyenne	WY	82003	307-772-8044	

589 PHARMACY BENEFITS MANAGEMENT SERVICES

A Pharmacy Benefits Management Service (Pbm) Is A Company That Manages Various Pharmacy-Related Aspects Of A Health Insurance Plan, Such As The Assignment Of Pharmacy Cards, Claims Filing And Processing, Formulary Management, Etc. For The Most Part, Pbm Clients Are Insurance Companies, Hmos, Or Ppos Rather Than Individuals Or Pharmacies.

	City	State	Zip	Phone	Fax
BeneScript Services Inc 3720 DaVinci Ct *TF:* 800-345-3189	Norcross	GA	30092	770-448-4344	448-4516
BioScrip Inc 100 Clearbrook Rd *NASDAQ: BIOS* ■ *TF:* 888-818-3939	Elmsford	NY	10523	914-460-1600	460-1670
Caremark Rx Inc PO Box 832407 *NYSE: CMX* ■ *TF:* 800-552-8159 ■ *Web:* www.caremark.com	Richardson	TX	75083	877-460-7766	
CoreSource Inc 400 Field Dr *TF:* 800-832-3332 ■ *Web:* www.coresource.com	Lake Forest	IL	60045	847-604-9200	615-3900
CuraScript Inc 6272 Lee Vista Blvd *TF:* 888-773-7376 ■ *Web:* www.curascript.com	Orlando	FL	32822	888-773-7376	773-7386
Express Scripts Inc 13900 Riverport Dr *NASDAQ: ESRX* ■ **Fax:* Hum Res ■ *TF:* 800-332-5455 ■ *Web:* www.express-scripts.com	Maryland Heights	MO	63043	314-702-7173	919-4649*
Health Smart Rx 2291 Riverfront Pkwy Suite 201 **Fax Area Code:* 330 ■ *TF:* 800-681-6912 ■ *Web:* www.ameriscript.com	Cuyahoga Falls	OH	44221	800-681-6912	926-9755*
Maxor National Pharmacy Services Corp 320 S Polk St Suite 100 *TF:* 800-658-6146 ■ *Web:* www.maxor.com	Amarillo	TX	79101	806-324-5400	324-5495
Medco Health Solutions Inc 100 Parsons Pond Dr *NYSE: MHS* ■ *TF Cust Svc:* 800-248-2268 ■ *Web:* www.medcohealth.com	Franklin Lakes	NJ	07417	201-269-3400	269-1222
MedImpact Healthcare Systems Inc 10680 Treena St Suite 500 *TF:* 800-788-2949 ■ *Web:* www.medimpact.com	San Diego	CA	92131	858-566-2727	790-6454
PharmaCare Management Services Inc 695 George Washington Hwy *TF:* 888-862-2699 ■ *Web:* www.pharmacare.com	Lincoln	RI	02865	401-334-0069	334-4995
Prescription Solutions 3515 Harbor Blvd **Fax Area Code:* 800 ■ *TF:* 800-562-6223 ■ *Web:* www.prescriptionsolutions.com	Costa Mesa	CA	92626	714-825-3600	483-7093*
Prime Therapeutics Inc 1305 Corporate Ctr Dr *TF:* 800-858-0723 ■ *Web:* www.primetherapeutics.com	Eagan	MN	55121	651-286-4000	286-4404
RxAmerica LLC 221 N Charles Lindbergh Dr *TF:* 800-770-8014 ■ *Web:* www.rxamerica.com	Salt Lake City	UT	84116	801-961-6000	961-6330
ScripNet 10050 Banburry Cross Dr Suite 290 **Fax Area Code:* 888 ■ *TF:* 888-880-8562 ■ *Web:* www.scripnet.com	Las Vegas	NV	89144	702-248-2692	245-1745*
Script Care Inc 6380 Folsom Dr *TF:* 800-880-9988 ■ *Web:* www.scriptcare.com	Beaumont	TX	77706	409-833-9061	832-3109
ScriptSave 4911 E Broadway Blvd # 200 *TF:* 800-347-5985 ■ *Web:* www.scriptsave.com	Tucson	AZ	85711	520-888-8070	888-8069
Serve You Custom Prescription Management 10201 Innovation Dr Suite 600 *TF:* 888-243-6890 ■ *Web:* www.serve-you-rx.com	Milwaukee	WI	53226	414-410-8100	410-8181
Walgreens Health Services 1411 Lake Cook Rd *Web:* www.walgreenshealth.com	Deerfield	IL	60015	847-374-2640	374-2645
WellPoint Pharmacy Management 8407 Fallbrook Ave	West Hills	CA	91304	818-313-5127	

590 PHARMACY MANAGEMENT SERVICES

Companies That Provide Long-Term Care Pharmacy Services To Individuals With Special Needs (E.G., Chronic Disease Or Advanced Age); And Those That Provide Pharmacy Management Services To Hospitals Or Other Institutions.

Company	City	State	Zip	Phone	Fax
Accredo Health Group Inc					
1640 Century Ctr Pkwy Suite 101	Memphis	TN	38134	901-385-3688	385-3689
TF: 877-222-7336 ■ *Web:* www.accredo.com					
Fisher Bio Svc Inc 14665 Rothgeb Dr.	Rockville	MD	20850	301-315-8460	838-9320
Web: www.fisherbioservices.com					
McKesson Pharmaceutical 1 Post St.	San Francisco	CA	94104	415-983-8300	983-7160
TF: 800-571-2889 ■ *Web:* www.mckesson.com					
MedExpress Pharmacy Ltd 1431 W Innes St	Salisbury	NC	28144	704-633-3113	633-3353
TF Cust Svc: 800-808-8060					
Omnicare Inc					
1600 River Ctr II, 100 E RiverCenter Blvd.	Covington	KY	41011	859-392-3300	392-3333
NYSE: OCR ■ *TF:* 800-342-5627 ■ *Web:* www.omnicare.com					
Pharmacy Systems Inc					
5050 Bradenton Ave PO Box 130	Dublin	OH	43017	614-766-0101	766-4448
Web: www.pharmacysystems.com					
PharMerica Inc 3625 Queen Palm Dr	Tampa	FL	33619	813-318-6000	318-6167
TF: 877-975-2273 ■ *Web:* www.pharmerica.com					

591 PHOTO PROCESSING & STORAGE

Company	City	State	Zip	Phone	Fax
ABC Photo & Imaging Services Inc					
9016 Prince William St.	Manassas	VA	20110	703-369-1906	631-8064
TF: 800-368-4044					
Advanced Photographic Solutions LLC					
1525 Hardeman Ln NE	Cleveland	TN	37312	423-479-5481	479-8077
TF: 800-241-9234 ■ *Web:* www.advancedphoto.com					
Burrell Imaging 1311 Merrillville Rd.	Crown Point	IN	46307	219-663-3210	662-0915
TF: 800-348-8732 ■ *Web:* www.burrellprolabs.com					
Candid Color Systems Inc					
1300 Metropolitan Ave	Oklahoma City	OK	73108	405-947-8747	951-7353
TF: 800-336-4550 ■ *Web:* www.candid.com					
Dale Laboratories 2960 Simms St	Hollywood	FL	33020	954-925-0103	922-3008
TF: 800-327-1776 ■ *Web:* www.dalelabs.com					
District Photo Inc 10501 Rhode Island Ave	Beltsville	MD	20705	301-937-5300	937-5627
Web: www.districtphoto.com					
dotPhoto Inc					
111 Silvia St					
American Enterprise Pk at Ewing	West Trenton	NJ	08628	609-434-0340	434-0344
Web: www.dotphoto.com					
Express Digital Graphics Inc					
9200 Panorama Cir Suite 150.	Englewood	CO	80112	303-790-1004	790-1443
TF: 888-584-0089 ■ *Web:* www.expressdigital.com					
FLM Graphics 123 Lehigh Dr.	Fairfield	NJ	07004	973-575-9450	575-6424
TF: 800-257-9757 ■ *Web:* www.flmgraphics.com					
FotoTime Inc 3803 Cibola Trail	Carrollton	TX	75007	469-361-3441	
TF: 888-705-0389 ■ *Web:* www.fototime.com					
Gamma Imaging Co 222 N DesPlaines	Chicago	IL	60661	312-441-0091	441-0092
TF: 877-441-4830 ■ *Web:* www.gammaphoto.com					
H & H Color Lab Inc					
8906 E 67th St PO Box 219080	Raytown	MO	64133	816-358-6677	313-1480
TF: 800-821-1305 ■ *Web:* www.hhcolorlab.com					
iMemories 9181 E Bell Rd	Scottsdale	AZ	85260	480-767-2510	767-2511
TF: 800-845-7986 ■ *Web:* www.imemories.com					
Kodak Imaging Network Inc					
1480 64th St Suite 300.	Emeryville	CA	94608	510-229-1200	229-2700
TF: 800-360-9098 ■ *Web:* www.kodakgallery.com					
McKenna Pro Imaging 2800 Falls Ave.	Waterloo	IA	50701	319-235-6265	235-1121
TF: 800-238-3456 ■ *Web:* www.mckennapro.com					
Meisel Visual Imaging 2019 McKenzie Dr	Carrollton	TX	75006	214-688-4950	688-4950
TF: 800-527-5186 ■ *Web:* www.meisel.com					
National Graphx & Imaging LLC					
9240 W Belmont Ave	Franklin Park	IL	60131	847-671-1122	671-1144
TF: 800-211-7978 ■ *Web:* www.nationalgraphx.com					
Photo USA 3736 Franklin Rd	Roanoke	VA	24014	540-344-0961	344-3509
TF: 888-234-6320 ■ *Web:* www.photousa.com					
PNI Digital Media Inc					
425 Carrall St Suite 590.	Vancouver	BC	V6B6E3	604-893-8955	893-8966
Web: www.pnidigitalmedia.com					
Prolab Visual Imaging Services Inc					
123 NW 36th St	Seattle	WA	98107	206-547-5447	547-5448
TF: 800-426-6770					
Quantity Photo Co 119 W Hubbard St	Chicago	IL	60610	312-644-8288	644-8299
Shutterfly.com					
2800 Bridge Pkwy Suite 101.	Redwood City	CA	94065	650-610-5200	654-1299
Web: www.shutterfly.com					
Snapfish 303 2nd St S Tower Suite 500	San Francisco	CA	94107	301-595-5308	975-3708*
**Fax Area Code:* 415 ■ *Web:* www.snapfish.com					
Yahoo! Photos 701 1st Ave	Sunnyvale	CA	94089	408-349-3300	349-3301
TF: 888-267-7574 ■ *Web:* www.photos.yahoo.com					

592 PHOTOCOPYING EQUIPMENT & SUPPLIES

SEE ALSO Business Machines - Whol p. 1549

Company	City	State	Zip	Phone	Fax
Canon USA Inc 1 Canon Plaza	Lake Success	NY	11042	516-328-5000	328-5069*
**Fax:* Hum Res ■ *TF:* 800-828-4040 ■ *Web:* www.usa.canon.com					
Coast to Coast Business Equipment Inc					
8 Vanderbilt PO Box 57077	Irvine	CA	92618	949-457-7300	457-7365
Web: www.ctcbe.com					
Eastman Kodak Co 343 State St.	Rochester	NY	14650	585-724-4000	724-0663
NYSE: EK ■ *Web:* www.kodak.com					
Konica Minolta Business Solutions USA Inc					
101 Williams Dr	Ramsey	NJ	07446	201-825-4000	
Web: www.kmbs.konicaminolta.us					
Kyocera Mita Corp 225 Sand Rd PO Box 40008	Fairfield	NJ	07004	973-808-8444	882-6008
Web: www.kyoceramita.com					
Miller's Inc 610 E Jefferson	Pittsburg	KS	66762	620-231-8050	231-6783
Web: www.millerslab.com					
Oce-USA Inc 5450 N Cumberland Ave 6th Fl	Chicago	IL	60656	773-714-8500	693-7634
TF: 800-877-6232 ■ *Web:* www.oceusa.com					
Ricoh Corp 5 Dedrick Pl.	West Caldwell	NJ	07006	973-882-2000	244-2605*
**Fax:* Mail Rm ■ *TF:* 800-637-4264 ■ *Web:* www.ricoh-usa.com					
Sharp Electronics Corp 1 Sharp Plaza.	Mahwah	NJ	07430	201-529-8200	529-8413
TF: 800-237-4277 ■ *Web:* www.sharpusa.com					
Toshiba America Inc					
1251 Avenue of the Americas Suite 4100	New York	NY	10020	212-596-0600	593-3875
TF: 800-457-7777 ■ *Web:* www.toshiba.com					
Xerox Canada Ltd 5650 Yonge St.	North York	ON	M2M4G7	416-229-3769	733-6811
TF: 800-275-9376 ■ *Web:* www.xerox.ca					
Xerox Corp 45 Glover Ave PO Box 4505	Norwalk	CT	06856	203-968-3000	968-3218
NYSE: XRX ■ *TF:* 800-842-0024 ■ *Web:* www.xerox.com					

593 PHOTOGRAPH STUDIOS - PORTRAIT

Company	City	State	Zip	Phone	Fax
Alderman Studios 325 Model Farm Rd.	High Point	NC	27263	336-889-6121	889-7717
Bryn-Alan Studios Inc 606 W Kennedy Blvd	Tampa	FL	33606	813-253-2891	251-6548
TF: 800-749-2796 ■ *Web:* www.bryn-alan.com					
CPI Corp 1706 Washington Ave	Saint Louis	MO	63103	314-231-1575	231-2398*
NYSE: CPY ■ **Fax:* Hum Res ■ *TF:* 800-669-9699 ■ *Web:* www.cpicorp.com					
Gartner Studios Inc 220 Myrtle St E.	Stillwater	MN	55082	651-351-7700	351-1408
Web: www.gartnerstudios.com					
Jostens Inc 3601 Minnesota Ave Suite 400	Minneapolis	MN	55435	952-830-3300	830-3309*
**Fax:* Hum Res ■ *TF:* 800-235-4774 ■ *Web:* www.jostens.com					
Lifetouch Inc 11000 Viking Dr	Eden Prairie	MN	55344	952-826-4000	826-5982*
**Fax:* Cust Svc ■ *Web:* www.lifetouch.com					
Olan Mills Inc 4325 Amnicola Hwy	Chattanooga	TN	37406	423-622-5141	629-8106
TF: 800-251-6320 ■ *Web:* www.olanmills.com					
PCA International Inc					
815 Mathews Mint Hill Rd	Matthews	NC	28105	704-847-8011	847-8010
TF Cust Svc: 877-763-4456 ■ *Web:* www.pcaintl.com					
Shugart Studios Inc 812 College Ave.	Levelland	TX	79336	806-894-4322	894-7388
TF: 800-888-4322 ■ *Web:* www.shugartstudios.com					

594 PHOTOGRAPHIC EQUIPMENT & SUPPLIES

SEE ALSO Cameras & Related Supplies - Retail p. 1552

Company	City	State	Zip	Phone	Fax
3M Electro Solutions Div					
6801 River Pl Blvd 3M Austin Ctr.	Austin	TX	78726	800-328-1371	984-6550*
**Fax Area Code:* 512 ■ *TF:* 800-328-1371 ■ *Web:* www.3m.com/meetings					
Advance Reproductions Corp					
100 Flagship Dr	North Andover	MA	01845	978-685-2911	685-1771
Web: www.advancerepro.com					
Agfa Corp 100 Challenger Rd.	Ridgefield Park	NJ	07660	201-440-2500	342-4742
TF: 800-581-2432 ■ *Web:* www.agfa.com/usa					
AIPTEK Inc 51 Discovery Suite 100	Irvine	CA	92618	949-585-9600	585-9345
Web: www.aiptek.com					
Alan Gordon Enterprises Inc					
5625 Melrose Ave.	Hollywood	CA	90038	323-466-3561	871-2193
TF: 800-825-6684 ■ *Web:* www.alangordon.com					
Anton/Bauer Inc 14 Progress Dr.	Shelton	CT	06484	203-929-1100	929-9935
TF: 800-422-3473 ■ *Web:* www.antonbauer.com					
Ballantyne Strong Inc 4350 McKinley St.	Omaha	NE	68112	402-453-4444	453-7238
AMEX: BTN ■ *TF:* 800-424-1215 ■ *Web:* www.strong-world.com					
Beta Screen Corp 707 Commercial Ave	Carlstadt	NJ	07072	201-939-2400	939-7656
TF: 800-272-7336 ■ *Web:* www.betascreen.com					
Canon USA Inc 1 Canon Plaza	Lake Success	NY	11042	516-328-5000	328-5069*
**Fax:* Hum Res ■ *TF:* 800-828-4040 ■ *Web:* www.usa.canon.com					
Carr Corp 1547 11th St.	Santa Monica	CA	90401	310-587-1113	395-9751
TF: 800-952-2398 ■ *Web:* www.carrcorporation.com					
Casio Inc 570 Mt Pleasant Ave	Dover	NJ	07801	973-361-5400	537-8910*
**Fax:* Hum Res ■ *TF Cust Svc:* 800-634-1895 ■ *Web:* www.casio.com					
Ceiva Logic Inc 214 E Magnolia Blvd	Burbank	CA	91502	818-562-1495	562-1491
TF Tech Supp: 877-693-7263 ■ *Web:* www.ceiva.com					
Champion Photochemistry					
7895 Tranmere Dr Unit 203	Mississauga	ON	L5S1V9	905-670-7900	670-2581
Web: www.championphotochemistry.com					
Da-Lite Screen Co Inc 3100 N Detroit St	Warsaw	IN	46581	574-267-8101	267-7804
TF: 800-622-3737 ■ *Web:* www.da-lite.com					
Douthitt Corp 245 Adair St	Detroit	MI	48207	313-259-1565	259-6806
TF: 800-368-8448 ■ *Web:* www.douthittcorp.com					
Draper Shade & Screen Co 411 S Pearl St	Spiceland	IN	47385	765-987-7999	987-7999
TF: 800-238-7999 ■ *Web:* www.draperinc.com					
DRS Data & Imaging Systems Inc 138 Bauer Dr	Oakland	NJ	07436	201-337-3800	337-2704
Web: www.drs.com					
Dukane Communication Systems					
2900 Dukane Dr	Saint Charles	IL	60174	630-584-2300	584-2300
Web: www.dukane.com					
Eastman Kodak Co 343 State St.	Rochester	NY	14650	585-724-4000	724-0663
NYSE: EK ■ *Web:* www.kodak.com					
Egoltronics Corp Inc 1265 Brants Teets Rd	Baker	WV	26801	304-897-6359	897-6556
Web: www.egoltronics.com					
Fuji Photo Film USA Inc 200 Summit Lake Dr.	Valhalla	NY	10595	914-789-8100	789-8295
TF: 800-755-3854 ■ *Web:* www.fujifilm.com					
Geosystems Inc 210 S Washington Ave	Titusville	FL	32796	321-383-9585	747-0601
Web: www.geosystemsinc.com					
Id Group Inc The 280 Trace Colony.	Ridgeland	MS	39157	601-982-2651	982-2653
TF: 800-280-2651 ■ *Web:* www.idgroup.net					
Identatronics Inc					
165 N Lively Blvd	Elk Grove Village	IL	60007	847-437-2654	437-2660
TF Cust Svc: 800-323-5403 ■ *Web:* www.identatronics.com					
InFocus Corp 13190 SW 68th Pkwy Suite 200	Portland	OR	97223	503-207-4700	207-1937
NASDAQ: INFS ■ *TF:* 877-388-8385 ■ *Web:* www.infocus.com					

				Phone	Fax
Matthews Studio Equipment Group 2405 W Empire Ave *Fax Area Code: 323 ■ TF: 800-237-8263 ■ Web: www.msegrip.com	Burbank	CA	91504	818-843-6715	849-1525*
Mustek Inc 15271 Barranca Pkwy TF: 800-308-7226 ■ Web: www.mustek.com	Irvine	CA	92618	949-790-3800	788-3670
Mvm Products LLC 940 Calle Amanecer Suite K TF: 888-246-5832 ■ Web: www.ink-jet.com	San Clemente	CA	92673	949-366-1470	498-2958
Navitar Inc 200 Commerce Dr TF Cust Svc: 800-828-6778 ■ Web: www.navitar.com	Rochester	NY	14623	585-359-4000	359-4999
Neumade Products Corp 30 Pecks Ln # 40 TF: 800-645-6687 ■ Web: www.neumade.com	Newtown	CT	06470	203-270-1100	270-7778
Neumade Products Corp Xetron Theatre Products Div 30-40 Pecks Ln TF: 800-526-0722	Newtown	CT	06470	203-270-1100	270-7778
Nikon Inc 1300 Walt Whitman Rd TF Cust Svc: 800-645-6687 ■ Web: www.nikonusa.com	Melville	NY	11747	631-547-4200	547-0299
OConnor Engineering 2701 N Ontario St Web: www.ocon.com	Burbank	CA	91504	818-847-8666	847-1205
Panavision Inc 6219 DeSoto Ave TF: 800-367-7262 ■ Web: www.panavision.com	Woodland Hills	CA	91367	818-316-1000	316-1111
Peter Pepper Products Inc 17929 S Susana Rd TF: 800-496-0204 ■ Web: www.peterpepper.com	Compton	CA	90221	310-639-0390	639-6013
Phase One Inc 200 Broadhollow Rd Suite 312 TF: 888-742-7366 ■ Web: www.phaseone.com	Melville	NY	11747	631-757-0400	547-9898
Pic-Mount Imaging Corp 2300 Arrowhead Dr TF: 800-458-6875	Carson City	NV	89706	775-887-5100	887-5138
Polaroid Corp 1265 Main St Suite W-3 *Fax: Hum Res ■ TF Cust Svc: 800-343-5000 ■ Web: www.polaroid.com	Waltham	MA	02451	781-386-2000	386-9698*
QuickSet International Inc 3650 Woodhead Dr TF Orders: 800-247-6563 ■ Web: www.tripods.com	Northbrook	IL	60062	847-498-0700	498-1258
Redlake MASD LLC 3440 E Britannia Dr TF: 800-453-1223 ■ Web: www.redlake.com	Tucson	AZ	85706	520-547-2772	547-2697
Reprographics One Inc 36060 Industrial Rd TF: 800-968-7788 ■ Web: www.reprographicsone.com	Livonia	MI	48150	734-542-8800	542-8480
Research Technology International Inc 4700 W Chase Ave TF Sales: 800-323-7520 ■ Web: www.rti-us.com	Lincolnwood	IL	60712	847-677-3000	677-1311
Ricoh Corp 5 Dedrick Pl *Fax: Mail Rm ■ TF: 800-637-4264 ■ Web: www.ricoh-usa.com	West Caldwell	NJ	07006	973-882-2000	244-2605*
Sanyo Fisher Co 21605 Plummer St Web: us.sanyo.com	Chatsworth	CA	91311	818-998-7322	701-4194
Schneider Optics Century Div 7701 Haskell Ave TF: 800-228-1254 ■ Web: www.centuryoptics.com	Van Nuys	CA	91406	818-766-3715	505-9865
Sharp Electronics Corp 1 Sharp Plaza TF: 800-237-4277 ■ Web: www.sharpusa.com	Mahwah	NJ	07430	201-529-8200	529-8413
Sony Corp of America 550 Madison Ave TF: 800-282-2848 ■ Web: www.sony.com	New York	NY	10022	212-833-6800	
Stewart Filmscreen Corp 1161 W Sepulveda Blvd TF: 800-762-4999 ■ Web: www.stewartfilm.com	Torrance	CA	90502	310-784-5300	326-6870
Tamron USA Inc 10 Austin Blvd TF: 800-827-8880 ■ Web: www.tamron.com/en	Commack	NY	11725	631-858-8400	543-5666
Tiffen Co LLC 90 Oser Ave TF: 800-645-2522 ■ Web: www.tiffen.com	Hauppauge	NY	11788	631-273-2500	273-2557
Toshiba America Inc 1251 Avenue of the Americas Suite 4100 TF: 800-457-7777 ■ Web: www.toshiba.com	New York	NY	10020	212-596-0600	593-3875
Universal Blueprint Paper Co 327 Bryan Ave Web: www.universalblue.com	Fort Worth	TX	76104	817-332-9634	332-5406
Visual Departures Ltd PO Box 427 TF: 800-628-2003 ■ Web: www.visualdepartures.com	Riverside	CT	06878	203-487-0789	487-0791
Vivitar Corp 195 Carter Dr *Fax Area Code: 805 ■ TF: 800-637-1090 ■ Web: www.vivitar.com	Edison	NJ	08817	800-637-1090	981-2421*
Vutec Corp 2741 NE 4th Ave TF: 800-770-4700 ■ Web: www.vutec.com	Pompano Beach	FL	33064	954-545-9000	545-9011
Waterhouse Inc 670 Queen St Suite 200	Honolulu	HI	96813	808-592-4800	592-4820
Wein Products Inc 115 W 25th St Web: www.weinproducts.com	Los Angeles	CA	90007	213-749-6049	749-6250

595 PHOTOGRAPHY - COMMERCIAL

				Phone	Fax
Image Inc 1100 S Lynndale Dr Web: www.imagestudios.com	Appleton	WI	54914	920-738-4080	738-4089
Kinetic The Technology Agency 200 Distillery Commons Suite 200 Web: kinetic.thetechnologyagency.com/Default.aspx	Louisville	KY	40206	502-719-9500	719-9509
Sport Graphics PO Box 95 *Fax Area Code: 877 ■ Web: www.sportgraphics.com	Shrewsbury	MA	01545	508-842-3345	330-7774*
Universal Image 7121 Grand National Dr Suite 104 TF: 800-553-5499 ■ Web: www.universalphoto.com	Orlando	FL	32819	407-352-5302	351-5163

596 PHOTOGRAPHY - STOCK

				Phone	Fax
Alaska Stock Images 2505 Fairbanks St TF: 800-487-4285 ■ Web: www.alaskastock.com	Anchorage	AK	99503	907-276-1343	258-7848
Bygone Designs PO Box 229 Web: www.bygones.com	Newport	MN	55055	651-451-6737	
Corbis Corp 710 2nd Ave Suite 200 TF: 800-260-0444 ■ Web: www.corbisimages.com	Seattle	WA	98104	206-373-6000	373-6100
Custom Medical Stock Photo Inc 3660 W Irving Pk Rd TF: 800-373-2677 ■ Web: www.cmsp.com	Chicago	IL	60618	773-267-3100	267-6071
Film & Video Stock Shots 10442 Burbank Blvd TF: 888-436-6824 ■ Web: www.stockshots.com	North Hollywood	CA	91601	818-760-2098	760-3294
George Hall Check Six 426 Greenwood Beach Rd Web: www.check-6.com	Tiburon	CA	94920	415-381-6363	383-4935
George Hall Code Red 426 Greenwood Beach Rd Web: www.code-red.com	Tiburon	CA	94920	415-381-6363	383-4935
Great American Stock 1375 N Barker Rd *Fax Area Code: 800 ■ Web: www.greatamericanstock.com	Brooksfield	WI	53045	262-782-6000	782-6222*
Highway Images 3160 Walnut St PO Box 72249	Thorndale	PA	19372	610-380-0342	380-0315
Image Works 1679 Rt 212 TF: 800-475-8801 ■ Web: www.theimageworks.com	Woodstock	NY	12498	845-679-8500	679-0606
ImageState New York 29 E 19th St 4th Fl TF: 800-821-9600 ■ Web: www.imagestate.com	New York	NY	10003	212-505-2500	358-9101
ImagiGraphics Inc 20 Mills St	Kalamazoo	MI	49048	269-345-6999	
Jupiterimages Corp 8280 Greensboro Dr Suite 520 TF: 800-764-7427 ■ Web: www.jupiterimages.com	McLean	VA	22102	703-770-5350	770-5349
Mountain Light Photography Inc 106 S Main St Web: www.mountainlight.com	Bishop	CA	93514	760-873-7700	873-3980
Photo Researchers Inc 307 5th Ave 3rd FL TF: 800-833-9033 ■ Web: www.photoresearchers.com	New York	NY	10016	212-758-3420	355-0731
Photo Resource Hawaii 111 Hekili St Suite 241 TF: 888-599-7773 ■ Web: www.photoresourcehawaii.com	Kailua	HI	96734	808-599-7773	
Rainbow 61 Entrada TF: 800-810-3686 ■ Web: www.rainbowimages.com	Santa Fe	NM	87507	505-820-3434	
Silver Image Photo Agency 4104 NW 70th Terr Web: www.images.silverimagephotoagency.com	Gainesville	FL	32606	352-373-5771	374-4074
Stockyard Photos 2500 Summer St Suite 12-A Web: www.stockyard.com	Houston	TX	77007	713-520-0898	227-0399

597 PIECE GOODS & NOTIONS

SEE ALSO Fabric Stores p. 1837

				Phone	Fax
A Meyers & Sons Corp 325 W 38th St TF: 800-666-5577 ■ Web: www.safetypins.com	New York	NY	10018	212-279-6632	594-4093
American Tape Measures Inc 4001 N Ravenswood Ave Suite 604 Web: www.americantapemeasures.com	Chicago	IL	60613	773-327-6667	327-6318
Aplix Inc 12300 Steele Creek Rd TF: 800-438-0424 ■ Web: www.aplix.com	Charlotte	NC	28273	704-588-1920	588-1941
Associated Fabrics Corp 15-01 Pollitt Dr Unit 7 *Fax Area Code: 866 ■ Web: www.afc-fabrics.com	Fair Lawn	NJ	07410	800-232-4077	710-3850*
B Berger Co 1380 Highland Rd TF Cust Svc: 800-288-8400	Macedonia	OH	44056	330-425-3838	425-9797
Baum Textile Mills Inc 812 Jersey Ave TF: 866-842-7631 ■ Web: www.baumtextile.com	Jersey City	NJ	07310	201-659-0444	659-9719
Blank Textiles Inc 2 Bridge St Suite 220 TF: 800-237-3717	Irvington	NY	10533	914-478-3100	478-4456
Blumenthal Lansing Co 1 Palmer Terr TF: 800-448-9749 ■ Web: www.buttonsplus.com	Carlstadt	NJ	07072	201-935-6220	935-0055
Bob Barker Co Inc PO Box 429 TF: 800-334-9880 ■ Web: www.bobbarker.com	Fuquay Varina	NC	27526	919-552-3431	552-5097
Brookwood Cos Inc 25 W 45th St # 11 TF: 800-426-5468 ■ Web: www.brookwoodcos.net	New York	NY	10036	212-551-0100	686-5626
Brunschwig & Fils 75 Virginia Rd TF: 800-538-8280 ■ Web: www.brunschwig.com	North White Plains	NY	10603	914-684-5800	684-5842
Burch Fabrics Group 4200 Brockton Dr SE TF: 800-841-8111 ■ Web: www.burchfabrics.com	Grand Rapids	MI	49512	616-698-2800	698-0011
Carolyn Fabrics Inc 1948 W Green Dr TF: 800-333-8400 ■ Web: www.carolynfabrics.com	High Point	NC	27261	336-887-3101	887-2895
Criterion Thread Co Inc 21744 98th Ave TF: 800-695-0080 ■ Web: www.cthread.com	Queens Village	NY	11429	718-464-4200	464-3310
Custom Metal Crafters Inc 815 N Mountain Rd TF: 800-262-3140 ■ Web: www.custom-metal.com	Newington	CT	06111	860-953-4210	953-1746
Design/Craft Fabrics Corp 2230 Ridge Dr Web: www.design-craft.com	Glenview	IL	60025	847-904-7000	904-7102
Dunlap Industries Inc 123 State St TF: 800-251-7214 ■ Web: www.dunlapworld.com	Dunlap	TN	37327	423-949-4021	949-3648
Duralee Fabrics Ltd Inc 1775 5th Ave *Fax Area Code: 800 ■ *Fax: Cust Svc ■ TF Cust Svc: 800-275-3872 ■ Web: www.duralee.com	Bay Shore	NY	11706	631-273-8800	275-3297*
Eagle Button Co Inc 700-76 Broadway 318 Web: www.eaglebutton.com	Westwood	NJ	07675	201-652-4063	652-2003
Edgar Fabrics Inc 50 Commerce Dr	Hauppauge	NY	11788	631-435-8989	435-9151
EE Schenck Co 6000 N Cutter Cir TF: 800-433-0722 ■ Web: www.eeschenck.com	Portland	OR	97217	503-284-4124	288-4475
Glick Textiles 2327 SW Fwy TF: 800-231-7246 ■ Web: www.glicktextiles.com	Houston	TX	77098	713-942-8585	942-9292
Grove Textiles Inc 150 E Grove St	Scranton	PA	18510	570-344-1174	344-1177
Hanes Cos Inc 500 N McLin Creek Rd TF: 800-438-9124 ■ Web: www.hanesindustries.com	Conover	NC	28613	828-464-4673	464-0459
Hoffman California Fabrics Inc 25792 Obrero Dr TF: 800-547-0100 ■ Web: www.hoffmanfabrics.com	Mission Viejo	CA	92691	949-770-2922	770-4022
Ideal Fastener Corp 603 W Industry Dr TF: 800-334-6653 ■ Web: www.idealfastener.com	Oxford	NC	27565	919-693-3115	693-3118
Jaftex Corp 49 W 37th St	New York	NY	10018	212-686-5194	545-0058
Janlynn Corp 2070 Westover Rd TF: 800-445-5565 ■ Web: www.janlynn.com	Chicopee	MA	01022	413-206-0002	206-0060
JHB International Inc 1955 S Quince St TF: 800-525-9007 ■ Web: www.buttons.com	Denver	CO	80231	303-751-8100	751-3131
Kaplan-Simon Co Inc 115 Messina Dr	Braintree	MA	02184	781-848-6500	848-6506
Keyston Bros 2801 Academy Way Suite A TF: 800-453-1112 ■ Web: www.keystonbros.com	Sacramento	CA	95815	916-646-1834	646-6392

Company	City	State	ZIP	Phone	Fax
Kravet Fabrics Inc 225 Central Ave S *TF Cust Svc:* 800-648-5728 ■ *Web:* www.kravet.com	Bethpage	NY	11714	516-293-2000	293-2737
Lew Jan Textile Corp 366 Veterans Memorial Hwy *TF:* 800-899-0531 ■ *Web:* www.lewjan.com	Commack	NY	11725	631-543-0531	543-0561
Majilite Corp 1530 Broadway Rd *Web:* www.majilite.com	Dracut	MA	01826	978-441-6800	441-0826
Marcus Bros Textiles Inc 980 Avenue of the Americas *TF:* 800-548-8295 ■ *Web:* www.marcusbrothers.com	New York	NY	10018	212-354-8700	768-0799
McKee Button Co Inc PO Box 230 *TF Cust Svc:* 800-553-9662 ■ *Web:* www.mckeesurfaces.com	Muscatine	IA	52761	563-263-2421	264-5365
Merrimac Textile 3 Edgewater Dr *Web:* www.barrowindustries.com	Norwood	MA	02062	781-440-2666	440-2667
Miami Corp The 720 Anderson Ferry Rd *TF:* 800-543-0448 ■ *Web:* www.miamicorp.com	Cincinnati	OH	45238	513-451-6700	451-7998
Miroglio Textiles USA Inc 1430 Broadway 6th Fl	New York	NY	10018	212-382-2020	382-2609
Peachtree Fabrics Inc 1400 English St *TF:* 800-732-2437 ■ *Web:* www.peachtreefabrics.com	Atlanta	GA	30318	404-351-5400	351-5270
Pine Cone Hill Inc 125 Pecks Rd *TF:* 800-556-4593 ■ *Web:* www.pineconehill.com	Pittsfield	MA	01201	413-499-9926	629-2400
Prym-Dritz Corp 950 Brisack Rd **Fax:* Cust Svc ■ *TF Cust Svc:* 800-255-7796 ■ *Web:* www.dritz.com	Spartanburg	SC	29303	864-576-5050	587-3352*
Raylon Corp 1430 Broadway	New York	NY	10018	212-221-3633	921-2947
Raytex Fabrics Inc 130 Crossways Pk Dr *Web:* www.raytexindustries.com	Woodbury	NY	11797	516-584-1111	584-1034
Richloom Fabrics Group 261 5th Ave	New York	NY	10016	212-685-5400	696-4407
Robert Allen Fabrics Inc 225 Foxboro Blvd **Fax:* Sales ■ *TF:* 800-333-3777 ■ *Web:* www.robertallendesign.com	Foxboro	MA	02035	800-333-3777	332-8256*
Robert Kaufman Co Inc PO Box 59266 *TF:* 800-877-2066 ■ *Web:* www.robertkaufman.com	Los Angeles	CA	90059	310-538-3482	538-9235
Rockville Fabrics Corp 99 W Hawthorne Ave *Web:* www.rockvillefabrics.com	Valley Stream	NY	10580	516-561-9810	
Rome Fastener Corp 257 Depot Rd *Web:* www.romefast.com	Milford	CT	06460	203-874-6719	877-0201
Safety Zone LLC The 39 Industrial Pk PO Box 85 *TF:* 800-821-5702 ■ *Web:* www.safety-zone.com	Centerbrook	CT	06409	860-767-2600	767-0205
Scher Fabrics Inc 224 W 35th St Suite 1008 *TF:* 800-289-0025	New York	NY	10001	212-382-2266	869-0920
Schott International Inc 2850 Gilchrist Rd *TF:* 877-661-2121 ■ *Web:* www.schotttextiles.com	Akron	OH	44305	330-794-2121	794-2122
Scovill Fasteners Inc 1802 Scovill Dr **Fax:* Cust Svc ■ *TF Cust Svc:* 800-756-4734 ■ *Web:* www.scovill.com	Clarkesville	GA	30523	706-754-1000	754-4000*
Spradling International Inc 200 Cahaba Valley Pkwy PO Box 1668 *TF:* 800-333-0955 ■ *Web:* www.spradlingvinyl.com	Pelham	AL	35124	205-985-4206	985-9176
Symphony Fabrics Corp 229 W 36th St 2nd Fl	New York	NY	10018	212-244-4686	736-0123
Tiger Button Co Inc 307 W 38th St 4th Fl *TF:* 800-223-2754 ■ *Web:* www.tigerbutton.com	New York	NY	10018	212-594-0570	695-0265
Tingue 535 N Midland Ave *Web:* www.tinguebrownco.com	Saddle Brook	NJ	07663	201-796-5233	
Titan Textile Co Inc 53 E 34th St **Fax:* Hum Res ■ *Web:* www.titantextile.com	Paterson	NJ	07514	973-684-1600	684-2610*
Trimtex Saint Louis Trimming Div 400 Pk Ave *TF:* 800-326-9135 ■ *Web:* www.trimtex.com	Williamsport	PA	17701	570-326-9135	326-4250
Twin Dragon Marketing Inc 14600 S Broadway St *Web:* www.twindragonmarketing.com	Gardena	CA	90248	310-715-7070	
United Notions Inc 13800 Hutton St **Fax Area Code:* 800 ■ *TF:* 800-527-9447 ■ *Web:* www.unitednotions.com	Dallas	TX	75234	972-484-8901	468-4209*
US Button Corp 328 Kennedy Dr *TF:* 800-243-1842 ■ *Web:* www.usbutton.com	Putnam	CT	06260	860-928-2707	928-2847
Valley Forge Fabrics Inc 2981 Gateway Dr *Web:* www.valleyforge.com	Pompano Beach	FL	33069	954-971-1776	968-1775
Velcro USA Inc 406 Brown Ave *TF:* 800-225-0180 ■ *Web:* www.velcro.com	Manchester	NH	03103	603-669-4880	669-9271
Waterbury Button Co 1855 Peck Ln *TF:* 800-431-4433 ■ *Web:* www.waterburybutton.com	Cheshire	CT	06410	203-271-9055	271-9852
Weber & Sons Button Co Inc PO Box 96	Muscatine	IA	52761	563-263-9451	264-3953
Westgate Interiors LLC 418 Chandler Dr **Fax Area Code:* 972 ■ *TF:* 800-527-6666 ■ *Web:* www.westgatefabrics.com	Gaffney	SC	29340	800-527-6666	602-8143*
YKK Snap Fasteners America Inc PO Box 240 **Fax:* Sales ■ *TF:* 800-786-2561 ■ *Web:* www.ykksnap-america.com	Lawrenceburg	KY	40342	502-839-6971	839-6525*
YKK USA Inc 1251 Valley Brook Ave *Web:* www.ykkfastening.com	Lyndhurst	NJ	07071	201-935-4200	964-0123
Zabin Industries Inc 3957 S Hill St *Web:* www.zabin.com	Los Angeles	CA	90037	213-749-1215	747-6162

598 PIPE & PIPE FITTINGS - METAL (FABRICATED)

SEE ALSO Metal Tube & Pipe p. 2240

Company	City	State	ZIP	Phone	Fax
Acme Mfg Co 7601 State Rd *TF Cust Svc:* 800-899-2850	Philadelphia	PA	19136	215-338-2850	335-1905
Advanced Tubing Technology Inc 150 Intercraft Dr *Web:* www.tubetec.net	Statesville	NC	28625	704-924-7020	924-7030
Airdrome Precision Components 3251 E Airport Way	Long Beach	CA	90806	562-426-9411	492-6909
Allegan Tubular Products Inc 1276 Lincoln Rd *Web:* www.allegantube.com	Allegan	MI	49010	269-673-6636	673-2477
Allied Chucker & Engineering Co 3529 Scheele Dr	Jackson	MI	49202	517-787-1370	787-2878
Alloy Stainless Products Co 611 Union Blvd *TF:* 800-631-8372 ■ *Web:* www.alloystainless.com	Totowa	NJ	07512	973-256-1616	256-5256
Atlas Industrial Holdings LLC 5275 Sinclair Rd *Web:* www.atlascos.com	Columbus	OH	43229	614-841-4500	841-4510
AY McDonald Mfg Co 4800 Chavenelle Rd PO Box 508 *TF Cust Svc:* 800-292-2737 ■ *Web:* www.aymcdonald.com	Dubuque	IA	52002	563-583-7311	588-0720
Beck Mfg 330 E 9th St *TF:* 800-742-6621 ■ *Web:* www.beckmfg.com	Waynesboro	PA	17268	717-762-9141	762-9153
Bent Tube Inc 9649 Van Buren Rd *TF:* 888-797-1931 ■ *Web:* www.benttube.com	Fowlerville	MI	48836	517-521-4330	521-4850
Betts Industries Inc 1800 Pennsylvania Ave W *Web:* www.bettsind.com	Warren	PA	16365	814-723-1250	723-7030
Campbell Mfg Inc 127 E Spring St *TF:* 800-523-0224 ■ *Web:* www.campbellmfg.com	Bechtelsville	PA	19505	610-367-2107	369-3580
Carpenter Powder Products 600 Mayer St *TF:* 866-790-9092 ■ *Web:* www.cartech.com	Bridgeville	PA	15017	412-257-5102	257-5058
Central Pipe Supply Inc 101 Ware Rd PO Box 5470 *TF:* 800-844-7700 ■ *Web:* www.centralpipe.com	Pearl	MS	39288	601-939-3322	932-8944
Champion Mfg Industries Inc 6021 N Galena Rd *TF:* 800-452-7473 ■ *Web:* www.championmfg.com	Peoria	IL	61614	309-685-1031	685-1088
Cobra Pipe Supply Inc 13 Homomick Rd *TF:* 877-474-7332	Colchester	CT	06415	860-537-5489	537-5489
Colonial Engineering Inc 6400 Corporate Ave *TF:* 800-374-0234 ■ *Web:* www.colonialengineering.com	Portage	MI	49002	269-323-2495	323-0630
Continental Industries Inc 4102 S 74th E Ave **Fax Area Code:* 800 ■ *TF:* 800-558-1373 ■ *Web:* www.conind.com	Tulsa	OK	74145	918-627-5210	788-1668*
Controls Southeast Inc PO Box 7500 *Web:* www.csiheat.com	Charlotte	NC	28241	704-588-3030	644-5100
Core Pipe 170 Tubeway Dr *Web:* www.gerlin.com	Carol Stream	IL	60188	630-690-7000	690-9701
Douglas Bros 423 Riverside Industrial Pkwy *TF:* 800-341-0927 ■ *Web:* www.douglasbrothers.com	Portland	ME	04103	207-797-6771	797-8385
Elkhart Products Corp 1255 Oak St *TF:* 800-284-4851 ■ *Web:* www.elkhartproducts.com	Elkhart	IN	46514	574-264-3181	264-4835
Empire Industries Inc 180 Olcott St *TF:* 800-243-4844 ■ *Web:* www.empireindustries.com	Manchester	CT	06040	860-647-1431	647-1160
Excelsior Mfg & Supply Corp 1465 E Industrial Dr **Fax:* Cust Svc ■ *TF:* 800-548-8135 ■ *Web:* excelsiorhvac.com	Itasca	IL	60143	630-773-5500	773-1612*
General Plug & Mfg Co Inc 455 Main St *TF:* 800-289-7584 ■ *Web:* www.generalplug.com	Grafton	OH	44044	440-926-2411	926-3305
Griffin Pipe Products Co 1400 Opus Pl Suite 700 *Web:* www.griffinpipe.com	Downers Grove	IL	60515	630-719-6500	719-2252
H-P Products Inc 512 W Gorgas St *TF:* 800-822-8356 ■ *Web:* www.hpproducts.net	Louisville	OH	44641	330-875-5556	875-7584
Hackney Ladish Inc 5945 Belt Line Rd Suite 290 *TF:* 800-527-4500 ■ *Web:* www.hackneyladish.com	Dallas	TX	75254	214-269-5600	269-5601
Highfield Mfg Co 380 Mountain Grove St *Web:* www.highfield-mfg.com	Bridgeport	CT	06605	203-384-2281	368-3906
Hydro Tube Enterprises Inc 137 Artino St *Web:* www.hydrotube.com	Oberlin	OH	44074	440-774-1022	774-1482
JB Smith Mfg Co 6618 Navigation Blvd *Web:* www.jbsmith.com	Houston	TX	77011	713-928-5711	928-5219
Kelly Pipe Co LLC 11680 Bloomfield Ave *TF:* 800-305-3559 ■ *Web:* www.kellypipe.com	Santa Fe Springs	CA	90670	562-868-0456	863-4695
Kraftube Inc 925 E Church Ave *Web:* www.kraftube.com	Reed City	MI	49677	231-832-5562	832-2937
Markovitz Enterprises Inc PO Box 7027 **Fax:* Sales ■ *TF:* 800-245-0354 ■ *Web:* www.flowlinefittings.com	New Castle	PA	16107	724-658-3711	658-6117*
McWane Inc 2900 Hwy 280 Suite 300 *Web:* www.mcwane.com	Birmingham	AL	35223	205-414-3100	414-3170
MicroGroup Inc 7 Industrial Pk Rd *TF:* 800-255-8823 ■ *Web:* www.microgroup.com	Medway	MA	02053	508-533-4925	533-5691
Mid States Pipe Fabricating Inc 205 Louis Hurley Rd *Web:* www.m-p-f.com	El Dorado	AR	71730	870-862-5167	862-4234
Mills Iron Works Inc 14834 Maple Ave **Fax Area Code:* 310 ■ *TF:* 800-421-2281 ■ *Web:* www.millsiron.com	Gardena	CA	90248	323-321-6520	532-0476*
Milwaukee Valve Co Inc 16550 W Stratton Dr *TF:* 800-348-6544 ■ *Web:* www.milwaukeevalve.com	New Berlin	WI	53151	262-432-2800	432-2801
Morton Industries LLC 70 Commerce Dr *Web:* www.mortonwelding.com	Morton	IL	61550	309-263-2590	263-0862
National Tube Form Inc 3405 Engle Rd *TF:* 800-752-1458 ■ *Web:* www.nationaltubeform.com	Fort Wayne	IN	46809	260-478-2363	478-1043
NIBCO Inc 1516 Middlebury St *TF:* 800-234-0227 ■ *Web:* www.nibco.com	Elkhart	IN	46515	574-295-3000	295-3307
Nor-Cal Products Inc 1967 S Oregon St **Fax:* Sales ■ *TF:* 800-824-4166 ■ *Web:* www.n-c.com	Yreka	CA	96097	530-842-4457	842-9130*
Norca Corp 185 Great Neck Rd 4th Fl *Web:* www.norcaprecision.com	Great Neck	NY	11022	516-466-9500	466-9588
Parker Hannifin Corp Brass Products Div 100 Parker Dr *TF:* 800-272-7537 ■ *Web:* www.parker.com	Otsego	MI	49078	269-694-9411	694-4614
Parker Hannifin Corp Instrumentation Products Div 1005 A Cleaner Way *Web:* www.parker.com	Huntsville	AL	35805	256-885-3800	885-3853
Penn Machine Co 106 Stn St *TF:* 800-763-0406 ■ *Web:* www.pennusa.com	Johnstown	PA	15905	814-288-1547	288-2260
Perma-Pipe Inc 7720 N Lehigh Ave *Web:* www.permapipe.com	Niles	IL	60714	847-966-2235	470-1204
Pioneer Pipe Inc 2021 Hanna Rd *Web:* www.pioneerpipeinc.com	Marietta	OH	45750	740-376-2400	373-8964
Piping Technology & Products Inc 3701 Holmes Rd PO Box 34506 *TF:* 866-746-9172 ■ *Web:* www.pipingtech.com	Houston	TX	77051	713-422-2271	731-8640
Propipe Technologies Inc 1800 Clayton Ave	Middletown	OH	45042	513-424-5311	424-5095
R & B Wagner Inc PO Box 423 *TF:* 888-243-6914 ■ *Web:* www.wagnercompanies.com	Butler	WI	53007	414-214-0444	214-0450

Phone | Fax

Richards Industries Inc 3170 Wasson Rd Cincinnati OH 45209 513-533-5600 871-0105*
*Fax: Sales ■ TF Cust Svc: 800-543-7311 ■ Web: www.richardsind.com
Robert Mfg Co Inc 10667 Jersey Blvd Rancho Cucamonga CA 91730 909-987-4654 989-6911
TF: 800-877-6237 ■ Web: www.robertmfg.com
Romac Industries Inc 21919 20th Ave SE Bothell WA 98021 425-951-6200 951-6201
TF: 800-426-9341 ■ Web: www.romac.com
Roscoe Moss Co 4360 Worth St Los Angeles CA 90063 323-261-4185 263-4497
TF: 800-767-2634 ■ Web: www.roscoemoss.com
Rovanco Piping Systems Inc
20535 SE Frontage Rd Joliet IL 60431 815-741-6700 741-4229
Web: www.rovanco.com
Shaw Group Inc The 4171 Essen Ln Baton Rouge LA 70809 225-932-2500 932-2661
NYSE: SHAW ■ TF: 800-747-3322 ■ Web: www.shawgrp.com
Snap-Tite Inc 8325 Hessinger Dr Erie PA 16509 814-838-5700 833-0145
Web: www.snap-tite.com
Spitzer Industries Inc 11250 Tanner Rd Houston TX 77041 713-466-1518 482-2780
Web: www.spitzerind.com
Star Pipe LLC 4018 Westhollow Pkwy Houston TX 77082 281-558-3000
TF: 800-999-3009 ■ Web: www.starpipeproducts.com
Steel Forgings Inc 1810 Barton Dr Shreveport LA 71107 318-222-3295 222-6185
Web: www.steelforgings.com
Swagelok Co 29500 Solon Rd Solon OH 44139 440-248-4600 519-1089
Web: www.swagelok.com
Synalloy Corp
2155 W Croft Cir PO Box 5627 Spartanburg SC 29304 864-585-3605 596-1501
NASDAQ: SYNL ■ TF Orders: 800-763-1001 ■ Web: www.synalloy.com
Tate Andale Inc 1941 Lansdowne Rd Baltimore MD 21227 410-247-8700 247-9672
TF: 800-296-8283 ■ Web: www.tateandale.com
Texas Steel Conversion Inc 3101 Holmes Rd Houston TX 77051 713-733-6013
Web: www.texassteelconversion.com
Thermacor Process LP
1670 Hicks Field Rd E Fort Worth TX 76179 817-847-7300 847-7222
Web: www.thermacor.com
Tolco Inc 1375 Sampson Ave Corona CA 92879 951-737-5599 737-0330
TF: 888-233-1887 ■ Web: www.nibco.com
Tru-Flex Metal Hose Corp
2391 S State Rd 263 West Lebanon IN 47991 765-893-4403 893-4114
TF: 800-255-6291
Tube Forming Inc 2101 W Belt Line Rd Carrollton TX 75006 972-512-2400 512-2401
TF: 800-513-0022
Tube Processing Corp
604 E Le Grande Ave Indianapolis IN 46203 317-787-1321 787-5384
TF: 800-776-4119 ■ Web: www.tubeproc.com
Twin Bros Marine LLC
Port of W St Mary Hwy 83 Saint Louisa LA 70538 337-923-4981 923-4349
Web: www.tbmc.com
Universal Tube Inc 2607 Bond St Rochester Hills MI 48309 248-853-5100 853-7365
TF: 800-394-8823 ■ Web: www.universaltube.com
US Pipe & Foundry Co
3300 1st Ave N PO Box 10406 Birmingham AL 35202 205-254-7000 254-7149
TF: 866-347-7473 ■ Web: www.uspipe.com
Vacco Industries Inc 10350 Vacco St South El Monte CA 91733 626-443-7121 442-6943
Web: www.vacco.com
Victaulic Co 4901 Kesslersville Rd Easton PA 18040 610-559-3300 250-8817
TF Sales: 800-523-9864 ■ Web: www.victaulic.com
Watson McDaniel Co
428 Jones Blvd
Limerick Airport Business Ctr Pottstown PA 19464 610-495-5131 495-5134
Web: www.watsonmcdaniel.com
Webster Valve Co 583 S Main St Franklin NH 03235 603-934-5110 934-1390
Wellstream International Ltd
520 Skyview Dr Panama City Beach FL 32408 850-636-4800 234-6874
Web: www.wellstream.com
Woolf Aircraft Products Inc 6401 Cogswell Rd Romulus MI 48174 734-721-5330 721-3490
TF: 800-367-5475 ■ Web: www.woolfaircraft.com
World Wide Fittings Co Inc 7501 N Natchez Ave Niles IL 60714 847-588-2200 588-2212
Web: www.worldwidefittings.com

599 PIPE & PIPE FITTINGS - PLASTICS

Phone | Fax

Advanced Drainage Systems Inc
4640 Trueman Blvd Hilliard OH 43026 614-658-0050 658-0204
TF: 800-821-6710 ■ Web: www.ads-pipe.com
Ameron International Corp
245 S Los Robles Ave Pasadena CA 91101 626-683-4000 683-4060
NYSE: AMN ■ Web: www.ameron.com
Ameron International Fiberglass-Composite Pipe Group
9720 Cypress Wood Dr Suite 325 Houston TX 77070 832-912-8282 912-9393
TF: 800-542-4070 ■ Web: www.ameronfpd.com
Bakersfield Pipe & Supply Inc
2903 Patton Way Bakersfield CA 93308 661-589-9141 589-3739
Web: www.onlinepipe.com
CANTEX Inc 202 Progress Rd Auburndale FL 33823 863-967-4161 967-4541
TF: 800-765-8704
Centron International Inc
600 FM 1195 S PO Box 490 Mineral Wells TX 76068 940-325-1341 325-9681
Web: www.centrongre.com
CertainTeed Corp 750 E Swedesford Rd Valley Forge PA 19482 610-341-7000 341-7797
TF Prod Info: 800-782-8777 ■ Web: www.certainteed.com
CertainTeed Corp Pipe & Plastics Div
750 E Swedesford Rd PO Box 860 Valley Forge PA 19482 610-341-7000 341-7413
TF: 800-274-8530 ■ Web: www.certainteed.com
Charlotte Pipe & Foundry Co Plastics Div
4210 Old Charlotte Hwy PO Box 1339 Monroe NC 28111 704-289-2531 348-6406
TF Sales: 800-438-6091
Chemtrol Div NIBCO Inc 1516 Middlebury St Elkhart IN 46516 574-295-3000 295-3307
TF: 800-234-0227 ■ Web: www.nibco.com/cms.do?id=2&pld=1
Chevron Phillips Chemical Co Performance Pipe Div
5085 W Pk Blvd Suite 500 Plano TX 75093 972-599-6600 599-7348
TF: 800-527-0662 ■ Web: www.cpchem.com/enu/performance_pipe.asp
Cresline-West Inc 600 Crosspointe Blvd Evansville IN 47715 812-428-9300 428-9353
TF: 800-528-5687 ■ Web: www.cresline.com
Crumpler Plastic Pipe Inc (CPP)
Hwy 24 W PO Box 2068 Roseboro NC 28382 910-525-4046 525-5801
TF: 800-334-5071 ■ Web: www.cpp-pipe.com
Diamond Plastics Corp
1212 Johnstown Rd PO Box 1608 Grand Island NE 68802 308-384-4400 384-9345
TF: 800-782-7473 ■ Web: www.dpcpipe.com
Dura Plastics Products Inc 533 E 3rd St Beaumont CA 92223 951-845-3161 845-7644
TF: 800-854-2323 ■ Web: www.duraplastics.com
Endot Industries Inc 60 Green Pond Rd Rockaway NJ 07866 973-625-8500 625-4087
TF: 800-443-6368 ■ Web: www.endot.com
Excalibur Extrusions Inc
110 E Crowther Ave Placentia CA 92870 714-528-8834 524-7453
TF: 800-648-6804 ■ Web: www.excaliburextrusions.com
Fernco PlumbQwik Inc 300 S Dayton St Davison MI 48423 810-653-9626 653-8714
TF: 800-521-1283 ■ Web: www.fernco.com
Fusibond Piping Systems Inc
2615 Curtiss St Downers Grove IL 60515 630-969-4488 969-2355
Web: www.fusibond.com
Genova Products Inc 7034 E Ct St Davison MI 48423 810-744-4500 744-1653
TF: 800-521-7488 ■ Web: www.genovaproducts.com
Genova-Minnesota Inc 500 12th St NW Faribault MN 55021 507-332-7421 332-2344
TF: 800-744-4500 ■ Web: www.genovaproducts.com
Hancor Inc PO Box 1047 Findlay OH 45839 419-422-6521 424-8300
Web: www.hancor.com
Hobas Pipe USA LP 1413 E Richey Rd Houston TX 77073 281-821-2200 821-7715
TF: 800-856-7473 ■ Web: www.hobaspipe.com
Isco Industries 926 Baxter Ave PO Box 4545 Louisville KY 40204 502-583-6591 238-8165
TF: 800-345-4726 ■ Web: www.isco-pipe.com
Lasco Fittings Inc
414 Morgan St PO Box 116 Brownsville TN 38012 731-772-3180 772-0835
TF: 800-776-2756 ■ Web: www.lascofittings.com
Maloney Technical Products
1300 E Berry St Fort Worth TX 76119 817-923-3344 923-1339
TF: 800-231-7236 ■ Web: www.maloneytech.com
Mueller Plastics Corp 3070 E Cedar Ontario CA 91761 909-930-2060 930-2070
TF: 800-348-8464 ■ Web: www.muellerindustries.com
National Pipe & Plastics Inc 3421 Vestal Rd Vestal NY 13850 607-729-9381 729-6130
TF: 800-836-4350 ■ Web: www.nationalpipe.com
Nebraska Plastics Inc 700 W Hwy 30 Cozad NE 69130 308-784-2500 784-3216
TF: 800-445-2887 ■ Web: www.countryestate.com
Normandy Industries Inc
1150 Freeport Rd PO Box 38805 Pittsburgh PA 15238 412-826-1825 826-1731
TF: 800-322-9463 ■ Web: www.normandyproducts.com
North American Pipe Corp
2801 Post Oak Blvd Suite 600 Houston TX 77056 713-840-7473 552-0087
Web: www.northamericanpipe.com
Oil Creek Plastics Inc
45619 State Hwy 27 PO Box 385 Titusville PA 16354 814-827-3661 827-9599
TF: 800-537-3661 ■ Web: www.oilcreek.com
Pyramid Industries 1422 Irwin Dr Erie PA 16505 814-455-7587 459-8094
Web: www.pyramidind.com
Resistoflex Co 1 Quality Way Marion NC 28752 828-724-4000 724-9469
Web: www.resistoflex.com
Silver-Line Plastics 900 Riverside Dr Asheville NC 28804 828-252-8755 285-8901
Web: www.slpipe.com
Smith Fibercast Div Fiber Glass Systems LP
25 S Main St Sand Springs OK 74063 918-245-6651 245-7566
TF: 800-331-4406 ■ Web: www.altius.coventryhealthcare.com
Special Plastics Systems Inc
385 W Valley St San Bernardino CA 92401 909-888-2531 888-8931
TF: 800-423-4422 ■ Web: www.spscompany.com
Teel Plastics Inc 1315 Lake St Baraboo WI 53913 608-355-3080 355-3088
Web: www.teel.com
Texas United Pipe Inc
11627 N Houston Rosslyn Rd Houston TX 77086 281-448-3276 448-6983
TF Sales: 800-966-8741 ■ Web: www.texasunitedpipe.com
USPoly Co 4501 W 49th St Tulsa OK 74107 918-446-4471 446-9369
TF: 800-962-1514 ■ Web: www.uspolycompany.com
Vinylplex Inc 1800 Atkinson Ave Pittsburg KS 66762 620-231-8290 232-8547
TF: 877-779-7473 ■ Web: www.vinylplex.com/main.html
Vinyltech Corp 201 S 61st Ave Phoenix AZ 85043 602-233-0071 272-4847
Web: www.vtpipe.com
Weiler Welding Co Inc 324 E 2nd St Dayton OH 45402 937-222-8312 222-2729
TF: 800-526-9353 ■ Web: www.weilerwelding.com
Wellstream International Ltd
520 Skyview Dr Panama City Beach FL 32408 850-636-4800 234-6874
Web: www.wellstream.com
Winrock Enterprises
2222 Cottondale Ln Suite 300 Little Rock AR 72201 501-663-5340 663-4456

600 PIPELINES (EXCEPT NATURAL GAS)

Phone | Fax

Alyeska Pipeline Service Co
The Alaska Corp
900 E Benson St PO Box 196660 Anchorage AK 99519 907-787-8700 787-8611
Belle Fourche Pipeline 455 N Poplar St Casper WY 82601 307-237-9301 266-0252
Web: www.truecos.com/bfpl
BP Exploration (Alaska) Inc (BPXA)
PO Box 196612 Anchorage AK 95519 907-561-5111
Web: www.bp.com
BP Plc 28100 Torch Pkwy Warrenville IL 60555 630-420-5111 298-0738*
NYSE: BP ■ *Fax Area Code: 281 ■ TF: 866-427-6947 ■ Web: www.bp.com
Buckeye Partners LP
5 Radnor Corporate Ctr
100 Matsonford Rd Suite 500 Radnor PA 19087 484-232-4000 254-4625*
NYSE: BPL ■ *Fax Area Code: 610 ■ *Fax: Mktg ■ Web: www.buckeye.com

Phone Fax

Buckeye Partners LP
1 Greenway Plaza Suite 600 . . . . Houston TX 77046 832-615-8600
Web: www.buckeye.com

Chevron Pipe Line Co 4800 Fournace Pl . . . . Bellaire TX 77401 713-432-6000
Web: www.chevron.com/prodserv/cpl

CITGO Pipeline Co 1293 Eldridge Pkwy . . . . Houston TX 77077 832-486-4000
Web: www.citgo.com

Collins Pipeline Co Hwy 588 E PO Box 1027. . . . . Collins MS 39428 601-765-6593 765-8648

Colonial Pipeline Co
1185 Sanctuary Pkwy # 100 . . . . Alpharetta GA 30009 678-762-2200 762-2883
TF: 800-275-3004 ■ *Web:* www.colpipe.com

Country Mark Co-op 1200 Refinery Rd . . . . Mount Vernon IN 47620 812-838-4341 838-8196
TF: 800-832-5490 ■ *Web:* www.countrymark.com

Dixie Pipeline Co
1117 Perimeter Ctr W Suite 301 W. . . . . Atlanta GA 30338 770-396-2994 396-4276
Web: www.dixiepipeline.com

Enbridge Energy Co Inc 119 N 25th St . . . . Superior WI 54880 715-394-1400 394-1475

Enbridge Energy Partners LP
1100 Louisiana Suite 3300. . . . . Houston TX 77002 713-821-2000 650-3232
NYSE: EEP ■ *TF:* 888-650-8900 ■ *Web:* www.enbridgepartners.com

Enbridge Inc 3000 Fifth Ave Pl 425 1st St SW. . . . . Calgary AB T2P3L8 403-231-3900 231-3920
NYSE: ENB ■ *Web:* www.enbridge.com

Express Pipeline 800 Werner Ct Suite 230. . . . . Casper WY 82601 307-577-6002 577-6014

ExxonMobil Pipeline Co 800 Bell St Rm 653A . . . . Houston TX 77002 713-656-6885 656-9586
Web: www.exxonmobilpipeline.com

Genesis Energy LP 919 Milam Suite 2100 . . . . Houston TX 77002 713-860-2500 860-2640
NYSE: GEL ■ *TF:* 800-284-3365 ■ *Web:* www.genesiscrudeoil.com

Gulf Central Pipeline Co Inc PO Box 2256 . . . . Wichita KS 67201 316-828-5500 828-5327

Hess Pipeline Co Inc 420 Hook Rd . . . . Bayonne NJ 07002 201-437-1017 437-8845*

Imperial Oil Resources Ltd
237 4th Ave SW PO Box 2480 Stn M . . . . Calgary AB T2P3M9 403-237-3737 237-2072
TF: 800-567-3776 ■ *Web:* www.imperialoil.ca

Jayhawk Pipeline LLC 2000 S Main St . . . . McPherson KS 67460 620-241-9270 241-9215
Web: www.jayhawkpl.com

Kaneb Pipe Line Partners LP
2435 N Central Expy Suite 700. . . . . Richardson TX 75080 972-699-4000 699-4025
TF: 866-769-2987 ■ *Web:* www.kaneb.com

Kaneb Services LLC
2435 N Central Expy Suite 700. . . . . Richardson TX 75080 972-699-4000 699-4025
Web: www.kaneb.com

Kinder Morgan Energy Partners LP
500 Dallas St Suite 1000 . . . . Houston TX 77002 713-369-9000 369-9411*
NYSE: KMP ■ **Fax:* Hum Res ■ *TF:* 888-844-5657 ■ *Web:* www.kindermorgan.com

Kinder Morgan Management LLC
500 Dallas St 1 Allen Ctr Suite 1000 . . . . Houston TX 77002 713-369-9000 369-9100
NYSE: KMR ■ *TF:* 800-324-2900 ■ *Web:* www.kindermorgan.com

Koch Pipeline Co Inc 4111 E 37th St N. . . . . Wichita KS 67220 316-828-5500
Web: www.kochpipeline.com

Magellan Midstream Partners LP 1 Williams Ctr. . . . . Tulsa OK 74172 918-574-7000 573-6714*
NYSE: MMP ■ **Fax:* Mail Rm ■ *TF:* 800-574-6671 ■ *Web:* www.magellanlp.com

Marathon Pipe Line LLC (MPL)
539 S Main St Rm 7614 . . . . Findlay OH 45840 419-422-2121 425-7040
Web: www.marathonpipeline.com

MarkWest Energy Partners LP
1515 Arapahoe St, Tower 1 Suite 1600. . . . . Denver CO 80202 303-925-9200 290-8769
AMEX: MWE ■ *TF:* 800-730-8388 ■ *Web:* www.markwest.com

Navajo Pipeline Co 311 W Quay . . . . Artesia NM 88210 505-397-5857 397-5827

Olympic Pipeline Co 2201 Lind Ave Suite 270. . . . . Renton WA 98055 425-235-7736 271-5320
TF: 877-659-7473 ■ *Web:* www.olympicpipeline.com

Pioneer Pipe Line Co Inc
245 E 1100 N . . . . North Salt Lake UT 84054 801-299-3610 299-3630

Plains All American Pipeline LP
333 Clay St Suite 1600. . . . . Houston TX 77002 713-646-4100 646-4305
NYSE: PAA ■ *TF Mktg:* 800-564-3036 ■ *Web:* www.plainsallamerican.com

Plantation Pipe Line Co
1435 Windward Concourse . . . . Alpharetta GA 30005 770-751-4000 751-4050
Web: www.plantation-ppl.com

Sunoco Inc 1735 Market St Suite LL . . . . Philadelphia PA 19103 215-977-3000 977-3409
NYSE: SUN ■ *TF:* 800-786-6261 ■ *Web:* www.sunocoinc.com

Sunoco Logistics Partners LP
525 Fritztown Rd. . . . . Sinking Spring PA 19103 610-670-3281
NYSE: SXL ■ *Web:* www.sunocologistics.com

Teppco Crude Oil LP
210 Pk Ave Suite 1600 . . . . Oklahoma City OK 73102 405-239-7191 605-2051*
**Fax:* Mktg ■ *Web:* www.teppco.com

United Brine Pipeline Corp 4800 San Felipe . . . . Houston TX 77056 713-877-1778 877-2605

Valero LP 1 Valero Way . . . . San Antonio TX 78249 210-592-2000 370-2646
NYSE: VLI ■ *TF:* 800-333-3377 ■ *Web:* www.valero.com

601 PLANETARIUMS

Phone Fax

Abrams Planetarium
Michigan State University. . . . . East Lansing MI 48824 517-355-4676 432-3838
Web: www.pa.msu.edu/abrams

Adler Planetarium & Astronomy Museum
1300 S Lake Shore Dr. . . . . Chicago IL 60605 312-922-7827 322-2257
Web: www.adlerplanetarium.org

Albert Einstein Planetarium
Independence Ave & 6th St SW . . . . Washington DC 20560 202-633-1000

Aldrin Planetarium
4801 Dreher Trail N. . . . . West Palm Beach FL 33405 561-832-1988 833-0551
Web: www.sfsm.org

Andrus Planetarium
511 Warburton Ave Hudson River Museum . . . . Yonkers NY 10701 914-963-4550 963-8558
Web: www.hrm.org/planetarium.html

Arnim D Hummel Planetarium
Eastern Kentucky University . . . . Richmond KY 40475 859-622-1547 622-6666
Web: www.planetarium.eku.edu

Phone Fax

Astronaut Memorial Planetarium & Observatory
1519 Clearlake Rd Brevard Community College. . . . . Cocoa FL 32922 321-433-7373
Web: www.brevard.cc.fl.us/planet

ASU School of Earth & Space Exploration
550 E Tyler Mall PO Box 871404 . . . . Tempe AZ 85287 480-965-6891 965-7331
Web: www.sese.asu.edu

Bays Mountain Planetarium & Observatory
853 Bays Mountain Pk Rd . . . . Kingsport TN 37660 423-229-9447 224-2589
Web: www.baysmountain.com/planetdept/astronomy.html

Berea College Weatherford Planetarium
101 Chestnut St . . . . Berea KY 40404 859-985-3000 985-3351

Buehler Planetarium & Observatory
3501 SW Davie Rd . . . . Davie FL 33314 954-201-6681 475-2858
Web: www.broward.edu/locations/central/buehler.jsp

Casper Planetarium 904 N Poplar St. . . . . Casper WY 82601 307-577-0310

Cernan Earth & Space Ctr
2000 N 5th Ave Triton College . . . . River Grove IL 60171 708-456-0300 583-3153
Web: www.triton.edu

Charles Hayden Planetarium 1 Science Pk . . . . Boston MA 02114 617-723-2500 589-0362
Web: www.mos.org

Chesapeake Planetarium 312 Cedar Rd. . . . . Chesapeake VA 23322 757-547-0153 547-0252

Christa McAuliffe Planetarium 2 Institute Dr . . . . Concord NH 03301 603-271-7827 271-7832
Web: www.starhop.com

Clark Planetarium 110 S 400 W. . . . . Salt Lake City UT 84101 801-456-7827
Web: www.clarkplanetarium.net

Community College of Southern Nevada Planetarium & Observatory
3200 E Cheyenne Ave. . . . . North Las Vegas NV 89030 702-651-4759 651-4825
Web: www.csn.edu/planetarium

Cormack Planetarium
Roger Williams Pk 1000 Elmwood Ave. . . . . Providence RI 02907 401-785-9457 461-5146
Web: www.providenceri.com\museum

Downing Planetarium
5320 N Maple Ave MS DP132
California State University Fresno. . . . . Fresno CA 93740 559-278-4121 278-4070
Web: www.downing-planetarium.org

Dreyfuss Planetarium 49 Washington St. . . . . Newark NJ 07102 973-596-6529 642-0459
Web: www.newarkmuseum.org

Ethyl IMAX Dome & Planetarium
2500 W Broad St . . . . Richmond VA 23220 804-864-1400 864-1488
TF: 800-659-1727

Fiske Planetarium 2414 Regent Dr . . . . Boulder CO 80309 303-492-5002 492-1725
Web: www.colorado.edu

Fleischmann Planetarium & Science Ctr
University of Nevada. . . . . Reno NV 89557 775-784-4811 784-4822
Web: planetarium.unr.nevada.edu

Gheens Science Hall & Rauch Planetarium
Rauch Planetarium
University of Louisville. . . . . Louisville KY 40292 502-852-6664 852-0831
Web: louisville.edu/planetarium

Hayden Planetarium 81st St & Central Park W . . . . New York NY 10024 212-769-5900 496-3500
Web: www.haydenplanetarium.org

Henry Buhl Jr Planetarium & Observatory
1 Allegheny Ave . . . . Pittsburgh PA 15212 412-237-3397 237-3395
TF: 877-975-6787 ■ *Web:* www.buhlplanetarium.org

Hopkins Planetarium 1 Market Sq. . . . . Roanoke VA 24011 540-342-5710 224-1240
Web: www.smwv.org

Hyde Memorial Observatory
70th St Normal Blvd . . . . Lincoln NE 68506 402-441-8708 441-6468
Web: www.hydeobservatory.info

JI Holcomb Observatory & Planetarium
702 W Lake Rd Butler University . . . . Indianapolis IN 46208 317-940-8333 940-9951
Web: www.butler.edu/holcomb

John Deere Planetarium
820 38th St Augustana College . . . . Rock Island IL 61201 309-794-7327 794-7564

Kenner Planetarium & MegaDome Cinema
2020 4th St. . . . . Kenner LA 70062 504-468-7231 471-2159
Web: www.rivertownkenner.com/planetarium.html

Kitt Peak National Observatory
950 N Cherry Ave. . . . . Tucson AZ 85719 520-318-8600 318-8724
Web: www.noao.edu/kpno

Lafayette Natural History Museum & Planetarium
433 Jefferson St . . . . Lafayette LA 70501 337-291-5544 291-5464
Web: www.lafayettesciencemuseum.org

Lake Afton Public Observatory 1845 Fairmount . . . . Wichita KS 67260 316-978-3170 978-3350
Web: www.webs.wichita.edu/lapo

Lick Observatory Mt Hamilton Rd. . . . . San Jose CA 95140 408-274-5061
Web: www.ucolick.org

Lodestar Astronomy Ctr
1801 Mountain Rd NW . . . . Albuquerque NM 87104 505-841-2800 841-5999
Web: www.nmnaturalhistory.org

Longway Planetarium 1310 E Kearsley St. . . . . Flint MI 48503 810-237-3400 237-3417
Web: www.sloanlongway.org

Lowell Observatory 1400 W Mars Hill Rd . . . . Flagstaff AZ 86001 928-774-3358 774-6296
Web: www.lowell.edu

Maria Mitchell Observatory 3 Vestal St. . . . . Nantucket MA 02554 508-228-9273 228-1031
Web: www.mmo.org/museums

Maynard F Jordan Planetarium & Observatory
5781 Wingate Hall Maynard F Jordan Planetarium. . . . . Orono ME 04469 207-581-1341 581-1314
Web: www.umainesky.com

Montreal Planetarium 1000 St Jacques St W . . . . Montreal QC H3C1G7 514-872-4530 872-8102
Web: www.planetarium.montreal.qc.ca

Moody Planetarium
3301 4th St Museum of Texas Tech University . . . . Lubbock TX 79409 806-742-2432 742-1136
Web: www.depts.ttu.edu/museumttu

Morehead Planetarium
250 E Franklin St
UNC Chapel Hill CB 3480 . . . . Chapel Hill NC 27599 919-962-1236 962-1238
Web: www.moreheadplanetarium.org

MT Brackbill Planetarium
1200 Pk Rd Eastern Mennonite University . . . . Harrisonburg VA 22802 540-432-4400 432-4488

Mueller Planetarium
University of Nebraska 210 Morrill Hall . . . . Lincoln NE 68588 402-472-2641 472-8899
Web: www.spacelaser.com

	City	State	Zip	Phone	Fax
Ott Planetarium 2508 University Ci Weber State University *Web:* community.weber.edu/planetarium	Ogden	UT	84408	801-626-6855	
Perkins Observatory PO Box 449 *Web:* www.perkins-observatory.org	Delaware	OH	43015	740-363-1257	363-1258
Pontchartrain Astronomy Society Observatory 409 Williams Blvd Rivertown *Web:* www.pasnola.org	Kenner	LA	70062	504-468-7231	471-2159
Portland Observatory 138 Congress St *Web:* www.portlandlandmarks.org/observatory.htm	Portland	ME	04101	207-774-5561	774-2509
Ritter Planetarium & Brooks Observatory 2801 W Bancroft MS 218 *Web:* www.utoledo.edu	Toledo	OH	43606	419-530-2650	530-5167
Roger B Chaffee Planetarium 272 Pearl St NW *Web:* www.grmuseum.org/planetarium	Grand Rapids	MI	49504	616-456-3977	456-3873
Russell C Davis Planetarium 201 E Pascagoula St *Web:* www.jacksonms.gov/visitors/planetarium	Jackson	MS	39201	601-960-1552	960-1555
Saint Petersburg College 6605 5th Ave N Science Bldg	Saint Petersburg	FL	33703	727-341-4320	
Sanford Museum & Planetarium 117 E Willow St *Web:* www.sanfordmuseum.org	Cherokee	IA	51012	712-225-3922	225-0446
Sharpe Planetarium 3050 Central Ave *Web:* www.memphismuseums.org	Memphis	TN	38111	901-636-2320	320-6391
Southworth Planetarium 96 Falmouth St *Web:* www.usm.maine.edu	Portland	ME	04104	207-780-4249	780-4051
Space Transit Planetarium 3280 S Miami Ave *Web:* www.miamisci.org	Miami	FL	33129	305-646-4400	646-4200
Strasenburgh Planetarium 663 E Ave Rochester Museum & Science Ctr *Web:* www.rmsc.org	Rochester	NY	14607	585-271-4320	271-5935
Tomchin Planetarium & Observatory West Virginia University 425 Hodges Hall PO Box 6315 *Web:* www.planetarium.wvu.edu	Morgantown	WV	26506	304-293-3422	293-5732
University of Arkansas at Little Rock 2801 S University Ave *Web:* www.ualr.edu	Little Rock	AR	72204	501-569-3275	569-3314
WA Gayle Planetarium 1010 Forest Ave *Web:* www.montgomery.troy.edu	Montgomery	AL	36106	334-241-4799	241-2301
Ward Beecher Planetarium Youngstown State University 1 University Plaza *Web:* www.cc.ysu.edu/physics-astro/planet.htm	Youngstown	OH	44555	330-941-3616	941-3121
William M Staerkel Planetarium 2400 W Bradley Ave Parkland College *Web:* www.parkland.edu	Champaign	IL	61821	217-351-2568	
Flandrau Science Center & Planetarium University of Arizona 1601 E University Blvd *Web:* www.flandrau.org	Tucson	AZ	85721	520-621-4515	621-8451
Rosicrucian Egyptian Museum & Planetarium 1342 Naglee Ave Rosicrucian Pk *Web:* www.rosicrucian.org	San Jose	CA	95191	408-947-3636	947-3677
Discovery Museum & Planetarium 4450 Pk Ave *Web:* www.discoverymuseum.org	Bridgeport	CT	06604	203-372-3521	374-1929
Science Factory Children's Museum & Planetarium 2300 Leo Harris Pkwy *Web:* www.sciencefactory.org	Eugene	OR	97401	541-682-7888	484-9027
Science Place The 1318 2nd Ave in Fair Pk *Web:* www.natureandscience.org	Dallas	TX	75210	214-428-5555	428-4356

602 PLASTICS - LAMINATED - PLATE, SHEET, PROFILE SHAPES

	City	State	Zip	Phone	Fax
American Renolit Corp 1207 E Lincolnway *Web:* www.americanrenolit.com	LaPorte	IN	46350	219-324-6886	324-5332
American Thermoplastic Extrusion Co 4851 NW 128th St Rd *TF:* 800-426-9605	Opa Locka	FL	33054	305-769-9566	769-1998
AMETEK Inc Westchester Plastics Div 42 Mountain Ave *Web:* www.ametek-westchesterplas.com	Nesquehoning	PA	18240	570-645-2191	645-6959
Applied Plastics Co Inc 7320 S 6th St *TF:* 800-959-0445 ■ *Web:* www.appliedplasticsinc.com	Oak Creek	WI	53154	414-764-2900	764-8606
Atlantis Plastics Inc Linear Films Div 6940 W 76th St S *TF Cust Svc:* 800-332-4437 ■ *Web:* www.atlantisplastics.com	Tulsa	OK	74131	918-446-1651	227-2454
Bourne Industries Inc 491 S Comstock St *Web:* www.bourneindustries.com	Corunna	MI	48817	989-743-3461	743-5481
C-K Composites Inc 361 Bridgeport Rd *Web:* www.ckcomposites.com	Mount Pleasant	PA	15666	724-547-4581	547-2890
California Combining Corp 5607 S Santa Fe Ave *Web:* www.californiacombining.com	Los Angeles	CA	90058	323-589-5727	585-8078
CCL Plastic Packaging 2501 W Rosecrans Ave *Web:* www.ccltube.com	Los Angeles	CA	90059	310-635-4444	635-6839
Columbus Cello-Poly Corp 4041 Roberts Rd *TF:* 800-837-1204 ■ *Web:* www.cello-poly.com	Columbus	OH	43228	614-876-1204	876-1072
Composite Technologies of America Inc 1331 S Chillicothe Rd *TF:* 800-692-5201 ■ *Web:* www.omegapultrusions.com	Aurora	OH	44202	330-562-5201	562-7452
Conimar Corp 1724 NE 22nd Ave *TF:* 800-874-9735 ■ *Web:* www.conimar.com	Ocala	FL	34470	352-732-7235	732-6888
Connecticut Laminating Co Inc 162 James St *TF:* 800-753-9119 ■ *Web:* www.ctlaminating.com	New Haven	CT	06513	203-787-2184	787-4073
Current Inc 30 Tyler St PO Box 120183 *TF:* 877-436-6542 ■ *Web:* www.currentcomposites.com	East Haven	CT	06512	203-469-1337	467-8435
DuPont Surfaces 4417 Lancaster Pike CRP 728/3105 *TF:* 800-448-9835 ■ *Web:* www2.dupont.com	Wilmington	DE	19805	302-774-1000	
Dynea Overlays Inc 2144 Milwaukee Way *Web:* www.dyneaoverlays.com	Tacoma	WA	98421	253-572-5600	627-2896
Edlon Inc 150 Pomeroy Ave *TF Sales:* 800-753-3566 ■ *Web:* www.edlon.com	Avondale	PA	19311	610-268-3101	268-8898
Fiberesin Industries Inc 37031 E Wisconsin Ave PO Box 88 *Web:* www.fiberesin.com	Oconomowoc	WI	53066	262-567-4427	567-4814
Formica Corp 10155 Reading Rd *TF:* 800-367-6422 ■ *Web:* www.formica.com	Cincinnati	OH	45241	513-786-3400	
Franklin Fibre-Lamitex Corp 903 E 13th St *TF:* 800-233-9739 ■ *Web:* www.franklinfibre.com	Wilmington	DE	19802	302-652-3621	571-9754
Hartson-kennedy Cabinet Top Co Inc 522 W 22nd St PO Box 3095 *TF:* 800-388-8144 ■ *Web:* www.hartson-kennedy.com	Marion	IN	46953	765-668-8144	662-3452
Insulfab Plastics Inc 834 Hayne St *TF:* 800-845-7599 ■ *Web:* www.insulfab.com	Spartanburg	SC	29301	864-582-7506	582-5215
Insultab Inc 45 Industrial Pkwy *TF Cust Svc:* 800-468-4822 ■ *Web:* www.insultab.com	Woburn	MA	01801	781-935-0800	935-0879
Iten Industries 4602 Benefit Ave *TF Orders:* 800-227-4836 ■ *Web:* www.itenindustries.com	Ashtabula	OH	44004	440-997-6134	992-3614
Klockner Pentaplast of America Inc 3585 Klockner Rd PO Box 500 *TF:* 800-446-3007 ■ *Web:* www.kpafilms.com	Gordonsville	VA	22942	540-832-1400	832-1405
Lakeland Plastics Inc 1550 McCormick Blvd *TF:* 800-225-2508 ■ *Web:* www.lakelandplastics.com	Mundelein	IL	60060	847-680-1550	680-1595
Lamart Corp 16 Richmond St *TF:* 800-526-2789 ■ *Web:* www.lamartcorp.com	Clifton	NJ	07015	973-772-6262	772-3673
Laminating Co of America 20322 Windrow Dr *Web:* www.lcoa.com	Lake Forest	CA	92630	949-587-3371	454-0066
Lamsco West Inc PO Box 802050 *Web:* www.lamscowest.com	Santa Clarita	CA	91380	661-295-8620	295-8626
LSI Corp of America Inc 2100 Xenium Ln N *Web:* www.lsi-casework.com	Plymouth	MN	55441	763-559-4664	559-4395
Madico Inc 64 Industrial Pkwy *TF:* 800-456-4331 ■ *Web:* www.madico.com	Woburn	MA	01801	781-935-7850	935-6841
Mar-Bal Inc 16930 Munn Rd *Web:* www.mar-bal.com	Chagrin Falls	OH	44023	440-543-7526	543-4374
Miniature Precision Components Inc 820 Wisconsin St *Web:* www.mpc-inc.com	Walworth	WI	53184	262-275-5791	275-6346
Olon Industries Inc 42 Armstrong Ave *TF:* 800-387-2319 ■ *Web:* www.olon.com	Georgetown	ON	L7G4R9	905-877-7300	877-7383
Petro Plastics Co Inc 450 S Ave *TF:* 800-486-4738 ■ *Web:* www.petroplastics.com	Garwood	NJ	07027	908-789-1200	789-1381
Reef Industries Inc 9209 Almeda Genoa Rd *TF:* 800-231-6074 ■ *Web:* www.reefindustries.com	Houston	TX	77075	713-507-4200	507-4295
Rochling Engineered Plastics 120 Rochling St PO Box 2729 *TF Cust Svc:* 800-541-4419 ■ *Web:* www.roechling.com	Gastonia	NC	28053	704-922-7814	922-7651
Rotuba Extruders Inc 1401 S Pk Ave *Web:* www.rotuba.com	Linden	NJ	07036	908-486-1000	486-0874
Rowmark Inc 2040 Industrial Dr *TF:* 800-243-3339 ■ *Web:* www.rowmark.com	Findlay	OH	45840	419-425-2407	425-2927
Sabin Corp 3800 Constitution Ave PO Box 788 *TF:* 800-264-4510 ■ *Web:* www.cookgroup.com	Bloomington	IN	47403	812-323-4500	339-3395
Schneller Inc 6019 Powdermille Rd *Web:* www.schneller.com	Kent	OH	44240	330-673-1400	676-7122
Schneller Inc 6200 49th St N *Web:* www.schneller.com	Pinellas Park	FL	33781	727-521-2393	525-7384
Spaulding Composites Co 55 Nadeau Dr *TF:* 800-801-0560 ■ *Web:* www.spauldingcom.com	Rochester	NH	03867	603-332-0555	332-5357
Techniform Industries Inc 2107 Hayes Ave *TF:* 800-691-2816 ■ *Web:* www.techniform-plastics.com	Fremont	OH	43420	419-332-8484	334-5222
Universal Laminates 14753 Aetna St *Web:* www.universallaminates.net	Van Nuys	CA	91411	818-782-3424	782-5134
V-T Industries Inc 1000 Industrial Pk *TF:* 800-827-1615 ■ *Web:* www.vtindustries.com	Holstein	IA	51025	712-368-4381	368-4111
Vytech Industries Inc 5201 Old Pearman Dairy Rd *TF:* 800-225-8531 ■ *Web:* www.vytech.com	Anderson	SC	29625	864-224-8771	224-8410
Wilmington Fibre Specialty Co 700 Washington St *TF:* 800-220-5132 ■ *Web:* www.wilmfibre.com	New Castle	DE	19720	302-328-7525	328-6630
Wilsonart International Inc 2400 Wilson Pl *TF Cust Svc:* 800-433-3222 ■ *Web:* www.wilsonart.com	Temple	TX	76504	254-207-7000	207-2545

603 PLASTICS - UNSUPPORTED - FILM, SHEET, PROFILE SHAPES

SEE ALSO Blister Packaging p. 1529

	City	State	Zip	Phone	Fax
3M Traffic Safety Systems Div 3M Ctr Bldg 235-3A-09 *TF:* 800-553-1380 ■ *Web:* www.3m.com/product/business-units/traffic-safety.html	Saint Paul	MN	55144	800-553-1380	591-9293
Advance Bag & Packaging Technologies 5720 Williams Lake Rd *TF:* 800-475-2247 ■ *Web:* www.advancepac.com	Waterford	MI	48329	248-674-3126	674-2630
AEP Industries Inc 125 Phillips Ave *NASDAQ: AEPI* ■ *TF:* 800-999-2374 ■ *Web:* www.aepinc.com	South Hackensack	NJ	07606	201-641-6600	807-2443
Allen Extruders Inc 1305 Lincoln Ave *TF:* 800-833-1305 ■ *Web:* www.allenx.com	Holland	MI	49423	616-392-9004	394-0100
Anaheim Custom Extruders 4640 E La Palma Ave *TF Cust Svc:* 800-229-2760	Anaheim	CA	92807	714-693-8508	693-9531

Company / Address	City	State	ZIP	Phone	Fax
Applied Extrusion Technologies Inc 15 Reads Way	New Castle	DE	19720	302-326-5500	326-5501
TF: 800-688-2044 ■ *Web:* www.aetfilms.com					
Arlon Adhesives & Films 2811 S Harbor Blvd	Santa Ana	CA	92704	714-540-2811	431-4305
TF: 800-540-2811 ■ *Web:* www.arlon.com					
Atlantis Plastics Inc 1870 The Exchange Suite 200	Atlanta	GA	30339	800-497-7659	618-7080*
NASDAQ: ATPL ■ **Fax Area Code: 770* ■ *TF:* 800-497-7659 ■ *Web:* www.atlantisplastics.com					
Atlas Roofing Falcon Foam Div 8240 Byron Ctr Rd SW	Byron Center	MI	49315	616-878-1568	878-9942
TF: 800-917-9138 ■ *Web:* www.falconfoam.com					
Avery Dennison Automotive Products Div 15939 Industrial Pkwy	Cleveland	OH	44135	216-267-8700	
Web: www.iapna.averydennison.com					
Avery Dennison Engineered Films Div 7600 Auburn Rd Bldg 18	Concord	OH	44077	440-358-4600	358-4684
Web: www.efd.averydennison.com					
Avery Dennison Performance Films Div 650 W 67th Ave	Schererville	IN	46375	219-322-5030	322-3236
Web: www.pfd.averydennison.com					
Avery Dennison Worldwide Graphics Div 250 Chester St Bldg 6	Painesville	OH	44077	440-358-3700	358-3665
TF: 800-443-9380 ■ *Web:* www.averygraphics.com					
Bemis Co Inc 1 Neenah Ctr 4th Fl PO Box 669	Neenah	WI	54957	920-727-4100	
NYSE: BMS ■ *Web:* www.bemis.com					
Bemis Co Inc Bemis Polyethylene Packaging Div 1350 N Fruitridge Ave PO Box 905	Terre Haute	IN	47808	812-460-6200	460-6370
TF: 800-457-0861 ■ *Web:* www.bemisppd.com					
Bixby International Corp 1 Preble Rd	Newburyport	MA	01950	978-462-4100	465-5184
TF: 800-466-4102 ■ *Web:* www.bixbyintl.com					
Brandywine Investment Group Homalite Div 11 Brookside Dr	Wilmington	DE	19804	302-652-3686	652-4578
TF: 800-346-7802 ■ *Web:* www.homalite.com					
Bunzl Extrusion Inc 1625 Ashton Pk Dr	Colonial Heights	VA	23834	804-518-1124	
TF: 800-755-7528 ■ *Web:* www.bunzlextrusion.com					
Catalina Graphic Films Inc 27001 Agoura Rd Suite 100	Calabasas Hills	CA	91301	818-880-8060	880-1144
TF: 800-333-3136 ■ *Web:* www.catalinagraphicfilms.com					
Chase Facile Holdings Inc 4 - 22 Erie St	Paterson	NJ	07524	973-684-1000	684-2749
Web: www.chasecorp.com					
Clopay Plastic Products Co 8585 Duke Blvd	Mason	OH	45040	513-770-4800	770-3863
TF: 800-282-2260 ■ *Web:* www.clopayplastics.com					
Coburn Corp 1650 Corporate Rd W	Lakewood	NJ	08701	732-367-5511	367-2908
Web: www.coburn.com					
Conwed Corp 1300 Godward St NE # 5000	Minneapolis	MN	55413	612-623-1700	623-2501
TF: 800-426-0149 ■ *Web:* www.conwedplastics.com					
CUE Inc 11 Leonberg Rd	Cranberry Township	PA	16066	724-772-5225	772-5280
TF: 800-283-4621 ■ *Web:* www.cue-inc.com					
CYRO Industries 100 Enterprise Dr	Rockaway	NJ	07866	973-442-6000	442-6114*
**Fax:* Hum Res ■ *Web:* www.cyro.com					
D & B Plastics Inc 706 Highland Ct Dr PO Box 26	Fairmont	MN	56031	507-235-5950	235-6048
TF: 800-405-2247 ■ *Web:* www.dandbplastics.com					
Danafilms Inc 5 Otis St PO Box 624	Westborough	MA	01581	508-366-8884	898-0106
TF: 800-634-8289 ■ *Web:* www.danafilms.com					
Dielectrics Industries Inc 300 Burnett Rd	Chicopee	MA	01020	413-594-8111	594-2343
TF: 800-472-7286 ■ *Web:* www.dielectrics.com					
Dunmore Corp 145 Wharton Rd	Bristol	PA	19007	215-781-8895	781-9293
TF: 800-444-0242 ■ *Web:* www.dunmore.com					
E S Robbins Corp 2802 Avalon Ave	Muscle Shoals	AL	35661	256-383-0124	383-4987
TF: 866-934-6018 ■ *Web:* www.esrobbins.com					
Enflo Corp 315 Lake Ave	Bristol	CT	06010	860-589-0014	589-7179
TF: 888-887-4093 ■ *Web:* www.enflo.com					
Favorite Plastic Corp 1465 Utica Ave	Brooklyn	NY	11234	718-253-7000	377-1918
TF Cust Svc: 800-221-8077 ■ *Web:* www.favoriteplastics.com					
Film Technologies International Inc 2630 Fairfield Ave S	Saint Petersburg	FL	33712	727-327-2544	327-7132
TF: 800-777-1770 ■ *Web:* www.filmtechnologies.com					
FLEXcon Co Inc 1 Flexcon Industrial Pk	Spencer	MA	01562	508-885-8200	885-8400
Web: www.flexcon.com					
Fluoro Plastics Inc 3601 G St	Philadelphia	PA	19134	215-425-5500	425-5521
TF Cust Svc: 800-262-1910 ■ *Web:* www.fluoro-plastics.com					
Francesville Drain Tile Corp 4385 S 1450 W	Francesville	IN	47946	219-567-9133	567-9296
Web: www.fratco.com					
Gary Plastic Packaging Corp 1340 Viele Ave	Bronx	NY	10474	718-893-2200	378-2141
TF: 800-221-8150 ■ *Web:* www.plasticboxes.com					
General Formulations Inc 309 S Union St	Sparta	MI	49345	616-887-7387	887-0537
TF: 800-253-3664 ■ *Web:* www.generalformulations.com					
Glasforms Inc 1226 Lincoln Ave	San Jose	CA	95125	408-297-9300	297-0601
TF: 888-297-3800 ■ *Web:* www.glassforms.com					
GSE Lining Technology Inc 19103 Gundle Rd	Houston	TX	77073	281-443-8564	875-6010
TF: 800-435-2008 ■ *Web:* www.gseworld.com					
Holm Industries Inc Saint Charles Div 315 N 9th St	Saint Charles	IL	60174	630-584-1880	584-8972
TF: 800-221-2209					
Interfilm Holdings Inc 223 Pine Rd	Easley	SC	29642	864-269-4690	269-5048
TF: 800-648-4828 ■ *Web:* www.interfilm-usa.com					
Kama Corp 600 Dietrich Ave	Hazleton	PA	18201	570-455-2022	
TF: 800-628-7598 ■ *Web:* www.alcoa.com/kama					
Kayline Processing Inc 31 Coates St	Trenton	NJ	08611	609-695-1449	989-1094
TF Sales: 800-367-5546 ■ *Web:* www.kayline.com					
Kendall Packaging Corp 10200 N Port Washington Rd	Mequon	WI	53092	262-404-1200	404-1221
TF: 800-237-0951 ■ *Web:* www.kendallpkg.com					
Kepner Plastics Fabricators Inc 3131 Lomita Blvd	Torrance	CA	90505	310-325-3162	326-8560
Web: www.kepnerplastics.com					
Kimoto Tech Inc PO Box 1783	Cedartown	GA	30125	770-748-2643	748-2648
Web: www.kimototech.com					
Latham International Inc 787 Watervliet Shaker Rd	Latham	NY	12110	518-783-7776	783-0004
Web: www.pacificpools.com					
Lavanture Products Co 22825 Gallatin Way	Elkhart	IN	46514	574-264-0658	264-6601
TF: 800-348-7625 ■ *Web:* www.lavanture.com					
Llc Shield Pack 411 Downing Pines Rd	West Monroe	LA	71292	318-387-4743	325-4800
TF: 800-551-5185 ■ *Web:* www.shieldpack.com					
Louisiana Plastic Industries 501 Downing Pines Rd	West Monroe	LA	71292	318-388-4562	387-5642
McNeel International Corp 5401 W Kennedy Blvd Suite 751	Tampa	FL	33609	813-286-8680	286-1535
Mitsubishi Polyester Film LLC 2001 Hood Rd	Greer	SC	29650	864-879-5000	879-5006*
**Fax:* Mktg ■ *TF:* 800-845-2009 ■ *Web:* www.m-petfilm.com					
MPI Technologies 37 E St	Winchester	MA	01890	781-729-8300	729-9093
TF: 888-674-8088 ■ *Web:* www.mpirelease.com					
Natvar 8720 US 70 W	Clayton	NC	27520	919-553-4151	553-4156
TF: 800-395-6288 ■ *Web:* www.natvar.com					
New Hampshire Plastics Inc 1 Bouchard St	Manchester	NH	03103	603-669-8523	622-4888
TF: 800-258-3036					
Northland Plastics Inc 1420 S 16th St PO Box 290	Sheboygan	WI	53082	920-458-0732	458-4881
TF: 800-776-7163 ■ *Web:* www.northlandplastics.com					
Orcon Corp 1570 Atlantic St	Union City	CA	94587	510-489-8100	489-6436
TF: 800-227-0505 ■ *Web:* www.orconproducts.com					
Paragon Films Inc 3500 W Tacoma	Broken Arrow	OK	74012	918-250-3456	355-3456
Web: www.paragon-films.com					
Penn Fibre Plastics 2434 Bristol Rd	Bensalem	PA	19020	215-702-9551	702-9552
TF Cust Svc: 800-662-7366 ■ *Web:* www.pennfibre.com					
Performance Coating International 600 Murray St	Bangor	PA	18013	610-588-7900	588-7901
Web: pcoatingsintl.com					
Performance Materials Corp 1150 Calle Suerte	Camarillo	CA	93012	805-482-1722	482-8776
Web: www.performancematerials.com					
Petoskey Plastics Inc 1 Petoskey St	Petoskey	MI	49770	231-347-2602	347-2878
TF: 800-999-6556 ■ *Web:* www.petoskeyplastics.com					
Plaskolite Inc 1770 Joyce Ave	Columbus	OH	43219	614-294-3281	297-7287
TF: 800-848-9124 ■ *Web:* www.plaskolite.com					
Polyvinyl Films Inc PO Box 753	Sutton	MA	01590	508-865-3558	865-1562
Web: www.stretchtite.com					
Primex Plastics Corp 1235 N 'F' St	Richmond	IN	47374	765-966-7774	935-1083
TF: 800-222-5116 ■ *Web:* www.primexplastics.com					
Prinsco Inc 108 W Hwy 7 PO Box 265	Prinsburg	MN	56281	320-978-4116	978-8602
TF: 800-992-1725 ■ *Web:* www.prinsco.com					
Professional Packaging Co Inc 22360 Royalton Rd	Strongsville	OH	44149	440-572-1771	
TF: 800-336-2766 ■ *Web:* www.a-roo.com					
Quality Films Inc 321 Duncan St PO Box 459	Schoolcraft	MI	49087	269-679-5263	679-4261
TF: 800-306-5263					
Raven Industries Inc 205 E 6th St	Sioux Falls	SD	57104	605-336-2750	335-0268
NASDAQ: RAVN ■ *TF:* 800-227-2836 ■ *Web:* www.ravenind.com					
Ross & Roberts Inc 1299 W Broad St	Stratford	CT	06615	203-378-9363	377-8841
TF: 800-822-4220					
Ryko Plastics Products Inc 12903 Jurupa Ave	Fontana	CA	92337	951-749-2411	749-2414
Sheffield Plastics Inc 119 Salisbury Rd	Sheffield	MA	01257	413-229-8711	229-8717
TF Cust Svc: 800-254-1707 ■ *Web:* www.sheffieldplasticsinc.com					
Shepherd CE Co Inc 2221 Canada Dry St	Houston	TX	77023	713-928-3763	928-2324
TF: 800-324-6733 ■ *Web:* www.ceshepherd.com					
Sigma Plastics Group Page & Schuyler Aves Bldg 8	Lyndhurst	NJ	07071	201-933-6000	933-6429
Web: www.sigmaplastics.com					
Sinclair & Rush Inc 123 Manufacturers Dr	Arnold	MO	63010	636-282-6800	282-6888
TF: 800-408-7125 ■ *Web:* www.sinclair-rush.com					
SLM Mfg Corp 215 Davidson Ave	Somerset	NJ	08873	732-469-7500	469-5546
TF: 800-526-3708 ■ *Web:* www.slmcorp.com					
Soliant LLC 1872 Hwy 9 Bypass	Lancaster	SC	29720	803-285-9401	313-8331
TF: 800-288-9401 ■ *Web:* www.paintfilm.com					
Southern Film Extruders Inc 2319 English Rd	High Point	NC	27262	336-885-8091	885-1221
TF: 800-334-6101 ■ *Web:* www.southernfilm.com					
Southwall Technologies Inc 3788 Fabian Way	Palo Alto	CA	94303	650-798-1200	798-1406
TF: 800-365-8794 ■ *Web:* www.southwall.com					
Sto-Cote Products Inc 218 S Rd	Genoa City	WI	53128	262-279-6000	279-6744
TF: 800-435-2621					
Summit Plastics Inc 107 S Laurel St	Summit	MS	39666	601-276-7500	276-2400
TF: 800-790-7117 ■ *Web:* www.summitplastics.us					
Sunlite Plastics Inc W 194 N 11340 McCormick Dr	Germantown	WI	53022	262-253-0600	253-0601
Web: www.sunliteplastics.com					
Tee Group Films 605 N Main St	Ladd	IL	61329	815-894-2331	894-3387
Web: www.tee-group.com					
Thatcher Tubes LLC 1005 Courtaulds Dr	Woodstock	IL	60098	815-334-1200	334-1230
TF: 888-842-8243 ■ *Web:* www.thatchertubes.com					
Thermoplastic Processes Inc 1268 Valley Rd	Stirling	NJ	07980	908-561-3000	753-6749
TF: 888-554-6400 ■ *Web:* www.thermoplasticprocesses.com					
Tredegar Corp Film Products Div 1100 Boulders Pkwy	Richmond	VA	23225	804-330-1222	330-1201
TF: 800-411-7441 ■ *Web:* www.tredegarfilms.com					
Tri-Seal International Inc 900 Bradley Hill Rd	Blauvelt	NY	10913	845-353-3300	353-3376
Web: www.tekni-plex.com					
Tulox Plastics Corp 401 S Miller Ave	Marion	IN	46953	765-664-5155	664-0257
TF Cust Svc: 800-234-1118 ■ *Web:* www.tulox.com					
Valley Decorating Co 2829 E Hamilton Ave	Fresno	CA	93721	559-495-1100	495-1195
TF: 800-245-2817 ■ *Web:* www.pomponcentral.com					
VCF Films Inc 1100 Sutton Ave	Howell	MI	48843	517-546-2300	546-2984
TF: 888-823-4141 ■ *Web:* www.vcffilm.com					
Vinylex Corp 2636 Byington Rd	Knoxville	TN	37931	865-690-2211	691-6273*
**Fax:* Cust Svc ■ *TF:* 800-624-4435 ■ *Web:* www.vinylex.com					
VPI Corp 3123 S 9th St	Sheboygan	WI	53081	920-458-4664	458-1368
TF Orders: 800-874-4240 ■ *Web:* www.vpicorp.com					
Watersaver Co Inc 5870 E 56th Ave	Commerce City	CO	80022	303-289-1818	287-3136
TF: 800-525-2424 ■ *Web:* www.watersaver.com					

				Phone	Fax
Winzen Engineering					
23350 Southport PO Box 692108	San Antonio	TX	78269	210-415-5041	
Winzen Film Inc 1212 Elm St	Sulphur Springs	TX	75482	903-885-7595	885-4702
TF: 800-779-7595 ■ *Web:* www.winzen.com					
Zippertubing Co 13000 S Broadway	Los Angeles	CA	90061	310-527-0488	767-1714
TF: 800-321-8178 ■ *Web:* www.zippertubing.com					

604 PLASTICS FOAM PRODUCTS

				Phone	Fax
Action Products Co Inc 1 Action Rd PO Box 100	Odessa	MO	64076	816-633-5514	230-8122
TF: 800-733-5514 ■ *Web:* www.actionp.com					
Allied Aerofoam Products LLC 216 Kelsey Ln	Tampa	FL	33619	813-626-0090	569-0629
TF: 800-338-9140 ■ *Web:* www.alliedaerofoam.com					
American Converters Inc 5360 Main St NE	Fridley	MN	55421	763-574-1044	574-1015
TF: 888-360-8050 ■ *Web:* www.amconvas.com					
American Excelsior Co					
850 Ave H E PO Box 5067	Arlington	TX	76005	817-640-1555	649-7816
TF: 800-777-7645 ■ *Web:* www.amerexcel.com					
Astrofoam Molding Co Inc 4117 Calle Tesoro	Camarillo	CA	93012	805-482-7276	482-6599
TF: 800-339-0967 ■ *Web:* www.astrofoam.com					
Bontex Inc 1 Bontex Dr	Buena Vista	VA	24416	540-261-2181	261-3784
PINK: BOTX ■ *TF:* 800-733-4234 ■ *Web:* www.bontex.com					
Carpenter Co 5016 Monument Ave	Richmond	VA	23230	804-359-0800	353-0694
TF: 800-288-3830 ■ *Web:* www.carpenter.com					
Cellofoam North America Inc					
1917 Rockdale Industrial Blvd	Conyers	GA	30012	770-929-3688	929-3608
TF: 800-241-3634 ■ *Web:* www.cellofoam.com					
Cellox Corp 1200 Industrial St	Reedsburg	WI	53959	608-524-2316	524-2362
TF: 888-217-6631 ■ *Web:* www.cellox.com					
Chestnut Ridge Foam Inc PO Box 781	Latrobe	PA	15650	724-537-9000	537-9003
TF Cust Svc: 800-234-2734 ■ *Web:* www.chestnutridgefoam.com					
Clark Foam Products Corp					
655 Remington Blvd	Bolingbrook	IL	60440	630-226-5900	226-5959
TF: 888-284-2290 ■ *Web:* www.clarkfoam.net					
Clayton Corp 866 Horan Dr	Fenton	MO	63026	636-349-5333	349-5335
TF Cust Svc: 800-325-6180 ■ *Web:* www.claytoncorp.com					
Createc Corp 6835 Guion Rd	Indianapolis	IN	46268	317-566-0022	566-0022
TF: 800-428-7483 ■ *Web:* www.createc.com					
Creative Foam Corp 300 N Alloy Dr	Fenton	MI	48430	810-629-4149	629-7368
TF: 800-837-0630 ■ *Web:* www.creativefoam.com					
Crest Foam Industries Inc 100 Carol Pl	Moonachie	NJ	07074	201-807-0809	807-1113
Web: www.crestfoam.com					
Custom Pack Inc 650 Pennsylvania Dr	Exton	PA	19341	610-524-4222	524-4777
TF: 800-722-7005 ■ *Web:* www.custompackinc.com					
Cyclics Corp 2135 Technology Dr	Schenectady	NY	12308	518-881-1440	881-1439
Web: www.cyclics.com					
Dart Container Corp 500 Hogsback Rd	Mason	MI	48854	517-676-3800	676-3883
TF: 800-248-5960 ■ *Web:* www.dart.biz					
Dow Thermoset Systems 1881 W Oak Pkwy	Marietta	GA	30062	770-428-2684	428-9431
TF: 800-735-3129 ■ *Web:* www.dow.com					
Duraco Inc 7400 W Industrial Dr	Forest Park	IL	60130	708-488-1025	488-1215
TF: 800-852-1025 ■ *Web:* www.duracoinc.com					
E-A-R Specialty Composites					
7911 Zions Rd	Indianapolis	IN	46268	317-692-6666	692-6624
TF: 800-544-5180 ■ *Web:* www.earsc.com					
Edge-Sweets Co 2887 Three-Mile Rd NW	Grand Rapids	MI	49544	616-453-5458	453-5458
Web: www.edge-sweets.com					
Elliott Co of Indianapolis Inc					
9200 Zionsville Rd	Indianapolis	IN	46268	317-291-1213	291-1213
TF Orders: 800-545-1213 ■ *Web:* www.elliottfoam.com					
Fairmont Corp 2245 W Pershing Rd	Chicago	IL	60609	773-376-1300	376-3037
TF: 800-621-6907					
Federal Foam Technologies Inc					
600 Wisconsin Dr	New Richmond	WI	54017	715-246-9500	246-9500
TF: 800-898-9559 ■ *Web:* www.federalfoam.com					
Flexible Packaging Co Inc PO Box 4321	Bayamon	PR	00958	787-622-7225	622-7245
Web: www.flepak.com					
Flexpak Corp 3720 W Washington St	Phoenix	AZ	85009	602-269-7648	269-7640
Web: www.flexpakcorp.com					
Flextron Industries Inc 720 Mt Rd	Aston	PA	19014	610-459-4600	459-5379
TF: 800-633-2181 ■ *Web:* www.flextronindustries.com					
FM Corp 3535 Hudson Rd	Rogers	AR	72756	479-636-3540	631-2392
Web: www.fmplastics.com					
Foam Fabricators Inc 950 Progress Blvd	New Albany	IN	47150	812-948-1696	948-2450
Web: www.foamfabricatorsinc.com					
Foam Molders & Specialty Corp					
20004 State Rd	Cerritos	CA	90703	800-378-8987	924-2168*
**Fax Area Code:* 562 ■ *TF:* 800-378-8987 ■ *Web:* www.foammolders.com					
Foam Rubber Products Inc 2000 Troy Ave	New Castle	IN	47362	765-521-2000	521-2759
TF: 800-878-3774					
Foamade Industries Inc 2550 Auburn Ct	Auburn Hills	MI	48326	248-852-6010	853-3442
TF: 800-221-7388 ■ *Web:* www.foamade.com					
Fomo Products Inc 2775 Barber Rd	Norton	OH	44203	330-753-4585	753-9566*
**Fax:* Cust Svc ■ *TF:* 800-321-5585 ■ *Web:* www.fomo.com					
Free Flow Packaging International Inc					
1090 Mills Way	Redwood City	CA	94063	650-261-5300	361-1713
TF: 800-866-9946 ■ *Web:* www.fpintl.com					
Future Foam Inc 400 N 10th St	Council Bluffs	IA	51503	712-323-6718	323-7163
TF: 800-733-8067					
FXI					
Rose Tree Corporate Ctr II, 1400 Providence Rd					
Suite 2000	Media	PA	19063	610-744-2300	859-3035
TF: 800-355-3626 ■ *Web:* www.foamex.com					
Fypon Ltd 960 W Barre Rd	Archbold	OH	43502	800-446-3040	446-9373
TF: 800-955-5748 ■ *Web:* www.fypon.com					
G & T Industries Inc 1001 76th St SW	Byron Center	MI	49315	800-968-6035	583-1524*
**Fax Area Code:* 616 ■ *TF:* 800-968-6035 ■ *Web:* www.gtindustries.com					
Gaco Western Inc 200 W Mercer St # 202	Seattle	WA	98119	206-575-0450	575-0587
TF: 800-456-4226 ■ *Web:* www.gaco.com					
General Foam Plastics Corp					
3321 E Princess Anne Rd	Norfolk	VA	23502	757-857-0153	857-0033
Web: www.genfoam.com					
General Plastics Mfg Co 4910 S Burlington Way	Tacoma	WA	98409	253-473-5000	473-5104
TF: 800-806-6051 ■ *Web:* www.generalplastics.com					
Gilman Bros Co PO Box 38	Gilman	CT	06336	860-889-8444	889-5226
TF: 800-852-4220					
Guardian Packaging Inc 3615 Security St	Garland	TX	75042	214-349-1500	349-1584
TF: 800-259-1502 ■ *Web:* www.guardianpackaging.com					
Hibco Plastics Inc 1820 Us 601 Hwy	Yadkinville	NC	27055	336-463-2391	463-5591
TF: 800-849-8683					
Houston Foam Plastics Inc PO Box 1615	Houston	TX	77251	713-224-3484	
Web: www.houstonfoam.com					
Innovative Plastics Corp 400 Rt 303	Orangeburg	NY	10962	845-359-7500	359-0237
Intertrade Industries Ltd					
15632 Commerce Ln	Huntington Beach	CA	92649	714-894-5566	894-3927
TF: 800-944-9277 ■ *Web:* www.intertradeindustries.com					
King & Co Inc PO Box 10	Clarksville	AR	72830	479-754-6090	754-8445
TF Cust Svc: 800-643-9530 ■ *Web:* www.thermo-tile.com					
M & H Industries Inc 32500 Capitol St	Livonia	MI	48150	734-261-7560	261-9210
Mg International Inc 90 International Pkwy	Dallas	GA	30157	770-505-0004	943-4474
Minnesota Diversified Products Inc					
9091 County Rd 50	Rockford	MN	55373	763-477-5854	477-5863
TF: 800-669-0100 ■ *Web:* www.diversifoam.com					
Mossberg Industries Inc 204 N 2nd St	Garrett	IN	46738	260-357-5141	357-5144
Web: www.mossbergindustries.com					
Munot Plastics Inc 2935 W 17th St	Erie	PA	16505	814-838-7721	833-2095
Web: www.munotplastics.com					
North Carolina Foam Industries Inc					
1515 Carter St	Mount Airy	NC	27030	336-789-9161	789-9586
TF: 800-346-8229 ■ *Web:* www.ncfi.com					
Nu-Foam Products Inc					
220 S Elizabeth St PO Box 126	Spencerville	OH	45887	419-647-4191	647-4202
OPCO Inc PO Box 101	Latrobe	PA	15650	724-537-9300	537-9349
TF: 800-229-6726					
Pacific Packaging Products Inc					
24 Industrial Way	Wilmington	MA	01887	978-657-9100	658-4933
TF: 800-777-0300 ■ *Web:* www.pacificpkg.com					
Perry Chemical & Mfg Co Inc PO Box 6419	Lafayette	IN	47903	765-474-3404	474-3423
TF: 800-592-6614 ■ *Web:* www.perrychemical.com					
Plastomer Corp 37819 Schoolcraft Rd	Livonia	MI	48150	734-464-0700	464-4792
Web: www.plastomer.com					
PMC Global Inc 12243 Branford St	Sun Valley	CA	91352	818-896-1101	686-2531
TF: 800-423-5632 ■ *Web:* www.pmcglobalinc.com					
Poly Foam Inc 116 Pine St S	Lester Prairie	MN	55354	320-395-2551	395-2702
Web: www.polyfoaminc.com					
Poly Molding LLC 96 4th Ave	Haskell	NJ	07420	973-835-7161	835-2438
TF: 800-229-7161					
Polycel Structural Foam Inc					
68 County Line Rd	Somerville	NJ	08876	908-722-5254	722-7457
Web: www.polycel.com					
Premier Bldg Systems 4609 70th Ave E	Fife	WA	98424	253-926-2020	926-3992
TF: 800-275-7086 ■ *Web:* www.premiersips.com					
Radnor Holdings Corp					
150 Radnor Chester Rd Radnor Financial Ctr	Radnor	PA	19087	610-341-9600	995-2697
Web: www.radnorholdings.com					
Radva Corp PO Box 2900	Radford	VA	24143	540-639-2458	731-3731
Web: www.radva.com					
Republic Packaging Corp 9160 S Green St	Chicago	IL	60620	773-233-6530	233-6005
Web: www.repco.com					
RL Adams Plastics Inc					
5955 Crossroads Commerce	Wyoming	MI	49517	616-261-4400	249-8955
TF: 800-968-2241 ■ *Web:* www.adamsplasticsinc.com					
Robbie Mfg Inc 10810 Mid America Ave	Lenexa	KS	66219	913-492-3400	492-1543
TF: 800-255-6328 ■ *Web:* www.robbieflexibles.com					
Rogers Foam Corp 20 Vernon St	Somerville	MA	02145	617-623-3010	629-2585
Rubberlite Inc 2501 Guyan Ave	Huntington	WV	25703	304-525-3116	523-4316
Web: www.rubberlite.com					
Sekisui America Corp Voltek Div					
100 Shepard St	Lawrence	MA	01843	978-685-2557	685-9861
TF Cust Svc: 800-225-0668 ■ *Web:* www.voltek.com					
Spectratek Technologies Inc					
5405 Jandy Pl	Los Angeles	CA	90066	310-822-2400	822-2660
TF: 888-442-6567 ■ *Web:* www.spectratek.net					
Spongex Corp 6 Bridge St	Shelton	CT	06484	203-924-9335	924-0412
TF: 800-782-7749					
Storopack Inc 12007 S Woodruff Ave	Downey	CA	90241	562-803-1584	803-4462
TF: 800-829-1491 ■ *Web:* www.storopackinc.com					
Styrotek Inc 545 Rd 176	Delano	CA	93215	661-725-4957	725-7064
TF: 800-936-2611 ■ *Web:* www.styrotek.com					
ThermoSafe Brands					
3930 N Ventura Dr Suite 450	Arlington Heights	IL	60004	847-398-0110	398-0653
TF: 800-323-7442 ■ *Web:* www.thermosafe.com					
ThermoServ 3901 Pipestone Rd	Dallas	TX	75212	214-631-0307	631-0566
TF: 800-635-5559 ■ *Web:* www.thermoserv.com					
TMP Technologies Inc 1200 Northland Ave	Buffalo	NY	14215	716-895-6100	895-6396
Web: www.tmptech.com					
Topp Industries Inc					
420 N State Rd 25 PO Box 420	Rochester	IN	46975	574-223-3681	223-6106
TF: 800-354-4534 ■ *Web:* www.toppindustries.com					
UFP Technologies Inc 172 E Main St	Georgetown	MA	01833	978-352-2200	352-7169
NASDAQ: UFPT ■ *TF:* 800-372-3172 ■ *Web:* www.ufpt.com					
Unique Fabricating Inc					
800 Standard Pkwy	Auburn Hills	MI	48326	248-853-2333	853-7720
Web: www.uniquefab.com					
WinCup 4640 Lewis Rd	Stone Mountain	GA	30083	770-938-5281	
TF: 800-292-2877 ■ *Web:* www.wincup.com					
Woodbridge Foam Corp					
4240 Sherwoodtowne Blvd	Mississauga	ON	L4Z2G6	905-896-3626	896-9262
Web: www.woodbridgegroup.com					

605 PLASTICS MACHINING & FORMING

SEE ALSO Plastics Molding - Custom p. 2428

Company	City	State	ZIP	Phone	Fax
Akra Plastic Products Inc 1504 E Cedar St	Ontario	CA	91761	909-930-1999	930-1948
Bardes Plastics Inc 5225 W Clinton Ave	Milwaukee	WI	53223	414-354-5300	354-6331
TF Cust Svc: 800-558-5161 ■ *Web:* www.bardesplastics.com					
Bo-Mer Mfg Co 13 Pulaski St	Auburn	NY	13021	315-252-7216	252-7450
TF: 800-221-6563 ■ *Web:* www.bo-mer.com					
Cal Plastics 2050 E 48th St	Los Angeles	CA	90058	323-581-6194	581-1805
Comco Plastics Inc 98-34 Jamaica Ave	Woodhaven	NY	11421	718-849-9000	441-5361
TF: 800-849-0731 ■ *Web:* www.comcoplastics.com					
Conroy & Knowlton Inc 320 S Montebello Blvd	Montebello	CA	90640	323-665-5288	722-4670
TF: 888-295-9500 ■ *Web:* www.conroyknowlton.com					
East Jordan Plastics Inc PO Box 575	East Jordan	MI	49727	231-536-2243	536-7090
Web: www.eastjordanplastics.com					
Empire West Inc 9270 Graton Rd PO Box 511	Graton	CA	95444	707-823-1190	823-8531
TF: 800-521-4261 ■ *Web:* www.empirewest.com					
Engineered Plastics Inc 212 Chase St	Gibsonville	NC	27249	336-449-4121	449-6352
TF: 800-711-1740 ■ *Web:* www.engplas.com					
Fabri-Form Co 200 S Friendship Dr	New Concord	OH	43762	740-826-5000	826-5001
TF: 800-837-2574 ■ *Web:* www.fabri-form.com					
Fabri-Kal Corp 600 Plastics Pl	Kalamazoo	MI	49001	269-385-5050	385-0197
TF: 800-888-5054 ■ *Web:* www.fabri-kal.com					
Filtrona Richmond Inc 1625-A Ashton Pk Dr	Colonial Heights	VA	23834	804-275-2631	743-0321
Web: www.fibrtec.com					
FNW Industrial Plastics Inc 12500 Jefferson Ave PO Box 2778	Newport News	VA	23602	360-835-2129	835-3521
TF: 800-634-5082 ■ *Web:* www.ferguson.com					
Formall Inc 3908 Fountain Valley Dr	Knoxville	TN	37918	865-922-7514	922-3941
TF: 800-643-3676 ■ *Web:* www.formall.com					
Formed Plastics Inc 207 Stonehinge Ln	Carle Place	NY	11514	516-343-2300	334-2679
Web: www.formedplastics.com					
Gage Industries Inc 6710 McEwan Rd	Lake Oswego	OR	97035	503-639-2177	624-1070
TF: 800-443-4243 ■ *Web:* www.gageindustries.com					
Graham Machinery Group 1203 Eden Rd	York	PA	17402	717-848-3755	848-3916
Web: www.grahammachinerygroup.com					
Gregstrom Corp 64 Holton St	Woburn	MA	01801	781-935-6600	935-4905
Web: www.gregstrom.com					
Harvel Plastics Inc 300 Kuebler Rd	Easton	PA	18040	610-252-7355	253-4436
Web: www.harvel.com					
Inline Plastics Corp 42 Canal St	Shelton	CT	06484	203-924-5933	924-0370
TF: 800-826-5567 ■ *Web:* www.inlineplastics.com					
Innovize Inc 500 Oak Grove Pkwy	Saint Paul	MN	55127	651-490-0000	490-1651
TF: 877-605-6580 ■ *Web:* www.innovize.com					
Jamestown Plastics Inc 98 Highland Ave	Brocton	NY	14716	716-792-4144	792-4154
Web: www.jamestownplastics.com					
Lamar Plastic Packaging Ltd 216 N Main St	Freeport	NY	11520	516-378-2500	378-6192
Mack Prototype Inc 424 Main St	Gardner	MA	01440	978-632-3700	632-3777
Web: www.mackprototype.com					
Mantex Corp 611 Industrial Pkwy	Imlay City	MI	48444	810-721-2100	721-9911
TF: 800-666-2689					
McNeal Enterprises Inc 2031 Ringwood Ave	San Jose	CA	95131	408-922-7290	922-7299
TF: 800-562-6325 ■ *Web:* www.mcnealplasticmachining.com					
Meyer Plastics Inc 5167 E 65th St	Indianapolis	IN	46220	317-259-4131	252-4687
TF: 800-968-4131 ■ *Web:* www.meyerplastics.com					
Morgan Hill Plastics Inc 640 E Dunne Ave	Morgan Hill	CA	95037	408-779-2118	779-0322
TF: 800-449-0322 ■ *Web:* www.morganhillplastics.com					
New Concept Mfg LLC 320 Busser Rd PO Box 297	Emigsville	PA	17318	717-741-0840	741-4301
Web: www.newconceptmfg.com					
Panterra Engineered Plastics 68 Southfield Ave 2 Stamford Landing Suite 100	Stamford	CT	06902	203-921-0345	921-0344
Web: www.ptonline.com/index.html					
Paradise Plastics PO Drawer Y	Plant City	FL	33563	813-752-1155	754-3168
Web: www.paradiseplastics.com					
Paramount Plastics Inc 15160 New Ave	Lockport	IL	60441	815-834-4100	834-1920
Web: www.paramountplastics.net					
Parkway Products Inc 10293 Burlington Rd	Cincinnati	OH	45231	513-851-5550	851-1926
Web: www.parkwayproducts.com					
Parsons Mfg Corp 1055 O'Brien Dr	Menlo Park	CA	94025	650-324-4726	324-3051
TF: 800-221-0823 ■ *Web:* www.espis.com/parsons/index.html					
Parsons Precision Products Inc 3333 Main St	Parsons	KS	67357	620-421-3400	421-2301
Web: www.parsonsprecision.com					
Perkasie Industries Corp PO Box 179	Perkasie	PA	18944	215-257-6581	453-1703
TF Sales: 800-523-6747					
Placon Corp 6096 McKee Rd	Madison	WI	53719	608-271-5634	271-3162
TF: 800-541-1535 ■ *Web:* www.placon.com					
Polygon Co 103 Industrial Pk Dr PO Box 176	Walkerton	IN	46574	574-586-3145	586-7336
TF: 800-918-9261 ■ *Web:* www.polygoncomposites.com					
Precision Molding Inc 5500 Roberts Matthews Hwy	Sparta	TN	38583	931-738-8376	738-8429
Web: www.precision-molding.com					
Prent Corp 2225 Kennedy Rd	Janesville	WI	53545	608-754-0276	754-2410
Web: www.prent.com					
Productive Plastics Inc 103 W Pk Dr	Mount Laurel	NJ	08054	856-778-4300	234-3310
Web: www.productiveplastics.com					
Progress Plastic Products Inc 420 Monroe St	Bellevue	OH	44811	419-483-3538	483-4850
Web: www.progressplastic.com					
PSC Mfg Inc 3424 De La Cruz Blvd	Santa Clara	CA	95054	408-988-5115	988-4044
Quadrant Engineering Plastic Products USA 2120 Fairmont Ave PO Box 14235	Reading	PA	19612	610-320-6600	320-6868*
**Fax:* Sales ■ *TF:* 800-366-0300 ■ *Web:* www.quadrantepp.com					
Ray Products Co Inc 1700 Chablis Ave	Ontario	CA	91761	909-390-9906	390-9984
TF: 800-423-7859 ■ *Web:* www.rayplastics.com					
Roncelli Plastics Inc 330 W Duarte Rd	Monrovia	CA	91016	626-359-2551	358-4329
Web: www.roncelli.com					
Ronningen Research & Development Co 6700 E 'YZ' Ave	Vicksburg	MI	49097	269-649-0520	649-0526
Web: www.ronningenresearch.com					
Soroc Products Inc Plastics Div 4349 S Dort Hwy	Burton	MI	48529	810-743-2660	743-5922
Web: www.sorocproducts.com					
Spaulding Composites Co Fab Div 55 Nadeau Dr	Rochester	NH	03867	603-332-0555	332-5357
TF: 800-964-0555 ■ *Web:* www.spauldingcom.com					
Speck Plastics Inc PO Box 421	Nazareth	PA	18064	610-759-1807	759-3916
TF: 800-755-2922 ■ *Web:* www.speckplastics.com					
Stewart Industries Inc 16 S Idaho St	Seattle	WA	98134	206-652-9110	652-9123
Sur-Flo Plastics & Engineering Inc 24358 Groesbeck Hwy	Warren	MI	48089	586-773-0400	773-8946
Web: www.sur-flo.com					
Teak Isle Mfg Inc 401 Capitol Court PO Box 417	Ocoee	FL	34761	407-656-8885	656-2344
Web: www.teakisle.com					
Tetralene Inc 875 Wakefield Dr	Houston	TX	77018	713-695-4011	699-0479
Web: www.tetralene.com					
Thermo-Fab Corp 76 Walker Rd	Shirley	MA	01464	978-425-2311	425-2305
Web: www.thermofab.com					
Topcraft precision Molders Inc 301 Ivyland Rd	WARMINSTER	PA	18974	215-441-4700	441-0847
TF: 800-441-4710 ■ *Web:* www.topcraft.com					
Total Plastics Inc 3316 Pagosa Ct	Indianapolis	IN	46226	317-543-3540	543-3553
TF: 800-382-4635 ■ *Web:* www.totalplastics.com					
Tri-Town Precision Plastics Inc 12 Bridge St	Deep River	CT	06417	860-526-3200	526-4848
Web: www.ttplastics.com					
Underwood Mold Co Inc 104 Dixie Dr PO Box 1607	Woodstock	GA	30188	770-926-2465	926-6565
Web: www.underwoodmoldco.com					
Western Fibre Products Inc 10924 Vulcan St	South Gate	CA	90280	562-861-6665	862-9692

606 PLASTICS MATERIALS - WHOL

Company	City	State	ZIP	Phone	Fax
A Daigger & Co Inc 620 Lakeview Pkwy	Vernon Hills	IL	60061	847-816-5060	320-7200*
**Fax Area Code:* 800 ■ *TF:* 800-621-7193 ■ *Web:* www.daigger.com					
Aetna Plastics Corp 1702 St Clair Ave	Cleveland	OH	44114	216-781-4421	781-4474
TF: 800-634-3074 ■ *Web:* www.aetnaplastics.com					
AIN Plastics Inc 1750 E Heights Dr	Madison Heights	MI	48071	248-356-4000	542-3920
TF Cust Svc: 800-521-1757 ■ *Web:* www.ainplastics.com					
All American Containers Inc 9330 NW 110th Ave	Miami	FL	33178	305-887-0797	888-4133
Web: www.americancontainers.com					
Allpak Co 1010 Lake St	Oak Park	IL	60301	708-383-7200	383-7206
Aztec Supply Co 954 N Batavia St	Orange	CA	92867	714-771-6580	771-3013
Web: www.aztecblaze.com					
Bamberger Polymers Inc 2 Jericho Plaza Suite 109	Jericho	NY	11753	516-622-3600	622-3610
TF: 800-888-8959 ■ *Web:* www.bambergerpolymers.com					
Buckley Industries Inc 1850 E 53rd St N	Wichita	KS	67219	316-744-7587	744-8463
TF: 800-835-2779 ■ *Web:* www.buckleyind.com					
Calsak Corp 1225 W 190th St Suite 375	Gardena	CA	90248	310-719-9500	719-1300
TF: 800-743-2595 ■ *Web:* www.calsak.com					
Cope Plastics Inc 4441 Industrial Dr	Godfrey	IL	62035	618-466-0221	467-7751*
**Fax:* Acctg ■ *TF:* 800-851-5510 ■ *Web:* www.copeplastics.com					
El Mar Plastics Inc 303 W Artesia Blvd	Compton	CA	90220	310-928-0205	928-0207
TF: 800-255-5210 ■ *Web:* www.elmarplastics.com					
GE Polymerland 9930 Kincey Ave	Huntersville	NC	28078	704-992-5100	752-7842*
**Fax Area Code:* 888 ■ *TF:* 800-752-7842					
H Muehlstein & Co Inc 800 Connecticut Ave	Norwalk	CT	06854	203-855-6000	855-6221
TF: 800-257-3746 ■ *Web:* www.muehlstein.com					
H Sattler Plastics Co Inc 5410 W Roosevelt Rd	Chicago	IL	60644	312-733-2900	733-5290
Web: www.sattlerplastics.com					
Laird Plastics Inc 6800 Broken Sound Pkwy Suite 150	Boca Raton	FL	33487	561-443-9100	443-9108
TF: 800-610-1016 ■ *Web:* www.lairdplastics.com					
Louisiana Utilities Supply PO Box 3531	Baton Rouge	LA	70821	225-383-8916	387-5256
TF: 800-743-8916					
M Holland Co 400 Skokie Blvd Suite 600	Northbrook	IL	60062	847-272-7370	272-0525
TF: 800-872-7370 ■ *Web:* www.m-holland.com					
Momentum Technologies Inc (MTI) 1507 Boettler Rd	Uniontown	OH	44685	330-896-5900	896-9943
TF: 800-720-0261 ■ *Web:* www.momentumtech.net					
Multi-Plastics Inc 7770 N Central Dr	Lewis Center	OH	43035	740-548-4894	548-5177
Web: www.multi-plastics.com					
Nytef Plastics Ltd Inc 6643 42nd Ter N	West Palm Beach	FL	33407	561-840-9499	638-7674*
**Fax Area Code:* 215 ■ *TF:* 800-646-9833 ■ *Web:* www.nytefplastics.com					
Orange County Industrial Plastics Inc 4811 E La Palma Ave	Anaheim	CA	92807	714-632-9450	630-6489
TF: 800-974-6247 ■ *Web:* www.ocip.com					
Pacific Nursery Pots Inc PO Box 580	Morgan Hill	CA	95038	408-778-3426	778-6294
TF: 800-468-8686					
Pilcher Hamilton Corp 6845 Kingery Hwy	Willowbrook	IL	60527	630-655-8100	655-9948
Web: www.pilcherhamilton.com					
Plastic Sales Southern Inc 6490 Fleet St	Los Angeles	CA	90040	323-728-8309	722-4221
TF: 800-257-7747					
PlastiFab Inc 1425 Palomares Ave	La Verne	CA	91750	909-596-1927	596-3020
TF: 800-421-9880 ■ *Web:* www.plastifabonline.com					
Port Plastics Inc 15325 Fairfield Ranch Rd Suite 150	Chino Hills	CA	91709	909-393-5894	597-0116
TF: 800-800-0039 ■ *Web:* www.portplastics.com					
Regal Plastic Supply Co 111 E 10th Ave	North Kansas City	MO	64116	816-421-6290	421-8206
TF: 800-627-2102 ■ *Web:* www.regalplastic.com					
Regal Plastic Supply Co Southern Div 2356 Merrell Rd	Dallas	TX	75229	972-484-0741	484-0746
TF: 800-441-1553 ■ *Web:* www.regal-plastics.com					

Company	City	State	ZIP	Phone	Fax
Ryan Herco Products Corp 3010 N San Fernando Blvd *TF:* 800-848-1141 ■ *Web:* www.ryanherco.com	Burbank	CA	91504	818-841-1141	973-2600
Seelye Plastics Inc 9700 Newton Ave S **Fax:* Sales ■ *TF:* 800-328-2728 ■ *Web:* www.seelye-plastics.com	Bloomington	MN	55431	952-881-2658	881-3503*
Sekisui America Corp 100 Gaither Dr Suite A *TF:* 800-866-4005 ■ *Web:* www.sekisui-corp.com	Mount Laurel	NJ	08054	856-235-5115	235-0097
Superior Oil Co Inc 1402 N Capitol Ave # 100 *TF:* 800-553-5480 ■ *Web:* www.superioroil.com	Indianapolis	IN	46202	317-781-4400	781-4401
Targun Plastics Co 899 Skokie Blvd	Northbrook	IL	60062	847-509-9355	509-9359
Tech Products Inc 1264-D La Quinta Dr *Web:* www.techprod.com	Orlando	FL	32809	407-447-6108	447-6115
Tekra Corp 16700 W Lincoln Ave *TF:* 800-448-3572 ■ *Web:* www.tekra.com	New Berlin	WI	53151	262-784-5533	797-3276

607 PLASTICS MOLDING - CUSTOM

Company	City	State	ZIP	Phone	Fax
A M A Plastics 350 W Rincon St *Web:* www.amaplastics.com	Corona	CA	92880	951-734-5600	734-5666
Akron Porcelain & Plastics Co 2739 Cory Ave PO Box 15157 *Web:* www.akronporcelain.com	Akron	OH	44314	330-745-2159	745-6688
Aline Components Inc 1830 Tomlinson Rd PO Box 263 *Web:* www.alinecomponents.com	Kulpsville	PA	19443	215-368-0300	361-1400
Alladin Plastics Inc 140 Industrial Dr *TF:* 800-960-2351 ■ *Web:* www.alladinplastics.com	Surgoinsville	TN	37873	423-345-2351	345-3772
American Metal & Plastics Inc 450 32nd St SW *Web:* www.ampi-gr.com	Grand Rapids	MI	49548	616-452-6061	452-3835
American Plastic Molding Corp 965 S Elm St *TF:* 877-527-8427 ■ *Web:* www.apmc.com	Scottsburg	IN	47170	812-752-7000	752-5155
American Plastics Group Inc 715 W Pk Rd *TF:* 800-325-9927	Union	MO	63084	636-583-2584	583-4357
American Urethane Inc 1905 Betson Ct *Web:* www.americanurethane.com	Odenton	MD	21113	410-672-2100	672-2191
Ams Plastics Inc 1530 Hilton Head Rd Suite 205 *Web:* www.amsplastics.com	El Cajon	CA	92019	619-713-2000	713-2975
Apollo Plastics Corp 5333 N Elston Ave	Chicago	IL	60630	773-282-9222	282-2763
Applied Composites Corp 333 N 6th St *TF:* 877-653-9577 ■ *Web:* www.appliedcompositescorp.birkey.com	Saint Charles	IL	60174	877-653-9577	653-9576
Applied Tech Products 565 Swedesford Rd Suite 315 *Web:* www.appliedtechproducts.com	Wayne	PA	19087	610-688-2200	688-1534
Arkay Industries Inc 220 American Way *Web:* www.arkayindustries.com	Monroe	OH	45050	513-360-0390	
Arrowhead Plastic Engineering Inc 2909 S Hoyt Ave *Web:* www.arrowheadinc.com	Muncie	IN	47302	765-286-0533	286-1681
ASK Plastics Inc 9750 Ashton Rd *Web:* www.askplastics.com	Philadelphia	PA	19114	215-969-0800	969-2164
B & S Plastics Inc 2200 Sturgis Rd *TF:* 888-772-5387 ■ *Web:* www.waterwayplastics.com	Oxnard	CA	93030	805-981-0262	981-9403
Bain Mfg Co Inc 2 Main St	Grenada	MS	38901	662-226-7921	226-7701
Bekum America Corp 1140 W Grand River Ave PO Box 567 *Web:* www.bekumamerica.com	Williamston	MI	48895	517-655-4331	655-4121
Berry Plastics Corp 101 Oakley St *TF:* 800-234-1930 ■ *Web:* www.berryplastics.com	Evansville	IN	47710	812-424-2904	424-0128
BMJ Mold & Engineering Co Inc 1104 Touby Pike *TF:* 800-238-7785 ■ *Web:* www.bmjmold.com	Kokomo	IN	46901	765-457-1166	459-3664
C & J Industries 760 Water St *Web:* www.cjindustries.com	Meadville	PA	16335	814-724-4950	724-4959
C Brewer Co 3630 E Miraloma Ave *Web:* www.cbrewer.com	Anaheim	CA	92806	714-630-6810	630-5527
Canton Mfg 120 E 2nd St	Canton	PA	17724	570-673-5145	673-6819
Capsonic Group 495 Renner Dr *Web:* www.capsonic.com	Elgin	IL	60123	847-888-7300	888-7543
Centro Inc 950 N Bend Dr *Web:* www.centroinc.com	North Liberty	IA	52317	319-626-3200	626-3203
Commercial Plastics Co 800 E Allanson Rd *Web:* www.ecommercialplastics.com	Mundelein	IL	60060	847-566-1700	566-4737
Confer Plastics Inc (CPI) 97 Witmer Rd *TF:* 800-635-3213 ■ *Web:* www.conferplastics.com	North Tonawanda	NY	14120	716-693-2056	694-3102
Connor Corp 10633 Coldwater Rd # 200 *Web:* www.connorcorp.com	Fort Wayne	IN	46845	260-424-1601	422-7202
Core Molding Technologies Inc (CMT) 800 Manor Pk Dr *AMEX:* CMT ■ *Web:* www.coremt.com	Columbus	OH	43228	614-870-5000	870-5051
Cosmo Corp 30201 Aurora Rd *Web:* www.cosmocorp.com	Cleveland	OH	44139	440-498-7500	498-7515
Cuyahoga Molded Plastics Corp 1265 Babbitt Rd *TF:* 800-805-9549 ■ *Web:* www.cuyahogaplastics.com	Cleveland	OH	44132	216-261-2744	261-3537
D & M Plastic Corp 150 French Rd PO Box 158 *Web:* www.dmplastics.com	Burlington	IL	60109	847-683-2054	683-2731
D-M-E Co 29111 Stephenson Hwy *TF:* 800-626-6653 ■ *Web:* www.dme.net	Madison Heights	MI	48071	248-398-6000	544-5705
Design & Molding Services Inc 25 Howard St	Piscataway	NJ	08854	732-752-0300	752-9672
Dickten & Masch LLC N 44 W 33341 Watertown Plank Rd *Web:* www.dicktenplastics.com	Nashotah	WI	53058	262-367-5200	367-5630
Diemolding Corp 125 Rasbach St *Web:* www.diemolding.com	Canastota	NY	13032	315-697-2221	697-2221
Double H Plastics Inc 50 W St Rd *TF:* 800-523-3932 ■ *Web:* www.doublehplastics.com	Warminster	PA	18974	215-674-4100	674-4109
EFP Corp 223 Middleton Run Rd *TF:* 800-205-8537 ■ *Web:* www.efpcorp.com	Elkhart	IN	46516	574-295-4690	295-6512
Eifel Mold & Engineering 31071 Fraser Dr *Web:* www.eifel-inc.com	Fraser	MI	48026	586-296-9640	296-7280
Elgin Molded Plastics 909 Grace St **Fax Area Code:* 800 ■ *TF:* 800-548-5483 ■ *Web:* www.elginmolded.com	Elgin	IL	60120	847-931-2455	524-0087*
Engineered Plastic Components 53150 N Main St *Web:* www.alcoa.com	Mattawan	MI	49071	269-668-3397	668-3276
Erie Plastics 844 Rt 6	Corry	PA	16407	814-664-4661	664-4661
Evans Industries Inc 200 Renaissance Ctr Suite 3150	Detroit	MI	48243	313-259-2266	259-4687
Evco Plastics Inc 100 W N St *TF:* 800-507-6000 ■ *Web:* www.evcoplastics.com	DeForest	WI	53532	608-846-6000	846-6050
Falcon Plastics Inc 1313 Western Ave *Web:* www.falconplastics.com	Brookings	SD	57006	605-696-2500	696-2585
Fawn Industries Inc 1920 Greenspring Dr Suite 140 *Web:* www.fawn-ind.com	Timonium	MD	21093	410-308-9200	308-9201
Filtertek Inc 11411 Price Rd *TF:* 800-248-2461 ■ *Web:* www.filtertek.com	Hebron	IL	60034	815-648-2416	648-2929
Flambeau Inc 15981 Valplast Rd *TF:* 800-457-5252 ■ *Web:* www.flambeau.com	Middlefield	OH	44062	440-632-1631	632-1581
FPI Thermoplastic Technologies PO Box 1907 *TF:* 800-932-0715	Morristown	NJ	07962	973-539-4200	539-4200
Graber-Rogg Inc 22 Jackson Dr *Web:* www.graber-rogg.com	Cranford	NJ	07016	908-272-4422	272-0134
Green Tokai Co Ltd 55 Robert Wright Dr *Web:* www.greentokai.com	Brookville	OH	45309	937-833-5444	833-2087
Gruber Systems Inc 25636 Ave Stanford *TF:* 800-257-4070 ■ *Web:* www.gruber-systems.com	Valencia	CA	91355	661-257-4060	257-4791
Guardian Automotive Trim Inc 601 N Congress Ave *Web:* www.srgglobalinc.com	Evansville	IN	47715	812-473-6200	473-6320
GW Plastics Inc 239 Pleasant St *Web:* www.gwplastics.com	Bethel	VT	05032	802-234-9941	234-9940
Hampson Industries PLC 802 Ave J E PO Box 534036 *Web:* www.texstars.com	Grand Prairie	TX	75053	972-647-1366	606-0232
Hoffer Plastics Corp 500 N Collins St *Web:* www.hofferplastics.com	South Elgin	IL	60177	847-741-5740	741-3086
Industrial Molding Corp 616 E Slaton Rd *Web:* www.indmolding.com	Lubbock	TX	79404	806-474-1000	474-1168
Injectech Industries Inc 501 Welham Rd *Web:* www.injectech.com	Barrie	ON	L4N8Z6	705-737-2242	737-4523
Injectronics Inc 1 Union St *TF:* 888-368-8701 ■ *Web:* www.injectronics.com	Clinton	MA	01510	978-368-8701	368-7941
Innovative Injection Technologies Inc 2360 Grand Ave *Web:* www.i2-tech.com	West Des Moines	IA	50265	515-225-6707	225-9673
Intec Group Inc 666 S Vermont St *Web:* www.intecgrp.com	Palatine	IL	60067	847-358-0088	358-4391
Ironwood Industries Inc 115 S Bradley Rd *Web:* www.ironind.com	Libertyville	IL	60048	847-362-8681	362-9190
Jarden Plastic Solutions PO Box 2750 *TF:* 888-291-5757 ■ *Web:* www.jardenplasticsolutions.com	Greenville	SC	29602	864-879-7600	877-4976
Jones & Vining Inc 1115 W Chestnut St *Web:* www.jonesandvining.com	Brockton	MA	02301	508-232-7470	232-7477
Jones Plastic & Engineering Co LLC 2410 S Plantside Dr *Web:* www.jonesplastic.com	Louisville	KY	40299	502-491-3785	499-2185
Jordan Specialty Plastics Inc 1751 Lake Cook Rd ArborLake Ctr Suite 550 *Web:* www.jordanindustries.com	Deerfield	IL	60015	847-945-5591	945-9645
Juno Inc 1100 McKinley St *Web:* www.junoinc.com	Anoka	MN	55303	763-553-1312	553-1360
Kennerley Spratling Inc 2116 Farallon Dr	San Leandro	CA	94577	510-351-8230	352-9240
Kenro Inc 200 Industrial Dr	Fredonia	WI	53021	262-692-2411	692-9141
Key Plastics Inc 21700 Haggerty Rd Suite 100-N *Web:* www.keyplastics.com	Northville	MI	48167	248-449-6100	449-4105
KI Industries Inc 5540 McDermott Dr *Web:* www.kiindustries.com	Berkeley	IL	60163	708-449-1990	449-1997
Kurz-Kasch Inc 511 Byers Rd *Web:* www.kurz-kasch.com	Miamisburg	OH	45342	937-299-0990	299-9292
Kyowa America Corp 14600 Hoover St *Web:* www.kyowaamerica.com	Westminster	CA	92683	714-889-6600	889-6699
Lacks Enterprises 5460 Cascade Rd SE *Web:* www.lacksenterprises.com	Grand Rapids	MI	49546	616-949-6570	285-2367
Lakeland Tool & Engineering Inc 2939 6th Ave *Web:* www.lte.biz	Anoka	MN	55303	763-422-8866	422-8867
Lehigh Valley Plastics Inc 187 N Commerce Way *TF:* 800-354-5344 ■ *Web:* www.lehighvalleyplastics.com	Bethlehem	PA	18017	484-893-5500	893-5513
Lenco Inc - PMC 10240 Deer Pk Rd PO Box 590 *TF:* 800-457-5612 ■ *Web:* www.lencopmc.com	Waverly	NE	68462	402-786-2000	786-2096
Leon Plastics Inc 4901 Clay Ave SW *TF:* 800-285-5366 ■ *Web:* www.leonplastics.com	Grand Rapids	MI	49548	616-531-7970	531-3393
LMC Industries Inc 100 Manufacturers Dr *Web:* www.lmcindustries.com	Arnold	MO	63010	636-282-8080	282-7114
M & Q Plastic Products 1120 Welsh Rd Suite 170 *TF:* 877-726-7287 ■ *Web:* www.mqplasticproducts.com	North Wales	PA	19454	267-498-4000	498-0030
Mack Molding Co Inc 608 Warm Brook Rd **Fax:* Hum Res ■ *Web:* www.mack.com	Arlington	VT	05250	802-375-2511	375-0792*
Makray Mfg Co 4400 N Harlem Ave *Web:* www.makray.com	Norridge	IL	60706	708-456-7100	456-7178

Company / Address	City	State	Zip	Phone	Fax
Mar-Lee Cos 55 Marshall St *Web:* www.mar-leecompanies.com	Leominster	MA	01453	978-534-8305	534-0472
Marland Mold Inc 12 Betnr Industrial Dr *Web:* www.marlandmold.com	Pittsfield	MA	01201	413-443-4481	443-1095
Master Molded Products Corp 1000 Davis Rd *Web:* www.mastermolded.com	Elgin	IL	60123	847-695-9700	695-9707
Meridian Automotive Systems Inc 999 Republic Dr	Allen Park	MI	48101	313-336-4182	336-4184
Midwest Plastic Components 7309 W 27th St *Web:* www.spectrumplasticsgroup.com	Minneapolis	MN	55426	952-929-3312	929-8404
Miner Elastomer Products Corp 1200 E State St PO Box 471 *Web:* www.minerelastomer.com	Geneva	IL	60134	630-232-3000	232-3172
Molded Fiber Glass Cos 2925 MFG Pl PO Box 675 *TF:* 800-860-0196 ■ *Web:* www.moldedfiberglass.com	Ashtabula	OH	44005	440-997-5851	994-5162
Molding Corp of America 10349 Norris Ave *TF:* 800-423-2747 ■ *Web:* www.moldingcorp.com	Pacoima	CA	91331	818-890-7877	890-7885
Mullinix Packages Inc 3511 Engle Rd *Web:* www.mullinixpackages.com	Fort Wayne	IN	46809	260-747-3149	747-1598
MXL Industries Inc 1764 Rohrerstown Rd *TF:* 800-233-0159 ■ *Web:* www.mxl-industries.com	Lancaster	PA	17601	717-569-8711	569-8716
National Molding Corp Security Plastics Div 14427 NW 60th Ave *TF:* 800-327-3787 ■ *Web:* www.securityplastics.com	Miami Lakes	FL	33014	305-823-5440	557-1431
Norland Plastics Co 117 Baughman Ave	Haysville	KS	67060	316-522-4887	522-1603
Nyloncraft Inc 616 W McKinley Ave *Web:* www.nyloncraft.com	Mishawaka	IN	46545	574-256-1521	255-3278
Nypro Inc 101 Union St *Web:* www.nypro.com	Clinton	MA	01510	978-365-9721	365-4352
NYX Inc 36111 Schoolcraft Rd *Web:* www.natplastics.com	Livonia	MI	48150	734-462-2385	
PECO Mfg Co Inc PO Box 82189 *Web:* www.pecomanufacturing.com	Portland	OR	97282	503-233-6401	233-6407
Pelham Products Inc 46 Payne Rd	Bethel	CT	06801	203-792-1515	798-1892
Plaspros Inc 1143 Ridgeview Dr *Web:* www.plaspros.com	McHenry	IL	60050	815-430-2300	430-2260
Plastech Corp 5481 St Croix Trail Suite 200 *TF:* 800-223-0462 ■ *Web:* www.plastechcorporation.com	North Branch	MN	55056	651-407-5700	407-5650
Plastek Group 2425 W 23rd St *Web:* www.plastekgroup.com	Erie	PA	16506	814-878-4400	878-4529
Plastic Components Inc N 116 W 18271 Morse Dr *Fax Area Code: 262 ■ *TF:* 877-253-1496 ■ *Web:* www.plasticcomponents.com	Germantown	WI	53022	877-253-1496	253-3682*
Plastic Design International Inc 111 Industrial Pk Rd *Web:* www.plasticdesign.com	Middletown	CT	06457	860-632-2001	632-1776
Plastic Molded Concepts Inc PO Box 490 *Web:* www.pmcplastics.com	Eagle	WI	53119	262-594-5050	594-5075
Plastic Moldings Co LLC 2181 Grand Ave *TF:* 800-927-5040 ■ *Web:* www.pmcsmartsolutions.com	Cincinnati	OH	45214	513-921-5040	921-5883
Plastic Products Co Inc 30355 Akerson St *Web:* www.plasticproductsco.com	Lindstrom	MN	55045	651-257-5980	257-9774
Plastic-Plate Inc 5460 Cascade Rd SE	Grand Rapids	MI	49546	616-949-6570	285-2367
Plastics Group Inc 7409 S Quincy St *Web:* www.theplasticsgroup.net	Willowbrook	IL	60527	630-325-1210	325-1393
Plastics Molding Co Inc 4211 N Broadway	Saint Louis	MO	63147	314-241-2479	241-3757
Polymer Corp 180 Pleasant St *Web:* www.polymerdesign.com	Rockland	MA	02370	781-871-4606	871-5460
Port Erie Plastics Inc 909 Troupe Rd *Web:* www.porterie.com	Harborcreek	PA	16421	814-899-7602	899-7854
Precision Plastics Inc 900 W Connexion Way *Web:* www.pplastic.com	Columbia City	IN	46725	260-244-6114	244-5995
Premix Inc US Rt 20 PO Box 281 *Web:* www.premix.com	North Kingsville	OH	44068	440-224-2181	224-2766
Product Miniature Co 627 Capitol Dr *Web:* www.pmplastic.com	Pewaukee	WI	53072	262-691-1700	691-4405
Proper Mold & Engineering Inc 13870 E 11-Mile Rd	Warren	MI	48089	586-779-8787	779-4530
PTA Corp 148 Christian St *Web:* www.ptacorp.com	Oxford	CT	06478	203-888-0585	888-1757
Putnam Precision Molding Inc 11 Danco Rd *TF:* 800-752-7865 ■ *Web:* www.putnamprecisionmolding.com	Putnam	CT	06260	860-928-7911	928-2229
QMR Plastics 434 Highland Dr *Web:* www.mnrubber.com/qmrplastics	River Falls	WI	54022	715-426-4700	426-5115
Quality Mold Inc 2200 Massillon Rd *Web:* www.qualitymold.com	Akron	OH	44312	330-645-6653	645-2493
R & R Technologies LLC 7560 E County Line Rd *Web:* www.rrtech.com	Edinburgh	IN	46124	812-526-2655	526-9294
Recto Molded Products Inc (RMP) 4425 Appleton St *Web:* www.rectomolded.com	Cincinnati	OH	45209	513-871-5544	871-8495
REO Plastics Inc 11850 93rd Ave N *Web:* www.reoplastics.com	Maple Grove	MN	55369	763-425-4171	425-0735
Rodgard 92 Msgr Valente Dr *Web:* www.rodgard.com	Buffalo	NY	14206	716-823-1411	852-7690
Royal Plastics Inc 9410 Pineneedle Dr *TF:* 800-533-2163 ■ *Web:* www.royalplastics.com	Mentor	OH	44060	440-352-1357	352-6681
Sabin Corp 3800 Constitution Ave PO Box 788 *TF:* 800-264-4510 ■ *Web:* www.cookgroup.com	Bloomington	IN	47403	812-323-4500	339-3395
Sajar Plastics Inc 15285 S State Ave PO Box 37 *Web:* www.sajarplastics.com	Middlefield	OH	44062	440-632-5203	632-1848
Schiffmayer Plastics Corp 1201 Armstrong St *TF:* 800-621-1092 ■ *Web:* www.schiffmayerplastics.com	Algonquin	IL	60102	847-658-8140	658-0863
Seitz Corp PO Box 1398 *TF:* 800-243-5115 ■ *Web:* www.seitzcorp.com	Torrington	CT	06790	860-489-0476	482-6616
Shape Global Technology Inc 90 Community Dr *TF Sales:* 800-627-5836 ■ *Web:* www.shapenet.com	Sanford	ME	04073	207-324-5200	324-0875
Steere Enterprises Inc 285 Commerce St *TF:* 800-875-4926 ■ *Web:* www.steere.com	Tallmadge	OH	44278	330-633-4926	633-3921
Stelrema Corp 4055 E 250 N *Web:* www.gettig.com/Stelrema.html	Knox	IN	46534	574-772-2103	772-5628
Sturgis Molded Products Co 1950 Clark St *Web:* www.smpco.com	Sturgis	MI	49091	269-651-9381	651-9224
Tech Group Inc The 14677 N 74th St *Web:* www.techgrp.com	Scottsdale	AZ	85260	480-281-4500	281-4502
Tech II Inc 1765 W County Line Rd PO Box 1468 *Web:* www.techii.com	Springfield	OH	45501	937-969-7000	969-8156
Thermotech Co 1302 S 5th St *Web:* www.thermotech.com	Hopkins	MN	55343	952-933-9400	933-9412
Tigerpoly Mfg Inc 6231 Enterprise Pkwy *Web:* www.tigerpoly.com	Grove City	OH	43123	614-871-0045	871-2576
Toledo Molding & Die Inc 4 E Laskey Rd *TF:* 800-437-5116 ■ *Web:* www.tmdinc.com	Toledo	OH	43612	419-476-0581	476-6053
Tri-Star Plastics Inc 1915 E Via Burton *Web:* www.tri-starplastics.com	Anaheim	CA	92806	714-533-7360	533-4383
Tricon Industries Inc 2325 Wisconsin Ave *Web:* www.triconinc.com	Downers Grove	IL	60515	630-964-2330	964-5179
Tricon Industries Inc Electromechanical Div 2325 Wisconsin Ave *Web:* www.triconinc.com	Downers Grove	IL	60515	630-964-2330	964-5179
Trimold LLC 200 Pittsburgh Rd	Circleville	OH	43113	740-474-7591	474-1053
Tubed Products LLC 44 O'Neill St *Web:* www.ksplastic.com	EastHampton	MA	01027	413-527-1250	529-1275
Tuthill Corp Plastics Group 2050 Sunnydale Blvd *TF:* 800-447-5278 ■ *Web:* www.tuthill.com	Clearwater	FL	33765	727-446-8593	446-8595
United Plastics Group Inc 1520 Kensington Rd Suite 313 *Web:* www.unitedplasticsgroup.com	Oakbrook	IL	60523	630-706-5500	706-5510
Universal Plastic Mold Inc 13245 Los Angeles St *Web:* www.upminc.com	Baldwin Park	CA	91706	626-962-4001	960-7166
ValTech LLC 1667 Emerson St *Web:* www.thevaltechgroup.com	Rochester	NY	14606	585-647-2300	647-6123
Vaupell Inc 1144 NW 53rd St *TF:* 800-426-7738 ■ *Web:* www.vaupell.com	Seattle	WA	98107	206-784-9050	784-9708
Venture Plastics Inc 4000 Warren Rd PO Box 249 *Web:* www.ventureplastics.com	Newton Falls	OH	44444	330-872-5774	872-3597
W-L Molding Co The 8212 Shaver Rd *Web:* www.wlmolding.com	Portage	MI	49024	269-327-3075	323-8416
Westlake Plastics Co PO Box 127 *TF:* 800-999-1700 ■ *Web:* www.westlakeplastics.com	Lenni	PA	19052	610-459-1000	459-1084
Williams Industries Inc 2201 E Michigan Rd *TF:* 800-383-4701 ■ *Web:* www.williamsindustries.com	Shelbyville	IN	46176	317-392-4701	398-3561
Winzeler Gear Inc 7355 W Wilson Ave *Web:* www.winzelergear.com	Harwood Heights	IL	60706	708-867-7971	867-7974
WM Plastics Inc 5151 Bolger Ct *Web:* www.wmplastics.com	McHenry	IL	60050	815-578-8888	578-8818

608 PLASTICS & OTHER SYNTHETIC MATERIALS

608-1 Synthetic Fibers & Filaments

Company / Address	City	State	Zip	Phone	Fax
Buckeye Technologies Inc 1001 Tillman St *NYSE: BKI* ■ *Web:* www.bkitech.com	Memphis	TN	38112	901-320-8100	320-8204
Carlee Corp 28 Piermont Rd *TF:* 800-822-7533 ■ *Web:* www.carlee.com	Rockleigh	NJ	07647	201-768-6800	768-7614
Color-Fi Inc 320 Neeley St *TF:* 800-843-6382 ■ *Web:* www.colorfi.com	Sumter	SC	29150	803-436-4200	436-4220
Consolidated Fibers 8100 S Blvd PO Box 240416 *TF:* 800-243-8621 ■ *Web:* www.consolidatedfibers.com	Charlotte	NC	28224	704-554-8621	554-7782
Deltech Corp 11911 Scenic Hwy *Web:* www.deltechcorp.com	Baton Rouge	LA	70807	225-775-0150	358-3149
DuPont Advanced Fibers Systems 5401 Jefferson Davis Hwy *TF:* 800-441-7515 ■ *Web:* www2.dupont.com	Richmond	VA	23234	804-383-2000	383-4077
DuPont Canada Inc 7070 Mississauga Rd *TF:* 800-268-3943 ■ *Web:* www2.dupont.com	Mississauga	ON	L5N7J8	905-821-5953	821-5230
EDO Fiber Science 506 N Billy Mitchell Rd *Web:* www.edocorp.com	Salt Lake City	UT	84116	801-537-1800	363-9554
Fairfield Processing Corp 88 Rose Hill Ave *TF:* 800-980-8000 ■ *Web:* www.poly-fil.com	Danbury	CT	06810	203-744-2090	792-9710
Hexcel Corp 281 Tresser Blvd 2 Stamford Plaza 16th Fl *NYSE: HXL* ■ *TF:* 800-444-3923 ■ *Web:* www.hexcel.com	Stamford	CT	06901	203-969-0666	
Honeywell Specialty Materials 101 Columbia Rd *TF:* 800-222-0094 ■ *Web:* www.acwax.com	Morristown	NJ	07962	973-455-2145	455-6154
International Fiber Corp 50 Bridge St *TF:* 888-698-1936 ■ *Web:* www.ifcfiber.com	North Tonawanda	NY	14120	716-693-4040	693-3528
InterTech Group Inc 4838 Jenkins Ave *Web:* www.theintertechgroup.com	North Charleston	SC	29405	843-744-5174	747-4092

Company	City	State	ZIP	Phone	Fax
INVISTA 4123 E 37th St N *TF:* 877-446-8478 ■ *Web:* www.invista.com	Wichita	KS	67220	316-828-1000	
Noble Fiber Technologies 300 Palm St *TF:* 877-978-2842 ■ *Web:* www.noblefiber.com	Scranton	PA	18505	570-558-5309	558-5351
Nylon Corp of America 333 Sundial Ave *TF:* 800-851-2001 ■ *Web:* www.nycoa.net	Manchester	NH	03103	603-627-5150	627-5154
Performance Fibers 16905 Northcross Dr *Web:* www.performancefibers.com	Huntersville	NC	23834	704-765-3700	
Polymer Dynamics Inc 2200 S 12th St PO Box 4400 *TF:* 800-287-4466 ■ *Web:* www.pdi-usa.com	Allentown	PA	18103	610-798-2200	798-2222
RadiciSpandex Corp 3145 NW Blvd *Web:* www.radicigroup.com	Gastonia	NC	28052	704-864-5495	836-3143
Stein Fibers Ltd 4 Computer Dr W Suite 200 *TF:* 888-489-2790 ■ *Web:* www.steinfibers.com	Albany	NY	12205	518-489-5700	489-5713
TenCate Grass North America 1131 Broadway St *TF:* 800-251-1033 ■ *Web:* www.tencate.com	Dayton	TN	37321	423-775-0792	775-4460
Toray Industries America Inc 461 5th Ave 9th Fl *Web:* www.toray.com	New York	NY	10017	212-697-8150	972-4279
United Plastic Fabricating Inc 165 Flagship Dr *Web:* www.unitedplastic.com	North Andover	MA	01845	800-638-8265	966-4520
Waltrich Plastic Corp 3005 Airport Rd PO Box D *Web:* www.waltrich.com	Walthourville	GA	31333	912-368-9341	369-3544
William Barnet & Son Inc 1300 Hayne St *TF:* 800-922-7638 ■ *Web:* www.barnet.com	Arcadia	SC	29320	864-576-7154	574-7261

608-2 Synthetic Resins & Plastics Materials

Company	City	State	ZIP	Phone	Fax
A Schulman Inc 3550 W Market St *NASDAQ: SHLM* ■ *TF:* 800-662-3751 ■ *Web:* www.aschulman.com	Akron	OH	44333	330-666-3751	668-7204
Akcros Chemicals America 500 Jersey Ave *TF Cust Svc:* 800-500-7890 ■ *Web:* www.akcros.com	New Brunswick	NJ	08903	732-247-2202	247-2287
Albis Plastics Corp 19901 SW Fwy *Web:* www.albis.com	Sugar Land	TX	77479	281-207-5467	207-5471
Alloy Polymers Inc (AP) 3310 Deepwater Terminal Rd *Web:* www.alloypolymers.com	Richmond	VA	23234	804-232-8000	230-0386
AlphaGary Corp 170 Pioneer Dr *TF:* 800-232-9741 ■ *Web:* www.alphagary.com	Leominster	MA	01453	978-537-8071	840-5005
AOC LLC 955 Tennessee 57 *Web:* www.aoc-resins.com	Collierville	TN	38017	901-854-2800	854-1183
Asahi Kasei America Inc 535 Madison Ave 33rd Fl *Web:* www.ak-america.com	New York	NY	10022	212-371-9900	371-9050
Asahi Kasei Plastics North America Inc 1 Thermofil Way *TF:* 800-444-4408 ■ *Web:* www.asahikaseiplastics.com	Fowlerville	MI	48836	517-223-2000	223-2002
Bayer Corp 100 Bayer Rd *TF:* 800-422-9374 ■ *Web:* www.bayerus.com	Pittsburgh	PA	15205	412-777-2000	778-4430
Bayer Inc 77 Belfield Rd **Fax:* Hum Res ■ *TF:* 800-622-2937 ■ *Web:* www.bayer.ca	Toronto	ON	M9W1G6	416-248-0771	248-1297*
Bayer MaterialScience LLC 100 Bayer Rd *TF:* 800-662-2927 ■ *Web:* www.polymers-usa.bayer.com	Pittsburgh	PA	15205	412-777-2000	
Capital Resin Corp 324 Dering Ave *Web:* www.capitalresin.com	Columbus	OH	43207	614-445-7177	445-7290
CL Hauthaway & Sons Corp 638 Summer St *Web:* www.hauthaway.com	Lynn	MA	01905	781-592-6444	599-9565
Colorite Specialty Resins PO Box 116 *TF:* 800-215-1497 ■ *Web:* www.coloritepolymers.com	Burlington	NJ	08016	609-386-9200	386-3415
Crossfield Products Corp 3000 E Harcourt St *Web:* www.crossfieldproducts.com	Rancho Dominguez	CA	90221	310-886-9100	886-9119
Cytec Engineered Materials 2085 E Technology Cir Suite 300 *Web:* www.cytec.com	Tempe	AZ	85284	480-730-2000	730-2088
Daikin America Inc 20 Olympic Dr *TF Cust Svc:* 800-365-9570 ■ *Web:* www.daikin-america.com	Orangeburg	NY	10962	845-365-9500	365-9515
Dow Chemical Co 2030 Dow Ctr *NYSE: DOW* ■ *TF Cust Svc:* 800-422-8193 ■ *Web:* www.dow.com	Midland	MI	48674	989-636-1463	636-1830
DSM Engineering Plastics Inc 2267 W Mill Rd **Fax:* Cust Svc ■ *TF:* 800-333-4237 ■ *Web:* www.dsm.com	Evansville	IN	47720	812-435-7500	435-7706*
DuPont Engineering Polymers Lancaster Pike Rt 141 Barley Mill Plaza Bldg 22 *TF:* 800-441-7515 ■ *Web:* www.dupont.com	Wilmington	DE	19805	302-999-4592	
Eastman Chemical Co 200 S Wilcox Dr *NYSE: EMN* ■ **Fax:* Mktg ■ *TF Cust Svc:* 800-327-8626 ■ *Web:* www.eastman.com	Kingsport	TN	37660	423-229-2000	229-1194*
Engineered Polymer Solutions Inc 1400 N State St *TF:* 800-654-4242 ■ *Web:* www.epscca.com	Marengo	IL	60152	815-568-3020	568-4155
Esterline Technologies Corp 500 108th Ave NE Suite 1500 *NYSE: ESL* ■ *Web:* www.esterline.com	Bellevue	WA	98004	425-453-9400	453-2916
ExxonMobil Chemical Co 13501 Katy Fwy *Web:* www.exxonmobilchemical.com	Houston	TX	77079	281-870-6000	870-6661
Ferro Corp Filled & Reinforced Plastics Div 5001 O'Hara Dr *Web:* www.ferro.com	Evansville	IN	47711	812-423-5218	423-5218
Formosa Plastics Corp USA 9 Peach Tree Hill Rd **Fax:* Hum Res ■ *Web:* www.fpcusa.com	Livingston	NJ	07039	973-992-2090	716-7456*
Gallagher Corp 3908 Morrison Dr *TF:* 800-524-8597 ■ *Web:* www.gallaghercorp.com	Gurnee	IL	60031	847-249-3440	249-3473
Goldsmith & Eggleton Inc 300 1st St *TF:* 800-321-0954 ■ *Web:* www.goldsmith-eggleton.com	Wadsworth	OH	44281	330-336-6616	334-4709
Heritage Plastics Inc 1002 Hunt St *TF:* 800-245-4623 ■ *Web:* www.heritage-plastics.com	Picayune	MS	39466	601-798-8663	798-1946
Hexion Specialty Chemicals Inc 180 E Broad St *Web:* www.hexionchem.com	Columbus	OH	43215	614-225-4000	
Huntsman Corp 500 Huntsman Way *NYSE: HUN* ■ *TF:* 800-421-2411 ■ *Web:* www.huntsman.com	Salt Lake City	UT	84108	801-584-5700	584-5781
Industrial Dielectrics Inc 407 S 7th St PO Box 357 *Web:* www.idiplastic.com	Noblesville	IN	46061	317-773-1766	773-3877
Interplastic Corp 1225 Wolters Blvd *TF:* 800-736-5497 ■ *Web:* www.interplastic.com	Saint Paul	MN	55110	651-481-6860	481-9834
Kraton Performance Polymers Inc 15710 John F Kennedy Blvd Suite 300 *NYSE: KRA* ■ *TF:* 800-457-2866 ■ *Web:* www.kraton.com	Houston	TX	77032	281-504-4950	504-4743
Landec Corp 3603 Haven Ave *NASDAQ: LNDC* ■ *Web:* www.landec.com	Menlo Park	CA	94025	650-306-1650	368-9818
Lewcott Corp 86 Providence Rd *TF Sales:* 800-225-7725 ■ *Web:* www.lewcott.com	Millbury	MA	01527	508-865-1791	865-0302
Lord Corp 111 Lord Dr *TF:* 800-524-2885 ■ *Web:* www.lord.com	Cary	NC	27511	919-468-5979	
Markel Corp 435 School Ln **Fax:* Sales ■ *Web:* www.markelcorporation.com	Plymouth Meeting	PA	19462	610-272-8960	270-3138*
Marval Industries Inc 315 Hoyt Ave *Web:* www.marvalindustries.com	Mamaroneck	NY	10543	914-381-2400	381-2259
Michael Day Enterprises Inc PO Box 179 *TF:* 800-758-0960 ■ *Web:* www.mdayinc.com	Wadsworth	OH	44281	330-336-7611	336-2143
Minova USA Inc 150 Carley Ct *TF:* 800-626-2948 ■ *Web:* www.minovausa.com	Georgetown	KY	40324	502-863-6800	863-6805
Mitsui Chemicals America Inc 800 Westchester Ave **Fax:* PR ■ *TF:* 800-682-2377 ■ *Web:* www.mitsuichemicals.com	Rye Brook	NY	10573	914-253-0777	253-0790*
Modern Dispersions Inc 78 Marguerite Ave *TF:* 800-633-6434 ■ *Web:* www.moderndispersions.com	Leominster	MA	01453	978-534-3370	537-6065
MRC Polymers Inc 3307 S Lawndale Ave *Web:* www.mrcpolymers.com	Chicago	IL	60623	773-890-9000	890-9007
Neville Chemical Co 2800 Neville Rd *TF Cust Svc:* 877-704-4200 ■ *Web:* www.nevchem.com	Pittsburgh	PA	15225	412-331-4200	771-0226
NOVA Chemicals Corp 1000 7th Ave SW PO Box 2518 *TF:* 866-289-6682 ■ *Web:* www.novachem.com	Calgary	AB	T2P5C6	403-750-3600	269-7410
Ouimet Corp 2967 Sidco Dr *TF:* 800-326-5152	Nashville	TN	37204	615-242-5478	244-6823
Parker Hannifin Corp Chomerics Div 77 Dragon Ct *Web:* www.parker.com	Woburn	MA	01801	781-935-4850	933-4318
Perstorp Polyols Inc 600 Matzinger Rd *TF Cust Svc:* 800-537-0280 ■ *Web:* www.perstorppolyols.com	Toledo	OH	43612	419-729-5448	729-3291
Plastics Color & Compounding Inc 349 Lake Rd *TF:* 888-549-7820 ■ *Web:* www.plasticscolor.com	Dayville	CT	06241	860-774-3770	779-7320
Plastics Engineering Co Inc 3518 Lake Shore Rd *Web:* www.plenco.com	Sheboygan	WI	53083	920-458-2121	458-1923
PolyOne Corp 33587 Walker Rd *NYSE: POL* ■ *TF:* 866-765-9663 ■ *Web:* www.polyone.com	Avon Lake	OH	44012	440-930-1000	930-3064
PSC Fabricating Co 1100 W Market St *Web:* www.pscofky.com	Louisville	KY	40203	502-625-7700	625-7837
Reichhold Inc 2400 Ellis Rd *TF:* 800-448-3482 ■ *Web:* www.reichhold.com	Durham	NC	27703	919-990-7500	990-7711
Resinall Corp 3065 High Ridge Rd *TF Cust Svc:* 800-421-0561 ■ *Web:* www.resinall.com	Stamford	CT	06905	203-329-7100	329-0167
Rhe Tech Inc 1500 E N Territorial Rd *TF:* 800-869-1230 ■ *Web:* www.rhetech.com	Whitmore Lake	MI	48189	734-769-0585	769-3565
Rimtec Corp 1702 Beverly Rd *Web:* www.rimtec.com	Burlington	NJ	08016	609-387-0011	387-0282
Rogers Corp 1 Technology Dr *NYSE: ROG* ■ *TF:* 800-227-6437 ■ *Web:* www.rogerscorp.com	Rogers	CT	06263	860-774-9605	779-5509
Rohm & Haas Co 100 Independence Mall W **Fax:* Hum Res ■ *Web:* www.rohmhaas.com	Philadelphia	PA	19106	215-592-3000	592-3377*
Rondy & Co Inc 255 Wooster Rd N *Web:* www.rondy.net	Barberton	OH	44203	330-745-9016	745-4886
RTP Co 580 E Front St **Fax:* Hum Res ■ *TF:* 800-433-4787 ■ *Web:* www.rtpcompany.com	Winona	MN	55987	507-454-6900	452-6286*
Rubicon Inc 9156 Hwy 75 PO Box 517 *Web:* www.huntsman.com	Geismar	LA	70734	225-673-6141	673-6442
Rutland Plastic Technologies 10021 Rodney St *TF:* 800-438-5134 ■ *Web:* www.rutlandinc.com	Pineville	NC	28134	704-553-0046	552-6589
S & E Specialty Polymers LLC 140 Leominster-Shirley Rd *Web:* www.sespoly.com	Lunenburg	MA	01462	978-537-8261	537-5310
Sartomer Co 502 Thomas Jones Way *TF:* 800-345-8247 ■ *Web:* www.sartomer.com	Exton	PA	19341	610-363-4100	363-4140
Scientific Polymer Products Inc 6265 Dean Pkwy *Web:* www.scientificpolymer.com	Ontario	NY	14519	585-265-0413	265-1390
Shintech Inc 3 Greenway Plaza Suite 1150 *Web:* www.shintechinc.com	Houston	TX	77046	713-965-0713	965-0629
Shuman Plastics Inc 35 Neoga St *Web:* www.shuman-plastics.com	Depew	NY	14043	716-685-2121	685-3236
SI Group Inc 2750 Balltown Rd *Web:* www.siigroup.com	Schenectady	NY	12301	518-370-4200	346-6908
Soluol Chemical Co Inc PO Box 112 *Web:* www.soluol.com	West Warwick	RI	02893	401-821-8100	823-6673
Solutia Inc 575 Maryville Centre Dr **Fax:* Hum Res ■ *TF:* 800-325-4330 ■ *Web:* www.solutia.com	Saint Louis	MO	63141	314-674-1000	674-1585*
Spartech Corp 120 S Central Ave Suite 1700 *NYSE: SEH* ■ *TF:* 888-721-4242 ■ *Web:* www.spartech.com	Clayton	MO	63105	314-721-4242	721-1543
Spraylat Corp 143 Sparks Ave *TF:* 800-642-3595 ■ *Web:* www.spraylat.com	Pelham	NY	10803	914-738-1600	712-2838

	City	State	ZIP	Phone	Fax
Sterling Fibers Inc 5005 Sterling Way *TF Cust Svc:* 800-342-3779 ■ *Web:* www.sterlingfibers.com	Pace	FL	32571	850-994-5311	994-2579
Talco Plastics Inc 1000 W Rincon St *Web:* www.talcoplastics.com	Corona	CA	92880	951-531-2000	531-2058
Teijin Kasei America Inc 5555 Triangle Pkwy Suite 275 *Web:* www.teijinkasei.com	Norcross	GA	30092	770-346-8949	346-7610
Texas Polymer Services Inc 6522 IH-10 W	Orange	TX	77632	409-883-4331	883-3013
Thermoclad Co 361 W 11th St *Web:* www.thermoclad.com	Erie	PA	16501	814-456-1243	459-2853
Ticona LLC 8040 Dixie Hwy **Fax:* Sales ■ *TF:* 800-833-4882 ■ *Web:* www.ticona.com	Florence	KY	41042	859-372-3244	372-3125*
Vi-Chem Corp 55 Cottage Grove St SW *TF:* 800-477-8501 ■ *Web:* www.vichem.com	Grand Rapids	MI	49507	616-247-8501	247-8703
Westlake Chemical Corp 2801 Post Oak Blvd Suite 600 *NYSE:* WLK ■ *TF:* 888-953-3623 ■ *Web:* www.westlakechemical.com	Houston	TX	77056	713-960-9111	963-1562
WTE Corp 7 Alfred Cir *Web:* www.wte.com	Bedford	MA	01730	781-275-6400	275-8612

608-3 Synthetic Rubber

	City	State	ZIP	Phone	Fax
AirBoss of America Corp Rubber Compounding 101 Glasgow St *TF:* 800-294-5723 ■ *Web:* www.airbossrubbercompounding.com	Kitchener	ON	N2G4X8	519-576-5565	576-1315
Akrochem Corp 255 Fountain St *TF:* 800-321-2260 ■ *Web:* www.akrochem.com	Akron	OH	44304	330-535-2100	535-8947
Bryant Rubber Corp 1112 Lomita Blvd *Web:* www.bryantrubber.com	Harbor City	CA	90710	310-530-2530	530-9143
Elementis Specialities Inc 329 Wyckoffs Mill Rd PO Box 700 *TF Cust Svc:* 800-418-5196 ■ *Web:* www.elementisspecialities.com	Hightstown	NJ	08520	609-443-2500	443-2422
Goodyear Tire & Rubber Co 1144 E Market St *NYSE:* GT ■ **Fax:* Cust Svc ■ *TF Cust Svc:* 800-321-2136 ■ *Web:* www.goodyear.com	Akron	OH	44316	330-796-2121	796-2222*
Lanxess Corp 111 RIDC Pk W Dr *TF:* 800-526-9377 ■ *Web:* www.lanxess.com	Pittsburgh	PA	15275	412-809-1000	
Midwest Elastomers Inc 700 Industrial Dr PO Box 412 *TF:* 800-786-3539 ■ *Web:* www.midwestelastomers.com	Wapakoneta	OH	45895	419-738-8844	738-4411
Preferred Rubber Compounding Corp 1020 Lambert St *Web:* www.preferredrubber.com	Barberton	OH	44203	330-798-4790	798-4795
R & S Processing Co Inc 15712 Illinois Ave PO Box 2037 *Web:* www.rsprocessing.com	Paramount	CA	90723	562-531-1403	531-4318
Teknor Apex Co 505 Central Ave *TF:* 800-556-3864 ■ *Web:* www.teknorapex.com	Pawtucket	RI	02861	401-725-8000	725-8095
Textile Rubber & Chemical Co Inc 1300 Tiarco Dr SW *TF:* 800-727-8453 ■ *Web:* www.trcc.com	Dalton	GA	30721	706-277-1300	277-3738

609 PLASTICS PRODUCTS - FIBERGLASS REINFORCED

	City	State	ZIP	Phone	Fax
Crane Composites Inc 23525 W Eames St **Fax:* Hum Res ■ *TF:* 800-435-0080 ■ *Web:* www.cranecomposites.com	Channahon	IL	60410	815-467-8600	467-8666*
Ershigs Inc 742 Marine Dr *TF:* 888-377-4447 ■ *Web:* www.ershigs.com	Bellingham	WA	98225	360-733-2620	733-2628
Fibergrate Composite Structures Inc 5151 Beltline Rd Suite 700 *TF:* 800-527-4043 ■ *Web:* www.fibergrate.com	Dallas	TX	75254	972-250-1633	250-1530
Formed Fiber Technologies Inc 125 Allied Rd PO Box 1300 *Web:* www.formedfiber.com	Auburn	ME	04211	207-784-1118	784-1137
Glastic Corp 4321 Glenridge Rd *TF:* 800-360-1319 ■ *Web:* www.glastic.com	Cleveland	OH	44121	216-486-0100	486-1091
GMI Composites Inc 1355 W Sherman Blvd *TF:* 800-330-4045 ■ *Web:* www.gmicomposites.com	Muskegon	MI	49441	231-755-1611	755-1613
Haysite Reinforced Plastics 5599 Perry Hwy *Web:* www.haysite.com	Erie	PA	16509	814-868-3691	864-7803
McClarin Plastics Inc 15 Industrial Dr PO Box 486 *TF:* 800-233-3189 ■ *Web:* www.mcclarinplastics.com	Hanover	PA	17331	717-637-2241	637-2091
Peterson Products Inc 1325 Old County Rd *Web:* www.petersonproducts.com	Belmont	CA	94002	650-591-7311	591-7498
Red Ewald Inc 2669 S Hwy 181 *TF:* 800-242-3524 ■ *Web:* www.redewald.com	Karnes City	TX	78118	830-780-3304	780-4272
Strongwell 400 Commonwealth Ave *Web:* www.strongwell.com	Bristol	VA	24201	276-645-8000	645-8132

610 PLASTICS PRODUCTS - HOUSEHOLD

	City	State	ZIP	Phone	Fax
A & E Products/Mainetti 104 Carnegie Ctr Dr *Web:* www.aehangers.com	Princeton	NJ	08540	609-806-2500	806-2502
Aero Plastics Inc 163 Pioneer Dr *TF:* 800-458-0116	Leominster	MA	01453	978-537-4363	537-9927
Contico International LLC 305 Rock Industrial Pk Dr **Fax Area Code:* 800 ■ *TF:* 800-831-7077 ■ *Web:* www.contico.com	Bridgeton	MO	63044	314-656-4349	327-5492*
Eagle Affiliates Inc 1000 S 2nd St *TF:* 800-221-0434 ■ *Web:* www.eagleaffiliates.com	Plainfield	NJ	07063	908-757-4464	769-7599
GT Water Products Inc 5239 N Commerce Ave *TF:* 800-862-5647 ■ *Web:* www.gtwaterproducts.com	Moorpark	CA	93021	805-529-2900	529-4558
Home Products International Inc 4501 W 47th St *TF:* 800-327-3534 ■ *Web:* www.hpii.com	Chicago	IL	60632	773-890-1010	890-0523
Igloo Products Corp 777 Igloo Rd *TF:* 800-364-5566 ■ *Web:* www.igloocoolers.com	Katy	TX	77494	713-584-6800	465-2009
Iris USA Inc PO Box 581910 *TF:* 800-320-4747 ■ *Web:* www.irisusainc.com	Pleasant Prair	WI	53158	262-612-1000	612-1010
Jet Plastica Inc 1100 Schwab Rd *TF:* 800-220-5381 ■ *Web:* www.jetplastica.com	Hatfield	PA	19440	215-362-1501	362-5018
King Plastics Inc 840 N Elm St	Orange	CA	92867	714-997-7540	997-0491
Kraftware Corp 270 Cox St *TF Cust Svc:* 800-221-1728 ■ *Web:* www.kraftwarecorp.com	Roselle	NJ	07203	908-259-8883	259-8885
Maryland Plastics Inc 251 E Central Ave *TF Cust Svc:* 800-544-5582 ■ *Web:* www.marylandplastics.com	Federalsburg	MD	21632	410-754-5566	754-8882
Newell Rubbermaid Inc Cleaning & Organization Group 3124 Valley Ave *TF:* 800-347-9800 ■ *Web:* www.newellrubbermaid.com	Winchester	VA	22601	540-667-8700	542-8583
Prolon Inc 305 Industrial Ave **Fax Area Code:* 888 ■ *TF:* 800-628-7749 ■ *Web:* www.prolon.biz	Port Gibson	MS	39150	601-437-4211	480-9828*
Sterilite Corp PO Box 524 *TF:* 800-225-1046 ■ *Web:* www.sterilite.com	Townsend	MA	01469	978-597-8702	597-1195
TAP Plastics Inc 6475 Sierra Ln *TF:* 800-894-0827 ■ *Web:* www.tapplastics.com	Dublin	CA	94568	925-829-4889	829-6921
Thermos Co 2550 Golf Rd # 800 *TF:* 800-243-0745 ■ *Web:* www.thermos.com	Rolling Meadows	IL	60008	847-439-7821	593-5570
Tupperware Corp 14901 S Orange Blossom Trail *NYSE:* TUP ■ *TF Cust Svc:* 800-772-4001 ■ *Web:* www.order.tupperware.com	Orlando	FL	32837	407-847-3111	826-8489
Union Products Inc 511 Lancaster St	Leominster	MA	01453	978-537-1631	537-0050
US Acrylic Inc 1320 Harris Rd *TF:* 800-232-2600 ■ *Web:* www.usacrylic.com	Libertyville	IL	60048	847-837-4800	837-1955
Venturi Inc 2299 Traversefield Dr *TF:* 800-968-0104 ■ *Web:* www.venturi-inc.com	Traverse City	MI	49686	231-929-7732	929-7735
Zyliss USA Corp 1 Post Suite 100 *TF:* 888-794-7623 ■ *Web:* www.zylissusa.com	Irvine	CA	92618	949-699-1884	699-1788

611 PLASTICS PRODUCTS (MISC)

	City	State	ZIP	Phone	Fax
Acry Fab Inc 584 Progress Way *TF:* 800-747-2279 ■ *Web:* www.acryfab.com	Sun Prairie	WI	53590	608-837-0045	837-1031
Advent Tool & Mold Inc 999 Ridgeway Ave *Web:* www.adventtool.com	Rochester	NY	14615	585-254-2000	254-3000
Agape Plastics Inc 11474 1st Ave NW *Web:* www.agapeplastics.com	Grand Rapids	MI	49534	616-735-4091	735-4392
Aigner Index Inc 23 Mac Arthur Ave *TF:* 800-242-3919 ■ *Web:* www.holdex.com	New Windsor	NY	12553	845-562-4510	562-2638
Ajax United Patterns & Molds Inc 34585 7th St *Web:* www.ajaxmfg.com	Union City	CA	94587	510-476-8000	476-8001
All States Inc 602 N 12th St *TF Cust Svc:* 800-621-5837	Saint Charles	IL	60174	773-728-0525	728-6410
American Window & Glass Inc 2715 Lynch Rd *Web:* www.americanwindowandglass.com	Evansville	IN	47711	812-464-9400	464-3131
Amerimade Technology Inc 449 Mountain Vista Pkwy *TF:* 800-938-3824 ■ *Web:* www.amerimade.com	Livermore	CA	94551	925-243-9090	243-9266
Armstrong Systems & Consulting 5101 Tremont Ave Suite A *Web:* www.armstrongsystems.com	Davenport	IA	52807	563-386-9090	391-2237
Ashland Hardware Systems 790 W Commercial Ave **Fax Area Code:* 800 ■ *Web:* www.ashlandhardware.com	Lowell	IN	46356	219-696-5950	626-1758*
Associated Packaging Enterprises Inc 1 Dickinson Dr Suite 100 *Web:* www.aptechnologies.com	Chadds Ford	PA	19317	484-785-1120	
Avery Dennison Fastener Div 224 Industrial Rd *TF:* 800-225-5913 ■ *Web:* www.fastener.averydennison.com	Fitchburg	MA	01420	800-225-5913	848-2169
Bay Polymer Corp 44530 S Grimmer Blvd *Web:* www.baypolymer.com	Fremont	CA	94538	510-490-1791	490-5914
Beemak Plastics Inc 13921 Bettencourt St **Fax:* Orders ■ *TF:* 800-421-4393 ■ *Web:* www.beemak.com	Cerritos	CA	90703	310-886-5880	764-0330*
Bemis Mfg Co 300 Mill St *TF:* 800-558-7651 ■ *Web:* www.bemismfg.com	Sheboygan Falls	WI	53085	920-467-4621	467-8573
Blackmore Co Inc 10800 Blackmore Ave *TF:* 800-874-8660 ■ *Web:* www.blackmoreco.com	Belleville	MI	48111	734-483-8661	483-5454
Bowie Mfg Inc 313 Jennings Ave *TF:* 800-831-0960 ■ *Web:* www.bowiemfg.com	Lake City	IA	51449	712-464-3191	464-8601
Bruce Plastics Inc PO Box 4547 *Web:* www.bruceplastics.com	Pittsburgh	PA	15205	412-922-9888	922-2380
Bunzl Distribution USA Inc 701 Emerson Rd Suite 500 *TF:* 888-997-5959 ■ *Web:* www.bunzldistribution.com	Saint Louis	MO	63141	314-997-5959	997-1405
C. L. Smith Co 1311 S 39th St *TF:* 800-264-1202 ■ *Web:* www.clsmith.com	Saint Louis	MO	63110	314-771-1202	771-3351
Cascade Engineering Inc The Learning Community 3400 Innovation Ct SE *TF:* 877-975-4950 ■ *Web:* www.cascadeng.com	Grand Rapids	MI	49512	616-975-4800	254-4174
Concept Plastics Inc 1210 Hickory Chapel Rd *TF:* 800-225-9553 ■ *Web:* www.cpico.com	High Point	NC	27260	336-889-2001	889-5752
Coverbind Corp 3200 Corporate Dr *TF:* 800-366-6060 ■ *Web:* www.coverbind.com	Wilmington	NC	28405	910-799-4116	799-3935
Cpc Of Vermont Inc PO Box 706 *Web:* www.cpcofvermont.com	Middlebury	VT	05753	802-388-6381	388-2545
Craftech EDM Corp 2941 E La Jolla St *Web:* www.craftechcorp.com	Anaheim	CA	92806	714-630-8117	630-7959
Crystal-Like Plastics 2547 N Ontario St *TF:* 800-554-6091 ■ *Web:* www.crystal-likeplastics.com	Burbank	CA	91504	818-846-1818	846-0877
Custom Accents 1940 Lunt Ave *TF:* 888-553-6789 ■ *Web:* www.customaccents.com	Elk Grove Village	IL	60007	847-640-4725	572-0674

Company	City	State	Zip	Phone	Fax
Daramic Inc 5525 US Hwy 60 E *Web:* www.daramic.com	Owensboro	KY	42303	270-683-1561	686-9226
DelStar Technologies Inc 220 E St Elmo Rd *TF:* 800-531-5112 ■ *Web:* www.delstarinc.com	Austin	TX	78745	512-447-7000	447-7444
Den Hartog Industries Inc 4010 Hospers Dr S PO Box 425 *TF:* 800-342-3408 ■ *Web:* www.denhartogindustries.com	Hospers	IA	51238	712-752-8432	752-8222
Dreco Inc 7887 Root Rd *Web:* www.drecoinc.com	North Ridgeville	OH	44039	440-327-6021	327-6865
Dutchland Plastics Corp 1026 De Master Rd *Web:* www.dutchlandplastics.com	Oostburg	WI	53070	920-564-2356	564-3337
E & O Tool & Plastics Inc 19178 Industrial Blvd NW *Web:* www.eoplastics.com	Elk River	MN	55330	763-441-6100	441-6452
Easley Custom Plastics Inc (ECP) 2930 Greenville Hwy PO Box 2369 *Web:* www.ecpsc.com	Easley	SC	29641	864-859-7548	850-8051
Engineered Polymers Corp (EPC) 1020 Maple Ave E *Web:* www.epcmolding.com	Mora	MN	55051	320-679-3232	679-2323
Epsilon Products Co LLC Post Rd & Blueball Ave	Marcus Hook	PA	70051	610-497-8850	494-3792
Exotic Automation & Supply Inc 34700 Grand River Ave *Web:* www.exoticautomation.com	Farmington Hills	MI	48335	248-477-2122	477-0427
Fiberglass Specialties Inc PO Box 1340 *TF:* 800-527-1459 ■ *Web:* www.fsiweb.com	Henderson	TX	75653	903-657-6522	657-2318
Flagship Converters Inc 205 Shelter Rock Rd *Web:* www.flagshipconverters.com	Danbury	CT	06810	203-792-0034	797-0410
Flotation Technologies Inc 20 Morin St *TF:* 800-639-7806 ■ *Web:* www.flotec.com	Biddeford	ME	04005	207-282-7749	284-8098
Fox Lite Inc 8300 Dayton Rd **Fax Area Code:* 513 ■ *Web:* www.foxlite.com	Fairborn	OH	45324	937-864-1966	864-7010*
Gabriel Mfg Co Inc 125 S Liberty Dr *TF:* 800-454-3387 ■ *Web:* www.4gabriel.com	Stony Point	NY	10980	845-942-0100	942-0159
Garner Industries Inc 7201 N 98th St *TF:* 800-228-0275 ■ *Web:* www.garnerindustries.com	Lincoln	NE	68507	402-434-9100	434-9133
General Polymeric Corp 1136 Morgantown Rd *TF:* 800-654-4391	Reading	PA	19607	610-374-5171	374-4990
Gkn Aerospace Transparency Systems Inc 12122 Western Ave *Web:* www.gkntransparencysystems.com	Garden Grove	CA	92841	714-893-7531	898-8150
Goodrich Corp Engineered Polymer Products Div 6061 Goodrich Blvd *TF:* 800-366-8945 ■ *Web:* www.goodrich.com/Goodrich/Businesses/Engineered-Polymer-Products	Jacksonville	FL	32226	904-757-3660	757-7116
Gorell Enterprises Inc 1380 Wayne Ave *TF:* 800-527-4723 ■ *Web:* www.gorell.com	Indiana	PA	15701	724-465-1800	465-1894
Gpk Products Inc 1601 43rd St NW *TF:* 800-437-4670 ■ *Web:* www.gpk-fargo.com	Fargo	ND	58102	701-277-3225	277-9286
Gregory Holdings Inc PO Box 247 *Web:* www.partnersinplastics.com	Sharon Center	OH	44274	330-239-0202	239-0211
H.Q.c Inc 230 Kendall Pt Dr *Web:* www.hqcinc.com	Oswego	IL	60543	630-820-5550	820-5549
Habasit America 805 Satellite Blvd *TF:* 800-458-6431 ■ *Web:* www.habasitamerica.com	Suwanee	GA	30024	678-288-3600	288-3651
Hanscom Inc 331 Market St *TF:* 866-941-1455 ■ *Web:* www.hanscominc.com	Warren	RI	02885	401-247-1999	247-4575
Henry Plastic Molding Inc 41703 Albrae St *Web:* www.henryplastic.com	Fremont	CA	94538	510-490-7991	490-3548
Hygolet Inc 349 SE 2nd Ave *TF:* 800-494-6538 ■ *Web:* www.hygolet.com	Deerfield Beach	FL	33441	954-481-8601	481-8669
Jatco Inc 725 Zwissig Way *Web:* www.jatco.com	Union City	CA	94587	510-487-0888	487-1880
Kalwall Corp 1111 Candia Rd *TF:* 800-258-9777 ■ *Web:* www.kalwall.com	Manchester	NH	03109	603-627-3861	627-7905
King Plastic Corp 1100 N Toledo Blade Blvd *Web:* www.kingplastic.com	North Port	FL	34288	941-493-5502	497-3274
Lakeside Plastics Inc 450 W 33rd Ave PO Box 2384 *Web:* www.lakesideplastics.net	Oshkosh	WI	54903	920-235-3620	235-6545
Lamvin Inc 4675 N Ave *TF:* 800-446-6329 ■ *Web:* www.lamvin.com	Oceanside	CA	92056	760-806-6400	806-3200
Landmark Plastic Corp 1331 Kelly Ave *Web:* www.landmarkplastic.com	Akron	OH	44306	330-785-2200	785-9200
Leaktite Corp 40 Francis St *TF:* 800-392-0039 ■ *Web:* www.leaktite.com	Leominster	MA	01453	978-537-8000	534-3539
Lsp Products Group Inc 3689 Arrowhead Dr *TF:* 800-854-3215 ■ *Web:* www.lspproducts.com	Carson City	NV	89706	800-854-3215	243-1777
Majors Plastics Inc 10117 I St *Web:* www.majorsplastics.com	Omaha	NE	68127	402-331-1660	331-9041
Mc Pherson Plastics Inc PO Box 58 *Web:* www.mcpherson-plastics.com	Otsego	MI	49078	269-694-9487	694-6662
Micro Plastics Inc 11 Industry Ln Hwy 178 N PO Box 149 *TF:* 800-466-1467 ■ *Web:* www.secure.microplastics.com/default.aspx	Flippin	AR	72634	870-453-2261	453-8676
Microdyne Plastics Inc 1901 E Cooley Dr *Web:* www.microdyneplastics.com	Colton	CA	92324	909-503-4010	503-4011
Middlefield Plastics Inc PO Box 708 *Web:* www.middlefieldplastics.com	Middlefield	OH	44062	440-834-4638	834-1247
MOCAP Inc 13100 Manchester Rd *TF:* 800-633-6775 ■ *Web:* www.mocap.com	Saint Louis	MO	63131	314-543-4000	543-4111
Mold-Rite Plastics LLC 1 Plant St PO Box 160 *Web:* www.mrpcap.com	Plattsburgh	NY	12901	518-561-1812	561-0017
Mylan Technologies Inc 110 Lake St *TF:* 800-848-0461 ■ *Web:* www.mylantech.com	Saint Albans	VT	05478	304-598-5430	
Neil Enterprises Inc 450 E Bunker Ct *TF:* 800-621-5584 ■ *Web:* www.neilenterprises.com	Vernon Hills	IL	60061	847-549-7627	
New Boston Rtm Inc 19155 Shook Rd *Web:* www.newbostonrtm.com	New Boston	MI	48164	734-753-9956	753-9221
Newell Rubbermaid Inc Cleaning & Organization Group 3124 Valley Ave *TF:* 800-347-9800 ■ *Web:* www.newellrubbermaid.com	Winchester	VA	22601	540-667-8700	542-8583
Nishiba Industries Corp 2360 Marconi Ct *Web:* www.nishiba.com	San Diego	CA	92154	619-661-8866	482-1585
Nissen Chemitec America 350 E High St *Web:* www.londonind.com	London	OH	43140	740-852-3200	852-4547
Oscoda Plastics Inc PO Box 189 *TF:* 800-544-9538 ■ *Web:* www.oscodaplastics.com	Oscoda	MI	48750	989-739-6900	739-1494
PI Inc 213 Dennis St *TF:* 800-951-3542 ■ *Web:* www.pi-inc.com	Athens	TN	37303	423-745-6213	746-1310
Piolax Corp 139 Etowah Industrial Ct *Web:* www.piolaxusa.com	Canton	GA	30114	770-479-2227	479-2399
Plastikon Industries Inc 688 Sandoval Way *Web:* www.plastikon.com	Hayward	CA	94544	510-400-1010	400-1133
Plastomer Technologies 23 Friends Ln *TF:* 800-798-1288 ■ *Web:* www.plastomertech.com	Newtown	PA	18940	215-968-5011	968-7640
Plastpro Inc 5200 W Century Blvd 9F *TF:* 800-779-0561 ■ *Web:* www.plastproinc.com	Los Angeles	CA	90045	310-693-8600	693-8620
Pleiger Plastics Co PO Box 1271 *TF:* 800-753-4437 ■ *Web:* www.pleiger.com	Washington	PA	15301	724-228-2244	228-2253
Ply Gem Holdings Inc 5020 Weston Pkwy Suite 400 *Web:* www.plygem.com	Cary	NC	27513	919-677-3900	
Porex Technologies Corp 500 Bohannon Rd *TF Cust Svc:* 800-241-0195 ■ *Web:* www.porex.com	Fairburn	GA	30213	770-964-1421	969-0954
PRA Co 1415 W Cedar St *Web:* www.vantageplastics.com	Standish	MI	48658	989-846-1029	846-0939
Precision Thermoplastic Components Inc PO Box 1296 *TF:* 800-860-4505 ■ *Web:* www.ptclima.com	Lima	OH	45802	419-227-4500	
Preferred Plastics Inc 800 E Bridge St *Web:* www.preferredplastics.net	Plainwell	MI	49080	269-685-5873	685-1148
Protomold Co Inc The 1757 Halgren Rd *TF:* 877-479-3680 ■ *Web:* www.protomold.com	Maple Plain	MN	55359	763-479-3680	479-2679
PSI Inc 10630 Marina Dr *TF:* 866-638-7926	Olive Branch	MS	38654	662-895-8777	895-8796
Rayner Covering Systems Inc 665 Schneider Dr *TF:* 800-648-0757 ■ *Web:* www.raynercovering.com	South Elgin	IL	60177	847-695-2264	695-2363
Richco Inc 8145 River Dr *TF:* 800-466-8301 ■ *Web:* www.richco-inc.com	Morton Grove	IL	60053	773-539-4060	539-6770
Rogan Corp 3455 Woodhead Dr *TF:* 800-423-1543 ■ *Web:* www.rogancorp.com	Northbrook	IL	60062	847-498-2300	498-2334
Rohrer Corp 717 Seville Rd PO Box 1009 *Web:* www.rohrer.com	Wadsworth	OH	44282	330-335-1541	336-5147
Rubbermaid Commercial Products (RCP) 3124 Valley Ave *TF:* 800-347-9800 ■ *Web:* www.rubbermaidcommercial.com	Winchester	VA	22601	540-667-8700	542-8770
Semco Plastic Co 5301 Old Baumgartner Rd *Web:* www.semcoplastics.com	Saint Louis	MO	63129	314-487-4557	487-4724
Seville Flexpack Corp 9905 S Ridgeview Dr *Web:* www.sevilleflexpack.com	Oak Creek	WI	53154	414-761-2751	761-3140
Shakespeare Monofilaments & Specialty Polymers PO Box 4060 *TF:* 800-845-2110 ■ *Web:* www.skpplastics.com	Columbia	SC	29240	803-754-7011	754-7991
Smith McDonald Corp 304 Sonwil Dr *TF:* 800-753-8548	Buffalo	NY	14225	716-684-7200	684-2053
Spears Mfg Co PO Box 9203 *TF:* 800-862-1499 ■ *Web:* www.spearsmfg.com	Sylmar	CA	91392	818-364-1611	367-3014
Spilltech Environmental Inc 1627 Odonoghue St *Web:* www.spilltech.com	Mobile	AL	36615	800-228-3877	
Spir-It Inc 200 Brickstone Sq Suite G-05 *TF:* 800-343-0996 ■ *Web:* www.spir-it.com	Andover	MA	01810	978-964-1551	964-1552
Spiratex Co Inc 1916 Frenchtown Ctr Dr *Web:* www.spiratex.com	Monroe	MI	48162	734-289-4800	289-4804
Standridge Color Corp 1196 E Hightower Trail *Web:* www.standridgecolor.com	Social Circle	GA	30025	770-464-3362	464-2202
Stant Corp 1620 Columbia Ave *TF:* 800-822-3121 ■ *Web:* www.stant.com	Connersville	IN	47331	765-825-3121	825-2875
Sunrise Windows Ltd. LLC 200 Enterprise Dr *Web:* www.sunrisewindows.com	Temperance	MI	48182	734-847-8778	847-7758
Syndicate Sales Inc PO Box 756 *TF:* 800-428-0515 ■ *Web:* www.syndicatesales.com	Kokomo	IN	46903	765-457-7277	454-6748
Syracuse Plastics LLC 7400 Morgan Rd *Web:* www.syracuseplastics.com	Liverpool	NY	13090	315-637-9881	637-9260
Tessy Plastics Corp 488 Rt 5 W *Web:* www.tessy.com	Elbridge	NY	13060	315-689-3924	689-6595
Thombert Inc 316 E 7th St N *TF:* 800-433-3572 ■ *Web:* www.thombert.com	Newton	IA	50208	641-792-4449	792-2390
Transparent Container Co Inc 625 Thomas Dr **Fax Area Code:* 630 ■ *Web:* www.transparentcontainer.com	Bensenville	IL	60106	708-449-8520	860-3651*
Tray-Pak Corp PO Box 14804 *TF:* 888-926-1777 ■ *Web:* www.traypak.com	Reading	PA	19612	610-926-5800	926-9140
Triad Products Co 1801 W 'B' St *TF:* 888-253-4227 ■ *Web:* www.triadproducts.net	Hastings	NE	68901	402-462-2181	462-2246
Trude Iso- Inc 1705 Eaton Dr *Web:* www.isotrude.com	Grand Haven	MI	49417	616-844-2888	844-2892
Tse Industries Inc 4370 112th Ter N *TF:* 800-237-7634 ■ *Web:* www.tse-industries.com	Clearwater	FL	33762	727-573-7676	572-0487
U S Farathane Corp 38000 Mound Rd *Web:* www.usfarathane.com	Sterling Heights	MI	48310	586-978-2800	268-5542
Ultra-Poly Corp 102 Demi Rd PO Box 330 *Web:* www.ultra-poly.com	Portland	PA	18351	570-897-7500	897-7510
Unette Corp 88 N Main St *Web:* www.unette.com	Wharton	NJ	07885	973-328-6800	537-1010
Univenture Inc 13311 Industrial Pkwy **Fax Area Code:* 937 ■ *TF:* 800-992-8262 ■ *Web:* www.univenture.com	Marysville	OH	43040	800-992-8262	645-4700*
Value Plastics Inc 3325 S Timberline Rd *TF:* 888-404-5837 ■ *Web:* www.valueplastics.com	Fort Collins	CO	80525	970-267-5200	223-0953
Ven-Tel Plastics Corp 11311 74th St N *Web:* www.ventelplastics.com	Largo	FL	33773	727-546-7470	546-7480

	City	State	Zip	Phone	Fax
Versatile Card Technology Inc 5200 Thatcher Rd *TF:* 800-445-4888 ■ *Web:* www.vct.com	Downers Grove	IL	60515	630-852-5600	852-5817
Vinyl Window Technologies Inc PO Box 588 *Web:* www.viwintech.com	Paducah	KY	42002	270-443-9622	
Vitec LLC 2627 Clark St *Web:* www.vitec-usa.com	Detroit	MI	48210	313-297-6676	843-1298
Viwinco Inc PO Box 499 *Web:* www.viwinco.com	Morgantown	PA	19543	610-286-8884	286-8877
Viziflex Seels Inc 221 Gracie Pl **Fax Area Code:* 201 ■ *TF:* 800-627-7752 ■ *Web:* www.viziflex.com	Hackensack	NJ	07601	800-627-7752	487-3266*
Wausaukee Composites Inc 837 Cedar St *Web:* www.wauscomp.com	Wausaukee	WI	54177	715-856-6321	856-5567
Williamston Products Inc 845 Progress Ct *Web:* www.wpius.com	Williamston	MI	48895	517-655-2131	655-2607
ZAGG INC 3855 S 500 W Suite J *TF:* 800-700-9244 ■ *Web:* www.zagg.com	Salt Lake City	UT	84115	801-263-0699	

612 PLUMBING FIXTURES & FITTINGS - METAL

	City	State	Zip	Phone	Fax
Accurate Partitions Corp 8000 Joliet Rd PO Box 287 *Web:* www.accuratepartitions.com	McCook	IL	60525	708-442-6800	442-7439
Acorn Engineering Co 15125 Proctor Ave PO Box 3527 *TF:* 800-488-8999 ■ *Web:* www.acorneng.com	City of Industry	CA	91744	626-336-4561	961-2200
Alsons Corp 3010 Mechanic Rd *TF:* 800-421-0001 ■ *Web:* www.alsons.com	Hillsdale	MI	49242	517-439-1411	439-9644
American Brass Mfg Co 5000 Superior Ave *TF:* 800-431-6440 ■ *Web:* www.americanbrass.com	Cleveland	OH	44103	216-431-6565	431-9420
American Specialties Inc (ASI) 441 Saw Mill River Rd *Web:* www.americanspecialties.com	Yonkers	NY	10701	914-476-9000	476-0688
Ames Fire & Waterworks 1427 N Market Blvd Suite 9 *Web:* www.amesfirewater.com	Sacramento	CA	95834	916-928-0123	928-9333
Anderson Copper & Brass Co 4325 Frontage Rd *TF:* 800-323-5284	Oak Forest	IL	60452	708-535-9030	535-9038
Bootz Industries PO Box 18010 *Web:* www.bootz.com	Evansville	IN	47719	812-423-5401	429-2254
Bradley Corp W 142 N 9101 Fountain Blvd *TF:* 800-272-3539 ■ *Web:* www.bradleycorp.com	Menomonee Falls	WI	53051	262-251-6000	251-5817
Brass-Craft Mfg Co 39600 Orchard Hill Pl **Fax:* Sales ■ *Web:* www.brasscraft.com	Novi	MI	48375	248-305-6000	305-6012*
Brasstech Inc 2001 E Carnegie Ave *TF:* 888-436-0805 ■ *Web:* www.brasstech.com	Santa Ana	CA	92705	949-417-5207	417-5297
Central Brass Mfg Co Inc 2950 E 55th St *TF:* 800-321-8630 ■ *Web:* www.centralbrass.com	Cleveland	OH	44127	216-883-0220	883-0875
Champion-Arrowhead LLC 5147 Alhambra Ave *Web:* www.arrowheadbrass.com	Los Angeles	CA	90032	323-221-9137	221-2579
Chicago Faucets A Geberit Co 2100 S Clearwater Dr **Fax:* Sales ■ *TF:* 800-323-5060 ■ *Web:* www.chicagofaucets.com	Des Plaines	IL	60018	847-803-5000	298-3101*
Delta Faucet Co 55 E 111th St *Web:* www.deltacom.deltafaucet.com	Indianapolis	IN	46280	317-848-1812	
Elias Industries Inc 605 Epsilon Dr **Fax Area Code:* 800	Pittsburgh	PA	15238	412-782-4300	223-1067*
Eljer Plumbingware Inc 14801 Quorum Dr 3rd Fl *TF:* 800-423-5537 ■ *Web:* www.eljer.com	Dallas	TX	75254	972-560-2000	560-2268
Elkay Mfg Co 2222 Camden Ct *Web:* www.elkay.com	Oak Brook	IL	60523	630-574-8484	574-5012
Fisher Mfg Co PO Box 60 *TF:* 800-421-6162 ■ *Web:* www.fisher-mfg.com	Tulare	CA	93275	800-421-6162	832-8238
Fluidmaster Inc 30800 Rancho Viejo Rd *TF:* 800-631-2011 ■ *Web:* www.fluidmaster.com	San Juan Capistrano	CA	92675	949-728-2000	728-2205
Fortune Brands Home & Hardware Inc 520 Lake Cook Rd *Web:* www.fortunebrands.com	Deerfield	IL	60015	847-484-4400	
Gerber Plumbing Fixtures LLC 2500 International Pkwy *TF:* 888-648-6466 ■ *Web:* www.gerberonline.com	Woodridge	IL	60517	630-679-1420	679-1430
Global Partitions 2171 Liberty Hill Rd *Web:* www.globalpartitions.com	Eastanollee	GA	30538	706-827-2700	827-2710
Grohe America Inc 241 Covington Dr *TF:* 800-444-7643 ■ *Web:* www.groheamerica.com	Bloomingdale	IL	60108	630-582-7711	582-7722
Hansgrohe Inc 1490 Bluegrass Lakes Pkwy *TF:* 800-334-0455 ■ *Web:* www.hansgrohe-usa.com	Alpharetta	GA	30004	770-360-9880	360-9885
In-Sink-Erator 4700 21st St *TF:* 800-558-5712 ■ *Web:* www.insinkerator.com	Racine	WI	53406	262-554-5432	554-3546
Josam Co 525 W US Hwy 20 **Fax Area Code:* 800 ■ *TF:* 800-365-6726 ■ *Web:* www.josam.com	Michigan City	IN	46360	219-872-5531	627-0008*
Keeney Mfg Co 1170 Main St **Fax:* Cust Svc ■ *TF Cust Svc:* 800-243-0526 ■ *Web:* www.keeneymfg.com	Newington	CT	06111	860-666-3342	665-0374*
Keystone Maax PO Box 544 *TF:* 800-355-5397	SouthHampton	PA	18966	215-355-0660	355-6881
Kohler Canada Co 180 Creditview Rd *TF:* 800-456-4537 ■ *Web:* www.ca.kohler.com	Vaughan	ON	L4L9N4	905-762-6599	850-2356
Kohler Plumbing North America 444 Highland Dr **Fax:* Sales ■ *TF:* 800-456-4537 ■ *Web:* www.us.kohler.com	Kohler	WI	53044	920-457-4441	459-1658*
Ldr Industries Inc 600 N Kilbourn Ave *TF:* 800-545-5230 ■ *Web:* www.ldrind.com	Chicago	IL	60624	773-265-3000	265-3130
Macristy Industries 206 Newington Ave *TF:* 800-966-6964	New Britain	CT	06051	860-225-4637	229-4328
Masco Corp 21001 Van Born Rd *NYSE:* MAS ■ *Web:* www.masco.com	Taylor	MI	48180	313-274-7400	792-6135
Microphor Inc 452 E Hill Rd *TF Orders:* 800-358-8280 ■ *Web:* www.microphor.com	Willits	CA	95490	707-459-5563	459-6617
Moen Inc 25300 Al Moen Dr **Fax:* Hum Res ■ *TF Cust Svc:* 800-289-6636 ■ *Web:* www.moen.com	North Olmsted	OH	44070	440-962-2000	962-2089*
Moen Inc CSI Bath Accessories Div 25300 Al Moen Dr *TF:* 800-321-8809 ■ *Web:* www.moen.com	North Olmsted	OH	44070	440-962-2000	962-2145
Norman Supply Co 825 SW 5th St *TF:* 800-375-3457 ■ *Web:* www.normansupply.com	Oklahoma City	OK	73109	405-235-9511	232-2645
Oatey Co 4700 W 160th St **Fax Area Code:* 800 ■ *TF Cust Svc:* 800-321-9532 ■ *Web:* www.oatey.com	Cleveland	OH	44135	216-267-7100	321-9535*
Pan-Pacific Plumbing Co 17911 Mitchell S *Web:* www.panpacplumbing.com	Irvine	CA	92614	949-474-9170	474-4274
Price Pfister Inc 19701 Da Vinci St *TF:* 800-732-8238 ■ *Web:* www.pfisterfaucets.com	Lake Forest	CA	92610	949-672-4000	672-4000
Quality Metal Finishing Co Inc 421 N Walnut St *Web:* www.qmfco.com	Byron	IL	61010	815-234-2711	234-2243
SH Leggitt Co 1000 Civic Ctr Loop *TF:* 800-877-2495 ■ *Web:* www.marshallgas.com	San Marcos	TX	78666	512-396-0707	396-2619
Sloan Valve Co 10500 Seymour Ave *TF:* 800-982-5839 ■ *Web:* www.sloanvalve.com	Franklin Park	IL	60131	847-671-4300	671-6944
Speakman Co 400 Anchor Mill Rd **Fax Area Code:* 800 ■ *TF:* 800-537-2107 ■ *Web:* www.speakmancompany.com	New Castle	DE	19720	302-764-9100	977-2747*
Sterling Plumbing 444 Highland Dr *TF Cust Svc:* 888-783-7546 ■ *Web:* www.sterlingplumbing.com	Kohler	WI	53044	920-457-4441	453-5851
Symmons Industries Inc 31 Brooks Dr *TF:* 800-796-6667 ■ *Web:* www.symmons.com	Braintree	MA	02184	781-848-2250	843-3849
T & S Brass & Bronze Works Inc PO Box 1088 *TF Cust Svc:* 800-476-4103 ■ *Web:* www.tsbrass.com	Travelers Rest	SC	29690	864-834-4102	834-3518
Water Pik Inc 1730 East Prospect Rd *NYSE:* PIK ■ *TF:* 800-525-2774 ■ *Web:* www.waterpik.com	Fort Collins	CO	80553	800-525-2774	
Water Saver Faucet Co 701 W Erie St 2nd Fl *TF Parts:* 800-973-7278 ■ *Web:* www.wsflab.com	Chicago	IL	60610	312-666-5500	666-8597
Waterworks Operating Co LLC 60 Backus Ave *TF:* 800-899-6757 ■ *Web:* www.waterworks.com	Danbury	CT	06810	203-546-6000	
William Steinen Mfg Co 29 E Halsey Rd *TF:* 800-724-3343 ■ *Web:* www.steinen.com	Parsippany	NJ	07054	973-887-6400	887-4632
Woodford Mfg Co 2121 Waynoka Rd *TF Sales:* 800-621-6032 ■ *Web:* www.woodfordmfg.com	Colorado Springs	CO	80915	719-574-0600	574-7699

613 PLUMBING FIXTURES & FITTINGS - PLASTICS

	City	State	Zip	Phone	Fax
American Shower & Bath Corp (ASB) 540 Glen Ave *Web:* www.asbcorp.com	Moorestown	NJ	08057	856-235-7700	222-1637
Belding Tank Technologies Inc 200 N Gooding St PO Box 160 *TF:* 800-253-4252 ■ *Web:* www.beldingtank.com	Belding	MI	48809	616-794-1130	794-3666
Dispensing Dynamics International 1020 Bixby Dr *TF:* 800-888-3698 ■ *Web:* www.dispensingdynamics.com	City of Industry	CA	91745	626-961-3691	330-5266
Ez-flo International Inc 2750 E Mission Blvd *Web:* www.ez-flo.net	Ontario	CA	91761	909-947-5256	947-5775
Florestone Products Co Inc 2851 Falcon Dr *TF:* 800-446-8827 ■ *Web:* www.florestone.com	Madera	CA	93637	559-661-4171	661-2070
Kohler Canada Co Hytec Plumbing Products Div 4150 Spallumcheen Dr *TF:* 800-871-8311 ■ *Web:* www.hytec.net	Armstrong	BC	V0E1B6	250-546-3067	546-8677
L B Plastics Inc PO Box 907 *TF:* 800-752-7739 ■ *Web:* www.lbplastics.com	Mooresville	NC	28115	704-663-1543	664-2989
Maax Corp 160 St Joseph Blvd *TF:* 888-201-8308 ■ *Web:* www.maax.com	Lachine	QC	H8S2L3	514-634-8981	985-4155
Nupla Corp 11912 Sheldon St *TF:* 800-872-7661 ■ *Web:* www.nuplacorp.com	Sun Valley	CA	91352	818-768-6800	546-8752
Olsonite Corp 25 Dart Rd **Fax Area Code:* 800 ■ *TF:* 800-521-8266	Newnan	GA	30265	770-253-3930	342-1276*
Resin Systems Corp 62 Rt 101a Suite 1 *Web:* www.resinsystems.com	Amherst	NH	03031	603-673-1234	673-4512
Softub Inc 27615 Ave Hopkins *TF Sales:* 800-554-1120 ■ *Web:* www.softub.com	Valencia	CA	91355	661-702-1401	702-0732
Swan Corp 1 City Ctr Suite 2300 *TF:* 800-325-7008 ■ *Web:* www.theswancorp.com	Saint Louis	MO	63101	314-231-8148	231-8165
Thetford Corp 7101 Jackson Ave PO Box 1285 *TF:* 800-521-3032 ■ *Web:* www.thetford.com	Ann Arbor	MI	48106	734-769-6000	769-2023
Thetford Corp Recreational Vehicle Group 2901 E Bristol St Suite B *TF:* 800-831-1076 ■ *Web:* www.rvbusiness.com	Elkhart	IN	46514	574-266-7980	266-7984

614 PLUMBING FIXTURES & FITTINGS - VITREOUS CHINA & EARTHENWARE

	City	State	Zip	Phone	Fax
American Standard Cos Inc Bath & Kitchen Products Div 1 Centennial Ave PO Box 6820 *TF:* 800-223-0068 ■ *Web:* www.americanstandard-us.com	Piscataway	NJ	08855	732-980-3000	
Briggs Plumbing Products 300 Eagle Rd **Fax Area Code:* 800 ■ *TF:* 800-888-4458 ■ *Web:* www.briggsplumbing.com	Goose Creek	SC	29445	843-569-7887	627-4449*
Eljer Plumbingware Inc 14801 Quorum Dr 3rd Fl *TF:* 800-423-5537 ■ *Web:* www.eljer.com	Dallas	TX	75254	972-560-2000	560-2268
Gerber Plumbing Fixtures LLC 2500 International Pkwy *TF:* 888-648-6466 ■ *Web:* www.gerberonline.com	Woodridge	IL	60517	630-679-1420	679-1430
Kohler Canada Co 180 Creditview Rd *TF:* 800-456-4537 ■ *Web:* www.ca.kohler.com	Vaughan	ON	L4L9N4	905-762-6599	850-2356
Kohler Plumbing North America 444 Highland Dr **Fax:* Sales ■ *TF:* 800-456-4537 ■ *Web:* www.us.kohler.com	Kohler	WI	53044	920-457-4441	459-1658*
Mansfield Plumbing Products Inc 150 E 1st St PO Box 620 *TF:* 800-984-7802 ■ *Web:* www.mansfieldplumbing.com	Perrysville	OH	44864	419-938-5211	938-1427

Phone Fax

Microphor Inc 452 E Hill Rd .... Willits CA 95490 707-459-5563 459-6617
TF Orders: 800-358-8280 ■ *Web:* www.microphor.com

New Jersey Porcelain Lenape Products
600 Plum St .... Trenton NJ 08638 609-394-5376 394-0929
Web: www.lenapebath.com

Norman Supply Co 825 SW 5th St ....Oklahoma City OK 73109 405-235-9511 232-2645
TF: 800-375-3457 ■ *Web:* www.normansupply.com

Peerless Pottery Inc PO Box 145 .... Rockport IN 47635 812-649-6430 649-6429
TF: 800-457-5785 ■ *Web:* www.peerlesspottery.com

Sterling Plumbing 444 Highland Dr.................... Kohler WI 53044 920-457-4441 453-5851
TF Cust Svc: 888-783-7546 ■ *Web:* www.sterlingplumbing.com

Sunrise Specialty Co 930 98th Ave ....Oakland CA 94603 510-729-7277 729-7270
TF: 800-646-9117 ■ *Web:* www.sunrisespecialty.com

Toto USA Inc 1155 Southern Rd.......................Morrow GA 30260 770-282-8686 282-8701*
**Fax:* Cust Svc ■ *TF:* 888-295-8134 ■ *Web:* www.totousa.com

615 PLUMBING, HEATING, AIR CONDITIONING EQUIPMENT & SUPPLIES - WHOL

SEE ALSO Refrigeration Equipment - Whol p. 2532

Phone Fax

Aaron & Co Inc PO Box 8310 ....Piscataway NJ 08855 732-752-8200
TF: 800-734-4822 ■ *Web:* www.aaronco.com

AB Young Cos Inc 15305 Stony Creek Way.......... Noblesville IN 46060 317-565-5000 565-5010
TF: 800-886-7001 ■ *Web:* www.abyoung.com

ACR Group Inc 3200 Wilcrest Dr Suite 440.............Houston TX 77042 713-780-8532 780-4067
Web: www.acrgroup.com

Active Plumbing Supply Co
216 Richmond St ....Painesville OH 44077 440-352-4411 352-0096
TF: 800-949-4412 ■ *Web:* www.activeplumbing.com

Air Monitor Corp 1050 Hopper Ave................. Santa Rosa CA 95403 707-544-2706 526-9970
TF: 800-247-3569 ■ *Web:* www.airmonitor.com

American Granby Inc 7652 Morgan Rd ....Liverpool NY 13090 315-451-1100 451-1876*
**Fax:* Acctg ■ *TF:* 800-776-2266 ■ *Web:* www.americangranby.com

Applied Membranes Inc 2325 Cousteau Ct............... Vista CA 92081 760-727-3711 727-4427
TF: 800-321-9321 ■ *Web:* www.appliedmembranes.com

Aquatic Eco-Systems Inc
2395 Apopka Blvd Unit 100 .... Apopka FL 32703 407-886-3939 886-6787
TF: 877-347-4788 ■ *Web:* www.aquaticeco.com

Arizona Partsmaster Inc
15 N 57th Dr PO Box 23169.........................Phoenix AZ 85043 602-233-3580 233-3607
TF: 888-924-7278 ■ *Web:* www.azpartsmaster.com

Arizona Wholesale Supply Co
2020 E University Dr.............................Phoenix AZ 85034 602-258-7901 258-8335
TF: 800-877-4954 ■ *Web:* www.arizonawholesalesupply.com

Atlas Heating & Vent Co Ltd
340 Roebling Rd........................South San Francisco CA 94080 650-873-7000 266-8079
Web: www.atlasheat.com

Auburn Supply Co 3850 W 167th St.................Markham IL 60428 708-596-9800 596-0981
Web: www.auburnsupply.com

Baker Distributing Co 4255 Emerson St ....Jacksonville FL 32207 904-733-9633 407-4511
TF: 800-217-4698 ■ *Web:* www.bakerdist.com

Barnett Inc 801 W Bay St.......................Jacksonville FL 32204 904-384-6530 388-2723*
**Fax:* Mktg ■ *TF:* 800-288-2000 ■ *Web:* www.e-barnett.com

Bayonne Plumbing 250 Ave E...................... Bayonne NJ 07002 201-339-8000 339-2770
TF: 800-713-7473 ■ *Web:* www.bayonneplumbingsupply.com

Behler-Young Co 4900 Clyde Pk SW ....Grand Rapids MI 49509 616-531-3400 531-1453
Web: www.behler-young.com

Brauer Supply Co 4260 Forest Pk Ave .... Saint Louis MO 63108 314-534-7150 534-1816
TF: 800-392-8776 ■ *Web:* www.brauersupply.com

Broedell Plumbing Supply Inc
1601 Commerce Ln Suite 100 ....Jupiter FL 33458 561-747-8000 743-4644
TF: 800-683-6363 ■ *Web:* www.broedell.com

Bruce Supply Corp 8805 18th Ave .... Brooklyn NY 11214 718-259-4900 256-5082
Web: www.brucesupplyplumbing.com

Butcher Distributors Inc 101 Boyce Rd .... Broussard LA 70518 337-837-2088 837-2069
TF: 800-960-0008 ■ *Web:* www.butcherdistributors.com

Capitol Plumbing & Heating Supply Co Inc
3125 Cocker Ln ....Springfield IL 62711 217-793-4300 793-7637
TF: 800-477-8525

Caroplast Inc PO Box 668405...................... Charlotte NC 28266 704-394-4191
TF: 800-327-5797 ■ *Web:* www.caroplast.com

Caylor Industrial Sales Inc PO Box 4659.............. Dalton GA 30719 706-226-3198 278-4104
Web: www.caylorindustrial.com

Chicago Furnace Supply Co 4929 S Lincoln Ave.......... Lisle IL 60532 630-971-0400 971-0255
Web: www.chicagofurnace.com

Cleveland Plumbing Supply Co Inc
143 E Washington St ....Chagrin Falls OH 44022 440-247-2555 247-2116
TF: 800-331-1078 ■ *Web:* www.clevelandplumbing.com

Coburn Supply Co Inc 390 Pk St Suite 950 .... Beaumont TX 77701 409-838-6363 838-1920
TF: 800-832-8492 ■ *Web:* www.coburns.com

Comfort Supply Inc 407 Garden Oaks Blvd ....Houston TX 77018 713-845-4705 491-5080
TF: 800-281-7511 ■ *Web:* www.comfortsupply.com

Consolidated Supply Co 7337 SW Kable Ln............. Tigard OR 97224 503-620-7050 684-3254
TF: 800-929-5810 ■ *Web:* www.consolidatedsupply.com

Corr Tech Inc 4545 Homestead Rd ....Houston TX 77028 713-674-7887 674-0840
Web: www.corr-tech.com

Dana Kepner Co Inc 700 Alcott St ....Denver CO 80204 303-623-6161 623-1667
TF: 800-332-3079 ■ *Web:* www.danakepner.com

Duncan Supply Co Inc 910 N Illinois St............Indianapolis IN 46204 317-634-1335 264-6689
TF: 800-382-5528 ■ *Web:* www.duncansupply.com

Eastern Pennsylvania Supply Co
700 Scott St PO Box 1126 ....Wilkes-Barre PA 18773 570-823-1181 824-2514
TF: 800-432-8075 ■ *Web:* www.easternpenn.com

Emco Corp 1108 Dundas St E...................... London ON N5W3A7 519-453-9600 453-9432
TF: 800-265-1065 ■ *Web:* www.emcoltd.com

Emerson-Swan Inc 300 Pond St......................Randolph MA 02368 781-986-2000 986-2028
TF: 800-346-9219 ■ *Web:* www.emersonswan.com

Engineering & Equipment Co Inc
910 N Washington St ....Albany GA 31701 229-435-5601 435-1502
TF: 800-688-8816

Everett J Prescott Inc 32 Prescott St .... Gardiner ME 04345 207-582-1851 582-5637
TF: 800-876-1357 ■ *Web:* www.ejprescott.com

Ferguson Enterprises Inc
12500 Jefferson Ave..........................Newport News VA 23602 757-874-7795 989-2501
Web: www.ferguson.com

First Supply LLC 6800 Gisholt Dr .... Madison WI 53713 608-222-7799 223-6621
TF: 800-236-9795 ■ *Web:* www.1supply.com

Forrer Supply Co Inc PO Box 220 .... Germantown WI 53022 262-255-3030 255-4064
TF: 800-255-1030 ■ *Web:* www.forrersupply.com

Four Seasons Inc 1801 Waters Ridge Dr .... Lewisville TX 75057 972-316-8100 316-8220
TF: 800-433-7508 ■ *Web:* www.4s.com

Fresno Distributing Co Inc
2055 E McKinley Ave ....Fresno CA 93703 559-442-8800 264-3809
TF: 800-655-2542 ■ *Web:* www.fresnod.com

Frontier Supply Inc 981 Van Horn Rd ....Fairbanks AK 99701 907-374-3500 374-3570
TF: 800-478-7867 ■ *Web:* www.frontierplumbing.com

Fujikin of America Inc
4677 Old Ironsides Dr .... Santa Clara CA 95054 408-980-8269 980-0572
Web: www.fujikin.com

Gateway Supply Co Inc 1312 Hamrick St ....Columbia SC 29202 803-771-7160 376-5600
TF: 800-922-5312 ■ *Web:* www.gatewaysupply.net

General Plumbing Supply Co Inc
PO Box 4666 ....Walnut Creek CA 94596 925-939-4622 939-1548
Web: www.generalplumbingsupply.com

Gensco Inc 4402 20th St E........................... Tacoma WA 98424 253-620-8203 926-2073
TF: 800-729-3003 ■ *Web:* www.gensco.com

Goodin Co 2700 N 2nd St.......................Minneapolis MN 55411 612-588-7811 588-7820*
**Fax Area Code:* 763 ■ *TF:* 800-328-8433 ■ *Web:* www.goodinco.com

Granite Group Wholesalers LLC 6 Storrs St........... Concord NH 03301 603-224-1901 224-6821*
**Fax Area Code:* 602 ■ *TF:* 800-258-3690 ■ *Web:* www.thegranitegroup.com

GW Berkheimer Co Inc 6000 Southport Rd............. Portage IN 46368 219-764-5200 764-5203
Web: www.gwberkheimer.com

Habegger Corp 4995 Winton Rd .... Cincinnati OH 45232 513-681-6313 681-9892
Web: www.habeggercorp.com

Hajoca Corp 127 Coulter Ave........................ Ardmore PA 19003 610-649-1430 649-7258
TF: 800-284-3164 ■ *Web:* www.hajoca.com

Hajoca Corp Keenan Supply Div
1341 Philadelphia St ....Pomona CA 91766 909-613-1363 613-1173
TF: 800-437-6593 ■ *Web:* www.hajoca.com

Harri Plumbing & Heating Inc 809 W 12th St ....Juneau AK 99801 907-586-3190 586-4129
TF: 800-478-3190 ■ *Web:* www.harriplumbing.com

Harrison Piping Supply Co Inc
38777 Schoolcraft Rd............................. Livonia MI 48150 734-464-4400 464-6488
TF: 800-482-3929 ■ *Web:* www.harrisonco.com

Harry Cooper Supply Co Inc
605 N Sherman Pkwy ....Springfield MO 65802 417-865-8392 873-9146
TF: 800-426-6737 ■ *Web:* www.harrycooper.com

Hercules Industries Inc 1310 W Evans Ave ....Denver CO 80223 303-937-1000 937-0903
TF: 800-356-5350 ■ *Web:* www.herculesindustries.com

I D Booth Inc PO Box 579 .... Elmira NY 14902 607-733-9121 733-9111
TF: 888-432-6684 ■ *Web:* www.idbooth.com

ILLCO Inc 535 S River St............................ Aurora IL 60506 630-892-7904 892-0318
Web: www.illco.com

Indiana Supply Corp 3835 E 21st St...............Indianapolis IN 46218 317-359-5451 351-2135
TF: 800-686-0195 ■ *Web:* www.indianasupply.com

Irr Supply Centers Inc
908 Niagara Falls Blvd ....North Tonawanda NY 14120 716-692-1600 692-1611
Web: www.irrsupply.com

J & B Supply Inc 4915 S Zero St.................... Fort Smith AR 72903 479-649-4915 649-4911
TF: 800-345-5752 ■ *Web:* www.jandbsupply.com

JH Larson Co 10200 51st Ave N.................... Plymouth MN 55442 763-545-1717 545-1144
TF: 800-292-7970 ■ *Web:* www.jhlarson.com

John M Frey Co Inc 2735 62nd St Ct.............. Bettendorf IA 52722 563-332-9200 332-9880
TF: 800-397-3739 ■ *Web:* www.jmfcompany.com

Johnson Supply & Equipment Inc
10151 Stella Link Rd ....Houston TX 77025 713-830-2300 661-3684
TF: 800-833-5455 ■ *Web:* www.johnsonsupply.com

Keidel Supply Co 2026 Delaware Ave .... Cincinnati OH 45212 513-351-1600 351-9649
Web: www.keidel.com

Keller Supply Co Inc 3209 17th Ave W .... Seattle WA 98119 206-285-3300 283-8668*
**Fax:* Acctg ■ *TF:* 800-285-3302 ■ *Web:* www.kellersupply.com

Kelly's Pipe & Supply Co Inc
2124 Industrial Rd .... Las Vegas NV 89102 702-382-4957 382-4879
TF: 888-382-4957 ■ *Web:* www.kellyspipe.com

Koch Air LLC 1900 W Lloyd Expy PO Box 1167......... Evansville IN 47706 812-962-5200 962-5310
TF: 877-456-2422 ■ *Web:* www.kochair.com

Lee Supply Corp 6610 Guion Rd..................Indianapolis IN 46268 317-290-2500 290-2512
TF: 800-873-1103 ■ *Web:* www.leesupply.net

Longley Supply Co Inc 2018 Oleander Dr .... Wilmington NC 28403 910-762-7793 762-9178

Mdm Supply Inc PO Box 6018 ....Helena MT 59604 406-443-4012 442-4536
Web: www.mdmsupply.com

Mid-Lakes Distributing Inc 1029 W Adams St..........Chicago IL 60607 312-733-1033 733-1721
TF: 888-733-2700 ■ *Web:* www.mid-lakes.com

Mid-States Supply Co 1716 Guinotte Ave ....Kansas City MO 64120 816-842-4290 842-3630
TF: 800-825-1410 ■ *Web:* www.midcoonline.com

Milwaukee Stove & Furnace Supply Co
5070 W State St ....Milwaukee WI 53208 414-258-0300 258-8552
Web: www.mstove.com

Moore Supply Co 200 N Loop 336 W .... Conroe TX 77301 936-756-4445 441-8468
Web: www.mooresupply.com

Morley-Murphy Co
200 S Washington St Suite 305 .... Green Bay WI 54301 920-499-3171 499-9409
TF: 877-499-3171 ■ *Web:* www.morley-murphycompany.com

Morrison Supply Co Inc 311 E Vickery Blvd ....Fort Worth TX 76104 817-336-0451 338-1612
Web: www.morsco.com

Mountain States Pipe & Supply Co
111 W Las Vegas St...................... Colorado Springs CO 80903 719-634-5555 634-5551
TF: 800-777-7173 ■ *Web:* www.msps.com

Mountainland Supply Co 1505 W 130 S................ Orem UT 84058 801-224-6050 224-6058
TF: 800-666-5434 ■ *Web:* www.mtncom.net

Company / Address	City	State	Zip	Phone	Fax
Murray Supply Co LLC 500 Olive St	Winston Salem	NC	27103	336-765-9480	245-0686
Web: www.murraysupply.com					
NB Handy Co 65 10th St	Lynchburg	VA	24504	434-847-4495	847-2404
TF: 800-284-6242 ■ *Web:* www.nbhandy.com					
New York Replacement Parts Corp 19 School St	Yonkers	NY	10701	914-965-0122	965-3147
TF: 800-228-4718 ■ *Web:* www.nyrpcorp.com					
Northeastern Supply Co Inc 8323 Pulaski Hwy	Baltimore	MD	21237	410-574-0010	574-3315*
**Fax:* Sales ■ *TF:* 800-999-5664 ■ *Web:* www.northeastern.com					
Northwest Pipe Fittings Inc 33 S 8th St W	Billings	MT	59103	406-252-0142	248-8072
TF: 800-937-4737 ■ *Web:* www.northwestpipe.net					
O'Connor Sales Inc 16107 Piuma Ave	Cerritos	CA	90703	562-403-3848	403-3858
Web: www.oconnorsales.net					
Peabody Supply Co Inc PO Box 669	Peabody	MA	01960	978-532-2200	532-1463
TF: 800-445-5816 ■ *Web:* www.peabodysupply.com					
Plumb Supply Co 1622 NE 51st Ave	Des Moines	IA	50313	515-262-9511	262-9790
TF: 800-483-9511 ■ *Web:* www.plumbsupply.com					
Plumbers Supply Co 1000 E Main St	Louisville	KY	40206	502-582-2261	585-5521
TF: 800-626-5133 ■ *Web:* www.plumbers-supply-co.com					
Plumbing Distributors Inc 1025 Old Norcross Rd	Lawrenceville	GA	30045	770-963-9231	822-9509
TF: 800-262-9231 ■ *Web:* www.pdiplumbing.com					
Porter Pipe & Supply Co 303 S Rohlwing Rd	Addison	IL	60101	630-543-8145	543-6830
Web: www.porterpipe.com					
Redlon & Johnson 172 St John St # 174	Portland	ME	04102	207-773-4755	772-2957
TF: 800-905-5250 ■ *Web:* www.redlon-johnson.com					
Reeves-Wiedeman Co Inc 14861 W 100th St	Lenexa	KS	66215	913-492-7100	492-6962
Web: www.rwco.com					
Refrigeration Sales Corp 9450 Allen Dr Suite A	Valley View	OH	44125	216-881-7800	525-8196
TF: 866-525-8196 ■ *Web:* www.refrigerationsales.net					
Republic Plumbing Supply Co Inc 890 Providence Hwy	Norwood	MA	02062	800-696-3900	769-7842*
**Fax Area Code:* 781 ■ *TF:* 800-696-3900 ■ *Web:* www.republicsupplyco.com					
Roberts-Hamilton Co Inc 7300 Northland Dr	Brooklyn Park	MN	55428	763-315-0100	315-0199
TF: 800-888-2222 ■ *Web:* www.robertshamilton.com					
Robertson Heating Supply Co 2155 W Main St	Alliance	OH	44601	330-821-9180	821-8251
TF: 800-433-9532 ■ *Web:* www.robertsonheatingsupply.com					
Robertson Supply Inc PO Box 1366	Nampa	ID	83653	208-466-8907	466-8900
Web: www.robertsonsupply.com					
Rundle-Spence Mfg Co PO Box 510008	New Berlin	WI	53151	262-782-3000	782-5078
TF: 800-783-6060 ■ *Web:* www.rundle-spence.com					
Samon's Tiger Stores Inc 2511 Monroe St NE	Albuquerque	NM	87110	505-884-4615	884-1725
Sauna Warehouse Inc 6 Orchard St Suite 201	Lake Forest	CA	92630	949-609-2202	699-0830
TF: 800-906-2242 ■ *Web:* www.saunawarehouse.com					
Security Supply Corp 196 Maple Ave	Selkirk	NY	12158	518-767-2226	767-2065
TF: 800-333-2226 ■ *Web:* www.secsupply.com					
SG Supply Co 12900 S Throop St	Calumet Park	IL	60827	708-371-8800	371-2752
TF: 800-626-9130 ■ *Web:* www.sgsupply.com					
Shane Group Inc PO Box 765	Hillsdale	MI	49242	517-439-4316	439-9159
Web: www.shanegroup.com					
Shelton Winnelson Co PO Box 761	Shelton	CT	06484	203-929-6344	929-6346
Web: www.sheltonwinnelson.com					
Sid Harvey Industries Inc 605 Locust St	Garden City	NY	11530	516-745-9200	268-6542*
**Fax Area Code:* 800 ■ *Web:* www.sidharvey.com					
Solar Depot LLC 1240 Holm Rd	Petaluma	CA	94954	707-766-7727	
TF: 800-822-4041 ■ *Web:* www.solardepot.com					
SPS Cos Inc 6363 Minnesota 7	Saint Louis Park	MN	55416	952-929-1377	929-1862
Web: www.spscompanies.com					
Standard Air & Lite Corp 2406 Woodmere Dr	Pittsburgh	PA	15205	412-920-6505	733-0010
TF: 800-472-2458 ■ *Web:* www.stdair.com					
TBA LLC 6700 Enterprise Dr	Louisville	KY	40214	502-367-0222	361-0715
TF: 800-626-3525 ■ *Web:* www.tballc.com					
Temperature Equipment Corp 17725 Volbrecht Rd	Lansing	IL	60438	708-418-0900	418-5100
Web: www.tecmungo.com					
Temperature Systems Inc 5001 Voges Rd	Madison	WI	53718	608-271-7500	274-1609
TF: 800-366-0930 ■ *Web:* www.tsihvac.com					
Thermal Corp 1264 Slaughter Rd	Madison	AL	35758	256-837-1122	837-0265
TF: 800-633-2962 ■ *Web:* www.thermalcorp.com					
Thomas Somerville Co 16155 Trade Zone Ave	Upper Marlboro	MD	20774	301-390-9575	390-1108
Web: www.tsomerville.com					
Three States Supply Co LLC 666 EH Crump Blvd	Memphis	TN	38126	901-948-8651	948-2454
TF: 800-666-1565 ■ *Web:* www.threestates.com					
Torrington Supply Co Inc 100 N Elm St	Waterbury	CT	06723	203-756-3641	753-4317
TF: 800-445-9936 ■ *Web:* www.torringtonsupply.com					
United Pipe & Supply Co Inc 90099 Prairie Rd	Eugene	OR	97402	541-688-6511	688-8994
TF: 800-288-6511 ■ *Web:* www.unitedpipe.com					
UP Electric/Wittock Supply Co 2650 Trautner Dr	Saginaw	MI	48603	989-497-2100	497-2101
TF: 800-562-7102 ■ *Web:* www.wittock.com					
US Airconditioning Distributors 16900 Chestnut St	City of Industry	CA	91748	626-854-4500	854-4690*
**Fax:* Sales ■ *TF:* 800-937-7222 ■ *Web:* www.us-ac.com					
V P Supply Corp PO Box 23868	Rochester	NY	14692	585-272-0110	272-0547
TF: 800-289-2284 ■ *Web:* www.vpsupply.com					
Vamac Inc 4201 Jacque St	Richmond	VA	23230	804-353-7811	358-7855
TF: 800-768-2622 ■ *Web:* www.vamac.com					
WA Roosevelt Co 2727 Commerce St	La Crosse	WI	54603	608-781-2000	781-8360
TF: 800-279-2726 ■ *Web:* www.waroosevelt.com					
Waxman Industries Inc 24460 Aurora Rd	Bedford Heights	OH	44146	440-439-1830	439-8494*
**Fax:* Cust Svc ■ *TF:* 800-531-3342 ■ *Web:* www.waxmanind.com					
Western Nevada Supply Co 950 S Rock Blvd	Sparks	NV	89431	775-359-5800	359-4649
TF: 800-648-1230 ■ *Web:* www.wns1.com					
Wholesale Supply Group Inc 885 Keith St NW	Cleveland	TN	37320	423-478-1191	478-5120
Web: www.wsginc.com					
Wilmar Industries Inc 200 E Pk Dr Suite 200	Mount Laurel	NJ	08054	856-439-1222	439-1333
TF: 800-345-3000 ■ *Web:* www.wilmar.com					
Winnelson 3110 Kettering Blvd	Dayton	OH	45439	937-294-7242	294-6921
Web: www.winholesale.com					
WinWholesale Inc 3110 Kettering Blvd	Dayton	OH	45439	937-294-6878	293-9591
Woodhill Supply Inc 4665 Beidler Rd	Willoughby	OH	44094	440-269-1100	269-1027
TF: 800-362-6111 ■ *Web:* www.woodhillsupply.com					
Young Supply Co 888 W Baltimore St	Detroit	MI	48202	313-875-3280	875-3051
TF: 800-872-3280 ■ *Web:* www.youngsupply.com					

616 PLYWOOD & VENEERS

SEE ALSO Lumber & Building Supplies p. 1733; Home Improvement Centers p. 2024

Company / Address	City	State	Zip	Phone	Fax
Aetna Plywood Inc 1401 St Charles Rd	Maywood	IL	60153	708-343-1515	343-1616
Web: www.aetnaplywood.com					
Amos-Hill Assoc Inc 112 Shelby Ave PO Box 7	Edinburgh	IN	46124	812-526-2671	526-5865
Web: www.amoshill.com					
Anderson Hardwood Floors PO Box 1155	Clinton	SC	29325	864-833-6250	833-6664
Web: www.andersonfloors.com					
Arkansas Face Veneer Inc 706 Ctr St PO Box 706	Benton	AR	72018	501-778-7412	778-7414
Web: www.arkansasface.com					
Atlantic Veneer Corp 2457 Lennoxville Rd PO Box 660	Beaufort	NC	28516	252-728-3169	728-4203
TF: 800-334-7723					
Barmon Door & Plywood Inc 2508 Hartford Dr	Lake Stevens	WA	98258	425-334-1222	335-0404
Bradford Veneer & Panel Co 1143 Clark Pond Rd	North Haverhill	NH	03774	802-222-5241	222-5134
Web: www.bvpc.com					
Buffalo Veneer & Plywood Co Inc 501 6th Ave NE PO Box 95	Buffalo	MN	55313	763-682-1822	682-9769
California Panel & Veneer Co 14055 Artesia Blvd	Cerritos	CA	90703	562-926-5834	926-3139
TF: 800-451-1745 ■ *Web:* www.calpanel.com					
Capital Veneer Works Inc 2550 Jackson Ferry Rd	Montgomery	AL	36104	334-264-1401	264-6923
Capitol Plywood Inc 160 Commerce Cir	Sacramento	CA	95815	916-922-8861	922-0775
TF: 800-326-1505 ■ *Web:* www.capitolplywood.com					
Cleveland Plywood Co Inc 5900 Harvard Ave	Cleveland	OH	44105	216-641-6600	641-6600
TF: 800-727-2759 ■ *Web:* www.clevelandplywood.com					
Columbia Forest Products Inc 222 SW Columbia St Suite 1575	Portland	OR	97201	503-224-5300	224-5294
TF: 800-547-4261 ■ *Web:* www.columbiaforestproducts.com					
Columbia Forest Products Inc Columbia Plywood Div PO Box 1780	Klamath Falls	OR	97601	541-882-7281	882-7295
TF: 800-547-1791 ■ *Web:* www.cfpwood.com					
Columbia Panel Mfg Co 100 Giles St	High Point	NC	27263	336-861-4100	861-4700
Constantine's Wood Ctr 1040 E Oakland Pk Blvd	Fort Lauderdale	FL	33334	954-561-1716	565-8149
TF: 800-443-9667 ■ *Web:* www.constantines.com					
Cummings Veneers Inc 601 E 4th St	New Albany	IN	47150	812-944-2269	944-0212
Darlington Veneer Co Inc 225 4th St	Darlington	SC	29532	843-393-3861	393-8243
TF: 800-845-2388 ■ *Web:* www.darlingtonveneer.com					
David R Webb Co Inc 206 S Holland St PO Box 8	Edinburgh	IN	46124	812-526-2601	526-5842
Web: www.davidrwebb.com					
Davis Wood Products Inc 735 Main St	Hudson	NC	28638	828-728-8444	728-4601
Web: www.daviswoodproducts.com					
Eggers Industries Inc 1 Eggers Dr	Two Rivers	WI	54241	920-793-1351	793-2958
Web: www.eggersindustries.com					
Erath Veneer Corp of Virginia 80 Industrial Ave	Rocky Mount	VA	24151	540-483-5223	483-1580
Web: www.erathveneer.com					
Fiber-Tech Industries Inc 2000 Kenskill Ave	Washington Court House	OH	43160	740-335-9400	335-4843
TF: 800-879-4377 ■ *Web:* www.fiber-tech.net					
Flexible Materials Inc 1202 Port Rd	Jeffersonville	IN	47130	812-280-7000	280-7001
TF: 800-359-9663 ■ *Web:* www.flexwood.com					
Freeman Corp 145 Magnolia St	Winchester	KY	40391	859-744-4311	744-4363
Web: www.freemancorp.com					
Freres Lumber Co Inc PO Box 276	Lyons	OR	97358	503-859-2121	859-2112
G-L Veneer Co Inc 2224 E Slauson Ave	Huntington Park	CA	90255	323-582-5203	582-9681
TF: 800-588-5003 ■ *Web:* www.glveneer.com					
Hambro Forest Products Inc 445 Elk Valley Rd PO Box 129	Crescent City	CA	95531	707-464-6131	464-9375
Web: www.cresdek.com					
Harbor Sales 1000 Harbor Ct	Sudlersville	MD	21668	800-345-1712	868-9257
TF: 800-345-1712 ■ *Web:* www.harborsales.net					
Hardel Mutual Plywood Corp 143 Maurin Rd	Chehalis	WA	98532	360-740-0232	740-9570
TF: 800-562-6344 ■ *Web:* www.hardel.com					
Hasty Plywood Co 100 N Austin St	Maxton	NC	28364	910-844-5267	844-9483
Web: www.hasply.com					
Hood Industries Inc 15 Professional Pkwy # 8	Hattiesburg	MS	39402	601-264-2559	296-4755
Web: www.hoodindustries.com					
Hoquiam Plywood Co Inc 1000 Woodlawn Rd	Hoquiam	WA	98550	360-533-3060	532-6980
Inland Plywood Co 375 N Cass Ave	Pontiac	MI	48342	248-334-4706	338-7407
TF: 800-521-4355 ■ *Web:* www.inlandplywood.com					
J M McCormick Co Inc (JMMC) 521 S Enterprise Blvd	Lebanon	IN	46052	765-894-8282	471-8065*
**Fax Area Code:* 317 ■ *TF:* 800-878-4700 ■ *Web:* www.jmmccormick.com					
Louisiana-Pacific Corp 414 Union St Suite 2000	Nashville	TN	37219	615-986-5600	986-5666
NYSE: LPX ■ *TF:* 877-744-5600 ■ *Web:* www.lpcorp.com					
Marion Plywood Corp 222 S Parkview Ave PO Box 497	Marion	WI	54950	715-754-5231	754-2582
Web: www.marionplywood.com					
Murphy Hardwood Plywood 2350 Prairie Rd	Eugene	OR	97402	541-461-4545	461-4547
TF: 888-461-4545 ■ *Web:* www.murphyplywood.com					

				Phone	Fax
Murphy Plywood Co 2350 Prairie Rd *TF:* 888-461-4545 ■ *Web:* www.murphyplywood.com	Eugene	OR	97408	541-461-4545	461-4546
Norbord Inc 1 Toronto St Suite 600 *TSX: NBD* ■ *TF:* 888-667-2673 ■ *Web:* www.norbord.com	Toronto	ON	M5C2W4	416-365-0705	365-3292
North American Plywood Corp 12343 Hawkins St *TF Sales:* 800-421-1372	Santa Fe Springs	CA	90670	562-941-7575	944-8368
Pasquier Panel Products Inc 1510 Puyallup St PO Box 1170 *Web:* www.pasquierpanel.com	Sumner	WA	98390	253-863-6323	891-7993
Pavco Industries Inc 619 Delmas Ave *TF:* 800-346-7206 ■ *Web:* www.pavcoind.com	Pascagoula	MS	39568	228-762-3172	762-3108
Phillips Plywood Co Inc 13599 Desmond St *TF Cust Svc:* 800-649-6410 ■ *Web:* www.phillipsplywood.com	Pacoima	CA	91331	818-897-7736	897-6571
Plywood Supply Inc 7036 NE 175th St *TF:* 800-683-9663 ■ *Web:* www.plywoodsupply.com	Kenmore	WA	98028	425-485-8585	485-6195
Potlatch Corp 601 W 1st Ave Suite 1600 *NASDAQ: PCH* ■ *Web:* www.potlatchcorp.com	Spokane	WA	99201	509-835-1500	835-1555
Potlatch Corp Wood Products Div 805 Mill Rd PO Box 1388 *Web:* www.potlatchcorp.com	Lewiston	ID	83501	208-799-0123	799-1918
Robert Weed Plywood Corp 705 Maple St PO Box 487 *Web:* www.robertweedplywood.com	Bristol	IN	46507	574-848-4408	848-5679
Roseburg Forest Products Co PO Box 1088 *TF:* 800-548-5275 ■ *Web:* www.rfpco.com	Roseburg	OR	97470	541-679-3311	
RS Bacon Veneer Co 6951 High Grove Blvd *TF:* 800-443-7995 ■ *Web:* www.baconveneer.com	Burr Ridge	IL	60527	630-323-1414	323-1499
SDS Lumber Co PO Box 266 *Web:* www.sdslumber.com	Bingen	WA	98605	509-493-2155	493-2535
South Coast Lumber Co 885 Railroad Ave PO Box 670 *Web:* www.socomi.com	Brookings	OR	97415	541-469-2136	469-9105
States Industries Inc PO Box 7037 *TF:* 800-626-1981 ■ *Web:* www.statesind.com	Eugene	OR	97401	541-688-7871	
StemWood Corp 2710 Grant Line Rd *Web:* www.stemwood.com	New Albany	IN	47150	812-945-6646	945-7549
Stimson Lumber Co 520 SW Yamhill St Suite 700 *TF:* 800-445-9758 ■ *Web:* www.stimsonlumber.com	Portland	OR	97204	503-222-1676	295-1849
Stoll Bros Lumber Inc PO Box 367	Odon	IN	47562	812-636-4053	636-8025
Texas Plywood & Lumber Co Inc 1001 E Ave K *Web:* www.texasplywood.com	Grand Prairie	TX	75050	972-262-1331	624-2225
Trimac Panel Products 5201 SW Westgate Dr # 200 *Web:* www.trimacpanel.com	Portland	OR	97221	503-297-1826	297-9049
United Plywood & Lumber Inc 1640 Mims Ave SW *TF:* 800-272-6486 ■ *Web:* www.unitedplywoods.com	Birmingham	AL	35211	205-925-7601	923-9511
Wavell-Huber Wood Products Inc 180 N 170 W *Web:* www.wavell-huber.com	North Salt Lake	UT	84054	801-936-6080	936-6078
Westcoast Forest Products 19406 68th Dr NE	Arlington	WA	98223	360-435-2175	435-3232
Winnsboro Plywood Co PO Box 449	Winnsboro	SC	29180	803-635-4696	635-3023
Wisconsin Veneer & Plywood Inc PO Box 140	Mattoon	WI	54450	715-489-3611	489-3268
@pos Transaction Systems 3051 N 1st St	San Jose	CA	95134	408-468-5400	433-0774

617 POINT-OF-SALE (POS) & POINT-OF-INFORMATION (POI) SYSTEMS

				Phone	Fax
3M Digital Signage 600 Ericksen Ave NE Suite 200 *TF:* 888-460-8866 ■ *Web:* www.3mdigitalsignage.com	Bainbridge Island	WA	98110	206-855-2000	855-4930
Catuity Inc 300 Preston Ave Suite 302 *NASDAQ: CTTY* ■ **Fax Area Code:* 734	Charlottesville	VA	22902	434-979-0724	293-4213*
CeroView 3 Chrysler *Web:* www.ceroview.com	Irvine	CA	92618	949-454-6500	454-2323
Checkpoint Systems Inc 101 Wolf Dr *NYSE: CKP* ■ *TF:* 800-257-5540 ■ *Web:* www.checkpointsystems.com	Thorofare	NJ	08086	856-848-1800	848-0937
Comtrex Systems Corp 1247 N Church St Suite 7 *Web:* www.comtrex.com	Moorestown	NJ	08057	856-778-0090	778-9322
Datalogic Scanning 959 Terry St *TF:* 800-695-5700 ■ *Web:* www.datalogic.com	Eugene	OR	97402	541-683-5700	345-7140
Fujitsu Transaction Solutions Inc 2801 Network Blvd *TF:* 800-538-8716 ■ *Web:* www.fujitsu.com	Frisco	TX	75034	972-963-2300	963-2641
Hypercom Corp 8888 E Raintree Dr Suite 300 *NYSE: HYC* ■ *TF:* 800-577-5501 ■ *Web:* www.hypercom.com	Scottsdale	AZ	85260	480-642-5000	642-4655
Kiosk Information Systems Inc (KIS) 346 S Arthur Ave *TF:* 800-529-5471 ■ *Web:* www.kis-kiosk.com	Louisville	CO	80027	303-466-5471	466-6730
Micros Systems Inc 7031 Columbia Gateway Dr *NASDAQ: MCRS* ■ **Fax:* Sales ■ *TF:* 800-937-2211 ■ *Web:* www.micros.com	Columbia	MD	21046	443-285-6000	285-0455*
MTI Inc 1050 NW 229th Ave *TF:* 800-426-6844 ■ *Web:* www.mti-interactive.com	Hillsboro	OR	97124	503-648-6500	648-7500
Omron Systems Inc 55 E Commerce Dr *TF Tech Supp:* 800-706-6766 ■ *Web:* www.omronosi.com	Schaumburg	IL	60173	847-884-0322	884-1866
PAR Technology Corp 8383 Seneca Tpke *NYSE: PTC* ■ *TF:* 800-448-6505 ■ *Web:* www.partech.com	New Hartford	NY	13413	315-738-0600	738-0562
Radiant Systems Inc 3925 Brookside Pkwy *NASDAQ: RADS* ■ *TF:* 877-794-7237 ■ *Web:* www.radiantsystems.com	Alpharetta	GA	30022	770-576-6000	754-7790
SeePoint Technology LLC 2619 Manhattan Beach Blvd *Web:* www.seepoint.com	Redondo Beach	CA	90278	310-725-9660	535-9234
Toshiba TEC America Retail Information Systems Inc 4401-A Bankers Cir *Web:* www.toshibatecusa.com	Atlanta	GA	30360	770-449-3040	449-1152
TouchSystems Corp 220 Tradesmen Dr *TF:* 800-320-5944 ■ *Web:* www.touchsystems.com	Hutto	TX	78634	512-846-2424	846-2425
Transaction Printer Group Inc 5893 Oberlin Dr Suite 103 *TF:* 800-732-8950 ■ *Web:* www.tpgprinters.com	San Diego	CA	92121	858-638-0000	320-0335
UTC RETAIL Inc 100 Rawson Rd *TF:* 800-349-0546 ■ *Web:* www.utcretail.com	Victor	NY	14564	585-924-9500	924-1434
VeriFone Inc 2099 Gateway Pl Suite 600 *NYSE: PAY* ■ *TF:* 800-837-4366 ■ *Web:* www.verifone.com	San Jose	CA	95110	408-232-7800	232-7811

618 POLITICAL ACTION COMMITTEES

SEE ALSO Civic & Political Organizations p. 1417

				Phone	Fax
21st Century Freedom PAC 355 Lexington Ave Suite 1001	New York	NY	10017	212-599-2121	370-0064
Action Committee for Rural Electrification (ACRE) 4301 Wilson Blvd *Web:* www.nreca.org/programs/PoliticalAction/Pages/default.aspx	Arlington	VA	22203	703-907-5500	907-5516
Action Fund of Lehman Bros Holdings Inc 2001 K St NW Suite 1125	Washington	DC	20006	202-452-4720	452-4791
AFL-CIO Committee on Political Education 815 16th St NW *Web:* www.aflcio.org	Washington	DC	20006	202-637-5101	637-5058
Air Conditioning Contractors of America PAC (ACCA-PAC) 2800 Shirlington Rd Suite 300	Arlington	VA	22206	703-575-4477	575-4449
Aircraft Owners & Pilots Assn PAC 601 Pennsylvania Ave NW S Bldg Suite 875	Washington	DC	20004	202-737-7950	737-7951
American Academy of Ophthalmology PAC 1101 Vermont Ave NW Suite 700	Washington	DC	20005	202-737-6662	737-7061
American Academy of Physician Assistants (AAPA) 2318 Mill Rd Suite 1300 *Web:* www.aapa.org	Alexandria	VA	22314	703-836-2272	684-1924
American Airlines PAC (AAPAC) 4333 Amon Carter Blvd PO Box 619616 **Fax Area Code:* 202 ■ *Web:* www.aa.com/i18n/aboutUs/corporateResponsibility/profile/public-policy.jsp	Fort Worth	TX	76155	817-963-1234	496-5660*
American Apparel & Footwear Assn PAC 1601 N Kent St Suite 1200	Arlington	VA	22209	703-524-1864	522-6741
American Assn for Justice PAC 1050 31st St NW *Web:* www.justice.org	Washington	DC	20007	202-965-3500	
American Assn of Crop Insurers PAC 1 Massachusetts Ave NW Suite 800	Washington	DC	20001	202-789-4100	408-7763
American Assn of Nurse Anesthetists PAC (AANAPAC) 222 S Prospect Ave *Web:* www.aana.com/aboutaana.aspx?id=105	Park Ridge	IL	60068	847-692-7050	692-6968
American Assn of Orthodontists PAC 401 N Lindbergh Blvd *TF:* 800-424-2841	Saint Louis	MO	63141	314-993-1700	997-1745
American Bakers Assn PAC 1300 'I' St NW Suite 700-W	Washington	DC	20005	202-789-0300	898-1164
American Bankers Assn PAC (ABAPAC) 1120 Connecticut Ave NW *Web:* www.aba.com/default.htm	Washington	DC	20036	202-663-5113	663-7544
American Beverage Assn PAC 1101 16th St NW	Washington	DC	20036	202-463-6732	463-8178
American Chiropractic Assn PAC (ACA-PAC) 1701 Clarendon Blvd *TF:* 800-986-4636	Arlington	VA	22209	703-276-8800	243-2593
American Dental PAC 1111 14th St NW Suite 1100	Washington	DC	20005	202-898-2424	898-2437
American Express PAC PO Box 981540 **Fax Area Code:* 202 ■ *TF Cust Svc:* 800-582-4800	El Paso	TX	79998	212-640-2000	624-0775*
American Family Life Assurance Co PAC (AFLAC PAC) 1300 Pennsylvania Ave Suite 300 *NYSE: AFL* ■ *TF:* 800-992-3522 ■ *Web:* www.aflac.com	Washington	DC	20004	202-289-6401	289-6404
American Financial Services Assn PAC (AFSA PAC) 919 18th St NW Suite 300	Washington	DC	20006	202-296-5544	223-0321
American Frozen Food Institute (AFFI) 2000 Corporate Ridge Blvd Suite 1000 *Web:* www.affi.org	McLean	VA	22102	703-821-0770	821-1350
American Health Care Assn PAC 1201 L St NW	Washington	DC	20005	202-842-4444	842-3860
American Home Furnishings Alliance PAC 1250 Connecticut Ave NW Suite 200 **Fax Area Code:* 202 ■ *TF:* 877-278-2118 ■ *Web:* www.ahfa.us	Washington	DC	20036	336-884-5000	261-3508*
American Hospital Assn PAC (AHAPAC) 325 7th St NW	Washington	DC	20004	202-638-1100	626-2345
American Insurance Assn PAC 1130 Connecticut Ave NW Suite 1000	Washington	DC	20036	202-828-7100	293-1219
American Intellectual Property Law Assn PAC (AIPLA PAC) 241 18th St S Suite 700	Arlington	VA	22202	703-415-0780	415-0786
American Iron & Steel Institute PAC 1140 Connecticut Ave NW Suite 705 *Web:* www.steel.org	Washington	DC	20036	202-452-7100	463-6573
American Meat Institute PAC (AMIPAC) 1150 Connecticut Ave NW *Web:* www.meatami.com	Washington	DC	20036	202-587-4200	587-4300
American Medical Assn PAC 25 Massachusetts Ave NW # 600	Washington	DC	20001	202-789-7400	789-7485
American Motorcyclist Assn PAC 101 Constitution Ave NW Suite 800-W	Washington	DC	20001	202-742-4301	
American Moving & Storage Assn PAC 1611 Duke St *Web:* www.promover.org	Alexandria	VA	22314	703-683-7410	683-7527
American Nurses Assn PAC (ANA PAC) 8515 Georgia Ave Suite 400 *TF:* 800-274-4262 ■ *Web:* www.nursingworld.org	Silver Spring	MD	20910	301-628-5000	628-5001
American Pharmacists Assn PAC 2215 Constitution Ave NW *TF:* 800-237-2742 ■ *Web:* www.aphanet.org/govt/govaffair.html	Washington	DC	20037	202-628-4410	783-2351

				Phone	Fax
American Postal Workers Union PAC (COPA) 1300 L St NW	Washington	DC	20005	202-842-4200	842-4283
American Society of Anesthesiologists PAC 1501 M St NW # 300	Washington	DC	20005	202-289-2222	371-0384
American Society of Travel Agents PAC 1101 King St Suite 200 *TF:* 800-275-2782	Alexandria	VA	22314	703-739-2782	684-8319
American Sportfishing Assnn PAC (ASA PAC) 225 Reinekers Ln Suite 420 *Web:* www.asafishing.org	Alexandria	VA	22314	703-519-9691	519-1872
American Sugar Cane League PAC 206 E Bayon Rd	Thibodaux	LA	70301	985-448-3707	448-3722
American Supply Assn PAC (ASA PAC) 222 Merchandise Mart Plaza Suite 1400 *Web:* www.asa.net	Chicago	IL	60654	312-464-0090	464-0091
American Veterinary Medical Assn PAC 1910 Sunderland Pl NW	Washington	DC	20036	202-789-0007	842-4360
ArchiPAC 1735 New York Ave NW *Web:* archipac.org	Washington	DC	20006	202-626-7403	626-7426
Assn of Home Appliance Manufacturers PAC (AHAM PAC) 1111 19th St NW Suite 402	Washington	DC	20036	202-872-5955	872-9354
Associated Builders & Contractors PAC (ABC-PAC) 4250 N Fairfax Dr 9th Fl	Arlington	VA	22203	703-812-2000	812-8203
Associated General Contractors PAC (AGC PAC) 333 John Carlyle St Suite 200 *TF:* 800-242-1766	Alexandria	VA	22314	703-548-3118	548-3119
Bank of America PAC 1100 N King St	Wilmington	DE	19884	302-432-0956	432-0039
Blue PAC 1310 G St NW 12th Fl	Washington	DC	20005	202-626-4780	626-4833
Burlington Northern Santa Fe Corp RAILPAC (BNSF) 500 New Jersey Ave NW Suite 550 *Web:* www.bnsf.com	Washington	DC	20001	202-347-8662	347-8675
Business-Industry Political Action Committee (BIPAC) 888 16th St NW Suite 305 *Web:* www.bipac.org	Washington	DC	20006	202-833-1880	833-2338
BUSPAC 700 13th St NW Suite 575 *TF:* 800-283-2877	Washington	DC	20005	202-842-1645	842-0850
Campaign for Working Families 2800 S Shirlington Rd # 930 *Web:* www.campaignforfamilies.org	Arlington	VA	22206	703-671-8800	671-8899
Carpenter's Legislative Improvement Committee 101 Constitution Ave NW 10th Fl	Washington	DC	20001	202-546-6206	547-8979
Caterpillar Inc Employees PAC (CAT PAC) 100 NE Adams St	Peoria	IL	61629	309-675-4482	675-1753
COALPAC 101 Constitution Ave NW Suite 500E	Washington	DC	20001	202-463-2625	463-6152
Coca-Cola Nonpartisan Committee for Good Government PO Box 1734	Atlanta	GA	30301	404-676-5424	676-6792
College of American Pathologists PAC 1350 I St NW Suite 590 *TF:* 800-392-9994	Washington	DC	20005	202-354-7100	354-7155
Committee on Letter Carriers Political Education (COLCPE) 100 Indiana Ave NW	Washington	DC	20001	202-393-4695	756-7400
Consumer Specialty Products Assn PAC 900 17th St NW Suite 300	Washington	DC	20006	202-872-8110	872-8114
Cosmetic Toiletry & Fragrance Assn PAC (CTFA PAC) 1101 17th St NW Suite 300 *Web:* www.ctfa.org	Washington	DC	20036	202-331-1770	331-1969
Credit Union Legislative Action Council of CUNA (CULCAC) 601 Pennsylvania Ave NW S Bldg Suite 600 *Web:* www.cuna.org/pol_affairs/culac.html	Washington	DC	20004	202-638-5777	638-7734
CSX Corp Good Government Fund 1331 Pennsylvania Ave NW Suite 560	Washington	DC	20004	202-783-8124	783-5929
Dairy Farmers of America PAC 10220 N Ambassador Dr Northpointe Tower *TF:* 888-332-6455 ■ *Web:* www.dfamilk.com	Kansas City	MO	64153	816-801-6455	801-6456
Dealers Election Action Committee 8400 Westpark Dr 3rd Fl MS 3 *TF:* 877-501-3322	McLean	VA	22102	703-821-7110	442-3168
Democratic Leadership Council (DLC) 600 Pennsylvania Ave SE Suite 400 *Web:* www.dlc.org	Washington	DC	20003	202-546-0007	544-5002
DGA-PAC 7920 W Sunset Blvd *TF:* 800-421-4173 ■ *Web:* www.dga.org	Los Angeles	CA	90046	310-289-2000	289-2029
Direct Marketing Assn PAC 1111 19th St NW Suite 1100	Washington	DC	20036	202-955-5030	955-0085
DTE Energy Co PAC 2000 2nd Ave	Detroit	MI	48226	313-235-9195	235-6830
Electric Power Supply Assn PAC (EPSA PAC) 1401 New York Ave NW 11th Fl	Washington	DC	20005	202-628-8200	628-8260
Electrical Contractors PAC 3 Bethesda Metro Ctr Suite 1100 *Web:* www.necanet.org/government	Bethesda	MD	20814	301-657-3110	215-4500
ESOP Assn PAC 1726 M St NW Suite 501 *TF:* 866-366-3832 ■ *Web:* www.esopassociation.org	Washington	DC	20036	202-293-2971	293-7568
ExxonMobil Corp PAC 2000 K St NW Suite 710	Washington	DC	20006	202-862-0200	862-0267
FedEx Corp Government Affairs 942 S Shady Grove R *Web:* www.about.fedex.designcdt.com	Memphis	TN	38120	202-218-3800	218-3803
FedPAC PO Box 320276 *Web:* www.fedpac.org	Alexandria	VA	22320	703-548-9774	548-4224
FIREPAC 1750 New York Ave NW Suite 300 *Web:* www.iaff.org	Washington	DC	20006	202-737-8484	737-8418
FMC Corp PAC 1101 Pennsylvania Ave NW Suite 325	Washington	DC	20004	202-956-5200	956-5235
Food Marketing Institute PAC (FoodPAC) 2345 Crystal Dr Suite 800 *Web:* www.fmi.org	Arlington	DC	22202	202-220-0600	429-4519
Footwear Distributors & Retailers of America PAC 1319 F St NW Suite 700	Washington	DC	20004	202-737-5660	638-2615
Ford Motor Co Civic Action Fund 1350 'I' St NW Suite 1000	Washington	DC	20005	202-962-5381	336-7228
FRAN-PAC 1501 K St Suite 350 *TF:* 800-543-1038 ■ *Web:* www.franchise.org	Washington	DC	20005	202-628-8000	628-0812
Friends Committee on National Legislation 245 2nd St NE *Web:* www.fcnl.org	Washington	DC	20002	202-547-6000	547-6019
Friends of the Earth 1100 15th St NW 11th Fl *Web:* www.foe.org	Washington	DC	20005	202-783-7400	783-0444
GASPAC 400 N Capitol St NW *Web:* www.aga.org	Washington	DC	20001	202-824-7000	824-7115
General Dynamics Corp PAC 2941 Fairview Pk Dr	Falls Church	VA	22042	703-876-3000	876-3125
General Electric Co PAC 1299 Pennsylvania Ave NW Suite 900	Washington	DC	20004	202-637-4000	637-4006
General Motors Corp PAC 25 Massachusetts Ave Suite 400 *Web:* www.gmpac.com	Washington	DC	20001	202-775-5090	775-5045
Goodyear Tire & Rubber Co PAC 1420 New York Ave NW Suite 200	Washington	DC	20005	202-682-9250	682-1533
GOPAC 1101 16th St NW Suite 201 *Web:* www.gopac.org	Washington	DC	20005	202-464-5170	464-5177
Harris Corp PAC 1201 E Abingdon Dr Suite 300	Alexandria	VA	22314	703-739-1942	739-2775
HotelPAC 1201 New York Ave NW Suite 600 *Web:* www.ahla.com/default.aspx	Washington	DC	20005	202-289-3124	289-3185
HSBC PAC 1401 I St NW Suite 520	Washington	DC	20005	202-466-3561	466-3583
Human Rights Campaign PAC (HRCPAC) 1640 Rhode Island Ave NW *TF:* 800-777-4723 ■ *Web:* www.hrc.org	Washington	DC	20036	202-628-4160	347-5323
IATSE PAC 1430 Broadway 20th Fl *TF:* 800-223-6972 ■ *Web:* www.iatse-intl.org	New York	NY	10018	212-730-1770	730-7809
Ice Cream Milk & Cheese PAC 1250 H St NW Suite 900 *Web:* www.idfa.org	Washington	DC	20005	202-737-4332	331-7820
Independent Action Inc 1619 13th St NW *Web:* www.independentaction.org	Washington	DC	20009	202-783-2900	783-3477
Independent Community Bankers of America PAC 1615 L St Suite 900 *TF:* 800-422-8439	Washington	DC	20036	202-659-8111	659-9216
Independent Insurance Agents & Brokers of America PAC (INSURPAC) 412 1st St SE Suite 300	Washington	DC	20003	202-863-7000	863-7015
Information Technology Assn of America PAC 1401 Wilson Blvd Suite 1100	Arlington	VA	22209	703-522-5055	525-2279
International Brotherhood of Electrical Workers PAC 900 7th St NW	Washington	DC	20001	202-833-7000	728-7676
International Chiropractors Assn PAC 1110 N Glebe Rd Suite 650	Arlington	VA	22201	703-528-5000	528-5023
International Council of Cruise Lines PAC 2111 Wilson Blvd 8th Fl	Arlington	VA	22201	703-522-8463	522-3811
International Council of Shopping Centers PAC (ICSCPAC) 1221 Avenue of the Americas 41st Fl **Fax Area Code: 732* ■ *Web:* www.icsc.org/srch/government/pac.php	New York	NY	10020	646-728-3800	694-1755*
International Paper PAC 1101 Pennsylvania Ave NW Suite 200	Washington	DC	20004	202-628-1223	628-1368
Investment Co Institute PAC 1401 H St NW 12th Fl	Washington	DC	20005	202-326-5800	326-5985
Ironworkers Political Action League 1750 New York Ave NW Suite 400 *TF:* 800-368-0105 ■ *Web:* www.ironworkers.org/organization/PoliticalAction.aspx	Washington	DC	20006	202-383-4800	638-4856
JP Morgan Chase & Co PAC 270 Pk Ave 9th Fl	New York	NY	10017	212-270-7260	622-4825
Koch Industries PAC 600 14th St NW # 800	Washington	DC	20005	202-737-1977	737-8111
Lockheed Martin PAC 1550 Crystal Dr Suite 300	Arlington	VA	22202	703-413-5996	413-5846
Magazine Publishers of AmNAerica PAC 1211 Connecticut Ave NW Suite 610	Washington	DC	20036	202-296-7277	296-0343
Manufactured Housing Institute PAC (MHI PAC) 2111 Wilson Blvd Suite 100 *TF:* 800-505-5500 ■ *Web:* www.manufacturedhousing.org	Arlington	VA	22201	703-558-0400	558-0401
MassMutual PAC 1295 State St *TF:* 800-272-2216 ■ *Web:* www.massmutual.com/pac/pacHome.do	Springfield	MA	01111	413-788-8411	744-6005
Mechanical Contractors Assn of America PAC 1385 Piccard Dr *Web:* www.mcaa.org	Rockville	MD	20850	301-869-5800	990-9690
MinePAC 101 Constitution Ave NW Suite 500 E	Washington	DC	20001	202-463-2625	463-2666
Morgan Stanley PAC 1585 Broadway *Web:* www.morganstanley.com	Washington	DC	20004	202-654-2000	654-2100
Mortgage Bankers Assn PAC (MORPAC) 1717 Rhode Island Ave NW Suite 400 *Web:* www.morpac.org	Washington	DC	20036	202-557-2700	721-0249
Motion Picture Assn of America PAC 1600 'I' St NW	Washington	DC	20006	202-293-1966	293-7674
Motorola PAC 600 N US Hwy 45 **Fax Area Code: 202* ■ *Web:* www.motorola.com	Libertyville	IL	60048	847-523-5000	842-3578*
NA for Home Care & Hospice PAC (NAHC PAC) 228 7th St SE *Web:* www.nahc.org/home.html	Washington	DC	20003	202-547-7424	547-3540
NA of Chain Drug Stores PAC (NACDS PAC) 413 N Lee St *TF:* 800-678-6223	Alexandria	VA	22314	703-549-3001	836-4869
NA of Dental Plans PAC 8111 LBJ Fwy Suite 935	Dallas	TX	75251	972-458-6998	458-2258
NA of Home Builders PAC 1201 15th St NW *TF:* 800-368-5242 ■ *Web:* www.nahb.org	Washington	DC	20005	202-266-8200	266-8400
NA of Insurance & Financial Advisors PAC 2901 Telestar Ct *Web:* www.naifa.org/advocacy/ifapac	Falls Church	VA	22042	703-770-8100	770-8151
NA of REALTORS PAC (RPAC) 500 New Jersey Ave NW	Washington	DC	20001	202-383-1000	383-7563
NA of Retired Federal Employees 606 N Washington St *TF:* 800-627-3394 ■ *Web:* www.narfe.org	Alexandria	VA	22314	703-838-7760	838-7785
NA of Water Cos PAC (NAWC PAC) 2001 L St NW Suite 850 *Web:* www.nawc.org	Washington	DC	20036	202-833-8383	331-7442

Organization	City	State	ZIP	Phone	Fax
NA of Wheat Growers PAC 415 2nd St NE Suite 300 *Web:* www.wheatworld.org	Washington	DC	20002	202-547-7800	546-2638
NAADAC PAC 901 N Washington St Suite 600 *TF:* 800-548-0497	Alexandria	VA	22314	703-741-7686	741-7698
NARAL Pro-Choice America PAC 1156 15th St NW Suite 700 *Web:* www.prochoiceamerica.org/elections	Washington	DC	20005	202-973-3000	973-3096
NASBIC PAC 1100 H St NW Suite 610 *Web:* www.nasbic.org/?page=FAQ_about_NASBICPAC	Washington	DC	20005	202-628-5055	628-5080
National Air Traffic Controllers Assn PAC (NATCA PAC) 1325 Massachusetts Ave NW *TF:* 800-266-0895 ■ *Web:* www.natca.org	Washington	DC	20005	202-628-5451	628-5767
National Beer Wholesalers Assn PAC (NBWA PAC) 1101 King St Suite 600	Alexandria	VA	22314	703-683-4300	683-8965
National Cable & Telecommunications Assn PAC (Cable PAC) 25 Massachusetts Ave NW *Web:* www.ncta.com	Washington	DC	20001	202-222-2516	222-2517
National Cattlemen's Beef Assn PAC 1301 Pennsylvania Ave NW Suite 300 *Web:* hill.beef.org	Washington	DC	20004	202-347-0228	638-0607
National Committee for an Effective Congress 122 C St NW Suite 650 *Web:* www.ncec.org	Washington	DC	20001	202-639-8300	639-5038
National Confectioners Assn PAC 8320 Old Courthouse Rd Suite 300 *TF:* 800-433-1200	Vienna	VA	22182	703-790-5750	790-5752
National Court Reporters Assn PAC 8224 Old Courthouse Rd *TF:* 800-272-6272 ■ *Web:* www.ncraonline.org	Vienna	VA	22182	703-556-6272	556-6291
National Federation of Independent Business SAFE Trust 1201 F St NW Suite 200 *TF:* 800-552-6342	Washington	DC	20004	202-554-9000	554-0496
National Fisheries Institute PAC 7918 Jones Branch Dr Suite 700	McLean	VA	22102	703-524-8880	524-4619
National Funeral Directors Assn PAC 400 C St NE	Washington	DC	20002	202-547-0441	547-0726
National Grain & Feed Assn PAC 1250 'I' St NW Suite 1003 *Web:* www.ngfa.org	Washington	DC	20005	202-289-0873	289-5388
National Ground Water Assn PAC 601 Dempsey Rd *TF:* 800-551-7379	Westerville	OH	43081	614-898-7791	898-7786
National Milk Producers Federation PAC (NMPF PAC) 2101 Wilson Blvd Suite 400 *Web:* nmpf.org	Arlington	VA	22201	703-243-6111	841-9328
National Multi Housing Council PAC 1850 M St NW Suite 540 *Web:* www.nmhc.org	Washington	DC	20036	202-974-2300	775-0112
National Organization for Women PAC (NOWPAC) 1100 H St NW Suite 300 *Web:* www.nowpacs.org	Washington	DC	20005	202-628-8669	785-8576
National Pest Management Assn PAC 10460 N St	Fairfax	VA	22030	703-352-6762	352-3031
National Pork Producers Council PAC 122 C St NW Suite 875 *TF:* 866-701-6388 ■ *Web:* www.nepork.org	Washington	DC	20001	202-347-3600	347-5265
National Propane Gas Assn PAC (NPGAPAC) 1899 L St NW Suite 350 *Web:* www.npga.org/i4a/pages/index.cfm?pageid=1707	Washington	DC	20036	202-466-7200	466-7205
National Restaurant Assn PAC 1200 17th St NW *TF:* 800-424-5156 ■ *Web:* www.restaurant.org/advocacy/action/nrapac	Washington	DC	20036	202-331-5900	331-2429
National Right to Life PAC 512 10th St NW *Web:* www.nrlc.org	Washington	DC	20004	202-626-8808	393-5433
National Roofing Contractors Assn PAC (NRCAPAC) 324 4th St NE	Washington	DC	20002	202-546-7584	546-9289
National Stone Sand & Gravel Assn PAC 1605 King St	Alexandria	VA	22314	703-525-8788	525-7782
National Sunflower Assn PAC 4023 State St *TF:* 888-718-7033	Bismarck	ND	58503	701-328-5100	328-5101
National Tour Assn PAC 546 E Main St	Lexington	KY	40508	859-226-4250	226-4263
National Turkey Federation PAC 1225 New York Ave NW Suite 400	Washington	DC	20005	202-898-0100	898-0203
National Venture Capital Assn (NVCA) 1655 N Fort Myer Dr Suite 850 *Web:* www.nvca.org	Arlington	VA	22209	703-524-2549	524-3940
NATSO PAC 1737 King St Suite 200	Alexandria	VA	22314	703-549-2100	684-4525
NCFC Co-op PAC 50 F St NW Suite 900 *Web:* www.ncfc.org	Washington	DC	20001	202-626-8700	626-8722
NEA Fund for Children & Public Education 1201 16th St NW *Web:* www.neafund.org	Washington	DC	20036	202-833-4000	822-7974
New Century Project (NCP) 2021 E Dublin-Granville Rd Suite 161 *Web:* www.newcenturyproject.org	Columbus	OH	43229	614-785-1600	785-1611
Northrop Grumman Corp PAC 1000 Wilson Blvd Suite 2300	Arlington	VA	22209	703-875-8400	276-0711
Northwest Airlines PAC 122 New York Ave NW Suite 200	Washington	DC	20005	202-842-3193	289-6834
NRA Institute for Legislative Action 11250 Waples Mill Rd *TF:* 800-672-3888 ■ *Web:* www.nraila.org	Fairfax	VA	22030	703-267-1000	267-3918
Nuclear Energy Institute Federal PAC 1776 I St NW Suite 400 *Web:* www.nei.org	Washington	DC	20006	202-739-8000	785-4019
Outdoor Adv Assn of America Inc (OAAA) 1850 M St NW Suite 1040 *Web:* www.oaaa.org	Washington	DC	20036	202-833-5566	833-1522
Outdoor Amusement Business Assn PAC (OABA-PAC) 1035 S Semoran Blvd Suite 1045A *Web:* www.oaba.org	Winter Park	FL	32792	407-681-9444	681-9445
Peace PAC 322 4th St NE	Washington	DC	20002	202-543-4100	543-6297
Petroleum Marketers Assn of America's Small Business Community 1901 N Fort Myer Dr Suite 500 *TF:* 800-300-7622	Arlington	VA	22209	703-351-8000	351-9160
PG & E Corp PAC 1 Market Spear Tower Suite 2400	San Francisco	CA	94105	415-267-7000	267-7268
Planned Parenthood Action Fund Inc 1780 Massachusetts Ave NW *Web:* www.ppaction.org/ppvotes	Washington	DC	20036	202-785-3351	296-3763
Print PAC 601 13th St NW Suite 360-N *TF:* 800-742-2666 ■ *Web:* www.printpaconline.org	Washington	DC	20005	202-730-7970	730-7987
PTPAC 1111 N Fairfax St	Alexandria	VA	22314	703-684-2782	684-7343
Recording Industry Assn of America (RIAA) 1025 F St NW 10th Fl *Web:* www.riaa.com	Washington	DC	20004	202-775-0101	775-7253
REITPAC 1875 'I' St NW Suite 600 *TF:* 800-362-7348 ■ *Web:* www.reit.com	Washington	DC	20006	202-739-9400	739-9401
SBC Communications Inc Employee Federal PAC (SBC EMPAC) 1133 21st St NW Suite 900	Washington	DC	20036	202-463-4100	
Securities Industry Assn PAC (SIA-PAC) 1425 K St NW 7th Fl *Web:* www.sia.com/political_action	Washington	DC	20005	202-216-2000	216-2119
Sierra Club PAC 85 2nd St 2nd Fl	San Francisco	CA	94105	415-977-5500	977-5797
Society of American Florists PAC 1601 Duke St *TF:* 800-336-4743	Alexandria	VA	22314	703-836-8700	836-8705
Southwest Airlines PAC 2702 Love Field Fr *TF:* 800-435-9792	Dallas	TX	75235	214-792-4000	792-5015
Textron Inc PAC 1101 Pennsylvania Ave NW Suite 400 *NYSE:* TXT	Washington	DC	20004	202-637-3800	637-3865
Title Industry PAC (TIPAC) 1828 L St NW Suite 705 *TF:* 800-787-2582 ■ *Web:* www.tipac.org	Washington	DC	20036	202-296-3671	223-5843
Truck PAC 430 1st St SE 2nd Fl *Web:* www.truckline.com	Washington	DC	20003	202-544-6245	675-6568
UAW Voluntary Community Action Program (UAW V-CAP) 8000 E Jefferson Ave	Detroit	MI	48214	313-926-5531	926-5691
United Technologies Corp PAC 1401 'I' St NW Suite 600	Washington	DC	20005	202-336-7400	336-7529
USAA Group PAC 9800 Fredericksburg Rd	San Antonio	TX	78288	210-498-2211	498-9940
UST Inc Executives Administrators & Managers PAC (USTeamPAC) 100 W Putnam Ave	Greenwich	CT	06830	203-661-1100	622-3493
Water PAC 2915 S 13th St *Web:* www.nrwa.org	Duncan	OK	73533	580-252-0629	255-4476
Wine & Spirits Wholesalers of America PAC 805 15th St NW Suite 430	Washington	DC	20005	202-371-9792	789-2405

POLITICAL LEADERS

SEE US Senators, Representatives, Delegates p. 1991; Governors - State p. 1999

619 POLITICAL PARTIES (MAJOR)

SEE ALSO Civic & Political Organizations p. 1417

Organization	City	State	ZIP	Phone	Fax
Communist Party USA 235 W 23rd St 7th Fl *Web:* www.cpusa.org	New York	NY	10011	212-989-4994	
Democratic National Committee 430 S Capitol St SE *TF:* 800-934-8683 ■ *Web:* www.democrats.org	Washington	DC	20003	202-863-8000	863-8063
Democratic Socialists of America 75 Maiden Ln Suite 505 *Web:* www.dsausa.org	New York	NY	10038	212-727-8610	
Libertarian Party 2600 Virginia Ave NW Suite 200 *TF:* 800-682-1776 ■ *Web:* www.lp.org	Washington	DC	20037	202-333-0008	333-0072
Republican National Committee 310 1st St *TF:* 800-445-5768 ■ *Web:* www.gop.org	Washington	DC	20003	202-863-8500	863-8820
Socialist Labor Party of America PO Box 218 *Web:* www.slp.org	Mountain View	CA	94042	408-280-7266	280-6964
Socialist Party USA 339 Lafayette St Suite 303 *Web:* socialistparty-usa.org	New York	NY	10012	212-982-4586	982-4586

619-1 Democratic State Committees

Organization	City	State	ZIP	Phone	Fax
Alabama Democratic Party 501 Adams Ave *TF:* 800-995-3386 ■ *Web:* www.aladems.org	Montgomery	AL	36104	334-262-2221	262-6474
Alaska Democratic Party 2602 Fairbanks St *Web:* www.alaskademocrats.org	Anchorage	AK	99503	907-258-3050	258-1626
Arkansas Democratic Party 1300 W Capitol Ave *Web:* www.arkdems.org	Little Rock	AR	72201	501-374-2361	376-8409
California Democratic Party 1401 21st St Suite 200 *Web:* www.cadem.org	Sacramento	CA	95811	916-442-5707	
Colorado Democratic Party 777 Santa Fe Dr *Web:* www.coloradodems.org	Denver	CO	80204	303-623-4762	623-2443
Connecticut Democratic Party 179 Allyn St *Web:* www.ctdems.org	Hartford	CT	06103	860-560-1775	560-1522
Delaware Democratic Party 19 E Commons Blvd 2nd Fl *Web:* www.deldems.org	New Castle	DE	19720	302-328-9036	328-9386
Florida Democratic Party 214 S Bronough St *TF:* 800-925-3411 ■ *Web:* www.fladems.com	Tallahassee	FL	32301	850-222-3411	222-0916
Georgia Democratic Party 1100 Spring St Suite 710 *TF:* 800-894-1996 ■ *Web:* www.democraticpartyofgeorgia.org	Atlanta	GA	30309	404-870-8201	873-4396

				Phone	Fax
Hawaii Democratic Party 770 Kapiolani Blvd Suite 115 *Web:* www.hawaiidemocrats.org	Honolulu	HI	96813	808-596-2980	596-2985
Idaho Democratic Party 1509 S Tyrell Ln # 108 *TF:* 800-542-4737 ■ *Web:* www.idaho-democrats.org	Boise	ID	83706	208-336-1815	336-1817
Indiana Democratic Party 115 W Washington St # 1165 *TF:* 800-223-3387 ■ *Web:* www.indems.org	Indianapolis	IN	46204	317-231-7100	231-7129
Iowa Democratic Party 5661 Fleur Dr. *Web:* www.iowademocrats.org	Des Moines	IA	50321	515-224-7292	244-5051
Kansas Democratic Party 700 SW Jackson St # 706 *Web:* www.ksdp.org	Topeka	KS	66603	785-234-0425	234-8420
Kentucky Democratic Party 190 Democrat Dr *Web:* www.kydemocrat.com	Frankfort	KY	40601	502-695-4828	695-7629
Louisiana Democratic Party 701 Government St. *Web:* www.lademo.org	Baton Rouge	LA	70802	225-336-4155	336-0046
Maine Democratic Party PO Box 5258 *Web:* www.mainedems.org	Augusta	ME	04332	207-622-6233	622-2657
Maryland Democratic Party 188 Main St Suite 1 *Web:* www.mddems.org	Annapolis	MD	21401	410-280-8818	280-8882
Massachusetts Democratic Party 10 Granite St 4th Fl. *Web:* www.massdems.org	Quincy	MA	02169	617-472-0637	472-4391
Michigan Democratic Party 606 Townsend St. *Web:* www.mi-democrats.com	Lansing	MI	48933	517-371-5410	371-2056
Minnesota Democratic Farmer Labor Party 255 E Plato Blvd *TF:* 800-999-7457 ■ *Web:* www.dfl.org	Saint Paul	MN	55107	651-293-1200	251-6325
Mississippi Democratic Party PO Box 1583 *TF:* 888-674-3367 ■ *Web:* www.msdemocrats.net	Jackson	MS	39215	601-969-2913	354-1599
Missouri Democratic Party PO Box 719 *Web:* www.missouridems.org	Jefferson City	MO	65102	573-636-5241	634-8176
Montana Democratic Party PO Box 802 *Web:* www.montanademocrats.org	Helena	MT	59624	406-442-9520	442-9534
Nebraska Democratic Party 633 S 9th St Suite 201 *TF:* 800-677-7068 ■ *Web:* www.nebraskademocrats.org	Lincoln	NE	68508	402-434-2180	434-2188
New Hampshire Democratic Party 105 N State St. *Web:* nhdp.org	Concord	NH	03301	603-225-6899	225-6797
New Jersey Democratic State Committee 196 W State St *Web:* www.njdems.org	Trenton	NJ	08608	609-392-3367	396-4778
New Mexico Democratic Party 1301 San Pedro Dr NE *Web:* www.dpnm.org	Albuquerque	NM	87110	505-830-3650	830-3645
New York State Democratic Committee 461 Pk Ave S 10th Fl *Web:* www.nydems.org	New York	NY	10016	212-725-8825	725-8867
North Carolina Democratic Party 220 Hillsborough St *TF:* 800-229-3367 ■ *Web:* www.ncdp.org	Raleigh	NC	27603	919-821-2777	821-4778
North Dakota Democratic Party 1902 E Divide Ave. *Web:* www.demnpl.com	Bismarck	ND	58501	701-255-0460	255-7823
Ohio Democratic Party 340 East Fulton St *Web:* www.ohiodems.org	Columbus	OH	43215	614-221-6563	221-0721
Oklahoma Democratic Party 4100 N Lincoln Blvd. *Web:* www.okdemocrats.org	Oklahoma City	OK	73105	405-427-3366	427-1310
Oregon Democratic Party 232 NE 9th Ave *Web:* www.dpo.org	Portland	OR	97232	503-224-8200	224-5335
Pennsylvania Democratic Party 300 N 2nd St 8th Fl *Web:* www.padems.com	Harrisburg	PA	17101	717-920-8470	901-7829
Puerto Rico Democratic Party PO Box 9065788	San Juan	PR	00906	787-721-2004	977-2045
Rhode Island Democratic Party 151 Broadway Suite 310 *Web:* www.ridemocrats.org	Providence	RI	02903	401-272-3367	272-3368
South Carolina Democratic Party PO Box 5965 *TF:* 800-841-1817 ■ *Web:* www.scdp.org	Columbia	SC	29250	803-799-7798	765-1692
South Dakota Democratic Party 335 N Main Ave Suite 200 *Web:* www.sddp.org	Sioux Falls	SD	57104	605-271-5405	
Tennessee Democratic Party 1900 Church St Suite 203 *Web:* www.tndp.org	Nashville	TN	37203	615-327-9779	327-9759
Texas Democratic Party 505 W 12th St Suite 200 *Web:* www.txdemocrats.org	Austin	TX	78701	512-478-9800	480-2500
Utah Democratic Party 455 S 300 E Suite 301 *Web:* www.utdemocrats.org	Salt Lake City	UT	84111	801-328-1212	328-1238
Vermont Democratic Party 73 Main St Suite 36 PO Box 1220 *Web:* www.vtdemocrats.org	Montpelier	VT	05601	802-229-1783	229-1784
Virginia Democratic Party 1710 E Franklin St 2nd Fl *TF:* 800-322-1144 ■ *Web:* www.vademocrats.org	Richmond	VA	23223	804-644-1966	343-3642
Washington Democratic Party PO Box 4027 *Web:* www.wa-democrats.org	Seattle	WA	98194	206-583-0664	583-0301
West Virginia Democratic Party 717 Lee St Suite 214 *Web:* www.wvdemocrats.com	Charleston	WV	25301	304-342-8121	342-8122
Wisconsin Democratic Party 110 King St Suite 203 *Web:* www.wisdems.org	Madison	WI	53703	608-255-5172	255-8919
Wyoming Democratic Party 201 E 2nd St # 25 *TF:* 800-729-3367 ■ *Web:* www.wyomingdemocrats.com	Casper	WY	82601	307-473-1457	473-1459

619-2 Republican State Committees

				Phone	Fax
Alabama Republican Party 3415 Independence Dr Suite 219 *TF:* 877-919-2002 ■ *Web:* www.algop.org	Birmingham	AL	35209	205-212-5900	212-5910
Alaska Republican Party 1001 W Fireweed Ln. *Web:* www.alaskarepublicans.com	Anchorage	AK	99503	907-276-4467	276-0425
Arizona Republican State Committee 3501 N 24th St *TF:* 800-844-4065 ■ *Web:* www.azgop.org	Phoenix	AZ	85016	602-957-7770	224-0932
Arkansas Republican Party 1201 W 6th St *Web:* www.arkansasgop.org	Little Rock	AR	72201	501-372-7301	372-1656
California Republican Party 1903 W Magnolia Blvd *Web:* www.cagop.org	Burbank	CA	91506	818-841-5210	841-6668
Colorado Republican Party 5950 S Willow Dr Suite 302 *Web:* www.cologop.org	Greenwood Village	CO	80111	303-758-3333	
Connecticut Republican Party 97 Elm St Rear *TF:* 888-982-8467 ■ *Web:* www.ctgop.org	Hartford	CT	06106	860-547-0589	278-8563
Delaware Republican Party 3301 Lancaster Pike Suite 4B *Web:* www.delawaregop.com	Wilmington	DE	19805	302-651-0260	651-0270
District of Columbia Republican Committee 1275 K St NW Suite 102 *Web:* www.dcgop.com	Washington	DC	20005	202-289-8005	289-2197
Florida Republican Party PO Box 311 *TF:* 800-777-7920 ■ *Web:* www.rpof.org	Tallahassee	FL	32302	850-222-7920	681-0184
Georgia Republican Party 3110 Maple Dr Suite 200-E *TF:* 877-464-2467 ■ *Web:* www.gagop.org	Atlanta	GA	30305	404-257-5559	257-0779
Hawaii Republican Party 725 Kapiolani Blvd Suite C105 *Web:* www.gophawaii.com	Honolulu	HI	96813	808-593-8180	593-7742
Idaho Republican State Committee 802 W Bannock St # Lp103 *TF:* 800-658-3898 ■ *Web:* www.idgop.org	Boise	ID	83702	208-343-6405	343-6414
Illinois Republican State Committee 320 S 4th St *Web:* www.ilgop.org	Springfield	IL	62701	217-525-0011	753-4712
Indiana Republican Party 47 S Meridian St Suite 200 *TF:* 800-466-1087 ■ *Web:* www.indgop.org	Indianapolis	IN	46204	317-635-7561	632-8510
Iowa Republican Party 621 E 9th St *Web:* www.iowagop.org	Des Moines	IA	50309	515-282-8105	282-9019
Kansas Republican Party 2025 SW Gage Blvd. *TF:* 888-482-9051 ■ *Web:* www.ksgop.org	Topeka	KS	66604	785-234-3456	228-0353
Kentucky Republican Party PO Box 1068 *Web:* www.rpk.org	Frankfort	KY	40602	502-875-5130	223-5625
Louisiana Republican Party 530 Lake Land Rd *Web:* www.lagop.com	Baton Rouge	LA	70802	225-389-4495	389-4493
Maine Republican Party 9 Higgins St. *Web:* www.mainegop.com	Augusta	ME	04330	207-622-6247	623-5322
Maryland Republican Party 15 W St *Web:* www.mdgop.org	Annapolis	MD	21401	410-269-0113	269-5937
Massachusetts Republican State Committee 85 Merrimac St Suite 400 *Web:* www.massgop.com	Boston	MA	02114	617-523-5005	523-6311
Michigan Republican State Committee 520 Seymour Ave *TF:* 877-644-6704 ■ *Web:* www.migop.org	Lansing	MI	48933	517-487-5413	487-0090
Minnesota Republican Party 525 Pk St Suite 250 *Web:* www.mngop.org	Saint Paul	MN	55103	651-222-0022	224-4122
Mississippi Republican Party 415 Yazoo St # 200 *Web:* www.msgop.org	Jackson	MS	39201	601-948-5191	354-0972
Missouri Republican Party 204 E Dunklin St. *Web:* www.mogop.org	Jefferson City	MO	65101	573-636-3146	636-3273
Montana Republican Party 921 Euclid Ave *Web:* www.mtgop.org	Helena	MT	59601	406-442-6469	442-3293
Nebraska Republican Party 1610 N St. *TF:* 800-829-3459 ■ *Web:* www.negop.org	Lincoln	NE	68508	402-475-2122	475-3541
Nevada Republican Party 6330 McLeod Dr Suite 1 *Web:* www.nevadagop.org	Las Vegas	NV	89120	702-258-9182	258-9186
New Hampshire Republican State Committee 10 Water St. *Web:* www.nhgop.org	Concord	NH	03301	603-225-9341	225-7498
New Jersey Republican State Committee 150 W State St Suite 230 *Web:* www.njgop.org	Trenton	NJ	08608	609-989-7300	989-8685
New Mexico Republican Party 5150 San Francisco Rd NE # A *Web:* www.gopnm.org	Albuquerque	NM	87109	505-298-3662	292-0755
New York Republican State Committee 315 State St *Web:* www.nygop.org	Albany	NY	12210	518-462-2601	449-7443
North Carolina Republican Party PO Box 12905 *Web:* www.ncgop.org	Raleigh	NC	27605	919-828-6423	899-3815
North Dakota Republican Party PO Box 1917 *Web:* www.ndgop.org	Bismarck	ND	58502	701-255-0030	255-7513
Ohio Republican Party 211 S 5th St *Web:* www.ohiogop.org	Columbus	OH	43215	614-228-2481	228-1093
Oklahoma Republican State Committee 4031 N Lincoln Blvd. *Web:* www.okgop.com	Oklahoma City	OK	73105	405-528-3501	521-9531

Organization	City	State	Zip	Phone	Fax
Pennsylvania Republican State Committee 301 Market St *Web:* www.pagop.org	Harrisburg	PA	17101	717-234-4901	231-3828
Rhode Island Republican Party 1800 Post Rd Suite 17-I *Web:* www.rigop.org	Warwick	RI	02886	401-732-8282	633-7362
South Carolina Republican Party The 1913 Marion St *Web:* www.scgop.com	Columbia	SC	29201	803-988-8440	988-8444
South Dakota Republican State Central Committee PO Box 1099 *Web:* www.southdakotagop.com	Pierre	SD	57501	605-224-7347	224-7349
Tennessee Republican Party 2424 21st Ave Suite 200 *Web:* www.tngop.org	Nashville	TN	37212	615-269-4260	269-4261
Texas Republican Party 900 Congress Ave Suite 300 *Web:* www.texasgop.org	Austin	TX	78701	512-477-9821	480-0709
Utah Republican Party 117 E S Temple St *TF:* 800-230-8824 ■ *Web:* www.utahgop.org	Salt Lake City	UT	84111	801-533-9777	533-0327
Vermont Republican State Committee 141 Main St Suite 3 PO Box 70 *Web:* www.vtgop.org	Montpelier	VT	05602	802-223-3411	229-1864
Virginia Republican Party 115 E Grace St *Web:* www.rpv.org	Richmond	VA	23219	804-780-0111	343-1060
West Virginia Republican State Committee 5019 MacCorkle Ave SW *Web:* www.wvgop.org	South Charleston	WV	25303	304-768-0493	768-6083
Wisconsin Republican Party 148 E Johnson St *Web:* www.wisgop.org	Madison	WI	53701	608-257-4765	257-4141
Wyoming Republican Party 400 E 1st St Suite 314 *Web:* www.wygop.org	Casper	WY	82601	307-234-9166	473-8640

620 PORTALS - VOICE

Voice Portals Permit Users To Access Web-Based Messaging As Well As Various Types Of Internet Information (E.G., Weather, Stock Quotes, Driving Directions, Etc.) Via The Telephone (Wired Or Wireless).

Organization	City	State	Zip	Phone	Fax
Genesys Telecommunications Laboratories Inc 1380 Rodrck Rd *Web:* www.genesyslab.com	Markham	ON	L3R4G5	905-968-3300	968-3400
GoSolo Technologies Inc 1901 Ulmerton Rd Suite 400 *TF:* 888-551-7656 ■ *Web:* www.gosolo.com	Clearwater	FL	33762	727-821-6565	898-9315
HeyAnita Inc 303 N Glenoaks Blvd Suite 500 *Web:* www.heyanita.com	Burbank	CA	91502	818-556-4400	556-4466
InternetSpeech.com 6980 Santa Teresa Blvd Suite 201 *Web:* www.internetspeech.com	San Jose	CA	95119	408-360-7730	360-7726
Tellme Networks Inc 1310 Villa St *TF:* 800-555-8355 ■ *Web:* www.tellme.com	Mountain View	CA	94041	650-930-9000	930-9101

621 PORTS & PORT AUTHORITIES

SEE ALSO Airports p. 1391; Cruise Lines p. 1779

Organization	City	State	Zip	Phone	Fax
Alabama State Port Authority PO Box 1588 *Web:* www.asdd.com	Mobile	AL	36633	251-441-7200	441-7216
Ashtabula County Port Authority 17 N Market St	Jefferson	OH	44047	440-576-6069	576-5003
Bridgeport Port Authority 330 Water St *Web:* www.portofbridgeport.com	Bridgeport	CT	06604	203-384-9777	384-9686
Cleveland-Cuyahoga County Port Authority 1375 E 9th St Suite 2300 *Web:* www.portofcleveland.com	Cleveland	OH	44114	216-241-8004	241-8016
Cordova Harbor & Port 114 Nicholoff Way *Web:* www.cityofcordova.net	Cordova	AK	99574	907-424-6400	424-6446
Delaware River Port Authority 1 Port Center 2 Riverside Dr PO Box 1949 *Fax: Hum Res ■ *Web:* www.drpa.org	Camden	NJ	08101	856-968-2000	968-2242*
Detroit-Wayne County Port Authority 8109 E Jefferson Ave *TF:* 800-249-7678 ■ *Web:* www.portdetroit.com	Detroit	MI	48214	313-331-3842	331-5457
Eastport Port Authority 3 Madison St *Web:* www.portofeastport.org	Eastport	ME	04631	207-853-4614	853-9584
Erie-Western Pennsylvania Port Authority 208 E Bayfront Pkwy Suite 201 *Web:* www.porterie.org	Erie	PA	16507	814-455-7557	455-8070
Georgia Ports Authority PO Box 2406 *TF:* 800-342-8012 ■ *Web:* www.gaports.com	Savannah	GA	31402	912-964-3811	964-3921
Greater Lafourche Port Commission PO Box 490 *Web:* www.portfourchon.com	Galliano	LA	70354	985-632-6701	632-6703
Haines Harbor 22 Beach Rd	Haines	AK	99827	907-766-2448	766-3010
Halifax Port Authority 1215 Marginal Rd PO Box 336 *Web:* www.portofhalifax.ca	Halifax	NS	B3J2P6	902-426-8222	426-7335
Hamilton Port Authority 605 James St N 6th Fl *TF:* 800-263-2131 ■ *Web:* www.hamiltonport.ca	Hamilton	ON	L8L1K1	905-525-4330	528-6554
Hawaii Dept of Transportation Harbors Div 79 S Nimitz Hwy *Web:* www.hawaii.gov	Honolulu	HI	96813	808-587-1927	587-1982
Humboldt Bay Harbor District 601 Startare Dr *Web:* www.portofhumboldtbay.org	Eureka	CA	95501	707-443-0801	443-0800
Illinois International Port District 3600 E 95th St *TF:* 800-843-7678 ■ *Web:* www.illinoisinternationalportdistrict.com	Chicago	IL	60617	773-646-4400	221-7678
Indiana Port Commission 150 W Market St Suite 100 *TF:* 800-232-7678 ■ *Web:* www.portsofindiana.com	Indianapolis	IN	46204	317-232-9200	232-0137
International Port of Dutch Harbor 748 Ballyhoo Rd *Web:* www.ci.unalaska.ak.us	Unalaska	AK	99685	907-581-1254	581-2519
Juneau Harbor 155 S Seward St *Web:* www.juneau.org/harbors	Juneau	AK	99801	907-586-5255	586-2507
Ketchikan Ports & Harbors Dept 2933 Tongass Ave *Web:* www.city.ketchikan.ak.us	Ketchikan	AK	99901	907-228-5632	247-3610
Key West Port Authority 201 William St Second Fl PO Box 6434 *Web:* www.keywestcity.com	Key West	FL	33040	305-293-6439	293-6438
Kodiak Port & Harbor 403 Marine Way	Kodiak	AK	99615	907-486-8080	486-8090
Manatee County Port Authority 300 Tampa Bay Way *Web:* www.portmanatee.com	Palmetto	FL	34221	941-722-6621	729-1463
Massachusetts Port Authority 1 Harborside Dr Suite 200S *Web:* www.massport.com	East Boston	MA	02128	617-568-8989	
Mississippi State Port Authority at Gulfport 2510 14th St # 1450 *TF:* 877-881-4367 ■ *Web:* www.shipmspa.com	Gulfport	MS	39501	228-865-4300	865-4335
Montreal Port Authority Port of Montreal Bldg 2100 Pierre-Dupuy Ave Wing 1 *Web:* www.port-montreal.com	Montreal	QC	H3C3R5	514-283-7011	283-0829
Nanaimo Port Authority 104 Front St *Web:* www.npa.ca	Nanaimo	BC	V9R5H7	250-753-4146	753-4899
New Bedford Harbor Development Commission 106 Co-Op Wharf	New Bedford	MA	02740	508-961-3000	979-1517
New Hampshire State Port Authority 555 Market St *Web:* www.portsmouthnh.com	Portsmouth	NH	03801	603-436-8500	436-2780
North Carolina State Ports Authority 2202 Burnett Blvd PO Box 9002 *TF:* 800-334-0682 ■ *Web:* www.ncports.com	Wilmington	NC	28402	910-763-1621	343-6225
Ogdensburg Bridge & Port Authority 1 Bridge Plaza *Web:* www.ogdensport.com	Ogdensburg	NY	13669	315-393-4080	393-7068
Oregon International Port of Coos Bay 125 Central Ave Suite 300 PO Box 1215 *Web:* www.portofcoosbay.com	Coos Bay	OR	97420	541-267-7678	269-1475
Oshawa Harbour Commission 1050 Farewell Ave *Web:* www.oshawaportauthority.com	Oshawa	ON	L1H6N6	905-576-0400	576-5701
Panama City Port Authority 5321 W Hwy 98 *Web:* www.portpanamacityusa.com	Panama City	FL	32401	850-767-3220	767-3235
Philadelphia Regional Port Authority 3460 N Delaware Ave 2nd Fl *Web:* www.philaport.com	Philadelphia	PA	19134	215-426-2600	426-6800
Plaquemines Port Authority 124 Edna Lafrance Rd	Braithwaite	LA	70040	504-682-7920	682-0649
Port Alberni Port Authority 2750 Harbour Rd *Web:* portalberniportauthority.ca	Port Alberni	BC	V9Y7X2	250-723-5312	723-1114
Port Authority of New York/New Jersey 225 Pk Ave S 15th Fl *Web:* www.panynj.gov	New York	NY	10003	212-435-7000	
Port Canaveral 445 Challenger Rd *TF:* 888-767-8226 ■ *Web:* www.portcanaveral.org	Cape Canaveral	FL	32920	321-783-7831	784-6223
Port Everglades 1850 Eller Dr *Web:* www.porteverglades.org	Fort Lauderdale	FL	33316	954-523-3404	525-1910
Port Freeport PO Box 615 *TF:* 800-362-5473 ■ *Web:* www.portfreeport.com	Freeport	TX	77542	979-233-2667	233-5625
Port Metro Vancouver 100 The Pt 999 Canada Pl *Fax Area Code: 866 ■ *Web:* www.portmetrovancouver.com	Vancouver	BC	V6C3T4	604-665-9000	284-4271*
Port of Albany *Albany Port District Commission* 106 Smith Blvd *Web:* www.portofalbany.us	Albany	NY	12202	518-463-8763	463-8767
Port of Anacortes 100 Commercial Ave *Web:* www.portofanacortes.com	Anacortes	WA	98221	360-293-3134	293-9608
Port of Anchorage 2000 Anchorage Port Rd *Web:* www.muni.org	Anchorage	AK	99501	907-343-6200	277-5636
Port of Astoria 422 Gateway Ave *TF:* 800-860-4093 ■ *Web:* www.portofastoria.com	Astoria	OR	97103	503-325-4521	325-4525
Port of Baltimore *Maryland Port Administration* 401 E Pratt St World Trade Ctr *TF:* 800-638-7519 ■ *Web:* www.mpa.state.md.us	Baltimore	MD	21202	410-385-4484	333-3402
Port of Beaumont 1225 Main St *Web:* www.portofbeaumont.com	Beaumont	TX	77701	409-835-5367	835-0512
Port of Bellingham 1801 Roeder Ave *Web:* www.portofbellingham.com	Bellingham	WA	98225	360-676-2500	671-6411
Port of Brownsville 1000 Foust Rd *TF:* 800-378-5395 ■ *Web:* www.portofbrownsville.com	Brownsville	TX	78521	956-831-4592	831-5006
Port of Burns Harbor 6625 S Boundary Dr *Web:* www.portsofindiana.com	Portage	IN	46368	219-787-8636	787-8842
Port of Corpus Christi 222 Power St *TF:* 800-580-7110 ■ *Web:* www.portofcorpuschristi.com	Corpus Christi	TX	78401	361-882-5633	882-7110
Port of Duluth *Duluth Seaway Port Authority* 1200 Port Terminal Dr *TF:* 800-232-0703 ■ *Web:* www.duluthport.com	Duluth	MN	55802	218-727-8525	727-6888
Port of Everett 2911 Bond St Suite 202 *TF:* 800-729-7678 ■ *Web:* www.portofeverett.com	Everett	WA	98201	425-259-3164	252-7366

				Phone	Fax
Port of Galveston 123 25th St *Web:* www.portofgalveston.com	Galveston	TX	77550	409-765-9321	766-6107
Port of Grays Harbor 111 S Wooding St *Web:* www.portofgraysharbor.com	Aberdeen	WA	98520	360-533-9528	533-9505
Port of Greater Baton Rouge *Greater Baton Rouge Port Commission* 2425 Ernest Wilson Dr PO Box 380 *Web:* www.portgbr.com	Port Allen	LA	70767	225-342-1660	342-1666
Port of Homer 4350 Homer Spit Rd *Web:* www.port.ci.homer.ak.us	Homer	AK	99603	907-235-3160	235-3152
Port of Houston 111 E Loop N *TF Cust Svc:* 800-688-3625 ■ *Web:* www.portofhouston.com	Houston	TX	77029	713-670-2400	670-2429
Port of Hueneme 333 Ponoma St PO Box 608 *Web:* www.portofhueneme.org	Port Hueneme	CA	93044	805-488-3677	488-2620
Port of Iberia 4611 S Lewis St PO Box 9986 *Web:* www.portofiberia.com	New Iberia	LA	70562	337-364-1065	364-3136
Port of Jacksonville *Jacksonville Port Authority* 2831 Talleyrand Ave PO Box 3005 *Web:* www.jaxport.com	Jacksonville	FL	32206	904-357-3000	357-3060
Port of Kalama 380 W Marine Dr *Web:* www.portofkalama.com	Kalama	WA	98625	360-673-2325	673-1503
Port of Lake Charles 150 Marine St *TF:* 800-845-7678 ■ *Web:* www.portlc.com	Lake Charles	LA	70601	337-439-3661	493-3523
Port of Long Beach 925 Harbor Plaza *Web:* www.polb.com	Long Beach	CA	90801	562-437-0041	901-1725
Port of Longview 10 Port Way *Web:* www.portoflongview.com	Longview	WA	98632	360-425-3305	425-8650
Port of Los Angeles 425 S Palos Verdes St **Fax:* Hum Res ■ *Web:* www.portoflosangeles.org	San Pedro	CA	90731	310-732-7678	831-0439*
Port of Miami 1015 N America Way *Web:* www.co.miami-dade.fl.us/portofmiami	Miami	FL	33132	305-371-7678	347-4843
Port of Milwaukee 2323 S Lincoln Memorial Dr *Web:* www.port.mil.wi.us	Milwaukee	WI	53207	414-286-3511	286-8506
Port of Mobile *Alabama State Docks Dept* 250 N Water St *Web:* www.asdd.com	Mobile	AL	36602	251-441-7203	441-7216
Port of Monroe *Monroe Port Commission* 2929 E Front St PO Box 585 *Web:* www.portofmonroe.com	Monroe	MI	48161	734-241-6480	241-0813
Port of New London *Connecticut Bureau of Aviation & Ports* State Pier Rd	New London	CT	06320	860-443-3856	437-7251
Port of New Orleans 990 Port of New Orleans Pl *TF:* 800-776-6652 ■ *Web:* www.portno.com	New Orleans	LA	70123	504-522-2551	524-4156
Port of Newport 600 SE Bay Blvd *Web:* www.portofnewport.com	Newport	OR	97365	541-265-7758	265-4235
Port of Nome 307 Belmont St *Web:* www.nomealaska.org	Nome	AK	99762	907-443-6619	443-5473
Port of Oakland *Oakland Board of Port Commissioners* 530 Water St *Web:* www.portofoakland.com	Oakland	CA	94607	510-627-1100	839-5104
Port of Olympia 915 Washington St NE *Web:* www.portolympia.com	Olympia	WA	98501	360-528-8000	528-8090
Port of Orange *Orange County Navigation Port District* 1201 Childers Rd *Web:* www.portoforange.com	Orange	TX	77630	409-883-4363	883-5607
Port of Oswego Authority 1 E 2nd St PO Box 387 *Web:* www.portoswego.com	Oswego	NY	13126	315-343-4503	343-5498
Port of Palm Beach 1 E 11th St Suite 400 *Web:* www.portofpalmbeach.com	Riviera Beach	FL	33404	561-842-4201	842-4240
Port of Pascagoula *Jackson County Port Authority* 3033 Pascagoula St *Web:* www.portofpascagoula.com	Pascagoula	MS	39567	228-762-4041	762-7476
Port of Pensacola 700 S Barracks St *Web:* www.portofpensacola.com	Pensacola	FL	32502	850-436-5070	436-5076
Port of Philadelphia & Camden 1 Port Ctr 2 Riverside Dr PO Box 1949 *Web:* www.drpa.org	Camden	NJ	08101	856-968-2054	968-2056
Port of Pittsburgh 425 6th Ave Suite 2990 *TF:* 877-609-9870 ■ *Web:* www.port.pittsburgh.pa.us	Pittsburgh	PA	15219	412-201-7330	201-7337
Port of Port Angeles 338 W 1st St PO Box 1350 *Web:* www.portofpa.com	Port Angeles	WA	98362	360-457-8527	452-3959
Port of Port Arthur 221 Houston Ave *Web:* www.portofportarthur.com	Port Arthur	TX	77640	409-983-2011	985-9312
Port of Port Lavaca-Point Comfort *Calhoun County Navigation District* PO Box 397 *Web:* www.calhounport.com	Point Comfort	TX	77978	361-987-2813	987-2189
Port of Portland 121 NW Everett St *TF:* 800-547-8411 ■ *Web:* www.portofportland.com	Portland	OR	97209	503-944-7000	944-7222
Port of Portland 389 Congress St *TF:* 800-773-7050 ■ *Web:* www.portofportlandmaine.com	Portland	ME	04101	207-541-6900	541-6905
Port of Prescott 3035 County Rd 2 PO Box 520 *Web:* www.portofprescott.com	Prescott	ON	K0E1T0	613-925-4228	925-5022
Port of Redwood City 675 Seaport Blvd *Web:* www.redwoodcityport.com	Redwood City	CA	94063	650-306-4150	369-7636
Port of Richmond Commission 5000 Deepwater Terminal Rd	Richmond	VA	23234	804-646-2020	271-1524

				Phone	Fax
Port of Sacramento 1110 W Capitol Ave *TF:* 888-258-7969 ■ *Web:* www.portofsacramento.com	West Sacramento	CA	95691	916-371-8000	372-4802
Port of Saint Helens 100 E St *Web:* www.portsh.org	Columbia City	OR	97018	503-397-2888	397-6924
Port of San Diego 3165 Pacific Hwy *TF:* 800-854-2757 ■ *Web:* www.portofsandiego.org	San Diego	CA	92101	619-686-6200	686-6400
Port of San Francisco Pier 1 The Embarcadero *Web:* www.sfport.com	San Francisco	CA	94111	415-274-0400	732-0400
Port of Seattle PO Box 1209 *TF:* 800-426-7817 ■ *Web:* www.portseattle.org	Seattle	WA	98111	206-728-3000	728-3280
Port of Sept-Iles 1 Quai Mgr-Blanche *Web:* www.portsi.com	Sept-Iles	QC	G4R5P3	418-968-1231	962-4445
Port of Seward PO Box 167 *Web:* www.cityofseward.net	Seward	AK	99664	907-224-3138	224-7187
Port of South Louisiana 171 Belle Terre Blvd Suite 100 *TF:* 888-752-7678 ■ *Web:* www.portsl.com	LaPlace	LA	70069	985-652-9278	652-9518
Port of Stockton 2201 W Washington St *TF:* 800-344-3213 ■ *Web:* www.portofstockton.com	Stockton	CA	95203	209-946-0246	465-7244
Port of Tacoma 1 Sitcum Way *Web:* www.portoftacoma.com	Tacoma	WA	98421	253-383-5841	593-4570
Port of Valdez 412 Ferry Terminal Way *Web:* www.ci.valdez.ak.us	Valdez	AK	99686	907-835-4564	835-4479
Port of Vancouver 3103 NW Lower River Rd *Web:* www.portvanusa.com	Vancouver	WA	98660	360-693-3611	735-1565
Port of Virginia 600 World Trade Ctr *TF:* 800-446-8098 ■ *Web:* www.vaports.com	Norfolk	VA	23510	757-683-8000	683-2573
Port of Wilmington 1 Hausel Rd *Web:* www.portofwilmingtonde.com	Wilmington	DE	19801	302-472-7678	472-7740
Prince Rupert Port Authority 200-215 Cow Bay Rd *Web:* www.rupertport.com	Prince Rupert	BC	V8J1A2	250-627-8899	627-8980
Quebec Port Authority 150 Dalhousie St PO Box 80 Stn Haute-Ville *Web:* www.portquebec.ca	Quebec	QC	G1R4M8	418-648-3640	648-4160
Saguenay Port Authority 6600 Quai-Marcel-Dionne Rd *Web:* www.portsaguenay.ca	La Baie	QC	G7B3N9	418-697-0250	697-0243
Saint Bernard Port Harbor & Terminal District 200 Marlin Dr PO Box 1331 *Web:* www.stbernardport.com	Chalmette	LA	70043	504-277-8418	277-8471
Saint John Port Authority 111 Water St *Web:* www.sjport.com	Saint John	NB	E2L0B1	506-636-4869	636-4443
Saint John's Port Authority PO Box 6178 *Web:* www.sjpa.com	Saint John's	NL	A1C5X8	709-738-4782	738-4784
Sitka Harbor 617 Katlian St	Sitka	AK	99835	907-747-3439	747-6278
South Carolina State Ports Authority 176 Concord St *TF:* 800-845-7106 ■ *Web:* www.scspa.com	Charleston	SC	29401	843-723-8651	577-8626
South Jersey Port Corp 2nd & Beckett Sts *Web:* www.southjerseyport.com	Camden	NJ	08103	856-757-4969	757-4903
Tampa Port Authority 1101 Channelside Dr *TF:* 800-741-2297 ■ *Web:* www.tampaport.com	Tampa	FL	33602	813-905-7678	905-5109
Thunder Bay Port Authority 100 Main St *Web:* www.portofthunderbay.com	Thunder Bay	ON	P7B6R9	807-345-6400	345-9058
Toledo-Lucas County Port Authority 1 Maritime Plaza *Web:* www.toledoportauthority.org	Toledo	OH	43604	419-243-8251	243-1835
Toronto Port Authority 60 Harbour St *Web:* www.torontoport.com	Toronto	ON	M5J1B7	416-863-2000	863-0495
Trois-Rivieres Port Authority 1545 Du Fleuve St Suite 300 *Web:* www.porttr.com	Trois-Rivieres	QC	G9A6K4	819-378-2887	378-2487
Vancouver Port Authority 100 The Pt 999 Canada Pl **Fax Area Code:* 866 ■ *TF:* 888-767-8826 ■ *Web:* www.portvancouver.com	Vancouver	BC	V6C3T4	604-665-9000	284-4271*
Virginia Port Authority 600 World Trade Ctr *Web:* www.vaports.com	Norfold	VA	23510	757-683-8000	683-8500
Waukegan Port District 55 S Harbor Pl PO Box 620 *Web:* www.waukeganport.com	Waukegan	IL	60085	847-244-3133	244-1348
Windsor Port Authority 251 Goyeau St Suite 502 *Web:* www.portwindsor.com	Windsor	ON	N9A6V2	519-258-5741	258-5905
Wrangell Harbor 1096 Outer Dr *Web:* www.wrangell.com	Wrangell	AK	99929	907-874-3736	874-3197

622 POULTRY PROCESSING

SEE ALSO Meat Packing Plants p. 2225

				Phone	Fax
Allen Family Foods Inc 126 N Shipley St *TF:* 800-477-9136 ■ *Web:* www.allenfamilyfoods.com	Seaford	DE	19973	302-629-9163	629-9532
American Dehydrated Foods Inc 3801 E Sunshine PO Box 4087 *TF:* 800-456-3447 ■ *Web:* www.adfinc.com	Springfield	MO	65809	417-881-7755	881-4963
Amick Farms Inc PO Box 2309 **Fax:* Sales ■ *TF:* 800-926-4257 ■ *Web:* www.amickfarms.com	Batesburg-Leesville	SC	29070	803-532-1400	532-1492*
Barber's Poultry Inc 4851 W 120th Ave *Web:* www.barberspoultry.com	Broomfield	CO	80020	303-466-7338	466-6960
Bell & Evans 154 W Main St PO Box 39 *Web:* www.bellandevans.com	Fredericksburg	PA	17026	717-865-6626	865-7046
Brakebush Bros Inc N4993 6th Dr *TF:* 800-933-2121 ■ *Web:* www.brakebush.com	Westfield	WI	53964	608-296-2121	296-3192
Brown Produce Co PO Box 265	Farina	IL	62838	618-245-3301	
Butterball LLC 215 W Diehl Rd *Web:* www.butterball.com	Naperville	IL	60563	630-857-1000	512-1139
Butterfield Foods Co 225 Hubbard Ave	Butterfield	MN	56120	507-956-5103	956-5751

Company	City	State	Zip	Phone	Fax
Cagle's Inc 1385 Collier Rd NW AMEX: CGL.A ■ TF: 800-476-2820 ■ Web: www.cagles.net	Atlanta	GA	30318	404-355-2820	350-9605
Cal-Maine Foods Inc 3320 Woodrow Wilson Dr PO Box 2960 NASDAQ: CALM ■ Web: www.calmainefoods.com	Jackson	MS	39209	601-948-6813	969-0905
Cargill Inc North America 15407 McGinty Rd TF: 800-227-4455	Wayzata	MN	55391	952-742-7575	
Cargill Kitchen Solutions 206 W 4th St TF: 800-872-3447 ■ Web: www.sunnyfresh.com	Monticello	MN	55362	763-271-5600	271-5711
Case Farms Inc 121 Rand St	Morganton	NC	28655	828-438-6900	437-5205
Claxton Poultry Farms PO Box 428 Web: www.claxtonpoultory.com	Claxton	GA	30417	912-739-3181	739-2144
Culver Duck Farms Inc PO Box 910 TF: 800-825-9225 ■ Web: www.culverduck.com	Middlebury	IN	46540	574-825-9537	825-2613
Dutch Quality House 4110 Continental Dr *Fax Area Code: 770 ■ TF: 800-392-0844 ■ Web: www.dutchqualityhouse.com	Oakwood	GA	30566	678-450-3100	534-9281*
Echo Lake Farm Produce Co 33102 S Honey Lake Rd PO Box 279 TF: 800-888-3447 ■ Web: www.echolakefoods.com	Burlington	WI	53105	262-763-9551	763-4593
Empire Kosher Poultry Inc Rd 5 PO Box 228 TF: 800-233-7177 ■ Web: www.empirekosher.com	Mifflintown	PA	17059	717-436-5921	436-7070
Far Best Foods Inc 4689 S 400 W PO Box 480 Web: www.farbestfoods.com	Huntingburg	IN	47542	812-683-4200	683-4226
Fieldale Farms Corp 555 Broiler Blvd TF: 800-241-5400 ■ Web: www.fieldale.com	Baldwin	GA	30511	706-778-5100	778-3767
Foster Farms Inc 1000 Davis St PO Box 457 Web: www.fosterfarms.com	Livingston	CA	95334	209-394-7901	394-6342
Georges Inc PO Drawer G	Springdale	AR	72765	479-927-7000	927-7200
Gold'n Plump Poultry 309 Lincoln Ave SE TF: 800-328-8236 ■ Web: www.goldnplump.com	Saint Cloud	MN	56304	320-251-6568	240-6250
Harrison Poultry Inc Star St PO Box 550	Bethlehem	GA	30620	770-867-7511	867-0999
Henningsen Foods Inc 14334 Industrial Rd *Fax Area Code: 420 ■ Web: www.henningsenfoods.com	Omaha	NE	68144	402-330-2500	330-0875*
Holmes Foods Inc 101 S Liberty Ave	Nixon	TX	78140	830-582-1551	582-1090
House of Raeford Farms Inc 520 E Central Ave TF: 800-888-7539 ■ Web: www.houseofraeford.com	Raeford	NC	28376	910-875-5161	875-8300
ISE America Inc 33335 Galena Sassafras TF: 800-343-7926	Galena	MD	21635	410-755-6300	755-6367
Jennie-O Turkey Store 2505 Willmar Ave SW TF: 800-328-1756 ■ Web: www.jennieo.com	Willmar	MN	56201	320-235-2622	231-7100
JFC Inc PO Box 1106 TF: 800-328-8236	Saint Cloud	MN	56302	320-251-3570	240-6250
Keystone Foods LLC 300 Bar Harbor Dr Suite 600, 5 Tower Bridge Web: www.keystonefoods.com	West Conshohocken	PA	19428	610-667-6700	667-1460
Koch Foods Inc 1300 Higgins Rd Suite 100 TF: 800-837-2778 ■ Web: www.kochfoods.com	Park Ridge	IL	60068	847-384-5940	384-5961
Koch Foods Inc 3500 Western Blvd TF: 800-277-2473	Montgomery	AL	36108	334-281-0400	284-2998
Mar-Jac Poultry Inc 1020 Aviation Blvd PO Box 1017 Web: www.marjacpoultry.com	Gainesville	GA	30501	770-531-5007	531-5049
Marshall Durbin Co 2830 Commerce Blvd TF: 800-245-8204 ■ Web: www.marshalldurbin.com	Birmingham	AL	35210	205-956-3505	956-3505
Michael Foods Inc 301 Carlson Pkwy Suite 400 TF: 800-325-4270 ■ Web: www.michaelfoods.com	Minnetonka	MN	55305	952-258-4000	258-4940
Mountaire Farms 17269 NC Hwy 71 N *Fax: Hum Res ■ TF: 800-968-0720 ■ Web: www.mountaire.com	Lumber Bridge	NC	28357	910-843-5942	843-8840*
Northern Pride Inc PO Box 598	Thief River Falls	MN	56701	218-681-1201	681-7183
OK Foods Inc PO Box 1787 TF: 800-635-9441 ■ Web: www.okfoods.com	Fort Smith	AR	72902	479-783-0244	784-1280
Olymel LP 2200 Pratte Ave Pratte Web: www.olymel.com	Saint-Hyacinthe	QC	J2S4B6	450-771-0400	771-0519
Oskaloosa Food Products Corp 546 9th Ave E	Oskaloosa	IA	52577	641-673-3487	673-8684
Park Farms Inc 1925 30th St NE TF: 800-683-6511 ■ Web: www.parkfarms.com	Canton	OH	44705	330-455-0241	455-5820
PECO Foods Inc 3701 Kauloosa Ave Web: www.pecofoods.com	Tuscaloosa	AL	35403	205-345-3955	343-2401
Pennfield Corp 711 Rohrerstown Rd TF: 800-732-0467 ■ Web: www.dairyfeed.com	Lancaster	PA	17604	717-299-2561	295-8783
Perdue Farms Inc 31149 Old Ocean City Rd TF: 800-457-3738 ■ Web: www.perdue.com	Salisbury	MD	21804	410-543-3000	543-3212
Petaluma Poultry Inc PO Box 7368 TF: 800-556-6789 ■ Web: www.petalumapoultry.com	Petaluma	CA	94955	707-763-1904	763-3924
Pilgrim's Corp 1770 Promontory Cir NYSE: PPC ■ TF: 800-727-5366 ■ Web: www.pilgrimspride.com	Greeley	CO	80634	800-727-5366	
Pilgrims Pride 244 Perimeter Ctr Pkwy NE Web: www.pilgrimspride.com	Atlanta	GA	30346	770-393-5000	393-5262
Randall Foods Inc 2905 E 50th St *Fax: Hum Res ■ TF: 800-372-6581	Vernon	CA	90058	323-587-2383	586-1587*
Rose Acre Farms Inc 351 Ronthor Dr Web: www.goodegg.com	Social Circle	GA	30025	770-464-0813	464-2998
Sanderson Farms Inc PO Box 988 NASDAQ: SAFM ■ TF: 800-844-4030 ■ Web: www.sandersonfarms.com	Laurel	MS	39441	601-426-1454	425-0704
Simmons Industries Inc 601 N Hico St TF: 888-831-7007 ■ Web: www.simfoods.simmonsglobal.com	Siloam Springs	AR	72761	479-524-8151	524-6562
Sonstegard Foods Inc 707 E 41st St Suite 107 TF: 800-533-3184 ■ Web: www.sonstegard.com	Sioux Falls	SD	57105	605-338-4642	338-9765
Tip Top Poultry Inc 327 Wallace Rd TF: 800-241-5230 ■ Web: www.tiptoppoultry.com	Marietta	GA	30062	770-973-8070	973-6897
Townsends Inc 22855 DuPont Blvd Web: www.products.townsends.com	Georgetown	DE	19947	302-855-7100	777-6660
Turkey Valley Farms 112 S 6th St PO Box 200 Web: www.turkeyvalleyfarms.com	Marshall	MN	56258	507-337-3100	337-3009
Tyson Foods Inc 2210 W Oaklawn Dr PO Box 2020 NYSE: TSN ■ *Fax: Hum Res ■ TF: 800-643-3410 ■ Web: www.tyson.com	Springdale	AR	72762	479-290-4000	290-4217*
Valley Fresh Inc 680 D St PO Box 339 TF: 800-526-3189	Turlock	CA	95381	209-668-3695	668-0770
Wayne Farms Enterprises LLC 1020 County Rd 114 TF: 800-223-2569	Jack	AL	36346	334-897-3435	897-1000
West Liberty Foods LLC 228 W 2nd St TF: 888-511-4500 ■ Web: www.wlfoods.com	West Liberty	IA	52776	319-627-2126	627-6334

623 POWER TRANSMISSION EQUIPMENT - MECHANICAL

SEE ALSO Bearings - Ball & Roller p. 1517

Company	City	State	Zip	Phone	Fax
Adams Co 8040 Chavenelle Rd Web: www.theadamscompany.com	Dubuque	IA	52002	563-583-3591	583-8048
Allied-Locke Industries 1088 Corregidor Rd TF: 800-435-7752 ■ Web: www.alliedlocke.com	Dixon	IL	61021	815-288-1471	288-7945
American Metal Bearing Co 7191 Acacia Ave TF: 800-888-3048 ■ Web: www.ambco.net	Garden Grove	CA	92841	714-892-5527	898-3217
Ameridrives Couplings 1802 Pittsburgh Ave PO Box 4000 TF: 800-352-0141 ■ Web: www.ameridrives.com	Erie	PA	16512	814-480-5000	453-5891
AmeriDrives International 1802 Pittsburgh Ave TF: 800-352-0141 ■ Web: www.ameridrives.com	Erie	PA	16502	814-480-5100	453-5891
Barden Corp 200 Pk Ave TF: 800-243-1060 ■ Web: www.bardenbearings.com	Danbury	CT	06810	203-744-2211	744-3756
Beemer Precision Inc 230 New York Dr PO Box 3080 TF: 800-836-2340 ■ Web: www.oilite.com	Fort Washington	PA	19034	215-646-8440	283-3397
Bird Precision 1 Spruce St PO Box 540569 TF Cust Svc: 800-454-7369 ■ Web: www.birdprecision.com	Waltham	MA	02454	781-894-0160	894-6308
Bishop-Wisecarver Corp 2104 Martin Way TF: 888-580-8272 ■ Web: www.bwc.com	Pittsburg	CA	94565	925-439-8272	439-5931
Buckeye Power Sales Co Inc 6850 Commerce Ct Dr PO Box 489 TF: 800-523-3587 ■ Web: www.buckeyepowersales.com	Blacklick	OH	43004	614-861-6000	861-2291
Cangro Industries Long Island Transmission Co 495 Smith St TF: 800-899-2264 ■ Web: www.cangroindustries.com	Farmingdale	NY	11735	631-454-9000	454-9155
Capitol Stampings Corp 2700 W N Ave Web: www.capitolstampings.com	Milwaukee	WI	53208	414-372-3500	372-3535
Carlyle Johnson Machine Co (CJM) 291 Boston Tpke TF: 888-629-4867 ■ Web: www.cjmco.com	Bolton	CT	06043	860-643-1531	646-2645
Certified Power Inc 970 Campus Dr TF: 800-877-8350 ■ Web: www.certifiedpower.com	Mundelein	IL	60060	847-573-3800	573-3832
Deublin Co 2050 Norman Dr W Web: www.deublin.com	Waukegan	IL	60085	847-689-8600	689-8690
Diamond Chain Co 402 Kentucky Ave TF Cust Svc: 800-872-4246 ■ Web: www.diamondchain.com	Indianapolis	IN	46225	317-638-6431	638-6431
Don Dye Co Inc 524 NW 20th Ave PO Box 107 TF: 800-901-3131 ■ Web: www.dondyeco.com	Kingman	KS	67068	620-532-3131	532-2141
Drives Inc 901 19th Ave TF: 800-435-0782 ■ Web: www.drivesinc.com	Fulton	IL	61252	815-589-2211	589-4420
Eaton Corp 1111 Superior Ave Eaton Ctr NYSE: ETN ■ Web: www.eaton.com	Cleveland	OH	44114	216-523-5000	523-4787
EC Styberg Engineering Co Inc 1600 Gold St PO Box 788 Web: www.styberg.com	Racine	WI	53401	262-637-9301	637-1319
Elliott Mfg Inc 11 Beckwith Ave PO Box 733 Web: www.elliottmfg.com	Binghamton	NY	13901	607-772-0404	772-0431
Entek International LLC 250 N Hansard Ave PO Box 127 Web: www.entek-international.com	Lebanon	OR	97355	541-259-3901	259-3932
Force Control Industries Inc 3660 Dixie Hwy TF: 800-829-3244 ■ Web: www.forcecontrol.com	Fairfield	OH	45014	513-868-0900	868-2105
General Bearing Corp 44 High St TF Sales: 800-431-1766 ■ Web: www.generalbearing.com	West Nyack	NY	10994	845-358-6000	358-6277
GGB North America 700 Mid Atlantic Pkwy PO Box 189 *Fax: Sales ■ TF: 800-222-0147 ■ Web: www.ggbearings.com	Thorofare	NJ	08086	856-848-3200	848-5115*
GKN Rockford Inc 1200 Windsor Rd *Fax: Sales ■ Web: www.rockfordpowertrain.com	Loves Park	IL	61111	815-633-7460	633-1311*
Hebeler Corp 2000 Military Rd TF: 800-486-4709 ■ Web: www.hebeler.com	Tonawanda	NY	14150	716-873-9300	873-7538
Helical Products Co Inc 901 W McCoy Ln PO Box 1069 Web: www.heli-cal.com	Santa Maria	CA	93456	805-928-3851	928-2369
Hilliard Corp 100 W 4th St Web: www.hilliardcorp.com	Elmira	NY	14902	607-733-7121	733-3009
Horton Inc 2565 Walnut St TF: 800-843-7445 ■ Web: www.hortonww.com	Roseville	MN	55113	651-361-6400	361-6804
Iberdrola Renewables Inc 1125 NW Couch Suite 700 Web: www.iberdrolarenewables.us	Portland	OR	97209	503-796-7000	796-6901
Industrial Clutch 1701-3 Pearl St Web: www.indclutch.com	Waukesha	WI	53186	262-547-3357	547-2949
John Deere Coffeyville Works Inc PO Box 577 TF: 800-844-1337	Coffeyville	KS	67337	620-251-3400	252-3252
Kamatics Corp 1330 Blue Hills Ave TF: 800-468-4735 ■ Web: www.kamatics.com	Bloomfield	CT	06002	860-243-9704	243-7993
Kingsbury Inc 10385 Drummond Rd TF: 800-898-8912 ■ Web: www.kingsbury.com	Philadelphia	PA	19154	215-824-4000	824-4999
Linn Gear Co 100 N 8th St PO Box 397 TF: 800-547-2471 ■ Web: www.linngear.com	Lebanon	OR	97355	541-259-1211	259-1299
Lovejoy Inc 2655 Wisconsin Ave TF: 800-334-9659 ■ Web: www.lovejoy-inc.com	Downers Grove	IL	60515	630-852-0500	
Magtrol Inc 70 Gardenville Pkwy W TF: 800-828-7844 ■ Web: www.magtrol.com	Buffalo	NY	14224	716-668-5555	668-8705

				Phone	Fax
Marland Clutch 485 S Frontage Rd Suite 330	Burr Ridge	IL	60527	800-216-3515	216-3001*
*Fax Area Code: 877 ■ TF: 800-216-3515 ■ Web: www.marland.com					
Martin Sprocket & Gear Inc 3100 Sprocket Dr PO Box 91588	Arlington	TX	76015	817-258-3000	258-3333
Web: www.martinsprocket.com					
Maurey Mfg Corp 410 Industrial Pk Rd	Holly Springs	MS	38635	662-252-1898	252-6364
TF: 800-284-2161 ■ Web: www.maurey.com					
Metallized Carbon Corp 19 S Water St	Ossining	NY	10562	914-941-3738	941-4050
Web: www.metcar.com					
Midwest Control Products Corp 590 E Main St	Bushnell	IL	61422	309-772-3163	772-2266
Web: www.midwestcontrol.com					
Nook Industries 4950 E 49th St	Cleveland	OH	44125	216-271-7900	271-7020
TF: 800-321-7800 ■ Web: www.nookindustries.com					
North American Clutch Corp 4360 N Green Bay Ave	Milwaukee	WI	53209	414-267-4000	267-4024
Web: www.noramclutch.com					
NSK Corp 4200 Goss Rd	Ann Arbor	MI	48105	734-761-9500	913-7500
TF: 888-446-5675 ■ Web: www.nskamericas.com/cps/rde/xchg/na_en/hs.xsl/index.html					
NTN Bearing Corp of America 1600 E Bishop Ct	Mount Prospect	IL	60056	847-298-7500	699-9744
TF: 800-323-2358 ■ Web: www.ntnamerica.com					
OPW Engineered Systems 2726 Henkle Dr	Lebanon	OH	45036	513-932-9114	932-9845*
*Fax: Cust Svc ■ TF Cust Svc: 800-547-9393 ■ Web: www.opw-es.com					
Ormat Technologies Inc 6225 Neil Rd Suite 300	Reno	NV	89511	775-356-9029	356-9039
NYSE: ORA ■ Web: www.ormat.com					
Peer Bearing Co 2200 Norman Dr S	Waukegan	IL	60085	847-578-1000	578-1200*
*Fax: Orders ■ TF: 800-433-7337 ■ Web: www.peerbearing.com					
Pic Design Corp 86 Benson Rd PO Box 1004	Middlebury	CT	06762	203-758-8272	758-8271
TF: 800-243-6125 ■ Web: www.pic-design.com					
Ramsey Products Corp 3701 Performance Rd PO Box 668827	Charlotte	NC	28266	704-394-0322	394-9134
Web: www.ramseychain.com					
RBC Transport Dynamics Corp 3131 W Segerstrom Ave PO Box 1953	Santa Ana	CA	92704	714-546-3131	545-9885
TF: 800-854-3922 ■ Web: www.rbcbearings.com					
Real Goods Solar 833 W S Boulder Rd	Louisville	CO	80027	303-222-8950	222-3786
NASDAQ: RSOL ■ TF: 888-567-6527 ■ Web: www.realgoodssolar.com					
Reell Precision Mfg Corp 1259 Willow Lake Blvd	Saint Paul	MN	55110	651-484-2447	484-3867
Web: www.reell.com					
Regal-Beloit Corp 200 State St	Beloit	WI	53511	608-364-8800	364-8818
NYSE: RBC ■ Web: www.regalbeloit.com					
Renold Ajax Inc 100 Bourne St	Westfield	NY	14787	716-326-3121	326-6121
Web: www.renold.com					
Rollease Inc 200 Harvard Ave	Stamford	CT	06902	203-964-1573	358-5865
Web: www.rollease.com					
Schaeffler Group USA Inc 308 Springhill Farm Rd	Fort Mill	SC	29715	803-548-8500	548-8599
Web: www.ina.com/us					
Siemens Power Transmission & Distribution Inc 7000 Siemens Rd	Wendell	NC	27591	919-365-2200	346-2777*
*Fax Area Code: 518 ■ TF: 800-347-6659					
SKF USA Inc 1111 Adams Ave	Norristown	PA	19403	610-630-2800	630-2801
Web: www.skfusa.com					
Solaria Corp 6200 Paseo Padre Pkwy	Fremont	CA	94555	510-270-2500	793-8388
Web: www.solaria.com					
Solomon Corp 103 W Main PO Box 245	Solomon	KS	67480	785-655-2191	655-2502
TF: 800-234-2867 ■ Web: www.solomoncorp.com					
Speed Selector Inc 17050 Munn Rd	Chagrin Falls	OH	44023	440-543-8233	543-8527
Web: www.speedselector.com					
SS White Technologies Inc 151 Old New Brunswick Rd	Piscataway	NJ	08854	732-752-8300	752-8315
TF: 800-872-2673 ■ Web: www.sswt.com					
Stock Drive Products/Sterling Instrument 2101 Jericho Tpke	New Hyde Park	NY	11040	516-328-3300	326-8827
TF: 800-737-7436 ■ Web: www.sdp-si.com					
TB Wood's Inc 440 N 5th Ave	Chambersburg	PA	17201	717-264-7161	264-6420
NASDAQ: TBWC ■ TF: 888-829-6637 ■ Web: www.tbwoods.com					
Tuthill Linkage Group 2110 Summit St	New Haven	IN	46774	260-749-5105	493-2387
Twin Disc Inc 1328 Racine St	Racine	WI	53403	262-638-4000	
NASDAQ: TWIN ■ Web: www.twindisc.com					
Universal Bearings Inc 431 N Birkey St	Bremen	IN	46506	574-546-2261	546-5085
Web: www.univbrg.com					
US Tsubaki Inc 301 E Marquardt Dr	Wheeling	IL	60090	847-459-9500	459-9515
TF: 800-323-7790 ■ Web: www.ustsubaki.com					
Warner Electric 449 Gardner St	South Beloit	IL	61080	815-389-3771	
TF: 800-234-3369 ■ Web: www.warnernet.com					
Waukesha Bearings Corp W 231 N 2811 Roundy Cir E Suite 200	Pewaukee	WI	53072	262-506-3000	506-3001
Web: www.waukbearing.com					
Wheeler Industries 7261 Investment Dr	North Charleston	SC	29418	843-552-1251	552-4790
TF: 800-343-0803 ■ Web: www.wheelerfluidfilmbearings.com					
Whittet-Higgins Co 33 Higginson Ave PO Box 8	Central Falls	RI	02863	401-728-0700	728-0703
Web: www.whittet-higgins.com					
Zero-Max Inc 13200 6th Ave N	Plymouth	MN	55441	763-546-4300	546-8260
TF: 800-533-1731 ■ Web: www.zero-max.com					

624 PRECISION MACHINED PRODUCTS

SEE ALSO Aircraft Parts & Auxiliary Equipment p. 1387; Machine Shops p. 2190

				Phone	Fax
A-1 Production Inc 5809 E Leighty Rd	Kendallville	IN	46755	260-347-0960	347-4727
Web: www.a1production.com					
Abbott Interfast Corp 190 Abbott Dr	Wheeling	IL	60090	847-459-6200	459-4076
TF: 800-877-0789 ■ Web: www.abbott-interfast.com					
Accellent Inc 200 W 7th Ave	Collegeville	PA	19426	610-489-0300	489-1150
TF: 800-321-6285 ■ Web: www.accellent.com					
Afco Products Inc 2074 S Mannheim Rd	Des Plaines	IL	60018	847-299-1055	299-8455
Web: www.afco-products.com					
AHF Ducommun Inc 268 E Gardena Blvd	Gardena	CA	90248	310-380-5390	380-5238
Air-Matic Products Co Inc 22218 Telegraph Rd	Southfield	MI	48033	248-356-4200	356-0738
Web: www.air-matic.com					
Alco Mfg Corp 10584 Middle Ave	Elyria	OH	44035	440-458-5165	458-6821
Web: www.alcomfgcorp.com					
Alger Mfg Co Inc 724 S Bon View Ave	Ontario	CA	91761	909-986-4591	983-3351
TF: 800-854-9833 ■ Web: www.alger1.com					
Allan Tool & Machine Co Inc 1822 E Maple Rd	Troy	MI	48083	248-585-2910	585-7728
Allied Screw Products Inc 815 E Lowell Ave	Mishawaka	IN	46545	574-255-4718	255-4173
Web: www.aspi-nc.com					
Allmetal Screw Products Corp 94 E Jefryn Blvd # A	Deer Park	NY	11729	631-243-5200	243-5307
Web: www.allmetalcorp.com					
Alpha Grainger Mfg Inc 20 Discovery Way	Franklin	MA	02038	508-520-4005	520-4185
Web: www.agmi.com					
American Products Co Inc 610 Rahway Ave	Union	NJ	07083	908-687-4100	687-0037
Web: www.amerprod.com					
American Turned Products Inc 7626 Klier Dr	Fairview	PA	16415	814-474-4200	474-4718
Web: www.atpteam.com					
Amsco-Wire Products Co 610 Grand Ave	Ridgefield	NJ	07657	201-945-5700	945-5618
Amtec Precision Products Inc 1355 Holmes Rd	Elgin	IL	60123	847-695-8030	695-8295
Web: www.amtecprecision.com					
Anchor Coupling Inc 5520 13th St	Menominee	MI	49858	906-863-2671	863-3242
TF: 800-662-5520 ■ Web: www.anchorcoupling.com					
Anderson Automatics Inc 6401 Welcome Ave N	Minneapolis	MN	55429	763-533-2206	533-0320
Web: www.andersonautomatics.com					
Anderson Precision Inc 20 Livingston Ave	Jamestown	NY	14701	716-484-1148	484-7779
Web: www.andersonprecision.com					
Ashley Ward Inc 7490 Easy St	Mason	OH	45040	513-398-1414	398-1125
Web: www.ashleyward.com					
Astro Seal Inc 827 Palmyrita Ave # B	Riverside	CA	92507	951-787-6670	787-6677
Web: www.astroseal.com					
ATEC Inc 12600 Executive Dr	Stafford	TX	77477	281-276-2700	240-2682
Web: www.atec.com					
Athanor Group Inc 921 E California Ave	Ontario	CA	91761	909-467-1205	467-1208
Auer Precision Inc 1050 W Birchwood Ave	Mesa	AZ	85210	480-834-4637	964-8237
Web: www.auerprecision.com					
Automatic Machine Products Co 17 Wall St	Attleboro	MA	02703	508-222-2300	222-2307
Web: www.ampcomp.com					
Automatic Products Corp 2735 Forest Ln	Garland	TX	75042	972-272-6422	494-0533
Web: www.ap-corp.com					
Avanti Engineering Inc 200 W Lake Dr	Glendale Heights	IL	60139	630-260-1333	260-1762
Web: www.avantiengineering.com					
Barber-Nichols Inc 6325 W 55th Ave	Arvada	CO	80002	303-421-8111	420-4679
Web: www.barber-nichols.com					
Barton Precision Components LLC PO Box 1060	West Bend	WI	53095	262-334-5583	334-0639
Web: www.bartonproducts.com					
Bay Swiss Mfg Co Inc 5 Airpark Vista Blvd	Dayton	NV	89403	775-246-7100	246-7104
TF: 800-247-3207 ■ Web: www.bayswiss.com					
Berkley Screw Machine Products Inc 2100 Royce Haley Dr	Rochester Hills	MI	48309	248-853-0044	853-1532
Berkshire Industries Inc 109 Apremont Way	Westfield	MA	01085	413-568-8676	562-0061
Web: www.berkshireindustries.com					
Betar Inc 1524 Millstone River Rd	Hillsborough	NJ	08844	908-359-4200	359-1010
TF: 800-841-8841 ■ Web: www.betar.net					
Betty Machine Co 324 Freehill Rd	Hendersonville	TN	37075	615-826-6004	826-6262
TF: 800-264-3480 ■ Web: www.bettymachine.com					
Biddle Precision Components Inc 701 S Main St	Sheridan	IN	46069	317-758-4451	758-5260
TF: 800-428-4387 ■ Web: www.bpcinc.biz					
Birken Mfg Co 3 Old Windsor Rd	Bloomfield	CT	06002	860-242-2211	242-2749
Web: www.birken.net					
Blackhawk Machine Products Inc 6 Industrial Dr	Smithfield	RI	02917	401-232-7563	732-0770
Web: www.blackhawk-machine.com					
BMI Inc 4541 Preslyn Dr	Raleigh	NC	27616	919-878-7776	878-0580
Web: www.bmi-inc.com					
Bracalente Mfg Group 20 W Creamery Rd PO Box 570	Trumbauersville	PA	18970	215-536-3077	536-4844
Web: www.bracalente.com					
Burgess-Norton Mfg Co 737 Peyton St	Geneva	IL	60134	630-232-4100	232-3700*
*Fax: Hum Res ■ Web: www.burgessnorton.com					
Bystrom Bros Inc 2200 Snelling Ave S	Minneapolis	MN	55404	612-721-7511	721-6745
Web: www.bystrombros.com					
Camcraft Inc 1080 Muirfield Dr	Hanover Park	IL	60133	630-582-6000	582-6019
Web: www.camcraft.com					
Cape Industries Inc 24055 Mound Rd	Warren	MI	48091	586-754-0898	754-7030
Cass Screw Machine Products Co 4800 N Lilac Dr	Minneapolis	MN	55429	763-535-0501	535-9238
Web: www.csmp.com					
CE Holden Inc 938 Rt 910	Cheswick	PA	15024	412-767-5050	767-9922
Web: www.ceholdeninc.com					
Celina Aluminum Precision Technology Inc (CAPT) 7059 Staeger Rd	Celina	OH	45822	419-586-2278	586-6474
Web: www.capt-celina.com					
Charleston Metal Products Inc 350 Grant St	Waterloo	IN	46793	260-837-8211	837-8101
Web: www.charlestonmetal.com					
CNW Inc 4710 Madison Rd	Cincinnati	OH	45227	513-321-2775	321-2013
TF: 800-327-5900 ■ Web: www.cnwinc.com					
Cole Screw Machine Products Inc 88 Great Hill Rd PO Box 1007	Naugatuck	CT	06770	203-723-1418	723-1252
Web: www.colescrew.com					
Contour Tool Inc 588 Ternes Ave	Elyria	OH	44035	440-365-7333	365-7335
Web: www.contourtool.com					
Corlett-Turner Co 2500 104th Ave	Zeeland	MI	49464	616-772-9082	772-1235

Company	City	State	ZIP	Phone	Fax
Cox Mfg Co 5500 N Loop 1604 E TF: 800-900-7981 ■ Web: www.coxmanufacturing.com	San Antonio	TX	78247	210-657-7731	657-2345
CPI Aerostructures Inc 60 Heartland Blvd. AMEX: CVU ■ Web: www.cpiaero.com	Edgewood	NY	11717	631-586-5200	586-5814
Curtis Screw Co Inc 50 Thielman Dr TF: 800-914-6276 ■ Web: www.curtisscrew.com	Buffalo	NY	14206	716-898-7800	898-7880
D-Velco Mfg of Arizona 401 S 36th St Web: www.dvelco.com	Phoenix	AZ	85034	602-275-4406	275-4406
Dabko Industries Inc 50 Emmett St Web: www.rgdtech.com	Bristol	CT	06010	860-589-0756	585-0874
Davies Molding LLC 350 Kehoe Blvd TF: 800-554-9208 ■ Web: www.daviesmolding.com	Carol Stream	IL	60188	630-510-8188	510-9944
DCG Precision Mfg Corp 9 Trowbridge Dr Web: www.dcgprecision.com	Bethel	CT	06801	203-743-5525	791-1737
Dearborn Precision Tubular Products Inc 6 Dearborn Dr PO Box 126 Web: www.dearbornprecision.com	Fryeburg	ME	04037	207-935-2171	935-2908
Delo Screw Products Co 700 London Rd Web: www.deloscrew.com	Delaware	OH	43015	740-363-1971	363-0042
Devon Precision Industries Inc 251 Munson Rd. Web: www.devonprecision.com	Wolcott	CT	06716	203-879-1437	879-5556
Dirksen Screw Products Co 14490 23-Mile Rd Web: www.dirksenscrew.com	Shelby Township	MI	48315	586-247-5400	247-9507
Diversified Machine Inc 28059 Ctr Oaks Ct Web: www.divmi.com	Wixom	MI	48393	248-277-4400	277-4399
Dow Screw Products 3810 Paule Ave Web: www.dowscrew.com	Saint Louis	MO	63125	314-638-5100	638-4838
Duffin Mfg Co 316 Warden Ave PO Box 4036 Web: www.duffinmfg.com	Elyria	OH	44036	440-323-4681	323-7389
DuPage Machine Products Inc 311 Longview Dr	Bloomingdale	IL	60108	630-690-5400	690-5504
Efficient Machine Products Corp 12133 Alameda Dr Web: www.efficientmachineprod.com	Strongsville	OH	44149	440-268-0205	268-0215
EJ Basler Co 9511 Ainslie St Web: www.ejbasler.com	Schiller Park	IL	60176	847-678-8880	678-8896
Elyria Mfg Corp 145 Northrup St. Web: www.elyriamfg.com	Elyria	OH	44035	440-365-4171	365-4000
Engineered Sinterings & Plastics Inc 140 Commercial St.	Watertown	CT	06795	860-274-7546	274-7546
Enoch Mfg Co 14242 SE 82nd Dr PO Box 98 TF: 888-659-6565 ■ Web: www.enochmfg.com	Clackamas	OR	97015	503-659-2660	659-4439
Fairchild Auto-mated Parts Inc 10 White St TF: 800-927-2545 ■ Web: www.fairchildparts.com	Winsted	CT	06098	860-379-2725	379-5340
Farrar Corp 142 W Burns St. Web: www.farrarusa.com	Norwich	KS	67118	620-478-2212	478-2200
FC Phillips Inc 471 Washington St Web: www.fcphillips.com	Stoughton	MA	02072	781-344-9400	344-3440
FCI Inc 4661 Giles Rd Web: www.fci-usa.com	Cleveland	OH	44135	216-251-5200	251-5206
Federal Screw Works 20229 Nine-Mile Rd Web: www.federalscrew.com	Saint Clair Shores	MI	48080	586-443-4200	443-4210
Fischer Special Mfg Co 1188 Industrial Rd Web: www.fischerspecial.com	Cold Spring	KY	41076	859-781-1400	781-4702
Form Cut Industries Inc 195 Mt Pleasant Ave Web: www.formcut.com	Newark	NJ	07104	973-483-5154	483-4512
Fraen Machining Corp 324 New Boston St Web: www.swisstronics.com	Woburn	MA	01801	781-205-5400	205-5472
Gates Albert Inc 3434 Union St Web: www.gatesalbert.com	North Chili	NY	14514	585-594-9401	594-4305
General Automotive Mfg LLC 5215 W Airways Ave. Web: www.gamfg.com	Franklin	WI	53132	414-423-6400	423-6415
General Engineering Works 1515 W Wrightwood Ct Web: www.gewinc.com	Addison	IL	60101	630-543-8000	543-8005
Gormac Products Inc 1836 Oakdale Ave TF: 800-596-0156 ■ Web: www.gormacproducts.com	Racine	WI	53406	262-637-9146	637-1519
Grand Traverse Machine Co (GTM) 1247 Boon St Web: www.gtmachine.com	Traverse City	MI	49686	231-946-8006	946-6606
Greystone of Lincoln Inc 7 Wellington Rd	Lincoln	RI	02865	401-333-0444	334-5745
Griner Engineering Inc 2500 N Curry Pike Web: www.griner.com	Bloomington	IN	47404	812-332-2220	332-2229
H & H Swiss Screw Machine Products Co Inc 1478 Chestnut Ave TF: 800-826-9985 ■ Web: www.hhswiss.com	Hillside	NJ	07205	908-688-6390	688-3503
H & L Tool Co Inc 32701 Dequindre Rd. Web: www.hltool.com	Madison Heights	MI	48071	248-585-7474	585-5774
Hadady Corp 510 W 172nd St Web: hadadycorp.com	South Holland	IL	60473	708-596-5168	596-7563
Hall Industries Inc 514 Mecklem Ln TF: 800-828-5519 ■ Web: www.hallind.com	Ellwood City	PA	16117	724-752-2000	758-1558
Herker Industries Inc N57 W13760 Carmen Ave. Web: www.herker.com	Menomonee Falls	WI	53051	262-781-4220	781-0931
Hi-Shear Corp 2600 Skypark Dr. Web: www.hi-shear.com	Torrance	CA	90509	310-326-8110	784-4144
High Precision Grinding & Machining Inc 1130 Pioneer Way.	El Cajon	CA	92020	619-440-0303	440-2148
High Precision Inc 375 Morse St Web: www.highprecisioninc.com	Hamden	CT	06517	203-777-5395	773-1976
Highland Machine & Screw Products Co 700 5th St PO Box 329 Web: www.highlandmachine.com	Highland	IL	62249	618-654-2103	654-8016
Horizon Mfg Industries Inc 11417 Cyrus Way Suite 1 Web: www.horizonman.com	Mukilteo	WA	98275	425-493-1220	493-0042
Horspool & Romine Mfg Inc 5850 Marshall St. TF: 800-446-2263 ■ Web: www.horspool.com	Oakland	CA	94608	510-652-1844	652-3455
Huron Automatic Screw Co PO Box 610068 Web: www.huronauto.com	Port Huron	MI	48061	810-364-6636	364-6639
Huron Inc 6554 Lakeshore Rd.	Lexington	MI	48450	810-359-5344	359-7521
Hyland Screw Machine Products 1900 Kuntz Rd Web: www.hylandmach.com	Dayton	OH	45404	937-233-8600	233-7067
Insaco Inc 1365 Canary Rd TF: 800-497-4531 ■ Web: www.insaco.com	Quakertown	PA	18951	215-536-3500	536-7750
Intat Precision Inc 2148 N State Rd 3 PO Box 488 Web: www.intat.com	Rushville	IN	46173	765-932-5323	932-3032
Iseli Co 402 N Main St	Walworth	WI	53184	262-275-2108	275-6094
J T M Technologies Inc 204 Industrial Ct TF: 877-586-8324 ■ Web: www.jtmtechnologies.com	Wylie	TX	75098	972-429-6575	429-3774
Jay Sons Screw Machine Products Inc 197 Burritt St PO Box 674 Web: www.jaysons.com	Milldale	CT	06467	860-621-0141	621-0142
Jessen Mfg Co Inc 1409 W Beardsley Ave PO Box 1729 Web: www.jessenmfg.com	Elkhart	IN	46515	574-295-3836	522-2962
Jet Products Corp 9106 Balboa Ave. Web: www.senioraerospace.com/Jet_Products	San Diego	CA	92123	858-430-2203	278-8768
John J Steuby Co 6002 N Lindbergh Blvd. Web: www.steuby.com	Hazelwood	MO	63042	314-895-1000	895-9814
K & K Screw Products LLC 99 Internationale Blvd Web: www.kksp.com	Glendale Heights	IL	60139	630-260-1735	260-4091
Kaddis Mfg Corp 1100 Beahan Rd PO Box 92985 Web: www.kaddis.com	Rochester	NY	14692	585-464-9000	464-0008
Kenlee Precision Corp 1701 Inverness Ave. TF: 800-969-5278 ■ Web: www.kenlee.com	Baltimore	MD	21230	410-525-3800	646-3278
Kerr Lakeside Inc 26841 Tungsten Rd TF: 800-487-5377 ■ Web: www.kerrlakeside.com	Euclid	OH	44132	216-261-2100	261-9798
Keystone Engineering 6310 Sidney St Web: www.keystoneeng.com	Houston	TX	77021	713-747-1478	
Komet Of America Inc 2050 Mitchell Blvd. TF: 800-865-6638 ■ Web: www.komet.com	Schaumburg	IL	60193	847-923-8400	923-2126
Lakeshore Automatic Products Inc 1865 Industrial Pk Dr TF: 800-851-6411 ■ Web: www.lakeshore-automatic.com	Grand Haven	MI	49417	616-846-5090	846-0790
Liberty Brass Turning Co Inc 38-01 Queens Blvd. TF: 800-345-5939 ■ Web: www.libertybrass.com	Long Island City	NY	11101	718-784-2911	784-2038
Lofts Precision Grinding LLC 459 Pulaski St 475	Syracuse	NY	13204	315-471-6143	471-7132
LSC Co 100 Herrmann Rd	Pittsburgh	PA	15239	412-795-6400	795-6442
M & S Mfg Co Inc 550 E Main St	Hudson	MI	49247	517-448-2026	448-7200
Machine Specialties Inc (MSI) 6511 Franz Warner Pkwy Web: www.machspec.com	Whitsett	NC	27377	336-603-1919	303-1920
Maddox Foundry & Machine Works Inc 13370 SW 170th St TF: 800-347-0789 ■ Web: www.maddoxfoundry.com	Archer	FL	32618	352-495-2121	495-3962
Mantel Machine Products Inc W141 N9350 Fountain Blvd Web: www.mantelmachine.com	Menomonee Falls	WI	53051	262-255-6780	255-9724
Manth-Brownell Inc 1120 Fyler Rd Web: www.manth.com	Kirkville	NY	13082	315-687-7263	687-6856
MarathonNorco Aerospace Inc 8301 Imperial Dr Web: www.mnaerospace.com	Waco	TX	76712	254-776-0650	776-6558
Marox Corp 373 Whitney Ave. Web: www.marox.com	Holyoke	MA	01040	413-536-1300	534-1829
Marshall Mfg Corp 611 Hawkins Dr PO Box 1729	Lewisburg	TN	37091	931-359-2573	359-5099
Marvel Screw Machine Products 58 Lafayette St TF: 800-394-6767	Waterbury	CT	06708	203-756-7058	754-0318
Meaden Precision Machined Products Co 16W210 83rd St Web: www.meaden.com	Burr Ridge	IL	60527	630-655-0888	655-3012
Mennie's Machine Co (MMC) Rt 71 & Mennie Dr PO Box 110 Web: www.mennies.com	Mark	IL	61340	815-339-2226	339-6550
Metric Machining Co 1425 S Vineyard Ave. Web: www.metricorp.com	Ontario	CA	91761	909-947-9222	923-1796
Micro-Matics Corp 8050 Ranchers Rd. Web: www.micro-matics.com	Minneapolis	MN	55432	763-780-2700	780-2706
Microbest Inc 670 Captain Neville Dr Web: www.microbest.com	Waterbury	CT	06705	203-597-0355	597-0655
Midwest Screw Products Inc 34700 Lakeland Blvd Web: www.midwestllc.com	Eastlake	OH	44095	440-951-2333	951-2336
Mitchel & Scott Machine Co Inc 1841 Ludlow Ave Web: www.mitsco.com	Indianapolis	IN	46201	317-639-5331	684-8245
MKM Machine Tool Co Inc 100 Technology Way. Web: www.mkmmachine.com	Jeffersonville	IN	47130	812-282-6627	284-5709
Modern Machine & Engineering Corp 1707 Jefferson St NE TF: 800-218-8838	Minneapolis	MN	55413	612-781-3347	781-0030

				Phone	Fax
Mold-Masters Injectioneering LLC					
103 Peyerk Ct Suite E	Romeo	MI	48065	586-752-6551	752-6552
TF: 800-387-2483 ■ *Web:* www.moldmasters.com					
Mount Vernon Screw Products Inc					
1020 N Canal St PO Box 250	Mount Vernon	IN	47620	812-838-5501	838-4038
TF: 800-880-5502 ■ *Web:* www.mvscrew.com					
MSK Precision Parts Inc					
4100 NW 10th Ave	Fort Lauderdale	FL	33309	954-776-0770	776-3780
TF: 800-992-5018 ■ *Web:* www.mskprecision.com					
Multimatic Products Inc 390 Oser Ave	Hauppauge	NY	11788	631-231-1515	231-1625
TF: 800-767-7633 ■ *Web:* www.multimaticproducts.com					
National Technologies Inc 7641 S 10th St	Oak Creek	WI	53154	414-571-1000	571-1010
Web: www.nationaltechnologies.com					
New Castle Industries Inc PO Box 7359	New Castle	PA	16107	724-656-5600	656-5620
TF: 800-897-2830					
Northern Screw Machine Co Inc					
300 Atwater St	Saint Paul	MN	55117	651-488-2568	488-6232
Northwest Swiss-Matic Inc					
8400 89th Ave N	Minneapolis	MN	55445	763-544-4222	544-6873
TF: 800-966-0178 ■ *Web:* www.nwswissmatic.com					
Ntn-bower Corp 707 Bower Rd	Macomb	IL	61455	309-837-0440	837-0438
Web: www.ntnbower.com					
Ohio Screw Products Inc 818 Lowell St	Elyria	OH	44035	440-322-6341	322-0750
Web: www.ohioscrew.com					
Pacific Aerospace & Electronics Inc					
434 Olds Stn Rd	Wenatchee	WA	98801	509-667-9600	667-5311
Web: www.pacaero.com					
Pacific Rim Inc 4120 SE International Way	Portland	OR	97222	503-654-9543	654-8050
Web: www.pacificrimmfg.com					
Palladin Precision Products Inc					
57 Bristol St	Waterbury	CT	06708	203-574-0246	756-9478
Web: www.palladin.com					
Peerless Screw Products Corp					
286 Sandbank Rd	Cheshire	CT	06410	203-272-6413	271-2269
Peterson Tool Co Inc					
739 Fesslers Ln PO Box 100830	Nashville	TN	37224	615-242-7341	242-7362
Web: www.petersontool.com					
Pohlman Inc 140 Long Rd	Chesterfield	MO	63005	636-537-1909	537-1930
Web: www.pohlman.com					
Powin Corp 20550 SW 115th Ave	Tualatin	OR	97062	503-598-6659	598-3941
Web: www.powin.com					
Precision Machine Works Inc 2024 Puyallup Ave	Tacoma	WA	98421	253-272-5119	272-6921
Web: www.pmwinc.com					
Precision Metal Products Co					
353 Garden Ave PO Box 1047	Holland	MI	49422	616-392-3109	392-3100
Web: www.pmpc1.com					
Precision Plus Inc 840 Kootman Ln PO Box 168	Elkhorn	WI	53121	262-743-1700	743-1701
Web: www.preplus.com					
Precision Screw Machine Products Inc					
20 Gooch St	Biddeford	ME	04005	207-283-0121	283-4824
Web: www.psmp.com					
Precisionform Inc 148 W Airport Rd	Lititz	PA	17543	717-560-7610	569-4792
TF: 800-233-3821 ■ *Web:* www.precisionform.com					
Prime Engineered Components					
1012 Buckingham St PO Box 359	Watertown	CT	06795	860-274-6773	274-7939
Web: www.primeeci.com					
Production Products Co					
6176 E Molloy Rd	East Syracuse	NY	13057	315-431-7200	431-7201
TF: 800-800-6652 ■ *Web:* www.ppc-online.com					
Quality Control Corp					
7315 W Wilson Ave	Howard Heights	IL	60706	708-867-5400	887-5009
Web: www.qccorp.com					
R G Ray Corp 3227 N Wilke Rd	Arlington Heights	IL	60004	847-459-5900	459-3473
Web: www.rgrayclamps.com					
R. & R. Mfg Co Inc 95 Silvermine Rd	Seymour	CT	06483	203-888-6441	888-9860
Web: www.rafhdwe.com					
Rable Machine Inc					
30 Paragon Pkwy PO Box 1583	Mansfield	OH	44901	419-525-2255	525-2371
Web: www.rablemachineinc.com					
RB Royal Industries Inc					
1350 S Hickory St PO Box 1168	Fond du Lac	WI	54936	920-921-1550	921-4713
Web: www.rbroyal.com					
Rima Mfg Co 3850 Munson Hwy	Hudson	MI	49247	517-448-8921	448-7142
Web: www.rimamfg.com					
Robert A Main & Sons Inc 555 Goffle Rd	Wyckoff	NJ	07481	201-447-3700	447-0302
Web: www.ramsco-inc.com					
Roberts Automatic Products Inc					
880 Lake Dr	Chanhassen	MN	55317	952-949-1000	949-9240
TF: 800-879-9837 ■ *Web:* www.robertsautomatic.com					
Rollin J Lobaugh Inc					
240 Ryan Way	South San Francisco	CA	94080	650-583-9682	583-0445
Web: www.rjlobaugh.com					
Roseland Metal Products Co 14753 Greenwood Rd	Dolton	IL	60419	708-841-4400	841-6234
Royal Screw Machine Products Co					
PO Box 1325	Waterbury	CT	06721	203-755-6565	575-9001
RW Screw Products Inc 999 Oberlin Ave SW	Massillon	OH	44647	330-837-9211	837-9223
Selflock Screw Products Inc					
114 Marcy St	East Syracuse	NY	13057	315-437-3367	463-7131
Web: www.selflockscrew.com					
Skyway Precision Inc 41225 Plymouth Rd	Plymouth	MI	48170	734-454-3550	455-9659
Web: www.skywayprecision.com					
Smith & Richardson Mfg Co PO Box 589	Geneva	IL	60134	630-232-2581	232-2610
TF: 800-426-0876 ■ *Web:* www.smithandrichardson.com					
Smithfield Mfg Inc 237 Kraft St	Clarksville	TN	37040	931-552-4327	648-4460
Web: www.smithfieldmfg.com					

				Phone	Fax
Sorenson Engineering Inc 32032 Dunlap Blvd	Yucaipa	CA	92399	909-795-2434	795-7190
Web: www.sorensoneng.com					
Specialty Screw Machine Products Inc					
1028 Dillerville Rd PO Box 4185	Lancaster	PA	17604	717-397-2867	397-5912
Web: www.ssmp-online.com					
Sperry Automatics Co Inc					
1372 New Haven Rd PO Box 717	Naugatuck	CT	06770	203-729-4589	729-7787
Web: www.sperryautomatics.com					
Stadco Corp 1931 N Broadway	Los Angeles	CA	90031	323-227-8888	222-0053
Web: www.stadco.com					
Standby Screw Machine Products Co Inc					
1122 W Bagley Rd	Berea	OH	44017	440-243-8200	243-8310
Sumitomo Metal Industries Ltd					
1815 Sandusky St	Fostoria	OH	44830	419-435-0411	435-3881
Superior Products Inc 3786 Ridge Rd	Cleveland	OH	44144	216-651-9400	651-4071
TF: 800-651-9490 ■ *Web:* www.superiorprod.com					
Supreme Machined Products Co Inc					
18686 172nd Ave	Spring Lake	MI	49456	616-842-6550	842-4481
Web: www.supreme1.com					
Supreme-Lake Mfg Inc					
455 Atwater St PO Box 19	Plantsville	CT	06479	860-621-8911	628-9746
Web: www.supremelake.com					
T & L Automatics Inc 770 Emerson St	Rochester	NY	14613	585-647-3717	647-1126
Web: www.tandlautomatics.com					
Talladega Machinery & Supply Co Inc					
301 N Johnson Ave PO Box 736	Talladega	AL	35161	256-362-4124	761-2565
TF Cust Svc: 800-289-8672 ■ *Web:* www.tmsco.com					
Tamer Industries 185 Riverside Ave	Somerset	MA	02725	508-677-0900	677-2242
TF: 800-882-6348 ■ *Web:* www.tamerind.com					
Tanko Screw Products Corp 515 Thomas Dr	Bensenville	IL	60106	630-787-0504	787-0507
Taylor Machine Products Inc 21300 Eureka Rd	Taylor	MI	48180	734-287-3550	287-4737
Taylor Metalworks Inc					
3925 California Rd	Orchard Park	NY	14127	716-662-3113	662-1096
Web: www.taylorcnc.com					
Theis Precision Steel Corp 300 Broad St	Bristol	CT	06010	860-589-5511	589-7411
Web: www.theis-usa.com					
Thorrez Industries Inc 4909 W Michigan Ave	Jackson	MI	49201	517-750-3160	750-1792
Web: www.thorrez.com					
Tomco Products Inc					
405 Centura Ct PO Box 4866	Spartanburg	SC	29303	864-574-7966	587-5608
Web: www.tomcoquickcouplers.com					
Tompkins Products Inc 1040 W Grand Blvd	Detroit	MI	48208	313-894-2222	894-2901
Web: www.tompkinsproducts.com					
Torco Inc 1330 Old 41 Hwy NW	Marietta	GA	30060	770-427-3704	426-9369
Web: www.torcoinc.com					
Trace-A-Matic Inc (T-A-M) 1570 Commerce Ave	Brookfield	WI	53045	262-797-7300	797-9434
TF: 877-375-0217 ■ *Web:* www.traceamatic.com					
Tri Tool Inc 3041 Sunrise Blvd	Rancho Cordova	CA	95742	916-288-6100	288-6160
TF: 800-345-5015 ■ *Web:* www.tritool.com					
Triumph Components 203 N Johnson Ave	El Cajon	CA	92020	619-440-2504	440-2509
Web: www.triumphgroup.com					
Triumph Corp 2130 S Industrial Pk Ave	Tempe	AZ	85282	480-967-3337	921-0446
Web: www.triumphcorp.com					
V-S Industries Inc 900 Chaddick Dr	Wheeling	IL	60090	847-520-1800	520-0269
Web: www.v-s.com					
Vallorbs Jewel Co					
2599 Old Philadelphia Pike	Bird-in-Hand	PA	17505	717-392-3978	392-8947
Vanamatic Co 701 Ambrose Dr	Delphos	OH	45833	419-692-6085	692-3260
Web: www.vanamatic.com					
Winslow Automatic Inc 23 St Clair Ave	New Britain	CT	06051	860-225-6321	224-1733
Xaloy Inc 1399 Countyline Rd	New Castle	PA	16101	800-897-2830	656-5620*
**Fax Area Code: 724* ■ *TF:* 800-897-2830 ■ *Web:* www.xaloy.com					
Yoder 4899 Commerce Pkwy	Cleveland	OH	44128	216-292-4460	831-7948
TF: 800-631-0520 ■ *Web:* www.krasnykaplan.com					

625 PREPARATORY SCHOOLS - BOARDING

SEE ALSO Preparatory Schools - Non-boarding p. 2449

Schools Listed Here Are Independent, College-Preparatory Schools That Provide Housing Facilities For Students And Teachers. All Are Members Of The Association Of Boarding Schools (Tabs), And Many Are Considered To Be Among The Top Prep Schools In The United States.

				Phone	Fax
Academie Ste Cecile International School (ASCIS)					
925 Cousineau Rd	Windsor	ON	N9G1V8	519-969-1291	969-7953
Web: www.stececile.ca					
Admiral Farragut Academy					
501 Pk St N	Saint Petersburg	FL	33710	727-384-5500	347-5160
Web: www.farragut.org					
Albert College 160 Dundas St W	Belleville	ON	K8P1A6	613-968-5726	968-9651
Web: www.albertc.on.ca					
American Boychoir School 19 Lambert Dr	Princeton	NJ	08540	609-924-5858	924-5812
Web: www.americanboychoir.org					
Andrews School 38588 Mentor Ave	Willoughby	OH	44094	440-942-3606	954-5020
TF: 800-753-4683 ■ *Web:* www.andrews-school.org					
Annie Wright School 827 N Tacoma Ave	Tacoma	WA	98403	253-272-2216	572-3616
TF: 800-847-1582 ■ *Web:* www.aw.org					
Appleby College 540 Lakeshore Rd W	Oakville	ON	L6K3P1	905-845-4681	845-9505
Web: www.appleby.on.ca					
Army & Navy Academy					
2605 Carlsbad Blvd PO Box 3000	Carlsbad	CA	92018	760-729-2385	434-5948
TF: 888-762-2338 ■ *Web:* www.armyandnavyacademy.org					
Ashbury College 362 Mariposa Ave	Ottawa	ON	K1M0T3	613-749-5954	749-9724
Web: www.ashbury.on.ca					

School / Address	City	State	ZIP	Phone	Fax
Asheville School 360 Asheville School Rd *Web:* www.ashevilleschool.org	Asheville	NC	28806	828-254-6345	252-8666
Athenian School 2100 Mt Diablo Scenic Blvd *Web:* www.athenian.org	Danville	CA	94506	925-837-5375	831-1120
Avon Old Farms School 500 Old Farms Rd *TF:* 800-464-2866 ■ *Web:* www.avonoldfarms.com	Avon	CT	06001	860-404-4100	675-6051
Balmoral Hall School 630 Westminster Ave *Web:* www.balmoralhall.com	Winnipeg	MB	R3C3S1	204-784-1600	774-5534
Baylor School 177 Baylor School Rd *TF:* 800-222-9567 ■ *Web:* www.baylorschool.org	Chattanooga	TN	37405	423-267-5902	757-2525
Bement School 94 Main St *Web:* www.bement.org	Deerfield	MA	01342	413-774-7061	774-7863
Ben Lippen School 7401 Monticello Rd *TF:* 888-236-5476 ■ *Web:* www.benlippen.com	Columbia	SC	29203	803-786-7200	744-1387
Berkshire School 245 N Undermountain Rd *Web:* www.berkshireschool.org	Sheffield	MA	01257	413-229-8511	229-1016
Bethany Hills School 727 Bethany Hills Rd PO Box 10	Bethany	ON	L0A1A0	705-277-2866	277-1279
Bishop Strachan School 298 Lonsdale Rd *Web:* www.bss.on.ca	Toronto	ON	M4V1X2	416-483-4325	481-5632
Bishop's College School 80 Moulton Hill Rd PO Box 5001 *Web:* www.bishopscollegeschool.com	Lennoxville	QC	J1M1Z8	819-566-0227	822-8917
Blair Academy 2 Pk St PO Box 600 *Web:* www.blair.edu	Blairstown	NJ	07825	908-362-2024	362-7975
Blue Ridge School Rt 627 *Web:* www.blueridgeschool.com	Saint George	VA	22935	434-985-2811	985-7215
Bolles School 7400 San Jose Blvd *Web:* www.bolles.org	Jacksonville	FL	32217	904-733-5952	739-9929
Brandon Hall School 1701 Brandon Hall Dr *Web:* www.brandonhall.org	Atlanta	GA	30350	770-394-8177	804-8821
Branksome Hall 10 Elm Ave *Web:* www.branksome.on.ca	Toronto	ON	M4W1N4	416-920-9741	920-5390
Brehm Preparatory School 1245 E Grand Ave *Web:* www.brehm.org	Carbondale	IL	62901	618-457-0371	549-1248
Brenau Academy 500 Washingtron St SE *Web:* www.brenauacademy.org	Gainesville	GA	30501	770-534-6140	534-6298
Brentwood College School 2735 Mt Baker Rd *Web:* www.brentwood.bc.ca	Mill Bay	BC	V0R2P1	250-743-5521	743-2911
Brewster Academy 80 Academy Dr *TF:* 800-842-9961 ■ *Web:* www.brewsteracademy.org	Wolfeboro	NH	03894	603-569-7200	569-7272
Bridgton Academy PO Box 292 *Web:* www.bridgtonacademy.org	North Bridgton	ME	04057	207-647-3322	647-8513
Brooks School 1160 Great Pond Rd *Web:* www.brooksschool.org	North Andover	MA	01845	978-686-6101	725-6298
Cambridge School of Weston 45 Georgian Rd *Web:* www.csw.org	Weston	MA	02493	781-642-8650	899-3870
Canterbury School 105 Aspetuck Ave *Web:* www.cbury.org	New Milford	CT	06776	860-210-3800	350-1120
Canyonville Christian Academy 250 E 1st St PO Box 1100 *TF:* 888-222-6379 ■ *Web:* www.canyonville.net	Canyonville	OR	97417	541-839-4401	839-6228
Cardigan Mountain School 62 Alumni Dr *Web:* www.cardigan.org	Canaan	NH	03741	603-523-3510	523-3565
Carson Long Military Institute 200 N Carlisle St PO Box 98 *Web:* www.carsonlong.org	New Bloomfield	PA	17068	717-582-2121	582-8763
Cate School 1960 Cate Mesa Rd *Web:* www.cate.org	Carpinteria	CA	93013	805-684-4127	684-8940
CFS the School at Church Farm PO Box 2000 *Web:* www.gocfs.net	Paoli	PA	19301	610-363-7500	280-6746
Chaminade College Preparatory School 425 S Lindbergh Blvd *TF:* 877-378-6847 ■ *Web:* www.chaminademo.com	Saint Louis	MO	63131	314-993-4400	993-5732
Chapel Hill-Chauncy Hall School 785 Beaver St *Web:* www.chch.org	Waltham	MA	02452	781-894-2644	894-5205
Chatham Hall 800 Chatham Hall Cir *Web:* www.chathamhall.org	Chatham	VA	24531	434-432-2941	432-2405
Cheshire Academy 10 Main St *Web:* www.cheshireacademy.org	Cheshire	CT	06410	203-272-5396	250-7209
Choate Rosemary Hall 333 Christian St *Web:* www.choate.edu	Wallingford	CT	06492	203-697-2239	697-2629
Christ School 500 Christ School Rd *TF:* 800-422-3212 ■ *Web:* www.christschool.org	Arden	NC	28704	828-684-6232	684-4869
Christchurch School 49 Seahorse Ln *TF:* 800-296-2306 ■ *Web:* www.christchurchschool.org	Christchurch	VA	23031	804-758-2306	758-0721
Colorado Rocky Mountain School 1493 County Rd 106 *Web:* www.crms.org	Carbondale	CO	81623	970-963-2562	963-9865
Concord Academy 166 Main St *Web:* www.concordacademy.org	Concord	MA	01742	978-402-2200	402-2210
Cotter High School 1115 W Broadway *Web:* www.winonacotter.org	Winona	MN	55987	507-453-5000	453-5406
Cranbrook Schools 39221 Woodward Ave *Web:* www.schools.cranbrook.edu	Bloomfield Hills	MI	48304	248-645-3610	645-3025
Crested Butte Academy 505 Whiterock Ave PO Box 1180 *TF:* 888-633-0222 ■ *Web:* www.crestedbutteacademy.com	Crested Butte	CO	81224	970-349-1805	349-0997
Culver Academies 1300 Academy Rd *TF:* 800-528-5837 ■ *Web:* www.culver.org	Culver	IN	46511	574-842-7000	842-8066
Cushing Academy 39 School St PO Box 8000 *Web:* www.cushing.org	Ashburnham	MA	01430	978-827-7000	827-6253
Dana Hall School 45 Dana Rd PO Box 9010 *Web:* www.danahall.org	Wellesley	MA	02482	781-235-3010	235-0577
Darlington School 1014 Cave Spring Rd *TF:* 800-368-4437 ■ *Web:* www.darlingtonschool.org	Rome	GA	30161	706-235-6051	232-3600
Darrow School 110 Darrow Rd *Web:* www.darrowschool.org	New Lebanon	NY	12125	518-794-6000	794-7065
Deerfield Academy 7 Boyden Ln *Web:* www.deerfield.edu	Deerfield	MA	01342	413-772-0241	772-1100
Devereux Glenholme School 81 Sabbaday Ln *Web:* www.theglenholmeschool.org	Washington	CT	06793	860-868-7377	868-7894
Dublin School 18 Lehmann Way PO Box 522 *Web:* www.dublinschool.org	Dublin	NH	03444	603-563-8584	563-8671
Dunn School 2555 Hwy 154 PO Box 98 *TF:* 800-287-9197 ■ *Web:* www.dunnschool.org	Los Olivos	CA	93441	805-688-6471	686-2078
Eagle Hill School 242 Old Petersham Rd PO Box 116 *Web:* www.eaglehillschool.com	Hardwick	MA	01037	413-477-6000	477-6837
Eaglebrook School 271 Pine Nook Rd *Web:* www.eaglebrook.org	Deerfield	MA	01342	413-774-9111	774-9119
Emma Willard School 285 Pawling Ave *Web:* www.emmawillard.org	Troy	NY	12180	518-833-1300	833-1805
Episcopal High School 1200 N Quaker Ln *TF:* 877-933-4347 ■ *Web:* www.episcopalhighschool.org	Alexandria	VA	22302	703-933-4062	933-3016
Ethel Walker School 230 Bushy Hill Rd *Web:* www.ethelwalker.org	Simsbury	CT	06070	860-408-4200	408-4201
Fay School 48 Main St *TF:* 800-933-2925 ■ *Web:* www.fayschool.org	Southborough	MA	01772	508-485-0100	481-7872
Fessenden School 250 Waltham St *Web:* www.fessenden.org	West Newton	MA	02465	617-630-2300	630-2303
Flintridge Sacred Heart Academy 440 St Katherine Dr *Fax: Admissions ■ *Web:* www.fsha.org	La Canada	CA	91011	626-685-8333	685-8520*
Forman School 12 Norfolk Rd PO Box 80 *Web:* www.formanschool.org	Litchfield	CT	06759	860-567-1802	567-3501
Fountain Valley School of Colorado 6155 Fountain Valley School Rd *Web:* www.fvs.edu	Colorado Springs	CO	80911	719-390-7035	390-7762
Fox River Country Day School 1600 Dundee Ave *Web:* www.frcds.org	Elgin	IL	60120	847-888-7910	888-7947
Foxcroft School 22407 Foxhound Ln *TF:* 800-858-2364 ■ *Web:* www.foxcroft.org	Middleburg	VA	20117	540-687-5555	687-3627
Fryeburg Academy 745 Main St *TF:* 877-935-2013 ■ *Web:* www.fryeburgacademy.org	Fryeburg	ME	04037	207-935-2013	935-4292
Garrison Forest School 300 Garrison Forest Rd *Web:* www.gfs.org	Owings Mills	MD	21117	410-363-1500	363-6841
George School 1690 Newtown-Langhorne Rd *Web:* www.georgeschool.org	Newtown	PA	18940	215-579-6547	579-6549
Georgetown Preparatory School 10900 Rockville Pike *Web:* www.gprep.org	North Bethesda	MD	20852	301-493-5000	493-6128
Gilmour Academy 34001 Cedar Rd *Web:* www.gilmour.org	Gates Mills	OH	44040	440-442-1104	473-8010
Girard College 2101 S College Ave Suite 311 *TF:* 877-344-7273 ■ *Web:* www.girardcollege.com	Philadelphia	PA	19121	215-787-2600	787-4457
Gould Academy PO Box 860 *Web:* www.gouldacademy.org	Bethel	ME	04217	207-824-7777	824-2926
Governor Dummer Academy 1 Elm St *Web:* www.thegovernorsacademy.org	Byfield	MA	01922	978-499-3120	462-1278
Gow School 2491 Emery Rd PO Box 85 *Web:* www.gow.org	South Wales	NY	14139	716-652-3450	652-3457
Grand River Academy 3042 College St PO Box 222 *Web:* www.grandriver.org	Austinburg	OH	44010	440-275-2811	275-1825
Greenwood School 14 Greenwood Ln *Web:* www.thegreenwoodschool.org	Putney	VT	05346	802-387-4545	387-5396
Grenville Christian College PO Box 610 *Web:* www.grenvillecc.ca	Brockville	ON	K6V5V8	613-345-5521	345-3826
Grier School Rt 453 PO Box 308 *Web:* www.grier.org	Tyrone	PA	16686	814-684-3000	684-2177
Groton School 282 Farmers Row PO Box 991 *Web:* www.groton.org	Groton	MA	01450	978-448-7510	448-9623
Gunnery The 99 Green Hill Rd *Web:* www.gunnery.org	Washington	CT	06793	860-868-7334	868-1614
Hackley School 293 Benedict Ave *Web:* www.hackleyschool.org	Tarrytown	NY	10591	914-631-0128	
Hampshire Country School 28 Patey Cir *Web:* www.hampshirecountryschool.org	Rindge	NH	03461	603-899-3325	899-6521
Happy Valley School PO Box 850 *TF:* 800-900-0437 ■ *Web:* www.hvalley.org	Ojai	CA	93024	805-646-4343	464-6431
Hargrave Military Academy (HMA) 200 Military Dr *TF:* 800-432-2480 ■ *Web:* www.hargrave.edu	Chatham	VA	24531	434-432-2481	432-3129
Harvey School 260 Jay St *Web:* www.harveyschool.org	Katonah	NY	10536	914-232-3161	232-6034
Havergal College 1451 Ave Rd *Web:* www.havergal.on.ca	Toronto	ON	M5N2H9	416-483-3519	483-6796
Hawaii Preparatory Academy 65-1692 Kohala Mountain Rd *Web:* www.hpa.edu	Kamuela	HI	96743	808-881-4007	881-4045

School	City	State	Zip	Phone	Fax
Hebron Academy Rt 119 PO Box 309 *TF:* 888-432-7664 ■ *Web:* www.hebronacademy.org	Hebron	ME	04238	207-966-2100	966-1111
High Mowing School 222 Isaac Frye Hwy *Web:* www.highmowing.org	Wilton	NH	03086	603-654-2391	654-6588
Hill School 717 E High St *TF:* 888-445-5150 ■ *Web:* www.thehill.org	Pottstown	PA	19464	610-326-1000	705-1753
Hillside School 404 Robin Hill Rd *Web:* www.hillsideschool.net	Marlborough	MA	01752	508-485-2824	485-4420
Hockaday School 11600 Welch Rd *Web:* www.hockaday.org	Dallas	TX	75229	214-363-6311	265-1649
Holderness School Chapel Ln PO Box 1879 *Web:* www.holderness.org	Plymouth	NH	03264	603-536-1747	536-2125
Hoosac School 14 Pine Valley Rd *Web:* www.hoosac.com	Hoosick	NY	12089	518-686-7331	686-3370
Hotchkiss School 11 Interlaken Rd PO Box 800 *Web:* www.hotchkiss.org	Lakeville	CT	06039	860-435-3102	435-0042
Houghton Academy 9790 Thayer St *Web:* www.houghtonacademy.org	Houghton	NY	14744	585-567-8115	567-8048
Howe Military School PO Box 240 *TF:* 888-462-4693 ■ *Web:* www.howemilitary.com	Howe	IN	46746	260-562-2131	562-3678
Hun School of Princeton 176 Edgerstoune Rd *Web:* www.hunschool.org	Princeton	NJ	08540	609-921-7600	279-9398
Hyde School 150 Rt 169 PO Box 237 *Web:* www.hyde.edu	Woodstock	CT	06281	860-963-4736	928-0612
Hyde School 616 High St *Web:* www.hyde.edu	Bath	ME	04530	207-443-5584	442-9346
Idyllwild Arts Academy 52500 Temecula Rd PO Box 38 *Web:* www.idyllwildarts.org	Idyllwild	CA	92549	951-659-2171	659-2058
Incarnate Word High School 727 E Hildebrand Ave *Web:* www.incarnatewordhs.org	San Antonio	TX	78212	210-829-3100	829-3101
Indian Mountain School 211 Indian Mountain Rd *Web:* www.indianmountain.org	Lakeville	CT	06039	860-435-0871	435-0641
Indian Springs School 190 Woodward Dr *TF:* 888-843-3477 ■ *Web:* www.indiansprings.org	Indian Springs	AL	35124	205-988-3350	988-3797
Kent School PO Box 2006 *TF:* 800-538-5368 ■ *Web:* www.kent-school.edu	Kent	CT	06757	860-927-6111	927-6109
Kents Hill School Rt 17 PO Box 257 *Web:* www.kentshill.org	Kents Hill	ME	04349	207-685-4914	685-9529
Kildonan School 425 Morse Hill Rd *Web:* www.kildonan.org	Amenia	NY	12501	845-373-8111	373-2004
Kimball Union Academy 54 Main St *Web:* www.kua.org	Meriden	NH	03770	603-469-2000	469-2040
Kiski School 1888 Brett Ln *TF:* 877-547-5448 ■ *Web:* www.kiski.org	Saltsburg	PA	15681	724-639-3586	639-8596
Knox School 541 E Long Beach Rd *Web:* www.knoxschool.org	Saint James	NY	11780	631-686-1600	686-1651
La Lumiere School 6801 N Wilhelm Rd *Web:* www.lalumiere.org	La Porte	IN	46350	219-326-7450	325-3185
Lake Forest Academy 1500 W Kennedy Rd *Web:* www.lfanet.org	Lake Forest	IL	60045	847-234-3210	615-3202
Lakefield College School 4391 County Rd 29 *Web:* www.lakefieldcs.on.ca	Lakefield	ON	K0L2H0	705-652-3324	652-6320
Landmark School 429 Hale St PO Box 227 *Web:* www.landmarkschool.org	Prides Crossing	MA	01965	978-236-3010	927-7268
Lawrence Academy Powderhouse Rd PO Box 992 *Web:* www.lacademy.edu	Groton	MA	01450	978-448-6535	448-9208
Lawrenceville School 2500 Main St PO Box 6008 *TF:* 800-735-2030 ■ *Web:* www.lawrenceville.org	Lawrenceville	NJ	08648	609-896-0400	895-2217
Lee Academy 26 Winn Rd *TF:* 888-433-2852 ■ *Web:* www.leeacademy.lee.me.us	Mee	ME	04455	207-738-2255	738-3257
Leelanau School 1 Old Homestead Rd *TF:* 800-533-5262 ■ *Web:* www.leelanau.org	Glen Arbor	MI	49636	231-334-5800	334-5898
Linden Hall School for Girls 212 E Main St *TF:* 800-258-5778 ■ *Web:* www.lindenhall.org	Lititz	PA	17543	717-626-8512	627-1384
Linden Hill School 154 S Mountain Rd *TF:* 888-254-6336 ■ *Web:* www.lindenhs.org	Northfield	MA	01360	413-498-2906	498-2908
Linsly School 60 Knox Ln *Web:* www.linsly.org	Wheeling	WV	26003	304-233-1436	234-4614
Loomis Chaffee School 4 Batchelder Rd *Web:* www.loomischaffee.org	Windsor	CT	06095	860-687-6400	298-8756
Lowell Whiteman School 42605 RCR 36 *Web:* www.lws.edu	Steamboat Springs	CO	80487	970-879-1350	879-0506
MacDuffie School 1 Ames Hill Dr *Web:* www.macduffie.com	Springfield	MA	01105	413-734-4971	734-6693
Madeira School 8328 Georgetown Pike *Web:* www.madeira.org	McLean	VA	22102	703-556-8200	
Maine Central Institute 125 S Main St *Web:* www.mci-school.org	Pittsfield	ME	04967	207-487-3355	487-3512
Marianapolis Preparatory School Rt 200 PO Box 304 *Web:* www.marianapolis.org	Thompson	CT	06277	860-923-9565	923-3730
Marvelwood School 476 Skiff Mountain Rd PO Box 3001 *TF:* 800-440-9107 ■ *Web:* www.themarvelwoodschool.net	Kent	CT	06757	860-927-0047	927-0021
Massanutten Military Academy 614 S Main St *Web:* www.militaryschool.com	Woodstock	VA	22664	540-459-2167	459-5421
Masters School The 49 Clinton Ave *Web:* www.themastersschool.com	Dobbs Ferry	NY	10522	914-479-6400	693-1230
Maur Hill-Mount Academy 1000 Green St *Web:* www.maurhillmountacademy.com	Atchison	KS	66002	913-367-5482	367-5096
McCallie School 500 Dodds Ave *TF:* 800-234-2163 ■ *Web:* www.mccallie.org	Chattanooga	TN	37404	423-624-8300	493-5426
Mercersburg Academy 300 E Seminary St *Web:* www.mercersburg.edu	Mercersburg	PA	17236	717-328-6173	328-6319
Mid-Pacific Institute 2445 Kaala St *Web:* www.midpac.edu	Honolulu	HI	96822	808-973-5000	973-5099
Middlesex School 1400 Lowell Rd *Web:* www.mxschool.edu	Concord	MA	01742	978-369-2550	402-1400
Midland School 5100 Figueroa Mountain Rd PO Box 8 *Web:* www.midland-school.org	Los Olivos	CA	93441	805-688-5114	686-2470
Millbrook School 131 Millbrook School Rd *Web:* www.millbrook.org	Millbrook	NY	12545	845-677-8261	677-1265
Miller School 1000 Samuel Miller Loop *Web:* www.millerschool.org	Charlottesville	VA	22903	434-823-4805	823-6617
Milton Academy 170 Centre St *Web:* www.milton.edu	Milton	MA	02186	617-898-1798	898-1701
Milton Hershey School PO Box 830 *TF:* 800-322-3248 ■ *Web:* www.mhs-pa.org	Hershey	PA	17033	717-520-2100	520-2117
Miss Hall's School 492 Holmes Rd *Web:* www.misshalls.org	Pittsfield	MA	01201	413-443-6401	448-2994
Miss Porter's School 60 Main St *Web:* www.missporters.org	Farmington	CT	06032	860-409-3530	409-3531
Monte Vista Christian School 2 School Way *Web:* www.mvcs.org	Watsonville	CA	95076	831-722-8178	722-6003
Montverde Academy 17235 7th St *Web:* www.montverde.org	Montverde	FL	34756	407-469-2561	469-3711
National Sports Academy 821 Mirror Lake Dr *Web:* www.nationalsportsacademy.com	Lake Placid	NY	12946	518-523-3460	523-3488
New Hampton School 70 Main St PO Box 579 *Web:* www.newhampton.org	New Hampton	NH	03256	603-677-3400	677-3481
New York Military Academy 78 Academy Ave *TF:* 888-275-6962 ■ *Web:* www.nyma.org	Cornwall-on-Hudson	NY	12520	845-534-3710	534-7699
North Country School 4382 Cascade Rd *Web:* www.nct.org	Lake Placid	NY	12946	518-523-9329	523-4858
Northfield Mount Hermon School 206 Main St *Web:* www.nmhschool.org	Northfield	MA	01360	413-498-3227	498-3152
Northwest School 1415 Summit Ave *Web:* www.northwestschool.org	Seattle	WA	98122	206-682-7309	328-1776
Northwood School PO Box 1070 *Web:* www.northwoodschool.com	Lake Placid	NY	12946	518-523-3382	523-2073
Oak Grove School 220 W Lomita Ave *Web:* www.oakgroveschool.com	Ojai	CA	93023	805-646-8236	646-6509
Oak Hill Academy 2635 Oak Hill Rd *Web:* www.oak-hill.net	Mouth of Wilson	VA	24363	276-579-2619	579-4722
Oakwood Friends School 22 Spackenkill Rd *TF:* 800-843-3341 ■ *Web:* www.oakwoodfriends.org	Poughkeepsie	NY	12603	845-462-4200	462-4251
Ojai Valley School 723 El Paseo Rd *TF:* 800-433-4687 ■ *Web:* www.ovs.org	Ojai	CA	93023	805-646-1423	646-0362
Oldfields School 1500 Glencoe Rd *Web:* www.oldfieldsschool.org	Glencoe	MD	21152	410-472-4800	472-6839
Olney Friends School 61830 Sandy Ridge Rd *TF:* 800-303-4291 ■ *Web:* www.olneyfriends.org	Barnesville	OH	43713	740-425-3655	425-3202
Oregon Episcopal School 6300 SW Nicol Rd *Web:* www.oes.edu	Portland	OR	97223	503-246-7771	768-3140
Orme School HC 63 PO Box 3040 *Web:* www.ormeschool.org	Mayer	AZ	86333	928-632-7601	632-7601
Oxford Academy 1393 Boston Post Rd *Web:* www.oxfordacademy.net	Westbrook	CT	06498	860-399-6247	399-6805
Peddie School 201 S Main St *Web:* www.peddie.org	Hightstown	NJ	08520	609-490-7500	944-7901
Pennington School 112 W Delaware Ave *Web:* www.pennington.org	Pennington	NJ	08534	609-737-1838	730-1405
Perkiomen School 200 Seminary St PO Box 130 *Web:* www.perkiomen.org	Pennsburg	PA	18073	215-679-9511	679-1146
Phelps School 583 Sugartown Rd *Web:* www.thephelpsschool.org	Malvern	PA	19355	610-644-1754	644-6679
Phillips Academy 180 Main St *Web:* www.andover.edu	Andover	MA	01810	978-749-4000	749-4068
Phillips Exeter Academy 20 Main St *Web:* www.exeter.edu	Exeter	NH	03833	603-772-4311	777-4399
Pickering College 16945 Bayview Ave *Web:* www.pickeringcollege.on.ca	Newmarket	ON	L3Y4X2	905-895-1700	895-9076
Piney Woods School 5096 Hwy 49 S PO Box 69 *Web:* www.pineywoods.org	Piney Woods	MS	39148	601-845-2214	845-2604
Pomfret School 398 Pomfret St PO Box 128 *Web:* www.pomfretschool.org	Pomfret	CT	06258	860-963-6100	963-2042
Portsmouth Abbey School 285 Cory's Ln *Web:* www.portsmouthabbey.org	Portsmouth	RI	02871	401-683-2000	683-6766
Proctor Academy 204 Main St PO Box 500 *Web:* www.proctoracademy.org	Andover	NH	03216	603-735-6000	735-6284
Purnell School 51 Pottersville Rd PO Box 500 *Web:* www.purnell.org	Pottersville	NJ	07979	908-439-2154	439-4088

School	City	State	Zip	Phone	Fax
Putney School 418 Houghton Brook Rd *Web:* www.putneyschool.org	Putney	VT	05346	802-387-5566	387-6278
Rabun Gap-Nacoochee School 339 Nacoochee Dr *TF:* 800-543-7467 ■ *Web:* www.rabungap.org	Rabun Gap	GA	30568	706-746-7467	746-2594
Randolph-Macon Academy 200 Academy Dr *TF:* 800-272-1172 ■ *Web:* www.rma.edu	Front Royal	VA	22630	540-636-5200	636-5419
Rectory School 528 Pomfret St PO Box 68 *Web:* www.rectoryschool.org	Pomfret	CT	06258	860-928-7759	928-4961
Ridley College 2 Ridley Rd PO Box 3013 *Web:* www.ridley.on.ca	Saint Catharines	ON	L2R7C3	905-684-1889	684-8875
Riverside Military Academy 2001 Riverside Dr *Fax Area Code: 678 ■ *TF:* 800-462-2338 ■ *Web:* www.cadet.com	Gainesville	GA	30501	770-532-6251	291-3364*
Rock Point School 1 Rock Pt Rd *Web:* www.rockpoint.org	Burlington	VT	05408	802-863-1104	863-6628
Rosseau Lake College 1967 Bright St *Web:* www.rosseaulakecollege.com	Rosseau	ON	P0C1J0	705-732-4351	732-6319
Rumsey Hall School 201 Romford Rd *Web:* www.rumseyhall.org	Washington Depot	CT	06794	860-868-0535	868-7907
Saint Andrew's College 15800 Yonge St *TF:* 877-378-1899 ■ *Web:* www.sac.on.ca	Aurora	ON	L4G3H7	905-727-3178	727-9032
Saint Andrew's School 350 Noxontown Rd *Web:* www.standrews-de.org	Middletown	DE	19709	302-285-4231	378-7120
Saint Andrew's School 3900 Jog Rd *Web:* www.saintandrewsschool.net	Boca Raton	FL	33434	561-226-0214	487-4655
Saint Andrew's School 63 Federal Rd *Web:* www.standrews-ri.org	Barrington	RI	02806	401-246-1230	246-0510
Saint Andrew's-Sewanee School 290 Quintard Rd *Web:* www.sasweb.org	Sewanee	TN	37375	931-598-5651	598-0039
Saint Anne's-Belfield School 2132 Ivy Rd *Web:* www.stab.org	Charlottesville	VA	22903	434-296-5106	979-1486
Saint Anthony's Catholic High School 3200 McCullough Ave *Web:* www.sachs.org	San Antonio	TX	78212	210-832-5600	832-5633
Saint Bernard Preparatory School 1600 St Bernard Dr SE *TF:* 800-722-0999 ■ *Web:* www.stbernardprep.com	Cullman	AL	35055	256-739-6682	734-2925
Saint Catherine's School 6001 Grove Ave *TF:* 800-648-4982 ■ *Web:* www.st.catherines.org	Richmond	VA	23226	804-288-2804	285-8169
Saint George's School 372 Purgatory Rd *Web:* www.stgeorges.edu	Middletown	RI	02842	401-842-6600	842-6600
Saint George's School 3851 W 29th Ave *Web:* www.stgeorges.bc.ca	Vancouver	BC	V6S1T6	604-224-1304	224-5820
Saint James School 17641 College Rd *Web:* www.stjames.edu	Saint James	MD	21740	301-733-9330	739-1310
Saint John's Military School 110 E Otis Ave PO Box 5020 *TF:* 866-704-5294 ■ *Web:* www.sjms.org	Salina	KS	67402	785-823-7231	823-7236
Saint John's Northwestern Military Academy 1101 N Genesee St *TF:* 800-752-2338 ■ *Web:* www.sjnma.org	Delafield	WI	53018	262-646-7115	646-7128
Saint John's Preparatory School 1857 Watertower Rd PO Box 4000 *TF:* 800-525-7737 ■ *Web:* www.sjprep.net	Collegeville	MN	56321	320-363-3321	363-3322
Saint John's-Ravenscourt School 400 S Dr *TF:* 800-437-0040 ■ *Web:* www.sjr.mb.ca	Winnipeg	MB	R3T3K5	204-477-2400	477-2429
Saint Johnsbury Academy 1000 Main St PO Box 906 *Web:* www.stjohnsburyacademy.org	Saint Johnsbury	VT	05819	802-751-2130	748-5463
Saint Margaret's School 444 Water Ln PO Box 158 *Web:* www.sms.org	Tappahannock	VA	22560	804-443-3357	443-6781
Saint Mark's School 25 Marlborough Rd *Web:* www.stmarksschool.org	Southborough	MA	01772	508-786-6000	786-6120
Saint Mary's School 900 Hillsborough St *TF:* 800-948-2557 ■ *Web:* www.saint-marys.edu	Raleigh	NC	27603	919-424-4100	424-4122
Saint Michael's University School 3400 Richmond Rd *TF:* 800-661-5199 ■ *Web:* www.smus.bc.ca	Victoria	BC	V8P4P5	250-592-2411	592-2812
Saint Paul's Preparatory Academy PO Box 32650 *Web:* www.stpaulsacademy.com	Phoenix	AZ	85064	602-956-9090	956-3018
Saint Paul's School 325 Pleasant St *Web:* www.sps.edu	Concord	NH	03301	603-229-4600	229-4772
Saint Stanislaus College 304 S Beach Blvd *TF:* 800-517-6257 ■ *Web:* www.ststan.com	Bay Saint Louis	MS	39520	228-467-9057	466-2972
Saint Stephen's Episcopal School 2900 Bunny Run *TF:* 888-377-7937 ■ *Web:* www.sstx.org	Austin	TX	78746	512-327-1213	327-6771
Saint Thomas Choir School 202 W 58th St *Web:* www.choirschool.org	New York	NY	10019	212-247-3311	247-3393
Saint Thomas More School 45 Cottage Rd *Web:* www.stthomasmoreschool.com	Oakdale	CT	06370	860-823-3861	823-3863
Saint Timothy's School 8400 Greenspring Ave *TF:* 800-467-8846 ■ *Web:* www.sttims-school.org	Stevenson	MD	21153	410-486-7400	486-1167
Salem Academy 500 E Salem Ave *TF:* 877-407-2536 ■ *Web:* www.salemacademy.org	Winston-Salem	NC	27101	336-721-2643	917-5340
Salisbury School 251 Canaan Rd *Web:* www.salisburyschool.org	Salisbury	CT	06068	860-435-5732	435-5750
San Domenico School 1500 Butterfield Rd *Web:* www.sandomenico.org	San Anselmo	CA	94960	415-258-1905	258-1906
San Marcos Baptist Academy 2801 Ranch Rd 12 *TF:* 800-428-5120 ■ *Web:* www.smba.org	San Marcos	TX	78666	512-753-8000	753-8031
Sandy Spring Friends School 16923 Norwood Rd *Web:* www.ssfs.org	Sandy Spring	MD	20860	301-774-7455	924-1115
Santa Catalina School 1500 Mark Thomas Dr *Web:* www.santacatalina.org	Monterey	CA	93940	831-655-9300	655-7535
Scattergood Friends School 1951 Delta Ave *TF:* 888-737-4636 ■ *Web:* www.scattergood.org	West Branch	IA	52358	319-643-7628	643-7638
Sedbergh School 810 Cote Azelie	Montebello	QC	J0V1L0	819-423-5523	423-5769
Shady Side Academy 423 Fox Chapel Rd *Web:* www.shadysideacademy.org	Pittsburgh	PA	15238	412-968-3000	968-3213
Shattuck-Saint Mary's School 1000 Shumway Ave PO Box 218 *TF:* 800-421-2724 ■ *Web:* www.s-sm.org	Faribault	MN	55021	507-333-1616	333-1661
Shawnigan Lake School (SLS) 1975 Renfrew Rd *Web:* www.shawnigan.ca	Shawnigan Lake	BC	V0R2W1	250-743-5516	743-6200
Solebury School 6832 Phillips Mill Rd *Web:* www.solebury.org	New Hope	PA	18938	215-862-5261	862-3366
South Kent School 40 Bull's Bridge Rd *Web:* www.southkentschool.net	South Kent	CT	06785	860-927-3539	927-1161
Southwestern Academy 2800 Monterey Rd *Web:* www.southwesternacademy.edu	San Marino	CA	91108	626-799-5010	799-0407
Stanstead College 450 Dufferin St *Web:* www.stansteadcollege.com	Stanstead	QC	J0B3E0	819-876-2223	876-5891
Stevenson School 3152 Forest Lake Rd *Web:* www.rlstevenson.org	Pebble Beach	CA	93953	831-625-8300	625-5208
Stoneleigh-Burnham School 574 Bernardston Rd *Web:* www.sbschool.org	Greenfield	MA	01301	413-774-2711	772-2602
Stony Brook School 1 Chapman Pkwy *Web:* www.stonybrookschool.org	Stony Brook	NY	11790	631-751-1800	751-4211
Storm King School 314 Mountain Rd *TF:* 800-225-9144 ■ *Web:* www.sks.org	Cornwall-on-Hudson	NY	12520	845-534-9860	534-9860
Stuart Hall School 235 E Frederick St PO Box 210 *TF:* 888-306-8926 ■ *Web:* www.stuart-hall.org	Staunton	VA	24402	540-885-0356	886-2275
Subiaco Academy 405 N Subiaco Ave *TF:* 800-364-7824 ■ *Web:* www.subi.org	Subiaco	AR	72865	479-934-1025	934-1033
Suffield Academy 185 N Main St PO Box 999 *Web:* www.suffieldacademy.org	Suffield	CT	06078	860-668-7315	668-2966
Tabor Academy 66 Spring St *Web:* www.taboracademy.org	Marion	MA	02738	508-748-2000	748-0353
Taft School 110 Woodbury Rd *Web:* www.taftschool.org	Watertown	CT	06795	860-945-7777	945-7808
Tallulah Falls School 201 Campus Dr PO Box 10 *Web:* www.tallulahfalls.org	Tallulah Falls	GA	30573	706-754-0400	754-3595
Texas Military Institute (TMI) 20955 W Tejas Trail *Web:* www.community.tmi-sa.org	San Antonio	TX	78257	210-698-7171	698-0715
Thacher School 5025 Thacher Rd *Web:* www.thacher.org	Ojai	CA	93023	805-640-3210	640-9377
Thomas Jefferson School 4100 S Lindbergh Blvd *Web:* www.tjs.org	Saint Louis	MO	63127	314-843-4151	843-3527
Thomas More Prep-Marian 1701 Hall St *Web:* www.tmp-m.org	Hays	KS	67601	785-625-6577	625-3912
Tilton School 30 School St *Web:* www.tiltonschool.org	Tilton	NH	03276	603-286-4342	286-1705
Trafalgar Castle School 401 Reynolds St *Web:* www.castle-ed.com	Whitby	ON	L1N3W9	905-668-3358	668-4136
Trinity College School 55 Deblaquire St N *Web:* www.tcs.on.ca	Port Hope	ON	L1A4K7	905-885-4565	885-7444
Trinity-Pawling School 700 Rt 22 *Web:* www.trinitypawling.org	Pawling	NY	12564	845-855-3100	855-3816
Universal Ballet Academy 4301 Harewood Rd NE *Web:* www.ubacademy.org	Washington	DC	20017	202-832-1087	526-4274
Upper Canada College 200 Lonsdale Rd *Web:* www.ucc.on.ca	Toronto	ON	M4V1W6	416-488-1125	484-8611
Vanguard School 22000 US Hwy 27 *Web:* www.vanguardschool.org	Lake Wales	FL	33859	863-676-6091	676-8297
Verde Valley School 3511 Verde Valley School Rd *Web:* www.verdevalleyschool.org	Sedona	AZ	86351	928-284-2272	284-0432
Vermont Academy PO Box 500 *TF:* 800-560-1876 ■ *Web:* www.vermontacademy.org	Saxtons River	VT	05154	802-869-6229	869-6242
Villanova Preparatory School 12096 N Ventura Ave *Web:* www.villanovaprep.org	Ojai	CA	93023	805-646-1464	646-4430
Virginia Episcopal School 400 VES Rd PO Box 408 *Web:* www.ves.org	Lynchburg	VA	24503	434-385-3607	385-3603
Wasatch Academy 120 S 100 W *TF:* 800-634-4690 ■ *Web:* www.wacad.org	Mount Pleasant	UT	84647	435-462-1400	462-3380

Name / Address	City	State	Zip	Phone	Fax
Washington Academy 66 High St	East Machias	ME	04630	207-255-8301	255-8303
Web: www.washingtonacademy.org					
Wayland Academy 101 N University Ave	Beaver Dam	WI	53916	920-885-3373	887-3373
TF: 800-860-7725 ■ *Web:* www.wayland.org					
Webb School PO Box 488	Bell Buckle	TN	37020	931-389-9322	389-6657
TF: 888-733-9322 ■ *Web:* www.thewebbschool.com					
Webb Schools 1175 W Baseline Rd	Claremont	CA	91711	909-482-5214	621-4582
Web: www.webb.org					
West Nottingham Academy 1079 Firetower Rd	Colora	MD	21917	410-658-5556	658-9264
TF: 800-962-1744 ■ *Web:* www.wna.org					
Western Reserve Academy 115 College St	Hudson	OH	44236	330-650-9717	650-9722
TF: 800-784-3776 ■ *Web:* www.wra.net					
Westminster School 995 Hopmeadow St	Simsbury	CT	06070	860-408-3060	408-3042
Web: www.westminster-school.org					
Westover School PO Box 847	Middlebury	CT	06762	203-758-2423	577-4588
Web: www.westoverschool.org					
Westtown School PO Box 1799	Westtown	PA	19395	610-399-0123	399-3760
Web: www.westtown.edu					
White Mountain School 371 W Farm Rd	Bethlehem	NH	03574	603-444-2928	444-5568
TF: 800-545-7813 ■ *Web:* www.whitemountain.org					
Wilbraham & Monson Academy 423 Main St	Wilbraham	MA	01095	413-596-6811	596-2448
Web: www.wmacademy.org					
Williston Northampton School 19 Payson Ave	EastHampton	MA	01027	413-529-3241	527-9497
Web: www.williston.com					
Winchendon School 172 Ash St	Winchendon	MA	01475	978-297-4476	297-0911
Web: www.winchendon.org					
Wolfeboro Camp School 93 Hill School Camp Rd	Wolfeboro	NH	03894	603-569-3451	569-4080
Web: www.wolfeboro.org					
Woodhall School 58 Harrison Ln PO Box 550	Bethlehem	CT	06751	203-266-7788	266-5896
Web: www.woodhallschool.org					
Woodlands Academy of the Sacred Heart 760 E Westleigh Rd	Lake Forest	IL	60045	847-234-4300	234-0865
Web: www.woodlandsacademy.org					
Woodside Priory School 302 Portola Rd	Portola Valley	CA	94028	650-851-8221	851-2839
Web: www.woodsidepriory.com					
Worcester Academy 81 Providence St	Worcester	MA	01604	508-754-5302	752-2382
Web: www.worcesteracademy.org					
Wyoming Seminary 201 N Sprague Ave	Kingston	PA	18704	570-270-2160	270-2191
TF: 877-996-7364 ■ *Web:* www.wyomingseminary.org					
Valley Forge Military Academy & College 1001 Eagle Rd	Wayne	PA	19087	610-989-1300	688-1545*
**Fax:* Admissions ■ *TF:* 800-234-8362 ■ *Web:* www.vfmac.edu					

626 PREPARATORY SCHOOLS - NON-BOARDING

SEE ALSO Preparatory Schools - Boarding p. 2445

The Schools Listed Here Are Among The Leading Private Elementary And Secondary Schools In The U.S. None Of These Schools Are Boarding Schools.

Name / Address	City	State	Zip	Phone	Fax
Albuquerque Academy 6400 Wyoming Blvd NE	Albuquerque	NM	87109	505-828-3200	828-3320
Web: www.aa.edu					
Blake School 110 Blake Rd S	Hopkins	MN	55343	952-988-3400	988-3455
Web: www.blakeschool.org					
Brearley School 610 E 83rd St	New York	NY	10028	212-744-8582	472-8020
Web: www.brearley.org					
Chapin School 100 E End Ave	New York	NY	10028	212-744-2335	
Web: www.chapin.edu					
Glen Mills Schools PO Box 5001	Concordville	PA	19331	610-459-8100	558-1493
Web: www.glenmillsschool.org					
Iolani School 563 Kamoku St	Honolulu	HI	96826	808-949-5355	943-2297
Web: www.iolani.org					
Kinkaid School The 201 Kinkaid School Dr	Houston	TX	77024	713-782-1640	782-3543
Web: www.kinkaid.org					
Latin School of Chicago 59 W N Blvd	Chicago	IL	60610	312-582-6000	
Web: www.latinschool.org					
Mary Institute & Saint Louis Country Day School 101 N Warson Rd	Saint Louis	MO	63124	314-993-5100	
Web: www.micds.org					
National Cathedral School 3609 Woodley Rd NW	Washington	DC	20016	202-537-6339	537-5743
Web: www.ncs.cathedral.org					
North Shore Country Day School 310 Green Bay Rd	Winnetka	IL	60093	847-446-0674	446-0675
Web: www.nscds.org					
Orchard School 615 W 64th St	Indianapolis	IN	46260	317-251-9253	254-8454
Web: www.orchard.org					
Punahou School 1601 Punahou St	Honolulu	HI	96822	808-944-5711	944-5779
Web: www.punahou.edu					
Roxbury Latin School 101 St Theresa Ave	West Roxbury	MA	02132	617-325-4920	325-3585
Web: www.roxburylatin.org					
Saint Albans School Mount St Alban	Washington	DC	20016	202-537-6435	537-5613
Web: www.staweb.sta.cathedral.org					
Saint Stephen's & Saint Agnes School 1000 St Stephen's Rd	Alexandria	VA	22304	703-751-2700	683-5930
Web: www.sssas.org					
Sidwell Friends School 3825 Wisconsin Ave NW	Washington	DC	20016	202-537-8100	537-8138
Web: www.sidwell.edu					
University School Hunting Valley Campus 2785 SOM Ctr Rd	Hunting Valley	OH	44022	216-831-2200	292-7810
Web: www.us.edu					
University School of Milwaukee 2100 W Fairy Chasm Rd	Milwaukee	WI	53217	414-352-6000	352-8076
Web: www.usm.k12.wi.us					
Westminster Schools 1424 W Paces Ferry Rd NW	Atlanta	GA	30327	404-355-8673	355-6606
Web: www.westminster.net					

627 PRESS CLIPPING SERVICES

Name / Address	City	State	Zip	Phone	Fax
Allen's Press Clipping Bureau 657 Mission St Rm 602	San Francisco	CA	94105	415-392-2353	362-6208
BurrellesLuce 75 E Northfield Rd	Livingston	NJ	07039	973-992-6600	992-7675
TF: 800-631-1160 ■ *Web:* www.burrellesluce.com					
Cision US Inc 332 S Michigan Ave Suite 900	Chicago	IL	60604	312-922-2400	922-3126*
**Fax:* Cust Svc ■ *TF:* 866-639-5087 ■ *Web:* www.us.cision.com					
Colorado Press Clipping Service 1336 Glenarm Pl	Denver	CO	80204	303-571-5117	571-1803
Web: www.coloradopressassociation.com					
CompetitivEdge 196 S Main St	Colchester	CT	06415	860-537-6731	
Florida Newsclips LLC PO Box 2190	Palm Harbor	FL	34682	727-726-5000	736-5005
TF: 800-442-0332 ■ *Web:* www.newsclipsonweb.com					
Kentucky Press Assn 101 Consumer Ln	Frankfort	KY	40601	502-223-8821	226-3867
TF Cust Svc: 800-264-5721 ■ *Web:* www.kypress.com					
Magnolia Clipping Service 298 Commerce Pk Dr Suite A	Ridgeland	MS	39157	601-856-0911	856-3340
Web: www.magnoliaclips.com					
New England Newsclip Agency Inc 5 Auburn St	Framingham	MA	01701	508-879-4460	620-1719
TF: 800-235-3879					
New Jersey Clipping Service 75 E Northfield Rd	Livingston	NJ	07039	212-227-5570	533-6042*
**Fax Area Code:* 973					
New York State Clipping Service 200 Central Pk Ave N	Hartsdale	NY	10530	914-948-2525	948-3534
TF: 800-772-5477					
Oklahoma Press Service Inc 3601 N Lincoln Blvd	Oklahoma City	OK	73105	405-524-4421	524-2201
Web: www.okpress.com					
South Carolina Press Services Inc 421 Zimal Crest PO Box 11429	Columbia	SC	29211	803-750-9561	551-0903
TF: 888-727-7377 ■ *Web:* www.scpress.org					
South Dakota Newspaper Services 527 Main Ave Suite 202	Brookings	SD	57006	605-692-4300	692-6388
TF: 800-658-3697 ■ *Web:* www.sdna.com					
Virginia Press Services Inc 11529 Nuckols Rd	Glen Allen	VA	23059	804-521-7570	521-7590
TF: 800-849-8717 ■ *Web:* www.vpa.net					
West Virginia Press Services Inc 3422 Pennsylvania Ave	Charleston	WV	25302	304-342-6908	343-5879
TF: 800-235-6881 ■ *Web:* www.wvpress.org					

628 PRINTED CIRCUIT BOARDS

SEE ALSO Electronic Components & Accessories - Mfr p. 1811; Semiconductors & Related Devices p. 2651

Name / Address	City	State	Zip	Phone	Fax
3Dlabs Inc Ltd 1901 McCarthy Blvd	Milpitas	CA	94035	408-432-6700	432-6701
TF: 800-464-3348 ■ *Web:* www.3dlabs.com					
Abelconn LLC 9210 Science Ctr Dr	New Hope	MN	55428	763-533-3533	536-0349
Web: www.abelconn.com					
Acromag Inc 30765 S Wixom Rd	Wixom	MI	48393	248-624-1541	624-9234
TF: 800-881-0268 ■ *Web:* www.acromag.com					
Adaptec Inc 691 S Milpitas Blvd	Milpitas	CA	95035	408-945-8600	262-2533
NASDAQ: ADPT ■ *TF:* 800-959-7274 ■ *Web:* www.adptco.com					
Advanced Circuits Inc 21101 E 32nd Pkwy	Aurora	CO	80011	303-576-6610	224-3291*
**Fax Area Code:* 888 ■ *TF:* 800-979-4722 ■ *Web:* www.4pcb.com					
AMDTechnologies Inc 1 Commerce Valley Dr E	Markham	ON	L3T7X6	905-882-2600	882-2620
Web: www.amd.com					
American Board Assembly Inc 5456 Endeavour Ct	Moorpark	CA	93021	805-523-0274	523-1185
Web: www.americanboard.com					
Amitron Inc 2001 Landmeier Rd	Elk Grove Village	IL	60007	847-290-9800	290-9823
Web: www.amitroncorp.com					
Ansen Corp 100 Chimney Pt Dr	Ogdensburg	NY	13669	315-393-3573	393-7638
Web: www.ansencorp.com					
Antex Electronics Corp 19821 Hamilton Ave	Torrance	CA	90502	310-532-3092	532-8509
TF: 800-338-4231 ■ *Web:* www.antex.com					
Apex Micro Corp 8128 River Way	Delta	BC	V4G1K5	604-946-9666	952-0689
Web: www.apexmicromfg.com					
Apsco International 3700 Ln Rd	Perry	OH	44081	440-352-8961	354-7306
Web: www.apscoinc.com					
Arc-tronics Inc 1150 Pagni Dr	Elk Grove Village	IL	60007	847-437-0211	437-0181
Web: www.arc-tronics.com					
ASUSTeK Computer International 800 corporate wy	Fremont	CA	94539	510-739-3777	608-4555
Web: www.asus.com					
Benchmark Electronics Inc 3000 Technology Dr	Angleton	TX	77515	979-849-6550	848-5271
NYSE: BHE ■ *Web:* www.bench.com					
Bicom Inc 755 Main St	Monroe	CT	06468	203-268-4484	268-3404
Web: www.bicom-inc.com					
Bourns Inc 1200 Columbia Ave	Riverside	CA	92507	951-781-5690	781-5006
TF: 877-426-8767 ■ *Web:* www.bourns.com					

Company	City	State	Zip	Phone	Fax
Cal Quality Electronics 2700 S Fairview St. *Web:* www.calquality.com	Santa Ana	CA	92704	714-545-8886	545-4975
Centon Electronics Inc 15 Argonaut **Fax Area Code:* 948 ■ *TF:* 800-836-1986 ■ *Web:* www.centon.com	Aliso Viejo	CA	92656	949-855-9111	586-8778*
Circuit Express Inc 229 S Clark Dr *Web:* www.circuitexpress.com	Tempe	AZ	85281	480-966-5895	966-5896
Compunetics Inc 700 Seco Rd *TF:* 800-879-4266 ■ *Web:* www.compunetics.com	Monroeville	PA	15146	412-373-8110	373-8060
Computer Modules Inc 11409 W Bernardo Ct. *Web:* www.computermodules.com	San Diego	CA	92127	858-613-1801	613-1815
Creative Labs Inc 1901 McCarthy Blvd *TF Cust Svc:* 800-998-1000 ■ *Web:* www.us.creative.com	Milpitas	CA	95035	408-428-6600	428-6611
Crucial Technology 3475 E Commercial Ct *TF:* 800-336-8915 ■ *Web:* www.crucial.com	Meridian	ID	83642	208-363-5790	363-5501
CyOptics Inc 9999 Hamilton Blvd *Web:* www.cyoptics.com	Breinigsville	PA	18031	484-397-2000	397-3592
Cytec Corp 1017 William D Tate Ave Suite 107 *TF:* 888-349-8881 ■ *Web:* www.cytecsys.com	Grapevine	TX	76051	214-349-8881	
Data Translation Inc 100 Locke Dr *TF:* 800-525-8528 ■ *Web:* www.datatranslation.com	Marlborough	MA	01752	508-481-3700	481-3700
Dataram Corp PO Box 7528 *NASDAQ: DRAM* ■ *TF:* 800-328-2726 ■ *Web:* www.dataram.com	Princeton	NJ	08543	609-799-0071	799-6734
DDi Corp 1220 Simon Cir *NASDAQ: DDIC* ■ *Web:* www.ddiglobal.com	Anaheim	CA	92806	714-688-7200	688-7500
Diversified Technology Inc 476 Highland Colony Pkwy *TF:* 800-443-2667 ■ *Web:* www.dtims.com	Ridgeland	MS	39157	601-856-4121	856-2888
DRS Laurel Technologies 246 Airport Rd *Web:* www.drs.com	Johnstown	PA	15904	814-534-8900	534-8815
Dynaco Corp 3020 S Pk Dr *Web:* www.dynacocorp.com	Tempe	AZ	85282	602-437-8003	437-8015
Dynatem Inc 23263 Madero Suite C *TF:* 800-543-3830 ■ *Web:* www.dynatem.com	Mission Viejo	CA	92691	949-855-3235	770-3481
EDGE Tech Corp 327 E 14th St *Web:* www.edgetechcorp.com	Ada	OK	74820	580-332-6581	310-6518
EI Microcircuits Inc 1651 Pohl Rd *Web:* www.eimicro.com	Mankato	MN	56001	507-345-5786	345-7559
Electropac Co Inc 252 Willow St *Web:* www.electropac.com	Manchester	NH	03103	603-622-3711	622-3711
Federal Electronics Inc 75 Stamp Farm Rd *Web:* www.federalelec.com	Cranston	RI	02921	401-944-6200	946-6280
Flex Technologies 5479 Gundy Dr PO Box 400 *Web:* www.flextechnologies.com	Midvale	OH	44653	740-922-5992	922-4416
GE Fanuc Embedded Systems Inc 7401 Snaproll NE *TF:* 877-832-4727 ■ *Web:* www.ge-ip.com	Albuquerque	NM	87109	505-875-0600	
Gigabyte Technology Inc 17358 Railroad St *Web:* www.giga-byte.com	City of Industry	CA	91748	626-854-9338	854-9339
GoldenRAM Computer Products 13 Whatney *TF:* 800-222-8861 ■ *Web:* www.goldenram.com	Irvine	CA	92618	949-460-9000	460-7600
Hauppauge Computer Works Inc 91 Cabot Ct. *TF:* 800-443-6284 ■ *Web:* www.hauppauge.com	Hauppauge	NY	11788	631-434-1600	434-3198
Hauppauge Digital Inc 91 Cabot Ct. *NASDAQ: HAUP* ■ *TF:* 800-443-6284 ■ *Web:* www.hauppauge.com	Hauppauge	NY	11788	631-434-1600	434-3198
I-Bus Corp 3350 Scott Blvd Bldg 54 *TF:* 877-777-4287 ■ *Web:* www.ibus.com	Santa Clara	CA	95054	408-450-7880	450-7881
IEC Electronics Corp 105 Norton St. *Web:* www.iec-electronics.com	Newark	NY	14513	315-331-7742	331-3547
Intel Corp 2200 Mission College Blvd *NASDAQ: INTC* ■ *TF Cust Svc:* 800-628-8686 ■ *Web:* www.intel.com	Santa Clara	CA	95052	408-765-8080	
Jabil Circuit Inc 10560 ML King St N *NYSE: JBL* ■ *TF:* 877-217-6328 ■ *Web:* www.jabil.com	Saint Petersburg	FL	33716	727-577-9749	803-5401
Kca Electronics Inc 223 N Crescent Way *TF:* 888-433-9406 ■ *Web:* www.kcamerica.com	Anaheim	CA	92801	714-239-2433	
Killdeer Mountain Mfg Inc (KMM) 233 Rodeo Dr PO Box 450 *Web:* www.kmmnet.com	Killdeer	ND	58640	701-764-5651	764-5427
Kimball Electronics Group 1038 E 15th St. **Fax:* Sales ■ *TF:* 800-634-4005 ■ *Web:* www.kegroup.com	Jasper	IN	47549	812-634-4200	634-4330*
Kontron Communications Inc 616 Cure-Boivin *TF:* 800-387-4222 ■ *Web:* www.kontron.com	Boisbriand	QC	J7G2A7	450-437-5682	437-8053
Leadtek Research Inc 910 Auburn Ct *Web:* www.leadtek.com	Fremont	CA	94538	510-490-8076	490-7759
Leda Corp 7080 Kearny Dr *Web:* www.ledacorp.net	Huntington Beach	CA	92648	714-841-7821	842-3683
Libra Industries Inc 7770 Division Dr *TF:* 800-825-1674 ■ *Web:* www.libraind.com	Mentor	OH	44060	440-974-7770	974-7779
M-Wave Inc 475 Industrial Dr *Web:* www.mwav.com	West Chicago	IL	60185	630-562-5550	562-2430
Macrolink Inc 1500 N Kellogg Dr *Web:* www.macrolink.com	Anaheim	CA	92807	714-777-8800	777-8807
Masterwork Electronics Inc 630 Martin Ave *Web:* www.masterworkelectronics.com	Rohnert Park	CA	94928	707-588-9906	588-9908
McDonald Technologies International Inc 1920 Diplomat Dr *TF:* 800-678-7046 ■ *Web:* www.mcdonald-tech.com	Farmers Branch	TX	75234	972-243-6767	241-2643
Merix Corp 1521 Poplar Ln *NASDAQ: MERX* ■ *Web:* www.merix.com	Forest Grove	OR	97116	503-359-9300	357-1504
Micro Industries Corp 8399 Green Meadow Dr N *TF:* 800-722-1845 ■ *Web:* www.microindustries.com	Westerville	OH	43081	740-548-7878	548-6184
Microboard Processing Inc 4 Progress Ave *Web:* www.microboard.com	Seymour	CT	06483	203-881-4300	881-1590
Micron Technology Inc 8000 S Federal Way *NYSE: MU* ■ *Web:* www.micron.com	Boise	ID	83707	208-368-4000	368-4617
Micron Technology Inc SpecTek Div 8000 S Federal Way PO Box 6 *Web:* www.spectek.com	Boise	ID	83707	208-368-4000	
Modular Components National Inc 105 E Jarrettsville Rd PO Box 453 *Web:* www.modularcomp.com	Forest Hill	MD	21050	410-879-6553	638-7359
MSI Computer Corp 901 Canada Ct **Fax:* Sales ■ *TF Cust Svc:* 888-447-6564 ■ *Web:* www.us.msi.com	City of Industry	CA	91748	626-913-0828	913-0818*
Mti Electronics Inc W133 N5139 Campbell Dr *Web:* www.mtielectronics.com	Menomonee Falls	WI	53051	262-783-6080	783-4959
Natel Engineering Co Inc 9340 Owensmouth Ave *TF:* 800-866-3590 ■ *Web:* www.natelengr.com	Chatsworth	CA	91311	818-734-6500	734-6530
National Semiconductor Corp 2900 Semiconductor Dr *NYSE: NSM* ■ *Web:* www.national.com	Santa Clara	CA	95051	408-721-5000	732-4880
National Technology Inc 1101 Carnegie St *Web:* www.nationaltech.com	Rolling Meadows	IL	60008	847-506-1300	506-1340
Nitto Denko America Inc 48500 Fremont Blvd *TF:* 800-356-4880 ■ *Web:* www.nittousa.com	Fremont	CA	94538	510-445-5400	445-5480
NVIDIA Corp 2701 San Tomas Expy *NASDAQ: NVDA* ■ *TF:* 877-768-4342 ■ *Web:* www.nvidia.com	Santa Clara	CA	95050	408-486-2000	486-2200
Oncore Mfg Services LLC 225 Carando Dr *Web:* www.oncorems.com	Springfield	MA	01104	413-736-2121	736-6373
Osi Electronics Inc 2385 Pleasant Valley Rd *Web:* www.osielectronics.com	Camarillo	CA	93012	805-499-6877	499-4072
Parallax Inc 599 Menlo Dr Suite 100 *TF:* 888-512-1024 ■ *Web:* www.parallax.com	Rocklin	CA	95765	916-624-8333	624-8003
Park Electrochemical Corp 48 S Service Rd Suite 300 *NYSE: PKE* ■ *Web:* www.parkelectro.com	Melville	NY	11747	631-465-3600	465-3100
Parlex Corp 1 Parlex Pl *Web:* www.parlex.com	Methuen	MA	01844	978-685-4341	685-8809
Pentek Inc 1 Pk Way **Fax:* Acctg ■ *Web:* www.pentek.com	Upper Saddle River	NJ	07458	201-818-5900	818-5692*
Philway Products Inc 701 Virginia Ave **Fax:* Sales ■ *Web:* www.philway.com	Ashland	OH	44805	419-281-7777	289-3447*
Pioneer Circuits Inc (PCI) 3000 S Shannon St *Web:* www.pioneercircuits.com	Santa Ana	CA	92704	714-641-3132	641-3120
Plexus Corp 1 Plexus Way PO Box 156 *NASDAQ: PLXS* ■ *Web:* www.plexus.com	Neenah	WI	54957	920-722-3451	751-5395
PNC Inc 115 E Centre St *Web:* www.pnconline.com	Nutley	NJ	07110	973-284-1600	284-1925
Precision Contract Mfg Inc 280 Clinton St *TF:* 866-462-4385 ■ *Web:* www.pcmanufacturing.com	Springfield	VT	05156	802-885-6208	885-6210
Printed Circuits Assembly Corp 13221 SE 26th St Suite E *Web:* www.pcacorporation.com	Bellevue	WA	98005	425-644-7754	644-6430
Progress Instruments Inc 807 NW Commerce Dr *TF:* 800-580-9881 ■ *Web:* www.progressinstruments.com	Lees Summit	MO	64086	816-524-4442	246-4556
Promise Technology Inc 580 Cottonwood Dr *TF Sales:* 800-888-0245 ■ *Web:* www.promise.com	Milpitas	CA	95035	408-228-1400	228-1100
Qual-pro Corp 18510 S Figueroa St *Web:* www.qual-pro.com	Gardena	CA	90248	310-329-7535	
Quality Circuits Inc 1102 Progress Dr *Web:* www.qciusa.com	Fergus Falls	MN	56537	218-739-9707	739-9705
Quality Systems Integrated Corp 6720 Cobra Way *Web:* www.qsic.com	San Diego	CA	92121	858-587-9797	
Quatech Inc 5675 Hudson Industrial Pkwy *TF:* 800-553-1170 ■ *Web:* www.quatech.com	Hudson	OH	44236	330-655-9000	655-9010
RadiSys Corp 5445 NE Dawson Creek Dr *NASDAQ: RSYS* ■ *TF:* 800-950-0044 ■ *Web:* www.radisys.com	Hillsboro	OR	97124	503-615-1100	615-1115
Reptron Electronics Inc 13700 Reptron Blvd *TF:* 800-800-5441 ■ *Web:* www.reptronmfg.com	Tampa	FL	33626	813-854-2000	891-4056
Riverside Electronics Ltd 1 Riverside Dr *Web:* www.rellew.com	Lewiston	MN	55952	507-523-3220	523-2831
Sabtech Industries Inc 23231 La Palma Ave *Web:* www.sabtech.com	Yorba Linda	CA	92887	714-692-3800	692-3838
SAE Circuits Colorado Inc 4820 N 63rd St *TF:* 800-234-9001 ■ *Web:* www.saecircuits.com	Boulder	CO	80301	303-530-1900	530-0210
Sanmina-SCI Corp 2700 N 1st St *NASDAQ: SANM* ■ *Web:* www.sanmina-sci.com	San Jose	CA	95134	408-964-3500	964-3636
Saturn Electronics & Engineering Inc 2120 Austin Ave *Web:* www.saturnee.com	Rochester Hills	MI	48309	248-853-5724	299-8514
Saturn Electronics Corp 28450 Northline Rd *Web:* www.saturnelectronics.com	Romulus	MI	48174	734-941-8100	941-3707
Servatron Inc 15520 E Fairview Ave *Web:* www.servatron.com	Spokane	WA	99216	509-321-9500	321-9510
Siemens Mfg Co Inc 410 W Washington St PO Box 61 *Web:* www.siemensmfg.com	Freeburg	IL	62243	618-539-3000	539-6172

Phone Fax

Sigma Designs Inc 1221 California Cir ... Milpitas CA 95035 408-262-9003 957-9740
NASDAQ: SIGM ■ TF Sales: 800-845-8086 ■ Web: www.sdesigns.com

SigmaTron International Inc
2201 Landmeier Rd ... Elk Grove Village IL 60007 847-956-8000 956-9410*
NASDAQ: SGMA ■ *Fax: Hum Res ■ TF: 800-700-9095 ■ Web: www.sigmatronintl.com

SIIG Inc 6078 Stewart Ave ... Fremont CA 94538 510-657-8688 657-5962
Web: www.siig.com

Socket Mobile Inc 39700 Eureka Dr ... Newark CA 94560 510-933-3000 933-3030
NASDAQ: SCKT ■ TF: 800-552-3300 ■ Web: www.socketmobile.com

Sopark Corp 3300 S Pk Ave ... Buffalo NY 14218 716-822-0434 822-5062
TF: 866-576-7275 ■ Web: www.sopark.com

Spectrum Signal Processing by Vecima
2700 Production Way Suite 300 ... Burnaby BC V5A4X1 604-676-6700 421-1764
TF: 800-663-8986 ■ Web: www.spectrumsignal.com

Suntron Corp 2401 W Grandview Rd ... Phoenix AZ 85023 602-789-6600 789-6600
TF: 888-520-3382 ■ Web: www.suntroncorp.com

Supermicro Computer Inc (SMCI) 980 Rock Ave ... San Jose CA 95131 408-503-8000 503-8008
NASDAQ: SMCI ■ Web: www.supermicro.com

TechWorks 4030 W Braker Ln Suite 120 ... Austin TX 78759 512-794-8533 794-8520
TF Cust Svc: 800-688-7466 ■ Web: www.techworks.com

Tekram USA 2861 Saturn St Suite B ... Brea CA 92821 714-961-0800 961-0899
Web: www.tekram.com

TYAN Computer Corp USA 3288 Laurelview Ct ... Fremont CA 94538 510-651-8868 651-7688
Web: www.tyan.com

Unicircuit Inc 8192 Southpark Ln ... Littleton CO 80120 303-730-0505 730-0606
TF: 800-648-6449 ■ Web: www.unicircuit.com

Unigen Corp 45388 Warm Springs Blvd ... Fremont CA 94539 510-668-2088 661-4889
TF: 800-826-0808 ■ Web: www.unigen.com

Universal Scientific of Illinois Inc
2101 Arthur Ave ... Elk Grove Village IL 60007 847-228-6464 228-0523
Web: www.usipcb.com

Viasystems Group Inc
101 S Hanley Rd Suite 400 ... Saint Louis MO 63105 314-727-2087 746-2233
Web: www.viasystems.com

Victron Inc 6600 Stevenson Blvd ... Fremont CA 94538 510-360-2222 445-2000
Web: www.victron.com

Viking Components Inc
30200 Avenida de Las Banderas ... Rancho Santa Margarita CA 92688 949-643-7255 643-7250
TF: 800-338-2361 ■ Web: www.vikingcomponents.com

VisionTek Inc 1610 Colonial Pkwy ... Inverness IL 60067 224-836-3000 836-3600
Web: www.visiontek.com

VM Services Inc 6701 Mowry Ave ... Newark CA 94560 510-744-3720 744-3730

Voyetra Turtle Beach Inc
150 Clearbrook Rd Suite 162 ... Elmsford NY 10523 914-345-2255 345-2266
Web: www.turtlebeach.com

Westak Inc 1225 Elko Dr ... Sunnyvale CA 94089 408-734-8686 734-3592
Web: www.westak.com

Western Electronics LLC 1550 S Tech Ln ... Meridian ID 83642 208-955-9700 955-9752
TF: 888-857-5775 ■ Web: www.westernelectronics.com

Wintec Industries Inc 4280 Technology Dr ... Fremont CA 94538 510-360-6300 770-9338*
*Fax: Tech Supp ■ Web: www.wintecindustries.com

Yun Industrial Co Ltd 161 Selandia Ln ... Carson CA 90746 310-715-1898 532-8128
Web: www.yic-assm.com

Zendex Corp 6780 Sierra Ct Suite A ... Dublin CA 94568 925-828-3000 828-1574
Web: www.zendex.com

629 PRINTING COMPANIES - BOOK PRINTERS

Phone Fax

Adair Printing Technologies 7850 2nd St ... Dexter MI 48130 734-426-2822 426-4360
TF: 800-637-5025 ■ Web: www.adairprinting.com

Bang Printing Inc 3323 Oak St ... Brainerd MN 56401 218-829-2877 829-7145
TF: 800-328-0450 ■ Web: www.bangprinting.com

Berryville Graphics
25 Jack Enders Blvd PO Box 272 ... Berryville VA 22611 540-955-2750 955-2633
Web: www.bvgraphics.com

Bertelsmann Printing & Mfg Corp
1540 Broadway ... New York NY 10036 212-782-7676 782-7600

Bradford & Bigelow Inc
1 Electronic Ave Danvers Industrial Pk ... Danvers MA 01923 978-777-1200 774-4021
TF: 800-882-9503 ■ Web: www.bradford-bigelow.com

Cadmus Communications Port City Press Div
1323 Greenwood Rd ... Baltimore MD 21208 410-486-3000 486-0706
TF: 800-858-7678 ■ Web: www.cadmus.com

CJK 3962 Virginia Ave ... Cincinnati OH 45227 513-271-6035 271-6082
TF: 800-598-7808 ■ Web: www.cjkusa.com

Claitor's Law Books & Publishing Inc
3655 Perkins Rd ... Baton Rouge LA 70808 225-344-0476 344-0480
TF: 800-274-1403 ■ Web: www.claitors.com

Command Web Offset Inc 100 Castle Rd ... Secaucus NJ 07094 201-863-8100 863-6693
TF: 800-466-2932

Consolidated Printers Inc 2630 8th St ... Berkeley CA 94710 510-843-8524 486-0580
Web: www.consoprinters.com

Cookbook Publishers Inc 10800 Lakeview Ave ... Lenexa KS 66219 913-492-5900 492-5947
TF: 800-227-7282 ■ Web: www.cookbookpublishers.com

Courier Corp 15 Wellman Ave ... North Chelmsford MA 01863 978-251-6000 251-6000
NASDAQ: CRRC ■ Web: www.courier.com

Courier Kendallville Inc 2500 Marion Dr ... Kendallville IN 46755 978-251-6000 347-3507*
*Fax Area Code: 260 ■ Web: www.courier.com

Cushing-Malloy Inc 1350 N Main St ... Ann Arbor MI 48104 734-663-8554 663-5731
TF: 888-295-7244 ■ Web: www.cushing-malloy.com

Darby Printing Co 6215 Purdue Dr ... Atlanta GA 30336 404-344-2665 346-3332
TF: 800-241-5292 ■ Web: www.darbyprinting.com

Deaton-Kennedy Co Inc 927 Gardner St ... Joliet IL 60433 815-726-6234 726-1379
TF: 800-435-4068 ■ Web: www.deatonkennedy.com

Edwards Bros Inc 2500 S State St ... Ann Arbor MI 48104 734-769-1000 913-1338*
*Fax: Cust Svc ■ Web: www.edwardsbrothers.com

Fannon Fine Printing 1712 Mt Vernon Ave ... Alexandria VA 22301 703-683-5600 683-2502
Web: www.fannonprinting.com

Friesens Corp 1 Printers Way ... Altona MB R0G0B0 204-324-6401 324-1333
Web: www.friesens.com

Gospel Publishing House
1445 N Boonville Ave ... Springfield MO 65802 417-862-2781 862-8558
TF Orders: 800-641-4310 ■ Web: www.gospelpublishing.com

Griffin Publishing Group 18022 Cowan ... Irvine CA 92614 949-263-3733 263-3734
TF: 800-472-9741 ■ Web: www.griffinpublishing.com

Hamilton Printing Co Inc PO Box 232 ... Rensselaer NY 12144 518-732-4491 732-7714
TF: 800-242-4222

Joe Christensen Inc 1540 Adams St ... Lincoln NE 68521 402-476-7535 476-3094
TF: 800-228-5030

John Henry Co 5800 W Grand River Ave ... Lansing MI 48906 517-323-9000 323-4707
TF: 800-748-0517 ■ Web: www.jhc.com

Jostens Inc 3601 Minnesota Ave Suite 400 ... Minneapolis MN 55435 952-830-3300 830-3309*
*Fax: Hum Res ■ TF: 800-235-4774 ■ Web: www.jostens.com

Kirby Lithographic Co Inc 2900 S Eads St ... Arlington VA 22202 703-684-7600 683-5918
TF: 800-932-3594

Library Reproduction Service
14214 S Figueroa St ... Los Angeles CA 90061 310-354-2610 354-2601
TF: 800-255-5002 ■ Web: www.largeprintschoolbooks.com

Malloy Inc 5411 Jackson Rd PO Box 1124 ... Ann Arbor MI 48103 734-665-6113 665-2326
TF: 800-722-3231 ■ Web: www.malloy.com

Maple-Vail Book Mfg Group 480 Willow Springs Ln ... York PA 17406 717-764-5911 764-4702
Web: www.maple-vail.com

McAdams Graphics Inc 7200 S First St ... Oak Creek WI 53154 414-768-8080 768-8099
Web: www.mcadamsgraphics.com

MCB Printing Inc 230 Walnut Hill Ln ... Havertown PA 19083 610-446-6011 446-6013
Web: www.mcbprinting.com

McNaughton & Gunn Inc 960 Woodland Dr ... Saline MI 48176 734-429-5411 677-2665*
*Fax Area Code: 800 ■ Web: www.mcnaughton-gunn.com

Moran Printing Inc 5425 Florida Blvd ... Baton Rouge LA 70806 225-923-2550 923-1078
TF: 800-211-8335 ■ Web: www.moranprinting.com

Offset Paperback Manufacturers Inc
101 Memorial Hwy ... Dallas PA 18612 570-675-5261 675-8714
Web: www.opm.com

Page Litho Inc 6445 E Vernor Hwy ... Detroit MI 48207 313-921-6880 921-6771
Web: www.pagelithoinc.com

Phoenix Color Corp
540 Western Maryland Pkwy ... Hagerstown MD 21740 301-733-0018 791-9560
TF: 800-632-4111 ■ Web: www.phoenixcolor.com

Print Communications Inc
2457 E Washington St ... Indianapolis IN 46201 317-266-8208
Web: www.pciprint.com

Publishers Press Inc
100 Frank E Simon Ave ... Shepherdsville KY 40165 502-955-6526 543-8808
TF: 800-627-5801 ■ Web: www.pubpress.com

RCL Enterprises 206 E Bethany Dr ... Allen TX 75002 972-390-6400 688-8356*
*Fax Area Code: 800 ■ TF: 877-275-4725 ■ Web: www.rclweb.com

Rose Printing Co Inc
2503 Jackson Bluff Rd ... Tallahassee FL 32304 850-576-4151 576-4153
TF: 800-227-3725 ■ Web: www.roseprinting.com

RR Donnelley 4411 Old Berwick Rd ... Bloomsburg PA 17815 570-784-7394 784-3129
Web: www.rrdonnelley.com

RR Donnelley & Sons Co 111 S Wacker Dr ... Chicago IL 60601 312-326-8000 326-8543*
NYSE: RRD ■ *Fax: Mail Rm ■ Web: www.rrdonnelley.com

Schneidereith & Sons Inc
2905 Whittington Ave ... Baltimore MD 21230 410-525-0300 525-3797
TF: 800-327-1982 ■ Web: www.schneidereith.com

Sheridan Books Inc 613 E Industrial Dr ... Chelsea MI 48118 734-475-9145 475-7337
TF: 800-999-2665 ■ Web: www.sheridan.com

Sheridan Group
11311 McCormick Rd Suite 260 ... Hunt Valley MD 21031 410-785-7277 785-7217
Web: www.sheridan.com

Smith-Edwards-Dunlap Co
2867 E Allegheny Ave ... Philadelphia PA 19134 215-425-8800 425-9110
TF: 800-829-0020 ■ Web: www.sed.com

Stinehour Press 853 Lancaster Rd ... Lunenburg VT 05906 802-328-2507 328-3960
TF: 800-331-7753

Thomson-Shore Inc 7300 W Joy Rd ... Dexter MI 48130 734-426-3939 706-4545*
*Fax Area Code: 800 ■ Web: www.thomsonshore.com

Transcontinental Printing Inc
395 Lebeau Blvd ... Saint-Laurent QC H4N1S2 514-337-8560 339-5230
TF: 800-337-8560 ■ Web: www.transcontinental-gtc.com

Tweddle Litho Co
24700 Maplehurst Dr ... Clinton Township MI 48036 586-307-3700 307-3708
Web: www.tweddle.com

Typecraft Wood & Jones Inc 2040 E Walnut St ... Pasadena CA 91107 626-795-8093 795-2423
Web: www.typecraft.com

United Graphics Inc 516 N Ogden Ave Suite 130 ... Chicago IL 60642 312-850-3317 277-2386
Web: www.bookmanufacturing.com

Versa Press Inc 1465 Springbay Rd ... East Peoria IL 61611 309-822-8272 822-8141
TF: 800-447-7829 ■ Web: www.versapress.com

Vicks Lithograph & Printing Co
5166 Commercial Dr PO Box 270 ... Yorkville NY 13495 315-736-9344 736-1901
Web: www.vicks.biz

Victor Graphics Inc 1211 Bernard Dr ... Baltimore MD 21223 410-233-8300 233-8304
TF: 800-899-8303 ■ Web: www.victorgraphics.com

Webcrafters Inc 2211 Fordem Ave ... Madison WI 53704 608-244-3561 244-5120
TF: 800-356-8200 ■ Web: www.webcrafters-inc.com

Whitehall Printing Co 4244 Corporate Sq ... Naples FL 34104 800-321-9290 643-6439*
*Fax Area Code: 239 ■ TF: 800-321-9290 ■ Web: www.whitehallprinting.com

Worzalla Publishing Co
3535 Jefferson St PO Box 307 ... Stevens Point WI 54481 715-344-9600 344-2578
Web: www.worzalla.com

Wright Color Graphics 9051 Sunland Blvd ... SunValley CA 91352 818-246-8877 246-8984
TF: 877-246-8877 ■ Web: www.wrightcolor.com

630 PRINTING COMPANIES - COMMERCIAL PRINTERS

Phone Fax

AdPlex Inc 650 Century Plaza Dr Suite 120 ... Houston TX 77073 281-443-4301 443-1040
Web: www.adplex.com

AlphaGraphics Inc
268 S State St Suite 300 ... Salt Lake City UT 84111 801-595-7270 595-7271
TF: 800-955-6246 ■ Web: www.alphagraphics.com

American Banknote Corp 2200 Fletcher Ave ... Fort Lee NJ 07024 201-592-3400 224-2762
Web: www.americanbanknote.com

American Press LLC 1 American Pl ... Gordonsville VA 22942 540-832-2253 832-7253
TF: 800-289-4602 ■ Web: www.american-press.com

Company	City	State	ZIP	Phone	Fax
American Spirit Graphics Corp 801 SE 9th St *Web:* www.asgc.com	Minneapolis	MN	55414	612-623-3333	623-9314
American Stationery Co Inc 100 N Pk Ave *TF Sales:* 800-822-2577 ■ *Web:* www.americanstationery.com	Peru	IN	46970	765-473-4438	472-8510
Amidon Graphics 1966 Benson Ave *TF:* 800-328-6502 ■ *Web:* www.amidongraphics.com	Saint Paul	MN	55116	651-690-2401	690-4009
Arandell Inc N 82 W 13118 Leon Rd *TF:* 800-558-8724 ■ *Web:* www.arandell.com	Menomonee Falls	WI	53051	262-255-4400	253-3166
Arcade Marketing Inc 1700 Broadway Suite 2500 *Web:* www.arcadeinc.com	New York	NY	10019	212-541-2600	489-3026
Ares Printing & Packaging Corp 63 Flushing Ave Unit 224 *Web:* www.aresny.com	Brooklyn	NY	11205	718-858-8760	
Art Dreams Home Inc 2433 Eastman Ave *Web:* www.artdreamshome.com	Ventura	CA	93003	805-642-6444	642-9781
B H G Inc PO Box 309 *TF:* 800-658-3485 ■ *Web:* www.nd-bhginc.com	Garrison	ND	58540	701-463-2201	
Balmar Inc 2818 Fallfax Dr **Fax:* Cust Svc ■ *Web:* www.balmar.com	Falls Church	VA	22042	703-289-9000	876-9606*
Beckmanxmo 376 Morrison Rd *TF:* 800-864-2232 ■ *Web:* beckmanxmo.com	Columbus	OH	43213	614-864-2232	864-3305
Berlin Industries Inc 175 Mercedes Dr *Web:* www.berlinindustries.com	Carol Stream	IL	60188	630-682-0600	682-3093
Bfc Forms Service Inc 1051 N Kirk Rd *TF:* 800-774-6840 ■ *Web:* www.bfcprint.com	Batavia	IL	60510	630-879-9240	
Bibbero Systems Inc 1300 N McDowell Blvd *TF:* 800-242-2376 ■ *Web:* www.bibbero.com	Petaluma	CA	94954	707-778-3131	778-0824
Bolger LLC 3301 Como Ave SE *TF:* 866-264-3287 ■ *Web:* www.bolgerinc.com	Minneapolis	MN	55414	651-645-6311	645-1750
Branch-Smith Resources PO Box 1868 *TF:* 800-315-4110 ■ *Web:* www.branchsmith.com	Fort Worth	TX	76101	817-882-4110	882-4111
Burton & Mayer Inc W140 N9000 Lilly Rd *TF:* 800-236-1770 ■ *Web:* www.burtonmayer.com	Menomonee Falls	WI	53051	262-781-0770	781-9598
Cadmus Communications Corp Whitehall Group Div 2750 Whitehall Pk Dr **Fax:* Sales ■ *TF:* 800-733-4318 ■ *Web:* www.cadmuswhitehall.com	Charlotte	NC	28273	704-583-6600	583-6781*
Cadmus Professional Communications 1801 Bayberry Ct Suite 200 *TF:* 877-422-3687 ■ *Web:* cjs.cadmus.com	Richmond	VA	23226	804-287-5680	287-5691
CadmusMack 2901 Byrdhill Rd *TF:* 800-888-2973 ■ *Web:* www.cadmus.com	Richmond	VA	23228	804-264-2711	515-5711
Canadian Bank Note Co Ltd (CBNC) 145 Richmond Rd *Web:* www.cbnco.com	Ottawa	ON	K1Z1A1	613-722-3421	722-2548
Canfield & Tack Inc 925 Exchange St *TF:* 800-836-0861 ■ *Web:* www.canfieldtack.com	Rochester	NY	14608	585-235-7710	235-4166
Cenveo Color-Art 10300 Watson Rd *TF:* 800-800-8845 ■ *Web:* www.colorart.com	Saint Louis	MO	63127	314-966-2000	966-4725
Cenveo Inc 201 Broad St 1 Canterberry Green *NYSE: CVO* ■ *Web:* www.cenveo.com	Stamford	CT	06901	203-595-3000	595-3070
Challenge Printing Co Inc The 2 Bridewell Pl *TF:* 800-654-1234 ■ *Web:* www.challprint.com	Clifton	NJ	07014	973-471-4700	471-5211
Champion Graphics 3901 Virginia Ave	Cincinnati	OH	45227	513-271-3800	271-5963
Champion Industries Inc 2450-90 First Ave PO Box 2968 *NASDAQ: CHMP* ■ *TF:* 800-624-3431 ■ *Web:* www.champion-industries.com	Huntington	WV	25728	304-528-2700	528-2765
ColorDynamics 200 E Bethany Dr *TF:* 800-445-0017 ■ *Web:* www.colordynamics.com	Allen	TX	75002	972-390-6500	390-6699
ColorGraphics Inc 150 N Myers St *Web:* www.colorgraphics.com	Los Angeles	CA	90033	323-261-7171	261-7077
Concord Litho Group 92 Old Tpke Rd *TF:* 800-258-3662 ■ *Web:* www.concordlitho.com	Concord	NH	03301	603-225-3328	225-6120
Conley Publishing Group Ltd 119 Monroe St	Beaver Dam	WI	53916	920-885-7800	887-0439
Consolidated Graphics Group Inc 1614 E 40th St *TF:* 888-884-9191 ■ *Web:* www.cgginc.com	Cleveland	OH	44103	216-881-9191	881-3442
Consolidated Graphics Inc 5858 Westheimer Rd Suite 200 *NYSE: CGX* ■ *Web:* www.cgx.com	Houston	TX	77057	713-787-0977	787-5013
Continental Web Press Inc 1430 Industrial Dr *Web:* www.continentalweb.com	Itasca	IL	60143	630-773-1903	773-1903
COP Communications Inc 620 W Elk Ave *Web:* www.copprints.com	Glendale	CA	91204	818-291-1100	291-1190
Cosmos Communications Inc 11-05 44th Dr *TF:* 800-223-5751 ■ *Web:* www.cosmoscommunications.com	Long Island City	NY	11101	718-482-1800	482-1968
Courier Printing 1 Courier Pl *TF:* 800-467-0444 ■ *Web:* www.courierprinting.com	Smyrna	TN	37167	615-355-4000	355-4088
Coyle Reproductions Inc 14949 Firestone Blvd *TF:* 866-269-5373 ■ *Web:* www.coylerepro.com	La Mirada	CA	90638	714-690-8200	690-8219
Darwill Inc 11900 Roosevelt Rd *Web:* www.darwill.com	Hillside	IL	60162	708-236-4900	236-5820
Disc Graphics Inc 10 Gilpin Ave *Web:* www.discgraphics.com	Hauppauge	NY	11788	631-234-1400	234-1460
Document Security Systems Inc 28 E Main St Suite 1525 *AMEX: DMC* ■ *TF:* 877-276-0293 ■ *Web:* www.documentsecurity.com	Rochester	NY	14614	585-325-3610	325-2977
Dupli Graphics Corp 1 Dupli Pk Dr PO Box 11500 *TF:* 800-724-2477 ■ *Web:* www.duplionline.com	Syracuse	NY	13218	315-472-1316	
DuraColor 1840 Oakdale Ave *TF:* 877-899-7900 ■ *Web:* www.duracolor.net	Racine	WI	53406	262-636-0040	636-0040
E & D Web Inc 4633 W 16th St **Fax Area Code:* 815 ■ *TF:* 800-323-5733 ■ *Web:* www.eanddweb.com	Cicero	IL	60804	708-656-6600	562-6600*
EarthColor 527 W 34th St *Web:* www.earthcolor.com	New York	NY	10001	212-967-9720	564-2500
EBSCO Media 801 5th Ave S *TF:* 800-765-0852 ■ *Web:* www.ebscomedia.com	Birmingham	AL	35233	205-323-1508	226-8400
Emerald City Graphics 23328 66th Ave S *TF:* 877-631-5178 ■ *Web:* www.emeraldcg.com	Kent	WA	98032	253-520-2600	520-2607
EU Services 649 N Horners Ln *TF:* 800-230-3362 ■ *Web:* www.euservices.com	Rockville	MD	20850	301-424-3300	424-3696
FB Johnston Graphics 300 E Boundary St PO Box 280 *TF:* 800-800-8160 ■ *Web:* www.fbjohnston.com	Chapin	SC	29036	803-345-5481	345-5512
FCL Graphics Inc 4600 N Olcott Ave *Web:* www.fclgraphics.com	Harwood Heights	IL	60706	708-867-5500	867-7768
Flagship Press Inc 150 Flagship Dr *TF:* 800-733-1520 ■ *Web:* www.flagshippress.com	North Andover	MA	01845	978-975-3100	975-0635
Forest Corp 1665 Enterprise Pkwy *TF:* 800-637-6434 ■ *Web:* www.forestcorporation.com	Twinsburg	OH	44087	330-425-3805	425-9604
Fort Dearborn Co 6035 W Gross Pt Rd *TF:* 888-332-7746 ■ *Web:* www.fortdearborn.com	Niles	IL	60714	773-774-4321	774-9105
Fundcraft Publishing Inc PO Box 340 *TF:* 800-964-5715 ■ *Web:* www.fcpromotions.com	Collierville	TN	38027	901-853-7070	853-6196
Gannett Offset 6883 Commercial Dr *TF:* 800-255-1457 ■ *Web:* www.gannettoffset.com	Springfield	VA	22159	703-750-8643	750-8717
Gazette Publishing Inc 1114 Broadway *TF:* 800-567-8303 ■ *Web:* www.mnnews.com	Wheaton	MN	56296	320-563-8146	563-8147
Gincop Inc 8410-B Tuscany Way *Web:* www.ginnysprinting.com	Austin	TX	78754	512-454-6874	453-2178
Grand River Printing Inc 8455 Haggerty Rd *TF:* 800-334-6857 ■ *Web:* www.grpinc.com	Belleville	MI	48111	734-394-1400	
Harty Press Inc The PO Box 324 *TF:* 800-654-0562 ■ *Web:* www.hartynet.com	New Haven	CT	06513	203-776-8196	782-9168
Hennegan Co 7455 Empire Dr *Web:* www.hennegan.com	Florence	KY	41042	859-282-3600	282-3601
Hickory Printing Group Inc 725 Reese Dr SW *TF:* 800-442-5679 ■ *Web:* www.hickoryprinting.com	Conover	NC	28613	828-465-3431	465-2517
IGI Earth Color Group 527 W 34th St *Web:* www.earthcolor.com	New York	NY	10001	212-967-9720	967-2965
IntegraColor 3210 Innovative Way *TF:* 800-933-9511 ■ *Web:* www.integracolor.com	Mesquite	TX	75149	972-289-0705	285-4881
Intelligencer Printing Co 330 Eden Rd *TF:* 800-233-0107 ■ *Web:* www.intellprinting.com	Lancaster	PA	17601	717-291-3100	569-2752
Interprint LLC 7111 Hayvenhurst Ave *TF:* 800-926-9873 ■ *Web:* www.interprintusa.com	Van Nuys	CA	91406	818-989-3600	989-4600
Iris Group Inc The 1675 Faraday Ave *TF:* 800-959-8365 ■ *Web:* www.modernpostcard.com	Carlsbad	CA	92008	760-431-7084	268-1730
J & A Printing Inc PO Box 457 *TF:* 800-793-1781 ■ *Web:* www.japrinting.com	Hiawatha	IA	52233	319-393-1781	
Japs-Olson Co 7500 Excelsior Blvd *TF:* 800-548-2897 ■ *Web:* www.japsolson.com	Saint Louis Park	MN	55426	952-932-9393	912-1900
John Roberts Co 9687 E River Rd *TF:* 800-551-1534 ■ *Web:* www.johnroberts.com	Coon Rapids	MN	55433	763-755-5500	754-4400
Journal Printing Co Inc 4848 Industrial Pk Rd *Web:* www.journalprinting.com	Stevens Point	WI	54481	715-344-4084	344-0829
K/P Corp 12647 Alcosta Blvd Suite 425 *TF:* 877-957-2677 ■ *Web:* www.kpcorporation.com	San Ramon	CA	94583	925-543-5200	543-5252
Kay Toledo Tag Inc PO Box 5038 *TF:* 800-822-8247 ■ *Web:* www.kaytag.com	Toledo	OH	43611	419-729-5479	729-0315
Keller Crescent Co Inc 1100 E Louisiana St **Fax:* Cust Svc ■ *TF:* 800-457-3837 ■ *Web:* www.kellercrescent.com	Evansville	IN	47711	812-464-2461	426-7601*
Kirkwood Printing Co Inc 904 Main St *Web:* www.kirkwoodprinting.com	Wilmington	MA	01887	978-658-4200	658-5547
Knepper Press Corp 2251 Sweeney Dr *Web:* www.knepperpress.com	Clinton	PA	15026	724-899-4200	899-1331
Lake County Press Inc 98 Noll St *TF:* 800-369-4333 ■ *Web:* www.lakecountypress.com	Waukegan	IL	60085	847-336-4333	336-5846
Lane Press Inc 87 Meadowland Dr PO Box 130 *TF:* 800-733-3740 ■ *Web:* www.lanepress.com	Burlington	VT	05402	802-863-5555	264-1485
Lew A. Cummings Co Inc PO Box 16495 *TF:* 800-647-0035 ■ *Web:* www.cummingsprinting.com	Hooksett	NH	03106	603-625-6901	623-5132
Litho-Krome Co 5700 Old Brim Dr *TF:* 800-572-8028 ■ *Web:* www.lithokrome.com	Midland	GA	31820	706-225-6600	225-6639
Lithographix Inc 12250 Crenshaw Blvd *TF:* 800-848-2449 ■ *Web:* www.lithographix.com	Hawthorne	CA	90250	323-770-1000	720-6000
Livewire Printing Co 310 Second St PO Box 208 *Web:* www.livewireprinting.com	Jackson	MN	56143	507-847-3771	847-5822
Lowen Corp PO Box 1528 *TF:* 800-835-2365 ■ *Web:* www.lowen.com	Hutchinson	KS	67504	620-663-2161	663-1429
M & R Sales & Service Inc 1n 372 Main St *Web:* www.mrprint.com	Glen Ellyn	IL	60137	630-858-6101	858-6134
M. Lee Smith Publishers LLC PO Box 5094 *TF:* 800-274-6774 ■ *Web:* www.mleesmith.com	Brentwood	TN	37024	615-373-7517	373-5183
Marketing Services By Vectra Inc 3950 Business Pk Dr *TF:* 800-862-2341 ■ *Web:* www.msbv.com	Columbus	OH	43204	614-351-6868	351-6877
Master Print Inc 8401 Terminal Rd *Web:* www.master-print.com	Newington	VA	22122	703-550-9555	550-9673
Merrill Corp 1 Merrill Cir *TF:* 800-688-4400 ■ *Web:* www.merrillcorp.com	Saint Paul	MN	55108	651-646-4501	649-3838
Merrill/Daniels Printing Co 40 Commercial St *TF:* 800-553-7733 ■ *Web:* www.merrillcorp.com	Everett	MA	02149	617-389-7900	389-5520
Meyers Printing Cos Inc The 7277 Boone Ave N *TF:* 800-927-9709 ■ *Web:* www.meyers.com	Brooklyn Park	MN	55428	763-533-9730	531-5771
Midland Information Resources Co 5440 Corporate Pk Dr *TF:* 800-232-3696 ■ *Web:* www.midlandcorp.com	Davenport	IA	52807	563-359-3696	359-1333
Minuteman Press International Inc 61 Executive Blvd *TF:* 800-645-3006 ■ *Web:* www.minutemanpress.com	Farmingdale	NY	11735	631-249-1370	249-5618
Monarch Litho Inc 1501 Date St *Web:* www.monarchlitho.com	Montebello	CA	90640	323-727-0300	720-1169
Nahan Printing Inc 7000 Saukview Dr PO Box 697 *Web:* www.nahan.com	Saint Cloud	MN	56302	320-251-7611	259-1378
National Graphics Inc					

Company / Address	City	State	Zip	Phone	Fax
248 Branford Rd # 1	North Branford	CT	06471	203-481-2351	483-0256
Web: www.natgraphics.com					
National Mail Graphics Corp 300 Old Mill Ln	Exton	PA	19341	610-524-1600	524-7638
Web: www.nmgcorp.com					
Nationwide Graphics Inc 2500 W Loop S Suite 500	Houston	TX	77027	713-961-4700	961-4701
Web: www.nationwidegraphics.com					
Naylor Inc 350 Great SW Pkwy	Atlanta	GA	30336	404-739-7299	739-7284
Web: www.naylorinc.com					
NCL Graphic Specialties Inc N29 w 22960 Marjean Ln	Waukesha	WI	53186	262-832-6100	
Web: www.nclgraphicspecialties.com					
Nebraska Printing Co Inc 4411 W Tampa Bay Blvd	Tampa	FL	33614	813-873-7117	873-1193
TF: 800-683-2056 ■ *Web:* www.nebcofl.com					
Network Communications Inc 2305 New Pt Pkwy	Lawrenceville	GA	30043	770-962-7220	822-4301
TF: 800-841-3401 ■ *Web:* www.livingchoices.com					
Newsweb Corp 1645 W Fullerton	Chicago	IL	60614	773-975-0400	975-6975
Web: www.newswebchicago.com					
Nielsen Co 7405 Industrial Rd	Florence	KY	41042	800-877-7405	525-7654*
**Fax Area Code:* 859 ■ *TF:* 800-877-7405 ■ *Web:* www.rrdonnelley.com					
Outlook Group Corp 1180 American Dr PO Box 748	Neenah	WI	54956	920-727-7999	727-8529
Web: www.outlookgroup.com					
Panel Prints Inc 1001 Moosic Rd	Old Forge	PA	18518	570-457-8334	457-6440
TF: 800-557-2635 ■ *Web:* www.panelprints.com					
PBM Graphics Inc PO Box 13603	Durham	NC	27709	919-544-6222	544-6695
TF: 800-849-8100 ■ *Web:* www.pbmgraphics.com					
Penn Lithographics Inc 16221 Author St	Cerritos	CA	90703	562-926-0455	926-8955
Web: www.pennlitho.com					
Perry Judd's Inc 575 W Madison St	Waterloo	WI	53594	920-478-3551	478-1800
TF: 800-737-7948					
Pictorial Offset Corp 111 Amor Ave PO Box 157	Carlstadt	NJ	07072	201-935-7100	935-3254
Web: www.pictorialoffset.com					
PIP Printing & Document Services Inc 26722 Plaza Dr Suite 200	Mission Viejo	CA	92691	949-282-3800	282-3899
Web: www.pip.com					
Polytype America Corp 10 Industrial Ave	Mahwah	NJ	07430	201-995-1000	995-1080
Web: www.polytypeamerica.com					
Print Direction Inc 1600 Indian Brook Way	Norcross	GA	30093	877-435-1672	
Web: www.printdirection.com					
Printer Inc The 1220 Thomas Beck Rd	Des Moines	IA	50315	515-288-7241	288-9234
Web: www.the-printer.com					
Prisma Graphic Corp 2937 E Broadway Rd	Phoenix	AZ	85040	602-243-5777	268-4804
TF: 800-379-5777 ■ *Web:* www.prismagraphic.com					
Pro Document Solutions Inc PO Box 2428	Paso Robles	CA	93447	805-238-6680	238-6819
TF: 800-726-0080 ■ *Web:* www.prodocumentsolutions.com					
Production Press Inc 307 E Morgan St	Jacksonville	IL	62650	217-243-3353	245-0400
TF: 800-231-3880 ■ *Web:* www.productionpress.com					
ProForma 8800 E Pleasant Valley Rd	Independence	OH	44131	216-520-8400	520-8444
TF: 800-825-1525 ■ *Web:* www.proforma.com					
Progress Printing Co 2677 Waterlick Rd	Lynchburg	VA	24502	434-239-9213	237-1618
TF: 800-572-7804 ■ *Web:* www.progprint.com					
Publication Printers Corp 2001 S Platte River Dr	Denver	CO	80223	303-936-0303	934-6712
TF: 888-824-0303 ■ *Web:* www.publicationprinters.com					
Publishers Printing Co 100 Frank E Simon Ave	Shepherdsville	KY	40165	502-543-2251	955-5586
TF: 800-627-5801 ■ *Web:* www.pubpress.com					
Quad/Graphics Inc N63 W23075 Main St	Sussex	WI	53089	414-566-6000	566-4646*
**Fax:* Hum Res ■ *Web:* www.qg.com					
Raff Printing Inc PO Box 42365	Pittsburgh	PA	15203	412-431-4044	
Web: www.raffprinting.com					
Regal Press Inc The 129 Guild St	Norwood	MA	02062	781-769-3900	769-7361
TF: 800-447-3425 ■ *Web:* www.regalpress.com					
Robin Enterprises Co PO Box 6180	Westerville	OH	43086	614-891-0250	891-4398
Web: www.robinent.com					
Rogers Printing Inc PO Box 215	Ravenna	MI	49451	231-853-2244	853-6558
TF: 800-622-5591 ■ *Web:* www.rogersprinting.net					
RR Donnelley & Sons Co 111 S Wacker Dr	Chicago	IL	60601	312-326-8000	326-8543*
NYSE: RRD ■ **Fax:* Mail Rm ■ *Web:* www.rrdonnelley.com					
Saint Ives Cleveland Inc 4437 E 49th St	Cleveland	OH	44125	216-271-5300	271-6203
TF: 800-634-1262 ■ *Web:* www.st-ives-usa.com/clevmain.htm					
Saint Ives Inc 2025 McKinley St	Hollywood	FL	33020	954-920-7300	926-4885*
**Fax:* Cust Svc ■ *Web:* www.st-ives-usa.com					
Sandy Alexander Inc 200 Entin Rd	Clifton	NJ	07014	973-470-8100	470-9269
Web: www.sandyinc.com					
Schawk Inc 1695 S River Rd	Des Plaines	IL	60018	847-827-9494	827-1264
NYSE: SGK ■ *TF:* 800-621-1909 ■ *Web:* www.schawk.com					
Schmidt Printing Inc 1101 Frontage Rd NW	Byron	MN	55920	507-775-6400	775-6655
Web: www.schmidt.com					
Schumann Printers Inc 701 S Main St	Fall River	WI	53932	920-484-3348	484-3661
Web: www.spiweb.com					
Sennett Security Products 4212A Technology Ct	Chantilly	VA	20151	703-803-8880	803-8884
Shakopee Valley Printing 5101 Valley Industrial Blvd S	Shakopee	MN	55379	952-445-8260	445-5805
TF: 800-752-9906					
Sheridan Group 11311 McCormick Rd Suite 260	Hunt Valley	MD	21031	410-785-7277	785-7217
Web: www.sheridan.com					
Shorewood Packaging Corp 277 Pk Ave 30th Fl	New York	NY	10172	212-371-1500	223-3815
Web: www.internationalpaper.com/US/EN/Business/Shorewood.html					
Sir Speedy Inc 26722 Plaza Dr	Mission Viejo	CA	92691	949-348-5000	348-5010
TF: 800-854-8297 ■ *Web:* www.sirspeedy.com					
Smith Litho Inc 1029 E Gude Dr	Rockville	MD	20850	301-424-1400	762-2080
TF: 800-622-2577 ■ *Web:* www.smith-litho.com					
Solar Communications Inc 1120 Frontenac Rd	Naperville	IL	60563	630-983-1400	983-1494
TF: 800-323-2751 ■ *Web:* www.solarcommunications.com					
Solo Printing Inc 7860 NW 66th St	Miami	FL	33166	305-594-8699	599-5245
TF: 800-325-0118 ■ *Web:* www.soloprinting.com					
Spectra Print 2301 Country Club Dr PO Box 247	Stevens Point	WI	54481	715-344-5175	344-7227
Web: www.spectraprint.com					
Spencer Press Inc 90 Spencer Dr	Wells	ME	04090	207-646-9926	646-5021
TF: 800-765-0039 ■ *Web:* www.spencerpress.com					
Sprint-Denver Inc 4999 Kingston St	Denver	CO	80239	303-371-0566	371-2341
TF: 800-377-4958 ■ *Web:* www.sprintdenver.com					
St Joseph Communications 50 MacIntosh Blvd	Concord	ON	L4K4P3	905-660-3111	660-9737
TF: 877-660-3111 ■ *Web:* www.stjoseph.com					
Stevens Graphics Inc 713 Rd Abernathy Blvd	Atlanta	GA	30310	404-753-1121	752-0514
Web: www.stevensgraphicsinc.com					
Strathmore Co 2000 Gary Ln	Geneva	IL	60134	630-232-9677	232-0198
Web: www.strath.com					
Strine Printing Co Inc 30 Grumbacher Rd	York	PA	17406	717-767-6602	764-3459
TF: 800-477-8746 ■ *Web:* www.strine.com					
Suncraft Technologies Inc 1301 Frontenac Rd	Naperville	IL	60563	630-369-7900	639-7070
Web: www.suncraft-tech.com					
Super Color Digital LLC 16761 Hale Ave	Irvine	CA	92606	949-622-0010	622-0050
TF: 800-979-4446 ■ *Web:* www.supercolordigital.com					
Synergy Graphics Inc 14505 27th Ave N	Plymouth	MN	55447	763-586-3700	
Web: www.synergy-graphics.com					
TanaSeybert LLC 525 W 52nd St	New York	NY	10019	212-453-9300	633-9621
TF: 800-606-6876 ■ *Web:* www.tanaseybert.com					
Thames Printing Co Inc 1 Wisconsin Ave	Norwich	CT	06360	860-887-3541	887-3064
TF: 800-553-0931 ■ *Web:* www.thamesprinting.com					
Times Printing Co Inc 100 Industrial Dr	Random Lake	WI	53075	920-994-4396	994-2059*
**Fax:* Cust Svc ■ *TF:* 800-236-4396 ■ *Web:* www.timesprintingco.com					
Toppan Printing Co America Inc 1100 Randolph Rd	Somerset	NJ	08873	732-469-8400	469-1868*
**Fax:* Sales ■ *Web:* www.ta.toppan.com					
Transcontinental Inc 1 pl Ville Marie Bureau 3315	Montreal	QC	H3B3N2	514-954-4000	954-4016
TSE: TCL.A ■ *Web:* www.transcontinental.com					
Trend Offset Printing Services Inc 3791 Catalina St	Los Alamitos	CA	90720	562-598-2446	430-2373*
**Fax:* Cust Svc ■ *Web:* www.trendoffset.com					
Ultra Flex Packaging Corp 975 Essex St	Brooklyn	NY	11208	718-272-9100	
Web: www.ultraflex.com					
Uni-Graphic Inc 110 Commerce Way Suite 6	Woburn	MA	01801	781-231-7200	938-7727
Web: www.uni-graphic.com					
Universal Printing Co 1234 S Kings Hwy	Saint Louis	MO	63110	314-771-6900	771-7987
Web: www.universalprintingco.com					
Valassis Communications Inc 19975 Victor Pkwy	Livonia	MI	48152	734-591-3000	591-4994*
NYSE: VCI ■ **Fax:* Hum Res ■ *TF:* 800-437-0479 ■ *Web:* www.valassis.com					
Vertis Inc 250 W Pratt St 18th Fl	Baltimore	MD	21201	410-528-9800	528-9289
TF: 800-577-3569 ■ *Web:* www.vertisinc.com					
Watson Label Products Corp 10616 Trenton Ave	Saint Louis	MO	63132	314-493-9300	493-9390
TF: 800-678-6715 ■ *Web:* www.wlp.com					
Weldon Williams & Lick Inc 711 N A St	Fort Smith	AR	72901	479-783-4113	783-7050
TF: 800-242-4995 ■ *Web:* www.wwlinc.com					
Westland Printers Inc 14880 Sweitzer Ln	Laurel	MD	20707	301-384-7700	384-2616
Web: www.westlandprinters.com					
Wetmore Printing 1645 W Sam Houston Pkwy N	Houston	TX	77043	713-468-7175	468-8021
TF: 800-444-7175 ■ *Web:* www.rrdonnelley.com/wetmore					
Whitmore Group 1982 Moreland Pkwy	Annapolis	MD	21401	410-263-6660	263-6833
TF: 800-327-1982 ■ *Web:* www.whitmore.com					
Williamson Printing Corp 6700 Denton Dr	Dallas	TX	75235	214-904-2100	352-1842
TF: 800-843-5423 ■ *Web:* www.twpc.com					
Z Three- Printing Co 902 W Main St	Teutopolis	IL	62467	217-857-3153	857-3010
Web: www.threez.com					

631 PRINTING & PHOTOCOPYING SUPPLIES

Company / Address	City	State	Zip	Phone	Fax
Abco Distribution Inc 6282 Proprietors Rd	Worthington	OH	43085	614-848-4899	848-4897
TF: 800-821-9435 ■ *Web:* www.printingbyabco.com					
American Ribbon & Toner Co 6500 NW 15th Ave Suite 300	Fort Lauderdale	FL	33309	954-971-2999	971-2004
TF: 800-327-1013					
Automated Office Products Inc 9730-EE ML King Jr Hwy	Lanham	MD	20706	301-731-4000	459-2783
TF: 800-929-2528 ■ *Web:* www.automatedonline.com					
Buckeye Business Products Inc 3830 Kelley Ave	Cleveland	OH	44114	216-391-6300	881-6105
TF: 800-837-4323 ■ *Web:* www.buckeyebusiness.com					
Canon USA Inc 1 Canon Plaza	Lake Success	NY	11042	516-328-5000	328-5069*
**Fax:* Hum Res ■ *TF:* 800-828-4040 ■ *Web:* www.usa.canon.com					
Chromaline Corp 4832 Grand Ave	Duluth	MN	55807	218-628-2217	628-3245
TF: 800-328-4261 ■ *Web:* www.chromaline.com					
Color Imaging Inc 4350 Peachtree Industrial Blvd Suite 100	Norcross	GA	30071	770-840-1090	783-9010*
**Fax Area Code:* 800 ■ *TF:* 800-783-1090					
Curtis-Young Corp 2704 Cindel Dr	Cinnaminson	NJ	08077	856-665-6650	786-1705
TF Cust Svc: 800-282-6650					
DuraLine Imaging Inc 110 Commercial Blvd	Flat Rock	NC	28731	828-692-1301	
TF: 800-982-3872 ■ *Web:* www.duralineimaging.com					
Encore Ribbon Inc 1010 N Dutton Ave	Santa Rosa	CA	95401	707-206-9600	206-9600
TF: 800-431-4969					

	City	State	ZIP	Phone	Fax
Frye Tech Inc 110 Industrial Rd.	New Windsor	NY	12553	845-561-6040	561-0415
Graphic Controls LLC 400 Exchange St	Buffalo	NY	14204	800-669-1535	347-2420
TF: 800-669-1535 ■ *Web:* www.graphiccontrols.com					
Guy Brown Products 9003 Overlook Blvd	Brentwood	TN	37027	615-777-1500	777-1501
TF: 877-794-5906 ■ *Web:* www.guybrown.com					
Hurst Chemical Co 231 W Pedregosa St	Santa Barbara	CA	93101	800-723-2004	723-2005
TF: 800-723-2004 ■ *Web:* www.hurstchemical.com					
Image One Corp 13201 Capital Ave.	Oak Park	MI	48237	248-414-9955	414-9955
TF: 800-799-5377 ■ *Web:* www.imageoneway.com					
ImageTek Corp 420 E Easy St Suite 2	Simi Valley	CA	93065	805-584-2100	584-1370
TF: 800-584-2503					
Ink Technology Corp 18320 Lanken Ave	Cleveland	OH	44119	216-486-6720	486-6003
TF: 800-633-2826 ■ *Web:* www.inktechnology.com					
ITW Coding Products 111 W Pk Dr	Kalkaska	MI	49646	231-258-5521	258-6120
Web: www.codingproducts.com					
Ko-Rec-Type Div Barouh Eaton Allen Corp					
67 Kent Ave.	Brooklyn	NY	11211	718-782-2601	486-6340
TF: 800-366-6767 ■ *Web:* www.korectype.com					
LexJet Corp 1680 Fruitville Rd 3rd Fl	Sarasota	FL	34236	941-330-1210	330-1220
TF: 800-453-9538 ■ *Web:* www.lexjet.com					
Light Impressions PO Box 2100	Santa Fe Springs	CA	90670	714-441-4539	786-7939*
**Fax Area Code:* 800 ■ *TF:* 800-828-6216 ■ *Web:* www.lightimpressionsdirect.com					
Micro Solutions Enterprises (MSE)					
8201 Woodley Ave	Van Nuys	CA	91406	818-407-7500	407-7575
TF: 800-673-4968 ■ *Web:* www.mse-usa.com					
MKG Cartridge Systems Inc					
1090 Lorimar Dr	Mississauga	ON	L5S1R8	905-564-9218	564-9225
TF: 800-881-7545					
NER Data Products Inc 307 S Delsea Dr	Glassboro	NJ	08028	856-881-5524	637-2217*
**Fax Area Code:* 800 ■ *TF:* 800-257-5235 ■ *Web:* www.nerdata.com					
Oasis Imaging Products Inc 460 Amherst St	Nashua	NH	03063	603-880-3991	598-4277
Perfecopy Co 103 W 61st St	Westmont	IL	60559	630-769-9901	769-1057
TF Cust Svc: 800-323-4030					
Rayven Inc 431 Griggs St N	Saint Paul	MN	55104	651-642-1112	642-9497
TF Cust Svc: 800-878-3776 ■ *Web:* www.rayven.com					
Ricoh Printing Systems America Inc					
2390 Ward Ave # A	Simi Valley	CA	93065	805-578-4000	578-4001
TF: 800-887-8848 ■ *Web:* www.rpsa.ricoh.com					
Texas Lift-Off Correction Ribbon					
1700 Surveyor Blvd Suite 110	Carrollton	TX	75006	972-416-8100	416-9690
Tomoegawa USA Inc 742 Glenn Ave.	Wheeling	IL	60090	847-541-3001	541-3021
Web: www.tomoegawa.com					
Western Numerical Control					
41102 N Hudson Trail	Anthem	AZ	85086	623-594-4602	594-3769
TF: 800-538-5108 ■ *Web:* www.westnc.com					

632 PRINTING & PUBLISHING EQUIPMENT & SYSTEMS

SEE ALSO Printers p. 1672

	City	State	ZIP	Phone	Fax
Apex Machine Co 3000 NE 12th Ter	Fort Lauderdale	FL	33334	954-566-1572	563-2844
Web: www.apexmachine.com					
Awt World Trade Inc 4321 N Knox Ave	Chicago	IL	60641	773-777-7100	777-0909
Web: www.awt-gpi.com					
Baldwin Technology Co Inc					
2 Trap Falls Rd Suite 402	Shelton	CT	06484	203-402-1000	402-5500
AMEX: BLD ■ *Web:* www.baldwintech.com					
Bmp America Inc 11625 Maple Ridge Rd	Medina	NY	14103	585-798-0950	798-4272
Web: www.bmpworldwide.com					
Brackett Inc 6700 SW Topeka Blvd	Topeka	KS	66619	785-862-2205	862-1127
TF: 800-255-3506 ■ *Web:* www.brackett-inc.com					
Brandtjen & Kluge Inc					
539 Blanding Woods Rd	Saint Croix Falls	WI	54024	715-483-3265	483-1640
TF: 800-826-7320 ■ *Web:* www.brandtjenandkluge.com					
Burgess Industries Inc (BII) 2700 Campus Dr	Plymouth	MN	55441	763-553-7800	553-9289
TF Cust Svc: 800-233-2589 ■ *Web:* www.burgessind.com					
CODA Inc 30 Industrial Ave	Mahwah	NJ	07430	201-825-7400	825-8133
Web: www.codamount.com					
Craftsmen Machinery Co 840 Main St Suite 208	Millis	MA	02054	508-376-2001	376-2003
Day International Inc 130 W 2nd St Suite 1700	Dayton	OH	45401	937-224-4000	226-1466
Web: www.dayintl.com					
Delphax Technologies Inc 6100 W 110th St.	Bloomington	MN	55338	952-939-9000	939-0798*
NASDAQ: DLPX ■ **Fax:* Cust Svc ■ *Web:* www.delphax.com					
Diamond Roller					
Pamarco Global Graphics 150 Marr Ave	Marietta	GA	30060	770-424-6828	795-9323
TF: 800-247-5290 ■ *Web:* www.diamondroller.com					
Goss International Corp 3 Territorial Ct	Bolingbrook	IL	60440	630-755-9300	755-9301
Web: www.gossinternational.com					
Graphic Innovators Inc					
855 Morse Ave	Elk Grove Village	IL	60007	847-718-1516	718-1517
Web: www.graphicinnovators.com					
Gravograph-New Hermes Inc 2200 Northmont Pkwy	Duluth	GA	30096	770-623-0331	533-7637*
**Fax Area Code:* 800 ■ *TF:* 800-843-7637 ■ *Web:* www.gravograph.com					
Heidelberg USA Inc 1000 Gutenberg Dr.	Kennesaw	GA	30144	770-419-6500	419-6550
TF Cust Svc: 888-472-9655 ■ *Web:* www.us.heidelberg.com					
Kodak's Graphic Communications Group Canada					
3700 Gilmore Way	Burnaby	BC	V5G4M1	604-451-2700	437-9891
TF: 877-387-2736 ■ *Web:* www.graphics.kodak.com					
Konica Minolta Graphic Imaging USA Inc					
4150 Danvers Ct SE	Grand Rapids	MI	49512	616-575-2800	285-7108
TF: 800-282-5752 ■ *Web:* www.gi.konicaminolta.us					
LasscoWizer Inc 485 Hague St	Rochester	NY	14606	585-436-1934	464-8665
TF: 800-854-6595 ■ *Web:* www.lasscowizer.com					
MAN Roland Inc 800 E Oak Hill Dr	Westmont	IL	60559	630-920-2000	920-9146
TF: 800-700-2344 ■ *Web:* www.manroland.us.com					
Mark Andy Inc					
18081 Chesterfield Airport Rd	Chesterfield	MO	63005	636-532-4433	532-4701*
**Fax:* Cust Svc ■ *TF:* 800-700-6275 ■ *Web:* www.markandy.com					
Pamarco Global Graphics 235 E 11th Ave	Roselle	NJ	07203	908-241-1200	241-4237
TF: 800-526-2180 ■ *Web:* www.pamarcoglobal.com					
Presstek Inc 55 Executive Dr.	Hudson	NH	03051	603-595-7000	546-4234
NASDAQ: PRST ■ *TF:* 877-862-2227 ■ *Web:* www.presstek.com					
Rosback Co 125 Hawthorne Ave	Saint Joseph	MI	49085	269-983-2582	983-2516
TF: 800-542-2420 ■ *Web:* www.rosbackcompany.com					
Stevens Technology LLC 5700 E Belknap St	Fort Worth	TX	76117	817-759-4000	759-4080
Web: www.stevenstechnology.com					
Stolle Machinery Co LLC 6949 S Potomac St	Centennial	CO	80112	303-708-9044	708-9045
TF: 800-228-4593 ■ *Web:* www.stollemachinery.com					
Web Press Corp 22023 68th Ave S	Kent	WA	98032	253-383-2584	395-4492
TF: 800-424-1411 ■ *Web:* www.webpresscorp.com					
Xerox Corp 45 Glover Ave PO Box 4505	Norwalk	CT	06856	203-968-3000	968-3218
NYSE: XRX ■ *TF:* 800-842-0024 ■ *Web:* www.xerox.com					

633 PRISON INDUSTRIES

Prison Industries Are Programs Established By Federal And State Governments That Provide Work For Inmates While They Are Incarcerated As Well As On-The-Job Training To Help Them Become Employable On Release. At The Same Time, Prison Industries Provide Quality Goods And Services At Competitive Prices.

	City	State	ZIP	Phone	Fax
Alabama Correctional Industries					
1400 Lloyd St.	Montgomery	AL	36107	334-261-3600	240-3162
TF: 800-224-7007 ■ *Web:* www.aci.alabama.gov					
Arizona Correctional Industries					
3701 W Cambridge Ave	Phoenix	AZ	85009	602-272-7600	255-3108
Web: www.adc.state.az.us					
Arkansas Correctional Industries (ACI)					
2403 E Harding St	Pine Bluff	AR	71601	870-850-8434	850-8440
TF: 877-635-7213 ■ *Web:* www.acicatalog.com					
Badger State Industries (BSI)					
3099 E Washington Ave PO Box 8990	Madison	WI	53708	608-240-5200	240-3320
TF: 800-862-1086 ■ *Web:* www.buybsi.com					
California Prison Industry Authority					
560 E Natoma St.	Folsom	CA	95630	916-358-2727	358-2660*
**Fax:* Cust Svc ■ *Web:* www.pia.ca.gov					
Cornhusker State Industries					
800 Pioneers Blvd	Lincoln	NE	68502	402-471-4597	471-1236
TF: 800-348-7537 ■ *Web:* www.corrections.state.ne.us/csi					
Correctional Enterprises of Connecticut					
24 Wolcott Hill Rd.	Wethersfield	CT	06109	860-263-6839	263-6838
TF: 800-842-1146 ■ *Web:* www.ct.gov					
Delaware Prison Industries 245 McKee Rd	Dover	DE	19904	302-739-5601	739-1608
Federal Prison Industries Inc					
320 1st St NW	Washington	DC	20534	202-305-3501	
Web: www.unicor.gov					
Georgia Correctional Industries					
2984 Clifton Springs Rd	Decatur	GA	30034	404-244-5100	244-5141
TF: 800-282-7130 ■ *Web:* www.gci-ga.com					
Idaho Correctional Industries					
1299 N Orchard St Suite 110	Boise	ID	83706	208-658-2175	658-2160
Web: www.ci.state.id.us					
Iowa Prison Industries (IPI)					
1445 E Grand Ave.	Des Moines	IA	50316	515-242-5770	242-5779
TF: 800-670-4537 ■ *Web:* www.iaprisonind.com					
Kansas Correctional Industries PO Box 2	Lansing	KS	66043	913-727-3249	727-2331
Web: www.165.201.143.141/shop					
Kentucky Correctional Industries					
1041 Leestown Rd	Frankfort	KY	40601	502-573-1040	573-1050
TF: 800-828-9524 ■ *Web:* www.kci.ky.gov					
Louisiana Prison Enterprises					
PO Box 44314	Baton Rouge	LA	70804	225-342-6633	342-5556
TF General: 888-399-6633					
Maryland Correctional Enterprises (MCE)					
7275 Waterloo Rd	Jessup	MD	20794	410-540-5454	540-5570
Web: www.mce.md.gov/mce					
Massachusetts Correctional Industries					
One Industries Dr Bldg A PO Box 188	Norfolk	MA	02056	508-850-1070	850-1091
TF: 800-222-2211 ■ *Web:* www.mass.gov					
Michigan State Industries 5656 S Cedar St	Lansing	MI	48909	517-373-4277	241-9063*
**Fax:* Hum Res ■ *Web:* www.michigan.gov					
MINNCOR Industries					
1450 Energy Pk Dr Suite 110	Saint Paul	MN	55108	651-603-0118	603-0119
TF: 800-646-6267 ■ *Web:* www.minncor.com					
Mississippi Prison Industries Corp					
663 N State St.	Jackson	MS	39202	601-969-5750	969-5757
Web: www.mpic.net					
Missouri Vocational Enterprises					
1717 Industrial Dr PO Box 1898	Jefferson City	MO	65102	573-751-6663	751-9197
TF Sales: 800-392-8486 ■ *Web:* www.doc.mo.gov					
New Hampshire Correctional Industries					
281 N State St PO Box 14	Concord	NH	03302	603-271-1875	271-1116
Web: www.nh.gov/nhdoc/nhci					
New Jersey Bureau of State Use Industries					
163 N Olden Ave PO Box 867	Trenton	NJ	08625	609-633-8100	633-2495
TF: 800-321-6524 ■ *Web:* www.state.nj.us/deptcor					
New Mexico Correctional Industries					
4337 SR 14	Santa Fe	NM	87508	505-827-8838	827-8689*
**Fax:* Cust Svc ■ *TF:* 800-568-8789					
New York Correctional Industries 550 Broadway	Albany	NY	12204	518-436-6321	436-6007
TF: 800-436-6321 ■ *Web:* www.corcraft.org					
North Carolina Correction Enterprises					
2020 Yonkers Rd	Raleigh	NC	27604	919-716-3600	716-3974
Web: www.doc.state.nc.us					
Ohio Penal Industries (OPI) 1221 McKinley Ave.	Columbus	OH	43222	614-752-0287	752-0303
TF: 800-237-3454 ■ *Web:* www.opi.state.oh.us					
Oklahoma Correctional Industries					
3402 ML King Blvd.	Oklahoma City	OK	73111	405-425-7500	425-2838*
**Fax:* Cust Svc ■ *TF:* 800-522-3565 ■ *Web:* www.ocisales.com					
PEN Products 2010 E New York St.	Indianapolis	IN	46201	317-388-8580	280-3001

	City	State	Zip	Phone	Fax
Pennsylvania Bureau of Correctional Industries PO Box 47 *TF:* 877-673-3724 ■ *Web:* www.pci.state.pa.us	Camp Hill	PA	17001	717-731-7132	425-7291
Prison Rehabilitative Industries & Diversified Enterprises Inc (PRIDE) 9400 4th St N Suite 200 *TF:* 877-283-6819 ■ *Web:* www.prideestore.com	Saint Petersburg	FL	33720	727-572-1987	570-3366
Rhode Island Correctional Industries 40 Howard Ave *Web:* www.doc.ri.gov	Cranston	RI	02920	401-462-1000	462-2135
Rough Rider Industries 3303 E Main Ave *TF:* 800-732-0557 ■ *Web:* www.roughriderindustries.com	Bismarck	ND	58506	701-328-6161	328-6164
Silver State Industries 3955 W Russell Rd *Web:* www.ssi.nv.gov	Las Vegas	NV	89118	702-682-3147	486-9908
South Carolina Prison Industries 4444 Broad River Rd **Fax:* Cust Svc ■ *Web:* www.doc.sc.gov	Columbia	SC	29210	803-896-8516	896-2173*
Tennessee Rehabilitative Initiative in Correction (TRICOR) 240 Great Cir Rd Suite 310 *TF:* 800-958-7426 ■ *Web:* www.tricor.org	Nashville	TN	37228	615-741-5705	741-2747
Texas Correctional Industries PO Box 4013 *TF:* 800-883-4302 ■ *Web:* www.tci.tdcj.state.tx.us	Huntsville	TX	77342	936-437-6048	437-6040
Utah Correctional Industries 14072 S Pony Express Rd *Web:* uci.utah.gov	Draper	UT	84020	801-576-7700	523-9753
Vermont Correctional Industries 37 Commercial Dr *Web:* www.vowp.com	Waterbury	VT	05676	802-241-2268	241-1475
Virginia Correctional Enterprises 8030 White Bark Terr *Web:* www.vcedigitalworks.com/vce	Richmond	VA	23237	804-743-4100	743-2206
Washington Correctional Industries 801 88th Ave SE *Web:* www.washingtonci.com	Tumwater	WA	98501	360-725-9100	753-0219
West Virginia Correctional Industries 617 Leon Sullivan Way *TF:* 800-525-5381 ■ *Web:* www.state.wv.us	Charleston	WV	25301	304-558-6054	558-6056

634 PROFESSIONAL EMPLOYER ORGANIZATIONS (PEOS)

Companies Listed Here Contractually Assume Human Resources Responsibilities For Client Companies In Exchange For A Fee, Thus Allowing The Client Company To Focus On Its True Company Business. The Peo Establishes And Maintains An Employer Relationship With The Workers Assigned To Its Client Companies, With The Peo And The Client Company Each Having Specific Rights And Responsibilities Toward The Employees.

	City	State	Zip	Phone	Fax
Accord Human Resources Inc 210 Pk Ave Suite 1200 *TF:* 800-725-4004 ■ *Web:* www.accordhr.com	Oklahoma City	OK	73102	405-232-9888	232-9899
Adams Keegan Inc 6055 Primacy Pkwy Suite 300 *TF:* 800-621-1308 ■ *Web:* www.adamskeegan.com	Memphis	TN	38119	901-683-5353	683-5392
ADP TotalSource Co 10200 Sunset Dr **Fax:* Hum Res ■ *TF:* 800-447-3237 ■ *Web:* www.adptotalsource.com	Miami	FL	33173	305-630-1000	630-3006*
AdvanTech Solutions 4890 W Kennedy Blvd Suite 500 *TF:* 888-340-9442	Tampa	FL	33609	813-289-9442	636-8238
Alcott Group 71 Executive Blvd *TF:* 888-425-2688 ■ *Web:* www.alcottgroup.com	Farmingdale	NY	11735	631-420-0100	420-1894
Allied Employer Group 4400 Buffalo Gap Rd Suite 4500 *TF:* 800-729-7823 ■ *Web:* www.coemployer.com	Abilene	TX	79606	325-695-5822	692-9660
AlphaStaff Inc 800 Corporate Dr Suite 600 **Fax Area Code:* 866 ■ *TF:* 888-335-9545 ■ *Web:* www.alphastaff.com	Fort Lauderdale	FL	33334	954-267-1760	632-8090*
ALTRES Inc 967 Kapiolani Blvd *TF:* 888-425-8737 ■ *Web:* www.altres.com	Honolulu	HI	96814	808-591-4940	591-4914
AmStaff Human Resources Inc 6723 Plantation Rd *TF:* 800-888-0472 ■ *Web:* www.lindrumprofessional.com	Pensacola	FL	32504	850-477-7022	478-4088
Assent Consulting Inc 10054 Pasadena Ave *TF:* 800-747-0940 ■ *Web:* www.assentconsulting.com	Cupertino	CA	95014	408-366-8820	366-8821
Axiom HR Solutions *Axet* 8345 Lenexa Dr Suite 100 *TF:* 800-801-7557 ■ *Web:* www.axethrsolutions.com	Lenexa	KS	66214	913-383-2999	383-2949
Barrett Business Services Inc 8100 NE Pkwy Dr Suite 200 *NASDAQ: BBSI* ■ *TF:* 800-494-5669 ■ *Web:* www.barrettbusiness.com	Vancouver	WA	98662	360-828-0700	828-0701
Beacon Hill Staffing Group LLC 152 Bowdoin St *Web:* www.beaconhillsg.com	Boston	MA	02108	617-326-4000	227-1220
Bowles Group of Cos 1903 Central Dr Suite 200 *TF:* 800-522-9778 ■ *Web:* www.workforcepeo.com	Bedford	TX	76021	817-868-7277	868-7210
Burnett Cos Consolidated Inc 9800 Richmond Ave Suite 800 *Web:* www.burnettstaffing.com	Houston	TX	77042	713-977-4777	977-7533
Century II Staffing Inc 278 Franklin Rd Suite 350 *TF:* 800-972-9630 ■ *Web:* www.centuryii.net	Brentwood	TN	37027	615-665-9060	665-1833
Ceridian Corp 3311 E Old Shakopee Rd *TF:* 800-767-4969 ■ *Web:* www.ceridian.com	Minneapolis	MN	55425	952-853-8100	
Chipton-ross Inc 343 Main St *TF:* 800-927-9318 ■ *Web:* www.chiptonross.com	El Segundo	CA	90245	310-414-7800	414-7808
Co-Advantage Resources 111 W Jefferson St Suite 100 *TF:* 888-278-6055 ■ *Web:* www.coadvantage.com	Orlando	FL	32801	407-422-8448	422-4382
Diversified Human Resources Inc 3020 E Camelback Rd Suite 213 **Fax Area Code:* 602 ■ *TF:* 888-870-5588 ■ *Web:* www.dhr.net	Phoenix	AZ	85016	480-941-5588	553-4684*
Doherty Employment Group 7625 Parklawn Ave *TF:* 800-910-8822 ■ *Web:* www.dohertyeg.com	Edina	MN	55435	952-832-8383	832-8371
Employee & Family Resources Inc (EFR) 505 5th Ave Suite 600 *Web:* www.efr.org	Des Moines	IA	50309	515-288-9020	288-4534
Employee Benefits Data Services Inc (EBDS) 420 Fort Duquesne Blvd 1 Gateway Ctr Suite 1250 *TF:* 800-472-2738	Pittsburgh	PA	15222	412-394-6300	394-6300
Employee Management Services 435 Elm St *TF:* 888-651-1536 ■ *Web:* www.emshro.com	Cincinnati	OH	45202	513-651-3244	381-2764
Employee Professionals 6320 Trail Blvd *TF:* 888-592-9700 ■ *Web:* www.employeepro.com	Naples	FL	34108	239-592-9700	592-9100
Employer's Human Resources Inc (EHRI) 75899 State Hwy 16 *TF:* 800-878-0515	Wagoner	OK	74467	918-485-9404	485-9317
G4S PLC 1395 University Blvd **Fax:* Hum Res ■ *Web:* www.g4s.com	Jupiter	FL	33458	561-622-5656	691-6591*
Genesis Consolidated Services Inc 76 Blanchard Rd *TF:* 800-367-8367 ■ *Web:* www.genesis-cos.com	Burlington	MA	01803	781-272-4900	273-6644
HR Affiliates 1930 Bishop Ln # 111 *Web:* www.hraffiliates.com	Louisville	KY	40218	502-485-9675	485-1242
Human Capital 18831 W 12 Mile Rd *TF:* 888-736-9071 ■ *Web:* www.human-capital.com	Southfield	MI	48076	248-353-3444	353-3829
Human Resources Inc 2127 Espey Ct Suite 306 *Web:* www.hri-online.com	Crofton	MD	21114	410-451-4202	451-4206
Iconma Llc 850 Stephenson Hwy Suite 612 **Fax Area Code:* 800 ■ *TF:* 888-451-2519 ■ *Web:* www.iconma.com	Troy	MI	48083	888-451-2519	489-8046*
Jackson Healthcare LLC 2655 Northwinds Pkwy *Web:* www.jacksonhealthcare.com	Alpharetta	GA	30009	770-643-5500	
Lazy Days RV Center Inc 6130 Lazy Days Blvd *TF:* 888-500-5299 ■ *Web:* www.lazydays.com	Seffner	FL	33584	813-246-4999	246-4408
Legacy Engineering LLC 18662 Macarthur Blvd Suite 457 *Web:* www.legacyeng.com	Irvine	CA	92612	949-794-5860	794-5866
Manpower Holding Corp 8170 W Sahara Ave Suite 207 *Web:* www.manpowerlv.com	Las Vegas	NV	89117	702-363-2626	363-0461
Marvel Consultants Inc 28601 Chagrin Blvd Suite 210 *TF:* 800-338-1257 ■ *Web:* www.marvelconsultants.com	Cleveland	OH	44122	216-292-2855	292-7207
Merit Resources Inc 4165 120th St *TF:* 800-336-1931 ■ *Web:* www.meritresources.com	Des Moines	IA	50323	515-278-1931	276-3813
Miss Paige Ltd 8430 W Bryn Mawr Suite 625 *Web:* www.paigepersonnel.com	Chicago	IL	60631	773-693-0480	693-0481
Mitchell Martin Inc 307 W 38th St Suite 1305 *Web:* www.mitchellmartin.com	New York	NY	10018	212-943-1404	943-0041
Moresource Inc 401 Vandiver Dr *Web:* www.moresource-inc.com	Columbia	MO	65202	573-443-1234	441-1225
Mountain Ltd 19 Yarmouth Dr Suite 301 *TF:* 800-322-8627 ■ *Web:* www.mountainltd.com	New Gloucester	ME	04260	207-688-6200	688-6212
NESCO Inc Service Group 6140 Parkland Blvd	Mayfield Heights	OH	44124	440-461-6000	449-3111
Netpixel Inc 370 7th Ave Suite 422 *Web:* www.netpixel.com	New York	NY	10001	212-279-1550	279-1556
Oasis Outsourcing Inc 2054 vista Pkwy Suite 300 *TF:* 800-627-4735 ■ *Web:* www.oasisoutsourcing.com	West Palm Beach	FL	33411	888-627-4735	274-4419
Odyssey OneSource Inc 204 N Ector Dr *TF:* 866-508-7361 ■ *Web:* www.odysseyonesource.com	Euless	TX	76039	817-267-6090	508-7362
Pay Plus Benefits Inc 1110 N Ctr Pkwy Suite B *TF:* 888-531-5781 ■ *Web:* www.payplusbenefits.com	Kennewick	WA	99336	509-735-1143	735-7668
PaySource Inc 251 New Karner Rd *TF:* 888-452-9743	Albany	NY	12205	518-452-9743	452-0472
PayTech 640 E Purdue Dr Suite 102 *TF:* 866-972-6064 ■ *Web:* www.pay-tech.com	Phoenix	AZ	85020	602-788-1317	971-6022
Pencom Systems Inc 152 Remsen St **Fax Area Code:* 718 ■ *TF:* 800-736-2664 ■ *Web:* www.pencom.com	Brooklyn	NY	11201	212-513-7777	923-6066*
People Lease Inc 689 Town Ctr Blvd Suite B PO Box 3303 *TF:* 800-723-3025 ■ *Web:* www.peoplelease.com	Ridgeland	MS	39158	601-987-3025	987-3029
Personnel Management Inc PO Box 6657 *TF:* 800-259-4126 ■ *Web:* www.pmiresource.com	Shreveport	LA	71136	318-869-4555	841-4350
Professional Group Plans Inc (PGP) 225 Wireless Blvd Suite 200 *Web:* www.pgpbenefits.com	Hauppauge	NY	11788	631-951-9200	951-9623
Professional Staff Management Inc 224 S 5th St *TF:* 800-967-5515 ■ *Web:* www.psmin.com	Richmond	IN	47374	765-935-1515	962-6732
Progressive Employer Services 3106 Alternate 19 *TF:* 800-741-7848 ■ *Web:* www.progressiveemployer.com	Palm Harbor	FL	34683	727-712-9121	712-8051
Qualified Resources International LLC 78 Kenwood St *Web:* www.qristaffing.com	Cranston	RI	02907	401-946-0946	946-9205
Recon Management Services Inc 3649 S Beglis Pkwy *TF:* 888-301-4662 ■ *Web:* www.recon-group.com	Sulphur	LA	70665	337-583-4662	583-7565
Reserves Network The 22021 Brookpark Rd *TF:* 866-876-2020 ■ *Web:* www.trnstaffing.com	Fairview Park	OH	44126	440-779-1400	779-1493
Resource Management Inc 281 Main St Suite 5 *TF Cust Svc:* 800-508-0048 ■ *Web:* www.rmi-solutions.com	Fitchburg	MA	01420	978-343-6018	343-0719
Response Personnel Inc 23 E 39th St *Web:* www.responseco.com	New York	NY	10016	212-983-8870	983-9492
RMPersonnel Inc 4707 Montana Ave *Web:* www.rmpersonnel.com	El Paso	TX	79903	915-565-7674	565-7687
Rwr Enterprises Inc 24 Greenway Plaza *TF:* 800-364-7979 ■ *Web:* www.rwr.com	Houston	TX	77046	713-629-6681	627-1736
Sequent Inc 4700 Lakehurst Ct Suite 200 **Fax Area Code:* 888 ■ *TF:* 888-456-3627 ■ *Web:* www.sequent.biz	Columbus	OH	43235	614-436-5880	456-3627*
Staff Management Inc 5919 Spring Creek Rd *TF:* 800-535-3518 ■ *Web:* www.staffmgmt.com	Rockford	IL	61114	815-282-3900	282-0826

				Phone	Fax
Staff One Inc 8111 LBJ Fwy *TF:* 800-771-7823 ■ *Web:* www.staffone.com	Dallas	TX	75251	580-920-1212	920-0863
Staff Resources Inc 870 Manzanita Ct Suite A *TF Sales:* 888-835-5774 ■ *Web:* www.staffresources.com	Chico	CA	95926	530-345-2487	894-8767
Staffing Plus 7425 ganes Ave Suite 201 *TF:* 800-782-3346 ■ *Web:* www.staffingplus.com	wood ridge	IL	60517	630-515-0500	515-0510
Strategic Outsourcing Inc 5260 PkwyPlaza Blvd Suite 140 *TF:* 800-426-1121 ■ *Web:* www.soi.net	Charlotte	NC	28217	704-523-2191	523-2158
Strom Aviation Inc 109 S Elm St *Web:* www.stromaviation.com	Waconia	MN	55387	952-544-3611	544-3948
Summit Technical Services Inc 355 Centerville Rd *TF:* 800-643-7372 ■ *Web:* www.summit-technical.com	Warwick	RI	02886	401-736-8323	738-3341
TekPartners 5810 Coral Ridge Dr Suite 250 *Web:* www.tekpartners.com	Coral Springs	FL	33076	954-656-8600	282-6070
TeleSearch Staffing Solutions 251 Re 206 *TF:* 800-499-8367 ■ *Web:* www.telesearchstaffing.com	Flanders	NJ	07836	973-927-7870	927-7880
Tilson HR Inc 1530 American Way # 200 *TF:* 800-276-3976 ■ *Web:* www.tilsonhr.com	Greenwood	IN	46143	317-885-3838	807-1039
Training Assoc Corp The 289 Tpke Rd *TF:* 800-241-8868 ■ *Web:* www.thetrainingassociates.com	Westborough	MA	01581	508-890-8500	890-8658
TriNet Group Inc 1100 San Leandro Blvd Suite 300 *TF:* 800-638-0461 ■ *Web:* www.trinet.com	San Leandro	CA	94577	510-352-5000	352-6480

635 PUBLIC BROADCASTING ORGANIZATIONS

SEE ALSO Radio Networks p. 2478; Television Networks - Broadcast p. 2689

				Phone	Fax
Alabama Educational Television Commission 2112 11th Ave S Suite 400 *TF:* 800-239-5233 ■ *Web:* www.aptv.org	Birmingham	AL	35205	205-328-8756	251-2192
Alabama Public Television (APT) 2112 11th Ave S Suite 400 *TF:* 800-239-5233 ■ *Web:* www.aptv.org	Birmingham	AL	35205	205-328-8756	251-2192
Alaska One PO Box 755620 *TF:* 800-727-6543 ■ *Web:* www.alaskaone.org	Fairbanks	AK	99775	907-474-7491	474-5064
Alaska Public Broadcasting Inc 135 Cordova St *Web:* www.akpb.org	Anchorage	AK	99520	907-277-6300	586-5692
American Public Television (APT) 55 Summer St 4th Fl *Web:* www.aptvs.org	Boston	MA	02110	617-338-4455	338-5369
Annenberg Media c/o Learner Online 1301 Pennsylvania Ave NW Suite 302 *TF:* 800-532-7637 ■ *Web:* www.learner.org	Washington	DC	20004	202-783-0500	783-0333
Arkansas Educational Television Network (AETN) 350 S Donaghey Ave *TF:* 800-662-2386 ■ *Web:* www.aetn.org	Conway	AR	72034	501-682-2386	682-4122
Assn of Independents in Radio (AIR) 42 Charles St 2nd Fl *Web:* www.airmedia.org	Dorchester	MA	02125	617-825-4400	
Assn of Minnesota Public & Educational Radio Stations 525 Park St Suite 310 *Web:* www.ampers.org	Saint Paul	MN	55103	651-293-0229	293-1709
Assn of Public Television Stations (APTS) 2100 Crystal Dr Suite 700 *Web:* www.apts.org	Arlington	VA	22202	202-654-4200	654-4236
BBC Worldwide Americas 747 3rd Ave *TF:* 800-888-4741 ■ *Web:* www.bbcworldwide.com	New York	NY	10017	212-705-9300	888-0576
Blue Ridge Public Television 1215 McNeil Dr *TF:* 888-332-7788 ■ *Web:* www.blueridgepbs.org	Roanoke	VA	24015	540-344-0991	344-2148
Boise State Radio 1910 University Dr *TF:* 888-859-5278 ■ *Web:* www.radio.boisestate.edu	Boise	ID	83725	208-426-3663	344-6631
California Public Radio 4100 Vachell Ln *Web:* www.kcbx.org	San Luis Obispo	CA	93401	805-781-3020	781-3025
Capitol Steps Productions Inc 210 N Washington St *TF:* 800-733-7837 ■ *Web:* www.capsteps.com	Alexandria	VA	22314	703-683-8330	
Commonwealth Club of California 595 Market St 2nd Fl *TF:* 800-933-7548 ■ *Web:* www.commonwealthclub.org	San Francisco	CA	94105	415-597-6700	597-6729
Commonwealth Public Broadcasting 23 Sesame St *Web:* www.ideastations.org	Richmond	VA	23235	804-320-1301	320-8729
Connecticut Public Broadcasting Inc (CPBI) 1049 Asylum Ave *TF:* 800-683-2112 ■ *Web:* www.cpbn.org	Hartford	CT	06105	860-278-5310	244-9624
Corporation for Public Broadcasting (CPB) 401 9th St NW *TF:* 800-272-2190 ■ *Web:* www.cpb.org	Washington	DC	20004	202-879-9600	879-9700
Development Exchange Inc (DEI) 1645 Hennepin Ave # 312 *TF:* 888-454-2314 ■ *Web:* www.deiworksite.org	Minneapolis	MN	55403	612-677-1505	677-1508
East Tennessee Public Communications Corp 1611 E Magnolia Ave *TF:* 800-595-0220 ■ *Web:* www.easttennesseepbs.org	Knoxville	TN	37917	865-595-0220	595-0300
Empresas Bechara Inc Bldg Business Bechara Ave Santa Teresa Journet S 637 PO Box 1194 *Web:* www.empresasbechara.com	Mayaguez	PR	00680	787-834-6666	834-8380
eTech Ohio Commission 2470 N Star Rd *Web:* www.etech.ohio.gov/about-us	Columbus	OH	43221	614-644-1714	644-3112
Florida Public Radio Network (FPRN) 1600 Red Barber Plaza *Web:* www.fsu.edu/wfsu_fm/fpr/index.htm	Tallahassee	FL	32310	850-487-3194	487-3293
Georgia Public Broadcasting (GPB) 260 14th St NW *TF:* 800-222-4788 ■ *Web:* www.gpb.org	Atlanta	GA	30318	404-685-4788	685-2431
GPB Education 260 14th St NW *TF:* 888-501-8960 ■ *Web:* www.gpb.org	Atlanta	GA	30318	404-685-2550	685-2556
Hawaii Public Television 2350 Dole St *TF:* 800-238-4847 ■ *Web:* www.pbshawaii.org	Honolulu	HI	96822	808-973-1000	973-1090
Idaho Public Television (IPTV) 1455 N Orchard St *TF:* 800-543-6868 ■ *Web:* www.idptv.state.id.us	Boise	ID	83706	208-373-7220	373-7245
Independent Television Service (ITVS) 651 Brannan St Suite 410 *Web:* www.itvs.org	San Francisco	CA	94107	415-356-8383	356-8391
Indiana Higher Education Telecommunication System (IHETS) 714 N Senate Ave Rm 0100 *TF:* 800-776-4438 ■ *Web:* www.ihets.org	Indianapolis	IN	46202	317-263-8900	263-8831
Indiana Public Broadcasting Stations Inc Ball State University Telecommunications Dept *Web:* www.ipbs.org	Muncie	IN	47306	765-285-2466	285-1490
Iowa Public Television (IPTV) 6450 Corporate Dr PO Box 6450 *TF:* 800-532-1290 ■ *Web:* www.iptv.org	Johnston	IA	50131	515-242-3100	242-5830
Kentucky Educational Television (KET) 600 Cooper Dr *TF:* 800-432-0951 ■ *Web:* www.ket.org	Lexington	KY	40502	859-258-7000	258-7399
Louisiana Educational Television Authority 7733 Perkins Rd *TF:* 800-272-8161	Baton Rouge	LA	70810	225-767-5660	767-4299
Louisiana Public Broadcasting (LPB) 7733 Perkins Rd *TF:* 800-272-8161 ■ *Web:* www.beta.lpb.org	Baton Rouge	LA	70810	225-767-5660	767-4288
Maine Public Broadcasting Network (MPBN) 65 Texas Ave *TF:* 800-884-1717 ■ *Web:* www.mpbn.net	Bangor	ME	04401	207-941-1010	942-2857
Maryland Public Television (MPT) 11767 Owings Mills Blvd *TF:* 800-223-3678 ■ *Web:* www.mpt.org	Owings Mills	MD	21117	410-356-5600	581-4338
Metropolitan Indianapolis Public Broadcasting Corp 1401 N Meridian St *Web:* www.wfyi.org	Indianapolis	IN	46202	317-636-2020	633-7418
Michigan Public Media 535 W William St Suite 110 *Web:* www.michiganradio.org	Ann Arbor	MI	48103	734-764-9210	647-3348
Minnesota Public Radio (MPR) 480 Cedar St *TF:* 800-228-7123 ■ *Web:* www.minnesota.publicradio.org	Saint Paul	MN	55101	651-290-1212	290-1260
Mississippi Public Broadcasting 3825 Ridgewood Rd *TF:* 800-922-9698 ■ *Web:* www.etv.state.ms.us	Jackson	MS	39211	601-432-6565	432-6311
Montana Public Radio 32 Campus Dr University of Montana *TF:* 800-325-1565 ■ *Web:* www.mtpr.org	Missoula	MT	59812	406-243-4931	243-3299
Montana Public Television PO Box 173340 *TF:* 800-426-8243 ■ *Web:* www.montanapbs.org	Bozeman	MT	59717	406-994-3437	994-6545
National Captioning Institute Inc (NCI) 1900 Gallows Rd Suite 3000 *Web:* www.ncicap.org	Vienna	VA	22182	703-917-7600	917-9878
National Educational Telecommunications Assn (NETA) 939 S Stadium Rd *Web:* www.netaonline.org	Columbia	SC	29201	803-799-5517	771-4831
National Public Radio (NPR) 635 Massachusetts Ave NW *Web:* www.npr.org	Washington	DC	20001	202-513-3232	513-3329
National Public Radio New York Bureau 11 W 42nd St 19th Fl *Web:* www.npr.org	New York	NY	10036	212-880-3500	
Nebraska Educational Telecommunications (NET) 1800 N 33rd St *TF:* 800-634-6788 ■ *Web:* netdb.unl.edu	Lincoln	NE	68503	402-472-3611	472-1785
New Hampshire Public Television (NHPTV) 268 Mast Rd *TF:* 800-639-8408 ■ *Web:* www.nhptv.org	Durham	NH	03824	603-868-1100	868-7552
New Mexico Commission on Public Broadcasting 2020 Coal Ave SE	Albuquerque	NM	87106	505-242-7163	244-0260
NJN Public Television & Radio PO Box 777 *TF:* 800-792-8645 ■ *Web:* www.njn.net	Trenton	NJ	08625	609-777-5000	633-2912
North Carolina Agency for Public Telecommunications 1316 Mail Service Ctr *Web:* www.ncapt.tv	Raleigh	NC	27699	919-733-6341	715-3569
NPR West 9909 Jefferson Blvd *Web:* www.npr.org	Culver City	CA	90232	310-815-4200	815-4329
Oklahoma Educational TV Authority (OETA) 7403 N Kelley St *TF:* 800-879-6382 ■ *Web:* www.oeta.onenet.net	Oklahoma City	OK	73111	405-848-8501	841-9216
Oregon Public Broadcasting Inc (OPB) 7140 SW Macadam Ave *Web:* www.opb.org	Portland	OR	97219	503-244-9900	293-1919
Pennsylvania Public Television Network (PPTN) 24 NE Dr	Hershey	PA	17033	717-533-6011	533-4236
Prairie Public Broadcasting Inc 207 N 5th St *TF:* 800-359-6900 ■ *Web:* www.prairiepublic.org	Fargo	ND	58102	701-241-6900	239-7650
Public Broadcast Marketing Inc (PBM) 1202 Lexington Ave Suite 307 *Web:* pbmnyc.com	New York	NY	10028	212-688-3530	888-0175
Public Broadcasting Council of Central New York 506 Old Liverpool Rd PO Box 2400 *TF:* 800-451-9269 ■ *Web:* www.wcny.org	Syracuse	NY	13220	315-453-2424	451-8824
Public Broadcasting Northwest Pennsylvania 8425 Peach St *TF:* 800-727-8854 ■ *Web:* www.wqln.org	Erie	PA	16509	814-864-3001	864-4077

Organization	City	State	Zip	Phone	Fax
Public Broadcasting Service (PBS) 2100 Crystal Dr *Web:* www.pbs.org	Arlington	VA	22202	703-739-5000	739-0775
Radio Research Consortium Inc (RRC) PO Box 1309 *Web:* www.rrconline.org	Olney	MD	20830	301-774-6686	774-0976
Rhode Island PBS 50 Pk Ln *TF:* 800-613-8836 ■ *Web:* www.ripbs.org	Providence	RI	02907	401-222-3636	222-3407
Rocky Mountain Public Broadcasting Network (RMPB) 1089 Bannock St *TF:* 800-274-6666 ■ *Web:* www.rmpbs.org	Denver	CO	80204	303-892-6666	620-5600
Small Station Assn KRWG-TV PO Box 30001 MSCPB 22 *Web:* www.krwg.org	Las Cruces	NM	88003	575-646-2222	646-1974
Smoky Hills Public Television (SHPTV) 604 Elm St *Web:* www.shptv.org	Bunker Hill	KS	67626	785-483-6990	483-4605
South Carolina Educational Television Commission (ETV) 1101 George Rogers Blvd *Web:* www.scetv.org	Columbia	SC	29201	803-737-3200	737-3526
South Dakota Public Broadcasting (SDPB) 555 N Dakota St PO Box 5000 *TF:* 800-456-0766 ■ *Web:* www.sdpb.org	Vermillion	SD	57069	605-677-5861	677-5010
Station Resource Group (SRG) 6935 Laurel Ave Suite 202 *Web:* www.srg.org	Takoma Park	MD	20912	301-270-2617	270-2618
Texas Public Radio (TPR) 8401 Datapoint Dr Suite 800 *TF:* 800-622-8977 ■ *Web:* www.tpr.org	San Antonio	TX	78229	210-614-8977	614-8983
ThinkTV 110 S Jefferson St *TF:* 800-247-1614 ■ *Web:* www.thinktv.org	Dayton	OH	45402	937-220-1600	220-1642
TRAC Media Services 3961 E Speedway Blvd Suite 410 *TF:* 888-299-1866 ■ *Web:* www.tracmedia.org	Tucson	AZ	85712	520-299-1866	577-6077
Twin Cities Public Television Inc 172 E 4th St *TF:* 866-229-1300 ■ *Web:* www.tpt.org	Saint Paul	MN	55101	651-222-1717	229-1282
University of North Carolina Center for Public Television (UNC-TV) 10 TW Alexander Dr PO Box 14900 *TF:* 800-906-5050 ■ *Web:* www.unctv.org	Research Triangle Park	NC	27709	919-549-7000	549-7201
Vermont Public Television (VPT) 204 Ethan Allen Ave *TF:* 800-639-7811 ■ *Web:* www.vpt.org	Colchester	VT	05446	802-655-4800	655-6593
WAMC/Northeast Public Radio 318 Central Ave *TF:* 800-323-9262 ■ *Web:* www.wamc.org	Albany	NY	12206	518-465-5233	432-6974
West Central Illinois Educational Telecommunications Corp PO Box 6248 *TF:* 800-232-3605 ■ *Web:* www.networkknowledge.tv	Springfield	IL	62708	217-483-7887	483-1112
West Tennessee Public Television Council Inc PO Box 966 *TF:* 800-366-9558 ■ *Web:* www.wljt.org	Martin	TN	38237	731-881-7561	881-7566
WGBH Educational Foundation 1 Guest St Brighton Landing *Web:* www.wgbh.org	Boston	MA	02135	617-300-2000	300-1026
Wisconsin Educational Communications Board 3319 W Beltline Hwy *Web:* www.ecb.org	Madison	WI	53713	608-264-9600	264-9622
Wisconsin Public Radio (WPR) 821 University Ave *TF:* 800-747-7444 ■ *Web:* www.wpr.org	Madison	WI	53706	608-263-2121	263-9763
Wisconsin Public Television (WPT) 821 University Ave *TF:* 800-422-9707 ■ *Web:* www.wpt.org	Madison	WI	53706	608-263-2121	263-9763
Wyoming Public Television 2660 Peck Ave *TF:* 800-495-9788 ■ *Web:* www.wyoptv.org	Riverton	WY	82501	307-856-6944	856-3893

636 PUBLIC INTEREST RESEARCH GROUPS (PIRGS) - STATE

SEE ALSO Consumer Interest Organizations p. 1421

Organization	City	State	Zip	Phone	Fax
Alaska Public Interest Research Group (AkPIRG) 737 W 5th Ave # 206 *Web:* www.akpirg.org	Anchorage	AK	99501	907-278-3661	278-9300
California Public Interest Research Group (CAPIRG) 1107 9th St Suite 601 *Web:* www.calpirg.org	Sacramento	CA	95814	916-448-4516	448-4560
Colorado Public Interest Research Group (COPIRG) 1536 Wynkoop St Suite 10-D *Web:* www.copirg.org	Denver	CO	80202	303-573-7474	573-3780
Connecticut Public Interest Research Group (CONNPIRG) 198 Pk Rd 2nd Fl *Web:* www.connpirg.org	West Hartford	CT	06119	860-233-7554	233-7574
Florida Public Interest Research Group 926 E Pk Ave *Web:* www.floridapirg.org	Tallahassee	FL	32301	850-224-3321	224-1310
Georgia Public Interest Research Group 1447 Peachtree St NE Suite 304 *Web:* www.georgiapirg.org	Atlanta	GA	30309	404-892-3573	892-5201
Indiana Student Public Interest Research Group (INPIRG) IMU Rm 470A Indiana University *Web:* www.inpirg.org	Bloomington	IN	47405	812-856-4128	
Iowa Public Interest Research Group 3209 Ingersoll Ave *Web:* www.iowapirg.org	Des Moines	IA	50312	515-282-4193	282-4196
Maryland Public Interest Research Group (MaryPIRG) 3121 St Paul St Suite 26 *Web:* www.marylandpirg.org	Baltimore	MD	21218	410-467-0439	366-2051
Massachusetts Public Interest Research Group (MASSPIRG) 44 Winter St 4th Fl *Web:* www.masspirg.org	Boston	MA	02108	617-292-4800	292-4800
Montana Public Interest Research Group (MontPIRG) 360 Corbin Hall *Web:* www.montpirg.org	Missoula	MT	59812	406-243-2908	243-2910
New Hampshire Public Interest Research Group (NHPIRG) 80 N Main St *Web:* www.nhpirg.org	Concord	NH	03301	603-229-3222	229-3221
New Mexico Public Interest Research Group (NMPIRG) 135 Harvard Dr SE *Web:* www.nmpirg.org	Albuquerque	NM	87106	505-254-1244	254-2280
New York Public Interest Research Group (NYPIRG) 9 Murray St *Web:* www.nypirg.org	New York	NY	10007	212-349-6460	349-1366
North Carolina Public Interest Research Group (NCPIRG) 112 S Blount St *Web:* www.ncpirg.org	Raleigh	NC	27601	919-833-2070	839-0767
Oregon State Public Interest Research Group (OSPIRG) 1536 SE 11th Ave *Web:* www.ospirg.org	Portland	OR	97214	503-231-4181	231-4007
Pennsylvania Public Interest Research Group (PennPIRG) 1420 Walnut St Suite 650 *Web:* www.pennpirg.org	Philadelphia	PA	19107	215-732-3747	732-4599
Public Interest Research Group In Michigan (PIRGIM) 103 E Liberty St Suite 202 *Web:* www.pirgim.org	Ann Arbor	MI	48104	734-662-6597	662-8393
Rhode Island Public Interest Research Group (RIPIRG) 298 W Exchange St *Web:* www.ripirg.org	Providence	RI	02903	401-421-6578	
Texas Public Interest Research Group (TexPIRG) 700 W Ave *Web:* www.texpirg.org	Austin	TX	78701	512-479-7287	479-0400
US Public Interest Research Group (US PIRG) 218 D St SE *Web:* www.uspirg.org	Washington	DC	20003	202-546-9707	546-2461
Vermont Public Interest Research Group (VPIRG) 141 Main St Suite 6 *Web:* www.vpirg.org	Montpelier	VT	05602	802-223-5221	223-6855
Washington State Public Interest Research Group (WashPIRG) 3240 Eastlake Ave E Suite 100 *Web:* www.washpirg.org	Seattle	WA	98102	206-568-2850	568-2858
Wisconsin Public Interest Research Group (WISPIRG) 210 N Bassett St Suite 200 *Web:* www.wispirg.org	Madison	WI	53703	608-251-1918	287-0865

637 PUBLIC POLICY RESEARCH CENTERS

Organization	City	State	Zip	Phone	Fax
A Alfred Taubman Center for State & Local Government Harvard Univ John F Kennedy School of Government 79 JFK St *Web:* www.hks.harvard.edu/centers/taubman	Cambridge	MA	02138	617-495-2199	496-1722
AARP Public Policy Institute 601 E St NW *TF:* 888-687-2277 ■ *Web:* www.aarp.org/ppi	Washington	DC	20049	202-434-2277	434-7599
Acton Institute for the Study of Religion & Liberty 161 Ottawa Ave NW Suite 301 *TF:* 800-345-2286 ■ *Web:* www.acton.org	Grand Rapids	MI	49503	616-454-3080	454-9454
Allegheny Institute for Public Policy 305 Mt Lebanon Blvd Suite 208 *Web:* www.alleghenyinstitute.org	Pittsburgh	PA	15234	412-440-0079	440-0085
American Assembly 475 Riverside Dr Suite 456 *Web:* www.americanassembly.org	New York	NY	10115	212-870-3500	870-3555
American Enterprise Institute for Public Policy Research (AEI) 1150 17th St NW Suite 1100 *TF:* 800-862-5801 ■ *Web:* www.aei.org	Washington	DC	20036	202-862-5800	862-7177
Ashbrook Ctr 401 College Ave Ashland University *TF:* 877-289-5411 ■ *Web:* www.ashbrook.org	Ashland	OH	44805	419-289-5411	289-5425
Aspen Institute 1 DuPont Cir NW Suite 700 *Web:* www.aspeninstitute.org	Washington	DC	20036	202-736-5800	467-0790
Atlantic Council of the United States 1101 15th St NW 11th Fl *Web:* www.acus.org	Washington	DC	20005	202-463-7226	463-7241
Belfer Center for Science & International Affairs (BCSIA) Harvard Univ John F Kennedy School of Government 79 JFK St *Web:* www.belfercenter.ksg.harvard.edu	Cambridge	MA	02138	617-495-1400	495-8963
Benton Foundation 1625 K St NW 11th Fl *Web:* www.benton.org	Washington	DC	20006	202-638-5770	638-5771
Berkeley Roundtable on the International Economy (BRIE) Univ of California Berkeley 2234 Piedmont Ave MC 2322 *Web:* www.brie.berkeley.edu	Berkeley	CA	94720	510-642-3067	643-6617
Brookings Institution 1775 Massachusetts Ave NW *TF:* 800-275-1447 ■ *Web:* www.brookings.edu	Washington	DC	20036	202-797-6000	797-6004
Capital Research Ctr 1513 16th St NW *TF:* 800-459-3950 ■ *Web:* www.capitalresearch.org	Washington	DC	20036	202-483-6900	483-6902
Carnegie Council for Ethics in International Affairs (CCEIA) Merrill House 170 E 64th St *Web:* www.carnegiecouncil.org	New York	NY	10065	212-838-4120	752-2432
Carnegie Endowment for International Peace 1779 Massachusetts Ave NW *Web:* www.carnegieendowment.org	Washington	DC	20036	202-483-7600	483-1840
Carr Center for Human Rights Policy Harvard Univ John F Kennedy School of Government 79 JFK St *Web:* www.hks.harvard.edu/cchrp	Cambridge	MA	02138	617-495-5819	495-4297
Carter Ctr 1 Copenhill Ave 453 Freedom Pkwy *Web:* www.cartercenter.org	Atlanta	GA	30307	404-331-3900	331-0283
Cascade Policy Institute 4850 SW Scholls Ferry Rd # 103 *Web:* www.cascadepolicy.org	Portland	OR	97225	503-242-0900	242-3822
Cato Institute 1000 Massachusetts Ave NW *Web:* www.cato.org	Washington	DC	20001	202-842-0200	842-3490

Phone | Fax

Center for American Progress
1333 H St NW 10th Fl. Washington DC 20005 202-682-1611 682-1867
Web: www.americanprogress.org

Center for Animals & Public Policy
Tufts Univ School of Veterinary Medicine
200 Westboro Rd North Grafton MA 01536 508-839-7920 839-2953
Web: www.tufts.edu/vet/cfa

Center for Arts & Culture
4350 N Fairfax Dr Suite 740 Arlington VA 22203 703-248-0430 248-0414
Web: www.culturalpolicy.org

Center for Business & Government
Harvard Univ John F Kennedy School of Government
Weil Hall 79 JFK St. Cambridge MA 02138 617-496-0587 496-6104
Web: www.ksg.harvard.edu/cbg

Center for Cognitive Liberty & Ethics
PO Box 73481 Davis CA 95617 530-750-7912
Web: www.cognitiveliberty.org

Center for Defense Information
1779 Massachusetts Ave NW Suite 615 Washington DC 20036 202-332-0600 462-4559
Web: www.cdi.org

Center for Equal Opportunity (CEO)
14 Pidgeon Hill Dr Suite 500 Sterling VA 20165 703-421-5443 421-6401
TF: 800-819-2343 ■ *Web:* www.ceousa.org

Center for Immigration Studies
1522 K St NW Suite 820 Washington DC 20005 202-466-8185 466-8076
Web: www.cis.org

Center for International Development at Harvard University (CID)
Harvard Univ John F Kennedy School of Government
1 Eliot St Bldg 79 JFK St Cambridge MA 02138 617-495-4112 496-8753
Web: www.hks.harvard.edu/centers/cid

Center for International Private Enterprise
1155 15th St NW Suite 700 Washington DC 20005 202-721-9200 721-9250
Web: www.cipe.org

Center for Law & Social Policy (CLASP)
1015 15th St NW Suite 400 Washington DC 20005 202-906-8000 842-2885
Web: www.clasp.org

Center for Mathematical Studies in Economics & Management Sciences
Northwestern University
2001 Sheridan Rd Leverone Hall Rm 580 Evanston IL 60208 847-491-3527 491-2530
Web: www.kellogg.northwestern.edu/research/math

Center for Media & Public Affairs
2100 L St NW Suite 300 Washington DC 20037 202-223-2942 872-4014
Web: www.cmpa.com

Center for National Policy
1 Massachusetts Ave NW Suite 333 Washington DC 20001 202-682-1800 682-1818
Web: www.centerfornationalpolicy.org

Center for Neighborhood Technology
2125 W N Ave Chicago IL 60647 773-278-4800 278-3840
Web: www.cnt.org

Center for Nonproliferation Studies
460 Pierce St Monterey CA 93940 831-647-4154 647-3519
Web: www.cns.miis.edu

Center for Policy Research
Syracuse University 426 Eggers Hall Syracuse NY 13244 315-443-3114 443-1081
Web: www.maxwell.syr.edu

Center for Public Integrity
910 17th St NW 7th Fl Washington DC 20006 202-466-1300 466-1101
Web: www.iwatchnews.org

Center for Public Leadership
Harvard Univ John F Kennedy School of Government
79 JFK St Cambridge MA 02138 617-496-8866 496-3337
Web: www.centerforpublicleadership.org

Center for Responsive Politics
1101 14th St NW Suite 1030 Washington DC 20005 202-857-0044 857-7809
Web: www.opensecrets.org

Center for Security Policy 1920 L St NW Washington DC 20036 202-835-9077 835-9066
Web: www.centerforsecuritypolicy.org

Center for Strategic & International Studies
1800 K St NW Suite 400 Washington DC 20006 202-887-0200 775-3199
Web: www.csis.org

Center of the American Experiment (CAE)
12 S 6th St 1024 Plymouth Bldg Minneapolis MN 55402 612-338-3605 338-3621
Web: www.amexp.org

Center on Budget & Policy Priorities
820 1st St NE Suite 510 Washington DC 20002 202-408-1080 408-1056
Web: www.cbpp.org

Century Foundation The 41 E 70th St New York NY 10021 212-535-4441 879-9197
Web: www.tcf.org

Chicago Council on Global Affairs The (CCGA)
332 S Michigan Ave Suite 1100 Chicago IL 60604 312-726-3860 821-7555
Web: www.thechicagocouncil.org

Claremont Institute
937 W Foothill Blvd Suite E Claremont CA 91711 909-621-6825 626-8724
Web: www.claremont.org

Committee for Economic Development
2000 L St NW Suite 700 Washington DC 20036 202-296-5860 223-0776
Web: www.ced.org

Commonwealth Institute 186 Hampshire St Cambridge MA 02139 617-547-4474 868-1267
Web: www.comw.org

Consortium for Policy Research in Education (CPRE)
University of Pennsylvania
3440 Market St Suite 560 Philadelphia PA 19104 215-573-0700 573-7914
Web: www.cpre.org

Council for Excellence in Government
1301 K St NW Suite 450 W Washington DC 20005 202-728-0418 728-0422
Web: www.excelgov.org

Council on Foreign Relations Inc
Harold Pratt House 58 E 68th St New York NY 10021 212-434-9400 434-9800
Web: www.cfr.org

Discovery Institute 208 Columbia St Seattle WA 98104 206-292-0401 682-5320
Web: www.discovery.org

Phone | Fax

Earth Policy Institute
1350 Connecticut Ave NW Suite 403 Washington DC 20036 202-496-9290 496-9325
Web: www.earth-policy.org

EastWest Institute (EWI) 1 E 26th St 20th Fl New York NY 10010 212-824-4100 824-4149
Web: www.ewi.info

Economic Policy Institute
1333 H St NW Suite 300 E Tower Washington DC 20005 202-775-8810 775-0819
Web: www.epi.org

Economic Strategy Institute
3050 K St NW Suite 220 Washington DC 20007 202-965-9484 965-1104
Web: www.econstrat.org

Employee Benefit Research Institute (EBRI)
1100 13th St NW Suite 878 Washington DC 20005 202-659-0670 775-6312
Web: www.ebri.org

Employment Policies Institute
1090 Vermont Ave NW Suite 800 Washington DC 20005 202-463-7650 463-7107
Web: www.epionline.org

Ethics & Public Policy Ctr 1730 M St NW Washington DC 20036 202-682-1200 408-0632
Web: www.eppc.org

Faith & Reason Institute
1413 K St NW Suite 1000 Washington DC 20005 202-289-8775 289-2502
Web: www.frinstitute.org

Food & Agricultural Policy Research Institute (FAPRI)
Iowa State University 578 Heady Hall Ames IA 50011 515-294-1183 294-6336
Web: www.fapri.iastate.edu

Foreign Policy Institute
Johns Hopkins Univ
1619 Massachusetts Ave NW Washington DC 20036 202-663-5773 663-5769
Web: www.sais-jhu.edu

Foreign Policy Research Institute (FPRI)
1528 Walnut St Suite 610 Philadelphia PA 19102 215-732-3774 732-4401
Web: www.fpri.org

Foundation for Economic Education (FEE)
30 S Broadway Irvington-on-Hudson NY 10533 914-591-7230 591-8910
TF: 800-960-4333 ■ *Web:* www.fee.org

Free Congress Foundation 717 2nd St NE Washington DC 20002 202-546-3000 543-5605
Web: www.freecongress.org

George Mason School of Public Policy
4400 University Dr Fairfax VA 22030 703-993-2280 993-2284
Web: www.policy.gmu.edu

Goldwater Institute 500 E Coronado Rd Phoenix AZ 85004 602-462-5000 256-7045
Web: www.goldwaterinstitute.org

Hauser Center for Nonprofit Organizations
Harvard Univ John F Kennedy School of Government
79 JFK St Cambridge MA 02138 617-496-5675 495-0996
Web: www.hks.harvard.edu/hauser

Heartland Institute 19 S LaSalle St Suite 903 Chicago IL 60603 312-377-4000 377-5000
Web: www.heartland.org

Heritage Foundation
214 Massachusetts Ave NE Washington DC 20002 202-546-4400 546-8328
TF: 800-546-2843 ■ *Web:* www.heritage.org

Hoover Institution on War Revolution & Peace
Stanford University 434 Galvez Mall Stanford CA 94305 650-723-1754 723-1687
TF: 877-466-8374 ■ *Web:* www.hoover.org

Hudson Institute 1015 15th St NW Suite 600 Washington DC 20005 202-974-2400 974-2410
TF: 800-483-7660 ■ *Web:* www.hudson.org

Independent Institute 100 Swan Way Oakland CA 94621 510-632-1366 568-6040
TF: 800-927-8733 ■ *Web:* www.independent.org

Institute for Food & Development Policy
398 60th St Oakland CA 94618 510-654-4400 654-4551
Web: www.foodfirst.org

Institute for Foreign Policy Analysis Inc
675 Massachusetts Ave 10th Fl Cambridge MA 02139 617-492-2116 492-8242
Web: www.ifpa.org

Institute for Health Policy Studies
University of California San Francisco
PO Box 0534 San Francisco CA 94118 415-476-4921 476-0705

Institute for Humane Studies
3301 N Fairfax Dr Suite 440 Arlington VA 22201 703-993-4880 993-4890
TF: 800-697-8799 ■ *Web:* www.theihs.org

Institute for International Economics
1750 Massachusetts Ave NW Washington DC 20036 202-328-9000 328-5432
Web: www.iie.com

Institute for Justice
901 N Glebe Rd Suite 900 Arlington VA 22203 703-682-9320 682-9321
Web: www.ij.org

Institute for Philosophy & Public Policy
Maryland School of Public Policy
3111 Van Munching Hall College Park MD 20742 301-405-4753 314-9346
Web: www.puaf.umd.edu/IPPP

Institute for Policy Studies (IPS)
1112 16th St NW Suite 600 Washington DC 20036 202-234-9382 387-7915
Web: www.ips-dc.org

Institute for Research on the Economics of Taxation (IRET)
1710 Rhode Island Ave NW 11th Fl Washington DC 20036 202-463-1400 463-6199
Web: www.iret.org

Institute for the Future
124 University Ave Palo Alto CA 94301 650-854-6322 854-7850
Web: www.iftf.org

Institute for the North 935 W 3rd Ave Anchorage AK 99501 907-343-2444 343-2466
Web: www.institutenorth.org

Institute of Government & Public Affairs
Univ of Illinois 1007 W Nevada St Urbana IL 61801 217-333-3340 244-4817
TF: 866-794-3340 ■ *Web:* www.igpa.uiuc.edu

Institute of World Politics
1521 16th St NW Washington DC 20036 202-462-2101 464-0335
TF: 888-566-9497 ■ *Web:* www.iwp.edu

Institute on Education & the Economy
525 W 120th St # 439 New York NY 10027 212-678-3091 678-3699
Web: www.tc.columbia.edu

Inter-American Dialogue
1211 Connecticut Ave NW Suite 510 Washington DC 20036 202-822-9002 822-9553
Web: www.thedialogue.org

	City	State	Zip	Phone	Fax
International Center for Alcohol Policies (ICAP) 1519 New Hampshire Ave NW *Web:* www.icap.org	Washington	DC	20036	202-986-1159	986-2080
International Food Policy Research Institute (IFPRI) 2033 K St NW *Web:* www.ifpri.org	Washington	DC	20006	202-862-5600	467-4439
Joan Shorenstein Center on the Press Politics & Public Policy Harvard Univ John F Kennedy School of Government 79 John F Kennedy St *Web:* www.hks.harvard.edu/presspol	Cambridge	MA	02138	617-495-8269	495-8696
Joint Center for Housing Studies 1033 Massachusetts Ave *Web:* www.jchs.harvard.edu	Cambridge	MA	02138	617-495-7908	496-9957
Joint Center for Political & Economic Studies 1090 Vermont Ave NW Suite 1100 *Web:* www.jointcenter.org	Washington	DC	20005	202-789-3500	789-6385
Keystone Ctr 1628 St John Rd *Web:* www.keystone.org	Keystone	CO	80435	970-513-5800	262-0152
Leon & Sylvia Panetta Institute for Public Policy California State University Monterey Bay 100 Campus Ctr Bldg 86E *Web:* www.panettainstitute.org	Seaside	CA	93955	831-582-4200	582-4082
Levy Economics Institute of Bard College Blithewood Rd Bard College *Web:* www.levyinstitute.org	Annandale-on-Hudson	NY	12504	845-758-7700	758-1149
Malcolm Wiener Center for Social Policy John F Kennedy School of Government Harvard University 79 John F Kennedy St *Web:* www.hks.harvard.edu	Cambridge	MA	02138	617-496-4082	496-9053
Manhattan Institute for Policy Research 52 Vanderbilt Ave 3rd Fl *Web:* www.manhattan-institute.org	New York	NY	10017	212-599-7000	599-3494
Manpower Demonstration Research Corp 16 E 34th St 19th Fl *TF:* 800-221-3165 ■ *Web:* www.mdrc.org	New York	NY	10016	212-532-3200	684-0832
Margaret Chase Smith Policy Ctr University of Maine York Complex Suite 4 *Web:* www.umaine.edu	Orono	ME	04469	207-581-1648	581-1266
Mathematica Inc PO Box 2393 *Web:* www.mathematica-mpr.com	Princeton	NJ	08543	609-799-3535	799-0005
Mershon Ctr 1501 Neil Ave *Web:* www.mershoncenter.osu.edu	Columbus	OH	43201	614-292-1681	292-2407
Milken Institute 1250 4th St *Web:* www.milkeninstitute.org	Santa Monica	CA	90401	310-570-4600	570-4601
National Academy on an Aging Society 1220 L St NW Suite 901 *Web:* www.agingsociety.org	Washington	DC	20005	202-408-3375	842-1150
National Center for Policy Analysis 12770 Coit Rd Suite 800 *Web:* www.ncpa.org	Dallas	TX	75251	972-386-6272	386-0924
National Center for Public Policy Research (NCPPR) 501 Capitol Ct NE Suite 200 *Web:* www.nationalcenter.org	Washington	DC	20002	202-543-4110	543-5975
National Center on Institutions & Alternatives 7222 Ambassador Rd *Web:* www.ncianet.org	Baltimore	MD	21244	410-265-1490	597-9656
National Defense Council Foundation (NDCF) 515 King St Suite 315 **Fax Area Code:* 703 ■ *Web:* www.ndcf.org	Alexandria	VA	22314	571-216-1928	807-2073*
Nelson A Rockefeller Institute of Government 411 State St *Web:* www.rockinst.org	Albany	NY	12203	518-443-5522	443-5788
New America Foundation 1899 L St NW *Web:* www.newamerica.net	Washington	DC	20036	202-986-2700	986-3696
Nixon Ctr 1615 L St NW Suite 1250 *Web:* www.nixoncenter.org	Washington	DC	20036	202-887-1000	887-5222
Northeast-Midwest Institute (NMI) 50 F St NW Suite 950 *Web:* www.nemw.org	Washington	DC	20001	202-544-5200	544-0043
Pacific Research Institute for Public Policy (PRI) 1 Embarcadero Ctr *Web:* www.pacificresearch.org	San Francisco	CA	94111	415-989-0833	989-2411
Pepper Institute on Aging & Public Policy Florida State Univ 207 Pepper Ctr 636 W Call St *Web:* www.pepperinstitute.org	Tallahassee	FL	32306	850-644-2831	644-2304
Phoenix Center for Advanced Legal & Economic Public Policy Studies 5335 Wisconsin Ave NW Suite 440 *Web:* www.phoenix-center.org	Washington	DC	20015	202-274-0235	244-8257
Princeton Institute for International & Regional Studies (PIIRS) Princeton University Bendheim Hall *Web:* www.princeton.edu/piirs	Princeton	NJ	08544	609-258-4852	258-3988
Progress & Freedom Foundation (PFF) 1444 Eye St NW Suite 500 *Web:* www.pff.org	Washington	DC	20005	202-289-8928	289-6079
Progressive Policy Institute (PPI) 600 Pennsylvania Ave SE Suite 400 *TF:* 800-546-0027 ■ *Web:* www.ppionline.org	Washington	DC	20003	202-547-0001	544-5014
Public Agenda 6 E 39th St *Web:* www.publicagenda.org	New York	NY	10016	212-686-6610	889-3461
RAND Corp 1776 Main St *Web:* www.rand.org	Santa Monica	CA	90401	310-393-0411	393-4818
Reason Public Policy Institute 3415 S Sepulveda Blvd Suite 400 *Web:* www.reason.org	Los Angeles	CA	90034	310-391-2245	391-4395
Renewable Energy Policy Project (REPP) 1612 K St NW Suite 202 *Web:* www.repp.org	Washington	DC	20006	202-293-2898	293-5857
Resources for the Future 1616 P St NW *Web:* www.rff.org	Washington	DC	20036	202-328-5000	939-3460
Robert J Dole Institute of Politics 2350 Petefish Dr *Web:* www.doleinstitute.org	Lawrence	KS	66045	785-864-4900	864-1414
Rockford Institute 928 N Main St *TF:* 800-383-0680 ■ *Web:* www.rockfordinstitute.org	Rockford	IL	61103	815-964-5053	964-9403
Schneider Institute for Health Policy Brandeis University 415 S St *Web:* sihp.brandeis.edu	Waltham	MA	02454	781-736-3964	
Science & Environmental Policy Project 1600 S Eads St Suite 712-S *Web:* www.sepp.org	Arlington	VA	22202	703-920-2744	
Smith Center for Private Enterprise Studies California State Univ E Bay College of Business & Economics *Web:* www.thesmithcenter.org	Hayward	CA	94542	510-885-2640	885-4222
Social Science Research Council (SSRC) 810 7th Ave *Web:* www.ssrc.org	New York	NY	10019	212-377-2700	377-2727
Tellus Institute 11 Arlington St *Web:* www.tellus.org	Boston	MA	02116	617-266-5400	266-8303
Urban Institute 2100 M St NW *Web:* www.urban.org	Washington	DC	20037	202-833-7200	331-9747
Weatherhead Center for International Affairs Harvard Univ 1737 Cambridge St *Web:* www.wcfia.harvard.edu	Cambridge	MA	02138	617-495-4420	495-8292
Winrock International 2101 Riverfront Dr *Web:* www.winrock.org	Little Rock	AR	72202	501-727-5435	280-3090
Woodrow Wilson International Center for Scholars 1 Woodrow Wilson Plaza 1300 Pennsylvania Ave NW *Web:* wilsoncenter.org	Washington	DC	20004	202-691-4000	691-4001
World Policy Institute (WPI) 220 5th Ave 9th Fl *Web:* www.worldpolicy.org	New York	NY	10001	212-481-5005	481-5009
World Resources Institute (WRI) 10 G St NE Suite 800 *Web:* www.wri.org	Washington	DC	20002	202-729-7600	729-7610
Worldwatch Institute 1776 Massachusetts Ave NW *TF:* 877-539-9946 ■ *Web:* www.worldwatch.org	Washington	DC	20036	202-452-1999	296-7365

638 PUBLIC RECORDS SEARCH SERVICES

SEE ALSO Investigative Services p. 2128

	City	State	Zip	Phone	Fax
Accufax 9432 E 51st St **Fax Area Code:* 866 ■ *TF:* 800-256-8898 ■ *Web:* www.accufax-us.com	Tulsa	OK	74153	918-627-2226	936-3027*
All-Search & Inspection Inc 1108 E S Union Ave *TF:* 800-227-3152 ■ *Web:* www.all-search.com	Midvale	UT	84047	801-984-8160	984-8170
American Background Information Services Inc 629 Cedar Creek Grade Suite C *TF:* 800-669-2247 ■ *Web:* www.americanbackground.com	Winchester	VA	22601	540-665-8056	722-4771
American Driving Records Inc 2860 Gold Tailings Ct PO Box 1970 *TF:* 800-766-6877 ■ *Web:* www.mvrs.com	Rancho Cordova	CA	95670	916-456-3200	456-3332
Ameridex Information Systems Inc PO Box 51314 *Web:* www.ameridex.com	Irvine	CA	92619	714-731-2546	
AmRent PO Box 771176 *TF:* 800-324-4595 ■ *Web:* www.amrent.com	Houston	TX	77215	713-266-1870	260-1290
Applicant Insight Ltd PO Box 458 *TF:* 800-771-7703 ■ *Web:* www.ainsight.com	New Port Richey	FL	34656	800-771-7703	890-6454
Apscreen Inc PO Box 80639 **Fax Area Code:* 888 ■ *TF:* 800-277-2733 ■ *Web:* www.apscreen.com	Rancho Santa Margarita	CA	92688	949-646-4003	277-2733*
Background Bureau Inc 2019 Alexandria Pike *TF:* 800-854-3990 ■ *Web:* www.backgroundbureau.com	Highland Heights	KY	41076	859-781-3400	781-9540
Background Information Services Inc 1800 30th St Suite 204 *TF:* 800-433-6010 ■ *Web:* www.bisi.com	Boulder	CO	80301	303-442-3960	442-1004
Barry Shuster Information Services 1157 Tucker Rd **Fax Area Code:* 877 ■ *TF:* 877-852-2507	North Dartmouth	MA	02747	508-999-5436	852-7531*
Best Reports Inc 209 W Jackson Blvd Suite 402 *TF:* 877-452-3781 ■ *Web:* www.bestreports.net	Chicago	IL	60606	312-427-0900	427-0500
Canadian Securities Registration Systems (CSRS) 4126 Norland Ave Suite 200 *TF:* 866-873-9780 ■ *Web:* www.csrs.ca	Burnaby	BC	V5G3S8	604-637-4000	637-4001
Capitol Lien Records & Research Inc 1010 N Dale St *Web:* www.capitollien.com	Saint Paul	MN	55117	651-488-0100	488-0200
Capitol Services Inc 800 Brazos St Suite 1100 *TF:* 800-345-4647 ■ *Web:* www.capitolservices.com	Austin	TX	78701	800-345-4647	432-3622
CARCO Group Inc 5000 Corporate Ct *TF:* 800-645-4556 ■ *Web:* www.carcogroup.com	Holtsville	NY	11742	631-862-9300	584-7094
CCH Washington Service Bureau Inc 1015 15th St NW 10th Fl *TF:* 800-955-5219 ■ *Web:* www.wsb.com	Washington	DC	20005	202-312-6600	962-0152
CDI Credit Inc 6160 Peachtree Dunwoody Rd NE Suite B-210 *TF:* 800-633-3961 ■ *Web:* www.cdicredit.com	Atlanta	GA	30328	770-350-5070	394-2197
Charles Jones Inc PO Box 8488 *TF:* 800-792-8888 ■ *Web:* www.cji.com	Trenton	NJ	08650	609-538-1000	883-0677
Colby Attorneys Service Co Inc 41 State St Suite 106 *TF:* 800-832-1220 ■ *Web:* www.colbyservice.com	Albany	NY	12207	518-463-4426	434-2574
CoreLogic SafeRent 7300 Westmore Rd Suite 3 **Fax Area Code:* 240 ■ *TF:* 800-999-0350 ■ *Web:* www.fadvsaferent.com	Rockville	MD	20850	301-881-8400	715-1212*
CT Corsearch 345 Hudson St **Fax:* Sales ■ *TF:* 800-233-2986 ■ *Web:* www.ctcorsearch.com	New York	NY	10014	917-408-5000	408-5006*
CT Lien Solutions 2727 Allen Pkwy Suite 1000 **Fax Area Code:* 877 ■ *TF:* 800-833-5778 ■ *Web:* www.uccdirect.com	Houston	TX	77019	800-833-5778	850-5194*

Company	City	State	Zip	Phone	Fax
Doc-U-Search Inc 63 Pleasant St PO Box 777	Concord	NH	03301	603-224-2871	224-2794
TF: 800-332-3034 ■ *Web:* www.docusearchinc.com					
Driving Records Facilities PO Box 1086	Glen Burnie	MD	21061	410-761-5510	760-5837
TF: 800-772-5510 ■ *Web:* www.dr-rec-fac.com					
Edge Information Management Inc					
1682 W Hibiscus Blvd	Melbourne	FL	32901	321-722-3343	780-3299*
**Fax Area Code: 800* ■ *TF:* 800-725-3343 ■ *Web:* www.edgeinformation.com					
Employment Screening Services Inc					
627 E Sprague St Suite 100	Spokane	WA	99202	509-624-3851	321-2905*
**Fax Area Code: 800* ■ *TF:* 800-473-7778 ■ *Web:* www.employscreen.com					
Explore Information Services LLC					
2945 Lone Oak Dr Suite 150	Eagan	MN	55121	651-681-4460	681-4476
TF: 800-531-9125 ■ *Web:* www.exploredata.com					
Federal Research Corp					
1023 15th St NW Suite 401	Washington	DC	20005	202-783-2700	783-0145
TF: 800-846-3190 ■ *Web:* www.federalresearch.com					
Fidelifacts 42 Broadway 15th Fl	New York	NY	10004	212-425-1520	248-5619
TF: 800-509-8496 ■ *Web:* www.fidelifacts.com					
Fidelity National Information Solutions Inc					
601 Riverside Ave	Jacksonville	FL	32204	904-854-8100	854-4282
TF: 888-934-3354 ■ *Web:* www.fnis.com					
First Advantage Corp					
100 Carillon Pkwy	Saint Petersburg	FL	33716	866-400-3238	214-3410*
**Fax Area Code: 727* ■ *TF:* 800-321-4473 ■ *Web:* www.fadv.com					
Government Liaison Services Inc (GLS)					
200 N Glebe Rd Suite 321	Arlington	VA	22203	703-524-8200	525-8451
TF: 800-642-6564 ■ *Web:* www.trademarkinfo.com					
HireRight Inc 5151 California Ave	Irvine	CA	74134	949-428-5800	224-6020
TF: 800-400-2761 ■ *Web:* www.hireright.com					
HRPlus 2902 Evergreen Pkwy	Evergreen	CO	80439	303-670-8177	670-8906
TF: 800-827-2479 ■ *Web:* www.hrplus.com					
Human Resource Profile Inc					
8506 Beechmont Ave	Cincinnati	OH	45255	513-388-4300	388-4320
TF: 800-969-4300 ■ *Web:* www.hrprofile.com					
IMI Data Search Inc					
275 E Hillcrest Dr Suite 102	Thousand Oaks	CA	91360	805-495-1149	495-0310
TF: 800-860-7779 ■ *Web:* www.imidatasearch.com					
Information Management Systems Inc					
114 W Main St Suite 202	New Britain	CT	06050	860-229-1119	225-5524
TF: 888-403-8347 ■ *Web:* www.imswebb.com					
InfoTrack Information Services Inc					
111 Deerlake Rd	Deerfield	IL	60015	847-444-1177	274-5594*
**Fax Area Code: 800* ■ *TF:* 800-275-5594 ■ *Web:* www.infotrackinc.com					
Insured Aircraft Title Service Inc					
6449 Denning Ave	Oklahoma City	OK	73169	405-681-6663	681-9299
TF: 800-654-4882 ■ *Web:* www.insuredaircraft.com					
KnowX LLC 730 Peachtree St Suite 700	Atlanta	GA	30303	404-541-0221	541-0244
TF: 877-317-5000 ■ *Web:* www.knowx.com					
Kress Employment screening					
320 Westcott St Suite 108	Houston	TX	77007	713-880-3693	880-3694
TF: 888-636-3693 ■ *Web:* www.kressinc.com					
Kroll Background America Inc					
1900 Church St Suite 300	Nashville	TN	37203	615-320-9800	321-9585
TF: 800-697-7189 ■ *Web:* www.baionline.net					
Laborchex Co The 2506 Lakeland Dr Suite 200	Jackson	MS	39232	601-664-6760	844-2722*
**Fax Area Code: 800* ■ *TF:* 800-880-0366 ■ *Web:* www.laborchex.com					
Legal Data Resources Inc					
2816 W Summerdale Ave	Chicago	IL	60625	773-561-2468	561-2488
TF: 800-735-9207 ■ *Web:* www.ldrsearch.com					
LegalEase Inc 211 E 43rd St # 2203	New York	NY	10017	212-393-9070	393-9796
TF: 800-393-1277 ■ *Web:* www.legaleaseinc.com					
LocatePLUS Inc 100 Cummings Ctr Suite 235M	Beverly	MA	01915	978-921-2727	524-8767
TF: 888-746-3463 ■ *Web:* www.locateplus.com					
Merlin Information Services					
220 S Complex Dr	Kalispell	MT	59901	406-755-8550	755-8568
TF: 800-367-6646 ■ *Web:* www.merlindata.com					
MicroPatent LLC 250 Dodge Ave	East Haven	CT	06512	203-466-5055	466-5054
TF: 800-648-6787 ■ *Web:* www.micropatent.com					
MLQ Attorney Services					
2000 River Edge Pkwy Suite 885	Atlanta	GA	30328	770-984-7007	984-7049
TF: 800-446-8794 ■ *Web:* www.mlqattorneyservices.com					
National Public Records Inc					
4426 Hugh Howell Rd Suite B314	Tucker	GA	30084	770-938-1050	808-8081
Web: www.findtherecord.com					
Nationwide Information Services Inc					
52 James St 5th Fl	Albany	NY	12207	518-449-8429	449-8522
TF: 800-873-3482					
OPENonline 1650 Lake Shore Dr Suite 350	Columbus	OH	43204	614-481-6999	481-6980
TF: 888-381-5656 ■ *Web:* www.openonline.com					
Orange Tree Employment Screening					
7275 Ohms Ln	Minneapolis	MN	55439	952-941-9040	941-9041
TF: 800-886-4777 ■ *Web:* www.orangetreescreening.com					
Pacific Corporate & Title Services					
914 S St	Sacramento	CA	95811	916-558-4988	441-2217
TF: 800-230-4988 ■ *Web:* www.paccorp.com					
Parasec Inc 640 Bercut Dr Suite A	Sacramento	CA	95814	916-441-1001	603-5868*
**Fax Area Code: 800* ■ *TF:* 800-533-7272 ■ *Web:* www.parasec.com					
Penncorp Servicegroup Inc					
600 N 2nd St Suite 401	Harrisburg	PA	17101	717-234-2300	264-1137*
**Fax Area Code: 800* ■ *TF:* 800-544-9050					
Property Owners Exchange Inc					
6630 Baltimore National Pike Suite 208	Baltimore	MD	21228	410-719-0100	719-6715
TF: 800-869-3200 ■ *Web:* www.poeknows.com					
Public Data Corp (PDC) 519 8th Ave Suite 811	New York	NY	10018	212-519-3063	519-3097
Web: www.pdcny.com					
Questel Orbit 1725 Duke St Suite 625	Alexandria	VA	22314	703-519-1820	519-1821
TF: 800-456-7248 ■ *Web:* www.questel.orbit.com					
Quick Search 4155 Buena Vista	Dallas	TX	75204	214-358-2840	358-6057
TF: 800-473-2840 ■ *Web:* www.quicksi.com					
Record Search America Inc 5327 Kendall St	Boise	ID	83706	208-375-1906	322-5469
Rental Research Services Inc					
7525 Mitchell Rd Suite 301	Eden Prairie	MN	55344	952-935-5700	935-9212
TF: 800-328-0333 ■ *Web:* www.rentalresearch.com					
Search Co International					
1535 Grant St Suite 140	Denver	CO	80203	303-863-1800	863-7767
TF: 800-727-2120 ■ *Web:* www.searchcompanyintl.com					
Search Network Ltd					
1503 42nd St Suite 210	West Des Moines	IA	50266	515-223-1153	223-2814
TF: 800-383-5050 ■ *Web:* www.searchnetworkltd.com					
SearchTec Inc 314 N 12th St # 100	Philadelphia	PA	19107	215-963-0888	851-8775
TF: 800-762-5018 ■ *Web:* www.searchtec.com					
Securitech Inc 8230 E Broadway Suite E-10	Tucson	AZ	85710	520-721-0305	721-7706
TF: 800-805-4473 ■ *Web:* www.hiresafe.com					
Security Search & Abstract Co					
111 Presidential Blvd Suite 159	Bala Cynwyd	PA	19004	610-664-5912	343-4294*
**Fax Area Code: 800* ■ *TF:* 800-345-9494 ■ *Web:* www.securitysearchabstract.com					
Sterling Infosystems Inc					
249 W 17th St 6th Fl	New York	NY	10011	212-736-5100	736-0683
TF: 800-899-2272 ■ *Web:* www.sterlinginfosystems.com					
Superior Information Services Inc					
300 Phillips Blvd Suite 500	Trenton	NJ	08618	609-883-7000	883-0677
TF: 800-792-8888 ■ *Web:* www.superiorinfo.com					
TABB Inc PO Box 10	Chester	NJ	07930	908-879-2323	879-8675
TF: 800-887-8222 ■ *Web:* www.tabb.net					
Thomson CompuMark 500 Victory Rd	North Quincy	MA	02171	617-479-1600	786-8273
TF: 800-692-8833 ■ *Web:* www.compumark.thomson.com					
Title First Agency Inc					
555 S Front St Suite 400	Columbus	OH	43215	614-224-9207	224-1423
TF: 800-837-4032 ■ *Web:* www.titlefirst.com					
TML Information Services Inc					
116-55 Queens Blvd Suite 210	Forest Hills	NY	11375	718-793-3737	544-2853
UCC Filing & Search Services Inc					
1574 Village Sq Blvd Suite 100	Tallahassee	FL	32309	850-681-6528	681-6528
Unisearch Inc 1780 Barnes Blvd SW	Tumwater	WA	98512	360-956-9500	531-1717*
**Fax Area Code: 800* ■ *TF:* 800-722-0708 ■ *Web:* www.unisearch.com					
US Search.com Inc					
600 Corporate Pointe Suite 220	Culver City	CA	90230	310-302-6300	822-7898
TF: 877-327-2450 ■ *Web:* www.ussearch.com					
USIS 7799 Leesburg Pike Suite 1100-S	Falls Church	VA	22043	703-448-0178	
TF: 888-270-8978 ■ *Web:* www.usis.com					
Verified Credentials Inc					
20890 Kenbridge Ct	Lakeville	MN	55044	952-985-7200	985-7212
TF: 800-473-4934 ■ *Web:* www.verifiedcredentials.com					
Westlaw Court Express					
1100 13th St NW Suite 300	Washington	DC	20005	877-362-7387	737-2640*
**Fax Area Code: 888* ■ *TF:* 800-916-8493					

639 PUBLIC RELATIONS FIRMS

SEE ALSO Advertising Agencies p. 1370

Company	City	State	Zip	Phone	Fax
Access Communications 101 Howard St	San Francisco	CA	94105	415-904-7070	904-7055
TF: 800-393-7737 ■ *Web:* www.accesspr.com					
Ackermann Public Relations & Marketing					
1111 Northshore Dr Suite N-400	Knoxville	TN	37919	865-584-0550	588-3009
TF: 888-414-7787 ■ *Web:* www.ackermannpr.com					
APCO Worldwide 700 12th St	Washington	DC	20005	202-778-1000	466-6002
Web: www.apcoworldwide.com					
B & B Media Group 109 S Main St	Corsicana	TX	75110	903-872-0517	872-0518
TF: 800-927-0517 ■ *Web:* www.tbbmedia.com					
Bender/Helper Impact					
11500 W Olympic Blvd Suite 655	Los Angeles	CA	90064	310-473-4147	478-4727
Web: www.bhimpact.com					
Bite Communications					
345 Spear St Suite 750	San Francisco	CA	94105	415-365-0222	365-0223
TF: 888-329-7059 ■ *Web:* www.bitepr.com					
Bohle Co					
1900 Avenue of the Stars Suite 200	Los Angeles	CA	90067	310-785-0515	277-2066
Web: www.bohle.com					
Brodeur Worldwide 399 Boylston St	Boston	MA	02116	617-587-2800	587-2828
Web: www.brodeur.com					
Brotman-Winter-Fried Communications					
111 Pk Pl	Falls Church	VA	22046	703-534-4600	536-2255
Web: www.specialevent.com					
Burson-Marsteller 230 Pk Ave S	New York	NY	10003	212-614-4000	598-5320
TF: 800-342-5692 ■ *Web:* www.burson-marsteller.com					
Calysto Communications					
3577 Chamblee Tucker Rd Suite A PO Box 275	Atlanta	GA	30341	404-266-2060	266-2041
Web: www.calysto.com					
Carmichael Lynch Spong 110 N 5th St	Minneapolis	MN	55403	612-334-6000	375-8501
TF: 800-835-9624 ■ *Web:* www.carmichaellynchspong.com					
Cary Francis Group Inc PO Box 321050	Franklin	WI	53132	414-304-6400	
Web: www.thecfg.com					
Cerrell Assoc Inc 320 N Larchmont Blvd	Los Angeles	CA	90004	323-466-3445	466-8653
Web: www.cerrell.com					
Chandler Chicco Agency 450 W 15th St 7th Fl	New York	NY	10011	212-229-8400	229-8496
Web: www.ccapr.com					
Charles Ryan Assoc Inc					
300 Summer St Suite 1100	Charleston	WV	25301	304-342-0161	342-1941
TF: 877-342-0161 ■ *Web:* www.cryanassoc.com					
Cohn & Wolfe 292 Madison Ave 9th Fl	New York	NY	10017	212-798-9700	329-9900
Web: www.cohnwolfe.com					
Cone Inc 855 Boylston St	Boston	MA	02116	617-227-2111	227-2111
TF: 877-531-5578 ■ *Web:* www.coneinc.com					
Connect PR 580 Howard St Suite 204	San Francisco	CA	94105	415-222-9691	222-9694
Web: www.connectpr.com					
Connors Communications 30 W 21st St	New York	NY	10010	212-807-7500	807-7503
Web: www.connors.com					
Cramer-Krasselt 246 E Chicago St	Milwaukee	WI	53202	414-227-3500	
Web: www.c-k.com					

Company	City	State	Zip	Phone	Fax
Creative Entertainment Services Inc 2550 N Hollywood Way *Web:* www.acreativegroup.com	Burbank	CA	91505	818-748-4800	847-8625
CRT/tanaka 101 W Commerce Rd *Web:* www.crt-tanaka.com	Richmond	VA	23224	804-675-8100	675-8183
Dan Klores Communications (DKC) 386 Pk Ave S 10th Fl *Web:* www.dkcnews.com	New York	NY	10016	212-685-4300	685-9024
DeVries Public Relations 30 E 60th St 14th Fl *Web:* www.devries-pr.com	New York	NY	10022	212-891-0400	644-0291
Dix & Eaton Inc 200 Public Sq Suite 1400 *Web:* www.dix-eaton.com	Cleveland	OH	44114	216-241-0405	241-3070
Duffey Communications Inc 3379 Peachtree Rd NE Suite 350 *Web:* www.duffey.com	Atlanta	GA	30326	404-266-2600	262-3198
Dye Van Mol & Lawrence 209 7th Ave N *Web:* www.dvl.com	Nashville	TN	37219	615-244-1818	780-3396
Edelman Public Relations Worldwide 200 E Randolph Dr Suite 6300 *Web:* www.edelman.com	Chicago	IL	60601	312-240-3000	240-2900
Environics Communications Inc 33 Bloor St E Suite 900 *TF:* 888-863-3377 ■ *Web:* www.eci.environics.net	Toronto	ON	M4W3H1	416-920-9000	920-1822
Equals Three Communications 7910 Woodmont Ave Suite 200 *Web:* www.equals3.com	Bethesda	MD	20814	301-656-3100	652-5264
Euro RSCG Magnet 200 Madison Ave # 2 *Web:* www.magnet.com	New York	NY	10016	212-367-6800	367-7154
FD Morgen-Walke 88 Pine St	New York	NY	10005	212-850-5600	850-5790
Fleishman-Hillard Inc 200 N Broadway *Web:* www.fleishmanhillard.com	Saint Louis	MO	63102	314-982-1700	231-2313
French West Vaughan 112 E Hargett St *Web:* www.swv-us.com	Raleigh	NC	27601	919-832-6300	832-8322
Gibbs & Soell Public Relations 60 E 42nd St # 44 *Web:* www.gibbs-soell.com	New York	NY	10165	212-697-2600	697-2646
Golin/Harris International 111 E Wacker Dr 11th Fl *Web:* www.golinharris.com	Chicago	IL	60601	312-729-4000	729-4367
GPC International 100 Queen St *Web:* www.gpcinternational.com	Ottawa	ON	K1P1J9	613-238-2090	238-9380
GS Schwartz & Co Inc 470 Pk Ave S 10th Fl *Web:* www.schwartz.com	New York	NY	10016	212-725-4500	725-9188
Hawthorn Group LC 625 Slaters Ln # 100 *Web:* www.hawthorngroup.com	Alexandria	VA	22314	703-299-4499	299-4488
Hill & Knowlton Inc 825 3rd Ave *Web:* www.hillandknowlton.com	New York	NY	10022	212-885-0300	885-0570
HLB Communications Inc 875 N Michigan Ave Suite 1340 *Web:* www.hlbcomm.com	Chicago	IL	60611	312-649-0371	649-1119
Hoffman Agency 70 N 2nd St *Web:* www.hoffman.com	San Jose	CA	95113	408-286-2611	286-0133
Horn Group Inc 612 Howard St *Web:* www.horngroup.com	San Francisco	CA	94105	415-905-4000	905-4001
Hunter Public Relations 41 Madison Ave 5th Fl *Web:* www.hunterpr.com	New York	NY	10010	212-679-6600	679-6607
IMG Worldwide 767 5th Ave *Web:* www.imgworld.com	New York	NY	10153	646-558-8357	558-8399
Jasculca/Terman & Assoc (JTPR) 730 N Franklin Suite 510 *Web:* www.jtpr.com	Chicago	IL	60654	312-337-7400	337-8189
KCSA Public Relations Worldwide 880 3rd Ave # 6 *Web:* www.kcsa.com	New York	NY	10022	212-682-6300	697-0910
Kemper Lesnik Communications 500 Skokie Blvd Suite 444 *Web:* www.klc.com	Northbrook	IL	60062	847-291-9666	291-0271
Ketchum 1285 Avenue of the Americas *Web:* www.ketchum.com	New York	NY	10019	646-935-3900	935-4499
LaForce & Stevens 132 W 21st St 8th Fl *Web:* www.laforce-stevens.com	New York	NY	10011	212-242-9353	242-9565
Lois Paul & Partners (LPP) 150 Presidential Way *Web:* www.loispaul.com	Woburn	MA	01801	781-782-5000	782-5999
M Booth & Assoc Inc 300 Pk Ave S 12th Fl *Web:* www.mbooth.com	New York	NY	10010	212-481-7000	481-9440
Makovsky & Co Inc 575 Lexington Ave 15th Fl *Web:* www.makovsky.com	New York	NY	10022	212-508-9600	751-9710
Manning Selvage & Lee 1675 Broadway 9th Fl *Web:* www.mslworldwide.com	New York	NY	10019	212-468-4200	
Marx Layne & Co 31420 Northwestern Hwy Suite 100 *Web:* www.marxlayne.com	Farmington Hills	MI	48334	248-855-6777	855-6719
McNeely Pigott & Fox 611 Commerce St Suite 2800 *TF:* 800-818-6953 ■ *Web:* www.mpf.com	Nashville	TN	37203	615-259-4000	259-4040
MCS Public Relations 1420 US Hwy 206 Suite 100 *TF:* 800-477-9626 ■ *Web:* www.mcspr.com	Bedminster	NJ	07921	908-234-9900	470-4490
Merkle Group Inc 7001 Columbia Gateway Dr **Fax Area Code:* 301 ■ *Web:* www.merkleinc.com	Columbia	MD	21046	443-542-4000	459-8431*
Montesquieu Corp 8221 Arjons Dr Suite F *TF:* 877-705-5669 ■ *Web:* www.montesquieu.com	San Diego	CA	92126	877-705-5669	
Morgan & Myers Inc N 16 W 23233 Stone Ridge Dr Suite 200 *Web:* www.morganmyers.com	Weukesha	WI	53188	262-650-7260	650-7261
MWW Group 1 Meadowlands Plaza 6th Fl *TF:* 800-724-7602 ■ *Web:* www.mwwpr.com	East Rutherford	NJ	07073	201-507-9500	507-0092
Ogilvy Public Relations Worldwide 636 11th Ave *Web:* www.ogilvypr.com	New York	NY	10036	212-880-5200	370-4636
Oliver Russell & Assoc Inc 217 S 11th St *Web:* www.oliverrussell.com	Boise	ID	83702	208-344-1734	344-1211
Pacifico Inc 3880 S Bascom Ave Suite 215 *Web:* www.pacifico.com	San Jose	CA	91524	408-559-8880	
Padilla Speer Beardsley Inc 1101 W River Pkwy Suite 400 *Web:* www.psbpr.com	Minneapolis	MN	55415	612-455-1700	455-1060
PainePR 19000 MacArthur Blvd 8th Fl *TF:* 866-724-6377 ■ *Web:* www.painepr.com	Irvine	CA	92612	949-809-6700	260-1116
PAN Communications 300 Brickstone Sq *Web:* www.pancommunications.com	Andover	MA	01810	978-474-1900	474-1903
PCG Campbell 3200 Greenfield St Suite 280 *Web:* www.pcgcampbell.com	Dearborn	MI	48120	313-336-9000	336-9029
PepperCom Inc 470 Pk Ave S 5th Fl *Web:* www.peppercom.com	New York	NY	10016	212-681-1333	931-6159
Plesser Holland Assoc 171 E 84th St Ground Fl *Web:* www.plesserholland.com	New York	NY	10028	212-420-8383	
Porter Novelli International 75 Varick St 6th Fl *Web:* www.porternovelli.com	New York	NY	10013	212-601-8000	601-8101
Prr 1109 1st Ave Suite 300 *Web:* www.prrbiz.com	Seattle	WA	98101	206-623-0735	623-0781
Public Communications Inc 35 E Wacker Dr Suite 1254 *Web:* www.pcipr.com	Chicago	IL	60601	312-558-1770	558-5425
Publicis Inc 14185 N Dallas Pkwy Suite 400	Dallas	TX	75254	972-628-7500	628-7864
Rendon Group Inc 1875 Conn Ave NW *Web:* www.rendon.com	Washington	DC	20009	202-745-4900	745-0215
RMR Assoc Inc 5870 Hubbard Dr *Web:* www.rmr.com	Rockville	MD	20852	301-230-0045	230-0046
Rogers Group The 1875 Century Pk E Suite 200 *TF:* 800-554-6901 ■ *Web:* www.rogerspr.com	Los Angeles	CA	90067	310-552-6922	552-9052
Rubin Communications Group 421 Cedar Mountain Rd *Web:* www.rubincomm.com	Dahlonega	GA	30533	706-867-0278	867-0408
Ruder Finn 301 E 57th St 4th Fl *Web:* www.ruderfinn.com	New York	NY	10022	212-593-6400	593-6397
S&S Public Relations Inc 2700 Patriot Blvd Suite 430 *Web:* www.sspr.com	Glenview	IL	60026	847-955-0700	955-7720
San Francisco Wine Exchange Inc The 620 Folsom St Suite 300 *Web:* www.sfwe.com	San Francisco	CA	94107	415-546-0484	243-0636
Schwartz Communications Inc 230 3rd Ave *Web:* www.schwartzcomm.com	Waltham	MA	02451	781-684-0770	684-6500
SHIFT Communications LLC 275 Washington St Suite 410 *Web:* www.shiftcomm.com	Newton	MA	02458	617-779-1800	779-1899
Sitrick & Co 1840 Century Pk E Suite 800 *TF:* 800-288-8809 ■ *Web:* www.sitrick.com	Los Angeles	CA	90067	310-788-2850	788-2855
Sloane & Co 7 Times Sq 17th Fl *Web:* www.sloanepr.com	New York	NY	10022	212-486-9500	702-9103
Southard Communications Inc 515 W 20th St # 6E *Web:* www.southardinc.com	New York	NY	10011	212-777-2220	777-7458
Stanton Public Relations & Marketing 880 Third Ave *Web:* www.stantonprm.com	New York	NY	10022	212-366-5300	
Strat@comm 1 Thomas Cir NW 10th Fl *Web:* www.stratacomm.net	Washington	DC	20005	202-289-2001	289-1327
Taylor Global Inc 350 Fifth Ave *Web:* www.taylorstrategy.com	New York	NY	10118	212-714-1280	695-5685
Text 100 North America 77 Maiden Ln 3rd Fl *Web:* www.text100.com	San Francisco	CA	94108	415-593-8400	593-8401
Tierney Communications 200 S Broad St 10th Fl *Web:* www.hellotierney.com	Philadelphia	PA	19102	215-790-4100	790-4363
Townsend Agency Ltd 9700 W Higgins Rd Suite 600 *Web:* www.townagcy.com	Rosemont	IL	60018	847-318-9010	318-9036
Tunheim Partners 8009 34th Ave S Suite 1100 *Web:* www.tunheim.com	Minneapolis	MN	55425	952-851-1600	851-1610
Vollmer Public Relations 808 Travis St Suite 501 *Web:* www.vollmerpr.com	Houston	TX	77002	713-970-2100	970-2140
Waggener Edstrom 3 Ctr Pt Dr Suite 300 *Web:* www.waggeneredstrom.com	Lake Oswego	OR	97035	503-443-7000	443-7001
Walt & Co Communications 2105 S Bascom Ave Suite 240 *Web:* www.walt.com	Campbell	CA	95008	408-369-7200	369-7201
Weber Shandwick Worldwide 640 5th Ave 8th Fl *Web:* www.webershandwick.com	New York	NY	10019	212-445-8000	445-8001
Widmeyer Communications 1129 20th St NW Suite 200 *Web:* www.widmeyer.com	Washington	DC	20036	202-667-0901	667-0902
Zeno Group 200 Pk Ave S Suite 1603 *Web:* www.zenogroup.com	New York	NY	10003	212-299-8888	462-1026
Zimmerman Agency 1821 Miccosukee Commons *Web:* www.zimmerman.com	Tallahassee	FL	32308	850-668-2222	656-4622

PUBLICATIONS

SEE Magazines & Journals p. 2194; Newsletters p. 2298; Newspapers p. 2305

640 PUBLISHING COMPANIES

SEE ALSO Book Producers p. 1535; Literary Agents p. 2180; Magazines & Journals p. 2194; Newsletters p. 2298; Newspapers p. 2305

640-1 Atlas & Map Publishers

				Phone	Fax
DeLorme 2 DeLorme Dr PO Box 298	Yarmouth	ME	04096	207-846-7000	561-5105*
*Fax Area Code: 800 ■ TF Sales: 800-452-5931 ■ Web: www.delorme.com					
George F Cram Co Inc 4719 W 62nd St	Indianapolis	IN	46268	317-612-3901	329-3305
TF: 800-227-4199 ■ Web: www.georgefcram.com					
MARCOA Publishing Inc 9955 Black Mountain Rd	San Diego	CA	92126	858-695-9600	695-9641
TF: 800-854-2935 ■ Web: www.marcoa.com					
Nystrom 4719 W 62nd St	Indianapolis	IN	46268	317-612-3901	329-3305
TF: 800-621-8086 ■ Web: www.nystromnet.com					
Rand McNally & Co 8255 N Central Pk Ave	Skokie	IL	60076	847-329-8100	673-9935*
*Fax: Cust Svc ■ TF: 800-333-0136 ■ Web: www.randmcnally.com					
Simon & Schuster Interactive 1230 Avenue of the Americas	New York	NY	10020	212-698-7000	632-8099
TF: 800-223-2348 ■ Web: www.simonandschuster.biz					
Universal Map 40 Skippack Pike	Fort Washington	PA	19034	800-829-6277	873-3011*
*Fax Area Code: 386 ■ TF: 800-829-6277 ■ Web: www.universalmap.com					

640-2 Book Publishers

				Phone	Fax
ABC-CLIO Inc 130 Cremona Dr	Santa Barbara	CA	93117	805-968-1911	685-9685
TF: 800-368-6868 ■ Web: www.abc-clio.com					
Alfred A Knopf Inc 1745 Broadway	New York	NY	10019	212-782-9000	
TF: 888-264-1745 ■ Web: www.randomhouse.com/knopf					
Algonquin Books PO Box 2225	Chapel Hill	NC	27515	919-967-0108	933-0272
Web: www.algonquinbooksblog.com					
American Biographical Institute 5126 Bur Oak Cir	Raleigh	NC	27612	919-781-8710	781-8712
Web: www.abiworldwide.com					
American Printing House for the Blind 1839 Frankfort Ave PO Box 6085	Louisville	KY	40206	502-895-2405	899-2274
TF: 800-223-1839 ■ Web: www.aph.org					
Antique Collectors' Club 116 Pleasant St Suite 18 Eastworks Bldg	EastHampton	MA	01027	413-529-0861	529-0862
TF: 800-252-5231 ■ Web: www.antiquecc.com					
Applewood Books Inc PO Box 365	Bedford	MA	01730	781-271-0055	271-0056
TF: 800-277-5312 ■ Web: www.awb.com					
Aspen Publishers Inc 111 8th Ave 7th Fl	New York	NY	10011	212-771-0600	771-0885
TF Orders: 800-447-1717 ■ Web: www.aspenpublishers.com					
Atlantic Publishing Co 1108 E 5th St	Tabor City	NC	28463	910-653-3153	653-9440
TF: 800-672-1022 ■ Web: www.atlantic-pub.com					
Auerbach Publications 6000 Broken Sound Pkwy NW Suite 300	Boca Raton	FL	33487	561-994-0555	989-9732
Web: www.auerbach-publications.com					
Author House 1663 Liberty Dr Suite 200	Bloomington	IN	47403	812-339-6000	339-6554
TF: 888-728-8467 ■ Web: www.authorhouse.com					
Avalon Travel Publishing 1700 4th St	Berkeley	CA	94710	510-595-3664	595-4228
Web: www.avalontravelbooks.com					
Barron's Educational Series Inc 250 Wireless Blvd	Hauppauge	NY	11788	631-434-3311	434-3723
TF: 800-645-3476 ■ Web: www.barronseduc.com					
Bartleby.com Inc PO Box 13	New York	NY	10034	646-522-2474	
Web: www.bartleby.com					
Beacon Press Inc 25 Beacon St	Boston	MA	02108	617-742-2110	723-3097
Web: www.beacon.org					
Bertelsmann Publishing Group Inc 1745 Broadway	New York	NY	10019	212-782-1000	782-1010
Web: www.bertelsmann.com					
Black Classic Press PO Box 13414	Baltimore	MD	21203	410-242-6954	242-6959
TF: 800-476-8870 ■ Web: www.blackclassic.com					
BOA Editions Ltd 250 N Goodman St Suite 306	Rochester	NY	14607	585-546-3410	546-3913
Web: www.boaeditions.org					
BRB Publications Inc PO Box 27869	Tempe	AZ	85285	480-829-7475	929-4981*
*Fax Area Code: 800 ■ TF: 800-929-3811 ■ Web: www.brbpub.com					
Brillacademic Publishers Inc 112 Water St Suite 400	Boston	MA	02109	617-742-5277	263-2324
TF: 800-337-9255 ■ Web: www.brill.nl					
British American Publishing Ltd 4 British American Blvd	Latham	NY	12110	518-786-6000	786-6001
Web: www.bapublish.com					
Brooks/Cole Publishing Co *Cengage Learning Inc* 10 Davis Dr	Belmont	CA	94002	650-595-2350	
TF: 800-354-0092 ■ Web: www.brookscole.com					
Browntrout Publishers Inc PO Box 280070	San Francisco	CA	94128	310-607-9010	607-9011
TF: 800-777-7812 ■ Web: www.browntrout.com					
Bureau of National Affairs Inc 1801 S Bell St	Arlington	VA	22202	703-341-3000	341-1634
TF: 800-372-1033 ■ Web: www.bna.com					
Bureau of National Affairs Inc BNA Books Div 1801 S Bell St	Arlington	VA	22202	703-341-5777	341-1610
TF Sales: 800-960-1220 ■ Web: www.bna.com/bnabooks					
Candlewick Press Inc 99 Dover St	Somerville	MA	02144	617-661-3330	661-0565
Web: www.candlewick.com					
Carroll Publishing Co 4701 Sangamore Rd Suite S-155	Bethesda	MD	20816	301-263-9800	263-9801
TF: 800-336-4240 ■ Web: www.carrollpub.com					
CCH Inc 2700 Lake Cook Rd	Riverwoods	IL	60015	847-267-7000	267-2516
TF Cust Svc: 800-835-5224 ■ Web: www.cch.com					
Cengage Learning 10650 Tobben Dr	Independence	KY	41051	800-544-0550	647-4599*
*Fax Area Code: 859 ■ TF: 800-354-9706 ■ Web: www.cengage.com					
Cengage Learning Inc PO Box 6904	Florence	KY	41022	800-423-0563	487-8488
TF: 800-423-0563 ■ Web: www.cengage.com/highered					
Charles C Thomas Publisher 2600 S 1st St PO Box 19265	Springfield	IL	62704	217-789-8980	789-9130
TF Sales: 800-258-8980 ■ Web: www.ccthomas.com					
Children's Press 557 Broadway	New York	NY	10012	212-343-6100	
Web: www.scholastic.com					
Chronicle Books 680 2nd St	San Francisco	CA	94107	415-537-4200	537-4460
TF: 800-722-6657 ■ Web: www.chroniclebooks.com					
Clarion Books 215 Pk Ave S	New York	NY	10003	212-420-5800	420-5855
Web: www.hmco.com					
Cornell Maritime Press PO Box 456	Centreville	MD	21617	410-758-1075	758-1075
TF: 800-638-7641					
Corwin Press Inc 2455 Teller Rd	Thousand Oaks	CA	91320	805-499-9734	499-0871
TF Orders: 800-233-9936 ■ Web: www.corwin.com					
CRC Press LLC 6000 Broken Sound Pkwy NW Suite 300	Boca Raton	FL	33487	561-994-0555	374-3401*
*Fax Area Code: 800 ■ *Fax: Cust Svc ■ TF Cust Svc: 800-272-7737 ■ Web: www.crcpress.com					
Creative Communications For The Parish Inc 1564 Fencorp Dr	Fenton	MO	63026	636-305-9777	305-9333
TF: 800-325-9414 ■ Web: www.creativecommunications.com					
Curriculum Assoc Inc 153 Rangeway Rd	North Billerica	MA	01862	800-225-0248	225-0248
TF: 800-225-0248 ■ Web: www.curriculumassociates.com					
D & B 103 JFK Pkwy	Short Hills	NJ	07078	973-921-5500	921-5501
NYSE: DNB ■ TF: 800-234-3867 ■ Web: www.dnb.com					
Dalmation Press 3101 Clairmont Rd Suite C	Atlanta	GA	30329	404-214-4300	
TF: 866-418-2572 ■ Web: www.dalmatianpress.com					
Delacorte Press 1745 Broadway	New York	NY	10019	212-782-9000	302-7985
TF: 800-200-3552 ■ Web: www.randomhouse.com					
Disney Consumer Products 500 S Buena Vista St	Burbank	CA	91521	818-560-1000	560-1930*
*Fax: Cust Svc ■ TF PR: 800-723-4763					
Disney Publishing Worldwide Inc 114 5th Ave	New York	NY	10011	212-633-4400	633-4811
Web: www.corporate.disney.go.com/corporate/overview.html					
Dolan Media Co 222 S 9th St # 2300	Minneapolis	MN	55402	612-317-9420	321-0563
Web: www.dolanmedia.com					
Donning Co Publishers 184 Business Pk Dr Suite 206	Virginia Beach	VA	23462	757-497-1789	497-2542
TF: 800-296-8572 ■ Web: www.donning.com					
Dorling Kindersley Publishing 375 Hudson St	New York	NY	10014	646-674-4000	674-4047
TF Cust Svc: 800-631-8571 ■ Web: us.dk.com					
Doubleday Broadway Publishing Group 1745 Broadway	New York	NY	10019	212-782-9000	659-2436*
*Fax Area Code: 800 ■ *Fax: Cust Svc ■ TF: 800-726-0600 ■ Web: www.randomhouse.com					
Educators Publishing Service Inc PO Box 9031	Cambridge	MA	02139	617-547-6706	547-6706
TF: 800-225-5750 ■ Web: www.eps.schoolspecialty.com					
EMC-Paradigm Publishing Co 875 Montreal Way	Saint Paul	MN	55102	651-290-2800	328-4564*
*Fax Area Code: 800 ■ TF: 800-328-1452 ■ Web: www.emcp.com					
Encyclopaedia Britannica Inc 331 N La Salle St	Chicago	IL	60610	312-347-7159	294-2104*
*Fax: PR ■ TF: 800-323-1229 ■ Web: www.britannica.com					
FA Davis Co 1915 Arch St	Philadelphia	PA	19103	215-568-2270	568-5065
TF: 800-323-3555 ■ Web: www.fadavis.com					
Feminist Press at the City University of New York 365 5th Ave 5th Fl	New York	NY	10016	212-817-7922	817-1593
Web: www.feministpress.org					
Financial Publishing Co PO Box 570	South Bend	IN	46624	574-243-6040	243-6060
TF Cust Svc: 800-433-0090 ■ Web: www.financial-publishing.com					
Fodor's Travel 1745 Broadway	New York	NY	10019	212-782-9000	
TF: 800-726-0600 ■ Web: www.fodors.com					
Forbes Inc 60 5th Ave	New York	NY	10011	212-620-2200	206-5534
TF: 800-888-9896 ■ Web: www.forbes.com					
Franklin Watts 557 Broadway	New York	NY	10012	212-343-6100	
Web: www.scholastic.com					
Gale Cengage Learning 27500 Drake Rd	Farmington Hills	MI	48331	248-699-4253	363-4253*
*Fax Area Code: 877 ■ TF Cust Svc: 800-877-4253 ■ Web: www.gale.cengage.com					
Garland Publishing Inc 270 Madison Ave	New York	NY	10016	212-216-7800	564-7854
TF: 800-797-3803 ■ Web: www.garlandpub.com					
Glencoe/McGraw-Hill 8787 Orion Pl	Columbus	OH	43240	614-430-4000	
TF: 800-437-3715 ■ Web: www.glencoe.com					
Golden Books 1745 Broadway	New York	NY	10019	212-782-9000	
TF: 888-264-1745 ■ Web: www.randomhouse.com/golden					
Good Will Publishers Inc PO Box 269	Gastonia	NC	28053	704-865-1256	861-1085
Web: www.goodwillpublishers.com					
Goodheart-Willcox Publisher 18604 W Creek Dr	Tinley Park	IL	60477	708-687-5000	409-3900*
*Fax Area Code: 888 ■ TF: 800-323-0440 ■ Web: www.g-w.com					
Government Research Service 1516 SW Boswell Ave	Topeka	KS	66604	785-232-7720	232-1615
TF: 800-346-6898 ■ Web: www.thinktankdirectory.com					
Grade Finders Inc PO Box 944	Exton	PA	19341	610-524-7070	269-7077
Web: www.gradefinders.com					
Greenwillow Books 1350 Avenue of the Americas	New York	NY	10019	212-261-6500	822-4090*
*Fax Area Code: 800 ■ TF: 800-242-7737 ■ Web: www.harpercollins.com					
Greenwood Publishing Group Inc 88 Post Rd W	Westport	CT	06881	203-226-3571	222-1502
TF Orders: 800-225-5800 ■ Web: www.greenwood.com					
Greenwood-Heinemann 361 Hanover St	Portsmouth	NH	03801	603-431-7894	431-7840
TF: 800-541-2086 ■ Web: www.heinemann.com					
Grey House Publishing 4919 Rt 22 PO Box 56	Amenia	NY	12501	518-789-8700	789-0556
TF: 800-562-2139 ■ Web: www.greyhouse.com					
Grove/Atlantic Inc 841 Broadway 4th Fl	New York	NY	10003	212-614-7860	614-7886
Web: www.groveatlantic.com					
Hachette Book Group 237 Pk Ave	New York	NY	10017	800-759-0190	331-1664
TF: 800-759-0190 ■ Web: www.hachettebookgroup.com					
Haights Cross Communications 136 Madison Ave 8th Fl	New York	NY	10016	212-209-0500	209-0501
Web: www.haightscross.com					
Harcourt Inc 6277 Sea Harbor Dr	Orlando	FL	32887	407-345-2000	345-3016*
*Fax: Cust Svc ■ TF: 800-782-4479 ■ Web: www.harcourtbrace.com					

Phone | Fax

Harlequin Enterprises Ltd
225 Duncan Mill Rd ... Don Mills ON M3B3K9 416-445-5860 445-8655
TF: 888-343-9777 ■ *Web:* www.eharlequin.com

Harlequin-Silhouette Books
233 Broadway Suite 1001 ... New York NY 10279 212-553-4200 227-8969
Web: www.eharlequin.com

HarperCollins Canada Ltd 1995 Markham Rd ... Scarborough ON M1B5M8 416-321-2241 668-5788*
**Fax Area Code:* 800 ■ *TF:* 800-387-0117 ■ *Web:* www.harpercollins.com

HarperCollins Publishers 10 E 53rd St ... New York NY 10022 212-207-7000 822-4090*
**Fax Area Code:* 800 ■ *TF:* 800-242-7737 ■ *Web:* www.harpercollins.com

HarperCollins Publishers Inc 10 E 53rd St ... New York NY 10022 212-207-7000 207-6998
TF: 800-242-7737 ■ *Web:* www.harpercollins.com

Harris Connect LLC 1511 Rt 22 Suite C-25 ... Brewster NY 10509 800-516-4915 940-0801*
**Fax Area Code:* 845 ■ *TF:* 800-877-6554 ■ *Web:* www.harrisconnect.com

Harry N Abrams Inc 115 W 18th St 6th Fl ... New York NY 10011 212-206-7715 519-1210
TF: 800-345-1359 ■ *Web:* www.abramsbooks.com

Health Communications Inc (HCI)
3201 SW 15th St ... Deerfield Beach FL 33442 954-360-0909 360-0034
TF Cust Svc: 800-441-5569 ■ *Web:* www.hcibooks.com

Holt Rinehart & Winston Inc
10801 N MoPac Expy Bldg 3 ... Austin TX 78759 512-721-7000 721-7770
TF: 800-992-1627 ■ *Web:* www.hrw.com

Holtzbrinck Publishers 175 5th Ave ... New York NY 10010 646-307-5151 420-9314*
**Fax Area Code:* 212 ■ *TF:* 800-221-7945 ■ *Web:* www.holtzbrinck.com/eng/index.html

Houghton Mifflin Co School Div
222 Berkeley St ... Boston MA 02116 617-351-5000 351-1100
Web: www.eduplace.com

Houghton Mifflin Co Trade & Reference Div
222 Berkeley St ... Boston MA 02116 617-351-5000 351-1100
Web: www.houghtonmifflinbooks.com

Houghton Mifflin Harcourt 10801 N MO Pac Expy ... Austin TX 78759 877-866-2586 265-2730
TF: 877-866-2586 ■ *Web:* www.saxonpublishers.com

Human Kinetics 1607 N Market St ... Champaign IL 61820 217-351-5076 351-2674
TF: 800-747-4457 ■ *Web:* www.humankinetics.com

HW Wilson Co 950 University Ave ... Bronx NY 10452 718-588-8400 590-1617
TF: 800-367-6770 ■ *Web:* www.hwwilson.com

Hyperion Books 77 W 66th St 11th Fl ... New York NY 10023 212-456-0100 456-0176
Web: www.hyperionbooks.com

Inner Traditions International 1 Pk St ... Rochester VT 05767 802-767-3174 767-3726
TF: 800-246-8648 ■ *Web:* www.innertraditions.com

iScribe
101 Redwood Shores Pkwy Suite 101 ... Redwood City CA 94065 650-381-2076
TF: 800-326-3784 ■ *Web:* www.iscribe.co.in

Island Press
1718 Connecticut Ave NW Suite 300 ... Washington DC 20009 202-232-7933 234-1328
TF: 800-828-1302 ■ *Web:* www.islandpress.org

iUniverse 1663 Liberty Dr ... Bloomington IN 47403 800-288-4677 349-0745*
**Fax Area Code:* 812 ■ *TF:* 800-288-4677 ■ *Web:* www.iuniverse.com

Jane's Information Group
110 N Royal St Suite 200 ... Alexandria VA 22314 703-683-3700 836-0029
TF: 800-824-0768 ■ *Web:* www.janes.com

Jeppesen Sanderson Inc 55 Inverness Dr E ... Englewood CO 80112 303-799-9090 353-2107
TF: 800-621-5377 ■ *Web:* www.jeppesen.com

Jist Publishing Inc 8902 Otis Ave ... Indianapolis IN 46216 317-613-4200 613-4309
TF: 800-648-5478 ■ *Web:* www.jist.com

John Wiley & Sons Inc 111 River St ... Hoboken NJ 07030 201-748-6000 748-6088
NYSE: JW.A ■ *TF Sales:* 800-225-5945 ■ *Web:* www.as.wiley.com

Jossey-Bass & Pfeiffer
989 Market St 5th Fl ... San Francisco CA 94103 415-782-3100 433-0499
Web: www.josseybass.com

Judaica Press Inc 123 Ditmas Ave ... Brooklyn NY 11218 718-972-6200 972-6204
TF: 800-972-6201 ■ *Web:* www.judaicapress.com

Kalmbach Publishing Co 21027 Crossroads Cir ... Waukesha WI 53186 262-796-8776 796-1615
TF Cust Svc: 800-446-5489 ■ *Web:* www.kalmbach.com

Kendall/Hunt Publishing Co
4050 Westmark Dr PO Box 1840 ... Dubuque IA 52002 563-589-1000 772-9165*
**Fax Area Code:* 800 ■ **Fax:* Cust Svc ■ *TF Cust Svc:* 800-228-0810 ■ *Web:* www.kendallhunt.com

Kensington Publishing Corp 119 W 40th St ... New York NY 10018 212-407-1500 935-0699
TF: 800-221-2647 ■ *Web:* www.kensingtonbooks.com

Key Curriculum Press 1150 65th St ... Emeryville CA 94608 510-595-7000 541-2442*
**Fax Area Code:* 800 ■ *TF:* 800-995-6284 ■ *Web:* www.keypress.com

Klutz 450 Lambert Ave ... Palo Alto CA 94306 650-857-0888 857-9110
TF: 800-737-4123 ■ *Web:* www.klutz.com

Lark Books 67 Broadway St ... Asheville NC 28801 828-253-0467 253-7952
Web: www.larkcrafts.com

Lawyers Diary & Manual
240 Mulberry St PO Box 50 ... Newark NJ 07102 973-642-1440 642-4280*
**Fax:* Cust Svc ■ *TF:* 800-444-4041 ■ *Web:* www.lawdiary.com

Leadership Directories Inc
104 5th Ave 3rd Fl ... New York NY 10011 212-627-4140 645-0931
Web: www.leadershipdirectories.com

Lerner Publishing Group
1251 Washington Ave N ... Minneapolis MN 55401 800-328-4929 332-1132
TF: 800-328-4929 ■ *Web:* www.lernerbooks.com

LexisNexis Matthew Bender 744 Broad St ... Newark NJ 07102 973-820-2000 820-2007
TF: 800-252-9257 ■ *Web:* www.lexisnexis.com

Lightning Source 1246 Heil Quaker Blvd ... La Vergne TN 37086 615-213-5815 213-4426
Web: www.lightningsource.com

Linden Publishing 2006 S Mary St ... Fresno CA 93721 559-233-6633 233-6933
TF Sales: 800-345-4447 ■ *Web:* www.woodworkerslibrary.com

Lippincott Williams & Wilkins
530 Walnut St ... Philadelphia PA 19106 215-521-8300 521-8902
Web: www.lww.com

Little Brown & Co 237 Pk Ave ... New York NY 10017 212-364-1100 522-0885
TF Cust Svc: 800-759-0190 ■ *Web:* www.hachettebookgroup.com

Llewellyn Worldwide Inc 2143 Wooddale Dr ... Woodbury MN 55125 651-291-1970 291-1908
TF: 800-843-6666 ■ *Web:* www.llewellyn.com

Lonely Planet Publications 50 Linden St ... Oakland CA 94607 510-893-8555 893-8572
TF: 800-275-8555 ■ *Web:* www.lonelyplanet.com

LRP Publications 360 Hiatt Dr ... Palm Beach Gardens FL 33418 561-622-6520 622-2423
TF: 800-621-5463 ■ *Web:* www.lrp.com

Marlin Co 10 Research Pkwy ... North Haven CT 06473 203-294-9800 294-9900
TF: 800-344-5901 ■ *Web:* www.themarlincompany.com

Phone | Fax

Marquis Who's Who
300 Connell Dr Suite 2000 ... Berkeley Heights NJ 07922 908-673-1000 673-1189
TF: 800-473-7020 ■ *Web:* www.marquiswhoswho.com

Martha Stewart Living Omnimedia Inc
11 W 42nd St 25th Fl ... New York NY 10036 212-827-8000 827-8188
NYSE: MSO ■ *TF:* 800-999-6518 ■ *Web:* www.marthastewart.com

Mc Farland & Co Inc PO Box 611 ... Jefferson NC 28640 336-246-4460 246-5018
TF: 800-253-2187 ■ *Web:* www.mcfarlandpub.com

McGraw-Hill Cos Inc
1221 Avenue of the Americas ... New York NY 10020 212-512-2000
NYSE: MHP ■ *Web:* www.mcgraw-hill.com

McGraw-Hill Higher Education Group
1333 Burr Ridge Pkwy ... Burr Ridge IL 60527 630-789-4000 755-5654*
**Fax Area Code:* 614 ■ *TF:* 800-634-3963 ■ *Web:* www.mhhe.com

McGraw-Hill Professional Publishing Group
2 Penn Plaza 11th Fl ... New York NY 10121 212-904-2000 904-4070
TF: 800-262-4729 ■ *Web:* www.mhprofessional.com

ME Sharpe Inc 80 Business Pk Dr Suite 202 ... Armonk NY 10504 914-273-1800 273-2106
TF Orders: 800-541-6563 ■ *Web:* www.mesharpe.com

Mel Bay Publications Inc 4 Industrial Dr ... Pacific MO 63069 636-257-3970 257-5062
TF: 800-863-5229 ■ *Web:* www.melbay.com

Meredith Corp 1716 Locust St ... Des Moines IA 50309 515-284-3000 284-3806
NYSE: MDP ■ *Web:* www.meredith.com

Merriam-Webster Inc PO Box 281 ... Springfield MA 01102 413-734-3134 731-5979
TF: 800-201-5029 ■ *Web:* www.m-w.com

Microsoft Press 1 Microsoft Way ... Redmond WA 98052 425-882-8080 936-7329
TF Cust Svc: 800-642-7676 ■ *Web:* www.microsoft.com/mspress

Midwest Plan Service 122 Davidson Hall ISU ... Ames IA 50011 515-294-4337 294-9589
TF: 800-562-3618 ■ *Web:* www.mwps.org

Mike Murach & Assoc Inc 4340 N Knoll ... Fresno CA 93722 559-440-9071 440-0963
TF: 800-221-5528 ■ *Web:* www.murach.com

Moody's Corp
250 Greenwich St 7 World Trade Ctr ... New York NY 10007 212-553-0300 553-5376
NYSE: MCO ■ *Web:* www.moodys.com

National Academy Press
500 5th St NW PO Box 285 ... Washington DC 20055 202-334-3313 334-2451*
**Fax:* Sales ■ *TF:* 800-624-6242 ■ *Web:* www.nap.edu

National Braille Press Inc 88 St Stephen St ... Boston MA 02115 617-266-6160 437-0456
TF: 888-965-8965 ■ *Web:* www.nbp.org

National Register Publishing Co
890 Mountain Ave Suite 4 ... New Providence NJ 07974 908-673-1000 673-1189
TF: 800-473-7020 ■ *Web:* www.nationalregisterpub.com

National Underwriter Co 5081 Olympic Blvd ... Erlanger KY 41018 859-692-2100 692-2246
TF: 800-543-0874 ■ *Web:* www.nationalunderwriter.com

Nerdy Books 135 Main St ... Flemington NJ 08822 908-788-4676 788-7097
TF: 866-843-8477 ■ *Web:* www.nerdybooks.com

New Generation Research Inc
225 Friend St Suite 801 ... Boston MA 02114 617-573-9550 573-9554
TF: 800-468-3810 ■ *Web:* www.turnarounds.com

New Readers Press 1320 Jamesville Ave ... Syracuse NY 13210 315-422-9121 894-2100*
**Fax Area Code:* 866 ■ *TF:* 800-448-8878 ■ *Web:* www.newreaderspress.com

Newkirk Products Inc 15 Corporate Cir ... Albany NY 12203 518-862-3200 862-3399
TF: 800-525-4237 ■ *Web:* www.newkirk.com

Nielsen Business Media
The Nielsen Co 770 Broadway ... New York NY 10003 646-654-5500 654-5518
TF: 800-451-1741 ■ *Web:* www.nielsen.com

Nightingale-Conant Corp 6245 W Howard St ... Niles IL 60714 847-647-0300 647-5989
TF Cust Svc: 800-323-3938 ■ *Web:* www.nightingale.com

No Starch Press Inc 38 Ringold St ... San Francisco CA 94103 415-863-9900 863-9950
TF: 800-420-7240 ■ *Web:* www.nostarch.com

Nolo.com 950 Parker St ... Berkeley CA 94710 800-728-3555 645-0895
TF: 800-728-3555 ■ *Web:* www.nolo.com

Oceana Publications Inc 198 Madison Ave ... New York NY 10016 212-726-6000 726-6458
TF Orders: 800-451-7556 ■ *Web:* www.oceanalaw.com

Omnigraphics Inc PO Box 31-1640 ... Detroit MI 48231 313-961-1340 961-1383
TF: 800-234-1340 ■ *Web:* www.omnigraphics.com

Open Court Publishing Co
70 E Lake St Suite 300 ... Chicago IL 60601 312-701-1720 701-1728
TF: 800-852-0790 ■ *Web:* www.opencourtbooks.com

Out Rider Press Inc 937 Patricia Ln ... Crete IL 60417 219-322-7270 672-5820*
**Fax Area Code:* 708 ■ *TF:* 866-510-6735 ■ *Web:* www.outriderpress.com/publishing.html

Overlook Press 141 Wooster St ... New York NY 10012 212-673-2210 673-2296
Web: www.overlookpress.com

Oxmoor House Inc 2100 Lakeshore Dr ... Birmingham AL 35209 205-445-6000
TF: 800-633-4910 ■ *Web:* www.oxmoorhouse.com

Parachute Publishing LLC
156 5th Ave Suite 302 ... New York NY 10010 212-691-1422 645-8769
Web: www.parachutepublishing.com

Pathway Press 1080 Montgomery Ave NE ... Cleveland TN 37311 423-476-4512 546-7590*
**Fax Area Code:* 800 ■ **Fax:* Sales ■ *TF Sales:* 800-553-8506 ■ *Web:* www.pathwaypress.org

Peachpit Press 1249 8th St ... Berkeley CA 94710 510-524-2178 524-2221
TF: 800-283-9444 ■ *Web:* www.peachpit.com

Pearson Education Inc 1 Lake St ... Upper Saddle River NJ 07458 201-236-7000 767-2993*
**Fax:* Cust Svc ■ *TF Cust Svc:* 800-922-0579 ■ *Web:* www.pearsoned.com

Pearson Education School Div
1900 E Lake Ave ... Glenview IL 60025 847-729-3000 841-8939*
**Fax Area Code:* 800 ■ **Fax:* Cust Svc ■ *TF Cust Svc:* 800-554-4411 ■ *Web:* www.pearsonschool.com

Pencor Services Inc 613 3rd St ... Palmerton PA 18071 610-826-9190 826-7626
TF: 800-634-6572 ■ *Web:* www.pencor.com

Penguin Books Canada Ltd
90 Eglent Ave E Suite 700 ... Toronto ON M4P2Y3 416-925-2249 925-0068
TF: 800-810-3104 ■ *Web:* www.penguin.ca

Penguin Group (USA) Inc 375 Hudson St ... New York NY 10014 212-366-2000 366-2933
TF Sales: 800-847-5515 ■ *Web:* us.penguingroup.com

Peoples Educational Holdings Inc
299 Market St ... Saddle Brook NJ 07663 201-712-0090 712-0045
NASDAQ: PEDH ■ *TF:* 800-822-1080 ■ *Web:* www.peopleseducation.com

Perseus Books Group The 387 Pk Ave S 12th Fl ... New York NY 10016 212-340-8100 351-5073*
**Fax Area Code:* 800 ■ *TF:* 800-343-4499 ■ *Web:* www.perseusbooksgroup.com/perseus/index.jsp

Peter Lang Publishing Inc 29 Broadway 18 ... New York NY 10006 212-509-5094 647-7707
Web: www.peterlang.com

				Phone	Fax
Peterson's Guides Inc					
Princeton Pike Corporate Ctr					
2000 Lenox Dr	Lawrenceville	NJ	08648	609-896-1800	896-1811
TF: 800-338-3282 ■ *Web:* www.petersons.com					
Pike & Fischer					
1010 Wayne Ave Suite 1400	Silver Spring	MD	20910	301-562-1530	562-1521
TF: 800-255-8131 ■ *Web:* www.pf.com					
Pocket Books					
1230 Avenue of the Americas 13th Fl	New York	NY	10020	212-698-7000	
TF Cust Svc: 800-223-2336					
Praeger Publishers 88 Post Rd W	Westport	CT	06881	203-226-3571	222-1502
TF: 800-225-5800 ■ *Web:* www.praeger.com					
Prentice-Hall Inc 1 Lake St	Upper Saddle River	NJ	07458	201-236-7000	236-3400
Web: www.pearsonhighered.com					
Price Books & Forms Inc					
531 E Sierra Madre Ave	Glendora	CA	91741	800-423-8961	768-2162*
**Fax Area Code:* 626 ■ *TF:* 800-423-8961 ■ *Web:* www.autopricebooks.com					
PublicAffairs 250 W 57th St Suite 1321	New York	NY	10107	212-397-6666	397-4277
Web: www.publicaffairsbooks.com					
Publications International Ltd					
7373 N Cicero Ave	Lincolnwood	IL	60712	847-676-3470	676-3671
TF: 800-745-9299 ■ *Web:* www.pubint.com					
Quebecor Media Inc 612 Rue St Jacques	Montreal	QC	H3C4M8	514-597-2231	594-8844
Web: www.quebecor.com					
Rand McNally & Co 8255 N Central Pk Ave	Skokie	IL	60076	847-329-8100	673-9935*
**Fax:* Cust Svc ■ *TF:* 800-333-0136 ■ *Web:* www.randmcnally.com					
Random House Inc 1745 Broadway	New York	NY	10019	212-782-9000	
TF Cust Svc: 800-733-3000 ■ *Web:* www.randomhouse.com					
Bantam Dell Publishing Group 1745 Broadway	New York	NY	10019	212-782-9000	
TF: 800-726-0600 ■ *Web:* bantam-dell.atrandom.com					
Random House Reference & Information Publishing					
1745 Broadway	New York	NY	10019	212-751-2600	572-4997
TF: 800-733-3000 ■ *Web:* www.randomhouse.com					
Reader's Digest Assn Inc					
Reader's Digest Rd	Pleasantville	NY	10570	914-238-1000	244-7653
NYSE: RDA ■ *TF:* 800-635-5006 ■ *Web:* www.rd.com					
Regnery Publishing Inc					
1 Massachusetts Ave NW	Washington	DC	20001	202-216-0600	216-0612
TF: 888-219-4747 ■ *Web:* www.regnery.com					
RIA Group 195 Broadway	New York	NY	10007	212-367-6300	337-4207
TF: 800-323-8724 ■ *Web:* ria.thomsonreuters.com					
Rizzoli International Publications Inc					
300 Pk Ave S 3rd Fl	New York	NY	10010	212-387-3400	387-3434
Web: www.rizzoliusa.com					
Rodale Inc 33 E Minor St	Emmaus	PA	18098	610-967-5171	813-6627*
**Fax Area Code:* 800 ■ **Fax:* Cust Svc ■ *TF Cust Svc:* 800-848-4735 ■ *Web:* www.rodale.com					
Rosen Publishing Group Inc The 29 E 21st St	New York	NY	10010	800-237-9932	436-4643*
**Fax Area Code:* 888 ■ *Web:* www.rosenpublishing.com					
Rowman & Littlefield Publishers Inc					
4501 Forbes Blvd Suite 200	Lanham	MD	20706	301-459-3366	429-5748
TF: 800-462-6420 ■ *Web:* www.rowmanlittlefield.com					
RR Bowker LLC 630 Central Ave	New Providence	NJ	07974	908-286-1090	219-0098*
**Fax:* Cust Svc ■ *TF:* 888-269-5372 ■ *Web:* www.bowker.com					
Rutledge Hill Press					
15 Century Blvd Lakeview #2 Bldg	Nashville	TN	37214	615-889-9000	902-2340
TF: 800-251-4000 ■ *Web:* www.rutledgehillpress.com					
Sage Publications Inc 2455 Teller Rd	Thousand Oaks	CA	91320	805-499-9774	499-0871
TF: 800-818-7243 ■ *Web:* www.sagepub.com					
Saint Martin's Press Inc 175 5th Ave	New York	NY	10010	646-307-5151	420-9314*
**Fax Area Code:* 212 ■ *TF:* 800-221-7945 ■ *Web:* us.macmillan.com					
Sams Technical Publishing					
9850 E 30th St	Indianapolis	IN	46229	317-396-9850	552-3910*
**Fax Area Code:* 800 ■ *TF Cust Svc:* 800-428-7267 ■ *Web:* www.samswebsite.com					
Santillana USA Publishing Co 2023 NW 84th Ave	Doral	FL	33122	305-591-9522	248-9518*
**Fax Area Code:* 888 ■ *TF:* 800-245-8584 ■ *Web:* www.santillanausa.com					
School Annual Publishing Co					
500 Science Pk Rd Suite B	State College	PA	16803	814-278-6600	436-6048*
**Fax Area Code:* 800 ■ *TF:* 800-436-6030 ■ *Web:* www.schoolannual.com					
Slack Inc 6900 Grove Rd	Thorofare	NJ	08086	856-848-1000	848-6091
TF: 800-257-8290 ■ *Web:* www.slackinc.com					
Sourcebooks Inc					
1935 Brookdale Rd Suite 139	Naperville	IL	60563	630-961-3900	961-2168
TF: 800-432-7444 ■ *Web:* www.sourcebooks.com					
SRDS 1700 Higgins Rd	Des Plaines	IL	60018	847-375-5000	375-5001
TF: 800-851-7737 ■ *Web:* www.srds.com					
Stackpole Books 5067 Ritter Rd	Mechanicsburg	PA	17055	717-796-0411	796-0412
TF Sales: 800-732-3669 ■ *Web:* www.stackpolebooks.com					
Standard & Poor's Corp 55 Water St	New York	NY	10041	212-438-1000	438-2000
Web: www.standardandpoors.com					
Steck-Vaughn Co 10801 N MoPac Expy Bldg 3	Austin	TX	78759	877-866-2586	265-2730
TF: 877-866-2586 ■ *Web:* www.steck-vaughn.com					
Sterling Publishing Co Inc					
387 Pk Ave S 5th Fl	New York	NY	10016	212-532-7160	213-2495
TF Cust Svc: 800-367-9692 ■ *Web:* www.sterlingpublishing.com					
Storey Publishing LLC 210 Mass Moca Way	North Adams	MA	01247	413-346-2100	346-2199*
**Fax:* Edit ■ *TF:* 800-827-7444 ■ *Web:* www.storey.com					
Sunset Publishing Corp 80 Willow Rd	Menlo Park	CA	94025	650-321-3600	327-7537*
**Fax:* Edit ■ *TF:* 800-227-7346 ■ *Web:* www.sunset.com					
Taylor & Francis Group LLC					
6000 Broken Sound Pkwy NW Suite 300	Boca Raton	FL	33487	561-994-0555	361-6075
TF: 800-272-7737 ■ *Web:* www.taylorandfrancisgroup.com					
Taylor Publishing Co 1550 W Mockingbird Ln	Dallas	TX	75235	214-637-2800	819-5005
TF: 800-677-2800 ■ *Web:* www.taylorpub.com					
Technology Marketing Corp 1 Technology Plaza	Norwalk	CT	06854	203-852-6800	866-3326
TF Cust Svc: 800-243-6002 ■ *Web:* www.tmcnet.com					
TFH Publications Inc					
3rd & Union Aves 1 TFH Plaza	Neptune	NJ	07753	732-988-8400	988-5466
TF: 800-631-2188 ■ *Web:* www.tfh.com					
Thomas Publishing Co 5 Penn Plaza	New York	NY	10001	212-695-0500	290-7365
TF: 800-699-9822 ■ *Web:* www.thomaspublishing.com					
Thorndike Press 295 Kennedy Memorial Dr	Waterville	ME	04901	207-859-1000	859-1008
TF: 800-223-1244 ■ *Web:* www.gale.com					

				Phone	Fax
Tor Books 175 5th Ave 14th Fl	New York	NY	10010	212-388-0100	388-0191
Web: www.tor.com					
Torstar Corp 1 Yonge St Suite 600	Toronto	ON	M5E1P9	416-869-4010	869-4183
TSE: TS.B ■ *Web:* www.torstar.com					
Townsend Press 439 Kelley Dr	West Berlin	NJ	08091	856-753-0554	225-8894*
**Fax Area Code:* 800 ■ *TF:* 800-772-6410 ■ *Web:* www.townsendpress.com					
Triumph Learning 136 Madison Ave	New York	NY	10016	800-221-9372	805-5723*
**Fax Area Code:* 866 ■ **Fax:* Cust Svc ■ *TF:* 800-221-9372 ■ *Web:* www.triumphlearning.com					
Tuttle Publishing					
364 Innovation Dr					
Airport Industrial Pk	North Clarendon	VT	05759	802-773-8930	329-8885*
**Fax Area Code:* 800 ■ *TF Sales:* 800-526-2778 ■ *Web:* www.tuttlepublishing.com					
Unisystems Inc 155 E 55th St	New York	NY	10022	212-826-0850	759-9069
Web: www.modernpublishing.com					
United Nations Publications					
2 UN Plaza Suite DC2-853	New York	NY	10017	212-963-8302	
TF: 800-253-9646 ■ *Web:* www.un.org/Pubs					
University Press of America					
4501 Forbes Blvd Suite 200	Lanham	MD	20706	301-459-3366	429-5746
TF: 800-462-6420 ■ *Web:* www.univpress.com					
Uniworld Business Publications Inc					
6 Seward Ave	Beverly	MA	01915	978-927-0219	927-0219
Web: www.uniworldbp.com					
US Government Printing Office (GPO)					
732 N Capitol St NW	Washington	DC	20401	202-512-1800	512-2104
TF: 866-512-1800 ■ *Web:* www.gpoaccess.gov					
Vantage Press Inc 419 Pk Ave S 18th Fl	New York	NY	10016	212-736-1767	736-2273
TF: 877-736-5403 ■ *Web:* www.vantagepress.com					
Verso Books 20 Jay St Suite 1010	Brooklyn	NY	11201	718-246-8160	246-8165
Web: www.versobooks.com					
Walch Education 40 Walch Dr	Portland	ME	04103	207-772-2846	772-3105
TF: 800-558-2846 ■ *Web:* www.walch.com					
Walsworth Publishing Co 306 N Kansas Ave	Marceline	MO	64658	660-376-3543	258-7798*
**Fax:* Hum Res ■ *TF:* 800-369-2646 ■ *Web:* www.walsworthyearbooks.com					
West Group 610 Opperman Dr	Eagan	MN	55123	651-687-7000	687-7551
TF Cust Svc: 800-328-4880 ■ *Web:* www.west.thomson.com					
Western Psychological Services					
12031 Wilshire Blvd	Los Angeles	CA	90025	310-478-2061	478-7838
TF: 800-648-8857 ■ *Web:* www.portal.wpspublish.com					
WH Freeman & Co 41 Madison Ave 35th Fl	New York	NY	10010	212-576-9400	689-2383
TF: 800-903-3019 ■ *Web:* www.whfreeman.com					
Wheatmark Inc 610 E Delano St Suite 104	Tucson	AZ	85705	520-798-0888	798-3394
TF: 888-934-0888 ■ *Web:* www.wheatmark.com					
White Wolf Publishing Co					
2075 W Pk Pl Blvd Suite G-50	Stone Mountain	GA	30087	404-292-1819	413-3025*
**Fax Area Code:* 770 ■ *TF Orders:* 800-454-9653 ■ *Web:* www.white-wolf.com					
Wilderness Press					
2204 First Ave S Suite 102	Birmingham	AL	35233	800-443-7227	326-1012*
**Fax Area Code:* 205 ■ *TF:* 800-604-4537 ■ *Web:* www.wildernesspress.com					
Wiley Publishing Inc 111 River St	Hoboken	NJ	07030	201-748-6000	748-6088
TF: 800-225-5945 ■ *Web:* www.wiley.com					
William B Eerdmans Publishing Co					
2140 Oak Industrial Dr NE	Grand Rapids	MI	49505	616-459-4591	459-6540
TF: 800-253-7521 ■ *Web:* www.eerdmans.com					
William H Sadlier Inc 9 Pine St	New York	NY	10005	212-227-2120	312-6080
TF: 800-582-5437 ■ *Web:* www.sadlier.com					
William Morrow & Co 10 E 53rd St	New York	NY	10022	212-207-7000	207-7145*
**Fax:* Edit ■ *TF:* 800-242-7737 ■ *Web:* www.harpercollins.com					
William S Hein & Co Inc 1285 Main St	Buffalo	NY	14209	716-882-2600	883-8100
TF: 800-828-7571 ■ *Web:* www.wshein.com					
Wilshire Book Co 9731 Variel Ave	Chatsworth	CA	91311	818-700-1522	700-1527
Web: www.mpowers.com					
Wimmer Cookbooks 4650 Shelby Air Dr	Memphis	TN	38118	901-362-8900	363-1771
TF: 800-548-2537 ■ *Web:* www.wimmerco.com					
Wolters Kluwer US Corp 2700 Lake Cook Rd	Riverwood	IL	60015	847-580-5000	
Web: www.wolterskluwer.com					
Workman Publishing 225 Varick St	New York	NY	10014	212-254-5900	254-8098
TF: 800-722-7202 ■ *Web:* www.workman.com					
World Almanac Education Group The					
512 7th Ave 21st Fl	New York	NY	10018	646-312-6893	312-6838*
**Fax:* Cust Svc ■ *Web:* www.worldalmanac.com					
World Book Publishing					
233 N Michigan Ave Suite 2000	Chicago	IL	60601	312-729-5800	729-5600
Web: www.worldbook.com					
Wright Group/McGraw-Hill					
130 E Randolph St Suite 400	Chicago	IL	60601	312-233-6500	233-6511
TF: 800-648-2970 ■ *Web:* www.wrightgroup.com					
WW Norton & Co Inc 500 5th Ave 6th Fl	New York	NY	10110	212-354-5500	869-0856
TF: 800-223-2584 ■ *Web:* www.wwnorton.com					
Zaner-Bloser Inc 1201 Dublin Rd	Columbus	OH	43215	614-486-0221	487-2699
TF: 800-421-3018 ■ *Web:* www.zaner-bloser.com					
Zebra Books					
Kensington Publishing Corp 119 W 40th St	New York	NY	10018	212-407-1500	
TF: 800-221-2647 ■ *Web:* www.kensingtonbooks.com					

640-3 Book Publishers - Religious & Spiritual Books

				Phone	Fax
Abbey Press Inc 1 Hill Dr	Saint Meinrad	IN	47577	812-357-6611	357-8388
TF: 800-962-4760 ■ *Web:* www.abbeypress.com					
American Bible Society 1865 Broadway	New York	NY	10023	212-408-1200	408-1512
TF: 800-322-4253 ■ *Web:* www.americanbible.org					
Augsburg Fortress Publishers					
100 S 5th St # 600	Minneapolis	MN	55402	612-330-3300	330-3455
TF: 800-426-0115 ■ *Web:* www.augsburgfortress.org					
Baker Book House Co Inc 6030 E Fulton St	Ada	MI	49301	616-676-9185	676-9573
TF Orders: 800-877-2665 ■ *Web:* www.bakerbooks.com					
Baker Book House Co Inc Revell Div					
6030 E Fulton St	Ada	MI	49301	616-676-9185	676-9573
TF Orders: 800-877-2665 ■ *Web:* www.bakerpublishinggroup.com					

				Phone	Fax
Bethany House Publishers 11400 Hampshire Ave S **Fax Area Code:* 616 ■ *TF:* 800-328-6109 ■ *Web:* www.bethanyhouse.com	Bloomington	MN	55438	800-328-6109	676-9573*
Brethren Press 1451 Dundee Ave *TF:* 800-441-3712 ■ *Web:* www.brethrenpress.com	Elgin	IL	60120	847-742-5100	742-5100
Broadman & Holman Publishers 127 Ninth Ave N MSN 114 **Fax Area Code:* 615 ■ *TF:* 800-448-8032 ■ *Web:* www.bhpublishinggroup.com	Nashville	TN	37234	800-448-8032	251-3914*
Concordia Publishing House Inc 3558 S Jefferson Ave *TF Cust Svc:* 800-325-3040 ■ *Web:* www.cph.org	Saint Louis	MO	63118	314-268-1000	268-1329
Cook Communications Ministries 4050 Lee Vance View *TF:* 800-708-5550 ■ *Web:* www.davidccook.com	Colorado Springs	CO	80918	719-536-0100	536-3265
CRC Publications Co 2850 Kalamazoo Ave SE **Fax Area Code:* 888 ■ *TF:* 800-333-8300 ■ *Web:* www.crcpublications.org	Grand Rapids	MI	49560	616-224-0808	642-8606*
Deseret Book Co 45 W S Temple **Fax Area Code:* 800 ■ *TF:* 800-453-4532 ■ *Web:* www.deseretbook.com	Salt Lake City	UT	84144	801-534-1515	453-3876*
DeVore & Sons Inc PO Box 780189 *TF Sales:* 800-676-2448 ■ *Web:* www.firesidecatholic.com	Wichita	KS	67278	316-267-3211	267-1850
E-Church Depot 3825 Hartzdale Dr *TF Orders:* 800-233-4443 ■ *Web:* www.echurchdepot.com	Camp Hill	PA	17011	717-761-7044	761-7273
Gospel Light Publications 1957 Eastman Ave **Fax:* Mktg ■ *TF:* 800-446-7735 ■ *Web:* www.gospellight.com	Ventura	CA	93003	805-644-9721	677-6818*
Hay House Inc PO Box 5100 **Fax Area Code:* 800 ■ *TF:* 800-654-5126 ■ *Web:* www.hayhouse.com	Carlsbad	CA	92018	760-431-7695	650-5115*
Jewish Publication Society 2100 Arch St 2nd Fl *TF:* 800-234-3151 ■ *Web:* www.jewishpub.org	Philadelphia	PA	19103	215-832-0600	568-2017
NavPress PO Box 35002 *TF:* 800-366-7788 ■ *Web:* www.navpress.com	Colorado Springs	CO	80935	800-366-7788	343-3902
Nelson Bibles 501 Nelson Pl PO Box 141000 *TF:* 800-251-4000 ■ *Web:* www.nelsonbibles.com	Nashville	TN	37214	615-889-9000	902-1897
New Leaf Publishing Group PO Box 726 *TF:* 800-999-3777 ■ *Web:* www.newleafpublishinggroup.com	Green Forest	AR	72638	870-438-5288	438-5120
New World Library 14 Pamaron Way *TF:* 800-972-6657 ■ *Web:* www.newworldlibrary.com	Novato	CA	94949	415-884-2100	884-2199
Northwestern Publishing House 1250 N 113th St *TF Orders:* 800-662-6022 ■ *Web:* online.nph.net	Milwaukee	WI	53226	414-475-6600	475-7695
Oregon Catholic Press (OCP) 5536 NE Hassalo St **Fax Area Code:* 800 ■ *TF:* 877-596-1653 ■ *Web:* www.ocp.org	Portland	OR	97213	503-281-1191	462-7329*
Our Sunday Visitor Inc 200 Noll Plaza *TF:* 800-348-2440 ■ *Web:* www.osv.com	Huntington	IN	46750	260-356-8400	359-0029
Pauline Books & Media 50 St Paul's Ave *TF Sales:* 800-876-4463 ■ *Web:* www.pauline.org	Boston	MA	02130	617-522-8911	524-8035
Review & Herald Publishing Assn 55 W Oak Ridge Dr *TF:* 800-456-3991 ■ *Web:* www.rhpa.org	Hagerstown	MD	21740	301-393-3000	393-4055
Standard Publishing Co 8805 Governors Hill Dr Suite 400 **Fax Area Code:* 877 ■ *TF Orders:* 800-543-1353 ■ *Web:* www.standardpub.com	Cincinnati	OH	45249	513-931-4050	867-5751*
Standex International Corp Consumer Group 8805 Governors Hill Dr Suite 400 *TF:* 800-543-1353 ■ *Web:* www.standex.com	Cincinnati	OH	45249	513-931-4050	931-4045
Thomas Nelson Inc 501 Nelson Pl PO Box 141000 *TF:* 800-251-4000 ■ *Web:* www.thomasnelson.com	Nashville	TN	37214	615-889-9000	889-5940
Tommy Nelson 15 Century Blvd Lakeview Bldg 2 5th Fl *TF:* 800-251-4000 ■ *Web:* www.tommynelson.com	Nashville	TN	37214	615-889-9000	902-2219
Tyndale House Publishers Inc 351 Executive Dr *TF:* 800-323-9400 ■ *Web:* www.tyndale.com	Carol Stream	IL	60188	800-323-9400	684-0247
United Methodist Publishing House 201 8th Ave S *TF:* 800-672-1789 ■ *Web:* www.umph.org	Nashville	TN	37203	615-749-6000	
Whitaker House/Anchor Distributors 1030 Hunt Valley Cir *TF Orders:* 800-444-4484 ■ *Web:* www.whitakerhouse.net	New Kensington	PA	15068	724-334-7000	334-1200
Zondervan 5300 Patterson Ave SE **Fax Area Code:* 800 ■ *TF Cust Svc:* 800-727-1309 ■ *Web:* www.zondervan.com	Grand Rapids	MI	49530	616-698-6900	934-6381*

640-4 Book Publishers - University Presses

				Phone	Fax
Associated University Presses 2010 Eastpark Blvd *Web:* www.aupresses.com	Cranbury	NJ	08512	609-655-4771	655-8366
Cambridge University Press 32 Avenue of the Americas 18th Fl **Fax:* Hum Res ■ *TF:* 800-221-4512 ■ *Web:* www.cambridge.org	New York	NY	10013	212-924-3900	691-3239*
Catholic University of America Press 620 Michigan Ave NE 240 Leahy Hall *TF:* 800-537-5487 ■ *Web:* www.cua.edu	Washington	DC	20064	202-319-5052	319-4985
Columbia University Press 61 W 62nd St 3rd Fl *TF:* 800-944-8648 ■ *Web:* www.columbia.edu	New York	NY	10023	212-459-0600	459-3677
Cornell University Press 750 Cascadilla St PO Box 6525 *TF Sales:* 800-666-2211 ■ *Web:* www.cornellpress.cornell.edu	Ithaca	NY	14850	607-277-2338	277-6292
Duke University Press 905 W Main St Suite 18-B **Fax Area Code:* 888 ■ **Fax:* Cust Svc ■ *TF Cust Svc:* 888-651-0122 ■ *Web:* www.dukeupress.edu	Durham	NC	27701	919-687-3600	651-0124*
Edwin Mellen Press 415 Ridge St *Web:* www.mellenpress.com	Lewiston	NY	14092	716-754-2266	754-4056
Gallaudet University Press 800 Florida Ave NE *Web:* gupress.gallaudet.edu	Washington	DC	20002	202-651-5488	651-5489
Harvard Business School Publishing 60 Harvard Way *TF:* 800-545-7685 ■ *Web:* www.harvardbusiness.org	Boston	MA	02163	617-783-7400	783-7664
Harvard University Press 79 Garden St **Fax Area Code:* 800 ■ *TF:* 800-405-1619 ■ *Web:* www.hup.harvard.edu	Cambridge	MA	02138	617-495-2600	406-9145*
Indiana University Press 601 N Morton St *TF:* 800-842-6796 ■ *Web:* www.iupress.indiana.edu	Bloomington	IN	47404	812-855-8817	855-8507
Johns Hopkins University Press 2715 N Charles St **Fax:* Orders ■ *TF Orders:* 800-537-5487 ■ *Web:* www.press.jhu.edu	Baltimore	MD	21218	410-516-6900	516-6998*
Mercer University Press 1400 Coleman Ave *TF:* 800-637-2378 ■ *Web:* www.mupress.org	Macon	GA	31207	478-301-2880	301-2264
Michigan State University Press 1405 S Harrison Rd Suite 25 Manly Miles Buildin *Web:* www.msupress.msu.edu	East Lansing	MI	48823	517-355-9543	432-2611
MIT Press The 55 Hayward St *Web:* www.mitpress.mit.edu	Cambridge	MA	02142	617-253-0080	253-1709
Naval Institute Press 291 Wood Rd *TF:* 800-233-8764 ■ *Web:* www.usni.org/press/press.html	Annapolis	MD	21402	410-268-6110	295-1049
Ohio State University Press 1070 Carmack Rd Pressey Hall Rm 180 *Web:* www.ohiostatepress.org	Columbus	OH	43210	614-292-6930	292-2065
Ohio University Press 19 Cir Dr The Ridges *TF Sales:* 800-621-2736 ■ *Web:* www.ohioswallow.com	Athens	OH	45701	740-593-1154	593-4536
Oregon State University Press 121 The Valley Library *TF Orders:* 800-426-3797 ■ *Web:* www.oregonstate.edu	Corvallis	OR	97331	541-737-3166	737-3170
Oxford University Press 198 Madison Ave **Fax:* PR ■ *TF:* 800-334-4249 ■ *Web:* www.oup.com/us	New York	NY	10016	212-726-6000	726-6447*
Pennsylvania State University Press 820 N University Dr USB1 Suite C *TF:* 800-326-9180 ■ *Web:* www.psupress.org	University Park	PA	16802	814-865-1327	863-1408
Princeton University Press 41 William St *Web:* www.press.princeton.edu	Princeton	NJ	08540	609-258-4900	258-6305
Purdue University Press 504 W State St Stewart Ctr 370 *TF Orders:* 800-247-6553 ■ *Web:* www.thepress.purdue.edu	West Lafayette	IN	47907	765-494-2038	496-2442
Rutgers University Press 100 Joyce Kilmer Ave *Web:* rutgerspress.rutgers.edu	Piscataway	NJ	08854	732-445-7762	445-7039
Southern Illinois University Press 1915 University Press Dr *Web:* www.siu.edu/siupress	Carbondale	IL	62901	618-453-2281	453-3787
Stanford University Press 1450 Page Mill Rd *TF:* 800-621-2736 ■ *Web:* www.sup.org	Palo Alto	CA	94304	650-723-9434	725-3457
State University of New York Press (SUNY) 22 Corporate Woods Blvd 3rd Fl *TF:* 866-430-7869 ■ *Web:* www.sunypress.edu	Albany	NY	12211	518-472-5000	472-5038
Temple University Press 1601 N Broad St USB 305 **Fax:* Edit ■ *TF:* 800-447-1656 ■ *Web:* www.temple.edu/tempress	Philadelphia	PA	19122	215-204-8787	204-4719*
Texas A & M University Press John H Lindsey Bldg 4354 TAMU *TF Orders:* 800-826-8911 ■ *Web:* www.tamu.edu	College Station	TX	77843	979-845-1436	847-8752
Texas Tech University Press 2903 4th St *TF:* 800-832-4042 ■ *Web:* www.ttup.ttu.edu	Lubbock	TX	79409	806-742-2982	742-2979
University of Alabama Press The 200 Hackberry Ln 2nd Fl PO Box 870380 *TF Orders:* 800-621-2736 ■ *Web:* www.uapress.ua.edu	Tuscaloosa	AL	35487	205-348-5180	348-9201
University of Alaska Press 794 University Ave # 220 *TF:* 888-252-6657 ■ *Web:* www.uaf.edu	Fairbanks	AK	99709	907-474-5831	474-5502
University Of Arizona Press The 1510 E University Blvd PO Box 210055 *TF:* 800-426-3797 ■ *Web:* www.uapress.arizona.edu	Tucson	AZ	85721	520-621-1441	621-8899
University of Arkansas Press McIlroy House 105 McIlroy *TF:* 800-626-0090 ■ *Web:* www.uapress.com	Fayetteville	AR	72701	479-575-3246	575-6044
University of California Press 2120 Berkeley Way *TF:* 800-822-6657 ■ *Web:* www.ucpress.edu	Berkeley	CA	94704	510-642-4247	643-7127
University of Chicago Press 1427 E 60th St *TF Sales:* 800-621-2736 ■ *Web:* www.press.uchicago.edu	Chicago	IL	60637	773-702-7700	702-9756
University of Delaware Press 181 S College Ave Rm 200-A *Web:* www2.lib.udel.edu/udpress	Newark	DE	19717	302-831-1149	831-6549
University of Hawaii Press 2840 Kolowalu St **Fax Area Code:* 800 ■ *TF:* 888-847-7377 ■ *Web:* www.uhpress.hawaii.edu	Honolulu	HI	96822	808-956-8255	650-7811*
University of Illinois Press 1325 S Oak St *Web:* www.press.uillinois.edu	Champaign	IL	61820	217-333-0950	244-8082
University of Iowa Press 119 W Pk Rd 100 Kuhl House *TF:* 800-621-2736 ■ *Web:* www.uiowapress.org	Iowa City	IA	52242	319-335-2000	335-2055
University of Massachusetts Press PO Box 429 *Web:* www.umass.edu/umpress	Amherst	MA	01004	413-545-2217	545-1226
University of Michigan Press 839 Greene St *Web:* www.press.umich.edu	Ann Arbor	MI	48104	734-764-4388	615-1540
University of Minnesota Press 111 Third Ave S Suite 290 *Web:* www.upress.umn.edu	Minneapolis	MN	55401	612-627-1970	627-1980
University of Missouri Press 2910 LeMone Blvd *TF:* 800-828-1894 ■ *Web:* press.umsystem.edu	Columbia	MO	65201	573-882-7641	884-4498
University of Nebraska Press 1111 Lincoln Mall **Fax:* Cust Svc ■ *TF Orders:* 800-755-1105 ■ *Web:* www.nebraskapress.unl.edu	Lincoln	NE	68508	402-472-3581	472-6208*
University of Nevada Press 206 N Virginia St *TF:* 877-682-6657 ■ *Web:* www.nvbooks.nevada.edu	Reno	NV	89501	775-784-6573	784-6200
University of New Mexico Press (UNM) 1717 Roma Ave NE **Fax Area Code:* 800 ■ *TF Orders:* 800-249-7737 ■ *Web:* www.unmpress.com	Albuquerque	NM	87106	505-277-7777	622-8667*

	City	State	Zip	Phone	Fax
University of North Carolina Press 116 S Boundary St *TF:* 800-848-6224 ■ *Web:* www.uncpress.unc.edu	Chapel Hill	NC	27514	919-966-3561	966-3829
University of North Texas Press 1155 Union Cir Suite 311336 *TF:* 800-826-8911 ■ *Web:* www.unt.edu/untpress	Denton	TX	76203	940-565-2142	565-4590
University of Oklahoma Press 2800 Venture Dr. *TF Orders:* 800-627-7377 ■ *Web:* www.oupress.com	Norman	OK	73069	405-325-2000	364-5798
University of Pennsylvania Press 3902 Spruce St. *TF Cust Svc:* 800-537-5487 ■ *Web:* www.upenn.edu/pennpress	Philadelphia	PA	19104	215-898-6261	898-0404
University of Pittsburgh Press 3400 Forbes Ave 5th Fl. *TF Sales:* 800-666-2211 ■ *Web:* www.upress.pitt.edu	Pittsburgh	PA	15261	412-383-2456	383-2466
University of South Carolina Press 1600 Hampton St 5th Fl *TF Orders:* 800-768-2500 ■ *Web:* www.sc.edu/uscpress	Columbia	SC	29208	803-777-5243	777-0160
University of Tennessee Press 600 Henley St. *Web:* www.utpress.org	Knoxville	TN	37902	865-974-3321	974-3724
University of Texas Press 2100 Comal St. *TF Sales:* 800-252-3206 ■ *Web:* www.utexas.edu/utpress	Austin	TX	78722	512-471-7233	232-7178
University of the South Press 735 University Ave Fulford Hall *TF:* 800-289-4919	Sewanee	TN	37383	931-598-1286	598-1667
University of Utah Press 1795 E S Campus Dr Suite 101 *Web:* www.uofupress.com	Salt Lake City	UT	84112	801-581-6771	581-3365
University of Washington Press 4333 Brooklyn Ave NE *TF:* 800-537-5487 ■ *Web:* www.washington.edu	Seattle	WA	98195	206-543-4050	543-3932
University of Wisconsin Press 1930 Monroe St 3rd Fl *Web:* www.wisc.edu	Madison	WI	53711	608-263-1110	263-1132
University Press of Colorado 5589 Arapahoe Ave Suite 206C *TF:* 800-627-7377 ■ *Web:* www.upcolorado.com	Boulder	CO	80303	720-406-8849	406-3443
University Press of Florida 15 NW 15th St *TF Sales:* 800-226-3822 ■ *Web:* www.upf.com	Gainesville	FL	32611	352-392-1351	392-7302
University Press of Kansas 2502 Westbrooke Cir *Web:* www.kansaspress.ku.edu	Lawrence	KS	66045	785-864-4154	864-4586
University Press of Kentucky 663 S Limestone St **Fax:* Mktg ■ *TF Sales:* 800-839-6855 ■ *Web:* www.kentuckypress.com	Lexington	KY	40508	859-257-8400	257-8481*
University Press of Mississippi 3825 Ridgewood Rd *TF:* 800-737-7788 ■ *Web:* www.upress.state.ms.us	Jackson	MS	39211	601-432-6205	432-6217
University Press of New England (UPNE) 1 Ct St Suite 250 *TF Orders:* 800-421-1561 ■ *Web:* www.upne.com	Lebanon	NH	03766	603-448-1533	448-9429
University Press of Virginia 210 Sprigg Ln. *TF Orders:* 800-831-3406 ■ *Web:* www.upress.virginia.edu	Charlottesville	VA	22904	434-924-3469	982-2655
Vanderbilt University Press 2014 Broadway Suite 320 *Web:* www.vanderbiltuniversitypress.com	Nashville	TN	37203	615-322-3585	343-8823
Wesleyan University Press 215 Long Ln *TF:* 800-421-1561 ■ *Web:* www.wesleyan.edu	Middletown	CT	06459	860-685-7711	685-7712
Yale University Press 302 Temple St. *TF Sales:* 800-405-1619 ■ *Web:* www.yale.edu	New Haven	CT	06511	203-432-0960	432-0948
Yeshiva University Press 500 W 185th St. *Web:* www.yu.edu	New York	NY	10033	212-960-5400	960-0043

640-5 Comic Book Publishers

	City	State	Zip	Phone	Fax
Archie Comic Publications Inc 325 Fayette Ave. *Web:* www.archiecomics.com	Mamaroneck	NY	10543	914-381-5155	381-4015
Dark Horse Comics Inc 10956 SE Main St *TF:* 800-862-0052 ■ *Web:* www.darkhorse.com	Milwaukie	OR	97222	503-652-8815	654-9440
DC Comics 1700 Broadway. **Fax:* Mktg ■ *Web:* www.dccomics.com	New York	NY	10019	212-636-5400	636-5599*
Diamond Comic Distributors Inc 1966 Greenspring Dr Suite 300 *TF:* 800-452-6642 ■ *Web:* www.diamondcomics.com	Timonium	MD	21093	410-560-7100	560-7148
Fantagraphics Books 7563 Lake City Way NE. *TF:* 800-657-1100 ■ *Web:* www.fantagraphics.com	Seattle	WA	98115	206-524-1967	524-2104
Image Comics Inc 1942 University Ave Suite 305 *Web:* www.imagecomics.com	Berkeley	CA	94704	510-644-4980	
Viz Media 295 Bay St. *Web:* www.viz.com	San Francisco	CA	94133	415-546-7073	546-7086

640-6 Directory Publishers

	City	State	Zip	Phone	Fax
1-800-ATTORNEY Inc 1601 W Airport Fwy **Fax Area Code:* 386 ■ *TF:* 800-288-6763 ■ *Web:* www.1800attorney.com	Euless	TX	76040	877-321-2899	228-0290*
ASD Data Services LLC PO Box 1184 *TF:* 877-742-7297 ■ *Web:* www.asd.com	Manchester	TN	37349	877-742-7297	
Bresser's Cross Index Directory Co 684 W Baltimore St. *TF:* 800-878-3333 ■ *Web:* www.bressers.com	Detroit	MI	48202	313-874-0570	874-3510
BurrellesLuce 75 E Northfield Rd *TF:* 800-631-1160 ■ *Web:* www.burrellesluce.com	Livingston	NJ	07039	973-992-6600	992-7675
Cincinnati Bell Directory Inc (CBYP) 312 Plum St Suite 900 *Web:* www.cbyp.com	Cincinnati	OH	45202	513-768-6555	784-1613
Cision US Inc 332 S Michigan Ave Suite 900 **Fax:* Cust Svc ■ *TF:* 866-639-5087 ■ *Web:* www.us.cision.com	Chicago	IL	60604	312-922-2400	922-3126*
Cole Information Services 3401 NW 39th St **Fax Area Code:* 800 ■ *TF:* 877-414-3332 ■ *Web:* www.coleinformation.com	Lincoln	NE	68524	402-323-3500	533-6591*
Contractors Register Inc 800 E Main St PO Box 500 **Fax Area Code:* 914 ■ *TF:* 800-922-9962 ■ *Web:* www.thebluebook.com	Jefferson Valley	NY	10535	800-431-2584	243-0287*
CSG Information Services 3922 Coconut Palm Dr **Fax Area Code:* 813 ■ *TF:* 800-927-9292 ■ *Web:* www.csgis.com	Tampa	FL	33619	800-927-9292	627-6888*
DAG Media Inc 125-10 Queens Blvd Suite 14 *NASDAQ: DAGM* ■ *TF:* 800-261-2799 ■ *Web:* www.newyellow.com	Kew Gardens	NY	11415	718-263-8454	793-2522
Dickman Directories Inc 6145 Columbus Pike *TF:* 877-836-4154	Lewis Center	OH	43035	740-548-6130	548-2217
Genesis Publisher Services 2025 E Beltline Ave SE *Web:* www.genesispubservices.com	Grand Rapids	MI	49546	616-831-2800	831-0831
Haines & Co Inc 8050 Freedom Ave *TF:* 800-843-8452 ■ *Web:* www.haines.com	North Canton	OH	44720	330-494-9111	494-3862
Harris InfoSource 2057 E Aurora Rd. **Fax Area Code:* 800 ■ *TF:* 800-888-5900 ■ *Web:* www.harrisinfo.com	Twinsburg	OH	44087	330-425-9000	643-5997*
HealthLeaders-InterStudy 1 Vantage Way Suite B-300 *TF:* 800-643-7600 ■ *Web:* www.hl-isy.com	Nashville	TN	37228	615-385-4131	385-4979
Hill-Donnelly Information Services - Info USA City Directories 5711 S 86th Cir *TF:* 866-478-8104 ■ *Web:* www.infousacity.com	Omaha	NE	68127	402-593-4500	537-7901
Hoover's Inc 5800 Airport Blvd *TF:* 800-486-8666 ■ *Web:* www.hoovers.com	Austin	TX	78752	512-374-4500	374-4501
Idearc Media 2200 W Airfield Dr. *TF:* 800-888-8448 ■ *Web:* www.supermedia.com	DFW Airport	TX	75261	800-555-4833	
LexisNexis Martindale-Hubbell 121 Chanlon Rd **Fax Area Code:* 908 ■ **Fax:* Sales ■ *TF:* 800-526-4902 ■ *Web:* www.martindale.com	New Providence	NJ	07974	800-526-4902	665-3593*
Local Insight Yellow Pages 100 Executive Pkwy *Web:* www.localinsightmedia.com	Hudson	OH	44236	330-650-7100	655-4508
Manufacturers Group Inc PO Box 4310 *TF:* 800-264-3303 ■ *Web:* www.industrysearch.com	Lexington	KY	40544	859-223-6703	223-6709
Marc Publishing Co 600 Germantown Pike Suite B *TF:* 800-432-5478 ■ *Web:* www.marcpub.com	Lafayette Hill	PA	19444	610-834-8585	834-7707
Oxbridge Communications Inc 186 5th Ave 6th Fl *TF:* 800-955-0231 ■ *Web:* www.oxbridge.com	New York	NY	10010	212-741-0231	633-2938
Real Yellow Pages Online 754 Peachtree St. **Fax Area Code:* 404 ■ *TF:* 866-326-7200 ■ *Web:* www.realpageslive.com	Atlanta	GA	30308	877-573-2597	986-9425*
RH Donnelley Corp 1001 Winstead Dr *NYSE: RHD* ■ *TF:* 866-527-4550 ■ *Web:* www.dexone.com	Cary	NC	27513	919-297-1600	297-1600
Rich's California Business Directories Inc 1820 Gateway Blvd Suite 170 **Fax Area Code:* 650 ■ *TF:* 800-969-7424 ■ *Web:* www.norcalcompanies.com	San Mateo	CA	94404	800-969-7424	350-4084*
Stewart Directories Inc 10540 York Rd # J *TF:* 800-311-0786 ■ *Web:* www.stewartdirectories.com	Cockeysville	MD	21030	410-628-5988	683-3153
SunShine Pages 1 Galleria # 1900 *TF:* 800-259-9835 ■ *Web:* www.sunshinepages.com	Metairie	LA	70001	504-832-9835	832-9931
Taylor & Francis Group LLC 6000 Broken Sound Pkwy NW Suite 300 *TF:* 800-272-7737 ■ *Web:* www.taylorandfrancisgroup.com	Boca Raton	FL	33487	561-994-0555	361-6075
United Yellow Pages Inc 12442 Knott St 2nd Fl.	Garden Grove	CA	92841	714-889-5304	889-5312
University Directories 88 VilCom Cir **Fax Area Code:* 800 ■ *TF:* 800-743-5556 ■ *Web:* www.universitydirectories.com	Chapel Hill	NC	27514	919-968-0225	743-0009*
Valley Yellow Pages 1850 N Gateway Blvd *TF:* 800-350-8887 ■ *Web:* www.myyp.com	Fresno	CA	93727	559-251-8888	253-9729
West Legal Directory 610 Opperman Dr *TF:* 800-328-9378 ■ *Web:* www.lawyers.findlaw.com	Eagan	MN	55123	651-687-7000	
Worldwide Chamber of Commerce Directory Inc 1717 Madison Ave Suite 3 *TF:* 888-883-3231 ■ *Web:* www.worldchamberdirectoryonline.com	Loveland	CO	80538	970-663-3231	663-6187
Yellow Book USA 398 RXR Plaza **Fax:* Hum Res ■ *TF:* 877-512-7710 ■ *Web:* www.yellowbook.com	Uniondale	NY	11556	516-730-1900	730-1950*

640-7 Music Publishers

	City	State	Zip	Phone	Fax
Alfred Publishing Co 16320 Roscoe Blvd Suite 100. *TF:* 800-292-6122 ■ *Web:* www.alfred.com	Van Nuys	CA	91406	818-891-5999	891-2369
Brentwood Benson Music Publishing 2555 Meridian Blvd *Web:* www.brentwoodbenson.com	Franklin	TN	37067	615-261-6500	261-3385
Carl Fischer Inc 65 Bleecker St 8th Fl. *TF:* 800-762-2328 ■ *Web:* www.carlfischer.com	New York	NY	10012	212-777-0900	477-6996
EMI Music Publishing 75 9th Ave 4th Fl *Web:* www.emimusicpub.com	New York	NY	10011	212-492-1200	492-1865
G Schirmer Inc 257 Pk Ave S 20th Fl *Web:* www.schirmer.com	New York	NY	10010	212-254-2100	254-2013
Hal Leonard Corp 960 E Mark St. *TF:* 800-321-3408 ■ *Web:* www.halleonard.com	Winona	MN	55987	507-454-2920	454-8334
Lorenz Corp 501 E 3rd St. *TF:* 800-444-1144 ■ *Web:* www.lorenz.com	Dayton	OH	45402	937-228-6118	223-2042
Malaco Music Group Inc 3023 W Northside Dr *TF Cust Svc:* 800-272-7936 ■ *Web:* www.malaco.com	Jackson	MS	39213	601-982-4522	982-4528
Mel Bay Publications Inc 4 Industrial Dr *TF:* 800-863-5229 ■ *Web:* www.melbay.com	Pacific	MO	63069	636-257-3970	257-5062
Sony/ATV Music Publishing LLC 550 Madison Ave 5th Fl *Web:* www.sonyatv.com	New York	NY	10022	212-833-7730	
Theodore Presser Co 588 N Gulph Rd. *Web:* www.presser.com	King of Prussia	PA	19406	610-592-1222	592-1229

Phone Fax

Universal Music Publishing
8750 Wilshire Blvd. Beverly Hills CA 90211 310-358-4300

Walt Disney Music Publishing
500 S Buena Vista St MC 6174 Burbank CA 91521 818-567-5128 567-5178
Web: www.corporate.disney.go.com

Warner/Chappell Music Inc
10585 Santa Monica Blvd. Los Angeles CA 90025 310-441-8600 441-8780
Web: www.warnerchappell.com

640-8 Newspaper Publishers

Phone Fax

ABC Inc 77 W 66th St New York NY 10023 212-456-7777 456-2795
Web: www.abc.go.com

Ada Evening News Corp PO Box 489 Ada OK 74821 580-310-7500 332-8734
Web: www.adaeveningnews.com

Advance Publications Inc
950 Fingerboard Rd Staten Island NY 10305 718-981-1234 981-5679
Web: www.advance.net

Afro-American Newspapers Co
2519 N Charles St Baltimore MD 21218 410-554-8200 570-9297*
**Fax Area Code:* 877 ■ *TF:* 800-237-6892 ■ *Web:* www.afro.com

Alameda Times-Star
7677 Oakport St Suite 950 PO Box 28884 Oakland CA 94604 510-208-6300 208-6304
TF: 800-595-9595 ■ *Web:* www.info.bayareanewsgroup.com

Albany Herald Publishing Co Inc
126 N Washington St Albany GA 31702 229-888-9300 888-9357
TF: 800-685-4639 ■ *Web:* www.albanyherald.com

Albert Lea Tribune The
808 W Front St PO Box 60 Albert Lea MN 56007 507-373-1411 373-0333
TF: 800-657-4996 ■ *Web:* www.albertleatribune.com

Arizona Publishing Cos PO Box 1950 Phoenix AZ 85001 602-444-8000 444-8340
TF: 800-331-9303 ■ *Web:* www.azcentral.com

Athens Messenger The 9300 Johnson Rd. Athens OH 45701 740-592-6612 592-4647
Web: www.athensmessenger.com

Athens Newspaper Inc PO Box 912 Athens GA 30603 706-549-0123 208-2246
Web: www.onlineathens.com

Auburn Publishers Inc 25 Dill St. Auburn NY 13021 315-253-5311 253-6031
TF: 800-878-5311 ■ *Web:* www.auburnpub.com

Austin Daily Herald Inc 310 NE 2nd St Austin MN 55912 507-433-8851 437-8644
Web: www.austindailyherald.com

Beckley Newspapers Inc 801 N Kanawha St. Beckley WV 25801 304-255-4400 255-4427
TF Cust Svc: 800-950-0250

Bee Publishing Co Inc PO Box 5503 Newtown CT 06470 203-426-3141 426-5169
Web: www.thebee.com

Belo Corp Newspaper Group 400 S Record St Dallas TX 75202 214-977-6606 977-6603
TF: 800-431-0010 ■ *Web:* www.belo.com

Bliss Communications Inc PO Box 5001 Janesville WI 53547 608-754-3311 755-8393
TF: 800-362-6712 ■ *Web:* www.blissnet.net

BMH Books 1104 Kings Hwy Winona Lake IN 46590 574-372-3098 267-4745
TF: 800-348-2756 ■ *Web:* www.bmhbooks.com

Boone Newspapers Inc
15222 Freeman's Bend Rd Northport
PO Box 2370 Tuscaloosa AL 35403 205-330-4100 330-4140
Web: www.boonenewspapers.com

Booth Michigan
55 Michigan St NW PO Box 2168 Grand Rapids MI 49501 616-222-5824 222-5318
TF: 800-886-5529 ■ *Web:* www.boothnewspapers.com

Breese Publishing Co
8060 Old Hwy 50 PO Box 405 Breese IL 62230 618-526-7211 526-2590
TF: 888-648-4616 ■ *Web:* www.breesepub.com

Breeze Newspaper 2510 Del Prado Blvd Cape Coral FL 33904 239-574-1110 574-3403
Web: www.breezenewspapers.com

Brehm Communications Inc
16644 W Bernardo Dr # 300 San Diego CA 92127 858-451-6200 451-3814
Web: www.brehmcommunications.com

Burlington Hawk Eye Co
800 S Main St PO Box 10 Burlington IA 52601 319-754-8461 754-6824
TF: 800-397-1708

Calkins Media Inc 8400 Rt 13 Levittown PA 19057 215-949-4011 949-4021

Capital City Press Inc PO Box 588 Baton Rouge LA 70821 225-383-1111 388-0397*
**Fax:* Hum Res ■ *Web:* www.2theadvocate.com

Capital Gazette Communications LLC
2000 Capital Dr PO Box 911 Annapolis MD 21401 410-268-5000 280-5953
Web: www.hometownannapolis.com

Capital Newspapers 805 Pk Ave PO Box 558 Beaver Dam WI 53916 920-887-0321 887-8790*
**Fax:* Cust Svc ■ *Web:* www.wiscnews.com

Casa Grande Valley Newspaper Inc
PO Box 15002 Casa Grande AZ 85130 520-836-7461 836-0343
TF: 800-821-1746 ■ *Web:* www.trivalleycentral.com

Casiano Communications Inc
1700 Fernandez Juncos Ave PO Box 12130 San Juan PR 00909 787-728-3000 268-1001
Web: www.casiano.com

Chattanooga Publishing Co Inc
400 E 11th St Chattanooga TN 37403 423-756-6900 757-6383
TF: 800-733-2637 ■ *Web:* www.timesfreepress.com

Cheyenne Newspaper Inc 702 W Lincolnway Cheyenne WY 82001 307-634-3361 633-3189
TF: 800-561-6268 ■ *Web:* www.wyomingnews.com

Christian Science Publishing Society
210 Massachusetts Ave P02-15 Boston MA 02115 617-450-2000
TF: 800-288-7090 ■ *Web:* www.csmonitor.com

Citizen Publishing Co Inc 260 10th St Windom MN 56101 507-831-3455 831-3740
Web: www.windomnews.com

Coffee News USA 120 Linden St. Bangor ME 04401 207-941-0860 941-1050
Web: www.coffeenewsusa.com

Columbia Star PO Box 5955 Columbia SC 29250 803-771-0219 254-9056
TF: 888-447-2732 ■ *Web:* www.thecolumbiastar.com

Community Newspaper Co 254 2nd Ave. Needham MA 02494 781-433-6700 433-7879*
**Fax:* Edit ■ *Web:* www.metrowest.com

Community Newspaper Co Inc 72 Cherry Hill Dr. Beverly MA 01915 978-739-1300 739-8501
Web: www.wickedlocal.com

Phone Fax

Community Newspaper Holdings Inc
3500 Colonnade Pkwy Suite 600 Birmingham AL 35243 205-298-7100 298-7102
TF: 800-951-2644 ■ *Web:* www.cnhi.com

Community Newspapers Inc 6605 SE Lake Rd. Portland OR 97222 503-684-0360 620-3433
Web: www.portlandtribune.com

Community Press Newspapers 4910 Para Dr Cincinnati OH 45237 513-242-4300 242-2649
Web: www.communitypress.cincinnati.com

Consolidated Publishing Co PO Box 189 Anniston AL 36202 256-236-1551 241-1991
Web: www.annistonstar.com

Contra Costa Newspapers Inc 1700 Cavallo Rd Antioch CA 94509 925-757-2525 706-2305
Web: www.contracostatimes.com

Coulter Press Inc 156 Church St Clinton MA 01510 978-368-0176 368-1151

Country Media Inc 2640 Lazelle Rd Sturgis SD 57785 605-347-2585 347-2525
TF: 800-253-3656 ■ *Web:* www.tsln.com

Courier Publications Inc
301 Pk St PO Box 249 Rockland ME 04841 207-594-4401 596-6981
TF: 800-499-4401 ■ *Web:* www.courierpub.com

Cox Media Group 6205 Peachtree Dunwoody Dr Atlanta GA 30328 678-645-0000 645-5002
TF: 800-950-3739 ■ *Web:* www.coxmediagroup.com

CTV Globemedia Inc 9 Ch Nine Ct. Toronto ON M1S4B5 416-332-5700 291-5537
Web: www.ctv.ca

Cumberlink Publishers PO Box 130 Carlisle PA 17013 717-243-2611 243-3121

Daily Globe The 118 E McLeod Ave PO Box 548 Ironwood MI 49938 906-932-2211 932-4211
TF: 800-236-2887 ■ *Web:* www.yourdailyglobe.com

Daily Herald Co The
1213 California St PO Box 930 Everett WA 98206 425-339-3000 339-3017
Web: www.heraldnet.com

Daily Journal Corp 915 E 1st St Los Angeles CA 90012 213-229-5300 229-5481
NASDAQ: DJCO ■ *Web:* www.dailyjournal.com

Daily Progress 685 W Rio Rd Charlottesville VA 22902 434-978-7200 978-7252
Web: www2.dailyprogress.com

Daily Record Co 11 E Saratoga St Baltimore MD 21202 443-524-8100 524-8100
TF: 800-296-8181 ■ *Web:* www.thedailyrecord.com

Daily Record Inc 6 Century Dr Parsippany NJ 07054 973-428-6200 428-6666
TF: 800-398-8991 ■ *Web:* www.dailyrecord.com

Daily Reflector Inc PO Box 1967 Greenville NC 27835 252-752-6166 752-9583
TF: 800-849-6166 ■ *Web:* www.reflector.com

Danbury Publishing Co 333 Main St Danbury CT 06810 203-744-5100 792-8730
Web: www.newstimes.com

Day Publishing Co 47 Eugene O'Neill Dr New London CT 06320 860-442-2200 442-5599
TF: 800-542-3354 ■ *Web:* www.theday.com

Dayton Newspapers Inc 116 S Main St. Dayton OH 45409 937-225-2000 225-2043*
**Fax:* Mktg ■ *Web:* www.daytondailynews.com

Delphos Herald Inc 405 N Main St. Delphos OH 45833 419-695-0015 692-7704
TF: 800-589-6950 ■ *Web:* www.delphosherald.com

Denver Newspaper Agency 101 W Colfax Ave Denver CO 80202 303-954-1010 954-1010
TF: 800-336-7678 ■ *Web:* www.denverpost.com

Derrick Publishing Co 1510 W 1st St Oil City PA 16301 814-676-7444 677-8351
TF: 800-352-1002 ■ *Web:* www.thederrick.com

Desert Sun Publishing Co PO Box 2734 Palm Springs CA 92263 760-322-8889 322-8889
TF Advertising: 800-233-3741 ■ *Web:* www.mydesert.com

Detroit Legal News Co 2001 W Lafayette Blvd. Detroit MI 48216 313-961-3949 961-3949
TF: 800-875-5275 ■ *Web:* www.legalnews.com

Diocese of Steubenville Catholic Charities
PO Box 969 Steubenville OH 43952 740-282-3631 282-3327
Web: www.diosteub.org

Dispatch Printing Co 34 S 3rd St. Columbus OH 43215 614-461-5000 461-7580
TF: 800-282-0263 ■ *Web:* www.dispatch.com

Dow Jones & Co Inc
1211 Avenue of the Americas New York NY 10281 212-416-2000 416-2658
Web: www.dowjones.com

Eagle Publishing Co 75 S Church St Pittsfield MA 01201 413-447-7311 447-7311
TF: 800-245-0254 ■ *Web:* www.berkshireeagle.com

East Coast Newspapers Inc PO Box 11707 Rock Hill SC 29731 803-329-4000 329-4021
Web: www.mcclatchy.com

East Hampton Star Inc The
153 Main St PO Box 5002 East Hampton NY 11937 631-324-0002 324-7943
Web: www.easthamptonstar.com

Eau Claire Press Co 701 S Farwell St Eau Claire WI 54701 715-833-9200 833-9244
TF: 800-236-8808 ■ *Web:* www.leadertelegram.com

ECM Publishers Inc 1201 14th Ave S. Princeton MN 55371 763-389-4710 389-5228
Web: www.ecm-inc.com

Edward A Sherman Publishing Co
101 Malbone Rd Newport RI 02840 401-849-3300 849-3306
TF: 800-320-2378 ■ *Web:* www.newportdailynews.com

Evening Post Publishing Co
134 Columbus St Charleston SC 29403 843-577-7111
Web: www.evepost.com

EW Scripps Co 312 Walnut St Suite 2800 Cincinnati OH 45202 513-977-3000 977-3720*
NYSE: SSP ■ **Fax:* Hum Res ■ *TF:* 800-888-3000 ■ *Web:* www.scripps.com

Express-News Corp PO Box 2171 San Antonio TX 78297 210-250-3000 250-3121
TF: 800-555-1551 ■ *Web:* www.mysanantonio.com

Feather Publishing Co Inc 287 Lawrence St. Quincy CA 95971 530-283-0800 283-3952
Web: www.plumasnews.com

Findlay Publishing Co 701 W Sandusky St Findlay OH 45840 419-422-5151 422-2937
Web: www.thecourier.com

Finger Lakes Printing Co
218 Genesee St PO Box 393 Geneva NY 14456 315-789-3333 789-4077
TF: 800-388-6652 ■ *Web:* www.fltimes.com

Flashes Publishers Inc 595 Jenner Dr Allegan MI 49010 269-673-2141 673-4761
TF: 800-968-4415 ■ *Web:* www.flashespublishers.com

Fort Wayne Newspapers Inc
600 W Main St PO Box 100 Fort Wayne IN 46802 260-461-8290 461-8817
TF: 800-444-3303 ■ *Web:* www.fortwayne.com

Forum Communications Co 101 5th St N Fargo ND 58102 701-451-5629 451-5633
TF: 800-747-7311 ■ *Web:* www.forumcomm.com

Forward Publishing 125 Maiden Ln New York NY 10038 212-889-8200 447-6406
TF: 800-266-0773 ■ *Web:* www.forward.com

Frankfort Publishing Co LLC
1216 Wilkinson Blvd Suite 40 Frankfort KY 40601 502-227-4556 227-2831
Web: www.state-journal.com

Company	City	State	ZIP	Phone	Fax
Freedom Communications Inc 17666 Fitch *Web:* www.freedom.com	Irvine	CA	92614	949-253-2300	474-7675
Galesburg Printing & Publishing Co 140 S Prairie St *Web:* www.galesburg.com	Galesburg	IL	61401	309-343-7181	343-2382
GateHouse Media Inc 350 Willowbrook Office Pk *Web:* www.gatehousemedia.com	Fairport	IL	14450	585-598-0030	248-2631
Gateway Newspapers 610 Beatty Rd *Web:* www.gatewaynewspapers.com	Monroeville	PA	15146	412-856-7400	856-7954
Gazette Newspapers Inc 9030 Comprint Ct **Fax:* Hum Res ■ *TF:* 888-670-7100 ■ *Web:* www.gazette.net	Gaithersburg	MD	20877	301-948-3120	670-7138*
George J Foster Co Inc 150 Venture Dr *TF:* 800-660-8310 ■ *Web:* www.fosters.com	Dover	NH	03820	603-742-4455	749-7079
George W Prescott Publishing Co Inc 400 Crown Colony Dr	Quincy	MA	02169	617-786-7000	786-7025
Gilmer Mirror Co 214 E Marshall St *Web:* www.gilmermirror.com	Gilmer	TX	75644	903-843-2503	843-5123
Glastonbury Citizen Inc PO Box 373 *Web:* www.glcitizen.com	Glastonbury	CT	06033	860-633-4691	657-3258
Glendale News Press 221 N Brand Ave *Web:* www.glendalenewspress.com	Glendale	CA	91203	818-637-3200	241-1975
Gray Television Inc 4370 Peachtree Rd NE *NYSE: GTN* ■ *Web:* www.graycommunications.com	Atlanta	GA	30319	404-504-9828	261-9607
Greater Media Inc 35 Braintree Hill Pk Suite 300 *Web:* www.greater-media.com	Braintree	MA	02184	781-348-8600	348-8695
Guard Publishing Co PO Box 10188 *Web:* www.registerguard.com	Eugene	OR	97440	541-485-1234	984-4699
Harris Enterprises Inc 1 N Main St # 616	Hutchinson	KS	67501	620-694-5830	694-5837
Hastings & Sons Publishing 38 Exchange St *Web:* www.itemlive.com	Lynn	MA	01901	781-593-7700	598-2891
Hearst Corp 300 W 57th St *Web:* www.hearst.com	New York	NY	10019	212-649-2275	
Hearst Newspapers 300 W 57th St 41st Fl *Web:* www.hearst.com/newspapers	New York	NY	10005	212-649-2275	
Herald Publishing Co PO Box 153 *Web:* www.jhvonline.com	Houston	TX	77001	713-630-0391	630-0404
Herald Publishing Co 1 Herald Sq *Web:* www.newbritainherald.com	New Britain	CT	06050	860-225-4601	225-2611
Herald Publishing Co 132 W Main St *TF:* 800-697-4111 ■ *Web:* www.heraldonline.com	Rock Hill	SC	29730	803-329-4000	329-4021
Herald-Mail Co The 100 Summit Ave PO Box 439 *TF:* 800-626-6397 ■ *Web:* www.herald-mail.com	Hagerstown	MD	21741	301-733-5131	739-7518
Herald-Star 401 Herald Sq *TF:* 800-526-7987 ■ *Web:* www.hsconnect.com	Steubenville	OH	43952	740-283-4711	284-7355
Herald-Sun Newspapers The 2828 Pickett Rd *TF:* 800-672-0061 ■ *Web:* www.heraldsun.com/durham	Durham	NC	27705	919-419-6500	419-6889
Herald-Times Inc PO Box 909 *Web:* www.heraldtimesonline.com	Bloomington	IN	47402	812-332-4401	331-4285
Heritage Newspapers Inc 1 Heritage Pl Suite 100 *Web:* www.heritagenews.com	Southgate	MI	48195	734-246-0800	246-2727
Hersam Acorn Newspapers 16 Bailey Ave *TF:* 800-372-2790 ■ *Web:* www.acorn-online.com	Ridgefield	CT	06877	203-438-6544	438-3395
Hi-Desert Publishing Co 56445 29 Palms Hwy *Web:* www.hidesertstar.com	Yucca Valley	CA	92284	760-365-3315	365-2650
High Plains Publishers Inc 1500 W Wyatt Earp Blvd *TF:* 800-452-7171 ■ *Web:* www.hpj.com	Dodge City	KS	67801	620-227-7171	227-7173
Hills Newspapers 1516 Oak St *Web:* www.insidebayarea.com	Alameda	CA	94501	510-748-1683	748-1680
Home News Enterprises 333 2nd St *TF:* 800-876-7811 ■ *Web:* homenewsenterprises.com	Columbus	IN	47201	812-372-7811	379-5706
Housatonic Publications 65 Bank St	New Milford	CT	06776	860-354-2261	354-8706
Hubbard Publishing Co 127 E Chillicothe Ave PO Box 40 *Web:* www.examiner.org	Bellefontaine	OH	43311	937-592-3060	592-4463
Huse Publishing Co PO Box 977 *TF:* 877-371-1020 ■ *Web:* www.norfolkdailynews.com	Norfolk	NE	68702	402-371-1020	371-5802
Hutchinson Leader Inc 36 Washington Ave W *Web:* www.hutchinsonleader.com	Hutchinson	MN	55350	320-587-5000	587-6104
Illini Media Co 512 E Green St *Web:* www.dailyillini.com	Champaign	IL	61820	217-337-8300	244-3001
Independent Newspapers Inc PO Box 737 *TF:* 800-282-8586 ■ *Web:* www2.newszap.com	Dover	DE	19903	302-674-3600	760-7440
Independent Publishing Co 1000 Williamston Rd *TF:* 800-859-6397 ■ *Web:* www.independentmail.com	Anderson	SC	29621	864-224-4321	260-1276
Indiana Printing & Publishing Co 899 Water St PO Box 10 *Web:* www.indianagazette.com	Indiana	PA	15701	724-465-5555	465-8267
Indianapolis Newspapers Inc 307 N Pennsylvania St *TF:* 800-669-7827 ■ *Web:* www.ndstar.com	Indianapolis	IN	46204	317-444-4000	444-6600
Journal & Topics Newspapers 622 Graceland Ave *Web:* www.journal-topics.com	Des Plaines	IL	60016	847-299-5511	298-8549
Journal Communications Inc 333 W State St *NYSE: JRN* ■ *TF:* 800-456-5943 ■ *Web:* www.journalcommunications.com	Milwaukee	WI	53201	414-224-2000	224-2469
Journal Graphics Inc 2840 NW 35th Ave Suite B *Web:* www.journalgraphics.com	Portland	OR	97210	503-790-9100	790-9043
Journal News Publishing Co Inc PO Box 998	Ephrata	WA	98823	509-754-4636	754-0996
Journal Publishing Co 1242 S Green St *TF:* 800-264-6397	Tupelo	MS	38804	662-842-2611	842-2233
Journal Register Co 790 Township Line Rd Suite 300 *Web:* www.journalregister.com	Yardley	PA	19067	215-504-4200	504-4201
Keene Publishing Corp PO Box 546 *TF:* 800-765-9994 ■ *Web:* www.sentinelsource.com	Keene	NH	03431	603-352-1234	352-0437
Knight Publishing Co 600 S Tryon St **Fax:* Hum Res ■ *TF:* 800-332-0686 ■ *Web:* www.charlotte.com	Charlotte	NC	28202	704-358-5000	358-5707*
Lake Charles American Press Inc PO Box 2893 *TF:* 800-737-2283 ■ *Web:* www.americanpress.com	Lake Charles	LA	70602	337-433-3000	494-4008
Lakeville Journal Co LLC 33 Bissell St *Web:* www.tcextra.com	Lakeville	CT	06039	860-435-9873	435-4802
Lakeway Publishers Inc PO Box 625	Morristown	TN	37815	423-581-5630	581-3061
Lancaster Newspapers Inc 8 W King St *TF:* 800-809-4666 ■ *Web:* www.lancasteronline.com	Lancaster	PA	17603	717-291-8811	291-8728
Landmark Community Newspapers Inc 601 Taylorsville Rd *TF:* 800-939-9322 ■ *Web:* www.lcni.com	Shelbyville	KY	40065	502-633-4334	633-4447
Law Bulletin Publishing Co 415 N State St *Web:* www.lawbulletin.com	Chicago	IL	60654	312-644-7800	644-4255
Lawrence Daily Journal-World Co 609 New Hampshire St PO Box 888 *TF:* 800-578-8748 ■ *Web:* www2.ljworld.com	Lawrence	KS	66044	785-843-1000	843-4512
Leader Union The 229 S 5th St *Web:* www.leaderunion.com	Vandalia	IL	62471	618-283-3374	283-0977
Leaf Chronicle Co 200 Commerce St *Web:* www.theleafchronicle.com	Clarksville	TN	37040	931-552-1808	648-8001
Lee Enterprises Inc 201 N Harrison St Suite 600 *NYSE: LEE* ■ *Web:* www.lee.net	Davenport	IA	52801	563-383-2100	328-4331
Lee Publications Inc 6113 State Hwy 5 *TF:* 888-355-5080 ■ *Web:* www.leepub.com	Palatine Bridge	NY	13428	518-673-8005	673-3245
Lehman Communications Corp 350 Terry St *TF:* 800-796-8201	Longmont	CO	80501	303-776-2244	678-8615
Lewiston Daily Sun Corp 104 Pk St *TF:* 800-482-0753 ■ *Web:* www.sunjournal.com	Lewiston	ME	04240	207-784-5411	777-3436
Livingston County Daily Press & Argus 323 E Grand River Ave **Fax Area Code:* 248 ■ *TF:* 888-999-1288 ■ *Web:* www.livingstondaily.com	Howell	MI	48843	517-548-2000	437-9460*
Los Angeles Newspaper Group 21860 Burbank Blvd Suite 200 PO Box 4200 *TF:* 800-346-6397 ■ *Web:* www.losangelesnewspapergroup.com	Woodland Hills	CA	91367	818-713-3000	713-0058
Lowell Sun Publishing Co 491 Dutton St **Fax:* Edit ■ *TF:* 800-694-7100 ■ *Web:* www.lowellsun.com	Lowell	MA	01854	978-458-7100	970-4600*
Madison Newspapers Inc 1901 Fish Hatchery Rd *TF Sales:* 800-252-7723 ■ *Web:* www.host.madison.com	Madison	WI	53713	608-252-6200	252-6119
Magic Valley Newspapers 132 Fairfield St W *TF:* 800-658-3883 ■ *Web:* www.magicvalley.com	Twin Falls	ID	83301	208-733-0931	734-5538
Manhattan Media LLC 79 Madison Ave 16th Fl *Web:* www.manhattanmedia.com	New York	NY	10016	212-268-8600	268-0614
Marshall Independent 508 W Main St PO Box 411 *Web:* www.marshallindependent.com	Marshall	MN	56258	507-537-1551	537-1557
Maverick Media Inc 123 W 17th St **Fax Area Code:* 800 ■ *Web:* www.ncnewspress.com	Syracuse	NE	68446	402-269-2135	456-5158*
McClatchy Co 2100 Q St *NYSE: MNI* ■ *Web:* www.mcclatchy.com	Sacramento	CA	95816	916-321-1855	321-1869
McClatchy Interactive 1100 Situs Ct *Web:* www.mcclatchyinteractive.com	Raleigh	NC	27606	919-861-1200	861-1300
McClatchy Newspapers 2100 Q St *Web:* www.mcclatchy.com	Sacramento	CA	95816	916-321-1000	321-1869
Media General Inc 333 E Franklin St *NYSE: MEG* ■ *Web:* www.media-general.com	Richmond	VA	23219	804-649-6000	
MediaNews Group Inc 101 W Colfax Ave Suite 1100 *Web:* www.medianewsgroup.com	Denver	CO	80202	303-954-6360	954-6320
Memphis Publishing Co 495 Union Ave *TF Cust Svc:* 800-444-6397 ■ *Web:* www.comercialappeal.com	Memphis	TN	38103	901-529-2211	529-2211
Meridian Star Inc 814 22nd Ave *TF Cust Svc:* 800-232-2525 ■ *Web:* www.meridianstar.com	Meridian	MS	39301	601-693-1551	485-1275
Metro Group Inc PO Box 790 *TF:* 866-638-7623 ■ *Web:* www.metrowny.com	Buffalo	NY	14225	716-668-5223	668-4526
MetroActive Publishing Inc 550 S 1st St *Web:* www.metroactive.com	San Jose	CA	95113	408-298-8000	298-0602
Mid-America Publishing Corp 9 2nd St NW *TF:* 800-558-1244 ■ *Web:* www.hamptonchronicle.com	Hampton	IA	50441	641-456-2585	456-2587
Milford Daily News Co 159 S Main St *Web:* www.milforddailynews.com	Milford	MA	01757	508-473-1111	634-7514
Mineral Daily News Tribune Inc 24 Armstrong St *TF:* 800-788-4026 ■ *Web:* www.newstribune.info	Keyser	WV	26726	304-788-3333	788-3398
Minnesota Sun Publications 10917 Valley View Rd *Web:* www.mnsun.com	Eden Prairie	MN	55344	952-829-0797	392-6868
Missouri Lawyers Media 319 N 4th St *TF:* 800-635-5297 ■ *Web:* www.molawyersmedia.com	Saint Louis	MO	63102	314-421-1880	421-0436
Missourian Publishing Co 14 W Main St *TF:* 888-239-7701 ■ *Web:* www.emissourian.com	Washington	MO	63090	636-239-7701	239-0915
Mobile Press Register Inc 401 Water St N *Web:* www.mobileregister.com/archive.htm	Mobile	AL	36652	251-219-5343	
Moline Dispatch Publishing Co 1720 5th Ave	Moline	IL	61265	309-764-4344	797-0317
Morning Call Inc 101 N 6th St **Fax:* Mktg ■ *TF:* 800-666-5492 ■ *Web:* www.mcall.com	Allentown	PA	18101	610-820-6500	820-6175*
Morris Communications Co LLC 725 Broad St *TF:* 800-622-6358 ■ *Web:* www.morris.com	Augusta	GA	30901	706-724-0851	828-3830
Morris Multimedia Inc 27 Abercorn St *Web:* www.morrismultimedia.com	Savannah	GA	31401	912-233-1281	232-4639
Natchez Newspapers Inc 503 N Canal St *TF:* 888-878-9101 ■ *Web:* www.natchezdemocrat.com	Natchez	MS	39120	601-442-9101	442-7315
Native American Times PO Box 411 *Web:* www.nativetimes.com	Tahlequah	OK	74465	918-708-5838	431-0213
New Mass Media Inc 121 Wawarme Ave *Web:* www.newmassmedia.com	Hartford	CT	06114	860-548-9300	548-9335

Company	City	State	ZIP	Phone	Fax
New Mexico Newspapers Inc PO Box 450 *TF:* 800-395-6397 ■ *Web:* www.daily-times.com	Farmington	NM	87499	505-325-4545	564-4630
New York News LP 450 W 33rd St 3rd Fl *Web:* www.nydailynews.com	New York	NY	10001	212-210-2100	643-7831
New York Times Co 620 Eighth Ave *NYSE: NYT* ■ *Web:* www.nytco.com	New York	NY	10018	212-556-1234	556-7389
Newhouse Newspapers 950 Fingerboard Rd	Staten Island	NY	10305	718-981-1234	981-1456
News Journal Co PO Box 15505 *TF:* 800-235-9100 ■ *Web:* www.delawareonline.com	Wilmington	DE	19850	302-324-2500	324-5509
News Publishing Co 305 E 6th Ave PO Box 1633 *Web:* www.npco.com	Rome	GA	30162	706-290-5330	
News-Journal Corp 901 6th St *Web:* www.news-journalonline.com	Daytona Beach	FL	32120	386-252-1511	258-8465
Newspaper Agency Corp 5600 W 4770 S *Web:* www.nacorp.com/NAC2/index.html	West Valley City	UT	84118	801-204-6100	237-2941
Newspapers of New England Inc PO Box 1177 *Web:* www.concordmonitor.com	Concord	NH	03302	603-224-5301	224-6949
Northwest Herald Inc PO Box 250 *TF:* 800-589-8910 ■ *Web:* www.nwherald.com	Crystal Lake	IL	60039	815-459-4040	459-5640
Northwest Publications 99 E State St **Fax:* Edit ■ *TF:* 800-383-7827 ■ *Web:* www.rrstar.com	Rockford	IL	61104	815-987-1200	987-1365*
Oakland Press Co 48 W Huron St *TF:* 800-686-2236 ■ *Web:* www.theoaklandpress.com	Pontiac	MI	48342	248-332-8181	253-9952
Observer & Eccentric Newspapers 615 W Lafayette 2nd Level *TF:* 866-887-2737 ■ *Web:* www.hometownlife.com	Detroit	MI	48226	734-591-2300	591-7279
Observer Dispatch Inc 221 Oriskany Plaza **Fax:* Cust Svc ■ *Web:* www.uticaod.com	Utica	NY	13501	315-797-9150	792-5138*
Observer Publishing Co 122 S Main St *TF:* 800-222-6397 ■ *Web:* www.observer-reporter.com	Washington	PA	15301	724-222-2200	225-2077
Ogden Newspapers Inc 1500 Main St *Web:* www.oweb.com	Wheeling	WV	26003	304-233-0100	233-9397
Ojai Valley News Inc 408 Bryant Cir # A *Web:* www.ojaivalleynews.com	Ojai	CA	93023	805-646-1476	646-4281
Oklahoma Publishing Co 9000 N Broadway Ext *TF:* 800-375-3450 ■ *Web:* www.newsok.com	Oklahoma City	OK	73114	405-475-3300	475-3513
Oshkosh Northwestern Co 224 State St *TF:* 800-924-6168 ■ *Web:* www.thenorthwestern.com	Oshkosh	WI	54901	920-235-7700	235-1527
Our Sunday Visitor Inc 200 Noll Plaza *TF:* 800-348-2440 ■ *Web:* www.osv.com	Huntington	IN	46750	260-356-8400	359-0029
Owatonna Peoples Press 135 W Pearl St *Web:* www.owatonna.com	Owatonna	MN	55060	507-451-2840	444-2382
Pacific Palisades Post Co 839 Via de la Paz *Web:* www.palisadespost.com	Pacific Palisades	CA	90272	310-454-1321	454-1078
Pacific Publishing Co 4000 Aurora Ave N Suite 100 *Web:* www.pacificpublishingcompany.com	Seattle	WA	98105	206-461-1300	461-1289
Paddock Publications Inc 155 E Algonquin Rd *Web:* www.dailyherald.com	Arlington Heights	IL	60005	847-427-4300	427-1301
Paducah Newspapers Inc 408 Kentucky Ave PO Box 2300	Paducah	KY	42002	502-443-1771	
Palm Beach Newspapers Inc PO Box 24700 *TF:* 800-432-7595 ■ *Web:* www.palmbeachpost.com	West Palm Beach	FL	33416	561-820-4100	820-4407
Papers Inc 206 S Main St *TF:* 800-733-4111 ■ *Web:* www.the-papers.com	Milford	IN	46542	574-658-4111	658-4701
Patuxent Publishing Co 10750 Little Patuxent Pkwy **Fax:* News Rm ■ *TF:* 800-884-8797	Columbia	MD	21044	410-730-3620	997-4564*
Paxton Media Group PO Box 1680	Paducah	KY	42002	270-575-8614	442-8188
Pennysaver 26522 La Alameda *TF:* 800-873-5548 ■ *Web:* www.pennysaverusa.com	Mission Viejo	CA	92691	949-614-2600	614-2727
PG Publishing Co 34 Blvd of the Allies *TF Cust Svc:* 800-228-6397 ■ *Web:* www.post-gazette.com	Pittsburgh	PA	15222	412-263-1100	263-1703
Philadelphia Tribune Co 520 S 16th St *Web:* www.phillytrib.com	Philadelphia	PA	19146	215-893-4050	735-3612
Phoenix Media Communications Group 126 Brookline Ave *TF:* 800-292-1017 ■ *Web:* www.thephoenix.com	Boston	MA	02215	617-536-5390	536-1463
Phoenix Newspapers Inc 200 E Van Buren St *NYSE: GCI* ■ *TF Cust Svc:* 800-331-9303	Phoenix	AZ	85004	602-444-8000	444-8044
Pioneer Group 115 N Michigan Ave *TF:* 800-968-1114 ■ *Web:* www.pioneergroup.com	Big Rapids	MI	49307	231-796-4831	796-1152
Pioneer Newspapers Inc 221 1st Ave W Suite 405 *Web:* www.pioneernewspapers.com	Seattle	WA	98119	206-284-4424	282-2143
Pioneer Press Inc 3701 W Lake Ave *Web:* www.pioneerlocal.com	Glenview	IL	60026	847-486-9200	486-7451
Pipestone Publishing Co PO Box 277 *TF:* 800-325-6440 ■ *Web:* www.pipestonestar.com	Pipestone	MN	56164	507-825-3333	825-2168
Pomerado Publishing Co PO Box 685 *Web:* www.pomeradonews.com	Poway	CA	92074	858-748-2311	748-7695
Ponca City Publishing Inc PO Box 191 *TF:* 866-765-3311 ■ *Web:* www.poncacitynews.com	Ponca City	OK	74602	580-765-3311	762-6397
Post Publishing Co 131 W Innes St *TF:* 800-633-8957 ■ *Web:* www.salisburypost.com	Salisbury	NC	28144	704-633-8950	639-0003
Press Community Newspapers East & Northeast Group 394 Wards Corner Suite 170 *Web:* www.communitypress.cincinnati.com/apps/pbcs.dll/section?Category=communities	Loveland	OH	45140	513-248-8600	248-1938
Press of Atlantic City Media Group 11 Devins Ln *Web:* www.pressofatlanticcity.com	Pleasantville	NJ	08232	609-272-7000	272-7724
Press-Enterprise Co PO Box 792 *TF:* 800-794-6397 ■ *Web:* www.pe.com	Riverside	CA	92502	951-684-1200	368-9023
Press-Enterprise Inc 3185 Lackawanna Ave *TF:* 800-228-3483 ■ *Web:* www.enterpe.com	Bloomsburg	PA	17815	570-784-2121	784-9226
Princeton Packet The 300 Witherspoon St PO Box 350 *Web:* centraljersey.com	Princeton	NJ	08542	609-924-3244	921-2714
Progressive Communications Corp 18 E Vine St PO Box 791 *Web:* www.mountvernonnews.com	Mount Vernon	OH	43050	740-397-5333	397-1321
Progressive Publishing Co PO Box 291 *Web:* www.theprogressnews.com	Clearfield	PA	16830	814-765-5581	765-5165
Quebecor Media Inc 612 Rue St Jacques *Web:* www.quebecor.com	Montreal	QC	H3C4M8	514-597-2231	594-8844
Quincy Newspapers Inc 130 S 5th St *TF:* 800-373-9444 ■ *Web:* www.whig.com	Quincy	IL	62301	217-223-5100	223-9757
Recorder Publishing Co PO Box 687	Bernardsville	NJ	07924	908-766-3900	766-6365
Reminder Press Inc 130 Old Town Rd PO Box 27 *TF:* 888-456-2211 ■ *Web:* www.remindernet.com	Vernon	CT	06066	860-875-3366	875-2089
Republican Co 1860 Main St *Web:* www.repub.com	Springfield	MA	01103	413-788-1000	788-1301
Republican-American Inc 389 Meadow St *TF:* 800-992-3232 ■ *Web:* www.rep-am.com	Waterbury	CT	06702	203-574-3636	596-9277
Richmond Newspapers Inc PO Box 85333 *TF:* 800-468-3382 ■ *Web:* www2.timesdispatch.com	Richmond	VA	23293	804-649-6000	819-1216
Rivertown Newspaper Group 2760 N Service Dr PO Box 15 *TF:* 800-535-1660 ■ *Web:* www.republican-eagle.com	Red Wing	MN	55066	651-388-8235	388-3404
Rock Valley Publishing LLC 11512 N 2nd St *Web:* www.rvpublishing.com	Machesney Park	IL	61115	815-877-4044	654-4857
Rome Sentinel Co 333 W Dominick St *Web:* www.romesentinel.com	Rome	NY	13440	315-337-4000	339-6281
Rust Publishing ID Lc PO Box 1330 *Web:* www.mountainhomenews.com	Mountain Home	ID	83647	208-587-3331	587-9205
Saint Joseph News Press & Gazette Co PO Box 29 *TF:* 800-779-6397	Saint Joseph	MO	64502	816-271-8500	271-8692
Saint Lawrence County Newspapers PO Box 409 *Web:* www.ogd.com	Ogdensburg	NY	13669	315-393-1000	393-5108
San Angelo Standard Times Inc PO Box 5111 *TF:* 800-588-1884 ■ *Web:* www.gosanangelo.com	San Angelo	TX	76902	325-653-1221	659-8173
San Gabriel Valley Newspaper Group 1210 N Azusa Canyon Rd *Web:* www.sgvn.com	West Covina	CA	91790	626-962-8811	338-9157
Santa Barbara News-Press Publishing Co 715 Anacapa St *TF:* 800-654-3292 ■ *Web:* www.newspress.com	Santa Barbara	CA	93101	805-564-5200	966-6258
Scotsman Publishing Co 234 S Main St *Web:* www.isanticountynews.com	Cambridge	MN	55008	763-689-1981	689-4372
Scranton Printing Co (SPCO) 1225 Penn Ave **Fax Area Code:* 570 ■ *TF:* 800-290-5283 ■ *Web:* www.scrantonprinting.com	Scranton	PA	18509	800-290-5283	347-0406*
Scripps Howard Inc PO Box 5380 **Fax:* PR ■ *TF:* 800-888-3000 ■ *Web:* www.scripps.com	Cincinnati	OH	45202	513-977-3000	977-3721*
Select Newspaper Group 138 Main St *Web:* www.losaltosonline.com	Los Altos	CA	94022	650-948-4489	948-6647
Singapore Press Holdings 529 14th St NW National Press Bldg Suite 916 *Web:* www.sph.com.sg	Washington	DC	20045	202-662-8726	662-8729
Sonoma Index-Tribune Inc 117 W Napa St *Web:* www.sonomanews.com	Sonoma	CA	95476	707-938-2111	938-1600
Sound Publishing Inc 19351 8th Ave Suite 106 *Web:* www.soundpublishing.com	Poulsbo	WA	98370	360-394-5800	394-5841
Southern Connecticut Newspapers Inc 9 Riverbend Dr S Bldg 9-A *Web:* www.stamfordadvocate.com	Stamford	CT	06907	203-964-2200	964-2345
Southern Newspapers Inc 5701 Woodway Dr Suite 300 *Web:* www.sninews.com	Houston	TX	77057	713-266-5481	266-1847
SouthtownStar The 18312 S W Creek Dr *Web:* southtownstar.suntimes.com	Tinley Park	IL	60477	708-633-4800	633-5999
Star-News Newspapers PO Box 840 *Web:* www.starnewsonline.com	Wilmington	NC	28402	910-343-2000	343-2210
Star-News Publishing Co 296 3rd Ave *Web:* www.thestarnews.com	Chula Vista	CA	91910	619-427-3000	426-6346
Stephens Media Group 1111 W Bonanza Rd *Web:* www.stephensmedia.com	Las Vegas	NV	89106	702-383-0211	
Stonebridge Press Inc 25 Elm St *TF:* 800-536-5836 ■ *Web:* www.stonebridgepress.com	Southbridge	MA	01550	508-764-4325	764-8015
Suburban Chicago Newspapers 1500 W Ogden Ave *Web:* www.suburbanchicagonews.com/sunpub	Naperville	IL	60540	630-355-0063	416-5163
Suburban Life Publications 1101 W 31st St Suite 100 *Web:* www.mysuburbanlife.com	Downers Grove	IL	60515	630-368-1100	969-0228
Suburban News Publications 5257 Sinclair Rd *Web:* www.snponline.com	Columbus	OH	43229	614-785-1212	842-4760
Suffolk Life Newspapers PO Box 9167	Riverhead	NY	11901	631-369-0800	591-5190
Sun Co 4030 N Georgia Blvd *TF:* 800-548-5448 ■ *Web:* www.sbsun.com	San Bernardino	CA	92407	909-889-9666	885-1253
Sun Media Corp 333 King St E *TF:* 877-786-8227 ■ *Web:* www.sunmedia.ca	Toronto	ON	M5A3X5	416-350-6379	947-1664
Sun Newspapers 5510 Cloverleaf Pkwy *TF:* 800-362-8008 ■ *Web:* www.sunnews.com	Cleveland	OH	44125	216-986-2600	986-2380
Sun Post Newspaper Group 1688 Meridian Ave Suite 404 *Web:* www.miamisunpost.com	Miami Beach	FL	33139	305-538-9700	538-6077
Sun Publications 4370 W 109 St Suite 300 *Web:* www.kccommunitynews.com	Overland Park	KS	66211	913-381-1010	381-9889
Sun-Sentinel Co 200 E Las Olas Blvd *TF:* 800-548-6397 ■ *Web:* www.sun-sentinel.com	Fort Lauderdale	FL	33301	954-356-4000	356-4559
Tacoma News Inc 1950 S State St *Web:* www.thenewstribune.com	Tacoma	WA	98405	253-597-8742	597-8274
TB Butler Publishing Co 410 W Erwin St *TF:* 800-333-9141 ■ *Web:* www.tylerpaper.com	Tyler	TX	75702	903-597-8111	595-0335
TDN Publishing Co 224 S Market St *Web:* www.tdn-net.com	Troy	OH	45373	937-335-5634	335-3552

	City	State	Zip	Phone	Fax
Tennessee Valley Printing Co Inc PO Box 2213 — *TF:* 888-353-4612 ■ *Web:* www.decaturdaily.com	Decatur	AL	35609	256-353-4612	340-2392
This Week Community Newspapers 7801 N Central Dr PO Box 608 — *Web:* www.thisweeknews.com	Lewis Center	OH	43035	740-888-6000	888-6006
Time-Press Publishing Co 110 W Jefferson St — *Web:* www.mywebtimes.com	Ottawa	IL	61350	815-433-2000	672-9322
Times & News Publishing Co 1570 Fairfield Rd PO Box 3669 — *Web:* www.gettysburgtimes.com	Gettysburg	PA	17325	717-334-1131	334-4243
Times Herald Inc 410 Markley St PO Box 591 — *TF:* 800-887-2501 ■ *Web:* www.timesherald.com	Norristown	PA	19404	610-272-2500	272-0660
Times News Publishing Co 707 S Main St — *TF:* 800-488-0085 ■ *Web:* www.thetimesnews.com	Burlington	NC	27215	336-227-0131	228-1889
Times Publishing Co 222 Lake St — *TF:* 800-525-4335 ■ *Web:* www.shreveporttimes.com	Shreveport	LA	71130	318-459-3200	459-3578
Times Publishing Co 490 First Ave S PO Box 1121 — *TF Cust Svc:* 800-888-7012 ■ *Web:* www.tampabay.com	Saint Petersburg	FL	33731	727-893-8111	893-8675
Times-Citizen Communications Inc 406 Stevens St PO Box 640 — *Web:* www.timescitizen.com	Iowa Falls	IA	50126	641-648-2521	648-4765
Tribune Review Publishing Co 622 Cabin Hill Dr — *TF:* 800-433-3045	Greensburg	PA	15601	724-834-1151	838-5171
Truth Publishing Co Inc 421 S 2nd St — *TF:* 800-585-5416 ■ *Web:* www.etruth.com	Elkhart	IN	46516	574-294-1661	294-3895
Village Voice Media Holdings LLC 36 Cooper Sq — *Web:* www.villagevoicemedia.com	New York	NY	10003	212-475-3333	475-8944
Wappingers Falls Shopper Inc 84 E Main St	Wappingers Falls	NY	12590	845-297-3723	297-6810
Warrick Publishing Inc 204 W Locust St PO Box 266 — *Web:* www.tristate-media.com	Boonville	IN	47601	812-897-2330	897-3703
Wave Newspaper Group 1730 W Olympic Blvd Suite 500 — **Fax Area Code:* 213 ■ *Web:* www.wavenewspapers.com	Los Angeles	CA	90015	323-556-5720	835-0584*
Wayne Printing Co Inc 310 N Berkeley Blvd — *Web:* www.newsargus.com	Goldsboro	NC	27534	919-778-2211	778-5408
West Virginia Newspaper Publishing Co 1251 Earl L Core Rd — *TF:* 800-654-4676	Morgantown	WV	26505	304-292-6301	291-2326
Western Communications Inc 1777 SW Chandler Ave — *Web:* www.bendbulletin.com	Bend	OR	97702	541-382-1811	383-0372
Western States Weeklies Inc PO Box 600600 — *TF:* 800-280-2985 ■ *Web:* www.navydispatch.com	San Diego	CA	92160	619-280-2985	280-2989
Whitcom Partners Inc 375 Pk Ave Suite 3800	New York	NY	10152	212-582-2300	582-2310
Wick Communications Inc 333 W Wilcox Dr Suite 302 — *Web:* www.wickcommunications.com	Sierra Vista	AZ	85635	520-458-0200	458-6166
William J Kline & Son Inc 1 Venner Rd — *TF:* 800-453-6397 ■ *Web:* www.recordernews.com	Amsterdam	NY	12010	518-843-1100	843-1338
Wooster Republican Printing Co 212 E Liberty St — *TF:* 800-686-2958 ■ *Web:* www.the-daily-record.com	Wooster	OH	44691	330-264-1125	264-3756
Worcester Telegram & Gazette Inc 20 Franklin St PO Box 15012 — *TF:* 800-678-6680 ■ *Web:* www.telegram.com	Worcester	MA	01615	508-793-9100	793-9313
World Publishing Co 315 S Boulder Ave — *Web:* www.tulsaworld.com	Tulsa	OK	74102	918-583-2161	581-8353
Yankton Press & Dakotan 319 Walnut St PO Box 56 — *TF:* 800-743-2968 ■ *Web:* www.yankton.net	Yankton	SD	57078	605-665-7811	665-1721
York Newspaper Co 1891 Loucks Rd — *TF:* 800-559-3520 ■ *Web:* www.inyork.com	York	PA	17408	717-767-6397	764-6233
Your Houston News 523 N Sam Houston Pkwy E Suite 600 — *Web:* www.yourhoustonnews.com	Houston	TX	77060	281-668-1100	

640-9 Periodicals Publishers

	City	State	Zip	Phone	Fax
1105 Media Inc 9201 Oakdale Ave Suite 101 — *Web:* www.1105media.com	Chatsworth	CA	91311	818-734-1520	734-1522
ABC Inc 77 W 66th St — *Web:* www.abc.go.com	New York	NY	10023	212-456-7777	456-2795
Access Intelligence LLC 4 Choke Cherry Rd 2nd Fl — *TF:* 800-777-5006 ■ *Web:* www.accessintel.com	Rockville	MD	20850	301-354-2000	738-8453
Advanstar Veterinary Healthcare Communications 8033 Flint St — *TF:* 800-255-6864 ■ *Web:* www.veterinarymedicine.dvm360.com	Lenexa	KS	66214	913-871-3808	871-3808
Advantage Business Media 100 Enterprise Dr Suite 600 PO Box 912 — **Fax:* Hum Res ■ *TF:* 800-222-0289 ■ *Web:* www.advantagebusinessmedia.com	Rockaway	NJ	07866	973-920-7000	920-7542*
Advertising Specialties Institute 4800 St Rd — *TF:* 800-546-1350 ■ *Web:* www.asicentral.com	Trevose	PA	19053	215-942-8600	953-3045
Advisor Media Inc 4849 Viewridge Ave — *Web:* advisor.com	San Diego	CA	92123	858-278-5600	
Adweek Directories 770 Broadway — *Web:* www.adweek.com	New York	NY	10003	646-654-5000	654-5362
Affinity Group Inc 2575 Vista Del Mar — *Web:* www.affinitygroup.com	Ventura	CA	93001	805-667-4100	667-4298
Affinity Media 6420 Sycamore Ln N Suite 100 — *TF:* 800-848-6247 ■ *Web:* www.ehlertmedia.com	Maple Grove	MN	55369	763-383-4400	383-4499
Agora Publishing Inc 14 W Monument St — *TF:* 800-433-1528 ■ *Web:* www.agora-inc.com	Baltimore	MD	21201	410-783-8499	

	City	State	Zip	Phone	Fax
AHC Media LLC 3525 Piedmont Rd NE Bldg 6 Suite 400 — **Fax:* Cust Svc ■ *TF Cust Svc:* 800-688-2421 ■ *Web:* www.ahcmedia.com	Atlanta	GA	30305	404-262-5476	262-5560*
Alexander Communications Group Inc 712 Main St Suite 187-B — *TF:* 800-232-4317 ■ *Web:* www.alexcommgrp.com	Boonton	NJ	07005	973-265-2300	402-6056
Alexander Hamilton Institute Inc 70 Hilltop Rd — *TF Orders:* 800-879-2441 ■ *Web:* www.ahipubs.com	Ramsey	NJ	07446	201-825-3377	825-8696
American Banker 1 State St Plaza 27th Fl — *TF:* 800-362-3807 ■ *Web:* www.americanbanker.com	New York	NY	10004	212-803-8200	843-9600
American Banker Newsletters 1 State St Plaza 27th Fl — *TF:* 800-221-1809 ■ *Web:* www.americanbanker.com	New York	NY	10004	212-803-8200	
American City Business Journals Inc 120 W Morehead St # 400 — *Web:* www.bizjournals.com	Charlotte	NC	28202	704-973-1000	973-1001
American Lawyer Media Inc (ALM) 120 Broadway 5th Fl — **Fax Area Code:* 646 ■ *TF:* 800-888-8300 ■ *Web:* www.alm.com	New York	NY	10271	212-457-9400	417-7705*
American Media Inc 1000 American Media Way — *TF:* 800-749-7733	Boca Raton	FL	33464	561-997-7733	998-7235
American Psychiatric Publishing Inc 1000 Wilson Blvd Suite 1825 — *TF:* 800-368-5777 ■ *Web:* www.appi.org	Arlington	VA	22209	703-907-7322	907-1091
Amos Press Inc 911 S Vandemark Rd — *TF:* 866-468-1622 ■ *Web:* www.amospress.com	Sidney	OH	45365	937-498-0850	498-0812
Anb International Inc PO Box 390 — *Web:* www.clairemurray.com	Ascutney	VT	05030	802-674-6017	674-6045
Annual Reviews 4139 El Camino Way — *TF:* 800-523-8635 ■ *Web:* www.annurev.org	Palo Alto	CA	94303	650-493-4400	855-9815
APN Media LLC PO Box 20113 — *Web:* www.ohranger.com	New York	NY	10023	212-581-3380	245-4226
AS Pratt & Sons 805-15th St NE 3rd Fl — **Fax Area Code:* 202 ■ *TF Cust Svc:* 800-456-2340 ■ *Web:* www.aspratt.com	Washington	DC	20005	800-524-2003	739-9511*
Aspen Publishers Inc 111 8th Ave 7th Fl — *TF Orders:* 800-447-1717 ■ *Web:* www.aspenpublishers.com	New York	NY	10011	212-771-0600	771-0885
Athlon Sports Communications Inc 220 25th Ave N Suite 200 — *Web:* www.athlonsports.com	Nashville	TN	37203	615-327-0747	327-1149
Atlantic Information Services Inc 1100 17th St NW Suite 300 — *TF:* 800-521-4323 ■ *Web:* www.aishealth.com	Washington	DC	20036	202-775-9008	331-9542
Augsburg Fortress Publishers 100 S 5th St # 600 — *TF:* 800-426-0115 ■ *Web:* www.augsburgfortress.org	Minneapolis	MN	55402	612-330-3300	330-3455
Babcox Publications Inc 3550 Embassy Pkwy — *Web:* www.babcox.com	Akron	OH	44333	330-670-1234	670-0874
Bauer Publishing Co LP 270 Sylvan Ave — *Web:* www.bauerpublishing.com	Englewood Cliffs	NJ	07632	201-569-6699	569-5303
BCC Research LLC 49 Walnut Pk Bldg 2 — *TF:* 866-285-7215 ■ *Web:* www.bccresearch.com	Wellesley	MA	02481	781-489-7301	489-7308
Becker Communications 119 Merchant St Suite 300 — *Web:* www.beckercommunications.com	Honolulu	HI	96813	808-533-4165	537-4990
Benjamin Franklin Literary & Medical Society Inc 1100 Waterway Blvd — *TF:* 800-558-2376	Indianapolis	IN	46202	317-636-8881	637-0126
Bertelsmann Publishing Group Inc 1745 Broadway — *Web:* www.bertelsmann.com	New York	NY	10019	212-782-1000	782-1010
Bloomberg LP 731 Lexington Ave — *Web:* www.bloomberg.com	New York	NY	10022	212-318-2000	893-5000
Boardroom Inc 281 Tresser Blvd 8th Fl — *Web:* www.boardroom.com	Stamford	CT	06901	203-973-5900	967-3086
Bobit Business Media 3520 Challenger St — **Fax:* Hum Res ■ *Web:* www.bobit.com	Torrance	CA	90503	310-533-2400	533-2508*
Bureau of National Affairs Inc 1801 S Bell St — *TF:* 800-372-1033 ■ *Web:* www.bna.com	Arlington	VA	22202	703-341-3000	341-1634
Business & Legal Reports Inc (BLR) 141 Mill Rock Rd E — *TF:* 800-727-5257 ■ *Web:* www.blr.com	Old Saybrook	CT	06475	860-510-0100	510-7225
Business News Publishing Co 2401 W Big Beaver Rd Suite 700 — *TF:* 800-837-7370 ■ *Web:* www.bnpmedia.com	Troy	MI	48084	248-362-3700	362-0317
Business Publishers Inc 2222 Sedwick Dr Suite 101 — *TF:* 800-223-8720 ■ *Web:* www.bpinews.com	Durham	NC	27713	800-223-8720	508-2592
Buyers Laboratory Inc 20 Railroad Ave — *Web:* www.buyerslab.com	Hackensack	NJ	07601	201-488-0404	488-0461
Cabot Heritage Corp 176 N St PO Box 2049 — *TF:* 800-654-1514 ■ *Web:* www.cabot.net	Salem	MA	01970	978-745-5532	745-1283
Careers & Colleges 2 LAN Dr Suite 100 — *Web:* www.careersandcolleges.com	Westford	MA	01886	978-692-5092	692-4174
CCH Inc 2700 Lake Cook Rd — *TF Cust Svc:* 800-835-5224 ■ *Web:* www.cch.com	Riverwoods	IL	60015	847-267-7000	267-2516
CD Publications 8204 Fenton St — *TF:* 800-666-6380 ■ *Web:* www.cdpublications.com	Silver Spring	MD	20910	301-588-6380	588-0519
Challenge Publications Inc 9509 Vassar Ave Suite A — *TF:* 800-562-9182 ■ *Web:* www.challengeweb.com	Chatsworth	CA	91311	818-700-6868	700-6282
Christian Board of Publication 1221 Locust St Suite 670 — *TF:* 800-366-3383 ■ *Web:* www.cbp21.com	Saint Louis	MO	63103	314-231-8500	231-8524
Christianity Today International 465 Gundersen Dr — *Web:* www.christianitytoday.com	Carol Stream	IL	60188	630-260-6200	260-0114
Cobblestone Publishing Co 30 Grove St Suite C — *TF:* 800-821-0115 ■ *Web:* www.cobblestonepub.com	Peterborough	NH	03458	603-924-7209	924-7380

	City	State	ZIP	Phone	Fax
CollegeBound Network 1200 S Ave Suite 202	Staten Island	NY	10314	718-761-4800	761-3300
Web: www.collegebound.net					
Commodity Information Systems Inc 3030 NW Expy Suite 725	Oklahoma City	OK	73112	405-604-8726	604-8726
TF: 800-231-0477 ■ *Web:* www.cis-okc.com					
Computer Economics Inc 2082 Business Ctr Dr Suite 240	Irvine	CA	92712	949-831-8700	442-7688
Web: www.computereconomics.com					
Conde Nast Publications Inc 4 Times Sq.	New York	NY	10036	212-286-2860	
TF: 800-690-6115 ■ *Web:* www.condenast.com					
Connell Communications Inc 86 Elm St	Peterborough	NH	03458	603-924-7271	924-7013
TF: 800-677-8847					
Consumers Digest Inc 520 Lake Cook Rd Suite 500	Deerfield	IL	60015	847-607-3000	
Consumers Union of US Inc 101 Truman Ave	Yonkers	NY	10703	914-378-2000	378-2915
TF: 800-695-4051 ■ *Web:* www.consumersunion.org					
Cook Communications Ministries 4050 Lee Vance View	Colorado Springs	CO	80918	719-536-0100	536-3265
TF: 800-708-5550 ■ *Web:* www.davidccook.com					
Cox Auto Trader Publishing Co 100 W Plume St	Norfolk	VA	23510	757-531-7700	
Web: www.traderonline.com					
Crain Communications Inc 1155 Gratiot Ave	Detroit	MI	48207	313-446-6000	259-8454*
**Fax:* Hum Res ■ *TF:* 888-288-6954 ■ *Web:* www.crain.com					
CRC Press LLC 6000 Broken Sound Pkwy NW Suite 300	Boca Raton	FL	33487	561-994-0555	374-3401*
**Fax Area Code:* 800 ■ **Fax:* Cust Svc ■ *TF Cust Svc:* 800-272-7737 ■ *Web:* www.crcpress.com					
Cutter Information Corp 37 Broadway Suite 1	Arlington	MA	02474	781-648-8700	648-8707
TF: 800-964-5118 ■ *Web:* www.cutter.com					
Cygnus Business Media Inc 1233 Janesville Ave	Fort Atkinson	WI	53538	631-845-2700	845-7109
TF: 800-547-7377 ■ *Web:* www.cygnusb2b.com					
Data Advantage Corp 1515 Story Ave	Louisville	KY	40206	502-587-9500	587-9582
Web: www.data-advantage.com					
DataTrends Publications Inc PO Box 3221	Leesburg	VA	20177	571-313-9916	771-9091*
**Fax Area Code:* 703 ■ *Web:* www.datatrendspublications.com					
Deal LLC The 20 Broad St	New York	NY	10005	212-313-9200	545-8442
TF Cust Svc: 888-667-3325 ■ *Web:* www.thedeal.com					
Dell Magazines 267 Broadway 4th Fl	New York	NY	10007	212-686-7188	686-7414
Web: www.pennydellpuzzles.com					
Desert Homes Magazine 303 N Indian Canyon Dr PO Box 2724	Palm Springs	CA	92262	760-325-2333	
Web: www.palmspringslife.com					
Desktop Engineering 1283 Main St PO Box 1039	Dublin	NH	03444	603-563-1631	563-8192
Web: www.deskeng.com					
Disney Consumer Products 500 S Buena Vista St	Burbank	CA	91521	818-560-1000	560-1930*
**Fax:* Cust Svc ■ *TF PR:* 800-723-4763					
Diversified Business Communications 121 Free St	Portland	ME	04101	207-842-5400	842-5505
TF: 800-842-5404 ■ *Web:* www.divbusiness.com					
Doane Advisory Services 77 Westport Plaza Suite 250	Saint Louis	MO	63146	314-569-2700	569-1083
TF: 800-535-2342 ■ *Web:* www.doane.com					
E H Publishing Inc PO Box 989	Framingham	MA	01701	508-663-1500	663-1599
Web: www.ehpub.com					
Earl G Graves Ltd 130 5th Ave 10th Fl	New York	NY	10011	212-242-8000	886-9532
TF Cust Svc: 800-727-7777 ■ *Web:* www.blackenterprise.com					
Economist Intelligence Unit 111 W 57th St 7th Fl	New York	NY	10019	212-554-0600	586-1181
TF: 800-938-4685 ■ *Web:* www.eiu.com					
Editorial Projects in Education 6935 Arlington Rd Suite 100	Bethesda	MD	20814	301-280-3100	280-3200
Web: www.edweek.org					
EGW.com Inc 4075 Papazian Way Suite 208	Fremont	CA	94538	510-668-0268	668-0280
TF Cust Svc: 800-546-4754 ■ *Web:* www.egw.com					
Eli Journals 2272 Airport Rd	Naples	FL	34112	239-280-2307	508-2592*
**Fax Area Code:* 800 ■ *TF:* 800-508-2582 ■ *Web:* www.elementkjournals.com					
Elliott Wave International (EWI) PO Box 1618	Gainesville	GA	30503	770-536-0309	536-2514
TF Cust Svc: 800-336-1618 ■ *Web:* www.elliottwave.com					
Elsevier Science Ltd 360 Pk Ave S	New York	NY	10010	212-989-5800	633-3990
TF: 888-437-4636 ■ *Web:* www.elsevier.com					
Energy Intelligence Group 5 E 37th St 5th Fl	New York	NY	10016	212-532-1112	616-0800*
**Fax Area Code:* 646 ■ *TF:* 888-427-7496 ■ *Web:* www.energyintel.com					
Entrepreneur Media Inc 2445 McCabe Way Suite 400	Irvine	CA	92614	949-261-2325	261-7729
Web: www.entrepreneur.com					
EPM Communications Inc 19 W 21st St # 301	New York	NY	10010	212-941-0099	941-1622
TF: 888-852-9467 ■ *Web:* www.epmcom.com					
Ernst Publishing Co LLC 1937 Delaware Tpke Suite B	Clarksville	NY	12041	800-345-3822	252-0906
TF: 800-345-3822 ■ *Web:* www.ernstpublishing.com					
Essence Communications Inc 135 W 50th St 4th Fl	New York	NY	10020	212-642-0600	921-5173
TF Sales: 800-274-9398 ■ *Web:* www.essence.com					
Euromoney Institutional Investor PLC 225 Pk Ave S	New York	NY	10003	212-224-3300	224-3171
Web: www.institutionalinvestor.com					
F & W Publications Inc 4700 E Galbraith Rd	Cincinnati	OH	45236	513-531-2690	531-2690
TF Sales: 800-289-0963 ■ *Web:* www.fwmedia.com					
Farm Progress Co Inc 255 38th Ave	Carol Stream	IL	60188	630-690-5600	462-2869
TF: 800-441-1410 ■ *Web:* www.farmprogress.com					
FDAnews 300 N Washington St Suite 200	Falls Church	VA	22046	703-538-7600	538-7676
TF: 888-838-5578 ■ *Web:* www.fdanews.com					
Forbes Inc 60 5th Ave	New York	NY	10011	212-620-2200	206-5534
TF: 800-888-9896 ■ *Web:* www.forbes.com					
Forecast International 22 Commerce Rd	Newtown	CT	06470	203-426-0800	426-1964
TF: 800-451-4975 ■ *Web:* www.forecastinternational.com					
Forum Publishing Co 383 E Main St	Centerport	NY	11721	631-754-5000	754-0630
TF: 800-635-7654 ■ *Web:* www.forum123.com					
Frequent Flyer Services 1930 Frequent Flyer Pt	Colorado Springs	CO	80915	719-597-8889	597-6855
TF: 800-209-2870 ■ *Web:* www.frequentflyerservices.com					
Gardner Publications Inc 6915 Valley Ave	Cincinnati	OH	45244	513-527-8800	527-8801
TF: 800-950-8020 ■ *Web:* www.gardnerweb.com					
Grace Communion International PO Box 5005	Glendora	CA	91740	626-650-2300	
TF: 800-423-4444 ■ *Web:* www.gci.org					
Grand View Media Group Inc (GVMG) 200 Croft St Suite 1	Birmingham	AL	35242	205-408-3700	408-3797
TF: 888-431-2877 ■ *Web:* www.gvmg.com					
Grass Roots Publishing Co Inc Hochman Assoc 908 Oaktree Rd Suite H	South Plainfield	NJ	07080	908-222-1811	222-8228
TF: 877-207-9007					
Greater Washington Publishing Inc 1919 Gallows Rd Suite 200	Vienna	VA	22182	703-992-1100	893-8356
Web: www.gwpi.net					
Gulf Publishing Co Inc 2 Greenway Plaza Suite 1020	Houston	TX	77046	713-529-4301	520-4433
TF: 800-231-6275 ■ *Web:* www.gulfpub.com					
Hachette Filipacchi Media US Inc 1633 Broadway	New York	NY	10019	212-767-6000	767-5600
Web: www.hfmus.com					
Hanley-Wood LLC 1 Thomas Cir NW Suite 600	Washington	DC	20005	202-452-0800	785-1974
TF: 800-636-0336 ■ *Web:* www.hanleywood.com					
Hart Publications Inc 1616 S Voss Rd Suite 1000	Houston	TX	77057	713-260-6400	840-8585
TF: 800-874-2544 ■ *Web:* www.hartenergy.com					
Hatton Brown Publishers Inc 225 Hanrick St	Montgomery	AL	36104	334-834-1170	834-4525
TF: 800-669-5613 ■ *Web:* www.hattonbrown.com					
Health Forum 1 N Franklin St 28th Fl	Chicago	IL	60606	312-893-6800	422-4506
TF: 800-621-6902					
Healthy Directions LLC 7811 Montrose Rd	Potomac	MD	20854	301-340-2100	251-3758*
**Fax:* Hum Res ■ *TF:* 800-777-5015 ■ *Web:* www.healthydirections.com					
Hearst Magazines Div 300 W 57th St	New York	NY	10019	212-649-2275	
TF: 800-678-7767 ■ *Web:* www.hearst.com					
Highlights for Children Inc 1800 Watermark Dr	Columbus	OH	43215	614-486-0631	487-2700
TF Cust Svc: 800-255-9517 ■ *Web:* www.highlights.com					
Hli Properties Inc PO Box 1052	Fort Dodge	IA	50501	515-955-1600	574-2125
TF: 800-247-2000 ■ *Web:* www.hlipublishing.com					
Hobsons CollegeView 50 E Business Way Suite 300	Cincinnati	OH	45241	800-927-8439	891-8531
TF: 800-927-8439 ■ *Web:* www.collegeview.com					
Homes & Land Magazine Affiliates LLC 1830 E Pk Ave	Tallahassee	FL	32301	850-574-2111	575-9567
TF: 800-726-6683 ■ *Web:* www.homesandland.com					
Honolulu Publishing Co Ltd 707 Richards St Suite 525	Honolulu	HI	96813	808-524-7400	531-2306
TF: 800-272-5245 ■ *Web:* www.honolulupublishing.com					
Horizon House Publications Inc (HHP) 685 Canton St	Norwood	MA	02062	781-769-9750	762-9071
TF: 800-225-9977 ■ *Web:* www.horizonhouse.com					
House of White Birches Inc 306 E Parr Rd	Berne	IN	46711	260-589-8741	589-8093
Web: www.whitebirches.com					
IEEE Computer Society Press 10662 Los Vaqueros Cir PO Box 3014	Los Alamitos	CA	90720	714-816-2165	821-4010
TF: 800-272-6657 ■ *Web:* www.computer.org/cspress					
Information Today Inc 143 Old Marlton Pike	Medford	NJ	08055	609-654-6266	654-6760
TF: 800-300-9868 ■ *Web:* www.infotoday.com					
InfoWorld Media Group Inc 501 2nd St Suite 120	San Francisco	CA	94107	415-243-4344	453-2200
TF: 800-227-8365 ■ *Web:* www.infoworld.com					
Inside Washington Publishers Inc 1919 S Eads St Suite 201	Arlington	VA	22202	703-416-8500	416-8543
TF: 800-424-9068 ■ *Web:* www.iwpnews.com					
Institute of Management & Administration Inc (IOMA) 1 Washington Pk Suite 1300	Newark	NJ	07102	973-718-4700	622-0595
TF: 800-401-5937 ■ *Web:* www.ioma.com					
Institutional Investor Newsletters 225 Pk Ave S 8th Fl	New York	NY	10003	212-224-3300	224-3491*
**Fax:* Cust Svc ■ *TF:* 800-715-9197 ■ *Web:* www.iinews.com					
International Data Group Inc (IDG) 699 Boylston St # 15	Boston	MA	02116	617-534-1200	859-8642
Web: www.idg.com					
International Scientific Communications Inc (ISC Inc) 30 Controls Dr PO Box 870	Shelton	CT	06484	203-926-9300	926-9310
Web: www.iscpubs.com					
Internet Business Network 303 Ross Dr	Mill Valley	CA	94941	415-377-2255	380-8245
Web: www.interbiznet.com					
Johnson Publishing Co Inc 820 S Michigan Ave	Chicago	IL	60605	312-322-9200	322-0951
Web: www.johnsonpublishing.com					
Jossey-Bass & Pfeiffer 989 Market St 5th Fl	San Francisco	CA	94103	415-782-3100	433-0499
Web: www.josseybass.com					
Journal of Commerce Group 33 Washington St 13th Fl	Newark	NJ	07102	973-848-7000	848-7167*
**Fax:* Edit ■ *TF Cust Svc:* 800-223-0243 ■ *Web:* www.joc.com					
JR O'Dwyer Co 271 Madison Ave 6th Fl	New York	NY	10016	212-679-2471	683-2750
TF: 866-395-7710 ■ *Web:* www.odwyerpr.com					
Kalmbach Publishing Co 21027 Crossroads Cir	Waukesha	WI	53186	262-796-8776	796-1615
TF Cust Svc: 800-446-5489 ■ *Web:* www.kalmbach.com					
Kennedy Information 1 Phoenix Mill Ln 3rd Fl	Peterborough	NH	03458	603-924-1006	924-4460
TF: 800-531-0007 ■ *Web:* www.kennedyinfo.com					
Kiplinger Washington Editors Inc 1729 H St NW	Washington	DC	20006	202-887-6400	496-1817
TF: 800-544-0155 ■ *Web:* www.kiplinger.com					
Krause Publications Inc 700 E State St	Iola	WI	54990	715-445-2214	445-4087
TF: 800-258-0929 ■ *Web:* www.krausebooks.com					
Lakeside Publishing LLC 990 Grove St 4th Fl	Evanston	IL	60201	847-491-6440	491-0459
Web: www.centurysports.net					

Company	City	State	Zip	Phone	Fax
Laurin Publishing Co Inc 2 S St *Web:* www.photonics.com	Pittsfield	MA	01202	413-499-0514	442-3180
Lawrence Ragan Communications Inc 111 E Wacker Dr Suite 500 *TF:* 800-878-5331 ■ *Web:* www.ragan.com	Chicago	IL	60601	312-960-4100	960-4105
Lebhar-Friedman Inc 425 Pk Ave 6th Fl **Fax:* Hum Res ■ *Web:* www.lf.com	New York	NY	10022	212-756-5000	756-5124*
LFP Inc 8484 Wilshire Blvd Suite 900 *Web:* www.lfp.com	Beverly Hills	CA	90211	323-651-5400	651-3525
Liberation Publications Inc PO Box 4371 *Web:* www.advocate.com	Los Angeles	CA	90078	323-871-1225	467-0173
Lippincott Williams & Wilkins 530 Walnut St *Web:* www.lww.com	Philadelphia	PA	19106	215-521-8300	521-8902
Liturgical Publications Inc 2875 S James Dr *TF:* 800-876-4574 ■ *Web:* www.4lpi.com	New Berlin	WI	53151	262-785-1188	785-9567
LRP Publications 360 Hiatt Dr *TF:* 800-621-5463 ■ *Web:* www.lrp.com	Palm Beach Gardens	FL	33418	561-622-6520	622-2423
MAC Publishing LLC 501 2nd St *Web:* www.macworld.com	San Francisco	CA	94107	415-243-0505	882-0936
Mary Ann Liebert Publishers Inc 140 Huguenot St 3rd Fl *TF:* 800-654-3237 ■ *Web:* www.liebertpub.com	New Rochelle	NY	10801	914-740-2100	740-2101
McGraw-Hill Cos Inc 1221 Avenue of the Americas *NYSE: MHP* ■ *Web:* www.mcgraw-hill.com	New York	NY	10020	212-512-2000	
McKnight's Long-Term Care News 1 Northfield Plaza Suite 521 *TF:* 800-558-1703 ■ *Web:* www.mcknights.com	Northfield	IL	60093	847-784-8706	784-9346
Meister Media Worldwide 37733 Euclid Ave *TF Orders:* 800-572-7740 ■ *Web:* www.meistermedia.com	Willoughby	OH	44094	440-942-2000	942-0662
Meredith Corp 1716 Locust St *NYSE: MDP* ■ *Web:* www.meredith.com	Des Moines	IA	50309	515-284-3000	284-3806
Mergent Inc 477 Madison Ave # 410 *TF:* 888-411-0893 ■ *Web:* www.mergent.com	New York	NY	10022	212-413-7700	413-7670
Merion Publications Inc 2900 Horizon Dr *TF:* 800-355-1088 ■ *Web:* www.advanceweb.com	King of Prussia	PA	19406	610-278-1400	278-1425
Metal Bulletin Inc 230 Pk Ave S 12th Fl *TF:* 800-638-2525 ■ *Web:* www.metalbulletin.com	New York	NY	10003	212-213-6202	213-6273
Miles Media Group Inc 6751 Professional Pkwy W Suite 200 *TF:* 800-683-0010 ■ *Web:* www.see-florida.com	Sarasota	FL	34240	941-342-2300	907-0300
Miller Publishing Co 12400 Whitewater Dr Suite 160	Minnetonka	MN	55343	952-931-0211	938-1832
Monarch Services Inc 4517 Harford Rd	Baltimore	MD	21214	410-254-9200	254-0991
Moody's Corp 250 Greenwich St 7 World Trade Ctr *NYSE: MCO* ■ *Web:* www.moodys.com	New York	NY	10007	212-553-0300	553-5376
National Auto Research Inc 2620 Barrett Rd **Fax Area Code:* 800 ■ *TF:* 800-554-1026	Gainesville	GA	30507	770-532-4111	357-3444*
National Braille Press Inc 88 St Stephen St *TF:* 888-965-8965 ■ *Web:* www.nbp.org	Boston	MA	02115	617-266-6160	437-0456
National Catholic Reporter Publishing Co 115 E Armour Blvd **Fax:* Edit ■ *TF:* 800-333-7373 ■ *Web:* www.natcath.com	Kansas City	MO	64111	816-531-0538	968-2280*
National Journal Group Inc 600 New Hampshire Ave NW *TF:* 800-613-6701 ■ *Web:* www.nationaljournal.com	Washington	DC	20037	202-739-8400	833-8069
Nelson Publishing 2500 Tamiami Trail N *TF:* 800-226-6113 ■ *Web:* www.nelsonpub.com	Nokomis	FL	34275	941-966-9521	966-2590
New York Times Co 620 Eighth Ave *NYSE: NYT* ■ *Web:* www.nytco.com	New York	NY	10018	212-556-1234	556-7389
News Corp 1211 Avenue of the Americas 2nd Fl *NASDAQ: NWS* ■ *Web:* www.newscorp.com	New York	NY	10036	212-301-3000	
Newsweek Inc 251 W 57th St *TF Cust Svc:* 800-634-6842 ■ *Web:* www.newsweek.com	New York	NY	10019	212-445-4000	445-4120
North American Publishing Co (NAPCO) 1500 Springarden St 12th Fl *TF:* 800-627-2689 ■ *Web:* www.napco.com	Philadelphia	PA	19130	215-238-5300	238-5457
Northstar Travel Media LLC 100 Lighting Way **Fax:* Hum Res ■ *TF:* 800-742-7076 ■ *Web:* www.northstartravelmedia.com	Secaucus	NJ	07094	201-902-2000	902-2037*
Open Horizons Publishing Co PO Box 2887 *Web:* www.bookmarket.com	Taos	NM	87571	505-751-3398	751-3100
Our Sunday Visitor Inc 200 Noll Plaza *TF:* 800-348-2440 ■ *Web:* www.osv.com	Huntington	IN	46750	260-356-8400	359-0029
Pace Communications Inc 1301 Carolina St Suite 200 *Web:* www.pacecommunications.com	Greensboro	NC	27401	336-378-6065	378-8271
Pacific Press Publishing Assn 1350 N Kings Rd *TF Cust Svc:* 800-545-2449	Nampa	ID	83687	208-465-2500	465-2531
Paisano Publications LLC 28210 Dorothy Dr *TF:* 800-323-3484 ■ *Web:* www.easyriders.com	Agoura Hills	CA	91301	818-889-8740	889-4726
Parade Publications Inc 711 3rd Ave *Web:* www.parade.com	New York	NY	10017	212-450-7000	450-7287
PC World Communications Inc 501 2nd St *TF:* 800-997-2967 ■ *Web:* www.pcworld.com	San Francisco	CA	94107	415-243-0500	442-1891
PennWell Publishing Co 1421 S Sheridan Rd *TF:* 800-331-4463 ■ *Web:* www.pennwell.com	Tulsa	OK	74112	918-835-3161	831-9497
Penton Media 249 W 17th St *Web:* www.penton.com	New York	NY	10011	913-967-1710	
Penton Media Inc 1300 E 9th St *Web:* www.penton.com	Cleveland	OH	44114	216-696-7000	696-1752
Photosource International 1910 35th Rd Pine Lake Farm *TF:* 800-624-0266 ■ *Web:* www.photosource.com	Osceola	WI	54020	715-248-3800	248-3800
Pike & Fischer 1010 Wayne Ave Suite 1400 *TF:* 800-255-8131 ■ *Web:* www.pf.com	Silver Spring	MD	20910	301-562-1530	562-1521
Platts 2 Penn Plaza 25th Fl *TF:* 800-752-8878 ■ *Web:* www.platts.com	New York	NY	10121	212-904-3070	
Playboy Enterprises Inc 680 N Lake Shore Dr *NYSE: PLA* ■ *TF:* 800-999-4438 ■ *Web:* www.playboyenterprises.com	Chicago	IL	60611	312-751-8000	751-2818
Pohly Co 99 Bedford St 5th Fl *TF:* 877-687-6459 ■ *Web:* www.pohlyco.com	Boston	MA	02111	617-451-1700	338-7767
PRIMEDIA Inc 3585 Engineering Dr Suite 100 *NYSE: PRM* ■ **Fax Area Code:* 212 ■ *TF:* 800-216-1423 ■ *Web:* www.primedia.com	Norcross	GA	30092	678-421-3000	745-0121*
PRIMEDIA Inc & Consumer Source Inc 3585 Engineering Dr Suite 100 *TF:* 800-216-1423 ■ *Web:* www.primedia.com/divisions/cmmg	Norcross	GA	30092	678-421-3000	
Professional Sports Publications 519 8th Ave 25th Fl **Fax Area Code:* 646 ■ *Web:* www.pspsports.com	New York	NY	10018	212-697-1460	753-9481*
Progressive Impressions 1 Hardman Dr **Fax Area Code:* 954 ■ *TF:* 800-641-9251	Bloomington	IL	61701	800-644-0444	971-4884*
Publications & Communications Inc 13581 Pond Springs Rd Suite 450 *TF:* 800-678-9724 ■ *Web:* www.pcinews.com	Austin	TX	78729	512-250-9023	331-3900
Publications International Ltd 7373 N Cicero Ave *TF:* 800-745-9299 ■ *Web:* www.pubint.com	Lincolnwood	IL	60712	847-676-3470	676-3671
Publishing Group of America Inc 341 Cool Springs Blvd Suite 400 *TF:* 800-720-6323 ■ *Web:* www.pubgroupofamerica.com	Franklin	TN	37067	615-468-6000	468-6100
Putman Media Inc 555 W Pierce Rd Suite 301 **Fax:* Hum Res ■ *TF:* 800-984-7644 ■ *Web:* www.putman.net	Itasca	IL	60143	630-467-1301	467-0153*
Quebecor Media Inc 612 Rue St Jacques *Web:* www.quebecor.com	Montreal	QC	H3C4M8	514-597-2231	594-8844
Randall-Reilly Publishing Co 3200 Rice Mine Rd NE *TF Cust Svc:* 800-633-5953 ■ *Web:* www.randallpub.com	Tuscaloosa	AL	35406	205-349-2990	349-3765
Reader's Digest Assn Inc Reader's Digest Rd *NYSE: RDA* ■ *TF:* 800-635-5006 ■ *Web:* www.rd.com	Pleasantville	NY	10570	914-238-1000	244-7653
Reiman Publications 5400 S 60th St *TF:* 800-344-6913 ■ *Web:* www.reimanpub.com	Greendale	WI	53129	414-423-0100	423-1143
Review & Herald Publishing Assn 55 W Oak Ridge Dr *TF:* 800-456-3991 ■ *Web:* www.rhpa.org	Hagerstown	MD	21740	301-393-3000	393-4055
Rodale Inc 33 E Minor St **Fax Area Code:* 800 ■ **Fax:* Cust Svc ■ *TF Cust Svc:* 800-848-4735 ■ *Web:* www.rodale.com	Emmaus	PA	18098	610-967-5171	813-6627*
Sage Publications Inc 2455 Teller Rd *TF:* 800-818-7243 ■ *Web:* www.sagepub.com	Thousand Oaks	CA	91320	805-499-9774	499-0871
Saint Croix Press Inc 1185 S Knowles Ave *TF:* 800-826-6622 ■ *Web:* www.stcroixpress.com	New Richmond	WI	54017	715-246-5811	246-2486
Sandhills Publishing 120 W Harvest Dr *TF:* 800-331-1978 ■ *Web:* www.sandhills.com	Lincoln	NE	68521	402-479-2181	479-2195
Saturday Evening Post Society 1100 Waterway Blvd *TF:* 800-558-2376 ■ *Web:* www.saturdayeveningpost.com	Indianapolis	IN	46202	317-634-1100	637-0126
Schaeffer's Investment Research Inc 5151 Pfeiffer Rd Suite 250 *TF:* 800-448-2080 ■ *Web:* www.schaeffersresearch.com	Cincinnati	OH	45242	513-589-3800	589-3810
Scholastic Corp 557 Broadway *NASDAQ: SCHL* ■ *TF Cust Svc:* 800-724-6527 ■ *Web:* www.scholastic.com	New York	NY	10012	212-343-6100	
Simba Information 60 Long Ridge Rd Suite 300 *TF:* 888-297-4622 ■ *Web:* www.simbainformation.com	Stamford	CT	06902	203-325-8193	325-8915
Simmons-Boardman Publishing Corp 345 Hudson St 12th Fl *TF:* 800-895-4389 ■ *Web:* www.simmonsboardman.com	New York	NY	10014	212-620-7200	633-1165
Singapore Press Holdings 529 14th St NW National Press Bldg Suite 916 *Web:* www.sph.com.sg	Washington	DC	20045	202-662-8726	662-8729
Sky Publishing Corp 90 Sherman St *TF:* 800-253-0245 ■ *Web:* www.skyandtelescope.com/aboutsky	Cambridge	MA	02140	617-864-7360	864-6117
Slack Inc 6900 Grove Rd *TF:* 800-257-8290 ■ *Web:* www.slackinc.com	Thorofare	NJ	08086	856-848-1000	848-6091
Smithsonian Institution Business Ventures Div 600 Maryland Ave SW Suite 6001 *TF:* 877-240-1183 ■ *Web:* www.si.edu	Washington	DC	20024	202-633-6080	633-6093
SNL Financial 1 SNL Plaza PO Box 2124 *Web:* www.snl.com	Charlottesville	VA	22902	434-977-1600	977-4466
Source Media Inc 1 State St Plaza 27th Fl *TF:* 800-221-1809 ■ *Web:* www.sourcemedia.com	New York	NY	10004	212-803-8200	
ST Media Group International Inc 11262 Cornell Pk Dr *TF:* 800-925-1110 ■ *Web:* www.stmediagroup.com	Cincinnati	OH	45242	513-421-2050	421-5144
Stamats Communications Inc 615 5th St SE *TF:* 800-553-8878 ■ *Web:* www.stamats.com	Cedar Rapids	IA	52401	319-364-6167	365-5421
Standard Publishing Co 8805 Governors Hill Dr Suite 400 **Fax Area Code:* 877 ■ *TF Orders:* 800-543-1353 ■ *Web:* www.standardpub.com	Cincinnati	OH	45249	513-931-4050	867-5751*
State Capitals Newsletters PO Box 7376	Alexandria	VA	22307	703-768-9600	768-9690
Strafford Publications Inc PO Box 13729 *TF:* 800-926-7926 ■ *Web:* www.straffordpub.com	Atlanta	GA	30324	404-881-1141	881-0074
Strang Communications 600 Rinehart Rd *Web:* www.charismamedia.com	Lake Mary	FL	32746	407-333-0600	333-7100
Sunset Publishing Corp 80 Willow Rd **Fax:* Edit ■ *TF:* 800-227-7346 ■ *Web:* www.sunset.com	Menlo Park	CA	94025	650-321-3600	327-7537*
Sys-con Media Inc 577 Chestnut Ridge Rd **Fax:* Cust Svc ■ *Web:* www.sys-con.com	Woodcliff Lake	NJ	07677	201-802-3000	782-9600*
Taunton Press Inc 63 S Main St PO Box 5506 *Web:* www.taunton.com	Newtown	CT	06470	203-426-8171	203-3434
Tax Management Inc 1801 S Bell St *TF:* 800-372-1033 ■ *Web:* www.bnatax.com	Arlington	VA	22202	703-341-3000	341-1623

Company / Address	City	State	Zip	Phone	Fax
Testa Communications 25 Willowdale Ave *TF:* 800-937-7678 ■ *Web:* www.testa.com	Port Washington	NY	11050	516-767-2500	767-9335
Thompson Publishing Group Inc 805 15th St NW 3rd Fl *TF Cust Svc:* 800-677-3789 ■ *Web:* www.thompson.com	Washington	DC	20005	202-872-4000	296-1091
Time Inc 1271 Avenue of the Americas *Web:* www.timeinc.com	New York	NY	10020	212-522-1212	522-0555
Transcontinental Inc 1100 Rene-Levesque Blvd W 24th Fl *TF:* 800-361-5479 ■ *Web:* www.transcontinentalmedia.com	Montreal	QC	H3B4X9	514-392-9000	
TransWorld Media 2052 Corte Del Nogal Suite 100 *TF General:* 800-788-7072	Carlsbad	CA	92011	760-722-7777	722-0653
Travelhost Inc 10701 N Stemmons Fwy *TF:* 800-527-1782 ■ *Web:* www.travelhost.com	Dallas	TX	75220	972-556-0541	432-8729
United Methodist Publishing House 201 8th Ave S *TF:* 800-672-1789 ■ *Web:* www.umph.org	Nashville	TN	37203	615-749-6000	
United Nations Publications 2 UN Plaza Suite DC2-853 *TF:* 800-253-9646 ■ *Web:* www.un.org/Pubs	New York	NY	10017	212-963-8302	
University of Chicago Press Journals Div PO Box 37005 *TF:* 877-705-1878 ■ *Web:* www.press.uchicago.edu	Chicago	IL	60637	773-753-3347	753-0811
Value Line Inc 220 E 42nd St *NASDAQ: VALU* ■ *TF Cust Svc:* 800-634-3583 ■ *Web:* www.valueline.com	New York	NY	10017	212-907-1500	818-9747
Vance Publishing Corp 400 Knightsbridge Pkwy *TF:* 800-621-2845 ■ *Web:* www.vancepublishing.com	Lincolnshire	IL	60069	847-634-2600	634-4379
Vendome Group LLC 149 5th Ave Suite 10 *TF:* 800-519-3692 ■ *Web:* www.vendomegrp.com	New York	NY	10010	212-812-8420	228-1308
Virgo Publishing Inc 3300 N Central Ave Suite 3000 *Web:* www.vpico.com	Phoenix	AZ	85012	480-990-1101	990-0819
Viz Media 295 Bay St *Web:* www.viz.com	San Francisco	CA	94133	415-546-7073	546-7086
Warren Communications News Inc 2115 Ward Ct NW *TF:* 800-771-9202 ■ *Web:* www.warren-news.com	Washington	DC	20037	202-872-9200	318-8350
Watt Publishing Co 303 N Main St Suite 500 *Web:* www.wattnet.com	Rockford	IL	61101	815-734-4171	966-6416
Wenner Media Inc 1290 Avenue of the Americas 2nd Fl	New York	NY	10104	212-484-1616	484-1621
Where International 79 Madison Ave 8th Fl *Web:* www.wheremagazine.com	New York	NY	10016	212-636-2700	636-2787
Whitaker Newsletters Inc PO Box 224 *TF:* 800-359-6049	Spencerville	MD	20868	301-384-1573	879-8803
WIL-FM 92.3 (Ctry) 11647 Olive Blvd	Saint Louis	MO	63141	317-582-1600	
William F Bland Co 709 Turmeric Ln *Web:* www.petrochemical-news.com	Durham	NC	27713	919-544-1717	544-1999
Windhover Information Inc 383 Main Ave *Web:* www.windhoverinfo.com	Norwalk	CT	06851	203-838-4401	838-3214
Wolters Kluwer US Corp 2700 Lake Cook Rd *Web:* www.wolterskluwer.com	Riverwood	IL	60015	847-580-5000	
Working Mother Media Inc 60 E 42nd St 27th *TF:* 800-627-0690 ■ *Web:* www.workingmother.com	New York	NY	10165	212-351-6400	351-6487
Yankee Publishing Inc PO Box 520 *TF:* 800-729-9265	Dublin	NH	03444	603-563-8111	563-8252
Ziff Davis Inc 28 E 28th St *TF:* 800-336-2423 ■ *Web:* www.ziffdavis.com	New York	NY	10016	212-503-3500	503-5696

640-10 Publishers (Misc)

Company / Address	City	State	Zip	Phone	Fax
AM Best Co Ambest Rd *TF:* 800-424-2378 ■ *Web:* www.ambest.com	Oldwick	NJ	08858	908-439-2200	439-3363
American Printing House for the Blind 1839 Frankfort Ave PO Box 6085 *TF:* 800-223-1839 ■ *Web:* www.aph.org	Louisville	KY	40206	502-895-2405	899-2274
Art Publishing Group 165 Chubb Ave *TF:* 800-760-3058 ■ *Web:* www.theartpublishinggroup.com	Lyndhurst	NJ	07071	201-842-8500	842-8546
Bernan Assoc 15200 NBN Way *TF:* 800-865-3457 ■ *Web:* www.bernan.com	Blue Ridge Summit	PA	17214	800-865-3457	865-3450
Brodart Co Automation Div 500 Arch St **Fax Area Code:* 800 ■ *TF:* 800-233-8467 ■ *Web:* www.brodart.com	Williamsport	PA	17701	570-326-2461	999-6799*
Cathedral Press Inc 600 NE 6th St *TF Cust Svc:* 800-874-8332 ■ *Web:* www.cathedralpress.com	Long Prairie	MN	56347	320-732-6143	732-3457
Chalk & Vermilion Fine Arts Inc 55 Old Post Rd # 2 *TF:* 800-877-2250 ■ *Web:* www.chalk-vermilion.com	Greenwich	CT	06830	203-869-9500	869-9520
Channing Bete Co 1 Community Pl **Fax Area Code:* 800 ■ **Fax:* Cust Svc ■ *TF:* 800-477-4776 ■ *Web:* www.channingbete.com	South Deerfield	MA	01373	413-665-7611	499-6464*
Clement Communications Inc 10 LaCrue Ave *TF:* 888-358-5858 ■ *Web:* www.clement.com	Concordville	PA	19331	610-459-4200	459-0936
Coastal Training Technologies Corp 500 Studio Dr *TF:* 888-776-8268 ■ *Web:* www.coastal.com	Virginia Beach	VA	23452	757-498-9014	498-3657
CSS Industries Inc 1845 Walnut St Suite 800 *NYSE: CSS* ■ *Web:* www.cssindustries.com	Philadelphia	PA	19103	215-569-9900	569-9979
Drivers License Guide Co 1492 Oddstad Dr *TF:* 800-227-8827 ■ *Web:* www.driverslicenseguide.com	Redwood City	CA	94063	650-369-4849	364-8740
EBSCO Publishing Inc 10 Estes St *TF:* 800-653-2726 ■ *Web:* www.ebscohost.com	Ipswich	MA	01938	978-356-6500	356-6500
Edmunds.com Inc 2401 Colorado Ave *Web:* www.edmunds.com	Santa Monica	CA	90404	310-309-6300	309-6400
Encyclopedia Britannica Inc 331 N Las Salle St *TF Cust Svc:* 800-747-8503 ■ *Web:* www.britannica.com	Chicago	IL	60654	312-347-7159	294-2104
Entertainment Publications Inc 1414 E Maple Rd *TF:* 800-926-0565 ■ *Web:* www.entertainment.com	Troy	MI	48083	248-404-1000	404-1916
Flyer.Com 201 Kelsey Ln	Tampa	FL	33619	813-626-9430	
Forecast International 22 Commerce Rd *TF:* 800-451-4975 ■ *Web:* www.forecastinternational.com	Newtown	CT	06470	203-426-0800	426-1964
Frames Data Inc 16269 Laguna Canyon Rd Suite 100 *TF:* 800-821-6069 ■ *Web:* www.framesdata.com	Irvine	CA	92618	949-788-0150	
Hadley House Co 4816 Nicollet Ave S *TF:* 800-927-0880 ■ *Web:* www.hadleyhouse.com	Minneapolis	MN	55419	952-943-8474	943-8098
Imagination Publishing 600 W Fulton St Suite 600 *TF:* 800-482-0776 ■ *Web:* www.imaginepub.com	Chicago	IL	60661	312-887-1000	887-1003
Imaginova 470 Pk Ave S 9th Fl *Web:* www.imaginova.com	New York	NY	10016	212-703-5800	703-5900
InfoCommerce Group Inc 2 Bala Plaza Suite 300 *Web:* www.infocommercegroup.com	Bala Cynwyd	PA	19004	610-649-1200	645-5360
Interactive Data Corp 32 Crosby Dr *Web:* www.interactivedata.com	Bedford	MA	01730	781-687-8500	687-8005
Krames Communication/Staywell 780 Township Line Rd **Fax Area Code:* 866 ■ *TF Sales:* 800-333-3032 ■ *Web:* www.krames.com	Yardley	PA	19067	267-685-2300	722-4377*
Lifetouch Church Directories 1371 Portland Way N *TF:* 800-521-4611	Galion	OH	44833	419-468-4739	462-5688
Majesco Entertainment Co 160 Raritan Ctr Pkwy *NASDAQ: COOL* ■ *Web:* www.majescoentertainment.com	Edison	NJ	08837	732-225-8910	225-8408
Mergent FIS Inc 580 Kingsley Pk Dr **Fax Area Code:* 704 ■ *TF:* 800-342-5647 ■ *Web:* www.mergent.com	Fort Mill	SC	29715	800-342-5647	559-6945*
New York Graphic Society Ltd 129 Glover Ave *TF:* 800-677-6947 ■ *Web:* www.nygs.com	Norwalk	CT	06850	203-847-2000	846-4869
Nielson Co 770 Broadway *Web:* www.nielsen.com	New York	NY	10003	646-654-5500	654-5835
O'neil & Assoc Inc 495 Byers Rd *Web:* www.oneil.com	Miamisburg	OH	45342	937-865-0800	865-5858
OAG Worldwide 3025 Highland Pkwy Suite 200 *TF:* 800-323-3537 ■ *Web:* www.oag.com	Downers Grove	IL	60515	630-515-5300	515-3933
OneSource Information Services Inc 300 Baker Ave *TF:* 800-333-8036 ■ *Web:* www.onesource.com	Concord	MA	01742	978-318-4300	318-4690
Post Asylum Inc 5642 Dyer St *Web:* www.postasylum.com	Dallas	TX	75206	214-363-0162	363-8871
San Dieguito Printers 1880 Diamond St *TF:* 800-321-5794 ■ *Web:* www.sd-print.com	San Marcos	CA	92078	760-744-0910	744-5811
Serif Inc 17 Hampshire Dr Suite 1 & 2 *TF Sales:* 800-489-6721 ■ *Web:* www.serif.com	Hudson	NH	03051	603-889-8650	889-1127
Somerset Fine Arts PO Box 869 *TF Sales:* 800-444-2540 ■ *Web:* www.somersetfineart.com	Fulshear	TX	77441	713-932-6847	932-7861
TechTarget 117 Kendrick St Suite 800 *TF:* 888-274-4111 ■ *Web:* www.techtarget.com	Needham	MA	02494	781-657-1000	657-1100
Thomson CenterWatch Inc 100 N Washington St Suite 301 *TF Cust Svc:* 800-765-9647 ■ *Web:* www.centerwatch.com	Boston	MA	02114	617-948-5100	948-5101
Washington Publishing Co 747 177th Ln NE **Fax Area Code:* 775 ■ *Web:* www.wpc-edi.com	Bellevue	WA	98008	425-562-2245	239-2061*
Winn Devon Art Group 6311 Westminster Hwy Unit 110 **Fax Area Code:* 888 ■ *TF:* 800-663-1166 ■ *Web:* www.winndevon.com	Richmond	BC	V7C4V4	604-276-4551	744-8275*
Wonderlic Inc 400 Lakeview Pkwy Suite 200 *TF:* 877-605-9496 ■ *Web:* www.wonderlic.com	Vernon Hills	IL	60061	847-680-4900	680-9492
Zagat Survey LLC 4 Columbus Cir 3rd Fl *TF:* 800-333-3421 ■ *Web:* www.zagat.com	New York	NY	10019	212-977-6000	977-6488

640-11 Technical Publishers

Company / Address	City	State	Zip	Phone	Fax
Aircraft Technical Publishers 101 S Hill Dr **Fax:* Sales ■ *TF:* 800-227-4610 ■ *Web:* www.atp.com	Brisbane	CA	94005	415-330-9500	468-1596*
American Chemical Society Publications 1155 16th St NW Publications Support Services *TF:* 800-227-5558 ■ *Web:* www.pubs.acs.org	Washington	DC	20036	202-872-4600	872-6060
American Technical Publishers Inc 1155 175th St *TF:* 800-323-3471 ■ *Web:* www.go2atp.com	Homewood	IL	60430	708-957-1100	957-1101
Applied Computer Research Inc (ACR) PO Box 41730 *TF:* 800-234-2227 ■ *Web:* www.itmarketintelligence.com	Phoenix	AZ	85080	602-937-4700	548-4800
Belltown Media PO Box 980955 *Web:* www.linuxjournal.com	Houston	TX	77098	713-344-1956	589-2677
Books24x7.com Inc 100 River Ridge Dr *Web:* www.books24x7.com	Norwood	MA	02062	781-440-0550	440-0560
Buyers Laboratory Inc 20 Railroad Ave *Web:* www.buyerslab.com	Hackensack	NJ	07601	201-488-0404	488-0461
Cambridge Information Group (CIG) 111 W 57th St *Web:* www.cambridgeinformationgroup.com	New York	NY	10019	212-897-6635	897-6640
Faulkner Information Services 7905 Browning Rd Suite 116 *TF:* 800-843-0460 ■ *Web:* www.faulkner.com	Pennsauken	NJ	08109	856-662-2070	662-0905
Health Forum 1 N Franklin St 28th Fl *TF:* 800-621-6902	Chicago	IL	60606	312-893-6800	422-4506
Information Gatekeepers Inc (IGI) 1340 Soldiers Field Rd Suite 2 *TF:* 800-323-1088 ■ *Web:* www.igigroup.com	Boston	MA	02135	617-782-5033	782-5735
JJ Keller & Assoc Inc 3003 Breezewood Ln **Fax Area Code:* 800 ■ *TF:* 800-558-5011 ■ *Web:* www.jjkeller.com	Neenah	WI	54956	920-722-2848	727-7516*

				Phone	Fax
Ken Cook Co 9929 W Silver Springs Dr. *Web:* www.kencook.com	Milwaukee	WI	53225	414-466-6060	466-0840
knovel.com 13 Eaton Ave. *TF:* 888-238-1626 ■ *Web:* www.knovel.com	Norwich	NY	13815	607-337-5600	334-9097
McGraw-Hill Osborne 100 Powell St 10th Fl *TF:* 800-227-0900 ■ *Web:* www.osborne.com	Emeryville	CA	94608	800-227-0900	
Miles-Samuelson Inc 475 Franklin Ave *Web:* www.miles-samuelson.com	Franklin Square	NY	11010	516-437-7330	488-8013
Mitchell 1 14145 Danielson St Suite A *Fax: Sales ■ *TF:* 888-724-6742 ■ *Web:* www.mitchell1.com	Poway	CA	92064	858-391-5000	746-5250*
Mitchell International Inc 6220 Greenwich Dr. *TF:* 800-854-7030 ■ *Web:* www.mitchell.com	San Diego	CA	92122	858-578-6550	578-4752
O'Reilly & Assoc Inc 1005 Gravenstein Hwy N *TF:* 800-998-9938 ■ *Web:* www.oreilly.com	Sebastopol	CA	95472	707-829-0515	829-0104
TeleGeography Inc 1909 K St NW Suite 380 *Web:* www.telegeography.com	Washington	DC	20006	202-741-0020	741-0021
Thompson Publishing Group Inc 805 15th St NW 3rd Fl *TF Cust Svc:* 800-677-3789 ■ *Web:* www.thompson.com	Washington	DC	20005	202-872-4000	296-1091
United Communications Group (UCG) 9737 Washingtonian Blvd Suite 100. *TF:* 888-275-2264 ■ *Web:* www.ucg.com	Gaithersburg	MD	20878	301-287-2700	287-2039

641 PULP MILLS

SEE ALSO Paper Mills p. 2337; Paperboard Mills p. 2339

				Phone	Fax
Alberta-Pacific Forest Industries Inc PO Box 8000 *TF:* 800-661-5210 ■ *Web:* www.alpac.ca	Boyle	AB	T0A0M0	780-525-8000	525-8028
Boise Paper Solutions Corp 222 NE Pk Plaza Dr Suite 105 *Web:* www.bc.com	Vancouver	WA	98684	360-891-8787	
Brant Allen Industries 80 Field Pt Rd 3rd Fl.	Greenwich	CT	06830	203-661-3344	661-3349
Canadian Forest Products Ltd 5162 Northwood Pulp Mill Rd PO Box 9000 *Fax: Acctg ■ *Web:* www.canfor.com	Prince George	BC	V2L4W2	250-962-3500	962-3533*
Daishowa America Co Ltd PO Box 271 *TF Sales:* 800-331-6314	Port Angeles	WA	98362	360-457-4474	452-9004
International Paper Co 6400 Poplar Ave. *NYSE:* IP ■ *TF Prod Info:* 800-223-1268 ■ *Web:* www.internationalpaper.com	Memphis	TN	38297	901-419-7000	
Kimberly-Clark Corp 351 Phelps Dr. *NYSE:* KMB ■ *TF:* 800-544-1847 ■ *Web:* www.kimberly-clark.com	Irving	TX	75038	972-281-1200	281-1435
Longview Fibre Paper & Packaging Inc 300 Fibre Way PO Box 639. *Web:* www.longviewfibre.com	Longview	WA	98632	360-425-1550	230-5135
Ohio Pulp Mills Inc 2100 Losantiville Ave	Cincinnati	OH	45237	513-731-0208	351-2129
Parsons & Whittemore Inc 4 International Dr	Rye Brook	NY	10573	914-937-9009	937-2259
Pope & Talbot Inc 1500 SW 1st Ave Suite 200. *NYSE:* POP ■ *Web:* www.poptal.com	Portland	OR	97201	503-228-9161	228-9161
Potlatch Corp 601 W 1st Ave Suite 1600 *NASDAQ:* PCH ■ *Web:* www.potlatchcorp.com	Spokane	WA	99201	509-835-1500	835-1555
Potlatch Corp Pulp & Paperboard Div 805 Mill Rd. *Fax: Hum Res ■ *Web:* www.potlatchcorp.com	Lewiston	ID	83501	208-799-1429	750-7809*
Southern Cellulose Products Inc PO Box 2278	Chattanooga	TN	37409	423-821-1561	821-2624

642 PUMPS - MEASURING & DISPENSING

				Phone	Fax
Aptargroup Inc Stratford 125 Access Rd *Web:* www.emsargroup.com	Stratford	CT	06615	203-377-8100	377-0500
Bennett Pump Co 1218 Pontaluna Rd. *TF:* 800-423-6638 ■ *Web:* www.bennettusa.com	Spring Lake	MI	49456	231-798-1310	799-6202
Dresser Inc Wayne Div 3814 Jarrett Way. *Fax: Cust Svc ■ *TF:* 888-929-6327 ■ *Web:* www.dresserwayne.com	Austin	TX	78728	512-388-8311	388-8429*
Gasboy International Inc 7300 W Friendly Ave. *Fax Area Code: 800 ■ *Fax: Cust Svc ■ *TF Sales:* 800-444-5579 ■ *Web:* www.gasboy.com	Greensboro	NC	27420	336-547-5000	444-5569*
Gilbarco Inc 7300 W Friendly Ave. *Fax: Mktg ■ *Web:* www.gilbarco.com	Greensboro	NC	27420	336-547-5000	547-5890*
O'Day Equipment Inc 1301 40th St NW *TF:* 800-654-6329 ■ *Web:* www.odayequipment.com	Fargo	ND	58102	701-282-9260	281-9770
Tuthill Transfer Systems 8825 Aviation Dr *Web:* www.tuthill.com	Fort Wayne	IN	46809	260-747-7529	747-3159

643 PUMPS & MOTORS - FLUID POWER

				Phone	Fax
Applied Energy Co Inc 11431 Chairman Dr. *TF:* 800-580-1171 ■ *Web:* www.appliedenergyco.com	Dallas	TX	75243	214-355-4200	355-4201
Bosch Rexroth Corp 5150 Prairie Stone Pkwy. *TF:* 800-860-1055 ■ *Web:* www.boschrexroth-us.com	Hoffman Estates	IL	60192	847-645-3600	645-6201
Bosch Rexroth Corp Piston Pump Div 8 Southchase Ct	Fountain Inn	SC	29644	864-967-2777	967-8900
Cross Mfg Inc 11011 King St Suite 210 *TF:* 800-542-7677 ■ *Web:* www.crossmfg.com	Overland Park	KS	66210	913-451-1233	451-1235
Delta Power Co 4484 Boeing Dr *Web:* www.delta-power.com	Rockford	IL	61109	815-397-6628	397-2526
Dynex Rivett Inc 770 Capitol Dr *Web:* www.dynexhydraulics.com	Pewaukee	WI	53072	262-691-0300	691-0312
Fluid Metering Inc 5 Aerial Way Suite 500. *TF:* 800-223-3388 ■ *Web:* www.fmipump.com	Syosset	NY	11791	516-922-6050	624-8261
Haldex Hydraulic Systems 2222 15th St. *TF:* 800-572-7867 ■ *Web:* www.haldex.com	Rockford	IL	61104	815-398-4400	398-5977
Howden Airdynamics 2616 Research Dr	Corona	CA	92882	951-734-0070	734-2594
Hydreco 1500 County Naple Blvd *Web:* www.hydreco.com	Charlotte	NC	28273	704-295-7575	295-7574
Jetstream of Houston LLP 4930 Cranswick *TF:* 800-231-8192 ■ *Web:* www.waterblast.com	Houston	TX	77041	713-462-7000	462-5387
Liquid Drive Corp 418 Hadley St. *TF:* 800-523-4443 ■ *Web:* www.liquiddrive.com	Holly	MI	48442	248-634-5382	634-5720
Milton Roy USA 201 Ivyland Rd. *Fax Area Code: 860 ■ *Web:* www.miltonroy.com	Ivyland	PA	18974	215-441-0800	998-4192*
Mte Hydraulics PO Box 5906 *Web:* www.mtehydraulics.com	Rockford	IL	61125	815-397-4701	399-5528
Oilgear Co 2300 S 51st St PO Box 343924 *Web:* www.oilgear.com	Milwaukee	WI	53219	414-327-1700	327-0532
Parker Hannifin Corp Hydraulic Pump/Motor Div 2745 Snapps Ferry Rd *Web:* www.parker.com	Greeneville	TN	37745	423-639-8151	787-2418
Parker Hannifin Corp Nichols Portland Div 2400 Congress St. *Web:* www.parker.com/nichport	Portland	ME	04102	207-774-6121	774-3601
Permco Inc 1500 Frost Rd *TF:* 800-628-2801 ■ *Web:* www.permco.com	Streetsboro	OH	44241	330-626-2801	626-2805
Sauer-Danfoss 2800 E 13th St. *Web:* www.sauer-danfoss.com	Ames	IA	50010	515-239-6000	239-6318
SPX Fluid Power 5885 11th St *Web:* www.spxfluidpower.com	Rockford	IL	61109	815-874-5556	874-7853
TII Network Technologies Inc 141 Rodeo Dr. *NASDAQ:* TIII ■ *TF:* 888-844-4720 ■ *Web:* www.tiinetworktechnologies.com	Edgewood	NY	11717	631-789-5000	789-5063
Viking Pump Inc 406 State St PO Box 8 *Web:* www.vikingpump.com	Cedar Falls	IA	50613	319-266-1741	273-8157
Voith Turbo Inc 25 Winship Rd *Web:* www.usa.voithturbo.com	York	PA	17406	717-767-3200	767-3210

644 PUMPS & PUMPING EQUIPMENT (GENERAL USE)

SEE ALSO Industrial Machinery, Equipment, & Supplies p. 2107

				Phone	Fax
Ace Pump Corp PO Box 13187 *Web:* www.acepumps.com	Memphis	TN	38113	901-948-8514	774-6147
Acme Dynamics Inc 3608 Sydney Rd PO Box 1780 *TF:* 800-622-9355 ■ *Web:* www.acmedynamics.com	Plant City	FL	33566	813-752-3137	752-4580
Aermotor Pumps Inc 293 Wright St. *TF:* 800-265-7241 ■ *Web:* www.aermotor.com	Delavan	WI	53115	800-230-1816	230-1816
Afton Pumps Inc 7335 Ave N *TF:* 800-829-9731 ■ *Web:* www.aftonpumps.com	Houston	TX	77011	713-923-9731	923-3902
American Machine & Tool Co Inc 400 Spring St. *TF:* 888-268-7867 ■ *Web:* www.amtpump.com	Royersford	PA	19468	610-948-3800	948-5300
Aqua-Dyne Inc 3620 W 11th St. *Web:* www.aqua-dyne.com	Houston	TX	77008	713-864-6929	864-0313
AR Wilfley & Sons Inc 7350 E Progress Pl Suite 200. *TF:* 800-525-9930 ■ *Web:* www.wilfley.com	Englewood	CO	80111	303-779-1777	779-1277
Armstrong International Inc 2081 SE Ocean Blvd 4th Fl. *Web:* www.armstronginternational.com	Stuart	FL	34996	772-286-7175	286-1001
ASM Industries Inc Pacer Pumps Div 41 Industrial Cir *TF Cust Svc:* 800-233-3861 ■ *Web:* www.pacerpumps.com	Lancaster	PA	17601	717-656-2161	656-0477
Autoform Tool & Mfg Inc PO Box 988 *Web:* www.autoformtool.com	Fremont	IN	46737	260-495-9641	495-2724
Barney's Pumps Inc 2965 Barney's Pumps Pl *Web:* www.barneyspumps.com	Lakeland	FL	33812	863-665-8500	666-3858
Baxa Corp 9540 S Maroon Cr Suite 400 *TF:* 800-494-2292 ■ *Web:* www.baxa.com	Englewood	CO	80112	303-690-4204	690-4804
Beckett Corp 3250 Skyway Cir N *TF:* 888-232-5388 ■ *Web:* www.beckettpumps.com	Irving	TX	75038	972-871-8000	871-8888
Berkeley Pumps 293 Wright St. *Fax Area Code: 800 ■ *Fax: Cust Svc ■ *TF Cust Svc:* 800-728-1240 ■ *Web:* www.berkeleypumps.com	Delavan	WI	53115	262-728-5551	426-9446*
Blackmer 1809 Century Ave. *Web:* www.blackmer.com	Grand Rapids	MI	49503	616-241-1611	241-3752
Buffalo Pumps Inc 874 Oliver St *Web:* www.buffalopumps.com	North Tonawanda	NY	14120	716-693-1850	693-6303
Calvert Engineering Inc 28606 Livingston Ave. *TF:* 800-225-1339 ■ *Web:* www.calpump.com	Valencia	CA	91355	661-257-7330	257-7331
Carver Pump Co 2415 Pk Ave *Web:* www.carverpump.com	Muscatine	IA	52761	563-263-3410	262-7688
Cascade Pump Co 10107 Norwalk Blvd *Web:* www.cascadepump.com	Santa Fe Springs	CA	90670	562-946-1414	941-3730
Cat Pumps 1681 94th Ln NE *Web:* www.catpumps.com	Minneapolis	MN	55449	763-780-5440	780-2958
Centrilift Inc 200 W Stuart Roosa Dr. *TF:* 800-633-5088 ■ *Web:* www.bakerhughes.com	Claremore	OK	74017	918-341-9600	342-0260
CIRCOR International Inc 25 Corporate Dr Suite 130 *NYSE:* CIR ■ *Web:* www.circor.com	Burlington	MA	01803	781-270-1200	270-1299
Coffin Turbo Pump Inc 326 S Dean St. *TF:* 800-568-9798 ■ *Web:* www.coffinturbopump.com	Englewood	NJ	07631	201-568-4700	568-4716
Colfax Corp 8730 Stony Pt Pkwy Suite 150. *Web:* www.colfaxcorp.com	Richmond	VA	23235	804-560-4070	560-4076
Corken Inc 3805 NW 36th St *TF:* 800-631-4929 ■ *Web:* www.corken.com	Oklahoma City	OK	73112	405-946-5576	948-6664

Company	City	State	Zip	Phone	Fax
Cornell Pump Co 16261 SE 130th Ave PO Box 6334 — *Web:* www.cornellpump.com	Portland	OR	97228	503-653-0330	653-0338
Crane Co 100 1st Stamford Pl 4th Fl — *NYSE: CR* ■ *Web:* www.craneco.com	Stamford	CT	06902	203-363-7300	363-7295
Crane Deming Pumps Co 420 Third St — *Web:* www.cranepumps.com	Piqua	OH	45356	937-778-8947	773-7157
Crane Pumps & Systems 420 3rd St — *Web:* www.cranepumps.com	Piqua	OH	45356	937-773-2442	773-2238
David Brown Union Pumps Co 4600 W Dickman Rd — *TF:* 800-877-7867	Battle Creek	MI	49037	269-966-4600	966-4649
Dempster Industries Inc 711 S 6th St PO Box 848 — *TF:* 800-777-0212 ■ *Web:* www.dempsterllc.com	Beatrice	NE	68310	402-223-4026	223-4026
Dosmatic USA/ International Inc 1230 Crowley Cir — *TF:* 800-344-6767 ■ *Web:* www.dosmatic.com	Carrollton	TX	75006	972-245-9765	245-9000
Ebara international corp 350 Salomon Cir — *Web:* www.ebaracryo.com	Sparks	NV	89434	775-356-2796	356-2884
Environment One Corp 2773 Balltown Rd — *Web:* www.eone.com	Niskayuna	NY	12309	518-346-6161	
Evans-Hydro 18128 S Santa Fe Ave — *TF:* 800-429-7867	Rancho Dominguez	CA	90221	310-608-5801	608-0685
Flint & Walling Inc 95 N Oak St — *TF Sales:* 800-927-0360 ■ *Web:* www.flintandwalling.com	Kendallville	IN	46755	260-347-1600	347-0909
Flowserve Corp 5215 N O'Connor Blvd Suite 2300 — *NYSE: FLS* ■ *Web:* www.flowserve.com	Irving	TX	75039	972-443-6500	443-6800
Gardner Denver Pump Div 4747 S 83rd E Ave — *TF:* 800-637-8099 ■ *Web:* www.gardnerdenver.com	Tulsa	OK	74145	918-664-1151	664-6225
GIW Industries Inc 5000 Wrightsboro Rd — *TF:* 800-241-2702 ■ *Web:* www.giwindustries.com	Grovetown	GA	30813	706-863-1011	860-5897
Gorman-Rupp Co 305 Bowman St PO Box 1217 — *AMEX: GRC* ■ *Web:* www.gormanrupp.com	Mansfield	OH	44901	419-755-1011	755-1263
Gorman-Rupp Industries 180 Hines Ave — *TF:* 800-998-3011 ■ *Web:* www.gripumps.com	Bellville	OH	44813	419-886-3001	886-2338
Goulds Pumps Inc 240 Fall St — **Fax:* Sales ■ *Web:* www.goulds.com	Seneca Falls	NY	13148	315-568-2811	568-2418*
Graco Inc 88 11th Ave NE PO Box 1441 — *NYSE: GGG* ■ **Fax:* Hum Res ■ *TF Cust Svc:* 800-328-0211 ■ *Web:* www.graco.com	Minneapolis	MN	55413	612-623-6000	623-6777*
Graymills Corp 3705 N Lincoln Ave — *Web:* www.graymills.com	Chicago	IL	60613	773-477-4100	477-4133
Great Plains Industries Inc 5252 E 36th St N — *TF Sales:* 800-835-0113 ■ *Web:* www.gpi.net	Wichita	KS	67220	316-686-7361	686-6746
Grundfos Pumps Corp 5900 E Shields Ave — *TF Cust Svc:* 800-333-1366 ■ *Web:* www.grundfos.com	Fresno	CA	93727	559-292-8000	348-9628
Gusher Pumps 115 Industrial Dr — *Web:* www.gusher.com	Williamstown	KY	41097	859-824-3100	824-7248
Hale Products Inc 700 Spring Mill Ave — **Fax:* Cust Svc ■ *TF:* 800-220-4253 ■ *Web:* www.haleproducts.com	Conshohocken	PA	19428	610-825-6300	825-6440*
Harben Inc 2010 Ronald Regan Blvd — *TF:* 800-327-5387 ■ *Web:* www.harben.com	Cumming	GA	30041	770-889-9535	887-9411
Haskel International Inc 100 E Graham Pl — **Fax:* Sales ■ *TF:* 800-743-2720 ■ *Web:* www.haskel.com	Burbank	CA	91502	818-843-4000	841-4291*
Hayward Tyler Inc 480 Roosevelt Hwy — *Web:* www.haywardtyler.com	Colchester	VT	05446	802-655-4444	655-4682
Houston Grinding & Mfg Inc 3544 W 12th St	Houston	TX	77008	713-869-3573	869-2660
Hypro 375 5th Ave NW — **Fax:* Sales ■ *TF Cust Svc:* 800-424-9776 ■ *Web:* www.hypropumps.com	New Brighton	MN	55112	651-766-6300	766-6600*
IDEX Corp 1925 W Field Ct Suite 400 — *NYSE: IEX* ■ *Web:* www.idexcorp.com	Northbrook	IL	60062	847-498-7070	498-3940
Imo Pump 1710 Airport Rd — **Fax:* Sales ■ *Web:* www.imo-pump.com	Monroe	NC	28110	704-289-6511	289-9273*
ITT A-C Pump N27 W 23293 Roundy Dr — *Web:* www.ittfluidbusiness.com	Pewaukee	WI	53072	262-548-8181	548-8170
ITT Corp 1133 Westchester Ave — **Fax:* Mktg ■ *Web:* www.bellgossett.com	White Plains	NY	10604	914-641-2000	696-2950*
ITT Industries Jabsco 666 E Dyer Rd — *TF:* 800-845-7000 ■ *Web:* www.ittflowcontrol.com	Santa Ana	CA	92705	714-557-4700	628-8478
Iwaki America Inc 5 Boynton Rd — *Web:* www.walchem.com	Holliston	MA	01746	508-429-1110	429-7433
Kemlon Products & Development Co 1424 N Main St — *Web:* www.kemlon.com	Pearland	TX	77581	281-997-3300	997-1300
Kerr Pump & Supply 12880 Cloverdale St — *TF:* 800-482-8259 ■ *Web:* www.kerrpump.com	Oak Park	MI	48237	248-543-3880	543-3236
Kimray Inc 52 NW 42nd St — *Web:* www.kimray.com	Oklahoma City	OK	73118	405-525-6601	525-7520
Kraft Fluid Systems Inc 14300 Foltz Pkwy — *TF:* 800-257-1155 ■ *Web:* www.kraftfluid.com	Strongsville	OH	44149	440-238-5545	238-5266
Lawrence Pumps Inc 371 Market St — **Fax:* Sales ■ *TF:* 800-434-5248 ■ *Web:* www.lawrencepumps.com	Lawrence	MA	01843	978-682-5249	975-4291*
Liquiflo Equipment Co 443 N Ave — *Web:* www.liquiflo.com	Garwood	NJ	07027	908-518-0777	518-1847
Maass Midwest Inc 11283 Dundee Rd PO Box 547 — **Fax Area Code:* 847 ■ *TF:* 800-323-6259 ■ *Web:* www.maassmidwest.com	Huntley	IL	60142	800-323-6259	669-3230*
Madden Mfg Inc PO Box 387 — **Fax:* Sales ■ *TF:* 800-369-6233 ■ *Web:* www.maddenmfg.com	Elkhart	IN	46515	574-295-4292	295-7562*
March Mfg Inc 1819 Pickwick Ave — *Web:* www.marchpump.com	Glenview	IL	60026	847-729-5300	729-7062
McNally Industries LLC 340 W Benson Ave PO Box 129 — *TF:* 800-473-0053 ■ *Web:* www.northern-pump.com	Grantsburg	WI	54840	715-463-8300	463-5261
Met-Pro Corp Dean Pump Div 6040 Guion Rd — *Web:* www.met-pro.com	Indianapolis	IN	46254	317-293-2930	297-7028
Met-Pro Corp Fybroc Div 700 Emlen Way — *TF:* 800-392-7621 ■ *Web:* www.fybroc.com	Telford	PA	18969	215-723-8155	723-2197
Met-Pro Corp Sethco Div 800 Emlen Way — *TF:* 800-645-0500 ■ *Web:* www.sethco.com	Telford	PA	18969	215-799-2577	799-0920

Company	City	State	Zip	Phone	Fax
Micropump Inc 1402 NE 136th Ave — *TF Sales:* 800-671-6269 ■ *Web:* www.micropump.com	Vancouver	WA	98684	360-253-2008	253-8294
Morgantown Machine & Hydraulics Inc 437 Goshen Rd — *Web:* www.swansonindustries.com	Morgantown	WV	26508	304-296-8371	
Moyno Inc 1895 W Jefferson St — **Fax:* Mktg ■ *TF:* 800-325-1331 ■ *Web:* www.moyno.com	Springfield	OH	45506	937-327-3111	327-3177*
MP Pumps Inc 34800 Bennett Dr — *TF:* 800-563-8006 ■ *Web:* www.mppumps.com	Fraser	MI	48026	586-293-8240	293-8469
MWI Corp 201 N Federal Hwy — *Web:* www.mwicorp.com	Deerfield Beach	FL	33441	954-426-1500	426-1582
Nagle Pumps Inc 1249 Ctr Ave — **Fax:* Sales ■ *Web:* www.naglepumps.com	Chicago Heights	IL	60411	708-754-2940	754-2944*
Neptune Chemical Pump Co PO Box 247 — *TF:* 800-255-4017 ■ *Web:* www.neptune1.com	Lansdale	PA	19446	215-699-8700	699-0370
Odessa Pumps & Equipment Inc 3209 N County Rd W — *Web:* www.odessapumps.com	Odessa	TX	79764	432-333-2817	333-2841
Oteco Inc PO Box 1849 — *Web:* www.oteco.com	Houston	TX	77251	713-695-3693	695-3520
Patterson Pump Co 2129 Ayersville Rd — *Web:* www.pattersonpumps.com	Toccoa	GA	30577	706-886-2101	886-0023
Peerless Pump Co 2005 ML King Jr St PO Box 7026 — *TF:* 800-879-0182 ■ *Web:* www.peerlesspump.com	Indianapolis	IN	46207	317-925-9661	924-7388
Pentair Inc 5500 Wayzata Blvd Suite 800 — *NYSE: PNR* ■ *TF:* 800-328-9626 ■ *Web:* www.pentair.com	Golden Valley	MN	55416	763-545-1730	656-5400
Pentair Water Pool & Spa 1620 Hawkins Ave — *TF:* 800-831-7133 ■ *Web:* www.pentairpool.com	Sanford	NC	27330	800-831-7133	284-4151
Procon Products Co 910 Ridgely Rd — *Web:* www.proconpumps.com	Murfreesboro	TN	37129	615-890-5710	896-7729
Pulsafeeder Inc 2883 Brighton-Henrietta Town Line Rd — *Web:* www.pulsa.com	Rochester	NY	14623	585-292-8000	424-5619
Robbins & Myers Inc 51 Plum St Suite 260 — *NYSE: RBN* ■ *Web:* www.robn.com	Dayton	OH	45440	937-458-6600	225-3314
Roper Pump Co 3475 Old Maysville Rd — *TF Sales:* 800-944-6769 ■ *Web:* www.roperpumps.com	Commerce	GA	30529	706-335-5551	335-5490
Roth Pump Co PO Box 4330 — *TF:* 888-444-7684 ■ *Web:* www.rothpump.com	Rock Island	IL	61204	309-787-1791	787-5142
RS Corcoran Co 500 N Vine St — *TF:* 800-637-1067 ■ *Web:* www.corcoranpumps.com	New Lenox	IL	60451	815-485-2156	485-2156
Scot Pump 6437 Pioneer Rd PO Box 286 — *TF:* 888-835-0600 ■ *Web:* www.scotpump.com	Cedarburg	WI	53012	262-377-7000	377-7330
seepex Inc 511 Speedway Dr — *TF:* 800-695-3659 ■ *Web:* www.seepex.com	Enon	OH	45323	937-864-7150	864-7157
Serfilco Ltd 2900 MacArthur Blvd — *TF:* 800-323-5431 ■ *Web:* www.serfilco.com	Northbrook	IL	60062	847-559-1777	559-1141
SHURflo Pump Mfg Co Inc 5900 Katella Ave Suite A — *TF:* 800-854-3218 ■ *Web:* www.shurflo.com	Cypress	CA	90630	562-795-5200	795-7554
SIHI Pumps Inc 303 Industrial Blvd — *Web:* www.sihi-pumps.com	Grand Island	NY	14072	716-773-6450	773-2330
Simflo Pumps Inc 754 E Maley St PO Box 849 — *Web:* www.simflo.com	Willcox	AZ	85644	520-384-2273	384-4042
SPX - Midwest Service Ctr 611 Sugar Creek Rd — *TF:* 800-252-5200 ■ *Web:* www.spxpe.com	Delavan	WI	53115	262-728-1900	728-4950
Standard Alloys & Mfg PO Box 969 — *TF:* 800-231-8240 ■ *Web:* www.standardalloys.com	Port Arthur	TX	77640	409-983-3201	983-7837
Sturm Rapid Response Ctr 1305 Main St — *TF:* 800-624-3485 ■ *Web:* www.sturm-inc.com	Barboursville	WV	25504	304-736-3476	736-4058
Sulzer Pumps (US) Inc 2800 NW Front Ave — *Web:* www.sulzerpumps.com	Portland	OR	97210	503-226-5200	226-5286
Syncroflo Inc 6700 Best Friend Rd — *Web:* www.syncroflo.com	Norcross	GA	30071	770-447-4443	448-5120
Systecon Inc 6121 Schumacher Pk Dr — *Web:* www.systecon.com	West Chester	OH	45069	513-777-7722	777-0259
Textron Fluid & Power Inc 40 Westminster St — *Web:* www.textron.com	Providence	RI	02903	401-588-3400	621-5045
Thompson Pump & Mfg Co Inc 4620 City Ctr Dr PO Box 291370 — *TF:* 800-767-7310 ■ *Web:* www.thompsonpumps.com	Port Orange	FL	32129	386-767-7310	761-0362
Tramco Pump Co 1500 W Adams St — **Fax:* Sales ■ *Web:* www.tramcopump.com	Chicago	IL	60607	312-243-5800	243-0702*
Tuthill Corp 8500 S Madison St — *TF:* 800-888-4455 ■ *Web:* www.tuthill.com	Burr Ridge	IL	60527	630-382-4900	382-4999
Tuthill Pump Group 12500 S Pulaski Rd — *Web:* www.pump.tuthill.com	Alsip	IL	60803	708-389-2500	388-0869
Vanton Pump & Equipment Corp 201 Sweetland Ave — *Web:* www.vanton.com	Hillside	NJ	07205	908-688-4216	686-9314
Vaughan Co Inc 364 Monte-Elma Rd — *TF:* 888-249-2467 ■ *Web:* www.chopperpumps.com	Montesano	WA	98563	360-249-4042	249-6155
Veeder-Root Red Jacket Div 125 Powder Forest Dr PO Box 2003 — *TF:* 800-873-3313 ■ *Web:* www.veeder.com	Simsbury	CT	06070	860-651-2700	651-7140
Viking Pump Inc 406 State St PO Box 8 — *Web:* www.vikingpump.com	Cedar Falls	IA	50613	319-266-1741	273-8157
Warren Rupp Inc 800 N Main St — *Web:* www.warrenrupp.com	Mansfield	OH	44902	419-524-8388	522-7867
Waterous Co 125 Hardman Ave — *TF:* 800-488-1228 ■ *Web:* www.waterousco.com	South Saint Paul	MN	55075	651-450-5000	450-5090
Waukesha Cherry-Burrell Corp (WCB) 611 Sugar Creek Rd — *TF:* 800-252-5200 ■ *Web:* www.gowcb.com	Delavan	WI	53115	262-728-1900	728-4904
Weil Pump Co 6337 Western Rd PO Box 887 — *Web:* www.weilpump.com	Cedarburg	WI	53012	262-377-1399	377-0515
Weir Minerals 225 N Cedar St — *Web:* www.weirminerals.com	Hazleton	PA	18201	570-455-7711	459-2586
Weir Slurry North America 2701 S Stoughton Rd	Madison	WI	53716	608-221-2261	221-5807

Company / Address	City	State	ZIP	Phone	Fax
Wilden Pump & Engineering Co 22069 Van Buren St *Web:* www.wildenpump.com	Grand Terrace	CA	92313	909-422-1730	783-3440
Yeomans Chicago Corp 3905 Enterprise Ct PO Box 6620 *Web:* www.yccpump.com	Aurora	IL	60504	630-236-5500	236-5511
Zoeller Co 3649 Kane Run Rd. *TF:* 800-928-7867 ■ *Web:* www.zoeller.com	Louisville	KY	40211	502-778-2731	774-3624

645 RACING & RACETRACKS

SEE ALSO Motor Speedways p. 2259

Company / Address	City	State	ZIP	Phone	Fax
Alameda County Fair Assn (ACFA) 4501 Pleasanton Ave *Web:* www.alamedacountyfair.com	Pleasanton	CA	94566	925-426-7600	426-7599
Arlington Park 2200 W Euclid Ave PO Box 7 *Web:* www.arlingtonpark.com	Arlington Heights	IL	60006	847-385-7500	385-7251
Atlantic City Racing Course 4501 Black Horse Pike	Mays Landing	NJ	08330	609-641-2190	645-8309
Balmoral Park 26435 S Dixie Hwy *Web:* www.balmoralpark.com	Crete	IL	60417	708-672-1414	672-5932
Batavia Downs 8315 Pk Rd. *TF:* 800-724-2000 ■ *Web:* www.westernotb.com	Batavia	NY	14020	585-343-3750	343-7773
Belmont Park 2150 Hempstead Tpke. **Fax:* Cust Svc ■ *Web:* www.nyra.com/index_belmont.html	Elmont	NY	11003	516-488-6000	488-6016*
Benton County Fairgrounds 1500 S Oak St Bldg 20 *Web:* www.bcfairgrounds.com	Kennewick	WA	99337	509-586-9211	582-1894
Beulah Park Race Track 3811 SW Blvd *Web:* www.beulahpark.com	Grove City	OH	43123	614-871-9600	871-0433
Brainerd International Raceway 5523 Birchdale Rd *TF:* 866-444-4455 ■ *Web:* www.brainerdraceway.com	Brainerd	MN	56401	218-824-7220	824-7240
Buffalo Raceway 5600 McKinley Pkwy *Web:* www.buffaloraceway.com	Hamburg	NY	14075	716-649-1280	649-0033
Calder Casino & Race Course 21001 NW 27th Ave PO Box 1808 *TF:* 800-333-3227 ■ *Web:* www.calderracecourse.com	Miami	FL	33056	305-625-1311	620-2569
Canterbury Park Holding Corp 1100 Canterbury Rd *TSE:* ECP ■ *TF:* 800-340-6361 ■ *Web:* www.canterburypark.com	Shakopee	MN	55379	952-445-7223	496-6400
Cassia County Fairgrounds 1101 Elba Ave.	Burley	ID	83318	208-678-9150	678-3612
Central Wyoming Fairgrounds 1700 Fairgrounds Rd *Web:* www.centralwyomingfair.com	Casper	WY	82604	307-235-5775	266-4224
Charlotte Motor Speedway 5555 Concord Pkwy S *TF:* 800-455-3267 ■ *Web:* www.charlottemotorspeedway.com	Concord	NC	28027	704-455-3200	455-2272
Churchill Downs Inc 700 Central Ave. *NASDAQ:* CHDN ■ *TF:* 800-283-3729 ■ *Web:* www.churchilldowns.com	Louisville	KY	40208	502-636-4400	636-4560
Coconino County Fair HCR 39 PO Box 3A.	Flagstaff	AZ	86001	928-679-8000	774-2572
Colonial Downs 10515 Colonial Downs Pkwy. **Fax:* PR ■ *TF:* 888-482-8722 ■ *Web:* www.colonialdowns.com	New Kent	VA	23124	804-966-7223	966-1565*
Columbus Races 822 15th St *TF:* 800-314-2983 ■ *Web:* www.agpark.com	Columbus	NE	68601	402-564-0133	564-0990
Dairyland Greyhound Park 5522 104th Ave *TF:* 800-233-3357	Kenosha	WI	53144	262-657-8200	657-8200
Del Mar Thoroughbred Club 2260 Jimmy Durante Blvd *Web:* www.dmtc.com	Del Mar	CA	92014	858-755-1141	755-1141
Delaware North Cos Gaming & Entertainment 40 Fountain Plaza *TF:* 800-828-7240 ■ *Web:* www.delawarenorth.com	Buffalo	NY	14202	716-858-5000	858-5926
Delaware Park Racetrack & Slots Casino 777 Delaware Pk Blvd. **Fax:* Hum Res ■ *TF:* 800-417-5687 ■ *Web:* www.delawarepark.com	Wilmington	DE	19804	302-994-2521	355-1298*
Delaware Racing Assn 777 Delaware Pk Blvd. *TF Mktg:* 800-441-5687 ■ *Web:* www.delpark.com	Wilmington	DE	19804	302-994-2521	994-3392
Delta Downs Racetrack 2717 Delta Downs Dr *TF:* 800-589-7441 ■ *Web:* www.deltadowns.com	Vinton	LA	70668	337-589-7441	589-2399
Dover Downs Casino 1131 N DuPont Hwy. *TF:* 800-711-5882 ■ *Web:* www.doverdowns.com	Dover	DE	19901	302-674-4600	857-3253
Dover Downs Gaming & Entertainment Inc 1131 N DuPont Hwy *NYSE:* DDE ■ *TF:* 800-711-5882 ■ *Web:* www.doverdowns.com	Dover	DE	19901	302-674-4600	734-3124
Dover International Speedway 1131 N DuPont Hwy PO Box 843 *TF:* 800-441-7223 ■ *Web:* www.doverspeedway.com	Dover	DE	19901	302-883-6500	672-0100
Dover Motorsports Inc 1131 N Dupont Hwy *NYSE:* DVD ■ *TF:* 800-441-7223 ■ *Web:* www.dovermotorsportsinc.com	Dover	DE	19901	302-674-4600	672-0100
Dubuque Greyhound Park & Casino 1855 Greyhound Pk Dr *TF:* 800-373-3647 ■ *Web:* www.dgpc.com	Dubuque	IA	52001	563-582-3647	582-9074
DuQuoin State Fair 655 Executive Dr *Web:* www.agr.state.il.us/dq	DuQuoin	IL	62832	618-542-1515	542-1541
Elko County Fairgrounds 13th St & Fairgrounds Rd	Elko	NV	89801	775-738-7925	778-3468
Eureka Downs 210 N Jefferson PO Box 228	Eureka	KS	67045	620-583-5528	583-5381
Fair Grounds Race Course 1751 Gentilly Blvd *TF:* 800-262-7983 ■ *Web:* www.fairgroundsracecourse.com	New Orleans	LA	70119	504-944-5515	948-1160
Fair Meadows at Tulsa 4609 E 21st St PO Box 4735	Tulsa	OK	74114	918-743-7223	743-8053
Fairmount Park 9301 Collinsville Rd **Fax Area Code:* 314 ■ *Web:* www.fairmountpark.com	Collinsville	IL	62234	618-345-4300	436-1516*
Finger Lakes Gaming & Race Track 5857 Rt 96 *Web:* www.fingerlakesracetrack.com	Farmington	NY	14425	585-924-3232	924-3967
Finger Lakes Racing Assn 5857 Rt 96 *Web:* www.fingerlakesgaming.com	Farmington	NY	14425	585-924-3232	924-3967
Fonner Park 700 E Stolley Pk Rd *Web:* www.fonnerpark.com	Grand Island	NE	68801	308-382-4515	384-2753
Fort Erie Race Track 230 Catherine St PO Box 1130 *TF:* 800-295-3770 ■ *Web:* www.forterieracing.com	Fort Erie	ON	L2A5N9	905-871-3200	994-3629
Freehold Raceway 130 Pk Ave PO Box 6669 *TF:* 800-836-0462 ■ *Web:* www.freeholdraceway.com	Freehold	NJ	07728	732-462-3800	462-2920
Fresno District Fair 1121 S Chance Ave *Web:* www.fresnofair.com	Fresno	CA	93702	559-650-3247	650-3226
Gillespie County Fairgrounds 530 Fair Dr PO Box 526 *Web:* www.gillespiefair.com	Fredericksburg	TX	78624	830-997-2359	997-4923
Golden Gate Fields 1100 Eastshore Hwy *Web:* www.goldengatefields.com	Berkeley	CA	94710	510-559-7300	559-7460
Goshen Historic Track Inc 44 Pk Pl PO Box 192 *Web:* www.goshenhistorictrack.com	Goshen	NY	10924	845-294-5333	294-3998
Grays Harbor Raceway 32 Elma McCleary Rd PO Box 768 *Web:* www.graysharborraceway.net	Elma	WA	98541	360-482-4374	892-6582
Greenetrack Inc 523 County Rd 208 PO Box 471 *TF:* 800-633-5942 ■ *Web:* www.greenetrackpaysyoumoney.com	Eutaw	AL	35462	205-372-9318	372-4569
Harrington Raceway 15 W Rider Rd. *TF:* 888-887-5687 ■ *Web:* www.casino.harringtonraceway.com	Harrington	DE	19952	302-398-7223	
Hawthorne Race Course 3501 S Laramie Ave. *TF:* 800-780-0701 ■ *Web:* www.hawthorneracecourse.com	Cicero	IL	60804	708-780-3700	780-3677
Hazel Park Raceway 1650 E 10 Mile Rd *Web:* www.hazelparkraceway.com	Hazel Park	MI	48030	248-398-1000	398-5236
Hollywood Casino at Charles Town Races 750 Hollywood Dr. *TF:* 800-795-7001 ■ *Web:* www.hollywoodcasinocharlestown.com	Charles Town	WV	25414	304-725-7001	725-6979
Hollywood Casino at Penn National Race Course 777 Hollywood Blvd *Web:* www.hollywoodpnrc.com	Grantville	PA	17028	717-469-2211	469-2910
Hoosier Park Racing & Casino 4500 Dan Patch Cir *TF:* 800-526-7223 ■ *Web:* www.hoosierpark.com	Anderson	IN	46013	765-642-7223	608-2754
Humboldt County Fair 1250 5th St *Web:* www.humboldtcountyfair.org	Ferndale	CA	95536	707-786-9511	786-9450
Illinois State Fairgrounds 801 E Sangamon Ave *Web:* www.agr.state.il.us	Springfield	IL	62702	217-782-4231	524-6194
Indiana State Fairgrounds 1202 E 38th St *Web:* www.in.gov	Indianapolis	IN	46205	317-927-7500	927-7695
Indianapolis Motor Speedway Corp 4600 W 16th St. *Web:* www.indyracingleague.com	Indianapolis	IN	46222	317-481-8500	492-6759
Jefferson County Kennel Club Inc 3079 N Jefferson St *Web:* www.jckcgreyhounds.com	Monticello	FL	32344	850-997-2561	997-3871
Jerome County Fairgrounds 200 N Fir St. *Web:* www.jeromecountyfair.com	Jerome	ID	83338	208-324-7209	324-7057
Josephine County Fairgrounds 1451 Fairgrounds Rd PO Box 672 *Web:* www.co.josephine.or.us	Grants Pass	OR	97527	541-476-3215	476-1027
Lake Erie Speedway 10700 Delmas Dr *Web:* www.lakeeriespeedway.com	North East	PA	16428	814-725-3303	725-3353
Laurel Park Rt 198 & Racetrack Rd Po Box 130. **Fax Area Code:* 410 ■ *TF:* 800-638-1859 ■ *Web:* www.laurelpark.com	Laurel	MD	20724	301-725-0400	792-7775*
Lebanon Raceway 665 N Broadway PO Box 58 *Web:* www.lebanonraceway.com	Lebanon	OH	45036	513-932-4936	932-7894
Lone Star Park at Grand Prairie 1000 Lone Star Pkwy *TF:* 800-795-7223 ■ *Web:* www.lonestarpark.com	Grand Prairie	TX	75050	972-263-7223	237-5505
Los Alamitos Race Course 4961 Katella Ave *Web:* www.losalamitos.com/laqhr	Los Alamitos	CA	90720	714-820-2800	820-2820
Los Angeles Turf Club Inc 285 W Huntington Dr	Arcadia	CA	91007	626-574-7223	446-9565
Maywood Park 8600 W N Ave. *TF:* 800-748-5782 ■ *Web:* www.maywoodpark.com	Melrose Park	IL	60160	708-343-4800	343-2564
Meadowlands Racetrack 50 Rt 120 *Web:* www.meadowlandsracetrack.com	East Rutherford	NJ	07073	201-843-2446	
Meadows Racetrack 210 Racetrack Rd *Web:* www.meadowsgaming.com	Washington	PA	15301	724-225-9300	225-0298
Melbourne Greyhound Park 1100 N Wickham Rd *Web:* www.mgpark.com	Melbourne	FL	32935	321-259-9800	259-3437
Midstate Raceway Inc 14 Ruth St PO Box 860 *TF:* 877-777-8559	Vernon	NY	13476	315-829-2201	829-2931
Mile High Racing & Entertainment/Mile High 6200 Dahlia St *Web:* www.mihiracing.com	Commerce City	CO	80022	303-751-5918	283-2482
Mohave County Fair Assn 2600 Fairgrounds Blvd *Web:* www.mcfairgrounds.org	Kingman	AZ	86401	928-753-2636	753-8383
Monmouth Park Racetrack 175 Oceanport Ave *TF:* 877-354-2563 ■ *Web:* www.monmouthpark.com	Oceanport	NJ	07757	732-222-5100	571-5226
Montana State Fair 400 3rd St NW *Web:* www.montanastatefair.com	Great Falls	MT	59404	406-727-8900	452-8955
Monticello Raceway 204 Rt 17B *TF:* 866-777-4263 ■ *Web:* www.monticelloraceway.com	Monticello	NY	12701	845-794-4100	794-4110
Mountaineer Racetrack & Gaming Resort PO Box 358 *TF:* 800-804-0468 ■ *Web:* www.mtrgaming.com	Chester	WV	26034	304-387-2400	387-0084
MTR Gaming Group Inc PO Box 358 *NASDAQ:* MNTG ■ *TF:* 800-804-0468 ■ *Web:* www.mtrgaming.com	Chester	WV	26034	304-387-8000	387-8001
Naples/Fort Myers Greyhound Track 10601 Bonita Beach Rd *Web:* www.naplesfortmyersdogs.com	Bonita Springs	FL	34135	239-992-2411	947-9244
New Mexico State Fair 6613 Central Ave NE	Albuquerque	NM	87108	505-265-1791	266-7784

	City	State	Zip	Phone	Fax
New York City Off-Track Betting Corp 1501 Broadway 12th Fl. *TF:* 800-862-9118	New York	NY	10036	212-221-5200	221-8025
New York Racing Assn (NYRA) 110-00 Rockaway Blvd PO Box 90 *Web:* www.nyra.com	Jamaica	NY	11420	718-641-4700	835-5246
Northville Downs 301 CadyCenter *Web:* www.northvilledowns.com	Northville	MI	48167	248-349-1000	348-8955
Northwest Montana Fair 265 N Meridian Rd *Web:* www.flathead.mt.gov/fairgrounds/2011	Kalispell	MT	59901	406-758-5810	756-8936
Oaklawn Park 2705 Central Ave *TF:* 800-625-5296 ■ *Web:* www.oaklawn.com	Hot Springs	AR	71901	501-623-4411	624-4950
Ocean Downs 10218 Racetrack Rd PO Box 11 *Web:* www.oceandowns.com	Berlin	MD	21811	410-641-0600	641-2711
Penn National Gaming Inc 825 Berkshire Blvd Suite 200 *NASDAQ: PENN* ■ *TF:* 877-565-2112 ■ *Web:* www.hollywoodpnrc.com	Wyomissing	PA	19610	610-373-2400	376-2842
Pensacola Greyhound Track 951 Dog Track Rd *TF:* 800-345-3997 ■ *Web:* www.pensacolagreyhoundtrack.com	Pensacola	FL	32506	850-455-8595	453-8883
Philadelphia Park Racetrack 2999 St Rd PO Box 100 *TF:* 800-523-6886 ■ *Web:* www.parxracing.com	Bensalem	PA	19020	215-639-9000	639-0337
Phoenix Greyhound Park 3801 E Washington St *Web:* www.phoenixgreyhoundpark.com	Phoenix	AZ	85034	602-273-7181	273-6176
Pinnacle Entertainment Inc 8918 Spanish Ridge Ave *NYSE: PNK* ■ *TF:* 877-764-8750 ■ *Web:* www.pnkinc.com	Las Vegas	NV	89169	702-784-7777	784-7778
Pocatello Downs 10560 N Fairgrounds Rd	Pocatello	ID	83202	208-238-1721	
Portland International Raceway 1940 N Victory Blvd *Web:* www.portlandraceway.com	Portland	OR	97217	503-823-7223	823-5896
Portland Meadows Horse Track 1001 N Schmeer Rd *Web:* www.portlandmeadows.com	Portland	OR	97217	503-285-9144	286-9763
Ravalli County Fair 100 Old Corvallis Rd *Web:* www.ravallicountyfair.com	Hamilton	MT	59840	406-363-3411	375-9152
Remington Park Race Track 1 Remington Pl *TF:* 866-456-9880 ■ *Web:* www.remingtonpark.com	Oklahoma City	OK	73111	405-424-1000	425-3297
Retama Park 1 Retama Pkwy *Web:* www.retamapark.com	Selma	TX	78154	210-651-7000	651-7097
Rockingham Park 79 Rockingham Pk Blvd *Web:* www.rockinghampark.com	Salem	NH	03079	603-898-2311	898-7163
Ruidoso Downs Race Track PO Box 449 *Web:* www.ruidownsracing.com	Ruidoso Downs	NM	88346	575-378-4431	378-4631
Sam Houston Race Park 7575 N Sam Houston Pkwy W *TF:* 800-807-7223 ■ *Web:* www.shrp.com	Houston	TX	77064	281-807-8700	807-8777
San Joaquin County Fair 1658 S Airport Way *Web:* www.sanjoaquinfair.com	Stockton	CA	95206	209-466-5041	466-5739
Santa Anita Park 285 W Huntington Dr *Web:* www.santaanita.com	Arcadia	CA	91007	626-574-7223	446-9565
Santa Cruz County Fair 3142 S Hwy 83 PO Box 85	Sonoita	AZ	85637	520-455-5553	455-5330
Saratoga Gaming & Raceway 342 Jefferson St PO Box 356 *Web:* www.saratogacasino.com	Saratoga Springs	NY	12866	518-584-2110	583-1269
Saratoga Race Course 267 Union Ave *Web:* www.saratogaracetrack.com	Saratoga Springs	NY	12866	718-641-4700	
Scarborough Downs 90 Payne Rd *Web:* www.scarboroughdowns.com	Scarborough	ME	04070	207-883-4331	883-2020
Solano County Fair 900 Fairgrounds Dr *Web:* www.scfair.com	Vallejo	CA	94589	707-551-2000	642-7947
Sonoma County Fairgrounds 1350 Bennett Valley Rd *Web:* www.sonomacountyfair.com	Santa Rosa	CA	95404	707-545-4200	573-9342
Sports Creek Raceway 4290 Morrish Rd *TF:* 800-635-4582 ■ *Web:* www.sportscreek.com	Swartz Creek	MI	48473	810-635-3333	635-9711
State Fair Park 1800 State Fair Pk Dr *Web:* www.statefair.org	Lincoln	NE	68508	402-473-4110	473-4114
Sunland Park Racetrack & Casino 1200 Futurity Dr *TF:* 800-572-1142 ■ *Web:* www.sunland-park.com	Sunland Park	NM	88063	575-874-5200	589-1518
Tampa Bay Downs Inc 11225 Racetrack Rd *TF:* 800-200-4434 ■ *Web:* www.tampabaydowns.com	Tampa	FL	33626	813-855-4401	854-3539
Tampa Greyhound Track 8300 N Nebraska Ave *Web:* www.tampadogs.com	Tampa	FL	33604	813-932-4313	932-5048
Thistledown Racing Club Inc 21501 Emery Rd *Web:* www.caesars.com	Cleveland	OH	44128	216-662-8600	662-5339
Tillamook County Fairgrounds 4603 E 3rd St PO Box 455 *Web:* www.tillamookfair.com	Tillamook	OR	97141	503-842-2272	842-3314
Turf Paradise Racetrack 1501 W Bell Rd *Web:* www.turfparadise.com	Phoenix	AZ	85023	602-942-1101	942-8659
Twin River Casino 100 Twin River Rd *TF:* 877-827-4837 ■ *Web:* www.twinriver.com	Lincoln	RI	02865	401-475-8505	
Walla Walla Racetrack 363 Orchard St *Web:* www.wallawallafairgrounds.com	Walla Walla	WA	99362	509-527-3247	527-3259
Western Montana Fair 1101 S Ave W *Web:* www.westernmontanafair.com	Missoula	MT	59801	406-721-3247	728-7479
Wyoming Downs 10180 Hwy 89 N *TF:* 800-225-8238	Evanston	WY	82930	307-789-0511	789-4614
Yavapai Downs at Prescott Valley 10501 Hwy 89A *Web:* www.yavapaidownsatpv.com	Prescott Valley	AZ	86314	928-775-8000	445-0408
Yonkers Raceway 810 Yonkers Ave *Web:* www.yonkersraceway.com	Yonkers	NY	10704	914-968-4200	968-4479
Yuma County Fair 2520 E 32nd St *Web:* www.yumafair.com	Yuma	AZ	85365	928-726-4420	344-3480
MetraPark PO Box 2514 *TF:* 800-366-8538 ■ *Web:* www.metrapark.com	Billings	MT	59103	406-256-2400	256-2479

646 RADIO COMPANIES

	City	State	Zip	Phone	Fax
Allegheny Mountain Network PO Box 247	Tyrone	PA	16686	814-684-3200	684-1220
American General Media 1400 Easton Dr Suite 144-B *Web:* www.liveradio.com	Bakersfield	CA	93309	661-328-1410	328-0873
Artistic Media Partners Inc 5520 E 75th St *Web:* www.artisticradio.com	Indianapolis	IN	46250	317-594-0600	594-9567
Astral Media Radio 2 St Clair Ave W Suite 1100 *Web:* www.astral.com	Toronto	ON	M4V1L6	416-323-5200	872-8683
Backyard Broadcasting 4237 Salisbury Rd Suite 225 *Web:* www.bybradio.com	Jacksonville	FL	32216	904-674-0260	854-4596
Beasley Broadcast Group Inc 3033 Riviera Dr Suite 200 *NASDAQ: BBGI* ■ *Web:* www.bbgi.com	Naples	FL	34103	239-263-5000	263-8191
Bi-Coastal Media LLC 140 N Main St *Web:* www.bicoastalmedia.com	Lakeport	CA	95453	707-263-6113	263-0939
Bible Broadcasting Network Inc 11530 Carmel Commons Blvd PO Box 7300 *TF:* 800-888-7077 ■ *Web:* www.bbnradio.org	Charlotte	NC	28226	704-523-5555	522-1967
Birach Broadcasting Corp 21700 Northwestern Hwy Tower 14 Suite 1190 *Web:* www.birach.com	Southfield	MI	48075	248-557-3500	557-2950
Bliss Communications Inc PO Box 5001 *TF:* 800-362-6712 ■ *Web:* www.blissnet.net	Janesville	WI	53547	608-754-3311	755-8393
Bonneville International Corp 55 N 300 W *Web:* www.bonneville.com	Salt Lake City	UT	84101	801-575-7500	575-7548
Border Media Partners LLC 8750 N Central Expy Suite 645 *Web:* www.bordermedia.com	Dallas	TX	75231	214-692-2000	361-0563
Bott Radio Network 10550 Barkley St Suite 100 *TF:* 800-875-1903 ■ *Web:* www.bottradionetwork.com	Overland Park	KS	66212	913-642-7770	642-1319
Brazos Valley Radio 1240 E Villa Maria Rd *Web:* www.barzosradios.com	Bryan	TX	77802	979-776-1240	776-6074
Brewer Broadcasting Inc 1305 Carter St *Web:* www.brewerradio.com	Chattanooga	TN	37402	423-265-9494	266-2335
Bristol Broadcasting Co Inc 901 E Valley Dr PO Box 1389 *TF:* 800-253-8112 ■ *Web:* www.bristolbroadcasting.com	Bristol	VA	24203	276-669-8112	669-0541
Buckley Broadcasting Corp 166 W Putnam Ave *Web:* www.buckleyradio.com	Greenwich	CT	06830	203-661-4307	622-7341
Canadian Broadcasting Corp (CBC) PO Box 3220 *Web:* www.cbc.radio-canada.ca	Ottawa	ON	K1Y1E4	613-288-6033	
CBS Radio Inc 1515 Broadway 46th Fl *Web:* www.cbsradio.com	New York	NY	10036	212-846-3939	846-2790
Cherry Creek Radio 501 S Cherry St Suite 480 *Web:* www.cherrycreekradio.com	Denver	CO	80246	303-468-6500	468-6555
Citadel Broadcasting Corp 7690 W Cheyenne Ave Suite 220 *Web:* www.citadelbroadcasting.com	Las Vegas	NV	89129	702-804-5200	804-8250
Clear Ch Radio 200 E Basse Rd *TF:* 888-937-6131 ■ *Web:* www.clearchannel.com	San Antonio	TX	78209	210-822-2828	822-2299
Crawford Broadcasting Co (CBC) 2821 S Parker Rd Suite 1205 *Web:* www.crawfordbroadcasting.com	Denver	CO	80014	303-433-5500	433-1555
Cromwell Group Inc 1824 Murfreesboro Rd 2nd Fl *Web:* www.cromwellradio.com	Nashville	TN	37217	615-361-7560	366-4313
Cumulus Media Inc 3280 Peachtree Rd Suite 2300 *NASDAQ: CMLS* ■ *Web:* www.cumulus.com	Atlanta	GA	30305	404-949-0700	949-0740
Curtis Media Group 3012 Highwoods Blvd Suite 200 *Web:* www.curtismedia.com	Raleigh	NC	27604	919-790-9392	790-8369
Delmarva Broadcasting Co PO Box 7492 *Web:* www.radiocenter.com	Wilmington	DE	19803	302-478-2700	
Eagle Communications Inc 2703 Hall St Suite 15 PO Box 817 *Web:* www.eaglecom.net	Hays	KS	67601	785-625-4000	625-8030
Eagle Radio Inc 2300 Hall PO Box 6 *TF:* 800-569-0144	Hays	KS	67601	785-625-2578	625-3632
Educational Media Foundation 2351 Sunset Blvd **Fax Area Code: 919* ■ *TF:* 800-525-5683 ■ *Web:* www.klove.com	Rocklin	CA	95765	916-251-1600	251-1650*
Emmis Communications Corp 40 Monument Cir 1 Emmis Plaza Suite 700 *NASDAQ: EMMS* ■ *Web:* www.emmis.com	Indianapolis	IN	46204	317-266-0100	631-3750
Entercom Communications Corp 401 City Ave Suite 809 *NYSE: ETM* ■ *Web:* www.entercom.com	Bala Cynwyd	PA	19004	610-660-5610	660-5620
Entravision Communications Corp 2425 Olympic Blvd Suite 6000 W *NYSE: EVC* ■ *Web:* www.entravision.com	Santa Monica	CA	90404	310-447-3870	447-3899
Family Radio 290 Hegenberger Rd *TF:* 800-543-1495 ■ *Web:* www.familyradio.com	Oakland	CA	94621	510-568-6200	562-0749
Far East Broadcasting Co Inc 15700 Imperial Hwy *TF:* 800-523-3480 ■ *Web:* www.febc.org	La Mirada	CA	90638	562-947-4651	943-0160
Flinn Broadcasting 6080 Mt Moriah Rd Ext *Web:* www.flinn.com	Memphis	TN	38115	901-375-9324	795-4454
Forever Broadcasting 1 Forever Dr *Web:* www.foreverradio.com	Hollidaysburg	PA	16648	814-941-9800	943-2754
Galaxy Communications LP 235 Walton St *Web:* www.galaxycommunications.com	Syracuse	NY	13202	315-472-9111	472-1888

Company	City	State	Zip	Phone	Fax
Georgia-Carolina Radiocasting Cos LLC 233 Big A Rd PO Drawer E *Web:* www.gacaradio.com	Toccoa	GA	30577	706-297-7264	297-7266
GHB Broadcasting Corp 1776 Briarcliff Rd NE Suite A	Atlanta	GA	30306	404-875-1110	875-1186
Great Scott Broadcasting 224 Maugers Mill Rd **Fax Area Code:* 610	Pottstown	PA	19464	484-524-8005	326-4809*
Greater Media Inc 35 Braintree Hill Pk Suite 300 *Web:* www.greater-media.com	Braintree	MA	02184	781-348-8600	348-8695
Hall Communications Inc 404 W Lime St PO Box 2038 *Web:* www.hallradio.com	Lakeland	FL	33815	863-682-8184	
Inner City Broadcasting Corp 3 Pk Ave 41st Fl *Web:* www.wbls.com	New York	NY	10016	212-447-1000	447-5194
International Broadcasting Bureau 330 Independence Ave SW *Web:* www.bbg.gov	Washington	DC	20237	202-203-4664	203-4612
Journal Broadcast Group Inc 333 W State St *Web:* www.journalbroadcastgroup.com	Milwaukee	WI	53203	414-332-9611	967-5400
Keymarket Communications LLC 123 Blaine Rd	Brownsville	PA	15417	724-938-2000	938-7824
Liberman Broadcasting Inc 1845 W Empire Ave *Web:* www.lbimedia.com	Burbank	CA	91504	818-729-5300	729-5678
Lincoln Financial Media 100 N Greene St PO Box 21008 *NYSE: LNC* ■ **Fax Area Code:* 704 ■ *Web:* www.lincolnfinancialmedia.com	Greensboro	NC	27420	336-691-3000	691-3938*
Lotus Communications Corp 3301 Barham Blvd Suite 200 *Web:* www.lotuscorp.com	Los Angeles	CA	90068	323-512-2225	512-2224
MacDonald Broadcasting Co 2000 Whittier St *Web:* www.98fmtcq.com	Saginaw	MI	48601	989-752-8161	752-8102
Magic Broadcasting LLC 7106 Laird St Suite 102 *Web:* www.magicbroadcasting.net	Panama City Beach	FL	32408	850-230-5855	230-6988
Mahaffey Enterprises Inc PO Box 4584 *TF:* 800-725-9180	Springfield	MO	65808	417-883-9180	883-9096
Main Line 25 Penncraft Ave # 4	Chambersburg	PA	17201	717-263-0813	263-9649
Mapleton Communications 60 Garden Ct Suite 300	Monterey	CA	93940	831-658-5200	658-5299
Maritime Broadcasting System (MBS) 5121 Sackville St 7th Fl *Web:* www.mbsradio.com	Halifax	NS	B3J1K1	902-425-1225	423-2093
Mel Wheeler Inc 5009 S Hulen St Suite 101	Fort Worth	TX	76132	817-294-7644	294-8519
Mid-America Radio Group Inc PO Box 1970	Martinsville	IN	46151	765-349-1485	342-3569
Midwest Communications Inc 904 Grand Ave **Fax:* Hum Res ■ *TF:* 877-903-2171 ■ *Web:* www.mwcradio.com	Wausau	WI	54403	715-842-1437	842-7061*
Midwest Family Broadcasting 319 E Battlefield Suite B *Web:* www.mwfmarketing.fm	Springfield	MO	65807	417-886-5677	886-2155
Millenium Radio Group 109 Walters Ave *Web:* www.mj1015.com	Trenton	NJ	08638	609-771-8181	406-7956
Miller Communications Inc 51 Commerce St *Web:* www.miller.fm	Sumter	SC	29151	803-775-2321	773-4856
Mortenson Broadcasting Co 3270 Blazer Pkwy Suite 100 *TF Acctg:* 866-406-6333 ■ *Web:* www.mortensonradio.com	Lexington	KY	40509	859-245-1000	245-1600
Mount Rushmore Broadcasting Inc 218 N Wolcott St *Web:* www.mrbradio.com	Casper	WY	82601	307-265-1984	266-3295
Multicultural Broadcasting Inc 449 Broadway *Web:* www.mrbi.net	New York	NY	10013	212-966-1059	966-9580
Nassau Broadcasting Partners LP 619 Alexander Rd 3rd Fl *Web:* www.nassaubroadcasting.com	Princeton	NJ	08540	609-419-0300	419-0143
New Northwest Broadcasters LLC 315 5th Ave S Suite 700 *Web:* www.nnbradio.com	Seattle	WA	98104	206-204-0213	204-0214
Newcap Radio (NCC) 745 Windmill Rd *Web:* www.ncc.ca	Dartmouth	NS	B3B1C2	902-468-7557	468-7558
Newfoundland Capital Corp Ltd 745 Windmill Rd *Web:* www.ncc.ca	Dartmouth	NS	B3B1C2	902-468-7557	468-7558
Newspaper Radio Corp 1201 18th St Suite 200 *Web:* www.nrcbroadcasting.com	Denver	CO	80202	303-675-4695	296-7030
NextMedia Group Inc 6312 S Fiddlers Green Cir Suite 205 *Web:* www.nextmediagroup.net	Greenwood Village	CO	80111	303-694-9118	694-4940
Northeast Broadcasting Corp 288 S River Rd	Bedford	NH	03110	603-668-6400	668-6470
Northern Star Broadcasting LLC 3250 Racquet Club Dr *TF:* 888-847-2346 ■ *Web:* www.nsbroadcasting.com	Traverse City	MI	49684	231-922-4981	922-3633
NRG Media 2875 Mt Vernon Rd SE *Web:* www.nrgmedia.com	Cedar Rapids	IA	52403	319-862-0300	286-9383
Pamal Broadcasting Ltd PO Box 310 **Fax:* Sales ■ *Web:* www.pamal.com	Beacon	NY	12508	845-831-6000	838-2109*
Perry Publishing & Broadcasting 1701 W Pine Ave *Web:* www.perrybroadcasting.net	Duncan	OK	73534	580-255-1350	470-9993
Quantum Communications Corp 1266 E Main St 6th Fl	Stamfort	CT	06902	203-388-0048	388-0054
Quarnstrom Media Group LLC 1104 Cloquet Ave *TF:* 888-404-9555	Cloquet	MN	55720	218-879-4534	879-1962
Radio One Inc 5900 Princess Garden Pkwy Suite 800 *NASDAQ: ROIA* ■ *Web:* www.radio-one.com	Lanham	MD	20706	301-306-1111	306-9609
Radio Training Network Inc PO Box 7217	Lakeland	FL	33807	863-644-3464	646-5326
Renda Broadcasting Corp 900 Parish St 4th Fl *Web:* www.rendabroadcasting.com	Pittsburgh	PA	15220	412-875-1800	875-1801
Results Radio LLC 1355 N Dutton Ave Suite 225	Santa Rosa	CA	95401	707-546-9185	546-9188
Route 81 Radio LLC 780 E Market St Suite 265	West Chester	PA	19382	610-696-8181	696-5072
Saga Communications Inc 73 Kercheval Ave *NYSE: SGA* ■ *TF:* 888-886-7070 ■ *Web:* www.sagacommunications.com	Grosse Pointe Farms	MI	48236	313-886-7070	886-7150
Salem Communications Corp 4880 Santa Rosa Rd *NASDAQ: SALM* ■ *Web:* www.salem.cc	Camarillo	CA	93012	805-987-0400	384-4511
Shamrock Communications Inc 149 Penn Ave *TF:* 800-228-4637 ■ *Web:* www.thetimes-tribune.com	Scranton	PA	18503	570-348-9100	348-9109
Simmons Media Group Inc 515 S 700 E *Web:* www.simmonsmedia.com	Salt Lake City	UT	84102	801-524-2600	521-9234
South Central Communications Corp PO Box 3848 *Web:* www.southcentralcommunications.net	Evansville	IN	47736	812-463-7950	463-7915
Spanish Broadcasting System Inc (SBS) 2601 S Bayshore Dr PH 2 *NASDAQ: SBSA* ■ *Web:* www.spanishbroadcasting.com	Coconut Grove	FL	33133	305-441-6901	446-5148
Tejas Broadcasting LLP 1300 Antelope St	Corpus Christi	TX	78401	361-883-1600	883-9303
Telesouth Communications Inc 6311 Ridgewood Rd *Web:* www.telesouth.com	Jackson	MS	39211	601-957-1700	956-5228
Three Eagles Communications Co 3800 Cornhusker Hwy *Web:* www.threeeagles.com	Lincoln	NE	68504	402-466-1234	467-4095
Townsquare Media Inc 240 Greenwich Ave *Web:* www.townsquaremedia.com	Greenwich	CT	06830	203-861-0900	
Triad Broadcasting Co LLC 2511 Garden Rd Bldg A Suite 104 *TF:* 888-333-6350 ■ *Web:* www.triadbroadcasting.com	Monterey	CA	93940	831-655-6350	655-6355
Univision Communications Inc 3102 Oak Lawn Ave Suite 215 *Web:* www.univision.net	Dallas	TX	75219	214-525-7700	525-7750
VerStandig Broadcasting 10960 John Wayne Dr PO Box 788 *Web:* www.verstandig.com	Greencastle	PA	17225	717-597-9200	597-9210
Waitt Corp LLC 1125 S 103rd St Suite 200 *TF:* 888-656-0634 ■ *Web:* www.waittcorp.com	Omaha	NE	68124	402-697-8011	697-8024
Walt Disney Co 500 S Buena Vista St *NYSE: DIS* ■ **Fax:* Mail Rm ■ *Web:* www.corporate.disney.go.com	Burbank	CA	91510	818-560-1000	553-7210*
West Virginia Radio Corp 1251 Earl L Core Rd	Morgantown	WV	26505	304-296-0029	296-3876
Willis Broadcasting 645 Church St Suite 400	Norfolk	VA	23510	757-622-4600	624-6515
Withers Broadcasting Co PO Box 1508 *TF:* 800-333-1577 ■ *Web:* www.mywithersradio.com/wmix	Mount Vernon	IL	62864	618-242-3500	242-2490
WTNI-AM 1640 (N/T) 2511 Garden Rd Suite 104A *Web:* www.triadbroadcasting.com	Monterey	CA	93940	831-655-6350	655-6355
Zimmer Radio Group 3215 Lemone Industrial Blvd Suite 200 *TF:* 800-455-1099 ■ *Web:* zimmerinteractive.com	Columbia	MO	65201	573-875-1099	875-2439

647 RADIO NETWORKS

Company	City	State	Zip	Phone	Fax
American Family Radio PO Drawer 2440 *TF:* 800-326-4543 ■ *Web:* www.afa.net	Tupelo	MS	38803	662-844-8888	842-6791
American Public Media 480 Cedar St *TF:* 877-276-8400 ■ *Web:* www.americanpublicmedia.publicradio.org	Saint Paul	MN	55101	651-290-1500	290-1415
AP Broadcast Services 1100 13th St NW Suite 700 *TF:* 800-821-4747 ■ *Web:* www.apbroadcast.com	Washington	DC	20005	202-641-9000	370-2712
BGC Partners Inc 499 Pk Ave *Web:* www.bgcpartners.com	New York	NY	10022	646-346-7000	346-6919
Black Radio Network 166 Madison Ave 4th Fl *Web:* www.blackradionetwork.com	New York	NY	10016	212-686-6850	686-7308
Bott Radio Network 10550 Barkley St Suite 100 *TF:* 800-875-1903 ■ *Web:* www.bottradionetwork.com	Overland Park	KS	66212	913-642-7770	642-1319
CBC Radio Canada 181 Queen St PO Box 3220 *Web:* www.cbc.ca	Ottawa	ON	K1P1K9	613-288-6000	
CBC Radio Two 181 Queen St PO Box 3220 Stn C **Fax:* Mktg ■ *Web:* www.cbc.ca/radio2	Ottawa	ON	K1P1K9	613-288-6000	724-5112*
CBS Corp 51 W 52nd St *NYSE: CBS* ■ *Web:* www.cbscorporation.com	New York	NY	10019	212-975-4321	975-4516
CBS Radio Network 524 W 57th St *Web:* www.cbsnews.com	New York	NY	10019	212-975-3615	975-6347
CNN en Espanol Radio 1 CNN Ctr *TF:* 800-331-7726 ■ *Web:* www.edition.cnn.com/espanol	Atlanta	GA	30303	404-827-1880	827-3294
CNN Radio Network 1 CNN Ctr *Web:* www.cnnradio.com	Atlanta	GA	30303	404-827-2750	827-1758
Crystal Media Networks 7201 Wisconsin Ave Suite 780	Bethesda	MD	20814	240-223-0846	
CSN International PO Box 391 *TF:* 800-357-4226 ■ *Web:* www.csnradio.com	Twin Falls	ID	83303	208-734-6633	736-1958
Dial Global Inc 1000 N 90th St Suite 105 *Web:* www.wrnonline.com	Omaha	NE	68114	402-952-7600	501-7060
ESPN Radio Network 545 Middle St *Web:* www.espn.go.com/espnradio	Bristol	CT	06010	860-766-2000	766-2213
Family Life Communications Inc PO Box 35300 *TF:* 800-776-1070 ■ *Web:* www.myflr.org	Tucson	AZ	85740	520-742-6976	742-6979
Far East Broadcasting Co Inc 15700 Imperial Hwy *TF:* 800-523-3480 ■ *Web:* www.febc.org	La Mirada	CA	90638	562-947-4651	943-0160
Fox News Radio Network 1211 Avenue of the Americas 18th Fl *TF:* 888-788-9913 ■ *Web:* www.foxnews.com/access/radio.html	New York	NY	10036	212-301-5439	301-5172

Name / Address	City	State	ZIP	Phone	Fax
Fox Sports Radio Network 15260 Ventura Blvd Suite 500 *TF:* 800-533-8686 ■ *Web:* www.foxsportsradio.com	Sherman Oaks	CA	91403	818-461-8289	461-8219
Hispanic Communications Network 1126 16th St NW Suite 350 *Web:* www.hcnmedia.com	Washington	DC	20036	202-637-8800	637-8801
Jones International Ltd 9697 E Mineral Ave *TF:* 800-525-7002 ■ *Web:* www.jones.com	Centennial	CO	80112	800-525-7002	
La Radio de Radio-Canada PO Box 3220 *Web:* www.radio-canada.ca	Ottawa	ON	K1Y1E4	613-288-6000	288-6770
Learfield Communications Inc 505 Hobbs Rd *Web:* www.learfield.com	Jefferson City	MO	65109	573-893-7200	893-2321
Marathon Media 980 N Michigan Ave Suite 1880	Chicago	IL	60611	312-204-9900	587-9466
Moody Broadcasting Network 820 N La Salle Blvd *Web:* www.mbn.org	Chicago	IL	60610	312-329-4460	329-4468
Motor Racing Network (MRN) 555 MRN Dr *Web:* www.origin.motorracingnetwork.com	Concord	NC	28027	704-262-6700	262-6811
Pacifica Radio Foundation 1925 ML King Jr Way *TF:* 800-436-7360 ■ *Web:* www.pacifica.org	Berkeley	CA	94704	510-849-2590	849-2617
Public Radio International (PRI) 401 2nd Ave N Suite 500 *Web:* www.pri.org	Minneapolis	MN	55401	612-338-5000	330-9222
Radio America 1100 N Glebe Rd Suite 900 **Fax Area Code:* 571 ■ *TF:* 800-807-4703 ■ *Web:* www.radioamerica.org	Arlington	VA	22201	703-302-1000	480-4141*
Radio Disney 500 S Buena Vista St *Web:* www.radio.disney.go.com	Burbank	CA	91521	818-973-4680	973-4155
Radio Free Asia 2025 M St NW Suite 300 *Web:* www.rfa.org	Washington	DC	20036	202-530-4900	530-7794
Radio Free Europe/Radio Liberty (RFE/RL) 1201 Connecticut Ave NW 4th Fl *Web:* www.rferl.org	Washington	DC	20036	202-457-6900	457-6992
Relevant Radio 1496 Bellevue St Suite 202 PO Box 10707 *TF:* 877-291-0123 ■ *Web:* www.relevantradio.com	Green Bay	WI	54311	920-884-1460	884-3170
Salem Communications Corp 4880 Santa Rosa Rd *NASDAQ: SALM* ■ *Web:* www.salem.cc	Camarillo	CA	93012	805-987-0400	384-4511
Salem Radio Network 6400 N Beltline Rd Suite 210 *Web:* www.srnonline.com	Irving	TX	75063	972-831-1920	831-8626
Sirius XM Radio Inc 1221 Avenue of the Americas *NASDAQ: SIRI* ■ *TF:* 888-539-7474 ■ *Web:* www.siriusradio.com	New York	NY	10020	212-584-5100	584-5200
Skylight Satellite Network 3003 Snelling Ave N *Web:* www.skylightcorp.us	Saint Paul	MN	55113	651-631-5000	631-5086
Sporting News Radio Network (SNR) *Mission Media Group* 6900 E Camelback Rd Suite 610 **Fax Area Code:* 480 ■ *Web:* www.sportingnewsradio.com	Scottsdale	AZ	85251	602-635-4177	945-0177*
Sports Byline USA 300 Broadway Suite 8 *TF:* 800-878-7529 ■ *Web:* www.sportsbyline1.com	San Francisco	CA	94133	415-434-8300	391-2569
SRN Broadcasting 307 E Washington PO Box 414 *Web:* www.internetfm.com	Lake Bluff	IL	60044	847-735-1995	735-1998
Tiger Financial News Network 601 Cleveland St Suite 618 *TF:* 877-518-9190 ■ *Web:* www.tfnn.com	Clearwater	FL	33755	727-518-9190	443-0869
Tribune Radio Network 435 N Michigan Ave *TF:* 800-654-8597 ■ *Web:* www.tribuneradio.com	Chicago	IL	60611	312-222-4700	222-4180
Trident Communications 31 Timber Ln *Web:* www.psaradio.com	Hilton Head Island	SC	29926	843-837-4978	
Triton Media Group LLC 15303 Ventura Blvd Suite 1500 *Web:* www.tritonmedianetworks.com	Sherman Oaks	CA	91403	818-528-8860	990-0930
United Stations Radio Network 1065 Avenue of the Americas 3rd Fl *Web:* www.unitedstations.com	New York	NY	10018	212-869-1111	869-1115
Voice of America Radio Network 330 Independence Ave SW Rm 1086 *Web:* www.voanews.com	Washington	DC	20237	202-203-4000	260-2579
Westwood One Inc 1166 Avenue of the Americas 10th Fl *NASDAQ: WWON* ■ *Web:* www.westwoodone.com	New York	NY	10036	212-641-2000	
WOR Radio Network 111 Broadway 3rd Fl *Web:* www.wor710.com	New York	NY	10006	212-642-4500	642-4486
Yesterday USA Radio Networks The 2001 Plymouth Rock Dr *Web:* www.yesterdayusa.com	Richardson	TX	75081	972-889-9872	889-2329

648 RADIO STATIONS

SEE ALSO Internet Broadcasting p. 2126

AAA	Adult Album Alternative	**NAC**	New Adult Contemporary
AC	Adult Contemporary	**Nost**	Nostalgia
Alt	Alternative	**NPR**	National Public Radio
CBC	Canadian Broadcasting Corp	**Oldies**	Oldies/80s
CHR	Contemporary Hit Radio	**Rel**	Religious
Clas	Classical	**Rock**	Rock
CR	Classic Rock	**Span**	Spanish
Ctry	Country	**Sports**	Sports
Ethnic	Multilingual	**Urban**	Urban
N/T	News/Talk	**Var**	Variety

Station / Address	City	State	ZIP	Phone	Fax
100.7 WLEV 2158 Ave C Suite 100 *Web:* www.wlevradio.com	Bethlehem	PA	18017	610-266-7600	231-0400
94.9 the Surf FM 429 Pine Ave *Web:* www.949thesurf.com	North Myrtle Beach	SC	29582	843-445-9491	445-9490
CBV-FM 106.3 (CBC) PO Box 18800 *Web:* www.cbc.radio-canada.ca	Québec City	QC	G1K9L4	418-654-1341	691-3610
CIDR-FM 93.9 (AC) 1640 Ouellette Ave *Web:* www.939theriverradio.com	Windsor	ON	N8X1L1	519-258-8888	258-0182
CIMX-FM 88.7 (Alt) 1640 Ouellette Ave *Web:* www.89xradio.com	Windsor	ON	N8X1L1	519-258-8888	258-0182
CING-FM 95.3 (Ctry) 875 Main St W Suite 900 *Web:* www.country953.com	Hamilton	ON	L8S4R1	905-521-9900	540-2452
CJXY-FM 107.9 (Rock) 875 Main St W Suite 900 *Web:* www.y108.ca	Hamilton	ON	L8S4R1	905-521-9900	540-2452
CKLW-AM 800 (N/T) 1640 Ouellette Ave *TF:* 866-554-5858 ■ *Web:* www.am800cklw.com	Windsor	ON	N8X1L1	519-258-8888	258-0182
CKWW-AM 580 (Nost) 1640 Ouellette Ave *Web:* www.am580radio.com	Windsor	ON	N8X1L1	519-258-8888	258-0182
KAAK-FM 98.9 (AC) 501 S Cherry St Suite 480 *Web:* www.cherrycreekradio.com	Denver	CO	80246	406-761-7600	761-5511
KAAM-AM 770 (Nost) 3201 Royalty Row *Web:* www.kaamradio.com	Irving	TX	75062	972-445-1700	438-6574
KABX-FM 97.5 (Oldies) 1020 W Main St *TF:* 800-350-3777 ■ *Web:* www.975kabx.com	Merced	CA	95340	209-723-2192	383-2950
KACL-FM 98.7 (Oldies) 4303 Memorial Hwy *TF:* 888-663-9870 ■ *Web:* www.cool987fm.com	Mandan	ND	58554	701-663-9898	663-8790
KADI-FM 99.5 (Rel) 5431 W Sunshine St *Web:* www.kadi.com	Brookline Station	MO	65619	417-831-0995	831-4026
KAJN-FM 102.9 (Rel) 110 W 3rd St *TF:* 800-364-7238 ■ *Web:* www.kajn.com	Crowley	LA	70526	337-783-1560	783-1674
KANE-AM 1240 (Cajun) 145 W Main St *Web:* www.kane1240.com	New Iberia	LA	70560	337-365-3434	365-9117
KANU-FM 91.5 (NPR) 1120 W 11th St Kansas Public Radio *TF:* 888-577-5268 ■ *Web:* www.kansaspublicradio.org	Lawrence	KS	66044	785-864-4530	864-5278
KAUS-FM 99.9 (Ctry) 18431 State Hwy 105	Austin	MN	55912	507-437-7666	437-7669
KAZU-FM 90.3 (NPR) 100 Campus Ctr Rm 317 PO Box 201 *TF:* 800-903-6624 ■ *Web:* www.kazu.org	Seaside	CA	93955	831-582-5298	582-5299
KBAQ-FM 89.5 (Clas) 2323 W 14th St *Web:* www.kbaq.org	Tempe	AZ	85281	480-833-1122	774-8475
KBBM-FM 100.1 (Alt) 503 Old Hwy 63 N *Web:* www.buzz.fm	Columbia	MO	65201	573-449-4141	449-7770
KBBY-FM 95.1 (AC) 1376 Walter St *Web:* www.b951.com	Ventura	CA	93003	805-642-8595	656-5838
KBCN-FM 104.3 (Ctry) 100 Bluebird St *TF:* 866-662-1043 ■ *Web:* www.kbcnradio.com	Harrison	AR	72601	870-743-1157	743-1168
KBCO-FM 97.3 (AAA) 2500 Pearl St Suite 315 *Web:* www.kbco.com	Boulder	CO	80302	303-444-5600	449-3057
KBHE-FM 89.3 (NPR) 555 N Dakota St PO Box 5000 *TF:* 800-456-0766 ■ *Web:* www.sdpb.org	Vermillion	SD	57069	605-677-5861	677-5010
KBIA-FM 91.3 (NPR) 409 Jesse Hall *TF:* 800-292-9136 ■ *Web:* www.kbia.org	Columbia	MO	65211	573-882-3431	882-2636
KBIG-FM 104.3 (AC) 3400 W Olive Ave Suite 550 *TF:* 866-544-6036 ■ *Web:* www.kbig104.com	Burbank	CA	91505	818-559-2252	955-8151
KBLV-FM 99.7 (CR) 7000 Squibb Rd	Mission	KS	66202	913-744-3600	944-3700
KBOK-AM 1310 (Ctry) 302 S Main	Malvern	AR	72104	501-332-6981	332-6984
KBON-FM 101.1 (Cajun) 109 S 2nd St *Web:* www.kbon.com	Eunice	LA	70535	337-546-0007	546-0097
KBRG-FM 100.3 (Span AC) 750 Battery St Suite 200 *TF:* 888-808-1003 ■ *Web:* recuerdo1003.univision.com	San Francisco	CA	94111	415-989-5765	733-5766
KBUE-FM 105.5 (Span) 1845 Empire Ave *Web:* www.aquisuena.com	Burbank	CA	91504	818-729-5300	729-5678
KBYZ-FM 96.5 (CR) 4303 Memorial Hwy *TF:* 888-663-9650 ■ *Web:* www.965thefox.com	Mandan	ND	58554	701-663-9600	663-8790
KCAQ-FM 104.7 (CHR) 2284 S Victoria Ave Suite 2G *Web:* www.q1047.com	Ventura	CA	93003	805-289-1400	644-7906
KCBI-FM 90.9 (Rel) 411 Ryan Plaza Dr *Web:* www.kcbi.org	Arlington	TX	76011	817-792-3800	277-9929
KCCV-AM 760 (Rel) 10550 Barkley St Suite 112 *Web:* www.bottradionetwork.com	Overland Park	KS	66212	913-642-7600	642-2424
KCFR-FM 90.1 (NPR) 7409 S Alton Ct *TF:* 800-722-4449 ■ *Web:* www.cpr.org	Centennial	CO	80112	303-871-9191	733-3319
KCFX-FM 101.1 (CR) 5800 Foxridge Dr 6th Fl *Web:* www.101thefox.net	Mission	KS	66202	913-514-3000	262-3946
KCHZ-FM 95.7 (CHR) 5800 Foxridge Dr Suite 600 *Web:* www.z957.net	Mission	KS	66202	913-514-3000	262-3946
KCJK-FM 105.1 (AC) 5800 Foxridge Dr 6th Fl *Web:* www.1051jackfm.com	Mission	KS	66202	913-514-3000	514-3009
KCLR-FM 99.3 (Ctry) 3215 Lemone Industrial Blvd Suite 200 *TF:* 800-455-5257 ■ *Web:* www.clear99.com	Columbia	MO	65201	573-875-1099	875-2439
KCLU-FM 88.3 (NPR) 60 W Olsen Rd Suite 4400 *Web:* www.kclu.org	Thousand Oaks	CA	91360	805-493-3900	
KCMO-AM 710 (N/T) 5800 Foxridge Dr 6th Fl *Web:* www.710kcmo.com	Mission	KS	66202	913-514-3000	262-3946
KCMO-FM 94.9 (Oldies) 5800 Foxridge Dr 6th Fl *Web:* www.949kcmo.com	Mission	KS	66202	913-514-3000	262-3946
KCMQ-FM 96.7 (CR) 3215 Lemone Industrial Blvd Suite 200 *TF:* 800-455-1967 ■ *Web:* www.kcmq.com	Columbia	MO	65201	573-875-1099	875-2439
KCOL-AM 600 (N/T) 4270 Byrd Dr *TF:* 866-888-5449 ■ *Web:* www.kcol.com	Loveland	CO	80538	970-461-2560	461-0118
KCRW-FM 89.9 (NPR) 1900 Pico Blvd *TF:* 888-600-5279 ■ *Web:* www.kcrw.com	Santa Monica	CA	90405	310-450-5183	450-7172
KCSD-FM 90.9 (NPR) 555 N Dakota St PO Box 5000 *TF:* 800-456-0766 ■ *Web:* www.sdpb.org	Vermillion	SD	57069	605-677-5861	677-5010
KCSM-FM 91.1 (Jazz) 1700 W Hillsdale Blvd *Web:* www.kcsm.org	San Mateo	CA	94402	650-574-6586	524-6975
KCSP-AM 610 (Sports) 7000 Squibb Rd *Web:* www.61sports.com	Mission	KS	66202	913-744-3600	744-3700
KCVI-FM 101.5 (Rock) 400 W Sunnyside *Web:* www.kbear.fm	Idaho Falls	ID	84401	208-523-3722	
KCXL-AM 1140 (N/T) 310 S La Frenz Rd *Web:* www.kcxl.com	Liberty	MO	64068	816-792-1140	792-8258
KDB-FM 93.7 (Clas) 414 E Cota St	Santa Barbara	CA	93101	805-966-4131	966-4788

Station / Address	City	State	Zip	Phone	Fax
Web: www.kdb.com					
KDKB-FM 93.3 (Rock) 1167 W Javelina Ave	Mesa	AZ	85210	480-897-9300	897-1964*
**Fax:* Sales ■ *Web:* www.kdkb.com					
KDON-FM 102.5 (CHR) 903 N Main St	Salinas	CA	93906	831-755-8181	755-8193
TF: 888-558-5366 ■ *Web:* www.kdon.com					
KEIN-AM 1310 (Nost) 3313 15th St N	Black Eagle	MT	59414	406-761-1310	454-3775
KESQ-AM 1400 (N/T) 42-650 Melanie Pl	Palm Desert	CA	92211	760-568-6830	568-3984
KEYY-AM 1450 (Rel) 307 S 1600 W	Provo	UT	84601	801-374-5210	374-2910
Web: www.keyy.com					
KEZA-FM 107.9 (AC)					
2049 E Joyce Blvd Suite 101	Fayetteville	AR	72703	479-582-1079	587-8255
Web: www.magic1079.com					
KEZN-FM 103.1 (AC) 72-915 Parkview Dr	Palm Desert	CA	92260	760-340-9383	340-5756
Web: www.ez103.com					
KFAX-AM 1100 (Rel) 39138 Fremont Blvd	Fremont	CA	94538	510-713-1100	505-1448
Web: www.kfax.com					
KFI-AM 640 (N/T) 3400 W Olive Ave Suite 550	Burbank	CA	91505	818-559-2252	729-2514
Web: www.kfi640.com					
KFJM-FM 90.7 (AAA) PO Box 8117	Grand Forks	ND	58202	701-777-4595	777-2810
TF: 800-359-4145 ■ *Web:* www.prairiepublic.org/kfjm					
KFMW-FM 107.9 (Rock) 514 Jefferson St	Waterloo	IA	50701	319-234-2200	233-4946*
**Fax:* News Rm ■ *Web:* www.rock108.com					
KFRG-FM 95.1 (Ctry)					
900 E Washington St Suite 315	Colton	CA	92324	909-825-9525	825-0441
TF: 888-431-3764 ■ *Web:* www.kfrog.com					
KFRU-AM 1400 (N/T) 503 Old Hwy 63 N	Columbia	MO	65201	573-449-4141	449-7770
Web: www.kfru.com					
KFSH-FM 95.9 (Rel)					
701 N Brand Blvd Suite 550	Glendale	CA	91203	818-956-5552	551-1110
TF: 866-347-4959 ■ *Web:* www.thefish959.com					
KFTZ-FM 103.3 (CHR) 400 W Sunnyside Rd	Idaho Falls	ID	83402	208-523-3722	525-2575
Web: www.z103.fm					
KFUO-FM 99.1 (Clas) 85 Founders Ln	Clayton	MO	63105	314-725-0099	725-3801
TF: 800-844-0524 ■ *Web:* www.classic99.com					
KGGO-FM 94.9 (CR) 4143 109th St	Urbandale	IA	50322	515-331-9200	331-9292
Web: www.kggo.com					
KGNU-FM 88.5 (Var) 4700 Walnut St	Boulder	CO	80301	303-449-4885	339-6340
TF: 800-737-3030 ■ *Web:* www.kgnu.org					
KGOU-FM 106.3 (NPR) 860 Van Vleet Oval Rm 300	Norman	OK	73019	405-325-3388	325-7129
Web: www.kgou.org					
KGPR-FM 89.9 (NPR) 2100 16th Ave S	Great Falls	MT	59403	406-268-3739	268-3736
Web: www.mtpr.net					
KGRT-FM 103.9 (Ctry)					
1355 California St PO Box 968	Las Cruces	NM	88004	575-525-9298	525-9419
Web: www.kgrt.com					
KGY-AM 1240 (AC) 1700 Marine Dr NE	Olympia	WA	98501	360-943-1240	352-1222
TF: 800-310-7625 ■ *Web:* www.kgyradio.com					
KGY-FM 96.9 (Ctry) 1700 Marine Dr NE	Olympia	WA	98501	360-943-1240	352-1222
TF: 800-962-5590 ■ *Web:* www.kgyradio.com					
KHAY-FM 100.7 (Ctry) 1376 Walter St	Ventura	CA	93003	805-642-8595	656-5838
Web: www.khay.com					
KHCC-FM 90.1 (NPR)					
815 N Walnut St Suite 300	Hutchinson	KS	67501	620-662-6646	
TF: 800-723-4657 ■ *Web:* www.radiokansas.org					
KHHT-FM 92.3 (Urban)					
3400 W Olive Blvd Suite 550	Burbank	CA	91505	818-559-2252	955-8178
Web: www.hot923.com					
KHJL-FM 92.7 (AC) 99 Long Ct Suite 200	Thousand Oaks	CA	91360	805-497-8511	497-8514
Web: www.927jillfm.com					
KHKI-FM 97.3 (Ctry) 4143 109th St	Urbandale	IA	50322	515-331-9200	331-9292
Web: www.973thehawk.com					
KHOZ-FM 102.9 (Ctry) 1111 Radio Ave	Harrison	AR	72601	870-741-2301	741-3299
TF: 800-553-6103 ■ *Web:* www.khoz.com					
KHQT-FM 103.1 (CHR)					
1355 California St PO Box 968	Las Cruces	NM	88004	575-525-9298	525-9419
Web: www.hot103.fm					
KIIS-FM 102.7 (CHR)					
3400 W Olive Ave Suite 550	Burbank	CA	91505	818-559-2252	729-2502
Web: www.kiisfm.com					
KIIX-AM 1410 (Sports) 4270 Byrd Dr	Loveland	CO	80538	970-461-2560	461-0118
Web: www.1410kiix.com					
KIXI-AM 880 (Nost)					
3650 131st Ave SE Suite 550	Bellevue	WA	98006	425-562-8964	653-1088
TF: 866-880-5494 ■ *Web:* www.kixi.com					
KIYX-FM 106.1 (AC) 51 Means Dr	Platteville	WI	53818	608-349-2000	349-2002
TF: 800-362-2224					
KJJY-FM 92.5 (Ctry) 4143 109th St	Urbandale	IA	50322	515-331-9200	331-9292
Web: www.kjjy.com					
KJLH-FM 102.3 (Urban) 161 N La Brea Ave	Inglewood	CA	90301	310-330-5550	330-5555
Web: www.kjlhradio.com					
KJZZ-FM 91.5 (NPR) 2323 W 14th St	Tempe	AZ	85281	480-834-5627	774-8475
Web: www.kjzz.org					
KKFN-FM 104.3 (Sports)					
7800 E Orchard Rd Suite 400	Greenwood Village	CO	80111	303-321-0950	321-3383
Web: www.fan950.com					
KKIM-FM 1000 (N/T) 4125 Carlisle Blvd NE	Albuquerque	NM	87107	505-878-0980	878-0098
Web: www.mykkim.com					
KKJZ-FM 88.1 (Jazz)					
1288 N Bellflower Blvd	Long Beach	CA	90815	562-985-2999	985-2982
TF: 800-767-3688 ■ *Web:* www.jazzandblues.org					
KKRQ-FM 100.7 (CR) 1 Stephen Atkins Dr	Iowa City	IA	52240	319-354-9500	354-9504
Web: www.thefox.net					
KKZZ-AM 1400 (N/T)					
2284 S Victoria Ave Suite 2G	Ventura	CA	93003	805-289-1400	644-7906
KLAC-AM 570 (Sports)					
3400 W Olive Ave Suite 550	Burbank	CA	91505	818-559-2252	260-9961
Web: www.570klac.com					
KLBB-AM 1220 (Nost) 104 N Main St	Stillwater	MN	55082	651-439-5006	439-5015
Web: www.klbbradio.com					
KLCE-FM 97.3 (AC) 400 W Sunnyside Rd	Idaho Falls	ID	83402	208-523-3722	525-2575
Web: www.klce.com					
KLHT-AM 1040 (Rel) 98 - 1016 Komo Mai Dr	Aiea	HI	96701	808-524-1040	487-1040
Web: www.klight.org					
KLOB-FM 94.7 (Span) 41601 Corporate Way	Palm Desert	CA	92260	760-341-5837	341-0951
TF: 800-420-2757 ■ *Web:* www.radiosuperestrella.com					
KLOZ-FM 92.7 (AC) 160 Hwy 42	Kaiser	MO	65047	573-348-1958	348-1923
TF: 800-613-9993 ■ *Web:* www.mix927.com					
KLTY-FM 94.9 (Rel)					
6400 N Beltline Rd Suite 120	Irving	TX	75063	972-870-9949	490-8361
Web: www.klty.com					
KLVE-FM 107.5 (Span AC)					
655 N Central Ave Suite 2500	Glendale	CA	91203	818-500-4500	500-4540
KMBR-FM 95.5 (Rock) 750 Dewey Blvd Suite 1	Butte	MT	59701	406-494-4442	494-6020
Web: www.955kmbr.com					
KMBZ-AM 980 (N/T) 7000 Squibb Rd	Mission	KS	66202	913-744-3600	744-3700
Web: www.kmbz.com					
KMFC-FM 92.1 (Rel) 1249 E Hwy 22	Centralia	MO	65240	573-682-5525	682-2744
TF: 800-769-5632 ■ *Web:* www.kmfc.com					
KMJJ-FM 99.7 (Urban AC) 270 Plaza Loop	Bossier City	LA	71111	318-549-8500	549-8505
Web: www.997kmjj.com					
KMJK-FM 107.3 (Urban)					
5800 Foxridge Dr Suite 600	Mission	KS	66202	816-576-7107	514-3004*
**Fax Area Code:* 913 ■ *Web:* www.magic1073.com					
KMKY-AM 1310 (Kids)					
963 Industrial Rd Suite I	San Carlos	CA	94070	650-637-8800	595-2296
Web: radio.disney.go.com					
KMVR-FM 104.9 (AC) 101 Perkins Dr	Las Cruces	NM	88005	575-527-1011	527-1100
Web: www.kmvrfm.com					
KNDR-FM 104.7 (Rel) 1400 NE 3rd St	Mandan	ND	58554	701-663-2345	663-2347
TF: 800-767-5095 ■ *Web:* www.kndr.fm					
KNOW-FM 91.1 (NPR) 480 Cedar St	Saint Paul	MN	55101	651-290-1500	290-1295
TF: 800-228-7123 ■ *Web:* minnesota.publicradio.org					
KNOX-AM 1310 (N/T) 1185 9th St NE	Thompson	ND	58278	701-775-4611	772-0540
Web: www.knoxradio.com					
KNOX-FM 94.7 (Ctry) 1185 9th St NE	Thompson	ND	58278	701-775-4611	772-0540
KNUS-AM 710 (N/T) 3131 S Vaughn Way Suite 601	Aurora	CO	80014	303-750-5687	696-8063
Web: www.710knus.com					
KNWI-FM 107.1 (Rel)					
3737 Woodland Ave Suite 111	West Des Moines	IA	50266	515-327-1071	327-1073
TF: 866-377-1071 ■ *Web:* www.knwi.nwc.edu					
KOBE-AM 1450 (N/T) 101 Perkins Dr	Las Cruces	NM	88005	575-527-1011	527-1100
Web: www.b1450.com					
KOCN-FM 105.1 (Urban) 903 N Main St	Salinas	CA	93906	831-755-8181	755-8193
TF: 888-896-5626 ■ *Web:* www.kocean105.com					
KOCP-FM 95.9 (CR)					
2284 S Victoria Ave Suite 2G	Ventura	CA	93003	805-289-1400	644-7906
Web: www.theoctopus959.com					
KOHL-FM 89.3 (CHR) 43600 Mission Blvd	Fremont	CA	94539	510-659-6221	659-6001
Web: www.kohlradio.com					
KOKZ-FM 105.7 (Oldies) 514 Jefferson St	Waterloo	IA	50701	319-234-2200	233-4946*
**Fax:* News Rm ■ *Web:* www.cool1057.com					
KOLA-FM 99.9 (Clas)					
1940 Orange Tree Ln Suite 200	Redlands	CA	92374	909-793-3554	793-7225
Web: www.kolafm.com					
KOPN-FM 89.5 (Var) 915 E Broadway	Columbia	MO	65201	573-874-1139	499-1662
TF: 800-895-5676 ■ *Web:* www.kopn.org					
KOQL-FM 106.1 (CHR) 503 Old Hwy 63 N	Columbia	MO	65201	573-449-4141	449-7770
Web: WWW.Q1061.COM					
KOST-FM 103.5 (AC) 3400 W Olive Ave Suite 550	Burbank	CA	91505	818-559-2252	260-9961
Web: www.kost1035.com					
KOZO-FM 89.7 (Rel) 301 Gibson Rd	Hollister	MO	65672	417-339-3388	339-3410
TF: 877-339-3388 ■ *Web:* www.oasisnetwork.org					
KPAW-FM 107.9 (CR) 4270 Byrd Dr	Loveland	CO	80538	970-461-2560	461-0118
Web: www.1079thebear.com					
KPCC-FM 89.3 (NPR) 1570 E Colorado Blvd	Pasadena	CA	91106	626-585-7000	585-7916
Web: www.scpr.org					
KPIG-FM 107.5 (AAA) 1110 Main St Suite 16	Watsonville	CA	95076	831-722-9000	722-7548
Web: www.kpig.com					
KPLA-FM 101.5 (AC) 503 Old 63 N	Columbia	MO	65201	573-442-3116	449-7770
Web: www.kpla.com					
KPLU-FM 88.5 (NPR) 12180 Pk Ave S	Tacoma	WA	98447	253-535-7758	535-8332
TF: 800-677-5758 ■ *Web:* www.kplu.org					
KPUL-FM 99.5 (Rel) 33365 335th St	Waukee	IA	50263	515-987-9995	987-9808
Web: www.pulse995.com					
KPVU-FM 91.3 (NPR)					
Prairie View A & M University MS 1415					
PO Box 159	Prairie View	TX	77446	936-261-3750	261-3769
Web: www.pvamu.edu/kpvu					
KPWR-FM 105.9 (CHR)					
2600 W Olive Ave Suite 850	Burbank	CA	91505	818-953-4200	848-0961
Web: www.power106.fm					
KQFX-FM 104.3 (Span) 2402 Broadmoor Bldg D-2	Bryan	TX	77802	806-355-1044	352-6525
Web: www.lamejorenvivo.com					
KQIS-FM 102.1 (AC) 320 N Parkerson Ave	Crowley	LA	70526	337-783-2520	783-5744
Web: www.kqis.com					
KQKS-FM 107.5 (Urban)					
7800 E Orchard Rd Suite 400	Greenwood Village	CO	80111	303-228-1075	321-3383
Web: www.ks1075.com					
KQMV-FM 92.5 (AC)					
3650 131st Ave SE Suite 550	Bellevue	WA	98006	425-653-9462	653-9464
TF: 866-668-4692 ■ *Web:* www.movin925.fm					
KQRC-FM 98.9 (Rock) 7000 Squibb Rd	Mission	KS	66202	913-744-3600	744-3700
Web: www.989therock.com					
KQST-FM 102.9 (CHR) 3405 SR 89 A Bldg A	Cottonwood	AZ	86326	928-634-2286	634-2295
KRAY-FM 103.5 (Span) 548 E Alisal St	Salinas	CA	93905	831-757-1910	757-8015
KRBZ-FM 96.5 (Alt) 7000 Squibb Rd	Mission	KS	66202	913-744-3600	744-3700
Web: www.965thebuzz.com					
KRCD-FM 103.9 (Span)					
655 N Central Ave Suite 2500	Glendale	CA	91203	818-500-4500	500-4329
Web: www.krcd.netmio.com					
KRDJ-FM 93.7 (AC) 202 Galbert Rd	Lafayette	LA	70506	337-232-1311	233-3779
Web: www.krdjfm.com					
KRKS-FM 94.7 (Rel) 3131 S Vaughn Way Suite 601	Aurora	CO	80014	303-750-5687	696-8063
Web: www.krks.com					

Station	City	State	ZIP	Phone	Fax
KRMD-AM 1340 (N/T) 270 Plaza Loop *Web:* www.supertalk1340.com	Bossier City	LA	71111	318-320-5655	549-8505
KRMD-FM 101.1 (Ctry) 270 Plaza Loop *Web:* www.krmd.com	Bossier City	LA	71111	318-549-8500	549-8505
KRNB-FM 105.7 (Urban) 621 NW 6th St *TF:* 800-310-1057 ■ *Web:* www.krnb.com	Grand Prairie	TX	75050	972-263-9911	558-0010
KROX-AM 1260 (Var) 208 S Main St *TF:* 800-450-1140 ■ *Web:* www.kroxam.com	Crookston	MN	56716	218-281-1140	281-5036
KRWG-FM 90.7 (NPR) PO Box 3000 *TF:* 800-245-5794 ■ *Web:* www.krwgfm.org	Las Cruces	NM	88003	575-646-4525	646-1974
KRWM-FM 106.9 (AC) 3650 131st Ave SE Suite 550 *Web:* www.warm1069.com	Bellevue	WA	98006	425-373-5536	653-1199
KSCA-FM 101.9 (Span) 655 N Central Ave Suite 2500 *Web:* www.lanueva1019.netmio.com	Glendale	CA	91203	818-500-4500	500-4440
KSCS-FM 96.3 (Ctry) 2221 E Lamar Blvd Suite 300 *Web:* www.kscs.com	Arlington	TX	76006	817-640-1963	429-5727
KSEA-FM 107.9 (Span) 229 Pajaro St Suite 302D *Web:* www.campesina.net	Salinas	CA	93901	831-754-1469	754-1563
KSEQ-FM 97.1 (CHR) 617 W Tulare Ave *Web:* www.q97.com	Visalia	CA	93277	559-627-9710	627-1590
KSKY-AM 660 (N/T) 6400 N Beltline Rd Suite 110 *TF:* 800-949-5973 ■ *Web:* www.ksky.com	Irving	TX	75063	214-561-9660	561-9662
KSME-FM 96.1 (CHR) 4270 Byrd Dr *TF:* 877-498-9600 ■ *Web:* www.kissfmcolorado.com	Loveland	CO	80538	970-461-2560	461-0118
KSNM-AM 570 (Var) 1355 California Ave PO Box 968 *Web:* www.ksnm570.am	Las Cruces	NM	88004	575-525-9298	525-9419
KSVN-AM 730 (Span) 4215 W 4000 S	West Haven	UT	84401	801-292-1799	820-9098
KTLK-AM 1150 (N/T) 3400 W Olive Ave Suite 550 *TF:* 866-987-8570 ■ *Web:* www.ktlk.com	Burbank	CA	91505	818-559-2252	
KTOM-FM 92.7 (Ctry) 903 N Main St *TF:* 888-660-5866 ■ *Web:* www.ktom.com	Salinas	CA	93906	831-755-8181	755-8193
KTRR-FM 102.5 (AC) 600 Main St *TF:* 800-964-1025 ■ *Web:* www.tri102.com	Windsor	CO	80550	970-686-2791	686-7491
KTSD-FM 91.1 (NPR) 555 N Dakota St PO Box 5000 *TF:* 800-456-0766 ■ *Web:* www.sdpb.org	Vermillion	SD	57069	605-677-5861	677-5010
KTTB-FM 96.3 (Urban) 5300 Edina Industrial Blvd Suite 200 *Web:* www.b96online.com	Edina	MN	55439	952-842-7200	842-3333
KTXY-FM 106.9 (AC) 3215 Lemone Industrial Blvd Suite 200 *TF:* 800-500-9107 ■ *Web:* www.y107.com	Columbia	MO	65201	573-875-1099	875-2439
KUAD-FM 99.1 (Ctry) 600 Main St *TF:* 800-500-2599 ■ *Web:* www.k99.com	Windsor	CO	80550	970-686-2791	686-7491
KUAF-FM 91.3 (NPR) 9 S School Ave *TF:* 800-522-5823 ■ *Web:* www.kuaf.org	Fayetteville	AR	72701	479-575-2556	575-8440
KUCR-FM 88.3 (Var) UC Riverside *Web:* www.kucr.org	Riverside	CA	92521	951-827-3737	827-3240
KUDL-FM 98.1 (AC) 7000 Squibb Rd *Web:* www.kudl.com	Mission	KS	66202	913-744-3600	677-8981
KUFM-FM 89.1 (NPR) 32 Campus Dr University of Montana *TF:* 800-325-1565 ■ *Web:* www.mtpr.net	Missoula	MT	59812	406-243-4931	243-3299
KUNA-FM 96.7 (Span) 42-650 Melanie Pl *Web:* www.kunamundo.com	Palm Desert	CA	92211	760-568-6830	568-3984
KUPD-FM 97.9 (Rock) 1900 W Carmen St *Web:* www.98kupd.com	Tempe	AZ	85283	480-838-0400	820-8469
KUSP-FM 88.9 (NPR) 203 8th Ave *TF:* 800-655-5877 ■ *Web:* www.kusp.org	Santa Cruz	CA	95062	831-476-2800	476-2802
KUWC-FM 91.3 (NPR) 1000 E University Ave PO Box 3984 *Web:* www.uwadmnweb.uwyo.edu	Laramie	WY	82071	307-766-4240	766-6184
KUWJ-FM 90.3 (NPR) 1000 E University Ave PO Box 3984 *Web:* www.uwadmnweb.uwyo.edu	Laramie	WY	82071	307-766-4240	766-6184
KUWR-FM 91.9 (NPR) 1000 E University Ave PO Box 3984 *Web:* www.uwadmnweb.uwyo.edu	Laramie	WY	82071	307-766-4240	766-6184
KUWS-FM 91.3 (NPR) 1805 Catlin Ave *TF:* 800-300-8530 ■ *Web:* www.kuws.fm	Superior	WI	54880	715-394-8530	394-8404
KVCM-FM 103.1 (Rel) PO Box 2426 *Web:* www.ynopradio.org	Havre	MT	59501	406-265-5845	265-8860
KVLC-FM 101.1 (Oldies) 101 Perkins Dr *TF:* 800-527-1170 ■ *Web:* www.101gold.com	Las Cruces	NM	88005	575-527-1111	527-1100
KVNA-FM 100.1 (AC) 3405 SR 89 A Bldg A *Web:* www.radioflagstaff.com/Sunny/sunny.htm	Cottonwood	AZ	86326	928-634-2286	634-2295
KVRP-FM 97.1 (Ctry) 1406 N 1st St *TF:* 800-460-5877 ■ *Web:* www.kvrp.com	Haskell	TX	79521	940-864-8505	864-8001
KWCR-FM 88.1 (CHR) 2188 University Cir *Web:* departments.weber.edu/kwcr	Ogden	UT	84408	801-626-6450	626-6935
KWIZ-FM 96.7 (Span) 3101 W 5th St *Web:* www.larockola967.com	Santa Ana	CA	92703	714-554-5000	554-9362
KWJZ-FM 98.9 (NAC) 3650 131st Ave SE Suite 550 *Web:* www.kwjz.com	Bellevue	WA	98006	425-373-5536	653-1133
KWWC-FM 90.5 (Jazz) 1200 E Broadway *Web:* www.stephens.edu/campuslife/kwwc	Columbia	MO	65215	573-876-7272	
KWWR-FM 95.7 (Ctry) 1705 E Liberty St *TF:* 800-264-5997 ■ *Web:* www.info.kwwr.com	Mexico	MO	65265	573-581-5500	581-1801
KWXY-FM 98.5 (Soft AC) 68700 Dinah Shore Dr *Web:* www.kwxy.com	Cathedral City	CA	92234	760-328-1104	328-7814
KWYR-FM 93.7 (AC) PO Box 491 *TF:* 800-388-5997 ■ *Web:* www.kwyr.com	Winner	SD	57580	605-842-3333	842-3875
KXFG-FM 92.9 (Ctry) 41593 Winchester Rd Suite 100 *Web:* www.kfrog.com	Temecula	CA	92590	951-695-8840	695-8550
KXTR-AM 1660 (Clas) 7000 Squibb Rd *Web:* www.kxtr.com	Mission	KS	66202	913-744-3600	744-3700
KXXO-FM 96.1 (AC) 119 NE Washington St *Web:* www.mixx96.com	Olympia	WA	98501	360-943-9937	352-3643
KYCK-FM 97.1 (Ctry) 1185 9th St NE *TF:* 800-659-5925 ■ *Web:* www.97kyck.com	Thompson	ND	58278	701-775-4611	772-0540
KYGO-FM 98.5 (Ctry) 7800 E Orchard Rd Suite 400 *Web:* www.kygo.com	Greenwood Village	CO	80111	303-321-0950	321-3383
KYSR-FM 98.7 (AC) 3400 W Olive Ave Suite 550 *Web:* www.star987.com	Burbank	CA	91505	818-559-2252	955-8178
KZGL-FM 95.9 (Rock) 3405 E Hwy 89 A Bldg A *Web:* www.radioflagstaff.com	Cottonwood	AZ	86326	928-634-2286	634-2295
La Nueva Mia 1430 10 Cabot Rd *Web:* www.mia1430.com	Medford	MA	02155	781-663-2548	290-0721
Super talk 1270 4303 Memorial Hwy *TF:* 888-663-1270 ■ *Web:* www.supertalk1270.com	Mandan	ND	58554	701-663-1270	663-8790
WAAF-FM 107.3 (Rock) 20 Guest St 3rd Fl **Fax:* Mktg ■ *Web:* www.waaf.com	Brighton	MA	02135	617-779-5800	779-5447*
WAEB-AM 790 (N/T) 1541 Alta Dr Suite 400 *Web:* www.waeb.com	Whitehall	PA	18052	610-434-1742	434-6288
WAEB-FM 104.1 (AC) 1541 Alta Dr Suite 400 *Web:* www.b104.com	Whitehall	PA	18052	610-434-1742	434-6288
WAEZ-FM 94.9 (CHR) 901 E Valley Dr *TF:* 888-937-4487 ■ *Web:* www.electric949.com	Bristol	VA	24201	276-669-8112	669-0541
WAFL-FM 97.7 (AC) 1666 Blairs Pond Rd *Web:* www.eagle977.com	Milford	DE	19963	302-421-1234	422-3069
WAFX-FM 106.9 (CR) 870 Greenbrier Cir Suite 399 *Web:* www.1069thefox.com	Chesapeake	VA	23320	757-366-9900	366-0022
WAJZ-FM 96.3 (Urban) 6 Johnson Rd *Web:* www.jamz963.com	Latham	NY	12110	518-786-6600	786-6610
WAKB-FM 100.9 (Urban) 411 Radio Stn Rd *Web:* www.1009magic.com	North Augusta	SC	29841	803-279-2330	279-8149
WAKS-FM 96.5 (CHR) 6200 Oak Tree Blvd S 4th Fl *Web:* www.kissfm965.com	Independence	OH	44131	216-520-2600	524-2600
WALK-FM 97.5 (AC) 66 Colonial Dr *Web:* www.walkradio.com	Patchogue	NY	11772	631-475-5200	475-9016
WAMR-FM 107.5 (Span AC) 2601 S Bayshore Dr PH2	Coconut Grove	FL	33133	305-447-1140	643-1075
WAMX-FM 106.3 (Rock) 134 4th Ave *Web:* www.x1063.com	Huntington	WV	25701	304-525-7788	525-6281
WAOR-FM 95.3 (CR) 237 W Edison Rd *Web:* www.waor.com	Mishawaka	IN	46545	574-258-5483	258-0930
WAPL-FM 105.7 (Rock) 2800 E College Ave *Web:* www.wapl.com	Appleton	WI	54915	920-734-9226	739-0494
WAPN-FM 91.5 (Rel) 1508 State Ave *Web:* www.wapn.net	Holly Hill	FL	32117	386-677-4272	673-3715
WAQI-AM 710 (Span N/T) 2601 S Bayshore Dr PH2	Coconut Grove	FL	33133	305-447-1140	442-7676
WAQY-FM 102.1 (CR) 45 Fisher Ave *Web:* www.rock102.com	East Longmeadow	MA	01028	413-525-4141	525-4334
WARF-AM 1350 (Sports) 7755 Freedom Ave *Web:* www.sportsradio1350.com	North Canton	OH	44720	330-836-4700	836-1350
WARO-FM 94.5 (CR) 2824 Palm Beach Blvd *Web:* www.classicrock945.com	Fort Myers	FL	33916	239-337-2346	332-0767
WASH-FM 97.1 (AC) 1801 Rockville Pike 5th Fl *TF:* 866-927-4361 ■ *Web:* www.washfm.com	Rockville	MD	20852	240-747-2700	
WAVA-AM 780 (Rel) 1901 N Moore St Suite 200 *TF:* 800-738-2356 ■ *Web:* www.wava.com	Arlington	VA	22209	703-807-2266	807-2248
WAVA-FM 105.1 (Rel) 1901 N Moore St Suite 200 *TF:* 888-293-9282 ■ *Web:* www.wava.com	Arlington	VA	22209	703-807-2266	807-2248
WAVZ-AM 1300 (Sports) 495 Benham St *Web:* www.wavz.com	Hamden	CT	06514	203-248-8814	281-2795
WAYJ-FM 88.7 (Rel) 1860 Boyscout Dr Suite 202 *TF:* 888-936-1929 ■ *Web:* www.wayj.wayfm.com	Fort Myers	FL	33907	239-936-1929	936-5433
WAYS-AM 1500 (Oldies) 3280 Peachtree Rd NW Suite 2300 *Web:* www.waysam.com	Atlanta	GA	30305	478-746-6286	749-1393
WAYV-FM 95.1 (CHR) 8025 Black Horse Pike Suite 100 *Web:* www.951wayv.com	Pleasantville	NJ	08232	609-484-8444	646-6331
WAYZ-FM 104.7 (Ctry) 10960 John Wayne Dr *TF:* 888-950-1047 ■ *Web:* www.wayz.com	Greencastle	PA	17225	717-597-9200	597-9210
WBAB-FM 102.3 (Rock) 555 Sunrise Hwy *Web:* www.wbab.com	West Babylon	NY	11704	631-587-1023	587-1282
WBAE-AM 1490 (Nost) 420 Western Ave *Web:* www.1490thebay.com	South Portland	ME	04106	207-774-4561	774-3788
WBAP-AM 820 (N/T) 2221 E Lamar Blvd Suite 300 *Web:* www.wbap.com	Arlington	TX	76006	817-640-1963	695-0018
WBBG-FM 106.1 (Oldies) 7461 S Ave *Web:* www.wbbgfm.com	Boardman	OH	44512	330-965-0057	729-9991
WBBN-FM 95.9 (Ctry) 4580 Hwy 15 N PO Box 6408 *Web:* www.b95country.com	Laurel	MS	39441	601-649-0095	649-8199
WBCI-FM 105.9 (Rel) 122 Main St *Web:* www.wbci.fm	Topsham	ME	04086	207-725-9224	725-2686
WBEB-FM 101.1 (AC) 10 Presidential Blvd *Web:* www.b101radio.com	Bala Cynwyd	PA	19004	610-667-8400	667-6795
WBEN-AM 930 (N/T) 500 Corporate Pkwy Suite 200 *Web:* www.wben.com	Amherst	NY	14226	716-843-0600	832-3080
WBGG-FM 105.9 (CR) 7601 Riviera Blvd *Web:* www.big1059.com	Miramar	FL	33023	954-862-2000	862-4212
WBGO-FM 88.3 (Jazz) 54 Pk Pl *Web:* www.wbgo.org	Newark	NJ	07102	973-624-8880	824-8888
WBGR-AM 860 (Rel) 918 Chesapeake Ave *Web:* www.familyradio.com	Annapolis	MD	21403	410-825-7700	268-0931
WBHT-FM 97.1 (CHR) 600 Baltimore Dr *TF:* 800-447-5000 ■ *Web:* www.97bht.com	Wilkes-Barre	PA	18702	570-824-9000	820-0520

Station / Address	City	State	ZIP	Phone	Fax
WBIG-FM 100.3 (Oldies) 1801 Rockville Pike 5th Fl *TF:* 800-493-1003 ■ *Web:* www.wbig.com	Rockville	MD	20852	240-747-2700	
WBLI-FM 106.1 (CHR) 555 Sunrise Hwy *Web:* www.wbli.com	West Babylon	NY	11704	631-587-1023	587-1282
WBON-FM 98.5 (Span) 3075 Veterans Memorial Hwy Suite 201 *Web:* www.lafiestali.com	Ronkonkoma	NY	11779	631-648-2500	648-2550
WBQI-FM 107.7 (Clas) 98 Main St	Ellsworth	ME	04605	207-667-9800	667-3900
WBRB-FM 101.3 (Ctry) 1065 Radio Pk Dr *Web:* www.1013thebear.com	Mount Clare	WV	26048	304-623-6546	623-6547
WBTT-FM 105.5 (Urban) 13320 Metro Pkwy Suite 1 *Web:* www.1055thebeat.com	Fort Myers	FL	33966	239-225-4300	225-4410
WBWB-FM 96.7 (CHR) 304 SR 446 PO Box 7797 *Web:* www.wbwb.com	Bloomington	IN	47407	812-336-8000	336-7000
WBYT-FM 100.7 (Ctry) 237 W Edison Rd *Web:* www.b100.com	Mishawaka	IN	46545	574-258-5483	258-0930
WBZN-FM 107.3 (CHR) 49 Acme Rd PO Box 100 *Web:* www.wbzn-fm.com	Brewer	ME	04412	207-989-5631	989-5685
WBZO-FM 103.1 (Oldies) 234 Airport Plaza Suite 5 *Web:* www.b103.com	Farmingdale	NY	11735	631-770-4200	770-0110
WCAR-AM 1090 (Rel) 32500 Pk Ln *TF:* 877-327-1090 ■ *Web:* www.catholicradio.org	Garden City	MI	48135	734-525-1111	525-3608
WCAT-AM 1390 (Sports) 372 Dorset St *TF:* 800-286-9537 ■ *Web:* www.wcat1390.com	South Burlington	VT	05403	802-863-1010	863-7256
WCAT-FM 102.3 (Ctry) 515 S 32nd St *TF:* 800-932-0505 ■ *Web:* www.red1023.com	Camp Hill	PA	17011	717-635-7000	635-7551
WCBK-FM 102.3 (Ctry) 1639 Burton Ln *Web:* www.wcbk.com	Martinsville	IN	46151	765-342-3394	342-5020
WCBM-AM 680 (N/T) 1726 Reisterstown Rd Suite 117 *Web:* www.wcbm.com	Pikesville	MD	21208	410-580-6800	580-6810
WCBN-FM 88.3 (Alt) University of Michigan 530 Student Activities Bldg *Web:* wcbn.org	Ann Arbor	MI	48109	734-763-3500	647-4127
WCGO-AM 1600 (Nost) 222 Vollmer Rd *Web:* www.wcgoradio.com	Chicago Heights	IL	60411	708-755-5900	755-5941
WCKT-FM 107.1 (Ctry) 13320 Metro Pkwy Suite 1 **Fax:* Hum Res ■ *Web:* www.wckt.com	Fort Myers	FL	33966	239-225-4300	225-4410*
WCLT-FM 100.3 (Ctry) PO Box 5150 *TF:* 800-837-9258 ■ *Web:* www.wclt.com	Newark	OH	43058	740-345-4004	345-5775
WCMR-AM 1270 (Rel) 25802 CR 26 *TF:* 800-522-9376 ■ *Web:* www.wfrn.com	Elkhart	IN	46517	574-875-5166	875-6662
WCMS-FM 94.5 (Ctry) PO Box 1897 *Web:* www.wcms.com	Kill Devil Hills	NC	27948	252-480-4655	441-4827
WCNK-FM 98.7 (Ctry) 30336 Overseas Hwy *Web:* www.conchcountry.com	Big Pine Key	FL	33043	305-872-9100	872-1603
WCNY-FM 91.3 (NPR) 506 Old Liverpool Rd *TF:* 800-451-9269 ■ *Web:* www.wcny.org	Liverpool	NY	13088	315-453-2424	451-8824
WCPV-FM 101.3 (CR) 265 Hegeman Ave *Web:* www.1013espn.com	Colchester	VT	05446	802-655-0093	655-6478
WCQR-FM 88.3 (Rel) 2312 Oak St *TF:* 888-477-5676 ■ *Web:* www.wcqr.org	Gray	TN	37615	423-477-5676	477-7060
WCRZ-FM 107.9 (AC) 3338 E Bristol Rd *Web:* wcrz.com	Burton	MI	48529	810-743-1080	742-5170
WCSX-FM 94.7 (CR) 1 Radio Plaza *Web:* www.wcsx.com	Ferndale	MI	48220	248-398-9470	541-9279
WCTL-FM 106.3 (Rel) 10912 Rt 19 N *Web:* www.wctl.org	Waterford	PA	16441	814-796-6000	796-3200
WCTO-FM 96.1 (Ctry) 2158 Ave C Suite 100 *Web:* www.catcountry96.com	Bethlehem	PA	18017	610-266-7600	231-0400
WCTZ-FM 96.7 (AC) 444 Westport Ave *Web:* 967thecoast.com	Norwalk	CT	06851	203-845-3030	845-3097
WCVT-FM 101.7 (Clas) PO Box 550 *Web:* www.wcvtradio.com	Waterbury	VT	05676	802-244-7321	244-1771
WCWM-FM 90.9 (Var) Campus Ctr PO Box 8795 College of William & Mary *Web:* www.wcwm.org	Williamsburg	VA	23187	757-221-3287	221-3451
WDAC-FM 94.5 (Rel) PO Box 3022 *Web:* www.wdac.com	Lancaster	PA	17604	717-284-4123	284-2300
WDAF-FM 106.5 (Ctry) 7000 Squibb Rd *Web:* www.wdaf.com	Mission	KS	66202	913-744-3600	443-3700
WDAI-FM 98.5 (Urban) 11640 Hwy 17 Bypass *Web:* www.985kissfm.net	Murrells Inlet	SC	29576	843-651-7869	651-3197
WDAS-FM 105.3 (Urban AC) 111 Presidential Blvd Suite 100 *TF:* 877-894-1053 ■ *Web:* www.wdasfm.com	Bala Cynwyd	PA	19004	610-784-3333	784-2098
WDCI-FM 104.1 (AC) PO Box 360	Bridgeport	WV	26330	304-842-8644	842-8653
WDDO-AM 1240 (Rel) 3280 Peachtree Rd NW Suite 2300 *Web:* www.wddoam.com	Atlanta	GA	30305	478-746-6286	749-1393
WDEA-AM 1370 (Nost) 49 Acme Rd PO Box 100 *Web:* www.am1370wdea.com	Brewer	ME	04412	207-989-5631	989-5685
WDEV-AM 550 (N/T) 9 Stowe St *Web:* www.wdevradio.com	Waterbury	VT	05676	802-244-7321	244-1771
WDFN-AM 1130 (Sports) 27675 Halsted Rd *Web:* www.wdfn.com	Farmington Hills	MI	48331	248-324-5800	324-0356
WDIY-FM 88.1 (NPR) 301 Broadway 3rd Fl *Web:* www.wdiyfm.org	Bethlehem	PA	18015	610-694-8100	954-9474
WDJA-AM 1420 (N/T) 2710 W Atlantic Ave *TF:* 877-278-1420 ■ *Web:* www.wdja.com	Delray Beach	FL	33445	561-278-1420	278-1898
WDRC-AM 1360 (N/T) 869 Blue Hills Ave *Web:* www.wdrc.com	Bloomfield	CT	06002	860-243-1115	286-8257
WDRC-FM 102.9 (Oldies) 869 Blue Hills Ave *Web:* www.drcfm.com	Bloomfield	CT	06002	860-243-1115	286-8257
WDRM-FM 102.1 (Ctry) 26869 Peoples Rd *Web:* www.wdrm.com	Madison	AL	35756	256-353-1750	350-2653
WDSD-FM 94.7 (Ctry) 920 W Basin Rd Suite 400 *TF:* 877-947-9373 ■ *Web:* www.wdsd.com	New Castle	DE	19720	302-395-9800	
WDTW-FM 106.7 (Cty) 27675 Halsted Rd *Web:* www.foxspacelive.com	Farmington Hills	MI	48331	248-324-5800	324-0356
WEDR-FM 99.1 (Urban) 2741 N 29th Ave *Web:* www.wedr.com	Hollywood	FL	33020	305-444-4404	444-4404
WEEI-AM 850 (Sports) 20 Guest St 3rd Fl *TF:* 888-525-0850 ■ *Web:* www.weei.com	Brighton	MA	02135	617-779-3500	779-3557
WEIB-FM 106.3 (NAC) 8 N King St *Web:* www.weibfm.com	NorthHampton	MA	01060	413-585-1112	585-9138
WEKU-FM 88.9 (Clas) 521 Lancaster Ave 102 Perkins Bldg-EKU *TF:* 800-621-8890 ■ *Web:* www.weku.fm	Richmond	KY	40475	859-622-1660	622-6276
WELI-AM 960 (N/T) 495 Benham St *Web:* www.weli.com	Hamden	CT	06514	203-248-8814	281-2795
WEMU-FM 89.1 (NPR) 1000 College Pl *TF:* 888-299-8910 ■ *Web:* www.wemu.org	Ypsilanti	MI	48197	734-487-2229	487-1015
WERU-FM 89.9 (Var) 1186 Acadia Hwy *TF:* 800-643-6273 ■ *Web:* www.weru.org	East Orland	ME	04431	207-469-6600	469-8961
WETA-FM 90.9 (NPR) 2775 S Quincy St *Web:* www.weta.org/fm	Arlington	VA	22206	703-998-2600	998-3401
WETH-FM 89.1 (NPR) 2775 S Quincy St *Web:* www.weta.org/fm	Arlington	VA	22206	703-998-2600	998-3401
WEVO-FM 89.1 (N/T) 2 Pillsbury St Suite 600 *TF:* 800-262-1816 ■ *Web:* www.nhpr.org	Concord	NH	03301	603-228-8910	224-6052
WEZF-FM 92.9 (AC) 265 Hegeman Ave *TF:* 866-865-7827 ■ *Web:* www.star929.com	Colchester	VT	05446	802-655-0093	655-0478
WEZL-FM 103.5 (Ctry) 950 Houston Northcutt Blvd Suite 201 *Web:* www.wezlfm.com	Mount Pleasant	SC	29464	843-884-2534	884-1218
WEZN-FM 99.9 (AC) 440 Wheelers Farm Rd Suite 302 *Web:* star999.com	Milford	CT	06461	203-783-8200	783-8399
WEZQ-FM 92.9 (AC) 49 Acme Rd PO Box 100 *Web:* www.wezq-fm.com	Brewer	ME	04412	207-989-5631	989-5685
WFBY-FM 102.3 (CR) 1065 Radio Pk Dr **Fax:* News Rm ■ *Web:* www.wfby.com	Mount Clare	WV	26408	304-623-6546	623-6547*
WFCF-FM 88.5 (Var) Flagler College PO Box 1027	Saint Augustine	FL	32085	904-819-6449	826-0094
WFCR-FM 88.5 (NPR) University of Massachusetts 131 County Cir *Web:* www.wfcr.org	Amherst	MA	01003	413-545-0100	545-2546
WFDM-FM 95.9 (N/T) 645 Industrial Dr *Web:* www.freedom959.com	Franklin	IN	46131	317-736-4040	736-4781
WFHB-FM 91.3 (Var) 108 W 4th St *Web:* www.wfhb.org	Bloomington	IN	47404	812-323-1200	323-0320
WFHM-FM 95.5 (Rel) 4 Summit Park Dr Suite 150 *Web:* www.955thefish.com	Cleveland	OH	44131	216-901-0921	901-5517
WFHN-FM 107.1 (CHR) 22 Sconticut Neck Rd *Web:* www.fun107.com	Fairhaven	MA	02719	508-999-6690	999-1420
WFIU-FM 103.7 (Clas) Indiana University 1229 E 7th St *TF:* 877-285-9348 ■ *Web:* www.wfiu.org	Bloomington	IN	47405	812-855-1357	855-5600
WFLC-FM 97.3 (AC) 2741 N 29th Ave *Web:* www.coastfm.com	Hollywood	FL	33020	954-584-7117	847-3240
WFLF-FM 540 (N/T) 2500 Maitland Ctr Pkwy Suite 401 *Web:* www.540wfla.com	Maitland	FL	32751	407-916-7800	916-7406
WFLY-FM 92.3 (CHR) 6 Johnson Rd *Web:* www.fly92.com	Latham	NY	12110	518-786-6600	786-6610
WFMP-FM 107.1 (N/T) 3415 University Ave *Web:* www.fm107.fm	Saint Paul	MN	55114	651-642-4107	646-5367
WFNT-AM 1470 (N/T) 3338 E Bristol Rd *Web:* wfnt.com	Burton	MI	48529	810-743-1080	742-5170
WFNX-FM 101.7 (Alt) 25 Exchange St *Web:* fnxradio.com	Lynn	MA	01901	781-595-6200	595-3810
WFOY-AM 1240 (N/T) PO Box 3847 *Web:* www.1240news.com	Saint Augustine	FL	32085	904-797-1955	797-3446
WFPG-FM 96.9 (AC) 950 Tilton Rd Suite 200 *TF:* 800-969-9374 ■ *Web:* www.literock969.com	Northfield	NJ	08225	609-645-9797	272-9228
WFRE-FM 99.9 (Ctry) 5966 Grove Hill Rd *TF:* 877-999-9373 ■ *Web:* www.wfre.com	Frederick	MD	21703	301-663-4181	682-8018
WFUV-FM 90.7 (Var) 441 E Fordham Rd Fordham University *Web:* www.wfuv.org	Bronx	NY	10458	718-817-4550	365-9815
WFXA-FM 103.1 (Urban) 411 Radio Stn Rd *Web:* www.wfxa103jamz.com	North Augusta	SC	29841	803-279-2330	819-3781
WFXH-AM 1130 (Sports) 1 St Augustine Pl	Hilton Head Island	SC	29928	843-785-9569	842-3369
WFXH-FM 106.1 (Rock) 1 St Augustine Pl *TF:* 800-394-1061 ■ *Web:* www.rock1061.com	Hilton Head Island	SC	29928	843-785-9569	842-3369
WGAR-FM 99.5 (Ctry) 6200 Oak Tree Blvd S 4th Fl **Fax:* Sales ■ *Web:* www.wgar.com	Independence	OH	44131	216-520-2600	524-2600*
WGBG-FM 98.5 (CR) 20200 DuPont Blvd *TF:* 888-780-0970 ■ *Web:* www.bigclassicrock.com	Georgetown	DE	19947	302-856-2567	856-7633
WGBZ-FM 105.5 (CHR) 8025 Black Horse Pike Suite 100 *Web:* www.993kiss.fm	Pleasantville	NJ	08232	609-484-8444	646-6331
WGCU-FM 90.1 (NPR) 10501 FGCU Blvd S *TF:* 888-824-0030 ■ *Web:* www.wgcu.org	Fort Myers	FL	33965	239-590-2300	590-2310
WGEZ-AM 1490 (Oldies) 622 Public Ave *Web:* www.1490trueoldies.com	Beloit	WI	53511	608-365-8865	365-8867
WGGY-FM 101.3 (Ctry) 305 Hwy 315 *Web:* www.froggy101.com	Pittston	PA	18640	570-883-9850	883-9851

Station / Address	City	State	ZIP	Phone	Fax
WGMD-FM 92.7 (N/T) PO Box 530	Rehoboth Beach	DE	19971	302-945-2050	945-3781
TF: 800-933-9027 ■ *Web:* www.wgmd.com					
WGNA-FM 107.7 (Ctry) 1241 Kings Rd	Schenectady	NY	12303	518-881-1515	881-1516
TF: 800-476-1077 ■ *Web:* www.wgna.com					
WGNE-FM 99.9 (Ctry) 6440 Atlantic Blvd	Jacksonville	FL	32211	904-727-9696	721-9322
Web: www.999gatorcountry.com					
WGOC-AM 1320 (Ctry) 162 Freehill Rd PO Box 8668	Gray	TN	37615	423-477-1000	477-4747
Web: www.wgoc.com					
WGPA-AM 1100 (Var) 528 N New St	Bethlehem	PA	18018	610-866-8074	866-9381
Web: www.wgpasunny1100.com					
WGR-AM 550 (Sports) 500 Corporate Pkwy Suite 200	Amherst	NY	14226	716-843-0600	832-3080
Web: www.wgr550.com					
WGSL-FM 91.1 (Rel) 5375 Pebble Creek Tr	Loves Park	IL	61111	815-654-1200	282-7779
Web: www.radio91.com					
WGTS-FM 91.9 (Rel) 7600 Flower Ave	Takoma Park	MD	20912	301-891-4200	270-9191
TF: 877-948-7919 ■ *Web:* www.wgts.org					
WGTY-FM 107.7 (Ctry) 1560 Fairfield Rd PO Box 3179	Gettysburg	PA	17325	717-334-3101	334-5822
TF: 800-366-9489 ■ *Web:* www.wgty.com					
WGY-AM 810 (N/T) 1203 Troy-Schenectady Rd Suite 201 Riverhill Ctr	Latham	NY	12110	518-452-4800	452-4813
TF: 800-825-5949 ■ *Web:* www.wgy.com					
WGZR-FM 106.9 (Ctry) 1 St Augustine Pl	Hilton Head Island	SC	29928	843-785-9569	842-3369
TF: 866-469-1069 ■ *Web:* www.104.9thegator.com					
WHB-AM 810 (Sports) 6721 W 121st St	Overland Park	KS	66209	913-344-1500	344-1599
Web: www.810whb.com					
WHCC-FM 105.1 (Ctry) 304 State Rd 446 PO Box 7797	Bloomington	IN	47401	812-336-8000	336-7000
Web: www.whcc105.com					
WHDR-FM 93.1 (Rock) 2741 N 29th Ave	Hollywood	FL	33020	305-444-4404	847-3201
Web: 93rock.com					
WHFS-AM 1580 (N/T) 4200 Parliament Pl Suite 300	Latham	MD	20706	301-918-0955	731-1583
TF: 888-432-1580 ■ *Web:* www.bigtalker1580.com					
WHFS-FM 105.7 (Sports) 1423 Clarkview Rd Suite 100	Balitmore	MD	21209	410-828-7722	821-8256
Web: www.whfs.com					
WHLI-AM 1100 (Nost) 234 Airport Plaza Suite 5	Farmingdale	NY	11735	631-770-4200	770-0110
Web: www.whli.com					
WHNN-FM 96.1 (Oldies) 1740 Champagne Dr N	Saginaw	MI	48604	989-776-2100	754-9600
TF: 877-479-9466 ■ *Web:* www.whnn.com					
WHQT-FM 105.1 (Urban) 2741 N 29th Ave	Hollywood	FL	33020	305-444-4404	847-3223*
**Fax Area Code:* 954 ■ *Web:* www.hot105fm.com					
WHRB-FM 95.3 (Var) 389 Harvard St	Cambridge	MA	02138	617-495-4818	
Web: www.whrb.org					
WHVR-AM 1280 (Ctry) 275 Radio Rd	Hanover	PA	17331	717-637-3831	637-9006
WHYI-FM 100.7 (CHR) 7601 Riviera Blvd	Miramar	FL	33023	954-862-2000	862-4212
Web: www.y100miami.com					
WICO-AM 1320 (N/T) 919 Ellegood St PO Box 909	Salisbury	MD	21801	410-219-3500	
Web: www.wicoam.com					
WILK-AM 980 (N/T) 305 Hwy 315	Pittston	PA	18640	570-883-9850	883-9851
Web: www.wilknetwork.com					
WILL-FM 90.9 (NPR) 300 N Goodwin Ave Campbell Hall	Urbana	IL	61801	217-333-0850	244-9586
Web: www.will.uiuc.edu					
WINK-FM 96.9 (AC) 2824 Palm Beach Blvd	Fort Myers	FL	33916	239-337-2346	332-0767
Web: www.winkfm.com					
WIOQ-FM 102.1 (CHR) 111 Presidential Blvd Suite 100	Bala Cynwyd	PA	19004	610-784-3333	
TF: 800-521-1021 ■ *Web:* www.q102philly.com					
WISN-AM 1130 (N/T) 12100 W Howard Ave	Greenfield	WI	53228	414-545-8900	546-9654
Web: www.newstalk1130.com					
WIWF-FM 969 (Ctry) 4230 Faber Pl Dr Suite 100	North Charleston	SC	29405	843-277-1200	277-1212
Web: www.969thewolf.com					
WJAB-FM 90.9 (Jazz) Alabama A&M University Telecommunications Ctr PO Box 1687	Normal	AL	35762	256-372-5722	372-5907
TF: 800-845-9746 ■ *Web:* www.aamu.edu/wjab					
WJBX-FM 99.3 (Alt) 20125 S Tamiami Trail	Estero	FL	33928	239-495-2100	992-8165
TF: 800-937-7465 ■ *Web:* www.99xwjbx.com					
WJCW-AM 910 (N/T) 162 Freehill Rd	Gray	TN	37615	423-477-1000	477-4747
Web: www.wjcw.com					
WJDA-AM 1300 (N/T) 90 Everett Ave	Chelsea	MA	02150	617-884-4500	884-4515
Web: www.wjda1300.com					
WJFK-FM 106.7 (N/T) 10800 Main St	Fairfax	VA	22030	703-691-1900	352-0111
TF: 800-636-1067 ■ *Web:* www.wjfk.com					
WJIB-AM 740 (AC) 443 Concord Ave	Cambridge	MA	02138	617-868-7400	
WJKK-FM 98.7 (AC) 265 Highpoint Dr	Ridgeland	MS	39157	601-956-0102	978-3980
Web: www.mix987.com					
WJMH-FM 102.1 (Urban) 7819 National Service Rd Suite 401	Greensboro	NC	27409	336-605-5200	605-5221
Web: www.102jamz.com					
WJMI-FM 99.7 (Urban) 731 S Pear Orchard Rd Suite 27	Ridgeland	MS	39157	601-957-1300	956-0516
Web: www.wjmi.com					
WJMN-FM 94.5 (Urban) 10 Cabot Rd Suite 302	Medford	MA	02155	781-290-0009	290-0722
Web: www.jamn945.com					
WJOX-FM 100.5 (Sports) 244 Goodwin Crst Dr Suite 300	Birmingham	AL	35209	205-945-4646	945-3999
TF: 800-239-9569 ■ *Web:* www.wjox1005fm.com					
WJOY-AM 1230 (Nost) 70 Joy Dr	South Burlington	VT	05403	802-658-1230	862-0786
Web: www.wjoy.com					
WJPT-FM 106.3 (Nost) 20125 S Tamiami Trail	Estero	FL	33928	239-495-2100	948-0785
Web: www.wjpt.com					
WJQK-FM 99.3 (Rel) 425 Centerstone Ct	Zeeland	MI	49464	616-931-9930	931-1280
TF: 888-993-1260 ■ *Web:* www.jq99.com					

Station / Address	City	State	ZIP	Phone	Fax
WJRR-FM 101.1 (Alt) 2500 Maitland Ctr Pkwy Suite 401	Maitland	FL	32751	407-916-7800	916-7406
Web: www.wjrr.com					
WJSE-FM 102.7 (Alt) 1601 New Rd	Linwood	NJ	08221	609-653-1400	601-0450
Web: www.wjse.com					
WJXQ-FM 106.1 (Rock) 2495 N Cedar St	Holt	MI	48842	517-699-0111	699-1880
Web: www.q106fm.com					
WJYY-FM 105.5 (CHR) Village W Bldg Suite 1 PO Box 7326	Gilford	NH	03249	603-225-1160	528-5185
Web: www.wjyy.com					
WKAR-AM 870 (NPR) Michigan State University 283 Communications Arts & Sciences Bldg	East Lansing	MI	48824	517-432-9527	353-7124
Web: www.wkar.org					
WKAR-FM 90.5 (NPR) Michigan State University 283 Comm Arts & Sciences Bldg	East Lansing	MI	48824	517-432-9527	353-7124
Web: www.wkar.org					
WKBN-AM 570 (N/T) 7461 S Ave	Boardman	OH	44512	330-965-0057	729-9991
TF: 800-777-5700 ■ *Web:* www.570wkbn.com					
WKCI-FM 101.3 (CHR) 495 Benham St	Hamden	CT	06514	203-248-8814	281-2795
Web: www.kc101.com					
WKCQ-FM 98.1 (Ctry) 2000 Whittier St	Saginaw	MI	48601	989-752-8161	752-8102
TF: 800-262-0098 ■ *Web:* www.98fmkcq.com					
WKDD-FM 98.1 (AC) 7755 Freedom Ave	North Canton	OH	44720	330-836-4700	836-1350
Web: www.wkdd.com					
WKGM-AM 940 (Rel) 13379 Great Spring Rd	Smithfield	VA	23430	757-357-9546	365-0412
TF: 800-706-4769					
WKKG-FM 101.5 (Ctry) 3212 Washington St	Columbus	IN	47203	812-372-4448	372-1061
Web: www.wkkg.com					
WKKV-FM 100.7 (Urban) 12100 W Howard Ave	Greenfield	WI	53228	414-321-1007	546-9654
Web: www.v100.com					
WKLC-FM 105.1 (Rock) 100 Kanawha Terr	Saint Albans	WV	25177	304-722-3308	727-1300
Web: www.wklc.com					
WKLI-FM 100.9 (Nost) 6 Johnson Rd	Latham	NY	12110	518-786-6600	786-6610
Web: www.albanymagic.com					
WKOS-FM 104.9 (Oldies) 162 Freehill Rd	Gray	TN	37615	423-477-1000	477-4747
Web: www.wkos.com					
WKOX-AM 1200 (Span) 10 Cabot Rd Suite 302	Medford	MA	02155	781-396-1430	
Web: www.talk1200.com					
WKPT-AM 1400 (Nost) 222 Commerce St	Kingsport	TN	37660	423-246-9578	247-9836
Web: www.wkptam.com					
WKPX-FM 88.5 (Alt) 8000 NW 44th St	Sunrise	FL	33351	754-322-1721	322-1830
WKQI-FM 95.5 (CHR) 27675 Halsted Rd	Farmington Hills	MI	48331	248-324-5800	324-0356
Web: www.channel955.com					
WKRR-FM 92.3 (CR) 192 E Lewis St	Greensboro	NC	27406	336-274-8042	274-5745
TF: 800-762-5923 ■ *Web:* www.rock92.com					
WKRZ-FM 98.5 (CHR) 305 Hwy 315	Pittston	PA	18640	570-883-9850	883-9851
Web: www.wkrz.com					
WKSE-FM 98.5 (CHR) 500 Corporate Pkwy Suite 200	Amherst	NY	14226	716-843-0600	832-3080
Web: www.kiss985.com					
WKSU-FM 89.7 (NPR) 1613 E Summit St	Kent	OH	44242	330-672-3114	672-4107
TF: 800-672-2132 ■ *Web:* www.wksu.org					
WKTO-FM 88.9 (Rel) 900 Old Mission Rd	New Smyrna Beach	FL	32168	386-427-1095	427-8970
TF: 877-541-9586					
WKTX-AM 830 (Var) 11906 Madison Ave	Lakewood	OH	44107	216-221-0330	221-3638
WKVV-FM 101.7 PO Box 2098	Omaha	NE	68103	800-525-5683	
TF: 800-525-5683 ■ *Web:* www.klove.com					
WKXI-FM 107.5 (Urban) 731 S Pear Orchard Rd Suite 27	Ridgeland	MS	39157	601-957-1300	956-0516
Web: www.kixie107.com					
WKXN-FM 95.9 (Urban) 563 Manningham Rd	Greenville	AL	36037	334-382-6555	382-7770
Web: www.wkxn.com					
WKYS-FM 93.9 (Urban) 5900 Princess Garden Pkwy 8th Fl	Lanham	MD	20706	301-306-1111	306-9540
Web: www.939wkys.com					
WKZL-FM 107.5 (CHR) 192 E Lewis St	Greensboro	NC	27406	336-274-8042	274-5745
TF: 800-682-1075 ■ *Web:* www.1075kzl.com					
WKZW-FM 94.3 (AC) 4580 Hwy 15 N PO Box 6408	Laurel	MS	39441	601-649-0095	649-8199
Web: www.kz94.com					
WLBR-AM 1270 (N/T) 440 Rebecca St	Lebanon	PA	17046	717-272-7651	274-0161
WLBW-FM 92.1 (Oldies) 351 Tilghman Rd	Salisbury	MD	21804	410-742-1923	742-2329
TF: 800-762-0105 ■ *Web:* www.isurfthewave.com					
WLCO-AM 1530 (N/T) 3338 E Bristol Rd	Burton	MI	48529	810-743-1080	742-5170
WLDB-FM 93.3 (AC) N 72 W 12922 Good Hope Rd	Menomonee Falls	WI	53051	414-778-1933	771-3036
Web: www.b933fm.com					
Wlev100.7 2158 Ave C Suite 100	Bethlehem	PA	18017	610-266-7600	
Web: www.wlevradio.com					
WLIF-FM 101.9 (AC) 1423 Clarkview Rd Suite 100	Baltimore	MD	21209	410-296-1019	821-5482
Web: www.1019litefm.com					
WLKE-FM 99.1 (Ctry) 184 Target Industrial Cir	Ellsworth	ME	04605	207-947-9100	942-8039
WLKX-FM 95.9 (Rel) 15226 W Fwy Dr	Forest Lake	MN	55025	651-464-6796	464-3638
Web: www.spirit.fm					
WLLL-AM 930 (Rel) PO Box 11375	Lynchburg	VA	24506	434-385-9555	385-6073
TF Cust Svc: 888-224-9809 ■ *Web:* www.wlllradio.com					
WLNO-AM 1060 (Rel) 401 Whitney Ave Suite 160	Gretna	LA	70056	504-362-9800	362-5541
Web: www.wlno.com					
WLOQ-FM 103.1 (NAC) 2301 Lucien Way Suite 180	Maitland	FL	32751	407-647-5557	647-4495
Web: www.wloq.com					
WLOW-FM 107.9 (AC) 1 St Augustine Pl	Hilton Head Island	SC	29928	843-785-9569	842-3369
TF: 888-802-1079					
WLUM-FM 102.1 (Rock) N 72 W 12922 Good Hope Rd	Menomonee Falls	WI	53051	414-771-1021	771-3036
Web: www.fm1021milwaukee.com					
WLVE-FM 93.9 (NAC) 7601 Riviera Blvd	Miramar	FL	33023	954-862-2000	862-4212
TF: 877-456-8394 ■ *Web:* www.love94.com					

Station	City	State	ZIP	Phone	Fax
WLXC-FM 98.5 (Urban) 1801 Charleston Hwy Suite J *Web:* www.kiss985fm.com	Cayce	SC	29033	803-796-7600	796-5502
WLZX-FM 99.3 (Rock) 45 Fisher Ave *Web:* www.lazer993.com	East Longmeadow	MA	01028	413-525-4141	525-4334
WMAG-FM 99.5 (AC) 2-B PAI Pk *Web:* www.wmagradio.com	Greensboro	NC	27409	336-822-2000	887-0104
WMBR-FM 88.1 (Var) 3 Ames St *Web:* www.wmbr.org	Cambridge	MA	02142	617-253-4000	232-1384
WMBS-AM 590 (Oldies) 44 S Mt Vernon Ave *TF:* 866-590-9627 ■ *Web:* www.wmbs590.com	Uniontown	PA	15401	724-438-3900	438-2406
WMEZ-FM 94.1 (AC) 6085 Quinette Rd *TF:* 888-741-0941 ■ *Web:* www.softrock941.com	Pace	FL	32571	850-994-5357	994-4169
WMGC-FM 105.1 (AC) 1 Radio Plaza *Web:* www.detroitmagic.com	Ferndale	MI	48220	248-414-5600	524-7700
WMGE-FM 94.9 (Span CHR) 7601 Riviera Blvd *TF:* 877-634-2949 ■ *Web:* www.mega949.com	Miramar	FL	33023	954-862-2000	862-4212
WMGF-FM 107.7 (AC) 2500 Maitland Ctr Pkwy Suite 401 *Web:* www.magic107.com	Maitland	FL	32751	407-916-7800	916-7406
WMGK-FM 102.9 (CR) 1 Bala Plaza Suite 339 *Web:* www.wmgk.com	Bala Cynwyd	PA	19004	610-667-8500	664-9610
WMGL-FM 101.7 (Urban) 4230 Faber Pl Dr Suite 100 *Web:* www.magic1017.com	North Charleston	SC	29405	843-277-1200	277-1212
WMGM-FM 103.7 (CR) 1601 New Rd *Web:* www.wmgm1037.com	Linwood	NJ	08221	609-653-1400	601-0450
WMGS-FM 92.9 (AC) 600 Baltimore Dr *TF:* 800-447-5000 ■ *Web:* www.magic93fm.com	Wilkes-Barre	PA	18702	570-824-9000	820-0520
WMGX-FM 93.1 (AC) 420 Western Ave *Web:* www.wmgx.com	South Portland	ME	04106	207-774-4561	774-3788
WMIB-FM 103.5 (Urban) 7601 Riviera Blvd *Web:* www.thebeatmiami.com	Miramar	FL	33023	954-862-2000	862-4212
WMID-AM 1340 (Nost) 8025 Black Horse Pike Suite 100 *Web:* www.classicoldieswmid.com	West Atlantic City	NJ	08232	609-484-8444	646-6331
WMIL-FM 106.1 (Ctry) 12100 W Howard Ave *Web:* www.fm106.com	Greenfield	WI	53228	414-545-8900	327-3200
WMIT-FM 106.9 (Rel) PO Box 159 *TF:* 800-330-9648 ■ *Web:* www.wmit.org	Black Mountain	NC	28711	828-285-8477	298-0117
WMJI-FM 105.7 (Oldies) 6200 Oak Tree Blvd S 4th Fl *Web:* www.wmji.com	Independence	OH	44131	216-520-2600	524-2600
WMKK-FM 93.7 (Var) 20 Guest St 3rd Fl *Fax: Sales ■ *Web:* www.937mikefm.com	Brighton	MA	02135	617-779-5800	779-5375*
WMMJ-FM 102.3 (Urban AC) 5900 Princess Garden Pkwy 8th Fl *Web:* www.majic1023.com	Lanham	MD	20706	301-306-1111	306-9540
WMMR-FM 93.3 (Rock) 1 Bala Plaza Suite 424 *Web:* www.wmmr.com	Bala Cynwyd	PA	19004	610-771-0933	771-9610
WMPI-FM 105.3 (Ctry) 22 E McClain Ave *TF:* 800-441-1053 ■ *Web:* www.i1053online.com	Scottsburg	IN	47170	812-752-3688	752-2345
WMUM-FM 89.7 (NPR) 243 Carey Salem Rd *TF:* 800-222-4788 ■ *Web:* www.gpb.org/radio/stations/wmum	Cochran	GA	31014	478-301-5760	
WMVX-FM 106.5 (AC) 6200 Oak Tree Blvd S 4th Fl *TF:* 800-829-1065 ■ *Web:* www.wmvx.com	Independence	OH	44131	216-520-2600	524-2600
WMWX-FM 95.7 (AC) 1 Bala Plaza Suite 339 *TF:* 866-957-2363 ■ *Web:* www.957benfm.com	Bala Cynwyd	PA	19004	610-667-8500	771-9610
WMXU-FM 106.1 (Urban) 200 6th St N Suite 205 *Web:* www.mymix1061.com	Columbus	MS	39702	662-327-1183	328-1122
WMYJ-AM 1540 (Rel) 1639 Burton Ln *Web:* www.indianabroadcasters.org	Martinsville	IN	46151	765-342-3394	342-5020
WMYX-FM 99.1 (AC) 11800 W Grange Ave *NYSE: ETM* ■ *Web:* www.99wmyx.com	Hales Corners	WI	53130	414-529-1250	529-2122
WMZQ-FM 98.7 (Ctry) 1801 Rockville Pike 5th FL *TF:* 800-505-0098 ■ *Web:* www.wmzq.com	Rockville	MD	20852	240-747-2700	
WNCL-FM 101.3 (Oldies) 1666 Blairs Pond Rd *Web:* www.wxpz.com	Milford	DE	19963	302-422-7575	422-3069
WNCS-FM 104.7 (AAA) 169 River St *TF:* 877-367-6468 ■ *Web:* www.pointfm.com	Montpelier	VT	05602	802-223-5275	223-1520
WNCW-FM 88.7 (AAA) PO Box 804 *Web:* www.wncw.org	Spindale	NC	28160	828-287-8000	287-8012
WNIC-FM 100.3 (AC) 27675 Halsted Rd *Web:* www.fresh100.com	Farmington Hills	MI	48331	248-324-5800	324-0356
WNIJ-FM 89.5 (NPR) 801 N 1st St *Web:* www.northernpublicradio.org	DeKalb	IL	60115	815-753-9000	753-9938
WNIO-AM 1390 (Nost) 7461 S Ave *Web:* www.wnio.com	Boardman	OH	44512	330-740-9300	729-9991
WNIU-FM 90.5 (Clas) 801 N 1st St *Web:* www.northernpublicradio.org	DeKalb	IL	60115	815-753-9000	753-9938
WNNH-FM 99.1 (Oldies) 501 S St	Bow	NH	03304	603-225-1160	
WNOG-AM 1270 (N/T) 2824 Palm Beach Blvd *Web:* www.tunein.com/radio/WNOG-1270-s21511	Fort Myers	FL	33916	239-479-5524	
WNOR-FM 98.7 (Rock) 870 Greenbrier Cir Suite 399 *Web:* www.fm99.com	Chesapeake	VA	23320	757-366-9900	366-0022
WNSN-FM 101.5 (AC) 1301 E Douglas Rd *Web:* www.sunny1015.com	Mishawaka	IN	46545	574-233-3141	239-4231
WNST-AM 1570 (Sports) 1550 Hart Rd *Web:* www.wnst.net	Towson	MD	21286	410-821-9678	828-4698
WNSX-FM 97.7 (AC) 409 High St	Ellsworth	ME	04605	207-667-0002	667-0627
WNUE-FM 98.1 (Span) 523 Douglas Ave *Web:* www.mega981.com	Altamonte Springs	FL	32714	407-331-1777	830-6223
WNWV-FM 107.3 (NAC) 538 W Broad St 4th Fl *Web:* www.wnwv.com	Elyria	OH	44036	440-322-3761	284-3189
WOCQ-FM 103.9 (CHR) 20200 DuPont Blvd *Web:* www.oc104.com	Georgetown	DE	19947	302-856-2567	856-7633
WODE-FM 99.9 107 Paxinosa Rd W *Web:* www.999thehawk.com	Easton	PA	18040	610-258-6155	253-3384
WOGG-FM 94.9 (Ctry) 123 Blaine Rd *TF:* 866-937-6449 ■ *Web:* www.froggyland.com	Brownsville	PA	15417	724-938-2000	938-7824
WOGH-FM 103.5 (Ctry) 320 Market St *Web:* www.froggyland.com	Steubenville	OH	43952	740-283-4747	283-3655
WOGL-FM 98.1 (Oldies) 2 Bala Plaza Suite 800 *TF:* 800-942-8998 ■ *Web:* wogl.radio.com	Bala Cynwyd	PA	19004	610-668-5900	667-1904
WOI-AM 640 (NPR) Iowa State University 2022 Communications Bldg *TF:* 800-861-8000 ■ *Web:* www.iowapublicradio.org	Ames	IA	50011	515-294-8603	294-1544
WOI-FM 90.1 (NPR) Iowa State University 2022 Communications Bldg *TF:* 800-861-8000 ■ *Web:* www.iowapublicradio.org	Ames	IA	50011	515-294-8603	294-1544
WOKO-FM 98.9 (Ctry) 70 Joy Dr *TF:* 800-354-9890 ■ *Web:* www.woko.com	South Burlington	VT	05403	802-658-1230	862-0786
WOKQ-FM 97.5 (Ctry) 292 Middle Rd PO Box 576 *Web:* www.wokq.com	Dover	NH	03821	603-749-9750	749-1459
WOKY-AM 920 (Oldies) 12100 W Howard Ave *Web:* www.am920woky.com	Greenfield	WI	53228	414-545-8900	546-9654
WOL-AM 1450 (N/T) 5900 Princess Garden Pkwy 8th Fl *Web:* www.wolam.com	Lanham	MD	20706	301-306-1111	306-9540
WOLC-FM 102.5 (Rel) 11890 Crisfield Ln PO Box 130 *TF:* 877-569-9652 ■ *Web:* www.wolc.org	Princess Anne	MD	21853	410-543-9652	651-9652
WOLZ-FM 95.3 (AC) 13320 Metro Pkwy Suite 1 *Web:* www.wolz.com	Fort Myers	FL	33966	239-225-4300	225-4410
WOMC-FM 104.3 (Oldies) 2201 Woodward Heights *Web:* www.womc.com	Ferndale	MI	48220	248-546-9600	546-5446
WOMP-AM 1290 (Sports) 56325 High Ridge Rd *Web:* www.wompam.com	Bellaire	OH	43906	740-676-5661	676-2742
WOND-AM 1400 (N/T) 1601 New Rd *Web:* www.1400wond.com	Linwood	NJ	08221	609-653-1400	601-0450
WONQ-AM 1030 (Span AC) 1355 E Altamonte Dr	Altamonte Springs	FL	32701	407-830-0800	260-6100
WORK-FM 107.1 (AC) 41 Jacques St *Web:* www.1071workfm.com	Barre	VT	05641	802-476-4168	479-5893
WOSM-FM 103.1 (Rel) 4720 Radio Rd	Ocean Springs	MS	39564	228-432-1032	875-6461
WPCV-FM 97.5 (Ctry) 404 W Lime St *TF:* 800-227-9797 ■ *Web:* www.wpcv.com	Lakeland	FL	33815	863-682-8184	683-2409
WPDX-FM 104.9 (Ctry) 59 Mountain Pk Dr *Web:* www.wpdxcountry.com	Whitehall	WV	26554	304-624-6425	363-3852
WPEN-AM 950 (Sports) 1 Bala Plaza Suite 339 *Web:* www.wpen.com	Bala Cynwyd	PA	19004	610-667-8500	664-9610
WPFB-FM 105.9 (Ctry) 4505 Central Ave *TF:* 888-723-4667 ■ *Web:* www.1059therebel.com	Middletown	OH	45044	513-422-3625	424-9732
WPGC-FM 95.5 (CHR) 4200 Parliament Pl Suite 300 *TF:* 877-955-5267 ■ *Web:* www.wpgc955.com	Lanham	MD	20706	301-918-0955	459-9557
WPHI-FM 100.3 (Urban) 1000 River Rd Suite 400 *TF:* 800-232-1003 ■ *Web:* www.1003thebeatphilly.com	Conshohocken	PA	19428	610-276-1100	276-1139
WPHT-AM 1210 (N/T) 2 Bala Plaza Suite 800 *Web:* www.thebigtalker1210.com	Bala Cynwyd	PA	19004	610-668-5800	668-5885
WPLK-AM 800 (Nost) 1428 St Johns Ave *Web:* www.wplk.com	Palatka	FL	32177	386-325-5800	328-8725
WPLM-FM 99.1 (AC) 17 Columbus Rd *TF:* 877-327-9991 ■ *Web:* www.easy991.com	Plymouth	MA	02360	508-746-1390	830-1128
WPLR-FM 99.1 (Rock) 440 Wheelers Farm Rd Suite 302 *Web:* wplr.com	Milford	CT	06461	203-783-8200	783-8399
WPMZ-AM 1110 (Span) 1270 Mineral Springs Ave	North Providence	RI	02904	401-726-8413	726-8649
WPOR-FM 101.9 (Ctry) 420 Western Ave *Web:* www.wpor.com	South Portland	ME	04106	207-774-4561	774-3788
WPRO-AM 630 (N/T) 1502 Wampanoag Trail *TF:* 800-321-9776 ■ *Web:* www.630wpro.com	East Providence	RI	02915	401-433-4200	433-5967
WPRO-FM 92.3 (CHR) 1502 Wampanoag Trail *TF:* 800-638-0092 ■ *Web:* www.92profm.com	East Providence	RI	02915	401-433-4200	433-5967
WPRS-FM 104.1 (Rel) 5900 Princess Garden Pkwy 8th FL	Lanham	MD	20706	301-306-1111	306-9540
WPST-FM 94.5 (AC) 619 Alexander Rd 3rd Fl *Web:* www.wpst.com	Princeton	NJ	08540	609-419-0300	419-0143
WPUR-FM 107.3 (Ctry) 950 Tilton Rd Suite 200 *Web:* www.catcountry1073.com	Northfield	NJ	08225	609-645-9797	272-9228
WPWX-FM 92.3 (Urban) 6336 Calumet Ave *Fax Area Code: 219 ■ *Web:* www.power92chicago.com	Hammond	IN	46324	773-734-4455	933-0323*
WPYX-FM 106.5 (CR) 1203 Troy-Schenectady Rd Suite 201 Riverhill Ctr *TF:* 877-476-1065 ■ *Web:* www.pyx106.com	Latham	NY	12110	518-452-4800	452-4813
WQAM-AM 560 (Sports) 20295 NW 2nd Ave 3rd Fl *Web:* www.wqam.com	Miami	FL	33169	305-653-6796	770-1456
WQBA-AM 1140 (N/T) 2601 S Bayshore Dr PH2	Coconut Grove	FL	33133	305-447-1140	441-2454
WQBK-FM 103.9 (Rock) 1241 Kings Rd *Web:* www.wqbk.com	Schenectady	NY	12303	518-881-1515	881-1516
WQBW-FM 97.3 (CR) 12100 W Howard Ave *Web:* www.973thebrew.com	Greenfield	WI	53228	414-545-8900	546-9654
WQCB-FM 106.5 (Ctry) 49 Acme Rd PO Box 100 *Web:* www.wqcb-fm.com	Brewer	ME	04412	207-989-5631	989-5685
WQFL-FM 100.9 (Rel) 5375 Pebble Creek Trail *Web:* www.101qfl.com	Loves Park	IL	61111	815-654-1200	282-7779
WQHQ-FM 104.7 (AC) 351 Tilghman Rd *TF:* 800-762-0105 ■ *Web:* www.q105fm.com	Salisbury	MD	21804	410-742-1923	742-2329

Station	City	State	Zip	Phone	Fax
WQJZ-FM 97.1 (NAC) 919 Ellegood St *Web:* www.wqjz.com	Salisbury	MD	21801	410-219-3500	548-1543
WQLZ-FM 92.7 (Rock) 1510 N 3rd St *Web:* www.wqlz.com	Riverton	IL	62561	217-629-7077	629-7952
WQTX-FM 92.1 (Oldies) 2495 N Cedar St *Web:* www.wqtx.net	Holt	MI	48842	517-699-0111	699-1880
WQUN-AM 1220 (Nost) 3085 Whitney Ave *Web:* www.quinnipiac.edu	Hamden	CT	06518	203-582-8984	582-5372
WQUT-FM 101.5 (CR) 162 Freehill Rd *Web:* www.wqut.com	Gray	TN	37615	423-477-1000	477-4747
WQXA-FM 105.7 (Rock) 515 S 32nd St *TF:* 800-932-0505 ■ *Web:* www.1057.com	Camp Hill	PA	17011	717-635-7000	635-7551
WRBR-FM 103.9 (Rock) 237 W Edison Rd *Web:* www.wrbr.com	Mishawaka	IN	46545	574-258-5483	258-0930
WRCH-FM 100.5 (AC) 10 Executive Dr *Web:* www.wrch.com	Farmington	CT	06032	860-677-6700	677-5483
WRDW-FM 96.5 (Urban) 555 City Line Ave Suite 330 *Web:* www.wired965.com	Bala Cynwyd	PA	19004	610-667-9000	667-2972
WRDX-FM 92.9 (CR) 920 W Basin Rd Suite 400 *Web:* www.wrdx.com	New Castle	DE	19720	302-395-9800	395-9808
WRFQ-FM 104.5 (CR) 950 Houston Northcutt Blvd Suite 201 *Web:* www.wrfq.com	Mount Pleasant	SC	29464	843-884-2534	884-1218
WRIT-FM 95.7 (CR) 12100 W Howard Ave *Web:* www.oldies957.com	Greenfield	WI	53228	414-545-8900	546-9654
WRKO-AM 680 (N/T) 20 Guest St 3rd Fl *TF:* 877-469-4322 ■ *Web:* www.wrko.com	Brighton	MA	02135	617-779-3400	779-5447
WROW-AM 590 (N/T) 6 Johnson Rd *Web:* www.wrow.com	Latham	NY	12110	518-786-6600	786-6610
WROZ-FM 101.3 (AC) 1996 Auction Rd *Web:* www.roseradio.com	Manheim	PA	17545	717-653-0800	653-0122
WRTO-FM 98.3 (Span) 2601 S Bayshore Dr PH2	Coconut Grove	FL	33133	305-447-1140	443-4701
WRVE-FM 99.5 (AC) 1203 Troy-Schenectady Rd Suite 201 Riverhill Ctr *TF:* 800-995-9783 ■ *Web:* www.wrve.com	Latham	NY	12110	518-452-4800	452-4855
WRVM-FM 102.7 (Rel) PO Box 212 *TF Cust Svc:* 888-225-9786 ■ *Web:* www.wrvm.org	Suring	WI	54174	920-842-2839	842-2704
WRZK-FM 95.9 (Alt) 222 Commerce St *Web:* www.wrzk.com	Kingsport	TN	37660	423-246-9578	247-9836
WSAN-AM 1470 (Sports) 1541 Alta Dr Suite 400 *Web:* www.fox1470.com	Whitehall	PA	18052	610-434-1742	434-6288
WSBY-FM 98.9 (Urban AC) 351 Tilghman Rd *TF:* 800-762-0105 ■ *Web:* www.wsby.com	Salisbury	MD	21804	410-742-1923	742-2329
WSCI-FM 89.3 (NPR) 1101 George Rogers Blvd *Web:* www.myetv.org/radio	Columbia	SC	29201	803-737-3545	737-3552
WSCL-FM 89.5 (NPR) PO Box 2596 *TF:* 800-543-6895 ■ *Web:* www.delmardapublicradio.net	Salisbury	MD	21802	410-543-6895	548-3000
WSEN-FM 92.1 (CR) 8456 Smokey Hollow Rd PO Box 1050 *Web:* www.wsenfm.com	Baldwinsville	NY	13027	315-635-3971	635-3490
WSGL-FM 104.7 (AC) 10915 K-Nine Dr *Web:* www.1047mixfm.com	Bonita Springs	FL	34135	239-495-8383	495-0883
WSHU-FM 91.1 (NPR) 83 Jefferson St *TF:* 800-937-6045 ■ *Web:* www.wshu.org	Fairfield	CT	06825	203-365-6604	371-7991
WSIC-AM 1400 (N/T) 1117 Radio Rd *Web:* www.wsicweb.com	Statesville	NC	28677	704-872-6348	873-6921
WSMK-FM 99.1 (Urban) 925 N 5th St *Web:* www.wsmkradio.com	Niles	MI	49120	269-683-4343	683-7759
WSMS-FM 99.9 (CR) 200 6th St N Suite 205 *TF:* 866-999-9767 ■ *Web:* www.999thefoxrocks.com	Columbus	MS	39701	662-327-1183	654-6510
WSRS-FM 96.1 (AC) 96 Stereo Ln *Web:* www.wsrs.com	Paxton	MA	01612	508-757-9696	757-1779
WSSX-FM 95.1 (CHR) 4230 Faber Pl Dr Suite 100 *TF:* 888-303-9579 ■ *Web:* www.95sx.com	North Charleston	SC	29405	843-277-1200	277-1212
WSTC-AM 1400 (N/T) 444 Westport Ave *Web:* wstcwnlk.com	Norwalk	CT	06851	203-845-3030	845-3097
WSYN-FM 103.1 11640 Hwy 17 Bypass	Murrells Inlet	SC	29576	843-651-1065	
WSYN-FM 106.5 (Oldies) 11640 Hwy 17 Bypass	Murrells Inlet	SC	29576	843-626-9103	
WTAG-AM 580 (N/T) 96 Stereo Ln *Web:* www.wtag.com	Paxton	MA	01612	508-795-0580	757-1779
WTAK-FM 106.1 (CR) 26869 Peoples Rd *Web:* www.wtak.com	Madison	AL	35756	256-309-2410	350-2653
WTAM-AM 1100 (N/T) 6200 Oak Tree Blvd S 4th Fl *Web:* www.wtam.com	Independence	OH	44131	216-520-2600	524-2600
WTFM-FM 98.5 (AC) 222 Commerce St *Web:* www.wtfm.com	Kingsport	TN	37660	423-246-9578	247-9836
WTHZ-FM 94.1 (AC) 200 Radio Dr *Web:* majic941.com	Lexington	NC	27292	336-248-2716	248-2800
WTIC-AM 1080 (N/T) 10 Executive Dr *Web:* www.wtic.com	Farmington	CT	06032	860-677-6700	284-9842
WTIC-FM 96.5 (AC) 10 Executive Dr *Web:* www.ticfm.com	Farmington	CT	06032	860-677-6700	284-9650
WTIX-FM 94.3 (Oldies) 4539 N I-10 Service Rd 3rd Fl *TF:* 877-398-9849 ■ *Web:* www.wtixfm.com	Metairie	LA	70006	504-454-9000	454-9002
WTJK-AM 1380 (Sports) 1 Parker Pl Suite 485 *Web:* www.espn1380.com	Janesville	WI	53545	608-758-9025	758-9550
WTKE-FM 98.1 (Sports) 21 Miracle Strip Pkwy *TF:* 877-981-0981 ■ *Web:* www.sportstalktheticket.com	Fort Walton Beach	FL	32548	850-244-1400	243-1471
WTKU-FM 98.3 (Oldies) 1601 New Rd *Web:* www.kool983.com	Linwood	NJ	08221	609-653-1400	601-0450
WTKZ-AM 1320 (Sports) 107 Paxinosa Rd W *Web:* www.espnlv.com	Easton	PA	18040	610-258-6155	253-3384

Station	City	State	Zip	Phone	Fax
WTLN-AM 950 (Rel) 1188 Lakeview Dr *Web:* www.wtln.com	Altamonte Springs	FL	32714	407-682-9494	682-7005
WTMA-AM 1250 (N/T) 4230 Faber Pl Dr Suite 100 *Web:* www.wtma.com	North Charleston	SC	29405	843-277-1200	277-1212
WTMD-FM 89.7 (AAA) 8000 York Rd Towson University *Web:* wwwnew.towson.edu	Towson	MD	21252	410-704-8938	704-2609
WTPL-FM 107.7 (N/T) 501 S St 3rd Fl *Web:* www.wtplfm.com	Bow	NH	03304	603-545-0777	545-0781
WTQR-FM 104.1 (Ctry) 2-B PAI Pk *Web:* www.wtqr.com	Greensboro	NC	27409	336-822-2000	887-0104
WTRY-FM 98.3 (Oldies) 1203 Troy-Schenectady Rd Suite 201 Riverhill Ctr *Web:* www.wtry.com	Latham	NY	12110	518-452-4800	452-4855
WTSR-FM 91.3 (Alt) College of New Jersey Kendall Hall PO Box 7718 *Web:* www.wtsr.org	Ewing	NJ	08628	609-771-3200	637-5113
WTSS-FM 102.5 (AC) 500 Corporate Pkwy Suite 200 *Web:* www.mystar1025.com	Amherst	NY	14226	716-843-0600	832-3080
WTSU-FM 89.9 (NPR) Troy University Wallace Hall *TF:* 800-800-6616	Troy	AL	36082	334-670-3268	670-3934
WTTH-FM 96.1 (Urban) 8025 Black Horse Pike Suite 100 *Web:* www.961wtth.com	Pleasantville	NJ	08232	609-484-8444	646-6331
WTTS-FM 92.3 (AAA) 400 One City Centre *TF:* 800-923-9887 ■ *Web:* www.wttsfm.com	Bloomington	IN	47404	812-332-3366	331-4570
WTWR-FM 98.3 (CHR) 14930 LaPlaisance Rd Suite 113 *TF:* 888-578-0098 ■ *Web:* www.tower983.com	Monroe	MI	48161	734-242-6600	242-6599
WTZR-FM 99.3 (Alt) 901 E Valley Dr *TF:* 866-770-7625 ■ *Web:* www.zrock993.com	Bristol	VA	24201	276-669-8112	669-0541
WUFM-FM 88.7 (Rel) 116 County Line Rd W *Web:* www.radiou.com	Westerville	OH	43082	614-890-9977	839-1329
WUMP-AM 730 (Sports) 1717 Hwy 72 E *TF:* 866-485-9867 ■ *Web:* www.730ump.com	Athens	AL	35611	256-830-8300	232-6842
WUNC-FM 91.5 (NPR) University of N Carolina PO Box 0915 *TF:* 800-962-9862 ■ *Web:* www.wunc.org	Chapel Hill	NC	27599	919-966-5454	
WUSJ-FM 96.3 (Ctry) 265 Highpoint Dr *Web:* www.us963.com	Ridgeland	MS	39157	601-956-0102	978-3980
WUSL-FM 99 (Urban) 111 Presidential Blvd Suite 100 *Web:* www.power99.com	Bala Cynwyd	PA	19004	610-784-3333	784-2075
WVBZ-FM 100.3 (Rock) 2-B PAI Park *Web:* www.buzzardrocks.com	Greensboro	NC	27409	336-822-2000	887-0104
WVCH-AM 740 (Rel) PO Box A *Web:* www.wvch.com	Brookhaven	PA	19015	610-872-8861	872-8865
WVFJ-FM 93.3 (Rel) 120 Peachtree E Shopping Ctr *Web:* www.j933.com	Peachtree City	GA	30269	770-487-4500	486-6400
WVIA-FM 89.9 (NPR) 100 WVIA Way *Web:* www.wvia.org	Pittston	PA	18640	570-826-6144	655-1180
WVMV-FM 98.7 (NAC) 26495 American Dr *Web:* www.v987.com	Southfield	MI	48034	248-455-7200	455-7369
WVNI-FM 95.1 (Rel) PO Box 1628 *Web:* www.spirit95fm.com	Bloomington	IN	47402	812-335-9500	335-8880
WVNN-AM 770 (N/T) 1717 Hwy 72 E *TF:* 866-494-9866 ■ *Web:* www.wvnn.com	Athens	AL	35611	256-830-8300	232-6842
WVPE-FM 88.1 (NPR) 2424 California Rd *TF:* 888-399-9873 ■ *Web:* www.wvpe.org	Elkhart	IN	46514	574-262-5660	262-5700
WVPS-FM 107.9 (NPR) 365 Troy Ave *TF:* 800-639-2192 ■ *Web:* www.vpr.net	Colchester	VT	05446	802-655-9451	655-2799
WVRB-FM 95.3 (Rel) 700 Lemons Mill Rd *TF:* 888-937-2471 ■ *Web:* www.air1.com	Georgetown	KY	40324	502-868-8879	868-9979
WWBN-FM 101.5 (Rock) 3338 E Bristol Rd *Web:* banana1015.com	Burton	MI	48529	810-743-1080	742-5170
WWDC-FM 101.1 (Rock) 1801 Rockville Pike 5th Fl **Fax Area Code:* 301 ■ *TF:* 866-913-2101 ■ *Web:* www.dc101.com	Rockville	MD	20852	240-747-2700	587-0225*
WWDE-FM 101.3 (AC) 236 Clearfield Ave Suite 206 *Web:* www.2wd.com	Virginia Beach	VA	23462	757-497-2000	456-5458
WWFG-FM 99.9 (Ctry) 351 Tilghman Rd *TF:* 800-664-3764 ■ *Web:* www.froggy999.com/main.html	Salisbury	MD	21804	410-742-1923	742-2329
WWFY-FM 100.9 (Ctry) 41 Jacques St *Web:* www.froggy1009.com	Barre	VT	05641	802-476-4168	479-5893
WWGR-FM 101.9 (Ctry) 10915 K-Nine Dr *TF:* 877-787-1019 ■ *Web:* www.gatorcountry1019.com	Bonita Springs	FL	34135	239-495-8383	495-0883
WWJ-AM 950 (N/T) 26495 American Dr *Web:* wwj.com	Southfield	MI	48034	248-455-7200	304-4970
WWKA-FM 92.3 (Ctry) 4192 N John Young Pkwy *TF:* 800-749-9292 ■ *Web:* k92fm.com	Orlando	FL	32804	407-298-9292	299-4947
WWKB-AM 1520 (Oldies) 500 Corporate Pkwy Suite 200 *Web:* kb1520.com	Amherst	NY	14226	716-843-0600	832-3080
WWKX-FM 106.3 (Urban) 1502 Wampanoag Trail *TF:* 888-224-1063 ■ *Web:* www.hot1063.com	East Providence	RI	02915	401-433-4200	433-5967
WWLI-FM 105.1 (AC) 1502 Wampanoag Trail *Web:* www.lite105.com	East Providence	RI	02915	401-433-4200	433-5967
WWMJ-FM 95.7 (CR) 49 Acme Rd PO Box 100 *Web:* www.wwmj-fm.com	Brewer	ME	04412	207-989-5631	989-5685
WWRV-AM 1330 (Span Rel) 419 Broadway *Web:* www.radiovision.net	Paterson	NJ	07501	973-881-8700	881-8324
WWTC-AM 1280 (N/T) 2110 Cliff Rd *Web:* www.am1280thepatriot.com	Eagan	MN	55122	651-405-8800	405-8222
WWUS-FM 104.1 (CR) 30336 Overseas Hwy *Web:* www.us1radio.com	Big Pine Key	FL	33043	305-872-9100	872-1603

Station	City	State	ZIP	Phone	Fax
WWWS-AM 1400 (Urban) 500 Corporate Pkwy Suite 200 *Web:* www.am1400solidgoldsoul.com	Amherst	NY	14226	716-843-0600	832-3080
WWWZ-FM 93.3 (Urban) 4230 Faber Pl Dr Suite 100 *Web:* www.z93jamz.com	North Charleston	SC	29405	843-277-1200	277-1212
WXBM-FM 102.7 (Ctry) 6085 Quintette Rd *TF:* 800-626-9926 ■ *Web:* www.wxbm.com	Pace	FL	32571	850-994-5357	994-4169
WXBQ-FM 96.9 (Ctry) 901 E Valley Dr PO Box 1389 *TF:* 800-332-3697 ■ *Web:* www.wxbq.com	Bristol	VA	24201	276-669-8112	669-0541
WXCY-FM 103.7 (Ctry) 707 Revolution St *Web:* www.wxcyfm.com	Havre de Grace	MD	21078	410-939-1100	939-1104
WXGM-FM 99.1 (AC) PO Box 634	Gloucester	VA	23061	804-693-9946	693-2182
WXHB-FM 96.5 (Rel) 4580 Hwy 15 N PO Box 6408 *Web:* www.solidgospel.com	Laurel	MS	39441	601-649-0095	649-8199
WXIS-FM 103.9 (Urban) 101 Riverview Rd *TF:* 866-923-1039 ■ *Web:* www.jammin9231039.com	Erwin	TN	37650	423-743-6123	743-6122
WXJN-FM 105.9 (Ctry) PO Box 909 *Web:* www.catcountryradio.com	Salisbury	MD	21801	410-219-3500	
WXKB-FM 103.9 (CHR) 20125 S Tamiami Trail *Web:* www.b1039.com	Estero	FL	33928	239-495-2100	948-0785
WXKS-FM 107.9 (CHR) 10 Cabot Rd *Web:* www.kiss108.com	Medford	MA	02155	781-396-1430	290-0722
WXKU-FM 92.7 (Ctry) PO Box 806	Seymour	IN	47274	812-522-1390	522-9541
WXLY-FM 102.5 (Oldies) 950 Houston Northcutt Blvd Suite 201 *Web:* www.wxly.com	Mount Pleasant	SC	29464	843-884-2534	884-1218
WXRL-AM 1300 (Ctry) 5426 Williams St PO Box 170 *Web:* www.wxrl.com	Lancaster	NY	14086	716-681-1313	681-7172
WXRR-FM 104.5 (Rock) 4580 Hwy 15 N PO Box 6408 *Web:* www.rock104fm.com	Laurel	MS	39441	601-649-0095	649-8199
WXRV-FM 92.5 (AAA) 30 How St *Web:* www.wxrv.com	Haverhill	MA	01830	978-374-4733	373-8023
WXSS-FM 103.7 (CHR) 11800 W Grange Ave *Web:* www.1037kissfm.com	Hales Corners	WI	53130	414-529-1250	529-2122
WXTU-FM 92.5 (Ctry) 555 City Line Ave Suite 330 *Web:* www.wxtu.com	Bala Cynwyd	PA	19004	610-667-9000	667-5978
WXXL-FM 106.7 (CHR) 2500 Maitland Ctr Pkwy Suite 401 *Web:* www.wxxl106.7.com	Maitland	FL	32751	407-916-7800	916-7406
WXXX-FM 95.5 (CHR) 118 Malletts Bay Ave *Web:* www.95triplex.com	Colchester	VT	05446	802-655-9550	655-1329
WXYT-AM 1270 (Sports) 31555 W 14 Mile Rd Suite 102	Farmington Hills	MI	48334	248-855-5100	855-1302
WXYT-FM 97.1 (Sports) 31555 W 14 Mile Rd Suite 102 *Web:* www.wxyt.com	Farmington Hills	MI	48334	248-855-5100	855-1302
WYCB-AM 1340 (Rel) 5900 Princess Garden Pkwy 8th Fl *Web:* www.wycb1340.com	Lanham	MD	20706	301-306-1111	306-9540
WYCR-FM 98.5 (AC) 275 Radio Rd *Web:* www.98ycr.com	Hanover	PA	17331	717-637-3831	637-9006
WYCS-FM 91.5 (Rel) 7330 George Washington Memorial Hwy Bldg J	Yorktown	VA	23692	757-886-7490	
WYGM-AM 740 (Span) 2500 Maitland Ctr Pkwy Suite 401 *TF:* 800-729-8255 ■ *Web:* www.740thegame.com	Maitland	FL	32751	407-916-7800	916-7406
WYJB-FM 95.5 (AC) 6 Johnson Rd *Web:* www.b95.com	Latham	NY	12110	518-786-6600	786-6610
WYJK-FM 100.5 (Var) 56325 High Ridge Rd *Web:* www.wyjkfm.com	Bellaire	OH	43906	740-676-5661	676-2742
WYNZ-FM 100.9 (Oldies) 420 Western Ave *Web:* www.wynz.com	South Portland	ME	04106	207-774-4561	774-3788
WYOY-FM 101.7 (CHR) 265 Highpoint Dr *Web:* www.y101.com	Ridgeland	MS	39157	601-956-0102	978-3980
WYUS-AM 930 (Span) 1666 Blairs Pond Rd *Web:* www.wyusam.com	Milford	DE	19963	302-422-7575	422-3069
WZBA-FM 100.7 (CR) 11350 McCormick Rd Executive Plaza 3 Suite 701 *Web:* www.wzbathebay.com	Hunt Valley	MD	21031	410-771-8484	771-1616
WZBC-FM 90.3 (Var) Boston College 107 McElroy Commons *Web:* www.wzbc.org	Chestnut Hill	MA	02467	617-552-3511	552-1738
WZBH-FM 93.5 (Rock) 20200 DuPont Blvd *TF:* 800-234-9350 ■ *Web:* www.max925.com	Georgetown	DE	19947	302-856-2567	856-7633
WZBT-FM 91.1 (Alt) 300 N Washington St Gettysburg College	Gettysburg	PA	17325	717-337-7288	
WZEB-FM 101.7 (AC) 20200 DuPont Blvd *TF:* 800-595-7525 ■ *Web:* www.musicontheb.com	Georgetown	DE	19947	302-856-2567	856-7633
WZLX-FM 100.7 (CR) 83 Leo Birmingham Pkwy *Web:* www.wzlx.com	Brighton	MA	02135	617-746-5100	746-5105
WZMX-FM 93.7 (Urban) 10 Executive Dr *Web:* www.hot937.com	Farmington	CT	06032	860-677-6700	674-8427
WZOC-FM 94.3 (Oldies) 112 W Washington St *TF:* 888-943-6539	Plymouth	IN	46563	574-936-4096	936-6776
WZTK-FM 101.1 (N/T) 1109 Tower Dr *TF:* 866-482-1011 ■ *Web:* www.fmtalk1011.com	Burlington	NC	27215	336-584-0126	584-0739
WZXL-FM 100.7 (Rock) 8025 Black Horse Pike Suite 100 *Web:* www.wzxl.com	West Atlantic City	NJ	08232	609-484-8444	646-6331
WZYP-FM 104.3 (CHR) 1717 Hwy 72 E *TF:* 866-476-1043 ■ *Web:* www.wzyp.net	Athens	AL	35611	256-830-8300	232-6842
WZZO-FM 95.1 (Rock) 1541 Alta Dr Suite 400 *Web:* www.wzzo.com	Whitehall	PA	18052	610-434-1742	434-6288
WZZR-FM 94.3 (N/T) 3771 SE Jennings Rd *TF:* 877-927-6969 ■ *Web:* www.wzzr.com	Port Saint Lucie	FL	34952	772-335-9300	335-3291
XLTN-FM 104.5 (Span AC) 2403 Hoover Ave *Web:* www.1045radiolatina.com	National City	CA	91950	619-336-7800	420-1092

648-1 Abilene, TX

Station	City	State	ZIP	Phone	Fax
KACU-FM 89.7 (NPR) ACU PO Box 27820 *Web:* www.kacu.org	Abilene	TX	79699	325-674-2441	674-2417
KBCY-FM 99.7 (Ctry) 2525 S Danville Dr *Web:* www.kbcy.com	Abilene	TX	79605	325-793-9700	692-1576
KCDD-FM 103.7 (CHR) 2525 S Danville Dr *Web:* www.power103.com	Abilene	TX	79605	325-793-9700	692-1576
KEAN-FM 105.1 (Ctry) 3911 S 1st St *TF:* 800-588-5326 ■ *Web:* www.keanradio.com	Abilene	TX	79605	325-676-7711	676-3851
KEYJ-FM 107.9 (Rock) 3911 S 1st St *Web:* www.keyj.com	Abilene	TX	79605	325-676-7711	676-3851
KFGL-FM 100.7 (Oldies) 3911 S 1st St *Web:* trueoldiesabilene.com	Abilene	TX	79605	325-676-5100	676-3851
KGNZ-FM 88.1 (Rel) 542 Butternut St *TF:* 800-588-8801 ■ *Web:* www.kgnz.com	Abilene	TX	79602	325-673-3045	672-7938
KGXL-FM 96.1 (Var) 1740 N 1st St *Web:* www.myxl96.com	Abilene	TX	79603	325-437-9596	673-1819
KHXS-FM 102.7 (CR) 2525 S Danville Dr *Web:* www.102thebear.com	Abilene	TX	79605	325-793-9700	692-1576
KKHR-FM 106.3 (Span) 402 Cypress St Suite 510 *Web:* www.radioabilene.com	Abilene	TX	79601	325-672-5442	672-6128
KORQ-FM 95.1 (CHR) 1740 N 1st St *Web:* www.95q.fm	Abilene	TX	79603	325-437-9596	673-1819
KTLT-FM 98.1 (Alt) 2525 S Danville Dr *Web:* www.98thelight.com	Abilene	TX	79605	325-793-9700	692-1576
KULL-FM 92.5 (Oldies) 3911 S 1st St *TF:* 800-659-1965 ■ *Web:* mymix92.com	Abilene	TX	79605	325-676-7711	676-3851
KZQQ-AM 1560 (Sports) 402 Cypress St Suite 510 *Web:* www.radioabilene.com	Abilene	TX	79601	325-673-1455	672-6128

648-2 Akron, OH

Station	City	State	ZIP	Phone	Fax
WAKR-AM 1590 (N/T) 1795 W Market St *TF:* 800-994-9973 ■ *Web:* www.wakr.net	Akron	OH	44313	330-869-9800	864-6799
WAPS-FM 91.3 (AAA) 65 Steiner Ave *Web:* www.913thesummit.com	Akron	OH	44301	330-761-3099	761-3103
WNIR-FM 100.1 (N/T) PO Box 2170 *Web:* www.wnir.com	Akron	OH	44309	330-673-2323	673-0301
WONE-FM 97.5 (Rock) 1795 W Market St *TF:* 800-994-9973 ■ *Web:* www.wone.net	Akron	OH	44313	330-869-9800	864-6799
WQMX-FM 94.9 (Ctry) 1795 W Market St *TF:* 800-994-9973 ■ *Web:* www.wqmx.com	Akron	OH	44313	330-869-9800	864-6799
WZIP-FM 88.1 (Rock) 302 E Buchtel Ave *Web:* www.wzip.fm	Akron	OH	44325	330-972-7105	972-5521

648-3 Albany, NY

Station	City	State	ZIP	Phone	Fax
WAMC-FM 90.3 (NPR) 318 Central Ave *TF:* 800-323-9262 ■ *Web:* www.wamc.org	Albany	NY	12206	518-465-5233	432-6974
WCDB-FM 90.9 (Var) 1400 Washington Ave SUNY Campus Ctr Rm 316 *Web:* www.wcdbfm.com	Albany	NY	12222	518-442-5234	442-4366

648-4 Albuquerque, NM

Station	City	State	ZIP	Phone	Fax
KABG-FM 98.5 (Oldies) 4125 Carlisle Ave NE *Web:* www.bigoldies.net	Albuquerque	NM	87107	505-878-0980	889-0619
KAGM-FM 106.3 (Ctry) 4125 Carlisle Blvd NE *Web:* www.1063therange.com	Albuquerque	NM	87107	505-878-0980	889-0619
KANW-FM 89.1 (NPR) 2020 Coal Ave SE *Web:* www.kanw.com	Albuquerque	NM	87106	505-242-7163	
KBQI-FM 107.9 (Ctry) 5411 Jefferson St NE Suite 100 *Web:* www.bigi1079.com	Albuquerque	NM	87109	505-830-6400	830-6543
KHFM-FM 95.5 (Clas) 4125 Carlisle Blvd NE *Web:* www.classicalkhfm.com	Albuquerque	NM	87107	505-878-0980	889-0619
KKOB-AM 770 (N/T) 500 4th St NW Suite 500 *Web:* 770kkob.com	Albuquerque	NM	87102	505-767-6700	767-6767
KKOB-FM 93.3 (AC) 500 4th St NW Suite 500 *Web:* www.kobfm.com	Albuquerque	NM	87102	505-767-6700	767-6767
KKSS-FM 97.3 (CHR) 8009 Marble Ave NE *Web:* www.mykiss973.com	Albuquerque	NM	87110	505-262-1142	254-7108
KMGA-FM 99.5 (AC) 500 4th St NW Suite 500 *Web:* www.995magicfm.com	Albuquerque	NM	87102	505-767-6700	767-6767
KNML-AM 610 (Sports) 500 4th St NW Suite 500 *TF:* 888-922-0610 ■ *Web:* www.610thesportsanimal.com	Albuquerque	NM	87102	505-767-6700	767-6767
KRST-FM 92.3 (Ctry) 500 4th St NW Suite 500 *Web:* www.92.3krst.com	Albuquerque	NM	87102	505-767-6700	767-6767

	City	State	ZIP	Phone	Fax
KUNM-FM 89.9 (NPR) 1University of New Mexico MSC 06 3520 *Web:* www.kunm.org	Albuquerque	NM	87131	505-277-4806	277-6393
KZRR-FM 94.1 (Rock) 5411 Jefferson St NE Suite 100 *Web:* www.94rock.com	Albuquerque	NM	87109	505-830-6400	830-6543

648-5 Allentown, PA

	City	State	ZIP	Phone	Fax
WHOL-AM 1600 (Span) 1125 Colorado St **Fax Area Code:* 484 ■ *Web:* www.whol1600.com	Allentown	PA	18103	610-434-4801	223-0088*

648-6 Amarillo, TX

	City	State	ZIP	Phone	Fax
KACV-FM 89.9 (Alt) 2408 S Jackson St *TF:* 800-766-0176 ■ *Web:* www.kacvfm.org	Amarillo	TX	79109	806-371-5228	371-5258
KARX-FM 95.7 (CR) 301 S Polk St Suite 100 *Web:* www.karx.com	Amarillo	TX	79101	806-342-5200	342-5202
KATP-FM 101.9 (Ctry) 6214 W 34th St *Web:* www.katcountry1019.com	Amarillo	TX	79109	806-355-9777	355-5832
KBZD-FM 99.7 (Span) 3639 Wolflin Ave.	Amarillo	TX	79102	806-355-1044	457-0642
KGNC-AM 710 (N/T) 3505 Olsen Blvd Suite 117 *TF:* 800-285-0710 ■ *Web:* www.kgncam.com	Amarillo	TX	79109	806-355-9801	354-8779
KGNC-FM 97.9 (Ctry) 3505 Olsen Blvd Suite 117 *TF:* 877-765-9790 ■ *Web:* www.kgncfm.com	Amarillo	TX	79109	806-355-9801	354-8779
KIXZ-AM 940 (News) 6214 W 34th St. *Web:* www.newsradio940.com	Amarillo	TX	79109	806-355-9777	355-5832
KMXJ-FM 94.1 (AC) 6214 W 34th St *Web:* www.mix941kmxj.com	Amarillo	TX	79109	806-355-9777	355-5832
KPRF-FM 98.7 (CHR) 6214 W 34th St *TF:* 866-930-5225 ■ *Web:* 987jackfm.com	Amarillo	TX	79109	806-355-9777	
KPUR-FM 107.1 (Oldies) 301 S Polk St Suite 100 *Web:* www.kpur107.com	Amarillo	TX	79101	806-342-5200	342-5202
KQIZ-FM 93.1 (CHR) 301 S Polk St Suite 100 *Web:* www.931thebeat.com	Amarillo	TX	79101	806-342-5200	342-5202
KXSS-FM 96.9 (CHR) 6214 W 34th St. *Web:* www.969kmml.com	Amarillo	TX	79109	806-355-9777	355-5832
KZRK-FM 107.9 (Rock) 301 S Polk St Suite 100 *Web:* www.amarillosrockstation.com	Amarillo	TX	79101	806-342-5200	342-5202

648-7 Anchorage, AK

	City	State	ZIP	Phone	Fax
KASH-FM 107.5 (Ctry) 800 E Dimond Blvd Suite 3-370 *Web:* www.kash1075.com	Anchorage	AK	99515	907-522-1515	743-5186
KATB-FM 89.3 (Rel) 6401 E Northern Lights Blvd. *Web:* www.katb.org	Anchorage	AK	99504	907-333-5282	333-9851
KBBO-FM 92.1 (AC) 833 Gambell St. *Web:* www.921bob.fm	Anchorage	AK	99501	907-344-4045	522-6053
KBFX-FM 100.5 (CR) 800 E Dimond Blvd Suite 3-370 *Web:* www.1005thefox.com	Anchorage	AK	99515	907-522-1515	743-5186
KBRJ-FM 104.1 (Ctry) 301 Arctic Slope Ave Suite 200 *Web:* www.kbrj.com	Anchorage	AK	99518	907-344-9622	349-3299
KDBZ-FM 102.1 (AC) 833 Gambell St. *Web:* www.buzz1021.com	Anchorage	AK	99501	907-344-4045	522-6053
KEAG-FM 97.3 (Oldies) 301 Arctic Slope Ave Suite 200 *Web:* www.kool973.com	Anchorage	AK	99518	907-344-9622	349-3299
KENI-AM 650 (N/T) 800 E Dimond Blvd Suite 3-370 *Web:* www.650keni.com	Anchorage	AK	99515	907-522-1515	743-5186
KFAT-FM 92.9 (Urban) 833 Gambell. *Web:* www.kfat929.com	Anchorage	AK	99501	907-344-4045	522-6053
KFQD-AM 750 (N/T) 301 Arctic Slope Ave Suite 200 *Web:* www.kfqd.com	Anchorage	AK	99518	907-344-9622	344-0742
KGOT-FM 101.3 (CHR) 800 E Dimond Blvd Suite 3-370 *Web:* www.kgot.com	Anchorage	AK	99515	907-272-5945	743-5183
KHAR-AM 590 (Nost) 301 Arctic Slope Ave Suite 200 *TF:* 800-896-1669 ■ *Web:* www.khar590.com	Anchorage	AK	99518	907-344-9622	349-7326
KLEF-FM 98.1 (Clas) 4700 Business Pk Blvd Suite 44-A *Web:* www.klef.com	Anchorage	AK	99503	907-561-5556	562-4219
KMXS-FM 103.1 (AC) 301 Arctic Slope Ave *Web:* www.kmxs.com	Anchorage	AK	99518	907-344-9622	344-1276
KNBA-FM 90.3 (NPR) 3600 San Geronimo Dr Suite 480 *TF:* 888-278-5622 ■ *Web:* www.knba.org	Anchorage	AK	99508	907-793-3500	793-3536
KNIK-FM 105.7 (NAC) 4700 Business Park Blvd Bldg E Suite 44A *Web:* www.knik.com	Anchorage	AK	99503	907-522-1018	522-1027
KSKA-FM 91.1 (NPR) 3877 University Dr *Web:* www.kska.org	Anchorage	AK	99508	907-550-8400	550-8403
KWHL-FM 106.5 (Rock) 301 Arctic Slope Ave *Web:* www.kwhl.com	Anchorage	AK	99518	907-344-9622	344-0742
KXLW-FM 96.3 (Rock) 833 Gambell St. *Web:* www.963thewolf.com	Anchorage	AK	99501	907-344-4045	522-6053
KYMG-FM 98.9 (AC) 800 E Dimond Blvd Suite 3-370 *Web:* www.magic989fm.com	Anchorage	AK	99515	907-522-1515	743-5186

648-8 Ann Arbor, MI

	City	State	ZIP	Phone	Fax
WCBN-FM 88.3 (Alt) University of Michigan 530 Student Activities Bldg. *Web:* wcbn.org	Ann Arbor	MI	48109	734-763-3500	647-4127
WFUM-FM 91.1 (NPR) 535 W William St Suite 110 *TF:* 800-728-9386 ■ *Web:* www.michiganradio.org	Ann Arbor	MI	48103	734-764-9210	647-3488
WQKL-FM 107.1 (AC) 1100 Victors Way Suite 100 *Web:* www.annarbors107one.com	Ann Arbor	MI	48108	734-302-8100	213-7508
WTKA-AM 1050 (N/T) 1100 Victors Way Suite 100 *TF:* 800-559-2657 ■ *Web:* www.wtka.com	Ann Arbor	MI	48108	734-302-8100	213-7508
WUOM-FM 91.7 (NPR) 535 W William St Suite 110 *Web:* www.michiganradio.org	Ann Arbor	MI	48103	734-764-9210	647-3488
WWWW-FM 102.9 (Ctry) 1100 Victors Way Suite 100 *Web:* www.w4country.com	Ann Arbor	MI	48108	734-302-8100	213-7508

648-9 Annapolis, MD

	City	State	ZIP	Phone	Fax
WBIS-AM 1190 (N/T) 1610 W St Suite 209 *Web:* www.wbis1190.com	Annapolis	MD	21401	410-269-0700	
WFSI-FM 107.9 (Rel) 918 Chesapeake Ave *Web:* www.familyradio.com	Annapolis	MD	21403	410-268-6200	268-0931
WNAV-AM 1430 (AC) PO Box 6726. *Web:* www.wnav.com	Annapolis	MD	21401	410-263-1430	268-5360
WRNR-FM 103.1 (AAA) 112 Main St 3rd Fl *Web:* www.wrnr.com	Annapolis	MD	21401	410-626-0103	267-7634

648-10 Asheville, NC

	City	State	ZIP	Phone	Fax
News Radio 570 WWNC 13 Summerlin Rd *Web:* www.880therevolution.com	Asheville	NC	28806	828-257-2700	255-7850
WCQS-FM 88.1 (NPR) 73 Broadway *TF:* 800-768-6698 ■ *Web:* www.wcqs.org	Asheville	NC	28801	828-210-4800	210-4801
WISE-AM 1310 (Sports) 1190 Patton Ave *Web:* www.1310bigwise.com	Asheville	NC	28806	828-259-9695	253-5619
WKJV-AM 1380 (Rel) 70 Adams Hill Rd *TF:* 800-809-9558 ■ *Web:* www.wkjv.com	Asheville	NC	28806	828-252-1380	259-9427
WKSF-FM 99.9 (Ctry) 13 Summerlin Rd. *TF:* 800-303-5477 ■ *Web:* www.99kisscountry.com	Asheville	NC	28806	828-257-2700	255-7850
WSKY-AM 1230 (Rel) 40 Westgate Pkwy Suite F *Web:* www.wilkinsradio.com	Asheville	NC	28806	828-251-2000	251-2135
WWNC-AM 570 (N/T) 13 Summerlin Rd *Web:* www.wwnc.com	Asheville	NC	28806	828-257-2700	255-7850

648-11 Atlanta, GA

	City	State	ZIP	Phone	Fax
WABE-FM 90.1 (NPR) 740 Bismark Rd NE *Web:* www.wabe.org	Atlanta	GA	30324	678-686-0321	686-0356
WACG-FM 90.7 (NPR) 260 14th St NW. *TF:* 800-222-4788 ■ *Web:* www.gpb.org/gpr	Atlanta	GA	30318	404-685-2690	685-2684
WALR-FM 104.1 (AC) 1601 W Peachtree St NE *Web:* www.kiss1041fm.com	Atlanta	GA	30309	404-897-7500	897-6495
WAMJ-FM 102.5 (Urban) 101 Marietta St 12th Fl *Web:* www.1025atlanta.com	Atlanta	GA	30303	404-765-9750	688-7686
WAOK-AM 1380 (N/T) 1201 Peachtree St NE Suite 800 *Web:* www.waok.com	Atlanta	GA	30361	404-898-8900	898-8909
WBTS-FM 95.5 (Urban) 1601 W Peachtree St *Web:* www.955thebeat.com	Atlanta	GA	30309	404-897-7500	876-7363
WCLK-FM 91.9 (Jazz) 111 James P Brawley Dr SW *Web:* www.wclk.com	Atlanta	GA	30314	404-880-8273	880-8869
WFSH-FM 104.7 (Rel) 2970 Peachtree Rd NW Suite 700. *Web:* www.thefishatlanta.com	Atlanta	GA	30305	404-995-7300	816-0748
WGST-AM 640 (N/T) 1819 Peachtree Rd NE Suite 700 *Web:* www.wgst.com	Atlanta	GA	30309	404-367-0640	367-1057
WHTA-FM 107.9 (Urban) 101 Marietta St 12th Fl. *Web:* www.hot1079atl.com	Atlanta	GA	30303	404-765-9750	688-7686
WJSP-FM 88.1 (NPR) 260 14th St NW *TF:* 800-222-4788 ■ *Web:* www.gpb.org/gpr	Atlanta	GA	30318	404-685-2400	685-2684
WJZZ-FM 107.5 (Jazz) 101 Marietta St 12th Fl. *Web:* www.1075wjzz.com	Atlanta	GA	30303	404-765-9750	688-7686
WKHX-FM 101.5 (Ctry) 210 I-North Pkwy 6th Fl *Web:* www.wkhx.com	Atlanta	GA	30339	404-521-1015	
WNNX-FM 99.7 (Alt) 780 Johnson Ferry Rd NE 5th Fl. *Web:* www.99x.com	Atlanta	GA	30342	404-497-4700	497-4735
WPZE-FM 97.5 (Rel) 101 Marietta St 12th Fl *Web:* www.praise975.com	Atlanta	GA	30303	404-765-9750	688-7686
WQXI-AM 790 (Sports) 3350 Peachtree Rd NE Suite 1610 *Web:* www.wqxi.com	Atlanta	GA	30326	404-237-0079	231-5923

				Phone	Fax
WRAS *Georgia State University* 33 Gilmer St MSC 2A1220 *Web:* www2.gsu.edu	Atlanta	GA	30303	404-651-3504	
WRFG-FM 89.3 (Var) 1083 Austin Ave NE *Web:* www.wrfg.org	Atlanta	GA	30307	404-523-3471	523-8990
WSB-AM 750 (N/T) 1601 W Peachtree St NE *Web:* www.wsbradio.com	Atlanta	GA	30309	404-897-7500	897-7363
WSB-FM 98.5 (AC) 1601 W Peachtree St NE *Web:* www.b985.com	Atlanta	GA	30309	404-897-7500	897-7363
WSRV-FM 97.1 (AC) 1601 W Peachtree St *Web:* www.971theriver.com	Atlanta	GA	30309	404-897-7500	897-7380
WSTR-FM 94.1 (CHR) 3350 Peachtree Rd NE Suite 1800 *Web:* www.star94.com	Atlanta	GA	30326	404-261-2970	365-9026
WVEE-FM 103.3 (Urban) 1201 Peachtree St NE Suite 800 *Web:* www.v-103.com	Atlanta	GA	30361	404-898-8900	898-8909
WWVA-FM 105.7 (Span) 1819 Peachtree Rd NE Suite 700 *Web:* www.viva1053.com	Atlanta	GA	30309	404-607-1336	367-1105
WYAY-FM 106.7 (Oldies) 210 I-North Pkwy 1st Fl *Web:* www.wyay.com	Atlanta	GA	30339	404-521-1067	
WZGC-FM 92.9 (CR) 1201 Peachtree St Suite 800 *Web:* www.929dave.fm	Atlanta	GA	30361	404-898-8900	898-8909

648-13 Augusta, GA

				Phone	Fax
WBBQ-FM 104.3 (AC) 2743 Perimeter Pkwy Bldg 100 Suite 300 *Web:* www.wbbq.com	Augusta	GA	30909	706-396-6000	396-6010
WCHZ-FM 95.1 (Rock) 4051 Jimmie Dyess Pkwy *Web:* www.95rock.com	Augusta	GA	30909	706-396-7000	396-7100
WEKL-FM 105.7 (CR) 2743 Perimeter Pkwy Bldg 100 Suite 300 *Web:* www.eagle1057.com	Augusta	GA	30909	706-396-6000	396-6010
WFAM-AM 1050 (Rel) 552 Laney Walker Blvd Ext	Augusta	GA	30901	706-722-6077	722-7066
WGAC-AM 580 (N/T) 4051 Jimmie Dyess Pkwy *Web:* www.wgac.com	Augusta	GA	30909	706-396-7000	396-7100
WGUS-FM 102.7 (Rel) 4051 Jimmie Dyess Pkwy *Web:* www.1027wgus.com	Augusta	GA	30907	706-396-7000	396-7100
WHHD-FM 98.3 (AC) 4051 Jimmie Dyess Pkwy *Web:* www.hd983.com	Augusta	GA	30909	706-396-7000	396-7100
WKXC-FM 99.5 (Ctry) 4051 Jimmie Dyess Pkwy *Web:* www.kicks99.com	Augusta	GA	30909	706-396-7000	396-7100
WPRW-FM 107.7 (Urban) 2743 Perimeter Pkwy Bldg 100 Suite 300 *Web:* www.power107.net	Augusta	GA	30909	706-396-6000	396-6010

648-14 Augusta, ME

				Phone	Fax
WEBB-FM 98.5 (Ctry) 56 Western Ave Suite 13 *Web:* www.b985.fm	Augusta	ME	04330	207-623-4735	626-5948
WFAU-AM 1280 (Sports) 125 Community Dr Suite 201	Augusta	ME	04330	207-623-9000	623-9007
WMME-FM 92.3 (CHR) 56 Western Ave Suite 13 *Web:* www.92moose.fm	Augusta	ME	04330	207-623-4735	626-5948

648-15 Austin, TX

				Phone	Fax
KAMX-FM 94.7 (AC) 4301 Westbank Dr Bldg B 3rd Fl *Web:* www.mix947.com	Austin	TX	78746	512-327-9595	329-6288
KASE-FM 100.7 (Ctry) 3601 S Congress Ave Bldg F *Web:* www.kase101.com	Austin	TX	78704	512-684-7300	684-7441
KAZI-FM 88.7 (Var) 8906 Wall St Suite 203 *Web:* www.kazifm.org	Austin	TX	78754	512-836-9544	836-9563
KDHT-FM 93.3 (Urban) 8309 N IH-35 *Web:* www.hot933.fm	Austin	TX	78753	512-832-4000	832-1579
KFIT-AM 1060 (Rel) 110 Wild Basin Rd Suite 375	Austin	TX	78746	512-328-8400	328-8437
KGSR-FM 107.1 (AAA) 8309 N IH-35 *Web:* www.kgsr.com	Austin	TX	78753	512-832-4000	832-1579
KHFI-FM 96.7 (CHR) 3601 S Congress Ave Bldg F *Web:* www.khfi.com	Austin	TX	78704	512-684-7300	684-7441
KIXL-AM 970 (Rel) 11615 Angus Rd Suite 102 *Web:* www.relevantradio.com	Austin	TX	78759	512-390-5495	241-0510
KJCE-AM 1370 (N/T) 4301 Westbank Dr Bldg B 3rd Fl *Web:* www.talkradio1370am.com	Austin	TX	78746	512-327-9595	329-6252
KKMJ-FM 95.5 (AC) 4301 Westbank Dr Bldg B 3rd Fl *Web:* www.majic.com	Austin	TX	78746	512-327-9595	329-6252
KLBJ-AM 590 (N/T) 8309 N IH-35 *Web:* www.590klbj.com	Austin	TX	78753	512-832-4000	832-4081
KLBJ-FM 93.7 (Rock) 8309 N IH-35 *Web:* www.klbjfm.com	Austin	TX	78753	512-832-4000	832-4081
KMFA-FM 89.5 (Clas) 3001 N Lamar Blvd Suite 100 *TF:* 866-472-2221 ■ *Web:* www.kmfa.org	Austin	TX	78705	512-476-5632	474-7463
KOOP-FM 91.7 (Var) PO Box 2116 *TF:* 888-917-5667 ■ *Web:* www.koop.org	Austin	TX	78768	512-472-1369	472-6149
KPEZ-FM 102.3 (Rel) 3601 S Congress Ave Bldg F *Web:* www.channel1023.com	Austin	TX	78704	512-684-7300	684-7441
KROX-FM 101.5 (Alt) 8309 N IH-35 *Web:* www.krox.com	Austin	TX	78753	512-832-4000	832-4071
KUT-FM 90.5 (NPR) University of Texas 1 University Stn PO Box A-0704 *TF:* 800-435-8836 ■ *Web:* www.kut.org	Austin	TX	78712	512-471-1631	471-3700
KVET-AM 1300 (Sports) 3601 S Congress Ave Bldg F *Web:* www.sportsradio1300.com	Austin	TX	78704	512-684-7300	684-7441
KXVT-FM 98.9 (Span) 912 S Capital of Texas Hwy Suite 400 *Web:* www.bmpradio.com	Austin	TX	78746	512-416-1100	314-7742

648-16 Bakersfield, CA

				Phone	Fax
KBFP-FM 105.3 (Span) 1100 Mohawk St Suite 280 *Web:* www.lapreciosa.com	Bakersfield	CA	93309	661-322-9929	283-2963
KCWR-FM 107.1 (Ctry) 3223 Sillect Ave *TF:* 800-962-5590	Bakersfield	CA	93308	661-326-1011	328-7503
KDFO-FM 98.5 (CR) 1100 Mohawk St Suite 280 *Web:* www.985thefox.com	Bakersfield	CA	93309	661-322-9929	322-9239
KERI-AM 1180 (Rel) 1400 Easton Dr Suite 144-B *Web:* www.keri.com	Bakersfield	CA	93309	661-328-1410	328-0873
KERN-AM 1410 (N/T) 1400 Easton Dr Suite 144-B *Web:* www.kernradio.com	Bakersfield	CA	93309	661-328-1410	328-0873
KGFM-FM 101.5 (AC) 1400 Easton Dr Suite 144-B *Web:* www.kgfm.com	Bakersfield	CA	93309	661-328-1410	328-0873
KHTY-AM 970 (Span) 1100 Mohawk St Suite 280	Bakersfield	CA	93309	661-322-9929	283-2963
KISV-FM 94.1 (CHR) 1400 Easton Dr Suite 144-B *Web:* www.hot941.com	Bakersfield	CA	93309	661-328-1410	328-0873
KIWI-FM 102.9 (Span) 5100 Commerce Dr *Web:* www.thespanishradio.com	Bakersfield	CA	93309	661-327-9711	327-0797
KKBB-FM 99.3 (Oldies) 3651 Pegasus Dr Suite 107 *Web:* www.groove993.com	Bakersfield	CA	93308	661-393-1900	393-1915
KKXX-FM 93.1 (Var) 1400 Easton Dr Suite 144-B *Web:* www.bakersfieldpirateradio.com	Bakersfield	CA	93309	661-328-1410	328-0873
KLHC-AM 1350 (Span) 3817 Wilson Rd Suite E *Web:* www.klhcradio.com	Bakersfield	CA	93309	661-847-1450	847-1452
KLLY-FM 95.3 (AC) 3651 Pegasus Dr Suite 107 *Web:* www.klly.com	Bakersfield	CA	93308	661-393-1900	393-1915
KMYX-FM 92.5 (Span) 6313 Schirra Ct *Web:* www.campesina.com	Bakersfield	CA	93313	661-837-0745	837-1612
KNZR-AM 1560 (N/T) 3651 Pegasus Dr Suite 107 *Web:* www.knzr.com	Bakersfield	CA	93308	661-393-1900	393-1915
KPSL-FM 92.1 (Span CHR) 5100 Commerce Dr *Web:* www.thespanishradio.com	Bakersfield	CA	93309	661-327-9711	327-0797
KRAB-FM 106.1 (Rock) 1100 Mohawk St Suite 280 *Web:* www.krab.com	Bakersfield	CA	93309	661-326-1122	377-1515
KSMJ-FM 97.7 (AC) 3651 Pegasus Dr Suite 107 *TF:* 866-977-5765 ■ *Web:* www.mix977fm.com	Bakersfield	CA	93308	661-393-1900	393-1915
KUZZ-FM 107.9 (Ctry) 3223 Sillect Ave *Web:* www.kuzzradio.com/home.shtml	Bakersfield	CA	93308	661-326-1011	328-7503

648-17 Baltimore, MD

				Phone	Fax
WBAL-AM 1090 (N/T) 3800 Hooper Ave *Web:* www.wbal.com	Baltimore	MD	21211	410-467-3000	338-6675
WBJC-FM 91.5 (Clas) 6776 Reisterstown Rd Suite 202 *Web:* www.wbjc.com	Baltimore	MD	21215	410-580-5800	
WCAO-AM 600 (Rel) 711 W 40th St Suite 350 *Web:* www.heaven600.com	Baltimore	MD	21211	410-366-7600	235-3899
WEAA-FM 88.9 (Jazz) 1700 E Cold Spring Ln *Web:* www.weaa.org	Baltimore	MD	21251	443-885-3564	885-8206
WERQ-FM 92.3 (Urban) 1705 Whitehead Rd *Web:* www.92qjams.com	Baltimore	MD	21207	410-944-7182	944-1282
WIYY-FM 97.9 (Rock) 3800 Hooper Ave *Web:* www.98online.com	Baltimore	MD	21211	410-889-0098	675-7946
WJFK-AM 1300 (N/T) 1423 Clarkview Rd Suite 100 *Web:* www.1300wjfk.com	Baltimore	MD	21209	410-321-9535	823-0816
WLIF-FM 101.9 (AC) 1423 Clarkview Rd Suite 100 *Web:* www.1019litefm.com	Baltimore	MD	21209	410-296-1019	821-5482

Station	City	State	ZIP	Phone	Fax
WPOC-FM 93.1 (Country) 711 W 40th St Suite 350 *Web:* www.wpoc.com	Baltimore	MD	21211	410-366-7600	235-3899
WQSR-FM 105.7 (Var) 1423 Clarkview Rd Suite 100 *Web:* www.wqsr.com	Baltimore	MD	21209	410-825-1000	821-8256
WRBS-FM 95.1 (Rel) 3500 Commerce Dr. *TF:* 800-899-0951 ■ *Web:* www.951shinefm.com	Baltimore	MD	21227	410-247-4100	247-4533
WWIN-AM 1400 (Rel) 1705 Whitehead Rd *Web:* www.spirit1400.com	Baltimore	MD	21207	410-332-8200	944-1282
WWMX-FM 106.5 (CHR) 1423 Clarkview Rd Suite 100 *Web:* www.mix1065.fm	Baltimore	MD	21209	410-825-1000	821-8256
WYPR-FM 88.1 (NPR) 2216 N Charles St. *TF:* 866-661-9308 ■ *Web:* www.wypr.org	Baltimore	MD	21218	410-235-1660	235-1161

648-18 Bangor, ME

Station	City	State	ZIP	Phone	Fax
WBFB-FM 104.7 (Ctry) 184 Target Industrial Cir *Web:* www.thenewbear.com	Bangor	ME	04861	207-947-9100	942-8039
WHCF-FM 88.5 (Rel) PO Box 5000 *TF:* 800-947-2577 ■ *Web:* www.whcffm.com	Bangor	ME	04402	207-947-2751	947-0010
WHSN-FM 89.3 (Alt) 1 College Cir *Web:* www.whsn-fm.com	Bangor	ME	04401	207-941-7116	947-3987
WKIT-FM 100.3 (CR) 861 Broadway *TF:* 800-287-1003 ■ *Web:* www.zoneradio.com/wkit	Bangor	ME	04401	207-990-2800	990-2444
WKSQ-FM 94.5 (AC) 184 Target Industrial Cir *TF:* 800-339-5477 ■ *Web:* www.wksqfm.com	Bangor	ME	04401	207-947-9100	942-8039
WMEH-FM 90.9 (NPR) 63 Texas Ave. *TF:* 800-884-1717 ■ *Web:* www.mpbn.net	Bangor	ME	04401	207-941-1010	761-0318
WVOM-FM 101.3 (N/T) 184 Target Industrial Cir *Web:* www.wvomfm.com	Bangor	ME	04861	207-947-9100	942-8039
WVOM-FM 103.9 (N/T) 184 Target Industrial Cir *TF:* 800-966-1039 ■ *Web:* www.wvomfm.com	Bangor	ME	04861	207-947-9100	942-8039
WZON-AM 620 (Sports) 861 Broadway *Web:* www.zoneradio.com/wzon	Bangor	ME	04401	207-990-2800	990-2444

648-19 Baton Rouge, LA

Station	City	State	ZIP	Phone	Fax
KNXX-FM 104.9 (Alt) 929-B Government St. *Web:* www.104thex.com	Baton Rouge	LA	70802	225-388-9898	499-9800
KQXL-FM 106.5 (Urban) 650 Wooddale Blvd *Web:* www.q106dot5.com	Baton Rouge	LA	70806	225-926-1106	928-1606
KRVE-FM 96.1 (AC) 5555 Hilton Ave Suite 500 **Fax:* News Rm ■ *Web:* www.961theriver.com	Baton Rouge	LA	70808	225-231-1860	231-1879*
WBKL-FM 92.7 (Rel) 7249 Florida Blvd *TF:* 800-525-5683 ■ *Web:* www.klove.com	Baton Rouge	LA	70806	225-612-4927	612-4928
WCDV-FM 103.3 (AC) 650 Wooddale Blvd *Web:* www.sunny1033.com	Baton Rouge	LA	70806	225-926-1106	
WDGL-FM 98.1 (CR) 929-B Government St. *Web:* www.eagle981.com	Baton Rouge	LA	70802	225-388-9898	499-9800
WEMX-FM 94.1 (Urban) 650 Wooddale Blvd *TF:* 800-499-9410 ■ *Web:* www.max94one.com	Baton Rouge	LA	70806	225-926-1106	928-1606
WFMF-FM 102.5 (CHR) 5555 Hilton Ave Suite 500 *Web:* www.wfmf.com	Baton Rouge	LA	70808	225-231-1860	231-1879
WJBO-AM 1150 (N/T) 5555 Hilton Ave Suite 500 *Web:* www.wjbo.com	Baton Rouge	LA	70808	225-231-1860	231-1879
WRKF-FM 89.3 (NPR) 3050 Valley Creek Dr. *TF:* 888-499-3050 ■ *Web:* www.wrkf.org	Baton Rouge	LA	70808	225-926-3050	926-3105
WSKR-AM 1210 (Sports) 5555 Hilton Ave Suite 500 *Web:* www.thescore1210.com	Baton Rouge	LA	70808	225-231-1860	231-1879
WXOK-AM 1460 (Rel) 650 Wooddale Blvd *Web:* www.heaven1460.com	Baton Rouge	LA	70806	225-926-1106	928-1606
WYNK-FM 101.5 (Ctry) 5555 Hilton Ave Suite 500 *Web:* www.wynk.com	Baton Rouge	LA	70808	225-231-1860	231-1879
WYPY-FM 100.7 (Ctry) 929-B Government St *Web:* www.newcountry1007.com	Baton Rouge	LA	70802	225-388-9898	499-9800

648-20 Billings, MT

Station	City	State	ZIP	Phone	Fax
KBLG-AM 910 (N/T) 2075 Central Ave. *Web:* www.kblg910.com	Billings	MT	59102	406-248-7777	
KBUL-AM 970 (N/T) 27 N 27th St 23rd Fl *Web:* www.newsradio970.com	Billings	MT	59101	406-248-7827	252-9577
KCTR-FM 102.9 (Ctry) 27 N 27th St 23rd Fl *Web:* kctr.com	Billings	MT	59101	406-248-7827	252-9577
KEMC-FM 91.7 (NPR) 1500 University Dr *TF:* 800-441-2941 ■ *Web:* www.yellowstonepublicradio.org	Billings	MT	59101	406-657-2941	657-2977
KGHL-FM 98.5 (Ctry) 222 N 32nd St 10th Fl *Web:* www.985thewolf.com	Billings	MT	59101	406-238-1000	238-1038
KKBR-FM 97.1 (Oldies) 27 N 27th St 23rd Fl. *Web:* kbear.com	Billings	MT	59101	406-245-9700	252-9577
KMHK-FM 103.7 (Var) 27 N 27th St 23rd Fl. *Web:* kmhk.com	Billings	MT	59101	406-294-1037	252-9577
KRKX-FM 94.1 (CR) 2075 Central Ave *Web:* www.941ksky.com	Billings	MT	59102	406-248-7777	
KRPM 107.5 (Rock) 222 N 32nd St 10th Fl *Web:* www.magic1075fm.com	Billings	MT	59101	406-238-1000	238-1038
KRSQ-FM 101.9 (Urban) 222 N 32nd St 10th Fl. *Web:* www.hot1019.com	Billings	MT	59101	406-238-1000	238-1038
KRZN-FM 96.3 (Rock) 2075 Central Ave *Web:* www.thezone963.com	Billings	MT	59102	406-652-8400	652-4899
KURL-AM 730 (Rel) 636 Haugen St. *Web:* www.kurlradio.com	Billings	MT	59101	406-245-3121	245-0822

648-21 Birmingham, AL

Station	City	State	ZIP	Phone	Fax
WAGG-AM 610 (Rel) 2700 Corporate Dr Suite 115 *Web:* wagg610.com	Birmingham	AL	35242	205-322-2987	322-2667
WAPI-AM 1070 (N/T) 244 Goodwin Crest Dr Suite 300 *Web:* www.wapi1070.com	Birmingham	AL	35209	205-945-4646	917-1906
WBHJ-FM 95.7 (Urban) 2700 Corporate Pkwy Suite 115 *Web:* 957jamz.com	Birmingham	AL	35242	205-322-2987	326-2526
WBHK-FM 98.7 (Urban) 2700 Corporate Pkwy Suite 115 *Web:* 987kiss.com	Birmingham	AL	35242	205-322-2987	326-2526
WBHM-FM 90.3 (NPR) 650 11th St S. *TF:* 800-444-9246 ■ *Web:* www.wbhm.org	Birmingham	AL	35294	205-934-2606	934-5075
WBPT-FM 106.9 (AC) 2700 Corporate Dr Suite 115 *Web:* birminghamseagle.com	Birmingham	AL	35242	205-916-1100	290-1061
WDJC-FM 93.7 (Rel) 120 Summit Pkwy *Web:* www.wdjconline.com	Birmingham	AL	35209	205-879-3324	941-1095
WDXB-FM 102.5 (Ctry) 600 Beacon Pkwy W Suite 400 *Web:* www.1025thebull.com	Birmingham	AL	35209	205-439-9600	439-8390
WERC-AM 960 (N/T) 600 Beacon Pkwy W Suite 400 *Web:* www.960werc.com	Birmingham	AL	35209	205-439-9600	439-8390
WJLD-AM 1400 (Var) PO Box 19123 *Web:* www.wjld1400.com	Birmingham	AL	35219	205-942-1776	942-4814
WJSR-FM 91.1 (CR) 2601 Carson Rd	Birmingham	AL	35215	205-856-7702	815-8499
WMJJ-FM 96.5 (AC) 600 Beacon Pkwy W Suite 400 *Web:* www.magic96fm.com	Birmingham	AL	35209	205-439-9600	439-8390
WNCB-FM 97.3 (Ctry) 2700 Corporate Dr Suite 115 *Web:* newcountry973.com	Birmingham	AL	35242	205-916-1100	290-1061
WQEN-FM 103.7 (CHR) 600 Beacon Pkwy W Suite 400 *Web:* www.1037theq.com	Birmingham	AL	35209	205-439-9600	439-8390
WSPZ-AM 690 (Sports) 244 Goodwin Crest Dr Suite 300 *Web:* www.690thesportsanimal.com	Birmingham	AL	35209	205-942-6690	917-1906
WVVB-FM 105.5 (Rock) 600 Beacon Pkwy W Suite 400 *Web:* www.1055thevulcan.com	Birmingham	AL	35209	205-439-9600	439-8390
WYSF-FM 94.5 (AC) 244 Goodwin Crest Dr Suite 300 *Web:* www.softrock945.com	Birmingham	AL	35209	205-945-4646	945-3994
WZRR-FM 99.5 (CR) 244 Goodwin Crest Dr Suite 300 *Web:* www.wzrr.com	Birmingham	AL	35209	205-945-4646	942-8959
WZZK-FM 104.7 (Ctry) 2700 Corporate Dr Suite 115 *Web:* wzzk.com	Birmingham	AL	35242	205-916-1100	290-1061

648-22 Bismarck, ND

Station	City	State	ZIP	Phone	Fax
KBMR-AM 1130 (Ctry) 3500 E Rosser Ave *TF:* 800-766-5267 ■ *Web:* www.kbmr.com	Bismarck	ND	58501	701-255-1234	222-1131
KCND-FM 90.5 (NPR) 1814 N 15th St. *TF:* 800-359-5566 ■ *Web:* www.prairiepublic.org	Bismarck	ND	58501	701-224-1700	224-0555
KKCT-FM 97.5 (CHR) 1830 N 11th St *Web:* www.hot975fm.com	Bismarck	ND	58501	701-250-6602	250-6632
KQDY-FM 94.5 (Ctry) 3500 E Rosser Ave PO Box 2156 *TF:* 800-825-5794 ■ *Web:* www.kqdy.com	Bismarck	ND	58501	701-255-1234	222-1131
KSSS-FM 101.5 (Rock) 3500 E Rosser Ave PO Box 2156 *TF:* 866-653-1015 ■ *Web:* www.1015.fm	Bismarck	ND	58501	701-255-1234	222-1131
KXMR-AM 710 (Sports) 3500 E Rosser Ave PO Box 2156 *TF:* 866-522-5710 ■ *Web:* www.espn710am.com/main.html	Bismarck	ND	58501	701-255-1234	222-1131
KYYY-FM 92.9 (AC) 3500 E Rosser Ave *TF:* 866-929-9393 ■ *Web:* www.y93.fm	Bismarck	ND	58501	701-250-9393	222-1131

648-23 Boise, ID

Station	City	State	ZIP	Phone	Fax
KAWO-FM 104.3 (Ctry) 827 E Pk Blvd Suite 201 *Web:* www.wow1043.com	Boise	ID	83712	208-344-6363	385-7385
KBSX-FM 91.5 (NPR) 1910 University Dr *TF:* 888-859-5278 ■ *Web:* www.boisestatepublicradio.org	Boise	ID	83725	208-947-5660	344-6631
KBXL-FM 94.1 (Rel) 1440 S Weideman Ave *Web:* www.myfamilyradio.com	Boise	ID	83709	208-377-3790	377-3792
KIDO-AM 580 (N/T) 827 E Pk Blvd Suite 201 *Web:* www.580kido.com	Boise	ID	83712	208-344-6363	385-7385
KIZN-FM 92.3 (Ctry) 1419 W Bannock St *Web:* www.kizn.com	Boise	ID	83702	208-336-3670	336-3734

Station	City	State	ZIP	Phone	Fax
KJOT-FM 105.1 (Rock) 5257 Fairview Ave Suite 260 *Web:* www.j105.com	Boise	ID	83706	208-344-3511	947-6765
KKGL-FM 96.9 (CR) 1419 W Bannock St. *Web:* www.96-9theeagle.com	Boise	ID	83702	208-336-3670	336-3734
KQFC-FM 97.9 (Ctry) 1419 W Bannock St *Web:* www.98kqfc.com	Boise	ID	83702	208-336-3670	336-3734
KQXR-FM 100.3 (Rock) 5257 Fairview Ave Suite 260 *Web:* www.xrock.com	Boise	ID	83706	208-344-3511	947-6765
KSAS-FM 103.3 (CHR) 827 E Pk Blvd Suite 201 *Web:* www.1033kissfm.com	Boise	ID	83712	208-344-6363	385-7385
KTIK-AM 1350 (Sports) 1419 W Bannock St *Web:* www.ktik.com	Boise	ID	83702	208-336-3670	336-3734

648-24 Boston, MA

Station	City	State	ZIP	Phone	Fax
WBCN-FM 104.1 (Alt) 83 Leo Birmingham Pkwy *Web:* www.wbcn.com	Boston	MA	02135	617-746-1400	746-1402
WBMX-FM 98.5 (AC) 1200 Soldiers Field Rd *Web:* www.mix985.com	Boston	MA	02134	617-779-2000	779-2002
WBOS-FM 92.9 (AAA) 55 Morrissey Blvd *Web:* www.wbos.com	Boston	MA	02125	617-822-9600	822-6759
WBUR-FM 90.9 (NPR) 890 Commonwealth Ave *TF:* 800-909-9287 ■ *Web:* www.wbur.org	Boston	MA	02215	617-353-0909	353-9380
WBZ-AM 1030 (N/T) 1170 Soldiers Field Rd *Web:* www.wbz1030.com	Boston	MA	02134	617-787-7000	787-7060
WGBH-FM 89.7 (NPR) 1 Guest St *Web:* www.wgbh.org	Boston	MA	02135	617-300-2000	300-1025
WKLB-FM 102.5 (Ctry) 55 Morrissey Blvd **Fax:* News Rm ■ *TF:* 888-784-0995 ■ *Web:* www.wklb.com	Boston	MA	02125	617-822-9600	822-6659*
WMJX-FM 106.7 (CHR) 55 Morrissey Blvd *Web:* www.magic1067.com	Boston	MA	02125	617-822-9600	822-6559
WODS-FM 103.3 (Oldies) 83 Leo Birmingham Pkwy *TF:* 800-336-1033 ■ *Web:* www.oldies1033.com	Boston	MA	02135	617-787-7500	787-7523
WRBB-FM 104.9 (Var) Northeastern University 360 Huntington Ave *Web:* wrbbradio.org	Boston	MA	02115	617-373-4338	373-5095
WROR-FM 105.7 (Oldies) 55 Morrissey Blvd. *Web:* www.wror.com	Boston	MA	02125	617-822-9600	822-6459
WTKK-FM 96.9 (N/T) 55 Morrissey Blvd. *Web:* www.969fmtalk.com	Boston	MA	02125	617-822-9600	822-6859
WUMB-FM 91.9 (Folk) 100 Morrissey Blvd *TF:* 800-573-2100 ■ *Web:* www.wumb.org	Boston	MA	02125	617-287-6900	287-6916

648-25 Branson, MO

Station	City	State	ZIP	Phone	Fax
KLFC-FM 88.1 (Rel) 205 W Atlantic St *TF:* 877-334-5532 ■ *Web:* www.klfcradio.com	Branson	MO	65616	417-334-5532	335-2437
KOMC-AM 1220 (Rel) 202 Courtney St. *TF:* 888-870-5035 ■ *Web:* www.hometownradioonline.com	Branson	MO	65616	417-334-6003	334-7141
KOMC-FM 100.1 (Nost) 202 Courtney St. *Web:* www.hometownradioonline.com	Branson	MO	65616	417-334-6003	334-7141
KRZK-FM 106.3 (Ctry) 202 Courtney St. *Web:* www.hometownradioonline.com	Branson	MO	65616	417-334-6003	334-7141

648-26 Buffalo, NY

Station	City	State	ZIP	Phone	Fax
WBFO-FM 88.7 (NPR) 3435 Main St 205 Allen Hall *TF:* 888-829-6000 ■ *Web:* www.wbfo.org	Buffalo	NY	14214	716-829-6000	829-2277
WBLK-FM 93.7 (Urban) 14 Lafayette Sq Suite 1300 *Web:* www.wblk.com	Buffalo	NY	14203	716-852-9393	852-9390
WBNY-FM 91.3 (Alt) 1300 Elmwood Ave *Web:* www.buffalostate.edu/wbny	Buffalo	NY	14222	716-878-5104	878-6600
WBUF-FM 92.9 (Var) 14 Lafayette Sq Suite 1300 *Web:* www.wbuf.com	Buffalo	NY	14203	716-852-9292	852-9290
WDCX-FM 99.5 (Rel) 625 Delaware Ave Suite 308 *Web:* www.wdcxfm.com	Buffalo	NY	14202	716-883-3010	883-3606
WEDG-FM 103.3 (Alt) 50 James E Casey Dr. *Web:* www.wedg.com	Buffalo	NY	14206	716-881-4555	884-2931
WGRF-FM 96.9 (CR) 50 James E Casey Dr *Web:* www.97rock.com	Buffalo	NY	14206	716-881-4555	884-2931
WHTT-FM 104.1 (AC) 50 James E Casey Dr *Web:* www.whtt.com	Buffalo	NY	14206	716-881-4555	884-2931
WJYE-FM 96.1 (AC) 14 Lafayette Sq Suite 1200 *Web:* www.wjye.com	Buffalo	NY	14203	716-852-7444	852-0537
WNED-AM 970 (NPR) 140 Lower Terr *Web:* www.wned.org	Buffalo	NY	14202	716-845-7000	845-7043
WYRK-FM 106.5 (Ctry) 14 Lafayette Sq Suite 1200 *Web:* www.wyrk.com	Buffalo	NY	14203	716-852-7444	852-5683

648-27 Burlington, VT

Station	City	State	ZIP	Phone	Fax
WBTZ-FM 99.9 (Alt) 255 S Champlain St PO Box 4489 *Web:* www.999thebuzz.com	Burlington	VT	05401	802-860-2440	860-1818
WIZN-FM 106.7 (Rock) 255 S Champlain St *TF:* 888-873-9496 ■ *Web:* www.wizn.com	Burlington	VT	05401	802-860-2440	860-1818
WRUV-FM 90.1 (Var) University of Vermont Davis Student Ctr. *Web:* www.uvm.edu	Burlington	VT	05405	802-656-0796	656-2281

648-28 Calgary, AB

Station	City	Prov	Postal Code	Phone	Fax
CBR-AM 1010 (N/T) 1724 Westmount Blvd NW **Fax:* News Rm ■ *Web:* www.cbc.ca/calgary	Calgary	AB	T2N3G7	403-521-6000	521-6262*
CBR-FM 102.1 (CBC) 1724 Westmount Blvd NW *TF:* 866-306-4636 ■ *Web:* www.cbc.ca/calgary	Calgary	AB	T2N3G7	403-521-6000	521-6262
CFAC-AM 960 (Sports) 2723 37th Ave NE Suite 240 *Web:* www.fan960.com	Calgary	AB	T1Y5R8	403-291-0000	291-4368
CFFR-AM 660 (N/T) 2723 37th Ave NE Suite 240 *Web:* www.660news.com	Calgary	AB	T1Y5R8	403-291-0000	246-4368
CHFM-FM 95.9 (AC) 2723 37th Ave NE Suite 240 *Web:* www.lite959.ca	Calgary	AB	T1Y5R8	403-291-0000	291-4368
CHQR-AM 770 (N/T) 630 3rd Ave SW Suite 105 *TF:* 800-563-7770 ■ *Web:* www.qr77.com	Calgary	AB	T2P4L4	403-716-6500	716-2111
CJAY-FM 92.1 (CR) 1110 Ctr St NE Suite 300 *Web:* www.cjay92.com	Calgary	AB	T2E2R2	403-240-5850	240-5801
CKIK-FM 107.3 (CHR) 630 3rd Ave SW Suite 105 *TF:* 800-563-7770 ■ *Web:* www.q107fm.ca	Calgary	AB	T2P4L4	403-716-6500	716-2111
CKMX-AM 1060 (Ctry) 1110 Ctr St NE Suite 300 *Web:* www.classiccountryam1060.com	Calgary	AB	T2E2R2	403-240-5850	240-5801

648-29 Casper, WY

Station	City	State	ZIP	Phone	Fax
KASS-FM 106.9 (CR) 218 N Wolcott St.	Casper	WY	82601	307-265-1984	266-3295
KHOC-FM 102.5 (AC) 218 N Wolcott St *Web:* www.wyomingradio.com/khoc	Casper	WY	82601	307-265-1984	266-3295
KMGW-FM 96.7 (AC) 150 N Nichols Ave *TF:* 800-832-0208 ■ *Web:* www.rock967online.com	Casper	WY	82601	307-266-5252	235-9143
KMLD-FM 94.5 (Oldies) 218 N Wolcott St *Web:* www.wyomingradio.com/kmld	Casper	WY	82601	307-265-1984	266-3295
KQLT-FM 103.7 (Ctry) 218 N Wolcott St.	Casper	WY	82601	307-265-1984	266-3295
KRVK-FM 107.9 (Rock) 150 N Nichols Ave *TF:* 800-832-0208 ■ *Web:* www.theriver1079.com	Casper	WY	82601	307-266-5252	235-9143
KTRS-FM 104.7 (CHR) 150 N Nichols Ave *TF:* 800-832-0208 ■ *Web:* www.kisscasper.com	Casper	WY	82601	307-266-5252	235-9143
KTWO-AM 1030 (Ctry) 150 N Nichols Ave *TF:* 800-832-0208 ■ *Web:* www.k2radio.com	Casper	WY	82601	307-266-5252	235-9143
KUYO-AM 830 (Rel) PO Box 50607 *Web:* www.kuyo.com	Casper	WY	82605	307-577-5896	
KVOC-AM 1230 (Nost) 218 N Wolcott St	Casper	WY	82601	307-265-1984	473-7461
KWYY-FM 95.5 (Ctry) 150 N Nichols Ave. *TF:* 800-832-0208 ■ *Web:* www.mycountry955.com	Casper	WY	82601	307-266-5252	235-9143

648-30 Cedar Rapids, IA

Station	City	State	ZIP	Phone	Fax
KCCK-FM 88.3 (Jazz) 6301 Kirkwood Blvd SW *TF:* 800-373-5225 ■ *Web:* www.kcck.org	Cedar Rapids	IA	52404	319-398-5446	398-5492
KDAT-FM 104.5 (AC) 425 2nd St SE 4th Fl *Web:* www.kdat.com	Cedar Rapids	IA	52401	319-365-9431	363-8062
KHAK-FM 98.1 (Ctry) 425 2nd St SE 4th Fl *TF:* 800-747-5425 ■ *Web:* www.khak.com	Cedar Rapids	IA	52401	319-365-9431	363-8062
KMRY-AM 1450 (Nost) 1957 Blairs Ferry Rd NE *Web:* www.kmryradio.com	Cedar Rapids	IA	52402	319-393-1450	393-1407
KRNA-FM 94.1 (Rock) 425 2nd St SE 4th Fl *Web:* www.krna.com	Cedar Rapids	IA	52401	319-365-9431	363-8062
KZIA-FM 102.9 (CHR) 1110 26th Ave SW *Web:* www.kzia.com	Cedar Rapids	IA	52404	319-363-2061	363-2948
WMT-AM 600 (N/T) 600 Old Marion Rd NE *TF:* 800-332-5401 ■ *Web:* www.wmtradio.com	Cedar Rapids	IA	52402	319-395-0530	393-9600
WMT-FM 96.5 (AC) 600 Old Marion Rd NE *TF:* 800-258-0096 ■ *Web:* www.mix965.com	Cedar Rapids	IA	52402	319-395-0530	393-9600

648-31 Champaign, IL

Station	City	State	ZIP	Phone	Fax
WBCP-AM 1580 (Urban) 904 N 4th St Suite D *Web:* www.wbsp1580.com	Champaign	IL	61820	217-359-1580	359-1583
WBGL-FM 91.7 (Rel) 2108 W Springfield Ave *TF Cust Svc:* 800-475-9245 ■ *Web:* www.wbgl.org	Champaign	IL	61822	217-359-8232	359-7374
WCFF-FM 92.5 (Oldies) 2603 W Bradley Ave *Web:* www.925thechief.com	Champaign	IL	61821	217-352-4141	352-1256
WDWS-AM 1400 (N/T) 2301 S Neil St. *TF:* 800-223-9397 ■ *Web:* www.wdws.com/wdws	Champaign	IL	61820	217-351-5300	351-5385
WEFT-FM 90.1 (Var) 113 N Market St *Web:* www.weft.org	Champaign	IL	61820	217-359-9338	
WGKC-FM 105.9 (CR) 4112 C Fieldstone Rd *Web:* www.wgkc.net	Champaign	IL	61822	217-367-1195	367-3291
WHMS-FM 97.5 (AC) 2301 S Neil St. *TF:* 800-223-9397 ■ *Web:* www.whms.com	Champaign	IL	61820	217-351-5300	351-5385
WIXY-FM 100.3 (Ctry) 2603 W Bradley Ave *Web:* www.wixy.com	Champaign	IL	61821	217-352-4141	352-1256
WLRW-FM 94.5 (CHR) 2603 W Bradley Ave *Web:* www.mix945.com	Champaign	IL	61821	217-352-4141	352-1256
WPCD-FM 88.7 (Rock) 2400 W Bradley Ave *Web:* www.parkland.edu/WPCD	Champaign	IL	61821	217-351-2450	
WPGU-FM 107.1 (Alt) 512 E Green St Suite 107 *Web:* www.wpgu.com	Champaign	IL	61820	217-337-3100	337-8303

648-32 Charleston, SC

Station	City	State	Zip	Phone	Fax
WAVF-FM101.7 (Alt) 2294 Clements Ferry Rd *Web:* www.1017chuckfm.com	Charleston	SC	29492	843-972-1100	972-1200
WQSC-AM 1340 (Sports) 60 Markfield Dr Unit 4 *Web:* www.real1340.net	Charleston	SC	29407	843-763-6631	766-1239
WXTC-AM 1390 (Rel) 2294 Clements Ferry Rd *Web:* www.heaven1390.com	Charleston	SC	29492	843-972-1100	972-1200
WYBB-FM 98.1 (Alt) 59 Windermere Blvd	Charleston	SC	29407	843-769-4799	769-4797

648-33 Charleston, WV

Station	City	State	Zip	Phone	Fax
WCHS-AM 580 (N/T) 1111 Virginia St E *Web:* www.58wchs.com	Charleston	WV	25301	304-342-8131	344-4745
WKAZ-FM 107.3 (Var) 1111 Virginia St E *Web:* www.1073kaz.com	Charleston	WV	25301	304-342-8131	344-4745
WKWS-FM 96.1 (Ctry) 1111 Virginia St E *TF:* 888-961-9653 ■ *Web:* www.961thewolf.com	Charleston	WV	25301	304-342-8131	344-4745
WQBE-FM 97.5 (Ctry) 817 Suncrest Pl *TF:* 800-222-3697 ■ *Web:* www.wqbe.com	Charleston	WV	25303	304-344-9700	342-3118
WVAF-FM 99.9 (AC) 1111 Virginia St E *Web:* www.v100.fm	Charleston	WV	25301	304-342-8131	344-4745
WVNP-FM 89.9 (NPR) 600 Capitol St *TF:* 888-596-9729 ■ *Web:* www.wvpubcast.org	Charleston	WV	25301	304-556-4900	556-4981
WVPN-FM 88.5 (NPR) 600 Capitol St *TF:* 888-596-9729 ■ *Web:* www.wvpubcast.org	Charleston	WV	25301	304-556-4900	556-4981
WVSR-FM 102.7 (CHR) 817 Suncrest Pl *Web:* www.electric102.com	Charleston	WV	25303	304-342-3136	342-3118
WZJO-FM 94.5 (Alt) 817 Suncrest Pl *Web:* www.zrock945.com	Charleston	WV	25303	304-342-3136	342-3118

648-34 Charlotte, NC

Station	City	State	Zip	Phone	Fax
WBAV-FM 101.9 (Urban AC) 1520 S Blvd Suite 300 *Web:* v1019.radio.com	Charlotte	NC	28203	704-342-2644	227-8985
WBT-AM 1110 (N/T) 1 Julian Price Pl *Web:* www.wbt.com	Charlotte	NC	28208	704-374-3500	374-3890
WEND-FM 106.5 (Alt) 801 Wood Ridge Ctr Dr *TF:* 800-332-1029 ■ *Web:* www.1065.com	Charlotte	NC	28217	704-714-9444	332-8805
WFAE-FM 90.7 (NPR) 8801 JM Keynes Dr Suite 91 *TF Cust Svc:* 800-876-9323 ■ *Web:* www.wfae.org	Charlotte	NC	28262	704-549-9323	547-8851
WFNZ-AM 610 (Sports) 1520 S Blvd Suite 300 *Web:* www.wfnz.com	Charlotte	NC	28203	704-342-2644	319-3934
WGIV-AM 1600 (Rel) 1520 S Blvd Suite 300	Charlotte	NC	28203	704-570-1672	
WKKT-FM 96.9 (Ctry) 801 Wood Ridge Ctr Dr *TF:* 800-332-1029 ■ *Web:* www.wkktfm.com	Charlotte	NC	28217	704-714-9444	332-8805
WLNK-FM 107.9 (AC) 1 Julian Price Pl *Web:* www.1079thelink.com	Charlotte	NC	28208	704-374-3500	374-3889
WLYT-FM 102.9 (AC) 801 Wood Ridge Ctr Dr *TF:* 800-332-1029 ■ *Web:* www.wlyt.com	Charlotte	NC	28217	704-714-9444	332-8805
WPEG-FM 97.9 (Urban) 1520 S Blvd Suite 300 *TF:* 800-525-0098 ■ *Web:* power98fm.radio.com	Charlotte	NC	28203	704-342-2644	227-8985
WRCM-FM 91.9 (Rel) PO Box 17069 *Web:* www.wrcm.org	Charlotte	NC	28227	704-821-9293	821-9285
WRFX-FM 99.7 (CR) 801 Wood Ridge Ctr Dr *TF:* 800-332-1029 ■ *Web:* www.wrfx.com	Charlotte	NC	28217	704-714-9444	332-8805
WSOC-FM 103.7 (Ctry) 1520 S Blvd Suite 300 *Web:* wsocfm.radio.com	Charlotte	NC	28203	704-342-2644	523-4800
WXRC-FM 95.7 (CR) 1515 Mockingbird Ln Suite 205 *TF:* 800-282-9570 ■ *Web:* www.957theride.com	Charlotte	NC	28209	704-527-0957	527-2720

648-35 Chattanooga, TN

Station	City	State	Zip	Phone	Fax
WBDX-FM 102.7 (Rel) 5512 Ringgold Rd Suite 214 *TF:* 877-262-5103 ■ *Web:* www.j103.com	Chattanooga	TN	37412	423-892-1200	892-1633
WDEF-AM 1370 (Sports) 2615 S Broad St *Web:* www.foxsportschattanooga.com	Chattanooga	TN	37408	423-321-6200	321-6270
WDEF-FM 92.3 (AC) 2615 S Broad St *Web:* www.sunny923.com	Chattanooga	TN	37408	423-321-6200	321-6270
WDOD-FM 96.5 (CHR) 2615 S Broad St *Web:* www.965themountain.com	Chattanooga	TN	37408	423-321-6200	321-6270
WGOW-FM 102.3 (N/T) 821 Pineville Rd *Web:* www.wgow.com	Chattanooga	TN	37405	423-756-6141	266-3629
WJTT-FM 94.3 (Urban) 1305 Carter St *Web:* www.power94.com	Chattanooga	TN	37402	423-265-9494	266-2335
WLND-FM 98.1 (Ctry) 7413 Old Lee Hwy *Web:* www.my981chattanooga.com	Chattanooga	TN	37421	423-892-3333	899-7224
WMBW-FM 88.9 (Rel) PO Box 73026 *TF:* 800-621-9629 ■ *Web:* www.wmbw.org	Chattanooga	TN	37407	423-629-8900	629-0021
WNOO-AM 1260 (Rel) 1108 Hendricks St *Web:* www.wnooradio.com	Chattanooga	TN	37406	423-698-8617	698-8796
WOGT-FM 107.9 (Ctry) 821 Pineville Rd *Web:* www.wogt.com	Chattanooga	TN	37405	423-756-6141	266-3629
WRXR-FM 105.5 (Rock) 7413 Old Lee Hwy *Web:* www.rock105.com	Chattanooga	TN	37421	423-892-3333	899-7224
WSKZ-FM 106.5 (Rock) 821 Pineville Rd *Web:* www.kz106.com	Chattanooga	TN	37405	423-756-6141	266-3629
WUSY-FM 101 7413 Old Lee Hwy *Web:* www.us101country.com	Chattanooga	TN	37421	423-892-3333	899-7224
WUTC-FM 88.1 (NPR) 615 McCallie Ave 104 Cadek Hall Dept 1151 *Web:* www.wutc.org	Chattanooga	TN	37403	423-425-4756	425-2379

648-36 Cheyenne, WY

Station	City	State	Zip	Phone	Fax
KFBC-AM 1240 (N/T) 1806 Capitol Ave *TF:* 877-388-7353 ■ *Web:* www.kfbcradio.com	Cheyenne	WY	82001	307-634-4462	632-8586
KGAB-AM 650 (N/T) 1912 Capitol Ave Suite 300 *Web:* www.kgab.com	Cheyenne	WY	82001	307-632-4400	632-1818
KIGN-FM 101.9 (Rock) 1912 Capitol Ave Suite 300 *Web:* www.kign.com	Cheyenne	WY	82001	307-632-4400	632-1818
KJUA-AM 1380 (Span) 415 E 3rd St Suite 205 *TF:* 888-896-1630	Cheyenne	WY	82007	307-635-8787	635-8788
KLEN-FM 106.3 (Ctry) 1912 Capitol Ave Suite 300 *Web:* www.1063klen.com	Cheyenne	WY	82001	307-632-4400	632-1818
KRAE-AM 1480 (Sports) 2109 E 10th St	Cheyenne	WY	82001	307-638-8921	638-8922
KRRR-FM 104.9 (Oldies) 2109 E 10th St *Web:* www.1049krrr.com	Cheyenne	WY	82001	307-638-8921	638-8922

648-37 Chicago, IL

Station	City	State	Zip	Phone	Fax
WBBM-AM 780 (N/T) 180 N Stetson Suite 1100 Prudential Plaza 2 *Web:* www.wbbm780.com	Chicago	IL	60601	312-297-7801	297-7822
WBBM-FM 96.3 (CHR) 180 N Stetson Suite 1100 Prudential Plaza 2 *Web:* www.b96.com	Chicago	IL	60601	312-297-7801	297-7822
WBEZ-FM 91.5 (NPR) 848 E Grand Ave Navy Pier *Web:* www.wbez.org	Chicago	IL	60611	312-948-4600	832-3158
WDRV-FM 97.1 (CR) 875 N Michigan Ave Suite 1510 *Web:* www.wdrv.com	Chicago	IL	60611	312-274-9710	274-1304
WFMT-FM 98.7 (Clas) 5400 N St Louis Ave *Web:* www.wfmt.com	Chicago	IL	60625	773-279-2000	279-2199
WGCI-FM 107.5 (Urban) 233 N Michigan Ave Suite 2800 **Fax:* Sales ■ *Web:* www.wgci.com	Chicago	IL	60601	312-540-2000	938-0692*
WGN Radio 720 (N/T) 435 N Michigan Ave *Web:* www.wgnradio.com	Chicago	IL	60611	312-222-4700	222-5165
WILV-FM 100.3 (AC) 130 E Randolph St 1 Prudential Plaza Suite 2780 *Web:* www.wilv.com	Chicago	IL	60601	312-297-5100	297-5155
WJMK-FM 104.3 (CR) 180 N Stetson Ave Suite 900 *Web:* www.wjmk.com	Chicago	IL	60601	312-870-6400	977-1859
WKSC-FM 103.5 (CHR) 233 N Michigan Ave Suite 2800 **Fax:* Sales ■ *Web:* www.wksc.com	Chicago	IL	60601	312-540-2000	938-0692*
WLEY-FM 107.9 (Span) 150 N Michigan Ave Suite 1040 **Fax:* PR ■ *Web:* www.laley1079.com	Chicago	IL	60601	312-920-9500	920-9515*
WLUP-FM 97.9 (CR) 222 Merchandise Mart Suite 230 *Web:* www.wlup.com	Chicago	IL	60654	312-440-5270	527-3620
WMBI-FM 90.1 (Rel) 820 N LaSalle Blvd *TF:* 800-600-9624 ■ *Web:* www.wmbi.org	Chicago	IL	60610	312-329-4300	329-4468
WMVP-AM 1000 (Sports) 190 N State St 7th Fl **Fax:* Sales ■ *Web:* www.espnradio1000.com	Chicago	IL	60601	312-980-1000	980-1010*
WNUA-FM 95.5 (NAC) 233 N Michigan Ave Suite 2800 *Web:* www.wnua.com	Chicago	IL	60601	312-540-2000	938-0111
WOJO-FM 105.1 (Span) 625 N Michigan Ave Suite 300 *TF:* 877-877-4786 ■ *Web:* quebuenachicago.univision.com	Chicago	IL	60611	312-981-1800	312-1840
WRTO-AM 1200 (Span) 625 N Michigan Ave Suite 300 *Web:* latremendachicago.univision.com	Chicago	IL	60611	312-981-1800	312-1840
WTMX-FM 101.9 (AC) 130 E Randolph St Suite 2700 1 Prudential Plaza *Web:* www.wtmx.com	Chicago	IL	60601	312-946-1019	946-4747
WUSN-FM 99.5 (Ctry) 2 Prudential Plaza Suite 1000 *Web:* www.us99.com	Chicago	IL	60601	312-649-0099	856-9586
WVAZ-FM 102.7 (Urban AC) 233 N Michigan Ave Suite 2700 *Web:* www.v103.com	Chicago	IL	60601	312-540-2000	938-4477
WVON-AM 1690 (N/T) 1000 E 87th St *Web:* www.wvon.com	Chicago	IL	60619	773-247-6200	247-5366
WWWN--FM 101.1 (Alt) 230 Merchandise Mart Plaza *Web:* www.q101.com	Chicago	IL	60654	312-527-8348	527-3620
WZZN-FM 94.7 (Oldies) 190 N State St 8th Fl *Web:* www.947chicago.com	Chicago	IL	60601	312-984-0890	984-5305

648-38 Cincinnati, OH

Station	City	State	Zip	Phone	Fax
WAKW-FM 93.3 (Rel) 6275 Collegevue Pl PO Box 24126 TF: 888-542-9393 ■ Web: www.mystar933.com	Cincinnati	OH	45224	513-542-9259	542-9333
WCKY-AM 1530 (N/T) 8044 Montgomery Rd Suite 650 Web: www.wcky.com	Cincinnati	OH	45236	513-686-8300	241-0358
WCVX-AM 1050 (Rel) 635 W 7th St Suite 400 Web: www.wcvx.com	Cincinnati	OH	45203	513-533-2500	533-2527
WEBN-FM 102.7 (Rock) 8044 Montgomery Rd Suite 650 TF: 800-616-9236 ■ Web: www.webn.com	Cincinnati	OH	45236	513-686-8300	749-3299
WGRR-FM 103.5 (Oldies) 4805 Montgomery Rd Suite 300 Web: www.wgrr.com	Cincinnati	OH	45212	513-241-9898	241-6689
WGUC-FM 90.9 (Clas) 1223 Central Pkwy Web: www.wguc.org	Cincinnati	OH	45214	513-241-8282	241-8456
WIZF-FM 101.1 (Urban) 705 Central Ave Web: wiznation.com	Cincinnati	OH	45202	513-679-6000	679-6014
WKFS-FM 107.1 (CHR) 8044 Montgomery Rd Suite 650 Web: www.kisscincinnati.com	Cincinnati	OH	45236	513-686-8300	421-3299
WKRC-AM 550 (N/T) 8044 Montgomery Rd Suite 650 Web: www.55krc.com	Cincinnati	OH	45236	513-686-8300	651-2555
WKRQ-FM 101.9 (CHR) 2060 Reading Rd Web: www.wkrq.com	Cincinnati	OH	45202	513-699-5102	699-5000
WLW-AM 700 (N/T) 8044 Montgomery Rd Suite 650 Web: www.700wlw.com	Cincinnati	OH	45236	513-686-8300	665-9700
WNNF-FM 94.1 (AC) 8044 Montgomery Rd Suite 650 Web: www.wvmx.com	Cincinnati	OH	45236	513-686-8300	421-3299
WRRM-FM 98.5 (AC) 4805 Montgomery Rd Suite 300 Web: www.warm98.com	Cincinnati	OH	45212	513-241-9898	241-6689
WUBE-FM 105.1 (Ctry) 2060 Reading Rd Web: www.wube.com	Cincinnati	OH	45202	513-699-5105	699-5000
WVXU-FM 91.7 (NPR) 1223 Central Pkwy Web: www.wvxu.org	Cincinnati	OH	45214	513-352-9170	241-8456
WYGY-FM 94.9 (Ctry) 2060 Reading Rd Web: www.theworldwidewolf.com	Cincinnati	OH	45202	513-699-5102	699-5000

648-39 Cleveland, OH

Station	City	State	Zip	Phone	Fax
WABQ-AM 1460 (Rel) 8000 Euclid Ave	Cleveland	OH	44103	216-231-8005	231-9803
WCLV-FM 104.9 (Clas) 26501 Renaissance Pkwy TF: 800-491-8863 ■ Web: www.wclv.com	Cleveland	OH	44128	216-464-0900	464-2206
WCPN-FM 90.3 (NPR) 1375 Euclid Ave Web: www.wcpn.org	Cleveland	OH	44115	216-916-6100	916-6101
WCRF-FM 103.3 (Rel) 9756 Barr Rd TF: 800-283-9273 ■ Web: www.wcrf.mbn.org	Cleveland	OH	44141	440-526-1111	526-1319
WDOK-FM 102.1 (AC) 2644 St Clair Ave TF: 888-633-5452 ■ Web: www.wdok.com	Cleveland	OH	44114	216-696-0123	363-7189
WENZ-FM 107.9 (Urban) 2510 St Clair Ave NE Web: www.z1079fm.com	Cleveland	OH	44114	216-579-1111	771-4164
WERE-AM 1490 (N/T) 2510 St Clair Ave NE Web: www.newstalk1490.com	Cleveland	OH	44114	216-579-1111	771-4164
WFHM-FM 95.5 (Rel) 4 Summit Park Dr Suite 150 Web: www.955thefish.com	Cleveland	OH	44131	216-901-0921	901-5517
WJMO-AM 1300 (Rel) 2510 St Clair Ave NE Web: www.praise1300.com	Cleveland	OH	44114	216-579-1111	771-4164
WKNR-AM 850 (Sports) 1301 E 9th St Suite 232 Web: www.espncleveland.com	Cleveland	OH	44114	216-583-9901	583-9550
WKRK-FM 92.3 (Alt) 1041 Huron Rd Web: www.krockcleveland.com	Cleveland	OH	44115	216-861-0100	696-3710
WMMS-FM 100.7 (Rock) 6200 Oak Tree Blvd S 4th Fl Web: www.wmms.com	Cleveland	OH	44131	216-520-2600	901-8166
WNCX-FM 98.5 (CR) 1041 Huron Rd Web: www.wncx.com	Cleveland	OH	44115	216-861-0100	696-0385
WQAL-FM 104.1 (AC) 1 Radio Ln *Fax Area Code: 213 ■ Web: www.q104.com	Cleveland	OH	44114	216-696-0123	363-7104*
WZAK-FM 93.1 (Urban) 2510 St Clair Ave NE Web: www.931wzak.com	Cleveland	OH	44114	216-579-1111	771-4164

648-40 Colorado Springs, CO

Station	City	State	Zip	Phone	Fax
KATC-FM 95.1 (Ctry) 6805 Corporate Dr Suite 130 Web: www.catcountry951.com	Colorado Springs	CO	80919	719-593-2700	573-2727
KBIQ-FM 102.7 (Rel) 7150 Campus Dr Suite 150 Web: www.kbiqradio.com	Colorado Springs	CO	80920	719-531-5438	531-5588
KCCY-FM 96.9 (Ctry) 2864 S Cir Dr Suite 300 Web: www.y969.com	Colorado Springs	CO	80906	719-540-9200	579-0882
KILO-FM 94.3 (Rock) 1805 E Cheyenne Rd TF: 800-727-5456 ■ Web: www.kilo943.com	Colorado Springs	CO	80905	719-634-4896	634-5837
KKFM-FM 98.1 (CR) 6805 Corporate Dr Suite 130 Web: www.kkfm.com	Colorado Springs	CO	80919	719-593-2700	593-2727
KKLI-FM 106.3 (AC) 2864 S Cir Dr Suite 150 Web: kkli.com	Colorado Springs	CO	80906	719-540-9200	579-0882
KKMG-FM 98.9 (CHR) 6805 Corporate Dr Suite 130 Web: www.989magicfm.com	Colorado Springs	CO	80919	719-593-2700	593-2727
KKPK-FM 92.9 (AC) 6805 Corporate Dr Suite 130	Colorado Springs	CO	80919	719-593-2700	592-2727
KRCC-FM 91.5 (NPR) 912 N Weber St TF: 800-748-2727 ■ Web: www.krcc.org	Colorado Springs	CO	80903	719-473-4801	473-7863
KRXP-FM 103.9 (Rock) 1805 E Cheyenne Rd TF: 866-952-7655 ■ Web: www.1039rxp.com	Colorado Springs	CO	80905	719-634-4896	634-5837
KSKX-FM 105.5 (N/T) 399 S 8th St Web: www.krdo.com	Colorado Springs	CO	80905	719-632-1515	635-8455
KVOR-AM 740 (N/T) 6805 Corporate Dr Suite 130 Web: www.kvor.com	Colorado Springs	CO	80919	719-593-2700	593-2727
KVUU-FM 99.9 (AC) 2864 S Cir Dr Suite 300 Web: www.my999radio.com	Colorado Springs	CO	80906	719-540-9200	579-0882

648-41 Columbia, SC

Station	City	State	Zip	Phone	Fax
WARQ-FM 93.5 (Rock) 1900 Pineview Rd Web: www.warq.com	Columbia	SC	29209	803-695-8680	695-8605
WCOS-AM 1400 (Sports) 316 Greystone Blvd Web: www.1400theteam.com	Columbia	SC	29210	803-343-1100	252-9267
WCOS-FM 97.5 (Ctry) 316 Greystone Blvd Web: www.wcosfm.com	Columbia	SC	29210	803-343-1100	748-9267
WEPR-FM 90.1 (NPR) 1101 George Rogers Blvd Web: www.myetv.org/radio	Columbia	SC	29201	803-737-3545	737-3552
WFMV-FM 95.3 (Rel) 2440 Milwood Ave Web: www.wfmv.com	Columbia	SC	29205	803-939-9530	939-9469
WHMC-FM 90.1 (NPR) 1101 George Rogers Blvd Web: www.scetv.org	Columbia	SC	29201	803-737-3545	737-3552
WHXT-FM 103.9 (Urban) 1900 Pineview Rd TF: 877-874-1039 ■ Web: www.hot1039fm.com	Columbia	SC	29209	803-376-1039	695-8605
WLTR-FM 91.3 (NPR) 1101 George Rogers Blvd Web: www.myetv.org/radio	Columbia	SC	29201	803-737-3545	737-3552
WLTY-FM 96.7 (AC) 316 Greystone Blvd Web: www.wlty.com	Columbia	SC	29210	803-343-1100	748-9267
WMFX-FM 102.3 (CR) 1900 Pineview Rd Web: www.fox102.com	Columbia	SC	29209	803-695-8680	695-8605
WNOK-FM 104.7 (CHR) 316 Greystone Blvd Web: www.wnok.com	Columbia	SC	29210	803-343-1100	779-7874
WOIC-AM 1230 (Sports) 1900 Pineview Rd Web: www.espn1230am.com	Columbia	SC	29209	803-695-8680	695-8605
WVOC-AM 560 (N/T) 316 Greystone Blvd Web: www.wvoc.com	Columbia	SC	29210	803-343-1100	256-5255
WWDM-FM 101.3 (Urban) 1900 Pineview Rd Web: www.thebigdm.com	Columbia	SC	29209	803-695-8680	695-8605

648-42 Columbus, GA

Station	City	State	Zip	Phone	Fax
WAGH-FM 98.3 (Urban) 1501 13th Ave Web: www.sunny100columbus.com	Columbus	GA	31901	706-576-3000	576-3010
WBFA-FM 98.3 (Urban) 1501 13th Ave Web: www.983thebeatonline.com	Columbus	GA	31901	706-576-3000	576-3010
WCGQ-FM 107.3 (AC) 1820 Wynnton Rd TF: 866-841-1077 ■ Web: www.q1073.com	Columbus	GA	31906	706-327-1217	596-4600
WDAK-AM 540 (N/T) 1501 13th Ave Web: www.newsradio540.com	Columbus	GA	31911	706-576-3000	576-3010
WFXE-FM 104.9 (Urban) 2203 Wynnton Rd Web: www.foxie105online.com	Columbus	GA	31906	706-576-3565	576-3683
WGSY-FM 100.1 (AC) 1501 13th Ave Web: www.sunny100columbus.com	Columbus	GA	31901	706-576-3000	576-3010
WHAL-AM 1460 (Span) 1501 13th Ave Web: www.foxsportsradio1460.com/main.html	Columbus	GA	31901	706-576-3000	576-3005
WIOL-AM 1580 (Rel) 2203 Wynnton Rd Web: www.1580thezone.com	Columbus	GA	31906	706-576-3565	576-3683
WKCN-FM 99.3 (Ctry) 1820 Wynnton Rd TF: 800-343-0993 ■ Web: www.kissin993.com	Columbus	GA	31906	706-327-1217	596-4600
WOKS-AM 1340 (Urban) 2203 Wynnton Rd Web: www.1340woks.com	Columbus	GA	31906	706-576-3565	576-3683
WRCG-AM 1420 (N/T) 1820 Wynnton Rd TF: 866-841-1077 ■ Web: www.1069rocks.com	Columbus	GA	31906	706-327-1217	596-4600
WRLD-FM 95.3 (Oldies) 1353 13th Ave Web: www.boomer.fm	Columbus	GA	31901	706-327-1217	596-4600
WSTH-FM 106.1 (Ctry) 1501 13th Ave TF: 800-445-4106 ■ Web: www.rooster106online.com	Columbus	GA	31901	706-576-3000	576-3010
WVRK-FM 102.9 (Rock) 1501 13th Ave Web: www.rock103online.com	Columbus	GA	31901	706-576-3000	576-3010

648-43 Columbus, OH

Station	City	State	Zip	Phone	Fax
WBNS-AM 1460 (Sports) 605 S Front St Suite 300 Web: www.1460thefan.com	Columbus	OH	43206	614-460-3850	460-2822
WBNS-FM 97.1 (AC) 605 S Front St Suite 300 TF: 800-210-6397 ■ Web: www.wbnsfm.com	Columbus	OH	43206	614-460-3850	460-2822
WCBE-FM 90.5 (NPR) 540 Jack Gibbs Blvd Web: www.wcbe.org	Columbus	OH	43215	614-365-5555	365-5060

Station	City	State	Zip	Phone	Fax
WCKX-FM 107.5 (Urban) 350 E 1st Ave Suite 100 *Web:* www.power1075.com	Columbus	OH	43201	614-487-1444	487-5862
WCOL-FM 92.3 (Ctry) 2323 W 5th Ave Suite 200 *Web:* www.wcol.com	Columbus	OH	43204	614-486-6101	487-2559
WHOK-FM 95.5 (Ctry) 280 N High St *Web:* www.whok.com	Columbus	OH	43215	614-225-9465	677-0116
WJYD-FM 106.3 (Rel) 350 E 1st Ave Suite 100 *Web:* www.joy106.com	Columbus	OH	43201	614-487-1444	487-5862
WJZA-FM 103.5 (NAC) 4401 Carriage Hill Ln *Web:* www.wjza.com	Columbus	OH	43220	614-451-2191	451-1831
WLVQ-FM 96.3 (Rock) 280 N High St 10th Fl *TF:* 877-736-9696 ■ *Web:* www.qfm96.com	Columbus	OH	43215	614-227-9696	461-1059
WMNI-AM 920 (Nost) 1458 Dublin Rd *Web:* www.wmni.com	Columbus	OH	43215	614-481-7800	481-8070
WNCI-FM 97.9 (CHR) 2323 W 5th Ave Suite 200 *Web:* www.wnci.com	Columbus	OH	43204	614-486-6101	487-2559
WNKK-FM 107.1 (Ctry) 280 N High St 10th Fl *Web:* www.wink1071.com	Columbus	OH	43215	614-255-9465	461-1059
WOSU-AM 820 (NPR) 2400 Olentangy River Rd *Web:* www.wosu.org	Columbus	OH	43210	614-292-9678	292-7625
WRKZ-FM 99.7 (Rock) 1458 Dublin Rd *Web:* www.997wrkz.com	Columbus	OH	43215	614-481-7800	481-8070
WSNY-FM 94.7 (AC) 4401 Carriage Hill Ln *Web:* www.sunny95.com	Columbus	OH	43220	614-451-2191	451-1831
WTDA-FM 103.9 (N/T) 1458 Dublin Rd *TF:* 800-821-1039	Columbus	OH	43215	614-481-7800	481-8070
WTVN-AM 610 (N/T) 2323 W 5th Ave Suite 200 *Web:* www.610wtvn.com	Columbus	OH	43204	614-486-6101	487-2559
WWCD-FM 101.1 (Alt) 503 S Front St Suite 101 *Web:* www.cd101.com	Columbus	OH	43215	614-221-9923	227-0021
WXMG-FM 98.9 (Urban) 350 E 1st Ave Suite 100 *Web:* www.magic989.com	Columbus	OH	43201	614-487-1444	487-5862
WYTS-FM 105.7 (N/T) 2323 W 5th Ave Suite 200 *Web:* www.1057thebrew.com	Columbus	OH	43204	614-486-6101	847-2559

648-44 Corpus Christi, TX

Station	City	State	Zip	Phone	Fax
KEDT-FM 90.3 (NPR) 4455 S Padre Island Dr Suite 38 *TF:* 800-307-5338 ■ *Web:* www.kedt.org	Corpus Christi	TX	78411	361-855-2213	855-3877
KEYS-AM 1440 (N/T) 2117 Leopard St *Web:* www.1440keys.com	Corpus Christi	TX	78408	361-882-7411	882-9767
KFTX-FM 97.5 (Ctry) 1520 S Port Ave *TF:* 866-975-5389 ■ *Web:* www.kftx.com	Corpus Christi	TX	78405	361-883-5987	883-3648
KKBA-FM 92.7 (AC) 2117 Leopard St *Web:* www.927kbay.com	Corpus Christi	TX	78408	361-883-3516	882-9767
KLTG-FM 96.5 (AC) 1300 Antelope St *Web:* www.thebeach965online.com	Corpus Christi	TX	78401	361-883-1600	883-9303
KLUX-FM 89.5 (AC) 1200 Lantana St *Web:* www.goccn.org	Corpus Christi	TX	78407	361-289-2487	289-1420
KMXR-FM 93.9 (Oldies) 501 Tupper Ln *Web:* www.mix939.com	Corpus Christi	TX	78417	361-289-0111	289-5035
KNCN-FM 101.3 (Rock) 501 Tupper Ln *Web:* www.c101.com	Corpus Christi	TX	78417	361-289-0111	289-5035
KOUL-FM 103.7 (Ctry) 1300 Antelope St	Corpus Christi	TX	78401	361-883-1600	883-9303
KRYS-FM 99.1 (Ctry) 501 Tupper Ln *Web:* www.krysfm.com	Corpus Christi	TX	78417	361-289-0111	289-5035
KSAB-FM 99.9 (Span) 501 Tupper Ln *Web:* www.ksabfm.com	Corpus Christi	TX	78417	361-289-0111	289-5035
KZFM-FM 95.5 (CHR) 2117 Leopard St *Web:* www.hotz95.com	Corpus Christi	TX	78408	361-883-3516	

648-45 Dallas/Fort Worth, TX

Station	City	State	Zip	Phone	Fax
KBFB-FM 97.9 (Urban) 13331 Preston Rd Suite 1180 *Web:* www.979thebeat.com	Dallas	TX	75240	972-331-5400	331-5560
KDGE-FM 102.1 (Alt) 14001 N Dallas Pkwy Suite 300 *Web:* www.kdge.com	Dallas	TX	75240	214-866-8000	866-8008
KDMX-FM 102.9 (AC) 14001 N Dallas Pkwy Suite 300 *Web:* www.mix1029.com	Dallas	TX	75240	214-866-8000	866-8008
KDXX-FM 107.1 (Span AC) 7700 John Carpenter Fwy *Web:* www.kdxx.netmio.com	Dallas	TX	75247	214-525-0400	631-1196
KEGL-FM 97.1 (Rock) 14001 N Dallas Pkwy Suite 300 *Web:* www.kegl.com	Dallas	TX	75240	214-866-8000	866-8008
KERA-FM 90.1 (NPR) 3000 Harry Hines Blvd *TF:* 800-456-5372 ■ *Web:* www.kera.org	Dallas	TX	75201	214-871-1390	754-0635
KESS-FM 107.9 (Span) 7700 John Carpenter Fwy *Web:* www.univision.com	Dallas	TX	75247	214-525-0400	631-1172
KHKS-FM 106.1 (CHR) 14001 N Dallas Pkwy Suite 300 *Web:* www.1061kissfm.com	Dallas	TX	75240	214-866-8000	866-8008
KJKK-FM 100.3 (Var) 4131 N Central Expy Suite 1000 *NYSE: CBS* ■ *Web:* www.jackontheweb.com	Dallas	TX	75247	214-525-7000	688-7760
KKDA-AM 730 (Oldies) 621 NW 6th St	Grand Prairie	TX	75050	972-263-9911	
KKDA-FM 104.5 (Urban) 621 NW 6th St *Web:* www.k104fm.com	Grand Prairie	TX	75050	972-263-9911	558-0010
KLIF-AM 570 (N/T) 3500 Maple Ave Suite 1600 *Web:* www.klif.com	Dallas	TX	75219	214-526-2400	520-4343
KLNO-FM 94.1 (Span) 7700 John Carpenter Fwy	Dallas	TX	75247	214-525-0400	631-1196
KLUV-FM 98.7 (Oldies) 4131 N Central Expy Suite 1000 *NYSE: CBS* ■ *Web:* www.kluv.com	Dallas	TX	75204	214-525-7000	688-7760
KMVK-FM 107.5 (Urban) 4131 N Central Expy Suite 1000 *Web:* www.movin1075.com	Dallas	TX	75204	214-525-7000	525-7145
KNON-FM 89.3 (Var) PO Box 710909 *Web:* www.knon.org	Dallas	TX	75371	214-828-9500	823-3051
KPLX-FM 99.5 (Ctry) 3500 Maple Ave Suite 1600 *Web:* www.995thewolf.com	Dallas	TX	75219	214-526-2400	520-4343
KRLD-AM 1080 (N/T) 4131 N Central Expy Suite 500 *TF:* 800-289-1080 ■ *Web:* www.krld.com	Dallas	TX	75204	214-525-7000	443-6572
KSOC-FM 94.5 (Urban) 13331 Preston Rd Suite 1180 *Web:* www.945ksoul.com	Dallas	TX	75240	972-331-5400	331-5560
KVIL-FM 103.7 (AC) 4131 N Central Expy Suite 1000 *NYSE: CBS* ■ *Web:* 1037litefm.com	Dallas	TX	75204	214-525-7000	688-7760
KVTT-FM 91.7 (Rel) 11061 Shady Trail *TF:* 866-787-1917 ■ *Web:* www.917thetruth.org	Dallas	TX	75229	214-351-6655	351-6809
KZPS-FM 92.5 (CR) 14001 N Dallas Pkwy Suite 300 *Web:* www.kzps.com	Dallas	TX	75240	214-866-8000	866-8008
WRR-FM 101.1 (Clas) PO Box 159001 *Web:* www.wrr101.com	Dallas	TX	75315	214-670-8888	670-8394

648-46 Dayton, OH

Station	City	State	Zip	Phone	Fax
WDHT-FM 102.9 (Urban) 717 E David Rd *Web:* www.hot1029.com	Dayton	OH	45429	937-294-5858	297-5233
WDKF-FM 94.5 (CHR) 101 Pine St *Web:* www.channeldayton.com	Dayton	OH	45402	937-224-1137	224-3667
WDPR-FM 88.1 (Clas) 126 N Main St *Web:* www.dpr.org	Dayton	OH	45402	937-496-3850	496-3852
WFCJ-FM 93.7 (Rel) PO Box 937 *Web:* www.wfcj.com	Dayton	OH	45449	937-866-2471	866-2062
WGTZ-FM 92.9 (CHR) 717 E David Rd *Web:* www.fly929.com	Dayton	OH	45429	937-457-4359	297-5233
WHIO-AM 1290 (N/T) 1414 Wilmington Ave *Web:* www.1290whio.com	Dayton	OH	45420	937-259-2111	259-2168
WHIO-FM 95.7 (N/T) 1414 Wilmington Ave *Web:* daytonspoint.com	Dayton	OH	45402	937-259-2111	259-2168
WHKO-FM 99.1 (Ctry) 1414 Wilmington Ave *Web:* www.k99online.com	Dayton	OH	45420	937-259-2111	259-2168
WING-AM 1410 (Sports) 717 E David Rd *Web:* www.wingam.com	Dayton	OH	45429	937-294-5858	297-5233
WLQT-FM 99.9 (AC) 101 Pine St *Web:* www.wlqt.com	Dayton	OH	45402	937-224-1137	224-3667
WMMX-FM 107.7 (AC) 101 Pine St *Web:* www.wmmx.com	Dayton	OH	45402	937-224-1137	224-3667
WONE-AM 980 (Sports) 101 Pine St *Web:* www.wone.com	Dayton	OH	45402	937-224-1137	224-5015
WROU-FM 92.1 (Urban AC) 717 E David Rd *Web:* www.921wrou.com	Dayton	OH	45429	937-294-5858	297-5233
WTUE-FM 104.7 (Rock) 101 Pine St *Web:* www.wtue.com	Dayton	OH	45402	937-224-1137	224-5015
WXEG-FM 103.9 (Alt) 101 Pine St *Web:* www.wxeg.com	Dayton	OH	45402	937-224-1137	224-5015

648-47 Daytona Beach, FL

Station	City	State	Zip	Phone	Fax
WHOG-FM 95.7 (CR) 126 W International Speedway Blvd *Web:* www.whog.fm	Daytona Beach	FL	32114	386-257-1150	238-6488
WKRO-FM 93.1 (Ctry) 126 W International Speedway Blvd *Web:* www.wkro.fm	Daytona Beach	FL	32114	386-255-9300	238-6488
WNDB-AM 1150 (N/T) 126 W International Speedway Blvd *Web:* www.daytonasun.com	Daytona Beach	FL	32114	386-355-9300	238-6488
WVYB-FM 103.3 (CHR) 126 W International Speedway Blvd *Web:* www.wvyb.fm	Daytona Beach	FL	32114	386-257-6900	238-6488

648-48 Denver, CO

Station	City	State	Zip	Phone	Fax
KALC-FM 105.9 (AC) 4700 S Syracuse Pkwy Suite 1050 *Web:* www.alice1059.com	Denver	CO	80237	303-967-2700	967-2747
KBPI-FM 106.7 (Rock) 4695 S Monaco St *Web:* www.kbpi.com	Denver	CO	80237	303-713-8000	713-8743
KEZW-AM 1430 (Nost) 4700 S Syracuse Pkwy Suite 1050 *Web:* www.kezw.com	Denver	CO	80237	303-967-2700	967-2747
KHOW-AM 630 (N/T) 4695 S Monaco St *Web:* www.khow.com	Denver	CO	80237	303-713-8000	713-8424
KIMN-FM 100.3 (AC) 1560 Broadway Suite 1100 *Web:* www.mix100.com	Denver	CO	80202	303-832-5665	832-7000
KJMN-FM 92.1 (Span AC) 777 Grant St 5th Fl *TF:* 888-874-2656 ■ *Web:* www.denverhispanicradio.com	Denver	CO	80203	303-832-0050	832-3410
KKZN-AM 760 (N/T) 4695 S Monaco St *Web:* www.am760.net	Denver	CO	80237	303-713-8000	713-8424
KMXA-AM 1090 (Span) 777 Grant St 5th Fl *Web:* www.somosnoticiascolorado.com	Denver	CO	80203	303-832-0050	832-3410
KOA-AM 850 (N/T) 4695 S Monaco Ave *Web:* www.850koa.com	Denver	CO	80237	303-713-8000	713-8424

Station	City	State	Zip	Phone	Fax
KOSI-FM 101.1 (AC) 4700 S Syracuse Pkwy Suite 1050 *Web:* www.kosi101.com	Denver	CO	80237	303-967-2700	967-2747
KPTT-FM 95.7 (CHR) 4695 S Monaco St *Web:* www.957theparty.com	Denver	CO	80237	303-713-8000	713-8734
KQMT-FM 99.5 (AAA) 4700 S Syracuse Pkwy Suite 1050 *Web:* www.995themountain.com	Denver	CO	80237	303-967-2700	967-2747
KRFX-FM 103.5 (CR) 4695 S Monaco St *Web:* www.thefox.com	Denver	CO	80237	303-713-8000	713-8743
KTCL-FM 93.3 (Alt) 4695 S Monaco St Suite 1300 *Web:* www.area93.com	Denver	CO	80237	303-713-8000	713-8743
KUVO-FM 89.3 (Jazz) 2900 Welton St # 200 *TF:* 800-574-5886 ■ *Web:* www.kuvo.org	Denver	CO	80205	303-480-9272	291-0757
KWLI-FM 92.5 (Ctry) 1560 Broadway Suite 1100 *Web:* www.willie925.com	Denver	CO	80202	303-832-5665	832-7000
KXKL-FM 105.1 (Oldies) 720 S Colorado Blvd Suite 1200 N *Web:* www.kool105.com	Denver	CO	80246	303-832-5665	832-7000
KXPK-FM 96.5 (Span) 777 Grant St 5th Fl *Web:* www.965tricolor.com	Denver	CO	80203	303-832-0050	832-3410

648-49 Des Moines, IA

Station	City	State	Zip	Phone	Fax
KAZR-FM 103.3 (Rock) 1416 Locust St *Web:* www.lazer1033.com	Des Moines	IA	50309	515-280-1350	280-3011
KDRB-FM 100.3 (AC) 2141 Grand Ave *Web:* www.thebusfm.com	Des Moines	IA	50312	515-245-8900	245-8902
KIOA-FM 93.3 (Oldies) 1416 Locust St *Web:* www.kioa.com	Des Moines	IA	50309	515-280-1350	280-3011
KKDM-FM 107.5 (AC) 2141 Grand Ave. *Web:* www.kkdm.com	Des Moines	IA	50312	515-245-8900	245-8902
KLTI-FM 104.1 (AC) 1416 Locust St *Web:* www.lite1041.com	Des Moines	IA	50309	515-280-1350	280-3011
KSTZ-FM 102.5 (AC) 1416 Locust St *Web:* www.star1025.com	Des Moines	IA	50309	515-280-1350	280-3011
WHO-AM 1040 (N/T) 2141 Grand Ave *Web:* www.whoradio.com	Des Moines	IA	50312	515-245-8900	245-8902

648-50 Detroit, MI

Station	City	State	Zip	Phone	Fax
WDET-FM 101.9 (NPR) 4600 Cass Ave Wayne State University *Web:* www.wdetfm.org	Detroit	MI	48201	313-577-4146	577-1300
WDMK-FM 105.9 (Urban) 3250 Franklin St *Web:* www.kissdetroit.com	Detroit	MI	48207	313-259-2000	259-7011
WDRQ-FM 93.1 (Var) 3011 W Grand Blvd Fisher Bldg Suite 800 *Web:* www.931dougfm.com	Detroit	MI	48202	313-871-9300	872-0190
WDVD-FM 96.3 (AC) 3011 W Grand Blvd Fisher Bldg Suite 800 *Web:* www.963wdvd.com	Detroit	MI	48202	313-871-3030	872-0190
WGPR-FM 107.5 (Urban) 3146 E Jefferson Ave *Web:* www.wgprdetroit.com	Detroit	MI	48207	313-259-8862	259-6662
WJR-AM 760 (N/T) 3011 W Grand Blvd Fisher Bldg Suite 800 *Web:* www.760wjr.com	Detroit	MI	48202	313-875-4440	875-9022
WMUZ-FM 103.5 (Rel) 12300 Radio Pl *Web:* www.wmuz.com	Detroit	MI	48228	313-272-3434	
WMXD-FM 92.3 (Urban) 645 Griswold St Suite 633 *Web:* www.mix923fm.com	Detroit	MI	48226	313-965-2000	965-3965
WRIF-FM 101.1 (Rock) 1 Radio Plaza Rd. *Web:* www.wrif.com	Detroit	MI	48220	248-547-0101	542-8800

648-51 Dubuque, IA

Station	City	State	Zip	Phone	Fax
KATF-FM 92.9 (AC) 346 W 8th St *TF:* 800-325-2836 ■ *Web:* www.katfm.com	Dubuque	IA	52001	563-690-0800	588-5688
KDTH-AM 1370 (N/T) 346 W 8th St PO Box 659 *TF:* 800-422-5384 ■ *Web:* www.kdth.com	Dubuque	IA	52001	563-690-0800	588-5688
KGRR-FM 97.3 (CR) 346 W 8th St. *TF:* 800-357-7625 ■ *Web:* www.973therock.com	Dubuque	IA	52001	563-690-0800	588-5688
KLYV-FM 105.3 (AC) 5490 Saratoga Rd *Web:* www.y105online.com	Dubuque	IA	52002	563-557-1040	583-4535
KXGE-FM 102.3 (CR) 5490 Saratoga Rd *Web:* www.eagle102rocks.com	Dubuque	IA	52002	563-557-1040	583-4535
WDBQ-AM 1490 (N/T) 5490 Saratoga Rd *Web:* www.wdbqam.com	Dubuque	IA	52002	563-557-1040	583-4535
WDBQ-FM 107.5 (Oldies) 5490 Saratoga Rd *Web:* www.myq1075.com	Dubuque	IA	52002	563-557-1040	583-4535
WJOD-FM 103.3 (Ctry) 5490 Saratoga Rd *Web:* www.103wjod.com	Dubuque	IA	52002	563-557-1040	583-4535

648-52 Duluth, MN

Station	City	State	Zip	Phone	Fax
KBMX-FM 107.7 (AC) 14 E Central Entrance *Web:* www.mix108.com	Duluth	MN	55811	218-727-2649	727-9356
KDAL-AM 610 (N/T) 715 E Central Entrance *TF:* 888-532-5610 ■ *Web:* www.kdal.am	Duluth	MN	55811	218-722-4321	722-5423
KDAL-FM 95.7 (AC) 715 E Central Entrance *TF:* 800-532-5610 ■ *Web:* www.kdal.fm	Duluth	MN	55811	218-722-4321	722-5423
KDNW-FM 97.3 (Rel) 1101 E Central Entrance *TF:* 888-322-5369 ■ *Web:* www.kdnw.nwc.edu	Duluth	MN	55811	218-722-6700	722-1092
KKCB-FM 105.1 (Ctry) 14 E Central Entrance. *TF:* 800-928-2105 ■ *Web:* www.kkcb.com	Duluth	MN	55811	218-727-4500	727-9356
KLDJ-FM 101.7 (Oldies) 14 E Central Entrance *Web:* www.kool1017.com	Duluth	MN	55811	218-727-5665	727-9356
KRBR-FM 102.5 (Rock) 715 E Central Entrance *TF:* 888-532-5610 ■ *Web:* www.krbr.com	Duluth	MN	55811	218-722-4321	722-5423
KTCO-FM 98.9 (Ctry) 715 E Central Entrance *TF:* 888-532-5610 ■ *Web:* www.ktco.fm	Duluth	MN	55811	218-722-4321	722-5423
KUMD-FM 103.3 (Var) 1201 Ordean Ct 130 Humanities Bldg Rm 130 *TF:* 800-566-5863 ■ *Web:* www.kumd.org	Duluth	MN	55812	218-726-7181	726-6571
WDSM-AM 710 (Sports) 715 E Central Entrance *TF:* 888-532-5610	Duluth	MN	55811	218-722-4321	722-5423
WEBC-AM 560 (Sports) 14 E Central Entrance *Web:* www.webc560.com	Duluth	MN	55811	218-727-4500	727-9356
WJRF-FM 89.5 (Rel) 4604 Airpark Blvd *TF:* 800-727-4487 ■ *Web:* www.refugeradio.com	Duluth	MN	55811	218-722-3017	
WSCN-FM 100.5 (NPR) 207 W Superior St Suite 224 *Web:* www.mpr.org	Duluth	MN	55802	218-722-9411	720-4900
WWJC-AM 850 (Rel) 1120 E McCuen St *TF:* 877-626-2738 ■ *Web:* www.wwjc.com	Duluth	MN	55808	218-626-2738	626-2585

648-53 Edmonton, AB

Station	City	Prov	Postal Code	Phone	Fax
CBX-AM 740 (CBC) 10062 102nd Ave 123 Edmonton City Ctr *Web:* www.cbc.ca/edmonton	Edmonton	AB	T5J2Y8	780-468-7500	468-7419
CBX-FM 90.9 (CBC) 10062 102nd Ave 123 Edmonton City Ctr *Web:* www.cbc.ca/edmonton	Edmonton	AB	T5J2Y8	780-468-7500	468-7419
CFBR-FM 100.3 (CR) 18520 Stony Plain Rd Suite 100 *Web:* www.thebearrocks.com	Edmonton	AB	T5S2E2	780-486-2800	489-6927
CFRN-AM 1260 (Sports) 18520 Stony Plain Rd Suite 100 *Web:* www.theteam1260.com	Edmonton	AB	T5S2E2	780-486-2800	489-6927
CHED-AM 630 (N/T) 5204 84th St *Web:* www.630ched.com	Edmonton	AB	T6E5N8	780-424-8800	469-5937
CHFA-AM 680 (CBC) 10062 102nd Ave 123 Edmonton City Ctr *Web:* www.radio-canada.ca	Edmonton	AB	T5J2Y8	780-468-7500	468-7849
CHQT-AM 880 (N/T) 5204 84th St *Web:* www.inews880.com	Edmonton	AB	T6E5N8	780-424-8800	469-5937
CIRK-FM 97.3 (CR) 8882 170th St 2394 W Edmonton Mall *Web:* www.k-rock973.com	Edmonton	AB	T5T4M2	780-437-4996	436-9803
CISN-FM 103.9 (Ctry) 5204 84th St *Web:* www.cisnfm.com	Edmonton	AB	T6E5N8	780-424-8800	469-5937
CKNG-FM 92.5 (CHR) 5204 84th St *Web:* www.joefm.ca	Edmonton	AB	T6E5N8	780-424-8800	469-5937
CKRA-FM 96.3 (Ctry) 8882 178th St 2394 W Edmonton Mall *Web:* www.963capitalfm.com	Edmonton	AB	T5T4M2	780-437-4996	436-9803
CKUA-AM 580 (Var) 10526 Jasper Ave 4th Fl *TF:* 800-494-2582 ■ *Web:* www.ckua.org	Edmonton	AB	T5J1Z7	780-428-7595	428-7624
CKUA-FM 94.9 (Var) 10526 Jasper Ave 4th Fl *TF:* 800-494-2582 ■ *Web:* www.ckua.org	Edmonton	AB	T5J1Z7	780-428-7595	428-7624

648-54 El Paso, TX

Station	City	State	Zip	Phone	Fax
KAMA-AM 750 (Span) 2211 E Missouri Ave Suite S-300 *TF:* 800-880-9797 ■ *Web:* kama.netmio.com	El Paso	TX	79903	915-544-9797	544-1247
KBNA-FM 97.5 (Span AC) 2211 E Missouri Ave Suite S-300 *TF:* 800-880-9797 ■ *Web:* kbna.netmio.com	El Paso	TX	79903	915-544-9797	544-1247
KELP-AM 1590 (Rel) 6900 Commerce St *Web:* www.kelpradio.com	El Paso	TX	79915	915-779-0016	779-6641
KHEY-FM 96.3 (Ctry) 4045 N Mesa St *Web:* www.khey.com	El Paso	TX	79902	915-351-5400	351-3136
KHRO-AM 1650 (N/T) 5426 N Mesa St *Web:* www.univision26.com	El Paso	TX	79912	915-581-1126	532-4970
KINT-FM 93.9 (Span) 5426 N Mesa St *Web:* www.univision26.com	El Paso	TX	79912	915-581-1126	532-4970
KLAQ-FM 95.5 (Rock) 4180 N Mesa St *Web:* www.klaq.com	El Paso	TX	79902	915-544-8864	532-3334
KOFX-FM 92.3 (Oldies) 5426 N Mesa St *Web:* www.923thefox.com	El Paso	TX	79912	915-581-1126	532-4970
KPRR-FM 102.1 (CHR) 4045 N Mesa St *Web:* www.kprr.com	El Paso	TX	79902	915-351-5400	351-3136
KROD-AM 600 (N/T) 4180 N Mesa St *Web:* www.krod.com	El Paso	TX	79902	915-544-8864	532-3334
KSII-FM 93.1 (AC) 4180 N Mesa St. *Web:* www.ksii.com	El Paso	TX	79902	915-544-8864	532-3334
KTEP-FM 88.5 (NPR) 500 W University Ave Cotton Memorial Bldg Rm 203 *Web:* www.ktep.org	El Paso	TX	79968	915-747-5152	747-5641
KTSM-AM 690 (N/T) 4045 N Mesa St *Web:* www.ktsmradio.com	El Paso	TX	79902	915-351-5400	351-3136
KTSM-FM 99.9 (AC) 4045 N Mesa St *Web:* www.sunny999fm.com	El Paso	TX	79902	915-351-5400	351-3136
XHNZ-FM 107.5 (Span) 2100 Trawood Dr *Web:* laradiodeneta.webs.com	El Paso	TX	79935	915-542-2969	542-2958

Phone *Fax*

XHTO-FM 104.3 (CHR) 2100 Trawood Dr . . . . El Paso TX 79936 915-542-2969 542-2958
Web: www.hitfmradio.com

648-55 Erie, PA

Phone *Fax*

WFNN-AM 1330 (Sports) 1 Boston Store Pl. . . . . Erie PA 16501 814-461-1000 874-0011
Web: www.sportsradio1330.com
WJET-AM 1400 (N/T) 1 Boston Store Pl . . . . Erie PA 16501 814-461-1000 461-1500
Web: www.jetradio1400.com
WQHZ-FM 102.3 (CR) 471 Robison Rd. Erie PA 16509 814-868-5355 868-1876
WQLN-FM 91.3 (NPR) 8425 Peach St . . . . Erie PA 16509 814-864-3001 864-4077
TF: 800-727-8854 ■ *Web:* www.wqln.org
WRIE-AM 1260 (Sports) 471 Robison Rd. . . . . Erie PA 16509 814-868-5355 868-1876
Web: www.am1260thescore.com
WRKT-FM 100.9 (Rock) 1 Boston Store Pl. . . . . Erie PA 16501 814-461-1000 455-1111
Web: www.rocket101.com
WRTS-FM 103.7 (CHR) 1 Boston Store Pl . . . . Erie PA 16501 814-461-1000 455-6000
Web: www.star104.com
WXBB-FM 94.7 (AC) 1 Boston Store Pl. Erie PA 16501 814-461-1000 874-0011
WXKC-FM 99.9 (AC) 471 Robison Rd. . . . . Erie PA 16509 814-868-5355 868-1876
Web: www.classy100.com
WXTA-FM 97.9 (Ctry) 471 Robison Rd. Erie PA 16509 814-868-5355 868-1876

648-56 Eugene, OR

Phone *Fax*

KDUK-FM 104.7 (CHR)
1500 Valley River Dr Suite 350. . . . . Eugene OR 97401 541-485-1120 484-5769
Web: www.kduk.com
KEUG-FM 105.5 (AC)
925 Country Club Rd Suite 200 . . . . Eugene OR 97401 541-484-9400 344-9424
Web: www.1055bobfm.com
KKNU-FM 93.3 (Ctry)
925 Country Club Rd Suite 200 . . . . Eugene OR 97401 541-484-9400 344-9424
Web: www.kknu.com
KLCC-FM 89.7 (NPR) 4000 E 30th Ave . . . . Eugene OR 97405 541-463-6000 463-6046
Web: www.klcc.org
KMGE-FM 94.5 (AC)
925 Country Club Rd Suite 200 . . . . Eugene OR 97401 541-484-9400 344-9424
Web: www.kmge.fm
KNRQ-FM 97.9 (Alt)
1200 Executive Pkwy Suite 440 . . . . Eugene OR 97401 541-284-8500 485-0969
Web: www.nrq.com
KODZ-FM 99.1 (CR)
1500 Valley River Dr Suite 350. . . . . Eugene OR 97401 541-485-1120 484-5769
Web: www.kool991.com
KUGN-AM 590 (N/T)
1200 Executive Pkwy Suite 440 . . . . Eugene OR 97401 541-284-8500 485-0969
TF: 800-590-5846 ■ *Web:* www.kugn.com
KZEL-FM 96.1 (CR)
1200 Executive Pkwy Suite 440 . . . . Eugene OR 97405 541-284-8500
Web: www.96kzel.com

648-57 Evansville, IN

Phone *Fax*

WABX-FM 107.5 (CR) 1162 Mt Auburn Rd. . . . . Evansville IN 47720 812-424-8284 426-7928
TF: 877-924-7625 ■ *Web:* www.wabx.net
WDKS-FM 106.1 (CHR) 1133 Lincoln Ave . . . . Evansville IN 47714 812-425-4226 428-5895
Web: www.kissfmevansville.com
WGBF-AM 1280 (N/T) 117 SE 5th St. . . . . Evansville IN 47708 812-425-4226
Web: www.newstalk1280.com
WGBF-FM 103.1 (Rock) 117 SE 5th St . . . . Evansville IN 47708 812-425-4226
Web: www.103gbfrocks.com
WIKY-FM 104.1 (AC) 1162 Mt Auburn Rd . . . . Evansville IN 47720 812-424-8284 426-7928
TF: 800-879-3172 ■ *Web:* www.wiky.com
WJLT-FM 105.3 (Oldies) 117 SE 5th St . . . . Evansville IN 47708 812-421-1117
Web: www.superhits1053.com
WKDQ-FM 99.5 (Ctry) 117 SE 5th St . . . . Evansville IN 47708 812-425-4226
Web: www.wkdq.com
WLFW-FM 93.5 (Ctry)
1162 Mt Auburn Rd PO Box 3848 . . . . Evansville IN 47720 812-424-8284 426-7928
TF: 800-879-3172 ■ *Web:* www.935thewolf.com
WNIN-FM 88.3 (NPR) 405 Carpenter St . . . . Evansville IN 47708 812-423-2973 428-7548
TF: 800-264-9646 ■ *Web:* www.wnin.org
WSTO-FM 96.1 (CHR)
1162 Mt Auburn Rd PO Box 3848 . . . . Evansville IN 47720 812-421-9696 421-3273
TF: 800-454-9459 ■ *Web:* www.wsto.com

648-58 Fairbanks, AK

Phone *Fax*

KAKQ-FM 101.1 (AC) 546 9th Ave . . . . .Fairbanks AK 99701 907-450-1000 457-2128
Web: www.101magic.com
KCBF-AM 820 (Sports) 819 1st Ave Suite A. . . . . .Fairbanks AK 99709 907-451-5910 451-5999
Web: www.820sports.com
KFAR-AM 660 (N/T) 819 1st Ave Suite A. . . . . .Fairbanks AK 99709 907-451-5910 451-5999
Web: kfar660.com
KFBX-AM 970 (N/T) 546 9th Ave. .Fairbanks AK 99701 907-450-1000 457-2128
Web: www.am970.com
KIAK-FM 102.5 (Ctry) 546 9th Ave. . . . . .Fairbanks AK 99701 907-450-1000 457-2128
Web: www.kiak.com
KKED-FM 104.7 (Rock) 546 9th Ave . . . . .Fairbanks AK 99701 907-450-1000 457-2128
Web: www.1047theedge.com
KSUA-FM 91.5 (Alt) 307 Capital Dr . . . . .Fairbanks AK 99709 907-474-7054 474-6314
Web: www.ksua.uaf.edu
KUAC-FM 89.9 (NPR)
312 Tanana Dr Suite 202 PO Box 755620. . . . . .Fairbanks AK 99775 907-474-7491 474-5064
TF: 800-727-6543 ■ *Web:* www.kuac.org
KWLF-FM 98.1 (CHR) 819 1st Ave Suite A . . . . .Fairbanks AK 99709 907-451-5910 451-5999
Web: www.wolf98fm.com
KXLR-FM 95.9 (CR) 819 1st Ave Suite A. . . . . .Fairbanks AK 99709 907-451-5910 451-5999
Web: www.xrock959.com

648-59 Fargo, ND

Phone *Fax*

KBVB-FM 95.1 (Cty) 1020 25th St S. .Fargo ND 58103 701-237-5346 237-0980
Web: www.bob95fm.com
KDSU-FM 91.9 (NPR) 207 5th St N. . . . . .Fargo ND 58102 701-241-6900 239-7651
TF: 800-359-6900 ■ *Web:* www.prairiepublic.org
KFGO-AM 790 (N/T) 1020 25th St S . . . . .Fargo ND 58103 701-237-5346 237-0908
Web: www.kfgo.com
KFNW-FM 97.9 (Rel) 5702 52nd Ave S. . . . . .Fargo ND 58104 701-282-5910 282-5781
TF: 800-979-1200 ■ *Web:* www.kfnw.org
KLTA-FM 105.1 (AC) 2720 7th Ave S .Fargo ND 58103 701-237-4500 235-9082
Web: www.fm1051.net
KPFX-FM 107.9 (CR) 2720 7th Ave S. . . . . .Fargo ND 58103 701-237-4500 237-5400
Web: www.1079thefox.com
KQWB-FM 98.7 (Rock) 2720 7th Ave S . . . . .Fargo ND 58103 701-237-4500 237-5400
Web: www.q98.com
KRWK-FM 101.9 (CR) 1020 25th St S . . . . .Fargo ND 58103 701-237-5346 235-4042
Web: www.rock102online.com
KVOX-FM 99.9 (Ctry) 2720 7th Ave S. . . . . .Fargo ND 58103 701-237-4500 235-9082
Web: www.froggyweb.com
WDAY-AM 970 (N/T) 301 8th St S . . . . .Fargo ND 58103 701-237-6500 241-5373
Web: www.wday.com
WDAY-FM 93.7 (CHR) 1020 25th St S. . . . . .Fargo ND 58103 701-237-5346 237-0980
Web: www.y94.com

648-60 Flagstaff, AZ

Phone *Fax*

KAFF-AM 930 (Ctry) 1117 W Rt 66. . . . . .Flagstaff AZ 86001 928-774-5231 779-2988
Web: www.kaff.com
KAFF-FM 92.9 (Ctry) 1117 W Rt 66 . . . . .Flagstaff AZ 86001 928-774-5231 779-2988
Web: www.kaff.com
KFLX-FM 105.1 (AAA) 112 E Rt 66 Suite 105. . . . . .Flagstaff AZ 86001 928-779-1177 774-5179
TF: 800-971-1051
KMGN-FM 93.9 (CR) 1117 W Rt 66. . . . . .Flagstaff AZ 86001 928-774-5231 779-2988
Web: www.kmgn.com
KNAU-FM 88.7 (NPR)
Bldg 83 NAU Campus PO Box 5764. . . . . .Flagstaff AZ 86011 928-523-5628 523-7647
TF: 800-523-5628 ■ *Web:* www.knau.org
KSED-FM 107.5 (Ctry)
2409 N 4th St Suite 101 . . . . .Flagstaff AZ 86004 928-779-1177 774-5179
TF: 800-799-5658 ■ *Web:* www.koltcountry.com

648-61 Flint, MI

Phone *Fax*

WDZZ-FM 92.7 (Urban) 6317 Taylor Dr . . . . .Flint MI 48507 810-238-7300 238-7310
Web: www.wdzz.com
WFBE-FM 95.1 (Ctry) G-4511 Miller Rd. . . . . .Flint MI 48507 810-720-9510 720-9513
Web: www.b95.fm
WFLT-AM 1420 (Rel) 317 S Averill Ave. . . . . .Flint MI 48506 810-239-5733 239-7134
WOWE-FM 98.9 (Urban) 444 Church St. . . . . .Flint MI 48502 810-234-4335 519-4809
WRSR-FM 103.9 (CR) 6317 Taylor Dr. .Flint MI 48507 810-238-7300 238-7310
Web: www.classicfox.com
WWCK-FM 105.5 (CHR) 6317 Taylor Dr . . . . .Flint MI 48507 810-238-7300 238-7310
Web: www.wwck.com

648-63 Fort Smith, AR

Phone *Fax*

KBBQ-FM 102.7 (Urban)
3101 Free Ferry Rd Suite E. . . . . Fort Smith AR 72903 479-452-0681 452-0873
Web: www.1027thevibe.com
KISR-FM 93.7 (CHR) 4 Glen Haven Dr . . . . Fort Smith AR 72901 479-785-2526 782-9127
Web: www.kisr.net
KKBD-FM 95.9 (CR) 311 Lexington Ave . . . . Fort Smith AR 72901 479-782-8888 785-5946
Web: www.bigdog959.com
KLSZ-FM 100.7 (Rock)
3101 Free Ferry Rd Suite E. . . . . Fort Smith AR 72903 479-452-0681 452-0873
Web: www.rock1007.com
KMAG-FM 99.1 (Ctry) 311 Lexington Ave . . . . Fort Smith AR 72901 479-782-8888 785-5946
Web: www.kmag991.com
KOMS-FM 107.3 (Ctry)
3101 Free Ferry Rd Suite E. . . . . Fort Smith AR 72903 479-452-0681 452-0873
Web: bigcountry1073.com
KREU-FM 92.3 (Span) 2201 1/2 N 58th St . . . . Fort Smith AR 72904 479-785-2526 782-9127
KTCS-FM 99.9 (Ctry) 5304 Hwy 45 E. . . . . Fort Smith AR 72916 479-646-6151 646-3509
Web: www.ktcs.com
KWHN-AM 1320 (N/T) 311 Lexington Ave. . . . . Fort Smith AR 72901 479-782-8888 785-5946
Web: www.kwhn.com

Station	City	State	ZIP	Phone	Fax
KZBB-FM 97.9 (CHR) 311 Lexington Ave .... Web: www.kzbb.com	Fort Smith	AR	72901	479-782-8888	785-5946
KZKZ-FM 106.3 (Rel) 6420 S Zero St .... TF: 800-583-7960 ■ Web: www.kzkzfm.com	Fort Smith	AR	72903	479-646-6700	646-1373

648-64 Fort Wayne, IN

Station	City	State	ZIP	Phone	Fax
98.9 the Bear WBYR 1005 Production Rd .... Web: www.989thebear.com	Fort Wayne	IN	46808	260-471-5100	471-5224
WAJI-FM 95.1 (AC) 347 W Berry St Suite 417 .... TF: 877-951-9254 ■ Web: www.waji.com	Fort Wayne	IN	46802	260-423-3676	422-5266
WBCL-FM 90.3 (Rel) 1025 W Rudisill Blvd .... Web: www.wbcl.org	Fort Wayne	IN	46807	260-745-0576	456-2913
WBNI-FM 89.1 (NPR) 3204 Clairmont Ct .... TF: 800-471-9264 ■ Web: www.wbni.org	Fort Wayne	IN	46808	260-452-1189	452-1188
WBTU-FM 93.3 (Ctry) 9604 Coldwater Rd Suite 201..................... Web: www.us933.us	Fort Wayne	IN	46825	260-482-9288	482-8655
WFWI 92.3 the Fort 1005 Production Rd............ Web: www.923thefort.com	Fort Wayne	IN	46808	260-471-5100	471-5224
WJFX-FM 107.9 (CHR) 9604 Coldwater Rd Suite 201..................... Web: www.hot1079online.com	Fort Wayne	IN	46825	260-482-9288	482-8655
WLDE-FM 101.7 (Oldies) 347 W Berry St Suite 417........................ TF: 888-450-1017 ■ Web: www.wlde.com	Fort Wayne	IN	46802	260-423-3676	422-5266
WMEE-FM 97.3 (AC) 2915 Maples Rd .... Web: www.wmee.com	Fort Wayne	IN	46816	260-447-5511	447-7546
WOWO-AM 1190 (N/T) 2915 Maples Rd............. TF: 800-333-1190 ■ Web: www.wowo.com	Fort Wayne	IN	46816	260-447-5511	447-7546
WQHK-FM 105.1 (Ctry) 2915 Maples Rd .... Web: www.k105fm.com	Fort Wayne	IN	46816	260-447-5511	447-7546
WXKE-FM 103.9 (CR) 2000 Lower Huntington Rd.......................	Fort Wayne	IN	46819	260-747-1511	747-3999

648-65 Fresno, CA

Station	City	State	ZIP	Phone	Fax
KALZ-FM 96.7 (AC) 83 E Shaw Ave Suite 150............. Web: www.allace967.com	Fresno	CA	93710	559-230-4300	243-4301
KBOS-FM 94.9 (CHR) 83 E Shaw Ave Suite 150........... Web: www.b95forlife.com	Fresno	CA	93710	559-230-4300	243-4301
KEZL-AM 1340 (Sports) 83 E Shaw Ave Suite 150.........	Fresno	CA	93710	559-230-4300	243-4301
KFIG-AM 1430 (Sports) 351 W Cromwell Ave Suite 108 .... Web: www.espn1430.com	Fresno	CA	93711	559-447-3570	447-3579
KFRR-FM 104.1 (Rock) 1066 E Shaw Ave	Fresno	CA	93710	559-230-0104	230-0177
KJWL-FM 99.3 (Nost) 675 Santa Fe Ave................. Web: www.kjwl.com	Fresno	CA	93721	559-497-5118	497-9760
KLBN-FM 101.9 (Span) 1110 E Olive Ave................	Fresno	CA	93728	559-497-1100	497-1125
KMGV-FM 97.9 (Oldies) 1071 W Shaw Ave............. Web: www.mega979.com	Fresno	CA	93711	559-490-0106	490-4199
KMJ-AM 580 (N/T) 1071 W Shaw Ave................... TF: 800-776-5858 ■ Web: www.kmj580.com	Fresno	CA	93711	559-490-5800	490-5878
KMJ-FM 105.9 (Var) 1071 W Shaw Ave.................. Web: www.kmj.com	Fresno	CA	93711	559-490-1019	490-5966
KPRX-FM 89.1 (NPR) 3437 W Shaw Ave Suite 101 .... TF: 800-275-0764 ■ Web: www.kvpr.org	Fresno	CA	93711	559-275-0764	275-2202
KRZR-FM 103.7 (Rock) 83 E Shaw Ave Suite 150 .... Web: www.krzr.com	Fresno	CA	93710	559-230-4300	243-4301
KSKS-FM 93.7 (Ctry) 1071 W Shaw Ave.................. TF: 800-767-5477 ■ Web: www.ksks.com	Fresno	CA	93711	559-490-5800	490-5889
KSOF-FM 98.9 (AC) 83 E Shaw Ave Suite 150 .... Web: www.softrock989.com	Fresno	CA	93710	559-230-4300	243-4301
KVPR-FM 89.3 (NPR) 3437 W Shaw Ave Suite 101 .... TF: 800-275-0764 ■ Web: www.kvpr.org	Fresno	CA	93711	559-275-0764	275-2202
KWYE-FM 101.1 (CHR) 1071 W Shaw Ave............... TF: 800-345-9101 ■ Web: www.y101hits.com	Fresno	CA	93711	559-490-1011	490-5990

648-66 Grand Forks, ND

Station	City	State	ZIP	Phone	Fax
KCNN-AM 1590 (N/T) PO Box 13638 .... Web: www.kcnn.com	Grand Forks	ND	58278	701-775-4611	772-0540
KFJM-FM 90.7 (AAA) PO Box 8117 .... TF: 800-359-4145 ■ Web: www.prairiepublic.org/kfjm	Grand Forks	ND	58202	701-777-4595	777-2810
KJKJ-FM 107.5 (Rock) 505 University Ave .... Web: www.kjkj.com	Grand Forks	ND	58203	701-746-1417	746-1410
KKXL-FM 92.9 (CHR) 505 University Ave .... Web: www.xl93.com	Grand Forks	ND	58203	701-746-1417	746-1410
KQHT-FM 96.1 (CR) 505 University Ave .... Web: www.961thefox.com	Grand Forks	ND	58203	701-746-1417	746-1410
KSNR-FM 100.3 (Ctry) 505 University Ave........... Web: www.ksnrfm100.com	Grand Forks	ND	58203	701-746-1417	746-1410
KZLT-FM 104.3 (AC) PO Box 13638 .... Web: www.leightonbroadcasting.com	Grand Forks	ND	58208	701-775-4611	772-0540

648-67 Grand Rapids, MI

Station	City	State	ZIP	Phone	Fax
WBBL-AM 1340 (Sports) 60 Monroe Ctr St NW 3rd Fl...................... TF: 866-828-4843 ■ Web: www.wbbl.com	Grand Rapids	MI	49503	616-456-5461	451-3299
WBCT-FM 93.7 (Ctry) 77 Monroe Ctr St NW Suite 1000................. TF: 800-633-9393 ■ Web: www.b93.com	Grand Rapids	MI	49503	616-459-1919	732-3330
WBFX-FM 101.3 (CR) 77 Monroe Ctr St NW Suite 1000................. TF: 888-399-9369 ■ Web: www.101thefoxrocks.com	Grand Rapids	MI	49503	616-459-1919	242-9373
WCSG-FM 91.3 (Rel) 1159 E Beltline Ave NE......................... TF: 800-968-4543 ■ Web: www.wcsg.org	Grand Rapids	MI	49525	616-942-1500	942-7078
WFGR-FM 98.7 (Oldies) 50 Monroe Ave NW Suite 500 .... Web: www.wfgr.com	Grand Rapids	MI	49503	616-451-4800	451-0113
WGRD-FM 97.9 (Rock) 50 Monroe Ave NW Suite 500 .... TF: 800-957-3979 ■ Web: www.wgrd.com	Grand Rapids	MI	49503	616-451-4800	451-0113
WGVU-FM 88.5 (NPR) 301 W Fulton St .... TF: 800-442-2771 ■ Web: www.wgvu.org	Grand Rapids	MI	49504	616-331-6666	331-6625
WLAV-FM 96.9 (CR) 60 Monroe Ctr St NW 3rd Fl..................... Web: www.wlav.com	Grand Rapids	MI	49503	616-456-5461	774-0351
WLHT-FM 95.7 (AC) 50 Monroe Ave NW Suite 500 .... Web: www.wlht.com	Grand Rapids	MI	49503	616-451-4800	451-0113
WOOD-AM 1300 (N/T) 77 Monroe Ctr St NW Suite 1000................. Web: www.woodradio.com	Grand Rapids	MI	49503	616-459-1919	242-9373
WOOD-FM 106.9 (AC) 77 Monroe Ctr St NW Suite 1000................. TF: 866-290-2899 ■ Web: www.ez1057.com	Grand Rapids	MI	49503	616-459-1919	732-3330
WSNX-FM 104.5 (CHR) 77 Monroe Ctr St NW Suite 1000................. Web: www.wsnx.com	Grand Rapids	MI	49503	616-459-1919	242-9373
WTNR-FM 94.5 (Ctry) 60 Monroe Ctr St NW 3rd Fl.....................	Grand Rapids	MI	49503	616-456-5461	774-0351

648-68 Great Falls, MT

Station	City	State	ZIP	Phone	Fax
KLFM-FM 92.9 (Oldies) 20 3rd St N Suite 231............................ Web: www.92coolradio.com	Great Falls	MT	59401	406-761-7600	761-5511
KMON-AM 560 (Ctry) 20 3rd St N Suite 231...........	Great Falls	MT	59401	406-761-7600	761-5511
KVVR-FM 97.9 (AC) 20 3rd St Suite 231..............	Great Falls	MT	59401	406-761-7600	761-5511

648-69 Green Bay, WI

Station	City	State	ZIP	Phone	Fax
WDUZ-AM 1400 (Sports) 810 Victoria St............. Web: www.thefan1075.com	Green Bay	WI	54302	920-468-4100	468-0250
WIXX-FM 101.1 (CHR) PO Box 23333 .... TF: 800-872-9499 ■ Web: www.wixx.com	Green Bay	WI	54305	920-435-3771	321-2300
WNCY-FM 100.3 (Ctry) PO Box 23333............... TF: 800-359-1003 ■ Web: www.wncy.com	Green Bay	WI	54305	920-435-3771	321-2300
WOGB-FM 103.1 (AC) 810 Victoria St............... Web: www.greenbayoldies.com	Green Bay	WI	54302	920-468-4100	468-0250
WPNE-FM 89.3 (NPR) 2420 Nicolet Dr............. TF: 800-654-6228 ■ Web: www.wpr.org	Green Bay	WI	54311	920-465-2444	465-2576
WQLH-FM 98.5 (AC) 810 Victoria St................ Web: www.star98.net	Green Bay	WI	54302	920-468-4100	468-0250
WTAQ-AM 1360 (N/T) PO Box 23333 .... TF: 888-455-1360 ■ Web: www.wtaq.com	Green Bay	WI	54305	920-435-3771	321-2300
WZNN-FM 106.7 (Alt) 810 Victoria St................	Green Bay	WI	54302	920-468-4100	468-0250

648-70 Greenville, SC

Station	City	State	ZIP	Phone	Fax
92.5 WESC-FM 101 N Main St Suite 1000 PO Box 100............... TF: 800-248-0863 ■ Web: www.wescfm.com	Greenville	SC	29601	864-242-4660	271-3830
WFBC-FM 93.7 (CHR) 25 Garlington Rd.............. Web: www.b937online.com	Greenville	SC	29615	864-271-9200	242-1567
WHZT-FM 98.1 (CHR) 220 N Main St Suite 402 .... TF: 866-639-4689 ■ Web: www.hot981.com	Greenville	SC	29601	864-232-9810	370-3403
WJMZ-FM 107.3 (Urban) 220 N Main St Suite 402 .... Web: www.1073jamz.com	Greenville	SC	29601	864-235-1073	370-3403
WLFJ-FM 89.3 (Rel) 2420 Wade Hampton Blvd .... TF: 800-447-7234 ■ Web: www.hisradio.com	Greenville	SC	29615	864-292-6040	292-8428
WMUU-FM 94.5 (Var) 920 Wade Hampton Blvd......... Web: www.wmuu.com	Greenville	SC	29609	864-242-6240	370-3829
WMYI-FM 102.5 (AC) 101 N Main St Suite 1000 PO Box 100............... TF: 800-248-0863 ■ Web: www.wmyi.com	Greenville	SC	29601	864-235-1025	271-3830
WORD-AM 1330 (N/T) 25 Garlington Rd.............. Web: www.newsradioword.com	Greenville	SC	29615	864-271-9200	242-1567
WROQ-FM 101.1 (CR) 25 Garlington Rd.............. TF: 800-476-9814 ■ Web: www.wroq.com	Greenville	SC	29615	864-271-9200	242-1567
WSPA-FM 98.9 (AC) 25 Garlington Rd .... Web: www.magic989online.com	Greenville	SC	29615	864-271-9200	242-1567
WSSL-FM 100.5 (Ctry) 101 N Main St Suite 1000 PO Box 100............... TF: 800-248-0863 ■ Web: www.wsslfm.com	Greenville	SC	29601	864-242-1005	271-9775
WTPT-FM 93.3 (Rock) 25 Garlington Rd .... Web: www.newrock933.com	Greenville	SC	29615	864-271-9200	242-1567

648-71 Gulfport/Biloxi, MS

Station	City	State	ZIP	Phone	Fax
WCPR-FM 97.9 (Rock) 1909 E Pass Rd Suite D-11 *TF:* 888-400-2771 ■ *Web:* www.979cprrocks.com	Gulfport	MS	39507	228-388-2771	896-9736
WGCM-FM 102.3 (Oldies) PO Box 2639 *Web:* www.coast102.com	Gulfport	MS	39505	228-896-5500	896-0458
WHGO-FM 105.9 (CR) 1909 E Pass Rd Suite D-11 *TF:* 800-280-7625 ■ *Web:* www.wxrgfm.com	Gulfport	MS	39507	228-388-2001	896-9736
WJZD-FM 94.5 (Urban) 10211 Southpark Dr *TF:* 866-945-9455 ■ *Web:* www.wjzd.com	Gulfport	MS	39503	228-896-5307	896-5703
WKNN-FM 99.1 (Ctry) 286 DeBuys Rd *TF:* 800-898-9900 ■ *Web:* www.k99fm.com	Biloxi	MS	39531	228-388-2323	388-2362
WMJY-FM 93.7 (AC) 286 DeBuys Rd *Web:* www.magic937.com	Biloxi	MS	39531	228-388-2323	388-2362
WXYK-FM 107.1 (CHR) 1909 E Pass Rd Suite D-11 *TF:* 800-847-7361 ■ *Web:* www.1071themonkey.net	Gulfport	MS	39507	228-388-1071	896-9736
WZKX-FM 107.9 (Ctry) 10250 Lorraine Rd *Web:* www.kicker108.com	Gulfport	MS	39503	228-896-5500	896-0458

648-72 Halifax, NS

Station	City	State	ZIP	Phone	Fax
CBH-FM 102.7 (CBC) PO Box 3000 *Web:* www.cbc.ca	Halifax	NS	B3J3E9	902-420-8311	420-4429
CBHA-FM 90.5 (CBC) PO Box 3000	Halifax	NS	B3J3E9	902-420-8311	420-4478
CFDR-AM 780 (Ctry) 2900 Agricola St	Halifax	NS	B3K6A7	902-453-2524	453-3132
CFRQ-FM 104.3 (CR) 2900 Agricola St *Web:* www.q104.ca	Halifax	NS	B3K6A7	902-453-2524	453-3132
CHAL-FM 89.9 (Oldies) PO Box 400	Halifax	NS	B3J2R2	902-422-1651	422-5330
CHFX-FM 101.9 (Ctry) PO Box 400	Halifax	NS	B3J2R2	902-422-1651	422-5330
CIOO-FM 100.1 (AC) 2900 Agricola St *Web:* www.c100fm.com	Halifax	NS	B3K6A7	902-453-2524	453-3132
CJCH-FM 101.3 (Urban) 2900 Agricola St *Web:* www.1013thebounce.com	Halifax	NS	B3K6A7	902-453-2524	453-3132

648-73 Harrisburg, PA

Station	City	State	ZIP	Phone	Fax
WHP-AM 580 (N/T) 600 Corporate Cir *TF:* 800-329-9562 ■ *Web:* www.whp580.com	Harrisburg	PA	17110	717-540-8800	540-9268
WITF-FM 89.5 (NPR) 4801 Lindle Rd *TF:* 800-366-9483 ■ *Web:* www.witf.org	Harrisburg	PA	17111	717-236-6000	704-3659
WKBO-AM 1230 (Rel) 600 Corporate Cir *TF:* 800-329-9562	Harrisburg	PA	17110	717-540-8800	540-9268
WNNK-FM 104.1 (AC) 2300 Vartan Way *Web:* www.wink104.com	Harrisburg	PA	17110	717-238-1041	234-4842
WRBT-FM 94.9 (Ctry) 600 Corporate Cir *TF:* 800-329-9562 ■ *Web:* www.bobradio.com	Harrisburg	PA	17110	717-540-8800	540-9268
WRVV-FM 97.3 (AC) 600 Corporate Cir *TF:* 800-329-9562 ■ *Web:* www.river973.cc	Harrisburg	PA	17110	717-540-8800	540-9268
WTPA-FM 93.5 (CR) 2300 Vartan Way *Web:* www.wtpafm.com	Harrisburg	PA	17110	717-238-1041	234-4842
WWKL-FM 92.1 (CHR) 2300 Vartan Way *Web:* www.hot92.com	Harrisburg	PA	17110	717-238-1041	234-4842

648-74 Hartford, CT

Station	City	State	ZIP	Phone	Fax
ESPN Radio 1410 10 Columbus Blvd *Web:* www.espnradio1410.com	Hartford	CT	06106	860-723-6000	723-6195
Kiss 95.7 10 Columbus Blvd *Web:* www.kiss957.com	Hartford	CT	06106	860-723-6000	723-6195
Rock 106.9 WCCC The 1039 Asylum Ave *Web:* www.wccc.com	Hartford	CT	06105	860-525-1069	246-9084
WEDW-FM 88.5 (NPR) 1049 Asylum Ave	Hartford	CT	06105	860-278-5310	275-7403*
WHCN-FM 105.9 (CR) 10 Columbus Blvd *Web:* www.whcn.com	Hartford	CT	06106	860-723-6000	723-6106
WLAT-AM 910 (Span) 135 Burnside Ave *TF:* 866-910-6342	Hartford	CT	06108	860-524-0001	524-0336
WPKT-FM 90.5 (NPR) 1049 Asylum Ave *Web:* www.wnpr.org	Hartford	CT	06105	860-278-5310	275-7403
WRTC-FM 89.3 (Var) Trinity College 300 Summit St *Web:* www.wrtcfm.com	Hartford	CT	06106	860-297-2439	297-5201
WTMI-AM 1290 (Clas) 1039 Asylum Ave *Web:* www.beethoven.com	Hartford	CT	06105	860-525-1069	246-9084
WWYZ-FM 92.5 (Ctry) 10 Columbus Blvd *Web:* www.wwyz.com	Hartford	CT	06106	860-723-6000	723-6159

648-75 Hattiesburg, MS

Station	City	State	ZIP	Phone	Fax
WFOR-AM 1400 (Sports) 6555 Hwy 98 W Suite 8 *TF:* 877-993-0993	Hattiesburg	MS	39402	601-296-9800	582-5481
WHER-FM 99.3 (Ctry) 6555 Hwy 98 W Suite 8 *TF:* 877-993-0993 ■ *Web:* www.eagle99.com	Hattiesburg	MS	39402	601-296-9800	582-5481
WJMG-FM 92.1 (Urban) 1204 Graveline St	Hattiesburg	MS	39401	601-544-1941	544-1947
WNSL-FM 100.3 (CHR) 6555 Hwy 98 W Suite 8 *TF:* 877-993-0993 ■ *Web:* www.sl100.com	Hattiesburg	MS	39402	601-296-9800	582-5481
WUSM-FM 88.5 (Var) 118 College Dr *Web:* www.wusm.usm.edu	Hattiesburg	MS	39406	601-266-4287	
WUSW-FM 103.7 (Rock) 6555 Hwy 98 W Suite 8 *TF:* 877-993-0993 ■ *Web:* www.thefoxrocks1037.com	Hattiesburg	MS	39402	601-296-9800	582-5481
WZLD-FM 106.3 (Urban) 6555 Hwy 98 W Suite 8 *TF:* 877-993-0993 ■ *Web:* www.wzldfm.com	Hattiesburg	MS	39402	601-296-9800	582-5481

648-76 Helena, MT

Station	City	State	ZIP	Phone	Fax
KBLL-AM 1240 (N/T) 110 E Broadway St	Helena	MT	59601	406-442-4490	442-7356
KBLL-FM 99.5 (Ctry) PO Box 4111	Helena	MT	59604	406-442-6620	
KHKR-FM 104.1 (AC) 110 E Broadway St	Helena	MT	59601	406-442-4490	442-7356
KKGR-AM 680 (Oldies) 1400 11th Ave	Helena	MT	59601	406-443-5237	442-6916
KMTX-FM 105.3 (AC) 516 Fuller Ave *Web:* www.hitsandfavorites.com	Helena	MT	59601	406-442-0400	442-0491
KZMT-FM 101.1 (CR) 110 E Broadway St	Helena	MT	59601	406-442-4490	442-7356

648-77 Honolulu, HI

Station	City	State	ZIP	Phone	Fax
KAIM-FM 95.5 (Rel) 1160 N King St 2nd Fl *Web:* www.thefishhawaii.com	Honolulu	HI	96817	808-533-0065	524-2104
KCCN-FM 100.3 (CHR) 900 Fort St Suite 700 *Web:* kccnfm100.com	Honolulu	HI	96813	808-536-2728	536-2528
KDDB-FM 102.7 (CHR) 765 Amana St Suite 200 *Web:* www.dabombhawaii.com	Honolulu	HI	96814	808-947-1500	947-1506
KDNN-FM 98.5 (Island) 650 Iwilei Rd Suite 400 *Fax: Sales ■ *Web:* www.island985.com	Honolulu	HI	96817	808-550-9200	550-9519*
KHPR-FM 88.1 (NPR) 738 Kaheka St Suite 101 *Web:* www.hawaiipublicradio.org	Honolulu	HI	96814	808-955-8821	946-3863
KHVH-AM 830 (N/T) 650 Iwilei Rd Suite 400 *Fax: Sales ■ *Web:* www.khvh830am.com	Honolulu	HI	96817	808-550-9200	550-9519*
KIKI-FM 93.9 (CHR) 650 Iwilei Rd Suite 400 *Fax: Sales ■ *Web:* www.i-94.net	Honolulu	HI	96817	808-550-9200	550-9519*
KINE-FM 105.1 (AC) 900 Fort St Suite 700 *Web:* hawaiian105.com	Honolulu	HI	96813	808-536-2728	536-2528
KKOL-FM 107.9 (Oldies) 1160 N King St 2nd Fl *Web:* www.oldies1079honolulu.com	Honolulu	HI	96817	808-533-0065	524-2104
KPHW-FM 104.3 (Urban) 900 Fort St Suite 700 *Web:* power1043.com	Honolulu	HI	96813	808-275-1000	536-2528
KPOI-FM 105.9 (CR) 765 Amana St Suite 200 *Web:* www.kpoifm.com/kpoi	Honolulu	HI	96814	808-947-1500	947-1506
KQMQ-FM 93.1 (CHR) 765 Amana St Suite 200 *Web:* www.kqmq.net	Honolulu	HI	96814	808-947-1500	947-1506
KRTR-FM 96.3 (AC) 900 Fort St Suite 700 *Web:* krater96.com	Honolulu	HI	96813	808-275-1000	536-2528
KSSK-AM 590 (AC) 650 Iwilei Rd Suite 400 *Fax: Sales ■ *Web:* www.ksskradio.com	Honolulu	HI	96817	808-550-9200	550-9519*
KSSK-FM 92.3 (AC) 650 Iwilei Rd Suite 400 *Web:* www.ksskradio.com	Honolulu	HI	96817	808-550-9200	550-9519
KUCD-FM 101.9 (Alt) 650 Iwilei Rd Suite 400 *Fax: Sales ■ *Web:* www.star1019fm.com	Honolulu	HI	96817	808-550-9200	550-9519*
KUMU-FM 94.7 (AC) 765 Amana St Suite 206 *Web:* www.kumu.com	Honolulu	HI	96814	808-947-1500	947-1506

648-78 Hot Springs, AR

Station	City	State	ZIP	Phone	Fax
KBHS-AM 1420 (Ctry) 208 Buena Vista Rd	Hot Springs	AR	71913	501-525-1420	525-4344
KHTO-FM 96.7 125 Corporate Terr *TF:* 866-425-9600 ■ *Web:* www.myhotsprings.com	Hot Springs	AR	71913	501-525-9700	525-9739
KLAZ-FM 105.9 (CHR) 208 Buena Vista Rd *Web:* www.klaz.com	Hot Springs	AR	71913	501-525-4600	525-4344
KLXQ-FM 101.9 (CR) 125 Corporate Terr *TF:* 800-442-0097 ■ *Web:* www.1019therocket.com	Hot Springs	AR	71913	501-525-9700	525-9739
KQUS-FM 97.5 (Ctry) 125 Corporate Terr *TF:* 800-442-0097 ■ *Web:* www.us97country.com	Hot Springs	AR	71913	501-525-9700	525-9739
KVRE-FM 92.9 (AC) 122 Desoto Ctr Dr	Hot Springs Village	AR	71909	501-624-5994	922-6626
KZNG-AM 1340 (N/T) 125 Corporate Terr *TF:* 800-442-0097 ■ *Web:* www.kzng.net	Hot Springs	AR	71913	501-525-9700	525-9739

648-79 Houston, TX

Station	City	State	ZIP	Phone	Fax
KAMA-FM 104.9 (Urban) 5100 SW Fwy *Web:* 1049tumusica.univision.com	Houston	TX	77056	713-965-2400	965-2401
KBME-AM 790 (Sports) 2000 W Loop S Suite 300 *Web:* www.sports790.com	Houston	TX	77027	713-212-8000	212-8790
KBXX-FM 97.9 (Urban) 24 Greenway Plaza Suite 900 *Web:* www.kbxx.com	Houston	TX	77046	713-623-2108	623-0344
KHJZ-FM 95.7 (NAC) 24 Greenway Plaza Suite 1900 *Web:* www.khjz.com	Houston	TX	77046	713-881-5100	881-5199
KHMX-FM 96.5 (CHR) 24 Greenway Plaza Suite 1900 *Web:* khmx.radio.com	Houston	TX	77046	713-212-5965	
KHPT-FM 106.9 (AC) 1990 Post Oak Blvd Suite 2300 *Web:* 1069thepoint.com	Houston	TX	77056	713-622-5533	993-9300
KHTC-FM 107.5 (Oldies) 1990 Post Oak Blvd Suite 2300 *Web:* www.1075khits.com	Houston	TX	77056	713-963-1200	622-5457
KKBQ-FM 92.9 (Ctry) 1990 Post Oak Blvd Suite 2300 *Web:* kkbq.com	Houston	TX	77056	713-622-5533	993-9300

Station	City	State	Zip	Phone	Fax
KKHT-FM 100.0 (Rel) 6161 Savoy Dr Suite 1200 *TF:* 800-808-5548 ■ *Web:* www.kkht.com	Houston	TX	77036	713-260-3600	260-3628
KKRW-FM 93.7 (CR) 2000 W Loop S Suite 300 *Web:* www.kkrw.com	Houston	TX	77027	713-212-8000	212-8963
KLAT-AM 1010 (Span N/T) 5100 SW Fwy *Web:* latremenda.netmio.com	Houston	TX	77056	713-407-1415	407-1400
KLOL-FM 101.1 (Span) 2000 W Loop S Suite 300 *Web:* mega101houston.com	Houston	TX	77027	713-212-8000	212-8101
KLTN-FM 102.9 (Span) 5100 SW Fwy *Web:* estereolatino.netmio.com	Houston	TX	77056	713-407-1415	965-2401
KMJQ-FM 102.1 (Urban) 24 Greenway Plaza Suite 900 *Web:* www.kmjq.com	Houston	TX	77046	713-623-2108	622-5267
KODA-FM 99.1 (AC) 2000 W Loop S Suite 300 *Web:* www.sunny99.com	Houston	TX	77027	713-212-8000	212-8963
KOVE-FM 106.5 (Span) 5100 SW Fwy *Web:* kove.netmio.com	Houston	TX	77056	713-407-1415	407-1400
KPRC-AM 950 (N/T) 2000 W Loop S Suite 300 *Web:* www.950kprc.com	Houston	TX	77027	713-212-8000	212-8963
KRBE-FM 104.1 (CHR) 9801 Westheimer Rd Suite 700 *Web:* www.krbe.com	Houston	TX	77042	713-266-1000	954-2344
KSEV-AM 700 (N/T) 11451 Katy Fwy Suite 215 **Fax Area Code:* 832 ■ *Web:* www.ksevradio.com	Houston	TX	77079	281-588-4800	358-9556*
KTBZ-FM 94.5 (Alt) 2000 W Loop S Suite 300 *Web:* www.thebuzz.com	Houston	TX	77027	713-212-8000	212-8963
KTHT-FM 1990 Post Oak Blvd Suite 2300 *Web:* www.countrylegends971.com	Houston	TX	77056	713-963-1200	622-5457
KTRH-AM 740 (N/T) 2000 W Loop S Suite 300 *Web:* www.ktrh.com	Houston	TX	77027	713-212-8000	212-8958
KUHF-FM 88.7 (Clas) 4343 Elgin St 3rd Fl *Web:* www.kuhf.org	Houston	TX	77204	713-743-0887	743-0868
SportsRadio 610 24 Greenway Plaza Suite 1900 *Web:* www.houston.cbslocal.com/station/sportsradio-610	Houston	TX	77046	713-881-5100	881-5250

648-80 Huntsville, AL

Station	City	State	Zip	Phone	Fax
WAHR-FM 99.1 (AC) 1555 the Boardwalk Suite 1 *Web:* rocketcitynews.com	Huntsville	AL	35816	256-536-1568	536-4416
WEUP-FM 103.1 (Urban) 2609 Jordan Ln NW *Web:* www.103weup.com	Huntsville	AL	35816	256-837-9387	837-9404
WJOU-FM 90.1 (Rel) 7000 Adventist Blvd *Web:* www.wjou.org	Huntsville	AL	35896	256-726-7420	726-7417
WLOR-AM 1550 (Oldies) 1555 the Boardwalk Suite 1 *Web:* www.jammin1550.am	Huntsville	AL	35816	256-536-1568	536-4416
WLRH-FM 89.3 (NPR) University of Alabama-Huntsville John Wright Dr *TF:* 800-239-9574 ■ *Web:* www.wlrh.org	Huntsville	AL	35899	256-895-9574	830-4577
WRSA-FM 96.9 (AC) 8402 Memorial Pkwy SW *Web:* www.lite969.com	Huntsville	AL	35802	256-885-9797	885-9796

648-81 Indianapolis, IN

Station	City	State	Zip	Phone	Fax
WFBQ-FM 94.7 (CR) 6161 Fall Creek Rd *Web:* www.wfbq.com	Indianapolis	IN	46220	317-257-7565	254-9619
WFMS-FM 95.5 (Ctry) 6810 N Shadeland Ave *Web:* www.wfms.com	Indianapolis	IN	46220	317-842-9550	577-3361
WFYI-FM 90.1 1630 N Meridian St *Web:* www.wfyi.org	Indianapolis	IN	46202	317-636-2020	283-6645
WHHH-FM 96.3 (CHR) 21 E St Joseph St *Web:* www.hot963.com	Indianapolis	IN	46204	317-266-9600	328-3870
WIBC-FM 93.1 (N/T) 40 Monument Cir Suite 400 *TF:* 800-571-9422 ■ *Web:* www.wibc.com	Indianapolis	IN	46204	317-266-9422	684-2022
WJJK-FM 104.5 (CR) 6810 N Shadeland Ave *Web:* www.1045wjjk.com	Indianapolis	IN	46220	317-842-9550	577-3361
WLHK-FM 97.1 (Ctry) 40 Monument Cir Suite 600 *Web:* www.hankfm.com	Indianapolis	IN	46204	317-266-9700	684-2021
WNDE-AM 1260 (Sports) 6161 Fall Creek Rd *Web:* www.wnde.com	Indianapolis	IN	46220	317-257-7565	254-9619
WNTR-FM 107.9 (AC) 9245 N Meridian St Suite 300 *Web:* www.1079thetrack.com	Indianapolis	IN	46260	317-816-4000	816-4060
WRWM-FM 93.9 (AC) 6810 N Shadeland Ave *Web:* warm939.com	Indianapolis	IN	46220	317-842-9550	577-3361
WRZX-FM 103.3 (Alt) 6161 Fall Creek Rd *Web:* www.x103.com	Indianapolis	IN	46220	317-257-7565	254-9619
WTLC-AM 1310 (Rel) 21 E St Joseph St *Web:* www.1310thelight.com	Indianapolis	IN	46204	317-266-9600	328-3870
WTLC-FM 106.7 (Urban) 21 E St Joseph St *Web:* www.wtlc.com	Indianapolis	IN	46204	317-266-9600	328-3870
WXNT-AM 1430 (N/T) 9245 N Meridian St Suite 300 *Web:* www.newstalk1430.com	Indianapolis	IN	46260	317-816-4000	816-4060
WYXB-FM 105.7 (AC) 40 Monument Cir Suite 600 *Web:* www.b1057.com	Indianapolis	IN	46204	317-266-9700	684-2021
WZPL-FM 99.5 (AC) 9245 N Meridian St Suite 300 *Web:* www.wzpl.com	Indianapolis	IN	46260	317-816-4000	816-4060

648-82 Jackson, MS

Station	City	State	Zip	Phone	Fax
WHLH-FM 95.5 (Rel) 1375 Beasley Rd *Web:* www.hallelujah955.com	Jackson	MS	39206	601-982-1062	362-1905
WJDX-AM 620 (Sports) 1375 Beasley Rd *Web:* www.wjdx.com	Jackson	MS	39206	601-982-1062	362-1905
WJSU-FM 88.5 (Jazz) 1400 Lynch St Blackburn Language Arts Bldg Rm 203 *Web:* www.wjsu.org	Jackson	MS	39217	601-979-2140	979-2878
WMAE-FM 89.5 (NPR) 3825 Ridgewood Rd *TF:* 800-922-9698 ■ *Web:* mpbonline.org	Jackson	MS	39211	601-432-6565	432-6746
WMAH-FM 90.3 (NPR) 3825 Ridgewood Rd *Web:* www.mpbonline.org	Jackson	MS	39211	601-432-6800	432-6806
WMPN-FM 91.3 (NPR) 3825 Ridgewood Rd *TF:* 866-262-9643 ■ *Web:* www.mpbonline.org	Jackson	MS	39211	601-432-6800	432-6806
WMSI-FM 102.9 (Ctry) 1375 Beasley Rd *Web:* www.miss103.com	Jackson	MS	39206	601-982-1062	362-1905
WSTZ-FM 106.7 (CR) 1375 Beasley Rd *Web:* www.z106.com	Jackson	MS	39206	601-982-1062	362-1905
WWJK-FM 94.7 (CR) 222 Beasley Rd *Web:* www.947jackfm.com	Jackson	MS	39206	601-957-3000	956-0370

648-83 Jacksonville, FL

Station	City	State	Zip	Phone	Fax
WAPE-FM 95.1 (CHR) 8000 Belfort Pkwy Suite 100 *TF:* 800-475-9595 ■ *Web:* wape951.com	Jacksonville	FL	32256	904-245-8500	245-8501
WAYL-FM 91.9 (AC) 4190 Belfort Rd Suite 450 *Web:* www.thepromisepraise.com	Jacksonville	FL	32216	904-829-9200	296-1683
WBOB-AM 1320 (N/T) 4190 Belfort Rd Suite 450 *Web:* www.1320wbob.com	Jacksonville	FL	32216	904-470-4615	296-1683
WCGL-AM 1360 (Rel) 3890 Dunn Ave Suite 804 *Web:* www.wcgl1360.com	Jacksonville	FL	32218	904-766-9955	765-9214
WEJZ-FM 96.1 (AC) 6440 Atlantic Blvd *Web:* www.wejz.com	Jacksonville	FL	32211	904-727-9696	721-9322
WFKS-FM 97.9 (CHR) 11700 Central Pkwy **Fax:* Sales ■ *Web:* www.979kissfm.cc	Jacksonville	FL	32224	904-636-0507	636-7971*
WFYV-FM 104.5 (CR) 8000 Belfort Pkwy Suite 100 *Web:* rock105i.com	Jacksonville	FL	32256	904-245-8500	245-8501
WJAX-AM 1220 (Nost) 5353 Arlington Expy *TF:* 800-896-1669 ■ *Web:* www.wktz.jones.edu	Jacksonville	FL	32211	904-371-1184	896-1669
WJBT-FM 93.3 (Urban) 11700 Central Pkwy **Fax:* Sales ■ *Web:* www.wjbt.com	Jacksonville	FL	32224	904-636-0507	636-7971*
WJCT-FM 89.9 100 Festival Pk Ave *Web:* www.wjct.org	Jacksonville	FL	32202	904-353-7770	358-6352
WJGL-FM 96.9 (CR) 8000 Belfort Pkwy *Web:* www.969theeagle.com	Jacksonville	FL	32256	904-245-8500	245-8501
WKTZ-FM 90.9 (AC) 5353 Arlington Expy *Web:* www.wktz.jones.edu	Jacksonville	FL	32211	904-371-1184	
WNCM-FM 88.1 (Rel) 4190 Belfort Rd Suite 450 *Web:* www.fm88.org	Jacksonville	FL	32216	904-641-9626	645-9626
WOKV-AM 690 (N/T) 8000 Belfort Pkwy Suite 100 *Web:* www.wokv.com	Jacksonville	FL	32256	904-245-8500	245-8501
WPLA-FM 107.3 (Alt) 11700 Central Pkwy **Fax:* Sales ■ *Web:* www.planet93.com	Jacksonville	FL	32224	904-636-0507	636-7971*
WQIK-FM 99.1 (Ctry) 11700 Central Pkwy **Fax:* Sales ■ *Web:* www.wqik.com	Jacksonville	FL	32224	904-636-0507	636-7971*
WSOL-FM 101.5 (Urban AC) 11700 Central Pkwy **Fax:* Sales ■ *Web:* www.v1015.com	Jacksonville	FL	32224	904-636-0507	636-7971*
WXXJ-FM 102.9 (AC) 8000 Belfort Pkwy *Web:* 1029i.com	Jacksonville	FL	32256	904-245-8500	245-8501
WZNZ-AM 1460 (Rel) PO Box 51585	Jacksonville Beach	FL	32240	904-241-3311	

648-84 Jefferson City, MO

Station	City	State	Zip	Phone	Fax
KATI-FM 94.3 (Ctry) 3109 S Ten-Mile Dr *TF:* 800-700-5284 ■ *Web:* kat943.com	Jefferson City	MO	65109	573-893-5696	893-4137
KJLU-FM 88.9 (Jazz) 1004 E Dunklin St *Web:* www.kjlu.com	Jefferson City	MO	65102	573-681-5301	681-5299
KJMO-FM 97.5 (Oldies) 1002 Diamond Ridge Ctr Suite 400 *TF:* 866-632-1240 ■ *Web:* www.kjmo.com	Jefferson City	MO	65109	573-893-5100	893-8330
KLIK-AM 1240 (N/T) 1002 Diamond Ridge Ctr Suite 400 *TF:* 866-632-1240 ■ *Web:* www.klik1240.com	Jefferson City	MO	65109	573-893-5100	893-8330
KWOS-AM 950 (N/T) 3109 S Ten-Mile Dr *TF:* 800-455-1099 ■ *Web:* www.kwos.com	Jefferson City	MO	65109	573-893-5696	893-4137

648-85 Johnson City, TN

Station	City	State	Zip	Phone	Fax
WETB-AM 790 (Rel) 231 Brandonwood Dr PO Box 4127	Johnson City	TN	37604	423-928-7131	928-8392
WETS-FM 89.5 (NPR) 89 Dr Suite 70630 *TF:* 888-895-9387 ■ *Web:* www.wets.org	Johnson City	TN	37614	423-439-6440	439-6449

648-86 Juneau, AK

Station	City	State	Zip	Phone	Fax
KINY-AM 800 (AC) 1107 W 8th St Suite 2 *Web:* www.kinyradio.com	Juneau	AK	99801	907-586-1800	586-3266
KJNO-AM 630 (N/T) 3161 Ch Dr Suite 202 *Web:* www.kjno.com	Juneau	AK	99801	907-586-3630	463-3685
KTKU-FM 105.1 (Ctry) 3161 Ch Dr Suite 2 *Web:* www.taku105.com	Juneau	AK	99801	907-586-3630	463-3685
KTOO-FM 104.3 (NPR) 360 Egan Dr *TF:* 800-870-5866 ■ *Web:* www.ktoo.org	Juneau	AK	99801	907-586-1670	586-3612

648-87 Kansas City, KS & MO

Station	City	State	Zip	Phone	Fax
KBEQ-FM 104.3 (Ctry) 508 Westport Rd Suite 202 *Web:* www.youngcountryq104.com	Kansas City	MO	64111	816-753-4000	753-4045
KCKC-FM 102.1 (AC) 508 Westport Rd Suite 202 *Web:* www.alice102.com	Kansas City	MO	64111	816-576-7102	753-4045
KCUR-FM 89.3 (NPR) 4825 Troost Ave Suite 202 *Web:* www.kcur.org	Kansas City	MO	64110	816-235-1551	235-2864
KFKF-FM 94.1 (Ctry) 508 Westport Rd Suite 202 *Web:* www.kfkf.com	Kansas City	MO	64111	816-753-4000	753-4045
KGGN-AM 890 (Rel) 1734 E 63rd St Suite 600 *TF:* 800-924-3177 ■ *Web:* www.kggnam.com	Kansas City	MO	64110	816-333-0092	363-8120
KKFI-FM 90.1 (Var) 3901 Main St Suite 203 *Web:* www.kkfi.org	Kansas City	MO	64171	816-931-3122	931-7078
KLJC-FM 88.5 (Rel) 15800 Calvary Rd *TF:* 800-466-5552 ■ *Web:* www.kljc.org	Kansas City	MO	64147	816-331-8700	331-3497
KMXV-FM 93.3 (CHR) 508 Westport Rd Suite 202 *Web:* www.mix93.com	Kansas City	MO	64111	816-753-4000	753-4045
KPRS-FM 103.3 (Urban) 11131 Colorado Ave *Web:* www.kprs.com	Kansas City	MO	64137	816-763-2040	966-1055
KPRT-AM 1590 (Rel) 11131 Colorado Ave *Web:* www.kprt.com	Kansas City	MO	64137	816-576-7400	966-1055

648-88 Key West, FL

Station	City	State	Zip	Phone	Fax
WAIL-FM 99.5 (Rock) 5450 MacDonald Ave Suite 10 *Web:* www.wail995.com	Key West	FL	33040	305-296-7511	296-0358
WEOW-FM 92.7 (CHR) 5450 MacDonald Ave Suite 10 *Web:* www.weow927.com	Key West	FL	33040	305-296-7511	296-0358
WIIS-FM 107.1 (Alt) 1075 Duval St Suite C17 *Web:* www.island107.com	Key West	FL	33040	305-292-1133	292-6936
WJIR-FM 90.9 (Rel) 1209 United St *Web:* www.sosradio.net	Key West	FL	33040	305-296-5773	294-9547
WKWF-AM 1600 (Sports) 5450 MacDonald Ave Suite 10 *Web:* www.sportsradio1600.com	Key West	FL	33040	305-296-7511	296-0358

648-89 Knoxville, TN

Station	City	State	Zip	Phone	Fax
WFIV-FM 105.3 (AAA) 517 Watt Rd *Web:* www.wfiv.com	Knoxville	TN	37934	865-675-4105	675-4859
WIMZ-FM 103.5 (CR) 1100 Sharps Ridge Memorial Pk Dr *Web:* www.wimz.com	Knoxville	TN	37917	865-525-6000	
WITA-AM 1490 (Rel) 7212 Kingston Pike *Web:* www.wwcr.com	Knoxville	TN	37919	865-588-2974	588-6720
WIVK-FM 107.7 (Ctry) 4711 Old Kingston Pike *Web:* www.wivk.com	Knoxville	TN	37919	865-588-6511	588-3725
WJBZ-FM 96.3 (Rel) 7101 Chapman Hwy *Web:* www.praise963.com	Knoxville	TN	37920	865-577-4885	579-4667
WJXB-FM 97.5 (AC) 1100 Sharps Ridge Rd PO Box 27100 *Web:* www.b975.com	Knoxville	TN	37917	865-525-6000	525-2000
WKGN-AM 1340 (Urban) 1017 Cox St	Knoxville	TN	37919	865-546-7900	546-7965
WMYU-FM 93.1 (Oldies) 1533 Amherst Rd *Web:* www.cool931fm.com	Knoxville	TN	37909	865-824-1021	824-1880
WNFZ-FM 94.3 (Alt) 1100 Sharps Ridge Memorial Pk Dr *Web:* www.943thex.com	Knoxville	TN	37917	865-525-6000	
WNML-AM 990 (Sports) 4711 Old Kingston Pike **Fax:* News Rm ■ *Web:* www.sportsanimal99.com	Knoxville	TN	37919	865-558-9900	558-4218*
WNML-FM 99.1 (Sports) 4711 Old Kingston Pike *Web:* www.wild987.net	Knoxville	TN	37919	865-588-6511	656-9453
WNOX-FM 100.3 (N/T) 4711 Old Kingston Pike **Fax:* News Rm ■ *Web:* www.wnoxnewstalk.com	Knoxville	TN	37919	865-558-9900	558-4218*
WUOT-FM 91.9 (NPR) 209 Communications Bldg University of Tennessee *Web:* www.wuot.org	Knoxville	TN	37996	865-974-5375	974-3941
WWST-FM 102.1 (CHR) 1533 Amherst Rd *Web:* www.star1021fm.com	Knoxville	TN	37909	865-824-1021	824-1880

648-90 Lafayette, LA

Station	City	State	Zip	Phone	Fax
KFTE-FM 96.5 (Rock) 1749 Bertrand Dr *Web:* www.planet965.com	Lafayette	LA	70506	337-233-6000	234-7360
KJCB-AM 770 (Urban) 604 St John St	Lafayette	LA	70501	337-233-4262	235-9681
KMDL-FM 97.3 (Ctry) 1749 Bertrand Dr *Web:* 973thedawg.com	Lafayette	LA	70506	337-233-6000	234-7360
KNEK-FM 104.7 (Urban) 202 Galbert Rd *TF:* 866-896-5635 ■ *Web:* www.knek.com	Lafayette	LA	70506	337-920-5635	233-3779
KPEL-AM 1420 (Sports) 1749 Bertrand Dr *Web:* espn1420.com	Lafayette	LA	70506	337-233-6000	234-7360
KPEL-FM 105.1 (N/T) 1749 Bertrand Dr *Web:* www.kpel1051news.com	Lafayette	LA	70506	337-233-6000	234-7360
KRKA-FM 107.9 (Urban) 1749 Bertrand Dr *Web:* 1079ishot.com	Lafayette	LA	70506	337-233-6000	234-7360
KRRQ-FM 95.5 (Urban) 202 Galbert Rd *Web:* www.krrq.com	Lafayette	LA	70506	337-232-1311	233-3779
KRVS-FM 88.7 (NPR) 231 Hebrard Blvd *TF:* 800-892-6827 ■ *Web:* www.krvs.org	Lafayette	LA	70503	337-482-5787	482-6101
KSMB-FM 94.5 (CHR) 202 Galbert Rd *TF:* 800-299-2100 ■ *Web:* www.ksmb.com	Lafayette	LA	70506	337-232-1311	233-3779
KTDY-FM 99.9 (AC) 1749 Bertrand Dr *Web:* 999ktdy.com	Lafayette	LA	70506	337-233-6000	234-7360
KVOL-AM 1330 (N/T) 3225 Ambassador Caffery Pkwy *Web:* www.kvol1330.com	Lafayette	LA	70506	337-993-5500	993-5510
KXKC-FM 99.1 (Ctry) 202 Galbert Rd *Web:* www.kxkc.com	Lafayette	LA	70506	337-232-1311	233-3779
KYBG-FM 102.1 PO Box 60571 *Web:* www.kqis.com	Lafayette	LA	70596	337-783-2521	267-4386

648-91 Lansing, MI

Station	City	State	Zip	Phone	Fax
WFMK-FM 99.1 (AC) 3420 Pine Tree Rd *Web:* www.99wfmk.com	Lansing	MI	48911	517-394-7272	394-3565
WHZZ-FM 101.7 (AC) 600 W Cavanaugh Rd *Web:* www.1017mikefm.com	Lansing	MI	48909	517-393-1320	393-0882
WILS-AM 1320 (N/T) 600 W Cavanaugh Rd *Web:* www.1320wils.com	Lansing	MI	48909	517-393-1320	393-0882
WITL-FM 100.7 (Ctry) 3420 Pine Tree Rd *Web:* www.witl.com	Lansing	MI	48911	517-394-7272	394-3565
WJIM-AM 1240 (N/T) 3420 Pine Tree Rd **Fax:* News Rm ■ *Web:* www.wjimam.com	Lansing	MI	48911	517-394-7272	394-3565*
WJIM-FM 97.5 (CHR) 3420 Pine Tree Rd *Web:* www.oldies975.com	Lansing	MI	48911	517-394-7272	394-3565
WLNZ-FM 89.7 (Var) 400 N Capitol Ave Suite 001 *Web:* www.lcc.edu	Lansing	MI	48933	517-483-1710	483-1894
WMMQ-FM 94.9 (CR) 3420 Pine Tree Rd *Web:* www.wmmq.com	Lansing	MI	48911	517-394-7272	394-3565
WQHH-FM 96.5 (Urban) 600 W Cavanaugh *Web:* www.power965fm.com	Lansing	MI	48910	517-393-1320	393-0882
WVFN-AM 730 (Sports) 3420 Pine Tree Rd *Web:* www.730amthefan.com	Lansing	MI	48911	517-394-7272	394-3565

648-92 Las Vegas, NV

Station	City	State	Zip	Phone	Fax
KCEP-FM 88.1 (Urban) 330 W Washington Ave *Web:* www.power88lv.com	Las Vegas	NV	89106	702-648-0104	647-0803
KCYE-FM 104.3 (Ctry) 1455 E Tropicana Ave Suite 800 *Web:* www.1027thecoyote.com	Las Vegas	NV	89119	702-730-0300	736-8447
KDWN-AM 720 (N/T) 1455 E Tropicana Ave Suite 800 *Web:* www.kdwn.com	Las Vegas	NV	89119	702-385-7212	736-8447
KENO-AM 1460 (Sports) 8755 W Flamingo Rd *Web:* www.foxsportsradio1460.com	Las Vegas	NV	89147	702-876-1460	876-6685
KKJJ-FM 100.5 (AC) 6655 W Sahara Ave Suite C216 *Web:* www.jackbaby.com	Las Vegas	NV	89146	702-889-5100	257-2936
KKLZ-FM 96.3 (CR) 1455 E Tropicana Ave Suite 800 *Web:* www.963kklz.com	Las Vegas	NV	89119	702-730-0300	736-8447
KKVV-AM 1060 (Rel) 3185 S Highland Dr Suite 13 *Web:* www.kkvv.com	Las Vegas	NV	89109	702-731-5588	731-5851
KLUC-FM 98.5 (CHR) 6655 W Sahara Ave Suite D208 *Web:* www.kluc.com	Las Vegas	NV	89146	702-253-9800	889-7373
KMXB-FM 94.1 (AC) 6655 W Sahara Ave Suite C216 *Web:* www.mix941.fm	Las Vegas	NV	89146	702-889-5100	257-2936
KNPR-FM 89.5 (NPR) 1289 S Torrey Pines Dr *TF:* 888-895-9895 ■ *Web:* www.knpr.org	Las Vegas	NV	89146	702-258-9895	258-5646
KOAS-FM 105.7 (NAC) 2725 E Desert Inn Rd Suite 180 *Web:* www.smoothjazz1057.com	Las Vegas	NV	89121	702-784-4000	784-4040
KOMP-FM 92.3 (Rock) 8755 W Flamingo Rd *Web:* www.komp.com	Las Vegas	NV	89147	702-876-1460	876-6685
KPLV-FM 93.1 (AC) 2880 Meade Ave Suite 250 *Web:* www.931theparty.com	Las Vegas	NV	89102	702-238-7300	732-4890

Station	City	State	Zip	Phone	Fax
KSNE-FM 106.5 (AC) 2880 Meade Ave Suite 250 *Web:* www.ksne.com	Las Vegas	NV	89102	702-238-7300	732-4890
KUNV-FM 91.5 (Jazz) 1515 E Tropicana Ave Suite 240 *Web:* www.kunv.unlv.edu	Las Vegas	NV	89119	702-798-9169	736-0983
KVEG-FM 97.5 (Urban) 3999 Las Vegas Blvd S Suite K *Web:* www.kvegas.com	Las Vegas	NV	89119	702-736-6161	736-2986
KWNR-FM 95.5 (Ctry) 2880 Meade Ave Suite 250 *Web:* www.kwnr.com	Las Vegas	NV	89102	702-238-7300	732-4890
KXNT-AM 840 (N/T) 6655 W Sahara Ave Suite D-110 *Web:* www.kxnt.com	Las Vegas	NV	89146	702-889-7300	889-7384
KXPT-FM 97.1 (CR) 8755 W Flamingo Rd *Web:* www.point97.com	Las Vegas	NV	89147	702-876-1460	876-6685
KXTE-FM 107.5 (Alt) 6655 W Sahara Ave Suite D-110 *Web:* www.xtremeradio.com	Las Vegas	NV	89146	702-257-1075	889-7575

648-93 Lexington/Frankfort, KY

Station	City	State	Zip	Phone	Fax
WBTF-FM 107.9 (Urban) 401 W Main St Suite 301 *Web:* www.1079thebeat.com	Lexington	KY	40507	859-233-1515	233-1517
WBUL-FM 98.1 (Ctry) 2601 Nicholasville Rd *TF:* 877-898-2855 ■ *Web:* www.wbul.com	Lexington	KY	40503	859-422-1000	422-1038
WFKY-FM 104.9 (Cty) 115 W Main St *Web:* www.myfroggy1049.com	Frankfort	KY	40601	502-875-1130	875-1225
WGKS-FM 96.9 (AC) 401 W Main St Suite 301 *Web:* www.wgks.com	Lexington	KY	40507	859-233-1515	233-1517
WKQQ-FM 100.1 (Rock) 2601 Nicholasville Rd *TF:* 866-525-9467 ■ *Web:* www.wkqq.com	Lexington	KY	40503	859-422-1000	422-1038
WKYL-FM 102.1 (NAC) 88 C Michael Davenport Blvd	Frankfort	KY	40601	502-839-1021	
WKYW-AM 1490 (N/T) 115 W Main St *Web:* www.talk1490.com	Frankfort	KY	40601	502-875-1130	875-1225
WLAP-AM 630 (N/T) 2601 Nicholasville Rd *Web:* www.wlap.com	Lexington	KY	40503	859-422-1000	422-1038
WLKT-FM 104.5 (CHR) 2601 Nicholasville Rd *Web:* www.wlkt.com	Lexington	KY	40503	859-422-1000	422-1038
WLXX-FM 92.9 (Ctry) 300 W Vine St *TF:* 877-777-9929 ■ *Web:* www.wlxxthebear.com	Lexington	KY	40507	859-253-5900	253-5940
WMKJ-FM 105.5 (Oldies) 2601 Nicholasville Rd. *Web:* www.magic1055.com	Lexington	KY	40503	859-422-1000	422-1038
WMXL-FM 94.5 (AC) 2601 Nicholasville Rd *Web:* www.wmxl.com	Lexington	KY	40503	859-422-1000	422-1038
WSTV-FM 103.7 (AC) 115 W Main St. *Web:* www.star1037.com	Frankfort	KY	40601	502-875-1130	875-1225
WUKY-FM 91.3 (NPR) 340 McVey Hall University of Kentucky *Web:* www.wuky.uky.edu	Lexington	KY	40506	859-257-3221	257-6291
WVLK-AM 590 (N/T) 300 W Vine St *TF:* 877-777-0590 ■ *Web:* www.wvlkam.com	Lexington	KY	40507	859-253-5900	253-5940
WXZZ-FM 103.3 (Rock) 300 W Vine St *Web:* www.zrock103.com	Lexington	KY	40507	859-253-5900	253-5940

648-94 Lincoln, NE

Station	City	State	Zip	Phone	Fax
KBBK-FM 107.3 (AC) 4343 'O' St *Web:* www.b1073.com	Lincoln	NE	68510	402-475-4567	479-1411
KFGE-FM 98.1 (Ctry) 4343 'O' St *Web:* www.froggy981.com	Lincoln	NE	68510	402-475-4567	479-1411
KFOR-AM 1240 (N/T) 3800 Cornhusker Hwy *Web:* www.kfor1240.com	Lincoln	NE	68504	402-466-1234	467-4095
KFRX-FM 106.3 (CHR) 3800 Cornhusker Hwy *Web:* www.kfrxfm.com	Lincoln	NE	68504	402-466-1234	467-4095
KIBZ-FM 104.1 (Rock) 3800 Cornhusker Hwy *Web:* www.kibz.com	Lincoln	NE	68504	402-466-1234	467-4095
KLNC-FM 105.3 (CR) 4343 'O' St *Web:* www.lincfm.com	Lincoln	NE	68510	402-475-4567	479-1411
KTGL-FM 92.9 (CR) 3800 Cornhusker Hwy *Web:* www.ktgl.com	Lincoln	NE	68504	402-466-1234	467-4095
KUCV-FM 91.1 (Var) 1800 N 33rd St *TF:* 888-638-7346 ■ *Web:* www.nprn.org	Lincoln	NE	68583	402-472-2200	472-2403
KZKX-FM 96.9 (Ctry) 3800 Cornhusker Hwy *Web:* www.kzkx.com	Lincoln	NE	68504	402-466-1234	467-4095

648-95 Little Rock, AR

Station	City	State	Zip	Phone	Fax
KABF-FM 88.3 (Var) 2101 Main St # 200 *Web:* www.kabf.org	Little Rock	AR	72206	501-372-6119	375-5965
KABZ-FM 103.7 (N/T) 2400 Cottondale Ln *TF:* 800-477-1037 ■ *Web:* www.1037thebuzz.com	Little Rock	AR	72202	501-664-9410	664-5871
KARN-AM 920 (N/T) 700 Wellington Hills Rd *Web:* www.920karn.com	Little Rock	AR	72211	501-401-0200	
KHLR-FM 94.9 (Rel) 10800 Colonel Glenn Rd *Web:* www.949hallelujah.com	Little Rock	AR	72204	501-217-5000	228-9547
KHTE-FM 96.5 (CHR) 400 Hardin Rd Suite 150 *Web:* www.hot965.com	Little Rock	AR	72211	501-219-1919	225-4610
KIPR-FM 92.3 (Urban) 700 Wellington Hills Rd *Web:* www.power923.com	Little Rock	AR	72211	501-401-0200	401-0366
KKPT-FM 94.1 (CR) 2400 Cottondale Ln. *TF:* 800-844-0094 ■ *Web:* www.kkpt.com	Little Rock	AR	72202	501-664-9410	664-5871
KLAL-FM 107.7 (CHR) 700 Wellington Hills Rd *Web:* www.alice1077.com	Little Rock	AR	72211	501-401-0200	
KMJX-FM 105.1 (CR) 10800 Colonel Glenn Rd *Web:* www.magic105fm.com	Little Rock	AR	72204	501-217-5000	228-9547
KOKY-FM 102.1 (Urban) 700 Wellington Hills Rd *Web:* www.koky.com	Little Rock	AR	72211	501-401-0200	
KSSN-FM 95.7 (Ctry) 10800 Colonel Glenn Rd *Web:* www.kssn.com	Little Rock	AR	72204	501-217-5000	228-9547
KUAR-FM 89.1 (NPR) 2801 S University Ave *TF:* 800-952-2528 ■ *Web:* www.ualr.edu/~kuar	Little Rock	AR	72204	501-569-8485	569-8488
KURB-FM 98.5 (AC) 700 Wellington Hills Rd *Web:* www.b98.com	Little Rock	AR	72211	501-401-0200	

648-96 Los Angeles, CA

Station	City	State	Zip	Phone	Fax
KABC-AM 790 (N/T) 3321 S La Cienega Blvd PO Box 790 *Web:* www.kabc.com	Los Angeles	CA	90016	310-840-4900	840-4921
KCBS-FM 93.1 (Var) 5901 Venice Blvd. *TF:* 866-931-5225 ■ *Web:* www.931jackfm.com	Los Angeles	CA	90034	323-937-9331	931-5198
KFWB-AM 980 (N/T) 5670 Wilshire Blvd Suite 200 *TF:* 866-900-5392 ■ *Web:* www.kfwb.com	Los Angeles	CA	90036	323-525-0980	464-6101
KKGO-FM 105.1 (Ctry) 1500 Cotner Ave *Web:* www.gocountry105.com	Los Angeles	CA	90025	310-478-5540	445-1439
KLAX-FM 97.9 (Span) 10281 W Pico Blvd *Web:* www.979laraza.com	Los Angeles	CA	90064	310-203-0900	203-8989
KLOS-FM 95.5 (CR) 3321 S La Cienega Blvd PO Box 955 *TF:* 800-955-5567 ■ *Web:* www.955klos.com	Los Angeles	CA	90016	310-840-4900	840-4921
KLSX-FM 97.1 (N/T) 5670 Wilshire Blvd Suite 200 *Web:* 971freefm.com	Los Angeles	CA	90036	323-971-9710	954-0971
KNX-AM 1070 (N/T) 5670 Wilshire Blvd Suite 200 *Web:* www.knx1070.com	Los Angeles	CA	90036	323-964-8351	964-8398
KROQ-FM 106.7 (Alt) 5901 Venice Blvd *TF:* 800-520-1067 ■ *Web:* www.kroq.com	Los Angeles	CA	90034	323-930-1067	931-1067
KRTH-FM 101.1 (Oldies) 5670 Wilshire Blvd Suite 200 *TF:* 800-232-5834 ■ *Web:* www.mykearth101.com	Los Angeles	CA	90036	323-936-5784	933-6072
KSPN-AM 710 (Sports) 800 W Olympic Blvd Suite 200 *TF:* 877-710-3776 ■ *Web:* espn.go.com/los-angeles/radio/index	Los Angeles	CA	90015	213-284-7100	
KSWD-FM 100.3 (Rock) 5900 Wilshire Blvd Suite 1900 *Web:* www.thesoundla.com	Los Angeles	CA	90036	323-634-1800	634-1888
KTWV-FM 94.7 (NAC) 5670 Wilshire Blvd Suite 200 *TF:* 800-520-9283 ■ *Web:* www.947wave.com	Los Angeles	CA	90036	323-937-9283	634-0947
KUSC-FM 91.5 (Clas) 1149 S Hill St # 150 *Web:* www.kusc.org	Los Angeles	CA	90007	213-225-7400	225-7410

648-97 Louisville, KY

Station	City	State	Zip	Phone	Fax
WAMZ-FM 97.5 (Ctry) 4000 One Radio Dr *Web:* www.wamz.com	Louisville	KY	40218	502-479-2222	479-2223
WDJX-FM 99.7 (CHR) 520 S 4th Ave 2nd Fl *Web:* www.wdjx.com	Louisville	KY	40202	502-625-1220	625-1253
WFPK-FM 91.9 (AAA) 619 S 4th St *Web:* www.wfpk.org	Louisville	KY	40202	502-814-6500	814-6599
WFPL-FM 89.3 (NPR) 619 S 4th St. *Web:* www.wfpl.org	Louisville	KY	40202	502-814-6500	814-6599
WGZB-FM 96.5 (Urban) 520 S 4th Ave 2nd Fl *Web:* www.b96jams.com	Louisville	KY	40202	502-625-1220	625-1253
WHAS-AM 840 (N/T) 4000 One Radio Dr. *TF:* 800-444-8484 ■ *Web:* www.whas.com	Louisville	KY	40218	502-479-2222	479-2308
WLOU-AM 1350 (Rel) 2001 W Broadway Suite 13 *Web:* www.wlouam.com	Louisville	KY	40203	502-776-1240	776-1250
WLRS-FM 105.1 (Alt) 520 S 4th Ave 2nd Fl *Web:* www.1051fmtalk.com	Louisville	KY	40202	502-625-1220	625-1253
WLUE-FM 100.5 (Var) 4000 One Radio Dr *Web:* www.louieonline.com	Louisville	KY	40218	502-479-2222	479-2227
WMJM-FM 101.3 (Oldies) 520 S 4th Ave 2nd Fl *Web:* www.1013online.com	Louisville	KY	40202	502-625-1220	625-1253
WQKC-AM 1450 (Sports) 9900 Corporate Campus Dr Suite 2600	Louisville	KY	40223	502-992-0939	992-0862
WQMF-FM 95.7 (CR) 4000 One Radio Dr *Web:* www.wqmf.com	Louisville	KY	40218	502-479-2222	479-2227
WQNU-FM 103.9 (Ctry) 612 S 4th Ave Suite 100 *Web:* newcountry1039.com	Louisville	KY	40202	502-589-4800	583-4820
WRKA-FM 103.1 (Ctry) 612 S 4th Ave Suite 100 *Web:* wrka.com	Louisville	KY	40202	502-589-4800	583-4820

	City	State	Zip	Phone	Fax
WSFR-FM 107.7 (CR) 612 S 4th Ave Suite 100 *Web:* 1077sfr.com	Louisville	KY	40202	502-589-4800	583-4820
WTFX-FM 93.1 (Rock) 4000 One Radio Dr *Web:* www.fox.com	Louisville	KY	40218	502-479-2222	479-2227
WTMT-AM 620 (Span) 4109 Bardstown Rd Suite 104 *Web:* www.wtmt.com	Louisville	KY	40218	502-583-6200	671-8743
WVEZ-FM 106.9 (AC) 612 S 4th Ave Suite 100 *TF:* 866-566-2456 ■ *Web:* lite1069.com	Louisville	KY	40202	502-589-4800	583-4820
WXMA-FM 102.3 (AC) 520 S 4th Ave 2nd Fl *Web:* www.themaxfm.com	Louisville	KY	40202	502-625-1220	625-1255

648-98 Lubbock, TX

	City	State	Zip	Phone	Fax
KFMX-FM 94.5 (Rock) 4413 82nd St Suite 300 *Web:* www.kfmx.com	Lubbock	TX	79424	806-798-7078	798-7052
KFYO-AM 790 (N/T) 4413 82nd St Suite 300 *Web:* www.kfyo.com	Lubbock	TX	79424	806-798-7078	798-7052
KKAM-AM 1340 (Sports) 4413 82nd St Suite 300 *Web:* www.kkam.com	Lubbock	TX	79424	806-798-7078	798-7052
KKCL-FM 98.1 (Oldies) 4413 82nd St Suite 300 *Web:* www.98kool.com	Lubbock	TX	79424	806-798-7078	798-7052
KLLL-FM 96.3 (Ctry) 33 Briercroft Office Pk *Web:* www.klll.com	Lubbock	TX	79412	806-762-3000	770-5363
KLZK-FM 104.3 (CHR) 9800 University Ave	Lubbock	TX	79423	806-770-5477	
KMMX-FM 100.3 (AC) 33 Briercroft Office Pk *Web:* www.kmmx.com	Lubbock	TX	79412	806-762-3000	770-5363
KOHM-FM 89.1 (NPR) 1901 University Ave Suite 603 B *Web:* www.kohm.org	Lubbock	TX	79410	806-742-3100	742-3716
KONE-FM 101.1 (Rock) 33 Briercroft Office Pk *Web:* www.rock101.fm	Lubbock	TX	79412	806-762-3000	770-5363
KQBR-FM 99.5 (Ctry) 4413 82nd St Suite 300 *Web:* www.kqbr.com	Lubbock	TX	79424	806-798-7078	798-7052
KRBL-FM 105.7 (Ctry) 916 Main St Suite 617 *Web:* www.krbl.net	Lubbock	TX	79401	806-749-1057	749-1177
KZII-FM 102.5 (CHR) 4413 82nd St Suite 300 *Web:* www.z102.com	Lubbock	TX	79424	806-798-7078	798-7052

648-99 Macon, GA

	City	State	Zip	Phone	Fax
WDEN-FM 99.1 (Ctry) 544 Mulberry St 5th Fl *Web:* www.wden.com	Macon	GA	31201	478-746-6286	749-1393
WFXM-FM 107.1 (Urban) 6174 Hwy 57 *Web:* www.powermacon.com	Macon	GA	31217	478-745-3301	742-2293
WIBB-FM 97.9 (Urban) 7080 Industrial Hwy *TF:* 800-813-8418 ■ *Web:* www.wibb.com	Macon	GA	31216	478-781-1063	781-6711
WLZN-FM 92.3 (Urban) 544 Mulberry St 5th Fl *Web:* www.blazin923.com	Macon	GA	31201	478-746-6286	749-1393
WMAC-AM 940 (N/T) 544 Mulberry St 5th Fl *Web:* www.wmac-am.com	Macon	GA	31201	478-746-6286	749-1393
WMGB-FM 95.1 (CHR) 544 Mulberry St 5th Fl *Web:* www.allthehitsb951.com	Macon	GA	31201	478-746-6286	749-1393
WPEZ-FM 93.7 (AC) 544 Mulberry St 5th Fl *Web:* www.z937.com	Macon	GA	31201	478-746-6286	749-1393
WPGA-FM 100.9 (AC) 1691 Forsyth St *TF:* 800-247-4487 ■ *Web:* wpga58.com	Macon	GA	31201	478-745-5858	745-5800
WRBV-FM 101.7 (Urban AC) 7080 Industrial Hwy *Web:* www.v1017.com	Macon	GA	31216	478-781-1063	781-6711
WZCH-FM 102.5 (CH) 7080 Industrial Hwy *Web:* www.newcountry1025.com	Macon	GA	31216	478-781-1063	781-6711

648-100 Madison, WI

	City	State	Zip	Phone	Fax
WCHY-FM 105.1 (Var) 7601 Ganser Way *Web:* www.1051charliefm.com	Madison	WI	53719	608-826-0077	826-1244
WERN-FM 88.7 (NPR) 821 University Ave *TF:* 800-747-7444 ■ *Web:* www.wpr.org	Madison	WI	53706	608-263-2121	263-9763
WHA-AM 970 (NPR) 821 University Ave *TF:* 800-747-7444 ■ *Web:* www.wpr.org	Madison	WI	53706	608-263-2121	263-9763
WIBA-AM 1310 (N/T) 2651 S Fish Hatchery Rd *Web:* www.wiba.com	Madison	WI	53711	608-274-5450	274-5521
WIBA-FM 101.5 (CR) 2651 S Fish Hatchery Rd *Web:* www.wibafm.com	Madison	WI	53711	608-274-5450	274-5521
WJJO-FM 94.1 (Rock) 730 Rayovac Dr *Web:* www.wjjo.com	Madison	WI	53711	608-273-1000	271-8182
WMAD-FM 96.3 (Ctry) 2651 S Fish Hatchery Rd *Web:* www.wmad.com	Madison	WI	53711	608-274-5450	274-5521
WMGN-FM 98.1 (AC) 730 Rayovac Dr *Web:* www.magic98.com	Madison	WI	53711	608-273-1000	441-0098
WMMM-FM 105.5 (AAA) 7601 Ganser Way *Web:* www.1055triplem.com	Madison	WI	53719	608-826-0077	826-1244
WTSO-AM 1070 (Sports) 2651 S Fish Hatchery Rd *Web:* www.thebig1070.com	Madison	WI	53711	608-274-5450	274-5521
WTUX-AM 1550 (Nost) 730 Rayovac Dr *Web:* www.wtux.com	Madison	WI	53711	608-273-1000	271-8182
WWQM-FM 106.3 (Ctry) 730 Rayovac Dr *Web:* www.q106.com	Madison	WI	53711	608-273-1000	271-8182
WXXM-FM 92.1 (N/T) 2651 S Fish Hatchery Rd *Web:* www.themic921.com	Madison	WI	53711	608-274-5450	274-5521
WZEE-FM 104.1 (CHR) 2651 S Fish Hatchery Rd *Web:* www.z104fm.com	Madison	WI	53711	608-274-5450	274-5521

648-101 Manchester, NH

	City	State	Zip	Phone	Fax
WFEA-AM 1370 (Nost) 500 Commercial St *Web:* www.wfea1370.com	Manchester	NH	03101	603-669-5777	669-4641
WGIR-AM 610 (N/T) 195 McGregor St Suite 810 *Web:* www.wgiram.com	Manchester	NH	03102	603-625-6915	625-9255
WGIR-FM 101.1 (Rock) 195 McGregor St Suite 810 *Web:* www.rock101wgir.com	Manchester	NH	03102	603-625-6915	625-9255
WMLL-FM 96.5 (CR) 500 Commercial St *Web:* www.themill965.com	Manchester	NH	03101	603-669-5777	669-4641
WZID-FM 95.7 (AC) 500 Commercial St *Web:* www.wzid.com	Manchester	NH	03101	603-669-5777	669-4641

648-102 Memphis, TN

	City	State	Zip	Phone	Fax
KJMS-FM 101.1 (Urban) 2650 Thousand Oaks Blvd Suite 4100 *Web:* www.myv101.com/main.html	Memphis	TN	38118	901-259-1300	259-6449
KWAM-AM 990 (N/T) 5495 Murray Rd *Web:* www.kwam990.com	Memphis	TN	38119	901-261-4200	261-4210
KXHT-FM 107.1 (Urban) 6080 Mt Moriah Rd Ext *Web:* www.hot1071.com	Memphis	TN	38115	901-375-9324	375-0041
WDIA-AM 1070 (Urban) 2650 Thousand Oaks Blvd Suite 4100 *Web:* www.am1070wdia.com	Memphis	TN	38118	901-259-1300	259-6449
WEGR-FM 102.7 (CR) 2650 Thousand Oaks Blvd Suite 4100 *Web:* www.rock103.com	Memphis	TN	38118	901-259-1300	259-6449
WGKX-FM 105.9 (Ctry) 5629 Murray Rd *Web:* www.kix106.com	Memphis	TN	38119	901-680-9898	767-9531
WHAL-FM 95.7 (Rel) 2650 Thousand Oaks Blvd Suite 4100 *Web:* www.hallelujahfm.com	Memphis	TN	38118	901-259-1300	259-6449
WHRK-FM 97.1 (Urban) 2650 Thousand Oaks Blvd Suite 4100 *Web:* www.k97fm.com	Memphis	TN	38118	901-259-1300	259-6449
WKIM-FM 98.9 (AC) 5629 Murray Rd *Web:* www.989kimfm.com	Memphis	TN	38119	901-680-9898	767-9531
WKNO-FM 91.1 (NPR) 900 Getwell Rd *TF:* 800-766-9566 ■ *Web:* www.wknofm.org	Memphis	TN	38124	901-325-6544	325-6506
WLOK-AM 1340 (Rel) 363 S 2nd St *Web:* www.wlok.com	Memphis	TN	38103	901-527-9565	528-0335
WMC-FM 99.7 (AC) 1960 Union Ave *Web:* www.fm100memphis.com	Memphis	TN	38104	901-767-0104	726-9580
WMFS-FM 92.9 (Alt) 1960 Union Ave *Web:* www.93xmemphis.com	Memphis	TN	38104	901-767-0104	726-9580
WRBO-FM 103.5 (Oldies) 5629 Murray Rd *Web:* www.soulclassics.com	Memphis	TN	38119	901-680-9898	767-9531
WREC-AM 600 (N/T) 2650 Thousand Oaks Blvd Suite 4100 *Web:* www.wrecradio.com	Memphis	TN	38118	901-259-1300	259-6449
WRVR-FM 104.5 (AC) 5904 Ridgeway Ctr Pkwy *Web:* www.wrvr.com	Memphis	TN	38120	901-767-0104	763-4290
WSMB-AM 680 (Sports) 5904 Ridgeway Ctr Pkwy *Web:* www.680wsmb.com	Memphis	TN	38120	901-767-0104	767-0582
WSNA-FM 94.1 (CHR) 5904 Ridgeway Ctr Pkwy *Web:* www.snap941.com	Memphis	TN	38120	901-767-0104	763-4290
WXMX-FM 98.1 (Rock) 5629 Murray Rd *Web:* www.981themax.com	Memphis	TN	38119	901-680-9898	767-9531

648-103 Miami/Fort Lauderdale, FL

	City	State	Zip	Phone	Fax
WCMQ-FM 92.3 (Span) 7007 NW 77th Ave *Web:* www.clasica92fm.com	Miami	FL	33166	305-444-9292	461-4951
WDNA-FM 88.9 (Jazz) 2921 Coral Way *TF:* 866-688-9362 ■ *Web:* www.wdna.org	Miami	FL	33145	305-662-8889	662-1975
WINZ-AM 940 (N/T) 7601 Riviera Blvd *Web:* www.am940southflorida.com	Miramar	FL	33023	954-862-2000	862-4212
WIOD-AM 610 (N/T) 7601 Riviera Blvd *Web:* www.newsradio610.com	Miramar	FL	33023	954-862-2000	862-4212
WKIS-FM 99.9 (Ctry) 194 NW 187th St *Web:* www.wkis.com	Miami	FL	33169	305-654-1700	654-1717
WLQY-AM 1320 (Var) 10800 Biscayne Blvd Suite 810	North Miami	FL	33161	305-891-1729	891-1583
WLRN-FM 91.3 (NPR) 172 NE 15th St *Web:* www.wlrn.org	Miami	FL	33132	305-995-1717	995-2299
WLYF-FM 101.5 (AC) 20450 NW 2nd Ave *TF:* 800-469-1015 ■ *Web:* www.wlyf.com	Miami	FL	33169	305-521-5100	521-1414
WMBM-AM 1490 (Rel) 13242 NW 7th Ave *TF:* 888-599-9626 ■ *Web:* www.wmbm.com	North Miami	FL	33168	305-769-1100	769-9975
WMXJ-FM 102.7 (Oldies) 20450 NW 2nd Ave *TF:* 800-924-1027 ■ *Web:* www.majic1027.com	Miami	FL	33169	305-521-5100	521-1414
WPOW-FM 96.5 (CHR) 20295 NW 2nd Ave 3rd Fl *Web:* www.power96.com	Miami	FL	33169	305-653-6796	770-1456
WRMA-FM 106.7 (Span AC) 7007 NW 77th Ave *Web:* www.romancefm.com	Miami	FL	33166	305-444-9292	883-1161
WSUA-AM 1260 (Span) 2100 Coral Way Suite 201 *TF:* 800-441-1260 ■ *Web:* www.caracol1260.com	Miami	FL	33145	305-285-7075	858-5907
WXDJ-FM 95.7 (Span) 7007 NW 77th Ave *Web:* www.elzol.com	Miami	FL	33166	305-444-9292	883-1341

648-104 Milwaukee, WI

Station	City	State	Zip	Phone	Fax
WAUK-AM 540 (Sports) 770 N Jefferson St *TF:* 888-273-3776	Milwaukee	WI	53202	414-273-3776	291-3776
WHAD-FM 90.7 (NPR) 310 W Wisconsin Ave Suite 750-E *TF:* 800-486-8655 ■ *Web:* www.wpr.org	Milwaukee	WI	53203	414-227-2040	227-2043
WHQG-FM 102.9 (Rock) 5407 W McKinley Ave *Web:* www.1029thehog.com	Milwaukee	WI	53208	414-978-9000	978-9001
WJMR-FM 98.3 (Urban) 5407 W McKinley Ave *Web:* www.wjmr.com	Milwaukee	WI	53208	414-978-9000	978-9001
WJYI-AM 1340 (Rel) 5407 W McKinley Ave *Web:* www.joy1340.com	Milwaukee	WI	53208	414-978-9000	978-9001
WKLH-FM 96.5 (CR) 5407 W McKinley Ave *Web:* www.wklh.com	Milwaukee	WI	53208	414-978-9000	978-9001
WLWK-FM 94.5 (AC) 720 E Capitol Dr *Web:* www.945lakefm.com	Milwaukee	WI	53212	414-332-9611	967-5266
WMCS-AM 1290 (Urban) 4222 W Capitol Dr *Web:* www.1290wmcs.com	Milwaukee	WI	53216	414-444-1290	444-1409
WTMJ-AM 620 (N/T) 720 E Capitol Dr *Web:* www.620wtmj.com	Milwaukee	WI	53212	414-332-9611	967-5298
WUWM-FM 89.7 (NPR) 111 E Wisconsin Ave Suite 700 *Web:* www.wuwm.com	Milwaukee	WI	53202	414-227-3355	270-1297
Wzbk FM 106.9 (Big Bubk Country) 5407 W McKinley Ave. *Web:* www.bigbuck1069.com	Milwaukee	WI	53208	414-978-9000	978-9001

648-105 Minneapolis/Saint Paul, MN

Station	City	State	Zip	Phone	Fax
KCMP-FM 89.3 (NPR) 480 Cedar St *Web:* minnesota.publicradio.org/radio	Saint Paul	MN	55101	651-290-1500	290-1295
KDWB-FM 101.3 (CHR) 1600 Utica Ave S Suite 400 *Web:* www.kdwb.com	Minneapolis	MN	55416	952-417-3000	417-3001
KEEY-FM 102.1 (Ctry) 1600 Utica Ave S Suite 400 *Web:* www.k102.com	Minneapolis	MN	55416	952-417-3000	417-3001
KFAN-AM 1130 (Sports) 1600 Utica Ave S Suite 400 *Web:* www.kfan.com	Minneapolis	MN	55416	952-417-3000	417-3001
KQQL-FM 107.9 (Oldies) 1600 Utica Ave S Suite 400 *Web:* www.kool108.com	Minneapolis	MN	55416	952-417-3000	417-3001
KQRS-FM 92.5 (CR) 2000 SE Elm St *Web:* www.92kqrs.com	Minneapolis	MN	55414	612-617-4000	676-8292
KSTP-AM 1500 (N/T) 3415 University Ave *TF:* 877-615-1500 ■ *Web:* www.am1500.com	Saint Paul	MN	55114	651-647-1500	647-2904
KSTP-FM 94.5 (AC) 3415 University Ave *Web:* www.ks95.com	Saint Paul	MN	55114	651-642-4141	642-4148
KTCZ-FM 97.1 (AAA) 1600 Utica Ave S Suite 400 *Web:* www.cities97.com	Minneapolis	MN	55416	952-417-3000	417-3001
KXXR-FM 93.7 (Rock) 2000 SE Elm St *Web:* www.93x.com	Minneapolis	MN	55414	612-617-4000	676-8293
KZJK-FM 104.1 (Var) 625 2nd Ave S *Web:* 1041jackfm.radio.com	Minneapolis	MN	55402	612-370-0611	612-0159
WCCO-AM 830 (N/T) 625 2nd Ave S Suite 200 *Web:* www.wccoradio.com	Minneapolis	MN	55402	612-370-0611	370-0159
WGVX-FM 105.7 (Alt) 2000 SE Elm St *Web:* www.love105.fm	Minneapolis	MN	55414	612-617-4000	676-8292
WLTE-FM 102.9 (AC) 625 2nd Ave S Suite 200 *Web:* wlte.radio.com	Minneapolis	MN	55402	612-370-0611	612-5653

648-106 Mobile, AL

Station	City	State	Zip	Phone	Fax
WABB-FM 97.5 (CHR) 1551 Springhill Ave. *Web:* www.wabb.com	Mobile	AL	36604	251-432-5572	438-4044
WBHY-FM 88.5 (Rel) PO Box 1328 *TF:* 888-473-8488 ■ *Web:* www.goforth.org	Mobile	AL	36633	251-473-8488	300-3149
WBLX-FM 92.9 (Urban) 2800 Dauphin St Suite 104 *Web:* www.thebigstation93blx.com	Mobile	AL	36606	251-652-2000	652-2001
WDLT-FM 98.3 2800 Dauphin St Suite 104 *TF:* 877-250-9898 ■ *Web:* www.983wdlt.com	Mobile	AL	36606	251-652-2000	652-2001
WGOK-AM 900 (Rel) 2800 Dauphin St Suite 104 *Web:* www.gospel900.com	Mobile	AL	36606	251-652-2000	652-2007
WHIL-FM 91.3 (NPR) 4000 Dauphin St. *TF:* 800-239-9445 ■ *Web:* www.whil.org	Mobile	AL	36608	251-380-4685	460-2189
WKSJ-FM 94.9 (Ctry) 555 Broadcast Dr 3rd Fl. *Web:* www.95ksj.com	Mobile	AL	36606	251-450-0100	479-3418
WMXC-FM 99.9 (AC) 555 Broadcast Dr 3rd Fl *Web:* www.litemix.com	Mobile	AL	36606	251-450-0100	479-3418
WNSP-FM 105.5 (Sports) 1100 Dauphin St Suite E *TF:* 888-560-9754 ■ *Web:* www.wnsp.com	Mobile	AL	36604	251-438-5460	438-5462
WNTM-AM 710 (N/T) 555 Broadcast Dr 3rd Fl *Web:* www.newsradio710.com	Mobile	AL	36606	251-450-0100	479-3418
WRKH-FM 96.1 (CR) 555 Broadcast Dr 3rd Fl *Web:* www.961therocket.com	Mobile	AL	36606	251-450-0100	479-3418

648-107 Modesto, CA

Station	City	State	Zip	Phone	Fax
KATM-FM 103.3 (Ctry) 1581 Cummins Dr Suite 135 *Web:* www.katm.com	Modesto	CA	95358	209-766-5000	522-2061
KCIV-FM 99.9 (Rel) 1031 15th St Suite 1 *TF:* 800-743-5248 ■ *Web:* www.bottradionetwork.com	Modesto	CA	95354	209-524-8999	524-9088
KESP-AM 970 (Sports) 1581 Cummins Dr Suite 135 *Web:* www.espnradio970.com	Modesto	CA	95358	209-766-5000	522-2061
KFIV-AM 1360 (N/T) 2121 Lancey Dr *Web:* www.kfiv1360.com	Modesto	CA	95355	209-551-1306	551-1359
KHKK-FM 104.1 (CR) 1581 Cummins Dr Suite 135 *Web:* www.104thehawk.com	Modesto	CA	95358	209-766-5000	522-2061
KHOP-FM 95.1 (CHR) 1581 Cummins Dr Suite 135 *Web:* www.khop.com	Modesto	CA	95358	209-766-5000	522-2061
KJSN-FM 102.3 (AC) 2121 Lancey Dr. *Web:* www.sunny102fm.com	Modesto	CA	95355	209-551-1306	551-1359
KMRQ-FM 96.7 (Rock) 2121 Lancey Dr. *TF:* 800-505-3967 ■ *Web:* www.rock967.com	Modesto	CA	95355	209-551-1306	551-1359
KOSO-FM 93.1 (AC) 2121 Lancey Dr. *TF:* 800-222-5693 ■ *Web:* www.b931.com	Modesto	CA	95355	209-551-1306	551-1359
KQOD-FM 100.1 (Oldies) 2121 Lancey Dr *TF:* 877-967-6342 ■ *Web:* www.mega100online.com	Modesto	CA	95355	209-551-1306	551-5319
KRVR-FM 105.5 (NAC) 961 N Emerald Ave Suite A *Web:* www.krvr.com	Modesto	CA	95351	209-544-1055	544-8105

648-108 Monterey, CA

Station	City	State	Zip	Phone	Fax
KBOQ-FM 103.9 (Clas) 60 Garden Ct Suite 300 *Web:* www.kbach.com	Monterey	CA	93940	831-658-5200	658-5299
KCDU-FM 101.7 (AC) 60 Garden Ct Suite 300 *Web:* www.1017thebeach.com	Monterey	CA	93940	831-658-5200	658-5299
KHIP-FM 104.3 (CR) 60 Garden Ct Suite 300 *TF:* 877-762-5104 ■ *Web:* www.thehippo.com	Monterey	CA	93940	831-658-5200	658-5299
KIDD-AM 630 (Nost) 5 Harris Ct Bldg C *Web:* www.magic63.com	Monterey	CA	93940	831-649-0969	649-3335
KKHK-FM 95.5 (Cty) 60 Garden Ct Suite 300 *Web:* www.hankcountry.com	Monterey	CA	93940	831-658-5200	658-5299
KLOK-FM 99.5 (Span) 67 Garden Ct. *TF:* 888-874-2656 ■ *Web:* www.tricolor995.com	Monterey	CA	93940	831-333-9735	373-6700
KSES-FM 107.1 (Span) 67 Garden Ct. *TF:* 800-420-2757 ■ *Web:* www.sesalinas.com	Monterey	CA	93942	831-333-9735	333-9750
KWAV-FM 96.9 (AC) 5 Harris Ct Bldg C *Web:* www.kwav.com	Monterey	CA	93940	831-649-0969	649-3335

648-109 Montgomery, AL

Station	City	State	Zip	Phone	Fax
WACV-AM 1170 (N/T) 4101-A Wall St *Web:* www.1170wacv.com	Montgomery	AL	36106	334-244-0961	279-9563
WBAM-FM 98.9 (Ctry) 4101-A Wall St. *Web:* www.bamacountry989.com	Montgomery	AL	36106	334-244-0961	279-9563
WHHY-FM 101.9 (CHR) 1 Commerce St Suite 300 *Web:* www.y102montgomery.com	Montgomery	AL	36104	334-240-9274	240-9219
WHLW-FM 104.3 (Rel) 203 Gunn Rd *Web:* www.1043hallelujahfm.com	Montgomery	AL	36117	334-274-6464	274-6465
WJWZ-FM 97.9 (Urban) 4101-A Wall St *Web:* www.979jamz.com	Montgomery	AL	36106	334-244-0961	279-9563
WLWI-FM 92.3 (Ctry) 1 Commerce St Suite 300 *TF:* 800-757-9594 ■ *Web:* www.wlwi.com	Montgomery	AL	36104	334-240-9274	240-9219
WMSP-AM 740 (Sports) 1 Commerce St Suite 300 *Web:* www.sportsradio740.com	Montgomery	AL	36104	334-240-9274	240-9219
WMXS-FM 103.3 (AC) 1 Commerce St Suite 300 *Web:* www.mix103.com	Montgomery	AL	36104	334-240-9274	240-9219
WVAS-FM 90.7 (Jazz) 915 S Jackson St PO Box 271 *Web:* www.wvasfm.org	Montgomery	AL	36101	334-229-4708	269-4995
WWMG-FM 97.1 (Urban) 203 Gunn Rd *Web:* www.mymagic97.com	Montgomery	AL	36117	334-274-6464	274-6465
WXFX-FM 95.1 (Rock) 1 Commerce St Suite 300 *Web:* www.wxfx.com	Montgomery	AL	36104	334-240-9274	240-9219
WXVI-AM 1600 (Rel) 912 S Perry St. *Web:* www.wxviradio.com	Montgomery	AL	36104	334-263-4141	263-9191
WZHT-FM 105.7 (Urban) 203 Gunn Rd *Web:* www.myhot105.com	Montgomery	AL	36117	334-274-6464	274-6465

648-110 Montreal, QC

Station	City	State	Zip	Phone	Fax
CFQR-FM 92.5 (AC) 800 De La Gauchetiere W Suite 1100 *Web:* www.q92fm.com	Montreal	QC	H5A1M1	514-787-7799	787-7979
CKOI-FM 96.9 (CHR) 800 Rue De La Gauchetiere Ouest Suite 1100 *Web:* www.ckoi.com	Montreal	QC	H5A1M1	514-787-7799	787-7982

648-111 Morgantown, WV

Station	City	State	Zip	Phone	Fax
WAJR-AM 1440 (N/T) 1251 Earl L Core Rd. *Web:* www.wajr.com	Morgantown	WV	26505	304-296-0029	296-3876
WCLG-FM 100.1 (Rock) PO Box 885 *Web:* www.wclg.com	Morgantown	WV	26507	304-292-2222	292-2224

Station	City	State	Zip	Phone	Fax
WKKW-FM 97.9 (Ctry) 1251 Earl L Core Rd *Web:* www.wkkwfm.com	Morgantown	WV	26505	304-296-0029	296-3876
WVAQ-FM 101.9 (CHR) 1251 Earl L Core Rd *Web:* www.wvaq.com	Morgantown	WV	26505	304-296-0029	296-3876
WVPM-FM 90.9 (NPR) 191 Scott Ave *TF:* 888-596-9729 ■ *Web:* www.wvpubcast.org	Morgantown	WV	26508	304-284-1440	284-1454
WWVU-FM 91.7 (Var) PO Box 6446 *Web:* u92.wvu.edu	Morgantown	WV	26506	304-293-3329	293-7363

648-112 Myrtle Beach, SC

Station	City	State	Zip	Phone	Fax
WEZV-FM 105.9 (AC) 3926 Wesley St Suite 301 *Web:* www.wezv.com	Myrtle Beach	SC	29579	843-903-9962	903-1797
WGTR-FM 107.9 (Ctry) 4841 Hwy 17 Bypass S *Web:* www.gator1079.com	Myrtle Beach	SC	29577	843-293-0107	293-1717
WKZQ-FM 96.1 (Rock) 1016 Ocala St *Web:* www.wkzq.net	Myrtle Beach	SC	29577	843-448-1041	626-5988
WMYB-FM 92.1 (AC) 1016 Ocala St *Web:* www.wmybstar92.net	Myrtle Beach	SC	29577	843-448-1041	626-5988
WQSD-FM 107.1 (Urban) 4841 Hwy 17 Bypass S *Web:* www.wqsdfm.com	Myrtle Beach	SC	29577	843-293-0107	293-1717
WRNN-FM 99.5 (N/T) 1016 Ocala St *Web:* www.wrnn.net	Myrtle Beach	SC	29577	843-448-1041	626-5988
WWXM-FM 97.7 (CHR) 4841 Hwy 17 Bypass S	Myrtle Beach	SC	29577	843-293-0107	293-1717
WYAV-FM 104.1 (CR) 1016 Ocala St *Web:* www.wave104.com	Myrtle Beach	SC	29577	843-448-1041	626-5988
WYNA-FM 104.9 (Oldies) 4841 Hwy 17 Bypass S *Web:* www.1049bobfm.com	Myrtle Beach	SC	29577	843-293-0107	293-1717

648-113 Naples, FL

Station	City	State	Zip	Phone	Fax
WAVV-FM 101.1 (AC) 11800 Tamiami Trail E *TF:* 866-310-9288 ■ *Web:* www.wavv101.com	Naples	FL	34113	239-775-9288	793-7000

648-114 Nashville, TN

Station	City	State	Zip	Phone	Fax
SuperTalk 99.7 WTN 10 Music Cir E *Web:* www.997wtn.com	Nashville	TN	37203	615-321-1067	321-5771
WAMB-AM 1200 (Nost) 1617 Lebanon Rd *Web:* www.wamb.net	Nashville	TN	37210	615-889-1960	902-9108
WBUZ-FM 102.9 (Alt) 1824 Murfreesboro Rd *Web:* www.1029thebuzz.com	Nashville	TN	37217	615-399-1029	361-9873
WCJK-FM 96.3 (Var) 504 Rosedale Ave *Web:* www.963jackfm.com	Nashville	TN	37211	615-259-9696	259-4594
WENO -AM 760 (Rel) 209 10th Ave S Suite 342 *Web:* www.760thegospel.com	Nashville	TN	37203	615-242-1411	242-3823
WFFH-FM 94.1 (Rel) 402 BNA Dr Suite 400 *TF:* 800-826-3637 ■ *Web:* www.94fmthefish.net	Nashville	TN	37217	615-367-2210	367-0758
WGFX-FM 104.5 (Sports) 506 2nd Ave S *Web:* www.1045thezone.com	Nashville	TN	37210	615-244-9533	259-1271
WJXA-FM 92.9 (AC) 504 Rosedale Ave *Web:* www.mix929.com	Nashville	TN	37211	615-259-9696	259-4594
WKDF-FM 103.3 (Ctry) 506 2nd Ave S *Web:* www.103wkdf.com	Nashville	TN	37210	615-244-9533	259-1271
WLAC-AM 1510 (N/T) 55 Music Sq W *Web:* www.wlac.com	Nashville	TN	37203	615-664-2400	744-4743
WNRQ-FM 105.9 (CR) 55 Music Sq W *Web:* www.1059.com	Nashville	TN	37203	615-664-2400	742-1059
WNSR-AM 560 (Sports) 435 37th Ave N *TF:* 888-228-6123 ■ *Web:* www.wnsr.com	Nashville	TN	37209	615-844-1039	777-2284
WPLN-FM 90.3 (NPR) 630 Mainstream Dr *TF:* 877-760-2903 ■ *Web:* www.wpln.org	Nashville	TN	37228	615-760-2903	760-2904
WQQK-FM 92.1 (Urban) 10 Music Cir E *Web:* www.92qnashville.com	Nashville	TN	37203	615-321-1067	321-5771
WRLT-FM 100.1 (AAA) 1310 Clinton St Suite 200 *Web:* www.wrlt.com	Nashville	TN	37203	615-242-5600	296-9039
WRQQ-FM 97.1 (Oldies) 10 Music Cir E *Web:* www.971rqq.com	Nashville	TN	37203	615-321-1067	321-5771
WRVW-FM 107.5 (CHR) 55 Music Sq W *Web:* www.1075theriver.com	Nashville	TN	37203	615-664-2400	664-2434
WSIX-FM 97.9 (Ctry) 55 Music Sq W *Web:* www.wsix.com	Nashville	TN	37203	615-664-2400	664-2470
WSM-AM 650 (Ctry) 2804 Opryland Dr *TF:* 877-878-4650	Nashville	TN	37214	615-889-6595	458-2445
WSM-FM 95.5 (Ctry) 10 Music Cir E *Web:* www.955thewolf.com	Nashville	TN	37203	615-321-1067	321-5771
WUBT-FM 101.1 (Urban) 55 Music Sq W *Web:* www.101thebeat.com	Nashville	TN	37203	615-664-2400	664-2406
WVNS-FM 102.5 (AC) 1824 Murfreesboro Rd *Web:* www.1025theparty.com	Nashville	TN	37217	615-399-1029	361-9873

648-115 New Haven, CT

Station	City	State	Zip	Phone	Fax
WYBC-AM 1340 (Var) 142 Temple St Suite 203 *Web:* www.wybc.com	New Haven	CT	06510	203-776-4118	776-2446
WYBC-FM 94.3 (Urban) 142 Temple St Suite 203 *Web:* www.943wybc.com	New Haven	CT	06510	203-776-4118	776-2446

648-116 New Orleans, LA

Station	City	State	Zip	Phone	Fax
KKND-FM 102.9 (Urban) 201 St Charles Ave Suite 201 *Web:* www.power1029.com	New Orleans	LA	70170	504-581-7002	566-4857
KMEZ-FM 106.7 (Oldies) 201 St Charles Ave Suite 201 *Web:* www.oldschool1067.com	New Orleans	LA	70170	504-581-7002	566-4857
WEZB-FM 97.1 (CHR) 400 Poydras St Suite 800 *Web:* www.b97.com	New Orleans	LA	70130	504-593-6376	593-2099
WKBU-FM 95.7 (Rock) 400 Poydras St Suite 800 *Web:* www.bayou957.com	New Orleans	LA	70130	504-593-6376	593-2099
WLMG-FM 101.9 (AC) 400 Poydras St Suite 800 *Web:* www.magic1019.com	New Orleans	LA	70130	504-593-6376	593-2099
WNOE-FM 101.1 (Ctry) 929 Howard Ave *TF:* 800-543-9663 ■ *Web:* www.wnoe.com	New Orleans	LA	70113	504-679-7300	679-7345
WODT-AM 1280 (Sports) 929 Howard Ave	New Orleans	LA	70113	504-679-7300	679-7345
WQUE-FM 93.3 (Urban) 929 Howard Ave *Web:* www.q93.com	New Orleans	LA	70113	504-679-7300	679-7345
WRKN-FM 92.3 (AC) 201 St Charles Ave Suite 201 *Web:* www.rock923neworleans.com	New Orleans	LA	70170	504-581-7002	566-4857
WRNO-FM 99.5 (N/T) 929 Howard Ave *Web:* www.wrno.com	New Orleans	LA	70113	504-679-7300	679-7345
WSHO-AM 800 (Rel) 365 Canal St Suite 1175 *Web:* www.wsho.com	New Orleans	LA	70130	504-527-0800	527-0881
WWL-AM 870 (N/T) 400 Poydras St Suite 800 *Web:* www.wwl.com	New Orleans	LA	70130	504-593-6376	593-2099
WWL-FM 105.3 N/T) 400 Poydras St Suite 800 *Web:* www.wwl.com	New Orleans	LA	70130	504-593-6376	593-2099
WWNO-FM 89.9 (NPR) University of New Orleans Lake Front Campus *TF:* 800-286-7002 ■ *Web:* www.wwno.org	New Orleans	LA	70148	504-280-7000	280-6061
WWOZ-FM 90.7 (Var) 1008 N Peters St *Web:* www.wwoz.org	New Orleans	LA	70116	504-568-1239	558-9332
WYLD-AM 940 (Rel) 929 Howard Ave *Web:* www.am940.com	New Orleans	LA	70113	504-679-7300	679-7345
WYLD-FM 98.5 (Urban) 929 Howard Ave *Web:* www.wyldfm.com	New Orleans	LA	70113	504-679-7300	679-7345

648-117 New York, NY

Station	City	State	Zip	Phone	Fax
WABC-AM 770 (N/T) 2 Penn Plaza 17th Fl *TF:* 800-848-9222 ■ *Web:* www.wabcradio.com	New York	NY	10121	212-613-3800	613-3866
WADO-AM 1280 (Span) 485 Madison Ave 3rd Fl *TF:* 800-999-1280 ■ *Web:* www.univision.com	New York	NY	10022	212-310-6000	888-3694
WAXQ-FM 104.3 (CR) 32 Avenue of the Americas *TF:* 888-872-1043 ■ *Web:* www.q1043.com	New York	NY	10013	212-377-7900	
WBAI-FM 99.5 (N/T) 120 Wall St 10th Fl *Web:* www.wbai.org	New York	NY	10005	212-209-2800	747-1698
WBBR-AM 1130 (N/T) 731 Lexington Ave *Web:* www.bloomberg.com/radio	New York	NY	10022	212-318-2000	940-1994
WBLS-FM 107.5 (Urban) 3 Pk Ave 41st Fl *Web:* www.wbls.com	New York	NY	10016	212-447-1000	447-5193
WCAA-FM 96.3 (Span) 485 Madison Ave 3rd Fl *TF:* 800-963-0963 ■ *Web:* www.univision.com	New York	NY	10022	212-310-6000	888-3694
WCBS-AM 880 (N/T) 524 W 57th St 8th Fl **Fax:* News Rm ■ *TF:* 877-987-9227 ■ *Web:* www.wcbs880.com	New York	NY	10019	212-975-2127	975-1907*
WCBS-FM 101.1 (Oldies) 40 W 57th St 15th Fl *Web:* wcbsfm.com	New York	NY	10019	212-314-9200	846-5188
WEMP-FM 101.9 (NAC) 395 Hudson St 7th Fl *TF:* 800-423-1019 ■ *Web:* www.1019rxp.com	New York	NY	10014	212-352-1019	929-8559
WEPN-AM 1050 (Sports) 2 Penn Plaza 17th Fl *TF:* 800-919-3776 ■ *Web:* www.1050espnradio.com	New York	NY	10121	212-613-3800	615-3246
WHTZ-FM 100.3 (CHR) 32 Avenue of the Americas *TF:* 800-242-0100 ■ *Web:* www.z100.com	New York	NY	10013	212-377-7900	239-2308
WINS-AM 1010 (N/T) 888 7th Ave 10th Fl *Web:* www.1010wins.com	New York	NY	10106	212-397-1010	247-7918
WKTU-FM 103.5 (CHR) 32 Avenue of the Americas *Web:* www.ktu.com	New York	NY	10013	212-377-7900	
WLTW-FM 106.7 (AC) 32 Avenue of the Americas 3rd Fl *TF:* 800-222-1067 ■ *Web:* www.1067litefm.com	New York	NY	10013	212-377-7900	
WNYC-AM 820 (NPR) 160 Varick St 7th Fl *Web:* www.wnyc.org	New York	NY	10013	646-829-4400	829-4171
WNYC-FM 93.9 (NPR) 160 Varick St 7th Fl *Web:* www.wnyc.org	New York	NY	10013	646-829-4400	829-4171
WOR-AM 710 (N/T) 111 Broadway 3rd Fl *Web:* www.wor710.com	New York	NY	10006	212-642-4500	642-4486
WPAT-FM 93.1 (Span AC) 26 W 56th St *TF:* 800-246-9393 ■ *Web:* www.931amor.com	New York	NY	10019	212-541-9200	541-8535
WPLJ-FM 95.5 (AC) 2 Penn Plaza 17th Fl *Web:* www.plj.com	New York	NY	10121	212-613-8900	613-8956
WQHT-FM 97.1 (Urban) 395 Hudson St 7th Fl *TF:* 800-223-9797 ■ *Web:* www.hot97.com	New York	NY	10014	212-229-9797	929-8559
WQXR-FM 96.3 (Clas) 122 5th Ave 3rd Fl *Web:* www.wqxr.com	New York	NY	10011	212-633-7600	633-7666

Station	City	State	Zip	Phone	Fax
WRKS-FM 98.7 (Urban) 395 Hudson St 7th Fl *TF:* 800-288-5477 ■ *Web:* www.987kissfm.com	New York	NY	10014	212-242-9870	242-0706
WSKQ-FM 97.9 (Span) 26 W 56th St *Web:* www.lamega.com	New York	NY	10019	212-541-9200	541-8535
WWPR-FM 105.1 (Urban) 32 Avenue of the Americas *TF:* 800-585-1051 ■ *Web:* www.power1051fm.com	New York	NY	10013	212-377-7900	
WXRK-FM 92.3 (Rock) 40 W 57th St 14th Fl *Web:* www.923freefm.com	New York	NY	10019	212-314-9230	314-9338

648-118 Norfolk/Virginia Beach, VA

Station	City	State	Zip	Phone	Fax
WCMS-AM 1310 (Sports) 5589 Greenwich Rd Suite 200 *Web:* www.espnradio1310.com	Virginia Beach	VA	23462	757-671-1000	671-1010
WGH-FM 97.3 (Ctry) 5589 Greenwich Rd Suite 200 *Web:* www.eagle97.com	Virginia Beach	VA	23462	757-671-1000	671-1010
WGPL-AM 1350 (Rel) 645 Church St Suite 400	Norfolk	VA	23510	757-622-4600	624-6515
WHRO-FM 90.3 (Clas) 5200 Hampton Blvd *Web:* www.whro.org	Norfolk	VA	23508	757-889-9400	489-0007
WHRV-FM 89.5 (NPR) 5200 Hampton Blvd *Web:* www.whro.org/radio/895	Norfolk	VA	23508	757-889-9400	489-0007
WJCD-FM 107.7 (AC) 1003 Norfolk Sq *Web:* www.wjcd.com	Norfolk	VA	23502	757-466-0009	466-7043
WKUS-FM 105.3 (Urban) 1003 Norfolk Sq *Web:* www.1053kiss.com	Norfolk	VA	23502	757-466-0009	466-7043
WNSB-FM 91.1 (Urban) 700 Pk Ave Suite 129 Spartan Stn *Web:* www.nsu.edu	Norfolk	VA	23504	757-823-9672	823-2385
WOWI-FM 102.9 (Urban) 1003 Norfolk Sq *Web:* www.103jamz.com	Norfolk	VA	23502	757-466-0009	466-7043
WPCE-AM 1400 (Rel) 645 Church St Suite 400 *Web:* www.wpce1400.com	Norfolk	VA	23510	757-622-4600	624-6515
WPTE-FM 94.9 (AC) 236 Clearfield Ave Suite 206 *Web:* www.pointradio.com	Virginia Beach	VA	23462	757-497-2000	518-1721
WVBW-FM 92.9 (Oldies) 5589 Greenwich Rd Suite 200 *Web:* www.929thewave.com	Virginia Beach	VA	23462	757-671-1000	671-1010
WXEZ-FM 94.1 (Rel) 5589 Greenwich Rd Suite 200 *Web:* www.wxez941.com	Virginia Beach	VA	23462	757-671-1000	671-1010

648-119 Ocean City, MD

Station	City	State	Zip	Phone	Fax
WOCM-FM 98.1 (AAA) Irie Radio 117 W 49th St *Web:* www.irieradio.com	Ocean City	MD	21842	410-723-3683	723-4347

648-120 Oklahoma City, OK

Station	City	State	Zip	Phone	Fax
KATT-FM 100.5 (Rock) 4045 NW 64th St Suite 600 *Web:* www.katt.com	Oklahoma City	OK	73116	405-848-0100	843-5288
KHBZ-FM 94.7 (Rock) 50 Penn Pl Suite 1000 *Web:* www.947thebuzz.com	Oklahoma City	OK	73118	405-840-5271	858-5333
KJYO-FM 102.7 (CHR) 1900 NW Expy # 1000 *Web:* www.kj103fm.com	Oklahoma City	OK	73118	405-840-5271	858-5333
KKNG-FM 93.3 (Ctry) 5101 S Shields Blvd *Web:* www.kkng.com	Oklahoma City	OK	73129	405-616-5500	616-5505
KKWD-FM 104.9 (CHR) 4045 NW 64th St Suite 600 *Web:* wild1049.static.com	Oklahoma City	OK	73116	405-848-0100	843-5288
KMGL-FM 104.1 (AC) 400 E Britton Rd *Web:* www.magic104.com	Oklahoma City	OK	73114	405-478-5104	475-7021
KOMA-FM 92.5 (Oldies) 400 E Britton Rd *Web:* www.komaradio.com	Oklahoma City	OK	73114	405-478-5104	475-7021
KQCV-AM 800 (Rel) 1919 N Broadway *TF:* 888-909-5728 ■ *Web:* www.bottradionetwork.com	Oklahoma City	OK	73103	405-521-0800	521-1391
KRXO-FM 107.7 (CR) 400 E Britton Rd *Web:* www.krxo.com	Oklahoma City	OK	73114	405-478-5104	475-7021
KTOK-AM 1000 (N/T) 50 Penn Pl Suite 1000 *Web:* www.ktok.com	Oklahoma City	OK	73118	405-840-5271	858-5333
KTST-FM 101.9 (Ctry) 50 Penn Pl Suite 1000 *Web:* www.thetwister.com	Oklahoma City	OK	73118	405-840-5271	858-5333
KVSP-FM 103.5 (Urban) 1528 NE 23rd St *Web:* www.kvsp.com	Oklahoma City	OK	73111	405-425-4100	424-8811
KXXY-FM 96.1 (Ctry) 50 Penn Pl Suite 1000 *Web:* www.kxy.com	Oklahoma City	OK	73118	405-840-5271	858-5333
KYIS-FM 98.9 (AC) 4045 NW 64th St Suite 600 *Web:* www.kyis.com	Oklahoma City	OK	73116	405-848-0100	843-5288
WWLS-AM 640 (Sports) 4045 NW 64th Suite 600 *Web:* www.thesportsanimal.com	Oklahoma City	OK	73116	405-848-0100	843-5288

648-121 Omaha, NE

Station	City	State	Zip	Phone	Fax
KEZO-FM 92.3 (Rock) 5030 N 72nd St **Fax:* Sales ■ *Web:* www.z92.com	Omaha	NE	68134	402-592-5300	592-9434*
KFAB-AM 1110 (N/T) 5010 Underwood Ave *Web:* www.kfab.com	Omaha	NE	68132	402-561-2000	556-8937
KGOR-FM 99.9 (Oldies) 5010 Underwood Ave *Web:* www.kgor.com	Omaha	NE	68132	402-561-2000	556-8937
KIOS-FM 91.5 (NPR) 3230 Burt St *Web:* www.kios.org	Omaha	NE	68131	402-557-2777	557-2559
KOOO-FM 101.9 (AC) 5011 Capitol Ave *Web:* www.literock1019.com	Omaha	NE	68132	402-342-2000	827-5293
KQBW-FM 96.1 (Rock) 5010 Underwood Ave	Omaha	NE	68132	402-558-9696	556-8937
KQCH-FM 94.1 (CHR) 5030 N 72nd St **Fax:* Sales ■ *Web:* www.channel941.com	Omaha	NE	68134	402-592-5300	592-9434*
KQKQ-FM 98.5 (CHR) 5011 Capitol Ave *Web:* www.sweet985.com	Omaha	NE	68132	402-342-2000	827-5293
KSRZ-FM 104.5 (AC) 5030 N 72nd St **Fax:* Sales ■ *Web:* www.104star.com	Omaha	NE	68134	402-592-5300	592-9434*
KTWI-FM 93.3 (Ctry) 5010 Underwood Ave *Web:* www.thedamstation.com	Omaha	NE	68132	402-561-2000	556-8937
KXKT-FM 103.7 (Ctry) 5010 Underwood Ave *Web:* www.thekat.com	Omaha	NE	68132	402-561-2000	556-8937

648-122 Orlando, FL

Station	City	State	Zip	Phone	Fax
WCFB-FM 94.5 (AC) 4192 N John Young Pkwy *TF:* 800-299-2945 ■ *Web:* www.star94fm.com	Orlando	FL	32804	407-294-2945	297-7595
WDBO-AM 580 (N/T) 4192 N John Young Pkwy *Web:* 580wdbo.com	Orlando	FL	32804	407-295-5858	291-4879
WHOO-AM 1080 (Sports) 1160 S Semoran Blvd Suite A *Web:* www.espn1080.com	Orlando	FL	32807	407-380-9255	382-7565
WHTQ-FM 96.5 (CR) 4192 N John Young Pkwy *Web:* whtq.com	Orlando	FL	32804	407-422-9696	422-0917
WJHM-FM 102 (Urban) 1800 Pembrook Dr Suite 400 *TF:* 877-919-0102 ■ *Web:* 102jamzorlando.radio.com	Orlando	FL	32810	407-919-1000	919-1329
WMFE-FM 90.7 (NPR) 11510 E Colonial Dr *Web:* www.wmfe.org/907	Orlando	FL	32817	407-273-2300	273-3613
WMMO-FM 98.9 (AC) 4192 N John Young Pkwy *Web:* www.wmmo.com	Orlando	FL	32804	407-422-9890	422-6538
WOCL-FM 105.9 (Rock) 1800 Pembrook Dr Suite 400 *TF:* 877-919-1059 ■ *Web:* www.orock1059.com	Orlando	FL	32810	407-919-1000	919-1190
WOMX-FM 105.1 (AC) 1800 Pembrook Dr Suite 400 *TF:* 877-919-1051 ■ *Web:* mix1051.radio.com	Orlando	FL	32810	407-919-1000	919-1190
WPYO-FM 95.3 (CHR) 4192 N John Young Pkwy *Web:* 953party.com	Orlando	FL	32804	407-295-9595	291-6912
WUCF-FM 89.9 (Jazz) 4000 Central Florida Blvd *Web:* www.wucf.ucf.edu	Orlando	FL	32816	407-823-0899	823-6364
WWKA-FM 92.3 (Ctry) 4192 N John Young Pkwy *TF:* 800-749-9292 ■ *Web:* k92fm.com	Orlando	FL	32804	407-298-9292	299-4947

648-123 Ottawa, ON

Station	City	State	Zip	Phone	Fax
CFGO-AM 1200 (Sports) 87 George St *TF:* 800-580-2372 ■ *Web:* www.team1200.com	Ottawa	ON	K1N9H7	613-789-2486	738-5024
CFRA-AM 580 (N/T) 87 George St *TF:* 800-580-2372 ■ *Web:* www.cfra.com	Ottawa	ON	K1N9H7	613-789-2486	738-5024
CHEZ-FM 106.1 (CR) 2001 Thurston Dr *Web:* www.chez106.com	Ottawa	ON	K1G6C9	613-736-2001	736-2002
CIWW-AM 1310 (Oldies) 2001 Thurston Dr *Web:* www.kissfm.com	Ottawa	ON	K1G6C9	613-736-2001	736-2002
CJMJ-FM 100.3 (AC) 87 George St *TF:* 800-580-2372 ■ *Web:* www.majic100.fm	Ottawa	ON	K1N9H7	613-789-2486	738-5024
CKBY-FM 101.1 (Ctry) 2001 Thurston Dr *Web:* www.y101.fm	Ottawa	ON	K1G6C9	613-736-2001	736-2002
CKKL-FM 93.9 (CHR) 87 George St *TF:* 800-580-2372 ■ *Web:* www.939bobfm.com	Ottawa	ON	K1N9H7	613-789-2486	738-5024

648-124 Oxnard, CA

Station	City	State	Zip	Phone	Fax
KDAR-FM 98.3 (Rel) 500 E Esplanade Dr # 1500 *Web:* www.kdar.com	Oxnard	CA	93036	805-485-8881	656-5330
KMLA-FM 103.7 (Span) 355 S 'A' St Suite 103 *Web:* www.lam1037.com	Oxnard	CA	93030	805-385-5656	385-5690
KXLM-FM 102.9 (Span) 200 S 'A' St Suite 400	Oxnard	CA	93030	805-487-0444	240-5960

648-125 Palm Springs, CA

Station	City	State	Zip	Phone	Fax
KCLB-FM 93.7 (Rock) 1321 N Gene Autry Trail *Web:* www.desertfun.com	Palm Springs	CA	92262	760-322-7890	322-5493
KDGL-FM 106.9 (AC) 1321 N Gene Autry Trail *Web:* www.theeagle1069.com	Palm Springs	CA	92262	760-322-7890	322-5493
KJJZ-FM 102.3 (NAC) 441 S Calle Encilia Suite 8 *Web:* www.102kjjz.com	Palm Springs	CA	92262	760-320-4550	320-3037

Station	City	State	Zip	Phone	Fax
KKUU-FM 92.7 (CHR) 1321 N Gene Autry Trail *Web:* www.927kkuu.com	Palm Springs	CA	92262	760-322-7890	322-5493
KMRJ-FM 99.5 (Alt) 1061 S Palm Canyon Dr *Web:* www.m995.com	Palm Springs	CA	92264	760-778-6995	778-1249
KNWZ-AM 970 (N/T) 1321 N Gene Autry Trail *Web:* www.desertfun.com	Palm Springs	CA	92262	760-322-7890	322-5493
KPLM-FM 106.1 (Ctry) 441 S Calle Encilia Suite 8 *Web:* www.thebig106.com	Palm Springs	CA	92262	760-320-4550	320-3037
KPSI-AM 920 (N/T) 2100 Tahquitz Canyon Way *Web:* www.newstalk920.com	Palm Springs	CA	92262	760-325-2582	325-4693
KPSI-FM 100.5 (AC) 2100 Tahquitz Canyon Way *TF:* 877-282-2648 ■ *Web:* www.mix1005.fm	Palm Springs	CA	92262	760-325-2582	322-3562

648-126 Pensacola, FL

Station	City	State	Zip	Phone	Fax
WBSR-AM 1450 (AC) 1601 N Pace Blvd *Web:* www.wbsr.com	Pensacola	FL	32505	850-438-4982	433-7932
WCOA-AM 1370 (N/T) 6565 N W St Suite 270 *Web:* www.wcoapensacola.com	Pensacola	FL	32505	850-478-6011	478-1846
WGCX-FM 95.7 (Rel) 2070 N Palafox St *Web:* www.praise95.net	Pensacola	FL	32501	850-434-1230	469-9698
WPCS-FM 89.5 (Rel) PO Box 18000 *TF:* 800-726-1191 ■ *Web:* www.rejoice.org	Pensacola	FL	32523	850-479-6570	969-1638
WPNN-AM 790 (N/T) 3801 N Pace Blvd *TF:* 888-433-1141 ■ *Web:* www.cnnpensacola.com	Pensacola	FL	32505	850-433-1141	433-1142
WRNE-AM 980 (Urban) 312 E Nine-Mile Rd Suite 29D *Web:* www.wrne980.com	Pensacola	FL	32514	850-478-6000	484-8080
WTKX-FM 101.5 (Rock) 6485 Pensacola Blvd *Web:* www.tk101.com	Pensacola	FL	32505	850-473-0400	473-0907
WUWF-FM 88.1 (NPR) 11000 University Pkwy *Web:* www.wuwf.org	Pensacola	FL	32514	850-474-2787	474-3283
WYCL-FM 107.3 (Oldies) 6485 Pensacola Blvd *TF:* 888-345-1073 ■ *Web:* www.cool107.com	Pensacola	FL	32505	850-473-0400	473-0907

648-127 Peoria, IL

Station	City	State	Zip	Phone	Fax
WCBU-FM 89.9 (NPR) 1501 W Bradley Ave *TF:* 888-488-9228 ■ *Web:* www.bradley.edu/wcbu	Peoria	IL	61625	309-677-3690	677-3462
WCIC-FM 91.5 (Rel) 3902 W Baring Trace *TF:* 877-692-9242 ■ *Web:* www.wcicfm.org	Peoria	IL	61615	309-282-9191	692-9241
WDQX-FM 102.3 (CR) 331 Fulton St Suite 1200 *Web:* www.eagleclassichits.com	Peoria	IL	61602	309-637-3700	272-1476
WFYR-FM 97.3 (Ctry) 120 Eaton St *TF:* 866-673-0973 ■ *Web:* www.973rivercountry.com	Peoria	IL	61603	309-673-0973	676-5000
WGLO-FM 95.5 (CR) 120 Eaton St *TF:* 888-676-9595 ■ *Web:* www.955glo.com	Peoria	IL	61603	309-676-9595	676-5000
WIXO-FM 105.7 (Rock) 120 Eaton St *TF:* 877-495-9496 ■ *Web:* www.99xrocks.com	Peoria	IL	61603	309-676-5000	676-2600
WMBD-AM 1470 (N/T) 331 Fulton St Suite 1200 *TF:* 800-698-1470 ■ *Web:* www.wmbdradio.com	Peoria	IL	61602	309-637-3700	686-8655
WPBG-FM 93.3 (CH) 331 Fulton St Suite 1200 *TF:* 800-310-0930 ■ *Web:* www.bigoldies933.com	Peoria	IL	61602	309-637-3700	686-8655
WSWT-FM 106.9 (AC) 331 Fulton St Suite 1200 *TF:* 800-597-1069 ■ *Web:* www.literock107.com	Peoria	IL	61602	309-637-3700	686-8655
WXCL-FM 104.9 (Ctry) 331 Fulton St 12th Fl *Web:* www.1049thewolf.com	Peoria	IL	61602	309-637-3700	272-1476

648-128 Philadelphia, PA

Station	City	State	Zip	Phone	Fax
KYW-AM 1060 (N/T) 400 Market St 10th Fl *Web:* www.kyw1060.com	Philadelphia	PA	19106	215-238-1060	238-4657
WEMG-AM 1310 (Span) 1341 N Delaware Ave Suite 509	Philadelphia	PA	19125	215-426-1900	426-1550
WHYY-FM 90.9 (NPR) 150 N 6th St *Web:* www.whyy.org	Philadelphia	PA	19106	215-351-9200	351-1211
WRTI-FM 90.1 (NPR) 1509 Cecil B Moore Ave 3rd Fl *TF:* 800-245-8776 ■ *Web:* www.wrti.org	Philadelphia	PA	19122	215-204-8405	204-7027
WXPN-FM 88.5 (AAA) 3025 Walnut St *Web:* www.xpn.org	Philadelphia	PA	19104	215-898-6677	898-0707
WYSP-FM 94.1 (Rock) 400 Market St 9th Fl *Web:* www.94wysp.com	Philadelphia	PA	19106	215-625-9460	625-6555

648-129 Phoenix, AZ

Station	City	State	Zip	Phone	Fax
KEDJ-FM 103.9 (Alt) 4745 N 7th St Suite 410 *Web:* www.theedge1039.com	Phoenix	AZ	85014	602-648-9800	283-0923
KESZ-FM 99.9 (AC) 4686 E Van Buren St Suite 300 *Web:* www.kez999.com	Phoenix	AZ	85008	602-374-6000	374-6035
KFYI-AM 550 (N/T) 4686 E Van Buren St Suite 300 *Web:* www.kfyi.com	Phoenix	AZ	85008	602-374-6000	374-6035
KGME-AM 910 (Sports) 4686 E Van Buren Suite 300 *Web:* www.xtrasports910.com	Phoenix	AZ	85008	602-374-6000	374-6035
KHOT-FM 105.9 (Span) 4745 N 7th St Suite 140 *Web:* khot.netmio.com	Phoenix	AZ	85014	602-308-7900	308-7979
KKFR-FM 98.3 (Urban) 4745 N 7th St Suite 410 *Web:* www.power983fm.com	Phoenix	AZ	85014	602-682-9200	283-0923
KMLE-FM 107.9 (Ctry) 840 N Central Ave *Web:* www.kmle108.com	Phoenix	AZ	85004	602-452-1000	
KMXP-FM 96.9 (AC) 4686 E Van Buren Suite 300 *Web:* www.mix969.com	Phoenix	AZ	85008	602-374-6000	374-6035
KNIX-FM 102.5 (Ctry) 4686 E Van Buren St Suite 300 *Web:* www.knixcountry.com	Phoenix	AZ	85008	602-374-6000	374-6035
KOMR-FM 106.3 (Span) 4745 N 7th St Suite 140 *Web:* kmrr.netmio.com	Phoenix	AZ	85014	602-308-7900	308-7979
KOOL-FM 94.5 (Oldies) 840 N Central Ave *Web:* www.koolradio.com	Phoenix	AZ	85004	602-956-9696	440-6530
KOY-AM 1230 (Nost) 4686 E Van Buren St Suite 300 *Web:* www.am1230koy.com	Phoenix	AZ	85008	602-374-6000	374-6035
KPKX-FM 98.7 (CR) 5300 N Central Ave *Web:* www.987thepeak.com	Phoenix	AZ	85012	602-274-6200	266-3858
KSLX-FM 100.7 (CR) 4343 E Camelback Rd Suite 200 **Fax Area Code:* 602 ■ **Fax:* Sales ■ *Web:* www.kslx.com	Phoenix	AZ	85018	480-941-1007	808-2288*
KXEG-AM 1280 (Rel) 2800 N 44th St Suite 100 *Web:* www.familyvaluesradio.net	Phoenix	AZ	85008	602-254-5001	296-3624
KYOT-FM 95.5 (NAC) 4686 E Van Buren St Suite 300 *Web:* www.kyot.com	Phoenix	AZ	85008	602-374-6000	374-6035
KZON-FM 101.5 (Urban) 840 N Central Ave *Web:* www.kzon.com	Phoenix	AZ	85004	602-452-1000	
KZZP-FM 104.7 (CHR) 4686 E Van Buren St Suite 300 *TF:* 877-937-1047 ■ *Web:* www.kzzp.com	Phoenix	AZ	85008	602-374-6000	374-6035

648-130 Pierre, SD

Station	City	State	Zip	Phone	Fax
JACK FM 95.3 106 W Capitol Ave *Web:* www.jackfm953.com	Pierre	SD	57501	605-224-1240	945-4270
KCCR-AM 1240 106 W Capitol Ave *Web:* www.todayskccr.com	Pierre	SD	57501	605-224-1240	945-4270
KGFX-AM 1060 (Ctry) 214 W Pleasant Dr *TF:* 800-658-3534 ■ *Web:* www.dakotaradiogroup.com	Pierre	SD	57501	605-224-8686	224-8984
KGFX-FM 92.7 (AC) 214 W Pleasant Dr *TF:* 800-658-3534 ■ *Web:* www.dakotaradiogroup.com	Pierre	SD	57501	605-224-8686	224-8984
KMLO-FM 100.7 (Ctry) 214 W Pleasant Dr *TF:* 800-658-5439 ■ *Web:* www.dakotaradiogroup.com	Pierre	SD	57501	605-224-8686	224-8984
KPLO-FM 94.5 (Ctry) 214 W Pleasant Dr *TF:* 800-658-3534 ■ *Web:* www.dakotaradiogroup.com	Pierre	SD	57501	605-224-8686	224-8984

648-131 Pittsburgh, PA

Station	City	State	Zip	Phone	Fax
KDKA-AM 1020 (N/T) 1 Gateway Ctr *Web:* www.kdkaradio.com	Pittsburgh	PA	15222	412-575-2200	575-2874
KQV-AM 1410 (N/T) 650 Smithfield St Suite 620 Centre City Towers *TF:* 800-424-1410 ■ *Web:* www.kqv.com	Pittsburgh	PA	15222	412-562-5900	562-5903
WAMO-AM 860 (Urban) 960 Penn Ave Suite 200 *TF:* 800-369-9266 ■ *Web:* www.wamo.com	Pittsburgh	PA	15222	412-456-4000	456-4077
WAMO-FM 106.7 (Urban) 960 Penn Ave Suite 200 *TF:* 800-369-9266 ■ *Web:* www.wamo.com	Pittsburgh	PA	15222	412-456-4000	456-4077
WBGG-AM 970 (Sports) 200 Fleet St *Web:* www.970espn.com	Pittsburgh	PA	15220	412-937-1441	937-0323
WBZW-FM 93.7 (CHR) 651 Holiday Dr Foster Plaza 2nd Fl *Web:* www.937krock.com	Pittsburgh	PA	15220	412-920-9400	920-9449
WDSY-FM 107.9 (Ctry) 651 Holiday Dr Foster Plaza 2nd Fl *Web:* www.y108.com	Pittsburgh	PA	15220	412-920-9400	920-9449
WDUQ-FM 90.5 (NPR) 600 Forbes Ave *Web:* www.wduq.org	Pittsburgh	PA	15219	412-396-6030	396-5061
WDVE-FM 102.5 (Rock) 200 Fleet St *Web:* www.dve.com	Pittsburgh	PA	15220	412-937-1441	923-0323
WJAS-AM 1320 (Nost) 900 Parish St 3rd Fl *Web:* www.1320wjas.com	Pittsburgh	PA	15220	412-875-9500	875-9474
WKST-FM 96.1 (CHR) 200 Fleet St 4th Fl *Web:* www.kissfm961.com	Pittsburgh	PA	15220	412-937-1441	937-0323
WLTJ-FM 92.9 (AC) 650 Smithfield St Suite 2200 *Web:* www.wltj.com	Pittsburgh	PA	15222	412-316-3342	316-3388
WORD-FM 101.5 (Rel) 875 Greentree Rd # 625 *Web:* www.wordfm.com	Pittsburgh	PA	15220	412-937-1500	937-1576
WPGB-FM 104.7 (N/T) 200 Fleet St *Web:* www.wpgb.com	Pittsburgh	PA	15220	412-937-1441	937-0323
WQED-FM 89.3 (Clas) 4802 5th Ave *TF:* 800-876-1316 ■ *Web:* www.wqed.org	Pittsburgh	PA	15213	412-622-1436	622-7073
WRRK-FM 96.9 (Var) 650 Smithfield St Suite 2200 *Web:* www.rrk.com	Pittsburgh	PA	15222	412-316-3342	316-3388
WSHH-FM 99.7 (AC) 900 Parish St 3rd Fl *Web:* www.wshh.com	Pittsburgh	PA	15220	412-875-9500	875-9474
WWSW-FM 94.5 (Oldies) 200 Fleet St 4th Fl *Web:* www.3wsradio.com	Pittsburgh	PA	15220	412-937-1441	937-0323

	City	State	Zip	Phone	Fax
WXDX-FM 105.9 (Alt) 200 Fleet St. *Web:* www.1059thex.com	Pittsburgh	PA	15220	412-937-1441	937-0323
WYEP-FM 91.3 (Var) 2313 E Carson St *TF:* 877-381-9900 ■ *Web:* www.wyep.org	Pittsburgh	PA	15203	412-381-9131	381-9126
WZPT-FM 100.7 (AC) 651 Holiday Dr 2nd Fl *Web:* www.1007.com	Pittsburgh	PA	15220	412-920-9400	920-9449

648-132 Pocatello, ID

	City	State	Zip	Phone	Fax
KISU-FM 91.1 (NPR) Idaho State University 921 So 8th Ave PO Box 8014 *Web:* www.isu.edu/kisufm	Pocatello	ID	83209	208-282-3691	282-4600
KLLP-FM 98.5 (AC) 259 E Ctr St *TF:* 800-582-1240 ■ *Web:* www.star985.com	Pocatello	ID	83201	208-233-1133	232-1240
KMGI-FM 102.5 (CR) 544 N Arthur Ave *Web:* www.102kmgi.com	Pocatello	ID	83204	208-233-2121	234-7682
KORR-FM 104.1 (AC) 436 N Main St *Web:* www.korr104.com	Pocatello	ID	83204	208-234-1290	234-9451
KOUU-AM 1290 (Ctry) 436 N Main St	Pocatello	ID	83204	208-234-1290	234-9451
KPKY-FM 94.9 (CR) 259 E Ctr St *TF:* 800-582-1240 ■ *Web:* www.kpky.com	Pocatello	ID	83201	208-233-1133	232-1240
KRTK-AM 1490 (Rel) 1633 Olympus Dr	Pocatello	ID	83201	208-237-9500	237-4600
KSEI-AM 930 (Sports) 544 N Arthur Ave *Web:* www.930espn.com	Pocatello	ID	83204	208-233-2121	234-7682
KZBQ-FM 93.7 (Ctry) 436 N Main St *Web:* www.kzbq.com	Pocatello	ID	83204	208-234-1290	234-9451

648-133 Portland, ME

	City	State	Zip	Phone	Fax
WBLM-FM 102.9 (CR) 1 City Ctr *Web:* www.wblm.com	Portland	ME	04101	207-774-6364	774-8707
WCYY-FM 94.3 (Alt) 1 City Ctr 3rd Fl. *Web:* www.wcyy.com	Portland	ME	04101	207-774-6364	774-8707
WHOM-FM 94.9 (AC) 1 City Ctr 3rd Fl *TF:* 800-228-1949 ■ *Web:* www.whom949.com	Portland	ME	04101	207-774-6364	774-8707
WJBQ-FM 97.9 (CHR) 1 City Ctr 3rd Fl. *Web:* www.wjbq.com	Portland	ME	04101	207-775-7979	774-8707
WRED-FM 95.9 (Urban) 779 Warren Ave *Web:* www.redhot959.com	Portland	ME	04106	207-773-9695	761-4406
WTHT-FM 99.9 (Ctry) 477 Congress St 3rd Fl Annex *TF:* 866-900-9653 ■ *Web:* www.999thewolf.com	Portland	ME	04101	207-797-0780	797-0368

648-134 Portland/Salem, OR

	City	State	Zip	Phone	Fax
KBNP-AM 1410 (N/T) 278 SW Arthur St *Web:* www.kbnp.com	Portland	OR	97201	503-223-6769	223-4305
KBOO-FM 90.7 (Var) 20 SE 8th Ave *Web:* www.kboo.fm	Portland	OR	97214	503-231-8032	231-7145
KBPS-FM 89.9 (Clas) 515 NE 15th Ave *TF:* 888-306-5277 ■ *Web:* www.allclassical.org	Portland	OR	97232	503-895-5727	802-9456
KBVM-FM 88.3 (Rel) 5000 N Willamette Blvd PO Box 5888 *TF:* 888-823-5286 ■ *Web:* www.kbvm.com	Portland	OR	97228	503-285-5200	285-3322
KBZY-AM 1490 (AC) 2659 Commercial St SE Suite 204 *Web:* www.kbzy.com	Salem	OR	97302	503-362-1490	362-6545
KEX-AM 1190 (N/T) 4949 SW Macadam Ave *TF:* 800-345-1190 ■ *Web:* www.1190kex.com	Portland	OR	97239	503-242-1190	323-6666
KFIS-FM 104.1 (Rel) 6400 SE Lake Rd Suite 350 *Web:* www.1041thefish.com	Portland	OR	97222	503-786-0600	786-1551
KGON-FM 92.3 (CR) 0700 SW Bancroft St *NYSE: ETM* ■ *TF:* 800-222-9236 ■ *Web:* www.kgon.com	Portland	OR	97239	503-223-1441	223-6909
KINK-FM 101.9 (AAA) 1211 SW 5th Ave *TF:* 877-567-5465 ■ *Web:* www.kink.fm	Portland	OR	97204	503-517-6000	517-6130
KKAD-AM 1550 (Oldies) 6605 SE Lake Rd. *TF:* 866-517-1550 ■ *Web:* www.1550kkad.com	Portland	OR	97222	503-228-5523	294-0074
KKCW-FM 103.3 (AC) 4949 SW Macadam Ave. *TF:* 800-333-0103 ■ *Web:* www.k103.com	Portland	OR	97239	503-222-5103	323-6664
KKRZ-FM 100.3 (CHR) 4949 SW Macadam Ave *TF:* 888-483-0100 ■ *Web:* www.z100portland.com	Portland	OR	97239	503-460-0100	323-6660
KLTH-FM 106.7 (AC) 222 SW Columbia Ave Suite 350 *Web:* www.khits1067.com	Portland	OR	97201	503-223-0300	517-6315
KNRK-FM 94.7 (Alt) 0700 SW Bancroft St *TF:* 800-777-0947 ■ *Web:* www.947.fm	Portland	OR	97239	503-223-1441	223-6909
KOOR-AM 1010 (Span) 5110 SE Stark St	Portland	OR	97251	503-234-5550	234-5583
KOPB-FM 91.5 (NPR) 7140 SW Macadam Ave. *Web:* www.opb.org	Portland	OR	97219	503-293-1905	
KPDQ-FM 93.9 (Rel) 6400 SE Lake Rd Suite 350 *TF:* 800-845-2162 ■ *Web:* www.kpdq.com	Portland	OR	97222	503-786-0600	786-1551
KPOJ-AM 620 (N/T) 4949 SW Macadam Ave *TF:* 866-452-0620 ■ *Web:* www.620kpoj.com	Portland	OR	97239	503-323-6400	323-6664
KQOL-FM 105.9 (Oldies) 4949 SW Macadam Ave *Web:* www.kool1059.com	Portland	OR	97239	503-323-6400	323-6664
KUFO-FM 101.1 (Rock) 2040 SW 1st Ave *TF:* 800-344-5836 ■ *Web:* www.kufo.com	Portland	OR	97201	503-222-1011	222-2047
KUPL-FM 98.7 (Ctry) 222 SW Columbia Ave Suite 350 *TF:* 800-533-5875 ■ *Web:* www.kupl.com	Portland	OR	97201	503-517-6200	517-6201
KWBY-AM 940 (Span) 1665 James St	Woodburn	OR	97071	503-981-9400	981-3561
KWJJ-FM 99.5 (Ctry) 0700 SW Bancroft St *TF:* 866-239-9653 ■ *Web:* www.thewolfonline.com	Portland	OR	97239	503-223-1441	223-6909
KXJM-FM 107.5 (AC) 2040 SW 1st Ave *TF:* 800-567-1075 ■ *Web:* www.jamminfm.com	Portland	OR	97201	503-222-1011	517-6401
KXJM-FM 95.5 (Sports) 2040 SW 1st Ave. *Fax: News Rm ■ *Web:* www.955thegame.com	Portland	OR	97201	503-517-6400	517-6401*
KXL-AM 750 (N/T) 1211 SW 5th Ave *TF:* 800-990-0750 ■ *Web:* www.kxl.com	Portland	OR	97204	503-243-7595	417-7661
KYKN-AM 1430 (N/T) PO Box 1430 *Web:* www.kykn.com	Salem	OR	97308	503-390-3014	390-3728

648-135 Providence, RI

	City	State	Zip	Phone	Fax
WBRU-FM 95.5 (Alt) 88 Benevolent St *Web:* www.wbru.com	Providence	RI	02906	401-272-9550	272-9278
WDOM-FM 91.3 (Var) 549 River Ave Providence College Slaven Center	Providence	RI	02918	401-865-2091	865-2522
WHJJ-AM 920 (N/T) 75 Oxford St 3rd Fl. *Web:* www.whjjam.com	Providence	RI	02905	401-781-9979	781-9329
WHJY-FM 94.1 (Rock) 75 Oxford St 3rd Fl. *Web:* www.whjy.com	Providence	RI	02905	401-781-9979	781-9329
WRNI-AM 1290 (NPR) 1 Union Stn. *Web:* www.wrni.org	Providence	RI	02903	401-351-2800	351-0246
WSNE-FM 93.3 (AC) 75 Oxford St 3rd Fl. *Web:* www.coast933.com	Providence	RI	02905	401-781-9979	781-9929
WWBB-FM 101.5 (Oldies) 75 Oxford St 3rd Fl *TF:* 800-808-2101 ■ *Web:* www.b101.com	Providence	RI	02905	401-781-9979	781-9329

648-136 Quebec City, QC

	City	State	Zip	Phone	Fax
CBVE-FM 104.7 (CBC) 888 Saint Jean St *Web:* www.cbc.radio-canada.ca	Quebec City	QC	G1K9L4	418-654-1341	691-3610
CHIK-FM 98.9 (CHR) 900 Dyouville 1st Fl	Quebec	QC	G1R3P7	418-687-9900	687-3106
CJMF-FM 93.3 (Var) 1305 ch Sainte-Foy Suite 402 *Fax: Sales ■ *Web:* www.fm93.com	Quebec	QC	G1S4Y5	418-687-9330	687-0211*
CKIA-FM 88.3 (Var) 600 Cote d'Abraham *Web:* www.ckiafm.org	Quebec	QC	G1R1A1	418-529-9026	529-4156

648-137 Raleigh/Durham, NC

	City	State	Zip	Phone	Fax
WBBB-FM 96.1 (Rock) 3012 Highwoods Blvd Suite 200 *Web:* www.96rockonline.com	Raleigh	NC	27604	919-876-3831	876-9213
WDCG-FM 105.1 (CHR) 3100 Smoketree Ct 7th Fl *Web:* www.g105.com	Raleigh	NC	27604	919-878-1500	876-8578
WFXC-FM 107.1 (Urban AC) 8001-101 Creedmoor Rd *TF:* 800-467-3699 ■ *Web:* www.foxyhits.com	Raleigh	NC	27613	919-848-9736	844-3947
WFXK-FM 104.3 (Urban AC) 8001-101 Creedmoor Rd *Web:* www.foxyhits.com	Raleigh	NC	27613	919-848-9736	844-3947
WKNC-FM 88.1 (Rock) NCSU PO Box 8607 343 Witherspoon Student Center *Web:* wknc.org	Raleigh	NC	27695	919-515-2401	513-2693
WKSL-FM 93.9 (CHR) 3100 Smoketree Ct 7th Fl *Web:* www.939kissfm.com	Raleigh	NC	27604	919-878-1500	876-2929
WNCU-FM 90.7 (NPR) PO Box 19875 *Web:* www.wncu.org	Durham	NC	27707	919-530-7445	530-5031
WNNL-FM 103.9 (Rel) 8001-101 Creedmoor Rd *TF:* 877-310-9665 ■ *Web:* www.thelight1039.com	Raleigh	NC	27613	919-848-9736	844-3947
WPTF-AM 680 (N/T) 3012 Highwoods Blvd Suite 200 *TF:* 800-662-7979 ■ *Web:* www.wptf.com	Raleigh	NC	27604	919-876-0674	790-8369
WQDR-FM 94.7 (Ctry) 3012 Highwoods Blvd Suite 201 *TF:* 800-233-9497 ■ *Web:* www.947qdr.com	Raleigh	NC	27604	919-876-6464	790-8893
WQOK-FM 97.5 (Urban) 8001-101 Creedmoor Rd *Web:* www.k975.com	Raleigh	NC	27613	919-848-9736	844-3947
WRAL-FM 101.5 (AC) 711 Hillsborough St. *TF:* 800-849-6101 ■ *Web:* www.wralfm.com	Raleigh	NC	27603	919-890-6101	890-6146
WRBZ-AM 850 (Sports) 4601 Six Forks Rd Suite 520 *Web:* www.850thebuzz.com	Raleigh	NC	27609	919-875-9100	510-6990
WRDU-FM 106.1 (Ctry) 3100 Smoketree Ct Suite 700 *Web:* www.1061rdu.com	Raleigh	NC	27604	919-878-1500	876-2929
WRJD-AM 1410 (Rel) 707 Leon St *Web:* www.1410wrjd.com	Durham	NC	27704	919-220-3226	220-0006
WRVA-FM 100.7 (AC) 3100 Smoketree Ct 7th Fl *Web:* www.1007theriver.com	Raleigh	NC	27604	919-878-1500	876-2929
WSHA-FM 88.9 (Jazz) 118 E S St. *TF:* 800-241-0421 ■ *Web:* www.wshafm.org	Raleigh	NC	27601	919-546-8430	546-8315
WWMY-FM 102.9 (Oldies) 3012 Highwoods Blvd Suite 201 *Web:* www.y1029.com	Raleigh	NC	27604	919-790-9392	790-8990
WXDU-FM 88.7 (Alt) PO Box 90689 *Web:* www.wxdu.duke.edu	Durham	NC	27708	919-684-2957	684-3260

648-138 Rapid City, SD

Station	City	State	Zip	Phone	Fax
KFXS-FM 100.3 (CR) 660 Flormann St Suite 100 *Web:* www.foxradio.com	Rapid City	SD	57701	605-348-1100	343-9012
KICK-FM 104.1 (Ctry) 3601 Canyon Lake Dr *TF:* 800-456-2613 ■ *Web:* www.kick104.com	Rapid City	SD	57702	605-343-0888	342-3075
KIMM-AM 1150 (Ctry) 11 Main St *TF:* 888-856-4312	Rapid City	SD	57701	605-342-1150	343-1096
KKLS-AM 920 (Oldies) 660 Flormann St Suite 100 *Web:* www.kkls.net	Rapid City	SD	57701	605-343-6161	343-9012
KKMK-FM 93.9 (AC) 660 Flormann St Suite 100 *Web:* www.magic939fm.com	Rapid City	SD	57701	605-343-6161	343-9012
KLMP-FM 88.3 (Rel) 1853 Fountain Plaza Dr *Web:* www.klmp.com	Rapid City	SD	57702	605-342-6822	342-0854
KOTA-AM 1380 (N/T) 518 St Joseph St *Web:* www.kotaradio.rapidnet.com	Rapid City	SD	57701	605-342-2000	342-7305
KOUT-FM 98.7 (Ctry) 660 Flormann St Suite 100 *Web:* www.katradio.com	Rapid City	SD	57701	605-348-1100	343-9012
KRCS-FM 93.1 (CHR) 660 Flormann St Suite 100 *Web:* www.hot931.com	Rapid City	SD	57701	605-343-6161	343-9012
KTOQ-AM 1340 (N/T) 3601 Canyon Lake Dr *TF:* 800-456-2613 ■ *Web:* www.ktalkam1340.com	Rapid City	SD	57702	605-343-0888	342-3075
KZLK-FM 106.3 (AC) 518 St Joseph St *Web:* www.kotaradio.com	Rapid City	SD	57701	605-342-2000	342-7305

648-139 Reno/Carson City, NV

Station	City	State	Zip	Phone	Fax
KBUL-FM 98.1 (Ctry) 595 E Plumb Ln *Web:* www.kbul.com	Reno	NV	89502	775-789-6700	789-6767
KDOT-FM 104.5 (Rock) 2900 Sutro St *Web:* www.kdot.com	Reno	NV	89512	775-329-9261	323-1450
KJFK-AM 1230 (N/T) 961 Matley Ln Suite 120 *Web:* www.1230kjfk.com	Reno	NV	89502	775-829-1964	825-3183
KLCA-FM 96.5 (Alt) 961 Matley Ln Suite 120 *Web:* www.alice965.com	Reno	NV	89502	775-829-1964	825-3183
KNIS-FM 91.3 (Rel) 6363 Hwy 50 E *TF:* 800-541-5647 ■ *Web:* www.pilgrimradio.com	Carson City	NV	89701	775-883-5647	
KODS-FM 103.7 (Oldies) 961 Matley Ln Suite 120 *Web:* www.river1037.com	Reno	NV	89502	775-829-1964	825-3183
KOZZ-FM 105.7 (CR) 2900 Sutro St *Web:* www.kozzradio.com	Reno	NV	89512	775-329-9261	323-1450
KRNO-FM 106.9 (AC) 961 Matley Ln Suite 120 *Web:* www.sunny1069.com	Reno	NV	89502	775-829-1964	825-3183
KRNV-FM 102.1 (Span) 300 S Wells Ave Suite 12 *Web:* www.pilgrimradio.com	Reno	NV	89502	775-333-1017	333-9046
KRZQ-FM 100.9 (Alt) 300 E 2nd St Suite 1400 *Web:* www.krzqfm.com	Reno	NV	89501	775-333-0123	322-7361
KTHX-FM 100.1 (AAA) 300 E 2nd St Suite 1400 *Web:* www.kthxfm.com	Reno	NV	89501	775-333-0123	322-7361
KUNR-FM 88.7 (NPR) University of Nevada-Reno MS-294 *Web:* www.kunr.org	Reno	NV	89557	775-327-5867	327-5386
KUUB-FM 94.5 (Ctry) 2900 Sutro St *Web:* www.cubcountry945.com	Reno	NV	89512	775-329-9261	323-1450

648-140 Richmond, VA

Station	City	State	Zip	Phone	Fax
WBBT-FM 107.3 (Oldies) 300 Arboretum Pl Suite 590 *Web:* www.1073bbt.com	Richmond	VA	23236	804-327-9902	327-9911
WBTJ-FM 106.5 (Urban) 3245 Basie Rd *Web:* www.wbtj.com	Richmond	VA	23228	804-474-0000	474-0096
WCDX-FM 92.1 (Urban) 2809 Emerywood Pkwy Suite 300 *Web:* www.power921jamz.com	Richmond	VA	23294	804-672-9299	672-9316
WCVE-FM 88.9 (NPR) 23 Sesame St *Web:* www.ideastations.org/wcvefm	Richmond	VA	23235	804-320-1301	320-8729
WFTH-AM 1590 (Rel) 227 E Belt Blvd *Web:* www.faith1590.com	Richmond	VA	23224	804-233-0765	233-3725
WKHK-FM 95.3 (Ctry) 812 Moorefield Pk Dr Suite 300 *Web:* k95country.com	Richmond	VA	23236	804-330-5700	330-4079
WKJM-FM 99.3 (Urban) 2809 Emerywood Pkwy Suite 300	Richmond	VA	23294	804-672-9299	672-9316
WKJS-FM 105.7 (Urban) 2809 Emerywood Pkwy Suite 300 *Web:* www.yestokiss.com	Richmond	VA	23294	804-672-9299	672-9316
WKLR-FM 96.5 (CR) 812 Moorefield Pk Dr Suite 300 *Web:* 965klr.com	Richmond	VA	23236	804-330-5700	330-4079
WLEE-AM 990 (N/T) 308 W Broad St *TF:* 877-953-3990 ■ *Web:* www.wlee990.am	Richmond	VA	23220	804-643-0990	643-4990
WLFV-FM 93.1 (Ctry) 300 Arboretum Pl Suite 590 *Web:* www.931thewolf.com	Richmond	VA	23236	804-327-9902	327-9911
WMXB-FM 103.7 (AC) 812 Moorefield Pk Dr Suite 300 *Web:* mix1037.com	Richmond	VA	23236	804-330-5700	330-4079
WRNL-AM 910 (Sports) 3245 Basie Rd *Web:* www.sportsradio910.com	Richmond	VA	23228	804-474-0000	474-0096
WRVA-AM 1140 (N/T) 3245 Basie Rd *Web:* www.wrva.com	Richmond	VA	23228	804-474-0000	474-0096
WRVQ-FM 94.5 (CHR) 3245 Basie Rd *Web:* www.wrvq94.com	Richmond	VA	23228	804-474-0000	474-0096
WRXL-FM 102.1 (Rock) 3245 Basie Rd *Web:* www.1021thex.com	Richmond	VA	23228	804-474-0000	474-0096
WTVR-FM 98.1 (AC) 3245 Basie Rd *Web:* www.lite98.com	Richmond	VA	23228	804-474-0000	474-0096
WVNZ-AM 1320 (Span) 308 W Broad St *Web:* www.davidsonmediagroup.com	Richmond	VA	23220	804-643-0990	643-4990
WXGI-AM 950 (Sports) 701 German School Rd *Web:* www.espn950am.com	Richmond	VA	23225	804-233-7666	233-7681

648-141 Riverside/San Bernardino, CA

Station	City	State	Zip	Phone	Fax
KCAL-AM 1410 (Span) 1950 S Sunwest Ln Suite 302 *Web:* www.radiolazer.com	San Bernardino	CA	92408	909-825-5020	884-5844
KCAL-FM 96.7 (Rock) 1940 Orange Tree Ln Suite 200 *Web:* www.kcalfm.com	Redlands	CA	92374	909-793-3554	798-6627
KCXX-FM 103.9 (Alt) 242 E Airport Dr Suite 106 *Web:* www.x1039.com	San Bernardino	CA	92408	909-890-5904	890-9035
KDIF-AM 1440 (Span) 2030 Iowa Ave Suite A *Web:* www.kdif.com	Riverside	CA	92507	951-684-1991	274-4911
KGGI-FM 99.1 (CHR) 2030 Iowa Ave Suite A **Fax:* Sales ■ *TF:* 866-991-5444 ■ *Web:* www.kggiradio.com	Riverside	CA	92507	951-684-1991	274-4911*
KKDD-AM 1290 (Kids) 2030 Iowa Ave Suite A **Fax:* Sales ■ *Web:* www.radiodisney.com	Riverside	CA	92507	951-684-1991	274-4911*
KPRO-AM 1570 (Rel) 7351 Lincoln Ave *Web:* www.bristar.com	Riverside	CA	92504	951-688-1570	688-7009
KSGN-FM 89.7 (Rel) 2048 Orange Tree Ln Suite 200 *TF:* 800-321-5746 ■ *Web:* www.ksgn.com	Redlands	CA	92374	909-583-2150	583-2170
KUCR-FM 88.3 (Var) UC Riverside *Web:* www.kucr.org	Riverside	CA	92521	951-827-3737	827-3240
KVCR-FM 91.9 (NPR) 701 S Mt Vernon Ave *Web:* www.kvcr.org	San Bernardino	CA	92410	909-384-4444	885-2116

648-142 Roanoke, VA

Station	City	State	Zip	Phone	Fax
WFIR-AM 960 (N/T) 3934 Electric Rd SW *Web:* wfir960.com	Roanoke	VA	24018	540-345-1511	342-2270
WJJS-FM 106.1 (CHR) 3807 Brandon Ave SW Suite 2350 *Web:* www.wjjs.com	Roanoke	VA	24018	540-725-1220	725-1245
WRIS-AM 1410 (Rel) 219 Luckett St NW	Roanoke	VA	24017	540-342-1410	342-5952
WROV-FM 96.3 (Rock) 3807 Brandon Ave SW Suite 2350 *TF:* 800-476-9603 ■ *Web:* www.rovrocks.com	Roanoke	VA	24018	540-725-1220	725-1245
WSLC-FM 94.9 (Ctry) 3934 Electric Rd SW *Web:* www.949starcountry.com	Roanoke	VA	24018	540-387-0234	342-2270
WSLQ-FM 99.1 (AC) 3934 Electric Rd SW *Web:* www.q99fm.com	Roanoke	VA	24018	540-387-0234	342-2270
WSNV-FM 93.5 (AC) 3807 Brandon Ave SW Suite 2350 *Web:* www.mysunnyfm.com	Roanoke	VA	24018	540-725-1220	725-1245
WVTF-FM 89.1 (NPR) 3520 Kingsbury Ln *TF:* 800-856-8900 ■ *Web:* www.wvtf.org	Roanoke	VA	24014	540-231-8900	776-2727
WXLK-FM 92.3 (CHR) 3934 Electric Rd SW *Web:* www.k92radio.com	Roanoke	VA	24018	540-774-9200	774-5667

648-143 Rochester, MN

Station	City	State	Zip	Phone	Fax
KFSI-FM 92.9 (Rel) 4016 28th St SE *Web:* www.kfsi.org	Rochester	MN	55904	507-289-8585	529-4017
KLSE-FM 91.7 (Clas) 206 S Broadway Suite 735 *TF:* 800-652-9700 ■ *Web:* www.mpr.org	Rochester	MN	55904	507-282-0910	282-2107
KNFX-AM 970 (Span) 1530 Greenview Dr SW Suite 200	Rochester	MN	55902	507-288-3888	288-7815
KOLM-AM 1520 (Sports) 122 SW 4th St *Web:* www.1520theticket.com	Rochester	MN	55902	507-286-1010	286-9370
KRCH-FM 101.7 (CR) 1530 Greenview Dr SW Suite 200 *Web:* www.laser1017.net	Rochester	MN	55902	507-288-3888	288-7815
KROC-AM 1340 (N/T) 122 SW 4th St *Web:* www.kroc.com	Rochester	MN	55902	507-286-1010	286-9370
KROC-FM 106.9 (CHR) 122 SW 4th St *Web:* www.kroc.com	Rochester	MN	55902	507-286-1010	286-9370
KWEB-AM 1270 (Sports) 1530 Greenview Dr SW Suite 200 *Web:* www.fan1270.com	Rochester	MN	55902	507-288-3888	288-7815
KWWK-FM 96.5 (Ctry) 122 SW 4th St *TF:* 888-599-5965 ■ *Web:* www.quickcountry.com	Rochester	MN	55902	507-286-1010	286-9370
KYBA-FM 105.3 (AC) 122 SW 4th St *Web:* www.y105fm.com	Rochester	MN	55902	507-286-1010	286-9370
KZSE-FM 90.7 (NPR) 206 S Broadway Suite 735 *TF:* 800-652-9700 ■ *Web:* www.mpr.org	Rochester	MN	55904	507-282-0910	282-2107

648-144 Rochester, NY

Station	City	State	Zip	Phone	Fax
WBEE-FM 92.5 (Ctry) 70 Commercial St *Web:* www.wbee.com	Rochester	NY	14614	585-423-2900	423-2947

	City	State	Zip	Phone	Fax
WBZA-FM 98.9 (CR) 70 Commercial St *Web:* www.rochesterbuzz.com	Rochester	NY	14614	585-423-2900	423-2947
WCMF-FM 96.5 (CR) 70 Commercial St *Web:* www.wcmf.com	Rochester	NY	14614	585-423-2900	399-5750
WDKX-FM 103.9 (Urban) 683 E Main St *Web:* www.wdkx.com	Rochester	NY	14605	585-262-2050	262-2626
WDVI-FM 100.5 (AC) 100 Chestnut St 17th Fl *Web:* www.mydrivefm.com	Rochester	NY	14604	585-454-4884	454-5081
WFXF-FM 95.1 (Rock) 100 Chestnut St 17th Fl *Web:* www.fox951.com	Rochester	NY	14604	585-454-4884	454-5081
WHAM-AM 1180 (N/T) 100 Chestnut St *Web:* www.wham1180.com	Rochester	NY	14604	585-454-4884	454-5081
WJZR-FM 105.9 (NAC) 1237 E Main St	Rochester	NY	14609	585-288-5020	
WKGS-FM 106.7 (CHR) 1700 Hsbc Plaza 100 Chestnut St *Web:* www.1067kiss.com	Rochester	NY	14604	585-454-4884	454-5081
WPXY-FM 97.9 (CHR) 70 Commercial St *Web:* www.98pxy.com	Rochester	NY	14614	585-423-2900	399-5750
WRMM-FM 101.3 (AC) 1700 HSBC Plaza Suite 1700 *Web:* www.warm1013.com	Rochester	NY	14604	585-399-5700	399-5750
WXXI-AM 1370 (NPR) PO Box 30021 *Web:* www.wxxi.org	Rochester	NY	14603	585-325-7500	258-0339
WXXI-FM 91.5 (Clas) PO Box 30021 *Web:* www.wxxi.org	Rochester	NY	14603	585-325-7500	258-0339
WZNE-FM 94.1 (Alt) 28 E Main St 8th Fl First Plaza *Web:* www.thezone941.com	Rochester	NY	14614	585-399-5700	399-5750

648-145 Rockford, IL

	City	State	Zip	Phone	Fax
WGFB-FM 103.1 (AC) 2830 Sandy Hollow Rd *Web:* www.b103fm.com	Rockford	IL	61109	815-874-7861	874-2202
WNTA-AM 1330 (N/T) 2830 Sandy Hollow Rd *Web:* www.wnta.com	Rockford	IL	61109	815-874-7861	874-2202
WROK-AM 1440 (N/T) 3901 Brendenwood Rd *Web:* www.1440wrok.com	Rockford	IL	61107	815-399-2233	484-2432
WXRX-FM 104.9 (Rock) 2830 Sandy Hollow Rd *Web:* www.wxrx.com	Rockford	IL	61109	815-874-7861	874-2202
WXXQ-FM 98.5 (Ctry) 3901 Brendenwood Rd *Web:* www.q985online.com	Rockford	IL	61107	815-399-2233	399-8148
WZOK-FM 97.5 (CHR) 3901 Brendenwood Rd *Web:* www.97zokonline.com	Rockford	IL	61107	815-399-2233	484-2432

648-146 Sacramento, CA

	City	State	Zip	Phone	Fax
Capital Public Radio Inc 7055 Folsom Blvd *TF:* 877-480-5900 ■ *Web:* www.capradio.org	Sacramento	CA	95826	916-278-8900	278-8989
KCTC-AM 1320 (Sports) 5345 Madison Ave *TF:* 800-375-7722	Sacramento	CA	95841	916-334-7777	339-4591
KDND-FM 107.9 (CHR) 5345 Madison Ave *Web:* www.endonline.com	Sacramento	CA	95841	916-334-7777	339-4591
KFBK-AM 1530 (N/T) 1440 Ethan Way Suite 200 *Web:* www.kfbk.com	Sacramento	CA	95825	916-929-5325	921-5555
KGBY-FM 92.5 (AC) 1440 Ethan Way Suite 200 *Web:* www.y92.com	Sacramento	CA	95825	916-929-5325	921-5555
KHHM-FM 103.4 (CHR) 1436 Auburn Blvd *NASDAQ:* EVC ■ *Web:* www.hot1035radio.com	Sacramento	CA	95815	916-646-4000	646-3237
KHTK-AM 1140 (Sports) 5244 Madison Ave *TF:* 800-920-1140 ■ *Web:* www.khtkam.com	Sacramento	CA	95841	916-338-9200	338-9208
KHYL-FM 101.1 (Oldies) 1440 Ethan Way Suite 200 *Web:* www.v1011fm.com	Sacramento	CA	95825	916-929-5325	921-5555
KKDO-FM 94.7 (NAC) 5345 Madison Ave *Web:* www.radio947.net	Sacramento	CA	95841	916-334-7777	339-4591
KKFS-FM 103.9 (Rel) 1425 River Pk Dr Suite 520 *Web:* www.1039thefish.com	Sacramento	CA	95815	916-924-0710	924-1587
KNCI-FM 105.1 (Ctry) 5244 Madison Ave *Fax: Sales ■ *TF:* 800-850-1051 ■ *Web:* www.kncifm.com	Sacramento	CA	95841	916-338-9200	338-9208*
KNTY-FM 101.9 (Ctry) 1436 Auburn Blvd *Web:* www.1019thewolf.com	Sacramento	CA	95815	916-646-4000	925-7969
KRXQ-FM 98.5 (Rock) 5345 Madison Ave *Web:* www.krxq.net	Sacramento	CA	95841	916-334-7777	339-4591
KSEG-FM 96.9 (CR) 5345 Madison Ave *Web:* www.eagle969.com	Sacramento	CA	95841	916-334-7777	339-4591
KSFM-FM 102.5 (Urban) 1750 Howe Ave Suite 500 *Web:* www.ksfm.com	Sacramento	CA	95825	916-920-1025	929-5341
KSTE-AM 650 (N/T) 1440 Ethan Way Suite 200 *Web:* www.kste.com	Sacramento	CA	95825	916-929-5325	921-5555
KTKZ-AM 1380 (N/T) 1425 River Pk Dr Suite 520 *Web:* www.ktkz.com	Sacramento	CA	95815	916-924-0710	924-1587
KUOP-FM 91.3 (NPR) 7055 Folsom Blvd *Web:* www.capradio.org	Sacramento	CA	95826	916-278-8900	278-8989
KWOD-FM 106.5 (Alt) 5345 Madison Ave *Web:* www.kwod.com	Sacramento	CA	95841	916-334-7777	339-4591
KXPR-FM 88.9 (Clas) 7055 Folsom Blvd *TF:* 877-480-5900 ■ *Web:* www.capradio.org	Sacramento	CA	95826	916-278-8900	278-8989
KXSE-FM 104.3 (Span AC) 1436 Auburn Blvd *NASDAQ:* EVC ■ *Web:* www.sesacramento.com	Sacramento	CA	95815	916-646-4000	646-3237
KYMX-FM 96.1 (AC) 280 Commerce Cir *Web:* www.kymx.com	Sacramento	CA	95815	916-923-6800	923-9696
KZZO-FM 100.5 (AC) 280 Commerce Cir *Web:* www.radiozone.com	Sacramento	CA	95815	916-923-6800	927-6468

648-147 Saint Louis, MO

	City	State	Zip	Phone	Fax
KATZ-AM 1600 (Rel) 1001 Highlands Plaza Dr W Suite 100 *Web:* www.gospel1600.com	Saint Louis	MO	63110	314-333-8000	692-5125
KATZ-FM 100.3 (Urban) 1001 Highlands Plaza Dr W Suite 100 *TF:* 800-541-0036 ■ *Web:* www.katzfm.com	Saint Louis	MO	63110	314-333-8300	333-8200
KEZK-FM 102.5 (AC) 3100 Market St *Web:* www.kezk.com	Saint Louis	MO	63103	314-531-0000	969-7638
KFNS-AM 590 (Sports) 8045 Big Bend Blvd *Fax: Sales ■ *Web:* www.kfns.com	Saint Louis	MO	63119	314-962-0590	962-7576*
KFNS-FM 100.7 (Sports) 8045 Big Bend Blvd *Web:* www.kfns.com	Saint Louis	MO	63119	314-962-0590	962-7576
KLOU-FM 103.3 (Oldies) 1001 Highlands Plaza Dr W *Web:* www.klou.com	Saint Louis	MO	63110	314-333-8000	333-8200
KMOX-AM 1120 (N/T) 1 Memorial Dr *Web:* www.kmox.com	Saint Louis	MO	63102	314-621-2345	444-3298
KPNT-FM 105.7 (Alt) 800 St Louis Union Stn *Web:* www.kpnt.com	Saint Louis	MO	63103	314-621-0095	621-3000
KSD-FM 93.7 (Ctry) 1001 Highlands Plaza Dr W Suite 100 *Web:* www.thebullrocks.com	Saint Louis	MO	63110	314-333-8000	333-8200
KSHE-FM 94.7 (Rock) 800 St Louis Union Stn *Web:* www.kshe95.com	Saint Louis	MO	63103	314-621-0095	621-3000
KSLZ 107.7 FM 1001 Highlands Plaza Dr W Suite 100 *Web:* www.z1077.com	Saint Louis	MO	63110	314-333-8000	333-8200
KTRS-AM 550 (N/T) 638 W Port Plaza *TF:* 888-550-5877 ■ *Web:* www.ktrs.com	Saint Louis	MO	63146	314-453-5500	453-9704
KWMU-FM 90.7 (NPR) 8001 Natural Bridge Rd *Web:* www.kwmu.org	Saint Louis	MO	63121	314-516-5968	516-5993
KYKY-FM 98.1 (AC) 3100 Market St *Web:* www.y98.com	Saint Louis	MO	63103	314-531-0000	531-9855
Magic 104.9 1001 Highlands Plaza Dr W Suite 100 *Web:* www.kmjm.com	Saint Louis	MO	63110	314-333-8000	333-8200
WARH-FM 106.5 (CR) 11647 Olive Blvd *Web:* www.1065thearch.com	Saint Louis	MO	63141	314-983-6000	994-9447
WEW-AM 770 (Var) 2740 Hampton Ave *Web:* www.wewradio.com	Saint Louis	MO	63139	314-781-9397	781-8545
WHHL-FM 104.1 (CHR) 9666 Olive Blvd Suite 610	Saint Louis	MO	63132	314-989-9550	989-9551
WVRV-FM 101.1 (AC) 11647 Olive Blvd	Saint Louis	MO	63141	314-983-6000	994-9447

648-148 Salt Lake City, UT

	City	State	Zip	Phone	Fax
KALL-AM 700 (Sports) 1903 W Research Way *TF:* 877-353-0700 ■ *Web:* www.hotticket700.com	Salt Lake City	UT	84119	801-470-0700	570-0700
KBEE-FM 98.7 (AC) 434 Bearcat Dr *Web:* www.b987.com	Salt Lake City	UT	84115	801-485-6700	487-5369
KBER-FM 101.1 (Rock) 434 Bearcat Dr *Web:* www.kber.com	Salt Lake City	UT	84115	801-485-6700	487-5369
KBZN-FM 97.9 (NAC) 257 E 200 S Suite 400 *TF:* 866-627-1430 ■ *Web:* www.kbzn.com	Salt Lake City	UT	84111	801-364-9836	364-8068
KCPW-FM 88.3 (NPR) 210 E 400 S Suite 10 PO Box 510730 *TF:* 888-359-5279 ■ *Web:* www.kcpw.org	Salt Lake City	UT	84151	801-359-5279	746-2708
KEGA-FM 101.5 (Ctry) 515 S 700 E Suite 1C *TF:* 866-551-1015 ■ *Web:* www.1015theeagle.com	Salt Lake City	UT	84102	801-524-2600	364-1811
KENZ-FM 107.5 (AAA) 434 Bearcat Dr	Salt Lake City	UT	84115	801-485-6700	487-5369
KFNZ-AM 1320 (Sports) 434 Bearcat Dr *Web:* www.1320kfan.com	Salt Lake City	UT	84115	801-485-6700	487-5369
KJMY-FM 99.5 (Rock) 2801 S Decker Lake Dr *Web:* www.my995fm.com	Salt Lake City	UT	84119	801-908-1300	908-1310
KJMYFM 105.7 (Ctry) 2801 S Decker Lake Dr *Web:* www.mycountry.com	Salt Lake City	UT	84119	801-908-1300	908-1310
KLO-AM 1430 (N/T) 257 E 200 S Suite 400 *TF:* 866-627-1430 ■ *Web:* www.kloradio.com	Salt Lake City	UT	84111	801-364-9836	364-8068
KNRS-AM 570 (N/T) 2801 S Decker Lake Dr *Web:* www.knrs.com	Salt Lake City	UT	84119	801-908-1300	908-1310
KODJ-FM 94.1 (Oldies) 2801 S Decker Lake Dr *Web:* www.kodj.com	Salt Lake City	UT	84119	801-908-1300	908-1415
KOSY-FM 106.5 (AC) 2801 S Decker Lake Dr *Web:* www.kosy.com	Salt Lake City	UT	84119	801-908-1300	908-1310
KRSP-FM 103.5 (CR) 55 N 300 W *Web:* www.arrow1035.com	Salt Lake City	UT	84180	801-595-1003	526-1070
KSFI-FM 100.3 (AC) 55 N 300 W *Web:* www.fm100.com	Salt Lake City	UT	84180	801-595-1003	526-1070
KSL-AM 1160 (N/T) 55 N 300 W PO Box 1160 *Web:* www.ksl.com	Salt Lake City	UT	84180	801-575-7600	575-5561

				Phone	Fax
KSL-FM 102.7 (N/T) 55 N 300 W *Web:* www.ksl.com	Salt Lake City	UT	84180	801-575-5555	575-5561
KSOP-AM 1370 (Ctry) 1285 W 2320 S	Salt Lake City	UT	84119	801-972-1043	974-0868
KSOP-FM 104.3 (Ctry) 1285 W 2320 S *Web:* www.ksopcountry.com	Salt Lake City	UT	84119	801-972-1043	974-0868
KUBL-FM 93.3 (Ctry) 434 Bearcat Dr *Web:* www.kbull93.com	Salt Lake City	UT	84115	801-485-6700	487-5369
KUER-FM 90.1 (NPR) 101 S Wasatch Dr Rm 270 *Web:* www.kuer.org	Salt Lake City	UT	84112	801-581-6625	581-6758
KUUU-FM 92.5 (Urban) 515 S 700 E Suite 1-C *Web:* www.u92online.com	Salt Lake City	UT	84102	801-524-2600	643-1811
KXRK-FM 96.3 (Alt) 515 S 700 E Suite 1C *Web:* www.x96.com	Salt Lake City	UT	84102	801-524-2600	521-9234
KZHT-FM 97.1 (CHR) 2801 S Decker Lake Dr *Web:* www.971zht.com	Salt Lake City	UT	84119	801-908-1300	908-1310
KZNS-AM 1280 (Sports) 515 S 700 E Suite 1C *TF:* 866-233-1280 ■ *Web:* www.1280kzn.com	Salt Lake City	UT	84102	801-524-2600	521-9234
KZNS-FM 97.5 (Rock) 515 S 700 E Suite 1-C *Web:* www.1280thezone.com	Salt Lake City	UT	84102	801-570-1280	

648-149 San Antonio, TX

				Phone	Fax
KAJA-FM 97.3 (Ctry) 6222 NW IH-10 *TF:* 800-707-5597 ■ *Web:* www.kj97.com	San Antonio	TX	78201	210-736-9700	735-8811
KBBT-FM 98.5 (Urban) 1777 NE Loop 410 Suite 400 *Web:* www.thebeatsa.com	San Antonio	TX	78217	210-829-1075	804-7825
KCYY-FM 100.3 (Ctry) 8122 Datapoint Dr Suite 600 *Web:* www.y100fm.com	San Antonio	TX	78229	210-615-5400	615-5331
KGSX-FM 95.1 (Span) 1777 NE Loop 410 Suite 400 *Web:* lakalle951.univision.com	San Antonio	TX	78217	210-829-1075	804-7825
KISS-FM 99.5 (Rock) 8122 Datapoint Dr Suite 600 *Web:* www.kissrocks.com	San Antonio	TX	78229	210-615-5400	615-5331
KJXK-FM 102.7 (Var) 4050 Eisenhauer Rd *Web:* www.hellojack.com	San Antonio	TX	78218	210-654-5100	855-5076
KKYX-AM 680 (Ctry) 8122 Datapoint Dr Suite 600 *Web:* www.kkyx.com	San Antonio	TX	78229	210-615-5400	615-5331
KLEY-FM 95.7 (Span) 4050 Eisenhower Rd *TF:* 888-424-4545	San Antonio	TX	78218	210-654-5100	855-5076
KLUP-AM 930 9601 McAllister Fwy Suite 1200 *TF:* 866-308-8867 ■ *Web:* www.klup.com	San Antonio	TX	78216	210-344-8481	340-1213
KONO-AM 860 (Oldies) 8122 Datapoint Dr Suite 600 *Web:* www.kono1011.com	San Antonio	TX	78229	210-615-5400	615-5300
KONO-FM 101.1 (Oldies) 8122 Datapoint Dr Suite 600 *Web:* www.kono1011.com	San Antonio	TX	78229	210-615-5400	615-5300
KPWT-FM 106.7 (Urban) 8122 Datapoint Dr Suite 600 *Web:* z1067fm.com	San Antonio	TX	78229	210-615-5400	615-5331
KQXT-FM 101.9 (AC) 6222 NW IH-10 *Web:* www.softrock1019.com	San Antonio	TX	78201	210-736-9700	735-8811
KROM-FM 92.9 (Span) 1777 NE Loop 410 Suite 400 *Web:* estereolatino929.univision.com	San Antonio	TX	78217	210-829-1075	804-7825
KSLR-AM 630 (Rel) 9601 McAllister Fwy Suite 1200 *TF:* 877-630-5757 ■ *Web:* www.kslr.com	San Antonio	TX	78216	210-344-8481	340-1213
KSMG-FM 105.3 (AC) 8122 Datapoint Dr Suite 600 *Web:* www.magic1053.com	San Antonio	TX	78229	210-615-5400	871-6116
KSTX-FM 89.1 (NPR) 8401 Datapoint Dr Suite 800 *TF:* 800-622-8977 ■ *Web:* www.tpr.org	San Antonio	TX	78229	210-614-8977	614-8983
KTKR-AM 760 (Sports) 6222 NW IH-10 *Web:* www.ticket760.com	San Antonio	TX	78201	210-736-9700	735-8811
KTSA-AM 550 (N/T) 4050 Eisenhauer Rd *TF:* 800-299-5872 ■ *Web:* www.ktsa.com	San Antonio	TX	78218	210-654-5100	855-5076
KXTN-FM 107.5 (Span) 1777 NE Loop 410 Suite 400 *Web:* www.kxtn.com	San Antonio	TX	78217	210-829-1075	804-7825
KXXM-FM 96.1 (CHR) 6222 NW IH-10 *Web:* www.mix961.com	San Antonio	TX	78201	210-736-9700	735-8811
KZEP-FM 104.5 (CR) 6222 I-10 W *Web:* www.kzep.com	San Antonio	TX	78201	210-736-9700	785-2698
WOAI-AM 1200 (N/T) 6222 NW IH-10 *TF:* 800-800-9700 ■ *Web:* radio.woai.com	San Antonio	TX	78201	210-736-9700	210-8811

648-150 San Diego, CA

				Phone	Fax
KBZT-FM 94.9 (Alt) 1615 Murray Canyon Rd Suite 710 *Web:* www.fm949sd.com	San Diego	CA	92108	619-291-9797	543-1353
KFMB-AM 760 (N/T) 7677 Engineer Rd *TF:* 800-760-5362 ■ *Web:* www.760kfmb.com	San Diego	CA	92111	858-292-7600	279-7676
KFMB-FM 100.7 (AC) 7677 Engineer Rd *Web:* www.sandiegojack.com	San Diego	CA	92111	858-292-7600	279-7676
KGB-FM 101.5 (CR) 9660 Granite Ridge Dr Suite 100 *Web:* www.101kgb.com	San Diego	CA	92123	858-292-2000	560-0742
KHTS-FM 93.3 (CHR) 9660 Granite Ridge Dr *Web:* www.channel933.com	San Diego	CA	92123	858-292-2000	294-2916
KIFM-FM 98.1 (NAC) 1615 Murray Canyon Rd Suite 710 *Web:* www.kifm.com	San Diego	CA	92108	619-291-9797	543-1353
KIOZ-FM 105.3 (Rock) 9660 Granite Ridge Dr Suite 100 *Web:* www.rock1053.com	San Diego	CA	92123	858-292-2000	560-0742
KLNV-FM 106.5 (Span) 600 W Broadway Suite 2150 *TF:* 866-702-1065 ■ *Web:* www.univision.com	San Diego	CA	92101	619-235-0600	744-4300
KLQV-FM 102.9 (Span AC) 600 W Broadway Suite 2150 *TF:* 877-702-1029 ■ *Web:* www.univision.com	San Diego	CA	92101	619-235-0600	744-4300
KLSD-AM 1360 (N/T) 9660 Granite Ridge Dr	San Diego	CA	92123	858-292-2000	715-3303
KMYI-FM 94.1 (AC) 9660 Granite Ridge Dr Suite 100 *Web:* www.star941sandiego.com	San Diego	CA	92123	858-292-2000	294-2916
KOGO-AM 600 (N/T) 9660 Granite Ridge Dr *Web:* www.kogo.com	San Diego	CA	92123	858-292-2000	715-3675
KPBS-FM 89.5 (NPR) San Diego State University 5200 Campanile Dr *Web:* www.kpbs.org	San Diego	CA	92182	619-594-8100	594-3812
KPRI-FM 102.1 (AAA) 9710 Scranton Rd Suite 200 *Web:* www.kprifm.com	San Diego	CA	92121	858-678-0102	320-7024
KSCF-FM 103.7 (N/T) 8033 Linda Vista Rd *Web:* www.1037freefm.com	San Diego	CA	92111	858-571-7600	571-0326
KSDS-FM 88.3 (Jazz) 1313 Pk Blvd *Web:* www.jazz88.org	San Diego	CA	92101	619-234-1062	230-2928
KSON-FM 97.3 (Ctry) 1615 Murray Canyon Rd Suite 710 *Web:* www.kson.com	San Diego	CA	92108	619-291-9797	543-1353
KUSS-FM 95.7 (Ctry) 9660 Granite Ridge Dr Suite 100 *Web:* www.us957.com	San Diego	CA	92123	858-292-2000	278-7957
KYXY-FM 96.5 (AC) 8033 Linda Vista Rd *Web:* www.kyxy.com	San Diego	CA	92111	858-571-7600	571-0326
XEMO-AM 860 (Span) 5030 Camino de la Siesta Suite 403 *Web:* www.uniradio.com	San Diego	CA	92108	619-497-0600	497-1019
XHRM-FM 92.5 (Oldies) 6160 Cornerstone Ct E Suite 150 *Web:* www.magic925.com	San Diego	CA	92121	858-888-7000	
XHTZ-FM 90.3 (Urban) 9660 Granite Ridge Dr Suite 200 *Web:* www.z90.com	San Diego	CA	92123	858-495-9100	499-1810
XTRA-FM 91.1 (Alt) 6160 Cornerstone Ct E Suite 150 *Web:* www.91x.com	San Diego	CA	92121	858-888-7000	

648-151 San Francisco, CA

				Phone	Fax
KALW-FM 91.7 (NPR) 500 Mansell St *Web:* www.kalw.org	San Francisco	CA	94134	415-841-4121	841-4125
KBLX-FM 102.9 (Urban AC) 55 Hawthorne St Suite 900 *TF:* 800-683-5259 ■ *Web:* www.kblxfm.com	San Francisco	CA	94105	415-284-1029	764-4959
KBWF-FM 95.7 (Ctry) 201 3rd St Suite 1200 *TF:* 888-266-9653 ■ *Web:* www.957thewolf.com	San Francisco	CA	94103	415-957-0957	356-8394
KCBS-AM 740 (N/T) 865 Battery St 3rd Fl *Web:* www.kcbs.com	San Francisco	CA	94111	415-391-9970	765-4146
KDFC-FM 102.1 (Clas) 201 3rd St Suite 1200 *Web:* www.kdfc.com	San Francisco	CA	94103	415-764-1021	777-2291
KFFG-FM 97.7 (CH) 55 Hawthorne St Suite 1100 *TF:* 800-300-5364 ■ *Web:* www.kfog.com	San Francisco	CA	94105	415-981-5726	995-6867
KFOG-FM 104.5 (CH) 55 Hawthorne St Suite 1100 *Web:* www.kfog.com	San Francisco	CA	94105	415-981-5726	995-6867
KFRC-AM 15.50 (Oldies) 865 Battery St 2nd Fl *TF:* 888-456-5372 ■ *Web:* www.kfrc.com	San Francisco	CA	94111	415-391-9970	765-4146
KGO-AM 810 (N/T) 900 Front St *Web:* www.kgoam810.com	San Francisco	CA	94111	415-954-8100	954-8686
KIOI-FM 101.3 (AC) 340 Townsend St 4th Fl *TF:* 800-800-1013 ■ *Web:* www.star1013fm.com	San Francisco	CA	94107	415-975-5555	538-1000
KISQ-FM 98.1 (Urban AC) 340 Townsend St 4th Fl *TF:* 888-354-7736 ■ *Web:* www.981kissfm.com	San Francisco	CA	94107	415-975-5555	538-1000
KITS-FM 105.3 (Alt) 865 Battery St *TF:* 800-696-1053 ■ *Web:* www.live105.com	San Francisco	CA	94111	415-391-9970	765-4146
KKSF-FM 103.7 (NAC) 340 Townsend St 4th Fl *TF:* 866-900-1037 ■ *Web:* www.oldies1037.com/main.html	San Francisco	CA	94107	415-975-5555	538-1000
KMEL-FM 106.1 (Urban) 340 Townsend St 4th Fl *TF:* 800-955-5635 ■ *Web:* www.106kmel.com	San Francisco	CA	94107	415-975-5555	538-1060
KMVQ-FM 99.7 (AC) 865 Battery St *TF:* 888-456-9970 ■ *Web:* www.kmvq.com	San Francisco	CA	94111	415-391-9970	765-4146
KNBR-AM 1050 (Sports) 55 Hawthorne St Suite 1100 *Web:* www.knbr.com	San Francisco	CA	94105	415-981-5726	995-6867

Station	City	State	Zip	Phone	Fax
KOIT-FM 96.5 (AC) 201 3rd St Suite 1200 *TF:* 800-564-8965 ■ *Web:* www.koit.com	San Francisco	CA	94103	415-777-0965	896-0965
KQED-FM 88.5 (NPR) 2601 Mariposa St *TF:* 800-864-2000 ■ *Web:* www.kqed.org	San Francisco	CA	94110	415-864-2000	553-2183
KSAN-FM 107.7 (Alt) 55 Hawthorne St Suite 1100 *TF:* 888-303-2663 ■ *Web:* www.1077thebone.com	San Francisco	CA	94105	415-981-5726	995-6867
KSFO-AM 560 (N/T) 900 Front St *Web:* www.ksfo560.com	San Francisco	CA	94111	415-954-7449	658-5401
KYLD-FM 94.9 (Urban) 340 Townsend St 4th Fl *TF:* 888-333-9490 ■ *Web:* www.wild949.com	San Francisco	CA	94107	415-975-5555	538-1000

648-152 San Jose, CA

Station	City	State	Zip	Phone	Fax
KBAY-FM 94.5 (AC) 190 Pk Ctr Plaza Suite 200 *TF:* 800-948-5229 ■ *Web:* www.kbay.com	San Jose	CA	95113	408-287-5775	293-3341
KCNL-FM 104.9 (Alt) 1420 Koll Cir Suite A *TF:* 800-509-1049 ■ *Web:* www.channel1049.com	San Jose	CA	95112	408-453-5400	452-1330
KRTY-FM 95.3 (Ctry) 750 Story Rd *Web:* www.krty.com	San Jose	CA	95122	408-293-8030	995-0823
KSJO-FM 92.3 (Span) 1420 Koll Cir Suite A *TF:* 888-820-6120 ■ *Web:* www.lapreciosa.com	San Jose	CA	95112	408-453-5400	452-1330
KUFX-FM 98.5 (CR) 1420 Koll Cir Suite A *TF:* 866-985-5369 ■ *Web:* www.kufx.com	San Jose	CA	95112	408-453-5400	452-1330

648-153 Santa Fe, NM

Station	City	State	Zip	Phone	Fax
KBAC-FM 98.1 (AAA) 2502 Camino Entrada Suite C *Web:* www.kbac.com	Santa Fe	NM	87507	505-988-5222	989-3881
KSWV-AM 810 (Span) 102 Taos St *TF:* 800-794-5798	Santa Fe	NM	87505	505-989-7441	989-7607
KTRC-AM 1260 (N/T) 2502 Camino Entrada Suite C *Web:* www.airamerica.com	Santa Fe	NM	87507	505-471-1067	473-2667

648-154 Savannah, GA

Station	City	State	Zip	Phone	Fax
WAEV-FM 97.3 (AC) 245 Alfred St *Web:* www.973kissfm.com	Savannah	GA	31408	912-964-7794	964-9414
WEAS-FM 93 (Urban) 214 Television Cir *TF:* 866-399-0093 ■ *Web:* www.e93fm.com	Savannah	GA	31406	912-961-9000	961-7070
WGCO-FM 98.3 (Var) 401 Mall Blvd Suite 101D *Web:* www.adventureradio.fm	Savannah	GA	31406	912-351-9830	352-4821
WGZO-FM 103.1 (AC) 401 Mall Blvd Suite 101D *Web:* www.1031thedrive.com	Savannah	GA	31406	912-351-9830	352-4821
WIXV-FM 95.5 (CR) 214 Television Cir *TF:* 866-399-9595 ■ *Web:* www.rockofsavannah.net	Savannah	GA	31406	912-961-9000	961-7070
WJCL-FM 96.5 (Ctry) 214 Television Cir *TF:* 866-999-9650 ■ *Web:* www.kix96.com	Savannah	GA	31406	912-961-9000	961-7070
WLVH-FM 101.1 (Urban AC) 245 Alfred St *Web:* www.love1011.com	Savannah	GA	31408	912-964-7794	964-9414
WQBT-FM 94.1 (Urban) 245 Alfred St *Web:* www.941thebeat.com	Savannah	GA	31408	912-964-7794	964-9414
WRHQ-FM 105.3 (Rock) 1102 E 52nd St *Web:* www.wrhq.com	Savannah	GA	31404	912-234-1053	354-6600
WSOK-AM 1230 (Rel) 245 Alfred St *Web:* www.1230wsok.com	Savannah	GA	31408	912-964-7794	964-9414
WSVH-FM 91.1 (NPR) 12 Ocean Science Cir *TF:* 800-673-7332 ■ *Web:* www.wsvh.org	Savannah	GA	31411	912-598-3300	
WTKS-AM 1290 (N/T) 245 Alfred St *Web:* www.newsradio1290wtks.com	Savannah	GA	31408	912-964-7794	964-9414
WYKZ-FM 98.7 (AC) 245 Alfred St *Web:* www.987theriver.com	Savannah	GA	31408	912-964-7794	964-9414

648-155 Scranton, PA

Station	City	State	Zip	Phone	Fax
WEJL-AM 630 (Sports) 149 Penn Ave *Web:* www.wejl-wbax.com	Scranton	PA	18503	570-346-6555	346-6038
WEZX-FM 106.9 (Rock) 149 Penn Ave *Web:* www.rock107.com	Scranton	PA	18503	570-346-6555	346-6038
WQFN-FM 92.1 (Var) 149 Penn Ave *Web:* www.fm921radio.com	Scranton	PA	18503	570-346-6555	346-6038
WVMW-FM 91.7 (Alt) 2300 Adams Ave *Web:* www.vmfm917.org	Scranton	PA	18509	570-348-6202	961-4769
WWRR-FM 104.9 (AC) 1049 N Sekol Rd *TF:* 888-577-4487 ■ *Web:* www.105theriver.net	Scranton	PA	18504	570-344-1221	344-0996

648-156 Seattle/Tacoma, WA

Station	City	State	Zip	Phone	Fax
KBKS-FM 106.1 (CHR) 1000 Dexter Ave N Suite 100 *TF:* 888-343-1061 ■ *Web:* www.kissfmseattle.com	Seattle	WA	98109	206-805-1110	805-0923
KCMS-FM 105.3 (Rel) 19319 Fremont Ave N *Web:* www.spirit1053.com	Shoreline	WA	98133	206-546-7350	289-7792
KHHO-AM 850 (Sports) 645 Elliott Ave W Suite 400 *Web:* www.foxsports850.com	Seattle	WA	98119	206-285-2295	286-2376
KING-FM 98.1 (Clas) 10 Harrison St Suite 100 *Web:* www.king.org	Seattle	WA	98109	206-691-2981	691-2982
KIRO-FM 97.3 (N/T) 1820 Eastlake Ave E *Web:* www.mynorthwest.com	Seattle	WA	98102	206-726-7000	726-5446
KISW-FM 99.9 (Rock) 1100 Olive Way Suite 1650 *TF:* 800-783-7625 ■ *Web:* www.kisw.com	Seattle	WA	98101	206-285-7625	215-9355
KJAQ-FM 96.5 (Var) 1000 Dexter Ave N Suite 100 *TF:* 866-416-5225 ■ *Web:* www.965jackfm.com	Seattle	WA	98109	206-805-1100	805-0932
KJR-AM 950 (Sports) 351 Elliott Ave W Suite 300 *TF:* 800-829-0950 ■ *Web:* www.kjram.com	Seattle	WA	98119	206-285-2295	286-2376
KMPS-FM 94.1 1000 Dexter Ave N Suite 100 PO Box 24888 *TF:* 800-464-9436 ■ *Web:* www.kmps.com	Seattle	WA	98109	206-805-0941	805-0911
KMTT-FM 103.7 (AAA) 1100 Olive Way Suite 1650 *Web:* www.kmtt.com	Seattle	WA	98101	206-233-1037	233-8979
KNDD-FM 107.7 (Alt) 1100 Olive Way Suite 1650 *TF:* 800-423-1077 ■ *Web:* www.1077theend.com	Seattle	WA	98101	206-622-3251	682-8349
KOMO-AM 1000 (N/T) 140 4th Ave N Suite 340 *Web:* komoradio.com	Seattle	WA	98109	206-404-4000	404-3646
KPLZ-FM 101.5 (AC) 140 4th Ave N Suite 340 *TF:* 888-821-1015 ■ *Web:* www.star1015.com	Seattle	WA	98109	206-404-4000	404-3644
KPTK-AM 1090 (N/T) 1000 Dexter Ave N Suite 100 *TF:* 877-753-1090 ■ *Web:* www.am1090seattle.com	Seattle	WA	98109	206-805-1100	805-0922
KUBE-FM 93.3 (AC) 351 Elliott Ave W Suite 300 *TF:* 877-933-9393 ■ *Web:* www.kube93.com	Seattle	WA	98119	206-285-2295	286-2376
KUOW-FM 94.9 (NPR) 4518 University Way NE Suite 310 *TF:* 800-289-5869 ■ *Web:* www.kuow.org	Seattle	WA	98105	206-543-2710	543-2720
KVI-AM 570 (N/T) 140 4th Ave N Suite 340 *TF:* 877-312-5757 ■ *Web:* www.570kvi.com	Seattle	WA	98109	206-404-4000	404-3648
KZOK-FM 102.5 (CR) 1000 Dexter Ave N Suite 100 *TF:* 800-252-1025 ■ *Web:* www.kzok.com	Seattle	WA	98109	206-421-1025	805-0919

648-157 Shreveport, LA

Station	City	State	Zip	Phone	Fax
KBTT-FM 103.7 (CHR) 208 N Thomas *Web:* www.1037thabeat.fm	Shreveport	LA	71137	318-222-3122	320-0957
KDAQ-FM 89.9 (NPR) 1 University Pl PO Box 5250 *TF:* 800-552-8502 ■ *Web:* www.redriverradio.org	Shreveport	LA	71115	318-797-5150	797-5265
KDKS-FM 102.1 (Urban) 208 N Thomas *Web:* www.kdks.fm	Shreveport	LA	71137	318-222-3122	320-0102
KEEL-AM 710 (N/T) 6341 W Port Ave *Web:* 710keel.com	Shreveport	LA	71129	318-688-1130	
KLKL-FM 95.7 (Oldies) 208 N Thomas *Web:* www.klkl.fm	Shreveport	LA	71137	318-222-3122	
KRUF-FM 94.5 (CHR) 6341 W Port Ave *Web:* k945.com	Shreveport	LA	71129	318-688-1130	
KTAL-FM 98.1 (CR) 208 N Thomas *Web:* www.98rocks.fm	Shreveport	LA	71137	318-222-3122	459-1493
KTUX-FM 98.9 (Rock) 6341 W Port Ave *Web:* www.ktux.com	Shreveport	LA	71129	318-688-1130	687-8574
KVKI-FM 96.5 (AC) 6341 W Port Ave *Web:* www.965kvki.com	Shreveport	LA	71129	318-688-1130	687-8574
KWKH-AM 1130 (Sports) 6341 W Port Ave *Web:* www.am1130thefan.com	Shreveport	LA	71129	318-688-1130	687-8574
KXKS-FM 93.7 (Ctry) 6341 W Port Ave *Web:* mykisscountry937.com	Shreveport	LA	71129	318-688-1130	

648-158 Sioux Falls, SD

Station	City	State	Zip	Phone	Fax
KELO-AM 1320 (N/T) 500 S Phillips Ave *TF:* 800-529-5356 ■ *Web:* www.keloam.com	Sioux Falls	SD	57104	605-331-5350	336-0415
KELO-FM 92.5 (AC) 500 S Phillips Ave *Web:* www.kelofm.com	Sioux Falls	SD	57104	605-331-5350	336-0415
KIKN-FM 100.5 (Ctry) 5100 S Tennis Ln *Web:* www.kikn.com	Sioux Falls	SD	57108	605-339-1140	339-2735
KKLS-FM 104.7 (CHR) 5100 S Tennis Ln *Web:* www.hot1047.com	Sioux Falls	SD	57108	605-339-1140	339-2735
KMXC-FM 97.3 (AC) 5100 S Tennis Ln *Web:* www.mix97-3.com	Sioux Falls	SD	57108	605-339-1140	339-2735
KNWC-AM 1270 (Rel) 6300 S Tallgrass Ave *Web:* www.knwc.org	Sioux Falls	SD	57108	605-339-1270	339-1271
KRRO-FM 103.7 (Rock) 500 S Phillips Ave *Web:* www.krro.com	Sioux Falls	SD	57104	605-331-5350	336-0415
KRSD-FM 88.1 (Clas) Augustana College PO Box 737	Sioux Falls	SD	57197	320-363-7702	363-4998
KSOO-AM 1140 (N/T) 5100 S Tennis Ln *Web:* www.ksoo.com	Sioux Falls	SD	57108	605-339-1140	339-2735
KTWB-FM 101.9 (Ctry) 500 S Phillips Ave *Web:* www.ktwb.com	Sioux Falls	SD	57104	605-331-5350	336-0415
KXRB-AM 1000 (Ctry) 5100 S Tennis Ln *Web:* www.kxrb.com	Sioux Falls	SD	57108	605-339-1140	339-2735
KYBB-FM 102.7 (CR) 5100 S Tennis Ln *Web:* www.b1027.com	Sioux Falls	SD	57108	605-339-1140	339-2735

648-159 South Bend, IN

Station	City	State	Zip	Phone	Fax
WHPZ-FM 96.9 (Rel) 61300 S Ironwood Rd *Web:* www.pulsefm.com	South Bend	IN	46614	574-291-8200	291-9043

Station	City	State	Zip	Phone	Fax
WNDV-FM 92.9 (CHR) 3371 Cleveland Rd Suite 300 *Web:* www.u93.com	South Bend	IN	46628	574-273-9300	273-9090

648-160 Spokane, WA

Station	City	State	Zip	Phone	Fax
KBBD-FM 103.9 (AC) 1601 E 57th Ave *Web:* www.1039bobfm.com	Spokane	WA	99223	509-448-1000	448-7015
KDRK-FM 93.7 (Ctry) 1601 E 57th Ave *Web:* www.937thecat.com	Spokane	WA	99223	509-448-1000	448-7015
KEYF-FM 101.1 (Oldies) 1601 E 57th Ave *Web:* www.oldies1011.com	Spokane	WA	99223	509-448-1000	448-7015
KGA-AM 1510 (N/T) 1601 E 57th Ave *Web:* www.1510kga.com	Spokane	WA	99223	509-448-1000	448-7015
KHTQ-FM 92.5 (Rock) 500 W Boone Ave *Web:* www.rock945.com	Spokane	WA	99201	509-324-4200	352-0676
KISC-FM 98.1 (AC) 808 E Sprague Ave *Web:* www.literockkiss.com	Spokane	WA	99202	509-242-2400	242-1160
KJRB-AM 790 (Sports) 1601 E 57th Ave *Web:* www.790kfan.com	Spokane	WA	99223	509-448-1000	448-7015
KKZX-FM 98.9 (CR) 808 E Sprague Ave *Web:* www.kkzx.com	Spokane	WA	99202	509-242-2400	242-1160
KPBX-FM 91.1 (NPR) 2319 N Monroe St *TF:* 800-328-5729 ■ *Web:* www.kpbx.org	Spokane	WA	99205	509-328-5729	328-5764
KPTQ-AM 1280 (N/T) 808 E Sprague Ave *Web:* www.1280kptq.com	Spokane	WA	99202	509-242-2400	242-1160
KXLY-AM 920 (N/T) 500 W Boone Ave *Web:* www.kxly.com	Spokane	WA	99201	509-324-4200	325-0676
KXLY-FM 99.9 (AC) 500 W Boone Ave *Web:* www.classy99.com	Spokane	WA	99201	509-324-4200	325-0676
KZBD-FM 105.7 (Rock) 1601 E 57th Ave *TF:* 800-718-7874 ■ *Web:* www.1057thepeak.com	Spokane	WA	99223	509-448-1000	448-7015
KZZU-FM 92.9 (CHR) 500 W Boone Ave *Web:* www.kzzu.com	Spokane	WA	99201	509-324-4200	325-0676

648-161 Springfield, IL

Station	City	State	Zip	Phone	Fax
WDBR-FM 103.7 (CHR) 3501 E Sangamon Ave *Web:* www.wdbr.com	Springfield	IL	62707	217-753-5400	753-7902
WFMB-AM 1450 (Sports) 3055 S 4th St *Web:* www.sportsradio1450.com	Springfield	IL	62703	217-544-9855	528-5348
WFMB-FM 104.5 (Ctry) 3055 S 4th St *Web:* www.wfmb.com	Springfield	IL	62703	217-544-9855	528-5348
WMAY-AM 970 (N/T) 210 S 5th St *Web:* www.wmay.com	Springfield	IL	62701	217-629-7970	629-7952
WNNS-FM 98.7 (AC) PO Box 460 *Web:* www.wnns.com	Springfield	IL	62705	217-629-5483	629-7952
WQQL-FM 101.9 (Oldies) 3501 E Sangamon Ave *Web:* www.cool1019.com	Springfield	IL	62707	217-753-5400	753-7902
WTAX-AM 1240 (N/T) 3501 E Sangamon Ave *Web:* www.wtax.com	Springfield	IL	62707	217-753-5400	753-7902
WUIS-FM 91.9 (NPR) University of Illinois at Springfield 1 University Plaza WUIS-130 *Web:* www.wuis.org	Springfield	IL	62703	217-206-6516	206-6527
WXAJ-FM 99.7 (CHR) 3055 S 4th St *Web:* www.997kissfm.com	Springfield	IL	62703	217-528-3033	528-5348
WYMG-FM 100.5 (CR) 3501 E Sangamon Ave *Web:* www.wymg.com	Springfield	IL	62707	217-753-5400	753-7902

648-162 Springfield, MA

Station	City	State	Zip	Phone	Fax
WHYN-AM 560 (N/T) 1331 Main St 4th Fl *TF:* 800-331-9496 ■ *Web:* www.whyn.com	Springfield	MA	01103	413-781-1011	734-4434
WHYN-FM 93.1 (AC) 1331 Main St 4th Fl *TF:* 888-293-9310 ■ *Web:* www.mix931.com	Springfield	MA	01103	413-781-1011	
WMAS-AM 1450 (Nost) 1000 W Columbus Ave *TF:* 800-937-9627 ■ *Web:* www.am1450wmas.com	Springfield	MA	01105	413-737-1414	737-1488
WMAS-FM 94.7 (AC) 1000 W Columbus Ave *TF:* 800-937-9627 ■ *Web:* www.947wmas.com	Springfield	MA	01105	413-737-1414	737-1488
WNNZ-AM 640 (NPR) 1331 Main St 4th Fl *Web:* www.wnnz.com	Springfield	MA	01103	413-781-1011	
WPKX-FM 97.9 (Ctry) 1331 Main St 4th Fl *TF:* 800-345-9759 ■ *Web:* www.kix979.com	Springfield	MA	01103	413-781-1011	734-4434
WRNX-FM 100.9 (AAA) 1331 Main St 4th Fl *TF:* 800-977-1009 ■ *Web:* www.wrnx.com	Springfield	MA	01103	413-781-1011	536-1153
WSCB-FM 89.9 (Urban) 263 Alden St *Web:* www.springfieldcollege.edu	Springfield	MA	01109	413-748-3131	748-3473
WTCC-FM 90.7 (Var) 1 Armory Sq *Web:* www.wtccfm.org	Springfield	MA	01105	413-781-6628	755-6305

648-163 Springfield, MO

Station	City	State	Zip	Phone	Fax
KGBX-FM 105.9 (AC) 1856 S Glenstone Ave *TF:* 800-445-1059 ■ *Web:* www.kgbx.com	Springfield	MO	65804	417-890-5555	890-5050
KGMY-AM 1400 (Sports) 1856 S Glenstone Ave *TF:* 800-996-9653 ■ *Web:* www.espn1400.com	Springfield	MO	65804	417-890-5555	890-5050
KKLH-FM 104.7 (CR) 319 E Battlefield St Suite B *Web:* www.kklh.fm	Springfield	MO	65807	417-886-5677	886-2155
KOSP-FM 105.1 (Oldies) 319 E Battlefield St Suite B *Web:* www.kosp.fm	Springfield	MO	65807	417-886-5677	886-2155
KSMS-FM 90.5 (NPR) Missouri State University 901 S National Ave *TF:* 800-767-5768 ■ *Web:* www.ksmu.org	Springfield	MO	65897	417-836-5878	836-5889
KSMU-FM 91.1 (NPR) Missouri State University 901 S National Ave *TF:* 800-767-5768 ■ *Web:* www.ksmu.org	Springfield	MO	65897	417-836-5878	836-5889
KSPW-FM 96.5 (CHR) 2330 W Grand St *Web:* www.power965jams.com	Springfield	MO	65802	417-865-6614	865-9643
KSWF-FM 100.5 (Ctry) 1856 S Glenstone Ave *TF:* 800-996-9653 ■ *Web:* www.1005thewolf.com	Springfield	MO	65804	417-890-5555	823-8505
KTOZ-FM 95.5 (AC) 1856 S Glenstone Ave *TF:* 800-757-9550 ■ *Web:* www.alice955.com	Springfield	MO	65804	417-890-5555	890-5050
KTTS-FM 94.7 (Ctry) 2330 W Grand St *TF:* 800-765-5887 ■ *Web:* www.ktts.com	Springfield	MO	65802	417-865-6614	865-9643
KTXR-FM 101.3 (AC) 3000 E Chestnut Expy *TF:* 800-749-8001 ■ *Web:* www.ktxrfm.com	Springfield	MO	65802	417-862-3751	869-7675
KWTO-AM 560 (N/T) 3000 E Chestnut Expy *TF:* 800-749-8001 ■ *Web:* www.newstalk560.com	Springfield	MO	65802	417-862-3751	869-7675
KXUS-FM 97.3 (CR) 1856 S Glenstone Ave *TF:* 800-494-8858 ■ *Web:* www.us97.com	Springfield	MO	65804	417-890-5555	890-5050

648-164 Stamford/Bridgeport, CT

Station	City	State	Zip	Phone	Fax
WCUM-AM 1450 (Span) 1862 Commerce Dr *Web:* www.radiocumbre.am	Bridgeport	CT	06605	203-335-1450	337-1216
WEBE-FM 108 (AC) 2 Lafayette Sq *TF:* 800-932-3108 ■ *Web:* www.webe108.com	Bridgeport	CT	06604	203-333-9108	384-0600
WICC-AM 600 (N/T) 2 Lafayette Sq *Web:* www.wicc600.com	Bridgeport	CT	06604	203-333-9108	384-0600
WPKN-FM 89.5 (Var) 244 University Ave *TF:* 888-331-9756 ■ *Web:* www.wpkn.org	Bridgeport	CT	06604	203-331-9756	331-1314

648-165 Stockton, CA

Station	City	State	Zip	Phone	Fax
KJOY-FM 99.3 (AC) 4643 Quail Lakes Dr Suite 100 *Web:* www.993kjoy.com	Stockton	CA	95207	209-476-1230	951-0033
KLVS -FM 107.3 (Span) 2171 Ralph Ave	Stockton	CA	95206	707-528-9236	528-9246
KSTN-AM 1420 (Oldies) 2171 Ralph Ave *Web:* www.kstn1420.com	Stockton	CA	95206	209-948-5786	
KWIN-FM 97.7 (CHR) 4643 Quail Lakes Dr Suite 100 *Web:* www.kwin.com	Stockton	CA	95207	209-476-1230	951-0030
KWNN-FM 98.3 (CHR) 4643 Quail Lakes Dr Suite 100 *Web:* www.kwin.com	Stockton	CA	95207	209-476-1230	951-0030
KYCC-FM 90.1 (Rel) 9019 W Ln *TF:* 800-654-5254 ■ *Web:* www.kycc.org	Stockton	CA	95210	209-477-3690	477-2762

648-166 Syracuse, NY

Station	City	State	Zip	Phone	Fax
WAER-FM 88.3 (Jazz) 795 Ostram Ave *Web:* www.waer.org	Syracuse	NY	13244	315-443-4021	443-2148
WAQX-FM 95.7 1064 James St *Web:* www.waqx.com	Syracuse	NY	13203	315-472-0200	472-1146
WBBS-FM 104.7 (Ctry) 500 Plum St Suite 100 *Web:* www.b1047.net	Syracuse	NY	13204	315-472-9797	472-2323
WHEN-AM 620 (Sports) 500 Plum St Suite 100 *Web:* www.sportsradio620.com	Syracuse	NY	13204	315-472-9797	472-2323
WJPZ-FM 89.1 (CHR) 316 Waverly Ave *Web:* www.z89online.com	Syracuse	NY	13210	315-443-4689	443-4379
WKRL-FM 100.9 (Alt) 235 Walton St *Web:* www.krock.com	Syracuse	NY	13202	315-472-9111	472-1888
WLTI-FM 105.9 1064 James St *Web:* www.lite1059.com	Syracuse	NY	13203	315-472-0200	478-5625
WMHR-FM 102.9 (Rel) 4044 Makyes Rd *TF:* 800-677-1881	Syracuse	NY	13215	315-469-5051	469-4066
WNTQ-FM 93.1 1064 James St *Web:* www.93q.com	Syracuse	NY	13203	315-472-0200	478-5625
WPHR-FM 106.9 (Urban) 500 Plum St Suite 100 *Web:* www.power1069.com	Syracuse	NY	13204	315-472-9797	472-2323
WSYR-AM 570 (N/T) 500 Plum St Suite 100 *Web:* www.wsyr.com	Syracuse	NY	13204	315-472-9797	472-2323
WTKW-FM 99.5 (CR) 235 Walton St *Web:* tk99.net	Syracuse	NY	13202	315-472-9111	472-1888
WYYY-FM 94.5 (AC) 500 Plum St Suite 100 *Web:* www.y94fm.com	Syracuse	NY	13204	315-472-9797	472-2323

648-167 Tallahassee, FL

Station	City	State	Zip	Phone	Fax
WAIB-FM 103.1 (Ctry) 3000 Olson Rd *Web:* www.1031thewolf.com	Tallahassee	FL	32308	850-386-8004	422-1897
WBZE-FM 98.9 (AC) 3411 W Tharpe St *Web:* www.mystar98.com	Tallahassee	FL	32303	850-201-3000	201-2329

Station	City	State	Zip	Phone	Fax
WFSQ-FM 91.5 (Clas) 1600 Red Barber Plaza; *TF:* 800-829-8809 ■ *Web:* www.wfsu.org	Tallahassee	FL	32310	850-487-3086	487-2611
WFSU-FM 88.9 (NPR) 1600 Red Barber Plaza; *TF:* 800-829-8809 ■ *Web:* www.wfsu.org	Tallahassee	FL	32310	850-487-3086	487-2611
WGLF-FM 104.1 (CR) 3411 W Tharpe St; *Web:* www.gulf104.com	Tallahassee	FL	32303	850-201-3000	201-2329
WHBX-FM 96.1 (Urban AC) 3411 W Tharpe St; *Web:* www.961jamz.com	Tallahassee	FL	32303	850-201-3000	205-3711
WHTF-FM 104.9 (CHR) 3000 Olsen Rd; *Web:* www.hot1049.com	Tallahassee	FL	32308	850-386-8004	422-1897
WNLS-AM 1270 (Sports) 325 John Knox Rd Bldg G; *Web:* www.wnls.com	Tallahassee	FL	32303	850-422-3107	383-0747
WQTL-FM 106.1 (Rock) 3000 Olson Rd; *Web:* www.q1061.fm	Tallahassee	FL	32308	850-386-8004	422-1897
WSLA-FM 100.7 (N/T) 325 John Knox Rd Bldg G; *Web:* www.wflafm.com	Tallahassee	FL	32303	850-422-3107	383-0747
WTLY-FM 107.1 (AC) 325 John Knox Rd Bldg G; *Web:* www.magic1071.com	Tallahassee	FL	32303	850-422-3107	383-0747
WTNT-FM 94.9 (Ctry) 325 John Knox Rd Bldg G; *Web:* www.wtntfm.com	Tallahassee	FL	32303	850-422-3107	383-0747
WXSR-FM 101.5 (Alt) 325 John Knox Rd Bldg G; *Web:* www.x1015.com	Tallahassee	FL	32303	850-422-3107	383-0747

648-168 Tampa/Saint Petersburg, FL

Station	City	State	Zip	Phone	Fax
WBTB-FM 95.7 (Urban) 4002 W Gandy Blvd; *Web:* www.957thebeat.com	Tampa	FL	33611	813-839-9393	831-3299
WDAE-AM 620 (Sports) 4002 W Gandy Blvd; *TF:* 888-546-4620 ■ *Web:* www.620wdae.com	Tampa	FL	33611	813-839-9393	837-0300
WDUV-FM 105.5 (AC) 11300 4th St N Suite 300; *TF:* 888-723-9388 ■ *Web:* www.wduv.com	Saint Petersburg	FL	33716	727-579-2000	579-2271
WFLA-AM 970 (N/T) 4002 W Gandy Blvd; *Web:* www.970wfla.com	Tampa	FL	33611	813-839-9393	837-0300
WFLZ-FM 93.3 (CHR) 4002 W Gandy Blvd; *Web:* www.933flz.com	Tampa	FL	33611	813-839-9393	831-3299
WFUS-FM 103.5 (Ctry) 4002 W Gandy Blvd; *Web:* www.us1035.com	Tampa	FL	33611	813-839-9393	831-3299
WGUL-AM 860 (N/T) 5211 W Laurel St Suite 101; *Web:* www.860wgul.com	Tampa	FL	33607	813-639-1903	639-1272
WHPT-FM 102.5 (CR) 11300 4th St N Suite 300; *TF:* 800-771-1025 ■ *Web:* www.theboneonline.com	Saint Petersburg	FL	33716	727-579-2000	579-2271
WLLD-FM 98.7 (CHR) 9721 Executive Ctr Dr N Suite 200; *Web:* www.wild987.com	Saint Petersburg	FL	33702	727-579-1925	579-9250
WMTX-FM 100.7 (AC) 4002 W Gandy Blvd; *Web:* www.mixmeansvariety.com	Tampa	FL	33611	813-839-9393	831-3299
WPOI-FM 101.5 (CR) 11300 4th St N Suite 300	Saint Petersburg	FL	33716	727-579-2000	
WQYK-AM 1010 (Ctry) 9721 Executive Ctr Dr N Suite 200; **Fax Area Code:* 813 ■ *Web:* www.wqyk.com	Saint Petersburg	FL	33702	727-579-1925	636-0995*
WQYK-FM 99.5 (Ctry) 9721 Executive Ctr Dr N Suite 200; **Fax Area Code:* 813 ■ *TF:* 800-992-1099 ■ *Web:* www.wqyk.com	Saint Petersburg	FL	33702	727-579-1925	636-0995*
WRBQ-FM 104.7 (Oldies) 9721 Executive Ctr Dr N Suite 200	Saint Petersburg	FL	33702	727-572-1047	
WRXB-AM 1590 (Urban) 3551 42nd Ave S Suite B-106; *TF:* 877-900-1590 ■ *Web:* www.wrxb.us	Saint Petersburg	FL	33711	727-865-1591	866-1728
WSJT-FM 94.1 (NAC) 9721 Executive Ctr Dr N Suite 200; *Web:* www.wsjt.com	Saint Petersburg	FL	33702	727-579-1925	579-9250
WSUN-FM 97.1 (Alt) 11300 4th St N Suite 300; *TF:* 877-327-9797 ■ *Web:* www.97xonline.com	Saint Petersburg	FL	33716	727-579-2000	579-2271
WTBN-AM 570 (Rel) 5211 W Laurel St Suite 101; *Web:* www.bayword.com	Tampa	FL	33607	813-639-1903	639-1272
WTMP-AM 1150 (Urban) 407 N Howard Ave; *Web:* www.wtmp.com	Tampa	FL	33609	813-259-9867	254-9867
WUSF-FM 89.7 (NPR) 4202 E Fowler Ave TVB 100; *TF:* 800-741-9090 ■ *Web:* www.wusf.usf.edu/wusf-fm	Tampa	FL	33620	813-974-8700	974-5016
WWRM-FM 94.9 (AC) 11300 4th St N Suite 300; *Web:* www.949online.com	Saint Petersburg	FL	33716	727-577-7131	578-1015
WXGL-FM 107.3 (AC) 11300 4th St N Suite 300; *TF:* 800-242-1073 ■ *Web:* www.1073theeagle.com	Saint Petersburg	FL	33716	727-579-2000	579-2271
WXTB-FM 97.9 (Rock) 4002 W Gandy Blvd; *Web:* www.98rock.com	Tampa	FL	33611	813-839-9393	831-3299
WYUU-FM 92.5 (Span) 9721 Executive Ctr Dr N Suite 200; *Web:* 925maxima.radio.com	Saint Petersburg	FL	33702	727-579-1925	

648-169 Toledo, OH

Station	City	State	Zip	Phone	Fax
WCWA-AM 1230 (Sports) 125 S Superior St; *Web:* www.wcwa.com	Toledo	OH	43604	419-244-8321	244-7631
WGTE-FM 91.3 (NPR) 1270 S Detroit Ave PO Box 30; *TF:* 800-243-9483 ■ *Web:* www.wgte.org	Toledo	OH	43614	419-380-4600	380-4710
WIOT-FM 104.7 (Rock) 125 S Superior St; *Web:* www.wiot.com	Toledo	OH	43604	419-244-8321	244-7631
WJUC-FM 107.3 (Urban) 5902 Southwyck Blvd Suite 101; *Web:* www.thejuice1073.com	Toledo	OH	43614	419-861-9582	861-2866
WKKO-FM 99.9 (Ctry) 3225 Arlington Ave; *Web:* www.k100country.com	Toledo	OH	43614	419-725-5700	725-5805
WLQR-AM 1470 (Sports) 3225 Arlington Ave; *Web:* www.1470theticket.com	Toledo	OH	43614	419-385-2507	385-2902
WRQN-FM 93.5 (Oldies) 3225 Arlington Ave; *Web:* www.935wrqn.com	Toledo	OH	43614	419-385-2507	385-2902
WRVF-FM 101.5 (AC) 125 S Superior St; *Web:* www.1015theriver.com	Toledo	OH	43604	419-244-8321	244-7631
WSPD-AM 1370 (N/T) 125 S Superior St; *TF:* 866-253-3993 ■ *Web:* www.wspd.com	Toledo	OH	43604	419-244-8321	244-7631
WVKS-FM 92.5 (CHR) 125 S Superior St; *TF:* 877-547-7366 ■ *Web:* www.925kissfm.com	Toledo	OH	43604	419-244-8321	244-7631
WWWM-FM 105.5 (AC) 3225 Arlington Ave; *Web:* www.star105toledo.com	Toledo	OH	43614	419-725-5700	725-5805
WXKR-FM 94.5 (CR) 3225 Arlington Ave; *TF:* 866-240-9945 ■ *Web:* www.wxkr.com	Toledo	OH	43614	419-725-5700	725-5805

648-170 Topeka, KS

Station	City	State	Zip	Phone	Fax
KDVV-FM 100.3 (CR) 825 S Kansas Ave Suite 100; *TF:* 866-297-1003 ■ *Web:* www.v100rocks.com	Topeka	KS	66612	785-272-2122	272-6219
KMAJ-AM 1440 (N/T) 825 S Kansas Ave Suite 100; *TF:* 877-297-1077 ■ *Web:* www.kmaj.com	Topeka	KS	66612	785-272-2122	272-6219
KMAJ-FM 107.7 (AC) 825 S Kansas Ave Suite 100; *TF:* 877-297-1077 ■ *Web:* www.kmaj.com	Topeka	KS	66612	785-272-2122	272-6219
KTPK-FM 106.9 (Ctry) 2121 SW Chelsea Dr; *TF:* 888-291-1069 ■ *Web:* www.ktpk1069.com	Topeka	KS	66614	785-273-1069	273-0123
KWIC-FM 99.3 (Oldies) 825 S Kansas Ave Suite 100; *Web:* www.eagle993.com	Topeka	KS	66612	785-272-2122	272-6219
WIBW-AM 580 (N/T) 1210 SW Executive Dr PO Box 1818; *Web:* www.am580wibw.com	Topeka	KS	66615	785-272-3456	228-7282
WIBW-FM 94.5 (Ctry) 1210 SW Executive Dr PO Box 1818; *Web:* www.94country.com	Topeka	KS	66601	785-272-3456	228-7282

648-171 Toronto, ON

Station	City	State	Zip	Phone	Fax
CBL-FM 94.1 (Clas) PO Box 500 Stn A; *TF:* 866-306-4636 ■ *Web:* www.cbc.ca/toronto	Toronto	ON	M5W1E6	416-205-3311	205-2344
CBLA-FM 99.1 (CBC) PO Box 500 Stn A; *TF:* 866-306-4636 ■ *Web:* www.cbc.ca/programguide/radio	Toronto	ON	M5W1E6	416-205-3311	205-6336
CFNY-FM 102.1 (Alt) 25 Dock Side Dr; *Web:* www.edge.ca	Toronto	ON	M5A0B5	416-221-0107	847-3300
CHIN-AM 1540 (Ethnic) 622 College St 4th Fl; *TF:* 888-944-2446 ■ *Web:* www.chinradio.com	Toronto	ON	M6G1B6	416-531-9991	531-5274
CHIN-FM 100.7 (Ethnic) 622 College St 4th Fl; *TF:* 888-944-2446 ■ *Web:* www.chinradio.com	Toronto	ON	M6G1B6	416-531-9991	531-5274
CHUM-AM 1050 (Oldies) 1331 Yonge St; *Web:* www.1050chum.com	Toronto	ON	M4T1Y1	416-925-6666	926-4026
CHUM-FM 104.5 (AC) 1331 Yonge St; *Web:* www.chumfm.com	Toronto	ON	M4T1Y1	416-925-6666	926-4026
CILQ-FM 107.1 (CR) 25 Dock Side Dr; *Web:* www.q107.com	Toronto	ON	M5A0B5	416-221-0107	847-3300

648-172 Trenton, NJ

Station	City	State	Zip	Phone	Fax
WBUD-AM 1260 (Oldies) 109 Walters Ave	Trenton	NJ	08638	609-882-4600	
WIMG-AM 1300 (Rel) 1842 S Broad St; *Web:* www.wimg1300.com	Trenton	NJ	08610	609-695-1300	278-1588
WKXW-FM 101.5 (N/T) 109 Walters Ave PO Box 5698; *TF:* 800-678-9599 ■ *Web:* www.nj1015.com	Trenton	NJ	08638	609-771-8181	406-7956
WNJN-FM 89.7 (NPR) PO Box 777; *TF:* 800-363-5151 ■ *Web:* www.njn.net/radio	Trenton	NJ	08625	609-777-5000	633-2927
WNJT-FM 88.1 (NPR) PO Box 777; *TF:* 800-363-5151 ■ *Web:* www.njn.net/radio	Trenton	NJ	08625	609-777-5000	777-5217
WWFM-FM 89.1 (Clas) PO Box B; *TF:* 888-232-1212 ■ *Web:* www.wwfm.org	Trenton	NJ	08690	609-587-8989	570-3863

648-173 Tucson, AZ

Station	City	State	Zip	Phone	Fax
KFMA-FM 92.1 (Alt) 3871 N Commerce Dr; *Web:* www.kfma.com	Tucson	AZ	85705	520-622-6711	407-4600
KHYT-FM 107.5 (CR) 575 W Roger Rd; *Web:* www.rock1075.com	Tucson	AZ	85705	520-887-1000	887-6397
KIIM-FM 99.5 (Ctry) 575 W Roger Rd; *Web:* www.kiimfm.com	Tucson	AZ	85705	520-887-1000	887-6397
KLPX-FM 96.1 (Rock) 3871 N Commerce Dr; *Web:* www.klpx.com	Tucson	AZ	85705	520-622-6711	407-4600
KMXZ-FM 94.9 (AC) 7280 E Rosewood; *Web:* www.mixfm.com	Tucson	AZ	85710	520-722-5486	
KNST-AM 790 (N/T) 3202 N Oracle Rd; *Web:* www.knst.com	Tucson	AZ	85705	520-618-2100	618-2135

Station	City	State	Zip	Phone	Fax
KOHT-FM 98.3 (Urban) 3202 N Oracle Rd *Web:* www.hot983.com	Tucson	AZ	85705	520-618-2100	618-2135
KRQQ-FM 93.7 (CHR) 3202 N Oracle Rd *Web:* www.krq.com	Tucson	AZ	85705	520-618-2100	618-2135
KTUC-AM 1400 (Nost) 575 W Roger Rd *Web:* www.1400ktuc.net	Tucson	AZ	85705	520-887-1000	887-6397
KUAT-FM 90.5 (Clas) PO Box 210067 *Web:* radio.azpm.org/classical	Tucson	AZ	85721	520-621-5828	621-3360
KUAZ-FM 89.1 (NPR) PO Box 210067 *TF:* 800-521-5828 ■ *Web:* www.kuaz.org	Tucson	AZ	85721	520-621-5828	621-3360
KWNTFM 92.9 (AAA) 3202 N Oracle Rd *Web:* www.929themountain.com	Tucson	AZ	85705	520-618-2100	618-2135

648-174 Tulsa, OK

Station	City	State	Zip	Phone	Fax
KBEZ-FM 92.9 (AC) 7030 S Yale Ave Suite 711 *Web:* www.kbez.com	Tulsa	OK	74136	918-492-2020	496-1937
KFAQ-AM 1170 (N/T) 4590 E 29th St *Web:* www.1170kfaq.com	Tulsa	OK	74114	918-743-7814	743-7613
KHTT-FM 106.9 (CHR) 7030 S Yale Ave Suite 711 *Web:* www.khits.com	Tulsa	OK	74136	918-492-2020	496-1937
KJSR-FM 103.3 (CR) 7136 S Yale Ave Suite 500 *Web:* www.star103fm.com	Tulsa	OK	74136	918-493-7400	493-2376
KMOD-FM 97.5 (Rock) 2625 S Memorial Dr *Web:* www.kmod.com	Tulsa	OK	74129	918-388-5100	665-0555
KMYZ-FM 104.5 (Alt) 5810 E Skelly Dr Suite 801 *Web:* www.edgetulsa.com	Tulsa	OK	74135	918-665-3131	663-6622
KQLL-FM 106.1 (Oldies) 2625 S Memorial Dr *Web:* www.kooltulsa.com	Tulsa	OK	74129	918-664-2810	665-0555
KRAV-FM 96.5 (AC) 7136 S Yale Ave Suite 500 *Web:* www.mix96tulsa.com	Tulsa	OK	74136	918-493-7400	
KRMG-AM 740 (N/T) 7136 S Yale Ave Suite 500 *Web:* www.krmg.com	Tulsa	OK	74136	918-493-7400	493-2376
KTBT-FM 92.1 (Urban) 2625 S Memorial Dr *Web:* www.921thebeat.com	Tulsa	OK	74129	918-664-2810	665-0555
KTBZ-AM 1430 (Sports) 2625 S Memorial Dr *Web:* www.1300thebuzz.com/main.html	Tulsa	OK	74129	918-664-2810	665-0555
KVOO-FM 98.5 (Ctry) 4590 E 29th St *Web:* www.kvoo.com	Tulsa	OK	74114	918-743-7814	743-7613
KWEN-FM 95.5 (Ctry) 7136 S Yale Ave Suite 500 *Web:* www.k955fm.com	Tulsa	OK	74136	918-493-7400	
KWGS-FM 89.5 (NPR) 800 Tucker Dr *TF:* 888-594-5947 ■ *Web:* www.kwgs.org	Tulsa	OK	74104	918-631-2577	631-3695
KXOJ-FM 100.9 (Rel) 2448 E 81st St Suite 5500 *Web:* www.kxoj.com	Tulsa	OK	74137	918-492-2660	492-8840

648-175 Tupelo, MS

Station	City	State	Zip	Phone	Fax
WAFR-FM 88.3 (Rel) PO Box 2440 *Web:* www.afr.net/newafr/default.asp	Tupelo	MS	38803	662-844-8888	842-6791
WATP-FM 90.7 (Rel) PO Box 2440 *Web:* www.afr.net	Tupelo	MS	38803	662-844-8888	842-6791
WBVV-FM 99.3 (Rel) 5026 Cliff Gooklin Blvd	Tupelo	MS	38801	662-842-1067	844-2887
WESE-FM 92.5 (Urban) 5026 Cliff Gookin Blvd *Web:* www.925jamz.com	Tupelo	MS	38801	662-842-1067	844-2887
WFTA-FM 101.9 (AC) 1241 Cliff Gookin Blvd	Tupelo	MS	38803	662-862-3191	842-9568
WSEL-FM 96.7 (Rel) PO Box 3788	Tupelo	MS	38803	662-489-0297	489-0297
WSYE-FM 93.3 (AC) 2214 S Gloster St *Web:* www.sunny933fm.com	Tupelo	MS	38801	662-842-7658	842-0197
WTUP-AM 1490 (Sports) 5026 Cliff Gookin Blvd *Web:* www.wtup1490.com	Tupelo	MS	38801	662-842-1067	844-2887
WWKZ-FM 103.9 (CHR) 5026 Cliff Gookin Blvd *Web:* www.kz103.com	Tupelo	MS	38801	662-842-1067	844-2887
WWMS-FM 97.5 (Ctry) 2214 S Gloster St *Web:* www.miss98.com	Tupelo	MS	38802	662-842-7658	842-0197
WWZD-FM 106.7 (Ctry) 5026 Cliff Gookin Blvd *Web:* www.wizard106.com	Tupelo	MS	38801	662-842-1067	844-2887
WZLQ-FM 98.5 (Rock) 2214 S Gloster St *Web:* www.z985.net	Tupelo	MS	38801	662-842-7658	842-0197

648-176 Tuscaloosa, AL

Station	City	State	Zip	Phone	Fax
WBEI-FM 101.7 (AC) 142 Skyland Blvd *Web:* www.b1017.fm	Tuscaloosa	AL	35405	205-345-7200	349-1715
WDGM-FM 99.1 (Oldies) 142 Skyland Blvd	Tuscaloosa	AL	35405	205-345-7200	349-1715
WQZZ-FM 104.3 (Urban AC) 601 Greensboro Ave Suite 507	Tuscaloosa	AL	35401	205-345-4787	345-4790
WRTR -AM 105.9 (Sports) 3900 11th Ave S *Web:* www.talkradio1059.com	Tuscaloosa	AL	35401	205-344-4589	366-9774
WRTR-FM 105.5 (Rock) 2121 9th St Suite B *Web:* www.rock105online.com	Tuscaloosa	AL	35402	205-344-4589	366-9774
WTBC-AM 1230 (N/T) 2110 McFarland Blvd E Suite C *TF:* 800-518-1977 ■ *Web:* www.wtbc1230.com	Tuscaloosa	AL	35404	205-758-5523	752-9696
WTSK-AM 790 (Rel) 142 Skyland Blvd	Tuscaloosa	AL	35405	205-345-7200	349-1715
WTUG-FM 92.9 (Urban) 142 Skyland Blvd *Web:* www.wtug.com	Tuscaloosa	AL	35405	205-345-7200	349-1715
WTXT-FM 98.1 (Ctry) 3900 11th Ave S *Web:* www.98txt.com	Tuscaloosa	AL	35401	205-344-4589	366-9774
WUAL-FM 91.5 (NPR) University of Alabama Phifer Hall Suite 166 *TF:* 800-654-4262 ■ *Web:* www.wual.ua.edu	Tuscaloosa	AL	35487	205-348-6644	
WWPG-AM 1280 (Rel) 601 Greensboro Ave Suite 507	Tuscaloosa	AL	35401	205-345-4787	345-4790
WZBQ-FM 94.1 (CHR) 3900 11th Ave S *Web:* www.941zbq.com	Tuscaloosa	AL	35401	205-344-4589	366-9774

648-177 Vancouver, BC

Station	City	Province	Postal Code	Phone	Fax
CHQM-FM 103.5 (AC) 380 W 2nd Ave Suite 300 *Web:* www.qmfm.com	Vancouver	BC	V5Y1C8	604-871-9000	871-2901
CKST-AM 1040 (Sports) 380 W 2nd Ave Suite 300 *Web:* www.teamradio.ca	Vancouver	BC	V5Y1C8	604-871-9000	871-2901
CSTE-AM 1410 380 W 2nd Ave Suite 300 *Web:* www.teamradio.ca	Vancouver	BC	V5Y1C8	604-871-9000	871-2901

648-178 Washington, DC

Station	City	State	Zip	Phone	Fax
WAMU-FM 88.5 (NPR) 4000 Brandywine St NW American University Radio *Web:* www.wamu.org	Washington	DC	20016	202-885-1200	885-1269
WHUR-FM 96.3 (Urban AC) 529 Bryant St NW *TF:* 800-221-9487 ■ *Web:* www.whur.com	Washington	DC	20059	202-806-3500	806-3522
WJZW-FM 105.9 (Oldies) 4400 Jenifer St NW 4th Fl *TF:* 800-779-1059 ■ *Web:* www.trueoldies1059.com	Washington	DC	20015	202-686-3100	686-3064
WMAL-AM 630 (N/T) 4400 Jenifer St NW 4th Fl *TF:* 888-630-9625 ■ *Web:* www.wmal.com	Washington	DC	20015	202-686-3100	686-3061
WRQX-FM 107.3 (AC) 4400 Jenifer St NW 4th Fl *Web:* www.mix1073fm.com	Washington	DC	20015	202-686-3100	686-3091
WTLP-FM 103.9(N/T) 3400 Idaho Ave NW *Web:* www.wtop.com	Washington	DC	20016	202-895-5000	895-5149
WTOP-FM 103.5 (N/T) 3400 Idaho Ave NW *Web:* www.wtopnews.com	Washington	DC	20016	202-895-5000	895-5149

648-179 West Palm Beach, FL

Station	City	State	Zip	Phone	Fax
WAYF-FM 88.1 (Rel) 800 Northpoint Pkwy Suite 881 *Web:* wayf.wayfm.com	West Palm Beach	FL	33407	561-881-1929	840-1929
WBZT-AM 1230 (N/T) 3071 Continental Dr *Web:* www.wbzt.com	West Palm Beach	FL	33407	561-616-6600	616-6677
WEAT-FM 104.3 (AC) 701 Northpoint Pkwy Suite 500 *TF:* 800-579-1043 ■ *Web:* www.sunny1043.com	West Palm Beach	FL	33407	561-686-9505	686-0157
WIRK-FM 107.9 (Ctry) 701 Northpoint Pkwy Suite 500 *TF:* 800-919-1079 ■ *Web:* www.wirk.com	West Palm Beach	FL	33407	561-686-9505	686-0157
WJNO-AM 1290 (N/T) 3071 Continental Dr *Web:* www.wjno.com	West Palm Beach	FL	33407	561-616-6600	616-6677
WKGR-FM 98.7 (CR) 3071 Continental Dr *Web:* www.gaterrocks.com	West Palm Beach	FL	33407	561-616-6600	616-6677
WLDI-FM 95.5 (CHR) 3071 Continental Dr *Web:* www.wild955.com	West Palm Beach	FL	33407	561-616-6600	616-6677
WMBX-FM 102.3 (Urban) 701 Northpoint Pkwy Suite 500 *TF:* 800-969-1023 ■ *Web:* www.thenewx1023.com	West Palm Beach	FL	33407	561-686-9505	686-0157
WOLL-FM 105.5 (AC) 3071 Continental Dr *TF:* 888-415-1055 ■ *Web:* www.kool1055.com	West Palm Beach	FL	33407	561-616-6600	616-6677
WPBZ-FM 103.1 (Alt) 701 Northpoint Pkwy Suite 500 *TF:* 866-954-7625 ■ *Web:* www.buzz103.radio.com	West Palm Beach	FL	33407	561-686-9505	686-0157
WRMF-FM 97.9 (AC) 477 S Rosemary Ave Suite 302 *Web:* www.wrmf.com	West Palm Beach	FL	33401	561-868-1100	868-1111
WXEL-FM 90.7 (NPR) PO Box 6607 *TF:* 800-915-9935 ■ *Web:* www.wxel.org	West Palm Beach	FL	33405	561-737-8000	369-3067

648-180 Wheeling, WV

Station	City	State	Zip	Phone	Fax
WBBD-AM 1400 (Nost) 1015 Main St *Web:* www.wheelingsrealoldies.com	Wheeling	WV	26003	304-232-1170	234-0036
WEGW-FM 107.5 (Rock) 1015 Main St *Web:* www.wegwfm.com	Wheeling	WV	26003	304-232-1170	234-0041
WKWK-FM 97.3 (AC) 1015 Main St *Web:* www.wk973.com	Wheeling	WV	26003	304-232-1170	234-0041
WOVK-FM 98.7 (Ctry) 1015 Main St *Web:* www.wovk.com	Wheeling	WV	26003	304-232-1170	234-0041
WVKF-FM 95.7 (CHR) 1015 Main St *Web:* www.kisswheeling.com	Wheeling	WV	26003	304-232-1170	234-0036
WWVA-AM 1170 (N/T) 1015 Main St *Web:* www.wwva.com	Wheeling	WV	26003	304-232-1170	234-0041

648-181 Wichita, KS

Station	City	State	ZIP	Phone	Fax
KDGS-FM 93.9 (CHR) 2120 N Woodlawn St Suite 352 *Web:* www.power939.com	Wichita	KS	67208	316-685-2121	685-1287
KEYN-FM 103.7 (Oldies) 2120 N Woodlawn St Suite 352 *Web:* www.keyn.com	Wichita	KS	67208	316-685-2121	685-3408
KFBZ-FM 105.3 (AC) 2120 N Woodlawn St Suite 352 *Web:* www.1053thebuzz.com	Wichita	KS	67208	316-685-2121	685-1287
KFDI-FM 101.3 (Ctry) 4200 N Old Lawrence Rd *Web:* www.kfdi.com	Wichita	KS	67219	316-838-9141	838-3607
KFH-AM 1240 (N/T) 2120 N Woodlawn St Suite 352 *Web:* www.kfhradio.com	Wichita	KS	67208	316-685-2121	685-3408
KFTI-AM 1070 (Ctry) 4200 N Old Lawrence Rd *Web:* www.kfdi.com	Wichita	KS	67219	316-838-9141	838-3607
KICT-FM 95.1 (Rock) 4200 N Old Lawrence Rd *Web:* www.t95.com	Wichita	KS	67219	316-838-9141	838-3607
KMUW-FM 89.1 (NPR) 3317 E 17th St N *Web:* www.kmuw.org	Wichita	KS	67208	316-978-6789	978-3946
KNSS-AM 1330 (N/T) 2120 N Woodlawn St Suite 352 *Web:* www.knssradio.com	Wichita	KS	67208	316-685-2121	685-3408
KRBB-FM 97.9 (AC) 9323 E 37th St N *Web:* www.b98fm.com	Wichita	KS	67226	316-494-6600	494-6730
KTHR-FM 107.3 (CR) 9323 E 37th St N *Web:* www.1073theroad.com	Wichita	KS	67226	316-494-6600	494-6730
KZCH-FM 96.3 (CHR) 9323 E 37th St N *Web:* www.channel963.com	Wichita	KS	67226	316-494-6600	494-6730
KZSN-FM 102.1 (Ctry) 9323 E 37th St N *Web:* www.kzsn.com	Wichita	KS	67226	316-494-6600	494-6730

648-182 Wilmington/Dover, DE

Station	City	State	ZIP	Phone	Fax
WDEL-AM 1150 (N/T) 2727 Shipley Rd *TF:* 800-544-1150 ■ *Web:* www.wdel.com	Wilmington	DE	19810	302-478-2700	478-0100
WDOV-AM 1410 (N/T) 1575 McKee Rd Suite 206 *Web:* www.wdov.com	Dover	DE	19904	302-674-1410	674-8621
WJBR-FM 99.5 (AC) 812 Philadelphia Pike *Web:* www.wjbr.com	Wilmington	DE	19809	302-765-1160	765-1192
WMPH-FM 91.7 (CHR) 5201 Washington St Ext. *Web:* www.wmph.org	Wilmington	DE	19809	302-762-7199	762-7042
WSTW-FM 93.7 (CHR) 2727 Shipley Rd *TF:* 800-544-9370 ■ *Web:* www.wstw.com	Wilmington	DE	19810	302-478-2700	478-0100

648-183 Winnipeg, MB

Station	City	Prov	Postal Code	Phone	Fax
CBW-AM 990 (CBC) 541 Portage Ave *Web:* www.cbc.ca/manitoba	Winnipeg	MB	R3B2G1	204-788-3222	788-3227
CBW-FM 98.3 (Clas) 541 Portage Ave *Web:* www.cbc.ca/manitoba	Winnipeg	MB	R3B2G1	204-788-3222	788-3227
CFQX-FM 104.1 (Ctry) 177 Lombard Ave 3rd Fl. *Web:* www.qx104fm.com	Winnipeg	MB	R3B0W5	204-944-1031	989-5291
CITI-FM 92.1 (CR) 4-166 Osborne St *NYSE:* RCI ■ *Web:* www.92citifm.ca	Winnipeg	MB	R3L1Y8	204-788-3400	788-3401
CJKR-FM 97.5 (Rock) 930 Portage Ave *Web:* www.power97.com	Winnipeg	MB	R3G0P8	204-786-2471	783-4512
CJOB-AM 680 (N/T) 930 Portage Ave *Web:* www.cjob.com	Winnipeg	MB	R3G0P8	204-786-2471	783-4512
CKMM-FM 103.1 (CHR) 177 Lombard Ave 3rd Fl *Web:* www.hot103live.com	Winnipeg	MB	R3B0W5	204-944-1031	989-5291
CKY-FM 102.3 (AC) 4-166 Osborne St *NYSE:* RCI ■ *Web:* www.102clearfm.com	Winnipeg	MB	R3L1Y8	204-788-3400	788-3401
Fab-FM 94.3 1445 Pembina Hwy. *Web:* www.fab943.com	Winnipeg	MB	R3T5C2	204-477-5120	453-0815
Sports Radio AM 129.0 1445 Pembina Hwy *Web:* www.sportsradio1290.com	Winnipeg	MB	R3T5C2	204-477-5120	453-0815

648-184 Winston-Salem, NC

Station	City	State	ZIP	Phone	Fax
WBFJ-FM 89.3 (Rel) 1249 Trade St *Web:* www.wbfj.org	Winston-Salem	NC	27101	336-721-1560	777-1032
WFDD-FM 88.5 (NPR) PO Box 8850 *TF:* 800-262-8850 ■ *Web:* www.wfdd.org	Winston-Salem	NC	27109	336-758-8850	758-3083
WSJS-AM 600 (N/T) 875 W 5th St. *Web:* www.wsjs.com	Winston-Salem	NC	27101	336-777-3900	777-3915

648-185 Worcester, MA

Station	City	State	ZIP	Phone	Fax
WCRN-AM 830 (N/T) 82 Franklin St *Web:* www.wcrnradio.com	Worcester	MA	01608	508-792-5803	770-0659
WCUW-FM 91.3 (Var) 910 Main St. *Web:* www.wcuw.com	Worcester	MA	01610	508-753-1012	
WICN-FM 90.5 (NPR) 50 Portland St *Web:* www.wicn.org	Worcester	MA	01608	508-752-0700	752-7518
WORC-AM 1310 (Span) 122 Green St Suite 2-R *Web:* www.power1310.com	Worcester	MA	01604	508-791-2111	752-6897
WVNE-AM 760 (Rel) 70 James St Suite 201 *Web:* www.wvne.net	Worcester	MA	01603	508-831-9863	831-7964
WWFX-FM 100.1 (CR) 250 Commercial St Suite 530 *Web:* www.worcesterpike.com	Worcester	MA	01608	508-752-1045	793-0824
WXLO-FM 104.5 (AC) 250 Commercial St *Web:* www.wxlo.com	Worcester	MA	01608	508-752-1045	793-0824

648-186 Youngstown, OH

Station	City	State	ZIP	Phone	Fax
WAKZ-FM 95.9 (CHR) 7461 S Ave *TF:* 877-827-5477 ■ *Web:* www.959kiss.com	Youngstown	OH	44512	330-965-0057	729-9991
WBBW-AM 1240 (Sports) 4040 Simon Rd *Web:* www.wbbw.com	Youngstown	OH	44512	330-783-1000	783-0060
WGFT-AM 1330 (N/T) 20 Federal Plaza W 1st Fl *Web:* www.1330wgft.com	Youngstown	OH	44503	330-744-5115	744-4020
WHOT-FM 101.1 (CHR) 4040 Simon Rd *TF:* 800-989-9468 ■ *Web:* www.hot101.com	Youngstown	OH	44512	330-783-1000	783-0060
WMXY-FM 98.9 (AC) 7461 S Ave *TF:* 800-801-9526 ■ *Web:* www.mix989.com	Youngstown	OH	44512	330-965-0057	729-9991
WNCD-FM 93.3 (Rock) 7461 S Ave *Web:* www.cd933.com	Youngstown	OH	44512	330-965-0057	729-9991
WQXK-FM 105.1 (Ctry) 4040 Simon Rd. *Web:* www.k105country.com	Youngstown	OH	44512	330-783-1000	783-0060
WRBP-FM 101.9 (Urban) 20 Federal Plaza W 1st Fl *Web:* www.jamz1019.com	Youngstown	OH	44503	330-744-5115	744-4020
WYFM-FM 102.9 (CR) 4040 Simon Rd. *TF:* 800-288-9103 ■ *Web:* www.y-103.com	Youngstown	OH	44512	330-783-1000	783-0060
WYSU-FM 88.5 (Clas) Youngstown State University 1 University Plaza *Web:* www.wysu.org	Youngstown	OH	44555	330-941-3363	941-1501

649 RADIO SYNDICATORS

Company	City	State	ZIP	Phone	Fax
Agrinet Farm Radio Network 176 Radio Rd *Web:* www.agrinetradio.com	Powells Point	NC	27966	252-491-2414	491-2939
American Urban Radio Networks 960 Penn Ave 4th Fl *TF:* 800-456-4211 ■ *Web:* www.aurn.com	Pittsburgh	PA	15222	412-456-4000	456-4040
AP Broadcast Services 1100 13th St NW Suite 700 *TF:* 800-821-4747 ■ *Web:* www.apbroadcast.com	Washington	DC	20005	202-641-9000	370-2712
BGC Partners Inc 499 Pk Ave *Web:* www.bgcpartners.com	New York	NY	10022	646-346-7000	346-6919
Business TalkRadio Network PO Box 4826 *Web:* www.businesstalkradio.net	Greenwich	CT	06831	203-323-7300	323-7302
Car Clinic Productions 5675 N Davis Hwy *TF:* 800-264-5454 ■ *Web:* www.carclinicnetwork.com	Pensacola	FL	32503	850-478-3139	477-0862
Crystal Media Networks 7201 Wisconsin Ave Suite 780	Bethesda	MD	20814	240-223-0846	
Environmental Media Broadcasting Radio Network PO Box 5832 *TF:* 800-963-9927 ■ *Web:* www.seeusonline.com	Whittier	CA	90607	562-945-6469	945-1802
FamilyNet 3836 Dekalb Technology Pkwy Bldg 3 *Web:* www.familynet.com	Atlanta	GA	30340	770-225-1400	936-2755
Jameson Broadcast Inc 1644 Hawthorne St *Web:* www.jamesonbroadcast.com	Sarasota	FL	34239	941-906-8800	906-8801
Joanna Langfield's Entertainment Reports 340 W 55th St Suite 8-C *Web:* www.themovieminute.com	New York	NY	10019	212-757-7654	
Jones MediaAmerica Inc 11 W 42nd St 11th Fl	New York	NY	10036	212-302-1100	556-9402
Lichtenstein Creative Media Inc 1 Broadway 14th Fl *Web:* www.lcmedia.com	Cambridge	MA	02142	617-682-3700	682-3710
Media Syndication Services 236 Massachusetts Ave NE Suite 510	Washington	DC	20002	202-544-4457	546-8435
MediaTracks Communications 2250 E Devon Ave Suite 151 *Web:* www.mediatracks.com	Des Plaines	IL	60018	847-299-9500	299-9501
New Dimensions Radio Broadcasting Network PO Box 569 *TF:* 800-935-8273 ■ *Web:* www.newdimensions.org	Ukiah	CA	95482	707-468-5215	
North American Network Inc 5335 Wisconsin Ave NW Suite 440 *Web:* www.radiospace.com	Washington	DC	20015	301-654-9810	654-9828
Pentacom Productions 1375 N Wetherly Dr	Los Angeles	CA	90069	310-276-7001	276-7002
Premiere Radio Networks Inc 15260 Ventura Blvd Suite 500 *TF:* 800-533-8686 ■ *Web:* www.premrad.com	Sherman Oaks	CA	91403	818-377-5300	377-5333
Radio America 1100 N Glebe Rd Suite 900 **Fax Area Code:* 571 ■ *TF:* 800-807-4703 ■ *Web:* www.radioamerica.org	Arlington	VA	22201	703-302-1000	480-4141*
Radio Express Inc 1415 W Magnolia Blvd Suite 201 *Web:* www.radioexpress.com	Burbank	CA	91506	818-295-5800	295-5801
Salem Radio Network 6400 N Beltline Rd Suite 210 *Web:* www.srnonline.com	Irving	TX	75063	972-831-1920	831-8626
Strand Media Group Inc 3955 Hwy 17 Bypass PO Box 1389 Suite D *Web:* www.somethingyoushouldknow.net	Murrells Inlet	SC	29576	843-626-8911	626-6452
Success Journal Corp 8700 Waukegan Rd Suite 250 *TF:* 800-743-1988	Morton Grove	IL	60053	847-583-9000	583-9025

Phone Fax

Superadio LLC 1661 Worcester Rd .... Framingham MA 01701 508-620-0006 628-1590
Web: www.superadio.com
Syndicated Solutions Inc PO Box 1078 .... Ridgefield CT 06877 203-431-0790 431-0792
Web: www.syndicatedsolutions.com
Talk Radio Network (TRN) PO Box 3755........... Central Point OR 97502 541-664-8827 664-6250
TF: 888-383-3733 ■ *Web:* www.trncorporate.com
TM Century Inc 2002 Academy Ln Suite 110 .... Dallas TX 75234 972-406-6800 406-6890
Web: www.tmstudios.com
Transmedia 719 Battery St...................... San Francisco CA 94111 415-956-3118 956-2595
TF: 800-229-7234 ■ *Web:* www.transmediasf.com
WCLV/Seaway Productions
1375 Euclid Ave Idea Ctr .... Cleveland OH 44115 216-464-0900 464-2206
TF: 800-491-8863 ■ *Web:* www.wclv.com
WestStar Talk Radio Networks 2711 N 24th St......... Phoenix AZ 85008 602-381-8200 381-8221
Web: www.weststar.com
Westwood One Inc
1166 Avenue of the Americas 10th Fl................. New York NY 10036 212-641-2000
NASDAQ: WWON ■ *Web:* www.westwoodone.com

650 RADIO & TELEVISION BROADCASTING & COMMUNICATIONS EQUIPMENT

SEE ALSO Audio & Video Equipment p. 1486; Telecommunications Equipment & Systems p. 2682

Phone Fax

AheadTek Inc 6410 Via Del Oro...................... San Jose CA 95119 408-226-9991 226-9195
TF: 800-971-9191 ■ *Web:* www.aheadtek.com
Airbiquity Inc 1011 Western Ave Suite 600............... Seattle WA 98104 206-219-2700 842-9259
TF: 888-334-7741 ■ *Web:* www.airbiquity.com
Alien Technology Corp
18220 Butterfield Blvd .... Morgan Hill CA 95037 408-782-3900 782-3910
TF: 800-372-4160 ■ *Web:* www.alientechnology.com
Andersen Mfg Inc 3125 N Yellowstone Hwy........... Idaho Falls ID 83401 208-523-6460 523-6562
TF: 800-635-6106 ■ *Web:* www.andersenin c.com
Antedo Inc PO Box 725 .... Cupertino CA 95015 408-253-1870 253-1871
Web: www.antedo.com
Antenna Products Corp 101 SE 25th Ave .... Mineral Wells TX 76067 940-325-3301 325-0716
Web: www.antennaproducts.com
Antennas for Communications 350 Cypress Rd .... Ocala FL 34472 352-687-4121 687-1203
Web: www.afcsat.com
Apex Airtronics Inc 2465 Atlantic Ave .... Brooklyn NY 11207 718-485-8560 485-8564
AR Worldwide 160 Schoolhouse Rd .... Souderton PA 18964 215-723-8181 723-5688
Web: www.ar-worldwide.com
ArrayComm LLC
1110 W Lk Cook Rd Suite 350 .... Buffalo Grove IL 60089 224-676-2619
Web: www.arraycomm.com
Arris 60 Decibel Rd .... State College PA 16801 814-238-2461 238-4065
TF: 800-233-2267 ■ *Web:* www.arrisi.com
Arris Group Inc 3871 Lakefield Dr.................... Suwanee GA 30024 678-473-2000 473-8470
NASDAQ: ARRS ■ *TF:* 866-362-7747 ■ *Web:* www.arrisi.com
Artel Video Systems Corp 5B Lyberty Way .... Westford MA 01886 978-263-5775 263-9755
TF: 800-225-0228 ■ *Web:* www.artel.com
Associated Industries
11347 Vanowen St .... North Hollywood CA 91605 818-760-1000 760-2142
Web: www.associated-ind.com
Atrex Inc 175 Industrial Loop S .... Orange Park FL 32073 904-264-9086 269-4916
TF: 800-874-4505 ■ *Web:* www.atrexinc.com
Avi Systems Inc 9675 W 76th St Suite 200........... Eden Prairie MN 55344 952-949-3700 949-6000
TF: 800-488-4954 ■ *Web:* www.avisystems.com
Avtech Corp 3400 Wallingford Ave N.................... Seattle WA 98103 206-695-8000 695-8011
Web: www.avtcorp.com
Axcera Corp 103 Freedom Dr........................ Lawrence PA 15055 724-873-8100 873-8105
TF: 800-215-2614 ■ *Web:* www.axcera.com
Ball Aerospace & Technologies Corp
1600 Commerce St............................... Boulder CO 80301 303-939-4000 460-2315*
**Fax:* Mail Rm ■ *Web:* www.ballaerospace.com
Barker & Williamson 603 Cidco Rd.................... Cocoa FL 32926 321-639-1510 445-6031
Web: www.bwantennas.com
Blonder Tongue Laboratories Inc
1 Jake Brown Rd.................................. Old Bridge NJ 08857 732-679-4000 679-4353
AMEX: BDR ■ *TF:* 800-523-6049 ■ *Web:* www.blondertongue.com
Broadcast Electronics Inc 4100 N 24th St.............. Quincy IL 62305 217-224-9600 224-9607
Web: www.bdcast.com
CalAmp Corp 1401 N Rice Ave......................... Oxnard CA 93030 805-987-9000 419-8498
NASDAQ: CAMP ■ *TF:* 888-767-7988 ■ *Web:* www.calamp.com
Cattron Group International
58 W Shenango St .... Sharpsville PA 16150 724-962-3571 962-4310
Web: www.cattron.com
Celerity Systems Inc
8401 Greensboro Dr Suite 500....................... McLean VA 22102 703-848-1900 848-2139
Web: www.celerity.com
Channell Commercial Corp
26040 Ynez Rd PO Box 9022 .... Temecula CA 92591 951-719-2600 296-2322
PINK: CHNL ■ *TF:* 800-423-1863 ■ *Web:* www.channellcomm.com
Chaparral Communications Inc
950 S Bascom Ave Suite 3111 .... San Jose CA 95128 408-294-2900 294-6969
Web: www.chaparral.net
Chelton Inc 1955 Lakeway Dr Suite 200 .... Lewisville TX 75057 972-221-1783 436-2716
Web: www.chelton.com
Cobra Electronics Corp 6500 W Cortland St............ Chicago IL 60707 773-889-8870 889-8870
NASDAQ: COBR ■ *Web:* www.cobra.com
Cohu Inc 12367 Crosthwaite Cir........................ Poway CA 92064 858-848-8100 848-8185
NASDAQ: COHU ■ *Web:* www.cohu.com
Cohu Inc Electronics Div 12367 Crosthwaite Cir .... Poway CA 92064 858-277-6700 277-0221
TF: 800-735-2648 ■ *Web:* www.cohu-cameras.com
Communications & Power Industries Inc Beverly Microwave Div
150 Sohier Rd.................................... Beverly MA 01915 978-922-6000 922-2736
Web: www.cpii.com/bmd
Comtech Systems Inc 2900 Titan Row Suite 142 .... Orlando FL 32809 407-854-1950 851-6960
Web: www.comtechsystems.com

Phone Fax

Comtech Telecommunications Corp
68 S Service Rd Suite 230 .... Melville NY 11747 631-962-7000 962-7001
NASDAQ: CMTL ■ *Web:* www.comtechtel.com
Concurrent 4375 River Green Pkwy Suite 100............. Duluth GA 30096 678-258-4000 258-4300
NASDAQ: CCUR ■ *TF:* 877-978-7363 ■ *Web:* www.ccur.com
Conolog Corp 5 Columbia Rd .... Somerville NJ 08876 908-722-8081 722-8081
NASDAQ: CNLG ■ *TF:* 800-526-3984 ■ *Web:* www.conolog.com
Continental Electronics Corp
4212 S Buckner Blvd .... Dallas TX 75227 214-381-7161 381-4949
TF: 800-733-5011 ■ *Web:* www.contelec.com
Dage-MTI Inc 701 N Roeske Ave................. Michigan City IN 46360 219-872-5514 872-5559
Web: www.dagemti.com
Datron World Communications Inc
3030 Enterprise Ct .... Vista CA 92081 760-579-1500 597-1510
TF Sales: 800-405-0744 ■ *Web:* www.dtwc.com
Dayton-Granger Inc 3299 SW 9th Ave .... Fort Lauderdale FL 33315 954-463-3451 761-3172
Web: www.daytongranger.com
Diamond Antenna & Microwave Corp
59 Porter Rd .... Littleton MA 01460 978-486-0039 486-0079
Web: www.diamondantenna.com
Digital Angel Corp 490 Villaume Ave .... South Saint Paul MN 55075 651-552-6301 455-0413
AMEX: DOC ■ *TF:* 800-328-0118 ■ *Web:* www.digitalangelcorp.com
DIRECTV Group Inc 2230 E Imperial Hwy............ El Segundo CA 90245 310-964-5000 535-5225
NYSE: DTV ■ *Web:* www.directv.com
DRS C3 & Aviation Co
767 Electronic Dr Suite A.......................... Horsham PA 19044 215-233-4100 233-9947
Web: www.drs.com
Eagle Comtronics Inc 7665 Henry Clay Blvd........... Liverpool NY 13088 315-622-3402 622-3800
TF: 800-448-7474 ■ *Web:* www.eaglecomtronics.com
Earmark LLC 1125 Dixwell Ave .... Hamden CT 06514 203-777-2130 777-2886
TF Cust Svc: 888-327-6275 ■ *Web:* www.earmark.com
EFJohnson Technologies 1440 Corporate Dr .... Irving TX 75038 972-819-0700 819-0639
TF: 800-328-3911 ■ *Web:* www.efjohnsontechnologies.com
Empower Rf Systems Inc 316 W Florence Ave .... Inglewood CA 90301 310-412-8100 412-9232
Web: www.empowerrf.com
EMS Technologies Inc 660 Engineering Dr............ Norcross GA 30092 770-263-9200 263-9207
NASDAQ: ELMG ■ *Web:* www.ems-t.com
Envivio Inc
400 Oyster Pt Blvd Suite 325 .... South San Francisco CA 94080 650-243-2700 243-2750
Web: www.envivio.com
Etm Electromatic Inc 35451 Dumbarton Ct............. Newark CA 94560 510-797-1100 797-4358
Web: www.etm-inc.com
Fidelity Technologies Corp 2501 Kutztown Rd.......... Reading PA 19605 610-929-3330 929-6861
Web: www.fidelitytech.com
GAI-Tronics Corp 400 E Wyomissing Ave.............. Mohnton PA 19540 610-777-1374 775-6540
TF: 800-492-1212 ■ *Web:* www.gai-tronics.com
General Dynamics SATCOM Technologies
1500 Prodelin Dr .... Newton NC 28658 828-464-4141 464-5725
TF: 888-836-1979 ■ *Web:* www.gdsatcom.com
Globecomm Systems Inc 45 Oser Ave............. Hauppauge NY 11788 631-231-9800 231-1557
NASDAQ: GCOM ■ *TF:* 888-231-9800 ■ *Web:* www.globecommsystems.com
Goodrich ISR Systems 6600 Gulton Ct NE.......... Albuquerque NM 87109 505-345-9031 344-9879
HAL Communications Corp
1201 W Kenyon Rd PO Box 365........................ Urbana IL 61803 217-367-7373 367-1701
Web: www.halcomm.com
Harmonic Inc 549 Baltic Way....................... Sunnyvale CA 94089 800-828-5521 542-2521*
NASDAQ: HLIT ■ **Fax Area Code:* 408 ■ *TF:* 800-828-5521 ■ *Web:* www.harmonicinc.com
Harris Corp 1025 W NASA Blvd..................... Melbourne FL 32919 321-727-9100
NYSE: HRS ■ *TF:* 800-442-7747 ■ *Web:* www.harris.com
Harris Corp Broadcast Communications Div
3200 Wismann Ln .... Quincy IL 62301 217-222-8200 221-7096
TF: 800-231-9673 ■ *Web:* www.broadcast.harris.com
Harris Corp Government Communication Systems Div
2400 Palm Bay Rd .... Palm Bay FL 32905 321-727-4000
Web: www.govcomm.harris.com
Harris Corp RF Communications Div
1680 University Ave .... Rochester NY 14610 585-244-5830 242-4755
TF: 800-288-4277 ■ *Web:* www.rfcomm.harris.com
Hitachi Kokusai Electric America Ltd
150 Crossways Pk Dr .... Woodbury NY 11797 516-921-7200 496-3718
Web: www.hitachikokusai.us
ICOM America Inc 2380 116th Ave NE................. Bellevue WA 98004 425-454-8155 454-1509
TF: 800-872-4266 ■ *Web:* www.icomamerica.com
ICx DAQ Electronics Inc
262B Old New Brunswick Rd .... Piscataway NJ 08854 732-981-0050 981-0058
Web: www.daq.icxt.com
ID Systems Inc 123 Tice Blvd Suite 101 .... Woodcliff Lake NJ 07677 201-996-9000 996-9144
NASDAQ: IDSY ■ *TF:* 866-410-0152 ■ *Web:* www.id-systems.com
Ikegami Electronics USA Inc 37 Brook Ave........... Maywood NJ 07607 201-368-9171 569-1626
TF: 800-368-9171 ■ *Web:* www.ikegami.com
Integral Systems Inc
6721 Columbia Gateway Dr .... Columbia MD 21046 443-539-5008 312-2705*
NASDAQ: ISYS ■ **Fax Area Code:* 410 ■ *Web:* www.integ.com
Intelect Technologies Inc
2200 10th St Suite 300.............................. Plano TX 75074 469-429-7800 429-7890
Web: www.intelectinc.com
Iteris Inc 1700 Carnegie Ave Suite 100 .... Santa Ana CA 92705 949-270-9400 270-9401
AMEX: ITI ■ *Web:* www.iteris.com
ITT Defense 1650 Tysons Blvd Suite 1700 .... McLean VA 22102 703-790-6300 790-6360
Web: www.defense.itt.com
Jampro Antennas Inc 6340 Sky Creek Dr .... Sacramento CA 95828 916-383-1177 383-1182
Web: www.jampro.com
Kenwood USA Corp 2201 E Dominguez St .... Long Beach CA 90810 310-639-9000 604-4488
TF: 800-536-9663 ■ *Web:* www.kenwoodusa.com
Kongsberg Maritime Inc
5373 W Sam Houston Pkwy N Suite 200 .... Houston TX 77041 713-329-5580 329-5581
Web: www.km.kongsberg.com
KVH Industries Inc 50 Enterprise Ctr .... Middletown RI 02842 401-847-3327 849-0045
NASDAQ: KVHI ■ *Web:* www.kvh.com
L-3 Communications Corp 600 3rd Ave 34-35 Fl .... New York NY 10016 212-697-1111 867-5249
NYSE: LLL ■ *TF:* 800-351-8483 ■ *Web:* www.l-3com.com
L-3 Communications ESSCO 90 Nemco Way .... Ayer MA 01432 978-568-5100 772-7581
Web: www.l-3com.com

	City	State	ZIP	Phone	Fax
L-3 Communications Telemetry East Div 1515 Grundy's Ln *Web:* www.l-3com.com	Bristol	PA	19007	267-545-7000	545-0100
L-3 Communications Telemetry West Div 9020 Balboa Ave *TF:* 800-351-8483 ■ *Web:* www.l-3com.com/tw	San Diego	CA	92123	858-694-7500	694-7538
Larcan Inc 228 Ambassador Dr *Web:* www.larcan.com	Mississauga	ON	L5T2J2	905-564-9222	564-9244
MCL Inc 501 S Woodcreek Rd *TF Support:* 800-743-4625 ■ *Web:* www.mcl.com	Bolingbrook	IL	60440	630-759-9500	759-5018
MDI Security Systems Inc 12500 Network Dr Suite 303 *NASDAQ: MDII* ■ *TF:* 866-435-7634 ■ *Web:* www.mdisecure.com	San Antonio	TX	78249	210-477-5400	477-5401
MFJ Enterprises Inc 300 Industrial Pk Rd *TF:* 800-647-1800 ■ *Web:* www.mfjenterprises.com	Starkville	MS	39759	662-323-5869	323-6551
Microphase Corp 587 Connecticut Ave *Web:* www.microphase.com	Norwalk	CT	06854	203-866-8000	866-6727
Millitech Inc 29 Industrial Dr E *Web:* www.millitech.com	NorthHampton	MA	01060	413-582-9620	
Minerva Networks Inc 2150 Gold St *TF:* 800-806-9594 ■ *Web:* www.minervanetworks.com	Santa Clara	CA	95054	408-567-9400	567-0747
Mirapoint Inc 1215 Bordeaux Dr *TF:* 800-937-8118 ■ *Web:* www.mirapoint.com	Sunnyvale	CA	94089	408-720-3700	720-3725
Mitsubishi International Corp 655 3rd Ave *Web:* www.micusa.com	New York	NY	10017	212-605-2000	
Morcom International Inc 3656 Centerview Dr Unit 1 *Web:* www.morcom.com	Chantilly	VA	20151	703-263-9305	263-9308
Moseley Assoc Inc 82 Coromar Dr *Web:* www.moseleysb.com	Santa Barbara	CA	93117	805-562-0550	685-9638
Motorola Inc Broadband Communications Sector 101 Tournament Dr *Web:* www.broadband.motorola.com	Horsham	PA	19044	215-323-1000	
Orbit/FR Inc 506 Prudential Rd *TF:* 800-672-4859 ■ *Web:* www.orbitfr.com	Horsham	PA	19044	215-674-5100	674-5108
ParkerVision Inc 7915 Baymeadows Way *NASDAQ: PRKR* ■ *TF:* 800-532-8034 ■ *Web:* www.parkervision.com	Jacksonville	FL	32256	904-737-1367	731-0958
Pelco 3500 Pelco Way *TF:* 800-289-9100 ■ *Web:* www.pelco.com	Clovis	CA	93612	559-292-1981	348-1120
Pico Macom Inc 6260 Sequence Dr *TF:* 800-421-6511 ■ *Web:* www.picomacom.com	San Diego	CA	92121	858-546-5050	546-5051
Powerwave Technologies Inc 1801 E St Andrew Pl *NASDAQ: PWAV* ■ *TF:* 888-797-9283 ■ *Web:* www.powerwave.com	Santa Ana	CA	92705	714-466-1000	466-5800
Prodelin Corp 1500 Prodelin Dr *TF:* 888-836-1979 ■ *Web:* www.gdsatcom.com/prodelin.php	Newton	NC	28658	828-464-4141	464-5725
PTS Corp 5233 Old Hwy 37 S **Fax:* Cust Svc ■ *TF:* 800-844-7871	Bloomington	IN	47401	812-824-9331	824-2848*
RA Miller Industries Inc 14500 168th Ave PO Box 858 *TF:* 888-845-9450 ■ *Web:* www.rami.com	Grand Haven	MI	49417	616-842-9450	842-2771
Radio Frequency Systems 200 Pondview Dr *Web:* www.rfsworld.com	Meriden	CT	06450	203-630-3311	634-2273
Radio Holland USA Inc 8943 Gulf Fwy *Web:* www.radiohollandusa.com	Houston	TX	77017	713-941-2290	378-2101
Rantec Microwave Systems Inc 24003 Ventura Blvd *Web:* www.rantecmdm.com	Calabasas	CA	91302	818-223-5000	223-5199
RELM Wireless Corp 7100 Technology Dr *AMEX: RWC* ■ *TF Cust Svc:* 800-648-0947 ■ *Web:* www.relm.com	West Melbourne	FL	32904	321-984-1414	676-4403
RF Products Inc 1500 Davis St *Web:* www.rfproductsinc.com	Camden	NJ	08103	856-365-5500	342-9757
RL Drake Co 230 Industrial Dr *Web:* www.rldrake.com	Franklin	OH	45005	937-746-4556	806-1510
Rockwell Collins Inc 400 Collins Rd NE *NYSE: COL* ■ **Fax:* PR ■ *TF:* 888-721-3094 ■ *Web:* www.rockwellcollins.com	Cedar Rapids	IA	52498	319-295-1000	295-9347*
Satcom Scientific Inc 5644 Commerce Dr *TF:* 800-741-5465 ■ *Web:* www.satcomscientific.com	Orlando	FL	32839	407-856-1050	855-7640
Satellite Systems Corp 101 Malibu Dr *Web:* www.satsyscorp.com	Virginia Beach	VA	23452	757-463-3553	463-3891
SEA Com Corp 7030 220th St SW *TF:* 800-426-1330 ■ *Web:* www.seacomcorp.com	Mountlake Terrace	WA	98043	425-771-2182	771-2650
SeaChange International Inc 50 Nagog Pk *NASDAQ: SEAC* ■ *TF:* 888-732-2641 ■ *Web:* www.schange.com	Acton	MA	01720	978-897-0100	897-0132
Secure Communication Systems Inc 1740 E Wilshire Ave *TF:* 866-926-2940 ■ *Web:* www.securecomm.com	Santa Ana	CA	92705	714-547-1174	953-8615
Sensor Systems Inc 8929 Fullbright Ave *Web:* www.sensorantennas.com	Chatsworth	CA	91311	818-341-5366	341-9059
Shively Labs 188 Harrison Rd PO Box 389 *TF:* 888-744-8359 ■ *Web:* www.shively.com	Bridgton	ME	04009	207-647-3327	647-8273
Space Systems/Loral 3825 Fabian Way *TF:* 800-332-6490 ■ *Web:* www.ssloral.com	Palo Alto	CA	94303	650-852-4000	
Sunair Electronics LLC 3131 SW 42 St *Web:* www.sunairhf.com	Fort Lauderdale	FL	33312	954-623-3131	623-3121
Talk-a-phone Co 7530 N Natchez Ave *Web:* www.talkaphone.com	Niles	IL	60714	773-539-1100	539-1241
TCI International Inc 3541 Gateway Blvd *TF:* 800-827-2661 ■ *Web:* www.tcibr.com	Fremont	CA	94538	510-687-6100	687-6101
Tecom Industries Inc 375 Conejo Ridge Ave *TF:* 800-959-0495 ■ *Web:* www.tecom-ind.com	Thousand Oaks	CA	91361	805-267-0100	267-0181
Telemobile Inc 19840 Hamilton Ave *Web:* www.telemobile.com	Torrance	CA	90502	310-538-5100	532-8526
Telephonics Corp 815 Broad Hollow Rd *TF:* 877-517-2327 ■ *Web:* www.telephonics.com	Farmingdale	NY	11735	631-755-7000	755-7200
Ten-Tec Inc 1185 Dolly Parton Pkwy *TF Cust Svc:* 800-833-7373 ■ *Web:* www.tentec.com	Sevierville	TN	37862	865-453-7172	428-4483
Thales Communications Inc 22605 Gateway Ctr Dr *TF:* 800-258-4420 ■ *Web:* www.thalescomminc.com	Clarksburg	MD	20871	240-864-7000	864-7920
Thomson Broadcast Inc 104 Feeding Hills Rd *TF:* 800-288-8364 ■ *Web:* www.thomson-broadcast.com	Southwick	MA	01077	413-998-1100	569-0679
TPL Communications 3370 San Fernando Rd Unit 206 *TF:* 800-447-6937 ■ *Web:* www.tplcom.com	Los Angeles	CA	90065	323-256-3000	254-3210
Ultra Electronics Flightline Systems Inc 7625 Omni Tech Pl *Web:* www.ultra-fei.com	Victor	NY	14564	585-924-4000	742-5397
Ultra Electronics-DNE Technologies Inc 50 Barnes Pk N *TF:* 800-370-4485 ■ *Web:* www.dnetech.com	Wallingford	CT	06492	203-265-7151	265-9101
Vicon Industries Inc 89 Arkay Dr *AMEX: VII* ■ *TF Sales:* 800-645-9116 ■ *Web:* www.vicon-security.com	Hauppauge	NY	11788	631-952-2288	951-2288
Wegener 11350 Technology Cir *PINK: WGNR* ■ *TF:* 800-848-9467 ■ *Web:* www.wegener.com	Duluth	GA	30097	770-623-4000	623-0698
Wilcom Inc 73 Daniel Webster Hwy PO Box 508 *TF:* 800-222-1898 ■ *Web:* www.wilcominc.com	Belmont	NH	03220	603-524-2622	524-3735
Winegard Co 3000 Kirkwood St *TF Cust Svc:* 800-288-8094 ■ *Web:* www.winegard.com	Burlington	IA	52601	319-754-0600	754-0787
Zetron Inc 12034 134th Ct NE *Web:* www.zetron.com	Redmond	WA	98052	425-820-6363	820-7031

651 RAIL TRANSPORT SERVICES

SEE ALSO Logistics Services (Transportation & Warehousing) p. 2183

	City	State	ZIP	Phone	Fax
Aberdeen & Rockfish Railroad Co 101 E Main St *TF:* 800-849-5713 ■ *Web:* www.aberdeen-rockfish.com	Aberdeen	NC	28315	910-944-2341	944-9738
AN Railway LLC 190 Railraod Shop Rd PO Box 250	Port Saint Joe	FL	32457	850-229-7411	229-2755
Angelina & Neches River Railroad 225 Spence St PO Box 1328 *Web:* www.anrrr.com	Lufkin	TX	75902	936-634-4403	639-3879
Apache Railway Co 13 W Hwy 277 PO Box 857	Snowflake	AZ	85937	928-536-4697	536-4260
Atlantic & Western Railway LP 136 S Steele St	Sanford	NC	27330	919-776-7521	774-4621
Bonneville Transloaders Inc (BTI) 642 S Federal Blvd *Web:* www.bonntran.com	Riverton	WY	82501	307-856-7480	856-4623
Buffalo & Pittsburgh Railroad Inc (BPRR) 1200-C Scottsville Rd Suite 200 **Fax Area Code:* 800 ■ *TF:* 800-603-3385 ■ *Web:* www.gwrr.com	Rochester	NY	14624	585-464-6650	477-4947*
Burlington Northern & Santa Fe Railway (BNSF) 2650 Lou Menk Dr **Fax Area Code:* 817 ■ *TF:* 800-795-2673 ■ *Web:* www.bnsf.com	Fort Worth	TX	76131	800-795-2673	352-7171*
Canadian National Railway Co 935 Rue de la Gauchetiere O *NYSE: CNI* ■ *TF:* 888-668-4626 ■ *Web:* www.cn.ca	Montreal	QC	H3B2M9	514-399-7212	
Canadian Pacific Railway Co 401 9 Ave SW Suite 500 *NYSE: CP* ■ **Fax:* Hum Res ■ *TF:* 888-333-6370 ■ *Web:* www.cpr.ca	Calgary	AB	T2P4Z4	403-319-7000	319-7479*
Cedar Rapids & Iowa City Railway Co 2330 12th St SW *Web:* www.crandic.com	Cedar Rapids	IA	52404	319-786-3698	
Chattahoochee Industrial Railroad Inc Hwy 370 PO Box 253	Cedar Springs	GA	39832	229-793-4530	793-4548
CHEP USA 8517 S Pk Cir *TF:* 800-432-2437 ■ *Web:* www.chep.com	Orlando	FL	32819	407-370-2437	355-6211
Chicago Southshore & South Bend Railroad 505 N Carroll Ave *TF:* 800-873-1486 ■ *Web:* www.southshorefreight.com	Michigan City	IN	46360	219-874-9000	879-3754
Columbus & Greenville Railway Co 201 19th St N PO Box 6000 *TF:* 888-601-1222	Columbus	MS	39703	662-327-8664	327-8664
Conrail Inc 2001 Market St 2 Commerce Sq 8th Fl *Web:* www.conrail.com	Philadelphia	PA	19103	215-209-5014	209-4819
CSX Transportation Inc 500 Water St *TF:* 877-744-7279	Jacksonville	FL	32202	904-359-3100	359-3100
Dardanelle & Russellville Railroad Co 4416 S Arkansas Ave *TF:* 800-530-7526	Russellville	AR	72801	479-968-6455	968-2634
Delray Connecting Railroad Co 7819 W Jefferson St	Detroit	MI	48209	313-841-2851	841-2470
El Dorado & Wesson Railway Co 900 S W Ave	El Dorado	AR	71730	870-863-7100	863-7130
Genesee & Wyoming Inc 66 Field Pt Rd *NYSE: GWR* ■ *TF:* 800-528-7296 ■ *Web:* www.gwrr.com	Greenwich	CT	06830	203-629-3722	661-4106
Georgetown Railroad Co 5300 S IH-35 PO Box 529 *TF:* 800-772-8272	Georgetown	TX	78627	512-863-2538	869-2649
Guilford Rail Systems Iron Horse Pk High St *TF:* 800-955-9208 ■ *Web:* www.guilfordrail.com	North Billerica	MA	01862	978-663-1130	
Illinois & Midland Railroad Inc 1500 N Grand Ave E *Web:* www.gwrr.com	Springfield	IL	62705	217-788-8601	788-8630
Iowa Interstate Railroad 5900 6th St SW *TF:* 800-321-3884 ■ *Web:* www.iaisrr.com	Cedar Rapids	IA	52404	319-298-5400	298-5454
Kansas City Southern Railway Co 427 W 12th St *TF:* 800-243-8624 ■ *Web:* www.kcsouthern.com	Kansas City	MO	64105	816-983-1303	983-1297
Lake State Railway Co 323 Newman St PO Box 232 *Web:* www.lsrc.com	East Tawas	MI	48730	989-362-0207	362-4677
Louisiana & Delta Railroad Inc (LDRR) 402 W Washington St *Web:* www.gwrr.com	New Iberia	LA	70560	337-364-9625	369-1487
McCloud Railway Co 801 Industrial Way PO Box 1500	McCloud	CA	96057	530-964-2141	964-2250

				Phone	Fax
Mississippi Export Railroad Co 4519 McInnis Ave *TF:* 866-353-3322 ■ *Web:* www.mserailroad.com	Moss Point	MS	39563	228-475-3322	475-3337
Modesto & Empire Traction Co 530 11th St *Web:* www.metrr.com	Modesto	CA	95354	209-524-4631	529-0336
Montana Rail Link Inc 101 International Way *TF:* 800-338-4750 ■ *Web:* www.montanarail.com	Missoula	MT	59808	406-523-1500	523-1493
Montreal Maine & Atlantic Railway Ltd 15 Iron Rd *TF:* 800-422-6760 ■ *Web:* www.mmarail.com	Hermon	ME	04401	207-848-4280	848-4232
New England Central Railroad 7411 Fullerton St Suite 300 *TF Cust Svc:* 800-800-3450 ■ *Web:* www.railamerica.com/railmaps/NECR.htm	acksonville	FL	32256	802-527-3450	527-3488
New York Susquehanna & Western Railway Corp (NYSW) 1 Railroad Ave *TF:* 800-366-6979 ■ *Web:* www.nysw.com	Cooperstown	NY	13326	607-547-2555	547-9834
Norfolk Southern Railway Co 3 Commercial Pl *TF:* 800-635-5768 ■ *Web:* www.nscorp.com	Norfolk	VA	23510	757-629-2600	
Paducah & Louisville Railway Inc 1500 Kentucky Ave *Web:* www.palrr.com	Paducah	KY	42003	270-444-4300	444-4388
Pioneer Railcorp 1318 S Johanson Rd *TF:* 800-914-3810 ■ *Web:* www.pioneer-railcorp.com	Peoria	IL	61607	309-697-1400	697-5387
Providence & Worcester Railroad Co 75 Hammond St *AMEX:* PWX ■ *TF:* 800-447-2003 ■ *Web:* www.pwrr.com	Worcester	MA	01610	508-755-4000	753-5548
Somerset Railroad Corp 7725 Lake Rd	Barker	NY	14012	716-795-9501	795-3654
Trans-Continental Systems Inc 10801 Evendale Dr *TF:* 800-525-8726 ■ *Web:* www.tcsohio.com	Cincinnati	OH	45241	513-769-4774	769-3215
Triple Crown Services 2720 Dupont Commerce Ct Suite 200 *TF:* 800-325-6510 ■ *Web:* www.triplecrownsvc.com	Fort Wayne	IN	46825	260-416-3600	416-3771
Union Pacific Railroad Co 1400 Douglas St **Fax Area Code:* 402 ■ *TF:* 888-870-8777 ■ *Web:* www.uprr.com	Omaha	NE	68179	888-870-8777	271-2256*
Union Railroad Co 1200 Penn Ave *Web:* www.tstarinc.com	Pittsburgh	PA	15222	412-433-7090	
Winston-Salem Southbound Railway Co 4550 Overdale Rd *TF:* 888-631-8223	Winston-Salem	NC	27107	336-788-9407	788-9085
Wisconsin & Southern Railroad Co 5300 N 33rd St PO Box 90229 *Web:* www.wsorrailroad.com	Milwaukee	WI	53209	414-438-8820	438-8826
York Railroad Co 2790 W Market St	York	PA	17404	717-792-1425	854-6275

652 RAIL TRAVEL

SEE ALSO Mass Transportation (Local & Suburban) p. 2220

				Phone	Fax
National Railroad Passenger Corp 60 Massachusetts Ave NE *TF:* 800-872-7245 ■ *Web:* www.amtrak.com	Washington	DC	20002	202-906-3741	906-3285
VIA Rail Canada Inc 3 Pl Ville-Marie Suite 500 *TF:* 800-681-2561 ■ *Web:* www.viarail.ca	Montreal	QC	H3B2C9	514-871-6000	871-6104

653 RAILROAD EQUIPMENT - MFR

SEE ALSO Transportation Equipment & Supplies - Whol p. 2728

				Phone	Fax
A Stucki Co 2600 Neville Rd *TF:* 800-771-7302 ■ *Web:* www.stucki.com	Pittsburgh	PA	15225	412-771-7300	771-7308
ACF Industries Inc 101 Clark St *Web:* www.acfindustries.com	Saint Charles	MO	63301	636-949-2399	949-2825
Adams & Westlake Ltd 940 N Michigan St PO Box 4524 *Web:* www.adlake.com	Elkhart	IN	46514	574-264-1141	264-1146
American Railcar Industries Inc 100 Clark St *NASDAQ:* ARII ■ *TF:* 800-933-7937 ■ *Web:* www.americanrailcar.com	Saint Charles	MO	63301	636-940-6000	940-6030
AMSTED Industries Inc 180 N Stetson St Suite 1800 **Fax:* Hum Res ■ *Web:* www.amsted.com	Chicago	IL	60601	312-645-1700	819-8504*
Barber Brake Beam LLC 4133 S M-139 *Web:* www.brakebeams.com	Saint Joseph	MI	49085	269-408-0011	408-0012
Bombardier Transportation North America 1101 Parent St *Web:* www.bombardier.com	Saint-Bruno	QC	J3V6E6	450-441-2020	441-1515
Cardwell Westinghouse Co 8400 S Stewart Ave **Fax:* Cust Svc ■ *Web:* www.wabtec.com	Chicago	IL	60620	773-483-7575	483-9302*
Curran Group Inc 7502 S Main St *Web:* www.currangroup.com	Crystal Lake	IL	60014	815-455-5100	455-7894
Dayton-Phoenix Group Inc 1619 Kuntz Rd *TF:* 800-657-0707 ■ *Web:* www.dayton-phoenix.com	Dayton	OH	45404	937-496-3807	496-3969
Electro-Motive Diesel Inc 9301 W 55th St *TF:* 800-255-5355 ■ *Web:* www.emdiesels.com	La Grange	IL	60525	708-387-6000	387-6626
FreightCar America Inc 17 Johns St *NASDAQ:* RAIL ■ **Fax Area Code:* 814 ■ *TF:* 800-458-2235 ■ *Web:* www.freightcaramerica.com	Johnstown	PA	15901	800-458-2235	533-5010*
GE Aviation 1 Neumann Way *Web:* www.geaviation.com	Cincinnati	OH	45215	513-243-2000	
GE Transportation Rail 2901 E Lake Rd **Fax:* Hum Res ■ *TF Prod Info:* 800-626-2000 ■ *Web:* www.getransportation.com	Erie	PA	16531	814-875-2234	875-2620*
Graham-White Mfg Co 1242 Colorado St PO Box 1099 *Web:* www.grahamwhite.com	Salem	VA	24153	540-387-5600	387-5697
Greenbrier Co 1 Centerpointe Dr Suite 200 *NYSE:* GBX ■ *TF:* 800-343-7188 ■ *Web:* www.gbrx.com	Lake Oswego	OR	97035	503-684-7000	684-7553
Harsco Track Technologies (HTT) 2401 Edmund Rd PO Box 20 *TF:* 800-345-9160 ■ *Web:* www.harscotrack.com	West Columbia	SC	29171	803-822-9160	822-7471
Holland Co 1000 Holland Dr *TF:* 800-899-7754 ■ *Web:* www.hollandco.com	Crete	IL	60417	708-672-2300	672-0119
Knorr Brake Corp 861 Baltimore Blvd **Fax:* Mktg ■ *Web:* www.knorrbrakecorp.com	Westminster	MD	21157	410-875-0900	875-1210*
LB Foster Co 415 Holiday Dr *NASDAQ:* FSTR ■ **Fax:* Sales ■ *TF:* 800-255-4500 ■ *Web:* www.lbfoster.com	Pittsburgh	PA	15220	412-928-3431	928-7891*
Loram Maintenance of Way 3900 Arrowhead Dr PO Box 188 *TF:* 800-328-1466 ■ *Web:* www.loram.com	Hamel	MN	55340	763-478-6014	478-6916
Miner Enterprises Inc 1200 E State St PO Box 471 *TF:* 800-323-0625 ■ *Web:* www.minerent.com	Geneva	IL	60134	630-232-3000	232-3055
MotivePower 4600 Apple St *TF:* 800-272-7702	Boise	ID	83716	208-947-4800	947-4820
National Railway Equipment Co (NREC) 14400 Robey Ave # 2 *TF:* 800-253-2905 ■ *Web:* www.nationalrailway.com	Dixmoor	IL	60426	708-388-6002	388-2487
New York Air Brake Co 748 Starbuck Ave **Fax:* Sales ■ *TF:* 888-836-6922 ■ *Web:* www.nyab.com	Watertown	NY	13601	315-786-5200	786-5675*
Nolan Co 1016 9th St SW *TF:* 800-298-2832 ■ *Web:* www.nolancompany.com	Canton	OH	44707	330-453-7922	453-7449
Plasser American Corp 2001 Myers Rd PO Box 5464 *Web:* www.plasseramerican.com	Chesapeake	VA	23324	757-543-3526	494-7186
Portec Rail Products Inc 900 Old Freeport Rd *Web:* www.portecrail.com	Pittsburgh	PA	15238	412-782-6000	782-1037
Racine Railroad Products Inc 1524 Frederick St PO Box 044577 *Web:* www.racinerailroad.com	Racine	WI	53404	262-637-9681	637-9069
Salco Products Inc 1385 101st St # A *TF:* 800-535-8990 ■ *Web:* www.salcoproducts.com	Lemont	IL	60439	630-783-2570	792-8186
Siemens Transportation Systems Inc 7464 French Rd *Web:* www.sts.siemens.com	Sacramento	CA	95828	916-681-3000	681-3006
Trackmobile Inc 1602 Executive Dr *Web:* www.trackmobile.com	LaGrange	GA	30240	706-884-6651	884-0390
Transco Railway Products Inc 820 Hopley Ave PO Box 231 *Web:* www.transcorailway.com	Bucyrus	OH	44820	419-562-1031	562-3684
Trinity Mining Service 109 48th St *TF:* 800-245-6206 ■ *Web:* www.trin-mine.com	Pittsburgh	PA	15201	412-682-4700	682-4725
Trinity Rail Group Inc 2525 N Stemmons Fwy *TF:* 800-631-4420 ■ *Web:* www.trinityrail.com	Dallas	TX	75207	214-631-4420	589-8501
Union Tank Car Co 175 W Jackson Blvd Suite 2100 *TF:* 800-635-3770 ■ *Web:* www.utlx.com	Chicago	IL	60604	312-431-3111	347-5020
Vapor Bus International 1010 Johnson Dr *TF:* 800-631-9200 ■ *Web:* www.vapordoors.com	Buffalo Grove	IL	60089	847-777-6400	520-2220
Vapor Rail 10655 Henri-Bourassa W *Web:* www.wabtec.com	Saint-Laurent	QC	H4S1A1	514-335-4200	335-4231
WABCO Freight Car Products Ltd 475 Seaman Dr **Fax Area Code:* 877 ■ *TF:* 877-757-2226 ■ *Web:* www.wabtec.com	Stoney Creek	ON	L8E2R2	905-561-8700	799-2819*
WABCO Locomotive Products 1001 Air Brake Ave *TF:* 800-784-6816 ■ *Web:* www.wabtec.com	Wilmerding	PA	15148	412-825-1000	825-1019
Wabtec Corp 1001 Air Brake Ave *NYSE:* WAB ■ *TF:* 800-784-6816 ■ *Web:* www.wabtec.com	Wilmerding	PA	15148	412-825-1000	825-1019
Wabtec Corp WABCO Transit Div PO Box 11 *Web:* www.wabtec.com	Spartanburg	SC	29304	864-433-5900	433-0176

654 RAILROAD SWITCHING & TERMINAL SERVICES

				Phone	Fax
Belt Railway Co of Chicago 6900 S Central Ave *Web:* www.beltrailway.com	Bedford Park	IL	60638	708-496-4000	496-3037
Central California Traction Co 2201 W Washington St Suite 12 *Web:* www.cctrailroad.com	Stockton	CA	95203	209-466-6927	466-1204
East Erie Commercial Railroad 1030 Lawrence Pkwy	Erie	PA	16511	814-875-6572	875-5858
Indiana Harbor Belt Railroad Co 2721 161st St *Web:* www.ihbrr.com	Hammond	IN	46323	219-989-4703	989-4707
Minnesota Commercial Railway 508 Cleveland Ave N	Saint Paul	MN	55114	651-646-2010	646-8337
OmniTRAX Inc 252 Clayton St # 400 *Web:* www.omnitrax.com	Denver	CO	80206	303-398-4500	398-4540
Portland Terminal Railroad Co 3500 NW Yeon Ave	Portland	OR	97210	503-241-9898	241-9885
Public Belt Railroad Commission 4822 Tchoupitulas St *TF Cust Svc:* 800-524-3421	New Orleans	LA	70115	504-896-7410	896-7452
Rail Link Inc 13901 Sutton Pk Dr S # 125 *TF:* 888-902-7245	Jacksonville	FL	32224	904-223-1110	223-8710
Railserve Inc 1691 Phoenix Blvd Suite 110 *TF:* 800-345-7245 ■ *Web:* www.railserveinc.com	Atlanta	GA	30349	770-996-6838	996-6830
Rescar Inc 1101 31st St Suite 250 *TF:* 800-851-5196 ■ *Web:* www.rescar.com	Downers Grove	IL	60515	630-963-1114	963-6342
Roadrunner Transportation Systems Inc 4900 S Pennsylvania Ave PO Box 8903 *NYSE:* RRTS ■ *Web:* www.rrts.com	Cudahy	WI	53110	414-615-1500	615-1513
Terminal Railroad Assn of Saint Louis 415 S 18th St # 200 *Web:* www.terminalrailroad.com	Saint Louis	MO	63103	314-231-5196	621-3673

655 REAL ESTATE AGENTS & BROKERS

Company	City	State	Zip	Phone	Fax
Allen Morris Co 121 Alhambra Plaza Suite 1600 *Web:* www.allenmorris.com	Coral Gables	FL	33134	305-443-1000	443-1462
Aronov Realty 3500 Eastern Blvd *Web:* www.aronov.com	Montgomery	AL	36116	334-277-1000	272-0747
Assist-2-Sell Inc 1610 Meadow Wood Ln. *TF:* 800-528-7816 ■ *Web:* www.assist2sell.com	Reno	NV	89502	775-688-6060	823-8823
Baird & Warner Inc 120 S LaSalle St Suite 2000 *Web:* www.bairdwarner.com	Chicago	IL	60603	312-368-1855	368-1490
Barletta & Assoc Inc 1313 Campbell Rd Suite F *Web:* www.barlettainc.com	Houston	TX	77055	713-464-7700	464-3696
Beco Management Inc 5410 Edson Ln Suite 200 *Web:* www.beconet.com	Rockville	MD	20852	301-816-1500	816-1501
Buy Owner 1192 E Newport Ctr Dr Suite 200 *TF:* 800-940-7777 ■ *Web:* www.buyowner.com	Deerfield Beach	FL	33442	954-771-7777	745-7777
Carlson Real Estate Co Inc 301 Carlson Pkwy Suite 100 *Web:* www.carlsonrealestate.org	Minnetonka	MN	55305	952-404-5000	404-5001
Cassidy Turley Co 200 S 6th St Suite 1400 *Web:* www.cassidyturley.com	Minneapolis	MN	55402	612-341-4444	347-9389
CB Richard Ellis Group Inc 100 N Sepulveda Blvd Suite 1050 *NYSE: CBG* ■ **Fax Area Code: 213* ■ *Web:* www.cbre.com	El Segundo	CA	90245	310-606-4700	613-3005*
Central Management Inc (CMI) 820 Gessner Rd Suite 1525 *Web:* www.cmirealestate.com	Houston	TX	77024	713-961-9777	961-5730
Century 21 Real Estate Corp 1 Campus Dr *TF:* 877-221-2765 ■ *Web:* www.century21.com	Parsippany	NJ	07054	973-428-9700	496-7564
Chelsea Moore Co 8940 Glendale Milford Rd *TF:* 888-621-1161 ■ *Web:* www.chelseamoore.com	Loveland	OH	45140	513-561-5454	561-5497
Cohen Financial LP 2 N LaSalle St Suite 800 *Web:* www.cohenfinancial.com	Chicago	IL	60602	312-346-5680	346-6669
Cohen-Esrey Real Estate Services LLC 6800 W 64th St *Web:* www.cohenesrey.com	Overland Park	KS	66202	913-671-3300	671-3301
Coldwell Banker Gundaker 2458 Old Dorsett Rd Suite 300 *TF:* 800-325-1978 ■ *Web:* www.cbgundaker.com	Maryland Heights	MO	63043	314-298-5000	298-5059
Coldwell Banker Residential Brokerage 600 Grant St Suite 925 *TF:* 800-525-3030 ■ *Web:* www.coloradohomes.com	Denver	CO	80203	303-409-1500	409-6336
Coldwell Banker Residential Real Estate 5951 Cattleridge Ave. *TF:* 800-624-5292 ■ *Web:* www.floridamoves.com	Sarasota	FL	34232	941-378-8211	378-8250
Colliers International 601 Union St Suite 4800 *Web:* www.colliers.com	Seattle	WA	98101	206-695-4200	
Colliers Pinkard 7172 Columbia Gateway Dr Suite 400 *Web:* www.colliers.com/Markets/Baltimore	Columbia	MD	21046	443-297-9000	543-0191
Commercial Realty & Resources Corp 1415 Wyckoff Rd PO Box 1468	Wall	NJ	07719	732-938-1111	938-6735
Cornish & Carey Commercial 2804 Mission College Suite 120 *Web:* www.ccarey.com	Santa Clara	CA	95054	408-727-9600	988-6340
Crye-Leike Inc 6525 N Quail Hollow Rd *Web:* www.crye-leike.com	Memphis	TN	38120	901-756-8900	758-5641
Curry Investment Co 2700 Kendallwood Pkwy Suite 208/106 *Web:* www.curryre.com	Gladstone	MO	64119	816-414-5200	452-4757
Cushman & Wakefield Inc 51 W 52nd St *Web:* www.cushwake.com	New York	NY	10019	212-841-7500	841-7867
Daum Commercial Real Estate Services 4675 MacArthur Ct *TF:* 888-659-3286 ■ *Web:* www.daumcommercial.com	Newport Beach	CA	92660	949-724-1900	474-1771
Divaris Real Estate Inc 1 Columbus Ctr Suite 700 *TF:* 888-373-0023 ■ *Web:* www.divaris.com	Virginia Beach	VA	23462	757-497-2113	497-1338
Emerald Cos Inc 400 Travis St *Web:* www.emeraldcompanies.com	Shreveport	LA	71101	318-425-7083	
ERA Franchise Systems Inc 1 Campus Dr *TF:* 800-869-1260 ■ *Web:* www.era.com	Parsippany	NJ	07054	973-407-5807	407-7354
First Properties of The Carolinas Inc 1 Executive Ct *TF:* 800-545-3342 ■ *Web:* www.firstproptc.com	Lake Wylie	SC	29710	803-831-2241	831-8299
FPI Management Inc 800 Iron Pt Rd *Web:* www.fpimgt.com	Folsom	CA	95630	916-357-5300	357-5310
Gerald A Teel Company 974 Campbell Rd Suite 204 *Web:* www.gateel.com	Houston	TX	77024	713-467-5858	467-0704
Grubb & Ellis Co 4 Hutton Centre Dr # 700 *TF:* 800-877-9066 ■ *Web:* www.grubb-ellis.com	Santa Ana	CA	92707	714-667-8252	667-6860
Grubb & Ellis/Harrison & Bates Inc 6606 W Broad St Suite 400 *Web:* www.harrison-bates.com	Richmond	VA	23230	804-788-1000	782-1145
GVA Advantis 101 W Main St Suite 900 *Web:* www.gvaadvantis.com	Norfolk	VA	23510	757-627-0661	627-1901
HABITAT CO LLC The 350 W Hubbard St Suite 500 *Web:* www.habitat.com	Chicago	IL	60610	312-527-5400	527-7440
Hart Corp 900 Jaymor Rd *TF:* 800-368-4278 ■ *Web:* www.hartcorp.com	SouthHampton	PA	18966	215-322-5100	322-5840
Help-U-Sell Real Estate PO Box 742 *Web:* www.helpusell.com	Colton	CA	92324	909-693-5403	
HomeGain.com Inc 6001 Shellmound St Suite 550 *TF:* 888-542-0800 ■ *Web:* www.homegain.com	Emeryville	CA	94608	510-655-0800	655-0848
HomeServices of America Inc 333 S 7th St 27th Fl **Fax Area Code: 612* ■ *TF:* 888-485-0018 ■ *Web:* www.homeservices.com	Minneapolis	MN	55402	888-485-0018	336-5590*
Inland Group Inc 2901 Butterfield Rd *TF:* 800-828-8999 ■ *Web:* www.inlandgroup.com	Oak Brook	IL	60523	630-218-8000	218-4917
Inland Real Estate Sales Inc 2901 Butterfield Rd *TF:* 800-828-8999 ■ *Web:* www.inlandgroup.com/ires	Oak Brook	IL	60523	630-218-8000	218-4917
Iowa Realty Co Inc 3501 Westown Pkwy *TF:* 800-247-2430 ■ *Web:* www.iowarealty.com	West Des Moines	IA	50266	515-453-6222	453-5786
Jack Conway 137 Washington St *TF:* 800-283-1030 ■ *Web:* www.jackconway.com	Norwell	MA	02061	781-871-0080	878-2632
Janet Mcafee Inc 9889 Clayton Rd *TF:* 888-991-4800 ■ *Web:* www.janetmcafee.com	Saint Louis	MO	63124	314-997-4800	997-0647
John Daugherty Realtors 520 Post Oak Blvd 6th Fl *TF:* 800-231-2821 ■ *Web:* www.jdaugherty.com	Houston	TX	77027	713-626-3930	963-9588
John L Scott Inc 3380 146th Pl SE Suite 450 *TF:* 800-368-4278 ■ *Web:* www.johnlscott.com	Bellevue	WA	98007	206-230-7600	230-7550
John Stewart Co Inc 1388 Sutter St Fl 11 *Web:* www.jsco.net	San Francisco	CA	94109	415-345-4400	614-9175
Jones Lang LaSalle & Staubach Retail 1843 Douglas Ave Suite 100 **Fax Area Code: 214* ■ *TF:* 800-944-0012 ■ *Web:* www.aarcorp.com	Dallas	TX	75225	972-361-5000	438-6101*
Jones Lang LaSalle Leasing & Management Services 200 E Randolph Dr Suite 4300 *Web:* www.joneslanglasalle.com	Chicago	IL	60601	312-782-5800	
Joyner Fine Properties (JFP) 2727 Enterprise Pkwy PO Box 31355 *TF:* 800-446-3858 ■ *Web:* www.joynerfineproperties.com	Richmond	VA	23294	804-270-9440	967-2770
Keller Williams Realty Inc 807 Las Cimas Pkwy Suite 200 *Web:* www.kw.com	Austin	TX	78746	512-327-3070	328-1433
Kiemle & Hagood Co 601 W Main Ave Suite 400 *Web:* www.khco.com	Spokane	WA	99201	509-838-6541	458-4014
Latter & Blum Inc 430 Notre Dame St *Web:* www.latterblum.com	New Orleans	LA	70130	504-525-1311	569-9336
Lechner Realty Group Inc 13421 Manchester Rd *Web:* www.lechnerrealty.com	Saint Louis	MO	63131	314-909-8100	909-8105
Lightstone Group The 460 Pk Ave Suite 1300 *Web:* www.lightstonegroup.com	New York	NY	10022	212-616-9969	
Long & Foster Realtors 14501 George Carter Way **Fax: Hum Res* ■ *TF:* 800-237-8800 ■ *Web:* www.longandfoster.com	Chantilly	VA	20151	703-653-8500	961-8101*
Lyon & Assoc Realtors 3640 American River Dr Suite 100 *TF:* 866-596-6466 ■ *Web:* www.golyon.com	Sacramento	CA	95864	916-484-5444	484-7683
MacPherson's Property Management Inc 18551 Aurora Ave N Suite 100 *TF:* 888-799-9788 ■ *Web:* www.macphersons.com	Seattle	WA	98133	206-567-9508	542-6566
Major Properties Real Estate 1200 W Olympic Blvd *Web:* www.majorproperties.com	Los Angeles	CA	90015	213-747-4151	749-7972
Mason-McDuffie Real Estate Inc 5724 W Las Positas Blvd Suite 100 *Web:* www.bhghome.com/homepage.aspx	Pleasanton	CA	94588	925-924-4600	924-1852
Me Cos Inc 635 Brooksedge Blvd *TF:* 800-229-1774 ■ *Web:* www.mecompanies.com	Westerville	OH	43081	614-818-4918	818-4901
Merin Hunter Codman Inc 1601 Forum Pl Suite 200 *Web:* www.mhcreal.com	West Palm Beach	FL	33401	561-471-8000	471-9992
Mitsui Fudosan America Inc 1251 Avenue of the Americas Suite 800 *Web:* www.mfamerica.com	New York	NY	10020	212-403-5600	403-5657
Mohawk Valley Ranch Inc 1137 Hwy 89	Clio	CA	96106	530-836-0394	836-4504
National Church Residences Inc 2335 N Bank Dr *TF:* 800-388-2151 ■ *Web:* www.ncr.org	Columbus	OH	43220	614-451-2151	451-0351
NP Dodge Real Estate 8701 W Dodge Rd Suite 300 *TF:* 800-642-5008 ■ *Web:* www.npdodge.com	Omaha	NE	68114	402-397-4900	
Oil & Gas Asset Clearinghouse LP The PO Box 671787 *TF:* 800-463-4558 ■ *Web:* www.ogclearinghouse.com	Houston	TX	77267	281-873-4600	873-0055
Olive Real Estate Group 102 N Cascade Ave Suite 250 *Web:* www.olivereg.com	Colorado Springs	CO	80903	719-598-3000	578-0089
Patterson-Schwartz & Assoc Inc 7234 Lancaster Pike Suite 200A *TF:* 877-456-4663 ■ *Web:* www.pattersonschwartz.com	Hockessin	DE	19707	302-234-5270	
PCRE LLC 520 Cromwell Ave *Web:* www.prudentialct.com	Rocky Hill	CT	06067	860-571-7000	571-7410
Phillips Property Management 6106 Macarthur Blvd Suite 102 *Web:* www.phillipspm.com	Bethesda	MD	20816	301-320-0422	229-0937
Preferred Properties of Venice Inc 325 W Venice Ave *Web:* www.veniceflproperties.com	Venice	FL	34285	941-493-1521	485-9604
Prudential Fox & Roach Realtors 431 W Lancaster Ave *Web:* www.prufoxroach.com	Devon	PA	19333	610-889-2700	672-9489
Prudential Northwest Real Estate 2497 Bethel Rd SE *TF:* 800-463-7768 ■ *Web:* www.pnwre.com	Port Orchard	WA	98366	360-876-5522	876-4833
Prudential Real Estate & Relocation Services Inc 3333 Michelson Dr Suite 1000 **Fax: Mktg* ■ *TF:* 800-666-6634 ■ *Web:* www.prudential.com/realestate	Irvine	CA	92612	949-794-7900	794-7036*
Re/MAX Equity Group Inc 8405 SW Nimbus Ave Suite C *TF:* 800-283-3358	Beaverton	OR	97008	503-670-3000	670-1138
RE/MAX International Inc 5075 S Syracuse St *TF Cust Svc:* 800-525-7452 ■ *Web:* www.remax.com	Denver	CO	80237	303-770-5531	796-3599
RE/MAX of Western Canada Inc 1060 Manhattan Dr Suite 340 *TF:* 800-563-3622 ■ *Web:* www.remax.ca	Kelowna	BC	V1Y9X9	250-860-3628	860-7424

				Phone	Fax
RE/MAX Ontario-Atlantic 7101 Syntex Dr. *TF:* 888-542-2499 ■ *Web:* www.remax-oa.com	Mississauga	ON	L5N6H5	905-542-2400	542-3340
RE/MAX Quebec Inc 1500 Cunard St *TF:* 800-361-9325 ■ *Web:* www.remax-quebec.com	Laval	QC	H7S2B7	450-668-7743	668-2115
Real Estate One Inc 25800 Northwestern Hwy Suite 100 *TF:* 800-521-0508 ■ *Web:* www.realestateone.com	Southfield	MI	48075	248-851-2600	263-5966
Real Living First Service Realty 13155 SW 42nd St Suite 200 *TF:* 800-899-8477 ■ *Web:* www.realliving.com	Miami	FL	33175	305-551-9400	551-4965
Real Living Inc 77 E Nationwide Blvd *TF:* 800-848-7400 ■ *Web:* www.realliving.com	Columbus	OH	43215	614-459-7400	457-6807
Realogy Corp 1 Campus Dr *Web:* www.realogy.com	Parsippany	NJ	07054	973-407-2000	407-7004
Realty Executives International Inc 2398 E Camelback Rd Suite 900 *TF:* 800-252-3366 ■ *Web:* www.realtyexecutives.com	Phoenix	AZ	85016	602-957-0747	224-5542
Rebman Properties Inc 1014 W Fairbanks Ave *Web:* www.rebmanproperties.com	Winter Park	FL	32789	407-875-8001	875-8004
Reece & Nichols Realtors 11500 Granada Ln *Web:* www.reeceandnichols.com	Leawood	KS	66211	913-491-1001	491-0930
Remax Villa Realtors 7505 Bergenline Ave *Web:* www.remax-villa.com	North Bergen	NJ	07047	201-868-3100	868-9440
Rose Assoc Inc 200 Madison Ave *Web:* www.rosenyc.com	New York	NY	10016	212-490-3090	210-6672
Ross Realty Investments Inc 3325 S University Dr Suite 210 *TF:* 800-370-4202 ■ *Web:* www.ross-realty.com	Davie	FL	33328	954-452-5000	452-4700
Royal LePage Estate Services Ltd 39 Wynford Dr *TF:* 877-757-4545 ■ *Web:* www.royallepage.ca	Don Mills	ON	M3C3K5	416-510-5800	510-5790
Sandy River Co 509 Forest Ave PO Box 110 *Web:* www.sandyrivercompany.com	Portland	ME	04112	207-879-5800	879-5810
Semonin Realtors 4967 US Hwy 42 Suite 200 *TF:* 800-548-1650 ■ *Web:* www.semonin.com	Louisville	KY	40222	502-425-4760	339-8950
Situs Inc 4665 SW Fwy *TF:* 877-270-6878 ■ *Web:* www.situscos.com	Houston	TX	77027	713-626-7700	355-5882
Slifer Smith & Frampton/Vail Assoc Ltd Inc PO Box 2820 *TF:* 888-773-8273 ■ *Web:* www.slifer.net	Avon	CO	81620	970-845-2000	845-2050
Sotheby's International Realty 38 E 61st St *TF:* 800-848-2541 ■ *Web:* www.sothebysrealty.com	New York	NY	10065	212-606-4100	606-4199
Steele Realty & Investment Co Inc 8900 Grant Line Rd *Web:* www.steelerealtyinc.com	Elk Grove	CA	95624	916-686-6500	686-8504
Stiles Realty Co 300 SE 2nd St *TF:* 800-398-0558 ■ *Web:* www.stiles.com	Fort Lauderdale	FL	33301	954-627-9300	627-9305
Studley Inc 399 Pk Ave 11th Fl *Web:* www.studley.com	New York	NY	10022	212-326-1000	326-1034
Taylor Morrison Inc 4900 N Scottsdale Rd Suite 2000 **Fax Area Code:* 941 ■ *Web:* www.taylormorrison.com	Scottsdale	AZ	85251	480-840-8100	554-3005*
Taylor Oil Co LLC 110 Oakwood Dr Suite 510	Winston Salem	NC	27103	336-725-9531	722-8372
Thalhimer Inc Morton G 11100 W Broad St *Web:* www.thalhimer.com	Glen Allen	VA	23060	804-648-5881	697-3479
Trammell Crow Co 2001 Ross Ave Suite 3400 *NYSE: TCC* ■ *Web:* www.trammellcrow.com	Dallas	TX	75201	214-863-4101	863-3138
Tri Commercial Real Estate Services Inc 1 Califorina St Suite 200 *Web:* www.tricommercial.com	San Francisco	CA	94111	415-268-2200	268-2299
Trimont Real Estate Advisors Inc 3424 Peachtree Rd Ne *Web:* www.trimontrea.com	Atlanta	GA	30326	404-420-5600	
United Commercial Development Inc 7001 Preston Rd Suite 500 *Web:* www.ucdcorp.com	Dallas	TX	75205	214-224-4600	219-2080
United Properties Inc 404 N 31st St Suite 100	Billings	MT	59101	406-255-7100	255-7125
Waterfront Properties & Club Communities 825 Pkwy Suite 8 *Web:* www.waterfront-properties.com	Jupiter	FL	33477	561-746-7272	
Watne Inc Realtors 408 N Broadway *TF:* 800-568-5311 ■ *Web:* www.minothomes.com	Minot	ND	58703	701-852-1156	839-8966
Watson Realty Co 5701 Truxtun Ave Suite 100 *Web:* www.watsonrealty.com	Bakersfield	CA	93309	661-327-5161	861-7474
Weichert Realtors 1625 Rt 10 E *Web:* www.weichert.com	Morris Plains	NJ	07950	973-984-1400	984-4075
Western Development Corp 3255 Grace St NW *Web:* www.westdev.com	Washington	DC	20007	202-338-5200	338-6014
Weston Cos 1715 Aaron Brenner Dr Suite 516 PO Box 17847 *Web:* www.westonco.com	Memphis	TN	38187	901-682-9100	684-6357
William C Smith & Co Inc 1100 New Jersey Ave SE *Web:* www.williamcsmith.com	Washington	DC	20003	202-863-1921	371-9410
ZipRealty Inc 2000 Powell St Suite 300 *NASDAQ: ZIPR* ■ *TF:* 800-225-5947 ■ *Web:* www.ziprealty.com	Emeryville	CA	94608	510-735-2600	735-2850

656 REAL ESTATE DEVELOPERS

SEE ALSO Construction - Building Contractors - Non-Residential p. 1703; Construction - Building Contractors - Residential p. 1710

				Phone	Fax
A & B Properties Inc 822 Bishop St *Web:* www.abprop.com	Honolulu	HI	96813	808-525-6676	525-8447
AG Spanos Cos 10100 Trinity Pkwy 5th Fl *Web:* www.agspanos.com	Stockton	CA	95219	209-478-7954	473-3703
AG Spanos Development Inc 10100 Trinity Pkwy 5th Fl *Web:* www.agspanos.com	Stockton	CA	95219	209-478-7954	478-3309
Al Neyer Inc 302 W 3rd St Suite 800 *TF:* 877-271-6400 ■ *Web:* www.neyer.com	Cincinnati	OH	45202	513-271-6400	271-1350
Allen & O'Hara Inc 530 Oak Ct Dr Suite 300 *Web:* www.aoinc.com	Memphis	TN	38117	901-259-2579	259-2543
Alter Group 5500 W Howard St *TF:* 800-637-4842 ■ *Web:* www.altergroup.com	Skokie	IL	60077	847-676-4300	676-4302
Amelia Island Co 1501 Lewis St *TF:* 888-261-6161 ■ *Web:* www.aipfl.com	Amelia Island	FL	32034	904-261-6161	277-5159
Amerco Real Estate Co 2727 N Central Ave Suite 500 *TF:* 877-213-1873 ■ *Web:* www.amercorealestate.com	Phoenix	AZ	85004	602-263-6555	277-5824
American Invsco Corp 1028 N Clark St *TF:* 800-340-3420 ■ *Web:* www.invsco.com	Chicago	IL	60610	312-431-8311	431-1125
American West Homes 250 Pilot Rd Suite 140 *Web:* www.americanwesthomes.com	Las Vegas	NV	89119	702-736-6434	736-7970
Amfac/JMB Hawaii LLC 700 Bishop St Suite 2002	Honolulu	HI	96813	808-543-8900	543-8918
AMLI Residential Properties Trust 125 S Wacker Dr Suite 3100 *NYSE: AML*	Chicago	IL	60606	312-443-1477	443-0909
AMREP Corp 300 Alexander Pk Suite 204 *NYSE: AXR* ■ *Web:* www.amrepcorp.com	Princeton	NJ	08540	609-716-8200	716-8255
AMREP Southwest Inc 333 Rio Rancho Dr NE **Fax:* Cust Svc ■ *Web:* www.amrepsouthwest.com	Rio Rancho	NM	87124	505-892-9200	896-9180*
Asset Plus Co 675 Bering Dr Suite 200 *Web:* www.assetpluscorp.com	Houston	TX	77057	713-782-5800	268-5111
Atlantic Builders Inc 7800 Belfort Pkwy Suite 200 *Web:* www.atlanticbuilders.net	Jacksonville	FL	32256	904-279-9500	279-9559
Ausherman Homes 721 Corporate Ct Suite B *Web:* www.dreeshomes.com	Frederick	MD	21703	301-663-6104	663-3929
Avatar Holdings Inc 201 Alhambra Cir 12th Fl *NASDAQ: AVTR* ■ *TF:* 800-736-6660 ■ *Web:* www.avatarhomes.com	Coral Gables	FL	33134	305-442-7000	448-9929
Beazer Homes 9202 N Meridian St Suite 300 *Web:* www.beazer.com	Indianapolis	IN	46260	317-843-9514	846-0398
Beazer Homes USA Inc 1000 Abernathy Rd Suite 1200 *NYSE: BZH* ■ *Web:* www.beazer.com	Atlanta	GA	30328	770-829-3700	481-0431
Belz Enterprises 100 Peabody Pl Suite 1400 *Web:* www.belz.com	Memphis	TN	38103	901-767-4780	271-7238
BPG Properties Ltd 1500 Market St 3200 Centre Sq W *Web:* www.bpgltd.com	Philadelphia	PA	19102	215-496-0400	496-0431
Brehm Cos 2714 Loker Ave W Suite 300 *TF:* 877-273-4622 ■ *Web:* www.brehmco.com	Carlsbad	CA	92010	760-448-2420	448-2421
Bresler & Reiner Inc 11200 Rockville Pike Suite 502 *Web:* www.breslerandreiner.com	Rockville	MD	20852	301-945-4300	945-4301
Brisben Cos 7800 E Kemper Rd *Web:* www.brisben.com	Cincinnati	OH	45249	513-489-1990	489-2780
Brooks Resources Corp 409 NW Franklin Ave Suite A *TF:* 888-773-7553 ■ *Web:* www.brooksresources.com	Bend	OR	97702	541-382-1662	385-3285
Brothers Property Corp 2 Alhambra Plaza Suite 1280 *Web:* www.brothersproperty.com	Coral Gables	FL	33134	305-285-1035	858-2733
Bruce Gunstra Builders Inc 2150 Elmwood Ave Suite 1	Lafayette	IN	47904	765-447-2134	447-0332
Butler Real Estate 1540 Genessee St *Web:* www.butlermfg.com	Kansas City	MO	64102	816-968-3000	968-3720
Cadillac Fairview Ltd 20 Queen St W 5th Fl *Web:* www.cadillacfairview.com	Toronto	ON	M5H3R4	416-598-8200	598-8578
Cafaro Co 2445 Belmont Ave *Web:* www.cafarocompany.com	Youngstown	OH	44505	330-747-2661	743-2902
California Pacific Homes 38 Executive Pk Suite 200 *TF:* 800-999-0629 ■ *Web:* www.calpacifichomes.com	Irvine	CA	92614	949-833-6000	833-6133
Capeletti Bros Inc 16401 NW 58th Ave PO Box 4944	Miami Lakes	FL	33014	305-823-9500	823-0943
Capo Group 1680 Michigan Ave PH 5 *Web:* www.bayresort.com	Miami	FL	33139	305-513-0501	673-5129
Cappelli Enterprises Inc 115 E Stevens Ave *Web:* www.cappelli-inc.com	Valhalla	NY	10595	914-769-6500	747-9268
Carl M Freeman Assoc Inc 18330 Village Ctr Dr 2nd Fl *Web:* www.freemancommunities.com	Olney	MD	20832	240-779-8000	779-8180
Carlisle Corp 263 Wagner Pl *Web:* www.carlislecorp.com	Memphis	TN	38103	901-526-5000	
Casden Properties 9090 Wilshire Blvd 3rd Fl	Beverly Hills	CA	90211	310-274-5553	276-6486
Castle & Cooke Inc 10900 Wilshire Blvd Suite 1600 *Web:* www.castlecooke.com	Los Angeles	CA	90024	310-208-3636	824-2159
Centex Real Estate Corp 2728 N Harwood St **Fax:* Sales ■ *Web:* www.centexhomes.com	Dallas	TX	75201	214-981-5000	981-6000*
Century Builders Group Inc 2301 NW 87 Ave 6th Fl *Web:* www.centuryhomebuilders.com	Doral	FL	33172	305-599-8100	470-1900
Century Homebuilders of South Florida 8812 SW 152 Ct *Web:* www.centurybuildersgroup.com	Miami	FL	33196	305-599-8100	470-1900

Company / Address	City	State	Zip	Phone	Fax
CFC Inc 320 W 8th St Suite 200 *Web:* www.cfcincorporated.com	Bloomington	IN	47402	812-332-0053	333-4680
Chelsea Investment Corp 5993 Avenida Encinas Suite 101 *Web:* www.chelseainvestco.com	Carlsbad	CA	92008	760-456-6000	456-6001
Choice Homes of Texas PO Box 1048 *Web:* www.choice-homes.com	Arlington	TX	76004	817-652-4900	633-3330
Christensen Group 4400 SE Columbia Way	Vancouver	WA	98661	360-696-0381	695-4762
Christopherson Homes Inc 1315 Airport Blvd *Web:* www.christophersonhomes.com	Santa Rosa	CA	95403	707-524-8222	524-8234
Colony Homes 110 Londonderry Ct Suite 136 **Fax Area Code:* 678 ■ *Web:* www.colonyhomes.com	Woodstock	GA	30188	770-928-0092	486-4584*
Comstock Homebulding Cos Inc 11465 Sunny Hills Rd 4th Fl *Web:* www.comstockhomebuilding.com	Reston	VA	20190	703-883-1700	760-1520
Connell Realty & Development Co 200 Connell Dr *TF:* 800-233-3240 ■ *Web:* www.connell-realestate.com	Berkeley Heights	NJ	07922	908-673-3700	673-3800
Conner Homes Co 846 108th Ave NE *Web:* www.connerhomes.com	Bellevue	WA	98004	425-455-9280	462-0426
Cooper Communities Inc 903 N 47th St *TF:* 800-648-6401 ■ *Web:* www.cooper-communities.com	Rogers	AR	72756	479-246-6500	
Coppenbarger Homes 7700 Sq Lake Blvd	Jacksonville	FL	32256	904-223-7470	363-1994
Corcoran Jennison Development Co 150 Mt Vernon St Bayside Office Ctr Suite 500 *Web:* www.corcoranjennison.com	Boston	MA	02125	617-822-7350	822-7352
Cornerstone Group 2100 Hollywood Blvd *TF:* 800-809-4099 ■ *Web:* www.theapartmentcorner.com	Hollywood	FL	33020	800-809-4099	
CountryTyme Inc 1660 Gateway Cir *TF:* 800-388-1349 ■ *Web:* www.countrytyme.com	Grove City	OH	43123	614-875-1423	875-1084
Craftmark Homes 6820 Elm St Suite 102 *Web:* www.craftmarkhomes.com	McLean	VA	22101	703-734-9855	749-9758
Crescent Resources Inc 227 W Trade St #1000 *Web:* www.crescent-resources.com	Charlotte	NC	28202	980-321-6000	
Crosswinds Communities 41050 Vincenti Ct *Web:* www.crosswinds.com	Novi	MI	48375	248-615-1313	615-4129
Darling Homes 2500 Legacy Dr Suite 100 *Web:* www.darlinghomes.com	Frisco	TX	75034	972-624-4100	624-4106
David Weekley Homes Inc 1111 N Post Oak Rd *Web:* www.davidweekleyhomes.com	Houston	TX	77055	713-963-0500	963-0322
Davis Homes Inc 3755 E 82nd St Suite 120 *TF:* 888-595-2800	Indianapolis	IN	46240	317-595-2800	595-2918
De Anza Land & Leisure Corp 1615 Cordova St	Los Angeles	CA	90007	323-734-9951	734-2531
Deltona Corp 8014 SW 135th St Rd *TF:* 800-935-6378 ■ *Web:* www.deltona.com	Ocala	FL	34473	352-347-2322	307-8103
Developers of Nevada 7448 W Sahara Ave Suite 101	Las Vegas	NV	89117	702-222-1410	227-0746
Development Services of America 4025 Delridge Way SW Suite 500 *TF:* 800-372-3663	Seattle	WA	98106	206-933-4888	933-4889
Dixon Builders & Developers Inc 7924 Jessie's Way *TF:* 877-442-5888 ■ *Web:* www.dixonbuilders.com	Hamilton	OH	45011	513-887-6400	887-6643
Dominion Homes Inc 4900 Tuttle Crossing Blvd *Web:* www.dominionhomes.com	Dublin	OH	43016	614-356-5000	761-6899
Donohoe Cos Inc 2101 Wisconsin Ave NW *TF:* 877-366-6463 ■ *Web:* www.donohoe.com	Washington	DC	20007	202-333-0880	342-3924
Double Diamond Co 10100 N Central Expy Suite 600 *TF:* 800-324-7438 ■ *Web:* www.ddresorts.com	Dallas	TX	75231	214-706-9801	706-9878
DR Horton Inc 301 Commerce St Suite 500 *NYSE: DHI* ■ *TF:* 800-846-7866 ■ *Web:* www.drhorton.com	Fort Worth	TX	76102	817-390-8200	390-1717
Duffel Financial & Construction Co 1430 Willow Pass Rd Suite 220	Concord	CA	94520	925-603-8444	603-8440
Eagle Hospitality Properties Trust Inc 100 E RiverCenter Blvd Suite 480 *Web:* www.eaglehospitality.com	Covington	KY	41011	859-292-5500	292-5599
EJM Development Co 9061 Santa Monica Blvd *Web:* www.ejmdevelopment.com	Los Angeles	CA	90069	310-278-1830	278-2965
Elan Development 211 Highland Cross Dr Suite 101	Houston	TX	77073	281-821-5556	482-1652
Elliott Homes 80 Iron Pt Cir Suite 110 *Web:* www.elliotthomes.com	Folsom	CA	95630	916-984-1300	984-1322
Embrey Partners Ltd 1020 NE Loop 410 Suite 700 *Web:* www.embreypropertiesltd.com	San Antonio	TX	78209	210-824-6044	824-7656
Emmer Group 2801 SW Archer Rd *Web:* www.emmergroup.com	Gainesville	FL	32608	352-376-2444	376-2260
Epoch Properties Inc 359 Carolina Ave *Web:* www.epochproperties.com	Winter Park	FL	32789	407-644-9055	644-9845
Ergon Properties Inc 2829 Lakeland Dr PO Box 23038 **Fax:* Hum Res ■ *TF:* 800-824-2626 ■ *Web:* www.ergonproperties.com	Jackson	MS	39232	601-933-3000	933-3355*
Estridge Cos 14300 Clay Terr Blvd # 200 *TF:* 800-473-7326 ■ *Web:* www.estridge.com	Carmel	IN	46032	317-846-7311	
Fairfield Homes 6420 E Tanque Verde Rd *TF:* 877-868-7125 ■ *Web:* www.fairfieldhomes.net	Tucson	AZ	85701	520-622-8771	622-8876
Fieldstone Communities Inc 14 Corporate Plaza *TF:* 800-665-0661 ■ *Web:* www.fieldstone-homes.com	Newport Beach	CA	92660	949-759-5810	759-5032
First Hartford Corp 149 Colonial Rd PO Box 1270 *TF:* 888-646-6555 ■ *Web:* www.firsthartford.com	Manchester	CT	06045	860-646-6555	646-8572
Flagship Properties Corp 1 Greenway Plaza Suite 750	Houston	TX	77046	713-623-6000	
Flournoy Development Co 900 Brookstone Ctr Pkwy *Web:* www.flournoycompanies.com	Columbus	GA	31904	706-324-4000	324-4150
Ford Motor Land Development Corp 330 Town Ctr Dr Suite 1100	Dearborn	MI	48126	313-323-3100	594-7215
Forecast Group 3536 Concours St Suite 100 *TF:* 800-229-4117 ■ *Web:* www.forecasthomes.com	Ontario	CA	91764	909-483-7320	980-7305
Forest City Commercial Group 50 Public Sq Terminal Tower Suite 1130 *Web:* www.forestcity.net/company/people/commercial/Pages/default.aspx	Cleveland	OH	44113	216-736-7646	
Forest City Enterprises Inc 50 Public Sq 1100 Terminal Tower *NYSE: FCEa* ■ **Fax:* Hum Res ■ *Web:* www.forestcity.net/Pages/default.aspx	Cleveland	OH	44113	216-621-6060	263-4808*
Forest City Land Group 50 Public Sq Terminal Tower Suite 1050 *Web:* www.forestcity.net/company/people/land/Pages/default.aspx	Cleveland	OH	44113	216-736-7646	
Forest City Ratner Cos (FCRC) 1 MetroTech Ctr N *Web:* www.forestcity.net	Brooklyn	NY	11201	718-923-8400	
Forest City Residential Development 50 Public Sq Terminal Tower Suite 1170 *Web:* www.forestcity.net/Contact/Pages/residential_development_inquiries.aspx	Cleveland	OH	44113	216-736-7646	
Forsberg Real Estate Co 2422 Jolly Rd Suite 200 *Web:* www.lansingrealestate.com	Okemos	MI	48864	517-349-9330	349-7131
Fox & Jacobs Homes 9229 LBJ Fwy Suite 100 **Fax Area Code:* 214 ■ **Fax:* Sales ■ *Web:* www.foxandjacobs.com	Dallas	TX	75243	972-416-1447	764-9920*
Fralin & Waldron Inc 2917 Penn Forest Blvd *TF:* 888-238-7459 ■ *Web:* www.fwinc.com	Roanoke	VA	24018	540-774-4415	774-4582
Friendswood Development Co 550 Greens Pkwy Suite 100	Houston	TX	77067	281-875-1552	872-4207
Gambone Bros Development Co 1030 W Germantown Pike PO Box 287 *Web:* www.gambone.com	Fairview Village	PA	19409	610-539-4700	539-2020
Gatehouse Group Inc The 120 Forbes Blvd *Web:* www.gatehousemgt.com	Mansfield	MA	02048	508-337-2500	
Gehan Homes Ltd 14901 Quorum Dr Suite 300 *Web:* www.gehanhomes.com	Dallas	TX	75254	972-383-4300	383-4399
General Real Estate Corp 8500 SW 8th St Suite 228	Miami	FL	33144	305-262-6533	262-4118
Gentry Homes Ltd 560 N Nimitz Hwy **Fax:* Sales ■ *Web:* www.gentryhawaii.com	Honolulu	HI	96809	808-599-5558	533-2949*
Gilbane Inc 7 Jackson Walkway *TF:* 800-445-2263 ■ *Web:* www.gilbaneco.com	Providence	RI	02903	401-456-5890	456-5996
Ginsburg Development Corp 245 Saw Mill River Rd *Web:* www.gdc-homes.com	Hawthorne	NY	10532	914-747-3600	747-1608
GL Homes of Florida Corp 1600 Sawgrass Corporate Pkwy Suite 300 *Web:* www.glhomes.com	Sunrise	FL	33323	954-753-1730	753-4509
Goldrich & Kest Industries 5150 Overland Ave *Web:* www.gkind.com	Culver City	CA	90230	310-204-2050	204-1900
Goodnight Homes Inc PO Box 276	Killeen	TX	76540	254-634-0491	634-5619
Grand Homes Inc 5150 Keller Springs Rd *Web:* www.grandhomes.com	Dallas	TX	75206	214-750-6528	750-6849
Grubb & Ellis Co 4 Hutton Centre Dr # 700 *TF:* 800-877-9066 ■ *Web:* www.grubb-ellis.com	Santa Ana	CA	92707	714-667-8252	667-6860
Haas & Haynie Corp 400 Oyster Pt Blvd Suite 123 *Web:* www.hh1898.com	South San Francisco	CA	94080	650-588-5600	873-9150
Hamilton Co The 39 Brighton Ave *Web:* www.thehamiltoncompany.com	Allston	MA	02134	617-783-0039	783-0568
Hamlet Homes 308 E 4500 S Suite 200 *Web:* www.hamlethomes.com	Salt Lake City	UT	84107	801-281-2223	281-2224
Harbour Homes 1300 Dexter Ave N Suite 550 *Web:* www.harbourhomes.com	Seattle	WA	98109	206-315-8130	315-8131
Hartz Construction Co Inc 9026 Heritage Pkwy *Web:* www.hartzhomes.com	Woodridge	IL	60517	630-228-3800	228-4800
Hartz Mountain Real Estate 400 Plaza Dr *Web:* www.hartzmountain.com	Secaucus	NJ	07094	201-348-1200	348-4358
Haubert Homes Inc 15 Central Blvd *Web:* www.hauberthomes.com	Camp Hill	PA	17011	717-761-7951	761-4125
Hayden Homes Inc 7 The Pines Ct Suite A *Web:* www.haydenhomes.com	Saint Louis	MO	63141	314-434-0995	434-5951
Hearn Co The 100 N Lasalle St Suite 2500 *Web:* www.hearncompany.com	Chicago	IL	60602	312-408-3000	
Henry Crown Co 222 N LaSalle St Suite 2000	Chicago	IL	60601	312-236-6300	984-1458
Heritage Development Group Inc 465 Heritage Rd PO Box 873	Southbury	CT	06488	203-264-8291	264-3347
Hff Inc 301 Grant St Suite 600 *NYSE: HF* ■ *Web:* www.hfflp.com	Pittsburgh	PA	15219	412-281-8714	281-2792
Highland Homes 12850 Hillcrest Rd Suite 200 *Web:* www.highlandhomes.com	Dallas	TX	75230	972-387-7905	385-0403
Hills Communities Inc 4901 Hunt Rd Suite 300 *Web:* www.hillsinc.com	Cincinnati	OH	45242	513-984-0300	618-7694
Hines Interest LP 2800 Post Oak Blvd 48th Fl *Web:* www.hines.com	Houston	TX	77056	713-621-8000	966-2055
HJ Kalikow Inc 101 Pk Ave 25th Fl *Web:* www.hjkalikow.com	New York	NY	10178	212-808-7000	573-6380
Hoffman Homes for Youth PO Box 4777 *Web:* www.hoffmanhomes.com	Gettysburg	PA	17325	717-359-7148	359-2600
Hofmann Co The 1380 Galaxy Way *Web:* www.hofmannhomes.com	Concord	CA	94520	925-682-4830	682-4771
Holiday Builders Inc 1801 Penn St Suite 1-A *Web:* www.holidaybuilders.com	Melbourne	FL	32901	321-259-3130	751-9198
Hovnanian Enterprises Inc 110 W Front St PO Box 500 *NYSE: HOV* ■ *Web:* www.khov.com	Red Bank	NJ	07701	732-747-7800	383-2942
Hunt Bldg Co Ltd 4401 N Mesa St *Web:* www.huntelp.com	El Paso	TX	79902	915-533-1122	545-2631
Hunt Midwest Enterprises Inc 8300 NE Underground Dr *TF:* 800-551-6877 ■ *Web:* www.huntmidwest.com	Kansas City	MO	64161	816-455-2500	
Hunt Midwest Residential Development 8300 NE Underground Dr *TF:* 800-551-6877 ■ *Web:* www.huntcommunities.com	Kansas City	MO	64161	816-455-2500	455-8701
IDI Group Cos 1700 N Moore St Suite 2020 *Web:* www.idigroup.com	Arlington	VA	22209	703-558-7300	558-7377
Inland Real Estate Development Corp 2901 Butterfield Rd *TF:* 800-828-8999 ■ *Web:* www.inlandgroup.com	Oak Brook	IL	60523	630-218-8000	218-4917
International Rivercenter					

	City	State	Zip	Phone	Fax
2 Poydras St 2nd Fl Riverside	New Orleans	LA	70140	504-584-3901	584-3955
Interstate General Co LP (IGC)					
105 W Washington St PO Box 1280	Middleburg	VA	20117	540-687-3177	687-3179
Web: www.iwtonline.com					
Intervest Construction Inc					
2379 Beville Rd	Daytona Beach	FL	32119	386-788-0820	
Web: www.icihomes.com					
Irvine Co 550 Newport Ctr Dr	Newport Beach	CA	92660	949-720-2000	720-2501*
**Fax:* Hum Res ■ *Web:* www.irvinecompany.com					
Ivory Homes 970 E Woodoak Ln	Salt Lake City	UT	84117	801-268-0700	747-7090
Web: www.ivoryhomes.com					
JJ Gumberg Co Inc 1051 Brinton Rd	Pittsburgh	PA	15221	412-244-4000	244-9133
Web: www.jjgumberg.com					
JMB Realty Corp 900 N Michigan Ave 14th Fl	Chicago	IL	60611	312-440-4800	915-2310
JMC Communities					
2201 4th St N Suite 200	Saint Petersburg	FL	33704	727-823-0022	821-2007
TF: 800-741-4106 ■ *Web:* www.jmccommunities.com					
John Buck Co 1 N Wacker Dr Suite 2400	Chicago	IL	60606	312-993-9800	993-0857
Web: www.tjbc.com					
John F Buchan Homes					
2821 Northup Way Suite 100	Bellevue	WA	98004	425-827-2266	827-0462
TF: 866-528-2426 ■ *Web:* www.buchan.com					
John F Long Properties LLLP					
5035 W Camelback Rd	Phoenix	AZ	85031	602-272-0421	846-7208*
**Fax Area Code:* 623 ■ *Web:* www.jflong.com					
John Wieland Homes & Neighborhoods Inc					
1950 Sullivan Rd	Atlanta	GA	30337	770-996-2400	904-3481
TF: 800-376-4663 ■ *Web:* www.jwhomes.com					
JPI 600 E Las Colinas Blvd Suite 1800	Irving	TX	75039	972-556-1700	444-2102
Web: www.jpi.com					
Jupiter Realty Corp					
401 Michigan Ave Suite 1300	Chicago	IL	60611	312-642-6000	642-2316
TF: 800-910-2276 ■ *Web:* www.jupiterrealty.com					
Kaiser Ventures LLC					
3633 Inland Empire Blvd # 48	Ontario	CA	91764	909-483-8500	944-6605
TF: 800-889-3652 ■ *Web:* www.kaiserventures.com					
Kapalua Land Co Ltd 200 Village Rd	Lahaina	HI	96761	808-669-5622	669-5454
TF Sales: 800-545-8439 ■ *Web:* www.mauiland.com					
KB Home 10990 Wilshire Blvd 7th Fl	Los Angeles	CA	90024	310-231-4000	231-4222
NYSE: KBH ■ *TF:* 800-344-6637 ■ *Web:* www.kbhome.com					
Kettler 1751 Pinnacle Dr Suite 700	McLean	VA	22102	703-641-9000	641-9630
Web: www.kettler.com					
Keystone Builders Resource Group Inc					
1207 Roseneath Rd Suite 200	Richmond	VA	23230	804-354-8830	358-6976
Web: www.keybuild.com					
Killearn Inc					
300 Lester Mill Rd Suite 110	Locust Grove	GA	30248	770-389-2020	389-2010
Web: www.killearn.com					
Knight Development Inc 9497 Thornton Blvd	Jonesboro	GA	30236	770-471-4751	603-0904
Web: www.knighthomes.com					
Kohner Properties Inc					
1034 S Brentwood Suite 1300	Saint Louis	MO	63117	314-862-5955	862-0839
Web: www.kohner.com					
Koren Development Inc					
9200 Rumsey Rd Suite 210	Columbia	MD	21045	410-740-1010	992-5573
Kravco Co 234 Mall Blvd	King of Prussia	PA	19406	610-768-6300	768-6444
Web: www.kravco.com					
Lakewood Homes					
2700 W Higgins Rd Suite 100	Hoffman Estates	IL	60195	847-884-8800	884-8986
Web: www.lakewoodhomes.com					
Lancia Construction 9430 Lima Rd Suite A	Fort Wayne	IN	46818	260-489-4433	489-0325
TF: 800-752-6242 ■ *Web:* www.lanciahomes.com					
LCOR Inc 100 Berwyn Pk Suite 110	Berwyn	PA	19312	610-251-9110	408-4420
Web: www.lcor.com					
LeCesse Development Corp					
650 S Northlake Blvd Suite 450	Altamonte Springs	FL	32701	407-645-5575	645-0553
Lefrak Organization 97-77 Queens Blvd	Rego Park	NY	11374	718-459-9021	575-4816
Web: www.lefrak.com					
Legend Homes Corp					
12755 SW 69th Ave Suite 100	Portland	OR	97223	503-620-8080	598-8900
Web: www.legendhomes.com					
Lennar Homes Inc 700 NW 107th Ave Suite 400	Miami	FL	33172	305-559-4000	226-4158
TF: 800-741-4663 ■ *Web:* www.lennar.com					
Lennar Homes of Arizona Inc					
5151 E Broadway Suite 1100	Tucson	AZ	85711	520-747-0997	
Web: www.lennar.com					
Lifestyle Homes Inc 17865 Georgetown Dr	Cold Springs	NV	89506	775-673-9000	674-4030
Web: www.woodlandvillagehomes.com					
Lord Baltimore Properties					
6225 Smith Ave Suite B100	Baltimore	MD	21209	410-415-7600	580-9250
Web: www.lordbaltimoreprop.com					
Lozier Homes Corp 1203 114th Ave SE	Bellevue	WA	98004	425-454-8690	646-8695
M/I Homes Inc 3 Easton Oval	Columbus	OH	43219	614-418-8000	418-8080
NYSE: MHO ■ *TF:* 888-644-4111 ■ *Web:* www.mihomes.com					
Maracay Homes Arizona I LLC					
15160 N Hayden Rd Suite 200	Scottsdale	AZ	85260	480-970-6000	970-8899
Web: www.maracayhomes.com					
Maui Land & Pineapple Co Inc					
120 Kane St PO Box 187	Kahului	HI	96733	808-877-3351	871-0953
NYSE: MLP ■ *Web:* www.mauiland.com					

	City	State	Zip	Phone	Fax
MBK Real Estate LLC					
175 Technology Dr Suite 200	Irvine	CA	92618	949-789-8300	789-9300
Web: www.mbk.com					
McGuyer Homebuilders Inc					
7676 Woodway Dr Suite 104	Houston	TX	77063	713-952-6767	952-5637
Web: www.mcguyerhomebuilders.com					
McKee Group 940 W Sproul Rd Suite 301	Springfield	PA	19064	610-604-9800	328-5023
Web: www.mckeebuilders.com					
McMillin Cos 2750 Womble Ave	San Diego	CA	92106	619-477-4117	794-1604
TF: 800-781-0401 ■ *Web:* www.mcmillin.com					
McStain Enterprises Inc					
400 Centennial Pkwy Suite 200	Louisville	CO	80027	303-494-5900	494-4933
Web: www.mcstain.com					
Mercedes Homes Inc					
6905 N Wickham Rd Suite 403	Melbourne	FL	32940	321-259-6972	242-1789
Web: www.mercedeshomes.com					
Meritage Homes Corp 17851 N 85th St Suite 300	Phoenix	AZ	85255	480-515-8100	
NYSE: MTH ■ *Web:* www.meritagehomes.com					
Mid-West Terminal Warehouse Co Inc					
1700 Universal Ave	Kansas City	MO	64120	816-231-8811	231-0020
Web: www.mwtco.com					
Miller & Smith Cos					
8401 Greensboro Dr Suite 300	McLean	VA	22102	703-821-2500	356-1933
Web: www.millerandsmith.com					
Minto Builders					
4400 W Sample Rd Suite 200	Coconut Creek	FL	33073	954-973-4490	974-7452
TF: 800-767-4490 ■ *Web:* www.minto.com					
Mission West Properties 10050 Bandley Dr	Cupertino	CA	95014	408-725-0700	725-1626
AMEX: MSW ■ *TF:* 800-222-5401 ■ *Web:* www.missionwest.com					
Mitchell Co Inc					
41 W I-65 Service Rd N					
Colonial Bank Ctr 3rd Fl	Mobile	AL	36608	251-380-2929	345-1264
Web: www.mitchellcompany.com					
Mitsubishi Estate NY Inc					
1221 Avenue of the Americas 17th Fl	New York	NY	10020	212-698-2200	698-2211
Web: www.mec.co.jp/index_ef.htm					
Moceri Development Corp					
3005 University Dr Suite 100	Auburn Hills	MI	48326	248-340-9400	340-9401
Web: www.moceri.com					
Montalbano Builders Inc					
1801 S Meyers Rd Suite 500	Oakbrook Terrace	IL	60181	630-613-2700	
Web: www.montalbanohomes.com					
Narragansett Improvement Co					
223 Allens Ave	Providence	RI	02903	401-331-7420	351-6444
Web: www.nicori.com					
NESCO Inc Real Estate Group					
6140 Parkland Blvd	Mayfield Heights	OH	44124	440-461-6000	449-3111
Newhall Land & Farming Co					
25124 Springfield Ct # 300	Valencia	CA	91355	661-255-4000	255-3960
TF: 800-342-3612 ■ *Web:* www.valencia.com					
Newmark Knight Frank 125 Pk Ave	New York	NY	10017	212-372-2000	372-2426
Web: www.newmarkkf.com					
Norwood Builders 7458 N Harlem Ave	Chicago	IL	60631	773-775-5400	775-4433
Web: www.norwoodbuilders.com					
NTS Development Co 10172 Linn Stn Rd	Louisville	KY	40223	502-426-4800	426-4994
Web: www.ntsdevelopment.com					
NTS Realty Holdings LP 10172 Linn Stn Rd	Louisville	KY	40223	502-426-4800	426-4994
AMEX: NLP ■ *Web:* www.ntsdevelopment.com					
O Hill Partners 1 Upper Newport Plaza	Newport Beach	CA	92660	949-752-0700	752-0885
Olympia Development LLC 2211 Woodward Ave	Detroit	MI	48201	313-983-6200	983-6049
Orleans Homebuilders Inc					
3333 St Rd 1 Greenwood Sq Suite 101	Bensalem	PA	19020	215-245-7500	
Web: www.orleanshomes.com					
Paparone Corp 702 N White Horse Pike	Stratford	NJ	08084	856-784-0550	627-0650
Web: www.paparonenewhomes.com					
Paramount Group Inc 1633 Broadway Suite 1801	New York	NY	10019	212-237-3100	237-3197
Web: www.paramount-group.com					
Park Square Enterprises Inc					
5200 Vineland Rd Suite 200	Orlando	FL	32811	407-529-3000	529-3100
Web: www.parksquarehomes.com					
Parker Lancaster Corp					
711 Moorefield Pk Dr Suite E	Richmond	VA	23236	804-323-3100	330-7198
Peebles Corp The					
One Alhambra Plaza Suite 1400	Coral Gables	FL	33134	305-442-4342	442-4345
Web: www.peeblescorp.com					
Peterson Cos					
10000 W 75th St Suite 100	Shawnee Mission	KS	66204	913-384-3800	384-9605
Phoenix Developers 605 Silverleaf Dr	Joliet	IL	60431	815-730-0008	730-6814
Web: www.phoenixdevelopers.com					
Picerne Real Estate Group					
75 Lambert Lind Hwy	Warwick	RI	02886	401-732-3700	738-6452
Web: www.picerne.com					
Pineloch Management Inc					
102 W Pineloch Ave Suite 10	Orlando	FL	32806	407-859-3550	650-0303
Web: www.pineloch.com					
Pitcairn Properties Inc					
165 Township Line Rd	Jenkintown	PA	19046	215-517-4040	690-3100
Web: www.pitcairnproperties.com					
Pizzuti Inc 2 Miranova Pl Suite 800	Columbus	OH	43215	614-280-4000	280-5000
TF: 877-749-9884 ■ *Web:* www.pizzuti.com					
Plaster Development Co Inc					
801 S Rancho Dr Suite E-4	Las Vegas	NV	89106	702-385-5031	385-6567
Web: www.signaturehomes.com					
Polygon Northwest Co					
11624 SE 5th St Suite 200	Bellevue	WA	98005	425-586-7700	688-0500
TF: 800-765-9466 ■ *Web:* www.polygonhomes.com					
Porten Cos 333 NE 2nd St	Delray Beach	FL	33483	561-819-1109	
Web: www.portencompanies.com					
Post Properties Inc					
4401 Northside Pkwy Suite 800	Atlanta	GA	30327	404-846-5000	846-6161*
NYSE: PPS ■ **Fax:* Hum Res ■ *Web:* www.postproperties.com					
Pringle Development Inc 2801 S Bay St	Eustis	FL	32726	352-483-8000	483-8001
TF: 800-325-4471 ■ *Web:* www.pringle.com					

Company	City	State	ZIP	Phone	Fax
Puget Western Inc 19515 N Creek Pkwy Suite 310	Bothell	WA	98011	425-487-6550	487-6565
Pulte Home Corp 100 Bloomfield Hills Pkwy Suite 300 — *TF:* 800-777-8583 ■ *Web:* www.pulte.com	Bloomfield Hills	MI	48304	248-644-7300	433-4598
Quadrangle Development Corp 1001 G St NW Suite 700-W — *Web:* www.quadrangledevcorp.com	Washington	DC	20001	202-393-1999	393-0548
Quadrant Corp 14725 SE 36 St Suite 300 — *Web:* www.quadranthomes.com	Bellevue	WA	98006	425-455-2900	646-8377
Questar Properties Inc 124 Slade Ave Suite 200 — **Fax:* Sales ■ *Web:* www.questar.net/qpi.html	Baltimore	MD	21208	410-486-1234	486-6346*
Realty Investment Co Ltd 345 Kekuanaoa St Suite 20 — *Web:* www.rinvest.com	Hilo	HI	96720	808-961-5252	935-8099
Redd Brown & Williams 201 Bridge St PO Box 1720 — *Web:* www.rbandw.com	Paintsville	KY	41240	606-789-8119	789-5414
Reeves-Williams Inc 7911 Sarah Ann Dr S	Southaven	MS	38671	662-349-4260	
Related Group of Florida 2828 Coral Way PH 1 — *Web:* www.relatedgroup.com	Miami	FL	33145	305-460-9900	460-9911
Related Midwest 350 W Hubbard St Suite 300 — *Web:* www.relatedmidwest.com	Chicago	IL	60610	312-595-7400	595-1898
Republic Properties Corp 1280 MD Ave SW Suite 280 — *Web:* www.republicpropertiescorp.com	Washington	DC	20024	202-863-0300	552-5320
Richman Group of Cos 599 W Putnam Ave — *TF:* 800-333-3509	Greenwich	CT	06830	203-869-0900	869-1034
Richmond American Homes Inc 4350 S Monaco St — *TF:* 888-402-4663 ■ *Web:* www.richmondamerican.com	Denver	CO	80237	303-773-2727	220-4492
Roberts Properties 450 Northridge Pkwy Suite 300	Atlanta	GA	30350	770-394-6000	396-0706
Robson Communities 9532 E Riggs Rd — *TF:* 800-732-9949 ■ *Web:* www.robson.com	Sun Lakes	AZ	85248	480-895-9200	895-0136
Rottlund Co Inc The 3065 Centre Pt Dr — *Web:* www.rottlundhomes.com	Roseville	MN	55113	651-638-0500	638-0501
Ryder Homes of Nevada Inc 985 Damonte Ranch Pkwy # 140 — *Web:* www.ryderhomes.com	Reno	NV	89521	775-823-3788	823-3799
Ryland Group Inc 24025 Pk Sorrento Suite 400 — *NYSE:* RYL ■ *TF:* 800-267-0998 ■ *Web:* www.ryland.com	Calabasas	CA	91302	818-223-7500	223-7667
S & A Custom Built Homes 2121 Old Gatesburg Rd Suite 200 — *Web:* www.sahomebuilder.com	State College	PA	16803	814-231-4780	272-8821
Sabey Corp 12201 Tukwila International Blvd 4th Fl — *Web:* www.sabey.com	Seattle	WA	98168	206-281-8700	282-9951
Santa Anita Race Track 285 W Huntington Dr — *Web:* www.santaanita.com	Arcadia	CA	91007	626-574-7223	446-9565
Schatten Properties Management Co Inc 1514 S St — *TF:* 800-892-1315 ■ *Web:* www.schattenproperties.com	Nashville	TN	37212	615-329-3011	327-2343
Schostak Bros & Co Inc 17800 Laurel Pk Dr N Suite 200C — *Web:* www.schostak.com	Livonia	MI	48152	248-262-1000	262-1814
Sea Pines Plantation Co Inc 32 Greenwood Dr — *TF:* 800-925-4653 ■ *Web:* www.seapines.com	Hilton Head Island	SC	29928	843-785-3333	842-1475
Sea Trail Corp 211 Clubhouse Rd — *TF:* 888-321-9076 ■ *Web:* www.seatrail.com	Sunset Beach	NC	28468	910-287-1100	287-1104
Seago Group Inc 3446 Marinatown Ln	North Fort Myers	FL	33903	239-997-7711	997-6407
SEDA Construction Co 2120 Corporate Sq Blvd Suite 3 — *Web:* www.sedaconstruction.com	Jacksonville	FL	32216	904-724-7800	727-9500
Shapell Industries Inc 8383 Wilshire Blvd Suite 700 — *TF:* 800-655-9502 ■ *Web:* www.shapellhomes.com	Beverly Hills	CA	90211	323-655-7330	655-4349
Shea Homes Inc 8800 N Gainey Ctr Dr Suite 350 — *Web:* www.sheahomes.com	Scottsdale	AZ	85258	480-348-6000	948-8806
Shelter Group The 218 N Charles St Suite 220 — *Web:* www.thesheltergroup.com	Baltimore	MD	21201	410-962-0595	347-0587
Shodeen Inc 17 N 1st St — *Web:* www.shodeen.com	Geneva	IL	60134	630-232-8570	232-8581
Simpson Housing LLLP (SHLP) 8110 E Union Ave Suite 200 — *Web:* www.simpsonhousing.com	Denver	CO	80237	303-283-4100	
Simpson Property Group LP (SPG) 8110 E Union Ave Suite 200 — *Web:* www.simpsonpropertygroup.com	Denver	CO	80237	303-283-4100	283-4258
Singh Homes Inc 7125 Orchard Lake Rd Suite 200 — *Web:* www.singhweb.com	West Bloomfield	MI	48322	248-865-1600	865-1630
Skanska USA Inc 16-16 Whitestone Expy — *Web:* www.skanska.com	Whitestone	NY	11357	718-767-2600	767-2663
South Shore Harbor Development Ltd 2525 S Shore Blvd Suite 205 — *Web:* www.southshoreharbour.com	League City	TX	77573	281-334-7501	334-7506
Space Center Inc 2501 Rosegate — *TF:* 800-548-9737 ■ *Web:* www.spacecenterinc.com	Saint Paul	MN	55113	651-604-4200	604-4222
Stanley Martin Cos 11111 Sunset Hills Rd Suite 200 — *TF:* 800-446-4807 ■ *Web:* www.stanleymartin.com	Reston	VA	20190	703-964-5000	715-8076
Steiner & Assoc Inc 4016 Townsfair Way — *Web:* www.steiner.com	Columbus	OH	43219	614-414-7300	414-7311
Stiles Corp 300 SE 2nd St — *Web:* www.stiles.com	Fort Lauderdale	FL	33301	954-627-9300	627-9305
Stiles Development Co 300 SE 2nd St — *Web:* www.stiles.com/development_about_us.htm	Fort Lauderdale	FL	33301	954-627-9300	627-9305
Stratus Properties Inc 212 Lavaca St Suite 300 — *NASDAQ:* STRS ■ *TF:* 800-690-0315 ■ *Web:* www.stratusproperties.com	Austin	TX	78701	512-478-5788	478-6340
Suarez Housing Corp 9950 Princess Palm Ave Suite 212 — *Web:* www.suarezhousing.com	Tampa	FL	33619	813-664-1100	622-6813
Sueba USA Corp 1800 W Loop S Suite 1300 — *Web:* www.suebausa.com	Houston	TX	77027	713-961-3588	961-1343
SunCor Development Co 80 E Rio Salado Pkwy Suite 410 — *Web:* www.suncoraz.com	Tempe	AZ	85281	480-317-6800	317-6934
Susquehanna Real Estate 140 E Market St — *Web:* www.susquehanna-realestate.com	York	PA	17401	717-848-5500	771-1430
Swerdlow Real Estate Group 3390 Mary St Suite 200 — *Web:* www.swerdlowgroup.com	Coconut Grove	FL	33133	305-476-0100	476-0108
Tak Construction 60 Walnut Ave Suite 400 — *Web:* www.takgroupinc.com	Clark	NJ	07066	732-340-0700	340-0850
Taylor-Morley Homes 17107 Chesterfield Airport Rd — *TF:* 888-297-3155	Chesterfield	MO	63005	314-434-9000	434-1390
TELACU 5400 E Olympic Blvd Third Fl — *Web:* www.telacu.com	Los Angeles	CA	90022	323-721-1655	724-3372
Tishman Speyer Properties Inc 520 Madison Ave — *Web:* www.tishmanspeyer.com	New York	NY	10022	212-715-0300	319-1745
Toll Bros Inc 250 Gibraltar Rd — *NYSE:* TOL ■ **Fax:* Mktg ■ *TF:* 800-289-8655 ■ *Web:* www.tollbrothers.com	Horsham	PA	19044	215-938-8000	938-8217*
Trammell Crow Co 2001 Ross Ave Suite 3400 — *NYSE:* TCC ■ *Web:* www.trammellcrow.com	Dallas	TX	75201	214-863-4101	863-3138
Trammell Crow Residential 2859 Paces Ferry Rd Suite 1100 — *Web:* www.tcresidential.com	Atlanta	GA	30339	770-801-1600	801-1256
TransCon Builders Inc 25250 Rockside Rd — *TF:* 800-362-0371 ■ *Web:* www.transconbuilders.com	Bedford Heights	OH	44146	440-439-3400	439-6710
Transeastern Properties Inc 3300 N University Dr Suite 001 — *TF:* 877-352-4635 ■ *Web:* www.transeasternhomes.com	Coral Springs	FL	33065	954-346-9700	346-9704
TW Lewis 850 W Elliot Rd Suite 101 — **Fax Area Code:* 602 ■ *Web:* www.twlewis.com	Tempe	AZ	85284	480-820-0807	820-1455*
Uniwell Corp 21172 Figueroa St — *Web:* www.milantile.com	Carson	CA	90745	310-782-8888	782-8500
US Home Corp 10707 Clay Rd — *Web:* www.lennar.com/ushome	Houston	TX	77041	713-877-2311	877-2452
Van Daele Homes 2900 Adams St Suite C-25 — *Web:* www.vandaele.com	Riverside	CA	92504	951-354-2121	354-2996
Van Metre Cos 5252 Lyngate Ct	Burke	VA	22015	703-425-2600	425-2261
Victory Housing Inc 5430 Grosvenor Ln Suite 210 — *Web:* www.victoryhousing.org	Bethesda	MD	20814	301-493-6000	493-9788
Village Builders 550 Greens Pkwy Suite 200 — *Web:* www.lennar.com	Houston	TX	77067	281-873-4663	872-4210
Village Green Cos 30833 Northwestern Hwy Suite 300 — *Web:* www.villagegreen.com	Farmington Hills	MI	48334	248-851-9600	851-6161
Village Homes of Colorado Inc 100 Inverness Terr Suite E-200 — *TF:* 866-752-2322 ■ *Web:* www.villagehomes.com	Englewood	CO	80112	303-795-1976	
Villages of Lake Sumter Inc 1100 Main St — **Fax:* Sales ■ *TF:* 800-346-4556 ■ *Web:* www.thevillages.com	The Villages	FL	32159	352-753-2270	753-6224*
Vineland Construction Co 71 W Pk Ave — *Web:* www.vinelandconstruction.com	Vineland	NJ	08360	856-794-4724	794-4721
Walt Disney Imagineering 500 S Vuenavista St — *NYSE:* DIF ■ *Web:* www.disneyworld.com	Burbank	CA	91521	818-544-6500	544-7995
Walton Associated Co Inc 2001 Financial Way Suite 200	Glendora	CA	91741	626-963-8505	914-7016
Warmington Group The 3090 Pullman St — *TF:* 800-925-9709 ■ *Web:* www.homesbywarmington.com	Costa Mesa	CA	92626	714-557-5511	641-9337
Waters Mcpherson Mcneill Pc 300 Lighting Way 7th Fl PO BOX 1560 — *Web:* www.lawwmm.com	Secaucus	NJ	07096	201-863-4400	863-2866
Wathen-Castanos Inc 7259 N 1st St Suite 101 — *Web:* www.wathen-castanos.com	Fresno	CA	93720	559-432-8181	432-8595
Watson Land Co 22010 S Wilmington Ave Suite 400 — *Web:* www.watsonlandcompany.com	Carson	CA	90745	310-952-6400	522-8788
WCI Communities Inc 24301 Walden Ctr Dr — **Fax:* Hum Res ■ *TF:* 800-924-2290 ■ *Web:* www.wcicommunities.com	Bonita Springs	FL	34134	239-498-8200	498-8278*
Weiss Homes Inc 828 E Jefferson Blvd — *TF:* 888-336-7373 ■ *Web:* www.weisshomes.com	South Bend	IN	46617	574-234-7373	282-2987
Wensmann Homes Inc 1895 Plaza Dr Suite 200	Eagan	MN	55122	651-406-4400	905-3678
Weston Cos 1715 Aaron Brenner Dr Suite 516 PO Box 17847 — *Web:* www.westonco.com	Memphis	TN	38187	901-682-9100	684-6357
Westrum Development Co Inc 370 Commerce Dr — *TF:* 800-937-8786 ■ *Web:* www.westrum.com	Fort Washington	PA	19034	215-283-2190	283-0991
Weyerhaeuser Co 33663 Weyerhaeuser Way S — *NYSE:* WY ■ *TF:* 800-525-5440 ■ *Web:* www.weyerhaeuser.com	Federal Way	WA	98003	253-924-2345	924-2685
Wilshire Homes 12401 Research Blvd # 1-300 — *Web:* www.buffingtonhomes.com	Austin	TX	78759	512-502-2050	338-4163
Wispark LLC 301 W Wisconsin Ave Suite 400 — *Web:* www.wispark.com	Milwaukee	WI	53203	414-274-4600	274-4640
Woodlands Operating Co LP PO Box 5050 — *TF:* 888-504-5050 ■ *Web:* www.thewoodlands.com	The Woodlands	TX	77387	281-719-6100	719-6177
Woodside Homes of Nevada 5888 W Sunset Rd Suite 200 — *Web:* www.woodside-homes.com	Las Vegas	NV	89118	702-889-7800	889-0801
Wooldridge Organization 395 Taylor Blvd Suite 120	Pleasant Hill	CA	94523	925-680-7979	680-7685

	City	State	Zip	Phone	Fax
Worthington Group The 9341 Marketplace Rd.	Fort Myers	FL	33912	239-561-4666	561-4676
TF: 877-560-4666 ■ *Web:* www.worthingtongroup.com					
Wynne Bldg Corp 12804 SW 122nd Ave.	Miami	FL	33186	305-235-3175	378-9716
Zaremba Group 14600 Detroit Ave.	Cleveland	OH	44107	216-221-6600	221-9742
TF: 800-252-3222 ■ *Web:* www.zarembagroup.com					
Zicka Homes 7861 E Kemper Rd	Cincinnati	OH	45249	513-247-3500	247-3512
TF: 800-652-1745 ■ *Web:* www.zickahomes.com					

657 REAL ESTATE INVESTMENT TRUSTS (REITS)

	City	State	Zip	Phone	Fax
Acadia Realty Trust 1311 Mamaroneck Ave Suite 260	White Plains	NY	10605	914-288-8100	428-2380
NYSE: AKR ■ *TF:* 800-227-5570 ■ *Web:* www.acadiarealty.com					
Affordable Residential Communities Inc 1981 N Broadway Suite 385	Walnut Creek	CA	94596	925-949-5100	949-5101
NYSE: ARC ■ *TF:* 800-245-5415 ■ *Web:* www.e-arc.com					
Alexandria Real Estate Equities Inc 385 E Colorado Blvd Suite 299	Pasadena	CA	91101	626-578-0777	578-0770
NYSE: ARE					
American Campus Communities Inc 12700 Hill Country Blvd Suite T-200	Austin	TX	78738	512-732-1000	732-2450
NYSE: ACC ■ *Web:* www.americancampus.com					
American Land Lease Inc (ANL) 380 Pk Pl Blvd Suite 200	Clearwater	FL	33759	727-726-8868	726-8885
NYSE: ANL ■ *TF:* 800-826-6069 ■ *Web:* www.americanlandlease.com					
AMLI Residential 200 W Monroe St Suite 2200	Chicago	IL	60606	312-283-4700	283-4720
Web: www.amli.com					
AmREIT 8 Greenway Plaza Suite 1000	Houston	TX	77046	713-850-1400	850-0498
TF: 800-888-4400 ■ *Web:* www.amreit.com					
Annaly Mortgage Management Inc 1211 Avenue of the Americas Suite 2902	New York	NY	10036	212-696-0100	696-9809
NYSE: NLY ■ *TF:* 800-487-9947 ■ *Web:* www.annaly.com					
Anworth Mortgage Asset Corp 1299 Ocean Ave 2nd Fl.	Santa Monica	CA	90401	310-255-4493	434-0070
NYSE: ANH ■ *Web:* www.anworth.com					
Apartment Investment & Management Co 4582 S Ulster St Pkwy Suite 1100	Denver	CO	80237	303-757-8101	759-3226
NYSE: AIV ■ *TF:* 888-789-8600 ■ *Web:* www.aimco.com					
Arbor Realty Trust Inc 333 Earle Ovington Blvd Suite 900	Uniondale	NY	11553	516-832-8002	832-8045
NYSE: ABR ■ *TF:* 800-272-6710 ■ *Web:* www.arborrealtytrust.com					
Ashford Hospitality Trust Inc 14185 Dallas Pkwy Suite 1100	Dallas	TX	75254	972-490-9600	980-2705
NYSE: AHT ■ *Web:* www.ahtreit.com					
AutoStar 180 Glastonbury Blvd Suite 201	Glastonbury	CT	06033	860-815-5900	815-5901
Web: www.autostar.com					
Benchmark Group 4053 Maple Rd	Amherst	NY	14226	716-833-4986	833-2954
TF: 800-876-0160 ■ *Web:* www.benchmarkgrp.com					
BioMed Realty Trust Inc 17190 Bernardo Ctr Dr	San Diego	CA	92128	858-485-9840	485-9843
NYSE: BMR ■ *Web:* www.biomedrealty.com					
Boardwalk Real Estate Investment Trust 1501 1st St SW Suite 200	Calgary	AB	T2P0W1	403-531-9255	531-9565
TSE: BEI.UN ■ *TF:* 888-231-8191 ■ *Web:* www.boardwalkreit.com					
BRE Properties Inc 525 Market St 4th Fl	San Francisco	CA	94105	415-445-6530	445-6505
NYSE: BRE ■ *Web:* www.breproperties.com					
BRT Realty Trust 60 Cutter Mill Rd Suite 303	Great Neck	NY	11021	516-466-3100	466-3132
NYSE: BRT ■ *TF:* 800-450-5816 ■ *Web:* www.brtrealty.com					
Cal-American Properties Trust 1109 westwood Blvd.	Los Angeles	CA	90024	310-277-6318	277-0738
TF General: 800-734-9811 ■ *Web:* www.calamerican.com					
Camden Property Trust 3 E Greenway Plaza Suite 1300	Houston	TX	77046	713-354-2500	354-2700*
NYSE: CPT ■ **Fax:* Mktg ■ *TF:* 800-922-6336 ■ *Web:* www.camdenliving.com					
Canadian Real Estate Investment Trust (CREIT) 175 Bloor St E Suite 500	Toronto	ON	M4W3R8	416-628-7771	628-7777
TSE: REF.UN ■ *Web:* www.creit.ca					
Capital Automotive Real Estate Services Inc 8270 Greensboro Dr Suite 950	McLean	VA	22102	703-288-3075	288-3375
TF: 877-422-7288 ■ *Web:* www.capitalautomotive.com					
Capital Lease Funding Inc 1065 Avenue of the Americas 19th Fl	New York	NY	10018	212-217-6300	217-6301
NYSE: LSE ■ *Web:* www.caplease.com					
Capital Trust Inc 410 Pk Ave 14th Fl	New York	NY	10022	212-655-0220	655-0044
NYSE: CT ■ *Web:* www.capitaltrust.com					
CAPREIT Inc 11200 Rockville Pike Suite 100	Rockville	MD	20852	301-231-8700	468-8392
Web: www.capreit.com					
Capstead Mortgage Corp 8401 N Central Expy Suite 800	Dallas	TX	75225	214-874-2323	874-2398
NYSE: CMO ■ *TF:* 800-358-2323 ■ *Web:* www.capstead.com					
CBL & Assoc Properties Inc CBL Ctr 2030 Hamilton Pl Blvd Suite 500	Chattanooga	TN	37421	423-855-0001	490-8662
NYSE: CBL ■ *TF:* 800-333-7310 ■ *Web:* www.cblproperties.com					
Cedar Shopping Centers Inc 44 S Bayles Ave Suite 304	Port Washington	NY	11050	516-767-6492	767-6497
NYSE: CDR ■ *TF:* 800-564-3128 ■ *Web:* www.cedarshoppingcenters.com					
Centro Properties Group 580 W Germantown Pike Suite 200	Plymouth Meeting	PA	19462	610-825-7100	834-8110
Web: www.centroprop.com					
Centro Properties Group 420 Lexington Ave 7th Fl	New York	NY	10170	646-344-8600	869-3989*
**Fax Area Code:* 212 ■ *TF:* 800-468-7526 ■ *Web:* www.centroprop.com					
Chesapeake Lodging Trust (CLT) 1997 Annapolis Exchange Pkwy Suite 410	Annapolis	MD	21401	800-698-2820	
NYSE: CHSP ■ *TF:* 800-698-2820 ■ *Web:* www.chesapeakelodgingtrust.com					
Choice Group 755 W Big Beaver Rd.	Troy	MI	48084	248-362-4150	362-4154
Web: www.choiceproperties.com					
Church Loans & Investment Trust 5305 W IH- 40	Amarillo	TX	79106	806-358-3666	358-1430
TF: 800-692-1111 ■ *Web:* www.churchloans.com					
Cogdell Spencer Inc 4401 Barclay Downs Dr Suite 300	Charlotte	NC	28209	704-553-5707	553-5825
NYSE: CSA ■ *Web:* www.cogdell.com					
Colonial Properties Trust 2101 6th Ave N Suite 750	Birmingham	AL	35203	205-250-8700	250-8890
NYSE: CLP ■ *TF:* 866-222-9877 ■ *Web:* www.colonialprop.com					
Commercial Properties Realty Trust 402 N Fourth St	Baton Rouge	LA	70802	225-924-7206	924-1235
TF: 800-648-9064 ■ *Web:* www.cprt.com					
Corporate Office Properties Trust 6711 Columbia Gateway Dr Suite 300	Columbia	MD	21046	443-285-5400	285-7650
NYSE: OFC ■ *Web:* www.copt.com					
Cousins Properties Inc 191 Peachtree St NE Suite 3600	Atlanta	GA	30303	404-407-1000	407-1002
NYSE: CUZ ■ *TF:* 800-926-8746 ■ *Web:* www.cousinsproperties.com					
CRIIMI MAE Inc 701 13th St NW Suite 1000	Washington	DC	20005	202-715-9500	
TF: 800-266-0535 ■ *Web:* www.cwcapital.com					
DiamondRock Hospitality Co (DRHC) 3 Bethesda Metro Ctr Suite 1500	Bethesda	MD	20814	240-744-1150	744-1199
NYSE: DRH ■ *Web:* www.drhc.com					
Digital Realty Trust Inc 560 Mission St Suite 2900	San Francisco	CA	94105	415-738-6500	738-6501
NYSE: DLR ■ *TF:* 877-357-7782 ■ *Web:* www.digitalrealtytrust.com					
Dividend Capital Trust 518 17th St Suite 1700	Denver	CO	80202	303-228-2200	228-0128
TF: 866-324-7348 ■ *Web:* www.dividendcapital.com					
Dmg Information Ltd (DMGI) 3 Stamford Landing, Suite 400 46 Southfield Ave	Stamford	CT	06902	203-973-2940	973-2995
Web: www.dmginfo.com					
Donahue Schriber Realty Group Inc 200 E Baker St Suite 100	Costa Mesa	CA	92626	714-545-1400	545-4222
Web: www.donahueschriber.com					
Duke Realty Corp 600 E 96th St Suite 100	Indianapolis	IN	46240	317-808-6000	808-6794
NYSE: DRE ■ *TF:* 800-875-3366 ■ *Web:* www.dukerealty.com					
Dupont Fabros Technology Inc 1212 New York Ave NW Suite 900	Washington	DC	20005	202-728-0044	728-0220
NYSE: DFT ■ *Web:* www.dft.com					
Dynex Capital Inc 4551 Cox Rd Suite 300	Glen Allen	VA	23060	804-217-5800	217-5860
NYSE: DX ■ *Web:* www.dynexcapital.com					
EastGroup Properties Inc 190 E Capitol St Suite 400	Jackson	MS	39201	601-354-3555	352-1441
NYSE: EGP ■ *TF:* 800-337-5602 ■ *Web:* www.eastgroup.net					
ECC Capital Corp 2600 E Coast Hwy Suite 250	Corona Del Mar	CA	92625	949-954-7060	
PINK: ECRO ■ *TF:* 800-899-0926 ■ *Web:* www.ecccapital.com					
Education Realty Trust Inc 530 Oak Ct Dr Suite 300	Memphis	TN	38117	901-259-2500	259-2594
NYSE: EDR ■ *Web:* www.edrtrust.com					
Equity International 2 N Riverside Plaza Suite 1500	Chicago	IL	60606	312-466-4001	466-3311
Web: www.equityinternational.com					
Equity Office Properties Trust 2 N Riverside Plaza Suite 2100	Chicago	IL	60606	312-466-3300	454-0332
NYSE: EOP ■ *Web:* www.equityoffice.com					
Essex Property Trust Inc 925 E Meadow Dr	Palo Alto	CA	94303	650-494-3700	494-8743
NYSE: ESS ■ *Web:* www.essexpropertytrust.com					
Federal Realty Investment Trust 1626 E Jefferson St.	Rockville	MD	20852	301-998-8100	998-3700
NYSE: FRT ■ *TF:* 800-658-8980 ■ *Web:* www.federalrealty.com					
FelCor Lodging Trust Inc 545 E John Carpenter Fwy Suite 1300	Irving	TX	75062	972-444-4900	444-4949
NYSE: FCH ■ *Web:* www.felcor.com					
Feldman Mall Properties Inc 2201 E Camelback Rd Suite 350	Phoenix	AZ	85016	602-277-5559	277-7774
NYSE: FMP ■ *TF:* 800-475-3716 ■ *Web:* www.feldmanmall.com					
First Industrial Realty Trust Inc 311 S Wacker Dr Suite 4000	Chicago	IL	60606	312-344-4300	922-6320
NYSE: FR ■ *TF:* 800-894-8778 ■ *Web:* www.firstindustrial.com					
First Potomac Realty Trust 7600 Wisconsin Ave Suite 1100	Bethesda	MD	20814	301-986-9200	986-5554
NYSE: FPO ■ *Web:* www.first-potomac.com					
First REIT of New Jersey 505 Main St	Hackensack	NJ	07602	201-488-6400	487-7881
Franklin Street Properties Corp 401 Edgewater Pl Suite 200	Wakefield	MA	01880	781-557-1300	246-2807
AMEX: FSP ■ *TF:* 877-686-9496 ■ *Web:* www.franklinstreetproperties.com					
Gables Residential Trust 777 Yamato Rd Suite 510	Boca Raton	FL	33431	561-997-9700	241-9506
Web: www.gables.com					
GE Capital Solutions Franchise Finance 450 S Orange Ave	Orlando	FL	32801	407-540-2000	540-2004
TF: 877-667-4769 ■ *Web:* www.gecapsol.com					
Ginkgo Residential LLC 301 S College St Suite 3850	Charlotte	NC	28202	704-944-0100	944-2039
Web: www.bnproperties.com					
Gramercy Capital Corp 420 Lexington Ave	New York	NY	10170	212-297-1000	297-1090
NYSE: GKK ■ *Web:* www.gramercycapitalcorp.com					
Health Care Property Investors Inc 3760 Kilroy Airport Way Suite 300	Long Beach	CA	90806	562-733-5100	733-5200
NYSE: HCP ■ *TF:* 888-604-1990 ■ *Web:* www.hcpi.com					
Health Care REIT Inc 1 SeaGate Suite 1500	Toledo	OH	43603	419-247-2800	247-2826
NYSE: HCN ■ *Web:* www.hcreit.com					
Healthcare Realty Trust Inc 3310 W End Ave Suite 700	Nashville	TN	37203	615-269-8175	269-8260
NYSE: HR ■ *Web:* www.healthcarerealty.com					
Highwoods Properties Inc 3100 Smoketree Ct Suite 600	Raleigh	NC	27604	919-872-4924	876-2448
NYSE: HIW ■ *TF:* 866-449-6637 ■ *Web:* www.highwoods.com					
HMG/Courtland Properties Inc 1870 S Bayshore Dr	Coconut Grove	FL	33133	305-854-6803	856-7342
AMEX: HMG					

Company	City	State	ZIP	Phone	Fax
Home Properties Inc 850 Clinton Sq *NYSE: HME* ■ *Web:* www.homeproperties.com	Rochester	NY	14604	585-546-4900	546-5433
Horizon Group Properties Inc 5000 Hakes Dr *Web:* www.horizongroup.com	Muskegon	MI	49441	231-798-9100	798-5100
Host Hotels & Resorts Inc 6903 Rockledge Dr Suite 1500 *NYSE: HST* ■ *TF:* 800-724-4268 ■ *Web:* www.hosthotels.com	Bethesda	MD	20817	240-744-1000	744-5125
Impac Mortgage Holdings Inc 19500 Jamboree Rd *NYSE: IMH* ■ *TF:* 800-597-4101 ■ *Web:* www.impaccompanies.com	Irvine	CA	92612	949-475-3600	
Income Opportunity Realty Investors Inc 1755 Wittington Pl Suite 340 *AMEX: IOT* ■ *TF:* 800-400-6407 ■ *Web:* www.incomeopp-realty.com	Dallas	TX	75234	469-522-4200	522-4299
ING Clarion Partners 230 Pk Ave 12th Fl *TF:* 800-776-4696 ■ *Web:* www.ingclarion.com	New York	NY	10169	212-883-2500	883-2700
Ing Real Estate Canada 202 Brownlow Ave Tower 2 Suite D200 *TF:* 866-786-6481 ■ *Web:* www.ingrealestate.com	Halifax	NS	B3B1T5	902-421-1222	420-0559
Inland Real Estate Corp 2901 Butterfield Rd *NYSE: IRC* ■ **Fax:* Investor Rel ■ *TF:* 888-331-4732 ■ *Web:* www.inlandrealestate.com	Oak Brook	IL	60523	630-218-8000	218-7357*
Innkeepers USA Trust 340 Royal Poinciana Plaza Suite 306 *Web:* www.innkeepersusa.com	Palm Beach	FL	33480	561-835-1800	835-0457
InnSuites Hospitality Trust 1615 E Northern Ave Suite 102 *AMEX: IHT* ■ *TF:* 800-842-4242 ■ *Web:* www.innsuitestrust.com	Phoenix	AZ	85020	602-944-1500	678-0281
Investors Real Estate Trust 3015 16th St SW Suite 100 PO Box 1988 *NASDAQ: IRET* ■ *TF:* 888-478-4738 ■ *Web:* www.iret.com	Minot	ND	58702	701-837-4738	838-7785
iStar Financial Inc 1114 Avenue of the Americas 39th Fl *NYSE: SFI* ■ *TF:* 888-335-3122 ■ *Web:* www.istarfinancial.com	New York	NY	10036	212-930-9400	930-9494
Kilroy Realty Corp 12200 W Olympic Blvd Suite 200 *NYSE: KRC* ■ *Web:* www.kilroyrealty.com	Los Angeles	CA	90064	310-481-8400	481-6501
Kimco Realty Corp 3333 New Hyde Pk Rd Suite 100 *NYSE: KIM* ■ *TF:* 800-645-6292 ■ *Web:* www.kimcorealty.com	New Hyde Park	NY	11042	516-869-9000	869-9001
Kite Realty Group Trust 30 S Meridian St Suite 1100 *NYSE: KRG* ■ *TF:* 888-577-5600 ■ *Web:* www.kiterealty.com	Indianapolis	IN	46204	317-577-5600	577-5605
KKR Asset Management LLC 555 California St Suite 5000 *NYSE: KFN*	San Francisco	CA	94104	415-315-3620	391-3077
LaSalle Hotel Properties 3 Bethesda Metro Ctr Suite 1200 *NYSE: LHO* ■ *Web:* www.lasallehotels.com	Bethesda	MD	20814	301-941-1500	941-1553
Lexington Corporate Properties Trust One Penn Plaza Suite 4015 *NYSE: LXP* ■ *TF:* 800-850-3948 ■ *Web:* www.lxp.com	New York	NY	10119	212-692-7200	594-6600
Lexington Realty Trust Inc 1 Penn Plaza Suite 4015 *Web:* www.lxp.com	New York	NY	10119	212-692-7200	594-6600
Liberty Property Trust 500 Chesterfield Pkwy *NYSE: LRY* ■ *Web:* www.libertyproperty.com	Malvern	PA	19355	610-648-1700	644-4129
Lillibridge Healthcare Real Estate Trust 200 W Madison St Suite 3200 *Web:* www.lillibridge.com	Chicago	IL	60606	312-408-1370	408-1415
LTC Properties Inc 2829 Townsgate Rd Suite 350 *NYSE: LTC* ■ *Web:* www.ltcproperties.com	Westlake Village	CA	91361	805-981-8655	981-8663
Macerich Co The 401 Wilshire Blvd Suite 700 *NYSE: MAC* ■ *TF:* 800-421-7237 ■ *Web:* www.macerich.com	Santa Monica	CA	90401	310-394-6000	395-2791
Mack-Cali Realty Corp 343 Thornall St *NYSE: CLI* ■ *Web:* www.mack-cali.com	Edison	NJ	08837	732-590-1000	205-8237
Madison Park Financial Corp 409 13th St 8th Fl *Web:* www.mpfcorp.com	Oakland	CA	94612	510-452-2944	452-2973
Medical Properties Trust Inc 1000 Urban Ctr Dr Suite 501 *NYSE: MPW* ■ *Web:* www.medicalpropertiestrust.com	Birmingham	AL	35242	205-969-3755	969-3756
Meredith Enterprises Inc 3000 Sand Hill Rd Bldg 2 Suite 120 *Web:* www.meredithreit.com	Menlo Park	CA	94025	650-233-7140	233-7160
MFA Mortgage Investments Inc 350 Pk Ave 21st Fl *NYSE: MFA* ■ *Web:* www.mfa-reit.com	New York	NY	10022	212-207-6400	207-6420
MHI Hospitality Corp 410 W Francis St Suite 201 *NASDAQ: MDH* ■ *Web:* www.mhihospitality.com	Williamsburg	VA	23185	757-229-5648	564-8801
Monmouth Real Estate Investment Corp (MREIC) 3499 Rt 9 N Suite 3C *NASDAQ: MNRTA* ■ *Web:* www.mreic.com	Freehold	NJ	07728	732-577-9996	577-9981
MPG Office Trust Inc 355 S Grand Ave Suite 3300 *NYSE: MPG* ■ *Web:* www.mpgoffice.com	Los Angeles	CA	90071	213-626-3300	687-4758
National Health Investors Inc 222 Robert Rose Dr *NYSE: NHI* ■ *Web:* www.nhinvestors.com	Murfreesboro	TN	37130	615-890-9100	225-3030
Nationwide Health Properties Inc 610 Newport Ctr Dr Suite 1150 *NYSE: NHP* ■ *TF:* 877-483-6827 ■ *Web:* www.nhp-reit.com	Newport Beach	CA	92660	949-718-4400	759-6876
NB Capital Corp 65 E 55th St	New York	NY	10022	212-632-8697	632-8789
New York Mortgage Trust Inc (NYMT) 52 Vanderbilt Ave Suite 403 *NASDAQ: NYMT* ■ *TF:* 800-491-6962 ■ *Web:* www.nymtrust.com	New York	NY	10017	212-792-0107	655-6269
Newcastle Investment Corp 1345 Avenue of the Americas 46th Fl *NYSE: NCT* ■ *Web:* www.newcastleinv.com	New York	NY	10105	212-798-6100	
NorthStar Realty Finance Corp 399 Pk Ave 18th Fl *NYSE: NRF* ■ *Web:* www.nrfc.com	New York	NY	10022	212-547-2600	547-2700
Novastar Financial Inc 2114 Central Suite 600 *NYSE: NFI* ■ *TF:* 800-591-1137 ■ *Web:* www.novastarfinancial.com	Kansas City	MO	64108	816-237-7000	
One Liberty Properties Inc 60 Cutter Mill Rd *NYSE: OLP* ■ *TF:* 800-450-5816	Great Neck	NY	11021	516-466-3100	466-3132
Parkway Properties Inc 188 E Capitol St Suite 1000 *NYSE: PKY* ■ *TF:* 800-748-1667 ■ *Web:* www.pky.com	Jackson	MS	39201	601-948-4091	949-4077
Pennsylvania Real Estate Investment Trust 200 S Broad St 3rd Fl *NYSE: PEI* ■ *TF:* 866-875-0700 ■ *Web:* www.preit.com	Philadelphia	PA	19102	215-875-0700	546-7311
Plum Creek Timber Co Inc 999 3rd Ave Suite 4300 *NYSE: PCL* ■ *TF:* 800-858-5347 ■ *Web:* www.plumcreek.com	Seattle	WA	98104	206-467-3600	467-3795
PMC Commercial Trust 17950 Preston Rd Suite 600 *AMEX: PCC* ■ *TF:* 800-486-3223 ■ *Web:* www.pmctrust.com	Dallas	TX	75252	972-349-3200	349-3265
Post Properties Inc 4401 Northside Pkwy Suite 800 *NYSE: PPS* ■ **Fax:* Hum Res ■ *Web:* www.postproperties.com	Atlanta	GA	30327	404-846-5000	846-6161*
Premium Outlets 105 Eisenhower Pkwy **Fax:* Hum Res ■ *Web:* www.premiumoutlets.com	Roseland	NJ	07068	973-364-6524	228-4746*
Presidential Realty Corp 180 S Broadway Suite 400 *AMEX: PDL/A* ■ *TF:* 800-948-2977	White Plains	NY	10605	914-948-1300	948-1327
ProLogis 4545 Airport Way *NYSE: PLD* ■ *TF:* 800-566-2706 ■ *Web:* www.prologis.com	Denver	CO	80239	303-375-9292	567-5600
PS Business Parks Inc 701 Western Ave *AMEX: PSB* ■ *TF:* 800-567-0759 ■ *Web:* www.psbusinessparks.com	Glendale	CA	91201	818-244-8080	242-0566
Public Storage Inc 701 Western Ave *NYSE: PSA* ■ **Fax:* Mail Rm ■ *TF Cust Svc:* 800-567-0759 ■ *Web:* www.publicstorage.com	Glendale	CA	91201	818-244-8080	291-1015*
RAIT Investment Trust 2929 Arch St Suite 1703 *NYSE: RAS* ■ *TF:* 800-826-6096 ■ *Web:* www.raitinvestmenttrust.com	Philadelphia	PA	19104	215-701-9555	701-8282
Ramco-Gershenson Properties Trust 31500 Northwestern Hwy Suite 300 *NYSE: RPT* ■ *TF:* 800-225-6765 ■ *Web:* www.ramcogershenson.com	Farmington Hills	MI	48334	248-350-9900	350-9925
Regency Centers 1 Independent Dr Suite 114 *NYSE: REG* ■ *TF:* 800-950-6333 ■ *Web:* www.regencyrealty.com	Jacksonville	FL	32202	904-598-7000	634-3428
Republic Property Trust 13861 Sunrise Valley Dr Suite 410 *NYSE: RPB* ■ *Web:* www.republicpropertytrust.com	Herndon	VA	20171	703-880-2900	880-2900
Resource Capital Corp 712 5th Ave 12th Fl *NYSE: RSO* ■ *Web:* www.resourcecapitalcorp.com	New York	NY	10019	212-506-3899	245-6372
Revenue Properties (America) Inc 2542 Williams Blvd *Web:* www.sizeler.net	Kenner	LA	70062	504-904-8500	904-8555
RioCan Real Estate Investment Trust 2300 Yonge St Suite 500 PO Box 2386 *TSE: REI.UN* ■ *TF:* 800-465-2733 ■ *Web:* www.riocan.com	Toronto	ON	M4P1E4	416-866-3033	866-3020
Roberts Realty Investors Inc 450 Northridge Pkwy Suite 302 *AMEX: RPI*	Atlanta	GA	30350	770-394-6000	551-5914
Royal Host Real Estate Investment Trust 808 42nd Ave SE Suite 103 *NYSE: RYL* ■ *Web:* www.royalhost.com	Calgary	AB	T2G1Y9	403-259-9800	259-8580
Simon Property Group Inc 225 W Washington St *NYSE: SPG* ■ **Fax:* Cust Svc ■ *Web:* www.simon.com	Indianapolis	IN	46204	317-636-1600	263-7658*
SL Green Realty Corp 420 Lexington Ave *NYSE: SLG* ■ *Web:* www.slgreen.com	New York	NY	10170	212-594-2700	216-1790
Spirit Finance Corp 14631 N Scottsdale Rd Suite 200 *TF:* 866-557-7474 ■ *Web:* www.spiritfinance.com	Scottsdale	AZ	85254	480-606-0820	606-0826
Starwood Hotels & Resorts Worldwide Inc 1111 Westchester Ave *NYSE: HOT* ■ *TF Cust Svc:* 877-443-4585 ■ *Web:* www.starwoodhotels.com	White Plains	NY	10604	914-640-8100	640-8310
Strategic Hotels & Resorts 200 W Madison St Suite 1700 *NYSE: BEE* ■ *Web:* www.strategichotels.com	Chicago	IL	60606	312-658-5000	658-5799
Sun Communities Inc 27777 Franklin Rd Suite 200 *NYSE: SUI* ■ *Web:* www.suncommunities.com	Southfield	MI	48034	248-208-2500	208-2640
Supertel Hospitality Inc 309 N 5th St PO Box 1448 *NASDAQ: SPPR* ■ *Web:* www.supertelinc.com	Norfolk	NE	68701	402-371-2520	371-5783
Tanger Factory Outlet Centers Inc 3200 Northline Ave Suite 360 *NYSE: SKT* ■ *TF:* 800-438-8474 ■ *Web:* www.tangeroutlet.com	Greensboro	NC	27408	336-292-3010	852-2096
Taubman Centers Inc 200 E Long Lake Rd Suite 300 *NYSE: TCO* ■ *TF:* 800-828-2626 ■ *Web:* www.taubman.com	Bloomfield Hills	MI	48303	248-258-6800	258-7683
Thayer Lodging Group 1997 Annapolis Exchange # 550 *Web:* www.thayerlodging.com	Annapolis	MD	21401	410-268-0515	268-1582
Transcontinental Realty Investors Inc 1800 Valley View Ln 1 Hickory Ctr *NYSE: TCI* ■ *TF:* 800-400-6407 ■ *Web:* www.transconrealty-invest.com	Dallas	TX	75234	469-522-4200	522-4299
United Mobile Homes Inc 3499 Rt 9 N Suite 3C *AMEX: UMH* ■ *Web:* www.umh.com	Freehold	NJ	07728	732-577-9997	577-9980
Universal Health Realty Income Trust Universal Corporate Ctr 367 S Gulph Rd PO Box 61558 *NYSE: UHT* ■ *Web:* www.uhrit.com	King of Prussia	PA	19406	610-265-0688	768-3336
Urstadt Biddle Properties Inc 321 Railroad Ave *NYSE: UBP* ■ *TF:* 800-323-8216 ■ *Web:* www.ubproperties.com	Greenwich	CT	06830	203-863-8200	861-6755
Vornado Realty Trust 888 Seventh Ave *NYSE: VNO* ■ **Fax Area Code:* 201 ■ *TF:* 800-242-4119 ■ *Web:* www.vno.com	New York	NY	10019	212-894-7000	587-0600*

Phone Fax

Washington Real Estate Investment Trust (WRIT)
6110 Executive Blvd Suite 800 . . . . . Rockville MD 20852 301-984-9400 984-9610
NYSE: WRE ■ *TF:* 800-565-9748 ■ *Web:* www.writ.com

Watson Land Co
22010 S Wilmington Ave Suite 400 . . . . . Carson CA 90745 310-952-6400 522-8788
Web: www.watsonlandcompany.com

Weingarten Realty Investors
2600 Citadel Plaza Dr Suite 300 . . . . . Houston TX 77008 713-866-6000 866-6049
NYSE: WRI ■ *TF:* 800-688-8865 ■ *Web:* www.weingarten.com

Wells Real Estate Funds Inc
6200 The Corners Pkwy PO Box 926040 . . . . . Norcross GA 30092 770-449-7800 243-8199
TF: 800-448-1010 ■ *Web:* www.wellsref.com

Westfield America Inc
11601 Wilshire Blvd 11th Fl . . . . . Los Angeles CA 90025 310-478-4456 478-1267
Web: www.westfield.com

Wilmorite Properties Inc
1265 Scottsville Rd . . . . . Rochester NY 14624 585-464-9400 464-0706
Web: www.wilmorite.com

Winthrop Realty Trust 7 Bulfinch Pl Suite 500 . . . . . Boston MA 02114 617-570-4614 570-4746
NYSE: FUR ■ *Web:* www.winthropreit.com

WP Carey & Co LLC
50 Rockefeller Plaza 2nd Fl . . . . . New York NY 10020 212-492-1100 492-8922
NYSE: WPC ■ *TF:* 800-972-2739 ■ *Web:* www.wpcarey.com

658 REAL ESTATE MANAGERS & OPERATORS

SEE ALSO Hotels & Hotel Companies p. 2081; Retirement Communities p. 2623

Phone Fax

Acadia Realty Trust
1311 Mamaroneck Ave Suite 260 . . . . . White Plains NY 10605 914-288-8100 428-2380
NYSE: AKR ■ *TF:* 800-227-5570 ■ *Web:* www.acadiarealty.com

Agree Realty Corp
31850 Northwestern Hwy . . . . . Farmington Hills MI 48334 248-737-4190 737-9110
NYSE: ADC ■ *Web:* www.agreerealty.com

Alexander Summer LLC E 80 Rt 4 Suite 300 . . . . . Paramus NJ 07652 201-712-1000 712-1274
Web: www.alexandersummer.com

Alexander's Inc 210 Rt 4 E . . . . . Paramus NJ 07652 201-587-8541 708-6214
NYSE: ALX ■ *Web:* www.alx-inc.com

Alexandria Real Estate Equities Inc
385 E Colorado Blvd Suite 299 . . . . . Pasadena CA 91101 626-578-0777 578-0770
NYSE: ARE

Allied Realty Co 20 26th St . . . . . Huntington WV 25703 304-525-9125 697-5511

American Assets Inc 11455 El Camino Real . . . . . San Diego CA 92130 858-350-2600 350-2620
Web: www.american-assets.com

American Golf Corp 2951 28th St . . . . . Santa Monica CA 90405 310-664-4000 664-6160
TF: 800-345-4259 ■ *Web:* www.americangolf.com

American Land Lease Inc (ANL)
380 Pk Pl Blvd Suite 200 . . . . . Clearwater FL 33759 727-726-8868 726-8885
NYSE: ANL ■ *TF:* 800-826-6069 ■ *Web:* www.americanlandlease.com

American Motel Management
2200 Northlake Pkwy Suite 277 . . . . . Tucker GA 30084 770-939-1801 939-1419
Web: www.americanmotelonline.com

American Realty Investors Inc
1800 Valley View Ln Suite 300 . . . . . Dallas TX 75234 469-522-4200 522-4299
NYSE: ARL ■ *TF:* 800-400-6407 ■ *Web:* www.amrealtytrust.com

American Spectrum Realty Inc
2401 Fountain View Suite 510 . . . . . Houston TX 77057 713-706-6200 706-6201
AMEX: AQQ ■ *Web:* www.americanspectrum.com

Amurcon Corp 30215 Southfield Rd Suite 200 . . . . . Southfield MI 48076 248-646-0202 646-0482

ANG Management Co 7779 New York Ln . . . . . Glen Burnie MD 21061 410-766-8900 766-6557

Apartment Investment & Management Co
4582 S Ulster St Pkwy Suite 1100 . . . . . Denver CO 80237 303-757-8101 759-3226
NYSE: AIV ■ *TF:* 888-789-8600 ■ *Web:* www.aimco.com

ARC Properties Inc 1401 Broad St 2nd Fl . . . . . Clifton NJ 07013 973-249-1000 249-1001
Web: www.arcproperties.com

Archstone-Smith Trust
9200 E Panorama Cir Suite 400 . . . . . Englewood CO 80112 303-708-5959 708-5999
NYSE: ASN ■ *TF:* 877-272-4786 ■ *Web:* www.archstoneapartments.com

Arden Realty Inc
11601 Wilshire Blvd Suite 400 . . . . . Los Angeles CA 90025 310-966-2600 966-2699
NYSE: ARI ■ *Web:* www.ardenrealty.com

Aronov Realty 3500 Eastern Blvd . . . . . Montgomery AL 36116 334-277-1000 272-0747
Web: www.aronov.com

Associated Estates Realty Corp
1 AEC Pkwy . . . . . Richmond Heights OH 44143 216-261-5000 289-9600
NYSE: AEC ■ *TF:* 800-440-2372 ■ *Web:* www.associatedestates.com

Belz Enterprises 100 Peabody Pl Suite 1400 . . . . . Memphis TN 38103 901-767-4780 271-7238
Web: www.belz.com

Ben Carter Properties LLC
950 E Paces Ferry Rd Suite 900 . . . . . Atlanta GA 30326 404-869-2700 869-7171
Web: www.bencarterproperties.com

Benderson Development Co Inc
8441 Cooper Creek Blvd . . . . . University Park FL 34201 941-359-8303 359-1836
Web: www.benderson.com

Berkshire Income Realty Inc
1 Beacon St Suite 1500 . . . . . Boston MA 02108 617-523-7722 646-2375
TF: 800-255-7877 ■ *Web:* www.berkshireincomerealty.com

Berkshire Property Advisors LLC
1 Beacon St Suite 1550 . . . . . Boston MA 02108 617-646-2300 646-2375
TF: 888-867-0100 ■ *Web:* www.berkshireapartments.com

Berwind Natural Resources Corp
1500 Market St 3000 Centre Sq W . . . . . Philadelphia PA 19102 215-563-2800 563-8347
Web: www.berwind.com

Blue Ridge Real Estate Co PO Box 707 . . . . . Blakeslee PA 18610 570-443-8433

Bob Harris Oil Co 905 S Main St . . . . . Cleburne TX 76031 817-641-4771 641-3074

Boston Properties Inc 800 Boylston St . . . . . Boston MA 02199 617-236-3300
NYSE: BXP ■ *Web:* www.bostonproperties.com

Boyle Investment Co 5900 Poplar Ave Suite 100 . . . . . Memphis TN 38119 901-767-0100 766-4299
TF: 888-862-6953 ■ *Web:* www.boyle.com

Bozzuto Group 7850 Walker Dr Suite 400 . . . . . Greenbelt MD 20770 301-220-0100 220-3738
TF: 800-718-0200 ■ *Web:* www.bozzuto.com

Phone Fax

Bradford Cos 9400 N Central Expy Suite 500 . . . . . Dallas TX 75231 972-776-7000 776-7083
Web: www.bradford.com

Brandywine Realty Trust
555 E Lancaster Ave Suite 100 . . . . . Radnor PA 19087 610-325-5600 325-5622
NYSE: BDN ■ *TF:* 866-426-5400 ■ *Web:* www.brandywinerealty.com

BRE Properties Inc 525 Market St 4th Fl . . . . . San Francisco CA 94105 415-445-6530 445-6505
NYSE: BRE ■ *Web:* www.breproperties.com

Bresler & Reiner Inc
11200 Rockville Pike Suite 502 . . . . . Rockville MD 20852 301-945-4300 945-4301
Web: www.bresler andreiner.com

Breslin Realty & Pinnacle Media LLC
500 Old Country Rd Suite 200 . . . . . Garden City NY 11530 516-741-7400 741-7128
Web: www.breslinrealty.com

Brookfield Office Properties Canada
181 Bay St Suite 330 PO Box 770 . . . . . Toronto ON M5J2T3 416-359-8555 359-8596
TSE: BOX ■ *Web:* www.brookfieldofficepropertiescanada.com

Brookfield Properties Corp (BOP)
181 Bay St Suite 330 . . . . . Toronto ON M5J2T3 416-369-2300 369-2301
TSE: BPO ■ *TF:* 800-465-4875 ■ *Web:* www.brookfieldofficeproperties.com

Brooklyn Navy Yard Development Corp
63 Flushing Ave Bldg 292 3rd Fl . . . . . Brooklyn NY 11205 718-907-5900 643-9296
Web: www.brooklynnavyyard.com

Cadillac Fairview Ltd 20 Queen St W 5th Fl . . . . . Toronto ON M5H3R4 416-598-8200 598-8578
Web: www.cadillacfairview.com

Calista Corp 301 Calista Ct Suite A . . . . . Anchorage AK 99518 907-279-5516 272-5060
TF: 800-277-5516 ■ *Web:* www.calistacorp.com

Camden Property Trust
3 E Greenway Plaza Suite 1300 . . . . . Houston TX 77046 713-354-2500 354-2700*
NYSE: CPT ■ **Fax:* Mktg ■ *TF:* 800-922-6336 ■ *Web:* www.camdenliving.com

Capital Properties Inc 717 5th Ave . . . . . New York NY 10022 212-980-0090 980-5669
PINK: CPTP ■ *Web:* www.capitalproperties.com

CAPREIT Inc 11200 Rockville Pike Suite 100 . . . . . Rockville MD 20852 301-231-8700 468-8392
Web: www.capreit.com

CASTO 191 W Nationwide Blvd Suite 200 . . . . . Columbus OH 43215 614-228-5331 469-8376
Web: www.donmcasto.com

CBL & Assoc Properties Inc
CBL Ctr 2030 Hamilton Pl Blvd Suite 500 . . . . . Chattanooga TN 37421 423-855-0001 490-8662
NYSE: CBL ■ *TF:* 800-333-7310 ■ *Web:* www.cblproperties.com

Cedar Shopping Centers Inc
44 S Bayles Ave Suite 304 . . . . . Port Washington NY 11050 516-767-6492 767-6497
NYSE: CDR ■ *TF:* 800-564-3128 ■ *Web:* www.cedarshoppingcenters.com

Cencor Realty Services Inc
3102 Maple Ave Suite 500 . . . . . Dallas TX 75201 214-954-0300 953-0860
TF: 800-256-5296 ■ *Web:* www.cencorrealty.com

CenterPoint Properties Trust 1808 Swift Dr . . . . . Oak Brook IL 60523 630-586-8000 586-8010
Web: www.centerpoint-prop.com

Centro Properties Group
580 W Germantown Pike Suite 200 . . . . . Plymouth Meeting PA 19462 610-825-7100 834-8110
Web: www.centroprop.com

Centro Properties Group 131 Dartmouth St . . . . . Boston MA 02116 617-247-2200 266-0885
Web: www.centroprop.com

Centro Properties Group
420 Lexington Ave 7th Fl . . . . . New York NY 10170 646-344-8600 869-3989*
**Fax Area Code:* 212 ■ *TF:* 800-468-7526 ■ *Web:* www.centroprop.com

Charles E Lakin Enterprises
8990 W Dodge Rd Suite 225 . . . . . Omaha NE 68114 402-393-5550

Charlwood International
1199 W Pender St Suite 900 . . . . . Vancouver BC V6E2R1 604-718-2600 718-2678

Chrisken Property Management LLC
345 N Canal St Suite 201 . . . . . Chicago IL 60606 312-454-1626 454-1627
Web: www.chrisken.com

Clover Financial Corp
4300 Haddonfield Rd
Suite 314 Fairway Corp Ctr 1 . . . . . Pennsauken NJ 08109 856-662-1116 662-6303

ClubCorp Inc 3030 Lyndon B Johnson Fwy # 600 . . . . . Dallas TX 75234 972-243-6191 888-7555
TF: 800-346-7621 ■ *Web:* www.clubcorp.com

ClubLink Corp 15675 Dufferin St . . . . . King City ON L7B1K5 905-841-3730 841-1134
TF: 800-661-1818 ■ *Web:* www.clublink.ca

Codding Enterprises
1400 Valley House Dr Suite 100
PO Box 3550 . . . . . Rohnert Park CA 94928 707-795-3550 665-2882
TF: 800-273-6833 ■ *Web:* www.codding.com

Coldwell Banker Commercial 1 Campus Dr . . . . . Parsippany NJ 07054 888-829-0221 407-5495*
**Fax Area Code:* 973 ■ *TF:* 888-829-0221 ■ *Web:* www.cbcworldwide.com

Colonial Properties Trust
2101 6th Ave N Suite 750 . . . . . Birmingham AL 35203 205-250-8700 250-8890
NYSE: CLP ■ *TF:* 866-222-9877 ■ *Web:* www.colonialprop.com

Combined Properties Inc 300 Commercial St . . . . . Malden MA 02148 781-321-7800 321-5144
Web: www.combinedproperties.com

CommonWealth REIT
255 Washington St 2 Newton Pl . . . . . Newton MA 02458 617-332-3990 332-2261
Web: www.cwhreit.com

Community Development Trust (CDT)
1350 Broadway Suite 700 . . . . . New York NY 10018 212-271-5080 271-5079
Web: www.cdt.biz

Continental Group Inc 2950 N 28th Terr . . . . . Hollywood FL 33020 954-378-2300 378-2298
Web: www.tcgmgt.com

Cornell & Assoc Inc 2633 E Lake Ave Suite 307 . . . . . Seattle WA 98102 206-329-0085 329-4110
Web: www.cornellandassociates.com

Corporate Office Properties Trust
6711 Columbia Gateway Dr Suite 300 . . . . . Columbia MD 21046 443-285-5400 285-7650
NYSE: OFC ■ *Web:* www.copt.com

Cousins Properties Inc
191 Peachtree St NE Suite 3600 . . . . . Atlanta GA 30303 404-407-1000 407-1002
NYSE: CUZ ■ *TF:* 800-926-8746 ■ *Web:* www.cousinsproperties.com

Crescent Real Estate Equities Co
777 Main St Suite 2000 . . . . . Fort Worth TX 76102 817-321-2100 321-2000
Web: www.crescent.com

Crombie REIT 115 King St . . . . . Stellarton NS B0K1S0 902-755-8100 755-6477
Web: www.crombieproperties.ca

Phone | Fax

Crye-Leike Property Management Inc
PO Box 17947 Memphis TN 38187 901-758-5678 758-5671
Web: www.cryeleikerentals.com

Curry Investment Co
2700 Kendallwood Pkwy Suite 208/106 Gladstone MO 64119 816-414-5200 452-4757
Web: www.curryre.com

Cushman & Wakefield Inc 51 W 52nd St New York NY 10019 212-841-7500 841-7867
Web: www.cushwake.com

Daniel Corp 3660 Grandview Pkwy Birmingham AL 35243 205-443-4500
Web: www.danielcorp.com

Developers Diversified Realty Corp
3300 Enterprise Pkwy Beachwood OH 44122 216-755-5500 755-1500
NYSE: DDR ■ *TF:* 800-258-7289 ■ *Web:* www.ddrc.com

Divaris Real Estate Inc
1 Columbus Ctr Suite 700 Virginia Beach VA 23462 757-497-2113 497-1338
TF: 888-373-0023 ■ *Web:* www.divaris.com

Donahue Schriber Realty Group Inc
200 E Baker St Suite 100 Costa Mesa CA 92626 714-545-1400 545-4222
Web: www.donahueschriber.com

Douglas Allred Co
11452 El Camino Real Suite 200 San Diego CA 92130 858-793-0202 793-5363
TF: 800-555-6214 ■ *Web:* www.douglasallredco.com

Douglas Elliman Property Management
675 3rd Ave 6th Fl New York NY 10017 212-350-2800 455-4726
Web: www.ellimanpm.com

Draper & Kramer Inc 33 W Monroe 19th Fl Chicago IL 60603 312-346-8600 346-8600
TF: 800-621-0776 ■ *Web:* www.draperandkramer.com

Duke Realty Corp 600 E 96th St Suite 100 Indianapolis IN 46240 317-808-6000 808-6794
NYSE: DRE ■ *TF:* 800-875-3366 ■ *Web:* www.dukerealty.com

DVL Inc 70 E 55th St 7th Fl New York NY 10022 212-350-9900 350-9911

EastGroup Properties Inc
190 E Capitol St Suite 400 Jackson MS 39201 601-354-3555 352-1441
NYSE: EGP ■ *TF:* 800-337-5602 ■ *Web:* www.eastgroup.net

Echelon Development LLC
235 3rd St S Suite 300 Saint Petersburg FL 33701 727-803-8200 803-8201
Web: www.echelonre.com

Ellman Cos 4040 E Camelback Rd Phoenix AZ 85018 602-840-3000 840-8101
Web: www.ellmanco.com

Emser International LLC
8431 Santa Monica Blvd Los Angeles CA 90069 323-650-2000 650-1589
Web: www.emser.com

Entertainment Properties Trust
909 Walnut Suite 200 Kansas City MO 64106 816-472-1700 472-5794
NYSE: EPR ■ *TF:* 888-377-7348 ■ *Web:* www.eprkc.com

Epoch Management Inc 359 Carolina Ave Winter Park FL 32789 407-629-5004 629-4264
Web: www.epochmanagement.com

Epoch Properties Inc 359 Carolina Ave Winter Park FL 32789 407-644-9055 644-9845
Web: www.epochproperties.com

Equity Lifestyle Properties Inc
2 N Riverside Plaza Suite 800 Chicago IL 60606 312-279-1400 279-1710
NYSE: ELS ■ *TF:* 800-274-7314 ■ *Web:* www.equitylifestyle.com

Equity Office Properties Trust
2 N Riverside Plaza Suite 2100 Chicago IL 60606 312-466-3300 454-0332
NYSE: EOP ■ *Web:* www.equityoffice.com

Equity One Inc
1696 NE Miami Gardens Dr North Miami Beach FL 33179 305-947-1664 947-1734
NYSE: EQY ■ *TF:* 800-867-2777 ■ *Web:* www.equityone.net

Equity Residential 2 N Riverside Plaza Chicago IL 60606 312-474-1300 454-8703
NYSE: EQR ■ *Web:* www.equityapartments.com

Essex Property Trust Inc 925 E Meadow Dr Palo Alto CA 94303 650-494-3700 494-8743
NYSE: ESS ■ *Web:* www.essexpropertytrust.com

Eugene Burger Management Corp
6600 Hunter Dr Rohnert Park CA 94928 707-584-5123 584-5124
Web: www.ebmc.com

Federal Realty Investment Trust
1626 E Jefferson St Rockville MD 20852 301-998-8100 998-3700
NYSE: FRT ■ *TF:* 800-658-8980 ■ *Web:* www.federalrealty.com

FelCor Lodging Trust Inc
545 E John Carpenter Fwy Suite 1300 Irving TX 75062 972-444-4900 444-4949
NYSE: FCH ■ *Web:* www.felcor.com

Festival Co 9841 Airport Blvd Suite 700 Los Angeles CA 90045 310-665-9600 665-9009
Web: www.festivalcos.com

First Industrial Realty Trust Inc
311 S Wacker Dr Suite 4000 Chicago IL 60606 312-344-4300 922-6320
NYSE: FR ■ *TF:* 800-894-8778 ■ *Web:* www.firstindustrial.com

First Realty Management Corp 151 Tremont St Boston MA 02111 617-423-7000 482-6617
Web: www.frmboston.com

First REIT of New Jersey 505 Main St Hackensack NJ 07602 201-488-6400 487-7881

First Republic Corp of America 302 5th Ave New York NY 10001 212-279-6100 629-6848
TF: 800-578-2254

FirstService Corp
1140 Bay St FirstService Bldg Suite 4000 Toronto ON M5S2B4 416-960-9500 960-5333
TSE: FSV ■ *Web:* www.firstservice.com

Flatley Co The 35 Braintree Hill Office Pk Braintree MA 02184 781-848-2000 849-4400
Web: www.flatleyco.com

Forest City Residential Group
50 Public Sq Terminal Tower Suite 1100 Cleveland OH 44113 216-736-7646
Web: www.forestcity.net/company/people/residential/Pages/default.aspx

Fortune International Realty 2666 Brickell Ave Miami FL 33129 305-856-2600 857-3636*
**Fax:* Hum Res ■ *Web:* www.fortunemiami.com

Freeport Center Assoc PO Box 160466 Clearfield UT 84016 801-825-9741 825-3587
Web: www.freeportcenter.com

G & L Realty Corp 439 N Bedford Dr Beverly Hills CA 90210 310-273-9930 248-2222
Web: www.glrealty.com

Gene B Glick Co Inc
8425 Woodfield Crossing Blvd
Suite 300-W Indianapolis IN 46240 317-469-0400 469-8142
Web: www.genebglick.com

General Growth Properties Inc
110 N Wacker Dr Chicago IL 60606 312-960-5000 960-5475
NYSE: GGP ■ *TF:* 888-395-8037 ■ *Web:* www.ggp.com

Ginkgo Residential LLC
301 S College St Suite 3850 Charlotte NC 28202 704-944-0100 944-2039
Web: www.bnproperties.com

Phone | Fax

Glimcher Realty Trust 180 E Broad St Columbus OH 43215 614-621-9000 621-9321
NYSE: GRT ■ *TF:* 800-987-8786 ■ *Web:* www.glimcher.com

Goodale & Barbieri Co
818 W Riverside Ave Suite 300 Spokane WA 99201 509-459-6109 325-7324
Web: www.g-b.com

Grady Management Inc
8630 Fenton St Suite 625 Silver Spring MD 20910 301-587-3330 588-5040*
**Fax:* Acctg ■ *TF:* 800-544-7239 ■ *Web:* www.gradymgt.com

Graham Cos 6843 Main St Miami Lakes FL 33014 305-821-1130 557-0313
Web: www.miamilakes.com

Great American Group Inc
21860 Burbank Blvd Suite 300 Woodland Hills CA 91367 818-884-3737 884-2976
OTC: GAMR ■ *Web:* www.greatamerican.com

Gundaker Property Management
2458 Old Dorsett Rd Suite 100 St. Louis MO 63043 314-298-5200 298-5096
TF: 800-325-1978 ■ *Web:* www.cbgundaker.com

GVA Advantis 101 W Main St Suite 900 Norfolk VA 23510 757-627-0661 627-1901
Web: www.gvaadvantis.com

Gyrodyne Co of America Inc
1 Flowerfield Suite 24 Saint James NY 11780 631-584-5400 584-7075
NASDAQ: GYRO ■ *Web:* www.gyrodyne.com

H & R Retail Inc
2800 Quarry Lake Dr Suite 320 Baltimore MD 21209 410-308-0800 486-2733
Web: www.hrretail.com

Hall Financial Group
6801 Gaylord Pkwy Suite 100 Frisco TX 75034 972-377-1100 377-6694
Web: www.hallfinancial.com

Harrison & Lear Inc 2310 Tower Pl Suite 105 Hampton VA 23666 757-825-9100 838-2574
TF: 800-229-6214 ■ *Web:* www.harrison-lear.com

Hawaii Reserves Inc 55-510 Kamehameha Hwy Laie HI 96762 808-293-9201 293-6456
Web: www.hawaiireserves.com

Health Care Property Investors Inc
3760 Kilroy Airport Way Suite 300 Long Beach CA 90806 562-733-5100 733-5200
NYSE: HCP ■ *TF:* 888-604-1990 ■ *Web:* www.hcpi.com

Health Care REIT Inc 1 SeaGate Suite 1500 Toledo OH 43603 419-247-2800 247-2826
NYSE: HCN ■ *Web:* www.hcreit.com

Healthcare Realty Trust Inc
3310 W End Ave Suite 700 Nashville TN 37203 615-269-8175 269-8260
NYSE: HR ■ *Web:* www.healthcarerealty.com

Heitman LLC 191 N Wacker Dr Suite 2500 Chicago IL 60606 312-855-5700 251-4807
TF: 800-225-5435 ■ *Web:* www.heitman.com

Helmsley-Spear Inc 770 Lexington Ave # 9 New York NY 10065 212-880-0100 687-6437
Web: www.helmsleyspear.com

Hemstreet Development Co
16100 NW Cornell Rd Suite 100 Beaverton OR 97006 503-531-4000 531-4001
Web: www.hemstreet.com

Herbert H Redl
80 Washington St Suite 100 Poughkeepsie NY 12601 845-471-3388 471-3851

Heritage Realty Management Inc
131 Dartmouth St Boston MA 02116 617-247-2200 266-0885
Web: www.heritage-realty.com

Hersha Enterprises 44 Hersha Dr Harrisburg PA 17102 717-236-4400 774-7383
Web: www.hersha.com

Hersha Hospitality Trust
510 Walnut St 9th Fl Philadelphia PA 17106 215-238-1046 238-0157
NYSE: HT ■ *Web:* www.hersha.com

Hickel Investment Co
939 W 5th Ave PO Box 101700 Anchorage AK 99510 907-343-2400 343-2211

Highwoods Properties Inc
3100 Smoketree Ct Suite 600 Raleigh NC 27604 919-872-4924 876-2448
NYSE: HIW ■ *TF:* 866-449-6637 ■ *Web:* www.highwoods.com

Holiday Retirement Corp 2250 McGilchrist St SE Salem OR 97302 503-370-7070 364-5716
TF: 800-322-0999 ■ *Web:* www.holidaytouch.com

Holladay Corp 3400 Idaho Ave NW Suite 500 Washington DC 20016 202-362-2400 364-0844

Home Properties 6 Garrison View Rd Owings Mills MD 21117 410-356-3320 356-0324
Web: www.homeproperties.com

Home Properties Inc 850 Clinton Sq Rochester NY 14604 585-546-4900 546-5433
NYSE: HME ■ *Web:* www.homeproperties.com

Horizon Group Properties Inc 5000 Hakes Dr Muskegon MI 49441 231-798-9100 798-5100
Web: www.horizongroup.com

Horning Bros
1350 Connecticut Ave NW Suite 800 Washington DC 20036 202-659-0700 659-9489
Web: www.horningbrothers.com

Hospitality Properties Trust
255 Washington St Newton MA 02458 617-964-8389 969-5730
NYSE: HPT ■ *Web:* www.hptreit.com

Hunt Midwest Enterprises Inc
8300 NE Underground Dr Kansas City MO 64161 816-455-2500
TF: 800-551-6877 ■ *Web:* www.huntmidwest.com

Imperial Realty Co Inc 4747 W Peterson Ave Chicago IL 60646 773-736-4100 736-4541
Web: www.imperialrealtyco.com

Inland Group Inc 2901 Butterfield Rd Oak Brook IL 60523 630-218-8000 218-4917
TF: 800-828-8999 ■ *Web:* www.inlandgroup.com

Inland Real Estate Corp
2901 Butterfield Rd Oak Brook IL 60523 630-218-8000 218-7357*
NYSE: IRC ■ **Fax:* Investor Rel ■ *TF:* 888-331-4732 ■ *Web:* www.inlandrealestate.com

Irvine Co Apartment Communities
110 Innovation Dr Irvine CA 92617 949-720-5500 720-5601
Web: www.rental-living.com

Jim Wilson & Assoc Inc
2660 E Chase Ln Suite 100 Montgomery AL 36117 334-260-2500 260-2533
Web: www.jwamalls.com

JJ Gumberg Co Inc 1051 Brinton Rd Pittsburgh PA 15221 412-244-4000 244-9133
Web: www.jjgumberg.com

JMG Realty Inc 5605 Glenridge Dr Suite 1010 Atlanta GA 30342 404-847-0111 995-1112
Web: www.jmgrealty.com

John F Long Properties LLLP
5035 W Camelback Rd Phoenix AZ 85031 602-272-0421 846-7208*
**Fax Area Code:* 623 ■ *Web:* www.jflong.com

Jonas Equities 725 Church Ave Brooklyn NY 11218 718-871-6020 871-4324
Web: www.jonasequities.com

	City	State	ZIP	Phone	Fax
Jones Lang LaSalle Inc					
200 E Randolph Dr Suite 4600	Chicago	IL	60601	312-782-5800	782-4339
NYSE: JLL ■ *Web:* www.joneslanglasalle.com					
Jones Lang LaSalle Leasing & Management Services					
200 E Randolph Dr Suite 4300	Chicago	IL	60601	312-782-5800	
Web: www.joneslanglasalle.com					
JPI 600 E Las Colinas Blvd Suite 1800	Irving	TX	75039	972-556-1700	444-2102
Web: www.jpi.com					
JW Mays Inc 9 Bond St	Brooklyn	NY	11201	718-624-7400	935-0378
NASDAQ: MAYS ■ *Web:* www.jwmays.com					
Kaempfer Co 1501 K St NW Suite 300	Washington	DC	20005	202-331-4300	331-4300
Web: www.kaempfer.com					
Kilroy Realty Corp					
12200 W Olympic Blvd Suite 200	Los Angeles	CA	90064	310-481-8400	481-6501
NYSE: KRC ■ *Web:* www.kilroyrealty.com					
Kimco Realty Corp					
3333 New Hyde Pk Rd Suite 100	New Hyde Park	NY	11042	516-869-9000	869-9001
NYSE: KIM ■ *TF:* 800-645-6292 ■ *Web:* www.kimcorealty.com					
KONOVER & Assoc Inc 135 S Rd	Farmington	CT	06032	860-284-7200	284-1176
TF: 877-566-6837 ■ *Web:* www.konover.com					
Koren Development Inc					
9200 Rumsey Rd Suite 210	Columbia	MD	21045	410-740-1010	992-5573
Kratsa Properties 2801 Freeport Rd	Pittsburgh	PA	15238	412-828-7711	828-9296
Web: www.kratsaproperties.com					
Kraus-Anderson Realty Co					
4210 W Old Shakopee Rd	Bloomington	MN	55437	952-881-8166	881-8114
TF: 800-399-4220 ■ *Web:* www.krausanderson.com					
Kravco Co 234 Mall Blvd	King of Prussia	PA	19406	610-768-6300	768-6444
Web: www.kravco.com					
L & B Realty Advisors LLP					
8750 N Central Expy Suite 800	Dallas	TX	75231	214-989-0800	989-0600
Web: www.lbgroup.com					
Levin Management Corp 893 Rt 22 W	North Plainfield	NJ	07060	908-755-2401	755-7194
TF: 800-488-0768 ■ *Web:* www.levinmgt.com					
Lexington Center Corp 430 W Vine St	Lexington	KY	40507	859-233-4567	253-2718
Web: www.lexingtoncenter.com					
Lexington Corporate Properties Trust					
One Penn Plaza Suite 4015	New York	NY	10119	212-692-7200	594-6600
NYSE: LXP ■ *TF:* 800-850-3948 ■ *Web:* www.lxp.com					
Liberty Property Trust 500 Chesterfield Pkwy	Malvern	PA	19355	610-648-1700	644-4129
NYSE: LRY ■ *Web:* www.libertyproperty.com					
Lillibridge Healthcare Real Estate Trust					
200 W Madison St Suite 3200	Chicago	IL	60606	312-408-1370	408-1415
Web: www.lillibridge.com					
Lincoln Property Co					
2000 McKinney Ave Suite 1000	Dallas	TX	75201	214-740-3300	740-3441
Web: www.lincolnproperty.com					
LNR Property Corp					
1601 Washington Ave Suite 800	Miami Beach	FL	33139	305-695-5600	695-5499
TF: 800-784-6380 ■ *Web:* www.lnrproperty.com					
Lomax Cos The 200 Highpoint Dr Suite 215	Chalfont	PA	18914	215-822-1550	997-9582
Web: www.thelomaxcos.com					
Lowe Enterprises					
11777 San Vicente Blvd Suite 900	Los Angeles	CA	90049	310-820-6661	207-1132
Web: www.loweenterprises.com					
Macerich Co The					
401 Wilshire Blvd Suite 700	Santa Monica	CA	90401	310-394-6000	395-2791
NYSE: MAC ■ *TF:* 800-421-7237 ■ *Web:* www.macerich.com					
Mack-Cali Realty Corp 343 Thornall St	Edison	NJ	08837	732-590-1000	205-8237
NYSE: CLI ■ *Web:* www.mack-cali.com					
Macklowe Properties Inc 767 5th Ave	New York	NY	10153	212-265-5900	554-5893
Web: www.macklowe.com					
Madison Marquette					
909 Montgomery St Suite 200	San Francisco	CA	94133	415-277-6800	217-5368
Web: www.madisonmarquette.com					
Madison Park Financial Corp					
409 13th St 8th Fl	Oakland	CA	94612	510-452-2944	452-2973
Web: www.mpfcorp.com					
Madison Square Garden Corp					
2 Pennsylvania Plaza 16th Fl	New York	NY	10121	212-465-6000	465-6026*
**Fax:* Hum Res ■ *Web:* www.thegarden.com					
Majestic Realty Co					
13191 Crossroads Pkwy N 6th Fl	City of Industry	CA	91746	562-692-9581	695-2329
Web: www.majesticrealty.com					
Maxus Realty Trust Inc					
104 Armour Rd PO Box 34729	North Kansas City	MO	64116	816-303-4500	221-1829
PINK: MRTI ■ *Web:* www.mrti.com					
Mericle Commercial Real Estate Services					
100 Baltimore Dr	Wilkes Barre	PA	18702	570-823-1100	823-8005
Web: www.mericle.com					
Merritt Properties LLC					
2066 Lord Baltimore Dr	Baltimore	MD	21244	410-298-2600	298-9644
Web: www.merrittproperties.com					
Mid-America Apartment Communities Inc (MAAC)					
6584 Poplar Ave Suite 300	Memphis	TN	38138	901-682-6600	682-6667
NYSE: MAA ■ *Web:* www.maac.net					
Milestone Properties Inc					
200 Congress Pk Dr Suite 103	Delray Beach	FL	33445	561-394-9533	394-6748
Web: www.milestonepropertiesinc.com					
Miller Valentine Group					
4000 Miller Valentine Ct	Dayton	OH	45439	937-293-0900	299-1564
TF: 877-684-7687 ■ *Web:* www.mvgse.com					
Monmouth Real Estate Investment Corp (MREIC)					
3499 Rt 9 N Suite 3C	Freehold	NJ	07728	732-577-9996	577-9981
NASDAQ: MNRTA ■ *Web:* www.mreic.com					
Moody Rambin Interests 3003 W Alabama St	Houston	TX	77098	713-271-5900	529-5310
Web: www.moodyrambin.com					
National Realty & Development Corp					
3 Manhattanville Rd	Purchase	NY	10577	914-694-4444	694-5448
TF: 800-932-7368 ■ *Web:* www.nrdc.com					
Nationwide Health Properties Inc					
610 Newport Ctr Dr Suite 1150	Newport Beach	CA	92660	949-718-4400	759-6876
NYSE: NHP ■ *TF:* 877-483-6827 ■ *Web:* www.nhp-reit.com					

	City	State	ZIP	Phone	Fax
NDC LLC 6312 S 27th St Suite 202	Oak Creek	WI	53154	414-761-2040	423-2280
Web: www.ndcllc.com					
NESCO Inc Real Estate Group					
6140 Parkland Blvd	Mayfield Heights	OH	44124	440-461-6000	449-3111
New England Development 1 Wells Ave	Newton	MA	02459	617-965-8700	243-7085
Web: www.nedevelopment.com					
Newcastle Investment Corp					
1345 Avenue of the Americas 46th Fl	New York	NY	10105	212-798-6100	
NYSE: NCT ■ *Web:* www.newcastleinv.com					
NTS Realty Holdings LP 10172 Linn Stn Rd	Louisville	KY	40223	502-426-4800	426-4994
AMEX: NLP ■ *Web:* www.ntsdevelopment.com					
Omega Healthcare Investors Inc					
200 International Cir9690 Deereco Rd					
Suite 3500	Hunt Valley	MD	21030	410-427-1700	427-8800
NYSE: OHI ■ *TF:* 866-226-6342 ■ *Web:* www.omegahealthcare.com					
One Liberty Properties Inc					
60 Cutter Mill Rd	Great Neck	NY	11021	516-466-3100	466-3132
NYSE: OLP ■ *TF:* 800-450-5816					
Oxford Development Co 301 Grant St	Pittsburgh	PA	15219	412-261-1500	642-7543
Web: www.oxford-pgh.com					
Pappas Properties Inc 655 Summer St	Boston	MA	02210	617-330-9797	439-9717
Parkway Properties Inc					
188 E Capitol St Suite 1000	Jackson	MS	39201	601-948-4091	949-4077
NYSE: PKY ■ *TF:* 800-748-1667 ■ *Web:* www.pky.com					
Peek Properties 258 E Arapaho Rd 160	Richardson	TX	75081	972-783-6040	669-0586
Penn Virginia Resource Partners LP					
5 Radnor Corporate Ctr Suite 500	Radnor	PA	19087	610-975-8204	975-8201
NYSE: PVR ■ *Web:* www.pvresource.com					
Pennsylvania Real Estate Investment Trust					
200 S Broad St 3rd Fl	Philadelphia	PA	19102	215-875-0700	546-7311
NYSE: PEI ■ *TF:* 866-875-0700 ■ *Web:* www.preit.com					
Perini Management Services Inc					
73 Mt Wayte Ave	Framingham	MA	01701	508-628-2000	628-2960
Web: www.perini.com/pmsi/specialized_body.htm					
Persis Corp 900 Fort St Mall Suite 1725	Honolulu	HI	96813	808-599-8000	526-4114
Web: www.persis.com					
Peterson Cos The					
12500 Fair Lakes Cir Suite 400	Fairfax	VA	22033	703-227-2000	631-6481
Web: www.petersoncos.com					
Picerne Real Estate Group					
75 Lambert Lind Hwy	Warwick	RI	02886	401-732-3700	738-6452
Web: www.picerne.com					
Pier 39 LP Inc					
Beach & Embarcadero Sts					
Stairway 2 Level 3	San Francisco	CA	94133	415-705-5500	981-8808
Web: www.pier39.com					
PM Realty Group 1000 Main St Suite 2400	Houston	TX	77002	713-209-5800	209-5702*
**Fax:* Hum Res ■ *Web:* www.pmrg.com					
Pocahontas Land Corp 800 Princeton Ave	Bluefield	WV	24701	304-324-2429	324-2461
Web: www.nscorp.com					
Polinger Shannon & Luchs Co					
5530 Wisconsin Ave Suite 1000	Chevy Chase	MD	20815	301-657-3600	986-9533
Web: www.recgov.org					
Portman Cos 303 Peachtree St NE Suite 575	Atlanta	GA	30303	404-614-5252	614-5400
Web: www.portmanholdings.com					
PRC Group 40 Monmouth Pk Hwy	West Long Branch	NJ	07764	732-222-5062	222-6410
Web: www.prcgroup.com					
Premium Outlets 105 Eisenhower Pkwy	Roseland	NJ	07068	973-364-6524	228-4746*
**Fax:* Hum Res ■ *Web:* www.premiumoutlets.com					
Price Edwards & Co					
210 Pk Ave Suite 1000	Oklahoma City	OK	73102	405-843-7474	236-1849
TF: 800-316-7811 ■ *Web:* www.priceedwards.com					
Prime Group Realty Trust					
330 N Wabash Ave Suite 2800	Chicago	IL	60611	312-917-1300	917-1310
Web: www.pgrt.com					
Prime Management Group Inc					
6300 Pk of Commerce Blvd	Boca Raton	FL	33487	561-997-4045	997-5684
Web: www.prime-mgt.com					
Professional Community Management Inc					
23726 Birtcher Dr	Lake Forest	CA	92630	949-768-7261	859-3729*
**Fax:* Cust Svc ■ *TF:* 800-369-7260					
ProLogis 4545 Airport Way	Denver	CO	80239	303-375-9292	567-5600
NYSE: PLD ■ *TF:* 800-566-2706 ■ *Web:* www.prologis.com					
Prudential Carruthers Realtors (PCR)					
3050 Chain Bridge Rd Suite 305	Fairfax	VA	22030	703-938-0909	615-2771
TF: 800-550-2364 ■ *Web:* www.prudentialcarruthers.com					
PS Business Parks Inc 701 Western Ave	Glendale	CA	91201	818-244-8080	242-0566
AMEX: PSB ■ *TF:* 800-567-0759 ■ *Web:* www.psbusinessparks.com					
Pyramid Cos 4 Clinton Sq	Syracuse	NY	13202	315-422-7000	472-4035
Web: www.pyramidmg.com					
Ramco-Gershenson Properties Trust					
31500 Northwestern Hwy Suite 300	Farmington Hills	MI	48334	248-350-9900	350-9925
NYSE: RPT ■ *TF:* 800-225-6765 ■ *Web:* www.ramcogershenson.com					
RD Management LLC 810 7th Ave 28th Fl	New York	NY	10019	212-265-6600	459-9133
Web: www.rdmanagement.com					
Realty Income Corp 600 La Terraza Blvd	Escondido	CA	92025	760-741-2111	741-8674
NYSE: O ■ *TF:* 877-924-6266 ■ *Web:* www.realtyincome.com					
Regency Centers					
1 Independent Dr Suite 114	Jacksonville	FL	32202	904-598-7000	634-3428
NYSE: REG ■ *TF:* 800-950-6333 ■ *Web:* www.regencyrealty.com					
Revenue Properties (America) Inc					
2542 Williams Blvd	Kenner	LA	70062	504-904-8500	904-8555
Web: www.sizeler.net					
Rex Corp Realty 625 Rex Corp Plaza	Uniondale	NY	11556	516-506-6000	506-6800
TF: 888-732-5766 ■ *Web:* www.rxrrealty.com					
Richard E Jacobs Group Inc					
25425 Ctr Ridge Rd	Cleveland	OH	44145	440-871-4800	808-6903
TF: 800-852-9558 ■ *Web:* www.rejacobsgroup.com					
Roberts Realty Investors Inc					
450 Northridge Pkwy Suite 302	Atlanta	GA	30350	770-394-6000	551-5914
AMEX: RPI					
Rochdale Village Inc 169-65 137th Ave	Jamaica	NY	11434	718-276-5700	723-0963

	City	State	ZIP	Phone	Fax
Rosen Assoc Management Corp 33 S Service Rd *Web:* www.rosenmgmt.com	Jericho	NY	11753	516-333-2000	333-7555
Rosenberg Investment Co 3400 E Bayaud Ave Suite 390	Denver	CO	80209	303-320-6067	320-0137
Rossmar & Graham Community Assn Management Co 9362 E Raintree Dr *Web:* www.rossmar.com	Scottsdale	AZ	85260	480-551-4300	551-6000
Royal American Group 30195 Chagrin Blvd Suite 210	Cleveland	OH	44124	216-289-0600	261-6716
Ruffin Cos 1522 S Florence St *Web:* www.ruffinco.com	Wichita	KS	67209	316-942-7940	942-0216
Sabey Corp 12201 Tukwila International Blvd 4th Fl *Web:* www.sabey.com	Seattle	WA	98168	206-281-8700	282-9951
Sares-Regis Group 18802 Bardeen Ave *Web:* www.sares-regis.com	Irvine	CA	92612	949-756-5959	756-5955
Saul Centers Inc 7501 Wisconsin Ave Suite 1500E *NYSE: BFS* ■ *Web:* www.saulcenters.com	Bethesda	MD	20814	301-986-6200	986-6079
Saxe Real Estate Management Service 1999 Van Ness Ave *Web:* www.saxerealestate.com	San Francisco	CA	94109	415-474-3171	447-8652
Schatten Properties Management Co Inc 1514 S St *TF:* 800-892-1315 ■ *Web:* www.schattenproperties.com	Nashville	TN	37212	615-329-3011	327-2343
Sea Island Co PO Box 30351 *TF:* 800-732-4752 ■ *Web:* www.seaisland.com	Sea Island	GA	31561	912-638-3611	634-3961
Selig Enterprises Inc 1100 Spring St NW Suite 550 *TF:* 800-830-9965 ■ *Web:* www.seligenterprises.com	Atlanta	GA	30309	404-876-5511	875-2629
Seligman & Assoc 1 Town Sq Suite 1913 *TF:* 866-864-9824	Southfield	MI	48076	248-862-8000	351-4888
Sen Plex Corp 938 Kohou St *TF:* 800-552-4553	Honolulu	HI	96817	808-848-0111	848-0210
Senior Housing Properties Trust 255 Washington St *NYSE: SNH* ■ *TF:* 866-511-5038 ■ *Web:* www.snhreit.com	Newton	MA	02458	617-796-8350	796-8349
Sentinel Real Estate Corp 1251 Avenue of the Americas *Web:* www.sentinelcorp.com	New York	NY	10020	212-408-2900	
Shorenstein Co LLC 555 California St Suite 4900 *Web:* www.shorenstein.com	San Francisco	CA	94104	415-772-7000	398-2280
Simon Property Group Inc 225 W Washington St *NYSE: SPG* ■ **Fax:* Cust Svc ■ *Web:* www.simon.com	Indianapolis	IN	46204	317-636-1600	263-7658*
SL Green Realty Corp 420 Lexington Ave *NYSE: SLG* ■ *Web:* www.slgreen.com	New York	NY	10170	212-594-2700	216-1790
SonomaWest Holdings Inc 2064 Hwy 116 N	Sebastopol	CA	95472	707-824-2534	829-4630
SR Weiner & Assoc Inc 1330 Boylston St *Web:* www.wsdevelopment.com	Chestnut Hill	MA	02467	617-232-8900	738-4661
Stadium Management Co 3600 Van Rick Dr *Web:* www.wingsstadium.com	Kalamazoo	MI	49001	269-345-1125	345-6452
Stanmar Inc 130 Boston Post Rd *Web:* www.stanmar-inc.com	Sudbury	MA	01776	978-443-9922	443-0479
Stiles Capital Group 300 SE 2nd St *Web:* www.stiles.com/capital_about_us.htm	Fort Lauderdale	FL	33301	954-627-9300	627-9399
Stiles Property Management 300 SE 2nd St *Web:* www.stiles.com/propmgt_about_us.htm	Fort Lauderdale	FL	33301	954-627-9300	627-9188
Stirling Properties 109 Northpark Blvd Suite 300 *TF:* 888-261-2022 ■ *Web:* www.stirlingprop.com	Covington	LA	70433	985-898-2022	898-2077
SUHRCO Management Inc 2010 156th Ave Ne Suite 100 *Web:* www.suhrco.com	Bellevue	WA	98007	425-455-0900	462-1943
Sun Communities Inc 27777 Franklin Rd Suite 200 *NYSE: SUI* ■ *Web:* www.suncommunities.com	Southfield	MI	48034	248-208-2500	208-2640
Supertel Hospitality Inc 309 N 5th St PO Box 1448 *NASDAQ: SPPR* ■ *Web:* www.supertelinc.com	Norfolk	NE	68701	402-371-2520	371-5783
Susquehanna Real Estate 140 E Market St *Web:* www.susquehanna-realestate.com	York	PA	17401	717-848-5500	771-1430
Tanger Factory Outlet Centers Inc 3200 Northline Ave Suite 360 *NYSE: SKT* ■ *TF:* 800-438-8474 ■ *Web:* www.tangeroutlet.com	Greensboro	NC	27408	336-292-3010	852-2096
Targa Real Estate Services Inc 720 S 348th St A2 *Web:* www.targarealestate.com	Federal Way	WA	98003	253-815-0393	815-0191
Taubman Centers Inc 200 E Long Lake Rd Suite 300 *NYSE: TCO* ■ *TF:* 800-828-2626 ■ *Web:* www.taubman.com	Bloomfield Hills	MI	48303	248-258-6800	258-7683
Topa Management Co 1800 Avenue of the Stars Suite 1400 *Web:* www.topamanagement.com	Los Angeles	CA	90067	310-203-9199	229-9788
Tower Properties Co 1000 Walnut St # 900 *Web:* www.towerproperties.com	Kansas City	MO	64106	816-421-8255	374-0624
Towne Properties 1055 St Paul Pl *Web:* www.towneprop.com	Cincinnati	OH	45202	513-381-8696	345-6971
Trammell Crow Co 2001 Ross Ave Suite 3400 *NYSE: TCC* ■ *Web:* www.trammellcrow.com	Dallas	TX	75201	214-863-4101	863-3138
Transcontinental Realty Investors Inc 1800 Valley View Ln 1 Hickory Ctr *NYSE: TCI* ■ *TF:* 800-400-6407 ■ *Web:* www.transconrealty-invest.com	Dallas	TX	75234	469-522-4200	522-4299
Transwestern Commercial Services 1900 W Loop S Suite 1300 *Web:* www.transwestern.net	Houston	TX	77027	713-270-7700	271-8063
Trillium Corp 4350 Cordata Pkwy *TF:* 800-546-7317 ■ *Web:* www.trilliumcorp.com	Bellingham	WA	98226	360-676-9400	676-7736
Tucson Realty & Trust Co 333 N Wilmont Rd Suite 340 *TF:* 877-254-5740 ■ *Web:* www.tucsonrealty.com	Tucson	AZ	85711	520-577-7000	918-3031
United Capital Corp 9 Pk Pl *AMEX: AFP* ■ *Web:* www.unitedcapitalcorp.net	Great Neck	NY	11021	516-466-6464	829-4301
United Mobile Homes Inc 3499 Rt 9 N Suite 3C *AMEX: UMH* ■ *Web:* www.umh.com	Freehold	NJ	07728	732-577-9997	577-9980
Universal Health Realty Income Trust Universal Corporate Ctr 367 S Gulph Rd PO Box 61558 *NYSE: UHT* ■ *Web:* www.uhrit.com	King of Prussia	PA	19406	610-265-0688	768-3336
University City Housing (UCH) 3418 Sansom St *Web:* www.universitycityhousing.com	Philadelphia	PA	19104	215-382-2986	222-5449
Urban Retail Properties Co 900 N Michigan Ave 13th Fl *Web:* www.urbanretail.com	Chicago	IL	60611	312-915-2000	
Urstadt Biddle Properties Inc 321 Railroad Ave *NYSE: UBP* ■ *TF:* 800-323-8216 ■ *Web:* www.ubproperties.com	Greenwich	CT	06830	203-863-8200	861-6755
USAA Real Estate Co 9830 Colonnade Blvd Suite 600 **Fax Area Code:* 210 ■ *TF:* 800-531-8182 ■ *Web:* www.usrealco.com	San Antonio	TX	78230	800-531-8182	641-8425*
Vann Realty Co 10330 Regency Pkwy Dr Suite 301 *Web:* www.vannrealtyco.com	Omaha	NE	68114	402-734-4800	734-5248
Ventas Inc 111 S Wacker Dr Suite 4800 *NYSE: VTR* ■ *TF:* 877-483-6827 ■ *Web:* www.ventasreit.com	Chicago	IL	60606	312-660-3800	660-3850
Vestar Development 2425 E Camelback Rd Suite 750 *Web:* www.vestar.com	Phoenix	AZ	85016	602-866-0900	955-2298
Village Green Cos 30833 Northwestern Hwy Suite 300 *Web:* www.villagegreen.com	Farmington Hills	MI	48334	248-851-9600	851-6161
Vinings Investment Properties Trust 2839 Paces Ferry Rd NW Suite 880 **Fax:* Cust Svc ■ *TF:* 800-849-5868	Atlanta	GA	30339	770-984-9500	984-1951*
Vornado Realty Trust 888 Seventh Ave *NYSE: VNO* ■ **Fax Area Code:* 201 ■ *TF:* 800-242-4119 ■ *Web:* www.vno.com	New York	NY	10019	212-894-7000	587-0600*
Wal-Mart Realty 2001 SE 10th St *TF:* 800-925-6278 ■ *Web:* www.wal-martrealty.com	Bentonville	AR	72716	479-273-4000	
Warren Properties Inc 140 N Escondido Blvd *TF:* 877-927-7361 ■ *Web:* www.warrenproperties.com	Escondido	CA	92025	760-480-6211	480-6404
Washington Real Estate Investment Trust (WRIT) 6110 Executive Blvd Suite 800 *NYSE: WRE* ■ *TF:* 800-565-9748 ■ *Web:* www.writ.com	Rockville	MD	20852	301-984-9400	984-9610
WC & AN Miller Development Co 4315 50th St NW	Washington	DC	20016	202-895-2700	895-2735
Weingarten Realty Investors 2600 Citadel Plaza Dr Suite 300 *NYSE: WRI* ■ *TF:* 800-688-8865 ■ *Web:* www.weingarten.com	Houston	TX	77008	713-866-6000	866-6049
Westcor Partners 11411 N Tatum Blvd *Web:* www.westcor.com	Phoenix	AZ	85028	602-953-6200	953-1964
Westfield America Inc 11601 Wilshire Blvd 11th Fl *Web:* www.westfield.com	Los Angeles	CA	90025	310-478-4456	478-1267
Westgate Management Co Inc 133 Franklin Corner Rd	Lawrenceville	NJ	08648	609-895-8890	895-0058
Weston Cos 1715 Aaron Brenner Dr Suite 516 PO Box 17847 *Web:* www.westonco.com	Memphis	TN	38187	901-682-9100	684-6357
White Co 1600 S Brentwood Blvd Suite 770 *Web:* www.white-co.com	Saint Louis	MO	63144	314-961-4480	961-5903
Winthrop Realty Trust 7 Bulfinch Pl Suite 500 *NYSE: FUR* ■ *Web:* www.winthropreit.com	Boston	MA	02114	617-570-4614	570-4746
Woodmont Real Estate Services (WRES) 1050 Ralston Ave *Web:* www.wres.com	Belmont	CA	94002	650-592-3960	591-4577
WP Carey & Co LLC 50 Rockefeller Plaza 2nd Fl *NYSE: WPC* ■ *TF:* 800-972-2739 ■ *Web:* www.wpcarey.com	New York	NY	10020	212-492-1100	492-8922
Wright Runstad & Co 1201 3rd Ave Suite 2700 *Web:* www.wrightrunstad.com	Seattle	WA	98101	206-447-9000	223-8791
Zamias Services Inc 300 Market St *Web:* www.zamias.com	Johnstown	PA	15901	814-535-3563	536-5505
Zions Securities Corp 5 Triad Ctr Suite 450 *Web:* www.zsc.com	Salt Lake City	UT	84180	801-321-8700	320-4600

659 REALTOR ASSOCIATIONS - STATE

SEE ALSO Real Estate Professionals Associations p. 1465

Listed Here Are The State Branches Of The National Association Of Realtors.

	City	State	ZIP	Phone	Fax
Alabama Assn of Realtors 2000 IH- Pk Dr *Web:* www.alabamarealtors.com	Montgomery	AL	36109	334-262-3808	263-9650
Alaska Assn of Realtors 4205 Minnesota Dr *Web:* www.alaskarealtors.com	Anchorage	AK	99503	907-563-7133	561-1779
Arizona Assn of Realtors 255 E Osborne Rd Suite 200 *TF:* 800-426-7274 ■ *Web:* www.aaronline.com	Phoenix	AZ	85012	602-248-7787	351-2474
Arkansas Realtors Assn 11224 Executive Ctr Dr *TF:* 888-333-2206 ■ *Web:* www.arkansasrealtors.com	Little Rock	AR	72211	501-225-2020	225-7131
California Assn of Realtors 525 S Virgil Ave *Web:* www.car.org	Los Angeles	CA	90020	213-739-8200	480-7724
Colorado Assn of Realtors 309 Inverness Way S *TF:* 800-944-6550 ■ *Web:* www.coloradorealtors.com	Englewood	CO	80112	303-790-7099	790-7299

Phone | Fax

Connecticut Assn of Realtors
111 Founders Plaza Suite 1101 .... East Hartford CT 06108 860-290-6601 290-6615
TF: 800-335-4862 ■ Web: www.ctrealtor.com
Delaware Assn of Realtors 9 E Loockerman St .... Dover DE 19901 302-734-4444 734-1341
TF: 800-305-4445 ■ Web: www.delawarerealtor.com
Florida Assn of Realtors
7025 Augusta National Dr. .... Orlando FL 32822 407-438-1400 438-1411
Web: www.floridarealtors.org
Georgia Assn of Realtors
3200 Presidential Dr. .... Atlanta GA 30340 770-451-1831 458-6992
TF: 866-280-0576 ■ Web: www.garealtor.com
Greater Capital Area Assn of Realtors
8757 Georgia Ave Suite 600 .... Silver Spring MD 20910 301-590-2000
Web: www.gcaar.com
Hawaii Assn of Realtors
1136 12th Ave Suite 220 .... Honolulu HI 96816 808-737-4000 737-4977
TF: 866-693-6767 ■ Web: www.hawaiirealtors.com
Idaho Assn of Realtors 301 S Capitol Blvd .... Boise ID 83702 208-342-3585 336-7958
TF: 800-621-7553 ■ Web: www.idahorealtors.com
Illinois Assn of Realtors 522 S Fifth St. .... Springfield IL 62701 217-529-2600 529-3904
Web: www.illinoisrealtor.org
Indiana Assn of Realtors
7301 N Shadeland Ave Suite A .... Indianapolis IN 46250 317-842-0890 842-1076
Web: www.indianarealtors.com
Iowa Assn of Realtors
1370 NW 114th St Suite 100 .... Clive IA 50325 515-453-1064 453-1070
TF: 800-532-1515 ■ Web: www.iowarealtors.com
Kansas Assn of Realtors 3644 SW Burlingame Rd. .... Topeka KS 66611 785-267-3610 267-1867
TF: 800-366-0069 ■ Web: www.kansasrealtor.com
Kentucky Assn of Realtors
161 Prosperous Pl .... Lexington KY 40509 859-263-7377 263-7565
TF: 800-264-2185 ■ Web: www.kar.com
Louisiana Realtors Assn
4639 Bennington Ave .... Baton Rouge LA 70808 225-923-2210 926-5922
TF: 800-266-8538 ■ Web: www.larealtors.org
Maine Assn of Realtors 19 Community Dr .... Augusta ME 04330 207-622-7501 623-3590
Web: www.mainerealtors.com
Maryland Assn of Realtors 2594 Riva Rd. .... Annapolis MD 21401 410-841-6080 261-8369*
*Fax Area Code: 301 ■ TF: 800-638-6425 ■ Web: www.mdrealtor.org
Massachusetts Assn of Realtors 256 2nd Ave .... Waltham MA 02451 781-890-3700 890-4919
TF: 800-725-6272 ■ Web: www.marealtor.com
Michigan Assn of Realtors
720 N Washington Ave .... Lansing MI 48906 517-372-8890 334-5568
TF: 800-454-7842 ■ Web: www.mirealtors.com
Minnesota Assn of Realtors 5750 Lincoln Dr .... Edina MN 55436 952-935-8313 835-3815
TF: 800-862-6097 ■ Web: www.mnrealtor.com
Mississippi Assn of Realtors PO Box 321000 .... Jackson MS 39232 601-932-9325 932-0382
TF: 800-747-1103 ■ Web: www.ms.living.net
Missouri Assn of Realtors
2601 Bernadette Pl .... Columbia MO 65203 573-445-8400 445-7865
TF: 800-403-0101 ■ Web: www.missourirealtor.org
Montana Assn of Realtors 1 S Montana Ave # M1 .... Helena MT 59601 406-443-4032 443-4220
TF: 800-477-1864 ■ Web: www.montanarealtors.org
Nebraska Realtors Assn 800 S 13th St # 200 .... Lincoln NE 68508 402-323-6500 323-6501
TF: 800-777-5231 ■ Web: www.nebraskarealtors.com
Nevada Assn of Realtors
760 Margrave Dr Suite 200 .... Reno NV 89502 775-829-5911 829-5915
TF: 800-748-5526 ■ Web: www.nvar.org
New Hampshire Assn of Realtors
115A Airport Rd .... Concord NH 03301 603-225-5549 228-0385
Web: nhar.org
New Jersey Assn of Realtors 295 Pierson Ave .... Edison NJ 08837 732-494-5616 494-4723
Web: www.njar.com
New York State Assn of Realtors
130 Washington Ave .... Albany NY 12210 518-463-0300 462-5474
TF: 800-422-2501 ■ Web: www.nysar.com
North Carolina Assn of Realtors Inc
4511 Weybridge Ln. .... Greensboro NC 27407 336-294-1415 299-7872
TF: 800-443-9956 ■ Web: www.ncrealtors.org
North Dakota Assn of Realtors
318 W Apollo Ave .... Bismarck ND 58503 701-355-1010 258-7211
TF: 800-279-2361 ■ Web: www.ndrealtors.com
Ohio Assn of Realtors 200 E Town St .... Columbus OH 43215 614-228-6675 228-2601
Web: www.ohiorealtors.org
Oklahoma Assn of Realtors
9807 N Broadway .... Oklahoma City OK 73114 405-848-9944 848-9947
TF: 800-375-9944 ■ Web: www.oklahomarealtors.com
Oregon Assn of Realtors 2110 Mission St SE .... Salem OR 97308 503-362-3645 362-9615
TF: 800-252-9115 ■ Web: www.oregonrealtors.org
Pennsylvania Assn of Realtors
4501 Chambers Hill Rd .... Harrisburg PA 17111 717-561-1303 561-8796
Web: www.parealtor.org
Realtors Assn of New Mexico
2201 Brothers Rd .... Santa Fe NM 87505 505-982-2442 983-8809
TF: 800-224-2282 ■ Web: www.nmrealtor.com
Rhode Island Assn of Realtors 100 Bignall St. .... Warwick RI 02888 401-785-9898 941-5360
Web: www.riliving.com
South Carolina Assn of Realtors
3780 Fernandina Rd .... Columbia SC 29210 803-772-5206 798-6650
TF: 800-233-6381 ■ Web: www.screaltors.com
South Dakota Assn of Realtors
204 N Euclid Ave .... Pierre SD 57501 605-224-0554 224-8975
Web: www.sdrealtor.org
Tennessee Assn of Realtors
901 19th Ave S Suite 201 .... Nashville TN 37212 615-321-1477 321-4905*
*Fax: Tech Supp ■ Web: www.tarnet.com
Texas Assn of Realtors
1115 San Jacinto Blvd Suite 200 .... Austin TX 78701 512-480-8200 370-2390
TF: 800-873-9155 ■ Web: www.texasrealtors.com
Utah Assn of Realtors
230 W Towne Ridge Pkwy Suite 500 .... Sandy UT 84070 801-676-5200 676-5225
TF: 800-594-8933 ■ Web: www.utahrealtors.com
Vermont Assn of Realtors 148 State St. .... Montpelier VT 05602 802-229-0513 229-0995
TF: 877-229-0523 ■ Web: www.vtrealtor.com
Virginia Assn of Realtors
10231 Telegraph Rd .... Glen Allen VA 23059 804-264-5033 262-0497
TF: 800-755-8271 ■ Web: www.varealtor.com
Washington Assn of Realtors
504 14th Ave SE # 200 .... Olympia WA 98501 360-943-3100 357-6627
TF: 800-562-6024 ■ Web: www.warealtor.com
West Virginia Assn of Realtors
2110 Kanawha Blvd E .... Charleston WV 25311 304-342-7600 343-5811
TF: 800-445-7600 ■ Web: www.wvrealtors.com
Wisconsin Realtors Assn
4801 Forest Run Rd Suite 201 .... Madison WI 53704 608-241-2047 241-2901
TF: 800-279-1972 ■ Web: www.wra.org
Wyoming Assn of Realtors
951 Werner Ct Suite 300 .... Casper WY 82601 307-237-4085 237-7929
TF: 800-676-4085 ■ Web: www.wyorealtors.com

660 RECORDING COMPANIES

Phone | Fax

A & M Records 2220 Colorado Ave. .... Santa Monica CA 90404 310-865-1000 865-5633
Web: www.interscope.com
Abkco Music & Records Inc
1700 Broadway Fl 41 .... New York NY 10019 212-399-0300 582-5090
Web: www.abkco.com
Alligator Records & Artist Management Inc
PO Box 60234 .... Chicago IL 60660 773-973-7736 973-2088
Web: www.alligator.com
American Gramaphone LLC 9130 Mormon Bridge Rd ..... Omaha NE 68152 402-457-4341 457-4332
TF: 800-348-3434 ■ Web: shop.mannheimsteamroller.com
Angel Records 150 5th Ave .... New York NY 10011 212-786-8600 253-3099*
*Fax: Mail Rm ■ Web: www.angelrecords.com
Astralwerks Records 104 W 29th St 4th Fl .... New York NY 10001 212-886-7500 643-5563
Web: www.astralwerks.com
Back Porch Records
4650 N Port Washington Rd .... Milwaukee WI 53212 414-961-8350 961-8351
TF: 800-966-3699 ■ Web: www.backporchrecords.com
Balboa Records Inc 10900 Washington Blvd. .... Culver City CA 90232 310-204-3792 204-0886
Web: www.balboarecords.com
Blue Note Records 150 5th Ave .... New York NY 10011 212-786-8600 253-3099*
*Fax: Mail Rm ■ Web: www.bluenote.com
BNA Records Label 1400 18th Ave S .... Nashville TN 37212 615-301-4400 301-4347
Web: www.bnarecords.com
Buena Vista Music Group 500 S Buena Vista St. .... Burbank CA 91521 818-560-1000 560-5737
Web: www.disneyworld.disney.go.com
Cambria Music PO Box 374 .... Lomita CA 90717 310-831-1322 833-7442
Web: www.cambriamus.com
Capitol Records Inc 1750 N Vine St .... Hollywood CA 90028 323-462-6252 871-5123
Web: www.capitolrecords.com
Capitol Records Nashville
3322 W End Ave 11th Fl .... Nashville TN 37203 615-269-2000 269-2023
Web: www.capitolnashville.com
Century Media 2323 W El Segundo Blvd .... Hawthorne CA 90250 323-418-1400 418-0118
TF: 800-250-4600 ■ Web: www.centurymedia.com
Columbia Records 550 Madison Ave .... New York NY 10022 212-833-8000
Web: www.columbiarecords.com
Curb Records 48 Music Sq E .... Nashville TN 37203 615-321-5080 321-5377*
*Fax: PR ■ Web: www.curb.com
Dualtone Music Group 203B N 11th St .... Nashville TN 37206 615-320-0620 320-0692
Web: www.dualtone.com
Eastern Standard Productions Inc
37 John Glenn Dr .... Buffalo NY 14228 716-691-7631 691-7632
TF: 800-527-9225 ■ Web: www.esp-cd.com
EMI Music Canada 3109 American Dr .... Mississauga ON L4V1B2 905-677-5050 677-1651
Web: www.emimusic.ca
Epic Records Group 550 Madison Ave 21st Fl .... New York NY 10022 212-833-8000
Web: www.epicrecords.com
Epitaph Records 2798 Sunset Blvd. .... Los Angeles CA 90026 213-355-5000 413-9678
Web: www.epitaph.com
Forefront Records PO Box 5085 .... Brentwood TN 37024 615-371-4300
Web: www.forefrontrecords.com
Geffen Records 2220 Colorado Ave .... Santa Monica CA 90404 310-865-4000
Web: www.interscope.com
HighBridge Audio 33 S 6th St CC-2205 .... Minneapolis MN 55402 612-304-7163 304-7175
TF: 800-755-8532 ■ Web: www.highbridgeaudio.com
Higher Octave Music
4650 N Port Washington Rd .... Milwaukee WI 53212 414-961-8350 961-8351
TF: 800-966-3699 ■ Web: www.higheroctave.com
Hollywood Records 500 S Buena Vista St .... Burbank CA 91521 818-560-5670 560-5737
Web: www.hollywoodrecords.go.com
Integrity Media Inc 1000 Cody Rd. .... Mobile AL 36695 251-633-9000 776-5134
TF Orders: 800-533-6912 ■ Web: www.integritymusic.com
Interscope Records 2220 Colorado Ave .... Santa Monica CA 90404 310-865-1000 865-7096
TF: 800-982-1812 ■ Web: www.interscope.com
Island Def Jam Music Group 825 8th Ave .... New York NY 10019 212-333-8000 603-7941*
*Fax: Mktg ■ Web: www.islanddefjam.com
Jive Records 550 Madison Ave Rm 2356 .... New York NY 10022 212-727-0016 645-3783
Web: www.jiverecords.com
Lava Records 1290 Avenue of the Americas .... New York NY 10104 212-707-2000 405-5561
Web: www.lavarecords.com
Legacy Recordings 550 Madison Ave .... New York NY 10022 212-833-8000
Web: www.legacyrecordings.com
Lost Highway Records
54 Music Sq E Suite 300 .... Nashville TN 37203 615-524-7500 524-7600
Web: www.umgnashville.com
Lyric Street Records
1100 Demonbreun St Suite 100 .... Nashville TN 37203 615-963-4848 963-4846
TF: 888-814-4934 ■ Web: www.lyricstreetrecords.com
Malaco Music Group Inc 3023 W Northside Dr .... Jackson MS 39213 601-982-4522 982-4528
TF Cust Svc: 800-272-7936 ■ Web: www.malaco.com

Company	City	State	ZIP	Phone	Fax
Matador Records 304 Hudson St # 700 *Web:* www.matadorrecords.com	New York	NY	10013	212-995-5882	995-5883
Mercury Nashville 54 Music Sq E Suite 300 *Web:* www.umgnashville.com	Nashville	TN	37203	615-524-7500	524-7600
Mosaic Records 35 Melrose Pl. *Web:* www.mosaicrecords.com	Stamford	CT	06902	203-327-7111	323-3526
Motown Record Co 1755 Broadway 7th Fl *Web:* www.motown.com	New York	NY	10019	212-373-0750	489-9096
Narada Productions Inc 4650 N Port Washington Rd *TF:* 800-966-3699 ■ *Web:* www.narada.com	Milwaukee	WI	53212	414-961-8350	961-8351
Naxos of America Inc 1810 Columbia Ave *TF:* 877-629-6723 ■ *Web:* www.naxos.com	Franklin	TN	37064	615-771-9393	771-6747
Nightingale-Conant Corp 6245 W Howard St *TF Cust Svc:* 800-323-3938 ■ *Web:* www.nightingale.com	Niles	IL	60714	847-647-0300	647-5989
Nitro Records 7071 Warner Ave Suite F-736 *Web:* www.nitrorecords.com	Huntington Beach	CA	92647	714-842-8897	
Nonesuch Records 1290 Avenue of the Americas 23rd Fl *Web:* www.nonesuch.com	New York	NY	10104	212-707-2900	707-3205
Putumayo World Music 8 W 25th St 5th Flr *TF:* 888-788-8629 ■ *Web:* www.putumayo.com	New York	NY	10010	212-625-1400	460-0095
RCA Records 550 Madison Ave *Web:* www.rcarecords.com	New York	NY	10022	212-833-8000	930-4447
Real World Records 4650 N Port Washington Rd *TF:* 800-966-3699 ■ *Web:* www.realworldusa.com	Milwaukee	WI	53212	414-961-8350	961-8351
Record Plant Inc 1032 N Sycamore Ave *Web:* www.recordplant.com	Hollywood	CA	90038	323-993-9300	466-8835
Reprise Records 3300 Warner Blvd *Web:* www.repriserec.com	Burbank	CA	91505	818-846-9090	846-8474
Rhino Records 3400 W Olive Ave *TF:* 800-827-4466 ■ *Web:* www.rhino.com	Burbank	CA	91505	818-238-6100	562-9231
Righteous Babe Records Ellicott Stn PO Box 95 *TF:* 800-664-3769 ■ *Web:* www.righteousbabe.com	Buffalo	NY	14205	716-852-8020	852-2741
Rounder Records 29 Camp St *TF:* 800-768-6337 ■ *Web:* www.rounder.com	Cambridge	MA	02140	617-354-0700	491-1970
Sire Records 1296 Avenue of the Americas *Web:* www.sirerecords.com	New York	NY	10104	212-707-3200	
Skaggs Family Records 329 Rockland Rd *Web:* www.skaggsfamilyrecords.com	Hendersonville	TN	37075	615-264-8877	264-8899
Smithsonian Folkways Recordings 600 Maryland Ave SW Suite 200 *TF:* 800-410-9815 ■ *Web:* www.folkways.si.edu	Washington	DC	20024	202-633-6450	633-6477
So So Def Records 137-139 W 25th St *Web:* www.soso-def.com	New York	NY	10001	212-727-0016	
Sony BMG Music Canada Inc 150 Ferrand Dr Suite 300 *Web:* www.sonybmg.ca	Toronto	ON	M6K3L5	416-589-3000	589-3001
Sony Music Entertainment 550 Madison Ave Suite 2356 **Fax:* Sales ■ *Web:* www.sonymusic.com	New York	NY	10022	212-833-8000	833-5828*
Sony Wonder 550 Madison Ave *Web:* www.sonywonder.com	New York	NY	10022	212-833-8100	833-5414
Sound of America Records (SOAR) 5200 Constitution Ave NE *TF:* 800-890-7627	Albuquerque	NM	87110	505-268-6110	268-0237
Sparrow Label Group 101 Winners Cir N *TF:* 800-347-4777 ■ *Web:* www.sparrowrecords.com	Brentwood	TN	37027	615-371-6800	371-6997
SubPop Records 2013 4th Ave 3rd Fl *Web:* www.subpop.com	Seattle	WA	98121	206-441-8441	441-8245
Sugar Hill Records 120 31st Ave N *TF:* 800-996-4455 ■ *Web:* www.sugarhillrecords.com	Nashville	TN	37203	615-297-6890	297-9945
Telarc International Corp 23307 Commerce Pk Rd *TF:* 800-801-5810 ■ *Web:* www.telarc.com	Cleveland	OH	44122	216-464-2313	360-9663
Universal Music Group 1755 Broadway *Web:* www.universalmusic.com	New York	NY	10019	212-373-0600	
Verity Records 137-139 W 25th St *Web:* www.verityrecords.com	New York	NY	10001	212-727-0016	
Verve Music Group The 1755 Broadway *Web:* www.vervemusicgroup.com	New York	NY	10019	212-373-0600	
Victory Records Inc 346 N Justine St 5th Fl *Web:* www.victoryrecords.com	Chicago	IL	60607	312-666-8661	666-8665
Virgin Records 150 5th Ave *Web:* www.virginrecords.com	New York	NY	10011	212-786-8200	253-3099
Walt Disney Records 500 S Buena Vista St *Web:* www.disney.go.com/DisneyRecords	Burbank	CA	91521	818-560-1000	
Warner Bros Records 3300 Warner Blvd *Web:* www.warnerbrosrecords.com	Burbank	CA	91505	818-846-9090	846-8474
Warner Music Group 75 Rockefeller Plaza 30th Fl *NYSE:* WMG ■ *Web:* www.wmg.com	New York	NY	10019	212-275-2000	
Warner Music Nashville 20 Music Sq E *Web:* www.warnermusicnashville.com	Nashville	TN	37203	615-214-1500	
Wind-up Records 72 Madison Ave 8th Fl *Web:* www.winduprecords.com	New York	NY	10016	212-251-9665	895-3200
Word Entertainment 25 Music Sq W *Web:* www.wordentertainment.com	Nashville	TN	37203	615-251-0600	252-8864

661 RECORDING MEDIA - MAGNETIC & OPTICAL

SEE ALSO Photographic Equipment & Supplies p. 2419

Company	City	State	ZIP	Phone	Fax
Allied Vaughn Inc 7951 Computer Ave *TF:* 800-323-0281 ■ *Web:* www.alliedvaughn.com	Bloomington	MN	55435	952-832-3200	832-3203
Americ Disc Inc 2525 Rue Canadien *TF:* 800-263-0419	Drummondville	QC	J2C6Z7	819-474-2655	478-4575
Ampex Corp 500 Broadway **Fax:* Hum Res ■ *TF:* 800-227-8333 ■ *Web:* www.ampex.com	Redwood City	CA	94063	650-367-2011	367-3077*
Athana Inc 1624 W 240 St *TF:* 800-421-1591 ■ *Web:* www.athana.com	Harbor City	CA	90710	310-539-7280	539-6596
Cine Magnetics Inc 100 Business Pk Dr Suite 1 *TF:* 800-431-1102 ■ *Web:* www.cinemagnetics.com	Armonk	NY	10504	914-273-7500	273-7575
Cinram International Inc 2255 Markham Rd *TF:* 800-387-5146 ■ *Web:* www.cinram.com	Scarborough	ON	M1B2W3	416-298-8190	298-0612
Demand Technology Software Inc Corporate Pk, 6300 NW 5th Way *TF:* 877-780-5111 ■ *Web:* www.datacore.com	Fort Lauderdale	FL	33309	954-377-6000	938-7953
Digigraphics Inc 2639 Minnehaha Ave S *TF:* 888-721-3259 ■ *Web:* www.digidigi.com	Minneapolis	MN	55406	612-721-2434	721-4855
Digital Excellence 300 York Ave *TF:* 800-608-8008 ■ *Web:* www.digx.com	Saint Paul	MN	55101	651-772-5100	771-5629
Duplication Factory Inc 4275 Norex Dr *TF:* 800-279-2009 ■ *Web:* www.duplicationfactory.com	Chaska	MN	55318	952-448-9912	448-3983
Farstone Technology Inc 1758-B N Shoreline Blvd **Fax Area Code:* 650 ■ *Web:* www.farstone.com	Mountain View	CA	94043	562-373-5370	969-4567*
Heritage Microfilm Inc 4049 21st Ave SW *TF:* 888-870-0484 ■ *Web:* www.heritagemicrofilm.com	Cedar Rapids	IA	52404	319-390-9442	396-4329
Imation Corp 1 Imation Pl *NYSE:* IMN ■ *TF:* 888-466-3456 ■ *Web:* www.imation.com	Oakdale	MN	55128	651-704-4000	704-7100
LaserCard Corp 1875 N Shoreline Blvd *Web:* www.lasercard.com	Mountain View	CA	94043	650-969-4428	969-3140
Maxell Corp of America 22-08 Rt 208 *TF:* 800-533-2836 ■ *Web:* www.maxell.com	Fair Lawn	NJ	07410	201-794-5900	796-8790
Mediostream Inc 4962 El Cmno Real 201 *Web:* www.mediostream.com	Los Altos	CA	94022	650-625-8900	625-9900
Optical Disc Solutions Inc 1767 Sheridan St *TF:* 800-704-7648 ■ *Web:* www.odiscs.com	Richmond	IN	47374	765-935-7574	935-0174
Peripheral Mfg Inc 4775 Paris St *TF:* 800-468-6888 ■ *Web:* www.periphman.com	Denver	CO	80239	303-371-8651	371-8643
TDK Electronics Corp 901 Franklin Ave *TF:* 800-835-8273 ■ *Web:* www.tdk.com	Garden City	NY	11530	516-535-2600	294-7931
TDK USA Corp 901 Franklin Ave PO Box 9302 **Fax:* Sales ■ *TF:* 800-835-8273 ■ *Web:* www.tdk.com	Garden City	NY	11530	516-535-2600	294-7751*
Transco Products Corp PO Box 1025 *TF:* 800-876-0039 ■ *Web:* www.transcousa.com	Linden	NJ	07036	908-862-0030	862-0035
US Optical Disc Inc 1 Eagle Dr *TF:* 800-743-1124	Sanford	ME	04073	207-324-1124	490-1707
USA Dubs 253 W 35th St *TF:* 800-872-3821 ■ *Web:* www.usadubs.com	New York	NY	10001	212-398-6400	398-4145
Verbatim Americas LLC 1200 W WT Harris Blvd *TF:* 800-538-8589 ■ *Web:* www.verbatim.com	Charlotte	NC	28262	704-547-6500	547-6767
VU Media Duplication 1420 Blake St *TF:* 800-637-4336 ■ *Web:* www.vumedia.com	Denver	CO	80202	303-534-5503	595-4630

662 RECREATION FACILITY OPERATORS

SEE ALSO Bowling Centers p. 1542

Company	City	State	ZIP	Phone	Fax
Clicks Billiards 3100 Monticello Ave Suite 350 *Web:* clicks.com	Dallas	TX	75205	214-521-7001	521-1449
Dave & Buster's Inc 2481 Manana Dr *TF:* 800-842-5369 ■ *Web:* www.daveandbusters.com	Dallas	TX	75220	214-357-9588	350-0941
Jeepers! Inc 800 S St *TF:* 800-533-7377	Waltham	MA	02453	781-890-1800	891-4916
Mt Bachelor 115 SW Columbia St *Web:* www.mtbachelor.com	Bend	OR	97702	541-382-2442	693-0210
Palace Entertainment Inc 4950 MacArthur Rd Suite 400 *Web:* www.palaceentertainment.com	Newport Beach	CA	92660	949-261-0404	261-1414
SEGA GameWorks LLC 600 N Brand Blvd 5th Fl *Web:* www.gameworks.com	Glendale	CA	91203	818-254-4263	254-4306

663 RECYCLABLE MATERIALS RECOVERY

Included Here Are Companies That Recycle Post-Consumer Trash, Tires, Appliances, Batteries, Etc. As Well As Industrial Recyclers Of Plastics, Paper, Wood, Glass, Solvents, And So On.

Company	City	State	ZIP	Phone	Fax
ACC Recycling Corp 1190 20th St N *TF:* 800-282-1153	Saint Petersburg	FL	33713	727-896-9600	822-4923
Active Recycling Co Inc 2000 W Slauson Ave	Los Angeles	CA	90047	323-295-7774	292-2114
Advanced Environmental Recycling Technologies Inc 914 N Jefferson St *OTC:* AERT ■ *TF:* 800-951-5117 ■ *Web:* www.aertinc.com	Springdale	AR	72764	479-756-7400	756-7410
All American Recycling Corp 2 Hope St	Jersey City	NJ	07307	201-656-3363	656-8188
Ambit Pacific Recycling Inc 16228 S Figueroa St *Web:* www.ambitpacific.com	Gardena	CA	90248	310-538-3798	327-7114
American Paper Recycling Corp 301 W Lake St *TF Cust Svc:* 800-762-6790	Northlake	IL	60164	708-344-6789	344-0262
Appliance Recycling Centers of America Inc 7400 Excelsior Blvd *NASDAQ:* ARCI ■ *TF:* 800-452-8680 ■ *Web:* www.arcainc.com	Minneapolis	MN	55426	952-930-9000	930-1800
Arrow-Intechra LLC PO Box 3226 *TF:* 800-393-7627 ■ *Web:* www.intechra.com	Ridgeland	MS	39158	800-393-7627	
Automated Material Handling Co 655 Christian Ln PO Box 7146	Kensington	CT	06037	860-223-3601	225-3166
Batliner Paper Stock Co 2501 E Front St *TF:* 800-821-8512 ■ *Web:* www.batlinerpaperstock.com	Kansas City	MO	64120	816-483-3343	241-9736

				Phone	Fax
Better Management Corp (BMC) 41738 Esterly Dr TF: 877-293-4300 ■ Web: www.bmcohio.com	Columbiana	OH	44408	330-482-7070	482-5929
Canusa Hershman Recycling Co 45 NE Industrial Rd Web: www.chrecycling.com	Branford	CT	06405	203-488-0887	488-9499
Clean Earth of North Jersey Inc 115 Jacobus Ave	South Kearny	NJ	07032	973-344-4004	344-8652
Community Recycling Inc 3840 NW 37th Ct	Miami	FL	33142	305-633-3100	634-4272
Continental Paper Grading Co Inc 1623 S Lumber St Web: www.cpgco.com	Chicago	IL	60616	312-226-2010	226-2025
Energy Answers Corp 79 N Pearl St Web: www.energyanswers.com	Albany	NY	12207	518-434-1227	436-6343
FCR LLC 809 W Hill St Web: www.casella.com/locations/fcr	Charlotte	NC	28208	704-697-2000	376-1625
Federal International Inc 7935 Clayton Rd TF: 800-972-7277 ■ Web: www.federalinternational.com	Saint Louis	MO	63117	314-721-3377	721-2007
Fritz Enterprises Inc 1650 W Jefferson Ave Web: www.fritzinc.com	Trenton	MI	48183	734-362-3200	362-3250
GreenMan Technologies Inc 7 Kimball Ln Bldg A Web: www.greenman.biz	Lynnfield	MA	01940	781-224-2411	224-0114
Hudson Baylor Corp 237 Dupont Ave PO Box 947 Web: www.hudsonbaylor.com	Newburgh	NY	12551	845-561-0160	562-8412
International Metals Reclamation Co Inc 1 Inmetco Dr Web: www.inmetco.com	Ellwood City	PA	16117	724-758-2800	758-2845
Jupiter Aluminum Corp 4825 Scott St Web: www.jupiteraluminum.com	Schiller Park	IL	60176	847-928-5930	928-0795
Macon Iron & Paper Stock Co Inc 950 Lower Poplar Rd TF: 800-342-1933 ■ Web: www.thescrapmarket.com	Macon	GA	31202	478-743-6773	743-9965
Marborg Industries 728 E Yanonali St TF: 800-798-1852 ■ Web: www.marborg.com	Santa Barbara	CA	93103	805-963-1852	962-0552
Mervis Industries Inc 3295 E Main St TF: 800-637-3016 ■ Web: www.mervis.com	Danville	IL	61834	217-442-5300	477-9245
Metro Recycling Co Inc 2424 Beekman St TF: 800-235-4843	Cincinnati	OH	45214	513-251-1800	251-5239
Minergy Corp 1512 S Commercial St Web: www.minergy.com	Neenah	WI	54956	920-727-1919	727-1418
North Shore Recycled Fibers Inc 53 Jefferson Ave	Salem	MA	01970	978-744-4330	744-8857
Pall Corp 2200 Northern Blvd NYSE: PLL ■ TF: 800-645-6532 ■ Web: www.pall.com	East Hills	NY	11548	516-484-5400	801-9754
Paper Tigers The 2201 Waukegan Rd Suite 270 TF: 800-621-1774 ■ Web: www.papertigers.com	Bannockburn	IL	60015	847-919-6500	919-6501
Potential Industries Inc 922 E E St	Wilmington	CA	90744	310-549-5901	513-1361
Strategic Materials Inc 16365 Pk Ten Pl Suite 200 Web: www.strategicmaterials.com	Houston	TX	77084	281-647-2700	647-2710
Sun Valley Paper Stock Inc 11166 Pendleton St	Sun Valley	CA	91352	818-767-8984	767-1323
Utah Metal Works Inc (UMW) 805 Everett Ave PO Box 1073 TF: 877-221-0099 ■ Web: www.umw.com	Salt Lake City	UT	84116	801-364-5679	364-5676
Veolia ES Solid Waste Inc 125 S 84th St Suite 200 Web: www.veoliaes-sw.com	Milwaukee	WI	53214	414-479-7800	479-7400
WTE Corp 7 Alfred Cir Web: www.wte.com	Bedford	MA	01730	781-275-6400	275-8612

664 RECYCLED PLASTICS PRODUCTS

SEE ALSO Flooring - Resilient p. 1849

				Phone	Fax
Allen Ventures Inc 517 State Farm Rd TF: 877-423-9800 ■ Web: www.allenventures.com	Deerfield	WI	53531	608-423-9800	423-9804
Amazing Recycled Products Inc PO Box 312 TF: 800-241-2174 ■ Web: www.amazingrecycled.com	Denver	CO	80201	303-699-7693	699-2102
American Recycled Plastic Inc 1500 Main St TF: 866-674-1525 ■ Web: www.itsrecycled.com	Palm Bay	FL	32905	321-674-1525	674-2365
Bedford Technology LLC 2424 Armour Rd PO Box 609 Web: www.bedfordtech.com	Worthington	MN	56187	507-372-5558	372-5726
Canopy Plastics 77 St David St TF: 888-255-1222 ■ Web: www.canopyplastics.com	Lindsay	ON	K9V1N8	705-878-5700	878-5702
Carefree Recycled Products 10290 S Progress Way Suite 102 Web: www.carefreerecycled.com	Parker	CO	80134	303-805-7809	805-7812
Everlast Plastic Lumber Inc 800 W Market St	Auburn	PA	17922	570-754-7440	754-7441
Harmon Assoc Corp 2 Jericho Plaza Suite 110 Web: www.eharmongp.com	Jericho	NY	11753	516-997-3400	997-3409
J-MacLumber Inc 4154 Faust St Web: www.maclumber.com	Bamberg	SC	29003	803-245-1700	245-1701
Koller Craft Plastic Products 1400 Old Rt 141 Web: www.koller-craft.com	Fenton	MO	63026	636-343-9220	343-1034
Parkland Plastics Inc 104 Yoder Dr PO Box 339 TF: 800-835-4110 ■ Web: www.parklandplastics.com	Middlebury	IN	46540	574-825-4336	825-4338
PlasTEAK 3563 Copley Rd PO Box 4290 TF: 800-320-1841 ■ Web: www.plasteak.com	Akron	OH	44321	330-668-2587	666-0844
Plastic Lumber Co Inc 115 W Bartges St TF: 800-886-8990 ■ Web: www.plasticlumber.com	Akron	OH	44311	330-762-8989	762-1613
Plastic Lumberyard LLC 220 E Washington St Web: www.plasticlumberyard.com	Norristown	PA	19401	610-277-3900	277-3970
Plastic Pilings Inc 1485 S Willow Ave Web: www.plasticpilings.com	Rialto	CA	92376	909-874-4080	874-4860
Plastic Recycling of Iowa Falls Inc 10252 Hwy 65 Web: www.hammersplastic.com	Iowa Falls	IA	50126	641-648-5073	648-5074
Plastiques Cascades Re-Plast 1350 ch Quatre-Saisons TF: 888-313-2440 ■ Web: www.perma-deck.com	Notre-Dame-du-Bon-Conseil	QC	J0C1A0	819-336-2440	336-2442
Plastival 1685 Holmes Rd TF: 800-585-4988 ■ Web: www.plastival.com	Elgin	IL	60123	847-931-4771	931-1771
Polymer Concentrates Inc 179 Woodlawn St PO Box 42 Web: www.polymerconcentrates.com	Clinton	MA	01510	978-365-7335	368-0438
Recycled Plastic Man Inc 5258 Linwood Rd TF: 800-253-7742 ■ Web: www.recycledplasticman.com	Placida	FL	33946	941-698-1060	698-1038
Renew Plastics 112 4th St PO Box 480 TF: 800-666-5207 ■ Web: www.renewplastics.com	Luxemburg	WI	54217	920-845-2326	845-2335
Resco Plastics Inc 93783 Newport Ln TF: 800-266-5097 ■ Web: www.rescoplastics.com	Coos Bay	OR	97420	541-269-5485	269-2572
Witt Industries Inc 4600 Mason-Montgomery Rd *Fax Area Code: 877 ■ TF: 800-543-7417 ■ Web: www.witt.com	Cincinnati	OH	45209	800-543-7417	891-8200*

665 REFRACTORIES - CLAY

				Phone	Fax
ANH Refractories Co 400 Fairway Dr Cherrington Corporate Ctr Web: www.hwr.com	Moon Township	PA	15108	412-375-6600	
BNZ Materials Inc 6901 S Pierce St Suite 260 TF: 800-999-0890 ■ Web: www.bnzmaterials.com	Littleton	CO	80128	303-978-1199	978-0308
DFC Ceramics Inc 515 S 9th St TF: 888-372-1876 ■ Web: www.dfcceramics.com	Canon City	CO	81212	719-275-7525	275-2051
Harbison-Walker Refractories Co *ANH Refractories Co* 400 Fairway Dr Web: www.hwr.com	Moon Township	PA	15108	412-375-6600	375-6962
Magneco/Metrel Inc 223 W I- Rd Web: www.magneco-metrel.com	Addison	IL	60101	630-543-6660	543-1479
MINTEQ International Inc 405 Lexington Ave 19th Fl TF: 888-801-1031 ■ Web: www.mineralstech.com/minteq.html	New York	NY	10174	212-878-1800	878-1952
Mount Savage Specialty Refractories Co 736 W Ingomar Rd PO Box 398 TF: 800-437-6777 ■ Web: www.mtsavage.com	Ingomar	PA	15127	412-367-9100	367-2228
Permatech Inc 911 E Elm St Web: www.permatech.net	Graham	NC	27253	336-578-0701	578-7758
RENO Refractories Inc 601 Reno Dr TF: 800-741-7366 ■ Web: www.renorefractories.com	Morris	AL	35116	205-647-0240	647-2115
RENO Refractories Inc Reftech Div 601 Reno Dr *Fax Area Code: 205 ■ TF: 800-741-7366 ■ Web: www.reftechnology.com	Morris	AL	35116	800-741-7366	647-2115*
Resco Products Inc 2 Penn Ctr W Suite 430 TF: 888-283-5505 ■ Web: www.rescoproducts.com	Pittsburgh	PA	15276	412-494-4491	494-4571
Riverside Refractories Inc 201 Truss Ferry Rd TF: 800-226-4542 ■ Web: www.riversiderefractories.com	Pell City	AL	35128	205-338-3366	338-7456
Saxonburg Ceramics Inc 100 N Isabella St PO Box 688 TF: 800-245-1270 ■ Web: www.saxonburgceramics.com	Saxonburg	PA	16056	724-352-1561	352-3580
Shenango Advanced Ceramics LLC 606 McCleary Ave Web: www.shenangoceramics.com	New Castle	PA	16101	724-652-6668	652-6664
Utah Refractories Corp 2200 N 1100 W TF Cust Svc: 800-345-6808	Lehi	UT	84043	801-768-3591	768-2684
Whitacre Greer Fireproofing Inc 1400 S Mahoning Ave TF Cust Svc: 800-947-2837 ■ Web: www.wgpaver.com	Alliance	OH	44601	330-823-1610	823-5502

666 REFRACTORIES - NONCLAY

				Phone	Fax
Allied Mineral Products Inc 2700 Scioto Pkwy Web: www.alliedmineral.com	Columbus	OH	43221	614-876-0244	876-0981
American Flux & Metal 352 E Fleming Pike PO Box 74	Winslow	NJ	08095	609-561-7500	561-3724
C-E Minerals Inc 901 E 8th Ave Web: www.ceminerals.com	King of Prussia	PA	19406	610-265-6880	337-8122
Fedmet Resources Corp 4060 St Catherine St W Suite 630 TF: 800-609-5711 ■ Web: www.fedmet.com	Montreal	QC	H3Z2Z3	514-931-5711	931-8378
Inland Refractories Co 38600 Chester Rd TF: 800-321-0767	Avon	OH	44011	440-934-6600	934-6601
Magnesita Refractories Co 425 S Salem Church Rd *Fax: Sales ■ TF General: 800-233-1991 ■ Web: www.magnesita.com	York	PA	17403	717-848-1501	793-5500*
Minco Inc 510 Midway Cir TF: 800-525-9753 ■ Web: www.mincoitc.com	Midway	TN	37809	423-422-6051	422-4802
MINTEQ International Inc 405 Lexington Ave 19th Fl TF: 888-801-1031 ■ Web: www.mineralstech.com/minteq.html	New York	NY	10174	212-878-1800	878-1952
Morganite Crucible Inc 22 N Plains Industrial Rd Suite 1 TF: 800-936-7550 ■ Web: www.morgancrucible.com	Wallingford	CT	06492	203-654-0586	
New Castle Refractories Co Inc 915 Industrial St Web: www.refractoriesinstitute.org	New Castle	PA	16102	724-654-7711	654-6322
Permatech Inc 911 E Elm St Web: www.permatech.net	Graham	NC	27253	336-578-0701	578-7758
Plibrico Co 1010 N Hooker St TF: 800-511-6203 ■ Web: www.plibrico-usa.com	Chicago	IL	60622	312-337-9000	337-9003

	City	State	Zip	Phone	Fax
Ransom & Randolph Co 3535 Briarfield Blvd TF: 800-800-7496 ■ Web: www.ransom-randolph.com	Maumee	OH	43537	419-865-9497	865-9997
RENO Refractories Inc 601 Reno Dr TF: 800-741-7366 ■ Web: www.renorefractories.com	Morris	AL	35116	205-647-0240	647-2115
RENO Refractories Inc Reftech Div 601 Reno Dr *Fax Area Code: 205 ■ TF: 800-741-7366 ■ Web: www.reftechnology.com	Morris	AL	35116	800-741-7366	647-2115*
Rex Roto Corp 5600 E Grand River PO Box 980 Web: www.rexmaterials.com	Fowlerville	MI	48836	517-223-3787	223-6806
TYK America Inc 301 Brickyard Rd TF: 800-569-9359 ■ Web: www.tykamerica.com	Clairton	PA	15025	412-384-4259	384-4242
Vesuvius McDanel Co 510 9th Ave Web: www.ceramics.com/vesuvius	Beaver Falls	PA	15010	724-843-8300	843-5644
Wahl Refractories Inc 767 SR 19 S TF: 800-837-9245 ■ Web: www.wahlref.com	Fremont	OH	43420	419-334-2658	334-9445
Wulfrath Refractories Inc 6th & Ctr Sts PO Box 28 TF: 800-245-1801	Tarentum	PA	15084	724-224-8800	224-3353

667 REFRIGERATION EQUIPMENT - MFR

SEE ALSO Air Conditioning & Heating Equipment - Commercial/Industrial p. 1382

	City	State	Zip	Phone	Fax
Advance Energy Technologies Inc 1 Solar Dr TF: 800-724-0198 ■ Web: www.advanceet.com	Clifton Park	NY	12065	518-371-2140	371-0737
Aluma Shield Industries Inc Butcher Boy Doors Div 725 Summerhill Dr TF: 888-882-5862	DeLand	FL	32724	386-626-6789	626-6884
American Panel Corp 5800 SE 78th St TF: 800-327-3015 ■ Web: www.americanpanel.com	Ocala	FL	34472	352-245-7055	245-0726
Applied Process Cooling Corp 1408 Grove St Web: www.apcco.net	Healdsburg	CA	95448	707-433-9471	433-1310
Arctic Star Refrigeration Mfg Co Inc 3540 W Pioneer Pkwy TF: 800-229-6562 ■ Web: www.arcticstar.com	Arlington	TX	76013	817-274-1396	277-4828
Berg Co 2160 Industrial Dr Web: www.berg-controls.com	Monona	WI	53713	608-221-4281	221-1416
Beverage-Air Corp 3779 Champion Blvd Web: www.beverage-air.com	Winston-Salem	NC	27105	336-245-6400	245-6453
Burch Industries Inc 16780 Airbase Rd TF: 800-322-3688 ■ Web: www.burchindustries.com	Maxton	NC	28364	910-844-3688	844-3689
Continental Materials Corp 200 S Wacker Dr Suite 4000 AMEX: CUO	Chicago	IL	60606	312-541-7200	541-8089
CrownTonka Inc 10700 Hwy 55 Suite 300 TF: 800-523-7337 ■ Web: www.crowntonka.com	Plymouth	MN	55441	763-541-1410	541-1563
Custom Coolers LLC 5609 Azle Ave TF: 800-627-0488 ■ Web: www.cccoolers.com	Fort Worth	TX	76114	817-626-3737	626-1213
Delfield Co 980 S Isabella Rd TF: 800-733-8821 ■ Web: www.delfield.com	Mount Pleasant	MI	48858	989-773-7981	773-3210
Dole Refrigerating Co 1420 Higgs Rd TF: 800-251-8990	Lewisburg	TN	37091	931-359-6211	359-8664
Edey Mfg Co Inc 2159 E 92nd St TF: 800-333-9634	Los Angeles	CA	90002	323-566-6151	566-0262
Eliason Corp 9229 Shaver Rd TF Cust Svc: 800-828-3655 ■ Web: www.eliasoncorp.com	Portage	MI	49024	269-327-7003	327-7006
Federal Industries Div Standex Corp 215 Federal Ave PO Box 290 TF: 800-356-4206 ■ Web: www.federalind.com	Belleville	WI	53508	608-424-3331	424-3234
Follett Corp 801 Church Ln TF Cust Svc: 800-523-9361 ■ Web: www.follettice.com	Easton	PA	18040	610-252-7301	250-0169
GEA FES Inc 3475 Board Rd PO Box 2306 Web: www.geafes.com	York	PA	17405	717-767-6411	767-9548
Harris Environmental Systems Inc 11 Connector Rd TF: 888-771-4200 ■ Web: www.harris-env.com	Andover	MA	01810	978-475-0104	475-7903
Haws Corp 1455 Kleppe Ln TF: 888-640-4297 ■ Web: www.hawsco.com	Sparks	NV	89431	775-359-4712	359-7424
Heatcraft Refrigeration Products 2175 W Pk Pl Blvd TF: 800-321-1881 ■ Web: www.heatcraftrpd.com	Stone Mountain	GA	30087	770-465-5600	465-5990
Hill PHOENIX Inc 1003 Sigman Rd TF: 800-518-6630 ■ Web: www.hillphoenix.com	Conyers	GA	30013	770-285-3264	285-3080
Howe Corp 1650 N Elston Ave Web: www.howecorp.com	Chicago	IL	60622	773-235-0200	235-1530
Hussmann Corp 12999 St Charles Rock Rd TF: 800-879-1152 ■ Web: www.hussmann.com	Bridgeton	MO	63044	314-291-2000	298-4756
Ice-O-Matic 11100 E 45th Ave TF: 800-423-3367 ■ Web: www.iceomatic.com	Denver	CO	80239	303-371-3737	371-6296
IMI Cornelius Inc 101 Broadway St W TF: 800-238-3600 ■ Web: www.cornelius.com	Osseo	MN	55369	763-488-8200	488-4298
International Cold Storage Co Inc 215 E 13th St TF: 800-835-0001 ■ Web: www.icsco.com	Andover	KS	67002	316-733-1385	733-2434
KDIndustries 1525 E Lake Rd TF: 800-840-9577 ■ Web: www.kold-draft.com	Erie	PA	16511	814-453-6761	455-6336
Kloppenberg & Co 2627 W Oxford Ave TF: 800-346-3246 ■ Web: www.kloppenberg.com	Englewood	CO	80110	303-761-1615	789-1741
Kolpak 2915 Tennessee Ave N TF: 800-826-7036 ■ Web: www.kolpak.com	Parsons	TN	38363	731-847-5328	847-5387
Kysor Panel Systems 4201 N Beach St TF: 800-633-3426 ■ Web: www.kysorpanel.com	Fort Worth	TX	76137	817-281-5121	281-5521
Lancer Corp 6655 Lancer Blvd TF: 800-729-1500 ■ Web: www.lancercorp.com	San Antonio	TX	78219	210-310-7000	310-7250
Leer LP 206 Leer St TF Cust Svc: 800-766-5337 ■ Web: www.leerlp.com	New Lisbon	WI	53950	608-562-7100	562-6022
Manitowoc Ice 2110 S 26th St *Fax: Sales ■ TF: 800-545-5720 ■ Web: www.manitowocice.com	Manitowoc	WI	54220	920-682-0161	683-7589*
McCann's Engineering & Mfg Co 4570 W Colorado Blvd TF: 800-423-2429 ■ Web: www.mccannseng.com	Los Angeles	CA	90039	818-637-7200	637-7222
Micro Matic USA Inc 10726 N 2nd St *Fax: Sales ■ TF: 800-435-6950 ■ Web: www.micro-matic.com	Machesney Park	IL	61115	815-968-7557	968-0363*
MicroMetl Corp 3035 N Shadeland Ave Suite 300 TF: 800-662-4822 ■ Web: www.micrometl.com	Indianapolis	IN	46226	317-524-5400	524-5499
Morris & Assoc Inc 803 Morris Dr Web: www.morris-associates.com	Garner	NC	27529	919-582-9200	582-9100
Mr Winter Inc 8080 W 26th Ct TF: 800-327-3371 ■ Web: www.mrwinterinc.com	Hialeah	FL	33016	305-556-6741	821-1084
Nor-Lake Inc 727 2nd St PO Box 248 TF: 800-388-5253 ■ Web: www.norlake.com	Hudson	WI	54016	715-386-2323	386-6149
Norcold Inc 600 S Kuther Rd PO Box 180 TF: 800-543-1219 ■ Web: www.norcold.com	Sidney	OH	45365	937-497-3080	497-3092
Perlick Corp 8300 W Good Hope Rd TF: 800-558-5592 ■ Web: www.perlick.com	Milwaukee	WI	53223	414-353-7060	353-7069
Scotsman Ice Systems 775 Corporate Woods Pkwy TF Cust Svc: 800-726-8762 ■ Web: www.scotsman-ice.com	Vernon Hills	IL	60061	847-215-4500	913-9844
Seattle Refrigeration & Mfg Co 1057 S Director St TF: 800-228-8881 ■ Web: www.seafrig.com	Seattle	WA	98108	206-762-7740	762-1730
Semco Mfg Co 705 E Business 83 Web: www.semcomfgco.com	Pharr	TX	78577	956-787-4203	781-0620
Silver King Refrigeration Inc 1600 Xenium Ln N TF: 800-328-3329 ■ Web: www.silverking.com	Minneapolis	MN	55441	763-923-2441	553-1209
Springer Penguin Inc 460 Grand Blvd TF: 800-529-4375 ■ Web: www.springer-penguin.com	Westbury	NY	11590	516-333-4400	333-4759
Starrett Corp 6203 Johns Rd Suite 8 TF: 800-237-8350 ■ Web: www.leerlp.com/starretm.html	Tampa	FL	53950	813-882-3616	882-3702
True Mfg Co 2001 E Terra Ln TF: 800-325-6152 ■ Web: www.truemfg.com	O'Fallon	MO	63366	636-240-2400	272-2408
Turbo Refrigerating LLC 1815 Shady Oaks Dr TF: 800-775-8648 ■ Web: www.vogtice.com	Denton	TX	76205	940-387-4301	382-0364
Victory Refrigeration Inc 110 Woodcrest Rd TF: 800-523-5008 ■ Web: www.victoryrefrigeration.com	Cherry Hill	NJ	08003	856-428-4200	428-7299
Vogt Ice 1000 W Ormsby Ave Suite 19 TF: 800-853-8648 ■ Web: www.vogtice.com	Louisville	KY	40210	502-635-3000	634-0479
WA Brown & Son Inc 209 Long Meadow Dr TF: 800-438-2316 ■ Web: www.wabrown.com	Salisbury	NC	28147	704-636-5131	637-0919

668 REFRIGERATION EQUIPMENT - WHOL

SEE ALSO Plumbing, Heating, Air Conditioning Equipment & Supplies - Whol p. 2434

	City	State	Zip	Phone	Fax
Abco Refrigeration Supply Corp 49-70 31st St TF: 800-786-2075 ■ Web: www.abcorefrig.com	Long Island City	NY	11101	718-937-9000	392-1296
Allied Supply Co Inc 1100 E Monument Ave TF: 800-589-5690 ■ Web: www.alliedsupply.com	Dayton	OH	45402	937-224-9833	224-5648
American Refrigeration Supplies 2632 E Chambers St Web: www.ars-net.com	Phoenix	AZ	85040	602-243-2792	243-2893
Automatic Ice & Beverage Inc PO Box 110159 TF: 800-476-4242	Birmingham	AL	35211	205-787-9640	787-9659
Baker Distributing Co 4255 Emerson St TF: 800-217-4698 ■ Web: www.bakerdist.com	Jacksonville	FL	32207	904-733-9633	407-4511
Broich Enterprises Inc 6440 City W Pkwy Suite 2 Web: www.arcticairco.com	Eden Prairie	MN	55344	952-941-2270	941-3066
Dennis Supply Co PO Box 3376 TF: 800-352-4618	Sioux City	IA	51102	712-255-1624	255-4913
Don Stevens Inc 980 Discovery Rd TF: 800-444-2299	Eagan	MN	55121	651-452-0872	452-4189
Ernest F Mariani Co Inc 573 W 2890 S TF: 800-453-2927	Salt Lake City	UT	84115	801-359-3744	531-9615
Gustave A Larson Co PO Box 910 TF: 800-829-9609 ■ Web: www.galarson.com	Pewaukee	WI	53072	262-542-0200	542-1400
Hart & Price Corp PO Box 36368 TF: 800-777-9129 ■ Web: www.hartprice.com	Dallas	TX	75235	214-521-9129	350-4143
Insco Distributing Inc 12501 Network Blvd TF: 800-203-8400 ■ Web: www.inscohvac.com	San Antonio	TX	78249	210-690-8400	690-1501
ISI Commercial Refrigeration LP 9136 Viscount Row TF: 800-777-5070 ■ Web: www.isi-texas.com	Dallas	TX	75247	214-631-7980	631-6813
Modern Ice Equipment & Supply Co 5709 Harrison Ave TF: 800-543-1581 ■ Web: www.modernice.com	Cincinnati	OH	45248	513-367-2101	367-5762
Preston Refrigeration Co Inc 3200 Fiberglass Rd TF: 800-621-1813 ■ Web: www.prestonrefrigeration.com	Kansas City	KS	66115	913-621-1813	621-6962
RE Lewis Refrigeration Inc 803 S Lincoln St PO Box 92 TF Cust Svc: 800-264-0767 ■ Web: www.relewisinc.com	Creston	IA	50801	641-782-8183	782-8156
Redico Inc 1850 S Lee Ct TF: 800-242-3920 ■ Web: www.redicoinc.com	Buford	GA	30518	770-614-1401	614-1403
Refricenter of Miami Inc 7101 NW 43rd St Web: www.refricenter.net	Miami	FL	33166	305-477-8880	599-9323
Rogers Supply Co Inc PO Box 740 TF: 800-252-0406 ■ Web: www.rogerssupply.com	Champaign	IL	61824	217-356-0166	356-1768
Sid Harvey Industries Inc 605 Locust St *Fax Area Code: 800 ■ Web: www.sidharvey.com	Garden City	NY	11530	516-745-9200	268-6542*

Company	City	State	Zip	Phone	Fax
Southern Refrigeration Corp 3140 Shenandoah Ave *TF:* 800-763-4433 ■ *Web:* www.southernrefcorp.com	Roanoke	VA	24017	540-342-3493	343-2163
Stafford-Smith Inc 3414 S Burdick St *TF:* 800-968-2442 ■ *Web:* www.staffordsmith.com	Kalamazoo	MI	49001	269-343-1240	343-2509
Supermarket Systems Inc PO Box 472513 *TF:* 800-553-1905	Charlotte	NC	28247	704-542-6000	542-6999
SWH Supply Co 242 E Main St *TF:* 800-866-6672 ■ *Web:* www.swhsupply.com	Louisville	KY	40202	502-589-9287	585-3812
Taylor Freezer Sales Co Inc 2032 Atlantic Ave *TF:* 800-768-6945 ■ *Web:* www.taylorfreezer.com	Chesapeake	VA	23324	757-545-7900	545-7908
Taylor Freezers of Southern California 6825 E Washington Blvd *TF:* 800-927-7704 ■ *Web:* www.taylorfreezers.com	Commerce	CA	90040	323-889-8700	888-9292
Thermo King of Houston LP 772 McCarty St *Web:* www.tkofhouston.net	Houston	TX	77029	713-671-2700	
Transport Refrigeration Inc 301 Lawrence Dr	De Pere	WI	54115	920-339-5700	339-5717
United Refrigeration Inc 11401 Roosevelt Blvd *TF:* 800-852-5132 ■ *Web:* www.uri.com	Philadelphia	PA	19154	215-698-9100	
Western Pacific Distributors Inc 1739 Sabre St *Web:* www.teamwpd.com	Hayward	CA	94545	510-732-0100	732-0155
Wittichen Supply Co Inc 1600 3rd Ave S *TF:* 800-239-5294 ■ *Web:* www.wittichen-supply.com	Birmingham	AL	35233	205-251-8203	251-9004

669 RELOCATION CONSULTING SERVICES

Company	City	State	Zip	Phone	Fax
Cartus Corp 40 Apple Ridge Rd *Web:* www.cartus.com	Danbury	CT	06810	203-205-3400	748-3704
Century 21 Real Estate Corp 1 Campus Dr *TF:* 877-221-2765 ■ *Web:* www.century21.com	Parsippany	NJ	07054	973-428-9700	496-7564
Coldwell Banker Gundaker 2458 Old Dorsett Rd Suite 300 *TF:* 800-325-1978 ■ *Web:* www.cbgundaker.com	Maryland Heights	MO	63043	314-298-5000	298-5059
Crye-Leike Inc 6525 N Quail Hollow Rd *Web:* www.crye-leike.com	Memphis	TN	38120	901-756-8900	758-5641
GMAC Global Relocation Services 900 S Frontage Rd **Fax Area Code:* 630 ■ *TF:* 800-589-7858 ■ *Web:* www.brookfieldgrs.com	Woodridge	IL	60517	866-465-0323	972-2287*
Hewitt Relocation Services Inc 7901 Stoneridge Dr Suite 390 *TF:* 800-831-3444	Pleasanton	CA	94588	925-734-3434	734-3440
Re/MAX International Relocation Services Inc 8390 E Crescent Pkwy Suite 500 *TF:* 800-442-3501 ■ *Web:* www.remax.com/corpreloc	Greenwood Village	CO	80111	303-770-5531	796-3599
RELO Direct Inc 161 N Clark St Suite 1250 *TF:* 800-621-7356 ■ *Web:* www.relodirect.com	Chicago	IL	60601	312-384-5900	384-5988
Relocation America 25800 Northwestern Hwy Suite 210 *Web:* www.relocationamerica.com	Southfield	MI	48075	248-208-2900	263-0093
Runzheimer International Runzheimer Pk *TF:* 800-558-1702 ■ *Web:* www.runzheimer.com	Rochester	WI	53167	262-971-2200	971-2254
SIRVA Inc 700 Oakmont Ln *TF:* 888-444-4765 ■ *Web:* www.sirva.com	Westmont	IL	60559	630-570-3047	570-3606
Windermere Relocation Inc 4040 Lake Washington Blvd NE Suite 201 *TF:* 800-735-7029 ■ *Web:* www.windermere.com	Kirkland	WA	98033	425-216-7100	216-7140

670 REMEDIATION SERVICES

SEE ALSO Environmental Organizations p. 1424; Consulting Services - Environmental p. 1736; Waste Management p. 2771

Remediation Services Include Clean-Up, Restorative, And Corrective Work To Repair Or Minimize Environmental Damage Caused By Lead, Asbestos, Mining, Petroleum, Chemicals, And Other Pollutants.

Company	City	State	Zip	Phone	Fax
Allstate Power Vac Inc 928 E Hazelwood Ave *TF:* 800-876-9699 ■ *Web:* www.allstatepv.com	Rahway	NJ	07065	732-815-0220	815-9892
Antea Group 5910 Rice Creek Pkwy Suite 100 *TF:* 800-477-7411 ■ *Web:* www.anteagroup.com	Saint Paul	MN	55126	651-639-9449	639-9473
Brook Environmental & Engineering Corp 11419 Cronridge Dr Suite 10 *TF:* 800-381-4434	Owings Mills	MD	21117	410-356-5073	
Carylon Corp 2500 W Arthington St *TF:* 800-621-4342 ■ *Web:* www.caryloncorp.com	Chicago	IL	60612	312-666-7700	666-5810
Chemical Waste Management Inc 1001 Fannin St Suite 4000 *TF:* 800-633-7871 ■ *Web:* www.wm.com	Houston	TX	77002	713-512-6200	513-6299
Clean Harbors Inc 42 Longwater Dr PO Box 9149 *NYSE: CLH* ■ *TF:* 800-282-0058 ■ *Web:* www.cleanharbors.com	Norwell	MA	02061	781-792-5000	
Clean Venture/Cycle Chem Inc 201 S 1st St *TF:* 800-347-7672 ■ *Web:* www.cyclechem.com	Elizabeth	NJ	07206	908-355-5800	355-0562
Commodore Applied Technologies Inc 2151 Jamieson Ave Suite 308 *Web:* www.commodore.com	Alexandria	VA	22314	703-567-1284	566-7526
Contaminant Recovery Systems 9 Rocky Hill Rd *Web:* www.conrec.net	Smithfield	RI	02917	401-231-3770	231-3360
Conti Cos 3001 S Clinton Ave *Web:* www.conticorp.com	South Plainfield	NJ	07080	908-561-7600	754-3283
Crosby & Overton Inc 1610 W 17th St *TF:* 800-827-6729 ■ *Web:* www.crosbyoverton.com	Long Beach	CA	90813	562-432-5445	436-7540
Ecology Control Industries Inc 255 Parr Blvd *TF:* 800-788-1393 ■ *Web:* www.ecologycontrol.com	Richmond	CA	94801	510-235-1393	235-3709
Environmental Enterprises Inc (EEI) 10163 Cincinnati Dayton Rd *TF:* 800-722-2818 ■ *Web:* www.eeienv.com	Cincinnati	OH	45241	513-772-2818	782-8950
Handex Group Inc *Handex Consulting & Remediation LLC* 1350 Orange Ave Suite 101 *TF:* 800-989-3753 ■ *Web:* www.hcr-llc.com	Winter Park	FL	32789	321-441-9801	594-2710
LVI Services Inc 150 W 30th St **Fax Area Code:* 212 ■ *Web:* www.lviservices.com	New York	NY	10001	201-370-2113	951-8930*
MCM Management Corp 35980 Woodward Ave Suite 210 *Web:* www.mcmmanagement.com	Bloomfield Hills	MI	48304	248-932-9600	932-9638
Pacific Ecosolutions Inc 2025 Battell Blvd	Richland	WA	99352	509-375-5160	375-0613
Pangea Inc 2604 S Jefferson St *Web:* www.pangea-group.com	Saint Louis	MO	63118	314-333-0600	333-0601
PDG Environmental Inc 1386 Beulah Rd Bldg 801 *TF:* 800-972-7341 ■ *Web:* www.flagshippdg.com	Pittsburgh	PA	15235	412-243-3200	243-4900
Perma-Fix Environmental Services Inc 8302 Dunwoody Pl Suite 250 *NASDAQ: PESI* ■ *TF:* 800-365-6066 ■ *Web:* www.perma-fix.com	Atlanta	GA	30350	770-587-9898	587-9937
Petroclean Inc PO Box 92 *TF:* 800-247-3592	Carnegie	PA	15106	412-279-9556	279-7082
PW Stephens Inc 15201 Pipeline Ln Unit B *TF:* 800-937-1521 ■ *Web:* www.pwstephensinc.com	Huntington Beach	CA	92649	714-892-2028	891-9807
Romic Environmental Technologies Corp 2081 Bay Rd *TF:* 800-766-4248	East Palo Alto	CA	94303	650-324-1638	462-2411
Safety-Kleen Corp 5400 Legacy Dr Cluster 2 Bldg 3 *TF:* 800-669-5740 ■ *Web:* www.safety-kleen.com	Plano	TX	75024	972-265-2000	265-2990
SEACOR Holdings Inc 2200 Eller Dr PO Box 13038 *NYSE: CKH* ■ *Web:* www.seacorholdings.com	Fort Lauderdale	FL	33316	954-523-2200	524-9185
Sevenson Environmental Services Inc 2749 Lockport Rd *TF:* 800-777-3836 ■ *Web:* www.sevenson.com	Niagara Falls	NY	14305	716-284-0431	284-1796
Sigma Environmental Services Inc 1300 W Canal St *TF:* 800-732-4671 ■ *Web:* www.thesigmagroup.com	Milwaukee	WI	53233	414-643-4200	643-4210
US Ecology 300 E Mallard Dr Suite 300 *NASDAQ: ECOL* ■ *TF:* 800-590-5220 ■ *Web:* www.americanecology.com	Boise	ID	83706	208-331-8400	331-7900
UXB International Inc 2020 Kraft Dr Suite 2100 *TF:* 800-422-4892 ■ *Web:* www.uxb.com	Blacksburg	VA	24060	540-443-3700	443-3790
Waste Control Specialists LLC 5430 LBJ Fwy Suite 1700 *Web:* www.wcstexas.com	Dallas	TX	75240	972-715-9800	448-1419
Winter Environmental 3350 Green Pointe Pkwy Suite 200 **Fax:* Hum Res ■ *Web:* www.winter-environmental.com	Norcross	GA	30092	404-588-3300	946-6494*
WRR Environmental Services Co Inc 5200 SR-93 *TF:* 800-727-8760 ■ *Web:* www.wrres.com	Eau Claire	WI	54701	715-834-9624	836-8785

671 RESEARCH CENTERS & INSTITUTIONS

SEE ALSO Market Research Firms p. 2218; Public Policy Research Centers p. 2457; Testing Facilities p. 2706

Company	City	State	Zip	Phone	Fax
Aaron Diamond AIDS Research Ctr 455 1st Ave 7th Fl *Web:* www.adarc.org	New York	NY	10016	212-448-5000	725-1126
Advanced Technology for Large Structural Systems Ctr (ATLSS) 117 ATLSS Dr *Web:* www.atlss.lehigh.edu	Bethlehem	PA	18015	610-758-3525	758-5902
Advion BioSciences Inc 19 Brown Rd *TF:* 877-523-8466 ■ *Web:* www.advion.com	Ithaca	NY	14850	607-266-0665	266-0749
Aerodyne Research Inc 45 Manning Rd *Web:* www.aerodyne.com	Billerica	MA	01821	978-663-9500	663-4918
Aeronautical Systems Ctr (ASC) 1865 4th St Bldg 20014 Rm 008 *Web:* www.wpafb.af.mil/asc	Wright-Patterson AFB	OH	45433	937-255-2079	656-7088
Aerospace Corp The 2310 E El Segundo Blvd PO Box 92957 *Web:* www.aero.org	Los Angeles	CA	90009	310-336-5000	336-7055
Air Force Office of Scientific Research (AFOSR) 875 N Randolph St Suite 325 Rm 3112 *Web:* www.wpafb.af.mil	Arlington	VA	22203	703-696-7551	696-9556
Air Force Research Laboratory (AFRL) AFRL/PA 1864 4th St Bldg 15 Rm 225 **Fax Area Code:* 937 ■ *TF:* 800-222-0336 ■ *Web:* www.afsbirsttr.com	Wright-Patterson AFB	OH	45433	800-222-0336	255-2219*
Air Resources Laboratory NOAA/OAR/ARL 1315 East-West Hwy Bldg 3 Rm 3316 *Web:* www.arl.noaa.gov	Silver Spring	MD	20910	301-713-0684	713-0119
Alaska Fisheries Science Ctr (AFSC) National Marine Fisheries Service 7600 Sand Pt Way NE Bldg 4 *Web:* www.afsc.noaa.gov	Seattle	WA	98115	206-526-4000	526-4004
Albany International Research Co 777 W St *TF:* 800-992-5017 ■ *Web:* www.ww3.albint.com	Mansfield	MA	02048	508-339-7300	339-4996
AMC Cancer Research Ctr 1600 Pierce St *TF:* 800-321-1557 ■ *Web:* www.amc.org	Denver	CO	80214	303-233-6501	239-3400

				Phone	Fax
American Institute for Cancer Research 1759 R St NW *TF:* 800-843-8114 ■ *Web:* www.aicr.org	Washington	DC	20009	202-328-7744	328-7226
American Institutes for Research 1000 Thomas Jefferson St NW *TF:* 877-334-3499 ■ *Web:* www.air.org	Washington	DC	20007	202-403-5000	403-5454
American Type Culture Collection (ATCC) 10801 University Blvd PO Box 1549 *TF Cust Svc:* 800-638-6597 ■ *Web:* www.atcc.org	Manassas	VA	20108	703-365-2700	365-2701
Ames Laboratory 111 TASF Iowa State University *Web:* www.ameslab.gov	Ames	IA	50011	515-294-9557	294-3226
Analytcal B Chemistry Laboratory Inc 7200 E ABC Ln *TF:* 800-538-5227 ■ *Web:* www.abclabs.com	Columbia	MO	65202	573-777-6000	443-9033
Annapolis Micro Systems Inc 190 Admiral Cochrane Dr *Web:* www.annapmicro.com	Annapolis	MD	21401	410-841-2514	841-2518
Applied Physics Laboratory University of Washington 1013 NE 40th St PO Box 355640 *Web:* www.apl.washington.edu	Seattle	WA	98105	206-543-1300	543-6785
Applied Research Laboratory Pennsylvania State University N Atherton St PO Box 30 *Web:* www.arl.psu.edu	State College	PA	16804	814-865-6531	865-3105
Aptima Inc 12 Gill St Suite 1400 *TF:* 866-461-7298 ■ *Web:* www.aptima.com	Woburn	MA	01801	781-935-3966	935-4385
Arca Biopharma Inc 8001 Arista Pl Suite 200 *NASDAQ: ABIO* ■ *Web:* www.arcabiopharma.com	Broomfield	CO	80021	720-940-2100	208-9261
Arctic Region Supercomputing Ctr UAF 909 Kayukuk Dr Suite 105 PO Box 756020 *Web:* www.arsc.edu	Fairbanks	AK	99775	907-450-8600	450-8601
Arctic Research Consortium of the US (ARCUS) 3535 College Rd Suite 101 *Web:* www.arcus.org	Fairbanks	AK	99709	907-474-1600	474-1604
Argonne National Laboratory (ANL) 9700 S Cass Ave *Web:* www.anl.gov	Argonne	IL	60439	630-252-2000	252-9396
Armed Forces Institute of Pathology (AFIP) 6825 16th St NW *Web:* www.afip.org	Washington	DC	20306	202-782-2100	782-9376
Armed Forces Radiobiology Research Institute (AFRRI) 8901 Wisconsin Ave *Web:* www.afrri.usuhs.mil	Bethesda	MD	20889	301-295-1953	295-4967
Arthropod-Borne Animal Diseases Research Laboratory USDA/ARS ABADRL College of Agriculture Dept 3354 1000 E University Ave *Web:* www.ars.usda.gov/npa/abadrl	Laramie	WY	82071	307-766-3600	766-3500
Atlantic Oceanographic & Meteorological Laboratory (AOML) 4301 Rickenbacker Cswy *Web:* www.aoml.noaa.gov	Miami	FL	33149	305-361-4300	361-4449
Autism Research Institute (ARI) 4182 Adams Ave *Web:* www.autism.com	San Diego	CA	92116	619-281-7165	563-6840
Aveo Pharmaceuticals Inc 75 Sidney St *NASDAQ: AVEO* ■ *Web:* www.aveopharma.com	Cambridge	MA	02139	617-299-5000	995-4995
Baker Institute for Animal Health Cornell University College of Veterinary Medicine Hungerford Hill Rd *Web:* www.bakerinstitute.vet.cornell.edu	Ithaca	NY	14853	607-256-5600	256-5608
Barbara Ann Karmanos Cancer Institute 4100 John R St *TF:* 800-527-6266 ■ *Web:* www.karmanos.org	Detroit	MI	48201	313-833-0710	831-6535
Barrios Technology Inc 16441 Space Ctr Blvd Suite B-100 *Web:* www.barrios.com	Houston	TX	77058	281-280-1900	280-1901
Battelle Memorial Institute Inc 505 King Ave *Web:* www.battelle.org	Columbus	OH	43201	614-424-6424	424-5263
Belle W Baruch Institute for Marine & Coastal Sciences University of S Carolina 607 EWS Bldg *Web:* www.cas.sc.edu/baruch	Columbia	SC	29208	803-777-5288	777-3935
Beltsville Agricultural Research Ctr (BARC) USDA/ARS 10300 Baltimore Ave *Web:* www.ars.usda.gov	Beltsville	MD	20705	301-504-6078	504-5863
Beltsville Human Nutrition Research Ctr USDA/ARS BARC-East Bldg 307-C Rm 117 10300 Baltimore Blvd *Web:* www.ars.usda.gov/main/site_main.htm?modecode=12-35-00-00	Beltsville	MD	20705	301-504-8157	504-9381
Bend Research Inc 64550 Research Rd *Web:* www.bendres.com	Bend	OR	97701	541-382-4100	382-2713
Berkeley Sensor & Actuator Ctr (BSAC) *University of California* 497 Cory Hall MC Suite 1774 *Web:* www-bsac.eecs.berkeley.edu	Berkeley	CA	94720	510-643-6690	643-6637
Bernard Schwartz Center for Economic Policy Analysis New School of Social Research 79 5th Ave 11th Fl *Web:* www.newschool.edu/cepa	New York	NY	10003	212-229-5717	229-5903
Bettis Laboratory 814 Pittsburgh-McKeesport Blvd **Fax:* Hum Res ■ *TF:* 800-296-5002 ■ *Web:* www.bettislab.com	West Mifflin	PA	15122	412-476-6000	476-7509*
Biotechnology Center for Agriculture & the Environment Rutgers The State University of New Jersey 59 Dudley Rd *Web:* www.biotech.rutgers.edu	New Brunswick	NJ	08901	732-932-8165	932-6535
Biotechnology Research & Development Corp 1815 N University St	Peoria	IL	61604	309-688-1188	688-1292
Boyce Thompson Institute for Plant Research Inc Cornell University Tower Rd *Web:* bti.cornell.edu	Ithaca	NY	14853	607-254-1234	254-1242
Brain Research Institute 695 Charles Young Dr S *Web:* www.bri.ucla.edu	Los Angeles	CA	90095	310-825-5061	206-5855
Brookhaven National Laboratory (BNL) PO Box 5000 *Web:* www.bnl.gov	Upton	NY	11973	631-344-8000	344-3000
Bureau of Economic Analysis (BEA) 1441 L St NW *Web:* www.bea.gov	Washington	DC	20005	202-606-9900	606-5311
Caelum Research Corp 1700 Research Blvd Suite 250 *Web:* www.caelum.com	Rockville	MD	20850	301-424-8205	424-8183
California National Primate Research Center 1 Shields Ave University of California *Web:* www.cnprc.ucdavis.edu	Davis	CA	95616	530-752-0447	752-2880
California Pacific Medical Center Research Institute 475 Brannan St Suite 220 *Web:* www.cpmc.org/professionals/research	San Francisco	CA	94107	415-600-1601	600-1753
Cancer Research Center of Hawaii University of Hawaii 1236 Lauhala St *Web:* www.crch.org	Honolulu	HI	96813	808-586-3013	586-3052
Cardiovascular Research Institute *University of California* MUE-418C PO Box 1303 *Web:* www.cvri.ucsf.edu	San Francisco	CA	94143	415-476-1884	353-2669
Carnegie Institution of Washington 1530 P St NW *Web:* www.carnegiescience.edu	Washington	DC	20005	202-387-6400	387-8092
Center for Advanced Biotechnology & Medicine *Rutgers The State University of New Jersey* 679 Hoes Ln *Web:* www2.cabm.rutgers.edu	Piscataway	NJ	08854	732-235-5310	235-5318
Center for Advanced Food Technology 63 Dudley Rd *Web:* www.foodsci.rutgers.edu	New Brunswick	NJ	08901	732-932-8306	932-8690
Center for Automation Research University of Maryland AV Williams Bldg 115 Rm 4413 *Web:* www.cfar.umd.edu	College Park	MD	20742	301-405-4526	314-9115
Center for Biofilm Engineering (CBE) Montana State University PO Box 173980 *Web:* www.biofilm.montana.edu	Bozeman	MT	59717	406-994-4770	994-6098
Center for Biophysical Sciences & Engineering (CBSE) University of Alabama CBSE 100 1530 3rd Ave S *Web:* www.cbse.uab.edu	Birmingham	AL	35294	205-934-5329	934-0480
Center for Crops Utilization Research Iowa State University 1041 Food Sciences Bldg *Web:* www.ag.iastate.edu/centers/ccur	Ames	IA	50011	515-294-0160	294-6261
Center for Education Rice University 320 IBC Bldg 6100 Main St MS 147 *Web:* www.centerforeducation.rice.edu	Houston	TX	77005	713-348-5145	348-4229
Center for Electromechanics University of Texas at Austin 10100 Burnet Rd Bldg 133 *Web:* www.utexas.edu/research/cem	Austin	TX	78758	512-471-4496	471-0781
Center for Engineering Logistics & Distribution (CELDi) University of Arkansas Dept of Industrial Engineering 4207 Bell Engineering Ctr *Web:* www.celdi.org	Fayetteville	AR	72701	479-575-2124	575-8431
Center for Global Change & Arctic System Research (CGC) *University of Alaska-Fairbanks* 930 Koyukuk Dr Rm 306 PO Box 757740 *Web:* www.cgc.uaf.edu	Fairbanks	AK	99775	907-474-5818	474-6722
Center for Global Change Science Massachusetts Institute of Technology 77 Massachusetts Ave *Web:* web.mit.edu/cgcs/www	Cambridge	MA	02139	617-253-4902	253-0354
Center for High Performance Software Research (HiPerSoft) Rice University 6100 Main St MS-41 *Web:* www.hipersoft.rice.edu	Houston	TX	77005	713-348-5186	348-3111
Center for Information Systems Research (CISR) Massachusetts Institute of Technology 5 Cambridge Ctr NE25, 7th Fl *Web:* cisr.mit.edu	Cambridge	MA	02142	617-253-2348	253-4424
Center for Integrative Toxicology Michigan State University 165C Food Safety & Toxicology Bldg *Web:* www.cit.msu.edu	East Lansing	MI	48824	517-353-6469	355-4603
Center for International Trade in Forest Products (CINTRAFOR) University of Washington PO Box 352100 *Web:* www.cintrafor.org	Seattle	WA	98195	206-543-8684	685-0790
Center for Lesbian & Gay Studies (CLAGS) *University of New York* 365 5th Ave Rm 7115 *Web:* www.web.gc.cuny.edu/clags	New York	NY	10016	212-817-1955	817-1567
Center for Medical Agricultural & Veterinary Entomology (CMAVE) 1700 SW 23rd Dr *Web:* www.ars.usda.gov/saa/cmave	Gainesville	FL	32608	352-374-5901	374-5852
Center for Nanophysics & Advanced Materials University of Maryland Physics Bldg 082 *Web:* www.csr.umd.edu	College Park	MD	20742	301-405-6129	405-3779
Center for Population Research NICHD 6100 Executive Blvd Rm 8B07D MSC 7510 *Web:* www.nichd.nih.gov/cpr	Rockville	MD	20852	301-496-1101	496-0962
Center for Radiophysics & Space Research Cornell University 314 Space Sciences Bldg *Web:* www.astro.cornell.edu	Ithaca	NY	14853	607-255-1955	255-3433

	City	State	ZIP	Phone	Fax
Center for Research for Mothers & Children National Institute of Child Health & Human Development 6100 Executive Blvd Rm 4B11A MSC 7510 *Web:* www.nichd.nih.gov/about/crmc	Rockville	MD	20852	301-496-5593	480-9791
Center for Research in Mathematics & Science Education San Diego State University 6475 Alvarado Rd Suite 206 *Web:* www.sci.sdsu.edu	San Diego	CA	92120	619-594-5090	594-1581
Center for Research on Education Diversity & Excellence (CREDE) University of California Berkeley 1640 Tolman Hall Graduate School of Education *Web:* www.crede.org	Berkeley	CA	94720	510-643-9024	
Center for Research on the Context of Teaching Stanford University Galvez Mall CERAS Bldg 520 Rm 411 *Web:* www.stanford.edu/group/CRC	Stanford	CA	94305	650-725-1845	736-2296
Center for Space Exploration Power Systems Auburn University Space Research Institute 231 Leach Ctr *Web:* www.auburn.edu/research/vpr/sri	Auburn	AL	36849	334-844-5894	844-5900
Center for Space Plasma & Aeronomic Research University of Alabama Huntsville *Web:* cspar.uah.edu	Huntsville	AL	35899	256-961-7403	961-7730
Center for Space Research University of Texas 3925 W Braker Ln Suite 200 *Web:* www.csr.utexas.edu	Austin	TX	78759	512-471-5573	471-3570
Center for Sustainable Environmental Technologies Iowa State University 1140 Biorenewables Research Laboratory *Web:* www.cset.iastate.edu	Ames	IA	50011	515-294-7936	294-3091
Center for the Study of Aging & Human Development Duke University Medical Ctr PO Box 3003 *Web:* www.geri.duke.edu	Durham	NC	27710	919-660-7500	684-8569
Center for the Study of Language & Information Stanford University Cordura Hall 210 Panama St *Web:* www-csli.stanford.edu	Stanford	CA	94305	650-725-3286	723-0758
Center for the Study of Teaching & Policy (CTP) University of Washington PO Box 353600 *Web:* www.depts.washington.edu	Seattle	WA	98195	206-221-4114	616-8158
Center for Transportation Research University of Tennessee 309 Conference Ctr Bldg 600 Henley St *Web:* www.ctr.utk.edu	Knoxville	TN	37996	865-974-5255	974-3889
Center on Drug & Alcohol Research (CDAR) University of Kentucky 643 Maxwelton Ct. *Web:* www.cdar.uky.edu	Lexington	KY	40506	859-257-2355	323-1193
Center on Education & Training for Employment Ohio State University 1900 Kenny Rd. *TF:* 800-848-4815 ■ *Web:* www.cete.org	Columbus	OH	43210	614-292-4353	292-1260
Center on Human Development & Disability University of Washington 1962 Columbia Rd PO Box 357920 *Web:* www.depts.washington.edu/chdd	Seattle	WA	98195	206-543-2832	543-3561
National Center for Environmental Health 4770 Buford Hwy Bldg 101 **Fax Area Code:* 770 ■ *TF:* 800-232-4636 ■ *Web:* www.cdc.gov	Chamblee	GA	30341	404-639-3311	488-0083*
National Institute for Occupational Safety & Health 200 Independence Ave SW *TF:* 800-356-4674 ■ *Web:* www.cdc.gov/niosh	Washington	DC	20201	404-639-3286	
Charles River Laboratories Inc 251 Ballardvale St. *NYSE: CRL* ■ **Fax Area Code:* 978 ■ *TF:* 800-522-7287 ■ *Web:* www.criver.com	Wilmington	MA	01887	781-222-6000	658-7132*
Charles Stark Draper Laboratory Inc 555 Technology Sq. *TF:* 800-676-1977 ■ *Web:* www.draper.com	Cambridge	MA	02139	617-258-1000	258-1131
Children's Nutrition Research Ctr USDA/ARS Baylor College of Medicine 1100 Bates St *Web:* www.bcm.edu/cnrc	Houston	TX	77030	713-798-7022	798-7046
Children's Research Institute Children's National Medical Ctr 111 Michigan Ave NW Research Fl 5 *TF:* 888-884-2327 ■ *Web:* www.childrensnational.org	Washington	DC	20010	202-476-2327	884-3985
Cincinnati Children's Hospital Research Foundation 3333 Burnet Ave *TF:* 800-344-2462 ■ *Web:* www.cincinnatichildrens.org/research	Cincinnati	OH	45229	513-636-4200	636-8453
Cleveland Biolabs Inc 73 High St *NASDAQ: CBLI* ■ **Fax Area Code:* 216 ■ *Web:* www.cbiolabs.com	Buffalo	NY	14203	716-849-6810	229-1764*
CNA Corp 4825 Mark Ctr Dr *TF:* 800-344-0007 ■ *Web:* www.cna.org	Alexandria	VA	22311	703-824-2000	824-2949
Co-op Institute for Arctic Research (CIFAR) University of Alaska Fairbanks PO Box 757740 *Web:* www.cifar.uaf.edu	Fairbanks	AK	99775	907-474-5818	474-6722
Coal Research Ctr Southern Illinois University 405 W Grand Ave MC 4623 *Web:* www.crc.siu.edu	Carbondale	IL	62901	618-536-5521	453-7346
Coastal & Marine Institute San Diego State University 5500 Campanile Dr. *Web:* www.sci.sdsu.edu/CMI	San Diego	CA	92182	619-594-5142	594-6381
Cold Spring Harbor Laboratory (CSHL) 1 Bungtown Rd *Web:* www.cshl.edu	Cold Spring Harbor	NY	11724	516-367-8800	367-8455
Colorado Center for Astrodynamics Research (CCAR) University of Colorado ECNT 323 UCB 431 *Web:* ccar.colorado.edu	Boulder	CO	80309	303-492-3105	492-2825
Columbia Environmental Research Ctr (CERC) 4200 New Haven Rd *Web:* www.cerc.usgs.gov	Columbia	MO	65201	573-875-5399	876-1896
Columbia Institute for Tele-Information (CITI) Columbia University 3022 Broadway Uris Hall Suite 1A *Web:* www4.gsb.columbia.edu/citi	New York	NY	10027	212-854-4222	854-1471
Computer Emergency Response Team (CERT) SEI Carnegie Mellon University 4500 5th Ave. *Web:* www.cert.org	Pittsburgh	PA	15213	412-268-7090	268-6989
Computer Science & Artificial Intelligence Laboratory (CSAIL) Massachusetts Institute of Technology 32 Vassar St Bldg 32 *Web:* www.csail.mit.edu	Cambridge	MA	02139	617-253-5851	258-8682
Conservation & Production Research Laboratory (CPRL) USDA/ARS PO Drawer 10. *Web:* www.cprl.ars.usda.gov	Bushland	TX	79012	806-356-5724	356-5750
Coriell Institute for Medical Research 403 Haddon Ave. *TF:* 800-752-3805 ■ *Web:* www.coriell.org	Camden	NJ	08103	856-966-7377	757-9737
Cornell NanoScale Science & Technology Facility (CNF) Cornell University 250 Duffield Hall *Web:* www.cnf.cornell.edu	Ithaca	NY	14853	607-255-2329	255-8601
Courant Institute of Mathematical Sciences (CIMS) *New York University* 251 Mercer St. *Web:* www.cims.nyu.edu	New York	NY	10012	212-998-3000	995-4121
Creare Inc 16 Great Hollow Rd. *Web:* www.creare.com	Hanover	NH	03755	603-643-3800	643-4657
CTC Inc Public Safety Technology Ctr 134 Flanders Rd Suite 375 *TF:* 800-328-8801 ■ *Web:* www.ctc.org	Westborough	MA	01581	508-870-0042	366-0101
CureSearch for Children's Cancer 440 E Huntington Dr Suite 600. *TF:* 800-458-6223 ■ *Web:* www.nccf.org	Bethesda	MD	20814	301-718-0047	
Curriculum Research & Development Group University of Hawaii 1776 University Ave *Web:* www.hawaii.edu/crdg	Honolulu	HI	96822	808-956-7961	956-9486
Dale Bumpers Small Farms Research Ctr USDA/ARS 6883 S State Hwy 23 *Web:* www.ars.usda.gov	Booneville	AR	72927	479-675-3834	675-2940
Dana-Farber Cancer Institute 44 Binney St. **Fax:* PR ■ *TF:* 800-757-3324 ■ *Web:* www.dana-farber.org	Boston	MA	02115	617-632-3000	632-5520*
Data Storage Systems Ctr (DSSC) *Carnegie Mellon University ECE Dept* 5000 Forbes Ave *Web:* www.dssc.ece.cmu.edu	Pittsburgh	PA	15213	412-268-6600	268-3497
Defense Advanced Research Projects Agency (DARPA) 3701 N Fairfax Dr *Web:* www.darpa.mil	Arlington	VA	22203	703-526-6630	528-3655
DEKA Research & Development Corp 340 Commercial St Suite 401. *Web:* www.dekaresearch.com	Manchester	NH	03101	603-669-5139	624-0573
Desert Research Institute 2215 Raggio Pkwy *Web:* www.dri.edu	Reno	NV	89512	775-673-7300	673-7397
Diabetes & Endocrinology Research Ctr (DERC) *University of California San Francisco* 513 Parnassus Ave	San Francisco	CA	94143	415-514-3734	502-1447
Diabetes Research Institute 1450 NW 10th Ave *Web:* www.diabetesresearch.org	Miami	FL	33136	305-243-5300	243-4404
Diversified Laboratories Inc 4150 Lafayette Ctr Dr *Web:* www.diversifiedlaboratories.com	Chantilly	VA	20151	703-222-8700	222-0786
Dryden Flight Research Ctr PO Box 273 *Web:* www.nasa.gov/centers	Edwards	CA	93523	661-276-3449	276-3566
Earth Sciences & Resources Institute 901 Sumter St Byrnes International Ctr Suite 402 *Web:* www.esri.sc.edu	Columbia	SC	29208	803-777-6484	777-6437
Earth System Research Laboratory NOAA/ESRL 325 Broadway *Web:* www.esrl.noaa.gov	Boulder	CO	80305	303-497-6643	497-6951
Eastern Regional Research Ctr (ERRC) 600 E Mermaid Ln *Web:* www.ars.usda.gov/main/site_main.htm?modecode=19350000	Wyndmoor	PA	19038	215-233-6400	233-6559
Edgewood Chemical Biological Ctr 5183 Blackhawk Rd Bldg E3330 *Web:* www.ecbc.army.mil	Aberdeen Proving Ground	MD	21010	410-436-3610	436-2014
Edison Biotechnology Institute Ohio University Konneker Research Laboratories The Ridges *Web:* www.ohiou.edu/biotech	Athens	OH	45701	740-593-4713	593-4795
ELORET Corp 465 S Mathilda Ave Suite 103 *Web:* www.eloret.com	Sunnyvale	CA	94086	408-732-3028	732-2482
Encorium Group Inc 1275 Drummers Ln Suite 100 *NASDAQ: ENCO* ■ *Web:* www.encorium.com	Wayne	PA	19087	610-975-9533	975-9556
Energy & Environmental Research Ctr (EERC) University of N Dakota 15 N 23rd St S- 9018 *Web:* www.eerc.und.nodak.edu	Grand Forks	ND	58202	701-777-5000	777-5181
Energy Institute Pennsylvania State University Coal Utilization Laboratory Rm C211 *Web:* www.energy.psu.edu	University Park	PA	16802	814-865-3093	863-7432
Engineering Research Center for Advanced Electronic Materials Processing *North Carolina State University* 2410 Campus Shore Dr Rm 421 MRC PO Box 7920	Raleigh	NC	27695	919-515-5153	515-5055
Engineering Research Center for Net Shape Mfg Ohio State University 1971 Neil Ave Rm 339 *Web:* nsmwww.eng.ohio-state.edu	Columbus	OH	43210	614-292-9267	292-9217
Enrico Fermi Institute University of Chicago 5640 S Ellis Ave. *Web:* efi.uchicago.edu	Chicago	IL	60637	773-702-7823	702-8038

Phone | Fax

Environmental & Occupational Health Sciences Institute (EOHSI)
170 Frelinghuysen Rd........Piscataway NJ 08854 732-445-0202 445-0131
Web: www.eohsi.rutgers.edu

Environmental Science Assoc
225 Bush St Suite 1700........San Francisco CA 94104 415-896-5900 896-0332
Web: www.esassoc.com

EPRI 3420 Hillview Ave........Palo Alto CA 94304 650-855-2000
Web: www.my.epri.com

Ernest B Yeager Center for Electrochemical Sciences
Case Western Reserve University
10900 Euclid Ave Dept of Chemistry........Cleveland OH 44106 216-368-1701
Web: electrochem.cwru.edu

Eunice Kennedy Shriver Ctr 200 Trapelo Rd........Waltham MA 02452 781-642-0001 642-0114
Web: www.umassmed.edu/shriver

Exponent Inc 149 Commonwealth Dr........Menlo Park CA 94025 650-326-9400 326-8072
NASDAQ: EXPO ■ *TF:* 888-656-3976 ■ *Web:* www.exponent.com

Families & Work Institute 267 5th Ave 2nd Fl........New York NY 10016 212-465-2044 465-8637
Web: www.familiesandwork.org

Federal Judicial Ctr
Thurgood Marshall Federal Judiciary Bldg
1 Columbus Cir NE........Washington DC 20002 202-502-4000 502-4099
Web: www.fjc.gov

Fels Institute for Cancer Research & Molecular Biology
Temple Univ School of Medicine
3400 N Broad St Rm 150........Philadelphia PA 19140 215-707-4300 707-4588
Web: www.temple.edu/medicine/departments_centers/research/fels.htm

Fermi National Accelerator Laboratory
PO Box 500........Batavia IL 60510 630-840-3000 840-4343
Web: www.fnal.gov

Florida Resources & Environmental Analysis Ctr
Florida State University UCC 2200 FSU........Tallahassee FL 32306 850-644-2007 644-7360
Web: www.freac.fsu.edu

Florida Solar Energy Ctr 1679 Clearlake Rd........Cocoa FL 32922 321-638-1000 638-1010
Web: www.fsec.ucf.edu

Food Research Institute
University of Wisconsin Madison
1550 Linden Dr........Madison WI 53706 608-263-7777 263-1114
Web: www.wisc.edu/fri

Forest Products Laboratory
1 Gifford Pinchot Dr........Madison WI 53726 608-231-9200 231-9592
Web: www.fpl.fs.fed.us

Fox Chase Cancer Ctr 333 Cottman Ave........Philadelphia PA 19111 215-728-6900 728-2682
TF: 888-369-2427 ■ *Web:* www.fccc.edu

Framingham Heart Study
73 Mt Wayte Ave Suite 2........Framingham MA 01702 508-935-3439 626-1262
Web: www.nhlbi.nih.gov/about/framingham

Francis Bitter Magnet Laboratory
Massachusetts Institute of Technology
150 Albany St NW 14........Cambridge MA 02139 617-253-5478 253-5405
Web: web.mit.edu/fbml

Fred Hutchinson Cancer Research Ctr
1124 Columbia St # S........Seattle WA 98104 206-667-5000 667-4051
Web: www.fhcrc.org

Friends Research Institute Inc
1040 Pk Ave # 103........Baltimore MD 21201 410-823-5116 823-5131
TF: 800-822-3677 ■ *Web:* www.friendsresearch.org
Social Research Ctr 1040 Pk Ave Suite 103........Baltimore MD 21201 410-837-3977 752-4218
Web: www.friendsresearch.org

Gas Technology Institute (GTI)
1700 S Mt Prospect Rd........Des Plaines IL 60018 847-768-0500 768-0501
Web: www.gastechnology.org

Gatorade Sports Science Institute
617 W Main St........Barrington IL 60010 847-381-1980
TF: 800-616-4774 ■ *Web:* www.gssiweb.com

General Atomics
3550 General Atomics Ct PO Box 85608........San Diego CA 92121 858-455-3000 455-3621
Web: www.ga.com

Geophysical Fluid Dynamics Laboratory
NOAA/OAR/GFDL 201 Forrestal Rd........Princeton NJ 08540 609-452-6500 987-5063
Web: www.gfdl.noaa.gov

Georgia Tech Fusion Research Ctr
900 Atlantic Dr Rm G106........Atlanta GA 30332 404-894-3758 894-3733
Web: www.frc.gatech.edu

Georgia Tech Research Institute (GTRI)
Georgia Institute of Technology
250 14th St NW........Atlanta GA 30318 404-407-7400 894-9875
Web: www.gtri.gatech.edu

Gerontology Research Ctr
Johns Hopkins Bayview Medical Ctr
5600 Nathan Shock Dr........Baltimore MD 21224 410-558-8110
Web: www.grc.nia.nih.gov

Glenn Research Ctr 21000 Brookpark Rd........Brookpark OH 44135 216-433-4000 433-8000
Web: www.nasa.gov/centers/glenn/home/index.html

Goddard Institute for Space Studies
2880 Broadway........New York NY 10025 212-678-5510 678-5552
Web: www.giss.nasa.gov

Goddard Space Flight Ctr 8800 Greenbelt Rd........Greenbelt MD 20771 301-286-2000 286-1707*
**Fax:* PR ■ *Web:* www.nasa.gov/centers/goddard

Grain Marketing & Production Research Ctr
1515 College Ave........Manhattan KS 66502 785-776-2701 776-2789
TF: 800-627-0388 ■
Web: www.ars.usda.gov/main/site_main.htm?modecode=54300000

Grand Forks Human Nutrition Research Ctr
USDA/ARS 2420 2nd Ave N PO Box 9034........Grand Forks ND 58202 701-795-8353 795-8395
Web: www.ars.usda.gov/Main/docs.htm?docid=3898

Great Lakes Environmental Research Laboratory (GLERL)
4840 S State St........Ann Arbor MI 48108 734-741-2235 741-2055
Web: www.glerl.noaa.gov

Gulf Coast Research Laboratory
703 E Beach Dr........Ocean Springs MS 39564 228-872-4200 872-4204
Web: www.coms.usm.edu

Phone | Fax

H Lee Moffitt Cancer Center & Research Institute
University of S Florida 12902 Magnolia Dr........Tampa FL 33612 813-972-4673 745-8495
TF: 800-456-3434 ■ *Web:* www.moffittcancercenter.com

Hamner Institutes for Health Sciences The
6 Davis Dr PO Box 12137........Research Triangle Park NC 27709 919-558-1200 558-1400
Web: www.thehamner.org

Harbor Branch Oceanographic Institution
5600 N Old Dixie Hwy........Fort Pierce FL 34946 772-465-2400 465-7156
Web: www.hboi.edu

Harry K Dupree Stuttgart National Aquaculture Research Ctr
USDA/ARS 2955 Hwy 130E PO Box 1050........Stuttgart AR 72160 870-673-4483 673-7710
Web: www.ars.usda.gov/main/site_main.htm?modecode=62251000

Harry Reid Center for Environmental Studies
University of Nevada 4505 Maryland Pkwy
PO Box 454030........Las Vegas NV 89154 702-895-3382 895-3094
Web: www.hrcweb.lv-hrc.nevada.edu

Harvard-Smithsonian Center for Astrophysics
60 Garden St........Cambridge MA 02138 617-495-7000 495-7468
Web: www.cfa.harvard.edu

Hatfield Marine Science Ctr
2030 SE Marine Science Dr........Newport OR 97365 541-867-0100 867-0138
Web: www.hmsc.oregonstate.edu

Hawaii Insitute of Geophysics & Planetology
University of Hawaii
1680 East-West Rd Post 602B........Honolulu HI 96822 808-956-8760 956-3188
Web: www.higp.hawaii.edu

Hazen Research Inc 4601 Indiana St........Golden CO 80403 303-279-4501 278-1528
Web: www.hazenusa.com

High Performance Computing Collaboratory
PO Box 9627........Mississippi State MS 39762 662-325-8278 325-7692
Web: www.erc.msstate.edu

Hill Top Research Inc
6088 Main & Mill Sts PO Box 138........Miamiville OH 45147 513-831-3114 831-1217
TF: 800-785-2693 ■ *Web:* www.hill-top.com

Holifield Radioactive Ion Beam Facility (HRIBF)
Oak Ridge National Laboratory Bldg 6000
PO Box 2008........Oak Ridge TN 37831 865-574-4114 574-1268
Web: www.phy.ornl.gov/hribf

Hopkins Population Ctr
Johns Hopkins University
615 N Wolfe St Suite E-4644........Baltimore MD 21205 410-955-7803 502-5831
Web: www.jhsph.edu/popcenter

Houston Advanced Research Ctr (HARC)
4800 Research Forest Dr........The Woodlands TX 77381 281-367-1348 363-7914
Web: www.harc.edu

Howard Hughes Medical Institute
4000 Jones Bridge Rd........Chevy Chase MD 20815 301-215-8500 215-8863
Web: www.hhmi.org

Human Resources Research Organization (HumRRO)
66 Canal Ctr Plaza Suite 400........Alexandria VA 22314 703-549-3611 549-9025
TF: 800-301-1508 ■ *Web:* www.humrro.org

Huntingdon Life Sciences Inc
Princeton Research Centre
Mettlers Rd PO Box 2360........East Millstone NJ 08875 732-873-2550 873-3992
Web: www.huntingdon.com

IBM Almaden Research Ctr 650 Harry Rd........San Jose CA 95120 408-927-1000 927-2100
Web: www.almaden.ibm.com

Idaho National Laboratory (INL)
2525 Fremont Ave PO Box 1625........Idaho Falls ID 83415 866-495-7440 526-5408*
**Fax Area Code:* 208 ■ *TF:* 866-495-7440 ■ *Web:* www.inl.gov

Ideas International Inc
800 Westchester Ave Suite N-337........Rye Brook NY 10573 914-937-4302 937-2485
TF: 800-253-1799 ■ *Web:* www.ideasinternational.com

IIT Research Institute (IITRI) 10 W 35th St........Chicago IL 60616 312-567-4000 567-4838*
**Fax:* Hum Res ■ *Web:* www.iitri.org

Immune Disease Institute 200 Longwood Ave........Boston MA 02115 617-278-3000 278-3493
TF: 800-850-2466 ■ *Web:* www.idi.harvard.edu

Indiana Molecular Biology Institute
Indiana University 915 E 3rd St........Bloomington IN 47405 812-855-4183 855-6082
Web: imbi.bio.indiana.edu

Industrial Partnership for Research in Interfacial & Materials Engineering (IPRIME)
University of Minnesota
151 Amundson Hall 421 Washington Ave SE........Minneapolis MN 55455 612-626-9509 626-7246
Web: www.iprime.umn.edu

Industrial Relations Ctr
University of Minnesota Carlson School of Management
321 19th Ave S........Minneapolis MN 55455 612-625-2553 624-8360

Innovative Nuclear Space Power & Propulsion Institute
University of Florida 2800 SW Archer Rd Bldg 554
PO Box 116502........Gainesville FL 32611 352-392-1427 392-8656

Institute for Astronomy
University of Hawaii 2680 Woodlawn Dr........Honolulu HI 96822 808-956-8312 988-2790
Web: www.ifa.hawaii.edu

Institute for Basic Research in Developmental Disabilities
1050 Forest Hill Rd........Staten Island NY 10314 718-494-0600 494-0833
Web: www.opwdd.ny.gov/ws/ws_ibr_resources.jsp

Institute for Biotechnology & Life Science Technologies
Cornell University Biotechnology Bldg Rm 130........Ithaca NY 14853 607-255-2300 255-6249
Web: www.biotech.cornell.edu

Institute for Defense Analyses (IDA)
4850 Mark Ctr Dr........Alexandria VA 22311 703-845-2000 845-2588
Web: www.ida.org

Institute for Diabetes Obesity & Metabolism
University of Pennsylvania
700 Clinical Research Bldg........Philadelphia PA 19104 215-898-4365 898-5408
Web: www.med.upenn.edu/pdc

Institute for Molecular Virology
University of Wisconsin
Bock Laboratories Rm 413 1525 Linden Dr........Madison WI 53706 608-262-4540 262-7414
Web: www.virology.wisc.edu/IMV

	Phone	Fax
Institute for Physical Research & Technology (IPRT) *Iowa State University* 2156 Gilman Hall. Ames IA 50011 *Web:* www.iprt.iastate.edu	515-294-3045	294-2361
Institute for Research on Poverty University of Wisconsin Madison 1180 Observatory Dr 3412 Social Science Bldg. Madison WI 53706 *Web:* www.irp.wisc.edu	608-262-6358	265-3119
Institute for Scientific Analysis 390 4th St 2nd Fl. San Francisco CA 94107 *Web:* www.scientificanalysis.org	415-777-2352	563-9940
Institute for Simulation & Training (IST) 3100 Technology Pkwy. Orlando FL 32826 *Web:* www.ist.ucf.edu	407-882-1300	658-5059
Institute for Social Behavioral & Economic Research University of California 2201 N Hall. Santa Barbara CA 93106 *Web:* www.isber.ucsb.edu	805-893-2548	893-7995
Institute for Social Research University of Michigan 426 Thompson St. Ann Arbor MI 48104 *Web:* www.isr.umich.edu	734-764-8363	936-9708
Institute for Systems Research University of Maryland 2173 AV Williams Bldg. College Park MD 20742 *Web:* www.isr.umd.edu	301-405-6615	314-9920
Institute for Telecommunications Sciences 325 Broadway. Boulder CO 80305 *Web:* www.its.bldrdoc.gov	303-497-5216	
Institute of Arctic & Alpine Research (INSTAAR) University of Colorado 1560 30th St PO Box 450. Boulder CO 80309 *Web:* instaar.colorado.edu	303-492-6387	492-6388
Institute of Behavioral Science University of Colorado 1416 Broadway. Boulder CO 80302 *Web:* www.colorado.edu/IBS	303-492-8147	492-6924
Institute of Ecosystem Studies (IES) 2801 Sharon Tpke PO Box AB. Millbrook NY 12545 *Web:* www.ecostudies.org	845-677-5343	677-5976
Institute of Education Sciences (IES) US Dept of Education 555 New Jersey Ave NW Rm 600. Washington DC 20208 *Web:* www.ies.ed.gov	202-219-1385	219-1466
Institute of Gerontology University of Michigan 300 N Ingalls St. Ann Arbor MI 48109 *TF:* 877-865-2167 ■ *Web:* www.iog.umich.edu	734-764-3493	936-2116
Institute of Human Origins (IHO) Arizona State Univ PO Box 874101. Tempe AZ 85287 *Web:* www.asu.edu/clas/iho	480-727-6580	727-6570
Institute of Marine Science University of Alaska Fairbanks. Fairbanks AK 99775 *Web:* www.ims.uaf.edu	907-474-7829	474-7204
Institute of Materials Science University of Connecticut 97 N Eagleville Rd. Storrs CT 06269 *Web:* www.ims.uconn.edu	860-486-4623	486-4745
Integrated Media Systems Ctr (USC IMSC) *University of Southern California* 3737 Watt Way. Los Angeles CA 90089 *Web:* www.imsc.usc.edu	213-740-8945	740-2539
International Arctic Research Ctr (IARC) 930 Koyukuk Dr PO Box 757340. Fairbanks AK 99775 *Web:* www.iarc.uaf.edu	907-474-6016	474-5662
International Center for Advanced Internet Research (iCAIR) 750 N Lake Shore Dr Suite 600. Chicago IL 60611 *Web:* www.icair.org	312-503-0735	
International Diabetes Center at Park Nicollet Park Nicollet Clinic - St Louis Pk 3800 Pk Nicollet Blvd. Saint Louis Park MN 55416 *TF:* 888-825-6315 ■ *Web:* www.parknicollet.com/diabetes	952-993-3393	993-1302
International Institute of Tropical Forestry (IITF) Jardin Botanico Sur 1201 Calle Ceiba. San Juan PR 00926 *Web:* www.fs.fed.us/global/iitf	787-766-5335	766-6302
Jackson Laboratory The 600 Main St. Bar Harbor ME 04609 *Web:* www.jax.org	207-288-6000	288-6076
James Cancer Hospital & Solove Research Institute The 300 W 10th Ave. Columbus OH 43210 *Web:* www.cancer.osu.edu	614-293-8000	293-3132
Jamie Whitten Delta States Research Ctr Experiment Stn Rd PO Box 225. Stoneville MS 38776 *Web:* www.ars.usda.gov/main/site_main.htm?modecode=64-02-00-00	662-686-5265	686-5459
Jean Mayer USDA Human Nutrition Research Center on Aging 711 Washington St. Boston MA 02111 *Web:* www.hnrc.tufts.edu	617-556-3136	556-3344
Jet Propulsion Laboratory (JPL) 1201 California Blvd. Pasadena CA 91101 *Web:* www.jpl.nasa.gov	818-354-4321	
John A Volpe National Transportation Systems Ctr 55 Broadway. Cambridge MA 02142 *Web:* www.volpe.dot.gov	617-494-2117	
John F. Kennedy Space Ctr. Kennedy Space Center FL 32899 *TF:* 800-561-8618 ■ *Web:* www.nasa.gov/centers/kennedy	321-867-5000	
John Wayne Cancer Institute (JWCI) 2200 Santa Monica Blvd. Santa Monica CA 90404 *TF:* 800-262-6259 ■ *Web:* www.jwci.org	310-449-5255	449-5259
Johns Hopkins University Applied Physics Laboratory 11100 Johns Hopkins Rd. Laurel MD 20723 *Web:* www.jhuapl.edu	240-228-5000	228-1093
Johnson Space Ctr 2101 NASA Pkwy. Houston TX 77058 *Web:* www.nasa.gov	281-483-0123	483-9192
Joint Institute for Laboratory Astrophysics (JILA) University of Colorado 440 UCB. Boulder CO 80309 *Web:* www.jila.colorado.edu	303-492-7789	492-5235

	Phone	Fax
Joint Institute for Marine & Atmospheric Research University of Hawaii at Manoa 1000 Pope Rd MSB Blg 312. Honolulu HI 96822 *Web:* ilikai.soest.hawaii.edu/JIMAR	808-956-8083	956-4104
Joint Institute for Marine Observations (JIMO) Scripps Institution of Oceanography -Univ of California 9500 Gilman Dr. La Jolla CA 92093 *Web:* www.jimo.ucsd.edu	858-534-4100	
Joseph Stokes Jr Research Institute Children's Hospital of Philadelphia 3615 Civic Center Blvd. Philadelphia PA 19104 *Web:* stokes.chop.edu	215-590-3800	590-3804
Joslin Diabetes Ctr 1 Joslin Pl. Boston MA 02215 *Web:* www.joslin.org	617-732-2400	732-2542
Kavali Institute for Astrophysics & Space Research Massachusetts Institute of Technology 77 Massachusetts Ave Bldg 37 Suite 287. Cambridge MA 02139 *Web:* space.mit.edu	617-253-7501	253-0861
Kendle International Inc 441 Vine St 1200 Carew Tower. Cincinnati OH 45202 *NASDAQ: KNDL* ■ *TF:* 800-733-1572 ■ *Web:* www.kendle.com	513-381-5550	381-5870
Kennedy Institute of Ethics Georgetown University Healy Hall 4th Fl 37th & 'O' St NW. Washington DC 20057 *Web:* www.kennedyinstitute.georgetown.edu	202-687-8099	687-8089
Keweenaw Research Ctr Michigan Technological University 1400 Townsend Dr. Houghton MI 49931 *Web:* www.mtukrc.org	906-487-2750	487-2202
Kika de la Garza Subtropical Agricultural Research Ctr 2413 E Hwy 83 Bldg 200. Weslaco TX 78596 *Web:* www.ars.usda.gov/spa/weslaco	956-447-6301	447-6345
Knolls Atomic Power Laboratory (KAPL) PO Box 1072. Schenectady NY 12301 *Web:* www.kaplinc.com	518-395-4000	395-4422
Kresge Hearing Research Institute (KHRI) University of Michigan Medical School 1150 W Medical Ctr Dr Rm 4605 Med Sci 2. Ann Arbor MI 48109 *Web:* www.khri.med.umich.edu	734-764-8110	764-0014
KU Center for Research on Learning (KUCRL) University of Kansas 1122 W Campus Rd Rm 521. Lawrence KS 66045 *Web:* www.ku-crl.org	785-864-4780	864-5728
Kurzweil Technologies Inc 15 Walnut St Suite 2. Wellesley Hills MA 02481 *TF:* 877-365-9633 ■ *Web:* www.kurzweiltech.com	781-263-0000	263-9999
Laboratory for Laser Energetics 250 E River Rd. Rochester NY 14623 *Web:* www.lle.rochester.edu	585-275-5101	275-5960
Laboratory for Nuclear Science Massachusetts Institute of Technology 77 Massachusetts Ave Bldg 26 Rm 505. Cambridge MA 02139 *Web:* web.mit.edu/lns	617-253-2395	253-0111
Lamont-Doherty Earth Observatory 61 Rt 9w. Palisades NY 10964 *Web:* www.ldeo.columbia.edu	845-359-2900	359-2931
Langley Research Ctr NASA ; Langley Research Ctr. Hampton VA 23681 *Web:* www.nasa.gov/centers/langley	757-864-1000	
Lawrence Berkeley National Laboratory (LBNL) 1 Cyclotron Rd. Berkeley CA 94720 *Web:* www.lbl.gov	510-486-4000	486-7000
Advanced Light Source 1 Cyclotron Rd MS 6-2100. Berkeley CA 94720 *Web:* www-als.lbl.gov	510-486-7745	486-4773
Lawrence Livermore National Laboratory (LLNL) 7000 E Ave PO Box 808. Livermore CA 94550 *Web:* www.llnl.gov	925-422-1100	422-1370
Learning Research & Development Ctr (LRDC) University of Pittsburgh 3939 O'Hara St. Pittsburgh PA 15260 *Web:* www.lrdc.pitt.edu	412-624-7020	624-9149
Learning Systems Institute 4600 University Ctr. Tallahassee FL 32306 *Web:* www.lsi.fsu.edu	850-644-2570	644-4952
Lerner Research Institute 9500 Euclid Ave. Cleveland OH 44195 *TF:* 800-223-2273 ■ *Web:* www.lerner.ccf.org	216-444-3900	444-3279
LIMRA International Inc 300 Day Hill Rd. Windsor CT 06095 *Web:* www.limra.com	860-688-3358	298-9555
Lincoln Laboratory Massachusetts Institute of Technology 244 Wood St. Lexington MA 02420 **Fax:* Hum Res ■ *Web:* www.ll.mit.edu	781-981-5500	981-7086*
Lipomics Technologies Inc 3410 Industrial Blvd Suite 103. West Sacramento CA 95691 *Web:* www.lipomics.com	916-371-7974	669-0475
Lodestar Research Corp 2400 Central Ave Suite P-5. Boulder CO 80301 *Web:* www.lodestar.com	303-449-9691	449-3865
Long Term Ecological Research Network (LTER) 1 University of New Mexico UNM Dept of Biology MSCo3 2020. Albuquerque NM 87131 *Web:* www.lternet.edu/sites/lno	505-277-2597	277-2541
Los Alamos National Laboratory (LANL) Bikini Atoll Rd SM 30 PO Box 1663. Los Alamos NM 87545 *TF:* 877-723-4101 ■ *Web:* www.lanl.gov	505-667-7000	
Los Angeles Biomedical Research Institute 1124 W Carson St. Torrance CA 90502 *TF:* 877-452-2674 ■ *Web:* www.labiomed.org	310-222-3616	222-3640
Lovelace Respiratory Research Institute (LRRI) 2425 Ridgecrest Dr SE. Albuquerque NM 87108 *Web:* www.lrri.org	505-348-9400	348-8541
Mahoney Institute of Neurological Sciences University of Pennsylvania School of Medicine Stemmler Hall Rm 215. Philadelphia PA 19104 *Web:* www.med.upenn.edu	215-898-0869	573-2015

	City	State	Zip	Phone	Fax
Mailman Research Ctr					
McLean Hospital 115 Mill St	Belmont	MA	02478	617-855-2000	855-3479
TF: 800-333-0338 ■ *Web:* www.mclean.harvard.edu/research/mrc					
Marine Biological Laboratory (MBL) 7 MBL St	Woods Hole	MA	02543	508-548-3705	540-6902
Web: www.mbl.edu					
Marine Environmental Research Institute (MERI)					
MERI Center for Marine Studies					
55 Main St PO Box 1652	Blue Hill	ME	04614	207-374-2135	374-2931
Web: www.meriresearch.org					
Marine Science Institute					
University of California	Santa Barbara	CA	93106	805-893-3765	893-8062
Web: www.msi.ucsb.edu					
Massey Cancer Ctr					
Virginia Commonwealth University					
401 College St PO Box 980037	Richmond	VA	23298	804-828-0450	828-8453
TF: 877-462-7739 ■ *Web:* www.massey.vcu.edu					
MBI International 3900 Collins Rd.	Lansing	MI	48910	517-337-3181	337-2122
Web: www.mbi.org					
McArdle Laboratory for Cancer Research					
University of Wisconsin Dept of Oncology					
1400 University Ave	Madison	WI	53706	608-262-8651	262-2824
Web: mcardle.oncology.wisc.edu					
McCrone Assoc Inc 850 Pasquinelli Dr	Westmont	IL	60559	630-887-7100	887-7417
Web: www.mccroneassociates.com					
MCEER Red Jacket Quadrangle	Buffalo	NY	14260	716-645-3391	645-3733
Web: www.mceer.buffalo.edu					
Measurement & Control Engineering Ctr					
509 E Stadium Hall	Knoxville	TN	37996	865-974-2375	974-4995
Web: www.nsf.gov/eng/iip/iucrc/directory/mcec.jsp					
Mechanical Technology Inc 431 New Karner Rd	Albany	NY	12205	518-533-2200	533-2201
NASDAQ: MKTY ■ *TF:* 800-828-8210 ■ *Web:* www.mechtech.com					
Membrane Technology & Research Inc					
1360 Willow Rd Suite 103	Menlo Park	CA	94025	650-328-2228	328-6580
Web: www.mtrinc.com					
Memorial Sloan-Kettering Cancer Ctr					
1275 York Ave.	New York	NY	10065	212-639-2000	432-2331*
**Fax:* Admitting ■ *TF:* 800-525-2225 ■ *Web:* www.mskcc.org					
Mental Retardation Research Ctr					
UCLA Neuropsychiatric Institute & Hospital					
760 Westwood Plaza Rm 58-258	Los Angeles	CA	90024	310-825-0404	206-5060
Web: www.mrrc.npi.ucla.edu					
Metrics Inc 1240 Sugg Pkwy.	Greenville	NC	27834	252-752-3800	758-8522
Web: www.metricsinc.com					
Miami Project to Cure Paralysis					
1095 NW 14th Terr Lois Pope LIFE Ctr.	Miami	FL	33136	305-243-6001	243-6017
TF: 800-782-6387 ■ *Web:* www.miamiproject.miami.edu					
Michigan Mfg Technology Ctr					
47911 Halyard Dr	Plymouth	MI	48170	888-414-6682	451-4201*
**Fax Area Code:* 734 ■ *TF:* 888-414-6682 ■ *Web:* www.mmtc.org					
Micro & Nanotechnology Laboratory					
University of Illinois Urbana-Champaign					
208 N Wright St	Urbana	IL	61801	217-333-3097	244-6375
Web: www.mntl.illinois.edu					
Mid-Continent Research for Education & Learning (McREL)					
4601 DTC Blvd Suite 500	Denver	CO	80237	303-337-0990	337-3005
Web: www.mcrel.org					
Midwest Research Institute (MRI)					
425 Volker Blvd	Kansas City	MO	64110	816-753-7600	753-8420
Web: www.mriresearch.org					
MIT Center for Materials Science & Engineering (CMSE)					
Massachusetts Institute of Technology					
77 Massachusetts Ave Bldg 13 Rm 2106	Cambridge	MA	02139	617-253-6850	258-6478
Web: web.mit.edu/cmse					
MIT Media Laboratory					
Massachusetts Institute of Technology					
77 Massachusetts Ave Bldg E15	Cambridge	MA	02139	617-253-5960	258-6264
Web: www.media.mit.edu					
MITRE Corp 202 Burlington Rd	Bedford	MA	01730	781-271-2000	271-2271
Web: www.mitre.org					
Monell Chemical Senses Ctr					
3500 Market St	Philadelphia	PA	19104	215-519-4700	898-2084
Web: www.monell.org					
Mote Marine Laboratory					
1600 Ken Thompson Pkwy	Sarasota	FL	34236	941-388-4441	388-4312
TF: 800-690-6083 ■ *Web:* www.mote.org					
MSU-DOE Plant Research Laboratory					
Michigan State University					
106 Plant Biology	East Lansing	MI	48824	517-353-2270	353-9168
Web: www.prl.msu.edu					
NAHB Research Ctr					
400 Prince Georges Blvd	Upper Marlboro	MD	20774	301-249-4000	430-6180
TF: 800-638-8556 ■ *Web:* www.nahbrc.org					
Nanotechnology Research Ctr					
Georgia Institute of Technology					
791 Atlantic Dr.	Atlanta	GA	30332	404-894-5100	894-5028
Web: www.mirc.gatech.edu					
Nathan S Kline Institute for Psychiatric Research					
140 Old Orangeburg Rd Bldg 35	Orangeburg	NY	10962	845-398-5500	398-5508
Web: www.rfmh.org/nki					
National Animal Disease Ctr (NADC)					
2300 Dayton Rd PO Box 70	Ames	IA	50010	515-337-7201	337-7677
Web: www.ars.usda.gov					
National Astronomy & Ionosphere Ctr (NAIC)					
Cornell University Space Sciences Bldg	Ithaca	NY	14853	607-255-3735	255-8803
Web: www.naic.edu					
National Biodynamics Laboratory (NBDL)					
University of New Orleans College of Engineering					
2000 Lakeshore Dr Rm 910	New Orleans	LA	70148	504-280-6328	280-7413
Web: www.coe.uno.edu					
National Bureau of Economic Research					
1050 Massachusetts Ave	Cambridge	MA	02138	617-868-3900	868-2742
Web: www.nber.org					
National Cancer Institute at Frederick					
1050 Boyles St PO Box B	Frederick	MD	21702	301-846-1108	846-1494
Web: www.ncifcrf.gov					
National Center for Agricultural Utilization Research					
USDA/ARS 1815 N University St	Peoria	IL	61604	309-685-4011	681-6686
Web: www.ars.usda.gov/Main/docs.htm?docid=3153					
National Center for Atmospheric Research (NCAR)					
1850 Table Mesa Dr PO Box 3000	Boulder	CO	80305	303-497-1000	497-8610*
**Fax:* PR ■ *Web:* www.ncar.ucar.edu					
National Center for Computational Toxicology					
US Environmental Protection Agency					
109 TW Alexander Dr	Research Triangle Park	NC	27709	919-541-3850	
Web: www.epa.gov					
National Center for Ecological Analysis & Synthesis (NCEAS)					
University of California Santa Barbara					
735 State St Suite 300	Santa Barbara	CA	93101	805-892-2500	892-2510
Web: www.nceas.ucsb.edu					
National Center for Electron Microscopy (NCEM)					
Lawrence Berkeley National Laboratory					
MS 72-150	Berkeley	CA	94720	510-486-6036	486-5888
Web: ncem.lbl.gov					
National Center for Genetic Resources Preservation					
USDA/ARS/NCGRP 1111 S Mason St	Fort Collins	CO	80521	970-495-3200	221-1427
Web: www.ars.usda.gov/npa/ftcollins/ncgrp					
National Center for Genome Resources					
2935 Rodeo Pk Dr E	Santa Fe	NM	87505	505-982-7840	995-4432
TF: 800-450-4854 ■ *Web:* www.ncgr.org					
National Center for Mfg Sciences (NCMS)					
3025 Boardwalk	Ann Arbor	MI	48108	734-995-0300	995-1150
TF: 800-222-6267 ■ *Web:* www.ncms.org					
National Center for Research on Evaluation Standards & Student Testing (CRESST)					
UCLA 300 Charles E Young Dr N					
Mail PO Box 951522	Los Angeles	CA	90095	310-206-1532	825-3883
Web: www.cse.ucla.edu					
National Center for Supercomputing Applications					
University of Illinois Urbana-Champaign					
1205 W Clark St Rm 1008 MC-257	Urbana	IL	61801	217-244-0072	244-8195
Web: www.ncsa.uiuc.edu					
National Center on Sleep Disorders Research					
National Heart Lung & Blood Institute					
31 Ctr Dr Bldg 31 Rm 5A52	Bethesda	MD	20892	301-435-0199	480-3451
Web: www.nhlbi.nih.gov/about/ncsdr					
National Development & Research Institutes Inc					
71 W 23rd St 8th Fl	New York	NY	10010	212-845-4400	438-0894*
**Fax Area Code:* 917 ■ *Web:* www.ndri.org					
National Energy Research Scientific Computing Ctr (NERSC)					
Lawrence Berkeley National Laboratory					
1 Cyclotron Rd MS 50C3396	Berkeley	CA	94720	510-486-5849	486-7520
TF: 800-847-6070 ■ *Web:* www.nersc.gov					
National Energy Technology Laboratory (NETL)					
3610 Collins Ferry Rd	Morgantown	WV	26505	304-285-4764	285-4919
TF: 800-432-8330 ■ *Web:* www.netl.doe.gov					
National Energy Technology Laboratory					
US Dept of Energy 626 Cochrans Mill Rd					
PO Box 10940	Pittsburgh	PA	15236	412-386-6000	386-6127
Web: www.netl.doe.gov					
National Exposure Research Laboratory					
US Environmental Protection Agency					
TW Alexander	Research Triangle Park	NC	27709	919-541-2106	541-0445
Web: www.epa.gov					
National Hansen's Disease Program (NHDP)					
1770 Physicians Pk Dr	Baton Rouge	LA	70816	225-756-3700	
TF: 800-642-2477					
National Health & Environmental Effects Research Laboratory					
US Environmental Protection Agency					
109 TW Alexander Dr	Research Triangle Park	NC	27709	919-541-2281	541-4324
Web: www.epa.gov/nheerl					
National High Magnetic Field Laboratory (NHMFL)					
1800 E Paul Dirac Dr	Tallahassee	FL	32310	850-644-0311	644-8350
Web: www.magnet.fsu.edu					
National Homeland Security Research Ctr					
US Environmental Protection Agency					
26 W Martin Luther King Dr	Cincinnati	OH	45268	513-569-7907	487-2555
Web: www.epa.gov					
National Institute of Standards & Technology (NIST)					
100 Bureau Dr Sp 1070	Gaithersburg	MD	20899	301-975-6478	926-1630
TF: 800-877-8339 ■ *Web:* www.nist.gov/index.html					
Boulder Laboratories 325 Broadway MS 104	Boulder	CO	80305	303-497-5507	497-6235
Web: www.boulder.nist.gov					
National Institute on Disability & Rehabilitation Research (NIDRR)					
400 Maryland Ave SW MS PCP-6056	Washington	DC	20202	202-245-7640	245-7323
Web: www.ed.gov/about/offices/list/osers/nidrr					
National Institutes of Health (NIH)					
9000 Rockville Pike	Bethesda	MD	20892	301-496-4000	
Web: www.nih.gov					
Clinical Ctr 10 Ctr Dr Bldg 10	Bethesda	MD	20892	301-496-2563	402-2984
Web: www.cc.nih.gov					
John E Fogarty International Ctr					
31 Ctr Dr MSC 2220	Bethesda	MD	20892	301-496-2075	594-1211
Web: www.fic.nih.gov					
National Cancer Institute					
Public Inquiries Office 6116 Executive Blvd					
Rm 3036A	Bethesda	MD	20892	301-435-3848	402-2594
TF: 800-422-6237 ■ *Web:* www.cancer.gov					
National Eye Institute 2020 Vision Pl.	Bethesda	MD	20892	301-496-5248	402-1065
Web: www.nei.nih.gov					
National Human Genome Research Institute					
31 Ctr Dr Bldg 31 Rm 4B09	Bethesda	MD	20892	301-402-0911	402-2218
Web: www.genome.gov					
National Institute of Allergy & Infectious Diseases					
6610 Rockledge Dr MSC 6612	Bethesda	MD	20892	301-496-5717	402-3573
TF: 866-284-4107 ■ *Web:* www.niaid.nih.gov					
National Institute of Arthritis & Musculoskeletal & Skin Diseases					
31 Ctr Dr MSC 2350 Bldg 31 Rm 4C02	Bethesda	MD	20892	301-496-8190	480-2814
Web: www.niams.nih.gov					
National Institute of Child Health & Human Development					
31 Ctr Dr Bldg 31 Rm 2A32	Bethesda	MD	20892	301-496-5133	496-7101
TF: 800-370-2943 ■ *Web:* www.nichd.nih.gov					
National Institute of Dental & Craniofacial Research					
31 Ctr Dr	Bethesda	MD	20892	301-496-3571	402-2185

				Phone	Fax
Web: www.nidcr.nih.gov					
National Institute of Environmental Health Sciences					
PO Box 12233	Research Triangle Park	NC	27709	919-541-3201	541-2260
Web: www.niehs.nih.gov					
National Institute of General Medical Sciences					
45 Ctr Dr MSC 6200	Bethesda	MD	20892	301-496-7301	
Web: www.nigms.nih.gov					
National Institute of Mental Health					
6001 Executive Blvd Rm 8184 MSC 9663	Bethesda	MD	20892	301-443-4513	443-4279
TF: 866-615-6464 ■ *Web:* www.nimh.nih.gov					
National Institute of Neurological Disorders & Stroke					
PO Box 5801	Bethesda	MD	20824	301-496-5751	
TF: 800-352-9424 ■ *Web:* www.ninds.nih.gov					
National Institute of Nursing Research					
31 Ctr Dr Bldg 31 Rm 5B05	Bethesda	MD	20892	301-496-8230	594-3405
Web: www.nih.gov/ninr					
National Institute on Aging					
31 Ctr Dr Bldg 31 Rm 5C27 MSC 2292	Bethesda	MD	20892	301-496-1752	496-1072
Web: www.nia.nih.gov					
National Institute on Alcohol Abuse & Alcoholism					
5635 Fishers Ln MSC 9304	Bethesda	MD	20892	301-443-3885	443-7043
Web: www.niaaa.nih.gov					
National Institute on Deafness & Other Communication Disorders					
31 Ctr Dr Bldg 31 Rm 3C35	Bethesda	MD	20892	301-496-7243	402-0018
TF: 800-241-1044 ■ *Web:* www.nidcd.nih.gov					
National Library of Medicine					
Lister Hill National Center for Biomedical Communications					
8600 Rockville Pike Bldg 38A 7th Fl	Bethesda	MD	20894	301-496-4441	480-3035
Web: www.lhncbc.nlm.nih.gov					
National Optical Astronomy Observatories					
950 N Cherry Ave	Tucson	AZ	85719	520-318-8002	318-8360
Web: www.noao.edu					
National Peanut Research Laboratory (NPRL)					
USDA/ARS 1011 Forrester Dr SE PO Box 509	Dawson	GA	39842	229-995-7400	995-7416
Web: www.ars.usda.gov					
National Protection Ctr (NPC)					
US Army Soldier Systems Ctr ATTN: PAO					
Kansas St	Natick	MA	01760	508-233-6959	
Web: www.nsrdec.natick.army.mil/about/index.htm					
National Radio Astronomy Observatory (NRAO)					
520 Edgemont Rd	Charlottesville	VA	22903	434-296-0211	296-0278
Web: www.nrao.edu					
National Renewable Energy Laboratory (NREL)					
1617 Cole Blvd	Golden	CO	80401	303-275-3000	275-4053
Web: www.nrel.gov					
National Research Center for Coal & Energy (NRCCE)					
West Virginia University					
385 Evansdale Dr PO Box 6064	Morgantown	WV	26506	304-293-2867	293-3749
TF: 800-624-8301 ■ *Web:* www.nrcce.wvu.edu					
National Research Center on English Learning & Achievement (CELA)					
School of Education University of Albany B9					
1400 Washington Ave	Albany	NY	12222	518-442-5026	442-5933
Web: www.albany.edu					
National Research Center on the Gifted & Talented (NRC/GT)					
University of Connecticut					
2131 Hillside Rd Unit 3007	Storrs	CT	06269	860-486-4676	486-2900
Web: www.gifted.uconn.edu/nrcgt.html					
National Risk Management Research Laboratory					
US Environmental Protection Agency					
26 Martin Luther King Dr	Cincinnati	OH	45268	513-569-7418	569-7680
Web: www.epa.gov/ordntrnt/ORD/NRMRL					
National Sedimentation Laboratory PO Box 1157	Oxford	MS	38655	662-232-2924	281-5706
Web: www.ars.usda.gov/main/site_main.htm?modecode=64-08-05-00					
National Severe Storms Laboratory (NSSL)					
120 David L Boren Blvd	Norman	OK	73072	405-325-6907	
Web: www.nssl.noaa.gov					
National Soil Dynamics Laboratory					
USDA/ARS 411 S Donahue Dr	Auburn	AL	36832	334-887-8596	887-8597
Web: www.ars.usda.gov					
National Soil Erosion Research Laboratory					
USDA/ARS 275 S Russell St	West Lafayette	IN	47907	765-494-8689	494-5948
Web: www.ars.usda.gov/main/site_main.htm?modecode=36021500					
National Soil Tilth Laboratory					
USDA/ARS 2110 University Blvd	Ames	IA	50011	515-294-5723	294-8125
Web: www.ars.usda.gov					
National Technical Information Service (NTIS)					
5285 Port Royal Rd	Springfield	VA	22161	703-605-6000	605-6900
TF Orders: 800-553-6847 ■ *Web:* www.ntis.gov					
National Technology Transfer Ctr					
316 Washington Ave	Wheeling	WV	26003	304-243-2455	243-2523
TF: 800-678-6882 ■ *Web:* www.nttc.edu					

				Phone	Fax
National Toxicology Program (NTP)					
PO Box 12233	Research Triangle Park	NC	27709	919-541-0530	541-3687
Web: ntp-server.niehs.nih.gov					
National Undersea Research Center for Hawaii & the Western Pacific					
University of Hawaii at Manoa					
1000 Pope Rd MSB Rm 303	Honolulu	HI	96822	808-956-6335	956-9772
Web: www.soest.hawaii.edu/HURL					
National Undersea Research Center for the Caribbean					
Perry Institute for Marine Science Caribbean Marine Research Ctr					
100 N US Hwy 1 Suite 202	Jupiter	FL	33477	561-741-0192	741-0193
Web: www.perryinstitute.org					
National Undersea Research Center for the Mid-Atlantic Bight					
Institute of Marine & Coastal Sciences					
Rutgers University 71 Dudley Rd	New Brunswick	NJ	08901	732-932-6555	932-8578
Web: www.marine.rutgers.edu					
National Undersea Research Center for the North Atlantic & Great Lakes (NURC)					
University of Connecticut at Avery Pt					
1080 Shennecossett Rd	Groton	CT	06340	860-405-9121	445-2969
Web: www.nurc.uconn.edu					
National Undersea Research Center for the Southeastern US & Gulf of Mexico (NURC)					
University of N Carolina at Wilmington					
5600 Marvin K Moss Ln	Wilmington	NC	28409	910-962-2300	962-2410
Web: www.uncwil.edu/nurc					
Florida Keys Research Program					
515 Caribbean Dr	Key Largo	FL	33037	305-451-0233	453-9719
Web: www.uncwil.edu/nurc					
National Undersea Research Center for the West Coast & Polar Regions					
University of Alaska-Fairbanks 209 O'Neill Bldg					
PO Box 757220	Fairbanks	AK	99775	907-474-5870	474-5804
Web: www.westnurc.uaf.edu					
National Water Resources Institutes Program (NWRI)					
US Geological Survey National Ctr					
12201 Sunrise Valley Dr	Reston	VA	20192	703-648-6800	
Web: wrri.nmsu.edu/niwr/niwr.html					
National Wetlands Research Ctr					
700 Cajundome Blvd	Lafayette	LA	70506	337-266-8500	266-8513
Web: www.nwrc.usgs.gov					
National Wildlife Health Ctr					
6006 Schroeder Rd	Madison	WI	53711	608-270-2400	270-2415
Web: www.nwhc.usgs.gov					
National Wildlife Research Ctr					
4101 LaPorte Ave	Fort Collins	CO	80521	970-266-6000	266-6032
Web: www.aphis.usda.gov					
Nationwide Children's Hospital					
700 Children's Dr	Columbus	OH	43205	614-722-2700	722-2716
Web: www.nationwidechildrens.org					
Natural Hazards Ctr					
University of Colorado CB 482	Boulder	CO	80309	303-492-6818	492-2151
Web: www.colorado.edu/hazards					
Natural Resource Ecology Laboratory					
Colorado State University					
Campus Delivery 1499	Fort Collins	CO	80523	970-491-1982	491-1965
Web: www.nrel.colostate.edu					
Natural Resources Research Institute (NRRI)					
University of Minnesota Duluth					
5013 Miller Trunk Hwy	Duluth	MN	55811	218-720-4294	720-4219
TF: 800-234-0054 ■ *Web:* www.nrri.umn.edu					
Naval Aerospace Medical Research Laboratory (NAMRL)					
280 Fred Bauer St Bldg 1811 Naval Air Stn	Pensacola	FL	32508	850-452-3486	452-9290
Web: www.namrl.navy.mil					
Naval Health Research Ctr (NHRC)					
140 Sylvester Rd	San Diego	CA	92106	619-553-8400	553-9389
Web: www.nhrc.navy.mil					
Naval Institute for Dental & Biomedical Research (NDRI)					
310-A B St Bldg 1-H	Great Lakes	IL	60088	847-688-4560	688-4279
Naval Medical Research Ctr (NMRC)					
503 Robert Grant Ave	Silver Spring	MD	20910	301-319-9646	319-7410
Web: www.med.navy.mil					
Naval Research Laboratory (NRL)					
4555 Overlook Ave SW Code 1000	Washington	DC	20375	202-767-3403	404-7419
Web: www.nrl.navy.mil					
Naval Submarine Medical Research Laboratory (NSMRL)					
PO Box 900	Groton	CT	06349	860-694-3822	694-4809
Web: www.med.navy.mil					
Naval Surface Warfare Ctr (NSWC)					
1333 Isaac Hull Ave SE MS 7101	Washington Navy Yard	DC	20376	202-781-5425	
Web: www.navsea.navy.mil/nswc/default.aspx					
Carderock Div 9500 MacArthur Blvd	West Bethesda	MD	20817	301-227-5040	227-3574
Dahlgren Div 6149 Welsh Rd Suite 203	Dahlgren	VA	22448	540-249-8291	
TF: 877-845-5656 ■ *Web:* www.navsea.navy.mil					
Naval Undersea Warfare Ctr (NUWC)					
1176 Howell St	Newport	RI	02841	401-832-7742	832-4396
Web: www.navsea.navy.mil/nuwc					
Keyport Div 610 Dowell St	Keyport	WA	98345	360-396-2699	396-2387
Web: www.navsea.navy.mil/nuwc/keyport/default.aspx					
Newport Div 1176 Howell St	Newport	RI	02841	401-832-7742	832-4661
Web: www.navsea.navy.mil/nuwc/default.aspx					
Navy Clothing & Textile Research Facility (NCTRF)					
15 Kansas St Bldg 86	Natick	MA	01760	508-233-4172	233-4783
Nebraska Center for Materials & Nanoscience					
University of Nebraska Brace Lab Rm 111	Lincoln	NE	68588	402-472-7886	472-2879
Web: www.unl.edu/ncmn					
NEC Laboratories America Inc					
4 Independence Way	Princeton	NJ	08540	609-520-1555	951-2481
Web: www.nec-labs.com					
New Brunswick Laboratory (NBL)					
9800 S Cass Ave Bldg 350	Argonne	IL	60439	630-252-2442	252-6256
Web: www.nbl.doe.gov					
New England Primate Research Ctr (NEPRC)					
1 Pine Hill Dr PO Box 9102	Southborough	MA	01772	508-624-8019	786-3317
Web: www.hms.harvard.edu					

Name / Address	City	State	ZIP	Phone	Fax
Noblis 3150 Fairview Pk Dr S *Web:* www.noblis.org	Falls Church	VA	22042	703-610-2000	
North American Science Assoc Inc 6750 Wales Rd *TF:* 866-666-9455 ■ *Web:* www.namsa.com	Northwood	OH	43619	419-666-9455	662-4386
North Central Agricultural Research Laboratory (NGIRL) USDA/ARS 2923 Medary Ave *Web:* www.ars.usda.gov/Main/docs.htm?docid=2357	Brookings	SD	57006	605-693-3241	693-5240
Northeast Fisheries Science Ctr 166 Water St *Web:* www.nefsc.noaa.gov	Woods Hole	MA	02543	508-495-2000	495-2258
Northern Plains Agricultural Research Laboratory USDA/ARS 1500 N Central Ave *Web:* www.ars.usda.gov	Sidney	MT	59270	406-433-2020	433-5038
Northern Prairie Wildlife Research Ctr 8711 37th St SE *Web:* www.npwrc.usgs.gov	Jamestown	ND	58401	701-253-5500	253-5553
Northern Research Station 11 Campus Blvd Suite 200 *Web:* www.nrs.fs.fed.us	Newtown Square	PA	19073	610-557-4017	557-4095
Northwest Fisheries Science Ctr 2725 Montlake Blvd E *Web:* www.nwfsc.noaa.gov	Seattle	WA	98112	206-860-3200	860-3217
Notre Dame Radiation Laboratory University of Notre Dame *Web:* www.rad.nd.edu	Notre Dame	IN	46556	574-631-6163	631-8068
Oak Ridge National Laboratory (ORNL) PO Box 2008 **Fax:* PR ■ *Web:* www.ornl.gov	Oak Ridge	TN	37831	865-576-2900	574-0595*
Oceanic Institute 41-202 Kalanianaole Hwy *Web:* www.oceanicinstitute.org	Waimanalo	HI	96795	808-259-7951	259-5971
Office of Naval Research (ONR) 1 Liberty Ctr 875 N Randolph St Suite 1425 *Web:* www.onr.navy.mil	Arlington	VA	22203	703-696-5031	696-5940
Office of Population Research Princeton University Wallace Hall 2nd Fl *Web:* www.opr.princeton.edu	Princeton	NJ	08544	609-258-4870	258-1039
Ohio State University Police The 1680 Madison Ave *Web:* www.oardc.ohio-state.edu	Wooster	OH	44691	330-287-0111	202-3579
Oklahoma Medical Research Foundation (OMRF) 825 NE 13th St *TF:* 800-522-0211 ■ *Web:* www.omrf.org	Oklahoma City	OK	73104	405-271-6673	271-7510
Omnicare Clinical Research 630 Alledale Rd *TF:* 800-290-5766 ■ *Web:* www.omnicarecr.com	King of Prussia	PA	19406	484-679-2400	679-2505
Oregon National Primate Research Ctr (ONPRC) Oregon Health & Science University 505 NW 185th Ave *Web:* www.onprc.ohsu.edu	Beaverton	OR	97006	503-645-1141	690-5532
Pacific Disaster Ctr 1305 N Holopono St Suite 2 *TF:* 888-808-6688 ■ *Web:* www.pdc.org	Kihei	HI	96753	808-891-0525	891-0526
Pacific Institute for Research & Evaluation 11720 Beltsville Dr Suite 900 *Web:* www.pire.org	Calverton	MD	20705	301-755-2738	755-2799
Pacific International Center for High Technology Research (PICHTR) 1440 Kapiolani Blvd Suite 1225 *Web:* www.pichtr.org	Honolulu	HI	96814	808-943-9581	943-9582
Pacific Island Ecosystems Research Ctr 677 Ala Moana Blvd Suite 615 *Web:* www.biology.usgs.gov/pierc	Honolulu	HI	96813	808-587-7452	587-7451
Pacific Marine Environmental Laboratory (PMEL) 7600 Sand Pt Way NE *Web:* www.pmel.noaa.gov	Seattle	WA	98115	206-526-6239	526-6815
Pacific Northwest National Laboratory (PNNL) 902 Battelle Blvd PO Box 999 **Fax:* Mail Rm ■ *TF:* 888-375-7665 ■ *Web:* www.pnl.gov	Richland	WA	99352	509-375-2121	375-2507*
Pacific Northwest Research Station 333 SW 1st Ave *Web:* www.fs.fed.us/pnw	Portland	OR	97204	503-808-2100	808-2130
Pacific Southwest Research Station 800 Buchanan St W Annex Bldg *Web:* www.fs.fed.us/psw	Albany	CA	94710	510-559-6300	559-6440
Palo Alto Research Center Inc (PARC) 3333 Coyote Hill Rd *Web:* www.parc.com	Palo Alto	CA	94304	650-812-4000	812-4970
PAREXEL International Corp 195 W St *NASDAQ: PRXL* ■ *TF:* 800-727-3935 ■ *Web:* www.parexel.com	Waltham	MA	02451	781-487-9900	487-0525
Parish Chemical Co Inc PO Box 277 *Web:* www.parishchemical.com	Orem	UT	84059	801-226-2018	226-8496
Patrick Center for Environmental Research 1900 Benjamin Franklin Pkwy *Web:* www.ansp.org/research/pcer	Philadelphia	PA	19103	215-299-1000	299-1079
Patuxent Wildlife Research Ctr 12100 Beech Forest Rd *Web:* www.pwrc.usgs.gov	Laurel	MD	20708	301-497-5500	497-5505
Pittsburgh Supercomputing Ctr 300 S Craig St *TF:* 800-221-1641 ■ *Web:* www.psc.edu	Pittsburgh	PA	15213	412-268-4960	268-5832
Plasma Science & Fusion Ctr Massachusetts Institute of Technology 167 Albany St NW 16-288 *Web:* www.psfc.mit.edu	Cambridge	MA	02139	617-253-8100	253-0238
Plum Island Animal Disease Ctr USDA/ARS PO Box 848 *Web:* www.ars.usda.gov/main/site_main.htm?modecode=19400000	Greenport	NY	11944	631-323-3200	323-2507
Polisher Research Institute Abramson Ctr for Jewish Life 1425 Horsham Rd *Web:* www.pgc.org/PRI	North Wales	PA	19454	215-371-1895	371-3015
Population Council 1 Dag Hammarskjold Plaza 9th Fl *Web:* www.popcouncil.org	New York	NY	10017	212-339-0500	755-6052
Population Research Ctr University of Chicago 1155 E 60th St *Web:* www.src.uchicago.edu/prc	Chicago	IL	60637	773-256-6302	256-6313
Population Research Institute Pennsylvania State University 601 Oswald Tower *Web:* www.pop.psu.edu	University Park	PA	16802	814-865-0486	863-8342
PPD Inc 929 N Front St *NASDAQ: PPDI* ■ *Web:* www.ppdi.com	Wilmington	NC	28401	910-251-0081	762-5820
Princeton Plasma Physics Laboratory (PPPL) James Forrestal Campus Princeton University PO Box 451 *Web:* www.pppl.gov	Princeton	NJ	08543	609-243-2750	243-2751
Public Health Research Institute (PHRI) International Ctr for Public Health 225 Warren St *Web:* www.phri.org	Newark	NJ	07103	973-854-3100	854-3101
QRDC Inc 125 Columbia Ct Suite 6 *Web:* www.qrdc.com	Chaska	MN	55318	952-556-5205	556-5206
Quintiles Transnational Corp 4820 Emperor Blvd *TF:* 800-875-2888 ■ *Web:* www.quintiles.com	Durham	NC	27703	919-998-2000	998-9113
Radiant Research Inc 11500 Northlake Dr Suite 320 *TF:* 866-232-8484 ■ *Web:* www.radiantresearch.com	Cincinnati	OH	45249	513-247-5500	247-5510
Red River Valley Agricultural Research Ctr USDA/ARS 1307 18th St N *Web:* www.ars.usda.gov/main/site_main.htm?modecode=54-42-00-00	Fargo	ND	58105	701-239-1384	239-1369
Regional Research Institute for Human Services Portland State University 1600 SW 4th Ave Suite 900	Portland	OR	97201	503-725-4040	725-4180
Renaissance Computing Institute (RENCI) 100 Europa Dr Suite 540 *Web:* www.renci.org	Chapel Hill	NC	27517	919-445-9640	445-9669
Research for Better Schools Inc 112 N Broad St *Web:* www.rbs.org	Philadelphia	PA	19102	215-568-6150	568-7260
Research Foundation of City University of New York The 230 W 41st St 7th Fl *Web:* www.rfcuny.org	New York	NY	10036	212-417-8300	
Research Institute for Advanced Computer Science (RIACS) NASA Ames Research Ctr MS T35-B-1 *Web:* www.riacs.edu	Moffett Field	CA	94035	650-966-5020	966-5021
Research Institute on Addictions (RIA) 1021 Main St *Web:* www.ria.buffalo.edu	Buffalo	NY	14203	716-887-2566	887-2252
Research Laboratory of Electronics Massachusetts Institute of Technology 77 Massachusetts Ave Rm 36-413 *Web:* www.rle.mit.edu	Cambridge	MA	02139	617-253-2519	253-1301
Research Triangle Institute 3040 Cornwallis Rd PO Box 12194 *TF:* 800-334-8571 ■ *Web:* www.rti.org	Research Triangle Park	NC	27709	919-541-6000	541-5985
Ricerca Biosciences LLC 7528 Auburn Rd PO Box 1000 *TF:* 888-742-3722 ■ *Web:* www.ricerca.com	Concord	OH	44077	440-357-3300	357-4939
Richard B Russell Agricultural Research Ctr USDA/ARS 950 College Stn Rd	Athens	GA	30605	706-546-3152	546-3367
Robert H Lurie Comprehensive Cancer Ctr Northwestern University 675 N St Clair 21st Fl *Web:* www.cancer.northwestern.edu/Home/Index.cfm	Chicago	IL	60611	312-695-0990	
Robotics Institute Carnegie Mellon University 5000 Forbes Ave *Web:* www.ri.cmu.edu	Pittsburgh	PA	15213	412-268-3818	268-6436
Rocky Mountain Research Station *US Forest Service* 240 W Prospec *Web:* www.fs.fed.us/rm	Fort Collins	CO	80526	970-498-1100	498-1010
Rodale Institute 611 Siegfriedale Rd *Web:* www.rodaleinstitute.org	Kutztown	PA	19530	610-683-1400	683-8548
Roman L Hruska US Meat Animal Research Ctr USDA/ARS 844 Rd 313 PO Box 166 *Web:* www.ars.usda.gov	Clay Center	NE	68933	402-762-4100	762-4148
Rose F. Kennedy Ctr *Albert Einstein College of Medicine* 1410 Pelham Pkwy S *Web:* www.einstein.yu.edu	Bronx	NY	10461	718-430-8500	918-7505
Roswell Park Cancer Institute 666 Elm St *TF:* 877-275-7724 ■ *Web:* www.roswellpark.org	Buffalo	NY	14263	716-845-2300	845-8335
Roy J Carver Biotechnology Ctr 2613 Institute for Genomic Biology 1206 W Gregory MC-195 *Web:* www.biotech.uiuc.edu	Urbana	IL	61801	217-333-1695	244-0466
Russell Sage Foundation 112 E 64th St *Web:* www.russellsage.org	New York	NY	10021	212-750-6000	371-4761
Rutgers Business School 1 Washington Pk Third Fl *Web:* www.business.rutgers.edu/default.aspx?id=645	Newark	NJ	07102	973-353-3587	
Safety Analysis & Forensic Engineering 6775 Hollister Ave Suite 100 *Web:* www.saferesearch.com	Goleta	CA	93117	805-964-0676	964-7669
Saint Jude Children's Research Hospital (SJCRH) 262 Danny Thomas Pl **Fax:* Admitting ■ *TF:* 866-278-5833 ■ *Web:* www.stjude.org	Memphis	TN	38105	901-495-3300	495-5297*
Salk Institute for Biological Studies PO Box 85800 *Web:* www.salk.edu	San Diego	CA	92186	858-453-4100	552-8285

Name / Address	City	State	Zip	Phone	Fax
San Diego Supercomputer Ctr (SDSC)					
9500 Gilman Dr	La Jolla	CA	92093	858-534-5000	534-5056
Web: www.sdsc.edu					
Sandia National Laboratories - California (SNL)					
7011 E Ave PO Box 969	Livermore	CA	94551	925-294-3000	
Web: www.ca.sandia.gov					
Sandia National Laboratories - New Mexico (SNL)					
1515 Eubank SE PO Box 5800	Albuquerque	NM	87123	505-844-5678	
Web: www.sandia.gov					
Sarnoff Corp 201 Washington Rd PO Box 5300	Princeton	NJ	08543	609-734-2000	734-2221
Web: www.sarnoff.com					
Savannah River National Laboratory					
Savannah River Site	Aiken	SC	29808	803-725-3994	725-1660
Web: srnl.doe.gov					
Sc&a Inc 1608 Spring Hill Rd Suite 400	Vienna	VA	22182	703-893-6600	821-8236
Web: www.scainc.com					
Schiefelbusch Institute for Life Span Studies					
Univ of Kansas Robert Dole Human Development Ctr					
1000 Sunnyside Ave Rm 1052	Lawrence	KS	66045	785-864-4295	864-5323
Web: www.lsi.ku.edu/lsi					
Science Applications International Corp					
10260 Campus Pt Dr	San Diego	CA	92121	858-826-6000	826-6634
Web: www.saic.com					
Scripps Institution of Oceanography (SIO)					
8622 Kennel Way	La Jolla	CA	92037	858-534-3624	
Web: www-sio.ucsd.edu					
Scripps Research Institute					
10550 N Torrey Pines Rd	La Jolla	CA	92037	858-784-1000	784-9004*
**Fax:* Hum Res ■ *Web:* www.scripps.edu					
SEDL 4700 Mueller Blvd	Austin	TX	78723	512-476-6861	476-2286
Web: www.sedl.org					
SEMATECH 2706 Montopolis Dr	Austin	TX	78741	512-356-3500	356-3086*
**Fax:* Hum Res ■ *Web:* www.sematech.org					
SERVE 5900 Summit Ave Suite 201	Browns Summit	NC	27214	336-315-7400	315-7457
TF: 800-755-3277 ■ *Web:* www.serve.org					
Sharp Laboratories Of America Inc					
5750 NW Pacific Rim Blvd	Camas	WA	98607	360-817-8400	817-8436
Web: www.sharplabs.com					
Shiley-Marcos Alzheimer's Disease Research Ctr					
8950 Villa La Jolla Dr Suite C129	La Jolla	CA	92037	858-622-5800	622-1012
Web: www.adrc.ucsd.edu					
Sidney Kimmel Comprehensive Cancer Center at Johns Hopkins					
401 N Broadway The Harry & Jeanette Weinberg Bldg					
Suite 1100	Baltimore	MD	21231	410-955-5222	955-6787
Web: www.hopkinsmedicine.org					
Siteman Cancer Ctr 4921 Parkview Pl	Saint Louis	MO	63110	314-362-5196	
TF: 800-600-3606 ■ *Web:* www.siteman.wustl.edu					
Smith-Kettlewell Eye Research Institute					
2318 Fillmore St	San Francisco	CA	94115	415-345-2000	345-8455
Web: www.ski.org					
Smithsonian Environmental Research Ctr					
647 Contees Wharf Rd PO Box 28	Edgewater	MD	21037	443-482-2200	482-2380
Web: www.serc.si.edu					
Smithsonian Tropical Research Institute (STRI)					
Quad Suite 3123 705 PO Box 37012	Washington	DC	20013	703-487-3770	786-2557*
**Fax Area Code:* 202 ■ *Web:* www.stri.org					
Snbl USA Ltd 6605 Merrill Creek Pkwy	Everett	WA	98203	425-407-0121	
Web: www.snblusa.com					
Social & Economic Sciences Research Ctr (SESRC)					
Washington State University					
Wilson Hall Rm 133 PO Box 644014	Pullman	WA	99164	509-335-1511	335-0116
TF: 800-932-5393 ■ *Web:* www.sesrc.wsu.edu					
Software Engineering Institute (SEI)					
4500 5th Ave	Pittsburgh	PA	15213	412-268-5800	268-6257*
**Fax:* Cust Svc ■ *TF:* 888-201-4479 ■ *Web:* www.sei.cmu.edu					
Software Engineering Services Corp					
1311 Fort Crook Rd S	Bellevue	NE	68005	402-292-8660	292-3271
TF: 800-244-1278 ■ *Web:* www.sessolutions.com					
Southeast Fisheries Science Ctr					
75 Virginia Beach Dr	Miami	FL	33149	305-361-4200	361-4219
Web: www.sefsc.noaa.gov					
Southern California Earthquake Ctr					
3651 Trousdale Pkwy Suite 169	Los Angeles	CA	90089	213-740-5843	740-0011
Web: www.scec.org					
Southern Plains Agricultural Research Ctr					
USDA/ARS 2881 F & B Rd	College Station	TX	77845	979-260-9372	260-9377
Web: www.sparc.ars.usda.gov					
Southern Regional Research Ctr (SRRC)					
1100 Robert E Lee Blvd PO Box 19687	New Orleans	LA	70179	504-286-4200	286-4419
Web: www.ars.usda.gov/main/site_main.htm?modecode=64350000					
Southern Research Institute					
2000 9th Ave S	Birmingham	AL	35205	205-581-2000	581-2726
TF: 800-967-6774 ■ *Web:* www.sri.org					
Southern Research Station					
USDA Forest Service 200 Weaver Blvd	Asheville	NC	28804	828-257-4300	257-4840
Web: www.srs.fs.usda.gov					
Southwest Fisheries Science Ctr					
National Marine Fisheries Service					
8604 La Jolla Shores Dr	La Jolla	CA	92037	858-546-7000	546-7003
Web: www.swfsc.noaa.gov					
Southwest National Primate Research Ctr (SNPRC)					
Texas Biomedical Research Institute					
PO Box 760549	San Antonio	TX	78245	210-258-9400	
Web: www.txbiomed.org/SNPRC/index.aspx					
Southwest Research Institute (SwRI)					
6220 Culebra Rd	San Antonio	TX	78238	210-684-5111	522-3990*
**Fax:* Hum Res ■ *Web:* www.swri.edu					
Space & Naval Warfare Systems Ctr					
53560 Hull St	San Diego	CA	92152	619-553-2717	553-2726
Web: www.public.navy.mil/SPAWAR/PACIFIC/PAGES/DEFAULT.ASPX					

Name / Address	City	State	Zip	Phone	Fax
Space Dynamics Laboratory					
1695 N Research Pkwy	North Logan	UT	84341	435-797-4600	797-4495
Web: www.sdl.usu.edu					
Space Physics Research Laboratory					
2455 Hayward St University of Michigan	Ann Arbor	MI	48109	734-936-7775	763-0437
Web: www.sprl.umich.edu					
Space Research Institute					
Auburn University 231 Leach Ctr	Auburn	AL	36849	334-844-5894	844-5900
Web: www.auburn.edu/research/vpr/sri					
Space Science & Engineering Ctr					
University of Wisconsin 1225 W Dayton St	Madison	WI	53706	608-262-0544	262-5974
Web: www.ssec.wisc.edu					
Space Telescope Science Institute					
3700 San Martin Dr	Baltimore	MD	21218	410-338-4700	338-4767
Web: www.stsci.edu					
SRI International 333 Ravenswood Ave	Menlo Park	CA	94025	650-859-2000	326-5512
Web: www.sri.com					
Stanford Cancer Ctr					
875 Lake Blake Wilbur Dr	Stanford	CA	94305	650-498-6000	725-9113
Web: www.cancer.stanford.edu					
Stanford Linear Accelerator Ctr (SLAC)					
2575 Sand Hill Rd	Menlo Park	CA	94025	650-926-3300	926-4999
Web: www.slac.stanford.edu					
Stanford Prevention Research Ctr					
Hoover Pavilion MC-5705 211 Quarry Rd	Stanford	CA	94305	650-723-6254	725-6906
Web: www.prevention.stanford.edu					
Stanford Synchrotron Radiation Lightsource (SSRL)					
2575 Sand Hill Rd MS 69	Menlo Park	CA	94025	650-926-2079	926-3600
Web: www-ssrl.slac.stanford.edu					
Stennis Space Ctr					
Blach Blvd Bldg 1100	Stennis Space Center	MS	39529	228-688-2211	688-1094*
**Fax:* PR ■ *Web:* www.nasa.gov					
Supercomputing Institute for Digital Simulation & Advanced Computation					
University of Minnesota					
599 Walter Library 117 Pleasant St SE	Minneapolis	MN	55455	612-625-1818	624-8861
Web: www.msi.umn.edu					
Synchrotron Radiation Ctr (SRC)					
3731 Schneider Dr	Stoughton	WI	53589	608-877-2000	877-2001
Web: www.src.wisc.edu					
Syntron Bioresearch Inc 2774 Loker Ave W	Carlsbad	CA	92010	760-930-2200	930-2212
Web: www.syntron.net					
Syracuse Research Corp (SRC)					
7502 Round Pond Rd	North Syracuse	NY	13212	315-452-8000	452-8090*
**Fax:* Hum Res ■ *TF:* 800-724-0451 ■ *Web:* www.syrres.com					
TCTI Hazardous Substance Research Ctr					
PO Box 10613	Beaumont	TX	77710	409-880-8768	880-2397
Technology Service Corp					
962 Wayne Ave Suite 800	Silver Spring	MD	20910	301-565-2970	565-0673
TERC 2067 Massachusetts Ave 2nd Fl	Cambridge	MA	02140	617-547-0430	349-3535
Web: www.terc.edu					
Texas Center for Superconductivity					
3201 Cullen Blvd # 202	Houston	TX	77204	713-743-8200	743-8201
Web: www.tcsuh.uh.edu					
Thomas Jefferson National Accelerator Facility					
12000 Jefferson Ave	Newport News	VA	23606	757-269-7100	269-7363
Web: www.jlab.org					
Thurston Arthritis Research Ctr					
University of N Carolina					
3330 Thurston Bldg CB 7280	Chapel Hill	NC	27599	919-966-0552	966-1739
Web: www.med.unc.edu/mac					
Transportation Research Center Inc (TRC Inc)					
10820 State Rt 347 PO Box B-67	East Liberty	OH	43319	937-666-2011	666-5066
TF: 800-837-7872 ■ *Web:* www.trcpg.com					
Transportation Technology Center Inc					
55500 DOT Rd PO Box 11130	Pueblo	CO	81001	719-584-0750	584-0711
Web: www.aar.com					
Trex Enterprises Corp 10455 Pacific Ctr Ct	San Diego	CA	92121	858-646-5300	646-5301
TF: 800-626-5885 ■ *Web:* www.trexenterprises.com					
Tulane National Primate Research Ctr (TNPRC)					
18703 Three Rivers Rd	Covington	LA	70433	985-862-8040	893-1352
Web: www.tpc.tulane.edu					
Turner-Fairbank Highway Research Ctr					
6300 Georgetown Pike	McLean	VA	22101	202-493-3022	493-3170
Web: www.fhwa.dot.gov					
UAB Comprehensive Cancer Ctr					
University of Alabama at Birmingham					
1824 6th Ave S	Birmingham	AL	35294	800-822-0933	
TF: 800-822-0933 ■ *Web:* www3.ccc.uab.edu					
UNC Neuroscience Ctr					
University of N Carolina					
115 Mason Farm Rd CB 7250	Chapel Hill	NC	27599	919-843-8536	966-1050
Web: www.med.unc.edu/neuroscience					
University of Chicago Cancer Research Ctr					
5841 S Maryland Ave MC1140	Chicago	IL	60637	773-834-7490	834-7855
Web: www.cancer.uchicago.edu					
University of Maryland Biotechnology Institute					
9600 Gudelsky Dr	Rockville	MD	20850	240-314-6000	314-6255
Web: www.umbi.umd.edu					
University of Maryland Center for Environmental Science (UMCES)					
2020 Horn Pt Rd	Cambridge	MD	21613	410-228-9250	228-3843
Web: www.umces.edu					
University of Michigan Transportation Research Institute (UMTRI)					
2901 Baxter Rd	Ann Arbor	MI	48109	734-764-6504	936-1081
Web: www.umtri.umich.edu					
University of Texas Institute for Geophysics (UTIG)					
JJ Pickle Research Campus Bldg 196					
10100 Burnet Rd (RR2200)	Austin	TX	78758	512-471-6156	471-8844
Web: www.ig.utexas.edu					
US Arid-Land Agricultural Research Ctr					
USDA/ARS 21881 N Cardon Ln	Mariposa	AZ	85239	520-316-6310	
Web: www.ars.usda.gov					
US Army Aeromedical Research Laboratory					
MCMR-UAC Bldg 6901	Fort Rucker	AL	36362	334-255-6920	255-6933
TF: 888-386-7635 ■ *Web:* www.usaarl.army.mil					

Phone | Fax

US Army Armament Research Development & Engineering Ctr (ARDEC)
Technical Research Ctr Bldg 59 .... Picatinny NJ 07806 973-724-5898 724-3044
Web: www.pica.army.mil

US Army Aviation & Missile Research Development & Engineering Ctr (AMRDEC)
5400 Bldg. .... Redstone Arsenal AL 35898 256-313-5742 876-9142
Web: www.redstone.army.mil/amrdec

US Army Benet Laboratories
Watervliet Arsenal
1 Buffington St AMSTA-AR-CCB, Bldg 40 .... Watervliet NY 12189 518-266-5418 266-3686
Web: www.benet.wva.army.mil

US Army Center for Environmental Health Research
ATTN: MCMR-CDE-Z 568 Doughten Dr .... Fort Detrick MD 21702 301-619-7685 619-7606
Web: www.usacehr.amedd.army.mil

US Army Communications-Electronics Research Development & Engineering Ctr (CERDEC)
ATTN: AMSRD-CER-D Myers Ctr Bldg 2700 ...... Fort Monmouth NJ 07703 732-532-5225 532-0749
Web: www.cerdec.army.mil

US Army Corps of Engineers Institute for Water Resources
Hydrologic Engineering Ctr 609 2nd St. .... Davis CA 95616 530-756-1104 756-8250
Web: www.hec.usace.army.mil

US Army Engineer Research & Development Ctr (ERDC)
3909 Halls Ferry Rd .... Vicksburg MS 39180 601-634-3188 634-2388
TF: 800-522-6937 ■ *Web:* www.erdc.usace.army.mil

US Army Institute of Surgical Research (USAISR)
3698 Chamber Pass .... Fort Sam Houston TX 78234 210-916-3219 227-8502
Web: www.usaisr.amedd.army.mil

US Army Medical Research & Materiel Command
504 Scott St .... Fort Detrick MD 21702 301-619-2736
Web: www.mrmc-www.army.mil

US Army Medical Research Institute of Chemical Defense
MCMR-CDZ
3100 Ricketts Point Rd .... Aberdeen Proving Ground MD 21010 410-436-3276 436-4160
Web: usamricd.apgea.army.mil

US Army Medical Research Institute of Infectious Diseases (USAMRIID)
ATTN: MCMR-UIZ-R 1425 Porter St. .... Frederick MD 21702 301-619-2285
Web: www.usamriid.army.mil

US Army Natick Research Development & Engineering Ctr
Kansas St .... Natick MA 01760 508-233-4514
Web: www.nsrdec.natick.army.mil

US Army Research Institute for the Behavioral & Social Sciences (ARI)
2511 Jefferson Davis Hwy .... Arlington VA 22202 703-602-8049
Web: www.hqda.army.mil/ari

US Army Research Institute of Environmental Medicine (USARIEM)
MCMR-UEMZ Bldg 42 Kansas St. .... Natick MA 01760 508-233-4811 233-5298
Web: www.usariem.army.mil

US Army Research Laboratory (ARL)
ATTN: AMSRD-ARL-O-PA 2800 Powder Mill Rd .... Adelphi MD 20783 301-394-2500 394-1174
TF: 800-276-9522 ■ *Web:* www.arl.army.mil

US Army Tank-Automotive Research Development & Engineering Ctr (TARDEC)
6501 E 11 Mile Rd .... Warren MI 48397 586-574-5494 574-6013
Web: www.tardec.army.mil

US Coast Guard Research & Development Ctr
1082 Shennecossett Rd .... Groton CT 06340 860-441-2600 441-2792
Web: www.uscg.mil/hq

US Dairy Forage Research Ctr (DFRC)
1925 Linden Dr W .... Madison WI 53706 608-890-0050
Web: www.dfrc.ars.usda.gov

US Horticultural Research Laboratory
2001 S Rock Rd .... Fort Pierce FL 34945 772-462-5800 462-5986
Web: www.ars.usda.gov/Main/docs.htm?docid=7376

US Salinity Laboratory
USDA/ARS 450 W Big Springs Rd .... Riverside CA 92507 951-369-4814 369-4818
Web: www.ars.usda.gov/AboutUs/AboutUs.htm?modecode=53-10-20-00

US Vegetable Laboratory
USDA/ARS 2700 Savannah Hwy. .... Charleston SC 29414 843-402-5300
Web: www.ars.usda.gov/Main/docs.htm?docid=5953

USC Information Sciences Institute
4676 Admiralty Way Suite 1001 .... Marina del Rey CA 90292 310-822-1511 823-6714

USGS Forest & Rangeland Ecosystem Science Ctr
777 NW 9th St Suite 400 .... Corvallis OR 97330 541-750-1030 750-1069
Web: fresc.usgs.gov

USGS Great Lakes Science Ctr 1451 Green Rd .... Ann Arbor MI 48105 734-994-3331 994-8780
Web: www.glsc.usgs.gov

USGS Leetown Science Ctr
11649 Leetown Rd .... Kearneysville WV 25430 304-724-4400 724-4410
Web: www.lsc.usgs.gov

USGS Northern Rocky Mountain Science Ctr (NRMSC)
2327 University Way Suite 2. .... Bozeman MT 59715 406-994-4293 994-6556
Web: www.nrmsc.usgs.gov

USGS Southwest Biological Science Ctr
2255 N Gemini Dr MS-9394. .... Flagstaff AZ 86001 928-556-7094 556-7092
Web: sbsc.wr.usgs.gov

USGS Upper Midwest Environmental Sciences Ctr
2630 Fanta Reed Rd .... La Crosse WI 54603 608-783-6451 783-6066
Web: www.umesc.usgs.gov

USGS Western Fisheries Research Ctr
US Geological Survey 6505 NE 65th St .... Seattle WA 98115 206-526-6282 526-6654
Web: www.wfrc.usgs.gov

Vanderbilt Kennedy Center for Research on Human Development
21st Ave S. .... Nashville TN 37203 615-322-8240 322-8236
Web: www.kc.vanderbilt.edu

Venture Design Services Inc 1051 S E St .... Anaheim CA 92805 714-765-3740
Web: www.venture.com.sg

Virginia Institute of Marine Science (VIMS)
1208 Greate Rd PO Box 1346. .... Gloucester Point VA 23062 804-684-7000 684-7097
Web: www.vims.edu

Visidyne Inc 10 Corporate Pl S Bedford St .... Burlington MA 01803 781-273-2820 272-1068
Web: www.visidyne.com

Wadsworth Ctr
Biggs Laboratory New York Dept of Health
Empire State Plaza PO Box 509 .... Albany NY 12201 518-474-2160
Web: www.wadsworth.org

Waisman Ctr
University of Wisconsin 1500 Highland Ave. .... Madison WI 53705 608-263-5940 263-0529
Web: www.waisman.wisc.edu

Walter Reed Army Institute of Research (WRAIR)
MCMR-UWZ 503 Robert Grant Ave .... Silver Spring MD 20910 301-319-9100 319-9227
Web: wrair-www.army.mil

Washington National Primate Research Ctr
1705 NE Pacific St PO Box 357330 .... Seattle WA 98195 206-543-0440 685-0305
Web: www.wanprc.org/WaNPRC

WestEd 730 Harrison St 5th Fl .... San Francisco CA 94107 415-565-3000 565-3012
TF: 877-493-7833 ■ *Web:* www.wested.org

Western Human Nutrition Research Ctr
WSDA/ARS/WHNRC 430 W Health Sciences 1 Shields Ave
University of California .... Davis CA 95616 530-752-5276 752-5271
Web: www.ars.usda.gov/main/site_main.htm?modecode=53-06-25-00

Western Regional Research Ctr (WRRC)
800 Buchanan St .... Albany CA 94710 510-559-5600 559-5963
Web: www.ars.usda.gov/Main/docs.htm?docid=5819

Western Research Institute 365 N 9th St .... Laramie WY 82072 307-721-2011 721-2345
Web: www.wri.uwyo.edu

Wisconsin Center for Education Research
University of Wisconsin Madison
1025 W Johnson St .... Madison WI 53706 608-263-4200 263-6448
Web: www.wcer.wisc.edu

Wisconsin National Primate Research Ctr
1220 Capitol Ct .... Madison WI 53715 608-263-3500 265-2067
Web: www.primate.wisc.edu

Wistar Institute 3601 Spruce St. .... Philadelphia PA 19104 215-898-3700 898-3715
TF: 800-724-6633 ■ *Web:* www.wistar.upenn.edu

WM Keck Center for Comparative & Functional Genomics
340 Edward R Madigan Laboratory
1201 W Gregory Dr. .... Urbana IL 61801 217-265-5057 265-5066
Web: www.biotec.uiuc.edu/centers/Keck

WM Keck Observatory 65-1120 Mamalahoa Hwy .... Kamuela HI 96743 808-885-7887 885-4464
Web: www.keckobservatory.org

Woods Hole Oceanographic Institution (WHOI)
86 Water St MS Suite 19 .... Woods Hole MA 02543 508-289-2282 457-2109*
**Fax:* Hum Res ■ *Web:* www.whoi.edu

Yale Child Study Ctr
Yale University 230 S Frontage Rd .... New Haven CT 06520 203-785-2540 785-7611
Web: www.medicine.yale.edu

Yerkes National Primate Research Ctr
Emory University 954 Gatewood Rd .... Atlanta GA 30322 404-727-7732 727-3108
Web: www.yerkes.emory.edu

672 RESORTS & RESORT COMPANIES

SEE ALSO Casinos p. 1558; Dude Ranches p. 1789; Hotels - Conference Center p. 2079; Hotels & Hotel Companies p. 2081; Spas - Hotel & Resort p. 2659

ALABAMA

Phone | Fax

Joe Wheeler Resort Lodge & Convention Ctr
4401 McLean Dr. .... Rogersville AL 35652 256-247-5461 247-5471
TF: 800-544-5639

Perdido Beach Resort
27200 Perdido Beach Blvd .... Orange Beach AL 36561 251-981-9811 981-5670
TF: 800-634-8001 ■ *Web:* www.perdidobeachresort.com

StillWaters Resort 797 Moonbrook Dr. .... Dadeville AL 36853 256-825-1353 825-4147
TF: 800-687-3732 ■ *Web:* www.stillwatersgolf.com

ALASKA

Phone | Fax

Alyeska Prince Hotel & Resort
1000 Arlberg Ave PO Box 249 .... Girdwood AK 99587 907-754-1111 754-2200
TF: 800-880-3880 ■ *Web:* www.alyeskaresort.com

Pybus Point Lodge PO Box 33497 .... Juneau AK 99801 907-790-4866 790-4866
Web: www.pybus.com

Whalers' Cove Lodge PO Box 101 .... Angoon AK 99820 907-788-3123 788-3104
TF: 800-423-3123 ■ *Web:* www.whalerscovelodge.com

ALBERTA

Phone | Fax

Delta Lodge at Kananaskis
1 Centennial Dr. .... Kananaskis Village AB T0L2H0 403-591-7711 591-7770
TF: 866-432-4322 ■
Web: www.deltahotels.com/hotels/hotels.php?hotelId=30

Fairmont Banff Springs PO Box 960. .... Banff AB T1L1J4 403-762-2211 762-5755
TF: 800-441-1414 ■ *Web:* www.fairmont.com

Fairmont Chateau Lake Louise
111 Lake Louise Dr. .... Lake Louise AB T0L1E0 403-522-3511 522-3834
TF: 800-441-1414 ■ *Web:* www.fairmont.com

Rimrock Resort Hotel The
300 Mountain Ave PO Box 1110. .... Banff AB T1L1J2 403-762-3356 762-4132
TF: 888-746-7625 ■ *Web:* www.rimrockresort.com

Waterton Lakes Lodge Resort
101 Clematis Ave PO Box 4 .... Waterton Park AB T0K2M0 403-859-2150 859-2229
TF: 888-985-6343 ■ *Web:* www.watertonlakeslodge.com

ARIZONA

Name / Address	City	State	Zip	Phone	Fax
Arizona Biltmore Resort & Spa 2400 E Missouri *TF:* 800-950-0086 ■ *Web:* www.arizonabiltmore.com	Phoenix	AZ	85016	602-955-6600	381-7600
Arizona Golf Resort & Conference Ctr 425 S Power Rd *TF:* 800-528-8282 ■ *Web:* www.arizonagolfresort.com	Mesa	AZ	85206	480-832-3202	981-0151
Arizona Grand Resort 8000 S Arizona Grand Pkwy *TF:* 866-267-1321 ■ *Web:* www.arizonagrandresort.com	Phoenix	AZ	85044	602-438-9000	431-6535
Boulders Resort & Golden Door Spa 34631 N Tom Darlington Dr PO Box 2090 *TF:* 866-397-6520 ■ *Web:* www.theboulders.com	Carefree	AZ	85377	480-488-9009	488-4118
Camelback Inn JW Marriott Resort Golf Club & Spa 5402 E Lincoln Dr *TF:* 800-242-2635 ■ *Web:* www.camelbackinn.com	Scottsdale	AZ	85253	480-948-1700	596-7029
Canyon Ranch Tucson 8600 E Rockcliff Rd *TF:* 800-742-9000 ■ *Web:* www.canyonranch.com/tucson	Tucson	AZ	85750	520-749-9000	749-1646
Chaparral Suites Resort & Conference Ctr 5001 N Scottsdale Rd *TF:* 800-528-1456 ■ *Web:* www.chaparralsuites.com	Scottsdale	AZ	85250	480-949-1414	947-2675
CopperWynd Resort & Club 13225 N Eagle Ridge Dr *TF:* 877-707-7760 ■ *Web:* www.copperwynd.com	Fountain Hills	AZ	85268	480-333-1900	333-1901
Doubletree Paradise Valley Resort 5401 N Scottsdale Rd *TF:* 800-222-8733 ■ *Web:* www.doubletree1.hilton.com	Scottsdale	AZ	85250	480-947-5400	443-9702
Enchantment Resort 525 Boynton Canyon Rd *TF:* 800-826-4180 ■ *Web:* www.enchantmentresort.com	Sedona	AZ	86336	928-282-2900	282-9249
Esplendor Resort at Rio Rico 1069 Camino Caralampi *TF:* 800-288-4746 ■ *Web:* www.esplendor-resort.com	Rio Rico	AZ	85648	520-281-1901	281-7132
Fairmont Scottsdale Princess 7575 E Princess Dr *TF:* 800-344-4758 ■ *Web:* www.fairmont.com	Scottsdale	AZ	85255	480-585-4848	585-0086
FireSky Resort & Spa 4925 N Scottsdale Rd *TF:* 800-528-7867 ■ *Web:* www.fireskyresort.com	Scottsdale	AZ	85251	480-945-7666	946-4056
Four Seasons Resort Scottsdale at Troon North 10600 E Crescent Moon Dr *TF:* 800-332-3442 ■ *Web:* www.fourseasons.com	Scottsdale	AZ	85262	480-515-5700	515-5599
Francisco Grande Hotel & Golf Resort 26000 Gila Bend Hwy *TF:* 866-589-3411 ■ *Web:* www.franciscogrande.com	Phoenix	AZ	85222	520-836-6444	421-0544
Gold Canyon Golf Resort 6100 S Kings Ranch Rd *TF:* 800-624-6445 ■ *Web:* www.gcgr.com	Gold Canyon	AZ	85218	480-982-9090	830-5211
Hacienda del Sol Guest Ranch Resort 5601 N Hacienda Del Sol Rd *TF:* 800-728-6514 ■ *Web:* www.haciendadelsol.com	Tucson	AZ	85718	520-299-1501	299-5554
Harrah's Ak-Chin Casino Resort 15406 Maricopa Rd *TF Sales:* 888-302-3293 ■ *Web:* www.totalrewards.com	Maricopa	AZ	85239	480-802-5000	802-5048
Hilton Sedona Resort & Spa 90 Ridge Trail Dr *TF:* 800-222-8733 ■ *Web:* www1.hilton.com	Sedona	AZ	86351	928-284-4040	284-6940
JW Marriott Desert Ridge Resort & Spa 5350 E Marriott Dr *TF:* 800-898-4527 ■ *Web:* www.marriott.com/hotels/travel/phxdr	Phoenix	AZ	85054	480-293-5000	293-3600
Lake Powell Resorts & Marinas 100 Lakeshore Dr *TF:* 800-528-6154 ■ *Web:* www.touroklahoma.com/parks.asp	Page	AZ	86040	928-645-2433	645-1031
Legacy Golf Resort 6808 S 32nd St *TF:* 888-828-3673 ■ *Web:* www.shellhospitality.com	Phoenix	AZ	85042	602-305-5500	305-5501
Lodge at Ventana Canyon - A Wyndham Luxury Resort 6200 N Clubhouse Ln *TF:* 800-828-5701 ■ *Web:* www.thelodgeatventanacanyon.com	Tucson	AZ	85750	520-577-1400	577-4065
Loews Ventana Canyon Resort 7000 N Resort Dr *TF:* 800-234-5117 ■ *Web:* www.loewshotels.com	Tucson	AZ	85750	520-299-2020	299-6832
Los Abrigados Resort 160 Portal Ln *TF:* 800-521-3131 ■ *Web:* www.losabrigados.com	Sedona	AZ	86336	928-282-1777	282-2614
Millennium Resort Scottsdale McCormick Ranch 7401 N Scottsdale Rd *TF:* 800-243-1332 ■ *Web:* www1.millenniumhotels.com	Scottsdale	AZ	85253	480-948-5050	991-5572
Omni Tucson National Golf Resort & Spa 2727 W Club Dr *Web:* www.tucsonnational.com	Tucson	AZ	85742	520-297-2271	297-7544
Orange Tree Golf & Conference Resort 10601 N 56th St *TF:* 866-729-7159 ■ *Web:* www.shellhospitality.com/hotels/orange_resort	Scottsdale	AZ	85254	480-948-6100	483-6074
Phoenician The 6000 E Camelback Rd *TF:* 800-888-8234 ■ *Web:* www.thephoenician.com	Scottsdale	AZ	85251	480-941-8200	947-4311
Pointe Hilton at Squaw Peak Resort 7677 N 16th St *TF:* 800-685-0550 ■ *Web:* www.pointehilton.com	Phoenix	AZ	85020	602-997-2626	997-2391
Pointe Hilton Resort at Tapatio Cliffs 11111 N 7th St *TF:* 800-876-4683 ■ *Web:* www.pointehilton.com	Phoenix	AZ	85020	602-866-7500	993-0276
Radisson Fort McDowell Resort 10438 N Fort McDowell Rd *TF:* 800-333-3333 ■ *Web:* www.radissonfortmcdowellresort.com	Scottsdale	AZ	85264	480-789-5300	836-5333
Rancho de los Caballeros 1551 S Vulture Mine Rd *TF:* 800-684-5030 ■ *Web:* www.ranchodeloscaballeros.com	Wickenburg	AZ	85390	928-684-5484	684-2267
Renaissance Scottsdale Resort 6160 N Scottsdale Rd	Scottsdale	AZ	85253	480-991-1414	951-3350
Ritz-Carlton Phoenix 2401 E Camelback Rd *TF:* 800-241-3333 ■ *Web:* www.ritzcarlton.com/hotels/phoenix	Phoenix	AZ	85016	602-468-0700	468-0793
Royal Palms Resort & Spa 5200 E Camelback Rd *TF:* 800-672-6011 ■ *Web:* www.royalpalmshotel.com	Phoenix	AZ	85018	602-840-3610	840-6927
Saguaro Lake Ranch 13020 Bush Hwy *Web:* www.saguarolakeranch.com	Mesa	AZ	85215	480-984-2194	380-1489
Sanctuary on Camelback Mountain 5700 E McDonald Dr *TF:* 800-245-2051 ■ *Web:* www.sanctuaryoncamelback.com	Paradise Valley	AZ	85253	480-948-2100	948-7314
Scottsdale Camelback Resort 6302 E Camelback Rd *TF:* 800-891-8585 ■ *Web:* www.scottsdalecamelback.com	Scottsdale	AZ	85251	480-947-3300	994-0594
Scottsdale Plaza Resort 7200 N Scottsdale Rd *TF:* 800-832-2025 ■ *Web:* www.scottsdaleplaza.com	Scottsdale	AZ	85253	480-948-5000	998-5971
Sedona Rouge Resort & Spa 2250 W Hwy 89A *TF:* 866-589-3411 ■ *Web:* www.sedonarouge.com	Sedona	AZ	86336	928-203-4111	203-9040
Sheraton San Marcos Golf Resort & Conference Ctr 1 San Marcos Pl *TF:* 800-528-8071 ■ *Web:* www.sanmarcosresort.com	Chandler	AZ	85225	480-812-0900	963-6777
Sheraton Wild Horse Pass Resort & Spa 5594 W Wild Horse Pass Blvd *TF:* 800-325-3535 ■ *Web:* www.wildhorsepassresort.com	Chandler	AZ	85226	602-225-0100	225-0300
Tanque Verde Guest Ranch 14301 E Speedway Blvd *TF:* 800-234-3833 ■ *Web:* www.tvgr.com	Tucson	AZ	85748	520-296-6275	721-9426
Westward Look Resort 245 E Ina Rd *TF:* 800-722-2500 ■ *Web:* www.westwardlook.com	Tucson	AZ	85704	520-297-1151	297-9023
Wigwam Golf Resort & Spa 300 E Wigwam Blvd *TF:* 800-327-0396 ■ *Web:* www.wigwamresort.com	Litchfield Park	AZ	85340	623-935-3811	935-3737
Xona Resort Suites of Scottsdale 7677 E Princess Blvd *TF:* 888-222-1059 ■ *Web:* www.resortsuites.com	Scottsdale	AZ	85255	480-585-1234	585-1457

ARKANSAS

Name / Address	City	State	Zip	Phone	Fax
Arlington Resort Hotel & Spa 239 Central Ave *TF:* 800-643-1502 ■ *Web:* www.arlingtonhotel.com	Hot Springs	AR	71901	501-623-7771	623-2243
Best Western Inn of the Ozarks 207 W Van Buren *TF:* 800-552-3785 ■ *Web:* www.bestwestern.com	Eureka Springs	AR	72632	479-253-9768	253-9768
Gaston's White River Resort 1777 River Rd *Web:* www.gastons.com	Lakeview	AR	72642	870-431-5202	431-5216
Lake Hamilton Resort 2803 Albert Pike Rd *TF:* 800-469-6130	Hot Springs	AR	71913	501-767-8606	767-8576

BRITISH COLUMBIA

Name / Address	City	State	Zip	Phone	Fax
Coast Hotels & Resorts Canada 1090 W Georgia St *Web:* www.coasthotels.com	Vancouver	BC	V6E3V7	604-682-7982	682-8942
Delta Victoria Ocean Pointe Resort & Spa 45 Songhees Rd *TF:* 800-667-4677 ■ *Web:* www.deltahotels.com	Victoria	BC	V9A6T3	250-360-2999	360-5871
Delta Whistler Village Suites 4308 Main St *TF:* 888-299-3987 ■ *Web:* www.deltahotels.com	Whistler	BC	V0N1B4	604-905-3987	938-6335
Echo Valley Ranch & Spa Clinton PO Box 16 **Fax Area Code: 778* ■ *TF:* 800-253-8831 ■ *Web:* www.evranch.com	Jesmond	BC	V0K1K0	604-988-3230	340-1077*
Fairmont Chateau Whistler 4599 Chateau Blvd *TF:* 800-441-1414 ■ *Web:* www.fairmont.com	Whistler	BC	V0N1B4	604-938-8000	938-2291
Four Seasons Resort Whistler 4591 Blackcomb Way *Web:* www.fourseasons.com/whistler	Whistler	BC	V0N1B4	604-935-3400	935-3455
Harrison Hot Springs Resort & Spa 100 Esplanade Ave *TF:* 800-663-2266 ■ *Web:* www.harrisonresort.com	Harrison Hot Springs	BC	V0M1K0	604-796-2244	796-3682
Hilton Whistler Resort & Spa 4050 Whistler Way *TF:* 800-515-4050 ■ *Web:* www.hiltonwhistler.com	Whistler	BC	V0N1B4	604-932-1982	966-5093
Holiday Inn SunSpree Resort Whistler Village 4295 Blackcomb Way *TF:* 800-229-3188 ■ *Web:* www.ichotelsgroup.com/h/d/hi/home	Whistler	BC	V0N1B4	604-938-0878	938-9943
Holiday Trails Resorts(Western) Inc 53730 Bridal Falls Rd *TF:* 800-663-2265 ■ *Web:* www.holidaytrailsresorts.com	Rosedale	BC	V0X1X0	604-794-7876	794-3756
Intrawest ULC 200 Burrard St Suite 800 *Web:* www.intrawest.com	Vancouver	BC	V6C3L6	604-669-9777	683-6778
Pan Pacific Whistler Mountainside 4320 Sundial Crescent *TF:* 888-905-9995 ■ *Web:* whistler.panpacific.com	Whistler	BC	V0N1B4	604-905-2999	905-2995
River Rock Casino Resort 8811 River Rd *TF:* 866-748-3718 ■ *Web:* www.riverrock.com	Richmond	BC	V6X3P8	604-247-8900	247-2641
Tantalus Resort Lodge 4200 Whistler Way *TF:* 888-633-4046 ■ *Web:* www.tantaluslodge.com	Whistler	BC	V0N1B4	604-932-4146	932-2405
Whistler Blackcomb Mountain Ski Resort 4545 Blackcomb Way *TF:* 800-766-0449 ■ *Web:* www.whistlerblackcomb.com	Whistler	BC	V0N1B4	604-932-3434	938-7527

CALIFORNIA

Name / Address	City	State	Zip	Phone	Fax
Alisal Guest Ranch & Resort 1054 Alisal Rd *TF:* 800-425-4725 ■ *Web:* www.alisal.com	Solvang	CA	93463	805-688-6411	688-2510
Alpine Meadows Ski Resort 2600 Alpine Meadows Rd PO Box 5279 *TF:* 800-441-4423 ■ *Web:* www.skialpine.com	Tahoe City	CA	96145	530-583-4232	583-0963
Bacara Resort & Spa 8301 Hollister Ave *TF:* 877-422-4245 ■ *Web:* www.bacararesort.com	Santa Barbara	CA	93117	805-968-0100	968-1800
Bahia Resort Hotel 998 W Mission Bay Dr *TF:* 800-576-4229 ■ *Web:* www.bahiahotel.com	San Diego	CA	92109	858-488-0551	488-7055
Balboa Bay Club & Resort 1221 W Coast Hwy *TF:* 888-445-7153 ■ *Web:* www.balboabayclub.com	Newport Beach	CA	92663	949-645-5000	630-4315
Barona Resort & Casino 1932 Wildcat Canyon Rd *TF:* 888-722-7662 ■ *Web:* www.barona.com	Lakeside	CA	92040	619-443-2300	443-1794
Bear Mountain Golf Course 43101 Gold Mine Dr PO Box 77 *Web:* www.bigbearmountainresorts.com	Big Bear Lake	CA	92315	909-585-2519	585-6805
Booth Creek Ski Holdings Inc 11025 Pioneer Trail Suite G100 *Web:* www.boothcreek.com	Truckee	CA	96161	530-550-7112	550-5116
Calistoga Ranch 580 Lommel Rd	Calistoga	CA	94515	707-254-2800	254-2825

	City	State	ZIP	Phone	Fax
TF: 800-942-4220 ■ *Web:* www.calistogaranch.com					
Carmel Valley Ranch Resort 1 Old Ranch Rd / *TF:* 866-282-4745 ■ *Web:* www.carmelvalleyranch.com	Carmel	CA	93923	831-625-9500	624-2858
Casa Palmero 1518 Cypress Dr / *TF:* 800-654-9300 ■ *Web:* www.pebble-beach.com	Pebble Beach	CA	93953	831-647-7500	644-7955
Catalina Canyon Resort & Spa 888 Country Club Dr PO Box 736 / *TF:* 888-478-7829 ■ *Web:* www.catalinacanyonresort.com	Avalon	CA	90704	310-510-0325	510-0900
Chaminade 1 Chaminade Ln / *TF:* 800-283-6569 ■ *Web:* www.chaminade.com	Santa Cruz	CA	95065	831-475-5600	476-4798
Claremont Resort & Spa 41 Tunnel Rd / *TF:* 800-551-7266 ■ *Web:* www.claremontresort.com	Berkeley	CA	94705	510-843-3000	848-6208
Costanoa Coastal Lodge & Camp 2001 Rossi Rd / *TF:* 877-262-7848 ■ *Web:* www.costanoa.com	Pescadero	CA	94060	650-879-1100	879-2275
Desert Hot Springs Spa Hotel 10805 Palm Dr / *TF:* 800-808-7727 ■ *Web:* www.dhsspa.com	Desert Hot Springs	CA	92240	760-329-6000	329-6915
Desert Springs Marriott Resort & Spa 74855 Country Club Dr / *TF:* 800-331-3112 ■ *Web:* www.desertspringsresort.com	Palm Desert	CA	92260	760-341-2211	341-1872
Doral Desert Princess Palm Springs Resort 67967 Vista Chino / *TF:* 888-386-4677 ■ *Web:* www.doralpalmsprings.com	Cathedral City	CA	92234	760-322-7000	322-6853
Double Eagle Resort & Spa 5587 Hwy 158 PO Box 736 / *Web:* www.doubleeagle.com	June Lake	CA	93529	760-648-7004	648-8225
Dr Wilkinson's Hot Springs Resort 1507 Lincoln Ave / *Web:* www.drwilkinson.com	Calistoga	CA	94515	707-942-4102	942-4412
Estancia La Jolla Hotel & Spa 9700 N Torrey Pines Rd / *Web:* www.estancialajolla.com	La Jolla	CA	92037	858-550-1000	550-1001
Fairmont Hotels & Resorts Inc 1 Beach St / *Web:* www.fairmont.com	San Francisco	CA	94133	415-772-7800	772-7805
Fairmont Sonoma Mission Inn & Spa The PO Box 1447 / *TF:* 866-540-4499 ■ *Web:* www.fairmont.com/sonoma	Sonoma	CA	95476	707-938-9000	938-4250
Fess Parker's Doubletree Resort (FPDTR) 633 E Cabrillo Blvd / *TF:* 800-222-8733 ■ *Web:* www.fessparkersantabarbarahotel.com	Santa Barbara	CA	93103	805-564-4333	564-4964
Flamingo Resort Hotel & Conference Ctr 2777 4th St / *TF:* 800-848-8300 ■ *Web:* www.flamingohotel.com	Santa Rosa	CA	95405	707-545-8530	528-1404
Four Seasons Resort Aviara 7100 Four Seasons Pt / *TF:* 800-332-3442 ■ *Web:* www.fourseasons.com/aviara	Carlsbad	CA	92009	760-603-6800	603-6801
Four Seasons Resort Santa Barbara 1260 Ch Dr / *TF:* 888-424-5866 ■ *Web:* www.fourseasons.com	Santa Barbara	CA	93108	805-969-2261	565-8321
Furnace Creek Inn & Ranch Resort Hwy 190 PO Box 187 / *Web:* www.furnacecreekresort.com	Death Valley	CA	92328	760-786-2345	786-2514
Grand Pacific Palisades Resort & Hotel 5805 Armada Dr / *TF:* 800-725-4723 ■ *Web:* www.grandpacificpalisades.com	Carlsbad	CA	92008	760-827-3200	827-3210
Greenhorn Creek Resort 711 McCauley Ranch Rd / *TF:* 888-736-5900 ■ *Web:* www.greenhorncreek.com	Angels Camp	CA	95222	209-736-6201	736-6210
Handlery Hotel & Resort 950 Hotel Cir N / *TF:* 800-676-6567 ■ *Web:* www.handlery.com	San Diego	CA	92108	619-298-0511	298-9793
Harrah's Rincon Casino & Resort 777 Harrah's Rincon Way / *TF:* 877-777-2457 ■ *Web:* www.totalrewards.com	Valley Center	CA	92082	760-751-3100	751-3200
Hilton San Diego Resort 1775 E Mission Bay Dr / *TF:* 877-414-8019 ■ *Web:* www.hilton.com	San Diego	CA	92109	619-276-4010	275-8944
Hilton Waterfront Beach Resort 21100 Pacific Coast Hwy / *Web:* www.hilton.com	Huntington Beach	CA	92648	714-845-8000	845-8424
Hotel Del Coronado 1500 Orange Ave / *TF:* 800-468-3533 ■ *Web:* www.hoteldel.com	Coronado	CA	92118	619-435-6611	522-8262
Indian Springs Resort & Spa 1712 Lincoln Ave / *Web:* www.indianspringscalistoga.com	Calistoga	CA	94515	707-942-4913	942-4919
Indian Wells Resort Hotel 76661 US Hwy 111 / *TF:* 800-248-3220 ■ *Web:* www.indianwellsresort.com	Indian Wells	CA	92210	760-345-6466	772-5083
Inn at Rancho Santa Fe 5951 Linea Del Cielo PO Box 869 / *TF:* 800-843-4661 ■ *Web:* www.theinnatrsf.com	Rancho Santa Fe	CA	92067	858-756-1131	759-1604
Inn at Spanish Bay The 2700 17-Mile Dr / *TF:* 800-654-9300 ■ *Web:* www.pebblebeach.com	Pebble Beach	CA	93953	831-647-7500	622-3603
Knott's Berry Farm Resort 7675 Crescent Ave / **Fax:* Resv ■ *TF:* 866-752-2444 ■ *Web:* www.radisson.com/buenaparkca	Buena Park	CA	90620	714-995-1111	952-9545*
L'Auberge Del Mar 1540 Camino del Mar PO Box 2880 / *TF:* 800-245-9757 ■ *Web:* www.laubergedelmar.com	Del Mar	CA	92014	858-259-1515	755-4940
La Costa Resort & Spa 2100 Costa del Mar Rd / *TF:* 800-854-5000 ■ *Web:* www.lacosta.com	Carlsbad	CA	92009	760-438-9111	438-3758
La Jolla Beach & Tennis Club 2000 Spindrift Dr / *TF:* 800-237-5211 ■ *Web:* www.ljbtc.com	La Jolla	CA	92037	858-454-7126	456-3805
La Quinta Resort & Club 49-499 Eisenhower Dr / *TF:* 800-598-3828 ■ *Web:* www.laquintaresort.com	La Quinta	CA	92253	760-564-4111	564-7625
Laguna Cliffs Marriott Resort 25135 Pk Lantern / *TF:* 800-228-9290 ■ *Web:* www.lagunacliffs.com	Dana Point	CA	92629	949-661-5000	661-5358
Lake Arrowhead Resort & Spa 27984 Hwy 189 / *TF:* 800-800-6792 ■ *Web:* www.laresort.com	Lake Arrowhead	CA	92352	909-336-1511	744-3088
Lakeland Village Beach & Mountain Resort 3535 Lake Tahoe Blvd / *TF:* 800-822-5969 ■ *Web:* www.lakeland-village.com	South Lake Tahoe	CA	96150	530-544-1685	541-6278
Lawrence Welks Desert Oasis 34567 Cathedral Canyon Dr / *TF:* 800-824-8224 ■ *Web:* www.welkresort.com	Cathedral City	CA	92234	760-321-9000	321-6200
Le Parker Meridien Palm Springs 4200 E Palm Canyon Dr / *Web:* www.starwoodhotels.com/lemeridien	Palm Springs	CA	92264	760-770-5000	324-2188
Leisure Sports Inc 7077 Koll Ctr Pkwy Suite 110 / *Web:* www.leisuresportsinc.com	Pleasanton	CA	94566	925-600-1966	600-1144
Lodge at Pebble Beach 1500 Cypress Dr / *TF Resv:* 800-654-9300	Pebble Beach	CA	93953	831-624-3811	625-8598
Lodge at Sonoma - A Renaissance Resort & Spa 1325 Broadway / *TF:* 866-263-0758 ■ *Web:* www.thelodgeatsonoma.com	Sonoma	CA	95476	707-935-6600	935-6829
Lodge at Torrey Pines Inn 11480 N Torrey Pines Rd / *Web:* www.lodgeattorreypines.com	La Jolla	CA	92037	858-453-4420	550-3908
Loews Coronado Bay Resort 4000 Coronado Bay Rd / *TF:* 800-815-6397 ■ *Web:* www.loewshotels.com/hotels/sandiego	Coronado	CA	92118	619-424-4000	424-4400
Mammoth Mountain Resort 1 Minaret Rd PO Box 24 / *TF:* 800-626-6684 ■ *Web:* www.mammothmountain.com	Mammoth Lakes	CA	93546	760-934-2571	934-0615
Meadowood Napa Valley 900 Meadowood Ln / *TF:* 800-458-8080 ■ *Web:* www.meadowood.com	Saint Helena	CA	94574	707-963-3646	963-3532
Miramonte Resort & Spa 45000 Indian Wells Ln / *TF:* 800-237-2926 ■ *Web:* www.miramonteresort.com	Indian Wells	CA	92210	760-341-2200	568-0541
Montage Resort & Spa 30801 S Coast Hwy / *TF:* 866-271-6953 ■ *Web:* www.montagelagunabeach.com	Laguna Beach	CA	92651	949-715-6001	715-6070
Montage Resort & Spa Laguna Beach 30801 S Coast Hwy / *Web:* www.montagelagunabeach.com	Laguna Beach	CA	92651	949-715-6000	715-6100
Morgan Run Resort & Club 5690 Cancha de Golf / *TF Resv:* 800-378-4653 ■ *Web:* www.clubcorp.com	Rancho Santa Fe	CA	92091	858-756-2471	756-3013
Morongo Casino Resort & Spa 49500 Seminole Dr / *TF:* 800-252-4499 ■ *Web:* www.morongocasinoresort.com	Cabazon	CA	92230	951-849-3080	755-5735
Mount Shasta Resort 1000 Siskiyou Lake Blvd / *TF:* 800-958-3363 ■ *Web:* www.mountshastaresort.com	Mount Shasta	CA	96067	530-926-3030	926-0333
Northstar-at-Tahoe PO Box 129 / *TF:* 800-466-6784 ■ *Web:* www.northstarattahoe.com	Truckee	CA	96160	530-562-1010	562-3812
Ojai Valley Inn & Spa 905 Country Club Rd / *TF:* 800-422-6524 ■ *Web:* www.ojairesort.com	Ojai	CA	93023	805-640-2068	646-0904
Pacific Palms Conference Resort 1 Industry Hills Pkwy / *TF Cust Svc:* 800-524-4557 ■ *Web:* www.pacificpalmsresort.com	City of Industry	CA	91744	626-810-4455	964-9535
Pala Casino Resort & Spa 35008 Pala-Temecula Rd / *TF:* 877-946-7252 ■ *Web:* www.palacasino.com	Pala	CA	92059	760-510-5100	510-5191
Pala Mesa Resort 2001 Old Hwy 395 / *TF:* 800-722-4700 ■ *Web:* www.palamesa.com	Fallbrook	CA	92028	760-728-5881	723-8292
Palm Mountain Resort & Spa 155 S Belardo Rd / *TF:* 800-622-9451 ■ *Web:* www.palmmountainresort.com	Palm Springs	CA	92262	760-325-1301	323-8937
Pan Pacific Hotels & Resorts 500 Post St / *TF:* 800-327-8585 ■ *Web:* www.panpacific.com	San Francisco	CA	94102	415-732-7747	732-5800
Paradise Point Resort & Spa 1404 W Vacation Rd / *TF:* 800-344-2626 ■ *Web:* www.paradisepoint.com	San Diego	CA	92109	858-274-4630	581-5929
Pechanga Resort & Casino 45000 Pechanga Pkwy / *TF:* 877-711-2946 ■ *Web:* www.pechanga.com	Temecula	CA	92592	951-693-1819	695-7410
Post Ranch Inn Hwy 1 PO Box 219 / **Fax:* Resv ■ *TF Resv:* 888-524-4787 ■ *Web:* www.postranchinn.com	Big Sur	CA	93920	831-667-2200	667-2512*
Quail Lodge Resort & Golf Club 8205 Valley Greens Dr / *TF:* 800-538-9516 ■ *Web:* www.quaillodge.com	Carmel	CA	93923	831-624-2888	624-3726
Rancho Bernardo Inn 17550 Bernardo Oaks Dr / *TF:* 877-517-9342 ■ *Web:* www.ranchobernardoinn.com	San Diego	CA	92128	858-675-8500	675-8501
Rancho Valencia Resort 5921 Valencia Cir PO Box 9126 / *TF:* 800-548-3664 ■ *Web:* www.ranchovalencia.com	Rancho Santa Fe	CA	92067	858-756-1123	756-0165
Renaissance Esmeralda Resort 44-400 Indian Wells Ln / *TF:* 800-552-4386 ■ *Web:* www.renaissanceesmeralda.com	Indian Wells	CA	92210	760-773-4444	346-9308
Resort at Squaw Creek 400 Squaw Creek Rd PO Box 3333 / *TF:* 800-327-3353 ■ *Web:* www.squawcreek.com	Olympic Valley	CA	96146	530-583-6300	581-6632
Ritz-Carlton Half Moon Bay 1 Miramontes Pt Rd / *TF:* 800-244-3333 ■ *Web:* www.ritzcarlton.com	Half Moon Bay	CA	94019	650-712-7000	712-7015
Ritz-Carlton Huntington Hotel & Spa 1401 S Oak Knoll Ave / *TF:* 800-241-3333 ■ *Web:* www.ritzcarlton.com	Pasadena	CA	91106	626-568-3900	568-3700

	City	State	Zip	Phone	Fax
Ritz-Carlton Laguna Niguel 1 Ritz Carlton Dr *TF:* 800-241-3333 ■ *Web:* www.ritzcarlton.com/resorts/laguna_niguel	Dana Point	CA	92629	949-240-2000	240-1061
Saint Regis Monarch Beach Resort & Spa 1 Monarch Beach Resort *TF:* 800-722-1543 ■ *Web:* www.stregismb.com	Dana Point	CA	92629	949-234-3200	234-3201
San Vicente Inn & Golf Course 24157 San Vicente Rd *TF:* 800-776-1289 ■ *Web:* www.sanvicenteresort.com	Ramona	CA	92065	760-789-8290	788-6115
San Ysidro Ranch 900 San Ysidro Ln *TF:* 800-368-6788 ■ *Web:* www.sanysidroranch.com	Montecito	CA	93108	805-565-1700	565-1995
Sea Venture Resort 100 Ocean View Ave *TF:* 800-662-5545 ■ *Web:* www.seaventure.com	Pismo Beach	CA	93449	805-773-4994	773-0924
Shadow Mountain Resort & Club 45-750 San Luis Rey *TF:* 800-472-3713 ■ *Web:* www.shadow-mountain.com	Palm Desert	CA	92260	760-346-6123	346-6518
Silverado Resort 1600 Atlas Peak Rd *TF:* 800-532-0500 ■ *Web:* www.silveradoresort.com	Napa	CA	94558	707-257-0200	257-2867
Snow Valley Mountain Resort 35100 State Hwy 18 PO Box 2337 *TF:* 800-680-7669 ■ *Web:* www.snow-valley.com	Running Springs	CA	92382	909-867-2751	867-7687
Spa Resort The 100 N Indian Canyon Dr *TF:* 800-854-1279 ■ *Web:* www.sparesortcasino.com	Palm Springs	CA	92262	760-325-1461	325-3344
Squaw Valley USA PO Box 2007 *TF:* 800-545-4350 ■ *Web:* www.squaw.com	Olympic Valley	CA	96146	530-583-6985	581-7106
Stonepine 150 E Carmel Valley Rd *Web:* www.stonepineestate.com	Carmel Valley	CA	93924	831-659-2245	659-5160
Sycuan Resort & Casino 3007 Dehesa Rd *TF:* 800-457-5568 ■ *Web:* www.sycuan.com/sycuan_resort	El Cajon	CA	92019	619-442-3425	442-9574
Tahoe Seasons Resort 3901 Saddle Rd PO Box 16300 *TF:* 800-540-4874 ■ *Web:* www.tahoeseasons.com	South Lake Tahoe	CA	96151	530-541-6700	541-0653
Temecula Creek Inn 44501 Rainbow Canyon Rd *TF:* 800-962-7335 ■ *Web:* www.temeculacreekinn.com	Temecula	CA	92592	951-694-1000	676-8961
Town & Country Resort & Convention Ctr 500 Hotel Cir N *TF:* 800-772-8527 ■ *Web:* www.towncountry.com	San Diego	CA	92108	619-291-7131	291-3584
Two Bunch Palms Resort & Spa 67425 Two Bunch Palms Trail *TF:* 877-839-3609 ■ *Web:* www.twobunchpalms.com	Desert Hot Springs	CA	92240	760-329-8791	329-1874
Ventana Inn 48123 Hwy 1 *TF:* 800-628-6500 ■ *Web:* www.ventanainn.com	Big Sur	CA	93920	831-667-2331	667-2419
Welk Resort San Diego 8860 Lawrence Welk Dr *TF Resv:* 800-932-9355 ■ *Web:* www.welkresort.com	Escondido	CA	92026	760-749-3000	749-9537
Winner's Circle Resort 550 Via de la Valle *Web:* www.winnerscircleresort.com	Solana Beach	CA	92075	858-755-6666	481-3706

COLORADO

	City	State	Zip	Phone	Fax
Aspen Meadows Resort 845 Meadows Rd *TF:* 800-452-4240	Aspen	CO	81611	970-925-4240	925-7790
Aspen Skiing Co 117 ABC *TF:* 800-308-6935 ■ *Web:* www.aspensnowmass.com	Aspen	CO	81611	970-925-1220	429-3219
Beaver Run Resort & Conference Ctr 620 Village Rd *TF:* 800-525-2253 ■ *Web:* www.beaverrun.com	Breckenridge	CO	80424	970-453-6000	453-2454
Breckenridge Ski Resort 351 County Rd 708 *TF:* 800-789-7669 ■ *Web:* www.breckenridge.com	Breckenridge	CO	80424	970-453-5000	453-3202
Broadmoor The 1 Lake Ave *TF:* 866-837-9520 ■ *Web:* www.broadmoor.com	Colorado Springs	CO	80906	719-577-5775	577-5738
C Lazy U Ranch 3640 Colorado Hwy 125 PO Box 379 *Web:* www.clazyu.com	Granby	CO	80446	970-887-3344	887-3917
Copper Mountain Resort 209 Ten Mile Cir PO Box 3001 *TF:* 888-219-2441 ■ *Web:* www.coppercolorado.com	Copper Mountain	CO	80443	970-968-2882	968-3300
Crested Butte Mountain Resort (CBMR) 12 Snowmass Rd PO Box 5700 *TF:* 800-810-7669 ■ *Web:* www.skicb.com/cbmr	Mount Crested Butte	CO	81225	970-349-2222	349-2250
Destination Hotels & Resorts Inc 10333 E Dry Creek Rd Suite 450 *TF:* 800-633-8347 ■ *Web:* www.destinationhotels.com	Englewood	CO	80112	303-799-3830	799-6011
Durango Mountain Resort 1 Skier Pl *TF:* 800-693-0175 ■ *Web:* www.durangomountainresort.com	Durango	CO	81301	970-247-9000	385-2106
Gold Lake Mountain Resort & Spa 3371 Gold Lake Rd *TF:* 800-450-3544 ■ *Web:* www.goldlake.com	Ward	CO	80481	303-459-3544	459-9077
Grand Lodge Crested Butte 12 Snowmass Rd *TF:* 888-823-4446 ■ *Web:* www.skicb.com/cbmr/grand-lodge.aspx	Crested Butte	CO	81224	970-349-2222	349-8050
Hot Springs Lodge & Pool 415 E 6th St PO Box 308 *TF:* 800-537-7946 ■ *Web:* www.hotspringspool.com	Glenwood Springs	CO	81602	970-945-6571	947-2950
Indian Hot Springs 302 Soda Creek Rd PO Box 1990 *Web:* www.indianhotsprings.com	Idaho Springs	CO	80452	303-989-6666	567-9304
Inverness Hotel & Golf Club 200 Inverness Dr W *TF:* 800-346-4891 ■ *Web:* www.invernesshotel.com	Englewood	CO	80112	303-799-5800	799-5874
Keystone Resort 21996 Hwy 6 PO Box 38 *TF:* 877-625-1556 ■ *Web:* www.keystone.snow.com	Keystone	CO	80435	970-496-2316	
Lion Square Lodge & Conference Ctr 660 W Lionshead Pl *TF:* 800-525-1943 ■ *Web:* www.lionsquare.com	Vail	CO	81657	970-476-2281	476-7423
Lodge at Tamarron 40292 Hwy 550 N Suite 425 *TF:* 800-678-1000	Durango	CO	81301	970-259-2000	382-7899
Lodge at Vail 174 E Gore Creek Dr *TF:* 800-331-5634 ■ *Web:* www.lodgeatvail.rockresorts.com	Vail	CO	81657	970-476-5011	476-7425
Manor Vail Lodge 595 E Vail Valley Dr *TF:* 800-950-8245 ■ *Web:* www.manorvail.com	Vail	CO	81657	970-476-5651	476-4982
Millennium Hotels & Resorts (MHR) 6560 Greenwood Plaza Blvd Suite 300 *Web:* www.millenniumhotels.com	Greenwood Village	CO	80111	303-779-2000	779-2001
Monarch Mountain Lodge 22720 W US Hwy 50 *TF:* 888-996-7669 ■ *Web:* www.monarchmountainlodge.com	Monarch	CO	81227	719-539-2581	539-7652
Mountain Lodge at Telluride 457 Mountain Village Blvd *TF:* 866-368-6867 ■ *Web:* www.mountainlodgetelluride.com	Telluride	CO	81435	970-369-5000	369-4317
Omni Interlocken Resort 500 Interlocken Blvd *TF:* 800-843-6664 ■ *Web:* www.omnihotels.com	Broomfield	CO	80021	303-438-6600	464-3236
Park Hyatt Beaver Creek Resort & Spa 136 E Thomas Pl *TF Cust Svc:* 800-233-1234 ■ *Web:* www.beavercreek.hyatt.com	Beaver Creek	CO	81620	970-949-1234	949-4164
Peaks Resort & Golden Door Spa 136 Country Club Dr **Fax Area Code:* 970 ■ *TF:* 866-282-4557 ■ *Web:* www.thepeaksresort.com	Telluride	CO	81435	800-789-2220	728-6175*
Ritz-Carlton Bachelor Gulch 0130 Daybreak Ridge *TF:* 800-241-3333 ■ *Web:* www.ritzcarlton.com	Avon	CO	81620	970-748-6200	343-1070
Saint Regis Resort Aspen 315 E Dean St *TF:* 888-454-9005 ■ *Web:* www.stregisaspen.com	Aspen	CO	81611	970-920-3300	925-8998
Snowmass Club PO Box G-2 *TF:* 800-525-0710 ■ *Web:* www.snowmassclub.com	Snowmass Village	CO	81615	970-923-5600	923-6944
Sonnenalp Resort of Vail 20 Vail Rd *TF:* 800-654-8312 ■ *Web:* www.sonnenalp.com	Vail	CO	81657	970-476-5656	476-1639
Steamboat Grand Resort Hotel & Conference Ctr 2300 Mt Werner Cir *TF:* 877-269-2628 ■ *Web:* www.steamboatgrand.com	Steamboat Springs	CO	80487	970-871-5500	871-5501
Steamboat Resorts 1847 Ski Times Sq Dr PO Box 772995 *TF:* 800-525-5502 ■ *Web:* www.steamboatresorts.com	Steamboat Springs	CO	80487	970-879-8000	879-8060
Steamboat Ski & Resort Corp 2305 Mt Werner Cir *TF:* 877-237-2628 ■ *Web:* www.steamboat.com	Steamboat Springs	CO	80487	970-879-6111	879-4757
Tall Timber Resort 1 Silverton Star *Web:* www.talltimberresort.com	Durango	CO	81301	970-259-4813	
Torian Plum Condo Resort 1855 Ski Time Sq Dr *TF:* 800-228-2458 ■ *Web:* www.resortquesteamboat.com	Steamboat Springs	CO	80487	970-879-8811	879-7374
Vail Cascade Resort & Spa 1300 Westhaven Dr *TF:* 800-420-2424 ■ *Web:* www.vailcascade.com	Vail	CO	81657	970-476-7111	479-7020
Vail Resorts Management Co 390 Interlocken Crescent Suite 1000 *NYSE:* MTN ■ *TF:* 800-842-8062 ■ *Web:* www.vailresorts.com	Broomfield	CO	80021	303-404-1800	404-6415
Village at Breckenridge Resort 535 S Pk Ave PO Box 8329 *TF:* 800-332-0424 ■ *Web:* www.breckresorts.com/villageatbreckenridge	Breckenridge	CO	80424	970-453-5192	453-5116
Winter Park Resort (WPR) 150 Alpenglobe Way PO Box 36 *TF:* 800-979-0332 ■ *Web:* www.winterparkresort.com	Winter Park	CO	80482	303-316-1590	316-1690

CONNECTICUT

	City	State	Zip	Phone	Fax
Foxwoods Resort Casino 39 Norwich Westerly Rd *TF:* 800-752-9244 ■ *Web:* www.foxwoods.com	Ledyard	CT	06339	860-312-3000	396-3639
Heritage Hotel 522 Heritage Rd *TF:* 800-932-3466 ■ *Web:* www.heritagesouthbury.com	Southbury	CT	06488	203-264-8200	264-5035
Interlaken Inn 74 Interlaken Rd Rt 12 *TF:* 800-222-2909 ■ *Web:* www.interlakeninn.com	Lakeville	CT	06039	860-435-9878	435-2980
Mohegan Sun Resort & Casino 1 Mohegan Sun Blvd *TF:* 888-226-7711 ■ *Web:* www.mohegansun.com	Uncasville	CT	06382	860-862-8000	862-7824
Saybrook Point Inn & Spa 2 Bridge St *TF:* 800-243-0212 ■ *Web:* www.saybrook.com	Old Saybrook	CT	06475	860-395-2000	388-1504
Water's Edge Resort & Spa 1525 Boston Post Rd PO Box 688 *TF:* 800-222-5901 ■ *Web:* www.watersedgeresortandspa.com	Westbrook	CT	06498	860-399-5901	399-8644

FLORIDA

	City	State	Zip	Phone	Fax
Admiral Lehigh Golf Resort & Spa 225 E Joel Blvd *TF:* 888-465-3222	Lehigh Acres	FL	33972	239-369-2121	368-1660
Alden Beach Resort 5900 Gulf Blvd *TF:* 800-237-2530 ■ *Web:* www.aldenbeachresort.com	Saint Pete Beach	FL	33706	727-360-7081	360-5957
Amelia Island Plantation 1501 Lewis St *TF:* 800-874-6878 ■ *Web:* www.aipfl.com	Amelia Island	FL	32034	904-261-6161	277-5159
Americano Beach Resort 1260 N Atlantic Ave *TF:* 800-874-1824 ■ *Web:* www.americanobeachresort.com	Daytona Beach	FL	32118	386-255-7431	253-9513
Bahia Mar Beach Resort & Yachting Ctr 801 Seabreeze Blvd *TF:* 888-802-2442 ■ *Web:* www.bahiamarhotel.com	Fort Lauderdale	FL	33316	954-764-2233	523-5424
Banana Bay Resort 2319 N Roosevelt Blvd *TF:* 800-226-2621 ■ *Web:* www.bananabay.com	Key West	FL	33040	305-296-6925	296-2004
Banyan Resort 323 Whitehead St *TF:* 800-853-9937 ■ *Web:* www.thebanyanresort.com	Key West	FL	33040	305-296-7786	294-1107
Bay Hill Golf Club & Lodge 9000 Bay Hill Blvd *TF:* 888-422-9445 ■ *Web:* www.bayhill.com	Orlando	FL	32819	407-876-2429	876-1035
Bay Point Resort Village Marriott Golf & Yacht Club 4200 Marriott Dr *TF:* 800-874-7105 ■ *Web:* www.marriotthotels.com/PFNBP	Panama City Beach	FL	32408	850-236-6000	236-6158
Beachcomber Resort Hotel & Villas 1200 S Ocean Blvd *TF:* 800-231-2423 ■ *Web:* www.beachcomberresort.com	Fort Lauderdale	FL	33062	954-941-7830	942-7680

Name / Address	City	State	Zip	Phone	Fax
Biltmore Hotel & Conference Center of the Americas 1200 Anastasia Ave. *TF Cust Svc:* 800-727-1926 ■ *Web:* www.biltmorehotel.com	Coral Gables	FL	33134	305-445-1926	913-3159
Bluewater Bay Resort 1950 Bluewater Blvd *TF:* 800-874-2128 ■ *Web:* www.bwresort.com	Niceville	FL	32578	850-897-3613	897-2424
Boca Raton Resort & Club 501 E Camino Real *TF:* 800-327-0101 ■ *Web:* www.bocaresort.com	Boca Raton	FL	33432	561-447-3000	394-3961
Breakers The 1 S County Rd *TF:* 800-833-3141 ■ *Web:* www.thebreakers.com	Palm Beach	FL	33480	561-655-6611	659-8403
Buena Vista Hospitality Group Inc 6750 Forum Dr Suite 316 *Web:* www.bvhg.com	Orlando	FL	32821	407-352-7161	352-2413
Buena Vista Palace Hotel & Spa 1900 N Buena Vista Dr *TF:* 866-397-6516 ■ *Web:* www.buenavistapalace.com	Lake Buena Vista	FL	32830	407-827-2727	827-6034
Casa Del Mar Beach Resort 621 S Atlantic Ave.	Ormond Beach	FL	32176	386-672-4550	672-1418
Casa Marina Resort & Beach Club 1500 Reynolds St *TF:* 888-303-5717 ■ *Web:* www.casamarinaresort.com	Key West	FL	33040	305-296-3535	296-4633
Casa Ybel Resort 2255 W Gulf Dr *TF:* 800-276-4753 ■ *Web:* www.casaybelresort.com	Sanibel Island	FL	33957	239-472-3145	472-2109
Castaways Beach Resort 2043 S Atlantic Ave. *TF:* 866-254-2722 ■ *Web:* www.castawaysbeachresort.com	Daytona Beach Shores	FL	32118	386-248-2525	253-9935
Charter Club Resort on Naples Bay 1000 10th Ave S *TF:* 800-494-5559 ■ *Web:* www.islandone.com	Naples	FL	34102	239-261-5559	261-6782
Cheeca Lodge & Spa MM 82 81801 Overseas Hwy *TF:* 800-327-2888 ■ *Web:* www.cheeca.com	Islamorada	FL	33036	305-664-4651	664-2893
Club Med Inc 75 Valencia Ave **Fax:* Mail Rm ■ *TF:* 800-258-2633 ■ *Web:* www.clubmed.com	Coral Gables	FL	33134	305-925-9000	443-0562*
Club Med Sandpiper 3500 SE Morningside Blvd. *TF:* 800-258-2633 ■ *Web:* www.clubmed.com	Port Saint Lucie	FL	34952	772-398-5100	398-5103
Colony Beach & Tennis Resort 1620 Gulf of Mexico Dr *TF:* 800-426-5669 ■ *Web:* www.colonybeachresort.com	Longboat Key	FL	34228	941-383-6464	383-7549
Deauville Beach Resort 6701 Collins Ave *TF:* 800-327-6656 ■ *Web:* www.deauvillebeachresort.com	Miami Beach	FL	33141	305-865-8511	865-8154
Diplomat Country Club & Spa 501 Diplomat Pkwy. *TF:* 800-327-1212 ■ *Web:* www.diplomatcountryclub.com	Hallandale Beach	FL	33009	954-883-4000	883-4009
Disney's All-Star Movies Resort 1901 W Buena Vista Dr. *Web:* disneyworld.disney.go.com/resorts/all-star-movies-resort	Lake Buena Vista	FL	32830	407-939-7000	939-7111
Disney's All-Star Music Resort 1801 W Buena Vista Dr. *Web:* disneyworld.disney.go.com	Lake Buena Vista	FL	32830	407-939-6000	939-7222
Disney's All-Star Sports Resort 1701 W Buena Vista Dr. *Web:* www.disneyworld.disney.go.com	Lake Buena Vista	FL	32830	407-939-5000	939-7333
Disney's Animal Kingdom Lodge 2901 Osceola Pkwy *Web:* disneyworld.disney.go.com/resorts/animal-kingdom-lodge	Lake Buena Vista	FL	32830	407-938-3000	938-4799
Disney's Beach Club Resort 1800 Epcot Resort Blvd *Web:* disneyworld.disney.go.com/resorts/beach-club-resort	Lake Buena Vista	FL	32830	407-934-8000	934-3850
Disney's BoardWalk Resort 2101 N Epcot Resort Blvd. *Web:* disneyworld.disney.go.com	Lake Buena Vista	FL	32830	407-939-5100	939-5150
Disney's BoardWalk Villas 2101 N Epcot Resort Blvd. *Web:* disneyworld.disney.go.com	Lake Buena Vista	FL	32830	407-939-5100	939-5150
Disney's Caribbean Beach Resort 900 Cayman Way *Web:* www.disneyworld.disney.go.com	Lake Buena Vista	FL	32830	407-934-3400	934-3288
Disney's Contemporary Resort 4600 N World Dr. *Web:* www.disneyworld.disney.go.com	Lake Buena Vista	FL	32830	407-824-1000	824-3539
Disney's Coronado Springs Resort 1000 W Buena Vista Dr. *Web:* www.disneyworld.disney.go.com	Lake Buena Vista	FL	32830	407-939-1000	939-1001
Disney's Fort Wilderness Resort & Campground 4510 Fort Wilderness Trail *Web:* www.disneyworld.disney.go.com	Lake Buena Vista	FL	32830	407-824-2900	824-3508
Disney's Grand Floridian Resort & Spa 4401 Floridian Way. *Web:* www.disneyworld.disney.go.com	Lake Buena Vista	FL	32830	407-824-3000	824-3186
Disney's Old Key West Resort 1510 N Cove Rd *Web:* disneyworld.disney.go.com/resorts/old-key-west-resort	Lake Buena Vista	FL	32830	407-827-7700	827-7710
Disney's Polynesian Resort 1600 Seven Seas Dr *Web:* www.disneyworld.disney.go.com	Lake Buena Vista	FL	32830	407-824-2000	824-3174
Disney's Pop Century Resort 1050 Century Dr.	Lake Buena Vista	FL	32830	407-938-4000	938-4040
Disney's Port Orleans Resort-French Quarter 2201 Orleans Dr *Web:* www.disneyworld.disney.go.com	Lake Buena Vista	FL	32830	407-934-5000	934-5353
Disney's Port Orleans Resort-Riverside 1251 Riverside Dr. *Web:* disneyworld.disney.go.com/resorts/port-orleans-resort-riverside	Lake Buena Vista	FL	32830	407-934-6000	934-5777
Disney's Wilderness Lodge 901 Timberline Dr. *Web:* disneyworld.disney.go.com/resorts/wilderness-lodge-resort	Lake Buena Vista	FL	32830	407-824-3200	824-3232
Disney's Yacht Club Resort 1700 EPCOT Resorts Blvd *Web:* www.disneyworld.disney.go.com	Lake Buena Vista	FL	32830	407-934-7000	934-3850
Don CeSar Beach Resort - A Loews Hotel 3400 Gulf Blvd **Fax:* Sales ■ *TF:* 866-563-9792 ■ *Web:* www.loewshotels.com	Saint Pete Beach	FL	33706	727-360-1881	360-1881*
Don Shula's Hotel & Golf Club 6842 Main St *TF:* 800-247-4852 ■ *Web:* www.donshulahotel.com	Miami Lakes	FL	33014	305-821-1150	820-8087
Doral Golf Resort & Spa 4400 NW 87th Ave *TF:* 800-713-6725 ■ *Web:* www.doralresort.com	Miami	FL	33178	305-592-2000	592-2000
Doubletree Grand Key Resort (DGKR) 3990 S Roosevelt Blvd *TF:* 888-844-0454	Key West	FL	33040	305-293-1818	296-6962
Eden Roc - A Renaissance Beach Resort & Spa 4525 Collins Ave *TF:* 800-319-5354	Miami Beach	FL	33140	305-531-0000	674-5555
Fairmont Turnberry Isle Resort & Club 19999 W Country Club Dr *TF:* 866-840-8069 ■ *Web:* www.fairmont.com	Miami	FL	33180	305-932-6200	933-6554
Fisher Island Club & Resort 1 Fisher Island Dr *TF Resv:* 800-537-3708 ■ *Web:* www.fisherislandclub.com	Fisher Island	FL	33109	305-535-6000	535-6003
Fishermen's Village 1200 W Retta Esplanade *TF:* 800-639-0020 ■ *Web:* www.fishville.com	Punta Gorda	FL	33950	941-639-8721	637-1054
Fontainebleau Hilton Resort 4441 Collins Ave *TF:* 800-548-8886	Miami Beach	FL	33140	305-538-2000	531-2845
Fort Lauderdale Grande Hotel & Yacht Club 1881 SE 17th St *TF:* 888-554-2131 ■ *Web:* www.fortlauderdalegrande.com	Fort Lauderdale	FL	33316	954-463-4000	527-6705
Four Seasons Resort Palm Beach 2800 S Ocean Blvd *TF:* 800-432-2335 ■ *Web:* www.fourseasons.com/palmbeach	Palm Beach	FL	33480	561-582-2800	547-1374
Galleon Resort & Marina 617 Front St *TF:* 800-544-3030 ■ *Web:* www.galleonresort.com	Key West	FL	33040	305-296-7711	296-0821
Gaylord Palms Resort & Convention Ctr 6000 W Osceola Pkwy *Web:* www.gaylordhotels.com	Kissimmee	FL	34746	407-586-0000	586-2199
Grand Palms Hotel & Golf Resort 110 Grand Palms Dr *TF:* 800-327-9246 ■ *Web:* www.grandpalmsresort.com	Pembroke Pines	FL	33027	954-431-8800	435-5988
Grenelefe Golf & Tennis Resort 3200 SR-546 *TF:* 888-808-7410 ■ *Web:* www.grenelefe.com	Haines City	FL	33844	863-422-7511	421-5000
Hard Rock Hotel at Universal Orlando Resort 5800 Universal Blvd *TF:* 888-430-4999 ■ *Web:* www.loewshotels.com	Orlando	FL	32819	407-503-2000	503-2010
Hawk's Cay Resort & Marina 61 Hawk's Cay Blvd *TF:* 800-432-2242 ■ *Web:* www.hawkscay.com	Duck Key	FL	33050	305-743-7000	743-5215
Hilton Longboat Key Beach Resort 4711 Gulf of Mexico Dr *Web:* www1.hilton.com	Longboat Key	FL	34228	941-383-2451	383-7979
Hilton Marco Island Beach Resort 560 S Collier Blvd *Web:* www1.hilton.com	Marco Island	FL	34145	239-394-5000	394-8410
Hilton Sandestin Beach Golf Resort & Spa 4000 Sandestin Blvd S *TF:* 800-559-1805 ■ *Web:* www.sandestinbeachhilton.com	Destin	FL	32550	850-267-9500	267-3076
Holiday Inn Express & Suites Oceanfront 3301 S Atlantic Ave. *TF:* 800-329-8662 ■ *Web:* www.hiexpress.com/hotels/us/en/daytona-beach-shores/dabaa/hoteldetail	Daytona Beach Shores	FL	32118	386-767-1711	271-0000
Holiday Inn Resort Lake Buena Vista 13351 SR 535 *TF:* 877-272-9985 ■ *Web:* www.hiresortlbv.com	Orlando	FL	32821	407-239-4500	239-7713
Holiday Isle Beach Resort & Marina 84001 Overseas Hwy *TF:* 800-327-7070 ■ *Web:* www.holidayisle.com	Islamorada	FL	33036	305-664-2321	664-2703
Innisbrook Resort & Golf Club 36750 US Hwy 19 N *TF:* 800-492-6899 ■ *Web:* www.innisbrookgolfresort.com	Palm Harbor	FL	34684	727-942-2000	942-5576
Inverrary Resort 3501 Inverrary Blvd *TF:* 800-241-0363 ■ *Web:* www.inverrary.org	Fort Lauderdale	FL	33319	954-485-0500	733-0236
Janus Hotels & Resorts Inc 2300 Corporate Blvd NW Suite 232 *Web:* www.janushotels.com	Boca Raton	FL	33431	561-997-2325	997-5331
Jupiter Beach Resort 5 N Hwy A1A *TF:* 800-228-8810 ■ *Web:* www.jupiterbeachresort.com	Jupiter	FL	33477	561-746-2511	744-1741
JW Marriott Orlando Grande Lakes Resort 4040 Central Florida Pkwy *TF:* 800-576-5750 ■ *Web:* www.grandelakes.com	Orlando	FL	32837	407-206-2300	206-2301
Key Largo Grande Resort & Beach Club 97000 S Overseas Hwy *TF:* 866-597-5397 ■ *Web:* www.keylargoresort.com	Key Largo	FL	33037	305-852-5553	852-8669
Key Largo Marriott Bay Resort 103800 Overseas Hwy *TF:* 866-849-3753 ■ *Web:* www.marriottkeylargo.com	Key Largo	FL	33037	305-453-0000	453-0093
La Cita Country Club 777 Country Club Dr *Web:* www.lacitacc.com	Titusville	FL	32780	321-383-2582	267-4209
La Playa Beach & Golf Resort 9891 Gulf Shore Dr. *TF:* 800-237-6883 ■ *Web:* www.laplayaresort.com	Naples	FL	34108	239-597-3123	597-6278
Lago Mar Resort & Club 1700 S Ocean Ln *TF:* 800-524-6627 ■ *Web:* www.lagomar.com	Fort Lauderdale	FL	33316	954-523-6511	524-6627
Le Meridien Sunny Isles Beach 18683 Collins Ave *Web:* www.starwoodhotels.com	Sunny Isles Beach	FL	33160	305-503-6000	503-6001
Little Palm Island Resort & Spa 28500 Overseas Hwy MM 28.5 *TF:* 800-343-8567 ■ *Web:* www.littlepalmisland.com	Little Torch Key	FL	33042	305-515-4004	872-4843
Lodge & Club at Ponte Vedra Beach 607 Ponte Vedra Blvd *TF:* 800-243-4304 ■ *Web:* www.pontevedra.com	Ponte Vedra Beach	FL	32082	904-273-9500	273-0210

	City	State	Zip	Phone	Fax
Longboat Key Club 301 Gulf of Mexico Dr *TF:* 800-237-8821 ■ *Web:* www.longboatkeyclub.com	Longboat Key	FL	34228	941-383-8821	383-5308
Marco Beach Ocean Resort 480 S Collier Blvd *TF:* 877-220-6642 ■ *Web:* www.marcoresort.com	Marco Island	FL	34145	239-393-1400	393-1401
Miami Beach Resort & Spa 4833 Collins Ave *TF:* 866-767-6060 ■ *Web:* www.miamibeachresortandspa.com	Miami Beach	FL	33140	305-532-3600	534-7409
Miccosukee Resort & Convention Ctr 500 SW 177th Ave *TF:* 877-242-6464 ■ *Web:* www.miccosukee.com	Miami	FL	33194	305-925-2555	925-2556
Mission Inn Resort & Club 10400 County Rd 48 *TF:* 800-874-9053 ■ *Web:* www.missioninnresort.com	Howey in the Hills	FL	34737	352-324-3101	324-2636
Naples Bay Resort 1500 5th Ave S *TF:* 866-605-1199 ■ *Web:* www.naplesbayresort.com	Naples	FL	34102	239-530-1199	436-8024
Naples Beach Hotel & Golf Club 851 Gulf Shore Blvd N *TF:* 800-237-7600 ■ *Web:* www.naplesbeachhotel.com	Naples	FL	34102	239-261-2222	261-7380
Naples Grande Resort & Club 475 Seagate Dr *TF:* 888-422-6177 ■ *Web:* www.naplesgranderesort.com	Naples	FL	34103	239-597-3232	594-6777
Nickelodeon Family Suites by Holiday Inn 14500 Continental Gateway *TF:* 877-387-5437 ■ *Web:* www.nickhotel.com	Orlando	FL	32821	407-387-5437	387-1488
Ocean Hammock Resort 105 16th Rd *TF:* 800-654-6538	Palm Coast	FL	32137	386-445-3000	445-2947
Ocean Key Resort & Spa Zero Duval St *TF:* 800-328-9815 ■ *Web:* www.oceankey.com	Key West	FL	33040	305-296-7701	292-7685
Ocean Manor Resort 4040 Galt Ocean Dr *TF:* 800-955-0444 ■ *Web:* www.oceanmanor.com	Fort Lauderdale	FL	33308	954-566-7500	564-3075
Ocean Sands Resort & Spa 1350 N Ocean Blvd *TF:* 800-583-3500 ■ *Web:* www.theoceansandsresortandspa.com	Pompano Beach	FL	33062	954-590-1000	590-1101
Omni Orlando Resort at Championsgate 1500 Masters Blvd *TF:* 800-843-6664 ■ *Web:* www.omnihotels.com	Champions Gate	FL	33896	407-390-6664	390-6600
Orange Lake Country Club Inc (OLCC) 8505 W Irlo Bronson Memorial Hwy *TF:* 800-877-6522 ■ *Web:* www.orangelake.com	Kissimmee	FL	34747	407-239-0000	239-1086
Palms The 3025 Collins Ave *TF:* 800-550-0505 ■ *Web:* www.thepalmshotel.com	Miami Beach	FL	33140	305-534-0505	534-0515
Park Shore Resort 600 Neapolitan Way *TF:* 800-548-2077 ■ *Web:* www.parkshorefl.com	Naples	FL	34103	239-263-2222	263-0946
PGA National Resort & Spa 400 Avenue of the Champions *TF:* 800-633-9150 ■ *Web:* www.pgaresort.com	Palm Beach Gardens	FL	33418	561-627-2000	227-2595
Pier House Resort Caribbean Spa 1 Duval St *TF:* 800-723-2791 ■ *Web:* www.pierhouse.com	Key West	FL	33040	305-296-4600	296-7569
Plantation Inn & Golf Resort 9301 W Fort Island Trail *TF:* 800-632-6262 ■ *Web:* www.plantationinn.com	Crystal River	FL	34429	352-795-4211	795-1156
Plaza Resort & Spa 600 N Atlantic Ave *TF:* 800-874-7420 ■ *Web:* www.plazaresortandspa.com	Daytona Beach	FL	32118	386-255-4471	238-7984
Ponte Vedra Inn & Club 200 Ponte Vedra Blvd *TF:* 800-234-7842 ■ *Web:* www.pontevedra.com	Ponte Vedra Beach	FL	32082	904-285-1111	285-1111
Portofino Bay Hotel at Universal Orlando - A Loews Hotel 5601 Universal Blvd *TF:* 800-232-7827 ■ *Web:* www.loewshotels.com	Orlando	FL	32819	407-503-1000	503-1010
Portofino Island Resort & Spa 10 Portofino Dr *TF:* 877-484-3405 ■ *Web:* www.portofinoisland.com	Pensacola Beach	FL	32561	850-916-5000	916-5010
Quality Inn & Suites Naples Golf Resort 4100 Golden Gate Pkwy *TF:* 800-277-0017 ■ *Web:* www.naplesgolfresort.com	Naples	FL	34116	239-455-1010	455-4038
Radisson Palm Beach Shores Resort & Vacation Villas 181 Ocean Ave *Web:* www.radisson.com	Palm Beach Shores	FL	33404	561-863-4000	845-3245
Radisson Resort Parkway 2900 PkwyBlvd *TF:* 800-333-3333 ■ *Web:* www.radisson.com	Kissimmee	FL	34747	407-396-7000	396-6792
Reach Resort 1435 Simonton St *TF:* 866-397-6427 ■ *Web:* www.reachresort.com	Key West	FL	33040	305-296-5000	296-2830
Renaissance Orlando Resort at SeaWorld 6677 Sea Harbor Dr *TF:* 800-327-6677 ■ *Web:* www.renaissancehotel.com/mcosr	Orlando	FL	32821	407-351-5555	351-9991
Renaissance Resort at World Golf Village 500 S Legacy Trail *TF:* 888-740-7020 ■ *Web:* www.worldgolfrenaissance.com	Saint Augustine	FL	32092	904-940-8000	940-8008
Renaissance Vinoy Resort & Golf Club 501 5th Ave NE *TF:* 800-468-3571 ■ *Web:* www.renaissancehotel.com/tpasr	Saint Petersburg	FL	33701	727-894-1000	822-2785
Resort & Club at Little Harbor 611 Destiny Dr *TF:* 800-327-2773 ■ *Web:* www.staylittleharbor.com	Ruskin	FL	33570	813-645-3291	641-1589
Resort at Singer Island 3800 N Ocean Dr *TF:* 800-325-3589	Singer Island	FL	33404	561-340-1700	340-1705
Ritz-Carlton Amelia Island 4750 Amelia Island Pkwy *TF:* 800-241-3333 ■ *Web:* www.ritzcarlton.com/resorts/amelia_island	Amelia Island	FL	32034	904-277-1100	261-9064
Ritz-Carlton Key Biscayne 455 Grand Bay Dr *TF:* 800-241-3333 ■ *Web:* www.ritzcarlton.com/resorts/key_biscayne	Key Biscayne	FL	33149	305-365-9575	365-4505
Ritz-Carlton Naples 280 Vanderbilt Beach Rd *TF:* 800-241-3333 ■ *Web:* www.ritzcarlton.com/resorts/naples	Naples	FL	34108	239-598-3300	598-6690
Ritz-Carlton Naples Golf Resort 2600 Tiburon Dr *TF:* 888-856-2164 ■ *Web:* www.ritzcarlton.com	Naples	FL	34109	239-593-2000	254-3300
Ritz-Carlton Orlando Grande Lakes 4012 Central Florida Pkwy *TF:* 800-576-5760 ■ *Web:* www.ritzcarlton.com	Orlando	FL	32837	407-206-2400	206-2401
Ritz-Carlton Palm Beach The 100 S Ocean Blvd *TF:* 800-241-3333 ■ *Web:* www.ritzcarlton.com/resorts/palm_beach	Manalapan	FL	33462	561-533-6000	588-4202
Ritz-Carlton Sarasota 1111 Ritz-Carlton Dr *TF:* 800-241-3333 ■ *Web:* www.ritzcarlton.com	Sarasota	FL	34236	941-309-2000	309-2100
Rosen Hotels & Resorts Inc 9840 International Dr *TF:* 800-204-7234 ■ *Web:* www.rosenhotels.com	Orlando	FL	32819	407-996-9840	996-0865
Royal Pacific Resort at Universal Orlando - A Loews Hotel 6300 Hollywood Way *TF:* 800-232-7827 ■ *Web:* www.loewshotels.com	Orlando	FL	32819	407-503-3000	503-3010
Saddlebrook Resort 5700 Saddlebrook Way *TF:* 800-729-8383 ■ *Web:* www.saddlebrook.com	Wesley Chapel	FL	33543	813-973-1111	973-4504
Safety Harbor Resort & Spa 105 N Bayshore Dr *TF:* 888-237-8772 ■ *Web:* www.safetyharborspa.com	Safety Harbor	FL	34695	727-726-1161	726-4268
Sandals Resorts International 4950 SW 72nd Ave **Fax:* PR ■ *TF:* 888-726-3257 ■ *Web:* www.sandals.com	Miami	FL	33155	305-284-1300	666-5332*
Sandestin Golf & Beach Resort 9300 Emerald Coast Pkwy W *TF:* 800-277-0800 ■ *Web:* www.sandestin.com	Sandestin	FL	32550	850-267-8000	267-8221
Sanibel Harbour Marriott Resort & Spa 17260 Harbour Pointe Dr *TF:* 800-767-7777 ■ *Web:* www.marriott.com	Fort Myers	FL	33908	239-466-4000	466-2266
Sawgrass Marriott Resort & Beach Club 1000 PGA Tour Blvd *TF:* 800-228-9290 ■ *Web:* www.marriott.com	Ponte Vedra Beach	FL	32082	904-285-7777	285-0906
Sea Gardens Beach & Tennis Resort 615 N Ocean Blvd *Web:* www.seagardens.com	Pompano Beach	FL	33062	954-943-6200	783-0047
Seabonay Beach Resort 1159 Hillsboro Mile *TF:* 800-777-1961	Hillsboro Beach	FL	33062	954-427-2525	427-3228
Seascape Resort 100 Seascape Dr *TF:* 800-874-9106 ■ *Web:* www.seascape-resort.com	Destin	FL	32550	850-837-9181	837-4769
Seminole Hard Rock Hotel & Casino Hollywood 1 Seminole Way *TF:* 800-937-0010 ■ *Web:* www.seminolehardrock.com	Hollywood	FL	33314	954-327-7625	364-4191
Sheraton Sand Key Resort 1160 Gulf Blvd *TF:* 800-325-3535 ■ *Web:* www.sheratonsandkey.com	Clearwater Beach	FL	33767	727-595-1611	596-8488
Sirata Beach Resort & Conference Ctr 5300 Gulf Blvd *TF:* 866-587-8538 ■ *Web:* www.sirata.com	Saint Pete Beach	FL	33706	727-363-5100	363-5195
South Seas Island Resort 5400 Plantation Rd *TF:* 877-205-1293 ■ *Web:* www.southseas.com	Captiva	FL	33924	239-472-5111	472-7541
Standard The 40 Island Ave *TF:* 800-327-8363 ■ *Web:* www.lidospa.com	Miami Beach	FL	33139	305-673-1717	673-8181
Summer Beach Resort 5456 First Coast Hwy *TF:* 800-862-9297 ■ *Web:* www.summerbeach.com	Amelia Island	FL	32034	904-277-0905	261-1065
Sundial Beach & Golf Resort 1451 Middle Gulf Dr *TF:* 866-565-5093 ■ *Web:* www.sanibelcollection.com	Sanibel	FL	33957	239-472-4151	472-8892
Sunset Beach Resort 3287 W Gulf Dr *TF:* 866-565-5091 ■ *Web:* www.sanibelcollection.com	Sanibel Island	FL	33957	239-472-1700	
Sunset Key Guest Cottages at Westin Resort 245 Front St *TF:* 800-937-8461 ■ *Web:* www.westinsunsetkeycottages.com	Key West	FL	33040	305-292-5300	292-5395
Trump International Sonesta Beach Resort 18001 Collins Ave *TF:* 800-766-3782 ■ *Web:* www.sonesta.com	Sunny Isles Beach	FL	33160	305-692-5600	692-5601
Vanderbilt Beach Resort 9225 Gulf Shore Dr N *TF:* 800-243-9076 ■ *Web:* www.vanderbiltbeachresort.com	Naples	FL	34108	239-597-3144	597-2199
Villas of Grand Cypress Golf Resort 1 N Jacaranda *TF:* 800-835-7377 ■ *Web:* www.grandcypress.com	Orlando	FL	32836	407-239-4700	239-7219
Walt Disney World Dolphin 1500 Epcot Resorts Blvd *TF:* 888-828-8850 ■ *Web:* www.swandolphin.com	Lake Buena Vista	FL	32830	407-934-4000	934-4884
Walt Disney World Resorts 4600 N World Dr PO Box 10000 *Web:* disneyworld.disney.go.com	Lake Buena Vista	FL	32830	407-824-2222	827-2096
Walt Disney World Swan 1200 Epcot Resorts Blvd *TF:* 888-828-8850 ■ *Web:* www.swandolphin.com	Lake Buena Vista	FL	32830	407-934-4000	934-4884
West Wind Inn 3345 W Gulf Dr *TF:* 800-824-0476 ■ *Web:* www.westwindinn.com	Sanibel	FL	33957	239-472-1541	472-8134
Westin Key West Resort & Marina 245 Front St *TF:* 866-716-8108 ■ *Web:* www.westinkeywestresort.com	Key West	FL	33040	305-294-4000	294-4086

GEORGIA

	City	State	Zip	Phone	Fax
Barnsley Gardens 597 Barnsley Gardens Rd *TF:* 877-773-2447 ■ *Web:* www.barnsleyresort.com	Adairsville	GA	30103	770-773-7480	773-1779
Brasstown Valley Resort 6321 US Hwy 76 *TF:* 800-201-3205 ■ *Web:* www.brasstownvalley.com	Young Harris	GA	30582	706-379-9900	379-9999
Callaway Gardens 17800 Hwy 27 *TF:* 800-225-5292 ■ *Web:* www.callawaygardens.com	Pine Mountain	GA	31822	706-663-2281	663-6812
Chateau Elan Resort & Conference Ctr 100 Rue Charlemagne *TF:* 800-233-9463 ■ *Web:* www.chateauelan.com	Braselton	GA	30517	678-425-0900	425-6000
Forrest Hills Mountain Resort & Conference Ctr 135 Forrest Hills Rd *TF:* 800-654-6313 ■ *Web:* www.foresths.com	Dahlonega	GA	30533	706-864-6456	864-0757
Jekyll Island Club Hotel 371 Riverview Dr *TF:* 800-535-9547 ■ *Web:* www.jekyllclub.com	Jekyll Island	GA	31527	912-635-2600	635-2818
King & Prince Beach & Golf Resort 201 Arnold Rd *TF:* 800-342-0212 ■ *Web:* www.kingandprince.com	Saint Simons Island	GA	31522	912-638-3631	638-7699

	City	State	ZIP	Phone	Fax
Lake Lanier Islands Resort 7000 Holiday Rd. *Fax Area Code: 678 ■ *TF:* 800-768-5253 ■ *Web:* www.lakelanierislands.com	Lake Lanier Islands	GA	30518	770-945-8787	318-2005*
Reynolds Plantation 100 Linger Longer Rd. *TF:* 888-298-3119 ■ *Web:* www.reynoldsplantation.com	Greensboro	GA	30642	706-467-0600	
Ritz-Carlton Lodge Reynolds Plantation 1 Lake Oconee Trail *TF:* 800-826-1945 ■ *Web:* www.ritzcarlton.com	Greensboro	GA	30642	706-467-0600	467-7124
Sea Palms Golf & Tennis Resort 5445 Frederica Rd *TF:* 800-841-6268 ■ *Web:* www.seapalms.com	Saint Simons Island	GA	31522	912-638-3351	634-8029
Sky Valley Golf Course Resort 696 Sky Valley Way *TF:* 800-437-2416 ■ *Web:* www.skyvalley.com	Sky Valley	GA	30537	706-746-5302	746-5198
Villas by the Sea Resort 1175 N Beachview Dr *TF:* 800-841-6262 ■ *Web:* www.jekyllislandga.com	Jekyll Island	GA	31527	912-635-2521	635-2569

HAWAII

	City	State	ZIP	Phone	Fax
Castle Group Inc *Castle Resorts & Hotels* 500 Ala Moana Blvd Suite 555 3 Waterfront Plaza *TF:* 800-733-7753 ■ *Web:* www.castleresorts.com	Honolulu	HI	96813	808-524-0900	521-9994
Fairmont Kea Lani Maui 4100 Wailea Alanui Dr *TF:* 800-659-4100 ■ *Web:* www.fairmont.com	Maui	HI	96753	808-875-4100	875-1200
Fairmont Orchid Hawaii 1 N Kaniku Dr *TF:* 800-845-9905 ■ *Web:* www.fairmont.com/orchid	Kohala	HI	96743	808-885-2000	885-5778
Four Seasons Resort Hualalai 100 Ka'upulehu Dr *TF:* 888-340-5662 ■ *Web:* www.fourseasons.com/hualalai	Ka'upulehu-Kona	HI	96740	808-325-8000	325-8200
Four Seasons Resort Maui at Wailea 3900 Wailea Alanui Dr *TF:* 800-334-6284 ■ *Web:* www.fourseasons.com	Wailea	HI	96753	808-874-8000	874-2244
Grand Hyatt Kauai Resort & Spa 1571 Poipu Rd. *TF:* 800-233-1234 ■ *Web:* kauai.hyatt.com	Koloa	HI	96756	808-742-1234	742-1557
Grand Wailea Resort & Spa 3850 Wailea Alanui Dr *TF:* 800-888-6100 ■ *Web:* www.grandwailea.com	Wailea	HI	96753	808-875-1234	879-4077
Hanalei Bay Resort & Suites 5380 Honoiki Rd. *TF:* 800-827-4427 ■ *Web:* www.hanaleibayresort.com	Princeville	HI	96722	808-826-6522	826-6680
Hapuna Beach Prince Hotel 62-100 Kauna'oa Dr. *TF:* 800-882-6060 ■ *Web:* www.princeresortshawaii.com	Kamuela	HI	96743	808-880-1111	880-3142
Hawaii Prince Hotel Waikiki The 100 Holomoana St *TF:* 888-977-4623 ■ *Web:* www.princeresortshawaii.com/hawaii-prince-hotel.php	Honolulu	HI	96815	808-956-1111	944-4491
Hilton Hawaiian Village 2005 Kalia Rd *TF:* 800-445-8667 ■ *Web:* www.hilton.com	Honolulu	HI	96815	808-949-4321	951-5458
Hilton Waikoloa Village 425 Waikoloa Beach Dr. *TF:* 866-223-6574 ■ *Web:* www.hiltonwaikoloavillage.com	Waikoloa	HI	96738	808-886-1234	886-2900
Hotel Hana-Maui 5031 Hana Hwy *TF:* 800-321-4262 ■ *Web:* www.hanacoast.com	Hana	HI	96713	808-248-8211	248-7202
Hyatt Regency Maui Resort & Spa 200 Nohea Kai Dr *TF:* 800-233-1234 ■ *Web:* www.maui.hyatt.com	Lahaina	HI	96761	808-661-1234	667-4497
JW Marriott Resort Ihilani 92-1001 Olani St *TF:* 800-626-4446 ■ *Web:* www.ihilani.com	Kapolei	HI	96707	808-679-0079	679-0080
Kapalua Resort 800 Kapalua Dr *TF:* 877-527-2582 ■ *Web:* www.kapaluamaui.com	Lahaina Maui	HI	96761	808-669-8044	669-4956
Kapalua Villas The 2000 Village Rd. *TF:* 800-545-0018 ■ *Web:* www.outrigger.com/hotels-resorts/hawaiian-islands/maui/the-kapalua-villas	Lahaina	HI	96761	808-665-5400	669-2702
Kona Village Resort Queen Kaahumanu Hwy *TF:* 800-367-5290 ■ *Web:* www.konavillage.com	Kaupulehu-Kona	HI	96740	808-325-5555	325-5124
Lodge at Koele 1 Keomoku Hwy *TF:* 800-321-4666 ■ *Web:* www.lodgeatkoele.com	Lanai City	HI	96763	808-565-7300	565-4561
Marriott Kaua'i Resort & Beach Club 3610 Rice St Kalapaki Beach *TF:* 800-220-2925 ■ *Web:* www.marriott.com	Lihue - Kauai	HI	96766	808-245-5050	245-5049
Mauna Kea Beach Hotel 62-100 Maunakea Beach Dr *TF:* 866-977-4589 ■ *Web:* www.maunakeabeachhotel.com	Kohala Coast	HI	96743	808-882-7222	882-5700
Mauna Lani Bay Hotel & Bungalows 68-1400 Mauna Lani Dr *TF:* 800-367-2323 ■ *Web:* www.maunalani.com	Kohala Coast	HI	96743	808-885-6622	881-7000
Napili Kai Beach Club 5900 Honoapiilani Rd *TF:* 800-367-5030 ■ *Web:* www.napilikai.com	Lahaina	HI	96761	808-669-6271	669-5740
Outrigger Hotels & Resorts 2375 Kuhio Ave *Fax: Sales ■ *TF:* 800-688-7444 ■ *Web:* www.outrigger.com	Honolulu	HI	96815	808-921-6941	926-4368*
Outrigger Kanaloa at Kona 78-261 Manukai St. *TF:* 800-688-7444 ■ *Web:* www.outrigger.com	Kailua-Kona	HI	96740	808-322-9625	322-3818
Outrigger Reef on the Beach 2169 Kalia Rd *TF:* 800-688-7444 ■ *Web:* www.outrigger.com	Honolulu	HI	96815	808-923-3111	924-4957
Prince Resorts Hawaii 100 Holomoana St *TF:* 888-977-4623 ■ *Web:* www.princeresortshawaii.com	Honolulu	HI	96815	808-956-1111	944-4491
Ritz-Carlton Kapalua 1 Ritz-Carlton Dr *TF Resv:* 800-262-8440 ■ *Web:* www.ritzcarlton.com/resorts/kapalua	Lahaina	HI	96761	808-669-6200	669-1566
Royal Hawaiian 2259 Kalakaua Ave *Web:* www.royal-hawaiian.com	Honolulu	HI	96815	808-923-7311	931-7098
Royal Lahaina Resort 2780 Kekaa Dr *TF:* 800-222-5642 ■ *Web:* www.hawaiianhotels.com	Lahaina	HI	96761	808-661-3611	661-6150
Sheraton Kauai Resort 2440 Hoonani Rd *TF:* 888-847-0208 ■ *Web:* www.sheraton-kauai.com	Koloa	HI	96756	808-742-1661	742-4041
Sheraton Maui Resort 2605 Kaanapali Pkwy *TF:* 888-782-9488 ■ *Web:* www.sheraton-maui.com	Lahaina	HI	96761	808-661-0031	661-0458
Sheraton Moana Surfrider 2365 Kalakaua Ave *TF:* 800-325-3535 ■ *Web:* www.moana-surfrider.com	Honolulu	HI	96815	808-922-3111	924-4799
Sheraton Waikiki 2255 Kalakaua Ave *TF:* 800-325-3535 ■ *Web:* www.sheraton-waikiki.com	Honolulu	HI	96815	808-922-4422	923-8785
Turtle Bay Resort 57-091 Kamehameha Hwy *TF:* 800-203-3650 ■ *Web:* www.turtlebayresort.com	Kahuku	HI	96731	808-293-8811	293-9147
Wailea Beach Marriott Resort & Spa 3700 Wailea Alanui Dr *TF:* 800-367-2960 ■ *Web:* www.marriott.com	Wailea	HI	96753	808-879-1922	874-7802

IDAHO

	City	State	ZIP	Phone	Fax
Aston Hotel & Resorts Sunvalley PO Box 659 *TF:* 800-635-4444 ■ *Web:* www.astonsunvalley.com	Sun Valley	ID	83353	208-622-6400	726-3999
Coeur d'Alene Resort 115 S 2nd St PO Box 7200 *TF:* 800-688-5253 ■ *Web:* www.cdaresort.com	Coeur d'Alene	ID	83814	208-765-4000	664-7276
Elkhorn Golf Club 1 Elkhorn Rd PO Box 6029 *TF:* 877-622-3350 ■ *Web:* www.elkhorngolfclub.com	Sun Valley	ID	83354	208-622-3300	622-7052
Red Lion Templin's Hotel on the River 414 E 1st Ave *TF:* 800-283-6754 ■ *Web:* www.redlion.rdln.com	Post Falls	ID	83854	208-773-1611	773-4192
Sun Valley Resort 1 Sun Valley Rd *TF:* 800-786-8259 ■ *Web:* www.sunvalley.com	Sun Valley	ID	83353	208-622-2001	622-2015

ILLINOIS

	City	State	ZIP	Phone	Fax
Eagle Ridge Inn & Resort 444 Eagle Ridge Dr *TF:* 800-892-2269 ■ *Web:* www.eagleridge.com	Galena	IL	61036	815-777-2444	777-4502
Eaglewood Resort & Spa 1401 Nordic Rd. *TF:* 877-285-6150 ■ *Web:* www.eaglewoodresort.com	Itasca	IL	60143	630-773-1400	773-1709
Indian Lakes Resort 250 W Schick Rd *TF:* 800-334-3417 ■ *Web:* www.indianlakesresort.com	Bloomingdale	IL	60108	630-529-0200	529-9271
Pheasant Run Resort & Spa 4051 E Main St *TF:* 800-999-3319 ■ *Web:* www.pheasantrun.com	Saint Charles	IL	60174	630-584-6300	584-4693

INDIANA

	City	State	ZIP	Phone	Fax
Belterra Casino Resort 777 Belterra Dr. *TF:* 888-235-8377 ■ *Web:* www.belterracasino.com	Florence	IN	47020	812-427-7777	427-7812
Brickyard Crossing Golf Resort & Inn 4400 W 16th St. *Web:* www.brickyardcrossing.com/hotel	Indianapolis	IN	46222	317-241-2500	492-2715
Eagle Pointe Golf Resort 2250 E Pointe Rd *TF:* 877-324-7683 ■ *Web:* www.eaglepointe.com	Bloomington	IN	47401	812-824-4040	824-6860
Fourwinds Resort & Marina 9301 Fairfax Rd *TF:* 800-824-2628 ■ *Web:* www.fourwindsresort.com	Bloomington	IN	47401	812-824-2628	824-9816
French Lick Resort 8670 W State Rd 56 *TF:* 888-936-9360 ■ *Web:* www.frenchlick.com	French Lick	IN	47432	812-936-9300	936-2100
Potawatomi Inn Pokagan State Pk 6 Ln 100A Lake James *TF:* 877-768-2928 ■ *Web:* www.in.gov/dnr/parklake/inns/potawatomi	Angola	IN	46703	260-833-1077	833-4087

IOWA

	City	State	ZIP	Phone	Fax
Grand Harbor Resort & Waterpark 350 Bell St *TF:* 866-690-4006 ■ *Web:* www.grandharborresort.com	Dubuque	IA	52001	563-690-4000	690-0558

KANSAS

	City	State	ZIP	Phone	Fax
Terradyne Resort Hotel & Country Club 1400 Terradyne Dr *Web:* www.terradyne-resort.com	Andover	KS	67002	316-733-2582	733-9149

KENTUCKY

	City	State	ZIP	Phone	Fax
General Butler State Resort Park 1608 US Hwy 227 *TF:* 866-462-8853 ■ *Web:* www.parks.ky.gov	Carrollton	KY	41008	502-732-4384	732-4270
Griffin Gate Marriott Resort 1800 Newtown Pike *TF:* 800-228-9290 ■ *Web:* www.marriotthotels.com/LEXKY	Lexington	KY	40511	859-231-5100	255-9944
Lake Cumberland State Resort Park 5465 State Pk Rd *TF:* 800-325-1709 ■ *Web:* www.state.ky.us	Jamestown	KY	42629	270-343-3111	343-5510
Park Mammoth Resort 22850 Louisville Rd PO Box 307 *Web:* www.parkmammothresort.us	Park City	KY	42160	270-749-4101	749-2524

LOUISIANA

	City	State	ZIP	Phone	Fax
Emerald Hills Golf Resort 42618 Hwy 171 S *TF:* 800-533-5031	Florien	LA	71429	318-586-4661	586-4804

MAINE

				Phone	Fax
Atlantic Oakes 119 Eden St *TF:* 800-336-2463 ■ *Web:* www.barharbor.com	Bar Harbor	ME	04609	207-288-5801	288-8402
Bar Harbor Inn Oceanfront Resort Newport Dr PO Box 7 *TF:* 800-248-3351 ■ *Web:* www.barharborinn.com	Bar Harbor	ME	04609	207-288-3351	288-8454
Bethel Inn & Country Club 21 Broad St PO Box 49 *TF:* 800-654-0125 ■ *Web:* www.bethelinn.com	Bethel	ME	04217	207-824-2175	824-2233
Black Point Inn Resort 510 Black Pt Rd *TF:* 800-258-0003 ■ *Web:* www.blackpointinn.com	Scarborough	ME	04074	207-883-2500	883-9976
Cliff House Resort & Spa 591 Shore Rd *Web:* www.cliffhousemaine.com	Cape Neddick	ME	03902	207-361-1000	361-2122
Colony Hotel 140 Ocean Ave *TF:* 800-552-2363 ■ *Web:* www.thecolonyhotel.com	Kennebunkport	ME	04046	207-967-3331	967-8738
Holiday Inn SunSpree Bar Harbor Regency Resort 123 Eden St *TF:* 800-234-6835 ■ *Web:* www.barharborregency.com	Bar Harbor	ME	04609	207-288-9723	288-3089
Inn by the Sea 40 Bowery Beach Rd *TF:* 800-888-4287 ■ *Web:* www.innbythesea.com	Cape Elizabeth	ME	04107	207-799-3134	799-4779
Samoset Resort 220 Warrenton St *TF:* 800-341-1650 ■ *Web:* www.samoset.com	Rockport	ME	04856	207-594-2511	594-0722
Sebasco Harbor Resort 29 Keynon Rd *TF:* 800-225-3819 ■ *Web:* www.sebasco.com	Sebasco Estates	ME	04562	207-389-1161	389-2004
Spruce Point Inn 88 Grandview Ave PO Box 237 *Web:* www.sprucepointinn.com	Boothbay Harbor	ME	04538	207-633-4152	633-7138
Stage Neck Inn 8 Stage Neck Rd Rt 1A PO Box 70 *TF:* 800-222-3238 ■ *Web:* www.stageneck.com	York Harbor	ME	03911	207-363-3850	363-2221
Sugarloaf/USA 5092 Access Rd *TF:* 800-843-5623 ■ *Web:* www.sugarloaf.com	Carrabassett Valley	ME	04947	207-237-2000	237-3768
Sunday River Ski Resort 15 S Ridge Rd PO Box 4500 *TF:* 800-543-2754 ■ *Web:* www.sundayriver.com	Newry	ME	04261	207-824-3000	824-5110

MARYLAND

				Phone	Fax
Coconut Malorie Resort 200 59th St *TF:* 800-767-6060 ■ *Web:* www.coconutmalorie.com	Ocean City	MD	21842	410-723-6100	524-9327
Francis Scott Key Family Resort 12806 Ocean Gateway PO Box 468 *TF:* 800-213-0088 ■ *Web:* www.fskmotel.com	Ocean City	MD	21842	410-213-0088	213-2854
Harbourtowne Golf Resort & Conference Ctr 9784 Martingham Dr *TF:* 800-446-9066 ■ *Web:* www.harbourtowne.com	Saint Michaels	MD	21663	410-745-9066	745-9124
Ritz-Carlton Hotel Co LLC The 4445 Willard Ave Suite 800 **Fax Area Code:* 801 ■ *Web:* www.ritzcarlton.com	Chevy Chase	MD	20815	301-547-4700	468-4069*
Turf Valley Resort & Conference Ctr 2700 Turf Valley Rd *TF:* 800-666-8873 ■ *Web:* www.turfvalley.com	Ellicott City	MD	21042	410-465-1500	465-9282
Wisp Mountain Resort Hotel & Conference Ctr Deep Creek Lake 290 Marsh Hill Rd *TF:* 800-462-9477 ■ *Web:* www.wispresort.com	McHenry	MD	21541	301-387-5581	542-0041

MASSACHUSETTS

				Phone	Fax
Bayside Resort Hotel 225 Massachusetts 28 *TF:* 800-243-1114 ■ *Web:* www.baysideresort.com	West Yarmouth	MA	02673	508-775-5669	775-8862
Blue Water Resort 291 S Shore Dr *TF:* 877-819-5014 ■ *Web:* www.redjacketresorts.com/resorts/blue-water-resort.php	South Yarmouth	MA	02664	508-619-4614	398-1010
Canyon Ranch Lenox 165 Kemble St *TF Resv:* 800-742-9000 ■ *Web:* www.canyonranch.com	Lenox	MA	01240	413-637-4100	637-0057
Cape Codder Resort & Spa 1225 Iyanough Rd Rt 132 Bearse"s Way *TF:* 888-297-2200 ■ *Web:* www.capecodderresort.com	Hyannis	MA	02601	508-771-3000	790-8145
Captain Gosnold Village 230 Gosnold St *Web:* www.captaingosnold.com	Hyannis	MA	02601	508-775-9111	
Chatham Bars Inn 297 Shore Rd *TF:* 800-527-4884 ■ *Web:* www.chathambarsinn.com	Chatham	MA	02633	508-945-0096	945-5491
Cranwell Resort Spa & Golf Club 55 Lee Rd *TF:* 800-272-6935 ■ *Web:* www.cranwell.com	Lenox	MA	01240	413-637-1364	637-4364
Harbor House Village South Beach St PO Box 1139 *TF:* 800-230-4134	Nantucket	MA	02554	508-228-1500	228-7639
New Seabury Resort 20 Red Brook Rd *TF:* 800-999-9033 ■ *Web:* www.newseabury.com	Mashpee	MA	02649	508-477-9111	539-8634
Ocean Edge Resort & Golf Club 2907 Main St *TF:* 800-343-6074 ■ *Web:* www.oceanedge.com	Brewster	MA	02631	508-896-9000	896-9123
Ocean Mist Resort 97 S Shore Dr *TF:* 800-248-6478 ■ *Web:* www.capecodtravel.com/oceanmist	South Yarmouth	MA	02664	508-398-2633	760-3151
Sea Crest Resort & Conference Ctr 350 Quaker Rd *TF:* 800-225-3110 ■ *Web:* www.seacrestbeachhotel.com	North Falmouth	MA	02556	508-540-9400	548-0556
Sonesta International Hotels Corp 116 Huntington Ave 9th Fl *NASDAQ: SNSTA* ■ *TF:* 800-766-3782 ■ *Web:* www.sonesta.com	Boston	MA	02116	617-421-5400	421-5402
Wequassett Inn Resort & Golf Club 2173 Rt 28 *TF:* 800-225-7125 ■ *Web:* www.wequassett.com	East Harwich	MA	02645	508-432-5400	432-1915

MICHIGAN

				Phone	Fax
Bay Valley Hotel & Resort 2470 Old Bridge Rd *TF:* 800-292-5028 ■ *Web:* www.bayvalley.com	Bay City	MI	48706	989-686-3500	686-6931
Boyne Highlands Resort 600 Highlands Dr *TF:* 800-462-6963 ■ *Web:* www.boyne.com	Harbor Springs	MI	49740	231-526-3000	526-3100
Boyne Mountain Resort 1 Boyne Mountain Rd PO Box 19 *TF:* 800-462-6963 ■ *Web:* www.boyneresorts.com	Boyne Falls	MI	49713	231-549-6000	549-6094
Crystal Mountain Resort 12500 Crystal Mountain Dr *TF:* 800-968-7686 ■ *Web:* www.crystalmountain.com	Thompsonville	MI	49683	231-378-2000	378-2998
Garland Resort 4700 N Red Oak Rd *TF:* 800-968-0042 ■ *Web:* www.garlandusa.com	Lewiston	MI	49756	989-786-2211	786-2254
Grand Traverse Resort & Spa 6300 US 31 N **Fax:* resv ■ *TF:* 800-748-0303 ■ *Web:* www.grandtraverseresort.com	Acme	MI	49610	231-534-6000	534-6670*
Homestead Resort The 1 Wood Ridge Rd *Web:* www.thehomesteadresort.com	Glen Arbor	MI	49636	231-334-5000	334-5246
Indianhead Mountain Resort 500 Indianhead Rd *TF:* 800-346-3426 ■ *Web:* www.indianheadmtn.com	Wakefield	MI	49968	906-229-2229	229-5134
Inn at Bay Harbor The 3600 Village Harbor Dr *TF:* 800-462-6963 ■ *Web:* www.innatbayharbor.com	Bay Harbor	MI	49770	231-439-4000	439-4094
Lakewood Shores Resort 7751 Cedar Lake Rd *TF:* 800-882-2493 ■ *Web:* www.lakewoodshores.com	Oscoda	MI	48750	989-739-2073	739-1351
Marsh Ridge Resort 4815 Old US Hwy 27 S *TF:* 800-743-7529 ■ *Web:* www.marshridge.com	Gaylord	MI	49735	989-732-5552	732-2134
McGuire's Resort 7880 Mackinaw Trail *TF:* 800-632-7302 ■ *Web:* www.mcguiresresort.com	Cadillac	MI	49601	231-775-9947	775-9621
Mission Point Resort 6633 Main St *TF:* 800-833-7711 ■ *Web:* www.missionpoint.com	Mackinac Island	MI	49757	906-847-3312	542-3868
Otsego Club 696 M-32 E Main St PO Box 556 *TF:* 800-752-5510 ■ *Web:* www.otsegoclub.com	Gaylord	MI	49734	989-732-5181	732-0497
Shanty Creek Resort 1 Shanty Creek Rd *TF:* 800-678-4111 ■ *Web:* www.shantycreek.com	Bellaire	MI	49615	231-533-8621	533-7020
Treetops Resort 3962 Wilkinson Rd *TF:* 800-444-6711 ■ *Web:* www.treetops.com	Treetops Village	MI	49735	989-732-6711	732-8459

MINNESOTA

				Phone	Fax
Arrowwood Resort & Conference Ctr 2100 Arrowwood Ln NW *TF Resv:* 866-386-5263 ■ *Web:* www.arrowwoodresort.com	Alexandria	MN	56308	320-762-1124	762-0133
Breezy Point Resort 9252 Breezy Pt Dr *TF:* 800-432-3777 ■ *Web:* www.breezypointresort.com	Breezy Point	MN	56472	218-562-7811	562-4510
Caribou Highlands Lodge 371 Ski Hill Rd PO Box 99 *TF:* 800-642-6036 ■ *Web:* www.caribouhighlands.com	Lutsen	MN	55612	218-663-7241	663-7920
Carlson *Radisson Hotels & Resorts* 701 Carlson Pkwy *TF:* 800-333-3333 ■ *Web:* www.carlson.com	Minnetonka	MN	55305	763-212-5000	
Cascade Lodge 3719 W Hwy 61 *TF:* 800-322-9543 ■ *Web:* www.cascadelodgemn.com	Lutsen	MN	55612	218-387-1112	387-1113
Cragun's Conference & Golf Resort 11000 Cragun's Dr *TF:* 800-272-4867 ■ *Web:* www.craguns.com	Brainerd	MN	56401	218-829-3591	829-9188
Eagle's Nest Resort 6103 Lavaque Rd *TF:* 800-348-4575	Duluth	MN	55803	218-721-4147	
Fair Hills Resort 24270 County Hwy 20 *TF resv:* 800-323-2849 ■ *Web:* www.fairhillsresort.com	Detroit Lakes	MN	56501	218-847-7638	532-2068
Grand Casino Hinckley 777 Lady Luck Dr *TF:* 800-472-6321 ■ *Web:* www.grandcasinomn.com	Hinckley	MN	55037	320-384-7777	384-4775
Grand Casino Mille Lacs 777 Grand Ave PO Box 343 *TF:* 800-626-5825 ■ *Web:* www.grandcasinomn.com	Onamia	MN	56359	320-532-7777	532-8103
Grand Portage Lodge & Casino 72 Casino Dr *TF:* 800-543-1384 ■ *Web:* www.grandportage.com	Grand Portage	MN	55605	218-475-2401	475-2309
Grand View Lodge 23521 Nokomis Ave *TF:* 866-801-2951 ■ *Web:* www.grandviewlodge.com	Nisswa	MN	56468	218-963-2234	963-2269
Izatys Golf & Yacht Club 40005 85th Ave *TF:* 800-533-1728 ■ *Web:* www.izatys.com	Onamia	MN	56359	320-532-4574	532-9072
Lake Breeze Motel Resort 9000 Congdon Blvd *TF:* 800-738-5884 ■ *Web:* www.lakebreeze.com	Duluth	MN	55804	218-525-6808	525-2986
Lutsen Resort 5700 W Hwy 61 PO Box 9 *TF:* 800-258-8736 ■ *Web:* www.lutsenresort.com	Lutsen	MN	55612	218-663-7212	663-0145
Madden's on Gull Lake 11266 Pine Beach Peninsula *TF:* 800-233-2934 ■ *Web:* www.maddens.com	Brainerd	MN	56401	218-829-2811	829-6583
Ruttger's Bay Lake Lodge 25039 Tame Fish Lake Rd PO Box 400 *TF:* 800-450-4545 ■ *Web:* www.ruttgers.com	Deerwood	MN	56444	218-678-2885	678-2864
Superior Shores Resort 1521 Superior Shores Dr *TF:* 800-242-1988 ■ *Web:* www.superiorshores.com	Two Harbors	MN	55616	218-834-5671	834-5677

MISSISSIPPI

				Phone	Fax
Beau Rivage Resort & Casino 875 Beach Blvd *TF:* 888-750-7111 ■ *Web:* www.beaurivage.com	Biloxi	MS	39530	228-386-7111	386-7414
Gulf Hills Hotel 13701 Paso Rd *TF:* 866-875-4211 ■ *Web:* www.gulfhillshotel.com	Ocean Springs	MS	39564	228-875-4211	875-4213
IP Casino Resort & Spa 850 Bayview Ave *TF:* 800-436-3000 ■ *Web:* www.ipbiloxi.com	Biloxi	MS	39530	228-436-3000	432-3260
Treasure Bay Casino & Hotel 1980 Beach Blvd *TF:* 800-747-2839 ■ *Web:* www.treasurebay.com	Biloxi	MS	39531	228-385-6000	385-6082

MISSOURI

Resort	City	State	ZIP	Phone	Fax
Best Western Dogwood Hills Resort Inn & Golf Club 1252 State Hwy KK *TF:* 800-528-1234 ■ *Web:* www.dogwoodhillsresort.com	Osage Beach	MO	65065	573-348-1735	348-0014
Big Cedar Lodge 612 Devil's Pool Rd *Web:* www.big-cedar.com	Ridgedale	MO	65739	417-335-2777	335-2340
Indian Point Resort 71 Dogwood Pk Trail *TF:* 800-888-1891 ■ *Web:* www.indianpoint.com	Branson	MO	65616	417-338-2250	338-3507
Lilleys' Landing Resort 367 River Ln *TF:* 800-284-2916 ■ *Web:* www.lilleyslanding.com	Branson	MO	65616	417-334-6380	334-6311
Lodge of Four Seasons Horseshoe Bend Pkwy PO Box 215 *TF Resv:* 888-265-5500 ■ *Web:* www.4seasonsresort.com	Lake Ozark	MO	65049	573-365-3000	
Peak Resorts 17409 Hidden Valley Dr. *Web:* www.peakresorts.com	Wildwood	MO	63025	636-938-7474	549-0064
Plantation at Fall Creek Resort 1 Fall Creek Dr *Web:* www.diamondresorts.com	Branson	MO	65616	417-336-3611	335-3255
Resort at Port Arrowhead The 3080 Bagnell Dam Blvd PO Box 1930 *TF:* 800-532-3575 ■ *Web:* www.lakeoftheozarksgetaway.com	Lake Ozark	MO	65049	573-365-2334	365-6887
Tan-Tar-A Resort Golf Club & Spa 494 Tantara Dr PO Box 188TT *TF Resv:* 800-826-8272 ■ *Web:* www.tan-tar-a.com	Osage Beach	MO	65065	573-348-3131	348-3206
Thousand Hills Golf Resort 245 S Wildwood Dr. *TF:* 877-262-0430 ■ *Web:* www.thousandhills.com	Branson	MO	65616	417-336-5873	337-5740
Welk Resort Branson 1984 State Hwy 165 *TF:* 800-505-9355 ■ *Web:* www.welkresortbranson.com	Branson	MO	65616	417-336-3575	339-3176

MONTANA

Resort	City	State	ZIP	Phone	Fax
Big EZ Lodge 7000 Beaver Creek Rd *TF:* 877-244-3299 ■ *Web:* www.bigezlodge.com	Big Sky	MT	59716	406-995-7000	995-7007
Big Sky Resort 1 Lone Mountain Trail PO Box 160001 *TF:* 800-548-4486 ■ *Web:* www.bigskyresort.com	Big Sky	MT	59716	406-995-5000	995-5001
Fairmont Hot Springs Resort 1500 Fairmont Rd *TF:* 800-332-3272 ■ *Web:* www.fairmontmontana.com	Fairmont	MT	59711	406-797-3241	797-3337
Glacier Park Inc PO Box 2025 *Web:* www.glacierparkinc.com	Columbia Falls	MT	59912	406-892-2525	892-1375
Meadow Lake Resort 100 St Andrews Dr *TF:* 800-321-4653 ■ *Web:* www.meadowlake.com	Columbia Falls	MT	59912	406-892-8700	892-0330
Rock Creek Resort 6380 US Hwy 212 *TF:* 800-667-1119 ■ *Web:* www.rockcreekresort.com	Red Lodge	MT	59068	406-446-1111	237-9851
Triple Creek Ranch 5551 W Fork Rd *Web:* www.triplecreekranch.com	Darby	MT	59829	406-821-4600	821-4666
Winter Sports Inc 3840 Big Mountain Rd PO Box 1400 *TF:* 800-858-3930 ■ *Web:* www.skiwhitefish.com	Whitefish	MT	59937	406-862-2900	862-2955

NEVADA

Resort	City	State	ZIP	Phone	Fax
Alexis Park Resort 375 E Harmon Ave *TF:* 800-582-2228 ■ *Web:* www.alexispark.com	Las Vegas	NV	89169	702-796-3300	796-3354
Aquarius Casino Resort 1900 S Casino Dr *TF:* 888-662-5825 ■ *Web:* www.aquariuscasinoresort.com	Laughlin	NV	89029	702-298-5111	
Atlantis Casino Resort 3800 S Virginia St *TF:* 800-723-6500 ■ *Web:* www.atlantiscasino.com	Reno	NV	89502	775-825-4700	332-2211
Bellagio Hotel & Casino 3600 Las Vegas Blvd S *TF:* 888-987-7111 ■ *Web:* www.bellagio.com	Las Vegas	NV	89109	702-693-7111	693-8585
Cal-Neva Resort Spa & Casino 2 Stateline Rd PO Box 368 *TF:* 800-225-6382 ■ *Web:* www.calnevaresort.com	Crystal Bay	NV	89402	775-832-4000	831-9007
Casablanca Resort 950 W Mesquite Blvd *TF:* 800-459-7529 ■ *Web:* www.casablancaresort.com	Mesquite	NV	89027	702-346-7529	346-6888
Club Cal Neva Hotel Casino The 38 E 2nd St PO Box 2071 *TF:* 877-777-7303 ■ *Web:* www.clubcalneva.com	Reno	NV	89501	775-323-1046	335-2614
Don Laughlin's Riverside Resort & Casino 1650 Casino Dr *TF:* 800-227-3849 ■ *Web:* www.riversideresort.com	Laughlin	NV	89029	702-298-2535	298-2695
Flamingo Las Vegas 3555 Las Vegas Blvd S *TF:* 800-902-9929 ■ *Web:* www.totalrewards.com	Las Vegas	NV	89109	702-697-2711	733-3528
Golden Nugget Hotel 129 E Fremont St *TF:* 800-634-3454 ■ *Web:* www.goldennugget.com	Las Vegas	NV	89101	702-385-7111	385-7111
Golden Nugget Laughlin 2300 S Casino Dr *TF:* 800-950-7700 ■ *Web:* www.goldennugget.com	Laughlin	NV	89029	702-298-7111	298-7122
Grand Sierra Resort & Casino 2500 E 2nd St *TF:* 800-501-2651 ■ *Web:* www.grandsierraresort.com	Reno	NV	89595	775-789-2000	789-1678
Hard Rock Hotel & Casino 4455 Paradise Rd *TF:* 800-693-7625 ■ *Web:* www.hardrockhotel.com	Las Vegas	NV	89169	702-693-5000	693-5557
Harrah's Las Vegas 3475 Las Vegas Blvd S *TF:* 800-214-9110 ■ *Web:* www.harrahslasvegas.com	Las Vegas	NV	89109	702-369-5000	369-6014
John Ascuaga's Nugget Hotel Casino 1100 Nugget Ave *Fax: Resv ■ *TF:* 800-648-1177 ■ *Web:* www.janugget.com	Sparks	NV	89431	775-356-3300	356-3434*
JW Marriott Resort Las Vegas 221 N Rampart Blvd *TF:* 877-869-8777 ■ *Web:* www.marriott.com	Las Vegas	NV	89145	702-869-7777	869-7339
Las Vegas Sands Corp 3355 Las Vegas Blvd S *NYSE: LVS* ■ *Web:* www.lasvegassands.com	Las Vegas	NV	89109	702-414-1000	414-4884
Loews Lake Las Vegas Resort 101 Montelago Blvd *TF:* 800-235-6397 ■ *Web:* www.loewshotels.com	Henderson	NV	89011	702-567-6000	567-6067
Mandalay Bay Resort & Casino 3950 Las Vegas Blvd S *TF:* 877-632-7800 ■ *Web:* www.mandalaybay.com	Las Vegas	NV	89119	702-632-7777	632-7234
MGM Grand Hotel & Casino 3799 Las Vegas Blvd S *TF:* 877-880-0880 ■ *Web:* www.mgmgrand.com	Las Vegas	NV	89109	702-891-1111	891-3036
Mirage The 3400 Las Vegas Blvd S *TF:* 800-627-6667 ■ *Web:* www.mirage.com	Las Vegas	NV	89109	702-791-7111	791-7414
Monarch Casino & Resort Inc 3800 S Virginia St *NASDAQ: MCRI* ■ *Web:* www.monarchcasino.com	Reno	NV	89509	775-335-4600	332-9171
Monte Carlo Resort & Casino 3770 Las Vegas Blvd S *TF:* 800-311-8999 ■ *Web:* www.montecarlo.com	Las Vegas	NV	89109	702-730-7777	730-7200
Planet Hollywood Resort & Casino 3667 Las Vegas Blvd S *TF:* 866-919-7472 ■ *Web:* www.planethollywoodresort.com	Las Vegas	NV	89109	702-785-5555	785-9600
Primm Valley Resort & Casino 31900 S Las Vegas Blvd *TF:* 800-386-7867 ■ *Web:* www.primmvalleyresorts.com	Primm	NV	89019	702-386-7867	679-5424
Ridge Tahoe 400 Ridge Club Dr PO Box 5790 *TF:* 800-334-1600 ■ *Web:* www.ridgetahoeresort.com	Stateline	NV	89449	775-588-3553	588-1551
Ritz-Carlton Lake Las Vegas 1610 Lake Las Vegas Pkwy *TF:* 800-241-3333 ■ *Web:* www.ritzcarlton.com	Henderson	NV	89011	702-567-4700	567-4777
Riviera Hotel & Casino 2901 Las Vegas Blvd S *TF Resv:* 800-634-6753 ■ *Web:* www.rivierahotel.com	Las Vegas	NV	89109	702-734-5110	794-9663
Sahara Hotel & Casino 2535 Las Vegas Blvd S *TF:* 888-696-2121 ■ *Web:* www.saharavegas.com	Las Vegas	NV	89109	702-737-2111	791-2027
Treasure Island Hotel & Casino 3300 Las Vegas Blvd S *TF:* 800-288-7206 ■ *Web:* www.treasureisland.com	Las Vegas	NV	89109	702-894-7111	894-7414
Tropicana Resort & Casino 3801 Las Vegas Blvd S *TF Resv:* 888-826-8767 ■ *Web:* www.troplv.com	Las Vegas	NV	89109	702-739-2222	739-3648
Venetian Resort Hotel & Casino 3355 Las Vegas Blvd S *TF:* 877-283-6423 ■ *Web:* www.venetian.com	Las Vegas	NV	89109	702-414-1000	414-1100
Wynn Resorts Ltd 3131 Las Vegas Blvd S *NASDAQ: WYNN* ■ *TF:* 877-321-9966 ■ *Web:* www.wynnresorts.com	Las Vegas	NV	89109	702-770-7555	770-1571

NEW BRUNSWICK

Resort	City	Province	Postal Code	Phone	Fax
Fairmont Algonquin 184 Adolphus St *TF:* 800-441-1414 ■ *Web:* www.fairmont.com	Saint Andrews	NB	E5B1T7	506-529-8823	529-7162

NEW HAMPSHIRE

Resort	City	State	ZIP	Phone	Fax
BALSAMS The 1000 Cold Springs Rd *TF:* 800-255-0600 ■ *Web:* www.thebalsams.com	Dixville Notch	NH	03576	603-255-3400	255-4221
Cranmore Mountain Resort 1 Skimobile Rd PO Box 1640 *TF:* 800-786-6754 ■ *Web:* www.cranmore.com	North Conway	NH	03860	603-356-5543	356-8526
Margate on Winnipesaukee The 76 Lake St *TF:* 800-627-4283 ■ *Web:* www.themargate.com	Laconia	NH	03246	603-524-5210	528-4485
Mount Washington Hotel & Resort Rt 302 *TF:* 800-314-1752 ■ *Web:* www.brettonwoods.com	Bretton Woods	NH	03575	603-278-1000	278-8828
Valley Inn Tecumseh Rd PO Box 1 *TF:* 800-343-0969 ■ *Web:* www.valleyinn.com	Waterville Valley	NH	03215	603-236-8425	236-4294
Waterville Valley Resort 1 Ski Area Rd PO Box 540 *TF:* 800-468-2553 ■ *Web:* www.waterville.com	Waterville Valley	NH	03215	603-236-8311	236-4344
White Mountain Hotel & Resort 2560 W Side Rd PO Box 1828 *TF:* 800-533-6301 ■ *Web:* www.whitemountainhotel.com	North Conway	NH	03860	603-356-7100	356-7100

NEW JERSEY

Resort	City	State	ZIP	Phone	Fax
Atlantic City Hilton Casino Resort Boston Ave & The Boardwalk *TF:* 800-257-7075 ■ *Web:* www.hiltonac.com	Atlantic City	NJ	08401	609-347-7111	340-7128
Bally's Atlantic City Park Pl & Boardwalk *TF:* 800-772-7777 ■ *Web:* www.ballysac.com	Atlantic City	NJ	08401	609-340-2000	340-1725
Caesars Atlantic City Hotel Casino 2100 Pacific Ave *TF:* 800-443-0104 ■ *Web:* www.totalrewards.com	Atlantic City	NJ	08401	609-348-4411	343-2405
Dolce International 28 W Grand Ave *TF:* 888-993-6523 ■ *Web:* www.dolce.com	Montvale	NJ	07645	201-307-8700	307-8837
Legends Resort & Country Club 430 Rt 517 PO Box 637 *TF:* 800-835-2555 ■ *Web:* www.golegends.com	McAfee	NJ	07428	973-827-6000	827-7198
Montreal Inn Beach Dr & Madison Ave *TF:* 800-525-7011 ■ *Web:* www.montreal-inn.com	Cape May	NJ	08204	609-884-7011	884-4559
Mountain Creek Resort 200 Rt 94 *Fax: Hum Res ■ *Web:* www.mountaincreek.com	Vernon	NJ	07462	973-827-2000	209-3342*
Ocean Place Resort & Spa 1 Ocean Blvd *TF:* 800-411-6493 ■ *Web:* www.oceanplace.com	Long Branch	NJ	07740	732-571-4000	229-0931
Resorts Casino Hotel 1133 Boardwalk *TF:* 800-334-6378 ■ *Web:* www.resortsac.com	Atlantic City	NJ	08401	800-334-6378	
Seaview Marriott Resort & Spa 401 S New York Rd *TF:* 800-205-6518 ■ *Web:* www.dolce-seaview-hotel.com	Galloway	NJ	08205	609-652-1800	652-6917
Tropicana Entertainment 2831 Boardwalk *TF:* 800-843-8767 ■ *Web:* www.tropicana.net	Atlantic City	NJ	08401	609-340-4000	340-4457

				Phone	Fax
Trump Taj Mahal Casino Resort 1000 Boardwalk & Virginia Ave *TF:* 800-825-8786 ■ *Web:* www.trumptaj.com	Atlantic City	NJ	08401	609-449-1000	449-6818

NEW MEXICO

				Phone	Fax
Angel Fire Resort PO Box 130 *TF:* 800-633-7463 ■ *Web:* www.angelfireresort.com	Angel Fire	NM	87710	505-377-6401	377-4200
El Monte Sagrado Living Resort & Spa 317 Kit Carson Rd *TF:* 888-213-4419 ■ *Web:* www.elmontesagrado.com	Taos	NM	87571	505-758-3502	737-2985
Inn of the Mountain Gods 287 Carrizo Canyon Rd *TF:* 800-545-9011 ■ *Web:* www.innofthemountaingods.com	Mescalero	NM	88340	505-464-5141	
La Posada de Santa Fe Resort & Spa 330 E Palace Ave *TF:* 800-727-5276 ■ *Web:* www.laposada.rockresorts.com	Santa Fe	NM	87501	505-986-0000	982-9646
Lifts West Condominium Resort Hotel PO Box 330 *TF:* 800-221-1859 ■ *Web:* www.redrivernm.com/liftswest	Red River	NM	87558	505-754-2778	754-6617
Lodge at Cloudcroft The 601 Corona Pl *TF:* 800-395-6343 ■ *Web:* www.thelodgeresort.com	Cloudcroft	NM	88317	505-682-2566	682-2715

NEW YORK

				Phone	Fax
Bonnie Castle Resort 31 Holland St *TF:* 800-955-4511 ■ *Web:* www.bonniecastle.com	Alexandria Bay	NY	13607	315-482-4511	482-9600
Canoe Island Lodge 3820 Lakeshore Dr. *Web:* www.canoeislandlodge.com	Diamond Point	NY	12824	518-668-5592	668-2012
Concord Resort & Golf Club 219 Concord Rd *TF:* 888-448-9686 ■ *Web:* www.concordresort.com	Kiamesha Lake	NY	12751	845-794-4000	794-6944
Doral Arrowwood Conference Resort 975 Anderson Hill Rd *TF:* 800-223-6725 ■ *Web:* www.arrowwood.com	Rye Brook	NY	10573	914-939-5500	323-5500
Friar Tuck Resort & Convention Ctr 4858 Rt 32 *TF:* 800-832-7600	Catskill	NY	12414	518-678-2271	678-2214
Gurney's Inn Resort & Spa 290 Old Montauk Hwy *TF:* 800-848-7639 ■ *Web:* www.gurneysinn.com	Montauk	NY	11954	631-668-2345	668-3576
Hilton Lake Placid Resort 1 Mirror Lake Dr *TF:* 800-755-5598	Lake Placid	NY	12946	518-523-4411	523-1120
Holiday Valley Resort PO Box 370 Rt 219 *TF:* 800-323-0020 ■ *Web:* www.holidayvalley.com	Ellicottville	NY	14731	716-699-2345	699-5204
Kutsher's Country Club Resort Kutchers Rd PO Box 432 *TF:* 800-431-1273 ■ *Web:* www.kutshers.com	Monticello	NY	12701	845-794-6000	794-0157
Mohonk Mountain House 1000 Mountain Rest Rd *TF:* 800-772-6646 ■ *Web:* www.mohonk.com	New Paltz	NY	12561	845-255-1000	256-2161
Montauk Yacht Club Resort & Marina 32 Star Island Rd *TF:* 888-692-8668 ■ *Web:* www.montaukyachtclub.com	Montauk	NY	11954	631-668-3100	668-6181
Nevele Grande Resort & Country Club 1 Nevele Rd *TF:* 800-647-6000	Ellenville	NY	12428	845-647-6000	647-9884
Otesaga The 60 Lake St *TF:* 800-348-6222 ■ *Web:* www.otesaga.com	Cooperstown	NY	13326	607-547-9931	547-9675
Peek 'n Peak Resort 1405 Olde Rd PO Box 360 *Web:* www.pknpk.com	Findley Lake	NY	14736	716-355-4141	355-4542
Pine Tree Point Resort 70 Anthony St PO Box 99 *TF:* 888-746-3229 ■ *Web:* www.pinetreepointresort.com	Alexandria Bay	NY	13607	315-482-9911	482-6420
Point The PO Box 1327 *TF:* 800-255-3530 ■ *Web:* www.thepointresort.com	Saranac Lake	NY	12983	518-891-5674	891-1152
Roaring Brook Ranch & Tennis Resort PO Box 671 *Web:* www.roaringbrookranch.com	Lake George	NY	12845	518-668-5767	668-4019
Rocking Horse Ranch Resort 600 Rt 44-55 *TF:* 800-647-2624 ■ *Web:* www.rhranch.com	Highland	NY	12528	845-691-2927	691-6434
Sagamore The 110 Sagamore Rd *TF:* 800-358-3585 ■ *Web:* www.thesagamore.com	Bolton Landing	NY	12814	518-644-9400	743-6036
Le Meridien 1111 Westchester Ave *TF:* 888-625-5144 ■ *Web:* www.starwoodhotels.com/lemeridien	White Plains	NY	10604	914-640-8100	640-8310
Saint Regis Hotels & Resorts 1111 Westchester Ave *Web:* www.starwoodhotels.com	White Plains	NY	10604	914-640-8100	640-8310
Thousand Islands Country Club 46433 CR 100 PO Box 290 *Web:* www.ticountryclub.com	Wellesley Island	NY	13640	315-482-9454	482-9321
Villa Roma Resort & Conference Ctr 356 Villa Roma Rd *TF:* 800-533-6767 ■ *Web:* www.villaroma.com	Callicoon	NY	12723	845-887-4880	887-4824
Whiteface Club & Resort 373 Whiteface Inn Ln *TF:* 800-422-6757 ■ *Web:* www.whitefaceclub.com	Lake Placid	NY	12946	518-523-2551	523-4278
Woodcliff Hotel & Spa 199 Woodcliff Dr *TF:* 800-365-3065 ■ *Web:* www.woodcliffhotelspa.com	Fairport	NY	14450	585-381-4000	381-2673

NORTH CAROLINA

				Phone	Fax
Ballantyne Resort Hotel 10000 Ballantyne Commons Pkwy *TF:* 866-248-4824 ■ *Web:* www.theballantynehotel.com	Charlotte	NC	28277	704-248-4000	248-4005
Chetola Resort PO Box 17 N Main St *TF:* 800-243-8652 ■ *Web:* www.chetola.com	Blowing Rock	NC	28605	828-295-5500	295-5529
Divi Resorts Inc 6340 Quadrangle Dr Suite 300 *TF:* 800-367-3484 ■ *Web:* www.diviresorts.com	Chapel Hill	NC	27517	919-419-3484	419-2075
Eseeola Lodge 175 Linville Ave PO Box 99 *TF:* 800-742-6717 ■ *Web:* www.eseeola.com	Linville	NC	28646	828-733-4311	733-3227
Fontana Village Resort 300 Woods Rd PO Box 68 *TF:* 800-849-2258 ■ *Web:* www.fontanavillage.com	Fontana Dam	NC	28733	828-498-2211	498-2345
Greystone Inn Greystone Ln *TF:* 800-824-5766 ■ *Web:* www.greystoneinn.com	Lake Toxaway	NC	28747	828-966-4700	862-5689
Grove Park Inn Resort & Spa 290 Macon Ave *TF:* 800-438-5800 ■ *Web:* www.groveparkinn.com	Asheville	NC	28804	828-252-2711	253-7053
High Hampton Inn & Country Club 1525 Hwy 107 S *TF:* 800-334-2551 ■ *Web:* www.highhamptoninn.com	Cashiers	NC	28717	828-743-2450	743-5991
Holiday Inn SunSpree Resort Wrightsville Beach 1706 N Lumina Ave *TF:* 877-330-5050 ■ *Web:* www.ichotelsgroup.com	Wrightsville Beach	NC	28480	910-256-2231	256-9208
Hound Ears Lodge & Club PO Box 188 *Web:* www.houndears.com	Blowing Rock	NC	28605	828-963-4321	963-8030
Maggie Valley Resort & Country Club 1819 Country Club Dr *TF:* 800-438-3861 ■ *Web:* www.maggievalleyclub.com	Maggie Valley	NC	28751	828-926-1616	926-2906
Mid Pines Inn & Golf Club 1010 Midland Rd *TF:* 800-323-2114 ■ *Web:* www.pineneedles-midpines.com	Southern Pines	NC	28387	910-692-2114	692-4615
Pine Needles Lodge & Golf Club PO Box 88 *TF:* 800-747-7272 ■ *Web:* www.pineneedles-midpines.com	Southern Pines	NC	28388	910-692-7111	692-5349
Pinehurst Resort & Country Club 80 Carolina Vista Dr *TF:* 800-487-4653 ■ *Web:* www.pinehurst.com	Pinehurst	NC	28374	910-295-6811	295-8466
Pinnacle Inn Resort 303 Pinnacle Inn Rd *TF:* 800-405-7888	Banner Elk	NC	28604	828-387-2231	387-3745
Sanderling Resort & Spa 1461 Duck Rd *TF:* 800-701-4111 ■ *Web:* www.sanderlinginn.com	Duck	NC	27949	252-261-4111	261-1638
Waynesville Inn Golf & Country Club The 176 Country Club Dr *TF:* 800-627-6250 ■ *Web:* www.thewaynesvilleinn.com	Waynesville	NC	28786	828-456-3551	456-3555
Wolf Ridge Ski Resort 578 Valley View Cir *TF:* 800-817-4111 ■ *Web:* www.skiwolfridgenc.com	Mars Hill	NC	28754	828-689-4111	689-9819

NORTH DAKOTA

				Phone	Fax
Prairie Knights Casino & Resort 7932 Hwy 24 *TF:* 800-425-8277 ■ *Web:* www.prairieknights.com	Fort Yates	ND	58538	701-854-7777	854-7786

NOVA SCOTIA

				Phone	Fax
Atlantica Hotel & Marina Oak Island 36 Treasure Dr PO Box 6 *TF:* 800-565-5075 ■ *Web:* www.oakislandresortandspa.com	Western Shore	NS	B0J3M0	902-627-2600	627-2020
Inverary Resort *Cape Breton Resorts* 368 Shore Rd PO Box 190 *TF:* 800-565-5660 ■ *Web:* www.capebretonresorts.com/inverary.asp	Baddeck	NS	B0E1B0	902-295-3500	295-3527
Pines Resort The 103 Shore Rd PO Box 70 *TF:* 800-667-4637 ■ *Web:* www.signatureresorts.com/pines	Digby	NS	B0V1A0	902-245-2511	245-6133

OHIO

				Phone	Fax
Atwood Lake Resort 2650 Lodge Rd *TF:* 800-362-6406 ■ *Web:* www.atwoodlakeresort.com	Sherrodsville	OH	44675	330-735-2211	735-2562
Avalon Inn & Resort 9519 E Market St *TF:* 800-828-2566 ■ *Web:* www.avaloninn.com	Warren	OH	44484	330-856-1900	856-2248
Deer Creek Resort & Conference Ctr 22300 State Pk Rd 20 PO Box 125 *TF:* 877-678-3777 ■ *Web:* www.deercreekstateparklodge.com	Mount Sterling	OH	43143	740-869-2020	869-4059
Glenmoor Country Club 4191 Glenmoor Rd *TF:* 888-456-6667 ■ *Web:* www.memberstatements.com	Canton	OH	44718	330-966-3600	966-3611
Hueston Woods Lodge & Conference Ctr 5201 Lodge Rd *Web:* www.huestonwoodsstateparklodge.com	College Corner	OH	45003	513-664-3500	523-1522
Renaissance Quail Hollow Resort 11080 Concord-Hambden Rd *TF:* 800-792-0258	Painesville	OH	44077	440-497-1100	497-1111
Sawmill Creek Resort 400 Sawmill Creek Dr. *TF:* 800-729-6455 ■ *Web:* www.sawmillcreek.com	Huron	OH	44839	419-433-3800	433-7610

OKLAHOMA

				Phone	Fax
Cherokee Casino & Resort 777 W Cherokee St *TF:* 800-760-6700 ■ *Web:* www.cherokeestarrewards.com	Catoosa	OK	74015	918-384-7800	266-3038
Fin & Feather Resort Inc Rt 1 PO Box 194 *Web:* www.finandfeatherresort.com	Gore	OK	74435	918-487-5148	487-5025
Lake Murray Resort Park 3323 Lodge Rd *TF:* 800-257-0322 ■ *Web:* www.touroklahoma.com	Ardmore	OK	73401	580-223-6600	226-9613
Lake Texoma Resort Park PO Box 248 *Web:* www.oklahomaparks.com	Kingston	OK	73439	580-564-2566	
Quartz Mountain Resort & Conference Ctr 22469 Lodge Rd *TF:* 877-999-5567 ■ *Web:* www.quartzmountainresort.com	Lone Wolf	OK	73655	580-563-2424	563-2422

ONTARIO

	City	State	Zip	Phone	Fax
Deerhurst Resort 1235 Deerhurst Dr *TF Sales:* 800-461-6522 ■ *Web:* www.deerhurstresort.com	Huntsville	ON	P1H2E8	705-789-6411	789-2431
Delta Hotels Ltd 70 University Ave 11th Fl *TF:* 800-268-1133 ■ *Web:* www.deltahotels.com	Toronto	ON	M5J2M4	416-874-2000	874-2001
Delta Meadowvale 6750 Mississauga Rd *TF:* 800-422-8238 ■ *Web:* www.deltahotels.com	Mississauga	ON	L5N2L3	905-821-1981	542-4036
Fallsview Casino Resort 6380 Fallsview Blvd *TF:* 888-325-5788 ■ *Web:* www.fallsviewcasinoresort.com	Niagara Falls	ON	L2G7X5	905-358-3255	371-7952
Pinestone Resort PO Box 809 *TF:* 800-461-0357 ■ *Web:* www.pinestone-resort.com	Haliburton	ON	K0M1S0	705-457-1800	457-1783

OREGON

	City	State	Zip	Phone	Fax
Black Butte Ranch 12930 Hawks Beard Rd PO Box 8000 *TF:* 866-901-2961 ■ *Web:* www.blackbutteranch.com	Black Butte Ranch	OR	97759	541-595-1252	595-2077
Gearhart By the Sea 1157 N Marion Ave *TF:* 800-547-0115 ■ *Web:* www.gearhartresort.com	Gearhart	OR	97138	503-738-8331	738-0881
Mount Bachelor Village Resort & Conference Ctr 19717 Mt Bachelor Dr *TF:* 800-547-5204 ■ *Web:* www.mtbachelorvillage.com	Bend	OR	97702	541-389-5900	388-7401
Resort at the Mountain 68010 E Fairway Ave *TF:* 800-669-7666 ■ *Web:* www.theresort.com	Welches	OR	97067	503-622-3101	622-2222
Salishan Lodge & Golf Resort PO Box 118 *TF:* 800-452-2300 ■ *Web:* www.salishan.com	Gleneden Beach	OR	97388	541-764-2371	764-3681
Seventh Mountain Resort 18575 SW Century Dr *TF:* 800-452-6810 ■ *Web:* www.seventhmountain.com	Bend	OR	97702	541-382-8711	382-3517
Sunriver Resort 17600 Ctr Dr PO Box 3609 *TF:* 800-547-3922 ■ *Web:* www.sunriver-resort.com	Sunriver	OR	97707	541-593-1000	593-4685
Timberline Lodge 88 Hwy 150 *TF:* 800-547-1406 ■ *Web:* www.timberlinelodge.com	Timberline Lodge	OR	97028	503-272-3311	622-0710
Village Green Resort & Gardens 725 Row River Rd *TF:* 800-343-7666 ■ *Web:* www.villagegreenresortandgardens.com	Cottage Grove	OR	97424	541-942-2491	942-2386

PENNSYLVANIA

	City	State	Zip	Phone	Fax
Allenberry Resort 1559 Boiling Springs Rd *TF:* 800-430-5468 ■ *Web:* www.allenberry.com	Boiling Springs	PA	17007	717-258-3211	960-5280
Caesars Cove Haven Resort 194 Lakeview Dr *TF:* 800-233-4141 ■ *Web:* www.caesarspoconoresorts.com	Lakeville	PA	18438	570-226-4506	226-4697
Caesars Paradise Stream Rt 940 Carlton Rd PO Box 99 *TF:* 800-233-4141 ■ *Web:* www.covepoconoresorts.com	Mount Pocono	PA	18344	570-839-8881	839-1842
Carroll Valley Golf Resort 121 Sanders Rd *TF:* 800-548-8504 ■ *Web:* www.carrollvalley.com	Fairfield	PA	17320	717-642-8211	642-5529
Cove Haven Pocono Palace 5241 Milford Rd *TF:* 800-233-4141 ■ *Web:* www.covepoconoresorts.com	Marshalls Creek	PA	18302	570-588-6692	588-0754
Felicita Resort 2201 Fishing Creek Valley Rd *TF:* 888-321-3713 ■ *Web:* www.felicitaresort.com	Harrisburg	PA	17112	717-599-5301	599-7714
Fernwood Resort & Country Club Rt 209 *TF:* 888-337-6966 ■ *Web:* resortsusa.com/fernwood.php	Bushkill	PA	18324	570-588-9500	588-0403
Heritage Hills Golf Resort & Conference Ctr 2700 Mt Rose Ave *TF:* 877-782-9752 ■ *Web:* www.hhgr.com	York	PA	17402	717-755-0123	812-9303
Hershey Entertainment & Resorts Co 27 W Chocolate Ave *TF:* 800-437-7439 ■ *Web:* www.hersheypa.com	Hershey	PA	17033	717-534-3131	534-3324
Hidden Valley Resort & Conference Ctr 1 Craighead Dr PO Box 4420 *TF:* 800-458-0175 ■ *Web:* www.hiddenvalleyresort.com	Hidden Valley	PA	15502	814-443-8000	443-1907
Hotel Hershey The 100 Hotel Rd *TF:* 800-533-3131 ■ *Web:* www.thehotelhershey.com	Hershey	PA	17033	717-533-2171	534-8887
Lancaster Host Resort 2300 Lincoln Hwy E *TF Resv:* 800-233-0121 ■ *Web:* www.lancasterhost.com	Lancaster	PA	17602	717-299-5500	295-5104
Liberty Mountain Resort & Conference Ctr 78 Country Club Trail *Web:* www.skiliberty.com	Carroll Valley	PA	17320	717-642-8282	
Mountain Laurel Resort & Spa Rt 940 PO Box 9 *TF:* 888-243-9300 ■ *Web:* www.mountainlaurelresort.com	White Haven	PA	18661	570-443-8411	443-5518
Nemacolin Woodlands Resort & Spa 1001 Lafayette Dr *TF:* 800-422-2736 ■ *Web:* www.nwlr.com	Farmington	PA	15437	724-329-8555	329-6198
Penn Hills Resort Rt 447 & 191 PO Box 309 *TF:* 800-233-8240 ■ *Web:* www.pennhillsresort.com	Analomink	PA	18320	570-421-6464	424-0310
Pocono Manor Golf Resort & Spa Rt 314 *TF:* 800-233-8150 ■ *Web:* www.poconomanor.com/pages	Pocono Manor	PA	18349	570-839-7111	839-3407
Seven Springs Mountain Resort 777 Waterwheel Dr *TF:* 800-452-2223 ■ *Web:* www.7springs.com	Champion	PA	15622	814-352-7777	352-2059
Shawnee Inn & Golf Resort 1 River Rd PO Box 67 *TF:* 800-742-9633 ■ *Web:* www.shawneeinn.com	Shawnee on Delaware	PA	18356	570-424-4000	424-9168
Skytop Lodge 1 Skytop *TF:* 800-345-7759 ■ *Web:* www.skytop.com	Skytop	PA	18357	570-595-7401	595-9618
Split Rock Resort 1 Lake Dr *TF:* 800-255-7625 ■ *Web:* www.splitrockresort.com	Lake Harmony	PA	18624	570-722-9111	722-8831
Tamiment Resort & Conference Ctr Bushkill Falls Rd *TF:* 800-532-8280	Tamiment	PA	18371	570-588-6652	
Toftrees Golf Resort & Conference Ctr 1 Country Club Ln *TF:* 800-252-3551 ■ *Web:* www.toftrees.com	State College	PA	16803	814-234-8000	238-4404
Willow Valley Resort & Conference Ctr 2416 Willow St Pike *TF:* 800-444-1714 ■ *Web:* www.willowvalley.com	Lancaster	PA	17602	717-464-2711	464-4784
Woodlands Inn & Resort 1073 Hwy 315 *TF:* 800-762-2222 ■ *Web:* www.thewoodlandsresort.com	Wilkes-Barre	PA	18702	570-824-9831	824-8865

PUERTO RICO

	City	State	Zip	Phone	Fax
Candelero Resort at Palmas Del Mar The 170 Candelero Dr *TF:* 800-725-6273 ■ *Web:* www.candelero-resort-puerto-rico.visit-puerto-rico.com	Humacao	PR	00791	787-852-6000	852-6370
Caribe Hilton Los Rosales St San Geronimo Grounds *TF:* 800-445-8667 ■ *Web:* www.caribehilton.com	San Juan	PR	00901	787-721-0303	725-8849
El Conquistador Resort & Golden Door Spa 1000 El Conquistador Ave *TF Resv:* 888-543-1282 ■ *Web:* www.elconresort.com	Fajardo	PR	00738	787-863-1000	863-6500
InterContinental San Juan Resort & Casino 5961 Isla Verde Ave *TF:* 800-443-2009 ■ *Web:* www.ichotelsgroup.com/h/d/ic/1/en/hd/sjuha	Carolina	PR	00979	787-791-6100	253-2510
Las Casitas Village & Golden Door Spa 1000 Avenida Conquistador *Web:* www.lascasitasvillage.com	Fajardo	PR	00738	787-863-1000	863-6831
Ritz-Carlton San Juan The 6961 Avenue of the Governors Isla Verde *TF:* 800-241-3333 ■ *Web:* www.ritzcarlton.com/en/Properties/SanJuan	Carolina	PR	00979	787-253-1700	253-1777

QUEBEC

	City	State	Zip	Phone	Fax
Fairmont Le Chateau Montebello 392 Notre Dame St *TF:* 800-441-1414 ■ *Web:* www.fairmont.com	Montebello	QC	J0V1L0	819-423-6341	423-1133
Hotel Cheribourg 2603 ch du Parc *TF:* 877-845-5344 ■ *Web:* www.hotelsvillegia.com	Orford	QC	J1X8C8	819-843-3308	843-2639
Hotel du Lac 121 Rue Cuttle *TF:* 800-567-8341 ■ *Web:* www.clubtremblant.com	Mont-Tremblant	QC	J8E1B9	819-425-2731	425-5617
Manoir du Lac Delage 40 du Lac Ave *TF:* 888-202-3242 ■ *Web:* www.lacdelage.com	Lac Delage	QC	G3C5C4	418-848-2551	848-6945
Westin Resort Tremblant 100 ch Kandahar *TF:* 800-937-8461 ■ *Web:* www.starwood.com/westin	Mont-Tremblant	QC	J8E1E2	819-681-8000	681-8001

RHODE ISLAND

	City	State	Zip	Phone	Fax
Castle Hill Inn & Resort 590 Ocean Dr *TF:* 888-466-1355 ■ *Web:* www.castlehillinn.com	Newport	RI	02840	401-849-3800	849-3885
Inn on Long Wharf 142 Long Wharf *TF:* 800-225-3522	Newport	RI	02840	401-847-7800	845-0127
Inn on the Harbor 359 Thames St *TF:* 800-225-3522 ■ *Web:* www.wyndhamvacationresorts.com	Newport	RI	02840	401-849-6789	849-2680

SOUTH CAROLINA

	City	State	Zip	Phone	Fax
Barefoot Resort & Golf 4980 Barefoot Resort Bridge Rd *TF:* 800-856-0501 ■ *Web:* www.barefootgolf.com	North Myrtle Beach	SC	29582	843-390-3200	390-3213
Bay Watch Resort & Conference Ctr 2701 S Ocean Blvd *TF:* 866-270-2172 ■ *Web:* www.patricia.com/myrtle-beach-resorts/bay-watch-resort	North Myrtle Beach	SC	29582	843-272-4600	272-4440
Beach Colony Resort 5200 N Ocean Blvd *TF:* 800-222-2141 ■ *Web:* www.beachcolony.com	Myrtle Beach	SC	29577	843-449-4010	449-2810
Bluewater Resort 2001 S Ocean Blvd *TF:* 800-845-6994 ■ *Web:* www.bluewaterresort.com	Myrtle Beach	SC	29577	843-626-8345	448-2310
Breakers Resort 2700 N Ocean Blvd *TF:* 800-952-4507 ■ *Web:* www.breakers.com	Myrtle Beach	SC	29577	843-444-4444	626-5001
Caravelle Resort Hotel & Villas 6900 N Ocean Blvd *TF:* 800-367-4518 ■ *Web:* www.thecaravelle.com	Myrtle Beach	SC	29572	843-918-8000	918-8199
Caribbean Resort & Villas 3000 N Ocean Blvd *TF:* 800-552-8509 ■ *Web:* www.caribbeanresort.com	Myrtle Beach	SC	29577	843-448-7181	448-3224
Compass Cove Ocean Resort 2311 S Ocean Blvd *TF:* 800-331-0934 ■ *Web:* www.compasscove.com	Myrtle Beach	SC	29577	843-448-8373	448-5444
Coral Beach Resort & Suites 1105 S Ocean Blvd *TF:* 800-556-1754 ■ *Web:* www.coralbeachmyrtlebeachresort.com	Myrtle Beach	SC	29577	843-448-8421	626-0156
Disney's Hilton Head Island Resort 22 Harborside Ln *Web:* www.disneyvacationclub.disney.go.com	Hilton Head Island	SC	29928	843-341-4100	341-4130
Hilton Charleston Harbor Resort & Marina 20 Patriots Pt Rd *TF:* 800-445-8667 ■ *Web:* www.charlestonharborresort.com	Mount Pleasant	SC	29464	843-856-0028	856-8333
Hilton Head Island Beach & Tennis Resort 40 Folly Field Rd *TF Resv:* 800-475-2631 ■ *Web:* www.hhibeachandtennis.com	Hilton Head Island	SC	29928	843-842-4402	842-3323
Hilton Myrtle Beach Resort 10000 Beach Club Dr *TF:* 877-887-9549 ■ *Web:* www.hilton.com	Myrtle Beach	SC	29572	843-449-5000	497-0168

			Phone	Fax
Hilton Oceanfront Resort Hilton Head Island 23 Ocean Ln . . . Hilton Head Island SC *TF:* 800-845-8001 ■ *Web:* www.hilton.com	29928		843-842-8000	341-8033
Holiday Inn Oceanfront at Surfside Beach 1601 N Ocean Blvd . . . Surfside Beach SC *TF:* 866-661-5139 ■ *Web:* www.ichotelsgroup.com	29575		843-238-5601	238-4758
Hotel Blue Beachfront Resort 705 S Ocean Blvd . . . Myrtle Beach SC *TF:* 800-843-3466 ■ *Web:* www.hotelbluemb.com	29577		843-448-4304	448-0015
Kiawah Island Golf Resort 1 Sancturay Beach Dr . . . Kiawah Island SC *Fax: Resv ■ *TF Resv:* 800-654-2924 ■ *Web:* www.kiawahresort.com/golf	29455		843-768-2121	768-2736*
Landmark Resort 1501 S Ocean Blvd . . . Myrtle Beach SC *TF:* 800-845-0658 ■ *Web:* www.landmarkresort.com	29577		843-448-9441	448-6701
Legends Resort 1500 Legends Dr PO Box 2038 . . . Myrtle Beach SC *TF:* 888-246-9809 ■ *Web:* www.legendsgolf.com	29578		843-236-9318	236-0516
Litchfield Beach & Golf Resort 14276 Ocean Hwy . . . Pawleys Island SC *TF:* 888-766-4633 ■ *Web:* www.litchfieldbeach.com	29585		843-237-3000	237-4282
Myrtle Beach Marriott Resort at Grande Dunes 8400 Costa Verde Dr . . . Myrtle Beach SC *Web:* www.marriott.com	29572		843-449-8880	449-8669
Myrtle Beach Resort Vacations 5905 S Kings Hwy PO Box 3936 . . . Myrtle Beach SC *TF:* 888-627-3767 ■ *Web:* www.myrtle-beach-resort.com	29578		843-238-1559	238-2424
Mystic Sea Resort 2105 S Ocean Blvd . . . Myrtle Beach SC *TF:* 800-443-7050 ■ *Web:* www.mysticsea.com	29577		843-448-8446	626-2024
Ocean Dunes Resort & Villas 201 75th Ave N . . . Myrtle Beach SC *TF:* 800-845-0635 ■ *Web:* www.sandsresorts.com/resorts/oceandunes	29578		843-449-7441	449-0558
Ocean Forest Villa Resort 5601 N Ocean Blvd . . . Myrtle Beach SC *TF:* 800-845-0347 ■ *Web:* www.sandsresorts.com/resorts/oceanforestvilla	29577		843-449-9661	449-9207
Ocean Reef Resort 7100 N Ocean Blvd . . . Myrtle Beach SC *TF:* 888-322-6411 ■ *Web:* www.oceanreefmyrtlebeach.com	29572		843-449-4441	497-3041
Palmetto Dunes Resort 4 Queen Folly Rd . . . Hilton Head Island SC *TF:* 800-845-6130 ■ *Web:* www.palmettodunes.com	29938		843-842-7000	842-4482
Palms Resort 2500 N Ocean Blvd . . . Myrtle Beach SC *TF:* 800-528-0451 ■ *Web:* www.palmsresort.com	29577		843-626-8334	448-1950
Patricia Grand Resort 2710 N Ocean Blvd . . . Myrtle Beach SC *TF:* 800-255-4763 ■ *Web:* www.oceanaresorts.com	29577		843-448-8453	448-3080
Pawleys Plantation 70 Tanglewood Dr . . . Pawleys Island SC *TF:* 800-367-9959 ■ *Web:* www.sandsresorts.com	29585		843-237-6009	237-0418
Player's Club Resort 35 Deallyon Ave . . . Hilton Head Island SC *TF:* 800-497-7529	29928		843-785-8000	785-9185
Reef Resort 2101 S Ocean Blvd . . . Myrtle Beach SC *TF Cust Svc:* 800-845-1212 ■ *Web:* www.reefmyrtlebeach.com	29577		843-448-1765	626-9971
Resort at Seabrook Island 3772 Seabrook Island Rd . . . Seabrook Island SC *Web:* www.discoverseabrook.com	29455		843-768-2500	768-7524
Sand Dunes Resort Hotel 201 74th Ave N . . . Myrtle Beach SC *TF:* 800-845-6701 ■ *Web:* www.sandsresorts.com	29572		843-449-3313	692-5178
Sea Mist Resort 1200 S Ocean Blvd . . . Myrtle Beach SC *TF:* 800-732-6478 ■ *Web:* www.myrtlebeachseamist.com	29577		843-448-1551	893-1108
Sea Pines Resort 32 Greenwood Dr . . . Hilton Head Island SC *TF:* 800-732-7463 ■ *Web:* www.seapines.com	29928		843-785-3333	842-1475
Seacrest Oceanfront Resort on the South Beach 803 S Ocean Blvd . . . Myrtle Beach SC *TF:* 888-889-8113 ■ *Web:* www.myrtlebeach-resorts.com	29577		843-913-5800	913-5801
Shore Crest Vacation Villas 4709 S Ocean Blvd . . . North Myrtle Beach SC *Web:* www.bluegreenrentals.com	29582		843-361-3600	361-3601
Wild Dunes Resort 5757 Palm Blvd . . . Isle of Palms SC *TF:* 800-845-8880 ■ *Web:* www.wilddunes.com	29451		843-886-6000	886-2916
Woodlands Resort & Inn 125 Parsons Rd . . . Summerville SC *TF:* 800-774-9999 ■ *Web:* www.woodlandsinn.com	29483		843-875-2600	875-2603
Wyndham Vacation Resorts King Cotton Villas 1 King Cotton Rd . . . Edisto Beach SC *TF:* 877-296-6335 ■ *Web:* www.wyndhamvacationresorts.com	29438		843-869-2561	869-2384

SOUTH DAKOTA

			Phone	Fax
Spearfish Canyon Resort 10619 Roughlock Falls Rd . . . Lead SD *TF:* 877-975-6343 ■ *Web:* www.spfcanyon.com	57754		605-584-3435	584-3990
Spring Creek Resort 28229 Spring Creek Pl . . . Pierre SD *Web:* www.springcreekventure.com	57501		605-224-8336	

TENNESSEE

			Phone	Fax
Blackberry Farm 1471 W Millers Cove Rd . . . Walland TN *TF:* 800-273-6004 ■ *Web:* www.blackberryfarm.com	37886		865-380-2260	681-7753
Brookside Resort 463 E Pkwy . . . Gatlinburg TN *TF:* 800-251-9597 ■ *Web:* www.brooksideresort.com	37738		865-436-5611	436-0039
Fairfield Glade Resort 109 Fairfield Blvd PO Box 1500 . . . Fairfield Glade TN	38558		931-484-7521	484-7521

TEXAS

			Phone	Fax
Bahia Mar Resort & Conference Ctr 6300 Padre Blvd . . . South Padre Island TX *TF:* 800-997-2373	78597		956-761-1343	761-6287
Barton Creek Conference Resort 8212 Barton Club Dr . . . Austin TX *TF:* 800-336-6158 ■ *Web:* www.bartoncreek.com	78735		512-329-4000	329-4597
Columbia Lakes Resort & Conference Ctr 188 Freeman Blvd . . . West Columbia TX *TF:* 800-231-1030 ■ *Web:* www.columbia-lakes.com	77486		979-345-5151	345-3049
Four Seasons Resort & Club Dallas at Las Colinas 4150 N MacArthur Blvd . . . Irving TX *TF:* 800-332-3442 ■ *Web:* www.fourseasons.com/dallas	75038		972-717-0700	717-2550
Hilton Galveston Island Resort 5400 Seawall Blvd . . . Galveston TX *TF:* 800-475-3386 ■ *Web:* www1.hilton.com	77551		409-744-5000	740-2209
Holiday Inn SunSpree Resort South Padre Island 100 Padre Blvd . . . South Padre Island TX *TF:* 800-531-7405	78597		956-761-5401	761-1560
Houstonian Hotel Club & Spa 111 N Post Oak Ln . . . Houston TX *TF:* 800-231-2759 ■ *Web:* www.houstonian.com	77024		713-680-2626	680-2992
Inn of the Hills River Resort 1001 Junction Hwy . . . Kerrville TX *TF:* 800-292-5690 ■ *Web:* www.innofthehills.com	78028		830-895-5000	895-6020
Quorum Hotels & Resorts 5429 Lyndon B Johnson Fwy #625 . . . Dallas TX *Web:* www.quorumhotels.com	75240		972-458-7265	991-5647
Rancho Viejo Resort & Country Club 1 Rancho Viejo Dr . . . Rancho Viejo TX *TF:* 800-531-7400 ■ *Web:* www.playrancho.com	78575		956-350-4000	350-5696
Rosewood Hotels & Resorts 500 Crescent Ct Suite 300 . . . Dallas TX *TF:* 888-767-3966 ■ *Web:* www.rosewoodhotels.com	75201		214-880-4200	880-4201
San Luis Resort Spa & Conference Ctr 5222 Seawall Blvd . . . Galveston Island TX *TF Cust Svc:* 800-445-0090 ■ *Web:* www.sanluisresort.com	77551		409-744-1500	744-8452
Silverleaf Resorts Inc 1221 Riverbend Dr Suite 120 . . . Dallas TX *NASDAQ: SVLF* ■ *TF:* 800-613-0310 ■ *Web:* www.silverleafresorts.com	75247		214-631-1166	637-0585
South Shore Harbour Resort & Conference Ctr 2500 S Shore Blvd . . . League City TX *TF resv:* 800-442-5005 ■ *Web:* www.sshr.com	77573		281-334-1000	334-1157
Tanglewood Resort Hotel & Conference Ctr 290 Tanglewood Cir . . . Pottsboro TX *TF:* 800-833-6569 ■ *Web:* www.tanglewoodresort.com	75076		903-786-2968	786-2128
Tapatio Springs Golf Resort & Conference Ctr PO Box 550 . . . Boerne TX *TF:* 800-999-3299 ■ *Web:* www.tapatio.com	78006		830-537-4611	537-4962
Waterwood National Resort 1 Waterwood Pkwy . . . Huntsville TX *TF:* 877-441-5211	77320		936-891-5211	891-5011

UTAH

			Phone	Fax
Alta Lodge PO Box 8040 . . . Alta UT *TF Cust Svc:* 800-707-2582 ■ *Web:* www.altalodge.com	84092		801-742-3500	742-3504
Brighton Ski Resort 12601 E Big Cottonwood Canyon Rd . . . Brighton UT *Fax Area Code: 435 ■ *TF:* 800-873-5512 ■ *Web:* www.brightonresort.com	84121		801-532-4731	649-1787*
Canyons Resort The 4000 The Canyons Resort Dr . . . Park City UT *TF:* 888-226-9667 ■ *Web:* www.thecanyons.com	84098		435-649-5400	649-7374
Deer Valley Resort Lodging PO Box 889 . . . Park City UT *TF:* 800-558-3337 ■ *Web:* www.deervalley.com	84060		435-649-4040	645-6538
Green Valley Resort 1871 W Canyon View Dr . . . Saint George UT *TF:* 800-237-1068 ■ *Web:* www.gvresort.com	84770		435-628-8060	673-4084
Homestead Resort 700 N Homestead Dr . . . Midway UT *TF:* 800-327-7220 ■ *Web:* www.homesteadresort.com	84049		435-654-1102	654-5087
Inn on the Creek 375 Rainbow Ln PO Box 1000 . . . Midway UT *TF:* 800-654-0892 ■ *Web:* www.innoncreek.com	84049		435-654-0892	654-5871
Little America Hotels & Resorts 500 S Main St . . . Salt Lake City UT *TF Resv:* 800-453-9450 ■ *Web:* www.littleamerica.com	84101		801-363-6781	596-5911
Park City Mountain Resort (PCMR) 1345 Lowell Ave PO Box 39 . . . Park City UT *TF:* 800-222-7275 ■ *Web:* www.parkcitymountain.com	84060		435-649-8111	647-5374
Premier Resorts International 1375 Deer Valley Dr S PO Box 4800 . . . Park City UT *TF:* 888-774-3533	84060		435-655-4800	655-4848
Rustler Lodge 10380 E Hwy 210 PO Box 8030 . . . Alta UT *TF:* 888-532-2582 ■ *Web:* www.rustlerlodge.com	84092		801-742-2200	742-3832
Snowbasin Ski Resort 3925 E Snowbasin Rd . . . Huntsville UT *TF:* 888-437-5488 ■ *Web:* www.snowbasin.com	84317		801-399-1135	620-1314
Snowbird Ski & Summer Resort Hwy 210 PO Box 929000 . . . Snowbird UT *TF:* 800-453-3000 ■ *Web:* www.snowbird.com	84092		801-742-2222	947-8227
Solitude Ski Resort 12000 Big Cottonwood Canyon . . . Solitude UT *TF:* 800-748-4754 ■ *Web:* www.skisolitude.com	84121		801-534-1400	517-7705
Stein Eriksen Lodge 7700 Stein Way . . . Park City UT *TF:* 800-453-1302 ■ *Web:* www.steinlodge.com	84060		435-649-3700	649-5825

VERMONT

			Phone	Fax
Ascutney Mountain Resort 485 Hotel Rd PO Box 699 . . . Brownsville VT *TF:* 800-243-0011 ■ *Web:* www.ascutney.com	05037		802-484-7711	484-3117
Basin Harbor Club 4800 Basin Harbor Rd . . . Vergennes VT *TF:* 800-622-4000 ■ *Web:* www.basinharbor.com	05491		802-475-2311	475-6545
Equinox The 3567 Main St Rt 7A . . . Manchester Village VT *TF:* 800-362-4747 ■ *Web:* www.equinoxresort.com	05254		802-362-4700	362-4861
Hawk Inn & Mountain Resort 75 Billings Rd . . . Plymouth VT *TF:* 800-685-4295 ■ *Web:* www.hawkresort.com	05056		802-672-3811	672-5585

Name / Address	City	State	ZIP	Phone	Fax
Inn at Stratton Mountain 61 Middle Ridge Rd *TF:* 800-777-1700 ■ *Web:* www.stratton.com	Stratton Mountain	VT	05155	802-297-2500	297-1778
Jay Peak Resort 4850 VT Rt 242 *TF:* 800-451-4449 ■ *Web:* www.jaypeakresort.com	Jay	VT	05859	802-988-2611	988-4049
Killington Resort & Pico Mountain 228 E Mountain Rd *TF:* 800-621-6867 ■ *Web:* www.killington.com	Killington	VT	05751	802-422-6200	422-6113
Lake Morey Resort 1 Clubhouse Rd. *TF:* 800-423-1211 ■ *Web:* www.lakemoreyresort.com	Fairlee	VT	05045	802-333-4311	333-4553
Smugglers' Notch Resort 4323 Vermont Rt 108 S. *TF:* 800-451-8752 ■ *Web:* www.smuggs.com	Jeffersonville	VT	05464	802-644-8851	644-1230
Stowe Mountain Resort 5781 Mountain Rd *TF:* 800-253-4754 ■ *Web:* www.summer.stowe.com	Stowe	VT	05672	802-253-3000	253-3406
Stoweflake Mountain Resort & Spa 1746 Mountain Rd PO Box 369 *TF:* 800-253-2232 ■ *Web:* www.stoweflake.com	Stowe	VT	05672	802-253-7355	253-6858
Sugarbush Resort & Inn 1840 Sugarbush Access Rd *TF:* 800-537-8427 ■ *Web:* www.sugarbush.com	Warren	VT	05674	802-583-6300	583-6390
Topnotch at Stowe Resort & Spa 4000 Mountain Rd *TF:* 800-451-8686 ■ *Web:* www.topnotch-resort.com	Stowe	VT	05672	802-253-8585	253-9263
Trapp Family Lodge 700 Trapp Hill Rd PO Box 1428 *TF:* 800-826-7000 ■ *Web:* www.trappfamily.com	Stowe	VT	05672	802-253-8511	253-5740
Tyler Place Family Resort 175 Old Dock Rd PO Box 254 *Web:* www.tylerplace.com	Highgate Springs	VT	05460	802-868-4000	868-5621
Woodstock Inn & Resort 14 The Green *TF:* 800-448-7900 ■ *Web:* www.woodstockinn.com	Woodstock	VT	05091	802-457-1100	457-6699

VIRGINIA

Name / Address	City	State	ZIP	Phone	Fax
Alamar Resort Inn 311 16th St *TF:* 800-346-5681 ■ *Web:* www.va-beach.com/alamarresort	Virginia Beach	VA	23451	757-823-4056	428-4857
Boar's Head Inn 200 Ednam Dr *TF:* 800-476-1988 ■ *Web:* www.boarsheadinn.com	Charlottesville	VA	22903	434-296-2181	972-6024
Breakers Resort Inn 16th & Oceanfront *TF:* 800-237-7532 ■ *Web:* www.breakersresort.com	Virginia Beach	VA	23451	757-428-1821	422-9602
Cavalier Hotel 4201 Atlantic Ave. *TF:* 800-446-8199 ■ *Web:* www.cavalierhotel.com	Virginia Beach	VA	23451	757-425-8555	425-0629
Crestline Hotels & Resorts 8405 Greensboro Dr Suite 500 *Web:* www.crestlinehotels.com	McLean	VA	22102	571-382-1800	382-1860
Great Wolf Lodge Williamsburg 549 E Rochambeau Dr *TF:* 800-551-9653 ■ *Web:* www.greatwolf.com	Williamsburg	VA	23188	757-229-9700	229-9780
Holiday Inn SunSpree Resort Virginia Beach 3900 Atlantic Ave *TF:* 800-942-3224 ■ *Web:* www.ichotelsgroup.com	Virginia Beach	VA	23451	757-428-1711	425-7872
Homestead The 7696 Sam Snead Hwy PO Box 2000 *TF:* 800-838-1766 ■ *Web:* www.thehomestead.com	Hot Springs	VA	24445	540-839-1766	839-7656
Kingsmill Resort & Spa 1010 Kingsmill Rd *TF:* 800-832-5665 ■ *Web:* www.kingsmill.com	Williamsburg	VA	23185	757-253-1703	253-8246
Lansdowne Resort 44050 Woodridge Pkwy *TF:* 800-541-4801 ■ *Web:* www.lansdowneresort.com	Leesburg	VA	20176	703-729-8400	729-4096
Massanutten Resort 1822 Resort Dr *Web:* www.massresort.com	McGaheysville	VA	22840	540-289-9441	289-6981
Shenvalee Golf Resort 9660 Fairway Dr PO Box 930 *TF:* 888-339-3181 ■ *Web:* www.shenvalee.com	New Market	VA	22844	540-740-3181	740-8931
Tides Resort 480 King Carter Dr *TF:* 800-843-3746 ■ *Web:* www.tidesinn.com	Irvington	VA	22480	804-438-5000	438-5222
Turtle Cay Resort 600 Atlantic Ave *TF:* 888-989-7788 ■ *Web:* www.turtlecay.com	Virginia Beach	VA	23451	757-437-5565	437-9104
Virginia Beach Resort Hotel & Conference Ctr 2800 Shore Dr *TF:* 800-468-2722 ■ *Web:* www.virginiabeachresort.com	Virginia Beach	VA	23451	757-481-9000	496-7429
Virginia Crossings Resort 1000 Virginia Ctr Pkwy *TF:* 888-444-6553 ■ *Web:* www.wyndhamvirginiacrossings.com	Glen Allen	VA	23059	804-727-1400	727-1690
Williamsburg Inn 136 E Francis St *TF:* 800-447-8679 ■ *Web:* www.colonialwilliamsburg.com	Williamsburg	VA	23185	757-229-1000	220-7096

WASHINGTON

Name / Address	City	State	ZIP	Phone	Fax
Alderbrook Resort & Spa 7101 E SR-106 *TF:* 800-622-9370 ■ *Web:* www.alderbrookresort.com	Union	WA	98592	360-898-2200	898-4610
Campbell's Resort 104 W Woodin Ave PO Box 278 *TF:* 800-553-8225 ■ *Web:* www.campbellsresort.com	Chelan	WA	98816	509-682-2561	682-2177
Carson Hot Mineral Springs Resort 372 St Martin Rd *TF:* 800-607-3678 ■ *Web:* www.carsonhotspringsresort.com	Carson	WA	98610	509-427-8292	427-7242
Coast Hotels & Resorts USA 2003 Western Ave Suite 500 *Web:* www.coasthotels.com	Seattle	WA	98121	206-826-2700	826-2701
Desert Canyon Golf Resort 1201 Desert Canyon Blvd *TF:* 800-258-4173 ■ *Web:* www.desertcanyon.com	Orondo	WA	98843	509-784-1111	784-2701
Freestone Inn at Wilson Ranch 31 Early Winters Dr. *TF:* 800-639-3809 ■ *Web:* www.freestoneinn.com	Mazama	WA	98833	509-996-3906	996-3907
Lake Quinault Lodge 345 S Shore Rd *TF:* 800-562-6672 ■ *Web:* www.olympicnationalparks.com	Quinault	WA	98575	360-288-2900	288-2901
Little Creek Casino Resort W 91 Hwy 108 *TF:* 800-667-7711 ■ *Web:* www.little-creek.com	Shelton	WA	98584	360-427-7711	427-7868
Polynesian Resort The 615 Ocean Shores Blvd NW *TF:* 800-562-4836 ■ *Web:* www.thepolynesian.com	Ocean Shores	WA	98569	360-289-3361	289-0294
Resort Semiahmoo 9565 Semiahmoo Pkwy *TF:* 800-770-7992 ■ *Web:* www.semiahmoo.com	Blaine	WA	98230	360-318-2000	318-2087
Rosario Resort & Spa 1400 Rosario Rd *TF:* 800-562-8820 ■ *Web:* www.rosarioresort.com	Eastsound	WA	98245	360-376-2222	376-2289
Salish Lodge & Spa 6501 Railroad Ave DE PO Box 1109 *TF:* 800-826-6124 ■ *Web:* www.salishlodge.com	Snoqualmie	WA	98065	425-888-2556	888-2533
Sun Mountain Lodge 604 Patterson Lake Rd PO Box 1000 *TF:* 800-572-0493 ■ *Web:* www.sunmountainlodge.com	Winthrop	WA	98862	509-996-2211	996-3133

WEST VIRGINIA

Name / Address	City	State	ZIP	Phone	Fax
Canaan Valley Resort & Conference Ctr 230 Main Lodge Rd *TF:* 800-622-4121 ■ *Web:* www.canaanresort.com	Davis	WV	26260	304-866-4121	866-2172
Coolfont Resort 3621 Cold Run Valley Rd *TF:* 800-888-8768	Berkeley Springs	WV	25411	304-258-4500	258-4500
Glade Springs Resort 255 Club Cir *TF:* 800-634-5233 ■ *Web:* www.gladesprings.com	Daniels	WV	25832	304-763-2000	763-3398
Greenbrier The 300 W Main St *TF:* 800-453-4858 ■ *Web:* www.greenbrier.com	White Sulphur Springs	WV	24986	304-536-1110	536-7854
Lakeview Golf Resort &Spa 1 Lakeview Dr *TF:* 800-624-8300 ■ *Web:* www.lakeviewresort.com	Morgantown	WV	26508	304-594-1111	594-9472
Oglebay Resort & Conference Ctr Rt 88 N Oglebay Pk. *TF:* 800-624-6988 ■ *Web:* www.oglebay-resort.com	Wheeling	WV	26003	304-243-4000	243-4070
Pipestem Resort State Park PO Box 150 *Web:* www.pipestemresort.com	Pipestem	WV	25979	304-466-1800	466-2803
Snowshoe Mountain Resort 10 Snowshoe Dr *TF:* 877-441-4386 ■ *Web:* www.snowshoemtn.com	Snowshoe	WV	26209	304-572-1000	572-5407
Stonewall Resort 940 Resort Dr *TF:* 888-278-8150 ■ *Web:* www.stonewallresort.com	Roanoke	WV	26447	304-269-7400	269-8818
Woods Resort & Conference Ctr Mountain Lake Rd PO Box 5 *TF:* 800-248-2222 ■ *Web:* www.thewoodsresort.com	Hedgesville	WV	25427	304-754-7977	754-8146

WISCONSIN

Name / Address	City	State	ZIP	Phone	Fax
Abbey Resort & Fontana Spa 269 Fontana Blvd *TF:* 800-709-1323 ■ *Web:* www.theabbeyresort.com	Fontana	WI	53125	262-275-9000	275-3264
Alpine Resort 7715 Alpine Rd PO Box 200 *Web:* www.alpineresort.com	Egg Harbor	WI	54209	920-868-3000	868-2576
American Club The 419 Highland Dr *TF:* 800-722-8435 ■ *Web:* www.destinationkohler.com	Kohler	WI	53044	920-457-8000	457-0299
Chanticleer Inn 1458 E Dollar Lake Rd *TF:* 800-752-9193 ■ *Web:* www.chanticleerinn.com	Eagle River	WI	54521	715-479-4486	479-0004
Chula Vista Theme Resort 25011 N River Rd *TF Cust Svc:* 800-388-4782 ■ *Web:* www.chulavistaresort.com	Wisconsin Dells	WI	53965	608-254-8366	254-7653
Devil's Head Resort & Convention Ctr S 6330 Bluff Rd *TF:* 800-472-6670 ■ *Web:* www.devilsheadresort.com	Merrimac	WI	53561	608-493-2251	493-2176
Fox Hills Resort & Convention Ctr 250 W Church St *TF:* 800-950-7615 ■ *Web:* www.foxhillsresort.com	Mishicot	WI	54228	920-755-2376	755-2186
Grand Geneva Resort & Spa 7036 Grand Geneva Way *TF:* 800-558-3417 ■ *Web:* www.grandgeneva.com	Lake Geneva	WI	53147	262-248-8811	249-4587
Great Wolf Resorts Inc 122 W Washington Ave *NASDAQ: WOLF* ■ *Web:* www.ir.greatwolfresorts.com	Madison	WI	53703	608-251-6400	661-4701
Heidel House Resort 643 Illinois Ave *TF:* 800-444-2812 ■ *Web:* www.heidelhouse.com	Green Lake	WI	54941	920-294-3344	294-6128
Holiday Acres Resort & Conference Ctr 4060 S Shore Dr PO Box 460 *TF:* 800-261-1500 ■ *Web:* www.holidayacres.com	Rhinelander	WI	54501	715-369-1500	369-3665
Lake Lawn Resort 2400 E Geneva St *TF:* 800-338-5253	Delavan	WI	53115	262-728-7950	728-2347
Landmark Resort 7643 Hillside Rd *TF:* 800-273-7877 ■ *Web:* www.thelandmarkresort.com	Egg Harbor	WI	54209	920-868-3205	868-2569
Maxwelton Braes Golf Resort 7670 Hwy 57 *Web:* www.maxwelton-braes.com	Baileys Harbor	WI	54202	920-839-2321	839-2729
Olympia Resort & Spa 1350 Royale Mile Rd *TF:* 800-558-9573 ■ *Web:* www.olympiaresort.com	Oconomowoc	WI	53066	262-567-0311	369-4998
Osthoff Resort The 101 Osthoff Ave PO Box 151 *TF:* 800-876-3399 ■ *Web:* www.osthoff.com	Elkhart Lake	WI	53020	920-876-3366	876-3228
Tundra Lodge Resort & Waterpark 865 Lombardi Ave. *TF:* 877-886-3725 ■ *Web:* www.tundralodge.com	Green Bay	WI	54304	920-405-8700	405-1997

WYOMING

Name / Address	City	State	ZIP	Phone	Fax
Amangani Resort 1535 NE Butte Rd *TF:* 877-734-7333 ■ *Web:* www.amanresorts.com	Jackson	WY	83001	307-734-7333	734-7332
Aramark Parks & Destinations 27655 Hwy 26 & 287 *TF:* 866-278-4245 ■ *Web:* www.togwoteelodge.com	Moran	WY	83013	307-543-2847	543-2391
Four Seasons Resort Jackson Hole 7680 Granite Loop Rd PO Box 544 *Web:* www.fourseasons.com/jacksonhole	Teton Village	WY	83025	307-732-5000	732-5001

				Phone	Fax
Grand Targhee Resort 3300 E Ski Hill Rd TF: 800-827-4433 ■ Web: www.grandtarghee.com	Alta	WY	83414	307-353-2300	353-8148
Grand Teton Lodge Co PO Box 240 *Fax: resv ■ TF resv: 800-628-9988 ■ Web: www.gtlc.com	Moran	WY	83013	307-543-3100	543-3046*
Jackson Hole Mountain Resort 3395 Cody Ln PO Box 290 TF: 888-333-7766 ■ Web: www.jacksonhole.com	Teton Village	WY	83025	307-733-2292	733-2660
Jackson HoleResort Lodging 3200 W McCollister Dri PO Box 510 TF: 800-443-8613 ■ Web: www.jhrl.com	Teton Village	WY	83025	307-733-3990	733-5551
Jackson Lake Lodge PO Box 250 TF: 800-628-9988 ■ Web: www.gtlc.com	Moran	WY	83013	307-543-2811	543-3143
Jenny Lake Lodge 5 Miles N of Moran Junction Hwy 89 TF: 800-628-9988 ■ Web: www.gtlc.com	Moran	WY	83013	307-733-4647	543-3358
Rusty Parrot Lodge & Spa PO Box 1657 TF: 800-458-2004 ■ Web: www.rustyparrot.com	Jackson	WY	83001	307-733-2000	733-5566
Signal Mountain Lodge PO Box 50 Web: www.signalmtnlodge.com	Moran	WY	83013	307-543-2831	543-2569
Snake River Lodge & Spa 7710 Granite Loop Rd TF: 800-445-4655 ■ Web: www.snakeriverlodge.rockresorts.com	Teton Village	WY	83025	307-733-3657	732-6009
Snow King Resort 400 E Snow King Ave PO Box SKI TF: 800-522-5464 ■ Web: www.snowking.com	Jackson	WY	83001	307-733-5200	733-4086
Teton Pines Resort & Country Club 3450 N Clubhouse Dr TF: 800-238-2223 ■ Web: www.tetonpines.com	Wilson	WY	83014	307-733-1005	733-2860

673 RESTAURANT COMPANIES

SEE ALSO Bakeries p. 1505; Food Service p. 1875; Franchises p. 1884; Ice Cream & Dairy Stores p. 2103

				Phone	Fax
94th Aero Squadron Restaurants 16320 Raymer St Web: www.94thvannuys.com/94thvannuys	Van Nuys	CA	91406	818-994-7437	
A & W Restaurants Inc 1441 Gardiner Ln Web: www.awrestaurants.com	Louisville	KY	40213	502-874-8300	874-3183
Abuelo's Mexican Food Embassy 2575 S Loop 289 Web: www.abuelos.com	Lubbock	TX	79423	806-785-8686	785-8866
Adf Cos 350 Passaic Ave 2nd Fl Web: www.adfcompanies.com	Fairfield	NJ	07004	973-808-9525	808-9526
Al Copeland Investments Inc 1001 Harimaw Ct S TF: 800-401-0401 ■ Web: www.alcopeland.com	Metairie	LA	70001	504-830-1000	832-8918
Ale House Management Inc (AHM) 612 N Orange Ave Suite C-6 TF: 866-743-2299	Jupiter	FL	33458	561-743-2299	744-3111
Aloha Restaurants Inc 17320 Redhill Ave Suite 190	Irvine	CA	92614	949-250-0331	250-5735
American Cafe The 340 S Washington St *Fax Area Code: 865 ■ TF: 800-325-0755 ■ Web: www.americancafe.com	Maryville	TN	37804	866-910-1394	273-2103*
American Restaurant Partners LP 3020 N Cypress Rd Suite 100	Wichita	KS	67226	316-634-1190	634-1662
Anthony's Seafood Group 5232 Lovelock St Web: www.gofishanthonys.com	San Diego	CA	92110	619-291-7254	298-1212
Arby's Restaurant Group Inc 1155 Perimeter Ctr W TF: 800-487-2729 ■ Web: www.arbys.com	Atlanta	GA	30338	678-514-4100	
Arctic Circle Restaurants Inc PO Box 339 Web: www.acburger.com	Midvale	UT	84047	801-561-3620	561-9646
Ark Restaurants Corp 85 5th Ave 14th Fl NASDAQ: ARKR ■ Web: www.arkrestaurants.com	New York	NY	10003	212-206-8800	206-8814
Aurelio's Pizza 18162 Harwood Ave Web: www.aureliospizza.com	Homewood	IL	60430	708-798-8050	798-6692
Azteca Mexican Restaurants 133 SW 158th St Web: www.aztecamex.com	Seattle	WA	98166	206-243-7021	246-0429
BAB Inc 500 Lake Cook Rd Suite 475 OTC: BABB ■ *Fax Area Code: 847 ■ TF: 800-251-6101 ■ Web: www.babcorp.com	Deerfield	IL	60015	800-251-6101	405-8140*
Back Bay Restaurant Group Inc 284 Newberry St TF: 800-367-2424 ■ Web: www.bbrginc.com	Boston	MA	02115	617-536-2800	236-4175
Back Yard Burgers Inc 500 Church St Suite 200 TF: 800-292-6939 ■ Web: www.backyardburgers.com	Nashville	TN	37219	615-620-2300	620-2301
Bahama Breeze 5900 Lake Ellenor Dr TF: 866-475-5666 ■ Web: www.bahamabreeze.com	Orlando	FL	32809	407-245-4000	245-5189
Bailey's Sports Grill 1551 N Waterfront Pkwy Suite 310 TF: 800-229-2118 ■ Web: www.shrg.com	Wichita	KS	67206	316-634-0505	634-6060
Baja Fresh Mexican Grill 5900-A Katella Ave Suite 101 *Fax Area Code: 805 ■ TF: 800-932-5309 ■ Web: www.bajafresh.com	Cypress	CA	90630	562-391-2400	374-1144*
Baker's Burgers Inc 1875 Business Ctr Dr Web: www.bakersdrivethru.com	San Bernardino	CA	92408	909-884-7241	885-4059
Barbato's Italian Restaurants 3512 Buffalo Rd Web: www.barbatos.com	Erie	PA	16510	814-899-3423	899-5293
Battleground Restaurant Group Inc 1337 Winstead Pl Web: www.brginc.com	Greensboro	NC	27408	336-272-9355	272-5568
Beef O'Bradys Inc 5510 W LaSalle St Suite 200 TF: 800-728-8878 ■ Web: www.beefobradys.com	Tampa	FL	33607	813-226-2333	226-0030
Bellacino's Corp 10096 Shaver Rd TF: 877-379-0700 ■ Web: www.bellacinos.com	Portage	MI	49024	269-329-0782	329-0930
Benihana Inc 8685 NW 53rd Terr Suite 201 NASDAQ: BNHN ■ TF: 800-327-3369 ■ Web: www.benihana.com	Miami	FL	33166	305-593-0770	592-6371
Bennett's Bar-B-Que Inc 3538 Peoria St Suite 508 Web: www.bennettsbbq.com	Aurora	CO	80110	303-792-3088	792-5801
Bennigan's 5151 Beltline Rd Suite 300 Web: www.bennigans.com	Dallas	TX	75254	469-248-4419	
Bertucci's Restaurant Corp 155 Otis St Web: www.bertuccis.com	Northborough	MA	01532	508-351-2500	393-1231
Beverly Hills Cafe Inc 18500 NE 5th Ave	North Miami Beach	FL	33179	305-652-7008	652-7017
BF Nashville 1101 Kermit Dr Suite 310	Nashville	TN	37217	615-399-9700	399-3373
Biaggi's Ristorante Italiano 1705 Clearwater Ave Web: www.biaggis.com	Bloomington	IL	61704	309-664-2148	664-2149
Bice Restaurant 7 E 54th St Web: www.bicenewyork.com	New York	NY	10022	212-688-1999	752-1329
Bickford's Family Restauarants Inc 37 Oak St Ext TF: 800-969-5653 ■ Web: www.bickfordsrestaurants.com	Brockton	MA	02301	617-782-4010	783-2554
Big Boy Restaurants International LLC 4199 Marcy St *Fax: Cust Svc ■ TF: 800-837-3003 ■ Web: www.bigboy.com	Warren	MI	48091	586-759-6000	755-8531*
Big Buck Brewery & Steakhouse Inc 550 S Wisconsin Ave Web: www.bigbuck.com	Gaylord	MI	49735	989-732-5781	732-3990
Big Town Hero Franchising Corp 333 SW Taylor St Suite 200 Web: www.bigtownhero.com	Portland	OR	97204	503-228-4376	228-8778
Bill Miller Bar-B-Q Inc 430 S Santa Rosa St PO Box 839925 *Fax: Sales ■ TF: 800-339-3111 ■ Web: www.billmillerbbq.com	San Antonio	TX	78207	210-225-4461	302-1533*
Biscuitville Inc 1414 Yanceyville St Web: www.biscuitville.com	Greensboro	NC	27405	336-553-3700	229-5246
BJ's Restaurants Inc 7755 Ctr Ave Suite 300 NASDAQ: BJRI ■ Web: www.bjsbrewhouse.com	Huntington Beach	CA	92647	714-500-2400	848-8287
Bob Evans Farms Inc 3776 S High St NASDAQ: BOBE ■ *Fax: Hum Res ■ TF: 800-272-7675 ■ Web: www.bobevans.com	Columbus	OH	43207	614-491-2225	497-4318*
Bobby Cox Cos Inc 4055 International Plaza Suite 450 TF: 800-897-8723 ■ Web: www.bobbycox.com	Fort Worth	TX	76109	817-377-6200	377-6201
Bobby Rubino's Place for Ribs 1990 E Sunrise Blvd	Fort Lauderdale	FL	33304	954-763-1478	
Boddie-Noell Enterprises Inc (BNEINC) 1021 Noell Ln PO Box 1908 Web: www.bneinc.com	Rocky Mount	NC	27804	252-937-2000	937-6991
Bojangles' Restaurants Inc 9432 Southern Pine Blvd TF: 800-366-9921 ■ Web: www.bojangles.com	Charlotte	NC	28273	704-527-2675	523-6676
Bonefish Grill 2202 N W Shore Blvd TF: 866-880-2226 ■ Web: www.bonefishgrill.com	Tampa	FL	33607	813-282-1225	282-1209
Bongos Cuban Cafe 420 Jefferson Ave Web: www.bongoscubancafe.com	Miami Beach	FL	33139	305-695-7072	695-7160
Bono's Pit Bar-B-Q 10645 Phillips Hwy Bldg 200 Web: www.bonosbarbq.com	Jacksonville	FL	32256	904-880-8310	880-8373
Boomerang Grille 1800 N IH- Dr Suite 200 Web: www.halsmithrestaurantgroup.com	Norman	OK	73072	405-321-2600	321-2992
Boston Beanery Restaurants Inc 689 Fairchance Rd Web: www.bostonbeanery.com	Morgantown	WV	26508	304-594-0095	594-0081
Boston Market Corp 14103 Denver W Pkwy TF: 800-877-2870 ■ Web: www.bostonmarket.com	Golden	CO	80401	303-278-9500	216-5335
Boston Pizza International Inc 5500 Parkwood Way Web: www.bostonpizza.com	Richmond	BC	V6V2M4	604-270-1108	270-4168
Boston Pizza Restaurants LP 1501 LBJ Fwy Suite 450 TF: 866-277-8721 ■ Web: www.bostons.com	Dallas	TX	75234	972-484-9022	484-7630
Boston Restaurant Assoc Inc 6 Kimball Ln Suite 210	Lynnfield	MA	01940	339-219-0466	
Boulder Creek Steakhouse 1701 Sunrise Hwy Web: www.bouldercreekbayshore.com	Bay Shore	NY	11706	631-968-9696	968-9698
BR Assoc Inc 4201 Mannheim Rd Suite A Web: www.brsidal.com	Jasper	IN	47546	812-482-3212	482-4013
Bravo! Development Inc 777 Goodale Blvd Suite 100 *Fax Area Code: 866 ■ TF: 888-452-7286 ■ Web: www.bestitalianusa.com	Columbus	OH	43212	614-326-7944	626-4009*
Breadeaux Pizza Inc 1806 Oakridge Cir TF: 800-835-6534 ■ Web: www.breadeauxpizza.com	Saint Joseph	MO	64506	816-364-1088	364-3739
Briad Group The 78 Okner Pkwy Web: www.briad.com	Livingston	NJ	07039	973-597-6433	597-6422
Brigantine Restaurants Inc 7889 Ostrow St Web: www.brigantine.com	San Diego	CA	92111	858-268-1030	268-5727
Brinker International Inc 6820 LBJ Fwy NYSE: EAT ■ TF: 800-983-4637 ■ Web: www.brinker.com	Dallas	TX	75240	972-980-9917	770-9593
Brio Tuscan Grille 777 Goodale Blvd Suite 100 *Fax Area Code: 866 ■ TF: 888-452-7286 ■ Web: www.brioitalian.com	Columbus	OH	43212	614-326-7944	626-4009*
Bristol Bar & Grill 8700 State Line Rd Web: www.houlihans.com	Leawood	KS	66206	913-901-2500	901-2651
Bristol Bar & Grille Inc 1308 Bardstown Rd PO Box 4607 Web: www.bristolbarandgrille.com	Louisville	KY	40204	502-456-6762	456-6784
Brock & Co Inc 257 Great Valley Pkwy TF: 866-468-2783 ■ Web: www.brockco.com	Malvern	PA	19355	610-647-5656	647-0867
Bruchi's Cheesesteaks & Subs 800 NE Tenney Rd TF: 877-488-9045 ■ Web: www.bruchis.com	Vancouver	WA	98685	360-882-8823	882-5988
Bubba Gump Shrimp Co LLC 1510 W Loop S TF: 877-729-4867 ■ Web: www.bubbagump.com	Houston	TX	77027	949-366-6260	366-6261

Company / Address	City	State	Zip	Phone	Fax
Buca di Beppo 1300 Nicollet Mall Suite 5003 *Web:* www.bucadibeppo.com	Minneapolis	MN	55403	612-225-3400	827-6446
Buca Inc 1300 Nicollet Mall Suite 5003 *NASDAQ: BUCA* ■ *TF:* 800-273-1388 ■ *Web:* www.bucadibeppo.com	Minneapolis	MN	55403	612-225-3400	827-6446
Buck's Pizza Franchising Corp Inc PO Box 405 *TF:* 800-310-8848 ■ *Web:* www.buckspizza.com	Du Bois	PA	15801	814-371-3076	371-4214
Buddy's Bar-B-Q 5806 Kingston Pike *Web:* www.buddysbarbq.com	Knoxville	TN	37919	865-584-1924	588-7211
Buffalo Wild Wings Inc 5500 Wayzata Blvd Suite 1600 *NASDAQ: BWLD* ■ *TF:* 800-499-9586 ■ *Web:* www.buffalowildwings.com	Minneapolis	MN	55416	952-593-9943	593-9787
Buffalo's Franchise Concepts Inc 707 Whitlock Ave SW Bldg H Suite 13 **Fax:* Cust Svc ■ *TF:* 800-459-4647 ■ *Web:* www.buffaloscafe.com	Marietta	GA	30064	770-420-1800	420-1810*
Buffets Inc 1020 Discovery Rd # 100 *Web:* www.buffet.com	Eagan	MN	55121	651-994-8608	365-2356
Bullets Corp of America Inc 13511 E Boundry Rd Sutie C	Midlothian	VA	23112	804-330-0837	330-5405
Burger King Corp 5505 Blue Lagoon Dr *TF:* 800-522-1278 ■ *Web:* www.bk.com	Miami	FL	33126	305-378-3000	
Burgerville USA 109 W 17th St *TF:* 866-264-2313 ■ *Web:* www.burgerville.com	Vancouver	WA	98660	360-694-1521	694-9114
Cafe Express LLC 675 Bering Dr # 600 *TF:* 800-552-1999 ■ *Web:* www.cafe-express.com	Houston	TX	77057	713-977-1922	977-9519
California Cafe Restaurants Old Town 50 University Ave Suite 260 *Web:* www.californiacafe.com	Los Gatos	CA	95030	408-354-8118	354-1400
California Pizza Kitchen Inc 6053 W Century Blvd Suite 1100 *NASDAQ: CPKI* ■ **Fax:* Hum Res ■ *TF:* 800-275-8255 ■ *Web:* www.cpk.com	Los Angeles	CA	90045	310-342-5000	342-4602*
Capital Grille 8215 Roswell Rd Bldg 600 *TF:* 800-434-6245 ■ *Web:* www.thecapitalgrille.com	Atlanta	GA	30350	770-399-9595	
Capital Restaurant Concepts Ltd (CRC) 1305 Wisconsin Ave NW *Web:* www.capitalrestaurants.com	Washington	DC	20007	202-339-6800	339-6801
Captain D's LLC 1717 Elm Hill Pike Suite A-1 *TF:* 800-314-4819 ■ *Web:* www.captainds.com	Nashville	TN	37210	615-391-5461	231-2309
Carey Hilliard's Restaurants 11111 Abercorn St	Savannah	GA	31419	912-925-2131	925-1699
Carlson Restaurants 4201 Marsh Ln *TF:* 800-374-3297 ■ *Web:* www.carlson.com	Carrollton	TX	75007	972-662-5400	
Carrabba's Italian Grill 2202 N Westshore Blvd Fl 5 *Web:* www.carrabbas.com	Tampa	FL	33607	813-288-8286	288-1779
Carrols Restaurant Group Inc 968 James St *NASDAQ: TAST* ■ **Fax:* Mktg ■ *Web:* www.carrols.com	Syracuse	NY	13203	315-424-0513	425-8874*
Carvers Steak & Chops 11940 Bernardo Plaza Dr *Web:* www.carverssteak.com	San Diego	CA	92128	858-485-1262	689-2289
Cask 'n' Cleaver 8689 9th St *Web:* www.caskncleaver.com	Rancho Cucamonga	CA	91730	909-981-5771	981-9734
Catalina Restaurant Group Inc 2200 Faraday Ave Suite 250 *Web:* www.catalinarestaurantgroup.com	Carlsbad	CA	92008	760-804-5750	476-5141
Cattle Baron Restaurants Inc 901 S Main St Suite A *Web:* www.cattlebaron.com	Roswell	NM	88203	505-622-3311	623-8801
CB & Potts 10013 59th Ave SW PO Box 99010 *TF:* 888-898-4050 ■ *Web:* www.cbpotts.com	Lakewood	WA	98499	253-588-1788	588-0713
CEC Entertainment Inc 4441 W Airport Fwy PO Box 152077 *NYSE: CEC* ■ *TF:* 888-778-7193 ■ *Web:* www.chuckecheese.com	Irving	TX	75062	972-258-8507	258-8545
Central Park America Inc 5751 Uptain Rd Suite 210 *Web:* www.centralparkamerica.com	Chattanooga	TN	37411	423-855-0991	899-5923
Champps Entertainment Inc 10375 Pk Meadows Dr Suite 560 *TF:* 800-461-5965 ■ *Web:* www.champps.com	Littleton	CO	80124	303-804-1333	804-8477
Chao Praya International 1880 Lakeland Dr Suite 3	Jackson	MS	39216	601-982-2863	982-2895
Char-O Chicken Systems Inc 2134 Main St Suite 220 *Web:* www.charochicken.com	Huntington Beach	CA	92648	714-960-2348	374-1889
Charleston's Restaurant 1800 N IH- Dr Suite 200 *Web:* www.halsmithrestaurantgroup.com	Norman	OK	73072	405-321-2600	321-2992
Charley's Eating & Drinking Saloon 284 Newbury St *TF:* 800-424-2753 ■ *Web:* www.backbayrestaurantgroup.com/bbrg/charleys.cfm	Boston	MA	02115	617-536-2800	236-4175
Charley's Grilled Subs 2500 Farmers Dr Suite 140 *TF:* 800-437-8325 ■ *Web:* www.charleys.com	Columbus	OH	43235	614-923-4700	923-4701
Charlie Brown's Steakhouse Inc 1450 Rt 22 W *TF:* 800-518-1855 ■ *Web:* www.charliebrowns.com	Mountainside	NJ	07092	908-518-1800	518-1509
Chart House Restaurants 1510 W Loop S *TF:* 800-552-6379 ■ *Web:* www.chart-house.com	Houston	TX	77027	713-850-1010	386-7707
Checkers Drive-In Restaurants Inc 4300 W Cypress St Suite 600 *TF:* 800-800-8072 ■ *Web:* www.checkers.com	Tampa	FL	33607	813-283-7000	283-7001
Cheddar's Casual Cafe 6600 Campus Cir Dr E Suite 560	Irving	TX	75063	214-596-6700	
Cheeburger Cheeburger Restaurants Inc 11595 Kelly Rd Suite 316 *TF:* 800-487-6211 ■ *Web:* www.cheeburger.com	Fort Myers	FL	33908	239-437-1611	437-1512
Cheesecake Factory Inc 26901 Malibu Hills Rd *NASDAQ: CAKE* ■ *Web:* www.cheesecakefactory.com	Calabasas Hills	CA	91301	818-871-3000	871-3100
Chefs International Inc 81 Ch Dr *Web:* www.jackbakerslobstershanty.com	Point Pleasant Beach	NJ	08742	732-899-6700	295-4514
Chelo's Inc 1725 Mendon Rd Suite 205 *Web:* www.chelos.com	Cumberland	RI	02864	401-312-6500	312-6501
Chesapeake Bay Seafood House Assoc LLC 1960 Gallows Rd Suite 200 *Web:* www.chesapeakerestaurants.com	Vienna	VA	22182	703-827-0320	893-1536
Chevys Inc 5660 Katella Ave Suite 100 *TF:* 800-424-3897 ■ *Web:* www.chevys.com	Cypress	CA	90631	562-346-1200	346-1470
Chick-fil-A Inc 5200 Buffington Rd **Fax:* Mktg ■ *TF:* 800-232-2677 ■ *Web:* www.chick-fil-a.com	Atlanta	GA	30349	404-765-8000	765-8140*
Chicken Out Rotisserie 15952 Shady Grove Rd *TF:* 800-328-4663 ■ *Web:* www.chickenout.com	Gaithersburg	MD	20877	301-921-0600	548-0024
China Grill Inc 60 W 53rd St 6th Ave *Web:* www.chinagrillmgt.com	New York	NY	10019	212-333-7788	581-9299
Chinese Cafes of America 4104 Aurora St *TF:* 800-662-1668 ■ *Web:* www.kellyscagungrill.com	Coral Gables	FL	33146	305-476-1611	476-9622
Chipotle Mexican Grill Inc 1543 Wazee St Suite 200 *NYSE: CMG* ■ *Web:* www.chipotle.com	Denver	CO	80202	303-595-4000	595-4014
Christo's Inc 782 Crescent St	Brockton	MA	02302	508-588-4200	583-6946
Chuck's Steak House Inc 1003 Boston Post Rd *Web:* www.chuckssteakhouse.com	West Haven	CT	06516	203-934-5300	934-3635
Chuy's Comida Deluxe 1623 Toomey Rd *TF:* 800-439-2489 ■ *Web:* www.chuys.com	Austin	TX	78704	512-473-2783	473-8684
CiCi Enterprises LP 1080 W Bethel Rd *Web:* www.cicispizza.com	Coppell	TX	75019	972-745-4200	745-4204
CKE Restaurants Inc 401 W Carl Karcher Way *NYSE: CKR* ■ **Fax:* Mail Rm ■ *TF:* 800-758-2275 ■ *Web:* www.ckr.com	Anaheim	CA	92803	714-774-5796	490-3630*
Claim Jumper Restaurants LLC 16721 Millikan Ave *TF:* 800-949-4538 ■ *Web:* www.claimjumper.com	Irvine	CA	92606	949-756-9001	757-7974
Clancy's Inc 15570 Stoney Creek Way	Noblesville	IN	46060	317-773-3284	776-6869
Clock Restaurants 902 Clint Moore Rd Suite 126	Boca Raton	FL	33487	561-994-3440	994-3655
Clyde's Restaurant Group 3236 M St NW *Web:* www.clydes.com	Washington	DC	20007	202-333-9180	625-7429
Coco's Bakery Restaurants 2200 Faraday Ave Suite 250 *Web:* www.cocosbakery.com	Carlsbad	CA	92008	760-804-5750	476-5141
Colter's Bar-B-Q 7502 Greenville Ave Suite 500 *TF:* 888-265-8377 ■ *Web:* www.coltersbbq.com	Dallas	TX	75231	214-987-5910	890-9230
Copeland's of New Orleans 1001 Harimaw Ct S *TF:* 800-401-0401 ■ *Web:* www.copelands.net	Metairie	LA	70001	504-620-3747	620-2016
Corporate Chefs Inc 22 Parkridge Rd *Web:* www.corporatechefs.com	Haverhill	MA	01835	978-372-7400	
Cosi Inc 1751 Lake Cook Rd Suite 600 *NASDAQ: COSI* ■ *TF:* 800-822-2076 ■ *Web:* www.getcosi.com	Deerfield	IL	60015	847-597-8800	597-8884
Cousins Submarines Inc N83 W13400 Leon Rd *TF:* 800-238-9736 ■ *Web:* www.cousinssubs.com	Menomonee Falls	WI	53051	262-253-7700	253-7710
Cozymels Restaurant 5720 LBJ Fwy Suite 190 *Web:* www.cozymels.com	Dallas	TX	75240	214-443-2000	443-2001
Crab House 1510 W Loop S *TF:* 800-552-6379 ■ *Web:* www.crabhouseseafood.com	Houston	TX	77027	713-850-1010	850-7274
Cracker Barrel Old Country Store Inc PO Box 787 *TF:* 800-333-9566 ■ *Web:* www.crackerbarrel.com	Lebanon	TN	37088	615-444-5533	444-5533
Cucina! Cucina! Italian Cafe Inc 555 116th Ave NE Suite 220	Bellevue	WA	98004	425-635-3575	637-7055
Culver Franchising System Inc 1240 Water St *Web:* www.culvers.com	Prairie du Sac	WI	53578	608-643-7980	643-7982
D'Angelo Sandwich Shops 600 Providence Hwy *TF:* 800-727-2446 ■ *Web:* www.dangelos.com	Dedham	MA	02026	781-461-1200	461-1896
Darden Restaurants Inc (DRI) 5900 Lake Ellenor Dr *NYSE: DRI* ■ *Web:* www.darden.com	Orlando	FL	32809	407-245-4000	245-5114
Darryl's Restaurant & Bar 8700 State Line Rd Suite 100 *Web:* www.houlihans.com	Leawood	KS	66206	913-901-2500	901-2651
Davanni's Inc 1100 Xenium Ln N *Web:* www.davannis.com	Plymouth	MN	55441	952-927-2300	927-2323
DavCo Restaurants Inc 1657 Crofton Blvd *TF:* 800-523-1411 ■ *Web:* www.wendavco.com	Crofton	MD	21114	410-721-3770	793-0754
Del Taco Inc 25521 Commercentre Dr Suite 200 *TF Cust Svc:* 800-852-7204 ■ *Web:* www.deltaco.com	Lake Forest	CA	92630	949-462-9300	462-7444
Deli Management Inc 2400 Broadway *Web:* www.jassondeli.com	Beaumont	TX	77702	409-838-1976	838-1906
Denny's Corp 203 E Main St *NASDAQ: DENN* ■ **Fax:* Mktg ■ *TF Cust Svc:* 800-733-6697 ■ *Web:* www.dennys.com	Spartanburg	SC	29319	864-597-8000	597-7230*
Denny's Inc 203 E Main St **Fax:* Mktg ■ *Web:* www.dennys.com	Spartanburg	SC	29319	864-597-8000	597-8780*
Desert Moon Cafe 612 Corporate Way Suite 1M *TF:* 877-564-6362 ■ *Web:* www.desertmooncafe.com	Valley Cottage	NY	10989	845-267-3300	267-2548
Diamond Dave's Mexican Restaurants 201 S Clinton St Suite 281 *Web:* www.diamonddaves.com	Iowa City	IA	52240	319-354-6794	337-4707
Dick's Last Resort 4514 Travis St Suite 220 *Web:* www.dickslastresort.com/domains/dallas/index.htm	Dallas	TX	75205	214-461-7197	
Dickey's Barbecue Restaurants Inc 4514 Cole Ave Suite 1100 *TF:* 866-340-6188 ■ *Web:* www.dickeys.com	Dallas	TX	75205	972-248-9899	248-8667
Dino's Pizza 11018 Southwalk Ln	Raleigh	NC	27614	919-676-1080	676-1081
Dixie Restaurants Inc 1215 Rebsamen Pk Rd *Web:* www.dixiecafe.com	Little Rock	AR	72202	501-666-3494	666-8900
Doctor's Assoc Inc 325 Bic Dr *TF:* 800-888-4848 ■ *Web:* www.subway.com	Milford	CT	06461	203-877-4281	783-7293

	City	State	ZIP	Phone	Fax
Dolly's Pizza Franchising Inc 1097 Union Lake Rd # B	White Lake	MI	48386	248-360-6440	360-7020
TF: 866-336-5597 ■ *Web:* www.dollyspizza.com					
Domino's Pizza Inc 30 Frank Lloyd Wright Dr	Ann Arbor	MI	48106	734-930-3030	930-3580*
NYSE: DPZ ■ **Fax:* Mail Rm ■ *TF:* 888-366-4667 ■ *Web:* www.express.dominos.com					
Don Cherry's Sports Grill Inc 72 James St	Parry Sound	ON	P2A1T5	866-821-0468	
TF: 866-821-0468 ■ *Web:* www.doncherryssportsgrill.com					
Don Pablo's Mexican Kitchen 150 Hancock St	Madison	GA	30650	706-342-4552	
TF: 800-765-7894 ■ *Web:* www.donpablos.com					
Don's Restaurants 8905 Lake Ave	Cleveland	OH	44102	216-961-6767	961-1966
Web: www.strangcorp.com					
Donatos Pizza 935 Taylor Stn Rd	Columbus	OH	43230	614-416-7700	416-7701
TF: 800-366-2867 ■ *Web:* www.donatos.com					
Drm Inc 5324 N 134th Ave	Omaha	NE	68164	402-573-1216	573-0171
Web: www.drmarbys.com					
Durango Steakhouse 2325 Ulmerton Rd Suite 20	Clearwater	FL	33762	727-576-6424	572-8342
TF: 800-525-8643 ■ *Web:* www.durangosteakhouse.com					
Dutchman Hospitality Group 4985 Walnut St PO Box 158	Walnut Creek	OH	44687	330-893-2926	893-2637
Web: www.dhgroup.com					
Dynaco Inc 10 Riverpark Pl E Suite 104	Fresno	CA	93720	559-485-8520	485-8520
TF: 800-230-4985 ■ *Web:* www.dynacofoods.com					
East of Chicago Pizza Co 512 E Tiffin St	Willard	OH	44890	419-935-3033	935-3278
Web: www.eastofchicago.com					
Eat at Joe's Ltd 670 White Plains Rd Suite 120	Scarsdale	NY	10583	914-725-2700	725-8663
Web: www.eatatjoesltd.com					
Eat'n Park Hospitality Group Inc 285 E Waterfront Dr PO Box 3000	Pittsburgh	PA	15120	412-461-2000	461-6000
TF: 800-947-4033 ■ *Web:* www.eatnpark.com					
Edo Japan International Inc 32 St SE Suite 4838	Calgary	AB	T2B2S6	403-215-8800	215-8801
TF: 888-336-9888 ■ *Web:* www.edojapan.com					
Eegee's Inc 3360 E Ajo Way	Tucson	AZ	85713	520-294-3333	889-4340
Web: www.eegees.com					
Einstein Noah Restaurant Group Inc 555 Zang St Suite 300	Lakewood	CO	80228	303-568-8000	
Web: www.newworldrestaurantgroup.com					
El Centro Foods Inc 6930 1/2 Tujunga Ave	North Hollywood	CA	91605	818-766-4395	766-1496
El Fenix Corp 11075 Harry Hines Blvd	Dallas	TX	75229	972-241-2171	241-3031
TF: 877-591-1918 ■ *Web:* www.elfenix.com					
El Pollo Loco 3535 Harbor Blvd Suite 100	Costa Mesa	CA	92626	714-599-5000	
TF: 877-375-4968 ■ *Web:* www.elpolloloco.com					
El Torito Restaurants Inc 5660 Katella Ave Suite 100	Cypress	CA	90630	562-346-1200	346-1470
TF: 800-858-6512 ■ *Web:* www.eltorito.com					
Elephant & Castle Group Inc 50 Congress St Suite 900	Boston	MA	02109	617-720-2100	720-2102
Web: www.elephantcastle.com					
Elephant Bar Restaurant 14241 Firestone Blvd Suite 315	La Mirada	CA	90638	562-207-6200	
Web: www.elephantbar.com					
Emeril's Homebase 829 St Charles Ave	New Orleans	LA	70130	504-524-4241	558-3937
Web: www.emerils.com					
Empress Chili 10592 Taconic Terr	Cincinnati	OH	45215	513-771-1441	771-1442
Erik's Deli Cafe 365 Coral St	Santa Cruz	CA	95060	831-458-1818	458-9797
Web: www.eriksdelicafe.com					
Escape Enterprises Ltd 222 Neilston St	Columbus	OH	43215	614-224-0300	224-6460
Web: www.steakescape.com					
Estefan Enterprises Inc 420 Jefferson Ave	Miami Beach	FL	33139	305-534-4330	534-5220
Family Sports Concepts Inc 5510 W La Salle St Suite 200	Tampa	FL	33607	813-226-2333	226-0030
TF: 800-728-8878 ■ *Web:* www.beefobradys.com					
Famous Dave's of America Inc 12701 Whitewater Dr Suite 200	Minnetonka	MN	55343	952-294-1300	294-0242
NASDAQ: DAVE ■ *TF:* 800-210-4040 ■ *Web:* www.famousdaves.com					
Famous Sam's Inc 16012 Metcalf Ave Suite 1	Overland Park	KS	66085	913-239-0266	239-9768
TF: 888-866-8808 ■ *Web:* www.famoussams.com					
Fatburger North America Inc 301 Arizona Ave Suite 200	Santa Monica	CA	90401	310-319-1850	319-1863
TF: 800-315-3901 ■ *Web:* www.fatburger.com					
Fatz Cafe 4324 Wade Hampton Blvd	Taylors	SC	29687	864-322-1331	322-1332
Web: www.fatzcafe.com					
Fausto's Fried Chicken Inc 905 E 4th St	Dequincy	LA	70633	337-786-7264	
Faz Restaurants Inc 5121 Hopyard Rd	Pleasanton	CA	94588	925-469-1600	469-1604
Web: www.fazrestaurants.com					
Fieldstone Restaurants Corp 1637 W Main St	Albert Lea	MN	56007	507-377-3805	377-8118
Web: www.fieldstonerestaurants.com					
Figaro's Italian Pizza Inc 1500 Liberty St SE Suite 160	Salem	OR	97302	503-371-9318	363-5364
TF: 888-344-2767 ■ *Web:* www.figaros.com					
Fired Up Inc 7500 Rialto Blvd Suite 250	Austin	TX	78735	512-263-0800	263-8055
Firehouse Restaurant Group Inc 3400 Kori Rd # 8	Jacksonville	FL	32257	904-886-8300	886-2111
TF: 800-388-3473 ■ *Web:* www.firehousesubs.com					
First Watch Restaurants Inc 9027 Town Ctr Pkwy	Bradenton	FL	94202	941-907-9800	907-8933
Web: www.firstwatch.com					
Flamers Charbroiled Hamburgers 1515 International Pkwy Suite 2013	Heathrow	FL	32746	407-574-8363	333-8852
TF: 866-749-4889 ■ *Web:* www.flamersgrill.com					
Flanigan's Enterprises Inc 5059 NE 18th Ave	Fort Lauderdale	FL	33334	954-377-1961	377-1980
AMEX: BDL ■ *Web:* www.flanigans.net					
Fogo de Chao 14881 Quorum Dr Suite 750	Dallas	TX	75254	972-960-9533	960-9877
Web: www.fogodechao.com					
Folks Southern Kitchen 1384 Buford Business Blvd Suite 500	Buford	GA	30518	770-904-6595	904-6805
Web: www.folkskitchen.com					
Food Concepts International LP 2575 S Loop 289	Lubbock	TX	79423	806-785-8686	785-8866
Web: www.abuelos.com					
Foodee's Franchising Inc 2 S Main St	Concord	NH	03301	603-225-3834	224-2421
Fosters Freeze LLC 8360 Red Oak Ave Suite 202	Rancho Cucamonga	CA	91730	909-944-0815	944-0895
Web: www.fostersfreeze.com					
Fox & Hound Restaurant Group 1551 N Waterfront Pkwy Suite 30	Wichita	KS	67206	316-634-0505	634-6060
TF: 800-229-2118 ■ *Web:* www.foxandhound.com					
Fox's Pizza Den Inc 4425 Willaim Penn Hwy	Murrysville	PA	15668	724-733-7888	325-5479
TF: 800-899-3697 ■ *Web:* www.foxspizza.com					
Fresh Choice Restaurants LLC 1310 65th St	Emeryville	CA	94608	510-420-8898	
TF: 800-859-8693 ■ *Web:* www.freshchoice.com					
Fresh Enterprises Inc 5900-A Katella Ave Suite 101	Cypress	CA	90630	562-391-2400	
TF: 877-225-2373 ■ *Web:* www.bajafresh.com					
Freshens Frozen Treats 1750 The Exchange	Atlanta	GA	30339	678-627-5400	627-5454
TF: 800-633-4519 ■ *Web:* www.freshens.com					
Friendly Ice Cream Corp 1855 Boston Rd	Wilbraham	MA	01095	413-543-2400	543-3966
TF: 800-966-9970 ■ *Web:* www.friendlys.com					
Frisch's Restaurants Inc 2800 Gilbert Ave	Cincinnati	OH	45206	513-961-2660	559-5160
AMEX: FRS ■ *TF:* 800-873-3633 ■ *Web:* www.frischs.com					
Frullati Cafe & Bakery 9311 E Via de Ventura	Scottsdale	AZ	85258	480-362-4800	362-4812
TF: 866-452-4252 ■ *Web:* www.frullati.com					
Garden Fresh Restaurant Corp 15822 Bernardo Ctr Dr Suite A	San Diego	CA	92127	858-675-1600	675-1616
TF: 800-874-1600 ■ *Web:* www.souplantation.com					
Garduno's 4604 Columbine Ne	Albuquerque	NM	87113	505-298-5514	298-5549
Web: www.gardunosrestaurants.com					
Garfield's Restaurant & Pub 1220 S Santa Fe Ave	Edmond	OK	73003	405-705-5000	705-5001
Gastronomy Inc 48 W Market St Suite 250	Salt Lake City	UT	84101	801-322-2020	363-5275
Web: www.gastronomyinc.com					
Gates Bar-B-Q 4621 Paseo Blvd	Kansas City	MO	64110	816-923-0900	923-3922
TF: 800-662-7427 ■ *Web:* www.gatesbbq.com					
Giorgio Restaurants 222 St Laurent Blvd	Montreal	QC	H2Y2Y3	514-845-4221	844-0071
Web: www.giorgio.ca					
Gold Star Chili 650 Lunken Pk Dr	Cincinnati	OH	45226	513-231-4541	624-4415
TF: 800-643-0465 ■ *Web:* www.goldstarchili.com					
Golden Corral Corp 5151 Glenwood Ave	Raleigh	NC	27612	919-781-9310	881-4485
TF: 800-284-5673 ■ *Web:* www.goldencorral.net					
Golden Franchising Corp 11488 Luna Rd Suite 100B	Dallas	TX	75234	972-831-0911	831-0401
Web: www.goldenchick.com					
Golden Griddle Corp The 305 Milner Ave Suite 900	Toronto	ON	M1B3V4	416-609-2200	609-2207
Web: www.goldengriddlecorp.com					
Good Eats Inc 12200 Stemmons Fwy Suite 100	Dallas	TX	75234	972-241-5500	888-8198
TF: 800-275-1337 ■ *Web:* www.goodeatsgrill.com					
Good Times Restaurants Inc 601 Corporate Cir	Golden	CO	80401	303-384-1400	273-0177
NASDAQ: GTIM ■ *Web:* www.goodtimesburgers.com					
Gordon Biersch Brewery Restaurants 2001 Riverside Dr Suite 3100	Chattanooga	TN	37406	423-424-2000	752-1973
Web: www.gordonbiersch.com					
Gorin's Homemade Ice Cream & Sandwiches 190 Marietta St NW	Atlanta	GA	30303	404-223-3502	
Granite City Food & Brewery Ltd 5500 Excelsior Blvd Suite 101	Saint Louis Park	MN	55416	952-746-9900	
NASDAQ: GCFB ■ *Web:* www.gcfb.net					
Great Steak & Potato Co 9311 E Via de Ventura	Scottsdale	AZ	85258	480-362-4800	362-4812
TF: 866-452-4252 ■ *Web:* www.thegreatsteak.com					
Great Wraps! Inc 4 Executive Pk E Suite 315	Atlanta	GA	30329	404-248-9900	248-0180
TF: 888-489-7277 ■ *Web:* www.greatwraps.com					
Greco Pizza Donair 105 Walker St PO Box 1040	Truro	NS	B2N5G9	902-220-1335	820-3109
TF: 800-565-4389 ■ *Web:* www.greco.ca					
Greek's Pizzeria 1600 University Ave	Muncie	IN	47303	765-284-5655	
Green Burrito 1325 N Anaheim Blvd	Anaheim	CA	92801	714-254-4500	490-3630
TF: 800-422-4141					
Green Mill Restaurants Inc 1342 Grand Ave Suite 215	St. Paul	MN	55105	651-203-3100	203-3101
Web: www.greenmill.com					
Griff's of America Inc 1202 Richardson Dr Suite 312	Richardson	TX	75080	972-238-9561	238-9564
Grill Concepts Inc 6300 Canoga Ave Suite 600	Woodland Hills	CA	91367	818-251-7000	999-4745
PINK: GLLC ■ *Web:* www.dailygrill.com					
Grindstone Charley's 15570 Stoney Creek Way	Noblesville	IN	46060	317-773-3284	776-6869
Grinner's Food Systems Ltd 105 Walker St PO Box 1040	Truro	NS	B2N4B1	902-893-4141	895-7635
Web: www.greco.ca					
Grotto Pizza Inc 20376 Coastal Hwy	Rehoboth Beach	DE	19971	302-227-3567	227-4566
Web: www.grottopizza.com					
Hacienda Mexican Restaurants 1501 N Ironwood Dr	South Bend	IN	46635	574-272-5922	272-6055
TF: 800-541-3227 ■ *Web:* www.haciendafiesta.com					
Haddad Restaurant Group Inc 4717 Grand Ave Suite 200	Kansas City	MO	64112	816-931-2261	931-9044
Hal Smith Restaurant Group Inc 1800 N IH- Dr Suite 200	Norman	OK	73072	405-321-2600	321-2992
Web: www.ehsrg.com					
Happy Chef Systems Inc 51646 US Hwy 169	Mankato	MN	56001	507-345-4571	345-4585
Happy Joe's Inc 2705 Happy Joe Dr	Bettendorf	IA	52722	563-332-8811	332-5822
Web: www.happyjoes.com					

Company	City	State	ZIP	Phone	Fax
Hard Rock Cafe International Inc 6100 Old Pk Ln *TF:* 800-235-7625 ■ *Web:* www.hardrock.com	Orlando	FL	32835	407-445-7625	445-7869
Hard Times Cafe Inc 6320 Augusta Dr Suite 801 *Web:* www.hardtimes.com	Springfield	VA	22150	703-451-7555	451-9292
Harman Management Corp 199 1st St Suite 212	Los Altos	CA	94022	650-941-5681	948-7532
Heart of America Restaurants & Inns LLC 1501 River Dr *Web:* www.hoari.com	Moline	IL	61265	309-797-9300	797-8700
Heartland Food Corp 1400 Opus Pl Suite 900 *Web:* www.heartlandfoodcorp.com	Downers Grove	IL	60515	630-598-3300	598-2211
Heidi's Family Restaurant Inc 106 E Adams St Suite 206	Carson City	NV	89706	775-884-1415	884-2091
High Plains Pizza Inc 7 W PkwyBlvd	Liberal	KS	67901	620-624-5638	624-5411
Hillstone Restaurant Group 147 S Beverly Dr *TF:* 800-230-9787 ■ *Web:* www.hillstone.com	Beverly Hills	CA	90212	310-385-7343	385-7119
Ho-Lee-Chow 2204 Danforth Ave *TF:* 800-465-3324 ■ *Web:* www.holeechow.com	Toronto	ON	M4C1K3	416-996-3333	778-6818
Hobee's California Restaurants 4224 El Camino Real *Web:* www.hobees.com	Palo Alto	CA	94306	650-493-7823	493-0756
Hof's Hut Restaurants Inc 2601 E Willow St *Web:* www.hofshut.com	Signal Hill	CA	90755	562-596-0200	430-0480
Holcomb Bridge at Grimes Bridge 690 Holcomb Bridge Rd *Web:* www.myfriendsplacedeli.com	Roswell	GA	30076	770-594-9117	
Holland Inc 109 W 17th St *Web:* www.hollandinc.com	Vancouver	WA	98660	360-694-1521	694-9114
Home Run Inn Inc 1300 Internationale Pkwy *TF:* 800-636-9696 ■ *Web:* www.homeruninn.com	Woodridge	IL	60517	630-783-9696	783-0069
Homestyle Dining LLC 3701 W Plano Pkwy Suite 200 *Web:* www.ponderosasteakhouses.com	Plano	TX	75093	972-244-8900	
HomeTown Buffet Restaurants 1460 Buffet Way *Web:* www.buffet.com	Eagan	MN	55121	651-994-8608	365-2356
Hooters Restaurants 1815 The Exchange **Fax:* Hum Res ■ *Web:* www.hooters.com	Atlanta	GA	30339	770-951-2040	618-7031*
Hops Grillhouse & Brewery 150 Hancock St *TF:* 888-865-4677 ■ *Web:* www.hopsrestaurants.com	Madison	GA	30650	706-342-4552	342-4057
Hoss's Steak & Sea House 170 Patchway Rd *TF:* 800-992-4677 ■ *Web:* www.hosss.com	Duncansville	PA	16635	814-695-7600	695-3865
Hot Dog on a Stick 5942 Priestly Dr *TF:* 800-321-8400 ■ *Web:* www.hotdogonastick.com	Carlsbad	CA	92008	760-930-0456	930-0420
Houlihan's Restaurant Group Inc 8700 State Line Rd Suite 100 *Web:* www.houlihans.com	Leawood	KS	66206	913-901-2500	901-2651
House of Blues Entertainment Inc 7060 Hollywood Blvd # 1100 *TF:* 800-843-2583 ■ *Web:* www.houseofblues.com	Hollywood	CA	90028	323-769-4600	769-4792
Huddle House Inc 5901 Peachtree Dunwoody Suite B450 *TF:* 800-418-9555 ■ *Web:* www.huddlehouse.com	Atlanta	GA	30328	770-325-1300	
Humperdink's Texas LLC PO Box 542465 *Web:* www.humperdinks.com	Dallas	TX	75354	214-353-0500	
Humpty's Restaurants International Inc 2505 Macleod Terr S *TF:* 800-661-7589 ■ *Web:* www.humptys.com	Calgary	AB	T2G5J4	403-269-4675	266-1973
Hungry Howie's Pizza & Subs Inc 30300 Stephenson Hwy Suite 200 *TF:* 800-624-8122 ■ *Web:* www.hungryhowies.com	Madison Heights	MI	48071	248-414-3300	414-3301
Hy's of Canada Ltd 333-610 Granville St 3rd Fl *Web:* www.hyssteakhouse.com	Vancouver	BC	V6C3T3	604-684-3311	684-3535
Hyde Park Restaurant Systems 26300 Chagrin Blvd Suite 1 *Web:* www.hydeparkrestaurants.com	Beachwood	OH	44122	216-464-0688	595-8267
IHOP Corp 450 N Brand Blvd *TF:* 800-241-4467 ■ *Web:* www.ihop.com	Glendale	CA	91203	818-240-6055	637-4730
Il Fornaio America Corp 770 Tamalpais Dr Suite 400 *TF:* 800-291-1505 ■ *Web:* www.ilfornaio.com	Corte Madera	CA	94925	415-945-0500	924-0906
Imo's Pizza 1610 Des Peres Rd Suite 160 *Web:* www.imospizza.com	Saint Louis	MO	63131	314-822-7227	822-5278
In-N-Out Burger Inc 4199 Campus Dr 9th Fl *TF Cust Svc:* 800-786-1000 ■ *Web:* www.in-n-out.com	Irvine	CA	92612	949-509-6200	509-6389
Interfoods of America Inc 9500 S Dadeland Blvd Suite 720 *TF:* 866-232-4401	Miami	FL	33156	305-670-0746	670-0767
International Dairy Queen Corp 7505 Metro Blvd *TF:* 866-793-7582 ■ *Web:* www.dairyqueen.com	Minneapolis	MN	55439	952-896-8696	830-0270
International Restaurant Management Group Inc 4104 Aurora St *TF:* 800-662-1668 ■ *Web:* www.kellyscagungrill.com	Coral Gables	FL	33146	305-476-1611	476-9622
Iron Hill Brewery 2502 W 6th St *Web:* www.ironhillbrewery.com	Wilmington	DE	19805	302-888-2739	652-4115
Isaac's Deli Inc 354 N Prince St Suite 220 *Web:* www.isaacsdeli.com	Lancaster	PA	17603	717-394-0623	393-0955
Islands Restaurants 5750 Fleet St Suite 120 *Web:* www.islandsrestaurants.com	Carlsbad	CA	92008	760-268-1800	918-1500
J & B Restaurant Partners Inc 3385 Veterans Memorial Hwy *Web:* www.jbrestaurants.com	Ronkonkoma	NY	11779	631-218-9067	218-8019
J & S Cafeteria Inc PO Box 5748 *Web:* www.jandscafeteria.com	High Point	NC	27262	336-884-0404	884-0815
J A Sutherland Inc 228 MN St *Web:* www.jasutherland.com	Red Bluff	CA	96080	530-529-1470	527-1959
J Alexander's Corp 3401 W End Ave Suite 260 *AMEX: JAX* ■ *TF:* 888-285-2539 ■ *Web:* www.jalexanders.com	Nashville	TN	37203	615-269-1900	269-1999
J Gilbert's Wood Fired Steaks 8700 State Line Rd Suite 100 *Web:* www.jgilberts.com	Leawood	KS	66206	913-901-2500	901-2673
Jack in the Box Inc 9330 Balboa Ave *TF:* 800-500-5225 ■ *Web:* www.jackinthebox.com	San Diego	CA	92123	858-571-2121	571-2101
Jack's Family Restaurants Inc 124 W Oxmoor Rd *TF:* 800-422-3893 ■ *Web:* www.eatatjacks.com	Birmingham	AL	35209	205-945-8167	945-9820
Jake's Over the Top 4605 Harrison Blvd The Centennial Bldg 3rd Fl *TF:* 800-207-5804	Ogden	UT	84403	801-476-9780	476-9788
Jake's Pizza Enterprises Inc 1931 Rohlwing Rd Suite B *TF:* 800-425-2537 ■ *Web:* www.jakespizza.com	Rolling Meadows	IL	60008	847-368-1990	368-1995
James Coney Island Inc 1750 Stebbins Dr *Web:* www.jamesconeyisland.com	Houston	TX	77043	713-932-1500	932-0061
Jan Cos 35 Sockanosset Cross Rd *TF:* 800-937-1800 ■ *Web:* www.jancompanies.com	Cranston	RI	02920	401-946-4000	946-4392
Jason Deli Co 2400 Broadway *TF:* 800-444-3354 ■ *Web:* www.jasonsdeli.com	Beaumont	TX	77702	409-838-1976	838-0370
Jerry's Famous Deli Inc 12711 Ventura Blvd Suite 400 *Web:* www.jerrysfamousdeli.com	Studio City	CA	91604	818-766-8311	766-8315
Jerry's Subs & Pizza 15942 Shady Grove Rd *TF:* 800-990-9176 ■ *Web:* www.jerrysusa.com	Gaithersburg	MD	20877	301-921-8777	948-3508
Jerry's Systems Inc 15942 Shady Grove Rd *TF:* 800-990-9176 ■ *Web:* www.jerrysusa.com	Gaithersburg	MD	20877	301-921-8777	948-3508
Jet's America Inc 37501 Mound Rd *TF:* 888-446-5870 ■ *Web:* www.jetspizza.com	Sterling Heights	MI	48130	586-268-5870	268-6762
Jim's Restaurants 8520 Crownhill Blvd *Web:* www.jimsrestaurants.com	San Antonio	TX	78209	210-828-1493	822-8606
Jimmy John's Franchise Inc 2212 Fox Dr *TF:* 800-546-6904 ■ *Web:* www.jimmyjohns.com	Champaign	IL	61820	217-356-9900	359-2956
Jocks & Jills & Frankie's Sports Grill 5600 Roswell Rd NE Suite 100-A *Web:* www.jocks-frankies.com	Atlanta	GA	30342	770-209-0920	
Joe's American Bar & Grille 284 Newbury St *Web:* www.backbayrestaurantgroup.com/bbrg/joesamerican.cfm	Boston	MA	02115	617-536-2800	236-4175
Joey's Only Seafood Franchising Corp 514-42nd Ave SE *TF:* 800-661-2123 ■ *Web:* www.joeys.ca	Calgary	AB	T2G1Y6	403-243-4584	243-8989
John Harvard's Brew House 33 Dunster St *Web:* www.johnharvards.com	Cambridge	MA	02138	617-868-3585	868-4341
Jonny Carino's Country Italian 7500 Rialto Blvd Suite 1-250 *Web:* www.carinos.com	Austin	TX	78735	512-263-0800	263-8055
JRN Inc 201 W 7th St *TF Cust Svc:* 800-251-8035	Columbia	TN	38401	931-381-3000	490-4801
K Bob's Steakhouse 141 E Palace Ave *Web:* www.kbobsusa.com	Santa Fe	NM	87505	505-982-3438	982-3468
K-Mac Enterprises Inc PO Box 6538 *TF:* 800-345-5622 ■ *Web:* www.kmaccorp.com	Fort Smith	AR	72906	479-646-2053	646-8748
Kahala Corp 9311 E Via de Ventura *TF:* 866-452-4252 ■ *Web:* www.blimpie.com	Scottsdale	AZ	85258	480-362-4800	362-4812
Kahunaville Island Restaurant & Party Bar 3300 Las Vegas Blvd S *TF:* 888-453-3990 ■ *Web:* www.kahunaville.com	Las Vegas	NV	89109	702-894-7390	
Keg Restaurants Ltd 10100 Shellbridge Way *Web:* www.kegsteakhouse.com	Richmond	BC	V6X2W7	604-276-0242	276-2681
KFC Corp 1441 Gardiner Ln *TF:* 800-544-5774 ■ *Web:* www.kfc.com	Louisville	KY	40213	502-874-8300	874-2759
Kimpton Hotel & Restaurant Group LLC 222 Kearny St Suite 200 *TF:* 800-546-2686 ■ *Web:* www.kimptonhotels.com	San Francisco	CA	94108	415-397-5572	296-8031
Kincaid's Fish Chop & Steak House 1818 N Northlake Way	Seattle	WA	98103	206-634-3082	632-3533
King Taco Restaurants Inc 3421 E 14th St *Web:* www.kingtaco.com	Los Angeles	CA	90023	323-268-2267	266-6565
King's Seafood Co 3185 Airway Ave Suite J *Web:* www.kingsseafood.com	Costa Mesa	CA	92626	714-432-0400	432-0111
Kings Family Restaurants 1180 Long Run Rd **Fax:* Hum Res ■ *Web:* www.kingsfamily.com	White Oak	PA	15131	412-751-0700	751-9008*
Kobe Japanese Steakhouse Inc 468 W Hwy 436 *Web:* www.kobesteakhouse.com	Altamonte Springs	FL	32714	407-862-6099	788-8887
Kona Grill Inc 7150 E Camelback Rd Suite 220 *NASDAQ: KONA* ■ *TF:* 866-328-5662 ■ *Web:* www.konagrill.com	Scottsdale	AZ	85251	480-922-8100	991-6811
Koo Koo Roo 5700 MopaC Expy S Bldg C Suite 300 *Web:* www.kookooroo.com	Austin	TX	78749	512-275-0400	275-0670
L & L Hawaiian Barbecue 931 University Ave Suite 202 *Web:* www.hawaiianbarbecue.com	Honolulu	HI	96826	808-951-9888	951-0888
La Salsa Inc 5900 Katella Ave Suite 125 *TF:* 866-452-7257 ■ *Web:* www.lasalsa.com	Cypress CA	CA	90630	562-391-2400	
LaBelle Management Inc 405 S Mission Rd *Web:* www.labellemgt.com	Mount Pleasant	MI	48858	989-772-2902	773-7521
Lambert's Cafe Inc 36 Papa Holler Ln *Web:* www.throwedrolls.com	Sikeston	MO	63801	573-471-8795	471-7563
Lamppost Pizza Franchise Corp 3002 Dow Ave Suite 320 *Web:* www.lamppostpizza.com	Tustin	CA	92780	714-731-6171	731-0951
Landry's Restaurants Inc 1510 W Loop S *NYSE: LNY* ■ *TF:* 800-552-6379 ■ *Web:* www.landrysrestaurants.com	Houston	TX	77027	713-850-1010	850-7205
LaRosa's Inc 2334 Boudinot Ave *Web:* www.larosas.com	Cincinnati	OH	45238	513-347-5660	922-2776

Company	City	State	ZIP	Phone	Fax
Lawry's Restaurants Inc 234 E Colorado Blvd Suite 500 *Web:* www.lawrysonline.com	Pasadena	CA	91101	626-440-5234	440-5232
LEDO Pizza System Inc 2001 Tidewater Colony Dr Suite 203 *Web:* www.ledopizza.com	Annapolis	MD	21401	410-721-6887	571-8395
Legal Sea Foods Inc 1 Seafood Way *TF:* 800-477-5342 ■ *Web:* www.legalseafoods.com	Boston	MA	02210	617-530-9000	530-9023
Leona's Pizzeria Inc 3215 N Sheffield Ave *Web:* www.leonas.com	Chicago	IL	60657	773-327-8861	
Lettuce Entertain You Enterprises Inc 5419 N Sheridan Rd *Web:* www.leye.com	Chicago	IL	60640	773-878-7340	878-7667
Levy Restaurants 980 N Michigan Ave Suite 400 *Web:* www.levyrestaurants.com	Chicago	IL	60611	312-664-8200	280-2739
Libby Hill Seafood Restaurants Inc 4517 W Market St # B *TF:* 800-452-2071 ■ *Web:* www.libbyhill.com	Greensboro	NC	27407	336-294-0505	292-6005
Little Caesars Inc 2211 Woodward Ave **Fax:* Cust Svc ■ *TF:* 800-722-3727 ■ *Web:* www.littlecaesars.com	Detroit	MI	48201	313-983-6000	983-6166*
Lobster Shanty 62 Broadway *Web:* www.jackpakerslobstershanty.com	Point Pleasant Beach	NJ	08742	732-295-0350	295-4514
Logan's Roadhouse Inc 3011 Armory Dr Suite 300 *TF:* 800-815-9056 ■ *Web:* www.logansroadhouse.com	Nashville	TN	37211	615-885-9056	346-6301
Lone Star Steakhouse & Saloon Inc 5055 W Pk Blvd Suite 500 *Web:* www.lonestarsteakhouse.com	Plano	TX	75093	972-295-8600	
Lone Star Texas Grill 472 Morden Rd Suite 101 *Web:* www.lonestartexasgrill.com	Oakville	ON	L6K3W4	905-845-5852	845-7091
Long John Silver's Restaurants Inc 1441 Gardiner Ln *Web:* www.ljsilvers.com	Louisville	KY	40213	502-874-8300	874-8306
LongHorn Steakhouse 8215 Roswell Rd Bldg 600 *TF:* 800-434-6245 ■ *Web:* www.longhornsteakhouse.com	Atlanta	GA	30350	770-399-9595	901-6628
Luby's Inc 13111 NW Fwy Suite 600 *NYSE: LUB* ■ *TF:* 800-886-4600 ■ *Web:* www.lubys.com	Houston	TX	77040	713-329-6800	
Lunan Corp 414 N Orleans St Suite 402 *Web:* www.arbysrestaurants.com	Chicago	IL	60610	312-645-9898	645-0654
Macayo Mexican Restaurants 3117 N 16th St *Web:* www.macayo.com	Phoenix	AZ	85016	602-264-1831	277-1795
Maggiano's Little Italy 8687 N Central Expy Suite 205 *Web:* www.maggianos.com	Dallas	TX	75225	214-360-0707	360-0756
Magic Time Machine 8520 Crownhill Blvd *Web:* www.magictimemachine.com	San Antonio	TX	78209	210-828-1493	822-8830
Malnati Organization Inc 3685 Woodhead Dr *TF:* 800-568-8646 ■ *Web:* www.loumalnatis.com	Northbrook	IL	60062	847-562-1814	562-1950
Mancha Development Co 2275 Sampson Ave Suite 201	Corona	CA	92879	951-271-4100	271-4110
Margaritaville Inc 424-A Fleming St *TF:* 800-262-6835 ■ *Web:* www.margaritaville.com	Key West	FL	33040	305-296-9089	296-1084
Marie Callender Restaurant & Bakery 27101 Puerta Real Suite 260 *TF:* 800-776-7437 ■ *Web:* www.mariecallender.com	Mission Viejo	CA	92691	949-448-5300	448-5315
Maui Tacos International Inc 145 Huguenot St Suite 320 *TF:* 866-388-3758 ■ *Web:* www.mauitacos.com	New Rochelle	NY	10801	866-388-3758	
Maui Wowi Inc 5445 DTC Pkwy Suite 1050 *Web:* www.mauiwowi.com	Greenwood Village	CO	80111	303-781-7800	781-2438
McAlister's Corp 731 S Pear Orchard Rd Suite 51 *TF:* 888-855-3354 ■ *Web:* www.mcalistersdeli.com	Ridgeland	MS	39157	601-952-1100	957-0964
McCormick & Schmick's Seafood Restaurant Inc 1414 NW Northrup Suite 700 *NASDAQ: MSSR* ■ *Web:* www.mccormickandschmicks.com	Portland	OR	97209	503-226-3440	228-5074
McDonald's Corp 1 McDonald's Plaza *NYSE: MCD* ■ *TF:* 800-234-6227 ■ *Web:* www.mcdonalds.com	Oak Brook	IL	60523	630-623-3000	623-5500
McDonald's Restaurants of Canada Ltd 1 McDonald's Pl *Web:* www.mcdonalds.ca	Toronto	ON	M3C3L4	416-443-1000	446-3443
McGrath's Fish House 1935 Davcor St SE *Web:* www.mcgrathsfishhouse.com	Salem	OR	97302	503-399-8456	391-2846
Me-N-Ed's-Bullard/West 1731 W Bullard Suite 101 *Web:* www.meneds.com	Fresno	CA	93711	559-431-7331	
Melting Pot Restaurants Inc 8810 Twin Lakes Blvd *TF:* 800-783-0867 ■ *Web:* www.meltingpot.com	Tampa	FL	33614	813-881-0055	889-9361
Meritage Hospitality Group Inc 3210 Eagle Run Dr NE Suite 100 *PINK: MHGU* ■ *Web:* www.meritagehospitality.com	Grand Rapids	MI	49525	616-776-2600	364-2810
Metz & Assoc Ltd 2 Woodland Dr *Web:* www.metzltd.com	Dallas	PA	18612	570-675-8100	675-0919
Mexican Restaurants Inc 1135 Edgebrook St *NASDAQ: CASA* ■ *TF:* 800-741-7574 ■ *Web:* www.mexicanrestaurantsinc.com	Houston	TX	77034	713-943-7574	943-9554
Mighty Taco Inc 9362 Transit Rd	East Amherst	NY	14051	716-636-1097	636-4520
Milio's Sandwiches 901 Deming Way Suite 202 *Web:* www.milios.com	Madison	WI	53717	608-662-3000	662-3001
Millie's 565 W Lambert Rd Suite C *Web:* www.millies.com	Brea	CA	92821	714-671-0772	671-7957
Mirabile Investment Corp 1900 Whitten Rd *Web:* www.mic-memphis.com	Memphis	TN	38133	901-324-0450	312-3280
Mitchco International Inc 4801 Sherburn Ln *Web:* www.mitchcointernational.com	Louisville	KY	40207	502-896-9653	896-2989
Mo's Restaurants 657 SW Bay Blvd *Web:* www.moschowder.com	Newport	OR	97365	541-265-7512	265-9323
Moe's Southwest Grill LLC 200 Glenridge Pt Pkwy Suite 200 **Fax Area Code:* 404 ■ *TF:* 877-667-7411 ■ *Web:* www.moes.com	Atlanta	GA	30342	877-667-7411	255-4978*
Monical Pizza Corp 530 N Kinzie Ave *TF:* 800-929-3227 ■ *Web:* www.monicalspizza.com	Bradley	IL	60915	815-937-1890	937-9828
Morgan's Foods Inc 4829 Galaxy Pkwy Suite S *TF:* 800-869-8691 ■ *Web:* www.morgansfoods.com	Cleveland	OH	44128	216-360-7500	360-0299
Morton's Restaurant Group Inc 3333 New Hyde Pk Rd Suite 210 *NYSE: MRT* ■ *Web:* www.mortons.com	New Hyde Park	NY	11042	516-627-1515	627-2050
Mr Gatti's Inc 5912 Balcones Dr *Web:* www.mrgattis.com	Austin	TX	78751	512-459-4796	454-4990
Mr Goodcents Franchise Systems Inc 8997 Commerce Dr *TF:* 800-648-2368 ■ *Web:* www.mrgoodcents.com	DeSoto	KS	66018	913-583-8400	583-3500
Mr Hero Restaurants 7010 Engle Rd Suite 100 *TF:* 888-860-5082 ■ *Web:* www.mrhero.com	Middleburg Heights	OH	44130	440-625-3080	625-3081
Mr Jim's Pizza Inc 2521 Pepperwood St *TF:* 800-583-5960 ■ *Web:* www.mrjimspizza.net	Farmers Branch	TX	75234	972-267-5467	267-5463
Mr Sub 4576 Yonge St Suite 600 *TF:* 800-668-7827 ■ *Web:* www.mrsub.ca	Toronto	ON	M2N6P1	416-225-5545	225-5536
Mrs Winner's Chicken & Biscuits 6055 Barfield Rd Suite 200 **Fax Area Code:* 678 ■ *TF:* 877-733-5577	Atlanta	GA	30328	404-459-5805	514-4677*
MTY Food Group Inc 3465 Thimens Blvd *CVE: MTY* ■ *TF:* 877-282-1011 ■ *Web:* www.mtygroup.com	Sainte-Laurent	QC	H4R1V5	514-336-8885	336-9222
Myriad Restaurant Group Inc 249 W Broadway *Web:* www.myriadrestaurantgroup.com	New York	NY	10013	212-219-9500	219-2380
Nancy's Pizzeria 8200 W 185th St Suite J *TF:* 800-626-2977 ■ *Web:* www.nancyspizza.com	Tinley Park	IL	60477	708-444-4411	444-4422
Nathan's Famous Inc One Jericho Plaza 2nd Fl *NASDAQ: NATH* ■ *TF:* 800-628-4267 ■ *Web:* www.nathansfamous.com	Jericho	NY	11753	516-338-8500	338-7220
National Coney Island Inc 27947 Groesback Hwy *Web:* www.nationalconeyisland.com	Roseville	MI	48066	586-771-7744	771-9578
Nature's Table 300 S Orange Ave Suite 1260 *TF:* 800-222-6090 ■ *Web:* www.naturestable.com	Orlando	FL	32801	407-481-2544	843-6057
New York Fries 1220 Yonge St Suite 400 *Web:* www.newyorkfries.com	Toronto	ON	M4T1W1	416-963-5005	963-4920
Newport Bay Restaurants 2865 NW Town Ctr Loop *Web:* www.newportbay.com	Portland	OR	97006	503-645-2526	620-6149
Nexdine LLC 100 Pleasant St *Web:* www.nexdine.com	Dracut	MA	01826	978-674-8464	
Nickels Restaurants 1955 Cote-de-liesse Suite 205 *Web:* www.nickelsrestaurants.com	Saint-Laurent	QC	H4N3A8	514-856-5555	856-6050
Ninety-Nine Restaurant & Pubs 160 Olympia Ave *Web:* www.99restaurants.com	Woburn	MA	01801	781-933-8999	933-0821
Noble Roman's Pizza Inc 1 Virginia Ave Suite 300 *TF:* 800-585-0669 ■ *Web:* www.nobleromans.com	Indianapolis	IN	46204	317-634-3377	636-3207
Noodles & Co 520 Zang St *Web:* www.noodles.com	Broomfield	CO	80021	720-214-1900	214-1933
Norsan Group Inc 4824 N Royal Atlanta Dr	Tucker	GA	30085	770-414-5026	414-5839
North Beach Pizza Inc 1462 Grant Ave *Web:* www.northbeachpizza.com	San Francisco	CA	94133	415-433-2444	433-7217
NPC International Inc 7300 W 129th St *Web:* www.npcinternational.com	Overland Park	KS	66213	913-327-5555	327-5850
O'Charley's Inc 3038 Sidco Dr *NASDAQ: CHUX*	Nashville	TN	37204	615-256-8500	782-5043
Office Beer Bar & Grill 1450 Rt 22 W *TF:* 800-518-1855 ■ *Web:* www.office-beerbar.com	Mountainside	NJ	07092	908-518-1800	518-1509
Old Chicago Restaurants 248 Centennial Pkwy *TF:* 800-273-9827 ■ *Web:* www.oldchicago.com	Louisville	CO	80027	303-664-4000	664-4199
Old Country Buffet Restaurants 1460 Buffet Way *Web:* www.buffet.com	Eagan	MN	55121	651-994-8608	365-2356
Old Spaghetti Factory Inc (OSF) 0715 SW Bancroft St *Web:* www.osf.com	Portland	OR	97239	503-225-0433	226-6214
Olga's Kitchen Inc 1940 Northwood Dr *TF:* 800-336-5427 ■ *Web:* www.olgas.com	Troy	MI	48084	248-362-0001	362-2013
Olive Garden 5900 Lake Ellenor Dr PO Box 695017 **Fax:* Mail Rm ■ *Web:* www.olivegarden.com	Orlando	FL	32869	407-245-4000	245-5389*
On the Border Mexican Cafe 6820 LBJ Fwy *TF:* 800-983-4637 ■ *Web:* www.ontheborder.com	Dallas	TX	75240	972-980-9917	770-9593
Orange Julius of America 7505 Metro Blvd PO Box 39286 **Fax:* Mktg ■ *TF:* 800-679-6556 ■ *Web:* www.dairyqueen.com	Minneapolis	MN	55439	952-830-0200	830-0480*
Original Pancake House Franchising Inc 8601 SW 24th Ave *Web:* www.originalpancakehouse.com	Portland	OR	97219	503-246-9007	
Outback Steakhouse Inc 2202 N W Shore Blvd 5th Fl *NYSE: OSI* ■ *TF:* 877-670-4329 ■ *Web:* www.outback.com	Tampa	FL	33607	813-282-1225	282-1209
PacPizza LLC 220 Porter Dr Suite 100	San Ramon	CA	94583	925-838-8567	838-5801
Palm Management Corp 1730 Rhode Island Ave NW Suite 900 *TF:* 800-388-7256 ■ *Web:* www.thepalm.com	Washington	DC	20036	202-775-7256	775-8292
Palm Restaurant 1730 Rhode Island Ave NW Suite 900 *TF:* 800-795-7256 ■ *Web:* www.thepalm.com	Washington	DC	20036	202-775-7256	775-8292
Palomino Euro-Bistro 1818 N Northlake Way	Seattle	WA	98103	206-634-0550	632-3533
Palomino Restaurant Rotisseria Bar 1420 Fifth Ave *Web:* www.palomino.com	Seattle	WA	98101	206-623-1300	547-4829
Panchero's Mexican Grill 2475 Coral Ct Suite B *TF:* 888-639-2378 ■ *Web:* www.pancheros.com	Coraville	IA	52241	319-545-6565	545-6570
Pancho's Management Inc 2855 Lamb Pl	Memphis	TN	38118	901-362-9691	362-8487

Company	City	State	ZIP	Phone	Fax
Pancho's Mexican Super Buffet 100 N Labarre *TF:* 877-558-2267 ■ *Web:* www.panchosmexicanbuffet.com	New Orleans	LA	70001	504-247-9220	247-9223
Panda Express 1683 Walnut Grove Ave PO Box 1159 *TF:* 800-487-2632 ■ *Web:* www.pandaexpress.com	Rosemead	CA	91770	626-799-9898	927-9888
Panda Restaurant Group Inc 1683 Walnut Grove Ave *TF:* 800-877-8988 ■ *Web:* www.pandarg.com	Rosemead	CA	91770	626-799-9898	927-9888
Papa Gino's Inc 600 Providence Hwy *TF:* 800-727-2446 ■ *Web:* www.papaginos.com	Dedham	MA	02026	781-461-1200	461-1896
Papa John's International Inc 2002 Papa John's Blvd *NASDAQ: PZZA* ■ **Fax:* Cust Svc ■ *TF:* 877-547-7272 ■ *Web:* www.papajohns.com	Louisville	KY	40299	502-261-7272	261-4331*
Papa Murphy's International Inc 8000 NE Pkwy Dr Suite 350 *Web:* www.papamurphys.com	Vancouver	WA	98662	360-260-7272	260-0500
Papa Razzi 284 Newbury St *TF:* 800-424-2753 ■ *Web:* www.backbayrestaurantgroup.com/bbrg/paparazzi.cfm	Boston	MA	02115	617-536-2800	236-4175
Papa's Pizza-To-Go Inc 4465 Commerce Dr Suite 101 *Web:* www.papaspizzatogo.com	Buford	GA	30518	770-614-6676	614-9095
Pappas Restaurants Inc 13939 NW Fwy *TF:* 877-277-2748 ■ *Web:* www.pappas.com	Houston	TX	77040	713-869-0151	869-1773
Pappas Seafood House 13939 NW Fwy *TF:* 877-277-2748 ■ *Web:* www.pappas.com	Houston	TX	77040	713-869-0151	869-4932
Pappasito's Cantina 13070 Hwy 290 *Web:* www.pappasitos.com	Houston	TX	77040	713-462-0246	
Pasta House Co 1143 Macklind Ave *TF:* 800-467-2782 ■ *Web:* www.pastahouse.com	Saint Louis	MO	63110	314-535-6644	531-2499
Pasta Pomodoro Inc 1550 Bryant St Suite 100 *Web:* www.pastapomodoro.com	San Francisco	CA	94103	415-431-2681	431-8940
Pat & Oscar's 1959 Palomar Oaks Way Suite 300 *Web:* www.breadstick.com	Carlsbad	CA	92011	858-695-8500	
Pat O'Brien's International Inc 718 St Peter St *TF:* 800-597-4823 ■ *Web:* www.patobriens.com	New Orleans	LA	70116	504-525-4823	582-6918
Patina Group 400 S Hope St Suite 950 *Web:* www.patinagroup.com	Los Angeles	CA	90071	213-239-2500	239-2501
Paul Revere's Pizza International Ltd 1570 42nd St NE *Web:* www.paulreverespizza.com	Cedar Rapids	IA	52402	319-395-9113	395-9115
Pei Wei 7676 E Pinnacle Peak Rd *Web:* www.peiwei.com	Scottsdale	AZ	85255	602-957-8986	957-8998
Penguin Point Franchise Systems Inc 2691 E US 30 PO Box 975 *TF:* 800-577-5755 ■ *Web:* www.penguinpoint.com	Warsaw	IN	46580	574-267-3107	267-3154
Pepe's Inc 1325 W 15th St *Web:* www.pepes.com	Chicago	IL	60608	312-733-2500	733-2564
Pepperoni Grill 1901 NW Hwy	Oklahoma City	OK	73132	405-848-4660	
Perkins Restaurant & Bakery 6075 Poplar Ave Suite 800 *TF:* 800-877-7375 ■ *Web:* www.perkinsrestaurants.com	Memphis	TN	38119	901-766-6400	766-6482
Peter Piper Inc 950 W Behrend Dr Suite 102 *TF:* 800-899-3425 ■ *Web:* www.peterpiperpizza.com	Phoenix	AZ	85027	480-609-6400	609-6520
PF Chang's China Bistro Inc 7676 E Pinnacle Peak Rd *NASDAQ: PFCB* ■ *TF:* 866-732-4264 ■ *Web:* www.pfchangs.com/index.aspx	Scottsdale	AZ	85255	480-888-3000	
Piatti Restaurant Co 625 Redwood Hwy *Web:* www.piatti.com	Mill Valley	CA	94941	415-380-2525	380-2530
Piccadilly Cafeterias Inc 3232 S Sherwood Forest Blvd *TF:* 800-535-9974 ■ *Web:* www.piccadilly.com	Baton Rouge	LA	70816	225-293-9440	296-8370
Piccadilly Circus Pizza 1007 Okoboji Ave PO Box 188 *TF:* 800-338-4340 ■ *Web:* www.pcpizza.com	Milford	IA	51351	712-338-2771	338-2263
Pick Up Stix Inc 1330 Calle Avanzado *TF:* 800-400-7849 ■ *Web:* www.pickupstix.com	San Clemente	CA	92673	949-361-3189	361-7749
Pitt Grill Inc 928 Shady Ln	Lake Charles	LA	70601	337-479-1320	582-4297
Pizza Boli's C/o Prosperity Systems 5725 Falls Rd **Fax Area Code:* 410 ■ *TF:* 800-234-2654 ■ *Web:* www.pizzabolis.com	Baltimore	MD	21209	800-234-2654	464-9226*
Pizza Factory Inc 49430 Rd 426 *TF:* 800-654-4840 ■ *Web:* www.pizzafactory.com	Oakhurst	CA	93644	559-683-3377	683-6879
Pizza Inn Inc 3551 Plano Pkwy *NASDAQ: PZZI* ■ *TF:* 800-880-9955 ■ *Web:* www.pizzainn.com	The Colony	TX	75056	469-384-5000	384-5054
Pizza King Inc 221 Farabee Dr	Lafayette	IN	47905	765-447-2172	447-5491
Pizza Pizza Ltd 580 Jarvis St *TF:* 800-265-9762 ■ *Web:* www.pizzapizza.ca	Toronto	ON	M4Y2H9	416-967-1010	967-0891
Pizza Plus Pizza Inc 299 Franklin Dr *TF:* 800-675-1220 ■ *Web:* www.pizzaplusinc.com	Blountville	TN	37617	423-279-9335	279-0532
Pizza Pro Inc 2107 N 2nd St PO Box 1285 *TF:* 800-777-7554 ■ *Web:* www.pizzapro.com	Cabot	AR	72023	501-605-1175	605-1204
Pizza Ranch Inc 204 19th St SE **Fax Area Code:* 712 ■ *TF:* 800-321-3401 ■ *Web:* www.pizzaranch.com	Orange City	IA	51041	800-321-3401	439-1125*
Pizzeria Regina 999 Broadway Suite 400 *Web:* www.pizzeriaregina.com	Saugus	MA	01906	781-231-7575	231-5225
Planet Hollywood International Inc 6052 Turkey Lake Rd Suite 201 *Web:* www.planethollywood.com	Orlando	FL	32819	407-903-5500	352-7310
PoFolks Restaurants 508 Harmon Ave *TF:* 888-876-3655 ■ *Web:* www.pofolks.com	Panama City	FL	32401	850-763-0501	872-0072
Popeyes Louisiana Kitchen 5555 Glenridge Connector NE Suite 300 *TF:* 866-232-4403 ■ *Web:* www.popeyes.com	Atlanta	GA	30342	404-459-4450	459-4533
Potbelly Sandwich Works 222 Merchandise Mart Plaza Suite 2300 *Web:* www.potbelly.com	Chicago	IL	60654	312-951-0600	951-0300
Pretzelmaker 1346 Oakbrook Dr Suite 170 *TF:* 877-639-2361 ■ *Web:* pretzelmaker.com	Norcross	GA	30093	877-639-2361	
Prime Pubs Inc 10 Kingsbridge Garden Cir Suite 600 *TF:* 800-361-3111 ■ *Web:* www.primepubs.com	Mississauga	ON	L5R3K6	905-568-0000	568-0080
Prime Restaurant Group Inc 10 Kingsbridge Garden Cir Suite 600 *TF:* 800-613-1111 ■ *Web:* www.primepubs.com	Mississauga	ON	L5R3K6	905-568-0000	568-0080
Prime Sirloin Steak House LLC 129 Fast Ln *TF:* 877-704-5939 ■ *Web:* www.primesirloin.com	Mooresville	NC	28117	704-660-5939	799-6199
Prism LP 101 Exchange Ave	Vaughan	ON	L4K5R6	416-739-2900	
Pry-Wing LLC 1265 IH- PkwySte B	Augusta	GA	30909	706-860-0510	860-4640
Qdoba Restaurant Corp 4865 Ward Rd Suite 500 *Web:* www.qdoba.com	Wheat Ridge	CO	80033	720-898-2300	898-2396
Quality Dining Inc 4220 Edison Lakes Pkwy *TF:* 800-589-3820 ■ *Web:* www.qdi.com	Mishawaka	IN	46545	574-271-4600	271-4612
Quick-Service Restaurant Chain 6307 Carpinteria Ave Suite A *Web:* www.carlsjr.com	Carpinteria	CA	93013	805-745-7500	
Quiznos Corp 1001 17th St Suite 200 *TF:* 866-486-2783 ■ *Web:* www.quiznos.com	Denver	CO	80202	720-359-3300	359-3399
Rafferty's Inc 1750 Scottsville Rd Suite 2 *Web:* www.raffertys.com	Bowling Green	KY	42104	270-781-2834	781-2860
Rainforest Cafe 1510 W Loop S *TF:* 800-552-6379 ■ *Web:* www.rainforestcafe.com	Houston	TX	77027	713-850-1010	850-7205
Ram International Ltd 10013 59th Ave SW PO Box 99010 *Web:* www.theram.com	Lakewood	WA	98499	253-588-1788	588-0713
Ram's Horn Restaurant Inc 24225 W Nine-Mile Rd	Southfield	MI	48034	248-350-3430	350-1024
Red Hot & Blue Restaurants Inc 1600 Wilson Blvd *TF:* 888-509-7100 ■ *Web:* www.redhotandblue.com	Arlington	VA	22209	703-276-7427	528-4789
Red Lobster 5900 Lake Ellenor Dr *TF:* 800-562-7837 ■ *Web:* www.redlobster.com	Orlando	FL	32809	407-245-4000	245-5389
Red Robin Gourmet Burgers Inc 6312 S Fiddlers Green Cir Suite 200-N *NASDAQ: RRGB* ■ *Web:* www.redrobin.com	Greenwood Village	CO	80111	303-846-6000	846-6013
Republic Foods Inc 5110 Rdgefield Rd Suite 401 *Web:* www.republicfoods.com	Bethesda	MD	20816	301-656-6687	656-3934
Restaurant Assoc Inc 330 5th Ave 5th Fl *Web:* www.restaurantassociates.com	New York	NY	10001	212-613-5500	
Restaurant Developers Corp 7010 Engle Rd Suite 100 *TF:* 888-860-5082 ■ *Web:* www.mrhero.com	Middleburg Heights	OH	44130	440-625-3080	
Restaurants Unlimited Inc 1818 N Northlake Way *TF:* 877-855-6106 ■ *Web:* www.r-u-i.com	Seattle	WA	98103	206-634-3084	547-4829
Rib Crib Corp 4535 S Harvard Ave *TF:* 800-275-9677 ■ *Web:* www.ribcrib.com	Tulsa	OK	74135	918-712-7427	728-6945
Rick's Cabaret International Inc 10959 Cutten Rd *NASDAQ: RICK* ■ *Web:* www.rickscabaret.com	Houston	TX	77066	281-397-6730	820-1445
Riscky's Barbecue 2314 Azle Ave	Fort Worth	TX	76106	817-624-8662	624-3777
Rock Bottom Restaurants Inc 1172 W Century Dr *TF:* 800-273-9827 ■ *Web:* www.rockbottom.com	Louisville	CO	80027	303-664-4000	664-4199
Rock-Ola Restaurants 1337 Winstad Pl *Web:* www.rock-olacafe.com	Greensboro	NC	27408	336-272-9355	272-5568
Rockfish Seafood Grill 801 E Campbell Rd Suite 450 *Web:* www.rockfishseafood.com	Richardson	TX	75081	214-887-9400	821-0138
Rocky Rococo 105 E Wisconsin Ave *TF:* 800-888-7625 ■ *Web:* www.rockyrococo.com	Oconomowoc	WI	53066	262-569-5580	569-5591
Romano's Macaroni Grill 6820 LBJ Fwy *TF:* 800-983-4637 ■ *Web:* www.macaronigrill.com	Dallas	TX	75240	972-980-9917	770-9593
Rosati's Pizza 28381 Davis Pkwy Suite 701 *Web:* www.rosatispizza.com	Warrenville	IL	60555	630-393-2280	393-2281
Rosebud Restaurant 1419 W Diversey Pkwy *Web:* www.rosebudrestaurants.com	Chicago	IL	60614	773-325-9700	325-9708
Roy's Restaurants 1300 Dove St Suite 105 *Web:* www.roysrestaurant.com	Newport Beach	CA	92660	949-261-2424	261-2626
Royal Fork Buffet Restaurant 6874 Fairview Ave	Boise	ID	83704	208-322-5600	322-0149
RPM Pizza LLC 15384 5th St *TF:* 800-622-6000 ■ *Web:* www.rpmpizza.com	Gulfport	MS	39503	228-832-4000	832-1092
Rubio's Restaurants Inc 1902 Wright Pl Suite 300 *NASDAQ: RUBO* ■ *TF:* 800-929-4199 ■ *Web:* www.rubios.com	Carlsbad	CA	92008	760-929-8226	929-8203
Ruby Tuesday Inc 150 W Church Ave *NYSE: RT* ■ **Fax:* Mktg ■ *TF:* 800-325-0755 ■ *Web:* www.rubytuesday.com	Maryville	TN	37801	865-379-5700	380-7639*
Runza Drive-Ins of America Inc PO Box 6042 *TF:* 800-929-2394 ■ *Web:* www.runza.com	Lincoln	NE	68506	402-423-2394	423-5726
Russ' Restaurants Inc 390 E 8th St *TF:* 800-521-1778 ■ *Web:* www.russrestaurants.com	Holland	MI	49423	616-396-6571	396-6755
Rusty Pelican 209 Avenida Fabricante Suite 200 *TF:* 877-729-4867	San Clemente	CA	92672	949-366-6260	366-6261
Rusty's Pizza Parlors Inc 228 W Carrillo St Suite F *Web:* www.rustyspizza.com	Santa Barbara	CA	93101	805-963-9127	962-5054
Ruth's Hospitality Group Inc 400 International Pkwy Suite 325 *NASDAQ: RUTH* ■ *TF:* 800-487-4785 ■ *Web:* www.ruthschris.com	Heathrow	FL	32746	407-333-7440	833-9625
Rws Enterprises Inc 4335 Brambleton Ave *Web:* www.countrycookin.com	Roanoke	VA	24018	540-774-0613	774-9554
Sagebrush Steakhouse 129 Fast Ln *TF:* 877-704-5939 ■ *Web:* www.sagebrushsteakhouse.com	Mooresville	NC	28117	704-660-5939	799-6199
Sandella's LLC 9 Brookside Pl *TF:* 888-544-9984 ■ *Web:* www.sandellas.com	West Redding	CT	06896	203-544-9984	544-9981

Company	City	State	ZIP	Phone	Fax
Sasnak Management Corp 1877 N Rock Rd *Web:* www.carlosokelleys.com	Wichita	KS	67206	316-683-2611	681-2481
Sbarro Inc 401 Broadhollow Rd *TF Cust Svc:* 800-766-4949 ■ *Web:* www.sbarro.com	Melville	NY	11747	631-715-4197	715-4181
Schwartz Bros Restaurants 325 118th Ave SE Suite 106 *Web:* www.schwartzbros.com	Bellevue	WA	98005	425-455-3948	451-3573
Select Restaurants Inc 2000 Auburn Dr 1 Chagrin Highlands *Web:* www.selectrestaurants.com	Cleveland	OH	44122	216-464-6606	464-8565
Selrico Services Inc 717 W Ashby Pl *Web:* www.selricoservices.com	San Antonio	TX	78212	210-737-8220	737-7994
Semolina International Pasta Restaurants Inc 8301 Oak St *Web:* www.semolina.com	New Orleans	LA	70118	504-486-4570	520-8426
Shakey's USA 2200 W Valley Blvd *TF:* 888-444-6686 ■ *Web:* www.shakeys.com	Alhambra	CA	91803	626-576-0737	576-2114
Shari's Restaurant & Pies 9400 SW Gemini Dr *TF:* 800-433-5334 ■ *Web:* www.sharis.com	Beaverton	OR	97008	503-605-4299	605-4260
Shoney's Restaurants Inc 1717 Elm Hill Pike Suite B1 *TF:* 877-474-6639 ■ *Web:* www.shoneys.com	Nashville	TN	37210	615-231-2333	231-2498
Shula's Steak House 6843 Main St *TF:* 800-247-4852 ■ *Web:* www.donshula.com	Miami Lakes	FL	33014	305-817-4072	817-4092
Silver Diner Inc 12276 Rockville Pike *TF:* 866-561-0518 ■ *Web:* www.silverdiner.com	Rockville	MD	20852	301-770-0333	770-2832
Simm's Restaurants 7985 Santa Monica Blvd Suite 200 **Fax Area Code:* 323	Los Angeles	CA	90046	818-997-1400	656-7898*
Sizzler Restaurants 6101 W Centinela Ave Suite 300 *Web:* www.sizzler.com	Culver City	CA	90230	310-846-8750	
Sizzling Wok International Inc 6551 #3 Rd Unit 1538	Richmond	BC	V6Y2B6	604-207-8871	207-9893
Skyline Chili Inc 4180 Thunderbird Ln *TF:* 800-443-4371 ■ *Web:* www.skylinechili.com	Fairfield	OH	45014	513-874-1188	874-3591
Slaymaker Group 404 E 4500 S Suite A-12	Salt Lake City	UT	84107	801-261-3700	261-1615
Small Sun Inc 2204 Danforth Ave *Web:* www.holeechow.com	Toronto	ON	M4C1K3	416-996-3333	
Smith & Wollensky Restaurant Group Inc 318 N State St *NASDAQ: SWRG* ■ *Web:* www.smithandwollensky.com	Chicago	IL	60654	312-670-9900	
Smith Bros Restaurant Corp 16 N Marengo Ave Suite 609 *Web:* www.smithbrothersrestaurants.com	Pasadena	CA	91101	626-577-2400	577-8330
Smitty's Canada Ltd 501 18th Ave SW Suite 600 *Web:* www.smittys.ca	Calgary	AB	T2S0C7	403-229-3838	229-3899
Smokey Bones BBQ 5900 Lake Ellenor Dr *TF:* 800-421-3035 ■ *Web:* www.darden.com	Orlando	FL	32809	407-245-4000	245-5189
Snappy Tomato Pizza Co 6111 A Burgundy Hill Dr *TF:* 888-463-7627 ■ *Web:* www.snappytomato.com	Burlington	KY	41005	859-525-4680	525-4686
Sobik's Subs 620 Crown Oak Ctr Dr Suite 104 *Web:* www.sobiks.com	Longwood	FL	32750	407-671-2600	671-0260
Sonic Corp 300 Johnny Bench Dr *NASDAQ: SONC* ■ *TF:* 800-569-6656	Oklahoma City	OK	73104	405-225-5000	225-5969
Sonic Drive-in Restaurants 300 Johnny Bench Dr *TF:* 800-569-6656 ■ *Web:* www.sonicdrivein.com	Oklahoma City	OK	73104	405-225-5000	225-5963
Sonny Bryan's Smokehouse 12720 Hilcrest Rd Suite 910 *Web:* www.sonnybryans.com	Dallas	TX	75230	214-350-1800	350-3738
Sonny's Franchise Co 2605 Maitland Ctr Pkwy Suite C *Web:* www.sonnysbbq.com	Maitland	FL	32751	407-660-8888	660-9050
Souplantation 15822 Bernardo Ctr Dr Suite A *TF:* 800-874-1600 ■ *Web:* www.soupplantation.com	San Diego	CA	92127	858-675-1600	675-1616
Southern Multifoods Inc 101 E Cherokee St *TF:* 800-810-0862	Jacksonville	TX	75766	903-586-1524	586-9644
Spaghetti Warehouse Inc 5525 MacArthur Blvd Suite 200 *Web:* www.meatballs.com	Irving	TX	75038	972-536-1901	550-0908
Spangles Inc 437 N Hillside St *Web:* www.spanglesinc.com	Wichita	KS	67214	316-685-8817	685-1671
Spear's Food Service Co 1930 N Woodlawn St	Wichita	KS	67208	316-686-5173	687-5253
Specialty Restaurants Corp 8191 E Kaiser Blvd *Web:* www.specialtyrestaurants.com	Anaheim	CA	92808	714-279-6100	998-7574
Spectra Hospitality Group Inc 389 W 6th Ave *Web:* www.spectragroup.com	Vancouver	BC	V5Y1L1	604-714-6500	730-5508
Stanford's Restaurant & Bar 7165 SW Fir Loop Suite 200 *Web:* www.stanfords.com	Portland	OR	97223	503-684-2803	620-6149
Star Buffet Inc 1312 N Scottsdale Rd *NASDAQ: STRZ*	Scottsdale	AZ	85257	480-425-0397	425-0494
Steak Escape 222 Neilston St *Web:* www.steakescape.com	Columbus	OH	43215	614-224-0300	224-6460
Steak N Shake Co 36 S Pennsylvania St Suite 500 *TF:* 800-437-2406 ■ *Web:* www.steaknshake.com	Indianapolis	IN	46204	317-633-4100	633-4105
Stockade Cos 113 E 3rd St *Web:* www.stockadecompanies.com	Taylor	TX	76574	512-352-5030	352-5200
Strang Corp 8905 Lake Ave *Web:* www.strangcorp.com	Cleveland	OH	44102	216-961-6767	961-1966
Strategic Restaurants Inc 3000 Executive Pkwy Suite 515 *Web:* www.strategicrestaurants.com	San Ramon	CA	94583	925-328-3300	328-3333
Stuart Anderson's Black Angus 4410 El Camino Real Suite 201 *TF:* 800-382-3852 ■ *Web:* www.stuartanderson.com	Los Altos	CA	94022	650-949-6400	949-6425
Stuckey's Corp 8555 16th St Suite 850 *TF:* 800-423-6171 ■ *Web:* www.stuckeyscorp.com	Silver Spring	MD	20910	301-585-8222	585-8997
Stuft Pizza Franchise Corp 50855 Washington St Suite 210 *Web:* www.stuftpizza.com	La Quinta	CA	92253	760-777-1660	777-1948
Sub Station II Inc PO Box 2260 *Web:* www.substationii.com	Sumter	SC	29151	803-773-4711	775-2220
Subway Restaurants 325 Bic Dr *TF:* 800-888-4848 ■ *Web:* www.subway.com	Milford	CT	06460	203-877-4281	
Summerwood Corp 14 Balligomingo Rd *TF:* 800-760-0950 ■ *Web:* www.summerwood.biz	Conshohocken	PA	19428	610-520-1000	
Super Subby's Inc 8924 N Dixie Dr *Web:* www.subbys.com	Dayton	OH	45414	937-898-0996	898-2367
Sushi Doraku 1104 Lincoln Rd *Web:* www.dorakusushi.com	Miami Beach	FL	33139	305-695-8383	695-1441
Sweet Tomatoes 15822 Bernardo Ctr Dr Suite A *TF:* 800-874-1600 ■ *Web:* www.soupplantation.com	San Diego	CA	92127	858-675-1600	675-1616
Tacala LLC 4268 Cahaba Heights Ct *Web:* www.tacala.com	Birmingham	AL	35243	205-443-9600	443-9796
Taco Bell Corp 1 Glen Bell Way *Web:* www.tacobell.com	Irvine	CA	92618	949-863-4000	863-2214
Taco Cabana Inc 8918 Tesoro Dr Suite 200 *TF:* 800-357-9924 ■ *Web:* www.tacocabana.com	San Antonio	TX	78217	210-804-0990	804-1970
Taco Mayo Inc 10405 Greenbriar Pl *TF:* 800-291-8226 ■ *Web:* www.tacomayo.com	Oklahoma City	OK	73159	405-691-8226	691-2572
Taco Tico Inc 11333 E Central *Web:* www.tacotico.com	Wichita	KS	67206	316-691-8060	
Taco Time International Inc 9311 E Via de Venutra *TF:* 866-452-4252 ■ *Web:* www.tacotime.com	Scottsdale	AZ	85258	480-362-4800	362-4812
Tacoma Inc 328 E Church St *TF:* 800-352-9417 ■ *Web:* www.gototaco.com	Martinsville	VA	24112	276-666-9417	666-9427
Tacos Mexico Inc 5120 E Olympic Blvd	Los Angeles	CA	90022	323-266-0482	266-1721
Tavistock Restaurants LLC 2200 Powell St Suite 750 *Web:* www.tavistockrestaurants.com	Emeryville	CA	94608	510-594-4262	654-8295
Ted's Hot Dogs 95 Roger Chaffee Dr *Web:* www.tedsonline.com	Amherst	NY	14228	716-691-3731	691-3776
Tee Jaye's Country Place Restaurants 1363 Parsons Ave PO Box 06359 *Web:* www.barnyardbuster.com	Columbus	OH	43206	614-443-9773	443-0613
Temple Square Hospitality Corp 15 E S Temple St 9th Fl *Web:* www.templesquarehospitality.com	Salt Lake City	UT	84150	801-539-3101	596-0107
Texas Land & Cattle Co 224 E Douglas Suite 700 **Fax Area Code:* 214	Wichita	KS	67202	316-264-8899	358-2826*
Texas Roadhouse Inc 6040 Dutchmans Ln Suite 400 *NASDAQ: TXRH* ■ *TF:* 800-839-7623 ■ *Web:* www.texasroadhouse.com	Louisville	KY	40205	502-426-9984	426-9924
Texas Steakhouse & Saloon 1324 Washington St *Web:* www.texassteakhouse.com	Louisville	KY	40206	502-561-2436	
TGI Friday's Inc 4201 Marsh Ln **Fax:* Mktg ■ *TF:* 800-374-3297 ■ *Web:* www.tgifridays.com	Carrollton	TX	75007	972-662-5400	662-5739*
Thompson Hospitality 505 Huntmar Pk Dr Suite 350 *TF:* 800-842-2737 ■ *Web:* www.thompsonhospitality.com	Herndon	VA	20170	703-964-5500	964-0505
Thundercloud Subs 1102 W 6th St *TF:* 800-256-7895 ■ *Web:* www.thundercloud.com	Austin	TX	78703	512-479-8805	479-8806
Tim Hortons Inc 874 Sinclair Rd *NYSE: THI* ■ *TF:* 888-601-1616 ■ *Web:* www.timhortons.com	Oakville	ON	L6K2Y1	905-845-6511	845-0265
Toarmina's Pizza Inc 673 Barbara St *Web:* www.toarminaspizza.com	Westland	MI	48185	734-729-9067	729-1882
TooJays Original Gourmet Deli 3654 Georgia Ave *Web:* www.toojays.com	West Palm Beach	FL	33405	561-659-9011	659-9703
Trader Vic's Inc 9 Anchor Dr *Web:* www.tradervics.com	Emeryville	CA	94608	510-653-3400	653-9384
Trail Dust Steak Houses Inc 2300 E Lamar Blvd *Web:* www.traildust.com	Arlington	TX	70006	817-640-6411	
Travaglini Enterprises 231 Chestnut St	Meadville	PA	16335	814-724-4880	337-2630
Trigild Inc 12707 High Bluff Dr Suite 300 *Web:* www.trigild.com	San Diego	CA	92130	858-720-6700	720-6707
Tripps Restaurants 1337 Winstead Pl *Web:* www.trippsrestaurants.com	Greensboro	NC	27408	336-272-9355	272-5568
Tropical Smoothie Cafe 12598 US Hwy 98 W *Web:* www.tropicalsmoothie.com	Destin	FL	32550	850-269-9850	269-9845
TS Restaurants of California & Hawaii 2530 Kekaa Dr Suite C2 *Web:* www.hulapie.com	Lahaina	HI	96761	808-667-4800	667-4802
TubbyÆs Grilled Submarines 18357 14 Mile Rd *TF:* 800-752-0644 ■ *Web:* www.tubby.com	Fraser	MI	48026	586-293-5099	293-5088
Tudor's Biscuit World 410 50th St SE *Web:* www.tudorsbiscuitworld.com	Charleston	WV	25304	304-343-4026	727-1111
Tumbleweed Inc 2301 River Rd Suite 200 *Web:* www.tumbleweedrestaurants.com	Louisville	KY	40206	502-893-0323	893-6676
Una Mas Restaurants Inc 461 S Milpitas Blvd Suite 1 *TF:* 888-862-2627 ■ *Web:* www.unamas.com	Milpitas	CA	95035	408-435-7800	435-7900
Uno Chicago Grill 100 Charles Pk Rd *TF:* 866-600-8667 ■ *Web:* www.unos.com	Boston	MA	02132	617-323-9200	469-3949
Uno Restaurant Corp 100 Charles Pk Rd *TF:* 866-600-8667 ■ *Web:* www.unos.com	Boston	MA	02132	617-323-9200	323-6906
V & J Holding Cos Inc 6933 W Brown Deer Rd *Web:* www.vjfoods.com	Milwaukee	WI	53223	414-365-9003	365-9467
Val Ltd Inc 2601 S 70th St *TF:* 800-556-8150 ■ *Web:* www.valentinos.com	Lincoln	NE	68506	402-434-9350	434-9325

Company	City	State	Zip	Phone	Fax
Valentino's 2601 S 70th St	Lincoln	NE	68506	402-434-9350	434-9325
TF: 888-240-8257 ■ *Web:* www.valentinos.com					
Villa Enterprises Management Ltd Inc 25 Washington St	Morristown	NJ	07960	973-285-4800	285-5252
Web: www.villapizza.com					
Village Inn 400 W 48th Ave	Denver	CO	80216	303-296-2121	672-2676*
**Fax:* Cust Svc ■ *TF:* 800-800-3644 ■ *Web:* www.villageinn.com					
Viva Burrito Co 860 E 16th St	Tucson	AZ	85718	520-882-8713	620-6468
Vocelli Pizza 1005 S Bee St	Pittsburgh	PA	15220	412-919-2100	937-9204
Web: www.vocellipizza.com					
Waffle House Inc 5986 Financial Dr	Norcross	GA	30071	770-729-5700	729-5758
TF: 800-882-9235 ■ *Web:* www.wafflehouse.com					
Wahoo's Fish Taco 2855 Pullman St	Santa Ana	CA	92705	949-222-0670	222-0750
Web: www.wahoos.com					
Ward's Food Systems Inc 5133 Lincoln Rd Ext	Hattiesburg	MS	39402	601-268-9273	268-9283
Web: www.wardsrestaurants.com					
Weathervane Seafood Restaurant 306 US Rt 1	Kittery	ME	03904	207-439-0330	439-7754
TF: 800-654-4639 ■ *Web:* www.weathervaneseafoods.com					
Wendy's International Inc 1 Dave Thomas Blvd	Dublin	OH	43017	614-764-3100	764-3459
Web: www.wendys.com					
Western Sizzlin Corp 416 S Jefferson St # 600	Roanoke	VA	24011	540-345-3195	345-0831
TF: 800-247-8325 ■ *Web:* www.western-sizzlin.com					
Whataburger Restaurants LP 300 Concord Plaza PO Box 791990	San Antonio	TX	78216	210-476-6000	
Web: www.whataburger.com					
White Castle Management Co 555 W Goodale St	Columbus	OH	43215	614-228-5781	464-0596
TF: 800-843-2728 ■ *Web:* www.whitecastle.com					
Willie G's 1605 Post Oak Blvd	Houston	TX	77056	713-850-1010	
Web: www.williegs.com					
Winger's Franchising Inc 404 E 4500 S Suite A-12	Salt Lake City	UT	84107	801-261-3700	261-1615
TF: 800-425-9784 ■ *Web:* www.wingers.info					
Wingstop Restaurants Inc 1101 E Arapaho Rd Suite 150	Richardson	TX	75081	972-686-6500	686-6502
Web: www.wingstop.com					
Wolfgang Puck Worldwide Inc 100 N Crescent Dr Suite 100	Beverly Hills	CA	90210	310-432-1500	432-1630
Web: www.wolfgangpuck.com					
Wolfgang Puck's Express 100 N Cresent Dr Suite 100	Beverly Hills	CA	90210	310-432-1500	432-1630
Web: www.wolfgangpuck.com/rest/index.html					
Woody's Bar-B-Q 4745 Sutton Pk Ct Suite 301	Jacksonville	FL	32224	904-992-0556	992-0551
Web: www.woodys.com					
World Wrapps 401 2nd Ave S Suite 150	Seattle	WA	98104	206-233-9727	233-0539
TF: 888-233-9727 ■ *Web:* www.worldwrapps.com					
Yard House 71 Fortune Dr	Irvine	CA	92618	949-753-9373	753-9372
Web: www.yardhouse.com					
Yaya's Flame Broiled Chicken 521 S Dort Hwy	Flint	MI	48503	810-235-6550	235-5210
TF: 800-754-1242 ■ *Web:* www.yayas.com					
Yogen Fruz 210 Shields Ct	Markham	ON	L3R8V2	905-479-8762	479-5235
TF: 800-528-0727 ■ *Web:* www.yogenfruz.com					
Yoshinoya Beef Bowl 991 Knox St	Torrance	CA	90502	310-527-6060	527-6050
TF: 800-576-8017 ■ *Web:* www.yoshinoyaamerica.com					
Yum! Brands Inc 1441 Gardiner Ln	Louisville	KY	40213	502-874-8300	454-2410
NYSE: YUM ■ *TF:* 800-225-5532 ■ *Web:* www.yum.com					
Zero's Subs 2859 Virginia Beach Blvd Suite 105	Virginia Beach	VA	23452	757-486-8338	486-9755
TF: 800-588-0782 ■ *Web:* www.zeros.com					
Zippy's Restaurant Inc 1765 S King	Honolulu	HI	96826	808-973-0880	955-7043
Web: www.zippys.com					
Zyng Inc RPO Atwater PO Box 72108	Montreal	QC	H3J2Z6	514-288-8800	939-8808
TF: 888-966-6353 ■ *Web:* www.zyng.com					
Morton's The Steakhouse 400 Post St	San Francisco	CA	94102	415-986-5830	986-5829
Web: www.mortons.com					

674 RESTAURANTS (INDIVIDUAL)

SEE ALSO Shopping/Dining/Entertainment Districts p. 1484; Restaurant Companies p. 2555

Individual Restaurants Are Organized By City Names Within State And Province Groupings. (Canadian Provinces Are Interfiled Among The Us States, In Alphabetical Order.)

ALABAMA

Restaurant	City	State	Zip	Phone	Fax
Bambi Nelli 2031 Cahaba Rd	Birmingham	AL	35223	205-871-2423	
Boque's Restaurant 3028 Clairmont Ave S	Birmingham	AL	35205	205-254-9780	
Bottega 2240 Highland Ave S	Birmingham	AL	35205	205-939-1000	939-1536
Daniel George 2837 Culver Rd	Birmingham	AL	35223	205-871-3266	871-7266
Web: www.birminghammenus.com/danielgeorge					
Dreamland BBQ 1427 14th Ave S	Birmingham	AL	35205	205-933-2133	933-9770
Web: www.dreamlandbbq.com					
Fire 212 Country Club Pk	Birmingham	AL	35213	205-802-1410	
Web: www.firebirmingham.com					
Fleming's Prime Steakhouse & Wine Bar 103 Summit Blvd	Birmingham	AL	35243	205-262-9463	262-9461
Web: www.flemingssteakhouse.com					
Golden Palace 7001 Crestwood Blvd	Birmingham	AL	35210	205-595-6868	595-6969
Highlands Bar & Grill 2011 11th Ave S	Birmingham	AL	35205	205-939-1400	939-1405
Web: www.highlandsbarandgrill.com					
Hot & Hot Fish Club 2180 11th Ct S	Birmingham	AL	35205	205-933-5474	933-6243
Web: www.birminghammenus.com					
Ichiban Japanese Steakhouse 620 Olde Town Rd	Birmingham	AL	35216	205-822-4646	822-4512
J Alexanders 3320 Galleria Cir	Birmingham	AL	35244	205-733-9995	733-8461
Web: www.jalexanders.com					
Jim-n-Nick's 1810 Montgomery Hwy S	Birmingham	AL	35244	205-733-1300	733-1314
Web: www.birminghammenus.com					
La Dolce Vita 1851 Montgomery Hwy	Birmingham	AL	35244	205-985-2909	
Little Savannah 3811 Clairmont Ave	Birmingham	AL	35222	205-591-1119	592-0415
Web: www.birminghammenus.com					
Los Angeles 2801 7th Ave S	Birmingham	AL	35233	205-328-7160	328-7161
Web: www.birminghammenus.com/losangeles					
Ming's Cuisine 514 Cahaba Pk Cir	Birmingham	AL	35242	205-991-3803	
Nabeel's Cafe 1706 Oxmoor Rd	Birmingham	AL	35209	205-879-9292	879-9291
Web: www.nabeels.com					
Niki's West 233 Finley Ave W	Birmingham	AL	35204	205-252-5751	252-8163
Web: www.nikiwest.com					
Ocean 1218 20th St S	Birmingham	AL	35205	205-933-0999	933-0998
Web: www.oceanbirmingham.com					
PF Chang's China Bistro 233 Summit Blvd	Birmingham	AL	35243	205-967-0040	967-3661
Web: www.pfchangs.com					
Ruth's Chris Steak House 2300 Woodcrest Pl	Birmingham	AL	35209	205-879-9995	879-8883
Web: www.ruthschris.com					
Sabor Latino 112 Green Springs Hwy	Birmingham	AL	35209	205-942-9480	942-9428
Shula's Steak House 1000 Riverchase Galleria	Birmingham	AL	35244	205-444-5750	987-0454
Web: www.donshula.com					
Sol Y Luna 2811 7th Ave S	Birmingham	AL	35233	205-322-1186	322-1708
Web: www.birminghammenus.com					
Standard Bistro 3 Mt Laurel Ave	Birmingham	AL	35242	205-995-0512	995-1854
Web: www.birminghammenus.com					
Stix 3250 Galleria Cir	Birmingham	AL	35244	205-982-3070	982-3073
Web: www.stixdining.com					
Surin West 1918 11th Ave S	Birmingham	AL	35205	205-324-1928	
Web: www.surinwest.com					
Taste of Thailand 3321 Lorna Rd	Birmingham	AL	35216	205-978-6863	978-6857
Village Tavern 101 Summit Blvd	Birmingham	AL	35243	205-970-1640	970-1641
Web: www.villagetavern.com					
Guido's 1709 Main St	Daphne	AL	36526	251-626-6082	
Roussos 5319 Hwy 90 W PO Box 308	Daphne	AL	36526	251-776-1121	666-1142
Web: www.roussosrestaurant.com					
Cocina Superior 587 Brookwood Village	Homewood	AL	35209	205-259-1980	259-1987
Web: www.thecocinasuperior.com					
801 Franklin 801 Franklin St	Huntsville	AL	35801	256-519-8019	519-6801
Web: www.801franklin.net					
Big Spring Cafe 2906 Governors Dr	Huntsville	AL	35805	256-539-9994	
Cafe 302 2700 Winchester Rd NE	Huntsville	AL	35811	256-852-3442	
Dreamland Bar-B-Que Ribs 3855 University Dr	Huntsville	AL	35816	256-539-7427	
Web: www.dreamlandbbq.com					
El Camino Real 4116 University Dr NW	Huntsville	AL	35816	256-830-1188	830-1188
La Alameda 3807 University Dr NW	Huntsville	AL	35816	256-539-6244	
Logan's Roadhouse 4249 Balmoral Dr SW	Huntsville	AL	35801	256-881-0584	881-3296
Web: www.logansroadhouse.com					
Mikato Japanese Steak House 4061 Independence Dr NW	Huntsville	AL	35816	256-830-1700	830-1873
Miyako 10013 S Memorial Pkwy	Huntsville	AL	35803	256-880-9879	
Rolo's Cafe 975 Airport Rd	Huntsville	AL	35802	256-883-7656	
Scrugg's Barbeque 7529 Moores Mill Rd	Huntsville	AL	35811	256-859-6800	
Thai Garden Restaurant Inc 800 Wellman Ave NE	Huntsville	AL	35801	256-534-0122	564-7341
Web: www.ilovethaigarden.com/I_Love_Thai_Garden/Thai_Garden_Restaurant.html					
WildFlour Bistro 501 Jordan Ln	Huntsville	AL	35805	256-722-9401	
Bama Belles Country Restaurant 3651 Government Blvd	Mobile	AL	36693	251-661-8700	
Brick Pit 5456 Old Shell Rd	Mobile	AL	36608	251-343-0001	
Web: www.brickpit.com					
Cafe 615 615 Dauphin St	Mobile	AL	36602	251-432-8434	433-9885
Cannon Grill 1850 Airport Blvd	Mobile	AL	36606	251-476-6777	476-9060
Delhi Palace 3674 Airport Blvd	Mobile	AL	36608	251-341-6171	341-6121
Downtowners 107 Dauphin St	Mobile	AL	36602	251-433-8868	433-8867
JR's Smokehouse 3843 Airport Blvd	Mobile	AL	36608	251-343-1853	
Web: www.jrssmokehouse.com					
Oliver's 251 Government St	Mobile	AL	36602	251-432-8000	405-5944
Web: www.admiralsemmeshotel.com					
Pillars The 1757 Government St	Mobile	AL	36604	251-471-3411	
Web: www.thepillarsmobile.com					
Ruth's Chris Steak House 2058 Airport Blvd	Mobile	AL	36606	251-476-0516	476-0518
Web: www.ruthschris.com					
Saucy-Q Bar B Que 1111 Government St	Mobile	AL	36604	251-433-7427	433-7428
Dreamland Bar-B-Que Ribs 101 Tallapoosa St	Montgomery	AL	36104	334-273-7427	273-7857
Web: www.dreamlandbbq.com					
Island Delight Caribbean Restaurant 323 Airbase Blvd	Montgomery	AL	36108	334-264-0041	
Ixtapa 6132 Atlanta Hwy	Montgomery	AL	36117	334-272-5232	
King Buffet 2727 Bell Rd	Montgomery	AL	36117	334-273-8883	273-8880
La Jolla 6854 E Chase Pkwy	Montgomery	AL	36117	334-356-2600	356-2610
Web: www.lajollarestaurant.com					
Lek's Taste of Thailand 5421 Atlanta Hwy	Montgomery	AL	36109	334-244-8994	
Mings Garden 1741 Eastern Bypass	Montgomery	AL	36117	334-277-8188	277-8266
Nobles Restaurant & Lounge 129 Montgomery St	Montgomery	AL	36104	334-262-3326	
Olive Room 121 Montgomery St	Montgomery	AL	36104	334-262-2763	
Peyton's Place 5344 Atlanta Hwy	Montgomery	AL	36109	334-396-3630	
Vintage Year 405 Cloverdale Rd	Montgomery	AL	36106	334-264-8463	269-5700
Zoes Kitchen 7218 EastChase Pkwy	Montgomery	AL	36117	334-270-9115	270-9116
Web: www.zoeskitchen.com					
Felix's Fish Camp at Pier 4 1530 Battleship Pkwy	Spanish Fort	AL	36527	251-626-6710	626-6794
Web: www.felixsfishcamp.com					
15th Street Diner 1036 15th St	Tuscaloosa	AL	35401	205-750-8750	758-4751
Web: www.dinerrestaurants.com					

Restaurant	City	State	ZIP	Phone	Fax
Baumhower's of Tuscaloosa 500 Harper Lee Dr	Tuscaloosa	AL	35404	205-556-5658	556-5639
Web: www.baumhowers.com					
Bento 1306 University Blvd Suite D	Tuscaloosa	AL	35401	205-758-7426	
Buffalo Phil's 1149 University Blvd.	Tuscaloosa	AL	35401	205-758-3318	758-3310
Cypress Inn The 501 Rice Mine Rd N	Tuscaloosa	AL	35406	205-345-6963	345-6997
Web: www.cypressinnrestaurant.com					
DePalma's Italian Cafe 2300 University Blvd	Tuscaloosa	AL	35401	205-759-1879	
Dreamland Bar-B-que 5535 15th Ave E	Tuscaloosa	AL	35401	205-758-8135	758-5158
Web: www.dreamlandbbq.com					
Epiphany Cafe 519 Greensborough Ave	Tuscaloosa	AL	35401	205-344-5583	344-5033
Evangeline's 1653 McFarland Blvd	Tuscaloosa	AL	35406	205-752-0830	752-0355
Web: www.evangelinesrestaurant.com					
Kozy's Restaurant 3510 Loop Rd	Tuscaloosa	AL	35404	205-556-0665	633-4034
Web: www.kozysrestaurant.com					
Los Tarascos 1759 Skyland Blvd	Tuscaloosa	AL	35401	205-553-8896	
Pottery Grill Hwy 11	Tuscaloosa	AL	35453	205-554-1815	
Rama Jama's 1000 Paul Bryant Dr	Tuscaloosa	AL	35401	205-750-0901	
Sol Azteca 1360 Montgomery Hwy Suite 128	Vestavia Hills	AL	35216	205-979-4902	979-9140
Casa Napoli 2215 US Hwy 231	Wetumpka	AL	36093	334-567-7777	
Web: www.napoli2.com					

ALASKA

Restaurant	City	State	ZIP	Phone	Fax
Aladdin's Fine Mediterranean 4240 Old Seward Hwy	Anchorage	AK	99503	907-561-2373	563-5117
Web: www.aladdinsalaska.com					
Bombay Deluxe 555 W Northern Lights Blvd.	Anchorage	AK	99503	907-277-1200	
Web: www.bombaydeluxe.com					
Bradley House 11321 Old Seward Hwy	Anchorage	AK	99517	907-336-7177	336-7178
Club Paris 417 W 5th Ave.	Anchorage	AK	99501	907-277-6332	277-6544
Web: www.clubparisrestaurant.com					
Corsair 944 W 5th Ave	Anchorage	AK	99501	907-278-4502	278-4515
Crow's Nest 939 W 5th Ave Hotel Captain Cook	Anchorage	AK	99501	907-276-6000	343-2211
Web: www.captaincook.com/restaurants.htm					
Don Jose's 2052 E Northern Lights Blvd	Anchorage	AK	99508	907-279-5111	279-2053
Web: www.alaskadonjoses.com					
Glacier Brew House 737 W 5th Ave	Anchorage	AK	99501	907-274-2739	277-1033
Web: www.glacierbrewhouse.com					
Gweenie's Old Alaska Restaurant 4333 Spenard Rd	Anchorage	AK	99517	907-243-2090	
Humpy's Great Alaskan Alehouse 610 W 6th Ave	Anchorage	AK	99501	907-276-2337	258-0780
Web: www.humpys.com					
Jen's Restaurant 701 W 36th Ave.	Anchorage	AK	99503	907-561-5367	561-5325
Web: www.jensrestaurant.com					
Kincaid Grill 6700 Jewel Lake Rd	Anchorage	AK	99502	907-243-0507	243-5110
Web: www.kincaidgrill.com					
Kumagoro Restaurant 533 W 4th Ave	Anchorage	AK	99501	907-272-9905	272-0573
La Cabana 312 E 4th Ave	Anchorage	AK	99501	907-272-0135	272-0137
Little Italy 2300 E 88th Ave	Anchorage	AK	99507	907-344-1515	344-1538
Los Arcos 2000 E Dowling St	Anchorage	AK	99507	907-562-0477	
Marx Bros Cafe 627 W 3rd Ave.	Anchorage	AK	99501	907-278-2133	258-6279
Web: www.marxcafe.com					
Mick's at the Inlet 1200 L St Inlet Towers Hotel	Anchorage	AK	99501	907-222-8787	258-4914
Orso Ristorante 737 W 5th Ave.	Anchorage	AK	99501	907-222-3232	792-3701
Web: www.orsoalaska.com					
Peking Wok 4000 W Dimond Blvd.	Anchorage	AK	99515	907-248-1648	245-2491
Phyllis' Cafe & Salmon Bake 436 D St	Anchorage	AK	99501	907-274-6576	
Sacks Cafe 328 G St	Anchorage	AK	99501	907-276-3546	
Web: www.sackscafe.com					
Sea Galley 4101 Credit Union Dr	Anchorage	AK	99503	907-563-3520	563-6382
Simon & Seafort's Saloon & Grill 420 L St	Anchorage	AK	99501	907-274-3502	274-2487
Web: www.simonandseaforts.com					
Snow Goose Restaurant 717 W 3rd Ave	Anchorage	AK	99501	907-277-7727	277-0606
Web: www.alaskabeers.com					
Sorrento's Restaurant 610 E Fireweed Ln	Anchorage	AK	99503	907-278-3439	258-2261
Sourdough Mining Co 5200 Juneau St.	Anchorage	AK	99518	907-563-2272	562-0161
Web: www.sourdoughmining.com					
Southside Bistro 1320 Huffman Pk Dr	Anchorage	AK	99515	907-348-0088	348-0089
Web: www.southsidebistro.com					
Villa Nova Restaurant 5121 Arctic Blvd Suite I	Anchorage	AK	99503	907-561-1660	
Alaska Salmon Bake In Alaskaland Airport Way & Peger Rd	Fairbanks	AK	99709	907-452-7274	456-6997
TF: 800-354-7274 ■ *Web:* www.akvisit.com/salmon.html					
Asiana Teriyaki 2001 Airport Way.	Fairbanks	AK	99701	907-457-3333	451-6689
Chena's Fine Dining & Deck 4200 Boat St.	Fairbanks	AK	99709	907-474-3644	474-8023
Cookie Jar 1006 Cadillac Ct.	Fairbanks	AK	99701	907-479-8319	479-8329
Web: www.fairbanks.com					
Gambardella's Pasta Bella 706 2nd Ave	Fairbanks	AK	99701	907-457-4992	456-3425
Web: www.gambardellas.com					
Geraldo's 701 College Rd.	Fairbanks	AK	99701	907-452-2299	452-7634
Ivory Jack's 2581 Goldstream Rd	Fairbanks	AK	99709	907-455-6665	455-4254
Web: www.ivoryjacks.alaskansavvy.com					
Lavelle's Bistro 575 1st Ave	Fairbanks	AK	99701	907-450-0555	450-0444
Web: www.lavellesbistro.com					
Pikes Landing 4438 Airport Way	Fairbanks	AK	99709	907-479-7113	479-6513
Pump House The 796 Chena Pump Rd	Fairbanks	AK	99709	907-479-8452	479-8432
Web: www.pumphouse.com					
Soapy Smith's Pioneer Restaurant 543 2nd Ave	Fairbanks	AK	99701	907-451-8380	451-8383
Thai House 412 5th Ave	Fairbanks	AK	99701	907-452-6123	452-6124
Turtle Club 10 Mile Old Steese Hwy.	Fairbanks	AK	99712	907-457-3883	457-4789
Vallata 2190 Goldstream Rd.	Fairbanks	AK	99709	907-455-6600	
Zach's 1717 University Ave S	Fairbanks	AK	99709	907-479-3650	479-7951
Seven Glaciers Restaurant 1000 Arlberg Ave	Girdwood	AK	99587	907-754-2237	754-2180
Web: www.alyeska.com					
Breakwater Inn Restaurant & Lounge 1711 Glacier Ave.	Juneau	AK	99801	907-586-6303	463-4820
TF: 888-586-6303 ■ *Web:* www.breakwaterinn.com					
Canton House 8585 Old Dairy Rd	Juneau	AK	99801	907-789-5075	790-2172
Web: www.cantonhouse.net					
Capital Cafe 127 N Franklin St	Juneau	AK	99801	907-586-2660	
DocWater's Pub 2 Marine Way Suite 225	Juneau	AK	99801	907-586-3627	
Web: www.docwaterspub.com					
El Sombrero 157 S Franklin St.	Juneau	AK	99801	907-586-6770	586-6772
Glacier Restaurant 1873 Shell Simmons Dr Suite 220	Juneau	AK	99801	907-789-9538	789-3090
Gold Room 127 N Franklin St.	Juneau	AK	99801	907-586-2660	586-8315
Web: www.westmarkhotels.com/juneau-food.php					
Grandma's Feather Bed Restaurant 2348 Mendenhall Loop Rd	Juneau	AK	99801	907-789-5005	789-2818
Hangar On The Wharf 2 Marine Way Suite 106	Juneau	AK	99801	907-586-5018	586-8173
Mi Casa 9200 Glacier Hwy	Juneau	AK	99801	907-789-3636	789-1969
Olivia's De Mexico 222 Seward St	Juneau	AK	99801	907-586-6870	
Red Dog Saloon 278 S Franklin St	Juneau	AK	99801	907-463-3658	463-5545
Web: www.reddogsaloon.cc					
Seong's Sushi Bar 740 W 9th St.	Juneau	AK	99801	907-586-4778	
Thane Ore House Salmon Bake 4400 Thane Rd.	Juneau	AK	99801	907-586-3442	
Mambo Grill Latin Cuisine 300 N Santa Clause Ln	North Pole	AK	99705	907-490-6868	490-6658

ALBERTA

Restaurant	City	Prov	Postal Code	Phone	Fax
Abruzzo Ristorante 402 8th St SW	Calgary	AB	T2P1Z9	403-237-5660	237-5661
Aida's Mediterranean Bistro 2208 4th St SW	Calgary	AB	T2S1W9	403-541-1189	228-5398
Antonio's Garlic Clove 2206 4th St SW.	Calgary	AB	T2S1S9	403-228-0866	
Web: www.garlicclove.net					
Belvedere The 107 8th Ave SW.	Calgary	AB	T2P1B4	403-265-9595	
Web: www.thebelvedere.ca					
Bonterra Trattoria 1016 8th St SW.	Calgary	AB	T2R1K2	403-262-8480	262-6541
Web: www.bonterra.ca					
Bow Bul Go Gui House 3515A 17th Ave SW.	Calgary	AB	T3E0B6	403-686-6826	
Broken Plate /Willow Park The 10816 MacLeod Trail SE Suite 590.	Calgary	AB	T2J5N8	403-225-9650	225-9691
Web: www.brokenplate.ca					
Buddha's Veggie Restaurant 5802 MacLeod Trail SW	Calgary	AB	T2J0J8	403-252-8830	
Web: www.buddhasveggie.com					
Buon Giorno Ristorante Italiano 823 17th Ave SW	Calgary	AB	T2T0A1	403-244-5522	244-5631
Cactus Club Cafe 7010 MacLeod Trail S	Calgary	AB	T2H0L3	403-255-1088	255-1049
Web: www.cactusclubcafe.com					
Caesar's Steak House 512 4th Ave SW	Calgary	AB	T2P0J6	403-264-1222	264-9933
Carver's Steakhouse 2620 32nd Ave NE	Calgary	AB	T1Y6B8	403-250-6327	
Catch Oyster Bar/Seafood Restaurant 100 8th Ave SE	Calgary	AB	T2G0K6	403-206-0000	206-0005
Web: www.catchrestaurant.ca					
Chianti Cafe 1438 17th Ave SW	Calgary	AB	T2T0C8	403-229-1600	229-1626
Web: www.chianticafe.ca					
China Rose Restaurant 228 28th St SE.	Calgary	AB	T2A6J9	403-248-2711	248-6810
Web: www.chinarose.ca					
Cilantro 338 17th Ave SW.	Calgary	AB	T2S0A8	403-229-1177	245-5239
Web: www.crmr.com/cilantro					
Co Do Vietnamese Restaurant 1411 17th Ave SW	Calgary	AB	T2T0C6	403-228-7798	228-7739
Coup The 924 17th Ave S W.	Calgary	AB	T2T0A2	403-541-1041	
Web: www.thecoup.ca					
Da Guido Ristorante 2001 Centre St N.	Calgary	AB	T2E2S9	403-276-1365	230-1002
Web: www.daguido.ca					
Ed's Restaurant 202 17th Ave SE	Calgary	AB	T2G1H4	403-262-3500	261-7810
Web: www.edsrestaurant.com					
Essence 320 4th Ave SW Westin Hotel.	Calgary	AB	T2P2S6	403-508-5165	265-7908
Web: www.western.com/calgary					
Fiore Cantina Italiana 638 17th Ave SW.	Calgary	AB	T2S0B4	403-244-6603	244-6615
Web: www.fiore.ca					
Hana Sushi 1803 4th St SW	Calgary	AB	T2S1W2	403-229-1499	229-1517
Il Sogno 24 4th St NE	Calgary	AB	T2E3R7	403-232-8901	232-8816
Web: www.ilsogno.org					
James Joyce Authentic Irish Pub 114 8th Ave SW	Calgary	AB	T2P1B3	403-262-0708	262-0709
Web: www.jamesjoycepub.com					
Joey Eau Claire 208 Barclay Parade SW Suite 200 Eau Claire Market	Calgary	AB	T2P4R5	403-263-6336	263-6385
Web: www.joeyrestaurants.com/food/eau-claire/menu					
Juan's Mexican Restaurante & Cantina 232 8th Ave SW Suite 7	Calgary	AB	T2P1B7	403-266-0045	266-0051
Web: www.juansrestaurante.com					
Kashmir 507 17th Ave SW	Calgary	AB	T2S0A9	403-244-2294	
Keg Steakhouse & Bar 7104 MacLeod Trail S.	Calgary	AB	T2H0L3	403-253-2534	253-2875
Web: www.kegsteakhouse.com					
King & I 822 11th Ave SW	Calgary	AB	T2R0E5	403-264-7241	264-8490
Web: www.kingandi.ca					
La Chaumiere Restaurant Ltd 17th Ave SW Suite 139.	Calgary	AB	T2S0A1	403-228-5690	228-4448
Web: www.lachaumiere.ca					
La Paella 800 6th Ave SW	Calgary	AB	T2P3E5	403-269-5911	269-5913
La Viena 2139 Kensington Rd NW	Calgary	AB	T2N3R8	403-283-3063	283-3032
Leo Fu's 511 70th Ave SW	Calgary	AB	T2V0P5	403-255-2528	255-2528
Limerick Traditional Public House 7304 MacLeod Trail SE.	Calgary	AB	T2E4Y7	403-252-9190	252-9174
Marathon Ethiopian Restaurant 130 10th St NW	Calgary	AB	T2N1V3	403-283-6796	283-1104
Melrose Cafe & Bar 730 17th Ave SW.	Calgary	AB	T2S0B7	403-228-3566	228-5708
Web: www.melrosecalgary.com					
Molly Malone's Irish Pub 1153 Kensington Crescent NW.	Calgary	AB	T2N1X7	403-296-3220	269-3229
Moti Mahal 1805 14 St SW	Calgary	AB	T2T3T1	403-228-9990	
Web: www.motimahal.ca					

Name / Address	City	State	Postal Code	Phone	Fax
Q Haute Cuisine 100 LaCaille Pl SW	Calgary	AB	T2P5E2	403-262-5554	237-6108
Web: www.qhautecuisine.com					
Rajdoot 2424 4th St SW	Calgary	AB	T2S2T4	403-245-0181	228-7194
Web: www.rajdoot.ca					
Redwater Rustic Grille 9223 MacLeod Trail S	Calgary	AB	T2J0P6	403-253-4266	253-9045
Web: www.redwatergrille.com					
River Cafe 25 Prince's Island Pk	Calgary	AB	T2P0R1	403-261-7670	261-8795
Web: www.river-cafe.com					
Rouge 1240 8th Ave SE	Calgary	AB	T2G0M7	403-531-2767	531-2768
Web: www.rougecalgary.com					
Sakana Grill 116 2nd Ave SW	Calgary	AB	T2P0B9	403-290-1118	290-1120
Salt & Pepper 6515 Bowness Rd NW	Calgary	AB	T3B0E8	403-247-4402	
Web: www.saltnpepper.ca					
Santorini Greek Taverna 1502 Centre St N	Calgary	AB	T2E2R9	403-276-8363	276-8399
Web: www.santorinirestaurant.com					
Silver Dragon Restaurant 106 3rd Ave SE	Calgary	AB	T2G0B6	403-264-5326	762-1575
Web: www.chomp.ca					
Singapore Sam's 555 11th Ave SW Suite 101	Calgary	AB	T2R1P6	403-234-8088	266-6883
Web: www.singaporesams.com					
Smuggler's Inn 6920 MacLeod Trail S	Calgary	AB	T2H0L3	403-253-5355	259-4787
Web: www.smugglers.ca					
Tandoori Hut 217 10th St NW	Calgary	AB	T2N1V5	403-270-4012	
Thai Sa-On 351 10th Ave SW	Calgary	AB	T2R0A5	403-264-3526	264-3526
Web: www.thai-sa-on.com					
Villa Firenze 610 1st Ave NE	Calgary	AB	T2E3B6	403-264-4297	365-1990
Vintage Chophouse & Tavern 322 11th Ave SW	Calgary	AB	T2R0C5	403-262-7262	262-7263
Web: www.vintagechophouse.com					
Wellington's 10325 Bonaventure Dr SE	Calgary	AB	T2J7E4	403-278-5250	271-3809
Allegro Italian Kitchen 10011-109 St	Edmonton	AB	T5J3S8	780-424-6644	424-8844
Web: www.allegroitaliankitchen.ca					
Ban Thai 15726 100th Ave	Edmonton	AB	T5P0L1	780-444-9345	484-8496
Web: www.banthai.com					
Barb & Ernie's 9906 72nd Ave	Edmonton	AB	T6E0Z3	780-433-3242	432-3244
Web: www.barbandernies.com					
Billingsgate Lighthouse Cafe 7331 104th St	Edmonton	AB	T6B4B9	780-433-0091	439-0099
Web: www.billingsgate.com					
Blue Pear 10643 123rd St NW	Edmonton	AB	T5N1P3	780-482-7178	
Web: www.thebluepear.com					
Bul-Go-Gi House 8813 92nd St	Edmonton	AB	T6C3P9	780-466-2330	
Web: www.bulgogi.ca					
Cafe Mosaics 10844 82nd Ave	Edmonton	AB	P6E2B3	780-433-9702	
Characters 10257 105th St	Edmonton	AB	T5J1E3	780-421-4100	425-1550
Web: www.characters.ca					
Chiante Cafe 10501 82nd Ave	Edmonton	AB	P6E2A4	780-439-9829	439-4071
Web: www.chiantecafe.ca					
Creperie The 10220 103rd St	Edmonton	AB	T5J0Y8	780-420-6656	426-5026
Web: www.thecreperie.com					
Dan Shing 15912 Stony Plain Rd	Edmonton	AB	P5P3Z8	780-483-1143	
Furusato 10012 82nd Ave	Edmonton	AB	T6E3Z1	780-439-1335	
Hardware Grill 9698 Jasper Ave	Edmonton	AB	T5H3V5	780-423-0969	423-4739
Web: www.hardwaregrill.com					
Il Pasticcio Trattoria 11520 100th Ave	Edmonton	AB	T5K0J7	780-488-9543	482-7956
Web: www.ilpasticcio.ca					
India Grill 4620 99th St	Edmonton	AB	T6E5H5	780-430-1900	438-2226
Web: www.indiangrill.ca					
Jack's Grill 5842 111th St	Edmonton	AB	T6H3G1	780-434-1113	433-0276
Web: www.jacksgrill.ca					
Japanese Village 10238 104th St	Edmonton	AB	T5J1B8	780-422-6083	425-0099
Julio's Barrio 10450 82nd Ave	Edmonton	AB	T6E2A2	780-431-0774	433-0575
Web: www.juliosbarrio.com					
Khazana 10177 107th St	Edmonton	AB	T5J1J5	780-702-0330	990-0342
Web: www.khazana.ab.ca					
Koutouki Restaurant 124th St NW Sutie 10719	Edmonton	AB	T5M0H2	780-452-5383	452-6220
Web: www.koutouki.ca					
Louisiana Purchase Restaurant 10320 111th St N W	Edmonton	AB	T5K1M9	780-420-6779	425-6659
Web: www.louisianapurchase.ca					
Noodle Noodle 10008 106th Ave	Edmonton	AB	T5H0N7	780-422-6862	424-8112
Web: www.noodlenoodle.ca					
Normand's 11639 A Jasper Ave	Edmonton	AB	T5K0M9	780-482-2600	488-3286
Web: www.normands.com					
Parkallen 7018 109th St	Edmonton	AB	T6H3C1	780-436-8080	430-0469
Web: www.parkallen.com					
Pearl River Restaurant 4728 99th St NW	Edmonton	AB	T6E5H5	780-435-2015	431-2758
Web: www.lusoft.ca/pearlriver					
Red Ox Inn 9420 91st St	Edmonton	AB	T6C3P4	780-465-5727	
Web: www.theredoxinn.com					
Sorrentino's On 95th 10844 95th St	Edmonton	AB	T5H2E4	780-425-0960	421-9123
Tasty Tom's Bistro 9965 82nd Ave NW	Edmonton	AB	T6E1Z1	780-437-5761	
Tropika Malaysian Cuisine 6004 104th St NW	Edmonton	AB	T6H2K3	780-439-6699	439-6644
Yianni's Taverna 10444 82nd Ave	Edmonton	AB	T6E2A2	780-433-6768	436-8883

ARIZONA

Name / Address	City	State	Zip	Phone	Fax
Haus Murphy's 5739 W Glendale Ave	Downtown Glendale	AZ	85301	623-939-2480	
Web: www.hausmurphys.com					
August Moon Chinese Restaurant 1300 S Milton Rd	Flagstaff	AZ	86001	928-774-5280	
Beaver Street Brewery 11 S Beaver St	Flagstaff	AZ	86001	928-779-0079	
Web: www.beaverstreetbrewery.com					
Black Barts Steakhouse Saloon 2760 E Butler Ave	Flagstaff	AZ	86004	928-779-3142	774-1113
TF: 800-574-4718 ■ *Web:* www.blackbartssteakhouse.com					
Brandy's 1500 E Cedar Ave Suite 40	Flagstaff	AZ	86004	928-779-2187	779-0004
Web: www.brandysrestaurant.com					
Buster's Restaurant & Bar 1800 S Milton Rd	Flagstaff	AZ	86001	928-774-5155	774-5156
Web: www.busters-restaurant.com					
Collins Irish Pub 2 N Laroux St	Flagstaff	AZ	86001	928-214-7363	226-7389
Cottage Place 126 W Cottage Ave	Flagstaff	AZ	86001	928-774-8431	774-0374
Web: www.cottageplace.com					
Dara Thai 14 S San Francisco St	Flagstaff	AZ	86001	928-774-0047	
Dehli Palace Cuisine of India 2700 S Woodlands Village Blvd	Flagstaff	AZ	86001	928-556-0019	
El Capitan Fresh Mexican Grill 1800 S Milton Rd Suite 21	Flagstaff	AZ	86001	928-774-1083	774-0447
Web: www.elcapitanfmg.com					
El Charro Cafe 409 S San Francisco St	Flagstaff	AZ	86001	928-779-0552	779-3034
Granny's Closet 218 S Milton Rd	Flagstaff	AZ	86001	928-774-8331	
Web: www.grannys-closet.com/site					
Horsemen Lodge 8500 Hwy 89 N	Flagstaff	AZ	86004	928-526-2655	526-1586
Web: www.horsemenlodge.com					
Josephine's 503 N Humphreys St	Flagstaff	AZ	86001	928-779-3400	226-0910
Web: www.josephinesrestaurant.com					
La Fonda 1900 N 2nd St	Flagstaff	AZ	86004	928-779-0296	773-9060
Little Thai Kitchen 1051 S Milton Rd	Flagstaff	AZ	86001	928-226-9422	226-9421
Mamma Luisa 2710 N Steves Blvd Suite 14	Flagstaff	AZ	86004	928-526-6809	526-6325
Miz Zips Cafe 2924 E Rt 66	Flagstaff	AZ	86001	928-526-0104	
Mountain Oasis 11 E Aspen Ave	Flagstaff	AZ	86001	928-214-9270	214-0020
Sakura 1175 W Rt 66	Flagstaff	AZ	86001	928-773-9118	773-0597
Web: www.radissonflagstaff.com					
Romeo's Euro Cafe 207 N Gilbert Rd Suite 105	Gilbert	AZ	85234	480-962-4224	558-2033
Web: www.eurocafe.com					
Ajo Al's *Arrowhead* 7458 W Bell Rd	Glendale	AZ	85308	623-334-9899	
Web: www.ajoals.com					
Babbo's 20211 N 67th Ave	Glendale	AZ	85308	623-566-9898	566-5561
Bitz-Ee Mama's 7023 N 58th Ave	Glendale	AZ	85301	623-931-0562	
Web: www.bitz-eemamas.com					
Black Bear Diner 6039 W Bell Rd	Glendale	AZ	85306	602-843-1921	
Web: www.blackbeardiner.com					
Caramba 5421 W Glendale Ave	Glendale	AZ	85301	623-934-8888	487-1934
Carvers Steakhouse 8172 W Bell Rd	Glendale	AZ	85308	623-412-0787	412-0454
Chanpen 13828 N 51st Ave	Glendale	AZ	85306	602-993-2046	993-2047
Kiss the Cook Restaurant 4915 W Glendale Ave	Glendale	AZ	85301	623-939-4663	939-2989
La Perla Cafe 5912 W Glendale Ave	Glendale	AZ	85301	623-939-7561	
Web: www.laperlacafe.net					
Mimi's Cafe 7450 W Bell Rd	Glendale	AZ	85308	623-979-4500	979-4339
Web: www.mimiscafe.com					
Pedro's 4938 W Glendale Ave	Glendale	AZ	85301	623-937-0807	551-8069
Rosario Ristorante 9250 N 43rd Ave	Glendale	AZ	85302	623-931-1810	
Ah-So 1919 S Gilbert Rd	Mesa	AZ	85204	480-497-1114	497-1115
Aloha Kitchen 2950 S Alma School Rd Suite 12	Mesa	AZ	85210	480-897-2451	897-7295
Web: www.alohakitchen.com					
Anzio Landing 2613 N Thunderbird Cir	Mesa	AZ	85215	480-832-1188	924-4954
Web: www.anziolanding.com					
Bavarian Point 4815 E Main St	Mesa	AZ	85205	480-830-0999	830-0530
Cafe Roma 2011 N Recker Rd	Mesa	AZ	85215	480-654-0558	
Golden Gate 2640 W Baseline Rd	Mesa	AZ	85202	480-897-1335	345-8416
Hodori 1116 S Dobson Rd	Mesa	AZ	85202	480-668-7979	668-9898
Ichi Ban 2015 S Alma School Rd	Mesa	AZ	85210	480-777-8433	777-8432
Julio's Too 1935 S Val Vista Dr	Mesa	AZ	85296	480-497-6600	497-6618
Landmark Restaurant 809 W Main St	Mesa	AZ	85201	480-962-4652	
Web: www.landmarkrestaurant.com					
On the Border Mexican Cafe 1710 S Power Rd	Mesa	AZ	85206	602-247-7510	654-6925*
**Fax Area Code: 480* ■ *Web:* www.ontheborder.com					
Rosa's Mexican Grill 328 E University Dr	Mesa	AZ	85201	480-964-5451	964-3273
Web: www.rosasmexicangrill.com					
SN Pacific Rim Asian Kitchen 1236 E Baseline Rd	Mesa	AZ	85204	480-892-0688	
Web: www.asiaaz.com					
Alexi's Grill 3550 N Central Ave Suite 120	Phoenix	AZ	85012	602-279-0982	279-0984
Alice Cooperstown 101 E Jackson St	Phoenix	AZ	85004	602-253-7337	253-4866
Web: www.alicecooperstown.com					
Avanti's 2728 E Thomas Rd	Phoenix	AZ	85016	602-956-0900	468-1913
Web: www.avanti-az.com					
Baby Kay's Cajun Kitchen 2119 E Camelback Rd	Phoenix	AZ	85016	602-955-0011	955-2288
Barrio Cafe 2814 N 16th St	Phoenix	AZ	85006	602-636-0240	636-0385
Web: www.barriocafe.com					
Bill Johnson's Big Apple 3757 E Van Buren St	Phoenix	AZ	85008	602-275-2107	
Web: www.billjohnsons.com					
Christopher's Crush 2502 E Camelback Rd	Phoenix	AZ	85016	602-522-2344	468-0314
Web: www.christophersaz.com					
Coronado Cafe 2201 N 7th St	Phoenix	AZ	85006	602-258-5149	258-7455
Coup des Tartes 4626 N 16th St	Phoenix	AZ	85016	602-212-1082	212-1138
Desert Jade 3215 E Indian School Rd	Phoenix	AZ	85018	602-954-0048	954-4038
Different Pointe of View 11111 N 7th St	Phoenix	AZ	85020	602-866-6350	866-6358
Web: www.pointehilton.com					
Durant's Restaurant 2611 N Central Ave	Phoenix	AZ	85004	602-264-5967	264-5112
Web: www.durantsaz.com					
George & Dragon 4240 N Central Ave	Phoenix	AZ	85012	602-241-0018	234-3841
Giuseppe's Italian Kitchen 2824 E Indian School Rd	Phoenix	AZ	85016	602-381-1237	381-3669
Web: www.giuseppes-restaurant.com					
Hard Rock Cafe 3 S 2nd St	Phoenix	AZ	85004	602-261-7625	261-7635
Web: www.hardrock.com					
India Palace 3202 E Greenbay Way	Phoenix	AZ	85032	602-942-4224	942-0719
La Pinata 3330 N 19th Ave	Phoenix	AZ	85015	602-279-1763	200-0931
Majerle's Sports Grill 24 N 2nd St	Phoenix	AZ	85004	602-253-9004	
Web: www.majerles.com					
Melting Pot of Ahwatukee The 3626 E Ray Rd	Phoenix	AZ	85044	480-704-9206	704-2973
Web: www.meltingpot.com					
Michelina's 3241 E Shea Blvd	Phoenix	AZ	85028	602-996-8977	996-9041
Web: www.michelinasrestaurant.com					
Morton's the Steakhouse 2501 E Camelback Rd	Phoenix	AZ	85016	602-955-9577	955-9670
Web: www.mortons.com					
Pizzeria Bianco 623 E Adams St	Phoenix	AZ	85004	602-258-8300	
Web: www.pizzeriabianco.com					
Roy's 5350 E Marriott Dr	Phoenix	AZ	85054	480-419-7697	419-7720
Web: www.roysrestaurant.com					
Ruth's Chris Steak House 2201 E Camelback Rd	Phoenix	AZ	85016	602-957-9600	224-1948
Web: www.ruthschris.com					
T Cook's 5200 E Camelback Rd	Phoenix	AZ	85018	602-808-0766	840-6927
Web: www.royalpalmshotel.com/restaurant					

Name / Address	City	State	ZIP	Phone	Fax
Tarbell's 3213 E Camelback *Web:* www.tarbells.com	Phoenix	AZ	85018	602-955-8100	955-8181
That's Italiano 3717 E Indian School Rd.	Phoenix	AZ	85018	602-778-9100	
Vincent Gueritthault on Camelback 3930 E Camelback Rd. *Web:* www.vincentsoncamelback.com	Phoenix	AZ	85018	602-224-0225	956-5400
Arcadia Farms Cafe 7014 E 1st Ave.	Scottsdale	AZ	85251	480-941-5665	
Atlas Bistro 2515 N Scottsdale Rd Suite 18. *Web:* www.azeats.com	Scottsdale	AZ	85257	480-990-2433	
Bandera Scottsdale 3821 N Scottsdale Rd	Scottsdale	AZ	85251	480-994-3524	
Bloom 8877 N Scottsdale Rd Suite 402.	Scottsdale	AZ	85253	480-922-5666	922-6556
Blue Adobe Grille 10885 Frank Lloyd Wright Blvd. *Web:* www.blueadobegrille.com	Scottsdale	AZ	85259	480-314-0550	
Bravo Bistro 4327 N Scottsdale Rd *Web:* www.bravobistro.com	Scottsdale	AZ	85251	480-481-7614	946-8205
Cowboy Ciao Wine Bar & Grill 7133 E Stetson Dr. *Web:* www.cowboyciao.com	Scottsdale	AZ	85251	480-946-3111	
Don & Charlie's 7501 E Camelback Rd *Web:* www.donandcharlies.com	Scottsdale	AZ	85251	480-990-0900	
Eddie V's Edgewater Grille 20715 N Pima Rd *Web:* www.eddiev.com	Scottsdale	AZ	85255	480-538-8468	
El Chorro Lodge 5550 E Lincoln Dr. *Web:* www.elchorrolodge.com	Scottsdale	AZ	85253	480-948-5170	
Fleming's Prime Steakhouse & Wine Bar 6333 N Scottsdale Rd. *Web:* www.flemingssteakhouse.com	Scottsdale	AZ	85250	480-596-8265	
George & Sons 11320 E Vfa Linda. *Web:* www.georgeandsons.com	Scottsdale	AZ	85259	480-312-7275	661-8104
J & G's Steakhouse 6000 E Camelback Rd.	Scottsdale	AZ	85251	480-423-2410	214-8001
Jalapeno's Mexican Cafe 23587 N Scottsdale	Scottsdale	AZ	85255	480-585-6442	
Kazimierz World Wine Bar 7137 E Stetson Dr. *Web:* www.kazbar.net	Scottsdale	AZ	85251	480-946-3004	
Kona Grill & Sushi Bar 7014 E Camelback Rd.	Scottsdale	AZ	85251	480-429-1100	
Los Olivos Mexican Patio 7328 E 2nd St *Web:* www.losolivosrestaurant.com	Scottsdale	AZ	85251	480-946-2256	
Mastro's Steakhouse 8852 E Pinnacle Peak Rd *Web:* www.mastrossteakhouse.com	Scottsdale	AZ	85255	480-585-9500	
Palm Court The 7700 E McCormick Pkwy.	Scottsdale	AZ	85258	480-596-7700	
Pane E Vino 8900 E Pinnacle Peak Rd	Scottsdale	AZ	85255	480-473-7900	
Pepin restaurant 7363 Scottsdale Mall *Web:* www.pepinrestaurant.com	Scottsdale	AZ	85251	480-990-9026	990-9073
PF Chang's China Bistro 7135 E Camelback Rd.	Scottsdale	AZ	85251	480-949-2610	
Rancho Pinot Grill 6208 N Scottsdale Rd. *Web:* www.ranchopinot.com	Scottsdale	AZ	85253	480-367-8030	443-7616
Remington's 7200 N Scottsdale Rd *Web:* www.scottsdaleplaza.com/dining_remingtons.htm	Scottsdale	AZ	85253	480-951-5101	951-5108
Roaring Fork 4800 N Scottsdale Rd Suite 1700. *Web:* www.eddiev.com	Scottsdale	AZ	85251	480-947-0795	994-1102
Roy's 7001 N Scottsdale Rd. *Web:* www.roysrestaurant.com	Scottsdale	AZ	85253	480-905-1155	
Ruth's Chris Steak House 7001 N Scottsdale Rd Suite 290. *Web:* www.ruthschris.com/Steak-House/3840/Scottsdale	Scottsdale	AZ	85253	480-991-5988	991-6850
Salt Cellar 550 N Hayden Rd *Web:* www.saltcellarrestaurant.com	Scottsdale	AZ	85257	480-947-1963	941-0929
Sapporo 14344 N Scottsdale Rd *Web:* www.sappororestaurant.com	Scottsdale	AZ	85254	480-607-1114	
Sassi Ristorante 10455 E Pinnacle Peak Pkwy *Web:* www.sassi.biz	Scottsdale	AZ	85255	480-502-9095	
Sushi on Shea 7000 E Shea Blvd.	Scottsdale	AZ	85254	480-483-7799	
Taggia 4925 N Scottsdale Rd *Web:* www.taggiascottsdale.com	Scottsdale	AZ	85251	480-424-6095	425-8966
Veneto Trattoria 6137 N Scottsdale Rd *Web:* www.venetotrattoria.com	Scottsdale	AZ	85250	480-948-9928	
L'Auberge de Sedona 301 L'Auberge Ln. *Web:* www.lauberge.com	Sedona	AZ	86336	928-282-1661	282-2885
Blue Nile Cafe 933 E University Dr Suite 112	Tempe	AZ	85281	480-377-1113	
Byblos Restaurant 3332 S Mill Ave *Web:* www.amdest.com	Tempe	AZ	85282	480-894-1945	
Caffe Boa 398 S Mill Ave. *Web:* www.cafeboa.com	Tempe	AZ	85281	480-968-9112	
Casey Moore's Oyster House 850 S Ash Ave	Tempe	AZ	85281	480-968-9935	968-6193
Cervantes 3318 S Mill Ave.	Tempe	AZ	85282	480-921-9113	
House of Tricks 114 E 7th St. *Web:* www.houseoftricks.com	Tempe	AZ	85281	480-968-1114	968-0080
John Henry's 909 E Elliot Rd *Web:* www.johnhenrysrestaurant.com	Tempe	AZ	85283	480-730-9009	831-2487
Monti's La Casa Vieja 100 S Mill Ave *Web:* www.montis.com	Tempe	AZ	85281	480-967-7594	967-8129
Pita Jungle 1250 E Apache Blvd	Tempe	AZ	85281	480-804-0234	
Rainforest Cafe 5000 S Arizona Mills Cir Suite 573 *Web:* www.rainforestcafe.com	Tempe	AZ	85282	480-752-9100	752-9101
Urban Cafe 1212 E Apache Blvd. *Web:* www.theurbancafe.com	Tempe	AZ	85281	480-968-8888	
Vincitorios Restaurant 1835 E Elliot Rd Suite C-109 *Web:* www.hstrial-vincitoriosre.intuitwebsites.com	Tempe	AZ	85284	480-820-2786	820-1987
Wong's Place 1825 E Baseline Rd.	Tempe	AZ	85283	480-838-8988	
Z'Tejas 20 W 6th St.	Tempe	AZ	85281	480-377-1170	377-1167
Anthony's in the Catalinas 6440 N Campbell Ave. *Web:* www.anthonyscatalinas.com	Tucson	AZ	85718	520-299-1771	299-6635

Name / Address	City	State	ZIP	Phone	Fax
Athens on Fourth Avenue 500 N 4th Ave *Web:* athenson4th.com	Tucson	AZ	85705	520-624-6886	
Cafe Poca Cosa 110 E Pennington St Suite 100.	Tucson	AZ	85701	520-622-6400	
Casa Molina 4240 E Grant Rd *Web:* www.casamolina.com	Tucson	AZ	85712	520-326-6663	326-9937
Char Thai 5039 5th St.	Tucson	AZ	85711	520-795-1715	
Delectables 533 N 4th Ave *Web:* www.delectables.com	Tucson	AZ	85705	520-884-9289	628-7948
El Charro 311 N Ct Ave. *Web:* www.elcharrorestaurant.com	Tucson	AZ	85701	520-622-1922	624-4118
El Corral 2201 E River Rd	Tucson	AZ	85718	520-299-6092	
Elle 2970 N Campbell Ave *Web:* www.ellerestaurant.com	Tucson	AZ	85719	520-327-0500	327-2353
Feast 3719 E Speedway *Web:* www.eatatfeast.com	Tucson	AZ	85712	520-326-9363	326-9245
Gandhi 150 W Fort Lowell Rd	Tucson	AZ	85705	520-292-1738	
Gold Room 245 E Ina Rd. *Web:* www.westwoodlook.com	Tucson	AZ	85704	520-297-1151	297-9023
Grill at Hacienda del Sol 5601 N Hacienda del Sol Rd. *Web:* www.haciendadelsol.com	Tucson	AZ	85718	520-529-3500	
J Bar 3770 E Sunrise Dr	Tucson	AZ	85718	520-615-6100	615-3334
Janos 3770 E Sunrise Dr. *Web:* www.janos.com	Tucson	AZ	85718	520-615-6100	615-3334
Jonathan's Tucson Cork 6320 E Tanque Verde Rd *Web:* www.jonathanscork.com	Tucson	AZ	85715	520-296-1631	296-0765
Kingfisher Bar & Grill 2564 E Grant Rd *Web:* www.kingfisherbarandgrill.com	Tucson	AZ	85716	520-323-7739	795-7810
Le Rendez-vous 3844 E Fort Lowell Rd. *Web:* www.lerendez-vous.com	Tucson	AZ	85716	520-323-7373	
Mi Nidito Restaurant 1813 S 4th Ave *Web:* www.minidito.net	Tucson	AZ	85713	520-622-5081	
Michelangelo 420 W Magee Rd *Web:* www.michelangelotucson.com	Tucson	AZ	85704	520-297-5775	
Pastiche Modern Eatery 3025 N Campbell Ave *Web:* www.pasticheme.com	Tucson	AZ	85718	520-325-3333	
PF Chang's China Bistro 1805 E River Rd. *Web:* www.pfchangs.com	Tucson	AZ	85718	520-615-8788	
Sushi Ten 4500 E Speedway Blvd	Tucson	AZ	85712	520-324-0010	
Thunder Canyon Brewery 7401 N La Cholla Blvd. *Web:* www.thundercanyonbrewery.com	Tucson	AZ	85741	520-797-2652	797-2589
Vivace 4310 N Campbell Rd	Tucson	AZ	85718	520-795-7221	
Wildflower 7037 N Oracle Rd.	Tucson	AZ	85704	520-219-4230	
Yoshimatsu 2660 N Campbell Ave. *Web:* www.yoshimatsuaz.com	Tucson	AZ	85719	520-320-1574	

ARKANSAS

Name / Address	City	State	ZIP	Phone	Fax
Calico County 2409 S 56th St Suite 116. *Web:* www.calicocounty.net	Fort Smith	AR	72903	479-452-4233	452-4286
Catfish Cove 1615 Phoenix Ave.	Fort Smith	AR	72901	479-646-8835	646-8835
Jerry Neel's Bar-B-Que 1823 Phoenix Ave.	Fort Smith	AR	72901	479-646-8085	696-0555
Taliano's Restaurant 201 N 14th St. *Web:* www.talianosrestaurant.com	Fort Smith	AR	72901	479-785-2292	785-2640
Back Porch Grill The 4810 Central Ave *Web:* www.backporchgrill.net	Hot Springs	AR	71901	501-525-0885	
Cafe 1217 1217 Malvern Ave	Hot Springs	AR	71901	501-318-1094	624-4931
Cajun Boilers 2806 Albert Pike Rd.	Hot Springs	AR	71913	501-767-5695	
Chef Paul's 4330 Central Ave Temperance Hill Sq.	Hot Springs	AR	71913	501-520-4187	520-4334
Chuck's Southern Bar-B-Que 1118 Airport Rd	Hot Springs	AR	71913	501-760-3223	
Don Juan 1311A Albert Pike Rd	Hot Springs	AR	71913	501-321-0766	
Hamilton House Estate Bed & Breakfast 132 Van Lyell Terr. *Web:* www.hamiltonhouseestate.com	Hot Springs	AR	71913	501-520-4040	520-4023
King's 3310 Central Ave	Hot Springs	AR	71903	501-318-1888	318-3888
Magnolia's on Central 510 Central Ave.	Hot Springs	AR	71901	501-624-5500	
McClard's Bar-B-Q 505 Albert Pike Rd *TF:* 866-622-5273 ■ *Web:* www.mcclards.com	Hot Springs	AR	71901	501-623-9665	622-2527
Mickey's CMB BBQ 1622 Pk Ave *Web:* www.mickeysbbq.net	Hot Springs National Park	AR	71901	501-624-1247	
1620 Restaurant 1620 Market St	Little Rock	AR	72212	501-221-1620	221-1921
Acadia 3000 Kavanaugh Blvd Suite 202 *Web:* www.acadiahillcrest.com	Little Rock	AR	72205	501-603-9630	603-0477
Anderson's Cajun Wharf 2400 Cantrell Rd *Web:* www.cajunswharf.com	Little Rock	AR	72202	501-375-5351	375-5354
Ashley's 111 W Markham St. *Web:* www.capitalhotels.com	Little Rock	AR	72201	501-374-7474	
Black Angus 10907 N Rodney Parham Rd.	Little Rock	AR	72212	501-228-7800	
Brave New Restaurant (BNR) 2300 Cottondale Ln Suite 105 *Web:* www.bravenewrestaurant.com	Little Rock	AR	72202	501-663-2677	
Buffalo Grill 1611 Rebsamen Pk Rd. *Web:* www.buffalogrilllr.com	Little Rock	AR	72202	501-296-9535	
Capers 14502 Cantrell Rd *Web:* www.capersrestaurant.com	Little Rock	AR	72223	501-868-7600	868-4294
Capriccio 200 W Markam. *Web:* www.peabodylittlerock.com	Little Rock	AR	72201	501-906-4000	399-8073
Dave's Place 210 Ctr St. *Web:* www.davesplacerestaurant.com	Little Rock	AR	72201	501-372-3283	
Doe's Eat Place 1023 W Marckham St *Web:* www.doeseatplace.net	Little Rock	AR	72201	501-376-1195	374-1190
El Chico 8409 IH- 30	Little Rock	AR	72209	501-562-3762	
Faded Rose 400 N Bowman Rd *Web:* www.thefadedrose.com	Little Rock	AR	72211	501-224-3377	224-4546
Fu Lin Chinese Restaurant 200 N Bowman Rd	Little Rock	AR	72211	501-225-8989	
Graffiti's Italian Restaurant 7811 Cantrell Rd.	Little Rock	AR	72227	501-224-9079	224-9161

Restaurant	City	State	Zip	Phone	Fax
Juanita's 1300 Main St *Web:* www.juanitas.com	Little Rock	AR	72202	501-372-1228	374-9735
Loca Luna 3519 Old Cantrell Rd *Web:* www.localuna.com	Little Rock	AR	72202	501-663-4666	664-4176
Markham Street Grill & Pub 11321 W Markham St *Web:* www.markhamstreetgrillandpub.com	Little Rock	AR	72211	501-224-2010	224-2519
Shogun Japanese Steak House 2815 Cantrell Rd *Web:* www.shogunlr.com	Little Rock	AR	72202	501-666-7070	666-7077
Shorty Small's Great American Restaurant 11100 N Rodney Parham Rd *Web:* www.shortysmalls.com	Little Rock	AR	72212	501-224-3344	
Sonny Williams' Steak Room 500 President Clinton Ave *Web:* www.sonnywilliamssteakroom.com	Little Rock	AR	72201	501-324-2999	324-4888
Trio's 8201 Cantrell Rd *Web:* www.triosrestaurant.com	Little Rock	AR	72227	501-221-3330	221-1002
Star of India 301 N Shackleford Rd Suite C4	West Little Rock	AR	72211	501-227-9900	

BRITISH COLUMBIA

Restaurant	City	State	Zip	Phone	Fax
Keg Steakhouse 10100 Shellbridge Way *Web:* www.kegsteakhouse.com	Richmond	BC	V6X2W7	604-276-0242	
Keg The 10100 Shellbridge Way *Web:* www.kegsteakhouse.com	Richmond	BC	V6X2W7	604-276-0242	
Accents 1967 W Broadway	Vancouver	BC	V6J1Z3	604-734-6660	734-0644
Afghan Horseman 1833 Anderson St	Vancouver	BC	V6H4E5	604-873-5923	
Athene's 3618 W Broadway	Vancouver	BC	V6R2B7	604-731-4135	
Bacchus Ristorante 845 Hornby St	Vancouver	BC	V6Z1V1	604-689-7777	608-5349
Banana Leaf 820 W Broadway *Web:* www.bananaleaf-vancouver.com	Vancouver	BC	V5Z1J8	604-731-6333	
Baru Latino Tapas Lounge 2535 Alma St *Web:* www.barulatino.com	Vancouver	BC	V6R3R8	604-222-9171	222-9171
Bin 941 Tapas Parlour 941 Davie St *Web:* www.bin941.com	Vancouver	BC	V6Z1B9	604-683-1246	683-1206
Bishop's 2183 W 4th Ave *Web:* www.bishopsonline.com	Vancouver	BC	V6K1N7	604-738-2025	738-4622
Bistro Pastis 2153 4th Ave W *Web:* www.bistropastis.com	Vancouver	BC	V6K1N7	604-731-5020	731-5039
Blue Water Cafe 1095 Hamilton St *Web:* www.bluewatercafe.net	Vancouver	BC	V6B5T4	604-688-8078	688-8978
Bridges Restaurant 1676 Duranleau St *Web:* www.bridgesrestaurant.com	Vancouver	BC	V6H3S4	604-687-4400	687-0352
C Restaurant 2-1600 Howe St *Web:* www.crestaurant.com	Vancouver	BC	V6Z1R8	604-681-1164	605-8263
Capone's 1141 Hamilton St	Vancouver	BC	V6B5P6	604-569-1770	
Cardero's 1583 Coal Harbour Quay *Web:* www.vancouverdine.com/carderos	Vancouver	BC	V6G3E7	604-669-7666	669-7609
Chambar 562 Beatty St *Web:* www.chambar.com	Vancouver	BC	V6B2L3	604-879-7119	879-7118
CinCin Ristorante 1154 Robson St 2nd Fl *Web:* www.cincin.net	Vancouver	BC	V6E1B5	604-688-7338	688-7339
Cioppino's Mediterranean Grill 1133&1129 Hamilton St *Web:* www.cioppinosyaletown.com	Vancouver	BC	V6B5P6	604-688-7466	688-7411
Cioppino's Mediterranean Grill & Enoteca 1133 Hamilton St *Web:* www.cioppinosyaletown.com	Vancouver	BC	V6B5P6	604-685-8462	688-7411
Cloud Nine Revolving Restaurant 1400 Robson St *Web:* www.cloud9restaurant.ca	Vancouver	BC	V6G1B9	604-687-0511	687-2801
Coast 1054 Alberni St *Web:* www.coastrestaurant.ca	Vancouver	BC	V6E1A3	604-685-5010	629-5014
Diva at the Met 645 Howe St *Web:* www.metropolitan.com/diva	Vancouver	BC	V6C2Y9	604-602-7788	643-7267
Five Sails Restaurant 999 Canada Pl Suite 410 *Web:* www.fivesails.ca	Vancouver	BC	V6C3E1	604-844-2855	682-6321
Glowbal Grill & Satay Bar 1079 Mainland St *Web:* www.glowbalgrill.com	Vancouver	BC	V6B5P9	604-602-0835	602-7523
Go Fish! Ocean Emporium 1505 W 1st Ave	Vancouver	BC	V6J1E8	604-730-5040	
Gotham Steakhouse & Cocktail Bar 615 Seymour St *Web:* www.gothamsteakhouse.com	Vancouver	BC	V6B3K3	604-605-8282	605-8285
Hy's Encore 637 Hornby St *Web:* www.hyssteakhouse.com	Vancouver	BC	V6C2G2	604-683-7671	683-1749
Imperial Chinese Seafood Restaurant 355 Burrard St *Web:* www.imperialrest.com	Vancouver	BC	V6C2G8	604-688-8191	688-8466
Kamei Royal 1030 W Georgia St	Vancouver	BC	V6E2Y3	604-687-8588	687-8488
La Bodega Restaurante & Tapa Bar 1277 Howe St *Web:* www.loopdeloop.ca/labodega	Vancouver	BC	V6Z1R3	604-684-8814	684-8814
Las Margaritas Restaurante 1999 W 4th Ave *Web:* www.lasmargaritas.com	Vancouver	BC	V6J1M7	604-734-7117	734-3528
Le Gavroche Restaurant 1616 Alberni St *Web:* www.legavroche.ca	Vancouver	BC	V6G1A6	604-685-3924	669-1885
Maurya Indian Cuisine 1643 W Broadway *Web:* www.mauryaindiancuisine.com	Vancouver	BC	V6J1W9	604-742-0622	
Mr Pickwick's 8620 Granville St	Vancouver	BC	V6P5A1	604-266-2340	
Original Tandoori Kitchen King 689 E 65th Ave	Vancouver	BC	V5X2P7	604-327-8900	327-8903
Ouisi Bistro 3014 Granville St *Web:* www.ouisibistro.com	Vancouver	BC	V6H3J8	604-732-7550	
Panos Greek Taverna 654 SE Marine Dr	Vancouver	BC	V5X2T4	604-322-7117	
Pink Pearl Chinese Seafood 1132 E Hastings St *Web:* www.pinkpearl.com	Vancouver	BC	V6A1S2	604-253-4316	253-4316
Raincity Grill 1193 Denman St *Web:* www.raincitygrill.com	Vancouver	BC	V6G2N1	604-685-7337	
Reef Caribbean Restaurants The 4172 Main St *Web:* www.thereefrestaurant.com	Vancouver	BC	V5V3P7	604-874-5375	
Sawasdee Thai 4250 Main St *Web:* www.sawasdeethairestaurant.com	Vancouver	BC	V5V3P9	604-876-4030	876-4035
Sequoia Grill at the Teahouse 1583 Coal Harbour Quay *Web:* www.vancouverdine.com	Vancouver	BC	V6G3E7	604-687-5684	669-7699
Simply Thai 1211 Hamilton St *Web:* www.simplythairestaurant.com	Vancouver	BC	V6B6K3	604-642-0123	
Stepho's 1124 Davie St	Vancouver	BC	V6E1N1	604-683-2555	
Sun Sui Wah Seafood Restaurant 3888 Main St	Vancouver	BC	V5V3N9	604-872-8822	876-1638
Tojo's *Tojo's Restaurant* 1133 W Broadway *Web:* www.tojos.com	Vancouver	BC	V6H1G1	604-872-8050	872-8060
Vij's Restaurant & Curry Art Gallery 1480 W 11th Ave	Vancouver	BC	V6H1L1	604-736-6664	
Yew Restaurant & Bar 791 W Georgia St 2nd Fl *Web:* www.fourseasons.com	Vancouver	BC	V6C2T4	604-692-4939	844-6749
Yuji Tapas 2059 4th Ave W	Vancouver	BC	V6J1N3	604-734-4990	

CALIFORNIA

Restaurant	City	State	Zip	Phone	Fax
Wood Ranch Barbecue & Grill Inc 28632 Roadside Dr Suite 100 *Web:* www.woodranch.com	Agoura Hills	CA	91301	818-889-9544	889-1345
Cuban Bistro 28 W Main St *Web:* www.cubanbistro.com	Alhambra	CA	91801	626-308-3350	308-3161
Anaheim White House 887 S Anaheim Blvd *Web:* www.anaheimwhitehouse.com	Anaheim	CA	92805	714-772-1381	772-7062
Catal Restaurant & Uva Bar 1580 S Disneyland Dr # 106 *Web:* www.patinagroup.com	Anaheim	CA	92802	714-774-4442	
Catch The 2100 E Katella Ave Suite 104 *Web:* www.catchanaheim.com	Anaheim	CA	92806	714-935-0101	935-0105
El Ortega's 2561 W Ball Rd	Anaheim	CA	92804	714-828-2830	
Hibachi Steak House 108 S Fairmont Blvd	Anaheim	CA	92807	714-998-4110	921-9926
JT Schmid's Restaurant & Brewery 2610 E Katella Ave *Web:* www.jtschmidsrestaurants.com	Anaheim	CA	92806	714-634-9200	634-9200
JW's Steakhouse 700 W Convention Way *Web:* www.anaheimmarriott.com	Anaheim	CA	92802	714-750-8000	750-9100
Merhaba 2801 W Ball Rd	Anaheim	CA	92804	714-826-8859	
Mr Stox 1105 E Katella Ave *Web:* www.mrstox.com	Anaheim	CA	92805	714-634-2994	634-0561
Napa Rose 1600 S Disneyland Dr	Anaheim	CA	92802	714-781-3463	
Naples 1550 S Disneyland Dr # 101 *Web:* www.patinagroup.com	Anaheim	CA	92802	714-776-6200	776-6340
Pepe's 2429 W Ball Rd	Anaheim	CA	92804	714-952-9410	
Rainforest Cafe 1515 S Disneyland Dr Downtown Disney *Web:* www.rainforestcafe.com	Anaheim	CA	92802	714-772-0413	772-3024
Ralph Brennan's Jazz Kitchen 1590 S Disneyland Dr Downtown Disney *Web:* www.rbjazzkitchen.com	Anaheim	CA	92802	714-776-5200	776-5300
Rosine's 721 S Weir Canyon Rd *Web:* www.rosines.com	Anaheim	CA	92808	714-283-5141	283-0158
Steakhouse 55 1150 Magic Way	Anaheim	CA	92802	714-956-6402	956-6597
Tortilla Jo's 1510 Disneyland Dr Downtown Disney *Web:* www.patinagroup.com/tortillaJos	Anaheim	CA	92803	714-535-5000	535-5700
Baci Trattoria 416 N Lakeview Ave *Web:* www.bacianaheim.com	Anaheim Hills	CA	92807	714-282-2220	
Benji's 4001 Rosedale Hwy	Bakersfield	CA	93308	661-328-0400	328-0423
Bill Lee's Bamboo Chopsticks 1203 18th St *Web:* www.billlees.com	Bakersfield	CA	93301	661-324-9441	324-7811
Bit Of Germany 1901 Flower St	Bakersfield	CA	93305	661-325-8874	872-0854
Buck Owens' Crystal Palace Steakhouse 2800 Buck Owens Blvd *Web:* www.buckowens.com	Bakersfield	CA	93308	661-328-7560	328-7565
Cactus Valley 4215 Rosedale Hwy	Bakersfield	CA	93308	661-633-1948	322-3234
Cafe Med Restaurant 4809 Scottdale Hwy *Web:* www.cafemedrestaurant.com	Bakersfield	CA	93309	661-834-4433	834-0188
Chalet Basque 200 Oak St *Web:* www.chaletbasque.net	Bakersfield	CA	93304	661-327-2915	
ChuyÆs Mesquite Broiler 2500 New Stine Rd	Bakersfield	CA	93309	661-833-3469	833-3130
Cope's Knotty Pine Cafe 1530 Norris Rd	Bakersfield	CA	93308	661-399-0120	
Imperial Chinese Restaurant 4525 Ming Ave	Bakersfield	CA	93309	661-836-0288	
Izumo Sushi 4412 Ming Ave	Bakersfield	CA	93309	661-398-0608	

Name / Address	City	State	ZIP	Phone	Fax
Jake's Tex-Mex Cafe 1710 Oak St	Bakersfield	CA	93301	661-322-6380	322-3731
Web: www.jakestexmex.com					
Las Costa Mariscos 716 21st St	Bakersfield	CA	93301	661-322-2655	
Mama Tosca's 9000 Ming Ave Suite K3	Bakersfield	CA	93309	661-831-1242	663-7436
Web: www.mamatoscas.com					
Mossman's Southwest 3610 Wible Rd	Bakersfield	CA	93309	661-832-5130	832-4783
Sorella Ristorante 7800 McNair Ct	Bakersfield	CA	93313	661-396-8603	396-9649
Tahoe Joe's 9000 Ming Ave	Bakersfield	CA	93311	661-664-8723	664-7732
Web: www.tahoejoes.com					
Uricchio's Trattoria 1400 17th St	Bakersfield	CA	93301	661-326-8870	326-8829
Wool Growers 620 E 19th St	Bakersfield	CA	93305	661-327-9584	
Belvedere The 9882 S Santa Monica Blvd	Beverly Hills	CA	90212	310-788-2306	788-2319
Crustacean 9646 Little Santa Monica Blvd	Beverly Hills	CA	90210	310-205-8990	271-0737
Lawry's the Prime Rib 100 N La Cienega Blvd	Beverly Hills	CA	90211	310-652-2827	657-5463
Web: www.lawrysonline.com					
Mastro's Steakhouse 246 N Canon Dr	Beverly Hills	CA	90210	310-888-8782	
Matsuhisa Restaurant 129 N La Cienega Blvd	Beverly Hills	CA	90211	310-659-9639	659-0492
Web: www.nobumatsuhisa.com					
Ruth's Chris Steak House 224 S Beverly Dr	Beverly Hills	CA	90212	310-859-8744	859-2576
Web: www.ruthschris.com					
Spago 176 N Canon Dr	Beverly Hills	CA	90210	310-385-0880	385-0880
Web: www.wolfgangpuck.com					
Tanzore 50 N La Cienega Blvd	Beverly Hills	CA	90211	310-652-3894	652-0163
Web: www.tanzore.com					
Anton & Michel Mission St	Carmel	CA	93921	831-624-2406	625-1542
Web: www.carmelsbest.com/antonmichel					
Bouchee Mission St	Carmel	CA	93921	831-626-7880	626-7883
Web: www.boucheecarmel.com					
Casanova 5th St-between Mission & San Carlos PO Box GG	Carmel	CA	93921	831-625-0501	625-9799
Web: www.casanovarestaurant.com					
Flying Fish Grill Mission St	Carmel	CA	93921	831-625-1962	
French Poodle The Junipero & 5th Ave	Carmel	CA	93921	831-624-8643	
Grasing's 6th & Mission Sts	Carmel	CA	93923	831-624-6562	624-7431
Web: www.grasings.com					
Pacific's Edge 120 Highland Dr	Carmel	CA	93923	831-622-5445	
Rio Grill 101 the Crossroads	Carmel	CA	93923	831-625-5436	625-2950
Web: www.riogrill.com					
Robata Grill 3658 The Barnyard	Carmel	CA	93923	831-624-2643	624-0360
Anthony's Fish Grotto 215 Bay Blvd	Chula Vista	CA	91910	619-425-4200	425-8370
Web: www.gofishanthonys.com					
Aunt Emma's 700 E St	Chula Vista	CA	91910	619-427-2722	727-4440
Web: www.auntemmaspancakes.com					
Meakwan 230 3rd Ave	Chula Vista	CA	91910	619-426-5172	
Web: www.meakwanthaicuisine.com					
Pescados y Mariscos Hector's 1177 Broadway Ave	Chula Vista	CA	91911	619-585-0773	585-7732
Web: www.pescadosymariscoshectors.com					
Zorba's Family Restaurant 100 Broadway	Chula Vista	CA	91910	619-422-8853	422-0104
Web: www.zorbasgreekbuffet.com					
Slocum House 7992 California Ave	Fair Oaks	CA	95628	916-961-7211	961-5710
Web: www.slocum-house.com					
Carmen & Family Bar-B-Q 41986 Fremont Blvd	Fremont	CA	94538	510-657-5464	657-9125
China Chili 39116 State St	Fremont	CA	95438	510-791-1688	791-5181
Country Way 5325 Mowry Ave	Fremont	CA	94536	510-797-3188	
El Patio Restaurant 37311 Fremont Blvd	Fremont	CA	94536	510-796-1733	796-0833
Web: www.elpatiooriginal.com					
Fremont Market Broiler 43406 Christy St	Fremont	CA	94538	510-791-8675	791-6172
Web: www.marketbroiler.com					
Ho Chow Restaurant 47966 Warm Springs Blvd	Fremont	CA	94539	510-657-0683	657-9026
Web: www.hochow.com					
Kimaree 39620 Mission Blvd	Fremont	CA	94539	510-742-5152	
Massimo's 5200 Mowry Ave	Fremont	CA	94538	510-792-2000	792-7041
Web: www.massimos.com					
Norman's Family Restaurant 4949 Stevenson Blvd	Fremont	CA	94538	510-226-7777	
Papillon Restaurant 37296 Mission Blvd	Fremont	CA	94536	510-793-6331	793-2789
Web: www.papillonrestaurant.com					
Southern Heritage BBQ 40645 Fremont Blvd Suite 23	Fremont	CA	94538	510-668-1850	
Star Buffett 34755 Ardenwood Blvd	Fremont	CA	94555	510-797-7181	797-7182
Campagnia 1185 E Champlain Dr	Fresno	CA	93720	559-433-3300	433-3066
Web: www.campagnia.net					
Chopsticks 4783 E Olive Ave	Fresno	CA	93702	559-255-0489	
Elbow Room 731 W San Jose Ave	Fresno	CA	93704	559-227-1234	227-1843
Web: www.elbow-room.com					
Giulia's 3050 W Shaw Ave	Fresno	CA	93711	559-276-3573	277-7552
Landmark The 644 E Olive Ave	Fresno	CA	93728	559-233-6505	233-9662
Livingstone's Restaurant & Pub 831 E Fern Ave	Fresno	CA	93728	559-485-5198	485-3439
Maxs Bistro 1784 W Bullard Ave	Fresno	CA	93711	559-439-6900	439-7206
Web: www.maxsbistro.com					
Ripe Tomato 5064 N Palm Ave	Fresno	CA	93704	559-225-1850	
Sequoia Brewing Co 777 E Olive St	Fresno	CA	93728	559-264-5521	
Thai House 1069 E Shaw Ave	Fresno	CA	93710	559-221-7245	
Tokyo Garden 1711 Fulton St	Fresno	CA	93721	559-268-3596	
Yoshino Restaurant 6226 N Blackstone Ave	Fresno	CA	93710	559-431-2205	431-0377
Azteca 12911 Main St	Garden Grove	CA	92840	714-638-3790	638-3737
Web: www.aztecamexicanrestaurant.org					
California Grill 11999 Harbor Blvd Hyatt Regency Orange County	Garden Grove	CA	92840	714-750-1234	740-0465
Carolina's 12045 Chapman Ave	Garden Grove	CA	92840	714-971-5551	971-5552
Casa De Soto 8562 Garden Grove Blvd	Garden Grove	CA	92844	714-530-4200	
Web: www.casadesoto.com					
Furiwa Seafood 13826 Brookhurst St	Garden Grove	CA	92843	714-534-3996	534-5327
Joe's Crab Shack 12011 Harbor Blvd	Garden Grove	CA	92840	714-703-0505	703-0252
Web: www.joescrabshack.com					
Pho 79 9941 Hazard Ave	Garden Grove	CA	92844	714-531-2490	
Seafood Cove 8547 Westminster Blvd	Garden Grove	CA	92844	714-895-7964	
Sun Spot Restaurant 12015 Harbor Blvd Anaheim Marriott Suites	Garden Grove	CA	92840	714-750-1000	383-6050
Tokyo Love 12565 S Harbor Blvd	Garden Grove	CA	92840	714-534-4751	534-4158
Vien Dong 14271 Brookhurst St	Garden Grove	CA	92843	714-531-8253	
Wong's 10642 Westminster Ave	Garden Grove	CA	92843	714-537-4920	
Barragan's 814 S Central Ave	Glendale	CA	91204	818-243-1103	243-2637
Carousel Restaurant 304 N Brand Blvd	Glendale	CA	91203	818-246-7775	246-6627
Web: www.carouselrestaurant.com					
Damon's Steak House 317 N Brand Blvd	Glendale	CA	91203	818-507-1510	240-0087
Web: www.damonsglendale.com					
Far Niente Ristorante 204 1/2 N Brand Blvd	Glendale	CA	91203	818-242-3835	242-2956
Fresco Ristorante 514 S Brand Blvd	Glendale	CA	91204	818-247-5541	247-1964
Web: www.frescoristorante.com					
Gauchos Village Churrascaria & Bar 411 N Brand Blvd	Glendale	CA	91203	818-550-1430	550-1429
Web: www.gauchosvillage.com					
Gennaro's Ristorante 1109 N Brand Blvd	Glendale	CA	91202	818-243-6231	254-0080
Web: www.gennarosristorante.com					
La Cabanita 3447 N Verdugo Rd	Glendale	CA	91208	818-957-2711	
Max's of Manila 313 W Broadway	Glendale	CA	91204	818-637-7751	637-2325
Notte Luna 113 N Maryland Ave	Glendale	CA	91206	818-552-4100	552-3522
Web: www.notteluna.com					
Panda Inn 111 E Wilson Ave	Glendale	CA	91206	818-502-1234	502-1730
Web: www.pandainn.com					
Scarantino's 1524 E Colorado St	Glendale	CA	91205	818-247-9777	247-5344
Web: www.scarantinos.com					
Shiraz 211 S Glendale Ave	Glendale	CA	91205	818-500-4948	
Tep Thai 209 W Wilson Ave	Glendale	CA	91203	818-246-0380	
Web: www.tepthai.com					
Two Guys From Italy 405 N Verdugo Rd	Glendale	CA	91206	818-240-0370	240-0972
Web: www.glendaletwoguysfromitaly.com					
Varouj's Kabobs 1110 S Glendale Ave	Glendale	CA	91205	818-243-9870	
Baci 18748 Beach Blvd	Huntington Beach	CA	92648	714-965-1194	965-4106
Web: www.bacirestaurant.com					
Baja Willie's 7891 Warner Ave	Huntington Beach	CA	92647	714-842-8955	842-6778
Web: www.bajawillies.net					
Beachfront 301 301 Main St	Huntington Beach	CA	92648	714-374-3399	374-1088
Web: www.beachfront301.com					
Bukhara Cuisine Of India 7594 Edinger Ave	Huntington Beach	CA	92647	714-842-3171	
Capone's Cucina 19688 Beach Blvd Suite 10	Huntington Beach	CA	92646	714-593-2888	705-0467
Web: www.caponescucina.com					
Hyatt Regency Huntington Beach Resort & Spa 21500 Pacific Coast Hwy	Huntington Beach	CA	92648	714-698-1234	845-4990
Web: huntingtonbeach.hyatt.com					
Longboard Restaurant & Pub 217 Main St	Huntington Beach	CA	92648	714-960-1896	960-8447
Web: www.longboardpub.com					
Lou's Red Oak BBQ Grill 21501 Brookhurst St	Huntington Beach	CA	92646	714-965-5200	
Web: www.lousbbq.com					
Mario's Restaurant 18603 Main St	Huntington Beach	CA	92648	714-842-5811	842-0292
Matsu Restaurant 18035 Beach Blvd	Huntington Beach	CA	92648	714-848-4404	842-4049
Pete's Sunset Grill & Bar 21500 Pacific Coast Hwy Hyatt Huntington Beach	Huntington Beach	CA	92648	714-698-1234	845-4990
TF: 800-233-1234 ■ *Web:* www.hyatt.com					
Ruby's Diner 1 Main St	Huntington Beach	CA	92648	714-969-7829	969-1630
Web: www.rubys.com					
Sea Siam Restaurant 16103 Bolsa Chica St	Huntington Beach	CA	92649	714-846-8986	846-4543
Shades Restaurant 21100 Pacific Coast Hwy	Huntington Beach	CA	92648	714-845-8000	845-8424
Web: www.waterfrontresort.com/dining/shades					
Spark Woodfire Grill 300 Pacific Coast Hwy Suite 202	Huntington Beach	CA	92648	714-960-0996	960-7332
Web: www.sparkwoodfiregrill.com					
Tsunami 17236 Pacific Coast Hwy	Huntington Beach	CA	92649	562-592-5806	592-4437
Tuna Town 221 Main St	Huntington Beach	CA	92648	714-536-3194	536-3473
Web: www.tunatownsushibar.com					
West Coast Club 21100 Pacific Coast Hwy Hilton Waterfront Beach Resort	Huntington Beach	CA	92648	714-845-8000	845-8425
Zubie's Dry Dock 9059 Adams Ave	Huntington Beach	CA	92646	714-963-6362	
Marine Room The 2000 Spindrift Dr	La Jolla	CA	92037	858-459-7222	551-4673
TF: 866-644-2351 ■ *Web:* www.marineroom.com					
Piatti 2182 Avenida de la Playa	La Jolla	CA	92037	858-454-1589	454-1799
Roppongi 875 Prospect St Suite 102	La Jolla	CA	92037	858-551-5252	551-7712
Web: www.roppongiusa.com					
Sky Room 1132 Prospect St	La Jolla	CA	92037	858-454-0771	
Tapenade 7612 Fay Ave	La Jolla	CA	92037	858-551-7500	551-9913
Web: www.tapenaderestaurant.com					
Duke's Huntington Beach 130 Kai Malina Pkwy	Lahaina	CA	96761	714-374-6446	374-6546
Web: www.hulapie.com					

Name / Address	City	State	Zip	Phone	Fax
Napoli Italian Restaurant 24960 Redlands Blvd	Loma Linda	CA	92354	909-796-3770	478-7756
555 East 555 E Ocean Blvd Web: www.555east.com	Long Beach	CA	90802	562-437-0626	
Alegria Cocina Latina Restaurant 115 Pine Ave Web: www.alegriacocinalatina.com	Long Beach	CA	90802	562-436-3388	436-9108
Bangkok Thai Cuisine 3426 E 4th St	Long Beach	CA	90814	562-433-0093	
Belmont Brewing Co 25 39th Pl Web: www.belmontbrewing.com	Long Beach	CA	90803	562-433-3891	434-0604
Cafe Piccolo 3222 E Broadway Web: www.cafepiccolo.com	Long Beach	CA	90803	562-438-1316	
Caffe La Strada 4716 E 2nd St	Long Beach	CA	90803	562-433-8100	
Christy's 3937 E Broadway Web: www.christysristorante.com	Long Beach	CA	90803	562-433-7133	621-1471
Crab Pot The 215 Marina Dr Web: www.thecrabpot.com	Long Beach	CA	90803	562-430-0272	799-0686
Frenchy's Bistro 4137 E Anaheim St Web: www.frenchysbistro.com	Long Beach	CA	90804	562-494-8787	494-1613
George's Greek Cafe 5316 E 2nd St	Long Beach	CA	90803	562-433-1755	
Green Field Churrascaria 5305 E Pacific Coast Hwy Web: www.greenfieldchurrascaria.com	Long Beach	CA	90804	562-597-0906	597-0916
Joe's Crab Shack 6550 E Marina Dr	Long Beach	CA	90803	562-594-6551	
Johnny Rebs' Southern Roadhouse 4663 Long Beach Blvd Web: www.johnnyrebs.com	Long Beach	CA	90805	562-423-7327	422-9681
Kelly's 5716 E 2nd St	Long Beach	CA	90803	562-433-4983	
Khoury's 110 N Marina Dr Web: www.khourys.net	Long Beach	CA	90803	562-598-6800	598-0079
King's Fish House 100 W Broadway Web: www.kingsfishhouse.com	Long Beach	CA	90802	562-432-7463	435-6143
L'Opera 101 Pine Ave Web: www.lopera.com	Long Beach	CA	90802	562-491-0066	436-1108
La Traviata 301 Cedar Ave Web: www.latraviata301.com	Long Beach	CA	90802	562-432-8022	432-6222
Lasher's 3441 E Broadway Web: www.lashersrestaurant.com	Long Beach	CA	90803	562-433-0153	433-2735
Lucille's Smokehouse Bar-B-Que 7411 Carson St Web: www.lucillesbbq.com	Long Beach	CA	90808	562-938-7427	627-1947
Madison 102 Pine Ave	Long Beach	CA	90802	562-628-8866	628-8870
McKenna's on the Bay 190 N Marina Dr Web: www.mckennasonthebay.com	Long Beach	CA	90803	562-342-9411	493-5399
Nino's 3853 Atlantic Ave	Long Beach	CA	90807	562-427-1003	427-3093
Parker's Lighthouse 435 Shoreline Village Dr Web: www.parkerslighthouse.com	Long Beach	CA	90802	562-432-6500	436-3551
Phil Trani's 3490 Long Beach Blvd	Long Beach	CA	90807	562-426-3668	426-1218
Reef Restaurant The 880 S Harbor Scenic Dr Web: www.reefrestaurant.com	Long Beach	CA	91344	562-435-8013	432-6823
Roscoe's House of Chicken & Waffles 730 E Broadway Web: www.roscoeschickenandwaffles.com	Long Beach	CA	90802	562-437-8355	437-2454
Sir Winston's Restaurant & Lounge 1126 Queens Hwy TF: 877-342-0738 ■ Web: www.queenmary.com	Long Beach	CA	90802	562-435-3511	
Sky Room 40 S Locust Ave	Long Beach	CA	90802	562-983-2703	
Sushi of Naples 5470 E 2nd St Web: www.sushiofnaples.com	Long Beach	CA	90803	562-434-1122	438-7520
Utopia 445 E 1st St Web: www.utopiarestaurant.net	Long Beach	CA	90802	562-432-6888	432-8687
Yard House 401 Shoreline Village Dr Web: www.yardhouse.com	Long Beach	CA	90802	562-628-0455	435-5544
Shenandoah at the Arbor 10631 Los Alamitos Blvd Web: www.shenandoahatthearbor.com	Los Alamitos	CA	90720	562-431-1990	431-1910
Amalfi 143 N Brea Ave Web: www.amalfiristorante.com	Los Angeles	CA	90036	323-938-2504	938-2252
Angeli Caffe 7274 Melrose Ave Web: www.angelicaffe.com	Los Angeles	CA	90046	323-936-9086	938-9873
Angelini Osteria 7313 Beverly Blvd Web: www.angeliniosteria.com	Los Angeles	CA	90036	323-297-0070	297-0072
Angelique Cafe 840 S Spring St	Los Angeles	CA	90014	213-623-8698	
AOC Wine Bar & Restaurant 8022 W 3rd St Web: www.aocwinebar.com	Los Angeles	CA	90048	323-653-6359	653-1390
Bamboo Restaurant 10835 Venice Blvd	Los Angeles	CA	90034	310-287-0668	287-0229
Ca'Brea 346 S La Brea Ave Web: www.cabrearestaurant.com	Los Angeles	CA	90036	323-938-2863	938-8659
Cafe Pinot 700 W 5th St Web: www.patinagroup.com	Los Angeles	CA	90071	213-239-6500	
Cafe Stella 3932-3936 Sunset Blvd	Los Angeles	CA	90029	323-666-0265	
Campanile 624 S La Brea Ave Web: www.campanilerestaurant.com	Los Angeles	CA	90036	323-938-1447	938-5840
Carlitos Gardel 7963 Melrose Ave Web: www.carlitosgardel.com	Los Angeles	CA	90046	323-655-0891	655-1576
Cha Cha Cha 656 N Virgil Ave Web: www.theoriginalchachacha.com	Los Angeles	CA	90004	323-664-7723	664-7769
Checkers 535 S Grand Ave Web: www.hiltoncheckers.com/diningCD.php	Los Angeles	CA	90071	213-624-0000	
Cicada 617 S Olive St Web: www.cicadarestaurant.com	Los Angeles	CA	90014	213-488-9488	488-9546
Cobras & Matadors 7615 Beverly Blvd	Los Angeles	CA	90036	323-932-6178	
Empress Pavilion 988 N Hill St Web: www.empresspavilion.com	Los Angeles	CA	90012	213-617-9898	617-8114
Encounter 209 World Way Web: www.encounterrestaurant.com	Los Angeles	CA	90045	310-215-5151	417-8478
Engine Co No 28 644 S Figueroa St Web: www.engineco.com	Los Angeles	CA	90017	213-624-6996	623-9278
Farfalla Trattoria 1978 Hillhurst Ave Web: www.farfallatrattoria.com	Los Angeles	CA	90027	323-661-7365	661-5956
Gardens 300 S Doheny Dr Four Seasons Hotel	Los Angeles	CA	90048	310-273-2222	786-2242
Genghis Cohen 740 N Fairfax Ave Web: www.genghiscohen.com	Los Angeles	CA	90046	323-653-0640	653-0701
Grace 7360 Beverly Blvd Web: www.gracerestaurant.com	Los Angeles	CA	90036	323-934-4400	934-0485
Gumbo Pot 6333 W 3rd St Web: www.thegumbopotla.com	Los Angeles	CA	90036	323-933-0358	932-6820
Hamasaku 11043 Santa Monica Blvd Web: www.hamasakula.com	Los Angeles	CA	90025	310-479-7636	479-3116
Harold & Belle's 2920 W Jefferson Blvd	Los Angeles	CA	90018	323-735-9023	735-8770
Hu's Szechwan Restaurant 10450 National Blvd Web: www.husrestaurant.com	Los Angeles	CA	90034	310-837-0252	
Il Grano 11359 Santa Monica Blvd	Los Angeles	CA	90025	310-477-7886	477-7775
India's Oven 7231 Beverly Blvd Web: www.indiasovenla.com	Los Angeles	CA	90036	323-936-1000	936-1792
India's Tandoori 5468 Wilshire Blvd Web: www.indiastandoori.net	Los Angeles	CA	90035	323-936-2050	936-0187
Ivy The 113 N Robertson Blvd	Los Angeles	CA	90048	310-274-8303	
JAR 8225 Beverly Blvd Web: www.thejar.com	Los Angeles	CA	90048	323-655-6566	655-6577
Jitlada 5233 1/2 W Sunset Blvd	Los Angeles	CA	90027	323-667-9809	663-3104
Kendall's Brasserie & Bar 135 N Grand Ave Web: www.patinagroup.com/kendallsBrasserie	Los Angeles	CA	90012	213-972-7322	972-7331
Kitchen The 4348 Fountain Ave Web: www.thekitchen-silverlake.com	Los Angeles	CA	90029	323-664-3663	
La Barca 2414 S Vermont Ave	Los Angeles	CA	90007	323-735-6567	735-0309
Little Door 8164 W 3rd St Web: www.thelittledoor.com	Los Angeles	CA	90048	323-951-1210	951-0487
Locanda Veneta 8638 W 3rd St Web: www.locandaveneta.net	Los Angeles	CA	90048	310-274-1893	274-4217
Loteria! Grill 6333 W 3rd St Web: www.loteriagrill.com	Los Angeles	CA	90036	323-930-2211	930-2282
Lucques 8474 Melrose Ave Web: www.lucques.com	Los Angeles	CA	90069	323-655-6277	655-3925
Marino 6001 Melrose Ave	Los Angeles	CA	90038	323-466-8812	466-9010
Mario's Peruvian 5786 Melrose Ave	Los Angeles	CA	90038	323-466-4181	
Marouch 4905 Santa Monica Blvd Web: www.marouchrestaurant.com	Los Angeles	CA	90029	323-662-9325	664-4229
Moishe's 6333 W 3rd St	Los Angeles	CA	90036	323-936-4998	
Mori Sushi 11500 W Pico Blvd Web: www.morisushi.org	Los Angeles	CA	90064	310-479-3939	479-2525
Morton's the Steakhouse 435 S La Cienega Blvd Web: www.mortons.com	Los Angeles	CA	90048	310-246-1501	246-1203
Nick & Stef's Steakhouse 330 S Hope St Web: www.patinagroup.com	Los Angeles	CA	90071	213-680-0330	680-0052
Ocean Seafood 750 N Hill St Web: www.oceansf.com	Los Angeles	CA	90012	213-687-3088	687-8549
Palms Thai 5900 Hollywood Blvd	Los Angeles	CA	90028	323-462-5073	
Pane e Vino 8265 Beverly Blvd Web: www.panevinola.com	Los Angeles	CA	90048	323-651-4600	966-2776
Papa Cristos 2771 W Pico Blvd Web: www.papacristo.com	Los Angeles	CA	90006	323-737-2970	737-3571
Patina 141 S Grand Ave Web: www.patinagroup.com	Los Angeles	CA	90012	213-972-3331	972-3531
R-23 923 E 2nd St Web: www.r23.com	Los Angeles	CA	90013	213-687-7178	687-7187
Rambutan Thai 2835 W Sunset Blvd Web: www.rambutanthai.com	Los Angeles	CA	90026	213-273-8424	413-0092
Seoul Jung 930 Wilshire Blvd Web: www.wilshiregrand.com	Los Angeles	CA	90017	213-688-7880	612-3976
Shabu Shabu House 127 Japanese Village Plaza Mall	Los Angeles	CA	90012	213-680-3890	810-1348
Simon LA 8555 Beverly Blvd Hotel Sofitel	Los Angeles	CA	90048	310-278-5444	
Sunnin 1776 Westwood Blvd Web: www.sunnin.com	Los Angeles	CA	90024	310-475-3358	
Tam O'Shanter Inn 2980 Los Feliz Blvd Web: www.lawrysonline.com	Los Angeles	CA	90039	323-664-0228	664-4915
Tantra 3705 W Sunset Blvd Web: www.tantrasunset.com	Los Angeles	CA	90026	323-663-8268	666-5522
Taylor's Steak House 3361 W 8th St Web: www.taylorssteakhouse.com	Los Angeles	CA	90005	213-382-8449	382-2372
Traxx 800 N Alameda St Web: www.traxxrestaurant.com	Los Angeles	CA	90012	213-625-1999	625-2999
Tuk Tuk Thai 8875 W Pico Blvd Web: www.tuktukla.com	Los Angeles	CA	90035	310-860-1872	492-0003
Vermont 1714 N Vermont Ave Web: www.vermontrestaurantonline.com	Los Angeles	CA	90027	323-661-6163	661-6206
Versailles 10319 Venice Blvd	Los Angeles	CA	90034	310-558-3168	558-1817
Water Grill 544 S Grand Ave Web: www.watergrill.com	Los Angeles	CA	90071	213-891-0900	629-1891
Zucca Ristorante 801 S Figueroa St Web: www.patinagroup.com	Los Angeles	CA	90017	213-614-7800	614-7887
Chi Dynasty 1813 Hillhurst Ave Web: www.chidynasty.com	Los Feliz	CA	90027	323-667-3388	667-3393
Nobu 3835 Crosscreek Rd Web: www.nobumatsuhisa.com	Malibu	CA	90265	310-317-9140	317-9136

Name / Address	City	State	ZIP	Phone	Fax
Appetez 825 W Roseburg Ave	Modesto	CA	95350	209-577-5099	577-5598
Web: www.appetez.com					
Dewz 1505 J St	Modesto	CA	95354	209-549-1101	549-0454
Web: www.dewzrestaunt.com					
El Rosal 3430 Tully Rd	Modesto	CA	95350	209-523-7871	
Fruit Yard The 7948 Yosemite Blvd	Modesto	CA	95357	209-577-3093	577-0600
Web: www.thefruityard.com					
Fuzio Universal Pasta 1020 10th St Suite 100	Modesto	CA	95354	209-557-9711	557-9717
Web: www.fuzio.com					
Galletto Ristorante 1101 J St	Modesto	CA	95354	209-523-4500	523-1213
Web: www.galletto.biz					
Hazel's Elegant Dining 431 12th St	Modesto	CA	95354	209-578-3463	578-0403
Marcella Restaurant 3507 Tully Rd	Modesto	CA	95350	209-577-3777	
MikiSushi 180 Leveland Ln	Modesto	CA	95350	209-524-3555	524-3555
Web: www.mikisushi.com					
Minnie's 107 McHenry Ave	Modesto	CA	95354	209-524-4621	524-6043
Noah's Hof Brau 1311 J St	Modesto	CA	95354	209-527-1090	527-8039
Orient House 609 Tully Rd	Modesto	CA	95350	209-577-2099	
Papachino's 1212 J St	Modesto	CA	95354	209-578-5225	
Papapavlo's 1320 Standiford Ave	Modesto	CA	95350	209-525-3995	525-3795
Pub Wexford's 3313 McHenry Ave	Modesto	CA	95350	209-576-7939	576-7934
Web: www.pwexpub.com					
Strings Italian Cafe 2601 Oakdale Rd	Modesto	CA	95355	209-578-9777	578-5266
Tasty Thai 1401 Coffee Rd	Modesto	CA	95355	209-571-8424	571-8164
Torii Japanese Restaurant 2401 E Orangeburg Ave Suite 590	Modesto	CA	95355	209-529-8697	
Velvet Grill & Creamery 2204 McHenry Ave	Modesto	CA	95350	209-544-9029	
Web: www.velvetgrill.net					
Verona's Cucina Italiana 1700 McHenry Ave	Modesto	CA	95354	209-549-8876	549-8869
Abalonetti Seafood Trattoria 57 Fisherman's Wharf Suite 1	Monterey	CA	93940	831-373-1851	373-2058
Web: www.restauranteur.com/abalonetti					
Bullwacker's 653 Cannery Row	Monterey	CA	93940	831-373-1353	373-0196
Web: www.bullwackers.com					
Cafe Fina 47 Fisherman's Wharf Suite 1	Monterey	CA	93940	831-372-5200	372-5209
Web: www.cafefina.com					
Chef Lee's 2031 N Fremont Blvd	Monterey	CA	93940	831-375-9551	656-9376
Domenico's on the Wharf 50 Fisherman's Wharf # 1	Monterey	CA	93940	831-372-3655	372-2073
Web: www.domenicosmonterey.com					
Duck Club The 400 Cannery Row	Monterey	CA	93940	831-646-1706	646-5425
Web: www.montereyplazahotel.com					
Epsilon Greek Restaurant 422 Tyler St	Monterey	CA	93940	831-655-8108	655-1791
Gilbert's on the Wharf 30 Fisherman's Wharf	Monterey	CA	93940	831-375-3113	375-3124
Indian Summer 220 Olivier St	Monterey	CA	93940	831-372-4744	
Montrio 414 Calle Principal	Monterey	CA	93940	831-648-8880	648-8241
Web: www.montrio.com					
Old Fishermans Grotto 39 Fishermans Wharf	Monterey	CA	93940	831-375-4604	375-0391
Web: www.oldfishermansgrotto.com					
Rosine's 434 Alvarado St	Monterey	CA	93940	831-375-1400	375-2636
Web: www.rosinesmonterey.com					
Sardine Factory The 701 Wave St	Monterey	CA	93940	831-373-3775	373-4241
Web: www.sardinefactory.com					
Stokes Restaurant & Bar 500 Hartnell St	Monterey	CA	93940	831-373-1110	373-1202
Web: www.stokesadobe.com					
Tarpy's Roadhouse 2999 Monterey-Salinas Hwy	Monterey	CA	93940	831-647-1444	
Web: www.tarpys.com					
Whaling Station Prime Steaks & Seafood 763 Wave St	Monterey	CA	93940	831-373-3778	373-2460
Web: www.whalingstationmonterey.com					
Fleming's Prime Steakhouse & Wine Bar 1300 Dove St Suite 105	Newport Beach	CA	92660	949-222-2223	222-0313
Web: www.flemingssteakhouse.com					
A Cote 5478 College Ave	Oakland	CA	94618	510-655-6469	655-6716
Web: www.acoterestaurant.com					
Banana Blossom Thai 4228 Pk Blvd	Oakland	CA	94602	510-336-0990	
Web: www.bananablossomthai.com					
Battambang 850 Broadway	Oakland	CA	94607	510-839-8815	
Bay Wolf Restaurant 3853 Piedmont Ave	Oakland	CA	94611	510-655-6004	
Web: www.baywolf.com					
Dopo/Adesso 4293 Piedmont Ave	Oakland	CA	94611	510-652-3676	597-0265
Web: www.dopoadesso.com/dopo					
El Huarache Azteca 3842 International Blvd	Oakland	CA	94601	510-533-2395	
Everett & Jones Barbeque 126 Broadway	Oakland	CA	94617	510-663-2350	663-8856
Web: www.eandjbbq.com					
Holy Land 677 Rand Ave	Oakland	CA	94610	510-272-0535	
La Taza de Cafe 3909 Grand Ave	Oakland	CA	94610	510-658-2373	658-2549
Web: www.latazadecafe.com					
Le Cheval Restaurant 1007 Clay St	Oakland	CA	94607	510-763-8495	763-7610
Web: www.lecheval.com					
Legendary Palace 708 Franklin St	Oakland	CA	94607	510-663-9188	663-3163
Mama's Royal Cafe 4012 Broadway	Oakland	CA	94611	510-547-7600	
Marica Seafood Restaurant 5301 College Ave	Oakland	CA	94618	510-985-8388	
Meritage 41 Tunnel Rd	Oakland	CA	94623	510-549-8510	
Mezze *Mezze Restaurant & Bar* 3407 Lakeshore Ave	Oakland	CA	94610	510-663-2500	
Web: www.mezze.com					
Milano Ristorante 3425 Grand Ave	Oakland	CA	94610	510-763-0300	763-1171
Nan Yang Rockridge Restaurant 6048 College Ave	Oakland	CA	94618	510-655-3298	
Oliveto Cafe & Restaurant 5655 College Ave	Oakland	CA	94618	510-547-5356	
Web: www.oliveto.com					
Pho84 354 17th St	Oakland	CA	94612	510-832-1338	
Quinn's Lighthouse 1951 Embarcadero Cove	Oakland	CA	94606	510-536-2050	535-1285
Web: www.quinnslighthouse.com					
Restaurant Peony 388 9th St Suite 288	Oakland	CA	94607	510-286-8866	286-8868
ScottÆs Seafood Grill & Bar *Jack London Square* 2 Broadway	Oakland	CA	94607	510-444-3456	302-0995
Web: www.scottsrestaurants.com					
Soi Four Bangkok Eatery 5421 College Ave	Oakland	CA	94618	510-655-0889	
Spettro 3355 Lakeshore Ave	Oakland	CA	94610	510-451-7738	
Uzen Japanese Cuisine 5415 College Ave	Oakland	CA	94618	510-654-7753	
PlumpJack Cafe 1920 Squaw Valley Rd PO Box 2407	Olympic Valley	CA	96146	530-583-1576	583-1734*
**Fax:* Hotel ■ *Web:* www.plumpjack.com					
Baja Fresh 2350 E Vineyard Ave	Oxnard	CA	93036	805-988-7878	988-7979
Web: www.bajafresh.com					
Big Daddy O's Beach BBQ 2333 Roosevelt Blvd	Oxnard	CA	93035	805-984-0014	
BJ's Restaurant & Brewery 461 Esplanade Dr	Oxnard	CA	93030	805-485-1124	485-5293
Web: www.bjsbrewhouse.com					
Cabo Seafood Grill & Cantina 1041 S Oxnard Blvd	Oxnard	CA	93030	805-487-6933	487-6954
Web: www.caboseafoodgrill.com					
El Ranchero 131 W 2nd St	Oxnard	CA	93030	805-486-5665	
Green Burrito 1801 E Ventura Blvd	Oxnard	CA	93030	805-983-7117	
Kampai Japanese Restaurant 2367 N Oxnard Blvd	Oxnard	CA	93036	805-983-3333	988-1482
Korean Barbeque Swan 2061 N Oxnard Blvd	Oxnard	CA	93030	805-278-9611	
Pepe's 200 Rossmore Dr	Oxnard	CA	93035	805-985-2880	
Pilar's Cafe 746 S 'A' St	Oxnard	CA	93030	805-487-1444	
Pirates Grub & Grog 450 S Victoria Ave	Oxnard	CA	93030	805-984-0046	382-6623
Web: www.piratesgrubngrog.net					
Plaza Grill 600 E Esplanade Dr	Oxnard	CA	93030	805-278-5070	485-2061
Favaloro's 545 Lighthouse Ave	Pacific Grove	CA	93950	831-373-8523	
Web: www.favalorosbignightbistro.com					
Passionfish 701 Lighthouse Ave	Pacific Grove	CA	93950	831-655-3311	655-3454
Web: www.passionfish.net					
Vito's 1180 Forest Ave	Pacific Grove	CA	93950	831-375-3070	
Pearl Dragon 15229 W Sunset Blvd	Pacific Palisades	CA	90272	310-459-9790	459-9560
Web: www.thepearldragon.com					
Al Dente Pasta 491 N Palm Canyon Dr	Palm Springs	CA	92262	760-325-1160	325-2199
Web: www.aldente-palmsprings.com					
Chop House 262 S Palm Canyon Dr	Palm Springs	CA	92262	760-320-4500	320-6940
El Mirasol Regional Cuisines of Mexico 140 E Palm Canyon Dr	Palm Springs	CA	92264	760-323-0721	323-0692
Europa Restaurant 1620 S Indian Trail	Palm Springs	CA	92264	760-327-2314	322-3794
TF: 800-245-2314 ■ *Web:* www.villaroyale.com					
Falls Prime Steakhouse 155 S Palm Canyon Dr 2nd Fl	Palm Springs	CA	92262	760-416-8664	416-8656
Web: www.thefallsprimesteakhouse.com					
Fisherman's Market & Grill 235 S Indian Canyon Dr	Palm Springs	CA	92262	760-327-1766	
Web: www.fishermans.com					
Johanne's 196 S Indian Canyon Dr	Palm Springs	CA	92262	760-778-0017	778-1447
Web: www.johannesrestaurants.com					
John Henry's Cafe 1785 E Tahquitz Canyon Way	Palm Springs	CA	92262	760-327-7667	
Kaiser Grille 205 S Palm Canyon Dr	Palm Springs	CA	92262	760-323-1003	
Las Casuelas Terraza 222 S Palm Canyon Dr	Palm Springs	CA	92262	760-325-2794	327-4174
Le Vallauris 385 W Tahquitz Canyon Way	Palm Springs	CA	92262	760-325-5059	325-7602
Web: www.palmsprings.com					
Leon's Bar & Grill 1100 Murray Canyon Dr	Palm Springs	CA	92264	760-416-4421	416-1902
Lyons English Grill 233 E Palm Canyon Dr	Palm Springs	CA	92264	760-327-1551	322-9833
Melvyn's 200 W Ramon Rd	Palm Springs	CA	92264	760-325-2323	325-0710
Web: www.inglesideinn.com					
Norma's 4200 E Palm Canyon Dr	Palm Springs	CA	92264	760-770-5000	342-2188
Web: www.starwoodhotels.com/lemeridien					
Sammy G's 265 S Palm Canyon Dr	Palm Springs	CA	92262	760-320-8041	
Spencer's Restaurant 701 W Barista Rd	Palm Springs	CA	92262	760-327-3446	327-5125
Web: www.spencersrestaurant.com					
Teriyaki Yogi 555 S Palm Canyon Dr	Palm Springs	CA	92264	760-323-1162	
Thai Smile 651 N Palm Canyon Dr	Palm Springs	CA	92262	760-320-5503	320-5584
Arroyo Chop House 536 S Arroyo Pkwy	Pasadena	CA	91105	626-577-7463	577-1089
Web: www.arroyochophouse.com					
Crocodile Cafe 140 S Lake Ave	Pasadena	CA	91101	626-449-9900	449-6968
Web: www.cafe140south.com					
Parkway Grill 510 S Arroyo Pkwy	Pasadena	CA	91105	626-795-1001	796-6221
Web: www.theparkwaygrill.com					
Texas Cattle Co 1429 N China Lake Blvd	Ridgecrest	CA	93555	760-446-6602	
Akina Sushi - Teppan Restaurant 195 E Alessandro Blvd	Riverside	CA	92508	951-789-0443	
Chen Ling Palace 9856 Magnolia Ave	Riverside	CA	92503	951-351-8511	351-8162
Ciao Bella 1630 Spruce St	Riverside	CA	92507	951-781-8840	781-1970
Web: www.ciaobellariverside.com					
City Cuisine The 2586 Main St	Riverside	CA	92501	951-682-9566	682-8649
Duane's 3649 Mission Inn Ave	Riverside	CA	92501	951-784-0300	683-1342
Web: www.missioninn.com					
Ho Ho 3411 Madison St	Riverside	CA	92504	951-637-2411	
Kountry Folks 3653 La Sierra Ave	Riverside	CA	92505	951-354-0437	354-7728
Web: www.kountry.com					
Las Campanas 3649 Mission Inn Ave	Riverside	CA	92501	951-784-0300	328-6915
Mario's Place 3646 Mission Inn Ave	Riverside	CA	92501	951-684-7755	
Web: www.mariosplace.com					
Sevilla Riverside 3252 Mission Inn Ave	Riverside	CA	92507	951-778-0611	530-0083
Web: www.cafesevilla.com					
33rd Street Bistro 3301 Folsom Blvd	Sacramento	CA	95816	916-455-2233	457-2189
Web: www.33rdstreetbistro.com					

Name / Address	City	State	ZIP	Phone	Fax
Aioli Bodega Espanola 1800 L St	Sacramento	CA	95814	916-447-9440	
Alamar Restaurant & Marina 5999 Garden Hwy	Sacramento	CA	95837	916-922-0200	
Web: www.alamarmarina.com					
Biba 2801 Capitol Ave	Sacramento	CA	95816	916-455-2422	455-0452
Web: www.biba-restaurant.com					
Caballo Blanco Restaurante 5604 Franklin Blvd	Sacramento	CA	95824	916-428-6706	
Casablanca 3516 Fair Oaks Blvd	Sacramento	CA	95864	916-979-1160	
El Novillero 4216 Franklin Blvd	Sacramento	CA	95820	916-456-4287	456-4149
Web: www.elnov.com					
Enotria Cafe & Wine Bar 1431 Del Paso Blvd	Sacramento	CA	95815	916-922-6792	
Ernesto's Mexican Food 1901 16th St	Sacramento	CA	95814	916-441-5850	441-2154
Web: www.ernestosmexicanfood.com					
Esquire Grill 1213 K St	Sacramento	CA	95814	916-448-8900	
Web: www.paragarys.com					
Firehouse The 1112 2nd St	Sacramento	CA	95814	916-442-4772	442-6617
Web: www.firehouseoldsac.com					
Gonuls J Street Cafe 3839 J St	Sacramento	CA	95816	916-457-1155	457-4492
Greek Village Inn 65 University Dr	Sacramento	CA	95864	916-922-6334	922-2321
House of Chang 1589 W El Camino Ave	Sacramento	CA	95833	916-925-2138	
Il Fornaio 400 Capitol Mall	Sacramento	CA	95814	916-446-4100	
Web: www.ilfornaio.com					
JR's Texas Bar-B-Que 180 Otto Cir	Sacramento	CA	95822	916-424-3520	424-9915
Web: www.jrtexasbbq.com					
Kamon 2210 16th St	Sacramento	CA	95818	916-443-8888	
Kaveri Madras Cuisine *NULL* 1148 Fulton Ave Suite A	Sacramento	CA	95825	916-481-9970	
Kitchen The 2225 Hurley Way	Sacramento	CA	95825	916-568-7171	
Lemon Grass 601 Munroe St	Sacramento	CA	95825	916-486-4891	486-1627
Web: www.lemongrassrestaurant.com					
Lucca Restaurant & Bar 1615 J St	Sacramento	CA	95814	916-669-5300	669-2848
Web: www.luccarestaurant.com					
MacQue's 8101 Elder Creek Rd	Sacramento	CA	95824	916-381-4119	381-3723
Web: www.macques.com					
Marrakech 1833 Fulton Ave	Sacramento	CA	95825	916-486-1944	
Web: www.marrakechrestaurant.com					
Nishiki Sushi 1501 16th St	Sacramento	CA	95814	916-446-3629	
PF Chang's China Bistro 1530 J St Suite 100	Sacramento	CA	95814	916-288-0970	288-0979
Web: www.pfchangs.com					
Piatti Ristorante & Bar Sacramento 571 Pavilions Ln	Sacramento	CA	95825	916-649-8885	649-8907
Web: www.piatti.com					
Rio City Cafe 1110 Front St	Sacramento	CA	95814	916-442-8226	
Web: www.riocitycafe.com					
Riverside Clubhouse 2633 Riverside Blvd	Sacramento	CA	95818	916-448-9988	448-9388
Web: www.riversideclubhouse.com					
Scott's Seafood Grill & Bar 545 Munroe St	Sacramento	CA	95825	916-489-1822	489-2447
Web: www.scottsseafood.net					
Tapa the World 2115 J St	Sacramento	CA	95816	916-442-4353	442-4348
Web: www.tapatheworld.com					
Texas West Bar-B-Que 1600 Fulton Ave	Sacramento	CA	95825	916-483-7427	483-8636
Web: www.texaswestbbq.com					
Thai Palms 943 Howe Ave	Sacramento	CA	95825	916-929-5915	
Tower Cafe 1518 Broadway	Sacramento	CA	95818	916-441-0222	
Web: www.towercafe.com					
Waterboy The 2000 Capitol Ave	Sacramento	CA	95811	916-498-9891	498-9893
Web: www.waterboyrestaurant.com					
Zinfandel Grille 2384 Fair Oaks Blvd	Sacramento	CA	95825	916-485-7100	484-7728
Costa Azul 7218 Franklin Blvd	Sacremento	CA	95823	916-424-9608	
Alfredo's Pizza & Pasta 251 W Baseline Rd	San Bernardino	CA	92410	909-885-0218	
Le Rendez-Vous 4775 N Sierra Way	San Bernardino	CA	92404	909-883-1231	
Web: www.lerendezvous.com					
Lotus Garden 111 E Hospitality Ln	San Bernardino	CA	92408	909-381-6171	381-1757
Manhattan Grill The 285 E Hospitality Ln	San Bernardino	CA	92408	909-889-0133	381-4299
Addison The Grand Del Mar 5200 Grand Del Mar Way	San Diego	CA	92130	858-314-1900	314-2001
Web: www.addisondelmar.com					
Albie's Beef Inn 1201 Hotel Cir S	San Diego	CA	92108	619-291-1103	
Alfiere Mediterranean Bistro 1590 Harbor Island Dr	San Diego	CA	92101	619-692-2778	
Web: www.alfiereonline.com					
Andiamo 5950 Santo Rd	San Diego	CA	92124	858-277-3501	
Andre's 1235 Morena Blvd	San Diego	CA	92110	619-275-4114	276-4245
Web: www.andresres.com					
Ashoka the Great 9474 Black Mountain Rd	San Diego	CA	92126	858-695-9749	695-9279
Bandar 845 4th Ave	San Diego	CA	92101	619-238-0101	232-7348
Web: www.bandarrestaurant.com					
Bernard'O Restaurant 12457 Rancho Bernardo Rd	San Diego	CA	92128	858-487-7171	487-7185
Web: www.bernardorestaurant.com					
Berta's 3928 Twiggs St	San Diego	CA	92110	619-295-2343	
Web: www.bertasinoldtown.com					
Bertrand at Mister A's 2550 5th Ave 12th Fl	San Diego	CA	92103	619-239-1377	239-1379
Web: www.bertrandatmisteras.com					
Blue Point Coastal Cuisine 565 5th Ave	San Diego	CA	92101	619-233-6623	
Buon Appetito 1609 India St	San Diego	CA	92101	619-238-9880	
Web: www.buonappetito.signosandiego.com					
Cafe Japengo 8960 University Ctr Ln	San Diego	CA	92122	858-450-3355	552-6104
Web: www.cafejapengo.com					
Cafe on Park 3831 Pk Blvd	San Diego	CA	92103	619-293-7275	
Cafe Pacifica 2414 San Diego Ave	San Diego	CA	92110	619-291-6666	291-0122
Web: www.panpacific.com					
Cafe Zucchero 1731 India St	San Diego	CA	92101	619-531-1731	
Web: www.cafezucchero.signonsandiego.com					
Candelas 416 3rd Ave	San Diego	CA	92101	619-702-4455	
Web: www.candelas-sd.com					
Celadon 3671 5th Ave	San Diego	CA	92103	619-297-8424	
Web: www.celadonrestaurant.com					
Chateau Orleans 926 Turquoise St	San Diego	CA	92109	858-488-6744	488-3745
Web: www.chateauorleans.com					
Cohn Restaurant Group 2790 Truxtun Rd Suite 120	San Diego	CA	92106	619-236-1299	236-1300
Web: www.cohnrestaurants.com					
Corvette Diner 3946 5th Ave	San Diego	CA	92103	619-542-1001	
Croce's Restaurant 802 5th Ave	San Diego	CA	92101	619-233-4355	232-9836
Web: www.croces.com					
De Medici 815 5th Ave	San Diego	CA	92101	619-702-7228	
Dobson's 956 Broadway Cir	San Diego	CA	92101	619-231-6771	
Web: www.dobsonsrestaurant.com					
Edgewater Grill 861 W Harbor Dr	San Diego	CA	92101	619-232-7581	
Web: www.edgewatergrill.com					
El Bizcocho 17550 Bernardo Oaks Dr	San Diego	CA	92128	858-675-8500	675-8501
Web: www.ranchobernardoinn.com					
Emerald Chinese Seafood Restaurant 3709 Convoy St	San Diego	CA	92111	858-565-6888	565-6688
Web: www.emeraldrestaurant.com					
Field The 544 5th Ave	San Diego	CA	92101	619-232-9840	232-9842
Web: www.thefield.com					
Fleming's Prime Steakhouse & Wine Bar 8970 University Ctr Ln	San Diego	CA	92122	858-535-0078	535-0096
French Market Grille 15717 Bernardo Heights Pkwy	San Diego	CA	92128	858-485-8055	673-5471
George's on Fifth 835 5th Ave	San Diego	CA	92101	619-702-0444	
Web: www.georgesonfifth.com					
Georgia's Greek Cuisine 3550 Rosecrans St	San Diego	CA	92110	619-523-1007	523-2455
Web: www.georgiasgreekcuisine.com					
Greek Palace 8878 Clairmont Mesa Blvd	San Diego	CA	92123	858-573-0155	573-9645
Web: www.greekpalace.com					
Greystone the Steakhouse 658 5th Ave	San Diego	CA	92101	619-232-0225	233-3606
Web: www.greystonethesteakhouse.com					
Gulf Coast Grill 4130 Pk Blvd	San Diego	CA	92103	619-295-2244	
Hob-Nob Hill 2271 1st Ave	San Diego	CA	92101	619-239-8176	
Humphreys Restaurant 2241 Shelter Island Dr	San Diego	CA	92106	619-224-3411	523-1064
Web: www.humphreysbythebay.com					
Ichiban 1449 University Ave	San Diego	CA	92103	619-299-7203	299-7514
Web: www.ichibansushisandiego.com					
Indigo Grill 1536 India St	San Diego	CA	92101	619-234-6802	234-6868
Web: www.cohnrestaurants.com					
Jack & Giulio's 2391 San Diego Ave	San Diego	CA	92110	619-294-2074	
Jasmine 4609 Convoy St	San Diego	CA	92111	858-268-0888	268-7729
JSix Restaurant 616 J St	San Diego	CA	92101	619-531-8744	393-0131
Web: www.jsixrestaurant.com					
Kemo Sabe 3958 5th Ave	San Diego	CA	92103	619-220-6802	
La Gran Tapa 611 B St	San Diego	CA	92101	619-234-8272	
Web: www.lagrantapa.com					
Lamont Street Grill 4445 Lamont St	San Diego	CA	92109	858-270-3060	
Lou & Mickey's 224 5th Ave	San Diego	CA	92101	619-237-4900	233-4977
Web: www.louandmickeys.com					
Mandarin Dynasty 1458 University Ave	San Diego	CA	92103	619-298-8899	298-5694
Marriott International Inc 11966 El Camino Real	San Diego	CA	92130	858-369-6005	369-6066
Web: www.arterrarestaurant.com					
Morton's the Steakhouse 285 J St	San Diego	CA	92101	619-696-3369	
Web: www.mortons.com					
Old Trieste 2335 Morena Blvd	San Diego	CA	92110	619-276-1841	
Web: www.oldtriesterestaurant.com					
Osteria Panevino 722 5th Ave	San Diego	CA	92101	619-595-7959	
Web: www.osteriapanevino.com					
Pampas Bar & Grill 8690 Aero Dr	San Diego	CA	92123	858-278-5971	278-9674
Web: www.pampasrestaurant.com					
Panda Inn 506 Horton Plaza	San Diego	CA	92101	619-233-7800	
Park House Eatery 4574 Pk Blvd	San Diego	CA	92116	619-295-7275	
Web: www.parkhouseeatery.com					
PF Chang's China Bistro 7077 Friars Rd	San Diego	CA	92108	619-260-8484	260-0808
Web: www.pfchangs.com					
Phil's BBQ 3750 Sports Arena Blvd	San Diego	CA	92110	619-226-6333	
Web: www.philsbbq.net					
Princess Pub & Grille 1665 India St	San Diego	CA	92101	619-702-3021	
Web: www.princesspub.com					
Rainwater's 1202 Kettner Blvd	San Diego	CA	92101	619-233-5757	
Rama 327 4th Ave	San Diego	CA	92101	619-501-8424	546-5304
Web: www.ramarestaurant.com					
Rei do Gado 939 4th Ave	San Diego	CA	92101	619-702-8464	
Web: www.reidogado.net					
Roy's 8670 Genesee Ave	San Diego	CA	92122	858-455-1616	455-7700
Web: www.roysrestaurant.com					
Ruth's Chris Steakhouse 1355 N Harbor Dr	San Diego	CA	92101	619-233-1422	
Web: www.ruthschris.com					
Saigon on Fifth 3900 5th Ave Suite 120	San Diego	CA	92103	619-220-8828	

				Phone	Fax
Shien of Osaka *akai hana* 16769 Bernardo Ctr Dr Suite K-11	San Diego	CA	92128	858-451-0074	451-2485
Star of India 423 F St *Web:* www.starofindia.com	San Diego	CA	92101	619-234-8000	
Star of the Sea 1360 N Harbor Dr *Web:* www.starofthesea.com	San Diego	CA	92101	619-232-7408	232-2128
Sushi Ota 4529 Mission Bay Dr	San Diego	CA	92109	858-270-5670	
Taka Restaurant 555 5th Ave *Web:* www.takasushi.com	San Diego	CA	92101	619-338-0555	
Tapas Picasso 3923 4th Ave *Web:* www.tapaspicasso.com	San Diego	CA	92103	619-294-3061	660-6888
Taste of Thai 527 University Ave	San Diego	CA	92103	619-291-7525	
Terra 7091 El Cajon Blvd *Web:* www.terrasd.com	San Diego	CA	92115	619-293-7088	293-7193
Tom Ham's Lighthouse 2150 Harbor Island Dr *Web:* www.tomhamslighthouse.com	San Diego	CA	92101	619-291-9110	
Trattoria La Strada 702 5th Ave *Web:* www.trattorialastrada.com	San Diego	CA	92101	619-239-3400	
Westgate Room The 1055 2nd Ave *TF:* 800-522-1564	San Diego	CA	92101	619-238-1818	
WineSellar & Brasserie 9550 Waples St Suite 115 *Web:* www.winesellar.com	San Diego	CA	92121	858-450-9557	
1550 Hyde Cafe & Wine Bar 1550 Hyde St	San Francisco	CA	94109	415-775-1550	
2223 Restaurant & Bar 2223 Market St *Web:* www.2223restaurant.com	San Francisco	CA	94114	415-431-0692	865-0836
Absinthe Brasserie & Bar 398 Hayes St *Web:* www.absinthe.com	San Francisco	CA	94102	415-551-1590	255-2385
Acquerello 1722 Sacramento St *Web:* www.acquerello.com	San Francisco	CA	94109	415-567-5432	567-6432
Albona Ristorante Istriano 545 Francisco St	San Francisco	CA	94133	415-441-1040	
Alfred's Steakhouse 659 Merchant St *Web:* www.alfredssteakhouse.com	San Francisco	CA	94111	415-781-7058	397-1928
Ana Mandara 891 Beach St *Web:* www.anamandara.com	San Francisco	CA	94109	415-771-6800	
Antica Trattoria 2400 Polk St	San Francisco	CA	94109	415-928-5797	
Anzu 222 Mason St Hotel Nikko *Web:* www.restaurantanzu.com	San Francisco	CA	94102	415-394-1100	394-1102
asiaSF 201 9th St *Web:* www.asiasf.com	San Francisco	CA	94103	415-255-2742	
Aziza 5800 Geary Blvd *Web:* www.aziza-sf.com	San Francisco	CA	94121	415-752-2222	
Betelnut 2030 Union St *Web:* www.betelnutrestaurant.com	San Francisco	CA	94123	415-929-8855	929-8894
Big Four Restaurant 1075 California St	San Francisco	CA	94108	415-771-1140	345-2891
Bistro Aix 3340 Steiner St *Web:* www.bistroaix.com	San Francisco	CA	94123	415-202-0100	202-0153
Bix Restaurant 56 Gold St *Web:* www.bixrestaurant.com	San Francisco	CA	94133	415-433-6300	433-4574
Blue Mermaid Chowder House & Bar 471 Jefferson St *Web:* www.bluemermaidsf.com	San Francisco	CA	94109	415-771-2222	447-4014
Blue Plate The 3218 Mission St *Web:* www.blueplatesf.com	San Francisco	CA	94110	415-282-6777	282-8053
Boulevard 1 Mission St *Web:* www.boulevardrestaurant.com	San Francisco	CA	94105	415-543-6084	495-2936
Cafe Kati 1963 Sutter St *Web:* www.cafekati.com	San Francisco	CA	94115	415-775-7313	
Campton Place Restaurant 340 Stockton St *Web:* www.camptonplacesf.com	San Francisco	CA	94108	415-781-5555	955-5559
Chappau 126 Clement St *Web:* www.chapeausf.com	San Francisco	CA	94118	415-387-0408	
Chaya Brasserie 132 The Embarcadero *Web:* www.thechaya.com	San Francisco	CA	94105	415-777-8688	247-9952
Chenery Park 683 Chenery St *Web:* www.chenerypark.com	San Francisco	CA	94131	415-337-8537	337-0390
Chez Papa Bistrot 1401 18th St *Web:* www.chezpapasf.com	San Francisco	CA	94107	415-824-8205	
Chez Spencer 82 14th St *Web:* www.chezspencer.net	San Francisco	CA	94103	415-864-2191	864-2199
Coco 500 500 Brannan St *Web:* www.coco500.com	San Francisco	CA	94107	415-543-2222	543-2999
Cosmopolitan Cafe 121 Spear St *Web:* www.cosmopolitansf.com	San Francisco	CA	94105	415-543-4001	
Crustacean 1475 Polk St 3rd Fl *Web:* www.anfamily.com	San Francisco	CA	94109	415-776-2722	
Delfina 3621 18th St *Web:* www.delfinasf.com	San Francisco	CA	94110	415-552-4055	552-4095
Dottie's True Blue Cafe 522 Jones St	San Francisco	CA	94102	415-885-2767	
Ebisu 1283 9th Ave *Web:* www.ebisusushi.com	San Francisco	CA	94122	415-566-1770	
Eos 901 Cole St *Web:* www.eossf.com	San Francisco	CA	94117	415-566-3063	
Farallon 450 Post St *Web:* www.farallonrestaurant.com	San Francisco	CA	94102	415-956-6969	834-1234
Fior D'Italia 2237 Mason St *Web:* www.fior.com	San Francisco	CA	94133	415-986-1886	
Firefly 4288 24th St *Web:* www.fireflyrestaurant.com	San Francisco	CA	94114	415-821-7652	821-1512
Fleur de Lys 777 Sutter St *Web:* www.fleurdelyssf.com	San Francisco	CA	94109	415-673-7779	
Foreign Cinema 2534 Mission St *Web:* www.foreigncinema.com	San Francisco	CA	94110	415-648-7600	648-7669

				Phone	Fax
Frascati 1901 Hyde St *Web:* www.frascatisf.com	San Francisco	CA	94109	415-928-1406	928-1983
Fringale 570 4th St *Web:* www.fringalesf.com	San Francisco	CA	94107	415-543-0573	
Garcon Restaurant 1101 Valencia St *Web:* www.garconsf.com	San Francisco	CA	94110	415-401-8959	401-8960
Garibaldis 347 Presidio Ave *Web:* www.garibaldisrestaurant.com	San Francisco	CA	94115	415-563-8841	563-3731
Grand Cafe 501 Geary St *Web:* www.grandcafe-sf.com	San Francisco	CA	94102	415-292-0101	292-0150
Greens Fort Mason Ctr Bldg A *Web:* www.greensrestaurant.com	San Francisco	CA	94123	415-771-6222	
Harris' Restaurant 2100 Van Ness Ave *Web:* www.harrisrestaurant.com	San Francisco	CA	94109	415-673-1888	673-8817
Hog Island Oyster Co & Bar 1 Ferry Bldg # 11A *Web:* www.hogislandoysters.com	San Francisco	CA	94111	415-391-7117	391-7118
House 1230 Grant Ave *Web:* www.thehse.com	San Francisco	CA	94133	415-986-8612	
House of Prime Rib 1906 Van Ness Ave	San Francisco	CA	94109	415-885-4605	
Hyde Street Seafood House 1509 Hyde St	San Francisco	CA	94109	415-931-3474	
Incanto 1550 Church St *Web:* www.incanto.biz	San Francisco	CA	94131	415-641-4500	641-4546
Indian Oven 233 Fillmore St *Web:* www.indianovensf.com	San Francisco	CA	94117	415-626-1628	553-3259
Isa 3324 Steiner St *Web:* www.isarestaurant.com	San Francisco	CA	94123	415-567-9588	409-1879
Jardiniere 300 Grove St *Web:* www.jardiniere.com	San Francisco	CA	94102	415-861-5555	861-5580
Kabuto Sushi 5121 Geary St	San Francisco	CA	94118	415-752-5652	
Kokkari Estiatorio 200 Jackson St *Web:* www.kokkari.com	San Francisco	CA	94111	415-981-0983	982-0983
Kyo-ya 2 New Montgomery St *Web:* www.sfpalace.com	San Francisco	CA	94105	415-546-5090	537-6299
La Folie 2316 Polk St *Web:* www.lafolie.com	San Francisco	CA	94109	415-776-5577	776-3431
Level 3 500 Post St *Web:* www.levelthreesf.com	San Francisco	CA	94102	415-771-8600	
Little Nepal 925 Cortland Ave *Web:* www.littlenepalsf.com	San Francisco	CA	94110	415-643-3881	643-8088
Manora's Thai Cuisine 1600 Folsom St *Web:* www.manorathai.com	San Francisco	CA	94103	415-861-6224	861-1731
Masa's Restaurant 648 Bush St *Web:* www.masasrestaurant.com	San Francisco	CA	94108	415-989-7154	989-3141
Maya 303 2nd St *Web:* www.mayasf.com	San Francisco	CA	94107	415-543-2928	543-6679
Maykadeh 470 Green St	San Francisco	CA	94133	415-362-8286	
Millennium 580 Geary St *Web:* www.millenniumrestaurant.com	San Francisco	CA	94102	415-345-3900	345-3941
Morton's The Steakhouse 400 Post St *Web:* www.mortons.com	San Francisco	CA	94102	415-986-5830	986-5829
One Market 1 Market St *Web:* www.onemarket.com	San Francisco	CA	94105	415-777-5577	
Ozumo 161 Steuart St *Web:* www.ozumosanfrancisco.com	San Francisco	CA	94105	415-882-1333	882-1794
Pane e Vino 1715 Union St *Web:* www.paneevinotrattoria.com	San Francisco	CA	94123	415-346-2111	
Park Grill 333 Battery St	San Francisco	CA	94111	415-296-2933	296-2919
Pesce Bar 2227 Polk St *Web:* www.pescebarsf.com	San Francisco	CA	94109	415-928-8025	928-8035
Piperade 1015 Battery St *Web:* www.piperade.com	San Francisco	CA	94111	415-391-2555	391-1159
Postrio 545 Post St *Web:* www.postrio.com	San Francisco	CA	94102	415-776-7825	
Puccini & Pinetti 129 Ellis St *Web:* www.pucciniandpinetti.com	San Francisco	CA	94102	415-392-5500	392-1635
Quince 470 Pacific Ave *Web:* www.quincerestaurant.com	San Francisco	CA	94133	415-775-8500	775-8501
Restaurant Gary Danko 800 N Pt St *Web:* www.garydanko.com	San Francisco	CA	94109	415-749-2060	
Ristorante Bacco 737 Diamond St	San Francisco	CA	94114	415-282-4969	282-1315
Roy's 575 Mission St *Web:* www.roysrestaurant.com	San Francisco	CA	94105	415-777-0277	777-0377
Ruth's Chris Steak House 1601 Van Ness Ave *Web:* www.ruthschris.com	San Francisco	CA	94109	415-673-0557	673-5309
Scala's Bistro 432 Powell St *Web:* www.scalasbistro.com	San Francisco	CA	94102	415-395-8555	395-8549
Schroeder's Cafe 240 Front St *Web:* www.schroederssf.com	San Francisco	CA	94111	415-421-4778	421-2217
Silks 222 Sansome St *TF:* 800-526-6566 ■ *Web:* www.mandarinoriental.com	San Francisco	CA	94104	415-986-2020	
Slanted Door 1 Ferry Bldg Sute 3 *Web:* www.slanteddoor.com	San Francisco	CA	94111	415-861-8032	
Sociale 3665 Sacramento St	San Francisco	CA	94118	415-921-3200	
South Park Cafe 108 S Pk St *Web:* www.southparkcafe.com	San Francisco	CA	94107	415-495-7275	
Straits Restaurant 845 Market St 4th Fl *Web:* www.straitsrestaurants.com	San Francisco	CA	94103	415-668-1783	668-3901
Tommy Toy's Cuisine Chinoise 655 Montgomery St *Web:* www.tommytoys.com	San Francisco	CA	94111	415-397-4888	397-0469
Town Hall 342 Howard St *Web:* www.townhallsf.com	San Francisco	CA	94105	415-908-3900	908-3700
Trattoria Contadina 1800 Mason St **Fax Area Code:* 418 ■ *Web:* www.trattoriacontadina.com	San Francisco	CA	94133	415-982-5728	982-5746*

	City	State	Zip	Phone	Fax
Tsunami Sushi & Sake Bar					
1306 Fulton St	San Francisco	CA	94117	415-567-7664	
Venticello 1257 Taylor St	San Francisco	CA	94108	415-922-2545	776-6583
Web: www.venticello.com					
Yabbies Coastal Kitchen 2237 Polk St	San Francisco	CA	94109	415-474-4088	
Web: www.yabbiesrestaurant.com					
Yank Sing 49 Stevenson St	San Francisco	CA	94105	415-541-4949	541-0308
Web: www.yanksing.com					
Zuni Cafe & Grill 1658 Market St	San Francisco	CA	94102	415-552-2522	
Web: www.zunicafe.com					
71 Sainte Peter 71 N San Pedro St	San Jose	CA	95110	408-971-8523	938-3440
Web: www.71saintpeter.com					
Amber India 377 Santana Row Suite 1140	San Jose	CA	95128	408-248-5400	248-5401
Web: www.amber-india.com					
Aqui Cal-Mex Grill 1145 Lincoln Ave	San Jose	CA	95125	408-995-0381	995-0385
Arcadia 100 W San Carlos St	San Jose	CA	95113	408-278-4555	278-4556
Bella Mia Restaurant & Bar 58 S First St	San Jose	CA	95113	408-280-1993	280-5624
Web: www.bellamia.com					
Blowfish 355 Santana Row Suite 1010	San Jose	CA	95128	408-345-3848	345-3855
Web: www.blowfishsushi.com					
ChaatCafe.com 834 Blossom Hill Rd	San Jose	CA	95123	408-225-2233	516-9059
Web: www.chaatcafes.com					
Cheesecake Factory South San Jose					
925 Blossom Hill Rd	San Jose	CA	95123	408-225-6948	225-6957
Web: www.thecheesecakefactory.com					
Emile's 545 S 2nd St	San Jose	CA	95112	408-289-1960	289-1960
Web: www.emiles.com					
Eulipia Restaurant 374 S 1st St	San Jose	CA	95113	408-280-6161	280-1639
Web: www.eulipia.com					
Gecko Grill 855 N 13th St	San Jose	CA	95112	408-971-1826	971-1809
Grill on The Alley The 172 S Market St	San Jose	CA	95113	408-294-2244	294-2255
Web: www.thegrill.com					
Henry's Hi-life 301 W St John St	San Jose	CA	95110	408-295-5414	295-5431
House of Siam 151 S 2nd St	San Jose	CA	95113	408-295-3397	
Korean Palace 2297A Stevens Creek Blvd	San Jose	CA	95128	408-947-8600	941-1887
Web: www.koreanpalace.com					
Krung Thai 640 S Winchester Ave	San Jose	CA	95128	408-260-8224	
La Foret 21747 Bertram Rd	San Jose	CA	95120	408-997-3458	
Web: www.laforetrestaurant.com					
La Pastaia 233 W Santa Clara St	San Jose	CA	95113	408-286-8686	286-8787
Web: www.lapastaia.com					
Le Papillon 410 Saratoga Ave	San Jose	CA	95129	408-296-3730	247-7812
Web: www.lepapillon.com					
Left Bank 377 Santana Row	San Jose	CA	95128	408-984-3500	984-0300
Web: www.leftbank.com					
Menara 41 E Gish Rd	San Jose	CA	95112	408-453-1983	
Original Joe's 301 S 1st St	San Jose	CA	97113	408-292-7030	
Web: www.originaljoes.com					
Pagoda The 170 S Market St	San Jose	CA	95113	408-998-3937	
Paolo's 333 W San Carlos St Suite 150	San Jose	CA	95110	408-294-2558	294-2595
Web: www.paolosrestaurant.com					
PF Chang's China Bistro 98 S 2nd St	San Jose	CA	95113	408-961-5250	961-5260
Web: www.pfchangs.com					
Picasso's 62 W Santa Clara St	San Jose	CA	95113	408-298-4400	
Web: www.picassostapas.com					
Rosy's Fish City 2882 Story Rd	San Jose	CA	95127	408-272-2088	272-2000
Straits Cafe 333 Santana Row Suite 1100	San Jose	CA	95128	408-246-6320	246-6397
Web: www.straitsrestaurants.com					
Sushi Factory Japanese Restaurant					
4632 Meridian Ave	San Jose	CA	95124	408-723-2598	723-2579
Web: www.sushifactorysj.com					
Teske's Germania 255 N 1st St	San Jose	CA	95113	408-292-0291	292-0347
Web: www.teskes-germania.com					
Tokyo Sushi 1716 Lundy Ave	San Jose	CA	95131	408-452-8868	452-8869
Tomisushi 4336 Moorpark Ave	San Jose	CA	95129	408-257-4722	
Web: www.tomisushi.us					
50 Forks 3601 W Sunflower Ave	Santa Ana	CA	92704	714-429-0918	
Antonello Ristorante 3800 S Plaza Dr	Santa Ana	CA	92704	714-751-7153	751-8650
Web: www.antonello.com					
Colima 130 N Fairview St	Santa Ana	CA	92703	714-836-1254	543-6169
Dayra Restaurant 3800 S Plaza Dr	Santa Ana	CA	92704	714-557-6600	
El Gallo Giro 1442 S Bristol St	Santa Ana	CA	92704	714-549-2011	
Favori 3502 W 1st St	Santa Ana	CA	92703	714-531-6838	
Web: www.favorirestaurant.com					
Ferdussi 3605 S Bristol St	Santa Ana	CA	92704	714-545-9096	545-8240
Web: www.ferdussi.com					
Gypsy Den 125 N Broadway Ave	Santa Ana	CA	92701	714-835-8840	
Web: www.gypsyden.com					
Hacienda The 1725 College Ave	Santa Ana	CA	92706	714-558-1304	
Web: www.the-hacienda.com					
Memphis 201 N Broadway	Santa Ana	CA	92701	714-564-1064	
Olde Ship The 1120 W 17th St	Santa Ana	CA	92706	714-550-6700	550-6702
Web: www.theoldeship.com					
Polly's 2660 N Main St	Santa Ana	CA	92705	714-547-9681	547-5302
Web: www.pollypies.com					
Royal Khyber 1621 W Sunflower Ave	Santa Ana	CA	92706	714-436-1010	436-9242
Web: www.royalkhyber.com					
Spoons California Grill 2601 Hotel Terr	Santa Ana	CA	92705	714-556-0700	957-8997
Web: www.spoonsoc.com					
Tangata 2002 N Main St	Santa Ana	CA	92706	714-550-0906	667-3471
Web: www.patinagroup.com					
Taqueria De Anda 1029 E 4th St	Santa Ana	CA	92701	714-558-0856	
Yellow Basket Restaurant 2860 S Main St	Santa Ana	CA	92707	714-545-8219	
Web: www.yellowbasket.com					
Border Grill					
Santa Monica 1445 4th St	Santa Monica	CA	90401	310-451-1655	394-2049
Web: www.bordergrill.com					
Chinois on Main 2709 Main St	Santa Monica	CA	90405	310-392-9025	396-5102
Web: www.wolfgangpuck.com					
Ivy at the Shore 1535 Ocean Ave	Santa Monica	CA	90401	310-393-3113	

	City	State	Zip	Phone	Fax
JiRaffe Restaurant					
502 Santa Monica Blvd	Santa Monica	CA	90401	310-917-6671	917-6677
Web: www.jirafferestaurant.com					
Josie 2424 Pico Blvd	Santa Monica	CA	90405	310-581-9888	581-4202
Web: www.josierestaurant.com					
Melisse 1104 Wilshire Blvd	Santa Monica	CA	90401	310-395-0881	395-3810
Web: www.melisse.com					
Ocean Avenue Seafood 1401 Ocean Ave	Santa Monica	CA	90401	310-394-5669	394-7322
Web: www.oceanave.com					
Valentino Santa Monica 3115 Pico Blvd	Santa Monica	CA	90405	310-829-4313	315-2791
Web: www.welovewine.com					
Delius Restaurant 2951 Cherry Ave	Signal Hill	CA	90755	562-426-0694	426-0694
Web: www.deliusrestaurant.com					
Thai Nakorn 11951 Beach Blvd	Stanton	CA	90680	714-799-2031	799-2032
Angelina's 1563 E Fremont St	Stockton	CA	95205	209-948-6609	948-2477
Web: www.angelinas.com					
Bangkok Restaurant 3255 W Hammer Ln Suite 18	Stockton	CA	95209	209-476-8616	
Basil's 2324 Grand Canal Blvd	Stockton	CA	95207	209-478-6290	
Breadfruit Tree 8095 Rio Blanco Rd	Stockton	CA	95219	209-952-7361	
Web: www.breadfruittree.com					
Bud's Seafood Grill 314 Lincoln Ctr	Stockton	CA	95207	209-956-0270	956-0275
Web: www.budsseafood.com					
China Palace 5052 W Ln	Stockton	CA	95210	209-955-0888	952-8871
Chitiva's Salsa & Sports Bar & Grille					
445 W Weber Ave	Stockton	CA	95203	209-941-8605	
Web: www.chitiva.net					
Cocoro Bistro & Sushi Bar 2105 Pacific Ave	Stockton	CA	95204	209-941-6053	
Dave Wong's 2828 W March Ln	Stockton	CA	95219	209-951-4152	951-5106
El Rancho Steak House 1457 E Mariposa Rd	Stockton	CA	95205	209-467-1529	467-1525
Garlic Bros 6629 Embarcadero Dr	Stockton	CA	95219	209-474-6585	474-0741
Web: www.garlic-brothers.com					
Hana Sushi 1101 E March Ln	Stockton	CA	95210	209-477-1667	
House of Shaw 227 Dorris Pl	Stockton	CA	95204	209-948-4300	
Le Bistro 3121 W Benjamin Holt Dr	Stockton	CA	95219	209-951-0885	951-3976
Web: www.lebistrostockton.com					
Le Kim's 631 N Ctr St	Stockton	CA	95202	209-943-0308	
Mi Ranchito Cafe 425 S Ctr St	Stockton	CA	95203	209-946-9257	939-0227
Miguel's 7555 Pacific Ave	Stockton	CA	95207	209-951-1931	
Papapavlos Mediterranean Bistro					
7555 Pacific Ave	Stockton	CA	95207	209-477-6855	
Saigon 1904 Pacific Ave	Stockton	CA	95204	209-463-2274	
Sho Mi 419 Lincoln Ctr	Stockton	CA	95207	209-951-3525	951-3628
Stockton Joe's 236 Lincoln Ctr	Stockton	CA	95207	209-951-2980	951-5900
Web: www.stocktonjoes.com					
Yasso Yani Restaurant 326 E Main St	Stockton	CA	95202	209-464-3108	
Pinot Bistro 12969 Ventura Blvd	Studio City	CA	91604	818-990-0500	990-0540
Web: www.patinagroup.com/restaurant.php?restaurants_id=60					
Sushi Nozawa 11288 Ventura Blvd Suite C	Studio City	CA	91604	818-508-7017	
Ca'del Sole 4100 Cahuenga Blvd	Toluka Lake	CA	91602	818-985-4669	985-5696
Web: www.cadelsole.com					
Rockenwagner					
3 Square Cafe + Bakery 1121 Abbot Kinney Blvd	Venice	CA	90291	310-399-6504	399-6518
Web: www.rockenwagner.com					
Chaya Brasserie 8741 Alden Dr	West Hollywood	CA	90048	310-859-8833	859-4991
Web: www.thechaya.com					
House of Blues 8430 W Sunset Blvd	West Hollywood	CA	90069	323-848-5100	
Web: www.houseofblues.com					
Madeo 8897 Beverly Blvd	West Hollywood	CA	90048	310-859-4903	859-0313
Vivoli Cafe & Trattoria of West Hollywood					
7994 Sunset Blvd	West Hollywood	CA	90046	323-656-5050	656-0419
Web: www.vivolicafe.com					
Eduardo's Border Grill					
1830 Westwood Blvd	West Los Angeles	CA	90025	310-475-2410	
Sushi Sasabune 12400 Wilshire Blvd	West Los Angeles	CA	90025	310-268-8380	820-6078
Bistro Jeanty 6510 Washington St	Yountville	CA	94599	707-944-0103	944-0370
Web: www.bistrojeanty.com					

COLORADO

	City	State	Zip	Phone	Fax
Cache Cache Bistro 205 S Mill St	Aspen	CO	81611	970-925-3835	544-8248
Web: www.cachecache.com					
Campo de Fiori 205 S Mill St	Aspen	CO	81611	970-920-7717	920-3098
Web: www.campodefiori.net					
China Thai Asian Cuisine					
Tang 308 S Hunter St	Aspen	CO	81611	970-544-9888	
Hickory House Ribs					
Aspen 730 W Main St	Aspen	CO	81611	970-925-2313	920-3819
Web: www.hickoryhouseribs.com					
Matsuhisa 303 E Main St	Aspen	CO	81611	970-544-6628	544-6630
Web: www.matushaspen.com					
Montagna 675 E Durant St	Aspen	CO	81611	970-920-6330	920-6328
TF: 888-843-6355					
Pine Creek Cookhouse PO Box 7817	Aspen	CO	81612	970-925-1044	925-7939
Web: www.pinecreekcookhouse.com					
Pinons 105 S Mill St	Aspen	CO	81611	970-920-2021	
Web: www.pinons.net					
Syzygy 520 E Hyman Ave	Aspen	CO	81611	970-925-3700	925-5593
Web: www.syzygyrestaurant.com					
Takah Sushi 320 S Mill St	Aspen	CO	81611	970-925-8588	925-4255
Web: www.takahsushi.com					

Name	City	State	ZIP	Phone	Fax
Aurora Summit Steak House & the Cabin Bar					
2700 S Havana St	Aurora	CO	80014	303-751-2112	369-8028
Web: www.aurorasummit.com					
Dozens 2180 S Havana St	Aurora	CO	80014	303-337-6627	
Web: www.dozensrestaurant.com					
East Cafe Chinese Restaurant					
15140 E Mississippi Ave	Aurora	CO	80012	303-369-6103	
El Alamo 1708 S Chambers Rd	Aurora	CO	80017	303-614-9806	
Emil-Lene's Sirloin House 16000 E Smith Rd	Aurora	CO	80017	303-366-6674	366-5795
Web: www.sirloinhouse.com					
Helga's German Restaurant					
14197 E Exposition Ave	Aurora	CO	80012	303-344-5488	344-5101
Web: www.helgasdeli.com					
La Cueva 9742 E Colfax Ave	Aurora	CO	80010	303-367-1422	367-4071
Web: www.lacueva.net					
Luigi's Bent Noodle 3055 S Parker Rd	Aurora	CO	80014	303-337-2733	751-1424
Web: www.bentnoodle.com					
Rock The 22934 E Smoky Hill Rd	Aurora	CO	80016	303-690-7934	690-1476
Royal Hilltop 18581 E Hampden Ave	Aurora	CO	80013	303-690-7738	690-7742
Web: www.royalhilltop.com					
Sam's No 3 2580 S Havana St	Aurora	CO	80014	303-751-0347	696-2025
Web: www.samsno3.com					
Senor Ric's 13200 E Mississippi Ave	Aurora	CO	80012	303-750-9000	750-9006
Web: www.senorrics.net					
Bacaro 921 Pearl St	Boulder	CO	80302	303-444-4888	445-2422
Web: www.bacaro.com					
Bombay Bistro 1800 Walnut St Suite 110	Boulder	CO	80302	303-444-4721	
Boulder ChopHouse & Tavern 921 Walnut St	Boulder	CO	80302	303-443-1188	443-4876
Web: www.chophouse.com					
Boulder Cork 3295 30th St	Boulder	CO	80301	303-443-9505	443-0193
Web: www.bouldercork.com					
Buff Restaurant 1725 28th St	Boulder	CO	80301	303-442-9150	442-8302
Web: www.buffrestaurant.com					
Carelli's of Boulder 645 30th St	Boulder	CO	80303	303-938-9300	938-4077
Web: www.carellis.com					
Casa Alvarez 3161 Walnut St	Boulder	CO	80301	303-546-0630	
Web: www.casaalvarezcolorado.com					
Chautauqua Dining Hall 900 Baseline Rd	Boulder	CO	80302	303-440-3776	440-0926
Web: www.chautauqua.com					
Chez Thuy 2655 28th St	Boulder	CO	80301	303-442-1700	
Web: www.chezthuy.com					
Dolan's Restaurant 2319 Arapahoe Ave	Boulder	CO	80302	303-444-8758	786-7197
Web: www.dolansrestaurant.com					
Falafel King Restaurant 1314 Pearl St	Boulder	CO	80302	303-449-9321	443-8965
Flagstaff House 1138 Flagstaff Rd	Boulder	CO	80302	303-442-4640	442-8924
Web: www.flagstaffhouse.com					
Greenbriar Inn The 8735 N Foothills Hwy	Boulder	CO	80302	303-440-7979	449-2054
Web: www.greenbriarinn.com					
Illegal Pete's 1447 Pearl St	Boulder	CO	80302	303-440-3955	440-6191
Japango 1136 Pearl St	Boulder	CO	80302	303-938-0330	938-0101
Web: www.boulderjapango.com					
Jax Fish House 928 Pearl St	Boulder	CO	80302	303-444-1811	444-1007
Web: www.jaxfishhouseboulder.com					
John's 2328 Pearl St	Boulder	CO	80302	303-444-5232	
Web: www.johnsrestaurantboulder.com					
L'Atelier 1739 Pearl St	Boulder	CO	80302	303-442-7233	652-3564
Web: www.latelierboulder.com					
Laudisio 1710 29th St	Boulder	CO	80301	303-442-1300	442-6617
Web: www.laudisio.com					
Lucile's 2124 14th St	Boulder	CO	80302	303-442-4743	939-9848
Web: www.luciles.com					
Pasta Jays 1001 Pearl St	Boulder	CO	80302	303-444-5800	
Web: www.pastajays.com					
Q's Restaurant 2115 13th St	Boulder	CO	80302	303-442-4880	442-4378
Web: www.qsboulder.com					
Ras Kassa's Ethiopian Restaurant					
2111 30th St	Boulder	CO	80301	303-447-2919	
Web: www.raskassas.com					
Red Lion Restaurant 38472 Boulder Canyon Dr	Boulder	CO	80301	303-442-9368	447-0986
Web: www.redlionrestaurant.com					
Sushi Tora 2014 10th St	Boulder	CO	80302	303-444-2280	
Web: www.sushitora.net					
Sushi Zanmai 1221 Spruce St	Boulder	CO	80302	303-440-0733	440-6676
Web: www.sushizanmai.com					
Taj Restaurant 2630 Baseline Rd	Boulder	CO	80303	303-494-5216	
Thyme on the Creek 1345 28th St	Boulder	CO	80302	303-998-3835	443-1480
Web: www.millenniumhotels.com					
Walnut Brewery 1123 Walnut St	Boulder	CO	80302	303-447-1345	447-0067
Web: www.walnutbrewery.com					
Walnut Cafe 3073 Walnut St	Boulder	CO	80301	303-447-2315	
Web: www.walnutcafe.com					
Zolo Grill 2525 Arapahoe Ave	Boulder	CO	80302	303-449-0444	447-0493
Web: www.zologrill.com					
Six89 Kitchen & Wine Bar 689 Main St	Carbondale	CO	81623	970-963-6890	
Web: www.six89.com					
Amanda's Fonda 3625 W Colorado Ave	Colorado Springs	CO	80904	719-227-1975	578-0285
Antonio's Italiano Ristorante					
301 E Garden Of the Gods Rd	Colorado Springs	CO	80907	719-531-7177	531-5622
Bamboo Court 4935 Centennial Blvd	Colorado Springs	CO	80919	719-599-7383	599-7098
Blue Star The 1645 S Tejon St	Colorado Springs	CO	80906	719-632-1086	632-6284
Web: www.thebluestar.net					
Cafe El Paso 3840 N Nevada Ave	Colorado Springs	CO	80907	719-634-3940	
China Town 326 S Nevada Ave	Colorado Springs	CO	80903	719-632-5151	
Chopsticks					
120 E Cheyenne Mountain Blvd	Colorado Springs	CO	80906	719-579-9111	579-9161
Edelweiss 34 E Ramona Ave	Colorado Springs	CO	80905	719-633-2220	471-8413
Web: www.restauranteur.com					
El Tesoro Restaurant					
10 N Sierra Madre St	Colorado Springs	CO	80903	719-471-0106	
Web: www.el-tesoro.com					
Flying W Ranch Inc					
3330 Chuckwagon Rd	Colorado Springs	CO	80919	719-598-4000	598-4600
TF: 800-232-3599 ■ *Web:* www.flyingw.com					
Fratelli 124 N Nevada Ave	Colorado Springs	CO	80903	719-575-9571	
Web: www.fratelliristorante.com					
Giuseppe's Old Depot Restaurant					
10 S Sierra Madre St	Colorado Springs	CO	80903	719-635-3111	444-0857
Web: www.giuseppesdepot.com					
Il Vicino 11 S Tejon St	Colorado Springs	CO	80903	719-475-9224	475-9466
Web: www.ilvicino.com					
Jake & Telly's 2616 W Colorado Ave	Colorado Springs	CO	80904	719-633-0406	473-1153
Web: www.jakeandtellys.com					
Jun Japanese Restaurant					
1760 Dublin Blvd	Colorado Springs	CO	80918	719-531-9368	
La Carreta 35 N Iowa Ave	Colorado Springs	CO	80909	719-477-1157	477-1157
La Creperie Bistro 204 N Tejon St	Colorado Springs	CO	80903	719-632-0984	
La Petite Maison					
1015 W Colorado Ave	Colorado Springs	CO	80904	719-632-4887	632-0340
Luigi's 947 S Tejon St	Colorado Springs	CO	80903	719-632-7339	
Web: www.luigiscoloradosprings.com					
MacKenzie's Chop House Restaurant					
128 S Tejon St	Colorado Springs	CO	80903	719-635-3536	635-1225
Web: www.mackenzieschophouse.com					
Marigold Cafe 4605 Centennial Blvd	Colorado Springs	CO	80919	719-599-4776	262-9521
Mason Jar The 2925 W Colorado Ave	Colorado Springs	CO	80904	719-632-4820	632-0392
Web: www.masonjarcolorado.com					
Penrose Room 1 Lake Ave	Colorado Springs	CO	80906	719-634-7711	
Web: www.broadmoor.com					
Pepper Tree The 888 W Moreno Ave	Colorado Springs	CO	80905	719-471-4888	471-0997
Web: www.peppertreecs.com					
PF Chang's China Bistro					
1725 Briargate Pkwy	Colorado Springs	CO	80920	719-593-8580	593-8836
Web: www.pfchangs.com					
Phantom Canyon Brewing Co					
2 E Pikes Peak Ave	Colorado Springs	CO	80903	719-635-2800	635-9930
Web: www.phantomcanyon.com					
Uwes German Restaurant					
31 N Iowa Ave	Colorado Springs	CO	80909	719-475-1611	
1515 On Market 1515 Market St	Denver	CO	80202	303-571-0011	
Web: www.1515restaurant.com					
Barolo Grill 3030 E 6th Ave	Denver	CO	80206	303-393-1040	333-9240
Web: www.barologrilldenver.com					
Bella Vista 127 E 20th Ave	Denver	CO	80205	303-297-9020	297-8866
Bistro Vendome 1420 Larimer St	Denver	CO	80202	303-825-3232	825-3240
Web: www.bistrovendome.com					
Broker The 821 17th St	Denver	CO	80202	303-292-5065	292-2652
Web: www.brokerrestaurant.com					
Cafe Brazil 4408 Lowell Blvd	Denver	CO	80211	303-480-1877	
Web: www.cafebrazildenver.com					
Capital Grille 1450 Larimer St	Denver	CO	80202	303-539-2500	539-2700
Web: www.thecapitalgrille.com					
Carmine's on Penn 92 S Pennsylvania St	Denver	CO	80209	303-777-6443	777-4129
Web: www.carminesonpenn.net					
Celtic Tavern The 1801 Blake St	Denver	CO	80202	303-308-1795	308-1576
Web: www.celtictavern.com					
Corkhouse The 4900 E Colfax Ave	Denver	CO	80220	303-355-4488	355-1336
Web: www.corkhousedenver.com					
Damascus 2276 S Colorado Blvd	Denver	CO	80222	303-757-3515	
Denver Chophouse & Brewery					
1735 19th St Suite 100	Denver	CO	80202	303-296-0800	296-2800
Web: www.chophouse.com					
El Taco de Mexico 714 Santa Fe Dr	Denver	CO	80204	303-623-3926	
Fado Irish Pub 1735 19th St Suite 150	Denver	CO	80202	303-297-0066	297-0055
Web: www.fadoirishpub.com					
Hapa Sushi Grill & Sake Bar 2780 E 2nd Ave	Denver	CO	80206	303-322-9554	355-3449
Web: www.hapasushi.com					
Highlands Garden Cafe 3927 W 32nd Ave	Denver	CO	80212	303-458-5920	477-6695
Web: www.highlandsgardencafe.com					
India's 7400 E Hampden Ave Suite F	Denver	CO	80231	303-755-4284	752-9814
Web: www.indiasrestaurant.com					
Jax Fish House 1539 17th St	Denver	CO	80202	303-292-5767	292-0530
Web: www.jaxfishhousedenver.com					
Le Central 112 E 8th Ave	Denver	CO	80203	303-863-8094	863-0219
Web: www.lecentral.com					
Little India 330 E 6th Ave	Denver	CO	80203	303-871-9777	871-1907
Web: www.littleindiadenver.com					
Luca d'Italia 711 Grant St	Denver	CO	80203	303-832-6600	823-3532
Web: www.lucadenver.com					
M & D's Bar-B-Que & Fish Palace					
2000 E 28th Ave	Denver	CO	80205	303-296-1760	296-1606
Maggiano's Little Italy					
500 16th St Pavilions Mall Suite 150	Denver	CO	80202	303-260-7707	260-7683
Web: www.maggianos.com					
Mizuna 225 E 7th Ave	Denver	CO	80203	303-832-4778	832-3532
Web: www.mizunadenver.com					
New Saigon 630 S Federal Blvd	Denver	CO	80219	303-936-4954	
Pagliacci's 1440 W 33rd Ave	Denver	CO	80211	303-458-0530	
Web: www.ipagliaccio.com					
Panzano 909 17th St	Denver	CO	80202	303-296-3525	
Web: www.panzano-denver.com					
Parisi 4401 Tennyson St	Denver	CO	80212	303-561-0234	480-5514
Web: www.parisidenver.com					
Pearl Street Grill 1477 S Pearl St	Denver	CO	80210	303-778-6475	778-0430
Web: www.pearlstreetgrilldenver.com					
PF Chang's China Bistro 1415 15th St	Denver	CO	80202	303-260-7222	260-7223
Web: www.pfchangs.com					
Pho Fusion 8800 E Hampden Ave	Denver	CO	80231	303-843-6080	
Web: www.phofusion.com					
Potager 1109 Ogden St	Denver	CO	80218	303-832-5788	861-8985
Web: www.potagerrestaurant.com					
Restaurant Kevin Taylor 1106 14th St	Denver	CO	80202	303-820-2600	893-1293
Web: www.restaurantkevintaylor.com					
Solera 5410 E Colfax Ave	Denver	CO	80220	303-388-8429	333-0553
Web: www.solerarestaurant.com					

Name / Address	City	State	Zip	Phone	Fax
Sullivan's Steakhouse 1745 Wazee St	Denver	CO	80202	303-295-2664	295-2678
Web: www.sullivansteakhouse.com					
Sushi Den 1487 S Pearl St	Denver	CO	80210	303-777-0826	777-3916
Web: www.sushiden.net					
Tamayo 1400 Larimer St	Denver	CO	80202	720-946-1433	946-1434
Web: www.richardsandoval.com					
Tuscany 4150 E Mississippi Ave	Denver	CO	80246	303-782-1600	639-1643
Venice Ristorante & Wine Bar 1700 Wynkoop St	Denver	CO	80202	303-534-2222	893-0560
Web: www.veniceristorante.com					
Wellshire Inn 3333 S Colorado Blvd	Denver	CO	80222	303-759-3333	759-3487
Wynkoop Brewing Co 1634 18th St	Denver	CO	80202	303-297-2700	297-2958
Web: www.wynkoop.com					
Yanni's 2223 S Monaco Pkwy	Denver	CO	80222	303-692-0404	
Zengo 1610 Little Raven St	Denver	CO	80202	720-904-0965	904-0966
Web: www.zengorestaurant.com					
Bar D Chuckwagon Suppers 8080 County Rd 250	Durango	CO	81301	970-247-5753	247-2010
TF: 888-800-5753 ■ *Web:* www.bardchuckwagon.com					
Brickhouse Cafe 1849 Main Ave	Durango	CO	81301	970-247-3760	
Web: www.brickhousecafe.com					
Carver Brewing Co 1022 Main Ave	Durango	CO	81301	970-259-2545	
Web: www.carverbrewing.com					
Christina's Grill & Bar 21382 Hwy 160 W	Durango	CO	81303	970-382-3844	382-3865
Web: www.christinasgrill.com					
Cyprus Cafe 725 E 2nd Ave	Durango	CO	81301	970-385-6884	
Web: www.cypruscafe.com					
East by Southwest 160 E College Dr	Durango	CO	81301	970-247-5533	247-2647
Web: www.eastbysouthwest.com					
Francisco's Restaurante y Cantina 619 Main Ave	Durango	CO	81301	970-247-4098	247-2008
Ken & Sue's 636 Main Ave	Durango	CO	81301	970-385-1810	385-1801
Web: www.kenandsues.com					
Lady Falconburgh's Barley Exchange 640 Main Ave	Durango	CO	81301	970-382-9664	382-9625
Web: www.ladyfalconburgh.biz					
Mahogany Grille 699 Main Ave	Durango	CO	81301	970-247-4433	259-2208
Web: www.mahoganygrille.com					
Randy's 152 E College Dr	Durango	CO	81301	970-247-9083	247-0191
Web: www.randysrestaurant.com					
Red Snapper 144 E 9th St	Durango	CO	80301	970-259-3417	259-3441
Web: www.redsnapperdurango.com					
Bisetti's Italian Restaurant 120 S College Ave	Fort Collins	CO	80524	970-493-0086	493-1701
Web: www.bisettis.com					
Enzio's Italian Kitchen 126 W Mountain Ave	Fort Collins	CO	80524	970-484-8466	484-8490
Web: www.enzios.com					
Jasmine Garden 2721 S College Rd	Fort Collins	CO	80525	970-223-6211	
Jay's Bistro 135 W Oak St	Fort Collins	CO	80524	970-482-1876	482-1897
Web: www.jaysbistro.net					
Los Tarascos 622 S College Ave	Fort Collins	CO	80524	970-416-0265	416-8455
Moot House 2626 S College Ave	Fort Collins	CO	80525	970-226-2121	
Web: www.themoothouse.com					
Nimo's 1220 W Elizabeth St	Fort Collins	CO	80521	970-221-1040	
Rainbow Restaurant 212 W Laurel St	Fort Collins	CO	80521	970-221-2664	221-2699
Renzio's 215 E Foothills Pkwy	Fort Collins	CO	80525	970-282-8818	
South China 4613 S Mason St Unit D-1	Fort Collins	CO	80525	970-225-6886	225-6802
SportsCaster Bar & Grill 165 E Boardwalk Dr	Fort Collins	CO	80525	970-223-3553	223-0838
Web: www.sportscasterbar.com					
Suehiro 223 Linden St	Fort Collins	CO	80524	970-482-3734	
Young's Cafe 3307 S College Rd	Fort Collins	CO	80525	970-223-8000	223-4923
Web: www.youngscafe.com					
Sam Taylor's Barbeque 435 S Cherry St	Glendale	CO	80246	303-388-9300	388-2230
240 Union 240 Union Blvd	Lakewood	CO	80228	303-989-3562	989-3565
Web: www.240union.com					
Casa Bonita 6715 W Colfax Ave	Lakewood	CO	80214	303-232-5115	232-7801
Web: www.casabonitadenver.com					
Briarhurst Manor 404 Manitou Ave	Manitou Springs	CO	80829	719-685-1864	314-4017
TF: 877-685-1448 ■ *Web:* www.briarhurst.com					
Krabloonik 4250 Divide Rd PO Box 5517	Snowmass Village	CO	81615	970-923-3953	923-0246
Web: www.krabloonik.com					

CONNECTICUT

Name / Address	City	State	Zip	Phone	Fax
Old Heidelberg 55 Stony Hill Rd	Bethel	CT	77057	203-797-1860	
Web: www.restaurantheidelberg.com					
Bloodroot 85 Ferris St	Bridgeport	CT	06605	203-576-9168	
Web: www.bloodroot.com					
Captain's Cove 1 Bostwick Ave	Bridgeport	CT	06605	203-335-7104	335-6793
Web: www.captainscoveseaport.com					
Field Restaurant & Bar The 3001 Fairfield Ave	Bridgeport	CT	06605	203-333-0043	331-1931
Web: www.fieldrestaurant.com					
Joseph's Steakhouse 360 Fairfield Ave	Bridgeport	CT	06604	203-337-9944	337-9996
Web: www.josephssteakhouse.com					
King & I 545 Broadbridge Rd	Bridgeport	CT	06610	203-374-2081	371-2293
Web: www.kingandict.com					
Ralph 'N Rich's 815 Main St	Bridgeport	CT	06604	203-366-3597	
Tony's Huntington Inn 437 Huntington Tpke	Bridgeport	CT	06610	203-374-5541	
Web: www.thpizza.com					
Tuscany 1084 Madison Ave	Bridgeport	CT	06606	203-331-9884	331-9885
Web: www.iliketuscany.com					
Vazzy's Brick Oven Restaurant 513 Broadbridge Rd	Bridgeport	CT	06610	203-371-8046	371-4293
Web: www.vazzysrest.com					
Barcelona Restaurant & Wine Bar 4180 Black Rock Tpke	Fairfield	CT	06824	203-255-0800	255-0225
Web: www.barcelonawinebar.com					
Saint Tropez Bistro 52 Sanford St	Fairfield	CT	06825	203-254-8094	254-8209
Web: www.saint-tropez-bistro.com					
Shiki Hana 222 Post Rd	Fairfield	CT	06824	203-259-5950	259-5428
Web: www.shikihanafaiefield.com					
Asiana Cafe 130 E Putnam Ave	Greenwich	CT	06830	203-622-6833	861-2680
Web: www.asianacafe.com					
Barcelona Restaurant & WIne Bar 18 W Putnam Ave	Greenwich	CT	06830	203-983-6400	983-6087
Web: www.barcelonawinebar.com					
Elm Street Oyster House 11 W Elm St	Greenwich	CT	06830	203-629-5795	629-8515
Web: www.elmstreetoysterhouse.com					
Jean-Louis 61 Lewis St	Greenwich	CT	06830	203-622-8450	
Web: www.restaurantjeanlouis.com					
L'Escale 500 Steamboat Rd	Greenwich	CT	06830	203-661-4600	661-4601
Web: www.lescalerestaurant.com					
Meli-Melo 362 Greenwich Ave	Greenwich	CT	06830	203-629-6153	422-5007
Morello Bistro 253 Greenwich Ave	Greenwich	CT	06830	203-661-3443	661-3588
Web: www.morellobistro.com					
Penang Grill 55 Lewis St	Greenwich	CT	06830	203-861-1988	861-0003
Polpo 554 Old Post Rd	Greenwich	CT	06830	203-629-1999	629-1718
Web: www.polporestaurant.com					
Tengda Asian Bistro 21 Field Pt Rd	Greenwich	CT	06830	203-625-5338	
Web: www.asianbistrogroup.com/greenwich					
Thomas Henkelmann Restaurant 420 Field Pt Rd	Greenwich	CT	06830	203-869-7500	869-7502
Web: www.homesteadinn.com					
Carbone's Ristorante 588 Franklin Ave	Hartford	CT	06114	860-296-9646	296-2785
Web: www.carbonesct.com					
Casa Mia Ristorante 381 Franklin Ave	Hartford	CT	06114	860-296-3441	563-4271
Web: www.tomad.net					
City Steam Brewery Cafe 942 Main St	Hartford	CT	06103	860-525-1600	244-2255
Web: www.citysteambrewerycafe.com					
Costa del Sol 901 Wethersfield Ave	Hartford	CT	06114	860-296-1714	296-9250
Web: www.costadelsolrestaurant.net					
Coyote Flaco 635 New Britain Ave	Hartford	CT	06106	860-953-1299	953-1954
Web: www.mycoyoteflaco.com					
Ficara's 577 Franklin Ave	Hartford	CT	06114	860-296-3238	296-3238
Web: www.ficarasrestaurant.com					
First & Last Tavern 939 Maple Ave	Hartford	CT	06114	860-956-6000	956-9783
Web: www.firstandlasttavern.com					
Hot Tomato's 1 Union Pl	Hartford	CT	06103	860-249-5100	524-8120
Web: www.hottomatos.net					
Ichiban Japanese Steak House 530 Farmington Ave	Hartford	CT	06105	860-236-5599	236-2669
Web: www.ichibanhartford.com					
Kashmir Restaurant 481 Wethersfield Ave	Hartford	CT	06114	860-296-9685	
King & I 1901 Pk St	Hartford	CT	06106	860-232-5471	
Koji 17 Asylum St	Hartford	CT	06103	860-247-5654	677-5359
Max Downtown 185 Asylum St	Hartford	CT	06103	860-522-2530	246-5279
Web: www.maxrestaurantgroup.com					
Museum Cafe at the Wadsworth Antheneum Museum of Art 600 Main St	Hartford	CT	06103	860-838-4042	
New Park 1615 Pk St	Hartford	CT	06106	860-232-1565	231-8776
Oporto 2074 Pk St	Hartford	CT	06106	860-233-3184	231-8112
Web: www.oportohartford.com					
Peppercorn's Grill 357 Main St	Hartford	CT	06106	860-547-1714	724-7612
Web: www.peppercornsgrill.com					
Szechuan Tokyo 1245 New Britain Ave	Hartford	CT	06110	860-561-0180	561-5992
Tapas on Ann 126 Ann St	Hartford	CT	06103	860-525-5988	525-5354
Web: www.tapasonline.com					
Trumbull Kitchen 150 Trumbull St	Hartford	CT	06103	860-493-7412	493-7416
Web: www.maxrestaurantgroup.com/home.html					
Vito's by the Park 26 Trumbull St	Hartford	CT	06103	860-244-2200	244-2210
Web: www.vitosct.com					
VIVO Seasonal Trattoria 200 Columbus Blvd	Hartford	CT	06103	860-760-2333	760-2330
Cavey's 45 E Ctr St	Manchester	CT	06040	860-643-2751	
Web: www.caveysrestaurant.com					
Adriana's 771 Grand Ave	New Haven	CT	06511	203-865-6474	865-4846
Akasaka 1450 Whalley Ave	New Haven	CT	06515	203-387-4898	397-3069
Archie Moore's Bar & Restaurant 188 1/2 Willow St	New Haven	CT	06511	203-773-9870	773-9799
Web: www.archiemoores.com					
Bangkok Garden 172 York St	New Haven	CT	06511	203-789-8684	789-0336
Web: www.bkkgardenct.com					
Bentara 76 Orange St	New Haven	CT	06510	203-562-2511	562-0892
Web: www.bentara.com					
Brazi's Italian Restaurant 201 Food Terminal Plaza	New Haven	CT	06511	203-498-2488	498-1652
Carmen Anthony Steakhouse 660 State St	New Haven	CT	06511	203-773-1444	772-4853
Web: www.carmenanthony.com					
Carmine's Tuscan Grill Ristorante 1500 Whalley Ave	New Haven	CT	06515	203-389-2805	389-1071
Web: www.nearhome.com					
Central Steakhouse 99 Orange St	New Haven	CT	06510	203-787-7885	787-9662
Web: www.centralsteakhouse.com					
Christopher Martin's 860 State St	New Haven	CT	06511	203-776-8835	777-8875
Web: www.christophermartins.com					
Claire's Corner Copia 1000 Chapel St	New Haven	CT	06510	203-562-3888	
Web: www.clairescornercopia.com					
Consiglio's 165 Wooster St	New Haven	CT	06511	203-865-4489	
Web: www.consiglios.com					
Fireside Restaurant 810 Woodward Ave	New Haven	CT	66512	203-466-1919	466-1589
Mamoun's Falafel Restaurant 85 Howe St	New Haven	CT	06511	203-562-8444	562-1474
Miya 68 Howe St	New Haven	CT	06511	203-777-9760	
Web: www.miyassushi.com					
Sage American Bar & Grill 100 S Water St	New Haven	CT	06519	203-787-3466	777-8274
Web: www.sageamerican.com					
Tre Scalini 100 Wooster St	New Haven	CT	06510	203-777-3373	787-5360
Web: www.trescalinirestaurant.com					
Union League Cafe 1032 Chapel St	New Haven	CT	06510	203-562-4299	562-6712
Web: www.unionleaguecafe.com					
Zaroka 148 York St	New Haven	CT	06511	203-776-8644	776-0051
Web: www.zaroka.com					
Zinc 964 Chapel St	New Haven	CT	06510	203-624-0507	624-9156
Web: www.zincfood.com					

	City	State	Zip	Phone	Fax
Ruth's Chris Steak House 2513 Berlin Tpke	Newington	CT	06111	860-666-2202	665-7246
Web: www.ruthschris.com					
Sabatiello Gourmet Pizza 1072 E Putnam Ave	Riverside	CT	09337	203-344-9339	
Web: www.pizzashops.info/Connecticut//Riverside/SabatielloGourmetPizza					
La Scogliera Restaurant 474 River Rd	Shelton	CT	06484	203-922-1179	922-1176
Web: www.lascoglierarestaurant.com					
Bobby Valentine's Sports Gallery Cafe 225 Main St	Stamford	CT	06901	203-348-0010	359-9395
Web: www.bobbyv.com					
Brasitas 954 E Main St	Stamford	CT	06902	203-323-3176	353-8102
Web: www.brasitas.com					
Chez Jean-Pierre 188 Bedford St	Stamford	CT	06901	203-357-9526	357-9618
Web: www.chezjeanpierre.com					
Columbus Park Trattoria 205 Main St	Stamford	CT	06901	203-967-9191	967-4724
Web: www.columbusparktrattoria.com					
Crab Shell 46 Southfield Ave	Stamford	CT	06905	203-967-7229	967-7233
Web: www.crabshell.com					
Eclisse Restaurant 700 Canal St	Stamford	CT	06902	203-325-3773	327-2308
Web: www.eclissestamford.com					
Grand Restaurant & Lounge 15 Bank St	Stamford	CT	06901	203-323-3232	323-3236
Web: www.stamfordgrand.com					
Hugo's Restaurant 161 Stillwater Ave	Stamford	CT	06902	203-323-5577	323-5574
Kotobuki 457 Summer St	Stamford	CT	06901	203-359-4747	357-7522
Web: www.kotobukijapaneserestaurant.com					
La Bretagne 2010 W Main St	Stamford	CT	06902	203-324-9539	
Minetto's 299 Long Ridge Rd	Stamford	CT	06902	203-964-9802	964-9804
Ole Mole 1030 High Ridge Rd	Stamford	CT	06905	203-461-9962	329-7438
Quattro Regali 245 Hope St	Stamford	CT	06906	203-964-1801	588-9188
Siena 519 Summer St	Stamford	CT	06901	203-351-0898	351-0899
Telluride 245 Bedford St	Stamford	CT	06901	203-357-7679	357-9817
Web: www.telluriderestaurant.com					
Arugula 953 Farmington Ave	West Hartford	CT	06107	860-561-4888	
Chengdu 179 Pk Rd	West Hartford	CT	06119	860-232-6455	232-3002
Grant's 977 Farmington Ave	West Hartford	CT	06107	860-236-1930	570-1431
Max's Oyster Bar 964 Farmington Ave	West Hartford	CT	06107	860-236-6299	233-6969
Web: www.maxrestaurantgroup.com					
Murasaki 23 LaSalle Rd	West Hartford	CT	06107	860-236-7622	236-7626
Web: www.murasakijapaneserestaurant.com					
Pond House Cafe 1555 Asylum Ave	West Hartford	CT	06117	860-231-8823	231-8731
Web: www.pondhousecafe.com					
Restaurant Bricco 78 LaSalle Rd	West Hartford	CT	06107	860-233-0220	233-7503
Web: www.billygrant.com					

DELAWARE

	City	State	Zip	Phone	Fax
Captain's Table Restaurant 20859 Coastal Hwy	Dewey Beach	DE	19971	302-227-6203	
Lighthouse Restaurant 124 Dickinson St	Dewey Beach	DE	19971	302-227-4333	226-2103
Rusty Rudder Restaurant 113 Dickinson St	Dewey Beach	DE	19971	302-227-3888	226-2402
Starboard Restaurant 2009 Hwy 1	Dewey Beach	DE	19971	302-227-4600	227-4601
Web: www.thestarboard.com					
Two Seas Restaurant Van Dyke Ave & Rt 1	Dewey Beach	DE	19971	302-227-2610	
Hibachi Japanese Steak House 691 N DuPont Hwy	Dover	DE	19901	302-734-5900	734-5671
Iron Gate Inn 1151 S Bay Rd	Dover	DE	19901	302-678-9666	
La Tolteca 859 N DuPont Hwy	Dover	DE	19901	302-734-3444	734-1777
Marimonti 107 Gagway W	Dover	DE	19904	302-674-0966	674-8070
Niko's 1115 S Governors Ave	Dover	DE	19904	302-730-3551	
Roma Italian Restaurant 3 President Dr	Dover	DE	19901	302-678-1041	678-1045
Web: www.romadover.com					
Schucker's Pier 13 Restaurant 889 N DuPont Hwy	Dover	DE	19901	302-674-1190	674-2965
Viet Kieu 510 Jefferic Blvd	Dover	DE	19901	302-744-9300	
Where Pigs Fly 617 E Loockerman St	Dover	DE	19901	302-678-0586	735-7675
Sambo's Tavern 283 Front St	Leipsic	DE	19901	302-674-9724	
Nonna Ristorante 4621 Stanton Ogleton Rd	Newark	DE	19713	302-737-9999	
Web: www.nonnaristorante.com					
1776 Eastern Shore Steakhouse & Bar 18585 Coastal Hwy	Rehoboth Beach	DE	19971	302-645-9355	645-0854
Web: www.1776steakhouse.net					
Adriatico Italian Restaurant 30 Baltimore Ave	Rehoboth Beach	DE	19971	302-227-9255	
Big Fish Grill 20298 Coastal Hwy	Rehoboth Beach	DE	19971	302-227-9007	227-1705
Web: www.bigfishgrill.com					
Blue Moon Restaurant 35 Baltimore Ave	Rehoboth Beach	DE	19971	302-227-6515	227-3702
Web: www.bluemoonrehoboth.com					
Dos Locos 208 Rehoboth Ave	Rehoboth Beach	DE	19971	302-227-3353	227-2213
Web: www.doslocos.com					
Jake's Seafood House Restaurant 29 Baltimore Ave	Rehoboth Beach	DE	19971	302-227-6237	226-5137
Web: www.jakesseafoodhouse.com					
Ristorante Zebra 32 Lake Ave	Rehoboth Beach	DE	19971	302-226-1160	226-4985
Roadhouse Steak Joint 4572 Hwy 1	Rehoboth Beach	DE	19971	302-645-8273	645-8275
Victoria's Restaurant 2 Olive Ave Boardwalk Plaza Hotel	Rehoboth Beach	DE	19971	302-227-0615	227-0516
Web: www.boardwalkplaza.com/restaurant.htm					
Yong Hua Chinese Restaurant 715 Rehoboth Ave	Rehoboth Beach	DE	19971	302-227-1549	
Bean Bag Cafe 913 N Market St	Wilmington	DE	19801	302-888-2444	427-2700
Blue Parrott Bar & Grille 1934 W 6th St	Wilmington	DE	19805	302-655-8990	655-9488
Web: www.blueparrotgrille.com					
Bonhouse 4713 Kirkwood Hwy	Wilmington	DE	19808	302-633-1218	633-3928
Brandywine Room 901 N Market St Suite 11	Wilmington	DE	19801	302-594-3156	594-3108
TF: 800-338-3404					
Bull's Eye Saloon & Restaurant 3734 Kirkwood Hwy	Wilmington	DE	19808	302-633-6557	998-9151
Web: www.bullseyesaloon.com					
Corner Bistro 3604 Silverside Rd	Wilmington	DE	19810	302-477-1778	477-1779
Web: www.mybistro.com					
Culinaria Branmar Plaza Marsh & Silverside Rd	Wilmington	DE	19810	302-475-4860	
Web: www.culinariarestaurant.com					
Deep Blue Bar & Grill 111 W 11th St	Wilmington	DE	19801	302-777-2040	777-1012
Web: www.deepbluebarandgrill.com					
Eclipse Bistro 1020 N Union St	Wilmington	DE	19805	302-658-1588	661-1080
Web: www.platinumdininggroup.com					
Golden Castle Diner-Restaurant 2722 Concord Pike	Wilmington	DE	19803	302-478-7701	478-7710
Green Room at the Hotel duPont 11th & Market St	Wilmington	DE	19801	302-594-3100	594-3108
TF: 800-441-9019 ■ *Web:* www.hoteldupont.com					
Harry's Savoy Grill 2020 Naamans Rd	Wilmington	DE	19810	302-475-3000	475-9990
Web: www.harrys-savoy.com					
Harry's Seafood Grill 101 S Market St	Wilmington	DE	19801	302-777-1500	777-2406
Web: www.harrysseafoodgrill.com					
Jimmy's Restaurant 703 Philadelphia Pike	Wilmington	DE	19809	302-764-1702	764-3199
LaTolteca 2209 Concord Pke	Wilmington	DE	19803	302-778-4646	
Web: www.authenticmex.com					
Luigi Vitrone's Pastabilities 415 N Lincoln St	Wilmington	DE	19805	302-656-9822	
Web: www.ljv-pastabilities.com					
Madeline's Italian Restaurant 531 N DuPont St	Wilmington	DE	19805	302-656-4505	
Web: www.madelinesitalianrestaurant.com					
Melting Pot The 1601 Concord Pike Suite 43-47 Independence Mall	Wilmington	DE	19803	302-652-6358	652-8101
Web: www.meltingpot.com					
Mexican Post 3100 Naamans Rd	Wilmington	DE	19810	302-478-3939	478-5599
Web: www.mexicanpost.com					
Mikimoto's 1212 N Washington St	Wilmington	DE	19801	302-656-8638	656-7423
Web: www.mikimotos.com					
Moro 1307 N Scott St	Wilmington	DE	19806	302-777-1800	777-2350
Web: www.mororestaurant.net					
Mrs Robino's Restaurant 520 N Union St	Wilmington	DE	19801	302-652-9223	658-8124
Web: www.mrsrobinos.com					
Piccolina Toscana 1412 N DuPont St	Wilmington	DE	19806	302-654-8001	654-8250
Web: www.piccolinatoscana.com					
Stanley's Tavern 2038 Foulk Rd	Wilmington	DE	19810	302-475-1887	475-0904
Web: www.stanleystavern.com					
Union City Grille 805 N Union St	Wilmington	DE	19805	302-654-9780	654-0238
Web: www.unioncitygrille.com					
Valle Cucina Italiana 4752 Limestone Rd	Wilmington	DE	19808	302-998-9999	
Web: www.vallecucina.com					
Walter's Steak House & Saloon 802 N Union St	Wilmington	DE	19805	302-652-6780	

DISTRICT OF COLUMBIA

	City	State	Zip	Phone	Fax
15 Ria 1515 Rhode Island Ave NW	Washington	DC	20005	202-742-0015	332-8436
Web: www.15ria.com					
1789 Restaurant 1226 36th St NW	Washington	DC	20007	202-965-1789	337-1541
Web: www.1789restaurant.com					
701 Restaurant 701 Pennsylvania Ave NW	Washington	DC	20004	202-393-0701	393-0242
Web: www.701restaurant.com					
Al Tiramisu 2014 P St NW	Washington	DC	20036	202-467-4466	467-4468
Web: www.altiramisu.com					
Ardeo 3311 Connecticut Ave NW	Washington	DC	20008	202-244-6750	244-8960
Web: www.ardeobardeo.com					
Bangkok Bistro 3251 Prospect St	Washington	DC	20007	202-337-2424	337-2222
Web: www.bangkokbistrodc.com					
Bistro Bis 15 E St NW	Washington	DC	20001	202-661-2700	661-2747
Web: www.bistrobis.com					
Bombay Club 815 Connecticut Ave NW	Washington	DC	20006	202-659-3727	659-5012
Web: www.bombayclubdc.com					
Cactus Cantina 3300 Wisconsin Ave NW	Washington	DC	20016	202-686-7222	362-5649
Web: www.cactuscantina.com					
Cafe Atlantico 405 8th St NW	Washington	DC	20004	202-393-0812	393-0555
Web: www.cafeatlantico.com					
Cashion's Eat Place 1819 Columbia Rd NW	Washington	DC	20009	202-797-1819	797-0048
Web: www.cashionseatplace.com					
Caucus Room 401 9th St NW	Washington	DC	20004	202-393-1300	393-6066
Web: www.thecaucusroom.com					
Ceiba 701 14th St NW	Washington	DC	20005	202-393-3983	393-1863
Web: www.ceibarestaurant.com					
Charlie Palmer Steak 101 Constitution Ave NW	Washington	DC	20001	202-547-8100	547-6607
Web: www.charliepalmer.com/steak_dc					
Citronelle 3000 M St NW	Washington	DC	20007	202-625-2150	339-6326
Web: www.citronelledc.com					
City Lights of China 1731 Connecticut Ave NW	Washington	DC	20009	202-265-6688	263-1369
Web: www.citylightsofchina.com					
Coeur de Lion 926 Massachusetts Ave NW	Washington	DC	20001	202-414-0500	414-0513
Web: www.henleypark.com					
Corduroy 1122 9th St NW	Washington	DC	20001	202-589-0699	589-0688
DC Coast 1401 K St NW	Washington	DC	20005	202-216-5988	371-2221
Web: www.dccoast.com					
Equinox 818 Connecticut Ave NW	Washington	DC	20006	202-331-8118	331-0809
Web: www.equinoxrestaurant.com					
Filomena Ristorante 1063 Wisconsin Ave NW	Washington	DC	20007	202-338-8800	338-8806
TF: 888-345-6636 ■ *Web:* www.filomenadc.com					
Hard Rock Cafe 999 E St NW	Washington	DC	20004	202-737-7625	628-6595
Web: www.hardrock.com					
Heritage India 1337 Connecticut Ave NW	Washington	DC	20036	202-331-1414	331-8788
Web: www.heritageindiausa.com					
I Ricchi 1220 19th St NW	Washington	DC	20036	202-835-0459	872-1220
Web: www.iricchi.net					
Ici Urban Bistro 806 15th St NW	Washington	DC	20005	202-737-8800	730-8500
Web: www.iciurbanbistro.com					
Indique 3512 Connecticut Ave NW	Washington	DC	20008	202-244-6600	244-6603
Web: www.indique.com					

Name / Address	City	State	Zip	Phone	Fax
Jaleo 480 7th St NW	Washington	DC	20004	202-628-7949	628-7952
Web: www.jaleo.com					
Johnny's Half Shell 400 N Capitol St NW	Washington	DC	20001	202-737-0400	737-3026
Web: www.johnnyshalfshell.net					
Jyoti 2433 18th St NW	Washington	DC	20009	202-518-5892	518-5892
Kaz Sushi Bistro 1915 I St NW	Washington	DC	20006	202-530-5500	530-5501
Web: www.kazsushibistro.com					
Kinkead's 2000 Pennsylvania Ave NW	Washington	DC	20006	202-296-7700	296-7688
Web: www.kinkead.com					
Komi 1509 17th St NW	Washington	DC	20036	202-332-9200	332-2265
Web: www.komirestaurant.com					
Lebanese Taverna 2641 Connecticut Ave NW	Washington	DC	20008	202-265-8681	483-3007
Web: www.lebanesetaverna.com					
Little Fountain Cafe 2339 18th St NW	Washington	DC	20009	202-462-8100	
Web: www.littlefountaincafe.com					
Makoto 4822 MacArthur Blvd NW	Washington	DC	20007	202-298-6866	625-6602
Marcel's 2401 Pennsylvania Ave NW	Washington	DC	20037	202-296-1166	296-6466
Web: www.marcelsdc.com					
Marrakesh 617 New York Ave NW	Washington	DC	20001	202-393-9393	737-3737
Web: www.marrakesh.us					
Mendocino Grille & Wine Bar 2917 M St NW	Washington	DC	20007	202-333-2912	625-7888
Web: www.mendocinodc.com					
Montmarte 327 7th St SE	Washington	DC	20003	202-544-1244	544-4038
Morton's the Steakhouse					
1050 Connecticut Ave NW	Washington	DC	20036	202-955-5997	955-5889
Web: www.mortons.com					
New Heights Restaurant 2317 Calvert St NW	Washington	DC	20008	202-234-4110	
Web: www.newheightsrestaurant.com					
Nora 2132 Florida Ave NW	Washington	DC	20008	202-462-5143	234-6232
Web: www.noras.com					
Obelisk 2029 P St NW	Washington	DC	20036	202-872-1180	
Oceanaire Seafood Room 1201 F St NW	Washington	DC	20004	202-347-2277	347-9858
Web: www.theoceanaire.com					
Old Ebbitt Grill 675 15th St NW	Washington	DC	20005	202-347-4800	347-6136
Web: www.ebbitt.com					
Palena 3529 Connecticut Ave NW	Washington	DC	20008	202-537-9250	
Web: www.palenarestaurant.com					
Palette 15th & M Sts NW	Washington	DC	20005	202-587-2700	587-2705
Peacock Cafe 3251 Prospect St NW	Washington	DC	20007	202-625-2740	625-1402
Web: www.peacockcafe.com					
Pesce Bistro 2016 P St NW	Washington	DC	20036	202-466-3474	466-8302
Prime Rib The 2020 K St NW	Washington	DC	20006	202-466-8811	466-2010
Web: www.theprimerib.com					
Rice 1608 14th St NW	Washington	DC	20009	202-234-2400	234-2737
Web: www.ricerestaurant.com					
Sakana 2026 P St NW	Washington	DC	20036	202-887-0900	
Sea Catch 1054 31st St NW	Washington	DC	20007	202-337-8855	337-7159
Web: www.seacatchrestaurant.com					
Smith & Wollensky 1112 19th St NW	Washington	DC	20036	202-466-1100	728-2020
Web: www.smithandwollensky.com					
Sushi Ko Glover Park					
2309 Wisconsin Ave NW	Washington	DC	20007	202-333-4187	333-7594
Web: www.sushikorestaurant.com					
Sushi Taro 1503 17th St NW	Washington	DC	20036	202-462-8999	328-3756
Web: www.sushitaro.com					
Tabard Inn 1739 N St NW	Washington	DC	20036	202-331-8528	785-6173
Web: www.tabardinn.com					
Taberna Del Alabardero 1776 I St NW	Washington	DC	20006	202-429-2200	775-3713
Web: www.alabardero.com					
Teatro Goldoni 1909 K St NW	Washington	DC	20006	202-955-9494	955-5584
Web: www.teatrogoldoni.com					
TenPenh 1001 Pennsylvania Ave NW	Washington	DC	20004	202-393-4500	393-4744
Web: www.tenpenh.com					
Tosca 1112 F St NW	Washington	DC	20004	202-367-1990	367-1999
Web: www.toscadc.com					
Vidalia 1990 M St NW	Washington	DC	20036	202-659-1990	223-8572
Web: www.vidaliadc.com					
Willard Room 1401 Pennsylvania Ave NW	Washington	DC	20004	202-637-7440	637-7326
Zaytinya 701 9th St NW	Washington	DC	20001	202-638-0800	638-6969
Web: www.zaytinya.com					
Zola 800 F St NW	Washington	DC	20004	202-654-0999	654-0974
Web: www.zoladc.com					

FLORIDA

Name / Address	City	State	Zip	Phone	Fax
Sandbar Seafood & Spirits 100 Spring Ave	Anna Maria	FL	34216	941-778-0444	778-3997
Chef Allen's 19088 NE 29th Ave	Aventura	FL	33180	305-935-2900	935-9062
Web: www.chefallens.com					
Addison The 2 E Camino Real	Boca Raton	FL	33432	561-372-0568	372-0570
Web: www.theaddison.com					
Arturo's 6750 N Federal Hwy	Boca Raton	FL	33487	561-997-7373	988-7259
Web: www.arturosrestaurant.com					
Kathy's Gazebo Cafe 4199 N Federal Hwy	Boca Raton	FL	33431	561-395-6033	395-6335
Web: www.kathysgazebo.com					
Ke-e Grill 17940 N Military Trail	Boca Raton	FL	33496	561-995-5044	995-5024
Le Vieux Paris 170 W Camino Real	Boca Raton	FL	33432	561-368-7910	368-9621
Lucca 501 E Camino Real	Boca Raton	FL	33432	561-447-5822	
Max's Grille 404 Plaza Real	Boca Raton	FL	33432	561-368-0080	392-1907
Web: www.maxsgrille.com					
New York Prime 2350 Executive Ctr Dr NW	Boca Raton	FL	33431	561-998-3881	998-5761
Web: www.newyorkprime.com					
Sapori 99 Royal Palm Plaza	Boca Raton	FL	33432	561-367-9779	367-9779
Uncle Tai's 5250 Town Ctr Cir	Boca Raton	FL	33486	561-368-8806	368-4569
Roy's 26831 S Bay Dr	Bonita Springs	FL	34134	239-498-7697	495-3985
Web: www.roysrestaurant.com					
Island Way Grill 20 Island Way	Clearwater Beach	FL	33767	727-461-6617	461-0158
Web: www.islandwaygrill.com					
Anokha 3324 Virginia Grove	Coconut Grove	FL	33133	786-552-1030	
Caffe Abbracci 318 Aragon Ave	Coral Gables	FL	33134	305-441-0700	441-0781
Web: www.caffeabbracci.com					
Caffe Vialetto 4019 S Le Jeune Rd	Coral Gables	FL	33134	305-446-5659	446-3532
Web: www.cafevialetto.com					
Christy's 3101 Ponce de Leon Blvd	Coral Gables	FL	33134	305-446-1400	446-3257
Web: www.christysrestaurant.com					
Francesco 325 Alcazar Ave	Coral Gables	FL	33134	305-446-1600	446-3364
Web: www.francescorestaurant.com					
Maroosh 223 Valencia Ave	Coral Gables	FL	33134	305-476-9800	476-3999
Web: www.maroosh.com					
Miss Saigon Bistro 148 Giralda Ave	Coral Gables	FL	33134	305-446-8006	446-3085
Web: www.missaigonbistro.com					
Ortanique 278 Miracle Mile	Coral Gables	FL	33134	305-446-7710	446-9895
Pascal's on Ponce					
2611 Ponce de Leon Blvd	Coral Gables	FL	33134	305-444-2024	444-9798
Web: www.pascalmiami.com					
Ruth's Chris Steak House					
2320 Salzedo St	Coral Gables	FL	33134	305-461-8360	461-8363
Web: www.ruthschris.com					
Runyon's 9810 W Sample Rd	Coral Springs	FL	33065	954-752-2333	752-2401
Web: www.runyonsofcoralsprings.com					
Islamorada Fish Co 200 Gulf Stream Way	Dania Beach	FL	33004	954-927-7737	924-5108
Web: www.ifcstonecrab.com					
Shorty's Bar-B-Q 5989 S University Dr	Davie	FL	33328	954-680-9900	
Web: www.shortys.com					
Angell & Phelps Cafe 156 S Beach St	Daytona Beach	FL	32114	386-257-2677	252-6515
Web: www.angellandphelpscafe.com					
Anna's Trattoria 304 Seabreeze Blvd	Daytona Beach	FL	32118	386-239-9624	
Caribbean Jack's 721 Ballough Rd	Daytona Beach	FL	32114	386-523-3000	252-7362
Web: www.caribbeanjacks.com					
Cellar The 220 Magnolia Ave	Daytona Beach	FL	32114	386-258-0011	258-0117
Web: www.thecellarrestaurant.com					
Chart House 100 Marina Pt Dr	Daytona Beach	FL	32114	386-255-9022	255-5362
Web: www.chart-house.com					
Gene's Steak House					
3674 W International Speedway Blvd	Daytona Beach	FL	32124	386-255-2059	255-5460
Gilly's Pub 44 Riverfront 115 Main St	Daytona Beach	FL	32118	386-226-3000	258-4700
Maria Bonita 1784 S Ridgwood Ave S	Daytona Beach	FL	32119	386-767-9512	
Ocean Deck 127 S Ocean Ave	Daytona Beach	FL	32118	386-253-5224	253-7226
Web: www.oceandeck.com					
Oyster Pub 555 Seabreeze Blvd	Daytona Beach	FL	32118	386-255-6348	258-7489
Web: www.oysterpub.com					
Pasha					
919 W International Speedway Blvd	Daytona Beach	FL	32114	386-257-7753	255-3421
Porto-Fino Restaurant					
3124 S Atlantic Ave	Daytona Beach	FL	32118	386-767-9484	
Top Of Daytona Restaurant					
2625 S Atlantic Ave	Daytona Beach	FL	32118	386-767-5791	322-1601
Web: www.topofdaytona.com					
Crabby Joe's Deck & Grill					
3701 S Atlantic Ave	Daytona Beach Shores	FL	32127	386-788-3364	756-9878
Web: www.sunglowpier.com					
Teauila's Hawaiian Dinner Theater					
2301 S Atlantic Ave	Daytona Beach Shores	FL	32118	386-255-5411	763-1901
Baja Cafe Dos 1310 S Federal Hwy	Deerfield Beach	FL	33441	954-596-1305	596-1306
Web: www.bajacafe.com					
Brooks 500 S Federal Hwy	Deerfield Beach	FL	33441	954-427-9302	427-9811
Web: www.brooks-restaurant.com					
Tamarind Asian Grill & Sushi Bar					
949 S Federal Hwy	Deerfield Beach	FL	33441	954-428-8009	418-0939
Web: www.tamarindgrill.com					
32 East 32 E Atlantic Ave	Delray Beach	FL	33444	561-276-7868	276-7894
Web: www.32east.com					
Fifth Avenue Grill 821 S Federal Hwy	Delray Beach	FL	33483	561-265-0122	272-0567
Web: www.fifthavenuegrill.net					
Old Calypso 900 E Atlantic Ave	Delray Beach	FL	33483	561-279-2300	279-0100
Shula's Steak House LLLP					
3020 NE 32nd Ave Suite 347	FL Lauderdale	FL	33014	954-393-1920	537-3313
Web: www.donshula.com					
15th Street Fisheries					
1900 SE 15th St	Fort Lauderdale	FL	33316	954-763-2777	763-2830
Web: www.15streetfisheries.com					
3030 Ocean 3030 Holiday Dr	Fort Lauderdale	FL	33316	954-765-3030	765-3136
Web: www.3030ocean.com					
Ambry 3016 E Commercial Blvd	Fort Lauderdale	FL	33308	954-771-7342	771-7378
Web: www.ambryrestaurant.com					
Bahia Mar Bar & Grill					
801 Seabreeze Blvd	Fort Lauderdale	FL	33316	954-764-2233	627-6313
Web: www.bahiamarhotel.com/recreation_dining.htm					
Bistro 17 1617 SE 17th St	Fort Lauderdale	FL	33316	954-626-1701	626-1717
Bistro Mezzaluna 741 SE 17th St	Fort Lauderdale	FL	33316	954-522-9191	
Web: www.bistromezzaluna.com					
Cafe Martorano					
3343 E Oakland Pk Blvd	Fort Lauderdale	FL	33308	954-561-2554	630-2082
Web: www.cafemartorano.com					
Cafe Seville 2768 E Oakland Pk Blvd	Fort Lauderdale	FL	33306	954-565-1148	
Web: www.cafeseville.com					
Cafe Vico 1125 N Federal Hwy	Fort Lauderdale	FL	33304	954-565-9681	565-6978
Web: www.cafevicorestaurant.com					
Canyon 1818 E Sunrise Blvd	Fort Lauderdale	FL	33304	954-765-1950	
Web: www.canyonfl.com					
Casa D'Angelo 1201 N Federal Hwy	Fort Lauderdale	FL	33304	954-564-1234	564-1235
Casablanca Cafe 3049 Alhambra St	Fort Lauderdale	FL	33304	954-764-3500	764-3815
Web: www.casablancacafeonline.com					
Eduardo de San Angel					
2822 E Commercial Blvd	Fort Lauderdale	FL	33308	954-772-4731	772-0794
Web: www.eduardodesanangel.com					
Grandma's Ice Cream & French Cafe					
3354 N Ocean Blvd	Fort Lauderdale	FL	33308	954-564-3671	206-0292
Web: www.grandmasfrenchcafe.com					
Greek Islands Taverna					
3300 N Ocean Blvd	Fort Lauderdale	FL	33308	954-565-5505	565-4675
Web: www.greekislandstaverna.com					
Grill Room On Las Olas					
620 E Las Olas Blvd Riverside Hotel	Fort Lauderdale	FL	33301	954-467-2555	462-2148

Name / Address	City	State	ZIP	Phone	Fax
Hi-Life Cafe 3000 N Federal Hwy *Web:* www.hilifecafe.com	Fort Lauderdale	FL	33306	954-563-1395	563-1615
Himmarshee Bar & Grille 210 SW 2nd St *Web:* www.himmarshee.com	Fort Lauderdale	FL	33301	954-524-1818	524-1813
Il Mulino 1800 E Sunrise Blvd *Web:* www.ilmulinofl.com	Fort Lauderdale	FL	33304	954-524-1800	524-3811
Johnny V 625 E Las Olas Blvd *Web:* www.johnnyvlasolas.com	Fort Lauderdale	FL	33301	954-761-7920	761-3495
Las Vegas 2807 E Oakland Pk Blvd *Web:* www.lasvegascubancuisine.com	Fort Lauderdale	FL	33334	954-564-1370	
Mango's 904 E Las Olas Blvd *Web:* www.mangosonlasolas.com	Fort Lauderdale	FL	33301	954-523-5001	523-5355
Max's Grille 330 SW 1st Ave	Fort Lauderdale	FL	33301	954-779-1800	
Nick's 3496 N Ocean Blvd *Web:* www.nicksitalian.com	Fort Lauderdale	FL	33308	954-563-6441	563-9232
PF Chang's China Bistro 2418 E Sunrise Blvd *Web:* www.pfchangs.com	Fort Lauderdale	FL	33304	954-565-5877	
Primavera Restaurant 830 E Oakland Pk Blvd	Fort Lauderdale	FL	33334	954-564-6363	564-0372
Rainbow Palace 2787 E Oakland Pk Blvd *Web:* www.rainbowpalace.com	Fort Lauderdale	FL	33306	954-565-5652	565-4175
Rustic Inn 4331 Ravenswood Rd *Web:* www.rusticinn.com	Fort Lauderdale	FL	33312	954-584-1637	581-4365
Sage 2378 N Federal Hwy *Web:* www.sagecafe.net	Fort Lauderdale	FL	33305	954-565-2299	565-3309
Sea Watch Restaurant 6002 N Ocean Blvd *Web:* www.seawatchontheocean.com	Fort Lauderdale	FL	33308	954-781-2200	783-0282
Sublime 1431 N Federal Hwy *Web:* www.sublimerestaurant.com	Fort Lauderdale	FL	33304	954-615-1431	335-3031
Sunfish Grill 2761 E Oakland Pk Blvd	Fort Lauderdale	FL	33306	954-645-6464	
Sushi Rock Cafe 1515 E Las Olas Blvd	Fort Lauderdale	FL	33301	954-462-5541	
Thai on the Beach 901 N Fort Lauderdale Beach Blvd	Fort Lauderdale	FL	33304	954-565-0015	
Thai Spice 1514 E Commercial Blvd *Web:* www.thaispicefla.com	Fort Lauderdale	FL	33334	954-771-4535	771-5678
Timpano Italian Chophouse 450 E Las Olas Blvd	Fort Lauderdale	FL	33301	954-462-9119	462-9109
Tokyo Sushi 1499 SE 17th St	Fort Lauderdale	FL	33316	954-767-9922	
Tom Jenkins' Bar-B-Q 1236 S Federal Hwy *Web:* www.tomjenkinsbbq.com	Fort Lauderdale	FL	33316	954-522-5046	522-7687
Trina 601 N Fort Lauderdale Beach Blvd *TF:* 877-567-8020 ■ *Web:* www.atlantichotelfl.com/dining/index.cfm	Fort Lauderdale	FL	33304	954-567-8020	567-8040
Zuckerello's 3017 E Commercial Blvd *Web:* www.zuckerellos.com	Fort Lauderdale	FL	33308	954-776-4282	776-6096
Alan's Cubana 1712 W University Ave	Gainesville	FL	32604	352-375-6969	373-6969
Amelia's 235 S Main St Suite 107 *Web:* www.ameliasgainesville.com	Gainesville	FL	32601	352-373-1919	374-8565
Bahn Thai 1902 SW 13th St *Web:* www.bahnthai.com	Gainesville	FL	32608	352-335-1204	335-1204
David's Barbecue 5121 NW 39th Ave	Gainesville	FL	32606	352-373-2002	372-8492
Emiliano's Cafe 7 SE 1st Ave *Web:* www.emilianoscafe.com	Gainesville	FL	32601	352-375-7381	
Joe's Place 5109 NW 39th Ave Suite J *Web:* www.panamajoesplace.com	Gainesville	FL	32606	352-377-1365	377-1008
La Fiesta 7038 NW 10th Pl	Gainesville	FL	32605	352-332-0878	332-0878
Las Margaritas 4401 NW 25th Pl	Gainesville	FL	32606	352-374-6699	264-8822
Leonardo's 706 706 W University Ave	Gainesville	FL	32601	352-378-2001	373-6239
Mildred's Big City Food 3445 W University Ave *Web:* www.mildredsbigcityfood.com	Gainesville	FL	32607	352-371-1711	371-3290
Miya Sushi 3222 SW 35th Blvd *Web:* miyasushi.net	Gainesville	FL	32608	352-335-3030	335-2288
Northwest Grille 5115 NW 39th Ave *Web:* www.nwgrille.com	Gainesville	FL	32606	352-376-0500	376-0018
Sushi Matsuri 3418 SW Archer Rd *Web:* www.matsuritime.com	Gainesville	FL	32608	352-335-1875	
Tim's Thai 501 NW 23rd Ave Suite A *Web:* www.timsthairestaurant.com	Gainesville	FL	32609	352-372-5424	372-5424
Tangelo's Grille 3121 Beach Blvd S *Web:* www.tangelosgrille.com	Gulfport	FL	33707	727-894-1695	821-7027
Flanigan's 1550 W 84th St *Web:* www.flanigans.net	Hialeah	FL	33014	305-821-0993	821-7012
Koky's Bar-B-Q Ranch 4950 W 12th Ave	Hialeah	FL	33012	305-558-5512	825-4928
Las Culebrinas 4590 W 12th Ave	Hialeah	FL	33012	305-823-5828	822-2341
Molina's 4090 E 8th Ave	Hialeah	FL	33013	305-687-0008	693-9255
Thai Cafe 6845 Main St	Hialeah	FL	33014	305-825-7752	
Dave & Buster's 3000 Oakwood Blvd *Web:* www.daveandbusters.com	Hollywood	FL	33020	954-923-5505	929-6643
Taverna Opa 800 N Ocean Dr *Web:* www.tavernaoparestaurant.com	Hollywood	FL	33019	954-922-2256	922-2258
bb's Restaurant & Bar 1019 Hendricks Ave *Web:* www.bbsrestaurant.com	Jacksonville	FL	32207	904-306-0100	306-0118
Biscotti's Restaurant 3556 St Johns Ave *Web:* www.biscottis.net	Jacksonville	FL	32205	904-387-2060	387-0051
Bistro Aix 1440 San Marco Blvd *Web:* www.bistrox.com	Jacksonville	FL	32207	904-398-1949	
Chart House 1501 Gulf Life Dr **Fax Area Code: 718* ■ *Web:* www.chart-house.com	Jacksonville	FL	32207	904-398-3353	877-3359*
Dave & Buster's 7025 Salisbury Rd *Web:* www.daveandbusters.com	Jacksonville	FL	32256	904-296-1525	296-9005
JJ's Bistro de Paris 7643 Gate Pkwy Suite 105 *Web:* www.jjbistro.com	Jacksonville	FL	32256	904-996-7557	996-7577
Marker 32 14549 Beach Blvd *Web:* www.marker32.com	Jacksonville	FL	32250	904-223-1534	223-7763
Matthew's 2107 Hendricks Ave *Web:* www.matthewsrestaurant.com	Jacksonville	FL	32207	904-396-9922	396-5222
Pastiche 4260 Herschel St *Web:* www.mypastiche.com	Jacksonville	FL	32210	904-387-6213	387-0609
Row The 1521 Riverside Ave	Jacksonville	FL	32204	904-354-5080	354-6854
Ruth's Chris Steak House 1201 Gulf Life Dr *Web:* www.ruthschris.com	Jacksonville	FL	32207	904-396-6200	396-4559
Wine Cellar 1314 Prudential Dr *Web:* www.winecellarjax.com	Jacksonville	FL	32207	904-398-8989	398-3964
Dwight's 1527 Penman Rd *Web:* www.dwightsbistro.com	Jacksonville Beach	FL	32250	904-241-4496	
Eleven South 216 11th Ave S *Web:* www.elevensouth.com	Jacksonville Beach	FL	32250	904-241-1112	241-1109
Thai Room 1286 3rd St S	Jacksonville Beach	FL	32250	904-249-8444	249-8844
A & B Lobster House 700 Front St *Web:* www.aandblobsterhouse.com	Key West	FL	33040	305-294-5880	294-6871
Ambrosia 1401 Simonton St	Key West	FL	33040	305-293-0304	
Antonia's 615 Duval St *Web:* www.antoniaskeywest.com	Key West	FL	33040	305-294-6565	294-3888
Bagatelle 115 Duval St *Web:* www.bagatellekeywest.com	Key West	FL	33040	305-296-6609	294-7304
Blue Heaven 729 Thomas St *Web:* www.blueheavenkw.homestead.com	Key West	FL	33040	305-296-8666	296-9052
BO's Fish Wagon 801 Caroline St	Key West	FL	33040	305-294-9272	
Cafe Marquesa 600 Fleming St *Web:* www.marquesa.com	Key West	FL	33040	305-292-1244	
Cafe Sole 1029 Southard St *Web:* www.cafesole.com	Key West	FL	33040	305-294-0230	296-8286
Camille's 1202 Simonton St *Web:* www.camilleskeywest.com	Key West	FL	33040	305-296-4811	294-8983
Chico's Cantina 5230 US Hwy 1 *Web:* www.chicoscantina.com	Key West	FL	33040	305-296-4714	296-1485
Conch Republic Seafood Co 631 Greene St *Web:* www.conchrepublicseafood.com	Key West	FL	33040	305-294-4403	296-4330
Duffy's Steak & Lobster House 1007 Simonton St	Key West	FL	33040	305-296-4900	294-4109
El Siboney 900 Catherine St *Web:* www.elsiboneyrestaurant.com	Key West	FL	33040	305-296-4184	296-8850
Grand Cafe Key West 314 Duval St *Web:* www.grandcafekeywest.com	Key West	FL	33040	305-292-4740	292-3002
Hard Rock Cafe Key West 313 Duval St *Web:* www.hardrock.com	Key West	FL	33040	305-293-0230	
Hog's Breath Saloon Key West 400 Front St Suite C *Web:* www.hogsbreath.com	Key West	FL	33040	305-296-4222	292-8472
Jimmy Buffet's Margaritaville 500 Duval St *Web:* www.margaritaville.com	Key West	FL	33040	305-292-1435	294-9147
Kelly's Caribbean Bar Grill & Brewery 301 Whitehead St *Web:* www.kellyskeywest.com	Key West	FL	33040	305-293-8484	296-0047
La Trattoria 524 Duval St *Web:* www.latrattoria.us	Key West	FL	33040	305-296-1075	296-4941
Latitudes Beach Cafe 245 Front St	Key West	FL	33040	305-292-5394	292-5395
Louie's Backyard 700 Waddell Ave *Web:* www.louiesbackyard.com	Key West	FL	33040	305-294-1061	294-0002
Mangia Mangia 900 Southard St *Web:* www.mangia-mangia.com	Key West	FL	33040	305-294-2469	
Mangoes 700 Duval St *Web:* www.mangoeskeywest.com	Key West	FL	33040	305-292-4606	292-7958
Meteor Smokehouse 404 Southard St	Key West	FL	33040	305-294-5602	294-9462
Michael's 532 Margaret St *Web:* www.michaelskeywest.com	Key West	FL	33040	305-295-1300	295-1378
Mo's 1116 White St	Key West	FL	33040	305-296-8955	
Opera 613 Duval St *Web:* www.operarestaurant.com	Key West	FL	33040	305-295-2705	
Pisces 1007 Simonton St *Web:* www.pisceskeywest.com	Key West	FL	33040	305-294-7100	
Seven Fish 632 Olivia St *Web:* www.7fish.com	Key West	FL	33040	305-296-2777	
Sloppy Joe's 201 Duval St *Web:* www.sloppyjoes.com	Key West	FL	33040	305-294-8585	
Square One 1075 Duval St Suite C12 *Web:* www.squareonerestaurant.com	Key West	FL	33040	305-296-4300	292-5039
Turtle Kraals Restaurant & Bar 231 Margaret St *Web:* www.turtlekraals.com	Key West	FL	33040	305-294-2640	
Artist Point 901 Timberline Dr *Web:* www.disneyworld.com	Lake Buena Vista	FL	32830	407-824-1081	824-5230
bluezoo 1500 Epcot Resorts Blvd PO Box 22653 *Web:* www.swandolphin.com/bluezoo	Lake Buena Vista	FL	32830	407-934-4000	934-4882
Boma 2901 Osceola Pkwy	Lake Buena Vista	FL	32830	407-938-4722	
Bongos Cuban Cafe 1498 E Buena Vista Dr *Web:* www.bongoscubancafe.com	Lake Buena Vista	FL	32830	407-828-0999	828-0955
California Grill 4600 N World Dr	Lake Buena Vista	FL	32830	407-824-1576	824-2444
Citricos 4401 Grand Floridian Way Disney's Grand Floridian Resort	Lake Buena Vista	FL	32830	407-824-3000	824-3186
House of Blues Orlando 1490 E Lake Buena Vista Dr *Web:* www.houseofblues.com	Lake Buena Vista	FL	32830	407-934-2583	934-1100
Ohana 1600 Seven Seas Dr	Lake Buena Vista	FL	32830	407-824-2000	824-3174
Planet Hollywood 1506 E Buena Vista Dr	Lake Buena Vista	FL	32830	407-827-7827	827-7847
Victoria & Albert's 4401 Floridian Way *Web:* www.victoria-alberts.com	Lake Buena Vista	FL	32830	407-939-3862	824-0093
Taqueria Elvira 3618 Lantana Rd	Lantana	FL	33462	561-965-2117	

Restaurant	City	State	ZIP	Phone	Fax
Blue Moon Fish Co 4405 W Tradewinds Ave *Web:* www.bluemoonfishco.com	Lauderdale-by-the-Sea	FL	33308	954-267-9888	267-9006
Rosey Baby 4587 N University Dr *Web:* www.roseybaby.com	Lauderhill	FL	33351	954-749-5627	749-5733
Cap's Place Island Restaurant 2765 NE 28th Ct *Web:* www.capsplace.com	Lighthouse Point	FL	33064	954-941-0418	941-2346
Le Bistro 4626 N Federal Hwy *Web:* www.lebistrorestaurant.com	Lighthouse Point	FL	33064	954-946-9240	
Seafood World 4602 N Federal Hwy *Web:* www.seafood-world.com	Lighthouse Point	FL	33064	954-942-0740	942-0771
Chart House 201 Gulf of Mexico Dr *Web:* www.chart-house.com	Longboat Key	FL	34228	941-383-5593	383-5879
Colony Dining Room The *Colony Beach & Tennis Resort* 1620 Gulf of Mexico Dr *TF:* 800-425-5669 ■ *Web:* www.colonybeachresort.com/dining	Longboat Key	FL	34228	941-383-5558	387-0250
Euphemia Haye 5540 Gulf of Mexico Dr *Web:* www.euphemiahaye.com	Longboat Key	FL	34228	941-383-3633	387-8336
Harry's Continental Kitchens 525 St Judes Dr *Web:* www.harryskitchen.com	Longboat Key	FL	34228	941-383-0777	383-2029
Pattigeorge's 4120 Gulf of Mexico Dr *Web:* www.pattigeorges.com	Longboat Key	FL	34228	941-383-5111	
Azul 500 Brickell Key Dr	Miami	FL	33131	305-913-8254	913-3825
Bali Cafe 109 NE 2nd Ave	Miami	FL	33132	305-358-5751	358-4777
Bizcaya Grill 3300 SW 27th Ave	Miami	FL	33133	305-644-4675	644-4681
Bongos Cuban Cafe 601 Biscayne Blvd *Web:* www.bongoscubancafe.com	Miami	FL	33132	786-777-2100	777-2107
Bubba Gump Shrimp Co 401 Biscayne Blvd Bayside Marketplace *Web:* www.bubbagump.com	Miami	FL	33132	305-379-8866	379-9699
Cafe Sambal 500 Brickell Key Dr Mandarin Oriental Hotel	Miami	FL	33131	305-913-8251	913-3825
Cancun Grill 15406 NW 77th Ct	Miami	FL	33016	305-826-8571	826-7994
Capital Grille 444 Brickell Ave *Web:* www.thecapitalgrille.com	Miami	FL	33131	305-374-4500	374-2777
Captain's Tavern Restaurant Inc 9625 S Dixie Hwy *Web:* www.captainstavernmiami.com	Miami	FL	33156	305-666-5979	665-9753
Casa Juancho 2436 SW 8th St *Web:* www.casajuancho.com	Miami	FL	33135	305-642-2452	642-2524
Casa Larios 7705 W Flagler St	Miami	FL	33144	305-266-5494	266-5894
Garcia's 398 NW N River Dr	Miami	FL	33128	305-375-0765	375-0167
Graziano's 9227 SW 40th St	Miami	FL	33165	305-225-0008	221-1949
La Loggia 68 W Flagler St *Web:* www.laloggiaristorante.com	Miami	FL	33130	305-373-4800	373-7350
Lan Pan Asian Cafe 8332 S Dixie Hwy	Miami	FL	33143	305-661-8141	661-7643
Las Culebrinas 4700 W Flagler St	Miami	FL	33134	305-445-2337	445-4320
Lombardi's 401 Biscayne Blvd	Miami	FL	33132	305-381-9580	381-9366
Melting Pot of Miami The 11520 Sunset Dr *Web:* www.meltingpot.com	Miami	FL	33173	305-279-8816	598-8931
Miyako 9533 S Dixie Hwy	Miami	FL	33156	305-668-9367	
Morton's The Steakhouse 1200 Brickell Ave *Web:* www.mortons.com	Miami	FL	33131	305-400-9990	400-9989
Old Lisbon 1698 SW 22nd St *Web:* www.oldlisbon.com	Miami	FL	33145	305-854-0039	854-3677
Pacific Time 35 NE 40th St *Web:* www.pacifictime.biz	Miami	FL	33137	305-722-7369	534-1607
Perricone's Marketplace & Cafe 15 SE 10th St *Web:* www.perricones.com	Miami	FL	33131	305-374-9449	371-6647
Romeo's Cafe 2257 SW 22nd St Coral Way *Web:* www.romeoscafe.com	Miami	FL	33145	305-859-2228	859-8566
Tony Chan's Water Club 1717 N Bayshore Dr *Web:* www.tonychans.com	Miami	FL	33132	305-374-8888	
Tropical Chinese Restaurant 7991 SW 40th St *Web:* www.tropicalchinesemiami.com	Miami	FL	33155	305-262-7576	262-1552
Tutto Pasta 1751 SW 3rd Ave *Web:* www.tuttopasta.com	Miami	FL	33129	305-857-0709	
Versailles 3555 SW 8th St	Miami	FL	33135	305-444-0240	444-0774
Zuperpollo 1247 Coral Way *Web:* www.zuperpollo.com	Miami	FL	33145	305-856-9494	859-9985
A Fish Called Avalon 700 Ocean Dr *Web:* www.afishcalledavalon.com	Miami Beach	FL	33139	305-532-1727	913-6818
AltaMar 1223 Lincoln Rd *Web:* www.altamarrestaurant.com	Miami Beach	FL	33139	305-532-3061	532-2177
Barton G 1427 W Ave *Web:* www.bartong.com	Miami Beach	FL	33139	305-672-8881	672-8781
Cafe Prima Pasta 414 71st St *Web:* www.primapasta.com	Miami Beach	FL	33141	305-867-0106	867-0761
Carpaccio 9700 Collins Ave Shops of Bal Harbour	Miami Beach	FL	33154	305-867-7777	
China Grill 404 Washington Ave *Web:* www.chinagrillmgt.com	Miami Beach	FL	33139	305-534-2211	534-2565
Emeril's Miami Beach 1601 Collins Ave *Web:* www.emerils.com	Miami Beach	FL	33139	305-695-4550	695-4551
Escopazzo 1311 Washington Ave *Web:* www.escopazzo.com	Miami Beach	FL	33139	305-674-9450	532-8770
Forge The 432 41st St *Web:* www.theforge.com	Miami Beach	FL	33140	305-538-8533	538-7733
Grillfish 1444 Collins Ave *Web:* www.grillfish.com	Miami Beach	FL	33139	305-538-9908	538-2203
Hosteria Romana 429 Espanola Way *Web:* www.hosteriaromana.com	Miami Beach	FL	33139	305-532-4299	673-2570
Icebox Cafe 1657 Michigan Ave *Web:* www.iceboxcafe.com	Miami Beach	FL	33139	305-538-8448	538-6405
Joe Allen 1787 Purdy Ave *Web:* www.joeallenrestaurant.com	Miami Beach	FL	33139	305-531-7007	531-7075
Joe's Stone Crab 11 Washington Ave *Web:* www.joesstonecrab.com	Miami Beach	FL	33139	305-673-0365	673-0295
Macaluso's 1747 Alton Rd	Miami Beach	FL	33139	305-604-1811	
Maiko Japanese Restaurant 1255 Washington Ave *Web:* www.maikosushi.com	Miami Beach	FL	33139	305-531-6369	672-2773
Myles Restaurant Group 100 Collins Ave *Web:* www.mylesrestaurantgroup.com	Miami Beach	FL	33139	305-532-4245	532-4187
Nemo 157 Collins Ave 2nd Fl *Web:* www.mylesrestaurantgroup.com	Miami Beach	FL	33139	305-538-9996	
News Cafe 800 Ocean Dr *Web:* www.newscafe.com	Miami Beach	FL	33139	305-538-6397	538-7817
Nikki Beach 1 Ocean Dr S Beach *Web:* www.nikkibeach.com/miami	Miami Beach	FL	33139	305-538-1111	779-5895
Nobu 1901 Collins Ave *Web:* www.noburestaurants.com	Miami Beach	FL	33139	305-695-3232	695-3246
Osteria Del Teatro 1443 Washington Ave	Miami Beach	FL	33139	305-538-7850	477-2830
Pelican Cafe 826 Ocean Dr *Web:* www.pelicanhotel.com	Miami Beach	FL	33139	305-673-1000	673-3255
Prime 112 112 Ocean Dr *Web:* www.mylesrestaurantgroup.com	Miami Beach	FL	33139	305-532-8112	674-7317
Shula's Steak House 5225 Collins Ave *Web:* www.donshula.com	Miami Beach	FL	33140	305-865-6500	341-6553
Spris 721 Lincoln Rd *Web:* www.spris.cc	Miami Beach	FL	33139	305-673-2020	532-1706
Sushi Rock Cafe 1351 Collins Ave	Miami Beach	FL	33139	305-532-2133	
SushiSamba 600 Lincoln Rd *Web:* www.sushisamba.com	Miami Beach	FL	33139	305-673-5337	673-5451
Tamarind Thai 946 Normandy Dr *Web:* www.tamarindthai.us	Miami Beach	FL	33141	305-861-6222	861-8822
Tantra 1445 Pennsylvania Ave	Miami Beach	FL	33139	305-672-4765	624-2084
Tap Tap 819 5th St *Web:* www.taptaprestaurant.com	Miami Beach	FL	33139	305-672-2898	672-0550
Toni's Sushi Bar 1208 Washington Ave *Web:* www.tonisushi.com	Miami Beach	FL	33139	305-673-9368	
Wish 801 Collins Ave *Web:* www.wishrestaurant.com	Miami Beach	FL	33139	305-674-9474	695-9539
World Resources 719 Lincoln Rd *Web:* www.worldresourcecafe.com	Miami Beach	FL	33139	305-535-8987	604-9673
Yuca 501 Lincoln Rd *Web:* www.yuca.com	Miami Beach	FL	33139	305-532-9822	673-8276
Beverly Hills Cafe 7321 Miami Lakes Dr *Web:* www.beverlyhills1.com	Miami Lakes	FL	33014	305-558-8201	822-2503
Canton Chinese Restaurant 16780 NW 67th Ave	Miami Lakes	FL	33015	305-821-1111	821-8711
El Novillo Restaurant 15450 New Barn Rd *Web:* www.elnovillorestaurant.com	Miami Lakes	FL	33014	305-819-2755	819-7570
Shula's Steak 2 6842 Main St *Web:* www.donshula.com	Miami Lakes	FL	33014	305-820-8047	820-8039
Bistro 821 821 5th Ave S *Web:* www.bistro821.com	Naples	FL	34102	239-261-5821	261-1972
Campiello 1177 3rd St S *Web:* www.campiello.damico.com	Naples	FL	34102	239-435-1166	435-1689
Chop's City Grill 837 5th Ave S *Web:* www.chopscitygrill.com	Naples	FL	34102	239-262-4677	430-2227
Cloyde's Steak & Lobster House 4050 Gulf Shore Blvd *Web:* www.cloydes.com	Naples	FL	34103	239-261-0622	261-7554
Dock at Crayton Cove 845 12th Ave S *Web:* www.dockcraytoncove.com	Naples	FL	34102	239-263-9940	
Jasmine 7231 Radio Rd	Naples	FL	34104	239-352-5528	352-5285
Lemonia 2600 Tiburon Dr	Naples	FL	34109	239-254-3373	598-6658
M Waterfront Grille 4300 Gulf Shore Blvd N *Web:* www.mwaterfrontgrille.com	Naples	FL	34103	239-263-4421	263-3509
McCabe's Irish Pub 699 5th Ave S	Naples	FL	34102	239-403-7170	403-8778
Pazzo! 853 5th Ave S	Naples	FL	34102	239-434-8494	430-2227
PF Chang's China Bistro 10840 Tamiami Trail N *Web:* www.pfchangs.com	Naples	FL	34108	239-596-2174	596-3369
Ristorante Ciao 835 4th Ave S *Web:* www.ristoranteciao.com	Naples	FL	34102	239-263-3889	263-3658
Shula's Steak House 5111 Tamiami Trail N *Web:* www.donshula.com	Naples	FL	34103	239-430-4999	430-8299
Watermark Grille 11280 Tamiami Trail N *Web:* www.watermarkgrille.com	Naples	FL	34110	239-596-1400	596-1402
Yabba Island Grill 711 5th Ave S *Web:* www.yabbaislandgrill.com	Naples	FL	34102	239-262-5787	262-7767
Heelsha 1550 NE 164th St *Web:* www.heelsha.com	North Miami Beach	FL	33162	305-919-8393	919-8339
Ruth's Chris Steak House 661 N Federal Hwy 1 *Web:* www.ruthschris.com	North Palm Beach	FL	33408	561-863-0660	863-3670
By Word of Mouth 3200 NE 12th Ave *Web:* www.bywordofmouthfoods.com	Oakland Park	FL	33334	954-564-3663	564-1901
Ayothaya Thai Cuisine 7555 W Sand Lake *Web:* www.ayothayathaicuisineoforlando.com	Orlando	FL	32819	407-345-0040	345-0495
Bahama Breeze 8849 International Dr *Web:* www.bahamabreeze.com	Orlando	FL	32819	407-248-2499	248-2494
Boheme The 325 S Orange Ave *Web:* www.grandbohemianhotel.com/theboheme	Orlando	FL	32801	407-313-9000	313-9001
Bravissimo Wine Bar & Cafe 337 N Shine Ave	Orlando	FL	32803	407-898-7333	
Bubbalou's Bodacious BBQ 5818 Conroy Rd *Web:* www.bubbalous.com	Orlando	FL	32835	407-295-1212	295-9090
Cafe Tu Tu Tango 8625 International Dr *Web:* www.cafetututango.com	Orlando	FL	32819	407-248-2222	352-3696
Capital Grille Offices The 1000 Darden Ctr Dr *Web:* www.thecapitalgrille.com	Orlando	FL	32837	202-737-6200	637-8821
Capital Grille The 1000 Darden Ctr Dr *Web:* www.thecapitalgrille.com	Orlando	FL	32837	407-245-4000	
Cariera's Cucina Italiana 7600 Dr Phillips Blvd Suite 12 *Web:* www.carierasorlando.com	Orlando	FL	32819	407-351-1187	351-1565
Cedar's 7732 W Sand Lake Rd *Web:* www.cedarsoforlando.com	Orlando	FL	32819	407-351-6000	355-0607
Charley's Steak House 8255 International Dr *Web:* www.talkofthetownrestaurants.com	Orlando	FL	32819	407-363-0228	354-4617

Restaurant	City	State	Zip	Phone	Fax
Chatham's Place Restaurant 7575 Doctor Philips Blvd Suite 150	Orlando	FL	32819	407-345-2992	345-0307
Web: www.chathamsplace.com					
Cheesecake Factory 4200 Conroy Rd	Orlando	FL	32839	407-226-0333	226-9020
Web: www.cheesecakefactory.com					
Christini's 7600 Dr Phillips Blvd	Orlando	FL	32819	407-345-8770	345-8700
Web: www.christinis.com					
Ciao Italia 6149 Westwood Blvd	Orlando	FL	32821	407-354-0770	370-0124
Web: www.ciaoitaliaonline.com					
Emeril's Orlando 6000 Universal Blvd Suite 702	Orlando	FL	32819	407-224-2424	224-2525
Web: www.emerils.com					
Emeril's Tchoup Chop 6300 Hollywood Way	Orlando	FL	32819	407-503-2467	503-3344
Web: www.emerils.com					
Hard Rock Cafe 6050 Universal Blvd	Orlando	FL	32819	407-351-7625	351-3983
Web: www.hardrock.com					
Hemingway's 1 Grand Cypress Blvd	Orlando	FL	32836	407-239-1234	239-3800
Hemisphere 9300 Airport Blvd	Orlando	FL	32827	407-825-1234	825-1270
Web: www.hyatt.com					
Hue Restaurant 629 E Central Blvd	Orlando	FL	32801	407-849-1800	872-3348
Web: www.huerestaurant.com					
Ichiban 19 S Orange Ave	Orlando	FL	32801	407-423-2688	423-3474
Web: www.orlandoichiban.com					
Journeys Restaurant 1831 W State Rd 434	Orlando	FL	32750	407-629-2221	
Julie's Waterfront 4201 S Orange Ave	Orlando	FL	32806	407-240-2557	857-5850
Web: www.julieswaterfront.com					
K Restaurant & Wine Bar 1710 Edgewater Dr	Orlando	FL	32804	407-872-2332	872-7988
Web: www.kwinebar.com					
La Coquina 1 Grand Cypress Blvd	Orlando	FL	32836	407-239-1234	239-3800
Le Coq Au Vin 4800 S Orange Ave	Orlando	FL	32806	407-851-6980	856-9805
Web: www.lecoqauvinrestaurant.com					
Linda's La Cantina 4721 E Colonial Dr	Orlando	FL	32803	407-894-4491	894-6415
Web: www.lindaslacantina.com					
Little Saigon 1106 E Colonial Dr	Orlando	FL	32803	407-423-8539	
McCormick & Schmick's 4200 Conroy Rd Suite 146	Orlando	FL	32839	407-226-6515	226-6516
Web: www.mccormickandschmicks.com					
Ming Court 9188 International Dr	Orlando	FL	32819	407-351-9988	
Web: www.ming-court.com					
MoonFish 7525 W Sand Lake Rd	Orlando	FL	32819	407-363-7262	345-0097
Web: www.talkofthetownrestaurants.com					
Morton's The Steakhouse 7600 Doctor Phillips Blvd	Orlando	FL	32819	407-248-3485	248-8559
Web: www.mortons.com					
Mount Fuji Sushi 6700 Conroy Rd	Orlando	FL	32835	407-298-2989	
Palm 5800 Universal Blvd Hard Rock Hotel	Orlando	FL	32819	407-503-7256	503-2383
Web: www.thepalm.com					
Roy's 7760 W Sand Lake Rd	Orlando	FL	32819	407-352-4844	352-3733
Web: www.roysrestaurant.com					
Ruth's Chris Steak House 7501 W Sand Lake Rd	Orlando	FL	32819	407-226-3900	226-3108
Web: www.ruthschris.com					
Seasons 52 7700 Sand Lake Rd	Orlando	FL	32819	407-354-5212	345-1109
Web: www.seasons52.com					
Sushi House of Orlando 1311 Florida Mall Ave	Orlando	FL	32809	407-812-9767	386-9986
Web: www.sushihouseint.com					
Thai House 2117 E Colonial Dr	Orlando	FL	32803	407-898-0820	898-1375
Web: www.thaihouseoforlando.net					
Trey Yuen Restaurant 6800 Visitors Cir	Orlando	FL	32819	407-352-6822	352-1212
Viet Garden 1237-1239 E Colonial Dr	Orlando	FL	32803	407-896-4154	896-4214
Web: www.vietgardenorlando.com					
Vito's Chop House 8633 International Dr	Orlando	FL	32819	407-354-2467	226-0914
Web: www.vitoschophouse.com					
Cafe Boulud 301 Australian Ave	Palm Beach	FL	33480	561-655-6060	655-5060
Web: www.danielnyc.com					
Cafe Cellini 2505 S Ocean Blvd	Palm Beach	FL	33480	561-588-1871	582-0335
Cafe L'Europe 331 S County Rd	Palm Beach	FL	33480	561-655-4020	659-6619
Web: www.cafeleurope.com					
Chez Jean-Pierre Bistro 132 N County Rd	Palm Beach	FL	33480	561-833-1171	835-0482
Echo 230A Sunrise Ave	Palm Beach	FL	33480	561-802-4222	802-3369
Web: www.echopalmbeach.com					
Flagler Steakhouse 2 S County Rd	Palm Beach	FL	33480	561-659-8471	659-8485
L'Escalier at the Florentine Room 1 S County Rd	Palm Beach	FL	33480	561-659-8480	655-2947
Restaurant The 2800 S Ocean Blvd	Palm Beach	FL	33480	561-547-1557	
Trevini 150 Worth Ave	Palm Beach	FL	33480	561-833-3883	835-9115
Web: www.treviniristorante.com					
Cafe Chardonnay 4533 PGA Blvd	Palm Beach Gardens	FL	33418	561-627-2662	627-3413
Web: www.cafechardonnay.com					
Ironwood Grill 400 Avenue of the Champions	Palm Beach Gardens	FL	33418	561-627-2000	624-3117
Web: www.pgaresortandspa.com					
River House The 2373 PGA Blvd	Palm Beach Gardens	FL	33410	561-694-1188	694-1204
Web: www.riverhouserestaurant.com					
Capriccio 2424 N University Dr	Pembroke Pines	FL	33024	954-432-7001	432-7560
Web: www.capriccios.net					
Angus The 1101 Scenic Hwy	Pensacola	FL	32503	850-432-0539	433-9060
Web: www.anguspensacola.com					
Brews Bros 847 N Navy Blvd	Pensacola	FL	32507	850-456-2537	
Fish House The 600 S Barracks St	Pensacola	FL	32502	850-470-0003	470-0694
Web: www.fishhouse.goodgrits.com					
Hall's Seafood 920 E Gregory St	Pensacola	FL	32502	850-438-9019	436-2676
Web: www.hallsseafoodrestaurant.com					
Horizen 3103 E Strong St	Pensacola	FL	32503	850-432-7899	436-7599
Jackson's Steakhouse 400 S Palafox St	Pensacola	FL	32501	850-469-9898	469-8198
Web: www.jacksons.goodgrits.com					
Los Rancheros 7250 Plantation Rd	Pensacola	FL	32504	850-476-1623	
McGuire's Irish Pub 600 E Gregory St	Pensacola	FL	32502	850-433-6789	
Web: www.mcguiresirishpub.com					
Melting Pot of Pensacola The 418 Gregory St Suite 500	Pensacola	FL	32501	850-438-4030	433-7664
Web: www.meltingpot.com					
Petrella's Italian Cafe 2174 W Nine Mile Rd	Pensacola	FL	32534	850-471-9444	417-9336
Web: www.petrellasitaliancafe.com					
Siam Thai 6403 N 9th Ave	Pensacola	FL	32504	850-479-2882	479-2769
Skopelos on the Bay 670 Scenic Hwy	Pensacola	FL	32503	850-432-6565	438-9396
Web: www.myskopelos.com					
Tokyo Japanese Steakhouse 312 E Nine Mile Rd	Pensacola	FL	32514	850-479-9111	479-5881
Web: www.tokyopensacola.com					
Vallarta 9101 Pensacola Blvd	Pensacola	FL	32534	850-476-5262	
Yamato Oriental Cuisine 131 N New Warrington Rd	Pensacola	FL	32506	850-453-3461	456-5967
Web: www.yamatodining.com					
Basha House of Sultana Grill 7821 W Sunrise Blvd	Plantation	FL	33322	954-236-9955	382-4027
India House 1711 N University Dr	Plantation	FL	33322	954-565-5701	565-6345
Web: www.indiahouserestaurant.com					
Cafe Maxx 2601 E Atlantic Blvd	Pompano Beach	FL	33062	954-782-0606	782-0648
Web: www.cafemaxx.com					
Booth's Bowery 3657 S Nova Rd	Port Orange	FL	32129	386-761-9464	761-7518
Web: www.boothsbowery.com					
Acapulco Mexican Restaurant 12 Avenida Menendez	Saint Augustine	FL	32084	904-808-9933	808-9937
Web: www.acabay.com					
Barnacle Bill's 14 Castillo Dr	Saint Augustine	FL	32084	904-824-3663	
Web: www.barnaclebillsonline.com					
Beachcomber Restaurant 2 A St	Saint Augustine	FL	32080	904-471-3744	
Cap's 4325 Myrtle St	Saint Augustine	FL	32084	904-824-8794	829-0709
TF: 888-647-0011 ■ *Web:* www.capsonthewater.com					
Columbia Restaurant 98 St George St	Saint Augustine	FL	32084	904-824-3341	824-1361
Web: www.columbiarestaurant.com					
Conch House Restaurant 57 Comares Ave Conch House Marina Resort	Saint Augustine	FL	32080	904-829-8646	
TF: 800-940-6256 ■ *Web:* www.conch-house.com/restrnt2.htm					
Cortesse's Bistro 172 San Marco Ave	Saint Augustine	FL	32084	904-825-6775	
TF: 866-409-4135 ■ *Web:* www.cortessesbistrostaugustine.com					
Creekside Dinery 160 Nix Boat Yard Rd	Saint Augustine	FL	32086	904-829-6113	829-6115
Fusion Point 237 San Marco Ave	Saint Augustine	FL	32084	904-823-1444	823-1445
Web: www.fusioncuisine.com					
Gypsy Cab Co 828 Anastasia Blvd	Saint Augustine	FL	32080	904-824-8244	829-9080
Web: www.gypsycab.com					
Kingfish Grill 252 Yacht Club Dr	Saint Augustine	FL	32084	904-824-2111	819-6765
Web: www.kingfishgrill.com					
Kings Head British Pub 6460 US Hwy 1 N	Saint Augustine	FL	32095	904-823-9787	823-1466
Le Pavillon 45 San Marco Ave	Saint Augustine	FL	32084	904-824-6202	824-1024
Web: www.lepav.com					
Manatee Cafe 525 SR 16 Suite 106 Westgate Plaza	Saint Augustine	FL	32084	904-826-0210	826-4080
Web: www.manateecafe.com					
Mikado Steak House 1092 S Ponce de Leon Blvd	Saint Augustine	FL	32086	904-824-7064	
O'Steen's 205 Anastasia Blvd	Saint Augustine	FL	32080	904-829-6974	
Oasis Deck & Restaurant 4000 A1A Ocean Trace Rd	Saint Augustine	FL	32080	904-471-3424	
Web: www.worldfamousoasis.com					
Opus 39 39 Cordova St	Saint Augustine	FL	32084	904-824-0402	824-5009
Raintree 102 San Marco Ave	Saint Augustine	FL	32084	904-824-7211	
Web: www.raintreerestaurant.com					
Reef The 4100 Coastal Hwy	Saint Augustine	FL	32082	904-824-8008	
Web: www.thereefstaugustine.com					
Salt Water Cowboy's 299 Dondanville Rd	Saint Augustine	FL	32084	904-471-2332	471-8997
Web: www.saltwatercowboys.com					
Santa Maria Restaurant 135 Avenida Menendez	Saint Augustine	FL	32084	904-829-6578	824-9214
South Beach Grill 45 Cubbedge Rd	Saint Augustine	FL	32086	904-471-8700	471-6762
Web: www.southbeachgrill.net					
Sunset Grill 421 A1A Beach Blvd	Saint Augustine	FL	32080	904-471-5555	
Amici's 1915 A1A S	Saint Augustine Beach	FL	32080	904-461-0102	461-3457
Web: www.amicistaugustine.com					
9 Bangkok Restaurant 571 Central Ave	Saint Petersburg	FL	33701	727-894-5990	826-6164
Arigato Japanese Steak House 3600 66th St N	Saint Petersburg	FL	33710	727-343-5200	343-2421
Web: www.dinearigato.com					
Athenian Garden 6940 22nd Ave N	Saint Petersburg	FL	33710	727-345-7040	345-0765
Chateau France Restaurant 136 4th Ave NE	Saint Petersburg	FL	33701	727-894-7163	894-0221
Web: www.chateaufrancecuisine.com					
Chattaway 358 22nd Ave S	Saint Petersburg	FL	33705	727-823-1594	
Fresco's Waterfront Bar & Grill 300 2nd Ave NE	Saint Petersburg	FL	33701	727-894-4429	894-0377
Garden Bistro 217 Central Ave	Saint Petersburg	FL	33701	727-896-3800	
Marchand's Grill 501 5th Ave NE Renaissance Vinoy Resort	Saint Petersburg	FL	33701	727-894-1000	824-5044
Melting Pot ST Petersburg The 2221 4th St N	Saint Petersburg	FL	33704	727-895-6358	894-7383
Web: www.meltingpot.com					
Pepin 4125 4th St N	Saint Petersburg	FL	33703	727-821-3773	822-5991
Web: www.pepinrestaurant.net					
Red Mesa Restaurant 4912 4th St N	Saint Petersburg	FL	33703	727-527-8728	537-4798
Web: www.redmesarestaurant.com					
Siam Garden 3125 Doctor Martin Luther King Junior St N	Saint Petersburg	FL	33704	727-822-0613	
Web: www.siamgardenthai1.com					
Ted Peter's 1350 Pasadena Ave S	Saint Petersburg	FL	33707	727-381-7931	
Tokyo Bay 5901 Sun Blvd	Saint Petersburg	FL	33715	727-867-0770	

Restaurant	City	State	ZIP	Phone	Fax
Bijou Cafe 1287 1st St	Sarasota	FL	34236	941-366-8111	366-7510
Web: www.bijoucafe.net					
Cafe Amici 1371 Main St	Sarasota	FL	34236	941-951-6896	951-6897
Web: www.cafeamicisrq.com					
Cafe Baci 4001 S Tamiami Trail	Sarasota	FL	34231	941-921-4848	923-8643
Web: www.cafebaci.net					
Cafe L'Europe 431 St Armands Cir	Sarasota	FL	34237	941-388-4415	388-2362
Web: www.cafeleurope.net					
Captain Brian's 8421 N Tamiami Trail	Sarasota	FL	34243	941-351-4492	355-1973
Chutney's Etc 1944 Hillview St	Sarasota	FL	34239	941-954-4444	954-0344
Web: www.chutneysetc.com					
Columbia 411 St Armands Cir	Sarasota	FL	34236	941-388-3987	388-3321
Web: www.columbiarestaurant.com					
Demetrio's 4410 S Tamiami Trail	Sarasota	FL	34231	941-922-1585	924-1395
Mediterraneo 1970 Main St	Sarasota	FL	34236	941-365-4122	954-0106
Michael's on East 1212 E Ave S	Sarasota	FL	34239	941-366-0007	953-3463
Morel Restaurant 3809 S Tuttle Ave	Sarasota	FL	34239	941-927-8716	922-3390
Web: www.morelrestaurant.com					
Old Salty Dog 1601 Ken Thompson Pkwy	Sarasota	FL	34236	941-388-4311	388-3902
Web: www.theoldsaltydog.com					
Patricks 1400 Main St	Sarasota	FL	34236	941-952-1170	955-2072
Phillippi Creek Village Restaurant & Oyster Bar 5353 S Tamiami Trail	Sarasota	FL	34231	941-925-4444	923-2861
Web: www.creekseafood.com					
Ruth's Chris Steak House 6700 S Tamiami Trail	Sarasota	FL	34231	941-924-9442	924-8982
TF: 800-544-0808 ■ *Web:* www.ruthschris.com					
Saga Japanese Steak House 8383 S Tamiami Trail	Sarasota	FL	34238	941-924-2800	
Selva Grill 1345 Main St	Sarasota	FL	34236	941-362-4427	362-2867
Web: www.selvagrill.com					
Tandoor 3440 Clark Rd	Sarasota	FL	34231	941-926-3077	
Zoria 1991 Main St Suite 118	Sarasota	FL	34236	941-955-4457	955-4328
Ophelia's on the Bay 9105 Midnight Pass Rd	Siesta Key	FL	34242	941-349-2212	349-3328
Web: www.opheliasonthebay.net					
El Rancho Grande 1626 Pennsylvania Ave	South Beach	FL	33139	305-673-0480	673-0424
Web: www.elranchograndemexicanrestaurant.com					
Martini's Chophouse 1815 S Ridgewood Ave	South Daytona	FL	32119	386-763-1090	788-0250
Web: www.martinischophouse.com					
Songkran Thai Restaurant 2309 S Ridgewood Ave	South Daytona Beach	FL	32119	386-760-0300	
Two Chefs 8287 S Dixie Hwy	South Miami	FL	33143	305-663-2100	663-0220
Rainforest Cafe 12801 W Sunrise Blvd	Sunrise	FL	33322	954-851-1015	851-1016
Web: www.rainforestcafe.com					
Cafe Ragazzi 9500 Harding Ave	Surfside	FL	33154	305-866-4495	866-8443
Andrew's 228 228 S Adams St	Tallahassee	FL	32301	850-222-3444	222-2433
Web: www.andrewsdowntown.com					
Bahn Thai Restaurant 1319 S Monroe St	Tallahassee	FL	32301	850-224-4765	
Barnacle Bill's 1830 N Monroe St	Tallahassee	FL	32303	850-385-8734	385-6298
Web: www.barnaclebills.com					
Bonefish Grill 3491 Thomasville Rd	Tallahassee	FL	32308	850-297-0460	585-5410*
**Fax Area Code: 866* ■ *Web:* www.bonefishgrill.com					
Cabo's Island Grill & Bar 1221 Apalachee Pkwy	Tallahassee	FL	32301	850-878-7707	878-7835
Web: www.cabosgrill.com					
Chez Pierre 1215 Thomasville Rd	Tallahassee	FL	32303	850-222-0936	681-3507
Web: www.chezpierre.com					
Clusters & Hops 707 N Monroe St	Tallahassee	FL	32303	850-222-2669	222-0469
Web: www.winencheese.com					
Crystal River Seafood 1968 W Tennessee St	Tallahassee	FL	32304	850-575-4418	575-0347
Cypress The 320 E Tennessee St	Tallahassee	FL	32301	850-513-1100	513-0020
Web: www.cypressrestaurant.com					
Food Glorious Food 1950 Thomasville Rd Betton Pl	Tallahassee	FL	32303	850-224-9974	224-4673
Web: www.foodgloriousfood.com					
Georgio's 3425 Thomasville Rd	Tallahassee	FL	32308	850-893-4161	668-2674
Julie's Place 2901 N Monroe St	Tallahassee	FL	32303	850-386-7181	422-3619
Web: www.juliesplace.net					
Kitcho 1415 Timberlane Rd Suite 121	Tallahassee	FL	32312	850-893-7686	
Web: www.kitchorestaurant.com					
Longhorn Steakhouse 2400 N Monroe St	Tallahassee	FL	32304	850-385-4028	383-0466
Los Compadres 2102 W Pensacola St	Tallahassee	FL	32304	850-576-8946	576-7900
Marie Livingston's Steakhouse & Saloon 2705 Apalachee Pkwy	Tallahassee	FL	32311	850-562-2525	270-9508
Melting Pot The 2727 N Monroe St	Tallahassee	FL	32303	850-386-7440	386-8410
Web: www.meltingpot.com					
Mom & Dad's 4175 Apalachee Pkwy	Tallahassee	FL	32311	850-877-4518	
Samrat 2529 Apalachee Pkwy	Tallahassee	FL	32301	850-942-1993	942-8091
San Miguel 200 W Tharpe St	Tallahassee	FL	32303	850-385-3346	
Web: www.sanmigueltally.com					
Z Bardhi 3596 Kinhega Dr	Tallahassee	FL	32312	850-894-9919	894-2466
Web: www.zbardhis.com					
Angithi 2047 E Fowler Ave	Tampa	FL	33612	813-979-4889	972-0401
Web: www.angithirestaurant.com					
Armani's Restaurant 2900 Bayport Dr	Tampa	FL	33607	813-207-6800	207-6709
Web: www.hyatt.com					
Bern's Steak House 1208 S Howard Ave	Tampa	FL	33606	813-251-2421	251-5001
Web: www.bernssteakhouse.com					
Boizao Steakhouse 4606 W Boy Scout Blvd	Tampa	FL	33607	813-286-7100	286-7113
Web: www.boizao.com					
Byblos Cafe 2832 S MacDill Ave	Tampa	FL	33629	813-805-7977	837-0951
Web: www.bybloscafe.com					
Caffe Paridiso 4205 S MacDill Ave	Tampa	FL	33611	813-835-6622	835-9773
Capdevila at Lateresita 3248 W Columbus Dr	Tampa	FL	33607	813-879-9704	871-2321
Charley's Steakhouse 4444 W Cypress St	Tampa	FL	33607	813-353-9706	353-9510
Columbia Restaurant 2025 E 7th Ave	Tampa	FL	33605	813-248-3000	247-5881
Web: www.columbiarestaurant.com					
Donatello 232 N Dale Mabry Hwy	Tampa	FL	33609	813-875-6660	875-6660
Web: www.donatellotampa.com					
Fleming's Prime Steakhouse & Wine Bar 4322 W Boy Scout Blvd	Tampa	FL	33607	813-874-9463	554-9931*
**Fax Area Code: 866* ■ *Web:* www.flemingssteakhouse.com					
Ichiban 2786A E Fowler Ave	Tampa	FL	33612	813-978-8095	972-8179
Jackson's Bistro 601 S Harbor Island Blvd	Tampa	FL	33602	813-277-0112	277-0114
Web: www.jacksonsbistro.com					
Jasmine 13248 N Dale Mabry Hwy	Tampa	FL	33618	813-968-1501	
Jimbo's Pit BBQ 4103 W Kennedy Blvd	Tampa	FL	33609	813-289-9724	289-1006
Web: www.jimbosbarbq.com					
Kojak's House of Ribs 2808 W Gandy Blvd	Tampa	FL	33611	813-837-3774	837-2179
Mangroves Bar & Grille 208 S Howard Ave	Tampa	FL	33602	813-258-3302	250-9802
Web: www.mangroves-restaurants.com					
Melting Pot of Tampa The 13164 N Dale Mabry Hwy	Tampa	FL	33618	813-962-6936	963-0125
Web: www.meltingpot.com					
Mise En Place 442 W Kennedy Blvd	Tampa	FL	33606	813-254-5373	254-3392
Web: www.miseonline.com					
Palm The 205 Westshore Plaza Dr	Tampa	FL	33609	813-849-7256	849-0878
Web: www.thepalm.com					
Roy's 4342 W Boy Scout Blvd	Tampa	FL	33607	813-873-7697	870-0447
Web: www.roysrestaurant.com					
Rusty Pelican 2425 N Rocky Pt Dr	Tampa	FL	33607	813-281-1943	289-3782
Web: www.therustypelican.com					
Ruth's Chris Steak House 1700 N Westshore Blvd	Tampa	FL	33607	813-282-1118	281-0982
Web: www.ruthschris.com					
Sam Seltzer's Steakhouse 4744 N Dale Mabry Hwy	Tampa	FL	33614	813-873-7267	879-4744
Sawatdee Thai Cuisine 10938 N 56th St	Tampa	FL	33617	813-985-2071	
Web: www.sawatdeethaitampa.com					
Shula's Steak House 4860 W Kennedy Blvd	Tampa	FL	33609	813-286-4366	286-4034
Web: www.donshula.com					
Sidebern's 2208 W Morrison Ave	Tampa	FL	33606	813-258-2233	259-9463
Web: www.sideberns.com					
Six Tables 4267 Henderson Blvd	Tampa	FL	33629	813-207-0527	
Web: www.sixtablestampa.com					
Taj Indian Cuisine 2734 E Fowler Ave	Tampa	FL	33612	813-971-8483	972-3587
Thai Terrace 2055-C N Dale Mabry Hwy	Tampa	FL	33607	813-877-8955	
Bimini Twist 8480 Okeechobee Blvd	West Palm Beach	FL	33411	561-784-2660	784-2660
Cabana 533 Clematis St	West Palm Beach	FL	33401	561-833-4773	514-0655
Web: www.cabanarestaurant.com					
Cafe Protege 2410 Metrocentre Blvd	West Palm Beach	FL	33407	561-687-2433	
City Cellar Wine Bar & Grill 700 S Rosemary Ave	West Palm Beach	FL	33401	561-366-0071	366-8541
La Sirena 6316 S Dixie Hwy	West Palm Beach	FL	33405	561-585-3128	585-3681
Web: www.lasirenaonline.com					
Leila 120 S Dixie Hwy	West Palm Beach	FL	33401	561-659-7373	659-5484
Maison Carlos 3010 S Dixie Hwy	West Palm Beach	FL	33405	561-659-6524	833-0856
Web: www.maisoncarlos.com					
Morton's the Steakhouse 777 S Flagler Dr	West Palm Beach	FL	33401	561-835-9664	835-4806
Web: www.mortons.com					
Okeechobee Steakhouse 2854 Okeechobee Blvd	West Palm Beach	FL	33409	561-683-5151	684-7402
Web: www.okeesteakhouse.com					
Raindancer Steak House 2300 Palm Beach Lakes Blvd	West Palm Beach	FL	33409	561-684-2810	689-4442
Web: www.raindancersteakhouse.com					
Rhythm Cafe 3800 S Dixie Hwy	West Palm Beach	FL	33405	561-833-3406	
Web: www.rhythmcafe.cc					
Stresa 2710 Okeechobee Blvd	West Palm Beach	FL	33409	561-615-0200	615-0200
Boondocks Restaurant 3948 S Peninsula Dr	Wilbur by the Sea	FL	32127	386-760-9001	
Old Florida Seafood House 1414 NE 26th St	Wilton Manors	FL	33305	954-566-1044	566-1048
Web: www.oldflaseafood.com					
Houston's 215 S Orlando Ave	Winter Park	FL	32789	407-740-4005	740-4050
Web: www.hillstone.com					

GEORGIA

Restaurant	City	State	ZIP	Phone	Fax
Di Paolo Cucina 8560 Holcomb Bridge Rd	Alpharetta	GA	30022	770-587-1051	587-1195
Web: www.dipaolorestaurant.com					
10 Degrees South 4183 Roswell Rd NE	Atlanta	GA	30342	404-705-8870	
Web: www.10degreessouth.com					
5 Seasons Brewing Co 5600 Roswell Rd Suite 21	Atlanta	GA	30342	404-255-5911	255-5966
Web: www.5seasonsbrewing.com					
Agave 242 Blvd SE	Atlanta	GA	30312	404-588-0006	588-0909
Web: www.agaverestaurant.com					
Anis Cafe & Bistro 2974 Grandview Ave	Atlanta	GA	30305	404-233-9889	233-4894
Web: www.anisbistro.com					
Annie's Thai Castle 3195 Roswell Rd	Atlanta	GA	30305	404-264-9546	
Anthony's Plantation Restaurant 3109 Piedmont Rd NE	Atlanta	GA	30305	404-262-7379	261-6009
Web: www.anthonysfinedining.com					
Antica Posta 519 E Paces Ferry Rd	Atlanta	GA	30305	404-262-7112	262-7335
Web: www.anticaposta.com					
Aria Restaurant 490 E Paces Ferry Rd NE	Atlanta	GA	30305	404-233-7673	262-5208
Web: www.aria-atl.com					
Atlanta Fish Market 265 Pharr Rd NE	Atlanta	GA	30305	404-262-3165	601-1315
Web: www.buckheadrestaurants.com					
Atlanta Grill 181 Peachtree St NE	Atlanta	GA	30303	404-221-6550	215-4672
Web: www.wisconsinhotel.com					
Atmosphere 1620 Piedmont Ave	Atlanta	GA	30324	678-702-1620	702-1621
Web: www.atmospherebistro.com					
Babette's Cafe 573 N Highland Ave	Atlanta	GA	30307	404-523-9121	523-7909
Web: www.babettescafe.com					
Bacchanalia 1198 Howell Mill Rd	Atlanta	GA	30318	404-365-0410	365-8020
Bangkok Thai 1492 Piedmont Ave NE	Atlanta	GA	30309	404-874-2514	
Baraonda 710 Peachtree St	Atlanta	GA	30308	404-879-9962	892-3973
Web: www.baraondaatlanta.com					
Basil's Restaurant & Bar 2985 Grandview Ave NE	Atlanta	GA	30305	404-233-9755	
Web: www.basils.net					

Name / Address	City	State	Zip	Phone	Fax
Beautiful Restaurant The 2260 Cascade Rd SW	Atlanta	GA	30311	404-752-5931	758-4767
Web: www.beautifulrestaurant-atlanta.com					
Benihana 229 Peachtree St NE	Atlanta	GA	30303	404-522-9629	525-4834
Web: www.benihana.com					
Blue Ridge Grill 1261 W Paces Ferry Rd	Atlanta	GA	30327	404-233-5030	233-5023
Web: www.blueridgegrill.com					
BluePointe 3455 Peachtree Rd	Atlanta	GA	30326	404-237-9070	237-2387
Web: www.buckheadrestaurants.com					
Bone's Restaurant 3130 Piedmont Rd NE	Atlanta	GA	30305	404-237-2663	233-5704
Web: www.bonesrestaurant.com					
Brasserie Le Coze 30 Ivan Allen Blvd	Atlanta	GA	30308	404-266-1440	266-1436
Web: www.fabatlanta.com					
Buckhead Diner 3073 Piedmont Rd NE	Atlanta	GA	30305	404-262-3336	262-3593
Web: www.buckheadrestaurants.com					
Cafe Prego 4279 Roswell Rd # 101	Atlanta	GA	30342	404-252-0032	
Web: www.cafeprego.net					
Cafe Sunflower 2140 Peachtree Rd	Atlanta	GA	30308	404-352-8859	352-2556
Web: www.cafesunflower.com					
Cafe The 3434 Peachtree Rd NE Ritz-Carlton Buckhead	Atlanta	GA	30326	404-237-2700	239-0078
Web: www.ritzcarlton.com					
Canoe 4199 Paces Ferry Rd NW	Atlanta	GA	30339	770-432-2663	433-2542
Web: www.canoeatl.com					
Capital Grille The 255 E Paces Ferry Rd	Atlanta	GA	30305	404-262-1162	262-1163
Web: www.thecapitalgrille.com					
Chequers Seafood Grill 236 Perimeter Ctr Pkwy	Atlanta	GA	30346	770-391-9383	394-2055
Web: www.chequersseafood.com					
China Cooks 215 Northwood Dr	Atlanta	GA	30342	404-252-6611	256-8221
Chops/Lobster Bar 70 W Paces Ferry Rd NW	Atlanta	GA	30305	404-262-2675	240-6645
Web: www.buckheadrestaurants.com					
Chopstix 4279 Roswell Rd	Atlanta	GA	30342	404-255-4868	
Web: www.chopstixatlanta.net					
City Grill 50 Hurt Plaza	Atlanta	GA	30303	404-524-2489	529-9474
Web: www.citygrillatlanta.com					
Eclipse di Luna 764 Miami Cir	Atlanta	GA	30324	404-846-0449	869-7418
Web: www.eclipsediluna.com					
Fat Matt's Rib Shack 1811 Piedmont Ave	Atlanta	GA	30324	404-607-1622	
Web: www.fatmattsribshack.com					
FGT Cafe & Bar 111 Perimeter Ctr W	Atlanta	GA	30346	770-280-0700	
Web: www.atlantaperimeterhotelandsuites.com					
Figo Pasta/Osteria del Figo 1170 Collier Rd NW # B	Atlanta	GA	30318	404-351-9667	351-9677
Web: www.figopasta.com					
Floataway Cafe 1123 Zonolite Rd Suite 15	Atlanta	GA	30306	404-892-1414	892-8833
Web: www.starprovisions.com					
Flying Biscuit Cafe 1655 McLendon Ave	Atlanta	GA	30307	404-687-8888	687-8838
Web: www.flyingbiscuit.com					
Fogo de Chao 3101 Piedmont Rd	Atlanta	GA	30305	404-266-9988	995-9983
Web: www.fogodechao.com					
Fritti 309 N Highland Ave	Atlanta	GA	30307	404-880-9559	880-0462
Web: www.frittirestaurant.com					
Fuego Spanish Grill 1136 Crescent Ave NE	Atlanta	GA	30309	404-389-0660	389-0662
Web: www.fuegocafe.com					
Georgia Grille 2290 Peachtree Rd	Atlanta	GA	30309	404-352-3517	841-9964
Web: www.thereynoldsgroupinc.com					
Goldfish 4400 Ashford Dunwoody Rd	Atlanta	GA	30346	770-671-0100	671-1887
Grand China Restaurant 2975 Peachtree Rd NE	Atlanta	GA	30305	404-231-8690	231-5415
Web: www.grandchinaatl.com					
Hal's on Old Ivy 30 Old Ivy Rd	Atlanta	GA	30342	404-261-0025	814-1248
Web: www.hals.net					
Harmony 4897 Buford Hwy	Atlanta	GA	30341	770-457-7288	
Harold's Barbecue 171 McDonough Blvd SE	Atlanta	GA	30315	404-627-9268	
Harry & Sons 820 N Highland Ave	Atlanta	GA	30306	404-873-2009	873-1940
Web: www.harryandsonsrestaurant.com					
Haven 1441 Dresden Dr NE Suite 100	Atlanta	GA	30319	404-969-0700	969-0701
Web: www.havenrestaurant.com					
Horseradish Grill 4320 Powers Ferry Rd	Atlanta	GA	30342	404-255-7277	847-0603
Web: www.horseradishgrill.com					
Hsu's Gourmet Chinese Restaurant 192 Peachtree Ctr Ave	Atlanta	GA	30303	404-659-2788	577-3456
Web: www.hsus.com					
Joel 3290 Northside Pkwy	Atlanta	GA	30327	404-233-3500	467-9450
Web: www.joelrestaurant.com					
Kyma 3085 Piedmont Rd	Atlanta	GA	30305	404-262-0702	841-9924
Web: www.buckheadrestaurants.com					
La Grotta 2637 Peachtree Rd	Atlanta	GA	30305	404-231-1368	231-1274
Web: www.la-grotta.com					
La Tavola Trattoria 992 Virginia Ave	Atlanta	GA	30306	404-873-5430	873-5410
Web: www.latavolatrattoria.com					
Le Giverny 1641 Clifton Rd	Atlanta	GA	30329	404-325-7252	325-8414
Web: www.legiverny.net					
Malaya 857 Collier Rd	Atlanta	GA	30318	404-609-9991	609-9892
Mali Restaurant 961 Amsterdam Ave NE	Atlanta	GA	30306	404-874-1411	874-5112
Web: www.malirestaurant.com					
McCormick & Schmick's 190 Marietta St NW	Atlanta	GA	30318	404-521-1236	521-1237
Web: www.mccormickandschmicks.com					
McKendrick's Steak House 4505 Ashford Dunwoody Rd	Atlanta	GA	30346	770-512-8888	379-1470
Web: www.mckendricks.com					
MF Sushibar 265 Ponce de Leon Ave	Atlanta	GA	30308	404-815-8844	872-2600
Web: www.mfsushibar.com					
Morton's The Steakhouse 303 Peachtree Ctr Ave	Atlanta	GA	30308	404-577-4366	577-4687
Web: www.mortons.com					
Mu Lan 824 Juniper St NE	Atlanta	GA	30308	404-877-5797	877-5798
Web: www.mulanatlanta.com					
Nakato 1776 Cheshire Bridge Rd NE	Atlanta	GA	30324	404-873-6582	874-7897
Web: www.nakatorestaurant.com					
Nam 931 Monroe Dr Suite A-101	Atlanta	GA	30308	404-541-9997	
Web: www.namrestaurant.com					
Nan Thai 1350 Spring St NW	Atlanta	GA	30309	404-870-9933	870-9955
Web: www.nanfinedining.com					
Nava 3060 Peachtree Rd	Atlanta	GA	30305	404-240-1984	240-1381
Web: www.buckheadrestaurants.com					
Nikolai's Roof 255 Courtland St	Atlanta	GA	30303	404-221-6362	221-6811
Web: www.nikolaisroof.com					
Nino's 1931 Chesire Bridge Rd	Atlanta	GA	30324	404-874-6505	874-3596
Web: www.ninosatlanta.com					
Nuevo Laredo 1495 Chattahoochee Ave	Atlanta	GA	30318	404-352-9009	352-9202
Web: www.nuevolaredocantina.com					
Oscar's Villa Capri 2090 Dunwoody Club Dr	Atlanta	GA	30350	770-392-7940	804-1503
Web: www.oscarsvillacapri.com					
Pacific Rim Bistro 303 Peachtree Ctr Ave	Atlanta	GA	30308	404-893-0018	893-0020
Web: www.pacificrimbistro.com					
Palm Restaurant 3391 Peachtree Rd NE	Atlanta	GA	30326	404-814-1955	814-1985
Web: www.thepalm.com					
Park 75 75 14th St	Atlanta	GA	30309	404-253-3840	253-3935
Paul's Restaurant 10 King Cir	Atlanta	GA	30305	404-231-4113	231-4710
Portofino 3199 Paces Ferry Pl	Atlanta	GA	30305	404-231-1136	231-4773
Web: www.portofinobistro.com					
Pricci 500 Pharr Rd	Atlanta	GA	30305	404-237-2941	261-0058
Web: www.buckheadrestaurants.com					
Prime 3393 Peachtree Rd	Atlanta	GA	30326	404-812-0555	812-0225
Pura Vida 656 N Highland Ave N E	Atlanta	GA	30306	404-870-9797	
Web: www.puravidatapas.com					
Rathbun's 112 Krog St Suite R	Atlanta	GA	30307	404-524-8280	524-8580
Web: www.kevinrathbun.com					
Ray's in the City 240 Peachtree St NW	Atlanta	GA	30303	404-524-9224	524-9229
Web: www.raysrestaurants.com					
Ritz-Carlton Dining Room 3434 Peachtree Rd	Atlanta	GA	30326	404-237-2700	239-0078
Rolling Bones Premium Pit BBQ 377 Edgewood Ave SE	Atlanta	GA	30312	404-222-2324	221-1174
Web: www.rollingbonesbbq.com					
Ruth's Chris Steak House 267 Marietta St	Atlanta	GA	30313	404-223-6500	223-1155
Web: www.ruthschrisatlanta.com					
Sip Wine Riverside 4403 Northside Pkwy NW	Atlanta	GA	30327	404-233-5455	233-3073
Web: www.riverroom.com					
Sotto Sotto Cucina Italiana 313 N Highland Ave	Atlanta	GA	30307	404-523-6678	880-0462
Web: www.sottosottorestaurant.com					
South City Kitchen 1144 Crescent Ave	Atlanta	GA	30309	404-873-7358	873-0317
Web: www.southcitykitchen.com					
Surin of Thailand 810 N Highland Ave NE	Atlanta	GA	30306	404-892-7789	892-8344
Web: www.surinofthailand.com					
Taka 385 Pharr Rd NE	Atlanta	GA	30305	404-869-2802	
Tamarind Seed 1197 Peachtree St NW Suite 110	Atlanta	GA	30361	404-873-4888	873-4886
Web: www.tamarindseed.com					
Thai Chili 2169 Briarcliff Rd NE	Atlanta	GA	30329	404-315-6750	315-9367
Web: www.thaichilicuisine.com					
Tierra Restaurant 1425 Piedmont Ave NE	Atlanta	GA	30309	404-874-5951	874-5235
Web: www.tierrarestaurant.com					
Top Spice 3007 N Druid Hills Rd NE	Atlanta	GA	30329	404-728-0588	728-1132
Web: www.topspiceatlanta.com					
Veni-Vidi-Vici 41 Fourteenth St	Atlanta	GA	30309	404-875-8424	875-6533
Web: www.buckheadrestaurants.com					
Vinings Inn 3011 Paces Mill Rd SE	Atlanta	GA	30339	770-438-2282	438-0653
Web: www.viningsinn.com					
Wisteria 471 N Highland Ave	Atlanta	GA	30307	404-525-3363	525-3313
Web: www.wisteria-atlanta.com					
Woodfire Grill 1782 Cheshire Bridge Rd	Atlanta	GA	30324	404-347-9055	347-9566
Web: www.woodfiregrill.com					
Augustino's 2 10th St	Augusta	GA	30901	706-823-6521	823-6523
Web: www.augustinos.net					
Bamboo Garden 819 15th St	Augusta	GA	30901	706-722-7300	
Beamie's 865 Reynolds St	Augusta	GA	30901	706-724-6593	724-7466
California Dreaming 3241 Washington Rd	Augusta	GA	30907	706-860-6206	860-4699
Web: www.centraarchy.com					
Calvert's Restaurant 475 Highland Ave	Augusta	GA	30909	706-738-4514	312-2121
Web: www.calvertsrestaurant.com					
Formosa's 3830 Washington Rd	Augusta	GA	30907	706-855-8998	855-9742
French Market Grille 425 Highland Ave	Augusta	GA	30909	706-737-4865	733-0275
Web: www.frenchmarketaugusta.com					
La Maison on Telfair 404 Telfair St	Augusta	GA	30901	706-722-4805	722-1753
Web: www.lamaisontelfair.com					
Luigi's 590 Broad St	Augusta	GA	30901	706-722-4056	
Web: www.luigisinc.com					
Ming Wah 920 Baker Ave	Augusta	GA	30904	706-733-0740	
Rhinehart's Oyster Bar 3051 Washington Rd	Augusta	GA	30907	706-860-2337	
Sconyer's Bar-B-Que 2250 Sconyers Way	Augusta	GA	30906	706-790-5411	790-1505
Shangri-La 3847 Washington Rd	Augusta	GA	30907	706-854-9791	
T's Restaurant 3416 Mike Pagett Hwy	Augusta	GA	30906	706-798-4145	793-8474
Web: www.tsrestaurant.com					
Verandah Grill 2110 Walton Way Partridge Inn	Augusta	GA	30904	706-737-8888	731-0826
Web: www.partridgeinn.com/dining					
Villa Europa 3044 Deans Bridge Rd	Augusta	GA	30906	706-798-6211	798-0066
Web: www.villaeuropa.com					
Cafe Amici 2301 Airport Thwy Suite E2	Columbus	GA	31904	706-653-6361	653-6357
Chef Lee's Peking Chinese Restaurant 4248 Buena Vista Rd	Columbus	GA	31907	706-568-7554	
Country's Barbecue 2016 12th Ave	Columbus	GA	31901	706-327-7702	324-5859
Web: www.countrysbarbecue.com					
Don Chuco's 5770 Milgen Rd	Columbus	GA	31907	706-561-3040	
Los Amigos Mexican Restaurant 5592 Whitesville Rd	Columbus	GA	31904	706-322-1993	
Macon Road Barbecue 2703 Avalon Rd	Columbus	GA	31907	706-563-0542	563-0208
Mikata Japanese Steakhouse 5300 Sidney Simons Blvd	Columbus	GA	31904	706-327-5100	
Web: www.mikatasteakhouse.com					
Panda Garden 5600 Milgen Rd	Columbus	GA	31907	706-569-8487	569-8467
Caliente's Burrito Shop 6255 Zebulon Rd Suite 260	Macon	GA	31210	478-471-8110	471-8148
Web: www.calientesburritoshop.com					

	City	State	ZIP	Phone	Fax
Dawson's Kitchen 3360 Brookdale Ave	Macon	GA	31204	478-742-9852	
Web: www.dawsonskitchen.com					
Downtown Grill 562 Mulberry St Ln	Macon	GA	31201	478-742-5999	742-9708
Web: www.macondowntowngrill.com					
El Azteca 169 Tom Hill Sr Blvd.	Macon	GA	31210	478-475-9199	475-4409
Fincher's Barbeque 5627 Houston Rd	Macon	GA	31216	478-781-6998	
Logan's Roadhouse 3933 Arkwright Rd	Macon	GA	31210	478-477-8806	477-8637
Web: www.logansroadhouse.com					
Marco 4581 Forsyth Rd.	Macon	GA	31210	478-405-5660	405-5668
Web: www.marcomacon.com					
Natalia's 201 N Macon St.	Macon	GA	31210	478-741-1380	743-9388
Saleem Fish Supreme 2198 Pio Nono Ave	Macon	GA	31206	478-788-8600	
Taj Indian Restaurant 5033 Brookhaven Rd	Macon	GA	31206	478-785-8540	785-0858
Monterrey 4018 Washington Rd.	Martinez	GA	30907	706-855-9949	855-6962
Aqua Blue 1564 Holcomb Bridge Rd	Roswell	GA	30076	770-643-8886	643-8851
Web: www.aquablueatl.com					
17 Hundred 90 Restaurant 307 E President St	Savannah	GA	31401	912-236-7122	236-7123
Web: www.17hundred90.com					
45 Bistro 123 E Broughton St.	Savannah	GA	31401	912-234-3111	233-9672
Web: www.marshallhouse.com					
Alligator Soul 114 Barnard St	Savannah	GA	31401	912-232-7899	232-7898
Belford's Savannah 315 W St Julian St	Savannah	GA	31401	912-233-2626	233-6741
Web: www.belfordssavannah.com					
Bistro Savannah 309 W Congress St	Savannah	GA	31401	912-233-6266	232-7957
Cancun 5500 Abercorn St Suite 30	Savannah	GA	31405	912-356-1333	
Casbah 118 E Broughton St	Savannah	GA	31401	912-234-6168	
Web: www.casbahrestaurant.com					
Elizabeth on 37th 105 E 37th St	Savannah	GA	31401	912-236-5547	232-1095
Web: www.elizabethon37th.net					
Exchange Tavern & Restaurant 201 E River St	Savannah	GA	31401	912-232-7088	
Garibaldi Cafe 315 W Congress St	Savannah	GA	31401	912-232-7118	232-7957
Huey's 115 E River St	Savannah	GA	31401	912-234-7385	234-7307
Il Pasticcio 2 E Broughton St.	Savannah	GA	31401	912-231-8888	231-8813
Web: www.ilpasticciosavannah.com					
Lady & Sons The 102 W Congress St	Savannah	GA	31401	912-233-2600	233-8283
Web: www.ladyandsons.com					
Loves Seafood & Steaks 6817 Basin Rd.	Savannah	GA	31419	912-925-3616	925-1900
Olde Pink House 23 Abercorn St.	Savannah	GA	31401	912-232-4286	231-1934
Pearl's Elegant Pelican 7000 LaRoche Ave	Savannah	GA	31406	912-352-8221	
Pirates' House 20 E Broad St	Savannah	GA	31401	912-233-5757	234-1212
Web: www.thepirateshouse.com					
River House Seafood Restaurant					
125 W River St	Savannah	GA	31401	912-234-1900	341-0277*
**Fax:* Orders ■ *TF:* 800-317-1912 ■ *Web:* www.riverhouseseafood.com					
Sapphire Grill 110 W St Julian St	Savannah	GA	31401	912-443-9962	443-9964
Web: www.sapphiregrill.com					
Shellhouse 8 Gateway Blvd	Savannah	GA	31419	912-927-3280	920-4814
Six Pence Pub 245 Bull St.	Savannah	GA	31401	912-233-3156	233-4576
Toucan Cafe 531 Stephenson Ave	Savannah	GA	31406	912-352-2233	352-2258
Web: www.toucancafe.com					
Tubby's Tank House 2909 River Dr.	Savannah	GA	31404	912-354-9040	354-1374
Web: www.savannahmenu.com					
Uncle Bubba's Oyster House					
104 Bryan Woods Rd	Savannah	GA	31410	912-897-6101	897-6811
Web: www.unclebubbas.com					
Wilkes Dining Room 107 W Jones St.	Savannah	GA	31401	912-232-5997	

HAWAII

	City	State	ZIP	Phone	Fax
Bravo 98-115 Kaonohi St	Aiea	HI	96701	808-487-5544	486-3837
Web: www.bravorestaurant.com					
3660 on the Rise 3660 Waialae Ave	Honolulu	HI	96816	808-737-1177	735-6105
Web: www.3660.com					
Alan Wong's 1857 S King St	Honolulu	HI	96826	808-949-2526	951-9520
Web: www.alanwongs.com					
Auntie Pasto's Restaurant					
1099 S Beretania St	Honolulu	HI	96814	808-523-8855	523-8857
Web: www.auntiepastos.com					
Bali By-the-Sea 2005 Kalia Rd	Honolulu	HI	96815	808-949-4321	947-7926
Bubba Gump Shrimp Co 1450 Ala Moana Blvd	Honolulu	HI	96814	808-949-4867	952-0400
Web: www.bubbagump.com					
Chef Mavro 1969 S King St	Honolulu	HI	96826	808-944-4714	944-3903
Web: www.chefmavro.com					
Chuck's Steak House 2335 Kalakaua Ave	Honolulu	HI	96815	808-923-1228	733-7503
Web: www.chuckshawaii.com					
Diamond Head Grill 2885 Kalakaua Ave	Honolulu	HI	96815	808-922-3734	922-1550
Duke's Waikiki Restaurant & Barefoot Bar					
2335 Kalakaua Ave	Honolulu	HI	96815	808-922-2268	923-5106
El Burrito 550 Piikoi St.	Honolulu	HI	96814	808-596-8225	
Genki Sushi Hawaii					
677 Ala Moana Blvd Suite 612	Honolulu	HI	96813	808-523-3315	523-3316
Web: www.genkisushiusa.com					
Gyotaku 1824 King St.	Honolulu	HI	96826	808-949-4584	946-6529
Web: www.gyotakuhawaii.com					
Hard Rock Cafe International Inc					
1837 Kapiolani Blvd	Honolulu	HI	96826	808-955-7383	949-6040
Web: www.hardrock.com					
Hee Hing 449 Kapahulu Ave	Honolulu	HI	96815	808-735-5544	732-6026
Web: www.heehinghawaii.com					
Hiroshi Eurasian Tapas 500 Ala Moana Blvd.	Honolulu	HI	96813	808-533-4476	536-0667
Web: www.hiroshihawaii.com					
Hoku's 5000 Kahala Ave	Honolulu	HI	96816	808-739-8779	739-8800
Web: www.kahalaresort.com					
Hy's Steak House 2440 Kuhio Ave	Honolulu	HI	96815	808-922-5555	926-5089
Web: www.hyshawaii.com					
Indigo 1121 Nuuanu Ave.	Honolulu	HI	96817	808-521-2900	537-4164
Web: www.indigo-hawaii.com					
Keo's 2028 Kuhio Ave	Honolulu	HI	96815	808-951-9355	953-2325
Web: www.keosthaicuisine.com					
Kincaid's Fish Chop & Steak House					
1050 Ala Moana Blvd	Honolulu	HI	96814	808-591-2005	591-2501
Web: www.kincaids.com					
Longhi's					
Ala Moana Shopping Ctr					
1450 Ala Moana Blvd Suite 3001	Honolulu	HI	96814	808-947-9899	944-3733
Web: www.longhis.com					
Mariposa 1450 Ala Moana Blvd	Honolulu	HI	96814	808-951-3420	951-3419
Michel's 2895 Kalakaua Ave Colony Surf Hotel	Honolulu	HI	96815	808-923-6552	926-6063
Web: www.michelshawaii.com					
Morton's The Steakhouse 1450 Ala Moana Blvd	Honolulu	HI	96814	808-949-1300	947-9512
Web: www.mortons.com					
Orchids 2199 Kalia Rd Halekulani Hotel	Honolulu	HI	96815	808-923-2311	931-5315
Ruth's Chris Steak House					
500 Ala Moana Blvd Suite 6C	Honolulu	HI	96813	808-599-3860	533-0786
Web: www.ruthschris.com					
Ryan's Grill at Ward Centre					
1200 Ala Moana Blvd	Honolulu	HI	96814	808-591-9132	591-0034
Web: www.ryansgrill.com					
Sansei Seafood Restaurant & Sushi Bar					
Waikiki Beach Marriot Resort & Spa					
2552 Kalakauna Ave.	Honolulu	HI	96815	808-931-6286	924-0667
Web: www.sanseihawaii.com					
Shorebird Beach Broiler					
2169 Kalia Rd Outrigger Reef Hotel	Honolulu	HI	96815	808-922-2887	926-5372
Web: www.shorebirdwaikiki.com					
Side Street Inn 1225 Hopaka St	Honolulu	HI	96814	808-591-0253	732-7333
Web: www.sidestreetinn.com					
Sorabol					
Sorabol Korean Restaurant 805 Keeaumoku St	Honolulu	HI	96814	808-947-3113	947-6861
Web: www.sorabolhawaii.com					
Stage Restaurant 1250 Kapiolani Blvd 2nd Fl	Honolulu	HI	96814	808-237-5429	956-1255
Web: www.stagerestauranthawaii.com					
Tanaka of Tokyo East 131 Kaiulani Ave 3rd Fl.	Honolulu	HI	96815	808-922-4233	922-6948
Web: www.tanakaoftokyo.com					
Willows The 901 Hausten St	Honolulu	HI	96826	808-952-9200	952-0050
Web: www.willowshawaii.com					
Assaggio 95-1249 Meheula Pkwy	Mililani	HI	96789	808-623-5115	623-4693
Web: www.assaggiohi.com					

IDAHO

	City	State	ZIP	Phone	Fax
Angell's Bar & Grill					
999 W Main St One Capital Ctr.	Boise	ID	83702	208-342-4900	342-3971
Web: www.angellsbarandgrill.com					
Barbacoa Grill 276 W Bobwhite Ct	Boise	ID	83706	208-338-5000	338-5004
Web: www.barbacoa-boise.com					
Bitter Creek Ale House 246 N 8th St.	Boise	ID	83702	208-345-1813	345-3788
Web: www.justeatlocal.com					
Brick Oven Bistro 801 Main St	Boise	ID	83702	208-342-3456	384-0266
Web: www.brickovenbistro.com					
Cazba Downtown Mediterranean & Greek Food					
211 N 8th St	Boise	ID	83702	208-381-0222	
Web: www.cazba.com					
Cottonwood Grille 913 W River St	Boise	ID	83702	208-333-9800	333-1450
Web: www.cottonwoodgrille.com					
Dong Khanh 111 Broadway Suite 139	Boise	ID	83702	208-345-0980	
Fujiyama 283 N Milwaukee St	Boise	ID	83704	208-672-8227	672-8247
Web: www.fujiyamaboise.com					
Gamekeeper 1109 Main St	Boise	ID	83702	208-343-4611	381-0695
Goodwood Barbecue Co 7849 W Spectrum Dr	Boise	ID	83709	208-658-7173	658-7176
Web: www.goodwoodbbq.com					
Joe's Crab Shack 2288 N Garden St.	Boise	ID	83706	208-336-9370	
Web: www.joescrabshack.com					
Mai Thai 750 W Idaho St	Boise	ID	83702	208-344-8424	344-2445
Web: www.maithaigroup.com					
Melting Pot The Sixth & Idaho St.	Boise	ID	83702	208-343-8800	343-4570
Web: www.meltingpot.com					
MilkyWay 205 N 10th St.	Boise	ID	83702	208-343-4334	319-0123
Reef 105 S 6th St	Boise	ID	83702	208-287-9200	287-9203
Web: www.reefboise.com					
Shige Japanese Cuisine 100 N 8th St Suite 215	Boise	ID	83702	208-338-8423	
Web: www.shigejapanesecuisine.food.officelive.com					
Smoky Mountain Pizzeria Grill 408 E 41st St	Boise	ID	83714	208-433-9596	433-9588
Web: www.smokymountainpizza.com					
Chapala 117 W Burnside Ave	Chubbuck	ID	83202	208-238-3365	237-1712
Bamboo Garden 1200 Yellowstone Ave.	Pocatello	ID	83201	208-238-2331	238-7662
Buddy's Italian Restaurant 626 E Lewis St	Pocatello	ID	83201	208-233-1172	
Butterburrs 917 Yellowstone Ave.	Pocatello	ID	83201	208-232-3296	478-0147
Mama Inez 390 Yellowstone Ave	Pocatello	ID	83201	208-234-7674	234-2707
Mandarin House 675 Yellowstone Ave Suite D	Pocatello	ID	83201	208-233-6088	233-6089
Web: www.mandarinhouse.takeout1.com					
Oliver's 130 S 5th Ave.	Pocatello	ID	83201	208-234-0672	234-4185
Remo's Steak Seafood & Pasta					
160 W Cedar St	Pocatello	ID	83201	208-233-1710	233-1438
Web: www.remosrestaurant.com					
Sandpiper 1400 Bench Rd	Pocatello	ID	83201	208-233-1000	233-1006
Web: www.sandpiperrestaurant.com					

ILLINOIS

	City	State	ZIP	Phone	Fax
Bacaro 113 N Walnut St	Champaign	IL	61820	217-398-6982	359-5922
Web: www.bacarowinelounge.com					
Empire Chinese Restaurant 410 E Green St.	Champaign	IL	61820	217-328-0832	
Fiesta Cafe 216 S 1st St	Champaign	IL	61820	217-352-5902	
Web: www.fiestacafe.com					
Kamakura 715 S Neil St	Champaign	IL	61820	217-351-9898	
Web: www.kamakurajapaneserestaurant.com					
Li'l Porgy's Bar-B-Q					
1917 W Springfield Ave	Champaign	IL	61821	217-398-6811	277-0002
Web: www.lilporgysbbq.com					

				Phone	Fax
Radio Maria 119 N Walnut St	Champaign	IL	61820	217-398-7729	398-4865
Ryan's Family Steak House 1004 W Anthony Dr *Web:* www.ryans.com	Champaign	IL	61821	217-352-7403	352-8344
Taffie's 301 S Mattis Ave	Champaign	IL	61821	217-359-4201	
A Tavola 2148 W Chicago Ave *Web:* www.atavolachicago.com	Chicago	IL	60622	773-276-7567	276-2519
Adobo Grill Chicago 1610 N Wells St *Web:* www.adobogrill.com	Chicago	IL	60614	312-266-7999	266-9299
Alinea 1723 N Halsted St *Web:* www.alinearestaurant.com	Chicago	IL	60614	312-867-0110	482-8192
Amarit Thai Restaurant 600 S Dearborn *Web:* www.amaritthai.com	Chicago	IL	60605	312-939-1179	939-1195
Angelina's 3561 N Broadway St *Web:* www.angelinasristorante.com	Chicago	IL	60657	773-935-5933	
Aria 200 N Columbus Dr *Web:* www.ariachicago.com	Chicago	IL	60601	312-444-9494	565-1143
Arun's 4156 N Kedzie Ave *Web:* www.arunsthai.com	Chicago	IL	60618	773-539-1909	539-2125
Atwood Cafe 1 W Washington St *Web:* www.atwoodcafe.com	Chicago	IL	60602	312-368-1900	357-2875
Avec Restaurant 615 W Randolph St *Web:* www.avecrestaurant.com	Chicago	IL	60661	312-377-2002	377-2008
Bacchanalia 2413 S Oakley Ave *Web:* www.bacchanaliachicago.com	Chicago	IL	60608	773-254-6555	254-6565
Ben Pao 52 W Illinois St *Web:* www.benpao.com	Chicago	IL	60654	312-222-1888	222-0925
BIN 36 339 N Dearborn St *Web:* www.bin36.com	Chicago	IL	60610	312-755-9463	755-9410
Bistrot Margot 1437 N Wells St *Web:* www.bistrotmargot.com	Chicago	IL	60610	312-587-3660	587-3668
Blackbird 619 W Randolph St *Web:* www.blackbirdrestaurant.com	Chicago	IL	60606	312-715-0708	715-0774
Bongo Room 1470 N Milwaukee Ave	Chicago	IL	60622	773-489-0690	489-0710
Brasserie Jo 59 W Hubbard St *Web:* www.brasseriejo.com	Chicago	IL	60610	312-595-0800	595-0808
Buona Terra 2535 N California Ave *Web:* www.buona-terra.com	Chicago	IL	60647	773-289-3800	289-3838
Cafe Absinthe 1954 W N Ave	Chicago	IL	60622	773-278-4488	278-5291
Caliterra 633 N St Clair St	Chicago	IL	60611	312-274-4444	
Capital Grille 633 N St Clair St *Web:* www.thecapitalgrille.com	Chicago	IL	60611	312-337-9400	337-1259
Charlie Trotter's 816 W Armitage Ave *Web:* www.charlietrotters.com	Chicago	IL	60614	773-248-6228	248-6088
Chicago Chop House 60 W Ontario St *Web:* www.chicagochophouse.com	Chicago	IL	60654	312-787-7100	787-3219
Coco Pazzo 300 W Hubbard St *Web:* www.cocopazzochicago.com	Chicago	IL	60654	312-836-0900	836-0257
Crofton on Wells 535 N Wells St *Web:* www.croftononwells.com	Chicago	IL	60610	312-755-1790	755-1850
Erwin 2925 N Halsted St *Web:* www.erwincafe.com	Chicago	IL	60657	773-528-7200	528-1931
Everest 1 S La Salle St # 4000 *Web:* www.everestrestaurant.com	Chicago	IL	60605	312-663-8920	663-8802
Fat Willy's 2416 W Schubert Ave *Web:* www.fatwillys.com	Chicago	IL	60647	773-782-1800	782-1818
Francesca's on Taylor 1400 W Taylor St *Web:* www.francescarestaurants.com	Chicago	IL	60607	312-829-2828	829-2831
Frontera Grill 445 N Clark St *Web:* www.rickbayless.com	Chicago	IL	60654	312-661-1434	661-1830
Geja's Cafe 340 W Armitage Ave *Web:* www.gejascafe.com	Chicago	IL	60614	773-281-9101	281-0849
Gene & Georgetti 500 N Franklin St *Web:* www.geneandgeorgetti.com	Chicago	IL	60642	312-527-3718	527-2039
Gibsons Steakhouse 1028 N Rush St *Web:* www.gibsonssteakhouse.com	Chicago	IL	60611	312-266-8999	266-3327
Green Zebra 1460 W Chicago Ave *Web:* www.greenzebrachicago.com	Chicago	IL	60642	312-243-7100	226-3360
Indian Garden 247 E Ontario St 2nd Fl *Web:* www.indiangardenchicago.com	Chicago	IL	60611	312-280-4910	280-4934
Japonais Chicago 600 W Chicago Ave *Web:* www.japonaischicago.com	Chicago	IL	60610	312-822-9600	822-9623
Jin Ju 5203 N Clark St	Chicago	IL	60640	773-334-6377	
Joe's Seafood Prime Steak & Stone Crab 60 E Grand Ave *Web:* www.leye.com	Chicago	IL	60611	312-379-5637	494-9787
Kiki's Bistro 900 N Franklin St *Web:* www.kikisbistro.com	Chicago	IL	60610	312-335-5454	335-0614
Klay Oven *Chicago* 414 N Orleans St *Web:* www.klayovenrestaurant.com	Chicago	IL	60610	312-527-3999	527-1563
L20 Restaurant 2300 N Lincoln Pk W *Web:* www.l2orestaurant.com	Chicago	IL	60614	773-868-0002	868-0001
La Petite Folie 1504 E 55th St *Web:* www.lapetitefolie.com	Chicago	IL	60615	773-493-1394	493-1450
Lawry's the Prime Rib 100 E Ontario St *Web:* www.lawrysonline.com	Chicago	IL	60611	312-787-5000	787-1264
Le Colonial 937 N Rush St *Web:* www.lecolonialchicago.com	Chicago	IL	60611	312-255-0088	255-1108
Les Nomades 222 E Ontario St *Web:* www.lesnomades.net	Chicago	IL	60611	312-649-9010	649-0608
Lobby The 108 E Superior St 5th Fl	Chicago	IL	60611	312-573-6760	573-6697
Merlo on Maple 16 W Maple St *Web:* www.merlochicago.com	Chicago	IL	60610	312-335-8200	335-8205
Mike Ditka's Restaurant 100 E Chestnut St *Web:* www.ditkasrestaurants.com	Chicago	IL	60611	312-587-8989	587-8980
Mirai Sushi 2020 W Division St	Chicago	IL	60622	773-862-8500	862-8510
MK Restaurant 868 N Franklin St *Web:* www.mkchicago.com	Chicago	IL	60610	312-482-9179	482-9171
Mon Ami Gabi 2300 N Lincoln Pk W *Web:* www.monamigabi.com	Chicago	IL	60614	773-348-8886	472-9077
Morton's the Steakhouse 325 N LaSalle St Suite 500 *TF:* 866-667-8667 ■ *Web:* www.mortons.com	Chicago	IL	60654	866-667-8667	
Morton's the Steakhouse 325 N LaSalle St Suite 500 *TF:* 866-667-8667 ■ *Web:* www.mortons.com	Chicago	IL	60654	866-667-8667	
Morton's the Steakhouse 1050 N State St *Web:* www.mortons.com	Chicago	IL	60610	312-266-4820	266-4852
N9ne 440 W Randolph St *Web:* www.n9negroup.com	Chicago	IL	60606	312-575-9900	575-9901
Nacional 27 325 W Huron St *Web:* www.leye.com	Chicago	IL	60654	312-664-2727	649-0256
Naha 500 N Clark St *Web:* www.naha-chicago.com	Chicago	IL	60657	312-321-6242	321-7561
Nick's Fishmarket 222 W Merchandise Mart Plaza #135 *Web:* www.nicksfishmarketchicago.com	Chicago	IL	60654	312-621-0200	621-1118
NoMI 800 N Michigan Ave *Web:* www.parkchicago.hyatt.com/hyatt/hotels/entertainment/restaurants/index.jsp#1705	Chicago	IL	60611	312-335-1234	239-4000
North Pond 2610 N Cannon Dr *Web:* www.northpondrestaurant.com	Chicago	IL	60614	773-477-5845	477-3224
One SixtyBlue 1400 W Randolph St *Web:* www.cornerstonerestaurants.com	Chicago	IL	60607	312-850-0303	829-3046
Pane Caldo 72 E Walton St *Web:* www.pane-caldo.com	Chicago	IL	60611	312-649-0055	274-0540
Parthenon The 314 S Halsted St *Web:* www.theparthenon.com	Chicago	IL	60661	312-726-2407	726-3203
Petterino's 150 N Dearborn St *Web:* www.petterinos.com	Chicago	IL	60601	312-422-0150	
PUBLIC CHICAGO 1301 N State Pkwy *Web:* www.publichotels.com	Chicago	IL	60610	312-787-3700	
Quartino 626 N State St *Web:* www.quartinochicago.com	Chicago	IL	60610	312-698-5000	
Rhapsody 65 E Adams St *Web:* www.rhapsodychicago.com	Chicago	IL	60603	312-786-9911	786-1718
Rise Sushi & Sake Lounge 3401 N Southport Ave *Web:* www.risesushi.com	Chicago	IL	60657	773-525-3535	525-3522
Rockwell's Neighborhood Grill 4632 N Rockwell St *Web:* www.rockwellsgrill.com	Chicago	IL	60625	773-509-1871	509-1877
Roy's 720 N State St *Web:* www.roysrestaurant.com	Chicago	IL	60610	312-787-7599	787-7297
Sabatino's 4441 W Irving Pk Rd *Web:* www.sabatinoschicago.com	Chicago	IL	60641	773-283-8331	283-0603
Sai Cafe 2010 N Sheffield Ave *Web:* www.saicafe.com	Chicago	IL	60614	773-472-8080	472-0699
Saloon Steakhouse The 200 E Chestnut St *Web:* www.saloonsteakhouse.com	Chicago	IL	60611	312-280-5454	280-6980
Salpicon 1252 N Wells St *Web:* www.salpicon.com	Chicago	IL	60610	312-988-7811	988-7715
Shanghai Terrace 108 E Superior St 4th Fl	Chicago	IL	60611	312-573-6744	573-6697
Shaw's Crab House Chicago 21 E Hubbard St *Web:* www.shawscrabhouse.com	Chicago	IL	60611	312-527-2722	527-4740
Soul Vegetarian East 205 E 75th St	Chicago	IL	60619	773-224-0104	224-6667
South Water Kitchen 225 N Wabash Ave *Web:* www.southwaterkitchen.com	Chicago	IL	60601	312-236-9300	960-8538
Spiaggia 980 N Michigan Ave *Web:* www.spiaggiarestaurant.com	Chicago	IL	60611	312-280-2750	943-8560
Suparossa 4256 N Central Ave *Web:* www.suparossa.com	Chicago	IL	60634	773-736-5828	736-1372
Sushi Loop 810 W Jackson Blvd	Chicago	IL	60607	312-714-1234	714-1120
Sushi Wabi 842 W Randolph St *Web:* www.sushiwabi.com	Chicago	IL	60607	312-563-1224	563-9579
Topolobampo 445 N Clark St *Web:* www.fronterakitchens.com	Chicago	IL	60654	312-661-1434	661-1830
Trattoria No 10 10 N Dearborn St *Web:* www.trattoriaten.com	Chicago	IL	60602	312-984-1718	984-1525
Tre Kronor 3258 W Foster Ave	Chicago	IL	60625	773-267-9888	
Tru 686 N St Clair St # 1 *Web:* www.trurestaurant.com	Chicago	IL	60611	312-202-0001	
University Club of Chicago 76 E Monroe St *Web:* www.ucco.com	Chicago	IL	60603	312-726-2840	726-0620
Vivere 71 W Monroe St *Web:* www.italianvillage-chicago.com	Chicago	IL	60603	312-332-4040	332-2656
West Town Tavern 1329 W Chicago Ave *Web:* www.westtowntavern.com	Chicago	IL	60622	312-666-6175	666-6178
Yoshi's Cafe 3257 N Halsted St *Web:* www.yoshiscafe.com	Chicago	IL	60657	773-248-6160	248-1860
Zealous Restaurant 419 W Superior St *Web:* www.zealousrestaurant.com	Chicago	IL	60654	312-475-9112	475-0165
Captain Merry Guesthouse & Fine Dining 399 Sinsinawa Ave *Web:* www.captainmerry.com	East Dubuque	IL	61025	815-747-3644	747-3645
Agatucci's 2607 N University St	Peoria	IL	61604	309-688-8200	
Carnegie's 501 Main St	Peoria	IL	61602	309-637-6500	
Fairview Farms 5911 Heuermann Rd *Web:* www.fairview-farm.com	Peoria	IL	61607	309-697-4111	697-1887
Fish House The 4919 N University St	Peoria	IL	61614	309-691-9358	
Flagstones 117 N Western Ave	Peoria	IL	61604	309-673-8040	
Flat Top Grill 5201 W War Memorial Dr *Web:* www.flattopgrill.com	Peoria	IL	61615	309-693-9966	693-9846
Jim's Downtown Steakhouse 110 SW Jefferson St *Web:* www.jimssteakhouse.net	Peoria	IL	61602	309-673-5300	673-9335
Ponte Vecchio 4125 N Sheridan Rd	Peoria	IL	61614	309-682-3994	
Sushigawa 2601 W Lake Ave	Peoria	IL	61615	309-679-9300	
Abreo 515 E State St *Web:* www.abreorockford.com	Rockford	IL	61104	815-968-9463	968-9792
Capri 313 E State St	Rockford	IL	61104	815-965-6341	965-8202
Cliffbreakers River Restaurant 700 W Riverside Blvd *Web:* www.cliffbreakers.com	Rockford	IL	61103	815-282-3033	282-6505

Name / Address	City	State	ZIP	Phone	Fax
Garrett's Cafe 1631 N Bell School Rd	Rockford	IL	61107	815-484-9473	397-7593
Web: www.garrettsrestaurantbar.com					
Giovanni's Restaurant & Convention Ctr 610 N Bell School Rd	Rockford	IL	61107	815-398-6411	398-6416
Web: www.giodine.com					
Great Wall Restaurant 4228 E State St	Rockford	IL	61108	815-226-0982	
Hoffman House 7550 E State St	Rockford	IL	61108	815-397-5800	397-0175
Web: www.hoffmanhouserockford.com					
Imperial Palace 3415 E State St	Rockford	IL	61108	815-227-1442	316-0721
JMK Nippon 2551 N Perryville Rd	Rockford	IL	61107	815-877-0505	877-0681
Maria's Italian Restaurant 828 Cunningham St	Rockford	IL	61102	815-968-6781	
Octane Interlounge 124 N Main St	Rockford	IL	61101	815-965-4012	965-1964
Web: www.octane.net					
Olympic Tavern 2327 N Main St	Rockford	IL	61103	815-962-8758	962-8760
Web: www.theolympictavern.com					
Perry Rock Pub 6957 Olde Creek Rd	Rockford	IL	61114	815-316-8600	
Web: www.table-13.com					
Rathskeller The 1132 Auburn St	Rockford	IL	61103	815-963-2922	963-9185
Web: www.derrathskeller.net					
Shogun 293 Executive Pkwy	Rockford	IL	61107	815-394-0007	394-0009
Web: www.shogunofrockford.com					
Alexander's 620 N Bruns Ln	Springfield	IL	62702	217-793-0440	793-0453
Augie's Front Burner 109 S 5th St	Springfield	IL	62701	217-544-6979	544-7088
Web: www.augiesfrontburner.com					
Chesapeake Seafood House 3045 Clear Lake Ave	Springfield	IL	62702	217-522-5220	522-5993
Web: www.chesapeakeseafoodhouse.com					
Fritz's Wagon Wheel Restaurant 2709 S MacArthur Blvd	Springfield	IL	62704	217-546-9888	726-5357
Golden Dragon 425 N Grand Ave E	Springfield	IL	62702	217-753-2996	
Indigo 3013 Lindbergh Blvd	Springfield	IL	62704	217-726-3487	726-4563
Web: www.indigocuisine.com					
Lime Street Cafe 951 S Durkin Dr	Springfield	IL	62704	217-793-1905	793-7860
Maldaner's 222 S 6th St	Springfield	IL	62701	217-522-4313	522-1720
Web: www.maldaners.com					
Sebastian's Hide-Out 221 S 5th St	Springfield	IL	62701	217-789-8988	525-5886
Web: www.sebastianshideout.com					
Taste Of Thai Restaurant 3053 S Dirksen Pkwy	Springfield	IL	62703	217-529-8393	
Tokyo of Japan 2225 Adlai Stevenson Dr	Springfield	IL	62703	217-585-0088	
Courier Cafe 111 N Race St	Urbana	IL	61801	217-328-1811	328-1880
Web: www.couriersilvercreek.com					
Kennedy's at Stone Creek 2560 Stone Creek Blvd	Urbana	IL	61802	217-384-8111	384-4823
Web: www.kennedysatstonecreek.com					
Miko Restaurant 407 W University Ave	Urbana	IL	61801	217-367-0822	367-0818
Web: www.mikorestaurant.com					
Milo's Restaurant 2870 S Philo Rd	Urbana	IL	61802	217-344-8946	344-8922
Web: www.milosurbana.com					
Timpone's 710 S Goodwin Ave	Urbana	IL	61801	217-344-7619	344-7648
Web: www.timpones-urbana.com					

INDIANA

Name / Address	City	State	ZIP	Phone	Fax
Buffa Louie's 114 S Indiana Ave	Bloomington	IN	47408	812-333-3030	334-3945
Web: www.buffalouies.com					
Cafe Django 116 N Grant St	Bloomington	IN	47408	812-335-1297	335-1821
Web: www.cafedjango.us					
Chapman's Restaurant 300 S State Rd 446	Bloomington	IN	47401	812-337-9999	336-0436
Web: www.chapmansrestaurant.com					
Crazy Horse 214 W Kirkwood Ave	Bloomington	IN	47404	812-336-8877	336-8011
Web: www.crazyhorseindiana.com					
Dragon Chinese Restaurant 3261 W 3rd St	Bloomington	IN	47404	812-332-6610	
Esan Thai 221 E Kirkwood Ave Suite D	Bloomington	IN	47408	812-333-8424	
Web: www.esanthairestaurant.com					
Fairfax Inn 8660 S Fairfax Rd	Bloomington	IN	47401	812-824-8552	824-2634
Web: www.thefairfaxinn.com					
Gratzi 106 W 6th St	Bloomington	IN	47401	812-323-0303	
Irish Lion 212 W Kirkwood Ave	Bloomington	IN	47404	812-336-9076	
Web: www.irishlion.com					
Laughing Planet Cafe 322 E Kirkwood Ave	Bloomington	IN	47408	812-323-2233	323-1336
Le Petit Cafe 308 W 6th St	Bloomington	IN	47404	812-334-9747	
Limestone Grille 2920 E Covenanter Dr	Bloomington	IN	47401	812-335-8110	
Web: www.limestonegrille.com					
Malibu Grill 106 N Walnut St	Bloomington	IN	47402	812-332-4334	333-2282
Web: www.malibugrill.net					
Michael's Uptown Cafe 102 E Kirkwood Ave	Bloomington	IN	47408	812-339-0900	331-6025
Web: www.the-uptown.com					
Mikado 895 S College Mall Rd	Bloomington	IN	47401	812-333-1950	333-1857
Web: www.btownmenus.com					
Nick's English Hut 423 E Kirkwood Ave	Bloomington	IN	47408	812-332-4040	339-0282
Web: www.nicksenglishhut.com					
Restaurant Tallent 208 N Walnut	Bloomington	IN	47404	812-330-9801	330-9803
Web: www.restauranttallent.com					
Scholars Inn Gourmet Cafe 717 N College Ave	Bloomington	IN	47404	812-332-1892	355-8785
TF: 800-765-3466 ■ *Web:* www.scholarsinn.com					
Trojan Horse 100 E Kirkwood Ave	Bloomington	IN	47408	812-332-1101	330-7092
Web: www.thetrojanhorse.com					
Upland Brewing Co 350 W 11th St	Bloomington	IN	47404	812-336-2337	330-7421
Web: www.uplandbeer.com					
Yogi's Grill & Bar 519 E 10th St	Bloomington	IN	47408	812-323-9644	323-8898
Web: www.yogis.com					
Glass Chimney 12901 Old Meridian St	Carmel	IN	46032	317-844-0921	574-1360
Web: www.glasschimneyanddeeters.com					
Angelo's 305 Main St	Evansville	IN	47708	812-428-6666	428-6699
Biaggi's 6401 E Lloyd Expy Suite 3	Evansville	IN	47715	812-421-0800	421-0801
Web: www.biaggis.com					
Canton Inn 947 N Pk Dr	Evansville	IN	47710	812-428-6611	
Chopstick House 5412 E Indiana St	Evansville	IN	47715	812-473-5551	
Web: www.chopstickhouserestaurant.net					
Hacienda 711 N 1st Ave	Evansville	IN	47710	812-423-6355	423-0884
Web: www.haciendafiesta.com					
Lorenzo's Bread Bistro 972 S Hebron Ave	Evansville	IN	47714	812-475-9477	475-9478
Web: www.lorenzosbistro.com					
Moe's Southwest Grill 6401 E Lloyd Expy Suite 5	Evansville	IN	47715	812-491-6637	491-6617
Web: www.moes.com					
Raffi's 1100 N Burkehardt Rd	Evansville	IN	47715	812-479-9166	491-0318
Web: www.raffis.us					
Raffis Italian Cuisine 1100 N Burkhart Rd	Evansville	IN	47715	812-479-9166	491-0318
Web: www.raffis.us					
Western Rib-Eye & Ribs 1401 N Boeke Rd	Evansville	IN	47711	812-476-5405	473-4850
Web: www.westernribeye.com					
Wolf's Bar-B-Q Restaurant 6600 N 1st Ave	Evansville	IN	47710	812-424-8891	424-8905
Web: www.wolfsbarbq.com					
Yen Ching 406 S Green River Rd	Evansville	IN	47715	812-474-0181	479-5561
Web: www.yenchingrestaurant.com					
Baan Thai 4634 Coldwater Rd	Fort Wayne	IN	46825	260-471-2929	471-2020
Bandido's Inc 6060 E State Blvd	Fort Wayne	IN	46815	260-493-0607	493-0806
Web: www.bandidos.com					
Biaggi's 4010 W Jefferson Blvd	Fort Wayne	IN	46804	260-459-6700	459-6701
Web: www.biaggis.com					
Casa Ristoranti 7539 W Jefferson Blvd	Fort Wayne	IN	46825	260-399-2455	745-5503
Web: www.casarestaurants.net					
Club Soda 235 E Superior St	Fort Wayne	IN	46802	260-426-3442	426-4214
Web: www.clubsodafortwayne.com					
Cork'N Cleaver 221 E Washington Ctr Rd	Fort Wayne	IN	46825	260-484-7772	482-8471
Don Hall's Old Gas House 305 E Superior St	Fort Wayne	IN	46802	260-426-3411	424-2903
Web: www.donhalls.com					
Double Dragon 117 W Wayne St	Fort Wayne	IN	46802	260-422-6426	
Eddie Merlot's 1502 Illinois Rd S	Fort Wayne	IN	46804	260-459-2222	459-8896
Web: www.eddiemerlots.com					
Flanagan's Restaurant & Pub 6525 Covington Rd	Fort Wayne	IN	46804	260-432-6666	432-6799
Web: www.eatatflanagans.com					
Logan's Roadhouse 6617 Lima Rd	Fort Wayne	IN	46818	260-487-9944	487-9943
Web: www.logansroadhouse.com					
Mi Pueblo IV 2419 W Jefferson Blvd	Fort Wayne	IN	46802	260-432-6462	459-2542
Rib Room 1235 E State Blvd	Fort Wayne	IN	46805	260-483-9767	
Web: www.theribroom.com					
Sakura 5828 W Jefferson Blvd	Fort Wayne	IN	46804	260-459-2022	
Taj Mahal 6410 W Jefferson Blvd	Fort Wayne	IN	46804	260-432-8993	432-8486
Takaoka of Japan 305 E Superior St	Fort Wayne	IN	46802	260-424-3183	
Agio 635 Massachusetts Ave	Indianapolis	IN	46204	317-488-0359	488-0361
Web: www.agiorestaurant.net					
Amalfi 1351 W 86th St	Indianapolis	IN	46260	317-253-4034	253-1267
Web: www.amalfiristoranteitaliano.com					
Amici's 601 E New York St	Indianapolis	IN	46202	317-634-0440	
Web: www.myfavoriteitalianrestaurant.com					
Bonefish Grill 4501 E 82nd St	Indianapolis	IN	46250	317-863-3474	863-0067
Web: www.bonefishgrill.com					
Canterbury Hotel 123 S Illinois St	Indianapolis	IN	46225	317-634-3000	685-2519
Web: www.canterburyhotel.com/go/restaurant.html					
Cheesecake Factory 8702 Keystone Xing # 4A	Indianapolis	IN	46240	317-566-0100	566-0200
Web: www.cheesecakefactory.com					
Circle City Bar & Grille 350 W Maryland St	Indianapolis	IN	46225	317-405-6100	822-1002
Dunaway's 351 S E St	Indianapolis	IN	46204	317-638-7663	638-7677
Web: www.dunaways.com					
El Jaripeo 10417 E Washington St	Indianapolis	IN	46229	317-898-3921	
Fujiyama Japanese Steakhouse 5149 Victory Dr	Indianapolis	IN	46203	317-787-7900	
Web: www.fujiyama-indy.com					
Greek Islands Restaurant 906 S Meridian St	Indianapolis	IN	46225	317-636-0700	636-2347
Web: www.greekislandsrestaurant.com					
Hard Rock Cafe Indianapolis 49 S Meridian St	Indianapolis	IN	46204	317-636-2550	636-2551
Web: www.hardrock.com					
Hollyhock Hill 8110 N College Ave	Indianapolis	IN	46240	317-251-2294	251-2295
Web: www.hollyhockhill.com					
Iaria's Italian Restaurant 317 S College Ave	Indianapolis	IN	46202	317-638-7706	687-9232
Web: www.iariasrestaurant.com					
India Garden 830 Broad Ripple Ave	Indianapolis	IN	46220	317-253-6060	253-2832
Web: www.indiagardenindy.com					
India Palace 4213 Lafayette Rd	Indianapolis	IN	46254	317-298-0773	298-1823
Web: www.indiapalaceindy.com					
Iron Skillet Restaurant The 2489 W 30th St	Indianapolis	IN	46222	317-923-6353	923-5209
Web: www.ironskillet.net					
Kona Jack's Fish Market & Sushi Bar 9419 N Meridian St	Indianapolis	IN	46260	317-843-1609	571-6987
Web: www.konajacksindy.com					
Maggiano's Little Italy 3550 E 86th St	Indianapolis	IN	46240	317-814-0700	814-0707
Web: www.maggianos.com					
Mama Carolla's Old Italian Restaurant 1031 E 54th St	Indianapolis	IN	46220	317-259-9412	
Web: www.mamacarollas.com					
Marker The 2544 Executive Dr	Indianapolis	IN	46241	317-381-6146	381-6170
Melting Pot of Indianapolis The 5650 E 86th St Suite A	Indianapolis	IN	46250	317-841-3601	841-1207
Web: www.meltingpot.com					
Mikado Japanese Restaurant 148 S Illinois St	Indianapolis	IN	46225	317-972-4180	972-4191
Web: www.mikadoindy.com					
Morton's the Steakhouse 41 E Washington St	Indianapolis	IN	46204	317-229-4700	229-4704
Web: www.mortons.com					

Phone | Fax

Oakley's Bistro 1464 W 86th St .... Indianapolis IN 46260 317-824-1231 824-0938
Web: www.oakleysbistro.com
Oceanaire Seafood Room The
30 S Meridian St Suite 100.................. Indianapolis IN 46204 317-955-2277 955-2278
Web: www.theoceanaire.com
Oh Yumm! Bistro 5615 N Illinois St .... Indianapolis IN 46208 317-251-5656 255-1840
Web: www.ohyummbistro.com
Palomino 49 W Maryland St Suite 189.................. Indianapolis IN 46204 317-974-0400 974-1865
Web: www.palomino.com
Plump's Last Shot 6416 Cornell Ave .... Indianapolis IN 46220 317-257-5867
R Bistro 888 Massachusetts Ave.................. Indianapolis IN 46204 317-423-0312 423-0348
Web: www.rbistro.com
Rathskeller Restaurant
401 E Michigan St .... Indianapolis IN 46204 317-636-0396 630-4652
Web: www.rathskeller.com
Rick's Cafe Boatyard 4050 Dandy Trail.................. Indianapolis IN 46254 317-290-9300 291-1043
Web: www.rickscafeboatyard.com
Ruth's Chris Steak House 9445 Threel Rd .... Indianapolis IN 46240 317-844-1155 574-9306
Web: www.ruthschris.com
Saint Elmo Steak House
127 S Illinois St .... Indianapolis IN 46225 317-635-0636 687-9162
Web: www.stelmos.com
Sakura 7201 N Keystone Ave .... Indianapolis IN 46240 317-259-4171 253-7846
Web: www.indysakura.com
Udupi Cafe 4225 Lafayette Rd .... Indianapolis IN 46254 317-299-2127
Yen Ching 9150 N Michigan Rd.................. Indianapolis IN 46268 317-228-0868 228-0886
Bonefish Grill 620 W Edison Ave Suite 100.................. Mishawaka IN 46545 574-259-2663 259-7725
Web: www.bonefishgrill.com
Hana Yori 3601 Grape Rd.................. Mishawaka IN 46545 574-258-5817 258-6045
Web: www.hanayori.com
Main Street Grille 112 N Main St.................. Mishawaka IN 46544 574-254-4995 254-4999
Web: www.mainstgrille.com
Backstage Grill The 222 S Michigan St.................. South Bend IN 46601 574-232-0222 234-5544
Web: www.222italiansteakhouse.com
Carriage House 24460 Adams Rd.................. South Bend IN 46628 574-272-9220 272-6179
Web: www.carriagehousedining.com
Frankie's Barbecue 1621 Cir Ave .... South Bend IN 46628 574-287-8993
Honkers 3939 S Michigan St .... South Bend IN 46614 574-291-2115 291-1145
LaSalle Grill 115 W Colfax Ave .... South Bend IN 46601 574-288-1155 288-2012
TF: 800-382-9323 ■ *Web:* www.lasallegrill.com
Matuba 2930 McKinley Ave .... South Bend IN 46615 574-251-0674 251-0675
Parisi's Italian Ristorante
1412 S Bend Ave .... South Bend IN 46617 574-232-4244 232-4257
Web: www.parisisrestaurant.com
Rocco's 537 N St Louis Blvd .... South Bend IN 46617 574-233-2464 288-0168
Simeri's Old Town Tap 1505 W Indiana Ave.................. South Bend IN 46613 574-289-1361
Tippecanoe Place 620 W Washington St.................. South Bend IN 46601 574-234-9077
Web: www.tippe.com
Volcano Restaurant 3700 Lincoln Way W.................. South Bend IN 46628 574-287-5775

IOWA

Phone | Fax

Biaggi's Ristorante 320 Collins Rd NE .... Cedar Rapids IA 52402 319-393-6593 393-6594
Bonanza Steakhouse 3505 16th Ave SW.................. Cedar Rapids IA 52404 319-396-1876
Web: www.bonanzasteakhouses.com
El Rancho 2747 16th Ave SW.................. Cedar Rapids IA 52404 319-298-8844 286-0048
Web: www.elranchomexican.com
Irish Democrat Pub 3207 1st Ave SE.................. Cedar Rapids IA 52402 319-364-9896 368-8020
Web: www.irishdemocrat.net
Olive Tree Restaurant 1500 20th St SW .... Cedar Rapids IA 52404 319-364-0781
Papa Juans 5505 Ctr Pt Rd NE.................. Cedar Rapids IA 52402 319-393-0258 378-8953
Texas Roadhouse 2605 Edgewood Rd SW .... Cedar Rapids IA 52404 319-396-3300 396-1500
Web: www.texasroadhouse.com
Third Base Sports Bar & Brewery
500 Blairs Ferry Rd NE.................. Cedar Rapids IA 52402 319-378-9090 378-9697
Web: www.thirdbasebrewery.com
Vernon Inn 2663 Mt Vernon Rd SE.................. Cedar Rapids IA 52403 319-366-7817 366-2109
Vino's 3611 1st Ave SE .... Cedar Rapids IA 52402 319-363-7550
Web: www.vinosristorante.com
Vito's 4100 River Ridge Dr NE.................. Cedar Rapids IA 52402 319-393-8727 393-3981
Web: www.vitoson42nd.com
Zio Johno's Spaghetti House
2925 Williams Blvd SW .... Cedar Rapids IA 52404 319-396-1700 365-1135
Web: www.ziojohnos.net
Cosi Cucina 1975 NW 86th St.................. Clive IA 50325 515-278-8148 278-2262
Web: www.cosicucina.biz
Taste of Italy 8421 University Blvd.................. Clive IA 50325 515-221-0743 309-3156
801 Steak & Chop House Ltd
801 Grand Ave Suite 200 .... Des Moines IA 50309 515-288-6000 288-4083
Web: www.801steakandchop.com
AK O'Connors 4050 Urbandale Ave .... Des Moines IA 50310 515-277-2227
Barattas 2320 S Union St.................. Des Moines IA 50315 515-243-4516 243-5324
Web: www.barattas.com
China Chef Restaurant 5010 SW 9th St .... Des Moines IA 50315 515-256-8005 256-1848
Chuck's Restaurant 3610 6th Ave .... Des Moines IA 50313 515-244-4104
Web: www.chucksdesmoines.com
Court Avenue Brewing Co 309 Ct Ave.................. Des Moines IA 50309 515-282-2739 282-3789
Web: www.courtavebrew.com
Gino's Restaurant & Lounge 2809 6th Ave.................. Des Moines IA 50313 515-282-4029 283-8230
Iowa Beef Steakhouse 1201 E Euclid Ave.................. Des Moines IA 50316 515-262-1138 288-3703
Web: www.iowabeefsteakhouse.com
Latin King 2200 Hubbell Ave .... Des Moines IA 50317 515-266-4466 264-1096
Web: www.tursislatinking.com
Manterrrey 8801 University Ave .... Des Moines IA 50325 515-457-8900 457-7964
Raccoon River Brewing Co 200 10th St.................. Des Moines IA 50309 515-362-5222 243-4317
Web: www.raccoonbrew.com
Thai Flavors 1254 E 14th St.................. Des Moines IA 50316 515-262-4658
Web: www.thaiflavorsiowa.com
Bridge Restaurant 31 Locust St.................. Dubuque IA 52001 563-557-7280
Web: www.bridgerest.com

Phone | Fax

Champps Americana
3100 Dodge St Best Western Midway.................. Dubuque IA 52003 563-690-2040
Web: www.champpsdubuque.com
Mario's Restaurant 13th Main St.................. Dubuque IA 52001 563-556-9424 582-0904
Web: www.mariosdubuque.com
Pepper Sprout 378 Main St.................. Dubuque IA 52001 563-556-2167 583-6428
Web: www.peppersprout.com
Yen Ching 926 Main St.................. Dubuque IA 52001 563-556-2574 556-2574
Trostel's Greenbrier Restaurant
5810 Merle Hay Rd.................. Johnston IA 50131 515-253-0124
Biaggi's 5990 University Ave .... West Des Moines IA 50266 515-221-9900 221-9901
Web: www.biaggis.com
Rock Bottom Restaurant & Brewery
4508 University Ave .... West Des Moines IA 50266 515-267-8900 267-1400
Web: www.rockbottom.com
Waterfront Seafood Market
2900 University Ave .... West Des Moines IA 50266 515-223-5106 224-9665
Web: www.waterfrontseafoodmarket.com

KANSAS

Phone | Fax

Arthur Bryant Barbecue
1702 Village W Pkwy .... Kansas City KS 66111 913-788-7500 788-2333
Web: www.arthurbryantsbbq.com
Casa De Hernandez 1817 Pk Dr.................. Kansas City KS 66102 913-342-6226 342-3981
Cheeseburger in Paradise
1705 Village W Pkwy .... Kansas City KS 66111 913-334-4500 334-4507
Web: www.cheeseburgerinparadise.com
Felitza's Fine Italian Cuisine
402 N 5th St.................. Kansas City KS 66101 913-281-1569 281-1522
Gates Bar-B-Que 1026 State Ave.................. Kansas City KS 66102 913-621-1134
Web: www.gatesbbq.com
Los Amigos 2610 State Ave.................. Kansas City KS 66102 913-281-4547
Oklahoma Joe's BBQ & Catering
3002 W 47th Ave .... Kansas City KS 66103 913-722-3366 722-6644
Web: www.oklahomajoesbbq.com
Rosedale Barbeque 600 SW Blvd .... Kansas City KS 66103 913-262-0343 262-1422
Sol Azteca Mexican Grill 542 SW Blvd.................. Kansas City KS 66103 913-362-0817 677-1699
Vietnam Cafe 2200 W 39th St.................. Kansas City KS 66103 913-262-8552 262-8193
Yukon Base Camp Restaurant
10300 Cabela Dr.................. Kansas City KS 66111 913-328-0322 328-0348
Fiorella's Jack Stack Barbecue
9520 Metcalf Ave .... Overland Park KS 66212 913-385-7427 385-5020
Web: www.jackstackbbq.com
Garozzo's 9950 College Blvd .... Overland Park KS 66210 913-491-8300 491-9797
Web: www.garozzos.com
Ruchi 11168 Antioch Rd .... Overland Park KS 66210 913-661-9088 338-3662
Web: www.ruchicuisine.com
Blind Tiger Brewery & Restaurant
417 SW 37th St .... Topeka KS 66611 785-267-2739 267-7527
Web: www.blindtiger.com
Boss Hawg's 2833 SW 29th St.................. Topeka KS 66614 785-273-7300 273-0077
Web: www.bosshawgsbbq.com
Casa 3320 SW Topeka Blvd.................. Topeka KS 66611 785-266-4503 266-4539
Web: www.topekacasa.com
New City Cafe 4005 SW Gage Ctr Dr.................. Topeka KS 66604 785-271-8646 271-8636
Web: www.newcityonline.biz
Paisano's 4043 SW 10th St .... Topeka KS 66604 785-273-0100 273-3674
Web: www.paisanoskansas.com
Pat's Pig 5900 SW Topeka Blvd .... Topeka KS 66619 785-862-7427
Web: www.patspigbbq.com
Pepe & Chela's 1001 SW Tyler St.................. Topeka KS 66612 785-357-8332
Web: www.pepeandchelas.com
Bamboo Stix 2243 N Tyler Rd Suite 101 .... Wichita KS 67205 316-722-8886 462-0888
Web: www.bamboostix.com
Cafe Bel Ami 229 E William St Suite 101 .... Wichita KS 67202 316-267-3433 267-3070
Web: www.cafebelami.biz
Chelsea Bar & Grill 2949 N Rock Rd .... Wichita KS 67226 316-636-1103
Web: www.chelseasbarandgrill.com
Cibola 1900 N Rock Rd.................. Wichita KS 67202 316-631-3700
Felipe's 2241 N Woodlawn.................. Wichita KS 67220 316-652-0027
Web: www.felipeswichita.com
Fox & Hound 1551 N Waterfront Pkwy Suite 310.................. Wichita KS 67206 316-634-0505 634-1741
TF: 800-229-2118 ■ *Web:* www.foxandhound.com
Great Wall 410 N Hillside Ave .... Wichita KS 67214 316-688-0881 612-4825
Harvest Kitchen & Bar 400 W Waterman.................. Wichita KS 67202 316-293-1234 293-1200
Il Vicino 4817 E Douglas .... Wichita KS 67218 316-612-7085
Web: www.ilvicino.com
Kwan Court 1443 N Rock Rd .... Wichita KS 67206 316-634-1828
Web: www.kwancourt.com
La Chinita 1451 N Broadway St .... Wichita KS 67214 316-267-1552 267-7097
Larkspur Restaurant & Grill 904 E Douglas St.................. Wichita KS 67202 316-262-5275 262-1292
Web: www.larkspuronline.com
Legends 2098 Airport Rd .... Wichita KS 67209 316-945-5272 945-7620
Nu Way Burgers 1416 W Douglas Ave.................. Wichita KS 67203 316-267-1131
Web: www.nuwaycafe.com
PF Chang's China Bistro 1401 Waterfront Pkwy .... Wichita KS 67206 316-634-2211 634-0480
Web: www.pfchangs.com
Sal's Japanese Steakhouse 6829 E Kellogg Dr .... Wichita KS 67207 316-682-8880
Savute's 3303 N Broadway St.................. Wichita KS 67219 316-838-0455
Web: www.360wichita.com
Sweet Basil 2424 N Woodlawn St .... Wichita KS 67220 316-651-0123 651-0220
Texas Roadhouse 6707 W Kellogg Dr.................. Wichita KS 67209 316-943-8722 943-8730
Web: www.texasroadhouse.com
Timberline Steakhouse & Grill
1445 N Rock Rd Suite 210.................. Wichita KS 67206 785-228-1155 228-1187
Web: www.timberlinesteakhouse.com
Tommy's Restaurant & Lounge 2121 N Tyler Rd .... Wichita KS 67212 316-722-7687
Yen Ching 430 N Rock Rd.................. Wichita KS 67206 316-686-9510 686-9510
Web: www.yenchingrestaurant.com

KENTUCKY

Name / Address	City	State	ZIP	Phone	Fax
Casa Fiesta 801 Louisville Rd	Frankfort	KY	40601	502-226-5010	696-0960
China Wok 111 E Wood Shopping Ctr	Frankfort	KY	40601	502-695-9388	695-0788
Web: www.chinawokky.com					
Jim's Seafood 950 Wilkinson Blvd	Frankfort	KY	40601	502-223-7448	227-7419
La Fiesta Grande 314 Versailles Rd	Frankfort	KY	40601	502-695-8378	695-8378
New China 1309 US Hwy 127 S	Frankfort	KY	40601	502-226-3400	226-3800
A La Lucie 159 N Limestone St	Lexington	KY	40507	859-252-5277	225-5027
Web: www.alalucie.com					
Billy's Hickory Pit Bar B-Q 101 Cochran Rd	Lexington	KY	40502	859-269-9593	266-7865
Web: www.billysbarbq.com					
Cheapside Bar & Grill 131 Cheapside St	Lexington	KY	40507	859-254-0046	233-2146
Web: www.cheapsidebarandgrill.com					
DeSha's 101 N Broadway	Lexington	KY	40507	859-259-3771	254-1602
Web: www.tavernrestaurantgroup.com					
Dudley's 380 S Mill St	Lexington	KY	40508	859-252-1010	253-9383
Web: www.dudleysrestaurant.com					
Durango's 2121 Richmond Rd	Lexington	KY	40502	859-268-0723	269-0396
Gratz Park Inn 120 W 2nd St	Lexington	KY	40507	859-231-1777	233-7593
TF: 800-752-4166 ■ *Web:* www.gratzparkinn.com					
Hunan 115 Southland Dr	Lexington	KY	40503	859-278-3811	
Jalapeno's 295 New Cir Rd NW	Lexington	KY	40505	859-299-8299	294-9739
Joe Bologna's 117 W Maxwell St	Lexington	KY	40508	859-259-0495	259-0496
Web: www.joebolognas.com					
Malone's					
Bluegrass Hospitality Group					
3347 Tates Creek Rd	Lexington	KY	40502	859-335-6500	335-1815
Web: www.bluegrasshospitality.com					
Mandarin Oriental Cafe					
2220 Nicholasville Rd	Lexington	KY	40503	859-275-1666	
Mansion at Griffin Gate 1800 Newtown Pike	Lexington	KY	40511	859-231-5100	288-6216
Web: www.mansionatgriffingate.com					
Merrick Inn 1074 Merrick Dr	Lexington	KY	40502	859-269-5417	269-5934
Web: www.themerican.com					
Natasha's Bistro & Bar 112 Esplanade	Lexington	KY	40507	859-259-2754	
TF: 888-901-8412 ■ *Web:* www.beetnik.com					
Panda Garden 531 W New Cir Rd	Lexington	KY	40511	859-299-9798	
Portofino 249 E Main St	Lexington	KY	40507	859-253-9300	258-2488
Web: www.portofinolexington.com					
Tachibana 785 Newtown Ct	Lexington	KY	40511	859-254-1911	231-3804
211 Clover Lane 211 Clover Ln	Louisville	KY	40207	502-896-9570	896-9591
610 Magnolia 610 Magnolia Ave	Louisville	KY	40208	502-636-0783	636-0787
Web: www.610magnolia.com					
August Moon 2269 Lexington Rd	Louisville	KY	40206	502-456-6569	456-4669
Web: www.augustmoonbistro.com					
Avalon 1314 Bardstown Rd	Louisville	KY	40204	502-454-5336	
Web: www.avalonfresh.com					
Bazo's Fresh Mexican Grill					
323 Wallace Ave	Louisville	KY	40207	502-899-9600	
Browning's Restaurant & Brewery					
401 E Main St Louisville Slugger Field	Louisville	KY	40220	502-515-0174	515-0175
Web: www.diningonmain.com					
Buck's 425 W Ormsby Ave	Louisville	KY	40203	502-637-5284	637-7883
Web: www.bucksrestaurantandbar.com					
Cafe Kilimanjaro 649 S 4th St	Louisville	KY	40202	502-583-4332	583-3143
Web: www.cafekilimanjaro.com					
De La Torre's 1606 Bardstown Rd	Louisville	KY	40205	502-456-4955	
Web: www.delatorres.com					
El Mundo 2345 Frankfort Ave	Louisville	KY	40206	502-899-9930	
Web: www.502elmundo.com					
English Grill 335 W Broadway St	Louisville	KY	40202	502-583-1234	587-7006
TF: 888-888-5252					
Equus 122 Sears Ave	Louisville	KY	40207	502-897-9721	897-0535
Web: www.equusrestaurant.com					
Kashmir 1285 Bardstown Rd	Louisville	KY	40204	502-473-8765	
Web: www.kashmirlouisville.com					
Lilly's 1147 Bardstown Rd	Louisville	KY	40204	502-451-0447	
Web: www.lillyslapeche.com					
Limestone Restaurant					
10001 Forest Green Blvd	Louisville	KY	40223	502-426-7477	426-7479
Web: www.limestonerestaurant.com					
Lynn's Paradise Cafe 984 Barret Ave	Louisville	KY	40204	502-583-3447	583-0211
Web: www.lynnsparadisecafe.com					
Oakroom The 500 S 4th St	Louisville	KY	40202	502-807-3463	585-9239
Pat's Steak House 2437 Brownsboro Rd	Louisville	KY	40206	502-896-9234	893-2062
Web: www.patssteakhouselouisville.com					
Patron The 3400 Frankfort Ave	Louisville	KY	40207	502-896-1661	896-1643
Porcini 2730 Frankfort Ave	Louisville	KY	40206	502-894-8686	899-1798
Web: www.porcinilouisville.com					
Ruth's Chris Steak House					
6100 Dutchman's Ln 16th Fl	Louisville	KY	40205	502-479-0026	451-5340
Web: www.ruthschris.com					
Shah's Mongolian Grill					
9148 Taylorsville Rd	Louisville	KY	40299	502-493-0234	495-1001
Web: www.shahsmongoliangrill.com					
Uptown Cafe 1624 Bardstown Rd	Louisville	KY	40205	502-458-4212	458-4252
Web: www.uptownlouisville.com					
Vincenzo's 150 S 5th St	Louisville	KY	40202	502-580-1350	580-1355
Web: www.vincenzositalianrestaurant.com					
White Oak Restaurant 620 E Market St	Louisville	KY	40202	502-583-4177	584-4178
Yang Kee Noodle Club 7900 Shelbyville Rd	Louisville	KY	40222	502-426-0800	426-9080
Web: www.yangkeenoodle.com					

LOUISIANA

Name / Address	City	State	ZIP	Phone	Fax
Albasha 5454 Bluebonnet Rd Suite G	Baton Rouge	LA	70809	225-292-7988	291-2739
Web: www.albashabr.com					
Boutin's 8322 Bluebonnet Blvd	Baton Rouge	LA	70810	225-819-9862	819-9759
Web: www.boutins.com					
Brunet's Cajun Restaurant					
135 S Flannery Rd	Baton Rouge	LA	70815	225-272-6226	272-0353
Web: www.brunetscajunrestaurant.com					
Chimes Restaurant & Tap Room					
3357 Highland Rd	Baton Rouge	LA	70802	225-383-1754	387-5413
Web: www.thechimes.com					
Copelands of New Orleans 4957 Essen Ln	Baton Rouge	LA	70809	225-769-1800	769-1812
Web: www.copelandsofneworleans.com					
Don's Seafood & Steak House					
6823 Airline Hwy	Baton Rouge	LA	70805	225-357-0601	357-9543
Gino's 4542 Bennington Ave	Baton Rouge	LA	70808	225-927-7156	927-7146
Web: www.ginosrestaurant.com					
India's 5230 Essen Ln	Baton Rouge	LA	70809	225-769-0600	769-2683
Juban's 3739 Perkins Rd	Baton Rouge	LA	70808	225-346-8422	387-2601
Web: www.jubans.com					
Koto of Japan 2562 Citiplace Blvd	Baton Rouge	LA	70808	225-456-5454	
Web: www.kotoofjapan.com					
Mansur's 5720 Corporate Blvd Suite A	Baton Rouge	LA	70808	225-923-3366	923-2976
Web: www.mansursontheboulevard.com					
Melting Pot The 5294 Corporate Blvd	Baton Rouge	LA	70808	225-928-5677	928-5622
Web: www.meltingpot.com					
Mike Anderson's Seafood Restaurant					
1031 W Lee Dr	Baton Rouge	LA	70809	225-766-7823	766-3205
Web: www.mikeandersonsseafood.com					
Ninfa's Restaurant 4738 Constitution Ave	Baton Rouge	LA	70808	225-924-0377	924-5620
Sullivan's Steakhouse					
5252 Corporate Blvd	Baton Rouge	LA	70808	225-925-1161	925-2348
Web: www.sullivansteakhouse.com					
Thai Kitchen 4335 Perkins Rd	Baton Rouge	LA	70808	225-346-1230	346-5113
Web: www.thaikitchenla.com					
L'Italiano 701 Barksdale Blvd	Bossier City	LA	71111	318-747-7777	
Ralph & Kacoo's					
1700 Old Minden Rd Suite 141	Bossier City	LA	71111	318-747-6660	747-9816
Web: www.ralphandkacoos.com					
Antoni's Italian Cafe					
1118 Coolidge Blvd Suite A	Lafayette	LA	70503	337-232-8384	232-4311
Web: www.antoniscafe.com					
Bailey's Seafood & Grill					
5520-A Johnston St	Lafayette	LA	70503	337-988-6464	988-6494
Web: www.baileyscss.com					
Cafe Vermilionville 1304 W Pinhook Rd	Lafayette	LA	70503	337-237-0100	233-5599
Web: www.cafev.com					
Casa Ole 2312 Kaliste Salocm Rd	Lafayette	LA	70508	337-993-9900	
Web: www.casaoleofacadiana.com					
Charley G's Seafood Grill					
3809 Ambassador Caffery Pkwy	Lafayette	LA	70503	337-981-0108	981-5899
Web: www.charleygs.com					
Don's Seafood & Steakhouse					
301 E Vermilion St	Lafayette	LA	70501	337-235-3551	235-6707
Web: www.donsdowntown.com					
Picante Mexican Restaurant					
3235 NW Evangeline Thwy	Lafayette	LA	70507	337-896-1200	896-1202
Web: www.picantesrestaurant.com					
Prejean's Restaurant					
3480 NE Evangeline Trwy	Lafayette	LA	70507	337-896-3247	896-3278
Web: www.prejeans.com					
Bozo's 3117 21st St	Metairie	LA	70002	504-831-8666	
Carreta's Grill 2320 Veterans Memorial Blvd	Metairie	LA	70002	504-837-6696	834-5428
Casa Garcia 8814 Veterans Memorial Blvd	Metairie	LA	70003	504-464-0354	
Deanie's Seafood 1713 Lake Ave	Metairie	LA	70005	504-834-1225	837-2166
Web: www.deanies.com					
Drago's 3232 N Arnoult Rd	Metairie	LA	70002	504-888-9254	888-9255
Web: www.dragosrestaurant.com					
Fausto's Bistro 530 Veterans Memorial Blvd	Metairie	LA	70005	504-833-7121	833-7632
Web: www.faustosbistro.com					
Impastato's 3400 16th St	Metairie	LA	70002	504-455-1545	833-1816
Web: www.impastatos.com					
Little Tokyo 1521 N Cswy Blvd	Metairie	LA	70001	504-831-6788	831-6672
Peppermill Restaurant 3524 Severn Ave	Metairie	LA	70002	504-455-2266	
Web: www.riccobonos.com					
Ruth's Chris Steak House					
3633 Veterans Memorial Blvd	Metairie	LA	70002	504-888-3600	885-6422
Web: www.ruthschris.com					
Siamese Thai Cuisine					
6601 Veterans Memorial Blvd Suite 29-30	Metairie	LA	70003	504-454-8752	454-8751
Web: www.siamesecuisine.com					
Sun Ray Grill 619 Pink St	Metairie	LA	70005	504-837-0055	835-2555
Web: www.sunraygrill.com					
Texas Bar-B-Que 3320 Houma Blvd	Metairie	LA	70006	504-456-2832	
Vega Tapas Cafe 2051 Metairie Rd	Metairie	LA	70005	504-836-2007	833-0907
Web: www.vegatapascafe.com					
Vincent's 4411 Chastant St	Metairie	LA	70006	504-885-2984	
Web: www.vincentsitaliancuisine.com					
Acme Oyster House 724 Iberville St	New Orleans	LA	70130	504-522-5973	524-1595
Web: www.acmeoyster.com					
Antoine's 713 St Louis St	New Orleans	LA	70130	504-581-4422	
Web: www.antoines.com					
Arnaud's 813 Bienville St	New Orleans	LA	70112	504-523-5433	355-5730
TF: 866-230-8895 ■ *Web:* www.arnauds.com					
August 301 Tchoupitoulas St	New Orleans	LA	70130	504-299-9777	299-1199
Web: www.rest-august.com					
Bacco 310 Chartres St	New Orleans	LA	70130	504-522-2426	521-8323
Web: www.bacco.com					
Bayona 430 Rue Dauphine	New Orleans	LA	70112	504-525-4455	522-0589
Web: www.bayona.com					
Begue's Restaurant 300 Bourbon St	New Orleans	LA	70130	504-553-2278	
Web: www.neworleansrestaurants.com/begues					
Bon Ton Cafe 401 Magazine St	New Orleans	LA	70130	504-524-3386	
Web: www.thebontoncafe.com					
Bourbon House Seafood & Oyster Bar					
144 Bourbon St	New Orleans	LA	70130	504-522-0111	522-0333
Web: www.bourbonhouse.com					

Name / Address	City	State	ZIP	Phone	Fax
Brigtsen's 723 Dante St *Web:* www.brigtsens.com	New Orleans	LA	70118	504-861-7610	866-7397
Broussard's Restaurant 819 Rue Conti *Web:* www.broussards.com	New Orleans	LA	70112	504-581-3866	581-3873
Byblos 3218 Magazine St *Web:* www.byblosrestaurants.com	New Orleans	LA	70115	504-894-1233	894-1239
Cafe Degas 3127 Esplanade Ave *Web:* www.cafedegas.com	New Orleans	LA	70119	504-945-5635	943-5255
Cafe Giovanni 117 Rue Decatur St *Web:* www.cafegiovanni.com	New Orleans	LA	70118	504-529-2154	529-3352
Ciro's Cote Sud 7918 Maple St *Web:* www.cotesudrestaurant.com	New Orleans	LA	70118	504-866-9551	
Clancy's 6100 Annunciation St	New Orleans	LA	70118	504-895-1111	
Cuvee 322 Magazine St *Web:* www.restaurantcuvee.com	New Orleans	LA	70130	504-587-9001	587-9006
Dick & Jenny's 4501 Tchoupitoulas St *Web:* www.dickandjennys.com	New Orleans	LA	70115	504-894-9880	895-5636
Elizabeth's 601 Gallier St *Web:* www.elizabeths-restaurant.com	New Orleans	LA	70117	504-944-9272	
Emeril's 800 Tchoupitoulas St *Web:* www.emerils.com	New Orleans	LA	70130	504-528-9393	558-3925
Emeril's Delmonico 1300 St Charles Ave *Web:* www.emerils.com	New Orleans	LA	70130	504-525-4937	595-2206
Galatoire's 209 Bourbon St *Web:* www.galatoires.com	New Orleans	LA	70130	504-525-2021	525-5900
Grill Room 300 Gravier St	New Orleans	LA	70130	504-522-1992	596-4513
GW Fins 808 Bienville St *Web:* www.gwfins.com	New Orleans	LA	70112	504-581-3467	565-5459
Herbsaint Bar & Restaurant 701 St Charles Ave *Web:* www.herbsaint.com	New Orleans	LA	70130	504-524-4114	522-1679
Horinoya 920 Poydras St	New Orleans	LA	70112	504-561-8914	561-8919
Irene's Cuisine 539 St Phillip St	New Orleans	LA	70116	504-529-8811	527-5273
Jacques-Imo's Cafe 8324 Oak St *Web:* www.jacquesimoscafe.com	New Orleans	LA	70118	504-861-0886	314-1585
K-Paul's Louisiana Kitchen 416 Chartres St *Web:* www.kpauls.com	New Orleans	LA	70130	504-596-2530	596-2540
Kyoto 4920 Prytania St	New Orleans	LA	70115	504-891-3644	891-3694
La Crepe Nanou 1410 Robert St *Web:* www.lacrepenanou.com	New Orleans	LA	70115	504-899-2670	
Le Meritage at the Maison Dupuy 1001 Rue Toulouse *Web:* www.lemeritagerestaurant.com	New Orleans	LA	70112	504-586-8000	525-5334
Liborio's 321 Magazine St *Web:* www.liboriocuban.com	New Orleans	LA	70130	504-581-9680	
Lilette 3637 Magazine St *Web:* www.liletterestaurant.com	New Orleans	LA	70115	504-895-1636	895-3622
Louisiana Bistro 337 Dauphine St	New Orleans	LA	70112	504-525-3335	
Martinique Bistro 5908 Magazine St *Web:* www.martiniquebistro.com	New Orleans	LA	70115	504-891-8495	891-2622
Mat & Naddie's Restaurant 937 Leonidas St *Web:* www.matandnaddies.com	New Orleans	LA	70118	504-861-9600	865-8094
Mr B's Bistro 201 Royal St *Web:* www.mrbsbistro.com	New Orleans	LA	70130	504-523-2078	521-8304
Muriel's 801 Chartres St *Web:* www.muriels.com	New Orleans	LA	70116	504-568-1885	568-9795
Ninja 8433 Oak St	New Orleans	LA	70118	504-866-1119	
NOLA 534 St Louis St *Web:* www.emerils.com	New Orleans	LA	70130	504-522-6652	524-6178
Orleans Grapevine Wine Bar & Bistro 718 - 720 Orleans Ave *Web:* www.orleansgrapevine.com	New Orleans	LA	70116	504-523-1930	523-1245
Palace Cafe 605 Canal St *Web:* www.palacecafe.com	New Orleans	LA	70130	504-523-1661	
Pelican Club 312 Exchange Alley *Web:* www.pelicanclub.com	New Orleans	LA	70130	504-523-1504	522-2331
Petunias 817 St Louis St	New Orleans	LA	70112	504-522-6440	528-9042
Port of Call 838 Esplanade Ave	New Orleans	LA	70116	504-523-0120	529-7678
Red Fish Grill 115 Bourbon St *Web:* www.redfishgrill.com	New Orleans	LA	70130	504-598-1200	598-1211
RioMar 800 S Peters St *Web:* www.riomarseafood.com	New Orleans	LA	70130	504-525-3474	
Sake Cafe 2830 Magazine St	New Orleans	LA	70115	504-894-0033	894-1546
Sara's 724 Dublin St *Web:* www.sarasrestaurant.com	New Orleans	LA	70118	504-861-0565	
Stella! 1032 Chartres St *Web:* www.restaurantstella.com	New Orleans	LA	70116	504-587-0091	587-0092
Sun Ray Grill 1051 Annunciation St *Web:* www.sunraygrill.com	New Orleans	LA	70130	504-566-0021	566-0041
Upperline 1413 Upperline St *Web:* www.upperline.com	New Orleans	LA	70115	504-891-9822	
Veranda Restaurant 444 St Charles Ave	New Orleans	LA	70130	504-525-5566	
Vincent's 7839 St Charles Ave *Web:* www.vincentsitaliancuisine.com	New Orleans	LA	70118	504-866-9313	861-8972
Bella Fresca Restaurant 6307 Line Ave *Web:* www.bellafresca.com	Shreveport	LA	71101	318-865-6307	865-6362
Bistro 6301 6301 Line Ave	Shreveport	LA	71106	318-865-6301	865-6306
Chianti Restaurant 6535 Line Ave	Shreveport	LA	71106	318-868-8866	865-7119
Copeland's of New Orleans 1665 E Industrial Loop *Web:* www.copelandsofneworleans.com	Shreveport	LA	71106	318-797-0143	797-7135
Ernest's Orleans Restaurant & Cocktail Lounge 1601 Spring St S *Web:* www.ernestsorleans.com	Shreveport	LA	71101	318-226-1325	425-0900
Mabry House 1540 Irving Pl	Shreveport	LA	71101	318-227-1121	227-1121
Ming Garden 1250 Shreveport Barksdale Hwy	Shreveport	LA	71105	318-861-2741	865-7222
Monjunis 1315 Louisiana Ave *Web:* www.monjunis.com	Shreveport	LA	71101	318-227-0847	227-9499
Superior Bar & Grill 6123 Line Ave *Web:* www.shreveport.superiorgrill.com	Shreveport	LA	71106	318-869-3243	868-7688
Trejo's 9122 Mansfield Rd	Shreveport	LA	71118	318-687-6192	687-8187
Village Grille 1313 Louisiana Ave	Shreveport	LA	71101	318-424-2874	

MAINE

Name / Address	City	State	ZIP	Phone	Fax
Capital Buffet 208 Western Ave	Augusta	ME	04330	207-623-8878	626-3568
Margaritas 390 Western Ave *Web:* www.margs.com	Augusta	ME	04330	207-622-7874	622-7908
Red Barn 455 Riverside Dr	Augusta	ME	04330	207-623-9485	623-9520
Riverfront Barbeque & Grill 300 Water St	Augusta	ME	04330	207-622-8899	
Senator Oyster Bar & Grill 284 Outer Western Ave	Augusta	ME	04330	207-622-0320	622-8803
Bugaboo Creek Steak House 24 Bangor Mall Blvd	Bangor	ME	04401	207-945-5515	945-5445
Captain Nick's 1165 Union St	Bangor	ME	04401	207-942-6444	947-8630
China Light 571 Broadway	Bangor	ME	04401	207-947-6759	
Geaghan's Restaurant & Pub 570 Main St *Web:* www.geaghanspub.com	Bangor	ME	04401	207-945-3730	941-6758
Ichiban 226 Union St	Bangor	ME	04401	207-262-9308	262-9310
Oriental Jade 555 Stillwater Ave *Web:* www.orientaljade.com	Bangor	ME	04401	207-947-6969	942-7170
Panda Garden 123 Franklin St	Bangor	ME	04401	207-942-2704	942-2704
Pepino's 570 Stillwater Ave *Web:* www.pepinosrestaurant.com	Bangor	ME	04401	207-947-1233	947-1233
Sea Dog Brewing Co 26 Front St *Web:* www.seadogbrewing.com	Bangor	ME	04401	207-947-8004	947-8720
Thistle's 175 Exchange St *Web:* www.thistlesrestaurant.com	Bangor	ME	04401	207-945-5480	990-3836
Whig & Courier Pub 18 Broad St	Bangor	ME	04401	207-947-4095	947-4095
Wright Bros American Grill & Lounge 308 Godfrey Blvd	Bangor	ME	04401	207-947-6721	941-9761
Cafe Blue Fish 122 Cottage St *Web:* www.cafebluefishbarharbor.com	Bar Harbor	ME	04609	207-288-3696	
China Joy 195 Main St	Bar Harbor	ME	04609	207-288-8666	288-8662
Geddy's Pub 19 Main St PO Box 955 *Web:* www.geddys.com	Bar Harbor	ME	04609	207-288-5077	288-9927
Havana 318 Main St	Bar Harbor	ME	04609	207-288-2822	
Maggie's Classic Scales 6 Summer St	Bar Harbor	ME	04609	207-288-9007	
Mama Di Matteo's 34 Kennebec Pl *Web:* www.mamadimatteos.com	Bar Harbor	ME	04609	207-288-3666	
Michelle's 194 Main St *Web:* www.ivymanor.com	Bar Harbor	ME	04609	207-288-0038	
Parkside Restaurant 185 Main St	Bar Harbor	ME	04609	207-288-3700	288-4929
Poor Boy's Gourmet 300 Main St *Web:* www.poorboysgourmet.com	Bar Harbor	ME	04609	207-288-4148	
Rosalie's 46 Cottage St	Bar Harbor	ME	04609	207-288-5666	
Route 66 21 Cottage St *Web:* barharborroute66.com	Bar Harbor	ME	04609	207-288-3708	
Rupununi Bar & Grill 119 Main St *Web:* www.rupununi.com	Bar Harbor	ME	04609	207-288-2886	
Stewman's Lobster Pound 35 W St *Web:* www.stewmanslobsterpound.com	Bar Harbor	ME	04609	207-288-9723	288-9723
West Street Cafe 76 W St *Web:* www.weststreetcafe.com	Bar Harbor	ME	04609	207-288-5242	
Ground Round 215 Whitten Rd PO Box 426 *Web:* www.sparetimerec.com	Hallowell	ME	04347	207-623-0022	621-2860
Hattie's Chowder House 103 Water St *Web:* www.hattieschowderhouse.com	Hallowell	ME	04347	207-621-4114	621-2622
Lucky Garden 218 Water St	Hallowell	ME	04347	207-622-3465	
Bar Harbor Lobster Bakes 10 State Hwy 3 PO Box 177 *Web:* www.barharborlobsterbakes.com	Hulls Cove	ME	04644	207-288-4055	288-5767
Back Bay Grill 65 Portland St *Web:* www.backbaygrill.com	Portland	ME	04101	207-772-8833	
Benkay 2 India St	Portland	ME	04101	207-773-5555	
Bintliff's American Cafe 98 Portland St *Web:* www.bintliffscafe.com	Portland	ME	04101	207-774-0005	774-2505
Blue Spoon 89 Congress St	Portland	ME	04101	207-773-1116	773-1119
Cinque Terre 36 Wharf St *Web:* www.cinqueterremaine.com	Portland	ME	04101	207-347-6154	347-6157
David's Creative Cuisine 22 Monument Sq **Fax:* Resv ■ *Web:* www.davidsrestaurant.com	Portland	ME	04101	207-773-4340	773-4425*
DiMillo's on the Water 25 Long Wharf *Web:* www.dimillos.com	Portland	ME	04101	207-772-2216	772-1081
Duckfat 43 Middle St *Web:* www.duckfat.com	Portland	ME	04101	207-774-8080	774-0262
Fore Street 288 Fore St	Portland	ME	04101	207-775-2717	
Fuji 29 Exchange St *Web:* www.fujimaine.com	Portland	ME	04101	207-773-2900	773-7096
Gilbert's Chowder House 92 Commercial St	Portland	ME	04101	207-871-5636	
Hugo's Restaurant 88 Middle St *Web:* www.hugos.net	Portland	ME	04101	207-774-8538	
Katahdin Restaurant 27 Forest Ave *Web:* www.katahdinrestaurant.com	Portland	ME	04101	207-774-1740	774-1740
Maria's 337 Cumberland Ave	Portland	ME	04101	207-772-9232	
Pat's Cafe 484 Stevens Ave *Web:* www.cafeatpats.com	Portland	ME	04103	207-874-0706	
Pepperclub 78 Middle St	Portland	ME	04101	207-772-0531	
Portland Lobster Co 180 Commercial St *Web:* www.portlandlobstercompany.com	Portland	ME	04112	207-775-2112	
Ri Ra Irish Pub & Restaurant 72 Commercial St *Web:* www.rira.com	Portland	ME	04101	207-761-4446	761-4447
Ribollita 41 Middle St	Portland	ME	04101	207-774-2972	
Roma Cafe The 769 Congress St	Portland	ME	04102	207-773-9873	756-6768
Sapporo 230 Commercial St *Web:* www.sappororestaurant.com	Portland	ME	04101	207-772-1233	871-9275
Siam City Cafe 339 Fore St *Web:* www.siamportland.com	Portland	ME	04101	207-773-8389	773-6369
Walter's Cafe 2 Portland Sq *Web:* www.waltersportland.com	Portland	ME	04101	207-871-9258	871-1018

Name / Address	City	State	Zip	Phone	Fax
Joe's Boathouse 1 Spring Pt Dr *Web:* www.joesboathouse.com	South Portland	ME	04106	207-741-2780	347-5718

MANITOBA

Name / Address	City	State	Postal Code	Phone	Fax
529 Wellington 529 Wellington Crescent	Winnipeg	MB	R2M5G8	204-487-8325	
Amici 326 Broadway *Web:* www.amiciwpg.com	Winnipeg	MB	R3C0S5	204-943-4997	943-0369
Bailey's 185 Lombard Ave *Web:* www.baileysprimedining.com	Winnipeg	MB	R3B0W4	204-944-1180	944-0449
Bella Vista 53 Maryland St	Winnipeg	MB	R3G1K6	204-775-4485	
Bombolini 326 Broadway	Winnipeg	MB	R3C0S5	204-943-5066	943-0369
Cafe Carlo 243 Lilac St *Web:* www.cafecarlo.com	Winnipeg	MB	R3M2S2	204-477-5544	477-1652
Dim Sum Garden 277 Rupert Ave	Winnipeg	MB	R3B0N5	204-942-8297	415-2972
East India Co 349 York Ave *Web:* www.eastindiaco.com	Winnipeg	MB	R3C3S9	204-947-3097	947-5019
Edohei 355 Ellice Ave *Web:* www.edohei.mb.ca	Winnipeg	MB	R3B1X8	204-943-0427	943-6104
Elephant & Castle/Delta Winnipeg Hotel 350 St Mary Ave *Web:* www.elephantcastle.com	Winnipeg	MB	R3C3J2	204-942-5555	947-0275
Fusion Grill 550 Academy Rd	Winnipeg	MB	R3N0E3	204-489-6963	
Gasthaus Gutenberger 2583 Portage Ave *Web:* www.gasthausgutenberger.com	Winnipeg	MB	R2Y0V3	204-888-3133	896-8358
Hy's Steakhouse & Cocktail Bar 1 Lombard Pl Main Fl Richardson Bldg *Web:* www.hyssteakhouse.com	Winnipeg	MB	R3B0X3	204-942-1000	947-3588
Ichiban 189 Carlton St *Web:* www.ichiban.ca	Winnipeg	MB	R3C3H7	204-925-7400	957-1697
King's Head Pub 120 King St *Web:* www.kingshead.ca	Winnipeg	MB	R3B1H9	204-957-7710	253-6520
Marigold 2591 Portage Ave	Winnipeg	MB	R3J0P5	204-888-5665	
Maxime 1131 St Mary's Rd **Fax Area Code: 207*	Winnipeg	MB	R2M3T9	204-257-1521	257-1521*
Mei Ji Sushi 454 River Ave *Web:* www.meijisushi.ca	Winnipeg	MB	R3L0C7	204-284-3996	452-3749
Mona Lisa 1697 Corydon Ave	Winnipeg	MB	R3N0J9	204-488-3687	489-1679
Mondragon 91 Albert St *Web:* www.a-zone.org/mondragon	Winnipeg	MB	R3B1G5	204-946-5241	956-1505
Pembina Village Restaurant 333 Pembina Hwy	Winnipeg	MB	R3L2E4	204-477-5439	284-3809
Restaurant Dubrovnik 390 Assiniboine Ave *Web:* www.restaurantdubrovnik.com	Winnipeg	MB	R3C1N2	204-944-0594	942-7074
Resto Gare 630 Des Meurons St *Web:* www.restogare.com	Winnipeg	MB	R2H2P9	204-237-7072	837-3624
Sawatdee 555 Osborne St *Web:* www.sawatdeeservice.ca	Winnipeg	MB	R3L2B3	204-284-8424	375-1123
Step'n Out Eclectic Cuisine 157 Provencher Blvd *Web:* www.stepnout.ca	Winnipeg	MB	R2H0G2	204-956-7837	237-1849
Toad in the Hole 112 Osborne St	Winnipeg	MB	R3L1Y5	204-284-7201	474-1490
Tre Visi 173 McDermot Ave *Web:* www.trevisirestaurant.com	Winnipeg	MB	R3B0S1	204-949-9032	943-7540
Tropikis 878 Ellice Ave	Winnipeg	MB	R3G0C5	204-788-4733	772-7935
Velvet Glove The 175 Portage Ave	Winnipeg	MB	R2C0A1	204-957-1350	956-1791
Wasabi Restaurant & Sushi Bistro 105-121 Osborne St	Winnipeg	MB	R3L1Y4	204-474-2332	
White Tower 3670 Roblin Blvd	Winnipeg	MB	R3R0E1	204-896-0406	837-3873

MARYLAND

Name / Address	City	State	Zip	Phone	Fax
Adam's Ribs East 921C Chesapeake Ave *Web:* www.adamsribseast.com	Annapolis	MD	21403	410-267-0064	626-1077
Aqua Terra 164 Main St *Web:* www.aquaterraofannapolis.com	Annapolis	MD	21401	410-263-1985	263-1986
Cafe Normandie 185 Main St *Web:* www.cafenormandie.com	Annapolis	MD	21401	410-263-3382	263-8824
Cantler's Riverside Inn 458 Forest Beach Rd *Web:* www.cantlers.com	Annapolis	MD	21409	410-757-1311	757-6784
Castlebay Irish Pub 193-A Main St *Web:* www.castlebayirishpub.com	Annapolis	MD	21401	410-626-0165	626-0827
Famous Dave's Barbeque 181 Jennifer Rd *Web:* www.famousdaves.com	Annapolis	MD	21401	410-224-2207	224-2088
Federal House Bar & Grille 22 Market Space	Annapolis	MD	21401	410-268-2576	280-0195
Galway Bay Irish Pub 63 Maryland Ave *Web:* www.galwaybayannapolis.com	Annapolis	MD	21401	410-263-8333	263-8989
Harry Browne's 66 State Cir *Web:* www.harrybrownes.com	Annapolis	MD	21401	410-263-4332	263-8049
Jalapenos 85 Forest Dr *Web:* www.jalapenosonline.com	Annapolis	MD	21401	410-266-7580	266-7582
Joss Cafe & Sushi Bar 195 Main St	Annapolis	MD	21401	410-263-4688	263-4764
Lebanese Taverna 2500 Solomons Island Rd *Web:* www.lebanesetaverna.com	Annapolis	MD	21401	410-897-1111	897-9099
Les Folies 2552 Riva Rd *Web:* www.lesfoliesbrasserie.com	Annapolis	MD	21401	410-573-0970	573-9131
Lewnes' Steakhouse 401 4th St *Web:* www.lewnessteakhouse.com	Annapolis	MD	21401	410-263-1617	
Main Ingredient 914 Bay Ridge Rd *Web:* www.themainingredient.com	Annapolis	MD	21403	410-626-0388	626-0204
Mangia 81 Main St	Annapolis	MD	21401	410-268-1350	268-6420
Melting Pot of Annapolis The 2348 Solomons Island Rd *Web:* www.meltingpot.com	Annapolis	MD	21401	410-266-8004	266-8431
O'Brien's Oyster Bar & Restaurant 113 Main St *Web:* www.obriensoysterbar.com	Annapolis	MD	21401	410-268-6288	267-7767
O'Leary's Seafood Restaurant 310 3rd St	Annapolis	MD	21403	410-263-0884	263-5859
Osteria 177 177 Main St *Web:* www.osteria177.com	Annapolis	MD	21401	410-267-7700	267-9999
Paul's Homewood Cafe 919 W St	Annapolis	MD	21401	410-267-7891	267-8004
Piccola Roma 200 Main St	Annapolis	MD	21401	410-268-7898	
Red Hot & Blue Restaurants Inc 200 Old Mill Bottom Rd S *Web:* www.redhotandblue.com	Annapolis	MD	21401	410-626-7427	757-5095
Reynolds Tavern 7 Church Cir *Web:* www.reynoldstavern.org	Annapolis	MD	21401	410-295-9555	295-9559
Rockfish The 400 6th St *Web:* www.rockfishmd.com	Annapolis	MD	21403	410-267-1800	
Ruth's Chris Steak House 301 Severn Ave *Web:* www.ruthschris.com	Annapolis	MD	21403	410-990-0033	269-6700
Sam's on the Waterfront 2020 Chesapeake Harbour Dr E *Web:* www.samsonthewaterfront.com	Annapolis	MD	21403	410-263-3600	263-3654
Abacrombie 58 W Biddle St *TF:* 888-922-3437 ■ *Web:* www.abacrombie.net	Baltimore	MD	21201	410-244-7227	837-6112
Akbar 823 N Charles St *Web:* www.akbar-restaurant.com	Baltimore	MD	21201	410-539-0944	539-0308
Aldo's 306 S High St *Web:* www.aldositaly.com	Baltimore	MD	21202	410-727-0700	625-3700
Ambassador Dining Room 3811 Canterbury Rd *Web:* www.ambassadordiningroom.com	Baltimore	MD	21218	410-366-1484	
Amicci's of Little Italy 231 S High St *Web:* www.amiccis.com	Baltimore	MD	21202	410-528-1096	685-6259
B - A Bolton Hill Bistro 1501 Bolton St *Web:* www.b-bistro.com	Baltimore	MD	21217	410-383-8600	383-1017
Ban Thai 340 N Charles St *Web:* www.banthai.us	Baltimore	MD	21201	410-727-7971	727-0125
Bicycle 1444 Light St *Web:* www.bicyclebistro.com	Baltimore	MD	21230	410-234-1900	878-7146
Birches 641 S Montford Ave *Web:* www.birchesrestaurant.com	Baltimore	MD	21224	410-732-3000	
Black Olive 814 S Bond St *Web:* www.theblackolive.com	Baltimore	MD	21231	410-276-7141	276-7143
Brewers Art 1106 N Charles St *Web:* www.thebrewersart.com	Baltimore	MD	21201	410-547-9310	547-7417
Brighton's 550 Light St	Baltimore	MD	21202	410-347-9750	659-5925
Carlyle Club 500 W University Pkwy	Baltimore	MD	21210	410-243-5454	
Chameleon Cafe 4341 Harford Rd *Web:* www.thechameleoncafe.com	Baltimore	MD	21214	410-254-2376	254-9437
Charleston 1000 Lancaster St *Web:* www.charlestonrestaurant.com	Baltimore	MD	21202	410-332-7373	332-8425
Cork's 1026 S Charles St *Web:* www.corksrestaurant.com	Baltimore	MD	21230	410-752-3810	752-0639
Da Mimmo Italian Cuisine 217 S High St *Web:* www.damimmo.com	Baltimore	MD	21202	410-727-6876	727-1927
Dalesio's of Little Italy 829 Eastern Ave *Web:* www.dalesios.com	Baltimore	MD	21202	410-539-1965	576-8749
Della Note Ristorante 801 Eastern Ave *Web:* www.dellanotte.com	Baltimore	MD	21202	410-837-5500	837-2600
Dukem 1100 Maryland Ave **Fax Area Code: 202* ■ *Web:* www.dukemrestaurant.com	Baltimore	MD	21201	410-385-0318	667-2488*
Faidley's Seafood 203 N Paca St *Web:* www.faidleyscrabcakes.com	Baltimore	MD	21201	410-727-4898	
Gertrude's 10 Art Museum Dr	Baltimore	MD	21218	410-889-3399	889-9689
Helmand The 806 N Charles St *Web:* www.helmand.com	Baltimore	MD	21201	410-752-0311	752-0511
Henninger's Tavern 1812 Bank St *Web:* www.henningerstavern.com	Baltimore	MD	21231	410-342-2172	
Holy Frijoles 908 W 36th St	Baltimore	MD	21211	410-235-2326	
Hull Street Blues 1222 Hull St *Web:* www.hullstreetblues.com	Baltimore	MD	21230	410-727-7476	576-2343
Ikaros 4805 Eastern Ave *Web:* www.ikarosrestaurant.com	Baltimore	MD	21224	410-633-3750	633-7881
Kali's Court 1606 Thames St *Web:* www.kaliscourt.com	Baltimore	MD	21231	410-276-4700	276-2420
Kali's Mezze 1606 Thames St *Web:* www.kalismezze.com	Baltimore	MD	21231	410-563-7600	276-2420
La Scala of Little Italy 1012 Eastern Ave *Web:* www.lascaladining.com	Baltimore	MD	21202	410-783-9209	783-5949
La Tavola 248 Albemarle St *Web:* www.la-tavola.com	Baltimore	MD	21202	410-685-1859	685-1891
Little Havana 1325 Key Hwy *Web:* www.littlehavanas.com	Baltimore	MD	21230	410-837-9903	332-0775
Louisiana Restaurant 1708 Aliceanna St *Web:* www.louisianasrestaurant.com	Baltimore	MD	21231	410-327-2610	327-0372
Mama's on the Half Shell 2901 O'Donnell St *Web:* www.mamasonthehalfshell.com	Baltimore	MD	21224	410-276-3160	327-7140
Matsuri Restaurant 1105 S Charles St *Web:* www.matsuri.us	Baltimore	MD	21230	410-752-8561	752-9919
Morton's the Steakhouse 300 S Charles St *Web:* www.mortons.com	Baltimore	MD	21201	410-547-8255	547-8244
Mughal Garden 920 N Charles St	Baltimore	MD	21201	410-547-0001	547-0002
Nacho Mama's 2907 O'Donnell St *Web:* www.nachomamascanton.com	Baltimore	MD	21224	410-675-0898	
Peter's Inn 504 S Ann St *Web:* www.petersinn.com	Baltimore	MD	21231	410-675-7313	
Petit Louis Bistro 4800 Roland Ave *Web:* www.petitlouis.com	Baltimore	MD	21210	410-366-9393	366-9019
Red Maple 930 N Charles St **Fax Area Code: 443* ■ *Web:* www.930redmaple.com	Baltimore	MD	21201	410-385-0520	524-1995*
Rocco's Capriccio 846 Fawn St	Baltimore	MD	21202	410-685-2710	
Ruth's Chris Steak House 600 Water St *Web:* www.ruthschris.com	Baltimore	MD	21202	410-783-0033	783-0049
Sabatino's 901 Fawn St *Web:* www.sabatinos.com	Baltimore	MD	21202	410-727-9414	837-6540
Saffron 802 N Charles St *Web:* www.saffronusa.com	Baltimore	MD	21201	410-528-1616	528-1310
Samos 600 Oldham St *Web:* www.samosrestaurant.com	Baltimore	MD	21224	410-675-5292	
San Sushi 2748 Lighthouse Pt	Baltimore	MD	21224	410-534-8888	534-8665

Name / Address	City	State	ZIP	Phone	Fax
Sascha's 527 527 N Charles St	Baltimore	MD	21201	410-539-8880	539-6105
Web: www.saschas.com					
Sotto Sopra 405 N Charles St	Baltimore	MD	21201	410-625-0534	625-2642
Web: www.sottosoprainc.com					
Suzie's Soba 1009 W 36th St	Baltimore	MD	21211	410-243-0051	243-3838
Tapas Teatro 1711 N Charles St	Baltimore	MD	21201	410-332-0110	323-1229
Web: www.tapasteatro.net					
Thai Arroy 1019 Light St	Baltimore	MD	21230	410-385-8587	
Web: www.thaiarroy.com					
Thai Landing 1207 N Charles St	Baltimore	MD	21201	410-727-1234	
Web: www.thailanding.us					
Thai Restaurant 3316-18 Greenmount Ave	Baltimore	MD	21218	410-889-6002	889-6003
Tio Pepe 10 E Franklin St	Baltimore	MD	21202	410-539-4675	837-7288
Viccino 1317 N Charles St	Baltimore	MD	21201	410-347-0349	783-1938
Web: www.viccino.com					
Angler Restaurant 312 Talbot St	Ocean City	MD	21842	410-289-7424	
Web: www.theangleroc.com					
BJ's On the Water 115 75th St	Ocean City	MD	21842	410-524-7575	524-7624
Web: www.bjsonthewater.com					
Bombora 1301 Atlantic Ave Beach Plaza Hotel	Ocean City	MD	21842	410-289-9121	289-3041
Web: www.bomboraoc.com					
Bonfire The 7009 Coastal Hwy	Ocean City	MD	21842	410-524-7171	524-4228
Web: www.thebonfirerestaurant.com					
Buxy's Salty Dog 2707 Philadelphia Ave	Ocean City	MD	21842	410-289-0973	289-0038
Web: www.buxyssaltydog.com					
Captain's Galley 12817 Harbor Rd	Ocean City	MD	21842	410-213-2525	213-0702
Coral Reef Restaurant 1701 Atlantic Ave	Ocean City	MD	21842	410-289-2612	289-3381
Fager's Island Restaurant 201 60th St	Ocean City	MD	21842	410-524-5500	723-2055
Web: www.fagers.com					
Galaxy Bar & Grille 66th St Bayside	Ocean City	MD	21842	410-723-6762	723-1387
Web: www.galaxy66barandgrille.com					
Hall's Restaurant 60th St Bayside	Ocean City	MD	21842	410-524-5008	524-5377
Web: www.halls-oc.com					
Harrison's Harbor Watch Restaurant 806 S Boardwalk	Ocean City	MD	21842	410-289-5121	
Web: www.harborwatchrestaurant.com					
Jonah & the Whale 26th St & Boardwalk	Ocean City	MD	21842	410-524-2722	
JR's Place for Ribs 131st St & Coastal	Ocean City	MD	21842	410-250-3100	250-3104
Web: www.jrsribs.com					
Jules 11805 Coastal Hwy	Ocean City	MD	21842	410-524-3396	
La Hacienda Restaurant 8003 Coastal Hwy	Ocean City	MD	21842	410-524-8080	
TF: 800-297-8081 ■ *Web:* www.beach-net.com/laha					
Macky's Bayside Bar & Grill 5311 Coastal Hwy	Ocean City	MD	21842	410-723-5565	723-4445
Web: www.mackys.com					
Marina Deck 306 Dorchester St	Ocean City	MD	21842	410-289-4411	289-6449
Web: www.marinadeckrestaurant.com					
Marlin Moon Grille 12806 Ocean Gateway	Ocean City	MD	21842	410-213-1618	
Web: www.marlinmoongrille.com					
Nick's Original House of Ribs 14410 Coastal Hwy	Ocean City	MD	21842	410-250-1984	250-2770
Web: www.nickshouseofribs.com					
Ocean Club 10100 Coastal Hwy	Ocean City	MD	21842	410-524-7500	
Phillips Crab House 2004 N Philadelphia Ave	Ocean City	MD	21842	410-289-6821	289-4258
Web: www.phillipsseafood.com					
Reflections Restaurant & Wine Bar 67th St & Coastal Hwy	Ocean City	MD	21842	410-524-5252	
Tequila Mockingbird 130th St Montego Bay Shopping Ctr	Ocean City	MD	21842	410-250-4424	
Web: www.octequila.com					
Tutti Gusti 3322 Coastal Hwy	Ocean City	MD	21842	410-289-3318	
Web: www.ocean-city.com/tuttigusti.htm					
Crab Alley 9703 Golf Course Rd	West Ocean City	MD	21842	410-213-7800	213-1048
Web: www.craballey.com					

MASSACHUSETTS

Name / Address	City	State	ZIP	Phone	Fax
Outermost Inn 81 Lighthouse Rd	Aquinnah	MA	02535	508-645-3511	645-3514
Web: www.outermostinn.com					
29 Newbury 29 Newbury St	Boston	MA	02116	617-536-0290	
Web: www.29newbury.com					
75 Chestnut 75 Chestnut St	Boston	MA	02108	617-227-2175	227-3675
Web: www.75chestnut.com					
Abe & Louie's 793 Boylston St	Boston	MA	02116	617-536-6300	437-6291
Web: www.abeandlouies.com					
Addis Red Sea 544 Tremont St	Boston	MA	02116	617-426-8727	695-3677
Web: www.addisredsea.com					
Antico Forno 93 Salem St	Boston	MA	02113	617-723-6733	
Web: www.anticofornoboston.com					
Aquitaine 569 Tremont St	Boston	MA	02118	617-424-8577	424-0249
Web: www.aquitaineboston.com					
Assaggio 29 Prince St	Boston	MA	02113	617-227-7380	742-3512
Web: www.assaggioboston.com					
Atlantic Fish Co 761 Boylston St	Boston	MA	02116	617-267-4000	267-0755
Web: www.backbayrestaurantgroup.com					
B & G Oysters 550 Tremont St	Boston	MA	02116	617-423-0550	423-3533
Web: www.bandgoysters.com					
Bangkok Blue 651 Boylston St	Boston	MA	02116	617-266-1010	266-9747
Web: www.bkkblueboston.com					
Bhindi Bazaar 95 Massachusetts Ave	Boston	MA	02115	617-450-0660	450-0320
Web: www.bhindibazaar.com					
Bin 26 Enoteca 26 Charles St	Boston	MA	02114	617-723-5939	
Web: www.bin26.com					
Blu 4 Avery St 4th Fl	Boston	MA	02111	617-375-8550	375-8201
Web: www.blurestaurant.com					
Bricco 241 Hanover St	Boston	MA	02113	617-248-6800	367-0666
Web: www.bricco.com					
Bristol The 200 Boylston St	Boston	MA	02116	617-338-4400	423-0154
Web: www.fourseasons.com					
Brown Sugar Cafe 1033 Commonwealth Ave	Boston	MA	02215	617-787-4242	783-1365
Web: www.brownsugarcafe.com					
Butcher Shop The 552 Tremont St	Boston	MA	02118	617-423-4800	423-4840
Web: www.thebutchershopboston.com					
Cantina Italiana 346 Hanover St	Boston	MA	02115	617-723-4577	723-6357
Web: www.cantinaitaliana.com					
Capital Grille 359 Newbury St	Boston	MA	02115	617-262-8900	262-9449
Web: www.thecapitalgrille.com					
Casa Romero 30 Gloucester St	Boston	MA	02115	617-536-4341	536-6191
Web: www.casaromero.com					
Clio 370A Commonwealth Ave	Boston	MA	02215	617-536-7200	578-0394
Web: www.cliorestaurant.com					
Davide 326 Commercial St	Boston	MA	02109	617-227-5745	227-8976
Web: www.daviderestaurant.com					
East Ocean City 27 Beach St	Boston	MA	02111	617-542-2504	348-2878
Web: www.eastoceancity.com					
Fleming's Prime Steakhouse & Wine Bar 217 Stuart St	Boston	MA	02116	617-292-0808	482-3025
Web: www.flemingssteakhouse.com					
Franklin Cafe 278 Shawmut Ave	Boston	MA	02118	617-350-0010	350-5115
Web: www.franklincafe.com					
Ginza 16 Hudson St	Boston	MA	02111	617-338-2261	426-3563
Grill 23 & Bar 161 Berkeley St	Boston	MA	02116	617-542-2255	896-1042
Web: www.grill23.com					
Grotto 37 Bowdoin St	Boston	MA	02114	617-227-3434	227-4616
Web: www.grottorestaurant.com					
Hamersley's Bistro 553 Tremont St	Boston	MA	02116	617-423-2700	
Web: www.hamersleysbistro.com					
India Quality 484 Commonwealth Ave	Boston	MA	02215	617-267-4499	267-4477
Web: www.indiaquality.com					
Kingfish Hall 188 Faneuil Hall Marketplace S Market Bldg	Boston	MA	02109	617-523-8862	523-8860
Web: www.toddenglish.com					
KO Prime 90 Tremont St	Boston	MA	02108	617-772-0202	772-5810
Web: www.koprimeboston.com					
L'Espalier 774-Bayleston St	Boston	MA	02115	617-262-3023	375-9297
Web: www.lespalier.com					
Lala Rokh 97 Mt Vernon St	Boston	MA	02108	617-720-5511	
Web: www.lalarokh.com					
Legal Sea Foods 26 Pk Plaza	Boston	MA	02116	617-426-4444	338-7629
Web: www.legalseafoods.com					
Les Zygomates 129 S St	Boston	MA	02111	617-542-5108	482-8806
Web: www.winebar.com					
Locke-Ober 3 Winter Pl	Boston	MA	02108	617-542-1340	542-6452
Web: www.lockeober.com					
Lucca 226 Hanover St	Boston	MA	02113	617-742-9200	723-2081
Web: www.luccaboston.com					
Mamma Maria's 3 N Sq	Boston	MA	02113	617-523-0077	523-4348
Web: www.mammamaria.com					
Mantra Restaurant 52 Temple Pl	Boston	MA	02111	617-542-8111	542-8666
Web: www.mantrarestaurant.com					
Meritage 70 Rowes Wharf	Boston	MA	02210	617-439-3995	439-0464
Web: www.meritagetherestaurant.com					
Metropolis Cafe 584 Tremont St	Boston	MA	02118	617-247-2931	247-2495
Web: www.metropolisboston.com					
Mistral 223 Columbus Ave	Boston	MA	02116	617-867-9300	351-2601
Web: www.mistralbistro.com					
Montien 63 Stuart St	Boston	MA	02116	617-338-5600	338-5348
Web: www.montien-boston.com					
Morton's The Steakhouse 699 Boylston at Exeter	Boston	MA	02116	617-266-5858	266-9521
No 9 PARK 9 Pk St	Boston	MA	02108	617-742-9991	742-9993
Web: www.no9park.com					
O Ya 9 E St	Boston	MA	02111	617-654-9900	654-9900
Web: www.oyarestaurantboston.com					
Oak Room 138 St James Ave	Boston	MA	02116	617-267-5300	867-8556
Web: www.theoakroom.com					
Oishii Boston 1166 Washington St	Boston	MA	02118	617-482-8868	482-8869
Web: www.oishiiboston.com					
Palm The 200 Dartmouth St	Boston	MA	02116	617-867-9292	867-0789
Web: www.thepalm.com					
Peach Farm 4 Tyler St	Boston	MA	02111	617-482-3332	482-1116
Piccola Venezia 263 Hanover St	Boston	MA	02113	617-523-3888	742-2960
Web: www.piccolaveneziaboston.com					
Pigalle 75 Charles St S	Boston	MA	02116	617-423-4944	423-6766
Web: www.pigalleboston.com					
Prezza 24 Fleet St	Boston	MA	02113	617-227-1577	227-1587
Web: www.prezza.com					
Radius 8 High St	Boston	MA	02110	617-426-1234	426-2526
Web: www.radiusrestaurant.com					
Ruby Room 155 Portland St	Boston	MA	02114	617-557-9950	557-0005
Web: www.rubyroomboston.com					
Sage Restaurant 1395 Washington St	Boston	MA	02118	617-248-8814	248-1879
Web: www.sageboston.com					
Sakurabana 57 Broad St	Boston	MA	02109	617-542-4311	542-2320
Web: www.sakurabanaonline.com					
Sonsie 327 Newbury St	Boston	MA	02115	617-351-2500	351-2565
Web: www.sonsieboston.com					
Strega 379 Hanover St	Boston	MA	02113	617-523-8481	523-2475
Web: www.stregaristorante.com					
Tapeo 268 Newbury St	Boston	MA	02116	617-267-4799	267-1602
Web: www.tapeo.com					
Taranta 210 Hanover St	Boston	MA	02113	617-720-0052	507-0492
Web: www.tarantarist.com					
Teatro 177 Tremont St	Boston	MA	02111	617-778-6841	778-6844
Web: www.teatroboston.com					
Terramia Ristorante 98 Salem St	Boston	MA	02113	617-523-3112	
Web: www.terramiaristorante.com					
Tresca 233 Hanover St	Boston	MA	02113	617-742-8240	742-8246
Web: www.trescanorthend.com					
Troquet 140 Boylston St	Boston	MA	02116	617-695-9463	
Web: www.troquetboston.com					

				Phone	Fax
Umbria 295 Franklin St	Boston	MA	02110	617-338-1000	338-4112
Web: www.umbriaristorante.com					
Union Bar & Grille 1357 Washington St	Boston	MA	02118	617-423-0555	423-6055
Web: www.unionrestaurant.com					
Via Matta 79 Pk Plaza	Boston	MA	02116	617-422-0008	422-0014
Web: www.viamattarestaurant.com					
Wagamama					
1183 Hancock St ; Quincy Ctr T Market	Boston	MA	02109	617-742-9242	
Web: www.wagamama.us					
Bramble Inn 2019 Main St	Brewster	MA	02631	508-896-7644	896-9332
Web: www.brambleinn.com					
Chillingsworth 2449 Main St	Brewster	MA	02631	508-896-3640	
Web: www.chillingsworth.com					
Fireplace 1634 Beacon St	Brookline	MA	02446	617-975-1900	975-1600
Web: www.fireplacerest.com					
East Coast Grill & Raw Bar					
1271 Cambridge St	Cambridge	MA	02114	617-491-6568	868-4278
Web: www.eastcoastgrill.net					
Elephant Walk 2067 Massachusetts Ave	Cambridge	MA	02140	617-492-6900	492-3907
Web: www.elephantwalk.com					
Harvest 44 Brattle St	Cambridge	MA	02138	617-868-2255	
Web: www.harvestcambridge.com					
Helmand 143 1st St	Cambridge	MA	02142	617-492-4646	497-6507
Web: www.helmandrestaurant.com					
Oleana Restaurant 134 Hampshire St	Cambridge	MA	02139	617-661-0505	661-3336
Web: www.oleanarestaurant.com					
Regatta of Cotuit at the Crocker House					
4631 Falmouth Rd Rt 28	Cotuit	MA	02635	508-428-5715	428-5742
Web: www.regattarestaurant.com					
Red Pheasant 905 Main St	Dennis	MA	02638	508-385-2133	
Web: www.redpheasantinn.com					
Nauset Beach Club 222 Main St	East Orleans	MA	02643	508-255-8547	255-8872
Web: www.nausetbeachclub.com					
Atria 137 Main St PO Box 561	Edgartown	MA	02539	508-627-5850	627-9389
Web: www.atriamv.com					
L'etoile 22 N Water St PO Box 2537	Edgartown	MA	02539	508-627-5187	
Web: www.letoile.net					
Water Street 131 N Water St	Edgartown	MA	02539	508-627-7000	627-8417
Web: www.harbour-view.com					
La Cucina Sul Mare 237 Main St	Falmouth	MA	02540	508-548-5600	
Web: www.lacucinasulmare.com					
Buca's Tuscan Roadhouse 4 Depot Rd	Harwich	MA	02645	508-432-6900	
Web: www.bucasroadhouse.com					
L'Alouette 787 Massachusetts 28	Harwich Port	MA	02646	508-430-0405	
Web: www.lalouettebistro.com					
Delaney House					
1 County Club Rd Rt 5 Smith's Ferry	Holyoke	MA	01040	413-532-1800	533-7137
Baxter's Boathouse Club 117 Pleasant St	Hyannis	MA	02601	508-775-4490	
Web: www.baxterscapecod.com					
Brazilian Grill 680 Main St	Hyannis	MA	02601	508-771-0109	771-1070
Web: www.braziliangrill-capecod.com					
Cooke's Seafood 1120 Rt 132	Hyannis	MA	02601	508-775-0450	
Web: www.cookesseafood.com					
Fazio's Trattoria 294 Main St	Hyannis	MA	02601	508-775-9400	
Web: www.fazio.net					
Misaki Sushi 379 W Main St	Hyannis	MA	02601	508-771-3771	771-4431
Web: www.misakisushi.com					
Naked Oyster Bistro & Raw Bar 410 main St	Hyannis	MA	02601	508-778-6500	778-5704
Web: www.nakedoyster.com					
Paddock The 20 Scudder Ave	Hyannis	MA	02601	508-775-7677	771-9517
Web: www.paddockcapecod.com					
Sam Diego's 950 Iyanough Rd Rt 132	Hyannis	MA	02601	508-771-8816	771-0174
Web: www.samdiegos.com					
Tiki Port 714 Iyanough Rd	Hyannis	MA	02601	508-771-5220	771-2775
Web: www.tikiport.com					
Centre Street Cafe 669 A Centre St	Jamaica Plain	MA	02130	617-524-9217	522-4028
Web: www.sites.google.com/site/centrestreetcafejp					
Beach Plum Inn 12 Menemsha Inn Rd PO Box 38	Menemsha	MA	02552	508-645-9454	645-9500
TF: 877-645-7398 ■ *Web:* www.beachpluminn.com					
Brant Point Grill 50 Easton St PO Box 1139	Nantucket	MA	02554	508-228-2500	
Web: www.nantucketislandresorts.com					
Co of the Cauldron 5 India St	Nantucket	MA	02554	508-228-4016	
Web: www.companyofthecauldron.com					
DeMarco 9 India St	Nantucket	MA	02554	508-228-1836	228-9437
Web: www.demarcorestaurant.com					
Le Languedoc Bistro 24 Broad St	Nantucket	MA	02554	508-228-2552	228-4682
Web: www.lelanguedoc.com					
Pearl The 12 Federal St	Nantucket	MA	02554	508-228-9701	
Web: www.boardinghouse-pearl.com					
Straight Wharf 6 Harbor Sq	Nantucket	MA	02554	508-228-4499	
Topper's 120 Wauwinet Rd	Nantucket	MA	02554	508-228-8768	
Woodbox The 36 Fair St	Nantucket	MA	02554	508-228-0587	
Lumiere 1293 Washington St	Newton	MA	02465	617-244-9199	796-9178
Web: www.lumiererestaurant.com					
Carmen 33 N Sq	North End	MA	02113	617-742-6421	742-1880
Web: www.carmenboston.com					
Abba 89 Old Colony Way	Orleans	MA	02653	508-255-8144	
Web: www.abbarestaurant.com					
Academy Ocean Grille 2 Academy Pl	Orleans	MA	02653	508-240-1585	240-1344
Web: www.academyoceangrille.com					
Captain Linnell House 137 Skaket Beach Rd	Orleans	MA	02653	508-255-3400	255-5377
Web: www.linnell.com					
Enzo 186 Commercial St	Provincetown	MA	02657	508-487-7555	487-6611
Web: www.enzolives.com					
Front Street 230 Commercial St	Provincetown	MA	02657	508-487-9715	487-7748
Web: www.frontstreetrestaurant.com					
Mews Restaurant & Cafe					
429 Commercial St	Provincetown	MA	02657	508-487-1500	487-3700
Web: www.mews.com					
Red Inn 15 Commercial St	Provincetown	MA	02657	508-487-7334	487-5115
Web: www.theredinn.com					
Ross' Grill					
237 Commercial St 2nd Fl PO Box 304	Provincetown	MA	02657	508-487-8878	
Web: www.rossgrille.com					
Daniel Webster Inn 149 Main St	Sandwich	MA	02563	508-888-3622	888-5156
TF: 800-444-3566 ■ *Web:* www.danlwebsterinn.com/dining.html					
Dali Restaurant 415 Washington St	Somerville	MA	02143	617-661-3254	661-2813
Web: www.dalirestaurant.com					
Ardeo 23V Whites Path	South Yarmouth	MA	02664	508-760-1500	760-1504
Web: www.dineardeo.com					
Riverway Lobster House 1338 Rt 28	South Yarmouth	MA	02664	508-398-2172	398-7111
Aqui-me-quedo Restaurant 13 Locust St	Springfield	MA	01108	413-737-2827	
Bamboo House 676 Belmont Ave	Springfield	MA	01108	413-732-0741	
Big Mamou 63 Liberty St	Springfield	MA	01103	413-732-1011	
Web: www.chefwaynes-bigmamou.com					
Cafe Lebanon 1390 Main St	Springfield	MA	01103	413-737-7373	737-5773
Web: www.cafelebanon.com					
Casa De Nana 995 Boston Rd	Springfield	MA	01119	413-783-1549	
Web: www.casadenana.com					
China Gourmet 1374 Allen St	Springfield	MA	01118	413-796-1888	439-0403
Lido's 555 Worthington St	Springfield	MA	01105	413-736-9433	781-7970
Web: www.lidosrestaurant.com					
Max's Tavern 1000 W Columbus Blvd	Springfield	MA	01105	413-746-6299	746-6211
Web: www.maxrestaurantgroup.com					
Pazzo Ristorante 1000 W Columbus Ave	Springfield	MA	01105	413-737-5800	737-0217
Web: www.pazzohof.com					
Pho Saigon 398 Dickinson St	Springfield	MA	01108	413-781-4488	
Salvatore's 1333 Boston Rd	Springfield	MA	01119	413-782-9968	796-7601
Web: www.salvatoresrestaurant.net					
Student Prince Cafe The 8 Fort St	Springfield	MA	01103	413-788-6628	739-7303
Web: www.studentprince.com					
Theodore's Booze Blues & BBQ					
201 Worthington St	Springfield	MA	01103	413-736-6000	
Web: www.theobbq.com					
Touch of Garlic 427 White St	Springfield	MA	01108	413-739-0236	
Typical Sicilian 497 Belmont Ave	Springfield	MA	01108	413-739-7100	
Web: www.typicalsicilian.com					
Wong Wok 749 Sumner Ave	Springfield	MA	01108	413-746-8084	
Il Capriccio 888 Main St	Waltham	MA	02451	781-894-2234	891-3227
Web: www.bostonchefs.com					
Blue Ginger 583 Washington St	Wellesley	MA	02484	781-283-5790	283-5772
Web: www.ming.com					
Bistro 5 5 Playstead Rd	West Medford	MA	02115	781-395-7464	395-0130
Web: www.bistro5.com					
Debbie Wong 878 Memorial Ave	West Springfield	MA	01089	413-781-1711	
111 Chop House 111 Shrewsbury St	Worcester	MA	01604	508-799-4111	
Web: www.111chophouse.com					
Boynton Family Restaurant 117 Highland St	Worcester	MA	01609	508-756-8458	756-8208
Coral Seafood Restaurant & Fish Market					
225 Shrewsbury St Suite A	Worcester	MA	01604	508-755-8331	791-9900
Web: www.coralseafood.com					
Dalat Restaurant 425 Pk Ave	Worcester	MA	01610	508-753-6036	
Dino's 13 Lord St	Worcester	MA	01604	508-753-9978	753-5646
Web: www.dineatdinos.com					
El Basha 424 Belmont St	Worcester	MA	01604	508-797-0884	
Web: www.elbasharestaurant.com					
Flying Rhino Cafe 278 Shrewsbury St	Worcester	MA	01604	508-757-1450	754-8102
Web: www.flyingrhinocafe.com					
Leo's Ristorante 11 Bracket Ct	Worcester	MA	01604	508-753-9490	797-5123
Web: www.leosristorante.net					
Maxwell Silverman's Toolhouse Lincoln Sq	Worcester	MA	01608	508-755-1200	753-8217
Web: www.maxwellmaxine.com					
Nancy Chang 372 Chandler St	Worcester	MA	01602	508-752-8899	798-6688
Web: www.nancychang.com					
O'Connor's Restaurant & Bar					
1160 W Boylston St	Worcester	MA	01606	508-853-0789	853-2879
Web: www.oconnorsrestaurant.com					
One Eleven Chop House 111 Shrewsbury St	Worcester	MA	01604	508-799-4111	791-7224
Web: www.111chophouse.com					
Sahara Cafe & Restaurant 143 Highland St	Worcester	MA	01609	508-798-2181	798-9164
Sole Proprietor The 118 Highland St	Worcester	MA	01609	508-798-3474	753-4889
Web: www.thesole.com					
Viva Bene 144 Commercial St	Worcester	MA	01608	508-799-9999	753-0434
Web: www.viva-bene.com					
Webster House Restaurant 1 Webster St	Worcester	MA	01603	508-757-7208	
Web: www.websterhouseweb.com					
Zipango Steak & Sushi 270 Shrewsbury St	Worcester	MA	01604	508-754-8047	
Web: www.zipango-sushi.com					
Inaho 157 Rt 6A	Yarmouth Port	MA	02675	508-362-5522	
Web: www.inahocapecod.com					
Colonial House Inn 277 Main St Rt 6A	Yarmouthport	MA	02675	508-362-4348	362-8034
TF: 800-999-3416 ■ *Web:* www.colonialhousecapecod.com/dine.html					

MICHIGAN

				Phone	Fax
Amadeus 122 E Washington St	Ann Arbor	MI	48104	734-665-8767	
Web: www.amadeusrestaurant.com					
Arbor Brewing Co 114 E Washington St	Ann Arbor	MI	48104	734-213-1393	213-2835
Web: www.arborbrewing.com					
Argiero's 300 Detroit St	Ann Arbor	MI	48104	734-665-0444	665-2653
Web: www.Argiero's.com					
Blue Nile Ethiopian Restaurant- Ann Arbor The					
221 E Washington St	Ann Arbor	MI	48104	734-998-4746	998-4750
Web: www.bluenilemi.com					
Chia Shiang 2016 Packard St	Ann Arbor	MI	48104	734-741-0778	
Chop House The 322 S Main St	Ann Arbor	MI	48104	734-669-9977	669-7177
Earle The 121 W Washington St	Ann Arbor	MI	48104	734-994-0211	994-3466
Web: www.theearle.com					
Gandy Dancer 401 Depot St	Ann Arbor	MI	48104	734-769-0592	769-0415
Web: www.muer.com					
Gratzi 326 S Main St	Ann Arbor	MI	48104	734-663-5555	668-7261

Name / Address	City	State	Zip	Phone	Fax
Great Lakes Chinese Seafood 2910 Carpenter Rd	Ann Arbor	MI	48108	734-973-6666	973-0030
Grizzly Peak Brewing Co 120 W Washington St	Ann Arbor	MI	48104	734-741-7325	741-4976
Web: www.grizzlypeak.net					
Jerusalem Garden 307 S 5th Ave	Ann Arbor	MI	48104	734-995-5060	995-9843
Web: www.jerusalemgarden.net					
Knight's Steak House 2324 Dexter Ave	Ann Arbor	MI	48103	734-665-8644	665-7948
Web: www.knightsrestaurants.com					
Mediteranno Restaurant 2900 S State St	Ann Arbor	MI	48104	734-332-9700	332-9702
Web: www.mediterrano.com					
Metzeger's 305 N Zeeb Rd	Ann Arbor	MI	48103	734-668-8987	668-9028
Middle Kingdom 332 S Main St	Ann Arbor	MI	48104	734-668-6638	668-6621
Miki Japanese Restaurant 106 S 1st St	Ann Arbor	MI	48104	734-665-8226	665-1301
Web: www.mikirestaurant.com					
MisSaigon 4085 Stoneschool Rd	Ann Arbor	MI	48108	734-971-8880	
Web: www.missaigononline.com					
Pacific Rim 114 W Liberty St	Ann Arbor	MI	48104	734-662-9303	662-8397
Web: www.pacificrimbykana.com					
Paesano's 3411 Washtenaw Ave	Ann Arbor	MI	48104	734-971-0484	971-0419
Web: www.paesanosannarbor.com					
Parthenon Restaurant 226 S Main St	Ann Arbor	MI	48104	734-994-1012	994-7073
Web: www.parthenonrestaurant.net					
Prickly Pear Southwest Cafe 328 S Main St	Ann Arbor	MI	48104	734-930-0047	930-1561
Raja Rani 400 S Division St	Ann Arbor	MI	48104	734-995-1545	995-5999
Sabor Latino 211 N Main St	Ann Arbor	MI	48104	734-214-7775	214-7776
Seoul Garden 3125 Boardwalk St	Ann Arbor	MI	48108	734-997-2120	
Web: www.aaseoulgarden.com					
Seva Restaurant 314 E Liberty St	Ann Arbor	MI	48104	734-662-1111	662-8447
Shalimar 307 S Main St	Ann Arbor	MI	48104	734-663-1500	929-9129
Web: www.shalimarrestaurant.com					
Smokehouse Blues 4855 Washtenaw Ave	Ann Arbor	MI	48108	734-434-5554	434-4969
Web: www.smokehouseblues.com					
Tuptim 4896 Washtenaw Ave	Ann Arbor	MI	48108	734-528-5588	528-2569
Web: www.tuptim.com					
Vinology 110 S Main St	Ann Arbor	MI	48104	734-222-9841	
Weber's 3050 Jackson Rd	Ann Arbor	MI	48103	734-665-3636	769-4743
Web: www.webersinn.com					
West End Grill 120 W Liberty Ave	Ann Arbor	MI	48104	734-747-6260	665-6493
Web: www.westendgrilla2.com					
Zingerman's Roadhouse 2501 Jackson Rd	Ann Arbor	MI	48103	734-663-3663	
Web: www.zingermansroadhouse.com					
Andiamo 400 Renaissance Ctr Suite A403	Detroit	MI	48243	313-567-6700	567-6701
Web: www.andiamoitalia.com					
Armando's Mexican Restaurant 4242 W Vernor Hwy	Detroit	MI	48209	313-554-0666	554-0667
Web: www.mexicantown.com					
Atlas Global Bistro 3111 Woodward Ave	Detroit	MI	48201	313-831-2241	831-4023
Web: www.atlasglobalbistro.com					
Atwater Brewing Co 237 Joseph Campau	Detroit	MI	48207	313-877-9205	877-9206
Caucus Club 150 W Congress St	Detroit	MI	48226	313-965-4970	
Clubhouse Tavern 3011 W Grand Blvd	Detroit	MI	48221	313-875-3663	
Web: www.theclubhousetavern.com					
Cuisine 670 Lothrop Rd	Detroit	MI	48202	313-872-5110	872-3801
Web: www.cuisinedetroit.com					
DaEdoardo Foxtown Grille 2203 Woodward Ave	Detroit	MI	48201	313-471-3500	471-3499
Web: www.daedoardo.com					
Dona Lola 1312 Springwells St	Detroit	MI	48209	313-843-4129	
El Comal 3456 W Vernor Ave	Detroit	MI	48216	313-841-7753	841-7071
El Zocalo Mexican Restaurant 3400 Bagley St	Detroit	MI	48216	313-841-3700	
Web: www.elzocalodetroit.com					
Evie's Tamales 3454 Bagley St	Detroit	MI	48216	313-843-5056	843-5143
Giovanni's Ristorante 330 S Oakwood Blvd	Detroit	MI	48217	313-841-0122	841-3947
Web: www.giovannisristorante.com					
Hard Rock Cafe 45 Monroe St	Detroit	MI	48226	313-964-7625	964-5064
Web: www.hardrock.com					
Hockeytown Cafe 2301 Woodward Ave	Detroit	MI	48201	313-965-9500	471-3466
Iridescence 2901 Grand River Ave	Detroit	MI	48201	313-237-7711	961-0966
La Dolce Vita 17546 Woodward	Detroit	MI	48203	313-865-0331	867-3568
Louisiana Creole Gumbo 2053 Gratiot Ave	Detroit	MI	48207	313-446-9639	396-1708
Mario's 4222 2nd Ave	Detroit	MI	48201	313-832-1616	832-1460
Web: www.mariosdetroit.com					
Opus One 565 E Larned St	Detroit	MI	48226	313-961-7766	961-9243
Web: www.opus-one.com					
Pegasus Taverna 558 Monroe St	Detroit	MI	48226	313-964-6800	964-0869
Rattlesnake Club 300 River Pl	Detroit	MI	48207	313-567-4400	567-2063
Web: www.rattlesnakeclub.com					
Roma Cafe 3401 Riopelle St	Detroit	MI	48207	313-831-5940	831-2253
Web: www.romacafe.com					
Sala Thai 1541 E Lafayette St	Detroit	MI	48207	313-567-8424	
Seldom Blues 400 Renaissance Ctr	Detroit	MI	48243	313-567-7301	567-7501
Web: www.seldomblues.com					
Small Plates 1521 Broadway St	Detroit	MI	48226	313-963-0497	963-0702
Web: www.smallplates.com					
Taqueria Mi Pueblo 7278 Dix St	Detroit	MI	48209	313-841-3315	841-3015
Web: www.mipueblorestaurant.com					
Union Street 4145 Woodward Ave	Detroit	MI	48201	313-831-3965	831-2553
Web: www.unionstreetdetroit.com					
Vincente's 1250 Library St	Detroit	MI	48226	313-962-8800	962-0898
Whitney The 4421 Woodward Ave	Detroit	MI	48201	313-832-5700	832-2159
Web: www.thewhitney.com					
Xochimilco Restaurant 3409 Bagley St	Detroit	MI	48216	313-843-0179	
Rose's on Reeds Lake 550 Lakeside Dr SE	East Grand Rapids	MI	49506	616-458-1122	458-3411
Beggar's Banquet 218 Abbott Rd	East Lansing	MI	48823	517-351-4540	351-3585
Web: www.beggarsbanquet.com					
Hershey's Steak & Seafood 2682 E Grand River	East Lansing	MI	48823	517-337-7324	337-8004
Web: www.hersheyssteakandseafood.com					
English Inn 677 S Michigan Rd	Eaton Rapids	MI	48827	517-663-2500	663-2643
TF: 800-858-0598 ■ *Web:* www.englishinn.com					
Blue Nile 545 W Nine-Mile Rd	Ferndale	MI	48220	248-547-6699	547-3165
Web: www.bluenilemi.com					
Badawest 4018 Corruna Rd	Flint	MI	48532	810-232-2479	232-3326
Canton Chinese Restaurant 5313 Fenton Rd	Flint	MI	48507	810-232-8710	
Churchill's Food & Spirits 340 S Saginaw St	Flint	MI	48502	810-238-3800	
Web: churchillsflint.com					
Golden Moon 4527 Miller Rd	Flint	MI	48507	810-733-7030	
Latina Restaurant & Pizzeria 1370 W Bristol Rd	Flint	MI	48507	810-767-8491	
Luigi's 2132 Davison Rd	Flint	MI	48506	810-234-9545	234-3153
Mario's G5227 Fenton Rd	Flint	MI	48507	810-232-6535	
Red Rooster Makuchs 3302 Davison Rd	Flint	MI	48506	810-742-9310	
Redwood Lodge 5304 Gateway Ctr Dr	Flint	MI	48507	810-233-8000	233-8833
Roma Pizzeria Flint G5227 N Saginaw St	Flint	MI	48505	810-787-1061	787-6788
Web: www.romaspizza.com					
Salvatore Scallopini Restaurant 3227 Miller Rd	Flint	MI	48507	810-732-1070	732-1538
Web: www.salvatorescallopini.com					
White Horse Tavern 621 W Ct St	Flint	MI	48503	810-234-3811	234-9073
Web: www.whitehorsetavern.net					
Bavarian Inn 713 S Main St	Frankenmuth	MI	48734	989-652-9941	652-3481
Web: www.bavarianinn.com					
Bangkok View 1233 28th St SW	Grand Rapids	MI	49509	616-531-8070	
Beltline Bar 16 28th St SE	Grand Rapids	MI	49548	616-245-0494	245-3955
Bentham's Riverfront Restaurant 187 Monroe Ave NW	Grand Rapids	MI	49503	616-774-2000	776-6489
Bistro Bella Vita 44 Grandville Ave SW	Grand Rapids	MI	49503	616-222-4600	222-4601
Web: www.bistrobellavita.com					
Bombay Cuisine 1420 Lake Dr	Grand Rapids	MI	49506	616-456-7055	
Brann's Steakhouse & Grille 401 Leonard St NW	Grand Rapids	MI	49504	616-454-9368	454-7702
Web: www.branns.com					
Charley's Crab Restaurant 63 Market St SW	Grand Rapids	MI	49503	616-459-2500	459-8142
Web: www.muer.com					
China Chef 4335 Lake Michigan Dr NW	Grand Rapids	MI	49544	616-791-4488	
Gill's Fish House 20 Monroe Ave NW	Grand Rapids	MI	49503	616-356-2000	493-2011
Hunan Chinese Restaurant 1740 44th St SW	Grand Rapids	MI	49509	616-530-3377	458-2130
Maggie's Kitchen 615 Bridge St NW	Grand Rapids	MI	49504	616-458-8583	458-1370
Web: www.gibsonsrestaurant.com					
Mikado 3971 28th St SE	Grand Rapids	MI	49512	616-285-7666	977-0509
Noto's Old World Italian 6600 28th St SE	Grand Rapids	MI	49546	616-493-6686	493-6682
Web: www.notosoldworld.com					
One Trick Pony 136 E Fulton St	Grand Rapids	MI	49503	616-235-7669	454-9809
Web: www.onetrick.biz					
San Chez 38 Fulton St W	Grand Rapids	MI	49503	616-774-8272	774-9954
Web: www.sanchezbistro.com					
Sayfee's 3555 Lake Eastbrook Blvd SE	Grand Rapids	MI	49546	616-949-5750	949-1446
Seoul Garden 3321 28th St	Grand Rapids	MI	49512	616-956-1522	956-1801
Spinnaker 4747 28th St SE	Grand Rapids	MI	49512	616-957-1111	
Taps Sports Bar 8 Ionia Ave SW	Grand Rapids	MI	49503	616-774-3338	774-7182
Tillman's 1245 Monroe Ave NW	Grand Rapids	MI	49505	616-451-9266	451-2227
Tokyo Grill 4478 Breton Rd SE	Grand Rapids	MI	49508	616-455-3433	455-0385
Tre Cugini 122 Monroe Ctr NW	Grand Rapids	MI	49503	616-235-9339	235-9449
Web: www.trecugini.com					
XO Asian Cuisine 58 Monroe Ctr NW	Grand Rapids	MI	49503	616-235-6969	235-2801
Web: www.xoasiancuisine.com					
Z's Bar & Restaurant 168 Louis Campau Promenade NW	Grand Rapids	MI	49503	616-454-3141	454-2075
Web: www.zsbar.com					
Apple Jade 300 N Clippert St	Lansing	MI	48912	517-332-8010	
Capitol City Grille 111 N Grand Ave Radisson Hotel Lansing	Lansing	MI	48933	517-267-3459	
Christie's Bistro 925 S Creyts Rd	Lansing	MI	48917	517-323-4190	323-2180
Web: www.lexingtonlansing.com/christies-bistro.aspx					
Clara's 637 E Michigan Ave	Lansing	MI	48912	517-372-7120	372-0157
Web: www.claras.com					
Deluca's Restaurant 2006 W Willow St	Lansing	MI	48917	517-487-6087	487-3633
Web: www.delucaspizza.com					
Emil's 2012 E Michigan Ave	Lansing	MI	48912	517-482-4430	482-9390
Firm Food & Spirits The 227 S Washington Sq	Lansing	MI	48933	517-487-3663	
Web: www.thefirmlounge.com					
House of Ing 4113 S Cedar St	Lansing	MI	48910	517-393-4848	393-6868
Web: www.houseofing.com					
Kelly's Downtown 203 S Washington Ave	Lansing	MI	48933	517-484-5007	
Knight Cap The 320 E Michigan Ave	Lansing	MI	48933	517-484-7676	
Web: www.theknightcap.com					
La Senorita 2706 Lake Lansing Rd	Lansing	MI	48912	517-485-0166	485-8350
Web: www.lasenorita.com					
Mitchell's Fish Market 2975 Preyde Blvd	Lansing	MI	48912	517-482-3474	482-3474
Web: www.cameronmitchell.com					
Piazzano's 1825 N Grand River Ave	Lansing	MI	48906	517-484-9922	484-2744
Web: www.piazzanos.com					
Dusty's Cellar 1839 W Grand River Ave	Okemos	MI	48864	517-349-8680	349-8416
Web: www.dustyscellar.com					

MINNESOTA

Name / Address	City	State	Zip	Phone	Fax
Kincaid's Fish Chop & Fish House 8400 Normandale Lake Blvd	Bloomington	MN	55437	952-921-2255	921-2252
Web: www.kincaids.com					
Angie's Cantina 11 E Buchanan St	Duluth	MN	55802	218-727-6117	727-8235
Web: www.grandmasrestaurants.com/littleangies					
Beijing Restaurant 1219 E Superior St	Duluth	MN	55802	218-724-2627	724-2578
Web: www.restaurantbeijing.net					
Bellisio's Italian Restaurant & Wine Bar 405 Lake Ave S	Duluth	MN	55802	218-727-4921	
Web: www.grandmasrestaurants.com					
Chinese Dragon 108 E Superior St	Duluth	MN	55802	218-723-4036	
Duluth Athletic Club Bar & Grill 21 N 4th Ave W	Duluth	MN	55802	218-720-4445	720-4689
Fitger's Brewery Complex 600 E Superior St	Duluth	MN	55802	218-722-8826	722-8826
TF: 888-348-4377 ■ *Web:* www.fitgers.com					

Name	City	State	Zip	Phone	Fax
Grandma's Saloon & Grill 522 Lake Ave S *Web:* www.grandmasrestaurants.com/gmas_cp.htm	Duluth	MN	55802	218-727-4192	723-1986
Grandma's Sports Garden Bar & Grill 425 Lake Ave S *Web:* www.grandmasrestaurants.com/sportsgarden/family.htm	Duluth	MN	55802	218-722-4724	720-3804
Green Mill Restaurant & Bar 340 Lake Ave S *Web:* www.greenmill.com	Duluth	MN	55802	218-727-7000	723-8510
Hacienda del Sol 319 E Superior St *Web:* www.hacienda-del-sol.com	Duluth	MN	55802	218-722-7296	
India Palace 319 W Superior St	Duluth	MN	55802	218-727-8767	
Jade Fountain 305 N Central Ave	Duluth	MN	55807	218-624-4212	624-4212
Lake Avenue Cafe 394 S Lake Ave # 107A *Web:* www.lakeavenuecafe.com	Duluth	MN	55802	218-722-2355	
Lakeview Castle Dining Room 5135 N Shore Dr *Web:* www.lakeviewcastleduluth.com	Duluth	MN	55804	218-525-1014	
Le Grand Supper Club 5906 Old Miller Trunk Hwy	Duluth	MN	55811	218-729-7973	729-1144
Maya Family Mexican Restaurant 4702 Miller Trunk Hwy	Duluth	MN	55811	218-722-0360	
New Scenic Cafe 5461 N Shore Dr *Web:* www.sceniccafe.com	Duluth	MN	55804	218-525-6274	525-0737
Old Chicago 327 Industrial Bldg *Web:* www.oldchicago.com	Duluth	MN	55802	218-720-2966	720-2930
Pickwick Restaurant & Pub 508 E Superior St *Web:* www.pickwickduluth.com	Duluth	MN	55802	218-727-8901	786-0228
Porter's 200 W 1st St	Duluth	MN	55802	218-727-6746	722-0233
Saigon Cafe 2224 Mountain Shadow Dr Suite 2400	Duluth	MN	55811	218-727-3987	
Sir Benedict's Tavern 805 E Superior St *Web:* www.sirbens.com	Duluth	MN	55802	218-728-1192	728-9878
Sneakers Sports Bar & Grill 207 W Superior St	Duluth	MN	55802	218-727-7494	
Thai Krathong 308 Lake Ave S *Web:* www.thaikrathong.com	Duluth	MN	55802	218-733-9774	
Timber Lodge Steakhouse 325 S Lake Ave *Web:* www.timberlodgesteakhouse.com	Duluth	MN	55802	218-722-2624	722-3844
Hubbell House Hwy 57 & 5th Ave *Web:* www.hubbellhouse.com	Mantorville	MN	55955	507-635-2331	635-5280
Alma 528 University Ave SE *Web:* www.restaurantalma.com	Minneapolis	MN	55414	612-379-4909	
Azia 2550 Nicollet Ave *Web:* www.aziarestaurant.com	Minneapolis	MN	55404	612-813-1200	870-8496
Black Forest Inn 1 E 26th St *Web:* www.blackforestinnmpls.com	Minneapolis	MN	55404	612-872-0812	872-0826
Brit's Pub & Eating Establishment 1110 Nicollet Mall *Web:* www.britspub.com	Minneapolis	MN	55403	612-332-3908	332-8032
Broders Southside Pasta Bar 5000 Penn Ave S *Web:* www.broders.com	Minneapolis	MN	55419	612-925-9202	
Cafe Barbette 1600 W Lake St *Web:* www.barbette.com	Minneapolis	MN	55408	612-827-5710	822-6305
Cafe Lurcat 1624 Harmon Pl *Web:* www.cafelurcat.com	Minneapolis	MN	55403	612-486-5500	
Cafe Twenty-Eight 2724 W 43rd St *Web:* www.cafetwentyeight.com	Minneapolis	MN	55410	612-926-2800	926-2804
California Cafe Bar & Grill 368 S Blvd	Minneapolis	MN	55425	952-854-2233	
Cave Vin 5555 Xerxes Ave S	Minneapolis	MN	55410	612-922-0100	
Christo's 2632 Nicollet Ave *Web:* www.christos.com	Minneapolis	MN	55408	612-871-2111	871-8129
Cosmos 601 1st Ave *Web:* www.cosmosrestaurant.com	Minneapolis	MN	55402	612-312-1158	677-1200
D'Amico Cucina 100 N 6th St Historic Butler Sq *Web:* www.damico.com	Minneapolis	MN	55403	612-338-2401	337-5130
Dakota Jazz Club & Restaurant 1010 Nicollet Ave *Web:* www.dakotacooks.com	Minneapolis	MN	55403	612-332-1010	332-7070
Erte Restaurant 323 13th Ave NE *Web:* www.ertedining.com	Minneapolis	MN	55413	612-623-4211	
Famous Dave's Bar-B-Que 3001 Hennepin Ave *Web:* www.famousdaves.com	Minneapolis	MN	55408	612-822-9900	822-9221
FireLake Grill House & Cocktail Bar 31 S 7th St *Web:* www.firelakerestaurant.com	Minneapolis	MN	55402	612-216-3473	547-6240
Fuji-Ya 600 W Lake St *Web:* www.fujiyasushi.com	Minneapolis	MN	55408	612-871-4055	
Gardens of Salonica 19 NE 5th St	Minneapolis	MN	55413	612-378-0611	378-0611
Joe's Garage 1610 Harmon Pl *Web:* www.joes-garage.com	Minneapolis	MN	55403	612-904-1163	904-1260
Khan's Mongolian Barbecue 500 E 78th St	Minneapolis	MN	55423	612-861-7991	
Kikugawa 43 Main St SE	Minneapolis	MN	55414	612-378-3006	
King & I 1346 La Salle Ave *Web:* www.kinganditahi.com	Minneapolis	MN	55403	612-332-6928	338-4293
La Belle Vie 510 Groveland Ave *Web:* www.labellevie.us	Minneapolis	MN	55403	612-874-6440	
Local The 931 Nicollet Mall *Web:* www.the-local.com	Minneapolis	MN	55402	612-904-1000	904-1005
Lucia's 1432 W 31st St *Web:* www.lucias.com	Minneapolis	MN	55408	612-825-1572	824-4553
Mandarin Kitchen 8766 Lyndale Ave S	Minneapolis	MN	55420	952-884-5356	
Manny's Steak House 825 Marquette Ave *Web:* www.mannyssteakhouse.com	Minneapolis	MN	55403	612-339-9900	341-2373
McCormick & Schmick's 800 Nicollet Mall *Web:* www.mccormickandschmicks.com	Minneapolis	MN	55402	612-338-3300	338-3314
Melting Pot The 80 S 9th St *Web:* www.meltingpot.com	Minneapolis	MN	55402	612-338-9900	312-2855
Mission American Kitchen 77 S 7th St *Web:* www.missionamerican.com	Minneapolis	MN	55402	612-339-1000	339-8700
Modern Cafe 337 13th Ave NE	Minneapolis	MN	55413	612-378-9882	
Morton's The Steakhouse 555 Nicollet Mall *Web:* www.mortons.com	Minneapolis	MN	55402	612-673-9700	673-0853
Murray's 26 S 6th St *Web:* www.murraysrestaurant.com	Minneapolis	MN	55402	612-339-0909	339-2310
Nami 251 N 1st Ave *Web:* www.namisushi.com	Minneapolis	MN	55402	612-333-1999	333-7449
Nicollet Island Inn 95 Merriam St *Web:* www.nicolletislandinn.com	Minneapolis	MN	55401	612-331-1800	331-6528
Oceanaire Seafood Room 1300 Nicollet Mall *Web:* www.theoceanaire.com	Minneapolis	MN	55403	612-333-2277	305-1923
Prima 5325 Lyndale Ave S *Web:* www.primamn.com	Minneapolis	MN	55419	612-827-7376	827-7534
Quang 2719 Nicollet Ave *Web:* www.quangrestaurant.com	Minneapolis	MN	55408	612-870-4739	879-4739
Rainbow Chinese 2739 Nicollet Ave S *Web:* www.rainbowrestaurant.com	Minneapolis	MN	55408	612-870-7084	872-6204
Rock Bottom Brewery 825 Hennepin Ave *Web:* www.rockbottom.com	Minneapolis	MN	55402	612-332-2739	332-1508
Ruth's Chris Steak House 920 2nd Ave S *Web:* www.ruthschris.com	Minneapolis	MN	55402	612-672-9000	672-9102
Salsa a la Salsa 1420 Nicollet Ave *Web:* www.salsaalasalsa.com	Minneapolis	MN	55403	612-813-1970	813-1972
Sapor Cafe & Bar 428 Washington Ave N	Minneapolis	MN	55401	612-375-1971	375-1974
Sawatdee 607 Washington Ave S *Web:* www.sawatdee.com	Minneapolis	MN	55415	612-338-6451	338-6498
Solera 900 Hennepin Ave *Web:* www.solera-restaurant.com	Minneapolis	MN	55403	612-338-0062	338-8871
True Thai 2627 E Franklin Ave *Web:* www.truethairestaurant.com	Minneapolis	MN	55406	612-375-9942	
VincentßA Restaurant 1100 Nicollet Mall *Web:* www.vincentarestaurant.com	Minneapolis	MN	55403	612-630-1189	343-5907
Zelo 831 Nicollet Mall	Minneapolis	MN	55402	612-333-7000	333-7707
Broken Axe The 700 1st Ave N *Web:* www.thebrokenaxe.com	Moorhead	MN	56560	218-287-0080	287-0090
Speak Easy 1001 30th Ave S	Moorhead	MN	56560	218-233-1326	233-6012
Canadian Honker 1203 2nd St SW *Web:* www.canadianhonker.com	Rochester	MN	55902	507-282-6572	
City Cafe 216 1st Ave SW Downtown *Web:* www.cccrmg.com/city_cafe.htm	Rochester	MN	55902	507-289-1949	
Fiesta Mexicana 1645 N Broadway	Rochester	MN	55906	507-288-1116	
Great China 4214 Hwy 52 N	Rochester	MN	55901	507-280-9092	
Hunan 844 S Broadway	Rochester	MN	55904	507-287-0002	287-0141
India Garden 1107 N Broadway	Rochester	MN	55906	507-288-6280	
Jaspers Alsatian Bistro & Wine Bar 14 Historic 3rd St SW	Rochester	MN	55902	507-280-6446	
Jenpachi Japanese Steak House 3160 Wellner NE	Rochester	MN	55906	507-292-1688	
Michael's 15 S Broadway *Web:* www.michaelsfinedining.com	Rochester	MN	55904	507-288-2020	288-5553
Redwood Room 300 1st Ave NW *Web:* www.cccrmg.com/redwoodroom	Rochester	MN	55902	507-281-2978	
Roscoe's Root Beer & Ribs 603 4th St SE	Rochester	MN	55904	507-285-0501	
Sky Dragon Buffet 34 17th Ave NW	Rochester	MN	55901	507-281-1813	
Timber Lodge Steakhouse 4144 Hwy 52 N *Web:* www.timberlodgesteakhouse.com	Rochester	MN	55901	507-252-8075	252-8074
Victoria's 7 1st Ave NW *Web:* www.victoriasmn.com	Rochester	MN	55902	507-280-6232	280-6288
Kahn's Mongolian Barbeque 2720 Snowing Ave	Roseville	MN	55113	651-631-3398	
128 Cafe 128 Cleveland Ave N	Saint Paul	MN	55104	651-645-4128	
Beirut Restaurant 1385 Robert St S *Web:* www.beirutrestaurantanddeli.com	Saint Paul	MN	55118	651-457-4886	
Cafe Latte 850 Grand Ave *Web:* www.cafelatte.com	Saint Paul	MN	55105	651-224-5687	
El Amanecer 194 Concord St *Web:* www.elamanecerrestaurant.com	Saint Paul	MN	55107	651-291-0758	225-1719
El Burrito Mercado 175 Concord St *Web:* www.elburritomercado.com	Saint Paul	MN	55107	651-227-2192	227-2411
Everest on Grand 1278 Grand Ave	Saint Paul	MN	55105	651-696-1666	698-6662
Forepaugh's 276 S Exchange St *Web:* www.forepaughs.com	Saint Paul	MN	55102	651-224-5606	224-5607
Fuji-Ya 465 N Wabasha St *Web:* www.fujiyasushi.com	Saint Paul	MN	55102	651-310-0111	
Heartland 289 E 5th St *Web:* www.heartlandrestaurant.com	Saint Paul	MN	55101	651-699-3536	
Kincaid's Fish Chop & Steak House 380 St Peters St Suite A *Web:* www.kincaids.com	Saint Paul	MN	55102	651-602-9000	602-9158
La Grolla 452 Selby Ave	Saint Paul	MN	55102	651-221-1061	
Lexington The 1096 Grand Ave *Web:* www.the-lexington.com	Saint Paul	MN	55105	651-222-5878	222-8230
Lindey's Prime Steak House 3610 Snelling Ave N	Saint Paul	MN	55112	651-633-9813	633-2222
Luci Ancora 2060 Randolph Ave	Saint Paul	MN	55105	651-698-6889	698-6696
Mai Village 394 University Ave	Saint Paul	MN	55103	651-290-2585	
Mancini's Char House 531 7th St W *Web:* www.mancinis.com	Saint Paul	MN	55102	651-224-7345	224-9367
Moscow on the Hill 371 Selby Ave *Web:* www.moscowonthehill.com	Saint Paul	MN	55102	651-291-1236	
Muffuletta Cafe 2260 Como Ave *Web:* www.muffuletta.com	Saint Paul	MN	55108	651-644-9116	644-5329
Pad Thai Grand Cafe 1681 Grand Ave	Saint Paul	MN	55105	651-690-1393	
Pazzaluna 360 St Peter St	Saint Paul	MN	55102	651-223-7000	227-1296
Peking Garden 1488 University Ave **Fax Area Code:* 651 ■ *Web:* www.pekinggardenmn.com	Saint Paul	MN	55104	612-623-3989	644-1738*
River Room 411 Cedar St	Saint Paul	MN	55101	651-292-5174	
Saji-Ya 695 Grand Ave *Web:* www.sajiya.com	Saint Paul	MN	55105	651-292-0444	225-4881
Sakura Japanese Restaurant 350 St Peter St *Web:* www.sakurastpaul.com	Saint Paul	MN	55102	651-224-0185	225-9350
St Paul Grill The 350 Market St *Web:* www.stpaulgrill.com	Saint Paul	MN	55102	651-224-7455	

Name / Address	City	State	Zip	Phone	Fax
Tavern on Grand 656 Grand Ave	Saint Paul	MN	55105	651-228-9030	229-0090
Web: www.tavernongrand.com					
Trattoria da Vinci 400 Sibley St	Saint Paul	MN	55101	651-222-4050	224-4545
Web: www.trattoriadavinci.com					
Wild Onion 788 Grand Ave	Saint Paul	MN	55105	651-291-2525	291-5215
Web: www.wild-onion.net					
Yang's 1568 Woodlane Dr	Saint Paul	MN	55125	651-731-3212	
Web: www.yangswoodbury.com					
Zander Cafe 525 Selby Ave	Saint Paul	MN	55102	651-222-5224	312-1193
Web: www.zandercafe.com					

MISSISSIPPI

Name / Address	City	State	Zip	Phone	Fax
Beau Rivage					
875 Beach Blvd Beau Rivage Resort & Casino	Biloxi	MS	39530	228-386-7111	
TF: 888-750-7111 ■ *Web:* www.beaurivage.com					
Jazzeppi's 195 B Porter Ave	Biloxi	MS	39530	228-374-9660	374-9692
Web: www.jazzeppis.net					
Mary Mahoney's 110 Rue Magnolia	Biloxi	MS	39530	228-374-0163	432-1387
Web: www.marymahoneys.com					
Mr Greek 1670 H Pass Rd	Biloxi	MS	39531	228-432-7888	432-8379
Blow Fly Inn 1201 Washington Ave	Gulfport	MS	39507	228-896-9812	248-0048
Web: www.blowflyinn.com					
El Mexicano Inn 1215 30th Ave	Gulfport	MS	39501	228-863-3691	
Emeril's Gulf Coast Fish House					
3300 W Beach Blvd	Gulfport	MS	39501	228-314-1515	
Lil Ray's 500A Courthouse Rd	Gulfport	MS	39501	228-896-9601	896-9622
South China 548 Courthouse Rd	Gulfport	MS	39507	228-896-9832	
206 Front 206 E Front St	Hattiesburg	MS	39401	601-545-5677	545-2025
Web: www.206front.com					
Cuco's Mexican Cafe 6104 Hwy 49 S	Hattiesburg	MS	39401	601-545-8241	545-8244
Donanelle's Bar & Grill 4321 U S Hwy 49	Hattiesburg	MS	39401	601-545-3860	545-7822
Web: www.donanelles.com					
Front Porch 205 Thornhill Dr	Hattiesburg	MS	39402	601-264-3536	268-0991
Garfield's 1000 Turtle Creek Dr	Hattiesburg	MS	39402	601-264-7000	
Web: www.eateries.inc					
La Fiesta Brava 4404 Hardy St	Hattiesburg	MS	39401	601-271-6070	271-8348
Web: www.lafiestabrava.net					
Leatha's Bar-B-Que Inn					
6374 US Hwy 98 Suite D	Hattiesburg	MS	39402	601-271-6003	
Web: www.leathas.com					
Purple Parrot Cafe 3810 Hardy St	Hattiesburg	MS	39402	601-264-0656	264-0681
Web: www.nsrg.com					
Rayner's Seafood House 7343 Hwy 49	Hattiesburg	MS	39402	601-268-2639	
Sakura 6194 Hwy 49	Hattiesburg	MS	39401	601-545-9393	545-9394
Walnut Circle Grill 115 Walnut St	Hattiesburg	MS	39401	601-544-2202	271-6004
Web: www.walnutcirclegrill.com					
Bonsai Japanese Steak House 1925 Lakeland Dr	Jackson	MS	39216	601-981-0606	
Bravo I-55 N Exit 100	Jackson	MS	39211	601-982-8111	981-1463
Web: www.bravobuzz.com					
CS's Restaurant 1359 1/2 N W St	Jackson	MS	39202	601-969-9482	969-9021
Elite Restaurant 141 E Capitol St	Jackson	MS	39201	601-352-5606	
Fenian's Pub 901 E Fortification St	Jackson	MS	39202	601-948-0055	948-1155
Web: www.fenianspub.com					
Hal & Mal's 200 S Commerce St	Jackson	MS	39204	601-948-0888	
Web: www.halandmals.com					
Keifer's 705 Poplar Blvd	Jackson	MS	39202	601-355-6825	355-0380
La Cazuela Mexican Grill					
1401 E Fortification St	Jackson	MS	39202	601-353-3014	353-3015
Nick's 3000 Old Canton Rd	Jackson	MS	39216	601-981-8017	982-9640
Web: www.nicksrestaurant.com					
Peking Chinese Restaurant 5315 I-55 N	Jackson	MS	39206	601-362-7000	
Que Sera Sera 2801 N State St	Jackson	MS	39216	601-981-2520	981-2522
Sakura Bana 4800 I-55 N LeFleur's Gallery	Jackson	MS	39211	601-982-3035	982-3075
Steak-Out 4680 I-55 N	Jackson	MS	39211	601-366-1100	366-4004
Web: www.steakout.com					
Thai House Restaurant 1405 Old Sq Rd	Jackson	MS	39211	601-982-9991	
Cancun Mexican Restaurant 201 N Gloster St	Tupelo	MS	38801	662-842-9557	
China Capital 530 N Gloster St	Tupelo	MS	38804	662-841-0484	
Harvey's 424 S.Gloster St	Tupelo	MS	38801	662-842-6763	844-4251
Web: www.eatwithus.com					
Ichiban Japanese Grill 603 N Gloster St	Tupelo	MS	38804	662-842-3838	
Las Margaritas 123 Industrial Rd	Tupelo	MS	38801	662-844-7399	
Web: www.lasmargaritas.com					
Logan's Roadhouse 3954 N Gloster St	Tupelo	MS	38804	662-840-7552	840-8308
Web: www.logansroadhouse.com					
Park Heights 335 E Main St	Tupelo	MS	38804	662-842-5665	844-7172
Web: www.eatwithus.com					
Sun Kai 775 E Main St	Tupelo	MS	38804	662-844-7047	
Tellini's 504 S Gloster St	Tupelo	MS	38801	662-620-9955	620-9951
Web: www.tellinis.com					
Vanelli's 1302 N Gloster St	Tupelo	MS	38804	662-844-4410	
Web: www.vanellis.com					
Woody's 619 N Gloster St	Tupelo	MS	38801	662-840-0460	

MISSOURI

Name / Address	City	State	Zip	Phone	Fax
Baldknobbers Restaurant					
2845 W 76 Country Blvd	Branson	MO	65616	417-334-7202	339-3505
Web: www.baldknobbers.com					
Branson Cafe 120 W Main St	Branson	MO	65616	417-334-3021	
BT Bones 2280 Shepherd Hill Expy	Branson	MO	65616	417-335-2002	338-8554
Web: www.btbones.com					
Buckingham's Restaurant & Oasis					
2820 W Hwy 76	Branson	MO	65616	417-337-7777	337-5335
Candlestick Inn 127 Taney St	Branson	MO	65616	417-334-3633	336-4348
Web: www.candlestickinn.com					
Casa Fuentes 1107 W Hwy 76	Branson	MO	65616	417-339-3888	
Web: www.casafuentes.com					
Charlie's Steak-Ribs-Ale 3009 W State Hwy 76	Branson	MO	65616	417-334-6090	336-4038
Chateau Grille 415 N State Hwy 265	Branson	MO	65616	417-334-1161	339-5566
TF: 888-333-5253 ■ *Web:* www.chateauonthelakebranson.com					
Farmhouse Restaurant 119 W Main St	Branson	MO	65616	417-334-9701	334-5222
Gilley's Texas Cafe 3457 W 76 Country Blvd	Branson	MO	65616	417-335-2755	335-2749
Web: www.gilleys.com					
Landry's Seafood House					
2900 W Missouri Hwy 76	Branson	MO	65616	417-339-1010	339-3801
Web: www.landrysseafood.com					
Plaza View 245 N Wildwood Dr	Branson	MO	65616	417-335-2798	
Rocky's Italian Restaurant 120 N Sycamore St	Branson	MO	65616	417-335-4765	
Sadies Sideboard Restaurant 2830 W Hwy 76	Branson	MO	65616	417-334-3619	334-5841
Whipper Snapper's 2421 W Hwy 76	Branson	MO	65616	417-334-3282	
Web: www.bransonsbestrestaurant.com					
Cardwell's 8100 Maryland Ave	Clayton	MO	63105	314-726-5055	726-1909
Web: www.cardwellsinclayton.com					
63 Diner The 5801 Hwy 763 N	Columbia	MO	65202	573-443-2331	815-0017
Web: www.63dinercolumbia.com					
Addison's An American Grill 709 Cherry St	Columbia	MO	65201	573-256-1995	256-2836
Web: www.addisonssophias.com					
Angelo's 4107 S Providence Rd	Columbia	MO	65203	573-443-6100	
Bambino's 203 Hitt St	Columbia	MO	65201	573-443-4473	443-6385
Web: www.bambinositaliancafe.com					
Bangkok Gardens 811 Cherry St	Columbia	MO	65201	573-874-3284	
Churchill's					
2200 I-70 Dr SW					
Holiday Inn Select Executive Ctr	Columbia	MO	65203	573-445-8531	445-7607
Web: www.holidayinnselect.com					
CJ's in Tiger Country 704 E Broadway	Columbia	MO	65201	573-442-7777	
Web: www.cjsintigercountry.com					
Ernie's Cafe 1005 E Walnut St	Columbia	MO	65201	573-874-7804	
Flat Branch Pub & Brewing Co 115 S 5th St	Columbia	MO	65201	573-499-0400	
Web: www.flatbranch.com					
Forge & Vine 119 W 7th St	Columbia	MO	65201	573-443-6743	
Web: www.forgeandvine.com					
Formosa Restaurant 913 E Broadway Suite A	Columbia	MO	65201	573-449-3339	
Web: www.formosatogo.com					
Gaucho's Churrascaria & Steakhouse					
10 Southampton	Columbia	MO	65203	573-443-3259	256-8566
Web: www.gauchos.us					
Hong Kong Restaurant 106 Business Loop 70 W	Columbia	MO	65203	573-442-7350	472-7360
Web: www.mizzoumenus.com					
India's Rasoi 1101 E Broadway	Columbia	MO	65201	573-817-2009	874-3018
International Cafe 209 Hitt St	Columbia	MO	65201	573-449-4560	499-1535
Italian Village Pizza					
711 Vandiver Dr Suite B	Columbia	MO	65202	573-442-8821	442-3571
Jack's Gourmet Restaurant					
1903 Business Loop 70 E	Columbia	MO	65201	573-449-3927	442-9881
Web: www.jacksgourmetrestaurant.com					
Jimmy's Family Steak House					
3101 S Providence Rd	Columbia	MO	65203	573-443-1796	
Murry's 3107 Green Meadows Way	Columbia	MO	65203	573-442-4969	
Osaka Japanese Restaurant					
120 E Nifong Blvd Suite A	Columbia	MO	65203	573-875-8588	875-8580
Pasta Factory 3013 W Broadway	Columbia	MO	65201	573-449-3948	815-0155
Q's Chinese Restaurant 4004 Peach Ct	Columbia	MO	65203	573-442-5342	
Web: www.qs-chinese.biz					
Taj Mahal 19 N 5th St	Columbia	MO	65201	573-256-6800	442-7146
Trattoria Strada Nova 21 N 9th St	Columbia	MO	65201	573-442-8992	
Wine Cellar & Bistro 505 Cherry St	Columbia	MO	65201	573-442-7281	441-8318
Web: www.winecellarbistro.com					
54th Street Grill 18700 E 38th Terr	Independence	MO	64057	816-795-7077	
Web: www.54thstreetgrill.com					
El Maguey 3738 S Noland Rd	Independence	MO	64055	816-252-6868	
Englewood Cafe 10904 E Winner Rd	Independence	MO	64050	816-461-9588	
Gates Bar-B-Q 10440 E Us Hwy 40	Independence	MO	64052	816-353-5880	923-3922
Web: www.gatesbbq.com					
Rheinland Restaurant 208 N Main St	Independence	MO	64050	816-461-5383	461-9159
Web: www.rheinlandrestaurant.com					
Samurai Chef Japanese Steakhouse & Sushi Bar					
12712 E Hwy 40	Independence	MO	64055	816-350-3777	350-3149
Web: www.kc-samuraichef.com					
South Chinese Restaurant					
1020 S Sterling Ave	Independence	MO	64054	816-461-3564	461-3572
V's Italiano Ristorante					
10819 E US Hwy 40	Independence	MO	64055	816-353-1241	353-0004
Web: www.vsrestaurant.com					
Zio's Italian Kitchen 3901 S Bolger Dr	Independence	MO	64055	816-350-1011	350-1211
Web: www.zios.com					
Alexandro's 2125 Missouri Blvd	Jefferson City	MO	65109	573-634-7740	
Cajun Catfish House 6819 Hwy 50 W	Jefferson City	MO	65109	573-893-4665	893-8580
Das Stein Haus 1436 S Ridge Dr	Jefferson City	MO	65109	573-634-3869	
Web: www.dassteinhaus.com					
Hunan Restaurant 1416 Missouri Blvd	Jefferson City	MO	65109	573-634-5253	634-8230
Madison's Cafe 216 Madison St	Jefferson City	MO	65101	573-634-2988	634-3740
Web: www.madisonscafe.com					
Park Place Restaurant					
415 W McCarty St	Jefferson City	MO	65101	573-635-1234	635-4565
Yen Ching Restaurant					
2208 Missouri Blvd	Jefferson City	MO	65109	573-635-5225	638-8893
Arthur Bryant's Barbeque					
1727 Brooklyn Ave	Kansas City	MO	64127	816-231-1123	421-7427
Web: www.arthurbryantsbbq.com					
BB's Lawnside Bar-B-Q 1205 E 85th St	Kansas City	MO	64131	816-822-7427	
Web: www.bbslawnsidebbq.com					
Benton's Steak & Chop House					
1 E Pershing Rd	Kansas City	MO	64108	816-391-4460	
Web: www.bentonskc.com					
Blue Bird Bistro 1700 Summit St	Kansas City	MO	64108	816-221-7559	221-7901
Bluestem 900 Westport Rd	Kansas City	MO	64111	816-561-1101	561-5726
Web: www.kansascitymenus.com/bluestem					
Bo Ling's 4800 Main St	Kansas City	MO	64112	816-753-1718	753-8819
Web: www.bolings.com					
Cafe Al Dente 412D Delaware	Kansas City	MO	64105	816-472-9444	472-9779

Name / Address	City	State	Zip	Phone	Fax
Californos 4124 Pennsylvania Ave *Web:* www.californos.com	Kansas City	MO	64111	816-531-7878	531-1894
Cascone's 3737 N Oak Trafficway *Web:* www.cascones.com	Kansas City	MO	64116	816-454-7977	454-8041
Cupini's Fresh Pasta & Panini 1809 Westport Rd *Web:* www.cupinis.com	Kansas City	MO	64111	816-753-7662	753-7564
Danny Edwards' Famous Kansas City Barbecue 1227 Grand Blvd	Kansas City	MO	64106	816-283-0880	
EBT Restaurant 1310 Carondelet Dr *Web:* www.ebtrestaurant.com	Kansas City	MO	64114	816-942-8870	941-8532
Europa! 323 E 55th St	Kansas City	MO	64113	816-523-1212	
Fiorella's Jack Stack Barbecue 13441 Holmes Rd *Web:* www.jackstackbbq.com	Kansas City	MO	64145	816-942-9141	941-8762
Garozzo's 526 Harrison St *Web:* www.garozzos.com	Kansas City	MO	64106	816-221-2455	221-7174
Grand Street Cafe 4740 Grand Ave *Web:* www.kansascitymenus.com	Kansas City	MO	64112	816-561-8000	561-9156
Grinders 417 E 18th St	Kansas City	MO	64108	816-472-5454	
Houston's 4640 Wornall Rd	Kansas City	MO	64112	816-561-8542	561-0423
Jardine's 4536 Main St *Web:* www.jardines4jazz.com	Kansas City	MO	64111	816-561-6480	561-2885
Jasper's 1201 W 103rd St *Web:* www.jasperskc.com	Kansas City	MO	64114	816-941-6600	941-4121
Jess & Jim's Steakhouse 517 E 135th St *Web:* www.jessandjims.com	Kansas City	MO	64145	816-941-9499	942-6348
JJ's Restaurant 910 W 48th St *Web:* www.jjs-restaurant.com	Kansas City	MO	64112	816-561-7136	561-5490
KatoSushi 6340 NW Barry Rd *Web:* www.katosushi.com	Kansas City	MO	64154	816-584-8883	
La Bodega 703 SW Blvd *Web:* www.kansascitymenus.com	Kansas City	MO	64108	816-472-8272	471-5250
Le Fou Frog 400 E 5th St *Web:* www.kansascitymenus.com	Kansas City	MO	64106	816-474-6060	474-3066
Lidia's Kansas City 101 W 22nd St *Web:* www.lidias-kc.com	Kansas City	MO	64108	816-221-3722	842-1960
Majestic Steakhouse 931 Broadway *Web:* www.kansascitymenus.com/majesticsteakhouse	Kansas City	MO	64105	816-471-8484	471-7906
Malay Cafe 6003 NW Barry Rd	Kansas City	MO	64154	816-741-3616	
McCormick & Schmick's 448 W 47th St *Web:* www.mccormickandschmicks.com	Kansas City	MO	64112	816-531-6800	531-2090
New Peking 540 Westport Rd	Kansas City	MO	64111	816-531-6969	531-9188
Osteria Il Centro 5101 Main St *Web:* www.osteria-ilcentro.com	Kansas City	MO	64111	816-561-2369	561-0511
Peach Tree 31 E 14th St *Web:* www.peachtreerestaurants.com	Kansas City	MO	64106	816-886-9800	886-9801
Pierpont's at Union Station 30 W Pershing Rd Suite 900 *Web:* www.herefordhouse.com	Kansas City	MO	64108	816-221-5111	221-9779
PotPie 904 Westport Rd *Web:* www.kcpotpie.com	Kansas City	MO	64111	816-561-2702	
Red Snapper 8430 Ward Pkwy *Web:* www.kcredsnapper.com	Kansas City	MO	64114	816-333-8899	333-8893
Ruth's Chris Steak House 700 W 47th St *Web:* www.ruthschris.com	Kansas City	MO	64112	816-531-4800	931-2094
Smokin' Guns BBQ 1218 Swift Ave *Web:* www.smokingunsbbq.com	Kansas City	MO	64116	816-221-2535	221-2606
Streetcar Named Desire 2450 Grand Ave	Kansas City	MO	64108	816-472-5959	
Stroud's Oak Ridge Manor 5410 NE Oak Ridge Rd *Web:* www.stroudsrestaurant.com	Kansas City	MO	64119	816-454-9600	454-0718
Taj Mahal 7521 Wornall Rd *Web:* www.kctajmahal.com	Kansas City	MO	64114	816-361-1722	361-1654
Thai Place 4130 Pennsylvania Ave *Web:* www.kcthaiplace.com	Kansas City	MO	64111	816-753-8424	753-5595
Thomas Restaurant 1815 W 39th St *Web:* www.thomaskc.com	Kansas City	MO	64111	816-561-3663	756-3265
Blue Owl Restaurant The 6116 2nd St *Web:* www.theblueowl.com	Kimmswick	MO	63053	636-464-3128	464-8108
Blue Water Grill 343 S Kirkwood Rd	Kirkwood	MO	63122	314-821-5757	821-4565
Chappell's Restaurant & Sports Museum 323 Armour Rd	North Kansas City	MO	64116	816-421-0002	472-7141
Al's Restaurant 1200 N 1st St *Web:* www.alsrestaurant.net	Saint Louis	MO	63102	314-421-6399	421-0357
An American Place 822 Washington Ave	Saint Louis	MO	63102	314-418-5800	
Bandana's Bar-B-Q 11750 Gravois Rd *Web:* www.bandanasbbq.com	Saint Louis	MO	63127	314-849-1162	729-1126
Bar Italian Ristorante-Caffe 13 Maryland Plaza *Web:* www.baritaliastl.com	Saint Louis	MO	63108	314-361-7010	361-6131
Broadway Oyster Bar 736 S Broadway *Web:* www.broadwayoysterbar.com	Saint Louis	MO	63102	314-621-8811	621-1995
Carmine's Steak House 20 S 4th St *Web:* www.lombardosrestaurants.com	Saint Louis	MO	63101	314-241-1631	231-2952
Chez Leon 4580 Laclede Ave *Web:* www.chezleon.com	Saint Louis	MO	63108	314-361-1589	
Clark Street Grill 811 Spruce St *Web:* www.clarkstreetgrill.com	Saint Louis	MO	63102	314-621-2000	552-5749
Crossing The 7823 Forsyth Blvd	Saint Louis	MO	63105	314-721-7375	721-3646
Cunetto House of Pasta 5453 Magnolia Ave *Web:* www.cunetto.com	Saint Louis	MO	63139	314-781-1135	781-5674
Dierdorf & Hart's Steak House 323 Westport Plaza *Web:* www.dierdorfharts.com	Saint Louis	MO	63146	314-878-1801	878-9056
Duff's 392 N Euclid Ave *Web:* www.dineatduffs.com	Saint Louis	MO	63108	314-361-0522	
Giovanni's 5201 Shaw Ave *Web:* www.giovannisonthehill.com	Saint Louis	MO	63110	314-772-5958	772-0343
Giuseppe's 4141 S Grand Blvd *Web:* www.giuseppesongrand.com	Saint Louis	MO	63118	314-832-8013	832-7598
Happy China 12921 Olive Arcade Plaza	Saint Louis	MO	63141	314-878-6660	
Harry's Restaurant & Bar 2144 Market St *Web:* www.harrysrestaurantandbar.com	Saint Louis	MO	63103	314-421-6969	241-2755
House of India 8501 Delmar Blvd *Web:* www.hoistl.com	Saint Louis	MO	63124	314-567-6850	567-5282
I Love Mr Sushi 9443 Olive Blvd	Saint Louis	MO	63132	314-432-8898	432-6590
Kemoll's 211 N Broadway *Web:* www.kemolls.com	Saint Louis	MO	63102	314-421-0555	436-9692
King & I 3157 S Grand Blvd *Web:* www.thaispicy.com	Saint Louis	MO	63118	314-771-1777	771-3265
Kreis' Restaurant 535 S Lindbergh Blvd *Web:* www.kreisrestaurant.com	Saint Louis	MO	63131	314-993-0735	993-3020
Liluma 236 N Euclid Ave	Saint Louis	MO	63108	314-361-7771	
Lorenzo's Trattoria 1933 Edwards St *Web:* www.lorenzostrattoria.com	Saint Louis	MO	63139	314-773-2223	773-0689
LoRusso's Cucina 3121 Watson Rd *Web:* www.lorussos.com	Saint Louis	MO	63139	314-647-6222	647-2821
Mike Shannon's 620 Market St *Web:* www.shannonsteak.com	Saint Louis	MO	63101	314-421-1540	241-5642
Modesto 5257 Shaw Ave *Web:* www.saucecafe.com/modesto	Saint Louis	MO	63110	314-772-8272	
Nobu's 8643 Olive Blvd	Saint Louis	MO	63132	314-997-2303	
Pho Grand 3195 S Grand Blvd *Web:* www.phogrand.com	Saint Louis	MO	63118	314-664-7435	771-5169
Saint Louis Fish Market 901 N 1st St *Web:* www.stlouisfishmarket.com	Saint Louis	MO	63102	314-621-4612	241-6513
Sam's Steakhouse 10205 Gravois Rd *Web:* www.samssteakhouse.com	Saint Louis	MO	63123	314-849-3033	849-0423
Sidney Street Cafe 2000 Sidney St *Web:* www.sidneystreetcafe.com	Saint Louis	MO	63104	314-771-5777	771-7016
Soulard's Restaurant 1731 S 7th St *Web:* www.soulards.com	Saint Louis	MO	63104	314-241-7956	241-7956
Spiro's 3122 Watson Rd *Web:* www.spiros-restaurant.com	Saint Louis	MO	63139	314-645-8383	781-0968
SqWire's 1415 S 18th St *Web:* www.sqwires.com	Saint Louis	MO	63104	314-865-3522	865-3524
Tenderloin Room 232 N Kingshighway Blvd *Web:* www.tenderloinroom.com	Saint Louis	MO	63108	314-361-0900	
Tony's 410 Market St *Web:* www.tonysstlouis.com	Saint Louis	MO	63102	314-231-7007	231-4740
Top of the Riverfront 200 S 4th St 28th Fl *Web:* www.milleniumhotels.com/stlouis	Saint Louis	MO	63102	314-241-3191	
Trattoria Marcella 3600 Watson Rd	Saint Louis	MO	63109	314-352-7706	352-0848
Tucker's Place *Historic Soulard* 2117 S 12th St *Web:* www.tuckersplacestl.com	Saint Louis	MO	63104	314-772-5977	773-3775
Vin de Set Rooftop Bar & Bistro 2017 Chouteau Ave *Web:* www.1111-m.com	Saint Louis	MO	63103	314-241-8989	621-5550
Yemanja Brasil 2900 Missouri Ave Pestalozzi St *Web:* www.yemanjabrasil.com	Saint Louis	MO	63118	314-771-7457	771-0296
Zia's 5256 Wilson Ave *Web:* www.zias.com	Saint Louis	MO	63110	314-776-0020	776-5778
Dominic's 5101 Wilson Ave *Web:* www.dominicsrestaurant.com	South Saint Louis	MO	63110	314-771-1632	771-1695
Bangkok City 1129 E Walnut St	Springfield	MO	65806	417-799-1221	
Bijan's Sea & Grille 209 E Walnut St	Springfield	MO	65806	417-831-1480	
Buckingham Smokehouse BBQ 2002 S Campbell Ave	Springfield	MO	65807	417-886-9979	
Canton Inn 205 W Sunshine St *Web:* www.cantoninnrestaurant.com	Springfield	MO	65807	417-862-5444	862-5934
China Star 1444 E Republic Rd	Springfield	MO	65804	417-887-9779	
Cielito Lindo Mexicano 2953 S National Ave	Springfield	MO	65804	417-886-3320	
Clary's 3014-A E Sunshine St *Web:* www.clarysrestaurant.com	Springfield	MO	65804	417-886-1940	227-9425
Gem of India 211 W Battlefield St	Springfield	MO	65807	417-881-9558	
Gilardi's 820 E Walnut St	Springfield	MO	65806	417-862-6400	
Hemingway's Blue Water Cafe 1935 S Campbell *Web:* restaurants.basspro.com	Springfield	MO	65898	417-891-5100	887-5204
Lucy's Chinese Food 3330 S Campbell Ave Suite C	Springfield	MO	65807	417-882-5383	
Metropolitan Grill 2931 E Battlefield	Springfield	MO	65804	417-889-4951	889-2728
Nonna's Italian American Cafe 306 S Ave	Springfield	MO	65806	417-831-1222	
Pappy's Place 943 N Main Ave	Springfield	MO	65802	417-866-8744	
Shanghai Inn 1937 N Glenstone Ave	Springfield	MO	65803	417-865-5111	
Springfield Brewing Co 305 S Market Ave *Web:* www.springfieldbrewingco.com	Springfield	MO	65806	417-832-8277	
Ziggie's Cafe 2222 S Campbell Ave *Web:* www.ziggiescafe.com	Springfield	MO	65807	417-883-0900	

MONTANA

Name / Address	City	State	Zip	Phone	Fax
Bistro Enzo 1502 Rehberg Ln *Web:* bistroenzobillings.com	Billings	MT	59102	406-651-0999	
Don Luis 15 N 26th St	Billings	MT	59101	406-256-3355	256-3359
Four Seas 1005 Grand Ave	Billings	MT	59102	406-254-1886	254-1186
Guadalajara Family Mexican 17 N 29th St	Billings	MT	59101	406-259-8930	259-8950
Jade Palace 2021 Overland Ave	Billings	MT	59102	406-656-8888	656-9993
Jake's 2701 1st Ave N	Billings	MT	59101	406-259-9375	259-1142
Juliano's 2912 7th Ave N	Billings	MT	59101	406-248-6400	
Montana Brewing Co 113 N 28th St	Billings	MT	59101	406-252-9200	259-3329
Rex The 2401 Montana Ave	Billings	MT	59101	406-245-7477	248-6469
Windmill Club 3921 1st Ave S	Billings	MT	59101	406-252-8100	651-0249
3-D International 1825 Smelter Ave	Black Eagle	MT	59414	406-453-6561	453-9947
Borrie's 1800 Smelter Ave	Black Eagle	MT	59414	406-761-0300	761-2021
Cattlemen's Cut Supper Club 369 Vaughn Frontage Rd S	Great Falls	MT	59404	406-452-0702	452-0408
Dante's Creative Cuisine 1325 8th Ave N	Great Falls	MT	59401	406-453-9599	453-9599

				Phone	Fax
Eddie's Supper Club 3725 2nd Ave N	Great Falls	MT	59401	406-453-1616	
El Comedor 1120 25th St S	Great Falls	MT	59405	406-761-5500	761-5502
Maple Garden 5401 9th Ave S	Great Falls	MT	59401	406-727-0310	452-5906
Prime Cut Restaurant 3219 10th Ave S	Great Falls	MT	59405	406-727-2141	
Sting The 1826 10th Ave S	Great Falls	MT	59405	406-727-7972	727-7972
Bert & Ernie's Saloon 361 N Last Chance Gulch	Helena	MT	59601	406-443-5680	443-7857
Web: www.bertanderniesofhelena.com					
Brewhouse Brew Pub & Grill 939 1/2 Getchell St	Helena	MT	59601	406-457-9390	457-9296
Chinese Kitchen & Oriental Shop 901 Euclid Ave	Helena	MT	59601	406-442-2302	
Jade Garden Helena 3128 N Montana Ave	Helena	MT	59602	406-443-8899	443-8390
Web: www.jadegardenhelena.com					
Jorgenson's 1720 11th Ave	Helena	MT	59601	406-442-6380	442-7693
Web: www.jorgensons.com					
Mediterranean Grill 42 S Pk Ave	Helena	MT	59601	406-495-1212	443-5252
Miller's Crossing 52 S Pk Ave	Helena	MT	59601	406-442-3290	442-1715
Web: www.millerscrossing.biz					
Montana Club 24 W 6th Ave	Helena	MT	59601	406-442-5980	442-0276
Web: www.mtclub.org					
On Broadway 106 Broadway	Helena	MT	59601	406-443-1929	
Windbag Saloon & Grill 19 S Last Chance Gulch	Helena	MT	59601	406-443-9669	
Marysville House 153 Main St	Marysville	MT	59601	406-443-6677	

NEBRASKA

				Phone	Fax
1st Ave Bar & Grill 2310 N 1st St	Lincoln	NE	68521	402-475-4600	475-1281
Billy's 1301 H St	Lincoln	NE	68508	402-474-0084	474-3391
Web: www.billysrestaurant.com					
Doozy's 101 N 14th St	Lincoln	NE	68508	402-438-1616	
El Sitio 17 Van Dorn St	Lincoln	NE	68502	402-476-0414	
El Toro 2600 S 48th St	Lincoln	NE	68506	402-488-3939	488-7746
Green Gateau 330 S 10th St	Lincoln	NE	68508	402-477-0330	477-0782
Web: www.greengateau.com					
Imperial Palace 701 N 27th St	Lincoln	NE	68503	402-474-2688	
La Paz *La PazMexican Restaurant* 321 N Cotner Blvd	Lincoln	NE	68505	402-466-9111	466-9244
Web: www.getintolapaz.com					
Lazlo's Brewery & Grill 210 N 7th St	Lincoln	NE	68508	402-434-5636	434-3291
Mazatlan 211 N 70th St	Lincoln	NE	68505	402-464-7201	464-7527
Misty's Steakhouse & Brewery 200 N 11th St	Lincoln	NE	68508	402-476-7766	476-7796
Web: www.mistyslincoln.com					
Oven The 201 N 8th St	Lincoln	NE	68508	402-475-6118	475-1281
Parthenon 5500 S 56th St	Lincoln	NE	68516	402-423-2222	423-2228
Web: www.theparthenon.net					
Rib Ranch 6440 'O' St	Lincoln	NE	68510	402-467-5110	467-5128
Sher-E-Punjab 1601 Q St	Lincoln	NE	68508	402-477-3090	477-2282
Shogun 3700 S 9th St Suite F	Lincoln	NE	68502	402-421-7100	421-0860
Skeeter Barnes 5800 S 58th St	Lincoln	NE	68516	402-421-3340	421-3504
Web: www.skeeterbarnes.com					
Steak House The 3441 Adams St	Lincoln	NE	68504	402-466-2472	466-4897
Web: www.thesteakhouselincoln.com					
Tandoor 3530 Village Dr	Lincoln	NE	68516	402-423-2007	423-2995
Terrace Grille 333 S 13th St	Lincoln	NE	68508	402-479-8292	474-1847
Tico's 317 S 17th St	Lincoln	NE	68508	402-475-1048	475-3291
Web: www.ticosoflincoln.com					
Vincenzo's 808 P St	Lincoln	NE	68505	402-435-3889	
Wind Chimes 3520 Village Dr Suite 100	Lincoln	NE	68516	402-420-7171	720-7172
Web: www.your-windchimes.com					
Ahmad's Persian 1006 Howard St	Omaha	NE	68102	402-341-9616	
Anthony's 7220 F St	Omaha	NE	68127	402-331-7575	331-1497
Web: www.anthonyssteakhouse.com					
Bangkok Cuisine 1905 Farnam St	Omaha	NE	68102	402-346-5874	
Biaggi's Ristorante Italiano 13655 California St	Omaha	NE	68154	402-965-9800	
Bohemian Cafe 1406 S 13th St	Omaha	NE	68108	402-342-9838	
Web: www.bohemiancafe.net					
Brother Sebastian's Steak House 1350 S 119th St	Omaha	NE	68144	402-330-0300	330-4814
Web: www.brothersebastians.com					
Caniglia's Venice Inn 6920 Pacific St	Omaha	NE	68106	402-556-3111	
Web: www.veniceinn.com					
Cascio's Steak House 1620 S 10th St	Omaha	NE	68108	402-345-8313	
Web: www.casciossteakhouse.com					
Charlie's on the Lake 4150 S 144th St	Omaha	NE	68137	402-894-9411	894-9415
Web: www.charliesonthelake.net					
Fleming's Prime Steakhouse & Wine Bar 140 Regency Pkwy	Omaha	NE	68114	402-393-0811	393-0958
Web: www.flemingssteakhouse.com					
Gorat's Steakhouse 4917 Ctr St	Omaha	NE	68106	402-215-0842	
Greek Islands 3821 Ctr St	Omaha	NE	68105	402-346-1528	345-7428
Hiro Sushi 3655 N 129th St	Omaha	NE	68164	402-933-0091	
Web: www.hiro88.com					
House of Hunan 2405 S 132nd St	Omaha	NE	68144	402-334-5382	
Indian Oven 1010 Howard St	Omaha	NE	68102	402-342-4856	342-2526
Jack & Mary's Restaurant 655 N 114th St	Omaha	NE	68154	402-496-2090	
Web: www.jackandmarysrestaurant.com					
Jaipur The 10922 Elm St	Omaha	NE	68144	402-392-7331	392-7338
Web: www.jaipurbrewhouse.com					
Jams American Grill 7814 Dodge St	Omaha	NE	68114	402-399-8300	392-1765
Web: www.jamseats.com					
Jazz A Louisiana Kitchen 1421 Farnam St	Omaha	NE	68102	402-342-3662	
Jim & Jennie's Greek Village 3026 N 90th St	Omaha	NE	68134	402-571-2857	
Johnny's Cafe 4702 S 27th St	Omaha	NE	68107	402-731-4774	731-6698
Web: www.johnnyscafe.com					
Lo Sole Mio 3001 S 32nd Ave	Omaha	NE	68105	402-345-5656	345-5859
Web: www.losolemio.com					
M's Pub 422 S 11th St	Omaha	NE	68102	402-342-2550	342-3035
Web: www.mspubomaha.com					
McFoster's Natural Kind Cafe 302 S 38th St	Omaha	NE	68131	402-345-7477	345-4585
Mediterranean Bistro 1712 N 120th St	Omaha	NE	68154	402-493-3080	493-3097
Web: www.medbistro.com					
Mimi's Cafe 301 N 175th Plaza	Omaha	NE	68118	402-289-9610	
Web: www.mimiscafe.com					
Mister C's Steakhouse 5319 N 30th St	Omaha	NE	68111	402-451-1998	451-1910
Web: www.mistercs.com					
Piccolo Pete's 2202 S 20th St	Omaha	NE	68108	402-342-9038	
Web: www.piccolopetesrestaurant.com					
Sean O'Casey's 10730 Q St	Omaha	NE	68127	402-593-1746	
Shanghai Garden 3118 Tower 24 St	Omaha	NE	68108	402-342-2244	
Taste of Thailand 15712 W Ctr Rd	Omaha	NE	68130	402-691-9991	
Web: www.totomaha.com					
Thai Spice 2933 N 108th St	Omaha	NE	68164	402-492-8808	492-8808
Web: www.thaispiceomaha.com					
Upstream Brewing Co 514 S 11th St	Omaha	NE	68102	402-344-0200	344-0451
Web: www.upstreambrewing.com					
Vincenzo's Ristorante 1207 Harney St	Omaha	NE	68102	402-342-4010	991-8149
Web: www.vincenzos-ne.com					

NEVADA

				Phone	Fax
Adele's 1112 N Carson St	Carson City	NV	89701	775-882-3353	882-0437
Web: www.adelesrestaurantandlounge.com					
B'Sghetti's 318 N Carson St	Carson City	NV	89701	775-887-8879	887-1942
Web: www.bsghettis.com					
China East 1810 Hwy 50 E	Carson City	NV	89701	775-885-6996	885-2138
Garibaldi's 307 N Carson St	Carson City	NV	89701	775-884-4574	246-4529
Glen Eagles 3700 N Carson St	Carson City	NV	89703	775-884-4414	884-4447
Web: www.gleneaglesrestaurant.com					
Grandma Hattie's 2811 S Carson St	Carson City	NV	89701	775-882-4900	
Heidi's 1020 N Carson St	Carson City	NV	89701	775-882-0486	884-2091
Ming's 2330 S Carson St	Carson City	NV	89701	775-887-8878	887-0570
Panda Kitchen 1986 Hwy 50 E	Carson City	NV	89701	775-882-8128	882-3236
Playa Azul 415 E William St	Carson City	NV	89701	775-883-2244	
Red's Old 395 Grill 1055 S Carson St	Carson City	NV	89701	775-887-0395	887-5640
Taqueria Uruaban 4601 Goni Rd	Carson City	NV	89706	775-883-7609	
Thurman's Ranch House 2943 Hwy 50 E	Carson City	NV	89701	775-883-1773	
Tito's 444 E William St	Carson City	NV	89701	775-885-0309	
America 3790 Las Vegas Blvd S	Las Vegas	NV	89119	702-740-6451	740-6453
Web: www.arkvegas.com					
Andre's 401 S 6th St	Las Vegas	NV	89101	702-385-5016	385-1742
Web: www.andrelv.com					
Archi's Thai Kitchen 6360 W Flamingo Rd	Las Vegas	NV	89103	702-880-5550	870-5551
Aureole 3950 Las Vegas Blvd S	Las Vegas	NV	89119	702-632-7401	632-7440
Web: www.charliepalmer.com					
Bartolotta Ristorante diMare 3131 Las Vegas Blvd S	Las Vegas	NV	89109	702-770-9966	
TF: 888-320-3305 ■ *Web:* www.wynnlasvegas.com					
Benihana 3000 Paradise Rd	Las Vegas	NV	89109	702-732-5755	732-5662
Web: www.benihana.com					
Border Grill Las Vegas 3950 Las Vegas Blvd S Mandalay Bay Resort & Casino	Las Vegas	NV	89119	702-632-7403	632-6945
Web: www.bordergrill.com					
Bouchon 3355 Las Vegas Blvd S	Las Vegas	NV	89109	702-414-6200	
Bradley Ogden at Caesar's Palace 3570 Las Vegas Blvd S	Las Vegas	NV	89109	702-731-7413	
Web: www.larkcreek.com/bolv.htm					
Buzio's 3700 W Flamingo Rd	Las Vegas	NV	89103	702-252-7697	777-7932
Caesar's Palace 3570 Las Vegas Blvd S Caesar's Palace	Las Vegas	NV	89109	702-731-7110	866-1700
TF: 800-634-6001 ■ *Web:* www.caesers.com					
Canaletta 3355 Las Vegas Blvd S	Las Vegas	NV	89109	702-733-0070	
Carluccio's Tivoli Gardens 1775 E Tropicana Ave	Las Vegas	NV	89119	702-795-3236	795-0283
Web: www.carlucciosvegas.com					
Charlie Palmer Steak Four Seasons Hotel 3960 Las Vegas Blvd S	Las Vegas	NV	89119	702-632-5120	632-7440
Web: www.charliepalmer.com					
Chicago Joe's 820 S 4th St	Las Vegas	NV	89101	702-382-5637	
Web: www.chicagojoesrestaurant.com					
China Grill 3950 Las Vegas Blvd S	Las Vegas	NV	89119	702-632-7404	632-6906
Web: www.chinagrillmgt.com/restaurants-and-bars/china-grill-las-vegas					
Craftsteak 3799 Las Vegas Blvd S	Las Vegas	NV	89109	702-891-7318	891-5899
Del Frisco's Double Eagle Steak House 3925 Paradise Rd	Las Vegas	NV	89109	702-796-0063	796-0081
Web: www.delfriscos.com					
Delmonico Steakhouse 3355 Las Vegas Blvd S Venetian Resort Hotel & Casino	Las Vegas	NV	89109	702-414-3737	414-3838
Web: www.emerils.com					
Eiffel Tower Restaurant 3655 Las Vegas Blvd S	Las Vegas	NV	89019	702-948-6937	942-0004
Web: www.eiffeltowerrestaurant.com					
Emeril's New Orleans Fish House 3799 Las Vegas Blvd S MGM Grand Hotel	Las Vegas	NV	89109	702-891-7374	891-7338
Web: www.emerils.com/restaurant/4/Emerils-New-Orleans-Fish-House					
Ferraro's 4480 Paradise Rd	Las Vegas	NV	89169	702-364-5300	871-2721
Web: www.ferraroslasvegas.com					
Fiamma Trattoria 3799 Las Vegas Blvd S	Las Vegas	NV	89109	702-891-7600	
Fleming's Prime Steakhouse & Wine Bar 8721 W Charleston Blvd	Las Vegas	NV	89117	702-838-4774	838-6639
Web: www.flemingssteakhouse.com					
Gandhi India's Cuisine 4080 Paradise Rd	Las Vegas	NV	89109	702-734-0094	734-3444
Web: www.gandhicuisine.com					
Grotto Ristorante 129 E Fremont St	Las Vegas	NV	89101	702-385-7111	
Web: www.goldennugget.com					
Hugo's Cellar 202 Fremont St	Las Vegas	NV	89101	702-385-4011	387-5120
Inka Si Senor 845 S Rainbow Blvd	Las Vegas	NV	89145	702-731-0826	731-9749
Jasmine 3600 Las Vegas Blvd S	Las Vegas	NV	89109	702-693-7111	
Le Cirque 3600 Las Vegas Blvd S	Las Vegas	NV	89109	702-693-8100	693-8106
Web: www.osteriadelcirco.com					

Name / Address	City	State	ZIP	Phone	Fax
Lillie's Asian Cuisine 129 E Fremont St	Las Vegas	NV	89101	702-385-7111	386-8351
Web: www.goldennugget.com/dining/lillies.asp					
Lotus of Siam 953 E Sahara Ave	Las Vegas	NV	89104	702-735-3033	735-3033
Web: www.saipinchutima.com					
Mayflower Cuisinier 4750 W Sahara Ave Suite 326	Las Vegas	NV	89102	702-870-8432	259-8493
Web: www.mayflowercuisinier.com					
McCormick & Schmick's 335 Hughes Ctr Dr	Las Vegas	NV	89109	702-836-9000	836-9500
Web: www.mccormickandschmicks.com					
Michael Mina 3600 Las Vegas Blvd S	Las Vegas	NV	89109	702-693-7223	693-8512
Web: michaelmina.net/restaurants/locations/mmlv.php					
Michael's 9777 Las Vegas Blvd S	Las Vegas	NV	89183	702-796-7111	797-8216
Web: www.southpointcasino.com					
Mon Ami Gabi 3655 Las Vegas Blvd S	Las Vegas	NV	89109	702-944-4224	
Web: www.monamigabi.com					
N9ne Steakhouse 4321 W Flamingo Rd	Las Vegas	NV	89103	702-933-9900	942-8072
Web: www.n9negroup.com					
Nob Hill 3799 Las Vegas Blvd S MGM Grand Hotel	Las Vegas	NV	89109	702-891-1111	891-3036
TF Resv: 800-929-1111 ■ *Web:* www.mgmgrand.com					
Okada 3131 Las Vegas Blvd S	Las Vegas	NV	89109	702-770-9966	
Olives 3600 Las Vegas Blvd S	Las Vegas	NV	89117	702-693-8181	
Onda Ristorante 3400 Las Vegas Blvd S	Las Vegas	NV	89109	702-791-7223	
Web: www.mirage.com					
Osaka 4205 W Sahara Ave	Las Vegas	NV	89102	702-876-4988	876-0259
Web: www.lasvegas-sushi.com					
Osteria Del Circo 3600 Las Vegas Blvd S	Las Vegas	NV	89109	702-693-8865	693-8106
TF: 866-259-7111 ■ *Web:* www.bellagio.com/restaurants/circo.aspx					
Pamplemousse 400 E Sahara Ave	Las Vegas	NV	89104	702-733-2066	733-9139
Web: www.pamplemousserestaurant.com					
PF Chang's China Bistro 3667 Las Vegas Blvd S	Las Vegas	NV	89128	702-836-0955	836-1963
Web: www.pfchangs.com					
Piero's Restaurant 355 Convention Ctr Dr	Las Vegas	NV	89109	702-369-2305	735-5699
Web: www.pieroscuisine.com					
Pinot Brasserie 3355 Las Vegas Blvd S	Las Vegas	NV	89109	702-414-8888	414-3885
Web: www.patinagroup.com/pinotBrasserie					
Postrio 3355 Las Vegas Blvd S	Las Vegas	NV	89109	702-796-1110	796-1112
Rosemary's 8125 W Sahara Ave Suite 110	Las Vegas	NV	89107	702-869-2251	869-2283
Web: www.rosemarysrestaurant.com					
Roy's 620 E Flamingo Rd	Las Vegas	NV	89119	702-691-2053	691-2072
Web: www.roysrestaurants.com					
Second Street Grill 200 E Fremont St	Las Vegas	NV	89125	702-385-6277	
Smith & Wollensky 3767 Las Vegas Blvd S	Las Vegas	NV	89109	702-862-4100	933-3931
Web: www.smithandwollensky.com					
Spago 3500 Las Vegas Blvd S Suite G1	Las Vegas	NV	89109	702-369-6300	369-0361
Web: www.wolfgangpuck.com					
Steak House 2880 Las Vegas Blvd S	Las Vegas	NV	89109	702-794-3767	
Sterling Brunch 3645 Las Vegas Blvd S	Las Vegas	NV	89109	702-739-4111	
STRIPSTEAK 3950 Las Vegas Blvd S Mandalay Bay Hotel	Las Vegas	NV	89119	702-632-7400	632-9196
Sushi Roku 3500 Las Vegas Blvd S	Las Vegas	NV	89109	702-733-7373	732-4455
Web: www.sushiroku.com					
SW Steakhouse 3131 Las Vegas Blvd S	Las Vegas	NV	89109	702-770-9966	770-1571
TF: 888-329-7110 ■ *Web:* www.winnlasvegas.com					
Thai Spice 4433 W Flamingo Rd	Las Vegas	NV	89103	702-362-5308	
Top of the World 2000 Las Vegas Blvd S	Las Vegas	NV	89101	702-380-7711	
Web: www.topoftheworldlv.com					
Trattoria Del Lupo 3950 Las Vegas Blvd S	Las Vegas	NV	89119	702-740-5522	740-5533
Web: www.wolfgangpuck.com/restaurants/fine-dining/3860					
Tsunami Asian Grill 3377 Las Vegas Blvd S	Las Vegas	NV	89109	702-414-1980	414-1981
Valentino Las Vegas 3355 Las Vegas Blvd S Venetian Resort Hotel & Casino	Las Vegas	NV	89109	702-414-3000	414-3099
Web: www.pieroselvaggio.com					
Verandah 3960 Las Vegas Blvd S	Las Vegas	NV	89119	702-632-5000	632-5195
Web: www.fourseasons.com					
Willy & Jose's Mexican Cantina 5111 Boulder Hwy	Las Vegas	NV	89122	702-456-7777	
Wolfgang Puck's Bar & Grill 3799 Las Vegas Blvd S	Las Vegas	NV	89109	702-891-3000	891-3263
Web: www.wolfgangpuck.com					
Zeffirino Ristorante 3377 Las Vegas Blvd S	Las Vegas	NV	89109	702-414-3500	
Web: www.zeffirinolasvegas.com					
Asian Garden 1945 S Virginia St	Reno	NV	89502	775-825-5510	825-1169
Atlantis Seafood Steakhouse 3800 S Virginia St Atlantis Casino Resort	Reno	NV	89502	800-723-6500	827-1518*
**Fax Area Code:* 775 ■ *TF:* 800-825-4700 ■ *Web:* www.atlantiscasino.com					
Bavarian World 595 Valley Rd	Reno	NV	89512	775-323-7646	
Beaujolais Bistro 130 W St	Reno	NV	89509	775-323-2227	
Web: www.beaujolaisbistro.com					
Bertha Miranda's 336 Mill St	Reno	NV	89502	775-786-9697	786-2525
Web: www.berthamirandas.com					
Beto's 575 W 5th St	Reno	NV	89503	775-324-0632	
Black Bear Diner 2323 S Virginia St	Reno	NV	89509	775-827-5570	
Web: www.blackbeardiner.com					
Brew House Pub & Grill 6395 S McCarran Blvd	Reno	NV	89509	775-828-2700	828-2716
Bricks 1695 S Virginia St	Reno	NV	89502	775-786-2277	
Cafe de Thai 7499 Longly Ln	Reno	NV	89511	775-829-8424	
China East Restaurant 1086 S Virginia St # A	Reno	NV	89502	775-348-7020	348-1956
Flowing Tide Pub 10580 N McCarran Blvd	Reno	NV	89503	775-747-7707	
Web: www.flowingtidepub.com					
Galena Forest Restaurant 17025 Mt Rose Hwy	Reno	NV	89501	775-849-2100	
Golden Flower 205 W 5th St	Reno	NV	89503	775-323-1628	
Harrah's Steak House 219 N Ctr St	Reno	NV	89501	775-788-2929	788-2962
TF: 800-427-7247					
India Garden 1565 S Virginia St	Reno	NV	89502	775-337-8002	379-8022
Johnny's 4245 W 4th St	Reno	NV	89503	775-747-4511	
La Strada 345 N Virginia St	Reno	NV	89501	775-348-9297	
Louis' Basque Corner 301 E 4th St	Reno	NV	89512	775-323-7203	
Paisan's 4826 Longley Ln	Reno	NV	89502	775-826-9444	856-9593
Web: www.paisancatering.com					
Palais de Jade 960 W Moana Ln	Reno	NV	89509	775-827-5233	
PF Chang's China Bistro 5180 S Kietzke Ln	Reno	NV	89511	775-825-9800	825-9825
Web: www.pfchangs.com					
Pho 777 Vietnamese Restaurant 201 E 2nd St	Reno	NV	89501	775-323-7777	
Pneumatic Diner 501 W 1st St	Reno	NV	89503	775-786-8888	
Rapscallion Seafood House 1555 S Wells Ave	Reno	NV	89502	775-323-1211	323-6096
Web: www.rapscallion.com					
Romanza 2707 S Virginia St Peppermill Hotel Casino	Reno	NV	89502	775-826-2121	
Silver Peak Grill & Taproom 135 N Sierra St	Reno	NV	89501	775-284-3300	284-3301
Sterling's Seafood Steakhouse 4th & Virginia Sts	Reno	NV	89505	775-325-7573	325-7580
TF: 800-687-7733 ■ *Web:* www.silverlegacy.com					
Sushi Club 294 E Moana Ln	Reno	NV	89502	775-828-7311	828-5426
Sushi Pier 1290 E Plumb Ln	Reno	NV	89502	775-825-6776	
Washoe Steakhouse 4201 W 4th St	Reno	NV	89503	775-786-1323	786-1314
Web: www.washoesteakhouse.com					
White Orchid 2707 S Virginia St	Reno	NV	89502	775-826-2121	

NEW HAMPSHIRE

Name / Address	City	State	ZIP	Phone	Fax
Bedford Village Inn 2 Olde Bedford Way	Bedford	NH	03110	603-472-2001	472-2379
Web: www.bedfordvillageinn.com					
Alan's Restaurant & Lounge 133 N Main St	Boscawen	NH	03303	603-753-6631	753-4890
Angelina's Ristorante Italiano 11 Depot St	Concord	NH	03301	603-228-3313	228-3775
Web: www.angelinasrestaurant.com					
Barley House 132 N Main St	Concord	NH	03301	603-228-6363	228-6565
Web: www.thebarleyhouse.com					
Cat N' Fiddle 118 Manchester St	Concord	NH	03301	603-228-8911	226-2350
Web: www.catnfiddle.com					
Cheers 17 Depot St	Concord	NH	03301	603-228-0180	226-3459
Web: www.cheersnh.com					
Common Man The 25 Water St	Concord	NH	03301	603-228-3463	224-5722
Web: www.thecman.com					
Corner View Restaurant 80 1/2 S St	Concord	NH	03301	603-229-4554	229-0932
Green Martini 6 Pleasant St Ext	Concord	NH	03301	603-223-6672	
Hermanos Cocina Mexicana 11 Hills Ave	Concord	NH	03301	603-224-5669	
Web: www.hermanosmexican.com					
Makris Lobster & Steak House 106 N Rd Rt 106	Concord	NH	03301	603-225-7665	224-4375
Web: www.eatalobster.com					
Man Yee Restaurant 79 S St	Concord	NH	03301	603-226-0001	226-0003
Margarita's 1 Bicentennial Sq	Concord	NH	03301	603-224-2821	224-3023
Web: www.margs.com					
Moritomo 32 Fort Eddy Rd	Concord	NH	03301	603-224-8363	224-8038
Red Blazer The 72 Manchester St	Concord	NH	03301	603-224-4101	224-7118
Web: www.theredblazer.com					
Siam Orchid 158 N Main St	Concord	NH	03301	603-228-1529	228-0571
Web: www.siamorchid.net					
Szechuan Garden Restaurant 108 Fisherville Rd	Concord	NH	03301	603-226-2650	226-2650
Tea Garden Restaurant 184 N Main St	Concord	NH	03301	603-228-4420	224-9820
Belmont Hall & Restaurant 718 Grove St	Manchester	NH	03103	603-625-8540	
Black Brimmer American Bar & Grill 1087 Elm St	Manchester	NH	03101	603-669-5523	
Web: www.blackbrimmer.com					
Cactus Jacks Southwest Grill 782 S Willow St	Manchester	NH	03103	603-627-8600	627-3200
Web: www.t-bones.com/cj_home.html					
Chateau Restaurant 201 Hanover St	Manchester	NH	03104	603-627-2677	
Commercial Street Fishery 33 S Commercial St	Manchester	NH	03101	603-296-0706	296-0710
Web: www.csfishery.com					
Cotton 75 Arms St	Manchester	NH	03101	603-622-5488	627-4529
Web: www.cottonfood.com/home.html					
Derryfield Restaurant The 625 Mammoth Rd	Manchester	NH	03104	603-623-2880	623-6850
Web: www.thederryfield.com					
Don Quijote 362 Union St	Manchester	NH	03103	603-622-2246	
Fratello's Ristorante Italiano 155 Dow St	Manchester	NH	03101	603-624-2022	629-9465
Web: www.fratellos.com					
India Palace 575 S Willow St	Manchester	NH	03103	603-641-8413	641-8583
La Carreta 545 Daniel Webster Hwy	Manchester	NH	03104	603-628-6899	628-6890
Web: www.lacarretamexican.com					
Lakorn Thai Restaurant 470 S Main St	Manchester	NH	03102	603-626-4545	626-4545
Piccola Italia 815 Elm St	Manchester	NH	03101	603-606-5100	
Web: www.piccolaitalianh.com					
Richard's Bistro 36 Lowell St	Manchester	NH	03101	603-644-1180	624-6082
Web: www.richardsbistro.com					
Shogun Japanese Steak House 545 Hooksett Rd	Manchester	NH	03104	603-669-8122	
Shorty's 1050 Bicentennial Dr	Manchester	NH	03104	603-625-1730	625-1770
Szechuan House 245 Maple St	Manchester	NH	03103	603-669-8811	622-7318
Taste of Europe 827 Elm St	Manchester	NH	03101	603-296-0292	
Thousand Crane 1000 Elm St	Manchester	NH	03101	603-634-0000	634-0040
Yard The 1211 S Mammoth Rd	Manchester	NH	03109	603-623-3545	625-8420
Web: www.theyardrestaurant.com					
Puritan Backroom Restaurant 245 Hooksett Rd	North Manchester	NH	03104	603-669-6890	623-3788
Web: www.puritanbackroom.com					

NEW JERSEY

Name / Address	City	State	ZIP	Phone	Fax
Rams Head Inn 9 W White Horse Pike	Absecon	NJ	08205	609-652-1700	652-2605
Web: www.ramsheadins.com					
Angelo's Fairmount Tavern 2300 Fairmount Ave	Atlantic City	NJ	08401	609-344-2439	348-1043
Web: www.angelosfairmounttavern.com					
Atlantic City Bar & Grill 1219 Pacific Ave	Atlantic City	NJ	08401	609-348-8080	348-8466
Web: www.acbarandgrill.com					

				Phone	Fax
Billy Ho's Imperial East					
7800 Ventnor Ave	Atlantic City	NJ	08402	609-487-1040	
Bobby Flay Steak 1 Borgata Way	Atlantic City	NJ	08401	609-317-1000	
Web: www.bobbyflaysteak.com					
Cuba Libre 2801 Pacific Ave	Atlantic City	NJ	08401	609-348-6700	348-6704
Web: www.cubalibrerestaurant.com					
Dock's Oyster House 2405 Atlantic Ave	Atlantic City	NJ	08401	609-345-0092	345-7893
Web: www.docksoysterhouse.com					
Girasole Ristorante & Lounge					
3108 Pacific Ave	Atlantic City	NJ	08401	609-345-5554	
Web: www.girasoleac.com					
Hard Rock Cafe					
Boardwalk at Virginia Ave	Atlantic City	NJ	08401	609-441-0007	449-1836
Web: www.hardrock.com					
Knife & Fork Inn The 3600 Atlantic Ave	Atlantic City	NJ	08401	609-344-1133	344-3533
Web: www.knifeandforkinn.com					
Los Amigos 1926 Atlantic Ave	Atlantic City	NJ	08401	609-344-2293	344-2373
Web: www.losamigosrest.com					
Mexico 3810 Ventor Ave	Atlantic City	NJ	08406	609-344-0366	
Mia Restaurant 2100 Pacific Ave	Atlantic City	NJ	08401	609-441-2345	441-2289
Web: www.miaac.com					
Palm The 2801 Pacific Ave	Atlantic City	NJ	08401	609-344-7256	
PF Chang's China Bistro					
2801 N Pacific Ave	Atlantic City	NJ	08401	609-348-4600	
Web: www.pfchangs.com					
Red Square 2801 Pacific Ave	Atlantic City	NJ	08401	609-344-9100	344-9105
Web: www.chinagrillmgt.com					
Sea Blue 1 Borgata Way	Atlantic City	NJ	08401	609-317-8220	317-1100
TF Cust Svc: 866-692-6742 ■ *Web:* www.theborgata.com					
Waterfront Buffet					
777 Harrah's Blvd					
Harrah""s Hotel & Casino	Atlantic City	NJ	08401	609-441-5576	
Wolfgang Puck American Grille					
1 Borgata Way	Atlantic City	NJ	08401	609-317-1000	
Sal Deforte's 1400 PkwyAve Serenity Plaza	Ewing	NJ	08628	609-406-0123	
Web: www.saldefortesristorante.com					
Banzai 3690 Quakerbridge Rd	Hamilton	NJ	08619	609-587-5454	
Web: www.banzairestaurant.com					
Oddfellows Rest 80 River St	Hoboken	NJ	07030	201-656-9009	656-0484
Web: www.oddfellowsrest.com					
Amelia's Bistro 187 Warren St	Jersey City	NJ	07303	201-332-2200	
Amiya					
160 Green St					
Harborside Financial Ctr Plaza 5	Jersey City	NJ	07311	201-433-8000	433-8866
Web: www.amiyarestaurant.com					
Baja 117 Montgomery St	Jersey City	NJ	07302	201-915-0062	915-1880
Web: www.bajamexicancuisine.com					
Casa Dante 737 Newark Ave	Jersey City	NJ	07306	201-795-2750	795-1225
Web: www.casadante.com					
Confucius Asian Bistro					
558 Washington Blvd	Jersey City	NJ	07306	201-386-8898	386-8896
Iron Monkey 97 Greene St	Jersey City	NJ	07302	201-435-5756	433-0762
Just Sonny 169 Sterling Ave	Jersey City	NJ	07305	201-434-9413	
Web: www.justsonny.com					
Komegashi 103 Montgomery St	Jersey City	NJ	07302	201-433-4567	333-8946
Web: www.komegashi.com					
Laico's 67 Terhune Ave	Jersey City	NJ	07305	201-434-9853	434-4116
Liberty House 76 Audrey Zapp Dr	Jersey City	NJ	07304	201-395-0300	395-0065
Web: www.libertyhouserestaurant.com					
Light Horse Tavern 199 Washington St	Jersey City	NJ	07302	201-946-2028	946-2029
Web: www.lighthorsetavern.com					
Madame Claude Cafe 364 1/2 4th St	Jersey City	NJ	07302	201-876-8800	
Web: www.madameclaudecafe.com					
Marco & Pepe 289 Grove St	Jersey City	NJ	07302	201-860-9688	
Web: www.marcoandpepe.com					
Marker's Restaurant					
153 Plaza II Harborside Financial Ctr	Jersey City	NJ	07311	201-433-6275	433-0399
Web: www.markersrestaurant.com					
Merchant The 279 Grove St	Jersey City	NJ	07302	201-200-0202	200-9945
Web: www.themerchantnj.com					
Nha Tranh Place 249 Newark Ave	Jersey City	NJ	07302	201-239-1988	
Pointe 2 Chapel Ave	Jersey City	NJ	07302	201-985-9854	
Puccini's 1064 Westside Ave	Jersey City	NJ	07306	201-432-4111	432-9026
Web: www.puccinisrestaurant.com					
Rita & Joe's 142 Broadway	Jersey City	NJ	07306	201-451-3606	
Web: www.rita-joes.com					
South City Grill 70 Town Sq Pl	Jersey City	NJ	07310	201-610-9225	610-1010
Web: www.southcitygrill.com					
Acacia 2637 Lawrenceville Rd	Lawrenceville	NJ	08648	609-895-9885	895-9874
Web: www.acaciacuisine.com					
Steve & Cookies By the Bay 9700 Amherst Ave	Margate	NJ	08402	609-823-1163	823-9571
Web: www.steveandcookies.com					
Adega Grill 130 Ferry St	Newark	NJ	07105	973-589-8830	741-0778
Web: www.adegagrill.com					
Brasilia Restaurante 132 Ferry St	Newark	NJ	07105	973-465-1227	
Campino Restaurant 70 Jabez St	Newark	NJ	07105	973-589-4004	
Casa Vasca 141 Elm St	Newark	NJ	07105	973-465-1350	465-7335
Don Pepe Restaurant & Catering					
844 McCarter Hwy	Newark	NJ	07102	973-623-4662	623-5402
Web: www.donpeperestaurant.com					
Fernandes Steak House 158 Fleming Ave	Newark	NJ	07105	973-589-4344	589-6312
Web: www.fernandessteakhouse.com					
Fornos of Spain 47 Ferry St	Newark	NJ	00751	973-589-4767	589-1482
Web: www.fornosrestaurant.com					
Iberia Peninsula Restaurant 67 Ferry St	Newark	NJ	07105	973-344-5611	344-2067
John's Place 24 Wright St	Newark	NJ	07114	973-824-9233	824-2038
Maize					
Maize Restaurant 50 Pk Pl	Newark	NJ	07102	973-639-2202	639-1600
Web: www.maizerestaurant.com					
Spain 419 Market St	Newark	NJ	07105	973-344-0994	344-2669
Web: www.spainrestaurant.com					

				Phone	Fax
Spanish Tavern 103 McWhorter St	Newark	NJ	07105	973-589-4959	589-4148
Web: www.spanishtavern.com					
Theater Square Grill 1 Ctr St	Newark	NJ	07102	973-642-1226	297-5877
Web: www.theatersquaregrill.com					
Tony da Caneca 72 Elm Rd	Newark	NJ	07105	973-589-6882	589-0036
Web: www.tonydacaneca.com					
Albasha 1076 Main St	Paterson	NJ	07503	973-345-3700	345-6001
Web: www.albashanj.com					
Bonfire 999 Market St	Paterson	NJ	07513	973-278-2400	278-1380
Web: www.bonfirerestaurant.com					
Brownstone House 351 W Broadway	Paterson	NJ	07522	973-595-8582	595-1141
Web: www.thebrownstone.com					
Cortina Ristorante 118 Berkshire Ave	Paterson	NJ	07502	973-942-1750	942-9590
Web: www.cortinarestaurant.com					
D'Classico 58-60 Ellison St	Paterson	NJ	07501	973-569-4300	
E & V Restaurant 320 Chamberlain Ave	Paterson	NJ	07502	973-942-4664	942-0060
Web: www.evrestaurant.com					
Getty Avenue Grill 169 Crooks Ave	Paterson	NJ	07503	973-278-7999	
Hacienda Restaurant 102 McLean Blvd	Paterson	NJ	07514	973-345-1255	345-5502
Web: www.haciendarestaurant.com					
Kikiriki 215 Market St	Paterson	NJ	07505	973-225-0336	
King Wok 712 Main St	Paterson	NJ	07503	973-881-8818	
Patsy's 72 7th Ave	Paterson	NJ	07524	973-742-9596	
Seven Bros Grill 846 Market St	Paterson	NJ	07513	973-684-2579	
Tierras Colombians 395 21st Ave	Paterson	NJ	07513	973-742-3736	742-3736
Big Fish Seafood Bistro 3535 US Rt 1 S	Princeton	NJ	08540	609-919-1179	919-0674
Blue Point Grill 258 Nassau St	Princeton	NJ	08542	609-921-1211	
Crab Trap 2 Broadway	Somers Point	NJ	08244	609-927-7377	927-5979
Web: www.thecrabtrap.com					
Amici Milano Restaurant 600 Chesnut Ave	Trenton	NJ	08611	609-396-6300	396-3926
Web: www.amicimilano.com					
Blue Danube 538 Adeline St	Trenton	NJ	08621	609-393-6133	
Casino Restaurant 15 Anderson St	Trenton	NJ	08611	609-393-5875	
Homestead Inn 800 Kuser Rd	Trenton	NJ	08619	609-890-9851	
Katmandu 50 Riverview Executive Pk	Trenton	NJ	08611	609-393-7300	695-8737
Web: www.katmandutrenton.com					
Malaga Spanish Restaurant 511 Lalor St	Trenton	NJ	08610	609-396-8878	396-5514
Web: www.malagarestaurant.com					
Marsilio's 541 Roebling Ave	Trenton	NJ	08611	609-695-1916	
Villa Maria 3800 Quakerbridge Rd	Trenton	NJ	08619	609-587-4445	587-6539
Yoshi Sono Japanese Restaurant					
643 Eagle Rock Ave Suite A	West Orange	NJ	07052	973-325-2005	
On the Border Mexican Cafe					
1738 US Rt 46 W	West Paterson	NJ	07424	973-785-9188	785-9226
Web: www.ontheborder.com					
Taste of China 500 McBride Ave	West Paterson	NJ	07424	973-523-8805	

NEW MEXICO

				Phone	Fax
66 Diner 1405 Central Ave NE	Albuquerque	NM	87106	505-247-1421	247-0882
Web: www.66diner.com					
ABQ Nick's Crossroads Cafe					
400 Central SW	Albuquerque	NM	87102	505-242-6447	242-8379
Ambrozia Cafe & Wine Bar					
108 Rio Grande Blvd NE	Albuquerque	NM	87104	505-242-6560	
Amerasia 301 Cornell Dr SE	Albuquerque	NM	87106	505-266-8400	
Antiquity 112 Romero St NW	Albuquerque	NM	87104	505-247-3545	
Artichoke Cafe 424 Central SE	Albuquerque	NM	87102	505-243-0200	243-3365
Web: www.artichokecafe.com					
Bangkok Cafe 5901 Central Ave NE	Albuquerque	NM	87108	505-255-5036	255-9177
Barry's Oasis Restaurant					
4451 Osuna Rd NE	Albuquerque	NM	87109	505-884-2324	
Web: www.barrysoasis.com					
Chama River Brewing Co					
4939 Pan American Fwy	Albuquerque	NM	87109	505-342-1800	342-2018
Web: www.chamariverbrewery.com					
Charlie's Front & Back Door					
8224 Menaul Blvd NE	Albuquerque	NM	87110	505-294-3130	
County Line 9600 Tramway Blvd NE	Albuquerque	NM	87122	505-856-7477	856-7479
Web: www.countyline.com					
El Pinto 10500 4th St NW	Albuquerque	NM	87114	505-898-1771	890-0498
Web: www.elpinto.com					
Forque					
330 Tijeras Ave NW					
Hyatt Regency Albuquerque	Albuquerque	NM	87102	505-842-1234	843-2710
Gardunos of Mexico 5400 Academy Rd NE	Albuquerque	NM	87109	505-821-3030	823-1628
Web: www.gardunosrestaurants.com					
Gold Street Caffe 218 Gold Ave SW	Albuquerque	NM	87102	505-765-1633	
High Finance Restaurant 40 Tramway Rd NE	Albuquerque	NM	87122	505-243-9742	247-8501
Il Vicino 3403 Central Ave NE	Albuquerque	NM	87106	505-266-7855	265-5133
Web: www.ilvicino.com					
India Kitchen 6910 Montgomery Blvd NE	Albuquerque	NM	87109	505-884-2333	
India Palace 4410Q Wyoming NE	Albuquerque	NM	87111	505-271-5009	271-5042
La Familiar 1611 4th St NW	Albuquerque	NM	87102	505-242-9661	
Lin's Restaurant 1035 Juan Tabo Blvd NE	Albuquerque	NM	87112	505-292-5438	
Melting Pot of Albuquerque The					
2011 Mountain Rd NW	Albuquerque	NM	87104	505-843-6358	883-3941
Web: www.meltingpot.com					
Monte Vista Fire Station					
3201 Central Ave NE	Albuquerque	NM	87106	505-255-2424	255-2521
Mr Powdrell's Barbeque House					
11301 Central Ave NE	Albuquerque	NM	87123	505-298-6766	298-0025
New Chinatown Restaurant					
5001 Central Ave NE	Albuquerque	NM	87108	505-265-8859	266-3324
Pelican's Restaurant					
9800 Montgomery Blvd NE	Albuquerque	NM	87111	505-298-7678	293-9953
Ragin' Shrimp 3624 Central Ave SE	Albuquerque	NM	87108	505-254-1544	
Web: www.raginshrimp.com					
Ranchers Club of New Mexico					
1901 University Blvd NE	Albuquerque	NM	87102	505-889-8071	
Web: www.theranchersclubofnm.com					

Name / Address	City	State	Zip	Phone	Fax
Robb's Ribbs Inc 3000-C San Pedro Dr NE	Albuquerque	NM	87110	505-884-7422	
Web: www.robbsribbs.com					
Sadie's 6230 4th St NW	Albuquerque	NM	87107	505-345-5339	345-9440
Web: www.sadiessalsa.com					
Samurai Grill & Sushi Bar 9500 Montgomery Blvd NE	Albuquerque	NM	87111	505-275-6601	275-4146
Web: www.abqsamurai.com					
Sandiago's Mexican Grill at the Tram 40 Tramway Rd NE	Albuquerque	NM	87122	505-856-6692	856-6364
Web: www.sandiapeakrestaurants.com					
Scalo Northern Italian Grill 3500 Central Ave SE	Albuquerque	NM	87106	505-255-8781	265-7850
Web: www.scalonobhill.com					
Seasons Rotisserie & Grill 2031 Mountain Rd NW	Albuquerque	NM	87104	505-766-5100	766-5252
Web: www.seasonsabq.com					
Yanni's Mediterranean Bar & Grill 3109 Central Ave NE	Albuquerque	NM	87106	505-268-9250	268-9178
Zinc Wine Bar & Bistro 3009 Central Ave NE	Albuquerque	NM	87106	505-254-9462	
Carillos Cafe 330 S Church St	Las Cruces	NM	88001	575-523-9913	
Cattle Baron 790 S Telshor Blvd	Las Cruces	NM	88001	575-522-7533	521-3300
Web: www.cattlebaron.com					
Chilito's 2405 S Valley Dr	Las Cruces	NM	88005	575-526-4184	532-1104
Web: chilitosrestaurant.net					
Farley's 3499 Foothills Dr	Las Cruces	NM	88011	575-522-0466	521-3523
Web: www.farleyspub.com					
Los Compas Cafe 603 S Nevarez St	Las Cruces	NM	88001	575-523-1778	527-5590
Mesilla Valley Kitchen 2001 E Lohman Ave Suite 103	Las Cruces	NM	88001	575-523-9311	
Meson de Mesilla 1803 Avenida de Mesilla PO Box 1537	Las Cruces	NM	88046	575-652-4953	652-4954
Web: www.mesondemesilla.com					
Mix Express 1001 E University Ave Suite D-3	Las Cruces	NM	88001	575-532-5553	532-2046
Web: www.themixexpress.com					
Nellie's Cafe 1226 W Hadley Ave	Las Cruces	NM	88005	575-524-9982	
Roberto's 908 E Amador Ave	Las Cruces	NM	88001	575-523-1851	
Si Senor Restaurant 1551 E Amador Ave	Las Cruces	NM	88001	575-527-0817	527-0412
Web: www.sisenor.com					
Spanish Kitchen 2960 N Main St	Las Cruces	NM	88001	575-526-4275	526-2275
Teriyaki Chicken House 805 El Paseo Rd	Las Cruces	NM	88001	575-541-1696	
Double Eagle Restaurant 2355 Calle de Guadelupe	Mesilla	NM	88046	505-523-6700	
Web: www.double-eagle-mesilla.com					
Anasazi 113 Washington Ave	Santa Fe	NM	87501	505-988-3236	
Andiamo 322 Garfield St	Santa Fe	NM	87501	505-995-9595	
Web: www.andiamoonline.com					
Annapurna Chai House 1620 St Michaels	Santa Fe	NM	87505	505-988-9688	988-9914
Web: www.chaishoppe.com					
Bull Ring 150 Washington Ave	Santa Fe	NM	87501	505-983-3328	982-8254
Chow's Contemporary Chinese Food 720 St Michaels Dr	Santa Fe	NM	87505	505-471-7120	
Web: www.mychows.com					
Coyote Cafe 132 W Water St	Santa Fe	NM	87501	505-983-1615	989-9026
Web: www.coyotecafe.com					
El Farol 808 Canyon Rd	Santa Fe	NM	87501	505-983-9912	
Web: www.elfarolsf.com					
Fuego 330 E Palace Ave	Santa Fe	NM	87501	505-986-0000	982-6850
TF Sales: 866-331-7625					
Geronimo 724 Canyon Rd	Santa Fe	NM	87501	505-982-1500	
Web: www.geronimorestaurant.com					
Harry's Roadhouse 96B Old Las Vegas Hwy	Santa Fe	NM	87505	505-989-4629	
Il Piatto 95 W Marcy St	Santa Fe	NM	87501	505-984-1091	983-6939
Web: www.ilpiattorestaurant.com					
Il Vicino 321 W San Francisco St	Santa Fe	NM	87501	505-986-8700	820-0524
Web: www.ilvicino.com					
India Palace 227 Don Gaspar Ave	Santa Fe	NM	87501	505-986-5859	986-5856
Web: www.indiapalace.com					
Kohnami 313 S Guadalupe St	Santa Fe	NM	87501	505-984-2002	
Maria's New Mexican Kitchen 555 W Cordova Rd	Santa Fe	NM	87501	505-983-7929	
Web: www.marias-santafe.com					
Mariscos La Playa 537 W Cordova Rd	Santa Fe	NM	87505	505-982-2790	
Mu Du Noodles 1494 Cerrillos Rd	Santa Fe	NM	87505	505-983-1411	
Web: www.mudunoodles.com					
Old House 309 W San Francisco St	Santa Fe	NM	87501	505-988-4455	995-4543
TF: 800-955-4455 ■ *Web:* www.eldoradohotel.com					
Rio Chama Steakhouse 414 Old Santa Fe Trail	Santa Fe	NM	87501	505-955-0765	955-8579
Web: www.riochamasteakhouse.com					
Santacafe 231 Washington Ave	Santa Fe	NM	87501	505-984-1788	
Web: www.santacafe.com					
Shed The 113 1/2 E Palace Ave	Santa Fe	NM	87501	505-982-9030	982-0902
Web: www.sfshed.com					
Tecolote Cafe 1203 Cerrillos Rd	Santa Fe	NM	87505	505-988-1362	
Tomasita's Santa Fe Station 500 S Guadalupe St	Santa Fe	NM	87501	505-983-5721	983-0780
Tortilla Flats 3139 Cerrillos Rd	Santa Fe	NM	87505	505-471-8685	471-8686
Web: www.santafenow.com/rest/tortilla					

NEW YORK

Name / Address	City	State	Zip	Phone	Fax
Cafe Capriccio 49 Grand St	Albany	NY	12207	518-465-0439	465-6822
Web: www.cafecapriccio.com					
Caffe Italia Ristorante 662 Central Ave	Albany	NY	12206	518-459-8029	482-9433
CH Evans Brewing Co at the Albany Pump Station 19 Quackenbush Sq	Albany	NY	12207	518-447-9000	465-1410
Web: www.evansale.com					
Desmond Albany Hotel The 660 Albany-Shaker Rd	Albany	NY	12211	518-869-8100	869-7659
TF: 800-448-3500 ■ *Web:* www.desmondhotelsalbany.com					
El Loco Mexican Cafe 465 Madison Ave	Albany	NY	12210	518-436-1855	
El Mariachi 144 Washington Ave	Albany	NY	12206	518-465-2568	463-1930
Gandhi 1 Central Ave	Albany	NY	12210	518-449-5577	449-8941
Web: www.albanygandhi.com					
Hiros 1933 Central Ave	Albany	NY	12205	518-456-1180	
Ichiban 338 Central Ave	Albany	NY	12206	518-432-0358	432-6038
Jack's Oyster House 42 State St	Albany	NY	12207	518-465-8854	434-2134
Web: www.jacksoysterhouse.com					
Justin's 301 Lark St	Albany	NY	12210	518-436-7008	432-4122
Web: www.justinsonlark.com					
Kirker's Steak & Seafood 959 New Loudon Rd	Albany	NY	12110	518-785-3653	
Miss Albany Diner 893 Broadway	Albany	NY	12207	518-465-9148	
Web: www.missalbanydiner.com					
My Linh 272 Delaware Ave	Albany	NY	12209	518-465-8899	465-8898
Web: www.mylinhrestaurant.com					
Nicole's Bistro 25 Quackenbush Sq	Albany	NY	12207	518-465-1111	465-3911
Web: www.nicolesbistro.com					
Pearl 1 Steuben Pl	Albany	NY	12207	518-694-3100	433-0012
Provence 1475 Western Ave Stuyvesant Plaza	Albany	NY	12203	518-689-7777	689-7780
Web: www.milano-restaurant.com/provence					
Real Seafood Co 195 Wolf Rd	Albany	NY	12205	518-458-2068	482-3471
Web: www.reelseafoodco.com					
Saso's Japanese Noodle House 218 Central Ave	Albany	NY	12205	518-436-7789	439-0159
Web: www.sasos.com					
Sushi House 6 New Scotland Ave	Albany	NY	12208	518-935-2270	462-3860
Bing's 1952 Kensington Ave	Amherst	NY	14215	716-839-5788	839-5336
Scotch & Sirloin 3999 Maple Rd	Amherst	NY	14226	716-837-4900	837-0987
Web: www.frontstreetrestaurant.com					
Roberto's 603 Crescent Ave	Bronx	NY	10458	718-733-9503	733-2724
Web: www.usmenuguide.com					
Elia 8611 3rd Ave	Brooklyn	NY	11209	718-748-9891	748-9879
Web: www.eliarestaurant.com					
Frankies 457 Court Street Spuntino 457 Ct St	Brooklyn	NY	11231	718-403-0033	403-9260
Web: www.frankies457.com					
Grocery The 288 Smith St	Brooklyn	NY	11231	718-596-3335	
Web: www.thegroceryrestaurant.com					
Ici Restaurant 246 DeKalb Ave	Brooklyn	NY	11205	718-789-2778	
Web: www.icirestaurant.com					
Peter Luger Steak House 178 Broadway	Brooklyn	NY	11211	718-387-7400	387-3523
Web: www.peterluger.com					
River Cafe 1 Water St	Brooklyn	NY	11201	718-522-5200	875-0037
Web: www.rivercafe.com					
Saul 140 Smith St	Brooklyn	NY	11201	718-935-9844	
Web: www.saulrestaurant.com					
Acropolis Family Restaurant 708 Elmwood Ave	Buffalo	NY	14222	716-886-2977	886-4802
Web: www.acropolisopa.com					
Ambrosia 467 Elmwood Ave	Buffalo	NY	14222	716-881-2196	881-2220
Bijou Grille The 643 Main St	Buffalo	NY	14203	716-847-1512	852-3041
Web: www.bijougrille.com					
Billy Ogden's Lovejoy Grill 1834 William St	Buffalo	NY	14206	716-896-8018	896-4932
Blackthorn Restaurant & Pub 2134 Seneca St	Buffalo	NY	14210	716-825-9327	
Duff's 3651 Sheridan Dr	Buffalo	NY	14226	716-834-6234	831-5513
Fat Bob's Smokehouse 41 Virginia Pl	Buffalo	NY	14202	716-887-2971	332-1201
Web: www.fatbobs.com					
Frank & Teressa's Anchor Bar & Restaurant 1047 Main St	Buffalo	NY	14209	716-886-8920	
Web: www.anchorbar.com					
Friar's Table 301 Cleveland Dr	Buffalo	NY	14215	716-833-5554	833-5560
Web: www.thefriarstable.com					
Gigi's Restaurant 257 E Ferry St	Buffalo	NY	14208	716-883-1438	
Harry's Harbour Place Grille 2192 Niagara St	Buffalo	NY	14207	716-874-5400	874-0132
Web: www.harrysharbour.com					
Hutch's 1375 Delaware Ave	Buffalo	NY	14209	716-885-0074	881-0222
Web: www.hutchsrestaurant.com					
Ilio DiPaolo's 3785 S Pk Ave	Buffalo	NY	14219	716-825-3675	825-1054
Web: www.iliodipaolos.com					
La Dolce Vita Caffe & Bistro 1472 Hertel Ave	Buffalo	NY	14216	716-446-5690	
Web: www.iloveladolcevita.com					
Left Bank 511 Rhode Island St	Buffalo	NY	14213	716-882-3509	881-5895
Web: www.leftbankrestaurant.com					
Marco's 1085 Niagara St	Buffalo	NY	14213	716-886-8776	885-4399
Mother's 33 Virginia Pl	Buffalo	NY	14202	716-882-2989	
Oliver's 2095 Delaware Ave	Buffalo	NY	14216	716-877-9662	877-8291
Web: www.oliverscuisine.com					
Pearl Street Grill & Brewery 76 Pearl St	Buffalo	NY	14202	716-856-2337	849-0839
Web: www.pearlstreetgrill.com					
Rue Franklin 341 Franklin St	Buffalo	NY	14202	716-852-4416	852-4470
Web: www.ruefranklin.com					
Santasiero's 1329 Niagara St	Buffalo	NY	14213	716-886-9197	884-9338
Web: www.santasieros.com					
Scharf's Schiller Park Restaurant 34 S Crossman St	Buffalo	NY	14211	716-895-7249	894-1992
Web: www.scharfsrest.com					
Tandoori at Transit 7740 Transit Rd	Buffalo	NY	14221	716-632-1112	632-1130
Web: www.tandooris.com					
Salvatore's Italian Gardens 6461 Transit Rd	Depew	NY	14043	716-683-7990	
TF: 877-456-4097 ■ *Web:* www.salvatores.net					
Horizons 199 Woodcliff Dr	Fairport	NY	14450	585-248-4825	381-5673
Jovi's 2795 Delaware Ave	Kenmore	NY	14217	716-874-9103	
Casa Mono 52 Irving Pl	Manhattan	NY	10017	212-253-2773	253-5318
CRU Wine Bar and Restaurant 24 5th Ave	Manhattan	NY	10011	212-529-1700	529-6300
Jewel Bako 239 E 5th St	Manhattan	NY	10003	212-979-1012	
Web: www.degustationnyc.com					
Kittichai 60 Thompson St	Manhattan	NY	10012	212-219-2000	925-2971
Web: www.kittichairestaurant.com					
Shanghai Pavilion 1378 3rd Ave	Manhattan	NY	10021	212-585-3388	288-9235
Sugiyama 251 W 55th St	Manhattan	NY	10019	212-956-0670	956-0671
Web: www.sugiyama-nyc.com					
Sushi Zen 108 W 44th St	Manhattan	NY	10036	212-302-0707	944-7710
Web: www.sushizen-ny.com					
Tomoe Sushi 172 Thompson St	Manhattan	NY	10012	212-777-9346	
Aki 181 W 4th St	New York	NY	10014	212-989-5440	

Name / Address	City	State	ZIP	Phone	Fax
Alain Ducasse at the Essex House					
145 W 58th St.	New York	NY	10019	212-265-7300	
Web: www.alain-ducasse.com					
Annisa 13 Barrow St	New York	NY	10014	212-741-6699	
Web: www.annisarestaurant.com					
Aquagrill 210 Spring St	New York	NY	10012	212-274-0505	274-0587
Web: www.aquagrill.com					
Aquavit 65 E 55th St	New York	NY	10022	212-307-7311	
Web: www.aquavit.org					
Artisanal 2 Pk Ave	New York	NY	10016	212-725-8585	481-5455
Web: www.artisanalbistro.com					
Asia de Cuba 237 Madison Ave	New York	NY	10016	212-726-7755	726-7755
Web: www.chinagrillmgt.com/restaurants-and-bars/asia-de-cuba-morgans					
Atelier 50 Central Pk S	New York	NY	10019	212-521-6125	
Atlantic Grill 1341 3rd Ave	New York	NY	10021	212-988-9200	452-1447
Web: www.atlanticgrill.com					
August 359 Bleecker St	New York	NY	10014	212-929-4774	
Web: www.augustny.com					
Aureole 135 W 42nd St.	New York	NY	10036	212-319-1660	750-8613
Web: www.charliepalmer.com					
Babbo 110 Waverly Pl	New York	NY	10011	212-777-0303	
Web: www.babbonyc.com					
Balthazar 80 Spring St.	New York	NY	10012	212-965-1414	
Web: www.balthazarny.com					
Bar Americain 152 W 52nd St.	New York	NY	10019	212-265-9700	
Web: www.baramericain.com					
Barbuto 775 Washington St	New York	NY	10014	212-924-9700	924-9300
Web: www.barbutonyc.com					
Beacon Restaurant & Bar 25 W 56th St.	New York	NY	10019	212-332-0500	
Web: www.beaconnyc.com					
Biltmore Room 290 8th Ave.	New York	NY	10001	212-807-0111	807-0074
Web: www.biltmore.inetgroup.com					
BLT Prime 111 E 22nd St	New York	NY	10010	212-995-8500	460-5881
Web: www.e2hospitality.com/blt-prime-new-york					
Blue Fin 1567 Broadway	New York	NY	10036	212-918-1400	918-1300
Blue Hill 75 Washington Pl.	New York	NY	10011	212-539-1776	539-0959
Web: www.bluehillnyc.com					
Blue Ribbon 97 Sullivan St	New York	NY	10012	212-274-0404	274-1318
Web: www.blueribbonrestaurants.com					
Blue Water Grill 31 Union Sq W	New York	NY	10003	212-675-9500	675-1899
Boom Restaurant 152 Spring St.	New York	NY	10012	212-431-3663	431-3643
Web: www.boomny.com					
Bouley 120 W Broadway	New York	NY	10013	212-964-2525	219-3443
Web: www.bouley.net					
Cafe Boulud 20 E 76th St.	New York	NY	10021	212-772-2600	772-7755
Web: www.danielnyc.com					
Cafe Carlyle 35 E 76th St.	New York	NY	10021	212-744-1600	717-4682
Cafe Centro 200 Pk Ave.	New York	NY	10166	212-818-1222	949-8266
Cafe Gray 10 Columbus Cir 3rd Fl	New York	NY	10019	212-823-6338	823-6221
Web: www.cafegray.com					
Capsouto Freres 451 Washington St	New York	NY	10013	212-966-4900	925-5296
Web: www.capsoutofreres.com					
Caviar Russe 538 Madison Ave 2nd Fl	New York	NY	10022	212-980-5908	871-1842
Web: www.caviarrusse.com					
Chanterelle 2 Harrison St	New York	NY	10013	212-966-6960	966-6143
Web: www.chanterellenyc.com					
China Grill 60 W 53rd St	New York	NY	10019	212-333-7788	581-9299
Churrascaria Plataforma 316 W 49th St.	New York	NY	10019	212-245-0505	974-8250
Web: www.churrascariaplataforma.com					
Craft 43 E 19th St	New York	NY	10003	212-780-0880	780-0580
Web: www.craftrestaurant.com					
Daniel 60 E 65th St	New York	NY	10065	212-288-0033	396-9014
Web: www.danielnyc.com					
Danube 30 Hudson St.	New York	NY	10013	212-791-3771	693-7490
Dawat 210 E 58th St	New York	NY	10022	212-355-7555	355-1735
db Bistro Moderne 55 W 44th St	New York	NY	10036	212-391-2400	391-1188
Web: www.danielnyc.com					
Del Frisco's Double Eagle Steak House					
1221 Avenue of the Americas	New York	NY	10020	212-575-5129	575-4873
Web: www.delfriscos.com					
Del Posto 85 10th Ave	New York	NY	10011	212-497-8090	
Web: www.delposto.com					
Devi 8 E 18th St.	New York	NY	10003	212-691-1300	691-1695
Web: www.devinyc.com					
Donguri 309 E 83rd St.	New York	NY	10028	212-737-5656	
Eleven Madison Park 11 Madison Ave	New York	NY	10010	212-889-0905	
Web: www.elevenmadisonpark.com					
Erminia 250 E 83rd St.	New York	NY	10028	212-879-4284	
Web: www.erminiaristorante.com					
Estiatorio Milos 125 W 55th St.	New York	NY	10019	212-245-7400	245-4828
Web: www.milos.ca					
Felidia 243 E 58th St	New York	NY	10022	212-758-1479	935-7687
Web: www.felidia.lidiasitaly.com					
Firebird 365 W 46th St.	New York	NY	10036	212-586-0244	957-2983
Web: www.firebirdrestaurant.com					
Four Seasons 99 E 52nd St	New York	NY	10022	212-754-9494	754-1077
Web: www.fourseasonsrestaurant.com					
Gordon Ramsay at the London 151 W 54th St.	New York	NY	10019	212-468-8888	
Web: www.thelondonnyc.com					
Gotham Bar & Grill 12 E 12th St.	New York	NY	10003	212-620-4020	627-7810
Web: www.gothambarandgrill.com					
Gramercy Tavern 42 E 20th St	New York	NY	10003	212-477-0777	
Web: www.gramercytavern.com					
Hangawi 12 E 32nd St	New York	NY	10016	212-213-0077	689-0780
Web: www.hangawirestaurant.com					
Harrison The 355 Greenwich St.	New York	NY	10013	212-274-9310	274-9376
Web: www.theharrison.com/harrison.php					
Il Mulino 86 W 3rd St.	New York	NY	10012	212-673-3783	673-9875
Web: www.ilmulino.com					
Il Palazzo 151 Mulberry St.	New York	NY	10013	212-343-7000	343-1508
Jean Georges 1 Central Pk W	New York	NY	10023	212-299-3900	
Web: www.jean-georges.com					
JoJo 160 E 64th St.	New York	NY	10021	212-223-5656	755-9038
Kai 822 Madison Ave 2nd Fl	New York	NY	10021	212-988-7277	507-4500
Web: www.itoen.com					
Kuruma Zushi 7 E 47th St 2nd Fl	New York	NY	10017	212-317-2802	317-2803
L'Absinthe Restaurant 227 E 67th St.	New York	NY	10065	212-794-4950	794-1589
Web: www.labsinthe.com					
L'Impero 45 Tudor City Pl	New York	NY	10017	212-599-5045	599-5043
Web: www.limpero.com					
La Grenouille 3 E 52nd St	New York	NY	10022	212-752-1495	593-4964
Web: www.la-grenouille.com					
Le Bernardin 155 W 51st St.	New York	NY	10019	212-489-1515	554-1100
Web: www.le-bernardin.com					
Le Perigord 405 E 52nd St.	New York	NY	10022	212-755-6244	486-3906
Web: www.leperigord.com					
Lupa Osteria Romana 170 Thompson St	New York	NY	10012	212-982-5089	982-5490
Web: www.luparestaurant.com					
Maloney & Porcelli 37 E 50th St	New York	NY	10022	212-750-2233	750-2252
Web: www.maloneyandporcelli.com					
Mas (Farmhouse) 39 Downing St	New York	NY	10014	212-255-1790	255-0279
Masa 10 Columbus Cir Time Warner Ctr 4th Fl.	New York	NY	10019	212-823-9800	
Web: www.masanyc.com					
Megu 62 Thomas St	New York	NY	10013	212-964-7777	
Web: www.megurestaurants.com					
Mercer Kitchen 99 Prince St.	New York	NY	10012	212-966-5454	965-3855
Web: www.jean-georges.com					
Mesa Grill 102 5th Ave.	New York	NY	10011	212-807-7400	989-0039
Web: www.mesagrill.com					
Metrazur					
Charlie Palmer					
404 Grand Central Terminal E Balcony	New York	NY	10017	212-687-4600	687-5671
Web: www.charliepalmer.com/metrazur					
Mexican Mama 525 Hudson St.	New York	NY	10014	212-924-4119	
Michael Jordan's Steak House					
23 Vanderbilt Ave	New York	NY	10017	212-655-2300	655-4915
Michael's New York 24 W 55th St	New York	NY	10019	212-767-0555	581-6778
Web: www.michaelsnewyork.com					
NIOS Restaurant & Wine Bar 130 W 46th St	New York	NY	10036	212-485-2999	485-2789
Web: www.niosrestaurant.com					
Nobu 105 Hudson St	New York	NY	10013	212-219-0500	219-1441
Web: www.noburestaurants.com					
Oceana 1221 Avenue of the Americas	New York	NY	10020	212-759-5941	759-6076
Web: www.oceanarestaurant.com					
Old Homestead Steakhouse 56 9th Ave	New York	NY	10011	212-242-9040	727-1637
Web: www.theoldhomesteadsteakhouse.com					
Olives New York 201 Pk Ave S	New York	NY	10003	212-353-8345	353-9592
Web: www.toddenglish.com					
One if by Land Two if by Sea 17 Barrow St.	New York	NY	10014	212-255-8649	304-2900*
**Fax Area Code:* 646 ■ *TF:* 800-228-0822 ■ *Web:* www.oneifbyland.com					
Ouest 2315 Broadway	New York	NY	10024	212-580-8700	580-1360
Web: www.ouestny.com					
Palm Restaurant 837 2nd Ave	New York	NY	10017	212-687-2953	983-4584
Web: www.thepalm.com					
Pampano 209 E 49th St	New York	NY	10017	212-751-4545	
Web: www.richardsandoval.com					
Park Avenue Summer 100 E 63rd St	New York	NY	10065	212-644-1900	688-0373
Web: www.parkavenuecafe.com					
Pearl Oyster Bar 18 Cornelia St	New York	NY	10014	212-691-8211	691-8210
Web: www.pearloysterbar.com					
Peasant 194 Elizabeth St	New York	NY	10012	212-965-9511	965-8174
Web: www.peasantnyc.com					
Per Se 10 Columbus Cir 4th Fl	New York	NY	10019	212-823-9335	823-9497
Web: www.perseny.com					
Periyali 35 W 20th St	New York	NY	10011	212-463-7890	924-9403
Web: www.periyali.com					
Petrossian 182 W 58th St	New York	NY	10019	212-245-2214	245-2812
Web: www.petrossian.com					
Picholine 35 W 64th St	New York	NY	10023	212-724-8585	875-8979
Web: www.picholinenyc.com					
Po 31 Cornelia St.	New York	NY	10014	212-645-2189	367-9448
Web: www.porestaurant.com					
Poke Restaurant 305 E 85th St.	New York	NY	10028	212-249-0569	
Post House The 28 E 63rd St	New York	NY	10021	212-935-2888	371-9264
Web: www.theposthouse.com					
Prime Grill 60 E 49th St	New York	NY	10017	212-692-9292	
Web: www.theprimegrill.com					
Remi 145 W 53rd St	New York	NY	10019	212-581-4242	581-5948
Rothmann's Steakhouse & Grill 3 E 54th St	New York	NY	10022	212-319-5500	319-5540
Web: www.rothmanns54.com					
Scalini Fedeli 165 Duane St	New York	NY	10013	212-528-0400	587-8773
Web: www.scalinifedeli.com					
Sea Grill Restaurant 19 W 49th St.	New York	NY	10020	212-332-7610	332-7677
Web: www.theseagrillnyc.com					
Shun Lee Palace 155 E 55th St.	New York	NY	10022	212-371-8844	752-1936
Web: www.shunleepalace.com					
Sparks Steak House 210 E 46th St.	New York	NY	10017	212-687-4855	557-7409
Web: www.sparkssteakhouse.com					
Spice Market 403 W 13th St	New York	NY	10014	212-675-2322	675-4365
Web: www.jean-georges.com					
Strip House 13 E 12th St	New York	NY	10003	212-328-0000	337-0233
Sushi of Gari 402 E 78th St	New York	NY	10021	212-517-5340	
Sushi Seki 1143 1st Ave.	New York	NY	10021	212-371-0238	
Sushi Yasuda 204 E 43rd St.	New York	NY	10017	212-972-1001	972-1717
Web: www.sushiyasuda.com					
Tabla 11 Madison Ave.	New York	NY	10010	212-889-0667	889-3865
Web: www.tablany.com					
Tamarind 43 E 22nd St # 42	New York	NY	10010	212-674-7400	674-4449
Web: www.tamarinde22.com					
Tavern on the Green					
W 67th St & Central Pk W	New York	NY	10023	212-873-3200	
Terrace in the Sky 400 W 119th St.	New York	NY	10027	212-666-9490	666-3471
Web: www.terraceinthesky.com					

Restaurant	City	State	ZIP	Phone	Fax
Thalia 828 8th Ave	New York	NY	10019	212-399-4444	399-3268
Web: www.restaurantthalia.com					
Tocqueville 1 E 15th St	New York	NY	10003	212-647-1515	647-7148
Web: www.tocquevillerestaurant.com					
Trattoria dell'Arte 900 7th Ave	New York	NY	10106	212-245-9800	265-3296
Web: www.trattoriadellarte.com					
Triomphe 49 W 44th St	New York	NY	10036	212-453-4233	827-0464
Web: www.triomphe-newyork.com					
Union Square Cafe 21 E 16th St	New York	NY	10003	212-243-4020	627-2673
Veritas 43 E 20th St	New York	NY	10003	212-353-3700	353-1632
Web: www.veritas-nyc.com					
Wallse 344 W 11th St	New York	NY	10014	212-352-2300	645-7127
Web: www.wallse.com					
Wolfgang's Steakhouse 4 Pk Ave	New York	NY	10016	212-889-3369	889-6845
Web: www.wolfgangssteakhouse.net					
Butcher Block Rt 3 & Exit 37	Plattsburgh	NY	12901	518-563-0920	566-1201
Web: www.butcherblockrestaurant.com					
Erawan 42-31 Bell Blvd	Queens	NY	11361	718-428-2112	428-2098
Web: www.erawanthai.com					
Sapori d'Ischia 55-15 37th Ave	Queens	NY	11377	718-446-1500	446-0134
Sripraphai 64-13 39th Ave	Queens	NY	11377	718-899-9599	
Web: www.sripraphai.com					
Agatina's 2967 Buffalo Rd	Rochester	NY	14624	585-426-0510	
Web: www.agatinas.com					
Aladdin's Natural Eatery 646 Monroe Ave	Rochester	NY	14607	585-442-5000	442-0550
Web: www.aladdinsnaturaleatery.com					
Bacco's 263 Pk Ave	Rochester	NY	14607	585-442-5090	
Bathtub Billy's 630 Ridge Rd W	Rochester	NY	14615	585-865-6510	865-6323
Web: www.bathtubbillys.com					
Benucci's 3349 Monroe Ave	Rochester	NY	14618	585-264-1300	264-1926
Web: www.benuccis.com					
Bernard's Grove 187 Long Pond Rd	Rochester	NY	14612	585-227-6405	723-5915
Web: www.bernardsgrove.com					
Brook House 3590 Ridge Rd W	Rochester	NY	14626	585-723-9988	723-9993
California Rollin' 274 N Goodman St	Rochester	NY	14607	585-271-8990	
Edibles Restaurant & Bar 704 University Ave	Rochester	NY	14607	585-271-4910	
Web: www.ediblesrochester.com					
Elmwood Inn The 1256 Mt Hope Ave	Rochester	NY	14620	585-271-5195	271-6689
Grill at Strathallan The 550 E Ave	Rochester	NY	14607	585-454-1880	
Web: www.strathallan.com					
Hogan's Hideaway 197 Pk Ave	Rochester	NY	14607	585-442-4293	461-4965
Web: www.hoganshideaway.com					
India House 998 S Clinton Ave	Rochester	NY	14620	585-461-0880	461-5918
Lucano 1815 E Ave	Rochester	NY	14610	585-244-3460	
Web: www.ristorantelucano.com					
Mamasan 309 University Ave	Rochester	NY	14607	585-262-4580	
Mario's Via Abruzzi 2740 Monroe Ave	Rochester	NY	14618	585-271-1111	
Web: www.mariosit.com					
Phillips European Restaurant 26 Corporate Woods	Rochester	NY	14623	585-272-9910	272-1778
Web: www.phillipseuropean.com					
Portofino Bistro & Catering 2171 W Henrietta Rd	Rochester	NY	14623	585-427-0410	424-1283
Web: www.portofinorochester.com					
Remington's 425 Merchants Rd	Rochester	NY	14609	585-482-4434	244-0710
Web: www.remingtonsrochester.com					
Salena's 247 N Goodman St	Rochester	NY	14607	585-256-5980	256-7428
Web: www.salenas.com					
1060 at the Genesee Grande 1060 E Genesee St	Syracuse	NY	13214	315-476-9000	
Alto Cinco 526 Westcott St	Syracuse	NY	13210	315-472-3633	
Web: www.altocinco.net					
Angotti's 725 Burnet Ave	Syracuse	NY	13203	315-472-8403	472-4149
Blue Tusk 165 Walton St	Syracuse	NY	13218	315-472-1934	
Web: www.bluetusk.com					
Casa Di Copani 3414 Burnet Ave	Syracuse	NY	13206	315-463-1031	
Daniel Jack's Entertainment Restaurant 218 Walton St	Syracuse	NY	13202	315-475-8357	
Delmonico's Italian Steakhouse Syracuse 2950 Erie Blvd E	Syracuse	NY	13224	315-445-1111	445-0257
Web: www.delmonicositaliansteakhouse.com					
Joey's Restaurant 6594 Thompson Rd	Syracuse	NY	13206	315-432-0315	
Juanita's Mexican Kitchen 600 Ct St	Syracuse	NY	13208	315-478-2185	
King David's 129 Marshall St	Syracuse	NY	13210	315-471-5000	
Web: www.kingdavids.com					
L'Adour Restaurant francais 110 Montgomery St	Syracuse	NY	13202	315-475-7653	471-9713
Web: www.ladour.com					
Lemon Grass 238 W Jefferson St	Syracuse	NY	13202	315-475-1111	475-3287
Web: www.lemongrassny.com					
Little Thai House 2863 1/2 Erie Blvd E	Syracuse	NY	13224	315-251-1366	
Luigi's 1524 Valley Dr	Syracuse	NY	13207	315-492-9997	
Mission The 304 E Onondaga St	Syracuse	NY	13202	315-475-7344	475-7340
Pascale Wine Bar & Restaurant 204 W Fayette St	Syracuse	NY	13202	315-637-8321	
Phoebe's 900 E Genesee St	Syracuse	NY	13210	315-475-5154	
Web: www.phoebessyracuse.com					
Redfield's 701 E Genesee St	Syracuse	NY	13210	315-479-7000	
Riley's 312 Pk St	Syracuse	NY	13203	315-471-7111	
Saratoga Steaks & Seafood 200 Waring Rd	Syracuse	NY	13224	315-445-1976	446-2094
Syracuse Suds Factory 320 S Clinton St	Syracuse	NY	13202	315-471-2253	
Web: www.sudsfactory.com					
Tokyo-Seoul 3180 Erie Blvd E	Syracuse	NY	13214	315-449-2688	
Jasmine 1330 Niagara Falls Blvd	Tonawanda	NY	14150	716-838-3011	332-0280
Web: www.jasminethairestaurant.com					
Ferrara's Seafood-Pasta Grill 2150 Central Pk Ave	Yonkers	NY	10710	914-961-8908	961-8908
Hunan Village Restaurant 1828 Central Pk Ave	Yonkers	NY	10710	914-779-2272	779-0164
Kang Suh 2375 Central Pk Ave	Yonkers	NY	10710	914-771-4066	
La Lanterna 23 Grey Oaks Ave	Yonkers	NY	10710	914-476-3060	375-7477
Web: www.lalanterna.com					
Louie's 187 S Broadway	Yonkers	NY	10701	914-969-8821	963-2418
Nyauta 27 Meyers Ave	Yonkers	NY	10704	914-476-1910	476-8878
Patang 2223 Central Pk Ave	Yonkers	NY	10710	914-793-8888	961-5300
Web: www.patangcuisine.com					
Renegades Bar & Grill 748 Yonkers Ave	Yonkers	NY	10704	914-375-2233	
Rory Dolan's 890 McLean Ave	Yonkers	NY	10704	914-776-2946	776-6538
Web: www.rorydolans.com					
Spiritoso 811 McLean Ave	Yonkers	NY	10704	914-237-4075	237-5713
Tombolino Restaurant 356 Kimball Ave	Yonkers	NY	10704	914-237-1266	237-1254
Web: www.tombolinorestaurant.com					
Ya Hala 326 S Broadway	Yonkers	NY	10705	914-476-4200	
Web: www.yahalarestaurant.com					
Zuppa 59 Main St	Yonkers	NY	10701	914-376-6500	376-4900
Web: www.zupparestaurant.com					

NORTH CAROLINA

Restaurant	City	State	ZIP	Phone	Fax
Blue Ridge Dining Room 290 Macon Ave	Asheville	NC	28804	828-252-2711	252-7053
Charlotte Street Grill & Pub 157 Charlotte St	Asheville	NC	28801	828-253-5348	
Web: www.charlottestreetgrill.com					
Cottonwood Cafe 122 College St	Asheville	NC	28801	828-281-0710	281-3549
Web: www.fioresasheville.com					
Doc Chey's Noodle House 37 Biltmore Ave	Asheville	NC	28801	828-252-8220	
Web: www.doccheys.com					
India Garden 156 S Tunnel Rd	Asheville	NC	28805	828-298-5001	298-5007
La Caterina Trattoria 39 Elm St	Asheville	NC	28801	828-254-1148	281-1051
Web: www.lacaterina.com					
Laughing Seed Cafe 40 Wall St	Asheville	NC	28801	828-252-3445	252-0104
Web: www.laughingseed.com					
Magnolia's Raw Bar & Grille 26 E Walnut St	Asheville	NC	28801	828-251-5211	
Market Place The 20 Wall St	Asheville	NC	28801	828-252-4162	253-3120
Web: www.marketplace-restaurant.com					
Moose Cafe 570 Brevard Rd	Asheville	NC	28806	828-255-0920	255-0042
Ristorante da Vincenzo 10 N Market St	Asheville	NC	28801	828-254-4698	
Web: www.vincenzos.com					
Salsa 6 Patton Ave	Asheville	NC	28801	828-252-9805	252-9805
Savoy Restaurant & Martini Bar 641 Merrimon Ave	Asheville	NC	28804	828-253-1077	252-6776
Web: www.savoyasheville.com					
Sorrento 875 Tunnel Rd	Asheville	NC	28805	828-299-1928	
Sunset Terrace 290 Macon Ave	Asheville	NC	28804	828-252-2711	252-6442
Web: www.groveparkinn.com					
Tripps 311 College St	Asheville	NC	28801	828-254-9163	252-8448
Tupelo Honey Cafe 12 College St	Asheville	NC	28801	828-255-4863	255-4864
Web: www.tupelohoneycafe.com					
Yoshida Japanese Steak House 4 Regent Pk Blvd	Asheville	NC	28806	828-252-5903	258-3514
Zambra! 85 W Walnut St	Asheville	NC	28801	828-232-1060	
Web: www.zambratapas.com					
Aria Tuscan Grill 100 N Tryon St	Charlotte	NC	28202	704-376-8880	344-2563
Web: www.sonomarestaurants.net					
Baoding 4722 Sharon Rd Suite F	Charlotte	NC	28210	704-552-8899	552-8828
Barrington's 7822 Fairview Rd	Charlotte	NC	28226	704-364-5755	364-5732
Web: www.barringtonsrestaurant.com					
Big Ben British Pub & Restaurant 2000 S Blvd	Charlotte	NC	28203	704-817-9697	
Web: www.bigbenpub.com					
Bill Spoon's Barbecue 5524 S Blvd	Charlotte	NC	28217	704-525-8865	
Blue Restaurant & Bar 206 N College St	Charlotte	NC	28202	704-927-2583	927-0555
Web: www.bluecharlotte.com					
Bonterra Dining & Wine Room 1829 Cleveland Ave	Charlotte	NC	28203	704-333-9463	372-9463
Web: www.bonterradining.com					
Cajun Queen 1800 E 7th St	Charlotte	NC	28204	704-377-9017	
Web: www.cajunqueen.net					
Carpe Diem 1535 Elizabeth Ave	Charlotte	NC	28204	704-377-7976	377-7975
Web: www.carpediemrestaurant.com					
Charleston House on the Plaza 3128 The Plaza	Charlotte	NC	28205	704-333-4441	
Frankie's 710 710 W Trade St	Charlotte	NC	28202	704-379-7555	379-7580
Web: www.sonomarestaurants.net					
Greek Isles 200 E Bland St	Charlotte	NC	28203	704-444-9000	373-2883
Web: www.greekislesrestaurant.com					
Ilios Noche 11508 Providence Rd	Charlotte	NC	28277	704-814-9882	
Jaimama Restaurant 1626 E Blvd	Charlotte	NC	28203	704-358-8188	
Jim Noble Restaurant 6801 Morrison Blvd	Charlotte	NC	28211	704-367-9463	367-9443
Web: www.noblesrestaurants.com					
Latorre's 118 W 5th St	Charlotte	NC	28202	704-377-4448	377-4449
LaVecchia's Seafood Grille 214 N Tryon St	Charlotte	NC	28202	704-370-6776	370-0016
Web: www.lavecchias.com					
Luce Ristorante & Bar 214 N Tryon St Suite J	Charlotte	NC	28202	704-344-9222	344-9909
Web: www.luceristorante.net					
Mama Ricotta's 601 S Kings Dr	Charlotte	NC	28204	704-343-0148	377-7461
Web: www.mamaricottasrestaurant.com					
McCormick & Schmick's 200 S Tryon St	Charlotte	NC	28202	704-377-0201	377-0208
Web: www.mccormickandschmicks.com					
McNinch House 511 N Church St	Charlotte	NC	28202	704-332-6159	376-0212
Web: www.mcninchhouserestaurant.com					
Melting Pot of Charlotte The 901 S Kings Dr Suite 140B	Charlotte	NC	28204	704-334-4400	334-0535
Web: www.meltingpot.com					
Mert's Heart & Soul 214 N College St	Charlotte	NC	28202	704-342-4222	342-4499
Web: www.uptown2go.com					
Mickey & Mooch The other Joint 8128 Providence Rd Suite 1200	Charlotte	NC	28277	704-752-8080	
Web: www.mickeyandmooch.com					
Mimosa Grill 327 S Tryon St	Charlotte	NC	28202	704-343-0700	343-9002
Web: www.harpersgroup.com					
Miro Spanish Grille 7804A Red Rd Suite A	Charlotte	NC	28277	704-540-7374	540-7388
Web: www.mirospanishgrille.com					

				Phone	Fax
Musashi 10110 Johnston Rd	Charlotte	NC	28210	704-543-5181	
Web: www.musashi-nc.com					
New South Kitchen & Bar 8140 Providence Rd Suite 300	Charlotte	NC	28277	704-541-9990	541-1163
Web: www.newsouthkitchen.com					
Nikko 325 Arlington Ave	Charlotte	NC	28203	704-370-0100	
Web: www.nikkosushibar.net					
Old Hickory House Restaurant 6538 N Tryon St	Charlotte	NC	28213	704-596-8014	596-0922
Patou French Bistro 1315 E Blvd	Charlotte	NC	28203	704-376-2233	376-8658
Web: www.patoubistro.com					
Pewter Rose Bistro 1820 S Blvd	Charlotte	NC	28203	704-332-8149	333-7075
Web: www.pewterrose.com					
Portofino 3124 Eastway Dr	Charlotte	NC	28205	704-568-7933	
Senor Tequila 6414 Rea Rd	Charlotte	NC	28277	704-543-0706	
Sullivan's Steakhouse 1928 S Blvd	Charlotte	NC	28203	704-335-8228	333-8797
Web: www.sullivansteakhouse.com					
Thai Orchid 4223 Providence Rd	Charlotte	NC	28211	704-364-1134	
Web: www.thaiorchidcharlotte.com					
Toscana 6401 Morrison Blvd	Charlotte	NC	28211	704-367-1808	367-0854
Upstream *Harper's Restaurant Group* 6902 Phillips Pl Ct	Charlotte	NC	28210	704-556-7730	552-2793
Web: www.harpersgroup.com/upstream.asp					
Villa Antonio 4707 S Blvd	Charlotte	NC	28217	704-523-1594	523-5697
Web: www.villaantonio.com					
Volare Ristorante Italiano 1523 Elizabeth Ave	Charlotte	NC	28204	704-370-0208	370-2584
Web: www.volareristoranteitaliano.com					
Zebra 4521 Sharon Rd	Charlotte	NC	28211	704-442-9525	442-9546
Web: www.zebrarestaurant.net					
Another Thyme 109 N Gregson St	Durham	NC	27701	919-682-5225	
Web: www.anotherthyme.com					
Bennett Pointe Grill 4625 Hillsborough Rd	Durham	NC	27705	919-382-9431	382-8073
Web: www.bpgrill.com					
Blue Corn Cafe 716 9th St	Durham	NC	27705	919-286-9600	416-0862
Web: bluecorncafedurham.com					
Bullock's Bar-B-Que 3330 Quebec Dr	Durham	NC	27705	919-383-3211	383-6202
Web: www.bullocksbbq.com					
Cafe Parizade 2200 W Main St	Durham	NC	27705	919-286-9712	416-9706
Web: www.parizadedurham.com					
El Rodeo 3404 Westgate Dr	Durham	NC	27707	919-402-9190	
Fairview Restaurant 3001 Cameron Blvd	Durham	NC	27705	919-493-6699	681-3514
Fishmonger's 806 W Main St	Durham	NC	27701	919-682-0128	
Web: www.fishmongers.net					
Four Square 2701 Chapel Hill Rd	Durham	NC	27707	919-401-9877	401-9878
Web: www.foursquarerestaurant.com					
Hog Heaven Bar-B-Q 2419 Guess Rd	Durham	NC	27705	919-286-7447	286-2829
Web: www.hogheavenbarbecue.com					
Jamaica Jamaica 4853 Hwy 55	Durham	NC	27713	919-544-1532	
Kanki Japanese House of Steaks 3504 Mt Moriah Rd	Durham	NC	27707	919-401-6908	401-6843
Web: www.kanki.com					
Kemp's Seafood House 115 Page Pt Cir	Durham	NC	27703	919-957-7155	957-0758
Kurama Seafood & Steakhouse 3644 Chapel Hill Blvd	Durham	NC	27707	919-489-2669	489-4400
Web: www.kuramadurham.com					
Magnolia Grill 1002 9th St	Durham	NC	27705	919-286-3609	
Web: www.magnoliagrill.net					
Nana's 2514 University Dr	Durham	NC	27707	919-493-8545	403-8487
Web: www.nanasdurham.com					
Neo-China 4015 University Dr	Durham	NC	27707	919-489-2828	489-9898
Web: www.neo-china.com					
Papas Grill 1821 Hillandale Rd	Durham	NC	27705	919-383-8502	382-9529
Web: www.papasgrille.com					
Pop's Italian Trattoria 810 W Peabody St	Durham	NC	27701	919-956-7677	688-0098
Web: www.pops-durham.com					
Q Shack The 2510 University Dr	Durham	NC	27707	919-402-4227	
Satisfaction Restaurant 905 W Main St Suite 37	Durham	NC	27701	919-682-7397	682-6642
Web: www.satisfactionrestaurant.com					
Shanghai Restaurant 3433 Hillsborough Rd	Durham	NC	27705	919-383-7581	383-7581
Web: www.shanghai.ypguides.net					
Shiki Sushi 207 W Nc Hwy 54	Durham	NC	27713	919-484-4108	484-4168
Web: www.shikisushionline.com					
Spice & Curry 2105 E Hwy 54	Durham	NC	27713	919-544-7555	544-7110
Web: www.spicencurry.net					
Torero's 800 W Main St	Durham	NC	27701	919-682-4197	682-2662
Tosca Ristorante Italiano 604 W Morgan St	Durham	NC	27701	919-680-6333	
Web: www.bluecorn-tosca.com/tr_home.asp					
Vin Rouge Bistro *GHG Restaurant Group* 2010 Hillsborough Rd	Durham	NC	27705	919-416-0406	
Web: www.vinrougerestaurant.com					
Acropolis Restaurant 416 N Eugene St	Greensboro	NC	27401	336-273-3306	273-3353
Anton's 1628 Battleground Ave	Greensboro	NC	27408	336-273-1386	273-1225
Asahi 4520 W Market St	Greensboro	NC	27407	336-855-8883	
Bangkok Cafe 1203-C S Holden Rd	Greensboro	NC	24707	336-855-9370	
Bert's Seafood Grille 4608 W Market St	Greensboro	NC	27407	336-854-2314	297-4885
Web: www.bertsseafoodgrille.com					
Bianca's 1901 Spring Garden St	Greensboro	NC	27403	336-273-8114	
Web: www.biancasitalianrestaurant.com					
Binh Minh 5211-C W Market St	Greensboro	NC	27409	336-851-1527	851-1552
Boba House 332 S Tate St	Greensboro	NC	27403	336-379-7444	
Web: www.bobahouse.com					
Bonefish Grill 2100 Koury Blvd	Greensboro	NC	27407	336-851-8900	851-8910
Web: www.bonefishgrill.com					
Cafe Pasta 305 State St	Greensboro	NC	27408	336-272-1308	272-1352
Web: www.cafepasta.com					
Casaldi's Cafe 1310 Westover Terr Suite 107	Greensboro	NC	27408	336-379-8191	379-0341
Cooper's Ale House 5340 W Market St	Greensboro	NC	27409	336-294-0575	292-8603
Web: www.coopers-ale-house.com					
Darryl's 3300 High Pt Rd	Greensboro	NC	27407	336-294-1781	294-2242
George K's Catering & Banquet Hall 2108 Cedar Fork Dr	Greensboro	NC	27407	336-854-0008	854-7841
Web: www.georgeks.net					
Green Valley Grill 622 Green Valley Rd	Greensboro	NC	27408	336-854-2015	544-9000
Web: www.greenvalleygrill.com					
Hugo's Food Sports & Spirits 3011-A Spring Garden St Suite A	Greensboro	NC	27403	336-852-9421	852-7061
Web: www.hugosmenu.com					
India Palace 413 Tate St	Greensboro	NC	27403	336-379-0744	
Leblon 4512 W Market St	Greensboro	NC	27407	336-294-2605	294-2606
Web: www.leblonbraziliansteakhouse.com					
Liberty Oak Restaurant & Bar 100 W Washington St # D	Greensboro	NC	27401	336-273-7057	273-7111
Web: www.libertyoakrestaurant.com					
Marisol 5834 High Pt Rd	Greensboro	NC	27407	336-852-3303	852-0347
Web: www.themarisol.com					
Melting Pot of Greensboro The 2924 Battleground Ave	Greensboro	NC	27408	336-545-6233	545-6448
Web: www.meltingpot.com					
Monterrey 3724 Battleground Ave	Greensboro	NC	27410	336-282-5588	282-7794
Rearn Thai Restaurant 5120 W Market St	Greensboro	NC	27409	336-292-5901	
Saigon 4205 High Pt Rd	Greensboro	NC	27407	336-294-9286	294-9994
Web: www.saigonrestaurant.net					
Sapporo Japanese Steak House 2939 C Battleground Ave	Greensboro	NC	27408	336-282-5345	282-5379
Southern Lights 2415 Lawndale Dr	Greensboro	NC	27408	336-379-9414	273-3875
Stamey's Barbecue 2206 High Pt Rd	Greensboro	NC	27403	336-299-9888	294-2599
Web: www.stameys.com					
Taste of Thai 1500 Mill St	Greensboro	NC	27408	336-273-1318	273-0180
Web: www.tasteofthaigreensboro.com					
Undercurrent The 327 Battleground Ave	Greensboro	NC	27401	336-370-1266	
Web: www.undercurrentrestaurant.com					
Village Tavern 1903 Westridge Rd	Greensboro	NC	27410	336-282-3063	545-1953
Web: www.villagetavern.com					
Villarosa Italian Restaurant & Grill 6010 Landmark Ctr Blvd	Greensboro	NC	27407	336-294-8688	294-8688
Web: www.villarosaitalian.com					
518 West 518 W Jones St	Raleigh	NC	27603	919-829-2518	829-0248
Web: www.518west.com					
Angus Barn 9401 Glenwood Ave	Raleigh	NC	27617	919-781-2444	783-5568
Web: www.angusbarn.com					
Bella Monica 3121 Edwards Mill Rd Suite 103	Raleigh	NC	27612	919-881-9778	881-1241
Web: www.bellamonica.com					
Bloomsbury Bistro 509-101 W Whitaker Mill Rd	Raleigh	NC	27608	919-834-9011	834-9096
Web: www.bloomsburybistro.com					
Caffe Luna 136 E Hargett St	Raleigh	NC	27601	919-832-6090	832-0176
Web: www.cafeluna.com					
Carvers Creek 2711 Capital Blvd	Raleigh	NC	27604	919-872-2300	
Web: www.carverscreek.com					
Cooper's Barbeque 109 E Davie St	Raleigh	NC	27601	919-832-7614	
Dalat 2109-120 Avent Ferry Rd	Raleigh	NC	27606	919-832-7449	832-9620
Duck & Dumpling The 222 S Blount St	Raleigh	NC	27601	919-838-0085	838-0087
Web: www.theduckanddumpling.com					
Frazier's Bistro 2418 Hillsborough St	Raleigh	NC	27607	919-828-6699	787-9994
Web: www.frazierswinebar.com					
Irregardless Cafe 901 W Morgan St	Raleigh	NC	27603	919-833-8898	
Kanki Japanese House of Steaks 4500 Old Wake Forest Rd	Raleigh	NC	27609	919-876-4157	876-7699
Web: www.kanki.com					
Melting Pot of Raleigh The 3100 Wake Forest Rd	Raleigh	NC	27609	919-878-0477	878-0815
Web: www.meltingpot.com					
Neo-Asia 6602 Glenwood Ave	Raleigh	NC	27612	919-783-8383	783-8353
Web: www.neo-china.com					
Nina's 8801 Lead Mine Rd	Raleigh	NC	27615	919-845-1122	
PF Chang's China Bistro 4325 Glenwood Ave	Raleigh	NC	27612	919-787-7754	787-7683
Web: www.pfchangs.com					
Prime Only 505 W Jones St	Raleigh	NC	27613	919-835-2649	844-1219
Web: www.primeonlydowntown.com					
Rey's 1130 Buck Jones Rd	Raleigh	NC	27606	919-380-0122	380-0411
Web: www.reysrestaurant.com					
Ruth's Chris Steakhouse 2010 Renaissance Pk Pl	Raleigh	NC	27513	919-677-0033	677-8633
Web: www.ruthschris.com					
Saint-Jacques 6112 Falls of the Neuse Rd	Raleigh	NC	27609	919-862-2770	862-2771
Second Empire 330 Hillsborough St	Raleigh	NC	27603	919-829-3663	
Web: www.second-empire.com					
ShabaShabu 3080 Wake Forest Rd	Raleigh	NC	27609	919-501-7755	501-7479
Sullivan's Steakhouse 414 Glenwood Ave Suite 103	Raleigh	NC	27603	919-833-2888	833-2889
Web: www.sullivansteakhouse.com					
Sushi Blues 301 Glenwood Ave	Raleigh	NC	27603	919-664-8061	664-8070
Web: www.sushibluescafe.com					
Waraji 5910 Duraleigh Rd Suite 147	Raleigh	NC	27612	919-783-1883	783-0693
Web: www.waraji.com					
Zely & Ritz 301 Glenwood Ave	Raleigh	NC	27603	919-828-0018	828-2937
Web: www.zelyandritz.com					
1703 Restaurant 1703 Robin Hood Rd	Winston-Salem	NC	27104	336-725-5767	725-5768
Web: www.1703restaurantws.com					
Arigato Japanese Steak House 585 Bethesda St	Winston-Salem	NC	27103	336-765-7798	765-4053
Bayberry The 420 High St	Winston-Salem	NC	27101	336-777-3000	
Bernardin's 373 Jonestown Rd	Winston-Salem	NC	27104	336-768-9365	
Web: www.bernardinsfinedining.com					
Cha-Da Thai 420-J Jonestown Rd	Winston-Salem	NC	27104	336-659-8466	659-8458
East China 216 Summit Sq Blvd	Winston-Salem	NC	27105	336-377-9191	
Forsyth Seafood Cafe 108 ML King Dr	Winston-Salem	NC	27101	336-748-0793	
Franco's 420 Jonestown Rd	Winston-Salem	NC	27104	336-659-7778	659-7778
Hill's Lexington Barbecue 4005 Patterson Ave	Winston-Salem	NC	27105	336-767-2184	
Ishi Japanese Restaurant 121 Stark St	Winston-Salem	NC	27103	336-774-0433	774-0451

Name / Address	City	State	Zip	Phone	Fax
Midtown Cafe & Dessertery 151 S Stratford Rd — Web: www.midtowncafews.com	Winston-Salem	NC	27104	336-724-9800	724-9830
Newab Indian Cuisine 129 S Stratford Rd	Winston-Salem	NC	27104	336-725-3949	725-8434
Newtown Bistro & Bar 420 Jonestown Rd Suite U — Web: www.newtownbistro.com	Winston-Salem	NC	27104	336-659-8062	659-9835
Noble's Grill 380 Knollwood St — Web: www.noblesrestaurant.com	Winston-Salem	NC	27103	336-777-8477	777-0322
Old Fourth Street Filling Station The 871 W 4th St — Web: www.theoldfourthstreetfillingstation.com	Winston-Salem	NC	27101	336-724-7600	724-6300
Par 3 Bistro 3870 Bethania Stn Rd	Winston-Salem	NC	27106	336-924-5850	
Paul's Fine Italian Dining 3443-B Robinhood Rd	Winston-Salem	NC	27106	336-768-2645	
Ryan's 719 Coliseum Dr — Web: www.ryansrestaurant.com	Winston-Salem	NC	27106	336-724-6132	724-5761
Sampan Chinese Restaurant 985 Peters Creek Pkwy	Winston-Salem	NC	27103	336-777-8266	
Sweet Potatoes 529 N Trade St — Web: www.sweetpotatoes-arestaurant.com	Winston-Salem	NC	27101	336-727-4844	727-4808
Szechuan Palace 3040 Healy Dr	Winston-Salem	NC	27103	336-768-7123	
Tequila 2802 Reynolda Rd	Winston-Salem	NC	27106	336-727-9547	
Tokyo Japanese Steakhouse 1111 Salisbury Ridge Rd — Web: www.tjsteakhouse.com	Winston-Salem	NC	27127	336-722-5009	722-5059
Village Tavern 2000 Griffith Rd — Web: www.villagetavern.com	Winston-Salem	NC	27103	336-760-8686	774-0001
Vincenzo's 3449 Robinhood Rd	Winston-Salem	NC	27106	336-765-3176	

NORTH DAKOTA

Name / Address	City	State	Zip	Phone	Fax
Bistro An American Cafe 1103 E Front Ave — Web: www.bistro1100.com	Bismarck	ND	58504	701-224-8800	224-0398
Captain Meriwether's Landing 1700 River Rd	Bismarck	ND	58501	701-258-0666	255-1598
China Garden 1929 N Washington St	Bismarck	ND	58501	701-224-0698	
DiDonna's 505 E Bismarck Expy	Bismarck	ND	58504	701-223-0012	
East 40 Chophouse & Tavern 1401 Interchange Ave	Bismarck	ND	58501	701-258-7222	258-7229
Famous Dave's 401 E Bismarck Expy — Web: www.famousdaves.com	Bismarck	ND	58504	701-530-9800	223-2485
Fortune Cookie 658 Kirkwood Mall	Bismarck	ND	58504	701-222-1518	222-1519
Hong Kong 1055 E I- Ave	Bismarck	ND	58501	701-223-2130	
Little Cottage Cafe 2513 E Main Ave	Bismarck	ND	58501	701-223-4949	
Los Amigos 431 S 3rd St	Bismarck	ND	58504	701-223-7580	
North American Steak Buffet 2000 N 12th St	Bismarck	ND	58501	701-223-1107	224-9921
Peacock Alley 422 E Main St — Web: www.peacock-alley.com	Bismarck	ND	58501	701-255-7917	255-7231
Seasons Cafe 800 S 3rd St	Bismarck	ND	58504	701-258-7700	224-8212
Space Aliens Grill & Bar 1304 E Century Ave — Web: www.spacealiens.cc	Bismarck	ND	58503	701-223-6220	223-2252
Walrus The 1136 Arrowhead Plaza — Web: www.thewalrus.com	Bismarck	ND	58502	701-250-0020	
Wood House Restaurant 1825 N 13th St	Bismarck	ND	58501	701-255-3654	
Bison Turf 1211 N University Dr	Fargo	ND	58102	701-235-9118	
Cafe Aladdin 530 6th Ave N	Fargo	ND	58102	701-298-0880	
Giant Panda 1331 Gateway Dr S	Fargo	ND	58103	701-298-8558	237-4511
Granite City Food & Brewery Ltd (GCFB) 1636 42nd St SW — Web: www.gcfb.com	Fargo	ND	58103	701-293-3000	492-0724
Great Wall 1617 University Dr S	Fargo	ND	58103	701-232-8288	
Juano's 402 Broadway	Fargo	ND	58102	701-232-3123	
Mexican Village 814 Main Ave — Web: www.fargoweb.com/mexicanvillage	Fargo	ND	58103	701-293-0120	298-2911
Nine Dragons Restaurant 4525 17th Ave S — Web: www.9dragonsrestaurant.com	Fargo	ND	58103	701-232-2411	
Paradiso 801 38th St SW	Fargo	ND	58103	701-282-5747	281-8570
Seasons at Rose Creek 1500 Rose Creek Pkwy E — Web: www.seasonsatrosecreek.com	Fargo	ND	58104	701-235-5000	235-3010
Shang Hai 3051 25th St SW	Fargo	ND	58103	701-280-5818	232-9433
Timberlodge Steakhouse 1111 38th St SW — Web: www.timberlodgesteakhouse.com	Fargo	ND	58103	701-282-8990	282-8987
Bronze Boot Steakhouse & Lounge 1804 N Washington St — Web: www.bronzeboot.com	Grand Forks	ND	58203	701-746-5433	
China Garden 2550 32nd Ave S	Grand Forks	ND	58201	701-772-0660	
Eagle's Crest Grill 5301 S Columbia Rd	Grand Forks	ND	58201	701-787-3491	787-3494
Italian Moon 810 S Washington St — Web: www.italianmoon.com	Grand Forks	ND	58201	701-772-7277	335-2493
Red Pepper 1011 University Ave — Web: www.redpepper.com	Grand Forks	ND	58203	701-775-9671	746-7268
Sanders 1907 22 S 3rd St — Web: www.sanders1907.com	Grand Forks	ND	58201	701-746-8970	
Shangri-La Restaurant 4220 5th Ave N	Grand Forks	ND	58203	701-775-5549	

NOVA SCOTIA

Name / Address	City	Prov	Postal Code	Phone	Fax
Baan Thai Restaurant 5234 Blowers St 2nd Fl — Web: www.baanthai.ca	Halifax	NS	B3J1J7	902-446-4301	446-4302
Chives Canadian Bistro 1537 Barrington St — Web: www.chives.ca	Halifax	NS	B3J1Z4	902-420-9626	422-7238
Cousin's Restaurant 3545 Robie St — Web: www.cousinsrestaurant.webs.com	Halifax	NS	B3K4S7	902-455-8931	
Da Maurizio *The Brewery Market* 1496 Lower Water St — Web: www.damaurizio.ca	Halifax	NS	B3J1R7	902-423-0859	496-5913
Dharma Sushi 1576 Argyle St — Web: www.dharmasushi.com	Halifax	NS	B3J2B3	902-425-7785	425-7250
Economy Shoe Shop Cafe & Bar 1663 Argyle St Suite 1661 — Web: www.economyshoeshop.ca	Halifax	NS	B3J2B5	902-423-7463	423-5880
Fid 1569 Dresden Row	Halifax	NS	B3J2K4	902-422-9162	422-0018
Five Fishermen Restaurant & Grill The 1740 Argyle St — Web: www.fivefishermen.com	Halifax	NS	B3J2W1	902-422-4421	422-4503
Great Wall 1649 Bedford Row — Web: www.thegreatwall.ca	Halifax	NS	B3J1T1	902-422-6153	
Hamachi House 5190 Morris St — Web: www.hamachihouse.com	Halifax	NS	B3J1B3	902-425-7711	444-4068
Jane's on the Common 2394 Robie St — Web: www.janesonthecommon.com	Halifax	NS	B3K4M7	902-431-5683	444-3608
McKelvie's 1680 Lower Water St — Web: www.mckelvies.com	Halifax	NS	B3J2Y3	902-421-6161	425-8949
Mexico Lindo 3635 Dutch Village Rd — Web: www.mexicolindo.ca	Halifax	NS	B3N2T1	902-445-0996	
Montana's Halifax 196B Chain Lake Dr — Web: www.montanas.ca	Halifax	NS	B3S1C5	902-450-1011	450-0253
Murphy's Cable Wharf 1751 Lower Water St PO Box 2378 — Web: www.mtcw.ca	Halifax	NS	B3J3E4	902-420-1015	423-7942
Onyx Dining Room & Cocktail Bar 5680 Spring Garden Rd — Web: www.onyxdining.com	Halifax	NS	B3J1H5	902-428-5680	428-5175
Taj Mahal 5175 S St — Web: www.tajmahal7wonders.com	Halifax	NS	B3J1A2	902-492-8251	
Wooden Monkey 1707 Grafton St — Web: www.thewoodenmonkey.ca	Halifax	NS	B3J2C6	902-444-3844	444-3693
Your Father's Moustache 5686 Spring Garden Rd — Web: www.yourfathersmoustache.ca	Halifax	NS	B3J1H5	902-423-6766	422-0054

OHIO

Name / Address	City	State	Zip	Phone	Fax
Bialy's at the Lake 493 Portage Lakes Dr	Akron	OH	44319	330-644-7177	644-1747
Bill Hwang's Restaurant 879 Canton Rd	Akron	OH	44312	330-784-7167	
Bricco 1 W Exchange St — Web: www.briccoakron.com	Akron	OH	44308	330-475-1600	475-1604
Dontino's La Vita Gardens 555 E Cuyahoga Falls Ave — Web: www.dontinos.com	Akron	OH	44310	330-928-9530	
Duffy's Restaurant 231 Darrow Rd	Akron	OH	44305	330-784-5043	
El Rincon 1485 S Arlington St	Akron	OH	44306	330-785-3724	785-2816
Gasoline Alley 870 N Cleveland Massillon Rd	Akron	OH	44333	330-666-2670	
House of Hunan 12 E Exchange St # 1	Akron	OH	44308	330-253-1888	
Hyde Park Grille 4073 Medina Rd — Web: www.hydeparkrestaurants.com	Akron	OH	44333	330-670-6303	670-6174
Ido Bar & Grille 1537 S Main St — Web: www.idobar.com	Akron	OH	44301	330-773-1724	
Ken Stewart's Grille 1970 W Market St — Web: www.kenstewartsgrille.com	Akron	OH	44313	330-867-2555	867-5858
Lanning's 826 N Cleveland-Massillon Rd — Web: www.lannings-restaurant.com	Akron	OH	44333	330-666-1159	
Larry's Main Entrance 1964 W Market St	Akron	OH	44313	330-864-8162	
Luigi's 105 N Main St	Akron	OH	44308	330-253-2999	762-9140
New Era Restaurant 10 Massillon Rd — Web: www.newerarestaurant.net	Akron	OH	44312	330-784-0087	784-7906
Olde Harbor Inn 562 Portage Lakes Dr — Web: www.theoldeharborinn.com	Akron	OH	44319	330-644-1664	644-1441
Otani Japanese Seafood & Steakhouse 1684 Merriman Rd	Akron	OH	44313	330-836-1500	
Papa Joe's 1561 Akron Peninsula Rd	Akron	OH	44313	330-923-7999	923-8009
Platinum Dragon 814 1/2 W Market St	Akron	OH	44303	330-434-8108	434-1908
Two Amigos Mexican Grill 804 W Market St	Akron	OH	44303	330-762-8226	
Vaccaro's Trattoria 1000 Ghent Rd — Web: www.vactrat.com	Akron	OH	44312	330-666-6158	666-4558
Antone's Italian Cafe 4837 Mahoning Ave	Austintown	OH	44515	330-793-0707	793-2857
Asuka 7381 Market St	Boardman	OH	44512	330-629-8088	629-6880
Blue Moon 79 S Main St — Web: www.bluemoonbistro.com	Centerville	OH	45458	937-436-3925	436-3921
Ambar 350 Ludlow Ave	Cincinnati	OH	45220	513-281-7000	281-7001
Amol India 354 Ludlow Ave	Cincinnati	OH	45220	513-961-3600	961-3665
Andy's Mediterranean Grille 906 Nassau St — Web: www.andyskabob.com	Cincinnati	OH	45206	513-281-9791	751-0416
Bacall's Cafe 6118 Hamilton Ave — Web: www.bacallscafe.com	Cincinnati	OH	45224	513-541-8804	541-8145
Ban Thai 792 Eastgate S Dr	Cincinnati	OH	45245	513-752-3200	752-8424
Barresi's 4111 Webster Ave — Web: www.barresis.com	Cincinnati	OH	45236	513-793-2540	
BBQ Revue 4725 Madison Rd — Web: www.bbqrevue.com	Cincinnati	OH	45227	513-871-3500	
Beluga 3520 Edwards Rd — Web: www.belugaone.com	Cincinnati	OH	45208	513-533-4444	533-0943
Big Art's BBQ 2796 Struble Rd	Cincinnati	OH	45251	513-825-4811	
Boca 3200 Madison Rd — Web: www.boca-restaurant.com	Cincinnati	OH	45209	513-542-2022	321-2366
Brown Dog Cafe 5893 Pfeiffer Rd — Web: www.browndogcafe.com	Cincinnati	OH	45242	513-794-1610	794-1613
Celestial Restaurant 1071 Celestial St — Web: www.thecelestial.com	Cincinnati	OH	45202	513-241-4455	241-4855
China Gourmet 3340 Erie Ave	Cincinnati	OH	45208	513-871-6612	
Cumin 3520 Erie Ave — Web: www.cuminrestaurant.com	Cincinnati	OH	45208	513-871-8714	871-3287
Daveed's at 934 934 Hatch St	Cincinnati	OH	45202	513-721-2665	721-0185
Delight Thai Cafe & Sushi Bar 11928 Montgomery Rd — Web: www.delightthaicafe.com	Cincinnati	OH	45249	513-677-6175	
El Coyote 7404 State Rd Off Five Mile Rd — Web: www.elcoyotecincy.com	Cincinnati	OH	45230	513-232-5757	232-3094
Grand Finale 3 E Sharon Rd — Web: www.grandfinale.info	Cincinnati	OH	45246	513-771-5925	772-3079

Name / Address	City	State	ZIP	Phone	Fax
Hibachi Master 8160 Beechmont Ave	Cincinnati	OH	45255	513-474-9888	
Iron Horse Inn 40 Village Sq	Cincinnati	OH	45246	513-772-3333	
Web: www.ironhorseinn.com					
Jean-Robert at Pigall's 127 W 4th St	Cincinnati	OH	45202	513-721-1345	352-6010
Web: www.jean-robertatpigalls.com					
Jeff Ruby's Steakhouse 700 Walnut St	Cincinnati	OH	45202	513-784-1200	723-4455
Web: www.jeffruby.com					
Morton's the Steakhouse 28 W 4th St	Cincinnati	OH	45202	513-241-4104	241-3666
Web: www.mortons.com					
Mt Adams Fish House 940 Pavilion St	Cincinnati	OH	45202	513-421-3250	421-1446
Web: www.mtadamsfishhouse.com					
Nectar Restaurant 1000 Delta Ave	Cincinnati	OH	45208	513-929-0525	929-0301
Web: www.dineatnectar.com					
Nicholson's Tavern & Pub 625 Walnut St	Cincinnati	OH	45202	513-564-9111	564-0123
Web: www.tavernrestaurantgroup.com					
Nicola's 1420 Sycamore St	Cincinnati	OH	45202	513-721-6200	721-1777
Web: www.nicolasrestaurant.com					
Palace The 601 Vine St	Cincinnati	OH	45202	513-381-6006	651-0256
Web: www.palacecincinnati.com					
Palomino Euro Bistro 505 Vine St	Cincinnati	OH	45202	513-381-1300	381-1303
Web: www.palomino.com					
PF Chang's China Bistro 2633 Edmondson Rd	Cincinnati	OH	45209	513-531-4567	531-4679
Web: www.pfchangs.com					
Primavista 810 Matson Pl	Cincinnati	OH	45204	513-251-6467	251-4669
Web: www.pvista.com					
Restaurant at the Phoenix 812 Race St	Cincinnati	OH	45202	513-721-8901	721-1475
Web: www.thephx.com/restaurant					
Shanghai Mama's 216 E 6th St	Cincinnati	OH	45202	513-241-7777	247-1309
Web: www.shanghaimamas.com					
Teak Thai 1049-51 St Gregory St	Cincinnati	OH	45202	513-665-9800	665-9861
Trio 7565 Kenwood Rd	Cincinnati	OH	45236	513-984-1905	984-3873
Web: www.triobistro.com					
Blue Point Grille 700 W St Clair Ave	Cleveland	OH	44113	216-875-7827	902-8175
Bo Loong Restaurant 3922 St Clair Ave	Cleveland	OH	44114	216-391-3113	391-8407
Cafe Limbo 12706 Larchmere Blvd	Cleveland	OH	44120	216-707-3333	
Web: www.cafelimbo.com					
China Jade 2190 Brookpark Rd	Cleveland	OH	44134	216-749-4720	
Don's Lighthouse Grille 8905 Lake Ave	Cleveland	OH	44102	216-961-6700	961-1966
Web: www.donslighthouse.com					
Fahrenheit 2417 Professor Ave	Cleveland	OH	44113	216-781-8858	781-8867
Web: www.fahrenheittremont.com					
Fat Cats 2061 W 10th St	Cleveland	OH	44113	216-579-0200	579-0588
Fire 13220 Shaker Sq	Cleveland	OH	44120	216-921-3473	921-1957
Web: www.firefoodanddrink.com					
Flying Fig 2523 Market St	Cleveland	OH	44113	216-241-4243	241-0255
Web: www.theflyingfig.com					
Frank Sterles Slovenian Restaurant 1401 E 55th St	Cleveland	OH	44103	216-881-4181	
Web: www.sterlescountryhouse.com					
Gene's Place 3730 Rocky River Dr	Cleveland	OH	44111	216-252-1741	252-1742
Ginza Sushi House 1105 Carnegie Ave	Cleveland	OH	44115	216-589-8503	589-9768
Great Lakes Brewing Co 2516 Market Ave	Cleveland	OH	44113	216-771-4404	771-4466
Web: www.greatlakesbrewing.com					
Gusto 12022 Mayfield Rd	Cleveland	OH	44106	216-791-9900	791-9903
Web: www.gustolittleitaly.com					
Harp The 4408 Detroit Ave	Cleveland	OH	44113	216-939-0200	939-0068
Web: www.the-harp.com					
Hyde Park Steakhouse 123 Prospect Ave W	Cleveland	OH	44115	216-344-2444	344-2726
Web: www.hydeparkrestaurants.com					
John Q's Steakhouse 55 Public Sq	Cleveland	OH	44113	216-861-0900	861-1237
Web: www.johnqssteakhouse.com					
Johnny's Bar on Fulton 3164 Fulton Rd	Cleveland	OH	44109	216-281-0055	631-6890
Johnny's Downtown 1406 W 6th St	Cleveland	OH	44113	216-623-0055	623-1248
Web: www.johnnyscleveland.com					
Lemon Grass 2179 Lee Rd	Cleveland	OH	44118	216-321-0210	321-2180
Light Bistro 2801 Bridge Ave	Cleveland	OH	44113	216-771-7130	771-8130
Web: www.lightbistro.com					
Lolita 900 Literary Rd	Cleveland	OH	44113	216-771-5652	771-5633
Web: www.lolabistro.com					
Mallorca 1390 W 9th St	Cleveland	OH	44113	216-687-9494	687-9493
Web: www.clevelandmallorca.com					
Momocho Mod Mex 1835 Fulton Rd	Cleveland	OH	44113	216-694-2122	
Web: www.momocho.com					
Mortons the Steakhouse 1600 W 2nd St	Cleveland	OH	44113	216-621-6200	621-7745
Web: www.mortons.com					
Parallax 2179 W 11th St	Cleveland	OH	44113	216-583-9999	583-0720
Web: www.parallaxtremont.com					
Phnom Penh 13124 Lorain Ave	Cleveland	OH	44111	216-251-0210	
Sans Souci 24 Public Sq	Cleveland	OH	44113	216-696-5600	696-0432
Web: www.sanssoucicleveland.com					
Sergio's in University Circle 1903 Ford Dr	Cleveland	OH	44106	216-231-1234	231-5700
Web: www.sergioscleveland.com					
Siam Cafe 3951 St Clair Ave	Cleveland	OH	44114	216-361-2323	361-9191
Sun Luck Garden 1901 S Taylor Rd	Cleveland	OH	44118	216-397-7676	289-4554
Sushi 86 144 Euclid Ave	Cleveland	OH	44114	216-621-8686	
Sushi Rock 1276 W 6th St	Cleveland	OH	44113	216-623-1212	623-1218
Web: www.sushirockohio.com					
Taytu 6125 St Clair Ave	Cleveland	OH	44103	216-391-9400	
Tommy's Restaurant 1824 Coventry Rd	Cleveland	OH	44118	216-321-7757	321-8377
Web: www.tommyscoventry.com					
Villa Y Zapata 8505 Madison Ave	Cleveland	OH	44102	216-961-4369	961-0574
Vivo Restaurant & Bar 347 Euclid Ave	Cleveland	OH	44114	216-621-4678	621-4802
XO Prime Steaks 500 W St Claire Ave	Cleveland	OH	44113	216-861-1919	861-0374
Cafe Tandoor 2096 S Taylor Rd	Cleveland Heights	OH	44118	216-371-8500	371-8560
Mad Greek 2466 Fairmount Blvd	Cleveland Heights	OH	44106	216-421-3333	421-8821
Web: www.madgreekcleveland.com					
Aladdin's Eatery 2931 N High St	Columbus	OH	43202	614-262-2414	262-2450
Web: www.aladdinseatery.com					
Alana's Food & Wine 2333 N High St	Columbus	OH	43202	614-294-6783	
Web: www.alanas.com					
Anna's Greek Cuisine 7370 Sawmill Rd	Columbus	OH	43235	614-799-2207	799-2549
Web: www.annasgreekcuisine.com					
Barcelona 263 E Whittier St	Columbus	OH	43206	614-443-3699	444-0539
Web: www.barcelonacolumbus.com					
Barley's Smokehouse & Brewpub 1130 Dublin Rd	Columbus	OH	43215	614-485-0227	485-0166
Web: www.barleysbrewing.com					
Basi Italia 811 Highland St	Columbus	OH	43215	614-294-7383	294-1236
Benevolence 41 W Swan St	Columbus	OH	43215	614-221-9330	
Web: www.benevolencecafe.com					
Brio Tuscan Grille 3993 Easton Stn St	Columbus	OH	43219	614-416-4745	416-4747
Web: www.brioitalian.com					
Cafe Istanbul 3983 Worth Ave	Columbus	OH	43219	614-473-9144	473-9133
Web: www.cafeistanbul.com					
Cafe Shish Kebab 1450 Bethel Rd	Columbus	OH	43220	614-273-4444	326-4668
Cap City 1299 Olentangy River Rd	Columbus	OH	43212	614-291-3663	291-0336
Web: www.cameronmitchell.com					
Columbus Fish Market 1245 Olentangy River Rd	Columbus	OH	43212	614-291-3474	291-7258
Due Amici 67 E Gay St	Columbus	OH	43215	614-224-9373	227-0015
Web: www.due-amici.com					
El Vaquero 2195 Riverside Dr	Columbus	OH	43221	614-486-4547	486-4050
G Michael's Bistro 595 S 3rd St	Columbus	OH	43215	614-464-0575	
Web: www.gmichaelsbistro.com					
Haiku Poetic Food & Art 800 N High St	Columbus	OH	43215	614-294-8168	294-3868
Web: www.haikupoeticfood.com					
Handke's Cuisine 520 S Front St	Columbus	OH	43215	614-621-2500	621-2626
Web: www.chefhandke.com					
Hunan House 2350 E Dublin Granville Rd	Columbus	OH	43229	614-895-3330	895-3073
Hyde Park Prime Steakhouse 569 N High St	Columbus	OH	43215	614-224-2204	
Indian Oven 427 E Main St	Columbus	OH	43215	614-220-9390	
Web: www.indianoven.com					
J Alexander's 7550 Vantage Dr	Columbus	OH	43235	614-847-1166	847-1332
Web: www.jalexanders.com					
Japanese Steak House 479 N High St	Columbus	OH	43215	614-228-3030	228-0504
Kikyo 3706 Riverside Dr	Columbus	OH	43221	614-457-5277	
Web: www.thekikyo.com					
L'Antibes 772 N High St Suite 106	Columbus	OH	43215	614-291-1666	
Web: www.lantibes.com					
Latitude 41 50 N 3rd St	Columbus	OH	43215	614-233-7541	
Web: www.latitude41restaurant.com					
Lemongrass 641 N High St	Columbus	OH	43215	614-224-1414	221-2535
Web: www.lemongrassfusion.com					
Lindey's 169 E Beck St	Columbus	OH	43206	614-228-4343	228-8920
Web: www.lindeys.com					
M at Miranova 2 Miranova PL Suite 100	Columbus	OH	43215	614-629-0000	221-5020
Web: www.matmiranova.com					
Martini Italian Bistro 445 N High St	Columbus	OH	43215	614-224-8259	224-8780
Web: www.martini-italian-bistro.com					
Mitchell's Ocean Club 4002 Easton Stn	Columbus	OH	43219	614-416-2582	416-2800
Web: www.mitchellsoceanclub.com					
Mitchell's Steakhouse 45 N 3rd St	Columbus	OH	43215	614-621-2333	621-2898
Web: www.mitchellssteakhouse.com					
Otani's Sushi & Karaoke Bar 5900 Roche Dr	Columbus	OH	43229	614-431-3333	840-9755
Web: www.otanisushi.com					
Refectory Resturant & Bistro 1092 Bethel Rd	Columbus	OH	43220	614-451-9774	451-4434
Web: www.therefectoryrestaurant.com					
Rigsby's Kitchen 698 N High St	Columbus	OH	43215	614-461-7888	228-5639
Web: www.rigsbyskitchen.com					
Rossi Bar & Kitchen 895 N High St	Columbus	OH	43201	614-299-2810	299-2801
Ruth's Chris Steak House 7550 High Cross Blvd	Columbus	OH	43235	614-885-2910	885-5740
Web: www.ruthschris.com					
Schmidt's Sausage Haus 240 E Kossuth St	Columbus	OH	43206	614-444-6808	449-4039
Shoku 1312 Grandview Ave	Columbus	OH	43212	614-485-9490	
Smith & Wollensky 4145 the Strand W Easton Town Ctr	Columbus	OH	43219	614-416-2400	416-2401
Web: www.smithandwollensky.com					
Thai Taste 1178 Kenny Centre Mall	Columbus	OH	43220	614-451-7605	
Trattoria Roma 1447 Grandview Ave	Columbus	OH	43212	614-488-2104	488-4452
Web: www.trattoria-roma.com					
Windward Passage 4739 Reed Rd	Columbus	OH	43220	614-451-2497	
Akashi Sushi Bar 2020 Harshman Rd	Dayton	OH	45424	937-233-8005	233-8845
Amber Rose 1400 Valley St	Dayton	OH	45404	937-228-2511	222-0479
Web: www.theamberrose.com					
Barnsider 5202 N Main St	Dayton	OH	45415	937-277-1332	277-0567
Cafe Blvd 329 E 5th St	Dayton	OH	45402	937-824-2722	824-2810
Web: www.cafeboulevard.com					
Citilites 109 N Main St Suite 305	Dayton	OH	45402	937-222-0623	222-1504
Dublin Pub 300 Wayne Ave	Dayton	OH	45410	937-224-7822	224-0355
Web: www.dubpub.com					
Elsa's 3618 Linden Ave	Dayton	OH	45410	937-252-9635	
Franco's Ristorante Italiano 824 E 5th St	Dayton	OH	45402	937-222-0204	222-1380
Web: www.francos-italiano.com					
I-Zu Japanese Restaurant & Grocery 5252 N Dixie Dr	Dayton	OH	45414	937-277-9596	
J Alexander's 7970 Washington Village	Dayton	OH	45459	937-435-4441	435-7723
Web: www.jalexanders.com					
Jay's Seafood Restaurant *The Woods Construction Co Inc* 225 E 6th St	Dayton	OH	45402	937-222-2892	222-7547
Web: www.jays.com					
North China 6090 Far Hills Ave	Dayton	OH	45459	937-433-6837	
Old Hickory 4029 N Main St	Dayton	OH	45405	937-276-2002	276-3001
Pine Club The 1926 Brown St	Dayton	OH	45409	937-228-7463	228-5371
Web: www.thepineclub.com					
Sake 7260 Miller Ln	Dayton	OH	45414	937-898-9834	898-9835
Thai9 11 Brown St	Dayton	OH	45402	937-222-3227	222-3235
Web: www.thai9restaurant.com					
La Petite France 3177 Glendale-Milford Rd	Evendale	OH	45241	513-733-8383	733-0038
Web: www.lapetitefrance.biz					
Max & Erma's 3750 W Market St	Fairlawn	OH	44333	330-666-1002	666-3001
Mama DiSalvo's 1375 E Stroop Rd	Kettering	OH	45429	937-299-5831	299-1752
Otani 1625 Golden Gate Plaza	Mayfield Heights	OH	44124	440-442-7098	442-7138
Web: www.otanicleveland.com					

Name / Address	City	State	ZIP	Phone	Fax
Montgomery Inn 9440 Montgomery Rd *Web:* www.montgomeryinn.com	Montgomery	OH	45242	513-791-3482	985-2049
356th Fighter Group 4919 Mt Pleasant Rd *Web:* www.356fg.com	North Canton	OH	44720	330-494-3500	494-5509
Cousino's Steak House 1842 Woodville Rd *Web:* www.cousinosrestaurants.com	Oregon	OH	43616	419-693-0862	
Saffron Patch 20600 Chagrin Blvd Tower E Bldg *Web:* www.thesaffronpatch.com	Shaker Heights	OH	44122	216-295-0400	295-1320
Avenue Bistro Restaurant 6710 W Central Ave	Toledo	OH	43615	419-841-5944	842-1435
Beirut 4082 Monroe St	Toledo	OH	43606	419-473-0885	473-8947
Cousino's Old Navy Bistro 26 Main St *Web:* www.cousinosrestaurants.com	Toledo	OH	43605	419-697-6289	697-6333
Dolly & Joe's 1045 S Reynolds St	Toledo	OH	43615	419-385-2441	
Dorr Street Cafe 5243 Dorr St	Toledo	OH	43615	419-531-4446	
Eddie Lee's 4700 Nantucket Dr	Toledo	OH	43623	419-882-0616	
El Camino Real 2500 W Sylvania Ave	Toledo	OH	43613	419-472-0700	
Fifi's 1423 Bernath Pkwy *Web:* www.fifisrestaurant.com	Toledo	OH	43615	419-866-6777	866-1661
Fritz & Alfredo's 3025 N Summit St	Toledo	OH	43611	419-729-9775	
Georgio's Cafe International 426 N Superior St *Web:* www.georgiostoledo.com	Toledo	OH	43604	419-242-2424	242-2155
Mancy's 953 Phillips Ave *Web:* www.mancys.com	Toledo	OH	43612	419-476-4154	
Mango Tree 217 S Reynolds Rd	Toledo	OH	43615	419-536-2883	
Manos Greek Restaurant & Bar 1701 Adams St *Web:* www.manosgreekrestaurant.com	Toledo	OH	43624	419-244-4479	255-8881
Real Seafood Co 22 Main St *Web:* www.realseafoodcorestaurant.com	Toledo	OH	43605	419-697-5427	697-4404
Rockwell's 27 Broadway *Web:* www.oliverhousetoledo.com	Toledo	OH	43602	419-241-1253	243-9256
Rose Thai 5333 Monroe St	Toledo	OH	43623	419-841-8467	843-6060
Shorty's Bar-B-Cue 5111 Monroe St *Web:* www.mancys.com	Toledo	OH	43623	419-841-9505	843-2158
Tony Packo's 1902 Front St *TF:* 866-472-2567 ■ *Web:* www.tonypacko.com	Toledo	OH	43605	419-691-1953	
Tropics Restaurant & Lounge 1583 Sylvania Ave	Toledo	OH	43612	419-478-8592	
Ventura's 7742 W Bancroft St	Toledo	OH	43617	419-841-7523	
Zia's 20 Main St *Web:* www.ziasrestaurant.com	Toledo	OH	43605	419-697-7138	697-4565
China Dynasty 1689 W Ln Ave *Web:* www.chinadynasty-cmh.com	Upper Arlington	OH	43221	614-486-7126	486-4131
Anthony's on the River 15 Oak Hill Ave	Youngstown	OH	44502	330-744-7888	
Blue Light Restaurant & Lounge 3136 Belmont Ave	Youngstown	OH	44505	330-759-8484	
Cedars Lounge & Restaurant 23 N Hazel St	Youngstown	OH	44503	330-743-6560	743-9686
Enterra Energy Trust 7098 Mahoning Ave *Web:* www.thefifthseasonrestaurant.com	Youngstown	OH	44513	330-799-3483	799-3485
Golden Dawn 1245 Logan Ave	Youngstown	OH	44505	330-746-0393	
Golden Hunan Restaurant 3309 Belmont Ave	Youngstown	OH	44505	330-759-7197	
Joe's Restaurant 2921 Belmont Ave	Youngstown	OH	44505	330-759-8890	
Lucianno's Restaurant 1732 S Raccoon Rd	Youngstown	OH	44515	330-792-5975	792-4711
Main Moon 1760 Belmont Ave	Youngstown	OH	44504	330-743-1638	743-8336
Nicolinni's 1912 S Raccoon Rd *Web:* www.nicolinnis.com	Youngstown	OH	44515	330-799-9999	
Station Square Restaurant 4250 Belmont Ave	Youngstown	OH	44505	330-759-8802	
Upstairs 4500 Mahoning Ave	Youngstown	OH	44515	330-793-5577	259-0658
Youngstown Crab Co 3917 Belmont Ave *Web:* www.youngstowncrabco.com	Youngstown	OH	44505	330-759-5480	759-7811

OKLAHOMA

Name / Address	City	State	ZIP	Phone	Fax
Ajanta 12215 N Pennsylvania Ave *Web:* www.ajantaokc.com	Oklahoma City	OK	73120	405-752-5283	
Alavarado's 11641 S Western Ave	Oklahoma City	OK	73170	405-692-2007	
Bangkok Restaurant 7906 N MacArthur Blvd	Oklahoma City	OK	73132	405-728-4822	
Bricktown Brewery 1 N Oklahoma Ave *Web:* www.bricktownbrewery.com	Oklahoma City	OK	73104	405-232-2739	601-8961
Charleston's 5907 NW Expy St *Web:* www.charlestons.com	Oklahoma City	OK	73132	405-721-0060	720-0039
Coach House 6437 Avondale Dr *Web:* www.thecoachhouseokc.com	Oklahoma City	OK	73116	405-842-1000	843-9777
Deep Fork Grill 5418 N Western Ave *Web:* www.deepforkgrill.com	Oklahoma City	OK	73118	405-848-7678	840-0624
Dot Wo 3101 N Portland Ave *Web:* www.dot-wo.com	Oklahoma City	OK	73112	405-942-1376	
Earl's Rib Place 6816 N Western Ave *Web:* www.earlsribpalace.com	Oklahoma City	OK	73116	405-843-9922	
Haunted House 7101 Miramar Blvd	Oklahoma City	OK	73111	405-478-1417	
Juniors Supper Club 2601 NW Expy St *Web:* www.juniorsokc.com	Oklahoma City	OK	73112	405-848-5597	848-5850
Kona Ranch Steakhouse 2037 S Meridian Ave *Web:* www.kona-ranch.com	Oklahoma City	OK	73108	405-681-1000	681-0265
Metro Wine Bar & Bistro 6418 N Western Ave *Web:* www.restaurant-row.org	Oklahoma City	OK	73116	405-840-9463	840-5963
Mickey Mantle's Steakhouse 7 Mickey Mantle Dr *Web:* www.mickeymantlesteakhouse.com	Oklahoma City	OK	73104	405-272-0777	232-7111
Musashi's Japanese Steakhouse 4315 N Western Ave *Web:* www.musashis.com	Oklahoma City	OK	73118	405-602-5575	602-4474
Papa Dio's 10712 N May Ave	Oklahoma City	OK	73120	405-755-2255	755-5522
Pearl's Oyster Bar 928 NW 63rd St *Web:* www.pearls.com	Oklahoma City	OK	73116	405-848-8008	840-0382
Pelicans 291 N Air Depot Blvd *Web:* www.pelicansrestaurantokc.com	Oklahoma City	OK	73110	405-732-4392	732-5700
PF Chang's China Bistro 13700 N Pennsylvania Ave *Web:* www.pfchangs.com	Oklahoma City	OK	73134	405-748-4003	748-5247
Redrock Canyon Grill 9221 Lake Hefner Pkwy *Web:* www.redrockcanyongrill.com	Oklahoma City	OK	73120	405-749-1995	749-2556
Royal Bavaria Brewery 3401 S Sooner Rd *Web:* www.royal-bavaria.com	Oklahoma City	OK	73165	405-799-7666	
Sushi Neko 4318 N Western Ave *Web:* www.sushineko.com	Oklahoma City	OK	73118	405-528-8862	521-9877
Ted's Cafe Escondido 2836 NW 68th St	Oklahoma City	OK	73116	405-848-8337	840-5865
Tokyo Japanese Restaurant 7516 N Western Ave *Web:* www.tokyookc.com	Oklahoma City	OK	73116	405-848-6733	
Trapper's Fishcamp & Grill 4300 W Reno St *Web:* www.funfresh.com	Oklahoma City	OK	73107	405-943-9111	942-0694
Zio's Italian Kitchen 2035 S Meridian Ave *Web:* www.zios.com	Oklahoma City	OK	73108	405-680-9999	685-7740
Albert G's Bar-BQ 2748 S Harvard Ave *Web:* www.albertgs.com	Tulsa	OK	74114	918-747-4799	747-6438
Avalon Steak House 6205 New Sapulpa Rd	Tulsa	OK	74131	918-446-9917	
Big Al's 3303 E 15th St	Tulsa	OK	74112	918-744-5085	
Binh-Le 5903 E 31st St	Tulsa	OK	74135	918-835-7722	
Bodean Seafood Restaurant 3376 E 51st St *Web:* www.bodean.net	Tulsa	OK	74135	918-749-1407	747-9352
Brookside by Day 3313 S Peoria Ave	Tulsa	OK	74105	918-745-9989	
Cardigan's in London Square 6000 S Lewis	Tulsa	OK	74105	918-749-9070	712-9843
Chalkboard The 1324 S Main St *Web:* www.thechalkboard-tulsa.com	Tulsa	OK	74119	918-582-1964	382-6013
Chimi's 1304 E 15th St	Tulsa	OK	74120	918-587-4411	587-0402
Doe's Eat Place 1350 E 15th St *Web:* www.doestulsa.com	Tulsa	OK	74120	918-585-3637	585-9309
Flavors 6104 E 71st St *Web:* www.flavorsrestaurant.com	Tulsa	OK	74136	918-492-7767	
French Hen The 7143 S Yale Ave *Web:* www.frenchhentulsa.net	Tulsa	OK	74136	918-492-2596	496-0160
Fuji 8226 E 71st St *Web:* www.fujisushibar.com	Tulsa	OK	74133	918-250-1821	459-5012
Green Onion 4532 E 51st St	Tulsa	OK	74135	918-481-3338	481-6952
In the Raw Sushi 3321 S Peoria *Web:* www.intherawsushi.com	Tulsa	OK	74105	918-744-1300	744-1311
India Palace Restaurant 6963 S Lewis Ave	Tulsa	OK	74136	918-492-8040	492-8350
Joe's Crab Shack 7646 E 61st St	Tulsa	OK	74133	918-252-1010	254-0319
Kilkenny's Irish Pub & Eatery 1413 E 15th St *Web:* www.tulsairishpub.com	Tulsa	OK	74120	918-582-8282	582-3931
Mahogany Prime Steak House 6823 S Yale Ave *Web:* www.mahogany.ehsrg.com	Tulsa	OK	74136	918-494-4043	494-0209
McGill's 1560 E 21st St	Tulsa	OK	74114	918-742-8080	742-8099
New Hong Kong Restaurant 2623 E 11th St	Tulsa	OK	74104	918-585-5328	
PF Chang's China Bistro 1978 E 21st St *Web:* www.pfchangs.com	Tulsa	OK	74114	918-747-6555	747-6575
Polo Grill 2038 Utica Sq *Web:* www.pologrill.com	Tulsa	OK	74114	918-744-4280	749-7082
Ricardo's 5629 E 41st St	Tulsa	OK	74135	918-622-2668	622-2669
Spudder The 6536 E 50th St *Web:* www.thespudder.com	Tulsa	OK	74145	918-665-1416	477-7719
Taste of China 11360 E 31st St	Tulsa	OK	74146	918-664-2252	
United States Beef Corp 4923 E 49th St *Web:* www.usbeefcorp.com	Tulsa	OK	74135	918-665-0740	610-2200
White Lion Pub 6927 S Canton Ave	Tulsa	OK	74136	918-491-6533	
Zio's 7111 S Mingo Rd	Tulsa	OK	74133	918-250-5999	252-1287

ONTARIO

Name / Address	City	Prov.	Postal Code	Phone	Fax
Mandarin 8 Clipper Crt *Web:* www.mandarinbuffet.com	Brampton	ON	L6W4T9	905-451-4100	456-3411
Capone's 1701 Woodroffe Ave *Web:* www.capones.com	Nepean	ON	K2G1W2	613-226-6947	226-7080
Beckta Dining & Wine 226 Nepean St *Web:* www.beckta.com	Ottawa	ON	K2P0B8	613-238-7063	231-7474
Black Tomato 11 George St *Web:* www.theblacktomato.com	Ottawa	ON	K1N8W5	613-789-8123	
Blue Cactus Bar & Grill 2 ByWard Market *Web:* www.bluecactusbarandgrill.com	Ottawa	ON	K1N7A1	613-241-7061	241-4504
Cafe Spiga 271 Dalhousie St *Web:* www.cafespiga.com	Ottawa	ON	K1N7E5	613-241-4381	
Coriander 282 Kent St	Ottawa	ON	K2P2A4	613-233-2828	
D'Arcy McGee's Irish Pub 44 Sparks St *Web:* www.ottawa.darcymcgees.com	Ottawa	ON	K1P5A8	613-230-4433	230-3849
Fratelli 749 Bank St *Web:* www.fratelli.ca	Ottawa	ON	K1S3V3	613-237-1658	237-1079
Giovanni's 362 Preston St *Web:* www.giovannis-restaurant.com	Ottawa	ON	K1S4M7	613-234-3156	
Golden Palace 2195 Carling Ave	Ottawa	ON	K2B7E8	613-820-8444	
Green Door 198 Main St *Web:* www.greendoor.ca	Ottawa	ON	K1S1C6	613-234-9597	234-6771
Green Papaya 256 Preston St *Web:* www.greenpapaya.ca	Ottawa	ON	K1R7R5	613-231-8424	231-1120
Haveli Restaurant 39 Clarence St *Web:* www.haveli.com	Ottawa	ON	K1N5P4	613-241-1700	
Heart & Crown 67 Clarence St *Web:* www.heartandcrown.ca	Ottawa	ON	K1N5P5	613-562-0674	562-3278
Horn of Africa 364 Rideau St	Ottawa	ON	K1N5Y8	613-789-0025	
Il Piccolino 449 Preston St *Web:* www.ilpiccolino.ca	Ottawa	ON	K1S4N5	613-236-8158	
Indian Biriyani House 1589 Bank St *Web:* www.ibiriyani.com	Ottawa	ON	K1H7Z3	613-260-3893	
Island Jerk 1800 Bank St	Ottawa	ON	K1V8Y5	613-737-5163	

Name / Address	City	State	Postal Code	Phone	Fax
Juniper 245 Richmond Rd *Web:* www.juniperdining.ca	Ottawa	ON	K1Z6W7	613-728-0220	728-3993
Kinki 41 York St *Web:* www.kinki.ca	Ottawa	ON	K1N5S7	613-789-7559	789-0505
Korea Garden 470 Rideau St	Ottawa	ON	K1N5Z4	613-789-5496	
Lemon Grass 331 Elgin St *Web:* www.ottawalemongrass.com	Ottawa	ON	K2P1M5	613-233-5000	
Luxe Bistro 47 York St *Web:* www.luxebistro.com	Ottawa	ON	K1N5S7	613-241-8805	241-8886
Mamma Grazzi's Kitchen 25 George St *Web:* www.mammagrazzis.com	Ottawa	ON	K1N8W5	613-241-8656	241-5738
Manx The 370 Elgin St	Ottawa	ON	K2P1N1	613-231-2070	
Mekong 637 Somerset St W *Web:* www.mekong.ca	Ottawa	ON	K1R5K3	613-237-7717	
Merlot Rooftop Grill 100 Kent St *Web:* www.merlotottawa.com	Ottawa	ON	K1P5R7	613-783-4212	783-4228
Mezzanotte Cafe 50 Murray St Byward Market *Web:* www.mezzanotte-bistro.com	Ottawa	ON	K1N9K1	613-562-3978	
Murray Street Kitchen 110 Murray St *Web:* www.murraystreet.ca	Ottawa	ON	K1N5M6	613-562-7244	562-9770
New Dubrovnik Dining Lounge 1170 Carling Ave *Web:* www.newdubrovnik.com	Ottawa	ON	K1Z7K2	613-722-1490	722-3249
New Mee Fung 350 Booth St	Ottawa	ON	K1R7K4	613-567-8228	
Nokham Thai 747 Richmond Rd	Ottawa	ON	K2A0G6	613-724-6135	724-6620
Pancho Villa 361 Elgin St	Ottawa	ON	K2P1M7	613-234-8872	234-7786
Pho Bo Ga 2 843 Somerset St W	Ottawa	ON	K1R6R6	613-234-7089	
Pub Italia 434 1/2 Preston St *Web:* www.pubitalia.ca	Ottawa	ON	K1S4N4	613-232-2326	
Royal Thai 272 Dalhousie St	Ottawa	ON	K1N7E6	613-562-8818	
Saigon 85 Clarence St	Ottawa	ON	K1N5P5	613-789-7934	
Sante Restaurant 45 Rideau St 2nd Fl *Web:* www.santerestaurant.com	Ottawa	ON	K1N5W8	613-241-7113	
Savana Cafe 431 Gilmour St *Web:* www.savanacafe.com	Ottawa	ON	K2P0R5	613-233-9159	
Shanghai Restaurant 651 Somerset St W *Web:* www.shanghaiottawa.com	Ottawa	ON	K1R5K3	613-233-4001	
Suisha Garden Japanese Restaurant 208 Slater St *Web:* www.japaninottawa.ca	Ottawa	ON	K1P5H8	613-236-9602	238-1691
Sweet Basil 1585 Bank St *Web:* www.thitaste.ca	Ottawa	ON	K1H7Z3	613-731-8424	
Sweetgrass Aboriginal Bistro 108 Murray St *TF:* 866-327-9338 ■ *Web:* www.sweetgrassbistro.ca	Ottawa	ON	K1N5M6	613-562-3683	562-4674
Tosca Ristorante 144 O'Connor St *Web:* www.tosca-ristorante.ca	Ottawa	ON	H2P2G7	613-565-3933	565-0312
Vietnam Palace Restaurant 819 Somerset St W	Ottawa	ON	K1R6R4	613-238-6758	
Vineyards Wine Bar Bistro 54 York St *Web:* www.vineyards.ca	Ottawa	ON	K1N5T1	613-241-4270	241-5538
Vittoria Trattoria 35 William St *Web:* www.vittoriatrattoria.com	Ottawa	ON	K1N6Z9	613-789-8959	730-5239
Yangtze Dining Lounge 700 Somerset W *Web:* www.yangtze.ca	Ottawa	ON	K1R6P6	613-236-0555	236-6825
360 Revolving Restaurant 301 Front St W *Web:* www.cntower.ca	Toronto	ON	M5V2T6	416-362-5411	
Acqua Fine Foods 671 The Queensway *Web:* www.acqua.ca	Toronto	ON	M5J2T3	416-368-7171	368-6171
Adega 33 Elm St *Web:* www.adegarestaurante.ca	Toronto	ON	M5G1H1	416-977-4338	977-9339
Bangkok Garden 18 Elm St *Web:* www.bangkokgarden.ca	Toronto	ON	M5G1G7	416-977-6748	977-8280
Barberian's Steak House 7 Elm St *Web:* www.barberians.com	Toronto	ON	M5G1H1	416-597-0335	597-1407
Biagio 155 King St E	Toronto	ON	M5C1G9	416-366-4040	366-4765
Big Daddy's 212 King St W *Web:* www.bigdaddys.ca	Toronto	ON	M5H1K5	416-599-5200	599-8582
Bodega Restaurant 30 Baldwin St *Web:* www.bodegarestaurant.com	Toronto	ON	M5T1L3	416-977-1287	408-1941
Cafe 668 885 Dundas St W *Web:* www.cafe668.com	Toronto	ON	M6J1V9	416-703-0668	
Carman's 26 Alexander St	Toronto	ON	M4Y1B4	416-924-8697	924-7638
Celestin 623 Mt Pleasant Rd *Web:* www.celestinrestaurant.com	Toronto	ON	M4S2M9	416-544-9035	544-8817
Centro Grill & Wine Bar 2472 Yonge St *Web:* www.centro.ca	Toronto	ON	M4P3E3	416-483-2211	483-2641
Chiado 864 College St *Web:* www.chiadorestaurant.com	Toronto	ON	M6H1A3	416-538-1910	538-8383
Coppi 3363 Yonge St *Web:* www.coppiristorante.com	Toronto	ON	M4N2M7	416-484-4464	
Corner House 501 Davenport Rd *Web:* www.cornerhouse.sites.toronto.com	Toronto	ON	M4W1B8	416-923-2604	923-0228
Courtyard Cafe 18 St Thomas St *TF Cust Svc:* 877-999-2767 ■ *Web:* www.windsorarmshotel.com	Toronto	ON	M5S3E7	416-921-2921	921-9121
Dhaba 309 King St W *Web:* www.dhaba.ca	Toronto	ON	M5V1J5	416-740-6622	740-4519
Easy & the Fifth 225 Richmond St W *Web:* www.thefifth.com	Toronto	ON	M5V1W2	416-979-3000	979-9877
EDO Sushi 484 Eglinton Ave W *Web:* www.edosushi.com	Toronto	ON	M5N1A5	416-322-3033	322-2272
Edo-ko 431 Spadina Rd *Web:* www.edosushi.com	Toronto	ON	M5P2W3	416-482-8973	
El Sol 1448 Danforth Ave	Toronto	ON	M4J1N4	416-405-8074	
Far Niente 187 Bay St PO Box 517 *Web:* www.farnienterestaurant.com	Toronto	ON	M5L1G5	416-214-9922	214-1895
Gandhi 554 Queen St W	Toronto	ON	M5V2B5	416-504-8155	
George 111C Queen St E *Web:* www.georgeonqueen.com	Toronto	ON	M5C1S2	416-863-6006	368-6093
Golden Thai 105 Church St *Web:* www.goldenthai.ca	Toronto	ON	M5C2G3	416-868-6668	868-0453
Grappa 797 College St *Web:* www.grapparestaurant.ca	Toronto	ON	M6G1C7	416-535-3337	
Harbour Sixty Steakhouse 60 Harbour St *Web:* www.harboursixty.com	Toronto	ON	M5J1B7	416-777-2111	777-2110
Hemispheres Restaurant & Bistro 108 Chestnut St *Web:* www.metropolitan.com	Toronto	ON	M5G1R3	416-599-8000	977-9513
Il Gatto Nero 720 College St *Web:* www.ilgattonero.ca	Toronto	ON	M6G1C4	416-536-3132	
Joso's 202 Davenport Rd *Web:* www.josos.com	Toronto	ON	M5R1J2	416-925-1903	925-6567
La Fenice 319 King St W *Web:* www.lafenice.ca	Toronto	ON	M5V1J5	416-585-2377	585-2709
Lai Wah Heen 108 Chestnut St *Web:* www.metropolitan.com/lwh	Toronto	ON	M5G1R3	416-977-9899	977-8027
Le Papillon on Front 69 Front St E *Web:* www.lepapillonfront.com	Toronto	ON	M5E1M1	416-367-0303	
Le Saint Tropez 315 King St W *TF:* 888-627-2357 ■ *Web:* www.marcels.com	Toronto	ON	M5V1J5	416-591-8600	591-7689
Marcel's 315 King St W *Web:* www.marcels.com	Toronto	ON	M5V1J5	416-591-8600	591-7689
Messis 97 Harbord St *Web:* www.messis.ca	Toronto	ON	M5S1G4	416-920-2186	
Morton's of Chicago 4 Ave Rd *Web:* www.mortons.com	Toronto	ON	M5R2E8	416-925-0648	925-7593
New Generation Sushi 493 Bloor St W	Toronto	ON	M5S1Y2	416-963-8861	
North 44 Degrees 2537 Yonge St *Web:* www.north44restaurant.com	Toronto	ON	M4P2H9	416-487-4897	487-2179
Opus 37 Prince Arthur Ave *Web:* www.opusrestaurant.com	Toronto	ON	M5R1B2	416-921-3105	921-9353
ORO Restaurant 45 Elm St *Web:* www.ororestaurant.com	Toronto	ON	M5G1H1	416-597-0155	597-2819
Panagaea Restaurant 1221 Bay St *Web:* www.pangaearestaurant.com	Toronto	ON	M5R3P5	416-920-2323	920-0002
Phil's Original BBQ 838 College St *Web:* www.philsoriginalbbq.com	Toronto	ON	M6H1A2	416-532-8161	
Prego della Piazza 150 Bloor St W *Web:* www.pregodellapiazza.ca	Toronto	ON	M5S2X9	416-920-9900	920-9949
Provence 12 Amelia St *Web:* www.provencerestaurant.com	Toronto	ON	M4X1E1	416-924-9901	924-9680
Red's Bistro & Bar 77 Adelaide St W *Web:* www.redsbistro.com	Toronto	ON	M5X1B1	416-862-7337	862-2615
Rodney's Oyster House 469 King St W *Web:* www.rodneysoysterhouse.com	Toronto	ON	M5V1K4	416-363-8105	363-6638
Rol San 323 Spadina Ave	Toronto	ON	M5T2E9	416-977-1128	
Rosewater Supper Club 19 Toronto St *Web:* www.libertygroup.com	Toronto	ON	M5C2R1	416-214-5888	214-2412
Ruth's Chris Steak House 145 Richmond St W Hilton Toronto Hotel **Fax Area Code:* 905 ■ *Web:* www.ruthschris.com	Toronto	ON	M5H2L2	416-955-1455	858-2860*
Sassafraz 100 Cumberland St *Web:* www.sassafraz.ca	Toronto	ON	M5R1A6	416-964-2222	964-2402
Scaramouche Restaurant 1 Benvenuto Pl *Web:* www.scaramoucherestaurant.com	Toronto	ON	M4V2L1	416-961-8011	961-1922
Segovia 5 St Nicholas St *Web:* www.segoviarestaurant.ca	Toronto	ON	M4Y1W5	416-960-1010	
Signatures 220 Bloor St W	Toronto	ON	M5S1T8	416-324-5885	
Southern Accent 595 Markham St *Web:* www.southernaccent.com	Toronto	ON	M6G2L7	416-536-3211	536-3548
Splendido's 88 Harbord St *Web:* www.splendido.ca	Toronto	ON	M5S1G6	416-929-7788	929-3501
Spuntini 116 Ave Rd *Web:* www.spuntini.ca	Toronto	ON	M5R2H4	416-962-1110	934-0179
Trattoria Nervosa 75 Yorkville Ave *Web:* www.eatnervosa.com	Toronto	ON	M5R1B8	416-961-4642	967-4642
Trattoria Sotto Sotto 116A Ave Rd *Web:* www.sottosotto.ca	Toronto	ON	M5R2H4	416-962-0011	962-2509
Young Thailand 936 King St W *Web:* www.youngthailand.com	Toronto	ON	M5V1P5	416-366-8424	
Zucca Trattoria 2150 Yonge St *Web:* www.zuccatrattoria.com	Toronto	ON	M4S2A8	416-488-5774	

OREGON

Name / Address	City	State	Postal Code	Phone	Fax
Ambrosia Restaurant 174 E Broadway *Web:* www.ambrosiarestaurant.com	Eugene	OR	97401	541-342-4141	345-6965
Anatolia's 992 Willamette St	Eugene	OR	97401	541-343-9661	
Beppe & Gianni's Tratorria 1646 E 19th Ave	Eugene	OR	97403	541-683-6661	485-9698
Broadway The 200 W Broadway	Eugene	OR	97401	541-685-0790	345-1235
Cafe Soriah 384 W 13th Ave *Web:* www.soriah.com	Eugene	OR	97401	541-342-4410	
Chao Praya 580 Adams St	Eugene	OR	97402	541-344-1706	344-1181
Chapala 136 Oakway Rd	Eugene	OR	97401	541-434-6113	434-6267
Fisherman's Market 830 W 7th Ave	Eugene	OR	97402	541-484-2722	
Iraila Mediterranean Rustica 2435 Hilyard *Web:* www.iraila.com	Eugene	OR	97405	541-684-8400	684-9800
Jade Palace 906 W 7th Ave	Eugene	OR	97402	541-344-9523	
Lotus Garden 810 Charnelton St	Eugene	OR	97401	541-344-1928	
Maple Garden 1275 Alder St	Eugene	OR	97401	541-683-8128	683-1126
Marche 296 E 5th Ave *Web:* www.marcherestaurant.com	Eugene	OR	97401	541-342-3612	342-3611
McGrath's Fish House 1036 Valley River Way *Web:* www.mcgrathsfishhouse.com	Eugene	OR	97401	541-342-6404	342-6079
Morning Glory Cafe 450 Willamette St	Eugene	OR	97401	541-687-0709	
Ocean Sky 1601 Chambers St	Eugene	OR	97402	541-342-4848	
Oregon Electric Station 27 E 5th Ave	Eugene	OR	97401	541-485-4444	484-6149
Red Agave 454 Willamette St	Eugene	OR	97401	541-683-2206	
Ring of Fire 1099 Chambers St *Web:* www.ringoffirerestaurant.com	Eugene	OR	97402	541-344-6475	684-0732
Sixth Street Grill 55 W 6th Ave *Web:* www.sixthstreetgrill.com	Eugene	OR	97401	541-485-2961	485-3080
Steelhead Brewery & Cafe 199 E 5th Ave *Web:* www.steelheadbrewery.com	Eugene	OR	97401	541-686-2739	342-5338
Sushi Station 199 E 5th Ave	Eugene	OR	97401	541-484-1334	

Name / Address	City	State	ZIP	Phone	Fax
Sustainable Table The 30 E Broadway *Web:* www.thesustainabletable.com	Eugene	OR	97401	541-344-6948	344-1266
Taste of India 2495 Hilyard St.	Eugene	OR	97405	541-485-9698	485-9698
Turtles Bar & Grill 2690 Willamette St	Eugene	OR	97405	541-465-9038	465-9051
Vintage Restaurant The 837 Lincoln St	Eugene	OR	97401	541-349-9181	
West Bros River Ranch Barbeque & Steaks 2123 Franklin Blvd	Eugene	OR	97403	541-686-2020	344-6564
3 Doors Down Cafe 1429 SE 37th St *Web:* www.3doorsdowncafe.com	Portland	OR	97214	503-236-6886	235-9221
Acadia 1303 NE Fremont St *Web:* www.creolapdx.com	Portland	OR	97212	503-249-5001	288-4383
Amalfi's 4703 NE Fremont St *Web:* www.amalfisrestaurant.com	Portland	OR	97213	503-284-6747	
Andina 1314 NW Glisan *Web:* www.andinarestaurant.com	Portland	OR	97209	503-228-9535	228-0788
Assaggio 7742 SE 13th Ave *Web:* www.assaggiorestaurant.com	Portland	OR	97202	503-232-6151	715-4981
Basta's Trattoria 410 NW 21st Ave. *Web:* www.bastastrattoria.com	Portland	OR	97209	503-274-1572	
Berlin Inn 3131 SE 12th Ave. *Web:* www.berlininn.com	Portland	OR	97202	503-236-6761	238-4068
Bluehour 250 NW 13th Ave *Web:* www.bluehouronline.com	Portland	OR	97209	503-226-3394	221-5005
Bombay Cricket Club Restaurant 1925 SE Hawthorne Blvd *Web:* www.bombaycricketclubrestaurant.com	Portland	OR	97214	503-231-0740	
Cafe Castagna 1758 SE Hawthorne Blvd. *Web:* www.castagnarestaurant.com	Portland	OR	97214	503-231-9959	231-7474
Cafe du Berry 6439 SW MacAdam Ave	Portland	OR	97201	503-244-5551	
Caffe Mingo 807 NW 21st Ave.	Portland	OR	97209	503-226-4646	295-2040
Campbell's Bar-B-Q 8701 SE Powell Blvd *Web:* www.campbellsbbq.com	Portland	OR	97266	503-777-9795	
Canton Grill 2610 SE 82nd Ave	Portland	OR	97202	503-774-1135	
Castagna 1752 SE Hawthorne Blvd *Web:* www.castagnarestaurant.com	Portland	OR	97214	503-231-7373	231-7474
Cha! Cha! Cha! 1208 NW Glisan St.	Portland	OR	97209	503-221-2111	
Chart House 5700 SW Terwilliger Blvd *Web:* www.chart-house.com	Portland	OR	97239	503-246-6963	246-8437
Clay's Smokehouse Grill 2932 SE Division St.	Portland	OR	97202	503-235-4755	
El Gaucho 319 SW Broadway *Web:* www.elgaucho.com	Portland	OR	97205	503-227-8794	227-3412
Esparza's Tex-Mex Cafe 2725 SE Ankeny St.	Portland	OR	97214	503-234-7909	234-7909
Fife 4440 NE Fremont St *Web:* www.fiferestaurant.com	Portland	OR	97213	971-222-3433	222-0042
Fratelli 1230 NW Hoyt St *Web:* www.fratellicucina.com	Portland	OR	97209	503-241-8800	
Giorgio's 1131 NW Hoyt St. *Web:* www.giorgiospdx.com	Portland	OR	97209	503-221-1888	
Giuseppe's 17937 SE Stark St	Portland	OR	97233	503-669-8767	492-4665
Heathman Restaurant 1001 SW Broadway *Web:* www.heathmanrestaurantandbar.com	Portland	OR	97205	503-790-7752	790-7105
Higgins Restaurant & Bar 1239 SW Broadway	Portland	OR	97205	503-222-9070	222-1244
Hugo's Cafe & Restaurant 2130 NE Broadway	Portland	OR	97232	503-287-7490	
Il Piatto 2348 SE Ankeny St *Web:* www.ilpiattopdx.com	Portland	OR	97214	503-236-4997	236-7233
Iron Horse 6034 SE Milwaukie Ave. *Web:* www.portlandironhorse.com	Portland	OR	97202	503-232-1826	236-3988
Jake's Famous Crawfish 401 SW 12th Ave SW Stark *TF:* 888-226-6212 ■ *Web:* www.mccormickandschmicks.com	Portland	OR	97205	503-226-1419	220-1856
Jake's Grill 611 SW 10th Ave. *TF:* 888-226-6212 ■ *Web:* www.mccormickandschmicks.com	Portland	OR	97205	503-220-1850	226-8365
Kell's 112 SW 2nd Ave *Web:* www.kellsirish.com	Portland	OR	97204	503-227-4057	593-1227
Koji Osakaya 606 SW Broadway *Web:* www.koji.com	Portland	OR	97205	503-294-1169	294-1169
Lemongrass 1705 NE Couch St	Portland	OR	97232	503-231-5780	
London Grill 309 SW Broadway *Web:* www.bensonhotel.com	Portland	OR	97205	503-295-4110	471-3924
Lucy's Table 704 NW 21st Ave. *Web:* www.lucystable.com	Portland	OR	97210	503-226-6126	274-7122
McCormick & Schmick's 235 SW 1st Ave *Web:* www.mccormickandschmicks.com	Portland	OR	97201	503-224-7522	220-1881
McCormick & Schmick's Harborside 0309 SW Montgomery *TF Resv:* 888-226-6212 ■ *Web:* www.mccormickandschmicks.com	Portland	OR	97201	503-220-1865	220-1855
Mint Restaurant & Bar 816 N Russell St. *Web:* www.mintand820.com	Portland	OR	97227	503-284-5518	284-5519
Mio Sushi 2271 NW Johnson St. *Web:* www.miosushi.com	Portland	OR	97210	503-221-1469	827-4932
Morton's the Steakhouse 213 SW Clay St *Web:* www.mortons.com	Portland	OR	97201	503-248-2100	218-2005
Mother's Bistro & Bar 212 SW Stark St. *Web:* www.mothersbistro.com	Portland	OR	97204	503-464-1122	525-5877
Noble Rot 1111 E Burnside St # 400 *Web:* www.noblerotpdx.com	Portland	OR	97214	503-233-1999	233-5999
Oba! 555 NW 12th Ave. *Web:* www.obarestaurant.com	Portland	OR	97209	503-228-6161	228-2673
OM Seafood Restaurant 7632 SE Powell Blvd	Portland	OR	97206	503-788-3128	471-2101
Paley's Place 1204 NW 21st Ave *Web:* www.paleysplace.net	Portland	OR	97209	503-243-2403	223-8041
Pambiche 2811 NE Glisan St *Web:* www.pambiche.com	Portland	OR	97232	503-233-0511	233-0495
Pho Van 1012 NW Glisan St	Portland	OR	97216	503-248-2172	
Piazza Italia 1129 NW Johnson St *Web:* www.piazzaportland.com	Portland	OR	97209	503-478-0619	227-5199
Plainfield's Mayur 852 SW 21st Ave *Web:* www.plainfields.com	Portland	OR	97205	503-223-2995	
Portland City Grill 111 SW 5th Ave Unico US Bank Tower 30th Fl *Web:* www.portlandcitygrill.com	Portland	OR	97204	503-450-0030	525-5265
Red Star Tavern & Roast House 503 SW Alder St *Web:* www.redstartavern.com	Portland	OR	97204	503-222-0005	417-3334
Ringside SteakHouse The 2165 W Burnside St *Web:* www.ringsidesteakhouse.com	Portland	OR	97210	503-223-1513	223-6908
Ruth's Chris Steak House 309 SW 3rd Ave. *Web:* www.ruthschris.com	Portland	OR	97204	503-221-4518	221-7766
Santorini 11525 SW Barns Rd	Portland	OR	97225	503-646-6889	671-0402
Saucebox 214 SW Broadway *Web:* www.saucebox.com	Portland	OR	97205	503-241-3393	
Sin Ju 1022 NW Johnson St *Web:* www.sinjurestaurant.com	Portland	OR	97209	503-223-6535	223-6536
Southpark Seafood Grill & Wine Bar 901 SW Salmon St *Web:* www.southparkseafood.com	Portland	OR	97205	503-326-1300	326-1301
Stickers Asian Cafe 6808 SE Milwaukie Ave *Web:* www.stickersasiancafe.com	Portland	OR	97217	503-239-8739	230-9884
Sweet Basil 3135 NE Broadway *Web:* www.sweetbasilor.com	Portland	OR	97232	503-281-8337	
Thai Orchid 10075 SW Barbur Blvd *Web:* www.thaiorchidrestaurant.com	Portland	OR	97219	503-452-2544	
Veritable Quandary 1220 SW 1st Ave *Web:* www.veritablequandry.com	Portland	OR	97204	503-227-7342	227-5142
Wildwood Restaurant & Bar 1221 NW 21st Ave *Web:* www.wildwoodrestaurant.com	Portland	OR	97209	503-248-9663	225-0030
Ya Hala 8005 SE Stark St *Web:* www.yahalarestaurant.com	Portland	OR	97215	503-256-4484	
Adam's Rib 1210 State St.	Salem	OR	97301	503-362-2194	362-2196
Almost Home Restaurant & Steakhouse 3310 Market St NE	Salem	OR	97301	503-378-0100	315-7155
Amadeus Cafe 5121 Skyline Village Loop S Suite 190.	Salem	OR	97306	503-362-8830	
Casa Baez 1292 Lancaster Dr NE	Salem	OR	97301	503-371-3867	371-9568
Da Vinci 180 High St	Salem	OR	97301	503-399-1413	
El Mirador East 1660 Lancaster Dr NE	Salem	OR	97301	503-566-7232	391-8244
Flight Deck Restaurant & Lounge 2680 Aerial Way *Web:* www.flightdeckrestaurant.com	Salem	OR	97302	503-581-5721	
India Palace 377 Ct St.	Salem	OR	97301	503-371-4808	
J James 325 High St SE *Web:* www.jjamesrestaurant.com	Salem	OR	97301	503-362-0888	362-8077
La Margarita Co 545 Ferry St SE	Salem	OR	97301	503-362-8861	
Los Arcos Mexican Grill 4120 Commercial St SE	Salem	OR	97302	503-581-2740	
Los Baez 2920 Commercial St SE.	Salem	OR	97302	503-363-3109	581-0701
Lucky Fortune 1401 Lancaster Dr NE	Salem	OR	97301	503-399-9189	581-7810
Lum-Yuen 3190 Portland Rd NE	Salem	OR	97303	503-581-2912	581-2903
Macedonia 189 Liberty St NE	Salem	OR	97301	503-316-9997	316-9997
Marco Polo Global Restaurant 210 Liberty St SE	Salem	OR	97301	503-364-4833	
McGrath's Fish House 350 Chemeketa St NE	Salem	OR	97301	503-362-0736	362-7306
Mortons Bistro Northwest 1128 Edgewater St NW	Salem	OR	97304	503-585-1113	
Soprano's Italian Steak House 189 Liberty St NE	Salem	OR	97302	503-364-1515	

PENNSYLVANIA

Name / Address	City	State	ZIP	Phone	Fax
Altland House Center Sq Rt 30 PO Box 448 *Web:* www.altlandhouse.com	Abbottstown	PA	17301	717-259-9535	259-9956
Aladdin 651 Union Blvd *Web:* www.thealaddinrestaurant.com	Allentown	PA	18103	610-437-4023	437-9841
Bay Leaf 935 W Hamilton St. *Web:* www.allentownbayleaf.com	Allentown	PA	18101	610-433-4211	433-2652
Brass Rail Restaurant 3015 Lehigh St *Web:* www.brassrailrestaurant.com	Allentown	PA	18103	610-797-1927	797-5530
Cheesesteak Louie's 1207 Chew St. *Web:* www.louiesrestaurant.com	Allentown	PA	18102	610-432-8411	
Federal Grill 536 W Hamilton St *Web:* www.federalgrill.com	Allentown	PA	18101	610-776-7600	776-3660
Gregory's 2201 Schoenersville Rd *Web:* www.gregoryssteakhouse.com	Allentown	PA	18109	610-264-9301	264-7394
Hunan Springs 4939 Hamilton Blvd.	Allentown	PA	18106	610-366-8338	366-7184
Ichiban 1916 Catasauqua Rd	Allentown	PA	18109	610-266-7781	266-7783
Jack Creek Steakhouse 1900 Catasauqua Rd In the Valley Plaza *Web:* www.jackcreeksteakhouse.com	Allentown	PA	18109	610-264-8888	264-0670
La Mexicana Grill 405 N 7th St	Allentown	PA	18102	610-776-1910	776-1910
New China Buffet 1680 S 4th St.	Allentown	PA	18103	610-797-7768	797-7781
Oasis Restaurant 2355 Schoenersville Rd	Allentown	PA	18103	610-264-1955	
Ritz Barbecue 302 17th St.	Allentown	PA	18104	610-432-0952	
Robata Of Tokyo 39 S 9th St. *Web:* www.web.me.com/robataoftokyo/site/home.html	Allentown	PA	18102	610-821-6900	
Sunset Grille 6751 Ruppsville Rd *Web:* www.sunset-grille.com	Allentown	PA	18106	610-395-9622	398-0697
Youell's Oyster House 2249 Walnut St *Web:* www.youellsoysterhouse.com	Allentown	PA	18104	610-439-1203	
Cashtown Inn Restaurant 1325 Old Rt 30 *TF:* 800-367-1797	Cashtown	PA	17310	717-334-9722	334-4679
Angelo Bistocchi's Restaurant 1120 Wheeler Ave.	Dunmore	PA	18510	570-961-9112	
Bertrand's 18 N Pk Row	Erie	PA	16501	814-871-6477	464-9029
Calamari's Squid Row 1317 State St *Web:* www.calamaris-squidrow.com	Erie	PA	16501	814-459-4276	455-5635
Colao's Ristorante 2826 Plum St	Erie	PA	16508	814-866-9621	
Colony Pub & Grille 2670 W 8th St	Erie	PA	16505	814-838-2162	838-9804
Danny's 5653 Peach St	Erie	PA	16509	814-868-4486	
El Canelo 2709 W 12th St	Erie	PA	16505	814-835-2290	836-0334
Hibachi Japanese Steak House 3000 W 12th St *Web:* www.hibachijapan.com	Erie	PA	16505	814-838-2495	
Hoss's Steak & Sea House 3302 W 26th St *Web:* www.hosss.com	Erie	PA	16506	814-838-6718	838-5071
Joe Roots Grill 2826 W 8th St.	Erie	PA	16505	814-836-7668	
Matthew's Trattoria 153 E 13th St *Web:* www.diningverse.com/matthewstrattoria	Erie	PA	16503	814-459-6458	452-2585

	City	State	Zip	Phone	Fax
Molly Brannigans 240 W 11th St Suite 401	Erie	PA	16501	814-453-2062	453-5885
Web: www.mollybrannigans.com					
Oscar's Pub & Restaurant 2147 W 12th St	Erie	PA	16505	814-454-4325	455-7659
Panos Restaurant 1504 W 38th St	Erie	PA	16508	814-866-0517	
Papermoon 1325 State St	Erie	PA	16501	814-455-7766	455-7768
Petra 3602 W Lake Rd	Erie	PA	16505	814-838-7197	833-9543
TF: 866-906-2931 ■ *Web:* www.petrarestaurant.com					
Pufferbelly 414 French St	Erie	PA	16507	814-454-1557	455-6138
Ricardo's 2112 E Lake Rd	Erie	PA	16511	814-455-4947	461-9177
Smokey Bones BBQ 2074 Interchange Rd	Erie	PA	16565	814-868-3388	864-9907
Web: www.smokeybones.com					
Sullivan's Pub & Eatery 301 French St	Erie	PA	16507	814-452-3446	
Syd's Place 2992 W Lake Rd	Erie	PA	16505	814-838-3089	
Valerio's 3205 Pittsburgh Ave	Erie	PA	16509	814-833-2959	
Waterfall Restaurant & Lounge 5735 E Lake Rd	Erie	PA	16511	814-899-8173	899-9895
Avenue Restaurant The 21 Steinwehr Ave	Gettysburg	PA	17325	717-334-3235	334-5209
Web: www.avenuerestaurant.net					
Blue Parrot Bistro 35 Chambersburg St	Gettysburg	PA	17325	717-337-3739	338-9345
Centuries on the Square 1 Lincoln Sq Best Western Gettysburg Hotel	Gettysburg	PA	17325	717-337-2000	337-2075
Dobbin House Inc 89 Steinwehr Ave	Gettysburg	PA	17325	717-334-2100	334-6905
Web: www.dobbinhouse.com/map.htm					
Dunlap's 90 Buford Ave	Gettysburg	PA	17325	717-334-4816	334-2053
Web: www.dunlapsrestaurant.com					
Ernie's Texas Lunch 58 Chambersburg St	Gettysburg	PA	17325	717-334-1970	
Farnsworth House Inn 401 Baltimore St	Gettysburg	PA	17325	717-334-8838	334-5862
Web: www.farnsworthhouseinn.com					
General Pickett's Buffet 571 Steinwehr Ave	Gettysburg	PA	17325	717-334-7580	334-3701
Gingerbread Man 217 Steinwehr Ave	Gettysburg	PA	17325	717-334-1100	
Herr Tavern & Public House 900 Chambersburg Rd	Gettysburg	PA	17325	717-334-4332	334-3332
TF: 800-362-9849 ■ *Web:* www.innatherrridge.com					
La Bella Italia 402 York St	Gettysburg	PA	17325	717-334-1978	334-0781
Mamma Ventura 13 Chambersburg St	Gettysburg	PA	17325	717-334-5548	334-7231
O'Rorke's Eatery & Spirits 44 Steinwehr Ave	Gettysburg	PA	17325	717-334-2333	
Ping's Cafe 34 Baltimore St	Gettysburg	PA	17325	717-334-2234	337-2289
Web: www.pingscafe.com					
Plaza Restaurant 2 Baltimore St	Gettysburg	PA	17325	717-334-1999	
Aangan Indian Cuisine 3500 Walnut St	Harrisburg	PA	17109	717-909-7777	909-7979
Web: www.aanganindiancuisine.net					
Appalachian Brewing Co 50 N Cameron St	Harrisburg	PA	17101	717-221-1080	221-1083
Web: www.abcbrew.com					
Benihana 2517 Paxton St	Harrisburg	PA	17111	717-232-6731	232-6740
Web: www.benihana.com					
El Rodeo 4659 Jonestown Rd	Harrisburg	PA	17109	717-652-5340	
Fuji Do Restaurant 1701 Paxton St	Harrisburg	PA	17104	717-561-1380	
Gabriella 3907 Jonestown Rd	Harrisburg	PA	17109	717-540-0040	
Golden Sheaf 1 N 2nd St	Harrisburg	PA	17101	717-237-6400	233-6271
Isaac's 421 Friendship Rd	Harrisburg	PA	17111	717-920-5757	920-3955
Web: www.isaacsdeli.com					
McGrath's Pub & Restaurant 202 Locust St	Harrisburg	PA	17101	717-232-9914	
Miyako 227 N 2nd St	Harrisburg	PA	17101	717-234-3250	
Molly Brannigans 31 N 2nd St	Harrisburg	PA	17101	717-260-9242	260-9244
Web: www.mollybrannigans.com					
Morgan's Place 4425 N Front St	Harrisburg	PA	17110	717-234-8103	260-0166
Web: www.morgans-place.com					
Passage to India 525 S Front St	Harrisburg	PA	17104	717-233-1202	
Pavone's 300 S Hershey Rd	Harrisburg	PA	17112	717-545-2338	671-9393
Scott's Bar & Grill 212 Locust St	Harrisburg	PA	17113	717-234-7599	901-9966
Stocks on Second 211 N 2nd St	Harrisburg	PA	17101	717-233-6699	441-1119
Web: www.stocksonsecond.com					
Ted's Bar & Grill 6197 Allentown Blvd	Harrisburg	PA	17112	717-652-3832	671-1806
Vietnamese Garden 304 Reily St	Harrisburg	PA	17102	717-238-9310	
Wharf The 6852 Derry St	Harrisburg	PA	17111	717-564-9920	
Web: www.thewharfbarandgrill.com					
Sullivan's Steakhouse 700 W DeKalb Pike	King of Prussia	PA	19406	610-878-9025	878-9248
Web: www.sullivansteakhouse.com					
Carr's Restaurant 50 W Grant St	Lancaster	PA	17603	717-299-7090	
Web: www.carrsrestaurant.com					
Damon's 680 Pk City Ctr	Lancaster	PA	17601	717-481-9800	481-9831
Web: www.damons.com					
El Serrano 2151 Columbia Ave	Lancaster	PA	17603	717-397-6191	397-6180
Web: www.elserrano.com					
Florentino's 1411 Columbia Ave	Lancaster	PA	17603	717-295-4964	
Gibraltar 931 Harrisburg Pike	Lancaster	PA	17603	717-397-2790	
La Fleur 2285 Lincoln Hwy E Continental Inn	Lancaster	PA	17602	717-299-0421	
Web: www.continentalinn.com/laFleur.asp					
Lancaster Brewing Co 302 N Plum St	Lancaster	PA	17602	717-391-6258	391-6015
Web: www.lancasterbrewing.com					
Lemon Grass Thai 2481 Lincoln Hwy E	Lancaster	PA	17602	717-295-1621	295-2419
Loft Restaurant The 201 W Orange St	Lancaster	PA	17603	717-299-0661	299-2010
Web: www.theloftlancaster.com					
Log Cabin 11 Lehoy Forest Dr	Lancaster	PA	17540	717-626-1181	626-1181
Web: www.logcabinrestaurant.com					
Lombardo's 216 Harrisburg Ave	Lancaster	PA	17603	717-394-3749	394-7179
Web: www.lombardosrestaurant.com					
Olde Greenfield Inn 595 Greenfield Rd	Lancaster	PA	17601	717-393-0668	393-0908
Web: www.thegreenfieldrestaurant.com					
Pressroom Restaurant 26 W King St	Lancaster	PA	17603	717-399-5400	399-5463
Web: www.pressroomrestaurant.com					
Symposium 125 S Centerville Rd	Lancaster	PA	17603	717-391-7656	391-0749
Web: www.symposiumrestaurant.com					
Taj Mahal 2080 Bennet Ave	Lancaster	PA	17601	717-295-1434	295-7413
Web: www.tajlancaster.com					
Tony Wang's 2217 Lincoln Hwy E	Lancaster	PA	17602	717-399-1915	399-8475
Amber 3505 Birney Ave	Moosic	PA	18507	570-344-7100	
Nana's Pasta House 1223 Springbrook Ave	Moosic	PA	18507	570-457-9612	
Hickory Bridge Farm 96 Hickory Bridge Rd	Orrtanna	PA	17353	717-642-5261	624-6419
TF: 800-642-1766 ■ *Web:* www.hickorybridgefarm.com					
Alma de Cuba 1623 Walnut St	Philadelphia	PA	19103	215-988-1799	988-0807
Web: www.almadecubarestaurant.com					
Barclay Prime 237 S 18th St	Philadelphia	PA	19103	215-732-7560	732-7560
Web: www.barclayprime.com					
Bistro Romano 120 Lombard St	Philadelphia	PA	19147	215-925-8880	925-9888
Web: www.bistroromano.com					
Buddakan 325 Chestnut St	Philadelphia	PA	19106	215-574-9440	574-8994
Web: www.buddakan.com					
Capital Grille The 1338 Chestnut St	Philadelphia	PA	19107	215-545-9588	545-6419
Web: www.thecapitalgrille.com					
Charles Plaza 234 N 10th St	Philadelphia	PA	19107	215-829-4383	
Chloe 232 Arch St	Philadelphia	PA	19106	215-629-2337	
Web: www.chloebyob.com					
Continental The 138 Market St	Philadelphia	PA	19106	215-923-6069	923-2955
Web: www.continentalmartinibar.com					
Cuba Libre Restaurant 10 S 2nd St	Philadelphia	PA	19106	215-627-0666	627-6193
Web: www.cubalibrerestaurant.com					
Cucina Forte 768 S 8th St	Philadelphia	PA	19147	215-238-0778	
Dahlak Restaurant inc 4708 Baltimore Ave	Philadelphia	PA	19143	215-726-6464	726-0996
Web: www.dahlakrestaurant.com					
El Vez 121 S 13th St	Philadelphia	PA	19107	215-928-9800	928-9889
Web: www.elvezrestaurant.com					
Fork 306 Market St	Philadelphia	PA	19106	215-625-9425	625-9435
Web: www.forkrestaurant.com					
Fountain Restaurant 1 Logan Sq	Philadelphia	PA	19103	215-963-1500	963-2748
Friday Saturday Sunday 261 S 21st St	Philadelphia	PA	19103	215-546-4232	940-1028
Web: www.frisatsun.com					
Hikaru 607 S 2nd St	Philadelphia	PA	19147	215-627-7110	
Il Cantuccio 701 N 3rd St	Philadelphia	PA	19123	215-627-6573	627-6573
Il Portico 1519 Walnut St	Philadelphia	PA	19102	215-587-7000	587-7005
Web: www.il-portico.com					
Jake's 4365 Main St	Philadelphia	PA	19127	215-483-0444	487-7122
Web: www.jakesrestaurant.com					
Karma 114 Chestnut St	Philadelphia	PA	19106	215-925-1444	925-1472
Web: www.thekarmarestaurant.com					
Kristian's 1100 Federal St	Philadelphia	PA	19147	215-468-0104	336-6229
Web: www.kristiansrestaurant.com					
L'Angolo 1415 Porter St	Philadelphia	PA	19145	215-389-4252	389-4525
L2 Restaurant & Bar 2201 S St	Philadelphia	PA	19146	215-732-7878	732-5278
Web: www.l2restaurant.com					
La Famiglia 8 S Front St	Philadelphia	PA	19106	215-922-2803	922-7495
Web: www.lafamiglia.com					
Lacroix at the Rittenhouse 210 W Rittenhouse Sq	Philadelphia	PA	19103	215-790-2533	546-9858
Web: www.rittenhousehotel.com					
Le Bar Lyonnais 1523 Walnut St	Philadelphia	PA	19102	215-567-1000	568-1151
Web: www.lebecfin.com					
Le Bec-Fin 1523 Walnut St	Philadelphia	PA	19102	215-567-1000	568-1151
Web: www.lebecfin.com					
Little Fish 600 Catherine St	Philadelphia	PA	19147	215-413-3464	
Web: www.littlefishphilly.com					
Los Catrines & Tequila's Bar 1602 Locust St	Philadelphia	PA	19103	215-546-0181	546-9953
Macaroni's 9315 Old Bustleton Ave	Philadelphia	PA	19115	215-464-3040	
Marrakesh 517 S Leithgow St	Philadelphia	PA	19147	215-925-5929	627-6107
Matyson 37 S 19th St	Philadelphia	PA	19103	215-564-2925	564-2926
Web: www.matyson.com					
McCormick & Schmick's 1 S Broad St	Philadelphia	PA	19107	215-568-6888	568-2066
Web: www.mccormickandschmicks.com					
Melograno 2201 Spruce St	Philadelphia	PA	19103	215-875-8116	
Meritage Philadelphia 500 S 20th St	Philadelphia	PA	19103	215-985-1922	985-0455
Web: www.meritagephiladelphia.com					
Morimoto 723 Chestnut St	Philadelphia	PA	19106	215-413-9070	413-9075
Web: www.morimotorestaurant.com					
Morning Glory Diner 735 S 10th St	Philadelphia	PA	19147	215-413-3999	
Web: www.themorninggPlorydiner.com					
Morton's The Steakhouse 1411 Walnut St	Philadelphia	PA	19106	215-557-0724	557-9741
Web: www.mortons.com					
Nan Restaurant 4000 Chestnut St	Philadelphia	PA	19104	215-382-0818	
Web: www.nanrestaurant.com					
Osaka 8605 Germantown Ave	Philadelphia	PA	19118	215-242-5900	242-4085
Palm Restaurant 200 S Broad St	Philadelphia	PA	19102	215-546-7256	546-3088
Web: www.thepalm.com					
Pod Restaurant 3636 Sansom St	Philadelphia	PA	19104	215-387-1803	387-1809
Web: www.podrestaurant.com					
Radicchio 402 Wood St	Philadelphia	PA	19106	215-627-6850	627-6801
Web: www.radicchio-cafe.com					
Rib Crib 6333 Germantown Ave	Philadelphia	PA	19144	215-438-6793	
Ristorante Panorama 14 N Front St	Philadelphia	PA	19106	215-922-7800	922-7642
Rose Tattoo Cafe 1847 Callowhill St	Philadelphia	PA	19130	215-569-8939	947-9786
Web: www.rosetattoocafe.com					
Ruth's Chris Steakhouse 260 S Broad St	Philadelphia	PA	19102	215-790-1515	790-9480
Web: www.ruthschris.com					
Saloon 750 S 7th St	Philadelphia	PA	19147	215-627-1811	627-6265
Web: www.saloonrestaurant.net					
Sansom Street Oyster House 1516 Sansom St	Philadelphia	PA	19102	215-567-7683	567-0476
Web: www.oysterhousephilly.com					
Scannicchio 2500 S Broad St	Philadelphia	PA	19145	215-468-3900	468-3900
Web: www.scannicchio.com					
Shiao Lan Kung 930 Race St	Philadelphia	PA	19107	215-928-0282	
Smith & Wollensky 210 W Rittenhouse Sq	Philadelphia	PA	19103	215-545-1700	545-8918
Web: www.smithandwollensky.com					
Standard Tap 901 N 2nd St	Philadelphia	PA	19123	215-238-0630	238-0493
Web: www.standardtap.com					
Susanna Foo 1512 Walnut St	Philadelphia	PA	19102	215-545-2666	546-9106
Web: www.susannafoo.com					
Swann Lounge 1 Logan Sq	Philadelphia	PA	19103	215-963-1500	963-9506
Web: www.fourseasons.com					
Sweet Lucy's Smokehouse 7500 State Rd	Philadelphia	PA	19136	215-333-9663	331-3185
Web: www.sweetlucys.com					

Name / Address	City	State	ZIP	Phone	Fax
Tai Lake Restaurant 134 N 10th St *Web:* www.tailakerestaurant.com	Philadelphia	PA	19107	215-922-0698	922-0347
Tangerine 232 Market St *Fax Area Code: 215 ■ *Web:* www.tangerinerestaurant.com	Philadelphia	PA	19106	267-886-1474	627-5117*
Tre Scalini 1915 Passyunk Ave	Philadelphia	PA	19148	215-551-3870	
Umbria 7131 Germantown Ave	Philadelphia	PA	19119	215-242-6470	
Valanni Restaurant & Lounge 1229 Spruce St *Web:* www.valanni.com	Philadelphia	PA	19107	215-790-9494	790-9642
Vetri 1312 Spruce St *Web:* www.vetrifamily.com	Philadelphia	PA	19107	215-732-3478	732-3487
Vientiane Cafe 4728 Baltimore Ave	Philadelphia	PA	19143	215-726-1095	
Vietnam Restaurant 221 N 11th St *Web:* www.eatatvietnam.com	Philadelphia	PA	19107	215-592-1163	
White Dog Cafe 3420 Sansom St *Web:* www.whitedog.com	Philadelphia	PA	19104	215-386-9224	
Ali Baba 404 S Craig St *Web:* www.alibabapittsburgh.com	Pittsburgh	PA	15213	412-682-2829	682-0926
Amel's 435 McNeilly Rd *Web:* www.amelsrestaurant.com	Pittsburgh	PA	15226	412-563-3466	
Cafe Allegro 51 S 12th St *Web:* www.cafeallegropittsburgh.com	Pittsburgh	PA	15203	412-481-7788	481-4520
Cafe du Jour 1107 E Carson St	Pittsburgh	PA	15203	412-488-9695	
Cafe Zao 649 Penn Ave	Pittsburgh	PA	15222	412-325-7007	
Carlton Restaurant 500 Grant St 1 Mellon Bank Ctr *Web:* www.thecarltonrestaurant.com	Pittsburgh	PA	15219	412-391-4099	281-1704
Casbah 229 S Highland Dr *Web:* www.bigburrito.com	Pittsburgh	PA	15206	412-661-5656	
Christos Mediterranean Grille 130 6th St	Pittsburgh	PA	15222	412-261-6442	
Church Brew Works 3525 Liberty Ave *Web:* www.churchbrew.com	Pittsburgh	PA	15201	412-688-8200	688-8201
Del's 4428 Liberty Ave *Web:* www.delsrest.com	Pittsburgh	PA	15224	412-683-1448	683-3863
Eleven 1150 Smallman St *Web:* www.bigburrito.com	Pittsburgh	PA	15222	412-201-5656	201-5655
Grand Concourse 100 W Stn Sq Dr *Web:* www.muer.com	Pittsburgh	PA	15219	412-261-1717	261-6041
Gypsy Cafe 1330 Bingham St *Web:* www.gypsycafe.net	Pittsburgh	PA	15203	412-381-4977	
India Garden 328 Atwood St *Web:* www.indiagarden.net	Pittsburgh	PA	15213	412-682-3000	682-3130
Kaya 2000 Smallman St *Web:* www.bigburrito.com	Pittsburgh	PA	15222	412-261-6565	261-1526
Kiku 225 W Stn Sq Dr *Web:* www.kikupittsburgh.com	Pittsburgh	PA	15219	412-765-3200	765-3202
Lidia's Italy 1400 Smallman St *Web:* www.lidias-pittsburgh.com	Pittsburgh	PA	15222	412-552-0150	
Mallorca 2228 E Carson St *Web:* www.mallorcarestaurant.com	Pittsburgh	PA	15203	412-488-1818	488-1320
Max's Allegheny Tavern 537 Suismon St *Web:* www.maxsalleghenytavern.com	Pittsburgh	PA	15212	412-231-1899	231-5099
Morton's The Steakhouse 625 Liberty Ave *Web:* www.mortons.com	Pittsburgh	PA	15222	412-261-7141	261-7151
Mullaney's Harp & Fiddle 24th St & Penn Ave *Web:* www.harpandfiddle.com	Pittsburgh	PA	15222	412-642-6622	
Nakama Japanese Steakhouse 1611 E Carson St *Web:* www.eatatnakama.com	Pittsburgh	PA	15203	412-381-6000	381-6643
Opus 107 6th St	Pittsburgh	PA	15222	412-992-2005	
Original Fish Market 1000 Penn Ave *Web:* www.originalfishmarket.com	Pittsburgh	PA	15222	412-227-3657	227-3658
Penn Brewery The 800 Vinial St *Web:* www.pennbrew.com	Pittsburgh	PA	15212	412-237-9402	
Pittsburgh Steak Co 1924 E Carson St *Web:* www.pghsteak.com	Pittsburgh	PA	15203	412-381-5505	488-6628
Pleasure Bar & Restaurant 4729 Liberty Ave	Pittsburgh	PA	15224	412-682-9603	
Primanti Bros 46 18th St *Web:* www.primantibrothers.com	Pittsburgh	PA	15222	412-263-2142	
Ruth's Chris Steak House 6 PPG Pl *Web:* www.ruthschris.com	Pittsburgh	PA	15222	412-391-4800	263-0121
Sesame Inn 715 Washington Rd *Web:* www.sesameinn.net	Pittsburgh	PA	15228	412-341-2555	341-6887
Soba 5847 Ellsworth Ave *Web:* www.bigburrito.com	Pittsburgh	PA	15232	412-362-5656	
Spice Island Tea House 253 Atwood St	Pittsburgh	PA	15213	412-687-8821	
Steelhead Grill 112 Washington Pl *Web:* www.steelhead-grill.com	Pittsburgh	PA	15219	412-394-3474	281-4797
Sushi Kim 1241 Penn Ave *Web:* www.sushikim.com	Pittsburgh	PA	15222	412-281-9956	281-9957
Tessaro's 4601 Liberty Ave	Pittsburgh	PA	15224	412-682-6809	
Thai Me Up 1925 E Carson St	Pittsburgh	PA	15203	412-488-8893	
Thai Place 5528 Walnut St *Web:* www.thaiplacepgh.com	Pittsburgh	PA	15232	412-687-8586	687-7970
Tram's Kitchen 4050 Penn Ave	Pittsburgh	PA	15224	412-682-2688	
Umi 5849 Ellsworth Ave	Pittsburgh	PA	15232	412-362-6198	
Wilson's Bar-B-Q 700 N Taylor Ave	Pittsburgh	PA	15212	412-322-7427	
Banshee 320 Penn Ave *Web:* www.thebansheepub.com	Scranton	PA	18503	570-969-4248	
Carmen's 700 Lackawanna Ave	Scranton	PA	18503	570-342-8300	
Cooper's Seafood House 701 N Washington Ave *Web:* www.coopers-seafood.com	Scranton	PA	18509	570-346-6883	
Foliage 122 N Main Ave	Scranton	PA	18504	570-347-1071	
Fresno's 914 Scranton Carbondale Hwy *Web:* www.fresnos.com	Scranton	PA	18508	570-383-9400	
Kelly's Pub & Eatery 1802 Cedar Ave	Scranton	PA	18505	570-346-9758	
La Trattoria 522 Moosic St	Scranton	PA	18505	570-961-1504	
Osaka 244 Adams Ave *Web:* www.osakacuisine.com	Scranton	PA	18503	570-341-9600	341-5777
Russell's 1918 Ash St	Scranton	PA	18510	570-961-8949	
Sibio's 1240 Quincy Ave	Scranton	PA	18510	570-961-9274	
Stirna's 120 W Market St	Scranton	PA	18508	570-343-5742	

QUEBEC

Name / Address	City	Prov	Postal Code	Phone	Fax
3 Amigos 1657 Suite Catherine W *Web:* www.3amigos.com	Montreal	QC	H3H1L9	514-939-3329	939-4194
Addict Restaurant 2171 Crescent St *Web:* www.addictrestaurant.com	Montreal	QC	H3G2C1	514-849-9333	849-9333
Arahova 266 St Viateur St W *Web:* www.arahova.com	Montreal	QC	H2V1X9	514-272-4681	272-4592
Ariel Restaurant 2072 Drummond St *Web:* arielrestaurant.com	Montreal	QC	H3G1W9	514-282-9790	288-0249
Bangkok Cuisine 1616 Sainte-Catherine St W	Montreal	QC	H3H1L7	514-935-2178	
Beijing 92 Rue de la Gauchetiere O *Web:* www.restaurantbeijing.net	Montreal	QC	H2Z1C1	514-861-2003	
Bombay Mahal 1001 Jean-Talon St W *Web:* www.restaurantbombaymahal.ca	Montreal	QC	H3N1T2	514-273-3331	
Buffet Maharaja 1481 Rene Levesque Blvd W *Web:* www.buffetmaharaja.com	Montreal	QC	H3G1T8	514-934-0655	934-0695
Carlos & Pepe's 1420 Peel St *Web:* www.carlosandpepes.com/en	Montreal	QC	H3A1S8	514-288-3090	288-3092
Casa Napoli 6728 E Freemont St	Montreal	QC	H2S3C7	514-274-4351	274-3602
Chao Praya 50 Laurier W	Montreal	QC	H2T2N4	514-272-5339	272-7793
Chez la Mere Michel 1209 Rue Guy St	Montreal	QC	H3H2K5	514-934-0473	939-0709
Chez Leveque 1030 Laurier W *Web:* www.chezleveque.ca	Montreal	QC	H2V2K8	514-279-7355	279-1737
Coco Rico 3907 St-Laurent Blvd	Montreal	QC	H2W1X9	514-849-5554	849-6677
Europea 1227 de la Montagne *Web:* www.europea.ca	Montreal	QC	H3G1Z2	514-397-9161	398-9718
Ferreira Cafe 1446 Peel St *Web:* www.ferreiracafe.com	Montreal	QC	H3A1S8	514-848-0988	848-9375
Frite Alors! 1562 Laurier St E *Web:* www.fritealors.com	Montreal	QC	H2J1H9	514-524-6336	
Globe Bar-Restaurant 3455 St Laurent Blvd *Web:* www.restaurantglobe.com	Montreal	QC	H2X2T6	514-284-3823	284-3531
Hwang-Kum 5908 Sherbrooke St W	Montreal	QC	H4A1X7	514-487-1712	
L'Entrecote St-Jean 2022 Peel St *Web:* www.lentrecotestjean.com	Montreal	QC	H3A2W5	514-281-6492	274-6411
L'Estaminet 1340 Fleury E *Web:* www.lestaminet.ca	Montreal	QC	H2C1R3	514-389-0596	
L'Express 3927 St Denis St	Montreal	QC	H2W2M4	514-845-5333	843-7576
La Buona Forchetta 2407 Mont-Royal E	Montreal	QC	H2H1L2	514-521-6766	
La Chronique 99 Laurier Ave W *Web:* www.lachronique.qc.ca	Montreal	QC	H2T2N6	514-271-3095	
La Colombe 554 Duluth E	Montreal	QC	H2L1A9	514-849-8844	879-6686
La Mer 1065 Papineau St	Montreal	QC	H2K4G9	514-522-2889	
La Sila 2040 St Denis St	Montreal	QC	H2X3K7	514-844-5083	282-6519
La Sirene de la Mer 114 Dresden St	Montreal	QC	H3P2B6	514-345-0345	345-0407
Laloux 250 Pine Ave E *Web:* www.laloux.com	Montreal	QC	H2W1P3	514-287-9127	281-0682
Le Mas Des Oliviers Restaurant 1216 Rue Bishop *Web:* www.lemasdesoliviers.ca	Montreal	QC	H3G2E3	514-861-6733	861-7838
Le Nil Bleu 3706 St-Denis	Montreal	QC	H2X3L7	514-285-4628	
Le Petit Moulinsart 139 St Paul W *Web:* www.lepetitmoulinsart.com	Montreal	QC	H2Y1Z5	514-843-7432	843-4779
Le Piemontais 1145A de Bullion *Web:* www.lepiemontais.com	Montreal	QC	H3X2Z2	514-861-8122	861-6041
Les Chenets 2075 Rue Bishop	Montreal	QC	H3G2E8	514-844-1842	844-0552
Maestro SVP 3615 St Laurent Blvd *Web:* www.maestrosvp.com	Montreal	QC	H2X1V5	514-842-6447	
Maison VIP 1077 Clark St	Montreal	QC	H2Z1K3	514-861-1943	
Mediterraneo Grill & Wine Bar 3500 St Laurent Blvd	Montreal	QC	H2X2V1	514-844-0027	844-9848
Milos 5357 du Parc Ave *Web:* www.milos.ca	Montreal	QC	H2V4G9	514-272-3522	272-0778
Moishes Steakhouse 3961 St Laurent Blvd *Web:* www.moishes.ca	Montreal	QC	H2W1Y4	514-845-3509	845-9504
Molivos 2310 Guy *Web:* www.molivos.qc.ca	Montreal	QC	H3H2M2	514-846-8818	846-1263
Mysore Indian Cuisine 4216 St Laurent	Montreal	QC	H2W1Z3	514-844-4733	
Nuances 1 du Casino Ave *Web:* www.casinosduquebec.com	Montreal	QC	H3C4W7	514-392-2708	864-4951
Oishii Sushi 277 Bernard St W	Montreal	QC	H2V1T5	514-271-8863	
Pho Bang New York 1001 St-Laurent Blvd	Montreal	QC	H2Z1J3	514-954-2032	
Restaurant Gandhi 230 Rue St Paul Oeust *Web:* www.restaurantgandhi.com	Montreal	QC	H2Y1Z9	514-845-5866	
Restaurant Jano Grillades 3883 St-Laurent Blvd *Web:* www.restaurantjano.com	Montreal	QC	H2W1X9	514-849-0646	849-3628
Ristorante Bar Luce 8693 St Denis St	Montreal	QC	H2P2H4	514-858-5823	858-5822
Ristorante DaVinci 1180 Bishop St *Web:* www.davinci.ca	Montreal	QC	H3G2E2	514-874-2001	874-9499
Rotisserie Chalet Bar-B-Q 5456 Sherbrooke St W *Web:* www.chaletbbq.com	Montreal	QC	H4A1V9	514-489-7235	
Rotisserie Italienne 1933 Sainte-Catherine St W	Montreal	QC	H3H1M3	514-935-4436	
Toque 900 Pl Jean-Paul Riopelle *Web:* www.restaurant-toque.com	Montreal	QC	H2Z2B2	514-499-2084	499-0292
Upstairs Jazz Bar & Grill 1254 MacKay St *Web:* www.upstairsjazz.com	Montreal	QC	H3G2H4	514-931-6808	931-5213
YOY Sushi Bar 4526 St Denis St W *Web:* www.yoysushi.ca	Montreal	QC	H2J2L3	514-844-9884	844-2535
Au Petit Coin Breton 1029 St Jean St	Quebec	QC	G1R1R9	418-694-0758	
Auberge du Tresor 20 Sainte-Anne St *TF:* 800-566-1876 ■ *Web:* www.aubergedutresor.com	Quebec	QC	G1R3X2	418-694-1876	694-0563
Auberge Louis-Hebert 668 Grande Allee E *Web:* www.louishebert.com	Quebec	QC	G1R2K5	418-525-7812	525-6294

Name / Address	City	State	Zip	Phone	Fax
Aux Anciens Canadiens 34 St Louis St PO Box 175 *Web:* www.auxancienscanadiens.qc.ca	Quebec	QC	G1R4P3	418-692-1627	692-5419
Cafe d'Europe 27 Sainte-Angele St	Quebec	QC	G1R4G5	418-692-3835	692-3192
Cafe de la Paix 44 des Jardins St *Web:* www.restoquebec.com/cafedelapaix	Quebec	QC	G1R4L7	418-692-1430	692-3949
Charles Baillairge 57 Sainte-Anne St *Web:* www.hotelclarendon.com	Quebec	QC	G1R3X4	418-692-2480	692-4652
Cochon Dingue Le 46 Champlain Blvd *Web:* www.cochondingue.com	Quebec	QC	G1K4H5	418-692-2013	692-4408
Cosmos Cafe 575 Grande Allee E	Quebec	QC	G1R2K4	418-640-0606	640-0520
Entrecote Saint Jean 1080 St Jean St *Web:* www.entrecotesaintjean.com	Quebec	QC	G1R1S4	418-694-0234	694-2172
Initiale 54 St-Pierre St *Web:* www.restaurantinitiale.com	Quebec	QC	G1K4A1	418-694-1818	694-2387
L'Astral 1225 Cours du General-de-Montcalm *Web:* www.lastral.ca	Quebec	QC	G1R4W6	418-647-2222	657-5817
L'Aviatic Club 450 de la Gare-du-Palais	Quebec	QC	G1K3X2	418-522-3555	522-6404
L'Echaude 73 Rue Sault-au-Matelot St *Web:* www.echaude.com	Quebec	QC	G1K3Y9	418-692-1299	692-1133
La Cremaillere 73 Sainte Anne St *Web:* www.cremaillere.qc.ca	Quebec	QC	G1R3X4	418-692-2216	692-5202
La Grolla 815 Cote d'Abraham *Web:* www.restaurantlagrolla.com	Quebec	QC	G1R1A4	418-529-8107	
Laurie Raphael 117 Dalhousie St *TF:* 877-876-4555 ■ *Web:* www.laurieraphael.com	Quebec	QC	G1K9C8	418-692-4555	692-4175
Le Beffroi Steakhouse 775 Honore-Mercier Ave	Quebec	QC	G1R6A5	418-380-2638	380-2563
Le Champlain 1 des Carrieres St	Quebec	QC	G1R4P5	418-692-3861	692-1751
Le Charbon 450 de la Gare-Du-Palais St	Quebec	QC	G1K3X2	418-522-0133	522-6404
Le Continental 26 St Louis St *Web:* www.restaurantlecontinental.com	Quebec	QC	G1R3Y9	418-694-9995	694-2109
Le Patriarche 17 St Stanislas St *Web:* www.lepatriarche.com	Quebec	QC	G1R4G7	418-692-5488	692-0370
Le Saint-Amour 48 Sainte-Ursule St *Web:* www.saint-amour.com	Quebec	QC	G1R4E2	418-694-0667	694-0967
Marie-Clarisse 12 du Petit-Champlain St *Web:* www.marieclarisse.qc.ca	Quebec	QC	G1K4H4	418-692-0857	692-5085
Parmesan 38 St Louis St	Quebec	QC	G1R3Z1	418-692-0341	692-4256
Pub Saint-Alexandre 1087 St Jean St *Web:* www.pubstalexandre.com	Quebec	QC	G1R1S3	418-694-0015	694-0178
Saint-James Resto Bistro 44 Cote du Palais	Quebec	QC	G1R4H8	418-692-1030	692-3822
Voodoo Grill 575 Grande Allee E *Web:* www.voodoogrill.com	Quebec	QC	G1R2K4	418-647-2000	647-4973
Apsara 71 D'Auteuil	Quebec City	QC	G1R4C3	418-694-0232	
Chez Rabelais 2 Rue Du Petit-Champlain	Quebec City	QC	G1K4H4	418-694-9460	
Ciccio Cafe 875 Claire-Fontaine	Quebec City	QC	G1R3A8	418-525-6161	
Il Teatro 972 St-Jean *Web:* www.lecapitole.com	Quebec City	QC	G1R1R5	418-694-9996	694-1916
Le Lapin Saute 52 ru du Petit-Champlain *Web:* www.lapinsaute.com	Quebec City	QC	G1K4H4	418-692-5325	692-2195
Mistral Gagnant 160 St-Paul	Quebec City	QC	G1K3W1	418-692-4260	
Poisson D'Avril 115 Quai St Andre *TF:* 877-692-1010 ■ *Web:* www.poissondavril.net	Quebec City	QC	G1K3Y3	418-692-1010	692-1664
Restaurant Le Graffiti 1191 Cartier Ave	Quebec City	QC	G1R2C9	418-529-4949	523-1956
Serge Bruyere 1200 St-Jean St	Quebec City	QC	G1R1S8	418-694-0618	694-2120
Pub St-Paul 124 St Paul St E *Web:* www.pubstpaul.com	Vieux-Montreal	QC	H2Y1G8	514-874-0485	874-9801
D'Orsay Restaurant Pub 65 Rue de Buade *Web:* www.dorsayrestaurant.com	Vieux-Quebec	QC	G1R4A2	418-694-1582	694-1587
Kaizen Sushi Bar 4075 Rue Sainte-Catherine Ouest *Web:* www.70sushi.com	Westmount	QC	H3Z3J8	514-707-8744	932-4274

RHODE ISLAND

Name / Address	City	State	Zip	Phone	Fax
Basta 2195 Broad St	Cranston	RI	02905	401-461-0330	
22 Bowen's 22 Bowen's Wharf *Web:* www.22bowens.com	Newport	RI	02840	401-841-8884	841-8883
Black Pearl The Bannister's Wharf *Web:* www.blackpearlnewport.com	Newport	RI	02840	401-846-5264	846-0360
Brick Alley Pub & Restaurant 140 Thames St *Web:* www.brickalley.com	Newport	RI	02840	401-849-6334	848-5640
Cafe Zelda 528 Lower Thames St *Web:* www.cafezelda.com	Newport	RI	02840	401-849-4002	846-4578
Christie's of Newport 14 Perry Mill Wharf *Web:* www.41north.com	Newport	RI	02840	401-847-5400	
Clarke Cooke House 1 Bannister's Wharf *Web:* www.bannistersnewport.com	Newport	RI	02840	401-846-4500	849-8750
Mamma Luisa 673 Thames St *Web:* www.mammaluisa.com	Newport	RI	02840	401-848-5257	849-8415
Mooring The Sayer's Wharf *Web:* www.mooringrestaurant.com	Newport	RI	02840	401-846-2260	846-8950
Red Parrot The 348 Thames St PO Box 340 *Web:* www.redparrotrestaurant.com	Newport	RI	02840	401-847-3800	845-2530
Restaurant Bouchard 505 Thames St *Web:* www.restaurantbouchard.com	Newport	RI	02840	401-846-0123	841-8565
Salas' Dining Room 345 Thames St	Newport	RI	02840	401-846-8772	846-7428
Salvation Cafe 140 Broadway *Web:* www.salvationcafe.com	Newport	RI	02840	401-847-2620	847-8967
Sardella's Restaurant 30 Memorial Blvd W *Web:* www.sardellas.com	Newport	RI	02840	401-849-6312	848-0190
Scales & Shells Restaurant & Raw Bar 527 Thames St *Web:* www.scalesandshells.com	Newport	RI	02840	401-846-3474	848-7706
Spiced Pear 117 Memorial Blvd	Newport	RI	02840	401-847-2244	847-3620
Thai Cuisine at Thames 517 Thames St	Newport	RI	02840	401-841-8822	845-8338
Tucker's Bistro 150 Broadway *Web:* www.tuckersbistro.com	Newport	RI	02840	401-846-3449	
White Horse Tavern 26 Marlborough St *Web:* www.whitehorsetavern.us	Newport	RI	02840	401-849-3600	849-7317
Al Forno Restaurant 577 S Main St	Providence	RI	02903	401-273-9760	
Andreas 268 Thayer St	Providence	RI	02906	401-331-7879	331-7300
Big Fish 370 Richmond St *Web:* www.bigfishri.com	Providence	RI	02903	401-751-3474	751-3495
Blue Grotto 210 Atwells Ave *Web:* www.bluegrottorestaurant.com	Providence	RI	02903	401-272-9030	272-4818
Cafe Nuovo 1 Citizens Plaza *Web:* www.cafenuovo.com	Providence	RI	02903	401-421-2525	621-7126
Camilles Restaurant 71 Bradford St *Web:* www.camillesonthehill.com	Providence	RI	02903	401-751-4812	
Capital Grille 1 Union Stn *Web:* www.thecapitalgrille.com	Providence	RI	02903	401-521-5600	331-8997
Capriccio 2 Pine St *Web:* www.capriccios.com	Providence	RI	02903	401-421-1320	331-8732
Cassarino's Restaurant 177 Atwells Ave *Web:* www.cassarinosri.com	Providence	RI	02903	401-751-3333	
CAV Restaurant 14 Imperial Pl *Web:* www.cavrestaurant.com	Providence	RI	02903	401-751-9164	274-9107
Chez Pascal 960 Hope St *Web:* www.chez-pascal.com	Providence	RI	02905	401-421-4422	
Chilangos 447 Manton Ave	Providence	RI	02909	401-383-4877	
Classic Cafe 865 Westminster St	Providence	RI	02903	401-273-0707	273-0757
Cuban Revolution 149 Washington St *Web:* www.thecubanrevolution.com	Providence	RI	02903	401-331-8829	
Don Jose Tequila's 351 Atwells Ave *Web:* www.donjoseteq.com	Providence	RI	02903	401-454-8951	
Downcity Food & Cocktails 50 Weybosett St *Web:* www.downcityfood.com	Providence	RI	02903	401-331-9217	331-7260
Gracie's Place 194 Washington St *Web:* www.grciestrov.com	Providence	RI	02903	401-272-7811	
Haruki East 172 Wayland Ave	Providence	RI	02906	401-223-0332	490-3243
Hemenway's Seafood Grille 121 S Main St Providence Washington Plaza *Web:* www.hemenwaysrestaurant.com	Providence	RI	02903	401-351-8570	331-8997
Julian's 318 Broadway *Web:* www.juliansprovidence.com	Providence	RI	02909	401-861-1770	831-3706
Lot 401 44 Hospital St *Web:* www.lot401.com	Providence	RI	02903	401-490-3980	
Mandarin Garden 555 Chalkstone Ave	Providence	RI	02908	401-751-0144	
Mill's Tavern 101 N Main St *Web:* www.millstavernrestaurant.com	Providence	RI	02903	401-272-3331	272-4453
New Rivers Restaurant 7 Steeple St *Web:* www.newriversrestaurant.com	Providence	RI	02903	401-751-0350	751-9669
Nick's on Broadway 500 Broadway	Providence	RI	02903	401-421-0286	
Not Just Snacks 833 Hope St	Providence	RI	02906	401-831-1150	351-1166
Opa Restaurant 230 Atwells Ave	Providence	RI	02903	401-351-8282	351-4666
Pakarang 303 S Main St *Web:* www.pakarangrestaurant.com	Providence	RI	02903	401-453-3660	453-3661
Pane E Vino 365 Atwells Ave *Web:* www.panevino.net	Providence	RI	02903	401-223-2230	223-4322
Parkside Rotisserie & Bar 76 S Main St *Web:* www.parksideprovidence.com	Providence	RI	02903	401-331-0003	454-1600
Pot Au Feu 44 Custom House St	Providence	RI	02903	401-273-8953	273-8963
Providence Oyster Bar 283 Atwells Ave *Web:* www.providenceoysterbar.com	Providence	RI	02903	401-272-8866	
Sawaddee Thai Restaurant 93 Hope St *Web:* www.sawaddeerestaurant.com	Providence	RI	02906	401-831-1122	831-1121
Taste of India 230 Wickenden St *Web:* www.tasteofindiari.com	Providence	RI	02903	401-421-4355	751-1432
Ten Prime Steak & Sushi 55 Pine St *Web:* www.tenprimesteakandsushi.com	Providence	RI	02903	401-453-2333	453-5217
Tokyo Restaurant 388 Wickenden St	Providence	RI	02903	401-331-5330	
Waterman Grille The 4 Richmond Sq *Web:* www.watermangrille.com	Providence	RI	02906	401-521-9229	521-9351
Wes' Rib House 38 Dike St *Web:* www.wesribhouse.com	Providence	RI	02909	401-421-9090	
XO Cafe 125 N Main St *Web:* www.xocafe.com	Providence	RI	02903	401-273-9090	
Tuscan Tavern 632 Metacom Ave *Web:* www.tuscantavern.net	Warren	RI	02885	401-247-9200	246-1755

SOUTH CAROLINA

Name / Address	City	State	Zip	Phone	Fax
39 Rue De Jean 39 John St *Web:* www.39ruedejean.com	Charleston	SC	29401	843-722-8881	722-8835
82 Queen 82 Queen St *TF:* 800-849-0082 ■ *Web:* www.82queen.com	Charleston	SC	29401	843-723-7591	577-7463
Anson's 12 Anson St *Web:* www.ansonrestaurant.com	Charleston	SC	29401	843-577-0551	720-1955
AW Shuck's 70 State St *Web:* www.a-w-shucks.com	Charleston	SC	29401	843-723-1151	720-2102
Basil *Basil Thai Restaurant* 460 King St *Web:* www.basilthairestaurant.com	Charleston	SC	29403	843-724-3490	724-3536
Blossom Restaurant 171 E Bay St	Charleston	SC	29401	843-722-9200	937-4019
Boathouse The 549 E Bay St *Web:* www.boathouserestaurants.com	Charleston	SC	29403	843-577-7171	577-7173
Bubba Gump Shrimp Co 99 S Market St *Web:* www.bubbagump.com	Charleston	SC	29401	843-723-5665	723-5220
California Dreaming 1 Ashley Pointe Dr *Web:* www.centraarchy.com	Charleston	SC	29407	843-766-1644	571-2232
Carolina's 10 Exchange St *Web:* www.carolinasrestaurant.com	Charleston	SC	29401	843-724-3800	722-9473
Charleston Grill 224 King St *Web:* www.charlestongrill.com	Charleston	SC	29401	843-577-4522	724-8405
Circa 1886 149 Wentworth St *Web:* www.circa1886.com	Charleston	SC	29401	843-853-7828	720-5292
Coast 39-D John St *Web:* www.coastbarandgrill.com	Charleston	SC	29403	843-722-8838	722-8835
Cru Cafe 18 Pinckney St *Web:* www.crucafe.com	Charleston	SC	29401	843-534-2434	534-2439
Cypress Lowcountry Grille 167 E Bay St *Web:* www.magnolias-blossom-cypress.com/cypresshome.asp?catID=20427	Charleston	SC	29401	843-727-0111	853-6073

Name / Address	City	State	ZIP	Phone	Fax
FIG restaurant 232 Meeting St	Charleston	SC	29401	843-805-5900	805-5996
Web: www.eatatfig.com					
Fish 442 King St	Charleston	SC	29403	843-722-3474	937-0406
Web: www.fishrestaurantcharleston.com					
Fulton Five 5 Fulton St	Charleston	SC	29401	843-853-5555	853-6212
Web: www.fultonfive.net					
Gaulart & Maliclet 98 Broad St	Charleston	SC	29401	843-577-9797	723-1018
Web: www.fastandfrench.org					
Great Wall Express 1077 King St	Charleston	SC	29403	843-722-8834	722-8834
Grill 225 225 E Bay St	Charleston	SC	29401	843-266-4222	723-4320
TF: 877-440-2250 ■					
Web: www.marketpavilion.com/?page=grill225&CFID=3120287&CFTOKEN=84109704					
Hank's Seafood Restaurant 10 Hayne St	Charleston	SC	29401	843-723-3474	
Web: www.hanksseafoodrestaurant.com					
Harbor View Restaurant 301 Savannah Hwy	Charleston	SC	29407	843-556-7100	556-6176
High Cotton Maverick Bar & Grill					
199 E Bay St	Charleston	SC	29401	843-724-3815	724-3816
Web: www.high-cotton.net					
Hominy Grill 207 Rutledge Ave	Charleston	SC	29403	843-937-0930	937-0931
Web: www.hominygrill.com					
Il Cortile Del Re 193A King St	Charleston	SC	29401	843-853-1888	
Jestine's Kitchen 251 Meeting St	Charleston	SC	29401	843-722-7224	722-1133
Kim's Korean Japanese Steak House					
1716 Hwy 171	Charleston	SC	29407	843-571-5100	
McCrady's 2 Unity Alley	Charleston	SC	29401	843-577-0025	577-3681
Web: www.mccradysrestaurant.com					
Middleton Place 4300 Ashley River Rd	Charleston	SC	29414	843-556-6020	766-4460
TF: 800-782-3608 ■ *Web:* www.middletonplace.org					
Mistral Restaurant 99 S Market St	Charleston	SC	29401	843-722-5708	
North Towne Grill & Seafood					
2093 Eagle Landing Rd	Charleston	SC	29464	843-863-1001	863-1002
Web: www.northtownegrill.com					
Peninsula Grill 112 N Market St	Charleston	SC	29401	843-723-0700	577-2125
Web: www.peninsulagrill.com					
Poogan's Porch 72 Queen St	Charleston	SC	29401	843-577-2337	577-2493
Web: www.poogansporch.com					
Robert's of Charleston 182 E Bay St	Charleston	SC	29401	843-577-7565	889-2953*
**Fax Area Code: 866* ■ *Web:* www.robertsofcharleston.com					
Slightly North of Broad 192 E Bay St	Charleston	SC	29401	843-723-3424	724-3811
Web: www.mavericksouthernkitchens.com					
Sticky Fingers 235 Meeting St	Charleston	SC	29401	843-853-7427	853-0132
Web: www.stickyfingers.com					
Sushi Hiro 298 King St	Charleston	SC	29401	843-723-3628	723-0199
Tristan 55 S Market St	Charleston	SC	29401	843-534-2155	254-2156
Web: www.tristandining.com					
Trotters Restaurant 2008 Savannah Hwy	Charleston	SC	29407	843-571-1000	766-9444
Vickery's Bar & Grill 15 Beaufain St	Charleston	SC	29401	843-577-5300	577-5020
Wasabi 61 State St	Charleston	SC	29401	843-577-5222	577-5001
Web: www.wasabicharleston.com					
Baan Sawan 2135 Devine St	Columbia	SC	29205	803-252-8992	
Bert's Grill & Diner 6820 Main St	Columbia	SC	29203	803-786-4432	
Blue Marlin 1200 Lincoln St	Columbia	SC	29201	803-799-3838	799-5606
Web: www.bluemarlincolumbia.com					
California Dreaming 401 S Main St	Columbia	SC	29201	803-254-6767	254-0158
Web: www.centraarchy.com					
Charleston Crab House 7205 Two Notch Rd	Columbia	SC	29223	803-462-1618	865-7363
Web: www.charlestoncrabhouse.com					
Delhi Palace 542 St Andrew Rd	Columbia	SC	29210	803-750-7760	750-7765
Web: www.delhipalacesc.com					
Dianne's on Devine 2400 Devine St	Columbia	SC	29205	803-254-3535	254-3445
Web: www.diannesondevine.com					
Eric's San Jose 6118 Garners Ferry Rd	Columbia	SC	29209	803-783-6650	
Gervais & Vine 620-A Gervais St	Columbia	SC	29201	803-799-8463	799-8442
Web: www.gervine.com					
Hampton Street Vineyard 1201 Hampton St	Columbia	SC	29202	803-252-0850	931-0193
Web: www.hamptonstreetvineyard.com					
Kyoto Japanese Steak House					
1999 N Beltline Blvd	Columbia	SC	29204	803-782-1064	
Melting Pot of Columbia The					
1410 Colonial Life Blvd	Columbia	SC	29210	803-731-8500	731-8569
Web: www.meltingpot.com					
Motor Supply Co Bistro 920 Gervais St	Columbia	SC	29201	803-256-6687	799-5146
Web: www.motorsupplycobistro.com					
Mr Friendly's New Southern Cafe					
2001 Greene St	Columbia	SC	29205	803-254-7828	254-8219
Web: www.mrfriendlys.com					
Palmetto Pig 530 Devine St	Columbia	SC	29201	803-733-2556	733-5860
SakiTumi Grill & Sushi Bar 807 Gervais St	Columbia	SC	29201	803-931-0700	799-7749
Saluda's 751 Saluda Ave	Columbia	SC	29205	803-799-9500	
Web: www.saludas.com					
Villa Tronco 1213 Blanding St	Columbia	SC	29201	803-256-7677	256-4336
Web: www.villatronco.com					
Village Gourmet					
1410 Colonial Life Blvd W Suite 150	Columbia	SC	29210	803-798-6300	798-2226
Web: www.thevillagegourmet.net					
Yamato Steak House of Japan					
360 Columbian Dr	Columbia	SC	29212	803-407-0033	
Web: www.yamatoinc.com					
Yesterday's Resturant & Tavern					
2030 Devine St 5 Pts	Columbia	SC	29205	803-799-0196	256-0860
Web: www.yesterdayssc.com					
Zorba's 6169 St Andrews Rd	Columbia	SC	29212	803-772-4617	772-0342
Lemongrass 106 N Main St	Downtown Greenville	SC	29601	864-241-9988	241-0503
Web: www.lemongrassthai.net					
Addy's Dutch Cafe & Restaurant					
17 E Coffee St	Greenville	SC	29601	864-232-2339	
Web: www.addys.net					
Augusta Grill 1818 Augusta Rd	Greenville	SC	29605	864-242-0316	232-0151
Web: www.augustagrill.com					
Blue Ridge Brewing Co 217 N Main St	Greenville	SC	29601	864-232-4677	232-4680
Web: www.blueridgebrewing.com					

Name / Address	City	State	ZIP	Phone	Fax
Caesar's Restaurant 225 S Pleasantburg Dr	Greenville	SC	29607	864-233-4094	233-5801
Web: www.caesarsrestaurant.net					
Chicora Alley 608B S Main St	Greenville	SC	29601	864-232-4100	
Web: www.chicoraalley.com					
Chophouse '47 36 Beacon Dr	Greenville	SC	29615	864-286-8700	286-8733
Web: www.centraarchy.com/chophouse47.php					
Greek Grille 3235 D-4 N Pleasantville Dr	Greenville	SC	29609	864-232-4033	232-7898
Henry's Smokehouse 240 Wade Hampton Blvd	Greenville	SC	29609	864-232-7774	232-7237
Web: www.henryssmokehouse.com					
Irashiai Sushi Pub & Japanese Restaurant					
420 N Pleasantburg Dr	Greenville	SC	29607	864-244-2008	
Web: www.irashiai.com					
Joy of Tokyo 215 Pelham Rd	Greenville	SC	29615	864-232-2888	232-4323
Kanpai of Tokyo 533 Haywood Rd	Greenville	SC	29607	864-234-0334	234-0165
Web: www.kanpaioftokyo.com					
Larkin's on the River 318 S Main St	Greenville	SC	29601	864-467-9777	467-3028
Web: www.larkinsontheriver.com					
Latitude 631 S Main St	Greenville	SC	29601	864-467-1101	467-0788
Web: www.latitude-westend.com					
Peter David's Fine Dining 921 Grove Rd	Greenville	SC	29605	864-242-0404	232-5028
Saskatoon 477 Haywood Rd	Greenville	SC	29607	864-297-7244	297-3614
Web: www.saskatoonrestaurant.com					
Soby's 207 S Main St	Greenville	SC	29601	864-232-7007	232-5282
Web: www.sobys.com					
Trattoria Giorgio 121 S Main St	Greenville	SC	29601	864-271-9166	271-9167
Web: www.trattoriagiorgio.net					
Alexander's Seafood Restaurant & Wine Bar					
76 Queens Folly Rd	Hilton Head Island	SC	29928	843-785-4999	785-2117
Web: www.alexandersrestaurant.com					
Alligator Grille Seafood & Sushi Bar					
33 Office Pk Rd	Hilton Head Island	SC	29928	843-842-4888	
Antonio's Restaurant					
1000 William Hilton Pkwy	Hilton Head Island	SC	29926	843-842-5505	842-8280
Web: www.antonios.net					
Aunt Chilada's Easy Street Cafe					
69 Pope Ave	Hilton Head Island	SC	29928	843-785-7700	842-9936
Charlie's L'Etoile Verte					
8 New Orleans Rd	Hilton Head Island	SC	29928	843-785-9277	
Web: www.charliesgreenstar.com					
CQ's Restaurant					
140-A Lighthouse Rd Harbour Town	Hilton Head Island	SC	29928	843-671-2779	671-6787
Web: www.cqsrestaurant.com					
Crane's Tavern & Steakhouse					
26 New Orleans Rd	Hilton Head Island	SC	29928	843-341-2333	341-3089
Crazy Crab 149 Lighthouse Rd	Hilton Head Island	SC	29928	843-363-2722	363-6025
Web: www.thecrazycrab.com					
Fiesta Fresh Mexican Grill					
51 New Orleans Rd Suite 4	Hilton Head Island	SC	29928	843-785-4788	
Harbourmaster's Restaurant					
1 Shelter Cove Ln	Hilton Head Island	SC	29928	843-785-3030	842-2252
Home Port The 107 Helmsman Way	Hilton Head Island	SC	29928	843-785-9666	
Web: www.hilton.head.island.diningchannel.com					
Hudson's Seafood House on the Docks					
1 Hudsons Rd	Hilton Head Island	SC	29926	843-681-2772	681-2774
Web: www.hudsonsonthedocks.com					
Jump & Phil's Bar & Grill					
7-B Greenwood Dr Suite 3	Hilton Head Island	SC	29928	843-785-9070	785-8298
Just Pasta 1 Coligny Plaza	Hilton Head Island	SC	29928	843-686-3900	
Kenny B's French Quarter Cafe					
70 Cir Ctr	Hilton Head Island	SC	29926	843-785-3315	785-3327
Kingfisher Seafood & Steak House					
18 Harborside Ln					
Shelter Cove Harbour	Hilton Head Island	SC	29928	843-785-4442	785-6792
Web: www.kingfisherseafood.com					
Mangiamo 1107 Main St	Hilton Head Island	SC	29926	843-682-2444	682-3355
Market Street Cafe					
1 N Forest Beach Blvd	Hilton Head Island	SC	29928	843-686-4976	
Web: www.marketstreetcafe.com					
Marley's Island Grille					
35 Office Pk Rd	Hilton Head Island	SC	29928	843-686-5800	686-4765
Web: www.marleyshhi.com					
Mi Tierra Mexican Restaurant					
160 William Hilton Pkwy Suite 6	Hilton Head Island	SC	29926	843-342-3409	
Michael Anthony's Cucina Italiana					
37 New Orleans Rd Suite L	Hilton Head Island	SC	29928	843-785-6272	671-3513
Web: www.michael-anthonys.com					
Old Fort Pub 65 Skull Creek Dr	Hilton Head Island	SC	29926	843-681-2386	681-9287
Old Oyster Factory					
101 Marshland Rd	Hilton Head Island	SC	29926	843-681-6040	
Web: www.oldoysterfactory.com					
Red Fish 8 Archer Rd	Hilton Head Island	SC	29928	843-686-3388	
Web: www.redfishofhiltonhead.com					
Sage Room 81 Pope Ave	Hilton Head Island	SC	29928	843-785-5352	785-5354
Web: www.thesageroom.com					
Salty Dog Cafe The					
232 S Sea Pines Dr	Hilton Head Island	SC	29928	843-671-5199	671-6498
Web: www.saltydog.com					
Santa Fe Cafe					
807 William Hilton Pkwy	Hilton Head Island	SC	29928	843-785-3838	785-2496
Scott's Fish Market Restaurant					
1 Shelter Cove Ln	Hilton Head Island	SC	29928	843-785-7575	785-6658
Signe's Bakery & Cafe 93 Arrow Rd	Hilton Head Island	SC	29928	843-785-9118	785-6144
Web: www.signesbakery.com					
Smokehouse The 102 Pope Ave	Hilton Head Island	SC	29928	843-842-4227	842-4245
Web: www.smokehousehhi.com					
Steamer Seafood Co					
1 N Forest Beach Dr					
Suite 28 Calligny Plaza	Hilton Head Island	SC	29928	843-785-2070	
Web: www.steamerseafood.com					
Studio The 20 Pope Executive Pk	Hilton Head Island	SC	29928	843-785-6000	785-5999
Web: www.studiodining.com					
Taste of Thailand					
807 William Hilton Pkwy	Hilton Head Island	SC	29928	843-341-6500	342-5327

Restaurant	City	State	Zip	Phone	Fax
Truffles Cafe PO Box 3189	Hilton Head Island	SC	29928	843-785-3130	785-3133
Web: www.trufflescafe.com					
Water Front Cafe 160 Lighthouse Rd	Hilton Head Island	SC	29928	843-671-3399	
Bovine's 3979 Hwy 17 Business	Murrells Inlet	SC	29576	843-651-2888	651-0211
Angelo's Steak & Pasta 2011 S Kings Hwy	Myrtle Beach	SC	29577	843-626-2800	
Bangkok House 318 N Kings Hwy	Myrtle Beach	SC	29577	843-626-5384	
Captain George's 1401 29th Ave	Myrtle Beach	SC	29577	843-916-2278	443-9097
Web: www.captaingeorges.com					
El Cerro Grande 108 S Kings Hwy	Myrtle Beach	SC	29577	843-946-9562	448-4431
Fiesta Del Burroloco 960 Jason Blvd	Myrtle Beach	SC	29577	843-626-1756	626-1860
Web: www.centraarchy.com					
Flamingo Grille 7050 N Kings Hwy	Myrtle Beach	SC	29572	843-449-5388	449-4551
Giant Crab 9597 N Kings Hwy	Myrtle Beach	SC	29572	843-449-1097	449-3575
Web: www.giantcrab.com					
J Edwards Great Ribs & More 2300 S Kings Hwy	Myrtle Beach	SC	29577	843-626-9986	626-9988
Web: www.jedwardsgreatribs.com					
Melting Pot The 5001 N Kings Hwy	Myrtle Beach	SC	29577	843-692-9003	692-9004
Web: www.meltingpot.com					
Miyabi 9732 N Kings Hwy	Myrtle Beach	SC	29572	843-449-9294	692-2274
New China Buffet 9601 N Kings Hwy	Myrtle Beach	SC	29572	843-497-0100	
Original Benjamin's The 9593 N Kings Hwy	Myrtle Beach	SC	29572	843-449-0821	
Web: www.originalbenjamins.com					
Sea Captain's House 3002 N Ocean Blvd	Myrtle Beach	SC	29577	843-448-8082	
Web: www.seacaptains.com					
Senor Frogs 1304 Celebrity Cir Bldg R-8	Myrtle Beach	SC	29577	843-444-5506	
Web: www.senorfrogs.com					
Spring House Restaurant 2600 N Kings Hwy	Myrtle Beach	SC	29577	843-626-5941	
Sugami 4813 N Kings Hwy	Myrtle Beach	SC	29577	843-692-7709	692-7639
Thoroughbreds 9706 N Kings Hwy	Myrtle Beach	SC	29572	843-497-2636	497-6474
Web: www.thoroughbredsrest.com					
Sea Blue 501 Hwy 17 N	North Myrtle Beach	SC	29582	843-249-8800	
Web: www.seablueonline.com					
Crabby Mike's Calabash Seafood 290 Hwy 17 N	Surfside Beach	SC	29575	843-444-2722	238-3526
Web: www.crabbymikes.com					

SOUTH DAKOTA

Restaurant	City	State	Zip	Phone	Fax
Cattleman's Club Steakhouse & Lounge 29608 SD Hwy 34	Pierre	SD	57501	605-224-9774	
Guadalajara 314 W Sioux Ave	Pierre	SD	57501	605-224-2771	224-2720
Jake's Good Time Place 620 S Cleveland	Pierre	SD	57501	605-945-0485	
La Minestra 106 E Dakota Ave	Pierre	SD	57501	605-224-8090	945-2696
Web: www.laminestra.com					
Longbranch Restaurant & Lounge 351 S Pierre St	Pierre	SD	57501	605-224-6166	945-2240
Mad Mary's Steakhouse & Saloon 110 E Dakota Ave	Pierre	SD	57501	605-224-6469	
Outpost Lodge 28229 Cow Creek Rd	Pierre	SD	57501	605-264-5450	264-5369
Web: www.theoutpostlodge.com					
Pier 347 Capitol Cafe 347 S Pierre St	Pierre	SD	57501	605-224-2400	
Saint Charles Restaurant & Cactus Lounge 207 E Capitol Ave	Pierre	SD	57501	605-224-4546	
Sunset Lodge Steakhouse 28181 182nd St	Pierre	SD	57501	605-264-5480	264-5487
Botticelli Italian Restaurant 523 Main St	Rapid City	SD	57701	605-348-0089	
Colonial House 2501 Mt Rushmore Rd	Rapid City	SD	57701	605-342-4640	341-0445
Web: www.colonialhousernb.com					
Diamond Dave's 2200 N Maple Ave	Rapid City	SD	57701	605-342-0556	
Web: www.diamonddaves.com					
Firehouse Brewing Co 610 Main St	Rapid City	SD	57701	605-348-1915	
Golden Phoenix 2421 W Main St	Rapid City	SD	57702	605-348-4195	
Great Wall 315 E N St	Rapid City	SD	57701	605-348-1060	
Hong Kong Buffet 927 E N St	Rapid City	SD	57701	605-716-4664	
Hunan 1720 Mt Rushmore Rd	Rapid City	SD	57701	605-341-3888	399-3203
Landmark Restaurant The 523 6th St	Rapid City	SD	57701	605-342-1210	
Web: www.alexjohnson.com/restaraunt.html					
Minerva's 2111 N Lacrosse St	Rapid City	SD	57701	605-394-9505	394-8945
Mongolian Grill 1415 N Lacrosse St # 1	Rapid City	SD	57701	605-388-3187	
Saigon 221 E N St	Rapid City	SD	57701	605-348-8523	
Casa Del Rey 901 W Russell St	Sioux Falls	SD	57104	605-338-6078	
Cherry Creek Grill 3104 E 26th St	Sioux Falls	SD	57103	605-336-2333	336-1999
CJ Callaway's 500 E 69th St	Sioux Falls	SD	57108	605-334-8888	334-1998
Web: www.cjcallaways.com					
Dynasty 5326 W 26th St	Sioux Falls	SD	57106	605-362-8888	
Falls Landing 200 E 8th St	Sioux Falls	SD	57103	605-336-2290	
Incas 3312 S Holly Ave	Sioux Falls	SD	57105	605-367-1992	367-1993
La Fiesta 2039 W 41st St	Sioux Falls	SD	57105	605-332-0330	332-5257
Minerva's 301 S Phillips Ave	Sioux Falls	SD	57104	605-334-0386	334-9585
Web: www.minervas.net					
River Walk 196 E 6th St	Sioux Falls	SD	57104	605-339-4824	274-0086
Sanaa's 401 E 8th St	Sioux Falls	SD	57104	605-275-2516	
Spezia 1716 S Western Ave	Sioux Falls	SD	57105	605-334-7491	334-7574
Web: www.ciaodown.com					
Sushi Masa 423 S Phillips Ave	Sioux Falls	SD	57104	605-977-6968	
Touch of Europe 337 S Phillips Ave	Sioux Falls	SD	57104	605-336-3066	

TENNESSEE

Restaurant	City	State	Zip	Phone	Fax
Corky's 100 Franklin Rd	Brentwood	TN	37027	615-373-1020	371-1638
Terra Nostra 105 Frazier Ave	Chattanoga	TN	37405	423-634-0238	634-0268
Web: www.terranostratapas.com					
212 Market Restaurant 212 Market St	Chattanooga	TN	37402	423-265-1212	267-6757
Web: www.212market.com					
Acropolis The 2213 Hamilton Pl Blvd	Chattanooga	TN	37421	423-899-5341	899-6587
Web: www.acropolisgrill.com					
Amigo Mexican Restaurant 3805 Ringgold Rd	Chattanooga	TN	37412	423-624-4345	
Broad Street Grille at the Chattanoogan 1201 Broad St	Chattanooga	TN	37402	423-424-3700	756-3404
Web: www.chattanooganhotel.com					
China Moon 5600 Brainerd Rd	Chattanooga	TN	37411	423-893-8088	
Chop House The 2011 Gunbarrel Rd	Chattanooga	TN	37421	423-892-1222	
Web: www.thechophouse.com					
Formosa Restaurant 5425 Hwy 153 N	Chattanooga	TN	37343	423-875-6953	875-4727
Web: www.formosa-restaurant.com					
India Mahal 5970 Brainerd Rd	Chattanooga	TN	37421	423-510-9651	
Kanpai of Tokyo 2200 Hamilton Pl Blvd	Chattanooga	TN	37421	423-855-8204	855-9687
Web: www.kanpaioftokyo.com					
Logan's Roadhouse 2119 Gunbarrel Rd	Chattanooga	TN	37421	423-499-4339	499-4350
Web: www.logansroadhouse.com					
Mount Vernon 3535 Broad St	Chattanooga	TN	37409	423-266-6591	
Na Go Ya 4921 Brainerd Rd	Chattanooga	TN	37411	423-899-9252	899-9252
Niko's Grill 1400 Cowart St	Chattanooga	TN	37408	423-266-9211	266-0927
Web: www.eatatnikos.com					
Porker's BBQ 1251 Market St	Chattanooga	TN	37402	423-267-2726	
Saint John's 1278 Market St	Chattanooga	TN	37402	423-266-4400	267-3004
Web: www.stjohnsrestaurant.com					
Sekisui of Chattanooga 200 Market St	Chattanooga	TN	37402	423-267-4600	267-4610
Web: www.sekisuiusa.com					
Southern Star 1206 Market St	Chattanooga	TN	37402	423-267-8899	
Web: www.southernstarrestaurant.com					
Station House 1400 Market St	Chattanooga	TN	37402	423-266-5000	
Sushi Nabe of Chattanooga 110 River St	Chattanooga	TN	37421	423-634-0171	
Web: www.sushinabechattanooga.com					
Sweet Basil 5845 Brainerd Rd	Chattanooga	TN	37411	423-485-8836	485-9545
Keg The 5760 SW Loop 820	Fort Worth	TN	76132	817-731-3534	732-2817
Web: www.kegsteakhouse.com					
Alta Cucina 1200 N Roan St	Johnson City	TN	37601	423-928-2092	928-3684
Amigo III 3211 Peoples St	Johnson City	TN	37604	423-952-0551	
Bello Vita 2927 N Roan St Bldg 2	Johnson City	TN	37601	423-282-8600	
Cafe 111 111 Broyles Dr	Johnson City	TN	37601	423-283-4633	283-0550
Cafe Pacific 1033 W Oakland Ave	Johnson City	TN	37604	423-610-0117	610-0117
Dixie Barbecue Co 3301 N Roan St	Johnson City	TN	37601	423-283-7447	
El Chico 2929 N Roan St	Johnson City	TN	37601	423-282-4080	282-0801
Web: www.elchico.com					
Firehouse Restaurant 627 W Walnut St	Johnson City	TN	37604	423-929-7377	929-2080
Web: www.thefirehouse.com					
Harbor House Seafood 2510 N Roan St	Johnson City	TN	37601	423-282-5122	282-0428
Web: www.harborhouseje.com					
Horseshoe Restaurant & Lounge 908 W Market St	Johnson City	TN	37604	423-928-8992	929-1511
Logan's Roadhouse 3112 Browns Mill Rd	Johnson City	TN	37604	423-915-1122	915-1022
Web: www.logansroadhouse.com					
Misaki Seafood & Steak House of Japan 3104 Bristol Hwy	Johnson City	TN	37601	423-282-5451	
Moto Japanese Restaurant 2607 N Roan St	Johnson City	TN	37601	423-282-6686	282-0132
Peerless Steak House 2531 N Roan St	Johnson City	TN	37601	423-282-2351	283-0439
Web: www.thepeerlessinc.com					
Red Pig Bar-B-Q 2201 Ferguson Rd	Johnson City	TN	37604	423-282-6585	282-6309
Sushi Blues Japanese Restaurant 1805 N Roan St Suite E-3	Johnson City	TN	37601	423-232-1289	
Baker-Peters Jazz Club 9000 Kingston Pike	Knoxville	TN	37923	865-690-8110	690-2044
Web: www.bakerpeters.com					
Bayou Bay Seafood House 7117 Chapman Hwy	Knoxville	TN	37920	865-573-7936	
Bistro by the Tracks 215 Brookview CentreáWay Suite 109	Knoxville	TN	37919	865-558-9500	584-7786
Web: www.bistrobythetracks.com					
Buddy's Bar-B-Q 4401 Chapman Hwy	Knoxville	TN	37920	865-579-1747	579-3315
Calhoun's 10020 Kingston Pk	Knoxville	TN	37922	865-673-3444	
Chesapeake's 500 Henley St	Knoxville	TN	37902	865-673-3433	673-3435
Web: www.coppercellar.com					
Chop House 9700 Kingston Pike	Knoxville	TN	37922	865-531-2467	693-4814
Copper Cellar 1807 Cumberland Ave PO Box 50370	Knoxville	TN	37916	865-673-3400	522-8526
Web: www.coppercellar.com/cc/index.htm					
Downtown Grill & Brewery 424 S Gay St	Knoxville	TN	37902	865-633-8111	633-8954
Web: www.downtownbrewery.com					
Italian Market & Grill 9648 Kingston Pike Suite 4	Knoxville	TN	37922	865-690-2600	539-4356
Web: www.italianmarketandgrill.com					
King Tut's Grill 4132 Martin Mill Pike	Knoxville	TN	37920	865-573-6021	
Litton's Market & Restaurant 2803 Essary Dr	Knoxville	TN	37918	865-687-8788	687-8788
Melting Pot The 111 N Central Ave	Knoxville	TN	37902	865-971-5400	971-3006
Web: www.meltingpot.com					
Miyabi Japanese Steakhouse 8207 Kingston Pike	Knoxville	TN	37919	865-691-3121	691-3218
Nama Sushi Bar 135 S Gay St	Knoxville	TN	37902	865-633-8539	633-8533
Web: www.namasushibar.com					
Naples Italian Restaurant 5500 Kingston Pike	Knoxville	TN	37919	865-584-5033	584-9415
Oodles 20 Market Sq	Knoxville	TN	37902	865-521-0600	546-2256
Orangery The 5412 Kingston Pike	Knoxville	TN	37919	865-588-2964	588-5499
Web: www.theorangeryrestaurant.com					
Pelanchos Mexican Grill 1516 Downtown W Blvd	Knoxville	TN	37919	865-694-9060	692-9666
Web: www.pelanchos.com					
Regas 318 N Gay St	Knoxville	TN	37917	865-637-3427	637-7799
Sam & Andy's Fountain City 4813 N Broadway	Knoxville	TN	37918	865-281-9539	281-9642
Savelli's 3055 Sutherland Ave	Knoxville	TN	37919	865-521-9085	
Sitar Indian Cuisine 6004 Kingston Pike	Knoxville	TN	37919	865-588-1828	588-1830
Web: www.sitarknox.com					
Sunspot 1909 Cumberland Ave	Knoxville	TN	37916	865-637-4663	637-4373
Taste of Thai 213 N Peters Rd	Knoxville	TN	37923	865-691-4442	
Tomato Head 12 Market Sq	Knoxville	TN	37902	865-637-4067	637-4019
Wasabi Japanese Steak House 226 Lovell Rd	Knoxville	TN	37922	865-675-0201	675-0202
Web: www.wasabi-steakhouse.com					
Ye Olde Steak House 6838 Chapman Hwy	Knoxville	TN	37920	865-577-9328	
Web: www.yeoldesteakhouse.com					
A Tan 3445 Poplar Ave	Memphis	TN	38111	901-452-4477	452-4484

	City	State	Zip	Phone	Fax
Automatic Slim's 83 S 2nd St *Web:* www.automaticslimsmemphis.com	Memphis	TN	38103	901-525-7948	526-6642
Bar-B-Q Shop The 1782 Madison Ave	Memphis	TN	38104	901-272-1277	272-9085
BB King's Blues Club & Restaurant 143 Beale St *Web:* www.bbkingsclub.com	Memphis	TN	38103	901-524-5464	524-5454
Benihana 912 Ridgelake Blvd *Web:* www.benihana.com	Memphis	TN	38120	901-683-7390	683-6946
Bhan Thai 1324 Peabody Ave *Web:* www.bhanthairestaurant.com	Memphis	TN	38104	901-272-1538	272-2487
Boscos Squared 827 S Main *Web:* www.boscosbeer.com	Memphis	TN	38106	901-278-0087	278-3040
Buckley's 5355 Poplar Ave *Web:* www.buckleysgrill.com	Memphis	TN	38119	901-683-4538	
Butcher Shop 101 S Front St	Memphis	TN	38103	901-521-0856	525-6657
Cafe 1912 243 So. Cooper at Peabody	Memphis	TN	38104	901-722-2700	
Cafe Society 212 N Evergreen St	Memphis	TN	38112	901-722-2177	722-2186
Celtic Crossing Irish Pub & Restaurant 903 S Cooper St *Web:* www.celticcrossingmemphis.com	Memphis	TN	38104	901-274-5151	274-5159
Central BBQ 2249 Central Ave	Memphis	TN	38104	901-272-9377	728-5850
Corky's Bar-B-Q 743 W Poplar Ave	Memphis	TN	38107	901-405-4999	273-2084
Cupboard The 1400 Union Ave *Web:* www.thecupboardrestaurant.com	Memphis	TN	38104	901-276-8015	728-5518
Dish Restaurant 948 S Cooper St *Web:* www.dishmemphis.com	Memphis	TN	38104	901-276-0002	276-7799
Erling Jensen Restaurant 1044 S Yates Rd *Web:* www.ejensen.com	Memphis	TN	38119	901-763-3700	763-3800
Folk's Folly Prime Steak House 551 S Mendenhall Rd *Web:* www.folksfolly.com	Memphis	TN	38117	901-762-8200	328-2287
Frank Grisanti's 1022 S Shady Grove Rd	Memphis	TN	38120	901-761-9462	761-2245
Golden India 2097 Madison Ave	Memphis	TN	38104	901-728-5111	728-5112
Grill83 83 Madison Ave *Web:* www.grill83.com	Memphis	TN	38103	901-333-1224	333-1210
Grove Grill 4550 Poplar Ave *Web:* www.thegrovegrill.com	Memphis	TN	38117	901-818-9951	818-9953
Huey's 1927 Madison Ave *Web:* www.hueyburger.com	Memphis	TN	38104	901-726-4372	278-9073
India Palace 1720 Poplar Ave *Web:* www.indiapalaceinc.com	Memphis	TN	38304	901-278-1199	278-1977
Jarrett's 5689 Quince Rd *Web:* www.jarretts.com	Memphis	TN	38119	901-763-2264	
Jim Neely's Interstate Barbeque 2265 S 3rd St *Web:* www.interstatebarbecue.com	Memphis	TN	38109	901-775-2304	775-3149
Jim's Place East 5560 Shelby Oaks Dr	Memphis	TN	38134	901-388-7244	383-9324
King's Palace Cafe 162 Beale St	Memphis	TN	38107	901-521-1851	
McEwen's on Monroe 120 Monroe Ave *Web:* www.mcewensonmonroe.com	Memphis	TN	38103	901-527-7085	527-0334
Melting Pot The 2828 Wolfcreek Pkwy *Web:* www.themeltingpot.com	Memphis	TN	38133	901-380-9500	380-9510
Mikasa Japan 6150 Poplar Ave *Web:* www.happymexican.con	Memphis	TN	38119	901-683-0000	683-0007
Mollie's La Casita Restaurant 2006 Madison Ave *Web:* www.mollyslacasita.com	Memphis	TN	38104	901-726-1873	726-1876
Owen Brennan's Restaurant 6150 Poplar Ave *Web:* www.brennansmemphis.com	Memphis	TN	38119	901-761-0990	761-9177
Paulette's 2110 Madison Ave *Web:* www.riverinnmemphis.com	Memphis	TN	38104	901-260-3300	726-5670
Pete & Sam's 3886 Pk Ave	Memphis	TN	38111	901-458-0694	458-9607
Rendezvous Restaurant The 52 S 2nd St *TF:* 888-464-7359 ■ *Web:* www.hogsfly.com	Memphis	TN	38103	901-523-2746	525-7688
Ronnie Grisanti & Sons 2855 Poplar Ave	Memphis	TN	38111	901-323-0007	323-0070
Saigon Le 51 N Cleveland St *Web:* www.saigon-le.com	Memphis	TN	38104	901-276-5326	
Salsa 6150 Poplar Ave Suite 129	Memphis	TN	38119	901-683-6325	767-4953
Sekisui 25 S Belvedere Blvd *Web:* www.sekisuiusa.com	Memphis	TN	38104	901-725-0005	
Sekisui Japanese Restaurant 50 Humphreys Ctr Suite 16 *Web:* www.sekisuiusa.com	Memphis	TN	38120	901-747-0001	747-2118
Silky O'Sullivan's 183 Beale St *Web:* www.silkyosullivans.com	Memphis	TN	38103	901-522-9596	522-8462
Stella 39 S Main St *Web:* www.stellamemphis.com	Memphis	TN	38103	901-526-4950	536-4941
Texas de Brazil 150 Peabody Pl Suite 103 *Web:* www.texasdebrazil.com	Memphis	TN	38103	901-526-7600	526-7615
Santa Fe Cantina 1824 Old Fort Pkwy	Murfreesboro	TN	37129	615-890-3030	
Acorn The 114 28th Ave N *Web:* www.theacornrestaurant.com	Nashville	TN	37203	615-320-4399	320-4397
Amerigo Nashville 1920 W End Ave *Web:* www.amerigo.net	Nashville	TN	37203	615-320-1740	320-0644
Anatolia 48 White Bridge Rd *Web:* www.anatolia-restaurant.com	Nashville	TN	37205	615-356-1556	356-1551
Antonios' of Nashville 7097 Old Harding Rd	Nashville	TN	37221	615-646-9166	
Big River Grille & Brewing Works 111 Broadway	Nashville	TN	37201	615-251-4677	742-3500
Blackstone Restaurant & Brewery 1918 W End Ave *Web:* www.blackstonebrewery.com	Nashville	TN	37203	615-327-9969	327-4131
Bound'ry 911 20th Ave S *Web:* www.pansouth.net/boundry-index.htm	Nashville	TN	37212	615-321-3043	321-0984
Chinatown 3900 Hillsboro Pike	Nashville	TN	37215	615-269-3275	
Cock of the Walk 2624 Music Valley Dr *Web:* www.cockofthewalkrestaurant.com	Nashville	TN	37214	615-889-1930	889-0047
Copper Kettle Cafe 4004 Granny White Pike	Nashville	TN	37204	615-383-7242	383-7949
F Scott's 2210 Crestmoor Rd *Web:* www.fscotts.com	Nashville	TN	37215	615-269-5861	269-8948
Finezza Trattoria 5405 Harding Rd	Nashville	TN	37205	615-356-9398	356-7256
Fleming's Prime Steakhouse & Wine Bar 2525 W End Ave *Web:* www.flemingssteakhouse.com	Nashville	TN	37203	615-342-0131	342-0134
Goten Japanese Steak & Sushi Bar 1719 W End Ave Suite 101W	Nashville	TN	37203	615-321-4537	321-3105
Hog Heaven 115 27th Ave N *Web:* www.hogheaven.com	Nashville	TN	37203	615-329-1234	
Horn of Africa 1041 Murfreesboro Pike *Web:* www.hornofafrica-restaurant.com	Nashville	TN	37217	615-366-3468	
Jack's Bar-B-Que 334 W Trinity Ln *Web:* www.jacksbarbque.com	Nashville	TN	37207	615-228-4600	228-4700
Jim 'N Nick's 7004 Charlotte Pike	Nashville	TN	37209	615-352-5777	
Jimmy Kelly's 217 Louise Ave *Web:* www.jimmykellys.com	Nashville	TN	37203	615-329-4349	320-7882
Kalamata's 3764 Hillsboro Rd *Web:* www.eatatkalamatas.com	Nashville	TN	37215	615-383-8700	383-8788
Ken's 2007 Division St *Web:* www.kensushi.com	Nashville	TN	37203	615-321-2444	321-2455
Kien Giang 5825 Charlotte Pike	Nashville	TN	37209	615-353-1250	
Kobe Steaks Nashville 210 25th Ave N Suite 100 *Web:* www.kobesteaks.net	Nashville	TN	37203	615-327-9081	327-9083
Korea House 6410 Charlotte Pike Suite 108	Nashville	TN	37209	615-352-2790	
La Paz Restaurante Cantina 2214 Elliston Pl Suite 102 *Web:* www.lapaz.com	Nashville	TN	37203	615-873-4435	873-4438
Mad Platter The 1239 6th Ave N	Nashville	TN	37208	615-242-2563	
Margot Cafe & Bar 1017 Woodland St	Nashville	TN	37206	615-227-4668	
Melting Pot The 166 2nd Ave N *Web:* www.meltingpot.com	Nashville	TN	37201	615-742-4970	726-6328
Midtown Cafe 102 19th Ave S *Web:* www.midtowncafe.com	Nashville	TN	37203	615-320-7176	320-0920
Morton's The Steakhouse 618 Church St *Web:* www.mortons.com	Nashville	TN	37219	615-259-4558	726-2760
Palm The 140 5th Ave S *Web:* www.thepalm.com	Nashville	TN	37206	615-742-7256	742-9028
Park Cafe 4403 Murphy Rd	Nashville	TN	37209	615-383-4409	383-4829
PF Chang's China Bistro 2525 W End Ave *Web:* www.pfchangs.com	Nashville	TN	37203	615-329-8901	329-8904
Rotier's 2413 Elliston Pl	Nashville	TN	37203	615-327-9892	
Royal Thai 120 19th Ave N	Nashville	TN	37203	615-321-6104	321-6108
Ru San's 505 12th Ave S	Nashville	TN	37203	615-252-8787	
Ruth's Chris Steak House 2100 W End Ave *Web:* www.ruthschris.com	Nashville	TN	37203	615-320-0163	329-0062
Shalimar 3711 Hillsboro Pike	Nashville	TN	37215	615-269-8577	292-0330
Siam Cafe 316 McCall St	Nashville	TN	37211	615-834-3181	
Sitar 116 21st Ave N *Web:* www.sitarnashville.com	Nashville	TN	37203	615-321-8889	321-2688
Sonobana Japanese Restaurant & Grocery 40 White Bridge Rd *Web:* www.sonobananashville.com	Nashville	TN	37205	615-356-6600	
South Street Restaurant 907 20th Ave S *Web:* pansouth.net/southstreet	Nashville	TN	37212	615-320-5555	327-0696
Sperry's 5109 Harding Pike *Web:* www.sperrys.com	Nashville	TN	37205	615-353-0809	353-0814
Sunset Grill 2001 Belcourt Ave *Web:* www.sunsetgrill.com	Nashville	TN	37212	615-386-3663	627-0078
Sylvan Park 4502 Murphy Rd	Nashville	TN	37209	615-292-9275	
Tayst 2100 21st Ave S *Web:* www.tayst.info	Nashville	TN	37212	615-383-1953	
Tin Angel 3201 W End Ave	Nashville	TN	37203	615-298-3444	
Valentino's 1907 W End Ave *Web:* www.valentinosnashville.com	Nashville	TN	37203	615-327-0148	327-9482
Yellow Porch 734 Thompson Ln	Nashville	TN	37204	615-386-0260	

TEXAS

	City	State	Zip	Phone	Fax
Alfredo's Mexican Food 2849 S 14th St	Abilene	TX	79605	325-698-0104	
Bedford Street Restaurant 1882 S Clack St	Abilene	TX	79605	325-695-1770	
Carino's 4157 Buffalo Gap Rd *Web:* www.carinos.com	Abilene	TX	79605	325-698-4950	698-0498
Catfish Corner 780 S Treadaway Blvd	Abilene	TX	79602	325-672-3620	672-4027
China Garden 2525 S 14th St	Abilene	TX	79605	325-692-3872	
Cotton Patch Cafe 3302 S Clack St *Web:* www.cottonpatch.com	Abilene	TX	79606	325-691-0509	691-1058
Cypress Street Station 158 Cypress St *Web:* www.cypress-street.com	Abilene	TX	79601	325-676-3463	676-6715
Eckos Restaurant 2701 S 1st St	Abilene	TX	79605	325-672-3792	
Fuji Japanese Steak House 3110 S 27th St	Abilene	TX	79605	325-695-9233	
Harold's 1305 Walnut St	Abilene	TX	79601	325-672-4451	
Joe Allen's Pit Bar-B-Que 303 S 11th St *Web:* www.joeallens.com	Abilene	TX	79602	325-672-6082	
Little Panda 1035 N Judge Ely Blvd *Web:* www.littlepandaonline.com	Abilene	TX	79601	325-670-9393	670-9392
Lytle Land & Cattle Co 1150 E S 11th St *Web:* www.lytlelandandcattle.com	Abilene	TX	79605	325-677-1925	677-0951
Spano's 4534 Buffalo Gap Rd	Abilene	TX	79606	325-698-3704	695-0598
Towne Crier Steak House 818 US Hwy 80 E *Web:* www.towneciersteakhouse.com	Abilene	TX	79601	325-673-4551	673-0065
Abuelo's Mexican Food Embassy 3501 W 45th Ave *Web:* www.abuelos.com	Amarillo	TX	79109	806-354-8294	
Amarillo Club 600 S Tyler St *Web:* www.amarilloclub.com	Amarillo	TX	79101	806-373-4361	372-2606
Big Texan Steak Ranch 7701 I-40 E *TF Cust Svc:* 800-657-7177 ■ *Web:* www.bigtexan.com	Amarillo	TX	79118	806-372-7000	371-0099
BL Bistro 2203 S Austin St *Web:* www.blbistro.com	Amarillo	TX	79109	806-355-7838	373-8481
Buns Over Texas 3440 Bell St	Amarillo	TX	79109	806-358-6808	
Cattle Call 4111 Wolflin Ave *Web:* www.cattlecall.com	Amarillo	TX	79102	806-353-1227	353-9084
Coyote Bluff Cafe 2417 S Grand St	Amarillo	TX	79103	806-373-4640	

Name / Address	City	State	ZIP	Phone	Fax
Doug's Hickory Pit Bar B Que 3313 S Georgia St	Amarillo	TX	79109	806-352-8471	
Golden Light Cafe 2908 W 6th Ave	Amarillo	TX	79106	806-374-0097	
Web: www.goldenlightcafe.com					
Hoffbrau Steaks 7203 IH- I-40 & Coulter	Amarillo	TX	79106	806-358-6595	354-8411
Web: www.hoffbrausteaks.com					
Hummer's Sports Cafe 2600 Paramount Blvd	Amarillo	TX	79109	806-353-0723	353-4249
Jorge's Taco Garcia Mexican Cafe 1100 S Ross St	Amarillo	TX	79102	806-371-0411	371-0538
Web: www.tacosgarcia.com					
Kabuki Japanese Steakhouse 8130 I 40 W	Amarillo	TX	79106	806-358-7799	
Web: www.kabukiromanca.com					
Macaroni Joe's 1619 S Kentucky St Suite 1500-D	Amarillo	TX	79102	806-358-8990	433-1325
Web: www.macaronijoes.com					
My Thai 2029 Coulter Dr	Amarillo	TX	79106	806-355-9541	379-9732
Pacific Rim 2061 Paramount Blvd	Amarillo	TX	79109	806-353-9179	
Web: www.pacificrimam.com					
Plaza Restaurant 3415 Bell St	Amarillo	TX	79109	806-358-4897	358-4038
Ruby Tequila's 2001 S Georgia	Amarillo	TX	79109	806-358-7829	358-0086
Web: www.rubytequilas.com					
Zen 721 616 S Polk St	Amarillo	TX	79101	806-372-1909	
Web: www.zen721.com					
Abuelo's Mexican Food Embassy 1041 IH- 20 W	Arlington	TX	76017	817-468-2622	468-7221
Web: www.abuelos.com					
Arlington Steak House 1724 W Division St	Arlington	TX	76012	817-275-7881	
Bigotes 1821 E Abram St	Arlington	TX	76010	817-274-1350	
Buck N' Loons Cafe 3517 S Cooper St	Arlington	TX	76015	817-466-2825	466-2900
Web: www.bucknloons.com					
Cacherel 2221 E Lamar Blvd	Arlington	TX	76006	817-640-9981	633-5737
Web: www.cacharel.net					
Candlelite Inn Restaurant 1202 E Division St	Arlington	TX	76011	817-275-9613	459-3288
Web: www.candlelite-inn.com					
La Isla 611 W Pk Row	Arlington	TX	76010	817-460-1180	
Mariano's 2614 Majesty Dr	Arlington	TX	76011	817-640-5118	633-3894
Web: www.marianosrestaurant.com					
Nagoya Japanese Restaurant 4040 S Cooper St	Arlington	TX	76015	817-466-3688	466-3684
Pappadeaux Seafood Kitchen 1304 E Copeland Rd	Arlington	TX	76011	817-543-0545	543-0548
Web: www.pappadeaux.com					
Pappasito's Cantina 321 Rd to Six Flags St W	Arlington	TX	76011	817-795-3535	795-5865
Web: www.pappas.com					
Piccolo Mondo 829 E Lamar Blvd	Arlington	TX	76011	817-265-9174	226-3474
Web: www.piccolomondo.com					
Piranha 851 NE Green Oaks Blvd	Arlington	TX	76006	817-261-1636	
Web: www.piranhakillersushi.com					
Portofino Ristorante 226 Lincoln Sq	Arlington	TX	76011	817-861-8300	861-1987
Web: www.portofinoristorante.com					
Simply Fondue 770 E Rd to Six Flags	Arlington	TX	76011	817-861-1144	861-1142
Web: www.simplyfondue.com					
Sukhothai 423 Fielder N Plaza	Arlington	TX	76012	817-860-4107	860-0421
Sushi Zone 915 E Rd to Six Flags	Arlington	TX	76011	817-226-4055	226-2265
Tandoor 532 N Fielder Rd	Arlington	TX	76012	817-261-6604	548-9026
Taste of Thai 2535 E Arkansas Ln	Arlington	TX	76010	817-543-0110	
Texas Land & Cattle Co 2009 E Copeland Rd	Arlington	TX	76011	817-461-1500	801-6600
Web: www.txlc.com					
TL Kowloon 100 W Pioneer Pkwy	Arlington	TX	76010	817-261-6699	
Alborz Persian Cuisine 3300 W Anderson Ln Suite 303	Austin	TX	78757	512-420-2222	
Web: www.alborzpersiancuisine.com					
Aquarelle 606 Rio Grande St	Austin	TX	78701	512-479-8117	206-0077
Web: www.aquarellerestaurant.com					
Asti Trattoria 408C E 43rd St	Austin	TX	78751	512-451-1218	451-2233
Web: www.astiaustin.com					
Austin Land & Cattle Co 1205 N LaMar Blvd	Austin	TX	78703	512-472-1813	472-1815
Web: www.austinlandandcattlecompany.com					
Bistro 88 2712 Bee Caves Rd	Austin	TX	78746	512-328-8888	328-1740
Web: www.bistro88.com					
Cafe at the Four Seasons 98 San Jacinto Blvd	Austin	TX	78701	512-478-4500	478-3117
Casa de Luz 1701 Toomey Rd	Austin	TX	78704	512-476-2535	476-0198
Web: www.casadeluz.org					
Chez Nous 510 Neches St	Austin	TX	78701	512-473-2413	236-8468
Chez Zee American Bistro 5406 Balcones Dr	Austin	TX	78731	512-454-2666	454-0034
Web: www.chez-zee.com					
Clay Pit 1601 Guadalupe St	Austin	TX	78701	512-322-5131	322-9514
Web: www.claypit.com					
Curra's Grill 614 E Oltorf St	Austin	TX	78704	512-444-0012	444-2542
Web: www.currasgrill.com					
Cypress Grill 4404 W William Cannon Dr Suite L	Austin	TX	78749	512-358-7474	358-7472
Web: www.cypressgrill.net					
Din Ho's Chinese BBQ 8557 Research Blvd	Austin	TX	78758	512-832-8788	
Dog & Duck Pub The 406 W 17th St	Austin	TX	78701	512-479-0598	
Web: www.dogandduckpub.com					
Driskill Grill 604 Brazos St	Austin	TX	78701	512-391-7162	391-7059
Web: www.driskillgrill.com					
Eastside Cafe 2113 Manor Rd	Austin	TX	78722	512-476-5858	477-5847
Web: www.eastsidecafeaustin.com					
Eddie V's Edgewater Grille 301 E 5th St	Austin	TX	78701	512-472-1860	477-9794
Web: www.eddiev.com					
El Sol Y La Luna 600 E 6th St	Austin	TX	78701	512-444-7770	444-4554
Emerald Restaurant 13614 Hwy 71 W	Austin	TX	78738	512-263-2147	
Fado's Irish Pub 214 W 4th St	Austin	TX	78701	512-457-0172	457-0519
Web: www.fadoirishpub.com					
Fonda San Miguel 2330 W N Loop Blvd	Austin	TX	78756	512-459-4121	459-5792
Web: www.fondasanmiguel.com					
Green Pastures 811 W Live Oak St	Austin	TX	78704	512-444-4747	444-3912
Web: www.greenpasturesrestaurant.com					
Habana 2728 S Congress Ave	Austin	TX	78704	512-443-4252	472-4042
Web: www.habana.com					
Hudson's on the Bend 3509 Ranch Rd 620 N	Austin	TX	78734	512-266-1369	266-1399
Web: www.hudsonsonthebend.com					
Hula Hut 3825 Lake Austin Blvd	Austin	TX	78703	512-476-4852	477-1604
Web: www.hulahut.com					
Hunan 1940 W William Cannon Dr	Austin	TX	78745	512-443-8848	
Web: www.hunanaustin.com					
Hyde Park Bar & Grill 4206 Duval St	Austin	TX	78751	512-458-3168	458-6722
Web: www.hpbng.com					
III Forks 111 Lavaca St	Austin	TX	78701	512-474-1776	
Web: www.3forks.com					
Jeffrey's Restaurant 1204 W Lynn St	Austin	TX	78703	512-477-5584	474-7279
Web: www.jeffreysofaustin.com					
Kenichi 419 Colorado St	Austin	TX	78701	512-320-8883	320-8882
Web: www.kenichiaustin.com					
Kim Phung 7601 N Lamar Blvd Suite I	Austin	TX	78752	512-451-2464	451-8083
Korea House 2700 W Anderson Ln	Austin	TX	78757	512-458-2477	
La Traviata 314 Congress Ave	Austin	TX	78701	512-479-8131	479-8545
Madam Mam's 2514 Guadalupe St	Austin	TX	78705	512-472-8306	236-4030
Madras Pavillion 9025 Research Blvd	Austin	TX	78758	512-719-5575	719-4527
Magnolia Cafe 2304 Lake Austin Blvd	Austin	TX	78703	512-478-8645	494-1722
Web: www.themagnoliacafe.com					
Marakesh Mediterranean Cafe 906 Congress Ave	Austin	TX	78701	512-476-7735	
Mikado Ryotei 9033 Research Blvd	Austin	TX	78758	512-833-8188	833-8145
Web: www.mikadoryotei.com					
Mirabelle 8127 Mesa Dr Suite A-100	Austin	TX	78759	512-346-7900	346-9900
Web: www.mirabellerestaurant.com					
Moonshine Patio Bar & Grill 303 Red River St	Austin	TX	78701	512-236-9599	236-8816
Web: www.moonshinegrill.com					
Musashino Sushi Dokoro 3407 Greystone Dr	Austin	TX	78731	512-795-8593	
Web: www.musashinosushi.com					
Oasis The 6550 Comanche Trail	Austin	TX	78732	512-266-2442	266-9296
Web: www.oasis-austin.com					
Rocco's Grill 900 Ranch Rd 620 S Suite A106	Austin	TX	78734	512-263-8204	263-5332
Web: www.roccosgrill.com					
Romeo's 1500 Barton Springs Rd	Austin	TX	78704	512-476-1090	476-5107
Web: www.romeosrestaurants.com					
Roy's 340 E 2nd St	Austin	TX	78701	512-391-1500	391-1514
Web: www.roysrestaurant.com					
Ruth's Chris Steak House 107 W 6th St	Austin	TX	78701	512-477-7884	
Satay 3202 W Anderson Ln	Austin	TX	78757	512-467-6731	467-9640
Web: www.satayusa.com					
Shoreline Grill 98 San Jacinto Blvd	Austin	TX	78701	512-477-3300	477-6392
Web: www.shorelinegrill.com					
Star of India 2900 W Anderson Ln Suite 12D	Austin	TX	78757	512-452-8199	
Web: www.starofindiaaustin.com					
Starlite 407 Colorado St	Austin	TX	78701	512-374-9012	299-9209
Sullivan's Steakhouse 300 Colorado St	Austin	TX	78701	512-495-6504	495-6509
Web: www.sullivansteakhouse.com					
Sunflower 8557 Research Blvd	Austin	TX	78758	512-339-7860	
Sushi Japon 6801 N IH-35	Austin	TX	78752	512-323-6663	323-6789
Web: www.sushijaponaustin.com					
Thai Noodles Etc House 2602 Guadelupe St	Austin	TX	78705	512-494-1011	474-2562
Threadgill's 6416 N Lamar Blvd	Austin	TX	78752	512-451-5440	451-5033
Web: www.threadgills.com					
Tien Hong 8301 Burnet Rd	Austin	TX	78757	512-458-2263	458-2268
Web: www.tienhong.net					
Uchi 801 S Lamar Blvd	Austin	TX	78704	512-916-4808	916-4806
Web: www.uchiaustin.com					
Umi Sushi Bar & Grill 5510 S IH-35 Suite 400	Austin	TX	78745	512-383-8681	383-8802
Veggie Heaven 1914 Guadalupe St	Austin	TX	78705	512-457-1013	
Vespaio 1610 S Congress Ave	Austin	TX	78704	512-441-6100	441-7746
Wink Restaurant 1014 N Lamar Blvd	Austin	TX	78703	512-482-8868	482-9477
Web: www.winkrestaurant.com					
Z Tejas Grill 9400-A Arboreum Blvd	Austin	TX	78759	512-346-3506	346-6328
Web: www.ztejas.com					
Zoot 11715 Bee Cave Rd	Bee Cave	TX	78738	512-477-6535	476-7649
Web: www.zootrestaurant.com					
Antonio's Mexican Village 840 Paredes Rd	Brownsville	TX	78521	956-542-6504	542-1125
Blue Mermaid Cafe 119 Billy Mitchell Blvd	Brownsville	TX	78521	956-544-2157	
Cobbleheads Bar & Grill 3154 Central Blvd	Brownsville	TX	78520	956-546-6224	546-6772
Web: www.cobbleheads.com					
Los Camperos 2500 N Expressway	Brownsville	TX	78520	956-546-8172	546-8506
Lotus Inn 905 N Expy	Brownsville	TX	78520	956-542-5715	541-6973
Lula's 2235 Central Blvd	Brownsville	TX	78520	956-541-4911	
Oyster Bar I 1057 E Levee St	Brownsville	TX	79520	956-542-9786	
Sylvia's Restaurant 1843 Southmost Rd	Brownsville	TX	78521	956-542-9220	
Vermillion The 115 Paredes Line Rd	Brownsville	TX	78521	956-542-9893	541-4221
Web: www.thevermillion.com					
Crawdaddy's 414 Starr St	Corpus Christi	TX	78401	361-883-5432	888-8892
D Noodlehouse 4701 Ayers St	Corpus Christi	TX	78415	361-855-6096	
El Rinconcitos 4025 Prescott St	Corpus Christi	TX	78416	361-851-8020	
Executive Surf Club 309 N Water St	Corpus Christi	TX	78401	361-884-7873	884-2865
Web: www.executivesurfclub.com					
Kiko's 5514 Everhart Rd	Corpus Christi	TX	78411	361-991-1211	
Kobe Japanese Seafood 5134 Carroll Ln	Corpus Christi	TX	78415	361-851-2555	851-2555
Little Manila Lumpia House 2124 Waldron Rd	Corpus Christi	TX	78418	361-937-5651	
Mamma Mia's 128 N Mesquite St	Corpus Christi	TX	78401	361-883-3773	
Peoples 9738 Up River Rd	Corpus Christi	TX	78410	361-241-8087	241-8089
Web: www.peoplesrestaurant.com					
Pier 99 2822 N Shoreline Blvd	Corpus Christi	TX	78402	361-887-0764	
Republic of Texas Bar & Grill 900 N Shoreline Blvd	Corpus Christi	TX	78401	361-886-3515	886-3530
Snoopy's Pier 13313 S Padre Island Dr	Corpus Christi	TX	78418	361-949-8815	
Thai Spice 523 N Water St	Corpus Christi	TX	78401	361-883-8884	883-8881
Web: www.thaispicecc.com					
Torch Restaurant 4425 S Alameda St	Corpus Christi	TX	78412	361-992-7491	
Two George's 5884 Everhart Rd	Corpus Christi	TX	78413	361-993-8008	993-0094
Web: www.2georgescc.com					

Name / Address	City	State	Zip	Phone	Fax
Vietnam Restaurant 701 N Water St	Corpus Christi	TX	78401	361-853-2682	
Web: www.vietnam-restaurant.com					
Water Street 309 N Water St	Corpus Christi	TX	78401	361-882-2211	888-7783
Web: www.waterstreetmarketcc.com					
Water Street Seafood Co 309 N Water St	Corpus Christi	TX	78401	361-882-2211	882-2835
2900 2900 Thomas Ave	Dallas	TX	75204	214-303-0400	
Web: www.2900restaurant.com					
Abacus *Kent Rathbun* 4511 McKinney Ave.	Dallas	TX	75205	214-559-3111	559-3113
Web: www.kentrathbun.com/abacus					
Al Biernat's 4217 Oak Lawn Ave	Dallas	TX	75219	214-219-2201	219-2093
Web: www.albiernats.com					
Ali Baba Cafe 1905 Greenville Ave	Dallas	TX	75206	214-823-8235	
Web: www.alibabacafe.com					
Amore 6931 Snider Plaza	Dallas	TX	75205	214-739-0502	739-0577
Anderson's BBQ House 5410 Harry Hines Blvd	Dallas	TX	75235	214-630-0735	630-1686
Web: www.mikeandersonsbbq.com					
Arcodoro & Pomodoro 2708 Routh St	Dallas	TX	75201	214-871-1924	871-3141
Web: www.arcodoro.com					
Asian Mint 11617 N Central Expy Suite 135	Dallas	TX	75243	214-363-6655	363-6686
Web: www.asianmint.com					
August Moon 15030 Preston Rd	Dallas	TX	75254	972-385-7227	385-7617
Web: www.guidelynx.net/augustmoon					
Aurora 4216 Oak Lawn Ave	Dallas	TX	75219	214-528-9400	528-9503
Web: www.auroradallas.net					
Avila's 4714 Maple Ave	Dallas	TX	75219	214-520-2700	
Aw Shucks restaurant 3601 Greenville Ave	Dallas	TX	75206	214-821-9449	821-4581
Web: www.awshucksdallas.com					
Blue Fish 3519 Greenville Ave	Dallas	TX	75206	214-824-3474	
Web: www.thebluefishsushi.com					
Bob's Steak & Chop House 4300 Lemmon Ave	Dallas	TX	75219	214-528-9446	526-8159
Web: www.bobs-steakandchop.com					
Cafe Istanbul 5450 W Lovers Ln	Dallas	TX	75209	214-902-0919	
Web: www.cafe-istanbul.net					
Cafe Izmir 3711 Greenville Ave	Dallas	TX	75206	214-826-7788	827-4359
Web: www.cafeizmir.com					
Cafe Madrid 4501 Travis St	Dallas	TX	75205	214-528-1731	522-8752
Web: www.cafemadrid-dallas.com					
Cafe Pacific 24 Highland Pk Village	Dallas	TX	75205	214-526-1170	526-0332
Web: www.cafepacificdalls.com					
Capital Grille The 500 Crescent Ct Suite 135	Dallas	TX	75201	214-303-0500	303-0523
Web: www.thecapitalgrille.com					
Celebration Restaurant & Catering 4503 W Lovers Ln PO Box 7330	Dallas	TX	75209	214-351-5681	904-1716
Web: www.celebrationrestaurant.com					
City Cafe 5757 W Lovers Ln	Dallas	TX	75209	214-351-2233	351-1936
Web: www.thecitycafedallas.com					
Cosmic Cafe 2912 Oak Lawn Ave	Dallas	TX	75219	214-521-6157	
Web: www.cosmiccafedallas.com					
Cuba Libre 2822 N Henderson Ave	Dallas	TX	75206	214-827-2820	827-2189
Web: consilientrestaurants.com					
Deep Sushi 2624 Elm St	Dallas	TX	75226	214-651-1177	
Web: www.deepsushi.com					
Del Frisco's of dallas 5251 Spring Valley Rd	Dallas	TX	75254	972-490-9000	934-0867
Web: www.delfriscos.com					
East Wind Vietnamese Restaurant 2800 Routh St	Dallas	TX	75201	214-745-5554	
Web: www.eastwinddallas.com					
Fadi's Mediterranean Grill 3001 Knox St	Dallas	TX	75205	214-528-1800	528-1807
Web: www.fadiscuisine.com					
Fearing's 2121 McKinney Ave	Dallas	TX	75201	214-922-4848	
Web: www.fearingsrestaurant.com					
French Room 1321 Commerce St	Dallas	TX	75202	214-742-8200	651-3575
Web: www.hoteladolphus.com					
Fuji Steakhouse & Sushi Bar 12817 Preston Rd	Dallas	TX	75230	972-661-5662	661-1751
Web: www.fujidallas.com					
Genghis Grill 4901 LBJ Fwy Suite 150	Dallas	TX	75244	214-774-4240	
TF: 888-436-4447 ■ *Web:* www.genghisgrill.com					
Grape The 2808 Greenville Ave	Dallas	TX	75206	214-828-1981	826-2187
Web: www.thegraperestaurant.com					
Green Papaya 3211 Oak Lawn Ave Suite B	Dallas	TX	75219	214-521-4811	521-4685
Web: www.greenpapayadallas.com					
Hibiscus 2927 N Henderson	Dallas	TX	75206	214-827-2927	
Web: www.hibiscusdallas.com					
Hotel St Germain 2516 Maple Ave	Dallas	TX	75201	214-871-2516	871-0740
Web: www.hotelstgermain.com					
III Forks Steakhouse 17776 Dallas Pkwy	Dallas	TX	75287	972-267-1776	267-1799
Web: www.iiiforks.com					
Il Sole 4514 Travis St Suite 201	Dallas	TX	75205	214-559-3888	559-3990
Web: www.ilsole-dallas.com					
India Palace Restaurant 12817 Preston Rd Suite 105	Dallas	TX	75230	972-392-0190	392-3188
Web: www.indiapalacedallas.com					
Jade Garden 4800 Bryan St	Dallas	TX	75204	214-821-0675	821-0675
Javier's Gourmet Mexicano 4912 Cole Ave	Dallas	TX	75205	214-521-4211	521-5239
Web: www.javiers.net					
Kathleen's Art Cafe 4424 Lovers Ln	Dallas	TX	75225	214-691-2355	691-3412
Web: www.skydinnerdallas.com					
La Duni Latin Cafe 4264 Oak Lawn Ave	Dallas	TX	75219	214-520-7300	520-7390
Web: www.laduni.com					
La Madeleine de Corps Inc 12201 Merit Dr Suite 900	Dallas	TX	75251	214-696-6962	696-0485
Web: www.lamadeleine.com					
Lavendou 19009 Preston Rd Suite 200	Dallas	TX	75252	972-248-1911	248-1660
Web: www.lavendou.com					
Luna de Noche 7927 Forest Ln	Dallas	TX	75230	972-233-1880	
Web: www.lunadenochetexmex.com					
May Dragon 4848 Beltline Rd	Dallas	TX	75254	972-392-9998	490-5023
Web: www.maydragon.com					
Mercury Grill The 11909 Preston Rd Suite 1418	Dallas	TX	75230	972-960-7774	960-7988
Web: www.mcrowd.com					
Monica's Aca Y Alla 2914 Main St	Dallas	TX	75226	214-748-7140	748-3291
Web: www.monicas.com					
Morton's The Steakhouse 2222 McKinney Ave	Dallas	TX	75201	214-741-2277	748-6360
Web: www.mortons.com					
Nana Restaurant 2201 Stemmons Fwy	Dallas	TX	75207	214-761-7470	761-7516
Web: www.nanarestaurant.com					
Nick & Sam's Grill 3008 Maple Ave	Dallas	TX	75201	214-871-7444	871-7663
Web: www.nick-sams.com					
Oceanaire Seafood Room 1334 Dallas Pkwy	Dallas	TX	75240	972-759-2277	759-0706
Web: www.theoceanaire.com					
Oishii 2525 Wycliff Ave	Dallas	TX	75219	214-599-9448	599-9468
Old Warsaw The 2610 Maple Ave	Dallas	TX	75201	214-528-0032	
Web: www.oldwarsaw.com					
Palm The Restaurant 701 Ross Ave	Dallas	TX	75202	214-698-0470	
Web: www.thepalm.com					
Palomino Euro Bistro 500 Crescent Ct Suite 165	Dallas	TX	75201	214-999-1222	999-1115
Web: www.palomino.com					
Pappadeaux Seafood Kitchen 3520 Oak Lawn Ave	Dallas	TX	75219	214-521-4700	521-4726
Web: www.pappadeaux.com					
Perry's 2911 Routh St	Dallas	TX	75201	214-871-9991	871-0302
Web: www.theplaceatperrys.com					
PF Chang's China Bistro 225 Northpark Ctr	Dallas	TX	75225	214-265-8669	265-8836
Web: www.pfchangs.com					
Primo's 3309 McKinney Ave	Dallas	TX	75204	214-220-0510	220-2786
Web: www.primosdallas.com					
Pyramid Grill 1717 N Akard St	Dallas	TX	75201	214-720-5249	720-5282
Web: www.pyramidrestaurant.com					
Rosewood Mansion on Turtle Creek 2821 Turtle Creek Blvd	Dallas	TX	75219	214-559-2100	528-4187
Web: www.rosewoodhotels.com					
Royal Thai 5500 Greenville Ave	Dallas	TX	75206	214-691-3555	
Ruth's Chris Steak House 17840 Dallas Pkwy	Dallas	TX	75287	972-250-2244	250-1590
Web: www.ruthschris.com					
S & D Oyster Co 2701 McKinney Ave	Dallas	TX	75204	214-880-0111	
Saint Martin's Wine Bistro 3020 Greenville Ave	Dallas	TX	75206	214-826-0940	826-1229
Web: www.stmartinswinebistro.com					
Sammy's Barbeque 2126 Leonard St	Dallas	TX	75201	214-880-9064	871-7597
Web: www.sammysbbq.com					
Sevy's Grill 8201 Preston Rd Suite 100	Dallas	TX	75225	214-265-7389	265-8949
Web: www.sevys.com					
Steel Restaurant & Lounge 3102 Oaklawn Ave	Dallas	TX	75219	214-219-9908	219-9929
Web: www.steeldallas.com					
Suze 4535 W NW Hwy	Dallas	TX	75220	214-350-6135	350-6178
Web: www.suzerestaurant.net					
Tei Tei Robata Bar 2906 N Henderson St	Dallas	TX	75206	214-828-2400	
Web: www.teiteirobata.com					
Tejano 110 W Davis St	Dallas	TX	75208	214-943-8610	946-4779
Teppo Yakitori & Sushi Bar 2014 Greenville Ave	Dallas	TX	75206	214-826-8989	826-1913
Web: www.teppo.com					
Tramontana 8220 Westchester Dr # B	Dallas	TX	75225	214-368-4188	
Web: www.mybistro.net					
Watel's 2207 Allen St	Dallas	TX	75204	214-720-0323	
YO Ranch Steakhouse 702 Ross Ave	Dallas	TX	75201	214-744-3287	748-7957
Web: www.yoranchsteakhouse.com					
Ziziki's Restaurant & Bar 4514 Travis St Suite 122	Dallas	TX	75205	214-521-2233	521-2722
Web: www.zizikis.com					
Salt Lick 18300 FM 1826	Driftwood	TX	78619	512-858-4959	858-2038
Web: www.saltlickbbq.com					
Azulejo's Restaurant 101 S El Paso St	El Paso	TX	79901	915-534-3020	
Bella Napoli 6331 N Mesa St	El Paso	TX	79912	915-584-3321	584-3466
Web: www.bellanapoliristorante.com					
Cafe Central 109 N Oregon St	El Paso	TX	79901	915-545-2233	545-2884
Web: www.cafecentral.com					
Cappetto's 2716 Montana Ave	El Paso	TX	79903	915-566-9357	
Web: www.cappettos.com					
Cattle Baron 1700 Airway Blvd	El Paso	TX	79925	915-779-6633	779-3147
Web: www.cattlebaron.com					
Dome The 101 S El Paso St	El Paso	TX	79901	800-769-4300	
TF: 800-769-4300					
Dominic's 6901 Montana Ave	El Paso	TX	79925	915-778-0011	778-0098
Web: www.dominicsitalianrestaurant.com					
Dona Lupe Cafe 2919 Pershing Dr	El Paso	TX	79903	915-566-9833	566-1175
Edge of Texas Steakhouse 8690 Edge of Texas	El Paso	TX	79934	915-822-3343	822-3348
Web: www.edgeoftexas.com					
Forti's Mexican Elder 321 Chelsea St	El Paso	TX	79905	915-772-0066	772-0067
Japanese Kitchen 4024 N Mesa St	El Paso	TX	79902	915-533-4267	542-1015
Jaxon's 4799 N Mesa St	El Paso	TX	79912	915-544-1188	577-0638
Web: www.jaxons.com					
Julio's Cafe Corona 8050 Gateway Blvd E	El Paso	TX	79907	915-591-7676	592-1294
L & J Cafe 3622 E Missouri St	El Paso	TX	79903	915-566-8418	566-4070
Web: www.l&jcafe.com					
Landry's Seafood House 6801 Gateway Blvd W	El Paso	TX	79925	915-779-2900	779-0600
TF: 800-394-3839					
Mediterranean Cuisine 4111 N Mesa St	El Paso	TX	79902	915-542-1012	
Michelinos 3615 Rutherglen St	El Paso	TX	79925	915-592-1700	
Web: www.michelinos.com					
New Clock Restaurant 8409 Dyer St	El Paso	TX	79904	915-751-6367	
Peking Garden 3306 Fort Blvd	El Paso	TX	79930	915-565-9090	565-9091
Pelican's West 130 Shadow Mountain Rd	El Paso	TX	79912	915-581-1392	
PF Chang's China Bistro 760 Sunland Pk Dr	El Paso	TX	79912	915-845-0166	845-0180
Web: www.pfchangs.com					
Pho Tre Bien 8838 Viscount Blvd	El Paso	TX	79925	915-598-0166	
Senor Fish 9530 Viscount Blvd Suite 1A	El Paso	TX	79925	915-598-3630	598-3608
State Line 1222 Sunland Pk Dr	El Paso	TX	79922	915-581-3371	833-4843
Web: www.airribs.com					
State Line The 1222 Sunland Pk Dr	El Paso	TX	79922	915-581-3371	
Web: www.countyline.com					
Trattoria Bella Sera 9449 Montana Ave	El Paso	TX	79925	915-598-7948	
Web: trattoriabellasera.com					

Name / Address	City	State	Zip	Phone	Fax
Cattleman's Steakhouse 4 1/2 Miles N Ih 10	Fabens	TX	79838	915-544-3200	764-4168
Web: www.cattlemanssteakhouse.com					
Bistro Louise 2900 S Hulen St	Fort Worth	TX	76109	817-922-9244	922-8148
Web: www.bistrolouise.com					
Blue Mesa Grill 1600 S University Dr	Fort Worth	TX	76107	817-332-6372	332-6398
Web: www.bluemesagrill.com					
Bonnell's 4259 Bryant Irvin Rd	Fort Worth	TX	76019	817-738-5489	
Web: www.bonnellsrestaurant.com					
Byblos Byblos Lebanese Restaurant 1406 N Main St	Fort Worth	TX	76106	817-625-9667	625-8319
Web: www.byblostx.com					
Cafe Aspen 6115 Camp Bowie Blvd	Fort Worth	TX	76116	817-738-0838	738-3217
Web: www.cafeaspen.com					
Cafe Modern 3200 Darnell St	Fort Worth	TX	76107	817-840-2157	735-1161
Web: www.themodern.org					
Caro's Restaurants Inc 3505 Bluebonnet Cir	Fort Worth	TX	76109	817-924-9977	394-2402
Web: www.pufftacodaddy.com					
Celaborelle Phoenician Buffet 2257 Hemphill St	Fort Worth	TX	76110	817-922-8118	
Web: www.celaborelle.com					
Del Frisco's Double Eagle Steak House 812 Main St	Fort Worth	TX	76102	817-877-3999	877-4499
Web: www.delfriscos.com					
Dixie House Cafe 6200 E Lancaster Ave	Fort Worth	TX	76112	817-451-6180	451-4763
Web: www.dixiehousecafe.com					
Edelweiss German Restaurant 3801 SW Blvd A	Fort Worth	TX	76116	817-738-5934	738-6946
Web: www.edelweissgermanrestaurant.com					
Fizzi 500 Commerce St	Fort Worth	TX	76102	817-336-3499	336-5696
Fort Worth Chop House 301 Main St	Fort Worth	TX	76102	817-336-4129	332-6773
Web: www.fortworthchophouse.com					
H3 Ranch 109 E Exchange Ave Stockyards Hotel	Fort Worth	TX	76106	817-624-1246	624-2571
Web: www.h3ranch.com					
Hui Chuan Sushi 6100 Camp Bowie Blvd Suite 12	Fort Worth	TX	76116	817-989-8886	
Joe T Garcia's 2201 N Commerce St	Fort Worth	TX	76164	817-626-4356	626-0581
Web: www.joets.com					
La Familia Restaurant 841 Foch St	Fort Worth	TX	76107	817-870-2002	
Web: www.lafamilia-fw.com					
Lanny's Alta Cocina Mexicana 3405 W 7th St	Fort Worth	TX	76107	817-850-9996	
Web: www.lannyskitchen.com					
Lonesome Dove Western Bistro 2406 N Main St	Fort Worth	TX	76164	817-740-8810	740-8632
Web: www.lonesomedovebistro.com					
Los Molcajetes 4320 Western Ctr Blvd	Fort Worth	TX	76137	817-306-9000	306-9033
Web: www.losmolcajetes.com					
Lucille's Stateside Bistro 4700 Camp Bowie Blvd	Fort Worth	TX	76107	817-738-4761	
Maharaja Restaurant 6308 Hulen Bend Blvd	Fort Worth	TX	76132	817-263-7156	
Mi Cocina 509 Main St	Fort Worth	TX	76102	817-877-3600	332-4182
Piranha 335 W 3rd St	Fort Worth	TX	76102	817-348-0200	
Web: www.piranhakillersushi.com					
Railhead Smokehouse 2900 Montgomery St	Fort Worth	TX	76107	817-738-9808	732-4059
Reata 310 Houston St	Fort Worth	TX	76102	817-336-1009	336-2661
Web: www.reata.net					
Ristorante La Piazza 1600 S University Dr	Fort Worth	TX	76107	817-334-0000	338-0945
Saint Emilion 3617 W 7th St	Fort Worth	TX	76107	817-737-2781	
Web: www.saint-emilionrestaurant.com					
Sapristi! 2418 Forest Pk Blvd	Fort Worth	TX	76110	817-924-7231	
Web: www.sapristibistro.com					
Sardines Ristorante Italiano 509 University Dr	Fort Worth	TX	76107	817-332-9937	332-6708
Silver Fox Steakhouse 1651 S University Dr	Fort Worth	TX	76107	817-332-9060	332-9073
Web: www.silverfoxcafe.com					
Spiral Diner 1314 W Magnolia Ave	Fort Worth	TX	76104	817-332-8834	
Web: www.spiraldiner.com					
Texas de Brazil 101 N Houston St	Fort Worth	TX	76102	817-882-9500	882-9503
Web: www.texasdebrazil.com					
Tokyo Cafe 5121 Pershing Ave	Fort Worth	TX	76107	817-737-8568	
Web: www.thetokyocafe.com					
Tres Jose's 4004 White Settlement Rd	Fort Worth	TX	76107	817-763-0456	763-0911
West Side Cafe 7950 Camp Bowie W	Fort Worth	TX	76116	817-560-1996	
Yum Yum 4954 Overton Ridge Blvd	Fort Worth	TX	76132	817-370-0688	
Web: www.yumyumrestaurant.com					
China City Restaurant 6022 Broadway Blvd	Garland	TX	75043	972-303-0373	
China Star 2425 W Walnut St Suite 222	Garland	TX	75042	972-487-8311	
Crazy Catfish 1410 W Buckingham Rd	Garland	TX	75042	972-487-2100	
Ernesto's 1202 NW Hwy	Garland	TX	75041	972-681-8112	
Fish City Grill 445 Coneflower Dr	Garland	TX	75040	972-675-1600	
Web: www.fishcitygrill.com					
General Pao Chinese Restaurant 1311 Plaza Dr	Garland	TX	75041	972-686-8691	686-8692
Lucky China Buffet 1102 NW Hwy	Garland	TX	75041	972-270-3430	270-8839
Luna de Noche 7602 N Jupiter Rd Suite 109A	Garland	TX	75044	469-246-8271	246-8274
Web: www.lunadenochetexmex.com					
On the Border Cafe 1350 NW Hwy	Garland	TX	75041	972-686-7867	613-0235
Pupusas Mama Tita 618 W Walnut St	Garland	TX	75042	972-272-5818	
Rick's Smoke House Barbecue 1417 Jupiter Rd	Garland	TX	75042	972-276-4353	487-1101
Web: www.rickssmokehousebbq.com					
Saigon Kitchen 3555 Walnut St	Garland	TX	75042	972-276-2214	
Soulman's Barbeque 3410 Broadway Blvd	Garland	TX	75043	972-271-6885	
Uncle Wing Chinese Restaurant 107 N 1st St	Garland	TX	75040	972-272-2775	
Web: www.letseat.at/UncleWing					
Yen China Cafe 1225 Belt Line Rd	Garland	TX	75040	972-495-9779	495-4929
Grey Moss Inn 19010 Scenic Loop Rd	Helotes	TX	78023	210-695-8301	695-3237
Web: www.grey-moss-inn.com					
Americas 1800 Post Oak Blvd Suite 164	Houston	TX	77056	713-961-1492	626-2701
Web: www.cordua.com/Americas_hm.htm					
Arcodoro 5000 Westheimer Rd Suite 120	Houston	TX	77056	713-621-6888	621-6886
Web: www.arcodoro.com					

Name / Address	City	State	Zip	Phone	Fax
Armandos 2630 Westheimer Rd	Houston	TX	77098	713-520-1738	520-5748
Web: www.armandosrestaurant.com					
Ashiana 12610 Briar Forest	Houston	TX	77070	281-679-5555	493-0981
Web: www.ashiana.cc					
Babin's Seafood House 17485 Tomball Pkwy	Houston	TX	77064	281-477-9300	477-9322
Web: www.babinsseafood.com					
Backstreet Cafe 1103 S Shepherd Dr	Houston	TX	77019	713-521-2239	520-5724
Web: www.backstreetcafe.net					
Baker's Ribs 2223 S Voss Rd	Houston	TX	77057	713-977-8725	
Web: www.bakersribs.com					
Benjy's 2424 Dunstan Rd Suite 125	Houston	TX	77005	713-522-7602	522-7655
Web: www.benjys.com					
Bistro Vino 819 W Alabama St	Houston	TX	77006	713-526-5500	526-7170
Web: www.bistrovino.net					
Bocados 1312 W Alabama St	Houston	TX	77006	713-523-5230	
Bonnie's Beef & Seafood Co 6867 Gulf Fwy	Houston	TX	77087	713-641-2397	641-4235
Web: www.bonniesbeefandseafood.com					
Brennan's of Houston 3300 Smith St	Houston	TX	77006	713-522-9711	522-9508
Web: www.brennanshouston.com					
Brenner's Steakhouse 10911 Katy Fwy	Houston	TX	77079	713-465-2901	877-3116
Web: www.brennerssteakhouse.com					
Cafe Rabelais 2442 Times Blvd	Houston	TX	77005	713-520-8841	526-6852
Web: www.caferabelais.com					
Cafe Red Onion 12041 NW Fwy	Houston	TX	77092	713-957-0957	957-1338
Carmelo's 14795 Memorial Dr	Houston	TX	77079	281-531-0696	
Web: www.carmelosrestaurant.com					
Charivari 2521 Bagby St	Houston	TX	77006	713-521-7231	521-4697
Web: www.charivarirest.com					
Churrasco's 2055 Westheimer Rd	Houston	TX	77098	713-527-8300	527-0847
Web: www.churrascos.com					
Da Marco 1520 Westheimer Rd	Houston	TX	77006	713-807-8857	807-8301
Web: www.damarcohouston.com					
Damian's Cucina Italiana 3011 Smith St	Houston	TX	77006	713-522-0439	522-4408
Web: www.damians.com					
El Tiempo Cantina 3130 Richmond Ave	Houston	TX	77098	713-807-1600	807-1616
Web: www.eltiempocantina.com					
Empire Turkish Grill 12448 Memorial Dr	Houston	TX	77024	713-827-7475	463-7719
Web: www.empiretrgrill.com					
Fabio's Bar & Grille 212 Westheimer Rd	Houston	TX	77006	713-528-4212	523-8212
Web: www.fabiosbarandgrill.com					
Fadi's Mediterranean Cuisine 8383 Westheimer Rd	Houston	TX	77063	713-532-0666	532-0677
Web: www.fadiscuisine.com					
Farrago 318 Gray St	Houston	TX	77002	713-523-6404	523-6405
Web: www.farrago.tv					
Felix 904 Westheimer Rd	Houston	TX	77006	713-529-3949	529-0508
Fogo de Chao 8250 Westheimer Rd	Houston	TX	77063	713-978-6500	978-6501
Web: www.fogodechao.com					
Frenchie's 1041 NASA Pkwy	Houston	TX	77058	281-486-7144	486-3952
Fuad's 6100 Westheimer Rd	Houston	TX	77057	713-785-0130	785-2215
Fung's Kitchen 7320 SW Fwy	Houston	TX	77074	713-779-2288	271-2288
Web: www.fungskitchen.com					
Goode Co Seafood 2621 Westpark Dr	Houston	TX	77098	713-523-7154	523-0774
Goode Co Texas Barbecue 5109 Kirby Dr	Houston	TX	77098	713-522-2530	522-3873
Web: www.goodecompany.com					
Hugo's 1600 Westheimer Rd	Houston	TX	77006	713-524-7744	524-7719
Web: www.hugosrestaurant.net					
Hunan Village 3311 S Shepherd Dr	Houston	TX	77098	713-528-4651	
Ibiza Food & Wine Bar 2450 Louisiana St	Houston	TX	77006	713-524-0004	524-5687
Web: www.ibizafoodandwinebar.com					
Indika 516 Westheimer Rd	Houston	TX	77006	713-524-2170	984-1755
Web: www.indikausa.com					
Jasmine Asian Cuisine 9938 Bellaire Blvd Suite D	Houston	TX	77036	713-272-8188	272-8187
Kam's 4500 Montrose Blvd	Houston	TX	77006	713-529-5057	529-5486
Kiran's Restaurant & Bar 4100 Westheimer Rd	Houston	TX	77027	713-960-8472	993-0739
Web: www.kiranshouston.com					
Kubo's Sushi Bar & Grill 2414 University Blvd 200	Houston	TX	77005	713-528-7878	528-9150
Web: www.kubos-sushi.com					
La Colombe D'Or 3410 Montrose Blvd	Houston	TX	77006	713-469-4750	524-8923
Web: www.lacolombedorhouston.com					
La Griglia 2002 W Gray St	Houston	TX	77019	713-526-4700	526-9249
Web: www.lagrigliarestaurant.com					
Lynn's Steakhouse 955 Dairy Ashford	Houston	TX	77079	281-870-0807	870-0888
Web: www.lynnssteakhouse.com					
Madras Pavilion 3910 Kirby Dr	Houston	TX	77098	713-521-2617	521-2647
Web: www.madraspavilion.us					
Maggiano's Little Italy Restaurant 2019 Post Oak Blvd	Houston	TX	77056	713-961-2700	961-4550
Web: www.maggianos.com					
Magic Island 2215 SW Fwy	Houston	TX	77098	713-526-2442	526-8309
Web: www.themagicisland.com					
Magnolia Bar & Grill 6000 Richmond Ave	Houston	TX	77057	713-781-6207	781-8061
Web: www.magnolia-grill.com					
Mark's American Cuisine 1658 Westheimer Rd	Houston	TX	77006	713-523-3800	523-9292
Web: www.marks1658.com					
Masraff's 1753 S Post Oak Ln	Houston	TX	77056	713-355-1975	355-1965
Web: www.masraffs.com					
Massa's 1160 Smith St	Houston	TX	77002	713-650-0837	650-0165
Web: www.massas.com					
Mockingbird Bistro 1985 Welch St	Houston	TX	77019	713-533-0200	533-0215
Web: www.mockingbirdbistro.com					
Morton's The Steakhouse 5000 Westheimer Rd	Houston	TX	77056	713-629-1946	629-4348
Web: www.mortons.com					
Nino's Vincent's Grappino di Nino 2817 W Dallas St	Houston	TX	77019	713-522-5120	528-1008
Web: www.ninos-vincents.com					
Noe Restaurant & Bar 4 Riverway	Houston	TX	77056	713-871-8177	871-0719
Osaka Japanese Restaurant 515 Westheimer Rd	Houston	TX	77006	713-533-9098	
Palm Restaurant 6100 Westheimer Rd	Houston	TX	77057	713-977-2544	977-3503
Web: www.thepalm.com					

Name / Address	City	State	ZIP	Phone	Fax
Pesce 3029 Kirby Dr *Web:* www.pescehouston.com	Houston	TX	77098	713-522-4858	522-9666
PF Chang's China Bistro 11685 Westheimer Rd *Web:* www.pfchangs.com	Houston	TX	77077	281-920-3553	920-3567
Piatto Ristorante 4925 W Alabama St *Web:* www.piattoristorante.com	Houston	TX	77056	713-871-9722	871-9190
Prego 2520 Amherst St *Web:* www.prego-houston.com	Houston	TX	77005	713-529-2420	526-3181
Prime Time Steakhouse 9275 FM 1960 W *Web:* www.primetimesteakhouse.com	Houston	TX	77070	281-469-1234	
Rainbow Lodge 2011 Ella Blvd *Web:* www.rainbow-lodge.com	Houston	TX	77008	713-861-8666	861-8405
Reef 2600 Travis St *Web:* www.reefhouston.com	Houston	TX	77006	713-526-8282	526-8266
Rio Ranch 9999 Westheimer Rd *Web:* www.magnetmail.net	Houston	TX	77042	713-952-5000	952-2263
Ruggles Grill 903 Westheimer Rd *Web:* www.rugglesgrill.com	Houston	TX	77006	713-527-9400	524-7396
Ruth's Chris Steak House 6213 Richmond Ave *Web:* www.ruthschris.com	Houston	TX	77057	713-789-2333	789-4136
Sabor! 5712 Bellaire Blvd	Houston	TX	77081	713-667-6001	
Saltgrass Steak House 520 Meyerland Plaza Mall	Houston	TX	77096	713-665-2226	877-3176
Shiva 2514 Times Blvd *Web:* www.shivarestaurant.com	Houston	TX	77005	713-523-4753	523-4754
Spanish Flower 4701 N Main St	Houston	TX	77009	713-869-1706	869-1734
Spindletop 1200 Louisiana St	Houston	TX	77002	713-375-4775	
T'afia 3701 Travis St *Web:* www.tafia.com	Houston	TX	77002	713-524-6922	524-9728
Taste of Texas Restaurant 10505 Katy Fwy *Web:* www.tasteoftexas.com	Houston	TX	77024	713-932-6901	461-6177
Tony Mandola's Gulf Coast Kitchen 1964 W Gray St # 204 *Web:* www.tonymandolas.com	Houston	TX	77019	713-528-3474	528-4438
Tony's 3755 Richmond Ave *Web:* www.tonyshouston.com	Houston	TX	77056	713-622-6778	626-1232
Vieng Thai 6929 Long Pt St	Houston	TX	77055	713-688-9910	
Zula 705 Main St Suite B *Web:* www.zulahouston.com	Houston	TX	77002	713-227-7052	227-7056
Benihana 5400 Whitehall St *Web:* www.benihana.com	Irving	TX	75038	972-550-0060	
Blue Fish 925 W John Carpenter Fwy *Web:* www.thebluefishsushi.com	Irving	TX	75039	972-385-3474	910-0130
Bruno's 9462 N MacArthur Blvd	Irving	TX	75063	972-556-2465	
Cafe Cipriani 220 Las Colinas Blvd E # 264 *Web:* www.cafecipriani.com	Irving	TX	75039	972-869-0713	869-2281
Cool River Cafe 1045 Hidden Ridge *Web:* www.coolrivercafe.com	Irving	TX	75038	972-871-8881	871-8882
Danal's Mexican Restaurant 508 N O'Connor Rd	Irving	TX	75061	972-254-2666	259-7483
Empress of China 2648 N Belt Line Rd *Web:* www.eocrestaurant.com	Irving	TX	75062	972-252-7677	258-6776
Hanasho Japanese Restaurant 2938 N Belt Line Rd *Web:* www.hanashojapaneserestaurant.com	Irving	TX	75062	972-258-0250	257-1243
I Fratelli 7701 N MacArthur Blvd *Web:* www.ifratelli.net	Irving	TX	75063	972-501-9700	501-9704
Italian Cafe 387 Las Colinas Blvd E	Irving	TX	75039	972-401-0000	401-9193
Jinbeh 301 E Las Colinas Blvd *Web:* www.jinbeh.com	Irving	TX	75039	972-869-4011	869-4311
Keg Steakhouse & Bar 859 W John Carpenter Fwy *Web:* www.kegsteakhouse.com	Irving	TX	75039	972-556-9188	506-0591
Midori Sushi 4020 N MacArthur Blvd	Irving	TX	75038	972-887-1818	717-3836
Pasand Indian Cuisine 2600 N Belt Line Rd *Web:* www.pasandrestaurant.com	Irving	TX	75062	972-594-0693	594-8935
Pei Wei Asian Diner 7600 N MacArthur Blvd	Irving	TX	75063	972-373-8000	
Piman Asian Bistro 4835 N O'Connor Rd *Web:* www.pimanasian.com	Irving	TX	75062	972-650-0001	
Rockfish Seafood Grill 7400 N MacArthur Blvd *Web:* www.rockfish.com	Irving	TX	75603	214-574-4111	
Sonny Bryan's Smoke House 4030 N MacArthur Blvd Suite 222 *Fax Area Code: 214 ■ *Web:* www.sonnybryans.com	Irving	TX	75038	972-650-9564	596-1081*
Spring Creek Barbeque 2340 W I- 20 Suite 100 *Fax Area Code: 972 ■ *TF:* 888-467-0505 ■ *Web:* www.springcreekbarbeque.com	Irving	TX	75062	817-467-0505	313-1174*
Texadelphia 7601 N MacArthur Blvd *Web:* www.texadelphia.com	Irving	TX	75063	972-432-0725	373-8810
Thai Chili 397 E Las Colinas Blvd	Irving	TX	75039	972-831-0797	
Trevi's 221 Las Colinas Blvd E	Irving	TX	75039	972-869-5550	
Via Real Restaurant 4020 N MacArthur Blvd *Web:* www.viareal.com	Irving	TX	75038	972-650-9001	541-0215
50 Yard Line Steakhouse 2549 Loop 289 S	Lubbock	TX	79423	806-745-3991	
Bless Your Heart 3701 19th St	Lubbock	TX	79410	806-791-2211	
Cagle Steaks 108 N FM 179 *Web:* www.caglesteaks.com	Lubbock	TX	79416	806-795-3879	
Cattle Baron 8201 Quaker Ave Suite 170 *Web:* www.cattlebaron.com	Lubbock	TX	79424	806-798-7033	
Choochai Thai Cuisine 2330 19th St	Lubbock	TX	79401	806-747-1767	
Fortune Cookie 7006 University Ave Suite 6	Lubbock	TX	79413	806-745-2205	
Gardski's 2009 Broadway *Web:* www.gardskislost.com	Lubbock	TX	79401	806-744-2391	744-0181
India palace 3021 34th St	Lubbock	TX	79407	806-799-6772	799-6772
Jake's Sports Cafe 5025 50th St *Web:* www.jakes-sportscafe.com	Lubbock	TX	79414	806-687-5253	
Jazz Restaurant 3703 19th St Suite C *Web:* www.jazzkitchen.com	Lubbock	TX	79410	806-799-2124	799-7870
Joe's Crab Shack 5802 W Loop S 289 *Web:* www.joescrabshack.com	Lubbock	TX	79414	806-797-8600	
Orlando's 2402 Ave Q *Web:* www.orlandos.com	Lubbock	TX	79405	806-747-5998	
Rudy's Country Store & Bar BQ 4930 S Loop 289 *Web:* www.rudys.com	Lubbock	TX	79414	806-797-1777	
Texas Cafe & Bar 3604 50th St	Lubbock	TX	79413	806-792-8544	
Texas Land & Cattle Steak House 7202 Indiana Ave *Web:* www.txlc.com	Lubbock	TX	79423	806-791-0555	
Thai Thai 5018 50th St	Lubbock	TX	79414	806-791-0024	
Tokyo Japanese Restaurant 4637 50th St	Lubbock	TX	79414	806-799-8998	
Bavarian Grill 221 W Parker Rd *Web:* www.bavariangrill.com	Plano	TX	75023	972-881-0705	
Big Easy New Orleans Style Sandwiches 1915 N Central Expy Suite 200 *Web:* www.bigeasyplano.com	Plano	TX	75075	972-424-5261	
Blue Goose Cantina 4757 W Pk Blvd *Web:* www.bluegoosecantina.com	Plano	TX	75093	972-596-8882	596-8722
Bob's Steak & Chop House 5760 Legacy Dr Suite B1 *Web:* www.bobs-steakandchop.com	Plano	TX	75024	972-608-2627	
Cathy's Wok 3948 Legacy Dr Suite 103 *Web:* www.cathyswok.com	Plano	TX	75023	972-491-7267	491-2621
Chettinaad Palace 2205 N Central Expy *Web:* www.chettinaadpalace.com	Plano	TX	75075	469-229-9100	229-9101
Covino's 3265 Independence Pkwy *Fax Area Code: 214	Plano	TX	75075	972-519-0345	778-2363*
Fishmonger's Seafood 1915 N Central Expy *Web:* www.fishmongersplano.com	Plano	TX	75075	972-423-3699	
Greek Isles Grille & Taverna 3309 N Central Expy Suite 370 In Ruisseau Village *Web:* greekislesgrille.com	Plano	TX	75023	972-423-7778	
Jade Palace 820 W Spring Creek Pkwy Suite 212	Plano	TX	75023	972-424-5578	
Japon Steak House & Sushi Bar 4021 Preston Rd *Web:* www.japonsteakhouseandsushi.com	Plano	TX	75093	972-781-2818	
Joe's Crab Shack 3320 N Central Expy	Plano	TX	75074	972-423-2800	
Jorg's Cafe Vienna 1037 E 15th St	Plano	TX	75074	972-509-5966	
Kirby's Steakhouse 3408 Preston Rd *Web:* www.kirbyssteakhouse.com	Plano	TX	75093	972-867-2122	
Kosta's Cafe 4621 W Pk Blvd Suite #100 *Web:* www.kostascafe.com	Plano	TX	75093	972-596-8424	
Love & War In Texas 601 E Plano Pkwy *Web:* www.loveandwarintexas.com	Plano	TX	75074	972-422-6201	
Mango's Thai Cuisine 4701 W Pk Blvd Suite 104	Plano	TX	75093	972-599-0289	599-7013
Nakamoto 3309 N Central Expy *Web:* www.nakamotosushi.com	Plano	TX	75023	972-881-0328	578-8965
Ojeda's 2001 Coit Rd Suite 102 *Web:* www.ojedasdallas.com	Plano	TX	75075	972-599-1300	
Osaka Sushi 5012 W Pk Blvd	Plano	TX	75093	972-931-8898	
Paesano's 1825 14th St *Web:* www.paesanosrestaurant.com	Plano	TX	75074	972-578-2727	578-1105
Patrizio's 1900 Preston Rd	Plano	TX	75093	972-964-2200	596-1743
Picasso's 3948 Legacy Dr *Web:* www.picassosrestaurant.us	Plano	TX	75023	972-618-4143	618-7339
Posados Cafe 3421 N Central Expy	Plano	TX	75023	972-509-4999	
Rockfish Seafood Grill 4701 W Pk Blvd Suite 105	Plano	TX	75093	972-599-2190	964-6898
Steve Fields Steak & Lobster Lounge 5013 W Pk Blvd *Web:* www.stevefieldsrestaurant.com	Plano	TX	75093	972-596-7100	599-3950
Taste of the Islands 909 W Spring Creek Pkwy	Plano	TX	75023	972-517-5900	
Tin Star 2208 Dallas Pkwy *Web:* www.tinstar.us	Plano	TX	75093	972-403-1765	
Vincent's 2432 Preston Rd *Web:* www.vincentsseafood.com	Plano	TX	75093	972-612-6208	612-0969
Alamo Cafe 10060 W IH-10 *Web:* www.alamocafe.com	San Antonio	TX	78230	210-691-8827	691-0056
Anaqua Grill 555 S Alamo St	San Antonio	TX	78205	210-229-1000	229-1418
Biga on the Banks 203 S St Mary's St *Web:* www.biga.com	San Antonio	TX	78205	210-225-0722	
Bistro Vatel 218 E Olmos Dr *Web:* www.bistrovatel.com	San Antonio	TX	78212	210-828-3141	
Boardwalk Bistro 4011 Broadway *Web:* www.boardwalkbistro.net	San Antonio	TX	78209	210-824-0100	
Bohanan's Prime Steaks & Seafood 219 E Houston St 2nd Fl *Web:* www.bohanans.com	San Antonio	TX	78205	210-472-2600	472-2276
Boudro's On the Riverwalk 421 E Commerce St *Web:* www.boudros.com	San Antonio	TX	78205	210-224-8484	225-2839
Cappy's 5011 Broadway St *Web:* www.cappysrestaurant.com	San Antonio	TX	78209	210-828-9669	828-3041
Cheesecake Factory 7400 San Pedro St *Web:* www.cheesecakefactory.com	San Antonio	TX	78216	210-798-2222	798-2232
Chris Madrid's 1900 Blanco Rd	San Antonio	TX	78212	210-735-3552	
County Line On I-10 10101 W IH-10 *Web:* www.countyline.com	San Antonio	TX	78230	210-641-1998	641-1345
Cove The 606 W Cypress St *Web:* www.thecove.us	San Antonio	TX	78212	210-227-2683	
Crumpets 3920 Harry Wurzbach St *Web:* www.crumpetsa.com	San Antonio	TX	78209	210-821-5600	821-5624
Demo's 2501 N St Mary's St *Web:* www.demosgreekfood.com	San Antonio	TX	78212	210-732-7777	731-9002
El Mirador 722 S St Mary's St	San Antonio	TX	78205	210-225-9444	271-3236
Fig Tree 515 Villita St *Web:* www.figtreerestaurant.com	San Antonio	TX	78205	210-224-1976	271-9180
Formosa Garden 1011 NE Loop 410 *Web:* www.formosagarden.com	San Antonio	TX	78209	210-828-9988	826-2566
Golden Wok 8822 Wurzbach Rd *Web:* www.golden-wok.com	San Antonio	TX	78240	210-615-8282	615-8285
Hard Rock Cafe 111 W Crocket St *Web:* www.hardrock.com	San Antonio	TX	78205	210-224-7625	224-7693
India Oven 1031 Patricia St Suite 106 *Web:* www.indiaoven.com	San Antonio	TX	78213	210-366-1030	366-1033
India Palace 8440 Fredericksburg Rd	San Antonio	TX	78229	210-692-5262	
La Fogata 2427 Vance Jackson Rd *Web:* www.lafogata.com	San Antonio	TX	78213	210-340-1337	349-6467

Name / Address	City	State	Zip	Phone	Fax
Little Rhein Steakhouse 231 S Alamo St	San Antonio	TX	78205	210-225-2111	271-9180
Web: www.littlerheinsteakhouse.com					
Lodge of Castle Hills The 1746 Lockhill Selma Rd	San Antonio	TX	78213	210-349-8466	
Melting Pot of San Antonio The 14855 Blanco Rd Suite 110	San Antonio	TX	78216	210-479-6358	479-8106
Web: www.meltingpot.com					
Meson European Dining 5999 De Zavala Rd	San Antonio	TX	78249	210-690-5811	
Web: www.mesoneuropeandining.com					
Mokara Hotels & Spas 212 W Crockett St	San Antonio	TX	78205	210-396-5800	
TF Resv: 866-605-1212 ■ *Web:* www.mokarahotels.com					
Old San Francisco Steak House 10223 Sahara Dr	San Antonio	TX	78216	210-342-2321	340-3135
Web: www.theoldsanfrancisco.com					
Paesano's 555 E Basse Rd	San Antonio	TX	78209	210-828-5191	828-6329
Web: www.prg-sa.com					
Pappadeaux Seafood Kitchen 76 NE Loop 410	San Antonio	TX	78216	210-340-7143	340-0572
Web: www.pappadeaux.com					
PF Chang's China Bistro 255 E Basse Rd	San Antonio	TX	78209	210-507-1000	507-1001
Web: www.pfchangs.com					
Piatti Ristorante & Bar San Antonio 255 E Basse Rd Suite 500	San Antonio	TX	78209	210-832-0300	832-0303
Web: www.piatti.com					
Picante Grill 3810 Broadway	San Antonio	TX	78209	210-822-3797	
Restaurant Le Reve 152 E Pecan St	San Antonio	TX	78205	210-212-2221	
Web: www.restaurantlereve.com					
Rio Rio Cantina 421 E Commerce St	San Antonio	TX	78205	210-226-8462	226-8443
Web: www.rioriocantina.com					
Ruth's Chris Steak House 7720 Jones-Maltsberger Rd	San Antonio	TX	78216	210-821-5051	821-5095
Web: www.ruthschris.com					
Silo 1133 Austin Hwy	San Antonio	TX	78209	210-824-8686	805-8452
Web: www.siloelevatedcuisine.com					
Sushi Zushi 9867 W I-10	San Antonio	TX	78230	210-691-3332	
Web: www.sushizushi.com					
Texas Land & Cattle Steak House 9911 W IH- 10	San Antonio	TX	78230	210-699-8744	
Web: www.txlc.com					
Thai Kitchen 100 Villita St	San Antonio	TX	78205	210-226-2970	
Zio's 12858 W IH-10	San Antonio	TX	78249	210-697-7222	697-7333
Web: www.zios.com					
Tamolly's 5940 Summerhill Rd	Texarkana	TX	75503	903-792-0732	
Web: www.tamollys.com					

UTAH

Name / Address	City	State	Zip	Phone	Fax
Athenian 252 25th St	Ogden	UT	84401	801-621-4911	395-2456
Bistro 258 258 25th St	Ogden	UT	84401	801-394-1595	
Web: www.bistro258.com					
Eastern Winds 3740 Washington Blvd	Ogden	UT	84403	801-627-2739	627-2739
El Matador 2564 Ogden Ave	Ogden	UT	84401	801-393-3151	
Golden Dynasty 3433 Washington Blvd	Ogden	UT	84401	801-621-6789	
Jasoh 195 25th St Suite 6	Ogden	UT	84404	801-399-0088	
Web: www.jasoh.com					
Javiers 703 Washington Blvd	Ogden	UT	84404	801-393-4747	
Jeremiah's 1307 W 1200 S	Ogden	UT	84404	801-394-3273	627-6579
Web: www.jeremiahsogden.com					
Prairie Schooner Restaurant 445 Pk Blvd	Ogden	UT	84401	801-392-2712	393-1626
Web: www.prairieschoonerrestaurant.com					
Rooster's 253 25th St	Ogden	UT	84401	801-627-6171	622-1353
Web: www.roostersbrewingco.com					
Ruby River Steak House 4286 Riverdale Rd	Ogden	UT	84405	801-622-2320	622-2420
Web: www.rubyriver.com					
Temari 3035 S Washington Blvd	Ogden	UT	84401	801-399-9536	
Timber Mine 1701 Pk Blvd	Ogden	UT	84401	801-393-2155	
Web: www.timbermine.com					
Tona 210 25th St	Ogden	UT	84401	801-622-8662	
Web: www.tonarestaurant.com					
Union Grill 2501 Wall Ave	Ogden	UT	84401	801-621-2830	621-7946
Web: www.uniongrillogden.com					
Windy's Sukiyaki 3809 Riverdale Rd	Ogden	UT	84405	801-621-4505	
Web: www.windyssukiyaki.com					
Yu's Maple Garden 3798 Washington Blvd	Ogden	UT	84403	801-621-1888	
Bombay House 463 N University Ave	Provo	UT	84601	801-373-6677	
Brick Oven 111 E 800 N	Provo	UT	84606	801-374-8800	
Web: www.brickovenrestaurants.com					
Demae Japanese Restaurant 82 W Ctr St	Provo	UT	84601	801-374-0306	373-3308
Web: www.provojapaneserestaurant.com					
Happy Sumo at the Riverwoods 4801 N University Ave	Provo	UT	84604	801-225-9100	
Web: www.happysumosushi.com					
Joe Vera's Mexican Fiestaurant 250 W Ctr St	Provo	UT	84601	801-375-6714	
Osaka Japanese Restaurant 46 W Ctr St	Provo	UT	84601	801-373-1060	
OZZ - Event and Fun Center 490 N Freedom Blvd	Provo	UT	84601	801-818-9000	
Web: www.ozzfun.com					
Ruby River Steakhouse 1454 S University Ave	Provo	UT	84601	801-371-0648	
Web: www.rubyriver.com					
Saigon Cafe 440 W 300 S	Provo	UT	84601	801-812-1173	
Web: www.saigoncafeprovo.com					
Sam Hawk 660 N Freedom Blvd	Provo	UT	84601	801-377-7766	
Tepanyaki Japanese Steak House 1240 N State St	Provo	UT	84604	801-374-0633	
Web: www.mytepanyaki.com					
Thai Ruby 744 E 820 N	Provo	UT	84606	801-375-6840	
Tucanos Brazilian Grill 4801 N University Ave Unit 790	Provo	UT	84604	801-224-4774	
Web: www.tucanos.com					
Aristo's 224 S 1300 E	Salt Lake City	UT	84102	801-581-0888	581-0890
Web: www.aristosgreekrestaurant.com					
Atlantic Cafe 325 S Main St	Salt Lake City	UT	84111	801-524-9900	
Baci Trattoria 134 W Pierpont Ave	Salt Lake City	UT	84101	801-328-1500	
Web: www.gastronomyinc.com					
Bambara Restaurant 202 S Main St	Salt Lake City	UT	84101	801-363-5454	363-5888
Web: www.bambara-slc.com					
Bangkok Thai 3142 S Highland Dr	Salt Lake City	UT	84106	801-582-8424	
Web: www.bangkokthai.com					
Benihana of Tokyo 165 S W Temple	Salt Lake City	UT	84101	801-322-2421	575-6415
Web: www.benihana.com					
Blue Iguana 165 S W Temple	Salt Lake City	UT	84101	801-533-8900	
Web: www.blueiguanarestaurant.net					
Bombay House 2731 Parleys Way	Salt Lake City	UT	84109	801-581-0222	
Web: www.bombayhouse.com					
Cafe Madrid 2080 E 3900 S	Salt Lake City	UT	84124	801-273-0837	
Cafe Rio 3025 E 3300 S	Salt Lake City	UT	84109	801-463-7250	
Web: www.caferio.com					
Cafe Trang 200 S 307 W	Salt Lake City	UT	84101	801-539-1638	328-1066
Web: www.cafetrangrestaurant.com					
Cafe Trio 6405 S 3000 E	Salt Lake City	UT	84121	801-944-8746	
Web: www.triodining.com					
Caffe Molise 55 W 100 S	Salt Lake City	UT	84101	801-364-8833	
Web: www.caffemolise.com					
Christopher's Seafood & Steak House 134 W Pierpont Ave	Salt Lake City	UT	84101	801-519-8515	
Cinegrill 344 S 300 E	Salt Lake City	UT	84111	801-328-4900	
Citris Grill 2991 E 3300 S	Salt Lake City	UT	84109	801-466-1202	
Web: www.citrisgrill.com					
Cucina Toscana 307 W Pierpont Ave	Salt Lake City	UT	84101	801-328-3463	
Web: www.cucina-toscana.com					
Desert Edge Brewery 273 Trolley Sq	Salt Lake City	UT	84102	801-521-8917	
Web: www.desertedgebrewery.com					
Em's 271 N Ctr St	Salt Lake City	UT	84101	801-596-0566	
Web: www.emsrestaurant.com					
Fleming's Prime Steakhouse & Wine Bar 20 S 400 W	Salt Lake City	UT	84101	801-355-3704	
Web: www.flemingssteakhouse.com					
Formosa Grill 2115 E 2100 S	Salt Lake City	UT	84109	801-461-0661	
Fresco Italian Cafe 1513 S 1500 E	Salt Lake City	UT	84105	801-486-1300	
Web: www.frescoitaliancafe.com					
Ginza 209 W 200 S	Salt Lake City	UT	84101	801-322-2224	
Hong Kong Tea House 565 W 200 S	Salt Lake City	UT	84101	801-531-7010	531-7033
Web: www.hongkongteahouse.com					
Ichiban Sushi & Japanese Cuisine 336 S 400 E	Salt Lake City	UT	84111	801-532-7522	
Koyo Restaurant 2275 E 33rd S	Salt Lake City	UT	84109	801-466-7111	
Web: www.koyoslc.com					
Lamb's Grill Cafe 169 S Main St	Salt Lake City	UT	84111	801-364-7166	355-1644
Web: www.lambsgrill.com					
Log Haven 6451 E Milcreek Canyon	Salt Lake City	UT	84109	801-272-8255	
Web: www.log-haven.com					
Lugano Restaurant 3364 S 2300 E	Salt Lake City	UT	84109	801-412-9994	
Web: www.luganorestaurant.com					
Market Street Broiler 260 S 1300 E	Salt Lake City	UT	84102	801-583-8808	
Market Street Oyster Bar 54 Market St	Salt Lake City	UT	84101	801-531-6044	
Mazza 1515 S 1500 E	Salt Lake City	UT	84105	801-484-9259	
Web: www.mazzacafe.com					
Metropolitan 173 W Broadway	Salt Lake City	UT	84101	801-364-3472	
Web: www.themetropolitan.com					
Michelangelo Ristorante 2156 S Highland Dr	Salt Lake City	UT	84106	801-466-0961	
New Yorker 60 Market St	Salt Lake City	UT	84101	801-363-0166	
Oasis Cafe 151 S 500 E	Salt Lake City	UT	84102	801-322-0404	
Old Salt City Jail 460 S 1000 E	Salt Lake City	UT	84102	801-359-6090	
Pagoda Restaurant 26 E St	Salt Lake City	UT	84103	801-355-8155	355-4617
Web: www.pagodaslc.com					
Paris Bistro 1500 S 1500 E	Salt Lake City	UT	85105	801-486-5585	
Web: www.theparis.net					
PF Chang's China Bistro 174 W 300 S	Salt Lake City	UT	84111	801-539-0500	
Web: www.pfchangs.com					
Red Iguana 736 W N Temple St	Salt Lake City	UT	84116	801-322-1489	322-4834
Web: www.rediguana.com					
Red Rock Brewing Co 254 S 200 W	Salt Lake City	UT	84101	801-521-7446	521-0908
Web: www.redrockbrewing.com					
Rino's 2302 E Parleys Way	Salt Lake City	UT	84109	801-484-0901	
Rio Grande Cafe 270 S Rio Grande St	Salt Lake City	UT	84101	801-364-3302	
Rodizio Grill 600 S 700 E	Salt Lake City	UT	84102	801-220-0500	
Web: www.rodiziogrill.com					
Rumbi Island Grill 358 S 700 E	Salt Lake City	UT	84102	801-530-1000	
Sage's Cafe 473 E Broadway	Salt Lake City	UT	84111	801-322-3790	
Web: www.sagescafe.com					
Sampan 675 E 2100 S	Salt Lake City	UT	84106	801-467-3663	466-4120
Web: www.esampan.com					
Shogun 321 S Main St	Salt Lake City	UT	84111	801-364-7142	
Spencer's for Steaks & Chops 255 S W Temple St	Salt Lake City	UT	84101	801-238-4748	
Web: www.spencersforsteaksandchops.com					
Squatter's Pub Brewery 147 W Broadway	Salt Lake City	UT	84101	801-363-2739	
Web: www.squatters.com					
Thai Siam 1435 S State St	Salt Lake City	UT	84115	801-474-3322	
Web: www.thaisiam.net					
Tuscany 2832 E 6200 S	Salt Lake City	UT	84121	801-277-9919	
Web: www.tuscanyslc.com					
La Caille at Quail Run 9565 Wasatch Blvd	Sandy	UT	84092	801-942-1751	944-8990
Web: www.lacaille.com					

VERMONT

Name / Address	City	State	Zip	Phone	Fax
Bangkok Bistro 144 Church St	Burlington	VT	05401	802-951-5888	
Bove's of Vermont 68 Pearl St	Burlington	VT	05401	802-864-6651	
Web: www.boves.com					
Cannon's 1127 N Ave Suite 20	Burlington	VT	05401	802-652-5151	652-5155
Web: www.cannonsitalian.com					

				Phone	Fax
Daily Planet 15 Ctr St	Burlington	VT	05401	802-862-9647	862-6693
Web: www.dailyplanet15.com					
Halvorson's Upstreet Cafe 16 Church St	Burlington	VT	05401	802-658-0278	
India House Restaurant 207 Colchester Ave	Burlington	VT	05401	802-862-7800	862-9191
L'Amante 126 College St	Burlington	VT	05401	802-863-5200	
Web: www.lamante.com					
Leunig's Bistro 115 Church St	Burlington	VT	05401	802-863-3759	658-6332
Web: www.leunigsbistro.com					
New World Tortilla 696 Pine St	Burlington	VT	05401	802-865-1058	
Web: www.newworldtortilla.com					
Parlima 185 Pearl St	Burlington	VT	05401	802-864-7917	
Pauline's 1834 Shelburne Rd	Burlington	VT	05403	802-862-1081	862-6842
Web: www.paulinescafe.com					
Ri Ra 123 Church St	Burlington	VT	05401	802-860-9401	
Web: www.rira.com					
Sakura 2 Church St	Burlington	VT	05401	802-863-1988	860-0496
Web: www.sakurabanavt.com					
Single Pebble 133 Bank St	Burlington	VT	05401	802-865-5200	
Web: www.asinglepebble.com					
Souza's 131 Main St	Burlington	VT	05401	802-864-2433	
Web: www.souzasrestaurant.com					
Sweetwaters 120 Church St	Burlington	VT	05401	802-864-9800	864-4913
Web: www.sweetwatersvt.com					
Trattoria Delia 152 St Paul St	Burlington	VT	05401	802-864-5253	
Web: www.trattoriadelia.com					
Black Door Bar & Bistro 44 Main St 2nd & 3rd Fls	Montpelier	VT	05602	802-223-7070	223-7070
Chef's Table 118 Main St	Montpelier	VT	05602	802-229-9202	
China Star Chinese Restaurant 15 Main St	Montpelier	VT	05602	802-223-0808	
House of Tang 114 River St	Montpelier	VT	05602	802-223-6020	223-3388
J Morgan's Steakhouse 100 State St	Montpelier	VT	05602	802-223-5252	229-5427
Web: www.jmorgans.com					
Julio's Restaurant 54 State St	Montpelier	VT	05602	802-229-9348	
Web: www.juliostantia.com					
Main Street Grill & Bar 118 Main St	Montpelier	VT	05602	802-223-3188	223-9285
Web: www.neci.edu					
McGillicuddy's Irish Pub 14 Langdon St	Montpelier	VT	05602	802-223-2721	
Royal Orchid 38 Elm St	Montpelier	VT	05602	802-223-0436	223-0457
Sarducci's 3 Main St	Montpelier	VT	05602	802-223-0229	
Web: www.sarduccis.com					
Orchid 5 Market St	South Burlington	VT	05403	802-658-3626	658-3513
Trader Duke's 1117 Williston Rd	South Burlington	VT	05403	802-660-7523	660-7516
Web: www.hilton.com					
Peking Duck House 79 W Canal St	Winooski	VT	05404	802-655-7474	
Web: www.pekingduckhousevt.com					

VIRGINIA

				Phone	Fax
219 Restaurant 219 King St	Alexandria	VA	22314	703-549-1141	549-0035
Web: www.219restaurant.com					
A La Lucia 315 Madison St	Alexandria	VA	22314	703-836-5123	548-9463
Web: www.alalucia.com					
Afghan Restaurant 2700 Jefferson Davis Hwy	Alexandria	VA	22301	703-548-0022	548-0673
Akasaka Japanese Restaurant 514-C S Van Dorn St	Alexandria	VA	22304	703-751-3133	751-3134
Atlantis Restaurant 3648 King St	Alexandria	VA	22302	703-671-0250	
Bistrot Lafayette 1118 King St	Alexandria	VA	22314	703-548-2525	548-0222
Web: www.bistrotlafayette.com					
Bombay Curry Co 3110 Mt Vernon Ave The Calvert Bldg	Alexandria	VA	22305	703-836-6363	
Web: www.bombaycurrycompany.com					
Cafe Monti 3250 Duke St	Alexandria	VA	22314	703-370-3632	
Web: www.cafemonti.com					
Chart House Restaurant 1 Cameron St	Alexandria	VA	22314	703-684-5080	684-7364
Web: www.chart-house.com					
Del Merei Grille 2419 Davis Ave	Alexandria	VA	22302	703-739-4335	739-4991
Web: www.delmereigrille.com					
Evening Star Cafe 2000 Mt Vernon Ave	Alexandria	VA	22301	703-549-5051	549-8520
Web: www.eveningstarcafe.net					
Finn & Porter 5000 Seminary Rd	Alexandria	VA	22311	703-379-2346	845-7662
Web: www.finnandporter.com					
Fish Market 105 King St	Alexandria	VA	22314	703-836-5676	684-9424
Web: www.fishmarketva.com					
Geranio Ristorante 722 King St	Alexandria	VA	22314	703-548-0088	548-0091
Web: www.geranio.net					
Grille at Morrison House The 116 S Alfred St	Alexandria	VA	22314	703-838-8000	519-7709
Web: www.thegrillealexandria.com					
Hana Tokyo Seafood & Steak House 4603 Duke St	Alexandria	VA	22304	703-823-3168	823-3161
Web: www.hanatokyo.com					
Hee Been 6231 Little River Tpke	Alexandria	VA	22312	703-941-3737	941-2721
Web: www.heebeen.com					
House of Dynasty 7550 Telegraph Rd	Alexandria	VA	22315	703-922-5210	922-5211
Web: www.houseofdynasty.com					
Il Porto Ristorante 121 King St	Alexandria	VA	22314	703-836-8833	836-8836
Web: www.ilporto.com					
La Bergerie 218 N Lee St	Alexandria	VA	22314	703-683-1007	519-6114
Web: www.labergerie.com					
La Piazza 535 E Braddock Rd	Alexandria	VA	22314	703-519-7711	
Web: www.lapiazzaoldtown.com					
Landini Bros 115 King St	Alexandria	VA	22314	703-836-8404	549-3596
Web: www.landinibrothers.com					
Las Tapas Restaurant 710 King St	Alexandria	VA	22314	703-836-4000	836-4668
Web: www.lastapas.us					
Le Refuge Restaurant 127 N Washington St	Alexandria	VA	22314	703-548-4661	
Web: www.lerefugealexandria.com					
Majestic Cafe 911 King St	Alexandria	VA	22314	703-837-9117	548-6681
Web: www.majesticcafe.com					
Mike's Italian Restaurant 8368 Richmond Hwy	Alexandria	VA	22309	703-780-5966	780-2604
Morrison House 116 S Alfred St	Alexandria	VA	22314	703-838-8000	684-6283
TF: 866-834-6628 ■ *Web:* www.morrisonhouse.com					
Murphy's Grand Irish Pub 713 King St	Alexandria	VA	22314	703-548-1717	739-4583
Web: www.murphyspub.com					
Potowmack Landing Restaurant 1 Marina Dr	Alexandria	VA	22314	703-548-0001	548-2296
Web: www.potowmacklanding.com					
Restaurant Eve 110 S Pitt St	Alexandria	VA	22314	703-706-0450	706-0968
Web: www.restauranteve.com					
Rocklands 25 S Quaker Ln	Alexandria	VA	22314	703-778-8000	778-8007
Web: www.rocklands.com					
RT's 3804 Mt Vernon Ave	Alexandria	VA	22305	703-684-6010	548-0417
Web: www.rtsrestaurant.net					
Satay Sarinah 512A S Van Dorn St	Alexandria	VA	22304	703-370-4313	370-9672
Web: www.sataysarinah.com					
Savio's 516 S Van Dorn St	Alexandria	VA	22304	703-212-9651	212-9652
Web: www.saviosrestaurant.com					
Shooter McGees 5239 Duke St	Alexandria	VA	22304	703-751-9266	
Web: www.shootermcgees.com					
Southside 815 815 S Washington St	Alexandria	VA	22314	703-836-6222	549-6985
Web: www.southside815.com					
Stardust Restaurant 608 Montgomery St	Alexandria	VA	22314	703-548-9864	548-4442
Taqueria el Poblano 2400B Mt Vernon Ave	Alexandria	VA	22310	703-548-8226	548-2824
Web: www.taqueriapoblano.com					
Taverna Cretekou 818 King St	Alexandria	VA	22314	703-548-8688	683-2739
Web: www.tavernacretekou.com					
Tempo Restaurant 4231 Duke St	Alexandria	VA	22304	703-370-7900	370-7902
Web: www.temporestaurant.com					
Thai Lemon Grass Restaurant 506 S Van Dorn St	Alexandria	VA	22304	703-751-4627	
Thai Old Town Restaurant 300 King St	Alexandria	VA	22314	703-684-6503	684-7979
Union Street Public House 121 S Union St	Alexandria	VA	22304	703-548-1785	548-0705
Web: www.unionstreetpublichouse.com					
Vermilion 1120 King St	Alexandria	VA	22314	703-684-9669	684-9614
Web: www.vermilionrestaurant.com					
Warehouse Bar & Grill 214 King St	Alexandria	VA	22314	703-683-6868	683-6928
Web: www.warehousebarandgrill.com					
Wharf The 119 King St	Alexandria	VA	22314	703-836-2836	836-2830
Web: www.wharfrestaurant.com					
Yamazato 6303 Little River Tpke	Alexandria	VA	22312	703-914-8877	914-8833
Web: www.yamazato.net					
Alpine Restaurant 4770 Lee Hwy	Arlington	VA	22207	703-528-7600	528-7625
Athena Pallas 556 22nd St S	Arlington	VA	22202	703-521-3870	521-3877
Web: www.athenapallas.com					
Bangkok 54 2919 Columbia Pike	Arlington	VA	22204	703-521-4070	521-4069
Web: www.bangkok54restaurant.com					
Cafe Asia 1550 Wilson Blvd	Arlington	VA	22209	703-741-0870	741-7666
Web: www.cafeasia.com					
Cafe Parisian Express 4520 Lee Hwy	Arlington	VA	22207	703-525-3332	525-3340
Caribbean Grill 5183 Lee Hwy	Arlington	VA	22207	703-241-8947	
Carlyle 4000 Campbell Ave	Arlington	VA	22206	703-931-0777	931-9420
Web: www.greatamericanrestaurants.com					
China Garden 1100 Wilson Blvd	Arlington	VA	22209	703-525-5317	525-5568
Clarendon Grill 1101 N Highland St	Arlington	VA	22201	703-524-7455	524-9598
Web: www.cgrill.com					
Crystal Thai 4819 1st St N	Arlington	VA	22203	703-522-1311	522-1331
Web: www.crystalthai.com					
El Paso Cafe 4235 N Pershing Dr	Arlington	VA	22203	703-243-9811	243-0064
El Pollo Rico 932 N Kenmore St	Arlington	VA	22201	703-522-3220	522-3282
Five 1250 S Hayes St	Arlington	VA	22202	703-415-5000	415-5060
Freddie's Beach Bar & Restaurant 555 23rd St S	Arlington	VA	22202	703-685-0555	685-0877
Guajillo 1727 Wilson Blvd	Arlington	VA	22201	703-807-0840	
Web: www.guajillogrill.com					
Harry's Tap Room 2800 Clarendon Blvd	Arlington	VA	22201	703-778-7788	778-8888
Web: www.harrystaproom.com					
Hunan Gate 4233 N Fairfax Dr	Arlington	VA	22203	703-243-5678	
Johnny Rockets 1100 S Hayes St	Arlington	VA	22202	703-415-3510	415-3510
Web: www.jhonnyrocket.com					
La Cote d'Or Cafe 6876 Lee Hwy	Arlington	VA	22213	703-538-3033	573-0409
Web: www.lacotedorcafe.com					
Laylalina Restaurant 5216 Wilson Blvd	Arlington	VA	22205	703-525-1170	525-6561
Web: www.layalinarestaurant.com					
Legal Sea Foods 2301 Jefferson Davis Hwy	Arlington	VA	22202	703-415-1200	415-1464
Web: www.legalseafoods.com					
McCormick & Schmick's 2010B Crystal Dr	Arlington	VA	22202	703-413-6400	413-7118
Web: www.mccormickandschmicks.com					
Melting Pot of Arlington The 1110 N Glebe Rd	Arlington	VA	22201	703-243-4490	243-4547
Web: www.meltingpot.com					
Mexicali Blues 2933 Wilson Blvd	Arlington	VA	22201	703-812-9352	
Web: www.mexicali-blues.com					
Minh's 2500 Wilson Blvd	Arlington	VA	22201	703-525-2828	525-2829
Pho 75 1721 Wilson Blvd	Arlington	VA	22209	703-525-7355	525-0597
Portabellos 2109 N Pollard St	Arlington	VA	22207	703-528-1557	528-2126
Web: www.portabellosrestaurant.com					
Ray's the Steaks 2300 Wilson Blvd	Arlington	VA	22209	703-841-7297	
Rhodeside Grill 1836 Wilson Blvd	Arlington	VA	22201	703-243-0145	243-8454
Web: www.rhodesidegrill.com					
Ristorante Murali 1201 S Joyce St	Arlington	VA	22202	703-415-0411	415-0410
Web: www.muraliva.com					
Ruth's Chris Steak House 2231 Crystal Dr 11th Fl	Arlington	VA	22202	703-979-7275	
Web: www.ruthschris.com					
SoBe Seafood Co 3100 Clarendon Blvd	Arlington	VA	22201	703-528-0033	832-8840
Taqureia el Poblano 2503 N Harrison St	Arlington	VA	22301	703-237-8250	237-9502
Web: www.taqueriapoblano.com					
Tara Thai 4001 N Fairfax Dr	Arlington	VA	22203	703-908-4999	408-9009
THAI 4029 Campbell Ave	Arlington	VA	22206	703-931-3203	
Web: www.thaiinshirlington.com					
Thaiphoon 1301 S Joy St	Arlington	VA	22202	703-413-8200	413-8868
Web: www.thaiphoon.com					

				Phone	Fax
Tutto Bene 501 N Randolph St	Arlington	VA	22203	703-522-1005	527-0863
Web: www.tuttobeneitalian.com					
Village Bistro The 1723 Wilson Blvd	Arlington	VA	22209	703-522-0284	522-7797
Web: www.villagebistro.com					
3 Amigos 200 N Battlefield Blvd	Chesapeake	VA	23320	757-548-4105	549-4295
Web: www.3amigosrestaurant.com					
Court House Cafe 350 S Battlefield Blvd	Chesapeake	VA	23322	757-482-7077	
Cugini's 1729 Parkview Dr	Chesapeake	VA	23320	757-366-9696	
Daikichi Sushi Japanese Bistro 1400 N Battlefield Blvd	Chesapeake	VA	23320	757-549-0200	549-0200
Web: www.welovesushi.net					
El Loro 801 Volvo Pkwy	Chesapeake	VA	23320	757-436-3415	436-3181
Grand China Buffet 1329 Battlefield Blvd	Chesapeake	VA	23320	757-549-6868	549-8383
Great Bridge BBQ 800 Battlefield Blvd S Suite 112	Chesapeake	VA	23322	757-546-2270	
Ho-Ho Chinese Restaurant 202 S Battlefield Blvd	Chesapeake	VA	23322	757-482-2242	
Jade Garden Restaurant 1200 Battlefield Blvd N	Chesapeake	VA	23320	757-436-1010	
Joe's Crab Shack 1568 Crossways Blvd	Chesapeake	VA	23320	757-420-8330	
Kyoto Japanese Steak House & Sushi Bar 1412 Greenbrier Pkwy Suite 129	Chesapeake	VA	23320	757-420-0950	420-0692
Nagoya Sushi 109 Gainsborough Sq	Chesapeake	VA	23320	757-549-7977	549-3458
Pirate's Cove 109 Gainsborough Sq	Chesapeake	VA	23320	757-549-7272	
Rancho Grande 1320 S Military Hwy	Chesapeake	VA	23320	757-366-5128	366-5241
Rose Bay 805 Battlefield Blvd N Suite 101	Chesapeake	VA	23320	757-548-9300	548-9318
Smokey Bones BBQ & Grill 1405 Greenbrier Pkwy	Chesapeake	VA	23320	757-361-6843	361-6849
Web: www.smokeybones.com					
Tida Thai Cuisine 1937 S Military Hwy	Chesapeake	VA	23320	757-543-9116	543-8872
Polo Grill 7784 Gunston Plaza Dr	Lorton	VA	22079	703-550-0002	550-0283
Web: www.pologrill.net					
Kabuto Steak House 13158 Midlothian Tpke	Midlothian	VA	23113	804-379-7979	
Alfresco 11710-A & B Jefferson Ave	Newport News	VA	23606	757-873-0644	873-2355
Web: www.alfrescoitalianrestaurant.com					
Barclay's 943 J Clyde Morris Blvd	Newport News	VA	23601	757-952-1122	596-6199
Bill's Seafood House 10900 Warwick Blvd	Newport News	VA	23601	757-595-4320	
Chung Oak 15320 A & B Warwick Blvd	Newport News	VA	23608	757-874-3505	
Das Waldcafe 12529 Warwick Blvd	Newport News	VA	23602	757-930-1781	
Japan Samurai 12233 Jefferson Ave	Newport News	VA	23602	757-249-4400	
Light Restaurant & Bar 3150 William Styron Sq N Port Warwick	Newport News	VA	23606	757-599-5800	599-5652
Mitty's Italian Ristorante 1000 Omni Blvd	Newport News	VA	23606	757-873-6664	873-1732
Port Arthur 11137 Warwick Blvd	Newport News	VA	23601	757-599-6474	
Web: www.portarthurva.com					
RJ's Restaurant & Sports Pub 12743 Jefferson Ave	Newport News	VA	23602	757-874-4246	
Schlesinger's Chop House 1106 William Styron Sq S	Newport News	VA	23606	757-599-4700	599-4707
Web: www.schlesingerssteaks.com					
So Ya Japanese Restaurant 12715 Warwick Blvd Suite J	Newport News	VA	23606	757-930-0156	930-2208
456 Fish 456 Granby St	Norfolk	VA	23507	757-625-4444	626-3692
Web: www.456fish.com					
Banque The 1849 E Little Creek Rd	Norfolk	VA	23518	757-480-3600	
Bodega 442 Granby St	Norfolk	VA	23510	757-622-8527	622-8529
Web: www.bodegaongranby.com					
Dawat Indian Cuisine 888 N Military Hwy	Norfolk	VA	23502	757-455-8080	
Domo Japanese Restaurant 273 Granby St	Norfolk	VA	23510	757-628-8282	724-8193*
**Fax Area Code: 888*					
Empire Little Bar & Bistro The 245 Granby St	Norfolk	VA	23510	757-626-3100	626-3124
Fellini's 3910 Colley Ave	Norfolk	VA	23508	757-625-3000	625-0717
Franco's 6200 N Military Hwy	Norfolk	VA	23518	757-853-0177	853-8377
Freemason Abbey 209 W Freemason St	Norfolk	VA	23510	757-622-3966	622-3592
Web: www.freemasonabbey.com					
Havana's 255 Granby St	Norfolk	VA	23227	757-627-5800	962-0296
Web: www.liquidassetsrestaurants.com					
Kin's Wok 222 W 21st St	Norfolk	VA	23517	757-623-2933	623-6780
Kotobuki 721 W 21st St	Norfolk	VA	23517	757-628-1025	628-9281
La Galleria Ristorante 120 College Pl	Norfolk	VA	23510	757-623-3939	623-9106
Luna Maya 2000 Colonial Ave	Norfolk	VA	23517	757-622-6986	
Max & Erma's Restaurant 1500 N Military Hwy	Norfolk	VA	23503	757-466-8000	
Web: www.maxandermas.com					
Mi Hogar 4201 Granby St	Norfolk	VA	23504	757-640-7705	640-1526
Omar's Carriage House 313 W Bute St	Norfolk	VA	23510	757-622-4990	622-8122
Orapax Inn 1300 Redgate Ave	Norfolk	VA	23507	757-627-8041	
Web: www.theorapax.com					
Rajput Indian Cuisine 742 W 21st St	Norfolk	VA	23517	757-625-4634	622-2955
Web: www.rajputonline.com					
Regino's 3816 E Little Creek Rd	Norfolk	VA	23518	757-588-4300	
Sai Gai Japanese Steakhouse 7521 Granby St	Norfolk	VA	23505	757-423-1000	
San Antonio Sams 1501 Colley Ave	Norfolk	VA	23517	757-623-0233	623-9577
Web: www.sanantoniosams.com					
Siam 21 742 W 21st St Suite F	Norfolk	VA	23517	757-624-2455	624-2457
Sirena 455 Granby St	Norfolk	VA	23510	757-623-6622	623-6623
Web: www.sirenanorfolk.com					
Todd Jurich's Bistro 150 W Main St Suite 100	Norfolk	VA	23510	757-622-3210	962-7638
Web: www.toddjurichsbistro.com					
Uptown Buffet 1050 N Military Hwy	Norfolk	VA	23502	757-893-9293	
Velvet 25 332 Granby St	Norfolk	VA	23510	757-961-7143	398-8740
Voila! 509 Botetourt St	Norfolk	VA	23510	757-640-0343	
Acacia 3325 W Cary St	Richmond	VA	23221	804-354-6060	
Web: www.acaciarestaurant.com					
Amici 3343 W Cary St	Richmond	VA	23221	804-353-4700	
Web: www.amiciristorante.net					
Bella Italia 6407 Iron Bridge Rd	Richmond	VA	23234	804-743-1116	
Web: www.bellaitalia.cc					
Capital Ale House 623 E Main St	Richmond	VA	23219	804-643-2537	
Web: www.capitalalehouse.com					
Cheesecake Factory 11800 W Broad St	Richmond	VA	23233	804-364-4300	
Web: www.thecheesecakefactory.com					
Copper Grill 11800 W Broad St	Richmond	VA	23233	804-364-9408	
Web: www.coppergrill.com					
Davis & Main 2501 W Main St	Richmond	VA	23220	804-353-6641	
Hana Zushi 1309 E Cary St	Richmond	VA	23219	804-225-8801	
Helen's 2527 W Main St	Richmond	VA	23220	804-358-4370	
India K'Raja 9051-5 W Broad St	Richmond	VA	23294	804-965-6345	
Kabab Grille 1580 W Koger Ctr Dr	Richmond	VA	23235	804-378-3394	378-3396
Web: www.kababgrille.com					
L'Italia 10610 Patterson Ave	Richmond	VA	23233	804-740-1165	790-9305
La Casita 5204 Brook Rd	Richmond	VA	23227	804-264-9896	
Web: www.lacasitarestaurant.com					
Lemaire 101 W Franklin St	Richmond	VA	23220	804-788-8000	
Web: www.lemairerestaurant.com					
Mamma 'Zu 501 S Pine St	Richmond	VA	23220	804-788-4205	
Mekong 6004 W Broad St	Richmond	VA	23230	804-288-8929	
Web: www.mekong-restaurant.com					
Melting Pot of Richmond The 9704 Gayton Rd	Richmond	VA	23233	804-741-3120	741-2781
Web: www.meltingpot.com					
Millie's 2603 E Main St	Richmond	VA	23223	804-643-5512	648-4321
Web: www.milliesdiner.com					
Old Original Bookbinder's 2306 E Cary St	Richmond	VA	23223	804-643-6900	
Palani Drive 401 Libbie Ave	Richmond	VA	23226	804-285-3200	
Web: www.palanidrive.com					
PF Chang's China Bistro 9212 Stony Pt	Richmond	VA	23235	804-253-0492	
Pomegranate 1209 E Cary St	Richmond	VA	23219	804-643-9354	
Roma's 6017 Nine Mile Rd	Richmond	VA	23223	804-737-3104	
Web: www.romaitalianrestaurant.com					
Sam Miller's Restaurant 1210 E Cary St	Richmond	VA	23219	804-643-1301	
Web: www.sammillers.com					
Sine Irish Pub & Restaurant 1327 E Cary St	Richmond	VA	23219	804-649-7767	649-0661
Web: www.sineirishpub.com/cms_richmond					
Skilligalee 5416 Glenside Dr	Richmond	VA	23228	804-672-6200	755-1312
Web: www.skilligalee.com					
Sticky Rice 2232 W Main St	Richmond	VA	23220	804-358-7870	
Web: www.ilovestickyrice.com					
Strawberry Street Cafe 421 N Strawberry St	Richmond	VA	23220	804-353-6860	
Web: www.strawberrystreetcafe.com					
Tobacco Co Restaurant 1201 E Cary St	Richmond	VA	23219	804-782-9555	788-8913
Web: www.thetobaccocompany.com					
White Dog The 2329 W Main St	Richmond	VA	23220	804-340-1975	
Web: www.thewhitedog.com					
Zeus Gallery Cafe 201 N Belmont Ave	Richmond	VA	23221	804-359-3219	
419 West 3865 Electric Rd	Roanoke	VA	24018	540-776-0419	
Alexander's 105 S Jefferson St	Roanoke	VA	24011	540-982-6983	
Awful Arthur's Seafood Co 108 Campbell Ave SE	Roanoke	VA	24011	804-559-4370	
Web: www.awfularthurs.com					
Carlos Brazilian International Cuisine 4167 Electric Rd SW	Roanoke	VA	24014	540-776-1117	
Web: www.carlosbrazilian.com					
Coach & Four 5206 Williamson Rd NW	Roanoke	VA	24012	540-362-4220	
Web: www.coachandfour.com					
DJ's Brasserie 117 Duke of Gloucester St	Roanoke	VA	24014	540-342-4773	
Double Dragon 7232 Williamson Rd	Roanoke	VA	24019	540-265-0393	
El Toreo 3790 Peter's Creek Rd Ext SW	Roanoke	VA	24018	540-342-7060	
Frankie Rowland's Steakhouse 104 Jefferson St	Roanoke	VA	24011	540-527-2333	
Kabuki Japanese Steak House 3503 Franklin Rd SW	Roanoke	VA	24014	540-981-0222	
Kobe Japanese Steak House 3214 Electric Rd	Roanoke	VA	24018	540-776-0008	
Luigi's 3301 Brambleton Ave SW	Roanoke	VA	24018	540-989-6277	
Metro! 14 Campbell Ave SE	Roanoke	VA	24011	540-345-6645	345-6647
Web: www.metroroanoke.com					
Montano's 3733 Franklin Rd SW	Roanoke	VA	24014	540-344-8960	
Web: www.montanos.com					
Nawab Indian Cuisine 118A Campbell Ave	Roanoke	VA	24011	540-345-5150	
Web: www.nawabonline.com					
Ragazzi's 3843 Electric Rd	Roanoke	VA	24018	540-989-9022	
Web: www.ragazzis.com					
Regency Room The 110 Shenandoah Ave	Roanoke	VA	24016	540-985-5900	853-8265
Web: www.roanokehotels.com					
Szechuan 5207 Bernard Dr	Roanoke	VA	24018	540-989-7947	
Texas Steak House & Saloon 5025 Valley View Blvd NW	Roanoke	VA	24012	540-265-1809	
Web: www.texassteakhouse.com					
Woo Lae Oak 8240 Leesburg Pike	Vienna	VA	22182	703-827-7300	827-7302
Web: www.woolaeoak.com					
22nd Street Raw Bar & Grill 202 22nd St	Virginia Beach	VA	23451	757-491-2222	
Aberdeen Barn 5805 Northampton Blvd	Virginia Beach	VA	23455	757-464-1580	
Web: www.aberdeenbarn.com					
Albie's 2401 Seaboard Rd	Virginia Beach	VA	23456	757-301-3326	
Aldo's Ristorante 1860 Laskin Rd	Virginia Beach	VA	23454	757-491-1111	
Alexander's on the Bay 4536 Ocean View Ave	Virginia Beach	VA	23455	757-464-4999	
Web: www.alexandersonthebay.com					
Angelo's By the Sea 2809 Atlantic Ave	Virginia Beach	VA	23451	757-425-0347	
Boulevard Cafe 2935 Virginia Beach Blvd	Virginia Beach	VA	23452	757-463-1311	
Bubba's Crabhouse Seafood Restaurant 3323 Shore Dr	Virginia Beach	VA	23451	757-481-0907	
Captain George's Seafood 2272 Old Pungo Ferry Rd	Virginia Beach	VA	23457	757-721-3463	
Coastal Grill 1427 N Great Neck Rd	Virginia Beach	VA	23454	757-496-3348	496-5619
Web: www.coastalgrill.com					
Coyote Cafe Cantina 972 Laskin Rd	Virginia Beach	VA	23451	757-425-8705	
Croc's Restaurant 620 19th St	Virginia Beach	VA	23451	757-428-5444	
Web: www.crocsrestaurant.com					
Ellington's on the Ocean 3301 Atlantic Ave	Virginia Beach	VA	23451	757-428-4585	
Ensenada 2824 Virginia Beach Blvd	Virginia Beach	VA	23452	757-631-1090	
Five 01 City Grill 501 N Birdneck Rd	Virginia Beach	VA	23451	757-425-7195	
Frederico 357 Independence Blvd	Virginia Beach	VA	23462	757-497-1445	

Name / Address	City	State	Zip	Phone	Fax
Hot Tuna Bar & Grill 2817 Shore Dr	Virginia Beach	VA	23451	757-481-2888	
Web: www.hottunavb.com					
Il Giardino 910 Atlantic Ave	Virginia Beach	VA	23451	757-422-6464	422-1175
Web: www.ilgiardino.com					
Imperial Palace 4878 Princess Anne Rd	Virginia Beach	VA	23462	757-493-8838	
Laverne's 701 Atlantic Ave	Virginia Beach	VA	23451	757-428-6836	
Lynnhaven Fish House 2350 Starfish Rd	Virginia Beach	VA	23451	757-481-0003	481-3474
Web: www.lynnhavenfishhouse.net					
Melting Pot of Virginia Beach The 1564 Laskin Rd	Virginia Beach	VA	23451	757-425-3463	
Web: www.meltingpot.com					
Mi Casita 3600 Bonney Rd	Virginia Beach	VA	23452	757-463-3819	
Mo Mo Sushi 1385 Fordham Dr	Virginia Beach	VA	23464	757-366-3188	
Nara Sushi 717 Independence Blvd	Virginia Beach	VA	23455	757-456-5111	490-0109
Web: www.getfoodtoday.com/nara					
One Fish - Two Fish 2109 W Great Neck Rd	Virginia Beach	VA	23451	757-496-4350	
Web: www.onefish-twofish.com					
Otani 1532 Laskin Rd	Virginia Beach	VA	23451	757-425-0404	
PF Chang's China Bistro 4551 Virginia Beach Blvd	Virginia Beach	VA	23462	757-473-9028	
Web: www.pfchangs.com					
Plaza Azteca 4292 Holland Rd	Virginia Beach	VA	23452	757-431-8135	
Reginella's 4000 Virginia Beach Blvd	Virginia Beach	VA	23452	757-498-9770	
Shogun Japanese Steakhouse 550 First Colonial Rd	Virginia Beach	VA	23451	757-422-5150	422-5158
Steinhilbers Thalia 653 Thalia Rd	Virginia Beach	VA	23452	757-340-1156	
Web: www.steinys.com					
Tautog's 205 23rd St	Virginia Beach	VA	23451	757-422-0081	
Web: www.tautogs.com					
Timbuktu 3107 Atlantic Ave	Virginia Beach	VA	23451	757-491-1800	
Tradewinds 2800 Shore Dr	Virginia Beach	VA	23451	757-481-9000	
Web: www.virginiabeachresorts.com					
Waterman's Grill 415 Atlantic Ave	Virginia Beach	VA	23451	757-428-3644	
Web: www.watermans.com					
Zia Marie 4497 Lookout Rd	Virginia Beach	VA	23455	757-460-0715	
Aberdeen Barn 1601 Richmond Rd	Williamsburg	VA	23185	757-229-6661	
Web: www.aberdeen-barn.com					
Blue Talon Bistro 420 Prince George St	Williamsburg	VA	23185	757-476-2583	
Web: www.bluetalonbistro.com					
Bray Bistro 1010 Kingsmill Rd	Williamsburg	VA	23185	757-253-1703	
TF: 800-832-5665 ■ *Web:* www.kingsmill.com/dining.html					
Captain George's Seafood Restaurant 5363 Richmond Rd	Williamsburg	VA	23188	757-565-2323	
Web: www.captaingeorges.com					
Christiana Campbell's Tavern Waller St	Williamsburg	VA	23185	757-229-2141	
Dining Room at Ford's Colony 240 Ford's Colony Dr	Williamsburg	VA	23188	757-258-4107	
Web: www.fordscolony.com/dining/dining.html					
Fat Canary 410 W Duke of Gloucester St	Williamsburg	VA	23185	757-229-3333	
Giuseppe's Italian Cafe 5601 Richmond Rd	Williamsburg	VA	23188	757-565-1977	
Jefferson Restaurant 1453 Richmond Rd	Williamsburg	VA	23185	757-229-2296	
Kitchen at Powhatan Plantation 3601 Ironbound Rd	Williamsburg	VA	23188	757-253-7893	
Web: www.kitchenatpowhatan.com					
La Tolteca 3048 Richmond Rd	Williamsburg	VA	23185	757-253-2939	
Le Yaca 1915 Pocahontas Trail	Williamsburg	VA	23185	757-220-3616	
Mirabella's 207 Bypass Rd	Williamsburg	VA	23185	757-253-8550	
Web: www.roccossmokehousegrill.com					
Nawab Indian Cuisine 204 Monticello Ave Monticello Shopping Ctr	Williamsburg	VA	23185	757-565-3200	
Web: www.nawabonline.com					
Old Chickahominy House 1211 Jamestown Rd	Williamsburg	VA	23185	757-229-4689	
Papillon Bistro 415 Richmond Rd Williamsburg Hospitality House	Williamsburg	VA	23185	757-229-4020	
Web: www.williamsburghopistalityhouse.com					
Peking 120 Waller Mill Rd	Williamsburg	VA	23185	757-229-2288	
Pierce's Pitt Bar-B-Que 477 E Rochambeau Dr	Williamsburg	VA	23185	757-565-2955	565-1548
Web: www.pierces.com					
Regency Room 136 E Francis St	Williamsburg	VA	23187	757-229-2141	565-8202
Sal's 1242 Richmond Rd	Williamsburg	VA	23185	757-220-2641	
Web: www.salsbyvictor.com					
Seafare The 1632 Richmond Rd	Williamsburg	VA	23185	757-229-0099	
Second Street Restaurant & Tavern 140 2nd St	Williamsburg	VA	23185	757-220-2286	
Web: www.secondst.com					
Trellis Restaurant 403 W Duke of Gloucester St	Williamsburg	VA	23185	757-229-8610	
Web: www.thetrellis.com					
Whaling Co The 494 McLaws Cir	Williamsburg	VA	23185	757-229-0275	229-2804
Web: www.thewhalingcompany.com					
Whitehall Restaurant 1325 Jamestown Rd	Williamsburg	VA	23185	757-229-4677	
Yorkshire Steak & Seafood Restaurant 700 York St	Williamsburg	VA	23185	757-229-9790	
Web: www.theyorkshirerestaurant.com					

WASHINGTON

Name / Address	City	State	Zip	Phone	Fax
Bavarian Corner 8910-D Martin Way E	Olympia	WA	98516	360-456-5066	
Budd Bay Cafe 525 N Columbia St	Olympia	WA	98501	360-357-6963	786-8474
Web: www.buddbaycafe.com					
Casa Mia 716 Plum St	Olympia	WA	98501	360-352-0440	
Web: www.casamiarestaurants.com					
El Sarape 4043 Martin Way E	Olympia	WA	98506	360-459-5525	
Emperor's Palace 400 Cooper Pt Rd SW	Olympia	WA	98502	360-352-0777	754-2188
Web: www.eprestaurant.com					
Fishbowl Brew Pub & Cafe 515 Jefferson St SE	Olympia	WA	98501	360-943-3650	943-6983
Web: www.fishbowl.com					
Gardner's Seafood & Pasta 111 Thurston Ave NW	Olympia	WA	98501	360-786-8466	
Koibito 1707 Harrison Ave NW	Olympia	WA	98502	360-352-4751	
Lemon Grass Restaurant 212 4th Ave W	Olympia	WA	98501	360-705-1832	
Mayan Family 4520 Pacific Ave SE	Olympia	WA	98503	360-491-8244	413-0564
Mekong 125 Columbia St NW	Olympia	WA	98501	360-352-9620	
Mercato 111 Market St NE	Olympia	WA	98501	360-528-3663	528-3665
Web: www.mercatorestaurant.com					
Oyster House 320 4th Ave W	Olympia	WA	98502	360-753-7000	753-7077
Web: www.oysterhouse.com					
Racha Noodles & Thai Cuisine 625 Black Lake Blvd SW	Olympia	WA	98502	360-943-8883	
Web: www.rachathai.com					
Ramblin Jack's 520 4th Ave E	Olympia	WA	98501	360-754-8909	
Web: www.ramblinjacks.com					
Saigon Rendez-vous 117 5th Ave SW	Olympia	WA	98501	360-352-1989	
Trinacria Ristorante 113 Capitol Way N	Olympia	WA	98501	360-352-8892	
Urban Onion 116 Legion Way SE	Olympia	WA	98501	360-943-9242	
13 Coins 125 Boren Ave N	Seattle	WA	98109	206-682-2513	
Web: www.13coins.com					
611 Supreme 611 E Pine St	Seattle	WA	98122	206-328-0292	
Agua Verde Cafe 1303 NE Boat St	Seattle	WA	98105	206-545-8570	
Web: www.aguaverde.com					
Al Boccalino 1 Yesler Way	Seattle	WA	98104	206-622-7688	622-1798
Alki Homestead 2717 61st Ave SW	Seattle	WA	98116	206-935-5678	
Andaluca 407 Olive Way	Seattle	WA	98101	206-382-6999	382-6997
Web: www.andaluca.com					
Anthony's Pier 66 2201 Alaskan Way	Seattle	WA	98121	206-448-6688	728-2500
Web: www.anthonys.com					
Assaggio Ristorante 2010 4th Ave	Seattle	WA	98121	206-441-1399	
Web: www.assaggioseattle.com					
Asteroid Cafe 1605 N 45th St	Seattle	WA	98103	206-547-2514	
Web: www.asteroidcafe.com					
Blue Onion Bistro 5801 Roosevelt Way NE	Seattle	WA	98105	206-729-0579	
Web: www.theblueonionbistro.com					
BluWater Bistro 1001 Fairview Ave N	Seattle	WA	98109	206-447-0769	447-6977
Web: www.bluwaterbistro.com					
Brad's Swingside Cafe 4212 Fremont Ave N	Seattle	WA	98103	206-633-4057	
Brasserie Margaux 401 Lenora St	Seattle	WA	98121	206-777-1990	
Web: www.margauxseattle.com					
Brooklyn Seafood Steak & Oyster House 1212 2nd Ave	Seattle	WA	98101	206-224-7000	224-7088
Cactus 4220 E Madison St	Seattle	WA	98112	206-324-4140	
Web: www.cactusrestaurants.com					
Cafe Flora 2901 E Madison St	Seattle	WA	98112	206-325-9100	
Web: www.cafeflora.com					
Cafe Lago 2305 24th Ave E	Seattle	WA	98112	206-329-8005	329-8053
Web: www.cafelago.com					
Campagne 86 Pine St	Seattle	WA	98101	206-728-2800	443-3804
Web: www.campagnerestaurant.com					
Canlis Restaurant 2576 Aurora Ave N	Seattle	WA	98109	206-283-3313	283-1766
Web: www.canlis.com					
Carmelita 7314 Greenwood Ave N	Seattle	WA	98103	206-706-7703	
Chandler's Crabhouse 901 Fairview Ave N	Seattle	WA	98109	206-223-2722	223-9380
Web: www.schwartzbros.com/chandlers.cfm					
Chez Shea 94 Pike St Suite 34	Seattle	WA	98101	206-467-9990	
Web: www.chezshea.com					
Chinook's at Salmon Bay 1900 W Nickerson St Suite 103	Seattle	WA	98119	206-283-4665	283-3705
Web: www.schinooks.com					
Chiso Restaurant 3520 Fremont Ave N	Seattle	WA	98103	206-632-3430	632-3429
Web: www.chisoseattle.com					
Chutney's Grille on the Hill 605 15th Ave E	Seattle	WA	98112	206-726-1000	
Coldwater Bar & Grill 1900 5th Ave Westin Seattle	Seattle	WA	98101	206-728-1000	
Cutters Bayhouse 2001 Western Ave	Seattle	WA	98121	206-448-4884	727-2194
Web: www.cuttersbayhouse.com					
Dahlia Lounge 2001 4th Ave	Seattle	WA	98121	206-682-4142	467-0568
Web: www.tomdouglas.com					
Daniel's Broiler 809 Fairview Pl N	Seattle	WA	98109	206-621-8262	748-7765
Web: www.schwartzbros.com					
Dulces Latin Bistro 1430 34th Ave	Seattle	WA	98122	206-322-5453	
Web: www.dulceslatinbistro.com					
Earth & Ocean 1112 4th Ave	Seattle	WA	98101	206-264-6060	264-6070
Web: www.earthocean.net					
El Gaucho 2505 1st Ave	Seattle	WA	98121	206-728-1337	728-4477
Web: www.elgaucho.com					
Elemental @ Gasworks 3309 Wallingford Ave	Seattle	WA	98103	206-547-2317	
Web: www.elementalatgasworks.com					
Elliott's Oyster House 1201 Alaskan Way Pier 56	Seattle	WA	98101	206-623-4340	224-0154
Web: www.elliottsoysterhouse.com					
Etta's Seafood 2020 Western Ave	Seattle	WA	98121	206-443-6000	443-0648
Web: www.tomdouglas.com					
Eva Restaurant 2227 N 56th St	Seattle	WA	98103	206-633-3538	
Flying Fish 300 Westlake Ave N	Seattle	WA	98109	206-728-8595	728-1551
Web: www.flyingfishseattle.com					
Galerias 611 Broadway E	Seattle	WA	98102	206-322-5757	
Web: www.galeriasgourmet.net					
Georgian Room 411 University St	Seattle	WA	98101	206-621-7889	
Harvest Vine 2701 E Madison St	Seattle	WA	98112	206-320-9771	
Web: www.harvestvine.com					
Hunt Club The 900 Madison St	Seattle	WA	98104	206-622-6400	343-6159
Icon Grill 1933 5th Ave	Seattle	WA	98101	206-441-6330	441-7037
Web: www.icongrill.net					
Il Bistro 93-A Pike St	Seattle	WA	98101	206-682-3049	223-0234
Web: www.ilbistro.net					
Il Terrazzo Carmine 411 1st Ave S	Seattle	WA	98104	206-467-7797	
Web: www.ilterrazzocarmine.com					
India Bistro 2301 NW Market St	Seattle	WA	98107	206-783-5080	297-9069
Web: www.seattleindiabistro.com					

Name / Address	City	State	ZIP	Phone	Fax
Ivar's Acres of Clams					
1001 Alaskan Way Pier 54	Seattle	WA	98104	206-624-6852	624-4895
Web: www.ivars.com					
JaK's Grill 3701 NE 45th St	Seattle	WA	98116	206-985-8545	985-8552
Web: www.jaksgrill.com					
Kabul Afghan Cuisine 2301 N 45th St	Seattle	WA	98103	206-545-9000	
Web: www.kabulrestaurant.com					
Kingfish Cafe 602 19th Ave E	Seattle	WA	98112	206-320-8757	320-0021
La Medusa 4857 Rainier Ave S	Seattle	WA	98118	206-723-2192	
Web: www.lamedusarestaurant.com					
La Rustica 4100 Beach Dr SW	Seattle	WA	98116	206-932-3020	
Web: www.larustica.com					
La Vita E Bella 2411 2nd Ave	Seattle	WA	98121	206-441-5322	
Web: www.lavitaebella.us					
Le Gourmand 425 NW Market St	Seattle	WA	98107	206-784-3463	789-4348
Web: www.legourmandrestaurant.com					
Le Pichet 1933 1st Ave	Seattle	WA	98101	206-256-1499	
Lola 2000 4th Ave	Seattle	WA	98121	206-441-1430	441-5224
Web: www.tomdouglas.com					
Madison Park Cafe 1807 42nd Ave E	Seattle	WA	98112	206-324-2626	328-0432
Web: www.madisonparkcafe.ypguides.net					
Maneki 304 6th Ave S	Seattle	WA	98122	206-622-2631	
Marco's Supperclub 2510 1st Ave	Seattle	WA	98121	206-441-7801	
Web: www.marcossupperclub.com					
Market Street Grill 1744 NW Market St	Seattle	WA	98107	206-789-6766	
Web: www.marketstreetgrill.net					
Matt's in the Market 94 Pike St Suite 32	Seattle	WA	98101	206-467-7909	
Web: www.mattsinthemarket.com					
McCormick's Fish House & Bar 722 4th Ave	Seattle	WA	98104	206-682-3900	667-0081
Web: www.mccormickandschmicks.com					
Metropolitan Grill 820 2nd Ave	Seattle	WA	98104	206-624-3287	389-0042
Web: www.themetropolitangrill.com					
Morton's The Steakhouse 1511 6th Ave	Seattle	WA	98101	206-223-0550	223-0507
Web: www.mortons.com					
Nell's 6804 E Green Lake Way N	Seattle	WA	98115	206-524-4044	
Web: www.nellsrestaurant.com					
Oceanaire Seafood Room 1700 7th Ave	Seattle	WA	98101	206-267-2277	
Web: www.theoceanaire.com					
Ototo Sushi 7 Boston St	Seattle	WA	98109	206-691-3838	691-3839
Web: www.ototosushi.com					
Pabla Indian Cuisine 1516 2nd Ave	Seattle	WA	98101	206-623-2868	
Web: www.pablaindiancuisine.com					
Palace Kitchen 2030 5th Ave	Seattle	WA	98121	206-448-2001	
Web: www.tomdouglas.com					
Palisade 2601 W Marina Pl	Seattle	WA	98199	206-285-1000	285-7087
Web: www.palisaderestaurant.com					
Palomino 1420 5th Ave	Seattle	WA	98101	206-623-1300	467-1386
Web: www.palomino.com					
Paseo 4225 Fremont Ave N	Seattle	WA	98103	206-545-7440	
PF Chang's China Bistro 400 Pine St Suite 136	Seattle	WA	98101	206-393-0070	393-0075
Web: www.pfchangs.com					
Phoenecia at Alki 2716 Alki Ave SW	Seattle	WA	98116	206-935-6550	
Pink Door The 1919 Post Alley	Seattle	WA	98101	206-443-3241	443-3341
Web: www.thepinkdoor.net					
Place Pigalle 81 Pike St	Seattle	WA	98101	206-624-1756	
Web: www.placepigalle-seattle.com					
Ponti Seafood Grill 3014 3rd Ave N	Seattle	WA	98109	206-284-3000	284-4768
Web: www.pontiseafoodgrill.com					
Queen City Grill 2201 1st Ave	Seattle	WA	98121	206-443-0975	973-5345
Web: www.queencitygrill.com					
Ray's Boathouse 6049 Seaview Ave NW	Seattle	WA	98107	206-789-3770	781-1960
Web: www.rays.com					
Restaurant Zoe 2137 2nd Ave	Seattle	WA	98121	206-256-2060	
Web: www.restaurantzoe.com					
Rock Salt Steak House 1232 Westlake Ave N	Seattle	WA	98109	206-284-1047	284-7856
Web: www.rocksaltlakeunion.com					
Rover's 2808 E Madison St	Seattle	WA	98112	206-325-7442	325-1092
Web: www.thechefinthehat.com					
Ruth's Chris Steak House 727 Pine St	Seattle	WA	98101	206-624-8524	624-6268
Web: www.ruthschris.com					
Salty's on Alki Beach 1936 Harbor Ave SW	Seattle	WA	98126	206-937-1600	937-1430
Web: www.saltys.com					
Serafina 2043 Eastlake Ave E	Seattle	WA	98102	206-323-0807	325-2766
Web: www.serafinaseattle.com					
Shiro's Sushi Restaurant 2401 2nd Ave	Seattle	WA	98121	206-443-9844	443-9974
Web: www.shiros.com					
SkyCity Restaurant 400 Broad St	Seattle	WA	98109	206-905-2100	
Web: www.spaceneedle.com					
Sostanza Trattoria 1927 43rd Ave E	Seattle	WA	98112	206-324-9701	324-9701
Sunfish 2800 Alki Ave SW	Seattle	WA	98116	206-938-4112	
Szmania's 3321 W McGraw St	Seattle	WA	98199	206-284-7305	283-7303
Web: www.szmanias.com					
Tango 1100 Pike St	Seattle	WA	98101	206-583-0382	
Ten Mercer 10 Mercer St	Seattle	WA	98109	206-691-3723	
Web: www.tenmercer.com					
Thai Heaven 352 Roy St	Seattle	WA	98109	206-285-1596	
Tilth Restaurant 1411 N 45th St	Seattle	WA	98103	206-633-0801	633-0801
Web: www.tilthrestaurant.com					
Tulio Ristorante 1100 5th Ave	Seattle	WA	98101	206-624-5500	
Web: www.tulio.com					
Typhoon! 1400 Western Ave	Seattle	WA	98101	206-262-9797	
Web: www.typhoonrestaurants.com					
Volterra 5411 Ballard Ave NW	Seattle	WA	98107	206-789-5100	
Web: www.volterrarestaurant.com					
Waterfront Seafood Grill					
2801 Alaskan Way Pier 70	Seattle	WA	98121	206-956-9171	956-8090
Web: www.waterfrontpier70.com					
Wild Ginger Asian Restaurant 1401 3rd Ave	Seattle	WA	98101	206-623-4450	623-8265
Web: www.wildginger.net					
Yanni's Restaurant 7419 Greenwood Ave N	Seattle	WA	98103	206-783-6945	
Azar's 2501 N Monroe St	Spokane	WA	99205	509-326-7171	
Azteca 245 W Spokane Falls Blvd	Spokane	WA	99206	509-456-0350	
Web: www.aztecamex.com					
Cafe Marron 144 Cannon St	Spokane	WA	99204	509-456-8660	
Web: www.cafemarronbrownes.com					
Catacombs Pub 110 S Monroe St	Spokane	WA	99201	509-838-4610	789-8345
Web: www.catacombspub.com					
Cathay Inn 3714 N Division St	Spokane	WA	99207	509-326-2226	
Web: www.cathayinn.com					
China Dragon 27 E Queen Ave	Spokane	WA	99207	509-483-5209	
Clinkerdagger 621 W Mallon Ave	Spokane	WA	99201	509-328-5965	
Web: www.clinkerdagger.com					
Cyrus O'Leary's 516 W Main Ave	Spokane	WA	99201	509-624-9000	
Web: www.cyrusolearys.com					
Downriver Grill 3315 W NW Blvd	Spokane	WA	99205	509-323-1600	326-3642
Web: www.downrivergrillspokane.com					
Elk Public House 1931 W Pacific Ave	Spokane	WA	99204	509-363-1973	
Europa 125 S Wall St	Spokane	WA	99201	509-455-4051	
Kim Do 2018 N Hamilton St	Spokane	WA	99207	509-487-7700	
Linnie Thai Cuisine 1301 W 3rd Ave	Spokane	WA	99201	509-838-0626	
Longhorn BBQ 2315 N Argonne Rd	Spokane	WA	99212	509-924-9600	
Web: www.longhornbarbecue.com					
Luigi's 245 W Main St	Spokane	WA	99201	509-624-5226	
Web: www.luigis-spokane.com					
Luna 5620 S Perry St	Spokane	WA	99223	509-448-2383	448-9765
Web: www.lunaspokane.com					
Mamma Mia's 420 W Francis Ave	Spokane	WA	99205	509-467-7786	467-7761
Ming Wah 1618 W 3rd Ave	Spokane	WA	99204	509-455-9474	
Mizuna 214 N Howard St	Spokane	WA	99201	509-747-2004	
Web: www.mizuna.com					
Mustard Seed 4750 N Division	Spokane	WA	99207	509-483-1500	
Web: www.mustardseedweb.com					
Niko's Greek Restaurant & Wine Bar					
725 W Riverside Ave	Spokane	WA	99201	509-624-7444	624-6854
Web: www.nikosspokane.com					
O'Doherty's Irish Grill					
525 W Spokane Falls Blvd	Spokane	WA	99201	509-747-0322	
Rancho Chico 2023 W NW Blvd	Spokane	WA	99205	509-327-2723	
Shogun 821 E 3rd Ave	Spokane	WA	99202	509-534-7777	
Spencer's 322 N Spokane Falls Ct	Spokane	WA	99220	509-744-2372	744-2396
Web: www.spencersforsteaksandchops.com					
Taste of India 3110 N Division St	Spokane	WA	99207	509-327-7313	327-1711
Tomato Street North 6220 N Division	Spokane	WA	99207	509-484-4500	484-1306
Web: www.tomatostreet.com					
Twigs Bistro & Bar 808 W Main Ave	Spokane	WA	99201	509-232-3376	
Web: www.twigsbistro.com					
Anthony's at Point Defiance					
5910 N Waterfront Dr	Tacoma	WA	98407	253-752-9700	752-1929
Web: www.anthonys.com					
Azteca 4801 Tacoma Mall Blvd	Tacoma	WA	98409	253-472-0246	
El Gaucho 2119 Pacific Ave	Tacoma	WA	98402	253-272-1510	
Web: www.elgaucho.com					
Europa Bistro 2515 N Proctor St	Tacoma	WA	98403	253-761-5660	
Web: www.europabistro.net					
Galanga 1129 Broadway	Tacoma	WA	98402	253-272-3393	
Web: www.galangathai.com					
Harmon Brewing Co 1938 Pacific Ave	Tacoma	WA	98402	253-383-2739	
Web: www.harmonbrewing.com					
Hidalgo 806 72nd St E	Tacoma	WA	98404	253-476-1097	
Indochine Asian Dining Lounge					
1924 Pacific Ave	Tacoma	WA	98402	253-272-8200	
Web: www.indochinedowntown.com					
Johnny's Dock 1900 E D St	Tacoma	WA	98421	253-627-3186	627-7457
Web: www.johnnysdock.com					
Kabuki Japanese Restaurant					
2919 S 38th St Suite B	Tacoma	WA	98409	253-474-1650	
La Costa Mexican Restaurant 928 Pacific Ave	Tacoma	WA	98402	253-272-0300	
Le-Le 1012 S Martin Luther King Jr Way	Tacoma	WA	98405	253-572-9491	
Lobster Shop South 4015 Ruston Way	Tacoma	WA	98402	253-759-2165	752-9640
Web: www.lobstershop.com					
Marzano 516 Garfield St S	Tacoma	WA	98444	253-537-4191	
Web: www.dinemarzano.com					
Mekong 2901 S 47th St	Tacoma	WA	98409	253-474-2728	
Melting Pot The 2121 Pacific Ave	Tacoma	WA	98402	253-535-3939	
Web: www.meltingpot.com					
Moctezuma's 4102 S 56th St	Tacoma	WA	98409	253-474-5593	
Web: www.moctezumas.com					
North China Garden 2303 6th Ave	Tacoma	WA	98403	253-572-5106	
Old House Cafe 2717 N Proctor St	Tacoma	WA	98407	253-759-7336	
Web: www.oldhousecafe.com					
Primo Grill 601 S Pine St	Tacoma	WA	98405	253-383-7000	
Web: www.primogrilltacoma.com					
Ravenous Restaurant 785 Broadway	Tacoma	WA	98402	253-572-6374	
Sakura Japanese Steakhouse 3630 S Cedar St	Tacoma	WA	98409	253-475-1300	
Skippers Seafood & Chowder House					
4710 Pacific Ave	Tacoma	WA	98408	253-475-5255	
Web: www.skippers.net					
Southern Kitchen 1716 6th Ave	Tacoma	WA	98405	253-627-4282	
Web: www.southernkitchenrestaurant.net					
Stanley & Seafort's 115 E 34th St	Tacoma	WA	98404	253-473-7300	471-1594
Web: www.stanleyandseaforts.com					
Sushi Tama 3919 6th Ave	Tacoma	WA	98406	253-761-1014	
Taqueria Guaymas 2630 S 38th St	Tacoma	WA	98409	253-471-2224	
Vuelve a la Vida 5310 Pacific Ave	Tacoma	WA	98408	253-473-7068	
Falls Terrace 106 S Deschutes Way	Tumwater	WA	98501	360-943-7830	
Web: www.fallsterrace.com					
Bacchus 3200 SE 16th Ave	Vancouver	WA	98683	360-882-9672	
Cactus Ya Ya 15704 SE Mill Plain Blvd	Vancouver	WA	98684	360-944-9292	
Canton Chinese Buffet 1118 NE 78th St	Vancouver	WA	98665	360-576-8699	
Carol's Corner Cafe 7800 NE St Johns Blvd	Vancouver	WA	98665	360-573-6357	
Dragon King 1401 NE 78th St	Vancouver	WA	98665	360-574-6684	
Hudson's Bar & Grill 7805 NW Greenwood Dr	Vancouver	WA	98662	360-816-6100	
Web: www.hudsonsbarandgrill.com					
Jerusalem Restaurant & Cafe					
106 E Evergreen Blvd	Vancouver	WA	98660	360-906-0306	

				Phone	Fax
Joe's Crab Shack 101 SE Columbia Way	Vancouver	WA	98661	360-693-9211	
Little Italy's Trattoria 901 Washington St	Vancouver	WA	98660	360-737-2363	
Web: www.littleitalystrattoria.com					
McMenamins on the Columbia 1801 S Access Rd	Vancouver	WA	98661	360-699-1521	
Namaste Indian Cuisine 6300 NE 117th Ave	Vancouver	WA	98662	360-891-5857	891-5906
Web: www.namasteindiancuisine.com					
Patrick's Hawaiian Cafe 316 SE 123rd Ave	Vancouver	WA	98683	360-885-0881	
Web: www.hawaiiancafe.com					
Thai Little Home 3214 E Fourth Plain Blvd	Vancouver	WA	98661	360-693-4061	
Thai Orchid 1004 Washington St	Vancouver	WA	98660	360-695-7786	
Web: www.thaiorchidrestaurant.com					
Tiger's Garden 312 W 8th St	Vancouver	WA	98660	360-693-9585	
Who-Song & Larry's 111 SE Columbia Way	Vancouver	WA	98661	360-695-1198	
Web: www.eltorito.com					
Beaches Restaurant & Bar 1919 SE Columbia River Dr	Vancover	WA	98661	360-699-1592	699-0724
Web: www.beachesrestaurantandbar.com					
Herbfarm The 14590 NE 145th St	Woodenville	WA	98072	425-485-5300	424-2925
Web: www.theherbfarm.com					

WEST VIRGINIA

				Phone	Fax
Aladdin 3024 Chesterfield Ave	Charleston	WV	25304	304-345-0052	343-3364
Fifth Quarter 201 Clendenin St	Charleston	WV	25301	304-345-3933	
Gratzi 1061 Charleston Town Ctr	Charleston	WV	25389	304-344-4824	344-4831
Web: www.gratzirestaurant.com					
Joe Fazio's 1008 Bullitt St	Charleston	WV	25301	304-344-3071	
Laury's 350 MacCorkle Ave SE	Charleston	WV	25314	304-343-0055	343-0078
Web: www.laurysrestaurant.com					
Leonoro's Spaghetti House 1507 Washington St E	Charleston	WV	25311	304-343-1851	
Rio Grande 60 Ct St	Charleston	WV	25301	304-344-8616	345-6458
Sitar of India 702 Lee St E	Charleston	WV	25301	304-346-3745	720-6260
Web: www.sibaraofindia.org					
Texas Steak House 2815 Mountaineer Blvd	Charleston	WV	25309	304-744-1255	744-1250
Web: www.texassteakhouse.com					
Tidewater Grill 1060 Charleston Town Ctr	Charleston	WV	25389	304-345-2622	345-5624
TF: 888-456-3463 ■ *Web:* www.tidewatergrillrestaurant.com					
Whitewater Grille 200 Lee St E	Charleston	WV	25301	304-353-3636	353-3727
Back Bay 1869 Mileground Rd	Morgantown	WV	26505	304-296-3027	
Cafe Bacchus 76 High St	Morgantown	WV	26505	304-296-9234	
Casa D'Amici 485 High St	Morgantown	WV	26507	304-292-4400	
Web: www.casadamici.com					
Flying Fish & Co 7000 Mid Atlantic Rd	Morgantown	WV	26508	304-225-3474	
Glasshouse Grille 709 Beechurst Ave	Morgantown	WV	26505	304-296-8460	
Web: www.theglasshousegrille.com					
Great Chinese Buffet 5000 Greenbag Rd	Morgantown	WV	26501	304-296-4050	
Hibachi Japanese Steak House 3091 University Ave	Morgantown	WV	26505	304-598-7140	
Web: www.mangoeskeywest.com					
Madeleine's Restaurant-Cellar 140 High St	Morgantown	WV	26505	304-296-6230	
Maxwell's 1 Wall St	Morgantown	WV	26505	304-292-0982	
Oliverio's Ristorante on the Wharf 52 Clay St	Morgantown	WV	26505	304-296-2565	296-2564
Web: www.oliverios.sites.morgantowns.com					
Peking House 1125 Van Voorhis Rd	Morgantown	WV	26505	304-598-3333	
Puglioni's 1137 Van Voorhis Rd	Morgantown	WV	26505	304-599-7521	
Voyagers Restaurant 110 Hartfield Rd	Morgantown	WV	26505	304-292-4701	
Web: www.alibabaexpress.com					
West Virginia Brewing Co 1293 University Ave	Morgantown	WV	26505	304-296-2739	296-2781
Web: www.mountainlair.com					
Wellington's 1 Dairy Rd	Poca	WV	25159	304-755-8219	755-3229
Colasante's 416 Fairmont Rd	Westover	WV	26505	304-296-7689	
Abbeys 145 Zane St	Wheeling	WV	26003	304-233-0729	
Bella Via 1 Burkham Ct	Wheeling	WV	26003	304-242-8181	242-8182
Coleman's Fish Market 2226 Centre Market	Wheeling	WV	26003	304-232-8510	
Figaretti's 1035 Mt de Chantel Rd	Wheeling	WV	26003	304-243-5625	
Generations Restaurant & Pub 338 National Rd	Wheeling	WV	26003	304-232-7917	233-8385
Web: www.generationswhg.com					
Golden Chopsticks 329 N York St	Wheeling	WV	26003	304-232-2888	
Panda Chinese Kitchen 1133 Market St	Wheeling	WV	26003	304-232-7572	
River City Ale Works 1400 Main St	Wheeling	WV	26003	304-233-4555	

WISCONSIN

				Phone	Fax
River Lane Inn 4313 W River Ln	Brown Deer	WI	53223	414-354-1995	
Brett Favre's Steakhouse 1004 Brett Favre Pass	Green Bay	WI	54304	920-499-6874	405-6896
Web: www.foodspot.com/brettfavressteakhouse					
China Palace 213 N Washington St	Green Bay	WI	54301	920-433-0688	433-9043
Eve's Supper Club 2020 Riverside Dr	Green Bay	WI	54301	920-435-1571	435-2899
Web: www.evessupperclub.com					
Grazies Pasta Co 2851 S Oneida St	Green Bay	WI	54304	920-499-6365	499-7983
Hinterland Brewery & Restaurant 313 Dousman St	Green Bay	WI	54303	920-438-8050	438-8053
TF: 800-604-2337 ■ *Web:* www.hinterlandbeer.com					
Kavarna 143 N Broadway	Green Bay	WI	54303	920-430-3200	
Web: www.kavarna.com					
Krolls West 1990 S Ridge Rd	Green Bay	WI	54304	920-497-1111	497-0237
Web: www.krollswest.com					
Legends Brewhouse & Eatery 2840 Shawano Ave	Green Bay	WI	54313	920-662-1111	
Little Tokyo 121B N Broadway	Green Bay	WI	54303	920-433-9323	433-9523
Los Banditos 1258 Main St	Green Bay	WI	54302	920-432-6460	
Web: www.foodspot.com/losbanditos					
Luigi's Italian Bistro 2733 Mantiwoc Rd	Green Bay	WI	54311	920-468-4900	
Mackinaws Grill & Spirits 2925 Voyager Dr	Green Bay	WI	54311	920-406-8000	406-8840
Web: www.mackinaws.com					
Mandarin Garden 2394 S Oneida St	Green Bay	WI	54304	920-499-4459	429-2992
Patrick's on the Bay 2607 Nicolet Dr	Green Bay	WI	54311	920-965-2483	965-2485
River's Bend 792 Riverview Dr	Green Bay	WI	54303	920-434-1383	434-9742
Web: www.riversbendrestaurant.com					
Rock Garden 1951 Bond St	Green Bay	WI	54303	920-497-4701	499-5242
Titletown Brewing Co 200 Dousman St	Green Bay	WI	54303	920-437-2337	437-2739
Web: www.titletownbrewing.com					
Wellington Restaurant 1060 Hansen Rd	Green Bay	WI	54304	920-499-2000	
Admiralty Room 666 Wisconsin Ave	Madison	WI	53703	608-256-9071	256-0910
TF: 800-922-5512					
Angelic Brewing Co 322 W Johnson St	Madison	WI	53703	608-257-2707	
Web: www.angelicbrewing.com					
Avenue Bar The 1128 E Washington Ave	Madison	WI	53703	608-257-6877	
Babe's Grill & Bar 5614 Schroeder Rd	Madison	WI	53711	608-274-7300	274-3201
Web: www.babesmadison.com					
Bahn Thai Restaurant 944 Williamson St	Madison	WI	53703	608-256-0202	
Web: www.bahnthai.741.com					
Bandung Indonesian Restaurant 600 Williamson St	Madison	WI	53703	608-255-6910	
Web: www.bandungrestaurant.com					
Biaggi's 601 Junction Rd	Madison	WI	53703	608-664-9288	664-0024
Web: www.biaggis.com					
Blue Marlin 101 N Hamilton St	Madison	WI	53703	608-255-2255	204-0043
Web: www.thebluemarlin.net					
Blue Moon Bar & Grill 2535 University Ave	Madison	WI	53705	608-233-0441	
Web: www.bluemoonbar.com					
Capitol Chophouse 9 E Wilson St	Madison	WI	53703	608-255-0165	260-2381
Chautara 334 State St	Madison	WI	53703	608-251-3626	
Eldorado Grill 744 Williamson St	Madison	WI	53703	608-280-9378	
Eno Vino Wine Bar & Bistro 601 Junction Rd	Madison	WI	53717	608-664-9565	664-9563
Web: www.eno-vino.com					
Essen Haus 514 E Wilson St	Madison	WI	53703	608-255-4674	258-8632
Web: www.essen-haus.com					
Famous Dave's Bar-B-Que 900 S Pk St	Madison	WI	53715	608-286-9400	286-9402
Web: www.famousdaves.com					
Husnu's 547 State St	Madison	WI	53703	608-256-0900	
Imperial Garden 4214 E Washington Ave	Madison	WI	53714	608-249-0466	249-1526
Johnny Delmonico's 130 S Pinckney St	Madison	WI	53703	608-257-8325	257-8324
Web: www.foodfightinc.com					
Jolly Bob's 1210 Williamson St	Madison	WI	53703	608-251-3902	
L'Etoile 1 S Pinckney St	Madison	WI	53703	608-251-0500	251-7577
Web: www.letoile-restaurant.com					
La Hacienda 515 S Pk St	Madison	WI	53715	608-255-8227	
Lao Laan-Xang 1146 Williamson St	Madison	WI	53703	608-280-0104	
Laredo's 694 S Whitney Way	Madison	WI	53711	608-278-0585	
Lombardino's 2500 University Ave	Madison	WI	53705	608-238-1922	218-9810
Web: www.lombardinos.com					
Maharaja 6713 Odana Rd	Madison	WI	53719	608-833-1824	803-2657
Mariner's Inn The 5339 Lighthouse Bay Dr	Madison	WI	53704	608-246-3120	
Nau-Ti-Gal 5360 Westport Rd	Madison	WI	53704	608-246-3130	
Web: www.nautigao.com					
Ocean Grill 117 MLK Jr Blvd	Madison	WI	53703	608-285-2582	
Web: www.foodfightinc.com					
Otto's Restaurant & Bar 6405 Mineral Pt Rd	Madison	WI	53705	608-274-4044	274-1358
Web: www.ottosrestaurant.com					
Pedro's Mexican Restaurante 3555 E Washington Ave	Madison	WI	53704	608-241-8110	241-8248
Web: www.pedrosmexicanrestaurant.com					
Porta Bella 425 N Frances St	Madison	WI	53703	608-256-3186	256-1210
Web: www.portabellarestaurant.biz					
Restaurant Magnus 120 E Wilson St	Madison	WI	53703	608-258-8787	
Web: www.restaurantmagnus.com					
Restaurant Muramoto 106 King St	Madison	WI	53703	608-260-2680	
Web: www.muramoto.biz					
Sa Bai Thong 2840 University Ave	Madison	WI	53705	608-238-3100	
Web: www.sabaithong.com					
Smokey Jon's No 1 B-B-Q 2310 Packers Ave	Madison	WI	53704	608-249-7427	249-7798
Smoky's Club 3005 University Ave	Madison	WI	53705	608-233-2120	
Web: www.smokys.com					
State Street Brats 603 State St	Madison	WI	53703	608-255-5544	
Web: www.statestreetbrats.com					
Taj Indian Restaurant 1256 S Pk St	Madison	WI	53715	608-268-0772	268-0774
Web: www.tajmadison.com					
Tornado Club Steak House 116 S Hamilton St	Madison	WI	53704	608-256-3570	
Tutto Pasta 305 State St	Madison	WI	53703	608-294-1000	255-2773
Web: www.foodspot.com					
Wasabi Japanese Restaurant 449 State St	Madison	WI	53703	608-255-5020	
Web: www.madisonwasabi.fc2web.com					
North Shore Bistro 8649 N Port Washington Rd	Mequon	WI	53217	414-351-6100	351-1443
Web: www.nsbbarandgrill.com					
Captain Bill's Seafood Co 2701 Century Harbor Rd	Middleton	WI	53562	608-831-7327	831-0634
Web: www.capbills.com					
African Hut 1107 N Old World 3rd St	Milwaukee	WI	53203	414-765-1110	765-0772
Web: www.africanpresentations.com					
Alioto's 3041 N Mayfair Rd	Milwaukee	WI	53222	414-476-6900	476-6902
Web: www.foodspot.com					
Apollo Cafe 1310 E Brady St	Milwaukee	WI	53202	414-272-2233	272-2344
Web: www.apollocafe.com					
Bacchus Restaurant 925 E Wells St	Milwaukee	WI	53202	414-765-1166	765-1161
Web: www.bacchusmke.com					
Beans & Barley 1901 E N Ave	Milwaukee	WI	53202	414-278-7878	278-6013
Web: www.beansandbarley.com					
Botanas 816 S 5th St	Milwaukee	WI	53204	414-672-3755	672-2771
Web: www.botanasrestaurant.com					
Caterina's Ristorante 9104 W Oklahoma Ave	Milwaukee	WI	53227	414-541-4200	541-4221
Web: www.caterinasrestaurant.com					
Cempazuchi 1205 E Brady St	Milwaukee	WI	53202	414-291-5233	291-5254
Web: www.cempazuchi.com					
Coast 931 E Wisconsin Ave	Milwaukee	WI	53202	414-727-5555	727-0777
Web: www.coastrestaurant.com					

				Phone	Fax
Coquette Cafe 316 N Milwaukee St	Milwaukee	WI	53202	414-291-2655	291-2657
Web: www.coquettecafe.com					
County Clare 1234 N Astor St	Milwaukee	WI	53202	414-272-5273	290-6300
Web: www.countyclare-inn.com					
Crawdaddy's 6414 W Greenfield Ave	Milwaukee	WI	53214	414-778-2228	778-0250
Web: www.foodspot.com/crawdaddys					
Eddie Martini's 8612 W Watertown Plank Rd	Milwaukee	WI	53226	414-771-6680	771-5034
Web: www.foodspot.com					
Elliot's Bistro 2321 N Murray Ave	Milwaukee	WI	53211	414-273-1488	273-1480
Web: www.elliotsbistro.com					
Elsa's on the Park 833 N Jefferson St	Milwaukee	WI	53202	414-765-0615	
Web: www.elsas.com					
Emperor of China Restaurant 1010 E Brady St	Milwaukee	WI	53202	414-271-8889	
Web: www.emperorofchinarestaurant.com					
Historic Turner Restaurant 1034 N 4th St	Milwaukee	WI	53203	414-276-4844	276-0442
Web: www.foodspot.com					
Il Mito 605 W Virginia St	Milwaukee	WI	53204	414-276-1414	276-2191
Web: www.ilmito.com					
Izumi's 2150 N Prospect Ave	Milwaukee	WI	53202	414-271-5278	287-0196
Web: www.izumis.com					
Jack Pandl's Whitefish Bay Inn 1319 E Henry Clay St	Milwaukee	WI	53217	414-964-3800	962-9309
Web: www.jackpandls.com					
Jackson Grill 3736 W Mitchell St	Milwaukee	WI	53215	414-384-7384	
Web: www.jacksongrill.com					
Karl Ratzsch's Old World Restaurant 320 E Mason St	Milwaukee	WI	53202	414-276-2720	276-3534
Web: www.karlratzsch.com					
Kegels German Inn 5901 W National Ave	Milwaukee	WI	53214	414-257-9999	774-4517
King & I The 830 N Old World 3rd St	Milwaukee	WI	53203	414-276-4181	276-4387
Web: www.kingandirestaurant.com					
La Fuente 625 S 5th St	Milwaukee	WI	53204	414-271-8595	271-8594
Web: www.ilovelafuente.com					
Louise's Trattoria 801 N Jefferson St	Milwaukee	WI	53202	414-273-4224	273-5225
Web: www.louiseswisconsin.com					
Mader's German Restaurant 1041 N Old World 3rd St	Milwaukee	WI	53203	414-271-3377	271-7914
Web: www.madersrestaurant.com					
Maharaja 1550 N Farwell Ave	Milwaukee	WI	53202	414-276-2250	
Web: www.restaurantmaharaja.com					
Milwaukee Chop House 633 N 5th St	Milwaukee	WI	53203	414-226-2467	390-4889
Web: www.chophouse411.com/milwaukee					
Mimma's Cafe 1307 E Brady St	Milwaukee	WI	53202	414-271-7337	272-4543
Web: www.mimmas.com					
Old Town 522 W Lincoln Ave	Milwaukee	WI	53207	414-672-0206	
Osteria del Mondo 1028 E Juneau Ave	Milwaukee	WI	53202	414-291-3770	291-0840
Web: www.getbianchini.com					
Packing House 900 E Layton Ave	Milwaukee	WI	53207	414-483-5054	483-3481
Web: www.foodspot.com/thepackinghouse					
Palms 221 N Broadway	Milwaukee	WI	53202	414-298-3000	
Safe House 779 N Front St	Milwaukee	WI	53202	414-271-2007	271-2676
Web: www.safe-house.com					
Sanford Restaurant 1547 N Jackson St	Milwaukee	WI	53202	414-276-9608	278-8509
Web: www.sanfordrestaurant.com					
Saraphino's 3074 E Layton Ave St Francis	Milwaukee	WI	53235	414-744-0303	
Web: www.saraphinos.com					
Saz's 5539 W State St	Milwaukee	WI	53208	414-453-2410	256-8778
Web: www.sazs.com					
Shahrazad 2847 N Oakland Ave	Milwaukee	WI	53211	414-964-5475	964-5471
Web: www.shahrazadrestaurant.com					
Speed Queen BBQ 1130 W Walnut St	Milwaukee	WI	53205	414-265-2900	265-7001
Web: www.foodspot.com					
Swig 1227 N Water St	Milwaukee	WI	53202	414-431-7944	
Web: www.swigmilwaukee.com					
Tandoor 1117 S 108th St	Milwaukee	WI	53214	414-777-1600	777-1577
Tess 2499 N Bartlett Ave	Milwaukee	WI	53211	414-964-8377	964-7790
Thai Palace 838 N Old World 3rd St	Milwaukee	WI	53203	414-224-7076	
Third Ward Caffe 225 E St Paul Ave	Milwaukee	WI	53202	414-224-0895	
Web: www.foodspot.com/thirdwardcaffe					
Three Bros 2414 S St Clair St	Milwaukee	WI	53207	414-481-7530	481-8652
Trocadero 1758 N Water St	Milwaukee	WI	53202	414-272-0205	272-0252
Web: www.ztrocadero.com					
Water Street Brewery 1101 N Water St	Milwaukee	WI	53202	414-272-1195	272-0406
Web: www.waterstreetbrewery.com					
Hammond Steakhouse 1402 N 5th St	Superior	WI	54880	715-392-3269	392-8374
Lan-Chi's Restaurant 1320 Belknap St	Superior	WI	54880	715-394-4496	395-2431
Filippo's 6915 W Lincoln Ave	West Allis	WI	53219	414-321-4040	
Singha Thai 2237 S 108th St	West Allis	WI	53227	414-541-1234	541-0683
Web: www.singhathaimilwaukee.com					

WYOMING

				Phone	Fax
303 Restaurant 303 S Wolcott St	Casper	WY	82601	307-233-4303	234-7005
Armor's Silver Fox Restaurant & Lounge 3422 S Energy Ln	Casper	WY	82604	307-235-3000	234-5324
Web: www.silverfoxrestaurant.ne					
Bosco's 847 E 'A' St	Casper	WY	82601	307-265-9658	235-4041
Dorn's Fireside 1745 Cy Ave	Casper	WY	82604	307-235-6831	235-6304
Goose Egg Inn 10580 Goose Egg Rd	Casper	WY	82604	307-473-8838	
Guadalajara 3355 Cy Ave	Casper	WY	82604	307-234-4699	234-5018
JS Chinese 116 W 2nd St	Casper	WY	82601	307-577-0618	577-0678
La Costa 1600 E 2nd St	Casper	WY	82601	307-235-6599	
Mongolian Grill 4801 E 2nd St Suite 110	Casper	WY	82609	307-473-1033	
Poor Boys Steakhouse 739 N Ctr St	Casper	WY	82601	307-237-8325	
Web: www.poorboyssteakhouse.net					
Sanford's Grub & Pub 241 Ctr St	Casper	WY	82601	307-234-4555	265-6449
Avanti 4620 Grandview Ave	Cheyenne	WY	82009	307-634-3432	
Casa de Trujillo 122 W 6th St	Cheyenne	WY	82007	307-635-1227	
Good Friends 507 E Lincolnway	Cheyenne	WY	82001	307-778-7088	
Guadalajara 1745 Dell Range Blvd	Cheyenne	WY	82009	307-432-6803	
Korean House 3219 Snyder Ave	Cheyenne	WY	82001	307-638-7938	
Little Bear Inn 1700 Little Bear Rd	Cheyenne	WY	82009	307-634-3684	
Los Amigos 620 Central Ave	Cheyenne	WY	82007	307-638-8591	
Renzios Greek Food 1400 Dell Range Blvd	Cheyenne	WY	82009	307-637-5411	
T-Joe's Steakhouse & Saloon 12700 I-80 Service Rd	Cheyenne	WY	82009	307-634-8750	
Twin Dragons 1809 Carey Ave	Cheyenne	WY	82001	307-637-6622	632-1168
Web: www.twindragons.com					
Bar-T-5 Covered Wagon Cook Out & Wild West Show 812 Cache Creek Dr	Jackson	WY	83001	307-733-5386	739-9183
Web: www.bart5.com					
Blue Lion Restaurant 160 N Millward St	Jackson	WY	83001	307-733-3912	733-3915
Web: www.bluelionrestaurant.com					
BonAppeThai 245 W Pearl St	Jackson	WY	83001	307-734-0245	
Bubba's 100 Flat Creek Dr	Jackson	WY	83001	307-733-2288	733-8990
Web: www.bubbasjh.com					
Bunnery The 130 N Cache Dr	Jackson	WY	83001	307-733-5474	
Cadillac Grille 55 N Cache St	Jackson	WY	83001	307-733-3279	739-0110
Calico Restaurant & Bar Teton Village Rd	Jackson	WY	83001	307-733-2460	734-0451
Web: www.calicorestaurant.com					
Chinatown 850 W Broadway	Jackson	WY	83001	307-733-8856	739-1904
Granary at Spring Creek Ranch The 1800 Spirit Dance Rd	Jackson	WY	83001	307-733-8833	733-1964
Web: www.springcreekranch.com/dining.html					
Grill The 1535 NE Butte Rd	Jackson	WY	83001	307-734-7333	734-7332
Gun Barrel Steak & Game House 862 W Broadway	Jackson	WY	83002	307-733-3287	733-6090
Web: www.gunbarrel.com					
Horse Creek Station 9800 S Hwy 89	Jackson	WY	83001	307-733-0810	
Nikai Sushi 225 N Cache St PO Box 14250	Jackson	WY	83001	307-734-6490	734-6488
Web: www.nikaisushi.com					
Ocean City 340 W Broadway	Jackson	WY	83001	307-734-9768	734-0454
Old Yellowstone Garage 175 Ctr St	Jackson	WY	83001	307-734-6161	734-6753
Snake River Brewing Co 265 S Millward St	Jackson	WY	83001	307-739-2337	739-2296
Web: www.snakeriverbrewing.com					
Snake River Grill 84 E Broadway	Jackson	WY	83001	307-733-0557	733-5767
Web: www.snakerivergrill.com					
Sweetwater Restaurant 85 King St	Jackson	WY	83001	307-733-3553	733-4463
Web: www.sweetwaterrest.com					
Teton Steakhouse 40 W Pearl St	Jackson	WY	83001	307-733-2639	739-4586
Web: www.tetonsteakhouse.com					
Thai Me Up 75 E Pearl St	Jackson	WY	85001	307-733-0005	
Rendezvous Bistro 380 S Broadway	Jackson Hole	WY	83001	307-739-1100	734-0494
Web: www.rendezvousbistro.com					
Mangy Moose 3285 McCollister Dr	Teton Village	WY	83025	307-733-4913	734-9436
Web: www.mangymoose.net					

675 RETIREMENT COMMUNITIES

SEE ALSO Long-Term Care Facilities p. 2185

Listed Here Are Senior Communities Where The Majority Of Residents Live Independently But Where Nursing Care And/Or Other Personal Care Is Available On-Site. The Listings In This Category Are Organized Alphabetically By State Names.

				Phone	Fax
Galleria Woods 3850 Galleria Woods Dr	Birmingham	AL	35244	205-985-7537	987-2146
Web: www.brookdaleliving.com					
Westminster Village 500 Spanish Fort Blvd	Spanish Fort	AL	36527	251-626-2900	626-8529
TF: 800-843-3740 ■ *Web:* www.westminstervillageal.com					
Atria Campana del Rio 1550 E River Rd	Tucson	AZ	85718	520-299-1941	529-2572
Web: www.atriaseniorliving.com					
Atria Chandler Villas 101 S Yucca St	Chandler	AZ	85224	480-899-7650	899-4485
Web: www.atriaseniorliving.com					
Beatitudes Campus of Care 1610 W Glendale Ave	Phoenix	AZ	85021	602-995-2611	995-4854
Web: www.beatitudescampus.org					
Forum at Desert Harbor 13840 N Desert Harbor Dr	Peoria	AZ	85381	623-972-0995	977-5271
Forum at Tucson 2500 N Rosemont Blvd	Tucson	AZ	85712	520-325-4800	319-4076
Friendship Village of Tempe 2645 E Southern Ave	Tempe	AZ	85282	480-831-5000	413-0285
TF: 800-824-1112 ■ *Web:* www.friendshipvillageaz.com					
Glencroft Retirement Community 8611 N 67th Ave	Glendale	AZ	85302	623-939-9475	842-9588
Web: www.glencroft.com					
La Posada at Park Centre 350 E Morningside Rd	Green Valley	AZ	85614	520-648-8131	648-8397
Web: www.laposadagv.com					
Terraces at Phoenix The 7550 N 16th St	Phoenix	AZ	85020	602-906-4024	371-9181
TF: 800-836-4281 ■ *Web:* www.theterracesphoenix.com					
Butterfield Trail Village 1923 E Joyce Blvd	Fayetteville	AR	72703	479-442-7220	442-2019
TF: 800-441-9996 ■ *Web:* www.butterfieldtrailvillage.com					
Alhambra Retirement Community 2400 S Fremont Ave	Alhambra	CA	91803	626-570-5290	570-5254
Web: www.alhretirement.org					
Atherton Baptist Homes 214 S Atlantic Blvd	Alhambra	CA	91801	626-289-4178	
Web: www.abh.org					
Bixby Knolls Towers 3737 Atlantic Ave	Long Beach	CA	90807	562-426-6123	426-2571
Web: www.bixbyknollstowers.org					
Carmel Valley Manor 8545 Carmel Valley Rd	Carmel	CA	93923	831-624-1281	622-4543
TF: 800-544-5546 ■ *Web:* www.cvmanor.com					
Casa Dorinda 300 Hot Springs Rd	Montecito	CA	93108	805-969-8011	969-8686
Web: www.casadorinda.com					
Castle Hill Retirement Village 3575 N Moorpark Rd	Thousand Oaks	CA	91360	805-492-2471	492-7431
Web: www.castlehill.com					
Channing House 850 Webster St	Palo Alto	CA	94301	650-327-0950	324-7585
Web: www.channinghouse.org					

				Phone	Fax
Covenant Village of Turlock 2125 N Olive Ave *TF:* 800-485-7844 ■ *Web:* www.covenantvillageofturlock.org	Turlock	CA	95382	209-216-5690	632-7885
Eskaton Inc 5105 Manzanita Ave *Web:* www.eskaton.org	Carmichael	CA	95608	916-334-0810	338-1248
Eskaton Village 3939 Walnut Ave *TF:* 800-300-3929 ■ *Web:* www.eskaton.org	Carmichael	CA	95608	916-974-2000	974-2022
Freedom Village 23442 El Toro Rd *TF:* 800-584-8084 ■ *Web:* www.freedomvillage.org	Lake Forest	CA	92630	949-472-4700	587-9711
Grand Lake Gardens 401 Santa Clara Ave **Fax Area Code:* 510 ■ *TF:* 800-840-1229 ■ *Web:* www.grandlakegardens.com	Oakland	CA	94610	800-416-6091	893-0114*
Hillcrest Homes 2705 Mountain View Dr *TF Mktg:* 800-566-4636 ■ *Web:* www.livingathillcrest.org	La Verne	CA	91750	909-392-4375	596-5538
Kensington Place 1580 Geary Rd	Walnut Creek	CA	94597	925-943-1906	
Lake Park Retirement Residences 1850 Alice St *Web:* www.lakeparkretirement.org	Oakland	CA	94612	510-835-5511	273-0529
Los Gatos Meadows (LGM) 110 Wood Rd *Web:* www.jtm-esc.org/lgm/index.html	Los Gatos	CA	95030	408-354-0211	354-4193
Morningside of Fullerton 800 Morningside Dr *TF:* 800-803-7597 ■ *Web:* www.morningsideoffullerton.com	Fullerton	CA	92835	714-529-2952	256-2469
Mount Miguel Covenant Village 325 Kempton St *TF:* 877-407-4790 ■ *Web:* www.mountmiguelcovenantvillage.org	Spring Valley	CA	91977	619-479-4790	479-2337
Mount San Antonio Gardens 900 E Harrison Ave	Pomona	CA	91767	909-624-5061	621-3327
O'Connor Woods 3400 Wagner Heights Rd *TF:* 800-249-6637 ■ *Web:* www.oconnorwoods.org	Stockton	CA	95209	209-956-3400	952-6201
Park Lane Classic Residence by Hyatt 200 Glenwood Cir *TF:* 800-782-5730	Monterey	CA	93940	831-373-6126	373-0863
Peninsula Regent The 1 Baldwin Ave *Web:* www.peninsularegent.com	San Mateo	CA	94401	650-579-5500	579-0446
Piedmont Gardens 110 41st St *Web:* www.piedmontgardens.com	Oakland	CA	94611	510-596-2600	
Plymouth Village 900 Salem Dr *TF:* 800-511-9304 ■ *Web:* www.plymouthvillage.org	Redlands	CA	92373	909-793-9195	798-5504
Quaker Gardens 12151 Dale St **Fax:* Mktg ■ *Web:* www.quakergardens.com	Stanton	CA	90680	714-530-9100	530-0945*
Rancho Park Villa 801 Cypress Way	San Dimas	CA	91773	626-339-5426	339-1755
Redwood Terrace *The Redwoods* 710 W 13th Ave **Fax Area Code:* 760 ■ *TF Mktg:* 800-842-6775 ■ *Web:* www.betheredwoods.org	Escondido	CA	92025	866-324-8792	480-2759*
Regents Point 19191 Harvard Ave **Fax Area Code:* 949 ■ *TF:* 800-278-8898 ■ *Web:* www.beregentspoint.org	Irvine	CA	92612	877-969-7376	725-9132*
Remington Club 16925 Hierba Dr	San Diego	CA	92128	858-673-6300	673-6318
Rosewood Retirement Community 1301 New Stine Rd *TF:* 800-984-4216 ■ *Web:* www.rosewoodretirement.org	Bakersfield	CA	93309	661-834-0620	834-0280
Saint Paul's Towers 100 Bay Pl *Web:* www.jtm-esc.org/spt	Oakland	CA	94610	510-891-8542	891-8018
Samarkand The 2550 Treasure Dr	Santa Barbara	CA	93105	805-687-0701	687-3386
San Joaquin Gardens 5555 N Fresno St	Fresno	CA	93710	559-439-4770	439-2457
Sequoias Portola Valley The *Northern California Presbyterian Homes & Services* 501 Portola Rd *Web:* www.ncphs.org	Portola Valley	CA	94028	650-851-1501	851-5007
Sequoias San Francisco 1400 Geary Blvd *Web:* www.ncphs.org	San Francisco	CA	94109	415-922-9700	567-2576
Smith Ranch Homes 400 Deer Valley Rd # L *TF:* 800-772-6264 ■ *Web:* www.smithranchhomes.com	San Rafael	CA	94903	415-491-4918	491-0254
Solheim Lutheran Home (SLH) 2236 Merton Ave *TF:* 888-257-7518 ■ *Web:* www.solheimlutheran.org	Eagle Rock	CA	90041	323-257-7518	255-3544
Spring Lake Village 5555 Montgomery Dr *TF:* 800-795-1267	Santa Rosa	CA	95409	707-538-8400	579-6997
Sunrise Villa Valencia 24552 Paseo de Valencia *Web:* www.sunriseseniorliving.com	Laguna Hills	CA	92653	949-581-6111	837-1082
Tamalpais The 501 Via Casitas *Web:* www.ncphs.org	Greenbrae	CA	94904	415-461-2300	461-0241
Terraces at Los Altos The 373 Pine Ln *TF:* 877-284-7635 ■ *Web:* www.abhow.com/multi/pilgrim_haven	Los Altos	CA	94022	650-948-8291	941-0372
Terraces of Los Gatos 800 Blossom Hill Rd *Web:* www.theterracesoflosgatos.com	Los Gatos	CA	95032	408-356-1006	356-9647
Valle Verde 900 Calle de los Amigos *TF:* 800-750-5089 ■ *Web:* www.valleverdesb.com	Santa Barbara	CA	93105	805-687-1571	687-5540
Villa Gardens 842 E Villa St *TF:* 800-958-4552 ■ *Web:* www.villagardens.org	Pasadena	CA	91101	626-463-5330	568-9606
Villa Marin 100 Thorndale Dr *Web:* www.villa-marin.com	San Rafael	CA	94903	415-492-2408	
Village The 2200 W Acacia Ave *TF:* 800-257-7888 ■ *Web:* www.thevillagehemet.com	Hemet	CA	92545	951-658-3369	658-4295
Vista del Monte 3775 Modoc Rd *TF:* 800-736-1333 ■ *Web:* www.vistadelmonte.org	Santa Barbara	CA	93105	805-687-0793	687-6350
White Sands of La Jolla 7450 Olivetas Ave *TF:* 800-892-7817	La Jolla	CA	92037	858-454-4201	450-5298
Englewood Meridian 3455 S Corona St *Web:* www.horizonbay.com	Englewood	CO	80113	303-761-0300	762-2154
Heritage Club 2020 S Monroe St *TF:* 877-756-0025 ■ *Web:* www.brookdaleliving.com/heritage-club-denver.aspx	Denver	CO	80210	303-756-0025	758-3738
Parkplace 111 Emerson St *Web:* www.brookdaleliving.com/parkplace-.aspx	Denver	CO	80218	303-744-1950	744-2118
Villa Pueblo Towers 1111 Bonforte Blvd	Pueblo	CO	81001	719-545-5911	544-1354
Villas at Sunny Acres 2501 E 104th Ave *TF:* 800-447-2092	Denver	CO	80233	303-452-4181	452-7993
Arbors of Hop Brook 403 W Ctr St *TF:* 888-227-2677 ■ *Web:* www.arborsct.com	Manchester	CT	06040	860-533-2520	647-7509
Ashlar Village 22 Masonic Ave PO Box 70 *Web:* www.masonicare.org	Wallingford	CT	06492	203-679-5900	679-6405
Covenant Village of Cromwell & Pilgrim Manor 52 Missionary Rd *Web:* www.covenantvillageofcromwell.org	Cromwell	CT	06416	860-635-2690	632-2407
Duncaster 40 Loeffler Rd *TF:* 800-545-5065 ■ *Web:* www.duncaster.org	Bloomfield	CT	06002	860-726-2000	242-8004
East Hill Woods 611 E Hill Rd **Fax:* Mktg ■ *TF:* 888-570-6659 ■ *Web:* www.watermarkcommunities.com/easthill	Southbury	CT	06488	203-262-6868	262-8002*
Elim Park Place 140 Cook Hill Rd *TF:* 800-994-1776 ■ *Web:* www.elimpark.org	Cheshire	CT	06410	203-272-3547	250-6282
Essex Meadows 30 Bokum Rd *TF:* 800-767-7201 ■ *Web:* www.essexmeadows.com	Essex	CT	06426	860-767-7201	767-0014
Evergreen Woods 88 Notch Hill Rd *TF:* 866-413-6378 ■ *Web:* www.branfordct.brightviewseniorliving.com/CommunityHome.aspx	North Branford	CT	06471	203-488-8000	488-9429
McAuley The 275 Steele Rd *Web:* www.themercycommunity.org/IndependentLiving/ContactTheMcAuley.aspx	West Hartford	CT	06117	860-236-6300	232-4077
Pomperaug Woods 80 Heritage Rd *TF:* 866-817-8935 ■ *Web:* www.pomperaugwoods.com	Southbury	CT	06488	203-262-6555	264-2155
Sterling Glen of Stamford (SG) 77 3rd St *TF:* 800-443-3245 ■ *Web:* www.sterlingglen.com	Stamford	CT	06905	203-327-4551	353-9105
Watermark at 3030 Park The 3030 Pk Ave *Web:* www.watermarkcommunities.com/3030Park	Bridgeport	CT	06604	203-502-7593	374-2871
Whitney Ctr 200 Leeder Hill Dr *TF:* 800-237-3847 ■ *Web:* www.whitneycenter.com	Hamden	CT	06517	203-848-2641	
Cokesbury Village 726 Loveville Rd	Hockessin	DE	19707	302-235-6000	239-2650
Methodist Country House 4830 Kennett Pike *Web:* www.actsretirement.org	Wilmington	DE	19807	302-654-5101	426-8108
Methodist Manor House 1001 Middleford Rd *TF:* 800-775-4593 ■ *Web:* www.actsretirement.org	Seaford	DE	19973	302-629-4593	629-6520
Stonegates 4031 Kennett Pike *Web:* www.stonegates.com	Greenville	DE	19807	302-658-6200	658-1510
Westminster Village 1175 Mckee Rd *TF:* 866-710-3101 ■ *Web:* www.presbyterianseniorliving.org	Dover	DE	19904	302-744-3600	674-8656
Ingleside Rock Creek 3050 Military Rd NW *Web:* www.ircdc.org	Washington	DC	20015	202-363-8310	363-0950
Knollwood 6200 Oregon Ave NW *TF:* 800-541-4255 ■ *Web:* www.armydistaff.org	Washington	DC	20015	202-541-0400	364-2856
Sunrise at Thomas Circle 1330 Massachusetts Ave NW *Web:* www.sunriseseniorliving.com	Washington	DC	20005	202-628-3844	628-3844
Abbey Delray 2000 Lowson Blvd *TF:* 800-936-7397 ■ *Web:* www.abbeydelray.com	Delray Beach	FL	33445	561-454-2000	278-8956
Atria Meridian Retirement Community 3061 Donnelly Dr	Lantana	FL	33462	561-965-7200	965-3542
Azalea Trace 10100 Hillview Dr *TF:* 800-828-8274 ■ *Web:* www.actsretirement.org	Pensacola	FL	32514	850-857-4950	474-0558
Bay Village 8400 Vamo Rd *Web:* www.bayvillage.org	Sarasota	FL	34231	941-966-5611	966-4040
Covenant Village of Florida 9201 W Broward Blvd *Web:* www.covenantretirement.com	Plantation	FL	33324	954-472-2860	472-5934
East Ridge Retirement Village 19301 SW 87th Ave *TF:* 800-605-7778 ■ *Web:* www.eastridgerc.com	Miami	FL	33157	305-238-2623	
Edgewater Pointe Estates 23315 Blue Water Cir *TF:* 888-339-2287 ■ *Web:* www.actsretirement.com/com-FL-ep.asp	Boca Raton	FL	33433	561-391-3114	367-8526
Fleet Landing Retirement Community 1 Fleet Landing Blvd *TF:* 800-215-1647 ■ *Web:* www.fleetlanding.com	Atlantic Beach	FL	32233	904-246-9900	246-9447
Florida Presbyterian Homes 16 Lake Hunter Dr *TF:* 866-294-3352 ■ *Web:* www.fphi.org	Lakeland	FL	33803	863-688-5521	682-4644
Freedom Village 6501 17th Ave W *TF:* 800-841-4676	Bradenton	FL	34209	941-798-8122	798-8193
Gulf Coast Village 1333 Santa Barbara Blvd **Fax:* Mktg ■ *Web:* www.gulfcoastvillage.com	Cape Coral	FL	33991	239-772-1333	772-0242*
Harbour's Edge 401 E Linton Blvd *TF:* 800-232-1358 ■ *Web:* www.harboursedge.com	Delray Beach	FL	33483	561-272-7979	243-0038
Indian River Estates 2250 Indian Creek Blvd W *TF Mktg:* 800-544-0277 ■ *Web:* www.actsretirement.com	Vero Beach	FL	32966	772-562-7400	778-7747
John Knox Village 651 SW 6th St *TF:* 800-998-5669 ■ *Web:* www.johnknoxvillage.com	Pompano Beach	FL	33060	954-783-4000	783-4044
Lake Seminole Square 8333 Seminole Blvd *TF:* 866-785-9025 ■ *Web:* www.brookdaleliving.com/lake-seminole-square.aspx	Seminole	FL	33772	727-391-0500	392-9497
Mayflower Retirement Community 1620 Mayflower Ct *TF:* 800-228-6518 ■ *Web:* www.themayflower.com	Winter Park	FL	32792	407-672-1620	671-6336
Mease Manor Retirement Living 700 Mease Plaza *Web:* www.measemanor.com	Dunedin	FL	34698	727-738-3000	
Moorings Park 120 Moorings Pk Dr *TF:* 866-802-4302 ■ *Web:* www.mooringspark.org	Naples	FL	34105	239-643-9111	262-7040
Oaks of Clearwater The 420 Bay Ave *TF:* 888-445-4862 ■ *Web:* www.theoaksofclearwater.com	Clearwater	FL	33756	727-445-4069	445-4011
Palace Renaissance & Royale 11355 SW 84th St *Web:* www.thepalace.org	Miami	FL	33173	305-270-7000	
Park Summit of Coral Springs 8500 Royal Palm Blvd	Coral Springs	FL	33065	954-752-9500	755-9559
Plymouth Harbor 700 John Ringling Blvd *Web:* www.plymouthharbor.org	Sarasota	FL	34236	941-365-2600	957-1812
Saint Andrews Estates 6152 Verde Trail N *TF Mktg:* 800-850-2287 ■ *Web:* www.actsretirement.org	Boca Raton	FL	33433	561-487-4728	883-3823
Saint Mark Village 2655 Nebraska Ave	Palm Harbor	FL	34684	727-785-2576	786-6835
Shell Point Village 15101 Shell Pt Blvd *TF Mktg:* 800-780-1131 ■ *Web:* www.shellpoint.org	Fort Myers	FL	33908	239-466-1131	454-2220
Stratford Court 45 Katherine Blvd *TF:* 800-772-2622 ■ *Web:* www.sunriseseniorliving.com	Palm Harbor	FL	34684	727-787-1500	787-1506
Village on the Green 500 Village Pl **Fax:* Mktg ■ *TF Mktg:* 800-432-8833 ■ *Web:* www.villageonthegreenrc.com	Longwood	FL	32779	407-788-2300	682-3893*
Village on the Isle 920 Tamiami Trail S	Venice	FL	34285	941-484-9753	484-0407

Name / Address	City	State	ZIP	Phone	Fax
Villages The 1000 Lake Sumter Landing TF: 800-245-1081 ■ Web: www.thevillages.com	The Villages	FL	32162	352-753-2270	
Waterford The 601 Universe Blvd TF: 866-791-7165 ■ Web: www.thewaterford.com	Juno Beach	FL	33408	561-627-3800	694-0242
Westminster Bradenton Manor 1700 21st Ave W TF: 866-846-8046	Bradenton	FL	34205	941-748-4161	748-6673
Westminster Oaks 4449 Meandering Way TF: 866-937-6257 ■ Web: www.westminsterretirement.com	Tallahassee	FL	32308	850-878-1136	942-4924
Westminster Towers 70 S Lucerne Cir W TF: 800-416-2612 ■ Web: www.westminsterretirement.com	Orlando	FL	32801	407-841-1310	849-0900
Winter Park Towers 1111 S Lakemont Ave TF: 866-647-4083 ■ Web: www.westminsterretirement.com	Winter Park	FL	32792	407-647-4083	645-4409
Clairmont Place 2100 Clairmont Lake	Decatur	GA	30033	404-633-8875	633-9417
Lenbrook 3747 Peachtree Rd NE TF: 866-629-5949 ■ Web: www.lenbrook-atlanta.com	Atlanta	GA	30319	404-264-3386	264-3380
Arcadia Retirement Residence 1434 Punahou St Web: www.arcadia-hi.org	Honolulu	HI	96822	808-941-0941	949-4965
Admiral at the Lake 1055 W Bryn Mawr Ave Suite 7 Web: www.admiralatthelake.com	Chicago	IL	60660	773-433-1800	561-2573
Church Creek 1250 W Central Rd Web: www.sunriseseniorliving.com	Arlington Heights	IL	60005	847-506-3200	506-2598
Clark-Lindsey Village 101 W Windsor Rd TF: 800-998-2581 ■ Web: www.clark-lindsey.com	Urbana	IL	61802	217-344-2144	344-9147
Covenant Retirement Communities Inc 5700 Old Orchard Rd Suite 100 TF: 800-255-8989 ■ Web: www.covenantretirement.com	Skokie	IL	60077	773-878-2294	
Fairview Village 200 Village Dr Web: www.lifeatfairview.com	Downers Grove	IL	60516	630-769-6100	769-6115
Friendship Manor 1209 21st Ave Web: www.friendshipmanor.org	Rock Island	IL	61201	309-786-9667	786-5611
Hallmark The 2960 N Lake Shore Dr NYSE: BKD ■ Web: www.brookdaleliving.com	Chicago	IL	60657	773-880-2960	880-2966
Holmstad The 700 W Fabyan Pkwy Web: www.covenantretirement.org	Batavia	IL	60510	630-879-4100	879-1153
Oak Crest DeKalb Area Retirement Ctr 2944 Greenwood Acres Dr Web: www.oakcrestdekalb.org	DeKalb	IL	60115	815-756-8461	756-6515
Providence Life Services 18601 N Creek Dr TF: 800-509-2800 ■ Web: www.providencelifeservices.com	Tinley Park	IL	60477	708-342-8100	342-8000
Senior Lifestyle Corp 111 E Wacker Dr Suite 2200 Web: www.seniorlifestyle.com	Chicago	IL	60601	312-673-4333	673-4440
Westminster Place 3200 Grant St TF: 800-896-9095 ■ Web: www.westminsterplace.org	Evanston	IL	60201	847-492-4800	492-2850
Westminster Village 2025 E Lincoln St	Bloomington	IL	61701	309-663-6474	663-1069
Concord Village 6723 S Anthony Blvd Web: www.lutheranhomefortwayne.org/concord	Fort Wayne	IN	46816	260-447-1591	447-7369
Four Seasons Retirement Ctr 1901 Taylor Rd Web: www.fourseasonsretirement.com	Columbus	IN	47203	812-372-8481	378-6184
Greencroft 1603 Eisenhower Dr N Web: www.greencroft.org	Goshen	IN	46526	574-537-4000	537-4185
Greenwood Village South 295 Village Ln Web: www.greenwoodvillagesouth.com	Greenwood	IN	46143	317-881-2591	881-1299
Hoosier Village 5300 W 96th St Web: www.hoosiervillage.com	Indianapolis	IN	46268	317-873-3349	873-8224
Marquette 8140 Township Line Rd Web: www.retirement-living.org	Indianapolis	IN	46260	317-875-9700	875-7504
Meadowood Retirement Community 2455 Tamarack Trail TF: 877-330-4370 ■ Web: www.meadowoodrc.com	Bloomington	IN	47408	812-336-7060	333-8917
Towne Centre 7250 Arthur Blvd	Merrillville	IN	46410	219-736-2900	736-2209
Towne House The 2209 St Joe Ctr Rd Web: www.townehouse.org	Fort Wayne	IN	46825	260-483-3116	969-8072
Wesley Manor 1555 N Main St Web: www.wesleymanor.org	Frankfort	IN	46041	765-659-1811	654-5596
Westminster Village 1120 E Davis Dr Web: www.westminstervillagein.com	Terre Haute	IN	47802	812-232-7533	232-3304
Friendship Village 600 Pk Ln Web: www.friendshipvillageiowa.com	Waterloo	IA	50702	319-291-8100	291-8324
Meth-Wick Community 1224 13th St NW Web: www.methwick.org	Cedar Rapids	IA	52405	319-365-9171	363-5312
Western Home Communities 420 E 11th St Web: www.westernhomecommunities.org	Cedar Falls	IA	50613	319-277-2141	268-8338
Aldersgate Village 7220 SW Asbury Dr Web: www.umhomes.org	Topeka	KS	66614	785-478-9440	478-9104
Brewster Place 1205 SW 29th St Web: www.brewsterplace.org	Topeka	KS	66611	785-267-3350	267-9355
Delmar Gardens of Lenexa Inc 9701 Monrovia St Web: www.delmargardens.com	Lenexa	KS	66215	913-492-1130	492-0586
Kansas Christian Home 1035 SE 3rd St	Newton	KS	67114	316-283-6600	283-6375
Larksfield Place 7373 E 29th St N TF: 877-636-1234 ■ Web: www.larksfieldplace.org	Wichita	KS	67226	316-858-3910	636-5790
Wesley Towers 700 Monterey Pl TF: 888-663-9175 ■ Web: www.wesleytowers.com	Hutchinson	KS	67502	620-663-9175	663-2961
Forum at Brookside 200 Brookside Dr	Louisville	KY	40243	502-245-3048	244-6327*
Treyton Oak Towers 211 W Oak St Web: www.treytonoaktowers.com	Louisville	KY	40203	502-589-3211	589-7263
Saint James Place 333 Lee Dr TF: 800-460-7007 ■ Web: www.stjamesplace.com	Baton Rouge	LA	70808	225-215-4500	215-4515
Seniorsplus 8 Falcon Rd PO Box 659 TF: 800-427-1241 ■ Web: www.seniorsplus.org	Lewiston	ME	04243	207-795-4010	795-4009
Asbury Methodist Village 201 Russell Ave TF: 800-327-2879 ■ Web: www.asburymethodistvillage.org	Gaithersburg	MD	20877	301-216-4100	
Bedford Court 3701 International Dr Web: www.sunriseseniorliving.com	Silver Spring	MD	20906	301-598-2900	598-8588
Broadmead 13801 York Rd Web: www.broadmead.org	Cockeysville	MD	21030	410-527-1900	527-0259
Carroll Lutheran Village 300 St Luke Cir TF: 877-848-0095 ■ Web: www.carrolllutheranvillage.org	Westminster	MD	21158	410-848-0090	848-8133
Charlestown Retirement Community (CCI) 715 Maiden Choice Ln TF: 800-917-8649 ■ Web: www.ericksonliving.com/ourcommunities/cci	Catonsville	MD	21228	410-242-2880	737-8854
Classic Residence by Hyatt 8100 Connecticut Ave TF: 888-595-0278 ■ Web: www.viliving.com/communities/chevychase	Chevy Chase	MD	20815	301-915-9219	
Collington Episcopal Community 10450 Lottsford Rd	Mitchellville	MD	20721	301-925-9610	925-7357
Edenwald 800 Southerly Rd Web: www.edenwald.org	Baltimore	MD	21286	410-339-6000	583-8786
Fairhaven 7200 3rd Ave TF: 800-241-9997 ■ Web: www.fairhavenccrc.org	Sykesville	MD	21784	410-795-8801	549-6788
Ginger Cove 4000 River Crescent Dr TF: 800-299-2683 ■ Web: www.gingercove.com	Annapolis	MD	21401	410-266-7300	266-6144
Glen Meadows 11630 Glen Arm Rd TF: 800-630-4689 ■ Web: www.glenmeadows.org	Glen Arm	MD	21057	410-592-5310	592-6175
Heron Point of Chestertown 501 E Campus Ave TF: 800-327-9138 ■ Web: www.actsretirement.org	Chestertown	MD	21620	410-778-7300	810-2915
Homewood at Williamsport 16505 Virginia Ave Web: www.homewood.com	Williamsport	MD	21795	301-582-1750	582-1805
Roland Park Place 830 W 40th St Web: www.rolandparkplace.org	Baltimore	MD	21211	410-243-5800	243-4929
Brookhaven at Lexington 1010 Waltham St Web: www.aboutbrookhaven.org	Lexington	MA	02421	781-863-9660	863-9944
Carleton-Willard Village (CWV) 100 Old Billerica Rd Web: www.cwvillage.org	Bedford	MA	01730	781-275-8700	275-5787
Epoch Senior Living 51 Sawyer Rd Suite 500 TF: 877-376-2475 ■ Web: www.epochsl.com	Waltham	MA	02453	781-891-0777	891-0774
Fox Hill Village 10 Longwood Dr Web: www.foxhillvillage.com	Westwood	MA	02090	781-329-4433	461-2464
Loomis Communities 246 N Main St TF: 800-865-7655 ■ Web: www.loomiscommunities.org	South Hadley	MA	01075	413-532-5325	532-8676
New Pond Village 180 Main St TF: 866-414-2520 ■ Web: www.norwoodma.brightviewseniorliving.com	Walpole	MA	02081	508-660-1555	668-8893
Willows The 1 Lyman St TF: 800-464-4730 ■ Web: www.salmonfamily.com	Westborough	MA	01581	508-366-3662	366-1930
Burcham Hills Retirement Ctr 2700 Burcham Dr	East Lansing	MI	48823	517-351-8377	351-1738
Friendship Village 1400 N Drake Rd TF: 800-613-3984 ■ Web: www.friendshipvillagemi.com	Kalamazoo	MI	49006	269-381-0560	381-5354
Glacier Hills 1200 Earhart Rd Web: www.glacierhills.org	Ann Arbor	MI	48105	734-769-6410	769-3092
Porter Hills 3600 E Fulton St Web: www.porterhills.org	Grand Rapids	MI	49546	616-949-4971	954-1795
Vista Grande Villa 2251 Springport Rd TF: 800-889-8499 ■ Web: www.vistagrandevilla.com	Jackson	MI	49202	517-787-0222	787-6909
Covenant Village of Golden Valley 5800 St Croix Ave TF: 800-296-4114 ■ Web: www.covenantvillageofgoldenvalley.org	Minneapolis	MN	55422	763-546-6125	546-8529
Friendship Village 8100 Highwood Dr Web: www.friendshipvillagemn.com	Bloomington	MN	55438	952-831-7500	830-9893
Armed Forces Retirement Home - Gulfport 1800 Beach Dr *Fax Area Code: 202 ■ TF: 800-332-3527 ■ Web: www.afrh.gov	Gulfport	MS	39507	228-604-2205	541-7519*
Trinity Place Retirement Community 300 Airline Rd Web: www.mss.org/trinityplace	Columbus	MS	39702	662-327-6716	327-3039
Friendship Village of South County 12503 Village Cir Dr Web: www.fvsunsethills.com	Saint Louis	MO	63127	314-842-6840	525-7500
John Knox Village 400 NW Murray Rd TF: 800-892-5669 ■ Web: www.johnknoxvillage.org	Lee's Summit	MO	64081	816-251-8000	246-4739
Kingswood Senior Living Community 10000 Wornall Rd *Fax: Sales ■ TF Sales: 888-942-2715 ■ Web: www.kingswoodathome.org	Kansas City	MO	64114	816-942-0994	942-2455*
Laclede Groves Retirement Community 723 S Laclede Stn Rd TF: 888-577-5484 ■ Web: www.lssliving.org/communities/laclede-groves	Saint Louis	MO	63119	314-968-5570	968-8504
Parkside Meadows Retirement Community 2150 W Randolph St Web: www.parksidemeadows.org	Saint Charles	MO	63301	636-946-4966	940-0214
Village North Retirement Community 11160 Village N Dr	Saint Louis	MO	63136	314-355-8010	653-4801
Eastmont Towers 6315 'O' St Web: www.eastmonttowers.com	Lincoln	NE	68510	402-486-2281	486-2331
Northfield Villa & Residency The Villa & Vista 2550 21st St Web: www.northfieldretirement.net	Gering	NE	69341	308-436-3101	436-3493
Skyline Retirement Community 7300 Graceland Dr # 120B	Omaha	NE	68134	402-572-5750	572-5777
Havenwood-Heritage Heights Havenwood Campus 33 Christian Ave TF: 800-457-6833 ■ Web: www.hhhinfo.com	Concord	NH	03301	603-224-5363	229-1188
Hillcrest Terrace 200 Alliance Way TF: 800-862-9490 ■ Web: www.hillcrestterrace.com	Manchester	NH	03102	603-669-1322	626-7724
Kendal at Hanover 80 Lyme Rd	Hanover	NH	03755	603-643-8900	643-7099
RiverMead Retirement Community 150 RiverMead Rd TF: 800-200-5433 ■ Web: www.rivermead.org	Peterborough	NH	03458	603-924-0062	924-6507
RiverWoods at Exeter 7 RiverWoods Dr TF: 800-688-9663 ■ Web: www.riverwoodsrc.org	Exeter	NH	03833	603-772-4700	778-9623
Applewood Estates 1 Applewood Dr TF Mktg: 800-438-0888 ■ Web: www.applewoodestates.com	Freehold	NJ	07728	732-303-7416	303-1240
Cadbury Retirement Community 2150 Rt 38 TF: 800-422-3287 ■ Web: www.cadbury.org	Cherry Hill	NJ	08002	856-667-4550	667-3653
Crestwood Manor 50 Lacey Rd TF General: 800-526-1665	Whiting	NJ	08759	732-849-4900	849-4342

				Phone	Fax
Evergreens The 309 Bridgeboro Rd *Fax: Mktg ■ TF: 800-371-4918 ■ Web: www.evergreens.org	Moorestown	NJ	08057	856-439-2000	439-2112*
Franciscan Oaks 19 Pocono Rd TF: 800-237-3330 ■ Web: www.franciscanoaks.com	Denville	NJ	07834	973-586-6000	586-6030
Harrogate 400 Locust St TF: 888-551-5531 ■ Web: www.harrogate-lifecare.org	Lakewood	NJ	08701	732-905-7070	905-2824
Medford Leas 1 Medford Leas Way TF: 800-331-4302 ■ Web: www.medfordleas.org	Medford	NJ	08055	609-654-3000	654-7894
Monroe Village 1 David Brainerd Dr TF: 866-859-2276 ■ Web: www.monroevillageonline.org	Monroe Township	NJ	08831	732-521-6400	521-6540
La Vida Llena 10501 Lagrima de Oro NE TF: 800-922-1344 ■ Web: www.lavidallena.com	Albuquerque	NM	87111	505-293-4001	291-3199
Montebello The 10500 Academy Rd NE	Albuquerque	NM	87111	505-294-9944	294-1808
Andrus on Hudson 185 Old Broadway	Hastings-on-Hudson	NY	10706	914-478-3700	478-3541
Fountains at Millbrook The 79 Flint Rd TF: 800-433-6092 ■ Web: www.watermarkcommunities.com/millbrook	Millbrook	NY	12545	845-677-8550	677-8630
Kendal at Ithaca 2230 N Triphammer Rd TF: 800-253-6325 ■ Web: www.kai.kendal.org	Ithaca	NY	14850	607-266-5300	266-5320
Arbor Acres 1240 Arbor Rd Web: www.arboracres.org	Winston-Salem	NC	27104	336-724-7921	721-0271
Bermuda Village 142 Bermuda Village Dr *Fax: Mktg ■ TF Mktg: 800-843-5433 ■ Web: www.bermudavillage.net	Advance	NC	27006	336-998-6535	940-2140*
Carol Woods Retirement Community 750 Weaver Dairy Rd TF: 800-518-9333 ■ Web: www.carolwoods.org	Chapel Hill	NC	27514	919-968-4511	918-3349
Carolina Meadows 100 Carolina Meadows TF: 800-458-6756 ■ Web: www.carolinameadows.org	Chapel Hill	NC	27517	919-942-4014	929-7808
Carolina Village 600 Carolina Village Rd Web: www.carolinavillage.com	Hendersonville	NC	28792	828-692-6275	692-7876
Covenant Village 1351 Robinwood Rd	Gastonia	NC	28054	704-867-2319	861-8893
Deerfield Episcopal Retirement Community 1617 Hendersonville Rd TF: 800-284-1531 ■ Web: www.deerfieldwnc.org	Asheville	NC	28803	828-274-1531	274-0238
Forest at Duke 2701 Pickett Rd Web: www.forestduke.com	Durham	NC	27705	919-490-8000	490-0887
Pines at Davidson 400 Avinger Ln Web: www.thepinesatdavidson.org	Davidson	NC	28036	704-896-1100	896-1119
Presbyterian Home of High Point 201 Greensboro Rd	High Point	NC	27260	336-883-9111	885-7215
Sharon Towers 5100 Sharon Rd Web: www.sharontowers.org	Charlotte	NC	28210	704-553-1670	553-1877
Springmoor Life Care Retirement Community 1500 Sawmill Rd Web: www.springmoor.com	Raleigh	NC	27615	919-848-7000	848-7392
Breckenridge Village 36851 Ridge Rd Web: www.oprs.org	Willoughby	OH	44094	440-942-4342	942-4150
First Community Village 1800 Riverside Dr TF: 888-328-9511 ■ Web: www.firstcommunityvillage.org	Columbus	OH	43212	614-324-4455	
Friendship Village 5800 Forest Hills Blvd Web: www.friendshipvillageoh.com	Columbus	OH	43231	614-890-8282	890-2661
Hilltop Village 25900 Euclid Ave Web: www.hilltopvillage.com	Euclid	OH	44132	216-261-8383	261-6816
Kendal at Oberlin 600 Kendal Dr TF Mktg: 800-548-9469 ■ Web: www.kao.kendal.org	Oberlin	OH	44074	440-775-0094	775-9880
Laurel Lake Retirement Community 200 Laurel Lake Dr *Fax Area Code: 330 ■ TF: 866-650-2100 ■ Web: www.laurellake.com	Hudson	OH	44236	866-650-2100	650-0576*
Llanfair Retirement Community 1701 Llanfair Ave Web: www.oprs.org/llanfair	Cincinnati	OH	45224	513-681-4230	681-0417
Maple Knoll Communities Inc 11100 Springfield Pike TF: 800-789-6008 ■ Web: www.mapleknoll.org	Cincinnati	OH	45246	513-782-2400	782-4324
Methodist ElderCare Services 5155 N High St Web: www.wesleyridge.com/wesleyglen_home.aspx	Columbus	OH	43214	614-396-4990	436-6012
Otterbein Retirement Living Communities 580 N SR 741 TF: 888-513-9131 ■ Web: www.otterbein.org	Lebanon	OH	45036	513-933-5400	932-1054
Renaissance The 26376 John Rd	Olmsted Township	OH	44138	440-235-7100	235-7115
Rockynol Retirement Community 1150 W Market St Web: www.oprs.org	Akron	OH	44313	330-867-2150	867-1642
Twin Towers 5343 Hamilton Ave	Cincinnati	OH	45224	513-853-2000	853-2703
Westlake Village 28550 Westlake Village Dr	Westlake	OH	44145	440-892-4200	892-4756
Westminster-Thurber Community 717 Neil Ave Web: www.westminsterthurber.org	Columbus	OH	43215	614-228-8888	228-8898
Epworth Villa 14901 N Pennsylvania Ave TF: 800-579-8776 ■ Web: www.epworthvilla.com	Oklahoma City	OK	73134	405-752-1200	755-4813
Golden Oaks Village 5801 N Oakwood Rd TF: 800-259-0914 ■ Web: www.goldenoaks.com	Enid	OK	73703	580-249-2600	
Spanish Cove 11 Palm Ave TF: 800-965-2683 ■ Web: www.spanishcove.com	Yukon	OK	73099	405-354-1901	354-4429
Capital Manor 1955 Dallas Hwy NW TF: 800-637-0327 ■ Web: www.capitalmanor.com	Salem	OR	97304	503-362-4101	371-9021
Friendsview Manor 1301 E Fulton St	Newberg	OR	97132	503-538-3144	538-6371
Mennonite Village 5353 Columbus St SE Web: www.mennonitevillage.org	Albany	OR	97322	541-928-7232	917-1399
Rogue Valley Manor 1200 Mira Mar Ave TF: 800-848-7868 ■ Web: www.retirement.org/rvm	Medford	OR	97504	541-857-7214	857-7599
Terwilliger Plaza 2545 SW Terwilliger Blvd TF: 800-875-4211 ■ Web: www.terwilligerplaza.com	Portland	OR	97201	503-226-4911	299-4231
Willamette View 12705 SE River Rd TF: 800-446-0670 ■ Web: www.willametteview.org	Milwaukie	OR	97222	503-654-6581	652-6260
Beaumont at Bryn Mawr 601 N Ithan Ave Web: www.beaumontretirement.com	Bryn Mawr	PA	19010	610-526-7000	525-0293
Bethany Village 325 Wesley Dr Web: www.bethanyvillage.org	Mechanicsburg	PA	17055	717-766-0279	766-0870
Brittany Pointe Estates 1001 Valley Forge Rd TF: 800-504-2287 ■ Web: www.actsretirement.org	Lansdale	PA	19446	215-855-3826	855-6137
Cross Keys Village 2990 Carlisle Pike PO Box 128 TF Mktg: 888-624-8242 ■ Web: www.crosskeysvillage.org	New Oxford	PA	17350	717-624-5350	624-5252
Foulkeways at Gwynedd 1120 Meetinghouse Rd Web: www.foulkeways.org	Gwynedd	PA	19436	215-643-2200	646-2917
Foxdale Village 500 E Marylyn Ave TF: 800-253-4951 ■ Web: www.foxdalevillage.org	State College	PA	16801	814-272-2117	238-2920
Friendship Village of South Hills 1290 Boyce Rd Web: www.friendshipvillagepa.com	Upper Saint Clair	PA	15241	724-941-3100	941-6331
Granite Farms Estates 1343 W Baltimore Pike TF: 888-499-2287 ■ Web: www.actsretirement.com/com-PA-gf.asp	Media	PA	19063	610-361-8221	558-9660
Kendal at Longwood & Crosslands PO Box 100 TF: 800-216-1920	Kennett Square	PA	19348	610-388-1441	388-5503
LAS Passavant Retirement Community 401 S Main St TF: 888-498-7753 ■ Web: www.lutheranseniorlife.org	Zelienople	PA	16063	724-452-5400	452-3684
Lebanon Valley Brethren Home 1200 Grubb Rd Web: www.lvbh.org	Palmyra	PA	17078	717-838-5406	838-3826
Lima Estates 411 N Middletown Rd	Lima	PA	19037	610-565-7020	565-7425
Lutheran Community at Telford 235 N Washington St Web: www.lctelford.org	Telford	PA	18969	215-723-9819	723-3623
Martins Run 11 Martins Run TF: 800-327-3875 ■ Web: www.martinsrun.org	Media	PA	19063	610-353-7660	353-4928
Meadowood 3205 Skippack Pike PO Box 670 Web: www.meadowood.net	Worcester	PA	19490	610-584-1000	584-3645
Menno Village 2075 Scotland Ave Web: www.mennohaven.org	Chambersburg	PA	17201	717-262-2373	263-6988
Messiah Village 100 Mt Allen Dr Web: www.messiahvillage.com	Mechanicsburg	PA	17055	717-697-4666	790-8200
Moravian Hall Square 175 W N St Web: www.moravian.com	Nazareth	PA	18064	610-746-1000	746-1023
Normandy Farms Estates 9000 Twin Silo Dr TF: 800-756-2287 ■ Web: www.actsretirement.com	Blue Bell	PA	19422	215-699-8721	699-2422
Philadelphia Protestant Home 6500 Tabor Rd Web: www.pphfamily.org	Philadelphia	PA	19111	215-697-8000	697-8137
Pine Run Community 777 Ferry Rd TF: 888-992-8992 ■ Web: www.pinerun.org	Doylestown	PA	18901	215-345-9000	340-5225
Quadrangle The 3300 Darby Rd Web: www.sunriseseniorliving.com	Haverford	PA	19041	610-642-3000	642-5743
Riddle Village 1048 W Baltimore Pike Web: www.riddlevillage.com	Media	PA	19063	610-891-3700	891-3671
Rydal Park 1515 The Fairway Web: www.rydalpark.org	Rydal	PA	19046	215-885-6800	885-4560
Sherwood Oaks 100 Norman Dr TF: 800-642-2217 ■ Web: www.sherwood-oaks.com	Cranberry Township	PA	16066	724-776-8100	776-8468
Simpson House 2101 Belmont Ave Web: www.simpsonhouse.org	Philadelphia	PA	19131	215-878-3600	878-6701
Spring House Estates 728 Norristown Rd TF: 888-365-2287 ■ Web: www.actsretirement.com/com-PA-sh.asp	Lower Gwynedd	PA	19002	215-628-8110	628-9701
Watermark at Logan Square 2 Franklin Town Blvd Web: www.watermarkcommunities.com/LoganSquare	Philadelphia	PA	19103	215-240-8915	
Waverly Heights 1400 Waverly Rd Web: www.waverlyheightsltd.org	Gladwyne	PA	19035	610-645-8600	645-8611
Westminster Village 803 N Wahneta St TF: 888-563-8147 ■ Web: www.wmvallentown.org	Allentown	PA	18109	610-782-8300	782-8398
White Horse Village 535 Gradyville Rd Web: www.whitehorsevillage.org	Newtown Square	PA	19073	610-558-5000	558-5001
Willow Valley Lakes Manor 300 Willow Valley Lakes Dr TF: 800-770-5445 ■ Web: www.willowvalleyretirement.com	Willow Street	PA	17584	717-464-0800	464-2560
Bethea Baptist Retirement Community 157 Home Ave	Darlington	SC	29532	843-393-2867	393-2458
Presbyterian Communities -The Village at Summerville 201 W 9th N St Unit #140 TF: 866-315-4725 ■ Web: www.preshomesc.org	Summerville	SC	29483	843-873-2550	851-2033
Westminster Towers 1330 India Hook Rd TF: 800-345-6026 ■ Web: www.westminstertowers.org	Rock Hill	SC	29732	803-328-5000	328-5140
White Oak Manor Inc 130 E Main St PO Box 3347 Web: www.whiteoakmanor.com	Spartanburg	SC	29304	864-582-7503	573-9107
Alexian Village 100 James Blvd TF: 800-251-4600	Signal Mountain	TN	37377	423-886-0100	886-0470
Brookdale Senior Living Inc 111 Westwood Pl Suite 200 TF: 866-785-9025 ■ Web: www.brookdaleliving.com	Brentwood	TN	37027	615-221-2250	221-2288
Army Residence Community 7400 Crestway Dr TF: 800-725-0083 ■ Web: www.armyresidence.com	San Antonio	TX	78239	210-646-5316	646-5313
Bayou Manor 4141 S Braeswood Blvd	Houston	TX	77025	713-666-2651	660-4800
Capital Senior Living Corp 14160 Dallas Pkwy Suite 300 NYSE: CSU ■ Web: www.capitalsenior.com	Dallas	TX	75254	972-770-5600	770-5666
Denton Good Samaritan Village 2500 Hinkle Dr	Denton	TX	76201	940-383-2651	382-9306
Forum at Lincoln Heights 311 W Nottingham Pl	San Antonio	TX	78209	210-824-2314	824-6556
Forum at Park Lane 7831 Pk Ln	Dallas	TX	75225	214-369-9902	373-1836
Grace Presbyterian Village 550 E Ann Arbor Ave Web: www.gracepresbyterianvillage.org	Dallas	TX	75216	214-376-1701	376-4350
John Knox Village of the Rio Grande Valley 1300 S Border Ave Web: www.johnknoxvillagergv.com	Weslaco	TX	78596	956-968-4575	968-4570
Manor Park Inc 2208 N Loop 250 W TF: 800-523-9898	Midland	TX	79707	432-689-9898	694-2551
Rolling Meadows 3006 McNiel Ave Web: www.rmeadows.com	Wichita Falls	TX	76309	940-691-7511	696-5154
Temple Meridian 4312 S 31st St Web: www.horizonbay.com	Temple	TX	76502	254-771-1226	774-7472
Westminster Manor 4100 Jackson Ave Web: www.westminstermanor.org	Austin	TX	78731	512-454-4643	371-7308

				Phone	Fax
Wake Robin 200 Wake Robin Dr	Shelburne	VT	05482	802-264-5103	985-8452
Web: www.wakerobin.com					
Brandermill Woods 14311 Brandermill Woods Trail	Midlothian	VA	23112	804-744-0141	744-4894
TF: 800-552-6579					
Colonnades The 2600 Barracks Rd	Charlottesville	VA	22901	434-963-4198	963-4108
Web: www.sunriseseniorliving.com					
Culpeper Baptist Retirement Community 12425 Village Loop	Culpeper	VA	22701	540-825-2411	825-5123
TF: 800-894-2411 ■ *Web:* www.vbh.org/culpeper					
Fairfax The 9140 Belvoir Woods Pkwy	Fort Belvoir	VA	22060	703-799-1200	781-2448
Goodwin House 4800 Fillmore Ave	Alexandria	VA	22311	703-578-1000	824-1379
Web: www.goodwinhouse.org					
Goodwin House Bailey's Crossroads 3440 S Jefferson St	Falls Church	VA	22041	703-820-1488	578-7519
Web: www.goodwinhouse.org					
Hermitage The 1600 Westwood Ave	Richmond	VA	23227	804-355-5721	358-0854
Jefferson The 900 N Taylor St	Arlington	VA	22203	703-516-9455	516-9459
Web: www.sunriseseniorliving.com					
Lakewood Manor 1900 Lauderdale Dr	Richmond	VA	23238	804-740-2900	740-3774
TF: 866-521-9100 ■ *Web:* www.lakewoodmanor.org					
Shenandoah Valley Westminster-Canterbury 300 Westminster-Canterbury Dr	Winchester	VA	22603	540-665-5914	665-9781
TF: 800-492-9463 ■ *Web:* www.svwc.org					
Virginian The 9229 Arlington Blvd	Fairfax	VA	22031	703-385-0555	383-1826
Web: www.thevirginian.org					
Washington House 5100 Fillmore Ave	Alexandria	VA	22311	703-379-9000	845-5140
Westminster-Canterbury of Lynchburg 501 VES Rd	Lynchburg	VA	24503	434-386-3500	386-3535
TF: 800-962-3520 ■ *Web:* www.wclynchburg.org					
Westminster-Canterbury on Chesapeake Bay 3100 Shore Dr	Virginia Beach	VA	23451	757-496-1100	496-1122
TF: 800-349-1722 ■ *Web:* www.wcbay.com					
Westminster-Canterbury Richmond 1600 Westbrook Ave	Richmond	VA	23227	804-264-6000	264-4579
TF: 800-445-9904 ■ *Web:* www.wcrichmond.org					
Williamsburg Landing 5700 Williamsburg Landing Dr	Williamsburg	VA	23185	757-565-6505	565-6537
TF: 800-554-5517 ■ *Web:* www.williamsburglanding.com					
Bayview Retirement Community 11 W Aloha St	Seattle	WA	98119	206-284-7330	284-9640
Web: www.bayviewcommunity.org					
Hearthstone The 6720 E Green Lake Way N	Seattle	WA	98103	206-525-9666	522-0190
Horizon House 900 University St	Seattle	WA	98101	206-624-3700	382-3728
Web: www.horizonhouse.org					
Judson Park 23600 Marine View Dr S	Des Moines	WA	98198	206-824-4000	878-6404
TF: 800-401-4113 ■ *Web:* www.judsonpark.com					
Panorama City 1751 Cir Ln SE	Lacey	WA	98503	360-456-0111	438-5901
TF: 800-999-9807 ■ *Web:* www.panoramacity.org					
Park Shore 1630 43rd Ave E	Seattle	WA	98112	206-329-0770	329-0227
Web: www.parkshore.org					
Rockwood Retirement Community 2903 E 25th Ave	Spokane	WA	99223	509-536-6650	536-6662
TF: 800-727-6650 ■ *Web:* www.rockwoodretirement.org					
Wesley Homes 815 S 216th St	Des Moines	WA	98198	206-824-5000	870-1209
TF: 866-937-5390 ■ *Web:* www.wesleyhomes.org					
Cedar Ridge Retirement Campus 113 Cedar Ridge Dr	West Bend	WI	53095	414-276-4370	
Fairhaven 435 W Starin Rd	Whitewater	WI	53190	262-473-2140	473-5468
TF: 877-624-2298 ■ *Web:* www.fairhaven.org					
Milwaukee Catholic Home 2330 & 2462 N Prospect Ave	Milwaukee	WI	53211	414-224-9700	224-1666
Web: www.milwaukeecatholichome.org					
Oakwood Village West 6165 Mineral Pt Rd	Madison	WI	53705	608-230-4000	230-3286
Web: www.oakwoodvillage.net					
Saint John's On the Lake 1840 N Prospect Ave	Milwaukee	WI	53202	414-831-7300	831-6760
Web: www.saintjohnsmilw.org					
Village at Manor Park The (VMP) 3023 S 84th St	Milwaukee	WI	53227	414-607-4100	607-4504
Web: www.vmpcares.com					

676 RETREATS - SPIRITUAL

The Facilities Listed Here Offer Basic Amenities And Services Such As Bed Linens, Food Preparation, Maid Service, Etc. Although Physical Activity May Play A Role In The Programs Offered, The Focus Is On The Spiritual.

				Phone	Fax
Ashram The PO Box 8009	Calabasas	CA	91372	818-222-6900	222-7393
Web: www.theashram.com					
Benedict Inn Retreat & Conference Ctr 1402 Southern Ave	Beech Grove	IN	46107	317-788-7581	782-3142
Web: www.benedictinn.org					
Bethany Retreat House 2202 Lituanica Ave	East Chicago	IN	46312	219-398-5047	398-9329
Web: www.bethanyretreathouse.org					
Bishop's Ranch 5297 Westside Rd	Healdsburg	CA	95448	707-433-2440	433-3431
Web: www.bishopsranch.org					
Bon Secours Spiritual Ctr 1525 Marriottsville Rd	Marriottsville	MD	21104	410-442-1320	442-8219
Web: www.bonsecours.org					
Bridge-Between Retreat Ctr 4471 Flaherty Ln	Denmark	WI	54208	920-864-7230	864-7044
Web: www.bridge-between.org					
Campion Renewal Ctr 319 Concord Rd	Weston	MA	02493	781-419-1337	894-5864
Web: www.campioncenter.org					
Cenacle Retreat House & Spirituality Ctr 29 W 012 Batavia Rd	Warrenville	IL	60555	630-393-1231	393-2646
TF: 800-240-6702 ■ *Web:* www.cenacle.org					
Chopra Center at La Costa Resort & Spa 2013 Costa del Mar Rd	Carlsbad	CA	92009	760-494-1600	494-1608
TF: 888-424-6772 ■ *Web:* www.chopra.com					
Christ the King Retreat Ctr 621 1st Ave S	Buffalo	MN	55313	763-682-1394	682-3453
Web: www.kingshouse.com					
Conception Abbey PO Box 501	Conception	MO	64433	660-944-2821	944-2811
Web: www.conceptionabbey.org					
Elat Chayyim 116 Johnson Rd	Falls Village	CT	06031	860-824-5991	824-7228
TF: 800-398-2630 ■ *Web:* www.elatchayyim.org					
Esalen Institute 55000 Hwy 1	Big Sur	CA	93920	831-667-3000	667-2724
Web: www.esalen.org					
Expanding Light 14618 Tyler Foote Rd	Nevada City	CA	95959	530-478-7518	478-7519
TF: 800-346-5350 ■ *Web:* www.expandinglight.org					
Franciscan Spirituality Ctr 920 Market St	La Crosse	WI	54601	608-791-5295	
Web: www.franciscanspiritualitycenter.org					
Genesis Spiritual Life Ctr 53 Mill St	Westfield	MA	01085	413-562-3627	572-1060
Web: www.westfield-ma.com					
Harbin Hot Springs 18424 Harbin Springs Rd PO Box 782	Middletown	CA	95461	707-987-2477	987-0616
Web: www.harbin.org					
Hollyhock PO Box 127	Mansons Landing	BC	V0P1K0	250-935-6576	935-6424
TF: 800-933-6339 ■ *Web:* www.hollyhock.bc.ca					
Holy Cross Abbey 901 Cool Spring Ln	Berryville	VA	22611	540-955-4383	955-1356
Web: www.hcava.org					
Holy Cross Monastery 1615 Rt 9W	West Park	NY	12493	845-384-6660	384-6031
Web: www.holycrossmonastery.com					
Jesuit Center for Spiritual Growth 501 N Church Rd	Wernersville	PA	19565	610-670-3642	670-3650
Web: www.jesuitspiritualcenter.org					
Jesuit Retreat House 300 Manresa Way	Los Altos	CA	94022	650-948-4491	948-0640
Web: www.elretiro.org					
Kalani Oceanside Retreat 12-6860 Kapoho Kalapana Rd	Pahoa	HI	96778	808-965-7828	965-0527
TF: 800-800-6886 ■ *Web:* www.kalani.com					
Kirkridge Retreat & Study Ctr 2495 Fox Gap Rd	Bangor	PA	18013	610-588-1793	588-8510
Web: www.kirkridge.org					
Kordes Retreat Ctr 841 E 14th St	Ferdinand	IN	47532	812-367-2777	367-2313
TF: 800-880-2777 ■ *Web:* www.thedome.org					
La Salette Retreat Ctr 947 Pk St	Attleboro	MA	02703	508-222-8530	236-9089
Web: www.lasalette-shrine.org					
Laity Lodge 719 Earl Garrett St PO Box 290670	Kerrville	TX	78029	830-792-1230	792-1237
Web: www.hebuttfoundation.org					
Laurelville Mennonite Church Ctr 941 Laurelville Ln	Mount Pleasant	PA	15666	724-423-2056	423-2096
TF: 800-839-1021 ■ *Web:* www.laurelville.org					
Linwood Spiritual Ctr 50 Linwood Rd	Rhinebeck	NY	12572	845-876-4178	876-1920
Web: www.linwoodspiritualctr.org					
Living Water Worship & Teaching Ctr 595 N Aspaas St	Cornville	AZ	86325	928-634-4421	634-0005
TF Mktg: 888-627-5631 ■ *Web:* www.livingwaterretreatcenter.com					
Louhelen Baha'i School 3208 S State Rd	Davison	MI	48423	810-653-5033	653-7181
TF: 800-894-9716 ■ *Web:* www.louhelen.org					
Loyola House 5420 Hwy 6 N	Guelph	ON	N1H6J2	519-824-1250	767-0994
Web: www.loyolahouse.ca					
Loyola Retreat House 161 James St	Morristown	NJ	07960	973-539-0740	898-9839
Web: www.loyola.org					
Loyola Retreat House 9270 Loyola Retreat Rd PO Box 9	Faulkner	MD	20632	301-392-0801	392-0808
Web: www.loyolaretreat.org					
Manna House of Prayer 323 E 5th St	Concordia	KS	66901	785-243-4428	243-4321
Web: www.mannahouse.org					
Marguerite Centre 700 Mackay St	Pembroke	ON	K8A1G6	613-732-9925	735-2048
Web: www.margueritecentre.com					
Marie Joseph Spiritual Center 10 Evans Rd	Biddeford	ME	04005	207-284-5671	286-1371
Web: www.mariejosephspiritual.org					
Marycrest Retreat & Conference Ctr 2851 W 52nd Ave	Denver	CO	80221	303-458-6270	433-5865
Web: www.marycrest.org					
Marywood Franciscan Spirituality Center 3560 Hwy 51 N	Arbor Vitae	WI	54568	715-385-3750	385-9118
Web: www.fspa.org/sponsoredministries/spiritualitycenters/marywood.html					
Mercy Center at Madison 167 Neck Rd PO Box 191	Madison	CT	06443	203-245-0401	245-8718
Web: www.mercyctrmadison.com					
Mercy Center for Healing the Whole Person 520 W Buena Ventura	Colorado Springs	CO	80907	719-633-2302	633-1031
Web: www.mercycenter.com					
Mercy Ctr 2300 Adeline Dr	Burlingame	CA	94010	650-340-7474	340-1299
Web: www.mercy-center.org					
Milford Spiritual Ctr 5361 S Milford Rd	Milford	OH	45150	513-248-3500	248-3503
Web: www.milfordspiritualcenter.org					
Monastery of Saint Gertrude 465 Keuterville Rd	Cottonwood	ID	83522	208-962-3224	962-7212
Web: www.rc.net					
Montserrat Jesuit Retreat House 600 N Shady Shores Dr PO Box 1390	Lake Dallas	TX	75065	940-321-6020	321-6040
Web: www.montserratretreat.org					
Mount Calvary Retreat House PO Box 1296	Santa Barbara	CA	93102	805-962-9855	962-4957
Web: www.mount-calvary.org					
Mount Carmel Ctr 4600 W Davis St	Dallas	TX	75211	214-331-6224	330-0844
Web: www.professionalwebs.com					
Mount Manresa Jesuit Retreat House 239 Fingerboard Rd	Staten Island	NY	10305	718-727-3844	727-4881
Web: www.manresasi.org					
Mount Saint Redemptorist Pastoral Ctr 1001 Broadway Rt 9W PO Box 219	Esopus	NY	12429	845-384-8000	384-8088
Web: www.mountsaintalphonsus.org					
Omega Institute for Holistic Studies 150 Lake Dr	Rhinebeck	NY	12572	845-266-4444	266-3769
TF: 800-944-1001 ■ *Web:* www.eomega.org					
Omega Retreat & Spirituality Ctr 216 W Highland	Boerne	TX	78006	830-816-8471	249-3327
Web: www.boernebenedictines.com					

Name / Address	City	State	Zip	Phone	Fax
Our Lady of Fatima Retreat House 5353 E 56th St *Web:* www.archindy.org	Indianapolis	IN	46226	317-545-7681	545-0095
Pecos Benedictine Monastery 143 Cowles Hwy *Web:* www.pecosabbey.org	Pecos	NM	87552	505-757-6415	757-2285
Pendle Hill 338 Plush Mill Rd *TF:* 800-742-3150 ■ *Web:* www.pendlehill.org	Wallingford	PA	19086	610-566-4507	566-3679
Priory Spirituality Ctr 500 College St NE *Web:* www.stplacid.org	Lacey	WA	98516	360-438-2595	438-9236
Pumpkin Hollow Farm 1184 Rt 11 *TF:* 877-325-3583 ■ *Web:* www.pumpkinhollow.org	Craryville	NY	12521	518-325-3583	325-5633
Quaker Hill Conference Ctr 10 Quaker Hill Dr *Web:* www.qhcc.org	Richmond	IN	47374	765-962-5741	
Redemptorist Retreat Ctr 1800 N Timber Trail Ln *Web:* www.redemptoristretreat.org	Oconomowoc	WI	53066	262-567-6900	567-0134
Rowe Camp & Conference Ctr 22 Kings Hwy Rd PO Box 273 *Web:* www.rowecenter.org	Rowe	MA	01367	413-339-4954	339-5728
Saint Andrew's Abbey 31001 N Valyermo Rd PO Box 40 *Web:* www.valyermo.com	Valyermo	CA	93563	661-944-2178	944-1076
Saint Anthony Retreat Ctr 300 E 4th St *Web:* www.sarcenter.com	Marathon	WI	54448	715-443-2236	443-2235
Saint Anthony Retreat Ctr 43816 Sierra Dr PO Box 249 *Web:* www.stanthonyretreat.org	Three Rivers	CA	93271	559-561-4595	561-4493
Saint Benedict's Retreat & Conference Centre 225 Masters Ave *Web:* www.mts.net	Winnipeg	MB	R4A2A1	204-339-1705	334-8840
Saint Columban Ctr 6892 Lake Shore Rd PO Box 816 *Web:* www.stcolumbancenter.org	Derby	NY	14047	716-947-4708	947-5759
Saint Edmund's Retreat PO Box 399 *Web:* www.endersisland.com	Mystic	CT	06355	860-536-0565	572-7655
Saint Francis Retreat Ctr 549 Mission Vineyard Rd *Web:* www.stfrancisretreat.com	San Juan Bautista	CA	95045	831-623-4234	623-9046
Saint Meinrad Archabbey 200 Hill Dr *Web:* www.saintmeinrad.edu	Saint Meinrad	IN	47577	812-357-6585	357-6325
San Damiano Retreat Ctr 710 Highland Dr PO Box 767 *Web:* www.sandamiano.org	Danville	CA	94526	925-837-9141	837-0522
Satchidananda Ashram Yogaville 180 Yogaville Way **Fax Area Code:* 804 ■ *Web:* yogaville.org	Buckingham	VA	23921	434-969-3121	969-1303*
Serra Retreat Ctr 3401 Serra Rd *Web:* www.serraretreat.com	Malibu	CA	90265	310-456-6631	456-9417
Shalom Prayer Ctr 840 S Main St *Web:* www.open.org	Mount Angel	OR	97362	503-845-6773	845-6585
Shambhala Mountain Ctr 4921 County Rd 68C *TF:* 888-788-7221 ■ *Web:* www.shambhalamountain.org	Red Feather Lakes	CO	80545	970-881-2184	881-2909
Siena Ctr 5635 Erie St	Racine	WI	53402	262-639-4100	639-9702
Song of the Morning Yoga Retreat Center 9607 Sturgeon Valley Rd *Web:* www.songofthemorning.org	Vanderbilt	MI	49795	989-983-4107	
Sophia Spirituality Ctr 751 S 8th St *Web:* www.mountosb.org	Atchison	KS	66002	913-360-6173	
Spiritual Life Center 7100 E 45th St N *Web:* www.slcwichita.org	Wichita	KS	67226	316-744-0167	744-8072
Spiritual Renewal Center Inc 6400 Coors Rd NW	Albuquerque	NM	87120	505-877-4211	890-4110
Still Life Retreat 394591 Concession 2 RR1 *TF:* 877-584-8880 ■ *Web:* www.spiritual-love-inn.com	Durham	ON	N0G1R0	519-369-3663	369-6676
Tabor Retreat Ctr 60 Anchor Ave *Web:* www.taborretreatcenter.org	Oceanside	NY	11572	516-536-3004	536-0214
Vivekananda Retreat Ridgely PO Box 321 *Web:* www.ridgely.org	Stone Ridge	NY	12484	845-687-4574	687-4578
Wainwright House 260 Stuyvesant Ave *Web:* www.wainwright.org	Rye	NY	10580	914-967-6080	967-6114
Weber Ctr 1257 E Siena Heights Dr *Web:* www.adriansisters.org/weber	Adrian	MI	49221	517-266-4000	266-4004
Wisdom House Retreat & Conference Ctr 229 E Litchfield Rd *Web:* www.wisdomhouse.org	Litchfield	CT	06759	860-567-3163	567-3166
WomanWell 1784 La Crosse Ave *Web:* www.womanwell.org	Saint Paul	MN	55119	651-739-7953	739-7475

677 ROLLING MILL MACHINERY

SEE ALSO Metalworking Machinery p. 2245

Name / Address	City	State	Zip	Phone	Fax
Abbey International Ltd 11140 Ave Rd *Web:* www.abbeyintl.com	Perrysburg	OH	43552	419-874-4301	874-8200
Ampco-Pittsburgh Corp 600 Grant St Suite 4600 *NYSE:* AP ■ *Web:* www.ampcopittsburgh.com	Pittsburgh	PA	15219	412-456-4400	456-4404
Bonell Mfg Co 13521 S Halsted St *TF:* 800-323-3110	Riverdale	IL	60827	708-849-1770	849-3434
Bradbury Co Inc 1200 E Cole *TF:* 800-397-6394 ■ *Web:* www.bradburygroup.net	Moundridge	KS	67107	620-345-6394	345-6381
Engel Industries Inc 5480 6 St SW **Fax Area Code:* 319 ■ *Web:* www.engelind.com	Saint Louis	MO	52404	314-638-0100	364-3436*
Fairfield Machine Co Inc 1143 Lower Elkton Rd PO Box 27 *Web:* www.fairfieldmachine.com	Columbiana	OH	44408	330-482-3387	482-5052
Formtek Metal Forming Inc 4899 Commerce Pkwy *TF:* 800-631-0520 ■ *Web:* www.formtekinc.com	Cleveland	OH	44128	216-292-4460	831-7948
Hegenscheidt-MFD Corp 6255 Ctr Dr *Web:* www.hegenscheidtmfd.com	Sterling Heights	MI	48312	586-274-4900	274-4916
Magnum Integrated Technologies Inc 200 1st Gulf Blvd *TF:* 800-830-0642 ■ *Web:* www.mit-world.com	Brampton	ON	L6W4T5	905-595-1998	455-0422
T Sendzimir Inc 269 Brookside Rd *Web:* www.sendzimir.com	Waterbury	CT	06708	203-756-4617	756-4610
WHEMCO Inc 5 Hot Metal St *TF:* 800-800-7686 ■ *Web:* www.whemco.com	Pittsburgh	PA	15203	412-390-2700	390-2737

678 ROYALTY TRUSTS

Name / Address	City	State	Zip	Phone	Fax
ARC Resources Ltd 308 4th Ave SW Suite 1200 *TSE:* ARX ■ *TF:* 888-272-4900 ■ *Web:* www.arcresources.com	Calgary	AB	T2P0H7	403-503-8600	
Cross Timbers Royalty Trust 901 Main St 17th Fl PO Box 830650 *NYSE:* CRT ■ *TF:* 877-228-5084 ■ *Web:* www.crosstimberstrust.com	Dallas	TX	75283	214-209-2400	209-2431
Dominion Resources Black Warrior Trust 901 Main St Bank of America Plaza 17th Fl *NYSE:* DOM ■ *TF General:* 800-365-6548 ■ *Web:* www.dom-dominionblackwarriortrust.com	Dallas	TX	75202	214-209-2400	209-2431
Freehold Royalties Ltd 144 4th Ave SW Suite 400 *TF:* 888-257-1873 ■ *Web:* www.freeholdtrust.com	Calgary	AB	T2P3N4	403-221-0800	221-0888
Great Northern Iron Ore Properties 332 Minnesota St Rm W1290 *NYSE:* GNI ■ *TF:* 800-468-9716 ■ *Web:* www.gniop.com	Saint Paul	MN	55101	651-224-2385	224-2387
Harvest Energy Trust 330 5th Ave SW Suite 2100 *TF:* 866-666-1178 ■ *Web:* www.harvestenergy.ca	Calgary	AB	T2P0L4	403-265-1178	266-3490
Hugoton Royalty Trust 901 Main St 17th Fl PO Box 830650 *NYSE:* HGT ■ *TF:* 877-228-5083 ■ *Web:* www.hugotontrust.com	Dallas	TX	75283	214-209-2400	209-2431
Marine Petroleum Trust 901 Main St Bank of America Plaza 17th Fl *NASDAQ:* MARPS ■ *TF:* 800-985-0794 ■ *Web:* www.marps-marinepetroleumtrust.com	Dallas	TX	75202	214-209-2400	
Mesa Royalty Trust 700 Lavaca St 2nd Fl	Austin	TX	78701	713-216-6369	216-5476
North European Oil Royalty Trust 43 W Front St Suite 19A *NYSE:* NRT ■ *TF:* 800-368-5948 ■ *Web:* www.neort.com	Red Bank	NJ	07701	732-741-4008	741-3140
Pengrowth Energy Trust 222 3rd Ave SW Suite 2100 *NYSE:* PGH ■ *TF:* 800-223-4122 ■ *Web:* www.pengrowth.com	Calgary	AB	T2P0B4	403-233-0224	265-6251
Penn West Energy Trust 425 1st St SW Suite 2200 *TF:* 866-693-2707 ■ *Web:* www.pennwest.com	Calgary	AB	T2P3L8	403-777-2500	777-2699
Permian Basin Royalty Trust 901 Main St Suite 1700 Bank of America Plaza *NYSE:* PBT ■ *TF:* 877-228-5085 ■ *Web:* www.pbt-permianbasintrust.com	Dallas	TX	75202	214-209-2400	209-2431
Sabine Royalty Trust 901 Main St 17th Fl Bank of America Plaza *NYSE:* SBR ■ *TF:* 800-365-6541 ■ *Web:* www.sbr-sabineroyalty.com	Dallas	TX	75202	214-209-2400	209-2431
San Juan Basin Royalty Trust 2525 Ridgmar Blvd Suite 100 *NYSE:* SJT ■ **Fax Area Code:* 817 ■ *TF:* 866-809-4553 ■ *Web:* www.sjbrt.com	Fort Worth	TX	76116	866-809-4553	735-0936*
TAQA North Ltd 5100 6th Ave SW Suite 150 *TF:* 877-968-7878 ■ *Web:* www.primewestenergy.com	Calgary	AB	T2P3Y7	403-724-5000	724-5001
TEL Offshore Trust 919 Congress Ave	Austin	TX	78701	512-236-6599	479-2553
Texas Pacific Land Trust 1700 Pacific Ave Suite 2770 *NYSE:* TPL ■ *Web:* www.tpltrust.com	Dallas	TX	75201	214-969-5530	871-7139
Tidelands Royalty Trust B PO Box 830650 *PINK:* TIRTZ ■ *TF:* 800-985-0794 ■ *Web:* www.tirtz-tidelandsroyaltytrust.com	Dallas	TX	75202	214-209-2400	209-2431
Torch Energy Royalty Trust 1221 Lamar Suite 1600 *NYSE:* TRU ■ **Fax Area Code:* 713 ■ *TF:* 800-536-7453 ■ *Web:* www.torchroyalty.com	Houston	TX	77010	800-536-7453	655-1866*
Williams Coal Seam Gas Royalty Trust PO Box 830650 *NYSE:* WTU ■ *TF:* 800-365-6544 ■ *Web:* www.wtu-williamscoalseamgastrust.com	Dallas	TX	75283	214-209-2364	209-2431

679 RUBBER GOODS

Name / Address	City	State	Zip	Phone	Fax
A & A Mfg Co Inc 2300 S Calhoun Rd *Web:* www.gortite.com	New Berlin	WI	53151	262-786-1500	786-3280
Aero Tec Labs Inc 45 Spear Rd Industrial Pk *TF:* 800-526-5330 ■ *Web:* www.atlinc.com	Ramsey	NJ	07446	201-825-1400	825-1962
Alliance Rubber Co 210 Carpenter Dam Rd *TF:* 800-626-5940 ■ *Web:* www.rubberband.com	Hot Springs	AR	71901	501-262-2700	262-8192
Apache Mills Inc 18 Passaic Ave Unit 1 *TF:* 800-456-7791	Fairfield	NJ	07004	973-227-9080	808-8330
Barry Controls 82 S St **Fax:* Sales ■ *TF:* 800-227-7962 ■ *Web:* www.barrycontrols.com	Hopkinton	MA	01748	508-417-7000	417-7223*
Biltrite Corp 51 Sawyer Rd *TF:* 800-877-8775 ■ *Web:* www.biltrite.com	Waltham	MA	02454	781-647-1700	647-4205
BRP Mfg Co 637 N Jackson St *TF:* 800-858-0482 ■ *Web:* www.brpmfg.com	Lima	OH	45801	419-228-4441	222-5010
Dawson Mfg Co 1042 N Crystal Ave PO Box 603 *Web:* www.dawsonmfg.com	Benton Harbor	MI	49023	269-925-0100	925-0997
Durable Products Inc PO Box 826 *TF:* 800-373-3502 ■ *Web:* www.durableproductsinc.com	Crossville	TN	38557	931-484-3502	456-7682
Eam World 5502 NW 37th Ave *Web:* www.theraft.com	Miami	FL	33142	305-871-4050	637-8632
Flexsys America LP 260 Springside Dr *TF:* 800-321-3416 ■ *Web:* www.flexsys.com	Akron	OH	44333	330-666-4111	668-8371
Griswold Corp 1 River St PO Box 638 *TF:* 800-472-8788 ■ *Web:* www.griswoldcorp.com	Moosup	CT	06354	860-564-3321	564-9103

	City	State	ZIP	Phone	Fax
HC Lien Rubber Co Inc 1223 E 63rd St *Web:* www.lienrubber.com	Los Angeles	CA	90001	323-846-8880	846-8886
Interstate Foam & Supply Inc PO Box 338 *Web:* www.interstatefoam.com	Conover	NC	28613	828-459-9700	459-0300
Itran Precision Rubber 375 Metuchen Rd **Fax:* Sales ■ *Web:* www.itran-tompkinsrubber.com	South Plainfield	NJ	07080	908-754-8100	757-1820*
Jet Rubber Co Inc 4457 Tallmadge Rd *Web:* www.jetrubber.com	Rootstown	OH	44272	330-325-1821	325-2876
Kent Elastomer Products Inc 1500 St Claire Ave *TF Cust Svc:* 800-331-4762 ■ *Web:* www.kentelastomer.com	Kent	OH	44240	330-673-1011	673-1351
Koneta Inc 1400 Lunar Dr *TF:* 800-331-0775 ■ *Web:* www.konetalrv.com	Wapakoneta	OH	45895	419-739-4200	739-4247
Kraco Enterprises Inc 505 E Euclid Ave *TF:* 800-678-1910 ■ *Web:* www.kraco.com	Compton	CA	90224	310-639-0666	604-9838
Ludlow Composites Corp 2100 Commerce Dr *TF:* 800-628-5463 ■ *Web:* www.ludlow-comp.com	Fremont	OH	43420	419-332-5531	332-7776
Mitchell Rubber Products Inc 10220 San Sevaine Way *Web:* www.mitchellrubber.com	Mira Loma	CA	91752	951-681-5655	681-1479
Mosites Rubber Co Inc PO Box 2115 *Web:* www.mositesrubber.com	Fort Worth	TX	76113	817-335-3451	870-1564
MSM Industries Inc 802 Swan Dr *TF:* 800-648-6648 ■ *Web:* www.msmind.com	Smyrna	TN	37167	615-355-4355	355-6874
Musson Rubber Co Inc 1320 E Archwood Ave *TF Cust Svc:* 800-321-2381 ■ *Web:* www.mussonrubber.com	Akron	OH	44306	330-773-7651	773-3254
National Rubber Technologies Corp 35 Cawthra Ave *TF:* 800-387-8501 ■ *Web:* www.knrubber.com	Toronto	ON	M6N5B3	416-657-1111	656-1231
Patch Rubber Co PO Box H *Web:* www.patchrubber.com	Roanoke Rapids	NC	27870	252-536-2574	536-4108
Pawling Corp 157 Charles Colman Blvd *TF:* 800-377-3820 ■ *Web:* www.pawling.com	Pawling	NY	12564	845-855-1000	855-1937
Philpott Rubber Co 1010 Industrial Pkwy *Web:* www.philpottrubber.com	Brunswick	OH	44212	330-225-3344	225-1999
Plasticoid Co 249 W High St *TF:* 800-398-2806 ■ *Web:* www.plasticoid.com	Elkton	MD	21921	410-398-2800	398-2803
Proco Products Inc PO Box 590 *TF:* 800-344-3246 ■ *Web:* www.procoproducts.com	Stockton	CA	95201	209-943-6088	943-0242
R & K Industrial Products Co 1945 7th St *TF:* 800-842-7655 ■ *Web:* www.rkwheels.com	Richmond	CA	94801	510-234-7212	234-1923
Regupol America 33 Keystone Dr **Fax Area Code:* 717 ■ *TF:* 800-537-8737 ■ *Web:* www.regupol.com	Lebanon	PA	17042	800-537-8737	675-2199*
Rex-Hide Inc 705 S Lyons Ave *TF:* 800-527-8403 ■ *Web:* www.rex-hide.com	Tyler	TX	75702	903-593-7387	592-0122
Rubber Industries Inc 200 Cavanaugh Dr *Web:* www.rubberindustries.com	Shakopee	MN	55379	952-445-1320	445-7934
Seismic Energy Products LP (SEP) 518 Progress Way *TF:* 800-603-8766 ■ *Web:* www.sepbearings.com	Athens	TX	75751	903-675-8571	677-4980
Shercon Inc 6262 Katella Ave *TF:* 800-228-3218 ■ *Web:* www.shercon.com	Cypress	CA	90630	714-548-3999	548-3991
SMR Technologies Inc 93 Nettie Fenwick Rd *TF:* 800-767-6899 ■ *Web:* www.smrtech.com	Fenwick	WV	26202	304-846-2554	846-2024
Star-Glo Industries LLC 2 Carlton Ave *Web:* www.starglo.com	East Rutherford	NJ	07073	201-939-6162	939-4054
Swarco Industries Inc PO Box 89 *Web:* www.swarco.com	Columbia	TN	38402	931-388-5900	388-4039
Teknor Apex Co 505 Central Ave *TF:* 800-556-3864 ■ *Web:* www.teknorapex.com	Pawtucket	RI	02861	401-725-8000	725-8095
Tennessee Mat Co Inc 1414 4th Ave S *TF:* 800-264-3030 ■ *Web:* www.wearwell.com	Nashville	TN	37210	615-254-8381	255-4428
Vulcan Corp 30 Garfield Pl Suite 1040 *TF Sales:* 800-447-1146 ■ *Web:* www.vulcorp.com	Cincinnati	OH	45202	513-621-2850	241-8199

680 RUBBER GOODS - MECHANICAL

Mechanical Rubber Goods Are Rubber Components Used In Machinery, Such As O-Rings, Sprockets, Sleeves, Roller Covers, Etc.

	City	State	ZIP	Phone	Fax
AGC Inc 106 Evansville Ave *Web:* www.agcincorporated.com	Meriden	CT	06451	203-235-3361	235-6543
AirBoss of America Corp 16441 Yonge St *TSE: BOS* ■ *Web:* www.airbossofamerica.com	Newmarket	ON	L3X2G8	905-751-1188	751-1101
American National Rubber Co Main & High St **Fax:* Sales ■ *TF Cust Svc:* 800-624-3410 ■ *Web:* www.anr-co.com	Ceredo	WV	25507	304-453-1311	453-2347*
American Roller Co 1440 13th Ave *Web:* www.americanroller.com	Union Grove	WI	53182	262-878-8665	878-1932
Ames Rubber Corp 19 Ames Blvd *TF:* 800-697-9101 ■ *Web:* www.amesrubber.com	Hamburg	NJ	07419	973-827-9101	827-8893
Applied Tech Products 565 Swedesford Rd Suite 315 *Web:* www.appliedtechproducts.com	Wayne	PA	19087	610-688-2200	688-1534
Armada Rubber Mfg Co 24586 Armada Ridge Rd PO Box 579 *TF:* 800-842-8311 ■ *Web:* www.armadarubber.com	Armada	MI	48005	586-784-9135	784-5023
Ashtabula Rubber Co 2751 W Ave *Web:* www.ashtabularubber.com	Ashtabula	OH	44004	440-992-2195	992-7829
Atlantic India Rubber Co 1437 Kentucky Rt 1428 *TF:* 800-476-6638 ■ *Web:* www.atlanticindia.com	Hager Hills	KY	41222	606-789-9115	789-9098
Avon Rubber & Plastics Inc 603 W 7th St	Cadillac	MI	49601	231-775-6571	775-8731
Boyd Corp 600 S McClure Rd *TF:* 800-554-0200 ■ *Web:* www.boydcorp.com	Modesto	CA	95357	209-236-1111	236-1154
Brc Rubber Group Inc PO Box 227 *Web:* www.brcrp.com	Churubusco	IN	46723	260-693-2171	693-6511
Buckhorn Rubber Products Inc 5151 Industrial Dr *Web:* www.buckhornrubber.com	Hannibal	MO	63401	573-221-8933	221-7144
Chicago Manifold Products Co 171 E Marquardt Dr *TF Sales:* 800-323-7735	Wheeling	IL	60090	847-459-6000	459-6277
Colonial Diversified Polymer Products LLC 2055 Forrest St Ext PO Box 930 *TF:* 800-303-3606 ■ *Web:* www.cdpp.colonialdpp.com	Dyersburg	TN	38025	731-287-3636	287-3691
Connor Corp 10633 Coldwater Rd # 200 *Web:* www.connorcorp.com	Fort Wayne	IN	46845	260-424-1601	422-7202
Cupples Rubber Industrial Products 903 W 13th St	Caruthersville	MO	63830	573-333-1585	333-1585
Da/Pro Rubber Inc 601 N Poplar Ave *Web:* www.daprorubber.com	Broken Arrow	OK	74012	918-258-9386	258-3286
Derby Cellular Products Inc 150 Roosevelt Dr *Web:* www.derbycellularproducts.com	Derby	CT	06418	203-735-4661	735-4661
Fabreeka International Inc 1023 Tpke St *TF Cust Svc:* 800-322-7352 ■ *Web:* www.fabreeka.com	Stoughton	MA	02072	781-341-3655	341-3983
Finzer Roller Co 129 Rawls Rd *TF:* 888-486-1900 ■ *Web:* www.finzerroller.com	Des Plaines	IL	60018	847-390-6200	390-6201
Flexan Corp 6626 W Dakin St *Web:* www.flexan.com	Chicago	IL	60634	773-685-6446	685-6630
Flexible Products Co 2600 Auburn Ct *Web:* www.flexible-products.com	Auburn Hills	MI	48326	248-852-5500	852-8620
Griffith Rubber Mills 2625 NW Industrial St *TF:* 800-321-9677	Portland	OR	97210	503-226-6971	226-6976
Hiawatha Rubber Co 1700 67th Ave N *TF:* 800-728-3845 ■ *Web:* www.hiawatharubber.com	Minneapolis	MN	55430	763-566-0900	566-9537
Holz Rubber Co Inc 1129 S Sacramento St *TF:* 800-285-1600 ■ *Web:* www.holzrubber.com	Lodi	CA	95240	209-368-7171	368-3246
IER Fujikura Inc 8271 Bavaria Rd *Web:* www.ierfujikura.com	Macedonia	OH	44056	330-425-7125	425-7596
International Rubber Products Inc 2600 Homestead Pl *TF:* 800-361-1915 ■ *Web:* www.mikronproducts.com	Rancho Dominguez	CA	90220	310-868-5200	868-5209
Jamak Fabrication Inc 1401 N Bowie Dr *TF:* 800-395-2625 ■ *Web:* www.jamak.com	Weatherford	TX	76086	817-594-8771	594-8324
Jasper Rubber Products Inc 1010 1st Ave W *TF:* 800-457-7457 ■ *Web:* www.jasperrubber.com	Jasper	IN	47546	812-482-3242	481-2702
Johnson Bros Rubber Inc 42 W Buckeye St	West Salem	OH	44287	419-853-4122	853-4062
Johnson Rubber Co 16025 Johnson St PO Box 67 *TF:* 800-362-1951 ■ *Web:* www.johnsonrubber.com	Middlefield	OH	44062	440-632-1611	
Jonal Laboratories Inc PO Box 743 *Web:* www.jonal.com	Meriden	CT	06450	203-634-4444	634-4448
Karman Rubber Co 2331 Copley Rd *Web:* www.karman.com	Akron	OH	44320	330-864-2161	864-2124
Kirkhill Mfg Co 12023 Woodruff Ave *Web:* www.rubbersales.com	Downey	CA	90241	562-803-1117	803-3117
Kirkhill-TA Co 300 E Cypress St *Web:* www.kirkhill-ta.com	Brea	CA	92821	714-529-4901	529-6775
Lauren Mfg 2228 Reiser Ave SE *TF:* 855-989-9090 ■ *Web:* www.lauren.com	New Philadelphia	OH	44663	330-339-3373	339-1515
Lavelle Industries Inc 665 McHenry St *TF:* 800-528-3553 ■ *Web:* www.lavelle.com	Burlington	WI	53105	262-763-2434	763-5607
Longwood Elastomers Inc 706 Green Valley Rd Suite 212 *TF:* 800-374-2837 ■ *Web:* www.longwood-elastomers.com	Greensboro	NC	27408	336-272-3710	272-3710
Lord Corp 111 Lord Dr *TF:* 800-524-2885 ■ *Web:* www.lord.com	Cary	NC	27511	919-468-5979	
Mantaline Corp 4754 E High St *TF:* 800-321-0948 ■ *Web:* www.mantaline.com	Mantua	OH	44255	330-274-2264	274-8850
Minnesota Rubber 1100 Xenium Ln N **Fax:* Sales ■ *TF:* 800-927-1422 ■ *Web:* www.mnrubber.com	Plymouth	MN	55441	952-927-1400	927-1470*
Minor Rubber Co Inc 49 Ackerman St *TF:* 800-433-6886 ■ *Web:* www.minorrubber.com	Bloomfield	NJ	07003	973-338-6800	893-1399
MOCAP Inc 13100 Manchester Rd *TF:* 800-633-6775 ■ *Web:* www.mocap.com	Saint Louis	MO	63131	314-543-4000	543-4111
Molded Rubber & Plastic Corp 13161 W Glendale Ave *TF:* 888-781-7122 ■ *Web:* www.mrpcorp.com	Butler	WI	53007	262-781-7122	781-5353
Neff-Perkins Co 16080 Industrial Pkwy *Web:* www.neffp.com	Middlefield	OH	44062	440-632-1658	632-1999
Paulstra CRC Corp 460 Fuller Ave NE PO Box 1886 *Web:* www.paulstra-purchasing.com	Grand Rapids	MI	49501	616-459-4541	588-5949
Precision Assoc Inc 3800 N Washington Ave *TF:* 800-394-6590 ■ *Web:* www.precisionassoc.com	Minneapolis	MN	55412	612-333-7464	342-2417
Precix Inc 744 Bellville Ave *Web:* www.precixinc.com	New Bedford	MA	02745	508-998-4000	998-4100
Prince Rubber & Plastics Co Inc 137 Arthur St *Web:* www.princerp.com	Buffalo	NY	14207	716-877-7400	877-0743
Quality Synthetic Rubber Inc 1700 Highland Rd *Web:* www.qsr-inc.com	Twinsburg	OH	44087	330-425-8472	425-7976
Reiss Mfg Inc 75 Mt Vernon Rd *Web:* www.reissbuilt.com	Englishtown	NJ	07726	732-446-6100	446-1394
RotaDyne Corp 8140 S Cass Ave *Web:* www.rotadyne.com	Darien	IL	60561	630-769-9700	769-9255
SETI Acme Machell Co Inc 2000 Airport Rd	Waukesha	WI	53188	262-521-2870	521-2894
SETI Mold-Ex Co 8052 Armstrong Rd	Milton	FL	32583	850-626-7211	626-7322
Sperry & Rice Mfg Co LLC 9146 US Hwy 52 *TF:* 800-541-9277 ■ *Web:* www.sperryrice.com	Brookville	IN	47012	765-647-4141	647-3302
Thermodyn Corp 3550 Silica Rd *TF:* 800-654-6518 ■ *Web:* www.thermodyn.com	Sylvania	OH	43560	419-841-7782	841-3139
Triangle Rubber Co Inc 1924 Elkhart Rd *Web:* www.trianglerubberco.com	Goshen	IN	46526	574-533-3118	534-0416
Trostel Ltd 901 Maxwell St *Web:* www.trostel.com	Lake Geneva	WI	53147	262-248-4481	248-6406
Universal Polymer & Rubber Ltd 15730 Madison Rd *TF:* 800-782-2375 ■ *Web:* www.universalpolymer.com	Middlefield	OH	44062	440-632-1691	632-5761

	City	State	Zip	Phone	Fax
Vail Rubber Works Inc 521 Langley Ave Web: www.vailrubber.com	Saint Joseph	MI	49085	269-983-1595	983-0155
Vernay Laboratories Inc 120 E S College St *Fax: Sales ■ TF: 800-837-6291 ■ Web: www.vernay.com	Yellow Springs	OH	45387	937-767-7261	767-7913*
Wabtec Rubber Products 269 Donohue Rd TF: 888-867-3539 ■ Web: www.wabtec.com	Greensburg	PA	15601	724-838-1317	832-5630
West American Rubber Co LLC 1413 Braden Ct Web: www.warco.com	Orange	CA	92868	714-532-3355	532-2238
YUSA Corp 151 Jamison Rd SW TF: 800-395-0335	Washington Court House	OH	43160	740-335-0335	335-0330

681 SAFETY EQUIPMENT - MFR

SEE ALSO Medical Supplies - Mfr p. 2229; Personal Protective Equipment & Clothing p. 2409

	City	State	Zip	Phone	Fax
ACR Electronics Inc 5757 Anglers Ave TF: 800-432-0227 ■ Web: www.acrelectronics.com	Fort Lauderdale	FL	33312	954-981-3333	983-5087
Adams Elevator Equipment Co 6310 W Howard St TF: 800-929-9247 ■ Web: www.adamselevator.com	Niles	IL	60714	847-581-2900	581-2949
Aerial Machine & Tool Corp 4298 Jeb Stuart Hwy PO Box 222 Web: www.aerialmachineandtool.com	Vesta	VA	24177	276-952-2006	952-2231
Air Cruisers Co PO Box 180 Web: www.aircruisers.com	Belmar	NJ	07719	732-681-3527	681-9163
ALP Industries Inc 1229 W Lincoln Hwy TF: 800-220-2515 ■ Web: www.alpind.com	Coatesville	PA	19320	610-384-1300	384-7300
Amerex Corp 7595 Gadsden Hwy PO Box 81 Web: www.amerex-fire.com	Trussville	AL	35173	205-655-3271	655-3279
AmSafe Inc 1043 N 47th Ave Web: www.amsafe.com	Phoenix	AZ	85043	602-850-2850	850-2812
Ancra International LLC 4880 W Rosecrans Ave TF: 800-973-5091 ■ Web: www.ancra-llc.com	Hawthorne	CA	90250	310-973-5000	973-1138
Autoliv Inc 3350 Airport Rd NYSE: ALV ■ Web: www.autoliv.com	Ogden	UT	84405	801-625-9200	629-9111
Badger Fire Protection 944 Glenwood Stn Ln Suite 303 *Fax Area Code: 800 ■ TF: 800-446-3857 ■ Web: www.badgerfire.com	Charlottesville	VA	22901	434-964-3206	248-7809*
Bradley Corp W 142 N 9101 Fountain Blvd TF: 800-272-3539 ■ Web: www.bradleycorp.com	Menomonee Falls	WI	53051	262-251-6000	251-5817
Buckeye Fire Equipment Co 110 Kings Rd PO Box 428 TF: 800-438-1028 ■ Web: www.buckeyef.com	Kings Mountain	NC	28086	704-739-7415	739-7418
Carsonite Composites LLC 19845 US Hwy 76 TF: 800-648-7916 ■ Web: www.carsonite.com	Newberry	SC	29108	803-321-1185	276-8940
Central Research Laboratories 3965 Pepin Ave Web: www.centres.com	Red Wing	MN	55066	651-388-3565	388-1232
Conax Florida Corp 2801 75th St N Web: www.conaxfl.com	Saint Petersburg	FL	33710	727-345-8000	345-4217
Cse Corp 600 Seco Rd TF: 800-245-2224 ■ Web: www.csecorporation.com	Monroeville	PA	15146	412-856-9200	856-9203
DBI/SALA & Protecta 3833 Sala Way TF: 800-328-6146 ■ Web: www.en.capitalsafety.us	Red Wing	MN	55066	651-388-8282	388-8282
Delta Scientific Corp 40355 Delta Ln Web: www.deltascientific.com	Palmdale	CA	93551	661-575-1100	575-1109
Encon Safety Products Co 6825 W Sam Houston Pkwy N PO Box 3826 TF: 800-283-6266 ■ Web: www.enconsafety.com	Houston	TX	77041	713-466-1449	466-1703
Energy Absorption Systems Inc 35 E Wacker Dr Suite 1100 Web: www.energyabsorption.com	Chicago	IL	60601	312-467-6750	467-1356
Gemtor Inc 1 Johnson Ave TF: 800-405-9048 ■ Web: www.gemtor.com	Matawan	NJ	07747	732-583-6200	290-9391
Hawkins Traffic Safety Supply 1255 E Shore Hwy TF: 800-772-3995	Berkeley	CA	94710	510-525-4040	525-2861
Herbert S Hiller Corp 401 Commerce Pt TF: 800-833-5211 ■ Web: www.hillercompanies.com	Harahan	LA	70123	504-736-0008	736-0030
Hoover Industries Inc 7260 NW 68th St	Miami	FL	33166	305-888-9791	887-4632
Key Safety Systems Inc 7000 Nineteen Mile Rd Web: www.keysafetyinc.com	Sterling Heights	MI	48314	586-726-3800	726-4150
Kidde Fire Fighting 180 Sheree Blvd Suite 390 Web: www.kidde-fire.com	Exton	PA	19341	610-363-1400	524-9073
Kidde Safety 1016 Corporate Pk Dr TF: 800-880-6788 ■ Web: www.kiddeus.com	Mebane	NC	27302	919-563-5911	563-3954
Labock Technologies Inc 1600 N Pk Dr Web: www.labock.com	Weston	FL	33326	954-335-3535	335-3525
Mercedes Textiles Ltd 5838 Cypihot St Web: www.mercedestextiles.com	Ville Saint Laurent	QC	H4S1Y5	514-335-4337	335-9633
Monaco Enterprises Inc 14820 E Sprague Ave PO Box 14129 Web: www.monaco.com	Spokane	WA	99216	509-926-6277	924-4980
North American Fire Hose 910 E Noble Way TF: 800-747-7075 ■ Web: www.northamericanfirehose.com	Santa Maria	CA	93454	805-922-7076	922-0086
Ocenco Inc 10225 82nd Ave TF: 800-932-2293 ■ Web: www.ocenco.com	Pleasant Prairie	WI	53158	262-947-9000	947-9020
Peck & Hale LLC 180 Division Ave Web: www.peckhale.com	West Sayville	NY	11796	631-589-2510	589-2925
Peerless Chain Co 1416 E Sanborn St TF: 800-533-8056 ■ Web: www.peerlesschain.com	Winona	MN	55987	507-457-9100	457-9252
Plastic Safety Systems Inc 2444 Baldwin Rd *Fax Area Code: 216 ■ TF: 800-662-6338 ■ Web: www.plasticsafety.com	Cleveland	OH	44104	800-662-6338	231-2702*
Potter-Roemer 17451 Hurley St TF: 800-366-3473 ■ Web: www.potterroemer.com	City of Industry	CA	91744	626-855-4890	937-4777
Reflexite North America 315 S St TF: 800-654-7570 ■ Web: www.reflexite.com	New Britain	CT	06051	860-223-9297	832-9267
Rite-Hite Corp 8900 N Arbon Dr TF: 800-456-0600 ■ Web: www.ritehite.com	Milwaukee	WI	53224	414-355-2600	355-9248
Rostra Precision Controls Inc 2519 Dana Dr TF Cust Svc: 800-782-3379 ■ Web: www.rostra.com	Laurinburg	NC	28352	910-276-4853	276-1354
Safety Components International Inc 41 Stevens St Web: www.safetycomponents.com	Greenville	SC	29605	864-240-2600	240-2728
Security Chain Co PO Box 949 TF: 800-547-6806 ■ Web: www.scc-chain.com	Clackamas	OR	97015	503-656-5400	656-4836
Simulaids 165 Malden Tpke Web: www.simulaids.com	Saugerties	NY	12477	845-679-2475	679-8996
Takata Inc 2500 Takata Dr Web: www.takata.com	Auburn Hills	MI	48326	248-373-8040	377-2897
Tread Corp 176 Eastpark Dr TF: 800-900-6881 ■ Web: www.treadcorp.com	Roanoke	VA	24019	540-982-6881	344-7536

682 SAFETY EQUIPMENT - WHOL

	City	State	Zip	Phone	Fax
Allstar Fire Equipment Inc 12328 Lower Azusa Rd TF: 800-425-5787 ■ Web: www.allstarfire.com	Arcadia	CA	91006	626-652-0900	652-0920
Alltype Fire Protection Co 9495 Page Ave PO Box 32432 TF: 800-369-7101	Saint Louis	MO	63132	314-426-7100	426-7782
American Cleanroom Supply LLC 1042-B El Camino Real Suite 414 *Fax Area Code: 760 ■ TF: 888-901-3220	Encinitas	CA	92024	888-901-3220	752-3238*
Arbill PO Box 820542 TF: 800-523-5367 ■ Web: www.arbill.com	Philadelphia	PA	19154	800-523-5367	426-5808
Brooks Equipment Co Inc 10926 David Taylor Dr Suite 300 *Fax Area Code: 800 ■ TF: 800-826-3473 ■ Web: www.brooksequipment.com	Charlotte	NC	28269	704-596-9438	433-9265*
Broward Fire Equipment & Service Inc 101 SW 6th St TF: 800-866-3473 ■ Web: www.browardfire.com	Fort Lauderdale	FL	33301	954-467-6625	467-6640
Calolympic Glove & Safety Co Inc 1720 Delilah St TF: 800-421-6630 ■ Web: www.caloly-safety.com	Corona	CA	92879	951-340-2229	340-3337
Choctaw-Kaul Distribution Co 3540 Vinewood Ave Web: www.choctawkaul.com	Detroit	MI	48208	313-894-9494	894-7977
Continental Safety Equipment Inc 899 Apollo Rd TF: 800-844-7003 ■ Web: www.csesafety.com	Eagan	MN	55121	651-454-7233	454-3217
Dunn Safety Products Inc 37 S Sangamon St TF: 800-451-3866 ■ Web: www.dunnsafety.com	Chicago	IL	60607	312-666-5800	666-5090
Empire Safety & Supply Inc 10624 Industrial Ave *Fax Area Code: 888 ■ TF: 800-995-1341 ■ Web: www.empiresafety.com	Roseville	CA	75678	916-781-3003	882-9060*
Fire Equipment Inc 88 Hicks Ave Web: www.firefire.com	Medford	MA	02155	781-391-8050	391-8835
Fire Fighters Equipment Co 5638 Commonwealth Ave TF: 800-488-8542 ■ Web: www.firefightersusa.com	Jacksonville	FL	32232	904-388-8542	384-2610
Fire Protection Service Inc 8050 Harrisburg Blvd Web: www.fps-usa.com	Houston	TX	77012	713-924-9600	923-6272
International Fire Equipment Corp 500 Telser Rd Web: www.intlfire.com	Lake Zurich	IL	60047	847-438-2343	438-1869
La Grand Industrial Supply Co PO Box 1959	Portland	OR	97207	503-224-5800	224-0639
Lab Safety Supply Inc 401 S Wright Rd *Fax Area Code: 800 ■ TF: 800-356-0783 ■ Web: www.labsafety.com	Janesville	WI	53546	608-754-2345	543-9910*
LaFrance Equipment Corp 516 Erie St TF: 800-873-8808 ■ Web: www.lafrance-equipment.com	Elmira	NY	14904	607-733-5511	733-0482
LN Curtis & Sons 1800 Peralta St TF: 800-443-3556 ■ Web: www.lncurtis.com	Oakland	CA	94607	510-839-5111	839-5325
McLean International Marketing Inc 5300 Elmhurst Rd PO Box 535 Web: www.mcleansafety.com	Mequon	WI	53092	262-242-0958	242-6644
Mid-Continent Safety LLC 2909 S Spruce St TF: 800-835-7233 ■ Web: www.midsafe.com	Wichita	KS	67216	316-522-0900	522-0956
Minnesota Conway 314 W 86th St Suite 101 TF: 800-223-2587 ■ Web: www.mnconway.com	Bloomington	MN	55420	952-345-3473	345-2499
Nardini Fire Equipment Co Inc 405 County Rd E W TF: 888-627-3464 ■ Web: www.nardinifire.com	Saint Paul	MN	55126	651-483-6631	483-6945
Orr Safety Corp 11601 Interchange Dr TF: 800-726-6789 ■ Web: www.orrsafety.com	Louisville	KY	40229	502-774-5791	776-8030
PK Safety Supply 2005 Clement Ave Bldg 9 TF: 800-829-9580 ■ Web: www.pksafety.com	Alameda	CA	94501	510-337-8880	337-8890
Reliable Fire Equipment Co 12845 S Cicero Ave Web: www.reliablefire.com	Alsip	IL	60803	708-597-4600	389-1150
Saf-T-Gard International Inc 205 Huehl Rd TF: 800-548-4273 ■ Web: www.saftgard.com	Northbrook	IL	60062	847-291-1600	291-1610
Safety Products Inc 3517 Craftsman Blvd *Fax Area Code: 800 ■ TF: 800-248-6860 ■ Web: www.spisafety.com	Lakeland	FL	33803	863-665-3601	330-0395*
Safety Solutions Inc 6161 Shamrock Ct PO Box 8100 TF: 800-232-7463 ■ Web: www.safetysolutions.com	Dublin	OH	43016	614-799-9900	799-9901
Safety Supply South Inc 100 Centrum Dr TF Cust Svc: 800-522-8344 ■ Web: www.safetysupplysouth.com	Irmo	SC	29063	803-732-1500	732-3696
Safeware Inc 3200 Hubbard Rd TF Cust Svc: 800-331-6707 ■ Web: www.safewareinc.com	Landover	MD	20785	301-683-1234	683-1200
Sanderson Safety Supply Co 1101 SE 3rd Ave TF: 800-547-0927 ■ Web: www.sandersonsafety.com	Portland	OR	97214	503-238-5700	238-6443
Skaggs Cos 3828 S Main St TF: 800-879-1787 ■ Web: www.skaggscompanies.com	Murray	UT	84115	801-261-4400	261-1580

Company	City	State	Zip	Phone	Fax
Stauffer Glove & Safety PO Box 45 *Web:* www.stauffersafety.com	Red Hill	PA	18076	215-679-4446	679-5053
Sun Devil Fire Equipment Inc 2929 W Clarendon Ave *Fax Area Code: 602 ■ *TF:* 800-536-3845 ■ *Web:* www.sundevilfire.com	Phoenix	AZ	85017	623-245-0636	495-9291*
United Fire Equipment Co 335 N 4th Ave *TF:* 800-362-0150 ■ *Web:* www.unitedfire.net/uf	Tucson	AZ	85705	520-622-3639	882-3991
Vanguard Distributors Inc 107 NE Lathrop Ave *Web:* www.vanguarddistributors.com	Savannah	GA	31415	912-236-1766	238-3072
Wayest Safety Inc 3750 N I-44 Service Rd *TF:* 800-256-1003 ■ *Web:* www.wayest.com	Oklahoma City	OK	73112	405-942-7101	942-5289
Wenaas AGS Inc 202 E Larkspur St *TF:* 888-576-2668 ■ *Web:* www.wenaasusa.com	Victoria	TX	77904	361-576-2668	576-2674
Wise El Santo Co Inc 11000 Linpage Pl *TF:* 800-727-8541 ■ *Web:* www.wiseelsanto.com	Saint Louis	MO	63132	314-428-3100	428-7017

683 SALT

SEE ALSO Spices, Seasonings, Herbs p. 1867

Companies Listed Here Produce Salt That May Be Used For A Variety Of Purposes, Including As A Food Ingredient Or For Deicing, Water Conditioning, Or Other Chemical Or Industrial Applications.

Company	City	State	Zip	Phone	Fax
Cargill Inc North America 15407 McGinty Rd *TF:* 800-227-4455	Wayzata	MN	55391	952-742-7575	
Cargill Salt Inc PO Box 5621 *TF:* 888-385-7258 ■ *Web:* www.cargill.com	Minneapolis	MN	55440	888-385-7258	
Compass Minerals International 9900 W 109th St Suite 600 *NYSE: CMP* ■ *TF Cust Svc:* 800-253-7934 ■ *Web:* www.compassminerals.com	Overland Park	KS	66210	913-344-9200	338-7919
Morton Salt Inc 123 N Wacker Dr *Fax Area Code: 312 ■ *Fax: Cust Svc ■ *TF:* 800-789-7258 ■ *Web:* www.mortonsalt.com	Chicago	IL	60606	800-789-7258	807-2899*
North American Salt Co 9900 W 109th St # 600 *Web:* www.nasalt.com	Overland Park	KS	66210	913-344-9100	345-0309
United Salt Corp 4800 San Felipe St *TF:* 800-554-8658 ■ *Web:* www.unitedsalt.com	Houston	TX	77056	713-877-2600	877-2604
US Salt Holdings LLC 2 Brush Creek Blvd Suite 200 *Fax Area Code: 816 ■ *TF:* 888-872-7258 ■ *Web:* www.ussaltllc.com	Kansas City	KS	64112	877-446-3749	531-0746*

684 SATELLITE COMMUNICATIONS SERVICES

SEE ALSO Cable & Other Pay Television Services p. 1552; Internet Service Providers (ISPs) p. 2128; Telecommunications Services p. 2684

Company	City	State	Zip	Phone	Fax
ARINC Inc 2551 Riva Rd *TF:* 800-492-2182 ■ *Web:* www.arinc.com	Annapolis	MD	21401	410-266-4000	266-4040
AssureSat Inc 2601 Ocean Pk Blvd Suite 316 *Web:* www.assuresat.com	Santa Monica	CA	90405	310-452-8300	399-7303
Broken Arrow Communications Inc 8316 Corona Loop NE *Web:* www.bacom-inc.com	Albuquerque	NM	87113	505-877-2100	877-2101
Bytemobile Inc 2860 De La Cruz Blvd 2nd Fl *Web:* www.bytemobile.com	Santa Clara	CA	95050	408-327-7700	327-7701
CapRock Communications Inc 4400 S Sam Houston Pkwy E *Web:* www.caprock.com	Houston	TX	77048	832-668-2300	668-2388
Clearwire Corp 4400 Carillon Pt *NASDAQ: CLWR* ■ *TF:* 866-877-3066 ■ *Web:* www.clearwire.com	Kirkland	WA	98033	425-216-7600	216-7900
Ellipso Inc 4410 Massachusetts Ave NW Suite 385 *Web:* www.ellipso.com	Washington	DC	20016	202-466-4488	466-4493
Force10 Networks Inc 1415 N McDowell Blvd *TF:* 866-600-5100 ■ *Web:* www.force10networks.com	Petaluma	CA	94954	707-665-4400	792-4938
Geoeye Inc 21700 Atlantic Blvd *NASDAQ: GEOY* ■ *TF:* 877-295-8616 ■ *Web:* www.geoeye.com	Dulles	VA	20166	703-480-7500	450-9570
Globalstar LP 461 S Milpitas Blvd Bldg 5 *TF:* 877-245-6225 ■ *Web:* www.globalstar.com	Milpitas	CA	95035	408-933-4000	933-4100
I Towerstream Inc 55 Hammarlund Way *NASDAQ: TWER* ■ *TF:* 866-848-5848 ■ *Web:* www.towerstream.com	Middletown	RI	02842	401-848-5848	848-5130
Intelsat Ltd 3400 International Dr NW *Web:* www.intelsat.com	Washington	DC	20008	202-944-6800	944-7898
International Satellite Services Inc 1004 Collier Ctr Way Suite 205 *TF:* 888-511-3403 ■ *Web:* www.issi-us.net	Naples	FL	34110	239-598-2241	598-9343
Level 3 Communications Inc 1 Technology Ctr *TF:* 800-364-0807 ■ *Web:* www.level3.com	Tulsa	OK	74103	918-547-5760	547-1114
Lightriver Technologies Inc 3732 Mt Diablo Blvd *TF:* 888-544-4825 ■ *Web:* www.lightriver.com	Lafayette	CA	94549	925-299-9520	299-9521
Loral Skynet Ltd 500 Hills Dr *Web:* www.loralskynet.com	Bedminster	NJ	07921	908-470-2300	470-2459
Mdu Communications International Inc 60 D Commerce Way *OTC: MDTV* ■ *TF:* 866-286-9638 ■ *Web:* www.mduc.com	Totowa	NJ	07512	973-237-9499	237-9243
Microspace Communications Corp 3100 Highwoods Blvd Suite 120 *Web:* www.microspace.com	Raleigh	NC	27604	919-850-4500	850-4518
MTN/ATC Teleports 3044 N Commerce Pkwy *TF:* 877-464-4686 ■ *Web:* www.mtnsat.com	Miramar	FL	33025	954-538-4000	431-4077
ORBCOMM LLC 21700 Atlantic Blvd *TF:* 800-672-2666 ■ *Web:* www.orbcomm.com	Dulles	VA	20166	703-433-6300	433-6400
Outerlink Corp 187 Ballardvale St Suite A260 *TF:* 877-688-3770 ■ *Web:* www.outerlink.com	Wilmington	MA	01887	978-856-0007	268-5444
SES World Skies 4 Research Way *Fax: Mktg ■ *TF Sales:* 800-273-0329 ■ *Web:* www.ses-americom.com	Princeton	NJ	08540	609-987-4000	987-4517*
SpaceCom Systems Inc 1950 E 71st St *Fax Area Code: 918 ■ *TF:* 800-950-6690 ■ *Web:* www.spacecom.com	Tulsa	OK	74136	800-950-6690	499-6060*
SpaceNet Inc 1750 Old Meadow Rd *Web:* www.spacenet.com	McLean	VA	22102	703-848-1000	848-1010
SS8 Networks Inc 750 Tasman Dr *Web:* www.ss8.com	Milpitas	CA	95035	408-944-0250	428-3732
StarBand Communciations Inc 1750 Old Meadow Rd *TF:* 800-478-2722 ■ *Web:* www.starband.net	McLean	VA	22102	703-287-3000	287-3010
Stratos Global Corp 6550 Rock Spring Dr Suite 650 *TSX: SGB* ■ *TF:* 800-563-2255 ■ *Web:* www.stratosglobal.com	Bethesda	MD	20817	301-214-8800	214-8801
Telesat 1601 Telesat Ct *Web:* www.telesat.ca	Gloucester	ON	K1B5P4	613-748-0123	748-8712
TerreStar Corp 12010 Sunset Hills Rd 6th Fl *Fax Area Code: 703 ■ *TF:* 877-878-2701 ■ *Web:* www.terrestar.com	Reston	VA	20190	877-878-2701	476-7143*
ViaSat Inc 6155 El Camino Real *NASDAQ: VSAT* ■ *TF:* 877-363-7396 ■ *Web:* www.viasat.com	Carlsbad	CA	92009	760-476-2200	929-3941
Xfone Inc 5307 W Loop 289 *AMEX: XFN* ■ *TF:* 877-407-8035 ■ *Web:* www.xfone.com	Lubbock	TX	79414	806-771-5212	788-3398

685 SAW BLADES & HANDSAWS

SEE ALSO Tools - Hand & Edge p. 2719

Company	City	State	Zip	Phone	Fax
Blount Outdoor Products Group 4909 SE International Way *TF:* 800-223-5168 ■ *Web:* www.blount.com/Cutsytm.html	Portland	OR	97222	503-653-8881	653-4201
California Saw & Knife Works 721 Brannan St *Web:* www.calsaw.com	San Francisco	CA	94103	415-861-0644	861-0406
Carlton Co 3901 SE Naef Rd	Milwaukie	OR	97267	503-659-8911	659-8616
Contour Saws Inc 1217 E Thacker St *TF:* 800-458-9034	Des Plaines	IL	60016	847-824-1146	803-9467
Diamond Saw Works Inc 12290 Olean Rd *TF:* 800-828-1180 ■ *Web:* www.diamondsaw.com	Chaffee	NY	14030	716-496-7417	496-8969
Disston Precision Inc 6795 State Rd *TF Cust Svc:* 800-238-1007 ■ *Web:* www.disstonprecision.com	Philadelphia	PA	19135	215-338-1200	338-7060
Great Neck Saw Mfg Inc 165 E 2nd St *TF Cust Svc:* 800-457-0600 ■ *Web:* www.greatnecksaw.com	Mineola	NY	11501	516-746-5352	746-5358
ICS Blount Inc 4909 SE International Way *TF:* 800-321-1240 ■ *Web:* www.icsbestway.com	Portland	OR	97222	503-653-8881	653-4201
LS Starrett Co 121 Crescent St *NYSE: SCX* ■ *TF:* 888-674-7443 ■ *Web:* www.starrett.com	Athol	MA	01331	978-249-3551	249-8495
Marvel Mfg Co Inc 3501 Marvel Dr *TF:* 800-472-9464 ■ *Web:* www.sawing.com	Oshkosh	WI	54902	920-236-7200	236-7209
MK Diamond Products Inc 1315 Storm Pkwy *TF:* 800-421-5830 ■ *Web:* www.mkdiamond.com	Torrance	CA	90501	310-539-5221	539-5158
MK Morse Co 1101 11th St SE *TF:* 800-733-3377 ■ *Web:* www.mkmorse.com	Canton	OH	44707	330-453-8187	453-1111
Simonds International 135 Intervale Rd *Fax Area Code: 800 ■ *TF:* 800-343-1616 ■ *Web:* www.simondsint.com	Fitchburg	MA	01420	978-343-3731	541-6224*

686 SAWMILLS & PLANING MILLS

Company	City	State	Zip	Phone	Fax
Anderson-Tully Co 775 Ridgelake Blvd Suite 1050 *Web:* www.andersontully.com	Memphis	TN	38120	901-576-1400	576-1484
Anthony Forest Products Co 309 N Washington Ave *TF:* 800-221-2326 ■ *Web:* www.anthonyforest.com	El Dorado	AR	71730	870-862-3414	863-4296
Anthony Timberlands Inc 111 S Plum St PO Box 137 *Web:* www.anthonytimberlands.com	Bearden	AR	71720	870-687-3611	687-2283
Balfour Lumber Co Inc 800 W Clay St PO Box 1337	Thomasville	GA	31799	229-226-0611	226-4297
Beadles Lumber Co Inc 900 6th St NE PO Box 3457 *TF:* 800-763-2400 ■ *Web:* www.beadleslumber.com	Moultrie	GA	31776	229-985-6996	890-6050
Begley Lumber Co PO Box 2800 *Web:* www.begleylumber.com	London	KY	40743	606-877-1228	877-1230
Bennett Lumber Products Inc 3759 Hwy 6 PO Box 130 *Web:* www.bennett-lumber.com	Princeton	ID	83857	208-875-1121	875-0191
Bibler Bros Inc 2401 S Arkansas Ave PO Box 490	Russellville	AR	72811	479-968-4986	968-5281
Buse Timber & Sales Inc 3812 28th Pl NE *TF:* 800-305-2577 ■ *Web:* www.busetimber.com	Everett	WA	98205	425-258-2577	259-6956
Buskirk Lumber Co 319 Oak St *TF:* 800-860-9663 ■ *Web:* www.buskirklumber.com	Freeport	MI	49325	616-765-5103	765-3380
Canadian Forest Products Ltd 5162 Northwood Pulp Mill Rd PO Box 9000 *Fax: Acctg ■ *Web:* www.canfor.com	Prince George	BC	V2L4W2	250-962-3500	962-3533*
Canfor Corp 1700 W 75th Ave *TSE: CFP* ■ *Web:* www.canfor.com	Vancouver	BC	V6P6G2	604-661-5241	661-5235
Catawissa Wood & Components Inc 1015 W Valley Ave *Web:* www.catlmbr.com	Elysburg	PA	17824	570-644-1928	644-0788

Company	City	State	ZIP	Phone	Fax
Cersosimo Lumber Co Inc 1103 Vernon St *TF:* 800-326-5647 ■ *Web:* www.cersosimolumber.com	Brattleboro	VT	05301	802-254-4508	254-5691
Claude Howard Lumber Co Inc 600 Pk Ave	Statesboro	GA	30458	912-764-5407	764-6279
Coastal Timbers Inc 1310 Jane St PO Box 10537 *Web:* www.coastaltimbers.com	New Iberia	LA	70562	337-369-3017	365-0003
Coe Mfg Inc 609 Bank St *Web:* www.coemfg.com	Painesville	OH	44077	440-352-9381	352-1487
Collins Cos 1618 SW 1st Ave Suite 500 *TF:* 800-329-1219 ■ *Web:* www.collinsco.com	Portland	OR	97201	503-471-2295	227-5349
Collum's Lumber Products LLC PO Box 535 *Web:* www.collumlumber.com	Allendale	SC	29810	803-584-3451	584-2783
Columbia Vista Corp PO Box 489 *Web:* www.columbiavistacorp.com	Vancouver	WA	98666	360-892-0770	944-8229
Cronland Lumber Co 1941 Hwy 73 E *Web:* www.cronlandlumber.com	Iron Station	NC	28080	704-735-6564	736-0284
Cumberland Lumber & Mfg Co 202 Red Rd	McMinnville	TN	37110	931-473-9542	473-6259
David R Webb Co Inc 206 S Holland St PO Box 8 *Web:* www.davidrwebb.com	Edinburgh	IN	46124	812-526-2601	526-5842
Deltic Timber Corp PO Box 7200 *NYSE: DEL* ■ *Web:* www.deltic.com	El Dorado	AR	71731	870-881-9400	881-6454
Domtar Corp 395 de Maisonneuve W *TF:* 877-848-4466 ■ *Web:* www.domtar.com	Montreal	QC	H3A1L6	514-848-5555	
DR Johnson Lumber Co 1991 Pruner Rd PO Box 66 *Web:* www.drjlumber.com	Riddle	OR	97469	541-874-2231	874-3337
Dwight Lewis Lumber Co Inc Rt 87 PO Box A	Hillsgrove	PA	18619	570-924-3507	924-4233
Fitzpatrick & Weller Inc 12 Mill St PO Box 490 *Web:* www.fitzweller.com	Ellicottville	NY	14731	716-699-2393	699-2893
Forest Products Mfg Co 51 E 30th St PO Box 606	Jasper	IN	47547	812-482-5625	482-9148
Frank Lumber Co Inc PO Box 79	Mill City	OR	97360	503-897-2371	897-3003
Fulghum Industries Inc 317 S Main St PO Box 909 *TF:* 800-841-5980 ■ *Web:* www.fulghum.com	Wadley	GA	30477	478-252-5223	252-0454
Gram Lumber Co 985 NW 2nd St	Kalama	WA	98625	360-673-5231	673-5558
Griffin Lumber Co 1603 Drayton Rd *Web:* www.griffinlumber.com	Cordele	GA	31015	229-273-3113	273-4909
Gulf Lumber Co Inc 1850 Conception St Rd PO Box 1663 *TF:* 800-496-3307 ■ *Web:* www.gulflumber.com	Mobile	AL	36633	251-457-6872	452-7110
Hampton Affiliates 9600 SW Barnes Rd Sunset Business Pk Suite 200 *TF:* 888-310-1464 ■ *Web:* www.hamptonaffiliates.com	Portland	OR	97225	503-297-7691	203-6604
Hankins Lumber Co Inc 496 Camp McCain Rd PO Box 1397	Grenada	MS	38902	662-226-2961	226-6404
Hardwoods Of Michigan Inc 430 Division St *TF:* 800-327-2812 ■ *Web:* www.hmilumber.com	Clinton	MI	49236	517-456-7431	456-4931
Hartzell Hardwoods Inc 1025 S Roosevelt Ave PO Box 919 *Web:* www.hartzellhardwoods.com	Piqua	OH	45356	937-773-7054	773-6160
Hassell & Hughes Lumber Co PO Box 68	Collinwood	TN	38450	931-724-9191	724-4714
Hedstrom Lumber Co Inc 1504 Gunflint Trail *Web:* www.hedstromlumber.com	Grand Marais	MN	55604	218-387-2995	387-2204
Hoge Lumber Co 701 S Main St PO Box 159 *Web:* www.hoge.com	New Knoxville	OH	45871	419-753-2263	753-2963
Hunt Forest Products 401 E Reynolds Dr PO Box 1263 *TF:* 800-390-8589 ■ *Web:* www.huntforpro.com	Ruston	LA	71273	318-255-2245	255-4048
Idaho Timber Corp 1299 N Orchard St Suite 300 *Web:* www.idahotimber.com	Boise	ID	83706	208-377-3000	377-1470
Independence Lumber Inc 407 Lumber Ln *Web:* www.indlbr.com	Independence	VA	24348	276-773-3744	773-3723
Indian Country Inc 791 Airport Rd	Deposit	NY	13754	607-467-3801	467-4559
Indiana Hardwoods 7988 Gardner Rd *TF:* 800-925-3344 ■ *Web:* www.indiana-hardwoods.com	Chandler	IN	47610	812-925-3343	925-2064
Industrial Timber & Lumber Corp (ITL) 23925 Commerce Pk Rd *TF:* 800-829-9663 ■ *Web:* www.itlcorp.com	Beachwood	OH	44122	216-831-3140	831-4734
Jerry G Williams & Sons Inc 524 Brogden Rd PO Box 2430 *Web:* www.jerrygwilliamsandsons.com	Smithfield	NC	27577	919-934-4115	934-4956
Jordan Lumber & Supply Inc 1939 NC Hwy 109 S PO Box 98 *Web:* www.jordanlumber.com	Mount Gilead	NC	27306	910-439-6121	439-6105
JW Jones Lumber Co Inc 1443 Northside Rd	Elizabeth City	NC	27909	252-771-2497	771-8252
Keadle Lumber Enterprises Inc 889 Railroad St *Web:* www.keadlelumber.com	Thomaston	GA	30286	706-647-8981	647-1392
Keener Lumber Co Inc 1209 W Market St PO Box 2323	Smithfield	NC	27577	919-934-1087	934-9999
Kitchens Bros Mfg Co 601 Carpenter St PO Box 217	Utica	MS	39175	601-885-6001	885-8501
Langdale Forest Products Co 1202 Madison Hwy PO Box 1088 *TF:* 800-864-6909 ■ *Web:* www.langdaleforest.com	Valdosta	GA	31603	229-242-7450	333-2533
Lewisohn Sales Co Inc 4001 Dell Ave # 15 *TF:* 800-631-3196 ■ *Web:* www.lewisohn.com	North Bergen	NJ	07047	201-864-0300	864-1266
Louisiana-Pacific Corp 414 Union St Suite 2000 *NYSE: LPX* ■ *TF:* 877-744-5600 ■ *Web:* www.lpcorp.com	Nashville	TN	37219	615-986-5600	986-5666
Manke Lumber Co Inc 1717 Marine View Dr *TF:* 800-426-8488 ■ *Web:* www.mankelumber.com	Tacoma	WA	98422	253-572-6252	383-2489
Matson Lumber Co Inc 132 Main St *Web:* www.matsonlumber.com	Brookville	PA	15825	814-849-5334	849-3811
MC Dixon Lumber Co Inc 605 W Washington St	Eufaula	AL	36027	334-687-8204	687-8208
Menominee Tribal Enterprises PO Box 10 *Web:* www.mtewood.com	Neopit	WI	54150	715-756-2311	799-4323
Merritt Bros Lumber 5400 E Hwy 54 PO Box 190 *TF:* 800-488-3321 ■ *Web:* www.merrittbros.com	Athol	ID	83801	208-683-3321	683-3328
Midwest Hardwood Corp 9540 83rd Ave N *Web:* www.midwesthardwood.com	Maple Grove	MN	55369	763-425-8700	391-6740
Moose River Lumber Co Inc 25 Talpey Rd PO Box 454 *Web:* www.mooseriverlumber.com	Moose River	ME	04945	207-668-4193	668-5381
North Amercian Forest Products Inc PO Box 600 *Web:* www.nafpinc.com	Edwardsburg	MI	49112	269-663-8500	663-2073
Ochoco Lumber Co 200 SE Combs Flat Rd PO Box 668 *Web:* www.ochocolumber.com	Prineville	OR	97754	541-447-6296	447-8992
Oregon Canadian Forest Products Inc 31950 Comml St NW PO Box 279 *Web:* www.ocfp.com	North Plains	OR	97133	503-647-5011	647-0910
Parton Lumber Co Inc 251 Parton Rd *TF:* 800-624-1501 ■ *Web:* www.partonlumber.com	Rutherfordton	NC	28139	828-287-4257	287-3308
Pike Lumber Co Inc PO Box 247 *TF:* 800-356-4554 ■ *Web:* www.pikelumber.com	Akron	IN	46910	574-893-4511	893-7400
Plum Creek Timber Co Inc 999 3rd Ave Suite 4300 *NYSE: PCL* ■ *TF:* 800-858-5347 ■ *Web:* www.plumcreek.com	Seattle	WA	98104	206-467-3600	467-3795
Potlatch Corp 601 W 1st Ave Suite 1600 *NASDAQ: PCH* ■ *Web:* www.potlatchcorp.com	Spokane	WA	99201	509-835-1500	835-1555
Potlatch Corp Wood Products Div 805 Mill Rd PO Box 1388 *Web:* www.potlatchcorp.com	Lewiston	ID	83501	208-799-0123	799-1918
Pyramid Mountain Lumber Inc 379 Boy Scout Rd PO Box 549 *Web:* www.pyramidlumber.com	Seeley Lake	MT	59868	406-677-2201	677-2509
Rajala Cos PO Box 217 *Web:* www.rajalacos.com	Deer River	MN	56636	218-246-8277	246-2802
Riley Creek Lumber Co 30 Riley Creek Pk Dr *Web:* www.rileycreek.com	Laclede	ID	83841	208-263-7574	265-6530
Robbins Inc 4777 Eastern Ave *TF:* 800-543-1913 ■ *Web:* www.robbinsfloor.com	Cincinnati	OH	45226	513-871-8988	871-7998
Robbins Lumber Inc 53 Ghent Rd *TF:* 800-287-5067 ■ *Web:* www.rlco.com	Searsmont	ME	04973	207-342-5221	342-5201
Rogers Lumber Co Inc 937 Hwy 7 N	Camden	AR	71701	870-574-0231	574-1206
Rosboro Lumber Co 2509 Main St *Web:* www.rosboro.com	Springfield	OR	97477	541-746-8411	726-8919
Roseburg Forest Products Co PO Box 1088 *TF:* 800-548-5275 ■ *Web:* www.rfpco.com	Roseburg	OR	97470	541-679-3311	
RSG Forest Products Inc 985 NW 2nd St *Web:* www.rsgfp.com	Kalama	WA	98625	360-673-2825	673-5558
Rushmore Forest Products 23848 Hwy 385 PO Box 619 *TF:* 866-466-5254	Hill City	SD	57745	605-574-2512	574-4154
Scotch Lumber Co 119 W Main St PO Box 38 *TF:* 800-936-4424	Fulton	AL	36446	334-636-4424	636-7107
Scott Industries Inc 1573 Hwy 136 W PO Box 7 *TF:* 800-951-9276 ■ *Web:* www.scott-mfg.com	Henderson	KY	42419	270-831-2037	831-2039
Seattle Snohomish Mill Co Inc 9525 Airport Way PO Box 949 *Web:* www.sea-sno.com	Snohomish	WA	98291	360-568-2171	568-1778
Sierra Pacific Industries 19794 Riverside Ave *Web:* www.sierrapacificind.com	Anderson	CA	96007	530-378-8000	378-8109
Simpson Timber Co 917 E 11th St *Web:* www.simpson.com	Tacoma	WA	98421	253-779-6400	280-9000
Smith Flooring Inc 1501 W Hwy 60 PO Box 99 *Web:* www.smithflooring.com	Mountain View	MO	65548	417-934-2291	934-2295
South Coast Lumber Co 885 Railroad Ave PO Box 670 *Web:* www.socomi.com	Brookings	OR	97415	541-469-2136	469-9105
Stimson Lumber Co 520 SW Yamhill St Suite 700 *TF:* 800-445-9758 ■ *Web:* www.stimsonlumber.com	Portland	OR	97204	503-222-1676	295-1849
Swaner Hardwood Co Inc 5 W Magnolia Blvd PO Box 4200 *TF:* 800-368-1108 ■ *Web:* www.swanerhardwood.com	Burbank	CA	91503	818-953-5350	846-3662
Taylor-Ramsey Corp PO Box 11888 *TF:* 800-368-3036 ■ *Web:* www.taylorramsey.com	Lynchburg	VA	24506	434-929-7443	929-6162
Tembec Inc 800 Boul Rene Levesque O Bureau 1050 *TSX: TBC* ■ *Web:* www.tembec.com	Montreal	QC	H3B1X9	514-871-0137	397-0896
Tolleson Lumber Co Inc 903 Jernigan St *TF:* 800-768-2105 ■ *Web:* www.tollesonlumber.com	Perry	GA	31069	478-988-3800	987-0160
TR Miller Mill Co Inc 215 Deer St PO Box 708 *TF:* 800-633-6740 ■ *Web:* www.trmillermill.com	Brewton	AL	36427	251-867-4331	867-6882
Tucker Lumber Cos LLC 601 N Pearl St	Pageland	SC	29728	843-672-6135	672-5393
Universal Forest Products Inc (UFPI) 2801 E Beltline Ave NE *NASDAQ: UFPI* ■ *TF:* 800-598-9663 ■ *Web:* www.ufpi.com	Grand Rapids	MI	49525	616-364-6161	361-7534
Warm Springs Forest Products Industries Hwy 26 Bldg 3270 PO Box 810 *Web:* www.wsfpi.com	Warm Springs	OR	97761	541-553-1148	553-1561
Welco Lumber Co Kkookum Div 780 W Hwy 108 **Fax:* Sales ■ *Web:* www.welcolumberusa.com	Shelton	WA	98584	360-426-9721	426-1935*
West Fraser Timber Co Ltd (WFT) 501-858 Beatty St Suite 501 *TSE: WFT* ■ *Web:* www.westfraser.com	Vancouver	BC	V6B1C1	604-895-2700	681-6061
Westervelt Co Inc PO Box 48999 **Fax:* Sales ■ *Web:* www.westervelt.com	Tuscaloosa	AL	35404	205-562-5000	562-5012*
Weyerhaeuser Canada Ltd 925 W Georgia St	Vancouver	BC	V6C3L2	604-661-8000	
Weyerhaeuser Co 33663 Weyerhaeuser Way S *NYSE: WY* ■ *TF:* 800-525-5440 ■ *Web:* www.weyerhaeuser.com	Federal Way	WA	98003	253-924-2345	924-2685

687 SCALES & BALANCES

SEE ALSO Laboratory Apparatus & Furniture p. 2142

Name / Address	City	State	Zip	Phone	Fax
Avery Weigh-Tronix Inc 1000 Armstrong Dr	Fairmont	MN	56031	507-238-4461	238-8258*
*Fax: Mktg ■ TF: 800-533-0456 ■ Web: www.wtxweb.com					
BRK Brands Inc 3901 Liberty St Rd	Aurora	IL	60504	630-851-7330	851-9015
TF: 800-323-9005 ■ Web: www.firstalert.com					
Cardinal Detecto Scale Mfg Co 203 E Daugherty St	Webb City	MO	64870	417-673-4631	673-5001
TF: 800-641-2008 ■ Web: www.cardet.com					
Detecto Scale Co 203 E Daugherty St PO Box 151	Webb City	MO	64870	417-673-4631	673-4631
TF: 800-641-2008 ■ Web: www.detecto.com					
Emery Winslow Scale Co 73 Cogwheel Ln	Seymour	CT	06483	203-881-9333	881-9477
Web: www.emerywinslow.com					
Fairbanks Scales Inc 821 Locust St	Kansas City	MO	64106	816-471-0231	471-0241
TF: 800-451-4107 ■ Web: www.fairbanks.com					
Industrial Data Systems Inc 3822 E La Palma Ave	Anaheim	CA	92807	714-921-9212	399-0286
TF: 800-854-3311 ■ Web: www.industrialdata.com					
Intercomp Co 3839 County Rd 116	Medina	MN	55340	763-476-2531	476-2613
TF: 800-328-3336 ■ Web: www.intercompco.com					
Johnson Scale Co 235 Fairfield Ave	West Caldwell	NJ	07006	973-226-2100	882-8068
TF: 800-572-2531 ■ Web: www.johnsonscale.com					
Measurement Specialties Inc 1000 Lucas Way	Hampton	VA	23666	757-766-1500	766-4297
NASDAQ: MEAS ■ TF: 800-236-6746 ■ Web: www.meas-spec.com					
Merrick Industries Inc 10 Arthur Dr	Lynn Haven	FL	32444	850-265-3611	265-9768*
*Fax: Hum Res ■ TF: 800-345-8440 ■ Web: www.merrick-inc.com					
Mettler-Toledo Hi-Speed Inc 5 Barr Rd	Ithaca	NY	14850	607-257-6000	266-5478
Web: www.hispeedcheckweigher.com					
Ohaus Corp 19-A Chapin Rd PO Box 2033	Pine Brook	NJ	07058	973-377-9000	944-7177
TF: 800-672-7722 ■ Web: www.ohaus.com					
Pennsylvania Scale Co 1042 New Holland Ave	Lancaster	PA	17601	717-295-6911	768-6350*
*Fax Area Code: 800 ■ TF: 800-233-0473 ■					
Web: www.temp.pennsylvaniascalecompanynet.officelive.com/default.aspx					
Premier Tech Industrial Equipment Group 1 Premier Ave	Rivere-du-Loup	QC	G5R6C1	418-867-8884	862-6642
Web: www.premiertechchronos.com					
Rice Lake Weighing Systems 230 W Coleman St	Rice Lake	WI	54868	715-234-9171	234-6967
TF: 800-472-6703					
Scale-Tronix Inc 200 E Post Rd	White Plains	NY	10601	914-948-8117	948-0581
TF: 800-873-2001 ■ Web: www.scale-tronix.com					
Schenck Trebel Corp 535 Acorn St	Deer Park	NY	11729	631-242-4010	242-5077
TF: 800-873-2357 ■ Web: www.schenck-usa.com					
Scientech Inc 5649 Arapahoe Ave	Boulder	CO	80303	303-444-1361	444-9229
TF: 800-525-0522 ■ Web: www.scientech-inc.com					
Setra Systems Inc 159 Swanson Rd	Boxborough	MA	01719	978-263-1400	264-0292
TF: 800-257-3872 ■ Web: www.setra.com					
Sunbeam Products Inc 2381 Executive Ctr Dr	Boca Raton	FL	33431	561-912-4100	912-4567
Web: www.sunbeam.com					
Tanita Corp of America Inc 2625 S Clearbrook Dr	Arlington Heights	IL	60005	847-640-9241	640-9261
Web: www.tanita.com					
TCI Scales 4208 Russell Rd Unit E	Mukilteo	WA	98275	425-353-4384	347-5845
TF: 800-522-2206 ■ Web: www.tciscales.com					
Thayer Scale Corp 91 Schoosett St	Pembroke	MA	02359	781-826-8101	826-0072*
*Fax: Cust Svc ■ TF: 800-225-0450 ■ Web: www.thayerscale.com					
Toroid Corp 225 Wynn Dr NW	Huntsville	AL	35805	256-837-7510	837-7512
Wisconsin Electrical Mfg Co Inc 2501 S Moorland Rd	New Berlin	WI	53151	262-782-2340	782-2653
Web: www.yamatocorp.com					
Yamato Corp 1775 S Murray Blvd	Colorado Springs	CO	80916	719-591-1500	591-1045
TF: 800-538-1762 ■ Web: www.yamatocorp.com					

688 SCHOOL BOARDS (PUBLIC)

Name / Address	City	State	Zip	Phone	Fax
A.C. White Transfer & Storage Co Inc 1775 Founders Pkwy	Alpharetta	GA	30009	770-325-9100	325-9180
Abbeville County School District 60 400 Greenville St	Abbeville	SC	29620	864-366-5427	
Web: www.acsd.k12.sc.us					
Aberdeen School District 5 216 N G St	Aberdeen	WA	98520	360-538-2000	
TF: 866-400-9275 ■ Web: www.asd5.org					
Acalanes Union High School Dist 1212 Pleasant Hill Rd	Lafayette	CA	94549	925-280-3900	932-2336
Web: www.acalanes.k12.ca.us					
Adair County Board of Education 1204 Greensburg St	Columbia	KY	42728	270-384-2476	
TF: 866-213-8739 ■ Web: www.adair.k12.ky.us					
Adams County School District 50 6933 Raleigh St	Westminster	CO	80030	303-428-3511	
Web: www.adams50.org					
Airport Community Schools 11270 Grafton Rd	Carleton	MI	48117	734-654-2414	654-3424
Web: www.acspublic.com					
Akron Public Schools 70 N Broadway Ave	Akron	OH	44308	330-761-1661	761-3225
Web: www.akronschools.com					
Alamance-Burlington School District 1712 Vaughn Rd	Burlington	NC	27217	336-570-6060	570-6218
Web: www.abss.k12.nc.us					
Albuquerque Public Schools (APS) 6400 Uptown Blvd NE	Albuquerque	NM	87110	505-880-3700	889-4883*
*Fax: Hum Res ■ Web: www.aps.edu					
Alisal Union Elementary School District 1205 E Market St	Salinas	CA	93905	831-753-5700	753-5702
Web: www.alisal.org					
Allegheny Valley School District 300 PEARL Ave	Cheswick	PA	15024	724-274-5300	274-8040
Web: www.avsd.k12.pa.us					
Allentown School District (ASD) 31 S Penn St	Allentown	PA	18105	484-765-4000	765-4140
Web: www.allentownsd.org					
Alpena Public Schools (inc) 2373 Gordon Rd	Alpena	MI	49707	989-358-5040	358-5041
Web: www.alpenaschools.com					
Alta Loma School District 9390 Baseline Rd	Alta Loma	CA	91701	909-484-5151	484-5195
Web: www.alsd.k12.ca.us					
Amador County Unified School District 217 Rex Ave	Jackson	CA	95642	209-223-1750	
Web: www.amadorcoe.org					
Amarillo Independent School District (AISD) 7200 I- 40 W	Amarillo	TX	79106	806-326-1000	354-4378*
*Fax: Hum Res ■ Web: www.amaisd.org					
American Quality Schools Corp 850 W Jackson Blvd	Chicago	IL	60607	312-226-3355	
Web: www.aqs.org					
Ames Community School District 415 Stanton Ave	Ames	IA	50014	515-268-6600	268-6633
TF: 800-798-4205 ■ Web: www.ames.k12.ia.us					
Anaheim City School District - Capital Facilities Corp 1001 S E St	Anaheim	CA	92805	714-517-7500	
Web: www.acsd.k12.ca.us					
Anaheim Union High School District PO Box 3520	Anaheim	CA	92803	714-999-3511	520-9752
Web: www.auhsd.k12.ca.us					
Anchor Bay School District 5201 County Line Rd Suite 100	Casco Twp	MI	48064	586-725-2861	725-0290
Web: www.anchorbay.misd.net					
Anchorage School District 3580 E Tudor Rd	Anchorage	AK	99507	907-742-4000	742-4176
Web: www.asdk12.org					
Anderson County Board of Education 103 N Main St	Lawrenceburg	KY	40342	502-839-3406	839-2501
TF: 866-425-7991 ■ Web: www.anderson.k12.ky.us					
Anoka-Hennepin Independent School District 11 11299 Hanson Blvd NW	Coon Rapids	MN	55433	763-506-1000	506-1003
Web: www.anoka.k12.mn.us					
Anthony Wayne Board of Education PO Box 2487	Whitehouse	OH	43571	419-877-5377	
Web: www.anthonywayneschools.org					
Apollo-Ridge School District PO Box 219	Spring Church	PA	15686	724-478-1141	
Web: www.apolloridge.com					
Apple Valley Unified School District (AVUSD) 12555 Navajo Rd	Apple Valley	CA	92308	760-247-8001	
Web: www.avusd.org					
Appling County Board of Education 249 Blackshear Hwy	Baxley	GA	31513	912-367-8600	
TF: 866-632-9992 ■ Web: www.appling.k12.ga.us					
Archway Programs Inc PO Box 668	Atco	NJ	08004	856-767-5757	
Web: www.archwayprograms.org					
Arlington Central School District 696 Dutchess Tpke	Poughkeepsie	NY	12603	845-486-4460	486-4457
TF: 800-808-1987 ■ Web: www.arlingtonschools.org					
Arlington School District 315 N French Ave	Arlington	WA	98223	360-618-6200	618-6221
TF: 888-535-0747 ■ Web: www.asd.wednet.edu					
Armstrong School District 410 Main St	Ford City	PA	16226	724-763-5200	763-7295
TF: 888-573-5733 ■ Web: www.asd.k12.pa.us					
Ashland Independent School District PO Box 3000	Ashland	KY	41105	606-327-2706	327-2705
TF: 800-752-6200 ■ Web: www.ashland.kyschools.us					
Ashtabula Area City School District PO Box 290	Ashtabula	OH	44005	440-993-2500	993-2626
Web: www.aacs.net					
Ashwaubenon School District 1055 Griffiths Ln	Green Bay	WI	54304	920-492-2900	492-2911
Web: www.ashwaubenon.k12.wi.us					
Athens City School District 25 S Plains Rd	The Plains	OH	45780	740-797-4544	
Web: www.athenscity.k12.oh.us					
Atkinson County School System 98 Roberts Ave E	Pearson	GA	31642	912-422-7373	422-7369
Web: www.atkinson.k12.ga.us					
Atlanta Public Schools 130 Trinity Ave SW	Atlanta	GA	30303	404-802-3500	802-1803
Web: www.atlanta.k12.ga.us					
Au Authum Ki Inc 665 E Morelos St Suite 101	Chandler	AZ	85225	480-497-1997	377-1143
Web: www.authumki.com					
Auburn City School District PO Box 3270	Auburn	AL	36831	334-887-2100	887-2107
TF: 866-277-9644 ■ Web: www.auburnschools.org					
Auburn Union School District 55 College Way	Auburn	CA	95603	530-885-7242	885-5170
Web: www.auburn.k12.ca.us					
Austin Independent School District 1111 W 6th St	Austin	TX	78703	512-414-1700	414-1486
Web: www.austin.isd.tenet.edu					
Avonworth School District 258 Josephs Ln	Pittsburgh	PA	15237	412-369-8738	369-8746
Web: www.avonworth.k12.pa.us					
Axis Construction Corp 125 Laser Ct	Hauppauge	NY	11788	631-243-5970	243-5973
Web: www.theaxisgroup.com					
B C C S Inc 1711 Dell Ave	Campbell	CA	95008	408-379-5500	379-3256
Web: www.sbci.com					
B.T. Trucking Inc 2600 S 25th Ave Suite K	Broadview	IL	60155	708-343-1598	343-6748
TF: 800-852-3183 ■ Web: www.bttrucking.com					
Bakersfield City School District 1300 Baker St	Bakersfield	CA	93305	661-631-4600	326-1485
Web: www.bcsd.com					
Baltimore City Public Schools 200 E N Ave	Baltimore	MD	21202	443-984-2000	545-0897*
*Fax Area Code: 410 ■ Web: www.baltimorecityschools.org					
Bank of Highland Park Financial Corp 1835 1st St PO Box 546	Highland Park	IL	60035	847-432-7800	433-2150
Web: www.firstbankhp.com					
Banks County Board of Education PO Box 248	Homer	GA	30547	706-677-2224	
Web: www.banks.k12.ga.us					

Name / Address	City	State	ZIP	Phone	Fax
Barbers Hill Isd (BHISD) 9600 Eagle Dr PO Box 1108 *Web:* www.bhisd.net	Mont Belvieu	TX	77580	281-576-2221	
Barberton City School District 479 Norton Ave. *Web:* www.barbertonschools.org	Barberton	OH	44203	330-753-1025	848-0884
Barnard & Sons Construction LLC 3054 Simpson Hwy 13 PO Box 517 *Web:* www.barnardandsons.com	Mendenhall	MS	39114	601-847-2420	847-0110
Barney Trucking Inc 235 SR- 24 *NYSE: BT* ■ **Fax Area Code: 435* ■ *Web:* www.barneytrucking.com	Salina	UT	84654	800-524-7930	529-7314*
Bath Central School District 25 Ellis Ave *Web:* www.bathcsd.org	Bath	NY	14810	607-776-3301	
Bay City Public Schools 910 N Walnut St *Web:* www.bcschools.net	Bay City	MI	48706	989-686-9700	686-7626
Beam Construction Co Inc 601 E Main St *Web:* www.beamconstruction.com	Cherryville	NC	28021	704-435-3206	435-8412
Beaufort County Board of Education 321 Smaw Rd *Web:* www.beaufort.k12.nc.us	Washington	NC	27889	252-946-6593	
Beaver Area School District 855 2nd St *Web:* www.basd.k12.pa.us	Beaver	PA	15009	724-774-0250	774-8770
Beavercreek Board of Education 3040 Kemp Rd *Web:* www.beavercreek.k12.oh.us	Dayton	OH	45431	937-426-1522	429-7517
Bedford Public Schools 1623 W Sterns Rd *Web:* www.bedford.k12.mi.us	Temperance	MI	48182	734-850-6000	850-6099
Beemac Trucking LLC 2747 Litionville Rd *TF:* 800-282-8781 ■ *Web:* www.beemac.com	Ambridge	PA	15003	724-266-8781	266-5638
Bellefonte Area School District 318 N Allegheny St *TF:* 866-632-9992 ■ *Web:* www.basd.net	Bellefonte	PA	16823	814-355-4814	
Belton School District 110 W Walnut St *Web:* www.beltonschools.org	Belton	MO	64012	816-348-1000	348-1068
Bemidji Ind School District 31 3300 Gillett Dr NW *Web:* www.bemidji.k12.mn.us	Bemidji	MN	56601	218-333-3110	
Berea City School District 390 Fair St *Web:* www.berea.k12.oh.us	Berea	OH	44017	216-898-8300	898-8551
Bernards Township Board of Education 101 Peachtree Rd *Web:* www.bernardsboe.com	Basking Ridge	NJ	07920	908-204-2600	
Bettendorf Community School District 800 23rd St *Web:* www.bettendorf.k12.ia.us	Bettendorf	IA	52722	563-359-3681	359-3685
Beverly Hills Unified School District 255 S Lasky Dr *Web:* www.beverlyhills.k12.ca.us	Beverly Hills	CA	90212	310-551-5100	277-6137
Bexley City School District 348 S Cassingham Rd *TF:* 866-800-1404 ■ *Web:* www.bexleyschools.org	Columbus	OH	43209	614-231-7611	
Big Spring Independent School District 708 E 11th Pl *Web:* www.bsisd.esc18.net	Big Spring	TX	79720	432-264-3600	264-3646
Biltmore Construction Co Inc 1055 Ponce De Leon Blvd *Web:* www.biltmoreconstruction.com	Belleair	FL	33756	727-585-2084	585-2088
Binghamton City School District (BCSD) 164 Hawley St PO Box 2126 *Web:* www.binghamtonschools.org	Binghamton	NY	13902	607-762-8100	
Birmingham City Schools (BCS) 2015 Pk Pl N *Web:* www.birmingham.schoolinsites.com	Birmingham	AL	35203	205-231-4600	231-4761
Black Horse Pike Regional School District 580 Erial Rd *Web:* www.bhprsd.org	Blackwood	NJ	08012	856-227-4105	227-6835
Blackfoot School District 55 270 E Bridge St *Web:* www.d55.k12.id.us	Blackfoot	ID	83221	208-785-8800	785-8809
Blast Intermediate Unit 17 2400 Reach Rd *Web:* www.iu17.org	Williamsport	PA	17701	570-323-8561	
Blue Mountain School District Inc PO Box 188 *Web:* www.bmsd.org	Orwigsburg	PA	17961	570-366-0515	
Boarder to Boarder Trucking Inc PO Box 328 *TF:* 800-678-8789 ■ *Web:* www.btbtrucking.com	Edinburg	TX	78541	956-316-4444	316-4445
Boise City Independent School District 8169 W Victory Rd *Web:* www.sd01.k12.id.us	Boise	ID	83709	208-854-4000	854-4003
Borton Lc 200 E 1st Ave *Web:* www.borton.biz	Hutchinson	KS	67501	620-669-8211	662-3225
Boston Public Schools 26 Ct St *Web:* www.bostonpublicschools.org	Boston	MA	02108	617-635-9000	635-9059
Bowling Green City Schools (BGCS) 137 Clough St *Web:* www.bgcs.k12.oh.us	Bowling Green	OH	43402	419-352-3576	352-1701
Bowling Green Independent School District 1211 Ctr St *Web:* www.b-g.k12.ky.us	Bowling Green	KY	42101	270-746-2200	
Bozeman School District 7 PO Box 520 *Web:* www.bsd7.org	Bozeman	MT	59771	406-522-6000	
Bradford Area School District Inc PO Box 375 *Web:* www.bradfordareaschools.org	Bradford	PA	16701	814-362-3841	
Breckinridge County School District 86 Airport Rd *TF:* 877-832-2457 ■ *Web:* www.breck.k12.ky.us	Hardinsburg	KY	40143	270-756-2186	
Brecksville Broadview Hts Csd 6638 Mill Rd *Web:* www.bbhcsd.org	Brecksville	OH	44141	440-526-4370	740-4004
Brentwood School 100 S Barrington Pl *Web:* www.bwscampus.com	Los Angeles	CA	90049	310-476-9633	476-4087
Bristol-Warren Regional School District 151 State St *Web:* www.bw.k12.ri.us	Bristol	RI	02809	401-253-4000	
Brookhaven School District PO Box 540 *Web:* www.brookhaven.k12.ms.us	Brookhaven	MS	39602	601-833-6661	833-4154
Broward County Public Schools 600 SE 3rd Ave *Web:* www.browardschools.com	Fort Lauderdale	FL	33301	754-321-0000	321-2701
Browning School Inc 52 E 62nd St *Web:* www.browning.edu	New York	NY	10065	212-838-6280	355-5602
Brownsville Area School Dist 1025 Lewis St *Web:* www.basd.org	Brownsville	PA	15417	724-785-2021	785-4333
Brownsville Independent School District 1900 E Price Rd *Web:* www.bisd.us	Brownsville	TX	78521	956-548-8000	548-8019
Brunswick City School District 3643 Ctr Rd *Web:* www.bcsoh.org	Brunswick	OH	44212	330-225-7731	273-0507
Brunswick County Board of Education 35 Referendum Dr *Web:* www.bcswan.net	Bolivia	NC	28422	910-253-2900	253-2983
Buckingham Browne & Nichols School 46 Belmont St *Web:* www.bbns.org	Watertown	MA	02472	617-800-2700	
Buckley School The 3900 Stansbury Ave *Web:* www.buckleyla.org	Sherman Oaks	CA	91413	818-783-1610	461-6714
Buffalo City School District 712 City Hall *Web:* www.buffaloschools.org	Buffalo	NY	14202	716-816-3500	851-3535
Bulloch County Board of Education 150 Williams Rd Suite A *Web:* www.bulloch.k12.ga.us	Statesboro	GA	30458	912-764-6201	764-8436
Bullock Creek Public Schools 1420 S Badour Rd *TF:* 877-706-2508 ■ *Web:* www.bcreek.k12.mi.us	Midland	MI	48640	989-631-9022	631-2882
Burke County Public Schools 789 Burke Veterans Pkwy *Web:* www.burke.k12.ga.us	Waynesboro	GA	30830	706-554-5101	554-8051
Butler Area School District 110 Campus Ln *Web:* www.butlerk12.com	Butler	PA	16001	724-287-8721	287-1802
Butler County Board of Education 215 Administrative Dr *Web:* www.butlerco.k12.al.us	Greenville	AL	36037	334-382-2665	
Butts County Board of Education 181 N Mulberry St *Web:* www.butts.k12.ga.us	Jackson	GA	30233	770-504-2300	504-2305
Byron Center Public Schools 2475 84th St SW *Web:* www.bcpsk12.net	Byron Center	MI	49315	616-878-6100	
Cabarrus County School District 4401 Old Airport Rd *Web:* www.ccsweb.cabarrus.k12.nc.us	Concord	NC	28025	704-786-6191	786-6141
Cabrillo Unified School District 498 Kelly Ave *Web:* www.cabrillo.k12.ca.us	Half Moon Bay	CA	94019	650-712-7100	726-0279
Cache County School District 2063 N 1200 E *Web:* www.ccsdut.org	N Logan	UT	84341	435-752-3925	753-2168
Caddo Parish School Board 1961 Midway Ave PO Box 32000 **Fax:* Hum Res ■ *Web:* www.caddo.k12.la.us	Shreveport	LA	71130	318-603-6300	603-6559*
Calhoun County Board of Education PO Box 2084 *Web:* www.calhoun.k12.al.us	Anniston	AL	36202	256-741-7400	237-5332
Calhoun School Inc The 160 W 74th St *Web:* www.calhoun.org	New York	NY	10023	212-497-6500	721-2025
Camden Central School District 51 3rd St *Web:* www.camdenschools.org	Camden	NY	13316	315-245-2500	
Campbell County Board of Education 101 Orchard Ln *TF:* 800-942-3767 ■ *Web:* www.campbellcountyschools.org	Alexandria	KY	41001	859-635-2173	448-2428
Campbell County Dept of Education PO Box 843 *Web:* www.campbell.k12.tn.us	Jacksboro	TN	37757	423-562-8377	566-7562
Campbell Union High School District 3235 Union Ave *Web:* www.cuhsd.org	San Jose	CA	95124	408-371-0960	
Campbell Union School District 155 N 3rd St *Web:* www.campbellusd.org	Campbell	CA	95008	408-364-4200	
Canandaigua City School District 143 N Pearl St *Web:* www.canandaiguaschools.org	Canandaigua	NY	14424	585-396-3700	
Canby School District 1130 S Ivy St *Web:* www.canby.k12.or.us	Canby	OR	97013	503-266-7861	266-0022
Canton Public School District 403 Lincoln St *Web:* www.cantonschools.net	Canton	MS	39046	601-859-4110	
Carlisle Carrier Corp PO Box 1549 *TF:* 800-628-7807 ■ *Web:* www.carlislecarrier.com	Mechanicsburg	PA	17055	717-691-8600	691-8559
Carlynton School District 435 Kings Hwy *Web:* www.carlynton.k12.pa.us	Carnegie	PA	15106	412-429-8400	
Cartersville School Board PO Box 3310 *Web:* www.cartersville.k12.ga.us	Cartersville	GA	30120	770-382-3666	
Centennial Independent School District No 12 4707 N Rd *Web:* www.centennial.k12.mn.us	Circle Pines	MN	55014	763-792-5000	
Centennial School District 18135 SE Brooklyn *Web:* www.centennial.k12.or.us	Portland	OR	97236	503-760-7990	762-3689
Centennial School District 433 Centennial Rd *Web:* www.centennialsd.org	Warminster	PA	18974	215-441-6000	441-5105
Center Independent School Dist 404 Mosby St *Web:* www.centerisd.org	Center	TX	75935	936-598-5642	
Central Islip Union Free School District 13 PO Box 9027 *TF:* 888-333-4988 ■ *Web:* www.centralislip.k12.ny.us	Central Islip	NY	11722	631-348-5112	348-0366

Name / Address	City	State	ZIP	Phone	Fax
Central Montcalm Public School 1480 S Sheridan Rd *Web:* www.central-montcalm.org	Stanton	MI	48888	989-831-5243	831-5580
Central Union High School District 351 W Ross Ave *Web:* www.cuhsd.net	El Centro	CA	92243	760-336-4500	353-3606
Chambers County School District 1298 Vocational Dr Po Box 408 *Web:* www.chambersk12.org	Lafayette	AL	36862	334-864-9343	864-0119
Champion Construction Corp 941 Forest Ave *Web:* www.championcc.homestead.com	Staten Island	NY	10310	718-818-8202	818-8238
Chariho Regional School District 455 Switch Rd *Web:* www.chariho.k12.ri.us	Wood River Junction	RI	02894	401-364-7575	415-6076
Charleston County School District (CCSD) 75 Calhoun St *Web:* www.ccsdschools.com	Charleston	SC	29401	843-937-6300	937-6300
Charlevoix Public Schools 104 E Saint Marys Dr *Web:* www.rayder.net	Charlevoix	MI	49720	231-547-3200	547-0556
Charlotte-Mecklenburg Schools 701 E ML King Jr Blvd *Web:* www.cms.k12.nc.us	Charlotte	NC	28202	980-343-3000	343-5661
Chatham Central School District 50 Woodbridge Ave *Web:* www.chathamcentralschools.com	Chatham	NY	12037	518-392-2400	
Cherokee County Board of Education PO Box 769 *TF:* 866-750-1367 ■ *Web:* www.cherokee.k12.ga.us	Canton	GA	30169	770-479-1871	
Cherokee County School District 1 PO Box 460 *Web:* www.cherokee1.k12.sc.us	Gaffney	SC	29342	864-902-3500	
Chester County School District 109 Hinton St *Web:* www.chester.k12.sc.us	Chester	SC	29706	803-385-6122	
Chicago Board of Education 125 S Clark St 6th Fl *Web:* www.cps.edu/about_cps/Pages/AboutCPS.aspx	Chicago	IL	60603	773-553-1600	553-1601
Chichester School District Inc PO Box 2100 *Web:* www.chichestersd.org	Boothwyn	PA	19061	610-485-6881	
Chico Unified School District 1163 E 7th St *Web:* www.chicousd.org	Chico	CA	95928	530-891-3000	891-3220
Christian County Public Schools 200 Glass Ave PO Box 609 *Web:* www.christian.kyschools.us	Hopkinsville	KY	42240	270-887-7000	887-1316
Churchill County School District 545 E Richards St *Web:* www.churchill.k12.nv.us	Fallon	NV	89406	775-423-5184	423-2959
Cincinnati Public Schools 2651 Burnet Ave PO Box 5381 *Web:* www.cpsboe.k12.oh.us	Cincinnati	OH	45201	513-363-0123	363-0055
Circleville City School District 388 Clark Dr *Web:* www.circlevillecityschools.org	Circleville	OH	43113	740-474-4340	474-6600
Citrus County School District 1007 W Main St *Web:* www.citrus.k12.fl.us	Inverness	FL	34450	352-726-1931	
Claiborne Parish School Board PO Box 600 *Web:* www.clairbornepsb.org	Homer	LA	71040	318-927-3502	
Clark County School District (CCSD) 5100 W Sahara Ave *Web:* www.ccsd.net	Las Vegas	NV	89146	702-799-5000	799-5125
Cleveland Municipal School District (CMSD) 1380 E 6th St *Fax: Hum Res ■ *Web:* www.cmsdnet.net	Cleveland	OH	44114	216-574-8500	574-8072*
Clinton Public School District PO Box 300 *Web:* www.clintonpublicschools.com	Clinton	MS	39060	601-924-7533	
Clio Area School District 430 N Mill St *TF:* 800-815-8477 ■ *Web:* www.clioschools.org	Clio	MI	48420	810-591-0500	
Clovis Unified School District 1450 Herndon Ave *Web:* www.cusd.com	Clovis	CA	93611	559-327-9000	327-9109
Clyde's Transfer Inc 8015 Industrial Park Rd *TF:* 800-342-8758 ■ *Web:* www.clydestransferinc.com	Mechanicsville	VA	23116	804-746-1135	746-8898
Coachella Valley Unified School District PO Box 847 *Web:* www.coachella.k12.ca.us	Thermal	CA	92274	760-399-5137	
Cobleskill-Richmondville Central School District 155 Washington Ave *Web:* www.crcs.k12.ny.us	Cobleskill	NY	12043	518-234-4032	
Cogun Inc 11369 Market St PO Box 704 *TF:* 800-258-5540 ■ *Web:* www.cogun.com	North Lima	OH	44452	330-549-5321	549-5328
Coil Construction Inc 209 E Broadway *Web:* www.coilconstruction.com	Columbia	MO	65203	573-874-1444	443-3039
Coldwater Community Schools 401 Sauk River Dr *Web:* www.coldwaterschools.org	Coldwater	MI	49036	517-279-5910	279-7651
Collier County School Board 5775 Osceola Trail *Web:* www.collier.k12.fl.us	Naples	FL	34109	239-377-0001	377-0336
Colorado Springs School District #11 1115 N El Paso St *Web:* www.cssd11.k12.co.us	Colorado Springs	CO	80903	719-520-2000	577-4546
Columbus City Schools 270 E State St *Web:* www.columbus.k12.oh.us	Columbus	OH	43215	614-365-5000	365-5652
Columbus County Schools PO Box 729 *Web:* www.columbus.k12.nc.us	Whiteville	NC	28472	910-642-5168	640-1010
Community High School District 99 6301 Springside Ave *Web:* www.csd99.org	Downers Grove	IL	60516	630-795-7100	
Community Unit School District 200 130 W Pk Ave *Web:* www.cusd200.org	Wheaton	IL	60189	630-682-2000	682-2227
Conestoga Valley School District 2110 Horseshoe Rd *Web:* www.cvsd.k12.pa.us	Lancaster	PA	17601	717-397-2421	397-0442
Conneaut School District 219 W School Dr *Web:* www.iu5.org	Linesville	PA	16424	814-683-5900	
Continental Development Corp 2041 Rosecrans Ave Suite 200 PO Box 916 *Web:* www.continentaldevelopment.com	El Segundo	CA	90245	310-640-1520	414-9279
Copperas Cove Independent School District 703 W Ave D *TF:* 866-632-9992 ■ *Web:* www.ccisd.com	Copperas Cove	TX	76522	254-547-1227	
Cornwall Lebanon School District 105 E Evergreen Rd *Web:* www.clsd.k12.pa.us	Lebanon	PA	17042	717-272-2031	274-2786
Corona-Norco Unified School District 2820 Clark Ave *Web:* www.cnusd.k12.ca.us	Norco	CA	92860	951-736-5000	
Corunna Public School District 124 N Shiawassee St *TF:* 866-632-9992 ■ *Web:* www.corunna.k12.mi.us	Corunna	MI	48817	989-743-6338	743-4474
Council Rock School District 30 N Chancellor St *Web:* www.crsd.org	Newtown	PA	18940	215-944-1000	
Cranford Board of Education (inc) 132 Thomas St *TF:* 877-900-6960 ■ *Web:* www.cranfordschools.org	Cranford	NJ	07016	908-272-9100	
Craven County School (CCS) 3600 Trent Rd *Web:* www.craven.k12.nc.us	New Bern	NC	28562	252-514-6300	514-6351
Crawford Ausable School District 1135 N Old 27 *Web:* www.casdk12.net	Grayling	MI	49738	989-344-3500	
Crawford Central School District 11280 Mercer Pike *Web:* www.craw.org	Meadville	PA	16335	814-724-3960	
Crawford County School District PO Box 8 *Web:* www.crawford.k12.ga.us	Roberta	GA	31078	478-836-3131	
Creative Contractors Inc 620 Drew St *Web:* www.creativecontractors.com	Clearwater	FL	33755	727-461-5522	447-4808
Crete-monee School District No 201-u 1500 S Sangamon St *Web:* www.cm201u.org	Crete	IL	60417	708-367-8300	
Crisp County Board of Education 201 7th St S PO Box 729 *Web:* www.crispcountyschools.org	Cordele	GA	31015	229-276-3400	276-3406
Crosby Independent School District 101906 14670 F.M.2100 PO Box 2009 *Web:* www.crosbyisd.org	Crosby	TX	77532	281-328-9247	328-9375
Crossroads School For Arts & Sciences 1714 21st St *Web:* www.xrds.org	Santa Monica	CA	90404	310-829-7391	828-5636
Cuba Rushford Central School 5476 Rt 305 *Web:* www.crcs.wnyric.org	Cuba	NY	14727	585-968-2650	968-2651
Cullman County Board of Education PO Box 1590 *Web:* www.ccboe.org	Cullman	AL	35056	256-734-2933	
Culver City Unified School District (CCUSD) 4034 Irving Pl *Web:* www.ccusd.org	Culver City	CA	90232	310-842-4220	842-4205
Cunningham-Limp Co 39300 W 12 Mile Rd Suite 200 *Web:* www.cunninghamlimp.com	Farmington Hills	MI	48331	248-489-2300	489-2310
Cupertino Union School District 10301 Vista Dr *Web:* www.cupertino.k12.ca.us	Cupertino	CA	95014	408-252-3000	253-8119
Currituck County Board of Education Hwy 168 *Web:* www.currituck.k12.nc.us	Currituck	NC	27929	252-232-2223	
Cypress-Fairbanks Independent School District PO Box 692003 *Web:* www.cfisd.net	Houston	TX	77269	281-897-4000	
D & T Trucking Inc 11530 Hudson Blvd N *Web:* www.dttruck.com	Lake Elmo	MN	55042	800-328-0858	
Dallas Center - Grimes Community School District 1414 Walnut St, Suite 200 PO Box 512 *Web:* www.dcgschools.com	Dallas Center	IA	50063	515-992-3866	992-3079
Dallas County Exchange Inc PO Box 1056 *Web:* www.dallask12.org	Selma	AL	36702	334-875-3440	
Dallas Independent School District 3700 Ross Ave *Web:* www.dallasisd.org	Dallas	TX	75204	972-925-3700	925-4201
Dallastown Area School District 700 New School Ln *Web:* www.dallastown.net	Dallastown	PA	17313	717-244-4021	
Dalton Public Schools 300 W Waugh St PO Box 1408 *Web:* www.daltonpublicschools.com	Dalton	GA	30722	706-278-8766	226-4583
Dassel-Cokato Public Schools PO Box 1700 *Web:* www.dc.k12.mn.us	Cokato	MN	55321	320-286-4100	
Davie County Schools 220 Cherry St *Web:* www.davie.k12.nc.us	Mocksville	NC	27028	336-751-5921	751-9013
Dawson County Board of Education The 517 Allen St *Web:* www.dawsoncountyschools.org	Dawsonville	GA	30534	706-265-3246	265-1226
Dayton City Schools 115 S Ludlow St *Web:* www.dps.k12.oh.us	Dayton	OH	45402	937-542-3000	542-3188
De Soto Public School District 73 610 Vineland School Rd *Web:* www.desoto.k12.mo.us	De Soto	MO	63020	636-586-1000	
Del Mar Union School District 225 9th St *Web:* district.dmusd.org	Del Mar	CA	92014	858-755-9301	755-4361
Delano Union School District 1405 12th Ave *Web:* www.duesd.org	Delano	CA	93215	661-721-5000	725-2446

	City	State	ZIP	Phone	Fax
Delaware City School District 248 N Washington St *Web:* www.dcs.k12.oh.us	Delaware	OH	43015	740-833-1100	833-1149
Delaware County Intermediate Unit 200 Yale Ave *Web:* www.dciu.org	Morton	PA	19070	610-938-9000	938-9887
Dennis-Yarmouth Regional School District 296 Stn Ave *Web:* www.dy-regional.k12.ma.us	South Yarmouth	MA	02664	508-398-7600	398-7622
Denver Public Schools 900 Grant St *Web:* www.communications.dpsk12.org	Denver	CO	80203	720-423-3200	423-3413
Des Moines Independent School District 901 Walnut St *Web:* www.dmps.k12.ia.us	Des Moines	IA	50309	515-242-7911	242-7579
Desoto County School District 5 E S St *Web:* www.desotocountyschools.org	Hernando	MS	38632	662-429-5271	
Desoto Parish School District 201 Crosby St	Mansfield	LA	71052	318-872-2836	
Destinta Theatres LLC 11 Kipp Ave *Web:* www.destinta.com	Lodi	NJ	07644	973-473-8002	473-8808
Detroit Public Schools 3031 W Grand Blvd *Web:* www.detroitk12.org	Detroit	MI	48202	313-873-7927	873-4564
Dickenson County School District PO Box 1127 *TF:* 866-632-9992 ■ *Web:* www.dickenson.k12.va.us	Clintwood	VA	24228	276-926-4643	926-6374
Dinwiddie County Public School 14016 Boydton Plank Rd PO Box 7 *Web:* www.dinwiddie.k12.va.us	Dinwiddie	VA	23841	804-469-4190	469-4197
District of Columbia Public Schools (DCPS) 1200 First St NE *Web:* www.dcps.dc.gov	Washington	DC	20002	202-442-5885	442-5026
Diversified Clinical Services Inc 4500 Salisbury Rd Suite 300 *TF:* 800-379-9774 ■ *Web:* www.diversifiedcs.com	Jacksonville	FL	32216	904-296-6526	296-3429
Donegal School District 1051 Koser Rd *Web:* www.donegal.k12.pa.us	Mount Joy	PA	17552	717-653-1447	
Douglas County Board of Education 9030 Hwy 5 PO Box 1077 *Web:* www.douglas.k12.ga.us	Douglasville	GA	30134	770-651-2000	920-4027
Duarte Unified School District 1620 Huntington Dr *Web:* www.duarte.k12.ca.us	Duarte	CA	91010	626-599-5000	599-5069
Dublin Unified School District 7471 Larkdale Ave *Web:* www.dublin.k12.ca.us	Dublin	CA	94568	925-828-2551	829-6532
Dufour Petroleum LP 1374 Hwy 11 N *Web:* www.dufourpetroleum.com	Petal	MS	39465	601-583-9991	583-9881
Durham Academy Inc 3130 Pickett Rd *TF:* 888-904-9149 ■ *Web:* www.da.org	Durham	NC	27705	919-489-9118	
Duval County School System 1701 Prudential Dr *Web:* www.duvalschools.org	Jacksonville	FL	32207	904-390-2000	390-2586
Earlimart School District PO Box 11970 *Web:* www.earlimart.org	Earlimart	CA	93219	661-849-3386	
Early County School District 11927 Columbia St *Web:* www.early.k12.ga.us	Blakely	GA	39823	229-723-4337	
East Aurora Union Free School District 430 Main St *Web:* www.eastauroraschools.org	East Aurora	NY	14052	716-687-2309	
East Baton Rouge Parish School Board 1050 S Foster Dr **Fax:* Hum Res ■ *Web:* www.ebrpss.k12.la.us	Baton Rouge	LA	70806	225-922-5400	922-5688*
East Cleveland Board of Education 14305 Shaw Ave *Web:* www.east-cleveland.k12.oh.us	Cleveland	OH	44112	216-268-6570	
East Maine School District 63 (EMSD) 10150 Dee Rd *Web:* www.emsd63.org	Des Plaines	IL	60016	847-299-1900	299-9963
East Penn School District 800 Pine St *TF:* 800-872-5327 ■ *Web:* www.eastpenn.k12.pa.us	Emmaus	PA	18049	610-966-8300	
East Ramapo Central School District 105 S Madison Ave *Web:* www.eram.k12.ny.us	Spring Valley	NY	10977	845-577-6000	577-6038
East Valley School District 361 12325 E Grace Ave *TF:* 800-795-3272 ■ *Web:* www.evsd.org	Spokane	WA	99216	509-924-1830	927-9500
Eastern Lancaster County School District 669 E Main St PO Box 609 *Web:* www.elanco.k12.pa.us	New Holland	PA	17557	717-354-1500	354-1512
Easton Area School District Inc 811 Northampton St *Web:* www.eastonsd.org	Easton	PA	18042	610-250-2433	
Eastside Union High School District 830 N Capitol Ave *Web:* www.esuhsd.org	San Jose	CA	95133	408-347-5000	347-5045
Eastside Union School District 45006 30th St E *Web:* www.eastside.k12.ca.us	Lancaster	CA	93535	661-952-1200	952-1220
Edcouch-Elsa Independent School District PO Box 127 *Web:* www.eeisd.org	Edcouch	TX	78538	956-262-6000	262-6032
Edwardsburg Public Schools 69410 Section St *Web:* www.edwardsburgpublicschools.org	Edwardsburg	MI	49112	269-663-1031	
Edwardsville Community School District 7 708 St Louis St *Web:* www.ecusd7.org	Edwardsville	IL	62025	618-656-1182	692-7423
El Campo Independent School District 700 W Norris St *Web:* www.ecisd.org	El Campo	TX	77437	979-543-6771	
El Centro Elementary School District 1256 Broadway St *Web:* www.ecesd.org	El Centro	CA	92243	760-352-5712	
El Monte City School District 3540 Lexington Ave *Web:* www.emcsd.org	El Monte	CA	91731	626-453-3700	
El Monte Union High School District 3537 Johnson Ave *Web:* www.emuhsd.k12.ca.us	El Monte	CA	91731	626-444-9005	448-8419
El Paso Independent School District 6531 Boeing Dr **Fax:* Hum Res ■ *Web:* www.episd.org	El Paso	TX	79925	915-779-3781	779-4280*
Elbert County Board of Education 50 Laurel Dr *Web:* www.elbert.k12.ga.us	Elberton	GA	30635	706-213-4000	
Elmont Union Free School District 135 Elmont Rd *Web:* www.elmontschools.org	Elmont	NY	11003	516-326-5500	326-5574
Elmore County Public School System 100 H H Robison Dr PO Box 817 *Web:* www.elmoreco.com	Wetumpka	AL	36092	334-567-1200	
Elzinga & Volkers 86 E 6th St *Web:* www.elzinga-volkers.com	Holland	MI	49423	616-392-2383	392-3752
Emanuel County Board of Education PO Box 130 *Web:* www.emanuel.k12.ga.us	Swainsboro	GA	30401	478-237-6674	237-3404
Encinitas Union School District Educational Facilities Corp 101 S Rancho Santa Fe Rd *Web:* www.eusd.k12.ca.us	Encinitas	CA	92024	760-944-4300	
Engineering Design Technologies Inc 1705 Entp Way SE Suite 200 *TF:* 877-728-1724 ■ *Web:* www.edtinc.net	Marietta	GA	30067	770-988-0400	988-0300
Ennis Independent School District 303 W Knox PO Box 1420 *Web:* www.ennis.k12.tx.us	Ennis	TX	75120	972-872-7000	875-8667
Erie 2-Chautauqua Cattaraugus Boces (ECCB) 8685 Erie Rd *TF:* 800-228-1184 ■ *Web:* www.e2ccb.org	Angola	NY	14006	716-549-4454	
Etiwanda School District (ESD) 6061 E Ave *Web:* www.etiwanda.k12.ca.us	Etiwanda	CA	91739	909-899-2451	899-1235
Eugene School District 4J 200 N Monroe St *Web:* www.4j.lane.edu	Eugene	OR	97402	541-687-3123	687-3691
Eureka Union School District 5455 Eureka Rd *Web:* www.eureka-usd.k12.ca.us	Granite Bay	CA	95746	916-791-4939	791-5527
Evanston/Skokie School District 65 1500 Mcdaniel Ave *Web:* www.district65.net	Evanston	IL	60201	847-859-8000	859-8707
Evergreen School District No 114 13501 NE 28th St PO Box 8910 *Web:* www.egreen.wednet.edu	Vancouver	WA	98668	360-604-4000	892-5307
Evesham Township Board of Education 25 S Maple Ave *Web:* www.evesham.k12.nj.us	Marlton	NJ	08053	856-983-1800	
Fannin County Board of Education 2290 E First St *TF:* 800-308-2145 ■ *Web:* www.fannin.k12.ga.us	Blue Ridge	GA	30513	706-632-3771	632-7583
Farwest Freight Systems Inc 4504 E Valley Hwy E	Sumner	WA	98390	253-804-0500	826-0350
Fayette County Board of Education 210 Stonewall Ave *Web:* www.fcboe.org	Fayetteville	GA	30214	770-460-3535	460-8191
Fayette County Public Schools 701 E Main St	Lexington	KY	40502	859-381-4100	381-4271*
Ferndale School District 502 6041 Vista Dr PO Box 698 *Web:* www.ferndale.wednet.edu	Ferndale	WA	98248	360-383-9200	383-9201
Ferry Transportation Inc 5 Thames Ave *Web:* www.ferrytrans.com	Laurel	MS	39440	601-425-5542	428-4749
First Farmers & Merchants National Bank 816 S Garden St PO Box 1148 *PINK:* FFMH ■ *TF:* 800-882-8378 ■ *Web:* www.fandmbank.com	Columbia	TN	38401	931-388-3145	380-8359
Flint Community Schools 923 E Kearsley St *Web:* www.flintschools.org	Flint	MI	48503	810-760-1000	760-6790
Floresville Independent School District 908 10th St *Web:* www.floresville.isd.tenet.edu	Floresville	TX	78114	830-393-5300	
Floyd Blinsky Trucking Inc 210 Keys Rd *Web:* www.blinsky.com	Yakima	WA	98901	509-457-3484	457-0832
Floyd County Board of Education 600 Riverside Pkwy NE *Web:* www.floydboe.net	Rome	GA	30161	706-234-1031	236-1824
Forest Hills Local School 7550 Forest Rd *Web:* www.foresthills.edu	Cincinnati	OH	45255	513-231-3600	
Forest Lake Area School District 6100 210th St N *Web:* www.forestlake.k12.mn.us	Forest Lake	MN	55025	651-982-8100	982-8137
Forney Independent School District (inc) 600 S Bois D ARC St *Web:* www.forneyisd.net	Forney	TX	75126	972-564-4055	
Forsyth County Board of Education 1120 Dahlonega Hwy *Web:* www.forsyth.k12.ga.us	Cumming	GA	30040	770-887-2461	781-6632
Fort Bragg Unified School District 312 S Lincoln St *TF:* 800-734-7793 ■ *Web:* www.fbusd.us	Fort Bragg	CA	95437	707-961-2850	
Fort Mill School District 4 120 E Elliott St *Web:* www.fort-mill.k12.sc.us	Fort Mill	SC	29715	803-548-2527	547-4696
Fort Wayne Community Schools (FWCS) 1200 S Clinton St	Fort Wayne	IN	46802	260-425-7272	467-1973
Fort Worth Independent School District 100 N University Dr *Web:* www.fortworthisd.org	Fort Worth	TX	76107	817-871-2000	871-2949

Name / Address	City	State	ZIP	Phone	Fax
Fox Chapel Area School District 611 Field Club Rd *Web:* www.fcasd.edu	Pittsburgh	PA	15238	412-967-2453	967-0697
Franklin Local School District PO Box 428 *TF:* 800-846-4976 ■ *Web:* www.franklin-local.k12.oh.us	Duncan Falls	OH	43734	740-674-5203	
Franklin Special School District 507 New Hwy 96 W *Web:* www.fssd.org	Franklin	TN	37064	615-794-6624	790-4716
Franklin-Pierce Schools 315 129th St S. *Web:* www.fp.k12.wa.us	Tacoma	WA	98444	253-298-3000	
Fredericksburg City Public Schools 817 Princess Anne St *Web:* www.cityschools.com	Fredericksburg	VA	22401	540-372-1130	372-1111
Fremont Public Schools 220 W Pine St *Web:* www.fremont.net	Fremont	MI	49412	231-924-2350	924-5264
Fremont Unified School District PO Box 5008 *TF:* 800-544-5248 ■ *Web:* www.fremont.k12.ca.us	Fremont	CA	94537	510-657-2350	770-9851
Fresno Unified School District 2309 Tulare St. *Fax: Hum Res ■ *Web:* www.fresno.k12.ca.us	Fresno	CA	93721	559-457-3000	457-3528*
Friendship House PO Box 3778 *Web:* www.friendshiphousepa.org	Scranton	PA	18505	570-342-8305	344-1178
Frontier Central School District 5120 Orchard Ave *Web:* www.frontier.wnyric.org	Hamburg	NY	14075	716-926-1710	
Fulton School District 58 2 Hornet Dr *Web:* www.fulton.k12.mo.us	Fulton	MO	65251	573-642-2206	
Gainesville City Schools 508 Oak St. *Web:* www.gcssk12.net	Gainesville	GA	30501	770-536-5275	287-2019
Galveston Independent School District (GISD) 3904 Ave PO Box 660 *Web:* www.gisd.org	Galveston	TX	77550	409-766-5100	762-8391
Garden Grove Unified School District 10331 Stanford Ave *TF:* 866-370-4740 ■ *Web:* www.ggusd.us	Garden Grove	CA	92840	714-663-6000	663-6100
Garland Independent School District (GISD) 501 S Jupiter PO Box 469026 *Web:* www.garlandisd.net	Garland	TX	75046	972-494-8201	485-4936
Gaston County School 943 Osceola St PO Box 1397 *Web:* www.gaston.k12.nc.us	Gastonia	NC	28054	704-866-6117	
Gateway Unified School Disrict 4411 Mountain Lakes Blvd *Web:* www.gateway-schools.org	Redding	CA	96003	530-245-7900	
Genesee Intermediate School District 2413 W Maple Ave *Web:* www.geneseeisd.org	Flint	MI	48507	810-591-4400	
Geneseo Community Unit School District 228 209 S College Ave *Web:* www.dist228.org	Geneseo	IL	61254	309-945-0450	945-0445
Geneva County Board of Education PO Box 250 *Web:* www.genevacounty.net	Geneva	AL	36340	334-684-5690	
Giddings Independent Schl Dst 2337 N Main PO Box 389 *Web:* www.giddings.net	Giddings	TX	78942	979-542-2854	542-9264
Gilroy Unified School District 7810 Arroyo Cir *Web:* www.gusd.k12.ca.us	Gilroy	CA	95020	408-847-2700	842-1158
Gladstone School District 115 17789 Webster Rd *TF:* 800-328-0272 ■ *Web:* www.gladstone.k12.or.us	Gladstone	OR	97027	503-655-2777	655-5201
Glen Ellyn School District 41 793 N Main St *Web:* www.d41.dupage.k12.il.us	Glen Ellyn	IL	60137	630-790-6400	790-1867
Glens Falls City School District 15 Quade St *Web:* www.gfsd.org	Glens Falls	NY	12801	518-792-1212	
Goleta Union School District 401 N Fairview Ave *Web:* www.goleta.k12.ca.us	Goleta	CA	93117	805-681-1200	
Goliad Independent School District PO Box 830 *TF:* 800-750-9911 ■ *Web:* www.goliadisd.org	Goliad	TX	77963	361-645-3259	
Gordon County Board of Education 205 Warrior Path PO Box 12001 *Web:* www.gcbe.org	Calhoun	GA	30703	706-629-7366	625-5671
Gordon Sevig Trucking Co (GSTC) 400 Hwy 151 E *Web:* www.gstcinc.com	Walford	IA	52351	319-846-5500	846-2713
Goshen County School District 1 626 W 25th Ave *Web:* www.goshen.k12.wy.us	Torrington	WY	82240	307-532-2171	532-7085
Grand Forks Public School District 1 PO Box 6000 *Web:* www.grand-forks.k12.nd.us	Grand Forks	ND	58206	701-746-2200	
Grand Haven Area Public Schools 1415 S Beechtree St *Web:* www.ghaps.org	Grand Haven	MI	49417	616-850-5000	
Grand Rapids Public Schools (GRPS) 1331 Franklin St SE PO Box 117 *Web:* www.grps.k12.mi.us	Grand Rapids	MI	49506	616-819-2500	819-2104
Grandview Heights City School District 1587 W 3rd Ave *Web:* www.grandviewschools.org	Columbus	OH	43212	614-481-3600	
Granite Falls School District 307 N Alder Ave *Web:* www.gfalls.wednet.edu	Granite Falls	WA	98252	360-691-7717	691-4459
Grant County Board of Education 820 Arnie Risen Blvd *TF:* 800-418-6423 ■ *Web:* www.grant.kyschools.us	Williamstown	KY	41097	859-824-3323	
Granville Bancshares Inc 328 S McCoy St PO Box 344 *TF:* 800-259-1383 ■ *Web:* www.gnbonline.com	Granville	IL	61326	815-339-2222	339-2123
Granville Central School District 58 Quaker St *Web:* www.granvillecsd.org	Granville	NY	12832	518-642-1051	642-4544
Gratiot-Isabella Regional Education Service District 1131 E Center St PO Box 310 *Web:* www.giresd.net/giresd/site/default.asp	Ithaca	MI	48847	989-875-5101	875-2858
Gray Transportation Inc 2459 GT Dr *TF:* 800-234-3930 ■ *Web:* www.graytran.com	Waterloo	IA	50703	319-234-3930	234-8841
Greencastle Antrim School District 500 Leitersburg St *TF:* 888-577-4722 ■ *Web:* www.greencastle.k12.pa.us	Greencastle	PA	17225	717-597-2187	
Greenfield Union School District 1624 Fairview Rd *Web:* www.gfusd.k12.ca.us	Bakersfield	CA	93307	661-837-6000	832-2873
Greenville County School District 301 Camperdown Way PO Box 2848 *Fax: Hum Res ■ *Web:* www.greenville.k12.sc.us	Greenville	SC	29602	864-241-3100	355-3975*
Greenwood School District 50 1855 Calhoun Rd PO Box 248 *Web:* www.gwd50.k12.sc.us	Greenwood	SC	29648	864-941-5400	941-5427
Grocery Haulers Inc 286 Homestead Ave. *TF:* 866-411-2444 ■ *Web:* www.groceryhaulers.com	Avenel	NJ	07001	732-499-3800	499-3812
Grosse Ile Township Schools 23276 E River Rd *Web:* www.gischools.org	Grosse Ile	MI	48138	734-362-2555	
Guilford County Schools 617 W Market St *Web:* www.gcsnc.com	Greensboro	NC	27401	336-370-8100	370-8398
Gulf Coast Bank & Trust Co 200 St Charles Ave *TF:* 800-223-2060 ■ *Web:* www.gulfbank.com	New Orleans	LA	70130	504-561-6100	556-5812
Gulf County School District 150 Middle School Rd *Web:* www.gulf.k12.fl.us	Port Saint Joe	FL	32456	850-229-8256	229-6089
Guy Shavender Trucking Inc PO Box 206. *TF:* 800-682-2447 ■ *Web:* www.shavender.com	Pantego	NC	27860	252-943-3379	943-6434
Habersham County Board of Education 132 W Stanford Mill Rd PO Box 70 *Web:* www.habershamschools.com	Clarkesville	GA	30523	706-754-2118	754-1549
Hale County Board of Education 1115 Powers St *Web:* www.halek12.org	Greensboro	AL	36744	334-624-8836	
Halifax County Public Schools 1030 Mary Bethune St PO Box 1849 *Web:* www.halifax.k12.va.us	Halifax	VA	24558	434-476-2171	476-1858
Hall County Schools 711 Green St NW Suite 100 *Web:* www.hallco.org	Gainesville	GA	30501	770-534-1080	535-7404
Hamblen County Board of Education 210 E Morris Blvd. *Web:* www.hcboe.net	Morristown	TN	37813	423-586-7700	586-7747
Hamburg Area School District (HASD) 701 Windsor St. *Web:* www.hasdhawks.org	Hamburg	PA	19526	610-562-2241	562-2634
Hamilton City School District (HCSD) 533 Dayton St PO Box 627 *Web:* www.hamiltoncityschools.com	Hamilton	OH	45012	513-887-5000	887-5014
Hamilton County Dept of Education 3074 Hickory Valley Rd *Fax: Hum Res ■ *Web:* www.hcde.org	Chattanooga	TN	37421	423-209-8400	209-8539*
Hamilton County Educational Service Ctr (HCESC) 11083 Hamilton Ave *Web:* www.hcesc.org	Cincinnati	OH	45231	513-674-4200	742-8339
Hanning Construction Inc 815 Swan St *Web:* www.hannigconstruction.com	Terre Haute	IN	47807	812-235-6218	235-1218
Hardee County School District PO Box 1678 *Web:* www.hardee.k12.fl.us	Wauchula	FL	33873	863-773-9058	
Harlem Children's Zone Inc 35 E 125th St *Web:* www.hcz.org	New York	NY	10035	212-360-3255	289-0661
Harnett County Board of Education PO Box 1029 *Web:* www.harnett.k12.nc.us	Lillington	NC	27546	910-893-8151	893-8839
Harrisburg School District Inc PO Box 2645 *Web:* www.hbgsd.k12.pa.us	Harrisburg	PA	17105	717-703-4000	
Hart County Board of Education PO Box 696 *Web:* www.hart.k12.ga.us	Hartwell	GA	30643	706-376-5141	376-7046
Hartford Public Schools 960 Main St *Fax: Hum Res ■ *Web:* www.hartfordschools.org	Hartford	CT	06103	860-695-8000	722-8454*
Haslett Public School 5593 Franklin St. *Web:* www.haslett.k12.mi.us	Haslett	MI	48840	517-339-8242	
Hatboro-Horsham School District 229 Meetinghouse Rd. *Web:* www.hatboro-horsham.org	Horsham	PA	19044	215-672-5660	420-5262
Hauppauge School District (HSP) 495 Hoffman Ln PO Box 6006 *Web:* www.hauppauge.k12.ny.us	Hauppauge	NY	11788	631-761-8225	
Hawaii Dept of Education Honolulu District Office 4967 Kilauea Ave *Web:* www.doe.k12.hi.us	Honolulu	HI	96816	808-733-4950	733-4953
Hays Consolidated I S D 21003 I- 35 *Web:* www.hayscisd.net	Kyle	TX	78640	512-268-2141	268-2147
Hayward Unified School District (HUSD) 24411 Amador St PO Box 5000 *Web:* www.husd.k12.ca.us	Hayward	CA	94540	510-784-2600	784-2641
Hebrew Academy of The Five Towns & Rockaway Inc 33 Washington Ave *Web:* www.haftr.org	Lawrence	NY	11559	516-569-3043	
Hemlock Public Schools District PO Box 260 *Web:* www.hemlock.k12.mi.us	Hemlock	MI	48626	989-642-5282	
Henry Carlson Co 1205 W Russell St PO Box 84010 *Web:* henrycarlson.com	Sioux Falls	SD	57118	605-336-2410	332-1314

	City	State	Zip	Phone	Fax
Hereford Independent School District 601 N 25 Mile Ave *Web:* www.herefordisd.net	Hereford	TX	79045	806-363-7600	363-7699
Hertford County School District PO Box 158 *Web:* www.hertford.k12.nc.us	Winton	NC	27986	252-358-1761	
Highland Central School District 320 Pancake Hollow Rd *Web:* www.highland-k12.org	Highland	NY	12528	845-691-1000	
Highland Falls-Ft Montgomery School District PO Box 287 *Web:* www.hffmcsd.org	Highland Falls	NY	10928	845-446-9575	
Hillsboro City Schools 338 W Main St *Web:* www.hillsboro.k12.oh.us	Hillsboro	OH	45133	937-393-3475	
Hillsboro Community Unit School District 3 1311 Vandalia Rd *Web:* www.hillsboroschools.net	Hillsboro	IL	62049	217-532-2942	532-3137
Hillsboro School District 3083 NE 49th Pl *Web:* www.hsd.k12.or.us	Hillsboro	OR	97124	503-844-1500	844-1540
Hillsborough County Public Schools 901 E Kennedy Blvd *Web:* www.sdhc.k12.fl.us	Tampa	FL	33602	813-272-4000	272-4073
Hillsborough Township Board of Education 379 S Branch Rd *Web:* www.hillsborough.k12.nj.us	Hillsborough	NJ	08844	908-431-6600	369-8286
Hinds County School District 13192 Hwy 18 *Web:* www.hinds.k12.ms.us	Raymond	MS	39154	601-857-5222	857-8548
Hiner Transport LLC 1350 S Jefferson St PO Box 621 *Web:* www.hinertransport.com	Huntington	IN	46750	260-356-8218	356-4664
Hingham School District 220 Central St *Web:* www.hingham-ma.com	Hingham	MA	02043	781-741-1500	
Hoffmeier Inc 3210 N Lewis Ave *Web:* www.hoffmeier.com	Tulsa	OK	74110	918-428-5823	428-0820
Holiday Express Corp 721 S 28th St *TF:* 800-831-5078 ■ *Web:* www.holidayxpress.net	Estherville	IA	51334	712-362-5812	362-3019
Holland Patent Central School District 9601 Main St *Web:* www.hpschools.org	Holland Patent	NY	13354	315-865-7200	
Holland Public Schools 156 W 11th St *Web:* www.hollandpublicschools.org	Holland	MI	49423	616-494-2000	392-8225
Holmes District School Board (HDSB) 701 E Pennsylvania Ave *Web:* www.hdsb.org	Bonifay	FL	32425	850-547-9341	547-3568
Homer Central School District PO Box 500 *Web:* www.homercentral.org	Homer	NY	13077	607-749-7241	
Hopkins County Board of Education 320 S Seminary St *Web:* www.hopkins.k12.ky.us	Madisonville	KY	42431	270-825-6000	825-6072
Houston Independent School District 228 McCarty St *Web:* www.houstonisd.org	Houston	TX	77029	713-556-6000	556-6006
Hueneme Elementary School Dist 205 N Ventura Rd *Web:* www.huensd.k12.ca.us	Port Hueneme	CA	93041	805-488-3588	488-1779
Humble Independent School District PO Box 2000 *Web:* www.humble.k12.tx.us	Humble	TX	77347	281-641-1000	641-1050
Huntington Union Free School District 3 PO Box 1500 *TF:* 866-723-3697 ■ *Web:* www.hufsd.edu	Huntington	NY	11743	631-673-2054	
Huntsville Board of Education 2820 Holmes Ave NW *Web:* www.hsv.k12.al.us	Huntsville	AL	35816	256-428-6800	428-6817
Hyde Park Central School District (inc) PO Box 2033 *Web:* www.hydeparkschools.org	Hyde Park	NY	12538	845-229-4000	
I E Miller Of Eunice Inc PO Box 472 *TF:* 800-567-0674 ■ *Web:* www.iemiller.com	Eunice	LA	70535	337-457-2216	457-4468
Idaho Falls School District 91 Education Foundation Inc 690 John Adams Pkwy *Web:* www.d91.k12.id.us	Idaho Falls	ID	83401	208-525-7500	525-7596
Ilex Construction & Woodworking 1425 Clarkview Rd *TF:* 866-551-4539 ■ *Web:* www.ilexconstruction.com	Baltimore	MD	21209	410-243-6796	243-6798
Independent School District 829 501 Elm Ave E *Web:* www.waseca.k12.mn.us	Waseca	MN	56093	507-835-2500	
Indianapolis Public Schools 120 E Walnut St	Indianapolis	IN	46204	317-226-4418	226-4936
Integrated Freight Corp 6371 Business Blvd Suite 200 *OTC: IFCR* ■ *Web:* www.integrated-freight.com	Sarasota	FL	34240	941-907-8372	
Iowa City Community School District 509 S Dubuque St *Web:* www.iowa-city.k12.ia.us	Iowa City	IA	52240	319-688-1000	
J.M. Bozeman Enterprises Inc 166 Seltzer Ln *TF:* 800-472-1836 ■ *Web:* www.jmbozemanint.com	Malvern	AR	72104	501-844-4060	844-4133
Jackson County Intermediate School District (JCISD) 6700 Browns Lake Rd *Web:* jacksoncisd.schoolwires.com/site/default.aspx?PageID=1	Jackson	MI	49201	517-768-5200	
Jackson County School District 6 300 Ash St *Web:* www.district6.org	Central Point	OR	97502	541-494-6200	664-1637
Jackson County School District 9 PO Box 548 *Web:* www.eaglepnt.k12.or.us	Eagle Point	OR	97524	541-830-1200	
Jackson County School System 1660 Winder Hwy *Web:* www.jackson.k12.ga.us	Jefferson	GA	30549	706-367-5151	367-9457
Jackson Public Schools 662 S President St *Web:* www.jackson.k12.ms.us	Jackson	MS	39201	601-960-8700	960-8713
Jacksonville Independent School District PO Box 631 *TF:* 888-863-5880 ■ *Web:* www.jisd.org	Jacksonville	TX	75766	903-586-6511	586-3133
Jacksonville School District 117 516 Jordan St *Web:* www.morgan.k12.il.us	Jacksonville	IL	62650	217-243-9411	243-6844
Jaffrey-Rindge School District 81 Fitzgerald Dr Unit 2 *Web:* www.sau47.k12.nh.us	Jaffrey	NH	03452	603-532-8100	
Jamesville-Dewitt Central School Dist (inc) 6845 Edinger Dr PO Box 606 *Web:* www.jamesvilledewitt.org	Fayetteville	NY	13066	315-445-8300	445-8477
Jefferson Area Local School District 906 W Main St *Web:* www.west-jefferson.k12.oh.us	West Jefferson	OH	43162	614-879-7654	
Jefferson County (KY) Public Schools PO Box 34020 *Web:* www.jefferson.k12.ky.us	Louisville	KY	40232	502-485-3011	485-3991
Jefferson Davis Parish Parish Schools 203 E Plaquemine St Po Box 640 *Web:* www.webserver.jeffersondavis.org	Jennings	LA	70546	337-824-1834	
Jefferson Schools 2400 N Dixie Hwy *Web:* www.jefferson.k12.mi.us	Monroe	MI	48162	734-289-5550	
Jenison Public Schools (JPS) 8375 20th Ave *Web:* www.jpsonline.org/index.php	Jenison	MI	49428	616-457-1402	457-8090
Jennings County Schools 34 W Main St *TF:* 866-346-3724 ■ *Web:* www.jenningscounty-in.gov	North Vernon	IN	47265	812-346-4483	
Johnston Community School District PO Box 10 *Web:* www.johnston.k12.ia.us	Johnston	IA	50131	515-278-0470	278-5884
Joliet Public School District 86 420 N Raynor Ave *Web:* www.joliet86.org	Joliet	IL	60435	815-740-3196	
Julian Charter School Inc 1704 Cape Horn *TF:* 866-853-0003 ■ *Web:* www.juliancharterschool.org	Julian	CA	92036	760-765-3847	
K12 Inc 2300 Corporate Pk Dr *NYSE: LRN* ■ *TF:* 866-512-2273 ■ *Web:* www.k12.com	Herndon	VA	20171	703-483-7000	483-7330
Kansas City Missouri School District 1211 McGee St *Web:* www2.kcmsd.net	Kansas City	MO	64106	816-418-7000	418-7766
Kbt Inc 3885 West Michigan Ave *TF:* 800-860-4055 ■ *Web:* www.kbt-inc.com	Sidney	OH	45365	937-498-1388	497-1870
Kelseyville Unified School District 4410 Konocti Rd *Web:* www.kusd.lake.k12.ca.us	Kelseyville	CA	95451	707-279-1511	
Kentwood Public Schools 5820 Eastern Ave SE *Web:* www.kentwoodps.org	Grand Rapids	MI	49508	616-455-4400	455-4476
Keppel Union School District PO Box 186 *Web:* www.keppel.k12.ca.us	Pearblossom	CA	93553	661-944-2155	944-2933
Kern County High School District 5801 Sundale Ave *Web:* www.khsd.k12.ca.us	Bakersfield	CA	93309	661-827-3100	827-3300
Kershaw County School District PO Box 7008 *Web:* www.kershaw.k12.sc.us	Camden	SC	29020	803-432-8416	425-8918
Keystone School District 451 Huston Ave *Web:* www.keyknox.com	Knox	PA	16232	814-797-5921	
King City Union Elementary School District 800 Broadway St *Web:* www.kcusd.org	King City	CA	93930	831-385-1144	385-7554
Kirkwood School District R-7 Inc 11289 Manchester Rd *Web:* www.kirkwoodschools.org	Saint Louis	MO	63122	314-213-6100	984-0002
Klamath County School District C U 600 10501 Washburn Way *TF:* 888-271-5983 ■ *Web:* www.kcsd.k12.or.us	Klamath Falls	OR	97603	541-883-5000	
Klein Independent School District 7200 Spring Cypress Rd *Web:* www.kleinisd.net	Spring	TX	77379	832-249-4000	
Knox County Public Schools 912 S Gay St **Fax:* Hum Res ■ *Web:* www.kcs.k12tn.net	Knoxville	TN	37901	865-594-1800	594-3758*
La Mesa-Spring Valley School District 4750 Date Ave *Web:* www.lmsvsd.k12.ca.us	La Mesa	CA	91941	619-668-5700	
Labette County Unified School District 506 PO Box 189 *Web:* www.506.k12.ks.us	Altamont	KS	67330	620-784-5326	784-5879
Lafayette Parish School System 113 Chaplin Dr *Web:* www.lpssonline.com	Lafayette	LA	70508	337-521-7000	
Laingsburg Community School District 205 S Woodhull Rd *Web:* www.laingsburg.k12.mi.us	Laingsburg	MI	48848	517-651-2705	651-9075
Lake Superior Ind Sch Dist 381 1640 2 Hwy *Web:* www.isd381.k12.mn.us	Two Harbors	MN	55616	218-834-8201	834-8239
Lake Travis Independent School District 3322 Ranch Rd 620 S *Web:* www.laketravis.txed.net	Austin	TX	78738	512-533-6000	533-6001
Lake Washington School District 414 16250 NE 74th St PO Box 97039 *Web:* www.lwsd.org	Redmond	WA	98073	425-936-1200	702-3213
Lake Worth Independent School District (LWISD) 6800 Telephone Rd *Web:* www.lwisd.org	Fort Worth	TX	76135	817-306-4200	
Lakewood School District 655 Princeton Ave *Web:* www.lakewood.k12.nj.us	Lakewood	NJ	08701	732-905-3600	364-1657
Lamesa Independent School District PO Box 261 *Web:* www.lamesa.esc17.net	Lamesa	TX	79331	806-872-5461	872-6220
Lamphere Schools 31201 Dorchester Ave *Web:* www.lamphere.k12.mi.us	Madison Heights	MI	48071	248-589-1990	589-2618
Lancaster City School District 345 E Mulberry St *TF:* 888-647-4729 ■ *Web:* www.lancaster.k12.oh.us	Lancaster	OH	43130	740-687-7300	

Name / Address	City	State	Zip	Phone	Fax
Lanier County Board of Education PO Box 158 *Web:* www.lanier.k12.ga.us	Lakeland	GA	31635	229-482-3966	482-3020
Lansing School District 517 W Kalamazoo *Web:* www.edline.net/pages/Lansing_SD	Lansing	MI	48933	517-755-1000	325-7345
Las Cruces Public Schools 505 S Main St Suite 249 **Fax:* Hum Res ■ *Web:* www.lcps.k12.nm.us	Las Cruces	NM	88001	575-527-5800	527-6658*
Laurel Highlands School District (LHSD) 304 Bailey Ave *Web:* www.lhsd.org	Uniontown	PA	15401	724-437-2821	437-8929
Laurens County Board of Education 467 Firetower Rd *Web:* www.lcboe.net	Dublin	GA	31021	478-272-4767	277-2619
Lawrence Public Schools 110 McDonald Dr *Web:* www.usd497.org	Lawrence	KS	66044	785-832-5000	832-5016
Leadership Public Schools 344 Thomas L. Berkley Way *Web:* www.leadps.org	Oakland	CA	94612	510-830-3780	225-2575
Lebanon City School District 700 Holbrook Ave *Web:* www.lebanon.k12.oh.us	Lebanon	OH	45036	513-934-5770	
Leflore County School District 1901 Hwy 82 W *Web:* www.leflorecountyschools.org	Greenwood	MS	38930	662-453-8566	
Lenoir County Public School (LCPS) 2017 W Vernon Ave PO Box 729 *Web:* www.lenoir.k12.nc.us	Kinston	NC	28504	252-527-1109	527-6884
Leon County Schools (LCS) 2757 W Pensacola St **Fax:* Hum Res ■ *Web:* www.leon.k12.fl.us	Tallahassee	FL	32304	850-487-7306	414-5146*
Lessors Inc 1056 Gemini Rd *TF:* 800-680-2911 ■ *Web:* www.lessorsinc.com	Saint Paul	MN	55122	651-789-9270	452-9510
Lewis S. Mills High School 24 Lyon Rd *Web:* www.region10ct.org	Burlington	CT	06013	860-673-0423	673-9128
Lexington City Board of Education 1010 Fair St *Web:* www.lexcs.org	Lexington	NC	27292	336-242-1527	
Lexington School District 4 607 E 5th St *Web:* www.lexington4.net	Swansea	SC	29160	803-568-1000	568-1020
Liberty Independent School District 1600 Grand Ave *Web:* www.libertyisd.net	Liberty	TX	77575	936-336-7215	
Liberty-Eylau Independent School District 2901 Leopard Dr *Web:* www.leisd.net	Texarkana	TX	75501	903-832-1535	838-9444
Libertyville School District 70 1381 W Lake St *Web:* www.d70.k12.il.us	Libertyville	IL	60048	847-362-8393	
Limestone County School District 300 S Jefferson St *Web:* www.lcsk12.org	Athens	AL	35611	256-232-5353	233-6461
Lincoln Public Schools PO Box 82889 **Fax:* Hum Res ■ *Web:* www.lps.org	Lincoln	NE	68510	402-436-1000	436-1620*
Lincoln Unified School District 2010 W Swain Rd *Web:* www.lusd.net	Stockton	CA	95207	209-953-8700	
Lincolnway Community High School District 210 1801 E Lincoln Hwy *Web:* www.lw210.org	New Lenox	IL	60451	815-462-2100	
Little Cypress-Mauriceville Cisd Inc 6586 FM 1130 *Web:* www.lcmcisd.org	Orange	TX	77632	409-883-2232	
Little Friends Inc 140 N Wright St *Web:* www.littlefriendsinc.com	Naperville	IL	60540	630-355-6533	
Little Rock School District 810 W Markham St **Fax:* Hum Res ■ *Web:* www.lrsd.org	Little Rock	AR	72201	501-447-1000	447-1162*
Locust Valley Central School District 22 Horse Hollow Rd *Web:* www.lvcsd.k12.ny.us	Locust Valley	NY	11560	516-277-5000	
Lompoc Unified School District PO Box 8000 *Web:* www.lusd.org	Lompoc	CA	93438	805-736-2371	
London City School District 60 S Walnut St *Web:* www.london.k12.oh.us	London	OH	43140	740-852-5700	
Long County Board of Education PO Box 428 *Web:* www.longcountyps.com	Ludowici	GA	31316	912-545-2367	545-2380
Longview School District 2715 Lilac St *Web:* www.longview.k12.wa.us	Longview	WA	98632	360-575-7000	575-7231
Los Alamitos Unified School District 10293 Bloomfield St *Web:* www.losal.org	Los Alamitos	CA	90720	562-799-4700	799-4711
Los Altos School District 201 Covington Rd *Web:* www.lasdschools.org	Los Altos	CA	94024	650-947-1150	947-0118
Los Angeles Unified School District (LAUSD) 333 S Beaudry Ave 25th Fl *Web:* www.notebook.lausd.net	Los Angeles	CA	90017	213-241-8220	241-8984
Los Gatos Union Elementary School District 17010 Roberts Rd *TF:* 866-986-1601 ■ *Web:* www.lgusd.k12.ca.us	Los Gatos	CA	95032	408-335-2000	
Louisville Municipal School District 112 S Columbus Ave PO Box 909 *Web:* www.louisville.k12.ms.us	Louisville	MS	39339	662-773-3411	773-4013
Lubbock-Cooper Independent School District 16302 Loop 493 *TF:* 800-546-9928 ■ *Web:* www.lcisd.net	Lubbock	TX	79423	806-863-2282	
Luling Independent School District 212 E Bowie St *Web:* www.luling.txed.net	Luling	TX	78648	830-875-3191	
Lyons Elementary School District 103 4100 Joliet Ave *Web:* www.sd103.com	Lyons	IL	60534	708-783-4100	
Macomb Community Unit School District 185 323 W Washington St *Web:* www.medfd.org	Macomb	IL	61455	309-833-4161	
Madera Unified School District 1902 Howard Rd *Web:* www.madera.k12.ca.us	Madera	CA	93637	559-675-4500	675-1186
Madison Local Board of Edcuation 1379 Grace St *Web:* www.madison-richland.k12.oh.us	Mansfield	OH	44905	419-589-2600	
Madison Metropolitan School District 545 W Dayton St **Fax:* Hum Res ■ *Web:* www.madison.k12.wi.us	Madison	WI	53703	608-663-1879	204-0346*
Mahanoy Area School District 1 Golden Bear Dr *Web:* www.mabears.net	Mahanoy City	PA	17948	570-773-3443	
Maine Endwell Central School 712 Farm To Market Rd *Web:* www.me.stier.org	Endwell	NY	13760	607-754-1400	
Malverne Union Free School District 12 301 Wicks Ln *Web:* www.malverne.k12.ny.us	Malverne	NY	11565	516-887-6400	
Mansfield Bancshares Inc 118 Jefferson St PO Box 1308 *TF:* 888-679-6246 ■ *Web:* www.communitybankofla.com	Mansfield	LA	71052	318-872-3831	872-9707
Maple Valley School District 11090 Nashville Hwy *Web:* www.mvs.k12.mi.us	Vermontville	MI	49096	517-852-9699	
Marana Unified School District 6 11279 W Grier Rd Suite 127 *Web:* www.maranausd.org	Marana	AZ	85653	520-682-4757	616-4515
Mardel Inc 7727 SW 44th St *Web:* www.mardel.com	Oklahoma City	OK	73179	405-745-1300	745-1337
Marinette School District 2139 Pierce Ave *Web:* www.marinette.k12.wi.us	Marinette	WI	54143	715-735-1406	
Marion Center Area School District PO Box 156 *Web:* www.mcasd.net	Marion Center	PA	15759	724-397-4911	
Marion County Board of Education Inc 200 Gaston Ave *Web:* www.marionboe.com	Fairmont	WV	26554	304-367-2100	
Mark Young Construction Inc 7200 Miller Pl *Web:* www.markyoungconstruction.com	Frederick	CO	80504	303-776-1449	776-1729
Marshall Independent School District (inc) 1305 E Pinecrest Dr *Web:* www.marshallisd.com	Marshall	TX	75670	903-927-8701	935-0203
Martinez Unified School District 921 Susana St *Web:* www.martinez.k12.ca.us	Martinez	CA	94553	925-335-5800	335-5960
Marysville School District 25 4220 80th St Ne *TF:* 800-999-1077 ■ *Web:* www.msvl.k12.wa.us	Marysville	WA	98270	360-653-7058	
Massillon City School District 207 Oak Ave SE *Web:* www.massillon.sparcc.org	Massillon	OH	44646	330-830-1810	
McCrory Construction Co LLC 1280 Assembly St PO Box 145 *Web:* www.mccroryconstruction.com	Columbia	SC	29201	803-251-8106	254-9800
McIntosh County Board of Education 200 Pine St *Web:* www.mcintosh.k12.ga.us	Darien	GA	31305	912-437-6645	
McLeod Express LLC 5002 Cundiff Ct *TF:* 800-709-3936 ■ *Web:* www.mcleodtrucking.com	Decatur	IL	62524	217-876-0570	875-7914
Mead School District 2323 E Farwell Rd *Web:* www.mead354.org	Mead	WA	99021	509-465-6000	465-6020
Mechanicsburg Area School District (inc) 100 E Elmwood Ave 2nd Fl *Web:* www.mbgsd.org	Mechanicsburg	PA	17055	717-691-4500	691-3438
Mecosta-Osceola Intermediate School District 15760 190th Ave *TF:* 877-488-8900 ■ *Web:* www.moisd.org	Big Rapids	MI	49307	231-796-3543	
Medford Township Board of Education 128 Rt 70 Suite 1 *Web:* www.medford.k12.nj.us	Medford	NJ	08055	609-654-6416	654-7436
Melvindale-Northern Allen Park Public Schools 18530 Prospect St *Web:* www.melnap.k12.mi.us	Melvindale	MI	48122	313-389-3300	389-3312
Memphis City Board of Education 2597 Avery Ave *Web:* www.mcsk12.net	Memphis	TN	38112	901-416-5300	416-5578
Meramec Valley R-3 School District 126 N Payne St *Web:* www.mvr3.k12.mo.us	Pacific	MO	63069	636-271-1400	271-1406
Meriwether County Schools 2100 Gaston St PO Box 70 *Web:* www.meriwether.k12.ga.us	Greenville	GA	30222	706-672-4297	
Metal Transportation Systems Inc 1850 County Rt 1	Oswego	NY	13126	315-342-5223	342-5318
Metropolitan Construction Services LLC 2803 Butterfield Rd Suite 100 *Web:* www.metroconstructionllc.com	Oak Brook	IL	60523	630-691-7200	691-7234
Metropolitan Nashville Public Schools (MNPS) 2601 Bransford Ave *TF:* 800-848-0298 ■ *Web:* www.mnps.org	Nashville	TN	37204	615-259-8531	214-8890
Miami-Dade County Public Schools (M-DCPS) 1450 NE 2nd Ave *Web:* www.dadeschools.net	Miami	FL	33132	305-995-1000	
Mid-East Career & Technology Centers 400 Richards Rd *Web:* www.mid-east.k12.oh.us	Zanesville	OH	43701	740-454-0101	454-0731
Middlebury Community Schools 57853 Northridge Dr *Web:* www.mcsin-k12.org	Middlebury	IN	46540	574-825-9425	825-9426

Name / Address	City	State	Zip	Phone	Fax
Middlesex County Educational Service Commission 1660 Stelton Rd *Web:* www.mresc.k12.nj.us	Piscataway	NJ	08854	732-777-9848	
Middlesex County Vocational & Technical High Schools PO Box 1070 *Web:* www.mcvts.net	East Brunswick	NJ	08816	732-257-3300	
Middleton Cross Plains Area School District 7106 S Ave *Web:* www.mcpasd.k12.wi.us	Middleton	WI	53562	608-829-9000	
Middletown Area School District (inc) 55 W Water St Suite 2 *Web:* www.raiderweb.org	Middletown	PA	17057	717-948-3300	948-3329
Middletown City School 1515 Girard Ave *Web:* www.middletowncityschools.com	Middletown	OH	45044	513-423-0781	420-4579
Midwestern Intermediate Unit Iv 453 Maple St *TF:* 800-942-8035 ■ *Web:* www.miu4.k12.pa.us	Grove City	PA	16127	724-458-6700	458-5083
Mifflin County School District 201 8th St *Web:* www.mcsdk12.org	Lewistown	PA	17044	717-248-0148	
Miken Builders Inc 32782 Cedar Dr Unit 1 *Web:* www.mikenbuilders.com	Millville	DE	19967	302-537-4444	537-4525
Milford Exempted Village School District 1039 St Rt 28 *Web:* www.milfordschools.org	Milford	OH	45150	513-831-9690	831-3208
Milwaukee Public Schools 5225 W Vliet St **Fax:* Hum Res ■ *Web:* www.mpsportal.milwaukee.k12.wi.us	Milwaukee	WI	53208	414-475-8393	475-8722*
Minisink Valley Central Sd PO Box 217 *Web:* www.minisink.com	Slate Hill	NY	10973	845-355-5100	
Minneapolis Public Schools 3345 Chicago Ave *Web:* www.mpls.k12.mn.us	Minneapolis	MN	55407	612-668-0000	668-0525
Minnehaha Academy 3100 W River Pkwy *Web:* www.minnehahaacademy.net	Minneapolis	MN	55406	612-729-8321	
Minnetonka Public School Service Ctr 5621 County Rd 101 *Web:* www.minnetonka.k12.mn.us	Minnetonka	MN	55345	952-401-5000	401-5083
Minot Public School District 1 215 2nd St SE *Web:* www.minot.k12.nd.us/education/components/scrapbook/default.php?sectionid=1	Minot	ND	58701	701-857-4400	857-4432
Mobile County Public Schools 1 Magnum Pass PO Box 180069 **Fax:* Hum Res ■ *Web:* www.mcpss.com	Mobile	AL	36618	251-221-4000	221-4545*
Modern Builders Inc PO Box 418	Janesville	IA	50647	319-987-2911	
Modesto City Schools 426 Locust St **Fax:* Hum Res ■ *Web:* www.mcs.monet.k12.ca.us/default.aspx	Modesto	CA	95351	209-576-4011	576-4846*
Monroe County Intermediate School District 1101 S Raisinville Rd *Web:* www.misd.k12.mi.us	Monroe	MI	48161	734-242-5454	
Monrovia Unified School District 325 E Huntington Dr *Web:* www.monroviaschools.net	Monrovia	CA	91016	626-471-2000	
Montebello Unified School District (MUSD) 123 S Montebello Blvd *Web:* www.montebello.k12.ca.us	Montebello	CA	90640	323-887-7900	
Montgomery Public Schools 307 S Decatur St PO Box 1991 *Web:* www.mps.k12.al.us	Montgomery	AL	36104	334-223-6700	269-3076
Monticello Central School District 237 Forestburgh Rd *TF:* 866-805-0990 ■ *Web:* www.monticelloschools.net	Monticello	NY	12701	845-794-7700	
Montrose County School District Re-1j Inc PO Box 10000 *Web:* www.mcsd.org	Montrose	CO	81402	970-249-7726	249-7173
Mooresville Graded School District 305 N Main St *Web:* www.mgsd.k12.nc.us	Mooresville	NC	28115	704-664-5553	663-3005
Morehouse Parish School Board PO Box 872 *Web:* www.mpsb.us	Bastrop	LA	71220	318-283-3415	281-1814
Morgan County Schools 1325 Pt Mallard Pkwy *Web:* www.morgank12.org	Decatur	AL	35601	256-353-6442	309-2180
Morris School District 31 Hazel St *Web:* www.morrisschooldistrict.org	Morristown	NJ	07960	973-292-2300	
Morris-Union Jointure Commission 340 Central Ave *Web:* www.mujc.org	New Providence	NJ	07974	908-464-7625	
Mountain Empire Unified School District 3291 Buckman Springs Rd *Web:* www.meusd.k12.ca.us	Pine Valley	CA	91962	619-473-9022	473-9728
Mountain View School District (MVSD) 3320 Gilman Rd *Web:* www.mtviewschools.com	El Monte	CA	91732	626-652-4000	652-4052
Mt Pleasant Central School District 825 Westlake Dr *Web:* www.mtplcsd.org	Thornwood	NY	10594	914-769-5500	769-3733
Mt. Lebanon School District 7 Horsman Dr *Web:* www.mtlsd.org	Pittsburgh	PA	15228	412-344-2000	344-2047
Mukwonago Area School District 385 County Rd NNßE *Web:* www.mukwonago.k12.wi.us	Mukwonago	WI	53149	262-363-6300	363-6272
Murray Co 1807 Park 270 Dr Suite 460 *TF:* 888-323-5560 ■ *Web:* www.murray-company.com	Saint Louis	MO	63146	314-576-2818	434-5780
Nashoba Regional School District Inc 50 Mechanic St *Web:* www.nrsd.net	Bolton	MA	01740	978-779-0539	
Nassau County School District 1201 Atlantic Ave *Web:* www.edline.net/pages/Nassau_County_School_District	Fernandina Beach	FL	32034	904-491-9900	
National Automobile Transporters Asso 2200 Mill Rd *Web:* www.carhaulers.org	Alexandria	VA	22314	703-838-7970	838-7994
National Children's Center Inc 6200 2nd St NW *TF:* 866-632-9992 ■ *Web:* www.nccinc.org	Washington	DC	20011	202-722-2319	
National Outdoor Leadership School 284 Lincoln St *TF:* 800-710-6657 ■ *Web:* www.nols.edu	Lander	WY	82520	307-332-5300	332-1220
National School District 1500 N Ave *Web:* www.nsd.us	National City	CA	91950	619-336-7500	336-7521
Nationwide Magazine & Book Distributors Inc PO Box 170746 *Web:* www.nationwidemagazine.com	Irving	TX	75017	972-438-2123	721-0613
New Brighton Area School District 3225 43rd St *Web:* www.nbasd.org	New Brighton	PA	15066	724-843-1795	843-6144
New Haven Public Schools (NHPS) 54 Meadow St *Web:* www.nhps.net	New Haven	CT	06519	203-946-8811	946-7107
New Haven Unified School District 34200 Alvarado Niles Rd *Web:* www.nhusd.k12.ca.us	Union City	CA	94587	510-471-1100	
New Lenox School District 122 (NLSD) 102 S Cedar Rd *Web:* www.nlsd122.org	New Lenox	IL	60451	815-485-2169	
New Trier Township High School District 203 7 Happ Rd *Web:* www.newtrier.k12.il.us	Northfield	IL	60093	847-446-7000	784-7500
New York City Dept of Education 65 Ct St *Web:* schools.nyc.gov	Brooklyn	NY	11201	718-935-2000	
Newberg School District 29 Jt 714 E 6th St *Web:* www.newberg.k12.or.us	Newberg	OR	97132	503-554-5000	538-4374
Newton-Conover City Sch Dist 605 N Ashe Ave *Web:* www.nccs.k12.nc.us	Newton	NC	28658	828-464-3191	
Niagara Fresh Fruit Co 5796 Wilson Burt Rd *Web:* niagarafreshfruit.com	Burt	NY	14028	716-778-7631	778-8768
Niles Community School 111 Spruce St *TF:* 877-622-2321 ■ *Web:* www.nilesschools.org	Niles	MI	49120	269-683-0734	
Niskayuna Central School District (NCSD) 1239 Van Antwerp Rd *Web:* www.niskyschools.org	Schenectady	NY	12309	518-377-4666	377-4074
Nordonia Hills School District 9370 Olde 8 Rd *Web:* www.nordoniaschools.org	Northfield	OH	44067	330-467-0580	
Norfolk Collegiate School 7336 Granby St *Web:* www.norfolkcollegiate.org	Norfolk	VA	23505	757-480-2885	
Norfolk Public Schools 800 E City Hall Ave *Web:* www.nps.k12.va.us	Norfolk	VA	23510	757-628-3843	628-3820
Normandy School District 3855 Lcas Hunt Rd Suite 100 *Web:* www.normandy.k12.mo.us	Saint Louis	MO	63121	314-493-0400	493-0414
North Hunterdon-Voorhees Regional High School District 1445 SR- 31 *Web:* www.nhvweb.net	Annandale	NJ	08801	908-735-2846	735-6914
North Mason School District Inc 71 E Campus Dr *Web:* www.nmsd.wednet.edu	Belfair	WA	98528	360-277-2300	
North Monterey County Unified School District 8142 Moss Landing Rd *Web:* www.nmcusd.org	Moss Landing	CA	95039	831-633-4286	633-2937
North Ridgeville City School District 5490 Mills Creek Ln *TF:* 877-644-6457 ■ *Web:* www.nrcs.k12.oh.us	North Ridgeville	OH	44039	440-327-4444	
North Rose-Wolcott Central School District 11669 Salter Colvin Rd *Web:* www.nrwcs.org	Wolcott	NY	14590	315-594-3141	594-2352
North Sanpete School District Inc 390 E 700 S *Web:* www.nsh.nsanpete.k12.ut.us	Mount Pleasant	UT	84647	435-462-2452	462-3112
North Santiam School District 29 J 1155 N 3rd Ave *Web:* www.nsantiam.k12.or.us	Stayton	OR	97383	503-769-6924	769-3578
North Schuylkill School District 15 Academy Ln *Web:* www.northschuylkill.net	Ashland	PA	17921	570-874-0466	874-3334
North Shore School Dst 112 (NSSD) 1936 Green Bay Rd *Web:* www.nssd112.org	Highland Park	IL	60035	847-681-6700	681-6712
Northampton County School District 701 N Church St PO Box 158 *Web:* www.northampton.k12.nc.us	Jackson	NC	27845	252-534-1371	534-4631
Northern Burlington County School District 160 Mansfield Rd E *Web:* www.nburlington.com	Columbus	NJ	08022	609-298-3900	
Northern Local School District 8700 Sheridan Dr *Web:* www.nlsd.k12.oh.us	Thornville	OH	43076	740-743-1303	743-3301
Northview Public School 4451 Hunsberger NE *Web:* www.nvps.net	Grand Rapids	MI	49525	616-363-4857	361-3494
Northwest Local School District (NWLSD) 3240 Banning Rd *Web:* www.nwlsd.org	Cincinnati	OH	45239	513-923-1000	923-3644
Northwest R-1 School District 2843 Community Ln *Web:* www.nwr1.k12.mo.us	High Ridge	MO	63049	636-677-3473	677-5480
Northwestern Lehigh Sch Dist 6493 Rt 309 *Web:* www.nwlehighsd.org	New Tripoli	PA	18066	610-298-8661	
Norwin School District 281 Mcmahon Dr *Web:* www.norwinsd.org	Irwin	PA	15642	724-861-3000	863-9467
Nye County School District Inc (NCSD) PO Box 113 *TF:* 800-796-6273 ■ *Web:* nyecounty.schoolinsites.com	Tonopah	NV	89049	775-482-6258	482-8573
Oak Creek-Franklin Joint School District 7630 S 10th St *Web:* www.oakcreek.k12.wi.us	Oak Creek	WI	53154	414-768-5886	768-6151
Oakland Schools Inc 2111 Pontiac Lake Rd *Web:* www.oakland.k12.mi.us	Waterford	MI	48328	248-209-2000	209-2206
Oakland Unified School District 1025 2nd Ave *TF:* 888-604-4636 ■ *Web:* www.ousd.k12.ca.us	Oakland	CA	94606	510-879-8582	

	City	State	ZIP	Phone	Fax
Oceanside Union Free School District 11 145 Merle Ave. *Web:* www.oceanside.k12.ny.us	Oceanside	NY	11572	516-678-1200	
Oconee County School District PO Box 146 *Web:* www.oconee.k12.ga.us	Watkinsville	GA	30677	706-769-5130	769-3500
Ohio County Board of Education PO Box 70 *Web:* www.ohio.k12.ky.us	Hartford	KY	42347	270-298-3249	
Oklahoma City Public Schools 2500 NE 30th St *Web:* www.okcps.org	Oklahoma City	OK	73111	405-587-1000	587-0043
Olympia School District 1113 Legion Way SE *Web:* www.osd.wednet.edu	Olympia	WA	98501	360-596-6100	596-6111
Omaha Public Schools 3215 Cuming St *Web:* www.ops.org	Omaha	NE	68131	402-557-2222	
Oneida City School District Inc 565 Sayles St *Web:* www.oneidacsd.org	Oneida	NY	13421	315-363-2550	363-6728
Orange County Public Schools 445 W Amelia St. **Fax:* Hum Res ■ *Web:* www.ocps.k12.fl.us	Orlando	FL	32801	407-317-3200	317-3392*
Orangeburg Consolidated School District 5 578 Ellis Ave. *Web:* www.ocsd5schools.org	Orangeburg	SC	29115	803-534-5454	533-7953
Oregon City School District 62 PO Box 2110 *Web:* www.orecity.k12.or.us	Oregon City	OR	97045	503-785-8000	
Orleans Parish School Board 3520 General DeGaulle Dr *Web:* www.nops.k12.la.us	New Orleans	LA	70114	504-304-3520	
Oroville Union High School District 2211 Washington Ave. *Web:* www.ouhsd.org	Oroville	CA	95966	530-538-2300	
Ossining Union Free School District 190 Croton Ave. *Web:* www.ossiningufsd.org	Ossining	NY	10562	914-941-7700	941-7291
Oswego Community Unit School District 308 4175 SR- 71 *Web:* www.oswego308.org	Oswego	IL	60543	630-554-3447	554-2168
Owosso Public Schools 1405 W N St PO Box 340 *Web:* www.owosso.k12.mi.us	Owosso	MI	48867	989-723-8131	723-7777
Oxford Academy & Central School 50 S Washington Ave PO Box 192 *Web:* www.oxac.org	Oxford	NY	13830	607-843-2025	843-3241
Oyster Bay-East Norwich Central School District 1 McCouns Ln *Web:* www.obenschools.org	Oyster Bay	NY	11771	516-624-6500	
Pacific Bldg Group 9752 Aspen Creek Ct Suite 150 *Web:* www.pacificbuildinggroup.com	San Diego	CA	92126	858-552-0600	552-0604
Paideia School Inc The 1509 Ponce De Leon Ave Ne. *Web:* www.paideiaschool.org	Atlanta	GA	30307	404-377-3491	377-0032
Palm Beach County School District The 3300 Forest Hill Blvd **Fax:* Hum Res ■ *TF:* 866-930-8402 ■ *Web:* www.palmbeach.k12.fl.us	West Palm Beach	FL	33406	561-434-8000	434-8899*
Palmerton Area School District 680 Fourth St *Web:* www.palmerton.k12.pa.us	Palmerton	PA	18071	610-826-7101	826-4958
Palmyra Area School District 1125 Pk Dr *Web:* www.palmyra.k12.pa.us	Palmyra	PA	17078	717-838-3144	
Paradise Valley Unified School District 15002 N 32nd St *Web:* www.pvschools.net	Phoenix	AZ	85032	602-867-5100	867-5251
Parent/Child Incorporated of San Antonio & Bexar County PO Box 830407 *TF:* 800-526-1960 ■ *Web:* www.parentchildinc.com	San Antonio	TX	78283	210-226-6232	
Parkland School District 1210 Springhouse Rd. *Web:* www.parklandsd.org	Allentown	PA	18104	610-351-5503	351-5509
Paul Risk Assoc Inc 11 W State St. *Web:* www.paulrisk.com	Quarryville	PA	17566	717-786-7308	786-2848
Pawling Central School District 515 Rt 22 *Web:* www.pawlingschools.org	Pawling	NY	12564	845-855-4600	
Pdq Transit Inc 1640 E Fifth Ave. *TF:* 877-840-0411 ■ *Web:* www.urbanexpress.biz	Columbus	OH	43219	614-253-7000	253-3010
Peach County School District Inc PO Box 1018 *Web:* www.peachschools.org	Fort Valley	GA	31030	478-825-5933	825-9970
Pembroke Hill School 400 W 51st St. *Web:* www.pembrokehill.org	Kansas City	MO	64112	816-936-1200	
Penn Hills School District 260 Aster St *Web:* www.phsd.k12.pa.us	Pittsburgh	PA	15235	412-793-7000	793-6402
Pennridge School District 1200 N 5th St *Web:* www.pennridge.org	Perkasie	PA	18944	215-257-5011	
Penns Grove-Carneys Point Regional Board of Education 100 Iona Ave. *Web:* www.pennsgrove.k12.nj.us	Penns Grove	NJ	08069	856-299-4250	299-5226
Perris Union High School District 155 E 4th St *Web:* www.puhsd.org	Perris	CA	92570	951-943-6369	
Person County Public Schools 304 S Morgan St. *TF:* 888-809-3724 ■ *Web:* www.person.k12.nc.us	Roxboro	NC	27573	336-599-2191	
Petaluma City Schools (PCS) 200 Douglas St *Web:* www.petalumacityschools.org	Petaluma	CA	94952	707-778-4813	
Petersburg Public Schools 255 S Bolevard E *Web:* www.petersburg.k12.va.us	Petersburg	VA	23805	804-732-0510	732-2154
Phillipsburg Board of Education 445 Marshall St *Web:* www.pburgsd.net	Phillipsburg	NJ	08865	908-454-3400	
Phoenix Elementary School District 1817 N 7th St **Fax:* Hum Res ■ *Web:* www.phxelem.k12.az.us	Phoenix	AZ	85006	602-257-3755	257-6077*
Phoenix Union High School District (PUHSD) 4502 N Central Ave. **Fax:* Hum Res ■ *Web:* www.phxhs.k12.az.us	Phoenix	AZ	85012	602-764-1100	271-3510*
Pickaway-Ross County Joint Vocational School District 895 Crouse Chapel Rd *Web:* www.pickawayross.com	Chillicothe	OH	45601	740-642-2550	
Pickens County School District (PCSD) 1348 Griffin Mill Rd *Web:* www.pickens.k12.sc.us	Easley	SC	29640	864-397-1000	855-8159
Pickerington Local School District 777 Long Rd. *Web:* www.pickerington.k12.oh.us	Pickerington	OH	43147	614-833-2110	833-2143
Pima County School Superintendent 130 W Congress St 4th Fl. **Fax:* Hum Res ■ *Web:* www.schools.pima.gov	Tucson	AZ	85701	520-740-8451	623-9308*
Pinckney Community Schools 2130 E MI 36 *Web:* www.pinckneyschools.org	Pinckney	MI	48169	810-225-3900	
Pine Grove Area School Dist 103 School St. *Web:* www.pgasd.com	Pine Grove	PA	17963	570-345-2731	
Pinelands Regional School District PO Box 248 *TF:* 866-850-0511 ■ *Web:* www.pinelandsregional.org	Tuckerton	NJ	08087	609-296-3106	
Pittsburgh Public Schools 341 S Bellefield Ave *Web:* www.pghboe.net/pps/site/default.asp	Pittsburgh	PA	15213	412-622-7920	
Pittsylvania County School Board 39 Bank St SE PO Box 232 *TF:* 888-440-6520 ■ *Web:* www.pcs.k12.va.us	Chatham	VA	24531	434-432-2761	432-9560
Placentia-Yorba Linda Unified School District (PYLUSD) 1301 E Orangethorpe Ave *Web:* www.pylusd.org	Placentia	CA	92870	714-996-2550	
Placer Union High School District PO Box 5048 *Web:* www.puhsd.k12.ca.us	Auburn	CA	95604	530-886-4400	886-4439
Plain Local School District 901 44th St NW *Web:* www.plainlocal.org	Canton	OH	44709	330-492-3500	493-5542
Plainfield Central School District 75 Canterbury Rd *Web:* www.plainfieldschools.org	Plainfield	CT	06374	860-564-6437	
Plainfield Community Consolidated School District 202 15732 S Howard St. *Web:* www.psd202.org	Plainfield	IL	60544	815-577-4000	436-7824
Plainwell Community School District 600 School Dr *Web:* www.plainwellschools.org	Plainwell	MI	49080	269-685-5823	685-1108
Plaquemines Parish School Board PO Box 69 *TF:* 877-453-2721 ■ *Web:* www.ppsb.org	Belle Chasse	LA	70037	504-392-4970	392-4973
Pleasant Valley Sch District 600 Temple Ave *Web:* www.pvsd.k12.ca.us	Camarillo	CA	93010	805-482-2763	987-5511
Pleasantville Union Free School District 60 Romer Ave *Web:* www.pleasantvillelacrosse.com	Pleasantville	NY	10570	914-741-1400	741-1499
Portage Community School District 904 De Witt St *Web:* www.portage.k12.wi.us	Portage	WI	53901	608-742-4867	
Portland Public Schools 501 N Dixon St *Web:* www.pps.k12.or.us	Portland	OR	97227	503-916-2000	916-3110
Positive Education Program Inc 3100 Euclid Ave *Web:* www.pepcleve.org	Cleveland	OH	44115	216-361-4400	361-8600
Poudre School District 2407 LaPorte Ave *Web:* www.psd.k12.co.us	Fort Collins	CO	80521	970-482-7420	490-3514
Powhatan County School District 2320 Skaggs Rd *Web:* www.powhatan.k12.va.us	Powhatan	VA	23139	804-598-5700	
Preble-Shawnee School District 124 Bloomfield St. *Web:* www.preble-shawnee.k12.oh.us	Camden	OH	45311	937-452-3323	
Prince Edward County School District 35 Eagle Dr. *Web:* www.pecps.k12.va.us	Farmville	VA	23901	434-315-2100	
Princeton Regional School District PO Box 711 *TF:* 877-652-2873 ■ *Web:* www.prs.k12.nj.us	Princeton	NJ	08540	609-806-4200	
Prior Lake-Savage Area Public School District 719 PO Box 539 *Web:* www.priorlake-savage.k12.mn.us	Prior Lake	MN	55372	952-226-0000	226-0049
Provo School District 280 W 940 N. *Web:* www.provo.edu	Provo	UT	84604	801-374-4800	374-4808
Puget Sound Educational Service District 800 Oakesdale Ave SW *TF:* 800-664-4549 ■ *Web:* www.psesd.org	Renton	WA	98057	425-917-7600	
Pulaski County School District (PCPS) 202 N Washington Ave *Web:* www.pcva.us	Pulaski	VA	24301	540-994-2550	994-2552
Pullman School District 267 240 SE Dexter St *Web:* www.psd267.org	Pullman	WA	99163	509-332-3581	334-0375
Putnam Valley School District Inc 146 Peekskill Hollow Rd *Web:* www.pvcsd.org	Putnam Valley	NY	10579	845-528-8143	528-8386
Quaker Valley School District 203 Graham St *Web:* www.qvsd.org	Sewickley	PA	15143	412-749-3600	
Queensbury Union Free School 429 Aviation Rd *Web:* www.queensburyschool.org	Queensbury	NY	12804	518-824-5699	
R.e. Crawford Construction Inc 6771 Professional Pkwy W Suite 100 *Web:* www.recrawford.com	Sarasota	FL	34240	941-907-0010	
Rabun County School District 41 Education St *Web:* www.rabun.k12.ga.us	Clayton	GA	30525	706-746-5376	746-3084

	City	State	Zip	Phone	Fax
Radnor Township School Authority 135 S Wayne Ave Suite 1 *Web:* www.rtsd.org	Wayne	PA	19087	610-688-8100	
Ramsey Board of Education 266 E Main St *Web:* www.ramsey.k12.nj.us	Ramsey	NJ	07446	201-785-2300	934-6623
Red Clay Consolidated School District 1502 Spruce Ave. *Web:* www.redclay.k12.de.us	Wilmington	DE	19808	302-552-3700	
Redmond School District 145 SE Salmon Ave *Web:* www.redmond.k12.or.us	Redmond	OR	97756	541-923-5437	923-5142
Redwood City School District (RCSD) 750 Bradford St *Web:* www.rcsd.k12.ca.us/site/default.aspx?PageID=1	Redwood City	CA	94063	650-423-2200	423-2294
Retail Construction Services Inc (RCS) 11343 39th St N *Web:* www.retailconstruction.com	Lake Elmo	MN	55042	651-704-9000	704-9100
Reynolds School District 7 Inc 1204 NE 201st Ave *Web:* www.reynolds.k12.or.us	Fairview	OR	97024	503-661-7200	667-6932
Reynoldsburg City Schools 7244 E Main St. **Fax Area Code:* 641 ■ *Web:* www.reyn.org	Reynoldsburg	OH	43068	614-501-1020	501-1050*
Rialto Unified School District School Facilities Corp 182 E Walnut Ave *Web:* www.rialto.k12.ca.us	Rialto	CA	92376	909-820-7700	873-0448
Richland County School District One 1616 Richland St **Fax:* Hum Res ■ *Web:* www.richlandone.org	Columbia	SC	29201	803-231-7000	231-7417*
Richmond City Public Schools 301 N 9th St *Web:* www.newweb.richmond.k12.va.us	Richmond	VA	23219	804-780-7700	780-4122
Richmond County School System 864 Broad St *Web:* www.rcboe.org/home.asp	Augusta	GA	30901	706-826-1000	
River View Local School District 26496 SR- 60 *Web:* www.river-view.k12.oh.us	Warsaw	OH	43844	740-824-3521	
Riverdale Country School 5250 Fieldston Rd *Web:* www.riverdale.edu	Bronx	NY	10471	718-549-8810	519-2795
Riverside Unified School District (RUSD) 3380 14th St PO Box 2800 *Web:* www.rusd.k12.ca.us	Riverside	CA	92501	951-788-7135	
Rochester City School District 131 W Broad St *Web:* www.rcsdk12.org	Rochester	NY	14614	585-262-8100	262-5151
Roman Catholic Diocese of Fresno 1550 N Fresno St *Web:* www.dioceseoffresno.org	Fresno	CA	93703	559-488-7400	
Rome City School District 508 E 2nd St *Web:* www.rcs.rome.ga.us	Rome	GA	30161	706-236-5050	802-4311
Romeo Community School District 316 N Main St *TF:* 888-427-6818 ■ *Web:* www.romeo.k12.mi.us	Romeo	MI	48065	586-752-0200	752-0228
Rose Tree Media School District 308 N Olive St *Web:* www.rtmsd.org	Media	PA	19063	610-627-6000	
Rosetta Stone Inc 1919 N Lynn St 7th Fl *NYSE:* RST ■ **Fax Area Code:* 540 ■ *TF:* 800-788-0822 ■ *Web:* www.rosettastone.com	Arlington	VA	22209	800-788-0822	432-0953*
Roseville Joint Union High School District Fin Corp 1750 Cirby Way *Web:* www.rjuhsd.k12.ca.us	Roseville	CA	95661	916-786-2051	786-2681
Ross Valley School District 110 Shaw Dr *TF:* 800-433-2611 ■ *Web:* www.rossvalleyschools.org	San Anselmo	CA	94960	415-454-2162	
Rush-Henrietta Central School District 2034 Lehigh Stn Rd *Web:* www.rhnet.org	Henrietta	NY	14467	585-359-5000	359-5045
S A Kennedy Inc 4255 Trotters Way Suite 1a *Web:* www.sakennedy.com	Alpharetta	GA	30004	770-667-3602	667-1430
Sachem Central School District At Holbrook 245 Union Ave *Web:* www.sachem.edu	Holbrook	NY	11741	631-471-1300	
Sacramento City Unified School District 5735 47th Ave. *Web:* www.scusd.edu	Sacramento	CA	95824	916-643-7400	643-9440
Safford Unified School District 1 734 W 11th St. *Web:* www.saffordusd.k12.az.us	Safford	AZ	85546	928-348-7000	
Saint Louis Public Schools 801 N 11th St **Fax:* Hum Res ■ *Web:* www.slps.org	Saint Louis	MO	63101	314-231-3720	345-2650*
Salem-Keizer Public Schools 2450 Lancaster Dr NE **Fax:* Hum Res ■ *Web:* www.salkeiz.k12.or.us	Salem	OR	97305	503-399-3000	375-7802*
Salin Bancshares Inc 8455 Keystone Xing *TF:* 800-320-7536 ■ *Web:* www.salin.com	Indianapolis	IN	46240	317-532-2265	532-2263
Saline Area Schools 7265 Saline Ann Arbor Rd. *Web:* www.salineschools.com	Saline	MI	48176	734-429-8000	429-8010
Salt Lake School District 440 E 100 S *Web:* www.slc.k12.ut.us	Salt Lake City	UT	84111	801-578-8599	578-8689
Sampson County Schools 437 Rowan Rd PO Box 439 *Web:* www.sampson.k12.nc.us	Clinton	NC	28329	910-592-1401	590-2445
San Antonio Independent School District (SAISD) 141 Lavaca St **Fax:* Hum Res ■ *Web:* www.saisd.net	San Antonio	TX	78210	210-554-2200	299-5600*
San Diego Jewish Academy 11860 Carmel Creek Rd *Web:* www.sdja.com	San Diego	CA	92130	858-704-3700	704-3750
San Diego Unified School District 4100 Normal St *Web:* www.sandi.net	San Diego	CA	92103	619-725-8000	725-8001
San Francisco Unified School District 555 Franklin St *Web:* www.sfusd.edu	San Francisco	CA	94102	415-241-6000	241-6429
San Jose Unified School District 855 Lenzen Ave. **Fax:* Hum Res ■ *Web:* www.sjusd.org	San Jose	CA	95126	408-535-6000	535-2377*
San Lorenzo Unified School District (SLZUSD) 15510 Usher St. *Web:* www.slzusd.org	San Lorenzo	CA	94580	510-317-4600	
San Ysidro School District 4350 Otay Mesa Rd *Web:* www.sysd.k12.ca.us	San Ysidro	CA	92173	619-428-4476	428-1505
Santa Barbara Unified School District 720 Santa Barbara St *Web:* www.sbsdk12.org	Santa Barbara	CA	93101	805-963-4338	
Santa Fe Independent School District PO Box 370 *Web:* www.sfisd.org	Santa Fe	TX	77510	409-925-3526	
Santa Maria-Bonita School Dist 708 S Miller St *Web:* www.smbsd.org	Santa Maria	CA	93454	805-928-1783	
Santee School District 9625 Cuyamaca St *Web:* www.santeesd.net	Santee	CA	92071	619-258-2300	
Saucon Valley School District 2097 Polk Valley Rd *TF:* 866-632-9992 ■ *Web:* www.sauconvalley.k12.pa.us	Hellertown	PA	18055	610-838-7026	
Savannah-Chatham County Public Schools 208 Bull St **Fax:* Hum Res ■ *Web:* www.savannah.chatham.k12.ga.us	Savannah	GA	31401	912-201-5600	201-7667*
Scarsdale Union Free School District 2 Brewster Rd *TF:* 888-886-9729 ■ *Web:* www.scarsdaleschools.k12.ny.us	Scarsdale	NY	10583	914-721-2410	
Schalmont Central School District 4 Sabre Dr *Web:* www.schalmont.org	Schenectady	NY	12306	518-355-9200	355-9203
School Board of Highlands County Florida PO Box 9300 *TF:* 877-357-7456 ■ *Web:* www.highlands.k12.fl.us	Sebring	FL	33871	863-471-5555	386-6179
School District of Cheltenham Township 2000 Ashbourne Rd *Web:* www.cheltenham.org	Elkins Park	PA	19027	215-886-9500	884-6929
School District of Hartford 675 E Rossman St *Web:* www.hartfordjt1.k12.wi.us	Hartford	WI	53027	262-673-3155	673-3548
School District of Philadelphia 440 N Broad St *Web:* www.phila.k12.pa.us	Philadelphia	PA	19130	215-400-4000	
School District of The Chathams 58 Meyersville Rd *Web:* www.chatham-nj.org	Chatham	NJ	07928	973-457-2500	701-0146
Schuylkill Haven Area School Authority 120 Haven St *Web:* www.haven.k12.pa.us	Schuylkill Haven	PA	17972	570-385-6705	
Schuylkill Valley School District 929 Lakeshore Dr *TF:* 888-883-8237 ■ *Web:* www.schuylkillvalley.org	Leesport	PA	19533	610-926-1706	926-8341
Scotch Plains-Fanwood Board of Education 2280 Evergreen Ave *Web:* www.spfk12.org	Scotch Plains	NJ	07076	908-889-5331	889-9332
Scotts Valley Unified School District Inc 4444 Scotts Vly Dr Suite 5b *Web:* www.svusd.santacruz.k12.ca.us	Scotts Valley	CA	95066	831-438-2312	
Scranton School District 425 N Washington Ave *Web:* www.scrsd.org	Scranton	PA	18503	570-348-3402	348-3563
Seaman Unified School District 345 901 NW Lyman Rd *Web:* www.usd345.com	Topeka	KS	66608	785-575-8600	575-8620
Seattle Public Schools PO Box 34165 *Web:* www.seattleschools.org	Seattle	WA	98124	206-252-0000	
Security Bancshares Co 735 11th St E PO Box 218 *Web:* www.security-banks.com	Glencoe	MN	55336	320-864-3171	864-5133
Sedalia School District 200 2806 Matthew Dr *Web:* www.sedalia200.com	Sedalia	MO	65301	660-829-6450	
Seguin Independent School District 1221 E Kingsbury St *Web:* www.seguin.k12.tx.us	Seguin	TX	78155	830-372-5771	379-0392
Seneca Falls School District 98 Clinton St *Web:* www.sfcs.k12.ny.us	Seneca Falls	NY	13148	315-568-5818	
Shelton City School District 382 Long Hill Ave *Web:* www.sheltonpublicschools.org	Shelton	CT	06484	203-924-1023	924-6851
Shikellamy School District 200 Island Blvd *Web:* www.shikbraves.org	Sunbury	PA	17801	570-286-3720	
Sidney Transportation Services 777 West Russell Rd PO Box 748 *TF:* 800-743-6391 ■ *Web:* www.sidneytransportationservices.com	Sidney	OH	45365	937-498-2323	492-4025
Sioux Falls School District 201 E 38th St **Fax:* Hum Res ■ *Web:* www.sf.k12.sd.us	Sioux Falls	SD	57105	605-367-7900	367-4637*
Siuslaw School District 97j 2111 Oak St *Web:* www.greatschools.org	Florence	OR	97439	541-997-2651	
Slaton Independent School District 140 E Panhandle St *Web:* www.slatonisd.net	Slaton	TX	79364	806-828-6591	
Snodgrass & Son's Construction Co Inc 2700 S George Washington Bldg *Web:* www.snodgrassconstruction.net	Wichita	KS	67210	316-687-3110	687-5853
Solanco School District 121 S Hess St *Web:* www.solanco.k12.pa.us	Quarryville	PA	17566	717-786-8401	786-8245
Sonoma Valley Unified School District 17850 Railroad Ave. *Web:* www.dunbarschool.com	Sonoma	CA	95476	707-935-6000	
Souderton Area School District 760 Lower Rd *Web:* www.soudertonsd.org	Souderton	PA	18964	215-723-6061	723-8897

Name / Address	City	State	Zip	Phone	Fax
South Bay Union School District 601 Elm Ave *Web:* www.sbusd.org	Imperial Beach	CA	91932	619-628-1600	628-1608
South Haven Public Schools Inc 554 Green St *Web:* www.shps.org	South Haven	MI	49090	269-637-0520	
South Kitsap School District 1962 Hoover Ave SE *Web:* www.skitsap.wednet.edu	Port Orchard	WA	98366	360-874-7000	874-7068
South Orangetown School District (inc) The 160 Van Wyck Rd *Web:* www.socsd.k12.ny.us	Blauvelt	NY	10913	845-680-1000	
South San Antonio Independent School District 5622 Ray Ellison Dr *Web:* www.southsanisd.net	San Antonio	TX	78242	210-977-7000	977-7021
South San Francisco Unified School District 398 B St *Web:* www.ssfusd.k12.ca.us	South San Francisco	CA	94080	650-877-8700	
South Summit School District 375 E 300 S *Web:* www.ssummit.k12.ut.us	Kamas	UT	84036	435-783-4301	
South Whidbey School Dist 206 PO Box 346 *Web:* www.sw.wednet.edu	Langley	WA	98260	360-221-6100	221-3835
Southern Lehigh School District 5775 Main St *Web:* www.slsd.org	Center Valley	PA	18034	610-282-3121	282-0193
Southern Regional High School District Board of Education 105 Cedar Bridge Rd *Web:* www.srsd.net	Manahawkin	NJ	08050	609-597-9481	978-0298
Southern Tioga School District 241 Main St. *Web:* www.southerntioga.org	Blossburg	PA	16912	570-638-2183	
Southgate Community School District 13305 Reeck Rd Suite 100 *Web:* www.southgateschools.com	Southgate	MI	48195	734-246-4600	283-6791
Southwest Local School District 230 S Elm St. *Web:* www.southwestschools.org	Harrison	OH	45030	513-367-4139	
Southwestern Central School District 600 Hunt Rd *Web:* www.swcs.wnyric.org	Jamestown	NY	14701	716-664-1881	
Southwick Tolland Regional SD 86 Powder Mill Rd *Web:* www.strsd.southwick.ma.us	Southwick	MA	01077	413-569-5391	
Spackenkill Union Free School Districts (inc) 15 Croft Rd *Web:* www.spackenkillschools.org	Poughkeepsie	NY	12603	845-463-7800	
Sparta Area Schools 465 S Union St *Web:* www.spartaschools.org	Sparta	MI	49345	616-887-8253	
Splendora Independent School District 23419 FM 2090 Rd *Web:* www.splendoraisd.org	Splendora	TX	77372	281-689-3128	689-7509
Spring-Ford Area School District 857 S Lewis Rd *Web:* www.spring-ford.net	Royersford	PA	19468	610-705-6000	705-6245
Springfield Public School District #186 1900 W Monroe St *Web:* www.springfield.k12.il.us	Springfield	IL	62704	217-525-3000	525-3005
Springfield Public Schools 1550 Main St. **Fax:* Hum Res ■ *Web:* www.sps.springfield.ma.us	Springfield	MA	01103	413-787-7100	787-7171*
Springfield Public Schools 1359 E St Louis St **Fax:* Mail Rm ■ *Web:* www.springfieldpublicschoolsmo.org	Springfield	MO	65802	417-523-0000	523-0196*
Stephenville Independent School District 2655 W Overhill Dr *Web:* www.sville.us	Stephenville	TX	76401	254-968-4141	
Stockton Unified School District 701 N Madison St. *Web:* www.stockton.k12.ca.us	Stockton	CA	95202	209-933-7000	933-7071
Stoughton Area School District 320 N St *Web:* www.stoughton.k12.wi.us	Stoughton	WI	53589	608-877-5000	
Stow-Munroe Falls City School District 4350 Allen Rd *Web:* www.stow.summit.k12.oh.us	Stow	OH	44224	330-689-5445	
Sugar Creek Board of Education 60 E S St *Web:* www.sugarcreek.k12.oh.us	Bellbrook	OH	45305	937-848-6251	
Sully Transport Inc PO Box 350	Sully	IA	50251	641-594-3435	594-4261
Sulphur Springs Union School District 17866 Sierra Hwy *Web:* www.sssd.k12.ca.us	Canyon Country	CA	91351	661-252-5131	
Summit Construction Co Inc 1107 Burdsal Pkwy PO Box 88126 *Web:* www.summitconst.com	Indianapolis	IN	46208	317-634-6112	264-2529
Sumner School District 1202 Wood Ave *Web:* www.sumner.wednet.edu	Sumner	WA	98390	253-891-6000	891-6098
Sunset Ridge School District 29 525 Sunset Ridge Rd *Web:* www.sunsetridge29.net	Northfield	IL	60093	847-446-6383	446-6388
Surry County School 209 N Crutchfield St PO Box 364 *Web:* www.surry.k12.nc.us	Dobson	NC	27017	336-386-8211	386-4279
Swan Valley School Dist 8380 Ohern Rd *Web:* www.swanvalley.k12.mi.us	Saginaw	MI	48609	989-921-3701	
Sweet Home Central School District 1901 Sweet Home Rd *Web:* www.sweethomeschools.com	Amherst	NY	14228	716-250-1402	
Sweet Home School District 55 1920 Long St *Web:* www.sweethome.k12.or.us	Sweet Home	OR	97386	541-367-7126	
Sweetwater County School District 2 320 Monroe Ave *Web:* www.sw2.k12.wy.us	Green River	WY	82935	307-872-5500	
Syracuse City School District The 725 Harrison St *Web:* www.syracusecityschools.com	Syracuse	NY	13210	315-435-4499	435-4023
Tacoma Public Schools The PO Box 1357 **Fax:* Hum Res ■ *Web:* www.tacoma.k12.wa.us	Tacoma	WA	98401	253-571-1000	571-1453*
Tahoe Truckee Unified School District (TTUSD) 11603 Donner Pass Rd *Web:* www.ttusd.org	Truckee	CA	96161	530-582-2500	582-7606
Talbot County Public Schools PO Box 1029 *Web:* www.tcps.k12.md.us	Easton	MD	21601	410-822-0330	820-4260
Tattnall County School 146 W Brazell St PO Box 157 *Web:* www.tattnallschools.org	Reidsville	GA	30453	912-557-4726	557-3036
Taylor Independent School District 911 602 W 12th St. *Web:* www.taylorisd.org	Taylor	TX	76574	512-352-6361	365-3800
Team Hardinger Transportation/Warehousing 1314 W 18th St. *Web:* www.team-h.com	Erie	PA	16502	814-453-6587	453-4919
Telfair County School District 212 W Huckabee St PO Box 240 *Web:* www.telfair.k12.ga.us	Mc Rae	GA	31055	229-868-5661	868-5549
Temecula Valley Unified School District School Facilities Corp 31350 Rancho Vista Rd *Web:* www.tvusd.k12.ca.us	Temecula	CA	92592	951-676-2661	695-7121
Templeton Unified School District 960 Old County Rd *Web:* tusd.ca.schoolloop.com	Templeton	CA	93465	805-434-5800	434-5879
Thornapple Kellogg Schools 10051 Green Lake Rd *Web:* www.tkschools.org	Middleville	MI	49333	269-795-3394	795-5492
Thunderbird School of Global Management 1 Global Pl *TF:* 800-848-9084 ■ *Web:* www.thunderbird.edu	Glendale	AZ	85306	602-978-7000	978-9663
Tipton County Schools 1580 Hwy 51 S *Web:* www.tipton-county.com	Covington	TN	38019	901-476-7148	476-4870
Toledo Public Schools 420 E Manhattan Blvd *Web:* www.tps.org	Toledo	OH	43608	419-729-8200	729-8425
Tomball Independent School District 221 W Main St *TF:* 877-382-4357 ■ *Web:* www.tomballisd.net	Tomball	TX	77375	281-357-3100	357-3128
Topeka School District (USD 501) 624 SW 24th St **Fax:* Hum Res ■ *Web:* www.topekapublicschools.net	Topeka	KS	66611	785-295-3000	575-6162*
Toppenish School District 202 306 Bolin Dr *Web:* www.toppenish.wednet.edu	Toppenish	WA	98948	509-865-4455	865-2067
Torrance Unified School District 2335 Plaza Del AMO *Web:* www.tusd.org	Torrance	CA	90501	310-972-6500	
Trenton Public School System 108 N Clinton Ave. *Web:* www.trenton.k12.nj.us	Trenton	NJ	08609	609-656-4900	989-2682
Tri-Valley Local School District PO Box 125 *Web:* www.tri-valley.k12.oh.us	Dresden	OH	43821	740-754-1442	754-6400
Trinity Area School District 231 Park Ave *Web:* www.trinitypride.k12.pa.us	Washington	PA	15301	724-225-9880	
Triway Local School District 3205 Shreve Rd *Web:* www.triway.k12.oh.us	Wooster	OH	44691	330-264-9491	262-3955
Tuckahoe Union Free School District 65 Siwanoy Blvd. *Web:* www.challengecamps.com	Eastchester	NY	10709	914-337-6600	
Tucson Unified School District No 1 1010 E 10th St *Web:* www.tusd1.org	Tucson	AZ	85719	520-225-6070	798-8767
Tulare Joint Union High School District 426 N Blackstone Ave *Web:* www.tulare.k12.ca.us	Tulare	CA	93274	559-688-2021	687-7317
Tulsa Public Schools 3027 S New Haven Ave **Fax:* Hum Res ■ *Web:* www8.tulsaschools.org	Tulsa	OK	74114	918-746-6517	746-6144*
Tupelo Public School District PO Box 557 *Web:* www.tupeloschools.com	Tupelo	MS	38802	662-841-8850	841-8887
Turner County Board of Education 423 N Cleveland St *Web:* www.turner.k12.ga.us	Ashburn	GA	31714	229-567-3338	567-3285
Tuscarora Intermediate Unit 11 2527 US 522 S Hwy **Fax Area Code:* 824 ■ *Web:* www.tiu11.org	Mc Veytown	PA	17051	717-899-7143	542-2569*
Twin Falls School District 411 201 Main Ave W *Web:* www.tfsd.k12.id.us	Twin Falls	ID	83301	208-733-6900	733-6987
Twin Rivers Unified School District 3222 Winona Way *Web:* www.twinriversusd.org	North Highlands	CA	95660	916-566-1628	566-3586
Unified School District 428 201 S Patton Rd *Web:* www.usd428.net	Great Bend	KS	67530	620-793-1500	
Unified School District 470 PO Box 1028 *Web:* www.arkcity.com	Arkansas City	KS	67005	620-441-2000	441-2009
Unified School District of Antigo 120 S Dorr St *TF:* 800-795-3272 ■ *Web:* www.antigo.k12.wi.us	Antigo	WI	54409	715-627-4355	623-3279
Union County Public Schools 510 S Mart St *Web:* www.union.kyschools.us	Morganfield	KY	42437	270-389-1694	389-9806
United Sales & Leasing Co Inc 3649 E Lke Rd PO Box 1338 *TF:* 800-283-7284 ■ *Web:* www.pathtrucklines.com	Dunkirk	NY	14048	716-366-6555	
Unlimited Construction Services Inc 1696 Haleukana St *Web:* www.unlimitedhawaii.com	Lihue	HI	96766	808-241-1400	245-6611
Upland Unified School District 390 N Euclid Ave *Web:* www.upland.k12.ca.us	Upland	CA	91786	909-985-1864	949-7863

Name / Address	City	State	Zip	Phone	Fax
Upper Dauphin Area School District 5668 SR- 209 *Web:* www.udasd.org	Lykens	PA	17048	717-362-8134	
Upper Freehold Regional Board of Education (inc) 27 High St *Web:* www.ufrsd.net	Allentown	NJ	08501	609-259-7292	
Upper Merion Area School District 435 Crossfield Rd *Web:* www.umasd.org	King of Prussia	PA	19406	610-337-6000	205-6433
Upper Perkiomen School District 2229 E Buck Rd Suite 2 *Web:* www.upsd.org	Pennsburg	PA	18073	215-679-7961	
US Special Delivery Inc 821 E Blvd *TF:* 800-821-6389 ■ *Web:* www.upspecial.com	Kingsford	MI	49802	906-774-1931	774-2032
Utica Community Schools (UCS) 11303 Greendale Dr *Web:* www.uticak12.org	Sterling Heights	MI	48312	586-797-1000	797-1001
Uvalde Consolidated Independent School District PO Box 1909 *Web:* www.ucisd.net	Uvalde	TX	78802	830-278-6655	591-4927
Val Verde Unified School District 975 Morgan St *TF:* 800-782-7463 ■ *Web:* www.valverde.edu	Perris	CA	92571	951-940-6100	
Valley Center-Pauma Unified School District 28751 Cole Grade Rd *Web:* www.vcpusd.net	Valley Center	CA	92082	760-749-0464	749-1208
Van Buren Public Schools (VBPS) 555 W Columbia Ave *Web:* www.vanburenschools.net	Belleville	MI	48111	734-697-9123	697-6385
Vernon Parish School Board 201 Belview Rd *TF:* 800-621-1742 ■ *Web:* www.vpsb.k12.la.us	Leesville	LA	71446	337-239-3401	392-2517
Vernon Township Board of Education (inc) PO Box 99 *Web:* www.vtsd.com	Vernon	NJ	07462	973-764-2900	
Vestal Central School District 201 Main St *Web:* www.vestal.stier.org	Vestal	NY	13850	607-757-2241	757-2227
Vestavia Hills Board of Education 1204 Montgomery Hwy *Web:* www.vestavia.k12.al.us	Birmingham	AL	35216	205-402-5100	
Victor Elementary School District (VESD) 15579 8th St *Web:* www.vesd.net	Victorville	CA	92392	760-245-1691	
Volmar Construction Inc 4400 2nd Ave *Web:* www.volmar.com	Brooklyn	NY	11232	718-832-2444	499-4045
W. N. Morehouse Truck Line Inc 4010 Dahlman Ave *TF:* 800-228-9378 ■ *Web:* www.morehousetruckline.com	Omaha	NE	68107	402-733-2200	733-6316
Wahluke School District 73 411 E Saddle Mt Dr *Web:* www.wsd73.wednet.edu	Mattawa	WA	99349	509-932-4565	
Wake County Public School System 3600 Wake Forest Rd *Web:* www.wcpss.net	Raleigh	NC	27609	919-850-1600	850-1819
Wakefield School District 60 Farm St *Web:* www.wakefield.k12.ma.us	Wakefield	MA	01880	781-246-6400	
Walbon & Co Inc 4230 Pine Bend Trial Suite A *Web:* www.walbon.com	Rosemount	MN	55068	651-437-2011	437-2087
Walker County Board of Education 1710 Alabama Ave PO Box 311 *Web:* www.walkercountyschools.com	Jasper	AL	35501	205-387-0555	221-5636
Wall Timber Products Inc 1825 Effingham Hwy *Web:* www.walltimber.com	Sylvania	GA	30467	912-863-5108	863-7478
Wallingford-Swarthmore School District 200 S Providence Rd *Web:* www.wssd.org	Wallingford	PA	19086	610-892-3470	
Wallkill Central School District (WCSD) 19 Main St PO Box 310 *Web:* www.wallkillcsd.k12.ny.us/education/district/district.php?sectionid=7785	Wallkill	NY	12589	845-895-7100	895-3630
Washington Co School District PO Box 716 *Web:* www.washington.k12.ga.us	Sandersville	GA	31082	478-552-3981	
Washington County Board of Education 802 Washington St *Web:* www.washingtonco.k12.nc.us	Plymouth	NC	27962	252-793-5171	
Washington International School 3100 Macomb St NW *Web:* www.wis.edu	Washington	DC	20008	202-243-1815	243-1695
Washington School District Inc 201 Allison Ave *Web:* www.washington.k12.pa.us	Washington	PA	15301	724-223-5085	223-5046
Washoe County School District 425 E 9th St *Web:* www.washoe.k12.nv.us	Reno	NV	89512	775-348-0200	348-0389
Watauga County Schools PO Box 1790 *Web:* www.watauga.k12.nc.us	Boone	NC	28607	828-264-7190	264-7196
Waterloo Community Unit School Dst 5 219 Pk St *Web:* www.wcusd5.net	Waterloo	IL	62298	618-939-3453	939-4578
Watertown-Mayer School District 1001 Hwy 25 Shls NW *Web:* www.wm.k12.mn.us	Watertown	MN	55388	952-955-0600	955-0251
Waxahachie Independent School District 411 N Gibson St *Web:* www.wisd.org	Waxahachie	TX	75165	972-923-4631	923-4759
Wayne Highlands School District 474 Grove St *Web:* www.waynehighlands.org	Honesdale	PA	18431	570-253-4661	253-9409
Wellsboro Area School District 2 Charles St *Web:* www.wellsborosd.k12.pa.us	Wellsboro	PA	16901	570-724-4424	
West Clermont Local School District 4350 Aicholtz Rd Suite 220 *Web:* www.westcler.k12.oh.us	Cincinnati	OH	45245	513-943-5000	752-6158
West Fargo School District 6 207 Main Ave W *Web:* www.west-fargo.k12.nd.us	West Fargo	ND	58078	701-356-2000	356-2009
West Genesee Central School District 300 Sanderson Dr *Web:* www.westgenesee.org	Camillus	NY	13031	315-487-4562	487-2999
West Irondequoit Central School District 321 List Ave *Web:* www.westirondequoit.org	Rochester	NY	14617	585-342-5500	
West Valley School District 208 8902 Zier Rd *Web:* www.wvsd208.org	Yakima	WA	98908	509-972-6000	
Western Placer Unified School District Finanacing Corp 600 6th St *Web:* www.wpusd.k12.ca.us	Lincoln	CA	95648	916-645-6350	
Westfield Board of Education Inc 302 Elm St *TF:* 877-900-6960 ■ *Web:* www.westfieldnjk12.org	Westfield	NJ	07090	908-789-4401	
Westminster School District 14121 Cedarwood St *Web:* www.wsd.k12.ca.us	Westminster	CA	92683	714-894-7311	899-2781
Wharton Independent School District 2100 N Fulton St *Web:* www.whartonisd.net	Wharton	TX	77488	979-532-3612	532-6228
Whittier City School District 7211 Whittier Ave *Web:* www.whittiercity.k12.ca.us	Whittier	CA	90602	562-789-3000	907-9425
Wichita Unified School District 259 201 N Water St *Web:* www.usd259.com	Wichita	KS	67202	316-973-4000	973-4595
Wicomico County Board of Education PO Box 1538 *TF:* 866-409-5734 ■ *Web:* www.wcboe.org	Salisbury	MD	21802	410-677-4400	677-4444
William B Meyer Inc 255 Long Beach Blvd *TF:* 800-727-5985 ■ *Web:* www.williambmeyer.com	Stratford	CT	06615	203-375-5801	375-9820
Williams Valley School District 10330 Rt 209 Rd *Web:* www.wvsd.k12.pa.us	Tower City	PA	17980	717-647-2167	
Williamsburg-James City County Educational Foundation Inc PO Box 8783 *Web:* www.wjcc.k12.va.us	Williamsburg	VA	23187	757-253-6777	253-0173
Williamsport Area School District 201 W 3rd St *TF:* 888-448-4642 ■ *Web:* www.wasd.org	Williamsport	PA	17701	570-327-5500	327-8122
Williamston Community Schools Inc PO Box 70 *Web:* www.wmston.k12.mi.us	Williamston	MI	48895	517-655-4361	
Willoughby Eastlake City Schools 37047 Ridge Rd *Web:* www.weschools.org	Willoughby	OH	44094	440-946-5000	946-4671
Wills Point Independent School Distric 338 W N Commerce St *Web:* www.wpisd.com	Wills Point	TX	75169	903-873-3161	873-2462
Wilson County Schools District 117 N Tarboro St *Web:* www.wilson.k12.nc.us	Wilson	NC	27893	252-399-7700	399-2776
Winchester-Thurston School 555 Morewood Ave *Web:* www.netclass.winchesterthurston.org	Pittsburgh	PA	15213	412-578-7500	578-7504
Windsor Central School District (WCSD) 1191 NY Rt 79 *Web:* www.windsor-csd.org	Windsor	NY	13865	607-655-8216	655-3553
Winston-Salem/Forsyth County Schools (WS/FCS) 1605 Miller St *Web:* www.wsfcs.k12.nc.us	Winston-Salem	NC	27103	336-727-2816	661-6572
Winton Woods City Schools 1215 W Kemper Rd *Web:* www.wintonwoods.org	Cincinnati	OH	45240	513-825-5700	619-2300
Woodland School District 50 1105 N Hunt Club Rd *Web:* www.dist50.net	Gurnee	IL	60031	847-596-5600	680-8266
Woodstock Community Unit School District 200 227 W Judd St *Web:* www.woodstockschools.org	Woodstock	IL	60098	815-338-8200	338-2005
Wooster City Board of Education 144 N Market St *Web:* www.woostercityschools.org	Wooster	OH	44691	330-264-0869	262-3407
Worcester Public Schools 20 Irving St *Web:* www.worcesterschools.org	Worcester	MA	01609	508-799-3115	799-3119
Worthington City School District 200 E Wilson Bridge Rd *Web:* www.worthington.k12.oh.us	Worthington	OH	43085	614-883-3000	
Wyoming Valley West School District 450 N Maple Ave *Web:* www.wvwspartans.org	Kingston	PA	18704	570-288-6551	288-1564
Yale School District 103 315 E Chicago Ave *Web:* www.yale.k12.ok.us	Yale	OK	74085	918-387-2434	387-2503
Yancey County Schools Foundation Inc The PO Box 190 *Web:* www.yanceync.net	Burnsville	NC	28714	828-682-6101	682-7110
Yough School District 915 Lowber Rd *Web:* www.yough.net	Herminie	PA	15637	724-446-7272	446-5017
Ypsilanti Pub School District 1885 Packard Rd *TF:* 877-433-7827 ■ *Web:* www.ypsd.org	Ypsilanti	MI	48197	734-714-1200	482-0857
Yuma Broadcasting Co Inc 1385 S Pacific Ave *Web:* www.kyma.com	Yuma	AZ	85365	928-782-1111	782-5401
Zachary Community School Board 4656 MN St *TF:* 800-256-3718 ■ *Web:* www.zacharyschools.org	Zachary	LA	70791	225-658-4969	
Zanesville City School Board 160 N 4TH St *TF:* 866-280-7377 ■ *Web:* www.zanesville.k12.oh.us	Zanesville	OH	43701	740-454-9751	

689 SCRAP METAL

SEE ALSO Recyclable Materials Recovery p. 2530

				Phone	Fax
A Tenenbaum Co Inc 4500 W Bethany Rd. Web: www.trg.net	North Little Rock	AR	72117	501-945-0881	945-3865
Adams Steel 3200 E Frontera St. TF: 800-468-7272 ■ Web: www.sarecycling.com	Anaheim	CA	92806	714-630-8901	630-5836
Addlestone International Corp PO Drawer 979	Charleston	SC	29402	843-577-9300	577-4141
Advantage Metals Recycling LLC 3005 Manchester Trfy. TF: 866-527-4733 ■ Web: www.advantagerecycling.com	Kansas City	MO	64129	816-861-2700	861-7670
Alco Iron & Metal Co 2140 Davis St. Web: www.alcometals.com	San Leandro	CA	94577	510-562-1107	562-1354
Allan Industries PO Box 999	Wilkes-Barre	PA	18703	570-826-0123	829-4099
Alter Trading Corp 700 Office Pkwy. TF: 888-337-2727 ■ Web: www.altertrading.com	Saint Louis	MO	63141	314-872-2400	872-2420
Amcep Inc 4484 E Tennessee St.	Tucson	AZ	85714	520-748-1900	748-2752
AMG Resources Corp 2 Robinson Plaza # 350. TF: 800-633-3606 ■ Web: www.amgresources.com	Pittsburgh	PA	15205	412-331-0770	331-4624
Azcon Corp 13733 S Ave O. Web: www.azcon.net	Chicago	IL	60633	773-646-2300	646-4121
Baker Iron & Metal Co Inc 740 Rock Castle Ave. TF: 800-398-2537 ■ Web: www.bakeriron.com	Lexington	KY	40505	859-255-5676	252-3590
Bollag International Corp 6924 Orr Rd PO Box 99. Web: www.bollagnet.com	Newell	NC	28213	704-596-2932	598-8478
Borg Compressed Steel Corp 1032 N Lewis Ave	Tulsa	OK	74110	918-587-2511	587-2520
Calbag Metals Co 2495 NW Nicolai St. TF: 800-398-3441 ■ Web: www.calbag.com	Portland	OR	97210	503-226-3441	228-0184
City Carton Co Inc 3 E Benton St. TF: 800-369-6112 ■ Web: www.citycarton.com	Iowa City	IA	52240	319-351-2848	351-3818
Cleveland Corp 42810 N Green Bay Rd. TF: 800-281-3464 ■ Web: www.clevelandcorp.com	Zion	IL	60099	847-872-7200	872-0827
Cohen Bros Inc 1723 Woodlawn Ave. TF: 800-878-3697 ■ Web: www.cohenbrothersinc.com	Middletown	OH	45044	513-422-3696	422-9018
Columbia Iron & Metal Co Inc 6600 Grant Ave.	Cleveland	OH	44105	216-883-4972	883-8548
Connell LP 1 International Pl 31st Fl. TF: 800-276-4746 ■ Web: www.connell-lp.com	Boston	MA	02110	617-737-2700	737-1617
Cycle Systems Inc 2580 Broadway SW PO Box 611. TF: 800-542-7000 ■ Web: www.cyclesystems.com	Roanoke	VA	24004	540-981-1211	981-0044
David J Joseph Co (DJJ) 300 Pike St. Web: www.djj.com	Cincinnati	OH	45202	513-419-6200	419-6222
Davis Industries Inc 9920 Richmond Hwy	Lorton	VA	22079	703-550-7402	550-5576
Duggan Industries Inc 3901 S Lamar St. TF Sales: 877-428-8336 ■ Web: www.dimcosteel.com	Dallas	TX	75215	214-428-8336	428-1929
Easton Iron & Metal Co 1100 Bushkill Dr. Web: www.eastonmetal.com	Easton	PA	18042	610-250-6300	250-6302
ELG Metals Inc 369 River Rd. Web: www.elgmetals.com	McKeesport	PA	15132	412-672-9200	672-0824
Fairway Salvage Inc 12428 Ctr St. Web: www.fairwaysalvage.com	South Gate	CA	90280	562-630-8766	630-5929
FPT Pontiac Div 500 Collier Rd	Pontiac	MI	48340	248-335-8141	335-8714
Franklin Iron & Metal Corp 1939 E 1st St. TF: 800-255-8184	Dayton	OH	45403	937-253-8184	253-2030
Gachman Metals & Recycling Co Inc 2600 Shamrock Ave. TF: 800-749-0423 ■ Web: www.gachman.com	Fort Worth	TX	76107	817-334-0211	877-1528
General Iron Industries Inc 1909 N Clifton Ave	Chicago	IL	60614	773-327-9600	327-8732
Gershow Recycling Corp 71 Peconic Ave PO Box 526. Web: www.gershow.com	Medford	NY	11763	631-289-6188	289-6368
Great Western Recycling Industries Inc 521 Barge Ch Rd. Web: www.northernmetalrecycling.com	Saint Paul	MN	55107	651-224-4877	224-4870
Grossman Iron & Steel 5 N Market St. TF: 800-969-9423 ■ Web: www.grossmaniron.com	Saint Louis	MO	63102	314-231-9423	231-6983
Iron & Metals Inc 5555 Franklin St. TF: 800-776-7910 ■ Web: www.ironandmetals.com	Denver	CO	80216	303-292-5555	292-0513
Jacobs Iron & Metal Co 3330 Pluto St.	Dallas	TX	75212	214-631-6740	631-7224
Joe Krentzman & Son Inc PO Box 508. TF: 800-543-2000	Lewistown	PA	17044	717-543-5635	543-6299
Joseph Behr & Sons Inc 1100 Seminary St PO Box 740. TF: 800-332-2347 ■ Web: www.jbehr.com	Rockford	IL	61105	815-987-2600	987-2606
Joseph Simon & Sons Inc 2202 E River St. TF: 800-562-8464 ■ Web: www.jsimonandsons.com	Tacoma	WA	98421	253-272-9364	838-1998
Keywell LLC 11900 S Cottage Grove Ave. Web: www.keywell.com	Chicago	IL	60628	773-660-2060	660-2064
Langley Recycling 503 SE Branner St. Web: www.langleyrecycling.com	Topeka	KS	66607	785-234-2691	354-8019
Liberty Iron & Metal Co PO Box 1391. TF: 800-836-0259 ■ Web: www.libertyiron.com	Erie	PA	16512	814-453-6758	456-6107
Lionetti Assoc 450 S Front St. TF: 800-734-0910 ■ Web: www.lorcopetroleum.com	Elizabeth	NJ	07202	908-820-8800	820-8412
Louis Padnos Iron & Metal Co PO Box 1979. TF: 800-442-3509 ■ Web: www.padnos.com	Holland	MI	49422	616-396-6521	396-7789
M Lipsitz & Co Inc 100 Elm St. Web: www.mlipsitzco.com	Waco	TX	76704	254-756-6661	754-7954
Mayer Pollock Steel Corp PO Box 759. TF: 800-323-5502 ■ Web: www.mayerpollock.com	Pottstown	PA	19464	610-323-5500	323-5506
Mervis Industries Inc 3295 E Main St. TF: 800-637-3016 ■ Web: www.mervis.com	Danville	IL	61834	217-442-5300	477-9245
Metal Exchange Corp 111 W Port Plaza Suite 700. Web: www.metalexchangecorp.com	Saint Louis	MO	63146	314-434-3500	434-2196
Metalico Annaco Inc 943 Hazel St. TF: 800-394-1300 ■ Web: www.annaco.com	Akron	OH	44305	330-376-1400	376-9696
Metalico Inc 186 N Ave E. AMEX: MEA ■ Web: www.metalico.com	Cranford	NJ	07016	908-497-9610	497-1097
Metalsco Inc 11775 Borman Suite 102. Web: www.metalsco.com	Saint Louis	MO	63146	314-997-5200	997-5921
Metro Metals Northwest 5611 NE Columbia Blvd. TF: 800-610-5680 ■ Web: www.metrometalsnw.com	Portland	OR	97218	503-287-8861	287-5569
Midland Davis Corp 3301 4th Ave. TF: 800-223-5942	Moline	IL	61265	309-764-6723	764-6729
Miller Compressing Co 1640 W Bruce St	Milwaukee	WI	53204	414-671-5980	671-3658
Minkin-Chandler Corp 13501 Sanders Ave	Detroit	MI	48217	313-843-5900	843-6782
Newell Recycling of San Antonio PO Box 830808	San Antonio	TX	78283	210-227-3141	227-8948
Northern Metal Recycling LLC 2800 Pacific St N. Web: www.northernmetalrecycling.com	Minneapolis	MN	55411	612-529-9221	529-2548
Omnisource Corp 2205 S Holt Rd. Web: www.omnisource.com	Indianapolis	IN	46241	317-381-5800	381-5810
OmniSource Corp 7575 W Jefferson Blvd. TF: 800-666-4789 ■ Web: www.omnisource.com	Fort Wayne	IN	46804	260-422-5541	423-8500
Pacific Coast Recycling Weiner Steel Div 1545 Gage Rd.	Montebello	CA	90640	323-723-8327	726-1988
Pascap Co Inc 4250 Boston Rd. Web: www.pascapco.net	Bronx	NY	10475	718-325-7200	325-7595
Philip Services Corp (PSC) 51 San Felipe Rd Suite 1600. TF: 800-726-1300 ■ Web: www.pscnow.com	Houston	TX	77056	713-623-8777	625-7185
Progress Rail Services 1600 Progress Dr PO Box 1037. TF: 800-476-8769 ■ Web: www.progressrail.com	Albertville	AL	35950	256-593-1260	593-1249
Recycle Metals Corp 407 Allen Wood Rd	Conshohocken	PA	19428	610-828-5553	828-5390
River Metals Recycling 2045 River Rd. Web: www.rmrecycling.com	Louisville	KY	40206	502-585-5331	587-8699
River Recycling Industries Inc 4195 Bradley Rd.	Cleveland	OH	44109	216-459-2100	749-8107
Riverside Scrap Iron 2993 6th St. TF: 800-399-4766 ■ Web: www.riversidemetalrecycling.com	Riverside	CA	92507	951-686-2120	686-8933
Rocky Mountain Recycling (RMR) 6510 Brighton Blvd. Web: www.mountainrecycling.com	Commerce City	CO	80022	303-288-6868	288-0250
Sadoff & Rudoy Industries LLP 240 W Arndt St. TF: 800-236-5700 ■ Web: www.sadoff.com	Fond du Lac	WI	54935	920-921-2070	921-1283
SD Richman Sons Inc 2435 Wheatsheaf Ln. TF: 800-648-3576 ■ Web: www.sdrichmansons.com	Philadelphia	PA	19137	215-535-5100	288-1043
Sefa Group Inc The 217 Cedar Rd. TF: 888-339-7332 ■ Web: www.sefagroup.com	Lexington	SC	29073	803-520-9000	794-4458
Shredded Products LLC 700 Commerce Rd.	Rocky Mount	VA	24151	540-489-7599	489-8431
Simon Resources Inc 2525 Trenton Ave.	Williamsport	PA	17701	570-326-9431	326-5028
Sims Bros Inc PO Box 1170. TF: 800-536-7461 ■ Web: www.simsbros.com	Marion	OH	43301	740-387-9041	387-0083
SLC Recycling Industries Inc 8701 E 8 Mile Rd.	Warren	MI	48089	586-759-6600	759-6518
Soave Enterprises LLC 3400 E Lafayette St. Web: www.soave.com	Detroit	MI	48207	313-567-7000	567-0966
Sol Tick & Co PO Box 1605.	Decatur	IL	62525	217-429-4148	429-7565
Sturgis Iron & Metal Co PO Box 579. TF: 800-446-0794	Sturgis	MI	49091	269-651-7851	651-4189
Sugar Creek Scrap Inc 1201 W National Ave. TF: 800-466-7462 ■ Web: www.sugarcreekscrap.com	West Terre Haute	IN	47805	812-533-2147	533-2140
Tennessee Valley Recycling LLC 821 W College St.	Pulaski	TN	38478	931-363-3593	363-8065
Thalheimer Bros Inc 5550 Whitaker Ave. Web: www.thalheimerbrothers.com	Philadelphia	PA	19124	215-537-5200	533-3993
Thermo Fluids Inc 4301 W Jefferson St. TF: 800-350-7565 ■ Web: www.thermofluids.com	Phoenix	AZ	85043	602-272-2400	
Tri-State Iron & Metal Co PO Box 775. TF: 800-773-8409	Texarkana	AR	71854	870-773-8409	772-3086
Tube City IMS Corp (TMS) 12 Monongahela Ave. NYSE: TMS ■ TF: 800-225-0478 ■ Web: www.tubecityims.com	Glassport	PA	15045	412-678-6141	675-8295
Tube City IMS Corp 1155 Business Ctr Dr. TF: 800-523-0781 ■ Web: www.tubecityims.com	Horsham	PA	19044	215-956-5500	
Upstate Shredding LLC 1 Recycle Dr Tioga Industrial Pk. Web: www.upstateshredding.com	Owego	NY	13827	607-687-7777	687-7746
Wabash Alloys LLC 4525 W Old 24. TF: 800-348-0571 ■ Web: www.wabashalloys.com	Wabash	IN	46992	260-563-7461	563-5997
Weiner Iron & Metal Corp PO Box 359. Web: www.weinermetals.com	Pottsville	PA	17901	570-622-6543	622-3175
Western Scrap Processing Co 3315 Drennan Industrial Loop S. Web: www.westernscrap.com	Colorado Springs	CO	80910	719-390-7986	390-3852
Wimco Metals Inc 401 Penn Ave	Pittsburgh	PA	15221	412-243-8000	243-2225
Wise Metals Group 857 Elkridge Landing Rd Suite 600. TF: 800-818-9473 ■ Web: www.wisemetals.com	Linthicum	MD	21090	410-636-6500	636-1564
Yaffe Cos Inc The PO Box 916. TF: 800-759-2333 ■ Web: www.yaffeco.net	Muskogee	OK	74402	918-687-7543	687-0053

690 SCREEN PRINTING

				Phone	Fax
Designer Decal Inc 1120 E 1st Ave. TF: 800-622-6333 ■ Web: www.designerdecal.com	Spokane	WA	99202	509-535-0267	535-1476
Eagle Eye Screen Printing LLC 8021 S Redwood Rd.	West Jordan	UT	84088	801-566-1681	566-1681
Empire Screen Printing Inc N5206 Marco Rd PO Box 218. Web: www.empirescreen.com	Onalaska	WI	54650	608-783-3301	783-3306

	City	State	Zip	Phone	Fax
Flow-Eze Co 3209 Auburn St TF: 800-435-4873 ■ Web: www.flow-eze.com	Rockford	IL	61101	815-965-1062	965-1329
Gill Studios Inc 10800 Lackman Rd TF: 888-455-4422	Lenexa	KS	66219	913-888-4422	841-2202
Innerworkings Inc 600 W Chicago Ave Suite 850 NASDAQ: INWK ■ Web: www.inwk.com	Chicago	IL	60610	312-642-3700	642-3704
Kay Automotive Graphics 57 Kay Industrial Dr TF: 800-443-0190 ■ Web: www.kayautomotive.com	Lake Orion	MI	48359	248-377-4999	377-2097
M & M Designs Inc PO Drawer 1049 TF: 800-627-0656 ■ Web: www.m-mdesigns.com	Huntsville	TX	77342	936-295-2682	295-9286
Motson Graphics Inc 1717 Bethlehem Pike TF: 800-972-1986 ■ Web: www.motson.com	Flourtown	PA	19031	215-233-0500	233-5014
Ram Graphics Inc 2408 S Pk Ave TF: 800-531-4656 ■ Web: www.ramgraphics.com	Alexandria	IN	46001	800-531-4656	551-6846
Screen Machine Inc 3855 Wabash Ave	San Diego	CA	92104	619-281-3355	281-2033
Serigraph Inc 3801 E Decorah Rd TF: 800-279-6060 ■ Web: www.serigraph.com	West Bend	WI	53095	262-335-7200	335-7699
Technigraph Corp 850 W 3rd St Web: www.technigraph.net	Winona	MN	55987	507-454-3830	454-6470
Trau & Loevner Inc 5817 Centre Ave TF: 800-245-6207 ■ Web: www.trau-loevner.com	Pittsburgh	PA	15206	412-361-7700	361-8221

691 SCREENING - WOVEN WIRE

	City	State	Zip	Phone	Fax
ACS Industries Inc 191 Social St TF: 800-237-1939 ■ Web: www.acsindustries.com	Woonsocket	RI	02895	401-769-4700	766-2191
Belleville Wire Cloth Inc 18 Rutgers Ave TF: 800-631-0490 ■ Web: www.bwire.com	Cedar Grove	NJ	07009	973-239-0074	239-3985
Buffalo Wire Works Co 1165 Clinton St TF: 800-828-7028 ■ Web: www.buffalowire.com	Buffalo	NY	14206	716-826-4666	826-8271
Cleveland Wire Cloth & Mfg Co 3573 E 78th St TF: 800-321-3234 ■ Web: www.wirecloth.com	Cleveland	OH	44105	216-341-1832	341-1876
Edward J Darby & Son Inc 2200 N 8th St PO Box 50049 TF: 800-875-6374 ■ Web: www.darbywiremesh.com	Philadelphia	PA	19133	215-236-2203	236-2203
Gerard Daniel Worldwide 34 Barnhart Dr TF: 800-233-3017 ■ Web: www.gerarddaniel.com	Hanover	PA	17331	717-637-5901	633-7095
Halliburton Screen Co 1815 Shearn St TF: 800-527-4772 ■ Web: www.halliburton.com	Houston	TX	77007	713-869-5771	869-0728
Hanover Wire Cloth 500 E Middle St Web: www.newyorkwireind.com	Hanover	PA	17331	717-637-3795	637-4766
Hoyt Wire Cloth Co PO Box 4647	Lancaster	PA	17604	717-394-6871	394-1640
Jelliff Corp 354 Pequot Ave TF: 800-364-9502 ■ Web: www.jelliff.com	Southport	CT	06890	203-259-1615	255-7908
King Wire Partitions Inc 6044 N Figueroa St Web: www.kingwireusa.com	Los Angeles	CA	90042	323-256-4848	256-1950
Metal Textiles 970 New Durham Rd *Fax: Sales ■ Web: www.metexcorp.com	Edison	NJ	08818	732-287-0800	287-8546*
National Wire Fabric 701 Arkansas St TF: 800-643-1558	Star City	AR	71667	870-628-4201	628-3700
New York Wire Co 152 Main St TF: 800-699-4732	Mount Wolf	PA	17347	717-266-5626	266-5871
Pittsfield Products Inc PO Box 1027	Ann Arbor	MI	48106	734-665-3771	665-3132
Sherman Wire Co 428 Gibbons Rd TF: 800-527-4637	Sherman	TX	75092	903-893-0191	868-9502
TWP Inc 2831 10th St TF: 800-227-1570 ■ Web: www.twpinc.com	Berkeley	CA	94710	510-548-4434	548-3073
United Capital Corp 9 Pk Pl AMEX: AFP ■ Web: www.unitedcapitalcorp.net	Great Neck	NY	11021	516-466-6464	829-4301
Universal Wire Cloth Co 16 N Steel Rd TF: 800-892-6374 ■ Web: www.uwcwirecloth.com	Morrisville	PA	19067	215-736-8981	736-8994
Wayne Wire Cloth Products Inc 200 E Dresden St TF: 800-654-7688 ■ Web: www.waynewire.com	Kalkaska	MI	49646	231-258-9187	258-5504
Western Wire Group 4025 NW Express Ave TF: 800-547-9192 ■ Web: www.thewesterngroup.com	Portland	OR	97210	503-222-1644	222-6843
Wire Cloth Filter Mfg Co 611 St Charles Rd	Maywood	IL	60153	708-410-1800	410-1807

692 SEATING - VEHICULAR

	City	State	Zip	Phone	Fax
Advanced Components Technologies Inc 91 - 16th St S Web: www.goact.net	Northwood	IA	50459	641-324-2231	324-1231
American Metal Fab Inc 55515 Franklin Dr Web: www.americanmetalfab.com	Three Rivers	MI	49093	269-279-5108	279-5356
Beloates Aircraft Trim Inc 4408 N Haltom Rd	Haltom City	TX	76117	817-485-5013	485-5014
Bostrom Seating Inc 50 Nances Creek Industrial Blvd TF: 800-459-7328 ■ Web: www.bostromseating.com	Piedmont	AL	36272	256-447-9051	447-2038
Bridgewater Interiors LLC 4617 W Fort St	Detroit	MI	48209	313-842-3300	842-3452
Custom Aircraft Interiors 3701 Industry Ave Web: www.customaircraftinteriors.com	Lakewood	CA	90712	562-426-5098	490-0213
Freedman Seating Co 4545 W Augusta Blvd TF: 800-443-4540 ■ Web: www.freedmanseating.com	Chicago	IL	60651	773-524-2440	252-7450
Gill Industries Inc 5271 Plainfield Ave NE Web: www.gill-industries.com	Grand Rapids	MI	49525	616-559-2700	559-8850
HO Bostrom Co Inc 818 Progress Ave TF: 800-332-5415 ■ Web: www.hobostrom.com	Waukesha	WI	53186	262-542-0222	542-3784
Johnson Controls Inc Automotive Systems Group 49200 Halyard Dr *Fax: Hum Res ■ Web: www.johnsoncontrols.com	Plymouth	MI	48170	734-254-5000	254-5843*
Knoedler Manufacturers Inc 7185 Tower Rd Web: www.knoedler.com	Battle Creek	MI	49014	269-969-7722	969-7720
Kustom Fit/Hi-Tech Seating 8990 Atlantic Ave Web: www.kustomfit.com	South Gate	CA	90280	323-564-4481	564-5754
Lear Corp 21557 Telegraph Rd NYSE: LEA ■ Web: www.lear.com	Southfield	MI	48034	248-447-1500	447-1722
Lear Seating Corp 4600 Nancy St	Detroit	MI	48212	313-852-7800	852-7852
Milsco Mfg Co 9009 N 51st St TF: 800-645-7261 ■ Web: www.milsco.com	Brown Deer	WI	53223	414-354-0500	354-0508
Precision Pattern Inc 1643 S Maize Rd TF: 800-448-5127	Wichita	KS	67209	316-721-3100	721-2053
Sears Mfg Co 1718 S Concord St PO Box 3667 TF Cust Svc: 800-553-3013 ■ Web: www.searsseating.com	Davenport	IA	52808	563-383-2800	383-2810
Seats Inc 1515 Industrial St PO Box 60 TF: 800-443-0615 ■ Web: www.seatsinc.com	Reedsburg	WI	53959	608-524-4316	524-6004
Weber Aircraft LP 2000 Weber Dr Web: www.weberair.com	Gainesville	TX	76240	940-668-4100	668-4195
Wise Co Inc 5828 Shelby Oaks Dr TF: 800-251-2622 ■ Web: www.wiseseats.com	Memphis	TN	38134	901-388-0155	373-8283

693 SECURITIES BROKERS & DEALERS

SEE ALSO Commodity Contracts Brokers & Dealers p. 1668; Electronic Communications Networks (ECNs) p. 1811; Investment Advice & Management p. 2129; Mutual Funds p. 2295

	City	State	Zip	Phone	Fax
AB Watley Inc 50 Broad St Suite 1728 *Fax Area Code: 212 ■ TF: 888-229-2853 ■ Web: www.abwatley.com	New York	NY	10004	646-753-9301	202-5204*
Allen & Co Inc 711 5th Ave 9th Fl	New York	NY	10022	212-832-8000	832-8023
Alps Holdings Inc 1290 Broadway Suite 1100 Web: www.alpsinc.com	Denver	CO	80203	303-623-2577	623-7850
Ameriprise Brokerage 70400 Ameriprise Financial Ctr *Fax Area Code: 800 ■ TF: 800-297-7378 ■ Web: www.ameriprise.com	Minneapolis	MN	55474	612-671-3131	624-2259*
Ameritas Investment Corp PO Box 81889 TF: 800-228-8712 ■ Web: www.aicinvest.com	Lincoln	NE	68501	402-466-4565	467-6945
Aronson + Johnson + Ortiz LP 230 S Broad St 20th Fl Web: www.ajopartners.com	Philadelphia	PA	19102	215-546-7500	546-7506
Baird Patrick & Co Inc 3 2nd St # 305 TF: 800-221-7747 ■ Web: www.bairdpatrick.com	Jersey City	NJ	07302	201-680-7300	680-7301
Barclays Capital Inc 200 Pk Ave *Fax: Hum Res ■ TF: 888-227-2275 ■ Web: www.barcap.com	New York	NY	10166	212-412-4000	412-6795*
Bernard L Madoff Investment Securities Co 885 3rd Ave 18th Fl TF: 800-334-1343 ■ Web: www.madoff.com	New York	NY	10022	212-230-2424	
Berthel Fisher & Co 701 Tama St Bldg B PO Box 609 TF: 800-356-5234 ■ Web: www.berthel.com	Marion	IA	52302	319-447-5700	447-4250
Blackstone Group 345 Pk Ave 31st Fl Web: www.blackstone.com	New York	NY	10154	212-583-5000	583-5749
Blaylock & Co Inc 780 3rd Ave 44th Fl Web: www.blaylockco.com	New York	NY	10017	212-715-6600	715-3300
BMO Nesbitt Burns Inc 1 First Canadian Pl PO Box 150 Web: www.bmo.com	Toronto	ON	M5X1H3	416-359-4000	359-4311
BNP Paribas 787 7th Ave Web: www.bnpparibas.com	New York	NY	10019	212-841-3000	841-2146
Boston Institutional Services Inc 60 State St TF: 800-325-5323 ■ Web: www.bostonis.com	Boston	MA	02109	617-223-5600	223-5650
Brean Murray & Co LLC 570 Lexington Ave 11th Fl Web: www.breanmurray.com	New York	NY	10022	212-702-6500	702-6649
BUYandHOLD.com Securities Corp PO Box 6498 *Fax Area Code: 732 ■ TF: 800-646-8212 ■ Web: www.buyandhold.com	Edison	NJ	08837	800-646-8212	934-3095*
Cabrera Capital Markets LLC 10 S La Salle St Suite 1050 TF: 800-291-2388 ■ Web: www.cabreracapital.com	Chicago	IL	60603	312-236-8888	236-8936
Calton & Assoc Inc 14497 N Dale Mabry Hwy TF: 800-942-0262 ■ Web: www.calton.com	Tampa	FL	33618	813-264-0440	962-8695
Cantor Fitzgerald LP 499 Pk Ave Web: www.cantor.com	New York	NY	10022	212-938-5000	829-5280
Charles Schwab & Co Inc 211 Main St *Fax: PR ■ TF Cust Svc: 800-648-5300 ■ Web: www.schwab.com	San Francisco	CA	94105	415-636-7000	636-5970*
City Securities Corp 30 S Meridian St # 600 TF: 800-800-2489 ■ Web: www.citysecurities.com	Indianapolis	IN	46204	317-634-4400	972-7150
Coastal Securities LP 5555 San Felipe St TF: 800-489-3232 ■ Web: www.coastalsecurities.com	Houston	TX	77056	713-435-4300	435-4444
Comerica Securities 201 W Fort St 3rd Fl *Fax: Cust Svc ■ TF: 800-232-6983 ■ Web: www.comerica.com/comerica/default.html	Detroit	MI	48226	313-222-5580	222-5098*
Credit Suisse 11 Madison Ave TF: 800-222-8977 ■ Web: www.credit-suisse.com	New York	NY	10010	212-325-2000	325-6665
Crowell Weedon & Co One Wilshire Blvd 26th Fl *Fax: Hum Res ■ TF: 800-227-0319 ■ Web: www.crowellweedon.com	Los Angeles	CA	90017	213-620-1850	244-9388*
DA Davidson & Co Inc 8 3rd St N TF: 800-332-5915 ■ Web: www.davidsoncompanies.com/indv	Great Falls	MT	59401	406-727-4200	791-7380
Davenport & Co LLC 901 E Cary St 11th Fl TF: 800-846-6666 ■ Web: www.davenportllc.com	Richmond	VA	23219	804-780-2000	780-2026
Development Corp For Israel 575 Lexington Ave Suite 600 TF: 888-519-4111 ■ Web: www.israelbonds.com	New York	NY	10022	212-644-2663	
Domestic Securities Inc 160 Summit Ave TF: 877-429-2111	Montvale	NJ	07645	201-782-0888	

Name / Address	City	State	Zip	Phone	Fax
Dougherty & Co LLC 90 S 7th St Suite 4300	Minneapolis	MN	55402	612-376-4000	338-7732
TF: 800-328-4085 ■ *Web:* www.doughertymarkets.com					
Dreyfus Corp 200 Pk Ave	New York	NY	10166	212-922-6500	922-7533
TF: 888-268-3036 ■ *Web:* www.dreyfus.com					
Duncan-Williams Inc 6750 Poplar Ave Suite 300	Memphis	TN	38138	901-260-6800	260-6994
TF: 800-827-0827 ■ *Web:* www.duncanw.com					
E*Trade Financial Corp 1271 Avenue of the Americas 14th Fl	New York	NY	10020	800-387-2331	
NASDAQ: ETFC ■ *TF:* 800-387-2331 ■ *Web:* www.us.etrade.com					
Eaton Vance Distributors Inc 255 State St	Boston	MA	02109	617-482-8260	482-2396
TF: 800-225-6265 ■ *Web:* www.eatonvance.com					
Edward Jones 12555 Manchester Rd	Saint Louis	MO	63131	314-515-2000	515-3269
Web: www.edwardjones.com					
Energynet.com Inc 7201 I-40 W Suite 319	Amarillo	TX	79106	806-351-2953	354-2835
Web: www.energynet.com					
Falcon Capital LLC 1111 Brickell Ave	Miami	FL	33131	305-913-7130	675-0925
Web: www.falconcapital.net					
Fidelity Brokerage Services Inc 155 Congress St	Boston	MA	02110	800-343-3548	
TF: 800-828-6680 ■ *Web:* www.fidelity.com					
Fidelity Personal Investments & Brokerage Group 82 Devonshire St	Boston	MA	02109	617-563-7000	
TF: 800-828-6680 ■ *Web:* www.fedility.com					
Financial Service Corp 2300 Windy Ridge Pkwy Suite 1100	Atlanta	GA	30329	770-916-6500	916-6563*
**Fax:* Mail Rm ■ *TF:* 800-352-4372 ■ *Web:* www.fscorp.com					
First Manhattan Co 437 Madison Ave	New York	NY	10022	212-756-3300	
Web: www.firstmanhattanco.com					
First New York Securities LLC 90 Pk Ave FL 5	New York	NY	10016	212-848-0600	888-3174
Web: www.firstny.com					
First Southwest Co 325 N St Paul St Suite 800	Dallas	TX	75201	214-953-4000	953-4065
TF: 800-678-3792 ■ *Web:* www.firstsw.com					
First Trust Portfolios LP 1001 Warrenville Rd	Lisle	IL	60532	630-241-4141	241-8650
TF: 800-621-1675 ■ *Web:* www.ftportfolios.com					
Franklin Templeton Investments 3344 Quality Dr	Rancho Cordova	CA	95670	650-312-2000	463-1125*
**Fax Area Code:* 916 ■ **Fax:* Cust Svc ■ *TF:* 800-632-2350 ■ *Web:* www.franklintempleton.com					
Freedom Investments Inc 375 Raritan Ctr Pkwy	Edison	NJ	08837	732-934-3113	934-3095
TF: 800-944-4033 ■ *Web:* www.freedominvestments.com					
Friedman Billings Ramsey Group Inc 1001 19th St N	Arlington	VA	22209	703-312-9500	312-9501
TF: 800-846-5050 ■ *Web:* www.fbr.com					
Gardner Rich & Co 401 S Financial Pl	Chicago	IL	60605	312-922-3333	922-2144
TF: 800-462-7324 ■ *Web:* www.gardnerrich.com					
George K Baum & Co 4801 Main St Suite 500 PO Box 20	Kansas City	MO	64112	816-474-1100	283-5180
TF: 800-821-7195 ■ *Web:* www.gkbaum.com					
Gilford Securities Inc 777 3rd Ave	New York	NY	10017	212-888-6400	826-9738
TF: 800-445-3673 ■ *Web:* www.gilfordsecurities.com					
Gleacher & Co LLC 660 Madison Ave 19th Fl	New York	NY	10021	212-418-4200	843-3828*
**Fax:* Hum Res ■ *Web:* www.gleacher.com					
Glickenhaus & Co 546 5th Ave 7th Fl	New York	NY	10036	212-953-7800	983-8436
Web: www.glickenhaus.com					
Goldman Sachs & Co 200 W St	New York	NY	10282	212-902-1000	
NYSE: GS ■ *TF:* 800-323-5678 ■ *Web:* www2.goldmansachs.com					
HC Wainwright & Co Inc 52 Vanderbilt Ave 12th Fl	New York	NY	10017	212-856-5700	856-5753
Web: www.hcwainwright.com					
Howe Barnes Investments Inc 222 S Riverside Plaza 7th Fl	Chicago	IL	60606	312-655-3000	655-2770*
**Fax:* Cust Svc ■ *TF:* 800-275-4693 ■ *Web:* www.howebarnes.com					
Huntleigh Securities Corp 7800 Forsyth Blvd FL 5	Saint Louis	MO	63105	314-236-2400	236-2401
TF: 800-727-5405 ■ *Web:* www.hntlgh.com					
ING Barings 1325 Avenue of the Americas	New York	NY	10019	646-424-6000	242-6060
TF: 800-221-5855					
Ingalls & Snyder 61 Broadway 31st Fl	New York	NY	10006	212-269-7800	269-7893
TF: 800-221-2598 ■ *Web:* www.ingalls.net					
Integrated Fund Services Inc 221 E 4th St Suite 300	Cincinnati	OH	45202	800-543-8721	362-8086*
**Fax Area Code:* 513 ■ *TF:* 800-543-8721					
Interactive Brokers Group LLC (IBG) 1 Pickwick Plaza	Greenwich	CT	06830	203-618-5800	618-5770
NASDAQ: IBKR ■ *Web:* www.interactivebrokers.com					
Investec Ernst & Co 1 Battery Pk Plaza 2nd Fl	New York	NY	10004	212-898-6200	895-3555
Web: www.investec.com					
Investment Technology Group 380 Madison Ave	New York	NY	10017	212-588-4000	
NYSE: ITG ■ *TF:* 800-215-4484 ■ *Web:* www.itginc.com					
Investors Capital Corp (ICC) 230 Broadway E Suite 205	Lynnfield	MA	01940	781-593-8565	593-9464
TF: 800-949-1422 ■ *Web:* www.investorscapital.com					
Investrade Discount Securities 950 N Milwaukee Ave Suite 102	Glenview	IL	60025	847-375-6080	367-8466*
**Fax Area Code:* 877 ■ **Fax:* Cust Svc ■ *TF Cust Svc:* 800-498-7120 ■ *Web:* www.investrade.com					
ITG Inc 380 Madison Ave 4th Fl	New York	NY	10017	212-588-4000	444-6292
TF: 800-215-4484 ■ *Web:* www.itginc.com					
Janney Montgomery Scott LLC 1801 Market St	Philadelphia	PA	19103	215-665-6000	977-8612*
**Fax:* Sales ■ *TF:* 800-526-6397 ■ *Web:* www.janneys.com					
Jefferies & Co Inc 11100 S Santa Monica Blvd # 10	Los Angeles	CA	90025	310-445-1199	914-1173
TF: 800-421-0160 ■ *Web:* www.jefco.com					
Jefferies Group Inc 520 Madison Ave 10th Fl	New York	NC	10022	212-284-2300	
NYSE: JEF ■ *Web:* www.jefco.com					
JJB Hilliard WL Lyons Inc 500 W Jefferson St	Louisville	KY	40202	502-588-8400	588-4154*
**Fax:* Hum Res ■ *TF:* 800-444-1854 ■ *Web:* www.hilliard.com					
Johnston Lemon & Co Inc 1101 Vermont Ave NW Suite 800	Washington	DC	20005	202-842-5500	842-7185
TF: 800-424-5158 ■ *Web:* www.johnstonlemon.com					
Kelso & Co Inc 320 Pk Ave 24th Fl	New York	NY	10022	212-751-3939	223-2379
Web: www.kelso.com					
Kent Financial Services Inc 376 Main St PO Box 74	Bedminster	NJ	07921	908-234-0078	234-9355
NASDAQ: KENT ■ *Web:* www.kentfinancialservices.com					
Knight Capital Group Inc 545 Washington Blvd	Jersey City	NJ	07310	201-222-9400	557-6853
NYSE: KCG ■ *TF:* 800-544-7508 ■ *Web:* www.knight.com					
Kohlberg Capital Corp 295 Madison Ave 6th Fl	New York	NY	10017	212-455-8300	983-7654
NASDAQ: KCAP ■ *Web:* www.kohlbergcapital.com					
Kohlberg Kravis Roberts & Co 9 W 57th St	New York	NY	10019	212-750-8300	750-0003
Web: www.kkr.com					
LaBranche & Co Inc 33 Whitehall St 8th Fl	New York	NY	10004	212-425-1144	248-7438
NYSE: LAB ■ *Web:* www.labranche.com					
Ladenburg Thalmann Financial Services Inc 4400 Biscayne Blvd 12th Fl	Miami	FL	33137	212-409-2000	572-4199*
AMEX: LTS ■ **Fax Area Code:* 305 ■ *TF:* 800-523-8425 ■ *Web:* www.ladenburg.com					
Lazard 30 Rockefeller Plaza 59th Fl	New York	NY	10020	212-632-6000	632-6051
NYSE: LAZ ■ *TF:* 877-266-8601 ■ *Web:* www.lazard.com					
Lebenthal & Co Inc 120 Broadway 12th Fl	New York	NY	10271	212-425-6116	482-1431
TF: 800-425-6116 ■ *Web:* www.lebenthal.com					
Legg Mason Inc (LMI) 100 International Dr	Baltimore	MD	21202	410-539-0000	454-3101*
NYSE: LM ■ **Fax:* Hum Res ■ *TF:* 800-368-2558 ■ *Web:* www.leggmason.com					
Lepercq de Neuflize & Co 40 W 57th St 19th Fl	New York	NY	10019	212-698-0700	262-0144
TF: 800-697-3863 ■ *Web:* www.lepercq.com					
Lincolnshire Management Inc 780 3rd Ave 40th Fl	New York	NY	10017	212-319-3633	755-5457
Web: www.lincolnshiremgmt.com					
Loop Capital Markets LLC 200 W Jackson Blvd 16th Fl	Chicago	IL	60606	312-913-4900	913-4928
TF: 888-294-8898 ■ *Web:* www.loopcap.com					
LPL Financial Services 1 Beacon St 22nd Fl	Boston	MA	02108	617-423-3644	
TF: 800-877-7210 ■ *Web:* www.joinlpl.com					
Meridian Capital LLC 2025 First Ave Suite 1170	Seattle	WA	98121	206-623-4000	623-8221
Web: www.meridianllc.com					
Merrill Lynch & Co Inc 250 Vessey St 4 World Financial Ctr N Tower	New York	NY	10080	212-449-1000	449-9418*
**Fax:* Mail Rm ■ *TF:* 800-637-7455 ■ *Web:* www.ml.com					
Mesirow Financial Inc 350 N Clark St	Chicago	IL	60610	312-595-6000	595-6035*
**Fax:* Hum Res ■ *TF:* 800-453-0600 ■ *Web:* www.mesirowfinancial.com					
Michael Saunders Securities Corp 1801 Main St	Sarasota	FL	34236	941-951-6660	
TF: 888-552-5228 ■ *Web:* www.michaelsaunders.com					
Mizuho Securities USA 111 River St 11th Fl	Hoboken	NJ	07030	201-626-1000	626-1577
Web: www.mizuhosecurities.com					
Morgan Keegan & Co Inc 50 N Front St Morgan Keegan Tower	Memphis	TN	38103	901-524-4100	524-4197
TF: 800-366-7426 ■ *Web:* www.morgankeegan.com					
Morgan Stanley 1585 Broadway	New York	NY	10036	212-761-4000	
NYSE: MWD ■ *TF:* 800-223-2440 ■ *Web:* www.morganstanley.com					
Morgan Stanley Investment Management 1221 Avenue of the Americas 5th Fl	New York	NY	10020	212-762-7400	762-7984
TF: 800-419-2861 ■ *Web:* www.morganstanley.com/im					
MR Beal & Co 110 Wall St 6th Fl	New York	NY	10005	212-983-3930	983-4539
Web: www.mrbeal.com					
Natexis Bleichroeder LLC 1345 Avenue of the Americas	New York	NY	10105	212-698-3000	299-4444
TF: 800-435-0336 ■ *Web:* www.blr.natixis.com					
Needham & Co Inc 445 Pk Ave 3rd Fl	New York	NY	10022	212-371-8300	371-8418
TF: 800-903-3268 ■ *Web:* www.needhamco.com					
New England Capital Partners Inc 1 Gateway Ctr Suite 405	Newton	MA	02458	617-964-7300	964-7301
Web: www.necapitalpartners.com					
New England Securities Corp 485 E Rt 1 S 4th Fl	Iselin	NJ	08830	800-472-7227	326-4051*
**Fax Area Code:* 732 ■ *TF:* 800-472-7227					
Nomura Securities International Inc 2 World Financial Ctr Bldg B	New York	NY	10281	212-667-9300	667-1016
Web: www.nomura.com					
Northeast Capital & Advisory Inc 7 Airport Pk Blvd 2nd Fl	Latham	NY	12110	518-426-0100	786-0105
Web: www.northeastcapital.net					
Northern Trust Securities 50 S La Salle St 12th Fl	Chicago	IL	60603	312-557-2000	630-6131
TF: 800-621-2253 ■ *Web:* www.northerntrust.com					
Nutmeg Securities Ltd 1960 Bronson Rd Bldg 2	Fairfield	CT	06824	203-255-3838	227-0425
TF: 800-288-5513 ■ *Web:* www.nutmegsecurities.com					
Nuveen Investments Inc 333 W Wacker Dr	Chicago	IL	60606	312-917-7700	
TF: 800-257-8787 ■ *Web:* www.nuveen.com					
NYLIFE Securities Inc 51 Madison Ave Rm 251	New York	NY	10010	800-695-4785	
TF: 800-695-4785 ■ *Web:* www.newyorklife.com					
Oberweis Securities Inc 3333 Warrenville Rd Suite 500	Lisle	IL	60532	630-577-2300	245-0467
TF: 800-323-6166 ■ *Web:* www.oberweis.net					
Olympic Cascade Financial Corp 120 Broadway 27th Fl	New York	NY	10271	212-417-8000	
Web: www.nationalsecurities.com					
Oscar Gruss & Son Inc 292 Madison Ave 4th Fl	New York	NY	10017	212-514-2400	514-2495
Web: www.oscargruss.com					
Pacific Crest Securities Inc 111 SW 5th Ave 42nd Fl	Portland	OR	97204	503-248-0721	227-3608
TF: 800-314-9837 ■ *Web:* www.pacific-crest.com					
Palladium Equity Partners LLC 1270 Avenue of the Americas	New York	NY	10020	212-218-5150	218-5155
Web: www.palladiumequity.com					
Paulson Capital Corp 811 SW Naito Pkwy Suite 200	Portland	OR	97204	503-243-6000	243-6018
NASDAQ: PLCC ■ *Web:* www.paulsoninvestment.com					

Phone Fax

Paulson Investment Co Inc
811 SW Naito Pkwy Suite 200 Portland OR 97204 503-243-6000 243-6018
Web: www.paulsoninvestment.com

PDI Financial Group 601 N Lynndale Dr. Appleton WI 54914 920-739-2303 739-2205
TF: 800-234-7341 ■ *Web:* www.pdifinancial.com

Pennsylvania Trust Co
5 Radnor Corp Ctr Suite 450 Radnor PA 19087 610-975-4300 975-4324
TF: 800-975-4316 ■ *Web:* www.penntrust.com

Penson Financial Services Inc
1700 Pacific Ave Suite 1400 Dallas TX 75201 214-765-1100 765-1164
TF: 800-696-3585 ■ *Web:* www.penson.com

People's Securities Inc
1000 Lafayette Blvd Bridgeport CT 06601 203-338-0800 338-3218*
**Fax:* Cust Svc ■ *TF:* 800-772-4400

Piper Jaffray Cos
800 Nicollet Mall Suite 800 Minneapolis MN 55402 612-303-6000 303-1309*
NYSE: PJC ■ **Fax:* PR ■ *TF:* 800-333-6000 ■ *Web:* www.piperjaffray.com

Questar Capital Corp
5701 Golden Hills Dr Minneapolis MN 55416 888-446-5872 765-5996*
**Fax Area Code:* 763 ■ *TF:* 888-446-5872 ■ *Web:* www.questarcapital.com

Ragen Mackenzie Group Inc
999 3rd Ave Suite 4000 Seattle WA 98104 206-343-5000 389-8245*
**Fax:* Hum Res ■ *TF:* 800-456-4457 ■ *Web:* www.wellsfargo.com/ragen_mackenzie/about

Raymond James Financial Inc
880 Carillon Pkwy Saint Petersburg FL 33716 727-567-1000 573-8622*
NYSE: RJF ■ **Fax:* Cust Svc ■ *TF:* 800-248-8863 ■ *Web:* www.raymondjames.com

RBC Capital Markets
200 Bay St 13th Fl N Tower Toronto ON M5J2J5 416-842-2000 842-8033*
**Fax:* Hum Res ■ *Web:* www.rbcds.com

RBC Capital Markets 1 Liberty Plaza New York NY 10006 212-428-6200 428-2329*
**Fax:* Hum Res ■ *TF:* 888-886-8296 ■ *Web:* www.rbccm.com

RBC Dain Rauscher Inc
60 S 6th St Dain Rauscher Plaza Minneapolis MN 55402 612-313-1234
Web: www.rbcdain.com

Rice Financial Products Co
17 State St 40th Fl New York NY 10004 212-908-9200 908-9299
Web: www.ricefinancialproducts.com

Robeco Investment Management
909 3rd Ave 32nd Fl New York NY 10022 212-908-9500 908-9672
Web: www.robecoinvest.com

Robert W Baird & Co Inc PO Box 672 Milwaukee WI 53201 414-765-3500 765-3600
TF: 800-792-2473 ■ *Web:* www.rwbaird.com

Roosevelt & Cross Inc
1 Exchange Plaza 55 Broadway 22nd Fl New York NY 10006 212-344-2500
TF: 800-348-3426 ■ *Web:* www.roosevelt-cross.com

Royal Alliance Assoc Inc
One World Financial Ctr 14th Fl New York NY 10281 800-821-5100
TF: 800-821-5100 ■ *Web:* www.royalalliance.com

Royal Securities Co
4095 Chicago Dr SW Suite 120 Grandville MI 49418 616-538-2550 538-3360
TF: 800-421-3518 ■ *Web:* www.royalsecurities.com

Ryan Beck & Co 18 Columbia Tpke Florham Park NJ 07932 973-549-4000
TF: 800-342-2325

Samuel A Ramirez & Co Inc
61 Broadway Suite 2924 New York NY 10006 212-248-0500 248-0528
TF: 855-726-4739 ■ *Web:* www.ramirezco.com

Sandler O'Neill + Partners LP
919 Third Ave Fl 6 New York NY 10022 212-466-7800 466-7888
TF: 800-635-6851 ■ *Web:* www.sandleroneill.com

SBK Brooks Investment Corp
820 Terminal Tower 50 Public Sq Cleveland OH 44113 216-861-6950 861-7619
Web: www.sbkbrooks.com

Schroder Investment Management North America Inc (SIMNA)
875 3rd Ave 22nd Fl New York NY 10022 800-730-2932 632-2954*
**Fax Area Code:* 212 ■ *TF:* 800-730-2932 ■ *Web:* www.schroders.com/us

Scotia Capital Markets 1 Liberty Plaza New York NY 10006 212-225-5000 225-5090
TF: 800-472-6842 ■ *Web:* www.scotiacapital.com

Scott & Stringfellow Inc 909 E Main St Richmond VA 23219 804-643-1811 649-2916
TF: 800-552-7757 ■ *Web:* www.scottstringfellow.com

Seasongood & Mayer LLC
414 Walnut St Suite 300 Cincinnati OH 45202 513-621-2000 621-5259
TF: 800-767-7207 ■ *Web:* www.seasongood.com

Seidler Cos Inc
515 S Figueroa St Suite 1100 Los Angeles CA 90071 213-683-4500 683-1247*
**Fax:* Hum Res ■ *TF:* 800-840-1090

SG Cowen Securities Corp
1221 Avenue of the Americas New York NY 10020 212-278-6000
TF: 800-221-5616 ■ *Web:* www.cowen.com

Siebert Brandford Shank & Co LLC
100 Wall St Suite 22 New York NY 10005 646-775-4863 576-9680
TF: 800-334-6800 ■ *Web:* www.sbsco.com

Smith Barney 388 Greenwich St 16th Fl New York NY 10013 212-816-1641 816-5944*
**Fax:* PR ■ *TF:* 800-221-3636 ■ *Web:* www.smithbarney.com

Standard & Poor's Securities Inc
55 Water St New York NY 10041 212-438-2000 438-6578*

Starshak Winzenburg & Co
55 W Monroe St Suite 2530 Chicago IL 60603 312-444-9367 444-9519
Web: www.swandco.com

Stephens Inc 111 Ctr St Little Rock AR 72201 501-377-2000 377-2666*
**Fax:* Mail Rm ■ *TF:* 800-643-9691 ■ *Web:* www.stephens.com

Sterne Agee & Leach Inc
800 Shades Creek Pkwy Suite 700 Birmingham AL 35209 205-949-3500 949-3607
TF: 800-240-1438 ■ *Web:* www.sterneagee.com

Stifel Financial Corp 501 N Broadway Saint Louis MO 63102 800-679-5446 342-2051*
NYSE: SF ■ **Fax Area Code:* 314 ■ *TF:* 800-488-0970 ■ *Web:* www.stifel.com

Stifel Nicolaus & Co Inc 501 N Broadway Saint Louis MO 63102 314-342-2000 342-2051
TF: 800-679-5446 ■ *Web:* www.stifel.com

SunTrust Robinson Humphrey Capital Markets
3333 Peachtree Rd NE Atlanta Financial Ctr Atlanta GA 30326 404-926-5000
TF: 877-266-6501 ■ *Web:* www.suntrustrh.com

Sws Financial Services Inc
1201 Elm St Suite 3500 Dallas TX 75270 214-859-1800 859-5500
TF: 800-562-8041 ■ *Web:* www.swsfinancial.net

Phone Fax

SWS Group Inc 1201 Elm St Suite 3500 Dallas TX 75270 214-859-1800 658-9312
NYSE: SWS ■ *TF:* 800-973-7977 ■ *Web:* www.swsgroupinc.com

Symphony Asset Management Inc
555 California St SAN FRANCISCO CA 94104 415-676-4000 676-2480
Web: www.symphonyasset.com

TD Ameritrade Inc PO Box 2760 Omaha NE 68103 402-331-2744 597-7759
TF Cust Svc: 866-468-6268 ■ *Web:* www.tdameritrade.com

TD Securities (USA) Inc 31 W 52nd St New York NY 10019 212-827-7000 827-7248*
**Fax:* Hum Res ■ *Web:* www.tdsecurities.com

Tejas Inc 8226 Bee Caves Rd Austin TX 78746 512-306-8222 306-1528
TF: 800-846-6803 ■ *Web:* www.tejassec.com

TradeStation Group Inc
8050 SW 10th St Suite 2000 Plantation FL 33324 954-652-7000 652-7899
NASDAQ: TRAD ■ *TF:* 800-871-3577 ■ *Web:* www.tradestation.com

TradeStation Securities Inc
8050 SW 10th St Suite 2000 Plantation FL 33324 954-652-7000 652-7300
TF: 800-515-3238 ■ *Web:* www.tradestation.com

Trading Direct 160 Broadway E Bldg 7th Fl New York NY 10038 212-766-0230 766-0914
TF: 800-925-8566 ■ *Web:* www.tradingdirect.com

UBS Capital Markets
111 Pavonia Ave E Newport Financial Ctr Jersey City NJ 07310 201-963-9100 963-2274
TF: 800-543-7995

UBS Financial Services Inc
1285 Avenue of the Americas New York NY 10019 212-713-2000
TF: 800-221-3260 ■ *Web:* www.financialservicesinc.ubs.com

UBS Warburg LLC 677 Washington Blvd Stamford CT 06901 203-719-3000 719-5499
TF: 800-221-3260 ■ *Web:* www.ubs.com

Utendahl Capital Management LP
30 Broad St 21st Fl New York NY 10004 212-797-2688 425-4199
TF: 877-941-4900 ■ *Web:* www.utendahl.com

Vanguard Brokerage Services PO Box 2600 Valley Forge PA 19482 610-669-1000 669-6366
TF: 800-992-8327 ■ *Web:* www.vanguard.com

Veronis Suhler Stevenson 350 Pk Ave 7th Fl New York NY 10022 212-935-4990 381-8168
Web: www.vss.com

vFinance Inc 1200 N Federal Hwy Suite 400 Boca Raton FL 33432 561-981-1000 283-0480
Web: www.vfinance.com

Walnut Street Securities Inc
260 Madison Ave 11th Fl New York NY 10016 212-354-8800 413-4966
TF: 800-873-7702

Wayne Hummer Investments LLC
222 S Riverside Pz 28th Fl Chicago IL 60606 312-431-1700 431-0704
TF: 800-621-4477 ■ *Web:* www.wintrustwealth.com

Wedbush Corp 1000 Wilshire Blvd Suite 830 Los Angeles CA 90017 213-688-8018 688-8095
Web: www.wedbushcapital.com

Wedbush Morgan Securities Inc
1000 Wilshire Blvd Suite 900 Los Angeles CA 90017 213-688-8000 688-6652*
**Fax:* Hum Res ■ *Web:* www.wedbush.com

Wells Fargo Investments
420 Montgomery St 5th Fl San Francisco CA 94104 415-396-0391 975-7150
TF: 800-621-7609 ■ *Web:* www.wellsfargo.com

William Blair & Co LLC 222 W Adams St Chicago IL 60606 312-236-1600 236-1875
TF: 800-621-0687 ■ *Web:* www.williamblair.com

WR Hambrecht & Co
539 Bryant St Suite 100 San Francisco CA 94107 415-551-8600 551-8686
TF Cust Svc: 877-673-6476 ■ *Web:* www.wrhambrecht.com

Ziegler Capital Markets Investment Services
200 S Wacker Chicago IL 60606 414-978-6400 334-3433*
**Fax Area Code:* 262 ■ **Fax:* Hum Res

Ziegler Cos Inc 250 E Wisconsin Ave Milwaukee WI 53202 414-978-6400 978-6401
Web: www.ziegler.com

694 SECURITIES & COMMODITIES EXCHANGES

Phone Fax

Arbinet Corp
120 Albany St Tower II 4th Fl New Brunswick NJ 08901 732-509-9100 509-9101
TF: 800-272-4638 ■ *Web:* www.arbinet.com

Chicago Board Options Exchange (CBOE)
400 S La Salle St Chicago IL 60605 312-786-5600 786-8818
TF: 800-678-4667 ■ *Web:* www.cboe.com

Chicago Stock Exchange 440 S LaSalle St Chicago IL 60605 312-663-2222 663-2058
Web: www.chx.com

CME Group Inc 20 S Wacker Dr Chicago IL 60606 312-930-1000 466-4410
NYSE: CME ■ *TF:* 866-716-7274 ■ *Web:* www.cmegroup.com

Ice Futures 1 N End Ave 13th Fl New York NY 10282 212-748-4000 742-6981
TF: 800-433-4348 ■ *Web:* www.theice.com

IntercontinentalExchange Inc
2100 Riverside Pkwy Suite 500 Atlanta GA 30328 770-857-4700 951-1307
NYSE: ICE ■ *Web:* www.theice.com

International Securities Exchange (ISE)
60 Broad St New York NY 10004 212-943-2400 425-4926
TF: 877-473-9989 ■ *Web:* www.iseoptions.com

Kansas City Board of Trade
4800 Main St Suite 303 Kansas City MO 64112 816-753-7500 753-3944
Web: www.kcbt.com

Minneapolis Grain Exchange
400 S 4th St Rm 130 Minneapolis MN 55415 612-321-7101 339-1155
TF: 800-827-4746 ■ *Web:* www.mgex.com

Montreal Exchange
800 Victoria Sq 3rd Fl PO Box 61 Montreal QC H4Z1A9 514-871-2424 871-3565
TF: 800-361-5353 ■ *Web:* www.m-x.ca

Nasdaq Stock Market Inc 165 Broadway New York NY 10006 212-401-8700
NASDAQ: NDAQ ■ *Web:* www.nasdaq.com

National Stock Exchange (NSX)
440 S LaSalle St Suite 2600 Chicago IL 60605 312-786-8803 939-7239
TF: 800-843-3924 ■ *Web:* www.nsx.com

NYSE Arce 115 Samsone St 3rd Fl San Francisco CA 94104 877-729-7291 393-7919*
**Fax Area Code:* 415 ■ *TF:* 877-729-7291 ■ *Web:* www.nyse.com

NYSE Euronext 11 Wall St New York NY 10005 212-656-3000 656-2126
NYSE: NYX ■ *TF:* 866-873-7422 ■ *Web:* www.nyse.com

				Phone	Fax
Toronto Stock Exchange 130 King St W	Toronto	ON	M5X1B8	416-947-4670	947-4662
TF: 888-873-8392 ■ *Web:* www.tmx.com					

695 SECURITY PRODUCTS & SERVICES

SEE ALSO Audio & Video Equipment p. 1486; Fire Protection Systems p. 1846; Signals & Sirens - Electric p. 2657

				Phone	Fax
A4S Security Inc 489 N Denver Ave	Loveland	CO	80537	970-461-0071	837-6765*
NASDAQ: SWAT ■ **Fax Area Code:* 888 ■ *TF:* 888-825-0247					
ADT Security Services Inc 14200 E Exposition Ave	Aurora	CO	80012	800-238-2455	238-3307*
**Fax Area Code:* 877 ■ **Fax:* Hum Res ■ *TF:* 800-238-2455 ■ *Web:* www.adt.com					
Advantor Systems Corp 12612 Challenger Pkwy Suite 300	Orlando	FL	32809	407-859-3350	857-1635*
**Fax:* Sales ■ *TF:* 800-523-1921 ■ *Web:* www.advantor.com					
AFA Protective Systems Inc 155 Michael Dr	Syosset	NY	11791	516-496-2322	496-2848
Web: www.afaprotectivesystems.com					
Akal Security Inc 7 Infinity Loop	Espanola	NM	87532	505-692-6600	753-8689
TF: 888-325-2527 ■ *Web:* www.akalsecurity.com					
Allied Fire & Security Inc 425 W 2nd Ave	Spokane	WA	99201	509-321-8778	321-8767*
**Fax:* Acctg ■ *TF Acctg:* 888-333-2632 ■ *Web:* www.allied-security.com					
AMAG Technology Inc 20701 Manhattan Pl	Torrance	CA	90501	310-518-2380	834-0685
TF: 800-889-9138 ■ *Web:* www.amagaccess.com					
American Dynamics Corp 6795 Flanders Dr	San Diego	CA	92121	858-642-2400	642-2440
TF: 800-854-2057 ■ *Web:* www.americandynamics.net					
American Locker Group Inc 815 S Main St	Grapevine	TX	76051	817-329-1600	421-8618
NASDAQ: ALGI ■ *TF:* 800-828-9118 ■ *Web:* www.americanlocker.com					
American Locker Security Systems Inc 608 Allen St	Jamestown	NY	14701	716-664-9600	664-2949
TF Sales: 800-828-9118 ■ *Web:* www.americanlocker.com					
American Science & Engineering Inc 829 Middlesex Tpke	Billerica	MA	01821	978-262-8700	262-8804
NASDAQ: ASEI ■ *TF:* 800-225-1608 ■ *Web:* www.as-e.com					
American Security Products Inc 11925 Pacific Ave	Fontana	CA	92337	951-685-9680	685-9685
TF: 800-421-6142 ■ *Web:* www.amsecusa.com					
APi Systems Group Inc 2609 National Cir	Garland	TX	75041	214-291-1200	291-1340
TF: 800-223-4922 ■ *Web:* www.apisystemsgroup.com					
Armor Safe Technologies LLC PO Box 560275	The Colony	TX	75056	972-624-5734	624-5735
TF: 800-487-2766 ■ *Web:* www.armorsafe.com					
Authentix Inc 4355 Excel Pkwy Suite 100	Addison	TX	75001	469-737-4400	737-4409
TF: 866-434-1402 ■ *Web:* www.authentix.com					
Baltimore Alarm & Security Inc 5314 Reistertown Rd	Baltimore	MD	21215	410-358-8600	358-6337
BI Inc 6400 Lookout Rd	Boulder	CO	80301	303-218-1000	218-1250
TF: 800-241-2911 ■ *Web:* www.bi.com					
Bosch Security Systems 130 Perinton Pkwy	Fairport	NY	14450	585-223-4060	223-9180
TF: 800-289-0096 ■ *Web:* www.boschsecurity.us					
Brink's Home Security Inc 8880 Esters Blvd	Irving	TX	75063	972-871-3500	871-3317*
**Fax:* Hum Res ■ *TF:* 800-874-1190 ■ *Web:* www.brinkshomesecurity.com					
Brivo Systems LLC 4350 E W Hwy Suite 201	Bethesda	MD	20814	301-664-5242	664-5264
TF Tech Supp: 866-692-7486 ■ *Web:* www.brivo.com					
Carter Bros LLC 100 Hartsfield Ctr Pkwy Suite 140	Atlanta	GA	30354	888-818-0152	767-2568*
**Fax Area Code:* 404 ■ *TF:* 888-818-0152 ■ *Web:* www.carterbrothers.com					
Central Signaling Inc 2033 Hamilton Rd	Columbus	GA	31904	706-322-3756	596-8552
TF Cust Svc: 800-554-1104 ■ *Web:* www.censignal.com					
Checkpoint Systems Inc 101 Wolf Dr	Thorofare	NJ	08086	856-848-1800	848-0937
NYSE: CKP ■ *TF:* 800-257-5540 ■ *Web:* www.checkpointsystems.com					
Collier Safe Co Inc 5104 W Hanna Ave	Tampa	FL	33634	813-920-0055	920-1221
TF: 800-307-9555 ■ *Web:* www.colliersafe.com					
Computerized Security Systems Inc 1950 Austin Dr	Troy	MI	48083	248-680-8484	680-8468
TF Sales: 877-272-3565 ■ *Web:* www.cssmain.com					
Corby Industries Inc 812 N Gilmore St	Allentown	PA	18109	610-433-1412	435-1963
TF: 800-652-6729 ■ *Web:* www.corby.com					
Detex Corp 302 Detex Dr	New Braunfels	TX	78130	830-629-2900	620-6711
TF: 800-729-3839 ■ *Web:* www.detex.com					
Diebold Inc 5995 Mayfair Rd	North Canton	OH	44720	330-490-4000	
NYSE: DBD ■ *TF:* 800-999-3600 ■ *Web:* www.diebold.com					
Digital Products of Delaware Inc 625 SW 9th Terr	Pompano Beach	FL	33069	954-941-0903	608-6627*
**Fax Area Code:* 888 ■ *TF:* 800-671-0299 ■ *Web:* www.digitaltechnologies-2000.com					
Digital Security Controls (DSC) 3301 Langstaff Rd	Concord	ON	L4K4L2	905-760-3000	760-3004
Web: www.dsc.com					
Directed Electronics Inc 1 Viper Way	Vista	CA	92081	760-598-6200	598-6400
NASDAQ: DEIX ■ *TF:* 800-876-0800 ■ *Web:* www.deiholdings.com					
Doyle Security Systems Inc 792 Calkins Rd	Rochester	NY	14623	585-244-3400	473-4991
TF: 800-836-9538 ■ *Web:* www.doylesecuritysystems.com					
Driven Technologies 2345 S Michigan Ave	Chicago	IL	60616	312-842-1880	842-6225
TF: 877-437-4836					
eDist 97 McKee Dr	Mahwah	NJ	07430	201-512-1400	391-5078*
**Fax Area Code:* 800 ■ *TF:* 800-800-6624 ■ *Web:* www.edist.com					
EMERgency 24 Inc 4179 W Irving Pk Rd	Chicago	IL	60641	773-777-0707	286-1992
TF: 800-877-3624 ■ *Web:* www.emergency24.com					
Engage Technologies Inc 8419 Sunstate St	Tampa	FL	33634	813-885-6615	886-7316
TF: 800-388-2219 ■ *Web:* www.engagetech.net					
Ez Electric Inc 1250 Birchwood Dr	Sunnyvale	CA	94089	408-734-4282	734-0798
Web: www.ez-electric.com					
Federal APD Inc (FAPD) 28100 Cabot Dr Suite 200	Novi	MI	48377	248-374-9600	374-9610
TF: 800-521-9330 ■ *Web:* www.federalapd.com					
Felts Lock & Alarm Co Inc 4000 E Indiana St	Evansville	IN	47715	812-473-4000	
Web: www.feltsonline.com					
FireKing Security Group 101 Security Pkwy	New Albany	IN	47150	812-948-8400	
TF: 800-457-2424 ■ *Web:* www.fireking.com					
First Action Security Security Team Inc 18702 Crestwood Dr	Hagerstown	MD	21742	301-797-2124	797-2189
TF Cust Svc: 800-342-4243 ■ *Web:* www.firstactionteam.com					
FMJ/Pad.Lock Computer Security Systems Inc 510 W Central Ave	Brea	CA	92821	714-990-3218	990-5409
TF: 800-872-9562 ■ *Web:* www.fmjpadlock.com					
Frisco Bay Industries Ltd 160 Graveline St	Saint-Laurent	QC	H4T1R7	514-738-7300	735-7039
TF: 800-463-7472 ■ *Web:* www.friscobay.com					
Frontier Systems Integrator LLC 2751 Prosperity Ave	Fairfax	VA	22031	703-289-9930	
Web: www.frontier-si.com					
Gentex Corp 600 N Centennial St	Zeeland	MI	49464	616-772-1800	772-7348
NASDAQ: GNTX ■ *TF:* 800-444-4689 ■ *Web:* www.gentex.com					
George Risk Industries Inc 802 S Elm St	Kimball	NE	69145	308-235-4645	235-2609
TF Sales: 800-523-1227 ■ *Web:* www.grisk.com					
Guardian Alarm Co 20800 Southfield Rd	Southfield	MI	48075	248-423-1000	423-3009
TF: 800-782-9688 ■ *Web:* www.stayout.com					
Hanchett Entry Systems Inc (HES) 22630 N 17th Ave	Phoenix	AZ	85027	623-582-4626	582-4641
TF: 800-626-7590 ■ *Web:* www.hesinnovations.com					
Honeywell Automation & Control Solutions 11 W Spring St	Freeport	IL	61032	815-235-5500	
Web: www.honeywell.com					
IDenticard Systems Inc 40 Citation Ln	Lititz	PA	17543	717-569-5797	569-2390
TF: 800-233-0298 ■ *Web:* www.identicard.com					
Intercon Security Ltd 40 Sheppard Ave W	Toronto	ON	M2N6K9	416-229-6811	229-1207
TF: 866-312-8960 ■ *Web:* www.interconsecurity.com					
International Electronics Inc 427 Tpke St	Canton	MA	02021	781-821-5566	821-4443
TF: 800-343-9502 ■ *Web:* www.ieib.com					
Johnson Controls Fire & Security Solutions 4100 Gardian St Suite 200	Simi Valley	CA	93063	805-522-5555	582-7899
TF: 800-229-4076 ■ *Web:* www.johnsoncontrols.com/security					
L-3 Communications Corp Security Systems Div 2005 Gandy Blvd N Suite 600	Saint Petersburg	FL	33702	727-556-0270	556-0271
Web: www.l-3com.com					
Linear LLC 1950 Camino Vida Roble Suite 150	Carlsbad	CA	92008	760-438-7000	931-1340
TF Cust Svc: 800-421-1587 ■ *Web:* www.linearcorp.com					
LoJack Corp 200 Lowder Brook Dr Suite 1000	Westwood	MA	02090	781-251-4700	326-7255
NASDAQ: LOJN ■ *TF:* 800-456-5225 ■ *Web:* www.lojack.com					
Mace Security International Inc 240 Gibraltar Rd Suite 220	Horsham	PA	19044	267-317-4009	672-8900*
NASDAQ: PINK ■ **Fax Area Code:* 215 ■ *Web:* www.corp.mace.com					
Matrix Systems Inc 1041 Byers Rd	Miamisburg	OH	45342	937-438-9033	438-0900
TF: 800-562-8749 ■ *Web:* www.matrixsys.com					
MDI Security Systems Inc 12500 Network Dr Suite 303	San Antonio	TX	78249	210-477-5400	477-5401
NASDAQ: MDII ■ *TF:* 866-435-7634 ■ *Web:* www.mdisecure.com					
MMF Industries Inc 1111 S Wheeling Rd	Wheeling	IL	60090	847-537-7890	537-1120
TF: 800-445-8293 ■ *Web:* www.mmfind.com					
Monitronics International Inc 2350 Valley View Ln	Dallas	TX	75234	972-243-7443	243-1064*
**Fax:* Cust Svc ■ *TF Cust Svc:* 800-447-9239 ■ *Web:* www.monitronics.com					
NAPCO Security Systems Inc 333 Bayview Ave	Amityville	NY	11701	631-842-9400	842-9137
NASDAQ: NSSC ■ *TF:* 800-645-9445 ■ *Web:* www.napcosecurity.com					
National Security Systems Inc 511 Manhasset Woods Rd	Manhasset	NY	11030	516-627-2222	
New England Security Inc 10 Industrial Dr PO Box 562	Westerly	RI	02891	401-596-0660	596-0108
TF: 800-556-7395					
Norment Security Group Inc 3224 Mobile Hwy	Montgomery	AL	36108	334-281-8440	288-5485
TF: 800-633-1968 ■ *Web:* www.normentsecurity.com					
Optex Inc 13661 Benson Ave Bldg C	Chino	CA	91710	909-993-5770	628-5560
TF: 800-966-7839 ■ *Web:* www.optexamerica.com					
OSI Systems Inc 12525 Chadron Ave	Hawthorne	CA	90250	310-978-0516	644-1727
NASDAQ: OSIS ■ *Web:* www.osi-systems.com					
Parking Products Inc 2517 Wyandotte Rd	Willow Grove	PA	19090	215-657-7500	657-4321
Web: www.parkingproducts.com					
Per Mar Security 1910 E Kimberly Rd	Davenport	IA	52807	563-326-6291	359-6700
TF: 800-473-7627 ■ *Web:* www.permarsecurity.com					
PerkinElmer Inc 45 William St	Wellesley	MA	02481	781-237-5100	237-9386
NYSE: PKI ■ *Web:* www.perkinelmer.com					
Protection One Inc 1035 N 3rd St Suite 101	Lawrence	KS	66044	785-856-5500	
TF: 800-438-4357 ■ *Web:* www.protectionone.com					
Qualys Inc 1600 Bridge Pkwy	Redwood Shores	CA	94065	650-801-6100	801-6101
TF: 866-801-6161 ■ *Web:* www.qualys.com					
Radiance Technologies Inc 350 Wynn Dr	Huntsville	AL	35805	256-704-3400	704-3412
Web: www.radiancetech.com					
Rapiscan Systems 3232 W El Segundo Blvd	Hawthorne	CA	80250	310-978-1457	349-2491
Web: www.rapiscansystems.com					
Seco-Larm USA Inc 16842 Millikan Ave	Irvine	CA	92606	949-261-2999	261-7326
TF: 800-662-0800 ■ *Web:* www.seco-larm.com					
Securitas Security Services USA Inc 2 Campus Dr	Parsippany	NJ	07054	973-267-5300	397-2534
TF: 800-325-6828 ■ *Web:* www.securitasinc.com					
Security Assoc International Inc 2101 S Arlington Heights Rd Suite 150	Arlington Heights	IL	60005	847-956-8650	956-9360
TF: 800-323-7601 ■ *Web:* www.sai-inc.com					
Security Corp 22325 Roethel Dr	Novi	MI	48375	248-374-5700	374-5750
TF: 888-374-5789 ■ *Web:* www.securitycorp.com					
Security Defense Systems Corp 160 Pk Ave	Nutley	NJ	07110	973-235-0606	235-0132
TF: 800-325-6339 ■ *Web:* www.securitydefense.com					
Security Signal Devices Inc 1740 N Lemon St	Anaheim	CA	92801	714-449-9900	
TF: 800-888-0444 ■ *Web:* www.ssdsystems.com					
Sensormatic Electronics Corp 6600 Congress Ave	Boca Raton	FL	33487	561-912-6000	912-6097
TF: 800-327-1765 ■ *Web:* www.sensormatic.com					
Sentry Group 900 Linden Ave	Rochester	NY	14625	585-381-4900	381-2940*
**Fax:* Cust Svc ■ *TF Cust Svc:* 800-828-1438 ■ *Web:* www.sentrysafe.com					

Company	City	State	Zip	Phone	Fax
Sentry Technology Corp 1881 Lakeland Ave TF: 800-645-4224 ■ Web: www.sentrytechnology.com	Ronkonkoma	NY	11779	631-739-2100	739-2124
SIRCHIE Finger Print Laboratories Inc 100 Hunter Pl TF: 800-356-7311 ■ Web: www.sirchie.com	Youngsville	NC	27596	919-554-2244	554-2266
Software House 70 Westview St TF: 800-550-6660 ■ Web: www.swhouse.com	Lexington	MA	02421	781-466-6660	466-9550
Sonitrol Corp 1000 Westlakes Dr Suite 150 *Fax Area Code: 610 ■ Web: www.sonitrol.com	Berwyn	PA	19312	215-238-9090	785-9707*
Southern Folger Detention Equipment Co 4634 S Presa St Web: www.southernfolger.com	San Antonio	TX	78223	210-533-1231	533-2211
Teletrac Inc 7391 Lincoln Way TF: 800-500-6009 ■ Web: www.teletrac.net	Garden Grove	CA	92841	714-897-0877	379-6378
Texas Industrial Security 101 Summit Ave Suite 404 Web: www.txsecurity.com	Fort Worth	TX	76102	817-335-3046	335-3048
Tyco Fire & Security 301 NE 51st St Web: www.tycofireandsecurity.com	Boca Raton	FL	33431	561-988-7200	
Tyco International Ltd 9 Roszel Rd NYSE: TYC ■ TF: 800-320-2350 ■ Web: www.tyco.com	Princeton	NJ	08540	609-720-4200	720-4208
Unisec Inc 2555 Nicholson St TF: 800-982-4587 ■ Web: www.ultrabarrier.com	San Leandro	CA	94577	510-352-5610	352-6707
Universal Security Instruments Inc 11407 cronhill Dr AMEX: UUU ■ TF: 800-390-4321 ■ Web: www.universalsecurity.com	Owings Mills	MD	21117	410-363-3000	363-2218
UTC Fire & Security 9 Farm Springs Rd Web: www.utcfireandsecurity.com	Farmington	CT	06037	860-284-3000	284-3149
VASCO Data Security International Inc 1901 S Meyers Rd Suite 210 NASDAQ: VDSI ■ Web: www.vasco.com	Oakbrook Terrace	IL	60181	630-932-8844	932-8852
Vector Security Inc 3400 McKnight E Dr Web: www.vectorsecurity.com	Pittsburgh	PA	15237	412-364-2600	364-2712
Verint Video Solutions 9101 Guilford Rd TF: 800-638-5969 ■ Web: www.verint.com	Columbia	MD	21046	301-483-8930	483-9790
W-b Holdings Inc PO Box 690830	San Antonio	TX	78269	210-691-2815	691-8407
William D White Co Inc 3505 Magnolia St	Oakland	CA	94608	510-658-8167	658-3503
Winner International LLC 32 W State St TF: 800-258-2321 ■ Web: www.winner-intl.com	Sharon	PA	16146	724-981-1152	981-1034

696 SECURITY & PROTECTIVE SERVICES

SEE ALSO Investigative Services p. 2128

Company	City	State	Zip	Phone	Fax
A & R Security Service Inc 2552 W 135th St Web: www.arsecurity.com	Blue Island	IL	60406	708-389-3830	389-3878
Accuvant Inc 621 17th St Suite 2425 TF: 800-574-0896 ■ Web: www.accuvant.com	Denver	CO	80293	303-298-0600	298-0868
AlliedBarton Security Services 150 S Warner Rd TF: 888-239-1104 ■ Web: www.alliedbarton.com	King of Prussia	PA	19406	610-239-1100	239-1108
Brink's Inc 555 Dividend Dr Suite 100 Web: www.brinksinc.com	Coppell	TX	75019	469-549-6000	549-6202
CastleRock Security Inc 2101 S Arlington Heights Rd Suite 150 TF: 800-705-7681 ■ Web: www.castlerocksecurity.com	Arlington Heights	IL	60005	847-768-6300	
Command Security Corp 1133 Rt 55 Suite D TF: 877-305-8254 ■ Web: www.commandsecurity.com	Lagrangeville	NY	12540	845-454-3703	454-3703
Diamond Group 13101 Preston Rd Suite 212 Web: www.thediamondgroup.ws	Dallas	TX	75240	972-788-1111	788-0077
Diversco Integrated Services Inc 105 Diversco Dr TF: 800-277-3420 ■ Web: www.diversco.com	Spartanburg	SC	29307	864-579-3420	579-9578
Garda World Security Corp 1390 Barre St TSX: GW ■ TF: 800-859-1599 ■ Web: www.gardaglobal.com	Montreal	QC	H3C1N4	514-281-2811	281-2811
Guard-Systems Inc 12124 Ramona Blvd TF: 800-307-0031 ■ Web: www.guardsystemsinc.com	El Monte	CA	91732	626-433-4999	433-4988
Guardian Alarm Co 20800 Southfield Rd TF: 800-782-9688 ■ Web: www.stayout.com	Southfield	MI	48075	248-423-1000	423-3009
Guardian Protection Services Inc 174 Thorn Hill Rd *Fax Area Code: 724 ■ TF Cust Svc: 877-314-7092 ■ Web: www.guardianprotection.com	Warrendale	PA	15086	412-788-2580	741-3537*
Guardsmark Inc 10 Rockefeller Plaza 12th Fl TF: 800-238-5878 ■ Web: www.guardsmark.com	New York	NY	10020	212-765-8226	
Hepaco Inc 2711 Burch Dr PO Box 26308 TF: 800-888-7689 ■ Web: www.hepaco.com	Charlotte	NC	28269	704-598-9782	598-7823
Huntleigh USA Corp 10332 Old Olive St Rd Web: www.icts-int.com	Saint Louis	MO	63141	314-997-6811	997-0401
IBI Armored Services Inc 37-06 61st St Web: www.ibiarmored.com	Woodside	NY	11377	718-458-4000	458-5371
Intercon Security Ltd 40 Sheppard Ave W TF: 866-312-8960 ■ Web: www.interconsecurity.com	Toronto	ON	M2N6K9	416-229-6811	229-1207
IPC International Corp 2111 Waukegan Rd TF: 800-323-1228 ■ Web: www.ipcinternational.com	Bannockburn	IL	60015	847-444-2000	444-2001
Law Enforcement Assoc Corp (LEA) 2609 Discovery Dr Suite 125 PINK: LAWE ■ TF: 800-354-9669 ■ Web: www.leacorp.com	Raleigh	NC	27616	919-872-6210	872-6431
Levy Security Corp 8750 W Bryn Mawr Ave Suite 1200 TF: 800-649-5389 ■ Web: www.levysecurity.com	Chicago	IL	60631	773-867-9204	714-1318
Maloney Security Inc 1055 Laurel St Web: www.maloneysecurity.com	San Carlos	CA	94070	650-593-0163	593-1101
Murray Guard Inc 58 Murray Guard Dr TF: 800-238-3830 ■ Web: www.murrayguard.com	Jackson	TN	38305	731-668-3400	664-8619
MVM Inc 44620 Guilford Dr Web: www.mvminc.com	Ashburn	VA	20147	571-223-4500	223-4474
Network Multi-Family Security Corp 4221 W John Carpenter Fwy TF: 800-645-2004 ■ Web: www.nmfc.com	Irving	TX	75063	214-277-7000	
Northwest Protective Service Inc 801 S Fidalgo 2nd Fl TF: 888-981-4040 ■ Web: www.nwprotective.com	Seattle	WA	98108	206-448-4040	448-2461
Smith Protective Services Inc 8918 John W Carpenter Fwy TF: 800-634-1381 ■ Web: www.smithprotective.com	Dallas	TX	75247	214-631-4444	631-4241
Trade Show Services 3511 S Eastern Ave Web: www.pro-tectsecurity.com	Las Vegas	NV	89109	702-735-0110	735-7793
Tyco International Ltd 9 Roszel Rd NYSE: TYC ■ TF: 800-320-2350 ■ Web: www.tyco.com	Princeton	NJ	08540	609-720-4200	720-4208
Universal Services of America Inc 1551 N Tustin Ave Suite 650 TF: 866-877-1965 ■ Web: www.universalpro.com	Santa Ana	CA	92705	714-619-9700	619-9701
US Security Assoc Inc 200 Mansell Ct 5th Fl TF: 800-241-0267 ■ Web: www.greatguards.com	Roswell	GA	30076	770-625-1400	625-1519
UTC Fire & Security 9 Farm Springs Rd Web: www.utcfireandsecurity.com	Farmington	CT	06037	860-284-3000	284-3149

697 SEED COMPANIES

SEE ALSO Farm Supplies p. 1841

Seed Production And Development Companies (Horticultural And Agricultural).

Company	City	State	Zip	Phone	Fax
AgriGold Hybrids RR 1 PO Box 203 TF: 800-262-7333 ■ Web: www.agrigold.com	Saint Francisville	IL	62460	618-943-5776	943-7333
Albert Lea Seed House 1414 W Main St TF: 800-352-5247 ■ Web: www.alseed.com	Albert Lea	MN	56007	507-373-3161	373-7032
Ampac Seed Co 32727 Hwy 99 E TF: 800-547-3230 ■ Web: www.ampacseed.com	Tangent	OR	97389	541-928-1651	928-2430
Applewood Seed Co 5380 Vivian St TF: 888-778-7333 ■ Web: www.applewoodseed.com	Arvada	CO	80002	303-431-7333	467-7886
Barenbrug USA Inc 33477 Hwy 99 E PO Box 239 *Fax: Sales ■ TF: 800-547-4101 ■ Web: www.barenbrug.com	Tangent	OR	97389	541-926-5801	926-9435*
Croplan Genetics PO Box 64281 TF: 800-328-9680 ■ Web: www.croplangenetics.com	Saint Paul	MN	55164	651-765-5712	765-5727
Foremostco Inc 8457 NW 66th St *Fax Area Code: 800 ■ Web: www.foremostco.com	Miami	FL	33166	305-592-8986	426-1362*
G & H Seed Co Inc 1110 W Mill St PO Box 321 Web: www.ghseed.com	Crowley	LA	70527	337-783-7762	783-9200
Gries Seed Farms Inc 2348 N 5th St TF: 800-472-4797	Fremont	OH	43420	419-332-5571	332-1817
Harris Moran Seed Co PO Box 4938 TF: 800-808-7333 ■ Web: www.harrismoran.com	Modesto	CA	95352	209-579-7333	527-5312
Johnny's Selected Seeds 955 Benton Ave TF: 877-564-6697 ■ Web: www.johnnyseeds.com	Winslow	ME	04901	207-861-3900	861-8363
Johnston Seed Co 319 W Chestnut St PO Box 1392 TF: 800-375-4613 ■ Web: www.jeinc.com	Enid	OK	73701	580-233-5800	249-5324
JW Jung Seed Co 335 S High St *Fax Area Code: 800 ■ TF: 800-297-3123 ■ Web: www.jungseed.com	Randolph	WI	53956	920-326-3121	692-5864*
Keithly-Williams Seeds Inc 420 Palm Ave PO Box 177 TF: 800-533-3465 ■ Web: www.keithlywilliams.com	Holtville	CA	92250	760-356-5533	356-2409
Latham Seed Co 131 180th St TF: 800-798-3258 ■ Web: www.lathamseeds.com	Alexander	IA	50420	641-692-3258	692-3250
Lebanon Seaboard Corp 1600 E Cumberland St TF: 800-233-0628 ■ Web: www.lebsea.com	Lebanon	PA	17042	717-273-1685	273-9466
Loft Seed Inc 9327 US Rt 1 Suite J TF: 800-732-3332	Laurel	MD	20723	301-362-5415	362-8548
Monsanto Co 800 N Lindbergh Blvd NYSE: MON ■ Web: www.monsanto.com	Saint Louis	MO	63167	314-694-1000	694-8506
Mycogen Seeds 9330 Zionsville Rd TF: 800-692-6436 ■ Web: www.mycogen.com	Indianapolis	IN	46268	800-692-6436	
Nunhems USA Inc 1200 Anderson Corner Rd *Fax: Cust Svc ■ TF Cust Svc: 800-733-9505 ■ Web: www.nunhemsusa.com	Parma	ID	83660	208-674-4000	674-4090*
Park Seed Co 1 Parkton Ave TF Orders: 800-845-3369 ■ Web: www.parkseed.com	Greenwood	SC	29647	864-223-8555	941-4502
Pennington Seed Inc 1280 AtlantaHwy TF: 800-277-1412 ■ Web: www.penningtonseed.com	Madison	GA	30650	706-342-1234	342-9644
Red River Commodities Inc 501 42nd St N TF: 800-437-5539 ■ Web: www.redriv.com	Fargo	ND	58102	701-282-2600	282-5325
Renee's Garden Seeds Inc 7389 W Zayante Rd TF: 888-880-7228 ■ Web: www.reneesgarden.com	Felton	CA	95018	831-335-7228	335-7227
Research Seeds Inc 812 1st St S PO Box 339 Web: www.foragegenetics.com	Nampa	ID	83653	208-466-3568	466-3684
Sakata Seed America Inc 18095 Serene Dr PO Box 880 Web: www.sakata.com	Morgan Hill	CA	95037	408-778-7758	778-7768
Sand Seed Service Inc 4765 Hwy 143 TF: 800-352-2228 ■ Web: www.sandsofiowa.com	Marcus	IA	51035	712-376-4135	376-4140
Schlessman Seed Co 11513 US Rt 250 TF: 888-534-7333 ■ Web: www.schlessman-seed.com	Milan	OH	44846	419-499-2572	499-2574
Seedway LLC 1734 Railroad Pl TF: 800-836-3710 ■ Web: www.seedway.com	Hall	NY	14463	585-526-6391	526-6832
Sharp Bros Seed Co 2005 S Sycamore TF: 800-462-8483 ■ Web: www.sharpseed.com	Healy	KS	67850	620-398-2231	398-2220
Stock Seed Farms 28008 Mill Rd TF: 800-759-1520 ■ Web: www.stockseed.com	Murdock	NE	68407	402-867-3771	867-2442
Stone Seed Farms Inc 5965 W SR 97 Web: www.stoneseed.com	Pleasant Plains	IL	62677	217-546-8006	546-8098
Stratton Seed Co 1530 Hwy 79 S PO Box 1088 TF: 800-264-4433 ■ Web: www.strattonseed.com	Stuttgart	AR	72160	870-673-4433	672-9837
Syngenta Seeds Inc Flowers Div 4343 Commerce Ct Suite 500 TF: 800-323-7253 ■ Web: www.greendemon.net	Lisle	IL	60532	630-969-6300	969-6373
Triumph Seed Co Hwy 62 Bypass PO Box 1050 TF: 800-530-4789 ■ Web: www.triumphseed.com	Ralls	TX	79357	806-253-2584	253-2820

Company	City	State	ZIP	Phone	Fax
W Atlee Burpee Co 300 Pk Ave *TF Cust Svc:* 800-333-5808 ■ *Web:* www.burpee.com	Warminster	PA	18974	215-674-4900	674-4170
Weeks Seed Co Inc 1050 Moye Blvd *TF:* 800-322-1234 ■ *Web:* www.weeksseeds.com	Greenville	NC	27834	252-757-1234	757-0978
Wetsel Inc 961 Liberty St *TF Cust Svc:* 800-572-4018 ■ *Web:* www.wetsel.com	Harrisonburg	VA	22802	540-434-6753	434-4894

698 SEMICONDUCTOR MANUFACTURING SYSTEMS & EQUIPMENT

Company	City	State	ZIP	Phone	Fax
Adcotron EMS Inc 12 Ch St Marine Industrial Pk *Web:* www.adcotron.com	Boston	MA	02210	617-598-3000	598-3001
Advanced Energy Industries Inc 1625 Sharp Pt Dr *NASDAQ: AEIS* ■ *TF:* 800-446-9167 ■ *Web:* www.advanced-energy.com	Fort Collins	CO	80525	970-221-4670	221-5583
Aehr Test Systems 400 Kato Terr *NASDAQ: AEHR* ■ *TF:* 800-522-7200 ■ *Web:* www.aehr.com	Fremont	CA	94539	510-623-9400	623-9450
AIXTRON Inc 1139 Karlstad Dr *TF:* 800-366-0989 ■ *Web:* www.aixtron.com	Sunnyvale	CA	94089	408-747-7140	747-7199
Akrion Systems LLC 6330 Hedgewood Dr Suite 150 **Fax:* Sales ■ *Web:* www.akrionsystems.com	Allentown	PA	18106	610-391-9200	391-1982*
Amistar Automation Inc 1269 Linda Vista *Web:* www.amistar.com	San Marcos	CA	92078	760-471-1700	471-9065
Amtech Systems Inc 131 S Clark Dr *NASDAQ: ASYS* ■ *Web:* www.amtechsystems.com	Tempe	AZ	85281	480-967-5146	968-3763
Applied Materials Inc 3050 Bowers Ave PO Box 58039 *NASDAQ: AMAT* ■ *Web:* www.appliedmaterials.com	Santa Clara	CA	95054	408-727-5555	748-9943
Applied Materials/Semitool 655 W Reserve Dr *TF:* 800-548-8495 ■ *Web:* www.semitool.com	Kalispell	MT	59901	406-752-2107	752-5522
ASM America Inc 3440 E University Dr *Web:* www.asm.com	Phoenix	AZ	85034	602-470-5700	437-1403
ASML US Inc 8555 S River Pkwy *TF:* 800-227-6462 ■ *Web:* www.asml.com	Tempe	AZ	85284	480-383-4422	383-3995
ATMI Inc 7 Commerce Dr *NASDAQ: ATMI* ■ *TF:* 800-766-2681 ■ *Web:* www.atmi.com	Danbury	CT	06810	203-794-1100	792-8040
Aviza Technology Inc 440 Kings Valley Rd *PINK: AVZAQ* ■ *Web:* www.avizatechnology.com	Scotts Valley	CA	95066	831-438-2100	439-6223
Axcelis Technologies Inc 108 Cherry Hill Dr *NASDAQ: ACLS* ■ *Web:* www.axcelis.com	Beverly	MA	01915	978-787-4000	787-4200
BOC Edwards 301 Ballardvale St *TF:* 800-848-9800	Wilmington	MA	01887	978-658-5410	658-5410
Brooks Automation Inc 15 Elizabeth Dr *NASDAQ: BRKS* ■ *Web:* www.brooks.com	Chelmsford	MA	01824	978-262-2400	262-2500
BTU International Inc 23 Esquire Rd *NASDAQ: BTUI* ■ *TF:* 800-998-0666 ■ *Web:* www.btu.com	North Billerica	MA	01862	978-667-4111	667-9068
Conceptronic Inc 1860 Smithtown Ave *Web:* www.conceptronic.com	Ronkonkoma	NY	11779	631-981-7081	981-7095
Contact Systems Inc 50 Miry Brook Rd *Web:* www.contactsystems.com	Danbury	CT	06810	203-743-3837	790-6322
CVD Equipment Corp 1860 Smithtown Ave *AMEX: CVV* ■ *Web:* www.cvdequipment.com	Ronkonkoma	NY	11779	631-981-7081	981-7095
Cymer Inc 17075 Thornmint Ct *NASDAQ: CYMI* ■ *Web:* www.cymer.com	San Diego	CA	92127	858-385-7300	385-7100
Data I/O Corp 6464 185th Ave NE Suite 101 *NASDAQ: DAIO* ■ *TF:* 800-426-1045 ■ *Web:* www.data-io.com	Redmond	WA	98052	425-881-6444	881-6444
DEK USA 8 Bartles Corner Rd *Web:* www.dek.com	Flemington	NJ	08822	908-782-4140	782-4774
Ebara Technologies Inc 51 Main Ave *TF:* 800-535-5376 ■ *Web:* www.ebaratech.com	Sacramento	CA	95838	916-920-5451	925-6654
EG Systems LLC 30974 Santana St *NASDAQ: EGLS* ■ *Web:* www.electroglas.com	Hayward	CA	94544	408-528-3000	528-3562
EMCORE Corp 10420 Research Rd SE *NASDAQ: EMKR* ■ *Web:* www.emcore.com	Albuquerque	NM	87123	505-332-5000	332-5038
Entegris Inc 129 Concord Rd Bldg 2 *TF:* 877-695-7654 ■ *Web:* www.entegris.com	Billerica	MA	01821	978-436-6500	436-6735
FormFactor Inc 7005 SouthFront Rd *NASDAQ: FORM* ■ *Web:* www.formfactor.com	Livermore	CA	94551	925-290-4000	290-4010
Fortrend Corp 687 N Pastoria Ave *Web:* www.fortrend.com	Sunnyvale	CA	94085	408-734-9311	734-4299
FSI International Inc 3455 Lyman Blvd *NASDAQ: FSII* ■ *TF:* 800-274-5440 ■ *Web:* www.fsi-intl.com	Chaska	MN	55318	952-448-5440	448-2825
Gem City Engineering & Mfg Co The 401 Leo St *Web:* www.gemcity.com	Dayton	OH	45404	937-223-5544	226-1908
Gem Services USA Inc 2880 Lakeside Dr Suite 203 *Web:* www.gemservices.com	Santa Clara	CA	95054	408-566-8866	566-8858
Global Communication Semiconductors Inc 23155 Kashiwa Ct *Web:* www.gcsincorp.com	Torrance	CA	90505	310-530-7274	530-7279
Goldfinger Technologies LLC 1241 E Dyer Rd Suite 100	Santa Ana	CA	92705	714-445-2000	445-2204
Hittite Microwave Corp 20 Alpha Rd *NASDAQ: HITT* ■ *Web:* www.hittite.com	Chelmsford	MA	01824	978-250-3343	250-3373
I.B.I.S. Inc 30 Technology Pkwy S Suite 400 *PINK: IBIS* ■ *Web:* www.ibis.com	Norcross	GA	30092	770-368-4000	368-1186
Imtec Acculine Inc 49036 Milmont Dr *Web:* www.imtecacculine.com	Fremont	CA	94538	510-770-1800	770-1400
JMAR Technologies Inc 10905 Technology Pl *PINK: JMAR* ■ *Web:* www.jmar.com	San Diego	CA	92127	858-312-7769	946-6899
KDF Electronic & Vacuum Services Inc 10 Volvo Dr *TF:* 877-533-3343 ■ *Web:* www.kdf.com	Rockleigh	NJ	07647	201-784-5005	784-0202
KLA-Tencor Corp One Technology Dr *NASDAQ: KLAC* ■ *TF:* 800-600-2829 ■ *Web:* www.kla-tencor.com	Milpitas	CA	95035	408-875-3000	875-4144
Kokusai Semiconductor Equipment Corp 2460 N 1st St # 290 *TF:* 800-800-5321 ■ *Web:* www.ksec.com	San Jose	CA	95131	408-456-2750	456-2760
Kulicke & Soffa Industries Inc (K&S) 100 Virginia Dr *NASDAQ: KLIC* ■ *TF:* 800-445-5671 ■ *Web:* www.kns.com	Fort Washington	PA	19034	215-784-6000	784-6001
Lam Research Corp 4650 Cushing Pkwy *NASDAQ: LRCX* ■ **Fax:* Cust Svc ■ *TF:* 800-526-7678 ■ *Web:* www.lamrc.com	Fremont	CA	94538	510-572-0200	572-1093*
Lansdale Semiconductor Inc 5245 S 39th St *Web:* www.lansdale.com	Phoenix	AZ	85040	602-438-0123	438-0138
Laurier Inc 10 Tinker Ave *Web:* www.besidiehandling.com	Londonderry	NH	03053	603-206-4800	626-4242
Leadis Technology Inc 800 W California Ave Suite 200 *NASDAQ: LDIS* ■ *Web:* www.leadis.com	Sunnyvale	CA	94086	408-331-8600	331-8601
Loranger International Corp 817 4th Ave *Web:* www.loranger.com	Warren	PA	16365	814-723-2250	723-5391
Mattson Technology Inc 47131 Bayside Pkwy *NASDAQ: MTSN* ■ *TF:* 800-628-8766 ■ *Web:* www.mattson.com	Fremont	CA	94538	510-657-5900	492-5911
MaxLinear Inc 2051 Palomar Airport Rd Suite 100 *NYSE: MXL* ■ *Web:* www.maxlinear.com	Carlsbad	CA	92011	760-692-0711	444-8598
MCT Worldwide LLC 121 S 8th St Suite 960 *TF:* 800-628-1628 ■ *Web:* www.mct.com	Minneapolis	MN	55402	612-436-3240	436-3242
Moore Technologies Inc 1905 N MacArthur Dr *Web:* www.mooretech.com	Tracy	CA	95376	209-833-0100	833-0410
N J R Corp 125 Nicholson Ln *Web:* www.njr.com	San Jose	CA	95134	408-321-0200	232-6060
Neutronix-Quintel (NXQ) 685 Jarvis Dr # A *Web:* www.neutronixinc.com	Morgan Hill	CA	95037	408-776-5190	776-1039
Novellus Systems Inc 4000 N 1st St *NASDAQ: NVLS* ■ *TF:* 800-800-3079 ■ *Web:* www.novellus.com	San Jose	CA	95134	408-943-9700	943-3422
Rudolph Technologies Inc One Rudolph Rd PO Box 1000 *NASDAQ: RTEC* ■ *TF:* 877-467-8365 ■ *Web:* www.rudolphtech.com	Flanders	NJ	07836	973-691-1300	691-4863
Semi-Kinetics Inc 20191 Windrow Dr Suite A *Web:* www.semi-kinetics.com	Lake Forest	CA	92630	949-830-7364	830-7385
Sensitron Semiconductor 221 W Industry Ct *Web:* www.sensitron.com	Deer Park	NY	11729	631-586-7600	586-6053
Shin-Etsu Microsi Inc 10028 S 51st St *Web:* www.microsi.com	Phoenix	AZ	85044	480-893-8898	893-8637
Siemens Dematic Electronics Assembly Systems Inc 3140 Northwoods Pkwy Suite 300 *TF:* 888-768-4357 ■ *Web:* www.ea.siemens-dematic.com	Norcross	GA	30071	770-797-3000	797-3096
SITE Services Inc 690 Aldo Ave *Web:* www.site.com	Santa Clara	CA	95054	408-980-1155	980-1267
Small Precision Tools Inc 1330 Clegg St *TF:* 800-346-4927 ■ *Web:* www.smallprecisiontools.com	Petaluma	CA	94954	707-765-4545	778-2271
Solid State Equipment Corp 185 Gibraltar Rd *Web:* www.ssecusa.com	Horsham	PA	19044	215-328-0700	328-9410
Solitec Wafer Processing Inc 1777 N Milpitas Blvd Suite 335 *TF:* 800-648-4040 ■ *Web:* www.solitec-wp.com	Milpitas	CA	95035	408-955-9939	955-0954
Spire Corp 1 Patriots Pk *NASDAQ: SPIR* ■ *TF:* 800-510-4815 ■ *Web:* www.spirecorp.com	Bedford	MA	01730	781-275-6000	275-7470
SPX Corp Kayex Div 1000 Millstead Way *Web:* www.kayex.com	Rochester	NY	14624	585-235-2524	436-2396
Tara Technologies Corp 305 Fentress Blvd *TF:* 866-669-8348 ■ *Web:* www.taratechnologies.com	Daytona Beach	FL	32114	386-253-0628	257-0122
Tegal Corp 2201 S McDowell Blvd *NASDAQ: TGAL* ■ *TF:* 800-828-3425 ■ *Web:* www.tegal.com	Petaluma	CA	94954	707-763-5600	765-9311
Tek-Vac Industries Inc 176 Express Dr S *Web:* www.tekvac.com	Brentwood	NY	11717	631-436-5100	436-5154
Tokyo Electron America Inc 2400 Grove Blvd *TF:* 800-828-6596 ■ *Web:* www.tel.com/eng/index.html	Austin	TX	78741	512-424-1000	424-1001
Trio-Tech International 14731 Califa St *AMEX: TRT* ■ *Web:* www.triotech.com	Van Nuys	CA	91411	818-787-7000	787-9130
Ultra Clean Holdings Inc 150 Independence Dr *NASDAQ: UCTT* ■ *Web:* www.uct.com	Menlo Park	CA	94025	650-323-4100	326-0929
Ultratech Inc 3050 Zanker Rd *NASDAQ: UTEK* ■ *TF:* 800-222-1213 ■ *Web:* www.ultratech.com	San Jose	CA	95134	408-321-8835	577-3378
United Memories Inc 4815 List Dr Suite 109 *Web:* www.unitedmemories.com	Colorado Springs	CO	80919	719-594-4238	
Universal Instruments Corp (UIC) 33 Broome Corporate Pk *TF:* 800-842-9732 ■ *Web:* www3.uic.com	Conklin	NY	13348	607-779-7522	779-4466
Varian Semiconductor Equipment Assoc Inc 35 Dory Rd *NASDAQ: VSEA* ■ *TF:* 800-447-1762 ■ *Web:* www.vsea.com	Gloucester	MA	01930	978-282-2000	282-7344
Veeco Instruments Inc 1 Terminal Dr *NASDAQ: VECO* ■ *TF:* 888-248-3326 ■ *Web:* www.veeco.com	Plainview	NY	11803	516-677-0200	714-1200

699 SEMICONDUCTORS & RELATED DEVICES

SEE ALSO Electronic Components & Accessories - Mfr p. 1811; Printed Circuit Boards p. 2449

Company	City	State	ZIP	Phone	Fax
8x8 Inc 810 W Maude Ave *NASDAQ: EGHT* ■ *TF:* 888-898-8733 ■ *Web:* www.8x8.com	Sunnyvale	CA	94085	408-727-1885	980-0432
Actel Corp 2061 Stierlin Ct *TF:* 800-262-1060 ■ *Web:* www.actel.com	Mountain View	CA	94043	650-318-4200	318-4600
Advanced Micro Devices Inc (AMD) 1 AMD Pl PO Box 3453 *NYSE: AMD* ■ *TF:* 800-538-8450 ■ *Web:* www.amd.com	Sunnyvale	CA	94088	408-749-4000	749-4291
Advanced Photonix Inc 2925 Boardwalk *AMEX: API* ■ *Web:* www.advancedphotonix.com	Ann Arbor	MI	48104	734-864-5600	998-3474
Aeroflex Inc 35 S Service Rd PO Box 6022 *NASDAQ: ARX* ■ *TF:* 800-843-1553 ■ *Web:* www.aeroflex.com	Plainview	NY	11803	516-694-6700	694-0658
Agilent Technologies Inc 5301 Stevens Creek Blvd *NYSE: A* ■ **Fax Area Code:* 408 ■ *TF:* 877-424-4536 ■ *Web:* www.home.agilent.com	Santa Clara	CA	95051	877-424-4536	345-8474*
Allegro Microsystems Inc 115 NE Cutoff *Web:* www.allegromicro.com	Worcester	MA	01606	508-853-5000	853-8378
Alliance Semiconductor Corp 4633 Old Ironsides Dr Suite 240 *PINK: ALSC* ■ *Web:* www.alsc.com	Santa Clara	CA	95054	408-855-4900	855-4999
Altera Corp 101 Innovation Dr	San Jose	CA	95134	408-544-7000	544-6403*

	City	St	Zip	Phone	Fax
NASDAQ: ALTR ■ **Fax:* Cust Svc ■ *TF Cust Svc:* 800-767-3753 ■ *Web:* www.altera.com					
American Arium 14811 Myford Rd	Tustin	CA	92780	714-731-1661	731-6344
TF: 877-508-3970 ■ *Web:* www.arium.com					
Amkor Technology Inc 1900 S Price Rd	Chandler	AZ	85248	480-821-5000	
NASDAQ: AMKR ■ *Web:* www.amkor.com					
ANADIGICS Inc 141 Mt Bethel Rd	Warren	NJ	07059	908-668-5000	668-5068
NASDAQ: ANAD ■ *Web:* www.anadigics.com					
Analog Devices Inc 3 Technology Way	Norwood	MA	02062	781-329-4700	461-3113
NYSE: ADI ■ *TF:* 800-262-5643 ■ *Web:* www.analog.com					
Apogee Technology Inc 129 Morgan Dr	Norwood	MA	02062	781-551-9450	440-9528
OTC: ATCS ■ *Web:* www.apogeemems.com					
Applied Micro Circuits Corp 215 Moffett Pk Dr	Sunnyvale	CA	94089	408-542-8600	542-8601
NASDAQ: AMCC ■ *TF:* 800-935-2622 ■ *Web:* www.apm.com					
ARM Inc 141 Caspian Ct	Sunnyvale	CA	94089	408-734-5600	734-5050
Web: www.arm.com					
ASAT Inc 490 N McCarthy Blvd Suite 200	Milpitas	CA	95035	408-964-7400	964-5535
Atheros Communications Inc 5480 Great American Pkwy	Santa Clara	CA	95054	408-773-5200	773-9909
NASDAQ: ATHR ■ *Web:* www.atheros.com					
Atmel Corp 2325 Orchard Pkwy	San Jose	CA	95131	408-441-0311	436-4200
NASDAQ: ATML ■ *Web:* www.atmel.com					
AuthenTec Inc 100 Rialto Pl # 100	Melbourne	FL	32901	321-308-1300	308-1430
Web: www.authentec.com					
Aware Inc 40 Middlesex Tpke	Bedford	MA	01730	781-276-4000	276-4001
NASDAQ: AWRE ■ *Web:* www.aware.com					
Axsun Technologies Inc 1 Fortune Dr	Billerica	MA	01821	978-262-0049	262-0035
TF: 866-462-9786 ■ *Web:* www.axsun.com					
AXT Inc 4281 Technology Dr	Fremont	CA	94538	510-438-4700	353-0668
NASDAQ: AXTI ■ *Web:* www.axt.com					
B & B Electronics Mfg Co PO Box 1040	Ottawa	IL	61350	815-433-5100	433-5109
TF: 800-346-3119 ■ *Web:* www.bb-elec.com					
Beceem Communications Inc 3960 Freedom Cir Fl 1	Santa Clara	CA	95054	408-387-5000	387-5099
Web: www.beceem.com					
BI Technologies Corp 4200 Bonita Pl	Fullerton	CA	92835	714-447-2300	447-2745
Web: www.bitechnologies.com					
BP Solar International LLC 630 Solarex Ct	Frederick	MD	21703	301-698-4200	698-4201
Web: www.bp.com					
Broadcom Corp 5300 California Ave	Irvine	CA	92617	949-926-5000	926-5203
NASDAQ: BRCM ■ *TF:* 877-577-2726 ■ *Web:* www.broadcom.com					
Celis Semiconductor Corp 4775 Centennial Blvd # 105	Colorado Springs	CO	80919	719-260-9133	593-8540
Web: www.celis-semi.com					
Cirrus Logic Inc 2901 Via Fortuna	Austin	TX	78746	512-851-4000	851-4977
NASDAQ: CRUS ■ *TF:* 800-888-5016 ■ *Web:* www.cirrus.com					
Clare Inc 78 Cherry Hill Dr	Beverly	MA	01915	978-524-6700	524-4700
Web: www.clare.com					
Conexant Systems Inc 4000 MacArthur Blvd	Newport Beach	CA	92660	949-483-4600	483-4078
TF: 888-855-4562 ■ *Web:* www.conexant.com					
Cree Inc 4600 Silicon Dr	Durham	NC	27703	919-313-5300	313-5451*
NASDAQ: CREE ■ **Fax:* Sales ■ *TF:* 800-533-2583 ■ *Web:* www.cree.com					
Cypress Semiconductor Corp 198 Champion Ct	San Jose	CA	95134	408-943-2600	943-4730*
NASDAQ: CY ■ **Fax:* Mktg ■ *TF:* 800-541-4736 ■ *Web:* www.cypress.com					
Dakota Systems Inc 1057 Broadway Rd Rte 113	Dracut	MA	01826	978-275-0600	275-0606
Web: www.dakotasystems.com					
Dallas Semiconductor Corp 4401 S Beltwood Pkwy	Dallas	TX	75244	972-371-4000	371-4470*
**Fax:* Cust Svc ■ *Web:* www.maxim-ic.com					
DayStar Technologies Inc 1010 S Milpitas Blvd	Milpitas	CA	95035	408-582-7100	907-4637
NASDAQ: DSTI ■ *Web:* www.daystartech.com					
Dialight Corp 1501 SR 34	Farmingdale	NJ	07727	732-919-3119	751-5778
Web: www.dialight.com					
Diodes Inc 15660 N Dallas Pkwy Suite 850	Dallas	TX	75248	972-385-2810	446-4850*
NASDAQ: DIOD ■ **Fax Area Code:* 805 ■ *Web:* www.diodes.com					
DSP Group Inc 2580 N First St Suite 460	San Jose	CA	95131	408-986-4300	986-4323
NASDAQ: DSPG ■ *Web:* www.dspg.com					
E/g Electro-graph Inc 2365 Camino Vida Roble	Carlsbad	CA	92011	760-438-9090	438-3923
TF: 800-824-8922 ■ *Web:* www.egraph.com					
EMCORE Corp 10420 Research Rd SE	Albuquerque	NM	87123	505-332-5000	332-5038
NASDAQ: EMKR ■ *Web:* www.emcore.com					
Enhanced Memory Systems Inc 1850 Ramtron Dr	Colorado Springs	CO	80921	719-481-7000	481-9170
TF: 800-545-3726 ■ *Web:* www.edram.com					
Enpirion Inc 53 Frontage Rd Suite 210	Hampton	NJ	08827	908-894-6000	894-6090
Web: www.enpirion.com					
Epson Electronics America Inc 150 River Oaks Pkwy	San Jose	CA	95134	408-922-0200	922-0238
TF: 800-228-3964 ■ *Web:* www.eea.epson.com					
Equator Technologies Inc 520 Pike St Suite 900	Seattle	WA	98101	206-267-4500	812-1285
Web: www.equator.com					
ESS Technology Inc 48401 Fremont Blvd	Fremont	CA	94538	510-492-1088	492-1098
Web: www.esstech.com					
Eudyna Devices USA Inc 2355 Zanker Rd	San Jose	CA	95131	408-232-9500	428-9111
Web: www.us.eudyna.com					
Evergreen Solar Inc 138 Bartlett St	Marlborough	MA	01752	508-357-2221	229-0747
NASDAQ: ESLR ■ *Web:* www.evergreensolar.com					
Exar Corp 48720 Kato Rd	Fremont	CA	94538	510-668-7000	668-7011
NASDAQ: EXAR ■ *Web:* www.exar.com					
Fairchild Imaging Inc 1801 McCarthy Blvd	Milpitas	CA	95035	408-433-2500	435-7352
TF: 800-325-6975 ■ *Web:* www.fairchildimaging.com					
Fairchild Semiconductor Corp 82 Running Hill Rd	South Portland	ME	04106	207-775-8100	761-6139
NYSE: FCS ■ *TF:* 800-341-0392 ■ *Web:* www.fairchildsemi.com					
Freescale Semiconductor Inc 6501 William Cannon Dr W	Austin	TX	78735	512-895-2000	
TF Tech Supp: 800-521-6274 ■ *Web:* www.freescale.com					
Gct Semiconductor Inc 2121 Ringwood Ave	San Jose	CA	95131	408-434-6040	434-6050
Web: www.gctsemi.com					
Gel-Pak LLC 31398 Huntwood Ave	Hayward	CA	94544	510-576-2220	576-2282
TF: 888-621-4147 ■ *Web:* www.gelpak.com					
Gennum Corp 4281 Harvestar Rd	Burlington	ON	L7L5M4	905-632-2996	632-2055
Web: www.gennum.com					
Global Solar Energy Inc 8500 S Rita Rd	Tucson	AZ	85747	520-546-6313	546-6318
TF: 800-810-9939 ■ *Web:* www.globalsolar.com					
GSI Technology Inc 2360 Owen St	Santa Clara	CA	95054	408-980-8388	980-8377
NASDAQ: GSIT ■ *Web:* www.gsitechnology.com					
HEI Inc 1495 Steiger Lake Ln	Victoria	MN	55386	952-443-2500	443-2668
NASDAQ: HEII ■ *TF:* 866-720-2397 ■ *Web:* www.heii.com					
Hitachi Canada Ltd 5750 Explore Dr Suit 301	Mississauga	ON	L4W0A9	905-821-4545	290-0141
TF: 800-906-4482 ■ *Web:* www.hitachi.ca					
Hitachi High Technologies America Inc 10 N Martingale Rd Suite 500	Schaumburg	IL	60173	847-273-4141	273-4407
Web: www.hii-hitachi.com					
Holt Integrated Circuits Inc 23351 Madero	Mission Viejo	CA	92691	949-859-8800	859-9643
Web: www.holtic.com					
Hynix Semiconductor America Inc 3101 N 1st St	San Jose	CA	95134	408-232-8000	232-8103
Web: www.hynix.com					
Hytel Group Inc 290 Industrial Dr	Hampshire	IL	60140	847-683-9800	683-7940
Web: www.hytel.com					
I-O Corp 1490 N 2200 W	Salt Lake City	UT	84116	801-973-6767	974-5683
Web: www.iocorp.com					
Ikanos Communications 47669 Fremont Blvd	Fremont	CA	94538	510-979-0400	979-0500
NASDAQ: IKAN ■ *Web:* www.ikanos.com					
Impinj Inc 701 N 34th St Suite 300	Seattle	WA	98103	206-517-5300	517-5262
TF: 866-467-4650 ■ *Web:* www.impinj.com					
Inabata America Corp 1270 Avenue of the Americas Suite 2212	New York	NY	10020	212-586-7764	245-2876
Web: www.inabataamerica.com					
Infineon Technologies Corp 640 N McCarthy Blvd	Milpitas	CA	95035	866-951-9519	
TF: 866-951-9519 ■ *Web:* www.infineon.com					
Integrated Device Technology Inc 6024 Silver Creek Valley Rd	San Jose	CA	95138	408-284-8200	284-2775
NASDAQ: IDTI ■ *TF:* 800-345-7015 ■ *Web:* www.IDT.com					
Integrated Silicon Solution Inc (ISSI) 1940 Zanker Rd	San Jose	CA	95112	408-969-6600	969-7800
NASDAQ: ISSI ■ *TF:* 800-379-4774 ■ *Web:* www.issi.com					
Intel Corp 2200 Mission College Blvd	Santa Clara	CA	95052	408-765-8080	
NASDAQ: INTC ■ *TF Cust Svc:* 800-628-8686 ■ *Web:* www.intel.com					
InterDigital Communications Corp 781 3rd Ave	King of Prussia	PA	19406	610-878-7800	992-9432
NASDAQ: IDCC ■ *TF:* 800-669-4737 ■ *Web:* www.interdigital.com					
International Rectifier Corp 101 N Sepulveda Blvd	El Segundo	CA	90245	310-322-3331	
NYSE: IRF ■ *Web:* www.irf.com					
Intersil Americas Inc 1001 Murphy Ranch Rd	Milpitas	CA	95035	408-432-3888	434-5351
TF: 888-468-3774 ■ *Web:* www.intersil.com					
Intersil Corp 1001 Murphy Ranch Rd	Milpitas	CA	95035	408-432-8888	434-5351
NASDAQ: ISIL ■ *TF:* 888-468-3774 ■ *Web:* www.intersil.com					
Invensense Inc 1197 Borregas Ave	Sunnyvale	CA	94089	408-988-7339	988-8104
Web: www.invensense.com					
IQE Inc 119 Technology Dr	Bethlehem	PA	18015	610-861-6930	861-5273
Web: www.iqep.com					
Irvine Sensors Corp 3001 Redhill Ave Bldg 3 Suite 108	Costa Mesa	CA	92626	714-549-8211	557-1260
NASDAQ: IRSN ■ *TF:* 800-468-4612 ■ *Web:* www.irvine-sensors.com					
IXYS Corp 3540 Bassett St	Santa Clara	CA	95054	408-982-0700	748-9788
NASDAQ: SYXI ■ *Web:* www.ixys.com					
Jazz Semiconductor Inc 4321 Jamboree Rd	Newport Beach	CA	92660	949-435-8000	435-8200
Web: www.jazzsemi.com					
Johnstech International Corp 1210 New Brighton Blvd	Minneapolis	MN	55413	612-378-2020	378-2030
Web: www.johnstech.com					
Judson Technologies LLC 221 Commerce Dr	Montgomeryville	PA	18936	215-368-6900	362-6107
Web: www.judsontechnologies.com					
Kawasaki Microelectronics America Inc 2550 N 1st St Suite 500	San Jose	CA	95131	408-570-0555	570-0567
Web: www.k-micro.us					
Kilopass Technology Inc 3333 Octavius Dr Suite 101	Santa Clara	CA	95054	408-980-8808	980-8856
Web: www.kilopass.com					
Kopin Corp 200 John Hancock Rd	Taunton	MA	02780	508-824-6696	822-1381
NASDAQ: KOPN ■ *Web:* www.kopin.com					
Kulite Semiconductor Products Inc 1 Willow Tree Rd	Leonia	NJ	07605	201-461-0900	461-0990
Web: www.kulite.com					
Kyocera America Inc 8611 Balboa Ave	San Diego	CA	92123	858-576-2600	569-9412
Web: www.americas.kyocera.com					
Kyocera Solar Inc 7812 E Acoma Dr Suite 2	Scottsdale	AZ	85260	480-948-8003	483-6431
TF: 800-544-6466 ■ *Web:* www.kyocerasolar.com					
Laser Diode Inc 4 Olsen Ave	Edison	NJ	08820	732-549-9001	906-1559
Web: www.laserdiode.com					

Company	City	State	Zip	Phone	Fax
Lattice Semiconductor Corp 5555 NE Moore Ct *NASDAQ: LSCC* ■ *TF:* 800-327-8636 ■ *Web:* www.latticesemi.com	Hillsboro	OR	97124	503-268-8000	268-8347
Linear Technology Corp 1630 McCarthy Blvd *NASDAQ: LLTC* ■ *Web:* www.linear.com	Milpitas	CA	95035	408-432-1900	434-0507
Logic Devices Inc 1375 Geneva Dr *PINK: LOGC* ■ *TF:* 800-233-2518 ■ *Web:* www.logicdevices.com	Sunnyvale	CA	94089	408-542-5400	542-0080
LSI Computer Systems Inc 1235 Walt Whitman Rd *Web:* www.lsicsi.com	Melville	NY	11747	631-271-0400	271-0405
LSI Logic Corp 1621 Barber Ln *NYSE: LSI* ■ *TF:* 800-372-2447 ■ *Web:* www.lsilogic.com	Milpitas	CA	95035	408-433-8000	433-7715
M Cubed Technologies Inc 921 Main St *Web:* www.mmmt.com	Monroe	CT	06468	203-452-2333	452-2335
M/A-COM Technology Solutions Inc 100 Chelmsford St *TF:* 800-366-2266 ■ *Web:* www.macomtech.com	Lowell	MA	01851	978-656-2500	
Macronix America Inc 680 N McCarthy Blvd *Web:* www.macronix.com	Milpitas	CA	95035	408-262-8887	262-8810
Marvell Technology Group Ltd 5488 Marvell Ln *NASDAQ: MRVL* ■ *Web:* www.marvell.com	Santa Clara	CA	95054	408-222-2500	988-8279
Maxim Integrated Products Inc 120 San Gabriel Dr *NASDAQ: MXIM* ■ *TF:* 800-659-5909 ■ *Web:* www.maxim-ic.com	Sunnyvale	CA	94086	408-737-7600	737-7194
Medtronic Microelectronics Ctr (MMC) 2343 W Medtronic Way *TF:* 800-633-8766	Tempe	AZ	85281	480-968-6411	921-6435
MEMC Electronic Materials Inc 501 Pearl Dr *NYSE: WFR* ■ **Fax:* Sales ■ *Web:* www.memc.com	Saint Peters	MO	63376	636-474-5000	474-5158*
Micrel Inc 2180 Fortune Dr *NASDAQ: MCRL* ■ *Web:* www.micrel.com	San Jose	CA	95131	408-944-0800	474-1000
Microchip Technology Inc 2355 W Chandler Blvd *NASDAQ: MCHP* ■ *TF:* 800-437-2767 ■ *Web:* www.microchip.com	Chandler	AZ	85224	480-792-7200	899-9210
Micropac Industries Inc 905 E Walnut St *OTC: MPAD* ■ *Web:* www.micropac.com	Garland	TX	75040	972-272-3571	487-6918
Microsemi Corp 2381 Morse Ave *NASDAQ: MSCC* ■ *TF:* 800-713-4113 ■ *Web:* www.microsemi.com	Irvine	CA	92614	949-221-7100	756-0308
Mindspeed Technologies Inc 4000 MacArthur Blvd *NASDAQ: MSPD* ■ *Web:* www.mindspeed.com	Newport Beach	CA	92660	949-579-3000	579-3200
Mini-Circuits Laboratories Inc 13 Neptune Ave *Web:* www.minicircuits.com	Brooklyn	NY	11235	718-934-4500	332-4661
MIPS Technologies Inc 955 E Arques Ave *NASDAQ: MIPS* ■ *Web:* www.mips.com	Sunnyvale	CA	94085	650-530-5000	530-5150
Monolithic Power Systems Inc (MPS) 6409 Guadalupe Mines Rd *NASDAQ: MPWR* ■ *Web:* www.monolithicpower.com	San Jose	CA	95120	408-826-0600	826-0601
Monolithic System Technology Inc (MoSys) 755 N Matilda Ave *NASDAQ: MOSY* ■ *Web:* www.mosysinc.com	Sunnyvale	CA	94085	408-731-1800	731-1893
Moschip Semiconductor Technology USA 3335 Kifer Rd *Web:* www.moschip.com	Santa Clara	CA	95051	408-737-7141	737-7708
National Semiconductor Corp 2900 Semiconductor Dr *NYSE: NSM* ■ *Web:* www.national.com	Santa Clara	CA	95051	408-721-5000	732-4880
NEC Electronics America Inc 2880 Scott Blvd *TF Tech Supp:* 800-366-9782 ■ *Web:* www.am.renesas.com	Santa Clara	CA	95052	408-588-6000	588-6130
NeoPhotonics Corp 2911 Zanker Rd *Web:* www.neophotonics.com	San Jose	CA	95134	408-232-9200	351-8899
NetLogic Microsystems Inc 3975 Freedom Cir *NASDAQ: NETL* ■ *Web:* www.netlogicmicro.com	Santa Clara	CA	95054	408-454-3000	454-3333
Nexx Systems Inc 900 Middlesex Tpke Bldg 6	Billerica	MA	01821	978-932-2000	932-2099
Nitto Denko America Inc 48500 Fremont Blvd *TF:* 800-356-4880 ■ *Web:* www.nittousa.com	Fremont	CA	94538	510-445-5400	445-5480
Nve Corp 11409 Valley View Rd *NASDAQ: NVEC* ■ *TF:* 800-467-7141 ■ *Web:* www.nve.com	Eden Prairie	MN	55344	952-829-9217	996-1600
O2Micro International Ltd 3118 Patrick Henry Dr *NASDAQ: OIIM* ■ *Web:* www.o2micro.com	Santa Clara	CA	95054	408-987-5920	987-5929
Oki Semiconductor 785 N Mary Ave *Web:* www.okisemi.com	Sunnyvale	CA	94085	408-720-1900	720-1918
OmniVision Technologies Inc 4275 Burton Dr *NASDAQ: OVTI* ■ *Web:* www.ovt.com	Santa Clara	CA	95054	408-542-3000	542-3001
ON Semiconductor Corp 5005 E McDowell Rd *NASDAQ: ONNN* ■ *TF:* 800-282-9855 ■ *Web:* www.onsemi.com	Phoenix	AZ	85008	602-244-6600	
Opnext Inc 46429 Landing Pkwy *NASDAQ: OPXT* ■ **Fax Area Code:* 732 ■ *Web:* www.opnext.com	Fremont	CA	94538	510-580-8828	544-3540*
Optek Technology Inc 1645 Wallace Dr *TF:* 800-341-4747 ■ *Web:* www.optekinc.com	Carrollton	TX	75006	972-323-2200	323-2396
OSI Systems Inc 12525 Chadron Ave *NASDAQ: OSIS* ■ *Web:* www.osi-systems.com	Hawthorne	CA	90250	310-978-0516	644-1727
Peregrine Semiconductor Corp 9380 Carroll Pk Dr *Web:* www.peregrine-semi.com	San Diego	CA	92121	858-731-9400	731-9499
Pericom Semiconductor Corp 3545 N 1st St *NASDAQ: PSEM* ■ *TF:* 800-435-2336 ■ *Web:* www.pericom.com	San Jose	CA	95134	408-435-0800	435-1100
PerkinElmer Inc 45 William St *NYSE: PKI* ■ *Web:* www.perkinelmer.com	Wellesley	MA	02481	781-237-5100	237-9386
Photronics Inc 15 Secor Rd *NASDAQ: PLAB* ■ **Fax:* Hum Res ■ *Web:* www.photronics.com	Brookfield	CT	06804	203-775-9000	740-5630*
Pixelworks Inc 224 Airport Pkwy Suite 400 *NASDAQ: PXLW* ■ *Web:* www.pixelworks.com	San Jose	CA	95110	408-200-9200	200-9201
Plascore Inc 615 N Fairview St *TF:* 800-630-9257 ■ *Web:* www.plascore.com	Zeeland	MI	49464	616-772-1220	772-1289
PLX Technology Inc 870 W Maude Ave *NASDAQ: PLXT* ■ *TF:* 800-759-3735 ■ *Web:* www.plxtech.com	Sunnyvale	CA	94085	408-774-9060	774-2169
PMC-Sierra Inc 1380 Bordeaux Dr *NASDAQ: PMCS* ■ *TF:* 866-268-7116 ■ *Web:* www.pmc-sierra.com	Sunnyvale	CA	94089	408-239-8000	492-1157
Power Integrations 5245 Hellyer Ave *NASDAQ: POWI* ■ *Web:* www.powerint.com	San Jose	CA	95138	408-414-9200	414-9201
Powerex Inc 173 Pavilion Ln *TF:* 800-451-1415 ■ *Web:* www.pwrx.com	Youngwood	PA	15697	724-925-7272	925-4393
Praxair Electronics 542 Rt 303 *TF:* 800-827-4387 ■ *Web:* www.praxair.com/semiconductor	Orangeburg	NY	10962	845-359-4200	359-0215
QLogic Corp 26650 Aliso Viejo Pkwy *NASDAQ: QLGC* ■ *TF:* 800-662-4471 ■ *Web:* www.qlogic.com	Aliso Viejo	CA	92656	949-389-6000	389-6114
QuickLogic Corp 1277 Orleans Dr *NASDAQ: QUIK* ■ *Web:* www.quicklogic.com	Sunnyvale	CA	94089	408-990-4000	990-4040
Rambus Inc 1050 Enterprise Way Suite 700 *NASDAQ: RMBS* ■ *TF:* 800-726-2879 ■ *Web:* www.rambus.com	Sunnyvale	CA	94089	408-462-8000	462-8001
Ramtron International Corp 1850 Ramtron Dr *NASDAQ: RMTR* ■ *TF:* 800-545-3726 ■ *Web:* www.ramtron.com	Colorado Springs	CO	80921	719-481-7000	481-9294
Raytek Inc 1201 Shaffer Rd Bldg 2 *TF:* 800-227-8074 ■ *Web:* www.raytek.com	Santa Cruz	CA	95060	831-458-1110	458-1239
Raytheon RF Components 350 Lowell St *Web:* www.raytheon.com	Andover	MA	01810	978-470-7509	470-4125
RF Micro Devices Inc 7628 Thorndike Rd *NASDAQ: RFMD* ■ *Web:* www.rfmd.com	Greensboro	NC	27409	336-664-1233	931-7454
Samsung Semiconductors Inc 3655 N 1st St *TF:* 800-726-7864 ■ *Web:* www.usa.samsungsemi.com	San Jose	CA	95134	408-544-4000	544-4980
SatCon Technology Corp 27 Dry Dock Ave *NASDAQ: SATC* ■ *TF:* 888-728-2760 ■ *Web:* www.satcon.com	Boston	MA	02210	617-897-2400	897-2401
Seiko Instruments USA Inc 1309 Rutherford Ln *TF:* 800-358-0880 ■ *Web:* www.seikoinstruments.com	Austin	TX	78753	512-349-3800	349-3000
Seiko Instruments USA Inc Electronic Components Div 2990 Lomita Blvd *Web:* www.seikoinstruments.com	Torrance	CA	90505	310-517-7771	517-7709
Semtech Corp 200 Flynn Rd *NASDAQ: SMTC* ■ *Web:* www.semtech.com	Camarillo	CA	93012	805-498-2111	498-3804
Sharp Microelectronics of the Americas 5700 NW Pacific Rim Blvd *Web:* www.sharpsma.com	Camas	WA	98607	360-834-2500	834-8903
Sheldahl Inc 1150 Sheldahl Rd *TF:* 800-533-0505 ■ *Web:* www.sheldahl.com	Northfield	MN	55057	507-663-8000	663-8545
Shin-Etsu Handotai America Inc PO Box 8965 *Web:* www.sehamerica.com	Vancouver	WA	98668	360-883-7000	254-6973
Showa Denko America Inc 489 5th Ave 18th Fl *Web:* www.sdasf.com	New York	NY	10017	212-370-0033	370-4566
Sigma Designs Inc 1221 California Cir *NASDAQ: SIGM* ■ *TF Sales:* 800-845-8086 ■ *Web:* www.sdesigns.com	Milpitas	CA	95035	408-262-9003	957-9740
Silicon Image Inc 1060 E Arques Ave *NASDAQ: SIMG* ■ *Web:* www.siliconimage.com	Sunnyvale	CA	94085	408-616-4000	830-9530
Silicon Laboratories Inc 400 W Cesar Chavez *NASDAQ: SLAB* ■ *TF:* 877-444-3032 ■ *Web:* www.silabs.com	Austin	TX	78701	512-416-8500	416-9669
Siliconix Inc 2201 Laurelwood Rd *Web:* www.vishay.com	Santa Clara	CA	95056	408-988-8000	567-8950
Siltronic Corp 7200 NW Front Ave **Fax:* Sales ■ *TF:* 800-922-5371 ■ *Web:* www.siltronic.com	Portland	OR	97210	503-243-2020	219-4509*
Skyworks Solutions Inc 20 Sylvan Rd *NASDAQ: SWKS* ■ *Web:* www.skyworksinc.com	Woburn	MA	01801	781-376-3000	376-3300
Solitron Devices Inc 3301 Electronics Way **Fax:* Mktg ■ *Web:* www.solitrondevices.com	West Palm Beach	FL	33407	561-848-4311	863-5946*
Sony Semiconductor 3300 Zanker Rd *Web:* products.sel.sony.com/semi	San Jose	CA	95134	408-432-1600	959-5176
Spectrolab Inc 12500 Gladstone Ave *TF:* 800-936-4888 ■ *Web:* www.spectrolab.com	Sylmar	CA	91342	818-365-4611	898-7534
SRS Labs Inc 2909 Daimler St *NASDAQ: SRSL* ■ *TF:* 800-243-2737 ■ *Web:* www.srslabs.com	Santa Ana	CA	92705	949-442-1070	852-1099
Standard Microsystems Corp 80 Arkay Dr *NASDAQ: SMSC* ■ *TF:* 800-443-7364 ■ *Web:* www.smsc.com	Hauppauge	NY	11788	631-435-6000	273-5550
Stretch Inc 1322 Orleans Dr *Web:* www.stretchinc.com	Sunnyvale	CA	94089	408-543-2700	747-5736
SunPower Corp 77 Rio Robles *NASDAQ: SPWRA* ■ *TF:* 800-786-7693 ■ *Web:* www.us.sunpowercorp.com	San Jose	CA	95134	408-240-5500	
Supertex Inc 1235 Bordeaux Dr *NASDAQ: SUPX* ■ *TF:* 800-487-8737 ■ *Web:* www.supertex.com	Sunnyvale	CA	94089	408-222-8888	222-4800
Symetrix Corp 5055 Mark Dabling Blvd *Web:* www.symetrixcorp.com	Colorado Springs	CO	80918	719-594-6145	598-3437
Taiwan Semiconductor Mfg Co Ltd (TSMC) 2585 Junction Ave *NYSE: TSM* ■ *TF:* 877-248-4237 ■ *Web:* www.tsmc.com	San Jose	CA	95134	408-382-8000	382-8008
TDK Semiconductor Corp 6440 Oak Canyon Suite 100 *Web:* www.tdksemiconductor.com	Irvine	CA	92618	714-508-8800	508-8875
Teledyne Electronics & Communications 1049 Camino Dos Rios *Web:* www.tet.com	Thousand Oaks	CA	91360	805-373-4545	
Tellurex Corp 1462 International Dr *Web:* www.tellurex.com	Traverse City	MI	49686	231-947-0110	947-5821
Tensilica Inc 3255 Scott Blvd # 6 *Web:* www.tensilica.com	Santa Clara	CA	95054	408-986-8000	986-8919
Tessera Technologies Inc 3099 Orchard Dr *NASDAQ: TSRA* ■ *Web:* www.tessera.com	San Jose	CA	95134	408-894-0700	894-0768
Texas Advanced Optoelectronic Solutions Inc (TAOS) 1001 Klein Rd Suite 300 *Web:* www.taosinc.com	Plano	TX	75074	972-673-0759	943-0610
Texas Instruments Inc 12500 TI Blvd *NYSE: TXN* ■ *TF Cust Svc:* 800-336-5236 ■ *Web:* www.ti.com	Dallas	TX	75243	972-995-3773	927-6377
Tezzaron Semiconductor Corp 1415 Bond St Suite 111 *Web:* www.tachyonsemi.com	Naperville	IL	60563	630-505-0404	505-9292
Thorlabs Quantum Electronics Inc 10335 Guilford Rd *TF:* 877-226-8342 ■ *Web:* www.covega.com	Jessup	MD	20794	240-456-7100	456-7200

				Phone	Fax
Toppan Photomasks Inc 131 Old Settlers Blvd *Web:* www.photomask.com	Round Rock	TX	78664	512-310-6500	310-6501
Toshiba America Electronic Components Inc 19900 MacArthur Blvd Suite 400 **Fax Area Code:* 949 ■ **Fax:* Hum Res ■ *TF:* 800-879-4963 ■ *Web:* www.toshiba.com/taec	Irvine	CA	92612	800-879-4963	581-9038*
Tosoh SMD Inc 3600 Gantz Rd *TF:* 800-678-8942 ■ *Web:* www.tosohsmd.com	Grove City	OH	43123	614-875-7912	875-0031
TranSwitch Corp 3 Enterprise Dr *NASDAQ: TXCC* ■ *Web:* www.transwitch.com	Shelton	CT	06484	203-929-8810	926-9453
Trident Microsystems Inc 1170 Kifer Rd *NASDAQ: TRID* ■ *Web:* www.tridentmicro.com	Sunnyvale	CA	94086	408-962-5000	
TriQuint Semiconductor Inc 2300 NE Brookwood Pkwy *NASDAQ: TQNT* ■ *Web:* www.triquint.com	Hillsboro	OR	97124	503-615-9000	615-8900
Tvia Inc 4800 Great America Pkwy Suite 405 *PINK: TVIA* ■ *Web:* www.tvia.com	Santa Clara	CA	95054	408-327-8033	982-8591
United Microelectronics Corp 488 De Guigne Dr *NYSE: UMC* ■ *Web:* www.umc.com	Sunnyvale	CA	94085	408-523-7800	733-8090
Universal Display Corp 375 Phillips Blvd *NASDAQ: PANL* ■ *Web:* www.universaldisplay.com	Ewing	NJ	08618	609-671-0980	671-0995
VIA Technologies Inc 940 Mission Ct *Web:* www.via.com.tw/en	Fremont	CA	94539	510-683-3300	687-4654
Vishay Intertechnology Inc 63 Lancaster Ave *NYSE: VSH* ■ *Web:* www.vishay.com	Malvern	PA	19355	610-644-1300	296-0657
Vishay Precision Group Inc 63 Lancaster Ave *NYSE: VPG* ■ *Web:* www.vishay.com	Malvern	PA	19355	484-321-5300	321-5301
Vitesse Semiconductor Corp 741 Calle Plano *NASDAQ: VTSS* ■ *TF:* 800-848-3773 ■ *Web:* www.vitesse.com	Camarillo	CA	93012	805-388-3700	987-5896
Vlsip Technologies Inc 750 Presidential Dr *Web:* www.vlsip.com	Richardson	TX	75081	972-437-5506	644-1286
Volterra Semiconductor Corp 47467 Fremont Blvd *NASDAQ: VLTR* ■ *Web:* www.volterra.com	Fremont	CA	94538	510-743-1200	743-1600
Wabash Technologies 1375 Swan St PO Box 829 **Fax:* Sales ■ *Web:* www.wabashtech.com	Huntington	IN	46750	260-356-8300	355-4265*
Wafertech LLC 5509 NW Parker St *Web:* www.wafertech.com	Camas	WA	98607	360-817-3000	817-3590
West Coast Quartz Corp (WCQ) 1000 Corporate Way PO Box 14066 *Web:* www.westcoastquartz.com	Fremont	CA	94539	510-249-2160	651-4617
Winbond Electronics Corp America 2727 N 1st St *TF:* 800-825-4473 ■ *Web:* www.winbond.com	San Jose	CA	95134	408-943-6666	474-1600
Winslow Automation Inc 905 Montague Expy *Web:* www.winslowautomation.com	Milpitas	CA	95035	408-986-0100	996-0199
X-fab Texas Inc 2301 N University Ave *Web:* www.xfab.com	Lubbock	TX	79415	806-747-4400	747-3111
Xilinx Inc 2100 Logic Dr *NASDAQ: XLNX* ■ *TF:* 800-494-5469 ■ *Web:* www.xilinx.com	San Jose	CA	95124	408-559-7778	559-7114
Zarlink Semiconductor Inc 400 March Rd *TSE: ZL* ■ *TF:* 800-325-4927 ■ *Web:* www.zarlink.com	Ottawa	ON	K2K3H4	613-592-0200	592-1010
ZiLOG Inc 1590 Buckeye Dr *TF:* 800-662-6211 ■ *Web:* www.zilog.com	Milpitas	CA	65035	408-513-1500	365-8535
Zoran Corp 1390 Kifer Rd *NASDAQ: ZRAN* ■ *Web:* www.zoran.com	Sunnyvale	CA	94086	408-523-6500	523-6501

700 SHEET METAL WORK

SEE ALSO Plumbing, Heating, Air Conditioning Contractors p. 1726; Roofing, Siding, Sheet Metal Contractors p. 1729

				Phone	Fax
AB Myr Industries Inc 39635 I-94 S Service Dr *TF:* 888-481-0446 ■ *Web:* www.abmyr.com	Belleville	MI	48111	734-941-2200	941-8332
Abalon Precision Mfg Corp 1040 Home St	Bronx	NY	10459	718-589-5682	589-0300
Abrams Airborne Mfg Inc 3735 N Romero Rd *Web:* www.abrams.com	Tucson	AZ	85705	520-887-1727	293-8807
Accurate Metal Fabricators Inc 1011 Seal Beach Blvd **Fax Area Code:* 562 ■ *Web:* www.amf1.com	Seal Beach	CA	90740	714-363-9206	596-6799*
Acme Mfg Co 7601 State Rd *TF Cust Svc:* 800-899-2850	Philadelphia	PA	19136	215-338-2850	335-1905
Aero Trades Mfg Corp 65 Jericho Tpke	Mineola	NY	11501	516-746-3360	746-3417
Air Comfort Corp 2550 Braga Dr *TF:* 800-466-3779 ■ *Web:* www.aircomfort.com	Broadview	IL	60155	708-345-1900	345-2730
Air Conditioning Products Co 30350 Ecorse Rd *Web:* www.acpshutters.com	Romulus	MI	48174	734-326-0050	326-9632
Air Vent Inc 4117 Tinnacle Pnt Dr *Web:* www.airvent.com	Dallas	TX	75211	214-630-6307	630-7413
Aircom Mfg Inc 6205 E 30th St *TF:* 800-925-2426 ■ *Web:* www.aircommfg.com	Indianapolis	IN	46219	317-545-5383	542-7365
Airolite Co LLC PO Box 410 *Web:* www.airolite.com	Schofield	WI	54476	715-841-8757	841-8773
Airtronics Metal Products Inc 1991 Senter Rd *Web:* www.airtronics.com	San Jose	CA	95112	408-977-7800	977-7810
Albers Mechanical Contractors Inc 200 W Plato Blvd *Web:* www.albersmechanical.com	Saint Paul	MN	55107	651-224-5428	224-1742
Aluminum Line Products Co 24460 Sperry Cir *TF:* 800-321-3154 ■ *Web:* www.aluminumline.com	Westlake	OH	44145	440-835-8880	835-8879
American Warming & Ventilating Inc 7301 International Dr *Web:* www.american-warming.com	Holland	OH	43528	419-865-5000	865-1375
Arizona Precision Sheet Metal 2140 W Pinnacle Peak Rd *TF:* 800-443-7039 ■ *Web:* www.apsm-jit.com	Phoenix	AZ	85027	623-516-3700	516-3701
Arrow United Industries 450 Riverside Dr PO Box 69 *Web:* www.arrowunited.com	Wyalusing	PA	18853	570-746-1888	746-9286
ASC Profiles Inc 2110 Enterprise Blvd *TF Cust Svc:* 800-726-2727 ■ *Web:* www.ascprofiles.com	West Sacramento	CA	95691	916-372-0933	372-2967
Associated Materials Inc 3773 State Rd *TF:* 800-257-4335 ■ *Web:* www.associatedmaterials.com	Cuyahoga Falls	OH	44223	330-929-1811	922-2296
Atlantic Ventilating & Equipment Co 25 Sebethe Dr	Cromwell	CT	06416	860-635-1300	632-7412
Atlas Mfg 2950 Weeks Ave SE *Web:* www.atlasmfg.com	Minneapolis	MN	55414	612-331-2566	331-1295
AW Mercer Inc 104 Industrial Dr PO Box 508 *Web:* www.awmercer.com	Boyertown	PA	19512	610-367-8460	367-7491
Basmat Inc 1531 240th St *Web:* www.mcstarlite.com	Harbor City	CA	90710	310-325-2063	325-9682
Berger Bldg Products Inc 805 Pennsylvania Blvd *TF Cust Svc:* 800-523-8852 ■ *Web:* www.bergerbros.com	Feasterville	PA	19053	215-355-1200	355-7738
Bert R Huncilman & Son 2072 McDonald Ave *Web:* www.huncilman.com	New Albany	IN	47150	812-945-3544	948-2133
BHW Sheet Metal Co 113 Johnson St	Jonesboro	GA	30236	770-471-9303	478-7923
Botner Mfg Inc 10000 Bigge St	San Leandro	CA	94577	510-569-2943	569-2942
Branch Mfg Co 6420 Pine St *Web:* www.branchmfg.com	North Branch	MN	55056	651-674-4441	674-4442
Bright Sheet Metal Co Inc 4212 W 71st Suite A	Indianapolis	IN	46268	317-291-7600	291-7604
California Chassis Inc 3356 E La Palma Ave *Web:* www.calchassis.com	Anaheim	CA	92806	714-666-8511	666-8509
Captive-aire Systems Inc 4641 Paragon Pk Rd *TF:* 800-334-9256 ■ *Web:* www.captiveaire.com	Raleigh	NC	27616	919-882-2410	554-4605
Cinnabar Solution Inc 155 Sunnynoll Ct Suite 300 *TF:* 800-782-2171 ■ *Web:* www.cinnabarsolutions.com	Winston-Salem	NC	27106	336-722-5195	722-5198
Clark Specialty Co Inc 8440 New York 54 *TF:* 888-569-2128 ■ *Web:* www.clarkspecialty.com	Hammondsport	NY	14840	607-569-2191	569-3694
Climatemp Inc 315 N May St	Chicago	IL	60607	312-829-3131	829-7510
Cody Co Inc 4200 N I-45 *Web:* www.codycompany.com	Ennis	TX	75119	972-875-5884	875-0308
Computer Components Corp 2751 S Hampton Rd *Web:* www.compcomp.com/ccc9	Philadelphia	PA	19154	215-676-7600	464-7876
Connell LP 1 International Pl 31st Fl *TF:* 800-276-4746 ■ *Web:* www.connell-lp.com	Boston	MA	02110	617-737-2700	737-1617
Consolidated Systems Inc 650 Rosewood Dr *TF:* 800-654-1912 ■ *Web:* www.csisteel.com	Columbia	SC	29202	803-771-7920	771-7920
Contech Construction Products Inc 9025 Centre Pointe Dr Suite 400 *TF:* 800-338-1122 ■ *Web:* www.contech-cpi.com	West Chester	OH	45069	513-645-7000	645-7993
Corchran Inc 1340 State St S *Web:* www.corchran.com	Waseca	MN	56093	507-835-3910	835-1382
Cortec Precision Sheet Metal Inc 2231 Will Wool Dr *Web:* www.cortecprecision.com	San Jose	CA	95112	408-278-8540	
Courtesy Mfg Co 1300 Pratt Blvd	Elk Grove Village	IL	60007	847-437-7500	437-7500
Crown Products Co Inc 6390 Phillips Hwy *TF:* 800-683-7144 ■ *Web:* www.crownproductsco.com	Jacksonville	FL	32216	904-737-7144	737-3533
CWR Mfg Corp 7000 Fly Rd *TF Sales:* 800-724-0311 ■ *Web:* www.cwronline.com	Syracuse	NY	13220	315-437-1032	437-1493
Daviess County Metal Sales Inc 9929 E US Hwy 50 *TF:* 800-279-4299 ■ *Web:* www.dcmetal.com	Cannelburg	IN	47519	812-486-4299	295-4344
Dawson Metal Co Inc 825 Allen St *TF:* 877-732-9766 ■ *Web:* www.dawsonmetal.com	Jamestown	NY	14701	716-664-3815	664-3485
Detronic Industries Inc 35800 Beattie Dr *Web:* www.detronic.com	Sterling Heights	MI	48312	586-977-5660	939-5340
Du-Mont Co 7800 N Pioneer Ct *Web:* www.du-mont.com	Peoria	IL	61615	309-692-7240	693-2937
Dura-Bilt Products Inc PO Box 188 *TF:* 800-233-4251 ■ *Web:* www.durabilt.com	Wellsburg	NY	14894	570-596-2000	596-3296
Durand Forms Inc 6200 Equitable Rd **Fax Area Code:* 989 ■ *TF:* 800-545-6342 ■ *Web:* www.durandforms.com	Kansas City	MO	64120	800-545-6342	288-2128*
Duray/JF Duncan Industries Inc 9301 Stewart & Gray Rd *Web:* www.duraynet.com	Downey	CA	90241	562-862-4269	869-1850
Eagle Cornice Co Inc 89 Pettaconsett Ave *Web:* www.eaglecornice.com	Cranston	RI	02920	401-781-5978	781-6570
Edco & Arrowhead Products Inc 8700 Excelsior Blvd *TF:* 800-333-2580 ■ *Web:* www.edcoproducts.com	Hopkins	MN	55343	952-938-6313	938-4950
Electro-Space Fabricators Inc 300 W High St *Web:* www.esfinc.com	Topton	PA	19562	610-682-7181	682-2133
Elixir Industries Inc 24800 Chrisanta Dr Suite 210 *TF:* 800-421-1942 ■ *Web:* www.elixirind.com	Mission Viejo	CA	92691	949-860-5000	860-5011
Epic Metals Corp 11 Talbot Ave *TF:* 877-696-3742 ■ *Web:* www.epicmetals.com	Rankin	PA	15104	412-351-3913	351-3913
Evansville Sheet Metal Works 1901 W Maryland St *Web:* www.esmw.com	Evansville	IN	47712	812-423-7871	423-7353
Experi-Metal Inc 6385 Wall St *Web:* www.experi-metal.com	Sterling Heights	MI	48312	586-977-7800	977-6981
Fabrication Concepts Corp 1800 E St Andrew Pl *Web:* www.fabcon.com	Santa Ana	CA	92705	714-881-2000	881-2001
Falstrom Co 147 Falstrom Ct	Passaic	NJ	07055	973-777-0013	777-6396
Flat Rock Metal Inc (FRM) 26601 W Huron River Dr PO Box 1090 *Web:* www.frm.com	Flat Rock	MI	48134	734-782-4454	782-5640
Floturn Inc 4236 Thunderbird Ln *Web:* www.floturn.com	Fairfield	OH	45014	513-860-8040	860-8044
Frank M Booth Inc 222 3rd St *TF:* 800-540-9369 ■ *Web:* www.frankbooth.com	Marysville	CA	95901	530-742-7134	742-8109
Fred Christen & Sons Co 714 George St *TF Cust Svc:* 800-243-4161	Toledo	OH	43608	419-243-4161	243-1292
G&g Steel Inc PO Box 179 *Web:* www.ggsteel.com	Russellville	AL	35653	256-332-6652	332-0143

Company / Address	City	State	Zip	Phone	Fax
Gary Metal Mfg LLC 2700 E 5th Ave	Gary	IN	46402	219-885-3232	885-0528
General Sheet Metal Corp 2330 Louisiana Ave N	Minneapolis	MN	55427	763-544-8747	544-6580
Gentek Bldg Products Inc 29325 Chagrin Blvd	Cuyahoga Falls	OH	44309	216-514-3501	922-2354*
**Fax Area Code:* 330 ■ *TF:* 800-548-4542 ■ *Web:* www.gentekinc.com					
Gerome Mfg Co Inc 135 Oliver Plaza	Uniontown	PA	15401	724-438-8544	437-5608
Web: www.geromemfg.com					
Gilbert Mechanical Contractors Inc 4451 W 76th St	Edina	MN	55435	952-835-3810	835-4765
TF: 800-701-0986 ■ *Web:* www.gilbertmech.com					
Global Power Equipment Group Inc 5119 N Mingo Rd	Tulsa	OK	74117	918-488-0828	488-8389
NASDAQ: GLPW ■ *Web:* www.globalpower.com					
Goldberg Bros Inc 8000 E 40th Ave	Denver	CO	80207	303-321-1099	388-0749
Web: www.goldbergbrothers.com					
Grayd-A Metal Fabricators 13233 Florence Ave	Santa Fe Springs	CA	90670	562-944-8951	944-2326
Web: www.grayd-a.com					
Greene Metal Products Inc 24500 Capital Blvd	Clinton Township	MI	48036	586-465-6800	465-0136
Web: www.greenemetal.com					
H & H Industrial Corp 7612 N Crescent Blvd	Pennsauken	NJ	08110	856-663-4444	663-4446
TF: 800-982-0341 ■ *Web:* www.hhindustrial.com					
Hamilton Form Co Ltd 7009 Midway Rd	Fort Worth	TX	76118	817-590-2111	595-1110
Web: www.hamiltonform.com					
HiMEC Mechanical 1400 7th St NW	Rochester	MN	55901	507-281-4000	281-5206
TF: 888-454-4632 ■ *Web:* www.himec.com					
HM White Inc 12855 Burt Rd	Detroit	MI	48223	313-531-8477	531-0522
Web: www.hmwhite.com					
Humanetics II Ltd 1700 Columbian Club Dr	Carrollton	TX	75006	972-416-1304	416-4163
Web: www.humanetics.com					
IMCO Inc 858 N Lenola Rd	Moorestown	NJ	08057	856-235-7540	727-1637
Industrial Air Inc 428 Edwardia Dr PO Box 8769	Greensboro	NC	27419	336-292-1030	855-7763
Web: www.industrialairinc.com					
Industrial Louvers Inc 511 7th St S	Delano	MN	55328	763-972-2981	972-2911
TF: 800-328-3421 ■ *Web:* www.industriallouvers.com					
Irving Tool & Mfg Co Inc 2249 Wall St	Garland	TX	75041	972-926-4000	926-4099
Jaquith Industries Inc 600 E Brighton Ave	Syracuse	NY	13210	315-478-5700	478-5707
Web: www.jaquith.com					
Jensen Bridge & Supply Co 400 Stoney Creek Dr	Sandusky	MI	48471	810-648-3000	648-3549
Web: www.jensenbridge.com					
John Sykes Co Inc PO Box 5189	Atlantic City	NJ	08404	609-345-1191	344-1952
John W McDougall Co Inc (JWMCD) 3731 Amy Lynn Dr	Nashville	TN	37218	615-321-3900	329-9069
TF: 800-264-1122 ■ *Web:* www.jwmcd.com					
Jones Metal Products Inc 3201 County Rd 5	Mankato	MN	56001	507-625-4436	625-2994
TF: 800-967-1750 ■ *Web:* www.jonesmetalproducts.com					
Jor-Mac Co Inc 155 E Main St	Lomira	WI	53048	920-269-8500	
Web: www.jor-mac.com					
Juniper Industries Inc 72-15 Metropolitan Ave PO Box 148	Middle Village	NY	11379	718-326-2546	326-3786
TF: 800-221-4664 ■ *Web:* www.juniperind.com					
Kirk Williams Co Inc 2734 Home Rd	Grove City	OH	43123	614-875-9023	875-9214
Web: www.kirkwilliamsco.com					
Klauer Mfg Co 1185 Roosevelt Ext PO Box 59	Dubuque	IA	52004	563-582-7201	582-2022
Web: www.klauer.com					
Krueger Sheet Metal Co 731 N Superior St	Spokane	WA	99202	509-489-0221	489-6539
TF: 800-777-9339					
KSM Industries Inc N 115 W 19025 Edison Dr	Germantown	WI	53022	262-251-9510	251-4865
Web: www.ksmindustries.com					
Kuest Corp PO Box 33007	San Antonio	TX	78265	210-655-1220	655-1220
Web: www.kuestcorp.com					
Landmark Mfg Corp 28100 Quick Ave	Gallatin	MO	64640	660-663-2185	663-2417
Web: www.landmarkfab.com					
LB Foster Co 415 Holiday Dr	Pittsburgh	PA	15220	412-928-3431	928-7891*
NASDAQ: FSTR ■ **Fax:* Sales ■ *TF:* 800-255-4500 ■ *Web:* www.lbfoster.com					
Limco Airepair Inc 5304 S Lawton Ave	Tulsa	OK	74107	918-445-4300	445-2210
Web: www.limcoairepair.com					
Link-Burns Mfg Co Inc 253 American Way	Voorhees	NJ	08043	856-429-6844	429-3734
Livers Bronze Co 4621 E 75th Terr	Kansas City	MO	64132	816-300-2828	300-0864
Web: www.liversbronze.com					
Maddox Metal Works Inc 4116 Bronze Way	Dallas	TX	75237	214-333-2311	337-8169
Web: www.maddoxmetalworks.com					
Mapes Panels LLC 2929 Cornhusker Hwy PO Box 80069	Lincoln	NE	68504	800-228-2391	737-6756
TF: 800-228-2391 ■ *Web:* mapes.com					
Mayco Industries LLC 18 W Oxmoor Rd	Birmingham	AL	35209	205-942-4242	945-8704
TF: 800-749-6061 ■ *Web:* www.maycoindustries.com					
Maysteel LLC N89 W14700 Patrita Dr PO Box 1240	Menomonee Falls	WI	53052	262-255-2400	255-2417
TF: 800-255-1247 ■ *Web:* www.maysteel.com					
Mayville Products Corp 403 Degner Ave	Mayville	WI	53050	920-387-3000	387-7196
TF: 800-230-0136 ■ *Web:* www.apwmayville.com					
McCorvey Sheet Metal Works LP 8610 Wallisvile Rd	Houston	TX	77029	713-672-7545	672-0509
TF: 800-580-7545 ■ *Web:* www.mccorvey.com					
McGill Airflow Corp 1 Mission Pk	Groveport	OH	43125	614-829-1200	829-1291
Web: www.mcgillairflow.com					

Company / Address	City	State	Zip	Phone	Fax
Mech-Tronics Corp 1635 N 25th Ave	Melrose Park	IL	60160	708-344-9823	344-0067
Web: www.mech-tronics.com					
Mercury Aircraft Inc 17 Wheeler Ave	Hammondsport	NY	14840	607-569-4632	569-4634
Web: www.mercurycorp.com					
Metal Trades Inc PO Box 129	Hollywood	SC	29449	843-889-6442	745-0474
Web: www.metaltrades.com					
Metal-Fab Inc 3025 May St	Wichita	KS	67213	316-943-2351	943-2717
TF: 800-835-2830 ■ *Web:* www.mtlfab.com					
Metalcraft Technologies Inc 526 N Aviation Way	Cedar City	UT	84720	435-586-3871	586-0289
Web: www.metalcraft.net					
Metaltech Inc 206 Prospect Ave	Kirkwood	MO	63122	314-965-4550	965-4234
TF: 800-325-9986 ■ *Web:* www.metaltechinc.org					
Metalworks Inc 902 E 4th St	Ludington	MI	49431	231-845-5136	845-1043
Metcam Inc 305 Tidwell Cir	Alpharetta	GA	30004	770-475-9633	442-3425
Web: www.metcam.com					
Micro Industries Inc 2990 S Main St	Salt Lake City	UT	84115	801-466-2232	466-1441
TF: 800-446-3902 ■ *Web:* www.microindustries.net					
Mid-Continent Engineering Inc 405 35th Ave NE	Minneapolis	MN	55418	612-782-1324	782-1320
Web: www.mid-continent.com					
Milbank Mfg Co Inc 4801 Deramus Ave	Kansas City	MO	64120	816-483-5314	483-6357
Web: www.milbankmfg.com					
Mitchell Metal Products Inc 19250 Hwy 12 E	Kosciusko	MS	39090	662-289-7110	289-7112
TF: 800-258-6137					
Modern Tool Inc 1200 Northdale Blvd	Coon Rapids	MN	55448	763-754-7337	754-7557
Web: www.moderntoolinc.com					
Morton Metalcraft Co 1021 W Birchwood St	Morton	IL	61550	309-266-7176	263-1866
Murray Sheet Metal Co Inc 3112 7th St	Parkersburg	WV	26101	304-422-5431	428-4623
TF: 800-464-8801 ■ *Web:* www.murraysheetmetal.com					
Napco Inc 125 McFann Rd	Valencia	PA	16059	724-898-1511	898-3357
TF: 800-786-2726 ■ *Web:* www.napcobuildingmaterials.com					
National Fabtronix Inc 28800 Hesperian Blvd	Hayward	CA	94545	510-785-3135	785-1253
Web: www.natfab.com					
National Metal Fabricators 2395 Greenleaf Ave	Elk Grove Village	IL	60007	847-439-5321	439-4774
TF: 800-323-8849 ■ *Web:* www.nmfrings.com					
New England Sheet Metal Works Inc PO Box 11158	Fresno	CA	93771	559-268-7375	268-5018
TF: 800-800-6376 ■ *Web:* www.nesmw.com					
Noll Mfg Co 1320 Performance Dr	Stockton	CA	95206	209-234-1600	234-5925
TF: 800-235-1014					
Nsa Industries LLC 815 Industrial Pkwy PO Box 54	Lyndonville	VT	05851	802-748-5007	748-0067
Web: www.nsaindustries.com					
Nu-Way Industries Inc 555 Howard Ave	Des Plaines	IL	60018	847-298-7710	635-8650
Web: www.nuwayindustries.com					
Owens Corning Fabricating Solutions 426 N Main St	Elkhart	IN	46516	574-522-8473	632-2935*
**Fax Area Code:* 877 ■ *TF:* 877-632-2935					
Pemberton Fabricators Inc 30 Indel Ave	Rancocas	NJ	08073	609-267-0922	261-2546
TF: 800-573-6322 ■ *Web:* www.pemfab.com					
Petersen Aluminum Corp 1005 Tonne Rd	Elk Grove Village	IL	60007	847-228-7150	722-7150*
**Fax Area Code:* 800 ■ *TF:* 800-323-1960 ■ *Web:* www.pac-clad.com					
Platt & Labonia Co 70 Stoddard Ave	North Haven	CT	06473	203-239-5681	234-7978
TF: 800-505-9099 ■ *Web:* www.plattlabonia.com					
Precise Metal Products Co 3839 N 39th Ave	Phoenix	AZ	85019	602-272-2625	233-2123
Quality Metal Products Inc 11500 W 13th Ave	Lakewood	CO	80215	303-232-4242	233-3944
Rangaire Co 501 S Wilhite St	Cleburne	TX	76031	817-556-6500	556-6549
RF Knox Co Inc 4865 Martin Ct SE	Smyrna	GA	30082	770-434-7401	433-1783
TF: 800-989-7401 ■ *Web:* www.rfknox.com					
RG Smith Co 1249 Dueber Ave SW	Canton	OH	44706	330-456-3415	456-9638
Web: www.rgscontractors.com					
Roll Forming Corp PO Box 369	Shelbyville	KY	40066	502-633-4435	633-5824
Rollex Corp 2001 Lunt Ave	Elk Grove Village	IL	60007	847-437-3000	437-7561
TF Cust Svc: 800-251-3300 ■ *Web:* www.rollex.com					
RTI Tradco 1701 W Main St	Washington	MO	63090	636-239-7816	239-3214
RuMar Mfg Corp 925 S St	Mayville	WI	53050	920-387-2104	387-2367
Web: www.rumar.com					
Ruskin Mfg Co 3900 Doctor Greaves Rd	Grandview	MO	64030	816-761-7476	765-8955
Web: www.ruskin.com					
Saint Regis Culvert Inc 202 Morrell St	Charlotte	MI	48813	517-543-3430	543-2313
TF: 800-527-4604 ■ *Web:* www.stregisculvert.com					
Serra Corp 3590 Snell Ave	San Jose	CA	95136	510-651-7333	657-5860
Web: www.serracorp.com					
Sheet Metal Engineers Inc PO Box 204627	Martinez	GA	30917	706-863-6575	863-8210
Simpson Dura-Vent Inc 877 Cotting Ct	Vacaville	CA	95688	707-446-1786	446-4740
TF: 800-835-4429 ■ *Web:* www.duravent.com					
SMT Inc 7300 ACC Blvd	Raleigh	NC	27617	919-782-4804	781-1498
Web: www.smtcoinc.com					
Southbridge Sheet Metal Works Inc 441 Main St	Sturbridge	MA	01566	508-347-7800	347-9118
Southwark Metal Mfg Co Inc 2800 Red Lion Rd	Philadelphia	PA	19114	215-735-3401	735-0411
TF: 800-523-1052					
Special Products & Mfg Inc 2625 Discovery Blvd	Rockwall	TX	75032	972-771-8851	722-0163
Web: www.spmfg.com					
Specialty Engineering Inc 1766 Hwy 36 E	Maplewood	MN	55109	651-777-8311	777-2707
Web: www.specialtyeng.com					
Standex International Corp Air Distribution Products Group 7601 State Rd	Philadelphia	PA	19136	215-338-2850	335-1905
TF: 800-899-2850 ■ *Web:* www.standexadp.com					
Streimer Sheet Metal Works Inc 740 N Knott St	Portland	OR	97227	503-288-9393	288-3327
TF: 888-288-3828 ■ *Web:* www.streimer.com					
Structures Unlimited Inc 88 Pine St	Manchester	NH	03103	603-645-6539	625-0798
TF: 800-225-3895 ■ *Web:* www.structuresunlimitedinc.com					
Swift-Cor Precision Inc 344 W 157th St	Gardena	CA	90248	310-354-1200	323-2029
Web: www.swiftcor.com					

Company / Address	City	State	Zip	Phone	Fax
Tella Tool & Mfg 1015 N Ridge Ave *Web:* www.tellatool.com	Lombard	IL	60148	630-495-0545	495-3056
Tenere Inc Oakdale Div 590 Hale Ave N *Web:* www.tenere.com	Oakdale	MN	55128	651-251-4674	251-8594
Thybar Corp 913 S Kay Ave *TF:* 800-666-2872 ■ *Web:* www.thybar.com	Addison	IL	60101	630-543-5300	543-5309
Trend Technologies LLC 4626 Eucalyptus Ave *Web:* www.trendtechnologies.com	Chino	CA	91710	909-597-7861	597-2284
Trinity Industries Inc Highway Safety Products Div 2525 N Stemmons Fwy *TF:* 800-527-6050 ■ *Web:* www.highway-safety.com	Dallas	TX	75207	214-589-8814	589-8423
United McGill Corp 1 Mission Pk *Web:* www.unitedmcgill.com	Groveport	OH	43125	614-829-1200	829-1291
Valley Joist 3019 Gault Ave N *TF:* 800-633-2258 ■ *Web:* www.valleyjoist.com	Fort Payne	AL	35967	256-845-2330	845-2597
Vent Products Co Inc 1901 S Kilbourn Ave *TF:* 800-368-8368 ■ *Web:* www.ventprod.com	Chicago	IL	60623	773-521-1900	521-5613
Vent-A-Hood Ltd 1000 N Greenville Ave *Web:* www.ventahood.com	Richardson	TX	75081	972-235-5201	231-0663
Voisard Mfg Inc 60 Scott St *Web:* www.voisard.com	Shiloh	OH	44878	419-896-3191	896-2127
Western Industries Inc Watertown Metal Products Div 1141 S 10th St *Web:* www.westernind.com	Watertown	WI	53094	920-261-0660	261-3832
Wisco Products Inc 109 Commercial St *TF:* 800-367-6570 ■ *Web:* www.wiscoproducts.com	Dayton	OH	45402	937-228-2101	228-2407
Wise Alloys LLC 4805 2nd St *TF Sales:* 800-437-4163 ■ *Web:* www.wisealloys.com	Muscle Shoals	AL	35661	256-386-6000	386-6980
Young & Bertke Air Systems Co 2118 Winchell Ave *Web:* www.youngbertke.com	Cincinnati	OH	45214	513-241-5566	421-1860
Young Custom Metal Fabrication 6205 St Louis St	Meridian	MS	39307	601-483-6281	693-6529

701 SHIP BUILDING & REPAIRING

Company / Address	City	State	Zip	Phone	Fax
Al Larson Boat Shop Inc 1046 S Seaside Ave	Terminal Island	CA	90731	310-514-4100	519-7183
Allied Shipyard Inc 310 Ledet Ln	Larose	LA	70373	985-693-3323	693-3687
Associated Naval Architects Inc (ANA) 3400 Shipwright St *Web:* www.anashipyard.com	Portsmouth	VA	23703	757-484-5320	483-1386
Atlantic Marine Inc 8500 Heckscher Dr **Fax:* Sales ■ *TF:* 800-395-6446 ■ *Web:* www.atlanticmarine.com	Jacksonville	FL	32226	904-251-1545	251-3500*
Bath Iron Works Corp 700 Washington St *Web:* www.gdbiw.com	Bath	ME	04530	207-443-3311	442-1567
Bay Ship & Yacht Co 310 W Cutting Blvd *TF:* 800-900-6646 ■ *Web:* www.bay-ship.com	Point Richmond	CA	94804	510-237-0140	237-0154
Bay Shipbuilding Co 605 N 3rd Ave PO Box 830 *Web:* www.manitowocmarine.com	Sturgeon Bay	WI	54235	920-743-5524	743-2371
Bender Shipbuilding & Repair 265 S Water St	Mobile	AL	36603	251-431-8000	432-2260
Boland Marine & Mfg Co Inc 1000 Tchoupitoulas St *TF:* 888-265-2631 ■ *Web:* www.bolandmarine.com	New Orleans	LA	70130	504-581-5800	581-5814
Bollinger Algiers Inc 434 Powder St *Web:* www.bollingershipyards.com	New Orleans	LA	70114	504-362-7960	361-1679
Bollinger Gretna 4640 Peters Rd	Harvey	LA	70058	504-367-8080	362-1938
Bollinger Shipyards Inc 8365 Louisiana 308 *Web:* www.bollingershipyards.com	Lockport	LA	70374	985-532-2554	532-7225
Bourg Drydock & Service Co PO Box 1852	Houma	LA	70361	985-594-5851	594-5992
Braswell Service Group Inc 2007 Cherry Hill Ln	Charleston	SC	29405	843-388-6136	
Cascade General Inc 5555 N Ch Ave **Fax:* Hum Res ■ *TF:* 800-505-1930 ■ *Web:* www.vigorindustrial.com	Portland	OR	97217	503-247-1828	247-6050*
Colonna's Shipyard Inc 400 E Indian River Rd *TF:* 800-265-6627 ■ *Web:* www.colonnaship.com	Norfolk	VA	23523	757-545-2414	545-5475
Conrad Industries Inc 1501 Front St *Web:* www.conradindustries.com	Morgan City	LA	70380	985-384-3060	385-4090
Continental Maritime of San Diego Inc 1995 Bay Front St *Web:* www.continentalmaritime.com	San Diego	CA	92113	619-234-8851	696-7358
Dakota Creek Industries Inc 820 4th St PO Box 218 *Web:* www.dakotacreek.com	Anacortes	WA	98221	360-293-9575	293-1372
Detyens Shipyards Inc 1670 Drydock Ave Bldg 236 Suite 200 *TF:* 800-745-2811 ■ *Web:* www.detyens.com	North Charleston	SC	29405	843-308-8000	308-8059
Earl Industries LLC 2 Harper Ave *Web:* www.earl-ind.com	Portsmouth	VA	23707	757-215-2500	215-2504
Electric Boat Corp (GDEB) 75 Eastern Pt Rd	Groton	CT	06340	860-433-3000	433-1400*
Elevating Boats LLC 201 Dean Ct *Web:* www.ebi-inc.com	Houma	LA	70363	985-868-9655	580-7974
Elmwood Marine Services 222 Bayou Rd	Belle Chasse	LA	70037	504-394-6230	392-8439
Essex Boat Works Inc Ferry St PO Box 37	Essex	CT	06426	860-767-8276	767-1729
First Wave Marine Inc 2616 S Loop W Suite 665 *TF:* 800-399-9283	Houston	TX	77054	713-847-4600	847-4601
Fraser Shipyards Inc 1 Clough Ave *Web:* www.frasershipyards.com	Superior	WI	54880	715-394-7787	394-2807
General Dynamics NASSCO 2798 E Harbor Dr *Web:* www.nassco.com	San Diego	CA	92113	619-544-3400	544-3541
Gladding-Hearn Shipbuilding 1 Riverside Ave PO Box 300 *Web:* www.gladding-hearn.com	Somerset	MA	02726	508-676-8596	672-1873
Goltens New York Corp 160 Van Brunt St *TF:* 877-204-1088 ■ *Web:* www.goltens.com	Brooklyn	NY	11231	718-855-7200	802-1147
Greenbrier Co 1 Centerpointe Dr Suite 200 *NYSE:* GBX ■ *TF:* 800-343-7188 ■ *Web:* www.gbrx.com	Lake Oswego	OR	97035	503-684-7000	684-7553
Gulf Copper & Mfg Corp 7200 Hwy 87 *Web:* www.gulfcopper.com	Port Arthur	TX	77642	409-983-1691	985-6349
Gulf Craft Inc 3904 Hwy 182 *Web:* www.gulfcraft.com	Patterson	LA	70392	985-395-5254	395-3657
Gulf Marine Repair Corp 1200 Sertoma Dr	Tampa	FL	33605	813-247-3153	247-4519
Huntington Ingalls Industries 4101 Washington Ave *Web:* www.huntingtoningalls.com	Newport News	VA	23607	757-380-2000	
J. M. Martinac Shipbuilding Corp 401 E 15th St *Web:* www.martinacship.com	Tacoma	WA	98421	253-572-4005	627-2816
Kvichak Marine Industries 469 NW Bowdoin Pl *Web:* www.kvichak.com	Seattle	WA	98107	206-545-8485	545-3504
Lake Union Drydock Co 1515 Fairview Ave E *Web:* www.ludd.com	Seattle	WA	98102	206-323-6400	324-0124
Leevac Shipyards Inc 111 Bunge St	Jennings	LA	70546	337-824-2210	824-2970
Lyon Shipyard Inc PO Box 2180 *Web:* www.lyonshipyard.com	Norfolk	VA	23501	757-622-4661	625-7137
MARCO Global 4259 22nd Ave W *Web:* www.marcoglobal.com	Seattle	WA	98199	206-285-3200	282-8520
Marine Hydraulics International Inc (MHI) 543 E Indian River Rd *Web:* www.mhi-shiprepair.com	Norfolk	VA	23523	757-545-6400	545-8169
Marinette Marine Corp 1600 Ely St	Marinette	WI	54143	715-735-9341	735-3516*
Metro Machine Corp 200 Ligon St PO Box 1860 **Fax:* Hum Res ■ *Web:* www.memach.com	Norfolk	VA	23501	757-543-6801	494-0445*
Mitsubishi Heavy Industries America Inc 630 5th Ave Suite 2650 *Web:* www.mitsubishitoday.com	New York	NY	10111	212-969-9000	262-3301
Newport Shipyard 1 Washington St *Web:* www.newportshipyard.com	Newport	RI	02840	401-846-6000	846-6001
Nichols Bros Boat Builders Inc 5400 Cameron Rd *Web:* www.nicholsboats.com	Freeland	WA	98249	360-331-5500	331-7484
North Florida Shipyards Inc PO Box 3255	Jacksonville	FL	32206	904-354-3278	353-2665
Northrop Grumman Newport News 13560 Jefferson Ave **Fax:* Hum Res ■ *TF:* 888-493-7386 ■ *Web:* www.newport-news.org	Newport News	VA	23603	757-886-7777	886-7920*
Ocean Shipholdings Inc 16211 Pk Ten Pl *Web:* www.oceanshipholdings.com	Houston	TX	77084	281-579-3700	
Orange Shipbuilding Co Inc 710 Market St *Web:* www.conradindustries.com	Orange	TX	77630	409-883-6666	882-0609
Pacific Fisherman Inc 5351 24th Ave NW	Seattle	WA	98107	206-784-2562	784-1986
Pacific Marine & Navitech Ltd 841 Bishop St Davies Pacific Ctr Suite 1110	Honolulu	HI	96813	808-531-7001	523-7668
Pacific Shipyards International LLC 1 Dry Dock Way Pier 41 PO Box 31328 *Web:* www.pacificshipyards.com	Honolulu	HI	96820	808-848-6211	848-6279
Pacord Inc 240 W 30th St *Web:* www.pacord.com	National City	CA	91950	619-336-2211	474-3422
Robishaw Engineering Inc 10106 Mathewson Ln *Web:* www.flexifloat.com	Houston	TX	77043	713-468-1706	468-5822
SeaArk Marine Inc 404 N Gabbert St *Web:* www.seaark.com	Monticello	AR	71655	870-367-9755	367-2120
Southwest Shipyard 18310 Market St Rd	Channelview	TX	77530	281-860-3200	860-3215
Swiftships Inc PO Box 2869 *Web:* www.swiftships.com	Morgan City	LA	70381	985-384-1700	384-0914
Tecnico Corp 831 Industrial Ave *TF:* 800-786-2207 ■ *Web:* www.tecnicocorp.com	Chesapeake	VA	23324	757-545-4013	545-4925
Trinity Marine Products Inc 2525 N Stemmons Fwy *Web:* www.trin.net/trinbusi/inlandbarge.html	Dallas	TX	75207	214-589-8446	589-8501
VT Halter Marine Inc 900 Bayou Casotte Pkwy *Web:* www.vthaltermarine.com	Pascagoula	MS	39581	228-696-6888	696-6928

702 SHUTTERS - WINDOW (ALL TYPES)

Company / Address	City	State	Zip	Phone	Fax
All Broward Hurricane & Aeicor Metal Products 472 W McNab Rd *TF:* 800-432-1803 ■ *Web:* www.aeicormetals.com	Fort Lauderdale	FL	33309	954-974-3300	973-3928
Atlantic Shutter Systems 3217 Hwy 301 S **Fax Area Code:* 843 ■ *TF:* 877-437-0608 ■ *Web:* www.atlanticshuttersystems.com	Latta	SC	29565	877-437-0608	752-0111*
Champion Window Mfg Inc 12121 Champion Way *TF:* 888-653-8479 ■ *Web:* www.championwindow.com	Cincinnati	OH	45241	513-346-4600	346-4614
Commonwealth Laminating & Coating Inc 345 Beaver Creek Dr *TF:* 888-321-5111 ■ *Web:* www.suntekfilms.com	Martinsville	VA	24112	276-632-4991	632-0173
Hurst Awning Co Inc 6865 NW 36th Ave	Miami	FL	33147	305-693-0600	634-9078
Perfect Shutters Inc 12213 Il Rt 173 *TF:* 800-548-3336 ■ *Web:* www.shuttersinc.com	Hebron	IL	60034	815-648-2401	648-4510
Roll Shutter Systems Inc 21633 N 14th Ave *TF:* 800-551-7655 ■ *Web:* www.rollshuttersystemsusa.com	Phoenix	AZ	85027	623-869-7057	581-3116
Roll-A-Way Inc 10601 Oak St *TF:* 800-683-9505 ■ *Web:* www.roll-a-way.com	Saint Petersburg	FL	33716	727-576-1143	579-9410
Rolladen Inc 550 Ansin Blvd *TF:* 800-748-8837 ■ *Web:* www.rolladen.com	Hallandale	FL	33009	954-525-3466	454-1577
Rolling Shield Inc 2500 NW 74th Ave *TF:* 800-474-9404 ■ *Web:* www.rollingshield.com	Miami	FL	33122	305-436-6661	436-5523
Rolsafe International 12801 Commonwealth Dr Suite 7 *TF:* 877-702-0320 ■ *Web:* www.rolsafe.com	Fort Myers	FL	33913	239-694-5400	694-8000
Shutter Mill Inc 8517 S Perkins Rd *TF:* 800-416-6455 ■ *Web:* www.kirtz.com	Stillwater	OK	74074	405-377-6455	377-1010
Storm Safe Shutters 3593 Veronica Shoemaker Blvd	Fort Myers	PA	33916	239-432-9181	337-7315
Sunburst Shutters 4094 Ponderosa Way *Web:* www.sunburstshutters.com	Las Vegas	NV	89118	702-870-4488	870-6070
Tapco Group 29797 Beck Rd **Fax Area Code:* 888 ■ *TF:* 800-521-8486 ■ *Web:* www.tapcogroup.com	Wixom	MI	48393	800-521-8486	459-3647*

				Phone	Fax
Vantage Products Corp 960 Almon Rd *TF:* 800-481-3303 ■ *Web:* www.vantageproducts.com	Covington	GA	30014	770-788-0136	788-0361

703 SIGNALS & SIRENS - ELECTRIC

				Phone	Fax
ADDCO Inc 240 Arlington Ave E *TF:* 888-616-4408 ■ *Web:* www.addcoinc.com	Saint Paul	MN	55117	651-488-8600	558-3600
ECCO 833 W Diamond St **Fax Area Code:* 800 ■ *TF:* 800-635-5900 ■ *Web:* www.eccolink.com	Boise	ID	83705	208-395-8000	688-3226*
Econolite Control Products Inc 25 Imclone Dr *Web:* www.econolite.com	Anaheim	CA	92806	714-630-3700	630-8576
Federal Signal Corp Emergency Products Div 2645 Federal Signal Dr *Web:* www.fedsig.com	University Park	IL	60466	708-534-3400	534-9050
GE-Harris Energy Control Systems PO Box 8900 **Fax:* Cust Svc ■ *TF:* 800-342-5434 ■ *Web:* www.getransportation.com	Melbourne	FL	32904	321-242-4000	435-7972*
Harrington Signal Co 2519 4th Ave *TF:* 800-577-5758 ■ *Web:* www.harringtonsignal.com	Moline	IL	61265	309-762-0731	762-8215
Rothenbuhler Engineering 524 Rhodes Rd PO Box 708 *Web:* www.rothenbuhlereng.com	Sedro Woolley	WA	98284	360-856-0836	856-2183
Safetran Systems Corp 2400 Nelson Miller Pkwy *TF:* 800-626-2710 ■ *Web:* www.safetran.com	Louisville	KY	40223	502-244-7400	244-7444
Safetran Traffic Systems Inc 1485 Garden of the Gods Rd *Web:* www.safetran-traffic.com	Colorado Springs	CO	80907	719-599-5600	599-3853
Siemens Intelligent Transportation Systems 8004 Cameron Rd *TF:* 800-388-6882 ■ *Web:* www.itssiemens.com	Austin	TX	78754	512-837-8310	837-0196
Union Switch & Signal Inc 1000 Technology Dr *TF:* 800-351-1520 ■ *Web:* www.ansaldo-sts.com	Pittsburgh	PA	15219	412-688-2400	688-2399
Western Cullen Hayes Inc 2700 W 36th Pl	Chicago	IL	60632	773-254-9600	254-1110
Whelen Engineering Co Inc 51 Winthrop Rd & Rt 145 *Web:* www.whelen.com	Chester	CT	06412	860-526-9504	526-4078
WL Jenkins Co 1445 Whipple Ave SW *TF:* 800-426-7021 ■ *Web:* www.wljenkinsco.com	Canton	OH	44710	330-477-3407	477-8404

704 SIGNS

SEE ALSO Displays - Exhibit & Trade Show p. 1785; Displays - Point-of-Purchase p. 1785; Signals & Sirens - Electric p. 2657

				Phone	Fax
ABC Letter Art 1623 S Vermont Ave	Los Angeles	CA	90006	323-733-0191	733-6505
Ace Sign Systems Inc 3621 W Royerton Rd *TF:* 800-607-6010 ■ *Web:* www.acesign.com	Muncie	IN	47304	765-288-1000	288-1010
Advance Corp Braille-Tac Div 8200 97th St S *TF:* 800-328-9451 ■ *Web:* www.advancecorp.com	Cottage Grove	MN	55016	651-771-9297	771-2121
Allen Industries Inc 6434 Burnt Poplar Rd *TF:* 800-967-2553 ■ *Web:* www.allenindustries.com	Greensboro	NC	27409	336-668-2791	668-7875
American Porcelain Enamel Co 203 W Church St *Web:* www.americanporcelain.com	Crandall	TX	75114	214-637-4775	631-5424
Artcraft Signs Co 1717 S Acoma St *TF:* 800-278-7771 ■ *Web:* www.artcraftsign.com	Denver	CO	80223	303-777-7771	778-7175
Atlantic Sign Media Inc 151 McArthur Ln *TF:* 800-948-3710	Burlington	NC	27217	336-584-1375	584-3848
Brady Corp 6555 W Good Hope Rd *NYSE: BRC* ■ **Fax Area Code:* 800 ■ **Fax:* Cust Svc ■ *TF Cust Svc:* 800-537-8791 ■ *Web:* www.bradycorp.com	Milwaukee	WI	53223	414-358-6600	292-2289*
California Neon Products Inc 4530 Mission Gorge Pl *TF:* 800-822-6366 ■ *Web:* www.cnpsigns.com	San Diego	CA	92120	619-283-2191	283-9503
Century Graphics & Metals Inc 550 S N Lake Blvd Suite 1000 *TF:* 800-327-5664 ■ *Web:* www.centurygraphics.com	Altamonte Springs	FL	32701	407-262-8290	262-8291
Clearr Corp 6325 Sandburg Rd *TF:* 800-948-3269 ■ *Web:* www.clearrcorp.com	Minneapolis	MN	55427	763-398-5400	398-0134
Colorado Time Systems 1551 E 11th St *TF:* 800-279-0111 ■ *Web:* www.colotime.com	Loveland	CO	80537	970-667-1000	667-5876
Couch & Philippi Inc 10680 Fern Ave PO Box A *TF Orders:* 800-854-3360 ■ *Web:* www.couchandphilippi.com	Stanton	CA	90680	714-527-2261	827-2077
Cummings Signs Inc 4560 Trousdale Dr *TF:* 800-489-7446 ■ *Web:* www.cummingssigns.com	Nashville	TN	37204	615-244-5555	782-6699
DeeSign Co 7950 Woodley Ave **Fax Area Code:* 818 ■ *TF:* 800-824-2565 ■ *Web:* www.deesignca.com	Van Nuys	CA	91406	800-732-7446	988-4511*
DiAZiT Co Inc 941 US 1 Hwy PO Box 276 *TF Cust Svc:* 800-334-6641 ■ *Web:* www.diazit.com	Youngsville	NC	27596	919-556-5188	556-3757
Douglas Corp 9650 Valley View Rd *Web:* www.douglascorp.com	Eden Prairie	MN	55344	952-941-2944	942-3124
Doyle Signs Inc 232 W IH- Rd *TF:* 800-344-9490 ■ *Web:* www.doylesigns.com	Addison	IL	60101	630-543-9490	543-9493
Dualite Sales & Service Inc 1 Dualite Ln *TF:* 800-543-7271 ■ *Web:* www.dualite.com	Williamsburg	OH	45176	513-724-7100	724-7100
Eastern Metal/USA-SIGN 1430 Sullivan St *TF Sales:* 800-872-7446 ■ *Web:* www.usa-sign.com	Elmira	NY	14901	607-734-2295	734-8783
Everbrite Inc 4949 S 110th St PO Box 20020 *TF:* 800-558-3888 ■ *Web:* www.everbrite.com	Greenfield	WI	53220	414-529-3500	529-7191
FASTSIGNS International Inc 2542 Highlander Way *TF:* 800-827-7446 ■ *Web:* www.fastsigns.com	Carrollton	TX	75006	972-447-0777	248-8201
Federal Heath Sign Co 4602 N Ave *Web:* www.federalheath.com	Oceanside	CA	92056	760-941-0715	941-0719
FLOORgraphics Inc 200 American Metro Blvd Suite 120 American Metro Ctr *TF:* 888-356-6723	Hamilton	NJ	08619	609-528-9200	689-0204
GableSigns Inc 7440 Fort Smallwood Rd *TF:* 800-854-0568 ■ *Web:* www.gablesigns.com	Baltimore	MD	21226	410-255-6400	437-5336
Gemini Inc 103 Mensing Way *TF:* 800-538-8377 ■ *Web:* www.signletters.com	Cannon Falls	MN	55009	507-263-3957	263-4887
Glolite Nudell LLC 125 Commerce Dr *TF:* 800-274-7824 ■ *Web:* www.nudell.com	Hauppauge	NY	11788	800-274-7824	
Gopher Sign Co 1310 Randolph Ave *TF:* 800-383-3156 ■ *Web:* www.gophersign.com	Saint Paul	MN	55105	651-698-5095	699-3727
Gordon Sign 2930 W 9th Ave *TF:* 800-323-6121 ■ *Web:* www.gordonsign.com	Denver	CO	80204	303-629-6121	629-1024
Grandwell Industries Inc 121 Quantum St *TF Cust Svc:* 800-338-6554 ■ *Web:* www.grandwell.com	Holly Springs	NC	27540	919-557-1221	552-9830
Graphic Specialties Inc 3110 Washington Ave N *TF:* 800-486-4605 ■ *Web:* www.signsbygsi.com	Minneapolis	MN	55411	612-522-5287	287-0952
Graphitek Inc 190 N St *TF:* 800-423-4371 ■ *Web:* www.graphitek.com	Bennington	VT	05201	802-440-8079	442-3184
Hall Signs Inc 4495 W Vernal Pike *TF:* 800-284-7446 ■ *Web:* www.hallsigns.com	Bloomington	IN	47404	812-332-9355	332-9816
Hawkins Traffic Safety Supply 1255 E Shore Hwy *TF:* 800-772-3995	Berkeley	CA	94710	510-525-4040	525-2861
Hi*Tech Electronic Displays 13900 US Hwy 19N *TF:* 800-723-9402	Clearwater	FL	33764	727-524-9130	524-6655
Highland Containers Inc 100 Ragsdale Rd *Web:* www.highlandcontainer.com	Jamestown	NC	27282	336-887-5400	887-5409
Hy-Ko Products Co 60 Meadow Ln *TF:* 800-292-0550 ■ *Web:* www.hy-ko.com	Northfield	OH	44067	330-467-7446	467-7442
Icon Identity Solutions 1418 Elmhurst Rd *TF:* 800-633-8181 ■ *Web:* www.iconid.com	Elk Grove Village	IL	60007	847-364-2250	364-1517
Image National Inc 16265 Star Rd *TF:* 800-592-8058 ■ *Web:* www.imagenational.com	Nampa	ID	83687	208-345-4020	336-9886
Insignia Systems Inc 8799 Brooklyn Blvd *NASDAQ: ISIG* ■ *TF:* 800-874-4648 ■ *Web:* www.insigniasystems.com	Minneapolis	MN	55445	763-392-6200	392-6222
International Display Systems Inc 5008 Veterans Memorial Hwy *TF:* 800-542-9779 ■ *Web:* www.idsmenus.com	Holbrook	NY	11741	631-218-1802	218-1801
International Patterns Inc 50 Inez Dr *TF:* 800-471-6368 ■ *Web:* www.internationalpatterns.com	Bay Shore	NY	11706	631-952-2000	952-7602
Interstate Highway Sign Corp 7415 Lindsey Rd *Web:* www.interstatesigns.com	Little Rock	AR	72206	501-490-4242	490-1090
Jarob Inc 2601 Elmridge Dr NW *TF:* 800-843-2508 ■ *Web:* www.jarob.com	Grand Rapids	MI	49534	616-453-5419	453-6362
JM Stewart Corp 2201 Cantu Ct Suite 217-218 *TF:* 800-237-3928 ■ *Web:* www.stewartsigns.com	Sarasota	FL	34232	941-378-4242	378-2765
Kieffer & Co Inc 3322 Washington Ave *TF:* 800-458-4394 ■ *Web:* www.kieffersigns.com	Sheboygan	WI	53081	920-458-4394	451-3360
Kux Architectural Products 45065 Michigan Ave *Web:* www.kux.com	Canton	MI	48188	734-394-0363	394-1846
LaFrance Corp 1 LaFrance Way PO Box 5002 *Web:* www.lafrancecorp.com	Concordville	PA	19331	610-361-4300	361-4301
Lake Shore Industries Inc 1817 Poplar St PO Box 59 *TF:* 800-458-0463 ■ *Web:* www.lsisigns.com	Erie	PA	16512	814-456-4277	453-4293
Lauretano Sign Group 1 Tremco Dr *Web:* www.lauretano.com	Terryville	CT	06786	860-582-0233	583-0949
Lawrence Sign Inc 945 Pierce Butler Rt *TF:* 800-998-8901 ■ *Web:* www.lawrencesign.com	Saint Paul	MN	55104	651-488-6711	488-6715
Leotek Electronics USA Corp 1330 Memorex Dr *TF:* 888-806-1188 ■ *Web:* www.leotek.com	Santa Clara	CA	95050	408-988-4668	980-0538
LSI Industries Inc 10000 Alliance Rd *NASDAQ: LYTS* ■ *TF:* 800-765-3454 ■ *Web:* www.lsi-industries.com	Cincinnati	OH	45242	513-793-3200	984-1335
Lyle Signs Inc 6294 Bury Dr *TF Sales:* 877-895-8816 ■ *Web:* www.lylesigns.com	Eden Prairie	MN	55346	952-934-7653	934-0406
Lynn Sign Co PO Box 1753 *TF:* 800-225-5764	Andover	MA	01810	978-470-1194	470-1198
M-R Sign Co Inc 1706 1st Ave N *TF:* 800-231-5564 ■ *Web:* www.mrsigncompany.com	Fergus Falls	MN	56537	218-736-5681	736-4070
Magnetsigns Adv Inc 4225 38th St *TF:* 800-219-8977 ■ *Web:* www.magnetsigns.com	Camrose	AB	T4V3Z3	780-672-8720	672-8716
McLoone 75 Sumner St *TF:* 800-624-6641 ■ *Web:* www.mcloone.com	La Crosse	WI	54603	608-784-1260	782-3711
Mulholland Harper Co Inc 24778 Meeting House Rd PO Box C *TF:* 800-882-3052 ■ *Web:* www.mulhollandharper.com	Denton	MD	21629	410-479-1300	479-0207
National Print Group Inc 2464 Amnicola Hwy PO Box 5968 *TF:* 800-624-0408 ■ *Web:* www.nationalposters.com	Chattanooga	TN	37406	423-622-2254	622-7623
National Sign Corp 1255 Westlake Ave N *Web:* www.nationalsigncorp.com	Seattle	WA	98109	206-282-0700	285-3091
National Stock Sign Co 1040 El Dorado Ave *TF:* 800-462-7726	Santa Cruz	CA	95062	831-476-2020	476-1734
O'Ryan Group Inc 4010 Pilot Suite 108 *TF:* 800-253-0750 ■ *Web:* www.oryangroup.com	Memphis	TN	38118	901-794-4610	794-3206
Pannier Graphics 345 Oak Rd *TF:* 800-544-8428 ■ *Web:* www.panniergraphics.com	Gibsonia	PA	15044	724-265-4900	265-4300
Pattison Sign Group 555 Ellesmere Rd *TF:* 866-233-2220 ■ *Web:* www.pattisonsign.com	Scarborough	ON	M1R4E8	416-759-1111	759-9560
Philadelphia Sign Co 707 W Spring Garden St *TF:* 800-355-1460 ■ *Web:* www.philadelphiasign.com	Palmyra	NJ	08065	856-829-1460	829-8549
Poblocki Sign Co LLC 922 S 70th St *TF:* 800-776-7064 ■ *Web:* www.poblocki.com	West Allis	WI	53214	414-453-4010	453-3070

Company	City	State	Zip	Phone	Fax
Precision Solar Controls Inc 2985 Market St. *TF:* 800-686-7414 ■ *Web:* www.precisionsolarcontrols.com	Garland	TX	75041	972-278-0553	271-9583
Prismaflex Inc 1645 Queens Way E. *TF:* 800-526-1488 ■ *Web:* www.prismaflex.com	Mississauga	ON	L4X3A3	905-279-9793	279-1330
Process Displays Inc 16333 W Rogers Dr. *TF:* 800-533-1764	New Berlin	WI	53151	262-782-3600	782-3857
Protection Services Inc 635 Lucknow Rd. *TF:* 866-489-1234 ■ *Web:* www.protectionservices.com	Harrisburg	PA	17110	717-236-9307	236-1281
Quality Mfg Inc 969 Labore Industrial Ct *TF:* 800-243-5473 ■ *Web:* www.qualitymanufacturing.com	Saint Paul	MN	55110	651-483-5473	483-1101
Quiel Bros Sign Co 272 S 'I' St *Web:* www.quielsigns.com	San Bernardino	CA	92410	909-885-4476	888-2239
SA-SO Co 4875 White Bear Pkwy PO Box 64784 *TF:* 800-527-2450 ■ *Web:* www.sa-so.com	Saint Paul	MN	55164	800-527-2450	752-4294
Safeway Sign Co 9875 Yucca Rd *TF:* 800-637-7233 ■ *Web:* www.safewaysign.com	Adelanto	CA	92301	760-246-7070	246-5512
Scioto Sign Co Inc 6047 US Rt 68 N *TF:* 800-572-4686 ■ *Web:* www.sciotosigns.com	Kenton	OH	43326	419-673-1261	675-3298
Scott Sign Systems Inc 7525 Pennsylvania Ave # 102 *TF:* 800-237-9447 ■ *Web:* www.scottsigns.com	Sarasota	FL	34243	941-355-5171	351-1787
Sign Builders Inc 4800 Jefferson Ave PO Box 28380 *TF:* 800-222-7330 ■ *Web:* www.signbuilders.com	Birmingham	AL	35221	205-925-9400	923-2124
Sign Designs Inc 204 Campus Way *TF:* 800-421-7446 ■ *Web:* www.signdesigns.com	Modesto	CA	95350	209-524-4484	521-0272
Sign Resource Inc 6135 District Blvd. *TF:* 800-423-4283 ■ *Web:* www.signresource.net	Maywood	CA	90270	323-771-2098	560-7143
Sign-A-Rama 2121 Vista Pkwy. *TF:* 800-776-8105 ■ *Web:* www.signarama.com	West Palm Beach	FL	33411	561-640-5570	640-5580
Signs by Tomorrow USA Inc 8681 Robert Fulton Dr *TF:* 800-765-7446 ■ *Web:* www.signsbytomorrow.com	Columbia	MD	21046	410-312-3600	312-3520
Signs First PO Box 11569 *TF:* 800-852-2163 ■ *Web:* www.signsfirst.net	Memphis	TN	38111	901-682-2264	327-7633
Signs Now 6976 Professional Pkwy E. **Fax Area Code:* 800 ■ *TF:* 800-356-3373 ■ *Web:* www.standoutinacrowdedworld.com	Sarasota	FL	34240	941-373-1958	992-2038*
Signtex Imaging LP 1225 Alma St Suite C *Web:* www.signtex.com	Tomball	TX	77375	281-351-2776	351-0170
Signtronix 1445 W Sepulveda Blvd **Fax Area Code:* 310 ■ **Fax:* Sales ■ *TF:* 800-729-4853 ■ *Web:* www.signtronix.com	Torrance	CA	90501	800-729-4853	539-3554*
Spectrum Corp 10048 Easthaven Blvd. *TF:* 800-392-5050 ■ *Web:* www.specorp.com	Houston	TX	77075	713-944-6200	944-1290
Stouse Inc 300 New Century Pkwy. *Web:* www.stouse.com	New Century	KS	66031	913-764-5757	764-0885
Stout Industries 6425 W Florissant Ave *TF:* 800-325-8530 ■ *Web:* www.stoutindustries.com	Saint Louis	MO	63136	314-385-4600	385-9412
Total Image Specialists LLC 1877 E 17th Ave *TF:* 800-366-7446	Columbus	OH	43219	614-564-1300	564-1399
Tube Art Displays Inc 1705 4th Ave S *TF:* 800-562-2854 ■ *Web:* www.tubeart.com	Seattle	WA	98134	206-223-1122	223-1123
Turnroth Sign Co Inc 1207 E Rock Falls Rd	Rock Falls	IL	61071	815-625-1155	625-1158
Vitachrome Graphics Group Inc 11517 Los Nietos Rd *TF:* 800-742-5507 ■ *Web:* www.vitachrome.com	Santa Fe Springs	CA	90670	562-692-9200	692-9055
Vomar Products Inc 7800 Deering Ave *Web:* www.vomarproducts.com	Canoga Park	CA	91304	818-610-5115	610-5123
Vomela Specialty Co 380 St Peter St Suite 705 *TF:* 800-645-1012 ■ *Web:* www.vomela.com	Saint Paul	MN	55102	651-228-2200	228-2295
Walter Haas & Sons Inc 123 W 23rd St *TF:* 800-552-3845 ■ *Web:* www.haasprint.com	Hialeah	FL	33010	305-883-2257	883-0598
Werner Tool & Mfg Co Inc 12301 E McNichols Rd. *Web:* www.trivision.com	Detroit	MI	48205	313-526-6020	526-6070
White Way Sign 451 Kingston Ct *TF:* 800-621-4122 ■ *Web:* www.whiteway.com	Mount Prospect	IL	60056	847-391-0200	391-0252
Worldwide Sign Systems 446 N Cecil St PO Box 338 **Fax Area Code:* 888 ■ *TF:* 800-874-3334 ■ *Web:* www.wwsign.com	Bonduel	WI	54107	715-758-2146	793-4455*
Young Electric Sign Co 2401 Foothill Dr. *Web:* www.yesco.com	Salt Lake City	UT	84109	801-464-4600	483-0998
Zumar Industries Inc 9719 Santa Fe Springs Rd *TF:* 800-654-7446 ■ *Web:* www.zumar.com	Santa Fe Springs	CA	90670	562-941-4633	941-4643

705 SILVERWARE

SEE ALSO Cutlery p. 1779; Metal Stampings p. 2238

Company	City	State	Zip	Phone	Fax
Empire Silver Co Inc 6520 New Utrecht Ave. *TF:* 800-255-9475 ■ *Web:* www.empiresilver.com	Brooklyn	NY	11219	718-232-3389	232-0680
Great American Products Inc 1661 S Seguin Ave *TF:* 800-341-4436 ■ *Web:* www.gap1.com	New Braunfels	TX	78130	830-620-4400	620-8430
Metallics Inc W7274 County Hwy Z PO Box 99 *Web:* www.metallics.net	Onalaska	WI	54650	608-781-5200	781-2254
Mikasa Inc 100 Plaza Dr *TF Cust Svc:* 800-833-4681 ■ *Web:* www.mikasa.com	Secaucus	NJ	07094	201-867-9210	867-0580
Old Newbury Crafters 36 Main St *TF:* 800-343-1388 ■ *Web:* www.silvercrafters.com	Amesbury	MA	01913	978-388-0983	388-8430
Olde Country Reproductions Inc 722 W Market St *TF Cust Svc:* 800-358-3997 ■ *Web:* www.pewtarex.com	York	PA	17405	717-848-1859	845-7129
Pfaltzgraff Co 140 E Market St **Fax:* Cust Svc ■ *TF:* 800-999-2811 ■ *Web:* www.pfaltzgraff.com	York	PA	17401	717-848-5500	771-1433*
Reed & Barton Silversmiths Corp 144 W Britannia St *TF:* 800-343-1383 ■ *Web:* www.reedbarton.com	Taunton	MA	02780	508-824-6611	822-7269
Rogers Lunt & Bowlen Co 298 Federal St *TF:* 800-242-2774 ■ *Web:* www.luntsilver.com	Greenfield	MA	01301	413-774-2774	774-4393
Salisbury inc 29085 Airpark Dr *TF:* 800-824-4708 ■ *Web:* www.salisburypewter.com	Easton	MD	21601	410-770-4901	770-4904
Towle Silversmiths 3501 Concord Rd *Web:* www.towlesilver.com	York	PA	17402	617-568-1300	568-9021
Tropar Mfg Inc 5 Vreeland Rd *Web:* www.airflyte.com	Florham Park	NJ	07932	973-822-2400	822-2891
Utica Cutlery Co 820 Noyes St PO Box 10527 *TF:* 800-879-2526 ■ *Web:* www.uticacutlery.com	Utica	NY	13503	315-733-4663	733-6602
Wallace Silversmiths Inc 3501 Concord Rd. *Web:* www.lifetimesterling.com	York	PA	17402	617-561-2200	569-8484
Woodbury Pewterers Inc 860 Main St S **Fax Area Code:* 800 ■ *TF:* 800-648-2014 ■ *Web:* www.woodburypewter.com	Woodbury	CT	06798	203-263-2668	819-9492*

706 SIMULATION & TRAINING SYSTEMS

Company	City	State	Zip	Phone	Fax
Bemco Inc 2255 Union Pl *Web:* www.bemcoinc.com	Simi Valley	CA	93065	805-583-4970	583-5033
CACI MTL Systems Inc 3481 Dayton-Xenia Rd *Web:* www.caci.com	Dayton	OH	45432	937-426-3111	426-8301
CAE Inc 8585 Cote de Liesse *NYSE: CAE* ■ *TF:* 866-999-6223 ■ *Web:* www.cae.com	Saint Laurent	QC	H4T1G6	514-341-6780	341-7699
Cubic Corp 9333 Balboa Ave PO Box 85587 *NYSE: CUB* ■ *Web:* www.cubic.com	San Diego	CA	92186	858-277-6780	505-1523
Cubic Defense Systems 9333 Balboa Ave. *Web:* www.cubic.com	San Diego	CA	92123	858-277-6780	505-1524
Cubic Simulation Systems 2001 W Oakridge Rd *TF:* 800-327-1020	Orlando	FL	32809	407-859-7410	855-4840
Doron Precision Systems Inc 174 Ct St. *TF:* 800-238-6766 ■ *Web:* www.doronprecision.com	Binghamton	NY	13901	607-772-1610	772-6760
DRS C3 Systems LLC 400 Professional Dr *TF:* 800-252-4734 ■ *Web:* www.drs.com	Gaithersburg	MD	20879	301-921-8100	921-8010
Energy Concepts Inc 404 Washington Blvd. *TF:* 800-621-1247	Mundelein	IL	60060	847-837-8191	837-8191
Environmental Tectonics Corp 125 James Way *OTC: ETCC* ■ *Web:* www.etcusa.com	SouthHampton	PA	18966	215-355-9100	357-4000
Evans & Sutherland Computer Corp 770 Komas Dr. *NASDAQ: ESCC* ■ **Fax:* Hum Res ■ *TF Sales:* 800-327-5707 ■ *Web:* www.es.com	Salt Lake City	UT	84108	801-588-1000	588-4500*
Faac Inc 1229 Oak Valley Dr *Web:* www.faac.com	Ann Arbor	MI	48108	734-761-5836	761-5368
Frasca International Inc 906 E Airport Rd *Web:* www.frasca.com	Urbana	IL	61802	217-344-9200	344-9207
Malwin Electronics Corp 52 E 22nd St. *Web:* www.malwin.com	Paterson	NJ	07514	973-881-1500	881-1686
Meggitt Training Systems Inc 296 Brogdon Rd. *TF:* 800-813-9046 ■ *Web:* www.meggitttrainingsystems.com	Suwanee	GA	30024	678-288-1090	288-1515
Nida Corp 300 S John Rodes Blvd *TF:* 800-327-6432 ■ *Web:* www.nida.com	Melbourne	FL	32904	321-727-2265	727-2655
Sensis Corp 85 Collamer Crossing *Web:* www.sensis.com	East Syracuse	NY	13057	315-445-0550	446-2209
Ternion Corp 2223 Drake Ave *Web:* www.ternion.com	Huntsville	AL	35805	256-881-9933	881-9957

707 SMART CARDS

Company	City	State	Zip	Phone	Fax
CardLogix 16 Hughes Suite 100 *Web:* www.cardlogix.com	Irvine	CA	92618	949-380-1312	380-1428
Clever Devices Ltd 137 Commercial St *TF:* 800-872-6129 ■ *Web:* www.cleverdevices.com	Plainview	NY	11803	516-433-6100	433-5088
Credit Card Systems Inc 180 Shepard Ave *TF:* 800-747-1269 ■ *Web:* www.ccsplastech.com	Wheeling	IL	60090	847-459-8320	459-1296
DataCard Corp 11111 Bren Rd W *TF:* 800-328-8623 ■ *Web:* www.datacard.com	Minnetonka	MN	55343	952-933-1223	933-7971
MDI Security Systems Inc 12500 Network Dr Suite 303 *NASDAQ: MDII* ■ *TF:* 866-435-7634 ■ *Web:* www.mdisecure.com	San Antonio	TX	78249	210-477-5400	477-5401
Perfect Plastic Printing Corp 311 Kautz Rd # 4 *Web:* www.perfectplastic.com	Saint Charles	IL	60174	630-584-1600	584-0648
QualTeq Inc 800 Montros Ave MS CN1037 *TF:* 800-257-5347 ■ *Web:* www.qualteq.com	South Plainfield	NJ	07080	908-668-0999	668-7976
Smart Card Integrators Inc (SCI) 2424 N Ontario St. *Web:* www.sci-s.com	Burbank	CA	91504	818-847-1022	847-1454
SPYRUS Inc 2355 Oakland Rd Suite 1 *TF:* 800-277-9787 ■ *Web:* www.spyrus.com	San Jose	CA	95131	408-953-0700	953-9835

708 SNOWMOBILES

SEE ALSO Sporting Goods p. 2664

Company	City	State	Zip	Phone	Fax
Arctic Cat Inc 601 Brooks Ave S. *NASDAQ: ACAT* ■ *TF:* 877-228-2687 ■ *Web:* www.arcticcat.com	Thief River Falls	MN	56701	218-681-8558	681-3162
Polaris Industries Inc 2100 Hwy 55 *NYSE: PII* ■ *Web:* www.polarisindustries.com	Medina	MN	55340	763-542-0500	542-0599
Yamaha Motor Corp USA 6555 Katella Ave *TF Cust Svc:* 800-962-7926 ■ *Web:* www.yamaha-motor.com	Cypress	CA	90630	714-761-7300	

SOFTWARE

SEE Computer Software p. 1679

709 SPAS - HEALTH & FITNESS

SEE ALSO Health & Fitness Centers p. 2008; Spas - Hotel & Resort p. 2659; Weight Loss Centers & Services p. 2774

Facilities Listed Here Provide Multi-Day Programs Designed To Increase Health And Well-Being. Types Of Programs Offered Include (But Are Not Limited To) Relaxation, Smoking Cessation, Weight Loss, And Physical Fitness.

Name / Address	City	State	Zip	Phone	Fax
Agavita Spa at Lajitas - the Ultimate Hideout HC 70 PO Box 400	Lajitas	TX	79852	432-424-5000	424-5001
AmorePacific Beauty Gallery & Spa 114 Spring St; *TF:* 877-552-6673 ■ *Web:* www.us.amorepacific.com	New York	NY	10012	212-966-0400	966-1190
Birdwing Spa 21398 575th Ave; *Web:* www.birdwingspa.com	Litchfield	MN	55355	320-693-6064	693-7026
Black Hills Health & Education Ctr PO Box 19; *TF Cust Svc:* 800-658-5433 ■ *Web:* www.bhhec.org	Hermosa	SD	57744	605-255-4101	255-4687
Bliss San Francisco 181 3rd St 4th Fl; *Web:* www.blissworld.com/spa	San Francisco	CA	94103	415-281-0990	
Body/Mind Restoration Retreats 56 Lieb Rd; *Web:* www.bodymindretreats.com	Spencer	NY	14883	607-272-0694	277-7801
Breitenbush Hot Springs Retreat & Conference Ctr 4 Service Rd 46 Mile Post 10 PO Box 578; *Web:* www.breitenbush.com	Detroit	OR	97342	503-854-3314	854-3319
Cal-a-Vie Spa 29402 Spa Havens Way; *TF:* 866-772-4283 ■ *Web:* www.cal-a-vie.com	Vista	CA	92084	760-945-2055	630-0074
Calistoga Spa Hot Springs 1006 Washington St; *TF:* 866-822-5772 ■ *Web:* www.calistogaspa.com	Calistoga	CA	94515	707-942-6269	942-4214
Cooper Wellness Program 12230 Preston Rd; *TF:* 800-444-5192 ■ *Web:* www.cooperaerobics.com/lif.htm	Dallas	TX	75230	972-386-4777	386-0039
Cornelia Day Resort 663 5th Ave 8th Fl; *TF:* 866-663-1700 ■ *Web:* www.cornelia.com	New York	NY	10022	212-871-3050	871-1028
Deerfield Spa 650 Resica Falls Rd; *TF:* 800-852-4494 ■ *Web:* www.deerfieldspa.com	East Stroudsburg	PA	18301	570-223-0160	223-8270
Duke Diet & Fitness Ctr (DFC) 501 Douglas St; *TF:* 800-235-3853 ■ *Web:* www.dukehealth.org/services/diet_and_fitness/about	Durham	NC	27705	919-688-3079	684-6176
Golden Door PO Box 463077; *TF:* 800-424-0777 ■ *Web:* www.goldendoor.com	Escondido	CA	92046	760-744-5777	471-2393
Green Mountain at Fox Run PO Box 164; *TF:* 800-448-8106 ■ *Web:* www.fitwoman.com	Ludlow	VT	05149	802-228-8885	228-8887
Green Valley Spa 1871 W Canyon View Dr; *TF:* 800-237-1068 ■ *Web:* www.greenvalleyspa.com	Saint George	UT	84770	435-628-8060	673-4084
Greenhouse Spa The PO Box 1144	Arlington	TX	76004	817-640-4000	649-0422
Healing Center of Arizona 25 Wilson Canyon Rd; *TF:* 877-723-2811	Sedona	AZ	86336	928-282-7710	282-6794
Heartland Spa 1237 E 1600 N Rd; **Fax Area Code:* 815 ■ *TF:* 800-545-4853 ■ *Web:* www.heartlandspa.com	Gilman	IL	60938	800-545-4853	683-2144*
Hills Health Ranch 4871 Caribou Hwy 97 PO Box 26; *TF:* 800-668-2233 ■ *Web:* www.spabc.com	108 Mile Ranch	BC	V0K2Z0	250-791-5225	791-6384
Hilton Head Health Institute 14 Valencia Rd; *TF:* 800-292-2440 ■ *Web:* www.hhhealth.com	Hilton Head Island	SC	29928	843-785-7292	686-5659
Himalayan Institute Center for Health & Healing 952 Bethany Tpke; *Web:* www.himalayaninstitute.org	Honesdale	PA	18431	570-253-5551	253-9078
Hippocrates Health Institute Life-Change Ctr 1443 Palmdale Ct; *TF:* 800-842-2125 ■ *Web:* www.hippocratesinst.org	West Palm Beach	FL	33411	561-471-8876	471-9464
Kerr House 17777 Beaver St PO Box 363; *Web:* www.thekerrhouse.com	Grand Rapids	OH	43522	419-832-1733	832-4303
Kohala Spa 425 Waikoloa Beach Dr; *Web:* www.kohalaspa.com	Waikoloa	HI	96738	808-886-2828	886-2953
Kripalu Center for Yoga & Health 57 Interlaken Rd; *TF:* 800-741-7353 ■ *Web:* www.kripalu.org	Stockbridge	MA	01262	413-448-3400	448-3384
Lifestyle Center of America Rt 1 PO Box 4001; *TF:* 800-213-8955 ■ *Web:* www.lifestylecenter.org	Sulphur	OK	73086	580-993-2327	993-3902
Lodge & Spa at Cordillera 2205 Cordillera Way; *TF:* 800-877-3529 ■ *Web:* www.cordilleralodge.com	Edwards	CO	81632	970-926-2200	926-2486
Miraval Life in Balance 5000 E Via Estancia Miraval; **Fax Area Code:* 520 ■ *TF:* 800-232-3969 ■ *Web:* www.miravalresort.com	Catalina	AZ	85739	800-232-3969	825-5163*
Mountain Trek Fitness Retreat & Health Spa Ltd 3800 N St; *TF:* 800-661-5161 ■ *Web:* www.hiking.com	Ainsworth Hot Springs	BC	V0G1A0	250-229-5636	229-5246
New Age Health Spa 7491 SR 55; *TF:* 800-682-4348 ■ *Web:* www.newagehealthspa.com	Neversink	NY	12765	845-985-7601	985-2467
New Life Hiking Spa 2617 Killington Rd PO Box 395; *TF:* 800-228-4676 ■ *Web:* www.newlifehikingspa.com	Killington	VT	05751	802-422-4302	422-3690
Northern Pines on Crescent Lake Bed & Breakfast Plus 31 Big Pine Rd; *Web:* www.maine.com/norpines	Raymond	ME	04071	207-655-7624	935-7574
Oaks at Ojai 122 E Ojai Ave; *TF:* 800-753-6257 ■ *Web:* www.oaksspa.com	Ojai	CA	93023	805-646-5573	640-1504
Ocean Waters Spa 600 N Atlantic Ave; *TF:* 800-767-4471 ■ *Web:* www.oceanwatersspa.com	Daytona Beach	FL	32118	386-267-1660	253-9307
Ojo Caliente Mineral Springs Resort 50 Los Banos Dr PO Box 68; *TF:* 800-222-9162 ■ *Web:* www.ojocalientesprings.com	Ojo Caliente	NM	87549	505-583-2233	583-2045
Optimum Health Institute 6970 Central Ave; *TF:* 800-993-4325 ■ *Web:* www.optimumhealth.org	Lemon Grove	CA	91945	619-464-3346	589-4098
Pritikin Longevity Center & Spa 8755 NW 36th St; **Fax:* Resv ■ *TF:* 800-327-4914 ■ *Web:* www.pritikin.com	Doral	FL	33178	305-935-7131	935-7371*
Raj The 1734 Jasmine Ave; *TF:* 800-248-9050 ■ *Web:* www.theraj.com	Fairfield	IA	52556	641-472-9580	472-2496
Regency House Natural Health Spa 2000 S Ocean Dr; *TF:* 800-454-0003 ■ *Web:* www.regencyhealthspa.com	Hallandale Beach	FL	33009	954-454-2220	454-4637
Sagestone Spa & Salon *Red Mountain Resort* 1275 E Red Mountain Cir; *TF:* 800-690-9215 ■ *Web:* www.redmountainspa.com	Ivins	UT	84738	800-690-9215	
Spa at Coeur d'Alene PO Box 7200; *TF:* 800-688-5253 ■ *Web:* www.cdaresort.com/spa	Coeur d'Alene	ID	83816	208-765-4000	664-7276
Spa at Disney Saratoga Springs Resort 1950-A Broadway; *Web:* www.relaxedyet.com	Lake Buena Vista	FL	32830	407-827-4455	827-4585
Spa at Grand Lake 1667 Exeter Rd; *TF:* 800-843-7721 ■ *Web:* www.thespaatgrandlake.com	Lebanon	CT	06249	860-642-4306	642-4799
Spa at Peninsula Beverly Hills 9882 S Santa Monica Blvd; *TF:* 800-462-7899 ■ *Web:* www.peninsula.com/beverly_hills/en	Beverly Hills	CA	90212	310-551-2888	788-2319
Spa at the Doral Forrestal 100 College Rd E; *Web:* www.marriottmodules.com	Princeton	NJ	08540	609-897-7520	897-7237
Spa at The Setai 2001 Collins Ave; *Web:* www.setai.com	Miami Beach	FL	33139	305-520-6900	520-6600
Spa Concept Bromont 90 Stanstead St; *TF:* 800-567-7727 ■ *Web:* www.spaconcept.ca	Bromont	QC	J2L1K6	450-534-2717	534-0599
Spa Radiance 3011 Fillmore St; *Web:* www.sparadiance.com	San Francisco	CA	94123	415-346-6281	346-6170
SpaHalekulani 2199 Kalia Rd; *TF:* 800-367-2343 ■ *Web:* www.halekulani.com/spa_halekulani	Honolulu	HI	96815	808-923-2311	926-8004
Structure House 3017 Pickett Rd; *TF:* 800-553-0052 ■ *Web:* www.structurehouse.com	Durham	NC	27705	919-493-4205	490-0191
Tennessee Fitness Spa 299 Natural Bridge Pk Rd; *TF:* 800-235-8365 ■ *Web:* www.tfspa.com	Waynesboro	TN	38485	931-722-5589	722-9113
Tracie Martyn Salon 59 5th Ave Suite 1; *Web:* www.traciemartyn.com	New York	NY	10003	212-206-9333	206-8399
Uchee Pines Lifestyle Ctr 30 Uchee Pines Rd PO Box 75; *Web:* www.ucheepines.org/lifestylecenter.htm	Seale	AL	36875	334-855-4764	855-9014
Vatra Mountain Valley Health Resort Rt 214 PO Box F; *TF:* 800-232-2772 ■ *Web:* www.vatraspa.com	Hunter	NY	12442	518-263-4919	263-4994
White Sulphur Springs Resort & Spa 3100 White Sulphur Springs Rd; *TF:* 800-593-8873 ■ *Web:* www.whitesulphursprings.com	Saint Helena	CA	94574	707-963-8588	963-2890
Wholistic Life Ctr 925 Life Ln	Washburn	MO	65772	417-435-2212	435-2211
Wiesbaden Hot Springs 625 5th St PO Box 349; *Web:* www.wiesbadenhotsprings.com	Ouray	CO	81427	970-325-4347	325-4358
Dr Wilkinson's Hot Springs Resort 1507 Lincoln Ave; *Web:* www.drwilkinson.com	Calistoga	CA	94515	707-942-4102	942-4412
Two Bunch Palms Resort & Spa 67425 Two Bunch Palms Trail; *TF:* 877-839-3609 ■ *Web:* www.twobunchpalms.com	Desert Hot Springs	CA	92240	760-329-8791	329-1874
Vail Cascade Resort & Spa 1300 Westhaven Dr; *TF:* 800-420-2424 ■ *Web:* www.vailcascade.com	Vail	CO	81657	970-476-7111	479-7020
Grand Wailea Resort & Spa 3850 Wailea Alanui Dr; *TF:* 800-888-6100 ■ *Web:* www.grandwailea.com	Wailea	HI	96753	808-875-1234	879-4077
El Monte Sagrado Living Resort & Spa 317 Kit Carson Rd; *TF:* 888-213-4419 ■ *Web:* www.elmontesagrado.com	Taos	NM	87571	505-758-3502	737-2985

710 SPAS - HOTEL & RESORT

SEE ALSO Spas - Health & Fitness p. 2659

Name / Address	City	State	Zip	Phone	Fax
100 Fountain Spa at the Pillar & Post Inn 48 John St PO Box 48; *TF:* 888-669-5566 ■ *Web:* www.vintage-hotels.com	Niagara-on-the-Lake	ON	L0S1J0	905-468-2123	468-3551
Abhasa Waikiki Spa at the Royal Hawaiian Hotel 2259 Kalakaua Ave; *Web:* www.abhasa.com	Honolulu	HI	96815	808-922-8200	922-3557
Agave the Arizona Spa at the Westin Kierland Resort & Spa 6902 E Greenway Pkwy; *TF:* 888-625-5144 ■ *Web:* www.kierlandresort.com	Scottsdale	AZ	85254	480-624-1500	624-1130
Allegria Spa at the Park Hyatt Beaver Creek 100 E Thomas Pl; *TF:* 800-233-1234 ■ *Web:* www.allegriaspa.com	Beaver Creek	CO	81620	970-748-7500	748-7501
Allegria Spa at the Ventana Inn & Spa Hwy 1; *TF:* 800-628-6500 ■ *Web:* www.ventanainn.com	Big Sur	CA	93920	831-667-4222	667-0573
Alvadora Spa at the Royal Palms Resort & Spa 5200 E Camelback Rd; *TF:* 800-672-6011 ■ *Web:* www.royalpalmshotel.com/spa.htm	Phoenix	AZ	85018	602-977-6400	840-6927
Amadeus Spa at the Marriott Napa Valley 3425 Solano Ave; *Web:* www.napavalleymarriott.com	Napa	CA	94558	707-254-3330	254-3333
Anara Spa at the Hyatt Regency Kauai 1571 Poipu Rd; *Web:* www.anaraspa.com	Koloa	HI	96756	808-240-6440	240-6599
Ancient Cedars Spa at the Wickaninnish Inn 500 Osprey Ln PO Box 250; *TF:* 800-333-4604 ■ *Web:* www.wickinn.com	Tofino	BC	V0R2Z0	250-725-3113	725-3110
Aquae Sulis Spa at the JW Marriott Resort Las Vegas 221 N Rampart Blvd; *TF:* 877-869-8777 ■ *Web:* www.marriott.com	Las Vegas	NV	89145	702-869-7807	869-7772

				Phone	Fax
Aquaterra Spa at the Surf & Sand Resort 1555 S Coast Hwy . . . . . Web: www.surfandsandresort.com	Laguna Beach	CA	92651	949-376-2772	376-2773
Aria Spa & Club at the Vail Cascade Resort 1300 Westhaven Dr. . . . . TF: 888-824-5772 ■ Web: www.vailcascade.com/spaclub.html	Vail	CO	81657	970-479-5942	476-7405
Au Naturel Wellness & Medical Spa at the Brookstreet Hotel 525 Legget Dr. . . . . TF: 888-826-2220 ■ Web: www.brookstreethotel.com	Ottawa	ON	K2K2W2	613-271-3393	271-3541
Avanyu Spa at the Equinox Resort 3567 Main St Rt 7-A. . . . . TF: 800-362-4747 ■ Web: www.rockresorts.com	Manchester Village	VT	05254	802-362-7881	362-7791
Avanyu Spa at the Rosario Resort 1400 Rosario Rd. . . . . TF: 800-562-8820 ■ Web: www.rosarioresort.com	Eastsound	WA	98245	360-376-2222	376-2289
Avanyu Spa at the Snake River Lodge 7710 Granite Loop Rd PO Box 348. . . . . TF: 800-445-4655 ■ Web: www.snakeriverlodge.rockresorts.com	Teton Village	WY	83025	307-732-6070	732-6069
Bathhouse at Calistoga Ranch 580 Lommel Rd . . . . . Web: www.calistogaranch.com	Calistoga	CA	94515	707-254-2820	254-2825
Boutique Spa at the Ritz-Carlton Georgetown 3100 S St NW. . . . . TF: 800-241-3333 ■ Web: www.ritzcarlton.com	Washington	DC	20007	202-912-4175	912-4199
Canyon Ranch SpaClub at the Gaylord Palms Resort 6000 W Osceola Pkwy . . . . . TF: 800-742-9000 ■ Web: www.canyonranch.com/spaclubs/gaylord	Kissimmee	FL	34746	407-586-2051	586-2061
Canyon Ranch SpaClub at the Venetian 3355 Las Vegas Blvd S Suite 1159. . . . . TF: 877-220-2688 ■ Web: www.canyonranch.com/spaclub	Las Vegas	NV	89109	702-414-3606	414-3801
Carefree Resort & Conference Ctr 37220 Mule Train Rd . . . . . TF: 888-692-4343 ■ Web: www.carefree-resort.com	Carefree	AZ	85377	480-488-5300	
Carneros Inn The 4048 Sonoma Hwy . . . . . TF: 888-400-9000 ■ Web: www.thecarnerosinn.com	Napa	CA	94559	707-299-4900	299-4950
Centre for Well-Being at the Phoenician 6000 E Camelback Rd. . . . . TF: 800-843-2392 ■ Web: www.shop.thephoenician.com	Scottsdale	AZ	85251	480-423-2452	423-2582
Century City Fitness Club & Spa 10220 Constellation Blvd . . . . . Web: www.equinox.com	Century City	CA	90067	310-286-2900	286-0208
Chateau Elan Spa at the Chateau Elan Atlanta 100 Rue Charlemagne . . . . . TF: 800-233-9463 ■ Web: www.chateauelan.com	Braselton	GA	30517	678-425-6064	425-6069
Cheeca Lodge & Spa 81801 Overseas Hwy Mile Marker 82. . . . . TF: 800-327-2888 ■ Web: www.cheeca.com	Islamorada	FL	33036	305-664-4651	664-2329
Chrysalis Inn & Spa The 804 10th St . . . . . TF: 888-808-0005 ■ Web: www.thechrysalisinn.com	Bellingham	WA	98225	360-756-1005	647-0342
Cliff Spa at Snowbird Hwy 210 PO Box 929000 . . . . . TF: 800-453-3000 ■ Web: www.snowbird.com	Snowbird	UT	84092	801-933-2225	933-2283
Cloister at Sea Island The 100 Hudson Pl . . . . . TF: 800-230-4134 ■ Web: www.seaisland.com/Accommodations/The-Cloister.aspx	Sea Island	GA	31561	912-638-5148	638-5894
Disney's Grand Floridian Spa 4111 N Floridian Way. . . . . Web: www.disneyworld.com	Lake Buena Vista	FL	32830	407-824-2332	824-2235
Elizabeth Arden Red Door Spa at Mystic Marriott Hotel & Spa 625 N Rd . . . . . TF: 866-449-7390 ■ Web: www.marriott.com	Groton	CT	06340	860-446-2500	446-2696
Elizabeth Arden Red Door Spa at the Seaview Marriott Resort & Spa 400 E Fairway Ln . . . . . TF: 800-205-6518 ■ Web: www.reddoorspas.com	Galloway	NJ	08205	609-404-4100	404-4110
Emerson Resort & Spa 5368 Rt 28 . . . . . TF: 877-688-2828 ■ Web: www.emersonresortandspa.com	Mount Tremper	NY	12457	845-688-7900	688-2789
Fairmont Orchid Hawaii The 1 N Kaniku Dr. . . . . TF: 866-540-4474 ■ Web: www.fairmont.com/orchid	Kohala Coast	HI	96743	808-885-2000	885-5778
Farmhouse Spa at Blackberry Farm 1471 W Millers Cove Rd. . . . . TF: 800-273-6004 ■ Web: www.blackberryfarm.com	Walland	TN	37886	865-379-9819	681-7753
Four Seasons Resort Scottsdale at Troon North The 10600 E Crescent Moon Dr . . . . . TF: 800-819-5053 ■ Web: www.fourseasons.com/scottsdale	Scottsdale	AZ	85262	480-513-5700	515-5599
Four Seasons Spa at the Four Seasons Hotel Las Vegas 3960 Las Vegas Blvd S. . . . . TF: 800-332-3442 ■ Web: www.fourseasons.com/lasvegas	Las Vegas	NV	89119	702-632-5302	632-5450
Four Seasons Spa at the Four Seasons Hotel Los Angeles at Beverly Hills 300 S Doheny Dr . . . . . TF: 800-819-5053 ■ Web: www.fourseasons.com/losangeles	Los Angeles	CA	90048	310-786-2229	860-8966
Four Seasons Spa at the Four Seasons Resort Aviara 7100 Four Seasons Pt . . . . . TF: 800-819-5053 ■ Web: www.fourseasons.com/aviara	Carlsbad	CA	92009	760-603-6902	603-3607
Four Seasons Spa at the Four Seasons Resort Jackson Hole 7680 Granite Loop Rd PO Box 544. . . . . TF: 800-819-5053 ■ Web: www.fourseasons.com/jacksonhole	Teton Village	WY	83025	307-732-5120	732-5121
Four Seasons Spa at the Four Seasons Resort Maui 3900 Wailea Alanui Dr . . . . . TF: 800-334-6284 ■ Web: www.fourseasons.com/maui	Wailea	HI	96753	808-874-2925	874-2269
Four Seasons Spa at the Four Seasons Resort Santa Barbara 1260 Ch Dr. . . . . TF: 800-819-5053 ■ Web: www.fourseasons.com/santabarbara	Santa Barbara	CA	93108	805-565-8250	565-8451
Fox Harb'r Resort & Spa 1337 Fox Harbour Rd. . . . . TF: 866-257-1801 ■ Web: www.foxharbr.com	Wallace	NS	B0K1Y0	902-257-1801	257-1852
Garden Spa at MacArthur Place 29 E MacArthur St . . . . . TF: 800-722-1866 ■ Web: www.macarthurplace.com	Sonoma	CA	95476	707-933-3193	933-9833
Glacial Waters Spa at Grand View Lodge 23521 Nokomis Ave . . . . . TF: 866-801-2951 ■ Web: www.grandviewlodge.com	Nisswa	MN	56468	218-963-2234	963-8791
Golden Door Spa at the Wyndham Peaks Resort 136 Country Club Dr PO Box 2702. . . . . TF: 800-772-5482 ■ Web: www.goldendoorspas.com	Telluride	CO	81435	970-728-2590	728-4779
Grand Hotel Marriott Resort Golf Club & Spa 1 Grand Blvd PO Box 639. . . . . TF: 800-544-9933 ■ Web: www.marriott.com	Point Clear	AL	36564	251-928-9201	928-1149
Health Spa at Meadowood Napa Valley The 900 Meadowood Ln . . . . . TF: 800-458-8080 ■ Web: www.meadowood.com	Saint Helena	CA	94574	707-967-1275	967-1270
Hibiscus Spa at the Myrtle Beach Marriott Resort at Grande Dunes 8400 Costa Verde Dr. . . . . Web: www.csspagroup.com	Myrtle Beach	SC	29572	843-692-3730	449-8669
Hilton Country Resort & Spa 9800 Westover Hills Blvd . . . . . Web: www.hilton.com	San Antonio	TX	78251	210-509-9800	509-9814
Hilton Short Hills 41 JFK Pkwy. . . . . TF: 800-445-8667 ■ Web: www.hiltonshorthills.com	Short Hills	NJ	07078	973-379-0100	379-6870
Hilton Suites Toronto/Markham Conference Centre & Spa 8500 Warden Ave . . . . . TF: 800-668-8800 ■ Web: www.torontomarkham.hilton.com	Markham	ON	L6G1C7	905-470-8500	477-8611
Hualalai Sports Club & Spa at the Four Seasons Resort Hualalai 100 Kaupulehu Dr. . . . . TF: 800-983-3880 ■ Web: www.fourseasons.com/hualalai	Kaupulehu-Kona	HI	96740	808-325-8440	325-8451
Hyatt Regency Scottsdale Resort at Gainey Ranch 7500 E Doubletree Ranch Rd . . . . . TF: 800-233-1234 ■ Web: scottsdale.hyatt.com	Scottsdale	AZ	85258	480-483-5558	483-5544
Indies Spa at the Hawks Cay Resort & Marina 61 Hawk's Cay Blvd . . . . . TF: 800-432-2232 ■ Web: www.hawkscay.com	Duck Key	FL	33050	305-289-4810	289-4811
Indulgence Spa at Taboo 1209 Muskoka Beach Rd . . . . . TF: 800-461-0236 ■ Web: www.tabooresort.com	Gravenhurst	ON	P1P1R1	705-687-2233	687-7474
Jurlique Spa 4925 N Scottsdale Rd . . . . . TF: 800-528-7867 ■ Web: www.fireskyresort.com	Scottsdale	AZ	85251	480-424-6072	424-6073
JW Starr Pass Resort & Spa 3800 W Starr Pass Blvd . . . . . TF: 800-690-8419 ■ Web: www.jwmarriottstarrpass.com	Tucson	AZ	85745	520-792-3500	792-3351
Kea Lani Spa at the Fairmont Kea Lani Maui 4100 Wailea Alanui Dr . . . . . TF: 800-659-4100 ■ Web: www.fairmont.com	Maui	HI	96753	808-875-2229	875-1200
Kohler Waters Spa 501 Highlands Dr. . . . . TF: 866-928-3777 ■ Web: www.americanclubresort.com	Kohler	WI	53044	920-457-7777	208-4934
Lafayette Park Hotel 3287 Mt Diablo Blvd . . . . . TF: 800-368-2468 ■ Web: www.lafayetteparkhotel.com	Lafayette	CA	94549	925-283-3700	284-1621
Lake Austin Spa Resort 1705 S Quinlan Pk Rd. . . . . TF: 800-847-5637 ■ Web: www.lakeaustin.com	Austin	TX	78732	512-372-7380	372-7382
Living Spa at El Monte Sagrado 317 Kit Carson Rd . . . . . TF: 888-213-4419 ■ Web: www.elmontesagrado.com	Taos	NM	87571	575-758-3502	737-2985
Lodge & Spa at Cordillera The 2205 Cordillera Way. . . . . TF: 800-877-3529 ■ Web: www.cordilleralodge.com	Edwards	CO	81632	970-926-2200	926-6419
Los Willows Inn & Spa 530 Stewart Canyon Rd . . . . . TF: 888-731-9400 ■ Web: www.loswillows.com	Fallbrook	CA	92028	760-731-9400	728-3622
Massage Center at Mohonk Mountain House 1000 Mountain Rest Rd . . . . . TF: 800-772-6646 ■ Web: www.mohonk.com	New Paltz	NY	12561	845-256-2751	256-2737
Mauna Lani Spa at Mauna Lani Resort 68-1365 Pauoa Rd . . . . . TF: 866-877-6982 ■ Web: www.maunalani.com	Kohala Coast	HI	96743	808-881-7922	885-4440
Mii Amo at Enchantment Resort 525 Boynton Canyon Rd. . . . . TF: 888-749-2137 ■ Web: www.miiamo.com	Sedona	AZ	86336	928-282-2900	282-9249
Mirbeau Inn & Spa 851 W Genesee St. . . . . TF: 877-647-2328 ■ Web: www.mirbeau.com	Skaneateles	NY	13152	315-685-5006	685-5150
Mirror Lake Inn Resort & Spa 77 Mirror Lake Dr. . . . . Web: www.mirrorlakeinn.com	Lake Placid	NY	12946	518-523-2544	523-2871
Mokara Hotel & Spa 212 W Crockett St. . . . . TF: 866-605-1212 ■ Web: www.mokarahotels.com	San Antonio	TX	78205	210-396-5800	226-0389
Moonlight Spa at Moonlight Lodge 1 Mountain Loop Rd. . . . . TF: 800-845-4428 ■ Web: www.moonlightbasin.com	Big Sky	MT	59716	406-995-7700	995-7632
Mountain Laurel Spa at Stonewall Resort 940 Resort Dr . . . . . TF: 888-278-8150 ■ Web: www.stonewallresort.com	Roanoke	WV	26447	304-269-8881	269-4358
Na Hoola Spa at Hyatt Regency Waikiki Resort 2424 Kalakaua Ave . . . . . TF: 800-233-1234 ■ Web: www.waikiki.hyatt.com	Honolulu	HI	96815	808-923-1234	926-3415
Nob Hill Spa at the Huntington Hotel 1075 California St. . . . . TF: 800-227-4683 ■ Web: www.huntingtonhotel.com	San Francisco	CA	94108	415-345-2888	345-2880
Old Edwards Inn & Spa The 445 Main St . . . . . TF: 866-526-8008 ■ Web: www.oldedwardsinn.com	Highlands	NC	28741	828-526-9887	787-2596
Portofino Spa at Portofino Island Resort 10 Portofino Dr. . . . . TF: 866-849-0223 ■ Web: www.portofinoisland.com	Pensacola	FL	32561	877-484-3405	
R Spa at the Renaissance ClubSport Walnut Creek Hotel 2805 Jones Rd . . . . . Web: www.marriott.com	Walnut Creek	CA	94597	925-942-6379	942-6348
Raindance Spa at the Lodge at Sonoma Renaissance Resort 1325 Broadway. . . . . TF: 888-710-8008 ■ Web: www.thelodgeatsonoma.com	Sonoma	CA	95476	707-931-2034	931-2137
Rancho Las Palmas Resort & Spa 41000 Bob Hope Dr . . . . . TF: 866-423-1195 ■ Web: www.rancholaspalmas.com/spa	Rancho Mirage	CA	92270	760-568-2727	837-2341
Red Door Lifestyle Spa 250 Racquet Club Rd . . . . . Web: www.reddoorlifestylespa.com	Weston	FL	33326	954-349-5500	
Revive Spa at the JW Marriott Desert Ridge Resort Phoenix 5350 E Marriott Dr . . . . . TF: 866-738-4834 ■ Web: www.jwdesertridgeresort.com	Phoenix	AZ	85054	480-293-3700	293-3725
Ritz-Carlton Tysons Corner The 1700 Tysons Blvd. . . . . TF: 800-241-3333 ■ Web: www.ritzcarlton.com	McLean	VA	22102	703-506-4300	506-2694

Name / Address	City	State	Zip	Phone	Fax
Saint Regis Aspen 315 E Dean St. TF: 888-625-5144 ■ Web: www.stregisaspen.com	Aspen	CO	81611	970-920-3300	544-7191
Sea Spa at Loews Coronado Bay Resort 4000 Coronado Bay Rd. Web: www.loewshotels.com/hotels/sandiego	Coronado	CA	92118	619-628-8770	628-8775
Secret Garden Spa at the Prince of Wales Hotel 6 Picton St PO Box 46 TF: 888-669-5566 ■ Web: www.vintage-hotels.com	Niagara-on-the-Lake	ON	L0S1J0	905-468-0515	468-9476
Senator Inn & Spa of Augusta 284 Western Ave TF: 877-772-2224 ■ Web: www.senatorinn.com	Augusta	ME	04330	207-622-8800	622-8803
ShaNah Spa at the Bishop's Lodge 1297 Bishop's Lodge Rd. TF: 800-974-2624 ■ Web: www.shanahspa.com	Santa Fe	NM	87501	505-819-4000	983-0832
Shui Spa at Crowne Pointe Historic Inn 82 Bradford St TF: 877-276-9631 ■ Web: www.shuispa.com	Provincetown	MA	02657	508-487-6767	487-5554
Spa & Athletic Club at the Lodge at Breckinridge 112 Overlook Dr TF: 800-736-1607 ■ Web: www.thelodgeatbreck.com	Breckenridge	CO	80424	970-453-4274	453-0625
Spa & Fitness Club at the Four Seasons Hotel Washington 2800 Pennsylvania Ave NW TF: 800-819-5053 ■ Web: www.fourseasons.com/washington	Washington	DC	20007	202-944-2022	944-2072
Spa at Bernardus Lodge 415 W Carmel Valley Rd. TF: 888-648-9463 ■ Web: www.bernardus.com	Carmel Valley	CA	93924	831-658-3514	659-3529
Spa at Big Cedar Lodge 612 Devil's Pool Rd. Web: www.bigcedar.com	Ridgedale	MO	65739	417-339-5201	335-2340
Spa at Eagle Crest Resort 1522 Cline Falls Hwy PO Box 1215 TF: 800-682-4786 ■ Web: www.eagle-crest.com	Redmond	OR	97756	541-923-9647	504-1420
Spa at Eden Roc A Renaissance Resort & Spa 4525 Collins Ave TF: 800-327-8337 ■ Web: www.ellespamiami.com	Miami Beach	FL	33140	305-674-5585	674-5595
Spa at Gurney's Inn Resort 290 Old Montauk Hwy TF: 800-848-7639 ■ Web: www.gurneysinn.com	Montauk	NY	11954	631-668-1892	668-3689
Spa at Kingsmill Resort 1010 Kingsmill Rd TF: 800-965-4772 ■ Web: www.kingsmill.com	Williamsburg	VA	23185	757-253-8230	258-1629
Spa at Le Merigot JW Marriott Beach Hotel Santa Monica 1740 Ocean Ave TF: 877-637-4468 ■ Web: www.marriott.com	Santa Monica	CA	90401	310-395-9700	395-9200
Spa at Montage Resort 30801 S Coast Hwy TF: 866-271-6953 ■ Web: www.montagelagunabeach.com	Laguna Beach	CA	92651	949-715-6010	715-6014
Spa at Monterey Plaza Hotel 400 Cannery Row TF: 800-334-3999 ■ Web: www.woodsidehotels.com	Monterey	CA	93940	831-645-4098	646-0285
Spa at Nemacolin Woodlands Resort 1001 Lafayette Dr TF: 800-422-2736 ■ Web: www.nwlr.com	Farmington	PA	15437	724-329-6772	329-6922
Spa at Pebble Beach 1518 Cypress Dr TF: 800-654-9300 ■ Web: www.pebblebeach.com	Pebble Beach	CA	93953	831-649-7615	622-6490
Spa at Pechanga Resort & Casino 45000 Pechanga Pkwy PO Box 9041 TF: 888-732-4264 ■ Web: www.pechanga.com	Temecula	CA	92592	951-693-1819	695-7410
Spa at Pinehurst Resort 1 Carolina Vista PO Box 4000 TF: 800-487-4653 ■ Web: www.pinehurst.com	Pinehurst	NC	28374	910-235-8320	235-8306
Spa at Silverado 1600 Atlas Peak Rd TF: 888-918-4772 ■ Web: www.silveradospa.com	Napa	CA	94558	707-257-5555	257-5550
Spa at the Amelia Island Plantation 60 Amelia Village TF: 877-843-7722 ■ Web: www.spaamelia.com	Amelia Island	FL	32034	904-432-2220	432-2214
Spa at the Arizona Biltmore Resort 2400 E Missouri Ave. TF: 800-950-0086 ■ Web: www.arizonabiltmore.com	Phoenix	AZ	85016	602-955-6600	954-2524
Spa at the Bacara Resort 8301 Hollister Ave Web: www.bacararesort.com	Santa Barbara	CA	93117	805-571-4210	571-3043
Spa at the Beau Rivage Resort & Casino 875 Beach Blvd. TF: 888-750-7111 ■ Web: www.beaurivage.com	Biloxi	MS	39530	228-386-7472	386-7918
Spa at The Beverly Wilshire The 9500 Wilshire Blvd TF: 800-545-4000 ■ Web: www.fourseasons.com	Beverly Hills	CA	90212	310-385-7023	385-3960
Spa at the Bodega Bay Lodge 103 Coast Hwy 1 TF: 888-875-2250 ■ Web: www.bodegabaylodge.com	Bodega Bay	CA	94923	707-875-3525	875-2428
Spa at the Breakers 1 S County Rd TF: 888-273-2537 ■ Web: www.thebreakers.com	Palm Beach	FL	33480	561-653-6656	653-6675
Spa at the Broadmoor 1 Lake Ave TF: 800-634-7711 ■ Web: www.broadmoor.com	Colorado Springs	CO	80906	719-577-5770	577-5766
Spa at the Buena Vista Palace Resort in the Walt Disney World Resort 1900 Buena Vista Dr PO Box 22206 TF: 866-397-6516 ■ Web: www.buenavistapalace.com/services_and_activities/spa.cfm	Lake Buena Vista	FL	32830	407-827-3200	827-3136
Spa at the Camelback Inn JW Marriott Resort Golf Club & Spa 5402 E Lincoln Dr. TF: 800-922-2635 ■ Web: www.camelbackspa.com	Scottsdale	AZ	85253	480-596-7040	596-7000
Spa at the Casa Madrona Hotel 801 Bridgeway Web: www.casamadrona.com	Sausalito	CA	94965	415-354-8308	332-0528
Spa at the Chattanoogan 1201 S Broad St TF: 800-619-0018 ■ Web: www.chattanooganhotel.com	Chattanooga	TN	37402	423-424-3779	756-3404
Spa at the CopperWynd Resort & Club 13225 N Eagle Ridge Dr TF: 877-707-1760 ■ Web: www.copperwynd.com	Fountain Hills	AZ	85268	480-333-1835	333-1901
Spa at the Delta Victoria Ocean Pointe Resort 45 Songhees Rd TF: 800-575-8882 ■ Web: www.deltahotels.com	Victoria	BC	V9A6T3	250-360-5858	360-5938
Spa at the Diplomat Country Club 501 Diplomat Pkwy. Web: www.diplomatresort.com	Hallandale	FL	33009	954-883-4905	883-4920
Spa at the Don CeSar Beach Resort 3400 Gulf Blvd TF: 866-728-2206 ■ Web: www.loewshotels.com	Saint Pete Beach	FL	33706	727-360-1883	
Spa at the Doral Golf Resort 8755 NW 36th St TF: 877-773-6725 ■ Web: www.marriott.com	Doral	FL	33178	305-717-6303	591-6630
Spa at the Fairmont Inn Sonoma Mission Inn 100 Boyes Blvd. TF: 877-289-7354 ■ Web: www.fairmont.com	Sonoma	CA	95476	707-938-9000	938-8012
Spa at the Hilton Sedona Resort 90 Ridge View Dr TF: 877-273-3762 ■ Web: www.hiltonsedonaspa.com	Sedona	AZ	86351	928-284-6900	284-6940
Spa at the Homestead Rt 220 Main St PO Box 2000 TF: 800-838-1766 ■ Web: www.thehomestead.com	Hot Springs	VA	24445	540-839-7547	839-7668
Spa at the Hotel Hershey 100 Hotel Rd TF: 877-772-9988 ■ Web: www.chocolatespa.com	Hershey	PA	17033	717-520-5888	520-5880
Spa at the JW Marriott Denver at Cherry Creek 2700 E 2nd Ave. Web: www.antoineduchez.com	Denver	CO	80206	303-320-6012	996-1061
Spa at the JW Marriott Desert Springs Resort Palm Desert 74855 Country Club Dr TF: 800-331-3112 ■ Web: www.marriott.com	Palm Desert	CA	92260	760-341-1856	862-1618
Spa at the JW Marriott Ihilani Resort 92-1001 Olani St TF: 800-626-4446 ■ Web: www.ihilani.com	Kapolei	HI	96707	808-679-3321	679-3871
Spa at the Kauai Marriott Resort & Beach Club 3610 Rice St TF: 800-220-2925 ■ Web: www.marriott.com	Lihue	HI	96766	808-246-4918	246-6518
Spa at the Laguna Cliffs Marriott Resort 25135 Pk Lantern TF: 866-526-7772 ■ Web: www.lagunacliffspa.com	Dana Point	CA	92629	949-487-7576	661-0874
Spa at the Lansdowne Resort 44050 Woodridge Pkwy TF: 877-509-8400 ■ Web: www.lansdowneresort.com	Leesburg	VA	20176	703-729-4036	729-4096
Spa at the Loews Santa Monica Beach Hotel 1700 Ocean Ave Web: www.loewshotels.com/hotels/losangeles	Santa Monica	CA	90401	310-899-4040	899-4045
Spa at the Loews Ventana Canyon Resort 7000 N Resort Dr Web: www.loewshotels.com/hotels/tucson	Tucson	AZ	85750	520-529-7830	529-7854
Spa at the Mandarin Oriental Miami 500 Brickell Key Dr. TF: 800-526-6566 ■ Web: www.mandarinoriental.com	Miami	FL	33131	305-913-8332	913-8326
Spa at the Marriott Harbor Beach Resort 3030 Holiday Dr TF: 866-303-0772 ■ Web: www.marriott.com	Fort Lauderdale	FL	33316	954-765-3032	766-6101
Spa at the Marriott Marco Island Resort Golf Club & Spa 400 S Collier Blvd TF: 800-438-4373 ■ Web: www.marcoislandmarriottspa.com	Marco Island	FL	34145	239-642-2686	389-6938
Spa at the Moody Gardens Hotel 7 Hope Blvd TF: 800-582-4673 ■ Web: www.moodygardenshotel.com	Galveston	TX	77554	409-683-4440	683-4936
Spa at the Norwich Inn 607 W Thames St. TF: 800-275-4772 ■ Web: www.thespaatnorwichinn.com	Norwich	CT	06360	860-886-2401	886-9299
Spa at the Omni Orlando Resort at Championsgate 1500 Masters Blvd TF: 800-843-6664 ■ Web: www.omnihotels.com	Champions Gate	FL	33896	407-390-6663	390-6600
Spa at the Orlando World Center Marriott Resort & Convention Ctr 8701 World Ctr Dr Web: www.marriott.com	Orlando	FL	32821	407-238-8705	238-8777
Spa at the PGA National Resort 450 Avenue of the Champions TF: 800-633-9150 ■ Web: www.pgaresort.com	Palm Beach Gardens	FL	33418	561-627-3111	627-6056
Spa at the Ponte Vedra Inn & Club 200 Ponte Vedra Blvd TF: 800-234-7842 ■ Web: www.pvspa.com	Ponte Vedra Beach	FL	32082	904-273-7700	273-7706
Spa at the Ritz-Carlton Amelia Island 4750 Amelia Island Pkwy TF: 800-241-3333 ■ Web: www.ritzcarlton.com	Amelia Island	FL	32034	904-277-1087	277-1071
Spa at the Ritz-Carlton Bachelor Gulch 0130 Daybreak Ridge TF: 800-241-3333 ■ Web: www.ritzcarlton.com	Avon	CO	81620	970-343-1138	343-1126
Spa at the Ritz-Carlton Coconut Grove 3300 SW 27th Ave TF: 800-241-3333 ■ Web: www.ritzcarlton.com	Coconut Grove	FL	33133	305-644-4680	644-4681
Spa at the Ritz-Carlton Half Moon Bay 1 Miramontes Pt Rd TF: 800-241-3333 ■ Web: www.ritzcarlton.com	Half Moon Bay	CA	94019	650-712-7040	712-7070
Spa at the Ritz-Carlton Huntington Hotel 1401 S Oak Knoll Ave TF: 800-241-3333 ■ Web: www.ritzcarlton.com	Pasadena	CA	91106	626-585-6414	585-6432
Spa at the Ritz-Carlton Key Biscayne 455 Grand Bay Dr TF: 800-241-3333 ■ Web: www.ritzcarlton.com	Key Biscayne	FL	33149	305-365-4158	365-4515
Spa at the Ritz-Carlton Naples 280 Vanderbilt Beach Rd. TF: 800-241-3333 ■ Web: www.ritzcarlton.com	Naples	FL	34108	239-514-6100	514-6160
Spa at the Ritz-Carlton New Orleans 921 Canal St. TF: 800-241-3333 ■ Web: www.ritzcarlton.com	New Orleans	LA	70112	504-670-2929	670-2930
Spa at the Ritz-Carlton Orlando Grande Lakes 4024 Central Florida Pkwy TF: 800-241-3333 ■ Web: www.ritzcarlton.com	Orlando	FL	32837	407-393-4200	393-4022
Spa at the Ritz-Carlton Reynolds Plantation 1 Lake Oconee Tr TF: 800-241-3333 ■ Web: www.ritzcarlton.com	Greensboro	GA	30642	706-467-7185	467-7188
Spa at the Ritz-Carlton Sarasota 1111 Ritz-Carlton Dr. TF: 800-241-3333 ■ Web: www.ritzcarlton.com	Sarasota	FL	34236	941-309-2000	309-2114
Spa at the Ritz-Carlton South Beach 1 Lincoln Rd TF: 800-241-3333 ■ Web: www.ritzcarlton.com	Miami Beach	FL	33139	786-276-4000	276-4100

Name / Address	City	State	Zip	Phone	Fax
Spa at the Saddlebrook Resort 5700 Saddlebrook Way *TF:* 800-729-8383 ■ *Web:* www.saddlebrook.com/spa1.html	Wesley Chapel	FL	33543	813-907-4419	907-4215
Spa at the Sagamore 110 Sagamore Rd *TF:* 800-358-3585 ■ *Web:* www.thesagamore.com	Bolton Landing	NY	12814	518-743-6081	743-6224
Spa at the Salish Lodge 6501 Railroad Ave PO Box 1109 *TF:* 800-272-5474 ■ *Web:* www.salishlodge.com	Snoqualmie	WA	98065	425-831-6535	888-2533
Spa at the Sanctuary on Camelback Mountain 5700 E McDonald Dr *TF:* 800-245-2051 ■ *Web:* www.slh.com/sanctuary	Paradise Valley	AZ	85253	480-948-2100	607-2335
Spa at the Sanderling Resort 1461 Duck Rd *TF:* 800-701-4111 ■ *Web:* www.thesanderling.com	Duck	NC	27949	252-261-7744	261-1352
Spa at the Stoweflake Mountain Resort 1746 Mountain Rd PO Box 369 *TF:* 800-253-2232 ■ *Web:* www.stoweflake.com	Stowe	VT	05672	802-760-1083	253-9264
Spa at the Vail Marriott Mountain Resort 715 W Lionshead Cir *TF:* 800-648-0720 ■ *Web:* www.marriott.com	Vail	CO	81657	970-479-5004	477-5671
Spa at the Villagio Inn 6481 Washington St *TF:* 800-351-1133 ■ *Web:* www.villagio.com	Yountville	CA	94599	707-948-5050	948-5054
Spa at Topnotch at Stowe Resort 4000 Mountain Rd *TF:* 800-451-8686 ■ *Web:* www.topnotchresort.com	Stowe	VT	05672	802-253-6463	253-6415
Spa at White Oaks Conference Resort 253 Taylor Rd *TF:* 800-263-5766 ■ *Web:* www.whiteoaksresort.com	Niagara-on-the-Lake	ON	L0S1J0	905-641-2599	641-2623
Spa du Soleil at the Auberge du Soleil 180 Rutherford Hill Rd *TF:* 800-348-5406 ■ *Web:* www.aubergedusoleil.com/html/spa.shtml	Rutherford	CA	94573	707-967-3159	967-3171
Spa Esmeralda at the Renaissance Esmeralda Resort 44400 Indian Wells Ln *TF:* 800-214-5524 ■ *Web:* www.renaissanceesmeralda.com	Indian Wells	CA	92210	760-836-1265	836-1295
Spa Fusion at the Hilton San Francisco 333 O'Farrell St	San Francisco	CA	94102	415-923-5014	202-7776
Spa Gaucin at the Saint Regis Monarch Beach 1 Monarch Beach Resort *TF:* 800-722-1543 ■ *Web:* www.spagaucin.com	Dana Point	CA	92629	949-234-3367	234-3365
Spa Grande at the Grand Wailea Resort Maui 3850 Wailea Alanui Dr *TF:* 800-772-1933 ■ *Web:* www.grandwailea.com/spa	Wailea	HI	96753	808-875-1234	874-2424
Spa Internazionale at Fisher Island Hotel & Resort 1 Fisher Island Dr *Web:* www.fisherisland.com	Miami	FL	33109	305-535-6030	535-6032
Spa La Quinta at La Quinta Resort 49499 Eisenhower Dr *TF:* 877-527-7721 ■ *Web:* www.laquintaresort.com	La Quinta	CA	92253	760-777-4800	564-5723
Spa Las Palmas at the Marriott Rancho Las Palmas Resort 41000 Bob Hope Dr *TF:* 877-843-7720 ■ *Web:* www.rancholaspalmas.com	Rancho Mirage	CA	92270	760-836-3106	862-4565
Spa Luana at Turtle Bay Resort 57-091 Kamehameha Hwy *TF:* 800-203-3650 ■ *Web:* www.turtlebayresort.com	Kahuku	HI	96731	808-293-8811	447-6742
Spa Moana at the Hyatt Regency Maui Resort & Spa 200 Nohea Kai Dr *TF:* 800-233-1234 ■ *Web:* www.maui.hyatt.com	Lahaina	HI	96761	808-667-4725	667-4503
Spa Moulay at Loews Lake Las Vegas Resort 101 Montelago Blvd *TF:* 800-235-6397 ■ *Web:* www.loewshotels.com	Henderson	NV	89011	702-567-6049	567-6067
Spa Olakino at the Waikiki Beach Marriott Resort 2552 Kalakaua Ave *TF:* 800-367-5370 ■ *Web:* www.spaolakino.com	Honolulu	HI	96815	808-924-2121	924-2255
Spa Pallazo at the Boca Raton Resort & Club 501 E Camino Real *TF:* 877-677-7347 ■ *Web:* www.bocaresort.com	Boca Raton	FL	33432	561-347-4772	447-3183
Spa Shiki at the Lodge of Four Seasons 315 Horseshoe Bend Pkwy *TF:* 800-843-5253 ■ *Web:* www.spashiki.com	Lake Ozark	MO	65049	573-365-8108	365-8101
Spa Suites at Kahala Hotel & Resort 5000 Kahala Ave *TF:* 800-367-2525 ■ *Web:* www.kahalaresort.com	Honolulu	HI	96816	808-739-8938	739-8939
Spa Terre at LaPlaya Beach & Golf Resort 9891 Gulf Shore Dr *Web:* www.laplayaresort.com	Naples	FL	34108	239-597-3123	597-6278
Spa Terre at Paradise Point Resort 1404 Vacation Rd *TF:* 800-344-2626 ■ *Web:* www.paradisepoint.com	San Diego	CA	92109	858-581-5998	490-6688
Spa Terre at the Hotel Viking 1 Bellevue Ave *TF:* 800-556-7126 ■ *Web:* www.hotelviking.com	Newport	RI	02840	401-847-3300	848-4864
Spa Terre at the Inn & Spa at Loretto 211 Old Santa Fe Trail *TF:* 800-727-5531 ■ *Web:* www.innatloretto.com	Santa Fe	NM	87501	505-984-7997	984-7907
Spa Terre at the Little Palm Island Resort 28500 Overseas Hwy *TF:* 800-343-8567 ■ *Web:* www.littlepalmisland.com	Little Torch Key	FL	33042	305-515-3028	515-3009
Spa Toccare at Borgata Hotel Casino 1 Borgata Way *TF:* 866-692-6742 ■ *Web:* www.theborgata.com	Atlantic City	NJ	08401	609-317-7555	317-1039
Spa Torrey Pines at the Lodge at Torrey Pines 11480 N Torrey Pines Rd *TF:* 800-656-0087 ■ *Web:* www.spatorreypines.com	La Jolla	CA	92037	858-777-6690	777-6698
Spa Vita di Lago at The Ritz Carlton Lake Las Vegas 1610 Lake Las Vegas Pkwy *TF:* 800-241-3333 ■ *Web:* www.ritzcarlton.com	Henderson	NV	89011	702-567-4600	567-4601
SpaHalekulani at the Halekulani Hotel 2199 Kalia Rd *TF:* 800-367-2343 ■ *Web:* www.halekulani.com	Honolulu	HI	96815	808-931-5322	931-5337
Stillwater Spa at the Hyatt Regency Coconut Point Resort 5001 Coconut Rd *Web:* www.coconutpoint.hyatt.com	Bonita Springs	FL	34134	239-444-1234	390-4344
Stillwater Spa at the Hyatt Regency Newport 1 Goat Island *TF:* 800-233-1234 ■ *Web:* www.newport.hyatt.com	Newport	RI	02840	401-851-3225	851-3201
Sunrise Springs 242 Los Pinos Rd *TF:* 800-955-0028 ■ *Web:* www.sunrisesprings.com	Santa Fe	NM	87507	505-471-3600	471-7365
Tamaya Spa at the Hyatt Regency Tamaya Resort 1300 Tuyuna Tr *Web:* tamaya.hyatt.com	Santa Ana Pueblo	NM	87004	505-771-6134	771-6232
Tampa Marriott Waterside Hotel & Marina 700 S Florida Ave *TF:* 888-268-1616 ■ *Web:* www.marriott.com	Tampa	FL	33602	813-204-6300	204-6373
Ten Thousand Waves Japanese Health Spa 3451 Hyde Pk Rd *Web:* www.tenthousandwaves.com	Santa Fe	NM	87501	505-982-9304	
Turtle Cove Spa at Mountain Harbor Resort 181 Club House Dr *TF:* 800-832-2276 ■ *Web:* www.turtlecovespa.com	Mount Ida	AR	71957	870-867-1220	867-4678
Vail Mountain Lodge & Spa The 352 E Meadow Dr *TF:* 888-794-0410 ■ *Web:* www.vailmountainlodge.com	Vail	CO	81657	970-476-0700	477-3225
Verandah Club & Spa at the Hilton Anatole 2201 Stemmons Fwy *Web:* www.verandahclub.com	Dallas	TX	75207	214-761-7878	761-7835
Village Bay Spa at Lake Arrowhead Resort 27984 Hwy 189 *TF:* 800-800-6792 ■ *Web:* www.laresort.com	Lake Arrowhead	CA	92352	909-744-3000	744-3023
Well Spa at Miramonte Resort 45000 Indian Wells Ln *TF:* 866-843-9355 ■ *Web:* www.miramonteresort.com	Indian Wells	CA	92210	760-837-1652	837-2330
Westglow Resort & Spa 224 Westglow Cir *TF:* 800-562-0807 ■ *Web:* www.westglowresortandspa.com	Blowing Rock	NC	28605	828-295-4463	295-5115
Westin Kierland Resort & Spa 6902 E Greenway Pkwy *TF:* 888-625-5144 ■ *Web:* www.kierlandresort.com	Scottsdale	AZ	85254	480-624-1000	624-1001
Westin Maui Resort & Spa The 2365 Kaanapali Pkwy *TF:* 866-716-8112 ■ *Web:* www.westinmaui.com	Lahaina	HI	96761	808-667-2525	661-5764
Westin Resort & Spa 4090 Whistler Way *TF:* 888-634-5577 ■ *Web:* www.westernwhistler.com	Whistler	BC	V0N1B4	604-905-5000	905-5640
Willow Stream Spa at Fairmont Scottsdale Princess 7575 E Princess Dr *TF:* 800-908-9540 ■ *Web:* www.willowstream.com	Scottsdale	AZ	85255	480-585-2732	585-0086
Willow Stream Spa at the Fairmont Banff Springs 405 Spray Ave *TF:* 800-404-1772 ■ *Web:* www.willowstream.com	Banff	AB	T1L1J4	403-762-1772	762-1766
Willow Stream Spa at the Fairmont Empress 633 Humboldt St *TF:* 866-854-7444 ■ *Web:* www.fairmont.com	Victoria	BC	V8W1A6	250-995-4650	995-4651
Willow Stream Spa at the Turnberry Isle Resort & Club 19999 W Country Club Dr *TF:* 866-840-8069 ■ *Web:* www.fairmont.com	Miami	FL	33180	305-932-6200	933-6554
Wintergreen Resort Rt 664 PO Box 706 *TF:* 800-266-2444 ■ *Web:* www.wintergreenresort.com	Wintergreen	VA	22958	434-325-8185	
ZaSpa at Hotel ZaZa 2332 Leonard St *TF:* 800-597-8399 ■ *Web:* www.hotelzaza.com	Dallas	TX	75201	214-550-9492	468-8397
Arizona Biltmore Resort & Spa 2400 E Missouri *TF:* 800-950-0086 ■ *Web:* www.arizonabiltmore.com	Phoenix	AZ	85016	602-955-6600	381-7600
Echo Valley Ranch & Spa Clinton PO Box 16 **Fax Area Code:* 778 ■ *TF:* 800-253-8831 ■ *Web:* www.evranch.com	Jesmond	BC	V0K1K0	604-988-3230	340-1077*
Estancia La Jolla Hotel & Spa 9700 N Torrey Pines Rd *Web:* www.estancialajolla.com	La Jolla	CA	92037	858-550-1000	550-1001
Indian Springs Resort & Spa 1712 Lincoln Ave *Web:* www.indianspringscalistoga.com	Calistoga	CA	94515	707-942-4913	942-4919
Montage Resort & Spa Laguna Beach 30801 S Coast Hwy *Web:* www.montagelagunabeach.com	Laguna Beach	CA	92651	949-715-6000	715-6100
Pala Casino Resort & Spa 35008 Pala-Temecula Rd *TF:* 877-946-7252 ■ *Web:* www.palacasino.com	Pala	CA	92059	760-510-5100	510-5191
Resort at Squaw Creek 400 Squaw Creek Rd PO Box 3333 *TF:* 800-327-3353 ■ *Web:* www.squawcreek.com	Olympic Valley	CA	96146	530-583-6300	581-6632
Omni Interlocken Resort 500 Interlocken Blvd *TF:* 800-843-6664 ■ *Web:* www.omnihotels.com	Broomfield	CO	80021	303-438-6600	464-3236
Peaks Resort & Golden Door Spa 136 Country Club Dr **Fax Area Code:* 970 ■ *TF:* 866-282-4557 ■ *Web:* www.thepeaksresort.com	Telluride	CO	81435	800-789-2220	728-6175*
Safety Harbor Resort & Spa 105 N Bayshore Dr *TF:* 888-237-8772 ■ *Web:* www.safetyharborspa.com	Safety Harbor	FL	34695	727-726-1161	726-4268
Cape Codder Resort & Spa 1225 Iyanough Rd Rt 132 Bearse's Way *TF:* 888-297-2200 ■ *Web:* www.capecodderresort.com	Hyannis	MA	02601	508-771-3000	790-8145
Cranwell Resort Spa & Golf Club 55 Lee Rd *TF:* 800-272-6935 ■ *Web:* www.cranwell.com	Lenox	MA	01240	413-637-1364	637-4364
Green Valley Ranch Resort Casino & Spa 2300 Paseo Verde Pkwy *TF:* 866-617-0777 ■ *Web:* www.greenvalleyranchresort.com	Henderson	NV	89052	702-617-7777	617-7778
Grove Park Inn Resort & Spa 290 Macon Ave *TF:* 800-438-5800 ■ *Web:* www.groveparkinn.com	Asheville	NC	28804	828-252-2711	253-7053
Felicita Resort 2201 Fishing Creek Valley Rd *TF:* 888-321-3713 ■ *Web:* www.felicitaresort.com	Harrisburg	PA	17112	717-599-5301	599-7714
Homestead Resort 700 N Homestead Dr *TF:* 800-327-7220 ■ *Web:* www.homesteadresort.com	Midway	UT	84049	435-654-1102	654-5087
Greenbrier The 300 W Main St *TF:* 800-453-4858 ■ *Web:* www.greenbrier.com	White Sulphur Springs	WV	24986	304-536-1110	536-7854
Abbey Resort & Fontana Spa 269 Fontana Blvd *TF:* 800-709-1323 ■ *Web:* www.theabbeyresort.com	Fontana	WI	53125	262-275-9000	275-3264

711 SPEAKERS BUREAUS

Company / Address	City	State	Zip	Phone	Fax
AEI Speakers Bureau 214 Lincoln St Suite 113	Boston	MA	02134	617-782-3111	782-3444
TF: 800-447-7325 ■ *Web:* www.aeispeakers.com					
Agricultural Speakers Network 10436 Oak Ridge Dr PO Box 810	Zionsville	IN	46077	317-873-9797	873-0800
TF Sales: 800-222-1556 ■ *Web:* www.agriculturalspeakers.com					
All-Star Agency Speakers Bureau 4829 Powell Rd	Fairfax	VA	22032	703-503-9438	503-5823
TF: 800-736-0031 ■ *Web:* www.allstaragency.com					
Ambassador Speakers Bureau PO Box 50358	Nashville	TN	37205	615-370-4700	661-4344
Web: www.ambassadorspeakers.com					
American Program Bureau Inc 36 Crafts St	Newton	MA	02458	617-965-6600	965-6610
TF: 800-225-4575 ■ *Web:* www.apbspeakers.com					
Atlantic Speakers Bureau 980 Rt 730	Scotch Ridge	NB	E3L5L2	506-465-0990	465-0813
TF: 866-465-0990 ■ *Web:* www.asb.nb.ca					
Barber & Assoc 1308 Sumac Dr PO Box 11669	Knoxville	TN	37939	865-546-0000	
Web: www.barberusa.com					
Brooks International Speakers Bureau 763 Santa Fe Dr	Denver	CO	80204	303-825-8700	825-8701
Web: www.brooksinternational.com					
Capitol City Speakers Bureau 1620 S 5th St	Springfield	IL	62703	217-544-8552	544-1496
TF: 800-397-3183 ■ *Web:* www.capcityspeakers.com					
Executive Speakers Bureau 8567 Cordes Cir	Germantown	TN	38139	901-754-9404	756-4237
TF: 800-754-9404 ■ *Web:* www.executivespeakers.com					
Five Star Speakers & Trainers LLC 7500 College Blvd	Overland Park	KS	66210	913-648-6480	648-6484
Web: www.fivestarspeakers.com					
Garrett Speakers International Inc 1203 Olde Towne Dr	Irving	TX	75061	972-513-0054	513-0540
TF: 800-787-2840 ■ *Web:* www.garrettspeakers.com					
Greater Talent Network Inc 437 5th Ave 7th Fl	New York	NY	10016	212-645-4200	627-1471
TF: 800-326-4211 ■ *Web:* www.greatertalent.com					
Harry Walker Agency Inc (HWA) 355 Lexington Ave 21st Fl	New York	NY	10017	646-227-4900	227-4901
Web: www.harrywalker.com					
High 5 Communications LLC 1375 E 150 S	Hyrum	UT	84319	435-750-0062	890-6157*
**Fax Area Code:* 888 ■ *Web:* www.high5communications.com					
IMG Speakers 825 7th Ave 8th Fl	New York	NY	10019	212-489-8300	246-1596
Web: www.imgspeakers.com					
International Speakers Bureau Inc 2128 Boll St	Dallas	TX	75204	214-744-3885	744-3888
TF: 800-842-4483 ■ *Web:* www.internationalspeakers.com					
Keppler Assoc Inc 4350 Fairfax Dr # 700	Arlington	VA	22203	703-516-4000	516-4819
Web: www.kepplerspeakers.com					
Key Speakers Bureau Inc 3500 E Coast Hwy Suite 6	Corona del Mar	CA	92625	949-675-7856	675-1478
TF: 800-675-1175 ■ *Web:* www.keyspeakers.com					
Leading Authorities Inc 1990 M St Suite 800	Washington	DC	20036	202-783-0300	783-0301
TF: 800-773-2537 ■ *Web:* www.leadingauthorities.com					
National Speakers Bureau 1663 W 7th Ave	Vancouver	BC	V6J1S4	604-734-3663	734-8906
TF: 800-661-4110 ■ *Web:* www.nsb.com					
National Speakers Bureau Inc 14047 W Petronalla Dr Suite 102	Libertyville	IL	60048	847-295-1122	367-5499
TF: 800-323-9442 ■ *Web:* www.nationalspeakers.com					
Professional Speakers Network 10436 Oak Ridge Dr PO Box 810	Zionsville	IN	46077	317-873-9797	873-0800
TF Sales: 800-222-1556 ■ *Web:* www.tillergroup.com/_psn					
Santa Barbara Speakers Bureau 145 Canon Dr	Santa Barbara	CA	93105	805-682-7474	563-1028
Web: www.sbsb.net					
Speak Inc Speakers Bureau 10680 Treena St Suite 230	San Diego	CA	92131	858-228-3771	228-3989
Web: www.speakinc.com					
Speakers Guild Inc PO Box 1540	Sandwich	MA	02563	508-888-6702	888-6771
TF: 800-343-4530 ■ *Web:* www.speakersguild.com					
Speakers Unlimited 5565 Woodridge Dr	Columbus	OH	43213	614-864-3703	864-3876
Web: www.speakersunlimited.com					
Speakers.com 130 Lubrano Dr Suite 110	Annapolis	MD	21401	410-897-1970	897-1971
Web: www.speakers.com					
Steven Barclay Agency 12 Western Ave	Petaluma	CA	94952	707-773-0654	778-1868
TF: 888-965-7323 ■ *Web:* www.barclayagency.com					
Walters International Speakers Bureau 18825 Hicrest Rd	Glendora	CA	91741	626-335-8069	335-6127
Web: www.walters-intl.com					
Washington Speakers Bureau 1663 Prince St	Alexandria	VA	22314	703-684-0555	684-9378
Web: www.washingtonspeakers.com					
World Class Speakers & Entertainers 5200 Kanan Rd Suite 210	Agoura Hills	CA	91301	818-991-5400	991-2226
Web: www.wcspeakers.com					

712 SPEED CHANGERS, INDUSTRIAL HIGH SPEED DRIVES, GEARS

SEE ALSO Aircraft Parts & Auxiliary Equipment p. 1387; Automotive Parts & Supplies - Mfr p. 1497; Controls & Relays - Electrical p. 1747; Machine Shops p. 2190; Motors (Electric) & Generators p. 2263; Power Transmission Equipment - Mechanical p. 2442

Company / Address	City	State	Zip	Phone	Fax
Ac Technology Corp 630 Douglas St	Uxbridge	MA	01569	508-278-9100	
TF: 800-217-9100 ■ *Web:* www.actech.com					
Altra Holdings Inc 14 Hayward St	Quincy	MA	02171	617-328-3300	479-6238
NASDAQ: AIMC ■ *TF Cust Svc:* 888-999-9860 ■ *Web:* www.altramotion.com					
Amarillo Gear Co 2401 W Sundown Ln	Amarillo	TX	79118	806-622-1273	622-3258
Web: www.amarillogear.com					
Auburn Gear Inc 400 E Auburn Dr	Auburn	IN	46706	260-925-3200	925-4725
Web: www.auburngear.com					
Bison Gear & Engineering Corp 3850 Ohio Ave	Saint Charles	IL	60174	630-377-4327	377-6777
TF: 800-282-4766 ■ *Web:* www.bisongear.com					
Charles Bond Co 11 Green St PO Box 105	Christiana	PA	17509	610-593-5171	593-5378
TF Cust Svc: 800-922-0125 ■ *Web:* www.bondgear.com					
Chicago Gear-DO James Corp 2823 W Fulton St	Chicago	IL	60612	773-638-0508	638-7161
Web: www.oc-gear.com					
Cleveland Gear Co 3249 E 80th St	Cleveland	OH	44104	216-641-9000	641-2731
TF: 800-423-3169 ■ *Web:* www.clevelandgear.com					
Columbia Gear Corp 530 County Rd 50	Avon	MN	56310	320-356-7301	356-2131
TF: 800-323-9838 ■ *Web:* www.columbiagear.com					
Cone Drive Operations Inc - A Textron Co 240 E 12th St	Traverse City	MI	49685	231-946-8410	907-2663*
**Fax Area Code:* 888 ■ *TF Sales:* 888-994-2663 ■ *Web:* www.textronpt.com					
Cotta Transmission Co LLC 1301 Prince Hall Dr	Beloit	WI	53511	608-368-5600	368-5605
Web: www.cotta.com					
Dalton Gear Co 212 Colfax Ave N	Minneapolis	MN	55405	612-374-2150	374-2467
TF: 800-328-7485 ■ *Web:* www.daltongear.com					
Danaher Motion 1500 Mittel Blvd	Wood Dale	IL	60191	630-860-7300	694-3305
TF: 866-993-2624 ■ *Web:* www.danahermotion.com					
Designatronics Inc 2101 Jericho Tpke	New Hyde Park	NY	11040	516-328-3300	326-8827
TF Orders: 800-345-1144 ■ *Web:* www.sdp-si.com					
Electro Sales Inc 100 Fellsway W	Somerville	MA	02145	617-666-0500	628-2800
TF: 888-789-0500 ■ *Web:* www.electrosales.com					
Emerson Control Techniques Drives Inc 12005 Technology Dr	Eden Prairie	MN	55344	952-995-8000	
Fairchild Industrial Products Co 3920 W Pt Blvd	Winston-Salem	NC	27103	336-659-3400	659-9323*
**Fax:* Sales ■ *TF:* 800-423-1093 ■ *Web:* www.fairchildproducts.com					
Fairfield Mfg Co Inc 2309 Concord Rd	Lafayette	IN	47909	765-772-4000	772-4001
Web: www.fairfieldmfg.com					
Gear Motions Inc 1750 Milton Ave	Syracuse	NY	13209	315-488-0100	488-0196
Web: www.gearmotions.com					
Gear Works The 500 S Portland St	Seattle	WA	98108	206-762-3333	762-3704
Web: www.thegearworks.com					
Geartronics Industries Inc 100 Chelmsford Rd	North Billerica	MA	01862	978-663-6566	667-3130
Web: www.geartronics.com					
Hankscraft Inc 300 Wengel Dr	Reedsburg	WI	53959	608-524-4341	524-4342
Web: www.hankscraft-motors.com					
Horsburgh & Scott Co 5114 Hamilton Ave	Cleveland	OH	44114	216-431-3900	432-5850
Web: www.horsburgh-scott.com					
Hub City Inc 2914 Industrial Ave	Aberdeen	SD	57401	605-225-0360	225-0567
TF: 800-482-2489 ■ *Web:* www.hubcityinc.com					
Imperial Electric Co 1503 Exeter Rd	Akron	OH	44306	330-734-3600	734-3601
Web: www.imperialelectric.com					
Industrial Motion Control LLC 1444 S Wolf Rd	Wheeling	IL	60090	847-459-5200	459-3064
Web: www.camcoindex.com					
Kurz Electric Solutions Inc 1325 McMahon Dr	Neenah	WI	54956	920-886-8200	886-8201
TF: 800-776-3629 ■ *Web:* www.kurz.com					
L & H Industrial Inc 913 L J Ct	Gillette	WY	82718	307-682-7238	686-1646
Web: www.lnh.net					
Leedy Mfg Co 210 Hall St SW	Grand Rapids	MI	49507	616-245-0517	245-3888
Web: www.leedymfg.com					
Leeson Electric Corp 2100 Washington St	Grafton	WI	53024	262-377-8810	
Web: www.leeson.com					
Martin Sprocket & Gear Inc 3100 Sprocket Dr PO Box 91588	Arlington	TX	76015	817-258-3000	258-3333
Web: www.martinsprocket.com					
Milwaukee Gear Co 5150 N Port Washington Rd	Milwaukee	WI	53217	414-962-3532	962-2774
TF: 800-959-1142 ■ *Web:* www.milwaukeegear.com					
Nixon Gear Inc 1750 Milton Ave	Syracuse	NY	13209	315-488-0100	488-0196
Web: www.gearmotions.com/nixongear.htm					
Nuttall Gear LLC 2221 Niagra Falls Blvd	Niagara Falls	NY	14304	716-298-4100	298-4101
TF: 800-432-0121 ■ *Web:* www.nuttallgear.com					
Oliver Gear Inc 1120 Niagara St	Buffalo	NY	14213	716-885-1080	885-1145
Web: www.gearmotions.com					
Peerless-Winsmith Inc 1401 W Market St	Warren	OH	44485	330-399-3651	393-6041
TF: 800-676-3651 ■ *Web:* www.winsmith.com					
Perfection Gear Inc 9 N Bear Creek Rd	Asheville	NC	28806	828-253-0000	253-2649
TF: 800-532-5314					
Piller Inc 45 Turner Rd	Middletown	NY	10941	845-695-5300	692-0295
TF: 800-597-6937 ■ *Web:* www.piller.com					
Regal-Beloit Corp 200 State St	Beloit	WI	53511	608-364-8800	364-8818
NYSE: RBC ■ *Web:* www.regalbeloit.com					
Regal-Beloit Corp Durst Div PO Box 298	Beloit	WI	53512	608-365-2563	365-2182
TF: 800-356-0775 ■ *Web:* www.durstdrives.com					
Rexnord Industries LLC 4701 Greenfield Ave	Milwaukee	WI	53214	414-643-3300	643-3078
TF: 800-852-3255 ■ *Web:* www.rexnord.com					
Richmond Gear PO Box 238	Liberty	SC	29657	864-843-9231	843-1276
TF Sales: 800-476-6446 ■ *Web:* www.richmondgear.com					
Rush Gears Inc 550 Virginia Dr	Fort Washington	PA	19034	215-542-9000	635-6273*
**Fax Area Code:* 800 ■ *TF:* 800-523-2576 ■ *Web:* www.rushgear.com					
Schafer Gear Works Inc 4701 Nimtz Pkwy	South Bend	IN	46628	574-234-4116	234-4115
Web: www.schafergear.com					
SEW-Eurodrive Inc 1295 Old Spartanburg Hwy	Lyman	SC	29365	864-439-7537	439-0566
Web: www.seweurodrive.com					
Sterling Electric Inc 7997 Allison Ave	Indianapolis	IN	46268	317-872-0471	872-0907
TF Cust Svc: 800-654-6220 ■ *Web:* www.sterlingelectric.com					
Sumitomo Machinery Corp of America 4200 Holland Blvd	Chesapeake	VA	23323	757-485-3355	485-7490
TF: 800-762-9256 ■ *Web:* www.smcyclo.com					
TECO-Westinghouse Motor Co 5100 N IH-35	Round Rock	TX	78681	512-255-4141	244-5512
TF: 800-451-8798 ■ *Web:* www.tecowestinghouse.com					
Textron Fluid & Power Inc 40 Westminster St	Providence	RI	02903	401-588-3400	621-5045
Web: www.textron.com					

	City	State	Zip	Phone	Fax
Westerman Cos The 245 N Broad St *TF:* 800-338-8265 ■ *Web:* www.westermancompanies.com	Bremen	OH	43107	740-569-4143	569-4111

713 SPORTING GOODS

SEE ALSO All-Terrain Vehicles p. 1394; Bicycles & Bicycle Parts & Accessories p. 1524; Boats - Recreational p. 1531; Cord & Twine p. 1763; Exercise & Fitness Equipment p. 1835; Firearms & Ammunition (Non-Military) p. 1846; Gym & Playground Equipment p. 2002; Handbags, Totes, Backpacks p. 2003; Motor Vehicles - Commercial & Special Purpose p. 2260; Personal Protective Equipment & Clothing p. 2409; Snowmobiles p. 2658; Swimming Pools p. 2680; Tarps, Tents, Covers p. 2682

	City	State	Zip	Phone	Fax
40-Up Tackle Co 16 Union Ave PO Box 442 *Web:* www.40uptackleco.com	Westfield	MA	01086	413-562-0385	
Abel Automatics Inc 165 Aviador St *TF:* 800-848-7335 ■ *Web:* www.abelreels.com	Camarillo	CA	93010	805-484-8789	482-0701
Acme Tackle Co Inc 77 Bucklin St *Web:* www.acmetackle.com	Providence	RI	02907	401-331-6437	272-7821
Acushnet Co 333 Bridge St **Fax:* Hum Res ■ *TF:* 800-225-8500 ■ *Web:* www.acushnet.com	Fairhaven	MA	02719	508-979-2000	979-3900*
AcuSport Corp 1 Hunter Pl **Fax:* Sales ■ *TF:* 800-543-3150 ■ *Web:* www.acusport.com	Bellefontaine	OH	43311	937-593-7010	592-5625*
Adams Golf 2801 E Plano Pkwy *TF:* 800-709-6142 ■ *Web:* www.adamsgolf.com	Plano	TX	75074	972-673-9000	398-8818
Adams USA Inc 610 S Jefferson Ave *TF:* 800-251-6857 ■ *Web:* www.adamsusa.com	Cookeville	TN	38501	931-526-2109	526-8357
Air Chair Inc 2175 N Kiowa Blvd Suite 101 *Web:* www.airchair.com	Lake Havasu City	AZ	86403	928-505-2226	505-2229
Aldila Inc 14145 Danielson St Suite B *PINK: ALDA* ■ *TF:* 800-854-2786 ■ *Web:* www.aldila.com	Poway	CA	92064	858-513-1801	513-1870
Alpine Archery 3101 N S Hwy PO Box 319 *Web:* www.alpinearchery.com	Lewiston	ID	83501	208-746-4717	746-1635
American Classic Sales 1142 S 2475 W *TF:* 888-733-5763 ■ *Web:* www.americanclassic.net	Salt Lake City	UT	84104	801-977-3935	977-0529
American Sports 74 Albe Dr Suite 1 *Web:* www.americansports.com	Newark	DE	19702	302-369-9480	250-4024
AMF Bowling Worldwide Inc 8100 AMF Dr *TF:* 800-342-5263 ■ *Web:* www.amf.com	Mechanicsville	VA	23111	804-730-4000	730-0923
Aqua-Leisure Industries Inc PO Box 239 **Fax Area Code:* 508 ■ *TF:* 866-807-3998 ■ *Web:* www.aqualeisure.com	Avon	MA	02322	866-807-3998	587-5318*
Aqualung America Inc 2340 Cousteau Ct *TF:* 800-635-3483 ■ *Web:* www.aqualung.com	Vista	CA	92083	760-597-5000	597-4900
Arrow Surfboards 1115 Thompson Ave Suite 7 *Web:* www.arrowsurfboards.com	Santa Cruz	CA	95062	831-462-2791	
Atomic Ski USA Inc 9 Columbia Dr	Amherst	NH	03031	603-880-6143	880-6099
Austin Surfboards 1244 Jensen Dr Suite 101 *Web:* www.austinsurfboards.com	Virginia Beach	VA	23451	757-425-6025	
Bankshot Sports Organization 303 Bradley Ave *TF:* 800-933-0140 ■ *Web:* www.bankshot.com	Rockville	MD	20851	301-309-0260	309-0263
Bare Sportswear Corp 1755 Grant Ave **Fax Area Code:* 604 ■ *TF:* 800-663-0111 ■ *Web:* www.baresports.com	Blaine	WA	98230	360-332-2700	530-8812*
Bauer Premium Fly Reels 585 Clover Ln # 1 *TF:* 888-484-4165 ■ *Web:* www.bauerflyreel.com	Ashland	OR	97520	541-488-8246	488-8244
Bear Creek Canoes Inc 72 Swamp Rd & Rt 107 *TF:* 800-241-2268 ■ *Web:* www.bearcreekcanoes.com	Sebago	ME	04029	207-647-5850	
Bell Sports Corp 6225 N State Hwy 161 Suite 300 **Fax Area Code:* 214 ■ *TF:* 866-525-2355 ■ *Web:* www.bellsports.com	Irving	TX	75038	469-417-6600	492-1639*
Big Rock Sports LLC 173 Hankison Dr *Web:* www.bigrocksports.com	Newport	NC	28570	252-808-3500	726-8352
Biscayne Rod Mfg Inc 425 E 9th St *TF:* 866-969-0808 ■ *Web:* www.biscaynerod.com	Hialeah	FL	33010	305-884-0808	884-3017
Bison Inc 603 L St **Fax Area Code:* 800 ■ *TF:* 800-247-7668 ■ *Web:* www.bisoninc.com	Lincoln	NE	68508	402-474-3353	638-0698*
Black Knight USA 5355 Sierra Rd *TF:* 800-535-3300 ■ *Web:* www.bksquash.com	San Jose	CA	95132	408-923-7777	923-7794
Bombardier Recreational Products (BRP) 565 de la Montagne *Web:* www.brp.com	Valcourt	QC	J0E2L0	450-532-2211	532-5133
Bravo Sports Corp 12801 Carmenita Rd *TF Cust Svc:* 800-234-9737 ■ *Web:* www.bravosportscorp.com	Santa Fe Springs	CA	90670	562-484-5100	484-5183
Bridgestone Golf Inc 15320 Industrial Pk Blvd NE *TF:* 800-358-6319 ■ *Web:* www.bridgestonegolf.com	Covington	GA	30014	770-787-7400	787-4915
Brine Inc 32125 Hollingsworth Ave **Fax Area Code:* 586 ■ **Fax:* Cust Svc ■ *TF:* 800-968-7845 ■ *Web:* www.brine.com	Warren	MI	48092	508-478-3250	446-1162*
Brunswick Bowling & Billiards 1 N Field Ct *Web:* www.brunswick.com	Lake Forest	IL	60045	847-735-4700	735-4501
Brunswick Corp 1 N Field Ct *NYSE: BC* ■ *Web:* www.brunswick.com	Lake Forest	IL	60045	847-735-4700	735-4765
Bullet Weights Inc 182 S Apollo St *TF:* 800-872-0131 ■ *Web:* www.bulletweights.com	Alda	NE	68810	308-382-7436	382-2906
Burton Snowboards Inc 80 Industrial Pkwy *TF:* 800-881-3138 ■ *Web:* www.global.burton.com	Burlington	VT	05401	802-862-4500	660-3250
Byrne Surfboards 3205 Production Ave Suite J *Web:* www.byrnesurf.com	Oceanside	CA	92058	760-721-6094	
Callaway Golf Co 2180 Rutherford Rd *NYSE: ELY* ■ *TF:* 800-588-9836 ■ *Web:* www.callawaygolf.com	Carlsbad	CA	92008	760-931-1771	931-8013
Carry-Lite Decoys PO Box 1587 *TF:* 800-531-1201 ■ *Web:* www.carrylitedecoys.com	Fort Smith	AR	72902	479-782-8971	782-5950
Carstens Industries Inc 105 N 8th Ave W *Web:* www.carstensindustries.com	Melrose	MN	56352	320-256-3919	256-4052
Cascade Designs Inc 4000 1st Ave S *TF Cust Svc:* 800-531-9531 ■ *Web:* www.cascadedesigns.com	Seattle	WA	98134	206-624-8573	505-9525
Caviness Woodworking Inc 200 N Aycock Ave PO Box 710 *TF:* 800-626-5195 ■ *Web:* www.cavinesspaddles.com	Calhoun City	MS	38916	662-628-5195	628-8580
Century Sports Inc 1995 Rutgers University Blvd *TF Sales:* 800-526-7548 ■ *Web:* www.centurysportsinc.com	Lakewood	NJ	08701	732-905-4422	901-7766
Century Tool & Mfg Co Inc 1462 US Rt 20 Bypass PO Box 188 *TF:* 800-435-4525 ■ *Web:* www.centurycamping.com	Cherry Valley	IL	61016	815-332-4951	332-2090
Champion Shuffleboard Ltd 7216 Burns St *TF:* 800-826-7856 ■ *Web:* www.championshuffleboard.com	Richland Hills	TX	76118	817-284-3499	595-1506
Cleveland Golf Co 5601 Skylab Rd *TF Cust Svc:* 800-999-6263 ■ *Web:* www.clevelandgolf.com	Huntington Beach	CA	92647	800-999-6263	831-6624
Cobra Mfg Co Inc 7909 E 148th St S *TF:* 800-352-6272 ■ *Web:* www.cobraarchery.com	Bixby	OK	74008	918-366-3634	
Coleman Co Inc 3600 N Hydraulic *TF Cust Svc:* 800-835-3278 ■ *Web:* www.coleman.com	Wichita	KS	67219	316-832-2653	832-3060
Colorado Classic Co 4030 N Sinton Rd *Web:* www.coloradoclassic.com	Colorado Springs	CO	80907	719-633-2064	633-2087
Columbia Industries Inc 5005 W Ave **Fax:* Hum Res ■ *TF Cust Svc:* 800-531-5920 ■ *Web:* www.columbia300.com	San Antonio	TX	78213	210-344-9211	349-8672*
Confluence Watersports Co 111 Kayaker Way *TF:* 800-311-7245 ■ *Web:* www.confluencewatersports.com	Easley	SC	29642	864-859-7518	855-5995
Connelly Billiard Mfg 1440 S Euclid Ave *TF:* 800-861-8619 ■ *Web:* www.connellybilliards.com	Tucson	AZ	85713	520-624-6000	624-0077
Connelly Skis Inc 20621 52nd Ave W *TF:* 800-234-7547 ■ *Web:* www.connellyskis.com	Lynnwood	WA	98036	425-775-5416	778-9590
Cortland Line Co Inc 3736 Kellogg Rd *TF:* 800-847-6787 ■ *Web:* www.cortlandline.com	Cortland	NY	13045	607-756-2851	753-8835
Coverstar LLC 1795 W 200 N *TF:* 800-617-7283 ■ *Web:* www.coverstar.com	Lindon	UT	84042	801-373-4777	373-5095
Creative Playthings Ltd 33 Loring Dr *Web:* www.creativeplaythings.com	Framingham	MA	01702	508-620-0900	872-3120
Current Designs PO Box 247 *TF:* 877-655-1822 ■ *Web:* www.cdkayak.com	Winona	MN	55987	507-454-5430	454-5448
Daisy Outdoor Products 400 W Stribling Dr *TF:* 800-643-3458 ■ *Web:* www.daisy.com	Rogers	AR	72756	479-636-1200	636-1601
Daiwa Corp 12851 Midway Pl *TF:* 800-736-4653 ■ *Web:* www.daiwa.com	Cerritos	CA	90703	562-802-9589	404-6212
DAKINE 408 Columbia St *TF:* 800-827-7466 ■ *Web:* www.dakine.com	Hood River	OR	97031	541-386-3166	386-6199
Donek Snowboards Inc 35907 E 88 Ave PO Box 580 *TF:* 877-533-6635 ■ *Web:* www.donek.com	Watkins	CO	80137	303-261-0100	261-9988
Douglas Industries Co 3441 S 11th Ave *TF:* 800-553-8907 ■ *Web:* www.douglas-sports.com	Eldridge	IA	52748	563-285-4162	285-4163
Dover Saddlery Inc 525 Great Rd PO Box 1100 *NASDAQ: DOVR* ■ *TF:* 800-406-8204 ■ *Web:* www.doversaddlery.com	Littleton	MA	01460	978-952-8062	952-8063
Dynastar/Lange 1441 Ute Blvd Suite 200 PO Box 981060 *TF:* 888-243-6722 ■ *Web:* www.dynastar.com	Park City	UT	84098	435-252-3300	252-3301
Eagle One Golf Products Inc 1340 N Jefferson St *TF:* 800-448-4409 ■ *Web:* www.eagleonegolf.com	Anaheim	CA	92807	714-983-0050	997-3400
Eagle Sports 7223 Wynnwood Ln *TF:* 800-862-4424 ■ *Web:* www.eaglesports.com	Houston	TX	77008	713-861-0427	861-0799
Eastaboga Tackle Mfg Co Inc 261 Mudd St *Web:* www.eastabogatackle.com	Eastaboga	AL	36260	256-831-9682	835-2524
Easton Sports Inc 7855 Haskell Ave Suite 200 *TF:* 800-632-7866 ■ *Web:* www.eastonsports.com	Van Nuys	CA	91406	818-782-6445	782-6445
Easton Tru-Flite LLC 2709 S Freeman Rd *TF:* 800-348-2224	Monticello	IN	47960	574-583-5131	583-9271
Easton-bell Sports Inc 7855 Haskell Ave Suite 200 *TF:* 800-632-7866 ■ *Web:* www.eastonbellsports.com	Van Nuys	CA	91406	818-902-5800	
Easy Rider Canoe & Kayak Co PO Box 88108 *Web:* www.easyriderkayaks.com	Seattle	WA	98138	425-228-3633	277-8778
Ebonite International Inc 1813 W 7th St *TF:* 800-626-8350 ■ *Web:* www.ebonite.com	Hopkinsville	KY	42240	270-881-1200	881-1201
Eddyline Kayaks 11977 W Star Ln *Web:* www.eddyline.com	Burlington	WA	98233	360-757-2300	757-2302
Ellett Bros Inc 267 Columbia Ave *TF Sales:* 800-845-3711 ■ *Web:* www.ellettbrothers.com	Chapin	SC	29036	803-345-3751	345-1820
Eppinger Mfg Co 6340 Schaefer Rd *TF:* 888-771-8277 ■ *Web:* www.eppinger.net	Dearborn	MI	48126	313-582-3205	582-0110
Escalade Inc 817 Maxwell Ave *NASDAQ: ESCA* ■ *TF Cust Svc:* 800-426-1421 ■ *Web:* www.escaladesports.com	Evansville	IN	47711	812-467-1200	467-1300
Everlast Worldwide Inc 183 Madison Ave Suite 1701 *Web:* www.everlast.com	New York	NY	10018	212-239-0990	239-4261
Facility Merchandising Inc 5959 Topanga Canyon Blvd Suite 125 *Web:* www.facilitymerchandising.com	Woodland Hills	CA	91367	818-703-6690	703-6576
Fly Logic Inc 511 Broadway Ave *TF:* 888-359-5644 ■ *Web:* www.flylogic.com	Melba	ID	83641	208-495-2090	495-2064
Folbot Inc 4209 Pace St *TF:* 800-533-5099 ■ *Web:* www.folbot.com	Charleston	SC	29405	843-744-3483	744-7783

	City	State	ZIP	Phone	Fax
Franklin Sports Inc 17 Campanelli Pkwy PO Box 508 *TF:* 800-225-8649 ■ *Web:* www.franklinsports.com	Stoughton	MA	02072	781-344-1111	341-3646
G & H Decoys Inc PO Box 1208 *TF Orders:* 800-443-3269 ■ *Web:* www.ghdecoys.com	Henryetta	OK	74437	918-652-3314	652-3400
G & S Surfboards Inc 7179 Construction Ct Unit A *Web:* www.gordonandsmith.com	San Diego	CA	92121	858-581-9212	
G Loomis Inc 1359 Down River Dr *TF:* 800-456-6647 ■ *Web:* www.gloomis.com	Woodland	WA	98674	360-225-6516	225-7169
Game Country Inc 2403 Commerce Ln *Web:* www.gamecountry.biz	Albany	GA	31707	229-883-4706	883-4766
Gamma Sports 200 Waterfront Dr *TF:* 800-333-0337 ■ *Web:* www.gammasports.com	Pittsburgh	PA	15222	412-323-0335	323-0317
Gared Sports Inc 707 N 2nd St Suite 220 *TF:* 800-325-2682 ■ *Web:* www.garedsports.com	Saint Louis	MO	63102	314-421-0044	421-6014
Gen-X Sports Inc - A Forzani Co 25 Vanley Crescent	Toronto	ON	M3J2B7	416-636-9993	636-7373
Gexco 3460 Vine St PO Box 6514 *TF:* 800-829-8222	Norco	CA	92860	951-735-4951	479-5154
Gill Athletics Inc 2808 Gemini Ct *TF Cust Svc:* 800-637-3090 ■ *Web:* www.gillathletics.com	Champaign	IL	61822	217-367-8438	367-8440
Goal Oriented Inc 7935 E 14th Ave *TF:* 888-393-0888 ■ *Web:* www.soccergoals.com	Denver	CO	80220	303-393-6040	
Goal Sporting Goods Inc 37 Industrial Pk Rd PO Box 236 *TF:* 800-334-4625 ■ *Web:* www.goalsports.com	Essex	CT	06426	860-767-9112	767-9121
Goals & Poles 7575 Jefferson Hwy *TF:* 800-275-0317 ■ *Web:* www.goalsandpoles.com	Baton Rouge	LA	70806	225-923-0622	926-0934
Goalsetter Systems Inc 1041 Cordova Ave *TF:* 800-362-4625 ■ *Web:* www.goalsettersystems.com	Lynnville	IA	50153	641-594-4625	594-3343
Golf Instruments Co 3210 Production Ave Unit A *Web:* www.golfinstruments.com	Oceanside	CA	92058	760-722-1129	
Golfsmith International Inc 11000 N IH-35 *TF Sales:* 800-396-0099 ■ *Web:* www.golfsmith.com	Austin	TX	78753	512-821-4050	837-1245
GolfWorks The 4820 Jacksontown Rd PO Box 3008 *TF:* 800-848-8358 ■ *Web:* www.golfworks.com	Newark	OH	43055	740-328-4193	323-0311
Green Grass Golf Corp 282 Newbridge Rd *Web:* www.greengrassgolf.com	Hicksville	NY	11801	516-935-6722	935-7064
Grundmann's Athletic Co 3018 Galleria Dr *Web:* www.grundmanns.com	Metairie	LA	70001	504-833-6602	833-6899
H O Sports Inc 17622 NE 67th Ct *TF:* 800-938-4040 ■ *Web:* www.hosports.com	Redmond	WA	98052	425-885-3505	867-5327
Harlick & Co Inc 893 American St *Web:* www.harlick.com	San Carlos	CA	94070	650-593-2093	593-9704
Harmony Sports 22 Village Dr *TF:* 800-882-3448 ■ *Web:* www.picskate.com	Riverside	RI	02915	401-490-9334	438-5419
HEAD USA Inc 1 Selleck St *TF:* 800-874-3235 ■ *Web:* www.head.com	Norwalk	CT	06855	203-855-8666	866-9573
HEAD/Penn Racquet Sports 306 S 45th Ave **Fax Area Code:* 888 ■ **Fax:* Cust Svc ■ *TF:* 800-289-7366 ■ *Web:* www.pennracquet.com	Phoenix	AZ	85043	602-269-1492	329-7366*
Hillerich & Bradsby Co Inc 800 W Main St *TF:* 800-282-2287 ■ *Web:* www.slugger.com	Louisville	KY	40202	502-585-5226	585-1179
Hireko Trading Co Inc 16185 Stephens St **Fax Area Code:* 888 ■ *TF:* 800-367-8912 ■ *Web:* www.hirekogolf.com	City of Industry	CA	91745	626-330-0121	367-8912*
Hobie Cat Co 4925 Oceanside Blvd *TF:* 800-462-4349 ■ *Web:* www.hobiecat.com	Oceanside	CA	92056	760-758-9100	758-1841
Hoops Sporting Equipment Inc 22047 Lutheran Church Rd *TF:* 800-294-4667 ■ *Web:* www.hoopshouston.com	Tomball	TX	77377	281-351-9822	357-4822
Hoyt USA 543 N Neil Armstrong Rd *Web:* www.hoytusa.com	Salt Lake City	UT	84116	801-363-2990	537-1470
Hunter Co Inc 3300 W 71st Ave *TF:* 800-676-4868 ■ *Web:* www.huntercompany.com	Westminster	CO	80030	303-427-4626	428-3980
Hunter's Specialties Inc 6000 Huntington Ct NE PO Box 10044 *Web:* www.hunterspec.com	Cedar Rapids	IA	52402	319-395-0321	395-0326
Innova Recreational Products 11782 Water Tank Rd *Web:* www.innovakayak.com	Burlington	WA	98233	360-707-2855	707-5435
International Billiards Inc 2311 Washington Ave *Web:* www.intlbilliards.com	Houston	TX	77007	713-869-3237	869-8420
Intex Recreation Corp 4000 Via Oro Ave Suite 210 PO Box 1440 *TF:* 800-234-6839 ■ *Web:* www.intexcorp.com	Long Beach	CA	90801	310-549-5400	513-6905
J & B Importers Inc 11925 SW 128th St *Web:* www.jbimporters.com	Miami	FL	33186	305-238-1866	235-8056
Jayhawk Bowling Supply Inc 355 N Iowa St PO Box 685 *TF:* 800-255-6436 ■ *Web:* www.jayhawkbowling.com	Lawrence	KS	66044	785-842-3237	842-9667
Jerry's Sport Center Inc 121 Main St **Fax Area Code:* 800 ■ *TF:* 800-234-2612 ■ *Web:* www.jerryssportscenter.com	Forest City	PA	18421	570-785-9400	388-8452*
Johnson Outdoors Inc 555 Main St *NASDAQ:* JOUT ■ *TF:* 800-299-2592 ■ *Web:* www.johnsonoutdoors.com	Racine	WI	53403	262-631-6600	631-6601
Jugs Sports 11885 SW Herman Rd *TF:* 800-547-6843 ■ *Web:* www.jugssports.com	Tualatin	OR	97062	503-692-1635	691-1100
K-2 Sports 4201 6th Ave S **Fax Area Code:* 800 ■ **Fax:* Cust Svc ■ *TF:* 800-972-1617 ■ *Web:* www.k2sports.com	Seattle	WA	98108	206-805-4800	972-4066*
Kalispel Case Line 418643 Sr 20 PO Box 267 *TF:* 800-398-0338	Cusick	WA	99119	509-445-1121	445-1082
Kangaroo Products Co 111 Kangaroo Dr PO Box 607 *TF:* 800-438-3011 ■ *Web:* www.kangaroogolf.com	Columbus	NC	28722	828-894-8241	894-2718
Kawasaki Motors Corp USA PO Box 25252 *Web:* www.kawasaki.com	Santa Ana	CA	92799	949-770-0400	460-5600
Kent Sporting Goods Co Inc 433 Pk Ave S *TF:* 800-537-2970	New London	OH	44851	419-929-7021	929-1769
KL Industries Inc 1790 Sun Dolphin Dr *TF:* 800-733-2727 ■ *Web:* www.klindustries.com	Muskegon	MI	49444	231-733-2725	739-4502
Klingbeil Shoe Labs Inc 145-01 Jamaica Ave *Web:* www.klingbeilskatingboots.com	Jamaica	NY	11435	718-297-6864	658-2396
Knight & Hale Game Calls PO Box 1587 *TF:* 800-500-9357 ■ *Web:* www.knightandhale.com	Fort Smith	AR	72901	479-782-8971	783-0234
Kolpin Outdoors Inc 205 N Depot St PO Box 107 **Fax:* Cust Svc ■ *TF:* 877-956-5746 ■ *Web:* www.kolpin.com	Fox Lake	WI	53933	920-928-3118	928-3687*
Kwik Goal Ltd 140 Pacific Dr **Fax Area Code:* 800 ■ *TF:* 800-531-4252 ■ *Web:* www.kwikgoal.com	Quakertown	PA	18951	215-536-2200	778-8869*
Lakes Mall LLC The 5600 Harvey St *Web:* www.thelakesmall.com	Muskegon	MI	49444	231-798-7104	798-7129
Lamartek Inc 175 NW Washington St *TF Orders:* 800-495-1046 ■ *Web:* www.diverite.com	Lake City	FL	32055	386-752-1087	755-0613
Lamiglas Inc 1400 Atlantic Ave *Web:* www.lamiglas.com	Woodland	WA	98674	360-225-9436	225-5050
Laughing Loon 344 Gardiner Rd *Web:* www.laughingloon.com	Jefferson	ME	04348	207-549-3531	
Life-Link International Inc 1240 Huff Ln *TF:* 800-443-8620 ■ *Web:* www.life-link.com	Jackson	WY	83001	307-733-2266	733-8469
Lifetime Products Inc 97 E 700 S *TF:* 800-242-3865 ■ *Web:* www.lifetime.com	Clearfield	UT	84015	801-776-1532	728-1959
Linden Surfboards 1027 S Cleveland St *Web:* www.lindensurfboards.com	Oceanside	CA	92054	760-722-8956	722-8972
Lindy Little Joe Inc 1110 Wright St *Web:* www.lindylittlejoe.com	Brainerd	MN	56401	218-829-1714	829-5426
Lobster Sports Inc 7340 Fulton Ave *TF:* 800-210-5992 ■ *Web:* www.lobsterinc.com	North Hollywood	CA	91605	818-764-6000	764-6061
Local Motion Inc 424 Sumner St *TF:* 800-841-7613 ■ *Web:* www.localmotionhawaii.com	Honolulu	HI	96817	808-523-7873	521-6413
Louisville Golf Club Co 2320 Watterson Trail *TF:* 800-456-1631 ■ *Web:* www.louisvillegolf.com	Louisville	KY	40299	502-491-5490	491-6189
MacNeill Engineering Co Inc 140 Locke Dr PO Box 735 *TF:* 800-652-4267 ■ *Web:* www.champspikes.com	Marlborough	MA	01752	508-481-8830	303-4923
Manns Bait Co 1111 State Docks Rd *TF:* 800-841-8435 ■ *Web:* www.mannsbait.com	Eufaula	AL	36027	334-687-5716	687-4352
Maravia Corp of Idaho 602 E 45th St *TF:* 800-223-7238 ■ *Web:* www.maravia.com	Boise	ID	83714	208-322-4949	322-5016
Marble Arms (MA) 420 Industrial Pk Dr *Web:* www.marblearms.com	Gladstone	MI	49837	906-428-3710	428-3711
Marble's Cutlery 420 Industrial Pk Dr	Gladstone	MI	49837	906-428-3710	428-3711
Mares America Corp 1 Selleck St *TF:* 800-874-3236 ■ *Web:* www.mares.com	Norwalk	CT	06855	203-855-0631	866-9573
Martin Archery Inc 3134 Heritage Rd *TF:* 800-541-8902 ■ *Web:* www.martinarchery.com	Walla Walla	WA	99362	509-529-2554	529-2186
Master Industries Inc 14420 Myford Rd *TF Cust Svc:* 800-854-3794 ■ *Web:* www.masterindustries.com	Irvine	CA	92606	949-660-0644	660-1678
Master Pitching Machine 4200 NE Birmingham Rd *TF:* 800-878-8228 ■ *Web:* www.masterpitch.com	Kansas City	MO	64117	816-452-0228	452-7581
Masterfit Golf Ltd 140 Phillips Hwy *TF:* 866-915-4800 ■ *Web:* www.masterfitgolfltd.com	Jacksonville Beach	FL	32256	904-866-4800	886-4805
Mitsven Surfboards 5151 Sante Fe St Suite B *Web:* www.mitsvensurfboards.com	San Diego	CA	92109	858-581-6220	581-6220
Mizuno USA 4925 Avalon Ridge Pkwy *TF:* 800-333-7888 ■ *Web:* www.mizunousa.com	Norcross	GA	30071	770-441-5553	448-3234
Moultrie Feeders 150 Industrial Rd *TF:* 800-653-3334 ■ *Web:* www.moultriefeeders.com	Alabaster	AL	35007	205-664-6700	664-6706
Murrey International Inc 14150 S Figueroa St *TF:* 800-421-1022 ■ *Web:* www.murrey.com	Los Angeles	CA	90061	310-532-6091	217-0504
Nash Mfg Inc 315 W Ripy St *TF:* 800-433-2901 ■ *Web:* www.nashmfg.com	Fort Worth	TX	76110	817-926-5223	924-5111
National Billiard Mfg Co 3315 Eugenia Ave *TF:* 800-543-0880 ■ *Web:* www.nationalbilliard.com	Covington	KY	41015	859-431-4129	431-4179
Natural Art Inc 2370 S Atlantic Ave *Web:* www.naturalart.com	Cocoa Beach	FL	32931	321-783-0764	783-3990
Nicklaus Golf Equipment LC 3875 Fiscal Ct Suite 300 *TF:* 800-322-1872 ■ *Web:* www.nicklausgolf.com/np/index.php	Riviera Beach	FL	33404	561-881-7981	881-8214
Nike Bauer Hockey Inc 100 Domain Dr *TF:* 800-362-3146 ■ *Web:* www.bauer.com	Exeter	NH	03833	603-430-2111	430-3010
Nitro USA 5 Commerce Ave *TF:* 877-648-7666	West Lebanon	NH	03784	603-298-9867	298-9872
Nocona Athletic Goods Co 105 Clay St **Fax Area Code:* 602 ■ *TF:* 800-433-0957 ■ *Web:* www.nokona.com	Nocona	TX	76255	940-825-3326	381-5658*
North Face The 14450 Doolittle Dr *TF:* 855-500-8639 ■ *Web:* www.thenorthface.com	San Leandro	CA	94577	510-618-3500	618-3531
O'Brien International 14615 NE 91st St *TF:* 800-662-7436 ■ *Web:* www.obrien.com	Redmond	WA	98052	425-202-2100	202-2199
O'Neill Wetsuits USA 1071 41st Ave PO Box 6300 *Web:* www.oneill.com	Santa Cruz	CA	95063	831-475-7500	475-0544
Ocean Kayak 125 Gilman Falls Ave Bldg B **Fax Area Code:* 207 ■ *TF:* 800-852-9257 ■ *Web:* www.oceankayak.com	Old Town	ME	04468	800-852-9257	827-3647*
Ocean Management Systems Inc PO Box 146 *Web:* www.omsdive.com	Montgomery	NY	12549	845-692-3600	692-3623
Oceanic USA 2002 Davis St *TF:* 800-435-3483 ■ *Web:* www.oceanicworldwide.com	San Leandro	CA	94577	510-562-0500	569-5404
Old Town Canoe Co 125 Gilman Falls Ave Bldg B PO Box 548 *TF:* 800-343-1555 ■ *Web:* www.oldtowncanoe.com	Old Town	ME	04468	207-827-5513	827-3647
Orlimar G-5140 Flushing Rd *TF:* 888-502-4653 ■ *Web:* www.orlimar.com	Flushing	MI	48433	810-732-0454	732-6662
Orvis International Travel 178 Conservation Way *TF:* 800-547-4322 ■ *Web:* www.orvis.com	Sunderland	VT	05250	802-362-8790	362-8795
Paragon Aquatics 1351 Rt 55 *TF:* 888-534-7946 ■ *Web:* www.paragonaquatics.com	Lagrangeville	NY	12540	845-463-7200	463-7291
Parker Compound Bows Inc PO Box 105 **Fax Area Code:* 800 ■ *Web:* www.parkerbows.com	Mint Spring	VA	24463	540-337-5426	332-2715*

Company	City	State	Zip	Phone	Fax
Penn Fishing Tackle Mfg Co 3028 W Hunting Pk Ave Web: www.pennreels.com	Philadelphia	PA	19132	215-229-9415	223-3017
Perception Inc 111 Kayaker Way TF: 800-595-2925 ■ Web: www.kayaker.com	Easley	SC	29642	888-525-2925	373-1220
Ping Inc 2201 W Desert Cove Ave PO Box 82000 *Fax: Cust Svc ■ TF: 800-474-6434 ■ Web: www.ping.com	Phoenix	AZ	85071	602-870-5000	687-4482*
Poolmaster Inc 770 Del Paso Rd TF: 800-854-1776 ■ Web: www.poolmaster.net	Sacramento	CA	95834	916-567-9800	567-9880
Powell Skate One Corp 30 S La Patera Ln TF: 800-884-3813 ■ Web: www.skateone.com	Santa Barbara	CA	93117	805-964-1330	964-0511
Precision Shooting Equipment Inc 2727 N Fairview Ave TF: 800-477-7789 ■ Web: www.pse-archery.com	Tucson	AZ	85705	520-884-9065	884-1479
Prince Sports Inc 1 Advantage Ct TF: 800-283-6647 ■ Web: www.princetennis.com	Bordentown	NJ	08505	609-291-5800	291-5900
Pure Fishing America 1900 18th St TF: 877-777-3850 ■ Web: www.purefishing.com	Spirit Lake	IA	51360	712-336-1520	336-5183
Pure Fishing USA 1900 18th St *Fax Area Code: 336 ■ TF: 800-243-9700 ■ Web: www.stren.com	Spirit Lake	IA	51360	866-447-8736	548-7836*
Quiet Flight Inc 109 N Orlando Ave	Cocoa Beach	FL	32931	321-783-1530	799-1643
Rapala-Normark Group 10395 Yellow Cir Dr TF: 800-874-4451 ■ Web: www.rapalaworld.com	Minnetonka	MN	55343	952-933-7060	933-0046
Rawlings Sporting Goods Co 510 Maryville University Rd Suite 110 TF: 800-729-5464 ■ Web: www.rawlings.com	Saint Louis	MO	63141	314-819-2800	
Reebok-CCM Hockey Inc 3400 Raymond Lasnir *Fax Area Code: 800 ■ Web: www.thehockeycompany.com	Montreal	QC	H4R3L3	514-461-8000	232-9226*
Resilite Sports Products PO Box 764 TF: 800-326-9307 ■ Web: www.resilite.com	Sunbury	PA	17801	570-473-3529	473-8988
Riedell Shoes Inc 122 Cannon River Ave TF: 800-698-6893 ■ Web: www.riedellskates.com	Red Wing	MN	55066	651-388-8251	385-5500
RIO Products International Inc 5050 S Yellowstone Hwy TF: 800-553-0838 ■ Web: www.rioproducts.com	Idaho Falls	ID	83402	208-524-7760	524-7763
RL Winston Rod Co 500 S Main St PO Box 411 TF: 866-946-7637 ■ Web: www.web.winstonrods.com	Twin Bridges	MT	59754	406-684-5674	684-5533
Roller Derby Skate Corp PO Box 930 Web: www.rollerderby.com	Litchfield	IL	62056	217-324-3961	324-2213
Rome Specialty Co Inc Rosco Div 501 W Embargo St TF: 800-794-8357 ■ Web: www.roscoinc.com	Rome	NY	13440	315-337-8200	339-2523
Ross Reels 1 Ponderosa Ct TF: 800-336-1050 ■ Web: www.rossreels.com	Montrose	CO	81401	970-249-1212	249-1834
Rossignol USA 1413 Ctr Dr PO Box 981060 TF: 888-243-6722 ■ Web: www.rossignol.com	Park City	UT	84098	435-252-3300	
Rsr Group Inc 4405 Metric Dr TF: 800-541-4867 ■ Web: www.rsrgroup.com	Winter Park	FL	32792	407-677-1000	677-4489
Sage Mfg Corp 8500 NE Day Rd TF: 800-533-3004 ■ Web: www.sageflyfish.com	Bainbridge Island	WA	98110	206-842-6608	842-6830
Saint Croix of Park Falls Ltd 856 4th Ave N PO Box 279 TF: 800-826-7042 ■ Web: www.stcroixrods.com	Park Falls	WI	54552	715-762-3226	762-3293
Sampo Inc 119 Remsen Rd Web: www.sampoinc.com	Barneveld	NY	13304	315-896-2606	896-6575
Saunders Archery Co 1874 14th Ave PO Box 1707 TF Cust Svc: 800-228-1408 ■ Web: www.sausa.com	Columbus	NE	68601	402-564-7176	564-3260
Schutt Sports 1200 E Union Ave PO Box 426 TF: 800-637-2047 ■ Web: www.schuttsports.com	Litchfield	IL	62056	217-324-2712	324-2732
Scott Fly Rod Co 2355 Air Pk Way *Fax Area Code: 970 ■ TF: 800-728-7208 ■ Web: www.scottflyrod.com	Montrose	CO	81401	800-728-7208	249-4172*
Scott USA Inc PO Box 2030 TF: 800-292-5874 ■ Web: www.scott-sports.com	Sun Valley	ID	83353	208-622-1000	622-1005
SCP Pool Corp 109 Northpark Blvd 4th Fl NASDAQ: POOL ■ Web: www.scppool.com	Covington	LA	70433	985-892-5521	801-5716
Sea Eagle Boats Inc 19 N Columbia St TF: 800-852-0925 ■ Web: www.seaeagle.com	Port Jefferson	NY	11777	631-473-7308	473-7398
Seeker Fishing Rods 1340 W Cowles St TF: 800-373-3537 ■ Web: www.seekerrod.com	Long Beach	CA	90813	562-491-0076	435-7599
Shakespeare Fishing Tackle Co 3801 Westmore Dr TF Cust Svc: 800-347-3759 ■ Web: www.shakespeare-fishing.com	Columbia	SC	29223	803-754-7000	754-7342
Sheldons' Inc 626 Ctr St Web: www.mepps.com	Antigo	WI	54409	715-623-2382	623-3001
Shimano American Corp 1 Holland Dr Web: www.shimano.com	Irvine	CA	92618	949-951-5003	768-0920
Sierra Designs Inc 2011 Cherry St Suite 202 TF: 800-635-0461 ■ Web: www.sierradesigns.com	Louisville	CO	80027	303-262-3050	262-3051
Simms Fishing Products Corp 101 Evergreen Dr TF: 866-585-3570 ■ Web: www.simmsfishing.com	Bozeman	MT	59715	406-585-3557	585-3562
Spalding 150 Brookdale Dr TF Cust Svc: 800-772-5346 ■ Web: www.spalding.com	Springfield	MA	01104	413-735-1400	735-1570
Sport Supply Group Inc 1901 Diplomat Dr TF: 800-527-7510 ■ Web: www.sportsupplygroup.com	Dallas	TX	75234	972-484-9484	243-0149
Sportco Sporting Goods Inc 2580 E Sunset Rd Web: www.sportcolasvegas.com	Las Vegas	NV	89120	702-739-9750	739-9021
SportRack 700 Bernard TF: 800-561-0716 ■ Web: www.sportrack.com	Granby	QC	J2J0H6	800-561-0716	
Standard Golf Co 6620 Nordic Dr TF: 800-553-1707 ■ Web: www.standardgolf.com	Cedar Falls	IA	50613	319-266-2638	266-9627
Stearns Inc 1100 Stearns Dr TF: 800-328-3208	Sauk Rapids	MN	56379	320-252-1642	252-4425
Stewart Surfboards 2102 S El Camino Real Web: www.stewartsurfboards.com	San Clemente	CA	92673	949-492-1085	492-2344
Stockli Ski USA Inc PO Box 370206 TF: 800-638-6284 ■ Web: www.stockli.com	Denver	CO	80237	303-220-9737	220-9745
Storm Products Inc 165 S 800 W TF: 888-450-6920 ■ Web: www.stormbowling.com	Brigham City	UT	84302	435-723-0403	734-0338
Straight Line Sports LLC 364 2nd St Suite 7 Web: www.slsports.com	Encinitas	CA	97230	760-943-8364	943-8972
Strikeforce Bowling LLC 2001 W Parkes Dr TF: 800-297-8555 ■ Web: www.krstrikeforce.com	Broadview	IL	60155	708-863-1200	222-1400
StrikeMaster Corp 17217 198 Ave Web: www.strikemaster.com	Big Lake	MN	55309	763-263-8999	263-8986
Summit Treestands LLC 715 Summit Dr Web: www.summitstands.com	Decatur	AL	35601	256-353-0634	353-9818
Sun Mountain Sports 301 N 1st St TF: 800-227-9224 ■ Web: www.sunmountain.com	Missoula	MT	59802	406-728-9224	728-8998
Talon 1552 Down River Dr PO Box 907 Web: www.talon-graphite.com	Woodland	WA	98674	360-225-8247	225-7737
TaylorMade - adidas Golf 5545 Fermi Ct TF Cust Svc: 800-456-8633 ■ Web: www.taylormadegolf.com	Carlsbad	CA	92008	760-918-6000	918-6014
Team Cobra Products 1750 Wadsworth Rd Rear Bldg *Fax Area Code: 866 ■ TF: 800-336-7784 ■ Web: www.cobraproducts.com	Akron	OH	44320	800-336-7784	755-0694*
Tecnica USA 19 Technology Dr TF: 800-258-3897 ■ Web: tecnicausa.com	West Lebanon	NH	03784	603-298-8032	298-5790
Toobs Inc 349 B Quintana Rd TF: 800-795-8662 ■ Web: www.toobs.com	Morro Bay	CA	93442	805-772-5742	772-5781
Top-Flite Golf Co 425 Meadow St TF: 866-834-6532 ■ Web: www.topflite.com	Chicopee	MA	01021	413-536-1200	322-2673
True Temper Sports 8275 Tournament Dr Suite 200 TF: 800-355-8783 ■ Web: www.truetemper.com	Memphis	TN	38125	901-746-2000	746-2160
Tubbs Snowshoe 4201 6th Ave S Web: www.snowshoes.com	Seattle	WA	98108	802-253-7398	253-9982
Tuf-Wear USA 1001 Industrial Ave TF: 800-445-5210	North Platte	NE	69101	308-532-0187	532-9133
Underwater Kinetics (UK) 13400 Danielson St TF: 800-852-7483 ■ Web: www.uwkinetics.com	Poway	CA	92064	858-513-9100	513-3602
Victoria Skimboards 2955 Laguna Canyon Rd Suite 1 Web: www.vicskim.com	Laguna Beach	CA	92651	949-494-0059	494-5485
Volkl Sport America 19 Technology Dr TF: 800-264-4579 ■ Web: www.volkl.com	West Lebanon	NH	03784	603-298-0314	298-6134
We-No-Nah Canoe 850 Louisa St Web: www.wenonah.com	Winona	MN	55987	507-454-5430	454-5448
Weed USA Inc 5780 Harrow Glen Ct TF: 800-933-3758 ■ Web: www.weedusa.com	Galena	OH	43021	740-548-3881	548-3882
West Coast Trends 17811 Jamestown Ln TF: 800-736-4568 ■ Web: www.clubglove.com	Huntington Beach	CA	92647	714-843-9288	843-9020
Wileys Custom Water Skis 1417 S Trenton TF: 800-962-0785 ■ Web: www.wileyski.com	Seattle	WA	98108	206-762-1300	762-7339
Wilson Sporting Goods Co 8750 W Bryn Mawr Ave Web: www.wilson.com	Chicago	IL	60631	773-714-6400	714-4565
Wittek Golf Supply Co Inc 3865 N Commercial Ave TF: 800-869-1800 ■ Web: www.wittekgolf.com	Northbrook	IL	60052	847-943-2399	412-9591
Worldwide Golf Shops Inc 1430 Village Way Suite T TF: 888-216-5252 ■ Web: www.rdgolf.com	Santa Ana	CA	92705	714-543-8284	
Worth Co The 214 Sherman Ave PO Box 88 TF: 800-944-1899 ■ Web: www.worthco.com	Stevens Point	WI	54481	715-344-6081	344-3021
Worth Sports 510 Maryville University Dr Suite 110 TF Cust Svc: 800-282-9637 ■ Web: www.worthsports.com	Saint Louis	MO	63141	314-819-2800	819-2990
Wright & McGill Co 4245 E 46th Ave *Fax Area Code: 303 ■ TF: 800-628-0108 ■ Web: www.wright-mcgill.com	Denver	CO	80216	720-941-8700	321-4750*
Yakima Bait Co Inc PO Box 310 TF: 800-527-2711 ■ Web: www.yakimabait.com	Granger	WA	98932	509-854-1311	854-2263
Yamaha Motor Corp USA 6555 Katella Ave TF Cust Svc: 800-962-7926 ■ Web: www.yamaha-motor.com	Cypress	CA	90630	714-761-7300	
Yonex Corp 20140 S Western Ave TF: 800-449-6639 ■ Web: www.yonex.com	Torrance	CA	90501	310-793-3800	793-3899
Zeagle Systems Inc 37150 Chancey Rd Web: www.zeagle.com	Zephyrhills	FL	33541	813-782-5568	782-5569
Zebco Corp 6101 E Apache St TF: 800-588-9030 ■ Web: www.zebco.com	Tulsa	OK	74115	918-836-5581	836-0154

714 SPORTING GOODS STORES

Company	City	State	Zip	Phone	Fax
2nd Swing Inc 13031 Ridgedale Dr Web: www.2ndswing.com	Minnetonka	MN	55305	952-546-1906	546-1908
2nd Wind Exercise Equipment Inc 7585 Equitable Dr Web: www.2ndwindexercise.com	Eden Prairie	MN	55344	952-544-5249	544-5053
Academy Sports & Outdoors 1800 N Mason Rd TF: 877-999-9856 ■ Web: www.academy.com	Katy	TX	77449	281-646-5200	646-5204
Adventure 16 Inc 4620 Alvarado Canyon Rd *Fax: Hum Res ■ TF: 800-854-2672 ■ Web: www.adventure16.com	San Diego	CA	92120	619-283-2362	283-7956*
Alpina Sports USA 93 Etna Rd TF: 800-425-7462 ■ Web: www.alpinasports.com	Lebanon	NH	03766	603-448-3101	448-1586
Altrec.com Inc 725 SW Umatilla Ave TF: 800-369-3949 ■ Web: www.altrec.com	Redmond	OR	97756	541-316-2400	
Any Mountain Ltd 71 Tamal Vista Blvd TF: 800-992-4844 ■ Web: www.anymountain.net	Corte Madera	CA	94925	415-927-2400	927-3388
Aspen Sports Ltd 408 E Cooper Ave TF: 800-544-6648 ■ Web: www.aspensports.com	Aspen	CO	81611	970-925-6331	925-2755
Athletic Supply Co 16101 NE 87th St Web: www.athleticsupply.com	Redmond	WA	98052	425-882-1456	497-4713
Austad's Golf Inc 2801 E 10th St TF: 800-444-1234 ■ Web: www.austads.com	Sioux Falls	SD	57103	605-332-3373	332-3373
Backwoods 127 E Riverside Dr Suite 101 Web: www.backwoods.com	Austin	TX	78704	512-370-3600	370-3636

Name / Address	City	State	Zip	Phone	Fax
Baseball Express Inc 1051 E Nakoma St *TF Cust Svc:* 800-937-4824 ■ *Web:* www.baseballexp.com	San Antonio	TX	78216	210-348-7000	525-9339
Bass Pro Shops Outdoor World 1935 S Campbell Ave *Web:* www.basspro.com	Springfield	MO	65807	417-887-7334	885-0072
Big 5 Sporting Goods Corp 2525 E El Segundo Blvd *NASDAQ: BGFV* ■ *TF:* 800-367-2445 ■ *Web:* www.big5sportinggoods.com	El Segundo	CA	90245	310-536-0611	297-7580
Big Bear Sports Centers Inc 2618 King Ave W	Billings	MT	59102	406-652-5777	652-1220
Bike Line Corp 700 Lawrence Dr *Web:* www.bikeline.com	West Chester	PA	19380	610-429-4370	429-4295
Bob Ward & Sons Inc 3015 Paxson St *TF:* 800-800-5083 ■ *Web:* www.bobwards.com	Missoula	MT	59801	406-728-3220	728-5230
Boyne Country Sports 1200 Bay View Rd *TF:* 800-462-6963 ■ *Web:* www.boyne.com	Petoskey	MI	49770	231-439-4906	439-4960
Brady's Sportsman's Surplus Inc 2315 Brooks St *TF:* 800-473-4867	Missoula	MT	59801	406-721-5500	728-1112
Busy Body Home Fitness 1000 Studebaker Rd Suite 1 *TF:* 800-466-3348 ■ *Web:* www.busybody.com	Long Beach	CA	90815	562-296-1095	493-3798
Cabela's Inc 1 Cabela Dr *NYSE: CAB* ■ **Fax:* Mktg ■ *TF:* 800-237-8888 ■ *Web:* www.cabelas.com	Sidney	NE	69160	308-254-5505	254-6102*
Campmor Inc 28 Pkwy *TF Orders:* 800-526-4784 ■ *Web:* www.campmor.com	Upper Saddle River	NJ	07458	201-825-8300	236-3601
Century Martial Art Supply Inc 1000 Century Blvd *TF Sales:* 800-626-2787 ■ *Web:* www.centurymartialarts.com	Midwest City	OK	73110	405-732-2226	737-8954
Champs Sports 311 Manatee Ave W **Fax:* Mktg ■ *TF:* 800-991-6813 ■ *Web:* www.champssports.com	Bradenton	FL	34205	941-748-0577	741-7582*
Christy Sports LLC 875 Parfet St *Web:* www.christysports.com	Lakewood	CO	80215	303-237-6321	233-5946
Crown Enterprises Inc 145 Hutton Ranch Rd *Web:* www.sportsmanskihaus.com	Kalispell	MT	59901	406-755-6484	758-7425
D & R Sports Center Inc 8178 W Main St *TF:* 800-992-1520 ■ *Web:* www.dandrsports.com	Kalamazoo	MI	49009	269-372-2277	372-9072
Dick's Sporting Goods Inc 300 Industry Dr *NYSE: DKS* ■ *TF:* 800-690-7655 ■ *Web:* www.dickssportinggoods.com	Pittsburgh	PA	15275	724-273-3400	695-2574
Dixie Gun Works Inc 1412 W Reelfoot Ave PO Box 130 *TF Orders:* 800-238-6785 ■ *Web:* www.dixiegun.com	Union City	TN	38281	731-885-0700	885-0440
Downtown Athletic Store Inc 199 Zan Rd *TF:* 888-889-6974 ■ *Web:* www.downtownathletic.com	Charlottesville	VA	22901	434-975-0750	975-0754
Eastern Mountain Sports 1 Vose Farm Rd *TF:* 888-463-6367 ■ *Web:* www.ems.com	Peterborough	NH	03458	603-924-9571	924-9138
Ed Shirley & Sons Sports Inc 5802 W Dempster St *Web:* www.fishtechmg.com	Morton Grove	IL	60053	847-966-5900	966-9174
Edwin Watts Golf Shops Inc 20 Hill Ave NW *TF:* 800-874-0146 ■ *Web:* www.edwinwattsgolf.com	Fort Walton Beach	FL	32548	850-244-2066	244-5217
Efinger Sporting Goods Co Inc 513 W Union Ave *Web:* www.efingersports.com	Bound Brook	NJ	08805	732-356-0604	356-0604
Erie Sport Store Inc 701 State St *TF Cust Svc:* 800-333-6812 ■ *Web:* www.eriesportstore.com	Erie	PA	16501	814-452-2289	453-5840
Fanzz 1832 W 2770 S Suite 10 *TF:* 888-326-9946 ■ *Web:* www.fanzz.com	Salt Lake City	UT	84119	801-325-2788	325-2736
Fitness Zone 7540 S Memorial Pkwy Suite D **Fax Area Code:* 256 ■ *TF Cust Svc:* 800-875-9145 ■ *Web:* www.fitnesszone.com	Huntsville	AL	35802	800-875-9145	883-2115*
Forzani Group Ltd 824 41st Ave NE *Web:* www.forzanigroup.com	Calgary	AB	T2E3R3	403-717-1400	717-1491
Gerry Cosby & Co Inc 3 Pennsylvania Plaza *TF:* 877-563-6464 ■ *Web:* www.cosbysports.com	New York	NY	10001	212-563-6464	967-0876
Golf Etc of America Inc 2201 Commercial Ln *TF:* 800-806-8633 ■ *Web:* www.golfetc.com	Granbury	TX	76048	817-279-7888	579-1793
Golf Shack Inc 1631 N Bell School Rd *TF:* 888-446-5390 ■ *Web:* www.golfshack.com	Rockford	IL	61107	815-397-3709	397-7593
Golf USA 7608 N Harvey Ave *TF:* 800-488-1107 ■ *Web:* www.golfusainc.com	Oklahoma City	OK	73116	405-751-0015	755-0065
Golfsmith International Inc 11000 N IH-35 *TF Sales:* 800-396-0099 ■ *Web:* www.golfsmith.com	Austin	TX	78753	512-821-4050	837-1245
Green Top Sporting Goods Corp PO Box 1015 *Web:* www.greentophuntfish.com	Glen Allen	VA	23060	804-550-2188	550-2693
Gregg's Greenlake Cycle 7007 Woodlawn Ave NE *Web:* www.greggscycles.com	Seattle	WA	98115	206-523-1822	523-5330
Gym Source 40 E 52nd St *TF:* 800-496-7687 ■ *Web:* www.gymsource.com	New York	NY	10022	212-688-4222	750-2886
Hibbett Sporting Goods Inc 451 Industrial Ln *NASDAQ: HIBB* ■ *Web:* www.hibbett.com	Birmingham	AL	35211	205-942-4292	912-7290
Hoigaards Inc 5425 Excelsior Blvd *TF:* 800-266-8157 ■ *Web:* www.hoigaards.com	Saint Louis Park	MN	55416	952-929-1351	929-2669
In The Swim Inc 320 Industrial Dr **Fax Area Code:* 800 ■ *TF:* 800-288-7946 ■ *Web:* www.intheswim.com	West Chicago	IL	60185	630-876-0040	766-5329*
Island Water Sports Inc 1985 NE 2nd St *TF:* 800-873-0375 ■ *Web:* www.islandwatersports.com	Deerfield Beach	FL	33441	954-427-4929	360-7873
Jan's Mountain Outfitters 1600 Pk Ave PO Box 280 *TF:* 800-745-1020 ■ *Web:* www.jans.com	Park City	UT	84060	435-649-4949	649-7511
Jay's Sporting Goods Inc 8800 S Clare Ave *Web:* www.jayssportinggoods.com	Clare	MI	48617	989-386-3475	386-3496
Kittery Trading Post 301 US 1 *TF:* 888-587-6246 ■ *Web:* www.kitterytradingpost.com	Kittery	ME	03904	207-439-2700	439-8001
Laacke & Joys Co 1433 N Water St *Web:* www.laackeandjoys.com	Milwaukee	WI	53202	414-271-7885	271-2330
Leslie's Swimming Pool Supplies 3925 E Broadway Rd Suite 100 *TF:* 800-233-8063 ■ *Web:* www.lesliespool.com	Phoenix	AZ	85040	602-366-3999	366-3944
Lombardi Sports Inc 1600 Jackson St *Web:* www.lombardisports.com	San Francisco	CA	94109	415-771-0600	771-1891
MC Sports 3070 Shaffer Ave SE *TF:* 800-626-1762 ■ *Web:* www.mcsports.com	Grand Rapids	MI	49512	616-942-2600	942-2786
Mel Cotton's Sales & Rentals Inc 1266 W San Carlos St *Web:* www.melcottons.com	San Jose	CA	95126	408-287-5994	298-3536
Modell's Sporting Goods 498 7th Ave 20th Fl *TF:* 800-250-7405 ■ *Web:* www.modells.com	New York	NY	10018	212-822-1000	822-1090
Nill Bros Sports 2814 S 44th St *Web:* www.nillbros.com	Kansas City	KS	66106	913-384-4242	384-0107
NRC Sports Inc 603 Pleasant St *TF:* 800-243-5033 ■ *Web:* www.nrcsports.com	Paxton	MA	01612	508-852-8206	852-8206
Olympia Sports 5 Bradley Dr *Web:* www.olympiasports.net	Westbrook	ME	04092	207-854-2794	854-4168
Paragon Sporting Goods Corp 867 Broadway 18th St *TF:* 800-961-3030 ■ *Web:* www.paragonsports.com	New York	NY	10003	212-255-8889	929-1831
Pedigree Ski Shop Inc 355 Mamaroneck Ave *Web:* www.pedigreeskishop.com	White Plains	NY	10605	914-948-2995	948-1599
Performance Inc 1 Performance Way *TF Cust Svc:* 800-727-2433 ■ *Web:* www.performancebike.com	Chapel Hill	NC	27514	919-933-9113	942-5431
Peter Glenn Ski & Sports 2901 W Oakland Pk Blvd *TF:* 800-818-0946 ■ *Web:* www.peterglenn.com	Fort Lauderdale	FL	33311	954-484-3606	739-5724
Pinch A Penny Inc 14480 62nd St N *TF:* 800-509-5571 ■ *Web:* www.pinchapenny.com	Clearwater	FL	33760	727-531-8913	536-8066
Play It Again Sports 4200 Dahlberg Dr Suite 100 *TF:* 800-433-2540 ■ *Web:* www.playitagainsports.com	Minneapolis	MN	55422	763-520-8500	520-8470
Pro Golf Inc 37735 Enterprise Ct Suite 600 *Web:* www.progolfamerica.com	Farmington Hills	MI	48331	248-994-0553	489-9334
Ramsey Outdoor Store 240 SR 17 N *Web:* www.ramseyoutdoor.com	Paramus	NJ	07652	201-261-5000	261-2742
Recreational Equipment Inc (REI) 6750 S 228th St *TF Orders:* 800-426-4840 ■ *Web:* www.rei.com	Kent	WA	98032	253-395-3780	395-4368
Ron Jon Surf Shop 3850 S Banana River Blvd *TF:* 888-757-8737 ■ *Web:* www.ronjonsurfshop.com	Cocoa Beach	FL	32931	321-799-8888	799-8805
Ski Stop 197 S Service Rd *Web:* www.skistop.com	Plainview	NY	11803	516-249-7980	249-5636
Special Tee Golf of Florida 620 E Altamonte Dr *Web:* www.specialteegolf.com	Altamonte Springs	FL	32701	407-834-1900	834-1689
Sport Chalet Inc One Sport Chalet Dr *NASDAQ: SPCHB* ■ *TF:* 888-801-9162 ■ *Web:* www.sportchalet.com	La Canada	CA	91011	818-949-5300	790-0087
Sports Endeavors Inc 431 US Hwy 70-A E *TF:* 800-955-3876 ■ *Web:* www.sportsendeavors.com	Hillsborough	NC	27278	919-644-6800	644-6808
Sports Promotion Network PO Box 200548 **Fax Area Code:* 866 ■ *TF:* 800-460-9989 ■ *Web:* www.gotospn.com	Arlington	TX	76006	800-460-9989	300-5333*
Sportsman's Warehouse 7035 S 185 W *Web:* www.sportsmanswarehouse.com	Midvale	UT	84047	801-566-6681	304-4301
Sun & Ski Sports 4001 Greenbriar St Suite 100 *Web:* www.sunandski.com	Stafford	TX	77477	281-340-5000	340-5020
Turner's Outdoorsman 11738 Sanmarino St Suite a *Web:* www.turners.com	cucamomga	CA	91730	909-923-3009	923-3022
Val Surf Inc 4810 Whitsett Ave *TF:* 888-825-7873 ■ *Web:* www.valsurf.com	Valley Village	CA	91607	818-769-6977	769-4318
Warrior Custom Golf Inc 15 Mason Suite A *TF:* 800-600-5113 ■ *Web:* www.warriorcustomgolf.com	Irvine	CA	92618	949-699-2499	
Western Power Sports Inc 601 E Gowen Rd *TF:* 800-999-3388 ■ *Web:* www.wps-inc.com	Boise	ID	83716	208-376-8400	375-8901
Wheel & Sprocket Inc 5722 S 108th St *TF:* 800-362-4537 ■ *Web:* wheelandsprocket.com	Hales Corners	WI	53130	414-529-6600	529-6605
World of Golf 4500 Tamiami Trail N *TF:* 800-505-9998 ■ *Web:* www.worldofgolf.com	Naples	FL	34103	239-263-4999	263-7423

715 SPORTS COMMISSIONS & REGULATORY AGENCIES - STATE

Name / Address	City	State	Zip	Phone	Fax
Arizona Racing Dept 1110 W Washington St Suite 260 *Web:* www.azracing.gov	Phoenix	AZ	85007	602-364-1700	364-1703
Arkansas Racing Commission 1515 W 7th St Rm 505 *Web:* www.state.ar.us/dfa/racing	Little Rock	AR	72203	501-682-1467	682-5273
California Athletic Commission 1430 Howe Ave *Web:* www.dca.ca.gov	Sacramento	CA	95825	916-263-2195	263-2197
California Horse Racing Board 1010 Hurley Way Rm 300 *Web:* www.chrb.ca.gov	Sacramento	CA	95825	916-263-6000	263-6042
Delaware Harness Racing Commission 2320 S Dupont Hwy *Web:* www.state.de.us/deptagri/harness	Dover	DE	19901	302-698-4599	697-6287
Delaware Thoroughbred Racing Commission 2320 S DuPont Hwy **Fax Area Code:* 512 ■ *Web:* www.state.de.us/deptagri/thoroughbred	Dover	DE	19901	302-698-4599	463-1376*
Florida State Boxing Commission 1940 N Monroe St *Web:* www.state.fl.us	Tallahassee	FL	32399	850-488-8500	922-2249
Idaho Racing Commission PO Box 700 *Web:* www.isp.state.id.us/race	Meridian	ID	83680	208-884-7080	884-7098
Illinois Racing Board 100 W Randolph St Suite 11-100 *Web:* www.state.il.us/agency/irb	Chicago	IL	60601	312-814-2600	814-5062
Indiana Horse Racing Commission 150 W Market St Suite 530 *Web:* www.in.gov	Indianapolis	IN	46204	317-233-3119	233-4470

	City	State	Zip	Phone	Fax
Kentucky Athletic Commission 500 Mero St # 5 *Web:* www.ppr.ky.gov	Frankfort	KY	40601	502-564-7760	564-3969
Kentucky Horse Racing Authority 4063 Iron Works Pkwy Bldg B *Web:* www.krc.ppr.ky.gov	Lexington	KY	40602	859-246-2040	246-2039
Louisiana Racing Commission 320 N Carrollton Ave Suite 2-B *Web:* www.horseracing.la.gov	New Orleans	LA	70119	504-483-4000	483-4898
Maryland Racing Commission 500 N Calvert St Rm 201 *Web:* www.dllr.state.md.us	Baltimore	MD	21202	410-230-6330	333-8308
Maryland State Athletic Commission 500 N Calvert St Rm 304 *Web:* www.dllr.state.md.us/license/occprof/athlet.html	Baltimore	MD	21202	410-230-6223	333-6314
Massachusetts State Boxing Commission 1 Ashburton Pl Rm 1301 *Web:* www.mass.gov/mbc	Boston	MA	02108	617-727-3200	727-5732
Massachusetts State Racing Commission 1 Ashurton Pl Rm 1313 *Web:* www.state.ma.us	Boston	MA	02108	617-727-2581	227-6062
Michigan Racing Commissioners Office 525 W Allegan St PO Box 30773 *Web:* www.michigan.gov	Lansing	MI	48909	517-335-1420	241-3018
Montana Horse Racing Board 1424 9th Ave *Web:* www.mt.gov	Helena	MT	59601	406-444-4287	444-4305
Nebraska State Racing Commission 301 Centennial Mall S 6th Fl PO Box 95014 *Web:* www.horseracing.state.ne.us	Lincoln	NE	68509	402-471-4155	471-2339
Nevada State Athletic Commission 555 E Washington Ave Suite 3300 *Web:* www.boxing.nv.gov	Las Vegas	NV	89101	702-486-2575	486-2577
New Jersey Racing Commission 140 E Front St *Web:* www.njpublicsafety.org	Trenton	NJ	08625	609-292-0613	599-1785
New Jersey State Athletic Control Board 140 E Front St *Web:* www.state.nj.us/lps/sacb	Trenton	NJ	08625	609-292-0317	292-3756
New Mexico Racing Commission 300 San Mateo NE Suite 110 *Web:* www.nmrc.state.nm.us	Albuquerque	NM	87108	505-841-6400	841-6413
New York Athletic Commission 123 William St 20th Fl *TF:* 866-269-3769 ■ *Web:* www.dos.state.ny.us	New York	NY	10038	212-417-5700	417-4987
North Dakota Racing Commission 500 N 9th St *Web:* www.ndracingcommission.com	Bismarck	ND	58501	701-328-4290	328-4300
Ohio Racing Commission 77 S High St 18th Fl *Web:* www.racing.ohio.gov	Columbus	OH	43215	614-466-2757	466-1900
Pennsylvania State Athletic Commission 2601 N 3rd St *Web:* dos.state.pa.us/portal/server.pt/community/state_athletic_commission/12431	Harrisburg	PA	17110	717-787-5720	783-0824
South Dakota Gaming Commission 221 W Capitol Ave Suite 101 *Web:* www.state.sd.us	Pierre	SD	57501	605-773-6050	773-6053
Tennessee Boxing & Racing Board 500 James Robertson Pkwy 2nd Fl	Nashville	TN	37243	615-741-2384	741-5995
Texas Racing Commission 8505 Cross Pk Dr Suite 110 *Web:* www.txrc.state.tx.us	Austin	TX	78754	512-833-6699	833-6907
Utah Sports Commission 201 S Main St Suite 2002 *Web:* www.utahsportscommission.com	Salt Lake City	UT	84111	801-328-2372	328-2389
Washington Horse Racing Commission 6326 Martin Way Suite 209 *Web:* www.whrc.wa.gov	Olympia	WA	98516	360-459-6462	459-6461
West Virginia Racing Commission 106 Dee Dr *Web:* www.wvf.state.wv.us	Charleston	WV	25311	304-558-2150	558-6319

SPORTS FACILITIES

SEE Motor Speedways p. 2259; Racing & Racetracks p. 2476; Stadiums & Arenas p. 2671

716 SPORTS TEAMS - BASEBALL

SEE ALSO Sports Organizations p. 1438

	City	State	Zip	Phone	Fax
Major League Baseball (Office of the Commissioner) 245 Park Ave 31st Fl **Fax:* PR ■ *TF Cust Svc:* 800-704-2937 ■ *Web:* www.mlb.com	New York	NY	10167	212-931-7800	949-5650*
Arizona Diamondbacks 401 E Jefferson St *Web:* diamondbacks.mlb.com	Phoenix	AZ	85004	602-462-6500	462-6600
Atlanta Braves PO Box 4064 *TF:* 800-326-4000 ■ *Web:* atlanta.braves.mlb.com	Atlanta	GA	30302	404-522-7630	614-1329
Boston Red Sox Fenway Pk 4 Yawkey Way *Web:* www.redsox.mlb.com	Boston	MA	02215	617-267-9440	236-6797
Chicago Cubs 1060 W Addison St # 1 **Fax:* PR ■ *Web:* www.chicago.cubs.mlb.com	Chicago	IL	60613	773-404-2827	404-4129*
Chicago White Sox US Cellular Field 333 W 35th St *Web:* www.chicago.whitesox.mlb.com	Chicago	IL	60616	312-674-1000	674-5109
Cincinnati Reds Great American Ballpark 100 Main St *Web:* www.reds.mlb.com	Cincinnati	OH	45202	513-765-7000	765-7342
Cleveland Indians Jacobs Field 2401 Ontario St **Fax:* Cust Svc ■ *Web:* www.indians.mlb.com	Cleveland	OH	44115	216-420-4200	420-4799*
Colorado Rockies Coors Field 2001 Blake St **Fax:* PR ■ *TF:* 800-388-7625 ■ *Web:* www.colorado.rockies.mlb.com	Denver	CO	80205	303-292-0200	296-2066*
Detroit Tigers Comerica Pk 2100 Woodward Ave **Fax:* PR ■ *Web:* www.tigers.mlb.com	Detroit	MI	48201	313-962-4000	471-2138*
Florida Marlins Dolphins Stadium 2267 Dan Marino Blvd *TF:* 877-627-5467 ■ *Web:* www.florida.marlins.mlb.com	Miami	FL	33056	305-626-7400	626-7428
Houston Astros Minute Maid Pk 501 Crawford St **Fax:* PR ■ *TF:* 800-278-7674 ■ *Web:* houston.astros.mlb.com	Houston	TX	77002	713-259-8000	259-8981*
Kansas City Royals Kauffman Stadium 1 Royal Way *TF Sales:* 800-676-9257 ■ *Web:* www.kansascity.royals.mlb.com	Kansas City	MO	64129	816-921-8000	921-5775
Los Angeles Angels of Anaheim Angel Stadium 2000 Gene Autry Way **Fax:* PR ■ *Web:* www.angels.mlb.com	Anaheim	CA	92806	714-940-2000	940-2205*
Los Angeles Dodgers Dodger Stadium 1000 Elysian Pk Ave **Fax:* PR ■ *Web:* www.losangeles.dodgers.mlb.com	Los Angeles	CA	90012	323-224-1500	224-1269*
Milwaukee Brewers Miller Pk 1 Brewers Way *TF:* 800-933-7890 ■ *Web:* www.brewers.mlb.com	Milwaukee	WI	53214	414-902-4400	902-4732
Minnesota Twins Hubert H Humphrey Metrodome 34 Kirby Puckett Pl *TF:* 800-338-9467 ■ *Web:* www.twins.mlb.com	Minneapolis	MN	55415	612-375-1366	375-7473
New York Mets Shea Stadium 123-01 Roosevelt Ave *TF:* 800-221-1155 ■ *Web:* www.mets.mlb.com	Flushing	NY	11368	718-507-6387	507-6395
New York Yankees Yankee Stadium 161st St & River Ave *Web:* www.newyork.yankees.mlb.com	Bronx	NY	10451	718-293-4300	293-8431
Oakland Athletics 7000 Coliseum Way McAphee Stadium *Web:* oaklandathletics.com	Oakland	CA	94621	510-638-4900	568-3770
Philadelphia Phillies Citizens Bank Pk 1 Citizens Bank Pk Way *Web:* philadelphia.phillies.mlb.com	Philadelphia	PA	19148	215-463-1000	
Pittsburgh Pirates PNC Pk 115 Federal St *TF:* 877-893-2827 ■ *Web:* www.pirates.mlb.com	Pittsburgh	PA	15212	412-323-5000	325-4409
Saint Louis Cardinals 420 S 8th St *Web:* stlouis.cardinals.mlb.com	Saint Louis	MO	63102	314-345-9600	345-9523
San Diego Padres Petco Pk 100 Park Blvd *Web:* padres.mlb.com	San Diego	CA	92101	619-795-5000	795-5035
San Francisco Giants AT & T Pk 24 Willie Mays Plaza *Web:* www.sfgiants.com	San Francisco	CA	94107	415-972-2000	947-2646
Seattle Mariners Safeco Field 1250 1st Ave S *Web:* seattle.mariners.mlb.com	Seattle	WA	98134	206-346-4000	346-4050
Tampa Bay Devil Rays Tropicana Field 1 Tropicana Dr **Fax:* PR ■ *TF:* 800-326-7297 ■ *Web:* www.tampabay.devilrays.mlb.com	Saint Petersburg	FL	33705	727-825-3137	825-3111*
Texas Rangers Rangers Ballpark in Arlington 1000 Ballpark Way *TF:* 888-968-3927 ■ *Web:* www.texas.rangers.mlb.com	Arlington	TX	76011	817-273-5222	273-5285
Toronto Blue Jays 1 Blue Jays Way Suite 3200 **Fax:* PR ■ *TF:* 888-654-6529 ■ *Web:* www.toronto.bluejays.mlb.com	Toronto	ON	M5V1J1	416-341-1000	341-1250*
Washington Nationals RFK Stadium 2400 E Capitol St SE *Web:* www.washington.nationals.mlb.com	Washington	DC	20003	202-349-0400	547-0025

717 SPORTS TEAMS - BASKETBALL

SEE ALSO Sports Organizations p. 1438

717-1 National Basketball Association (NBA)

	City	State	Zip	Phone	Fax
National Basketball Assn (NBA) 645 5th Ave *Web:* www.nba.com	New York	NY	10022	212-407-8000	832-3861
Atlanta Hawks Centennial Tower 101 Marietta St NW Suite 1900 *Web:* www.nba.com/hawks	Atlanta	GA	30303	404-828-3800	827-3880
Boston Celtics 226 Cswy St 4th Fl *Web:* www.nba.com	Boston	MA	02114	617-854-8000	367-4286
Charlotte Bobcats 333 E Trade St *Web:* www.nba.com/bobcats	Charlotte	NC	28202	704-688-8600	688-8732
Chicago Bulls 1901 W Madison St *Web:* www.nba.com	Chicago	IL	60612	312-455-4000	
Cleveland Cavaliers Quicken Loans Arena 1 Ctr Ct **Fax:* PR ■ *TF:* 800-332-2287 ■ *Web:* www.nba.com	Cleveland	OH	44115	216-420-2000	420-2298*
Dallas Mavericks 2909 Taylor St *Web:* www.nba.com	Dallas	TX	75226	214-747-6287	658-7121
Denver Nuggets 1000 Chopper Cir *Web:* www.nba.com	Denver	CO	80204	303-405-1100	575-1920
Detroit Pistons Palace at Auburn Hills 5 Championship Dr *Web:* www.nba.com	Auburn Hills	MI	48326	248-377-0100	377-4262
Golden State Warriors 1011 Broadway *TF:* 888-479-4667 ■ *Web:* www.nba.com	Oakland	CA	94607	510-986-2200	452-0132
Houston Rockets 1510 Polk St **Fax:* Hum Res ■ *Web:* www.nba.com/rockets	Houston	TX	77002	713-758-7200	758-7396*
Indiana Pacers Conseco Fieldhouse 125 S Pennsylvania St *Web:* www.nba.com/pacers	Indianapolis	IN	46204	317-917-2500	917-2599

				Phone	Fax
Los Angeles Clippers Staples Ctr 1111 S Figueroa St Suite 1100 *Web:* www.nba.com/clippers	Los Angeles	CA	90015	213-742-7100	742-7550
Los Angeles Lakers 555 N Nash St *Web:* www.nba.com/lakers	El Segundo	CA	90245	310-426-6000	426-6105
Memphis Grizzlies FedExForum 191 Beale St *Web:* www.nba.com/grizzlies	Memphis	TN	38103	901-205-1234	205-1235
Miami Heat American Airlines Arena 601 Biscayne Blvd *Web:* www.nba.com	Miami	FL	33132	786-777-1000	777-1609
Milwaukee Bucks Bradley Ctr 1001 N 4th St *Web:* www.nba.com	Milwaukee	WI	53203	414-227-0500	227-0543
Minnesota Timberwolves Target Ctr 600 1st Ave N *Web:* www.nba.com	Minneapolis	MN	55403	612-673-1600	673-1699
New Jersey Nets Nets Champion Ctr 390 Murray Hill Pkwy **Fax:* PR ■ *TF:* 800-765-6387 ■ *Web:* www.nba.com	East Rutherford	NJ	07073	201-935-8888	935-6691*
New Orleans Hornets 1250 Poydras St Fl 19 *Web:* www.nba.com	New Orleans	LA	70113	504-593-4900	
New York Knicks Madison Sq Garden 2 Pennsylvania Plaza 14th Fl **Fax:* PR ■ *Web:* www.nba.com/knicks	New York	NY	10121	212-465-6471	465-6498*
Orlando Magic 8701 Maitland Summit Blvd *Web:* www.nba.com	Orlando	FL	32810	407-916-2400	916-2884
Philadelphia 76ers 3601 S Broad St *Web:* www.nba.com	Philadelphia	PA	19148	215-339-7600	339-7615
Phoenix Suns US Airways Ctr 201 E Jefferson St *Web:* www.nba.com/suns	Phoenix	AZ	85004	602-379-7900	379-7990
Portland Trail Blazers 1 Ctr Ct Suite 200 *Web:* www.nba.com/blazers	Portland	OR	97227	503-234-9291	736-2187
Sacramento Kings ARCO Arena 1 Sports Pkwy *Web:* www.nba.com/kings	Sacramento	CA	95834	916-928-0000	928-0727
San Antonio Spurs 1 AT & T Ctr *Web:* www.nba.com/spurs	San Antonio	TX	78219	210-444-5000	444-5003
Seattle SuperSonics 1201 3rd Ave Suite 1000 *TF:* 800-743-7021 ■ *Web:* www.nba.com	Seattle	WA	98101	206-281-5800	281-5839
Toronto Raptors Air Canada Centre 40 Bay St Suite 400	Toronto	ON	M5J2X2	416-366-3865	359-9198
Utah Jazz 301 W S Temple St Energy Solutions Arena **Fax:* PR ■ *TF:* 800-358-7328 ■ *Web:* www.nba.com	Salt Lake City	UT	84101	801-325-2500	325-2578*
Washington Wizards Verizon Ctr 601 F St NW *TF:* 800-551-7328 ■ *Web:* www.nba.com	Washington	DC	20004	202-661-5000	

717-2 Women's National Basketball Association (WNBA)

				Phone	Fax
Women's National Basketball Assn (WNBA) 645 5th Ave *Web:* www.wnba.com	New York	NY	10022	212-688-9622	750-9622
Chicago Sky 20 W Kinzie St Suite 1000 *Web:* www.wnba.com	Chicago	IL	60610	312-828-9550	
Connecticut Sun 1 Mohegan Sun Blvd *TF:* 877-786-8499 ■ *Web:* www.wnba.com	Uncasville	CT	06382	860-862-4000	862-4010
Detroit Shock 5 Championship Dr Palace at Auburn Hills *Web:* www.wnba.com/shock	Auburn Hills	MI	48326	248-377-0100	377-3260
Houston Comets 1730 Jefferson St **Fax:* Hum Res ■ *Web:* www.wnba.com	Houston	TX	77003	713-739-7442	739-7709*
Indiana Fever Conseco Fieldhouse 125 S Pennsylvania St *Web:* www.wnba.com/fever	Indianapolis	IN	46204	317-917-2500	917-2899
Los Angeles Sparks 865 S Figueroa St # 104 *Web:* www.wnba.com	Los Angeles	CA	90017	213-929-1300	929-1325
Minnesota Lynx 600 1st Ave N Target Ctr *Web:* www.wnba.com/lynx	Minneapolis	MN	55403	612-673-1600	673-8407
New York Liberty Madison Sq Garden 2 Pennsylvania Plaza *Web:* www.wnba.com/liberty	New York	NY	10121	212-564-9622	465-6250
Phoenix Mercury US Airways Ctr 201 E Jefferson St *Web:* www.wnba.com/mercury	Phoenix	AZ	85004	602-514-8333	514-8303
Sacramento Monarchs ARCO Arena 1 Sports Pkwy *Web:* www.wnba.com/monarchs	Sacramento	CA	95834	916-928-0000	928-8109
San Antonio Silver Stars 1 AT & T Ctr *Web:* www.wnba.com/silverstars	San Antonio	TX	78219	210-444-5090	444-5003
Seattle Storm 351 Elliott Ave W Suite 500 *TF:* 800-743-7021 ■ *Web:* www.wnba.com	Seattle	WA	98119	206-281-5800	281-5839
Washington Mystics 627 N Glebe Rd Suite 850 *Web:* www.wnba.com	Arlington	VA	22203	202-266-2200	266-2220

718 SPORTS TEAMS - FOOTBALL

SEE ALSO Sports Organizations p. 1438

Phone Fax

718-1 Arena Football League (AFL)

				Phone	Fax
Arena Football League (AFL) 8700 W Bryn Mawr Ave Suite 120-S *Web:* www.arenafootball.com	Chicago	IL	60631	773-444-1000	444-1010
Arizona Rattlers 320 E McDowell Rd Suite 221 *Web:* www.azrattlers.com	Phoenix	AZ	85004	602-379-2320	379-2323
Dallas Desperados Cowboys Ctr 1 Cowboys Pkwy *Web:* 66.111.108.147/dd_community.cfm	Irving	TX	75063	972-556-9333	556-9910
Georgia Force 4400 Falcon Pkwy *Web:* www.georgiaforce.com	Flowery Branch	GA	30542	770-965-4344	965-4345
Grand Rapids Rampage 130 Fulton St W *TF:* 888-595-4878 ■ *Web:* www.rampagefootball.com	Grand Rapids	MI	49503	616-559-1871	742-5680
Kansas City Brigade 5366 W 95th St *Web:* www.kcbrigade.com	Prairie Village	KS	66207	913-383-8020	383-8386
Las Vegas Gladiators 4205 W Tompkins Suite 5	Las Vegas	NV	89103	702-731-4977	731-2921
Nashville Kats 1 Titans Way *Web:* www.katsonline.com	Nashville	TN	37213	615-565-4699	565-4252
New Orleans VooDoo 5800 Airline Dr *Web:* www.govoodoo.com	Metairie	LA	70003	504-733-0255	729-5598
New York Dragons 1535 Old Country Rd *TF:* 800-882-4753 ■ *Web:* www.newyorkdragons.com	Plainview	NY	11803	516-501-6700	501-6762
Orlando Predators 302 S Graham Ave *Web:* www.orlandopredators.com	Orlando	FL	32803	407-447-7337	999-5299
Philadelphia Soul 7 Penn Ctr 1635 Market St Suite 1700 *TF:* 888-744-5235 ■ *Web:* www.philadelphiasoul.com	Philadelphia	PA	19103	215-636-0421	636-0933
Tampa Bay Storm 401 Channelside Dr *Web:* www.tampabaystorm.com	Tampa	FL	33602	813-276-7300	276-7301
Utah Blaze 405 S Main St Suite 1100 *Web:* www.utahblaze.com	Salt Lake City	UT	84111	801-257-3555	257-3497

718-2 Canadian Football League (CFL)

				Phone	Fax
Canadian Football League 50 Wellington St E 3rd Fl *Web:* www.cfl.ca	Toronto	ON	M5E1C8	416-322-9650	322-9651
British Columbia Lions 10605 135th St *Web:* www.bclions.com	Surrey	BC	V3T4C8	604-930-5466	583-7882
Calgary Stampeders 1817 Crowchild Trail NW McMahon Stadium *Web:* www.stampeders.com	Calgary	AB	T2M4R6	403-289-0205	289-7850
Edmonton Eskimos 9023 111th Ave *TF:* 800-667-3757 ■ *Web:* www.esks.com	Edmonton	AB	T5B0C3	780-448-1525	429-3452
Hamilton Tiger-Cats 75 Balsam Ave N Ivor Wynne Stadium *TF:* 800-714-7627 ■ *Web:* www.ticats.ca	Hamilton	ON	L8L8C1	905-547-2418	549-6610
Montreal Alouettes 1260 University St Suite 100 *Web:* www.montrealalouettes.com	Montreal	QC	H3B3B9	514-871-2266	871-2277
Saskatchewan Roughriders 1910 Piffles Taylor Way PO Box 1966 *TF:* 888-474-3377 ■ *Web:* www.saskriders.com	Regina	SK	S4P3E1	306-569-2323	566-4280
Toronto Argonauts 1 Blue Jays Way Suite 3300 *Web:* www.argonauts.ca	Toronto	ON	M5V1J3	416-341-2700	341-0550
Winnipeg Blue Bombers 1465 Maroons Rd *Web:* www.bluebombers.com	Winnipeg	MB	R3G0L6	204-784-2583	783-5222

718-3 National Football League (NFL)

				Phone	Fax
National Football League (NFL) 280 Park Ave *Web:* www.nfl.com	New York	NY	10017	212-450-2000	681-7599
Arizona Cardinals 8701 S Hardy Dr *TF:* 800-999-1402 ■ *Web:* www.azcardinals.com	Tempe	AZ	85284	602-379-0101	379-1819
Atlanta Falcons 4400 Falcon Pkwy *TF:* 800-241-3489 ■ *Web:* www.atlantafalcons.com	Flowery Branch	GA	30542	770-965-3115	965-3185
Baltimore Ravens 1101 Russell St *Web:* www.baltimoreravens.com	Baltimore	MD	21230	410-261-7283	
Buffalo Bills Ralph Wilson Stadium 1 Bills Dr *TF:* 877-228-4257 ■ *Web:* www.buffalobills.com	Orchard Park	NY	14127	716-648-1800	649-6446
Carolina Panthers Bank of America Stadium 800 S Mint St *Web:* www.panthers.com	Charlotte	NC	28202	704-358-7000	358-7618
Chicago Bears 1000 Football Dr *Web:* www.chicagobears.com	Lake Forest	IL	60045	847-295-6600	295-8986
Cincinnati Bengals 1 Paul Brown Stadium *TF:* 866-621-8383 ■ *Web:* www.bengals.com	Cincinnati	OH	45202	513-621-3550	621-3570
Cleveland Browns 76 1st Ave *Web:* www.clevelandbrowns.com	Berea	OH	44017	440-891-5000	891-5009
Dallas Cowboys 1 Cowboys Pkwy *Web:* www.dallascowboys.com	Irving	TX	75063	972-556-9900	556-9304
Denver Broncos 13655 Broncos Pkwy *Web:* www.denverbroncos.com	Englewood	CO	80112	303-649-9000	649-9354
Detroit Lions 222 Republic Dr *TF:* 800-616-7627 ■ *Web:* www.detroitlions.com	Allen Park	MI	48101	313-216-4000	216-4226
Green Bay Packers 1265 Lombardi Ave PO Box 10628 *Web:* www.packers.com	Green Bay	WI	54304	920-569-7500	569-7301
Houston Texans 2 Reliant Pk *Web:* www.houstontexans.com	Houston	TX	77054	832-667-2000	667-2100
Indianapolis Colts 7001 W 56th St *TF:* 800-805-2658 ■ *Web:* www.colts.com	Indianapolis	IN	46254	317-297-2658	297-8971
Jacksonville Jaguars 1 Stadium Pl **Fax:* Mktg ■ *TF:* 877-452-4784 ■ *Web:* www.jaguars.com	Jacksonville	FL	32202	904-633-6100	633-6050*

	City	State	Zip	Phone	Fax
Kansas City Chiefs Arrowhead Stadium 1 Arrowhead Dr *Web:* www.kcchiefs.com	Kansas City	MO	64129	816-920-9300	920-4315
Miami Dolphins 7500 SW 30th St **Fax:* PR ■ *Web:* www.miamidolphins.com	Davie	FL	33314	954-452-7000	452-7055*
Minnesota Vikings 9520 Viking Dr *Web:* www.vikings.com	Eden Prairie	MN	55344	952-828-6500	828-6540
New England Patriots 1 Patriots Pl *Web:* www.patriots.com	Foxboro	MA	02035	508-543-8200	543-0285
New Orleans Saints 5800 Airline Dr *Web:* www.neworleanssaints.com	Metairie	LA	70003	504-733-0255	731-1768
New York Giants 50 State Hwy 120 Giants Stadium *Web:* www.giants.com	East Rutherford	NJ	07073	201-935-8111	939-4134
New York Jets 1000 Fulton Ave *Web:* www.newyorkjets.com	Hempstead	NY	11550	516-560-8100	560-8198
Oakland Raiders 1220 Harbor Bay Pkwy *TF:* 800-724-3377 ■ *Web:* www.raiders.com	Alameda	CA	94502	510-864-5000	864-5134
Philadelphia Eagles NovaCare Complex 1 NovaCare Way *Web:* www.philadelphiaeagles.com	Philadelphia	PA	19145	215-463-2500	339-5464
Pittsburgh Steelers 3400 S Water St *Web:* www.steelers.com	Pittsburgh	PA	15203	412-432-7800	432-7878
Saint Louis Rams 1 Rams Way *TF Cust Svc:* 800-246-7267 ■ *Web:* www.stlouisrams.com	Earth City	MO	63045	314-982-7267	770-9261
San Diego Chargers 4020 Murphy Canyon Rd *TF:* 877-242-7437 ■ *Web:* www.chargers.com	San Diego	CA	92123	858-874-4500	292-2760
San Francisco 49ers 4949 Centennial Blvd *Web:* www.sf49ers.com	Santa Clara	CA	95054	408-562-4949	727-4937
Seattle Seahawks 12 Seahawks Way *Web:* www.seahawks.com	Renton	WA	98056	888-635-4295	
Tampa Bay Buccaneers 1 Buccaneer Pl *Web:* www.buccaneers.com	Tampa	FL	33607	813-870-2700	878-0813
Tennessee Titans 460 Great Cir Rd *Web:* www.titansonline.com	Nashville	TN	37228	615-565-4000	565-4006
Washington Redskins 21300 Redskin Park Dr *Web:* www.redskins.com	Ashburn	VA	20147	703-726-7000	726-7086

719 SPORTS TEAMS - HOCKEY

SEE ALSO Sports Organizations p. 1438

	City	State	Zip	Phone	Fax
National Hockey League (NHL) 50 Bay St 11th Fl **Fax:* PR ■ *TF:* 800-363-4645 ■ *Web:* www.nhl.com	Toronto	ON	M5J2X8	416-359-7900	981-2779*
National Hockey League (NHL) 1185 Avenue of the Americas *Web:* www.nhl.com	New York	NY	10036	212-789-2000	789-2020
Anaheim Ducks 2695 E Katella Ave *TF:* 877-945-3946 ■ *Web:* www.ducks.nhl.com	Anaheim	CA	92806	714-704-2700	940-2953
Atlanta Thrashers Centennial Tower 101 Marietta St NW Suite 1900 *Web:* www.atlantathrashers.com	Atlanta	GA	30303	404-878-3800	827-5909
Boston Bruins 100 Legends Way *Web:* www.bostonbruins.com	Boston	MA	02114	617-624-1900	523-7184
Buffalo Sabres HSBC Arena 1 Seymour H Knox III Plaza *TF:* 888-467-2273 ■ *Web:* www.sabres.com	Buffalo	NY	14203	716-855-4444	855-4115
Calgary Flames Pengrowth Saddledome 555 Saddledome Rise SE **Fax:* PR ■ *Web:* www.calgaryflames.com	Calgary	AB	T2G2W1	403-777-2177	777-2195*
Carolina Hurricanes RBC Ctr 1400 Edwards Mill Rd *Web:* hurricanes.nhl.com	Raleigh	NC	27607	919-467-7825	462-7030
Chicago Blackhawks 1901 W Madison St **Fax:* PR ■ *Web:* www.chicagoblackhawks.com	Chicago	IL	60612	312-455-7000	455-7041*
Colorado Avalanche Pepsi Ctr 1000 Chopper Cir *Web:* www.coloradoavalanche.com	Denver	CO	80204	303-405-1100	575-1928
Columbus Blue Jackets Nationwide Arena 200 W Nationwide Blvd 3rd Fl *TF:* 800-645-2657 ■ *Web:* www.bluejackets.com	Columbus	OH	43215	614-246-4625	246-4007
Dallas Stars 2601 Avenue of the Stars *Web:* www.dallasstars.com	Frisco	TX	75034	214-387-5500	387-5599
Detroit Red Wings Joe Louis Arena 600 Civic Ctr Dr **Fax:* PR ■ *Web:* www.detroitredwings.com	Detroit	MI	48226	313-396-7544	567-0296*
Edmonton Oilers 11230 110th St *TF:* 866-414-4625 ■ *Web:* www.edmontonoilers.com	Edmonton	AB	T5G3H7	780-414-4000	409-5890
Florida Panthers BankAtlantic Ctr 1 Panther Pkwy **Fax:* Sales ■ *Web:* panthers.nhl.com	Sunrise	FL	33323	954-835-7000	835-7200*
Los Angeles Kings Staples Ctr 1111 S Figueroa St *TF:* 888-546-4752 ■ *Web:* www.lakings.com	Los Angeles	CA	90015	213-742-7100	742-4500
Minnesota Wild 150 Kellogg Blvd W *Web:* www.wild.com	Saint Paul	MN	55102	651-222-9453	222-1055
Montreal Canadiens Bell Centre 1260 de la Gauchetiere St W **Fax:* PR ■ *TF:* 800-663-6786 ■ *Web:* www.canadiens.com	Montreal	QC	H3B5E8	514-989-2841	989-3085*
Nashville Predators 501 Broadway *Web:* www.nashvillepredators.com	Nashville	TN	37203	615-770-7825	770-2341
New Jersey Devils Continental Airlines Arena 50 Rt 120N *TF:* 800-653-3845 ■ *Web:* www.newjerseydevils.com	East Rutherford	NJ	07073	201-935-6050	935-1407
New York Islanders 1535 Old Country Rd *TF:* 800-882-4753 ■ *Web:* www.newyorkislanders.com	Plainview	NY	11803	516-501-6700	501-6729
New York Rangers 2 Pennsylvania Plaza *Web:* www.newyorkrangers.com	New York	NY	10121	212-465-6486	465-6494
Ottawa Senators 1000 Palladium Dr Scotia Bank Pl *TF:* 800-444-7367 ■ *Web:* www.ottawasenators.com	Kanata	ON	K2V1A5	613-599-0100	599-0358
Philadelphia Flyers Wachovia Ctr 3601 S Broad St *Web:* www.philadelphiaflyers.com	Philadelphia	PA	19148	215-465-4500	389-9476
Phoenix Coyotes 6751 N Sunset Blvd Suite 200 *Web:* www.phoenixcoyotes.com	Glendale	AZ	85305	623-772-3200	772-3201
Pittsburgh Penguins 1 Chatham Ctr Suite 400 *TF:* 800-642-7367 ■ *Web:* www.pittsburghpenguins.com	Pittsburgh	PA	15219	412-642-1300	642-1859
Saint Louis Blues Savvis Ctr 1401 Clark Ave *Web:* www.stlouisblues.com	Saint Louis	MO	63103	314-622-5435	622-2582
San Jose Sharks HP Pavilion at San Jose 525 W Santa Clara St *TF:* 800-755-5050 ■ *Web:* www.sj-sharks.com	San Jose	CA	95113	408-287-7070	999-5797
Tampa Bay Lightning St Pete Times Forum 401 Channelside Dr *Web:* lightning.nhl.com	Tampa	FL	33602	813-301-6500	301-1482
Toronto Maple Leafs Air Canada Center 40 Bay St Suite 400 *Web:* mapleleafs.nhl.com	Toronto	ON	M5J2X2	416-815-5700	359-9205
Vancouver Canucks General Motors Pl 800 Griffiths Way *TF:* 888-446-7522 ■ *Web:* www.canucks.com	Vancouver	BC	V6B6G1	604-899-4600	899-7401
Washington Capitals 627 N Glebe Rd Suite 850 *Web:* www.washingtoncaps.com	Arlington	VA	22203	202-266-2200	266-2210

720 SPORTS TEAMS - SOCCER

SEE ALSO Sports Organizations p. 1438

	City	State	Zip	Phone	Fax
Major League Soccer (MLS) 420 5th Ave 7th Fl *Web:* www.mlsnet.com	New York	NY	10018	212-450-1200	
Chicago Fire 7000 S Harlem Ave *TF:* 888-657-3473 ■ *Web:* www.chicago-fire.com	Ridgeview	IL	60455	708-594-7200	496-6050
Club Deportivo Chivas USA *Home Depot Ctr* 18400 Avalon Blvd *TF:* 877-244-8271 ■ *Web:* chivas.usa.mlsnet.com	Carson	CA	90746	310-630-4550	630-4551
Colorado Rapids 6000 Victory Way *Web:* www.coloradorapids.com	Commerce City	CO	80266	303-727-3500	727-3536
Columbus Crew Crew Stadium 1 Black & Gold Blvd *TF:* 800-273-9326	Columbus	OH	43211	614-447-2739	447-4109
DC United 2400 E Capitol St SE *Web:* www.dcunited.com	Washington	DC	20003	202-587-5000	587-5400
FC Dallas 9200 World Cup Way Suite 202 *TF:* 888-323-4625 ■ *Web:* www.fcdallas.mlsnet.com	Frisco	TX	75034	214-705-6700	705-6799
Houston Dynamo 1415 Louisiana St Suite 3400 *Web:* www.houstondynamo.com	Houston	TX	77002	713-276-7500	276-7580
Kansas City Wizards 8900 State Line Rd *Web:* www.kcwizards.com	Leawood	KS	66206	913-387-3400	387-3401
Los Angeles Galaxy Home Depot Ctr 18400 Avalon Blvd Suite 200 *TF:* 877-342-5299 ■ *Web:* www.lagalaxy.com	Carson	CA	90746	310-630-2200	630-2250
New England Revolution Gillette Stadium 1 Patriot Pl *TF:* 877-438-7387 ■ *Web:* www.revolutionsoccer.net	Foxboro	MA	02035	508-543-5001	384-9128
New York Red Bulls 1 Harmon Plaza 8th Fl *TF:* 877-727-6223 ■ *Web:* www.newyorkredbulls.com	Secaucus	NJ	07094	201-583-7000	583-7055
Real Salt Lake 515 S 700 E #2R *Web:* www.realsaltlake.com	Salt Lake City	UT	84102	801-924-8585	933-4713
Toronto FC BMO Field 170 Princes' Blvd *Web:* toronto.fc.mlsnet.com	Toronto	ON	M6K3C3	416-263-5700	

721 SPRINGS - HEAVY-GAUGE

	City	State	Zip	Phone	Fax
Associated Spring Barnes Group Inc 80 Scott Swamp Rd *Web:* www.asbg.com	Farmington	CT	06032	860-678-0700	409-4611
Automatic Spring Products Corp 803 Taylor Ave *Web:* www.automaticspring.com	Grand Haven	MI	49417	616-842-7800	842-4380
Barnes Group Inc 123 Main St *NYSE:* B ■ *TF:* 800-877-8803 ■ *Web:* www.bginc.com	Bristol	CT	06011	860-583-7070	589-3507
Draco Spring Mfg Co PO Box 266086 *Web:* www.dracospring.com	Houston	TX	77207	713-645-4973	645-0480
General Wire Spring Co 1101 Thompson Ave *TF:* 800-245-6200 ■ *Web:* www.generalwirespring.com	McKees Rocks	PA	15136	412-771-6300	771-6317
HS Spring Group 3805 Business Pk Dr *Web:* www.hsspring.com	Louisville	KY	40213	502-962-6464	962-6410
MW Industries Inc 101 Godfrey St PO Box 7008 *Web:* www.mw-ind.com	Logansport	IN	46947	574-722-8242	722-8224
Pa-Ted Spring Co Inc 137 Vincent P Kelly Rd	Bristol	CT	06010	860-582-6368	583-1044
Perfection Spring & Stamping Corp 1449 E Algonquin Rd *Web:* www.pss-corp.com	Mount Prospect	IL	60056	847-437-3900	437-1322
Rockford Spring Co 3801 S Central Ave *Web:* www.rockfordspring.com	Rockford	IL	61102	815-968-3000	968-3100
Service Spring Corp 4370 Moline Martin Rd *TF:* 800-752-8522 ■ *Web:* www.sscorp.com	Millbury	OH	43447	419-838-6081	838-6071

	City	State	ZIP	Phone	Fax
Southern Spring & Stamping Inc 401 Sub Stn Rd *TF:* 800-450-5882 ■ *Web:* www.southernspring.com	Venice	FL	34292	941-488-2276	485-9156
Stanley Spring & Stamping Corp 5050 W Foster Ave *Web:* www.stanleyspring.com	Chicago	IL	60630	773-777-2600	777-3894

722 SPRINGS - LIGHT-GAUGE

	City	State	ZIP	Phone	Fax
AJ Kay Co 5406 N Elston Ave	Chicago	IL	60630	773-545-5955	545-2587
Alsco Co 1014 Clarkson Parma Town Ln Rd	Hilton	NY	14468	585-392-2585	392-1873
American Coil Spring Co Inc 1041 E Keating Ave	Muskegon	MI	49442	231-726-4021	726-2206
Atlantic Spring 137 Hwy 202 S *Web:* www.chestnutgroup.com	Ringoes	NJ	08551	908-788-5800	788-0511
Atlas Spring Mfg Corp 150 E 157th St	Gardena	CA	90248	310-660-0150	660-0172
Century Spring Corp 222 E 16th St *TF:* 800-237-5225 ■ *Web:* www.centuryspring.com	Los Angeles	CA	90015	213-749-1466	749-3802
Connecticut Spring & Stamping Corp 48 Spring Ln **Fax:* Cust Svc ■ *TF:* 800-255-8590 ■ *Web:* www.ctspringandstamping.com	Farmington	CT	06034	860-677-1341	677-7199*
Dudek & Bock Spring Mfg Co 5100 W Roosevelt Rd *Web:* www.dudek-bock.com	Chicago	IL	60644	773-379-4100	379-4715
Economy Spring & Stamping Co 29 DePaolo Dr PO Box 651 *Web:* www.economyspring.com	Southington	CT	06489	860-621-7358	621-7882
Exacto Spring Corp 1201 Hickory St *Web:* www.exacto.com	Grafton	WI	53024	262-377-3970	377-3854
Fennell Spring LLC PO Box 69	Horseheads	NY	14845	607-739-3541	739-7601
Flex-O-Lators Inc 1460 Jackson Dr *TF:* 800-641-4363	Carthage	MO	64836	417-358-4095	358-3019
General Wire Spring Co 1101 Thompson Ave *TF:* 800-245-6200 ■ *Web:* www.generalwirespring.com	McKees Rocks	PA	15136	412-771-6300	771-6317
Hickory Springs Mfg Co 235 2nd Ave NW *TF:* 800-438-5341 ■ *Web:* www.hickorysprings.com	Hickory	NC	28601	828-328-2201	328-5501
John Evans' Sons Inc 1 Spring Ave PO Box 885 *Web:* www.springcompany.com	Lansdale	PA	19446	215-368-7700	368-9019
Lee Spring Co Inc 140 58th St # 3C *TF:* 800-426-0272 ■ *Web:* www.leespring.com	Brooklyn	NY	11220	718-236-2222	236-3919
Leggett & Platt Inc Number 1 Leggett Rd PO Box 757 *NYSE:* LEG ■ *TF:* 800-888-4569 ■ *Web:* www.leggett.com	Carthage	MO	64836	417-358-8131	358-6996
Maryland Precision Spring Co 8900 Kelso Dr *Web:* www.mw-ind.com	Baltimore	MD	21221	410-391-7400	687-9223
Mastercoil Spring 4010 W Albany St *Web:* www.mastercoil.com	McHenry	IL	60050	815-344-0051	344-0071
Micromatic Spring & Stamping Co Inc 9325 King St *Web:* www.micromaticspring.com	Franklin Park	IL	60131	847-671-6600	671-3452
Mid-West Spring & Stamping Co 1404 Joliet Rd Unit C **Fax Area Code:* 888 ■ *TF:* 800-838-7812 ■ *Web:* www.mwspring.com	Romeoville	IL	60446	630-739-3800	643-9781*
Monticello Spring Corp 3137 Freeman Rd PO Box 705 *Web:* www.monticellospring.com	Monticello	IN	47960	574-583-8090	583-9299
Newcomb Spring Corp 235 Spring St *Web:* www.newcombspring.com	Southington	CT	06489	860-621-0111	621-7048
O & G Spring & Wire Forms Specialty Co 4500 W Division St *Web:* www.ogspring.com	Chicago	IL	60651	773-772-9331	772-6578
Pa-Ted Spring Co Inc 137 Vincent P Kelly Rd	Bristol	CT	06010	860-582-6368	583-1044
Perfection Spring & Stamping Corp 1449 E Algonquin Rd *Web:* www.pss-corp.com	Mount Prospect	IL	60056	847-437-3900	437-1322
Peterson Spring 21200 Telegraph Rd *Web:* www.pspring.com	Southfield	MI	48033	248-799-5400	357-3176
Plymouth Spring Co Inc 281 Lake Ave *Web:* www.plymouthspring.com	Bristol	CT	06010	860-584-0594	584-0943
Precision Coil Spring Co 10107 Rose Ave *Web:* www.pcspring.com	El Monte	CA	91731	626-444-0561	444-3712
Precision Products Group Inc 4205 Galleria Dr	Rockford	IL	61111	815-636-9800	636-8294
Precision Products Group Inc Michigan Spring Div 2700 Wickham Dr	Muskegon	MI	49441	231-755-1691	755-3449
QS/Togo Inc 355 Jay St *Web:* www.qsti.com	Coldwater	MI	49036	517-278-2391	279-4680
R & L Spring Co 1097 Geneva Pkwy *Web:* www.rlspring.com	Lake Geneva	WI	53147	262-249-7854	249-7866
Rockford Spring Co 3801 S Central Ave *Web:* www.rockfordspring.com	Rockford	IL	61102	815-968-3000	968-3100
Rowley Spring & Stamping Corp 210 Redstone Hill Rd *Web:* www.rowleyspring.com	Bristol	CT	06010	860-582-8175	589-8718
Southern Spring & Stamping Inc 401 Sub Stn Rd *TF:* 800-450-5882 ■ *Web:* www.southernspring.com	Venice	FL	34292	941-488-2276	485-9156
Spring Dynamics Inc 7378 Research Dr *TF:* 888-274-8432 ■ *Web:* www.springdynamics.com	Almont	MI	48003	810-798-2622	798-2902
Spring Engineers Inc 9740 Tanner Rd *TF:* 800-899-9488	Houston	TX	77041	713-690-9488	690-1199
Spring Suhm Works Inc 2710 McKinney St *TF:* 800-338-6903 ■ *Web:* www.suhm.net	Houston	TX	77003	713-224-9293	224-9418
Stanley Spring & Stamping Corp 5050 W Foster Ave *Web:* www.stanleyspring.com	Chicago	IL	60630	773-777-2600	777-3894
Sterling Spring Corp 5432 W 54th St *TF:* 800-969-7884 ■ *Web:* www.sterlingspring.com	Chicago	IL	60638	773-582-6464	582-0657
Twist Inc 47 S Limestone St *Web:* www.twistinc.com	Jamestown	OH	45335	937-675-9581	675-6781
Walker Corp 1555 Vintage Ave *Web:* www.walkercorp.com	Ontario	CA	91761	909-390-4300	390-4301
Wesco Spring Co 4501 S Knox Ave *Web:* www.wescospring.com	Chicago	IL	60632	773-838-3350	838-0018
Winamac Coil Spring Inc 512 N Smith St *Web:* www.winamaccoilspring.com	Kewanna	IN	46939	574-653-2186	653-2645
Wire Products Co Inc 14601 Industrial Pkwy *Web:* www.wire-products.com	Cleveland	OH	44135	216-267-0777	267-7972
Yost Superior Co PO Box 1487 *TF:* 800-544-4570 ■ *Web:* www.yostsuperior.com	Springfield	OH	45501	937-323-7591	323-5180

723 STADIUMS & ARENAS

SEE ALSO Convention Centers p. 1749; Performing Arts Facilities p. 2392

	City	State	ZIP	Phone	Fax
1st Mariner Arena 201 W Baltimore St *Web:* www.1stmarinerarena.com	Baltimore	MD	21201	410-347-2020	347-2042
Air Canada Centre 40 Bay St *Web:* www.theaircanadacentre.com	Toronto	ON	M5J2X2	416-815-5500	359-9231
Alamodome 100 Montana St *TF:* 800-884-3663 ■ *Web:* www.alamodome.com	San Antonio	TX	78203	210-207-3663	207-3646
Albert Lea City Arena 221 E Clark St *Web:* www.city.albertlea.org	Albert Lea	MN	56007	507-377-4374	
Allen County War Memorial Coliseum 4000 Parnell Ave *Web:* www.memorialcoliseum.com	Fort Wayne	IN	46805	260-482-9502	484-1637
Allstate Arena 6920 Mannheim Rd *Web:* www.allstatearena.com	Rosemont	IL	60018	847-635-6601	635-6606
Aloha Stadium 99-500 Salt Lake Blvd *Web:* www.alohastadium.hawaii.gov	Honolulu	HI	96818	808-483-2500	483-2823
American Airlines Arena 601 Biscayne Blvd **Fax:* Hum Res ■ *Web:* www.aaarena.com	Miami	FL	33132	786-777-1000	777-1230*
American Airlines Ctr 2500 Victory Ave *TF:* 800-745-3000 ■ *Web:* www.americanairlinescenter.com	Dallas	TX	75219	214-222-3687	
Amway Arena 600 W Amelia St *Web:* www.orlandovenues.net	Orlando	FL	32801	407-849-2000	849-2329
Angel Stadium 2000 Gene Autry Way *Web:* www.losangeles.angels.mlb.com	Anaheim	CA	92806	714-940-2000	940-2244
Arrowhead Stadium 1 Arrowhead Dr **Fax:* PR ■ *Web:* www.kcchiefs.com/arrowhead	Kansas City	MO	64129	816-920-9300	923-4719*
AT & T Park 24 Willie Mays Plaza *TF:* 877-473-4849 ■ *Web:* www.sanfrancisco.giants.mlb.com	San Francisco	CA	94107	415-972-1800	947-2925
AT&T Ctr 1 AT&TCtr *TF Resv:* 800-745-3000 ■ *Web:* www.attcenter.com	San Antonio	TX	78219	210-444-5000	444-5100
Bank of America Stadium 800 S Mint St *Web:* www.panthers.com	Charlotte	NC	28202	704-358-7000	358-7615
BankAtlantic Ctr 1 Panther Pkwy *Web:* www.bankatlanticcenter.com	Sunrise	FL	33323	954-835-7000	835-7200
Bell Centre 1260 de la Gauchetiere St W *Web:* www.centrebell.ca	Montreal	QC	H3B5E8	514-989-2800	989-2895
BI-LO Ctr 650 N Academy St *Web:* www.bilocenter.com	Greenville	SC	29601	864-241-3800	250-4939
Big Sandy Superstore Arena 1 Civic Ctr Plaza *Web:* www.bigsandyarena.com	Huntington	WV	25701	304-696-5990	696-4463
Blue Cross Arena at the War Memorial 1 War Memorial Sq *Web:* www.bluecrossarena.com	Rochester	NY	14614	585-758-5300	758-5327
Bradley Ctr 1001 N 4th St *Web:* www.bradleycenter.com	Milwaukee	WI	53203	414-226-2363	227-0497
British Columbia Place Stadium 777 Pacific Blvd *Web:* www.bcplacestadium.com	Vancouver	BC	V6B4Y8	604-669-2300	661-3412
Broome County Veterans Memorial Arena 1 Stuart St	Binghamton	NY	13905	607-778-1527	778-1529
Busch Stadium 700 Clark St *TF:* 800-352-0212 ■ *Web:* www.stlouis.cardinals.mlb.com	Saint Louis	MO	63102	314-345-9600	345-9523
Canal Park Stadium 300 S Main St *TF:* 800-972-3767	Akron	OH	44308	330-253-5151	253-3300
Charlotte Bobcats Arena 333 E Trade St *Web:* www.timewarnercablearena.com	Charlotte	NC	28202	704-424-4120	688-8733
Chase Field 401 E Jefferson St *TF:* 888-777-4664 ■ *Web:* www.arizona.diamondbacks.mlb.com	Phoenix	AZ	85004	602-462-6500	462-6600
Cincinnati Gardens 2250 Seymour Ave *Web:* www.cincygardens.com	Cincinnati	OH	45212	513-631-7793	351-5898
Citizens Bank Park 1 Citizens Bank Pk Way *Web:* www.philadelphia.phillies.mlb.com	Philadelphia	PA	19148	215-463-6000	389-3050
Cleveland Browns Stadium 100 Alfred Lerner Way *TF Sales:* 888-891-1999 ■ *Web:* www.clevelandbrowns.com/stadium	Cleveland	OH	44114	440-891-5000	
Columbus Civic Ctr 400 4th St *TF:* 800-711-3986 ■ *Web:* www.columbusciviccenter.org	Columbus	GA	31901	706-653-4482	653-4481
Comcast Spectacor LP 3601 S Broad St *Web:* www.comcast-spectacor.com	Philadelphia	PA	19148	215-336-3600	389-9506
Comerica Park 2100 Woodward Ave *Web:* www.detroit.tigers.mlb.com	Detroit	MI	48201	313-962-2000	471-2297
Conseco Fieldhouse 125 S Pennsylvania St *Web:* www.consecofieldhouse.com	Indianapolis	IN	46204	317-917-2500	917-2599
Coors Field 2001 Blake St *TF:* 800-388-7625 ■ *Web:* www.colorado.rockies.mlb.com	Denver	CO	80205	303-292-0200	312-2115
Cotton Bowl 3750 Midway Plaza	Dallas	TX	75315	214-939-2222	939-2224
Cowtown Coliseum 121 E Exchange Ave *TF:* 888-269-8696 ■ *Web:* www.cowtowncoliseum.com	Fort Worth	TX	76164	817-625-1025	625-1148
David S Palmer Arena 100 W Main St *Web:* www.palmerarena.com	Danville	IL	61832	217-431-2424	431-6444
Denver Coliseum 4600 Humboldt St *Web:* www.denvercoliseum.com	Denver	CO	80216	720-865-2475	865-2467
Dodger Stadium 1000 Elysian Pk Ave *Web:* www.losangeles.dodgers.mlb.com	Los Angeles	CA	90012	323-224-1500	224-1269

Name / Address	City	State	ZIP	Phone	Fax
Dunkin' Donuts Ctr 1 LaSalle Sq *Web:* www.dunkindonutscenter.com	Providence	RI	02903	401-331-0700	751-6792
Ed Smith Stadium 2700 12th St	Sarasota	FL	34237	941-954-4101	365-1587
Edward Jones Dome 701 Convention Plaza *Web:* www.stlouisrams.com	Saint Louis	MO	63101	314-342-5036	342-5040
Energy Solutions Arena 301 W S Temple *Fax: PR ■ *Web:* www.energysolutionsarena.com	Salt Lake City	UT	84101	801-325-2000	325-2578*
Family Arena 2002 Arena Pkwy *Web:* www.familyarena.com	Saint Charles	MO	63303	636-896-4242	896-4205
FARGODOME 1800 N University Dr *Web:* www.fargodome.com	Fargo	ND	58102	701-241-9100	237-0987
FedEx Field 1600 FedEx Way *Web:* www.redskins.com	Landover	MD	20785	301-276-6000	276-6001
FedEx Forum 191 Beale St *Web:* www.nba.com/grizzlies	Memphis	TN	38103	901-205-1234	205-1235
Fenway Park 4 Yawkey Way *TF:* 877-733-7699 ■ *Web:* www.redsox.com	Boston	MA	02215	617-267-9440	226-6682
Ford Ctr 100 W Reno Ave *Web:* www.okfordcenter.com	Oklahoma City	OK	73102	405-602-8700	
Ford Field 2000 Brush St Suite 200 *Web:* www.detroitlions.com	Detroit	MI	48226	313-262-2000	262-2808
Frank Erwin Ctr 1701 Red River PO Box 2929 *Web:* www.uterwincenter.com	Austin	TX	78701	512-471-7744	471-9652
Freeman Coliseum 3201 E Houston St *Web:* www.freemancoliseum.com	San Antonio	TX	78219	210-226-1177	226-5081
Garrett Coliseum 1555 Federal Dr *Web:* www.garrett.state.al.us	Montgomery	AL	36107	334-242-5597	240-3242
George M Sullivan Sports Arena 1600 Gambell St *Web:* www.sullivanarena.com	Anchorage	AK	99501	907-279-0618	274-0676
Georgia Dome 1 Georgia Dome Dr NW *Web:* www.gadome.com	Atlanta	GA	30313	404-223-9200	223-8011
Giants Stadium 50 State Hwy 120 *Fax: Hum Res ■ *Web:* www.giants.com	East Rutherford	NJ	07073	201-935-8500	935-4262*
Gillette Stadium 1 Patriots Pl *Web:* www.gillettestadium.com	Foxboro	MA	02035	508-543-8200	543-0285
Great American Ball Park 100 Joe Nuxhall Way *Web:* www.cincinnati.reds.mlb.com	Cincinnati	OH	45202	513-765-7000	765-7342
Greensboro Coliseum 1921 W Lee St *Web:* www.greensborocoliseum.com	Greensboro	NC	27403	336-373-7400	373-2170
Hampton Coliseum 1000 Coliseum Dr PO Box 7309 *Web:* www.hampton.gov/coliseum	Hampton	VA	23666	757-838-5650	838-2595
Heinz Field 100 Art Rooney Ave *Web:* www.steelers.com	Pittsburgh	PA	15212	412-697-7181	697-7701
Hersheypark Arena & Stadium 550 W Hersheypark Dr *Web:* www.hersheyparkstadium.com	Hershey	PA	17033	717-534-3911	534-8996
Honda Ctr 2695 E Katella Ave *TF:* 877-945-3946 ■ *Web:* www.hondacenter.com	Anaheim	CA	92806	714-704-2400	704-2443
HP Pavilion at San Jose 525 W Santa Clara St *TF:* 800-755-5050 ■ *Web:* www.hppsj.com	San Jose	CA	95113	408-287-7070	999-5797
HSBC Arena 1 Seymour Knox III Plaza *TF:* 888-467-2273 ■ *Web:* www.hsbcarena.com	Buffalo	NY	14203	716-855-4100	855-4122
Hubert H Humphrey Metrodome 900 S 5th St *Web:* www.msfc.com	Minneapolis	MN	55415	612-332-0386	332-8334
Husky Stadium 3800 Mont Lake Blvd	Seattle	WA	98105	206-543-2246	
i Wireless Ctr 1201 River Dr *Web:* www.iwirelesscenter.com	Moline	IL	61265	309-764-2001	764-2192
Independence Stadium 3301 Pershing Blvd	Shreveport	LA	71109	318-673-7758	673-7786
INVESCO Field at Mile High 1701 Bryant St *Web:* www.invescofieldatmilehigh.com	Denver	CO	80204	720-258-3000	258-3050
Izod Ctr 50 State Hwy 120 *TF:* 800-745-3000 ■ *Web:* www.meadowlands.com	East Rutherford	NJ	07073	201-935-8500	
Jacksonville Municipal Stadium 1 Stadium Pl *Fax: Mktg ■ *TF:* 877-452-4784 ■ *Web:* www.jaguars.com	Jacksonville	FL	32202	904-633-6000	633-6050*
Jacksonville Veterans Memorial Arena 300 A Philip Randolph Blvd *Web:* www.jaxevents.com	Jacksonville	FL	32202	904-630-3900	854-0601
Jobing.com Arena 9400 W Maryland Ave *Web:* www.jobingarena.com	Glendale	AZ	85305	623-772-3200	772-3201
Joe Louis Arena 600 Civic Ctr Dr *Web:* www.olympiaentertainment.com	Detroit	MI	48226	313-396-7444	396-7994
Kansas Coliseum 1229 E 85th St N	Valley Center	KS	67147	316-660-1000	755-2869
Kauffman Stadium 1 Royal Way *TF:* 800-676-9257 ■ *Web:* www.kcroyals.com	Kansas City	MO	64129	816-921-8000	921-5775
Kemper Arena 1800 Genessee St *TF:* 800-634-3942 ■ *Web:* www.kemperarenakc.com	Kansas City	MO	64102	816-513-4000	513-4001
Kentucky Fair & Expo Ctr 937 Phillips Ln *Web:* www.kyfairexpo.org	Louisville	KY	40209	502-367-5000	367-5139
Key Arena 305 Harrison St *Web:* www.seattlecenter.com	Seattle	WA	98109	206-684-7202	684-7343
Ladd-Peebles Stadium 1621 Virginia St *Web:* www.laddpeeblesstadium.com	Mobile	AL	36604	251-208-2500	208-2514
Lambeau Field Atrium 1265 Lombardi Ave *Web:* www.packers.com	Green Bay	WI	54304	920-569-7500	569-7301
Laredo Energy Arena 6700 Arena Blvd *Web:* www.learena.com	Laredo	TX	78041	956-791-9192	523-7777
LC Walker Arena & Conference Ctr 955 4th St *Web:* www.lcwalkerarena.com	Muskegon	MI	49440	231-726-2939	726-4620
Lincoln Financial Field 1 NovaCare Way *Fax Area Code: 267 ■ *Web:* www.lincolnfinancialfield.com	Philadelphia	PA	19145	215-463-2500	570-4040*
Long Beach Arena 300 E Ocean Blvd *Web:* www.longbeachcc.com/arena.htm	Long Beach	CA	90802	562-436-3636	436-9491
Los Angeles Memorial Coliseum 3939 S Figueroa St *Web:* www.lacoliseum.com	Los Angeles	CA	90037	213-747-7111	748-5828
Los Angeles Memorial Coliseum & Sports Arena 3939 S Figueroa St *Web:* www.lacoliseum.com	Los Angeles	CA	90037	213-748-6136	746-9346
Louis J Tullio Arena 809 French St *Web:* www.erieevents.com/tullio.html	Erie	PA	16501	814-452-4857	455-9931
Louisiana Superdome 1500 Girod St PO Box 52439 *TF:* 800-756-7074 ■ *Web:* www.superdome.com	New Orleans	LA	70112	504-587-3663	587-3848
LP Field 1 Titans Way *Web:* www.titansonline.com	Nashville	TN	37213	615-565-4300	565-4444
Lubbock Municipal Auditorium/Coliseum Brownfield Hwy & 4th St *Web:* lmcc.ci.lubbock.tx.us/facilities/auditoriumColiseum.aspx	Lubbock	TX	79415	806-775-2242	775-3240
Lucas Oil Stadium 500 S Capitol Ave *Web:* www.icclos.com	Indianapolis	IN	46225	317-262-8600	262-5700
M&T Bank Stadium 1101 Russell St *Web:* www.baltimoreravens.com	Baltimore	MD	21230	410-261-7283	
Macon Centreplex Coliseum 200 Coliseum Dr *TF:* 877-532-6144 ■ *Web:* www.maconcentreplex.com	Macon	GA	31217	478-751-9152	751-9154
Madison Square Garden 2 Pennsylvania Plaza *Fax: Sales ■ *Web:* www.thegarden.com	New York	NY	10121	212-465-6000	465-6092*
Martin Luther King Jr Arena 301 W Oglethorpe Ave *TF:* 800-351-7469 ■ *Web:* www.savannahcivic.com	Savannah	GA	31401	912-651-6550	651-6552
Meadowlands Sports Complex 50 State Hwy 120 *TF:* 800-745-3000 ■ *Web:* www.meadowlands.com	East Rutherford	NJ	07073	201-935-8500	935-4262
Mellon Arena 66 Mario Lemieux Pl *Web:* www.mellonarena.com	Pittsburgh	PA	15219	412-642-1800	642-1925
MetraPark Arena 308 6th Ave N *TF:* 800-366-8538 ■ *Web:* www.metrapark.com	Billings	MT	59101	406-256-2400	254-7991
MGM Grand Garden Arena 3799 Las Vegas Blvd S *Web:* www.mgmgrand.com	Las Vegas	NV	89109	702-891-1111	891-3036
Michigan Stadium 1201 S Main St University of Michigan *TF:* 866-296-6849 ■ *Web:* www.mgoblue.com	Ann Arbor	MI	48104	734-647-2583	764-3221
Minute Maid Park 501 Crawford St *TF:* 877-927-8767 ■ *Web:* www.mlb.mlb.com	Houston	TX	77002	713-259-8000	259-8981
Mississippi Veterans Memorial Stadium 2531 N State St *Web:* www.ms-veteransstadium.com	Jackson	MS	39216	601-354-6021	354-6019
Monster Park 602 Jamestown Ave	San Francisco	CA	94124	415-656-4949	467-3049
Mullins Ctr 200 Commonwealth Ave University of Massachusetts *Web:* www.mullinscenter.com	Amherst	MA	01003	413-545-3001	545-3005
Municipal Auditorium Arena 301 W 13th St *TF:* 800-821-7060 ■ *Web:* www.kcconvention.com	Kansas City	MO	64105	816-513-5000	513-5001
Nassau Veterans Memorial Coliseum 1255 Hempstead Tpke *Web:* www.nassaucoliseum.com	Uniondale	NY	11553	516-794-9300	794-9389
Nationwide Arena 200 W Nationwide Blvd *TF:* 800-645-2657 ■ *Web:* www.nationwidearena.com	Columbus	OH	43215	614-246-2000	246-4300
Neil S Blaisdell Center Arena 777 Ward Ave *Web:* www.blaisdellcenter.com	Honolulu	HI	96814	808-527-5400	527-5433
New Orleans Arena 1501 Girod St *TF:* 800-756-7074 ■ *Web:* www.neworleansarena.com	New Orleans	LA	70113	504-587-3663	587-3848
Norfolk Scope Arena 201 E Brambleton Ave Scope Arena *Web:* www.norfolkscope.com	Norfolk	VA	23510	757-664-6464	664-6990
North Charleston Coliseum & Convention Ctr 5001 Coliseum Dr *Web:* www.northcharlestoncoliseumpac.com	North Charleston	SC	29418	843-529-5050	529-5010
Oakland Arena & McAfee Coliseum 7000 Coliseum Way *Web:* www.coliseum.com	Oakland	CA	94621	510-569-2121	569-4246
Ohio Stadium 411 Woody Hayes Dr *Web:* www.ohiostatebuckeyes.com	Columbus	OH	43210	614-292-7572	292-0506
Olympic Center Arena 2634 Main St *TF:* 800-462-6236 ■ *Web:* www.orda.org	Lake Placid	NY	12946	518-523-1655	523-9275
Oriole Park at Camden Yards 333 Camden St *TF:* 888-848-2473 ■ *Web:* www.baltimore.orioles.mlb.com	Baltimore	MD	21201	410-547-6100	
Palace of Auburn Hills 5 Championship Dr *Fax: PR ■ *Web:* www.palacenet.com	Auburn Hills	MI	48326	248-377-0100	377-3260*
Paul Brown Stadium 1 Paul Brown Stadium *Web:* www.bengals.com/stadium/index.html	Cincinnati	OH	45202	513-621-3550	621-3570
Peoria Civic Center Arena 201 SW Jefferson St *Web:* www.peoriaciviccenter.com	Peoria	IL	61602	309-673-8900	673-9223
Pepsi Ctr 1000 Chopper Cir *Web:* www.pepsicenter.com	Denver	CO	80204	303-405-1100	405-1315
Perani Arena & Event Ctr 3501 Lapeer Rd *Web:* www.peraniarena.com	Flint	MI	48503	810-744-0580	744-2906
Percival Molson Memorial Stadium 475 Pine Ave W *Web:* www.montrealalouettes.com	Montreal	QC	H2W1S4	514-398-7014	
Petco Park 100 Pk Blvd *TF:* 888-487-3219 ■ *Web:* www.padres.com	San Diego	CA	92101	619-795-5000	795-5035
PGE Park 1844 SW Morrison St *Web:* www.pgepark.com	Portland	OR	97205	503-553-5400	553-5405
Philips Arena 1 Philips Dr *Web:* www.philipsarena.com	Atlanta	GA	30303	404-878-3000	878-3055
PNC Park 115 Federal St *TF:* 800-289-2827 ■ *Web:* www.pittsburgh.pirates.mlb.com	Pittsburgh	PA	15212	412-321-2827	325-4404
Power Balance Pavilion 1 Sports Pkwy *Web:* www.powerbalancepavilion.com	Sacramento	CA	95834	916-928-0000	928-0727
Progressive Field 2401 Ontario St *TF:* 800-388-7423 ■ *Web:* www.cleveland.indians.mlb.com	Cleveland	OH	44115	216-420-4444	420-4799
Qualcomm Stadium 9449 Friars Rd *Web:* www.sandiego.gov/qualcomm	San Diego	CA	92108	619-641-3100	283-0460
Quicken Loans Arena 1 Ctr Ct *TF:* 888-894-9424 ■ *Web:* www.theqarena.com	Cleveland	OH	44115	216-420-2000	420-2298
Qwest Arena 233 S Capitol Blvd *Web:* www.qwestarenaidaho.com	Boise	ID	83702	208-424-2200	424-2222

Phone Fax

Qwest Field 800 Occidental Ave S Suite 200 . . . . Seattle WA 98134 206-381-7555 381-7557
Web: www.seahawks.com/stadium.aspx?SecID=31
Ralph Wilson Stadium 1 Bills Dr . . . . Orchard Park NY 14127 716-648-1800 649-6446
Web: www.buffalobills.com
Rangers Ballpark in Arlington
1000 Ballpark Way Suite 400 . . . . Arlington TX 76011 817-273-5222 273-5285
TF: 888-968-3927 ■ *Web:* www.texas.rangers.mlb.com
Raymond James Stadium 4201 N Dale Mabry Hwy . . . . Tampa FL 33607 813-350-6500 673-4308
Web: www.tampasportsauthority.com
RBC Ctr 1400 Edwards Mill Rd . . . . Raleigh NC 27607 919-467-7825 861-2310
Web: www.rbccenter.com
Reliant Astrodome 1 Reliant Pk . . . . Houston TX 77054 832-667-1400 667-1748
Web: www.reliantpark.com
Reliant Park 1 Reliant Pk . . . . Houston TX 77054 832-667-1400
Web: www.reliantpark.com
Reliant Stadium 1 Reliant Pk . . . . Houston TX 77054 832-667-1400 667-1727
Web: www.reliantpark.com/reliant-stadium
Reunion Arena 777 Sports St . . . . Dallas TX 75207 214-800-3000 800-3040
Rexall Place 7300 116th Ave . . . . Edmonton AB T5B4X5 780-471-7210 471-8195
Web: www.rexall-place.com
Richmond Coliseum 601 E Leigh St . . . . Richmond VA 23219 804-780-4970 780-4606
Web: www.richmondcoliseum.net
Roanoke Civic Ctr 710 Williamson Rd . . . . Roanoke VA 24016 540-853-2241 853-2748
TF: 888-397-3100 ■ *Web:* www.roanokeciviccenter.com
Robert F Kennedy Stadium
2400 E Capitol St SE . . . . Washington DC 20003 202-547-9077 547-7460
Web: washington.nationals.mlb.com/NASApp/mlb/index.jsp?c_id=was
Roberts Stadium 2600 Division St . . . . Evansville IN 47711 812-476-1383 476-1881
Web: www.smgevansville.com/roberts.html
Rockford MetroCentre 300 Elm St . . . . Rockford IL 61101 815-968-5600 968-5451
Web: www.metrocentre.com
Roger Dean Stadium 4751 Main St . . . . Jupiter FL 33458 561-775-1818 691-6886
Web: www.rogerdeanstadium.com
Rogers Arena 800 Griffiths Way . . . . Vancouver BC V6B6G1 604-899-7400 899-7401
Web: www.rogersarena.ca
Rogers Centre 1 Blue Jays Way Suite 3000 . . . . Toronto ON M5V1J1 416-341-3663 341-3101
Web: www.rogerscentre.com
Rose Bowl 1001 Rose Bowl Dr . . . . Pasadena CA 91103 626-577-3100 405-0992
Web: www.rosebowlstadium.com
Rose Quarter Facilities 1 Ctr Ct Suite 200 . . . . Portland OR 97227 503-235-8771 736-2187
Web: www.rosequarter.com
Rupp Arena 430 W Vine St . . . . Lexington KY 40507 859-233-4567 253-2718
Web: www.rupparena.com
Safeco Field 1250 1st Ave S . . . . Seattle WA 98134 206-346-4000 346-4050
Web: seattle.mariners.mlb.com/index.jsp?c_id=sea
San Jose Municipal Stadium 588 E Alma Ave . . . . San Jose CA 95112 408-297-1435 297-1453
Web: www.sanjose.giants.milb.com
Scotiabank Place 1000 Palladium Dr . . . . Kanata ON K2V1A5 613-599-0100 599-0358
TF: 800-444-7367 ■ *Web:* www.scotiabankplace.com
Scottrade Ctr 1401 Clark Ave . . . . Saint Louis MO 63103 314-622-5400 622-5410
Web: www.scottradecenter.com
Scottsdale Stadium 7408 E Osborn Rd . . . . Scottsdale AZ 85251 480-312-2856 312-7729
Web: www.scottsdaleaz.gov/stadium
Selland Arena 700 M St . . . . Fresno CA 93721 559-445-8100 445-8110
Web: www.fresnoconventioncenter.com
Shea Stadium 123-01 Roosevelt Ave . . . . Flushing NY 11368 718-507-6387 639-3619
Web: www.newyork.mets.mlb.com
Show Me Ctr 1333 N Sprigg St . . . . Cape Girardeau MO 63701 573-651-2297 651-5054
Web: www.showmecenter.biz
Sioux Falls Arena 1201 N W Ave . . . . Sioux Falls SD 57104 605-367-7288 338-1463
TF: 800-338-3177 ■ *Web:* www.sfarena.com
Sky Sox Stadium 4385 Tutt Blvd . . . . Colorado Springs CO 80922 719-597-1449 597-2491
Web: www.coloradosprings.skysox.milb.com
Soldier Field 1410 S Museum Campus Dr . . . . Chicago IL 60605 312-235-7000 235-7030
Web: www.soldierfield.net
Sommet Ctr 501 Broadway . . . . Nashville TN 37203 615-770-2000 770-2010
Web: www.sommetcenter.com
Sovereign Bank Arena 81 Hamilton Ave . . . . Trenton NJ 08611 609-656-3200 656-3201
TF: 888-722-8499 ■ *Web:* www.sunnationalbankcenter.com
Spartan Stadium 1257 S 10th St . . . . San Jose CA 95112 408-924-1200 924-1169
Web: www.sjsuspartans.com
Spokane Arena 720 W Mallon Ave . . . . Spokane WA 99201 509-279-7000 279-7050
Web: www.spokanearena.com
St Pete Times Forum 401 Channelside Dr . . . . Tampa FL 33602 813-301-6500 301-1481
Web: www.sptimesforum.com
Staples Ctr 1111 S Figueroa St . . . . Los Angeles CA 90015 213-742-7100 742-7296
Web: www.staplescenter.com
Sun Bowl Stadium 2701 Sun Bowl Dr . . . . El Paso TX 79902 915-747-5265 747-5228
Web: www.sunbowl.org
Sun Devil Stadium
500 E Veterans Way Arizona State University . . . . Tempe AZ 85287 480-965-3482 965-1261
Web: www.asu.edu/tour/main/stad.html
Sun Life Stadium 2269 Dan Marino Blvd . . . . Miami Gardens FL 33056 305-623-6100 625-6403
Web: www.sunlifestadium.com
Taco Bell Arena 1910 University Dr . . . . Boise ID 83725 208-426-1900 426-1998
Web: www.tacobellarena.com
Tacoma Dome Arena & Exhibition Hall
2727 E 'D' St . . . . Tacoma WA 98421 253-272-3663 593-7620*
**Fax:* Mktg ■ *Web:* www.tacomadome.org
Target Center Arena 600 1st Ave N . . . . Minneapolis MN 55403 612-673-1300 673-1387
Web: www.targetcenter.com
TD Banknorth Garden 100 Legends Way . . . . Boston MA 02114 617-624-1050 624-1818
Web: www.tdgarden.com
Texas Stadium 1 Cowboys Pkwy . . . . Irving TX 75063 972-785-4000 785-4709
Web: www.dallascowboys.com
Thomas & Mack Center/Sam Boyd Stadium
4505 S Maryland Pkwy PO Box 450003 . . . . Las Vegas NV 89154 702-895-3761 895-1099
Web: www.unlvtickets.com
Times Union Ctr 51 S Pearl St . . . . Albany NY 12207 518-487-2000 487-2020
Web: www.timesunioncenter-albany.com
Toyota Ctr 1510 Polk St . . . . Houston TX 77002 713-758-7200 758-7315
TF: 866-446-8849 ■ *Web:* www.houstontoyotacenter.com

Phone Fax

Tropicana Field 1 Tropicana Dr . . . . Saint Petersburg FL 33705 727-825-3120 825-3204
TF: 888-326-7297 ■ *Web:* www.tampabay.rays.mlb.com
United Ctr 1901 W Madison St . . . . Chicago IL 60612 312-455-4500 455-4511
Web: www.unitedcenter.com
University of Phoenix Stadium
1 Cardinals Dr . . . . Glendale AZ 85305 623-433-7100
Web: www.azcardinalsstadium.com
US Airways Ctr 201 E Jefferson St . . . . Phoenix AZ 85004 602-379-2000 379-2093
Web: www.usairwayscenter.com
US Cellular Field 333 W 35th St . . . . Chicago IL 60616 312-674-1000 674-5104*
**Fax:* Hum Res ■ *Web:* chicago.whitesox.mlb.com/cws/ballpark/index.jsp
US Olympic Training Ctr
1750 E Boulder St 1 Olympic Plaza . . . . Colorado Springs CO 80909 719-632-5551 866-4677*
Web: www.teamusa.org/about-usoc/u-s-olympic-training-center-colorado-springs
US Olympic Training Ctr
196 Old Military Rd . . . . Lake Placid NY 12946 518-523-2600 523-4790
Web: www.teamusa.org/about-usoc/u-s-olympic-training-center-lake-placid
Valley View Casino Ctr
3500 Sports Arena Blvd . . . . San Diego CA 92110 619-224-4171 224-3010
Web: www.valleyviewcasinocenter.com
Van Andel Arena 130 Fulton St W . . . . Grand Rapids MI 49503 616-742-6600 742-6197
Web: www.vanandelarena.com
Verizon Arena 1 Alltel Arena Way . . . . North Little Rock AR 72114 501-340-5660 340-5668
Web: www.alltelarena.com
Verizon Ctr 601 F St NW . . . . Washington DC 20004 202-628-3200 661-5083
Web: www.verizoncenter.com
Verizon Wireless Arena 555 Elm St . . . . Manchester NH 03101 603-644-5000 644-1575
Web: www.verizonwirelessarena.com
Wachovia Ctr 3601 S Broad St . . . . Philadelphia PA 19148 215-336-3600 389-9506
Web: www.comcast-spectacor.com
War Memorial Stadium 1 Stadium Dr . . . . Little Rock AR 72205 501-663-6385 663-6387
Web: www.arkansas.gov/wms
Webster Bank Arena 600 Main St 2nd St . . . . Bridgeport CT 06604 203-345-2300 335-1719
TF: 800-745-3000 ■ *Web:* www.websterbankarena.com
Will Rogers Memorial Ctr
3401 W Lancaster Ave . . . . Fort Worth TX 76107 817-392-7469 392-8170
Web: www.fortworthgov.org
Winston-Salem Entertainment-Sports Complex
2825 University Pkwy . . . . Winston-Salem NC 27105 336-725-5635 727-2922
Web: www.ljvm.com
Wrigley Field 1060 W Addison St . . . . Chicago IL 60613 773-404-2827 404-4129
Web: www.chicago.cubs.mlb.com
Yankee Stadium 161st St & River Ave . . . . Bronx NY 10451 718-293-4300 293-8431
Web: www.newyork.yankees.mlb.com
Rabobank Arena Theater & Convention Ctr
1001 Truxtun Ave . . . . Bakersfield CA 93301 661-852-7300 861-9904
US Cellular Ctr 370 1st Ave E . . . . Cedar Rapids IA 52401 319-398-5211 362-2102
Web: www.uscellularcenter.com
DCU Ctr 50 Foster St . . . . Worcester MA 01608 508-755-6800 929-0111
Web: www.dcucenter.com
Greensboro Coliseum Complex 1921 W Lee St . . . . . . Greensboro NC 27403 336-373-7400 373-2170
Web: www.greensborocoliseum.com
Alerus Ctr 1200 42nd St S . . . . Grand Forks ND 58201 701-792-1200 746-6511
Web: www.aleruscenter.com
Golden Spike Event Ctr 1000 N 1200 W . . . . Ogden UT 84404 801-399-8544 392-1995
TF: 800-442-7362 ■ *Web:* www.goldenspikeeventcenter.com
Seattle Ctr 305 Harrison St . . . . Seattle WA 98109 206-684-7200 684-7342
Web: www.seattlecenter.com

724 STAFFING SERVICES

SEE ALSO Employment Offices - Government p. 1822; Employment Services - Online p. 1822; Executive Recruiting Firms p. 1834; Modeling Agencies p. 2253; Professional Employer Organizations (PEOs) p. 2455; Talent Agencies p. 2681

Phone Fax

Accountants International
111 Anza Blvd Suite 400 . . . . Burlingame CA 94010 650-579-1111 343-5485
Web: www.accountantsintl.com
Accounting Principals
1 Independent Dr Suite 215 . . . . Jacksonville FL 32202 904-360-2400 360-2394
Web: www.accountingprincipals.com
Ace Personnel 10000 W 75 St Suite 122 . . . . Overland Park KS 66204 913-384-1100 384-1102
Web: www.acepersonnel.com
Acentron Technologies Inc PO Box 78378 . . . . Charlotte NC 28271 704-335-0030 675-1061*
**Fax Area Code:* 864 ■ *Web:* www.acentron.com
Act-1 Group 1999 W 190th St . . . . Torrance CA 90504 310-750-3400 750-1100
TF: 800-365-2281 ■ *Web:* www.act-1.com
Adecco Inc 175 Broad Hollow Rd . . . . Melville NY 11747 631-844-7800 844-7022*
**Fax:* Mktg ■ *TF:* 877-632-9169 ■ *Web:* www.adeccousa.com
Advantage Resourcing 220 Norwood Pk S . . . . Norwood MA 02062 800-343-4314
TF: 800-343-4314 ■ *Web:* www.advhr.com
Aerotek Inc 7301 Pkwy Dr . . . . Hanover MD 21076 410-694-5100
TF: 800-237-6835 ■ *Web:* www.aerotek.com
All Medical Personnel
4651 Sheridan St Suite 350 . . . . Hollywood FL 33021 954-922-9696 927-0590
TF: 800-706-2378 ■ *Web:* www.allmedstaffing.com
Allegis Group Inc 7301 Pkwy Dr . . . . Hanover MD 21076 410-579-3000 540-7709
TF: 877-388-3823 ■ *Web:* www.allegisgroup.com
Allied Health Group LLC
145 Technology Pkwy NW . . . . Norcross GA 30092 800-741-4674 245-7142*
**Fax Area Code:* 678 ■ *TF:* 800-741-4674 ■ *Web:* www.alliedhealth.com
Allstaff Hr Group
6650 Sugarloaf Pkwy Suite 300 . . . . Duluth GA 30097 770-339-0000 339-4850
TF: 888-339-8211 ■ *Web:* www.allstaffhrgroup.com

				Phone	Fax
AllStates Technical Services					
1900 International Dr	Birmingham	AL	35243	877-972-5401	
TF: 800-432-8006 ■ *Web:* www.allstatestech.com					
ALTRES Inc 967 Kapiolani Blvd	Honolulu	HI	96814	808-591-4940	591-4914
TF: 888-425-8737 ■ *Web:* www.altres.com					
American Healthcare Services LLC					
1000 John R Suite 250	Troy	MI	48083	248-588-9700	588-2828
TF: 866-227-9998 ■ *Web:* www.americanhealthcareservices.com					
Ameritemps Inc 6100 Rockside Woods	Independence	OH	44131	216-447-9700	447-9788
Web: www.ameritemps.com					
AMN Healthcare Services Inc					
12400 High Bluff Dr Suite 100	San Diego	CA	92130	866-871-8519	282-1211*
NYSE: AHS ■ **Fax Area Code:* 800 ■ *TF:* 866-510-1904 ■ *Web:* www.amnhealthcare.com					
APEX Systems Inc 4400 Cox Rd Suite 100	Glen Allen	VA	23060	804-254-2600	254-7290
TF: 800-452-7391 ■ *Web:* www.apexsystemsinc.com					
AppleOne Employment Services Inc					
327 W Broadway	Glendale	CA	91204	818-240-8688	265-5514
TF: 800-872-2677 ■ *Web:* www.appleone.com					
AppleOne Employment Services Inc					
50 Paxman Rd Unit 8	Etobicoke	ON	M9C1B7	416-622-0100	622-6327
TF: 800-564-5644 ■ *Web:* www.appleone.com					
Aquent LLC 711 Boylston St	Boston	MA	02116	617-535-5000	535-5004
TF: 800-878-0900 ■ *Web:* www.aquent.com					
ARC Industries Inc 2879 Johnstown Rd	Columbus	OH	43219	614-475-7007	342-5680
TF: 800-734-7007 ■ *Web:* www.arcind.com					
Area Temps Inc 1228 Euclid Ave	Cleveland	OH	44115	216-781-5350	348-6395
Web: www.areatemps.com					
Artech Information Systems LLC					
240 Cedar Knolls Rd Suite 100	Cedar Knolls	NJ	07927	973-998-2500	998-2599
Web: www.artechinfo.com					
Aspire Group 711 Boylston St	Boston	MA	02116	800-487-2967	500-7284*
**Fax Area Code:* 617 ■ *TF:* 800-487-2967 ■ *Web:* www.aspiregroup.net					
Astrid Contract Technical Services Inc					
PO Box 429	New Ellenton	SC	29809	803-652-8600	
TF: 866-232-2287 ■ *Web:* www.actsincorporated.com					
ATC Travelers 1983 Marcus Ave Suite E122	Lake Success	NY	11042	866-562-7667	546-5616*
**Fax Area Code:* 800 ■ *TF:* 866-562-7667 ■ *Web:* www.atctravelers.com					
Atlantic Group 5426 Robin Hood Rd	Norfolk	VA	23513	757-857-6400	233-7491
TF: 800-446-8131 ■ *Web:* www.atlanticgroup.com					
ATS Services Inc					
9700 Phillips Hwy Suite 101	Jacksonville	FL	32256	904-645-9505	645-0390
TF: 800-346-5574 ■ *Web:* www.ats-services.com					
Attorney Resource 750 N St Paul St Suite 540	Dallas	TX	75201	214-922-8050	871-3041
Web: www.attorneyresource.com					
Bartech Group 17199 N Laurel Pk Dr Suite 224	Livonia	MI	48152	734-953-5050	
TF: 800-828-4410 ■ *Web:* www.bartechgroup.com					
Bay Area Anesthesia Inc					
617 S State St PO Box 1547	Ukiah	CA	95482	707-468-9301	
Web: www.fastgas.com					
Bergaila & Assoc Inc 16285 Pk 10 Pl Suite 150	Houston	TX	77077	281-496-0803	496-4705
Web: www.bergaila.com					
C & A Industries Inc 13609 California St	Omaha	NE	68154	402-891-0009	891-9461
TF: 800-574-9829 ■ *Web:* www.ca-industries.com					
Calian Technology Ltd 340 Legget Dr Suite 101	Ottawa	ON	K2K1Y6	613-599-8600	599-8650
PINK: CLNFF ■ *TF:* 877-225-4264 ■ *Web:* www.calian.com					
CareerBuilder.com 200 N LaSalle St Suite 1100	Chicago	IL	60601	773-527-3600	349-4467*
**Fax Area Code:* 877 ■ *TF:* 800-638-4212 ■ *Web:* www.careerbuilder.com					
CareerStaff Unlimited Inc 13105 NW Fwy	Houston	TX	77063	713-297-9000	622-8464
TF: 800-580-6090 ■ *Web:* www.careerstaff.com					
CDI Corp 1717 Arch St 35th Fl	Philadelphia	PA	19103	215-569-2200	569-1300
NYSE: CDI ■ *TF:* 800-996-7566 ■ *Web:* www.cdicorp.com					
Cejka Search Inc 4 CityPlace Dr Suite 300	Saint Louis	MO	63141	314-726-1603	726-0026
TF: 800-678-7858 ■ *Web:* www.cejkasearch.com					
Comforce Corp					
999 Stewart Ave Suite 100 PO Box 969	Bethpage	NY	11714	516-437-3300	437-3392
NYSE: CFS ■ *TF:* 877-266-3672 ■ *Web:* www.comforce.com					
Command Center Inc 3773 W 5th Ave	Post Falls	ID	83854	208-773-7450	773-7467
OTC: CCNI ■ *TF:* 866-464-5844 ■ *Web:* www.commandonline.com					
CompHealth Inc					
6440 S Millrock Dr Suite 175					
PO Box 713100	Salt Lake City	UT	84121	801-930-3000	930-4517
TF: 800-453-3030 ■ *Web:* www.comphealth.com					
Compunnel Software Group Inc					
12 Perrine Rd Suite 104	Monmouth Junction	NJ	08852	609-606-9010	452-0882
TF: 800-696-8128 ■ *Web:* www.compunnel.com					
Computer Consulting Assoc International Inc					
200 Pequot Ave	Southport	CT	06480	203-255-8966	255-8501
Web: www.ccaii.com					
Computer Enterprises Inc (CEI)					
1910 Cochran Rd, Manor Oak Two Suite 230	Pittsburgh	PA	15220	412-341-3541	341-0519
Web: www.ceiamerica.com					
Compuware Corp Professional Services Div					
11095 Viking Dr Suite 430	Eden Prairie	MN	55344	612-851-2200	851-2300
TF Cust Svc: 800-358-3048 ■ *Web:* www.compuware.com/services					
Consultis 4401 N Federal Hwy Suite 100	Boca Raton	FL	33431	561-362-9104	367-9802
TF: 800-275-2667 ■ *Web:* www.consultis.com					
Consultnet LLC					
10813 S River Front Pkwy Suite 150	South Jordan	UT	84095	801-208-3700	208-3643
TF: 888-215-9675 ■ *Web:* www.consult-net.com					
Continuum Legal 1651 Old Meadow Rd Suite 600	McLean	VA	22102	703-734-7474	734-8839
Web: www.continuumlegal.com					
CORESTAFF Services 1775 St James Pl Suite 300	Houston	TX	77056	713-438-1400	438-1763*
**Fax:* Mktg ■ *Web:* www.corestaff.com					
Corporate Personnel Network Inc					
3552 Green Ave Suite 201	Los Alamitos	CA	90720	562-493-1503	493-0314
Web: www.ppersonnel.com					
Corporate Services Group Holdings Inc					
1775 St James Pl	Houston	TX	77056	713-438-1411	376-4077*
**Fax Area Code:* 806					
CPC Logistics Inc					
14528 S Outer 40 Rd Suite 210	Chesterfield	MO	63017	314-542-2266	542-0666
TF: 800-274-3746 ■ *Web:* www.callcpc.com					

				Phone	Fax
Cross Country Healthcare Inc					
6551 Pk of Commerce Blvd	Boca Raton	FL	33487	561-998-2232	998-8533
NASDAQ: CCRN ■ *TF:* 800-347-2264 ■ *Web:* www.crosscountryhealthcare.com					
CyberStaff America Ltd 315 E 86th St # 8PE	New York	NY	10028	212-244-2300	244-1025
TF: 888-244-2300 ■ *Web:* www.cyberstaff.com					
Davis Cos 33 Boston Post Rd W	Marlborough	MA	01752	508-481-9500	481-8519
TF: 800-482-9494 ■ *Web:* www.daviscos.com					
Debbie's Staffing Services Inc					
4431 Cherry St Suite 50	Winston Salem	NC	27105	336-744-2393	776-1661
Web: www.debbiesstaffing.com					
Design Group Staffing Inc 10012 Jasper Ave	Edmonton	AB	T5J1R2	780-428-1505	428-7095
TF: 800-770-1228 ■ *Web:* www.designgroupstaffing.com					
Devon Consulting 950 W Valley Rd Suite 2602	Wayne	PA	19087	610-964-2700	964-2708
TF: 800-229-5709 ■ *Web:* www.devonconsulting.com					
Diversco Integrated Services Inc					
105 Diversco Dr	Spartanburg	SC	29307	864-579-3420	579-9578
TF: 800-277-3420 ■ *Web:* www.diversco.com					
Duran Human Capital Partners Inc					
300 Orchard City Dr Suite 142	Campbell	CA	95008	408-540-0070	540-0073
Web: www.duranhcp.com					
Durham Cos Inc 6300 Transit Rd	Depew	NY	14043	716-684-3333	681-7408
TF: 800-633-7724 ■ *Web:* www.durhamstaffing.com					
Durham Exchange Club Industries Inc					
1717 E Lawson St	Durham	NC	27703	919-596-1341	596-6380
Web: www.deci.org					
Eagle Professional Resources Inc					
67 Yonge St Suite 200	Toronto	ON	M5E1J8	416-861-0636	861-8401
TF: 800-281-2339 ■ *Web:* www.eagleonline.com					
EmCare 1717 Main St Suite 5200	Dallas	TX	75201	214-712-2000	712-2444
TF: 800-527-2145 ■ *Web:* www.emcare.com					
EmployBridge Inc					
222 W Las Colinas Blvd Suite 250	Irving	TX	75039	214-296-6885	
Web: www.employbridge.net					
Energy Services Group International Inc (ESG)					
3601 La Grange Pkwy	Toano	VA	23168	757-741-4040	741-4045
Web: www.esgi.net					
Enherent Corp 33 Wood Ave S Suite 400	Iselin	NJ	08830	732-603-3859	603-3868
TF: 877-778-4768 ■ *Web:* www.enherent.com					
Ensearch Management Consultants					
905 E Cotati Ave	Cotati	CA	94931	707-795-3800	795-6200
TF: 888-667-5627 ■ *Web:* www.ensearch.com					
Entech Personnel Services Inc					
363 W Big Beaver Rd	Troy	MI	48084	248-528-1444	528-6982
TF: 800-333-6832 ■ *Web:* www.entechpersonnel.com					
Entegee Inc 70 Blanchard Rd Suite 102	Burlington	MA	01803	781-221-5800	221-4544
TF: 800-368-3433 ■ *Web:* www.entegee.com					
EuroSoft Inc					
1705 S Capital of Texas Hwy Suite 200	Austin	TX	78746	512-329-8100	329-5150
TF: 888-329-8100 ■ *Web:* www.eurosoft-inc.com					
Execupharm Inc					
500 N Gulph Rd Suite 120	King Of Prussia	PA	19406	610-272-8771	272-8056
Web: www.execupharm.com					
Express Employment Professionals					
8516 NW Expy	Oklahoma City	OK	73162	405-840-5000	717-5665
TF: 800-222-4057 ■ *Web:* www.expresspros.com					
Falls City Placement Service Inc					
1941 Bishop Ln Suite 100	Louisville	KY	40218	502-456-2380	456-2389
Web: www.jcmalone.com					
G&A Partners 4801 Woodway Dr Suite 210W	Houston	TX	77056	713-784-1181	784-2705
TF: 800-253-8562 ■ *Web:* www.gnapartners.com					
General Employment Enterprises Inc					
1 Tower Ln Suite 2200	Oakbrook Terrace	IL	60181	630-954-0400	954-0447
AMEX: JOB ■ *Web:* www.generalemployment.com					
Gibson Arnold & Assoc					
1776 Yorktown St Suite 350	Houston	TX	77056	713-572-3000	572-4664
TF: 800-879-2007 ■ *Web:* www.gibsonarnold.com					
Hawkins Assoc Inc					
909 NE Loop 410 Suite 104	San Antonio	TX	78209	210-349-9911	349-3393
Web: www.hawkinspersonnel.com					
Headway Corporate Resources Inc					
317 Madison Ave 18th Fl	New York	NY	10017	212-672-6500	672-6599
Web: www.headwaycorp.com					
Info Technologies Inc					
187 Rt 36 Bldg A Suite 220	West Long Branch	NJ	07764	732-222-1250	222-4050
Web: www.infotechnologiesinc.com					
Integrity Staffing Solutions Inc					
750 Shipyard Dr Suite 300	Wilmington	DE	19801	302-661-8776	661-8779
TF: 888-458-8367 ■ *Web:* www.integritystaffing.com					
Inteliant Corp					
2650 Decker Lake Blvd Suite 500	Salt Lake City	UT	84119	801-484-4400	483-4283
Web: www.inteliant.com					
Interim HealthCare Inc					
1601 Sawgrass Corporate Pkwy	Sunrise	FL	33323	954-858-6000	858-2820
TF: 800-338-7786 ■ *Web:* www.interimhealthcare.com					
Ipc Technologies Inc					
7200 Glen Forest Dr Suite 100	Richmond	VA	23226	804-622-7288	
Web: www.ipctech.com					
Jean Simpson Personnel Services Inc					
1318 Shreveport Barksdale	Shreveport	LA	71105	318-869-3494	868-0790
Web: www.jeansimpson.com					
Joule Inc 1245 US Rt 1 S	Edison	NJ	08837	732-548-5444	632-9795
TF: 800-341-0341 ■ *Web:* www.jouleinc.com					
Judge Group Inc					
300 Conshohocken State Rd					
Suite 300	West Conshohocken	PA	19428	610-667-7700	667-1058
TF: 888-228-7162 ■ *Web:* www.judge.com					
Kelly Law Registry Inc 999 W Big Beaver Rd	Troy	MI	48084	248-244-5150	244-4483
Web: www.kellylawregistry.com					
Kelly Services Inc 999 W Big Beaver Rd	Troy	MI	48084	248-362-4444	244-5292*
NASDAQ: KELYA ■ **Fax:* Mail Rm ■ *Web:* www.kellyservices.com					
Kforce Inc 1001 E Palm Ave	Tampa	FL	33605	813-552-5000	552-2588
NASDAQ: KFRC ■ *TF:* 800-395-5575 ■ *Web:* www.kforce.com					

Company	City	State	ZIP	Phone	Fax
Kimco Staffing Services Inc 17872 Cowan Ave *TF:* 800-649-5627 ■ *Web:* www.kimco.com	Irvine	CA	92614	949-752-6996	752-1126
Labor Finders International Inc 11426 N Jog Rd *TF:* 800-864-7749 ■ *Web:* www.laborfinders.com	Palm Beach Gardens	FL	33418	561-627-6507	627-6556
Lakeshore Staffing Inc 1 N Franklin St Suite 600 *TF:* 877-666-0779 ■ *Web:* www.lakeshorestaffing.com	Chicago	IL	60606	312-251-7575	251-7580
LJ Gonzer Assoc Inc 14 Commerce Dr Suite 305 *TF:* 800-631-4218 ■ *Web:* www.gonzer.com	Cranford	NJ	07016	908-709-9494	709-9077
Lucas Assoc Inc 3384 Peachtree Rd Suite 900 *TF:* 800-515-0819 ■ *Web:* www.lucasgroup.com	Atlanta	GA	30326	404-239-5630	260-7290
Lumen Legal 1025 Campbell Rd *TF:* 877-933-1330 ■ *Web:* www.lumenlegal.com	Royal Oak	MI	48067	248-597-0400	597-0410
Magnum Staffing Services Inc 2900 Smith St Suite 250 *Web:* www.magnumstaffing.com	Houston	TX	77006	713-658-0068	523-3621
Major Legal Services 1301 E 9th St Suite 1414 *TF:* 800-808-3097 ■ *Web:* www.lawplacement.com	Cleveland	OH	44114	216-579-9782	579-1662
ManpowerGroup 100 Manpower Pl *NYSE: MAN* ■ *Web:* www.us.manpower.com	Milwaukee	WI	53212	414-961-1000	906-7822
Marketstar Corp 2475 Washington Blvd *TF:* 800-877-8259 ■ *Web:* www.marketstar.com	Ogden	UT	84401	801-393-1155	393-4115
Medical Staffing Assoc Inc 6731 Whittier Ave Suite A300 *TF:* 800-235-5105 ■ *Web:* www.medstaffer.com	McLean	VA	22101	703-893-1773	893-7358
Medical Staffing Network Holdings Inc 901 Yamato Rd Suite 110 *TF:* 800-676-8326 ■ *Web:* www.msnhealth.com	Boca Raton	FL	33431	561-322-1300	322-1200
Medical Staffing Network Inc 901 NW 51st St # 110 *TF:* 800-676-8326 ■ *Web:* www.intelistaf.com	Boca Raton	FL	33431	561-322-1300	322-1200
Medvantx Inc 5810 Nncy Rdge Dr Suite 100 *Web:* www.medvantx.com	San Diego	CA	92121	858-625-2990	625-2999
Midcom Corp 1056 N Tustin Ave *TF:* 800-737-1632 ■ *Web:* www.midcom.com	Anaheim	CA	92807	714-630-1999	459-7061
Minute Men Staffing Services 3740 Carnegie Ave *TF:* 877-873-8856 ■ *Web:* www.minutemeninc.com	Cleveland	OH	44115	216-426-9675	426-2246
Moody International Inc 24900 Pitkin Rd Suite 200 *Web:* www.moodyint.com	The Woodlands	TX	77386	281-367-8764	367-3496
Motion Recruitment Partners 206 Newbury St 3rd Fl *Web:* www.motionrecruitment.com	Boston	MA	02116	617-585-6500	536-9154
National Engineering Service Corp 72 Mirona Rd **Fax Area Code:* 800 ■ *TF:* 800-562-3463 ■ *Web:* www.nesc.com	Portsmouth	NH	03801	603-431-9740	637-2562*
Nextgen Information Services Inc 906 Olive St Suite 1100 *Web:* www.nextgen-is.com	Saint Louis	MO	63101	314-588-1212	588-1211
North Highland Co The 550 Pharr Rd Suite 850 *Web:* www.northhighland.com	Atlanta	GA	30305	404-233-1015	233-4930
Nursefinders Inc 524 E Lamar Blvd Suite 300 *TF:* 800-445-0459 ■ *Web:* www.nursefinders.com	Arlington	TX	76011	817-460-1181	462-9146
On Assignment Inc 26745 Malibu Hills Rd *NASDAQ: ASGN* ■ *TF:* 866-297-3856 ■ *Web:* www.assignment.net	Calabasas	CA	91301	818-878-7900	878-7930
Orion International Consulting Group Inc 912 Capital of Texas Hwy S Bldg 1 Suite 220 *TF:* 800-336-7466 ■ *Web:* www.orioninternational.com	Austin	TX	78746	512-327-7111	327-4286
Oxford Global Resources Inc 100 Cummings Ctr Suite 206L *TF:* 800-426-9196 ■ *Web:* www.oxfordcorp.com	Beverly	MA	01915	978-236-1182	236-1077
Peak Technical Services Inc 583 Epsilon Dr *TF:* 800-825-8088 ■ *Web:* www.peaktechnical.com	Pittsburgh	PA	15238	412-696-1080	696-1083
Pinnacle Staffing Inc 127 Tanner Rd PO Box 17589 *Web:* www.pinnaclestaffing.com	Greenville	SC	29606	864-297-4212	987-7351
Plus Group Inc 725 James Ave Suite 201 *TF:* 888-782-3346 ■ *Web:* www.theplusgroup.com	Woodridge	IL	60514	630-515-0500	515-0510
Premier Staffing Services of New York Inc 1 N Broadway Suite 801 *Web:* www.thepremiergroup.com	White Plains	NY	10601	914-428-2233	428-5547
Prime Staffing Inc 3806 N Cicero Ave *Web:* www.primestaffing.com	Chicago	IL	60641	773-685-9399	685-9565
Principal Technical Services Inc 9960 Research Dr Suite 200 *TF:* 888-787-3711 ■ *Web:* www.ptsstaffing.com	Irvine	CA	92618	949-268-4000	268-4040
Pro Staff Personnel Services 5001 American Blvd W Suite 300 *Web:* www.prostaff.com	Bloomington	MN	55437	952-842-8359	
Productive Data Solutions Inc (PDSINC) 7935 EßPrentice Ave Suite 210-W *TF:* 800-404-7165 ■ *Web:* www.productivedatasolutions.com	Greenwood Village	CO	80111	303-220-7165	220-7425
Professional Placement Inc 4040 E Camelback Suite 235 *Web:* www.proplacement.com	Phoenix	AZ	85018	602-955-0870	955-0604
Professional Staffing Group 89 Devonshire St *Web:* www.psgstaffing.com	Boston	MA	02109	617-250-1000	250-1099
Profiles International Inc 5205 Lake Shore Dr *TF:* 866-751-1644 ■ *Web:* www.profilesinternational.com	Waco	TX	76710	254-751-1644	776-5405
Progressive Software Computing Inc (PSCI) 3505 Silverside Rd Plaza Center Suite 201-B *Web:* www.psci.com	Wilmington	DE	19810	302-479-9700	479-7573
PRWT Services Inc 1835 Market St 8th Fl *Web:* www.prwt.com	Philadelphia	PA	19103	215-569-8810	569-9893
Randstad North America 2015 S Pk Pl *TF:* 888-726-3782 ■ *Web:* www.us.randstad.com	Atlanta	GA	30339	770-937-7000	
RCM Technologies Inc 2500 McClellan Ave Suite 350 *NASDAQ: RCMT* ■ *Web:* www.rcmt.com	Pennsauken	NJ	08109	856-356-4500	356-4600
Remedy Temp Inc 3820 State St *TF:* 800-688-6162 ■ *Web:* www.remedystaff.com	Santa Barbara	CA	93105	805-882-2200	898-7111
Research Pharmaceutical Services Inc 520 Virginia Dr *TF:* 866-777-1151 ■ *Web:* www.rpsweb.com	Fort Washington	PA	19034	215-540-0700	540-0770
Resources Global Professionals 17101 Armstrong Ave *NASDAQ: RECN* ■ *TF:* 800-900-1131 ■ *Web:* www.resourcesglobal.com	Irvine	CA	92614	714-430-6400	433-6100
Right at Home Inc 11949 Q St Suite 118 *TF:* 877-697-7537 ■ *Web:* www.rightathome.net	Omaha	NE	68137	402-697-7537	697-0289
Robert Half International Inc 2884 Sand Hill Rd Suite 200 *NYSE: RHI* ■ *Web:* www.rhi.com	Menlo Park	CA	94025	650-234-6000	854-9735
Robert Half International Inc Accountemps Div 2884 Sand Hill Rd Suite 200 **Fax:* Mktg ■ *Web:* www.accountemps.com	Menlo Park	CA	94025	650-234-6000	234-6915*
Robert Half International Inc Affiliates Div 2884 Sand Hill Rd Suite 200 *Web:* www.roberthalflegal.com	Menlo Park	CA	94025	650-854-9700	234-6930
Robert Half International Inc OfficeTeam Div 2884 Sand Hill Rd Suite 200 **Fax:* Mktg ■ *Web:* www.officeteam.com	Menlo Park	CA	94025	650-234-6000	234-6998*
Roth Staffing Cos LP 333 City Blvd W Suite 100 *TF:* 888-304-4684 ■ *Web:* www.rothstaffing.com	Orange	CA	92868	714-939-8600	939-8688
Sacramento Employment & Training Agency 925 Del Paso Blvd *Web:* www.seta.net	Sacramento	CA	95815	916-263-3800	263-3825
Salem Group The 2 TransAm Plaza Dr Suite 170 *Web:* www.saleminc.com	Oakbrook Terrace	IL	60181	630-932-7000	932-7010
Sapphire Technologies LP 10 Presidential Way *Web:* www.sapphire.com	Woburn	MA	01801	781-938-1910	935-6152
Seek Inc PO Box 148 *Web:* www.seekcareers.com	Grafton	WI	53024	262-377-8888	375-6677
Select Staffing 3820 State St *TF:* 800-688-6162 ■ *Web:* www.selectstaffing.com	Santa Barbara	CA	93105	805-882-2200	898-7111
Show Pros Entertainment Services Inc PO Box 12599 *Web:* www.showprostaff.com	Charlotte	NC	28220	704-525-3784	525-3785
Sigma Systems Inc 201 Boston Post Rd Suite 201 *TF:* 888-867-4462 ■ *Web:* www.sigmainc.com	Marlborough	MA	01752	508-357-6300	357-6301
Silicon Valley Staffing 2200 Powell St Suite 510 *TF:* 877-660-6000 ■ *Web:* www.siliconvalleystaffing.com	Emeryville	CA	94608	510-923-9898	923-9313
Snelling Personnel Services 12801 N Central Expy Suite 700 **Fax:* Cust Svc ■ *TF:* 800-766-7500 ■ *Web:* www.snelling.com	Dallas	TX	75243	972-239-7575	239-6879*
Softworld Inc 281 Winter St Suite 301 *TF:* 877-899-1166 ■ *Web:* www.softworldinc.com	Waltham	MA	02451	781-466-8882	466-8885
Solomon-Page Group LLC 260 Madison Ave *TF:* 800-296-7646 ■ *Web:* www.spgjobs.com	New York	NY	10016	212-403-6100	764-6003
SOS Staffing Services Inc 2650 S Decker Lake Blvd Suite 500 *TF:* 800-474-1722 ■ *Web:* www.sosstaffing.com	Salt Lake City	UT	84119	801-484-4400	483-4283
Southwest Medical Assoc Inc 638 E Market St PO Box 2168 *TF:* 800-929-4854 ■ *Web:* www.swmed.com	Rockport	TX	78382	361-729-0646	729-0954
Special Counsel Inc 1 Independent Dr Suite 112 *TF:* 800-737-3436 ■ *Web:* www.specialcounsel.com	Jacksonville	FL	32202	904-737-3436	360-2350
Spherion Corp 2050 Spectrum Blvd *NYSE: SFN* ■ *TF:* 866-435-7456 ■ *Web:* www.sfngroup.com	Fort Lauderdale	FL	33309	954-308-7600	351-8117
Spherion Corp Technology Group 2050 Spectrum Blvd *Web:* www.spherion.com	Fort Lauderdale	FL	33309	954-938-7600	308-7775
Staffing Now Inc 4600 Westown Pkwy Regency W 6 Suite 113 *TF:* 877-823-3669 ■ *Web:* www.staffingnow.com	West Des Moines	IA	50266	515-222-6350	222-6360
Staffmark 435 Elm St Suite 300 **Fax Area Code:* 501 ■ *TF:* 888-651-1536 ■ *Web:* www.staffmark.com	Cincinnati	OH	45202	888-651-1536	235-1199*
Sterling Computer Corp 1508 Sq Turn Blvd *Web:* www.sterlingcomputers.com	Norfolk	NE	68701	402-379-1030	379-2855
Stivers Staffing Services Inc 200 W Monroe St Suite 1300 **Fax:* Hum Res ■ *Web:* www.stivers.com	Chicago	IL	60606	312-558-3550	558-1934*
Stratus Services Group Inc 149 Ave at the Common Suite 4 *TF:* 800-777-1557	Shrewsbury	NJ	07702	732-866-0300	653-0292
Superior Design International Inc 1000 Corporate Dr Suite 410 *TF:* 800-850-4222 ■ *Web:* www.sdintl.com	Fort Lauderdale	FL	33334	954-938-5400	772-5061
Superior Technical Resources Inc 250 International Dr *TF:* 800-568-8310 ■ *Web:* www.superior-sdc.com	Williamsville	NY	14221	716-929-1400	633-2026
Surgical Staff Inc 120 St Matthews Ave PO Box 192 *TF:* 800-339-9599 ■ *Web:* www.surgicalstaff.com	San Mateo	CA	94401	650-558-3999	558-3949
TAJ Technologies Inc 1168 Northland Dr *TF:* 877-825-2801 ■ *Web:* www.tajtech.com	Mendota Heights	MN	55120	651-688-2801	688-8321
Team Health Inc 265 Brookview Ctr Way Suite 400 *TF:* 800-342-2898 ■ *Web:* www.teamhealth.com	Knoxville	TN	37919	865-693-1000	539-8030
TeamStaff Inc 1 Executive Dr Suite 130 *NASDAQ: TSTF* ■ *TF:* 866-352-5304 ■ *Web:* www.teamstaff.com	Somerset	NJ	08873	866-352-5304	
Technology & Management Staffing Inc 15245 Shady Grove Rd Suite 350 *Web:* www.t-msi.com	Rockville	MD	20850	301-840-8054	840-0828

Phone | Fax

TEKsystems Inc 7437 Race Rd .... Hanover MD 21076 410-540-7700 540-7556
TF: 888-519-0776 ■ *Web:* www.teksystems.com

Telesec Corestaff 1775 St James Pl Suite 300 .... Houston TX 77056 713-438-1400 438-1763
Web: www.corestaff.com/telesec.html

Temporary Solutions Inc 10515 Crestwood Dr .... Manassas VA 20109 703-368-3800 368-3594
TF: 888-222-0457

Thinkpath Inc
9080 Springboro Pike Suite 300 .... Miamisburg OH 45342 937-291-8374
Web: www.thinkpath.com

Thompson Technologies Inc
114 Townpark Dr Suite 100 .... Kennesaw GA 30144 770-794-8380 794-8381
TF: 888-794-7947 ■ *Web:* www.thompsontechnologies.com

Todays Office Professionals
600 N Pearl St Suite 2350 .... Dallas TX 75201 214-969-7207
TF: 800-422-3819 ■ *Web:* www.todays.com

Transforce Inc 6551 Loisdale Ct Suite 801 .... Springfield VA 22150 703-838-5580 838-5585
TF: 800-308-6989 ■ *Web:* www.transforce.com

TRC Staffing Services Inc
115 Perimeter Ctr Pl NE Suite 850 .... Atlanta GA 30338 770-392-1411 393-2742
TF: 800-488-8008 ■ *Web:* www.trcstaffing.com

True Blue Inc PO Box 2910 .... Tacoma WA 98401 253-383-9101 733-0399*
NYSE: TBI ■ **Fax Area Code:* 877 ■ *TF:* 800-610-8920 ■ *Web:* www.trueblueinc.com

TSR Inc 400 Oser Ave Suite 150 .... Hauppauge NY 11788 631-231-0333 435-1428
NASDAQ: TSRI ■ *Web:* www.tsrconsulting.com

UltraStaff 1818 Memorial Dr Suite 200 .... Houston TX 77007 713-522-7100 522-0744
TF: 800-522-7707 ■ *Web:* www.ultrastaff.com

US Legal Support Inc
363 N Sam Houston Pkwy E Suite 900 .... Houston TX 77060 713-653-7100 653-7171
TF: 800-567-8757 ■ *Web:* www.uslegalsupport.com

Vaco 5410 Maryland Way Suite 460 .... Brentwood TN 37027 615-324-8226 324-8245
Web: www.vaco.com

VMC Consulting Corp 11611 Willows Rd NE .... Redmond WA 98052 425-558-7700 558-7703
Web: www.vmc-consulting.com

Volt Services Group 477 Madison Ave .... New York NY 10022 212-719-7800 719-7850
TF: 800-367-8658 ■ *Web:* www.volt.com/staffing/profile.cfm

White Glove Placement Inc 85 Bartlett St .... Brooklyn NY 11206 718-387-8181 387-8359
TF: 866-387-8100 ■ *Web:* www.whiteglovecare.com

Winston Resources Inc 122 E 42nd St 3rd Fl .... New York NY 10168 212-557-5000 682-1056
TF: 800-494-6786 ■ *Web:* www.winstonresources.com

Wontawk 240 E 68th St .... New York NY 10065 212-869-3348 997-1127
Web: www.wontawk.com

Wood Personnel Services Inc
2 Intl Plaza Dr Suite 800 .... Nashville TN 37217 615-399-0019 399-1930
Web: www.wpscareers.com

Workstream Inc 485 N Keller Rd Suite 500 .... Maitland FL 32751 407-475-5500 475-5517
OTC: WSTMF ■ *TF:* 866-953-8800 ■ *Web:* www.workstreaminc.com

York Solutions LLC
1 Westbrook Corporate Ctr Suite 910 .... Westchester IL 60154 708-531-8362 531-8361
TF: 877-700-9675 ■ *Web:* www.yorksolutions.net

725 STAGE EQUIPMENT & SERVICES

Phone | Fax

Angstrom Lighting 837 N Cahuenga Blvd .... Hollywood CA 90038 323-462-4246 462-8190
TF: 866-275-9211 ■ *Web:* www.angstromlighting.com

Apollo Design Technology Inc
4130 Fourier Dr .... Fort Wayne IN 46818 260-497-9191 497-9192
TF: 800-288-4626 ■ *Web:* www.internetapollo.com

ARTEC Consultants Inc 114 W 26th St 10th Fl .... New York NY 10001 212-242-0120 706-7786*
**Fax Area Code:* 646 ■ *Web:* www.arteconsultants.com

Audio Visual Services Corp
111 W Ocean Blvd Suite 1110 .... Long Beach CA 90802 562-366-0620 366-0628
Web: www.avservicescorp.com

BlueScreen LLC
137 N Larchmont Blvd Suite 508 .... Los Angeles CA 90004 323-467-7572 220-2195*
**Fax Area Code:* 707 ■ *Web:* www.bluescreen.com

Chapman/Leonard Studio Equipment Inc
12950 Raymer St .... North Hollywood CA 91605 818-764-6726 764-6730
TF: 888-883-6559 ■ *Web:* www.chapman-leonard.com

Clair Bros Audio Systems Inc 1 Ellen Ave .... Lititz PA 17543 717-626-4000 625-4900
Web: www.clair-audio.com

Creative Stage Lighting Co Inc
149 Rt 28 N PO Box 567 .... North Creek NY 12853 518-251-3302 251-2908
Web: www.creativestagelighting.com

Dreamworld Backdrops
6450 Lusk Blvd Suite E-106 .... San Diego CA 92121 858-452-4922 453-2783
TF: 800-737-9869 ■ *Web:* www.dreamworldbackdrops.com

Fisher Dachs Assoc 22 W 19th St 6th Fl .... New York NY 10011 212-691-3020 633-1644
Web: www.fda-online.com

Grosh Scenic Rentals 4114 Sunset Blvd .... Hollywood CA 90029 323-662-1134 664-7526
TF: 877-363-7998 ■ *Web:* www.grosh.com

High End Systems Inc 2105 Gracy Farms Ln .... Austin TX 78758 512-836-2242 837-5290
TF: 800-890-8989 ■ *Web:* www.highend.com

Hollywood Rentals Production Services
12800 Foothill Blvd .... Sylmar CA 91342 818-407-7800 407-7875
TF: 800-233-7830 ■ *Web:* www.hollywoodrentals.com

Holzmueller Productions Corp
1000 25th St .... San Francisco CA 94107 415-826-8383 826-2608
Web: www.holzmueller.com

Janson Industries 1200 Garfield Ave SW .... Canton OH 44706 330-455-7029 455-5919
TF: 800-548-8982 ■ *Web:* www.jansonindustries.com

Lycian Stage Lighting Kings Hwy PO Box D .... Sugar Loaf NY 10981 845-469-2285 469-5355
Web: www.lycian.com

Musson Theatrical Inc 890 Walsh Ave .... Santa Clara CA 95050 408-986-0210 986-9552
TF: 800-843-2837 ■ *Web:* www.musson.com

Nmr Staging & Events 28 Abeel Rd .... Monroe Township NJ 08831 609-395-0550 395-7142
TF: 800-637-2496 ■ *Web:* www.nmrrents.com

Production Resource Group LLC
539 Temple Hill Rd .... New Windsor NY 12553 845-567-5700 567-5800
Web: www.prg.com

Phone | Fax

Rosco Laboratories Inc 52 Harbor View Ave .... Stamford CT 06902 203-708-8900 708-8919
TF: 800-767-2669 ■ *Web:* www.rosco.com

Schuler & Shook 750 N Orleans St Suite 400 .... Chicago IL 60654 312-944-8230 944-8297
Web: www.schulershook.com

Screen Works 2201 W Fulton St .... Chicago IL 60612 312-243-8265 243-8290
TF Cust Svc: 800-294-8111 ■ *Web:* www.thescreenworks.com

Secoa Inc 8650 109th Ave N .... Champlin MN 55316 763-506-8800 506-8844
TF: 800-328-5519 ■ *Web:* www.secoa.com

Syracuse Scenery & Stage Lighting Co Inc
101 Monarch Dr .... Liverpool NY 13088 315-453-8096 453-7897
TF: 800-453-7775 ■ *Web:* www.syracusescenery.com

Triangle Scenery Drapery & Lighting Co
1215 Bates Ave .... Los Angeles CA 90029 323-662-8129 662-8120
Web: www.tridrape.com

726 STEEL - MFR

Phone | Fax

A Finkl & Sons Co 2011 N Southport Ave .... Chicago IL 60614 773-975-2500 348-5347
TF: 800-343-2562 ■ *Web:* www.finkl.com

AK Steel Corp 1801 Crawford St .... Middletown OH 45044 513-425-6541
Web: www.aksteel.com

AK Steel Holding Corp
9227 Centre Pointe Dr .... West Chester OH 45069 513-425-5000 425-5220
NYSE: AKS ■ *TF:* 800-331-5050 ■ *Web:* www.aksteel.com

Aleris International Inc
25825 Science Pk Dr Suite 400 .... Beachwood OH 44122 216-910-3400 910-3650
TF: 866-266-2586 ■ *Web:* www.aleris.com

Allegheny Technologies Inc
1000 Six PPG Pl .... Pittsburgh PA 15222 412-394-2800 394-3034*
NYSE: ATI ■ **Fax:* Hum Res ■ *TF Sales:* 800-258-3586 ■ *Web:* www.alleghenytechnologies.com

American Tank & Fabricating Co (AT&F)
12314 Elmwood Ave .... Cleveland OH 44111 216-252-1500 251-4963
Web: www.amtank.com

ATI Allegheny Ludlum Corp 100 River Rd .... Brackenridge PA 15014 724-224-1000 394-2805*
**Fax Area Code:* 412 ■ *TF Sales:* 800-258-3586 ■ *Web:* www.alleghenyludlum.com

Bayou Steel Corp PO Box 5000 .... LaPlace LA 70069 985-652-0370 652-8450
TF: 800-535-7692 ■ *Web:* www.bayousteel.com

Block Steel Corp 6101 Oakton St Suite 2 .... Skokie IL 60077 847-966-3000 966-5906
Web: www.blocksteel.com

Calstrip Steel Corp 7140 Bandini Blvd .... Los Angeles CA 90040 323-726-1345 722-8269
Web: calstripsteel.com

Canam Group Inc
11505 1st Ave Bureau 500 .... Saint-Georges QC G5Y7X3 418-228-8031 227-5424
TSX: CAM ■ *TF:* 877-499-6049 ■ *Web:* www.canamgroup.ws

Carpenter Specialty Alloys Operations
101 W Bern St .... Reading PA 19601 610-208-2000 208-3716
TF: 800-654-6543 ■ *Web:* www.cartech.com/sao_products

Carpenter Technology Corp PO Box 14662 .... Reading PA 19612 610-208-2000 208-3716
NYSE: CRS ■ *TF:* 800-654-6543 ■ *Web:* www.cartech.com

Cascade Steel Rolling Mills Inc (CSRM)
3200 N Hwy 99 W PO Box 687 .... McMinnville OR 97128 503-472-4181 434-5739
TF: 800-283-2776 ■ *Web:* www.cascadesteel.com

Central Illinois Steel Co
21050 Rt 4 PO Box 78 .... Carlinville IL 62626 217-854-3251 854-4771

Charleston Steel & Metal Co
2700 Spruill Ave .... North Charleston SC 29405 843-722-7278 722-7287

Charter Mfg Co Inc 1212 W Glen Oaks Ln .... Mequon WI 53092 262-243-4700 243-4767
Web: www.chartermfg.com

Chicago Heights Steel Acquisition Corp
211 E Main St .... Chicago Heights IL 60411 708-754-0410 756-5628
TF: 800-424-4487 ■ *Web:* www.chs.com

Commercial Metals Co (CMC)
6565 N MacArthur Blvd Suite 800 .... Irving TX 75039 214-689-4300 689-4300
NYSE: CMC ■ *Web:* www.cmc.com

Corey Steel Co 2800 S 61st Ct .... Cicero IL 60804 708-735-8000 735-8100
TF: 800-323-2750 ■ *Web:* www.coreysteel.com

Creform Corp PO Box 830 .... Greer SC 29652 864-989-1700 877-3863
TF: 800-839-8823 ■ *Web:* www.creform.com

Crucible Compaction Metals 1001 Robb Hill Rd .... Oakdale PA 15071 412-923-2670 923-2670
TF: 888-923-2670

Crucible Materials Corp 575 State Fair Blvd .... Syracuse NY 13209 315-487-4111 470-9358*
**Fax:* Sales ■ *TF:* 800-365-1180 ■ *Web:* www.crucible.com

D-M-E Co 70 E Hillis St .... Youngwood PA 15697 724-925-7291 925-2424
TF: 800-626-6653

Dunkirk Specialty Steel Corp
830 Brigham Rd PO Box 319 .... Dunkirk NY 14048 716-366-1000 366-0478
TF: 800-916-9133 ■ *Web:* www.dunkirkspecialtysteel.com

E&h Steel Corp
3635 E Hwy 134 PO Box 1170 .... Midland City AL 36350 334-983-5636 983-6173
Web: www.ehsteel.com

Electralloy Corp 175 Main St .... Oil City PA 16301 814-678-4100 678-4100
TF: 800-458-7273 ■ *Web:* www.electralloy.com

F & D Head Co 3040 E Peden Rd .... Fort Worth TX 76179 817-236-8773 236-1061
TF Cust Svc: 800-451-2684 ■ *Web:* www.fwfdhead.com

Feroleto Steel Co Inc 300 Scofield Ave .... Bridgeport CT 06605 203-366-3263 366-8058
TF: 800-243-2839 ■ *Web:* www.feroletosteel.com

Georgetown Steel Corp 420 S Hazard St .... Georgetown SC 29440 843-546-2525 527-3134*
**Fax:* Sales ■ *TF Sales:* 800-472-7637

Gerdau AmeriSteel Corp
4221 W Boy Scout Blvd Suite 600 .... Tampa FL 33607 813-286-8383
NYSE: GNA ■ *TF Sales:* 800-876-7833 ■ *Web:* www.gerdauameristeel.com

Gibraltar Industries Inc 3556 Lakeshore Rd .... Buffalo NY 14219 716-826-6500 826-1589*
NASDAQ: ROCK ■ **Fax:* Sales ■ *TF:* 800-777-0675 ■ *Web:* www.gibraltar1.com

GO Carlson Inc
350 Marshallton Thorndale Rd .... Downingtown PA 19335 610-384-2800 383-3429
TF: 800-338-5622

Greer Steel Co 624 Blvd .... Dover OH 44622 330-343-8811 343-1700
TF Sales: 800-388-2868 ■ *Web:* www.greersteel.com

Gulf Coast Machine & Supply Co Inc
6817 Industrial Rd .... Beaumont TX 77705 409-842-1311 842-4621
TF: 800-231-3032 ■ *Web:* www.gulfco.com

Company	City	State	Zip	Phone	Fax
Harris Steel Co 1223 S 55th Ct *Web:* www.harrissteelco.com	Cicero	IL	60804	708-656-5500	656-0151
Heidtman Steel Products Inc 2401 Front St *Web:* www.heidtman.com	Toledo	OH	43605	419-691-4646	698-1150
Huron Valley Steel Corp 41000 E Huron River Dr *TF:* 800-783-3404	Belleville	MI	48111	734-697-3400	697-4445
Interstate Steel Co 1965 Pratt Blvd *TF:* 800-323-9800 ■ *Web:* www.interstatesteelco.com	Elk Grove Village	IL	60007	847-806-7676	806-7624
Intsel Steel Distributors LP 11310 W Little York *TF:* 800-762-3316 ■ *Web:* www.intselsteel.com	Houston	TX	77041	713-937-9500	937-1091
Jersey Shore Steel Co 70 Maryland Ave PO Box 5055 *TF:* 800-833-0277 ■ *Web:* www.jssteel.com	Jersey Shore	PA	17740	570-398-0220	753-3782
JFE Steel Corp 350 Pk Ave 27th Fl *Web:* www.jfe-steel.co.jp	New York	NY	10022	212-310-9320	308-9292
Kentucky Electric Steel LLC 2704 S Big Run Rd W *TF:* 800-333-3012 ■ *Web:* www.kentuckyelectricsteel.com	Ashland	KY	41102	606-929-1200	929-1219
Keystone Steel & Wire Co 7000 S Adams St *Web:* www.redbrand.com	Peoria	IL	61641	309-697-7020	697-7487
Kobe Steel USA Inc 535 Madison Ave 5th Fl *Web:* www.kobelco.co.jp/indexe.htm	New York	NY	10022	212-751-9400	355-5564
LeTourneau Inc PO Box 2307 *Web:* www.letourneau-inc.com	Longview	TX	74606	903-237-7000	237-7032
Lynchburg Steel & Specialty Co 275 Francis Ave *Web:* lynchburgsteel.com	Monroe	VA	24574	434-929-0951	929-2613
Metalex Corp 1530 Artaius Pkwy PO Box 399 *TF:* 800-323-0792 ■ *Web:* www.metlx.com	Libertyville	IL	60048	847-362-8300	362-7939
Mill Steel Co 5116 36th St SE *TF:* 800-247-6455 ■ *Web:* www.millsteel.com	Grand Rapids	MI	49512	616-949-6700	977-9300
Millerbernd Mfg Co PO Box 98 *Web:* www.millerberndmfg.com	Winsted	MN	55395	320-485-2111	485-4420
Neilsen Mfg Inc 3501 Portland Rd NE *TF:* 800-292-2495 ■ *Web:* www.neilsenmfg.com	Salem	OR	97303	503-585-0040	362-3814
New Technology Steel 12301 Hubbell St	Detroit	MI	48227	313-653-4746	653-4916
Niagara Corp 667 Madison Ave *NASDAQ: NIAG* ■ *Web:* www.niagaralasalle.com	New York	NY	10021	212-317-1000	317-1001
Nisshin USA LLC 1701 Golf Rd Continental Tower 3 Suite 1004 *Web:* www.nisshin-steel.co.jp	Rolling Meadows	IL	60008	847-290-5100	290-0826
NS Group Inc 530 W 9th St *TF:* 800-348-7751	Newport	KY	41071	859-292-6809	292-0593
Nucor Corp 1915 Rexford Rd *NYSE: NUE* ■ *Web:* www.nucor.com	Charlotte	NC	28211	704-366-7000	362-4208
Nucor Corp Cold Finish Div 2800 N Governor Williams Hwy **Fax:* Sales ■ *TF:* 800-333-0590 ■ *Web:* www.nucor.com	Darlington	SC	29540	843-395-8689	395-8759*
Nucor Corp Steel Div 1455 Hagan Ave **Fax:* Sales ■ *TF:* 888-466-8267 ■ *Web:* www.nucorsteel.com	Huger	SC	29450	843-336-6000	336-6150*
Nucor-Yamato Steel Co 5929 E State Hwy 18 *TF:* 800-289-6977 ■ *Web:* www.nucoryamato.com	Blytheville	AR	72315	870-762-5500	762-1130
Outokumpu Stainless 425 N Martingale Rd Suite 1600 *TF:* 800-833-8703 ■ *Web:* www.outokumpu.com	Schaumburg	IL	60173	847-517-4050	517-2950
Precision Rolled Products Inc 306 Columbia Tpke *TF Cust Svc:* 800-321-0135 ■ *Web:* www.thysfenkrupp-vdm-usa.com	Florham Park	NJ	07932	973-822-9100	822-0932
Quanex Corp 1900 W Loop S Suite 1500 *NYSE: NX* ■ *TF:* 800-231-8176 ■ *Web:* www.quanex.com	Houston	TX	77027	713-961-4600	439-1016
Rome Strip Steel Co Inc 530 Henry St PO Box 189 *Web:* www.romestripsteel.com	Rome	NY	13442	315-336-5500	336-5510
Sandmeyer Steel Co 1 Sandmeyer Ln *TF:* 800-523-3663 ■ *Web:* www.sandmeyersteel.com	Philadelphia	PA	19116	215-464-7100	677-1430
Schnitzer Steel Industries Inc 3200 NW Yeon Ave *NASDAQ: SCHN* ■ *TF:* 800-666-2992 ■ *Web:* www.schnitzersteel.com	Portland	OR	97210	503-224-9900	323-2804
Scion Steel Inc 21555 Mullin Ave *TF:* 800-288-2127 ■ *Web:* www.scionsteel.com	Warren	MI	48089	586-755-4000	755-4064
Sheffield Steel Corp 2300 Hwy S 97 *TF:* 800-331-3304	Sand Springs	OK	74063	918-245-1335	241-6931
Standard Steel LLC 500 N Walnut St *Web:* www.standardsteel.com	Burnham	PA	17009	717-248-4911	248-8050
Steel Dynamics Inc 7575 W Jefferson Blvd Suite 200 *NASDAQ: STLD* ■ *Web:* www.steeldynamics.com	Fort Wayne	IN	46804	260-969-3500	969-3590
Steel of West Virginia Inc 17th St & 2nd Ave *TF:* 800-624-3492 ■ *Web:* www.swvainc.com	Huntington	WV	25703	304-696-8200	529-1479
Tempel Steel Co 5500 N Wolcott Ave **Fax:* Cust Svc ■ *Web:* www.tempel.com	Chicago	IL	60640	773-250-8000	250-8910*
Tenaris 530-8th Ave SW Suite 400 *Web:* www.tenaris.com	Calgary	AB	T2P3S8	403-767-0100	767-0299
Texas Industries Inc 1341 W Mockingbird Ln Suite 700W *NYSE: TXI* ■ *Web:* www.txi.com	Dallas	TX	75247	972-647-6700	647-3878
Thomas Steel Strip Corp Delaware Ave NW *TF:* 800-321-7778 ■ *Web:* www.corusspecialstrip.com/tss	Warren	OH	44485	330-841-6429	841-6366
Thompson Steel Co Inc 120 Royall St *Web:* www.thompsonsteelco.com	Canton	MA	02021	781-828-8800	828-5082
ThyssenKrupp Materials NA Inc 22355 W 11-Mile Rd *Web:* www.tincna.com	Southfield	MI	48034	248-233-5600	233-5699
Tube Products Corp 14420 Ewing Ave S	Burnsville	MN	55306	952-894-2817	
TWB Co 1600 Nadeau Rd *Web:* www.twbcompany.com	Monroe	MI	48162	734-289-6400	289-6555

Company	City	State	Zip	Phone	Fax
Ulbrich Stainless Steels & Special Metals Inc (USSM) 57 Dodge Ave **Fax:* Sales ■ *TF:* 800-243-1676 ■ *Web:* www.ulbrich.com	North Haven	CT	06473	203-239-4481	239-7479*
Union Electric Steel Corp 726 Bell Ave *Web:* www.uniones.com	Carnegie	PA	15106	412-429-7655	276-1711
United Performance Metals 3475 Symmes Rd *TF:* 888-282-3292 ■ *Web:* www.fergusonmetals.com	Hamilton	OH	45015	513-860-6500	874-6857
US Steel Corp 600 Grant St *NYSE: X* ■ **Fax:* Hum Res ■ *Web:* www.ussteel.com	Pittsburgh	PA	15219	412-433-6791	433-6779*
USS-POSCO Industries 900 Loveridge Rd *TF:* 800-877-7672 ■ *Web:* www.ussposco.com	Pittsburg	CA	94565	925-439-6000	439-6506
Wheeling Corrugating Co 1134 Market St *TF Sales:* 800-922-3325 ■ *Web:* www.wheelingcorrugating.com	Wheeling	WV	26003	304-234-2332	234-2378
Wheeling-Pittsburgh Corp 1134 Market St *NASDAQ: WPSC* ■ *TF:* 800-441-8190	Wheeling	WV	26003	304-234-2400	234-2213
WHX Corp 444 Theodore Fremd Ave *Web:* www.whxcorp.com	Rye	NY	10580	914-925-4413	925-4498
Worthington Industries Inc 200 Old Wilson Bridge Rd *NYSE: WOR* ■ *TF:* 800-944-2255 ■ *Web:* www.worthingtonindustries.com	Columbus	OH	43085	614-438-3210	438-3256
Worthington Specialty Processing 4905 S Meridian Rd	Jackson	MI	49204	517-789-0200	789-0209
Worthington Steel Co 1127 Dearborn Dr **Fax:* Sales ■ *TF:* 800-944-3733	Columbus	OH	43085	614-438-3205	438-3283*

727 STONE (CUT) & STONE PRODUCTS

Company	City	State	Zip	Phone	Fax
Adam Ross Cut Stone Co 1003 Broadway *Web:* www.adamrosscutstone.com	Albany	NY	12204	518-463-6674	463-0710
Austin Countertops 11108 Bluff Bend Dr *Web:* www.austincountertops.com	Austin	TX	78753	512-835-5100	339-1796
Benson Stone Co 1100 11th St *Web:* www.bensonstone.com	Rockford	IL	61104	815-227-2000	227-2001
Biesanz Stone Co Inc 4600 Goodview Rd *TF:* 800-247-8322 ■ *Web:* www.biesanzstone.com	Winona	MN	55987	507-454-4336	454-8140
Briar Hill Stone Co 12470 SR 520 *Web:* www.briarhillstone.com	Glenmont	OH	44628	330-377-5100	377-5110
Bristol Memorial Works Inc 797 King St *TF:* 877-225-7626 ■ *Web:* www.rockofages.com	Bristol	CT	06010	860-583-1654	583-1655
Bybee Stone Co Inc 6293 N Matthews Dr *TF:* 800-457-4530 ■ *Web:* www.bybeestone.com	Ellettsville	IN	47429	812-876-2215	876-6329
C & H Stone Co Inc 4000 S Rockport Rd	Bloomington	IN	47403	812-336-2560	331-7292
Cold Spring Granite Inc 17482 Granite W Rd *TF:* 800-328-5040 ■ *Web:* www.coldspringgranite.com	Cold Spring	MN	56320	320-685-3621	685-8490
Columbus Marble Works Corp 2415 Hwy 45 N PO Box 791 *TF Cust Svc:* 800-647-1055 ■ *Web:* www.columbusmarbleworks.net	Columbus	MS	39703	662-328-1477	328-5002
Continental Cast Stone Mfg Inc 22001 W 83rd St *TF:* 800-989-7866 ■ *Web:* www.continentalcaststone.com	Shawnee	KS	66227	913-422-7575	422-7272
Dakota Granite Co 14964 484th Ave PO Box 1351 *TF:* 800-843-3333 ■ *Web:* www.dakgran.com	Milbank	SD	57252	605-432-5580	432-6155
Dakota Marble Inc 902 W 19th St *TF:* 800-697-7241 ■ *Web:* www.dakotamarble.com	Yankton	SD	57078	605-665-7241	665-7241
Daprato Rigali Inc 6030 N NW Hwy *Web:* www.dapratorigali.com	Chicago	IL	60631	773-763-5511	763-5522
Finger Lakes Stone Co Inc 33 Quarry Rd *Web:* www.fingerlakesstone.net	Ithaca	NY	14850	607-273-4646	273-4692
Glenrock International Inc 985 E Linden Ave *TF:* 800-442-6374 ■ *Web:* glenrock.com	Linden	NJ	07036	908-862-3433	862-0430
Harmony Blue Granite Co Inc 8 N Oliver St *TF:* 800-241-7000 ■ *Web:* www.harmonybluegranite.com	Elberton	GA	30635	706-283-3111	283-1008
Hilltop Slate Inc 3 County Rt 21 PO Box 201 *Web:* www.hilltopslate.com	Middle Granville	NY	12849	518-642-2270	642-1220
Intercontinental Marble Corp 8228 NW 56th St *Web:* www.intercontinentalmarble.com	Miami	FL	33166	305-591-2207	477-3237
Kollmann Monumental Works Inc 1915 W Division St *TF:* 800-659-8010 ■ *Web:* www.kollmann.com	Saint Cloud	MN	56301	320-251-8010	251-8019
Kotecki-Rock of Ages Inc 3636 Pearl Rd *TF:* 800-753-2880 ■ *Web:* www.rockofages.com	Cleveland	OH	44109	216-749-2880	749-7221
Little Falls Granite Works 10802 Hwy 10 PO Box 240	Little Falls	MN	56345	320-632-9277	632-3342
Mankato-Kasota Stone Inc 818 N Willow St *TF:* 800-437-7059 ■ *Web:* www.mankato-kasota-stone.com	Mankato	MN	56001	507-625-2746	625-2748
Milwaukee Marble & Granite Co Inc 4535 W Mitchell St *TF:* 877-645-6272 ■ *Web:* www.milwaukeemarble.com	Milwaukee	WI	53214	414-645-0305	645-2620
Monumental Sales Inc 537 22nd Ave N PO Box 667 *TF:* 800-442-1660 ■ *Web:* www.sunburstmemorials.com	Saint Cloud	MN	56302	320-251-6585	251-6547
North Carolina Granite Corp 151 Granite Quarry Trail PO Box 151 *TF:* 800-227-6242 ■ *Web:* www.ncgranite.com	Mount Airy	NC	27030	336-786-5141	719-2623
Northfield Block Co 1 Hunt Ct *TF:* 800-358-3003 ■ *Web:* northfieldblock.com	Mundelein	IL	60060	847-949-3600	816-9072
Northwestern Marble & Granite Co 7705 Bush Lake Rd Suite A *Web:* www.northwesternmarble.com	Edina	MN	55439	952-941-8601	941-0994
RJ Marshall Co 26776 W 12-Mile Rd Suite 201 *TF Cust Svc:* 800-338-7900 ■ *Web:* www.rjmarshallco.com	Southfield	MI	48034	248-353-4100	948-6460
Rock of Ages Corp 560 Graniteville Rd *TF:* 877-870-9057 ■ *Web:* www.rockofages.com	Graniteville	VT	05654	877-870-9057	
Royal Melrose Granite Co 17482 Granite W Rd **Fax Area Code:* 800 ■ *TF:* 800-328-7021 ■ *Web:* www.coldspringgranite.com	Cold Spring	MN	56320	320-685-5101	473-4881*

				Phone	Fax
Starrett Tru-Stone Technologies Div					
1101 Prosper Dr PO Box 430	Waite Park	MN	56387	320-251-7171	259-5073
TF: 800-959-0517 ■ *Web:* www.tru-stone.com					
Taylor Industries Inc 35 Anderson Rd	Parker Ford	PA	19457	610-495-5261	495-5934
Web: www.tere-stone.com					
Tri-State Cut Stone & Brick Co					
10333 Van's Dr	Frankfort	IL	60423	815-469-7550	464-5096
Web: www.stone-brick.com					
Vermont Structural Slate Co Inc					
3 Prospect St PO Box 98	Fair Haven	VT	05743	802-265-4933	265-3865
TF: 800-343-1900 ■ *Web:* www.vermontstructuralslate.com					
Vetter Stone Co (VSC) 23894 3rd Ave PO Box 38	Mankato	MN	56001	507-345-4568	345-4777
TF: 800-878-2850 ■ *Web:* www.vetterstone.com					
Waller Bros Stone Co					
744 McDermott Rushtown Rd PO Box 157	McDermott	OH	45652	740-259-2356	259-2308
Web: www.wallerbrothersstone.com					
WE Neal Slate Co 2840 Hwy 25	Watertown	MN	55388	952-955-3340	955-3341
Web: www.nealslate.com					
Winona Monument Co Inc 174 W 3rd St	Winona	MN	55987	507-452-4672	
TF: 800-657-4411					
WS Hampshire Inc 365 Keyes Ave	Hampshire	IL	60140	800-541-0251	683-4407*
**Fax Area Code:* 847 ■ *TF:* 800-541-0251 ■ *Web:* www.wshampshire.com					

728 STUDENT ASSISTANCE PROGRAMS

				Phone	Fax
Alabama Commission on Higher Education					
100 N Union St PO Box 302000	Montgomery	AL	36130	334-242-1998	242-0268
Web: www.ache.state.al.us/StudentAsst/Programs.htm					
Alabama Prepaid Affordable College Tuition (PACT) Program					
100 N Union St Suite 660	Montgomery	AL	36130	334-242-7514	242-7041
TF: 800-252-7228 ■ *Web:* www.treasury.state.al.us					
Alaska Commission on Postsecondary Education					
PO Box 110510	Juneau	AK	99811	907-465-2962	465-5316
TF: 800-441-2962 ■ *Web:* www.alaskaadvantage.state.ak.us					
Arkansas Financial Aid Office					
114 E Capitol St	Little Rock	AR	72201	501-371-2013	371-2001
TF: 800-547-8839 ■ *Web:* www.arkansashighered.com/financial.html					
California Student Aid Commission					
PO Box 419027	Rancho Cordova	CA	95741	916-526-8999	526-8002
TF: 888-224-7268 ■ *Web:* www.csac.ca.gov					
Coca-Cola Scholars Foundation					
1 Coca-Cola Plaza Bldg NAT 7th Fl PO Box 442	Atlanta	GA	30301	404-733-5420	733-5439
TF: 800-306-2653 ■ *Web:* www.coca-colascholars.org					
College Savings Plans Network					
2670 Research Pk Dr PO Box 11910	Lexington	KY	40578	859-244-8175	244-8053
Web: www.collegesavings.org					
Colorado CollegeInvest					
1560 Broadway Suite 1700	Denver	CO	80202	303-295-1981	296-4811
TF: 800-448-2424 ■ *Web:* www.collegeinvest.org					
Council for Opportunity in Education					
1025 Vermont Ave NW Suite 900	Washington	DC	20005	202-347-7430	347-0786
Web: www.coenet.us					
DC Tuition Assistance Grant Program					
810 First St NE	Washington	DC	20001	202-727-2824	727-2834
TF: 877-485-6751 ■ *Web:* www.osse.dc.gov					
Dollars for Scholars					
Scholarship America 1 Scholarship Way	Saint Peter	MN	56082	507-931-1682	931-9168
TF: 800-248-8080 ■ *Web:* www.scholarshipamerica.org					
EdVest PO Box 55244	Boston	MA	02205	608-264-7899	266-2647
TF: 888-338-3789 ■ *Web:* www.wellsfargoadvantagefunds.com					
FastWeb Inc 444 N Michigan Ave Suite 3000	Chicago	IL	60611	312-832-2312	467-0638
TF: 800-327-8932 ■ *Web:* www.fastweb.com					
FinAid Page LLC PO Box 2056	Cranberry Township	PA	16066	724-538-4500	538-4502
TF: 800-433-3243 ■ *Web:* www.finaid.org					
Florida Prepaid College Board					
PO Box 6448	Tallahassee	FL	32314	850-488-8514	309-1766*
**Fax:* Cust Svc ■ *TF:* 800-552-4723 ■ *Web:* www.myfloridaprepaid.com					
Florida Student Financial Assistance Office					
1940 N Monroe St Suite 70	Tallahassee	FL	32303	850-410-5200	488-3612
TF: 888-827-2004 ■ *Web:* www.floridastudentfinancialaid.org					
Free Application for Federal Student Aid (FAFSA)					
US Federal Student Aid Program					
PO Box 7001	Mount Vernon	IL	62864	319-337-5665	
TF: 800-433-3243 ■ *Web:* www.fafsa.ed.gov					
Georgia Student Finance Commission					
2082 E Exchange Pl Suite 200	Tucker	GA	30084	770-724-9000	724-9089
TF: 800-505-4732 ■ *Web:* www.gsfc.org					
Harry S Truman Scholarship Foundation					
712 Jackson Pl NW	Washington	DC	20006	202-395-4831	395-6995
Web: www.truman.gov					
Hawaii Postsecondary Education Commission					
2444 Dole St Bachman Hall Rm 209	Honolulu	HI	96822	808-956-8213	956-5156
Hispanic Scholarship Fund					
55 2nd St Suite 1500	San Francisco	CA	94105	415-808-2300	808-2301
TF: 877-473-4636 ■ *Web:* www.hsf.net					
Idaho Scholarship Office					
650 W State St Rm 307 PO Box 83720	Boise	ID	83720	208-334-2270	334-2632
Web: www.boardofed.idaho.gov					
Illinois Student Assistance Commission					
1755 Lake Cook Rd	Deerfield	IL	60015	847-948-8500	831-8549*
**Fax:* Cust Svc ■ *TF:* 800-899-4722 ■ *Web:* www.collegeillinois.org					
Indiana Students Assistance Commission					
150 W Market St Suite 500	Indianapolis	IN	46204	317-232-2350	232-3260
TF: 888-528-4719 ■ *Web:* www.in.gov					
Iowa College Student Aid Commission					
603 E 12th St FL 5th	Des Moines	IA	50319	515-725-3400	725-3401
TF: 800-383-4222 ■ *Web:* www.iowacollegeaid.gov					
James Madison Memorial Fellowship Foundation					
2000 K St NW Suite 303	Washington	DC	20006	202-653-8700	653-6045
Web: www.jamesmadison.com					
Kansas Student Financial Aid Div					
1000 SW Jackson St Suite 520	Topeka	KS	66612	785-296-3421	296-0983
Web: www.kansasregents.org					
Kentucky Higher Education Assistance Authority (KHEAA)					
PO Box 798	Frankfort	KY	40602	502-696-7200	696-7345
TF: 800-928-8926					
Louisiana Office of Student Financial Assistance (LOSFA)					
602 N 5th St PO Box 91202	Baton Rouge	LA	70802	225-922-1011	208-1496
TF: 800-259-5626 ■ *Web:* www.osfa.la.gov					
Maine Finance Authority of Maine (FAME)					
5 Community Dr PO Box 949	Augusta	ME	04332	207-623-3263	623-0095
TF: 800-228-3734 ■ *Web:* www.famemaine.com					
Maryland Student Financial Assistance Office					
839 Bestgate Rd Suite 400	Annapolis	MD	21401	410-260-4565	260-3200
TF: 800-974-0203 ■ *Web:* www.mhec.state.md.us					
Massachusetts Educational Financing Authority (MEFA)					
160 Federal St 4th Fl	Boston	MA	02110	617-261-9760	261-9765
TF: 800-449-6332 ■ *Web:* www.mefa.org					
Michigan Education Trust PO Box 30198	Lansing	MI	48909	517-335-4767	373-6967
TF: 800-638-4543 ■ *Web:* www.michigan.gov/treasury					
Michigan Student Financial Services Bureau					
Austin Bldg 430 W Allegan	Lansing	MI	48922	517-373-4897	
TF: 800-642-5626 ■ *Web:* www.michigan.gov/mistudentaid					
Minnesota Office of Higher Education					
1450 Energy Pk Dr Suite 350	Saint Paul	MN	55108	651-642-0567	642-0675
TF: 800-657-3866 ■ *Web:* www.ohe.state.mn.us					
Mississippi Student Financial Aid Office					
3825 Ridgewood Rd	Jackson	MS	39211	601-432-6997	432-6527
TF: 800-327-2980 ■ *Web:* www.ihl.state.ms.us/financialaid					
Mississippi Treasury Dept					
501 N W St Suite 1101	Jackson	MS	39201	601-359-5255	359-5234
TF: 800-987-4450 ■ *Web:* www.collegesavingsmississippi.com					
Missouri Student Assistance Resource Services (MOSTARS)					
205 Jefferson St PO Box 1469	Jefferson City	MO	65109	573-751-2361	751-6635
TF: 800-473-6757 ■ *Web:* www.dhe.mo.gov					
Montana Higher Education Board of Regents					
2500 Broadway St PO Box 203201	Helena	MT	59620	406-444-6570	444-1469
TF: 877-501-1722 ■ *Web:* www.mus.edu					
Morris K Udall Foundation 110 S Church # 3350	Tucson	AZ	85709	520-670-5529	670-5530
Web: www.udall.gov					
National Merit Scholarship Corp					
1560 Sherman Ave Suite 200	Evanston	IL	60201	847-866-5100	866-5113
Web: www.nationalmerit.org					
Nebraska Coordinating Commission for Postsecondary Educatio					
140 N 8th St Suite 300 PO Box 95005	Lincoln	NE	68509	402-471-2847	471-2886
Web: www.ccpe.state.ne.us					
New Hampshire Postsecondary Education Commission					
3 Barrell Ct Suite 300	Concord	NH	03301	603-271-2555	271-2696
TF: 800-735-2964 ■ *Web:* www.nh.gov					
New Jersey Higher Education Student Assistance Authority					
4 Quakerbridge Plaza PO Box 540	Trenton	NJ	08625	609-588-7944	588-7389
TF: 800-792-8670 ■ *Web:* www.hesaa.org					
New Mexico Financial Aid & Student Services Unit					
1068 Cerrillos Rd	Santa Fe	NM	87505	505-476-6500	476-6511
TF: 800-279-9777 ■ *Web:* www.hed.state.nm.us					
New York Higher Education Services Corp					
99 Washington Ave	Albany	NY	12255	518-473-1574	473-3749
TF: 888-697-4372 ■ *Web:* www.hesc.com					
North Carolina State Education Assistance Authority (NCSEAA)					
PO Box 14103	Research Triangle Park	NC	27709	919-549-8614	549-8481
TF: 800-700-1775 ■ *Web:* www.ncseaa.edu					
North Dakota Student Financial Assistance Program					
600 E Blvd Ave 10th Fl Dept 215	Bismarck	ND	58505	701-328-2960	328-2961
Web: www.ndus.nodak.edu					
Office of Federal Student Aid					
Union Ctr Plaza 830 1st St NE	Washington	DC	20202	202-377-3000	275-5000
TF: 800-433-3243 ■ *Web:* www.ed.gov/about/offices/list/fsa					
Federal Student Aid Information Ctr					
PO Box 84	Washington	DC	20044	800-433-3243	
TF: 800-433-3243 ■ *Web:* www.studentaid.ed.gov					
Ohio State Grants & Scholarships Office					
30 E Broad St 36th Fl PO Box 182452	Columbus	OH	43218	614-466-7420	752-5903
TF: 888-833-1133 ■ *Web:* regents.ohio.gov/sgs					
Ohio Tuition Trust Authority					
580 S High St Suite 208	Columbus	OH	43215	614-752-9400	466-4486
TF Cust Svc: 800-233-6734 ■ *Web:* www.collegeadvantage.com					
Oklahoma State Regents for Higher Education					
655 Research Pkwy Suite 200	Oklahoma City	OK	73104	405-225-9100	225-9235
Web: www.okhighered.org					
Oregon Student Assistance Commission					
1500 Valley River Dr Suite 100	Eugene	OR	97401	541-687-7400	687-7419
TF: 800-452-8807 ■ *Web:* www.osac.state.or.us					
Pennsylvania Higher Education Assistance Agency					
1200 N 7th St	Harrisburg	PA	17102	717-720-2860	720-3644
TF: 800-692-7392 ■ *Web:* www.pheaa.org					
Pennsylvania Tuition Account Plan (TAP 529)					
2005 Market St PO Box 42529	Philadelphia	PA	19103	866-244-9877	
TF: 866-244-9877 ■					
Web: www.lfg.com/LincolnPageServer?LFGPage=/lfg/pa5/index.html					
Scholarship America					
1 Scholarship Way PO Box 297	Saint Peter	MN	56082	507-931-1682	931-9168
TF: 800-537-4180 ■ *Web:* www.scholarshipamerica.org					
Scholarship Resource Network Inc					
600 Lexington Ave 3rd Fl	New York	NY	10022	800-926-2619	753-1190*
**Fax Area Code:* 212 ■ *TF:* 800-926-2619 ■ *Web:* www.srnexpress.com					
South Carolina Higher Education Tuition Grants Commission					
101 Business Pk Blvd Suite 2100	Columbia	SC	29203	803-896-1120	896-1126
Web: www.sctuitiongrants.com					
Tennessee Student Assistance Corp					
404 James Robertson Pkwy Suite 1510	Nashville	TN	37243	615-741-1346	741-6101
TF: 800-257-6526 ■ *Web:* www.state.tn.us/tsac					
Tennessee Treasurer					
Tennessee State Capitol					
1st Fl 600 Charlotte Ave	Nashville	TN	37243	615-741-2956	
Web: www.treasury.state.tn.us					
Texas Higher Education Coordinating Board					
1200 E Anderson Ln	Austin	TX	78752	512-427-6101	427-6169
Web: www.thecb.state.tx.us					
Thurgood Marshall Scholarship Fund					
80 Maiden Ln Suite 2204	New York	NY	10038	212-573-8888	573-8497
Web: www.thurgoodmarshallfund.net					

	City	State	Zip	Phone	Fax
Utah Higher Education Assistance Authority PO Box 145112 — TF: 877-336-7378 ■ Web: www.uheaa.org	Salt Lake City	UT	84114	801-321-7294	366-8430
Vermont Student Assistance Corp (VSAC) PO Box 2000 — TF: 800-642-3177 ■ Web: www.vsac.org	Winooski	VT	05404	802-655-9602	654-3765
Virginia College Savings Plan 9001 Arboretum Pkwy PO Box 607 — TF: 888-567-0540 ■ Web: www.virginia529.com	Richmond	VA	23236	804-786-0719	786-2453
Virginia State Council of Higher Education 101 N 14th St 9th Fl — Web: www.schev.edu	Richmond	VA	23219	804-225-2600	225-2604
Wisconsin Higher Educational Aids Board (HEAB) 131 W Wilson S PO Box 7885 — Web: www.heab.state.wi.us	Madison	WI	53707	608-267-2206	267-2808
Washington Higher Education Coordinating Board 917 Lakeridge Way PO Box 43430 — Web: www.hecb.wa.gov	Olympia	WA	98504	360-753-7800	753-7808
West Virginia Higher Education Policy Commission 1018 Kanawha Blvd E Suite 700 — TF: 888-825-5707 ■ Web: www.wvhepcnew.wvnet.edu	Charleston	WV	25301	304-558-2101	558-5719
Wyoming Community College Commission 2020 Carey Ave 8th Fl — Web: www.commission.wcc.edu	Cheyenne	WY	82002	307-777-7763	777-6567

729 SUBSTANCE ABUSE TREATMENT CENTERS

SEE ALSO Self-Help Organizations p. 1436; General Hospitals - Canada p. 2038; General Hospitals - US p. 2041; Psychiatric Hospitals p. 2071

	City	State	Zip	Phone	Fax
AdCare Hospital of Worcester 107 Lincoln St — TF: 800-345-3552 ■ Web: www.adcare.com	Worcester	MA	01605	508-799-9000	453-3064
Anchor Hospital 5454 Yorktowne Dr — Web: www.anchorhospital.com	Atlanta	GA	30349	770-991-6044	991-3843
Anthony Louis Ctr 115 Forestview Ln — Web: www.anthonylouiscenter.com	Plymouth	MN	55441	763-542-9212	542-9248
AREBA Casriel Inc (ACI) 500 W 57th St — TF: 800-724-4444 ■ Web: www.acirehab.org	New York	NY	10019	212-293-3000	293-3020
Arms Acres 75 Seminary Hill Rd — TF: 800-989-2676 ■ Web: www.armsacres.com	Carmel	NY	10512	845-225-3400	225-7581
Baltimore Behavioral Health 200 S Arlington Ave — Web: www.bbhtx.org	Baltimore	MD	21223	410-962-7180	962-7194
Betty Ford Ctr 39000 Bob Hope Dr — TF: 800-854-9211 ■ Web: www.bettyfordcenter.org	Rancho Mirage	CA	92270	760-773-4100	773-4126
Blue Hills Hospital 500 Vine St — Web: www.ct.gov	Hartford	CT	06112	860-293-6400	293-6470
Boniface Human Services 5886 W Fort St — Web: comnet.org/local/orgs/boniface	Detroit	MI	48209	313-842-5741	554-2039
Bradford Health Services 2101 Magnolia Ave S Suite 518 — TF: 800-217-2849 ■ Web: www.bradfordhealth.com	Birmingham	AL	35205	205-251-7753	251-7760
Brighton Hospital 12851 E Grand River Ave — TF Cust Svc: 800-523-8198 ■ Web: www.brightonhospital.org	Brighton	MI	48116	810-227-1221	227-1869
Central Dupage Hospital's Behavioral Health Services 27 W 350 High Lake Rd — Web: www.cdh.org	Winfield	IL	60190	630-653-4000	933-1933
Central Street Health Ctr 26 Central St — Web: www.cambridgehealthalliance.org	Somerville	MA	02143	617-591-6033	591-6452
Clear Brook Lodge 890 Bethel Hill Rd — Web: www.clearbrookinc.com	Shickshinny	PA	18655	570-864-3116	864-2812
Clear Brook Manor 1100 E Northampton St — TF: 800-582-6241 ■ Web: www.clearbrookinc.com	Laurel Run	PA	18706	570-823-1171	823-1582
Conifer Park 79 Glenridge Rd — TF: 800-989-6446 ■ Web: www.coniferpark.com	Glenville	NY	12302	518-399-6446	952-8228
Cornerstone Medical Arts Center Hospital 159-05 Union Tpke — TF: 800-233-9999 ■ Web: www.cornerstoneny.com	Fresh Meadows	NY	11366	718-906-6700	906-6840
Eagleville Hospital 100 Eagleville Rd — TF: 800-255-2019 ■ Web: www.eaglevillehospital.com	Eagleville	PA	19408	610-539-6000	539-6249
Fairbanks Hospital 8102 Clearvista Pkwy — TF: 800-225-4673	Indianapolis	IN	46256	317-849-8222	849-8222
Fellowship Hall Inc 5140 Dunstan Rd — TF: 800-659-3381 ■ Web: www.fellowshiphall.com	Greensboro	NC	27405	336-621-3381	621-7513
Florida Center for Addictions & Dual Disorders 100 W College Dr — Web: www.tchsonline.com	Avon Park	FL	33825	863-452-3858	452-3863
Friary of Lakeview Ctr The 4400 Hickory Shores Blvd — TF: 800-332-2271 ■ Web: www.thefriary.org	Gulf Breeze	FL	32563	850-932-9375	934-1281
Gateway Foundation Inc 55 E Jackson St Suite 1500 — Web: www.recovergateway.org	Chicago	IL	60604	312-663-1130	913-2344
Gaudenzia Inc Common Ground 2835 N Front St — TF: 888-237-8984	Harrisburg	PA	17110	717-238-5553	232-7362
Glenbeigh Health Source 2863 SR 45 — TF: 800-234-1001 ■ Web: www.glenbeigh.com	Rock Creek	OH	44084	440-563-3400	563-9619
Greenleaf Ctr 2209 Pineview Dr — TF: 800-247-2747	Valdosta	GA	31602	229-247-4357	244-6194
Griffin Memorial Hospital PO Box 151 — TF: 877-580-5044	Norman	OK	73070	405-321-4880	573-6652
Hanley Ctr 5200 E Ave — TF: 800-444-7008 ■ Web: www.hanleycenter.org	West Palm Beach	FL	33407	561-841-1000	841-1100
Hazelden Center for Youth & Families (HCYF) 11505 36th Ave N — TF: 800-257-7810 ■ Web: www.hazelden.org	Plymouth	MN	55441	763-509-3800	559-0149
Hazelden Chicago 867 N Dearborn St — TF: 800-257-7810 ■ Web: www.hazelden.org	Chicago	IL	60610	312-943-3534	943-3530
Hazelden Foundation 15251 Pleasant Valley Rd — TF: 800-257-7810 ■ Web: www.hazelden.org	Center City	MN	55012	651-213-4200	213-4411
Hazelden New York 322 8th Ave 12th Fl — TF: 800-257-7800 ■ Web: www.hazelden.org	New York	NY	10001	212-420-9520	420-9664
Hazelden Springbrook 1901 Esther St — TF: 866-866-4662 ■ Web: www.hazelden.org	Newberg	OR	97132	503-554-4300	537-7007
HealthSource Saginaw 3340 Hospital Rd — TF: 800-662-6848	Saginaw	MI	48603	989-790-7700	790-9297
Highland Ridge Hospital 7309 S 180 W — Web: www.highlandridgehospital.com	Midvale	UT	84047	801-569-2153	567-9006
Impact Drug & Alcohol Treatment Ctr 1680 N Fair Oaks Ave PO Box 93607 — TF: 888-400-4222 ■ Web: www.impacthouse.com	Pasadena	CA	91103	626-798-0884	798-6970
Julian F Keith Alcohol & Drug Abuse Treatment Ctr 201 Tabernacle Rd — Web: www.jfkadatc.net	Black Mountain	NC	28711	828-257-6200	257-6300
Keystone Ctr 2001 Providence Ave — TF: 800-558-9600 ■ Web: www.keystonecenter.net	Chester	PA	19013	610-876-9000	876-5441
La Hacienda Treatment Ctr 145 La Hacienda Way — TF: 800-749-6160 ■ Web: www.lahacienda.com	Hunt	TX	78024	830-238-4222	238-3120
Livengrin Foundation 4833 Hulmeville Rd — TF: 800-245-4746 ■ Web: www.livengrin.org	Bensalem	PA	19020	215-638-5200	638-2603
Malvern Institute 940 W King Rd — TF: 888-643-3869 ■ Web: www.malverninstitute.com	Malvern	PA	19355	610-647-0330	647-2572
Mount Regis Ctr 405 Kimball Ave — TF: 877-217-3447 ■ Web: www.mtregis.com	Salem	VA	24153	540-389-4761	389-6539
Mountain Manor Treatment Ctr 9701 Keysville Rd PO Box 136 — TF: 800-537-3422	Emmitsburg	MD	21727	301-447-2361	447-6504
New Directions Inc 30800 Chagrin Blvd — TF: 800-750-6709 ■ Web: www.newdirect.org	Cleveland	OH	44124	216-591-0324	591-1243
Phoenix House Foundation Inc (PHF) 164 W 74th St 4th Fl — TF: 800-262-2463 ■ Web: www.phoenixhouse.org	New York	NY	10023	212-595-5810	595-6365
Providence Behavioral Health Hospital 1233 Main St — TF: 800-274-7724 ■ Web: www.mercycares.com	Holyoke	MA	01040	413-536-5111	539-2992
Rimrock Foundation 1231 N 29th St — TF: 800-227-3953 ■ Web: www.rimrock.org	Billings	MT	59101	406-248-3175	248-3821
Riverside General Hospital *Houston Recovery Ctr* 4514 Lyons Ave — Web: riversidehospital.fifthwardhouston.org	Houston	TX	77020	713-331-2500	526-2441
Rivervalley Behavioral Health Hospital 1000 Industrial Dr — TF: 800-755-8477 ■ Web: www.rvbh.com	Owensboro	KY	42301	270-689-6800	689-6799
Rubicon Inc 1300 MacTavish Ave	Richmond	VA	23230	804-359-3255	359-5137
Saint Josephs Villa of Rochester 3300 Dewey Ave — Web: www.stjosephsvilla.com	Rochester	NY	14616	585-865-1550	865-5219
Samaritan Village 138-02 Queens Blvd — Web: www.samvill.org	Briarwood	NY	11435	718-206-2000	206-2399
Schick Shadel Hospital 12101 Ambaum Blvd SW — TF: 800-500-6395 ■ Web: www.schick-shadel.com	Seattle	WA	98146	206-244-8100	431-9142
Self Help Addiction Rehabilitation Corp 1852 W Grand Blvd	Detroit	MI	48208	313-894-8444	894-5542
Serenity Lane 616 E 16th Ave — TF: 800-543-9905 ■ Web: www.serenitylane.org	Eugene	OR	97401	541-687-1110	687-9041
Sierra Tucson Inc 39580 S Lago Del Oro Pkwy — TF: 800-842-4487 ■ Web: www.sierratucson.com	Tucson	AZ	85739	520-624-4000	818-5888
Spectrum Programs Inc 11031 NE 6th Ave — Web: www.mbhc.org	Miami	FL	33161	305-757-0602	757-2387
Spencer Recovery Centers Inc 1316 S Coast Hwy — TF: 800-334-0394 ■ Web: www.spencerrecovery.com	Laguna Beach	CA	92651	949-376-3705	376-6862
Starlite Recovery Ctr 230 Mesa Verde Dr PO Box 317 — TF: 866-220-1626 ■ Web: www.starliterecovery.com	Center Point	TX	78010	830-634-2212	634-2532
Substance Abuse Foundation 3125 E 7th St — TF: 888-476-2743 ■ Web: www.safinc.org	Long Beach	CA	90804	562-987-5722	438-6891
Talbott Recovery Campus 5448 Yorktowne Dr — TF: 800-445-4232 ■ Web: www.talbottcampus.com	Atlanta	GA	30349	770-994-0185	994-2024
Turning Point Hospital 3015 Veterans Pkwy PO Box 1177 — TF: 800-342-1075 ■ Web: www.turningpointcare.com	Moultrie	GA	31776	229-985-4815	890-1614
Turning Point of Tampa 6227 Sheldon Rd — TF: 800-397-3006 ■ Web: www.tptampa.com	Tampa	FL	33615	813-882-3003	885-6974
Twin Town Treatment Ctr 1706 University Ave	Saint Paul	MN	55104	651-645-3661	645-0959
Valley Forge Medical Center & Hospital 1033 W Germantown Pike — TF: 888-539-8500	Norristown	PA	19403	610-539-8500	539-0910
Village South Inc 3050 Biscayne Blvd 9th Fl — TF: 800-443-3784 ■ Web: www.villagesouth.com	Miami	FL	33137	305-573-3784	576-1348
Wabash Valley Alliance Inc 2900 N River Rd — TF: 800-859-5553 ■ Web: www.wvhmhc.org	West Lafayette	IN	47906	765-463-2555	497-3960
Wake County Alcoholism Treatment Ctr 3000 Falstaff Rd	Raleigh	NC	27610	919-250-1500	250-1597
Walter B Jones Alcohol & Drug Abuse Treatment Ctr 2577 W 5th St	Greenville	NC	27834	252-830-3426	830-8585

				Phone	Fax
Warwick Manor Behavioral Health 3680 Warwick Rd *TF:* 800-344-6423	East New Market	MD	21631	410-943-8108	943-3976
Willingway Hospital 311 Jones Mill Rd *TF:* 800-242-9455 ■ *Web:* www.willingway.com	Statesboro	GA	30458	912-764-6236	764-7063
Wilmington Treatment Ctr 2520 Troy Dr. *TF:* 877-762-3750 ■ *Web:* www.wilmingtontreatment.com	Wilmington	NC	28401	910-762-2727	762-7923

730 SURVEYING, MAPPING, RELATED SERVICES

SEE ALSO Engineering & Design p. 1823

				Phone	Fax
Bowman Consulting Group 14020 Thunderbolt Pl # 300 *Web:* www.bowmanconsulting.com	Chantilly	VA	20151	703-464-1000	481-8410
Cochrane Technologies Inc PO Box 81276 *TF:* 800-346-3745 ■ *Web:* www.cochranetech.com	Lafayette	LA	70598	337-837-3334	837-7134
Day & Zimmermann Group Inc 1818 Market St *TF:* 800-523-0786 ■ *Web:* www.dayzim.com	Philadelphia	PA	19103	215-299-8000	299-8030
Fugro Chance Inc 6100 Hillcroft St Suite 300 *Web:* www.fugrochance.com	Houston	TX	77081	713-346-3700	346-3671
Fugro Pelagos Inc 3574 Ruffin Rd *Web:* www.fugro-pelagos.com	San Diego	CA	92123	858-292-8922	292-5308
Greenhorne & O'Mara Inc 6110 Frost Pl. *TF:* 866-322-8905 ■ *Web:* www.g-and-o.com	Laurel	MD	20707	301-982-2800	220-2483
Huitt-Zollars Inc 1717 McKinney Ave Suite 1400 *Web:* www.huitt-zollars.com	Dallas	TX	75202	214-871-3311	871-0757
KCI Technologies Inc 936 Ridgebrook Rd *TF:* 800-572-7496 ■ *Web:* www.kci.com/tech	Sparks	MD	21152	410-316-7800	316-7817
L Robert Kimball & Assoc Inc 615 W Highland Ave *Web:* www.lrkimball.com	Ebensburg	PA	15931	814-472-7700	472-7712
Landiscor Inc 1710 E Indian School Rd Suite 201 *Web:* www.landiscor.com	Phoenix	AZ	85016	602-248-8989	266-8116
MacDonald Dettwiler & Assoc Ltd 13800 Commerce Pkwy *TSX: MDA* ■ *Web:* www.mda.ca	Richmond	BC	V6V2J3	604-278-3411	231-2768
Print-O-Stat Inc 1011 W Market St PO Box 15046 *Web:* www.printostat.com	York	PA	17404	717-854-7821	846-4084
Quantapoint Inc 275 Curry Hollow Rd *Web:* www.quantapoint.com	Pittsburgh	PA	15236	412-653-0100	653-2940
Sidwell Co Inc 675 Sidwell Ct *Web:* www.sidwellco.com	Saint Charles	IL	60174	630-549-1000	549-1111
Teletrac Inc 7391 Lincoln Way *TF:* 800-500-6009 ■ *Web:* www.teletrac.net	Garden Grove	CA	92841	714-897-0877	379-6378
Wade-Trim Group Inc 500 Griswold Ave Suite 2500 *TF:* 800-482-2864 ■ *Web:* www.wadetrim.com	Detroit	MI	48226	313-961-3650	961-0898

731 SWIMMING POOLS

				Phone	Fax
Anthony & Sylvan Pools Corp 3739 Easton Rd Rt 611 *TF:* 800-366-7958 ■ *Web:* www.anthony-sylvan.com	Doylestown	PA	18901	215-489-5600	489-5610
Delair Group LLC 8600 River Rd *TF:* 800-235-0185 ■ *Web:* www.delairgroup.com	Delair	NJ	08110	856-663-2900	663-1297
Fox Pool Corp 3490 Board Rd *TF:* 800-723-1011 ■ *Web:* www.foxpool.com	York	PA	17406	717-764-8581	764-4293
Gary Pools Inc 438 Sandau Rd *TF:* 800-966-9605 ■ *Web:* www.garypools.com	San Antonio	TX	78216	210-341-5153	341-5154
Hoffinger Industries Inc 315 N Sebastian *Web:* www.hoffinger.com	West Helena	AR	72390	870-572-3466	235-8011
Hornerxpress Inc 5755 Powerline Rd *TF:* 800-432-6966 ■ *Web:* www.hornerxpress.com	Fort Lauderdale	FL	33309	954-772-6966	772-6970
Imperial Pools Inc 33 Wade Rd *TF:* 800-444-9977 ■ *Web:* www.imperialpoolsb2b.com	Latham	NY	12110	518-786-1200	786-0954
Mission Pools of Escondido 755 W Grand Ave *Web:* www.missionpools.com	Escondido	CA	92025	760-743-2605	743-0384
Morgan Bldg Systems Inc 2800 McCree Rd *TF:* 800-935-0321 ■ *Web:* www.morganusa.com	Garland	TX	75041	972-864-7300	864-7307
Paddock Pools 6525 E Thomas Rd *Web:* www.paddockpoolsandspas.com	Scottsdale	AZ	85251	480-947-7261	970-7432
Radiant Pools Div Trojan Leisure Products LLC 440 N Pearl St *TF:* 866-697-5870 ■ *Web:* www.radiantpools.com	Albany	NY	12207	518-434-4161	432-6554
Viking Pools Inc 121 Crawford Rd PO Box 96 *TF:* 800-854-7665 ■ *Web:* www.vikingpools.net	Williams	CA	95987	530-473-5319	473-5393
Vogue Pool Products 7050 St Patrick St *TF:* 800-363-3232 ■ *Web:* www.piscinesvogue.com	LaSalle	QC	H8N1V2	514-363-3232	363-1772
Wagner Pool Co Inc 750 Wordin Ave *Web:* www.wagnerswimmingpools.com	Bridgeport	CT	06605	203-335-3960	331-9430

732 SWITCHGEAR & SWITCHBOARD APPARATUS

SEE ALSO Transformers - Power, Distribution, Specialty p. 2725; Wiring Devices - Current-Carrying p. 2776

				Phone	Fax
Atkinson Industries Inc 1801 E 27th St Terr *Web:* www.atkinsonindustries.com	Pittsburg	KS	66762	620-231-6900	231-7154
AZZ Inc 3100 W 7th St Suite 500 *Web:* www.azz.com	Fort Worth	TX	76107	817-810-0095	336-5354
Bel Fuse Inc 206 Van Vorst St *NASDAQ: BELFA* ■ *TF:* 800-235-3873 ■ *Web:* www.belfuse.com	Jersey City	NJ	07302	201-432-0463	432-9542
Cole Instrument Corp 2650 S Croddy Way **Fax:* Sales ■ *Web:* www.cole-switches.com	Santa Ana	CA	92704	714-556-3100	241-9061*
Components Corp of America 5950 Berkshire Ln # 1550 *Web:* www.components-corp-amer.com	Dallas	TX	75225	214-969-0166	969-5905
CW Industries 130 James Way *Web:* www.cwind.com	SouthHampton	PA	18966	215-355-7080	355-1088
E. A. Pedersen Co 3900 Dahlman Ave *Web:* www.eapedersen.com	Omaha	NE	68107	402-734-3900	734-0622
Eaton Cutler-Hammer Inc 1 Tuscarawas Rd *TF:* 800-354-2070	Beaver	PA	15009	724-775-2000	
Electroswitch Corp 180 King Ave *Web:* www.electroswitch.com	Weymouth	MA	02188	781-335-5200	335-4253
Grayhill Inc 561 W Hillgrove Ave *TF:* 800-244-0559 ■ *Web:* www.grayhill.com	La Grange	IL	60525	708-354-1040	354-2820
Guardian Electric Mfg Co Inc 1425 Lake Ave *TF:* 800-762-0369 ■ *Web:* www.guardian-electric.com	Woodstock	IL	60098	815-334-3600	337-0377
Indak Mfg Corp 1915 Techny Rd *Web:* www.indak.com	Northbrook	IL	60062	847-272-0343	272-0697
Instruments Inc 7263 Engineer Rd Suite G *Web:* www.instrumentsinc.com	San Diego	CA	92111	858-571-1111	571-0188
ITW Switches 2550 Mill Brook Dr *TF:* 800-544-3354 ■ *Web:* www.itwswitches.com	Buffalo Grove	IL	60089	847-876-9400	876-9440
Kasa Industrial Controls Inc 418 E Ave B *TF:* 800-755-5272 ■ *Web:* www.kasacontrols.com	Salina	KS	67401	785-825-7181	825-1663
Keystone Electrical Mfg Co 2511 Bell Ave *Web:* www.keystoneemc.com	Des Moines	IA	50321	515-283-2567	283-0418
Kraus & Naimer 760 New Brunswick Rd *TF:* 800-526-3966 ■ *Web:* www.krausnaimer.com	Somerset	NJ	08873	732-560-1240	560-8823
Littelfuse Inc 8755 W Higgins Rd Suite 500 *NASDAQ: LFUS* ■ *TF Sales:* 800-227-0029 ■ *Web:* www.littelfuse.com	Chicago	IL	60631	773-628-1000	
Lumitex Inc 8443 Dow Cir *TF:* 800-969-5483 ■ *Web:* www.lumitex.com	Strongsville	OH	44136	440-243-8401	845-6061
Mac Products Inc 60 Pennsylvania Ave PO Box 469 *Web:* www.macproducts.net	Kearny	NJ	07032	973-344-0700	344-5368
Marathon Special Products 13300 Van Camp Rd PO Box 468 *Web:* www.marathonsp.com	Bowling Green	OH	43402	419-352-8441	352-0875
Mersen Inc 374 Merrimac St *Web:* www.mersen.com	Newburyport	MA	01950	978-462-6662	462-7934
Meter Devices Co Inc 3359 Bruening Ave SW PO Box 6382 Stn B *TF:* 888-367-6383 ■ *Web:* www.meter-devices.com	Canton	OH	44706	330-455-0301	455-1461
Multitech Industries Inc 350 Village Dr *Web:* www.multitechind.com	Carol Stream	IL	60188	630-784-9200	784-9225
Otto Engineering Inc 2 E Main St *Web:* www.ottoexcellence.com	Carpentersville	IL	60110	847-428-7171	428-1956
Pacs Industries Inc 61 Steamboat Rd *Web:* www.pacsindustries.com	Great Neck	NY	11024	516-829-9060	829-9557
Powell Industries Inc 8550 Mosely Dr *NASDAQ: POWL* ■ *Web:* www.powellind.com	Houston	TX	77075	713-944-6900	947-4453
Powercon Corp PO Box 477 *TF:* 800-638-5055 ■ *Web:* www.powerconcorp.com	Severn	MD	21144	410-551-6500	551-8451
Professional Power Products Inc 448 W Madison St *Web:* www.professionalpowerproducts.com	Darien	WI	53114	262-882-9000	882-9010
Reliance Controls Corp 2001 Young Ct *TF:* 800-634-6155 ■ *Web:* www.reliancecontrols.com	Racine	WI	53404	262-634-6155	634-6436
Revere Control Systems Inc 2240 Rocky Ridge Rd *Web:* www.reverecontrol.com	Birmingham	AL	35216	205-824-0004	824-0439
Russelectric Inc 99 Industrial Pk Rd *TF:* 800-225-5250 ■ *Web:* www.russelectric.com	Hingham	MA	02043	781-749-6000	749-8077
S & C Electric Co 6601 N Ridge Blvd *TF:* 800-621-5546 ■ *Web:* www.sandc.com	Chicago	IL	60626	773-338-1000	338-3657
Satin American Corp 40 Oliver Terr *TF:* 800-272-7711 ■ *Web:* www.satinamerican.com	Shelton	CT	06484	203-929-6363	929-9684
Southwest Electric Co PO Box 82639 *Web:* www.swelectric.com	Oklahoma City	OK	73148	405-869-1100	869-1105
SPD Technologies 13500 Roosevelt Blvd *Web:* www.spdtech.com	Philadelphia	PA	19116	215-677-4900	677-1504
Superior Electric 28 Spring Ln Suite 3 *Web:* www.superiorelectric.com	Farmington	CT	06032	860-507-2025	507-2050
Tapeswitch Corp 100 Schmitt Blvd *TF:* 800-234-8273 ■ *Web:* www.tapeswitch.com	Farmingdale	NY	11735	631-630-0442	630-0454
TopWorx Inc 3300 Fern Valley Rd *TF:* 800-969-9020 ■ *Web:* www.topworx.com	Louisville	KY	40213	502-969-8000	969-5911

733 TABLE & KITCHEN SUPPLIES - CHINA & EARTHENWARE

				Phone	Fax
Bradshaw International Inc 9409 Buffalo Ave. *Web:* www.goodcook.com	Rancho Cucamonga	CA	91730	909-476-3884	476-3616
Dansk International Designs Ltd 1414 Radcliff St **Fax Area Code:* 609 ■ *TF Cust Svc:* 800-293-2675 ■ *Web:* www.dansk.com	Bristol PA	NJ	19007	267-525-7800	844-1576*
Hall China Co 1 Anna St PO Box 989 **Fax Area Code:* 800 ■ *TF Cust Svc:* 800-445-4255 ■ *Web:* www.hallchina.com	East Liverpool	OH	43920	330-385-2900	837-4950*
Heartland China Inc 2015 NE Grantville Rd PO Box 8156 *TF:* 888-383-3163 ■ *Web:* www.heartlandchina.com	Topeka	KS	66608	785-354-8080	242-8090
Heritage Mint Ltd PO Box 13750 *TF:* 888-860-6245 ■ *Web:* www.heritagemint.com	Scottsdale	AZ	85267	480-860-1300	860-8174
Homer Laughlin China Co 672 Fiesta Dr *TF:* 800-452-4462 ■ *Web:* www.hlchina.com	Newell	WV	26050	304-387-1300	387-4265

				Phone	Fax
Lenox Corp PO Box 2006 *TF:* 800-223-4311 ■ *Web:* www.lenox.com	Bristol	PA	19007	800-223-4311	
Lipper International Inc 235 Washington St *TF:* 800-243-3129 ■ *Web:* www.lipperinternational.com	Wallingford	CT	06492	203-269-8588	284-8637
Luna Garcia 201 San Juan Ave *TF:* 800-905-9975 ■ *Web:* www.lunagarcia.com	Venice	CA	90291	310-396-8026	
Martin's Herend Imports Inc 21440 Pacific Blvd PO Box 1178 *TF:* 800-643-7363 ■ *Web:* www.herendusa.com	Sterling	VA	20167	703-450-1601	450-1605
Mikasa Inc 100 Plaza Dr *TF Cust Svc:* 800-833-4681 ■ *Web:* www.mikasa.com	Secaucus	NJ	07094	201-867-9210	867-0580
Oneida Ltd 163-181 Kenwood Ave *TF:* 800-877-6667 ■ *Web:* www.oneida.com	Oneida	NY	13421	315-361-3000	361-3700
Original Hartstone Pottery The 1719 Dearborn St *TF:* 800-339-4278 ■ *Web:* www.hartstonepottery.com	Zanesville	OH	43701	740-452-9000	452-5369
Pfaltzgraff Co 140 E Market St **Fax:* Cust Svc ■ *TF:* 800-999-2811 ■ *Web:* www.pfaltzgraff.com	York	PA	17401	717-848-5500	771-1433*
Royal China & Porcelain Cos Inc 1265 Glen Ave *TF Orders:* 800-631-7120	Moorestown	NJ	08057	856-866-2900	866-2499
Syracuse China Co 2801 Ct St *TF:* 800-448-5711 ■ *Web:* www.libbey.com	Syracuse	NY	13208	315-455-5671	455-4532
True West 8549 PR 2414 PO Box 441 *Web:* www.truewesthome.com	Royse City	TX	75189	972-636-7922	635-2059
Waterford Wedgwood USA Inc 1330 Campus Pkwy *Web:* www.wwusa.com	Wall	NJ	07719	732-938-5800	938-6915
World Kitchen Inc 11911 Freedom Dr Suite 600 *TF Cust Svc:* 800-999-3436 ■ *Web:* www.worldkitchen.com	Reston	VA	20190	703-456-4700	456-2020

734 TALENT AGENCIES

SEE ALSO Literary Agents p. 2180; Modeling Agencies p. 2253

				Phone	Fax
Agency for the Performing Arts 405 S Beverly Dr *Web:* www.apa-agency.com	Beverly Hills	CA	90212	310-888-4200	888-4242
Artists Group 1650 Broadway Suite 610	New York	NY	10019	212-586-1452	586-0037
Blitz Models & Talents 487 Adelaide St W Suite 305	Toronto	ON	M5V1T4	416-703-5799	703-6232
Brillstein Grey Entertainment 9150 Wilshire Blvd Suite 350	Beverly Hills	CA	90212	310-275-6135	275-6180
Brookside Artist Management 250 W 57th St Suite 2303	New York	NY	10107	212-489-4929	489-9056
Buddy Lee Attractions Inc 38 Music Sq E Suite 300 *Web:* www.buddyleeattractions.com	Nashville	TN	37203	615-244-4336	726-0429
CAA Sports 801 W 47th St Suite 219 *Web:* www.caa.com	Kansas City	MO	64112	816-531-5777	753-2332
CESD Talent Agency Inc 10635 Santa Monica Blvd Suite 130/135 *Web:* www.cesdtalent.com	Los Angeles	CA	90025	310-475-2111	474-5307
CESD Voices 10635 Santa Monica Blvd Suites 130/135 *Web:* www.cedvoices.com	Los Angeles	CA	90025	310-475-2111	475-1929
CKX Inc 650 Madison Ave *NASDAQ: CKXE* ■ *Web:* www.ir.ckx.com	New York	NY	10022	212-838-3100	872-1473
CM Artists New York 127 W 96th St Suite 13 B *Web:* www.cmartists.com	New York	NY	10025	212-864-1005	864-1066
Columbia Artists Management LLC 1790 Broadway *Web:* www.cami.com	New York	NY	10019	212-841-9500	841-9744
Creative Artists Agency Inc (CAA) 2000 Avenue of the Stars *Web:* www.caa.com	Los Angeles	CA	90067	424-288-2000	288-2900
Don Buchwald & Assoc 6500 Wilshire Blvd Suite 2200 *Web:* www.buchwald.com	Los Angeles	CA	90048	323-655-7400	655-7470
Endeavor Agency 9601 Wilshire Blvd 3rd Fl	Beverly Hills	CA	90210	310-248-2000	285-9010
Gaylord Sports Management 13845 N Northsight Blvd Suite 200 *Web:* www.gaylordsports.com	Scottsdale	AZ	85260	480-483-9500	483-9598
Gersh Agency 9465 Wilshire Blvd *Web:* www.gershcomedy.com	Beverly Hills	CA	90212	310-274-6611	274-3923
Gersh Agency 41 Madison Ave 33rd Fl *Web:* www.gershcomedy.com	New York	NY	10010	212-997-1818	997-1978
Gorfaine/Schwartz Agency 4111 W Alameda Ave Suite 509 *Web:* www.gsamusic.com	Burbank	CA	91505	818-260-8500	260-8522
Great North Artists Management 350 Dupont St	Toronto	ON	M5R1V9	416-925-2051	925-3904
Hartig Hilepo Agency Ltd 54 W 21st St Suite 610	New York	NY	10010	212-929-1772	929-1266
HS International 9871 Irvine Ctr Dr *Web:* www.hsi.net	Irvine	CA	92618	949-753-9153	753-9253
IFA Talent Agency 8730 Sunset Blvd Suite 490	Los Angeles	CA	90069	310-659-5522	659-3344
IMG Artists 152 W 57th St # 5 *Web:* www.imgartists.com	New York	NY	10019	212-994-3500	994-3550
IMG Inc 1360 E 9th St IMG Ctr Suite 100 *Web:* www.imgworld.com	Cleveland	OH	44114	216-522-1200	522-1145
IMG Worldwide 767 5th Ave *Web:* www.imgworld.com	New York	NY	10153	646-558-8357	558-8399
Innovative Artists 1505 10th St *Web:* www.innovativeartists.com	Santa Monica	CA	90401	310-656-0400	656-0456
International Creative Management Inc 10250 Constellation Blvd *Web:* www.icmtalent.com	Los Angeles	CA	90067	310-550-4000	550-4100
International Creative Management Inc (ICM) 825 8th Ave 26th Fl *Web:* www.icmtalent.com	New York	NY	10019	212-556-5600	556-5665
Kraft-Engel Management 15233 Ventura Blvd Suite 200 *Web:* www.kraft-engel.com	Sherman Oaks	CA	91403	818-380-1918	380-2609
Legacy Sports Group 500 Newport Ctr Dr Suite 800	Newport Beach	CA	92660	949-721-6200	720-1331
Media Talent Group 9200 Sunset Blvd Suite 550	West Hollywood	CA	90069	310-275-7900	275-7910
Metropolitan Talent Agency (MTA) 4500 Wilshire Blvd *Web:* www.mta.com	Los Angeles	CA	90010	323-857-4500	857-4599
Monterey International 200 W Superior St Suite 202 *Web:* www.montereyinternational.net	Chicago	IL	60654	312-640-7500	640-7515
Monterey Peninsula Artists/Paradigm 509 Hartnell St	Monterey	CA	93940	831-375-4889	375-2623
Nettwerk 1650 W 2nd Ave *Web:* www.nettwerk.com	Vancouver	BC	V6J4R3	604-654-2929	654-1993
Nettwerk 1545 Wilcox Ave Suite 200 *Web:* www.nettwerk.com	Hollywood	CA	90028	323-301-4200	301-4199
Nettwerk 345 7th Ave 24th Fl *Web:* www.nettwerk.com	New York	NY	10001	212-760-1540	760-9719
One Entertainment 12 W 57th St PH	New York	NY	10019	212-974-3900	
Original Artists 826 Broadway 4th Fl	New York	NY	10003	212-254-1234	254-3121
Panacea Entertainment 13587 Andalusia Dr	Camarillo	CA	93012	805-491-9400	491-0406
Paradigm Talent & Literary Agency 360 N Crescent Dr N Bldg	Beverly Hills	CA	90210	310-288-8000	288-2000
Parseghian/Planco Management 23 E 22nd St 3rd Fl	New York	NY	10010	212-777-7786	777-8642
Peter Strain & Assoc 5455 Wilshire Blvd Suite 1812	Los Angeles	CA	90036	323-525-3391	525-0881
Peter Strain & Assoc 321 W 44th St Suite 805	New York	NY	10036	212-391-0380	391-1405
PMK/HBH 700 San Vicente Blvd Suite G910	West Hollywood	CA	90069	310-289-6200	289-6677
Prince Marketing Group 454 Prospect Ave Suite 74 *TF:* 800-987-7462 ■ *Web:* www.princemarketinggroup.com	West Orange	NJ	07052	973-325-0800	243-0037
Rogers & Cowan Pacific Design Ctr 8687 Melrose Ave 7th Fl *Web:* www.rogersandcowan.com	Los Angeles	CA	90069	310-854-8100	854-8106
Rosebud Agency PO Box 170429 *Web:* www.rosebudus.com	San Francisco	CA	94117	415-386-3456	386-0599
SFX Sports Group 5335 Wisconsin Ave NW Suite 850 *TF:* 800-776-7378	Washington	DC	20015	202-686-2000	686-5050
Shapiro/West & Assoc 141 El Camino Dr Suite 205	Beverly Hills	CA	90212	310-278-8896	278-7238
Shelly Finkel Management 110 Greene St # 403 *Web:* www.shellyfinkel.com	New York	NY	10012	212-682-9400	983-9028
SMS Talent Agency 8730 Sunset Blvd Suite 440	Los Angeles	CA	90069	310-289-0909	289-0990
Special Artists Agency Inc 9465 Wilshire Blvd Suite 890	Beverly Hills	CA	90212	310-859-9688	859-1842
Stone Manners Agency 9911 W Pico Blvd Suite 1400	Los Angeles	CA	90035	323-655-1313	389-1577
Susan Smith Co 1344 N Wetherly Dr	Los Angeles	CA	90069	310-276-4224	276-4343
TalentWorks 3500 W Olive Ave Suite 1400 *Web:* www.talentworks.us	Burbank	CA	91505	818-972-4300	955-6411
United Talent Agency Inc (UTA) 9560 Wilshire Blvd Suite 500 *Web:* www.unitedtalent.com	Beverly Hills	CA	90212	310-273-6700	247-1111
William Morris Agency 1325 Avenue of the Americas *Web:* www.wma.com	New York	NY	10019	212-586-5100	246-3583
William Morris Agency 1600 Division St Suite 300 *Web:* www.wma.com	Nashville	TN	37203	615-963-3000	963-3090
William Morris Agency 119 Washington Ave Suite 400 *Web:* www.wma.com	Miami Beach	FL	33139	305-938-2000	938-2002
William Morris Agency 1 William Morris Pl *Web:* www.wma.com	Beverly Hills	CA	90212	310-859-4000	859-4462

TAPE - ADHESIVE

SEE Medical Supplies - Mfr p. 2229

735 TAPE - CELLOPHANE, GUMMED, MASKING, PRESSURE SENSITIVE

SEE ALSO Medical Supplies - Mfr p. 2229

				Phone	Fax
3M Canada Co 300 Tartan Dr **Fax:* Library ■ *TF:* 800-479-4453 ■ *Web:* www.3m.com/ca	London	ON	N5Y4M9	519-451-2500	452-4714*
3M Personal Care Div 3M Ctr Bldg 0220-03-W-10 **Fax Area Code:* 651 ■ *TF:* 866-212-5083 ■ *Web:* www.3m.com/product/business-units/personal-care.html	Saint Paul	MN	55144	866-212-5083	737-4359*
Adchem Corp 1852 County Rd 58 *Web:* www.adchem.com	Riverhead	NY	11901	631-727-6000	727-6010
American Biltrite Inc 57 River St *AMEX: ABL* ■ *Web:* www.ambilt.com	Wellesley Hills	MA	02481	781-237-6655	237-6880
American Biltrite Inc Tape Products Div (ABI) 105 Whittendale Dr **Fax Area Code:* 888 ■ *Web:* www.abitape.com	Moorestown	NJ	08057	856-778-0700	224-6325*
Argent Automotive Systems 41016 Concept Dr *TF:* 800-223-9890 ■ *Web:* www.argent-automotive.com	Plymouth	MI	48170	734-582-9800	582-9999

Company	City	State	ZIP	Phone	Fax
Avery Dennison Corp 150 N Orange Grove Blvd *NYSE:* AVY ■ *TF Cust Svc:* 800-252-8379 ■ *Web:* www.averydennison.com	Pasadena	CA	91103	626-304-2000	304-2192
Avery Dennison Specialty Tapes Div 250 Chester St Bldg 5 *TF:* 866-462-8379 ■ *Web:* www.averydennison.com	Painesville	OH	44077	440-358-6000	358-3341
Beiersdorf North America 187 Danbury Rd **Fax:* Hum Res ■ *TF:* 800-233-2340 ■ *Web:* www.beiersdorf.com	Wilton	CT	06897	203-563-5800	854-8112*
Bemis Co Inc 1 Neenah Ctr 4th Fl PO Box 669 *NYSE:* BMS ■ *Web:* www.bemis.com	Neenah	WI	54957	920-727-4100	
Brady Coated Products 6555 W Good Hope Rd **Fax Area Code:* 800 ■ *TF:* 800-635-7557 ■ *Web:* www.coatedproducts.com	Milwaukee	WI	53223	414-358-6600	541-1686*
Brite-Line LLC 10660 E 51st Ave *TF:* 888-201-6448 ■ *Web:* www.brite-line.com	Denver	CO	80239	888-201-6448	208-0758
Canada Vibac Tape Corp 12250 Industrial Blvd *TF:* 800-557-0192 ■ *Web:* www.vibacgroup.com	Montreal	QC	H1B5M5	514-640-1599	640-1630
Cantec Industries Inc 455 Cote Vertu Rd *TF Orders:* 800-334-1567 ■ *Web:* www.cttgroup.com	Montreal	QC	H4N1E8	514-334-1510	745-0764
Compac Corp 103 Bilby Rd *TF:* 800-631-9350 ■ *Web:* www.compaccorp.com	Hackettstown	NJ	07840	908-498-0660	850-0272
Crowell Corp 1 Coral Rd PO Box 3227 *TF:* 800-441-7525 ■ *Web:* www.crowellcorp.com	Newport	DE	19804	302-998-0557	998-0626
Decker Tape Products Inc 6 Stewart Pl *TF:* 800-227-5252 ■ *Web:* www.deckertape.com	Fairfield	NJ	07004	973-227-5350	808-9418
DeWAL Industries Inc 15 Ray Trainor Dr *TF:* 800-366-8356 ■ *Web:* www.dewal.com	Narragansett	RI	02882	401-789-9736	783-6780
Dielectric Polymers Inc 218 Race St *TF:* 800-628-9007 ■ *Web:* www.dipoly.com	Holyoke	MA	01040	413-532-3288	533-9316
Eternabond 75 E Division St *TF:* 888-336-2663 ■ *Web:* www.eternabond.com	Mundelein	IL	60060	847-837-9400	837-9449
FiberMark Inc 161 Wellington Rd **Fax:* Sales ■ *Web:* www.fibermark.com	Brattleboro	VT	05301	802-257-0365	257-5907*
Forbo Adhesives LLC 523 Davis Dr Suite 400 *TF:* 800-213-4805 ■ *Web:* www.forbo.com	Durham	NC	27713	919-433-1300	433-1301
Gaska-Tape Inc 1810 W Lusher Ave *TF:* 800-423-1571 ■ *Web:* www.gaska.com	Elkhart	IN	46517	574-294-5431	293-4504
Harris Industries Inc 5181 Argosy Ave *TF:* 800-222-6866 ■ *Web:* www.harrisind.com	Huntington Beach	CA	92649	714-898-8048	898-7108
Hawkeye International Ltd 5760 VT Rt 100 *Web:* www.hawkeyeintl.com/home.htm	North Hyde Park	VT	05565	802-635-7500	635-7900
Holland Mfg Co Inc 15 Main St PO Box 404 *TF:* 800-345-0492 ■ *Web:* www.hollandmfg.com	Succasunna	NJ	07876	973-584-8141	584-6845
JHL Industries 10012 Nevada Ave *TF:* 800-255-6636 ■ *Web:* www.jhlindustries.com	Chatsworth	CA	91311	818-882-2233	882-4350
Kruse Adhesive Tape Inc 16582 Burke Ln *TF:* 800-992-7702 ■ *Web:* www.krusetape.com	Huntington Beach	CA	92647	714-596-0707	596-4887
M & C Specialties Co 90 James Way *TF Cust Svc:* 800-441-6996 ■ *Web:* www.mcspecialties.com	SouthHampton	PA	18966	215-322-1600	322-1620
Neptco Inc 30 Hamlet St *TF:* 800-354-5445 ■ *Web:* www.neptco.com	Pawtucket	RI	02861	401-722-5500	722-6378
Permacel PO Box 671 *TF:* 800-755-8273 ■ *Web:* www.permacel.com	New Brunswick	NJ	08903	732-418-2400	418-2474
Plymouth Rubber Co Inc 275 Tpke St Suite 310 *TF:* 800-458-0336 ■ *Web:* www.plymouthrubber.com	Canton	MA	02021	781-828-0220	828-6041
Presto Tape Inc 1626 Bridgewater Rd *TF:* 800-331-1373 ■ *Web:* www.prestotape.com	Bensalem	PA	19020	215-245-8555	245-8554
Pro Tapes & Specialties 100 Northfield Ave *TF:* 800-345-0234 ■ *Web:* www.protapes.com	Edison	NJ	08837	732-346-0900	346-0777
Quik-Tape Inc 6558 Holiday Rd *TF:* 800-462-8273 ■ *Web:* www.quik-tape.com	Buford	GA	30518	770-804-1244	698-0717
Shurtape Technologies Inc 1985 Tate Blvd SE *TF:* 800-438-5779 ■ *Web:* www.shurtape.com	Hickory	NC	28602	828-322-2700	322-4419
STA Overlaminations 100 S Puente St *Web:* www.sta-overlamination.com	Brea	CA	92821	714-255-7888	990-6851
Stik-II Products Inc 41 O'Neill St *TF:* 800-356-3572 ■ *Web:* www.stik-2.com	EastHampton	MA	01027	413-527-7120	527-7249
TapeSouth Inc 10302 Deerwood Pk Suite 125 *Web:* www.tapesouth.com	Jacksonville	FL	32256	904-642-1800	642-7006
Tesa Tape Inc 5825 Carnegie Blvd **Fax Area Code:* 800 ■ **Fax:* Cust Svc ■ *TF:* 800-873-8825 ■ *Web:* www.tesatape.com	Charlotte	NC	28209	704-554-0707	852-8831*
Thomas Tape Co 1713 Sheridan Ave *Web:* www.thomastape.com	Springfield	OH	45505	937-325-6414	325-2850
Tommy Tape Mfg Inc 135 Redstone St *Web:* www.tommytape.com	Southington	CT	06489	860-378-0111	378-0113
Venture Tape Corp 30 Commerce Rd *TF:* 800-343-1076 ■ *Web:* www.venturetape.com	Rockland	MA	02370	781-331-5900	871-0065
WTP Inc 100 Klitchman Dr PO Box 938 *TF:* 800-521-0731 ■ *Web:* www.wtp-inc.com	Coloma	MI	49038	269-468-3399	468-3391
Zepak Corp 26755 SW 95th Ave PO Box 789 *TF:* 800-248-7732 ■ *Web:* www.zepak.com	Wilsonville	OR	97070	503-682-1248	682-3599

736 TARPS, TENTS, COVERS

SEE ALSO Bags - Textile p. 1505; Sporting Goods p. 2664

Company	City	State	ZIP	Phone	Fax
Aero Industries Inc 4243 W Bradbury Ave *TF Sales:* 800-535-9545 ■ *Web:* www.aeroindustries.com	Indianapolis	IN	46241	317-244-2433	244-1311
American Pavilion 1706 Warrington Ave *Web:* www.americanpavilion.com	Danville	IL	61832	217-443-0800	443-9619
Anchor Industries Inc 1100 Burch Dr *TF:* 800-544-4445 ■ *Web:* www.anchorinc.com	Evansville	IN	47725	812-867-2421	867-1429
Bailey & Staub Inc 1 Bailey Cir	New London	CT	06320	860-442-5621	444-6622
Canvas Products Co 274 S Waterman St *TF:* 800-624-6671 ■ *Web:* www.canvaspc.com	Detroit	MI	48209	313-496-1000	496-1001
Canvas Specialty 7344 E Bandini Blvd *Web:* www.can-spec.com	Los Angeles	CA	90040	323-722-1156	724-3848
Carefree of Colorado 2145 W 6th Ave **Fax Area Code:* 800 ■ *TF:* 800-621-2617 ■ *Web:* www.carefreeofcolorado.com	Broomfield	CO	80020	303-469-3324	731-8600*
Clamshell Structures Inc 1101 Maulhardt Ave *TF:* 800-360-8853 ■ *Web:* www.clamshell.com	Oxnard	CA	93030	805-988-1340	988-2266
Commonwealth Canvas Corp 411 Electronics Ave *TF:* 877-922-6827 ■ *Web:* www.commonwealthcanvas.com	Danvers	MA	01923	978-646-9400	646-9260
CR Daniels Inc 3451 Ellicott Ctr Dr *TF:* 800-933-2638 ■ *Web:* www.crdaniels.com	Ellicott City	MD	21043	410-461-2100	461-2987
DC Humphrys Inc 5744 Woodland Ave *TF Sales:* 800-523-4503	Philadelphia	PA	19143	215-724-8181	724-8706
Diamond Brand Canvas Products 145 Cane Creek Industrial Pk Rd Suite 1 *TF Sales:* 800-258-9811 ■ *Web:* www.diamondbrand.com	Fletcher	NC	28732	828-684-9848	687-0965
Eide Industries Inc 16215 Piuma Ave *TF:* 800-422-6827 ■ *Web:* www.eideindustries.com	Cerritos	CA	90703	562-402-8335	924-2233
Estex Mfg Co Inc 402 E Broad St PO Box 368 *TF:* 800-749-1224 ■ *Web:* www.estexmfg.com	Fairburn	GA	30213	770-964-3322	964-7534
Fisher Canvas Products Inc 415 St Mary St *TF:* 800-892-6688 ■ *Web:* www.fishercanvas.com	Burlington	NJ	08016	609-239-2733	239-2728
Harry Miller Co Inc 850 Albany St *TF:* 800-225-5598 ■ *Web:* www.harrymiller.com	Boston	MA	02119	617-427-2300	442-1152
John Johnson Co 274 Waterman St *TF:* 800-991-1394 ■ *Web:* www.jjcompany.com	Detroit	MI	48209	313-496-0600	496-0252
Johnson Outdoors Inc 555 Main St *NASDAQ:* JOUT ■ *TF:* 800-299-2592 ■ *Web:* www.johnsonoutdoors.com	Racine	WI	53403	262-631-6600	631-6601
Loop-Loc Ltd 390 Motor Pkwy *TF:* 800-562-5667 ■ *Web:* www.looploc.com	Hauppauge	NY	11788	631-582-2626	582-2636
Mauritzon Inc 3939 W Belden Ave *TF:* 800-621-4352 ■ *Web:* www.mauritzononline.com	Chicago	IL	60647	773-235-6000	235-1479
Midwest Canvas Corp 4635 W Lake St *TF:* 800-433-4701 ■ *Web:* www.midwestcanvas.com	Chicago	IL	60644	773-287-4400	854-2017
North Sails Group LLC 125 Old Gate Ln *Web:* www.na.northsails.com	Milford	CT	06460	203-877-7621	874-6059
Outdoor Venture Corp Hwy 1651 PO Box 337	Stearns	KY	42647	606-376-5021	376-3341
Rainier Industries Ltd 18435 Olympic Ave S *TF:* 800-869-7162 ■ *Web:* www.rainierindustries.com	Tukwila	WA	98188	425-251-1800	251-5065
Robertson Mfg Inc 112 Woodland Ave *TF:* 800-260-5423	West Grove	PA	19390	610-869-9600	869-6365
Shur-Co Inc 2309 Shur-Lok St PO Box 713 *TF:* 800-437-4172 ■ *Web:* www.shurco.com	Yankton	SD	57078	605-665-6000	665-0501
Steele Canvas Basket Corp 201 William St PO Box 6267 IMCN *TF:* 800-541-8929 ■ *Web:* www.steele-canvas.com	Chelsea	MA	02150	617-889-0202	889-0524
Sullivan & Brampton Inc 1688 Abram Ct *TF:* 800-257-5900 ■ *Web:* www.sullivanandbrampton.com	San Leandro	CA	94577	510-483-7771	483-7723
Trimaco LLC 2800 Meridian Pkwy Suite 185 *TF:* 866-874-6226 ■ *Web:* www.trimaco.com	Durham	NC	27713	919-433-4010	433-4011
Troy Sunshade Co 607 Riffle Ave *TF:* 800-833-8769	Greenville	OH	45331	937-548-2466	548-6102
Universal Fabric Structures Inc 2200 Kumry Rd *TF:* 800-634-8368 ■ *Web:* www.ufsinc.com	Quakertown	PA	18951	215-529-9921	529-9936
Webb Mfg Co 1241 Carpenter St *TF:* 800-932-2634 ■ *Web:* www.webbmfg.com	Philadelphia	PA	19147	215-336-5570	336-4422

737 TAX PREPARATION SERVICES

Company	City	State	ZIP	Phone	Fax
DuCharme McMillen & Assoc Inc 6610 Mutual Dr *Web:* www.dmainc.com	Fort Wayne	IN	46825	260-484-8631	482-8152
Express Tax Franchise Corp 3030 Hartley Rd Suite 320 *TF:* 888-417-4461 ■ *Web:* www.expresstaxservice.com	Jacksonville	FL	32257	904-262-0031	262-2864
Fiducial 1370 Avenue of the Americas 31st Fl *TF:* 866-343-8242 ■ *Web:* www.fiducial.com	New York	NY	10019	212-207-4700	308-2613
Fiducial Franchising 10480 Little Patuxent Pkwy 3rd Fl *TF:* 800-323-9000 ■ *Web:* www.fiducial.com	Columbia	MD	21044	410-910-5885	910-5903
H & R Block Tax Services Inc 4400 Main St *TF:* 800-869-9220 ■ *Web:* www.hrblock.com	Kansas City	MO	64111	816-753-6900	753-5346
Jackson Hewitt Inc 3 Sylvan Way Suite 301 *NYSE:* JTX ■ *TF:* 800-234-1040 ■ *Web:* www.jacksonhewitt.com	Parsippany	NJ	07054	800-234-1040	
Liberty Tax Service Inc 1716 Corporate Landing Pkwy *TF Cust Svc:* 800-790-3863 ■ *Web:* www.libertytax.com	Virginia Beach	VA	23454	757-493-8855	493-0169

738 TELECOMMUNICATIONS EQUIPMENT & SYSTEMS

SEE ALSO Modems p. 1671; Radio & Television Broadcasting & Communications Equipment p. 2515

Company	City	State	ZIP	Phone	Fax
ABB Flexible Automation Inc 2487 S Commerce Dr *Web:* www.abb.com	New Berlin	WI	53151	262-785-3400	785-0342
ADTRAN Inc 901 Explorer Blvd *NASDAQ:* ADTN ■ *TF:* 800-923-8726 ■ *Web:* www.adtran.com	Huntsville	AL	35806	256-963-8000	963-8004
AirNet Communications Corp 3950 Dow Rd *TF:* 800-984-1990 ■ *Web:* www.aircom.com	Melbourne	FL	32934	321-984-1990	676-6734
Airspan Networks Inc 777 Yamato Rd Suite 105 *PINK:* AIRN ■ *Web:* www.airspan.com	Boca Raton	FL	33431	561-893-8670	893-8671
Alcatel Canada Inc 600 March Rd *TF:* 888-662-3425 ■ *Web:* www.alcatel-lucent.com	Ottawa	ON	K2K2E6	613-591-3600	591-3680

Company / Address	City	State	ZIP	Phone	Fax
AltiGen Communications Inc 410 E Plumeria Dr *NASDAQ: ATGN* ■ *TF:* 888-258-4436 ■ *Web:* www.altigen.com	San Jose	CA	95134	408-597-9000	597-9020
Alvarion Inc 2495 Leghorn St *NASDAQ: ALVR* ■ *Web:* www.alvarion.com	Mountain View	CA	94043	650-314-2500	967-3966
Amtelco 4800 Curtin Dr *TF:* 800-356-9148 ■ *Web:* www.amtelco.com	McFarland	WI	53558	608-838-4194	838-8367
Argon ST Inc 12701 Fair Lakes Cir Suite 800 *NASDAQ: STST* ■ *Web:* www.argonst.com	Fairfax	VA	22033	703-322-0881	322-0885
Aspect Software Inc 1310 Ridder Pk Dr *TF:* 800-391-2341 ■ *Web:* www.aspect.com	San Jose	CA	95131	408-325-2200	325-2260
Astrocom Corp 2950 Xenium Ln N Suite 140 *TF:* 800-669-6242 ■ *Web:* www.astrocorp.com	Plymouth	MN	55441	763-694-9949	551-0664
AT & T Inc 175 E Houston St *NYSE: T* ■ **Fax:* Hum Res ■ *TF:* 888-875-6388 ■ *Web:* www.att.com	San Antonio	TX	78205	210-821-4105	351-2274*
Audiovox Corp 180 Marcus Blvd *NASDAQ: VOXX* ■ *TF:* 800-645-4994 ■ *Web:* www.audiovox.com	Hauppauge	NY	11788	631-231-7750	434-3995
Axesstel Inc 6815 Flanders Dr Suite 210 *PINK: AXST* ■ *Web:* www.axesstel.com	San Diego	CA	92121	858-625-2100	625-2110
Bo-Sherrel Co Inc 3340 Tree Swallow Pl	Fremont	CA	94555	510-792-0354	797-2038
Call One Inc 400 Imperial Blvd PO Box 9002 *TF:* 800-749-3160 ■ *Web:* www.calloneonline.com	Cape Canaveral	FL	32920	321-783-2400	799-9222
Casabyte Inc 222 Williams Ave S *TF Cust Svc:* 888-352-9527 ■ *Web:* www.casabyte.com	Renton	WA	98055	425-254-9925	254-9926
Ceragon Networks Inc 10 Forest Ave *NASDAQ: CRNT* ■ *TF Tech Supp:* 877-342-3247 ■ *Web:* www.ceragon.com	Paramus	NJ	07652	201-845-6955	845-5665
Charles Industries Ltd 5600 Apollo Dr *TF:* 800-458-4747 ■ *Web:* www.charlesindustries.com	Rolling Meadows	IL	60008	847-806-6300	806-6231
CiDRA Corp 50 Barnes Pk N *TF:* 877-243-7277 ■ *Web:* www.cidra.com	Wallingford	CT	06492	203-265-0035	294-4211
CIENA Corp 1201 Winterson Rd *NASDAQ: CIEN* ■ *TF:* 800-921-1144 ■ *Web:* www.ciena.com	Linthicum	MD	21090	410-694-5700	694-5750
ClearOne Communications Inc 5225 Wiley Post Way *TF:* 800-945-7730 ■ *Web:* www.clearone.com	Salt Lake City	UT	84116	801-975-7200	977-0087
COM DEV International Ltd 155 Sheldon Dr. *TSE: CDV* ■ *Web:* www.comdev.ca	Cambridge	ON	N1R7H6	519-622-2300	622-1691
Comarco Inc 25541 Commerce Ctr Dr. *NASDAQ: CMRO* ■ *TF:* 800-792-0250 ■ *Web:* www.comarco.com	Lake Forest	CA	92630	949-599-7400	599-1415
Comarco Wireless Technologies Inc 25541 Commerce Ctr Dr. *TF Cust Svc:* 800-697-1500 ■ *Web:* www.comarco.com	Lake Forest	CA	92630	949-599-7400	599-1415
Communication Technologies Inc 14151 Newbrook Dr Suite 400 *TF:* 888-266-8358 ■ *Web:* www.comtechnologies.com	Chantilly	VA	20151	703-961-9080	961-1330
Communications Systems Inc 10900 Red Cir Dr *AMEX: JCS* ■ *Web:* www.commsystems.com	Minnetonka	MN	55343	952-996-1674	996-1693
Communications Test Design Inc 1339 Enterprise Dr *TF:* 800-223-3910 ■ *Web:* www.ctdi.com	West Chester	PA	19380	610-436-5203	436-6890
Compunetix Inc 2420 Mosside Blvd *TF:* 800-879-4266 ■ *Web:* www.compunetix.com	Monroeville	PA	15146	412-373-8110	373-2720
Comverse Network Systems Inc 200 Quannapowitt Pkwy *Web:* www.comverse.com	Wakefield	MA	01880	781-246-9000	224-8135
Comverse Technology Inc 100 Quannapowitt Pkwy *NASDAQ: CMVT* ■ *Web:* www.cmvt.com	Wakefield	MA	01880	781-246-9000	224-8135
Conklin Corp 199 W Rd *TF:* 800-266-5546	Pleasant Valley	NY	12569	845-635-2136	635-2136
Consolidated Communications Holdings Inc 121 S 17th St *NASDAQ: CNSL*	Mattoon	IL	61938	217-235-3311	235-3311
Convergent Networks Inc 9 Executive Pk Dr *Web:* www.convergentnet.com	North Billerica	MA	01862	978-323-3300	323-3500
CopperCom Inc 3600 FAU Blvd. *TF:* 866-267-7371 ■ *Web:* www.coppercom.com	Boca Raton	FL	33431	561-322-4000	322-4050
CopyTele Inc 900 Walt Whitman Rd. *Web:* www.copytele.com	Melville	NY	11747	631-549-5900	549-5974
Cyber Digital Inc 400 Oser Ave Suite 1650. *Web:* www.cyberdigitalinc.com	Hauppauge	NY	11788	631-231-1200	231-1446
Digital Lightwave Inc 5575 Rio Vista Dr *TF:* 800-548-9283 ■ *Web:* www.lightwave.com	Clearwater	FL	33760	727-442-6677	442-5660
Digital Voice Corp 1201 S Beltline Rd Suite 150 *TF Cust Svc:* 800-777-8329 ■ *Web:* www.digitalvoicecorp.com	Coppell	TX	75019	469-635-6500	635-6500
Ditech Networks Inc 825 E Middlefield Rd *NASDAQ: DITC* ■ *TF:* 800-234-0884 ■ *Web:* www.ditechcom.com	Mountain View	CA	94043	650-623-1300	564-9599
DynaMetric Inc 717 S Myrtle Ave *TF:* 800-525-6925 ■ *Web:* www.dynametric.com	Monrovia	CA	91016	626-358-2559	359-5701
Dynamic Concepts Inc 1730 17th St NE *Web:* www.dcihq.com	Washington	DC	20002	202-944-8787	526-7233
Eagle Telephonics Inc 3880 Veterans Memorial Hwy *Web:* www.eagletelephonics.com	Bohemia	NY	11716	631-471-3600	471-3600
ECI Telecom Ltd 1201 W Cypress Creek Rd *Web:* www.ecitele.com	Fort Lauderdale	FL	33309	954-351-4328	351-4404
Electronic Tele-Communications Inc 1915 MacArthur Rd *TF:* 888-746-4382 ■ *Web:* www.etcia.com	Waukesha	WI	53188	262-542-5600	542-1524
EMS Technologies Inc 660 Engineering Dr *NASDAQ: ELMG* ■ *Web:* www.ems-t.com	Norcross	GA	30092	770-263-9200	263-9207
eOn Communications Corp 1703 Sawyer Rd *NASDAQ: EONC* ■ *TF:* 800-955-5321 ■ *Web:* www.eoncc.com	Corinth	MS	38834	770-423-2200	423-2228
Ericsson Inc 6300 Legacy Dr. *TF:* 800-234-0730 ■ *Web:* www.ericsson.com	Plano	TX	75024	972-583-0000	
FleetBoss Global Positioning Solutions Inc 241 O'Brien Rd *TF:* 877-265-9559 ■ *Web:* www.fleetboss.com	Fern Park	FL	32730	407-265-9559	265-0365
Franklin Wireless Corp 5440 Morehouse Dr Suite 1000 *Web:* www.franklinwireless.com	San Diego	CA	92121	858-623-0000	623-0050
Fujitsu America Inc 1250 E Arques Ave. *TF:* 800-538-8460 ■ *Web:* www.fujitsu.com	Sunnyvale	CA	95085	408-746-6200	746-6260
GAI-Tronics Corp 400 E Wyomissing Ave *TF:* 800-492-1212 ■ *Web:* www.gai-tronics.com	Mohnton	PA	19540	610-777-1374	775-6540
General DataComm Inc 6 Rubber Ave *Web:* www.gdc.com	Naugatuck	CT	06770	203-729-0271	729-2883
Genesys Telecommunications Laboratories Inc 2001 Junipero Serra Blvd *TF:* 888-436-3797 ■ *Web:* www.genesyslab.com	Daly City	CA	94014	650-466-1100	466-1260
GN US Inc 77 Northeastern Blvd *TF:* 800-327-2230 ■ *Web:* www.jabra.com	Nashua	NH	03062	603-598-1100	598-1122
Harris Corp 1025 W NASA Blvd *NYSE: HRS* ■ *TF:* 800-442-7747 ■ *Web:* www.harris.com	Melbourne	FL	32919	321-727-9100	
Hughes Network Systems LLC 11717 Exploration Ln *Web:* www.hughes.com	Germantown	MD	20876	301-428-5500	428-1868
I Wireless 4135 NW Urbandale Dr *TF Cust Svc:* 888-550-4497 ■ *Web:* www.iwireless.com	Urbandale	IA	50322	515-258-7000	258-7100
iDirect Technologies Inc 13865 Sunrise Valley Dr Suite 100 *TF:* 888-362-5475 ■ *Web:* www.idirect.net	Herndon	VA	20171	703-648-8080	648-8014
Infinera Corp 140 Caspian Ct *NASDAQ: INFN* ■ *Web:* www.infinera.com	Sunnyvale	CA	94089	408-572-5200	572-5454
InnoMedia Inc 128 Baytech Dr *TF:* 888-251-6250 ■ *Web:* www.innomedia.com	San Jose	CA	95134	408-432-5400	432-5404
InterWorks Systems Inc 70 Corbin St Suite M *TF:* 800-814-9757 ■ *Web:* www.interworks.com	Bayshore	NY	11706	631-424-9757	424-9774
ISCO International LLC 1450 Arthur Ave Suite A *Web:* www.iscointl.com	Elk Grove Village	IL	60007	224-222-1666	222-1691
JDS Uniphase Corp 430 N McCarthy Blvd *NASDAQ: JDSU* ■ *TF:* 800-543-1550 ■ *Web:* www.jdsu.com	Milpitas	CA	95035	408-546-5000	546-4300
JTech Communications Inc 6413 Congress Ave Suite 150 *TF:* 800-321-6221 ■ *Web:* www.jtech.com	Boca Raton	FL	33487	561-997-0772	995-2260
Kyocera Wireless Corp 9520 Towne Centre Dr *Web:* www.kyocera-wireless.com	San Diego	CA	92121	858-882-2000	882-2010
L-3 Communications Corp 600 3rd Ave 34-35 Fl *NYSE: LLL* ■ *TF:* 800-351-8483 ■ *Web:* www.l-3com.com	New York	NY	10016	212-697-1111	867-5249
L-3 Communications ILEX Systems 246 Industrial Way W *Web:* www.l-3com.com	Eatontown	NJ	07724	732-380-9400	380-9401
Lantronix Inc 167 Technology Dr. *NASDAQ: LTRX* ■ *TF Orders:* 800-526-8766 ■ *Web:* www.lantronix.com	Irvine	CA	92618	949-453-3990	450-7249
LCC International Inc 4800 Westfields Blvd Suite 200 *Web:* www.lcc.com	Chantilly	VA	20151	703-873-2000	873-2100
Magnasync Corp 1135 N Mansfield Ave *TF:* 800-366-3564 ■ *Web:* www.magnasync.com	Hollywood	CA	90038	323-962-0382	962-8601
Matsushita Communication Industrial Corp of USA 776 Hwy 74 S *Web:* www.panasonic.com	Peachtree City	GA	30269	770-487-3356	487-3357
Metro-Tel Corp 11640 Arbor St Suite 100 *TF:* 888-998-8300 ■ *Web:* www.metrotelcorp.com	Omaha	NE	68144	402-498-2964	493-5100
Microlog Corp 20270 Goldenrod Ln *Web:* www.mlog.com	Germantown	MD	20876	301-540-5500	540-5557
Micronetics Inc 26 Hampshire Dr. *NASDAQ: NOIZ* ■ *Web:* www.micronetics.com	Hudson	NH	03051	603-883-2900	882-8987
Microphase Corp 587 Connecticut Ave. *Web:* www.microphase.com	Norwalk	CT	06854	203-866-8000	866-6727
Microsemi-RFIS 1000 Avenida Acaso *Web:* www.amlj.com	Camarillo	CA	93012	805-388-1345	484-2191
Mitel Networks Corp 350 Legget Dr PO Box 13089 *TF:* 800-267-6244 ■ *Web:* www.mitel.com	Kanata	ON	K2K2W7	613-592-2122	592-4724
Mobile Telesystems Inc 2 Metropolitan Ct # 6 *Web:* www.mti-usa.com	Gaithersburg	MD	20878	301-963-5970	963-4140
Molex Premise Networks 2222 Wellington Ct *TF:* 800-866-3827 ■ *Web:* www.molexpn.com	Lisle	IL	60532	630-969-4550	969-1352
Motorola Canada Ltd 8133 Warden Ave *TF:* 800-268-3395 ■ *Web:* www.motorola.ca	Markham	ON	L6G1B3	905-948-5200	948-5250
Motorola Inc Cellular Subscriber Sector 600 N US Hwy 45 *TF:* 800-331-6456	Libertyville	IL	60048	847-523-5000	525-4348
Motorola Inc iDEN Group 8000 W Sunrise Blvd *Web:* www.motorola.com	Plantation	FL	33322	954-723-5000	
Movius Interactive 11360 Lakefield Dr *TF Tech Supp:* 800-866-4002 ■ *Web:* www.moviuscorp.com	Duluth	GA	30097	770-283-1000	497-3982
NDS Americas 3500 Highland Ave. *TF:* 866-398-8749 ■ *Web:* www.nds.com	Costa Mesa	CA	92626	714-434-2100	434-2474
NEC America Inc 6555 N State Hwy 161 *TF Cust Svc:* 800-338-9549 ■ *Web:* www.necam.com	Irving	TX	75039	214-262-2000	262-2114
Net Optics Inc 5303 Betsy Ross Dr *Web:* www.netoptics.com	Santa Clara	CA	95054	408-737-7777	745-7719
Network Equipment Technologies Inc 6900 Paseo Padre Pkwy *NYSE: NWK* ■ *TF:* 888-828-8080 ■ *Web:* www.net.com	Fremont	CA	94555	510-713-7300	574-4000
NextIO Inc 8303 N MoPac Expwy Suite A210 *Web:* www.nextio.com	Austin	TX	78759	512-439-5350	439-5391
NICE Systems Inc 301 Rt 17 N 10th Fl *TF:* 888-577-6423 ■ *Web:* www.nice.com	Rutherford	NJ	07070	201-964-2600	964-2610
Noble Systems Corp 4151 Ashford Dunwoody *TF:* 888-866-2538 ■ *Web:* www.noblesys.com	Atlanta	GA	30319	404-851-1331	851-1421
Nokia Inc 102 Corporate Pk Dr. *NYSE: NOK* ■ *Web:* www.nokia.com	White Plains	NY	10604	914-368-0400	368-0501

Company	City	State	Zip	Phone	Fax
Norsat International Inc 110-4020 Viking Way *TF:* 888-830-4223 ■ *Web:* www.norsat.com	Richmond	BC	V6V2N2	604-821-2800	821-2801
Nortel Networks Corp 5945 Airport Rd Suite 360 *PINK: NRTLQ* ■ *Web:* www.nortel.com	Mississauga	ON	L4V1R9	905-863-7000	
Nortel Networks Corp 2221 Lakeside Blvd *Web:* www.nortelnetworks.com	Richardson	TX	75082	972-684-1000	684-3801
Notify Technology Corp 1054 S De Anza Blvd Suite 202 **Fax Area Code:* 330 ■ *Web:* www.notifycorp.com	San Jose	CA	95129	408-777-7930	533-0160*
Numerex Corp 1600 Parkwood Cir 5th Fl *NASDAQ: NMRX* ■ *TF:* 800-665-5686 ■ *Web:* www.numerex.com	Atlanta	GA	30339	770-693-5950	693-5951
Oki America Inc 785 N Mary Ave *TF:* 800-654-3282 ■ *Web:* www.oki.com	Sunnyvale	CA	94085	408-720-1900	720-1918
Oplink Communications Inc 46335 Landing Pkwy *NASDAQ: OPLK* ■ *Web:* www.oplink.com	Fremont	CA	94538	510-933-7200	933-7300
Orion Systems Inc 602 Masons Mill Business Pk *Web:* www.orionsystemsinc.net	Huntingdon Valley	PA	19006	215-659-1207	659-4234
OSRAM Sylvania Inc 100 Endicott St *Web:* www.sylvania.com	Danvers	MA	01923	978-777-1900	750-2152
Pics Telecom International Corp 1920 Lyell Ave *TF:* 800-521-7427 ■ *Web:* www.picstelecom.com	Rochester	NY	14606	585-295-2000	295-2020
Plantronics Inc 345 Encinal St *NYSE: PLT* ■ *TF:* 800-544-4660 ■ *Web:* www.plantronics.com	Santa Cruz	CA	95060	831-426-5858	426-6098
Polycom Inc 4750 Willow Rd *NASDAQ: PLCM* ■ **Fax:* Hum Res ■ *TF:* 866-476-5926 ■ *Web:* www.polycom.com	Pleasanton	CA	94588	925-924-6000	924-6101*
Protel Inc 4150 Kidron Rd *TF:* 800-925-8882 ■ *Web:* www.protelinc.com	Lakeland	FL	33811	863-644-5558	646-5855
Proxim Wireless Corp 1561 Buckeye Dr *TF:* 800-229-1630 ■ *Web:* www.proxim.com	Milpitas	CA	95035	408-383-7600	383-7680
Pulse Communications Inc 2900 Towerview Rd **Fax:* Cust Svc ■ *TF Cust Svc:* 800-381-1997 ■ *Web:* www.pulse.com	Herndon	VA	20171	703-471-2900	471-2951*
Pyott-Boone Electronics Inc PO Box 809 *Web:* www.pyottboone.com	Tazewell	VA	24651	276-988-5505	988-6820
Qualcomm Inc 5775 Morehouse Dr *NASDAQ: QCOM* ■ *Web:* www.qualcomm.com	San Diego	CA	92121	858-587-1121	658-2100
Quintron Systems Inc 2105 S Blosser Rd *Web:* www.quintron.com	Santa Maria	CA	93458	805-928-4343	928-5775
QuorTech Solutions Ltd Bay 3-3855 64th Ave SE *Web:* www.quortech.com	Calgary	AB	T2C2V5	403-516-2600	516-2620
RAD Data Communications Ltd 900 Corporate Dr *TF:* 800-444-7234 ■ *Web:* www.rad.com	Mahwah	NJ	07430	201-529-1100	529-1157
Redback Networks Inc 300 Holger Way *NASDAQ: RBAK* ■ *TF:* 866-727-5400	San Jose	CA	95134	408-750-5000	750-3599
Redback Networks Systems Canada Inc 4190 Still Creek Dr Suite 200 *TF:* 877-922-2847	Burnaby	BC	V5C6C6	604-629-7000	294-8830
Redcom Laboratories Inc 1 Redcom Ctr *Web:* www.redcom.com	Victor	NY	14564	585-924-7550	924-6572
RFL Electronics Inc 353 Powerville Rd *Web:* www.rflelect.com	Boonton	NJ	07005	973-334-3100	334-3863
Rochelle Communications Inc 8900 Shoal Creek Blvd Suite 129 *Web:* www.rochelle.com	Austin	TX	78757	512-339-8188	339-1299
SAJE Technology LLC 765 Dixon Ct *Web:* www.saje-tech.com	Hoffman Estates	IL	60195	847-756-7603	496-4515
Samsung Telecommunications America LLP 1301 E Lookout Dr *TF:* 800-726-7864 ■ *Web:* www.samsung.com	Richardson	TX	75082	972-761-7000	761-7001
Sanyo Fisher Co 21605 Plummer St *Web:* us.sanyo.com	Chatsworth	CA	91311	818-998-7322	701-4194
Siemens Canada Ltd 1550 Appleby Line *Web:* www.siemens.ca	Burlington	ON	L7L6X7	905-319-3600	319-7170
SmarTrunk Systems Inc 867 Bowsprit Rd *TF:* 866-870-9052 ■ *Web:* www.smartrunk.com	Chula Vista	CA	91914	619-426-3781	426-3788
Sola Communications Inc 113 N Patch St *TF:* 800-458-8301	Scott	LA	70583	337-235-1515	235-1515
Sonetronics Inc PO Box L *Web:* www.sonetronics.com	West Belmar	NJ	07719	732-681-5016	681-5216
Sonus Networks Inc 7 Technology Dr *NASDAQ: SONS* ■ *TF:* 888-391-3434 ■ *Web:* www.sonusnet.com	Westford	MA	01886	978-614-8100	614-8101
SPL Integrated Solutions 9180 Rumsey Rd Suite D-4 *TF:* 800-292-4125 ■ *Web:* www.splis.com	Columbia	MD	21045	410-992-0998	992-0758
SR Telecom Inc 8150 Trans-Canada Hwy *TSX: SRX* ■ *Web:* www.srtelecom.com	Saint-Laurent	QC	H4S1M5	514-335-1210	334-7783
Star Dynamics Corp 100 Outwater Ln *Web:* www.stardynamic.com	Garfield	NJ	07026	973-340-3883	340-1530
Startel Corp 17661 Cowan Ave *TF:* 800-782-7835 ■ *Web:* www.startelcorp.com	Irvine	CA	92614	949-863-8700	863-9650
STM Wireless Inc 2 Faraday *Web:* www.stmi.com	Irvine	CA	92618	949-753-7864	753-1122
Sunrise Telecom Inc 302 Enzo Dr *NASDAQ: SRTI* ■ *Web:* www.sunrisetelecom.com	San Jose	CA	95138	408-363-8000	363-8313
Superior Essex Communications LP 6120 Powers Ferry Rd Suite 150 *TF:* 800-551-8948 ■ *Web:* www.superioressex.com	Atlanta	GA	30339	770-657-6000	657-6652
Suttle 1001 E Hwy 212 *TF:* 800-852-8662 ■ *Web:* www.suttleonline.com	Hector	MN	55342	320-848-6711	848-6218
Symetrics Industries Inc 1615 W NASA Blvd *Web:* www.symetrics.com	Melbourne	FL	32901	321-254-1500	259-4122
Symmetricom Inc 2300 Orchard Pkwy *NASDAQ: SYMM* ■ *TF:* 888-367-7966 ■ *Web:* www.symmetricom.com	San Jose	CA	95131	408-433-0910	428-7998
Syntellect Inc 16610 N Black Canyon Hwy Suite 100 *TF:* 800-788-9733 ■ *Web:* www.syntellect.com	Phoenix	AZ	85053	602-789-2800	789-2899
System Engineering International Inc (SEI) 5115 Pegasus Ct Suite Q *TF:* 800-765-4734 ■ *Web:* www.seipower.com	Frederick	MD	21704	301-694-9601	694-9608
T-Systems Inc 701 Warrenville Rd *Web:* www.t-systems.com	Lisle	IL	60532	630-493-6100	493-6111
TAG Solutions LLC 12 Elmwood Rd *Web:* www.tagsolutions.com	Albany	NY	12204	518-292-6500	292-6510
Taylored Systems Inc 14701 Cumberland Rd Suite 100 *Web:* www.taylored.com	Noblesville	IN	46060	317-776-4000	776-4004
Technical Communications Corp 100 Domino Dr *Web:* www.tccsecure.com	Concord	MA	01742	978-287-5100	371-1280
Tekelec 5200 Paramount Pkwy *NASDAQ: TKLC* ■ *TF:* 800-835-3532 ■ *Web:* www.tekelec.com	Morrisville	NC	27560	919-460-5500	460-0877
Tel Electronics Inc 705 E 50 S *TF:* 800-564-9424 ■ *Web:* www.tel-electronics.com	American Fork	UT	84003	801-756-9606	756-9135
Telco Systems Inc 15 Berkshire Rd *TF:* 800-227-0937 ■ *Web:* www.telco.com	Mansfield	MA	02048	781-255-2120	255-2122
Telect Inc 23321 E Knox Ave *TF Cust Svc:* 800-551-4567 ■ *Web:* www.telect.com	Liberty Lake	WA	99019	509-926-6000	926-8915
Telekenex Inc 3221 20th St **Fax Area Code:* 866 ■ *TF:* 888-469-5100 ■ *Web:* www.telekenex.com	San Francisco	CA	94110	415-869-9000	726-1739*
Telemobile Inc 19840 Hamilton Ave *Web:* www.telemobile.com	Torrance	CA	90502	310-538-5100	532-8526
Tellabs Inc 1415 W Diehl Rd *NASDAQ: TLAB* ■ *TF:* 888-290-8377 ■ *Web:* www.tellabs.com	Naperville	IL	60563	630-798-8800	798-2000
Telrad Connegy Inc 400 Crossways Pk Dr *TF Cust Svc:* 800-628-3038 ■ *Web:* www.telradusa.com	Woodbury	NY	11797	516-730-3310	
Teltronics Inc 2511 Corporate Way *PINK: TELTQ* ■ *Web:* www.teltronics.com	Palmetto	FL	34221	941-753-5000	758-8469
Telular Corp 311 S Wacker Dr Suite 4300 *NASDAQ: WRLS* ■ *TF:* 800-229-2326 ■ *Web:* www.telular.com	Chicago	IL	60606	312-379-8397	379-8310
Texcom Inc 600 Washington St *Web:* www.texcominc.com	Portsmouth	VA	23704	757-397-0035	397-2813
Tollgrade Communications Inc 3120 Unionville Rd Suite 400 *TF Cust Svc:* 800-878-3399 ■ *Web:* www.tollgrade.com	Cranberry Township	PA	16066	412-820-1400	820-1530
Tone Commander Systems Inc 11609 49th Pl W *TF:* 800-524-0024 ■ *Web:* www.tonecommander.com	Mukilteo	WA	98275	425-349-1000	349-1010
Toshiba America Inc 1251 Avenue of the Americas Suite 4100 *TF:* 800-457-7777 ■ *Web:* www.toshiba.com	New York	NY	10020	212-596-0600	593-3875
Tricomm Services Corp 1247 N Church St Suite 8 *TF:* 800-872-2401 ■ *Web:* www.tricommcorp.com	Moorestown	NJ	08057	856-914-9001	914-9065
TSI Global Cos 700 Fountain Lakes Blvd *Web:* www.tsi-inc.com	Saint Charles	MO	63301	636-949-8889	925-2111
Tyco Telecommunications 60 Columbia Rd *Web:* www.tycotelecom.com	Morristown	NJ	07960	973-656-8000	656-8990
Uniden America Corp 4700 Amon Carter Blvd **Fax:* Hum Res ■ *TF Cust Svc:* 800-297-1023 ■ *Web:* www.uniden.com	Fort Worth	TX	76155	817-858-3300	858-3300*
UTStarcom Inc 48249 Lakeview Blvd Suite A *NASDAQ: UTSI* ■ *TF:* 866-663-3266 ■ *Web:* www.utstar.com	Fremont	CA	94538	510-864-8800	864-8802
Valcom Inc 5614 Hollins Rd *TF:* 800-825-2661 ■ *Web:* www.valcom.com	Roanoke	VA	24019	540-563-2000	362-9800
Vbrick Systems Inc 12 Beaumont Rd *TF:* 866-827-4251 ■ *Web:* www.vbrick.com	Wallingford	CT	06492	203-265-0044	265-6750
VCON Inc 578A Main St *Web:* www.vcon.com	Hackensack	NJ	07601	201-883-1220	883-1229
Vela Research LP 5540 Rio Vista Dr *Web:* www.vela.com	Clearwater	FL	33760	727-507-5300	507-5312
Veramark Technologies Inc 3750 Monroe Ave *Web:* www.veramark.com	Pittsford	NY	14534	585-381-6000	383-6800
Verint Systems Inc 330 S Service Rd *NASDAQ: VRNT* ■ *TF:* 800-967-1028 ■ *Web:* www.verint.com	Melville	NY	11747	631-962-9600	962-9300
Viseon Inc 17103 Preston Rd Suite 150-N *Web:* www.viseonvideo.com	Dallas	TX	75248	972-220-1500	
VTech Innovations LP 9590 SW Gemini Dr Suite 120 *TF:* 800-835-8023 ■ *Web:* www.vtechphones.com	Beaverton	OR	97008	503-596-1200	644-9887
Westell Technologies Inc 750 N Commons Dr *NASDAQ: WSTL* ■ **Fax:* Sales ■ *TF:* 800-323-6883 ■ *Web:* www.westell.com	Aurora	IL	60504	630-898-2500	375-4931*
Wireless Telecom Group Inc 25 Eastmans Rd *AMEX: WTT* ■ *Web:* www.wirelesstelecomgroup.com	Parsippany	NJ	07054	973-386-9696	386-9191
XETA Technologies Inc 1814 W Tacoma St *NASDAQ: XETA* ■ *TF Cust Svc:* 800-845-9145 ■ *Web:* www.xeta.com	Broken Arrow	OK	74012	918-664-8200	664-6876
Zhone Technologies Inc 7001 Oakport St *NASDAQ: ZHNE* ■ *TF:* 877-946-6320 ■ *Web:* www.zhone.com	Oakland	CA	94621	510-777-7000	777-7001

739 TELECOMMUNICATIONS SERVICES

Company	City	State	Zip	Phone	Fax
AboveNet Inc 360 Hamilton Ave 7th Fl *TF:* 866-859-6971 ■ *Web:* www.above.net	White Plains	NY	10601	914-421-6700	421-6777
ACC Business 400 W Ave *TF:* 800-456-6000 ■ *Web:* www.accbusiness.com	Rochester	NY	14611	585-987-3000	
Acceris Communications Inc 9530 Padgett St Suite 101 **Fax Area Code:* 877 ■ *Web:* www.acceris.com	San Diego	CA	92126	858-547-5700	547-5621*
Access America 673 Emory Valley Rd *TF:* 800-860-2140 ■ *Web:* www.accessam.com	Oak Ridge	TN	37830	865-482-2140	482-2306
Access Point Inc 1100 Crescent Green *TF:* 877-419-4274 ■ *Web:* www.accesspointinc.com	Cary	NC	27518	919-851-4838	
ACT Teleconferencing Inc 1526 Cole Blvd Bldg 3 Suite 300 *TF:* 800-228-2554 ■ *Web:* www.actconferencing.com	Lakewood	CO	80401	303-233-3500	238-0096
Advanced Communications Inc 5711 Research Dr *Web:* www.acidirect.com	Canton	MI	48188	734-467-8121	480-0911
Advanced Telecom Services Inc 996 Old Eagle School Rd Suite 1105 *Web:* www.advancedtele.com	Wayne	PA	19087	610-688-6000	964-9117

Company	City	State	ZIP	Phone	Fax
Alaska Communications Systems Group Inc 600 Telephone Ave *NASDAQ: ALSK* ■ *TF:* 800-478-7121 ■ *Web:* www.acsalaska.com	Anchorage	AK	99503	907-297-3000	297-3100
Allstream Corp 200 Wellington St W *TF:* 877-288-2345 ■ *Web:* www.allstream.com	Toronto	ON	M5V3G2	416-345-2000	345-2840
Amanda Co The 4079 Govenor Dr Suite 320 *TF:* 800-410-2745 ■ *Web:* www.taa.com	San Diego	CA	92122	800-410-2745	396-7218
AmeriCom Inc 870 E 9400 S **Fax Area Code: 775* ■ *TF:* 800-820-6296 ■ *Web:* www.americom.com	Sandy	UT	84094	801-571-2446	257-6643*
Aperto Networks Inc 598 Gibraltar Dr *TF:* 877-353-9586 ■ *Web:* www.apertonet.com	Milpitas	CA	95035	408-719-9977	719-9970
Arkansas Telephone Co Inc PO Box 69 *TF:* 800-482-1164 ■ *Web:* www.artelco.com	Clinton	AR	72031	501-745-2114	
AT & T Inc 175 E Houston St *NYSE: T* ■ **Fax:* Hum Res ■ *TF:* 888-875-6388 ■ *Web:* www.att.com	San Antonio	TX	78205	210-821-4105	351-2274*
ATI 30575 Trabuco Canyon Rd Suite 200 *TF:* 877-757-0000 ■ *Web:* www.ati1.com	Trabuco Canyon	CA	92679	949-265-2000	265-2001
ATSI Communications Inc 3201 Cherry Ridge *Web:* www.atsi.net	San Antonio	TX	78230	210-614-7240	614-7264
ATX Group Inc 8550 Freeport Pkwy *Web:* www.atxg.com	Irving	TX	75063	972-753-6200	753-6300
Auragan LLC PO Box 1501 *TF:* 866-644-2872 ■ *Web:* www.advection.net	New Canaan	CT	06840	866-644-2872	
Bell Aliant Regional Communications 6 S Maritime Centre 1505 Barrington St *TSX: BA.UN* ■ *TF:* 800-387-0825 ■ *Web:* www.bellaliant.ca	Halifax	NS	B3J3K5	902-487-4609	425-0708
Bell Canada 1000 Rue de la Gauchetiere O Bureau 3700 *TF:* 888-932-6666 ■ *Web:* www.bell.ca	Montreal	QC	H3B4Y7	514-870-8777	786-3962
BestNet Communications Corp 5075 Cascade Rd SE Suite A *Web:* www.bestnetcom.com	Grand Rapids	MI	49546	616-977-9933	977-9955
Big River Telephone Co LLC PO Box 1608 **Fax Area Code: 800* ■ *TF:* 855-244-7483 ■ *Web:* www.bigrivertelephone.com	Cape Girardeau	MO	63702	573-651-3373	455-4533*
Birch Telecom Inc 2300 Main St Suite 2300 *TF:* 888-422-4724 ■ *Web:* www.birch.com	Kansas City	MO	64108	816-300-3000	300-3291
Bledsoe Telephone Co-op Corp (BTC) 338 Cumberland Ave PO Box 609 *Web:* www.bledsoe.net	Pikeville	TN	37367	423-447-2121	447-2498
Bluegrass Cellular Inc 2902 Ring Rd PO Box 5012 *TF:* 800-928-2355 ■ *Web:* www.bluegrasscellular.com	Elizabethtown	KY	42702	270-769-0339	
Brazoria Telephone Co 314 W Texas St *Web:* www.btel.com	Brazoria	TX	77422	979-798-2121	798-3005
Broadcast International Inc 7050 Union Pk Ctr Suite 650 *TF:* 800-722-0400 ■ *Web:* www.brin.com	Midvale	UT	84047	801-562-2252	562-1773
Broadview Networks Holdings Inc 800 Westchester Ave Suite N-501 *TF:* 800-260-8766 ■ *Web:* www.broadviewnet.com	Rye Brook	NY	10573	914-922-7000	922-7001
CallWave Inc 136 W Canon Perdido St Suite A PO Box 609 *NASDAQ: CALL* ■ *TF:* 800-380-4341 ■ *Web:* www.callwave.com	Santa Barbara	CA	93101	805-690-4000	690-4200
Cap Rock Telephone Co-op Inc PO Box 300 *TF:* 800-692-4242 ■ *Web:* www.caprock-spur.com	Spur	TX	79370	806-271-3336	271-3601
Cavalier Telephone LLC 2134 W Laburnum Ave *TF:* 800-683-3944 ■ *Web:* www.cavtel.com	Richmond	VA	23227	804-422-4100	422-4392
Cbeyond Communications LLC 320 IH- N Pkwy SE Suite 300 *NASDAQ: CBEY* ■ *TF:* 866-424-2600 ■ *Web:* www.cbeyond.net	Atlanta	GA	30339	678-424-2400	424-2500
Century Interactive LLC 7502 Greenville Ave Suite 300 *TF:* 800-256-3159 ■ *Web:* www.centuryinteractive.com	Dallas	TX	75231	214-360-6280	360-6283
Cincinnati Bell Inc 221 E 4th St *NYSE: CBB* ■ *TF:* 800-422-1199 ■ *Web:* www.cincinnatibell.com	Cincinnati	OH	45202	513-397-9900	241-1264
Cinedigm Digital Cinema Corp 55 Madison Ave Suite 300 *Web:* www.accessitx.com	Morristown	NJ	07960	973-290-0080	290-0081
Citizens Telephone Co-Operative PO Box 137 *TF:* 800-941-0426 ■ *Web:* www.citizens.coop	Floyd	VA	24091	540-745-2111	745-3791
Co-op Communciations Inc 210 Clay Ave **Fax Area Code: 201* ■ *TF:* 800-833-2700 ■ *Web:* www.cooperativenet.com	Lyndhurst	NJ	07071	973-759-8100	531-0150*
Comcast Business Communications Inc 650 Centerton Rd *TF:* 888-205-5000	Moorestown	NJ	08057	856-638-4000	638-4051
Commonwealth Telephone Co 100 CTE Dr *TF:* 800-544-1530 ■ *Web:* www.ct-enterprises.com/ct.html	Dallas	PA	18612	570-675-1121	675-4205
Communication Services Inc 2151 E Broadway Rd *Web:* www.com-serv.com	Tempe	AZ	85282	480-905-8689	905-8818
Comporium Communications 332 E Main St *TF:* 866-922-5922 ■ *Web:* www.comporium.com	Rock Hill	SC	29730	803-324-9011	326-5708
Computer Consulting Operations Specialists Inc 600 Corporate Pointe *Web:* www.ccops.com	Culver City	CA	90230	310-568-5000	417-7991
Conference Plus Inc 1051 E Woodfield Rd *Web:* www.conferenceplus.com	Schaumburg	IL	60173	847-619-6100	
Convergent Media Systems Corp 190 Bluegrass Valley Pkwy 1 Convergent Ctr *TF:* 800-254-7463 ■ *Web:* www.convergent.com	Alpharetta	GA	30005	770-369-9000	369-9100
Corporate Telephone 184 W 2nd St *TF:* 800-274-1211 ■ *Web:* www.corporatetelephone.com	Boston	MA	02127	617-625-1200	625-1201
Covista Communications Inc 4803 Tennessee 58 *TF:* 800-805-1000 ■ *Web:* www.covista.com	Chattanooga	TN	37416	423-648-9700	648-9705
CPA2Biz Inc 100 Broadway 6th Fl *TF:* 888-777-7077 ■ *Web:* www.cpa2biz.com	New York	NY	10005	646-233-5000	233-5090
Criticom Inc 4211 Forbes Blvd *TF:* 877-274-8426 ■ *Web:* www.criticom.com	Lanham	MD	20706	301-306-0600	306-0605
Cypress Communications Inc 4 Piedmont Ctr Suite 600 *TF:* 888-205-6912 ■ *Web:* www.cypresscom.net	Atlanta	GA	30305	404-869-2500	869-2525
Dakota Central Telecommunications Co-op 630 5th St N *TF:* 800-771-0974 ■ *Web:* www.daktel.com	Carrington	ND	58421	701-652-3184	674-8121
Deltacom Inc 7037 Old Madison Pike *TF:* 800-239-3000 ■ *Web:* www.deltacom.com	Huntsville	AL	35806	256-382-5900	
deltathree Inc 75 Broad St *NASDAQ: DDDC* ■ *TF:* 888-335-8230	New York	NY	10004	212-500-4850	500-4888
DSLi Corp 5000 SW 75th Ave *TF:* 888-800-1303 ■ *Web:* www.dsli.com	Miami	FL	33155	305-779-7777	507-4329
Eagle Broadband Inc 101 Courageous Dr *PINK: EAGB* ■ *TF:* 800-628-3910	League City	TX	77573	281-538-6000	334-5302
Eastex Telephone Co-op Inc PO Box 150 *TF:* 800-232-7839 ■ *Web:* www.eastex.com	Henderson	TX	75653	903-854-1000	657-9703
EATELCORP Inc 913 S Burnside Ave *TF:* 800-621-4211	Gonzales	LA	70737	225-621-4300	621-4300
Eircom (US) Ltd 1 Landmark Sq Suite 1105 *TF:* 888-387-6731 ■ *Web:* www.eircomus.com	Stamford	CT	06901	203-363-7171	363-7176
Elantic Networks Inc 2134 W Laburnum Ave *TF:* 888-854-2138 ■ *Web:* www.elantictelecom.com	Richmond	VA	23227	804-422-4100	422-4392
Empire Telephone Corp PO Box 349 *Web:* www.northpenntelephone.net	Prattsburgh	NY	14873	607-522-3712	522-4228
Enventis Telecom Inc 21 W Superior St Suite 200 *TF:* 888-436-8683 ■ *Web:* www.enventis.com	Duluth	MN	55802	218-740-6111	720-2765
Etex Telephone Co-op Inc 801 Hwy 155 N *TF:* 877-482-3839 ■ *Web:* www.etex.net	Gilmer	TX	75644	903-797-2711	797-6666
Excel Telecommunications 433 Las Colinas Blvd Suite 400 *TF:* 800-589-5884 ■ *Web:* www.excel.com	Irving	TX	75039	972-910-1900	
Extend America Inc 1915 N Kavaney Dr Suite B *TF:* 877-356-9246 ■ *Web:* www.extendamerica.com	Bismarck	ND	58501	701-255-9500	255-9509
FairPoint Communications Inc 521 E Morehead St Suite 250 *PINK: FRCMQ* ■ *TF:* 800-240-5019 ■ *Web:* www.fairpoint.com	Charlotte	NC	28202	704-344-8150	344-8121
Farmers Telecommunications Co-op (FTC) 144 McCurdy Ave N PO Box 217 *Web:* www.farmerstel.com	Rainsville	AL	35986	256-638-2144	638-4830
Farmers Telephone Co-op Inc 1101 E Main St *TF:* 888-218-5050 ■ *Web:* www.ftc-i.net	Kingstree	SC	29556	843-382-2333	382-2333
Faxaway 417 2nd Ave W *TF:* 800-906-4329 ■ *Web:* www.faxaway.com	Seattle	WA	98119	206-301-7000	301-7500
FaxBack Inc 7409 SW Cardinal Ln Suite 105 *TF:* 800-329-2225 ■ *Web:* www.faxback.com	Portland	OR	97224	503-597-5350	597-5399
FDN Communications 2301 Lucien Way Suite 200 *TF:* 877-433-6435 ■ *Web:* www.windstreambusiness.com	Maitland	FL	32751	407-835-0300	835-1437
FiberTower Corp 185 Berry St Suite 4800 *NASDAQ: FTWR* ■ *Web:* www.fibertower.com	San Francisco	CA	94107	415-659-3500	659-0007
Filer Mutual Telephone Co PO Box 89 *Web:* www.filertel.com	Filer	ID	83328	208-326-4331	326-3190
Frontier Communications Corp 3 High Ridge Pk *NYSE: CZN* ■ *TF:* 800-877-4390 ■ *Web:* www.czn.net	Stamford	CT	06905	203-614-5600	614-4602
Frontier Corp 180 S Clinton Ave *TF:* 800-836-0342	Rochester	NY	14646	585-777-1000	
Fusion Telecommunications International Inc 420 Lexington Ave Suite 1718 *OTC: FSNN* ■ *TF:* 877-579-6453 ■ *Web:* www.fusiontel.com	New York	NY	10170	212-201-2407	972-7884
General Communication Inc 2550 Denali St Suite 1000 *NASDAQ: GNCMA* ■ *TF:* 800-770-7886 ■ *Web:* www.gci.com	Anchorage	AK	99503	907-265-5600	868-5676
Genesys Conferencing Inc 9139 S Ridgeline Blvd *TF:* 800-685-1995 ■ *Web:* www.genesys.com	Highlands,Ranch	CO	80129	303-267-1272	267-1287
Global Crossing Conferencing 1499 W 121 Ave *TF:* 800-525-8244 ■ *Web:* www.net.globalcrossing.com	Westminster	CO	80234	303-633-3000	633-3001
Global Domains International Inc 701 Palomar Airport Rd Suite 300 *Web:* www.worldsite.ws	Carlsbad	CA	92009	760-602-3000	602-3099
Global Telecom & Technology Inc 8484 Westpark Dr Suite 720 *OTC: GTLT* ■ *TF:* 866-767-2767 ■ *Web:* www.gt-t.net	McLean	VA	22102	866-767-2767	
Golden State Cellular 17400 High School Rd *TF:* 800-453-8255 ■ *Web:* www.goldenstatecellular.com	Jamestown	CA	95327	209-533-8844	533-8400
Golden West Telecommunications 415 Crown St PO Box 411 *TF:* 866-279-2161 ■ *Web:* www.goldenwest.com	Wall	SD	57790	605-279-2161	279-2727
Granite Telecommunications LLC 100 Newport Ave Ext *Web:* www.granitenet.com	Quincy	MA	02171	617-933-5500	328-0312
Graphnet Inc 40 Fultron St 28th Fl *TF:* 800-327-1800 ■ *Web:* www.graphnet.com	New York	NY	10038	212-994-1100	994-1150
Guadalupe Valley Telephone Co-op (GVTC) 36101 FM 3159 *TF:* 800-367-4882 ■ *Web:* www.gvtc.com	New Braunfels	TX	78132	830-885-4411	885-2400
Guidance Solutions Inc 4134 Del Rey Ave *TF:* 866-725-0403 ■ *Web:* www.guidance.com	Marina del Rey	CA	90292	310-754-4000	754-4010
Hargray Communications 856 William Hilton Pkwy PO Box 5986 *TF:* 800-726-1266 ■ *Web:* www.hargray.com	Hilton Head Island	SC	29938	843-341-1501	686-1152
Harrisonville Telephone Co 213 S Main St PO Box 149 *TF:* 888-482-8353 ■ *Web:* www.portal.htc.net	Waterloo	IL	62298	618-939-6112	939-4826
Hayneville Telephone Co Inc PO Box 175 *Web:* www.htcnet.net	Hayneville	AL	36040	334-548-2101	548-2051
Hitachi Communication Technologies America Inc 2280 Campbell Creek Blvd Suite 325 *Web:* www.hitachi-cta.com	Richardson	TX	30092	469-461-5400	

				Phone	Fax

Horry Telephone Co-op Inc (HTC)
3480 Hwy 701 N PO Box 1820 — Conway SC 29528 — 843-365-2151 — 365-0855
TF: 800-824-6779 ■ *Web:* www.htcinc.net

I C Interactive Inc
12325 Oracle Blvd Suite 100 — Colorado Springs CO 80921 — 719-593-7377 — 593-2996
TF: 888-235-3231 ■ *Web:* www.infopros.com

Ibahn Corp
2755 E Cottonwood Pkwy Suite 400 — Salt Lake City UT 84121 — 801-952-2000 — 952-2191
Web: www.ibahn.com

iBasis Inc 20 2nd Ave. — Burlington MA 01803 — 781-505-7500 — 505-7300
Web: www.ibasis.net

IDT Corp 520 Broad St — Newark NJ 07102 — 973-438-1000 — 438-1453
NYSE: IDT ■ *TF:* 800-225-5438 ■ *Web:* www.idt.net

ILD Telecommunications Inc
16200 Addison Rd Suite 180 — Addison TX 75001 — 972-267-0100 — 267-0105
TF: 800-749-1229 ■ *Web:* www.ildtelecommunications.com

Integra Telecom Inc
1201 NE Lloyd Blvd Suite 500 — Portland OR 97232 — 503-453-8000 — 453-8221
TF: 866-468-3472 ■ *Web:* www.integratelecom.com

Inter-Community Telephone Co (ICTC) PO Box 8 — Nome ND 58062 — 701-924-8815 — 924-8808
TF: 800-350-9137 ■ *Web:* www.ictc.com

Intercall Inc 8420 W Bryn Mawr Suite 400 — Chicago IL 60631 — 773-399-1600 — 399-1588
Web: www.intercall.com

Intrado Inc 1601 Dry Creek Dr. — Longmont CO 80503 — 720-494-5800 — 494-6600
Web: www.intrado.com

Iridium Satellite LLC 6701 Democracy Blvd — Bethesda MD 20817 — 301-571-6200 — 571-6250
Web: www.iridium.com

IVCi LLC 601 Old Willett Pastth Ave — Hauppauge NY 11788 — 631-273-5800 — 273-7277
TF: 800-224-7083 ■ *Web:* www.ivci.com

j2 Global Communications Inc
6922 Hollywood Blvd 8th Fl — Hollywood CA 90028 — 323-860-9200
NASDAQ: JCOM ■ *TF Sales:* 888-718-2000 ■ *Web:* www.j2global.com

Japan Telecom America Inc
100 Wall St Suite 1803 — New York NY 10020 — 212-422-4650 — 422-4653
Web: www.jt-america.com

Kaplan Telephone Co Inc PO Box 369 — Kaplan LA 70548 — 337-643-2255 — 643-6000
TF: 866-643-7171 ■ *Web:* www.ktconline.net

KDDI America Inc 825 3rd Ave 3rd Fl — New York NY 10022 — 212-295-1200 — 295-1080
Web: www.kddia.com/eng

Kennebec Telephone Co Inc 220 S Main St. — Kennebec SD 57544 — 605-869-2220 — 869-2221
TF: 888-868-3390 ■ *Web:* www.kennebectelephone.com

Knology Inc 1241 OG Skinner Dr. — West Point GA 31833 — 706-645-8553 — 645-1446
NASDAQ: KNOL ■ *TF:* 877-566-5649 ■ *Web:* www.knology.com

Leap Wireless International Inc
5887 Copley Dr — San Diego CA 92111 — 858-882-6000 — 882-6010
NASDAQ: LEAP ■ *TF:* 800-274-2538 ■ *Web:* www.leapwireless.com

Lexent Inc 90 White St. — New York NY 10013 — 212-981-0700 — 334-0847
Web: www.lexent.net

Liberty Global Inc 12300 Liberty Blvd — Englewood CO 80112 — 303-220-6600 — 220-6601
NASDAQ: LBTYA ■ *Web:* www.lgi.com

LICT Corp 401 Theodore Fremd Ave — Rye NY 10580 — 914-921-8821 — 921-6410
Web: www.lictcorp.com

Lightsquared Inc 10802 Parkridge Blvd — Reston VA 20191 — 212-730-7540 — 730-7541
TF: 877-678-2920 ■ *Web:* www.skyterra.com

Linkedin Corp 2029 Stierlin Ct — Mountain View CA 94043 — 650-687-3600 — 687-0505
Web: www.linkedin.com

M D Notify Inc 318 Seaboard Ln Suite 310 — Franklin TN 37067 — 615-778-6700 — 778-6770
TF: 800-696-0155 ■ *Web:* www.notifymd.com

Matanuska Telephone Assn Inc
1740 S Chugach St. — Palmer AK 99645 — 907-745-3211 — 761-2481
Web: www.mta-telco.com

MetroPCS Wireless Inc PO Box 601119 — Dallas TX 75360 — 214-265-2550 — 265-2570
TF Cust Svc: 888-863-8768 ■ *Web:* www.metropcs.com

Microserve Inc 276 5th Ave Suite 1011 — New York NY 10001 — 212-683-2811 — 696-0123
Web: www.mserve.com

Midcontinent Communications PO Box 5010 — Sioux Falls SD 57117 — 605-229-1775 — 330-4089*
**Fax:* Cust Svc ■ *TF:* 800-888-1300 ■ *Web:* www.midcocomm.com

Millington Telephone Co Inc 4880 Navy Rd. — Millington TN 38053 — 901-872-7772 — 873-0022
Web: www.millingtononline.com

Molalla Communications Co
211 Robbins St PO Box 360 — Molalla OR 97038 — 503-829-1100 — 829-7781
Web: www.molalla.net

Multiband Corp 9449 Science Ctr Dr — New Hope MN 55428 — 763-504-3000 — 504-3060
NASDAQ: MBND ■ *TF:* 866-577-6263 ■ *Web:* www.multibandusa.com

National Field Service Corp (NFS)
162 Orange Ave — Suffern NY 10901 — 845-368-1600 — 368-1989
Web: nfsco.com/newdesign/services.htm

Net Access Corp 9 Wing Dr — Cedar Knolls NJ 07927 — 973-590-5000 — 590-5080
TF: 800-638-6336 ■ *Web:* www.nac.net

Net2Phone Inc 520 Broad St. — Newark NJ 07102 — 973-438-3111 — 438-1829
TF: 800-386-6438 ■ *Web:* www.net2phone.com

Netwolves Corp 4710 Eisenhower Blvd Suite E-8 — Tampa FL 33634 — 813-579-3200 — 882-0209
Web: www.netwolves.com

Network Communications International Corp
606 E Magrill St — Longview TX 75601 — 903-757-4455 — 757-4899
TF: 888-686-3699 ■ *Web:* www.ncic.com

Network Management Corp (NMC) 111 Derek Pl — Roseville CA 95678 — 916-772-2020 — 772-2323
TF: 888-455-4662 ■ *Web:* www.netmgmt.com

Network Services LLC
525 S Douglas St Suite 250 — El Segundo CA 90245 — 310-615-6500 — 536-0900*
**Fax Area Code:* 800 ■ *TF:* 800-536-0700 ■ *Web:* www.networkservices.net

New Global Telecom Inc 600 12th St Suite 200 — Golden CO 80401 — 303-278-0700 — 278-0728
Web: www.ngt.com

New Ulm Telecom Inc 27 N Minnesota St — New Ulm MN 56073 — 507-354-4111 — 354-1982
OTC: NULM ■ *TF:* 877-664-0283 ■ *Web:* www.newulmtel.net

NII Holdings Inc 1875 Explorer St Suite 1000 — Reston VA 20190 — 703-390-5100 — 390-5149
NASDAQ: NIHD ■ *Web:* www.nii.com

North Central Telephone Co-op Corp
PO Box 70 — Lafayette TN 37083 — 615-666-2151 — 666-6772
TF: 888-882-1693 ■ *Web:* www.nctc.com

North State Communications 111 N Main St. — High Point NC 27261 — 336-886-3600 — 887-7418
Web: www.northstate.net

Novatel Ltd 11550 Ih 10 W Suite 110 — San Antonio TX 78230 — 210-698-8005 — 349-7562
Web: www.novatelnetworks.com

NTELOS Holdings Corp
401 Spring Ln Suite 300 PO Box 1990 — Waynesboro VA 22980 — 540-946-3500 — 946-3595
NASDAQ: NTLS ■ *TF:* 877-468-3567 ■ *Web:* www.ntelos.com

NTT America Inc 101 Pk Ave 41st Fl — New York NY 10178 — 212-661-0810 — 661-1078
Web: www.us.ntt.com

NTT DoCoMo USA Inc 101 Pk Ave 41st Fl — New York NY 10178 — 212-994-7222 — 994-7219
NYSE: DCM ■ *Web:* www.docomo-usa.com

01 Communications Inc 1515 K St Suite 100 — Sacramento CA 95814 — 916-554-2100 — 554-2180
TF: 888-444-1111 ■ *Web:* www.o1.com

One Communications Corp 100 Chestnut St. — Rochester NY 14604 — 585-246-4231
Web: www.onecommunications.com

Optimum Lightpath 1111 Stewart Ave — Bethpage NY 11714 — 516-803-2300
Web: www.optimumlightpath.com

Otelco Inc 505 3rd Ave E — Oneonta AL 35121 — 205-625-3591 — 625-3523
NASDAQ: OTT ■ *TF:* 800-286-4600 ■ *Web:* www.otelco.net

Otz Telephone Co-op Inc PO Box 324 — Kotzebue AK 99752 — 907-442-3114 — 442-2123
TF: 800-478-3111 ■ *Web:* www.otz.net

Oxford County Telephone & Telegraph Co Inc
491 Lisbon St — Lewiston ME 04240 — 207-333-6900 — 333-3489
TF: 800-520-9911 ■ *Web:* www.oxfordnetworks.com

Pac-West Telecomm Inc
201 Mission St Suite 720 — San Francisco CA 94105 — 877-626-4325 — 966-4043*
**Fax Area Code:* 800 ■ *TF:* 877-626-4325 ■ *Web:* www.pacwest.com

PaeTec Communications Inc
600 Willowbrook Office Pk — Fairport NY 14450 — 585-340-2500 — 340-2801
TF: 877-472-3832 ■ *Web:* www.paetec.com

Panhandle Telecommunication Systems Inc
2224 NW Hwy 64 — Guymon OK 73942 — 580-338-7525 — 338-4200
TF: 800-327-7525 ■ *Web:* www.ptsi.net

Penasco Valley Telecommunications (PVT)
4011 Main St — Artesia NM 88210 — 505-746-9844 — 746-4142*
**Fax Area Code:* 575 ■ *TF:* 866-746-9844 ■ *Web:* www.pvt.com

Piedmont Rural TelephoneCo-op Inc (PRTC)
PO Box 249 — Laurens SC 29360 — 864-682-3131 — 682-8888
Web: www.prtcnet.com

Pioneer Long Distance Inc PO Box 539 — Kingfisher OK 73750 — 405-375-0850
Web: www.pldi.net

Pioneer Telephone Assn Inc PO Box 707 — Ulysses KS 67880 — 620-356-3211 — 356-3242
TF: 800-308-7536 ■ *Web:* www.pioncomm.net

Pioneer Telephone Co-op Inc
108 E Roberts Ave PO Box 539 — Kingfisher OK 73750 — 405-375-4111 — 699-3053*
**Fax:* Mktg ■ *Web:* www.ptci.com

Powercom Corp 1807 N Ctr St — Beaver Dam WI 53916 — 920-887-3148 — 885-2879
TF Cust Svc: 800-444-4014 ■ *Web:* www.powercom.net

Pratt Communications 2913 Tech Ctr — Santa Ana CA 92705 — 714-540-6840 — 540-0506
TF: 800-980-2323 ■ *Web:* www.prattcommunications.com

Primus Telecommunications (PTGi)
7901 Jones Ranch Dr Suite 900 — McLean VA 22102 — 703-902-2800 — 902-2814
NASDAQ: PRTL ■ *TF:* 866-385-3360 ■ *Web:* www.ptgi.com

Proximity Inc 1526 Cole Blvd Suite 300 — Golden CO 80401 — 303-235-3500
TF: 800-433-2900 ■ *Web:* www.proximity.com

Puerto Rico Telephone Co PO Box 360998 — San Juan PR 00936 — 787-782-8282 — 792-8877
Web: www.telefonicapr.com

PWR LLC 6402 Deere Rd Suite 3 — Syracuse NY 13206 — 315-701-0210 — 701-0217
TF: 800-342-0878 ■ *Web:* www.pwrllc.com

Questar InfoComm Inc
180 E 100 S PO Box 45433 — Salt Lake City UT 84145 — 801-324-5856 — 324-5510
TF: 800-729-6790 ■ *Web:* www.questarpipeline.com

Reserve Telephone Co Inc PO Box T — Reserve LA 70084 — 985-536-1111 — 536-4815
TF: 888-611-6111 ■ *Web:* www.rtconline.com

Rnk Inc 333 Elm St Suite 310 — Dedham MA 02026 — 781-297-9831 — 297-2091
TF: 877-323-2486 ■ *Web:* www.rnktel.com

Rogers Communications Inc
333 Bloor St E 10th Fl — Toronto ON M4W1G9 — 416-935-7777 — 935-3599
NYSE: RCI ■ *Web:* www.rogers.com

Rogers Wireless Communications Inc
1 Mt Pleasant Rd 9th Fl — Toronto ON M4Y2Y5 — 416-935-6441 — 935-3339
TF: 800-268-7347 ■ *Web:* www.rogers.com

Rural Telephone Service Co Inc PO Box 158 — Lenora KS 67645 — 785-567-4281 — 567-4401
TF: 877-625-7872 ■ *Web:* www.ruraltelephone.com

Sage Telecom Inc
3300 E Renner Rd Suite 350, Bldg 2 — Richardson TX 75082 — 214-495-4700 — 495-4790
TF: 877-742-5622 ■ *Web:* www.sagetelecom.net

Sandhill TelephoneCo-op Inc PO Box 519 — Jefferson SC 29718 — 843-658-3434 — 658-7700
Web: www.shtc.net

Securus Technologies Inc
14651 Dallas Pkwy 6th Fl — Dallas TX 75254 — 972-277-0300 — 277-0301
TF: 800-559-1539 ■ *Web:* www.securustech.net

Shawnee Telephone Co PO Box 69 — Equality IL 62934 — 618-276-4211
TF: 800-461-3956 ■ *Web:* www.shawneetelco.com

Shenandoah Telecommunications Co
500 Shentel Way — Edinburg VA 22824 — 540-984-5224 — 984-3438
NASDAQ: SHEN ■ *TF:* 800-743-6835 ■ *Web:* www.shentel.com

Skyline Telephone Membership Corp
PO Box 759 — West Jefferson NC 28694 — 336-877-3111
TF: 877-475-9546 ■ *Web:* www.skyline.org

SkyTel Corp PO Box 2469 — Jackson MS 39225 — 601-944-1300 — 460-8736*
**Fax:* Hum Res ■ *TF Cust Svc:* 800-759-8737 ■ *Web:* www.skytel.com

Smart City Networks
5795 W Badura Ave Suite 110 — Las Vegas NV 89118 — 702-943-6000 — 943-6001
TF: 888-446-6911 ■ *Web:* www.smartcity.com

SMI International LLC
5520 Tech Ctr Dr. — Colorado Springs CO 80919 — 719-531-9090 — 536-3560
TF: 800-377-7765 ■ *Web:* www.aleutmgt.com

Smithville Communications Inc
1600 W Temperance St PO Box 728 — Ellettsville IN 47429 — 812-876-2211 — 876-9267
Web: www.smithville.net

Solarus 440 E Grand Ave. — Wisconsin Rapids WI 54494 — 715-421-8111 — 421-6081
TF: 800-421-9282 ■ *Web:* www.solarus.net

SoundBite Communications Inc 22 Crosby Dr — Bedford MA 01730 — 781-897-2500 — 897-2502
NASDAQ: SDBT ■ *TF:* 877-768-6324 ■ *Web:* www.soundbite.com

	City	State	Zip	Phone	Fax
South Central Rural Telephone Co-op Corp Inc PO Box 159 *TF:* 877-678-2111 ■ *Web:* www.scrtc.com	Glasgow	KY	42142	270-678-2111	678-2854
Southern Communications Services Inc 5555 Glenridge Connector Suite 500 *TF:* 800-406-0151 ■ *Web:* www.southernlinc.com	Atlanta	GA	30342	678-443-1500	443-1596
Spanlink Communications Inc 605 Hwy 169 N Suite 900 *TF:* 800-303-1241 ■ *Web:* www.spanlink.com	Minneapolis	MN	55441	763-971-2000	971-2300
Spirit Telecom 1500 Hampton St Suite 101 *TF:* 800-333-2949 ■ *Web:* www.spirittelecom.com	Columbia	SC	29201	803-771-7476	771-7436
Sprint PCS Group 6391 Sprint Pkwy *TF:* 800-829-0965 ■ *Web:* www.sprintpcs.com	Overland Park	KS	66251	800-829-0965	
Startec Global Communications Corp 7361 Calhoun Pl Suite 650 *TF:* 800-827-3374 ■ *Web:* www.startec.com	Rockville	MD	20855	301-610-4300	610-4301
SureWest Communications 211 Lincoln St PO Box 969 *NASDAQ: SURW* ■ *TF:* 866-787-3937 ■ *Web:* www.surewest.com	Roseville	CA	95678	916-786-1799	786-7170
Syniverse Technologies Inc 8125 Highwoods Palm Way *NYSE: SVR* ■ *TF:* 800-543-6741 ■ *Web:* www.syniverse.com	Tampa	FL	33647	813-637-5000	
T-Mobile USA Inc 12920 SE 38th St *TF:* 800-318-9270 ■ *Web:* www.t-mobile.com	Bellevue	WA	98006	425-383-4000	378-4040
T-Systems Inc 701 Warrenville Rd *Web:* www.t-systems.com	Lisle	IL	60532	630-493-6100	493-6111
TDS Telecommunications Corp 525 Junction Rd *TF:* 800-358-3648 ■ *Web:* www.tdstelecom.com	Madison	WI	53717	608-664-4000	830-5569
TelAlaska Inc 201 E 56th St *TF:* 888-570-1792 ■ *Web:* www.telalaska.com	Anchorage	AK	99518	907-563-2003	565-5539
Telefonica USA Inc 1111 Brickell Ave 10th Fl *Web:* www.us.telefonica.com	Miami	FL	33131	305-925-5300	373-1685
Telephone Service Co PO Box 408 *TF:* 800-743-5707 ■ *Web:* www.telserco.com	Wapakoneta	OH	45895	419-739-2200	739-2299
Telephone Systems International Inc (TSI) 4400 Marsh Landing Blvd Suite 3 *Web:* www.tsiglobe.com	Ponte Vedra Beach	FL	32082	904-686-1470	686-1709
Teletouch Communications Inc 5718 Airport Fwy *OTC: TLLE* ■ *TF:* 800-232-3888 ■ *Web:* www.teletouch.com	Fort Worth	TX	76117	817-654-6100	654-6220
Teligent Inc PO Box 105451 *TF:* 888-411-1175 ■ *Web:* www.teligent.com	Atlanta	GA	30348	888-411-1175	841-1957
TELUS Corp 3B-555 Robson St *NYSE: TU* ■ *TF:* 800-667-4871 ■ *Web:* www.telus.com	Vancouver	BC	V6B3K9	604-432-2151	899-9228
Time Warner Telecom Inc 10475 Pk Meadow Dr *NASDAQ: TWTC* ■ *TF:* 800-565-8982 ■ *Web:* www.twtelecom.com	Littleton	CO	80124	303-566-1000	516-1011
TNS Inc 11480 Commerce Pk Dr Suite 600 *NYSE: TNS* ■ *TF:* 800-240-2824 ■ *Web:* www.tnsi.com	Reston	VA	20191	703-453-8300	453-8599
TracFone Wireless Inc 9700 NW 112th Ave *Web:* www.tracfone.com	Miami	FL	33178	305-640-2000	640-2070
Trans National Communications International Inc (TNCI) 2 Charlesgate W Suite 500 *TF:* 800-900-5210 ■ *Web:* www.tncii.com	Boston	MA	02215	617-369-1000	369-1111
Twin Lakes Telephone Co-op 201 W Gore Ave *TF Cust Svc:* 800-644-8582 ■ *Web:* www.twlakes.net	Gainesboro	TN	38562	931-268-2151	268-2734
United Systems Access Inc 5 Bragdon Ln Suite 200 *TF:* 877-872-2800 ■ *Web:* www.savewithusa.com	Kennebunk	ME	04043	207-467-8000	467-8008
United Utilities Inc PO Box 92730 *Web:* www.unicom-alaska.com	Anchorage	AK	99509	907-561-1674	273-5322
Unitel Inc PO Box 165 *TF:* 888-760-1048 ■ *Web:* www.unitelme.com	Unity	ME	04988	207-948-3900	948-3021
Universal Service Administrative Co (USAC) 2000 L St NW Suite 200 *TF:* 888-641-8722 ■ *Web:* www.usac.org	Washington	DC	20036	202-776-0200	776-0080
Universal Service Administrative Co Rural Health Care Div 100 S Jefferson Rd *TF:* 800-229-5476 ■ *Web:* www.rhc.universalservice.org	Whippany	NJ	07981	973-581-5010	599-6514
Universal Service Administrative Co Schools & Libraries Div 2000 L St NW Suite 200 *TF:* 888-203-8100 ■ *Web:* www.usac.org	Washington	DC	20036	888-203-8100	276-8736
Upper Peninsula Telephone Co PO Box 86 *TF:* 800-950-8506 ■ *Web:* www.uptelephone.net	Carney	MI	49812	906-639-2111	639-9935
uReach Technologies Inc 2137 State Hwy 35 & Union Ave *TF:* 888-506-7790 ■ *Web:* www.ureachtech.com	Holmdel	NJ	07733	732-335-5400	335-8129
US Cellular Corp (USCC) 8410 W Bryn Mawr Ave Suite 700 *AMEX: USM* ■ *TF:* 888-944-9400 ■ *Web:* www.uscellular.com	Chicago	IL	60631	773-399-8900	399-8936
US LEC Corp 6801 Morrison Blvd 3 Morrocroft Ctr *NASDAQ: CLEC* ■ *TF:* 800-588-7380	Charlotte	NC	28211	704-319-1000	319-1040
Usa Datanet Corp 109 S Warren St Suite 602 *TF:* 800-566-8655 ■ *Web:* www.usadatanet.com	Syracuse	NY	13202	800-566-8655	
USA Mobility Inc 6677 Richmond Hwy *Web:* www.usamobility.com	Alexandria	VA	22306	703-660-6677	660-6994
Valley Telephone Co-op Inc 752 E Maley St *TF:* 800-421-5711 ■ *Web:* www.vtc.net	Willcox	AZ	85643	520-384-2231	384-2831
VarTec Telecom Inc 433 Las Colinas Blvd E Suite 1300 **Fax Area Code:* 214 ■ *TF:* 800-583-8832 ■ *Web:* www.vartec.com	Irving	TX	75039	800-779-2239	424-1144*
VeriSign Inc 350 Ellis St *NASDAQ: VRSN* ■ *TF Sales:* 866-893-6565 ■ *Web:* www.verisign.com	Mountain View	CA	94043	650-426-3100	961-7300
Verizon Business 1 Verizon Way *TF Cust Svc:* 866-232-4282 ■ *Web:* www.verizonbusiness.com	Basking Ridge	NJ	07920	800-339-9911	
Verizon Communications Inc 140 W St *NYSE: VZ* ■ *Web:* www.verizon.com	New York	NY	10007	212-395-2121	869-3265
Verizon Wireless 180 Washington Valley Rd **Fax:* Hum Res ■ *TF:* 800-922-0204 ■ *Web:* www.verizonwireless.com	Bedminster	NJ	07921	908-306-7000	306-6839*
Virgin Media Inc 909 Third Ave Suite 2863 *NASDAQ: VMED* ■ *Web:* www.virginmedia.com	New York	NY	10022	212-906-8440	397-5943
Virgin Mobile USA Inc 10 Independence Blvd *TF:* 888-322-1122 ■ *Web:* www.virginmobileusa.com	Warren	NJ	07059	908-607-4000	607-4822
Voice Power Telecommunications Inc PO Box 187 *TF:* 800-613-6470 ■ *Web:* www.vptnet.com	Austin	TX	78767	512-419-4600	419-4601
Voicecom 5900 Windward Pkwy Suite 500 **Fax Area Code:* 877 ■ *TF:* 800-384-4357 ■ *Web:* www.voicecom.com	Alpharetta	GA	30005	800-384-4357	761-1173*
Vonage Holdings Corp 23 Main St *NYSE: VG* ■ *TF:* 800-980-1455 ■ *Web:* www.vonage.com	Holmdel	NJ	07733	732-528-2600	834-0189
W3i Holdings LLC 1900 Medical Arts Ave S *Web:* www.freeze.com	Sartell	MN	56377	320-257-7500	253-2225
Wabash Telephone Co-Operative Inc PO Box 299 *TF:* 800-228-9824 ■ *Web:* www.wabashtelephone.coop	Louisville	IL	62858	618-665-3311	665-4188
Warwick Valley Telephone Co 47 Main St PO Bo 592 *NASDAQ: WWVY* ■ *TF Cust Svc:* 800-952-7642 ■ *Web:* www.wvtc.com	Warwick	NY	10990	845-986-8080	986-6699
Wave2Wave Communications Inc 433 Hackensack Ave Continental Plaza **Fax Area Code:* 201 ■ *TF:* 877-928-3292 ■ *Web:* www.wave2wave.com	Hackensack	NJ	07601	877-928-3292	968-1886*
Wavedivision Holdings LLC 401 Kirkland Prk Pl PO Box 34808 *TF:* 866-928-3123 ■ *Web:* www.wavebroadband.com	Kirkland	WA	98033	425-576-8200	576-8221
West River Co-op Telephone Co (WRCTC) 801 Coleman Ave PO Box 39 *Web:* www.sdplains.com	Bison	SD	57620	605-244-5213	244-7288
West River Telecommunications Co-op PO Box 467 *TF:* 800-748-7220 ■ *Web:* www.westriv.com	Hazen	ND	58545	701-748-2211	748-6800
West Texas Rural TelephoneCo-op Inc PO Box 1737 *Web:* www.wtrt.net	Hereford	TX	79045	806-364-3331	276-5219
Windstream Corp 4001 Rodney Parham Rd *NYSE: WIN* ■ *Web:* www.windstream.com	Little Rock	AR	72212	501-748-7000	
Working Assets Long Distance Service 101 Market St Suite 700 *TF Cust Svc:* 800-788-0898 ■ *Web:* www.workingforchange.com	San Francisco	CA	94105	415-369-2000	371-1048
WQN Inc 14911 Quorum Dr Suite 140 *NASDAQ: WQNI* ■ *TF:* 866-661-6176 ■ *Web:* www.wqn.com	Dallas	TX	75254	972-361-1980	980-8996
XO Communications Inc 13865 Sunrise Valley Dr *TF:* 800-900-6398 ■ *Web:* www.xo.com	Herndon	VA	20171	703-547-2000	547-2881
Yak Communications Corp 48 Yonge St Suite 1200 *TF:* 877-878-1100 ■ *Web:* www.yak.ca	Toronto	ON	M5E1G6	647-722-2752	722-2763
York Telecom Corp 81 Corbett Way *TF:* 866-836-8463 ■ *Web:* www.yorktel.com	Eatontown	NJ	07724	732-413-6000	413-6060

740 TELEMARKETING & OTHER TELE-SERVICES

Both Inbound And Outbound Telephone Marketing As Well As Other Tele-Services Are Included Here.

	City	State	Zip	Phone	Fax
Aegis Communications Group Inc 8201 Ridgepoint Dr *TF:* 800-830-1800 ■ *Web:* www.aegisglobal.com	Irving	TX	75063	972-830-1800	868-0220
AFFINA 2001 Ruppman Plaza **Fax:* Hum Res ■ *TF:* 800-787-7626 ■ *Web:* www.affina.com	Peoria	IL	61614	309-685-5901	679-4431*
Alta Resources 120 N Commercial St *TF:* 877-464-2582 ■ *Web:* www.altaresources.com	Neenah	WI	54956	920-727-9925	727-9954
American Home Base 428 Childers St *TF:* 800-422-4663 ■ *Web:* www.amhomebase.com	Pensacola	FL	32534	850-857-0860	484-8661
Ameridial Inc 4535 Strausser St NW *TF:* 800-445-7128 ■ *Web:* www.ameridial.com	North Canton	OH	44720	330-497-4888	497-5500
AnswerNet Network 2325 Marylane Rd **Fax Area Code:* 215 ■ *TF:* 800-411-5777 ■ *Web:* www.answernet.com	willowgroove	PA	19090	609-921-7450	659-6486*
APAC Customer Services Inc 2333 Waukegan Rd Suite 100 *NASDAQ: APAC* ■ *TF:* 800-776-2722 ■ *Web:* www.apaccustomerservices.com	Bannockburn	IL	60015	847-374-4980	374-4991
Bluestem Brands Inc 6509 Flying Cloud Dr *Web:* bluestembrands.silkroad.com	Eden Prairie	MN	55344	952-656-3700	
Calling Solutions By Phone Power Inc 2200 McCullough Ave *TF Cust Svc:* 800-321-8582 ■ *Web:* www.callingsolutions.com	San Antonio	TX	78212	210-822-7400	581-6541
Carlson Marketing Group 1405 Xenium Ln *TF:* 888-521-2200 ■ *Web:* www.carlsonmarketing.com	Plymouth	MN	55441	763-212-4000	212-1896
Connection The 11351 Rupp Dr *TF Sales:* 800-883-5777 ■ *Web:* www.the-connection.com	Burnsville	MN	55337	952-948-5488	948-5498
Convergys Corp 201 E 4th St *NYSE: CVG* ■ *TF:* 888-284-9900 ■ *Web:* www.convergys.com	Cincinnati	OH	45202	513-723-7000	
Dale Corp 28091 Dequindre *Web:* www.dalecorporation.com	Madison Heights	MI	48071	248-542-2400	542-6007
Data Services Direct LLC 959 US 46 Suite 302	Parsippany	NJ	07054	973-331-8101	331-8108
DialAmerica Marketing Inc 960 MacArthur Blvd *TF Cust Svc:* 800-526-4679 ■ *Web:* www.dialamerica.com	Mahwah	NJ	07495	201-327-0200	818-6242
EBSCO TeleServices 4150 Belden Village Ave NW Suite 401 *TF:* 800-456-5105 ■ *Web:* www.call-ets.com	Canton	OH	44718	330-492-5105	492-5205
Gage 10000 Hwy 55 *Web:* www.gage.com	Minneapolis	MN	55441	763-595-3800	595-3871
Global Response Corp 777 S SR-7 *TF:* 800-537-8000 ■ *Web:* www.globalresponse.com	Margate	FL	33068	954-973-7300	969-2407
Harte-Hanks Direct Marketing 260 Madison Ave # 20 *TF:* 800-543-2212 ■ *Web:* www.harte-hanks.com	New York	NY	10016	212-889-5000	696-9151
Harte-Hanks Response Management 2800 Wells Branch Pkwy *TF:* 800-333-3383 ■ *Web:* www.harte-hanks.com	Austin	TX	78728	512-434-1100	244-9222
Holden MSS 5000 Lima St *TF:* 888-714-3700	Denver	CO	80239	720-374-3700	374-3720

				Phone	Fax
InfoCision Management Corp 325 Springside Dr	Akron	OH	44333	330-668-1400	668-1401
TF: 800-210-6269 ■ *Web:* www.infocision.com					
Integretel Inc 5883 Rue Ferrari	San Jose	CA	95138	408-362-4000	362-2795
TF: 888-302-2750 ■ *Web:* www.integretel.com					
InterMedi@ Marketing Solutions					
204 Carter Dr	West Chester	PA	19382	610-696-4646	429-5137
TF: 800-835-3466 ■ *Web:* www.intermediamarketing.com					
iSky Inc 6100 Frost Pl	Laurel	MD	20707	240-456-4300	456-4335
TF: 800-351-5055 ■ *Web:* www.isky.com					
Lester Inc 19 Business Pk Dr	Branford	CT	06405	203-488-5265	483-0408
TF: 800-999-5265 ■ *Web:* www.lesterusa.com					
Lexicon Marketing Corp					
640 S San Vicente Blvd	Los Angeles	CA	90048	323-782-7400	782-7410
TF: 800-722-8888 ■ *Web:* www.lexiconmarketing.com					
Meyer Assoc Inc 14 7th Ave N	Saint Cloud	MN	56303	320-259-4000	259-4044
TF: 800-676-9233 ■ *Web:* www.callmeyer.com					
Midco Call Center Services					
4901 E 26th St	Sioux Falls	SD	57110	605-330-4125	910-5655*
**Fax Area Code:* 800 ■ *TF:* 800-843-8800 ■ *Web:* www.midcocall.com					
Millennium Teleservices LLC					
425 Raritan Ctr Pkwy	Edison	NJ	08837	877-877-7698	417-4435*
**Fax Area Code:* 732 ■ *TF:* 877-877-7698 ■ *Web:* www.mmtel.com					
NOVO 1 Inc 4301 Cambridge Rd	Fort Worth	TX	76155	817-355-8200	355-8505
TF: 800-325-2580 ■ *Web:* www.novo1.com					
One Call Systems Inc					
115 Evergreen Heights Dr	Pittsburgh	PA	15229	412-415-5000	415-5023
PRC LLC 8151 Peters Rd Suite 4000	Plantation	FL	33324	954-693-3700	693-3767
TF: 800-866-4443 ■ *Web:* www.prcnet.com					
ProCom Inc 28838 US Hwy 69 PO Box 27	Lamoni	IA	50140	641-784-8841	784-4100
TF: 800-433-9893 ■ *Web:* www.procom-inc.com					
Prosodie Interactive					
855 SW 78th Ave Suite 100	Plantation	FL	33324	954-343-5588	776-7634*
**Fax Area Code:* 866 ■ *TF:* 877-453-5700 ■ *Web:* www.prosodieinteractive.com					
Reese Teleservices Inc					
925 Penn Ave Suite 6	Pittsburgh	PA	15222	412-765-3100	
TF: 800-365-3500					
Results Telemarketing Inc					
499 Sheridan St 4th Fl	Dania Beach	FL	33004	954-921-2400	923-8070
TF: 800-284-5318 ■ *Web:* www.resultstel.com					
SITEL Corp					
2 American Ctr 3102 W End Ave Suite 1000	Nashville	TN	37203	615-301-7100	301-7150
TF: 800-445-6600 ■ *Web:* www.sitel.com					
TCIM Services Inc 1013 Centre Rd Suite 400	Wilmington	DE	19805	302-633-3000	633-3039
TF: 800-333-2255 ■ *Web:* www.tcim.com					
Tele Business USA 1945 Techny Rd Suite 3	Northbrook	IL	60062	877-315-8353	480-6055*
**Fax Area Code:* 847 ■ *TF:* 800-228-8353 ■ *Web:* www.tbiz.com					
Tele-Serve 409 Main St	Eau Claire	WI	54701	800-686-0162	615-4921
TF: 800-686-0162 ■ *Web:* www.tele-serve.net					
Telemarketing Co 3945 N Neenah	Chicago	IL	60634	773-545-0407	545-4034
Web: www.thetelemarketingco.com					
TeleNational Marketing 2918 N 72nd St	Omaha	NE	68134	402-548-1100	391-2044
TF Cust Svc: 800-333-6106 ■ *Web:* www.telenational.com					
Teleperformance USA 1991 S 4650 W	Salt Lake City	UT	84104	801-257-5800	257-6246
Web: www.teleperformance.com					
Telerx 723 Dresher Rd	Horsham	PA	19044	215-347-5700	347-5800
TF: 800-283-5379 ■ *Web:* www.valueofx.telerx.com					
TeleServices Direct					
5305 Lakeview Pkwy S Dr	Indianapolis	IN	46268	317-216-2240	216-2248
TF: 888-646-6626 ■ *Web:* www.teleservicesdirect.com					
TeleSystems Marketing Inc					
3600 S Gessner St Suite 250	Houston	TX	77063	713-784-3439	780-5931
TF: 800-622-0190					
TeleTech Holdings Inc 9197 S Peoria St	Englewood	CO	80112	303-397-8100	397-8695
NASDAQ: TTEC ■ *TF:* 800-835-3832 ■ *Web:* www.teletech.com					
TRG Customer Solutions					
1700 Pennsylvania Ave NW	Washington	DC	20006	202-289-9898	
TF: 888-767-1051 ■ *Web:* www.trgcustomersolutions.com					
USA 800 Inc 9808 E 66th Terr PO Box 16795	Raytown	MO	64133	816-358-1303	358-8845
TF: 800-821-7539 ■ *Web:* www.usa-800.com					
West Corp 11808 Miracle Hills Dr	Omaha	NE	68154	800-232-0900	573-1030*
**Fax Area Code:* 402 ■ *TF Sales & Marketing:* 800-841-9000 ■ *Web:* www.west.com					
Working Solutions					
1820 Preston Pk Blvd Suite 2000	Plano	TX	75093	972-964-4800	964-4802
Web: www.workingsol.com					
Young America Corp 5050 Lincoln Dr Suite 450	Edina	MN	55346	952-467-3366	294-8496
TF: 800-533-4529 ■ *Web:* www.young-america.com					

TELEVISION - CABLE

SEE Cable & Other Pay Television Services p. 1552; Television Networks - Cable p. 2689

741 TELEVISION COMPANIES

				Phone	Fax
Acme Communications Inc					
2101 E 4th St Suite 202	Santa Ana	CA	92705	714-245-9499	245-9494
NASDAQ: ACME ■ *Web:* www.acmecommunications.com					
Allbritton Communications Co					
1000 Wilson Blvd Suite 2700	Arlington	VA	22209	703-647-8700	647-8707
Barrington Broadcasting					
2500 W Higgins Rd Suite 155	Hoffman Estates	IL	60169	847-884-1178	755-3045
Web: www.barringtontv.com					
Belo Corp 400 S Record St	Dallas	TX	75202	214-977-6606	977-6603
TF: 800-431-0010 ■ *Web:* www.belo.com					
California Oregon Broadcasting Inc					
125 S Fir St	Medford	OR	97501	541-779-5555	779-5564
Web: www.kobi5.com					
Capitol Broadcasting Co Inc					
2619 Western Blvd	Raleigh	NC	27606	919-890-6000	890-6095
Web: www.cbc-raleigh.com					
CBS Television Stations Group 51 W 52nd St	New York	NY	10019	212-975-4321	655-2221*
**Fax Area Code:* 818 ■ *Web:* www.cbs.com					
Chambers Productions 2975 Chad Dr	Eugene	OR	97408	541-485-5614	342-1568
Web: www.cmc.net/~chambers					
Christian Television Network Inc (CTN)					
6922 142nd Ave N	Largo	FL	33771	727-535-5622	531-2497
Web: www.ctnonline.com					
Cisneros Group of Cos 36 E 61st St	New York	NY	10065	212-355-0620	838-1836
Web: www.cisneros.com					
Citadel Communications Co					
44 Pondfield Rd Suite 12	Bronxville	NY	10708	914-793-3400	793-3693
Communications Corp of America					
700 St John St Suite 300	Lafayette	LA	70501	337-237-1142	237-1373
TF: 800-237-1142					
Community Educational Television					
10902 S Wilcrest Dr	Houston	TX	77099	281-561-5828	561-9793
Web: www.communitytv.org					
CTV Globemedia Inc 9 Ch Nine Ct	Toronto	ON	M1S4B5	416-332-5700	291-5537
Web: www.ctv.ca					
CW Network LLC The 3300 Olive Ave	Burbank	CA	91505	818-977-2500	954-7667
Web: www.cwtv.com					
Diversified Business Communications					
121 Free St	Portland	ME	04101	207-842-5400	842-5505
TF: 800-842-5404 ■ *Web:* www.divbusiness.com					
Duhamel Broadcasting Enterprises Inc					
518 St Joseph St	Rapid City	SD	57701	605-342-2000	342-7305
Emmis Communications Corp					
40 Monument Cir 1 Emmis Plaza Suite 700	Indianapolis	IN	46204	317-266-0100	631-3750
NASDAQ: EMMS ■ *Web:* www.emmis.com					
Entravision Communications Corp					
2425 Olympic Blvd Suite 6000 W	Santa Monica	CA	90404	310-447-3870	447-3899
NYSE: EVC ■ *Web:* www.entravision.com					
EW Scripps Co 312 Walnut St Suite 2800	Cincinnati	OH	45202	513-977-3000	977-3720*
NYSE: SSP ■ **Fax:* Hum Res ■ *TF:* 800-888-3000 ■ *Web:* www.scripps.com					
Fisher Communications Inc					
140 4th Ave N Suite 500	Seattle	WA	98109	206-404-7000	404-6037
NASDAQ: FSCI ■ *Web:* www.fsci.com					
Flinn Broadcasting 6080 Mt Moriah Rd Ext	Memphis	TN	38115	901-375-9324	795-4454
Web: www.flinn.com					
Forum Communications Co 101 5th St N	Fargo	ND	58102	701-451-5629	451-5633
TF: 800-747-7311 ■ *Web:* www.forumcomm.com					
Fox Television Stations Inc					
1999 S Bundy Dr	Los Angeles	CA	90025	310-584-2000	584-2012
Web: www.myfoxla.com					
Freedom Communications Inc 17666 Fitch	Irvine	CA	92614	949-253-2300	474-7675
Web: www.freedom.com					
Gannett Co Inc 7950 Jones Branch Dr	McLean	VA	22107	703-854-6000	
Web: www.gannett.com					
Granite Broadcasting Corp					
767 3rd Ave 34th Fl	New York	NY	10017	212-826-2530	826-2858
Web: www.granitetv.com					
Gray Television Inc 4370 Peachtree Rd NE	Atlanta	GA	30319	404-504-9828	261-9607
NYSE: GTN ■ *Web:* www.graycommunications.com					
Groupe TVA Inc 1600 de Maisonneuve Blvd E	Montreal	QC	H2L4P2	514-526-9251	598-6085
Web: www.tva.canoe.com					
Hearst-Argyle Television Inc					
300 W 57th St 39th Fl	New York	NY	10019	212-887-6800	887-6855
NYSE: HTV ■ *Web:* www.hearsttelevision.com					
Hoak Media Corp 500 Crescent Ct Suite 220	Dallas	TX	75201	972-960-4848	960-4899
Web: www.hoak.net					
Hubbard Broadcasting Inc					
3415 University Ave	Saint Paul	MN	55114	651-646-5555	642-4314*
intermountian west communication stations					
1500 Foremaster Ln	Las Vegas	NV	89101	702-642-3333	657-3423
Web: www.minus3.com					
KYVM-TV 340 W Main St	Missoula	MT	59802	406-721-2063	721-2083
Web: www.nbcmontana.com					
LeSea Broadcasting Corp					
61300 S Ironwood Rd	South Bend	IN	46614	574-291-8200	291-9043
TF: 800-365-3732 ■ *Web:* www.lesea.com					
LIN TV Corp 1 W Exchange St Suite 5A	Providence	RI	02903	401-454-2880	454-6990
NYSE: TVL ■ *Web:* www.linmedia.com					
Max Media LLC 2200 Stephens Ave	Missoula	MT	59801	406-542-8900	728-4800
TF: 800-926-9952 ■ *Web:* www.maxmontana.com					
McGraw-Hill Cos Inc Broadcasting Group					
1301 Shoreway Rd Suite 300	Belmont	CA	94002	650-595-0610	
Web: www.mcgraw-hill.com					
McKinnon Broadcasting Co PO Box 719051	San Diego	CA	92171	858-571-5151	571-4852
Web: www.kusi.com					
Media General Broadcast Group 111 N 4th St	Richmond	VA	23219	804-649-6000	775-4601
Web: www.mediageneral.com					
Meredith Corp 1716 Locust St	Des Moines	IA	50309	515-284-3000	284-3806
NYSE: MDP ■ *Web:* www.meredith.com					
Morgan Murphy Broadcasting Group					
7025 Raymond Rd	Madison	WI	53719	608-271-4321	271-6111
Web: www.channel3000.com					
Morris Multimedia Inc 27 Abercorn St	Savannah	GA	31401	912-233-1281	232-4639
Web: www.morrismultimedia.com					
Newfoundland Broadcasting Co Ltd					
446 Logy Bay Rd PO Box 2020	Saint Johns	NL	A1C5S2	709-722-5015	726-5107
Web: www.ntv.ca					
Nexstar Broadcasting Group Inc					
5215 N OConnor Blvd Suite 1400	Irving	TX	75039	972-373-8800	
NASDAQ: NXST ■ *Web:* www.nexstar.tv					
Northwest Television Inc PO Box 1313	Eugene	OR	97440	541-342-4965	342-5436
Pappas Telecasting Cos 823 W Ctr Ave	Visalia	CA	93291	559-733-7800	733-7878
Web: www.pappastv.com					
Post-Newsweek Stations Inc					
550 W Lafayette Blvd	Detroit	MI	48226	313-223-2260	223-2263
Web: www.washpostco.com					
Quincy Newspapers Inc 130 S 5th St	Quincy	IL	62301	217-223-5100	223-9757
TF: 800-373-9444 ■ *Web:* www.whig.com					

Name / Address	City	State	Zip	Phone	Fax
Raycom Media Inc 201 Monroe St RSA Tower 20th Fl *Web:* www.raycommedia.com	Montgomery	AL	36104	334-206-1400	206-1555
Red River Broadcasting Co LLC 2001 London Rd *Web:* www.fox21online.com	Duluth	MN	55812	218-728-8930	728-8932
Reiten Television Inc PO Box 1686	Minot	ND	58702	701-852-2104	838-1050
Roberts Broadcasting Co 1408 N Kingshighway Blvd Suite 300 *Web:* www.robertstower.com	Saint Louis	MO	63113	314-367-4600	367-0174
Saga Communications Inc 73 Kercheval Ave *NYSE:* SGA ■ *TF:* 888-886-7070 ■ *Web:* www.sagacommunications.com	Grosse Pointe Farms	MI	48236	313-886-7070	886-7150
Sarkes Tarzian Inc PO Box 62	Bloomington	IN	47402	812-332-7251	331-4575
Sinclair Broadcast Group Inc 10706 Beaver Dam Rd *NASDAQ:* SBGI ■ *Web:* www.sbgi.net	Hunt Valley	MD	21030	410-568-1500	568-1533
Smith Broadcasting Group Inc 2315 Red Rose Way *Web:* www.smithtelevision.com	Santa Barbara	CA	93109	805-965-0400	
Telemundo Communications Group Inc 2290 W 8th Ave *Web:* www.telemundo.com	Hialeah	FL	33010	305-884-8200	
Tribune Co 435 N Michigan Ave Suite 1800 *Web:* www.tribune.com	Chicago	IL	60611	312-222-9100	329-0611
Univision Television Group Inc 5999 Ctr Dr *TF:* 800-594-5387 ■ *Web:* www.univision.com	Los Angeles	CA	90045	310-216-3434	348-5674
Weigel Broadcasting 26 N Halstead St *Web:* metvnetwork.com	Chicago	IL	60661	312-705-2600	705-2656
Wicks Group of Cos LLC 405 Pk Ave Suite 702 *Web:* www.wicksgroup.com	New York	NY	10022	212-838-2100	223-2109
WMFE 11510 E Colonial Dr *Web:* www.wmfe.org	Orlando	FL	32817	407-273-2300	273-3613
WYOMedia Inc 1856 Skyview Dr	Casper	WY	82601	307-577-5923	577-5928
Xanadoo Co 225 City Ave Suite 100 *TF:* 888-438-7488 ■ *Web:* www.xanadoo.com	Bala Cynwyd	PA	19004	610-934-7000	934-7121
ZGS Communications 2000 N 14th St Suite 400 *Web:* www.zgsgroup.com	Arlington	VA	22201	703-528-5656	526-0879

742 TELEVISION NETWORKS - BROADCAST

Name / Address	City	State	Zip	Phone	Fax
ABC Inc 77 W 66th St *Web:* www.abc.go.com	New York	NY	10023	212-456-7777	456-2795
CBS Broadcasting Inc 51 W 52nd St *Web:* www.cbs.com	New York	NY	10019	212-975-4321	
CBS Corp 51 W 52nd St *NYSE:* CBS ■ *Web:* www.cbscorporation.com	New York	NY	10019	212-975-4321	975-4516
Fox Broadcasting Co 10201 W Pico Blvd *Web:* www.fox.com	Los Angeles	CA	90035	310-369-1350	369-0468
NBC Television Network 30 Rockefeller Plaza *Web:* www.nbc.com	New York	NY	10112	212-664-4444	664-4085
Nstreams Technologies Inc 209 E Java Dr *Web:* www.nstreams.com	Sunnyvale	CA	94089	408-734-8889	734-8886
Public Broadcasting Service (PBS) 2100 Crystal Dr *Web:* www.pbs.org	Arlington	VA	22202	703-739-5000	739-0775
Univision Communications Inc 1999 Avenue of the Stars Suite 3050 *NYSE:* UVN ■ *Web:* www.univision.com	Los Angeles	CA	90067	310-556-7665	556-7615
@MAX 1100 Avenue of the Americas *Web:* www.cinemax.com	New York	NY	10036	212-512-1000	

743 TELEVISION NETWORKS - CABLE

Name / Address	City	State	Zip	Phone	Fax
5StarMAX 1100 Avenue of the Americas *Web:* www.cinemax.com	New York	NY	10036	212-512-1000	512-5570
A&E Television Networks LLC 235 E 45th St *Web:* www.aetn.com	New York	NY	10017	212-210-1400	210-1308
ABC Family Ch 500 S Buena Vista St *Web:* www.abcfamily.go.com	Burbank	CA	91521	818-560-1000	
ABS-CBN International 150 Shoreline Dr *TF:* 800-345-2465 ■ *Web:* www.abs-cbnglobal.com	Redwood City	CA	94065	650-508-6000	508-6001
Accent Health 5440 Beaumont Ctr Blvd Suite 400 **Fax Area Code:* 813 ■ *TF:* 800-235-4930 ■ *Web:* www.accenthealth.com	Tampa	FL	33634	800-235-4930	349-7299*
Access Television 1850 Stony Plain Rd *Web:* www.accesstv.ca	Edmonton	AB	T5S1A8	780-483-3311	486-4296
AMC Networks Inc 11 Penn Plaza 2nd Fl **Fax Area Code:* 516 ■ *Web:* www.amcnetworks.com	New York	NY	10001	212-324-8500	803-3003*
American Movie Classics (AMC) 11 Penn Plaza 15th Fl *Web:* www.amctv.com	New York	NY	10001	646-273-7105	
AmericanLife TV Network (ALN) 6565 N MacArthur Suite 400 **Fax Area Code:* 202 ■ *Web:* www.americanlifetv.com	Irving	TX	75039	214-444-7100	289-6632*
Animal Planet Canada 9 Ch Nine Ct *Web:* animalplanet.ca	Scarborough	ON	M1S4B5	416-332-5000	332-4275
Arts & Entertainment Network (A & E) 235 E 45th St 9th Fl *Web:* www.aetv.com	New York	NY	10017	212-210-1400	210-9755
Artv 1400 Rene-Levesque Blvd E Bureau A-53-1 *Web:* www.artv.ca	Montreal	QC	H2L2M2	514-597-3636	597-3633
Asian Television Network (ATN) 130 Pony Dr *Web:* www.asiantelevision.com	Newmarket	ON	L3Y7B6	905-836-6460	853-5212
Astral 355 Rue Sainte-Catherine Ouest *Web:* www.musiqueplus.com	Montreal	QC	H3B1A5	514-284-7587	284-1889
Astral Television Networks 181 Bay St Suite 100 PO Box 787 *Web:* www.astral.com	Toronto	ON	M5J2T3	416-956-2010	956-2018
Auto Ch 332 W Broadway Suite 1604 *Web:* www.theautochannel.com	Louisville	KY	40202	502-992-0200	992-0201
BBC America 747 3rd Ave 6th Fl *Web:* www.bbcamerica.com	New York	NY	10017	212-705-9300	705-9338
BET Networks & BET Interactive LLC 1235 W St NE *TF:* 800-626-9911 ■ *Web:* www.bet.com	Washington	DC	20018	202-608-2000	608-2599
Bloomberg Television 731 Lexington Ave *TF:* 800-955-4003 ■ *Web:* www.bloomberg.com/tv	New York	NY	10022	212-318-2000	617-5999
Boating Ch 2615 Deerfield Rd PO Box 1148	Sag Harbor	NY	11963	631-725-4440	
Book Television 299 Queen St W *Web:* www.booktelevision.com	Toronto	AB	M5V2Z5	416-591-7400	591-5117
Bpm:tv 105 Gordon Baker Rd Suite 800 *Web:* www.bpmtv.com	Toronto	ON	M2H3P8	416-756-5523	756-5526
Bravo 30 Rockefeller Plaza 14th Fl *Web:* www.bravotv.com	New York	NY	10112	212-664-4444	
Bravo! Canada 299 Queen St W *Web:* www.bravo.ca	Toronto	ON	M5V2Z5	416-591-5757	340-7482
Business News Network (BNN) 299 Queen St W *TF:* 877-284-7878 ■ *Web:* www.bnn.ca	Toronto	ON	M5V2Z5	416-384-8000	
C-SPAN Extra 400 N Capitol St NW Suite 650 *Web:* www.c-span.org	Washington	DC	20001	202-737-3220	737-3323
C-SPAN3 400 N Capitol St NW Suite 650 *Web:* www.c-span.org	Washington	DC	20001	202-737-3220	
Cable News Network (CNN) 1 CNN Ctr *Web:* www.cnn.com	Atlanta	GA	30303	404-878-2276	827-1995
Cable Public Affairs Ch (CPAC) 45 O'Connor St Suite 1750 PO Box 81099 **Fax Area Code:* 613 ■ *TF:* 877-287-2722 ■ *Web:* www.cpac.ca	Ottawa	ON	K1P1A4	877-287-2722	567-2749*
Cable Satellite Public Affairs Network (C-SPAN) 400 N Capitol St NW Suite 650 *Web:* www.c-span.org	Washington	DC	20001	202-737-3220	737-3323
Canal D 2100 Rue Sainte-Catherine O Bureau 700 *TF:* 800-361-5194 ■ *Web:* www.canald.com	Montreal	QC	H3H2T3	514-939-3150	939-3151
Canal Indigo 2100 Rue Sainte-Catherine Ouest Bureau 1000 *TF:* 800-361-1830 ■ *Web:* www.canalindigo.com	Montreal	QC	H3H2T3	514-939-5090	939-5098
Cartoon Network Inc The 1050 Techwood Dr *Web:* www.cartoonnetwork.com	Atlanta	GA	30318	404-827-1700	827-2559
Christian Broadcasting Network (CBN) 977 Centerville Tpke CBN Ctr *TF:* 800-759-0700 ■ *Web:* www.cbn.com	Virginia Beach	VA	23463	757-226-7000	226-2017
Cinemax 1100 Avenue of the Americas *Web:* www.cinemax.com	New York	NY	10036	212-512-1000	
Classic Arts Showcase PO Box 828 *Web:* www.classicartsshowcase.org	Burbank	CA	91503	323-878-0283	878-0329
CNBC Inc 900 Sylvan Ave *TF:* 800-788-2622 ■ *Web:* www.cnbc.com	Englewood Cliffs	NJ	07632	201-735-2622	
CNBC World 900 Sylvan Ave *TF:* 877-280-4548 ■ *Web:* www.cnbc.com	Englewood Cliffs	NJ	07632	201-735-2622	346-6527
CNN Headline News 1 CNN Ctr *Web:* www.us.cnn.com	Atlanta	GA	30303	404-827-1500	878-0891
CNN International 1 CNN Ctr *Web:* www.edition.cnn.com	Atlanta	CA	30303	404-827-1500	
College Sports Television 85 10th Ave 3rd Fl *TF:* 888-870-2788 ■ *Web:* www.cstv.com	New York	NY	10011	212-342-8700	342-8899
Comedy Central 1775 Broadway *Web:* www.comedycentral.com	New York	NY	10019	212-767-8600	767-8592
Comedy Network 299 Queen St W *Web:* www.thecomedynetwork.ca	Toronto	ON	M5V2Z5	416-591-7400	591-9317
Corus Entertainment Inc 64 Jefferson Ave Unit 18 *Web:* www.promos.treehousetv.com	Toronto	ON	M6K3H4	416-534-1191	
Country Music Television (CMT) 330 Commerce St *Web:* www.cmt.com	Nashville	TN	37201	615-335-8400	335-8628
Country Music Television Canada (CMTCA) 64 Jefferson Ave Unit 18 *Web:* www.cmt.ca	Toronto	ON	M6K3H4	416-534-1191	530-5206
CRN Digital Talk Radio 10487 Sunland Blvd *TF:* 800-336-2225 ■ *Web:* www.crntalk.com	Sunland	CA	91040	818-352-7152	352-3229
Cross TV 370 W Camino Gardens Blvd Suite 300 *Web:* www.crosstv.com	Boca Raton	FL	33432	561-367-7454	750-7959
Crown Media Holdings Inc 12700 Ventura Blvd Suite 200 *NASDAQ:* CRWN ■ *TF:* 800-522-5131 ■ *Web:* www.hallmarkchannel.com	Studio City	CA	91604	818-755-2400	755-2564
CTV Television Inc 9 Ch Nine Ct *TF:* 800-461-1542 ■ *Web:* www.ctv.ca	Toronto	ON	M1S4B5	416-332-5000	291-5337
Daystar Television Network 3901 Hwy 121 PO Box 610546 *TF:* 800-329-0029 ■ *Web:* www.daystar.com	Bedford	TX	76021	817-571-1229	571-7458
Deep Dish TV 339 Lafayette St 3rd Fl *Web:* www.deepdishtv.org	New York	NY	10012	212-473-8933	420-8332
Discovery Ch LLC 1 Discovery Pl *Web:* www.dsc.discovery.com	Silver Spring	MD	20910	240-662-2000	
Discovery Communications Inc 1 Discovery Pl *TF:* 800-762-2189 ■ *Web:* www.dsc.discovery.com	Silver Spring	MD	20910	240-662-2000	662-2000
Discovery Health Ch 1 Discovery Pl *Web:* www.health.discovery.com	Silver Spring	MD	20910	240-662-2000	
Discovery Home Ch 1 Discovery Pl *Web:* www.planetgreen.discovery.com	Silver Spring	MD	20910	240-662-2000	
Discovery Latin America 6505 Blue Lagoon Dr Suite 300	Miami	FL	33126	786-273-4700	
Discovery Science Canada 9 Ch Nine Ct *Web:* discoverycivilization.ca	Scarborough	ON	M1S4B5	416-332-5000	
Disney 500 S Buena Vista St *Web:* www.corporate.disney.go.com	Burbank	CA	91521	818-560-1000	567-4375
Documentary Ch 1207 16th Ave S *Web:* www.documentarychannel.com	Nashville	TN	37212	615-322-9333	

	City	State	Zip	Phone	Fax
E! Entertainment Television					
5750 Wilshire Blvd	Los Angeles	CA	90036	323-954-2400	954-2660
Web: www.eonline.com					
ESPN 545 Middle St	Bristol	CT	06010	860-585-2000	766-2213
Web: www.espn.go.com					
ESPN Classic Canada 9 Ch Nine Ct	Scarborough	ON	M1S4B5	416-332-5000	
Web: www.tsn.ca					
ESPN Classic Inc 935 Middle St	Bristol	CT	06010	860-585-2000	766-7273
ESPN Deportes 2 Alhambra Plaza 9th Fl	Coral Gables	FL	33134	305-567-3797	
TF: 800-337-6783 ■ *Web:* www.espndeportes.espn.go.com					
ESPNEWS 545 Middle St	Bristol	CT	06010	860-585-2000	585-2425*
**Fax:* Hum Res ■ *Web:* www.sports.espn.go.com					
Eternal Word Television Network (EWTN)					
5817 Old Leeds Rd	Irondale	AL	35210	205-271-2900	
Web: www.ewtn.com					
Family Ch 181 Bay St Suite 100 PO Box 787	Toronto	ON	M5J2T3	416-956-2010	956-2035
TF: 800-893-4862 ■ *Web:* www.family.ca					
FamilyNet 3836 Dekalb Technology Pkwy Bldg 3	Atlanta	GA	30340	770-225-1400	936-2755
Web: www.familynet.com					
Fashion Television Ch					
Bell Media Inc 299 Queen St W	Toronto	ON	M5V2Z5	416-384-7400	384-0080
Web: www.fashiontelevision.com					
Fox Deportes PO Box 900	Beverly Hills	CA	90213	310-369-1350	
Fox Movie Ch PO Box 900	Beverly Hills	CA	90213	310-369-1000	369-0468
Web: www.thefoxmoviechannel.com					
FOX News Ch 1211 Avenue of the Americas	New York	NY	10036	212-301-3000	301-8274*
**Fax:* News Rm ■ *Web:* www.foxnews.com					
FOX Sports Interactive Media LLC					
1000 Legion Pl Suite 1600	Orlando	FL	32801	407-648-1150	245-2521
Web: www.foxsportsflorida.com					
FOX Sports Net 10201 W Pico Blvd	Los Angeles	CA	90035	310-369-6000	
Web: www.msn.foxsports.com					
Free Speech TV 2900 Welton St # 300	Denver	CO	80205	303-442-8445	442-6472
Web: www.freespeech.org					
Fuel TV Inc					
1440 Sepulveda Blvd Suite 1900	Los Angeles	CA	90025	310-369-1000	444-8559
Web: www.fuel.tv					
Fuse 11 Penn Plaza 17th Fl	New York	NY	10001	646-273-7300	324-3445*
**Fax Area Code:* 212 ■ *Web:* www.fuse.tv					
FX Networks LLC					
10201 W Pico Blvd Bldg 103	Los Angeles	CA	90035	310-369-1000	969-4688
Web: www.fxnetworks.com					
G4 Media Inc 5750 Wilshire Blvd	Los Angeles	CA	90036	323-954-2400	
Web: www.g4tv.com					
Game Show Network LLC					
2150 Colorado Ave Suite 100	Santa Monica	CA	90404	310-255-6800	255-6810
Web: www.gsn.com					
God's Learning Ch (GLC) PO Box 61000	Midland	TX	79711	432-563-0420	563-1736
TF: 800-707-0420 ■ *Web:* www.glc.us.com					
Golf Ch 7580 Commerce Ctr Dr	Orlando	FL	32819	407-363-4653	363-7976
Web: www.thegolfchannel.com					
GolTV Inc 1666 JFK Cswy Suite 402	North Bay Village	FL	33141	786-866-3932	864-7299*
**Fax Area Code:* 305 ■ *Web:* www.goltv.tv					
Hallmark Ch 12700 Ventura Blvd Suite 200	Studio City	CA	91604	818-755-2400	755-2564
TF: 888-390-7474 ■ *Web:* www.hallmarkchannel.com					
HBO Comedy 1100 Avenue of the Americas	New York	NY	10036	212-512-1000	512-5570
Web: www.hbo.com/comedy/index.html					
HBO Family 1100 Avenue of the Americas	New York	NY	10036	212-512-1000	512-1182
Web: www.hbofamily.com					
HBO Latino 1100 Avenue of the Americas	New York	NY	10036	212-512-1000	512-5570
Web: www.hbolatino.com					
Hispanic Information & Telecommunications Network Inc					
63 Flushing Ave Unit 281	Brooklyn	NY	11205	212-966-5660	966-5725
Web: www.hitn.org					
Historia					
2100 Rue Sainte-Catherine O Bureau 700	Montreal	QC	H3H2T3	514-939-3150	938-3332
Web: www.historiatv.com					
History Ch					
A&E Television Networks LLC					
235 E 45th St 8th Fl	New York	NY	10017	212-210-1400	210-1308
Web: www.historychannel.com					
History International 235 E 45th St	New York	NY	10017	212-210-1400	
Web: www.historyinternational.com					
Home & Garden Television (HGTV)					
9721 Sherrill Blvd	Knoxville	TN	37932	865-694-2700	531-8933
Web: www.hgtv.com					
Home Box Office Inc (HBO)					
1100 Avenue of the Americas	New York	NY	10036	212-512-1000	
Web: www.hbo.com					
Idea Ch 2002 Filmore Ave Suite 1	Erie	PA	16506	814-833-7107	833-7415
TF: 800-388-0662 ■ *Web:* www.ideachannel.com					
iN DEMAND 345 Hudson St 17th Fl	New York	NY	10014	646-638-8200	486-0855
Web: www.indemand.com					
Independent Film Ch Canada					
121 Bloor St E 15th Fl	Toronto	ON	M4W3M5	416-967-1174	423-7862*
**Fax Area Code:* 902 ■ *TF:* 877-345-9195 ■ *Web:* www.ifctv.ca					
Independent Film Ch LLC The 11 Penn Plaza	New York	NY	10001	212-324-8500	
Web: www.ifc.com					
Ion Media Networks					
601 Clearwater Pk Rd	West Palm Beach	FL	33401	561-659-4122	655-7343*
**Fax:* PR ■ *TF:* 800-646-7296 ■ *Web:* www.ionline.tv					
Learning Ch The (TLC) 1 Discovery Pl	Silver Spring	MD	21279	240-662-2000	
Web: tlc.discovery.com					
Les Chaines Tele Astral					
1800, Ave McGill College Bureau 1600	Montreal	QC	H3A3J6	514-939-3150	939-3151
Web: www.astral.com					
Liberty Ch PO Box 10352	Lynchburg	VA	24506	434-582-2718	
TF: 800-332-1883 ■ *Web:* www.liberty.edu					
Lifetime Entertainment Services					
309 W 49th St	New York	NY	10019	212-424-7000	957-4110
Web: www.mylifetime.com					

	City	State	Zip	Phone	Fax
Mentv 121 Bloor St E Suite E	Toronto	ON	M4W3M5	204-926-4800	926-4853
Web: www.canada.com					
MeteoMedia					
1755 Boul Rene-Levesque E Bureau 251	Montreal	QC	H2K4P6	514-597-1700	597-2981
TF: 800-461-8368 ■ *Web:* www.meteomedia.com					
MoreMAX 1100 Avenue of the Americas	New York	NY	10036	212-512-1000	512-5570
Web: www.cinemax.com					
Movie Central 25 Dockside Dr	Toronto	ON	M5A0B5	416-479-6784	
Web: www.moviecentral.ca					
Mpix 181 Bay St Suite 100	Toronto	ON	M5J2T3	416-956-2010	956-5415
Web: www.mpix.ca					
MSG Network Two Pennsylvania Plaza	New York	NY	10121	212-465-6741	465-6024
Web: www.msg.com					
MSNBC 30 Rockefeller Plaza	New York	NY	10112	212-664-4444	413-5196
Web: www.msnbc.msn.com					
MTV Networks 1515 Broadway	New York	NY	10036	212-258-8000	258-8100
Web: www.mtv.com					
MTV Networks Latin America					
1111 Lincoln Rd 6th Fl	Miami Beach	FL	33139	305-535-3700	535-5377
Web: www.mtvla.com					
MTV Networks On Campus Inc (MTVU)					
1540 Broadway 33rd Fl	New York	NY	10036	212-654-6031	
Web: www.mtvu.com					
MTV2 1515 Broadway 10th Fl	New York	NY	10036	212-258-8000	422-6630*
**Fax Area Code:* 201 ■ *Web:* www.mtv2.com					
MuchLoud 299 Queen St W	Toronto	ON	M5V2Z5	416-591-5757	591-6824
Web: www.muchloud.com					
MuchMoreMusic					
Bell Media Inc 299 Queen St W	Toronto	ON	M5V2Z5	416-591-5757	
Web: www.muchmore.ca					
MuchMoreRetro 299 Queen St W	Toronto	ON	M5V2Z5	877-380-2511	591-0080*
**Fax Area Code:* 416 ■ *TF:* 877-380-2511 ■ *Web:* www.muchmoreretro.com					
MuchVibe 299 Queen St W	Toronto	ON	M5V2Z5	416-591-5757	
Web: www.muchvibe.ca					
Mun2 TV 2470 W 8th Ave	Hialeah	FL	33010	305-882-8700	889-7203
Web: www.mun2tv.com					
NASA TV 300 E St SW Suite 5K39	Washington	DC	20546	202-358-0001	358-4338
Web: www.nasa.gov/ntv					
National Geographic Ch (NGC) 1145 17th St NW	Washington	DC	20036	202-857-7000	912-6603
Web: www.nationalgeographic.com/channel					
New England Cable News (NECN) 160 Wells Ave	Newton	MA	02459	617-630-5000	630-5055
Web: www.necn.com					
New England Sports Network (NESN)					
480 Arsenal St Bldg 1	Watertown	MA	02472	617-536-9233	536-7814
Web: www.nesn.com					
News Central 10706 Beaver Dam Rd	Hunt Valley	MD	21030	410-568-1500	568-2121
NFL Network 280 Pk Ave	New York	NY	10017	212-450-2000	681-7599
Web: www.nfl.com/nflnetwork					
NHL Network Inc The 9 Ch Nine Ct	Scarborough	ON	M1S4B5	416-332-5000	
Web: www.tsn.ca/nhl_network					
Nick Jr 1515 Broadway 7th Fl	New York	NY	10019	212-654-7707	654-4879
Web: www.nickjr.com					
Nickelodeon 1515 Broadway 38th Fl	New York	NY	10036	212-258-8000	258-7705
Web: www.nick.com					
Oasis TV Inc 2029 Century Pk E Suite 1400	Los Angeles	CA	90067	310-553-4300	
Web: www.oasistv.com					
One: the Body Mind & Spirit Ch					
171 E Liberty St Suite 230	Toronto	ON	M6K3P6	416-368-3194	368-9774
Web: www.onebodymindspiritlove.com					
Oprah Winfrey Network Canada (OWN)					
25 Dockside Dr	Toronto	ON	M5A0B5	780-483-3311	486-4296
Outdoor Ch 43445 Business Pk Dr Suite 103	Temecula	CA	92590	951-699-6991	699-6313
NASDAQ: OUTD ■ *TF:* 800-770-5750 ■ *Web:* www.outdoorchannel.com					
Outdoor Life Network Canada					
545 Lakeshore Blvd W	Toronto	ON	M5V1A3	416-260-0047	260-3621
Web: www.oln.ca					
OuterMAX 1100 Avenue of the Americas	New York	NY	10036	212-512-1000	512-5570
Web: www.cinemax.com					
Ovation The Arts Network					
2850 Ocean Pk Blvd Suite 225	Santa Monica	CA	90405	310-430-7575	430-7591
TF: 800-682-8466 ■ *Web:* www.ovationtv.com					
Oxygen Media Inc 75 9th Ave 7th Fl	New York	NY	10011	212-651-2000	651-2099
Web: www.oxygen.com					
Pet Network 105 Gordon Baker Rd 8th Fl	Toronto	ON	M2H3P8	416-756-2404	756-5526
Web: www.thepetnetwork.tv					
Playboy Entertainment 2706 Media Ctr Dr	Los Angeles	CA	90065	323-276-4000	276-4500
Product Information Network					
2600 Michelson Dr Suite 1650	Irvine	CA	92612	949-263-9900	757-1526
Web: www.pinnet.com					
QVC Inc 1200 Wilson Dr	West Chester	PA	19380	484-701-1000	701-1138*
**Fax:* Cust Svc ■ *TF:* 800-367-9444 ■ *Web:* www.qvc.com					
Resort Sports Network					
Outside Television PO Box 7528	Portland	ME	04112	207-772-5000	775-3658
TF: 800-653-0697 ■ *Web:* www.outsidetelevision.com					
Rogers Sportsnet Inc 1 Mt Pleasant	Toronto	ON	M4Y3A1	416-764-6000	764-6001
TF: 888-451-6363 ■ *Web:* www.sportsnet.ca					
Roges Sports Network Canada 1 Mt Pleasant	Toronto	ON	M4Y3A1	416-764-6000	764-6001
TF: 888-451-6363 ■ *Web:* www.sportsnet.ca					
Science Ch 1 Discovery Pl	Silver Spring	MD	20910	240-662-2000	
Web: www.science.discovery.com					
SCOLA 21557 270th St	McClelland	IA	51548	712-566-2202	566-2502
Web: www.scola.org					
Score The 370 King St W Suite 435 PO Box 10	Toronto	ON	M5V1J9	416-977-6787	977-0238
Web: www2.thescore.com					
Scripps Networks LLC 9721 Sherrill Blvd	Knoxville	TN	37932	865-694-2700	531-8933
Web: www.diynetwork.com					
Shaw Media Inc 121 Bloor St E Suite 1500	Toronto	ON	M4W3M5	416-967-1174	967-0971
Web: www.bbccanada.com					
ShopNBC 6740 Shady Oak Rd	Eden Prairie	MN	55344	952-943-6000	943-6711*
**Fax:* Hum Res ■ *TF:* 800-676-5523 ■ *Web:* www.shopnbc.com					

Name / Address	City	State	ZIP	Phone	Fax
Shopping Ch The					
Credit Card Dept 59 Ambassador Dr	Mississauga	ON	L5T2P9	905-362-2020	362-7702
TF: 888-202-0888 ■ *Web:* www.theshoppingchannel.com					
Showcase 121 Bloor St E Suite 1500	Toronto	ON	M4W3M5	416-967-1174	960-0971
Web: www.showcase.ca					
Showcase Diva 121 Bloor St E Suite B-1	Toronto	ON	M4W3M5	416-967-0022	967-0044
Web: www.showcase.ca/diva					
Showtime Networks Inc 1633 Broadway 15th Fl	New York	NY	10019	212-708-1600	708-1530
Web: www.sho.com					
Si TV 3030 Andrita St	Los Angeles	CA	90065	323-256-8900	256-9888
Web: www.sitv.com					
SoapNet LLC 500 S Buena Vista St	Burbank	CA	91521	818-560-1000	
Web: soapnet.go.com					
Space: the Imagination Station					
299 Queen St W	Toronto	ON	M5V2Z5	416-591-5757	591-6619
Web: www.spacecast.com					
Spike TV 345 Hudson 3rd Fl	New York	NY	10014	212-767-4001	
Web: www.spiketv.com					
Starz Encore Group LLC 8900 Liberty Cir	Englewood	CO	80112	720-852-7700	852-7710
Web: www.starz.com					
Starz Entertainment LLC 8900 Liberty Cir	Englewood	CO	80112	720-852-7700	852-7710
Web: www.starz.com					
Starz LLC 8900 Liberty Cir	Englewood	CO	80112	720-852-7700	852-7710
Web: www.starz.com					
Starz! Family 8900 Liberty Cir	Englewood	CO	80112	720-852-7700	852-7710
Web: www.starz.com					
Stornoway Communications					
105 Gordon Baker Rd Suite 800	Toronto	ON	M2H3P8	416-756-2404	756-5526
Web: www.stornoway.com					
Sundance Ch 1633 Broadway 8th Fl	New York	NY	10019	212-708-8002	654-4724
Web: www.sundancechannel.com					
TBS Superstation Inc 1050 Techwood Dr NW	Atlanta	GA	30318	404-885-4488	
Web: www.tbs.com					
TCT Ministries Inc 11717 N Rt 37 PO Box 1010	Marion	IL	62959	618-997-4700	993-9778
Web: www.tct.tv					
Telelatino Network Inc (TLN) 5125 Steeles Ave W	Toronto	ON	M9L1R5	416-744-8200	744-0966
TF: 800-551-8401 ■ *Web:* www.tlntv.com					
Teletoon Canada Inc					
181 Bay St Suite 100 Brookfield Pl					
PO Box 787	Toronto	ON	M5J2T3	416-956-2060	956-2070
Web: www.teletoon.com					
Tennis Ch 2850 Ocean Pk Blvd Suite 150	Santa Monica	CA	90405	310-314-9400	314-9433
Web: www.tennischannel.com					
ThrillerMAX 1100 Avenue of the Americas	New York	NY	10036	212-512-1000	512-5570
Web: www.cinemax.com					
Total Living Network (TLN) 2880 Vision Ct	Aurora	IL	60506	630-801-3838	801-3839
Web: www.tln.com					
Travel Ch LLC					
5425 Wisconsin Ave Suite 500	Chevy Chase	MD	20815	301-244-7500	
Web: www.travelchannel.com					
Trinity Broadcasting Network (TBN) PO Box A	Santa Ana	CA	92711	714-832-2950	
TF: 888-731-1000 ■ *Web:* www.tbn.org					
truTV 600 3rd Ave 2nd Fl	New York	NY	10016	212-973-3227	692-7855*
**Fax:* News Rm ■ *Web:* www.trutv.com					
Turner Broadcasting System Inc (TBS) 1 CNN Ctr	Atlanta	GA	30303	404-827-1700	885-4326
Web: www.turner.com					
Turner Classic Movies (TCM) 1050 Techwood Dr NW	Atlanta	GA	30318	404-827-1717	
Web: www.tcm.turner.com					
Turner Network Television (TNT)					
1050 Techwood Dr NW	Atlanta	GA	30318	404-827-1717	
Web: www.tnt.tv					
TV Asahi America Inc 875 3rd Ave 3rd Fl	New York	NY	10022	212-644-6300	644-0003
TF: 800-272-4467 ■ *Web:* www.tvasahiamerica.com					
TV Guide Ch 11 W 42nd St 16th Fl	New York	NY	10036	212-626-2500	
Web: www.tvguide.com					
TV Land 1515 Broadway 48th Fl	New York	NY	10036	212-846-2550	
Web: www.tvland.com					
TV One 1010 Wayne Ave 10th Fl	Silver Spring	MD	20910	301-755-0400	755-2833
Web: www.tv-one.tv					
TVA Nouvelles					
1600 de Maisonneuve E PO Box 170 Stn C	Montreal	QC	H2L4P6	514-598-2869	598-6073
Web: tvanouvelles.ca					
USA Network 30 Rockefeller Plaza 21st Fl	New York	NY	10112	212-664-4444	413-6509
Web: www.usanetwork.com					
ValueVision Media Inc 6740 Shady Oak Rd	Eden Prairie	MN	55344	952-943-6000	943-6711
NASDAQ: VVTV ■ *TF:* 800-676-5523 ■ *Web:* www.shopnbc.com					
VH1 Classic 1515 Broadway 21st Fl	New York	NY	10036	212-258-6000	654-4743
Web: www.vh1.com					
Video Hits One (VH1) 1515 Broadway 20th Fl	New York	NY	10036	212-258-8000	846-1753*
**Fax:* Hum Res ■ *Web:* www.vh1.com					
VisionTV 171 E Liberty St Suite 230	Toronto	ON	M6K3P6	416-368-3194	368-9774
Web: www.visiontv.ca					
VRAK-TV					
2100 Rue Sainte-Catherine O Bureau 700	Montreal	QC	H3H2T3	514-939-3150	939-3151
TF: 800-361-5194 ■ *Web:* www.vrak.tv					
W Network 25 Dockside Dr Unit 18	Toronto	ON	M5A0B5	416-534-1191	530-2240
Web: www.wnetwork.com					
Weather Ch Inc The 300 IH- N Pkwy	Atlanta	GA	30339	770-226-0000	226-2702
Web: www.weather.com					
Weather Network The 2655 Bristol Cir	Oakville	ON	L6H7W1	905-829-1159	829-5800
Web: www.theweathernetwork.com					
WGN America 2501 W Bradley Pl	Chicago	IL	60618	773-528-2311	
Web: www.wgnamerica.com					
Women's Entertainment LLC					
11 Penn Plaza 19th Fl	New York	NY	10001	646-273-3500	273-7109*
**Fax:* Mktg ■ *Web:* www.we.tv					
Worship Network PO Box 428	Safety Harbor	FL	34695	727-536-0036	
TF: 800-728-8723 ■ *Web:* www.worship.net					
YTV Canada Inc PO Box 369 Stn C	Toronto	ON	M6J3N1	416-534-1191	
Web: www.ytv.com					
Ztele 2100 Rue Sainte-Catherine O Bureau 700	Montreal	QC	H3H2T3	514-939-3150	939-3151
TF: 800-361-5194 ■ *Web:* www.ztele.com					

744 TELEVISION STATIONS

SEE ALSO Internet Broadcasting p. 2126

ABC	American Broadcasting Co	**PBS**	Public Broadcasting Service
CBC	Canadian Broadcasting Corp	**QS**	Television Quatre Saisons
CBS	Columbia Broadcasting System	**SRC**	Societe Radio-Canada
CTV	Canadian Television Network	**TBN**	Trinity Broadcasting Network
Fox	Fox Broadcasting Co	**Tele**	Telemundo Communications Group
GTN	Global Television Network	**TVA**	Groupe TVA
Ind	Independent	**Uni**	Univision Television Network
NBC	National Broadcasting Co	**UPN**	United Paramount Network
PAX	Paxson Communications Corp	**WB**	Warner Bros Television

Name / Address	City	State	ZIP	Phone	Fax
CBET-TV Ch 9 (CBC) 825 Riverside Dr W	Windsor	ON	N9A5K9	519-255-3411	
Web: www.cbc.ca/windsor					
CFCM-TV Ch 4 (TVA) 1000 Myrand Ave	Sainte-Foy	QC	G1V2W3	418-688-9330	681-1252
CFGS-TV Ch 34 (QS) 171-A Jean Proulx St	Gatimeau	QC	J8Z1W5	819-770-1040	770-1490
CHAN-TV Ch 8 (GTN) 7850 Enterprise St	Burnaby	BC	V5A1V7	604-420-2288	422-6427
CHOT-TV Ch 40 (TVA) 171-A Jean Proulx St	Gatimeau	QC	J8Z1W5	819-770-1040	770-1490
CIVI-TV Ch 12 (Ind) 1420 Broad St	Victoria	BC	V8W2B1	250-381-2484	381-2484
TF: 866-242-2484 ■ *Web:* www.achannel.ca					
CKMI-TV Ch 20 (GTN) 1000 Myrand Ave	Sainte-Foy	QC	G1V2W3	418-682-2020	682-2620
CKVR-TV Ch 3 (Ind) 33 Beacon Rd PO Box 519	Barrie	ON	L4M4T9	705-734-3300	733-0302
Web: www.thenewvr.com					
KAAL-TV Ch 6 (ABC) 1701 10th Pl NE	Austin	MN	55912	507-437-6666	433-9560
TF: 800-234-0776 ■ *Web:* www.kaaltv.com					
KABC-TV Ch 7 (ABC) 500 Cir Seven Dr	Glendale	CA	91201	818-863-7777	863-7080
Web: www.abclocal.go.com					
KAET-TV Ch 8 (PBS) PO Box 871405	Tempe	AZ	85287	480-965-3506	965-1000
TF: 888-329-7088 ■ *Web:* www.azpbs.org					
KAFT-TV Ch 13 (PBS) 350 S Donaghey Ave	Conway	AR	72034	501-682-2386	682-4122
TF: 800-662-2386 ■ *Web:* www.aetn.org					
KAIL-TV Ch 7 1590 Alluvial Ave	Clovis	CA	93611	559-299-9753	299-1523
Web: www.kail.tv/my_index.html					
KARE-TV Ch 11 (NBC) 8811 State Hwy 55	Golden Valley	MN	55427	763-546-1111	546-8606
Web: www.kare11.com					
KAZT-TV Ch 7 (Ind) 3211 Tower Rd	Prescott	AZ	86305	928-778-6770	445-5210
KBHE-TV Ch 9 (PBS)					
555 N Dakota St PO Box 5000	Vermillion	SD	57069	800-333-0789	677-5010*
**Fax Area Code:* 605 ■ *TF:* 800-456-0766 ■ *Web:* www.sdpb.org					
KBYU-TV Ch 11 (PBS)					
2000 Ironton Blvd Brigham Young University	Provo	UT	84606	801-422-8450	422-8478
TF: 800-298-5298 ■ *Web:* www.kbyutv.org					
KCAH-TV Ch 25 (PBS) 1585 Schallenberger Rd	San Jose	CA	95131	408-795-5400	995-5446
Web: www.kteh.org					
KCAL-TV Ch 9 (Ind) 4200 Radford Ave	Studio City	CA	91604	818-655-2000	
Web: www.kcal9.com					
KCBA-TV Ch 35 (Fox) 1550 Moffett St	Salinas	CA	93905	831-422-3500	422-9365
TF: 800-321-5222 ■ *Web:* www.kcba.com					
KCBS-TV Ch 2 (CBS) 4200 Radford Ave	Studio City	CA	91604	818-655-2000	
Web: www.cbs2.com					
KCTV-TV Ch 5 (CBS) 4500 Shawnee Mission Pkwy	Fairway	KS	66205	913-677-5555	677-7243
Web: www.kctv.com					
KCWC-TV Ch 4 (PBS) 2660 Peck Ave	Riverton	WY	82501	307-856-6944	856-3893
Web: www.wyoptv.org					
KCWY-TV Ch 13 (NBC)					
141 Progress Cir PO Box 1450	Mills	WY	82644	307-577-0013	577-5251
Web: www.nbcforwyoming.com					
KDIN-TV Ch 11 (PBS) 6450 Corporate Dr	Johnston	IA	50131	515-242-3100	242-5830
TF: 800-532-1290 ■ *Web:* www.iptv.org					
KDOC-TV Ch 56 (Ind) 625 N Grand Ave	Santa Ana	CA	92701	949-442-9800	261-5956
Web: www.kdoctv.net					
KDTX-TV Ch 58 (TBN) 2823 W Irving Blvd	Irving	TX	75061	972-313-1333	790-5853
Web: www.tbn.org					
KESQ-TV Ch 3 (ABC) 42650 Melanie Pl	Palm Desert	CA	92211	760-568-6830	773-5107
TF: 877-564-9729 ■ *Web:* www.kesq.com					
KETG-TV Ch 9 (PBS) 350 S Donaghey Ave	Conway	AR	72034	501-682-2386	682-4122
TF: 800-662-2386 ■ *Web:* www.aetn.org					
KETS-TV Ch 2 (PBS) 350 S Donaghey Ave	Conway	AR	72034	501-682-2386	682-4122
TF: 800-662-2386 ■ *Web:* www.aetn.org					
KFBB-TV 3200 Old Havre Hwy PO Box 1139	Black Eagle	MT	59414	406-453-4377	
TF: 800-854-7720 ■ *Web:* www.kfbb.com					
KFPX-TV Ch 39 (I) 4570 114th St	Urbandale	IA	50322	515-331-3939	331-1312
Web: www.ionmedia.tv					
KGBT-TV Ch 4 (CBS) 9201 W Expy 83	Harlingen	TX	78552	956-421-4444	366-4494
Web: www.team4news.com					
KHIZ-TV Ch 64 (Ind) 15605 Village Dr	Victorville	CA	92394	760-241-6464	241-0056
Web: www.khiztv.com					
KICU-TV Ch 36 (Ind) 2102 Commerce Dr	San Jose	CA	95131	408-953-3636	953-3610
TF: 800-464-5428 ■ *Web:* www.ktvu.com					
KIDK-TV Ch 3 (CBS) 1255 E 17th St	Idaho Falls	ID	83404	208-522-5100	535-0946
Web: www.kidktv.com					
KIIN-TV Ch 12 (PBS) 6450 Corporate Dr	Johnston	IA	50131	515-242-3100	242-4113
TF: 800-532-1290 ■ *Web:* www.iptv.org					
KIMT-TV Ch 3 (CBS) 112 N Pennsylvania Ave	Mason City	IA	50401	641-423-2540	423-9309
TF: 877-546-8847 ■ *Web:* www.kimt.com					
KION-TV Ch 46 (CBS) 1550 Moffett St	Salinas	CA	93905	831-422-3500	422-9365
TF: 800-321-5222 ■ *Web:* www.kionrightnow.com					
KIVI-TV Ch 6 (ABC) 1866 E Chisholm Dr	Nampa	ID	83687	208-336-0500	381-6682
Web: www.6onyourside.com					
KMAX-TV Ch 31 (CBS) 2713 Kovr Dr	West Sacramento	CA	95605	916-374-1313	374-1304
TF: 800-374-8813 ■ *Web:* www.cbs13.com					
KMBH-TV Ch 60 (PBS) 1701 Tennessee St	Harlingen	TX	78551	956-421-4111	421-4150
Web: www.kmbh.org					
KMIR-TV Ch 6 (NBC) 72920 Parkview Dr	Palm Desert	CA	92260	760-568-3636	568-1176*
**Fax:* Sales ■ *Web:* www.kmir6.com					
KMIZ-TV Ch 17 (ABC) 501 Business Loop 70 E	Columbia	MO	65201	573-449-0917	875-7078
TF: 800-441-4485 ■ *Web:* www.kmiz.com					
KMOS-TV Ch 6 (PBS)					
University of Central Missouri	Warrensburg	MO	64093	660-543-4134	543-8863
TF: 800-753-3436 ■ *Web:* www.kmos.org					
KMSP-TV Ch 9 (Fox) 11358 Viking Dr	Eden Prairie	MN	55344	952-944-9999	942-0455
Web: www.kmsp.com					

Station / Address	City	State	Zip	Phone	Fax
KMTR-TV Ch 16 (NBC) 3825 International Ct *Web:* www.kmtr.com	Springfield	OR	97477	541-746-1600	747-0866
KNBC-TV Ch 4 (NBC) 3000 W Alameda Ave *Web:* www.nbc4.tv	Burbank	CA	91523	818-840-4444	840-3535
KNIN-TV Ch 9 (MNT) 1866 E Chisholm *Web:* www.knin.com	Nampa	ID	83687	208-336-0500	381-6682
KNTV-TV Ch 11 (NBC) 2450 N 1st St *Web:* www.nbcbayarea.com	San Jose	CA	95131	408-432-6221	
KNVO-TV Ch 48 (Uni) 801 N Jackson Rd	McAllen	TX	78501	956-687-4848	687-7784
KNWA-TV Ch 51 (NBC) 15 S Block St Suite 101 *Web:* www.knwa.com	Fayetteville	AR	72701	479-571-5100	571-8914
KOAA-TV Ch 5/30 (NBC) 2200 7th Ave *Web:* www.koaa.com	Pueblo	CO	81003	719-544-5781	295-6655
KOMU-TV Ch 8 (NBC) 5550 Hwy 63 S *TF:* 800-409-0292 ■ *Web:* www.komu.com	Columbia	MO	65201	573-884-6397	884-5353
KOVR-TV Ch 13 (CBS) 2713 Kovr Dr *Web:* www.kovr13.com	West Sacramento	CA	95605	916-374-1313	374-1304
KPDX-TV Ch 49 (MNT) 14975 NW Greenbrier Pkwy *TF:* 866-906-1249 ■ *Web:* www.kptv.com	Beaverton	OR	97006	503-906-1249	548-6920
KPLC-TV Ch 7 (NBC) 320 Division St *Web:* www.kplctv.com	Lake Charles	LA	70601	337-439-9071	437-7600
KPLO-TV Ch 6 (CBS) 501 S Phillips Ave *TF:* 800-888-5356 ■ *Web:* www.keloland.com	Sioux Falls	SD	57104	605-336-1100	336-0202
KPTV-TV Ch 12 (Fox) 14975 NW Greenbrier Pkwy *TF:* 866-906-1249 ■ *Web:* www.kptv.com	Beaverton	OR	97006	503-906-1249	548-6920
KPXC-TV Ch 59 (I) 3001 S Jamaica Ct Suite 200 *Web:* www.ionline.tv	Aurora	CO	80014	303-751-5959	751-5993
KPXD-TV Ch 68 (I) 600 Six Flags Dr Suite 652 *Web:* www.ionline.tv	Arlington	TX	76011	817-633-6843	633-3176
KPXE-TV Ch 50 (I) 4220 Shawnee Mission Pkwy *TF:* 800-646-7296 ■ *Web:* www.iontelevision.com	Fairway	KS	66205	913-722-0798	
KPXM-TV Ch 41 (I) 22601 176th St *Web:* www.ionline.tv	Big Lake	MN	55309	763-263-8666	263-6600
KRCA-TV Ch 62 (Ind) 1845 Empire Ave *Web:* www.krca62.tv	Burbank	CA	91504	818-563-5722	729-5678
KRCG-TV Ch 13 (CBS) 10188 Old Hwy 54 N *Web:* www.connectmidmissouri.com	New Bloomfield	MO	65063	573-896-5144	896-5193
KRGV-TV Ch 5 (ABC) PO Box 5 *Web:* www.newschannel5.tv	Weslaco	TX	78599	956-968-5555	973-5016
KRWG-TV Ch 22 (PBS) Jordan St PO Box 30001 MSC TV 22 *TF:* 866-457-9488 ■ *Web:* www.krwg-tv.org	Las Cruces	NM	88003	575-646-2222	646-1924
KSBW-TV Ch 8 (NBC) 238 John St *Web:* www.ksbw.com	Salinas	CA	93901	831-758-8888	424-3750
KSMO-TV Ch 62 (MNT) 4500 Shawnee Mission Pkwy *Web:* www.myksmotv.com	Fairway	KS	66205	913-677-5555	621-4703
KSMQ-TV Ch 15 (PBS) 2000 8th Ave NW *TF:* 800-658-2539 ■ *Web:* www.ksmq.org	Austin	MN	55912	507-433-0678	433-0670
KSPX-TV Ch 29 (I) 3352 Mather Field Rd *TF:* 888-467-2988 ■ *Web:* www.ionmedia.tv	Rancho Cordova	CA	95670	916-368-2929	368-0225
KSTS-TV Ch 48 (Tele) 2450 N 1st St *Web:* www.ksts.com	San Jose	CA	95131	408-944-4848	433-5921
KSTW-TV Ch 11 (CW) 602 Oakesdale Ave SW *TF:* 866-313-5789 ■ *Web:* www.kstw.com	Renton	WA	98055	206-441-1111	441-1116
KTBN-TV Ch 40 (TBN) 2442 Michelle Dr *TF:* 888-731-1000 ■ *Web:* www.tbn.org	Tustin	CA	92780	714-832-2950	665-2191
KTEH-TV Ch 54 (PBS) 1585 Schallenberger Rd *Web:* www.kteh.org	San Jose	CA	95131	408-795-5400	995-5446
KTLM-TV Ch 40 (Tele) 3900 N 10th St 7th Fl	McAllen	TX	78501	956-686-0040	686-0770
KTNL-TV Ch 13 (CBS/I) 520 Lake St *Web:* www.ktnl.tv	Sitka	AK	99835	907-747-5749	747-8440
KTRV-TV Ch 12 (Fox) 1 6th St N *Web:* www.fox12news.com	Nampa	ID	83687	208-466-1200	467-6958
KTSC-TV Ch 8 (PBS) 2200 Bonforte Blvd *Web:* www.ktsc.org	Pueblo	CO	81001	719-543-8800	549-2208
KTSD-TV Ch 10 (PBS) 555 N Dakota St PO Box 5000 **Fax Area Code:* 605 ■ *TF:* 800-456-0766 ■ *Web:* www.sdpb.org	Vermillion	SD	57069	800-333-0789	677-5010*
KTSF-TV Ch 26 (Ind) 100 Valley Dr *TF:* 800-488-6226 ■ *Web:* www.ktsf.com	Brisbane	CA	94005	415-468-2626	467-7559
KTVU-TV Ch 2 (Fox) 2 Jack London Sq *Web:* www.ktvu.com	Oakland	CA	94607	510-834-1212	272-9957
KUSD-TV Ch 2 (PBS) 555 N Dakota St PO Box 5000 **Fax Area Code:* 605 ■ *TF:* 800-456-0766 ■ *Web:* www.sdpb.org	Vermillion	SD	57069	800-333-0789	677-5010*
KUSM-TV Ch 9 (PBS) Visual Communications Bldg Rm 183 *TF:* 800-426-8243 ■ *Web:* www.montanapbs.org	Bozeman	MT	59717	406-994-3437	994-6545
KVEA-TV Ch 52 (Tele) 3000 W Alameda Ave *Web:* www.telemundola.com	Burbank	CA	91523	818-260-5700	260-5730
KVOS-TV Ch 12 (Ind) 1151 Ellis St *TF:* 800-488-5867 ■ *Web:* www.kvos.com	Bellingham	WA	98225	360-671-1212	647-0824
KVVU-TV Ch 5 (Fox) 25 TV 5 Dr *Web:* www.fox5vegas.com	Henderson	NV	89014	702-435-5555	451-4220
KWHD-TV Ch 53 (Ind) 12999 E Adams Aircraft Cir *TF:* 866-576-5353 ■ *Web:* www.kwhdtv53.com	Englewood	CO	80112	303-799-8853	792-5303
KWKB-TV Ch 20 (CW) 1547 Baker Ave *Web:* www.kwkb.com	West Branch	IA	52358	319-643-5952	643-3124
KWPX-TV Ch 33 (I) 8112C 304th Ave SW PO Box 426 *TF:* 888-467-2988 ■ *Web:* www.ionmedia.com	Preston	WA	98050	425-222-6010	222-6032
KWWL-TV Ch 7 (NBC) 500 E 4th St *Web:* www.kwwl.com	Waterloo	IA	50703	319-291-1200	291-1255
KWYB-TV Ch 18 (ABC) 505 W Pk St *Web:* www.kwyb.com	Butte	MT	59701	406-782-7185	723-9269
KXLF-TV Ch 4 (CBS) 1003 S Montana St *Web:* www.montanasnewsstation.com	Butte	MT	59701	406-782-0444	782-8906
UNC-TV Ch 4 (PBS) 10 TW Alexander Dr PO Box 14900 *TF:* 800-906-5050 ■ *Web:* www.unctv.org	Research Triangle Park	NC	27709	919-549-7000	549-7201
WADL-TV Ch 38 (Fox) 35000 Adell Dr *Web:* www.wadldetroit.com	Clinton Township	MI	48035	586-790-3838	790-3841
WAND-TV Ch 17 (ABC) 904 S Side Dr *Web:* www.wandtv.com	Decatur	IL	62521	217-424-2500	424-2583
WAOE-TV Ch 59 (MNT) 2907 Springfield Rd *Web:* www.upn59tv.com	East Peoria	IL	61602	309-698-2525	674-5959
WAPK-TV Ch 36 (MNT) 222 Commerce St *Web:* www.wapktv.com	Kingsport	TN	37660	423-246-9578	246-1863
WAQP-TV Ch 49 (Ind) 2865 Trautner Dr	Saginaw	MI	48604	989-249-5969	249-1220
WAVY-TV Ch 10 (NBC) 300 Wavy St *Web:* www.wavy.com	Portsmouth	VA	23704	757-393-1010	397-8279
WAZE-TV Ch 19 (CW) 1408 N Kings Hwy *Web:* www.cwaze.com	Saint Louis	MO	63113	314-256-4602	256-4683
WBDT-TV Ch 26 (CW) 2589 Corporate Pl *Web:* www.daytonswb.com	Miamisburg	OH	45342	937-384-9226	384-7392
WBIN TV 11 A St *Web:* www.wbintv.com	Derry	NH	03038	603-845-1000	434-8627
WBND-TV Ch 57 (Ind) 3665 Pk Pl W Suite 200 *Web:* www.abc57.com	Mishawaka	IN	46545	574-243-4316	243-4326
WBNX-TV Ch 55 (CW) 2690 State Rd *TF:* 800-367-8855 ■ *Web:* www.wbnx.com	Cuyahoga Falls	OH	44223	330-922-5500	929-9269
WBOC-TV Ch 16 (CBS) 1729 N Salisbury Blvd *Web:* www.wboc.com	Salisbury	MD	21801	410-749-1111	742-5190
WBRE-TV Ch 28 (NBC) 62 S Franklin St *TF:* 800-294-7261 ■ *Web:* www.wbre.com	Wilkes-Barre	PA	18701	570-823-2828	829-0440
WBUI-TV Ch 23 (CW) 101 S Main St *TF:* 888-440-9223 ■ *Web:* www.wb23tv.com	Decatur	IL	62523	217-428-2323	428-6455
WCAU-TV Ch 10 (NBC) 10 Monument Rd *Web:* www.nbcphiladelphia.com	Bala Cynwyd	PA	19004	610-668-5510	668-3700
WCAX-TV Ch 3 (CBS) 30 Joy Dr *Web:* www.wcax.com	South Burlington	VT	05403	802-658-6300	652-6399
WCBB-TV Ch 10 (PBS) 1450 Lisbon St *TF:* 800-884-1717 ■ *Web:* www.mpbc.org	Lewiston	ME	04240	207-783-9101	783-5193
WCBD-TV Ch 2 (NBC) 210 W Coleman Blvd *Web:* www.wcbd.com	Mount Pleasant	SC	29464	843-884-2222	881-3410
WCBI-TV Ch 4 (CBS) 201 5th St S *Web:* www.wcbi.com	Columbus	MS	39701	662-327-4444	328-5222
WCES-TV Ch 20 (PBS) 260 14th St NW *Web:* www.gpb.org/gptv	Atlanta	GA	30318	404-685-2400	685-2684
WCIA-TV Ch 3 (CBS) PO Box 20 *TF:* 800-929-3559 ■ *Web:* www.illinoishomepage.net	Champaign	IL	61824	217-356-8333	373-3663
WCLF-TV Ch 22 (Ind) PO Box 6922 *Web:* www.ctnonline.com	Clearwater	FL	33758	727-535-5622	531-2497
WCPB-TV CH 28 (PBS) 11767 Owings Mills Blvd *Web:* www.mpt.org	Owings Mills	MD	21117	410-581-4097	581-4338
WCTX-TV Ch 59 (MNT) 8 Elm St	New Haven	CT	06510	203-782-5900	782-5995
WCVB-TV Ch 5 (ABC) 5 TV Pl *Web:* www.thebostonchannel.com	Needham	MA	02494	781-449-0400	433-4510
WCWG-TV Ch 20 (CW) 622G Guilford College Rd	Greensboro	NC	27409	336-547-0020	547-8144
WCYB-TV Ch 5 (NBC) 101 Lee St *Web:* www.wcyb.tv	Bristol	VA	24201	276-645-1555	645-1554
WDAM-TV Ch 7 (NBC) PO Box 16269 *TF:* 800-844-9326 ■ *Web:* www.wdam.com	Hattiesburg	MS	39404	601-544-4730	584-9302
WDSC-TV Ch 15 (PBS) 1200 W International Speedway Blvd Bldg 400 *TF:* 800-638-9238 ■ *Web:* www.wceu.org	Daytona Beach	FL	32114	386-506-4415	506-4427
WEAO-TV Ch 49 (PBS) 1750 Campus Ctr Dr *TF:* 800-544-4549 ■ *Web:* www.pbs4549.org	Kent	OH	44240	330-677-4549	678-0688
WEAR-TV Ch 3 (ABC) 4990 Mobile Hwy *TF:* 866-856-9327 ■ *Web:* www.weartv.com	Pensacola	FL	32506	850-456-3333	455-8972
WECT-TV Ch 6 (NBC) 322 Shipyard Blvd *Web:* www.wect.com	Wilmington	NC	28412	910-791-8070	791-9535
WEEK-TV Ch 25 (NBC) 2907 Springfield Rd *Web:* www.week.com	East Peoria	IL	61611	309-698-2525	698-9335
WEHT-TV Ch 25 (ABC) 800 Marywood Dr *TF:* 800-879-8549 ■ *Web:* www.news25.us	Henderson	KY	42420	270-826-9566	827-0561
WELF-TV Ch 23 (TBN) 384 S Campus Rd *Web:* www.tbn.org	Lookout Mountain	GA	30750	706-820-1663	820-1735
WEMT-TV Ch 39 (Fox) 101 Lee St *TF:* 800-376-3939 ■ *Web:* www.wemt39.com	Bristol	VA	24201	276-821-9296	645-1510
WENH-TV Ch 11 (PBS) 268 Mast Rd *Web:* www.nhptv.org	Durham	NH	03824	603-868-1100	868-7552
WESH-TV Ch 2 (NBC) 1021 N Wymore Rd *Web:* www.wesh.com	Winter Park	FL	32789	407-645-2222	539-7948
WETA-TV Ch 26 (PBS) 2775 S Quincy St *Web:* www.weta.org	Arlington	VA	22206	703-998-1801	998-3401
WETK-TV Ch 33 (PBS) 204 Ethan Allen Ave *TF:* 800-639-7811 ■ *Web:* www.vpt.org	Colchester	VT	05446	802-655-4800	655-6593
WEYI-TV Ch 25 (NBC) 2225 W Willard Rd *Web:* www.nbc25.net	Clio	MI	48420	810-687-1000	687-4925
WEYS-TV Ch 22 (CBS) 525 Southard St	Key West	FL	33040	305-296-4969	296-1669
WFFF-TV Ch 44 (Fox) 298 Mountain View Dr *TF:* 888-400-4855 ■ *Web:* www.fox44now.com	Colchester	VT	05446	802-658-8022	660-8673
WFGX MyTV 35 PO Box 12278 *Web:* www.wfgxtv.com	Pensacola	FL	32591	850-456-3333	455-0159
WFMY-TV Ch 2 (CBS) 1615 Phillips Ave *Web:* www.wfmy.com	Greensboro	NC	27405	336-379-9369	273-9433
WFMZ-TV Ch 69 (Ind) 300 E Rock Rd *Web:* www.wfmz.com	Allentown	PA	18103	610-797-4530	791-9994
WFPX-TV Ch 62 (I) Drawer 62	Lumber Bridge	NC	28357	910-843-3884	843-2873
WFSB-TV Ch 3 (CBS) 333 Capital Blvd *Web:* www.wfsb.com	Rocky Hill	CT	06067	860-244-1740	728-0263
WFTC-TV Ch 29 (MNT) 11358 Viking Dr *Web:* www.upn29.com	Eden Prairie	MN	55344	952-944-9999	942-0455
WFXT-TV Ch 25 (Fox) 25 Fox Dr *Web:* www.fox25.com	Dedham	MA	02026	781-467-2525	467-7213
WGAL-TV Ch 8 (NBC) 1300 Columbia Ave *Web:* www.thewgalchannel.com	Lancaster	PA	17604	717-393-5851	295-7457

Station / Address	City	State	Zip	Phone	Fax
WGBH-TV Ch 2 (PBS) 1 Guest St. *TF:* 800-300-2000 ■ *Web:* www.wgbh.org	Brighton	MA	02135	617-300-2000	300-1026
WGCB-TV Ch 49 (Ind) PO Box 88 *Web:* www.wgcbtv.com	Red Lion	PA	17356	717-246-1681	244-9316
WGGS-TV Ch 16 (Ind) 3409 Rutherford Rd Ext *TF:* 800-849-3683 ■ *Web:* www.wggs16.com	Taylors	SC	29687	864-244-1616	292-8481
WGHP-TV Ch 8 (Fox) 2005 Francis St *TF:* 800-808-6397 ■ *Web:* www.fox8wghp.com	High Point	NC	27263	336-841-8888	841-5169
WGNO-TV Ch 26 (ABC) 1 Galleria Blvd # 850 *Web:* www.abc26.trb.com	Metairie	LA	70001	504-525-3838	619-6332
WGPX-TV Ch 16 (I) 1114 N O' Henry Blvd	Greensboro	NC	27405	336-272-9227	272-9298
WHFT-TV Ch 45 (TBN) 3324 Pembroke Rd *TF:* 888-731-1000	Pembroke Park	FL	33021	954-962-1700	962-2817
WHKY-TV Ch 14 (Ind) PO Box 1059 *Web:* www.whky.com	Hickory	NC	28603	828-322-5115	322-8256
WHLT-TV Ch 22 (CBS) 5912 Hwy 49 Cloverleaf Mall Suite A *Web:* www.cbs22thehub.com	Hattiesburg	MS	39401	601-545-2077	545-3589
WHMB-TV Ch 40 (Ind) 10511 Greenfield Ave *Web:* www.whmbtv.com	Noblesville	IN	46060	317-773-5050	776-4051
WHOI-TV Ch 19 (ABC) 500 N Stewart St *Web:* www.hoinews.com	Creve Coeur	IL	61610	309-698-1919	698-4817
WHPX-TV Ch 26 (I) Shaws Cove 3 Suite 226 *Web:* www.paxhartford.tv	New London	CT	06320	860-444-2626	440-2601
WICD-TV Ch 15 (ABC) 250 S Country Fair Dr *Web:* www.wicd15.com	Champaign	IL	61821	217-351-8500	351-6056
WILL-TV Ch 12 (PBS) 300 N Goodwin Ave *Web:* www.will.illinois.edu	Urbana	IL	61801	217-333-7300	333-7151
WITV-TV Ch 7 (PBS) 1101 Geroge Rogers Blvd *Web:* www.scetv.org	Columbia	SC	29201	803-737-3200	737-3476
WJAR-TV Ch 10 (NBC) 23 Kenney Dr *Web:* www.turnto10.com	Cranston	RI	02920	401-455-9100	455-9140
WJBK-TV Ch 2 (Fox) PO Box 2000 *Web:* www.wjbk.com	Southfield	MI	48037	248-557-2000	557-1199
WJLA-TV Ch 7 (ABC) 1100 Wilson Blvd *Web:* www.wjla.com	Arlington	VA	22209	703-236-9552	236-2331
WJWJ-TV Ch 16 (PBS) PO Box 1165 *Web:* www.wjwj.org	Beaufort	SC	29901	843-524-0808	524-1016
WJYS-TV Ch 62 (Ind) 18600 S Oak Pk Ave *Web:* www.wjystv62.com	Tinley Park	IL	60477	708-633-0001	633-0040
WKAR-TV Ch 23 (PBS) MSU 283 Communications Arts Bldg *Web:* wkar.org/tv	East Lansing	MI	48824	517-432-9527	353-7124
WKBD-TV Ch 50 (CW) 26905 W 11-Mile Rd *Web:* www.cw50detroit.com	Southfield	MI	48034	248-355-7000	355-7000
WKMJ-TV Ch 68 (PBS) 600 Cooper Dr *TF:* 800-432-0951 ■ *Web:* www.ket.org	Lexington	KY	40502	859-258-7000	258-7399
WKNO-TV Ch 10 (PBS) 7151 Cherry Farms Rd *Web:* www.wkno.org	Cordova	TN	38016	901-729-8765	729-8176
WKPC-TV Ch 15 (PBS) 600 Cooper Dr *TF:* 800-432-0951 ■ *Web:* www.ket.org	Lexington	KY	40502	859-258-7000	258-7399
WKPT-TV Ch 19 (ABC) 222 Commerce St *Web:* www.wkpttv.com	Kingsport	TN	37660	423-246-9578	246-1863
WKTC-TV Ch 63 (MNT) 120-A Pontiac Business Center Dr Suite A	Elgin	SC	29045	803-419-6363	419-6038
WLAE-TV Ch 32 (PBS) 3330 N Cswy Blvd Suite 345 *Web:* www.wlae.com	Metairie	LA	70002	504-866-7411	840-9838
WLGA-TV Ch 66 (CW) 1800 Pepperell Pkwy *Web:* www.wlgatv.com	Opelika	AL	36801	334-749-5766	749-5768
WLIW-TV Ch 21 (PBS) 1 Ch 21 Dr PO Box 21 *Web:* www.wliw.org	Plainview	NY	11803	516-367-2100	349-0760
WLLA-TV Ch 64 (Ind) PO Box 3157 *Web:* www.wlla.com	Kalamazoo	MI	49003	269-345-6421	345-5665
WLNY-TV Ch 55 (Ind) 270 S Service Rd Suite 55 *Web:* www.wlnytv.com	Melville	NY	11747	631-777-8855	420-4822
WLOV-TV Ch 27 (Fox) PO Box 1732 *Web:* www.wlov.com	Tupelo	MS	38802	662-842-2227	
WLOX-TV Ch 13 (ABC) 208 Debuys Rd **Fax:* News Rm ■ *Web:* www.wlox.com	Biloxi	MS	39531	228-896-1313	896-2596*
WLPX-TV Ch 29 (I) 600-C Prestige Pk Dr Suite C	Hurricane	WV	25526	304-760-1029	760-1036
WMDT-TV Ch 47 (ABC) 202 Downtown Plaza *Web:* www.wmdt.com	Salisbury	MD	21801	410-742-4747	742-5767
WMGM-TV Ch 40 (NBC) 1601 New Rd	Linwood	NJ	08221	609-927-4440	927-7014
WMHT-TV Ch 17 (PBS) 4 Global View *TF:* 800-477-9648 ■ *Web:* www.wmht.org	Troy	NY	12180	518-880-3400	880-3409
WMMP-TV Ch 36 (MNT) 4301 Arco Ln *Web:* www.wmmp36.com	North Charleston	SC	29418	843-744-2424	554-9649
WMPT-TV Ch 22 (PBS) 11767 Owings Mills Blvd *TF:* 800-223-3678 ■ *Web:* www.mpt.org	Owings Mills	MD	21117	410-356-5600	581-4338
WMPT-TV Ch 67 (PBS) 11767 Owings Mills Blvd *TF:* 800-223-3678 ■ *Web:* www.mpt.org	Owings Mills	MD	21117	410-356-5600	581-4338
WMTW-TV Ch 8 (ABC) 99 Danville Corner Rd *TF:* 800-248-6397 ■ *Web:* www.wmtw.com	Auburn	ME	04211	207-782-1800	783-7371
WMUR-TV Ch 9 (ABC) 100 S Commercial St *Web:* www.thewmurchannel.com	Manchester	NH	03101	603-669-9999	641-9005
WMYD-TV Ch 20 (MNT) 2777 Franklin Rd Suite 1220 *Web:* www.tv20detroit.com	Southfield	MI	48034	248-355-2020	355-0368
WNAC-TV Ch 64 (Fox) 25 Catamore Blvd	East Providence	RI	02914	401-438-7200	431-1012
WNEG-TV Ch 32 (PBS) 802 E Doyle St *Web:* www.wugatv.org	Toccoa	GA	30577	706-886-0032	583-0121
WNEM-TV Ch 5 (CBS) 107 N Franklin St *TF:* 800-522-9636 ■ *Web:* www.wnem.com	Saginaw	MI	48607	989-755-8191	758-2110
WNEO-TV Ch 45 (PBS) 1750 Campus Ctr Dr *TF:* 800-554-4549 ■ *Web:* www.pbs4549.org	Kent	OH	44240	330-677-4549	678-0688
WNEP-TV Ch 16 (ABC) 16 Montage Mountain Rd **Fax:* News Rm ■ *TF:* 800-982-4374 ■ *Web:* www.wnep.com	Moosic	PA	18507	570-346-7474	341-1344*
WNGS-TV Ch 67 (Ind) 9279 Dutch Hill Rd	West Valley	NY	14171	716-942-3000	942-3010
WNJT-TV Ch 52 (PBS) PO Box 777 *Web:* www.njn.net/television	Trenton	NJ	08625	609-777-5000	633-2927
WNJU-TV Ch 47 (Tele) 2200 Fletcher Ave 6th Fl *Web:* www.telemundo47.com	Fort Lee	NJ	07024	201-969-4247	969-4111
WNNE-TV Ch 31 (NBC) PO Box 1310 **Fax:* News Rm ■ *Web:* www.thechamplainchannel.com/wnne	White River Junction	VT	05001	802-295-3100	295-9056*
WNOL-TV Ch 38 (CW) 1 Galeria Blvd Suite 850 *Web:* www.nola38.com	Metairie	LA	70001	504-525-3838	569-0908
WNPB-TV Ch 24 (PBS) 600 Capitol St *TF:* 888-596-9729 ■ *Web:* www.wvpubcast.org	Charleston	WV	26301	304-556-4900	284-1454
WNPX-TV Ch 28 (I) 1281 N Mt Juliet Rd Suite L	Mount Juliet	TN	37122	615-773-6100	773-6106
WOFL-TV Ch 35 (Fox) 35 Skyline Dr *Web:* www.wofl.com	Lake Mary	FL	32746	407-644-3535	741-5189
WOI-TV Ch 5 (ABC) 3903 Westown Pkwy **Fax:* Sales ■ *Web:* www.woi-tv.com	West Des Moines	IA	50266	515-457-9645	457-1034*
WOTF-TV Ch 43 (Uni) 605 Third Ave 12th Fl **Fax Area Code:* 321 ■ *Web:* corporate.univision.com	New York	NY	10158	212-455-5331	254-9343*
WOUC-TV Ch 44 (PBS) 9 S College St *Web:* www.woub.org	Athens	OH	45701	740-593-1771	593-0240
WOWK-TV Ch 13 (CBS) 555 5th Ave *TF:* 800-234-9695 ■ *Web:* www.wowktv.com	Huntington	WV	25701	304-525-1313	523-0545
WPBF-TV Ch 25 (ABC) 3970 RCA Blvd Suite 7007 *Web:* www.wpbfnews.com	Palm Beach Gardens	FL	33410	561-694-2525	624-1089
WPDE-TV Ch 15 (ABC) 1194 Atlantic Ave *TF:* 800-698-9733	Conway	SC	29526	843-234-9733	234-9739
WPLG-TV Ch 10 (ABC) 3401 W Hallandale Beach Blvd **Fax:* News Rm ■ *Web:* www.local10.com	Pembroke Park	FL	33023	305-576-1010	325-2480*
WPME-TV Ch 35 (MNT) 4 Ledgeview Dr *Web:* www.mainesupn.com	Westbrook	ME	04092	207-774-0051	774-6849
WPMT-TV Ch 43 (Fox) 2005 S Queen St *TF:* 888-369-9768 ■ *Web:* fox43.trb.com	York	PA	17403	717-843-0043	843-9741
WPNE-TV Ch 38 (PBS) 821 University Ave *Web:* www.wpt.org	Madison	WI	53706	608-263-2121	263-1952
WPRI-TV Ch 12 (CBS) 25 Catamore Blvd *Web:* www.wpri.com	East Providence	RI	02914	401-438-7200	431-1012
WPTZ-TV Ch 5 (NBC) 5 Television Dr *Web:* www.thechamplainchannel.com	Plattsburgh	NY	12901	518-561-5555	561-1201
WPXA-TV Ch 14 (I) 200 N Cobb Pkwy Suite 114	Marietta	GA	30062	770-919-0575	919-9621
WPXC-TV Ch 21 (I) 7434 Blythe Island Hwy	Brunswick	GA	31523	912-267-0021	261-9582
WPXD-TV Ch 31 (I) 3975 Varsity Dr *TF:* 888-467-2988 ■ *Web:* www.iontelevision.com	Ann Arbor	MI	48108	734-973-7900	973-7906
WPXL-TV Ch 49 (I) 3900 Veterans Blvd Suite 202	Metairie	LA	70002	504-887-9795	887-1518
WPXP-TV Ch 67 (I) 13801 NW 14th St *Web:* www.ionline.tv	Sunrise	FL	33323	954-703-1921	858-1848
WPXQ-TV Ch 69 (I) 3 Shaws Cove	New London	CT	06320	860-444-2626	440-2601
WPXT-TV Ch 12 (CW) 4 Ledgeview Dr *Web:* www.maineswb.com	Westbrook	ME	04092	207-774-0051	774-6849
WPXW-TV Ch 66 (I) 6199 Old Arrington Ln	Fairfax Station	VA	22039	703-503-7966	503-1225
WQCW-TV Ch 30 (CW) 800 Gallia St Suite 430 *Web:* www.whcp-tv.com	Portsmouth	OH	45662	740-353-3391	353-3372
WRBW-TV Ch 65 (MNT) 35 Skyline Dr *Web:* www.wrbw.com	Lake Mary	FL	32746	407-644-3535	741-5189
WRGB-TV Ch 6 (CBS) 1400 Balltown Rd *Web:* www.wrgb.com	Schenectady	NY	12309	518-346-6666	346-6249
WRNN-TV Ch 62 (Ind) 800 Westchester Ave Suite S-640 *Web:* www.rnntv.com	Rye Brook	NY	10573	914-417-2700	696-0276
WSAZ-TV Ch 3 (NBC) PO Box 2115 *Web:* www.wsaz.com	Huntington	WV	25721	304-697-4780	690-3066
WSBK-TV Ch 38 (Ind) 1170 Soldiers Field Rd *Web:* www.upn38.com	Allston	MA	02134	617-787-7000	254-6383
WSBT-TV Ch 22 (CBS) 1301 E Douglas Rd *TF:* 800-872-3141 ■ *Web:* www.wsbt.com	Mishawaka	IN	46545	574-232-6397	289-0622
WSCV-TV Ch 51 (NBC) 15000 SW 27th St *Web:* www.telemundo51.com	Miramar	FL	33027	954-622-6000	622-7700
WSET-TV Ch 13 (ABC) 2320 Langhorne Rd *Web:* www.wset.com	Lynchburg	VA	24501	434-528-1313	847-0458
WSKY-TV Ch 4 (Ind) 920 Corporate Ln *TF:* 800-414-0911 ■ *Web:* www.wsky4.com	Chesapeake	VA	23320	757-382-0004	382-0365
WSPX-TV Ch 56 (I) 6508-B Basile Rowe	East Syracuse	NY	13057	315-414-0178	414-0482
WSRE-TV Ch 23 (PBS) 1000 College Blvd *Web:* www.wsre.org	Pensacola	FL	32504	850-484-1200	484-1255
WSYR-TV Ch 9 (ABC) 5904 Bridge St *Web:* www.wsyr.com	East Syracuse	NY	13057	315-446-9999	446-9283
WTAT-TV Ch 24 (Fox) 4301 Arco Ln *Web:* www.wtat24.com	North Charleston	SC	29418	843-744-2424	554-9649
WTGL-TV Ch 45 (Ind) 31 Skyline Dr *Web:* www.tv45.org	Lake Mary	FL	32746	407-215-6745	215-6789
WTIU-TV Ch 30 (PBS) 1229 E 7th St *TF:* 800-662-3311 ■ *Web:* www.wtiu.indiana.edu	Bloomington	IN	47405	812-855-5900	855-0729
WTJP-TV Ch 60 (TBN) 313 Rosedale Ave *Web:* www.tbn.org	Gadsden	AL	35901	256-546-8860	543-8623
WTKLF-TV Ch 57 (CW) 950 Commerce Blvd	Midway	FL	32343	850-576-4990	576-0200
WTLH-TV Ch 49 (Fox) 950 Commerce Blvd *Web:* www.fox49.com	Midway	FL	32343	850-576-4990	576-0200
WTLJ-TV Ch 54 (Ind) 10290 48th Ave *Web:* www.tct-net.org	Allendale	MI	49401	616-895-4154	892-4401
WTNH-TV Ch 8 (ABC) 8 Elm St **Fax:* Mktg ■ *Web:* www.wtnh.com	New Haven	CT	06510	203-784-8888	789-2010*
WTOV-TV Ch 9 (NBC) 9 Red Donley Plaza *TF:* 800-288-0799 ■ *Web:* www.wtov9.com	Mingo Junction	OH	43938	740-282-0911	282-0439
WTVA-TV Ch 9 (NBC) PO Box 350 *Web:* www.wtva.com	Tupelo	MS	38802	662-842-7620	
WTVJ-TV Ch 6 (NBC) 15000 SW 27th St *Web:* www.nbc6.net	Miramar	FL	33027	954-622-6000	622-6107

Station	City	State	Zip	Phone	Fax
WTXL-TV Ch 27 (ABC) 1620 Commerce Blvd *Web:* www.wtxl.com	Midway	FL	32343	850-893-3127	668-0423
WUNI-TV Ch 27 (Uni) 33 4th Ave. *Web:* www.wunitv.com	Needham	MA	02494	781-433-2727	433-2750
WUNL-TV Ch 26 (PBS) 10 TW Alexander Dr PO Box 14900 *Web:* www.unctv.org	Research Triangle Park	NC	27709	919-549-7000	
WUVC-TV Ch 40 (Uni) 230 Donaldson St	Fayetteville	NC	28301	910-323-4040	323-3924
WVBT-TV Ch 43 (Fox) 243 Wythe St. *Web:* www.wvbt.com	Portsmouth	VA	23704	757-393-4343	397-8279
WVIA-TV Ch 44 (PBS) 100 WVIA Way *Web:* www.wvia.org/tv	Pittston	PA	18640	570-344-1244	655-1180
WVIT-TV Ch 30 (NBC) 1422 New Britain Ave *TF:* 800-523-9848 ■ *Web:* www.nbc30.com	West Hartford	CT	06110	860-521-3030	521-3110
WVNY-TV Ch 22 (ABC) 298 Mountain View Dr *Web:* www.abc22.com	Colchester	VT	05446	802-660-9333	660-8673
WWJ-TV Ch 62 (CBS) 26905 W 11-Mile Rd *Web:* www.wwjtv.com	Southfield	MI	48034	248-355-7000	355-6292
WWMT-TV Ch 3 (CBS) 590 W Maple St *TF:* 800-875-3333 ■ *Web:* www.wwmt.com	Kalamazoo	MI	49008	269-388-3333	388-8322
WWOR-TV Ch 9 (MNT) 9 Broadcast Plaza *Web:* www.upn9.com	Secaucus	NJ	07096	201-348-0009	330-3777
WXPX-TV Ch 66 (I) 14444 66th St N *Web:* www.ionmedia.tv	Clearwater	FL	33764	727-479-1053	479-1055
WXTV-TV Ch 41 (Uni) 500 Frank W Burr Blvd 6th Fl *Web:* www.univision.com	Teaneck	NJ	07666	201-287-4141	287-9427
WXXV-TV Ch 25 (Fox) 14351 Hwy 49 N *Web:* www.wxxv25.com	Gulfport	MS	39503	228-832-2525	832-4442
WXYZ-TV Ch 7 (ABC) 20777 W 10-Mile Rd *TF:* 800-825-0770 ■ *Web:* www.wxyz.com	Southfield	MI	48037	248-827-7777	827-9444
WYES-TV Ch 12 (PBS) 111 Veterans Blvd Suite 250 *Web:* www.wyes.org	Metairie	LA	70005	504-486-5511	840-9954
WYOU-TV Ch 22 (CBS) 62 S Franklin St *TF:* 800-422-9968 ■ *Web:* www.pahomepage.com	Wilkes-Barre	PA	18701	570-961-2222	829-0440
WYPX-TV Ch 55 (I) 1 Charles Blvd	Guilderland	NY	12084	518-464-9842	464-0633
WYZZ-TV Ch 43 (Fox) 2714 E Lincoln St *Web:* www.wyzz43.com	Bloomington	IL	61704	309-662-4373	663-6943

744-1 Abilene, TX

Station	City	State	Zip	Phone	Fax
KIDZ-TV Ch 42 (MNT) 500 Chestnut St Suite 804 *Web:* www.kidzabilene.com	Abilene	TX	79602	325-672-5606	676-2437
KRBC-TV Ch 9 (NBC) 4510 S 14th St *Web:* www.krbctv.com	Abilene	TX	79605	325-692-4242	692-8265
KTAB-TV Ch 32 (CBS) 4510 S 14th St. *Web:* www.ktabtv.com	Abilene	TX	79605	325-695-2777	695-9922
KTXS-TV Ch 12 (ABC) 4420 N Clack St *Fax: News Rm ■ *TF:* 800-588-5897 ■ *Web:* www.ktxs.com	Abilene	TX	79601	325-677-2281	672-5307*
KXVA-TV Ch 15 (Fox) 500 Chestnut St Suite 804	Abilene	TX	79602	325-672-5606	676-2437

744-2 Albany, NY

Station	City	State	Zip	Phone	Fax
WNYT-TV Ch 13 (NBC) 715 N Pearl St *TF:* 800-999-9698 ■ *Web:* www.wnyt.com	Albany	NY	12204	518-436-4791	434-0659
WTEN-TV Ch 10 (ABC) 341 Northern Blvd *Fax: News Rm ■ *Web:* www.wten.com	Albany	NY	12204	518-436-4822	426-4792*
WXXA-TV Ch 23 (Fox) 28 Corporate Cir *Fax: News Rm ■ *TF:* 800-999-2882 ■ *Web:* www.fox23tv.com	Albany	NY	12203	518-862-2323	862-0930*

744-3 Albuquerque/Santa Fe, NM

Station	City	State	Zip	Phone	Fax
KASA-TV Ch 2 (Fox) 13 Broadcast Plaza SW *TF:* 800-283-4227 ■ *Web:* www.kasa.com	Albuquerque	NM	87104	505-243-2285	248-1464
KASY-TV Ch 50 (MNT) 8341 Washington St NE *Web:* www.upn50tv.com	Albuquerque	NM	87113	505-797-1919	344-1145
KLUZ-TV Ch 41 (Uni) 2725 F Broadbent Pkwy NE *Web:* www.kluz.tv	Albuquerque	NM	87107	505-342-4141	341-9264
KNAT-TV Ch 23 (TBN) 1510 Coors Blvd NW *Web:* www.tbn.org	Albuquerque	NM	87121	505-836-6585	831-8725
KNME-TV Ch 5 (PBS) 1130 University Blvd NE University of New Mexico *TF:* 800-328-5663 ■ *Web:* www.knmetv.org	Albuquerque	NM	87102	505-277-2121	277-2191
KOAT-TV Ch 7 (ABC) 3801 Carlisle Blvd NE *TF:* 800-421-6159 ■ *Web:* www.koat.com	Albuquerque	NM	87107	505-884-7777	884-6354
KOB-TV Ch 4 (NBC) 4 Broadcast Plaza SW *Web:* www.kobtv.com	Albuquerque	NM	87104	505-243-4411	764-2522
KRQE-TV Ch 13 (CBS) 13 Broadcast Plaza SW *TF:* 800-283-4227 ■ *Web:* www.krqe.com	Albuquerque	NM	87104	505-243-2285	842-8483
KTFQ-TV Ch 14 (Uni) 2725 F Broadbent Pkwy NE Suite F	Albuquerque	NM	87107	505-342-4141	344-8714
KWBQ-TV Ch 19 (CW) 8341 Washington St NE *Web:* www.wb19tv.com	Albuquerque	NM	87113	505-797-1919	344-1145

744-4 Amarillo, TX

Station	City	State	Zip	Phone	Fax
KACV-TV Ch 2 (PBS) PO Box 447 *TF:* 800-999-9243 ■ *Web:* www.kacvtv.org	Amarillo	TX	79178	806-371-5222	371-5258
KAMR-TV Ch 4 (NBC) 1015 S Fillmore St *Web:* www.kamr.com	Amarillo	TX	79101	806-383-3321	349-9083
KCIT-TV Ch 14 (Fox) 1015 S Fillmore St *Web:* www.fox14.tv	Amarillo	TX	79101	806-374-1414	349-9083
KCPN-TV Ch 31 (Ind) 1015 S Fillmore St *Web:* www.fox14.tv	Amarillo	TX	79101	806-374-1414	349-9083
KFDA-TV Ch 10 (CBS) 7900 Broadway *Web:* www.newschannel10.com	Amarillo	TX	79105	806-383-1010	381-9859
KVII-TV Ch 7 (ABC) 1 Broadcast Ctr *TF:* 800-777-5844 ■ *Web:* www.kvii.com	Amarillo	TX	79101	806-373-1787	371-7329

744-5 Anchorage, AK

Station	City	State	Zip	Phone	Fax
KAKM-TV Ch 7 (PBS) 3877 University Dr *Web:* www.publicbroadcasting.net	Anchorage	AK	99508	907-550-8400	550-8401
KIMO-TV Ch 13 (ABC) 2700 E Tudor Rd *TF:* 877-304-1313 ■ *Web:* www.youralaskalink.com	Anchorage	AK	99507	907-561-1313	561-8934
KTBY-TV Ch 4 (Fox) 440 E Benson Blvd Suite 1 *Web:* www.fox4ktby.com	Anchorage	AK	99503	907-274-0404	264-5180
KTUU-TV Ch 2 (NBC) 701 E Tudor Rd Suite 220 *Web:* www.ktuu.com	Anchorage	AK	99503	907-762-9202	563-3318
KTVA-TV Ch 11 (CBS) 1007 W 32nd Ave *Web:* www.ktva.com	Anchorage	AK	99503	907-562-3456	273-3189
KYES-TV Ch 5 (MNT) 3700 Woodland Dr Suite 800 *Web:* www.kyes.com	Anchorage	AK	99517	907-248-5937	339-3889

744-6 Asheville, NC/Greenville, SC/Spartanburg, SC

Station	City	State	Zip	Phone	Fax
WHNS-TV Ch 21 (Fox) 21 IH- Ct *Web:* www.whns.com	Greenville	SC	29615	864-288-2100	297-0728
WLOS-TV Ch 13 (ABC) 110 Technology Dr *TF:* 800-288-8813 ■ *Web:* www.wlos.com	Asheville	NC	28803	828-684-1340	651-4618
WMYA-TV Ch 40 (MNT) 110 Technology Dr *Fax Area Code: 864 ■ *TF:* 800-288-8813 ■ *Web:* www.my40.tv	Asheville	NC	28803	828-684-1340	297-8085*
WRET-TV Ch 49 (PBS) PO Box 4069 *Web:* www.scetv.org	Spartanburg	SC	29305	864-503-9371	503-3615
WSPA-TV Ch 7 (CBS) 250 International Dr *TF:* 800-207-6397 ■ *Web:* www.wspa.com	Spartanburg	SC	29303	864-576-7777	587-4480
WYCW-TV Ch 62 (CW) 250 International Dr *Web:* www.wasv.com	Spartanburg	SC	29303	864-576-7777	587-4480
WYFF-TV Ch 4 (NBC) 505 Rutherford St *TF:* 800-453-9933 ■ *Web:* www.wyff4.com	Greenville	SC	29609	864-242-4404	240-5305

744-7 Atlanta, GA

Station	City	State	Zip	Phone	Fax
Peachtree TV 1050 Techwood Dr NW *Web:* www.peachtreetv.com	Atlanta	GA	30318	404-575-7888	575-9720
WAGA-TV Ch 5 (Fox) 1551 Briarcliff Rd NE *Fax: News Rm ■ *Web:* www.fox5atlanta.com	Atlanta	GA	30306	404-875-5555	898-0169*
WATL-TV Ch 36 (MNT) 1 Monroe Pl NE *Web:* www.wb36.trb.com	Atlanta	GA	30324	404-892-1611	881-0675
WDCO-TV Ch 29 (PBS) 260 14th St NW *TF:* 800-222-6006 ■ *Web:* www.gpb.org/gptv	Atlanta	GA	30318	404-685-2400	685-2417
WGCL-TV Ch 46 (CBS) 425 14th St NW *Web:* www.cbsatlanta.com	Atlanta	GA	30318	404-327-3000	327-3004
WGTV-TV Ch 8 (PBS) 260 14th St NW *TF:* 800-222-6006 ■ *Web:* www.gpb.org/gptv	Atlanta	GA	30318	404-685-2400	685-2417
WJSP-TV Ch 28 (PBS) 260 14th St NW *TF:* 800-222-4788 ■ *Web:* www.gpb.org/gptv	Atlanta	GA	30318	404-685-2400	685-2591
WPBA-TV Ch 30 (PBS) 740 Bismark Rd NE *Web:* www.wpba.org	Atlanta	GA	30324	678-686-0321	686-0356
WSB-TV Ch 2 (ABC) 1601 W Peachtree St NE *Web:* www.wsbtv.com	Atlanta	GA	30309	404-897-7000	897-7370
WUPA-TV Ch 69 (CW) 2700 NE Expy Bldg A *Web:* cwatlantatv.com	Atlanta	GA	30345	404-325-6929	633-4567
WVAN-TV Ch 9 (PBS) 260 14th St NW *TF:* 800-222-6006 ■ *Web:* www.gpb.org/gptv	Atlanta	GA	30318	404-685-2400	685-2431
WXIA-TV Ch 11 (NBC) 1 Monroe Pl *Fax: News Rm ■ *Web:* www.11alive.com	Atlanta	GA	30324	404-892-1611	881-0675*

744-8 Augusta, GA

Station	City	State	Zip	Phone	Fax
WAGT-TV Ch 26 (NBC) 905 Broad St *TF:* 800-924-8639 ■ *Web:* www.nbc26news.com	Augusta	GA	30901	706-826-0026	724-4028
WFXG-TV Ch 54 (Fox) 3933 Washington Rd *Web:* www.wfxg.com	Augusta	GA	30907	706-650-5400	650-8411
WRDW-TV Ch 12 (CBS) PO Box 1212 *Web:* www.wrdw.com	Augusta	GA	30903	803-278-1212	279-8316

744-9 Austin, TX

Station	City	State	Zip	Phone	Fax
KEYE-TV Ch 42 (CBS) 10700 Metric Blvd *TF:* 800-563-9742 ■ *Web:* www.keyetv.com	Austin	TX	78758	512-835-0042	490-2111

Station	City	State	Zip	Phone	Fax
KLRU-TV Ch 18 (PBS) 2504-B Whitis Ave *Web:* www.klru.org	Austin	TX	78712	512-471-4811	475-9090
KNVA-TV Ch 54 (CW) 908 W ML King Jr Blvd *Web:* www.thecwaustin.com	Austin	TX	78701	512-478-5400	476-1520
KTBC-TV Ch 7 (Fox) 119 E 10th St *Web:* www.fox7.com	Austin	TX	78701	512-476-7777	495-7060
KVUE-TV Ch 24 (ABC) 3201 Steck Ave **Fax:* News Rm ■ *Web:* www.kvue.com	Austin	TX	78757	512-459-6521	533-2233*
KXAN-TV Ch 36 (NBC) 908 W Martin Luther King Jr Bl *Web:* www.kxan.com	Austin	TX	78701	512-476-3636	469-0630

744-10 Bakersfield, CA

Station	City	State	Zip	Phone	Fax
KABE-TV Ch 31 (Uni) 5801 Truxtun Ave *Web:* www.univision.com	Bakersfield	CA	93309	661-324-0031	334-2691
KBAK-TV Ch 29 (CBS) 1901 Westwind Dr *TF:* 800-229-6397 ■ *Web:* www.eyeoutforyou.com	Bakersfield	CA	93301	661-327-7955	327-5603
KERO-TV Ch 23 (ABC) 321 21st St **Fax:* News Rm ■ *Web:* www.turnto23.com	Bakersfield	CA	93301	661-637-2323	323-5538*
KGET-TV Ch 17 (NBC) 2120 L St *Web:* www.kget.com	Bakersfield	CA	93301	661-283-1700	283-1855
KUVI-TV Ch 45 (MNT) 5801 Truxtun Ave *Web:* www.kuvi45.com	Bakersfield	CA	93309	661-324-0045	334-2691

744-11 Baltimore, MD

Station	City	State	Zip	Phone	Fax
WBAL-TV Ch 11 (NBC) 3800 Hooper Ave *TF:* 800-677-9225 ■ *Web:* www.thewbalchannel.com	Baltimore	MD	21211	410-467-3000	338-6460
WBFF-TV Ch 45 (Fox) 2000 W 41st St *Web:* www.foxbaltimore.com	Baltimore	MD	21211	410-467-4545	467-5090
WJZ-TV Ch 13 (CBS) 3725 Malden Ave *Web:* www.wjz.com	Baltimore	MD	21211	410-466-0013	578-7502
WNUV-TV Ch 40 (CW) 2000 W 41st St *Web:* www.cwbaltimore.com	Baltimore	MD	21211	410-467-4545	467-5093
WUTB-TV Ch 24 (MNT) 4820 Seton Dr *Web:* www.upn24.com	Baltimore	MD	21215	410-358-2400	764-7232

744-12 Bangor, ME

Station	City	State	Zip	Phone	Fax
WABI-TV Ch 5 (CBS) 35 Hildreth St *Web:* www.wabi.tv	Bangor	ME	04401	207-947-8321	941-9378
WLBZ-TV Ch 2 (NBC) 329 Mt Hope Ave *TF:* 800-244-6306 ■ *Web:* www.wlbz.com	Bangor	ME	04401	207-942-4821	942-2109
WMEB-TV Ch 12 (PBS) 63 Texas Ave *Web:* www.mpbn.net	Bangor	ME	04401	207-941-1010	942-2857
WVII-TV Ch 7 (ABC) 371 Target Industrial Cir *TF:* 800-499-9844 ■ *Web:* www.localmaine.com	Bangor	ME	04401	207-945-6457	945-6864

744-13 Baton Rouge, LA

Station	City	State	Zip	Phone	Fax
KLPB-TV Ch 24 (PBS) 7733 Perkins Rd *TF:* 800-272-8161 ■ *Web:* www.lpb.org	Baton Rouge	LA	70810	225-767-5660	767-4421
KLTS-TV Ch 24 (PBS) 7733 Perkins Rd *Web:* www.lpb.org	Baton Rouge	LA	70810	225-767-5660	767-4299
KZUP-TV 19 (Ind) 10000 Perkins Rd	Baton Rouge	LA	70810	225-766-3233	768-9293
NBC 33 TV 10000 Perkins Rd *Web:* www.nbc33tv.com	Baton Rouge	LA	70810	225-766-3233	768-9293
WAFB-TV Ch 9 (CBS) 844 Government St **Fax:* News Rm ■ *TF:* 800-223-9232 ■ *Web:* www.wafb.com	Baton Rouge	LA	70802	225-383-9999	379-7880*
WBRL-TV Ch 21 (CW) 10000 Perkins Rd	Baton Rouge	LA	70810	225-769-0044	768-9293
WBRZ-TV Ch 2 (ABC) 1650 Highland Rd **Fax:* News Rm ■ *Web:* www.2theadvocate.com	Baton Rouge	LA	70802	225-387-2222	336-2347*
WGMB-TV Ch 44 (Fox) 10000 Perkins Rd *Web:* www.fox44.com	Baton Rouge	LA	70810	225-769-0044	768-9293
WLPB-TV Ch 27 (PBS) 7733 Perkins Rd **Fax:* News Rm ■ *TF:* 800-272-8161 ■ *Web:* www.lpb.org	Baton Rouge	LA	70810	225-767-5660	767-4421*

744-14 Billings, MT

Station	City	State	Zip	Phone	Fax
KHMT-TV Ch 4 (Fox) 445 S 24th St W *Web:* www.khmt.com	Billings	MT	59102	406-652-7366	652-6963
KSVI-TV Ch 6 (ABC) 445 S 24th St W *Web:* www.ksvi.com	Billings	MT	59102	406-652-4743	652-6963
KTVQ-TV Ch 2 (CBS) 3203 3rd Ave N *Web:* www.ktvq.com	Billings	MT	59101	406-252-5611	252-9938
KULR-TV Ch 8 (NBC) 2045 Overland Ave *Web:* www.kulr8.com	Billings	MT	59102	406-656-8000	652-8207

744-15 Birmingham, AL

Station	City	State	Zip	Phone	Fax
WABM-TV Ch 68 (MNT) 651 Beacon Pkwy W Suite 105 *Web:* www.wabm68.com	Birmingham	AL	35209	205-943-2168	290-2114
WBIQ-TV Ch 10 (PBS) 2112 11th Ave S Suite 400 *TF:* 800-239-5233 ■ *Web:* www.aptv.org	Birmingham	AL	35205	205-328-8756	251-2192
WBRC-TV Ch 6 (Fox) 1720 Valley View Dr *Web:* www.wbrc.com	Birmingham	AL	35209	205-322-6666	583-4356
WCFT-TV Ch 33 (ABC) 800 Concourse Pkwy Suite 200 **Fax:* News Rm ■ *Web:* www.abc3340.com	Birmingham	AL	35244	205-403-3340	982-3942*
WEIQ-TV Ch 42 (PBS) 2112 11th Ave S Suite 400 *TF:* 800-239-5233 ■ *Web:* www.aptv.org	Birmingham	AL	35205	205-328-8756	251-2192
WHIQ-TV Ch 24 (PBS) 2112 11th Ave S Suite 400 *TF:* 800-239-5233 ■ *Web:* www.aptv.org	Birmingham	AL	35205	205-328-8756	251-2192
WIAT-TV Ch 42 (CBS) PO Box 59496 *Web:* www.wiat.com	Birmingham	AL	35259	205-322-4200	320-2713
WPXH-TV Ch 44 (I) 2085 Golden Crust Dr	Birmingham	AL	35209	205-870-4404	870-0744
WTTO-TV Ch 21 (CW) 651 Beacon Pkwy W Suite 105 *Web:* www.wtto21.com/birmingham_al	Birmingham	AL	35209	205-943-2168	290-2114
WVTM-TV Ch 13 (NBC) 1732 Valley View Dr *Web:* www.nbc13.com	Birmingham	AL	35209	205-933-1313	323-3314

744-16 Bismarck, ND

Station	City	State	Zip	Phone	Fax
KBMY-TV Ch 17 (ABC) 1811 N 15th St *Web:* www.abc17.tv	Bismarck	ND	58502	701-223-1700	
KFYR-TV Ch 5 (NBC) 200 N 4th St *Web:* www.kfyrtv.com	Bismarck	ND	58501	701-255-5757	255-8220
KNDX-TV Ch 26 (Fox) 3130 E Broadway Ave *TF:* 877-563-9369 ■ *Web:* www.westdakotafox.com	Bismarck	ND	58501	701-355-0026	250-7244
KXMB-TV Ch 12 (CBS) 1811 N 15th St *TF:* 800-223-9197 ■ *Web:* www.kxmb.com	Bismarck	ND	58501	701-223-1700	355-9140

744-17 Boise, ID

Station	City	State	Zip	Phone	Fax
KAID-TV Ch 4 (PBS) 1455 N Orchard St *TF:* 800-543-6868 ■ *Web:* www.idahoptv.org	Boise	ID	83706	208-373-7220	373-7245
KBCI-TV Ch 2 (CBS) 140 N 16th St *Web:* www.kbcitv.com	Boise	ID	83702	208-336-5222	472-2212
KTVB-TV Ch 7 (NBC) 5407 Fairview *TF:* 800-559-7277 ■ *Web:* www.ktvb.com	Boise	ID	83706	208-375-7277	378-1762

744-18 Boston, MA

Station	City	State	Zip	Phone	Fax
WBPX-TV Ch 68 (I) 1120 Soldiers Field Rd *Web:* www.ionline.tv	Boston	MA	02134	617-787-6868	787-4114
WBZ-TV Ch 4 (CBS) 1170 Soldiers Field Rd *Web:* www.wbz4.com	Boston	MA	02134	617-787-7000	254-6383
WHDH-TV Ch 7 (NBC) 7 Bulfinch Pl *Web:* www2.whdh.com	Boston	MA	02114	617-725-0777	723-6117
WLVI-TV Ch 56 (CW) 7 Bulfinch Pl	Boston	MA	02114	617-265-5656	287-2872*

744-19 Brownsville, TX

Station	City	State	Zip	Phone	Fax
KLUJ-TV Ch 44 (TBN) 1920 Loop 499 Suite 117	Brownsville	TX	78550	956-425-4225	412-1740
KVEO-TV Ch 23 (NBC) 394 N Expy *Web:* www.kveo.com	Brownsville	TX	78521	956-544-2323	544-4636

744-20 Buffalo, NY

Station	City	State	Zip	Phone	Fax
WGRZ-TV Ch 2 (NBC) 259 Delaware Ave *TF:* 877-849-2200 ■ *Web:* www.wgrz.com	Buffalo	NY	14202	716-849-2200	849-7602
WIVB-TV Ch 4 (CBS) 2077 Elmwood Ave **Fax:* News Rm ■ *Web:* www.wivb.com	Buffalo	NY	14207	716-874-4410	874-8173*
WKBW-TV Ch 7 (ABC) 7 Broadcast Plaza **Fax:* News Rm ■ *TF:* 800-234-9529 ■ *Web:* www.wkbw.com	Buffalo	NY	14202	716-845-6100	856-8784*
WNED-TV Ch 17 (PBS) 140 Lower Terr Horizons Plaza *Web:* www.wned.org	Buffalo	NY	14202	716-845-7000	845-7036
WNYO-TV Ch 49 (MNT) 699 Hertel Ave Suite 100 *Web:* www.mytvbuffalo.com	Buffalo	NY	14207	716-447-3200	875-4919
WUTV-TV Ch 29 (Fox) 699 Hertel Ave Suite 100 *Web:* www.wutv.com	Buffalo	NY	14207	716-447-3200	875-4919

744-21 Calgary, AB

Station	City	State	Zip	Phone	Fax
CBRT-TV Ch 9 (CBC) 1724 Westmount Blvd NW *Web:* www.cbc.ca	Calgary	AB	T2N3G7	403-521-6000	521-6079
CFCN-TV Ch 3 (CTV) 80 Patina Rise SW *Web:* calgary.ctv.ca	Calgary	AB	T3H2W4	403-240-5600	240-5689
CICT-TV Ch 7 (GTN) 222 23rd St NE **Fax:* News Rm ■ *Web:* www.canada.com	Calgary	AB	T2E7N2	403-235-7709	248-3842*
CKAL-TV Ch 5 (Ind) 535 7th Ave SW *Web:* www.citytv.com/calgary	Calgary	AB	T2P0Y4	403-508-2222	508-3300

744-22 Casper, WY

Station	City	State	ZIP	Phone	Fax
KFNB-TV Ch 20 (Fox) 1856 Skyview Dr	Casper	WY	82601	307-577-5923	577-5928
KGWC-TV Ch 14 (CBS) 1856 Skyview Dr	Casper	WY	82601	307-234-1111	234-4005
KLWY-TV Ch 27 (Fox) 1856 Skyview Dr	Casper	WY	82601	307-577-5923	577-5928
KTWO-TV Ch 2 (ABC) 1896 Skyview Dr *Web:* www.k2tv.com	Casper	WY	82609	307-237-3711	234-9866

744-23 Cedar Rapids, IA

Station	City	State	ZIP	Phone	Fax
KCRG-TV Ch 9 (ABC) 501 2nd Ave SE *TF:* 800-332-5443 ■ *Web:* www.kcrg.com	Cedar Rapids	IA	52401	319-398-8422	398-8378
KFXA-TV Ch 28 (Fox) 600 Old Marion Rd NE *TF:* 800-642-6140 ■ *Web:* www.kfxa.tv	Cedar Rapids	IA	52402	319-393-2800	395-7028
KGAN-TV Ch 2 (CBS) 600 Old Marion Rd NE *TF:* 800-642-6140 ■ *Web:* www.kgan.com	Cedar Rapids	IA	52402	319-395-9060	395-0987
KPXR-TV Ch 48 (I) 1957 Blairs Ferry Rd NE *Web:* www.iontelevision.com	Cedar Rapids	IA	52402	319-378-1260	378-0076

744-24 Charleston, SC

Station	City	State	ZIP	Phone	Fax
WCIV-TV Ch 4 (ABC) PO Box 22165 **Fax:* News Rm ■ *Web:* www.abcnews4.com	Charleston	SC	29413	843-881-4444	849-2519*
WCSC-TV Ch 5 (CBS) 2126 Charlie Hall Blvd *Web:* www.wcsc.com	Charleston	SC	29414	843-577-6397	402-5744

744-25 Charleston, WV

Station	City	State	ZIP	Phone	Fax
WCHS-TV Ch 8 (ABC) 1301 Piedmont Rd *TF:* 888-696-9247 ■ *Web:* www.wchstv.com	Charleston	WV	25301	304-346-5358	346-4765
WPBY-TV Ch 33 (PBS) 600 Capitol St *TF:* 888-596-9729 ■ *Web:* www.wvpubcast.org	Charleston	WV	25301	304-556-4900	556-4960
WVAH-TV Ch 11 (Fox) 1301 Piedmont Rd *Web:* www.wvah.com	Charleston	WV	25301	304-346-5358	346-4765

744-26 Charlotte, NC

Station	City	State	ZIP	Phone	Fax
WAXN-TV Ch 64 (ABC) 1901 N Tryon St **Fax:* News Rm ■ *TF:* 800-367-9762 ■ *Web:* www.wsoctv.com/action64	Charlotte	NC	28206	704-338-9999	335-4736*
WBTV-TV Ch 3 (CBS) 1 Julian Price Pl *Web:* www.wbtv.com	Charlotte	NC	28208	704-374-3500	374-3671
WCCB-TV Ch 18 (Fox) 1 Television Pl *Web:* www.foxcharlotte.tv	Charlotte	NC	28205	704-372-1800	358-4841
WCNC-TV Ch 36 (NBC) 1001 Wood Ridge Ctr Dr *Web:* www.wcnc.com	Charlotte	NC	28217	704-329-3636	357-4975
WJZY-TV Ch 46 (CW) 3501 Performance Rd *Web:* www.wjzy.com	Charlotte	NC	28214	704-398-0046	944-3440
WMYT-TV Ch 12 (MNT) 3501 Performance Rd *Web:* www.wmyt12.com	Charlotte	NC	28214	704-398-0046	393-8407
WSOC-TV Ch 9 (ABC) 1901 N Tryon St *TF:* 800-367-9762 ■ *Web:* www.wsoctv.com	Charlotte	NC	28206	704-338-9999	335-4736
WTVI-TV Ch 42 (PBS) 3242 Commonwealth Ave *Web:* www.wtvi.org	Charlotte	NC	28205	704-372-2442	335-1358

744-27 Chattanooga, TN

Station	City	State	ZIP	Phone	Fax
WDEF-TV Ch 12 (CBS) 3300 Broad St *Web:* www.wdef.com	Chattanooga	TN	37408	423-785-1200	785-1271
WDSI-TV Ch 61 (Fox) 1101 E Main St *Web:* www.fox61tv.com	Chattanooga	TN	37408	423-265-0061	265-3636
WRCB-TV Ch 3 (NBC) 900 Whitehall Rd **Fax:* News Rm ■ *Web:* www.wrcbtv.com	Chattanooga	TN	37405	423-267-5412	756-3148*
WTCI-TV Ch 45 (PBS) 7540 Bonnie Shire Dr *Web:* www.wtci-tv45.com	Chattanooga	TN	37416	423-702-7800	702-7823
WTVC-TV Ch 9 (ABC) PO Box 60028 *Web:* www.newschannel9.com	Chattanooga	TN	37406	423-757-7320	757-7401

744-28 Cheyenne, WY

Station	City	State	ZIP	Phone	Fax
KGWN-TV Ch 5 (CBS) 2923 E Lincolnway *TF:* 877-672-8019 ■ *Web:* www.kgwn.tv	Cheyenne	WY	82001	307-634-7755	638-0182

744-29 Chicago, IL

Station	City	State	ZIP	Phone	Fax
WCIU-TV Ch 26 (Ind) 26 N Halsted St *Web:* www.wciu.com	Chicago	IL	60661	312-705-2600	660-8323
WCPX-TV Ch 38 (I) 333 S Desplaines St Suite 101 *Web:* www.ionline.tv	Chicago	IL	60661	312-376-8520	575-8735
WFLD-TV Ch 32 (Fox) 205 N Michigan Ave Ground Fl *Web:* www.foxchicago.com	Chicago	IL	60601	312-565-5532	819-1332
WGBO-TV Ch 66 (Uni) 541 N Fairbanks Ct 11th Fl	Chicago	IL	60611	312-670-1000	494-6492
WGN-TV Ch 9 (CW) 2501 W Bradley Pl *Web:* www.wgntv.trb.com	Chicago	IL	60618	773-528-2311	528-6050
WMAQ-TV Ch 5 (NBC) 454 N Columbus Dr NBC Tower *Web:* www.nbc5.com	Chicago	IL	60611	312-836-5555	527-5925
WPWR-TV Ch 50 (Fox) 205 N Michigan Ave *Web:* www.my50chicago.com	Chicago	IL	60601	312-565-5532	819-1332
WSNS-TV Ch 44 (Tele) 454 N Columbus Dr	Chicago	IL	60611	312-836-3000	836-3232
WTTW-TV Ch 11 (PBS) 5400 N St Louis Ave *Web:* www.wttw.com	Chicago	IL	60625	773-583-5000	583-3046
WYCC-TV Ch 20 (PBS) 6258 S Union Ave *Web:* www.wycc.org	Chicago	IL	60621	773-838-7878	783-2906

744-30 Cincinnati, OH

Station	City	State	ZIP	Phone	Fax
WCET-TV Ch 48 (PBS) 1223 Central Pkwy *Web:* www.wcet.org	Cincinnati	OH	45214	513-381-4033	381-7520
WCPO-TV Ch 9 (ABC) 1720 Gilbert Ave *Web:* www.wcpo.com	Cincinnati	OH	45202	513-721-9900	721-7717
WKRC-TV Ch 12 (CBS) 1906 Highland Ave *Web:* www.wkrc.com	Cincinnati	OH	45219	513-763-5500	421-3820
WLWT-TV Ch 5 (NBC) 1700 Young St *Web:* www.channelcincinnati.com	Cincinnati	OH	45202	513-412-5000	412-6121
WSTR-TV Ch 64 (MNT) 5177 Fishwick Dr *Web:* www.wb64.net	Cincinnati	OH	45216	513-641-4400	242-2633
WXIX-TV Ch 19 (Fox) 635 W 7th St 19 Broadcast Plaza *Web:* www.wxix.com	Cincinnati	OH	45203	513-421-1919	421-3022

744-31 Cleveland/Akron, OH

Station	City	State	ZIP	Phone	Fax
WDLI-TV Ch 17 (TBN) 1764 Wadsworth Rd *Web:* www.tbn.org	Akron	OH	44320	330-753-5542	753-4563
WEWS-TV Ch 5 (ABC) 3001 Euclid Ave *Web:* www.newsnet5.com	Cleveland	OH	44115	216-431-5555	431-3666
WJW-TV Ch 8 (Fox) 5800 S Marginal Rd *Web:* www.fox8cleveland.com	Cleveland	OH	44103	216-431-8888	391-9559
WKYC-TV Ch 3 (NBC) 1333 Lakeside Ave E *Web:* www.wkyc.com	Cleveland	OH	44114	216-344-3333	344-3314
WOIO-TV Ch 19 (CBS) 1717 E 12th St *TF:* 877-929-1943 ■ *Web:* www.woio.com	Cleveland	OH	44114	216-771-1943	515-7152
WQHS-TV Ch 61 (Uni) 2861 W Ridgewood Dr	Cleveland	OH	44134	440-888-0061	888-7023
WUAB-TV Ch 43 (MNT) 1717 E 12th St *TF:* 800-929-0132 ■ *Web:* www.wuab.com	Cleveland	OH	44114	216-771-1943	515-7152
WVIZ-TV Ch 25 (PBS) 1375 Euclid Ave *Web:* www.wviz.org	Cleveland	OH	44115	216-916-6100	916-6090

744-32 Colorado Springs, CO

Station	City	State	ZIP	Phone	Fax
KKTV-TV Ch 11 (CBS) 3100 N Nevada Ave *Web:* www.kktv.com	Colorado Springs	CO	80907	719-634-2844	634-3741
KXRM-TV Ch 21 (Fox) 560 Wooten Rd *Web:* www.kxrm.com	Colorado Springs	CO	80915	719-596-2100	591-4180

744-33 Columbia, SC

Station	City	State	ZIP	Phone	Fax
WACH-TV Ch 57 (Fox) 1400 Pickens St Suite 6 *Web:* www.wach.com	Columbia	SC	29201	803-252-5757	212-7270
WHMC-TV Ch 23 (PBS) 1101 George Rogers Blvd *Web:* www.scetv.org	Columbia	SC	29201	803-737-3200	737-3417
WIS-TV Ch 10 (NBC) 1111 Bull St *Web:* www.wistv.com	Columbia	SC	29201	803-758-1218	758-1155
WLTX-TV Ch 19 (CBS) 6027 Garner's Ferry Rd *Web:* www.wltx.com	Columbia	SC	29209	803-776-3600	695-3714
WOLO-TV Ch 25 (ABC) 5807 Shakespeare Rd *Web:* www.wolo.com	Columbia	SC	29223	803-754-7525	754-6147
WRLK-TV Ch 35 (PBS) 1101 George Rogers Blvd *TF:* 800-922-5437 ■ *Web:* www.scetv.org	Columbia	SC	29201	803-737-3200	737-3526

744-34 Columbus, GA

Station	City	State	ZIP	Phone	Fax
WLTZ-TV Ch 38 (NBC) 6140 Buena Vista Rd *Web:* www.wltz.com	Columbus	GA	31907	706-561-3838	563-8467
WRBL-TV Ch 3 (CBS) 1350 13th Ave *Web:* www.wrbl.com	Columbus	GA	31901	706-323-3333	323-0841
WTVM-TV Ch 9 (ABC) 1909 Wynnton Rd *Web:* www.wtvm.com	Columbus	GA	31906	706-324-6471	322-7527
WXTX-TV Ch 54 (Fox) 6524 Buena Vista Rd *Web:* www.wtvm.com	Columbus	GA	31907	706-568-2900	561-5965

744-35 Columbus, OH

Station	City	State	Zip	Phone	Fax
WBNS-TV Ch 10 (CBS) 770 Twin Rivers Dr *Fax: News Rm ■ *Web:* www.wbns10tv.com	Columbus	OH	43215	614-460-3700	460-2891*
WCMH-TV Ch 4 (NBC) 3165 Olentangy River Rd *Web:* www.nbc4i.com	Columbus	OH	43202	614-263-4444	263-0166
WOSU-TV Ch 34 (PBS) 2400 Olentangy River Rd *Web:* www.wosu.org/tv	Columbus	OH	43210	614-292-9678	292-7625
WSYX-TV Ch 6 (ABC) 1261 Dublin Rd *Fax: News Rm ■ *Web:* www.wsyx6.com	Columbus	OH	43215	614-481-6666	481-6624*
WTTE-TV Ch 28 (Fox) 1261 Dublin Rd *Web:* www.wtte28.com	Columbus	OH	43215	614-481-6666	481-6624
WWHO-TV Ch 53 (CW) 1160 Dublin Rd Suite 500 *Web:* www.wwhotv.com	Columbus	OH	43215	614-485-5300	485-5339

744-36 Corpus Christi, TX

Station	City	State	Zip	Phone	Fax
KDF-TV Ch 47 (Fox) 409 S Staples St *Web:* www.kristv.com	Corpus Christi	TX	78401	361-886-6100	886-6116
KEDT-TV Ch 16 (PBS) 4455 S Padre Island Dr Suite 38 *TF:* 800-307-5338 ■ *Web:* www.kedt.org	Corpus Christi	TX	78411	361-855-2213	855-3877
KIII-TV Ch 3 (ABC) 5002 S Padre Island Dr *TF:* 800-874-5705 ■ *Web:* www.kiiitv.com	Corpus Christi	TX	78411	361-986-8300	986-8440
KORO-TV Ch 28 (Uni) 102 N Mesquite St *Web:* www.korotv.com	Corpus Christi	TX	78401	361-883-2823	883-2931
KRIS-TV Ch 6 (NBC) 301 Artesian St *Web:* www.kristv.com	Corpus Christi	TX	78401	361-886-6100	886-6175
KZTV-TV Ch 10 (CBS) 301 Artesian St *Fax: News Rm ■ *Web:* www.kztv10.com	Corpus Christi	TX	78401	361-883-7070	884-8111*

744-37 Dallas/Fort Worth, TX

Station	City	State	Zip	Phone	Fax
KDAF-TV Ch 33 (CW) 8001 John Carpenter Fwy *TF:* 877-252-8233 ■ *Web:* www.wb33.trb.com	Dallas	TX	75247	214-252-9233	252-3379
KDFW-TV Ch 4 (Fox) 400 N Griffin St *Web:* www.kdfwfox4.com	Dallas	TX	75202	214-720-4444	720-3263
KERA-TV Ch 13 (PBS) 3000 Harry Hines Blvd *Web:* www.kera.org	Dallas	TX	75201	214-871-1390	754-6035
KFWD-TV Ch 52 (Ind) 606 Young St *Web:* www.kfwd.tv	Dallas	TX	75202	214-748-9631	977-6544
KTVT-TV Ch 11 (CBS) 5233 Bridge St *Web:* www.cbs11tv.com	Fort Worth	TX	76103	817-451-1111	496-7739
KTXA-TV Ch 21 (Ind) 10111 N Central Expy *Web:* www.upn21.com	Dallas	TX	75231	214-743-2100	743-2150
KXAS-TV Ch 5 (NBC) 3900 Barnett St *TF:* 800-232-5927 ■ *Web:* www.nbc5i.com	Fort Worth	TX	76103	817-429-5555	654-6325
KXTX-TV Ch 39 (Tele) 3100 McKinnon St Suite 800 *Web:* www.telemundodallas.com	Dallas	TX	75021	214-521-3900	523-5946
WFAA-TV Ch 8 (ABC) 606 Young St Communications Ctr *Web:* www.wfaa.com	Dallas	TX	75202	214-748-9631	977-6585

744-38 Dayton, OH

Station	City	State	Zip	Phone	Fax
WDTN-TV Ch 2 (NBC) 4595 S Dixie Ave *Web:* www.wdtn.com	Dayton	OH	45439	937-293-2101	296-7147
WHIO-TV Ch 7 (CBS) 1414 Wilmington Ave *Web:* www.whiotv.com	Dayton	OH	45420	937-259-2111	259-2005
WKEF-TV Ch 22 (ABC) 45 Broadcast Plaza *Web:* www.wkef22.com	Dayton	OH	45418	937-263-2662	263-9537
WPTD-TV Ch 16 (PBS) 110 S Jefferson St *TF:* 800-247-1614 ■ *Web:* www.thinktv.org	Dayton	OH	45402	937-220-1600	220-1642
WRGT-TV Ch 45 (Fox) 45 Broadcast Plaza *Web:* www.wkef22.com	Dayton	OH	45418	937-263-4500	263-9537

744-39 Denver, CO

Station	City	State	Zip	Phone	Fax
KBDI-TV Ch 12 (PBS) 2900 Welton St 1st Fl *TF:* 800-727-8812 ■ *Web:* www.kbdi.org	Denver	CO	80205	303-296-1212	296-6650
KCEC-TV Ch 50 (Uni) 777 Grant St 5th Fl *Web:* www.entravision.com	Denver	CO	80203	303-832-0050	832-3410
KCNC-TV Ch 4 (CBS) 1044 Lincoln St *Web:* www.cbs4denver.com	Denver	CO	80203	303-861-4444	830-6380
KDVR-TV Ch 31 (Fox) 100 E Speer Blvd *TF:* 888-369-4762 ■ *Web:* www.fox31news.com	Denver	CO	80203	303-595-3131	566-2931
KMGH-TV Ch 7 (ABC) 123 E Speer Blvd *Web:* www.thedenverchannel.com	Denver	CO	80203	303-832-7777	832-0119
KRMA-TV Ch 6 (PBS) 1089 Bannock St *TF:* 800-274-6666 ■ *Web:* www.krma.org	Denver	CO	80204	303-892-6666	620-5600
KUSA-TV Ch 9 (NBC) 500 Speer Blvd *Web:* www.kusa.com	Denver	CO	80203	303-871-9999	698-4700
KWGN-TV Ch 2 (CW) 100 E Speer Blvd *Web:* www.cw2.trb.com	Denver	CO	80203	303-595-3131	566-2931

744-40 Des Moines, IA

Station	City	State	Zip	Phone	Fax
KCCI-TV Ch 8 (CBS) 888 9th St *Web:* www.kcci.com	Des Moines	IA	50309	515-247-8888	244-0202
KDSM-TV Ch 17 (Fox) 4023 Fleur Dr *Web:* www.kdsm.com	Des Moines	IA	50321	515-287-1717	287-0064
WHO-TV Ch 13 (NBC) 1801 Grand Ave *Fax: News Rm ■ *TF:* 800-835-1313 ■ *Web:* www.whotv.com	Des Moines	IA	50309	515-242-3500	242-3796*

744-41 Detroit, MI

Station	City	State	Zip	Phone	Fax
WDIV-TV Ch 4 (NBC) 550 W Lafayette Blvd *TF:* 800-654-8221 ■ *Web:* www.clickondetroit.com	Detroit	MI	48226	313-222-0500	222-0592
WTVS-TV Ch 56 (PBS) 7441 2nd Ave *Web:* www.wtvs.org	Detroit	MI	48202	248-305-3788	

744-42 Duluth, MN

Station	City	State	Zip	Phone	Fax
KBJR-TV Ch 6 (NBC) 246 S Lake Ave *Web:* www.kbjr.com	Duluth	MN	55802	218-727-8484	720-9699
KDLH-TV Ch 3 (CBS) 246 S Lake Ave *Web:* www.kdlh.com	Duluth	MN	55802	218-720-9600	720-9660
KQDS-TV Ch 21 (Fox) 2001 London Rd *Web:* www.fox21online.com	Duluth	MN	55812	218-728-1622	728-1557
WDIO-TV Ch 10 (ABC) 10 Observation Rd *TF:* 800-477-1013 ■ *Web:* www.wdio.com	Duluth	MN	55811	218-727-6864	727-4415
WDSE-TV Ch 8 (PBS) 632 Niagara Ct *TF:* 888-563-9373 ■ *Web:* www.wdse.org	Duluth	MN	55811	218-724-8568	724-4269

744-43 Edmonton, AB

Station	City	State	Zip	Phone	Fax
CBXFT-TV Ch 11 (SRC) PO Box 555 *Web:* www.radio-canada.ca/television	Edmonton	AB	T5J2P4	780-468-7500	468-7779
CBXT-TV Ch 5 (CBC) 123 Edmonton City Centre 10062-102 Ave PO Box 555 *Web:* www.cbc.ca/edmonton	Edmonton	AB	T5J2Y8	780-468-7555	468-7510
CFRN-TV Ch 3 (CTV) 18520 Stony Plain Rd *Web:* edmonton.ctv.ca	Edmonton	AB	T5S1A8	780-483-3311	489-5883
CITV-TV Ch 13 (GTN) 5325 Allard Way *TF:* 877-307-1999	Edmonton	AB	T6H5B8	780-436-1250	989-4686
CKEM-TV Ch 51 (Ind) 10212 Jasper Ave	Edmonton	AB	T5J5A3	780-412-2783	412-2799*

744-44 El Paso, TX

Station	City	State	Zip	Phone	Fax
KCOS-TV Ch 13 (PBS) 9050 Viscount Blvd Suite A-440 *Web:* www.kcostv.org	El Paso	TX	79925	915-590-1313	594-5394
KDBC-TV Ch 4 (CBS) 2201 Wyoming Ave *Web:* www.kdbc.com	El Paso	TX	79903	915-496-4444	496-4593
KFOX-TV Ch 14 (Fox) 6004 N Mesa St *Web:* www.kfoxtv.com	El Paso	TX	79912	915-833-8585	833-8717
KINT-TV Ch 26 (Uni) 5426 N Mesa St *Web:* www.univision26.com	El Paso	TX	79912	915-581-1126	585-4642
KTDO-TV Ch 48 (Tele) 10033 Carnegie Ave	El Paso	TX	79925	915-591-9595	591-9896
KTFN-TV Ch 65 (Uni) 5426 N Mesa St *Web:* www.univision26.com	El Paso	TX	79912	915-581-1126	585-4642
KTSM-TV Ch 9 (NBC) 801 N Oregon St *Web:* www.ktsm.com	El Paso	TX	79902	915-532-5421	544-0536
KVIA-TV Ch 7 (ABC) 4140 Rio Bravo St *Fax: News Rm ■ *TF:* 800-580-5842 ■ *Web:* www.kvia.com	El Paso	TX	79902	915-496-7777	532-0505*

744-45 Erie, PA

Station	City	State	Zip	Phone	Fax
WFXP-TV Ch 66 (Fox) 8455 Peach St *TF:* 888-989-9538 ■ *Web:* www.fox66.tv	Erie	PA	16509	814-864-2400	864-5393
WICU-TV Ch 12 (NBC) 3514 State St *Web:* www.wicu12.com	Erie	PA	16508	814-454-5201	454-3753
WJET-TV Ch 24 (ABC) 8455 Peach St *Web:* www.wjettv.com	Erie	PA	16509	814-864-2400	868-3041
WQLN-TV Ch 54 (PBS) 8425 Peach St *TF:* 800-727-8854 ■ *Web:* www.wqln.org	Erie	PA	16509	814-864-3001	864-4077
WSEE-TV Ch 35 (CBS) 1220 Peach St *Web:* www.35wsee.com	Erie	PA	16501	814-455-7575	454-2564

744-46 Eugene, OR

Station	City	State	Zip	Phone	Fax
KEZI-TV Ch 9 (ABC) PO Box 7009 *Web:* www.kezi.com	Eugene	OR	97401	541-485-5611	343-9664
KLSR-TV Ch 34 (Fox) 2940 Chad Dr *Web:* www.klsrtvfox.com	Eugene	OR	97408	541-683-2525	683-8016
KVAL-TV Ch 13 (CBS) 4575 Blanton Rd PO Box 1313 *Web:* www.kval.com	Eugene	OR	97405	541-342-4961	342-2635

744-47 Evansville, IN

Station	City	State	Zip	Phone	Fax
WEVV-TV Ch 44 (CBS) 44 Main St *Web:* www.wevv.com	Evansville	IN	47708	812-464-4444	465-4559

Station	City	State	Zip	Phone	Fax
WFIE-TV Ch 14 (NBC) 1115 Mt Auburn Rd *TF:* 800-832-0014 ■ *Web:* www.14wfie.com	Evansville	IN	47720	812-426-1414	426-1945
WNIN-TV Ch 9 (PBS) 405 Carpenter St *Web:* www.wnin.org	Evansville	IN	47708	812-423-2973	428-7548
WTSN-TV Ch 63 (MNT) 44 Main St	Evansville	IN	47708	812-464-4463	465-4559

744-48 Fairbanks, AK

Station	City	State	Zip	Phone	Fax
KATN-TV Ch 2 (ABC) 516 2nd Ave Suite 400 *Web:* www.aksuperstation.com	Fairbanks	AK	99701	907-452-2125	456-8225
KFXF-TV Ch 7 (Fox) 3650 Bradock St Suite 2 *Web:* www.tvtv.com	Fairbanks	AK	99701	907-452-3697	456-3428
KTVF-TV Ch 11 (NBC) 3528 International St	Fairbanks	AK	99701	907-452-5121	458-1820
KUAC-TV Ch 9 (PBS) University of Alaska PO Box 755620 *TF:* 800-727-6543 ■ *Web:* www.alaskaone.org	Fairbanks	AK	99775	907-474-7491	474-5064
KXD-TV Ch 13 (CBS) 3650 Bradock St Suite 2 *Web:* www.cbsnews13.com	Fairbanks	AK	99701	907-452-3697	456-3428

744-49 Fargo/Grand Forks, ND

Station	City	State	Zip	Phone	Fax
KBME-TV Ch 3 (PBS) 207 N 5th St *TF:* 800-359-6900 ■ *Web:* www.prairiepublic.org	Fargo	ND	58102	701-241-6900	239-7650
KFME-TV Ch 13 (PBS) 207 N 5th St *TF:* 800-359-6900 ■ *Web:* www.prairiepublic.org	Fargo	ND	58102	701-241-6900	239-7650
KGFE-TV Ch 2 (PBS) 207 N 5th St *TF:* 800-359-6900 ■ *Web:* www.prairiepublic.org	Fargo	ND	58102	701-241-6900	239-7650
KVLY-TV Ch 11 (NBC) 1350 21st Ave S *TF:* 800-450-5844 ■ *Web:* www.kvlytv11.com	Fargo	ND	58103	701-237-5211	232-0493
KVRR-TV Ch 15 (Fox) PO Box 9115	Fargo	ND	58106	701-277-1515	277-1830
KXJB-TV Ch 4 (CBS) 1350 21st Ave S *Web:* www.kx4.com	Fargo	ND	58103	701-237-5211	232-0493
WDAY-TV Ch 6 (ABC) 301 S 8th St *Web:* www.in-forum.com	Fargo	ND	58103	701-237-6500	241-5358
WDAZ-TV Ch 8 (ABC) 2220 S Washington St *TF:* 800-732-4361 ■ *Web:* www.wdaz.com	Grand Forks	ND	58201	701-775-2511	746-4507

744-50 Flint, MI

Station	City	State	Zip	Phone	Fax
WFUM-TV Ch 28 (PBS) 303 E Kearsley St University of Michigan *TF:* 800-728-9386 ■ *Web:* www.wfum.org	Flint	MI	48502	810-762-3028	233-6017
WJRT-TV Ch 12 (ABC) 2302 Lapeer Rd **Fax:* News Rm ■ *Web:* www.abclocal.go.com	Flint	MI	48503	810-233-3130	257-2812*
WSMH-TV Ch 66 (Fox) 3463 W Pierson Rd *TF:* 800-244-4664 ■ *Web:* www.wsmh66.com	Flint	MI	48504	810-785-8866	785-8963

744-51 Fort Smith, AR

Station	City	State	Zip	Phone	Fax
KFSM-TV Ch 5 (CBS) 318 N 13th St *Web:* www.kfsm.com	Fort Smith	AR	72902	479-783-3131	783-3295
KHBS-TV Ch 40 (ABC) 2415 N Albert Pike *TF:* 800-870-4029 ■ *Web:* www.4029tv.com	Fort Smith	AR	72904	479-783-4040	785-5375

744-52 Fort Wayne, IN

Station	City	State	Zip	Phone	Fax
WANE-TV Ch 15 (CBS) 2915 W State Blvd *Web:* www.wane.com	Fort Wayne	IN	46808	260-424-1515	424-6054
WFWA-TV Ch 39 (PBS) 2501 E Coliseum Blvd *TF:* 888-484-8839 ■ *Web:* www.wfwa.org	Fort Wayne	IN	46805	260-484-8839	482-3632
WISE-TV Ch 33 (NBC) 3401 Butler Rd *Web:* www.wise33.com	Fort Wayne	IN	46808	260-422-7474	422-7702
WPTA-TV Ch 21 (ABC) 3401 Butler Rd *Web:* www.wpta.com	Fort Wayne	IN	46808	260-483-0584	483-2568

744-53 Fresno, CA

Station	City	State	Zip	Phone	Fax
KFSN-TV Ch 30 (ABC) 1777 G St *Web:* abclocal.go.com/kfsn	Fresno	CA	93706	559-442-1170	266-5024
KFTV-TV Ch 21 (Uni) 601 W Univision Plaza *TF:* 800-733-5388 ■ *Web:* www.univision.net	Fresno	CA	93650	559-222-2121	222-2890
KGPE-TV Ch 47 (CBS) 4880 N 1st St **Fax:* News Rm ■ *Web:* www.47cbs.com	Fresno	CA	93726	559-222-2411	225-5305*
KMPH-TV Ch 26 (Fox) 5111 E McKinley Ave *Web:* www.kmph.com	Fresno	CA	93727	559-453-8850	255-9626
KNXT-TV Ch 49 (Ind) 1550 N Fresno St *Web:* www.knxt.tv	Fresno	CA	93703	559-488-7440	488-7444
KSEE-TV Ch 24 (NBC) 5035 E McKinley Ave *TF:* 800-234-5733 ■ *Web:* www.ksee24.com	Fresno	CA	93727	559-454-2424	454-2485
KVPT-TV Ch 18 (PBS) 1544 Van Ness Ave *Web:* www.kvpt.org	Fresno	CA	93721	559-266-1800	650-1880

744-54 Grand Rapids, MI

Station	City	State	Zip	Phone	Fax
WGVU-TV Ch 35 (PBS) 301 W Fulton St *TF:* 800-442-2771 ■ *Web:* www.wgvu.org	Grand Rapids	MI	49504	616-331-6666	331-6625
WOOD-TV Ch 8 (NBC) 120 College Ave SE *Web:* www.woodtv.com	Grand Rapids	MI	49503	616-456-8888	456-5755
WOTV-TV Ch 4 (ABC) 120 College Ave *Web:* www.wotv.com	Grand Rapids	MI	49503	616-456-8888	456-9169
WXMI-TV Ch 17 (Fox) 3117 Plaza Dr NE *Web:* www.fox17.trb.com	Grand Rapids	MI	49525	616-364-8722	364-8506
WZPX-TV Ch 43 (I) 2610 Horizon Dr SE Suite E *TF:* 877-729-8843 ■ *Web:* www.wzpxtv.com	Grand Rapids	MI	49546	616-222-4343	493-2677
WZZM-TV Ch 13 (ABC) 645 3-Mile Rd NW *Web:* www.wzzm13.com	Grand Rapids	MI	49544	616-785-1313	785-1301

744-55 Great Falls, MT

Station	City	State	Zip	Phone	Fax
KRTV-TV Ch 3 (CBS) PO Box 2989 *Web:* www.krtv.com	Great Falls	MT	59403	406-453-2433	791-5479

744-56 Green Bay, WI

Station	City	State	Zip	Phone	Fax
WACY-TV Ch 32 (MNT) 1391 N Rd *TF:* 800-800-6619 ■ *Web:* www.mynew32.com	Green Bay	WI	54313	920-490-0320	494-7071
WBAY-TV Ch 2 (ABC) 115 S Jefferson St *TF:* 800-261-9229 ■ *Web:* www.wbay.com	Green Bay	WI	54301	920-432-3331	432-1190
WFRV-TV Ch 5 (CBS) 1181 E Mason St PO Box 19055 *Web:* www.wfrv.com	Green Bay	WI	54301	920-437-5411	437-4576
WGBA-TV Ch 26 (NBC) 1391 N Rd *Web:* www.wgba.com	Green Bay	WI	54313	920-494-2626	490-2500
WIWB-TV Ch 14 (CW) 975 Parkview Rd Suite 4 *TF:* 877-352-1000 ■ *Web:* www.wb14tv.com	Green Bay	WI	54304	920-983-9014	983-9424
WLUK-TV Ch 11 (Fox) 787 Lombardi Ave *TF:* 800-242-8067 ■ *Web:* www.wluk.com	Green Bay	WI	54304	920-494-8711	494-8782

744-57 Halifax, NS

Station	City	State	Zip	Phone	Fax
CBHT-TV Ch 3 (CBC) 1840 Bell Rd PO Box 3000 *Web:* www.cbc.ca/ns	Halifax	NS	B3J3E9	902-420-8311	420-4286
CIHF-TV Ch 8 (GTN) PO Box 1643 CRO	Halifax	NS	B3J2Z1	902-481-7400	481-7427
CJCH-TV Ch 5 (Ind) 2885 Robie St	Halifax	NS	B3J2Z4	902-454-3200	454-3280

744-58 Harrisburg, PA

Station	City	State	Zip	Phone	Fax
WHP-TV Ch 21 (CBS) 3300 N 6th St *Web:* www.whptv.com	Harrisburg	PA	17110	717-238-2100	238-4903
WHTM-TV Ch 27 (ABC) 3235 Hoffman St *Web:* www.whtm.com	Harrisburg	PA	17110	717-236-2727	236-1263
WITF-TV Ch 33 (PBS) 4801 Lindle Rd *TF:* 800-366-9483 ■ *Web:* www.witf.org	Harrisburg	PA	17111	717-704-3000	704-3659
WLYH-TV Ch 15 (CW) 3300 N 6th St *Web:* www.cw15.com	Harrisburg	PA	17110	717-238-2100	238-4903

744-59 Hartford, CT

Station	City	State	Zip	Phone	Fax
WEDH-TV Ch 24 (PBS) 1049 Asylum Ave *Web:* www.cptv.org	Hartford	CT	06105	860-278-5310	275-7406
WTIC-TV Ch 61 (Fox) 1 Corporate Ctr **Fax:* News Rm ■ *Web:* www.fox61.trb.com	Hartford	CT	06103	860-527-6161	293-0178*
WTXX-TV Ch 20 (CW) 1 Corporate Ctr *Web:* www.cw20.trb.com	Hartford	CT	06103	860-527-6161	293-0178
WUVN-TV Ch 18 (Uni) 1 Constitution Plaza 7th Fl *Web:* www.wuvntv.com	Hartford	CT	06103	860-278-1818	278-1811

744-60 Helena, MT

Station	City	State	Zip	Phone	Fax
KMTF-TV Ch 10 (CW) 100 W Lyndale Ave Suite B	Helena	MT	59601	406-457-1010	442-5106
KTVH-TV Ch 12 (NBC) 100 W Lyndale Ave *Web:* www.ktvh.com	Helena	MT	59601	406-457-1212	442-5106

744-61 Honolulu, HI

Station	City	State	Zip	Phone	Fax
KBFD-TV Ch 32 (Ind) 1188 Bishop St Suite PH 1 *Web:* www.kbfd.com	Honolulu	HI	96813	808-521-8066	521-5233
KGMB-TV Ch 9 (CBS) 1534 Kapiolani Blvd *Web:* www.kgmb.com	Honolulu	HI	96814	808-973-5462	944-5252
KHET-TV Ch 11 (PBS) 2350 Dole St *Web:* www.pbshawaii.org	Honolulu	HI	96822	808-973-1000	973-1090
KHNL-TV Ch 8 (NBC) 420 Waiakamilo Rd Suite 205 *Web:* www.khnl.com	Honolulu	HI	96817	808-847-3246	845-3616

				Phone	Fax
KHON-TV Ch 2 (Fox) 88 Piikoi St.	Honolulu	HI	96814	808-591-4278	593-2418
Web: www.khon2.com					
KIKU-TV Ch 20 (Ind) 737 Bishop St Mauka Tower Suite 1430	Honolulu	HI	96813	808-847-2021	841-3326
Web: www.kikutv.com					
KITV-TV Ch 4 (ABC) 801 S King St	Honolulu	HI	96813	808-535-0400	536-8993
Web: www.thehawaiichannel.com					
KPXO-TV Ch 66 (I) 875 Waimanu St Suite 630	Honolulu	HI	96813	808-591-1275	591-1409
KWHE-TV Ch 14 (Ind) 1188 Bishop St Suite 502	Honolulu	HI	96813	808-538-1414	526-0326
TF: 800-218-1414 ■ *Web:* www.kwhe.com					

744-62 Houston, TX

				Phone	Fax
KETH-TV Ch 14 (TBN) 10902 S Wilcrest Dr	Houston	TX	77009	281-561-5828	561-9793
Web: www.communityedtv.org					
KHOU-TV Ch 11 (CBS) 1945 Allen Pkwy	Houston	TX	77019	713-526-1111	520-7763
Web: www.khou.com					
KHWB-TV Ch 39 (CW) 7700 Westpark Dr	Houston	TX	77063	713-781-3939	787-0528
Web: khwbtv.trb.com					
KNWS-TV Ch 51 (Ind) 8440 Westpark Dr	Houston	TX	77063	713-974-5151	974-5188
Web: knws51.com					
KPRC-TV Ch 2 (NBC) 8181 SW Fwy	Houston	TX	77074	713-222-2222	771-4930
Web: www.click2houston.com					
KPXB-TV Ch 49 (I) 256 N Sam Houston Pkwy E Suite 49	Houston	TX	77060	281-820-4900	820-3916
Web: www.ionline.tv					
KRIV-TV Ch 26 (Fox) 4261 SW Fwy	Houston	TX	77027	713-479-2600	479-2859*
**Fax:* News Rm ■ *Web:* www.fox26.com					
KTBU-TV Ch 55 (Ind) 11150 Equity Dr	Houston	TX	77041	713-351-0755	351-0756
Web: www.thetube.net					
KTMD-TV Ch 47 (Tele) 1235 N Loop W Suite 125	Houston	TX	77008	713-974-4848	266-6397
Web: www.ktmd.com					
KTRK-TV Ch 13 (ABC) 3310 Bissonnet St.	Houston	TX	77005	713-666-0713	664-0013
Web: abclocal.go.com/ktrk					
KTXH-TV Ch 20 (MNT) 4261 SW Fwy	Houston	TX	77027	713-661-2020	479-2859
Web: www.ktxh.com					
KUHT-TV Ch 8 (PBS) 4343 Elgin St.	Houston	TX	77204	713-748-8888	743-8867
TF: 800-364-5848 ■ *Web:* www.houstonpbs.org					
KXLN-TV Ch 45 (Uni) 5100 SW Fwy	Houston	TX	77056	713-662-4545	965-2604
Web: univisionhouston.univision.com					

744-63 Huntsville, AL

				Phone	Fax
WAAY-TV Ch 31 (ABC) 1000 Monte Sano Blvd SE	Huntsville	AL	35801	256-533-3131	533-5191*
**Fax:* News Rm ■ *TF:* 877-799-9229 ■ *Web:* www.waaytv.com					
WAFF-TV Ch 48 (NBC) 1414 Memorial PkwyNW	Huntsville	AL	35801	256-533-4848	534-4101
Web: www.waff.com					
WHDF-TV Ch 15 (CW) 200 Andrew Jackson Way	Huntsville	AL	35801	256-536-1550	536-8286
Web: www.thevalleyscw.tv					
WHNT-TV Ch 19 (CBS) PO Box 19	Huntsville	AL	35804	256-533-1919	536-9468
TF: 800-533-8819 ■ *Web:* www.whnt.com					
WZDX-TV CH 54 (Fox) 1309 N Memorial Pkwy	Huntsville	AL	35801	256-533-5454	533-5315
Web: www.fox54.com					

744-64 Indianapolis, IN

				Phone	Fax
WFYI-TV Ch 20 (PBS) 1630 N Meridian St	Indianapolis	IN	46202	317-636-2020	253-6645
Web: www.wfyi.org					
WIPX-TV Ch 63 (I) 2441 Production Dr Suite 104	Indianapolis	IN	46241	317-486-0633	
WISH-TV Ch 8 (CBS) 1950 N Meridian St	Indianapolis	IN	46202	317-923-8888	931-2242
Web: www.wishtv.com					
WNDY-TV Ch 23 (MNT) 1950 N Meridian	Indianapolis	IN	46202	317-956-8888	931-2242
Web: www.wndy.com					
WRTV-TV Ch 6 (ABC) 1330 N Meridian St	Indianapolis	IN	46202	317-635-9788	269-1445*
**Fax:* News Rm ■ *Web:* www.theindychannel.com					
WTHR-TV Ch 13 (NBC) 1000 N Meridian St	Indianapolis	IN	46204	317-636-1313	636-3717
Web: www.wthr.com					
WTTV-TV Ch 4 (CW) 6910 Network Pl.	Indianapolis	IN	46278	317-632-5900	687-6556*
**Fax:* News Rm ■ *Web:* thecw4.trb.com					
WXIN-TV Ch 59 (Fox) 6910 Network Pl.	Indianapolis	IN	46278	317-632-5900	715-6251
Web: www.fox59.com					

744-65 Jackson, MS

				Phone	Fax
WAPT-TV Ch 16 (ABC) 7616 Ch 16 Way	Jackson	MS	39209	601-922-1607	922-1663
Web: www.wapt.com					
WJTV-TV Ch 12 (CBS) 1820 TV Rd.	Jackson	MS	39204	601-372-6311	372-8798
Web: www.wjtv.com					
WLBT-TV Ch 3 (NBC) 715 S Jefferson St.	Jackson	MS	39201	601-948-3333	355-7830
Web: www.wlbt.com					
WMAE-TV Ch 12 (PBS) 3825 Ridgewood Rd	Jackson	MS	39211	601-432-6565	432-6746
TF: 800-922-9698 ■ *Web:* www.mpbonline.org					
WMAH-TV Ch 19 (PBS) 3825 Ridgewood Rd	Jackson	MS	39211	601-432-6565	432-6135
TF: 800-922-9698 ■ *Web:* www.mpbonline.org					
WMPN-TV Ch 29 (PBS) 3825 Ridgewood Rd	Jackson	MS	39211	601-432-6565	432-6135
TF: 866-262-9643 ■ *Web:* www.mpbonline.org					
WUFX-TV Ch 35 (Fox) 1 Fox 40 News Pl	Jackson	MS	39209	601-922-1234	922-0268
Web: www.gomiss.com					

744-66 Jacksonville, FL

				Phone	Fax
WAWS-TV Ch 30 (Fox) 11700 Central Pkwy Unit 2	Jacksonville	FL	32224	904-642-3030	642-5665
Web: www.fox30online.com					
WCWJ-TV Ch 17 (CW) 9117 Hogan Rd	Jacksonville	FL	32216	904-641-1700	642-7201
Web: www.wjwb.com					
WJCT-TV Ch 7 (PBS) 100 Festival Pk Ave	Jacksonville	FL	32202	904-353-7770	354-6846
Web: www.wjct.org					
WJXT-TV Ch 4 (Ind) 4 Broadcast Pl.	Jacksonville	FL	32207	904-399-4000	393-9822*
**Fax:* News Rm ■ *Web:* www.news4jax.com					
WJXX-TV Ch 25 (ABC) 1070 E Adams St	Jacksonville	FL	32202	904-354-1212	633-8899*
**Fax:* News Rm ■ *TF:* 800-352-8812 ■ *Web:* www.firstcoastnews.com					
WTEV-TV Ch 47 (CBS) 11700 Central Pkwy Unit 2	Jacksonville	FL	32224	904-642-3030	642-5665
Web: www.wtev.com					
WTLV-TV Ch 12 (NBC) 1070 E Adams St.	Jacksonville	FL	32202	904-354-1212	633-8899*
**Fax:* News Rm ■ *TF:* 800-352-8812 ■ *Web:* www.firstcoastnews.com					

744-67 Jefferson City, MO

				Phone	Fax
KNLJ-TV Ch 25 (Ind) 311 W Dunklin	Jefferson City	MO	65101	573-896-5105	896-0251
TF: 800-228-5284 ■ *Web:* www.hereshelpnet.org					

744-68 Johnson City, TN

				Phone	Fax
WJHL-TV Ch 11 (CBS) 338 E Main St	Johnson City	TN	37601	423-926-2151	434-4537
TF: 800-606-9545 ■ *Web:* www.tricities.com					

744-69 Juneau, AK

				Phone	Fax
KATH-TV Ch 5 (NBC) 1107 W 8th St	Juneau	AK	99801	907-586-8384	586-8394
KJUD-TV Ch 8 (ABC) 175 S Franklin St Suite 320	Juneau	AK	99801	907-723-4500	463-3041
TF: 877-304-1313 ■ *Web:* www.aksuperstation.com					
KTOO-TV Ch 3 (PBS) 360 Egan Dr.	Juneau	AK	99801	907-586-1670	586-3612
TF: 800-870-5866 ■ *Web:* www.ktoo.org					

744-70 Kansas City, KS & MO

				Phone	Fax
KCPT-TV Ch 19 (PBS) 125 E 31st St	Kansas City	MO	64108	816-756-3580	931-2500
Web: www.kcpt.org					
KCWE-TV Ch 29 (CW) 6455 Winchester Ave	Kansas City	MO	64133	816-221-2900	421-4163*
**Fax:* Sales ■ *Web:* www.kmbc.com/kcwe/index.html					
KMBC-TV Ch 9 (ABC) 6455 Winchester Ave	Kansas City	MO	64133	816-221-9999	421-4163
Web: www.thekansascitychannel.com					
KMCI-TV Ch 38 (Ind) 4720 Oak St	Kansas City	MO	64112	816-753-4141	932-4145
Web: www.kmci.com					
KSHB-TV Ch 41 (NBC) 4720 Oak St.	Kansas City	MO	64112	816-753-4141	932-4145
Web: www.kshb.com					
WDAF-TV Ch 4 (Fox) 3030 Summit St.	Kansas City	MO	64108	816-753-4567	561-4181
Web: www.wdaftv4.com					

744-71 Knoxville, TN

				Phone	Fax
WATE-TV Ch 6 (ABC) 1306 Broadway	Knoxville	TN	37917	865-637-6666	525-4091
Web: www.wate.com					
WBIR-TV Ch 10 (NBC) 1513 Hutchinson Ave	Knoxville	TN	37917	865-637-1010	637-6380
Web: www.wbir.com					
WBXX-TV Ch 20 (CW) 10427 Cogdill Rd Suite 100	Knoxville	TN	37932	865-777-9220	777-9221
Web: www.wbxx.tv					
WETP-TV Ch 41 (PBS) 1611 E Magnolia Ave	Knoxville	TN	37917	865-595-0220	595-0220
TF: 800-595-0220 ■ *Web:* www.etptv.org					
WKOP-TV Ch 17 (PBS) 1611 E Magnolia Ave	Knoxville	TN	37917	865-595-0220	595-0300
TF: 800-595-0220 ■ *Web:* www.etptv.org					
WTNZ-TV Ch 43 (Fox) 9000 Executive Pk Dr Bldg D Suite 300	Knoxville	TN	37923	865-693-4343	691-6904
Web: www.wtnzfox43.com					
WVLT-TV Ch 8 (CBS) 6450 Papermill Dr	Knoxville	TN	37919	865-450-8888	450-8869
Web: www.volunteertv.com					

744-72 Lafayette, LA

				Phone	Fax
KADN-TV Ch 15 (Fox) 1500 Eraste Landry Rd.	Lafayette	LA	70506	337-237-1500	237-2237
TF: 800-738-6736 ■ *Web:* www.kadn.com					
KATC-TV Ch 3 (ABC) 1103 Eraste Landry Rd.	Lafayette	LA	70506	337-235-3333	235-9363
Web: www.katc.com					
KLFY-TV Ch 10 (CBS) 1808 Eraste Landry Rd PO Box 90665	Lafayette	LA	70509	337-981-4823	984-8323*
**Fax:* Sales ■ *Web:* www.klfy.com					

744-73 Lansing, MI

Station	City	State	Zip	Phone	Fax
WILX-TV Ch 10 (NBC) 500 American Rd *TF:* 800-968-9180 ■ *Web:* www.wilx.com	Lansing	MI	48911	517-393-0110	393-8555
WLAJ-TV Ch 3 (ABC) 5815 S Pennsylvania Ave *Web:* www.wlaj.com	Lansing	MI	48911	517-394-5300	887-0077
WLNS-TV Ch 6 (CBS) 2820 E Saginaw St *Web:* www.wlns.com	Lansing	MI	48912	517-372-8282	374-7610
WSYM-TV Ch 47 (Fox) 600 W St Joseph St Suite 47 *Web:* www.fox47news.com	Lansing	MI	48933	517-484-7747	484-3144

744-74 Las Vegas, NV

Station	City	State	Zip	Phone	Fax
KBLR-TV Ch 39 (Tele) 450 Fremont St Suite 310	Las Vegas	NV	89101	702-258-0039	258-0556
KINC-TV Ch 15 (Uni) 500 Pilot Rd Suite D *Web:* www.entravision.com	Las Vegas	NV	89119	702-434-0015	434-0527
KLAS-TV Ch 8 (CBS) 3228 Ch 8 Dr **Fax:* News Rm ■ *Web:* www.klas-tv.com	Las Vegas	NV	89109	702-792-8888	792-2977*
KLVX-TV Ch 10 (PBS) 3050 E Flamingo *Web:* www.klvx.org	Las Vegas	NV	89119	702-799-1010	799-5586
KTNV-TV Ch 13 (ABC) 3355 S Valley View Blvd *TF:* 800-463-9713 ■ *Web:* www.ktnv.com	Las Vegas	NV	89102	702-876-1313	876-2237
KVBC-TV Ch 3 (NBC) 1500 Foremaster Ln *Web:* www.kvbc.com	Las Vegas	NV	89101	702-642-3333	657-3152
KVMY-TV Ch 21 (CW) 3830 S Jones Blvd *Web:* www.sbgi.net	Las Vegas	NV	89103	702-382-2121	952-4683

744-75 Lexington, KY

Station	City	State	Zip	Phone	Fax
WDKY-TV Ch 56 (Fox) 836 Euclid Ave Suite 201 *Web:* www.foxlexington.com	Lexington	KY	40502	859-269-5656	293-1578
WKLE-TV Ch 46 (PBS) 600 Cooper Dr *TF:* 800-432-0951	Lexington	KY	40502	859-258-7000	258-7399
WKYT-TV Ch 27 (CBS) 2851 Winchester Rd **Fax:* News Rm ■ *Web:* www.wkyt.com	Lexington	KY	40509	859-299-0411	293-1578*
WLEX-TV Ch 18 (NBC) PO Box 1457 **Fax:* News Rm ■ *TF:* 800-255-4566 ■ *Web:* www.wlextv.com	Lexington	KY	40588	859-259-1818	254-2217*
WTVQ-TV Ch 36 (ABC) 6940 Man O War Blvd *Web:* www.wtvq.com	Lexington	KY	40509	859-294-3636	293-5002

744-76 Lincoln, NE

Station	City	State	Zip	Phone	Fax
KLKN-TV Ch 8 (ABC) 3240 S 10th St *Web:* www.klkntv.com	Lincoln	NE	68502	402-434-8000	436-2236
KOLN-TV Ch 10 (CBS) 840 N 40th *TF:* 800-475-1011 ■ *Web:* www.kolnkgin.com	Lincoln	NE	68503	402-467-4321	467-9210
NET Radio 1800 N 33rd St *TF:* 888-638-7346 ■ *Web:* www.netnebraska.org	Lincoln	NE	68583	402-472-6141	

744-77 Little Rock, AR

Station	City	State	Zip	Phone	Fax
KARK-TV Ch 4 (NBC) 1401 W Capitol Ave Suite 104 *Web:* www.arkansasmatters.com	Little Rock	AR	72201	501-340-4444	376-1852
KATV-TV Ch 7 (ABC) 401 S Main St *Web:* www.katv.com	Little Rock	AR	72201	501-372-7777	324-7852
KLRT-TV Ch 16 (Fox) 10800 Colonel Glenn Rd *TF:* 888-367-1615 ■ *Web:* www.fox16.com	Little Rock	AR	72204	501-225-0016	224-6162
KTHV-TV Ch 11 (CBS) 720 S Izard St *Web:* www.todaysthv.com	Little Rock	AR	72201	501-376-1111	376-1645

744-78 Los Angeles, CA

Station	City	State	Zip	Phone	Fax
KCET-TV Ch 28 (PBS) 4401 Sunset Blvd *Web:* www.kcet.org	Los Angeles	CA	90027	323-666-6500	953-5523
KCOP-TV Ch 13 (MNT) 1999 S Bundy Dr *Web:* www.upn13.com	Los Angeles	CA	90025	310-584-2000	584-2024
KJLA-TV Ch 57 (Ind) 2323 Corinth Ave *TF:* 800-588-5788 ■ *Web:* www.kjla.com	Los Angeles	CA	90064	310-943-5288	943-5299
KLCS-TV Ch 58 (PBS) 1061 W Temple St *Web:* www.klcs.org	Los Angeles	CA	90012	213-241-4000	481-1019
KMEX-TV Ch 34 (Uni) 5999 Ctr Dr **Fax:* News Rm ■ *Web:* www.kmex.com	Los Angeles	CA	90045	310-216-3434	348-3493*
KSCI-TV Ch 18 (Ind) 1990 S Bundy Dr Suite 850 *TF:* 800-841-1818 ■ *Web:* www.la18.tv	Los Angeles	CA	90025	310-478-1818	479-8118
KTLA-TV Ch 5 (CW) 5800 W Sunset Blvd *Web:* www.ktla.trb.com	Los Angeles	CA	90028	323-460-5500	460-5333
KTTV-TV Ch 11 (Fox) 1999 S Bundy Dr *Web:* www.fox11la.com	Los Angeles	CA	90025	310-584-2000	584-2024

744-79 Louisville, KY

Station	City	State	Zip	Phone	Fax
WAVE-TV Ch 3 (NBC) 725 S Floyd St PO Box 32970 *Web:* www.wave3.com	Louisville	KY	40203	502-585-2201	561-4115
WBKI-TV Ch 34 (CW) 6100 Dutchmans Ln *TF:* 877-541-3434 ■ *Web:* www.wbki.tv	Louisville	KY	40205	502-809-3400	266-6262
WBNA-TV Ch 21 (I) 3701 Fern Valley Rd *Web:* www.wbna-21.com	Louisville	KY	40219	502-964-2121	966-9692
WDRB-TV Ch 41 (Fox) 624 W Muhammad Ali Blvd *Web:* www.fox41.com	Louisville	KY	40203	502-584-6441	589-5559
WHAS-TV Ch 11 (ABC) 520 W Chestnut *Web:* www.whas11.com	Louisville	KY	40202	502-582-7711	582-7532
WLKY-TV Ch 32 (CBS) 1918 Mellwood Ave *Web:* www.wlky.com	Louisville	KY	40206	502-893-3671	896-0725

744-80 Lubbock, TX

Station	City	State	Zip	Phone	Fax
KAMC-TV Ch 28 (ABC) 7403 S University Ave *Web:* everythinglubbock.com	Lubbock	TX	79423	806-745-2828	748-2250
KCBD-TV Ch 11 (NBC) 5600 Ave A *Web:* www.kcbd.com	Lubbock	TX	79404	806-744-1414	749-1111
KJTV-TV Ch 34 (Fox) 9800 University Ave *Web:* www.foxkjtv34.com	Lubbock	TX	79423	806-745-3434	748-1949
KLBK-TV Ch 13 (CBS) 7403 S University Ave *Web:* everythinglubbock.com	Lubbock	TX	79423	806-745-2345	748-2250
KTXT-TV Ch 5 (PBS) Texas Tech Univ PO Box 42161 *Web:* www.ktxt.org	Lubbock	TX	79409	806-742-2209	742-1274

744-81 Macon, GA

Station	City	State	Zip	Phone	Fax
WGNM-TV Ch 64 (Ind) 178 Steven Dr *Web:* www.wgnm.com	Macon	GA	31210	478-474-8400	474-4777
WMAZ-TV Ch 13 (CBS) 1314 Gray Hwy *Web:* www.13wmaz.com	Macon	GA	31211	478-752-1313	752-1331
WMGT-TV Ch 41 (NBC) 301 Poplar St *TF:* 866-901-6397 ■ *Web:* www.wmgt.com	Macon	GA	31201	478-745-4141	742-2626
WPGA-TV Ch 58 (ABC) 1691 Forsyth St *TF:* 800-225-5222 ■ *Web:* wpga58.com	Macon	GA	31201	478-745-5858	745-5800

744-82 Madison, WI

Station	City	State	Zip	Phone	Fax
WBUW-TV Ch 57 (CW) 2814 Syene Rd *Web:* www.wb57.com	Madison	WI	53713	608-270-5700	270-5717
WHA-TV Ch 21 (PBS) 821 University Ave *Web:* www.wpt.org	Madison	WI	53706	608-263-2121	263-1952
WISC-TV Ch 3000 (CBS) 7025 Raymond Rd *Web:* www.channel3000.com	Madison	WI	53719	608-271-4321	271-0800
WKOW-TV Ch 27 (ABC) 5727 Tokay Blvd *Web:* www.wkowtv.com	Madison	WI	53719	608-274-1234	274-9514
WMSN-TV Ch 47 (Fox) 7847 Big Sky Dr *Web:* www.fox47.com	Madison	WI	53719	608-833-0047	274-9569
WMTV-Ch 15 (NBC) 615 Forward Dr *TF:* 800-894-4222 ■ *Web:* www.nbc15.madison.com	Madison	WI	53711	608-274-1515	271-5194

744-83 Memphis, TN

Station	City	State	Zip	Phone	Fax
WBUY-TV Ch 40 (TBN) 3447 Cazassa St	Memphis	TN	38116	901-396-9541	396-9585
WHBQ-TV Ch 13 (Fox) 485 S Highland St *Web:* www.foxmemphis.com	Memphis	TN	38111	901-320-1313	320-1366
WLMT-TV Ch 30 (CW) 2701 Union Ave Ext *Web:* www.upn30memphis.com	Memphis	TN	38112	901-323-2430	452-1820
WMC-TV Ch 5 (NBC) 1960 Union Ave *Web:* www.wmctv.com	Memphis	TN	38104	901-726-0555	278-7633
WPTY-TV Ch 24 (ABC) 2701 Union Ave Ext *Web:* www.abc24.com	Memphis	TN	38112	901-323-2430	452-1820
WREG-TV Ch 3 (CBS) 803 Ch Three Dr *Web:* www.wreg.com	Memphis	TN	38103	901-543-2333	543-2167

744-84 Miami/Fort Lauderdale, FL

Station	City	State	Zip	Phone	Fax
WBFS-TV Ch 33 (MNT) 8900 NW 18th Terr *Web:* upn33.com	Miami	FL	33172	305-591-4444	477-3040
WFOR-TV Ch 4 (CBS) 8900 NW 18th Terr *Web:* www.wfor.com	Miami	FL	33172	305-591-4444	477-3040
WLRN-TV Ch 17 (PBS) 172 NE 15th St *Web:* www.wlrn.org	Miami	FL	33132	305-995-1717	995-2299
WLTV-TV Ch 23 (Uni) 9405 NW 41st St	Miami	FL	33178	305-470-2323	471-4236
WPBT-TV Ch 2 (PBS) 14901 NE 20th Ave **Fax:* News Rm ■ *TF:* 800-222-9728 ■ *Web:* www.channel2.org	Miami	FL	33181	305-949-8321	949-9772*
WSFL-TV Ch 39 (CW) 200 E Las Olas Blvd 10th Fl *Web:* www.cwsfl.trb.com	Fort Lauderdale	FL	33301	954-627-7300	355-5200
WSVN-TV Ch 7 (Fox) 1401 79th St Cswy *Web:* www.wsvn.com	Miami	FL	33141	305-751-6692	757-2266

744-85 Milwaukee, WI

Station	City	State	ZIP	Phone	Fax
WCGV-TV Ch 24 (MNT) 4041 N 35th St	Milwaukee	WI	53216	414-874-1824	874-1899
Web: www.my24milwaukee.com					
WDJT-TV Ch 58 (CBS) 809 S 60th St	Milwaukee	WI	53214	414-777-5800	777-5802
Web: www.cbs58.com					
WISN-TV Ch 12 (ABC) 759 N 19th St	Milwaukee	WI	53233	414-342-8812	342-7505
Web: www.wisn.com					
WITI-TV Ch 6 (Fox) 9001 N Green Bay Rd	Milwaukee	WI	53209	414-355-6666	586-2141*
**Fax:* News Rm ■ *Web:* www.fox6now.com					
WMVS-TV Ch 10 1036 N 8th St	Milwaukee	WI	53233	414-271-1036	297-8549
Web: www.mptv.org					
WMVT-TV Ch 36 1036 N 8th St	Milwaukee	WI	53233	414-271-1036	297-7536
Web: www.mptv.org					
WPXE-TV Ch 55 (I) 6161 N Flint Rd Suite F	Milwaukee	WI	53209	414-247-0117	247-1302
Web: www.ionmedia.tv					
WTMJ-TV Ch 4 (NBC) 720 E Capitol Dr	Milwaukee	WI	53212	414-332-9611	967-5378
Web: www.touchtmj4.com					
WVCY-TV Ch 30 (Ind) 3434 W Kilbourn Ave	Milwaukee	WI	53208	414-935-3000	935-3015
TF: 800-729-9829 ■ *Web:* www.vcyamerica.org					
WVTV-TV Ch 18 (CW) 4041 N 35th St	Milwaukee	WI	53216	414-442-7050	203-2300
Web: www.cw18milwaukee.com					

744-86 Minneapolis/Saint Paul, MN

Station	City	State	ZIP	Phone	Fax
KSTP-TV Ch 5 (ABC) 3415 University Ave W	Saint Paul	MN	55114	651-646-5555	642-4409
Web: www.kstp.com					
KTCA-TV Ch 2 (PBS) 172 E 4th St	Saint Paul	MN	55101	651-222-1717	229-1282
Web: www.ktca.org					
KTCI-TV Ch 17 (PBS) 172 E 4th St	Saint Paul	MN	55101	651-222-1717	229-1282
Web: www.tpt.org					
WCCO-TV Ch 4 (CBS) 90 S 11th St	Minneapolis	MN	55403	612-339-4444	330-2767
TF: 800-444-9226 ■ *Web:* www.wcco.com					
WUCW-TV Ch 23 (CW) 1640 Como Ave	Saint Paul	MN	55108	651-646-2300	646-1220
Web: www.kmwb23.com					

744-87 Mobile, AL

Station	City	State	ZIP	Phone	Fax
WALA-TV Ch 10 (Fox) 1501 Satchel Paige Dr	Mobile	AL	36606	251-434-1010	434-1073
Web: www.fox10tv.com					
WKRG-TV Ch 5 (CBS) 555 Broadcast Dr	Mobile	AL	36606	251-479-5555	473-8130
Web: www.wkrg.com					
WMPV-TV Ch 21 (TBN) 1668 W I-65 Service Rd S	Mobile	AL	33693	251-661-2101	661-7121
Web: www.tbn.org					
WPMI-TV Ch 15 (NBC) 661 Azalea Rd	Mobile	AL	36609	251-602-1500	602-1550
Web: www.local15tv.com					

744-88 Monterey, CA

Station	City	State	ZIP	Phone	Fax
KSMS-TV Ch 67 (Uni) 67 Garden Ct	Monterey	CA	93940	831-373-6767	373-6700
Web: www.ksmstv.com					

744-89 Montgomery, AL

Station	City	State	ZIP	Phone	Fax
WAIQ-TV Ch 26 (PBS) 1255 Madison Ave	Montgomery	AL	36107	334-264-9900	264-7045
TF: 800-239-5239 ■ *Web:* www.aptv.org					
WAKA-TV Ch 8 (CBS) 3020 Eastern Blvd	Montgomery	AL	36116	334-271-8888	244-7859
TF: 800-467-0401 ■ *Web:* www.waka.com					
WCOV-TV Ch 20 (Fox) 1 W Cov Ave	Montgomery	AL	36111	334-288-7020	288-5414
Web: www.wcov.com					
WNCF-TV Ch 32 (ABC) 3251 Harrison Rd	Montgomery	AL	36109	334-270-3200	271-6348
Web: www.abc32.com					
WSFA-TV Ch 12 (NBC) 12 E Delano Ave	Montgomery	AL	36105	334-288-1212	613-8303*
**Fax:* News Rm ■ *Web:* www.wsfa.com					

744-91 Montreal, QC

Station	City	Province	Postal Code	Phone	Fax
CBFT-TV Ch 2 (SRC) 1400 Rene-Levesque Blvd E	Montreal	QC	H2L2M2	514-597-6000	597-5404
CBMT-TV Ch 6 (CBC) 1400 Rene-Levesque Blvd E Rm B 62-1	Montreal	QC	H2L2M2	514-597-6000	597-6354
Web: www.cbc.ca/montreal					
CBVE-TV Ch 5 (CBC) 1400 Rene-Levesque Blvd E	Montreal	QC	H2L2M2	514-597-6000	597-6354
CFCF-TV Ch 12 (CTV) 1205 Papineau Ave	Montreal	QC	H2K4R2	514-273-6311	276-9399
Web: www.cfcf12.ca					
CFJP-TV Ch 35 (QS) 612 St Jacques St Suite 100	Montreal	QC	H3C5R1	514-390-6035	390-0773
CFTM-TV Ch 10 (TVA) 1600 de Maisonneuve Blvd E	Montreal	QC	H2L4P2	514-526-9251	598-6073
CFTU-TV Ch 29 (Ind) 2200 Rue Sainte-Catherine Est	Montreal	QC	H2K2J1	514-509-2222	509-2299
TF: 888-640-2626 ■ *Web:* www.canalsavoir.tv					
CIVM-TV Ch 17 (Ind) 1000 Rue Fullum	Montreal	QC	H2K3L7	514-521-2424	873-7464
Web: www.telequebec.tv					

744-92 Myrtle Beach, SC

Station	City	State	ZIP	Phone	Fax
WBTW-TV Ch 13 (CBS) 101 McDonald Ct	Myrtle Beach	SC	29588	843-293-1301	293-7701
Web: www.wbtw.com					
WFXB-TV Ch 43 (Fox) 3364 Huger St	Myrtle Beach	SC	29577	843-828-4300	828-4343
Web: www.wfxb.com					

744-93 Naples/Fort Myers, FL

Station	City	State	ZIP	Phone	Fax
WBBH-TV Ch 20 (NBC) 3719 Central Ave PO Box 7578	Fort Myers	FL	33901	239-939-2020	936-7771
Web: www.nbc-2.com					
WFTX-TV Ch 4 (Fox) 621 SW Pine Island Rd	Cape Coral	FL	33991	239-574-3636	574-2025
Web: www.fox4florida.com					
WGCU-TV Ch 30 (PBS) 10501 FGCU Blvd	Fort Myers	FL	33965	239-590-2300	590-2310
TF: 888-824-0030 ■ *Web:* www.wgcu.org					
WINK-TV Ch 11 (CBS) 2824 Palm Beach Blvd	Fort Myers	FL	33916	239-334-1111	332-0767
Web: www.winktv.com					
WTVK-TV Ch 46 (CW) 2824 Palm Beach Blvd	Fort Myers	FL	33916	239-334-1111	332-0767
WZVN-TV Ch 26 (ABC) 3719 Central Ave PO Box 7578	Fort Myers	FL	33901	239-939-2020	936-7771
TF: 800-741-8820 ■ *Web:* www.wzvn.com					

744-94 Nashville, TN

Station	City	State	ZIP	Phone	Fax
WKRN-TV Ch 2 (ABC) 441 Murfreesboro Rd	Nashville	TN	37210	615-369-7222	369-7329
TF: 800-242-9576 ■ *Web:* www.wkrn.com					
WNAB-TV Ch 58 (CW) 631 Mainstream Dr PO Box 17	Nashville	TN	37228	615-259-5617	259-3962
Web: www.cw58.tv					
WNPT-TV Ch 8 (PBS) 161 Rains Ave	Nashville	TN	37203	615-259-9325	248-6120
Web: www.wnpt.net					
WSMV-TV Ch 4 (NBC) 5700 Knob Rd	Nashville	TN	37209	615-353-4444	353-2343
Web: www.wsmv.com					
WTVF-TV Ch 5 (CBS) 474 James Robertson Pkwy	Nashville	TN	37219	615-244-5000	244-9883*
**Fax:* News Rm ■ *Web:* www.newschannel5.com					
WUXP-TV Ch 30 (MNT) 631 Mainstream Dr PO Box 17	Nashville	TN	37228	615-259-5630	259-3962
Web: www.wuxp.com					
WZTV-TV Ch 17 (Fox) 631 Mainstream Dr PO Box 17	Nashville	TN	37228	615-244-1717	259-3962
Web: www.fox17.com					

744-95 New Orleans, LA

Station	City	State	ZIP	Phone	Fax
WDSU-TV Ch 6 (NBC) 846 Howard Ave	New Orleans	LA	70113	504-679-0600	679-0733
TF: 800-416-6397 ■ *Web:* www.wdsu.com					
WHNO-TV Ch 20 (Ind) 839 St Charles Ave	New Orleans	LA	70130	504-681-0120	681-0180
Web: www.whno.com					
WUPL-TV Ch 54 (MNT) 1024 N Rampart St	New Orleans	LA	70116	504-529-4444	529-6472
Web: www.wupltv.com					
WVUE-TV Ch 8 (Fox) 1025 S Jefferson Davis Pkwy	New Orleans	LA	70125	504-486-6161	483-1543
Web: www.fox8live.com					
WWL-TV Ch 4 (CBS) 1024 N Rampart St	New Orleans	LA	70116	504-529-4444	529-6472
Web: www.wwltv.com					

744-96 New York, NY

Station	City	State	ZIP	Phone	Fax
WABC-TV Ch 7 (ABC) 7 Lincoln Sq	New York	NY	10023	212-456-7000	456-2381*
**Fax:* News Rm ■ *Web:* www.abclocal.go.com					
WCBS-TV Ch 2 (CBS) 51 W 52th St	New York	NY	10019	212-975-4321	975-9387
Web: www.cbs2ny.com					
WNBC-TV Ch 4 (NBC) 30 Rockefeller Plaza	New York	NY	10112	212-664-4444	664-2994
Web: www.wnbc.com					
WNET-TV Ch 13 (PBS) 450 W 33rd St	New York	NY	10001	212-560-1313	560-1314
Web: www.thirteen.org					
WNYE-TV Ch 25 (PBS) 1 Ctr St 27th Fl	New York	NY	10007	212-669-7400	669-8448
Web: www.wnye.org					
WNYW-TV Ch 5 (Fox) 205 E 67th St	New York	NY	10065	212-452-5555	249-1182
Web: www.myfoxny.com					
WPIX-TV Ch 11 (CW) 220 E 42nd St	New York	NY	10017	212-949-1100	210-2591*
**Fax:* News Rm ■ *Web:* cw11.trb.com					
WPXN-TV Ch 31 (I) 1330 Avenue of the Americas 32nd Fl	New York	NY	10019	212-757-3100	956-0920
TF: 800-646-7296					
WTBY-TV Ch 54 (TBN) 17 Irving Pl	New York	NY	10003	212-777-2120	777-0405
Web: www.tbn.org					

744-97 Norfolk/Virginia Beach, VA

Station	City	State	ZIP	Phone	Fax
WHRO-TV Ch 15 (PBS) 5200 Hampton Blvd	Norfolk	VA	23508	757-889-9400	489-0007
Web: www.whro.org					

Phone Fax

WPXV-TV Ch 49 (I)
230 Clearfield Ave Suite 104 .... Virginia Beach VA 23462 757-499-1261 499-1679
Web: www.ionmedia.com
WTKR-TV Ch 3 (CBS) 720 Boush St .... Norfolk VA 23510 757-446-1000 446-1376
TF: 800-375-0901 ■ *Web:* www.wtkr.com
WTVZ-TV Ch 33 (MNT) 900 Granby St .... Norfolk VA 23510 757-622-3333 623-1541
Web: www.wtvz33.com
WVEC-TV Ch 13 (ABC) 613 Woodis Ave .... Norfolk VA 23510 757-625-1313 628-5855
Web: www.wvec.com

744-98 Oklahoma City, OK

Phone Fax

KAUT-TV Ch 43 (MNT) 444 E Britton Rd .... Oklahoma City OK 73114 405-478-4300 516-4343
Web: www.ok43.com
KETA-TV Ch 13 (PBS) PO Box 14190 .... Oklahoma City OK 73113 405-848-8501 841-9216
Web: www.oeta.onenet.net
KFOR-TV Ch 4 (NBC) 444 E Britton Rd .... Oklahoma City OK 73114 405-478-1212 478-6337
Web: www.kfor.com
KOCB-TV Ch 34 (CW)
1228 E Wilshire Blvd .... Oklahoma City OK 73111 405-843-2525 478-4343
Web: www.kocb.com
KOCO-TV Ch 5 (ABC) 1300 E Britton Rd .... Oklahoma City OK 73131 405-478-3000 478-6675
Web: www.channeloklahoma.com
KOKH-TV Ch 25 (Fox)
1228 E Wilshire Blvd .... Oklahoma City OK 73111 405-843-2525 478-4343
Web: www.kokh25.com
KOPX-TV Ch 62 (I) 13424 Railway Dr .... Oklahoma City OK 73114 405-478-9562 751-6867
Web: www.ionline.tv
KWTV-TV Ch 9 (CBS) 7401 N Kelley Ave........... Oklahoma City OK 73111 405-843-6641 841-9989*
**Fax:* News Rm ■ *Web:* www.newsok.com

744-99 Omaha, NE

Phone Fax

KETV-TV Ch 7 (ABC) 2665 Douglas St .... Omaha NE 68131 402-345-7777 522-7740
TF: 800-279-5388 ■ *Web:* www.ketv.com
KMTV-TV Ch 3 (CBS) 10714 Mockingbird Dr .... Omaha NE 68127 402-592-3333 592-4714
Web: www.km3news.com
KPTM-TV Ch 42 (Fox) 4625 Farnam St.................. Omaha NE 68132 402-554-1500 554-4290
Web: www.kptm.com
KXVO-TV Ch 15 (CW) 4625 Farnam St .... Omaha NE 68132 402-554-1500 554-4290
Web: www.kxvo.com
KYNE-TV Ch 26 (PBS) 6001 Dodge St.................. Omaha NE 68182 402-472-3611 554-2440
WOWT-TV Ch 6 (NBC) 3501 Farnam St.................. Omaha NE 68131 402-346-6666 233-7880
TF: 800-688-2431 ■ *Web:* www.wowt.com

744-100 Orlando, FL

Phone Fax

WFTV-TV Ch 9 (ABC) 490 E S St....................... Orlando FL 32801 407-841-9000 481-2891
Web: www.wftv.com
WKMG-TV Ch 6 (CBS) 4466 N John Young Pkwy .... Orlando FL 32804 407-291-6000 298-2122
TF: 888-853-6060 ■ *Web:* www.local6.com
WOPX-TV Ch 56 (I)
7091 Grand National Dr Suite 100 .... Orlando FL 32819 407-370-5600 363-1759
Web: www.ionmedia.tv

744-101 Ottawa, ON

Phone Fax

CBOFT-TV Ch 9 (CBC)
250 Lanark Ave CP 3220 Succ C .... Ottawa ON K1Y1E4 613-724-5550 724-5074*
CHRO-TV Ch 5 (Ind) 87 George St...................... Ottawa ON K1N9H7 613-789-0606 789-7197
TF: 800-461-2476
CJOH-TV Ch 13 (CTV) 87 George St .... Ottawa ON K2C3G6 613-224-1313 274-4301
Web: ottawa.ctv.ca

744-102 Peoria, IL

Phone Fax

WMBD-TV Ch 31 (CBS) 3131 N University St............. Peoria IL 61604 309-688-3131 686-8650
Web: www.wmbd.com
WTVP-TV Ch 47 (PBS) 101 State St .... Peoria IL 61602 309-677-4747 677-4730
TF: 800-837-4747 ■ *Web:* www.wtvp.org

744-103 Philadelphia, PA

Phone Fax

KYW-TV Ch 3 (CBS) 1555 Hamilton St .... Philadelphia PA 19130 215-977-5300 238-4545
Web: www.kyw.com
WHYY-TV Ch 12 (PBS) 150 N 6th St............... Philadelphia PA 19106 215-351-1200 351-3352
Web: www.whyy.org
WPHL-TV Ch 17 (MNT) 5001 Wynnefield Ave........ Philadelphia PA 19131 215-878-1700
Web: www.myphl17.com
WPPX-TV Ch 61 (I)
3901 B Main St Suite 301....................... Philadelphia PA 19127 215-482-4770 482-4777
Web: www.ionmedia.tv
WPSG-TV Ch 57 (CW) 1555 Hamilton St............ Philadelphia PA 19130 215-977-5700 977-5658
Web: www.cwphilly.com
WPVI-TV Ch 6 (ABC) 4100 City Line Ave .... Philadelphia PA 19131 215-878-9700 581-4530
Web: www.abclocal.go.com

Phone Fax

WTXF-TV Ch 29 (Fox) 330 Market St .... Philadelphia PA 19106 215-925-2929 982-5494*
**Fax:* News Rm ■ *Web:* www.myfoxphilly.com
WYBE-TV Ch 35 (Ind) 8200 Ridge Ave .... Philadelphia PA 19128 215-483-3900 483-6908
Web: www.wybe.org

744-104 Phoenix, AZ

Phone Fax

KASW-TV Ch 61 (CW) 5555 N 7th Ave .... Phoenix AZ 85013 480-661-6161 207-3277
KNXV-TV Ch 15 (ABC) 515 N 44th St .... Phoenix AZ 85008 602-273-1500 685-3000
TF: 800-803-3277 ■ *Web:* www.abc15.com
KPAZ-TV Ch 21 (TBN) 3551 E McDowell Rd............. Phoenix AZ 85008 602-273-1477 267-9427
Web: www.tbn.org
KPHO-TV Ch 5 (CBS) 4016 N Black Canyon Hwy .... Phoenix AZ 85017 602-264-1000 650-0761
Web: www.kpho.com
KPNX-TV Ch 12 (NBC) 1101 N Central Ave.............. Phoenix AZ 85004 602-257-1212 257-6619
Web: www.azcentral.com/12news
KPPX-TV Ch 17 (I)
2777 E Camelback Rd Suite 220....................... Phoenix AZ 85016 602-340-1466 808-8864
TF: 888-467-2988
KSAZ-TV Ch 10 (Fox) 511 W Adams St.................. Phoenix AZ 85003 602-257-1234 262-0177
TF: 888-369-4762 ■ *Web:* www.myfoxphoenix.com
KTVK-TV Ch 3 (Ind) 5555 N 7th Ave................... Phoenix AZ 85013 602-207-3333 207-3477
Web: www.azfamily.com
KTVW-TV Ch 33 (Uni) 6006 S 30th St.................. Phoenix AZ 85042 602-243-3333 276-8658
Web: www.univision.com
KUTP-TV Ch 45 (MNT) 511 W Adams.................... Phoenix AZ 85003 602-257-1234 262-0177
Web: www.kutp.com

744-105 Pittsburgh, PA

Phone Fax

KDKA-TV Ch 2 (CBS) 1 Gateway Ctr .... Pittsburgh PA 15222 412-575-2200 575-2871
Web: www.kdka.com
WPGH-TV Ch 53 (Fox) 750 Ivory Ave .... Pittsburgh PA 15214 412-931-5300 931-8135*
**Fax:* News Rm ■ *Web:* www.wpgh53.com/pittsburgh_pa
WPMY-TV Ch 22 (MNT) 750 Ivory Ave .... Pittsburgh PA 15214 412-931-5300 931-8135
Web: www.wcwb22.com
WPXI-TV Ch 11 (NBC) 4145 Evergreen Rd .... Pittsburgh PA 15214 412-237-1100 237-4900
TF: 800-237-9794 ■ *Web:* www.wpxi.com
WQED-TV Ch 13 (PBS) 4802 5th Ave .... Pittsburgh PA 15213 412-622-1300 622-6413
TF: 800-876-1316 ■ *Web:* www.wqed.org
WTAE-TV Ch 4 (ABC) 400 Ardmore Blvd.............. Pittsburgh PA 15221 412-242-4300 244-4628*
**Fax:* News Rm ■ *Web:* www.thepittsburghchannel.com

744-106 Pocatello, ID

Phone Fax

KFXP-TV Ch 31 (Fox) 902 E Sherman St............... Pocatello ID 83201 208-232-6666 233-6678
Web: www.kfxp.com
KIFI-TV Ch 8 (ABC)
1246 Yellowstone Ave Suite A-1...................... Pocatello ID 83201 208-233-8888 233-8932
Web: www.localnews8.com
KISU-TV Ch 10 (PBS)
Idaho State University CB 8111
921 S 8th Ave...................................... Pocatello ID 83209 208-282-2857 282-2848
TF: 800-543-6868 ■ *Web:* www.idahoptv.org
KPVI-TV Ch 6 (NBC) 902 E Sherman St................ Pocatello ID 83201 208-232-6666 233-6678
TF: 800-366-5784 ■ *Web:* www.kpvi.com

744-107 Portland, ME

Phone Fax

WCSH-TV Ch 6 (NBC) 1 Congress Sq .... Portland ME 04101 207-828-6666 828-6620
TF: 800-464-1213 ■ *Web:* www.wcsh6.com
WGME-TV Ch 13 (CBS) 81 Northport Dr................ Portland ME 04103 207-797-1313 878-3505
TF: 800-766-9330 ■ *Web:* www.wgme.com

744-108 Portland, OR

Phone Fax

KATU-TV Ch 2 (ABC) 2153 NE Sandy Blvd .... Portland OR 97232 503-231-4222 231-4263
TF: 800-777-5288 ■ *Web:* www.katu.com
KEPB-TV Ch 28 (PBS) 7140 SW Macadam Ave........... Portland OR 97219 503-244-9900 293-1919
TF: 800-241-8123 ■ *Web:* www.opb.org
KGW-TV Ch 8 (NBC) 1501 SW Jefferson St............. Portland OR 97201 503-226-5000 226-5059
TF: 800-288-5498 ■ *Web:* www.kgw.com
KOIN-TV Ch 6 (CBS) 222 SW Columbia St .... Portland OR 97201 503-464-0600 464-0717
Web: www.koin.com
KOPB-TV Ch 10 (PBS) 7140 SW Macadam Ave .... Portland OR 97219 503-244-9900 293-1919
TF: 800-241-8123 ■ *Web:* www.opb.org
KPXG-TV Ch 22 (I)
811 SW Naito Pkwy Suite 100 .... Portland OR 97204 503-222-2221 222-4613*
**Fax:* Sales ■ *Web:* www.ionmedia.tv

744-109 Providence, RI

Phone Fax

WLNE-TV Ch 6 (ABC) 10 Orms St .... Providence RI 02904 401-453-8000 331-4431
Web: www.abc6.com
WSBE-TV Ch 36 (PBS) 50 Pk Ln.................... Providence RI 02907 401-222-3636 222-3407
TF: 800-639-0036 ■ *Web:* www.ripbs.org

744-110 Quebec City, QC

Station / Address	City	State	Postal Code	Phone	Fax
CFAP-TV Ch 2 (QS) 330 St Vallier St E Office 025	Quebec	QC	G1K9C5	418-624-2222	624-3099

744-111 Raleigh/Durham, NC

Station / Address	City	State	ZIP	Phone	Fax
WLFL-TV Ch 22 (CW) 3012 Highwoods Blvd Suite 101 *Web:* www.wb22tv.com	Raleigh	NC	27604	919-872-9535	878-3697
WNCN-TV Ch 17 (NBC) 1205 Front St *Web:* www.nbc17.com	Raleigh	NC	27609	919-836-1717	836-1747
WRAL-TV Ch 5 (CBS) 2619 Western Blvd *TF:* 800-245-9725 ■ *Web:* www.wral.com	Raleigh	NC	27606	919-821-8555	821-8541
WRAZ-TV Ch 50 (Fox) 512 S Mangum St *TF:* 877-369-5050 ■ *Web:* www.fox50.com	Durham	NC	27701	919-595-5050	595-5028
WTVD-TV Ch 11 (ABC) 411 Liberty St *TF:* 800-467-4440 ■ *Web:* www.abclocal.go.com	Durham	NC	27701	919-683-1111	687-4373

744-112 Rapid City, SD

Station / Address	City	State	ZIP	Phone	Fax
KCLO-TV Ch 15 (CBS) 1719 W Main St *Web:* www.keloland.com	Rapid City	SD	57702	605-341-1500	348-5518
KEVN-TV Ch 7 (Fox) 2000 Skyline Dr PO Box 677 *Web:* www.blackhillsfox.com	Rapid City	SD	57709	605-394-7777	348-9128
KNBN-TV Ch 27 (NBC) 2424 S Plaza Dr *Web:* www.newscenter1.com	Rapid City	SD	57702	605-355-0024	355-9274
KOTA-TV Ch 3 (ABC) 518 St Joseph St *Web:* www.kotatv.com	Rapid City	SD	57701	605-342-2000	342-7305

744-113 Reno/Carson City, NV

Station / Address	City	State	ZIP	Phone	Fax
KAME-TV Ch 21 (MNT) 4920 Brookside Ct *Web:* www.foxreno.com	Reno	NV	89502	775-856-2121	856-2116
KNPB-TV Ch 5 (PBS) 1670 N Virginia St *Web:* www.knpb.org	Reno	NV	89503	775-784-4555	784-1438
KOLO-TV Ch 8 (ABC) 4850 Ampere Dr **Fax:* News Rm ■ *Web:* www.kolotv.com	Reno	NV	89502	775-858-8888	858-8855*
KRNV-TV Ch 4 (NBC) 1790 Vassar St *TF:* 877-377-0122 ■ *Web:* www.krnv.com	Reno	NV	89502	775-322-4444	785-1250
KRXI-TV Ch 11 (Fox) 4920 Brookside Ct *Web:* www.foxreno.com	Reno	NV	89502	775-856-1100	856-2116
KTVN-TV Ch 2 (CBS) 4925 Energy Way *Web:* www.ktvn.com	Reno	NV	89502	775-858-2222	861-4298

744-114 Richmond, VA

Station / Address	City	State	ZIP	Phone	Fax
WCVE-TV Ch 23 (PBS) 23 Sesame St *TF:* 800-476-8440 ■ *Web:* www.wcve.org	Richmond	VA	23235	804-320-1301	320-8729
WRIC-TV Ch 8 (ABC) 301 Arboretum Pl *Web:* www.wric.com	Richmond	VA	23236	804-330-8888	330-8881
WRLH-TV Ch 35 (Fox) 1925 Westmoreland St *Web:* www.fox35.com	Richmond	VA	23230	804-358-3535	358-1495
WTVR-TV Ch 6 (CBS) 3301 W Broad St **Fax:* Sales ■ *Web:* www.wtvr.com	Richmond	VA	23230	804-254-3600	342-3418*
WUPV-TV Ch 65 (CW) 5710 Midlothian Tpke *Web:* www.cwrichmond.tv	Richmond	VA	23225	804-230-1212	342-5746
WWBT-TV Ch 12 (NBC) 5710 Midlothian Tpke *Web:* www.nbc12.com	Richmond	VA	23225	804-230-1212	230-2793

744-115 Roanoke, VA

Station / Address	City	State	ZIP	Phone	Fax
WBRA-TV Ch 15 (PBS) 1215 McNeil Dr *TF:* 888-332-7788 ■ *Web:* www.blueridgepbs.org	Roanoke	VA	24015	540-344-0991	344-2148
WDBJ-TV Ch 7 (CBS) 2807 Hershberger Rd NW *TF:* 800-777-9325 ■ *Web:* www.wdbj7.com	Roanoke	VA	24017	540-344-7000	344-5097
WDRL-TV Ch 24 (Ind) 5002 Airport Rd NW *Web:* www.wdrl-tv.com	Roanoke	VA	24012	540-366-1825	366-7530
WFXR-TV Ch 27 (Fox) 2618 Colonial Ave SW *Web:* www.fox2127.com	Roanoke	VA	24015	540-344-2127	345-1912
WSLS-TV Ch 10 (NBC) PO Box 10 *TF:* 800-800-9757 ■ *Web:* www.wsls.com	Roanoke	VA	24022	540-981-9110	343-2059

744-116 Rochester, MN

Station / Address	City	State	ZIP	Phone	Fax
KTTC-TV Ch 10 (NBC) 6301 Bandel Rd NW *TF:* 800-288-1656 ■ *Web:* www.kttc.com	Rochester	MN	55901	507-288-4444	288-6324
KXLT-TV Ch 47 (Fox) 6301 Bandel Rd NW *TF:* 877-369-4788 ■ *Web:* www.fox47kxlt.com	Rochester	MN	55901	507-252-4747	252-5050

744-117 Rochester, NY

Station / Address	City	State	ZIP	Phone	Fax
WHAM-TV Ch 13 (ABC) 4225 W Henrietta Rd *Web:* www.13wham.com	Rochester	NY	14623	585-334-8700	334-8719
WHEC-TV Ch 10 (NBC) 191 E Ave *TF:* 800-284-9432 ■ *Web:* www.whec.com	Rochester	NY	14604	585-546-5670	546-5688
WROC-TV Ch 8 (CBS) 201 Humboldt St **Fax:* News Rm ■ *Web:* www.wroctv.com	Rochester	NY	14610	585-288-8400	288-1505*
WUHF-TV Ch 31 (Fox) 201 Humbolt St **Fax:* News Rm ■ *Web:* www.foxrochester.com	Rochester	NY	14610	585-232-3700	288-1505*
WXXI-TV Ch 21 (PBS) PO Box 30021 *Web:* www.wxxi.org	Rochester	NY	14603	585-325-7500	258-0335

744-118 Rockford, IL

Station / Address	City	State	ZIP	Phone	Fax
WIFR-TV Ch 23 (CBS) 2523 N Meridian Rd *Web:* www.wifr.com	Rockford	IL	61101	815-987-5300	965-0981
WQRF-TV Ch 39 (Fox) 1917 N Meridian Rd *Web:* www.mystateline.com	Rockford	IL	61101	815-963-5413	963-6113
WREX-TV Ch 13 (NBC) 10322 Auburn Rd **Fax:* News Rm ■ *Web:* www.wrex.com	Rockford	IL	61103	815-335-2213	335-2055*
WTVO-TV Ch 17 (ABC) 1917 N Meridian Rd *Web:* www.mystateline.com	Rockford	IL	61101	815-963-5413	963-6113

744-119 Sacramento, CA

Station / Address	City	State	ZIP	Phone	Fax
KCRA-TV Ch 3 (NBC) 3 Television Cir *Web:* www.kcra.com	Sacramento	CA	95814	916-446-3333	554-4688
KQCA-TV Ch 58 (MNT) 58 Television Cir *Web:* www.my58.com	Sacramento	CA	95814	916-447-5858	554-4658
KTXL-TV Ch 40 (Fox) 4655 Fruitridge Rd *Web:* www.fox40.com	Sacramento	CA	95820	916-454-4422	739-0559
KUVS-TV Ch 19 (Uni) 1710 Arden Way *Web:* www.univision.com	Sacramento	CA	95815	916-927-1900	614-1906
KVIE-TV Ch 6 (PBS) 2030 W El Camino Ave *TF:* 800-347-5843 ■ *Web:* www.kvie.org	Sacramento	CA	95833	916-929-5843	929-7215
KXTV-TV Ch 10 (ABC) 400 Broadway *Web:* www.news10.net	Sacramento	CA	95818	916-441-2345	447-6107

744-120 Saint Louis, MO

Station / Address	City	State	ZIP	Phone	Fax
KDNL-TV Ch 30 (ABC) 1215 Cole St *Web:* www.abcstlouis.com	Saint Louis	MO	63106	314-436-3030	
KETC-TV Ch 9 (PBS) 3655 Olive St *Web:* www.ketc.org	Saint Louis	MO	63108	314-512-9000	512-9005
KMOV-TV Ch 4 (CBS) 1 S Memorial Dr *TF:* 800-477-5668 ■ *Web:* www.kmov.com	Saint Louis	MO	63102	314-621-4444	621-4775
KNLC-TV Ch 24 (Ind) 1411 Locust St *Web:* www.knlc.tv	Saint Louis	MO	63103	314-436-2424	436-2434
KSDK-TV Ch 5 (NBC) 1000 Market St **Fax:* News Rm ■ *Web:* www.ksdk.com	Saint Louis	MO	63101	314-421-5055	444-5164*

744-121 Salt Lake City, UT

Station / Address	City	State	ZIP	Phone	Fax
KJZZ-TV Ch 14 (Ind) 301 W S Temple *Web:* www.kjzz.com	Salt Lake City	UT	84101	801-537-1414	238-6414
KPNZ-TV Ch 24 (Ind) 150 N Wright Bros Dr Suite 520 *Web:* www.kpnz24.tv	Salt Lake City	UT	84116	801-519-2424	359-1272
KSL-TV Ch 5 (NBC) PO Box 1160 *Web:* www.ksl.com	Salt Lake City	UT	84110	801-575-5555	575-5560
KSTU-TV Ch 13 (Fox) 5020 W Amelia Earhart Dr *Web:* www.fox13.com	Salt Lake City	UT	84116	801-532-1300	537-5335
KTVX-TV Ch 4 (ABC) 2175 W 1700 S *Web:* www.abc4.com	Salt Lake City	UT	84104	801-975-4444	973-4176
KUED-TV Ch 7 (PBS) 101 Wasatch Dr Rm 215 *TF:* 800-477-5833 ■ *Web:* www.kued.org	Salt Lake City	UT	84112	801-581-7777	585-5096
KUPX-TV Ch 16 (I) 466C Lawndale Dr *TF:* 888-467-2988 ■ *Web:* www.ionmedia.tv	Salt Lake City	UT	84115	801-474-0016	463-9667
KUTV-TV Ch 2 (CBS) 299 S Main St Suite 150 **Fax:* News Rm ■ *Web:* www.connect2utah.com	Salt Lake City	UT	84111	801-839-1234	839-1235*

744-122 San Antonio, TX

Station / Address	City	State	ZIP	Phone	Fax
KABB-TV Ch 29 (Fox) 4335 NW Loop 410 *Web:* www.kabb.com	San Antonio	TX	78229	210-366-1129	377-4758
KENS-TV Ch 5 (CBS) 5400 Fredericksburg Rd *Web:* www.kens5.com	San Antonio	TX	78229	210-366-5000	377-0740
KLRN-TV Ch 9 (PBS) 501 Broadway St *TF:* 800-627-8193 ■ *Web:* www.klrn.org	San Antonio	TX	78215	210-270-9000	270-9078
KMYS-TV Ch 35 (MNT) 4335 NW Loop 410 **Fax:* News Rm ■ *Web:* www.krrt.com	San Antonio	TX	78229	210-366-1129	377-4758*
KSAT-TV Ch 12 (ABC) 1408 N St Mary's St **Fax:* News Rm ■ *Web:* www.ksat.com	San Antonio	TX	78215	210-351-1200	351-1310*

	City	State	Zip	Phone	Fax
KVDA-TV Ch 60 (Tele) 6234 San Pedro Ave *Fax: News Rm ■ Web: www.msnlatino.telemundo.com	San Antonio	TX	78216	210-340-8860	341-2051*
KWEX-TV Ch 41 (Uni) 411 E Durango Blvd Web: www.univision.com	San Antonio	TX	78204	210-227-4141	227-0469
WOAI-TV Ch 4 (NBC) 1031 Navarro St Web: www.woai.com	San Antonio	TX	78205	210-226-4444	224-9898

744-123 San Diego, CA

	City	State	Zip	Phone	Fax
KFMB-TV Ch 8 (CBS) 7677 Engineer Rd Web: www.kfmb.com	San Diego	CA	92111	858-571-8888	560-0627
KGTV-TV Ch 10 (ABC) 4600 Airway Web: www.10news.com	San Diego	CA	92102	619-237-1010	527-0369
KNSD-TV Ch 39 (NBC) 225 Broadway Web: www.nbcsandiego.com	San Diego	CA	92101	619-231-3939	578-0202
KPBS-TV Ch 15 (PBS) 5200 Campanile Dr TF: 888-399-5727 ■ Web: www.kpbs.org	San Diego	CA	92182	619-594-1515	594-3812
KSWB-TV Ch 5 (Fox) 7191 Engineer Rd *Fax: News Rm ■ Web: www.fox5sandiego.com	San Diego	CA	92111	858-492-9269	268-0401*
KUSI-TV Ch 51 (Ind) 4575 Viewridge Ave Web: www.kusi.com	San Diego	CA	92123	858-571-5151	576-9317
XETV-TV Ch 6 (CW) 8253 Ronson Rd Web: www.sandiego6.com	San Diego	CA	92111	858-279-6666	279-0061

744-124 San Francisco, CA

	City	State	Zip	Phone	Fax
KBHK-TV Ch 44 (CW) 855 Battery St 4th Fl *Fax: PR ■ Web: www.cwbayarea.com	San Francisco	CA	94111	415-765-8144	765-8916*
KBWB-TV Ch 20 (Ind) 2500 Marin St Web: www.kofytv.com	San Francisco	CA	94124	415-821-2020	821-9158
KDTV-TV Ch 14 (Uni) 50 Fremont St 41st Fl Web: www.univision.com	San Francisco	CA	94105	415-538-8000	538-8053
KGO-TV Ch 7 (ABC) 900 Front St Web: www.abclocal.go.com	San Francisco	CA	94111	415-954-7777	956-6402
KQED-TV Ch 9 (PBS) 2601 Mariposa St Web: www.kqed.org	San Francisco	CA	94110	415-864-2000	553-2254
KRON-TV Ch 4 (Ind) 1001 Van Ness Ave Web: www.kron.com	San Francisco	CA	94109	415-441-4444	561-8136
KTNC-TV Ch 42 (Ind) 1700 Montgomery St Suite 400 Web: www.ktnc.com	San Francisco	CA	94111	415-398-4242	352-1800

744-125 San Juan, PR

	City	State	Zip	Phone	Fax
WKAQ-TV Ch 2 (Tele) PO Box 009366222	San Juan	PR	00936	787-758-2222	641-2179*

744-126 Savannah, GA

	City	State	Zip	Phone	Fax
WGSA-TV Ch 34 (CW) 401 Mall Blvd Suite 201-B	Savannah	GA	31406	912-692-8000	692-0400
WJCL-TV Ch 22 (ABC) 10001 Abercorn St Web: www.abc22tv.com	Savannah	GA	31406	912-925-0022	921-2235
WSAV-TV Ch 3 (NBC) 1430 E Victory Dr Web: www.wsav.com	Savannah	GA	31404	912-651-0300	651-0304
WTGS-TV Ch 28 (Fox) 10001 Abercorn St Web: www.wtgs.com	Savannah	GA	31406	912-925-2287	921-2235
WTOC-TV Ch 11 (CBS) 11 the News Pl PO Box 8086 *Fax: News Rm ■ Web: www.wtoctv.com	Savannah	GA	31412	912-234-1111	232-4945*

744-128 Seattle/Tacoma, WA

	City	State	Zip	Phone	Fax
KBTC-TV Ch 28 (PBS) 2320 S 19th St TF: 888-596-5282 ■ Web: www.kbtc.org	Tacoma	WA	98405	253-680-7700	680-7725
KCPQ-TV Ch 13 (Fox) 1813 Westlake Ave N Web: www.q13.trb.com	Seattle	WA	98109	206-674-1313	674-1777
KCTS-TV Ch 9 (PBS) 401 Mercer St TF: 800-443-9991 ■ Web: www.kcts.org	Seattle	WA	98109	206-728-6463	443-6691
KING-TV Ch 5 (NBC) 333 Dexter Ave N TF: 800-456-3975 ■ Web: www.king5.com	Seattle	WA	98109	206-448-5555	448-4525
KIRO-TV Ch 7 (CBS) 2807 3rd Ave TF: 800-777-5476 ■ Web: www.kirotv.com	Seattle	WA	98121	206-728-7777	441-4840
KMYQ-TV Ch 22 (MNT) 1813 Westlake Ave N Web: www.myq2.trb.com	Seattle	WA	98109	206-674-1313	674-1777
KOMO-TV Ch 4 (ABC) 140 4th Ave N Web: www.komotv.com	Seattle	WA	98109	206-404-4000	404-4422
KONG-TV Ch 16 (Ind) 333 Dexter Ave N Web: www.kongtv.com	Seattle	WA	98109	206-448-3166	448-3167

744-129 Shreveport, LA

	City	State	Zip	Phone	Fax
KMSS-TV Ch 33 (Fox) 3519 Jewella Ave TF: 800-631-5677 ■ Web: www.kmsstv.com	Shreveport	LA	71109	318-631-5677	631-4195
KSHV-TV Ch 45 (MNT) 3519 Jewella Ave Web: www.kshv.com	Shreveport	LA	71109	318-631-4545	621-8629
KSLA-TV Ch 12 (CBS) 1812 Fairfield Ave Web: www.ksla.com	Shreveport	LA	71101	318-222-1212	677-6703
KTAL-TV Ch 6 (NBC) 3150 N Market St TF: 866-665-6000 ■ Web: www.arklatexhomepage.com	Shreveport	LA	71107	318-629-6000	629-7171
KTBS-TV Ch 3 (ABC) 312 E Kings Hwy Web: www.ktbs.com	Shreveport	LA	71104	318-861-5800	219-4601

744-130 Sioux Falls, SD

	City	State	Zip	Phone	Fax
KDLT-TV Ch 46 (NBC) 3600 S Westport Ave TF: 800-727-5358 ■ Web: www.kdlt.com	Sioux Falls	SD	57106	605-361-5555	361-3982
KELO-TV Ch 11 (CBS) 501 S Phillips Ave *Fax: News Rm ■ TF: 800-888-5356 ■ Web: www.keloland.com	Sioux Falls	SD	57104	605-336-1100	336-0202*
KSFY-TV Ch 13 (ABC) 300 N Dakota Ave Suite 100 Web: www.ksfy.com	Sioux Falls	SD	57104	605-336-1300	336-2067
KTTW-TV Ch 7 (Fox) 2817 W 11th St TF: 800-759-8352 ■ Web: www.kttw.com	Sioux Falls	SD	57104	605-338-0017	338-7173

744-131 South Bend, IN

	City	State	Zip	Phone	Fax
WNDU-TV Ch 16 (NBC) PO Box 1616 Web: www.wndu.com	South Bend	IN	46634	574-284-3000	284-3009
WNIT-TV Ch 34 (PBS) 300 W Jefferson Blvd PO Box 7034 Web: www.wnit.org	South Bend	IN	46601	574-675-9648	289-3441
WSJV-TV Ch 28 (Fox) PO Box 28 TF: 800-975-8881 ■ Web: www.fox28.com	South Bend	IN	46624	574-679-9758	294-1267

744-132 Spokane, WA

	City	State	Zip	Phone	Fax
KAYU-TV Ch 28 (Fox) 4600 S Regal St Web: www.myfoxspokane.com	Spokane	WA	99223	509-448-2828	448-0926
KHQ-TV Ch 6 (NBC) 1201 W Sprague Ave Web: www.khq.com	Spokane	WA	99201	509-448-6000	448-4644
KREM-TV Ch 2 (CBS) 4103 S Regal St TF: 800-753-2000 ■ Web: www.krem.com	Spokane	WA	99223	509-448-2000	448-6397
KSKN-TV Ch 22 (CW) 4103 S Regal St TF: 800-753-2000 ■ Web: www.krem.com	Spokane	WA	99223	509-448-2000	448-6397
KSPS-TV Ch 7 (PBS) 3911 S Regal St TF: 800-735-2377 ■ Web: www.ksps.org	Spokane	WA	99223	509-354-7800	354-7757
KXLY-TV Ch 4 (ABC) 500 W Boone Ave Web: www.kxly.com	Spokane	WA	99201	509-324-4000	327-3932

744-133 Springfield, IL

	City	State	Zip	Phone	Fax
WICS-TV Ch 20 (ABC) 2680 E Cook St *Fax: News Rm ■ TF: 800-263-9720 ■ Web: www.wics.com	Springfield	IL	62703	217-753-5620	753-5681*
WRSP-TV Ch 55 (Fox) 3003 Old Rochester Rd Web: www.myfoxillnois.com	Springfield	IL	62703	217-523-8855	523-4410
WSEC-TV Ch 14 (PBS) PO Box 6248 TF: 800-232-3605 ■ Web: www.networkknowledge.tv	Springfield	IL	62708	217-483-7887	483-1112

744-134 Springfield, MA

	City	State	Zip	Phone	Fax
WGBY-TV Ch 57 (PBS) 44 Hampden St Web: www.wgby.org	Springfield	MA	01103	413-781-2801	731-5093
WGGB-TV Ch 40 (ABC) 1300 Liberty St Web: www.wggb.com	Springfield	MA	01104	413-733-4040	788-7640
WWLP-TV Ch 22 (NBC) PO Box 2210 Web: www.wwlp.com	Springfield	MA	01102	413-786-2200	377-2261

744-135 Springfield, MO

	City	State	Zip	Phone	Fax
KOLR-TV Ch 10 (CBS) 2650 E Division St Web: ozarksfirst.com	Springfield	MO	65803	417-862-1010	831-4209
KOZK-TV Ch 21 (PBS) 901 S National Ave TF: 866-684-5695 ■ Web: www.optv.org	Springfield	MO	65804	417-836-3500	836-3569
KSPR-TV Ch 33 (ABC) 1359 St Louis St TF: 800-220-8222 ■ Web: www.kspr.com	Springfield	MO	65802	417-831-1333	831-9358
KWBM-TV Ch 31 (MNT) 1736 E Sunshine Suite 831	Springfield	MO	65804	417-336-0031	877-9015
KYTV-TV Ch 3 (NBC) PO Box 3500 TF: 800-492-4335 ■ Web: www.ky3.com	Springfield	MO	65808	417-268-3000	268-3364

744-136 Syracuse, NY

	City	State	Zip	Phone	Fax
WCNY-TV Ch 24 (PBS) 506 Old Liverpool Rd PO Box 2400 Web: www.wcny.org	Syracuse	NY	13220	315-453-2424	451-8824
WNYS-TV Ch 43 (MNT) 1000 James St Web: www.wnys43.com	Syracuse	NY	13203	315-472-6800	471-8889

Station	City	State	Zip	Phone	Fax
WSTM-TV Ch 3 (NBC) 1030 James St *Web:* www.wstm.com	Syracuse	NY	13203	315-474-5000	474-5122
WSYT-TV Ch 68 (Fox) 1000 James St *Web:* www.wsyt68.com	Syracuse	NY	13203	315-472-6800	471-8889
WTVH-TV Ch 5 (CBS) 980 James St *Web:* www.wtvh.com	Syracuse	NY	13203	315-425-5555	425-0129

744-137 Tallahassee, FL

Station	City	State	Zip	Phone	Fax
WCTV-TV Ch 6 (CBS) 1801 Halstead Blvd *TF:* 800-375-4204 ■ *Web:* www.wctv6.com	Tallahassee	FL	32319	850-893-6666	668-3851
WFSU-TV Ch 11 (PBS) 1600 Red Barber Plaza *TF:* 800-322-9378 ■ *Web:* www.wfsu.org	Tallahassee	FL	32310	850-487-3170	487-3093
WTWC-TV Ch 40 (NBC) 8440 Deerlake Rd S *Web:* www.wtwc40.com	Tallahassee	FL	32312	850-893-4140	893-6974

744-138 Tampa/Saint Petersburg, FL

Station	City	State	Zip	Phone	Fax
WEDU-TV Ch 3 (PBS) 1300 N Blvd *Web:* www.wedu.org	Tampa	FL	33607	813-254-9338	253-0826
WFLA-TV Ch 8 (NBC) 200 S Parker St *TF:* 800-348-9352 ■ *Web:* www.wfla.com	Tampa	FL	33606	813-228-8888	225-2770
WFTS-TV Ch 28 (ABC) 4045 N Himes Ave *TF:* 800-234-9387 ■ *Web:* www.wfts.com	Tampa	FL	33607	813-354-2800	870-2828
WMOR-TV Ch 32 (Ind) 7201 E Hillsborough Ave *Web:* www.moretv32.com	Tampa	FL	33610	813-626-3232	626-1961
WTOG-TV Ch 44 (CW) 365 105th Terr NE *Web:* www.cw44.com	Saint Petersburg	FL	33716	727-576-4444	576-6155
WTSP-TV Ch 10 (CBS) 11450 Gandy Blvd N *TF:* 800-393-6610 ■ *Web:* www.wtsp.com	Saint Petersburg	FL	33702	727-577-1010	576-6924
WTTA-TV Ch 38 (MNT) 7622 Bald Cypress Pl *Web:* www.wtta38.com	Tampa	FL	33614	813-886-9882	880-8100
WTVT-TV Ch 13 (Fox) 3213 W Kennedy Blvd *Web:* www.wtvt.com	Tampa	FL	33609	813-876-1313	871-3135
WUSF-TV Ch 16 (PBS) 4202 E Fowler Ave *TF:* 800-654-3703 ■ *Web:* www.wusftv.usf.edu	Tampa	FL	33620	813-974-4000	974-4806

744-139 Toledo, OH

Station	City	State	Zip	Phone	Fax
WGTE-TV Ch 30 (PBS) PO Box 30 *TF:* 800-243-9483 ■ *Web:* www.wgte.org	Toledo	OH	43614	419-380-4600	380-4710
WLMB-TV Ch 40 (Ind) 825 Capital Commons Dr *Web:* www.wlmb.org	Toledo	OH	43615	419-874-8862	720-9563
WNWO-TV Ch 24 (NBC) 300 S Byrne Rd *Web:* www.wnwo.com	Toledo	OH	43615	419-535-0024	535-8936
WTOL-TV Ch 11 (CBS) 730 N Summit St *Web:* www.wtol.com	Toledo	OH	43604	419-248-1111	244-7104
WTVG-TV Ch 13 (ABC) 4247 Dorr St *Web:* abclocal.go.com/wtvg	Toledo	OH	43607	419-531-1313	534-3898
WUPW-TV Ch 36 (Fox) 4 Seagate *TF:* 866-369-6397 ■ *Web:* www.foxtoledo.com	Toledo	OH	43604	419-244-3600	725-1636

744-140 Topeka, KS

Station	City	State	Zip	Phone	Fax
KSNT-TV Ch 27 (NBC) 6835 NW Hwy 24 *Web:* www.ksnt.com	Topeka	KS	66618	785-582-4000	582-5283
KTKA-TV Ch 49 (ABC) 2121 SW Chelsea Dr *TF:* 800-279-3128 ■ *Web:* www.ktka.tv	Topeka	KS	66614	785-273-4949	273-7811
KTWU-TV Ch 11 (PBS) 1700 College *TF:* 800-866-5898 ■ *Web:* www.ktwu.org	Topeka	KS	66621	785-670-1111	670-1112
WIBW-TV Ch 13 (CBS) 631 SW Commerce Pl *Web:* www.wibw.com	Topeka	KS	66615	785-272-6397	272-1363

744-141 Toronto, ON

Station	City	State	Zip	Phone	Fax
CBLT-TV Ch 5 (CBC) PO Box 500 *TF:* 866-306-4636 ■ *Web:* www.cbc.ca/toronto	Toronto	ON	M5W1E6	416-205-3311	205-7166
CFMT-TV Ch 47 (Ind) 545 Lake Shore Blvd W *TF:* 888-260-0047 ■ *Web:* www.omni1.ca	Toronto	ON	M5V1A3	416-260-0047	260-3621
CFTO-TV Ch 9 (CTV) 9 Ch 9 Ct *TF:* 800-668-0060 ■ *Web:* www.cftonews.com	Toronto	ON	M1S4B5	416-332-5000	299-2273
CICA-TV Ch 19 (Ind) 2180 Yonge St Stn Q PO Box 200 *TF:* 800-613-0513 ■ *Web:* www.tvo.org	Toronto	ON	M4T2T1	416-484-2600	484-4234
CITY-TV Ch 57 (Ind) 33 Dundas St E *Web:* www.citytv.com/toronto	Toronto	ON	M5B1B8	416-599-2489	

744-142 Tucson, AZ

Station	City	State	Zip	Phone	Fax
KGUN-TV Ch 9 (ABC) 7280 E Rosewood St *Web:* www.kgun9.com	Tucson	AZ	85710	520-722-5486	733-7050
KHRR-TV Ch 40 (Tele) 5151 E Broadway Blvd Suite 600	Tucson	AZ	85711	520-396-2600	396-2640
KMSB-TV Ch 11 (Fox) 1855 N 6th Ave *Web:* www.fox11az.com	Tucson	AZ	85705	520-770-1123	629-7185
KOLD-TV Ch 13 (CBS) 7831 N Business Pk Dr *Web:* www.kold.com	Tucson	AZ	85743	520-744-1313	744-5235
KUAT-TV Ch 6 (PBS) University of Arizona PO Box 210067 *Fax: News Rm ■ *Web:* www.tv.azpm.org/kuat	Tucson	AZ	85721	520-621-5828	621-4122*
KVOA-TV Ch 4 (NBC) 209 W Elm PO Box 5188 *Web:* www.kvoa.com	Tucson	AZ	85703	520-792-2270	620-1309

744-143 Tulsa, OK

Station	City	State	Zip	Phone	Fax
KJRH-TV Ch 2 (NBC) 3701 S Peoria Ave *Web:* www.kjrh.com	Tulsa	OK	74105	918-743-2222	748-1436
KOKI-TV Ch 23 (Fox) 2625 S Memorial Dr *Web:* www.fox23.com	Tulsa	OK	74129	918-491-0023	491-6650
KOTV-TV Ch 6 (CBS) PO Box 6 *Web:* www.newson6.com	Tulsa	OK	74101	918-732-6000	732-6185
KTUL-TV Ch 8 (ABC) PO Box 8 *Web:* www.ktul.com	Tulsa	OK	74101	918-445-8888	445-9316
KWHB-TV Ch 47 (Ind) 8835 S Memorial Dr *Web:* www.kwhb.com	Tulsa	OK	74133	918-254-4701	254-5614

744-144 Vancouver, BC

Station	City	State	Zip	Phone	Fax
CBUFT-TV Ch 26 (SRC) 700 Hamilton St	Vancouver	BC	V6B4A2	604-662-6212	662-6229
CIVT-TV Ch 9 (CTV) 750 Burrard St Suite 300 *Web:* www.ctvbc.ctv.ca	Vancouver	BC	V6Z1X5	604-608-2868	608-2698
CKVU-TV Ch 10 (Ind) 180 W 2nd Ave *TF:* 888-336-9978 ■ *Web:* www.citytv.com/vancouver	Vancouver	BC	V5Y3T9	604-876-1344	876-3100

744-145 Washington, DC

Station	City	State	Zip	Phone	Fax
WDCA-TV Ch 20 (MNT) 5151 Wisconsin Ave NW *Web:* www.myfoxdc.com	Washington	DC	20016	202-895-3050	895-3340
WDCW-TV Ch 50 (CW) 2121 Wisconsin Ave NW Suite 350 *Web:* www.thecwdc.trb.com	Washington	DC	20007	202-965-5050	965-0050
WHUT-TV Ch 32 (PBS) 2222 4th St NW *Web:* www.howard.edu/tv	Washington	DC	20059	202-806-3200	806-3300
WRC-TV Ch 4 (NBC) 4001 Nebraska Ave NW *Web:* www.nbcwashington.com	Washington	DC	20016	202-885-4000	885-4104
WTTG-TV Ch 5 (Fox) 5151 Wisconsin Ave NW *Fax: News Rm ■ *TF:* 800-988-4885 ■ *Web:* www.fox5dc.com	Washington	DC	20016	202-244-5151	895-3132*
WUSA-TV Ch 9 (CBS) 4100 Wisconsin Ave NW *Web:* www.wusatv9.com	Washington	DC	20016	202-895-5999	364-6163

744-146 West Palm Beach, FL

Station	City	State	Zip	Phone	Fax
WFGC-TV Ch 61 (Ind) 1900 S Congress Ave Suite A *Web:* www.wfgc.com	West Palm Beach	FL	33406	561-642-3361	967-5961
WFLX-TV Ch 29 (Fox) 4119 W Blue Heron Blvd *Web:* www.wflxfox29.com	West Palm Beach	FL	33404	561-845-2929	863-1238
WPEC-TV Ch 12 (CBS) 1100 Fairfield Dr *Web:* www.wpecnews12.com	West Palm Beach	FL	33407	561-844-1212	842-1212
WPTV-TV Ch 5 (NBC) 1100 Banyan Blvd *NYSE: SSP* ■ *Fax: News Rm ■ *Web:* www.wptv.com	West Palm Beach	FL	33401	561-655-5455	653-5719*
WTVX-TV Ch 34 (CW) 1700 Palm Beach Lakes Blvd *Web:* www.upn34.com	West Palm Beach	FL	33401	561-681-3434	684-9193
WXEL-TV Ch 42 (PBS) PO Box 6607 *TF:* 800-915-9935 ■ *Web:* www.wxel.org	West Palm Beach	FL	33405	561-737-8000	369-3067

744-147 Wheeling, WV

Station	City	State	Zip	Phone	Fax
WTRF-TV Ch 7 (CBS) 96 16th St *Fax: News Rm ■ *TF:* 800-777-9873 ■ *Web:* www.wtrf.com	Wheeling	WV	26003	304-232-7777	233-5822*

744-148 Wichita, KS

Station	City	State	Zip	Phone	Fax
KAKE-TV Ch 10 (ABC) 1500 N W St *Web:* www.kake.com	Wichita	KS	67203	316-943-4221	943-5374
KPTS-TV Ch 8 (PBS) 320 W 21 St *TF:* 800-794-8498 ■ *Web:* www.kpts.org	Wichita	KS	67203	316-838-3090	838-8586
KSAS-TV Ch 24 (Fox) 316 N W St *Web:* www.foxkansas.com	Wichita	KS	67203	316-942-2424	942-8927
KSCC-TV Ch 36 (MNT) 316 N W St *Web:* www.mytvwichita.com	Wichita	KS	67203	316-942-2424	942-8927
KSCW-TV Ch 33 (CW) 2815 E 37th St N *Web:* www.kansascw.com	Wichita	KS	67219	316-838-1212	832-4090

Phone | Fax

KSNW-TV Ch 3 (NBC) 833 N Main St .... Wichita KS 67203 316-265-3333 292-1195
TF: 800-949-5769 ■ *Web:* www.ksn.com

KWCH-TV Ch 12 (CBS) 2815 E 37th St N .... Wichita KS 67219 316-838-1212 831-6193
TF: 888-512-6397 ■ *Web:* www.kwch.com

744-149 Winnipeg, MB

Phone | Fax

CBWF-TV Ch 3 (SRC) 541 Portage Ave ....Winnipeg MB R3B2G1 204-788-3222 788-3255
TF: 866-306-4636

CBWT-TV Ch 6 (CBC) 541 Portage Ave ....Winnipeg MB R3B2G1 204-788-3222 788-3643
TF: 866-306-4636 ■ *Web:* www.cbc.ca/manitoba

CKND-TV Ch 9 (GTN) 201 Portage Ave 30th Fl ....Winnipeg MB R3B3K6 204-233-3304 233-5615
Web: www.canada.com/winnipeg

CTV-TV Ch 5 (CTV) 345 Graham Ave Suite 400..........Winnipeg MB R3C5S6 204-788-3300 788-3399*
**Fax:* News Rm ■ *TF:* 800-461-1542 ■ *Web:* winnipeg.ctv.ca

744-150 Winston-Salem, NC

Phone | Fax

WMYV-TV Ch 48 (MNT) 3500 Myer Lee Dr........ Winston-Salem NC 27101 336-274-4848 723-8217
Web: www.upn48.com

WXII-TV Ch 12 (NBC) 700 Coliseum Dr .... Winston-Salem NC 27106 336-721-9944 721-0856
Web: www.wxii12.com

WXLV-TV Ch 45 (ABC) 3500 Myer Lee Dr......... Winston-Salem NC 27101 336-722-4545 723-8217
Web: www.abc45.com

744-151 Youngstown, OH

Phone | Fax

WFMJ-TV Ch 21 (NBC) 101 W Boardman St..........Youngstown OH 44503 330-744-8611 742-2472
TF: 800-488-9365 ■ *Web:* www.wfmj.com

WKBN-TV Ch 27 (CBS) 3930 Sunset Blvd............Youngstown OH 44512 330-782-1144 782-3504
Web: www.wkbn.com/default.aspx

WYFX-TV Ch 62 (Fox) 3930 Sunset Blvd ....Youngstown OH 44512 330-782-1114 782-3504
Web: www.foxyoungstown.com

WYTV-TV Ch 33 (ABC) 3930 Sunset Blvd............Youngstown OH 44512 330-783-2930 782-3504
TF: 800-686-2930 ■ *Web:* www.wytv.com/default.aspx

745 TELEVISION SYNDICATORS

Television Syndicators Are Companies That Produce Programming In-House And Market And Distribute The Programs To Networks On A National Or Regional Basis.

Phone | Fax

A Taste of New York Inc 10 Roberta Ln................Syosset NY 11791 516-677-0239
Web: www.tasteofny.com

ABC NewsOne 47 W 66th St 2nd Fl...................New York NY 10023 212-456-4110 456-2771

Access Television Network Inc
2600 Michelson Dr Suite 1650.........................Irvine CA 92612 949-263-9900 622-6295
Web: www.accesstv.com

American Public Television (APT)
55 Summer St 4th Fl...............................Boston MA 02110 617-338-4455 338-5369
Web: www.aptvs.org

AP Broadcast Services
1100 13th St NW Suite 700 ....Washington DC 20005 202-641-9000 370-2712
TF: 800-821-4747 ■ *Web:* www.apbroadcast.com

Babe Winkelman Productions PO Box 407............Brainerd MN 56401 218-822-4424 822-7436
TF: 800-333-0471 ■ *Web:* www.winkelman.com

Broadcast Center Studios Inc 30 Whyte Dr...........Voorhees NJ 08043 856-751-3500 751-7729

CBS Newspath 524 W 57th St........................New York NY 10019 212-975-2881 541-8630
NYSE: CBS ■ *Web:* www.newspath.cbs.com

CBS Television Distribution
2401 Colorado Ave Suite 110................... Santa Monica CA 90404 310-264-3300 264-3301
Web: www.cbstvd.com

CF Entertainment Inc
9903 Santa Monica Blvd Suite 418............... Beverly Hills CA 90212 310-277-3500 277-3511
Web: www.entertainmentstudios.com

Disney ABC Domestic Television
500 S Buena Vista St ....Burbank CA 91521 818-460-6552

Five Star Productions
6001 Pk of Commerce Blvd .... Boca Raton FL 34787 561-279-7827 279-4808
Web: www.vstar.com

Guthy-Renker Television Network
3340 Ocean Pk Blvd .... Santa Monica CA 90405 310-581-6250 581-3232
Web: www.guthy-renker.com

Hearst Entertainment & Syndication Group
300 W 57th St.................................New York NY 10019 212-969-7553
Web: www.hearst.com/entertainment/index.php

Independent Television Service (ITVS)
651 Brannan St Suite 410...................... San Francisco CA 94107 415-356-8383 356-8391
Web: www.itvs.org

Information Television Network
6650 Pk of Commerce Blvd .... Boca Raton FL 33487 561-997-5433 997-5208
TF: 800-463-6488 ■ *Web:* www.itvisus.com

Initiative Corp
5700 Wilshire Blvd Suite 400....................Los Angeles CA 90036 323-370-8000 370-8965
Web: www.im-na.com

Ivanhoe Broadcast News
2745 W Fairbanks Ave .... Winter Park FL 32789 407-740-0789 740-5320
Web: www.ivanhoe.com

Jameson Broadcast Inc 1644 Hawthorne St........... Sarasota FL 34239 941-906-8800 906-8801
Web: www.jamesonbroadcast.com

Litton Entertainment
884 Allbritton Blvd Suite 200 .... Mount Pleasant SC 29464 843-883-5060 883-9957
Web: www.litton.tv

Phone | Fax

McLaughlin Group The
1717 Rhode Island Ave NW Suite 640 ....Washington DC 20036 202-457-0870 296-2285
Web: www.mclaughlin.com

Medstar Television Inc 5920 Hamilton Blvd.......... Allentown PA 18106 610-395-1300 391-1556
Web: www.medstar.com

National Educational Telecommunications Assn (NETA)
939 S Stadium Rd................................Columbia SC 29201 803-799-5517 771-4831
Web: www.netaonline.org

NBC Enterprises 3000 W Alameda Ave.................Burbank CA 91523 818-526-6900 526-6922
Web: www.nbcenterprises.com

RCTV International 4380 NW 128th St................. Miami FL 33054 305-688-7475 685-5697
Web: www.rctvintl.com

Thomson Reuters 3 Times Sq.......................New York NY 10036 646-223-4000
Web: www.thomsonreuters.com

TV Japan 100 Broadway 15th Fl......................New York NY 10005 212-262-3377 262-5577
TF Cust Svc: 877-885-2726 ■ *Web:* www.tvjapan.net

TVA Productions 3950 Vantage Ave .... Studio City CA 91604 818-505-8300 505-8370
Web: www.tvaproductions.com

Warner Bros Domestic Television Distribution
4000 Warner Blvd.................................Burbank CA 91522 818-954-6000

WPT Enterprises Inc (WPTE)
5700 Wilshire Blvd Suite 350.....................Los Angeles CA 90036 323-330-9900 330-9901
NASDAQ: WPTE ■ *Web:* www.worldpokertour.com

746 TESTING FACILITIES

Phone | Fax

ABC Research Corp (ABCR) 3437 SW 24th Ave ....Gainesville FL 32607 352-372-0436 378-6483
Web: www.abcr.com

Accutest Laboratories 2235 Rt 130 Bldg B.............Dayton NJ 08810 732-329-0200 329-3499
TF: 800-329-0204 ■ *Web:* www.accutest.com

Adamson Analytical Laboratories Inc
200 Crouse Dr .... Corona CA 92879 951-549-9657 549-9659
Web: www.adamsonlab.com

AEDC Public Affairs
100 Kindell Dr Suite B-213....................... Arnold AFB TN 37389 931-454-5655 454-6720*
**Fax:* Hum Res ■ *Web:* www.arnold.af.mil

Air Force Flight Test Ctr
AFFTC/PA 1 S Rosamond Blvd...................Edwards AFB CA 93524 661-277-3510 277-2732
Web: www.edwards.af.mil

Aircraft X-Ray Labs Inc
5216 Pacific Blvd .... Huntington Park CA 90255 323-587-4141 588-6410
Web: www.aircraftxray.com

All Metals Processing of Orange County Inc
8401 Standustrial St.............................. Stanton CA 90680 714-828-8238 828-4552
TF: 800-894-4489 ■ *Web:* www.allmetalsprocessing.com

Altran Solutions USA 2525 Rt 130 S ....Cranbury NJ 08512 609-409-9790
Web: www.altransolutions.com

Alucid Solutions Inc
5887 Glenridge Dr Suite 350 ....Atlanta GA 30328 678-904-9490 904-9490

American Standards Testing Bureau Inc
PO Box 583 ....New York NY 10274 212-943-3160 825-2250
TF: 800-221-5170

Ana-Lab Corp PO Box 9000...........................Kilgore TX 75663 903-984-0551 984-5914
Web: www.ana-lab.com

Analysts Inc 22750 Hawthorne Blvd # 220 ....Torrance CA 90505 310-320-0070 320-0970
TF: 800-336-3637 ■ *Web:* www.analystsinc.com

Animal & Plant Health Inspection Service (APHIS)
National Veterinary Services Laboratories
2300 Dayton Ave ....Ames IA 50010 515-663-7200 663-7402
Web: www.aphis.usda.gov

Astro Pak Corp 270 E Baker St Suite 100 .... Costa Mesa CA 92626 866-492-7876 434-1376*
**Fax Area Code:* 714 ■ *TF:* 800-743-5444 ■ *Web:* www.astropak.com

Ballantine Laboratories Inc
312 Old Allerton Rd .... Annandale NJ 08801 908-713-7742 713-7743
Web: www.ballantinelabs.com

Bosch Automotive Proving Grounds
32104 State Rd 2 .... New Carlisle IN 46552 574-654-4000 654-8755
Web: www.bosch.us

Brook Environmental & Engineering Corp
11419 Cronridge Dr Suite 10...................Owings Mills MD 21117 410-356-5073
TF: 800-381-4434

Camin Cargo Control Inc 230 Marion Ave..............Linden NJ 07036 908-862-1899 523-0616*
**Fax:* Hum Res ■ *TF:* 800-756-8798 ■ *Web:* www.camincargo.com

Celsis International
6200 S Lindbergh Blvd......................... Saint Louis MO 63123 314-487-6776 487-8991
Web: www.celsis.com

Columbia Analytical Services Inc
1317 S 13th Ave...................................Kelso WA 98626 360-577-7222 425-9096
Web: www.caslab.com

Construction Testing & Engineering Inc
242 W Larch Rd Suite F .... Tracy CA 95304 209-839-2890 839-2895
TF: 800-576-2271 ■ *Web:* www.cte-inc.net

CTLGroup 5400 Old Orchard Rd......................... Skokie IL 60077 847-965-7500 965-6541
TF: 800-522-2285 ■ *Web:* www.ctlgroup.com

Dayton T Brown Inc 1175 Church St .... Bohemia NY 11716 631-589-6300 589-4046
TF: 800-232-6300 ■ *Web:* www.daytontbrown.com

Defiance Testing & Engineering Services Inc
1628 Northwood St..................................Troy MI 48084 248-458-5900 458-5901
Web: www.defiancetest.com

Detroit Testing Lab Inc
27485 George Merrelli Dr...........................Warren MI 48092 586-754-9000 754-9045
TF: 800-820-7009 ■ *Web:* www.dtl-inc.com

EDO Technical Services Operations
254 E Ave K-4...................................Lancaster CA 93535 661-723-7368 948-7003
Web: www.edotso.com

Engineering Dynamics Inc
3925 S Kalamath St ....Englewood CO 80110 303-761-4367 761-4379
Web: www.engdynamics.com

Environmental Enterprises Inc (EEI)
10163 Cincinnati Dayton Rd..................... Cincinnati OH 45241 513-772-2818 782-8950
TF: 800-722-2818 ■ *Web:* www.eeienv.com

Evans Analytical Group 810 Kifer Rd .... Sunnyvale CA 94086 408-530-3500 530-3501
Web: www.eaglabs.com

Froehling & Robertson Inc 3015 Dumbarton Rd ...... Richmond VA 23228 804-264-2701 264-1202
Web: www.fandr.com

GZA GeoEnvironmental Inc 1 Edgewater Dr .... Norwood MA 02062 781-278-3700 278-5701
Web: www.gza.com

Name / Address	City	State	Zip	Phone	Fax
Hoffman Engineering Corp PO Box 4430	Stamford	CT	06907	203-425-8900	425-8910
Web: www.hoffmanengineering.com					
Indyne Inc 11800 Sunrise Valley Dr Suite 250	Reston	VA	20191	703-903-6900	903-4997
Web: www.indyneinc.com					
InformationWEEK Labs 600 Community Dr	Manhasset	NY	11030	516-562-5000	562-5036
Web: www.informationweek.com					
Infoworld Test Ctr 501 2nd St Suite 120	San Francisco	CA	94107	415-243-4344	543-2200
Web: www.infoworld.com					
Institute For Clean & Secure Energy					
University of Utah					
155 S 1452 E Rm 380	Salt Lake City	UT	84112	801-585-1233	585-1456
Web: www.ices.utah.edu					
International Down & Feather Testing Laboratory					
1455 S 1100 E	Salt Lake City	UT	84105	801-467-7611	467-7711
Web: www.idfl.com					
Intertek Automotive Research					
5404 Bandera Rd	San Antonio	TX	78238	210-684-2310	684-6074
Web: www.intertek-cb.com					
Kett Engineering Corp					
15500 Erwin St Suite 1029	Van Nuys	CA	91411	818-908-5388	908-5323
TF: 877-372-6799 ■ *Web:* www.ketteng.com					
Keweenaw Research Ctr					
Michigan Technological University					
1400 Townsend Dr	Houghton	MI	49931	906-487-2750	487-2202
Web: www.mtukrc.org					
Lancaster Laboratories Inc					
2425 New Holland Pike PO Box 12425	Lancaster	PA	17605	717-656-2301	656-2681
Web: www.lancasterlabs.com					
Laucks Testing Laboratories Inc					
940 S Harney St	Seattle	WA	98108	206-767-5060	767-5063
Ledoux & Co Inc 359 Alfred Ave	Teaneck	NJ	07666	201-837-7160	837-1235
Web: www.ledoux.com					
LFR Inc 194 Forbes Rd Suite 100	Braintree	MA	02184	781-356-7300	356-2211
Web: www.lfr.com					
Magna Chek Inc 32701 Edward Ave	Madison Heights	MI	48071	248-597-0089	597-0440
TF: 800-582-8947 ■ *Web:* www.magnachek.com					
Magnetic Inspection Laboratory Inc					
1401 Greenleaf Ave	Elk Grove Village	IL	60007	847-437-4488	437-4538
Web: www.milinc.com					
Metcut Research Inc 3980 Rosslyn Dr	Cincinnati	OH	45209	513-271-5100	271-9511
TF: 800-966-2888 ■ *Web:* www.metcut.com					
Midwest Testing Laboratory Inc PO Box 3042	Fargo	ND	58108	701-282-9633	282-9635
Web: www.midwesttestinglabs.com					
Modern Industries Inc 613 W 11th St	Erie	PA	16501	814-455-8061	453-4382
Web: www.mi-erie.com					
MSE Technology Applications Inc					
200 Technology Way	Butte	MT	59701	406-494-7100	494-7230
Web: www.mse-ta.com					
Nanotechnology Research & Education Ctr					
University of S Florida Dept of Engineering					
4202 E Fowler Ave ENB 118	Tampa	FL	33620	813-974-2096	974-3610
Web: www.nnrc.eng.usf.edu					
National Air & Radiation Environmental Laboratory (NAREL)					
US Environmental Protection Agency					
540 S Morris Ave	Montgomery	AL	36115	334-270-3400	270-3454
Web: www.epa.gov/narel					
National Technical Systems Inc					
24007 Ventura Blvd Suite 200	Calabasas	CA	91302	818-591-0776	591-0899
NASDAQ: NTSC ■ *TF:* 800-879-9225 ■ *Web:* www.nts.com					
Naval Air Warfare Center Weapons Div (NAWCWD)					
575 I Ave Suite 1	Point Mugu	CA	93042	805-989-1023	
Web: www.nawcwpns.navy.mil					
Physical Science Laboratory					
Stewart & Espina Sts	Las Cruces	NM	88003	575-646-9100	646-9434
Northwest Labs of Seattle 241 S Holden St	Seattle	WA	98108	206-763-6252	763-3949
Web: www.nwlabs1896.com					
NU Laboratories Inc 312 Old Allerton Rd	Annandale	NJ	08801	908-713-9300	713-9001
Web: www.nulabs.com					
Owensby & Kritikos Inc 671 Whitney Ave Bldg B	Gretna	LA	70056	504-368-3122	362-4546
TF: 800-749-3122 ■ *Web:* www.ok-insp.com					
Penniman & Browne Inc					
6252 Falls Rd PO Box 65309	Baltimore	MD	21209	410-825-4131	321-7384
Web: www.pandbinc.com					
Performance Validation LLC					
2601 Fortune Cir					
Suite 200-C 1 Pk Fletcher	Indianapolis	IN	46241	317-248-8848	248-0464
TF: 800-875-8897 ■ *Web:* www.perfval.com					
Perry Technologies 100 E 17th St	Riviera Beach	FL	33404	561-842-5261	842-5303
Web: www.perrytech.com					
PPD Development Inc 929 N Front St	Wilmington	NC	28401	910-251-0081	762-5820
Web: www.ppdi.com					
Professional Service Industries Inc Pittsburgh Testing Lab Div					
2710 W 5th Ave	Eugene	OR	97402	541-484-9212	344-2735
TF: 800-324-5024 ■ *Web:* www.psiusa.com					
Radiometrics Midwest Corp					
12 E Devonwood Ave	Romeoville	IL	60446	815-293-0772	293-0820
Web: www.radiomet.com					
Retlif Inc Testing Laboratories					
795 Marconi Ave	Ronkonkoma	NY	11779	631-737-1500	737-1497
Web: www.retlif.com					
Rothe Development Inc 4614 Sinclair Rd	San Antonio	TX	78222	210-648-3131	648-4091
TF: 800-229-5209 ■ *Web:* www.rothe.com					
SGS Canada Inc 6490 Vipond Dr	Mississauga	ON	L5T1W8	905-364-3757	364-0344
TF: 800-636-0847 ■ *Web:* www.ca.sgs.com					
SGS Life Science Services 310 Brunel Rd	Mississauga	ON	L4Z2C2	905-890-4880	890-4890
Web: www.sgs.com/life_sciences					
SGS US Testing Co Inc 291 Fairfield Ave	Fairfield	NJ	07004	973-575-5252	575-7175
TF Cust Svc: 800-777-8378 ■ *Web:* www.us.sgs.com					
Sigma Test Labs 1480 W 178th St	Gardena	CA	90248	310-324-9465	532-6216
Web: www.sigmatestlabs.com					
Simco Electronics 1178 Bordeaux Dr	Sunnyvale	CA	94089	408-734-9750	734-9754
TF: 866-299-6029 ■ *Web:* www.simco.com					
Sonoscan Inc 2149 Pratt Blvd	Elk Grove Village	IL	60007	847-437-6400	437-1550
Web: www.sonoscan.com					
Southern Petroleum Lab Inc					
8880 Interchange Dr	Houston	TX	77054	713-660-0901	660-8975
TF: 800-969-6775 ■ *Web:* www.spl-inc.com					
Specialized Technology Resources Inc					
10 Water St	Enfield	CT	06082	860-749-8371	749-8234
TF: 800-729-8371 ■ *Web:* www.strquality.com					
Spectrum Analytical Inc 830 Silver St	Agawam	MA	01001	413-789-9018	789-4076
TF: 800-789-9115 ■ *Web:* www.spectrum-analytical.com					
Speedie & Assoc Inc 3331 E Wood St	Phoenix	AZ	85040	602-997-6391	943-5508
TF: 800-628-6221 ■ *Web:* www.speedie.net					
St Louis Testing Laboratories					
2810 Clark Ave	Saint Louis	MO	63103	314-531-8080	531-8085
Web: www.labinc.com					
Stennis Space Ctr					
Blach Blvd Bldg 1100	Stennis Space Center	MS	39529	228-688-2211	688-1094*
**Fax:* PR ■ *Web:* www.nasa.gov					
Stork Herron Testing Laboratories Inc					
5405 E Schaaf Rd	Cleveland	OH	44131	216-524-1450	524-1459
Web: www.storksmt.com					
Sypris Test & Measurement					
6120 Hanging Moss Rd	Orlando	FL	32807	407-678-6900	671-0664
TF: 800-775-2550 ■ *Web:* www.sypris.com/stm					
Teledyne Solutions Inc					
5000 Bradford Dr Suite 200	Huntsville	AL	35805	256-726-4444	
Web: www.teledynesolutions.com					
Terra Tek Inc 1935 S Fremont Dr	Salt Lake City	UT	84104	801-584-2400	584-2406
TF: 800-372-2522 ■ *Web:* www.terratek.com					
TestAmerica Laboratories Inc 122 Lyman St	Asheville	NC	28801	828-258-3746	258-1292*
**Fax:* Sales ■ *TF:* 800-344-5759 ■ *Web:* www.testamericainc.com					
Thornton Laboratories Testing & Inspection Services					
1145 E Cass St	Tampa	FL	33602	813-223-9702	223-9332
Web: www.thorntonlab.com					
Tolly Group 3701 Sau Blvd Suite 100	Boca Raton	FL	33431	561-391-5610	391-5810
Web: www.tolly.com					
Toxikon Corp 15 Wiggins Ave	Bedford	MA	01730	781-275-3330	271-1133
TF: 800-458-4141 ■ *Web:* www.toxikon.com					
Transportation Research Center Inc (TRC Inc)					
10820 State Rt 347 PO Box B-67	East Liberty	OH	43319	937-666-2011	666-5066
TF: 800-837-7872 ■ *Web:* www.trcpg.com					
Transportation Technology Center Inc					
55500 DOT Rd PO Box 11130	Pueblo	CO	81001	719-584-0750	584-0711
Web: www.aar.com					
Truesdail Laboratories Inc 14201 Franklin Ave	Tustin	CA	92780	714-730-6239	730-6462
Web: www.truesdail.com					
Twin City Testing 662 Cromwell Ave	Saint Paul	MN	55114	651-645-3601	659-7348
TF: 888-645-8378 ■ *Web:* www.storksmt.com					
Twining Laboratories of Southern California Inc					
3310 Airport Way	Long Beach	CA	90806	562-426-3355	426-6424
Web: www.twininglabs.com					
Underwriters Laboratories Inc (UL)					
2600 NW Lake Rd	Camas	WA	98607	877-854-3577	817-6278*
**Fax Area Code:* 360 ■ *TF:* 877-854-3577 ■ *Web:* www.ul.com					
US Army Aviation Technical Test Ctr					
Cairns Army Air Field Bldg 30601	Fort Rucker	AL	36362	334-255-8000	255-8232
TF: 888-838-1306					
US Army Electronic Proving Ground					
CSTE-DTC-EP-CO	Fort Huachuca	AZ	85613	520-533-8267	538-6361
Web: www.epg.army.mil					
US Army White Sands Missile Range					
Bldg 465 Rm 140	White Sands	NM	88002	575-678-2121	
Web: www.wsmr.army.mil					
US Army Yuma Proving Ground 301 C St	Yuma	AZ	85365	928-328-2163	328-6249
Web: www.yuma.army.mil					
Valley Lea Laboratories					
4609 Grape Rd Suite D-4	Mishawaka	IN	46545	574-272-8484	272-8485
TF: 800-822-1283					
Wadsworth Ctr					
Biggs Laboratory New York Dept of Health					
Empire State Plaza PO Box 509	Albany	NY	12201	518-474-2160	
Web: www.wadsworth.org					
Wallops Flight Facility					
Office of Public Affairs	Wallops Island	VA	23337	757-824-1579	824-1971
Web: www.wff.nasa.gov					
Westmoreland Mechanical Testing & Research Inc					
PO Box 388	Youngstown	PA	15696	724-537-3131	537-8664
Web: www.wmtr.com					
WIL Research Laboratories Inc 1407 George Rd	Ashland	OH	44805	419-289-8700	289-3650
TF Cust Svc: 800-221-9610 ■ *Web:* www.wilresearch.com					
Yulista Management Services Inc					
6613 Brayton Dr Suite C	Anchorage	AK	99507	907-258-2502	868-2494
Web: www.yulista.com					

747 TEXTILE MACHINERY

Name / Address	City	State	Zip	Phone	Fax
AB Carter Inc 4801 York Hwy PO Box 518	Gastonia	NC	28053	704-865-1201	864-8870
Web: www.abcarter.com					

	City	State	Zip	Phone	Fax
Advanced Innovative Technologies LLC 530 Wilbanks Dr. *Web:* www.aitequipment.com	Ball Ground	GA	30107	770-479-1900	479-4179
Andritz Kusters Inc 201 Zima Pk Dr *Web:* www.kuesters.com	Spartanburg	SC	29301	864-587-4848	576-2306
Barudan America Inc 29500 Fountain Pkwy *TF:* 800-627-4776 ■ *Web:* www.barudan.com	Solon	OH	44139	440-248-8770	248-8856
Belmont Textile Machinery Co 1212 W Catawba St PO Box 568 *Web:* www.btmc.com	Mount Holly	NC	28120	704-827-5836	827-8551
Bowman Hollis Mfg Inc 2925 Old Steele Creek Rd *TF:* 888-269-2358 ■ *Web:* www.bowmanhollis.com	Charlotte	NC	28208	704-374-1500	333-5520
Cobble/Tufting Machine Co Inc 1731 Kimberly Pk Dr *Web:* www.cobbleusa.com	Dalton	GA	30720	706-278-1857	226-8223
Custom Industries Inc 215 Aloe Rd *Web:* www.customindustries.com	Greensboro	NC	27409	336-299-2885	294-2472
Eastman Machine Co 779 Washington St *TF:* 800-872-5571 ■ *Web:* www.eastmancuts.com	Buffalo	NY	14203	716-856-2200	856-1140
Elliott Metal Works Inc 210 Old Piedmont Hwy PO Box 8675 *TF:* 800-726-1542	Greenville	SC	29604	864-269-8930	269-8930
Entec Composite Machines Inc 300 W 2975 S *Web:* www.entec.com	Salt Lake City	UT	84115	801-486-8721	484-4363
Gaston County Dyeing Machine Co PO Box 308 *Web:* www.gaston-county.com	Stanley	NC	28164	704-822-5000	822-0753
Gerber Technology Inc 24 Industrial Pk Rd W **Fax:* Mktg ■ *TF:* 800-826-3243 ■ *Web:* www.gerbertechnology.com	Tolland	CT	06084	860-871-8082	871-3779*
Gribetz International Inc 13800 NW 4th St *TF:* 800-326-4742 ■ *Web:* www.gsgcompanies.com/gribetz.htm	Sunrise	FL	33325	954-846-0300	846-0381
GTP Inc 1801 Rutherford Rd *Web:* www.globaltextilepartner.com	Greenville	SC	29609	864-288-5475	297-5081
Handy/Kenlin Group 1750 N 25th Ave *Web:* www.handykenlin.com	Melrose Park	IL	60160	708-450-9000	450-9047
HH Arnold Co Inc 529 Liberty St *Web:* www.hharnold.com	Rockland	MA	02370	781-878-0346	878-7944
Hirsch International Corp 50 Engineers Rd Suite 100 *NASDAQ: HRSH* ■ **Fax Area Code:* 800 ■ *TF:* 800-394-4426 ■ *Web:* www.hirschinternational.com	Hauppauge	NY	11738	631-436-7100	772-1788*
Hix Corp 1201 E 27th Terr *TF:* 800-835-0606 ■ *Web:* www.hixcorp.com	Pittsburg	KS	66762	620-231-8568	231-1598
Hollingsworth John D On Wheels Inc PO Box 516 *Web:* www.jdhow.com	Greenville	SC	29602	864-297-1000	297-2637
Ioline Corp 14140 NE 200th St *TF:* 800-598-0029 ■ *Web:* www.ioline.com	Woodinville	WA	98072	425-398-8282	398-8383
KMSCO Inc 42A Cindy Ln *TF:* 800-874-5646 ■ *Web:* www.logoknits.com	Ocean Township	NJ	07712	732-382-9898	382-9479
Lawson-Hemphill Inc 1658 G A R Hwy Suite 6 *Web:* www.lawsonhemphill.com	Swansea	MA	02777	508-679-5364	679-5396
Lummus Corp 1 Lummus Dr PO Box 4259 *TF:* 800-458-6687 ■ *Web:* www.lummus.com	Savannah	GA	31407	912-447-9000	447-9250
Mayer Industries Inc 3777 Industrial Blvd	Orangeburg	SC	29118	803-536-3500	536-2545
MB Industries Inc Hwy 64 W PO Box 1118	Rosman	NC	28772	828-862-4201	862-4297
McCoy-Ellison Inc 1101 Curtis St PO Box 967 *TF:* 800-811-5348 ■ *Web:* www.mccoy-ellison.com	Monroe	NC	28111	704-289-5413	283-0480
Morrison Berkshire Inc 865 S Church St *Web:* www.morrisonberkshire.com	North Adams	MA	01247	413-663-6501	664-8738
Petty Machine Co Inc 2403 Forbes Rd *TF All:* 800-343-0960	Gastonia	NC	28056	704-864-3254	861-1937
Pneumafil Corp Textile Systems Div 440-A Chesapeake Dr PO Box 16348 *TF:* 800-525-1560 ■ *Web:* www.pneumafil.com/td	Charlotte	NC	28297	704-399-7441	398-7516
Rando Machine Corp 1071 Rt 31 PO Box 614 *Web:* www.randomachine.com	Macedon	NY	14502	315-986-2761	986-7943
Standex International Corp Mullen Testers Div 939 Chicopee St *Web:* www.mullentesters.com	Chicopee	MA	01013	413-536-1311	536-1367
Stork Prints America Inc 3201 Rotary Dr *Web:* www.spgprints.com	Charlotte	NC	28269	704-598-7171	569-0858
Thermopatch Corp 2204 Erie Blvd E *TF Cust Svc:* 800-252-6555 ■ *Web:* www.thermopatch.com	Syracuse	NY	13224	315-446-8110	445-8046
Tidland Corp 2305 SE 8th Ave *TF:* 800-426-1000 ■ *Web:* www.tidland.com	Camas	WA	98607	360-834-2345	834-5865
Tompkins Bros Co Inc 623 Oneida St *Web:* www.tompkinsusa.com	Syracuse	NY	13202	315-422-8763	422-8762
TrimMaster 4860 N 5th St Hwy *TF:* 800-356-4237 ■ *Web:* www.trimmaster.com	Temple	PA	19560	610-921-0203	929-8833
Tubular Textile Machinery 113 Woodside Dr PO Box 2097 *TF:* 800-531-3715 ■ *Web:* www.navisglobal.com	Lexington	NC	27292	336-956-6444	956-8956
Tuftco Corp 2318 S Holtzclaw Ave *TF:* 800-288-3826 ■ *Web:* www.tuftco.com	Chattanooga	TN	37408	423-698-8601	698-0842
Tuftco Finishing Systems 100 W Industrial Blvd	Dalton	GA	30720	706-277-1110	277-4334
Vanguard Supreme 601 MacArthur Cir *TF:* 800-222-1971 ■ *Web:* www.vanguardsupreme.com	Monroe	NC	28110	704-283-8171	283-9257
VITAL Link Machine Group 2035 Soapstone Mountain Rd *TF Cust Svc:* 800-727-4244	Staley	NC	27355	336-209-0057	622-0854
Wardwell Braiding Machine Co 1211 High St *Web:* www.wardwell.com	Central Falls	RI	02863	401-724-8800	723-2690
West Point Industries 2021 Stateline Rd PO Box 589 *Web:* www.westpoint.com	West Point	GA	31833	706-643-2101	643-2100
Whirlaway Corp 720 Shiloh Ave *Web:* www.whirlawaycorporation.com	Wellington	OH	44090	440-647-4711	647-3962

748 TEXTILE MILLS

748-1 Broadwoven Fabric Mills

	City	State	Zip	Phone	Fax
Alice Mfg Co Inc 208 E 1st Ave *TF:* 800-695-2542 ■ *Web:* www.alicemfgco.com	Easley	SC	29640	864-859-6323	859-6328
American Cotton Growers Textile Div (ACG) 1926 FM 54 PO Box 430 *TF:* 800-333-8011 ■ *Web:* www.pcca.com/Denim	Littlefield	TX	79339	806-385-6401	385-5155
American Fiber & Finishing Inc PO Box 2488 *Web:* www.affinc.com	Albemarle	NC	28002	704-983-6102	985-1352
American Silk Mills Corp 75 Stark St *Web:* www.americansilk.com	Plains	PA	18705	570-822-7147	829-7044
Belding Hausman Inc 2130 E Main St *TF:* 800-350-2353	Lincolnton	NC	28092	704-735-2581	748-9863
Bloomsburg Mills Inc 111 W 40th St 10th Fl *Web:* www.bloomsburgmills.net	New York	NY	10018	212-221-6114	354-9375
Carpostan Industries Inc 205 W 12th Ave	Lake View	SC	29563	843-759-2105	759-2594
Central Textiles Inc 237 Mill Ave	Central	SC	29630	864-639-2491	639-4513
Circa 1801 1 Jacquard Dr *TF Cust Svc:* 800-462-9295	Connelly Springs	NC	28612	828-397-7003	397-1867
Cone Denim LLC 804 Green Valley Rd Suite 300 *TF:* 800-763-0123	Greensboro	NC	27408	336-379-6220	379-6043
Copland Fabrics Inc 1714 Carolina Mill Rd *Web:* www.coplandfabrics.com	Burlington	NC	27217	336-226-0272	229-9551
Covington Industries Inc 386 Pk Ave S 18th Fl *Web:* www.covington-industries.com	New York	NY	10016	212-689-2200	576-1167
Covington Upholstery Fabrics Inc 317 W High St 7th Fl *Web:* www.covington-industries.com	High Point	NC	27260	336-883-4141	889-6387
Craftex Mills Inc 450 Sentry Pkwy E *TF:* 866-992-5684 ■ *Web:* www.craftex.com	Blue Bell	PA	19422	610-941-1212	941-7171
Culp Inc 1823 E Chester Dr *NYSE: CFI* ■ *Web:* www.culpinc.com	High Point	NC	27265	336-889-5161	881-8615
Culp Woven Velvets Inc 414 W Hampton St	Anderson	SC	29624	864-226-2857	225-9006
Dan River Inc 700 Lanier Ave *TF:* 800-645-0880	Danville	VA	24541	434-799-7000	799-7000
Delta Woodside Industries Inc 700 N Woods Dr	Fountain Inn	SC	29644	864-255-4100	255-4100
DeRoyal Textiles 141 E York St PO Box 400 *TF:* 800-845-1062 ■ *Web:* www.deroyal.com	Camden	SC	29020	803-432-2403	424-5112
Dicey Mills Inc 430 Neisler St	Shelby	NC	28151	704-487-6324	482-1972
Egi Liquidating Co Ltd 3022 Franklin Ave *TF:* 800-327-9462 ■ *Web:* www.easygardener.com	Waco	TX	76710	254-753-5353	753-5372
Faribault Mills 1500 NW 2nd Ave PO Box 369 *TF:* 800-533-0444	Faribault	MN	55021	507-334-6444	334-6444
Fiberweb Simpsonville Inc 840 SE Main St *Web:* www.fiberweb.com	Simpsonville	SC	29681	864-967-5600	967-5695
Fortune Fabrics Inc *Wyoming Weavers* 315 Simpson St *Web:* www.wyomingweavers.com	Swoyersville	PA	18704	570-288-3667	283-2124
Garnet Hill Inc 231 Main St *TF:* 800-870-3513 ■ *Web:* www.garnethill.com	Franconia	NH	03580	603-823-5545	823-7034
Glen Raven Inc 142 Glen Raven Rd *TF:* 800-788-4413 ■ *Web:* www.glenraven.com	Glen Raven	NC	27217	336-227-6211	226-8133
Greenwood Mills Inc 300 Morgan Ave *TF:* 800-847-5929	Greenwood	SC	29646	864-229-2571	229-1111
Hamrick Mills Inc 515 W Buford St PO Box 48 *TF:* 800-297-6306 ■ *Web:* www.mvmills.com	Gaffney	SC	29342	864-489-4731	487-9946
Henry Glass & Co 11 E 36th St *TF:* 800-845-5933 ■ *Web:* www.henryglassfabrics.com	New York	NY	10016	212-213-8500	213-0076
Inman Mills 300 Pk Rd PO Box 207 *Web:* www.inmanmills.com	Inman	SC	29349	864-472-2121	472-0261
JB Martin Co 645 5th Ave Suite 400 *TF:* 800-223-0525 ■ *Web:* www.jbmartin.com	New York	NY	10022	212-421-2020	421-1460
Johnston Textiles Inc 3101 23rd Dr *TF:* 800-227-0192 ■ *Web:* www.johnstontextiles.com	Valley	AL	36854	334-768-1000	768-1047
Juniata Fabrics Inc 1301 Broadway *TF:* 800-654-2666 ■ *Web:* www.juniatafabrics.com	Altoona	PA	16601	814-944-9381	944-1938
Keystone Weaving Mills Inc 1349 Cumberland St	Lebanon	PA	17042	717-272-4665	272-4840
KM Fabrics Inc 2 Waco St	Greenville	SC	29611	864-295-2550	295-3356
Kuraray America Inc 101 E 52nd St 26th Fl *TF:* 800-879-1676 ■ *Web:* www.kurarayamerica.com	New York	NY	10022	212-986-2230	867-3543
Lantal Textiles Inc 1300 Langenthal Dr PO Box 965 **Fax:* Hum Res ■ *TF:* 800-334-3309 ■ *Web:* www.lantal.com	Rural Hall	NC	27045	336-969-9551	969-3810*
Leggett & Platt Inc Textile & Fiber Products Group 1410 Donelson Pike *TF:* 800-888-4136 ■ *Web:* www.lpfiber.com	Nashville	TN	37217	615-367-8900	360-8451
LW Packard & Co Inc 6 Mill St *Web:* www.lwpackard.com	Ashland	NH	03217	603-968-3351	968-7649
Milliken & Co 920 Milliken Rd **Fax:* Hum Res ■ *Web:* www.milliken.com	Spartanburg	SC	29303	864-503-2020	503-2100*
Mount Vernon Mills Inc 503 S Main St PO Box 100 *TF:* 800-845-8857 ■ *Web:* www.mvmills.com	Mauldin	SC	29662	864-688-7100	688-7215
Polartec LLC 46 Stafford St *TF:* 800-252-6688 ■ *Web:* www.polartec.com	Lawrence	MA	01841	978-685-6341	975-2595
Polymer Group Inc 9335 Harris Corners Pkwy *Web:* www.polymergroupinc.com	Charlotte	NC	28269	704-697-5100	697-5116
Precision Fabrics Group Inc 301 N Elm St Suite 600 *TF:* 800-284-8001 ■ *Web:* www.precisionfabrics.com	Greensboro	NC	27401	336-510-8000	510-8004
Ramtex Inc 1259 Foushee Rd	Ramseur	NC	27316	336-824-5600	824-5689

Company	City	State	ZIP	Phone	Fax
Raxon Fabrics Corp 261 5th Ave Suite 501	New York	NY	10016	212-532-6816	481-9361
Reeves Bros Inc 790 Reeves St. *Web:* www.reevesbrothers.com	Spartanburg	SC	29301	864-576-1210	595-2270
Scalamandre Silks Inc 350 Wireless Blvd. *TF:* 800-932-4361 ■ *Web:* www.scalamandre.com/contents.htm	Hauppauge	NY	11788	631-467-8800	467-9448
Stanwood Mills Inc 570 7th Ave	New York	NY	10018	212-944-4826	944-6485
Stonecutter Mills Corp 400 Spindale St *Web:* www.stonecuttermills.com	Spindale	NC	28160	828-286-2341	287-7280
Sunbury Textile Mills Inc 1200 Miller St PO Box 768	Sunbury	PA	17801	570-286-3800	286-8530
Tweave LLC 138 Barrows St PO Box AV *Web:* www.tweave.com	Norton	MA	02766	508-285-6701	285-2904
Valdese Weavers LLC 1000 Perkins Rd SE PO Box 70 *Web:* www.valdeseweavers.com	Valdese	NC	28690	828-874-2181	874-3920
Vectorply Corp 3500 Lakewood Dr *TF:* 800-577-4521 ■ *Web:* www.vectorply.com	Phenix City	AL	36867	334-291-7704	291-7743
Warm Co 5529 186th Pl SW *TF:* 800-234-9276 ■ *Web:* www.warmcompany.com	Lynnwood	WA	98037	425-248-2424	248-2422
WestPoint Home Inc 28 E 28th St 8th Fl *TF:* 800-533-8229 ■ *Web:* martex.com	New York	NY	10016	212-930-2000	

748-2 Coated Fabric

Company	City	State	ZIP	Phone	Fax
Adell Plastics Inc 4530 Annapolis Rd *TF:* 800-638-5218 ■ *Web:* www.adellplas.com	Baltimore	MD	21227	410-789-7780	789-2804
Alpha Assoc Inc 145 Lehigh Ave *TF:* 800-631-5399 ■ *Web:* www.alphainc.com	Lakewood	NJ	08701	732-634-5700	634-1430
Archer Rubber Co 213 Central St *Web:* www.archerrubber.com	Milford	MA	01757	508-473-1870	478-7078
Beckmann Converting Inc 14 Pk Dr PO Box 390 *Web:* www.beckmannconverting.com	Amsterdam	NY	12010	518-842-0073	842-0282
Bondcote Corp PO Box 729 *TF:* 800-368-2160 ■ *Web:* www.bondcote.com	Pulaski	VA	24301	540-980-2640	980-5636
Bradford Industries Inc 1857 Middlesex St *Web:* www.bradfordind.com	Lowell	MA	01851	978-459-4100	459-2597
Brookwood Laminating 275 Putnam Rd *Web:* www.brookwoodcos.com	Wauregan	CT	06387	860-774-5001	774-5002
Cellusuede Products Inc 500 N Madison St *Web:* www.cellusuede.com	Rockford	IL	61107	815-964-8619	964-7949
Cooley Group 50 Esten Ave *TF Cust Svc:* 800-333-3048 ■ *Web:* www.cooleygroup.com	Pawtucket	RI	02860	401-724-9000	726-8620
Dazian Inc 124 Enterprise Ave S *Web:* www.dazian.com	Secaucus	NJ	07094	201-549-1000	549-1055
Deccofelt Corp 555 S Vermont Ave *TF Cust Svc:* 800-543-3226 ■ *Web:* www.deccofelt.com	Glendora	CA	91740	626-963-8511	963-4981
Der-Tex Corp 1 Lehner Rd *TF:* 800-669-0364 ■ *Web:* www.dertexcorp.com	Saco	ME	04072	207-284-5931	669-9026
Duracote Corp 350 N Diamond St *TF:* 800-321-2252 ■ *Web:* www.duracote.com	Ravenna	OH	44266	330-296-9600	296-5102
Emtex Inc 42 Cherry Hill Dr # B *Web:* www.emtexinc.com	Danvers	MA	01923	978-907-4500	907-4555
Engineered Fabrics Corp 669 Goodyear St	Rockmart	GA	30153	770-684-7855	684-7855
Fabrite Laminating Corp 70 Passaic St	Wood Ridge	NJ	07075	973-777-1406	777-1406
Flexfirm Products Inc 2226 Chico Ave *Web:* www.flexfirmproducts.com	South El Monte	CA	91733	626-448-7627	579-5116
Haartz Corp 87 Hayward Rd *Web:* www.haartz.com	Acton	MA	01720	978-264-2600	264-2601
Herculite Products Inc 105 E Sinking Springs Ln *TF Cust Svc:* 800-772-0036 ■ *Web:* www.herculite.com	Emigsville	PA	17318	717-764-1192	764-5211
ICG/Holliston 905 Holliston Mills Rd PO Box 478 **Fax Area Code:* 800 ■ *TF:* 800-251-0451 ■ *Web:* www.icgholliston.com	Church Hill	TN	37642	423-357-6141	325-0351*
Middlesex Research Mfg Co Inc 27 Apsley St *TF:* 800-424-5188 ■ *Web:* www.middlesexresearch.com	Hudson	MA	01749	978-562-3697	562-7446
Noble Biomaterials Inc 300 Palm St *TF:* 877-978-2842 ■ *Web:* www.noblebiomaterials.com	Scranton	PA	18505	570-955-1800	955-1801
OMNOVA Solutions Inc 175 Ghent Rd *NYSE:* OMN ■ *Web:* www.omnova.com	Fairlawn	OH	44333	330-869-4200	869-4288
Polyguard Products Inc PO Box 755 *Web:* www.polyguardproducts.com	Ennis	TX	75120	972-875-8421	
Reflexite Corp 120 Darling Dr *TF:* 800-654-7570 ■ *Web:* www.reflexite.com	Avon	CT	06001	860-676-7100	676-7199
SanduskyAthol International 100 22nd St PO Box 105 *TF:* 800-282-6523 ■ *Web:* www.sanduskyathol.com	Butner	NC	27509	919-575-6523	575-9344
Seaman Corp 1000 Venture Blvd *TF:* 800-927-8578 ■ *Web:* www.seamancorp.com	Wooster	OH	44691	330-262-1111	263-6950
Swift Textile Metalizing LLC 23 Britton Dr PO Box 66 *Web:* www.swift-textile.com	Bloomfield	CT	06002	860-243-1122	243-0848
Taconic 136 Coonbrook Rd PO Box 69 *TF:* 800-833-1805 ■ *Web:* www.4taconic.com	Petersburgh	NY	12138	518-658-3202	658-3204
Twitchell Corp 4031 Ross Clark Cir NW *TF:* 800-633-7550 ■ *Web:* www.twitchellcorp.com	Dothan	AL	36304	334-792-0002	673-4120
Uniroyal Engineered Products LLC 1800 2nd St Suite 970 *Web:* www.naugahyde.com	Sarasota	FL	34236	941-906-8580	
Vintex Inc 1 Mt Forest Dr **Fax:* Sales ■ *TF Sales:* 800-846-8399 ■ *Web:* www.vintex.com	Mount Forest	ON	N0G2L2	519-323-0100	323-0333*
WL Gore & Assoc Inc 551 Papermill Rd *Web:* www.gore.com	Newark	DE	19711	302-738-4880	738-7710

748-3 Industrial Fabrics

Company	City	State	ZIP	Phone	Fax
Acme Group 550 Hulet Dr # 103 *TF:* 800-521-8565 ■ *Web:* www.acmemills.com	Bloomfield Hills	MI	48302	248-203-2000	454-9658
Albany International Corp 1373 Broadway PO Box 1907 *NYSE:* AIN ■ *TF:* 800-833-3836 ■ *Web:* www.albint.com	Albany	NY	12204	518-445-2200	445-2250
Amatex Corp 1032 Stambridge St *TF:* 800-441-9680 ■ *Web:* www.amatex.com	Norristown	PA	19404	610-277-6100	277-6106
AMETEK Inc Chemical Products Div 455 Corporate Blvd *TF Orders:* 800-441-7777 ■ *Web:* www.ametekfpp.com	Newark	DE	19702	302-456-4400	456-4444
AstenJohnson 4399 Corporate Rd *Web:* www.astenjohnson.com	Charleston	SC	29405	843-747-7800	202-6278
Belton Industries Inc 1205 Hanby Rd PO Box 127 *TF:* 800-845-8753 ■ *Web:* www.beltonindustries.com	Belton	SC	29627	864-338-5711	338-5594
BGF Industries Inc 3802 Robert Porcher Way *TF:* 800-476-4845 ■ *Web:* www.bgf.com	Greensboro	NC	27410	336-545-0011	545-0233
Carthage Mills 4243 Hunt Rd *TF Sales:* 800-543-4430 ■ *Web:* www.carthagemills.com	Cincinnati	OH	45242	513-794-1600	794-3434
Fablok Mills Inc 140 Spring St *Web:* www.fablokmills.com	Murray Hill	NJ	07974	908-464-1950	464-6520
FH Bonn Co 4300 Gateway Blvd *TF:* 800-323-0143 ■ *Web:* www.fhbonn.com	Springfield	OH	45502	937-323-7024	323-0388
Firestone Fibers & Textiles Co 100 Firestone Ln PO Box 1369 *TF:* 800-441-1336 ■ *Web:* www.firestonefibers.com	Kings Mountain	NC	28086	704-734-2132	734-2104
HFI LLC 2421 McGaw Rd	Columbus	OH	43207	614-491-0700	491-1899
Industrial Fabrics Corp 7160 Northland Cir N *TF:* 800-328-3036 ■ *Web:* www.ifcfabrics.com	Minneapolis	MN	55428	763-535-3220	535-6040
Mutual Industries Inc 707 W Grange St *TF:* 800-523-0888 ■ *Web:* www.mutualindustries.com	Philadelphia	PA	19120	215-927-6000	927-3388
Newtex Industries Inc 8050 Victor Mendon Rd *TF:* 800-836-1001 ■ *Web:* www.newtex.com	Victor	NY	14564	585-924-9135	924-4645
Sefar Printing Solutions Inc 120 Mt Holly Bypass *TF:* 800-289-8385 ■ *Web:* www.sefar.com	Lumberton	NJ	08048	609-613-5000	267-1750
Stern & Stern Industries Inc 188 Thacher St PO Box 556 *Web:* www.sternandstern.com	Hornell	NY	14843	212-972-4040	818-9230
TenCate Geosynthetics North America 365 S Holland Dr *TF:* 888-795-0808 ■ *Web:* www.tencate.com	Pendergrass	GA	30567	706-693-2226	693-4400
TenCate Protective Fabrics USA 6501 Mall Blvd *TF:* 800-241-8630 ■ *Web:* www.tencate.com	Union City	GA	30291	800-241-8630	
Tex-Tech Industries Inc 105 N Main St PO Box 8 *TF:* 800-441-7089 ■ *Web:* www.textechindustries.com	North Monmouth	ME	04265	207-933-4404	933-9266
Ultrafabrics LLC 303 S Broadway *TF:* 888-361-9216 ■ *Web:* www.ultrafabricsllc.com	Tarrytown	NY	10591	914-460-1730	347-1591
Weavexx 51 Flex Way *Web:* www.weavexx.com	Youngsville	NC	27596	919-556-7235	556-2432
Wellstone Mills 856 S Pleasantburg Dr *TF:* 877-867-6455 ■ *Web:* www.wellstonemills.com	Greenville	SC	29607	864-242-1293	242-1927
Wendell Fabrics Corp 108 E Church St PO Box 128 *Web:* www.wendellfabrics.com	Blacksburg	SC	29702	864-839-6341	839-2911

748-4 Knitting Mills

Company	City	State	ZIP	Phone	Fax
Alamac American Knits LLC 1885 Alamac Rd PO Box 1347 *Web:* www.alamacusa.com	Lumberton	NC	28358	910-618-2436	618-2292
Ames Textile Corp 710 Chelmsford St *Web:* www.amestextile.com	Lowell	MA	01851	978-458-3321	454-9149
Apex Mills Corp 168 Doughty Blvd *TF:* 800-989-2739 ■ *Web:* www.apexmills.com	Inwood	NY	11096	516-239-4400	239-4951
Asheboro Elastics Corp 150 N Pk St *Web:* www.asheboroelastics.com	Asheboro	NC	27203	336-629-2626	629-3782
Cellunet Mfg Co 1002 Jacksonville Rd	Burlington	NJ	08016	609-386-1147	386-8978
Charbert Inc 299 Church St *TF:* 800-570-2184	Alton	RI	02894	401-364-7751	364-3390
Clover Knits Inc 1075 Jackson Heights	Clover	SC	29710	803-222-3021	222-4105
Contempora Fabrics Inc 351 Contempora Dr *TF:* 800-346-3650 ■ *Web:* www.contemporafabrics.com	Lumberton	NC	28358	910-738-7131	738-9575
Darlington Fabrics Corp 1407 Broadway Suite 1220 *TF:* 800-556-7152 ■ *Web:* www.darlingtonfabrics.com	New York	NY	10018	212-938-1054	938-1025
Draper Knitting Co 28 Draper Ln *Web:* www.draperknitting.com	Canton	MA	02021	781-828-0029	828-3034
Elastic Fabrics of America 3112 Pleasant Garden Rd *Web:* www.elasticfabrics.com	Greensboro	NC	27406	336-275-9401	378-2631
Fab Industries Corp 98 Cutter Mill Rd Suite 412-N	Great Neck	NY	11021	516-498-3200	498-3200
Flexlon Fabrics Inc 174 Trollingwood Rd	Haw River	NC	27258	336-578-0111	578-8247
Gehring Textiles Inc 1225 Franklin Ave Suite 300 *Web:* www.gehringtextiles.com	Garden City	NY	11530	516-747-4555	747-8885
Hornwood Inc 766 HaileyÆs Ferry Rd *Web:* www.hornwoodinc.com	Lilesville	NC	28091	704-848-4121	848-4555
Klauber Bros Inc 980 Avenue of the Americas 2nd Fl *Web:* www.klauberlace.com	New York	NY	10018	212-686-2531	481-7194
Minnesota Knitting Mills 1450 Mendota Heights Rd *Web:* www.mnknit.com	Saint Paul	MN	55120	651-452-2240	452-8915
MoCaro Industries Inc 2201 Mocaro Dr *Web:* www.mocaro.com	Statesville	NC	28677	704-878-6645	873-6139

Phone *Fax*

Monterey Mills Inc 1725 E Delavan Dr . . . Janesville WI 53546 608-754-2866 754-3750
TF: 800-255-9665 ■ *Web:* www.montereymills.com
Paris Lace Inc 1500 Main Ave . . . Clifton NJ 07011 973-478-9035 478-9186
TF: 800-533-5223
Russ-Knits Inc 520 E Main St . . . Candor NC 27229 910-974-4114 974-4023
Westchester Lace & Textiles Inc
3901 Liberty Ave. . . . North Bergen NJ 07047 201-864-2150 864-2116
TF: 800-699-5223 ■ *Web:* www.westchesterlace.com

748-5 Narrow Fabric Mills

Phone *Fax*

Advance Fiber Technologies Corp
344 Lodi St. . . . Hackensack NJ 07601 201-488-2700 489-5656
TF: 800-631-1930
American Cord & Webbing Co 88 Century Dr . . . Woonsocket RI 02895 401-762-5500 762-5514
Web: www.acw1.com
Avery Dennison 950 German St PO Box 735. . . . Lenoir NC 28645 828-758-2338 758-2038
TF: 800-528-9591 ■ *Web:* www.paxar.com
Bally Ribbon Mills 23 N 7th St. . . . Bally PA 19503 610-845-2211 845-8013
Web: www.ballyribbon.com
Bo-Buck Mills Inc 921 E Blvd. . . . Chesterfield SC 29709 843-623-2158 623-6849
TF: 800-690-7474 ■ *Web:* www.bobuckmills.com
Carolina Narrow Fabric Co
1100 N Patterson Ave. . . . Winston-Salem NC 27101 336-631-3000 631-3060
Web: www.carolinanarrowfabric.com
Carson & Gebel Ribbon Co 17 Green Pond Rd . . . Rockaway NJ 07866 973-627-4200 627-1175
TF: 800-223-8283 ■ *Web:* www.cgribbon.com
Conrad-Jarvis Corp 217 Conant St. . . . Pawtucket RI 02860 401-722-8700 726-8860*
CT-Nassau Corp 4101 S NC 62 . . . Alamance NC 27201 336-570-0091 570-1519
ELC Industries
1439 Dave Lyle Blvd Suite 16-C. . . . Rock Hill SC 29730 803-980-7600 980-7676
TF Sales: 800-765-7423 ■ *Web:* www.ahrice.com
Fulflex Inc 701 E Church St. . . . Greenville TN 37745 423-638-5722 638-1298
TF: 800-283-2500 ■ *Web:* www.fulflex.com
Glencairn Mfg Co 5 Saunders St . . . Pawtucket RI 02860 401-723-9871 724-5340
Hickory Brands Inc 429 27th St NW. . . . Hickory NC 28601 828-322-2600 328-1700
TF: 800-438-5777 ■ *Web:* www.griffinshine.com
Hope Global Engineered Textile Solutions
50 Martin St . . . Cumberland RI 02864 401-333-8990 334-6442
TF: 800-634-1335 ■ *Web:* www.hopeglobal.com
JRM Industries Inc 1 Mattimore St. . . . Passaic NJ 07055 973-779-9340 779-8017
TF: 800-533-2697 ■ *Web:* www.jrm.com
Julius Koch USA Inc 387 Church St. . . . New Bedford MA 02745 508-995-9565 995-8434
TF Sales: 800-522-3652 ■ *Web:* www.jkusa.com
Moore Co 36 Beach St . . . Westerly RI 02891 401-596-2816 596-6801
Web: www.darlingtonfabrics.com
Murdock Webbing Co 27 Foundry St. . . . Central Falls RI 02863 401-724-3000 722-9730
TF: 800-375-2052 ■ *Web:* www.murdockwebbing.com
Name Maker Inc 4450 Commerce Cir PO Box 43821. . . . Atlanta GA 30336 404-691-2237 691-7711
TF: 800-241-2890 ■ *Web:* www.namemaker.com
Narricot Industries LP
928 Jaymore Rd Suite C150. . . . SouthHampton PA 18966 215-322-3900 322-3905
Web: www.narricot.com
Narrow Fabric Industries Inc
701 Reading Ave. . . . West Reading PA 19611 610-376-2891 376-2869
TF: 800-523-8118 ■ *Web:* www.narrowfabric.com
NFA Corp 850 Boylston St Suite 428. . . . Chestnut Hill MA 02467 617-232-6060
Paxar Corp Woven Labels Group
1600 Pollitt Dr . . . Fair Lawn NJ 07410 201-956-6100 956-6020
Premier Narrow Fabrics 455 Hwy 70 W . . . Columbiana AL 35051 205-669-3101 669-3101
TF: 800-633-4538
Rhode Island Textile Co 211 Columbus Ave. . . . Pawtucket RI 02861 401-722-3700 726-2840
TF: 800-556-6488 ■ *Web:* www.ritextile.com
Ross Matthews Mills Inc 657 Quarry St. . . . Fall River MA 02723 508-677-0601 676-9663
TF: 800-753-7677
Sequins International Inc 60-01 31st Ave . . . Woodside NY 11377 718-204-0002 204-0999
Web: www.sequins.com
Shelby Elastics Inc 639 N Post Rd. . . . Shelby NC 28150 704-487-4301 481-9348
TF: 800-562-4507 ■ *Web:* www.shelbyelastics.com
South Carolina Elastic Co
201 S Carolina Elastic Rd. . . . Landrum SC 29356 864-457-3388 457-3579
TF: 800-845-6700 ■ *Web:* www.scelastic.com
Southern Weaving Co 1005 W Bramlett Rd . . . Greenville SC 29611 864-233-1635 240-9302
TF: 800-849-8962 ■ *Web:* www.southernweaving.com
State Narrow Fabrics Inc
2902 Borden Ave . . . Long Island City NY 11101 718-392-8787 392-9421
TF: 800-221-7288 ■ *Web:* www.statenarrow.com
Sturges Mfg Co Inc 2030 Sunset Ave PO Box 59. . . . Utica NY 13502 315-732-6159 732-2314
Web: www.sturgesstraps.com
Sullivan-Carson Inc
1018 Laurel Oak Rd Suite 12 . . . Voorhees NJ 08043 856-784-4222 784-1151
Tape Craft Corporations 200 Tape Craft Dr. . . . Oxford AL 36203 256-236-2535 236-6718
TF Cust Svc: 800-521-1783 ■ *Web:* www.tapecraft.com
Trimtex Co Inc 400 Pk Ave . . . Williamsport PA 17701 570-326-9135 326-4250
TF: 800-326-9135 ■ *Web:* www.trimtex.com
Wayne Mills Co Inc 130 W Berkley St . . . Philadelphia PA 19144 215-842-2134 438-8599
TF: 800-220-8053 ■ *Web:* www.waynemills.com
William Wright Co 85 S St. . . . West Warren MA 01092 413-436-7732 436-9785
TF: 800-545-5740 ■ *Web:* www.wrights.com
Worldtex Inc PO Box 2187 . . . Hickory NC 28603 828-322-2242 327-6417

748-6 Nonwoven Fabrics

Phone *Fax*

Acme Felt Works Co 6500 Stanford Ave . . . Los Angeles CA 90001 323-752-3778 752-7164
Aetna Felt Corp 2401 W Emaus Ave. . . . Allentown PA 18103 610-791-0900 791-5791
TF: 800-526-4451 ■ *Web:* www.aetnafelt.com
Airtex Consumer Products a Div of Federal Foam Technologies
150 Industrial Pk Blvd . . . Cokato MN 55321 320-286-2696 286-2428
TF: 800-851-8887 ■ *Web:* www.airtex.com
American Felt & Filter Co 361 Walsh Ave . . . New Windsor NY 12553 845-561-3560 563-4422
Web: www.affco.com
American Nonwovens Corp 221 Fabritek Dr. . . . Columbus MS 39704 662-327-0745 327-8317
TF: 800-628-7961
BBA Nonwovens 70 Old Hickory Blvd. . . . Old Hickory TN 37138 615-847-7000 847-7068
TF: 800-847-7000 ■ *Web:* www.bbanonwovens.com
Berwick Offray LLC 2015 W Front St. . . . Berwick PA 18603 570-752-5934 759-0889
TF: 800-327-0350 ■ *Web:* www.berwickindustries.com
Boston Felt Co Inc
31 Front St PO Box 6258 . . . East Rochester NH 03868 603-332-7000 332-6049
Web: www.bostonfelt.com
Buffalo Batt & Felt 3307 Walden Ave . . . Depew NY 14043 716-683-4100 683-8928
Web: www.buffalobatt.com
Cerex Advanced Fabrics Inc
610 Chemstrand Rd . . . Cantonment FL 32533 850-968-0100 937-3342
TF: 800-572-3739 ■ *Web:* www.cerex.com
Clark-Cutler-McDermott Co
5 Fisher St PO Box 269 . . . Franklin MA 02038 508-528-1200 528-1406
TF: 800-922-3019 ■ *Web:* www.ccmcd.com
Fiber Bond Corp 110 Menke Rd . . . Michigan City IN 46360 219-879-4541 874-7502
Web: www.fiberbond.net
Fiberweb Inc 70 Old Hickory Blvd. . . . Old Hickory TN 37138 615-847-7000 847-7068
Web: www.fiberweb.com
Fisher Textiles Inc 139 Business Pk Dr. . . . Indian Trail NC 28079 704-821-8870 821-8880
TF: 800-554-8886 ■ *Web:* www.fishertextiles.com
Foss Mfg Co LLC
11 Merrill Industrial Dr PO Box 5000. . . . Hampton NH 03843 603-929-6000 929-6010
TF: 800-343-3277 ■ *Web:* www.fossmfg.com
Hobbs Bonded Fibers Inc 200 Commerce Dr . . . Waco TX 76710 254-741-0040 772-7238
TF: 800-433-3357 ■ *Web:* www.hobbsbondedfibers.com
Leggett & Platt Inc Textile & Fiber Products Group
1410 Donelson Pike. . . . Nashville TN 37217 615-367-8900 360-8451
TF: 800-888-4136 ■ *Web:* www.lpfiber.com
National Nonwovens 110 Pleasant St. . . . EastHampton MA 01027 413-527-3445 527-0456
TF: 800-333-3469 ■ *Web:* www.nationalnonwovens.com
Orr Felt Co 750 S Main St . . . Piqua OH 45356 937-773-0551 778-9670
Web: www.orrfelt.com
Sellars Nonwovens 808 Valley Ave. . . . Atglen PA 19310 610-593-5145 593-7000
Texollini Inc 2575 E El Presidio St. . . . Long Beach CA 90810 310-537-3400 537-3500
Web: www.texollini.com
Tietex International
3010 N Blackstock Rd. . . . Spartanburg SC 29301 864-574-0500 574-9440
TF: 800-843-8390 ■ *Web:* www.tietex.com
Trenton Mills LLC 400 Factory St PO Box 107 . . . Trenton TN 38382 731-855-1323 855-9000
Web: www.trentonmills.com

748-7 Textile Dyeing & Finishing

Phone *Fax*

Advanced Textile Composites 700 E Parker St . . . Scranton PA 18509 570-207-7000 207-7070
Web: www.advtextile.com
Albert Screen Print Inc 3704 Summit Rd . . . Norton OH 44203 330-753-1252 753-1612
TF: 800-759-2774 ■ *Web:* www.albertinc.com
Amerbelle Textiles LLC 104 E Main St PO Box 30 . . . Vernon CT 06066 860-979-0070 797-0072
Web: www.amerbelle.com
Aurora Textile Finishing Co
911 N Lake St PO Box 70 . . . Aurora IL 60507 630-892-7651 892-3215
TF: 800-864-0303 ■ *Web:* www.auroratextile.com
Bradford Dyeing Assoc Inc 460 Bradford Rd . . . Bradford RI 02808 401-377-2231 377-2234
Web: www.bdadye.com
Brittany Dyeing & Printing Corp
1357 E Rodney French Blvd . . . New Bedford MA 02744 508-999-3281 996-7001
Web: www.brittanyusa.com
Buckeye Fabric Finishing Co
1260 E Main St PO Box 216. . . . Coshocton OH 43812 740-622-3251 622-9317
Web: www.buckeyefabric.com
Carlisle Finishing
3863 Carlisle Chester Hwy . . . Carlisle SC 29031 864-427-6221 429-0330
Web: www.itg-global.com/companies/carlisle_finishing.html
Como Textile Prints Inc 193 E Railway Ave. . . . Paterson NJ 07503 973-279-2950 881-8450
Coral Dyeing & Finishing Corp 555 E 31st St . . . Paterson NJ 07513 973-278-0272 278-9490
Cosmo 12 Kent Way Suite 201 PO Box 737. . . . Byfield MA 01922 978-462-7311 465-6223
Web: www.cosmofabric.net
Cranston Print Works Co 1381 Cranston St . . . Cranston RI 02920 401-943-4800 943-3971
TF: 800-876-2756 ■ *Web:* www.cranstonvillage.com
Crystal Springs Print Works Inc
100 Longstreet Ave PO Box 750. . . . Chickamauga GA 30707 706-375-2121 375-5585
Web: www.cspwi.com
Deep River Dyeing & Finishing Co Inc
225 Poplar St PO Box 217 . . . Randleman NC 27317 336-498-4181 498-7252
DFP Acquisition LLC 1150 Ctr St. . . . Easton PA 18042 610-252-6181 559-9152
Duro Textiles LLC 110 Chace St . . . Fall River MA 02724 508-675-0101 677-6791
Web: www.duroindustries.com
GJ Littlewood & Son Inc 4044 Main St. . . . Philadelphia PA 19127 215-483-3970 483-6129
Web: www.littlewooddyers.com
Graphic Prints Inc 16540 S Main St. . . . Gardena CA 90248 310-768-0474 515-1164
Web: www.graphicprints.com
Hanes Cos Inc 600 W NW Blvd . . . Winston-Salem NC 27101 336-725-1391 777-3375
Web: www.hanesfinishing.com
Hanes Dye & Finish Inc 600 NW Blvd. . . . Winston-Salem NC 27101 336-725-1391 777-3375
Web: www.hanesfinishing.com
Harodite Industries Inc 66 S St. . . . Taunton MA 02780 508-824-6961 880-0696
TF: 800-328-5656 ■ *Web:* www.harodite.com
Holt Sublimation Printing & Products
2208 Air Pk Dr . . . Burlington NC 27215 336-222-3600 229-7580
TF: 800-544-4658 ■ *Web:* www.holtsublimation.com
Huffman Finishing Co
4919 Hickory Blvd PO Box 170 . . . Granite Falls NC 28630 828-396-1741 396-4235
Kenyon Industries Inc 36 Sherman Ave. . . . Shannock RI 02836 401-364-3400 364-6130
Web: www.kenyonindustries.net

Company	City	State	ZIP	Phone	Fax
Mastex Industries Inc 2-3 Bigelow St PO Box 1160	Holyoke	MA	01040	413-536-3614	532-6639
Meridian Dyed Yarn Group (MSYG) 312 Colombo St	Valdese	NC	28690	828-874-2151	874-3780
Web: www.msyg.com					
Microfibres Inc 1 Moshassuck St PO Box 1208	Pawtucket	RI	02862	401-725-4883	722-8520
Web: www.microfibres.com					
Parthenon Prints Inc PO Box 2505	Panama City	FL	32402	850-769-8321	769-5374
Web: www.parthenonprints.com					
Royal Carolina Corp 7305 Old Friendly Rd	Greensboro	NC	27410	336-292-8845	294-2396
Web: www.royalcarolina.com					
Russell Corp Fabrics Div 755 Lee St	Alexander City	AL	35010	256-500-4000	500-9036
Web: www.russell-brands.com					
TSG Inc 1400 Welsh Rd PO Box 1400	North Wales	PA	19454	215-628-2000	641-1325
Wade Mfg Co Hwy 74 E	Wadesboro	NC	28170	704-694-2131	694-6621
Westex Inc 2845 W 48th Pl	Chicago	IL	60632	773-523-7000	523-0965
TF: 866-493-7839 ■ *Web:* www.westexinc.com					
William J Dixon Co Inc 756 Springdale Dr	Exton	PA	19341	610-524-1131	524-7964
Web: www.wjdixon.com					
Wolfe Dye & Bleach Works Inc 25 Ridge Rd	Shoemakersville	PA	19555	610-562-7639	562-4462
Yates Bleachery Co 503 Flintstone Rd	Flintstone	GA	30725	706-820-1531	820-9459
Web: www.yatesbleachery.com					

748-8 Textile Fiber Processing Mills

Company	City	State	ZIP	Phone	Fax
A Sheftel & Sons Inc 2121 31st St SW	Allentown	PA	18103	610-797-9420	797-7272
TF Cust Svc: 800-542-2426					
Acordis Celluosic Fibers Ltd US Hwy 43 N PO Box 171	Axis	AL	36505	251-679-2200	679-2200
TF: 800-633-6720					
Blue Ridge Converting 100 Fairview Rd	Asheville	NC	28803	828-274-2100	274-0000
TF: 800-438-3893 ■ *Web:* www.slosman.com					
Buffalo Industries Inc 99 S Spokane St	Seattle	WA	98134	206-682-9900	682-9907
Web: www.buffaloindustries.com					
Charles House & Sons Inc 235 Singleton St	Woonsocket	RI	02895	401-769-0189	769-0192
TF: 800-243-7063					
Claremont Flock Corp 101 Scott Dr	Leominster	MA	01453	978-534-6191	534-8924
Web: www.claremontflock.com					
Fabri-Tech Inc 8236 N 600 W	McCordsville	IN	46055	317-335-9412	335-9413
TF Cust Svc: 800-332-4797					
Fiber Conversion Inc 15 E Elm St	Broadalbin	NY	12025	518-883-3431	883-8748
JE Herndon Co Inc 1020 J E Herndon Access Rd	Kings Mountain	NC	28086	704-739-4711	734-0621
TF: 800-277-0500					
Leggett & Platt Inc Textile & Fiber Products Group 1410 Donelson Pike	Nashville	TN	37217	615-367-8900	360-8451
TF: 800-888-4136 ■ *Web:* www.lpfiber.com					
Leigh Fibers Inc 1101 Syphrit Rd	Wellford	SC	29385	864-439-4111	439-4116
TF: 800-274-7707 ■ *Web:* www.leighfibers.com					
Lewis Industrial Supply Co 3307 N 6th St	Harrisburg	PA	17110	717-234-2409	233-4380
TF: 800-929-2400 ■ *Web:* www.lewisindustrialsupply.com					
Norman W Paschall Co Inc 1 Paschall Rd	Peachtree City	GA	30269	770-487-7945	487-0840
TF: 800-849-1820 ■ *Web:* www.paschall.com					
Oklahoma Waste & Wiping Rag Co Inc 2013 SE 18th St	Oklahoma City	OK	73129	405-670-3100	670-3993
TF Cust Svc: 800-232-4433					
Roddie Wool Scouring Co Inc 201 A L Reed St PO Box 30	Brady	TX	76825	325-597-2138	597-2797
Royal Processing Co 5710 Old Concord Rd	Charlotte	NC	28213	704-599-2804	599-2805
RSM Co 811 Pressley Rd PO Box 31605	Charlotte	NC	28231	704-525-6851	525-8368
Web: www.rsmcompany.com					
Spectro Coating Corp 101 Scott Dr	Leominster	MA	01453	978-534-1800	534-4155
Web: www.spectrocoating.com					
Triangle Textiles Ltd 1320 E Division St	Slaton	TX	79364	806-828-6573	828-5198
TF: 800-622-8299					

748-9 Yarn & Thread Mills

Company	City	State	ZIP	Phone	Fax
American & Efird Inc 22 American St PO Box 507	Mount Holly	NC	28120	704-827-4311	453-9060*
**Fax Area Code:* 800 ■ *TF:* 800-438-6781 ■ *Web:* www.amefird.com					
Brodnax Mills Inc 2 Kerr Dr PO Box A	Brodnax	VA	23920	434-729-2325	729-9581
Web: www.brodnaxmills.com					
Carolina Mills Inc 618 Carolina Ave	Maiden	NC	28650	828-428-9911	428-2335
Web: www.carolinamills.com					
Chargeurs Wool USA 178 Wool Rd	Jamestown	SC	29453	843-257-2212	257-4579
Charles Craft Inc 21381 Charles Craft Ln PO Box 1049	Laurinburg	NC	28352	910-844-3521	844-9846
TF: 800-277-1009 ■ *Web:* www.charlescraft.com					
Chesterfield Yarn Mills Inc 201 N Maple St	Pageland	SC	29728	843-672-7211	672-7210
Web: www.chesterfieldwraps.com					
Clover Yarns Inc 1030 Tanyard Branch Trail	Clover	VA	24534	434-454-7151	454-6725
Coats & Clark Inc 3430 Toringdon Way Suite 301	Charlotte	NC	28227	704-329-5800	329-5025
Coats North America 3430 Toringdon Way Suite 301	Charlotte	NC	28277	704-329-5800	329-5899
TF: 800-631-0965 ■ *Web:* www.coats.com					
Crescent Woolen Mills Co 1016 School St	Two Rivers	WI	54241	920-793-3331	793-3818
Dillon Yarn Inc 1019 Titan Rd	Dillon	SC	29536	843-774-7353	774-0338
DMC Corp 10 Basin Dr Suite 130	Kearny	NJ	07032	973-589-0606	589-8931
Web: www.dmc-usa.com					
EAM Inc 398 W Memorial Dr	Dallas	GA	30132	770-445-2776	445-2777
Eddington Thread Mfg Co PO Box 446	Bensalem	PA	19020	215-639-8900	639-8900
TF: 800-220-8901 ■ *Web:* www.edthread.com					
Glen Raven Inc 142 Glen Raven Rd	Glen Raven	NC	27217	336-227-6211	226-8133
TF: 800-788-4413 ■ *Web:* www.glenraven.com					
Grover Industries Inc 219 Laurel Ave PO Box 79	Grover	NC	28073	704-937-7434	937-7507
Web: www.groverindustries.com					
Hickory Yarns Inc 1025 10th St NE	Hickory	NC	28601	828-322-1550	322-1627
Web: www.hickoryyarns.com					
Interstock Premium Cabinets LLC 915 Pennsylvania Blvd	Feasterville	PA	19053	267-288-1200	288-1206
Web: www.interstockcabinets.com					
Jagger Bros Inc 5 Water St PO Box 188	Springvale	ME	04083	207-324-5622	490-2661
Web: www.jaggeryarn.com					
Jefferson Mills Inc 27 Valley St	Pulaski	VA	24301	540-980-1530	980-6388
TF Sales: 800-574-0069 ■ *Web:* www.jeffersonmills.com					
Jones Cos Ltd 312 S 14th St	Humboldt	TN	38343	731-784-2832	784-7131
Web: www.jonesyarn.com					
Kent Mfg Co 671 Runnymede Rd	Pickens	SC	29671	864-878-6367	878-2723
Liberty Throwing Co Inc 214 Pringle St PO Box 1387	Kingston	PA	18704	570-287-1114	283-3531
Web: www.libertythrowing.com					
Lion Brand Yarn Co 135 Kero Rd	Carlstadt	NJ	07072	212-243-8995	627-8154
TF: 800-795-5466 ■ *Web:* www.lionbrand.com					
Lorenzo Textile Mills Inc 417 Fillmore St	Lorenzo	TX	79343	806-634-5506	634-5775
Ludlow Textiles Co Inc 50 State St PO Box 559	Ludlow	MA	01056	413-583-5051	589-1415
TF: 800-628-9048 ■ *Web:* www.ludlowtextiles.com					
Meridian Specialty Yarns Inc 312 Colombo St SW	Valdese	NC	28690	828-874-2151	874-3780
Web: www.msyg.com					
National Spinning Co Inc 1140 Avenue of the Americas	New York	NY	10036	212-382-6400	382-6450
TF: 800-868-7764 ■ *Web:* www.natspin.com					
Parkdale Mills Inc 531 Cotton Blossom Cir	Gastonia	NC	28054	704-864-8761	874-5170
TF: 800-331-1843 ■ *Web:* www.parkdalemills.com					
Pharr Yarns LLC 100 Main St PO Box 1939	McAdenville	NC	28101	704-824-3551	824-0072
Web: www.pharryarns.com					
Regal Mfg Co Inc 990 3rd Ave SE PO Box 2363	Hickory	NC	28603	828-328-5381	328-4936
RL Stowe Mills Inc 100 N Main St	Belmont	NC	28012	704-825-6630	825-6630
Web: www.rlstowe.com					
Sapona Mfg Co Inc 2478 Cedar Falls Rd	Cedar Falls	NC	27230	336-625-2727	626-0876
Web: www.saponamfg.com					
Shuford Mills Inc 1985 Tate Blvd SE	Hickory	NC	28601	828-328-2131	328-5792*
**Fax:* Cust Svc ■ *TF:* 800-633-7649 ■ *Web:* www.shufordmills.com					
Spectrum Dyed Yarns Inc 136 Patterson Rd	Kings Mountain	NC	28086	704-739-7401	739-4754
TF: 800-221-9456 ■ *Web:* www.sdy.com					
Supreme Corp 325 Spence Rd	Conover	NC	28613	828-322-6975	322-7881
TF: 888-604-6975 ■ *Web:* www.ukisupreme.com					
Swift Spinning Inc 16 Corporate Ridge Pkwy PO Box 8767	Columbus	GA	31907	706-323-6303	571-0059
TF: 800-849-1252 ■ *Web:* www.swiftspinning.com					
Tuscarora Yarns Inc 8760 E Franklin St	Mount Pleasant	NC	28124	704-436-6527	436-9461
TF: 800-849-6527 ■ *Web:* www.tuscarorayarns.com					
Ultrafab Inc 1050 Hook Rd	Farmington	NY	14425	585-924-2186	924-7680
Web: www.ultrafab.com					
Unifi Inc 7201 W Friendly Ave	Greensboro	NC	27410	336-294-4410	316-5422
NYSE: UFI ■ *Web:* www.unifi.com					
Universal Fibers Inc 14401 County Rd 1717	Bristol	VA	24202	276-669-1161	669-3304
TF: 800-457-4759 ■ *Web:* www.universalfibers.com					
Waverly Mills Inc 23 3rd St	Laurinburg	NC	28352	910-276-1441	276-5826
TF Cust Svc: 800-496-9276					
Wehadkee Yarn Mills Inc 802 3rd Ave	West Point	GA	31833	706-645-1331	645-1373
TF: 800-996-9276 ■ *Web:* www.wehadkee.com					

749 TEXTILE PRODUCTS - HOUSEHOLD

Company	City	State	ZIP	Phone	Fax
1888 Mills 1581 Southern Dr PO Box 797	Griffin	GA	30224	770-229-2361	228-4732
Ado Corp 851 Simuel Rd	Spartanburg	SC	29301	864-574-2731	574-5835
TF Cust Svc: 800-845-0918 ■ *Web:* www.ado-usa.com					
Amana Woolen Mill 800 48th Ave	Amana	IA	52203	319-622-3432	622-6018
TF: 800-222-6430 ■ *Web:* www.amanawoolenmill.com					
American Textile Co 10 N Linden St	Duquesne	PA	15110	412-948-1020	948-1002
TF Cust Svc: 800-289-2826 ■ *Web:* www.americantextile.com					
American Woolen Co 4000 NW 30th Ave	Miami	FL	33142	305-635-4000	633-4997
Arden Cos 30400 Telegraph Rd Suite 200	Bingham Farms	MI	48025	248-415-8500	415-8520
Web: www.ardencompanies.com					
Arlee Home Fashions Inc 261 5th Ave 6th Fl	New York	NY	10016	212-689-0020	532-6428
Ascot Enterprises Inc 503 S Main St	Nappanee	IN	46550	574-773-7751	773-2894
Web: www.ascotent.com					
Bardwil Industries Inc 1071 Avenue of the Americas 4th Fl	New York	NY	10018	212-944-1870	869-3599
Web: www.bardwilhome.com					
Beacon Looms Inc 411 Alfred Ave	Teaneck	NJ	07666	201-833-1600	833-4053
Web: www.beaconlooms.com					
Biddeford Blankets 300 Terr Dr	Mundelein	IL	60060	847-566-7442	566-6431
TF: 800-789-6441 ■ *Web:* biddefordblankets.com					
Biederlack of America 11501 Bedford Rd NE	Cumberland	MD	21502	301-759-3633	759-3837
Web: www.biederlack.com					
Brentwood Originals Inc 20639 S Fordyce Ave	Long Beach	CA	90810	310-637-6804	639-9710
Web: www.brentwoodoriginals.com					
Carole Fabrics Inc 633 NW Frontage Rd	Augusta	GA	30907	706-863-4742	863-8186
TF: 800-241-0920 ■ *Web:* www.carolefabrics.com					
Carpenter Co Morning Glory Div 302 Highland Dr	Taylor	TX	76574	800-234-9105	352-6025*
**Fax Area Code:* 512 ■ *TF:* 800-234-9105 ■ *Web:* www.carpenter.com					
CHF Industries Inc 1 Pk Ave 9th Fl	New York	NY	10016	212-951-7800	951-8001
TF: 800-243-7090 ■ *Web:* www.chfindustries.com					
Cotton Goods Mfg Co 259 N California Ave	Chicago	IL	60612	773-265-0088	265-0096
Web: www.cottongoodsmfg.com					
Creative Bath Products 250 Creative Dr	Central Islip	NY	11722	631-582-8000	582-2020
Web: www.creativebath.com					

Company	City	State	ZIP	Phone	Fax
Crown Crafts Inc 916 S Burnside TF: 800-433-9560 ■ Web: www.crowncrafts.com	Gonzales	LA	70737	225-647-9100	647-8331
CS Brooks Inc 9 Benedict Pl Web: www.csbrooks.com	Greenwich	CT	06830	203-622-4171	622-4172
Curtain & Drapery Fashions Inc 100 Curtain Way Web: www.curtainanddraperyfashions.com	Lowell	NC	28098	704-823-1266	823-1270
Custom Drapery Blinds & Shutters 3402 E T C Jester Blvd TF: 800-929-9211 ■ Web: www.cdbas.com	Houston	TX	77018	713-225-9211	227-0808
Dorothy's Ruffled Originals Inc 6721 Market St TF: 800-367-6849 ■ Web: www.dorothysoriginals.com	Wilmington	NC	28405	910-791-1298	791-0729
Earle Industries Inc 17539 Hwy 64 PO Box 28 TF: 888-944-8667	Earle	AR	72331	870-792-8694	792-7100
Easy Way Leisure Corp 412 S Cooper Ave TF: 800-543-4532 ■ Web: www.easywayproducts.com	Cincinnati	OH	45215	513-731-5640	821-6470
Echota Fabrics Inc 1394 US 41 N Web: www.echotafabrics.com	Calhoun	GA	30701	706-629-9750	629-5229
Elrene Home Fashions Inc 261 5th Ave 10th Fl	New York	NY	10016	212-889-6376	481-1738
F Schumacher & Co 79 Madison Ave TF: 800-523-1200 ■ Web: www.fschumacher.com	New York	NY	10016	212-213-7900	213-7848
Franco Mfg Co Inc 555 Prospect St TF: 800-631-4663 ■ Web: www.francomfg.com	Metuchen	NJ	08840	732-494-0500	494-8270
Haleyville Drapery PO Box 695	Haleyville	AL	35565	205-486-9257	486-4788
Hedaya Home Fashions Inc 1111 Jefferson Ave	Elizabeth	NJ	07201	908-352-0808	352-4060
Hollander Home Fashions Corp 6560 W Rogers Cir Suite 19 TF: 800-233-7666 ■ Web: www.hollander.com	Boca Raton	FL	33487	561-997-6900	997-8738
Kaslen Textiles 5899 Downey Rd TF: 800-423-4448 ■ Web: www.kaslentextiles.com	Vernon	CA	90058	323-589-5337	588-7799
Kay Dee Designs Inc 177 Skunk Hill Rd *Fax Area Code: 800 ■ TF: 800-537-3433 ■ Web: www.kaydeedesigns.com	Hope Valley	RI	02832	401-539-2405	272-0724*
Kellwood Co 600 Kellwood Pkwy Web: www.kellwood.com	Chesterfield	MO	63017	314-576-3100	576-3460
Kennebunk Home Inc 25 Canal St TF: 800-242-1537 ■ Web: www.kennebunkhome.com	Suncook	NH	03275	603-485-7511	485-2054
Klear-Vu Corp 135 Alden St TF: 800-732-8723 ■ Web: www.klearvu.com	Fall River	MA	02723	508-674-5723	672-2027
Lafayette Venetian Blind Inc 3000 N 300 W TF: 800-342-5523 ■ Web: www.lafvb.com	West Lafayette	IN	47906	765-464-2500	464-2680
Lincoln Textile Products Co Inc 900 Conroy Pl Web: www.lincolntextile.com	Easton	PA	18040	610-438-2418	258-2791
Louis Hornick & Co Inc 117 E 38th St Web: www.louishornick.com	New York	NY	10016	212-679-2448	779-7098
Louisville Bedding Co 10400 Bunsen Way TF: 800-626-2594 ■ Web: www.loubed.com	Louisville	KY	40299	502-491-3370	495-5346
Manual Woodworkers & Weavers Inc 3737 Howard Gap Rd TF: 800-542-3139 ■ Web: www.manualww.com	Hendersonville	NC	28792	828-692-7333	696-2961
Marietta Drapery & Window Coverings Co Inc 22 Trammel St PO Box 569 *Fax: Mktg ■ TF Mktg: 800-762-4774 ■ Web: www.mariettadrapery.com	Marietta	GA	30064	770-428-3335	423-3398*
Miller Curtain Co Inc 211 New Laredo Hwy TF: 800-741-9020	San Antonio	TX	78211	210-483-1000	483-1509
Miller Industries Inc 7 Canal St PO Box 97	Lisbon Falls	ME	04252	207-353-4371	353-5900
Newport Layton Home Fashions Inc 8515 N Columbia Blvd TF Cust Svc: 800-752-2225 ■ Web: www.newportlayton.com	Portland	OR	97203	503-283-4864	283-4895
Pacific Coast Feather Co 1964 4th Ave S Web: www.pacificcoast.com	Seattle	WA	98134	206-624-1057	625-9783
Paramount Industrial Cos Inc 1112 Kingwood Ave TF: 800-777-5337 ■ Web: www.paramountsleep.com	Norfolk	VA	23502	757-855-3321	855-2029
Pendleton Woolen Mills Inc 220 NW Broadway TF: 800-760-4844 ■ Web: www.pendleton-usa.com	Portland	OR	97209	503-226-4801	535-5502
Perfect Fit Industries Inc 230 5th Ave # 1305 TF: 800-438-1516 ■ Web: www.perfectfitindustries.com	New York	NY	10001	212-679-6656	545-7241
Phoenix Down Corp 85 US Hwy 46 TF: 800-255-3696 ■ Web: www.phoenixdown.com	Totowa	NJ	07512	973-812-8100	812-9077
Quip Industries Inc 191 Methodist St TF: 800-851-4013	Carlyle	IL	62231	618-594-2437	594-4707
Riegel Consumer Products 51 Riegel Rd PO Box E TF: 800-845-3251 ■ Web: www.riegellinen.com	Johnston	SC	29832	803-275-2541	275-2219
S Lichtenberg & Co Inc 295 5th Ave Rm 918 TF Cust Svc: 800-682-1959 ■ Web: www.lichtenberg.com	New York	NY	10016	212-689-4510	689-4517
Samson Mfg Co 231 E 13th St PO Box 807 TF: 800-682-1959	Waynesboro	GA	30830	706-554-2129	554-6857
Saturday Knight Ltd 2100 Section Rd	Cincinnati	OH	45237	513-641-1400	242-2805
Springs Global US Inc PO Box 70 *Fax: Mktg ■ TF: 888-926-7888 ■ Web: www.springs.com	Fort Mill	SC	29716	803-547-1500	547-1579*
Standard Textile Co Inc Decorative Products One Knollcrest Dr TF: 800-888-5000 ■ Web: www.standardtextile.com	Cincinnati	OH	45237	513-761-9255	761-0467
Surefit Inc 6575 Snowdrift Rd Suite 101 TF: 800-305-5856 ■ Web: www.surefit.net	Allentown	PA	18106	610-264-7300	266-2690
TexStyle Inc 5555 Murray Ave Suite A TF: 800-875-8001	Cincinnati	OH	45227	513-272-1800	272-1817
Tuway American Group Inc The 2820 W Maple Rd Suite 101 Web: www.tuwaymops.com	Troy	MI	48084	248-649-8790	649-3666
Tweel Home Furnishings Inc 18 Beaver St	Newark	NJ	07102	973-286-1800	481-1911
United Feather & Down Inc 414 E Golf Rd TF: 800-932-3696 ■ Web: www.ufandd.com	Des Plaines	IL	60016	847-296-6500	296-6616
Wesco Fabrics Inc 4001 Forest St TF: 800-950-9372 ■ Web: www.wescofabrics.com	Denver	CO	80216	303-388-4101	388-3908

750 THEATERS - BROADWAY

SEE ALSO Performing Arts Facilities p. 2392; Theater Companies p. 2407; Theaters - Resident p. 2713

Company	City	State	ZIP	Phone	Fax
Al Hirschfeld Theatre 302 W 45th St TF: 800-432-7250	New York	NY	10036	212-239-6200	239-5801
Ambassador Theatre 215 W 49th St TF: 800-432-7250 ■ Web: ambassadortheater.com	New York	NY	10019	212-239-6200	239-5801
American Airlines Theatre 227 W 42nd St Web: www.roundabouttheatre.org	New York	NY	10036	212-719-1300	869-8817
August Wilson 245 W 52nd St TF: 800-432-7250 ■ Web: www.telecharge.com	New York	NY	10019	212-239-6200	239-5801
Belasco Theatre 111 W 44th St TF: 800-432-7250	New York	NY	10036	212-239-6200	
Biltmore Theatre 261 W 47th St Web: www.manhattantheatreclub.com	New York	NY	10036	212-399-3000	399-4329
Booth Theatre 222 W 45th St TF: 800-432-7250 ■ Web: www.telecharge.com	New York	NY	10036	212-239-6200	239-5801
Broadhurst Theatre 235 W 44th St TF: 800-432-7250 ■ Web: www.telecharge.com/BehindTheCurtain.aspx?prodid=7793	New York	NY	10036	212-239-6200	239-5801
Circle in the Square Theatre 1633 Broadway TF: 800-432-7250 ■ Web: www.telecharge.com	New York	NY	10019	212-239-6200	239-5801
Golden Theatre 252 W 45th St TF: 800-432-7250 ■ Web: www.telecharge.com	New York	NY	10036	212-239-6200	239-5801
Helen Hayes Theatre 240 W 44th St TF: 800-432-7250 ■ Web: www.telecharge.com/BehindTheCurtain.aspx?ProdID=8417	New York	NY	10036	212-239-6200	239-5801
Imperial Theatre 249 W 45th St TF: 800-432-7250 ■ Web: www.telecharge.com	New York	NY	10036	212-239-6200	239-5801
Jacobs Theatre 242 W 45th St TF: 800-432-7250 ■ Web: www.telecharge.com	New York	NY	10036	212-239-6200	239-5801
Longacre Theatre 220 W 48th St TF: 800-432-7250 ■ Web: www.telecharge.com	New York	NY	10036	212-239-6200	239-5801
Lyceum Theatre 149 W 45th St TF: 800-432-7250 ■ Web: www.telecharge.com	New York	NY	10036	212-239-6200	239-5801
Majestic Theatre 245 W 44th St TF: 800-432-7250 ■ Web: www.telecharge.com	New York	NY	10036	212-239-6200	239-5801
Minskoff Theatre 1515 Broadway TF: 800-755-4000 ■ Web: minskofftheatre.com	New York	NY	10036	212-307-4100	
Music Box Theatre 239 W 45th St TF: 800-432-7250 ■ Web: www.telecharge.com	New York	NY	10036	212-239-6200	239-5801
Palace Theatre 1564 Broadway Web: palacetheatreonbroadway.com	New York	NY	10036	212-730-8200	
Richard Rodgers Theatre 226 W 46th St TF: 800-755-4000 ■ Web: richardrodgerstheatre.com	New York	NY	10036	212-307-4100	
Roundabout Theatre Co 231 W 39th St Suite 1200 Web: www.roundabouttheatre.org	New York	NY	10018	212-719-9393	869-8817
Saint James Theatre 246 W 44th St TF: 800-432-7250 ■ Web: www.telecharge.com	New York	NY	10036	212-239-6200	239-5801
Shubert Theatre 225 W 44th St TF: 800-432-7250 ■ Web: www.telecharge.com	New York	NY	10036	212-239-6200	239-5801
Studio 54 Theatre 254 W 54th St Web: www.roundabouttheatre.org	New York	NY	10019	212-719-1300	956-9254
Walter Kerr Theatre 219 W 48th St TF: 800-432-7250 ■ Web: www.telecharge.com	New York	NY	10036	212-239-6200	239-5801

751 THEATERS - MOTION PICTURE

Company	City	State	ZIP	Phone	Fax
Allen Theaters 133 Wyatt Dr Suite 3 Web: www.allentheatresinc.com	Las Cruces	NM	88001	575-524-7933	527-0068
AMC Entertainment Inc 920 Main St TF: 800-326-2432 ■ Web: www.amctheatres.com	Kansas City	MO	64105	816-221-4000	480-4617
AMC Star Theatres 25333 W 12-Mile Rd TF: 888-262-4386 ■ Web: www.amctheatres.com	Southfield	MI	48034	248-368-1802	357-1151
American Multi-Cinema Inc 920 Main St TF: 800-326-2432 ■ Web: www.amctheatres.com	Kansas City	MO	64105	816-221-4000	480-4617
Carmike Cinemas Inc 1301 1st Ave NASDAQ: CKEC ■ TF: 800-241-0431 ■ Web: www.carmike.com	Columbus	GA	31901	706-576-3400	576-3880
Celebration! Cinema 2121 Celebration Ave Web: www.celebrationcinema.com	Grand Rapids	MI	49525	616-447-4200	447-4201
Chakeres Theatres Inc 222 N Murray St Web: www.chakerestheatres.com	Springfield	OH	45503	937-323-6447	325-1100
Cinemark USA Inc 3900 Dallas Pkwy Suite 500 NYSE: CNK ■ TF: 800-950-2872 ■ Web: www.cinemark.com	Plano	TX	75093	972-665-1000	665-1004
Cineplex Entertainment LP 1303 Yonge St TF: 800-333-0061 ■ Web: www.cineplex.com	Toronto	ON	M4T2Y9	416-323-6600	323-7228
Classic Cinemas 603 Rogers St Web: www.classiccinemas.com	Downers Grove	IL	60515	630-968-1600	968-1626
Clearview Cinema Group Inc 200 Pk Ave Suite 302 Web: www.clearviewcinemas.com	Florham Park	NJ	07932	908-918-2000	273-7157
De Anza Land & Leisure Corp 1615 Cordova St	Los Angeles	CA	90007	323-734-9951	734-2531
Dickinson Theaters Inc 6801 W 107th St Web: www.dtmovies.com	Overland Park	KS	66212	913-432-2334	432-9507
Eastern Federal Corp 901 E Blvd *Fax: Mktg ■ TF: 800-394-7368 ■ Web: www.easternfederal.com	Charlotte	NC	28203	704-377-3495	358-8427*
Empire Theatres Ltd 610 E River Rd Web: www.empiretheatres.com	New Glasgow	NS	B2H3S2	902-928-0550	755-7640

Name / Address	City	State	Zip	Phone	Fax
Goodrich Quality Theaters Inc 4417 Broadmoor SE *TF:* 800-473-3523 ■ *Web:* www.gqti.com	Grand Rapids	MI	49512	616-698-7733	698-7220
Harkins Amusement Enterprises Inc 7511 E McDonald Dr *Web:* www.harkinstheatres.com	Scottsdale	AZ	85250	480-627-7777	443-0950
Hollywood Theater Holdings Inc 919 SW Taylor St Suite 800 *Web:* www.gohollywood.com	Portland	OR	97205	503-221-7090	796-0229
IMAX Corp 2525 Speakman Dr *NYSE: IMAX* ■ *Web:* www.imax.com	Mississauga	ON	L5K1B1	905-403-6500	403-6450
Kerasotes ShowPlace Theatres LLC 224 N Des Plaines Ave Suite 200 *TF:* 877-293-2000 ■ *Web:* www.kerasotes.com	Chicago	IL	60661	312-775-3160	777-0480
Landmark Theaters 2222 S Barrington Ave *TF Cust Svc:* 888-724-6362 ■ *Web:* www.landmarktheatres.com	Los Angeles	CA	90064	310-473-6701	312-2364
Malco Theatres Inc 5851 Ridgeway Ctr Pkwy *Web:* www.malco.com	Memphis	TN	38120	901-761-3480	681-2044
Marcus Corp 100 E Wisconsin Ave *NYSE: MCS* ■ *TF:* 800-274-0099 ■ *Web:* www.marcuscorp.com	Milwaukee	WI	53202	414-905-1000	905-2129
Marcus Theatres Corp 100 E Wisconsin Ave Suite 19 *TF Cust Svc:* 800-274-0099 ■ *Web:* www.marcustheaters.com	Milwaukee	WI	53202	414-905-1000	905-2189
Metropolitan Theaters Corp 8727 W 3rd St *Web:* www.metrotheatres.com	Los Angeles	CA	90048	310-858-2800	858-2860
Muvico Theaters 3101 N Federal Hwy 6th Fl *TF:* 800-294-6585 ■ *Web:* www.muvico.com	Fort Lauderdale	FL	33306	954-564-6550	564-6553
National Amusements Inc 200 Elm St **Fax:* Mktg ■ *Web:* www.national-amusements.com	Dedham	MA	02026	781-461-1600	329-4670*
Northeast Cinemas LLC 500 Franklin Village Dr Suite 204 **Fax Area Code:* 508	Franklin	MA	02038	774-235-2300	520-3196*
Pacific Theatres Corp 120 N Robertson Blvd *Web:* www.pacifictheatres.com	Los Angeles	CA	90048	310-657-8420	855-9837
Rave Motion Pictures 3333 Welborn St Suite 100 *Web:* www.ravemotionpictures.com	Dallas	TX	75219	972-692-1700	692-1708
Reading International Inc 500 Citadel Dr Suite 300 *AMEX: RDI* ■ *Web:* www.readingrdi.com	Commerce	CA	90040	213-235-2240	235-2229
Regal Entertainment Group 7132 Regal Ln *NYSE: RGC* ■ *TF Cust Svc:* 877-835-5734 ■ *Web:* www.regmovies.com	Knoxville	TN	37918	865-922-1123	922-3188
WF Cinema Holdings LP 16530 Ventura Blvd Suite 500 *Web:* www.manntheatres.com	Encino	CA	91436	818-784-6266	784-8717
Wometco Enterprises Inc 3195 Ponce De Leon Blvd	Coral Gables	FL	33134	305-529-1400	529-1499

752 THEATERS - RESIDENT

SEE ALSO Performing Arts Facilities p. 2392; Theater Companies p. 2407; Theaters - Broadway p. 2712

All Of The Theaters Listed Here Are Members Of The League Of Resident Theatres (Lort). In Order To Become A Member Of Lort, Each Theater Must Be Incorporated As A Non-Profit, Irs-Approved Organization; Must Rehearse Each Self-Produced Production For A Minimum Of Three Weeks; Must Have A Playing Season Of 12 Weeks Or More; And Must Operate Under A Lort-Equity Contract.

Name / Address	City	State	Zip	Phone	Fax
Actors Theatre of Louisville 316 W Main St *TF:* 800-428-5849 ■ *Web:* www.actorstheatre.org	Louisville	KY	40202	502-584-1265	561-3300
Alabama Shakespeare Festival 1 Festival Dr *TF:* 800-841-4273 ■ *Web:* www.asf.net	Montgomery	AL	36117	334-271-5300	271-5348
Alliance Theatre Co 1280 Peachtree St NE Woodruff Arts Ctr *Web:* www.alliancetheatre.org	Atlanta	GA	30309	404-733-4650	733-4625
American Repertory Theatre (ART) 64 Brattle St *Web:* www.americanrepertorytheater.org	Cambridge	MA	02138	617-495-2668	495-1705
Arden Theatre Co 40 N 2nd St *Web:* www.ardentheatre.org	Philadelphia	PA	19106	215-922-8900	922-7011
Arkansas Repertory Theatre 601 Main St PO Box 110 *TF:* 866-684-3737 ■ *Web:* www.therep.org	Little Rock	AR	72201	501-378-0445	378-0012
Asolo Repertory Theatre 5555 N Tamiami Tr *TF:* 800-361-8388 ■ *Web:* www.asolorep.org	Sarasota	FL	34243	941-351-9010	351-5796
Barter Theatre 127 W Main St *Web:* www.bartertheatre.com	Abingdon	VA	24210	276-628-3991	619-3335
Berkeley Repertory Theatre 2025 Addison St *TF:* 888-427-8849 ■ *Web:* www.berkeleyrep.org	Berkeley	CA	94704	510-647-2949	647-2975
Berkshire Theatre Festival PO Box 797 *TF:* 866-811-4111 ■ *Web:* www.berkshiretheatre.org	Stockbridge	MA	01262	413-298-5576	298-3368
Capital Repertory Theatre 432 State St *Web:* www.capitalrep.org	Schenectady	NY	12305	518-462-4531	881-1823
Center Stage 700 N Calvert St *Web:* www.centerstage.org	Baltimore	MD	21202	410-986-4000	539-3912
City Theatre Co 1300 Bingham St *Web:* www.citytheatrecompany.org	Pittsburgh	PA	15203	412-431-4400	431-5535
Court Theatre 5535 S Ellis Ave *Web:* www.courttheatre.org	Chicago	IL	60637	773-702-7005	834-1897
Dallas Theater Ctr 3636 Turtle Creek Blvd *Web:* www.dallastheatercenter.org	Dallas	TX	75219	214-526-8210	521-7666
Delaware Theatre Co 200 Water St *Web:* www.delawaretheatre.org	Wilmington	DE	19801	302-594-1104	594-1107
Denver Center Theatre Co 1101 13th St *TF:* 800-641-1222 ■ *Web:* www.denvercenter.org	Denver	CO	80204	303-893-4000	595-9634
Florida Stage 262 S Ocean Blvd *TF:* 800-514-3837 ■ *Web:* www.floridastage.org	Manalapan	FL	33462	561-585-3404	588-4708
Ford's Theatre 511 10th St NW *TF:* 800-899-2367 ■ *Web:* www.fordstheatre.org	Washington	DC	20004	202-638-2941	347-6269
Geffen Playhouse 10886 Le Conte Ave *Web:* www.geffenplayhouse.com	Los Angeles	CA	90024	310-508-5454	208-8383
George Street Playhouse 9 Livingston Ave *Web:* www.georgestreetplayhouse.org	New Brunswick	NJ	08901	732-246-7717	247-9151
Georgia Shakespeare 4484 Peachtree Rd NE *Web:* www.gashakespeare.org	Atlanta	GA	30319	404-504-3400	504-3414
Goodspeed Musicals PO Box A *Web:* www.goodspeed.org	East Haddam	CT	06423	860-873-8664	873-2329
Great Lakes Theater Festival 1501 Euclid Ave Suite 300 *TF:* 800-766-6048 ■ *Web:* www.greatlakestheater.org	Cleveland	OH	44115	216-241-5490	241-6315
Hartford Stage Co 50 Church St *Web:* www.hartfordstage.org	Hartford	CT	06103	860-525-5601	247-8243
Huntington Theatre Co 264 Huntington Ave Boston University Theatre *Web:* www.huntingtontheatre.org	Boston	MA	02115	617-266-7900	353-8300
Kansas City Repertory Theatre 4949 Cherry St *TF:* 888-502-2700 ■ *Web:* www.kcrep.org	Kansas City	MO	64110	816-235-2727	235-5508
La Jolla Playhouse PO Box 12039 *Web:* www.lajollaplayhouse.com	La Jolla	CA	92039	858-550-1070	550-1075
Laguna Playhouse The 606 Laguna Canyon Rd PO Box 1747 *Web:* www.lagunaplayhouse.com	Laguna Beach	CA	92651	949-497-2787	497-6948
Lincoln Center Theater 150 W 65th St *Web:* www.lct.org	New York	NY	10023	212-362-7600	873-0761
Maltz Jupiter Theatre 1001 E Indiantown Rd *TF:* 800-445-1666 ■ *Web:* www.jupitertheatre.org	Jupiter	FL	33477	561-743-2666	743-0107
Manhattan Theatre Club Inc 311 W 43rd St 8th Fl *Web:* www.manhattantheatreclub.com	New York	NY	10036	212-399-3000	399-4329
Merrimack Repertory Theatre 132 Warren St *Web:* www.merrimackrep.org	Lowell	MA	01852	978-654-7550	654-7575
Milwaukee Repertory Theater 108 E Wells St *Web:* www.milwaukeerep.com	Milwaukee	WI	53202	414-224-1761	224-9097
Northlight Theatre 9501 Skokie Blvd *Web:* www.northlight.org	Skokie	IL	60077	847-679-9501	679-1879
Old Globe Theatre 1363 Old Globe Way *Web:* www.oldglobe.org	San Diego	CA	92101	619-231-1941	231-5879
Pasadena Playhouse The 39 S El Molino Ave *Web:* www.pasadenaplayhouse.org	Pasadena	CA	91101	626-356-7529	204-7399
People's Light & Theatre Co 39 Conestoga Rd *Web:* www.peopleslight.org	Malvern	PA	19355	610-647-1900	640-9521
Philadelphia Theatre Co 230 S Broad St Suite 1105 *Web:* www.philadelphiatheatrecompany.org	Philadelphia	PA	19102	215-985-1400	985-5800
Pittsburgh Public Theater 621 Penn Ave *Web:* www.ppt.org	Pittsburgh	PA	15222	412-316-8200	316-8219
PlayMakers Repertory Co 150 Country Club Rd **Fax Area Code:* 866 ■ *Web:* www.playmakersrep.org	Chapel Hill	NC	27599	919-962-7529	904-8396*
Portland Center Stage (PCS) 128 NW Eleventh Ave *Web:* www.pcs.org	Portland	OR	97205	503-445-3700	445-3701
Portland Stage Co PO Box 1458 *Web:* www.portlandstage.org	Portland	ME	04104	207-774-1043	774-0576
Prince Music Theater 1412 Chestnut St *Web:* www.princemusictheater.org	Philadelphia	PA	19102	215-569-9700	972-1020
Repertory Theatre of Saint Louis 130 Edgar Rd PO Box 191730 *Web:* www.repstl.org	Saint Louis	MO	63119	314-968-7340	968-9638
Roundabout Theatre Co 231 W 39th St Suite 1200 *Web:* www.roundabouttheatre.org	New York	NY	10018	212-719-9393	869-8817
San Jose Repertory Theatre 101 Paseo de San Antonio *Web:* www.sjrep.com	San Jose	CA	95113	408-367-7255	367-7236
Seattle Repertory Theatre (SRT) 155 Mercer St PO Box 900923 *TF:* 877-900-9285 ■ *Web:* www.seattlerep.org	Seattle	WA	98109	206-443-2210	443-2379
Shakespeare Theatre 516 8th St SE *TF:* 877-487-8849 ■ *Web:* www.shakespearetheatre.org	Washington	DC	20003	202-547-3230	547-0226
South Coast Repertory 655 Town Ctr Dr *Web:* www.scr.org	Costa Mesa	CA	92626	714-708-5500	708-5576
Syracuse Stage 820 E Genesee St *Web:* www.syracusestage.org	Syracuse	NY	13210	315-443-4008	443-9846
Theatre For A New Audience 154 Christopher St #3D *Web:* www.tfana.org	New York	NY	10014	212-229-2819	229-2911
TheatreWorks 1100 Hamilton Ct PO Box 50458 *Web:* www.theatreworks.org	Palo Alto	CA	94303	650-463-1950	463-1963
Trinity Repertory Co 201 Washington St *Web:* www.trinityrep.com	Providence	RI	02903	401-521-1100	751-5577
Virginia Stage Co 254 Granby St PO Box 3770 *Web:* www.vastage.com	Norfolk	VA	23510	757-627-6988	628-5958
Yale Repertory Theatre 1120 Chapel St PO Box 1257 *Web:* www.yale.edu/yalerep	New Haven	CT	06505	203-432-1234	432-6423
Arena Stage 1101 6th St SW *Web:* www.arenastage.org	Washington	DC	20024	202-554-9066	488-4056
Goodman Theatre 170 N Dearborn St *Web:* www.goodmantheatre.org	Chicago	IL	60601	312-443-3811	443-3821
Guthrie Theater 818 S 2nd St *TF:* 877-447-8243 ■ *Web:* www.guthrietheater.org	Minneapolis	MN	55415	612-377-2224	225-6004
McCarter Theatre 91 University Pl *Web:* www.mccarter.org	Princeton	NJ	08540	609-258-6500	497-0369
Geva Theatre Ctr 75 Woodbury Blvd *Web:* www.gevatheatre.org	Rochester	NY	14607	585-232-1366	232-4031
Wilma Theater 265 S Broad St *Web:* www.wilmatheater.org	Philadelphia	PA	19107	215-893-9456	893-0895
Clarence Brown Theatre *University of Tennessee* 206 McClung Tower *Web:* www.clarencebrowntheatre.com	Knoxville	TN	37996	865-974-5161	974-4867
Alley Theatre 615 Texas Ave *Web:* www.alleytheatre.org	Houston	TX	77002	713-228-9341	222-6542
A Contemporary Theatre (ACT) 700 Union St Kreielsheimer Pl	Seattle	WA	98101	206-292-7660	292-7670

				Phone	Fax
Web: www.acttheatre.org					

753 TICKET BROKERS

	City	State	Zip	Phone	Fax
Acteva Inc 100 Pine St 10th Fl *TF Cust Svc:* 877-855-8646 ■ *Web:* www.acteva.com	San Francisco	CA	94111	415-374-8222	358-4459
All American Ticket Service 2616 Philadelphia Pike Suite E *TF:* 800-669-0571 ■ *Web:* www.alltickets.com	Claymont	DE	19703	302-798-8556	798-6552
Americana Tickets NY 1535 Broadway *TF:* 800-833-3121 ■ *Web:* www.americanatickets.com	New York	NY	10036	212-581-6660	262-9627
Broadway.com 727 7th Ave 6th Fl *TF:* 800-276-2392 ■ *Web:* www.broadway.com	New York	NY	10019	212-541-8457	541-4892
Casual Apparel Inc 139 S Main St *Web:* www.casualapparel.com	Sparta	TN	38583	931-836-3004	836-2393
Front Row USA Entertainment Inc 18170 W Dixie Hwy 2nd Fl *TF:* 800-446-8499 ■ *Web:* www.frontrowusa.com	North Miami Beach	FL	33160	305-940-8499	936-2438
Global Entertainment Ticketing 4909 E McDowell Rd Suite 104 *Web:* www.gettix.net	Phoenix	AZ	85008	480-994-0772	994-0759
Good Time Tickets Inc 38 Hadden Field Rd *TF:* 800-774-8499 ■ *Web:* www.goodtimetickets.com	Palmyra	NJ	08065	856-829-3900	829-2797
Great Seats Inc 7338 Baltimore Ave Suite 108A *TF:* 800-664-5056 ■ *Web:* www.greatseats.com	College Park	MD	20740	301-985-6250	985-6254
HMR Enterprises Inc 14515 Ventura Blvd Suite 210 *TF:* 800-328-4253 ■ *Web:* www.viptickets.com	Sherman Oaks	CA	91403	818-907-1548	784-2359
Moviefone Inc 333 Westchester Ave 2nd Fl *TF Cust Svc:* 800-745-0009 ■ *Web:* www.moviefone.com	White Plains	NY	10604	914-872-0333	872-0066
Pacific Northwest Ticket Service 2864 77th Ave SE *TF:* 800-281-0753	Mercer Island	WA	98040	206-232-0150	232-0159
Select-A-Ticket Inc 25 Rt 23 S *TF:* 800-735-3288 ■ *Web:* www.selectaticket.com	Riverdale	NJ	07457	973-839-6100	839-0870
Shubert Ticketing 234 W 44th St *TF:* 800-938-8587 ■ *Web:* www.shubertticketing.com	New York	NY	10036	212-944-4160	944-4170
Theatre Development Fund 1501 Broadway 21st Fl *Web:* www.tdf.org	New York	NY	10036	212-221-0885	768-1563
Ticket Box 2125 Ctr Ave Suite 509 *TF:* 800-842-5440 ■ *Web:* www.theticketbox.com	Fort Lee	NJ	07024	201-461-8771	461-4606
Ticket Heaven Inc 600 S County Farm Rd Suite 144 *TF:* 800-260-6616	Wheaton	IL	60187	630-260-0626	260-4831
Ticket Pros USA 245 Peachtree Ctr Ave Suite M-39 *TF:* 800-962-2985 ■ *Web:* www.ticketmall.com	Atlanta	GA	30303	404-524-8491	614-0420
Ticket Source Inc 5516 E Mockingbird Ln Suite 100 *TF:* 800-557-6872 ■ *Web:* www.ticketsource.com	Dallas	TX	75206	214-821-9011	821-9060
Ticketfinder.com 236 W Portal Ave Suite 360 *TF:* 800-523-1515 ■ *Web:* www.ticketfinder.com	San Francisco	CA	94127	650-757-3514	
Ticketmaster 3701 Wilshire Blvd 7th Fl *TF:* 800-366-8652 ■ *Web:* www.ticketmaster.com	Los Angeles	CA	90010	213-381-2000	386-1244
Tickets Galore Inc 33 Haddon Ave *TF:* 888-849-9663 ■ *Web:* www.ticketsgalore.com	Westmont	NJ	08108	856-869-8499	869-2258
Tickets.com Inc 555 Anton Blvd 11th Fl *TF:* 800-352-0212 ■ *Web:* www.tickets.com	Costa Mesa	CA	92626	714-327-5400	327-5410
TicketWeb Inc PO Box 77250 **Fax Area Code:* 510 ■ *TF Cust Svc:* 866-468-7630 ■ *Web:* www.ticketweb.com	San Francisco	CA	94103	800-965-4827	649-9218*
TNT Tickets Inc 23881 Via Fabricante Suite 505 *TF:* 800-425-5849 ■ *Web:* www.tnttickets.com	Mission Viejo	CA	92691	949-458-5744	830-4504
Total Travel & Tickets Inc 5703 N Andrews Way *TF:* 800-493-8499 ■ *Web:* www.totaltickets.com	Fort Lauderdale	FL	33309	954-493-9151	493-8698
Up Front Tickets 915 Druid Hill Ave *Web:* www.upfronttickets.com	Pasadena	MD	21122	410-384-9104	384-9106
Western States Ticket Service 143 W McDowell Rd *TF:* 800-326-0331 ■ *Web:* www.wstickets.com	Phoenix	AZ	85003	602-254-3300	254-3387
Who Needs Two 707 Lake Cook Rd Suite 115 *TF Cust Svc:* 888-246-8499 ■ *Web:* www.ticketbrokers.com	Deerfield	IL	60015	847-564-8499	564-8855

754 TILE - CERAMIC (WALL & FLOOR)

	City	State	Zip	Phone	Fax
American Marazzi Tile Inc 359 Clay Rd *TF:* 877-832-8324 ■ *Web:* www.marazzitile.com	Sunnyvale	TX	75182	972-232-3801	226-5629
Ann Sacks Tile & Stone Inc 8120 NE 33rd Dr *TF:* 800-278-8453 ■ *Web:* www.annsacks.com	Portland	OR	97211	503-281-7751	287-8807
Armstrong World Industries Inc 2500 Columbia Ave **Fax:* Hum Res ■ *TF Cust Svc:* 800-233-3823 ■ *Web:* www.armstrong.com	Lancaster	PA	17603	717-397-0611	396-6133*
B & W Tile Mfg Co Inc 14600 S Western Ave *Web:* www.bwtile.com	Gardena	CA	90249	310-538-9579	538-2190
BolArt Custom Tile 6 Terr St *Web:* www.bolarttile.com	Alfred	NY	14802	607-587-9771	587-9110
Crossville Porcelain Stone/USA PO Box 1168 *Web:* www.crossvilleinc.com	Crossville	TN	38557	931-484-2110	484-2110
Curran Group Inc 7502 S Main St *Web:* www.currangroup.com	Crystal Lake	IL	60014	815-455-5100	455-7894
Dal-Tile International Inc 7834 Hawn Fwy *TF:* 800-933-8453 ■ *Web:* www.daltile.com	Dallas	TX	75217	214-398-1411	309-4553
Deutsche Steinzeug America Inc (DSA) 367 Curie Dr *Web:* www.deutsche-steinzeug.de	Alpharetta	GA	30005	770-442-5500	442-5502
Ege Seramik America Inc 5600 Oakbrook Pkwy Suite 280 *Web:* www.egeseramik-usa.com	Norcross	GA	30093	678-291-0888	291-0832
Endicott Tile LLC 57120 707 Rd *TF:* 800-927-9179 ■ *Web:* www.endicott.com	Endicott	NE	68350	402-729-3315	729-5804
Epro Tile Inc 10890 E CR 6 **Fax Area Code:* 866 ■ *TF:* 866-818-3776 ■ *Web:* www.eprotile.com	Bloomville	OH	44818	419-426-3561	343-8453*
Florida Tile Industries Inc 998 Governors Ln Suite 300 *TF Cust Svc:* 800-352-8453 ■ *Web:* www.floridatile.com	Lexington	KY	40513	859-219-5200	
Florim USA Inc 300 International Blvd *TF:* 877-356-7461 ■ *Web:* www.florimusa.com	Clarksville	TN	37040	931-645-5100	647-9934
Interceramic USA 2333 S Jupiter Rd *Web:* www.interceramicusa.com	Garland	TX	75041	214-503-5500	503-4890
Interstyle Ceramics & Glass Ltd 3625 Brighton Ave *TF:* 800-667-1566 ■ *Web:* www.interstyle.ca	Burnaby	BC	V5A3H5	604-421-7229	421-7544
Ironrock Capital Inc 1201 Millerton St SE *TF:* 800-325-3945 ■ *Web:* www.ironrock.com	Canton	OH	44707	330-484-4887	484-3584
Jefferson Ceramic Tile Co Inc 405 S Main St *Web:* www2.jctc.com	Jefferson	WI	53549	920-674-5725	674-3677
Laufen USA 4244 Mt Pleasant St NW Suite 100 *TF:* 800-321-0684	North Canton	OH	44720	330-649-5000	649-5055
ME Tile Co Inc 6463 Waveland Ave *Web:* www.metile.com	Hammond	IN	46320	219-554-1877	554-1880
Meredith Collection 1201 Millerton St SE *TF:* 800-325-3945 ■ *Web:* www.meredithtile.com	Canton	OH	44707	330-484-1656	484-9380
Metropolitan Ceramics 1201 Millerton St SE *TF:* 800-325-3945 ■ *Web:* www.metroceramics.com	Canton	OH	44707	330-484-4887	484-4880
Monarch Ceramic Tile 834 Richwood Ave *TF Cust Svc:* 800-289-8453 ■ *Web:* www.monarchceramictile.com	Florence	AL	35630	256-764-6181	718-4148
Nudo Products Inc 1500 Taylor Ave *TF:* 800-826-4132 ■ *Web:* www.nudo.com	Springfield	IL	62703	217-528-5636	528-8722
Sovereign Distributors Inc 2030 Springdale Rd *Web:* www.avaloncarpettile.com	Cherry Hill	NJ	08003	856-489-4996	489-6483
Summitville Tiles Inc SR-644 *Web:* www.summitville.com	Summitville	OH	43962	330-223-1511	223-1414
Talisman Handmade Tiles 4401 N Ravenswood Ave	Chicago	IL	60640	773-784-2628	784-2656
Twin City Tile & Marble Co 900 Montreal Way *Web:* www.tctm.com	Saint Paul	MN	55102	651-602-5800	602-5858
Wood Pro Inc 421 Washington St PO Box 363 *TF:* 877-668-6800 ■ *Web:* www.woodproinc.com	Auburn	MA	01501	508-832-3291	832-9847

755 TIMBER TRACTS

	City	State	Zip	Phone	Fax
Boething Treeland Farms Inc 23475 Long Valley Rd	Woodland Hills	CA	91367	818-883-1222	592-4955
Boise Cascade LLC 1111 W Jefferson St Suite 300 *Web:* www.bc.com	Boise	ID	83702	208-384-6161	384-7189
Crescent Resources Inc 227 W Trade St #1000 *Web:* www.crescent-resources.com	Charlotte	NC	28202	980-321-6000	
Deltic Timber Corp PO Box 7200 *NYSE:* DEL ■ *Web:* www.deltic.com	El Dorado	AR	71731	870-881-9400	881-6454
Haida Corp PO Box 89 *TF:* 800-478-3721 ■ *Web:* www.haidacorp.com	Hydaburg	AK	99922	907-285-3721	285-3944
Holiday Tree Farms Inc 800 NW Cornell Ave *TF:* 800-289-3684 ■ *Web:* www.holidaytreefarm.com	Corvallis	OR	97330	541-753-3236	757-8028
Industrial Timber & Lumber Corp (ITL) 23925 Commerce Pk Rd *TF:* 800-829-9663 ■ *Web:* www.itlcorp.com	Beachwood	OH	44122	216-831-3140	831-4734
JM Huber Corp 499 Thornall St 8th Fl **Fax:* Hum Res ■ *Web:* www.huber.com	Edison	NJ	08837	732-549-8600	549-2239*
Lester Group The 4 E Liberty St PO Box 4991 *Web:* www.lestergroup.com	Martinsville	VA	24115	276-632-2195	632-2117
McShan Lumber Co Inc PO Box 27 *TF:* 800-882-3712 ■ *Web:* www.mcshanlumber.com	McShan	AL	35471	205-375-6277	375-2773
MeadWestvaco Forest Resources 180 Westvaco Rd	Summerville	SC	29483	843-871-5000	873-2654
Murray Pacific Corp 1201 Pacific Ave Suite 1750	Tacoma	WA	98402	253-383-4911	383-3261
Musser Forests Inc 1800 119 Hwy N *TF:* 800-643-8319 ■ *Web:* www.musserforests.com	Indiana	PA	15701	724-465-5685	465-9893
Olympic Resource Management 19245 10th Ave NE *NASDAQ:* popec ■ *Web:* www.orminc.com	Poulsbo	WA	98370	360-697-6626	697-1156
Pike Lumber Co Inc PO Box 247 *TF:* 800-356-4554 ■ *Web:* www.pikelumber.com	Akron	IN	46910	574-893-4511	893-7400
Plum Creek Timber Co Inc 999 3rd Ave Suite 4300 *NYSE:* PCL ■ *TF:* 800-858-5347 ■ *Web:* www.plumcreek.com	Seattle	WA	98104	206-467-3600	467-3795

Phone Fax

Roy O Martin Lumber Co Inc
2189 Memorial Dr .... Alexandria LA 71301 318-448-0405 443-0159
Web: www.martco.com

Sierra Pacific Industries
19794 Riverside Ave.............................. Anderson CA 96007 530-378-8000 378-8109
Web: www.sierrapacificind.com

Starker Forests Inc 7240 SW Philomath Blvd .... Corvallis OR 97333 541-929-2477 929-2178
Web: www.starkerforests.com

Timber Resource Services 6400 Hwy 66 .... Klamath Falls OR 97601 541-884-2240 880-5472

Westervelt Co Inc PO Box 48999.................. Tuscaloosa AL 35404 205-562-5000 562-5012*
**Fax:* Sales ■ *Web:* www.westervelt.com

Weyerhaeuser Co 33663 Weyerhaeuser Way S........ Federal Way WA 98003 253-924-2345 924-2685
NYSE: WY ■ *TF:* 800-525-5440 ■ *Web:* www.weyerhaeuser.com

Yule Tree Farms 12704 Ehlen Rd NE .... Aurora OR 97002 503-678-2101 651-2663
Web: www.yuletreefarm.com

756 TIMESHARE COMPANIES

SEE ALSO Hotels & Hotel Companies p. 2081

Phone Fax

Bluegreen Corp
4960 Conference Way N Suite 100................. Boca Raton FL 33431 561-912-8000 912-8100
NYSE: BXG ■ *TF:* 800-456-2582 ■ *Web:* www.bluegreenonline.com

Celebrity Resorts 2800 N Poinciana Blvd............ Kissimmee FL 34746 407-997-5000 997-5225
TF: 800-423-8604 ■ *Web:* www.celebrityresorts.com

Central Florida Investments Inc
5601 Windhover Dr .... Orlando FL 32819 407-351-3350 352-8935
TF: 800-925-9999 ■ *Web:* www.westgateresorts.com

Club Intrawest 375 Water St Suite 326.............. Vancouver BC V6B5C6 604-689-8816 682-7842
TF: 800-767-2166 ■ *Web:* www.clubintrawest.com

Diamond Resorts Corp
3865 W Cheyenne Ave .... North Las Vegas NV 89032 702-804-8600 532-1075
NASDAQ: SNRR

Diamond Resorts International
3745 Las Vegas Blvd S........................... Las Vegas NV 89109 702-823-7700
Web: www.diamondresorts.com

Disney Vacation Club 200 Celebration Pl .... Celebration FL 34747 407-566-3100 566-3393
TF: 800-500-3990 ■ *Web:* www.disneyvacationclub.disney.go.com

Festiva Resorts 1 Vance Gap Rd.................... Asheville NC 28805 828-254-3378 254-2285*
**Fax:* Financial ■ *TF Resv:* 866-933-7848 ■ *Web:* www.festiva.travel

Four Seasons Hotels & Resorts 1165 Leslie St......... Toronto ON M3C2K8 416-449-1750 441-4374
TF: 800-332-3442 ■ *Web:* www.fourseasons.com

Grand Pacific Resorts
5900 Pasteur Ct Suite 200 .... Carlsbad CA 92008 760-431-8500 431-4580
TF: 800-444-3515 ■ *Web:* www.grandpacificresorts.com

Hilton Grand Vacations Co LLC
6355 Metro W Blvd Suite 180....................... Orlando FL 32835 407-521-3100 521-3112
TF: 800-521-3144 ■ *Web:* www.hiltongrandvacations.com

Hyatt Vacation Ownership Inc
140 Fountain Pkwy N # 570.................. Saint Petersburg FL 33716 727-803-9400 803-9401
TF: 800-926-4447 ■ *Web:* www.hyatt.com

Interval International Inc 6262 Sunset Dr PH 1.......... Miami FL 33143 305-666-1861 667-5948
TF: 800-828-8200 ■ *Web:* www.intervalworld.com

Island One Resorts 8680 Commodity Cir............... Orlando FL 32819 407-859-8900 240-9506
TF: 800-892-7523 ■ *Web:* www.islandone.com

Marriott Vacation Club International
6649 Westwood Blvd Suite 500 .... Orlando FL 32821 407-206-6000
TF: 800-307-7312 ■ *Web:* www.marriottvacationclub.com

Monarch Grand Vacations
23091 Mill Creek Dr........................... Laguna Hills CA 92653 949-609-2400 587-2499
TF: 800-828-4200 ■ *Web:* www.monarchgrandvacations.com

One Napili Way 5355 Lower Honoapiilani Hwy .... Lahaina HI 96761 808-669-2007 669-5103
TF Cust Svc: 800-841-6284 ■ *Web:* www.onenapiliway.com

Resort Condominiums International (RCI)
9998 N Michigan Rd................................ Carmel IN 46032 317-805-9000 805-9677*
**Fax:* Cust Svc ■ *TF:* 800-481-5738 ■ *Web:* www.rci.com

Royal Aloha Vacation Club
1505 Dillingham Blvd Suite 212..................... Honolulu HI 96817 808-847-8050 841-5467
TF: 800-367-5212 ■ *Web:* www.ravc.com

Shell Vacations Club
40 Skokie Blvd Suite 350 .... Northbrook IL 60062 847-564-4600 564-0703
Web: www.shellvacationsclub.com

Starwood Vacation Ownership Inc
Sheraton Vistana Resort 8800 Vistana Ctr Dr .... Orlando FL 32821 407-239-3100 239-3111
TF Resv: 800-847-8262 ■ *Web:* www.starwoodvo.com

Sunchaser Vacation Villas
5006 Fairmont Frontage Rd
PO Box 127 .... Fairmont Hot Springs BC V0B1L1 250-345-6321 345-6446
TF Resv: 800-663-6333 ■ *Web:* www.sunchaservillas.ca

Tempus Resorts International
7380 Sand Lake Rd Suite 600........................ Orlando FL 32819 407-226-1000
TF: 800-463-7256 ■ *Web:* www.tempusresorts.com

Vacation Internationale 1417 116th Ave NE .... Bellevue WA 98004 425-454-3065 454-4339
TF Cust Svc: 800-444-6633 ■ *Web:* www.vacationinternationale.com

WorldMark by Wyndham Inc 8427 S Park Cir .... Orlando FL 32819 888-648-7363
TF: 888-648-7363 ■ *Web:* www.worldmarkbywyndham.com

WorldMark the Club 9805 Willows Rd NE.............. Redmond WA 98052 425-498-1950 498-1968
TF: 800-722-3487 ■ *Web:* www.worldmarktheclub.com

Wyndham Vacation Resorts
8427 S Pk Cir Suite 500........................... Orlando FL 32819 407-662-1000 370-6328
TF Cust Svc: 800-251-8736 ■ *Web:* www.wyndhamvacationresorts.com/ffr/index.do

Silverleaf Resorts Inc
1221 Riverbend Dr Suite 120 .... Dallas TX 75247 214-631-1166 637-0585
NASDAQ: SVLF ■ *TF:* 800-613-0310 ■ *Web:* www.silverleafresorts.com

757 TIRES - MFR

Phone Fax

Bridgestone Americas Holding Inc
535 Marriott Dr.................................. Nashville TN 37214 615-937-5000 937-3621
TF Cust Svc: 800-543-7522 ■ *Web:* www.bridgestone-firestone.com

Callaghan Tire 1511 38th Ave E .... Bradenton FL 34208 941-746-6188
Web: www.callaghantire.com

Carlisle Tire & Wheel Mfg 23 Windham Blvd............. Aiken SC 29805 803-643-2919 643-2919
TF Sales: 800-827-1001 ■ *Web:* www.carlisletire.com

Continental Tire North America Inc
1800 Continental Blvd .... Charlotte NC 28273 704-583-3900 583-8947*
**Fax:* Mktg ■ *TF:* 800-478-1254 ■ *Web:* www.conti-online.com

Phone Fax

Cooper Tire & Rubber Co 701 Lima Ave .... Findlay OH 45840 419-423-1321 424-4108
NYSE: CTB ■ *TF:* 800-854-6288 ■ *Web:* www.coopertire.com

Denman Tire Corp 400 Diehl S Rd .... Leavittsburg OH 44430 330-675-4242 675-4242
TF Cust Svc: 800-334-5543

Dunlop Tire Corp PO Box 1109........................ Buffalo NY 14240 716-639-5200 639-5200*
**Fax:* Hum Res ■ *TF:* 800-845-8378 ■ *Web:* www.dunlopmotorcycle.com

Goodyear Tire & Rubber Co 1144 E Market St............ Akron OH 44316 330-796-2121 796-2222*
NYSE: GT ■ **Fax:* Cust Svc ■ *TF Cust Svc:* 800-321-2136 ■ *Web:* www.goodyear.com

Hankook Tire America Corp 1450 Valley Rd .... Wayne NJ 07470 973-633-9000 633-0028
TF: 800-426-8252 ■ *Web:* www.hankooktireusa.com

Hercules Tire & Rubber Co
16380 E US Rt 224 - 200 .... Findlay OH 45840 419-425-6400 425-6403
TF: 800-677-9535 ■ *Web:* www.herculestire.com

Kelly-Springfield Tire Co
12501 Willow Brook Rd SE...................... Cumberland MD 21502 301-777-6000 777-6008
Web: www.kelly-springfield.com

Maine Industrial Tires Ltd
107 Audubon Rd Bldg 2 Suite 205.................... Gorham ME 04038 207-856-6381 854-1029
TF Sales: 877-648-1949 ■ *Web:* www.industrialtires.com

Martin Wheel Co Inc 342 W Ave .... Tallmadge OH 44278 330-633-3278 633-3303
TF: 800-462-7846

Michelin North America Inc
1 PkwyS PO Box 19001 .... Greenville SC 29602 864-458-5000 423-2987*
**Fax Area Code:* 800 ■ **Fax:* Cust Svc ■ *TF Cust Svc:* 800-847-3435 ■ *Web:* www.michelin.com

Mickey Thompson Tires 4600 Prosper Dr................ Stow OH 44224 330-928-9092 928-0503
TF: 800-222-9092 ■ *Web:* www.mickeythompsontires.com

Mitchell Industrial Tire Co
2915 8th Ave PO Box 71839..................... Chattanooga TN 37407 423-698-4442 697-7143*
**Fax:* Sales ■ *TF:* 800-251-7226 ■ *Web:* www.mitco.com

Pensler Capital Corp 132 Elm Rd .... Princeton NJ 08540 609-688-8549 481-6271*
**Fax Area Code:* 212 ■ *Web:* www.penslercapital.com

Pirelli Tire North America
100 Pirelli Dr PO Box 700 .... Rome GA 30161 706-368-5800 368-5832
TF: 800-747-3554 ■ *Web:* www.us.pirelli.com

Purcell Tire & Rubber Co 301 N Hall St .... Potosi MO 63664 573-438-2133 438-2151*
**Fax:* Hum Res ■ *TF:* 800-326-8410 ■ *Web:* www.purcelltire.com

Robbins LLC PO Box 60.......................... Tuscumbia AL 35674 256-383-5441 383-9424*
**Fax:* Acctg ■ *TF:* 800-633-3312 ■ *Web:* www.robbinsllc.com

SolidBoss Worldwide Inc
200 Veterans Blvd............................ South Haven MI 49090 269-637-6356 637-6356
TF: 888-258-7252 ■ *Web:* www.solidboss.com

Specialty Tires of America Inc
1600 Washington St.............................. Indiana PA 15701 724-349-9010 349-8192
TF: 800-622-7327

Superior Tire & Rubber Corp
1818 Pennsylvania Ave W PO Box 308................. Warren PA 16365 814-723-2370 723-5123
TF Cust Svc: 800-289-1456 ■ *Web:* www.superiortire.com

Tech International 200 E Coshocton St .... Johnstown OH 43031 740-967-9015 967-1039
TF: 800-336-8324 ■ *Web:* www.techtirerepairs.com

Tech Supply
28300 Industrial Blvd Suite E PO Box 56747 .... Hayward CA 94545 510-783-7085 783-8741
TF: 800-245-8324 ■ *Web:* www.techinc.biz

Titan Tire Co 2345 E Market St .... Des Moines IA 50317 515-265-9200 265-9301
TF: 800-872-2327 ■ *Web:* www.titan-intl.com

Toyo Tire USA Corp 6261 Katella Ave Suite 2B........... Cypress CA 90630 800-678-3250 229-6184*
**Fax Area Code:* 714 ■ **Fax:* Mktg ■ *TF:* 800-678-3250 ■ *Web:* www.toyo.com

Vogue Tire & Rubber Co Inc
1101 Feehanville Dr .... Mount Prospect IL 60056 847-297-1900 375-9367
TF: 800-323-1466 ■ *Web:* www.voguetyre.com

Yokohama Tire Corp 601 S Acacia Ave .... Fullerton CA 92831 714-870-3800 870-3853
TF: 800-423-4544 ■ *Web:* www.yokohamatire.com

758 TIRES & TUBES - WHOL

Phone Fax

A & E Tire Inc 3855 E 52nd Ave........................ Denver CO 80216 303-308-6900
Web: www.aetire.com

Allied Oil & Supply Inc 2209 S 24th St .... Omaha NE 68103 402-344-4343 344-4360
TF: 800-333-3717 ■ *Web:* www.allied-oil.com

Ball Tire & Gas Inc 620 S Ripley Blvd .... Alpena MI 49707 989-354-4186 356-2080
TF: 800-322-3016

Barron's Wholesale Tire Inc
1302 Eastport Rd .... Jacksonville FL 32218 904-751-2449 751-2506
TF: 800-245-1899 ■ *Web:* www.barrontire.com

Bauer Built Inc PO Box 248 .... Durand WI 54736 715-672-4295 672-8452
TF: 800-999-0123 ■ *Web:* www.bauerbuilt.com

Ben Tire Distributors Ltd
203 E Madison St PO Box 158......................... Toledo IL 62468 217-849-3519 849-3019
TF: 800-252-8961 ■ *Web:* www.bentire.com

Bob Sumerel Tires & Service Inc
3646 E Broad St .... Columbus OH 43213 614-237-6325 237-6328
TF: 800-858-0421 ■ *Web:* www.bobsumereltire.com

Burggraf Corp 322 Main St .... Quapaw OK 74363 918-674-2281 674-2283
TF Cust Svc: 800-331-2617 ■ *Web:* www.burggraftire.com

Capital Tire Inc 1001-17 Cherry St...................... Toledo OH 43608 419-241-5111 241-7902
TF: 800-537-0190

Clark Tire & Auto Supply Co Inc 220 S Ctr St.......... Hickory NC 28602 828-322-2303 327-2783
TF: 800-968-3092 ■ *Web:* www.clarktire.com

Cross-Midwest Tire Inc 3570 Gardener Ave .... Kansas City MO 64120 816-231-6511 231-6393
Web: www.crossmidwest.com

Dapper Tire Co Inc 4025 Lockridge St .... San Diego CA 92102 619-266-1397 266-2384
TF: 800-266-7172 ■ *Web:* www.dappertire.com

Phone *Fax*

De Ronde Tire Supply Inc 95 Rapin Pl .... Buffalo NY 14211 716-897-6690 893-5716
TF: 800-227-4647 ■ *Web:* www.etrucktire.com
Dunlap & Kyle Co Inc 280 Eureka St .... Batesville MS 38606 662-563-7601 563-0019
TF: 800-647-6133 ■ *Web:* www.dktire.com
East Bay Tire Co 2200 Huntington Dr Unit C .... Fairfield CA 94533 707-437-4700 437-4800
TF: 800-831-8473 ■ *Web:* www.live.eastbaytire.com
Eddie's Tire Service Inc
3077 Valley Rd .... Berkeley Springs WV 25411 304-258-1368 258-1777
Falken Tire Corp 10404 6th St .... Rancho Cucamonga CA 91730 909-466-1116 466-1169
TF: 800-723-2553 ■ *Web:* www.falkentire.com
Free Service Tire Co Inc 126 Buffalo St .... Johnson City TN 37604 423-979-2250 979-2263
Web: www.freeservicetire.com
Friend Tire Co 11 N Industrial Dr .... Monett MO 65708 417-235-7836 235-3062
TF: 800-950-8473 ■ *Web:* www.friendtire.com
Gateway Tire Co Inc 4 W Crescentville Rd............ Cincinnati OH 45246 513-874-2500 874-7412
TF: 800-837-1405
Grismer Tire Co PO Box 337 .... Dayton OH 45401 937-224-9815 224-3800
Web: www.grismertire.com
Harris Tire Co 1100 S Brundidge St .... Troy AL 36081 334-566-2691 566-9511
Web: www.harristire.com
Ken Jones Tire Inc 73 Chandler St.................. Worcester MA 01609 508-755-5255 755-4397
TF: 800-225-9513 ■ *Web:* www.kenjones.com
Kenda USA 7095 Americana Pkwy .... Reynoldsburg OH 43068 614-866-9803 866-9805
TF: 866-536-3287 ■ *Web:* www.kendausa.com
Kost Tire Distributors Inc 335 Ct St............... Binghamton NY 13904 607-723-1230 771-8443
TF: 800-622-6672 ■ *Web:* www.kosttire.com
Kramer Tire Co Inc 1369 Azalea Garden Rd .... Norfolk VA 23502 757-857-1234 857-7339
Web: www.kramertire.com
Kumho Tire USA Inc 14605 Miller Ave .... Fontana CA 92336 909-428-3999 428-3988
TF: 800-445-8646 ■ *Web:* www.kumhotireusa.com
Lakin Tire West Inc
15305 Spring Ave.......................... Santa Fe Springs CA 90670 562-802-2752 802-7584
TF: 800-488-2752 ■ *Web:* www.lakintire.com
Laramie Tire Distributors Inc
2000 Campus Ln .... East Norristown PA 19403 610-615-8000 615-8001
TF: 800-523-0430
Michelin North America Inc
1 PkwyS PO Box 19001.......................... Greenville SC 29602 864-458-5000 423-2987*
**Fax Area Code:* 800 ■ **Fax:* Cust Svc ■ *TF Cust Svc:* 800-847-3435 ■ *Web:* www.michelin.com
Parrish Tire Co Inc 5130 Indiana Ave............ Winston-Salem NC 27106 336-767-0202 744-2716
TF: 800-849-8473 ■ *Web:* www.parrishtire.com
Phillips Tire Co Inc
1123 W Commonwealth Ave........................ Fullerton CA 92833 714-525-2306 525-1297
Web: www.phillipstire.com
Piedmont Truck Tires Inc PO Box 18228 .... Greensboro NC 27419 336-668-0091
TF: 800-274-8473 ■ *Web:* www.piedmonttrucktires.com
Pomps Tire Service Inc 1123 Cedar St .... Green Bay WI 54302 920-435-8301 431-7614
TF: 800-236-8911 ■ *Web:* www.pompstire.com
Radial Tire Wholesale Corp
PO Box 204 .... West Sacramento CA 95691 916-371-5190 371-0614
TF: 800-365-3265
Reliable Tire Co
805 N Blackhorse Pike PO Box 39 .... Blackwood NJ 08012 856-232-0700 232-6583
TF: 800-342-3426 ■ *Web:* www.reliabletire.com
Rott-Keller Supply Co Inc
6520 8th St PO Box 390.............................. Fargo ND 58107 701-235-0563 232-7900
TF: 800-342-4709 ■ *Web:* www.rottkeller.com
Snyder Wholesale Tire Co 401 Cadiz Rd .... Wintersville OH 43953 740-264-5543 264-1489
TF: 800-967-8473 ■ *Web:* www.snydertire.com
South Dade Automotive Inc 2875 NW 77th Ave.......... Miami FL 33122 305-718-6664 718-8908
Web: www.sdatire.com
Southeastern Wholesale Tire Co
4721 Trademark Dr............................... Raleigh NC 27610 919-832-3900 861-4357
TF General: 800-849-9215
Steepleton Tire Co 777 S Lauderdale St .... Memphis TN 38126 901-774-6440 774-6445
Terry's Tire Town Inc 2360 W Main St............. Alliance OH 44601 330-821-5022 829-1913
TF: 800-235-2921
Tire Centers LLC 310 Inglesby Pkwy.................. Duncan SC 29334 864-329-2700 329-2900
TF: 800-603-2430 ■ *Web:* www.tirecenters.com
Tire Group International Inc 6695 NW 36th Ave .... Miami FL 33147 305-696-0096 696-5926
Web: www.tiregroup.com
Tire Rack 7101 Vorden Pkwy .... South Bend IN 46628 574-287-2345 236-7707
TF: 800-428-8359 ■ *Web:* www.tirerack.com
Tire Warehouse Inc 7300 NW 41st St .... Miami FL 33166 305-592-9280 592-9280
Web: www.tirewarehouse.com
Tire Wholesalers Co Inc 1783 E 14-Mile Rd............... Troy MI 48083 248-589-9910 589-9919
Tire's Warehouse Inc 240 Teller St .... Corona CA 92879 951-808-0111 808-9062
Tire-Rama Inc
1401 Industrial Ave PO Box 23509.................... Billings MT 59104 406-245-4006 245-0257
TF: 800-828-1642 ■ *Web:* www.tirerama.com
TO Haas Tire Co Inc 2400 'O' St PO Box 81067.......... Lincoln NE 68501 402-323-4220 474-0336
Web: www.tohaastire.com
University Wholesalers Inc 1945 Main St .... Colchester VT 05446 802-655-8030 662-8294
TF Cust Svc: 800-852-5222 ■ *Web:* www.nokiantires.com
WD Tire Warehouse Inc 3805 E Livingston Ave........ Columbus OH 43227 614-461-8944 461-0136
TF: 800-634-7883
Wheels Etc 17521 Mesa St .... Hesperia CA 92345 909-350-8200 949-1000*
**Fax Area Code:* 760 ■ *TF:* 800-758-4737 ■ *Web:* www.wheels-etc.com
White Tire Distributors Inc
1513 Seibel Dr NE .... Roanoke VA 24012 540-342-3183 342-2341
TF: 800-476-9448 ■ *Web:* www.whitetire.com
Wholesale Tire Co PO Box 1637 .... Victoria TX 77902 361-578-2945 578-2967
TF: 800-950-8119
Wholesale Tire Inc PO Box 1660................... Clarksburg WV 26302 304-624-8465 624-8468*
**Fax:* Sales ■ *TF:* 800-772-5752
Woody Tire Co Inc 1606 50th St....................... Lubbock TX 79412 806-747-4556 747-7507
TF: 800-530-4818 ■ *Web:* www.woodytire.com

759 TOBACCO & TOBACCO PRODUCTS

Phone *Fax*

800-JR Cigar Inc 301 Rt 10 E .... Whippany NJ 07981 973-884-9555 457-3299*
**Fax Area Code:* 800 ■ **Fax:* Orders ■ *TF Cust Svc:* 800-572-4427 ■ *Web:* www.jrcigars.com
Abel Reel The 165 Aviador St .... Camarillo CA 93010 805-484-8789 482-0701
TF: 800-848-7335 ■ *Web:* www.abelreels.com
Albert H Notini & Sons Inc 225 Aiken St................ Lowell MA 01854 978-459-7151 458-7692
TF: 800-366-8464 ■ *Web:* www.ahnotini.com
Alliance One International Inc
8001 Aerial Ctr Pkwy PO Box 2009 .... Morrisville NC 27560 919-379-4300 379-4346
NYSE: AOI ■ *Web:* www.aointl.com
Altadis USA
5900 N Andrews Ave Suite 1100 .... Fort Lauderdale FL 33309 954-772-9000 938-7811
TF Orders: 800-446-5797 ■ *Web:* www.altadisusa.com
AMCON Distributing Co 7405 Irvington Rd .... Omaha NE 68122 402-331-3727 331-4834
AMEX: DIT ■ *TF:* 800-369-6200 ■ *Web:* www.amcon.com
American Snuff Co LLC PO Box 217 .... Memphis TN 38101 901-685-7267 727-0949*
**Fax Area Code:* 800 ■ *TF:* 800-238-2409 ■ *Web:* www.americansnuff.com
AW Marshall Co PO Box 16127.................. Salt Lake City UT 84116 801-328-4713 328-9600
TF: 800-273-4713
Burklund Distributors Inc
2500 N Main St Suite 3 .... East Peoria IL 61611 309-694-1900 694-6788
TF: 800-322-2876 ■ *Web:* www.burklund.com
Buyers Wholesale Distributors Inc
510 W Merrill St............................... Indianapolis IN 46225 317-684-7500 639-2591
TF: 800-284-6592 ■ *Web:* www.buyerswholesale.com
Carolina Group 714 Green Valley Rd................ Greensboro NC 27408 336-335-7000 335-7414
NYSE: CG ■ *TF:* 888-278-1133
Central America Tobacco Corp
7440 SW 50th Ter Suite 106.......................... Miami FL 33155 305-661-2707 661-9083
TF: 800-724-4277 ■ *Web:* www.torano.com
Cigar.com Inc 6771 Chrisphalt Dr......................... Bath PA 18014 800-357-9800 281-1025*
**Fax Area Code:* 484 ■ *TF:* 800-357-9800 ■ *Web:* www.cigar.com
Commonwealth Brands Inc PO Box 51587........ Bowling Green KY 42102 270-781-9100 781-7651
Web: www.commonwealthbrands.com
Conwood Co LP 46 Keel Ave PO Box 217 .... Memphis TN 38101 901-248-1700 526-3527
TF: 800-238-2409 ■ *Web:* www.cwdlp.com
Core-Mark International Inc
395 Oyster Pt Blvd Suite 415 .... South San Francisco CA 94080 650-589-9445 952-4284
TF: 800-622-1713 ■ *Web:* www.coremark.com
Domestic Tobacco Co 830 N Prince St .... Lancaster PA 17603 717-393-0613 397-2381
Web: www.amishcigar.com
Eby-Brown Co 280 W Shuman Blvd Suite 280.......... Naperville IL 60563 630-778-2800 778-2831
TF: 800-553-8249 ■ *Web:* www.eby-brown.com
Finck Cigar Co 414 Vera Cruz St................... San Antonio TX 78207 210-226-4191 226-2825
TF Orders: 800-221-0638 ■ *Web:* www.finckcigarcompany.com
Flue-Cured Tobacco Co-op 1304 Annapolis Dr .... Raleigh NC 27608 919-821-4560 821-4564
Web: www.ustobaccofarmer.com
General Cigar Co Inc 387 Pk Ave S .... New York NY 10016 212-448-3800 679-1450
TF: 800-273-8044 ■ *Web:* www.cigarworld.com
Holts Cigar Co 1522 Walnut St .... Philadelphia PA 19102 215-732-8500 732-4988
TF: 800-523-1641 ■ *Web:* www.holts.com
J Polep Distribution Services Inc
705 Meadow St.................................. Chicopee MA 01013 413-592-4141 592-5870
TF: 800-447-6537 ■ *Web:* www.jpolep.com
JC Newman Cigar Co 2701 16th St .... Tampa FL 33605 813-248-2124 247-2135
TF Orders: 800-477-1884 ■ *Web:* www.cigarfamily.com
Keilson-Dayton Co 107 Commerce Pk Dr................ Dayton OH 45404 937-236-1070 236-2124
TF: 800-759-3174
Klafter's Inc 216 N Beaver St.................... New Castle PA 16101 724-658-6561 658-8633
TF: 800-922-1233 ■ *Web:* www.cigarexpress.com
Kretek International Inc 5449 Endeavour Ct .... Moorpark CA 93021 800-532-4481
TF: 800-532-4481 ■ *Web:* www.pkcigar.com
Liggett Group Inc PO Box 490 .... Mebane NC 27302 212-687-8080
TF: 877-415-4100 ■ *Web:* www.liggettvectorbrands.com
Lorillard Tobacco Co PO Box 21688 .... Greensboro NC 27408 336-335-7000 335-7550
TF: 877-703-0386 ■ *Web:* www.lorillard.net
Macon Cigar & Tobacco Co Inc 575 12th St............ Macon GA 31201 478-743-2236 744-0903
TF: 800-637-0190 ■ *Web:* www.mctweb.com
National Cigar Corp 407 N Main St PO Box 97 .... Frankfort IN 46041 765-659-3326 654-6932
TF: 800-321-0247 ■ *Web:* www.broadleafcigars.com
National Tobacco Co LP
5201 Interchange Way .... Louisville KY 40229 502-778-4421 774-9235
TF Cust Svc: 800-331-5964
Philip Morris USA 2325 Bells Rd .... Richmond VA 23234 804-274-2000
TF: 800-343-0975 ■ *Web:* www.philipmorrisusa.com
Reynolds American Inc PO Box 2990........... Winston-Salem NC 27102 336-741-7693 741-0881
NYSE: RAI ■ *Web:* www.reynoldsamerican.com
RJ Reynolds Tobacco Co 401 N Main St......... Winston-Salem NC 27102 336-741-5000 741-4238
Web: www.rjrt.com
Saint Joe Distributing
5808 Corporate Dr .... Saint Joseph MO 64507 816-233-8213 233-5525
TF Cust Svc: 800-892-9072 ■ *Web:* www.saintjoedistributing.com
Sledd Co 100 E Cove Ext.......................... Wheeling WV 26003 304-243-1820 243-1209
TF: 800-333-0374 ■ *Web:* www.sleddco.com
Star Scientific Inc 801 Liberty Way .... Chester VA 23836 804-530-0535 530-8474
NASDAQ: STSI ■ *TF:* 800-867-6653 ■ *Web:* www.starscientific.com
Swisher International Group Inc
459 E 16th St PO Box 2230 .... Jacksonville FL 32203 904-353-4311 353-9175
TF: 800-843-3731 ■ *Web:* www.swisher.com
Taylor Bros Div Conwood Co LP
2415 Stratford Rd SW....................... Winston-Salem NC 27103 336-768-4630 768-4677
Thompson Cigar 5401 Hangar Ct .... Tampa FL 33634 800-237-2559 882-4605*
**Fax Area Code:* 813 ■ *TF:* 800-573-9099 ■ *Web:* www.thompsoncigar.com
Tobacco Superstores Inc
3550 Commerce Rd .... Forrest City AR 72335 870-633-0099 633-8279
Web: www.tobaccosuper.com
Universal Leaf Tobacco Co Inc
1501 N Hamilton St PO Box 25099 .... Richmond VA 23260 804-359-9311 254-3560*
**Fax:* Hum Res ■ *Web:* www.universalcorp.com

760 TOOL & DIE SHOPS

Company	City	State	ZIP	Phone	Fax
A & M Tool & Die Co Inc 64 Mill St.	Southbridge	MA	01550	508-764-3241	765-1377
TF: 800-848-4628 ■ *Web:* www.am-tool.com					
A Finkl & Sons Co 2011 N Southport Ave.	Chicago	IL	60614	773-975-2500	348-5347
TF: 800-343-2562 ■ *Web:* www.finkl.com					
ABA-PGT Inc 10 Gear Dr PO Box 8270	Manchester	CT	06040	860-649-4591	643-7619
Web: www.abapgt.com					
Abrasive-Form Inc 454 Scott Dr.	Bloomingdale	IL	60108	630-893-7800	893-6313
Web: www.abrasive-form.com					
Ahaus Tool & Engineering Inc PO Box 280	Richmond	IN	47375	765-962-3571	962-3426
TF: 800-962-3571 ■ *Web:* www.ahaus.com					
AIP Inc 1290 Maplelawn St.	Troy	MI	48084	248-649-7300	649-8079
TF: 800-247-5551 ■ *Web:* www.aippunch.com					
Alco Industries Inc					
820 Adams Ave Suite 130.	Norristown	PA	19403	610-666-0930	666-0752
Web: www.alcoind.com					
Alcona Tool & Machine Inc PO Box 340	Lincoln	MI	48742	989-736-8151	736-6717
Web: www.alconatool.com					
Alden Tool Co Inc 199 New Pk Dr.	Berlin	CT	06037	860-828-3556	828-8872
Web: www.aldentool.com					
Alliance Carolina Tool & Mold Corp					
125 Glenn Bridge Rd PO Box 686.	Arden	NC	28704	828-684-7831	687-0808
TF: 800-684-7831 ■ *Web:* www.alliance-carolina.com					
Alliance Precision Plastics 1220 Lee Rd.	Rochester	NY	14606	585-426-5310	426-5081
Web: www.allianceppc.com					
American Tool & Mold Inc 1700 Sunshine Dr	Clearwater	FL	33765	727-447-7377	447-0125
Web: www.a-t-m.com					
Anchor Lamina Inc 2590 Ouellette Ave.	Windsor	ON	N8X1L7	519-966-4431	972-6862
Web: www.anchorlamina.com					
Anchor Tool & Die Co 11830 Brookpark Rd	Cleveland	OH	44130	216-362-1850	265-7833
Web: www.anchor-mfg.com					
Apex Tool Works Inc 3200 Tollview Dr.	Rolling Meadows	IL	60008	847-394-5810	394-2739
Web: www.apextool.com					
Armin Industries 1500 N La Fox St.	South Elgin	IL	60177	847-742-1864	742-0253
TF: 800-427-3607 ■ *Web:* www.armin-ind.com					
Armstrong Mold Corp					
6910 Manlius Ctr Rd	East Syracuse	NY	13057	315-437-1517	437-9198
Web: www.armstrongmold.com					
Astro Tool & Machine Co Inc 810 Martin St	Rahway	NJ	07065	732-382-2454	382-6394
Web: www.astrotoolco.com					
Atlas Tool Inc 29880 Groesbeck Hwy	Roseville	MI	48066	586-778-3570	778-3931
Web: www.atlastool.com					
Austro Mold Inc 3 Rutter St.	Rochester	NY	14606	585-458-1410	458-0963
Web: www.austromold.com					
Autodie LLC 44 Coldbrook St NW	Grand Rapids	MI	49503	616-454-9361	356-1410
Web: www.autodie.com					
Bilco Tool Corp 30076 Dequindre Rd	Warren	MI	48092	586-574-9300	574-9340
Web: www.bilcotool.com					
Birdsall Tool & Gage Co					
24735 Crestview Ct	Farmington Hills	MI	48335	248-474-5150	474-5600
Web: www.birdsalltool.com					
Brinkman Tool & Die Inc 325 Kiser St.	Dayton	OH	45404	937-222-1161	222-2079
Web: www.brinkmantool.com					
C&a Tool Engineering Inc					
4100 N US 33 PO Box 94	Churubusco	IN	46723	260-693-2167	693-3633
Web: www.catool.com					
CA Spalding Co 1011 Cedar Ave	Croydon	PA	19021	267-550-9000	550-9008
Web: www.caspalding.com					
Caco-Pacific Corp 813 N Cummings Rd	Covina	CA	91724	626-331-3361	966-4219
Web: www.cacopacific.com					
Carlson Tool & Mfg Corp					
W 57 N 14386 Doerr PO Box 85.	Cedarburg	WI	53012	262-377-2020	377-1751
TF: 800-532-2252 ■ *Web:* www.carlsontool.com					
Carr Lane Mfg 4200 Carr Ln Ct.	Saint Louis	MO	63119	314-647-6200	647-5736
Web: www.carrlane.com					
Chicago Cutting Die Co 3555 Woodhead Dr.	Northbrook	IL	60062	847-509-5800	509-0355
TF: 800-747-3437 ■ *Web:* www.chicagocuttingdie.com					
Chicago Mold Engineering Co					
615 Stetson Ave	Saint Charles	IL	60174	630-584-1311	584-8695
Web: www.chicagomold.com					
Cleveland Punch & Die Co					
666 Pratt St PO Box 769.	Ravenna	OH	44266	888-451-4342	451-6877
TF: 888-451-4342 ■ *Web:* www.clevelandpunch.com					
Clifty Engineering & Tool Co Inc					
2949 Clifty Dr.	Madison	IN	47250	812-273-3272	273-3272
Web: www.cliftyengineering.com					
Coast Composites Inc 5 Burroughs.	Irvine	CA	92618	949-455-0665	455-0061
Web: www.coastcomposites.com					
Cockburn Enterprises Inc PO Box 2369.	Muscle Shoals	AL	35662	256-381-3620	381-9146
Web: www.ckbent.com					
Cole Tool & Die Co 241 Ashland Rd	Mansfield	OH	44905	419-522-1272	522-5506
Web: www.coletool.com					
Colonial Machine Co 1041 mogadore Rd	Kent	OH	44240	330-673-5859	673-5859
Web: www.colonial-machine.com					
Comet Die & Engraving Co 909 N Larch Ave	Elmhurst	IL	60126	630-833-5600	833-2644
Web: www.cometdie.com					
Composidie Inc 1295 SR- 380	Apollo	PA	15613	724-727-3466	727-3788
Web: www.composidie.com					
Cook Technologies Inc N 2nd St.	Green Lane	PA	18054	215-234-4535	234-5015
TF: 800-755-2856 ■ *Web:* www.cooktechnologies.com					
Crown Mold & Machine Inc 16959 Munn Rd.	Chagrin Falls	OH	44023	440-543-5090	708-2900
Web: www.crownmold.net					
Custom Mold Engineering Inc					
9780 S Franklin Dr	Franklin	WI	53132	414-421-5444	421-5444
TF: 800-448-2005 ■ *Web:* www.custommold.com					
D & D Mfg Inc 500 Territorial Dr	Bolingbrook	IL	60440	630-759-0015	759-0043
Web: www.ddmfg.com					
D-M-E Co 29111 Stephenson Hwy	Madison Heights	MI	48071	248-398-6000	544-5705
TF: 800-626-6653 ■ *Web:* www.dme.net					
Danly IEM 6779 Engle Rd Suite F.	Middleburg Heights	OH	44130	440-239-7600	833-2659*
**Fax Area Code:* 800 ■ *TF:* 800-243-2659 ■ *Web:* www.danly.com					
Dayton Progress Corp 500 Progress Rd	Dayton	OH	45449	937-859-5111	859-5353
Web: www.daytonprogress.com					
Decatur Mold Tool & Engineering Inc					
3330 N State Rd 7 PO Box 387.	North Vernon	IN	47265	812-346-5188	346-7357
Web: www.decaturmold.com					
Delaware Machinery & Tool 700 S Mulberry St.	Muncie	IN	47302	765-284-3335	289-7185
Web: www.delawaremachinery.com					
Delva Tool & Machine Corp					
1603 Industrial Hwy	Cinnaminson	NJ	08077	856-786-8700	786-8708
Web: www.delvatool.com					
Demmer Corp 1600 N Larch St # 1	Lansing	MI	48906	517-321-3600	321-7449
Web: www.demmercorp.com					
Detroit Tool & Engineering Co 441 W Elm St	Lebanon	MO	65536	417-532-2141	532-8367
Web: www.detroittool.com					
Diamond Die & Mold Co					
35401 Groesbeck Hwy	Clinton Township	MI	48035	586-791-0700	791-5419
Web: www.diamond-die.com					
Diamond Tool & Die Inc 508 29th Ave.	Oakland	CA	94601	510-534-7050	534-0454
TF: 800-227-1084 ■ *Web:* www.dtdjobshop.com					
Die Services International					
45000 Van Born Rd PO Box 339.	Belleville	MI	48112	734-699-3400	699-4081
Web: www.dieservicesinternational.com					
Diemasters Mfg Inc 2100 Touhy Ave	Elk Grove Village	IL	60007	847-640-9900	640-9900
Web: www.thediemasters.com					
Dominion Technologies Inc					
15736 Sturgeon St	Roseville	MI	48066	586-773-3303	773-2730
Web: www.dominiontec.com					
Ehrhardt Tool & Machine Co					
25 Central Industrial Dr	Granite City	IL	62040	618-452-5749	436-6905*
**Fax Area Code:* 314 ■ *Web:* www.ehrhardttool.com					
Electro-Magnetic Products Inc					
355 Crider Ave	Moorestown	NJ	08057	856-235-3011	722-0566
TF: 800-234-0071 ■ *Web:* www.empmags.com					
Elizabeth Carbide Die Co Inc					
601 Linden St.	McKeesport	PA	15132	412-751-3000	754-0755
Web: www.eliz.com					
Estee Mold & Die Inc 1467 Stanley Ave	Dayton	OH	45404	937-224-7853	228-0257
Web: www.esteemold.com					
Excel Tool Inc 2020 1st Ave	Seymour	IN	47274	812-522-6880	522-6524
Web: www.exceleti.com					
Ferriot Inc 1000 Arlington Cir	Akron	OH	44306	330-786-3000	786-3001
Web: www.ferriot.com					
First Tool Corp 612 Linden Ave.	Dayton	OH	45403	937-254-6197	254-0625
Web: www.firsttoolcorp.com					
Fischer Tool & Die Corp					
7155 Industrial Dr.	Temperance	MI	48182	734-847-4788	847-5027
Web: www.fischertool.com					
Fort Wayne Wire Die Inc 2424 American Way.	Fort Wayne	IN	46809	260-747-1681	747-4269
Web: www.fwwd.com					
Frizzelle & Parsons Die Sinking Co					
6602 John Deere Rd	Moline	IL	61265	309-796-1030	796-2935
Web: www.frizzelle-parsons.com					
Futuramic Tool & Engineering Co					
24680 Gibson Dr	Warren	MI	48089	586-758-2200	758-0641
Web: www.futuramic.com					
Future Products Tool Corp 885 Rochester Rd S	Clawson	MI	48017	248-588-1060	588-7303
TF: 800-237-5754 ■ *Web:* www.future-products.com					
Genca 9600 18th St N.	Saint Petersburg	FL	33716	727-524-3622	531-5700
TF: 800-237-5448 ■ *Web:* www.genca.com					
General Carbide Corp 1151 Garden St.	Greensburg	PA	15601	724-836-3000	836-6274
TF: 800-245-2465 ■ *Web:* www.generalcarbide.com					
General Tool Co 101 Landy Ln	Cincinnati	OH	45215	513-733-5500	733-5604
TF: 800-472-4406 ■ *Web:* www.gentool.com					
Gillette Machine & Tool Co					
955 Millstead Way	Rochester	NY	14624	585-436-0058	235-0016
Web: www.precisionpartnersinc.com					
Global Concepts Enterprise Inc					
785 Waverly Ct	Holland	MI	49423	616-355-7657	355-7662
Web: www.globalconcepts.com					
GlobalDie 1130 Minot Ave PO Box 1120	Auburn	ME	04211	800-910-3747	910-9187
TF: 800-910-3747 ■ *Web:* www.globaldie.com					
Goodrich Corp Sterling Die Div					
5565 Venture Dr Suite D.	Parma	OH	44130	216-267-1300	267-3356
TF: 800-533-1300 ■ *Web:* www.sterlingdie.com					
Greenville Tool & Die Co					
1215 S Lafayette St.	Greenville	MI	48838	616-754-5693	754-5500
Web: www.gtd.com					
Guill Tool & Engineering Co Inc					
10 Pike St	West Warwick	RI	02893	401-828-7600	823-5310
Web: www.guilltool.com					
H & J Tool & Die Co Inc 1565 Ocean Ave	Bohemia	NY	11716	631-589-7500	589-2951
Web: www.hjtooldie.com					
Harig Mfg Corp 5757 W Howard St.	Niles	IL	60714	847-647-9500	647-8351
Web: www.harigmfg.com					
Hercules Machine Tool & Die Co					
13920 E Ten-Mile Rd	Warren	MI	48089	586-778-4120	778-0070
Web: www.hmtd.com					
Hill Engineering Inc 373 Randy Rd	Carol Stream	IL	60188	630-834-4430	834-4755
Web: www.hillengr.com					
Howmet TMP Corp 3960 S Marginal Rd	Cleveland	OH	44114	216-361-5229	391-4842
Web: www.alcoa.com/howmet					
Hudson Tool & Die Co					
Hudson Technologies 1327 N US 1	Ormond Beach	FL	32174	386-672-2000	676-6212*
**Fax:* Sales ■ *Web:* www.hudsontool.com					
Hydro Carbide 4439 Pennsylvania 982	Latrobe	PA	15650	724-539-9701	539-8140
TF: 800-245-2476 ■ *Web:* www.hydrocarbide.com					
Hygrade Precision Technologies Inc					
329 Cooke St	Plainville	CT	06062	860-747-5773	747-3179
TF: 800-457-1666 ■ *Web:* www.hygrade.com					
Incoe Corp 1740 E Maple Rd	Troy	MI	48083	248-616-0220	616-0225
Web: www.incoe.com					

				Phone	Fax
Ivanhoe Tool & Die Co Inc 590 Thompson Rd	Thompson	CT	06277	860-923-9541	923-2497
Web: www.ivanhoetool.com					
Jade Corp 3063 Philmont Ave	Huntingdon Valley	PA	19006	215-947-3333	947-6838
TF: 800-628-4370 ■ *Web:* www.jadecorp.com					
Jasco Tools Inc					
1390 Mt Read Blvd PO Box 60497	Rochester	NY	14606	585-254-7000	254-2655
TF: 800-724-5497 ■ *Web:* www.jascotools.com					
Jennings International Corp					
3 Blue Heron Dr	Collegeville	PA	19426	610-272-1600	272-1737
Web: www.jenningsinternational.com					
Jo-Ad Industries Inc					
31465 Stephenson Hwy	Madison Heights	MI	48071	248-588-4810	588-3448
Web: www.jo-ad.com					
Jones Metal Products Co 200 N Ctr St	West Lafayette	OH	43845	740-545-6381	545-9690
TF: 800-552-3468					
Kell-Strom Tool Co 214 Church St	Wethersfield	CT	06109	860-529-6851	257-9694
TF: 800-851-6851 ■ *Web:* www.kell-strom.com					
Kenmode Tool & Engineering Co					
820 W Algonquin Rd	Algonquin	IL	60102	847-658-5041	658-9150
Kennedy Tool & Die Inc 325 W Main St	Birdsboro	PA	19508	610-582-8735	582-3150
Web: www.ktdmold.com					
Kirby Machine Co					
1709 E Cherry St PO Box 1776	Noblesville	IN	46060	317-773-6700	773-8031
Web: www.wckirby.com					
Lane Punch Corp 281 Ln Pkwy	Salisbury	NC	28146	704-633-3900	227-6725*
**Fax Area Code:* 800 ■ *Web:* www.lanepunch.com					
Lansing Tool & Engineering Inc					
1313 S Waverly Rd	Lansing	MI	48917	517-372-2550	372-1703
Web: www.lansingtool.com					
Leech Tool & Die Works Inc					
13144 Dickson Rd	Meadville	PA	16335	814-336-2141	337-0354
Web: www.leechind.com					
Lenhardt Tool & Die Co 3100 E Broadway	Alton	IL	62002	618-462-1075	462-6306
Web: www.lenhardttool.com					
Lou-Rich Machine Tool Inc 505 W Front St	Albert Lea	MN	56007	507-377-8910	373-7110
TF: 800-893-3235 ■ *Web:* www.lou-rich.com					
Luick Quality Gage & Tool 4401 S Delaware Dr	Muncie	IN	47302	765-288-1818	288-2346
Web: www.luick.com					
Mate Precision Tooling Inc 1295 Lund Blvd	Anoka	MN	55303	763-421-0230	421-0285
TF: 800-328-4492 ■ *Web:* www.matept.com					
May Tool & Mold Co Inc 2922 Wheeling Ave	Kansas City	MO	64129	816-923-6262	923-6277
Web: www.mayinc.com					
McAfee Tool & Die Inc 1717 Boettler Rd	Uniontown	OH	44685	330-896-9555	896-9549
Web: www.mcafeetool.com					
Metco Mfg Co Inc 1993 County Line Rd	Warrington	PA	18976	215-343-1993	343-7703
TF: 888-343-1993					
Metro Mold & Design Inc 20600 County Rd 81	Rogers	MN	55374	763-428-4690	428-4706
Web: www.metromold.com					
Microcast Technologies Corp (MTC)					
1611 W Elizabeth Ave	Linden	NJ	07036	908-523-9503	523-0910
Web: www.mtcnj.com					
Mid-State Machine Products Inc 83 Verti Dr	Winslow	ME	04901	207-873-6136	872-2017
TF: 800-341-4672 ■ *Web:* www.mid-statemachine.com					
Midwest Tool & Engineering Co 112 Webster St	Dayton	OH	45402	937-224-0756	224-0757
Web: www.themidwesttool.com					
Moeller Mfg Co Inc Punch & Die Div					
43938 Plymouth Oaks Blvd	Plymouth	MI	48170	734-416-0000	416-2200
TF: 800-521-7613 ■ *Web:* www.moellerpunch.com					
Mold Base Industries Inc 7501 Derry St	Harrisburg	PA	17111	717-564-7960	564-2250
TF: 800-241-6656 ■ *Web:* www.moldbase.com					
Mold Masters Intl Inc 7500 Clover Ave	Mentor	OH	44060	440-953-0220	953-1016
Web: www.moldmastersintl.com					
Mold-A-Matic Corp 147 River St	Oneonta	NY	13820	607-433-2121	432-7861
TF: 866-886-2626 ■ *Web:* www.mamco-molding.com					
MS Willett Inc 220 Cockeysville Rd	Cockeysville	MD	21030	410-771-0460	771-6972
Web: www.mswillett.com					
MTD Technologies Inc 5201 102nd Ave N	Pinellas Park	FL	33782	727-546-2446	541-3684
Mutual Tool & Die Inc 1350 Commerce Pk Dr	Tipp City	OH	45371	937-667-5818	667-4093
Web: www.mutualtool.com					
National Tool & Mfg Co Inc					
100-124 N 12th St	Kenilworth	NJ	07033	908-276-1600	276-8616
TF: 800-223-0926					
Northwestern Tools Inc 3130 Valleywood Dr	Dayton	OH	45429	937-298-9994	298-3715
TF: 800-236-3956 ■ *Web:* www.northwesterntools.com					
Nypromold Inc 144 Pleasant St	Clinton	MA	01510	978-365-4547	365-9375
Web: www.nypromold.com					
O Keller Tool Engineering Co					
12701 Inkster Rd	Livonia	MI	48150	734-425-4500	
Oberg Industries Inc					
2301 Silverville Rd PO Box 368	Freeport	PA	16229	724-295-2121	295-2588
TF: 800-286-1275 ■ *Web:* www.oberg.com					
Ontario Die Co of America 2735 20th St	Port Huron	MI	48060	810-987-5060	987-3688
Web: www.ontariodie.com					
Ort Tool & Die Corp 6555 S Dixie Hwy	Erie	MI	48133	734-848-6845	848-4308
Web: www.orttool.com					
Paragon Die & Engineering Co					
5225 33rd St SE	Grand Rapids	MI	49512	616-949-2220	949-2536
Web: www.paragondie.com					
Paslin Co 25411 Ryan Rd	Warren	MI	48091	586-758-0200	758-3322
TF: 877-972-7546 ■ *Web:* www.paslin.com					
PCS Co 34488 Doreka Dr	Fraser	MI	48026	586-294-7780	294-7799
TF: 800-521-0546 ■ *Web:* www.pcs-company.com					
Peddinghaus Corp 300 N Washington Ave	Bradley	IL	60915	815-937-3800	937-4003
TF: 800-786-2448 ■ *Web:* www.peddinghaus.com					
Penn State Tool & Die Corp					
7590 Rt 30	North Huntingdon	PA	15642	724-864-2626	864-5300
Web: www.pennstatetool.com					
Penn United Technology Inc 799 N Pike Rd	Cabot	PA	16023	724-352-1507	352-4970
Web: www.pennunited.com					
Pennsylvania Tool & Gages Inc PO Box 534	Meadville	PA	16335	814-336-3136	333-9131
TF: 877-827-8285 ■ *Web:* www.patool.com					
PHB Inc 7900 W Ridge Rd	Fairview	PA	16415	814-474-5511	474-2063
Web: www.phbcorp.com					
Phinney Tool & Die Co PO Box 270	Medina	NY	14103	585-798-3000	798-5612
Web: www.phinneytool.com					
Plasidyne Engineering & Mfg Inc					
3230 E 59th St	Long Beach	CA	90805	562-531-0510	531-1377
Web: www.plasidyne.com					
Porter Precision Products Inc					
2734 Banning Rd	Cincinnati	OH	45239	513-923-3777	923-1111
TF: 800-543-7041 ■ *Web:* www.porterpunch.com					
Power Brake Dies Inc 263 W 154th St	South Holland	IL	60473	708-339-5951	339-7737
Web: www.powerbrakedies.com					
Precision Component Industries					
5325 Southway St SW	Canton	OH	44706	330-477-6287	477-1052
Web: www.precision-component.com					
Precision Fasteners Tooling Inc					
11530 Western Ave	Stanton	CA	90680	714-898-8558	891-4988
Precision Tool Die & Machine Co Inc					
6901 Preston Hwy	Louisville	KY	40219	502-479-0800	635-2636
Web: www.nth-works.com					
Prikos & Becker Tool Co 8109 N Lawndale Ave	Skokie	IL	60076	847-675-3910	675-3913
Product Engineering Co 1480 14th St	Columbus	IN	47201	812-372-4421	372-2837
Producto Machine Co 800 Union Ave	Bridgeport	CT	06607	203-367-8675	367-0418
TF Cust Svc: 800-243-9898					
Prospect Mold Inc 1100 Main St	Cuyahoga Falls	OH	44221	330-929-3311	920-1338
TF: 800-683-3312 ■ *Web:* www.prospectmold.com					
Quality Metalcraft Inc 33355 Glendale St	Livonia	MI	48150	734-261-6700	261-5180
Web: www.qualitymetalcraft.com					
Rand Machine Products Inc PO Box 72	Falconer	NY	14733	716-665-5217	665-3374
Web: www.randmachine.com					
Ready Machine Tool & Die Corp					
PO Box 285	Connersville	IN	47331	765-825-3108	825-1176
Reddog Industries Inc 2012 E 33rd St	Erie	PA	16510	814-898-4321	899-5671
Web: www.reddog-erie.com					
Reed City Tool & Die Inc 603 E Church St	Reed City	MI	49677	231-832-5504	832-5270
Web: www.reedcitytool.com					
Reliance Tool & Mfg Co 617 N State St	Elgin	IL	60123	847-695-1234	695-0931
Web: www.reliancetool.com					
Remmele Engineering Inc 10 Old Hwy 8 SW	New Brighton	MN	55112	651-635-4100	635-4168
TF: 800-222-7737 ■ *Web:* www.remmele.com					
Reuther Mold & Mfg Co					
1225 Munroe Falls Ave	Cuyahoga Falls	OH	44221	330-923-5266	923-9930
Web: www.reuthermold.com					
Reynolds Mfg Co 501 38th St	Rock Island	IL	61201	309-788-7443	788-7715
Web: www.reynoldsmfg.com					
Richardson Mfg Co					
2209 Old Jacksonville Rd	Springfield	IL	62704	217-546-2249	546-9433
Web: www.rmc-bigcnc.com					
Rocheleau Tool & Die Co Inc					
117 Industrial Rd	Fitchburg	MA	01420	978-345-1723	345-5972
Web: www.rocheleautool.com					
Rocon Mfg Corp 606 Hague St	Rochester	NY	14606	585-436-8189	436-2188
Web: www.roconmfg.com					
Rome Tool & Die Co Inc 113 Hemlock St	Rome	GA	30161	706-234-6743	234-1242
TF: 800-241-3369 ■ *Web:* www.rometool.com					
Ronart Industries Inc 19365 Sherwood St	Detroit	MI	48234	313-893-4800	893-1440
Web: www.ronart.com					
RotoMetrics Group 800 Howerton Ln	Eureka	MO	63025	636-587-3600	587-3701
TF: 800-325-3851 ■ *Web:* www.rotometrics.com					
Sarcol Inc 3050 W Taylor St	Chicago	IL	60612	773-533-3000	533-3004
SB Whistler & Sons Inc PO Box 270	Medina	NY	14103	585-318-4630	798-5612
TF: 800-828-1010 ■ *Web:* www.sbwhistler.com					
Schoitz Engineering Inc PO Box 546	Waterloo	IA	50704	319-234-6615	234-0368
Web: www.schoitz.com					
Schroeder & Bogardus Die Co Inc					
1130 Red Gum St	Anaheim	CA	92806	714-630-2270	630-1739
Web: www.schroederinc.com					
Select Tool & Die Corp 60 Heid Ave	Dayton	OH	45404	937-233-9191	233-7640
TF: 800-797-4150 ■ *Web:* www.selecttoolcorp.com					
Sensus Precision Die Casting					
232 Hopkinsville Rd	Russellville	KY	42276	270-726-0235	726-6468
Web: www.sensuspdc.com					
Sidney Tool & Die Inc PO Box 849	Sidney	OH	45365	937-492-6121	498-9601
Web: www.sidneytool.com					
Specialty Design & Mfg Co PO Box 4039	Reading	PA	19606	610-779-1357	370-0269
Web: www.specialtydesign.com					
SPX Corp OTC Div 655 Eisenhower Dr	Owatonna	MN	55060	507-455-7000	455-7300*
**Fax: Hum Res* ■ *TF:* 800-533-6127 ■ *Web:* www.otctools.com					
Superior Die Set Corp 900 W Drexel Ave	Oak Creek	WI	53154	414-764-4900	657-0855*
**Fax Area Code:* 800 ■ *TF:* 800-558-6040 ■ *Web:* www.supdie.com					
Superior Die Tool & Machine Co					
2301 Fairwood Ave	Columbus	OH	43207	614-444-2181	444-8712
TF: 800-292-2181 ■ *Web:* www.superior-dietool.com					
Superior Jig Inc 1540 N Orangethorpe Way	Anaheim	CA	92801	714-525-4777	525-8798
Web: www.sji.net					
Swan Engineering & Machine Co					
2611 State St	Bettendorf	IA	52722	563-355-2671	355-5380
Taylors Industrial Services LLC HPM Div					
820 W Marion Rd	Mount Gilead	OH	43338	419-946-0222	946-2473
Web: www.taylorsind.com					
Tipp Machine & Tool Inc PO Box 280	Tipp City	OH	45371	937-667-8481	667-2818
Web: www.tippmachine.com					
Tom Smith Industries 500 Smith Dr	Clayton	OH	45315	937-832-1555	832-1577
Web: www.tomsmithindustries.com					
Toolcraft Products Inc 1265 Mc Cook Ave	Dayton	OH	45404	937-223-8271	223-1408
Web: www.toolcraftproducts.com					
Tools & Production Co					
4924 N Encinita Ave	Temple City	CA	91780	626-286-0213	286-3398
Web: www.toolsandproduction.com					
Triangle Tool Corp 8609 W Port Ave	Milwaukee	WI	53224	414-357-7117	357-7610
Tru-Cut Inc 1145 Allied Dr	Sebring	OH	44672	330-938-9806	938-9342
Web: www.trucut.com					

				Phone	Fax
Uniloy Milacron Inc 5550 S Occidental Rd Suite B	Tecumseh	MI	49286	517-424-8900	424-8992
TF: 800-419-7771 ■ *Web:* www.uniloymilacron.com					
Unipunch Products Inc 370 Babcock St	Buffalo	NY	14206	716-825-7960	825-0581
TF Sales: 800-828-7061 ■ *Web:* www.unipunch.com					
Walker Tool & Die Inc 2411 Walker Ave NW	Grand Rapids	MI	49544	616-453-5471	453-3765
TF: 888-925-5377 ■ *Web:* www.walkertool.com					
Wand Tool Co Inc 852 Seton Ct	Wheeling	IL	60090	847-459-2400	459-2421
Web: www.wandtool.com					
Western Supply Independent Dies Div 2930 Cass Ave	Saint Louis	MO	63106	314-531-4300	531-4401
Web: www.wsids.com					
Westland Corp 1735 S Maize Rd	Wichita	KS	67209	316-721-1144	721-1495
TF: 800-247-1144 ■ *Web:* www.westlandusa.com					
Wirtz Mfg Co Inc 1105 24th St PO Box 5006	Port Huron	MI	48061	810-987-7600	987-8135
Web: www.wirtzusa.com					
Yarema Die & Engineering Co Inc 300 Minnesota Rd	Troy	MI	48083	248-585-2830	616-1422
TF: 800-989-2830 ■ *Web:* www.yarema.com					

761 TOOLS - HAND & EDGE

SEE ALSO Lawn & Garden Equipment p. 2148; Metalworking Devices & Accessories p. 2244; Saw Blades & Handsaws p. 2631

				Phone	Fax
Adjustable Clamp Co 404 N Armour St	Chicago	IL	60622	312-666-0640	666-2723
Web: www.adjustableclamp.com					
Allway Tools Inc 1255 Seabury Ave	Bronx	NY	10462	718-792-3636	823-9640
TF: 800-422-5592 ■ *Web:* www.allwaytools.com					
Ames Taping Tools Inc 3350 Breckinridge Blvd # 100	Duluth	GA	30096	770-243-2637	243-2658
TF: 800-408-2801 ■ *Web:* www.amestools.com					
Ames True Temper Inc 465 Railroad Ave	Camp Hill	PA	17011	717-737-1500	730-2550
TF: 800-393-1846 ■ *Web:* www.ames.com					
Arrow Fastener Co Inc 271 Mayhill St	Saddle Brook	NJ	07663	201-843-6900	843-3911
Web: www.arrowfastener.com					
BARCO Industries Inc 1020 MacArthur Rd	Reading	PA	19605	610-374-3117	374-6320
TF Cust Svc: 800-234-8665 ■ *Web:* www.barcotools.com					
Bondhus Corp 1400 E Broadway St PO Box 660	Monticello	MN	55362	763-295-2162	295-4440
TF Cust Svc: 800-328-8310 ■ *Web:* www.bondhus.com					
Brunner & Lay Inc 9300 King Ave	Franklin Park	IL	60131	847-678-3232	678-0642
TF: 800-872-6899 ■ *Web:* www.brunnerlay.com					
Cal-Van Tools 4300 Waterleaf Ct	Greensboro	NC	27410	336-294-3259	299-4003
TF: 800-537-1077 ■ *Web:* www.calvantools.com					
Channellock Inc 1306 S Main St	Meadville	PA	16335	814-724-8700	337-3616
TF Cust Svc: 800-724-3018 ■ *Web:* www.channellock.com					
Charles GG Schmidt & Co Inc 301 W Grand Ave	Montvale	NJ	07645	201-391-5300	391-3565
TF: 800-724-6438 ■ *Web:* www.cggschmidt.com					
Consolidated Devices Inc (CDI) 19220 San Jose Ave	City of Industry	CA	91748	626-965-0668	810-2759
TF: 800-525-6319 ■ *Web:* www.cditorque.com					
Cooper Industries 600 Travis St Suite 5800	Houston	TX	77002	713-209-8400	209-8995
NYSE: CBE ■ *TF:* 866-853-4293 ■ *Web:* www.cooperindustries.com					
Cooper Tools Inc Apex Div 762 W Stewart St	Dayton	OH	45408	937-222-7871	228-0422
Web: www.coopertools.com					
Cornwell Quality Tools Co 667 County Hwy 16	Wadsworth	OH	44281	330-336-3506	336-3337
TF: 800-321-8356 ■ *Web:* www.cornwelltools.com					
CS Osborne & Co Inc 125 Jersey St	Harrison	NJ	07029	973-483-3232	484-3621
Web: www.csosborne.com					
CTA Mfg Corp 263 Veterans Blvd	Carlstadt	NJ	07072	201-896-1000	896-1378
Web: www.ctatools.com					
Danaher Corp 2200 Pennsylvania Ave NW Suite 800	Washington	DC	20037	202-828-0850	828-0860
NYSE: DHR ■ *TF:* 866-873-5600 ■ *Web:* www.danaher.com					
Daniels Mfg Corp PO Box 593872	Orlando	FL	32859	407-855-6161	855-6884
Web: www.dmctools.com					
Dasco Pro Inc 340 Blackhawk Pk Ave	Rockford	IL	61104	815-962-3727	
TF: 800-327-2690					
Duo-Fast Corp 2400 Galvin Dr	Elgin	IL	60123	847-783-5500	783-5500
TF Cust Svc: 888-386-3278 ■ *Web:* www.itwindfast.com					
Empire Level Mfg Corp 929 Empire Dr	Mukwonago	WI	53149	262-368-2000	368-2127
TF: 800-558-0722 ■ *Web:* www.empirelevel.com					
Emporium Specialties Co Inc 94 Foster St PO Box 65	Austin	PA	16720	814-647-8661	647-5536
Web: www.empspec.com					
Enderes Tool Co Inc 14925 Energy Way	Apple Valley	MN	55124	952-891-1200	891-1202
TF: 800-874-7776 ■ *Web:* www.enderes.com					
Estwing Mfg Co 2647 8th St	Rockford	IL	61109	815-397-9558	397-8665
Web: www.estwing.com					
Everhard Products Inc 1016 9th St SW	Canton	OH	44707	330-453-7786	
Web: www.everhard.com					
Fiskars Brands Inc 2537 Daniels St	Madison	WI	53718	608-259-1649	294-4790
TF: 866-348-5661 ■ *Web:* www.fiskars.com					
Fletcher-Terry Co Inc 65 Spring Ln	Farmington	CT	06032	860-677-7331	676-8858
TF Cust Svc: 800-843-3826 ■ *Web:* www.fletcherviscom.com					
General Machine Products Co Inc 3111 Old Lincoln Hwy	Trevose	PA	19053	215-357-5500	357-6216
TF Tech Supp: 800-345-6009 ■ *Web:* www.gmptools.com					
General Tools Mfg Co LLC 80 White St	New York	NY	10013	212-431-6100	431-6499
TF: 800-697-8665 ■ *Web:* www.generaltools.com					
Grobet File Co of America Inc 750 Washington Ave	Carlstadt	NJ	07072	201-939-6700	939-5067
TF: 800-847-4188 ■ *Web:* www.grobetusa.com					
Hastings Fiber Glass Products Inc 770 Cook Rd PO Box 218	Hastings	MI	49058	269-945-9541	945-4623
Web: www.hfgp.com					
Hexacon Electric Co 161 W Clay Ave	Roselle Park	NJ	07204	908-245-6200	245-6176
TF: 888-439-2266 ■ *Web:* www.hexaconelectric.com					
Huther Bros Inc 1290 University Ave	Rochester	NY	14607	585-473-9462	473-9476
TF: 888-448-8437 ■ *Web:* www.hutherbros.com					
Hyde tools co 54 Eastford Rd	Southbridge	MA	01550	508-764-4344	765-5250
TF: 800-872-4933 ■ *Web:* www.hydetools.com					
Johnson Level & Tool Mfg Co Inc 6333 W Donges Bay Rd	Mequon	WI	53092	262-242-1161	242-0189
Web: www.johnsonlevel.com					
Jonard Industries Corp 134 Marbledale Rd	Tuckahoe	NY	10707	914-793-0700	793-4527
Web: www.jonard.com					
Jore Corp 34837 Innovation Dr	Ronan	MT	59864	406-528-4350	676-8415
TF Sales: 888-809-5673 ■ *Web:* www.jorecorporation.com					
Kastar Inc 5501 21st St PO Box 1616	Racine	WI	53401	262-554-2300	598-2835
TF Cust Svc: 800-645-1142 ■ *Web:* www.aetools.com					
Ken-Tool Co 768 E N St	Akron	OH	44305	330-535-7177	872-4929*
**Fax Area Code:* 800 ■ *Web:* www.kentool.com					
Klein Tools Inc 7200 N McCormick Blvd PO Box 599033	Skokie	IL	60659	847-677-9500	677-4476
TF Cust Svc: 800-553-4676 ■ *Web:* www.kleintools.com					
Leatherman Tool Group Inc 12106 NE Ainsworth Cir	Portland	OR	97220	503-253-7826	253-7830
TF: 800-847-8665 ■ *Web:* www.leatherman.com					
Lisle Corp 813 E Main St	Clarinda	IA	51632	712-542-5101	542-6591
Web: www.lislecorp.com					
LS Starrett Co 121 Crescent St	Athol	MA	01331	978-249-3551	249-8495
NYSE: SCX ■ *TF:* 888-674-7443 ■ *Web:* www.starrett.com					
Mac Tools Inc 505 N Cleveland Ave	Westerville	OH	43082	614-755-7000	622-3295
TF: 800-622-8665 ■ *Web:* www.mactools.com					
Malco Products Inc 14080 State Hwy 55 NW PO Box 400	Annandale	MN	55302	320-274-8246	274-2269
TF: 800-328-3530 ■ *Web:* www.malcoproducts.com					
Mann Edge Tool Co PO Box 351	Lewistown	PA	17044	717-248-9628	248-4846
TF Sales: 800-248-8303 ■ *Web:* www.mannedge.com					
Marshalltown Co 104 S 8th Ave	Marshalltown	IA	50158	641-753-5999	753-6341
TF: 800-888-0127 ■ *Web:* www.marshalltown.com					
Matco Tools 4403 Allen Rd	Stow	OH	44224	330-929-4949	926-5320
TF: 800-368-6651 ■ *Web:* www.matcotools.com					
Mayhew Steel Products Inc 199 Industrial Blvd	Turners Falls	MA	01376	413-863-4860	863-8464
TF: 800-872-0037 ■ *Web:* www.mayhew.com					
MIBRO Group 111 Sinnott Rd	Toronto	ON	M1L4S6	416-285-9000	285-9500
TF: 866-941-9006 ■ *Web:* www.mibro.com					
Newell Rubbermaid Inc Irwin Tools Div 8935 Northpointe Executive Dr	Huntersville	NC	28078	704-987-4555	987-4506
TF: 800-866-5740 ■ *Web:* www.irwin.com					
Olympia Group Inc 505 S 7th Ave	City of Industry	CA	91746	626-336-4999	336-5399
TF: 800-888-8782 ■ *Web:* www.olympiaweb.com					
QEP Co Inc 1001 Broken Sound Pkwy NW Suite A	Boca Raton	FL	33487	561-994-5550	241-2830
TF Sales: 800-777-8665 ■ *Web:* www.qep.com					
Red Devil Inc 1437 S Boulder Suite 750, Boulder Towers	Tulsa	OK	74119	918-585-8111	585-8120
TF: 800-423-3845 ■ *Web:* www.reddevil.com					
Reed Mfg Co 1425 W 8th St	Erie	PA	16502	814-452-3691	455-1697
TF: 800-456-1697 ■ *Web:* www.reedmfgco.com					
Relton Corp 317 Rolyn Dr PO Box 60019	Arcadia	CA	91066	626-446-8201	446-9671
TF Cust Svc: 800-423-1505 ■ *Web:* www.relton.com					
Ridge Tool Co 400 Clark St	Elyria	OH	44035	440-323-5581	329-4853
Web: www.ridgid.com					
Ripley Co 46 Nooks Hill Rd	Cromwell	CT	06416	860-635-2200	635-3631
TF: 800-528-8665 ■ *Web:* www.ripley-tools.com					
Seymour Mfg Co Inc 500 N Broadway St	Seymour	IN	47274	812-522-2900	522-6109
TF: 800-457-1909 ■ *Web:* www.seymourmfg.com					
Skyo Industries Inc 171 Brook Ave	Deer Park	NY	11729	631-586-4702	586-4126
TF: 800-645-5535					
Snap-on Inc 2801 80th St	Kenosha	WI	53143	262-656-5200	656-5577
NYSE: SNA ■ *TF:* 877-762-7664 ■ *Web:* www.snapon.com					
Snow & Nealley Co PO Box 876	Bangor	ME	04402	207-947-6642	941-0857
TF: 800-933-6642 ■ *Web:* www.snowandnealley.com					
Stabila Inc 332 Industrial Dr	South Elgin	IL	60177	847-488-0050	488-0051
TF: 800-869-7460 ■ *Web:* www.stabila.com					
Stanley Fastening Systems LP Briggs Dr	East Greenwich	RI	02818	800-556-6696	842-9360
TF: 800-556-6696 ■ *Web:* www.bostitch.com					
Stanley Supply & Services Inc 335 Willow St	North Andover	MA	01845	978-682-2000	743-8141*
**Fax Area Code:* 800 ■ *TF Cust Svc:* 888-887-9473 ■ *Web:* www.stanleysupplyservices.com					
Stanley Tools Inc 480 Myrtle St	New Britain	CT	06053	860-225-5111	643-3756*
**Fax Area Code:* 800 ■ *TF Cust Svc:* 800-262-2161 ■ *Web:* www.stanleytools.com					
Stanley Tools Worldwide 480 Myrtle St	New Britain	CT	06053	860-225-5111	643-3756*
**Fax Area Code:* 800 ■ *TF Cust Svc:* 800-262-2161 ■ *Web:* www.stanleytools.com					
Stride Tool Inc Imperial Div 6300 W Howard St	Niles	IL	60714	847-581-3300	581-3380
TF: 888-467-8665 ■ *Web:* www.stridetool.com					
Stride Tool Inc Milbar Div 30333 Emerald Valley Pkwy	Glenwillow	OH	44139	440-247-4600	527-6383*
**Fax Area Code:* 800 ■ *TF Cust Svc:* 888-467-8665 ■ *Web:* www.milbar.com					
Superior Tool Co 100 Hayes Dr Unit C	Brooklyn Heights	OH	44131	216-398-8600	398-8691
TF Cust Svc: 800-533-3244 ■ *Web:* www.superiortool.com					
Tamco Inc 1466 Delberts Dr	Monongahela	PA	15063	724-258-6622	258-6692
TF: 800-826-2672 ■ *Web:* www.tamcotools.com					
Triumph Twist Drill Co Inc 301 Industrial Rd	Crystal Lake	IL	60039	815-459-6250	459-2804
Web: www.ttdonlineusa.com					
Ullman Devices Corp 664 Danbury Rd	Ridgefield	CT	06877	203-438-6577	431-9064
Web: www.users.ntplx.net/~ullman					
UnionTools Inc 390 W Nationwide Blvd	Columbus	OH	43215	614-222-4400	221-8397
TF: 800-848-6657					
Vaughan & Bushnell Mfg Co 11414 Maple Ave PO Box 390	Hebron	IL	60034	815-648-2446	648-4300
TF: 800-435-6000 ■ *Web:* www.hammernet.com					
Vermont American Corp 1961 Bishop Ln	Louisville	KY	40218	502-625-2000	625-2064
TF: 800-626-2834 ■ *Web:* www.vermontamerican.com					

Phone Fax

Wall Lenk Corp 1950 Dr Martin Luther King Jr .... Kinston NC 28501 252-527-4186 527-4189
TF: 888-527-4186 ■ Web: www.wlenk.com
Walter Meier Mfg Inc 427 New Sanford Rd .... La Vergne TN 37086 615-793-8900 793-8905
Web: www.wiltontool.com
Warner Mfg Co 13435 Industrial Pk Blvd .... Minneapolis MN 55441 763-559-4740 559-1364
TF: 800-234-7708 ■ Web: www.warnertool.com
Wheeler-Rex Inc
3744 Jefferson Rd PO Box 688 .... Ashtabula OH 44005 440-998-2788 992-2925
TF: 800-321-7950 ■ Web: www.wheelerrex.com
Wolfcraft Inc 333 Swift Rd .... Addison IL 60101 630-773-4777 268-9476
Web: www.wolfcraft.com
Wright Tool Co 1 Wright Dr .... Barberton OH 44203 330-848-3702 848-0619
TF: 800-321-2902 ■ Web: www.wrighttool.com
Zephyr Mfg Co Inc 201 Hindry Av .... Inglewood CA 90301 310-410-4907 410-2913
TF: 800-624-3944 ■ Web: www.zephyrtools.com

TOOLS - MACHINE

SEE Machine Tools - Metal Cutting Types p. 2192; Machine Tools - Metal Forming Types p. 2193

762 TOOLS - POWER

SEE ALSO Lawn & Garden Equipment p. 2148; Metalworking Devices & Accessories p. 2244

Phone Fax

Actuant Corp 13000 W Silver Spring Dr .... Butler WI 53007 414-352-4160 918-0033
NYSE: ATU ■ TF: 800-624-5242 ■ Web: www.actuant.com
Air Tool Service Co (ATSCO) 7722 Metric Dr .... Mentor OH 44060 440-942-4475 942-6387
TF: 800-321-3554 ■ Web: www.atsco.com
Alpine Power Systems Inc 24355 Capitol .... Redford MI 48239 313-531-6600 531-2950
TF: 877-769-3762 ■ Web: www.alpinepowersystems.com
American Pneumatic Tool Inc
9949 Tabor Pl .... Santa Fe Springs CA 90670 562-204-1555 204-1773
TF: 800-532-7402 ■ Web: www.apt-tools.com
Atlas Copco Tools & Assembly Systems
2998 Dutton Rd .... Auburn Hills MI 48326 248-373-3000 373-3001
TF: 800-859-3746 ■ Web: www.atlascopco.com/tools/us
Blackstone Industries Inc 16 Stoney Hill Rd .... Bethel CT 06801 203-792-8622 796-7861
TF: 800-441-0625 ■ Web: www.blackstoneind.com
Blount Inc Oregon Cutting Systems Div
4909 SE International Way .... Portland OR 97222 503-653-8881 653-4201
TF: 800-223-5168 ■ Web: www.oregonchain.com
Chicago Pneumatic Tool Co 1800 Overview Dr .... Rock Hill SC 29730 803-817-7000 228-9096*
*Fax Area Code: 800 ■ *Fax: Hum Res ■ TF: 800-624-4735 ■ Web: www.cp.com
Cooper Industries 600 Travis St Suite 5800 .... Houston TX 77002 713-209-8400 209-8995
NYSE: CBE ■ TF: 866-853-4293 ■ Web: www.cooperindustries.com
Dremel Inc 4915 21st St .... Racine WI 53406 262-554-1390 554-7654
TF: 800-437-3635 ■ Web: www.dremel.com
Dynabrade Inc 8989 Sheridan Dr .... Clarence NY 14031 716-631-0100 631-2073
TF Cust Svc: 800-828-7333 ■ Web: www.dynabrade.com
Enerpac 6101 N Baker Rd .... Milwaukee WI 53209 262-781-6600 781-1049*
*Fax: Cust Svc ■ TF Cust Svc: 800-433-2766 ■ Web: www.enerpac.com
Florida Pneumatic Mfg Corp 851 Jupiter Pk Ln .... Jupiter FL 33458 561-744-9500 575-9134
TF: 800-327-9403 ■ Web: www.florida-pneumatic.com
Greenlee Textron Inc 4455 Boeing Dr .... Rockford IL 61109 815-397-7070 397-8289
TF: 800-435-0786 ■ Web: www.greenlee.textron.com
Hilti Inc 5400 S 122nd E Ave .... Tulsa OK 74146 918-252-6000 252-0522
TF Cust Svc: 800-879-8000 ■ Web: www.us.hilti.com
Hougen Mfg Inc 3001 Hougen Dr .... Swartz Creek MI 48473 810-635-7111 635-8277
TF Orders: 800-462-7818 ■ Web: www.hougen.com
International Staple & Machine Co PO Box 629 .... Butler PA 16003 800-378-3430 827-4762
TF: 800-378-3430
Makita USA Inc 14930 Northam St Suite C .... La Mirada CA 90638 714-522-8088 522-8133
TF: 800-462-5482 ■ Web: www.makitausa.com
Master Appliance Corp 2420 18th St .... Racine WI 53403 262-633-7791 633-9745
TF: 800-558-9413 ■ Web: www.masterappliance.com
Milwaukee Electric Tool Corp
13135 W Lisbon Rd .... Brookfield WI 53005 262-781-3600 638-9582*
*Fax Area Code: 800 ■ *Fax: Orders ■ TF: 800-729-3878 ■ Web: www.milwaukeetool.com
P & F Industries Inc 445 Broadhollow Rd .... Melville NY 11747 631-694-9800 694-9804
NASDAQ: PFIN ■ Web: www.pfina.com
Paslode 888 Forest Edge Dr .... Vernon Hills IL 60061 847-634-1900 634-6602
TF Cust Svc: 800-682-3428 ■ Web: www.paslode.com
Pioneer Tool & Forge Inc 101 6th St .... New Kensington PA 15068 724-337-4700 337-4707
TF: 800-359-6408 ■ Web: www.breakersteel.com
Pneutek Inc 17 Friars Dr .... Hudson NH 03051 603-883-1660 882-9165
TF: 800-431-8665 ■ Web: www.pneutek.com
Powernail Co 1300 Rose Rd .... Lake Zurich IL 60047 847-634-3000 634-4943
TF: 800-323-1653 ■ Web: www.powernail.com
Ridge Tool Co 400 Clark St .... Elyria OH 44035 440-323-5581 329-4853
Web: www.ridgid.com
Robert Bosch Tool Corp
1800 W Central Rd .... Mount Prospect IL 60056 224-223-2000 232-2368
TF: 800-301-8255 ■ Web: www.boschtools.com
Ryobi Technologies Inc
1428 Pearman Dairy Rd .... Anderson SC 29625 864-226-6511 261-9435
TF: 800-525-2579 ■ Web: www.ryobitools.com
SENCO Products Inc 4270 Ivy Pt Blvd .... Cincinnati OH 45245 513-388-2000 388-2026
TF Tech Supp: 800-543-4596 ■ Web: www.sencobrands.com
Shopsmith Inc 6530 Poe Ave .... Dayton OH 45414 937-898-6070 722-3965*
*Fax Area Code: 800 ■ TF Cust Svc: 800-543-7586 ■ Web: www.shopsmith.com
Sioux Tools Inc 250 Snap-on Dr .... Murphy NC 28906 828-835-9765 835-9685
TF Orders: 800-722-7290 ■ Web: www.siouxtools.com
Speedgrip Chuck Inc 2000 E Industrial Pkwy .... Elkhart IN 46516 574-294-1506 294-2465
Web: www.speedgrip.com
Stanley Assembly Technologies Div
5335 Avion Pk Dr .... Cleveland OH 44143 440-461-5500 461-2710
Web: www.stanleyassembly.com
Stihl Inc 536 Viking Dr .... Virginia Beach VA 23452 757-486-9100 784-8576*
*Fax Area Code: 888 ■ TF Cust Svc: 888-784-8575 ■ Web: www.stihlusa.com

Phone Fax

Suhner Mfg Inc PO Box 1234 .... Rome GA 30162 706-235-8047 235-8045
TF: 800-323-6886 ■ Web: www.suhnerusa.com
Thomas C Wilson Inc 21-11 44th Ave .... Long Island City NY 11101 718-729-3360 361-2872
TF: 800-230-2636 ■ Web: www.tcwilson.com

763 TOUR OPERATORS

SEE ALSO Bus Services - Charter p. 1546; Travel Agencies p. 2729

Phone Fax

Abercrombie & Kent International Inc
1520 Kensington Rd Suite 212 .... Oak Brook IL 60523 630-954-2944 954-3324
TF: 800-323-7308 ■ Web: www.abercrombiekent.com
Academy Bus Tours Inc 111 Paterson Ave .... Hoboken NJ 07030 201-339-6000 420-8087
TF: 800-442-7272 ■ Web: www.academybus.com
ACIS Educational Tours
343 Congress St Suite 3100 .... Boston MA 02210 617-236-2051 450-5601
TF: 800-888-2247 ■ Web: www.acis.com
Adventure Alaska Tours Inc PO Box 64 .... Hope AK 99605 907-782-3730 782-3725
TF: 800-365-7057 ■ Web: www.adventurealaskatours.com
Adventure Center Inc
1311 63rd St Suite 200 .... Emeryville CA 94608 510-654-1879 654-4200
TF: 800-227-8747 ■ Web: www.adventurecenter.com
Adventure Challenge 8225 Oxer Rd .... Richmond VA 23235 804-276-7600 222-1709
Web: www.adventurechallenge.com
Adventure Connection PO Box 475 .... Coloma CA 95613 530-626-7385 626-9268
TF: 800-556-6060 ■ Web: www.raftcalifornia.com
Adventure Ctr 40 N Main St .... Ashland OR 97520 541-488-2819 482-5139
TF: 800-444-2819 ■ Web: www.raftingtours.com
Adventure Life South America
1655 S 3rd St W Suite 1 .... Missoula MT 59801 406-541-2677 541-2676
TF: 800-344-6118 ■ Web: www.adventure-life.com
Adventures Out West 15001 N 74th St .... Scottsdale AZ 85260 800-755-0935 996-4890*
*Fax Area Code: 602 ■ TF: 800-755-0935 ■ Web: www.advoutwest.com
Africa Adventure Co The
5353 N Federal Hwy Suite 300 .... Fort Lauderdale FL 33308 954-491-8877 491-9060
TF: 800-882-9453 ■ Web: www.africa-adventure.com
African Travel Inc 1100 E Broadway .... Glendale CA 91205 818-507-7893 507-5802
TF: 800-421-8907 ■ Web: www.africantravelinc.com
Agape Tours Inc 1210 US Hwy 281 .... Wichita Falls TX 76310 940-767-4935 692-8477*
*Fax: Sales ■ TF: 800-460-2641 ■ Web: www.agapetoursinc.com
AHI International Corp 6400 Shafer Ct .... Rosemont IL 60018 847-384-4500 318-5000
TF: 800-323-7373 ■ Web: www.ahitravel.com
Alaska! Bus Charters & Tours Inc
PO Box 190735 .... Anchorage AK 99519 706-743-5509 743-5929
Web: www.alaskabus.com
Alpha Omega Tours & Charters
419 N Jefferson St PO Box 97 .... Medical Lake WA 99022 509-299-5595 299-5545
TF: 800-351-1060 ■ Web: www.alphaomegatoursandcharters.com
Alpine Adventure Trails Tours Inc
7495 Lower Thomaston Rd .... Macon GA 31220 478-477-4004 477-4117
TF: 888-478-4004 ■ Web: www.swisshiking.com
Alyson Adventures Inc 923 White St .... Key West FL 33040 305-296-9935 292-9665
TF: 800-825-9766 ■ Web: www.alysonadventures.com
Ambassadors Group Inc 110 S Ferrall St .... Spokane WA 99202 509-534-6200 534-5245
NASDAQ: EPAX ■ TF: 800-669-7882 ■ Web: www.ambassadorsgroup.com
American Coach Lines Inc
2328 10th Ave N Suite 501 .... Lake Worth FL 33460 561-721-1170 721-2390
Web: www.americancoachlines.com
American Trails West (ATW) 92 Middle Neck Rd .... Great Neck NY 11021 516-487-2800 487-2855
TF: 800-645-6260 ■ Web: www.americantrailswest.com
AmericanTours International LLC (ATI)
6053 W Century Blvd .... Los Angeles CA 90045 310-641-9953 216-5807
TF: 800-800-8942 ■ Web: www.americantours.com
Ameritours 5018 William Flynn Hwy .... Gibsonia PA 15044 724-443-5600 443-7447
TF: 800-466-3868
Anderson Coach & Travel 1 Anderson Plaza .... Greenville PA 16125 724-588-8310 588-0257
TF: 800-345-3435 ■ Web: www.goanderson.com
Atlantis Submarines International Inc
210 W 6th Ave Suite 200 .... Vancouver BC V5Y1K8 604-875-1367 875-0833
Web: www.atlantisadventures.com
ATS Tours 300 Continental Blvd Suite 350 .... El Segundo CA 90245 310-643-0044 643-0032
TF: 888-410-5770 ■ Web: travel2-us.com
Australian Pacific Touring (USA) Ltd
4605 Lankershim Blvd Suite 712 .... North Hollywood CA 91602 818-755-6392 755-6396
TF: 888-299-1428 ■ Web: www.aptouring.com
Backroads 801 Cedar St .... Berkeley CA 94710 510-527-1555 527-1444
TF: 800-462-2848 ■ Web: www.backroads.com
Badger Coaches Inc 5501 Femrite Dr .... Madison WI 53718 608-255-1511 258-3484
TF: 800-442-8259 ■ Web: www.badgerbus.com
Banff Adventures Unlimited
211 Bear St Bison Courtyard .... Banff AB T1L1A8 403-762-4554 760-3196
TF: 800-644-8888 ■ Web: www.banffadventures.com
Beamers Hells Canyon Tours & Excursions
PO Box 1243 .... Lewiston ID 83501 509-758-4800 758-3643
TF: 800-522-6966 ■ Web: www.hellscanyontours.com
Bestway Tours & Safaris 8678 Greenall Ave .... Burnaby BC V5J3M6 604-264-7378 264-7774
TF: 800-663-0844 ■ Web: www.bestway.com
Big Five Tours & Expeditions 1551 SE Palm Ct .... Stuart FL 34994 772-287-7995 287-5990
TF: 800-244-3483 ■ Web: www.bigfive.com
Blue Grass Tours Inc 817 Enterprise Dr .... Lexington KY 40510 859-233-2152 255-4748
TF: 800-755-6956 ■ Web: www.bluegrasstours.com
Bombard Society Inc
605 Belvedere Rd # 15 .... West Palm Beach FL 33405 561-837-6610 837-6623
TF: 800-862-8537 ■ Web: www.buddybombard.com
Bonaventure Tours 8 Boudreau Ln .... Haute-Aboujagane NB E4P5N1 506-532-3674 532-6487
TF: 800-561-1213 ■ Web: www.aboutbonaventuretours.com
Borderland Tours 2550 W Calle Padilla .... Tucson AZ 85745 520-882-7650 792-9205
TF: 800-525-7753 ■ Web: www.borderland-tours.com

Name / Address	City	State	Zip	Phone	Fax
Boston Duck Tours Ltd 3 Copley Pl Suite 310 *TF:* 800-226-7442 ■ *Web:* www.bostonducktours.com	Boston	MA	02116	617-450-0068	
Branson Vacation Tours 1972 SR 165 Suite J *Web:* www.bvtamerica.com	Branson	MO	65616	417-336-6122	336-6126
Breakaway Tours 3300 Bloor St Suite 1800 *TF:* 800-465-4257 ■ *Web:* www.breakawaytours.com	Toronto	ON	M8X2X2	416-915-9880	915-9881
Brendan Vacations 21625 Prairie St *TF:* 800-421-8446 ■ *Web:* www.brendanvacations.com	Chatsworth	CA	91311	818-428-6000	772-6492
Brennan Vacations 5301 S Federal Cir *TF:* 800-237-7249 ■ *Web:* www.brennanvacations.com	Littleton	CO	80123	303-703-7549	703-7601
Brewster Rocky Mountain Adventures 208 Caribou St *TF:* 800-691-5085 ■ *Web:* www.brewsteradventures.com	Banff	AB	T1L1A9	403-762-5454	673-2100
Brewster Travel Canada 100 Gopher St PO Box 1140 *TF:* 866-606-6700 ■ *Web:* www.brewster.ca	Banff	AB	T1L1J3	403-762-6700	762-6750
Brown Tours 50 Venner Rd *TF:* 800-424-4700 ■ *Web:* www.browntours.com	Amsterdam	NY	12010	518-843-4700	843-3600
Burke International Tours Inc PO Box 890 *TF:* 800-476-3900 ■ *Web:* www.burkechristiantours.com	Newton	NC	28658	828-465-3900	465-3912
Butterfield & Robinson 70 Bond St Suite 300 *TF:* 866-551-9090 ■ *Web:* www.butterfield.com	Toronto	ON	M5B1X3	416-864-1354	915-8001
California Parlor Car Tours 500 Sutter St Suite 401 *TF:* 800-227-4250 ■ *Web:* www.calpartours.com	San Francisco	CA	94102	415-474-7500	673-1539
CampAlaska Tours PO Box 872247 *TF:* 800-376-9438 ■ *Web:* www.campalaska.com	Wasilla	AK	99687	907-376-9438	376-2353
Centennial Travelers 311 S College Ave *TF:* 800-223-0675 ■ *Web:* www.centennialtravel.com	Fort Collins	CO	80524	970-484-4988	484-0022
Chicago Supernatural Tours PO Box 557544 *Web:* www.ghosttours.com	Chicago	IL	60655	708-499-0300	
Churchill Nature Tours PO Box 429 *TF:* 877-636-2968 ■ *Web:* www.churchillnaturetours.com	Erickson	MB	R0J0P0	204-636-2968	636-2557
Classic Student Tours 75 Rhoads Ctr Dr *TF:* 800-860-0246	Dayton	OH	45458	937-439-0032	439-0041
Club Europa 802 W Oregon St *TF:* 800-331-1882 ■ *Web:* www.clubeuropatravel.com	Urbana	IL	61801	217-344-5863	344-4072
Coach Tours Ltd 475 Federal Rd *TF:* 800-822-6224 ■ *Web:* www.coachtour.com	Brookfield	CT	06804	203-740-1118	775-6851
Collette Travel Service Inc 162 Middle St *TF:* 800-832-4656 ■ *Web:* www.collettevacations.com	Pawtucket	RI	02860	401-728-3805	728-1380
Columbia River Safaris PO Box 2292 *TF:* 866-344-4931 ■ *Web:* www.columbiariversafaris.ca	Golden	BC	V0A1H0	250-344-4931	344-6140
Contemporary Tours 1400 Old Country Rd Suite 100 *TF:* 800-627-8873 ■ *Web:* www.contemporarytours.com	Westbury	NY	11590	516-484-5032	
Contiki Holidays 801 E Katella Ave 3rd Fl *TF:* 888-266-8454 ■ *Web:* www.ie.contiki.com	Anaheim	CA	92805	714-935-0808	935-2579
Cox & Kings 25 Davis Blvd *TF:* 800-999-1758 ■ *Web:* www.coxandkingsusa.com	Tampa	FL	33606	813-258-3323	258-3852
Cultural Experiences Abroad Inc (CEA) 1400 E Southern Ave Suite B-108 *TF:* 800-266-4441 ■ *Web:* www.gowithcea.com	Tempe	AZ	85282	480-557-7900	557-7926
Cyr Bus Tours 153 Gilman Falls Ave *TF:* 800-244-2335 ■ *Web:* www.cyrbustours.com/#tours	Old Town	ME	04468	207-827-2335	827-6763
Dash Tours 1024 Winnipeg St *TF:* 800-265-0000 ■ *Web:* www.dashtours.com	Regina	SK	S4R8P8	306-352-2222	757-4126
Dipert Travel & Transportation Ltd PO Box 580 *TF:* 800-433-5335 ■ *Web:* www.dandipert.com	Arlington	TX	76004	817-543-3710	543-3728
Discovery Charter & Tours 1558 Broughton Blvd *TF:* 888-468-6877	Port McNeil	BC	V0N2R0	250-956-3167	956-4285
Earthwatch Institute 114 Western Ave *TF:* 800-776-0188 ■ *Web:* www.earthwatch.org	Boston	MA	02134	978-461-0081	461-2332
Eco Park Resort at Mt. St. Helens Inc PO Box 350 *Web:* www.ecoparkresort.com/tours.htm	Toutle	WA	98649	360-274-7007	
Educational Tours 1123 Sterling Rd *TF:* 800-343-9003 ■ *Web:* www.edtours-us.com	Inverness	FL	34450	352-344-3589	344-0067
Educational Tours Inc PO Box 828 *TF:* 800-962-0060 ■ *Web:* www.educationaltours.com	Northbrook	IL	60065	847-509-0088	509-0011
Educational Travel Consultants 2876 Middleton Vista *TF:* 800-247-7969 ■ *Web:* www.educationaltravelconsultants.com	Hendersonville	NC	28791	828-693-0412	692-1591
Educational Travel Tours Inc PO Box 9028 *TF:* 800-959-9833 ■ *Web:* www.educationaltraveltours.com	Trenton	NJ	08650	609-587-1550	587-1550
EF Tours 1 Education St *TF:* 800-872-8439 ■ *Web:* www.eftours.com	Cambridge	MA	02141	617-619-1000	619-1901
Especially 4-U Tours & Travel 7165 E University Dr Suite 15 Sun Valley Office Pk *TF:* 800-331-4968 ■ *Web:* www.especially4utours.com	Mesa	AZ	85207	480-985-4200	355-4128
Esplanade Tours 160 Commonwealth Ave Suite L3 *TF:* 800-426-5492 ■ *Web:* www.esplanadetours.com	Boston	MA	02116	617-266-7465	262-9829
Explorica Inc 145 Tremont St *TF:* 888-310-7120 ■ *Web:* www.explorica.com	Boston	MA	02111	888-310-7120	310-7088
Fantastic Tours & Travel 6143 Jericho Tpke *TF:* 800-552-6262 ■ *Web:* www.fantastictours.com	Commack	NY	11725	631-462-6262	462-2311
Festive Holidays Inc 5501 New Jersey Ave *TF:* 800-257-8920 ■ *Web:* www.festiveholidays.com	Wildwood Crest	NJ	08260	609-522-6316	729-8606
Friendly Excursions Inc PO Box 69	Sunland	CA	91041	818-353-7726	353-3903
Frontiers International Travel PO Box 959 *TF:* 800-245-1950 ■ *Web:* www.frontierstravel.com	Wexford	PA	15090	724-935-1577	935-5388
Gadabout Vacations 1801 E Tahquitz Canyon Way Suite 100 *TF:* 800-952-5068 ■ *Web:* www.gadaboutvacations.com	Palm Springs	CA	92262	760-325-5556	325-5127
General Tours 53 Summer St *TF:* 800-221-2216 ■ *Web:* www.generaltours.com	Keene	NH	03431	603-357-5033	357-4548
Geographic Expeditions 1008 Gen Kennedy Ave PO Box 29902 *TF:* 800-777-8183 ■ *Web:* www.geoex.com	San Francisco	CA	94129	415-922-0448	346-5535
Gerber Tours Inc 1400 Old Country Rd Suite 100 *TF:* 800-645-9145 ■ *Web:* www.gerbertours.com	Westbury	NY	11590	516-826-5000	826-5044
Global Educational Tours 7216 Madison Ave # U *TF:* 888-508-6877 ■ *Web:* www.globaledtours.com	Indianapolis	IN	46227	317-787-2787	787-2765
GlobalQuest Journeys Ltd 185 Willis Ave 2nd Fl *TF:* 800-221-3254	Mineola	NY	11501	516-739-3690	739-8022
Globus 5301 S Federal Cir *TF:* 866-755-8581 ■ *Web:* www.globusjourneys.com	Littleton	CO	80123	303-797-2800	798-5441
Go Ahead Tours 1 Education St *TF:* 800-242-4686 ■ *Web:* www.goaheadtours.com	Cambridge	MA	02141	617-619-1000	619-1901
Go Next 8000 W 78th St Suite 345 *TF:* 800-842-9023 ■ *Web:* www.gonext.com	Minneapolis	MN	55439	952-918-8950	918-8975
Go West Adventures Inc PO Box 882319 *Web:* www.gowestadventures.com	Los Angeles	CA	90009	310-216-2522	216-2638
Go...With Jo! Tours & Travel Inc 910 Dixieland Rd *TF:* 800-999-1446 ■ *Web:* www.gowithjo.com	Harlingen	TX	78552	956-423-1446	421-5787
Good Time Tours 455 Corday St *TF:* 800-446-0886 ■ *Web:* www.goodtimetours.com	Pensacola	FL	32503	850-476-0046	476-7637
Good Times Travel Inc 17132 Magnolia St *TF:* 888-488-2287 ■ *Web:* www.goodtimestravel.com	Fountain Valley	CA	92708	714-848-1255	848-2855
Grand European Tours 6000 Meadows Rd Suite 520 *TF:* 877-622-9109 ■ *Web:* www.getours.com	Lake Oswego	OR	97035	503-718-2262	718-5198
Gray Line Worldwide 1835 Gaylord St *Web:* www.grayline.com	Denver	CO	80206	303-394-6920	394-6950
Green Tortoise Adventure Travel & Hostels 494 Broadway *TF:* 800-867-8647 ■ *Web:* www.greentortoise.com	San Francisco	CA	94133	415-834-1000	956-4900
Greene Coach Charters & Tours Inc 126 Bohannon Ave *TF:* 800-338-5469 ■ *Web:* www.greenecoach.com	Greeneville	TN	37745	423-638-8271	638-5541
Group Leaders of America Inc 420 E State St PO Box 129 *TF:* 800-628-0993 ■ *Web:* www.glamer.com	Salem	OH	44460	330-337-1027	337-1118
Gutsy Women Travel 101 Limekiln Pike *TF Resv:* 866-464-8879 ■ *Web:* www.gutsywomentravel.com	Glenside	PA	19038	215-572-7676	886-2228
Hesselgrave International PO Box 30768 *TF:* 800-457-5522 ■ *Web:* www.hesselgravetours.com	Bellingham	WA	98228	360-734-3570	734-3588
Historic Tours of America Inc 201 Front St Suite 224 *TF:* 800-868-7482 ■ *Web:* www.historictours.com	Key West	FL	33040	305-296-3609	292-8902
Holiday River Expeditions 544 E 3900 S *TF:* 800-624-6323 ■ *Web:* www.bikeraft.com	Salt Lake City	UT	84107	801-266-2087	266-1448
Holiday Tours Inc 10367 Randleman Rd *TF:* 800-733-9011 ■ *Web:* www.holidaytoursinc.com	Randleman	NC	27317	336-498-9000	498-2204
Holiday Travel Inc 2727 Henry Ave *TF:* 800-826-2266 ■ *Web:* www.holidayvacation.com	Eau Claire	WI	54701	715-834-5555	834-8554
Insight Vacations Inc 801 E Katella Ave **Fax Area Code:* 714 ■ *TF:* 800-582-8380 ■ *Web:* www.insightvacations.com	Anaheim	CA	92805	800-582-8380	937-4910*
International Expeditions Inc 1 Environs Pk *TF:* 800-234-9620 ■ *Web:* www.ietravel.com	Helena	AL	35080	205-428-1700	428-1714
International Student Tours 999 W Broadway Ave Suite 720 *TF:* 888-472-3933 ■ *Web:* www.istours.com	Vancouver	BC	V5Z1K5	604-714-1244	738-4080
Isram World of Travel Inc 233 Pk Ave S 10th Fl *TF:* 800-223-7460 ■ *Web:* www.isram.com	New York	NY	10003	212-661-1193	370-1477
JALPAK International Hawaii Inc 2270 Kalakaua Ave Suite 1600	Honolulu	HI	96815	808-926-4500	924-6797
Jasmine's China Adventure Tours 6044 Laguna Villa Way *Web:* www.jasminechina.com	Elk Grove	CA	95758	916-683-1790	
Julian Tours 1500 N Beauregard St Suite 110 *TF:* 800-541-7936 ■ *Web:* www.juliantours.com	Alexandria	VA	22311	703-379-2300	379-5030
Katmai Coastal Bear Tours PO Box 1503 *TF:* 800-532-8338 ■ *Web:* www.katmaibears.com	Homer	AK	99603	907-235-8337	
KE Adventure Travel PO Box 8910 **Fax Area Code:* 303 ■ *TF:* 800-497-9675 ■ *Web:* www.keadventure.com	Avon	CO	81620	970-949-0606	547-3768*
Ker & Downey Inc 6703 Hwy Blvd *TF:* 800-423-4236 ■ *Web:* www.kerdowney.com	Katy	TX	77494	281-371-2500	371-2514
Kincaid Coach Lines Inc 9207 Woodend Rd *TF:* 800-998-1901 ■ *Web:* www.kincaidcoach.com	Edwardsville	KS	66111	913-441-6200	441-0068
Knight Inlet Grizzly Bear Adventure Tours 8841 Driftwood Rd *Web:* www.grizzlytours.com	Black Creek	BC	V9J1A8	250-337-1953	337-1914
Kootenay River Runners PO Box 81 *TF:* 800-599-4399 ■ *Web:* www.raftingtherockies.com	Edgewater	BC	V0A1E0	250-347-9210	347-6598
Landmark Tours Inc 164 Demar Ave	Saint Paul	MN	55126	651-490-5408	490-1454
Lindblad Expeditions 96 Morton St 9th Fl *TF:* 800-397-3348 ■ *Web:* www.expeditions.com	New York	NY	10014	212-765-7740	265-3770
M & M Tours Inc 17 Spaulding Ln	Saugerties	NY	12477	845-246-3196	246-4450
Macy's Travel 700 Nicollet Mall *TF:* 800-316-6166 ■ *Web:* www.travel.carlsonwagonlit.com	Minneapolis	MN	55402	612-375-2884	
Magic Bus Co 520 Lakeshore Blvd E *TF:* 877-371-8747 ■ *Web:* www.magicbuscompany.com	Toronto	ON	M5A1C3	416-516-7827	516-6774
Martz Group 239 Old River Rd *TF:* 800-334-9608 ■ *Web:* www.martzgroup.com	Wilkes-Barre	PA	18702	570-821-3838	821-3835
Martz Tours 239 Old River Rd *TF:* 800-432-8069 ■ *Web:* www.martztours.com	Wilkes-Barre	PA	18702	570-821-3849	821-3811
Maupintour Inc 2690 Weston Rd Suite 200 *TF:* 800-255-4266 ■ *Web:* www.maupintour.com	Weston	FL	33331	954-653-3820	888-9082
Mayflower Tours Inc 1225 Warren Ave PO Box 490 *TF:* 800-323-7604 ■ *Web:* www.mayflowertours.com	Downers Grove	IL	60515	630-435-8500	960-3575

	City	State	ZIP	Phone	Fax
McKinzie Tours Inc 7835 W 151st St PO Box 23559 Web: www.mckinzietours.com	Overland Park	KS	66283	913-681-2202	681-2685
Meline's Lodge & Guide Service PO Box 82 TF: 800-561-3166 ■ Web: www.canadafishingtrips.com	Nestor Falls	ON	P0X1K0	807-484-2483	
Micato Safaris 15 W 26th St 11th Fl TF: 800-642-2861 ■ Web: www.micato.com	New York	NY	10010	212-545-7111	545-8297
Mid-American Coaches Inc 4530 Hwy 47 TF: 866-944-8687 ■ Web: www.mid-americancoaches.com	Washington	MO	63090	636-432-7860	660-1505
Midnight Sun Adventure Travel 1027 Pandora Ave TF: 800-255-5057 ■ Web: www.midnightsuntravel.com	Victoria	BC	V8V3P6	250-480-9409	483-7422
Monograms 5301 S Federal Cir TF: 866-270-9841 ■ Web: www.monogramstravel.com	Littleton	CO	80123	303-797-2800	798-5441
Montana River Outfitters 923 10th Ave N TF: 800-800-8218 ■ Web: www.montanariveroutfitters.com	Great Falls	MT	59401	406-761-1677	452-3833
Moose Travel Network 460 King St W Web: www.moosenetwork.com	Toronto	ON	M5V1L7	416-504-7514	504-7480
Mountain Travel Sobek 1266 66th St Suite 4 TF: 888-831-7526 ■ Web: www.mtsobek.com	Emeryville	CA	94608	510-594-6000	594-6001
Musiker Discovery Programs Inc 1326 Old Northern Blvd TF: 888-878-6637 ■ Web: www.summerdiscovery.com	Roslyn	NY	11576	516-621-3939	625-3438
Natural Habitat Adventures 2945 Ctr Green Ct TF: 800-543-8917 ■ Web: www.nathab.com	Boulder	CO	80301	303-449-3711	449-3712
New Horizons Tour & Travel Inc (NHTT) 2727 Spring Arbor Rd TF Cust Svc: 800-327-4695 ■ Web: www.nhtt.com	Jackson	MI	49203	517-788-6822	788-6847
New York Tours 1414 Grand St *Fax Area Code: 201 ■ TF: 800-735-8530 ■ Web: www.newyorktoursnyc.com	Hoboken	NJ	07030	800-735-8530	653-5498*
Nichols Five Star Charters & Tours PO Box 709	Fond du Lac	WI	54936	920-929-8030	929-8039
Northern Light Balloon Expeditions 455 Dry Creek Rd TF: 800-230-6222	Sedona	AZ	86336	928-282-2274	282-6173
Off the Beaten Path 7 E Beall St TF: 800-445-2995 ■ Web: www.offthebeatenpath.com	Bozeman	MT	59715	406-586-1311	587-4147
Olivia Cruises & Resorts 434 Brannan St TF: 800-631-6277 ■ Web: www.olivia.com	San Francisco	CA	94107	415-962-5700	962-5710
On Tour 201 Cortsen Rd	Pleasant Hill	CA	94523	925-930-9135	
Onondaga Coach Corp PO Box 277 TF: 800-451-1570 ■ Web: www.onondagacoach.com	Auburn	NY	13021	315-255-2216	255-0925
Orange Belt Stages PO Box 949 TF: 800-266-7433 ■ Web: www.orangebelt.com	Visalia	CA	93292	559-733-4408	733-0538
Overseas Adventure Travel 347 Congress St *Fax Area Code: 617 ■ TF: 800-221-0814 ■ Web: www.oattravel.com	Boston	MA	02210	800-221-0814	346-6700*
Pacific Delight Tours Inc 3 Pk Ave 38th Fl TF: 800-221-7179 ■ Web: www.pacificdelighttours.com	New York	NY	10016	212-818-1781	818-1743
Panorama Balloon Tours 2683 Via De La Valle 625G TF: 800-455-3592 ■ Web: www.gohotair.com	Del Mar	CA	92014	760-271-3467	
ParkEast Tours 1 Environs Pk TF: 800-234-9620 ■ Web: www.parkeast.com	Helena	AL	35080	205-428-1700	428-1714
Perillo Tours 577 Chestnut Ridge Rd TF: 800-431-1515 ■ Web: www.perillotours.com	Woodcliff Lake	NJ	07677	201-307-1234	307-1808
Pilgrim Tours & Travel Inc 3821 Main St PO Box 268 TF: 800-322-0788 ■ Web: www.pilgrimtours.com	Morgantown	PA	19543	610-286-0788	286-6262
Pitmar Tours 7549 140th St Suite 9 TF: 877-596-9670 ■ Web: www.pitmartours.com	Surrey	BC	V3W5J9	604-596-9670	596-3444
PML Travel & Tours 750 Rt 73 S Suite 204 TF: 800-872-4868 ■ Web: www.pmltours.com	Marlton	NJ	08053	856-983-1866	983-8434
Polynesian Adventure Tours Inc 2880 Kilihau St *Fax: Resv ■ TF: 800-622-3011 ■ Web: www.polyad.com	Honolulu	HI	96819	808-833-3000	833-3473*
Premier Tours 21 S 12th St 9th Fl TF: 800-545-1910 ■ Web: www.premiertours.com	Philadelphia	PA	19107	215-893-9966	893-0357
Presley Tours Inc 16 Presley Pk Dr PO Box 58 TF: 800-621-6100 ■ Web: www.presleytours.com	Makanda	IL	62958	618-549-0704	549-0404
Princess Tours 2815 2nd Ave Suite 400 TF: 800-426-0442 ■ Web: www.princess.com/news/article.jsp?newsArticleId=na209&submit=pk	Seattle	WA	98121	206-336-6000	336-6100
Rail Europe Group 44 S Broadway 11th Fl *Fax: Sales ■ TF: 800-848-7245 ■ Web: www.raileurope.com	White Plains	NY	10601	914-682-2999	681-3287*
Red Sail Sports Inc 5 Pier # 102 TF: 877-733-7245 ■ Web: www.redsail.com	San Francisco	CA	94111	415-981-4411	981-6203
REI Adventures PO Box 1938 TF: 800-622-2236 ■ Web: www.rei.com/adventures	Sumner	WA	98390	253-437-1100	395-8160
Richmond Tours 1828 Hylan Blvd TF: 800-766-3868	Staten Island	NY	10305	718-979-3111	979-7143
Rivers Oceans & Mountains Adventures Inc (ROAM) 7025 Beggs Rd TF: 888-639-1114 ■ Web: www.iroamtheworld.com	Nelson	BC	V1L5P6	250-229-2115	229-2119
Roberts Hawaii Inc 680 Iwilei Rd Dole Office Bldg Suite 700 TF: 800-831-5541 ■ Web: www.robertshawaii.com	Honolulu	HI	96817	808-523-7750	522-7872
Royal Coach Tours 630 Stockton Ave TF: 800-927-6925 ■ Web: www.royal-coach.com	San Jose	CA	95126	408-279-4801	286-1410
Royal Tours Inc PO Box 998 TF: 800-997-6925 ■ Web: www.royaltours.org	Randleman	NC	27317	336-629-9080	629-9011
RSVP Vacations 2535 25th Ave S TF: 800-328-7787 ■ Web: www.rsvpvacations.com	Minneapolis	MN	55406	612-729-1113	729-2809
Sanborn Tours Inc 2015 S 10th St PO Box 936 TF: 800-395-8482 ■ Web: www.sanborns.com	McAllen	TX	78505	956-682-9872	682-0016
Scenic Airlines Inc 3900 Paradise Rd Suite #185 TF: 866-235-9422 ■ Web: www.scenic.com	Las Vegas	NV	89169	702-638-3300	638-3275
Scholastic Tours Inc 3841 Nostrand Ave TF: 800-221-6209	Brooklyn	NY	11235	718-934-9400	891-8681
Seniors Unlimited LLC 53 W Huron St TF: 800-837-1333	Pontiac	MI	48342	248-338-1333	338-2637
Short Hills Tours 46 Chatham Rd PO Box 310 TF: 800-348-6871 ■ Web: www.shorthillstours.com	Short Hills	NJ	07078	973-467-2113	467-3353
Silver Fox Tours & Motorcoaches 3 Silver Fox Dr TF: 800-342-5998 ■ Web: www.silverfoxcoach.com	Millbury	MA	01527	508-865-6000	865-4660
Silverado Stages Inc 241 Prado Rd TF: 866-766-4937 ■ Web: www.silveradostages.com	San Luis Obispo	CA	93401	805-545-8400	545-8404
Sky High Red Rock Balloon Adventures 105 Canyon Diablo TF: 800-258-3754 ■ Web: www.redrockballoons.com	Sedona	AZ	86351	928-284-0040	284-1760
Smithsonian Journeys PO Box 23182 TF: 877-338-8687 ■ Web: www.smithsonianjourneys.org	Washington	DC	20077	202-357-4700	633-6088
South of the Border Tours 7937 E Coronado Rd	Tucson	AZ	85750	520-760-4000	760-3999
Specialty Tours Inc 3095 S Parker Rd Suite 150 TF: 800-342-4299	Aurora	CO	80014	303-337-7488	337-9257
Sports Leisure Vacations 9812 Old Winery Pl TF: 800-951-5556 ■ Web: www.sportsleisure.com	Sacramento	CA	95827	916-361-2051	361-7995
Sports Travel Inc 60 Main St PO Box 50 TF: 800-662-4424 ■ Web: www.sportstravelandtours.com	Hatfield	MA	01038	413-247-7678	247-5700
Storm Chasing Adventure Tours 4775 Deer Cr Web: www.stormchasing.com	Island Park	ID	83429	303-888-8629	
Straight A Tours & Travel 6881 Kingspointe Pkwy Suite 18 TF: 800-237-5440 ■ Web: www.straightatours.com	Orlando	FL	32819	407-896-1242	896-1151
Student Tours Inc 60 W Ave TF: 800-331-7093 ■ Web: www.studenttoursinc.com	Vineyard Haven	MA	02568	508-693-5078	693-8627
Student Travel Services Inc 1413 Madison Pk Dr TF: 800-648-4849 ■ Web: www.ststravel.com	Glen Burnie	MD	21061	410-859-4200	787-9580
Sunny Land Tours Inc 166 Main St1 Corporate Dr Suite 1-F TF: 800-783-7839 ■ Web: www.sunnylandtours.com	Palm Coast	FL	32127	386-449-0059	449-0060
Sunrise Fantasy Flights Inc 8710 W Hillsborough Ave Suite 189 Web: www.bigredballoon.com	Tampa	FL	33615	813-969-1518	886-5538
Suntrek Tours Inc *Intrepid Travel* 77 W 3rd St TF: 800-786-8735 ■ Web: www.suntrek.com	Santa Rosa	CA	95401	707-523-1800	523-1911
Super Holiday Tours 116 Gatlin Ave TF: 800-327-2116 ■ Web: www.superholiday.com	Orlando	FL	32806	407-851-0060	851-0071
Tag-A-Long Expeditions 452 N Main St TF: 800-453-3292 ■ Web: www.tagalong.com	Moab	UT	84532	435-259-8946	259-8990
Talbot Tours Inc 1952 Camden Ave TF: 800-662-9933 ■ Web: www.talbottours.com	San Jose	CA	95124	408-879-0101	879-0183
Tauck World Discovery 10 Norden Pl *Fax: Hum Res ■ TF: 800-468-2825 ■ Web: www.tauck.com	Norwalk	CT	06855	203-899-6500	899-6612*
TCS Expeditions 1000 2nd Ave # 1400 TF: 800-727-7477 ■ Web: www.tcs-expeditions.com	Seattle	WA	98104	206-727-7300	727-7309
Timberwolf Tours Ltd 51404 RR 264 Suite 34 *Fax Area Code: 866 ■ TF: 888-467-9697 ■ Web: www.timberwolftours.com	Spruce Grove	AB	T7Y1E4	780-470-4966	339-3960*
Toto Tours Ltd 1326 W Albion Ave TF: 800-565-1241 ■ Web: www.tototours.com	Chicago	IL	60626	773-274-8686	274-8695
Tourco Inc 16 E Pond Rd TF: 800-537-5378	Nobleboro	ME	04555	207-563-2288	563-3335
Travcoa 4340 Von Karman Ave Suite 400 TF: 800-992-2003 ■ Web: www.travcoa.com	Newport Beach	CA	92660	949-476-2800	476-2538
Travel Adventures Inc 1175 S Lapeer Rd TF: 800-356-2737 ■ Web: www.traveladventures.com	Lapeer	MI	48446	810-664-1777	664-1913
Travel Tours Inc 2111 W Hwy 51 PO Box 40 TF: 800-331-3192 ■ Web: www.traveltoursinc.com	Wagoner	OK	74477	918-485-4595	485-8216
TravelQuest International 305 Double D Dr TF: 800-830-1998 ■ Web: www.tq-international.com	Prescott	AZ	86303	928-445-7754	
TrekAmerica 115 Hibernia Ave TF: 800-221-0596 ■ Web: www.trekamerica.com	Rockaway	NJ	07866	973-983-1144	983-8551
Tri-State Travel PO Box 307 TF: 800-779-4869 ■ Web: www.tristatetravel.com	Galena	IL	61036	815-777-0820	777-8128
Tumlare Corp 2128 Bellmore Ave TF: 800-223-4664 ■ Web: www.tumlare.com	Bellmore	NY	11710	516-781-0322	781-0896
Upstate Tours & Travel 207 Geyser Rd TF: 800-237-5252 ■ Web: www.upstatetours.com	Saratoga Springs	NY	12866	518-584-5252	584-1092
USA Student Travel 5080 Robert J Mathews Pkwy TF: 800-448-4444 ■ Web: www.usastudenttravel.com	El Dorado Hills	CA	95762	916-939-6805	939-6806
VBT Bicycle Vacations 614 Monkton Rd TF: 800-245-3868 ■ Web: www.vbt.com	Bristol	VT	05443	802-453-4811	453-4806
VentureOut 575 Pierce St Suite 604 TF: 888-431-6789 ■ Web: www.venture-out.com	San Francisco	CA	94117	415-626-5678	626-5679
VIP Tour & Charter Bus Co 129-137 Fox St TF: 800-337-4457 ■ Web: www.vipchartercoaches.com	Portland	ME	04101	207-772-4457	772-7020
Visit America Inc 330 7th Ave 20th Fl Web: www.visitamerica.com	New York	NY	10001	212-683-8082	683-8501
Wade Tours Inc 797 Burdeck St TF: 800-955-9233 ■ Web: www.wadetours.com	Schenectady	NY	12306	518-355-4500	355-4942
Walking Adventures International 14612 NE Fourth Plain Rd # A TF: 800-779-0353 ■ Web: www.walkingadventures.com	Vancouver	WA	98682	360-260-9393	260-1131
West Coast Connection 318 Indian Trace Suite 336 TF: 800-767-0227 ■ Web: www.westcoastconnection.com	Weston	FL	33326	954-888-9780	888-9781
Western Discovery LLC 1175 Fairview Dr Suite M TF: 800-843-5061 ■ Web: www.westerndiscovery.com	Carson City	NV	89701	775-329-9933	329-1045
White Mountain Adventures 122 A Eagle Crescent PO Box 4259 TF: 800-408-0005 ■ Web: www.whitemountainadventures.com	Banff	AB	T1L1E6	403-760-4403	760-4409

				Phone	Fax
White Star Tours 26 E Lancaster Ave	Reading	PA	19607	610-775-5000	775-7155
TF: 800-437-2323 ■ *Web:* www.whitestartours.com					
Wilderness Travel 1102 9th St	Berkeley	CA	94710	510-558-2488	558-2489
TF: 800-368-2794 ■ *Web:* www.wildernesstravel.com					
Wings Tours Inc 11350 McCormick Rd Suite 703	Hunt Valley	MD	21031	410-771-0925	771-0928
TF: 800-869-4647					
WorldPass Travel Group LLC 5080 Robert J Matthews Pkwy	El Dorado Hills	CA	95838	916-939-6805	939-6806
TF: 888-877-4445 ■ *Web:* www.goworldpass.com					
WorldStrides 590 Peter Jefferson Pkwy Suite 300	Charlottesville	VA	22911	434-982-8600	982-8748
TF: 800-468-5899 ■ *Web:* www.worldstrides.com					

764 TOY STORES

				Phone	Fax
A2Z Science & Nature Store 57 King St	NorthHampton	MA	01060	413-586-1611	584-7253
TF: 877-261-6171 ■ *Web:* www.a-two-z.com					
Build-A-Bear Workshop Inc 1954 Innerbelt Business Ctr Dr	Saint Louis	MO	63114	314-423-8000	423-8188
NYSE: BBW ■ *TF:* 888-560-2327 ■ *Web:* www.buildabear.com					
Creative Kid Stuff 3939 E 46th St	Minneapolis	MN	55406	612-929-2431	929-6770
TF: 800-353-0710 ■ *Web:* www.creativekidstuff.com					
Discount School Supplies 2 Lower Ragsdale Rd Suite 125	Monterey	CA	93940	800-919-5238	919-5235
TF: 800-919-5238 ■ *Web:* www.discountschoolsupply.com					
FAO Schwarz 875 Avenue of the Americas 20th Fl	New York	NY	10001	800-426-8697	276-0170
TF: 800-426-8697 ■ *Web:* www.fao.com					
Galt Toys 900 N Michigan Ave	Chicago	IL	60611	312-440-9550	440-9258
Web: galttoysgaltbaby.com					
Hobbytown USA 1233 Libra Dr	Lincoln	NE	68512	402-434-5385	
TF Cust Svc: 800-869-0424 ■ *Web:* www.hobbytown.com					
Learning Express Inc 29 Buena Vista St	Devens	MA	01434	978-889-1000	889-1010
TF: 800-924-2296 ■ *Web:* www.learningexpress.com					
Mga Entertainment Inc 16300 Roscoe Blvd Suite 150	Van Nuys	CA	91406	818-894-2525	894-8094
TF: 800-222-4685 ■ *Web:* www.mgae.com					
Pun's Toy Shop 839 1/2 Lancaster Ave	Bryn Mawr	PA	19010	610-525-9789	527-5514
Right Start Inc 23622 Calabasas Rd Suite 339	Calabasas	CA	91302	818-707-7100	
Ting Ltd 878 Firetower Rd	Yanceyville	NC	27379	336-694-5665	694-5284
Web: www.wizardscauldron.com					
Toys 'R' Us Inc 1 Geoffrey Way	Wayne	NJ	07470	973-617-3500	617-4006
TF: 800-869-7787 ■ *Web:* www.toysrus.com					

765 TOYS, GAMES, HOBBIES

SEE ALSO Baby Products p. 1504; Bicycles & Bicycle Parts & Accessories p. 1524; Games & Entertainment Software p. 1684

				Phone	Fax
Action Products International Inc 1101 N Keller Rd Suite E	Orlando	FL	32810	407-660-7200	481-2781
NASDAQ: APII ■ *TF:* 800-772-2846					
Airmate Co Inc 16280 County Rd D	Bryan	OH	43506	419-636-3184	636-4210
TF: 800-544-3614 ■ *Web:* www.airmatecompany.com					
Alexander Doll Co Inc 615 W 131st St	New York	NY	10027	212-283-5900	283-4263
TF: 800-229-5192 ■ *Web:* www.madamealexander.com					
American Girl Inc 8400 Fairway Pl	Middleton	WI	53562	608-836-4848	836-0761
TF Orders: 800-845-0005 ■ *Web:* www.americangirl.com					
American Plastic Toys Inc 799 Ladd Rd	Walled Lake	MI	48390	248-624-4881	624-4918
TF: 800-521-7080 ■ *Web:* www.americanplastictoys.com					
Atlas Model Railroad Co Inc 378 Florence Ave	Hillside	NJ	07205	908-687-0880	687-8857
TF Orders: 800-872-2521 ■ *Web:* www.atlasrr.com					
Baby Einstein Co LLC 500 S Buena Vista St	Burbank	CA	91521	800-793-1454	549-2060*
**Fax Area Code:* 818 ■ *TF:* 800-793-1454 ■ *Web:* www.babyeinstein.com					
Bachmann Industries Inc 1400 E Erie Ave	Philadelphia	PA	19124	215-533-1600	744-4699
TF Cust Svc: 800-356-3910 ■ *Web:* www.bachmanntrains.com					
Back To Basics Toys Inc 610 Herdon Pkwy Suite 600	Herndon	VA	20170	719-948-1956	356-4174*
**Fax Area Code:* 800 ■ *TF:* 800-356-5360 ■ *Web:* www.backtobasicstoys.com					
Ball Bounce & Sport Inc/Hedstrom Plastics 100 Hedstrom Dr	Ashland	OH	44805	419-289-9310	281-3371
TF: 800-765-9665 ■ *Web:* www.hedstrom.com					
Bravo Sports Corp 12801 Carmenita Rd	Santa Fe Springs	CA	90670	562-484-5100	484-5183
TF Cust Svc: 800-234-9737 ■ *Web:* www.bravosportscorp.com					
Buffalo Games Inc 220 James E Casey Dr	Buffalo	NY	14206	716-827-8393	827-8163
Web: www.buffalogames.com					
Cardinal Industries Inc 21-01 51st Ave	Long Island City	NY	11101	718-784-3000	482-7877
Web: www.cardinalgames.com					
Cepia LLC 121 Hunter Ave Suite 103	Saint Louis	MO	63124	314-725-4900	725-4919
TF: 800-225-9319 ■ *Web:* www.cepiallc.com					
Commonwealth Toy & Novelty Co 45 W 25th St 5th Fl	New York	NY	10010	212-242-4070	645-4279
Community Products LLC 2032 Rt 213	Rifton	NY	12471	845-572-3410	336-5948*
**Fax Area Code:* 800 ■ **Fax:* Cust Svc ■ *TF:* 800-777-4244 ■ *Web:* www.communityplaythings.com					
Creativity for Kids 9450 Allen Dr	Cleveland	OH	44125	216-643-4660	643-4663
TF: 800-311-8684 ■ *Web:* www.creativityforkids.com					
Dentt Inc 4171 Marquis Way	Salt Lake City	UT	84124	801-277-7056	
Douglas Cuddle Toys Co Inc 69 Krif Rd PO Box D	Keene	NH	03431	603-352-3414	352-1248
TF: 800-992-9002 ■ *Web:* www.douglascuddletoy.com					
Effanbee Doll Co 459 Hurley Ave	Hurley	NY	12443	845-339-8246	339-8326
TF: 888-362-3655 ■ *Web:* www.effanbeedoll.com					
Electronic Arts Inc (EA) 209 Redwood Shores Pkwy	Redwood City	CA	94065	650-628-1500	628-1414
NASDAQ: ERTS ■ *TF Sales:* 877-324-2637 ■ *Web:* www.ea.com					
Erapro/Paris Co Inc 2500 Guenette St	Saint Laurent	QC	H4R2H2	514-335-0550	335-0571
TF: 877-372-9273 ■ *Web:* eragroup.ca					
Estes-Cox Corp 1295 H St	Penrose	CO	81240	719-372-6565	372-3419
TF: 800-525-7561 ■ *Web:* www.estesrockets.com					
Fisher-Price Inc 636 Girard Ave	East Aurora	NY	14052	716-687-3000	687-3476
TF: 800-432-5437 ■ *Web:* www.fisher-price.com					
Five Below Inc 1616 Walnut St Suite 400	Philadelphia	PA	19103	215-546-7909	546-8099
Web: www.fivebelow.com					
Gayla Industries Inc 6401 Antoine Dr	Houston	TX	77091	713-681-2411	682-1357
TF: 800-231-7508 ■ *Web:* www.gaylainc.com					
Goffa International Corp 930 Flushing Ave	Brooklyn	NY	11206	718-361-8883	361-0506
TF: 800-969-7864 ■ *Web:* www.goffausa.com					
Goldberger Co The 36 W 25th St 14th Fl	Brooklyn	NY	11237	212-924-1194	
TF: 800-452-3655 ■ *Web:* www.goldbergertoy.com					
Great Planes Model Distributors Co 1608 IH- Dr	Champaign	IL	61826	217-398-6300	398-1104
TF: 800-637-7660 ■ *Web:* www.greatplanes.com					
Guidecraft USA 66 Grand Ave Suite 207	Englewood	NJ	07631	201-894-5401	894-5405
TF: 800-544-6526 ■ *Web:* www.guidecraft.com					
Gund Inc 1 Runyons Ln	Edison	NJ	08817	732-248-1500	248-1968
TF Cust Svc: 800-448-4863 ■ *Web:* www.gund.com					
Hanover Accessories Inc 3500 Holly Ln N Suite 10	Plymouth	MN	55447	763-509-6100	551-9992
TF: 888-509-6100 ■ *Web:* www.hanoveraccessories.com					
Hasbro Inc 1027 Newport Ave	Pawtucket	RI	02861	401-431-8697	431-8082*
NYSE: HAS ■ **Fax:* Cust Svc ■ *TF:* 800-242-7276 ■ *Web:* www.hasbro.com					
Hasbro Inc Parker Bros Div 200 Narragansett Pk Dr	Pawtucket	RI	02862	888-836-7025	431-8082*
**Fax Area Code:* 401 ■ *TF:* 888-836-7025 ■ *Web:* www.hasbro.com/games					
Hasbro Inc Playskool Div 1027 Newport Ave	Pawtucket	RI	02861	401-431-8697	727-5544
NASDAQ: HAS ■ *TF:* 800-242-7276 ■ *Web:* www.hasbro.com					
Imperial Toy LLC 16641 Roscoe Pl	North Hills	CA	91343	818-536-6500	536-6501
Web: www.imperialtoy.com					
International Playthings Inc 75D Lackawanna Ave	Parsippany	NJ	07054	973-316-2500	316-5883
TF: 800-631-1272 ■ *Web:* www.intplay.com					
JAKKS Pacific Inc 22619 Pacific Coast Hwy Suite 250	Malibu	CA	90265	310-456-7799	317-8527
NASDAQ: JAKK ■ *TF:* 877-875-2557 ■ *Web:* www.jakkspacific.com					
K'NEX Industries Inc 2990 Bergey Rd	Hatfield	PA	19440	215-997-7722	996-4225
TF: 800-543-5639 ■ *Web:* www.brio.net					
Klutz 450 Lambert Ave	Palo Alto	CA	94306	650-857-0888	857-9110
TF: 800-737-4123 ■ *Web:* www.klutz.com					
LeapFrog Enterprises Inc 6401 Hollis St Suite 100	Emeryville	CA	94608	510-420-5000	420-5001
NYSE: LF ■ *TF:* 800-701-5327 ■ *Web:* www.shop.leapfrog.com					
Learning Curve International Inc 1111 W 22nd St Suite 320	Oak Brook	IL	60523	630-573-7200	573-7575
TF: 800-704-8697 ■ *Web:* www.learningcurve.com					
Learning Resources 380 N Fairway Dr	Vernon Hills	IL	60061	847-573-8400	573-8425
TF: 800-222-3909 ■ *Web:* www.learningresources.com					
LEGO Systems Inc 555 Taylor Rd	Enfield	CT	06082	860-763-6731	
TF: 800-243-4870 ■ *Web:* www.lego.com					
Lionel .com LLC 26750 23 Mile Rd	Chesterfield	MI	48051	586-949-4100	949-6757*
**Fax:* Hum Res ■ *TF:* 800-454-6635 ■ *Web:* www.lionel.com					
Little Tikes Co The 2180 Barlow Rd	Hudson	OH	44236	330-650-3000	
TF Cust Svc: 800-321-0183 ■ *Web:* www.littletikes.com					
Losi 4710 E Guasti Rd	Ontario	CA	91761	909-390-9595	390-5356
TF: 888-899-5674 ■ *Web:* www.teamlosi.com					
Lovee Doll & Toy Co Inc 200 5th Ave Suite 1210	New York	NY	10010	212-242-1545	242-4596
Mag-Nif Inc 8820 E Ave	Mentor	OH	44060	440-946-4308	974-0449
TF: 800-869-5463 ■ *Web:* www.magnif.com					
Maple City Rubber Co 55 Newton St PO Box 587	Norwalk	OH	44857	419-668-8261	668-1275
TF: 800-841-9434 ■ *Web:* www.maplecityrubber.com					
Marvel Enterprises Inc 417 5th Ave	New York	NY	10016	212-576-4000	
NYSE: MVL ■ *TF:* 800-217-9158 ■ *Web:* www.marvel.com					
Mattel Inc 333 Continental Blvd	El Segundo	CA	90245	310-252-2000	252-2179
NYSE: MAT ■ *TF:* 800-524-8697 ■ *Web:* www.mattel.com					
Mega Brands Inc 4505 Hickmore	Montreal	QC	H4T1K4	514-333-5555	333-4470
TF Cust Svc: 800-465-6342 ■ *Web:* www.megabloks.com					
Midwest Products Co Inc 400 S Indiana St	Hobart	IN	46342	219-942-1134	947-2347*
**Fax:* Sales ■ *TF Orders:* 800-348-3497 ■ *Web:* www.midwestproducts.com					
Model Rectifier Corp 80 Newfield Ave	Edison	NJ	08837	732-225-2100	225-0091
Web: www.modelrec.com					
Nintendo of America Inc 4820 150th Ave NE	Redmond	WA	98052	425-882-2040	882-3585
TF Cust Svc: 800-255-3700 ■ *Web:* www.nintendo.com					
Ohio Art Co 1 Toy St	Bryan	OH	43506	419-636-3141	636-7614
TF: 800-641-6226 ■ *Web:* www.world-of-toys.com					
Original Appalachian Artworks Inc 1721 Hwy 75 S PO Box 714	Cleveland	GA	30528	706-865-2171	865-5862
Web: www.cabbagepatchkids.com					
Patch Products Inc 1400 E Inman Pkwy	Beloit	WI	53511	608-362-6896	362-8178
TF: 800-524-4263 ■ *Web:* www.patchproducts.com					
Paul K Guillow Inc 40 New Salem St PO Box 229	Wakefield	MA	01880	781-245-5255	246-5017
Web: www.guillow.com					
Pepperball Technologies Inc 6142 Nncy Rdge Dr Suite 101	San Diego	CA	92121	858-638-0236	638-0781
TF: 877-887-3773 ■ *Web:* www.pepperball.com					
Pioneer National Latex Co 5000 E 29th St N	Wichita	KS	67220	316-685-2266	329-3864*
**Fax Area Code:* 800 ■ *TF:* 800-386-4438 ■ *Web:* www.pioneernational.com					
Plaid Enterprises Inc 3225 Westech Dr	Norcross	GA	30092	678-291-8100	291-8368*
**Fax:* Mktg ■ *TF:* 800-842-4197 ■ *Web:* www.plaidonline.com					
Playmobil USA Inc 26 Commerce Dr	Cranbury	NJ	08512	609-395-5566	409-1288
TF: 800-752-9662 ■ *Web:* www.playmobil.com					
Poof-Slinky Inc 45400 Helm St PO Box 701394	Plymouth	MI	48170	734-454-9552	454-9540
TF: 800-829-9502 ■ *Web:* www.poof-slinky.com					
Pop Rocket Inc 6330 San Vicente Blvd	Los Angeles	CA	90048	323-932-4300	932-4400
TF: 800-238-0798 ■ *Web:* www.poprocket.com					

	City	State	Zip	Phone	Fax
Pressman Toy Corp 121 New England Ave	Piscataway	NJ	08854	732-562-1590	562-1590
TF Cust Svc: 800-800-0298 ■ *Web:* www.pressmantoy.com					
Princess Soft Toys 7664 W 78th St	Minneapolis	MN	55439	952-829-5772	829-5596
TF: 800-252-7638 ■ *Web:* www.princesstoys.com					
Radica USA Ltd 13628-A Beta Rd	Dallas	TX	75244	972-490-4247	490-0765
NASDAQ: RADA ■ *TF:* 800-803-9611					
Radio Flyer Inc 6515 W Grand Ave	Chicago	IL	60707	773-637-7100	637-8874
TF: 800-621-7613 ■ *Web:* www.radioflyer.com					
RC2 Corp 1111 W 22nd St Suite 320	Oak Brook	IL	60523	630-573-7200	573-7575
NASDAQ: RCRC ■ *TF:* 800-704-8697 ■ *Web:* www.rc2.com					
SEGA of America Inc 650 Townsend St Suite 650	San Francisco	CA	94103	415-701-6000	701-6018
Web: www.sega.com					
SIG Mfg Co Inc 401 S Front St	Montezuma	IA	50171	641-623-5154	623-3922
TF Sales: 800-247-5008 ■ *Web:* www.sigmfg.com					
Sony Computer Entertainment America Inc 919 E Hillsdale Blvd Fl 2	Foster City	CA	94404	650-655-8000	655-8001
Web: www.us.playstation.com					
Spin Master Ltd 450 Front St W	Toronto	ON	M5V1B6	416-364-6002	364-8005
TF: 800-622-8339 ■ *Web:* www.spinmaster.com					
Steiff North America 425 Paramont Dr	Raynham	MA	02767	508-828-2377	821-4477
TF: 800-830-0429 ■ *Web:* www.steiffusa.com					
Swibco Inc 4810 Venture Rd	Lisle	IL	60532	630-968-8900	367-7943*
**Fax Area Code:* 800 ■ *TF:* 877-794-2261 ■ *Web:* www.swibco.com					
Tara Toy Corp 40 Adams Ave	Hauppauge	NY	11788	631-273-8697	273-8583
TF: 800-899-8272 ■ *Web:* www.taratoy.com					
Testor Corp 440 Blackhawk Pk Ave	Rockford	IL	61104	815-962-6654	962-7401
TF: 800-837-8677 ■ *Web:* www.testors.com					
Tonner Doll Co 459 Hurley Ave	Hurley	NY	12443	845-339-9537	339-1259
TF: 888-362-3655 ■ *Web:* www.tonnerdoll.com					
Trinity Products Inc 36 Meridian Rd	Edison	NJ	08820	732-635-1600	635-1640
Web: www.teamtrinity.com					
Troxel Co 11495 Hwy 57	Moscow	TN	38057	901-877-6875	877-3439
Web: www.troxel.com					
Twin Hills Inc 70 Hickory Rd	Hickory	KY	42051	270-856-2277	856-2249
TF: 888-918-7071 ■ *Web:* www.hdinc.biz					
Ty Inc 280 Chestnut Ave	Westmont	IL	60559	630-920-1515	920-1980*
**Fax:* Cust Svc ■ *TF Cust Svc:* 800-876-8000 ■ *Web:* www.world.ty.com					
Uncle Milton Industries Inc 5717 Corsa Ave	Westlake Village	CA	91362	818-707-0800	707-0878
TF: 800-869-7555 ■ *Web:* www.unclemilton.com					
Universal Mfg Co Inc 5450 Deramus Ave	Kansas City	MO	64120	816-231-2771	483-6842
TF: 800-821-2724					
University Games Corp 2030 Harrison St	San Francisco	CA	94110	415-503-1600	503-0085
TF: 800-347-4818 ■ *Web:* www.ugames.com					
Upper Deck Co LLC 5909 Sea Otter Pl	Carlsbad	CA	92010	760-929-6500	929-3512
TF Cust Svc: 800-873-7332 ■ *Web:* www.upperdeck.com					
US Playing Card Co 4590 Beech St	Cincinnati	OH	45212	513-396-5700	396-5878*
**Fax:* Mktg ■ *TF:* 800-832-0523 ■ *Web:* www.usplayingcard.com					
Vermont Teddy Bear Co Inc 6655 Shelburne Rd	Shelburne	VT	05482	802-985-3001	985-1304
TF: 800-988-8277 ■ *Web:* www.vermontteddybear.com					
VTech Electronics North America LLC 1155 W Dundee St Suite 130	Arlington Heights	IL	60004	847-400-3600	400-3601
TF: 800-521-2010 ■ *Web:* www.vtechkids.com					
Wham-O Inc 5903 Christie Ave	Emeryville	CA	94608	510-596-4202	596-4292
TF: 888-942-6650 ■ *Web:* www.wham-o.com					
Wiffle Ball Inc 275 Bridgeport Ave PO Box 193	Shelton	CT	06484	203-924-4643	924-9433
Web: www.wiffle.com					
William K Walthers Inc 5601 W Florist Ave	Milwaukee	WI	53218	414-527-0770	527-4423
TF: 800-877-7171 ■ *Web:* www.walthers.com					
Wizards of the Coast Inc 1600 Lind Ave SW # 400	Renton	WA	98057	425-226-6500	204-5818
TF: 800-324-6496 ■ *Web:* www.wizards.com					
World Wide Press Inc 801 River Dr S	Great Falls	MT	59405	406-727-7812	453-3711
TF: 800-548-9888					

TRAILERS - TRUCK

SEE Truck Trailers p. 2735

766 TRAILERS (TOWING) & TRAILER HITCHES

	City	State	Zip	Phone	Fax
Blessey Marine Services Inc 1515 River Oaks Rd E	Harahan	LA	70123	504-734-1156	734-1195
Web: www.blessey.com					
Bright Coop Inc 803 W Seale St	Nacogdoches	TX	75964	936-564-8378	564-3281
TF: 800-562-0730 ■ *Web:* www.brightcoop.com					
Cequent Towing Products 47774 Anchor Ct W	Plymouth	MI	48170	734-656-3000	656-3009
TF: 800-521-0510 ■ *Web:* www.draw-tite.com					
Cequent Trailer Products 1050 Indianhead Dr	Mosinee	WI	54455	715-693-1700	693-1799
TF: 800-604-9466 ■ *Web:* www.fultonperformance.com					
CM Trailers Inc 200 County Rd PO Box 680	Madill	OK	73446	580-795-5536	795-7263
TF: 888-268-7577 ■ *Web:* www.cmtrailers.com					
Com-Fab Inc 4657 Price Hilliards Rd	Plain City	OH	43064	740-857-1107	857-1757
Web: www.comfab-inc.com					
Creek Hill Welding 50 Mill St	Christiana	PA	17509	610-593-5321	593-5321
TF: 866-593-8188 ■ *Web:* www.creekhillwelding.com					
Dethmers Mfg Co Inc 4010 320th St	Boyden	IA	51234	712-725-2302	725-2380
TF: 800-543-3626 ■ *Web:* www.demco-products.com/index.html					
Eagle Trailers Inc 300 S Elm St	Homer	MI	49245	517-568-5372	568-5399
Web: www.eagletrailer.com					
Exiss Aluminum Trailers Inc 900 Exiss Blvd PO Box D	El Reno	OK	73036	405-262-6471	262-9277
TF: 877-993-9477 ■ *Web:* www.exiss.com					
EZ Loader Boat Trailers Inc 717 N Hamilton St	Spokane	WA	99202	509-489-0181	489-5729
TF: 800-398-5623 ■ *Web:* www.ezloader.com					
Gardner Cryogenics 2136 City Line Rd	Bethlehem	PA	18017	610-264-4523	266-3752
Web: www.gardnercryo.com					
Gooseneck Trailer Mfg Co 4400 E Hwy 21	Bryan	TX	77808	979-778-0034	778-0615
TF Cust Svc: 800-688-5490 ■ *Web:* www.gooseneck.net					
Hawkeye Leisure Trailers Ltd 1419 11th St N	Humboldt	IA	50548	515-332-1802	332-1833
TF: 888-874-9943 ■ *Web:* www.yachtclubtrailers.com					
Karavan Trailers Inc 100 Karavan Dr	Fox Lake	WI	53933	920-928-6200	928-6201
Web: www.karavantrailer.com					
Load Rite Trailers Inc 265 Lincoln Hwy	Fairless Hills	PA	19030	215-949-0500	949-1385
TF: 800-562-3783 ■ *Web:* www.loadrite.com					
Mac-Lander Inc 925 Furnas Dr	Osceola	IA	50213	641-342-6036	342-3508
Web: www.mac-lander.com					
Midwest Industries Inc 122 E State Hwy 175	Ida Grove	IA	51445	712-364-3365	364-3361
TF: 800-859-3028 ■ *Web:* www.shorelandr.com					
Performance Trailers Inc 6430 47th St N	Pinellas Park	FL	33781	727-527-8829	521-3701
Web: www.360boating.com					
Quality S Mfg Inc 3801 N 43rd Ave	Phoenix	AZ	85019	602-233-3499	233-9110
TF: 800-521-8181 ■ *Web:* www.quality-s.com					
Reese Products Inc 2602 College Ave	Goshen	IN	46528	574-537-6800	537-6986
TF: 800-326-1090 ■ *Web:* www.reeseprod.com					
Rigid Hitch Inc 3301 W Burnsville Pkwy	Burnsville	MN	55337	952-895-5001	895-9150
TF Cust Svc: 800-624-7630 ■ *Web:* www.rigidhitch.com					
Sundowner Trailers Inc 9805 S State Hwy 48	Coleman	OK	73432	580-937-4255	937-4440
TF: 800-654-3879 ■ *Web:* www.sundownertrailer.com					
Take 3 Trailers Inc 2007 Longwood Dr	Brenham	TX	77833	979-337-9568	337-9122
TF: 866-428-2533 ■ *Web:* www.take3trailers.com					
TriMas Corp 39400 Woodward Ave Suite 130	Bloomfield Hills	MI	48304	248-631-5450	631-5455
Web: www.trimascorp.com					
Unique Functional Products Corp 135 Sunshine Ln	San Marcos	CA	92069	760-744-1610	744-4709
TF: 800-854-1905 ■ *Web:* www.ufpnet.com					
Valley Automotive Inc 32501 Dequindre Rd	Madison Heights	MI	48071	248-588-6900	588-0027
TF Cust Svc: 800-344-3112					

767 TRAINING & CERTIFICATION PROGRAMS - COMPUTER & INTERNET

	City	State	Zip	Phone	Fax
DSI Inc PO Box 162652	Austin	TX	78716	512-327-6800	327-6838
Web: www.dsiinc.com					
Element K LLC 500 Canal View Blvd	Rochester	NY	14623	585-240-7500	240-7760
TF: 800-434-3466 ■ *Web:* www.elementk.com					
Global Knowledge Training LLC 9000 Regency Pkwy Suite 500	Cary	NC	27518	919-461-8600	461-8646
TF: 800-268-7737 ■ *Web:* www.globalknowledge.com					
Learning Tree International Inc 1831 Michael Faraday Dr	Reston	VA	20190	703-709-9119	337-0434*
NASDAQ: LTRE ■ **Fax Area Code:* 310 ■ *TF Cust Svc:* 800-843-8733 ■ *Web:* www.learningtree.com					
MeasureUp Inc 2325 Lakeview Pkwy Suite 175	Alpharetta	GA	30004	678-356-5000	777-0732*
**Fax Area Code:* 770 ■ *TF:* 800-649-1687 ■ *Web:* www.measureup.com					
Minact Inc 5220 Keele St	Jackson	MS	39206	601-362-1631	362-5771
Web: www.minact.com					
MindLeaders.com Inc 5500 Glendon Ct Suite 200	Dublin	OH	43016	614-781-7300	781-6510
TF: 800-223-3732 ■ *Web:* www.mindleaders.com					
New Horizons Computer Learning Centers Inc 1900 S State College Blvd Suite 450	Anaheim	CA	92806	714-940-8000	938-6002
TF: 888-222-3380 ■ *Web:* www.newhorizons.com					
New Horizons Worldwide Inc 1 W Elm St Suite 125	Conshohocken	CA	19428	484-567-3000	
Web: www.newhorizons.com					
Productivity Point International Inc 2950 Gateway Ctr Blvd	Morrisville	NC	27560	919-379-5611	379-5602
Sento Corp 420 E S Temple Suite 400	Salt Lake City	UT	84111	801-431-9200	492-2100
NASDAQ: SNTO ■ *TF:* 800-868-8448 ■ *Web:* www.sento.com					
Texas Engineering Extension Service 301 Tarrow St	College Station	TX	77840	979-458-6800	458-6910
TF: 877-833-9638 ■ *Web:* teexweb.tamu.edu					

768 TRAINING PROGRAMS - CORPORATE

	City	State	Zip	Phone	Fax
AchieveGlobal Inc 8875 Hidden River Pkwy Suite 400	Tampa	FL	33637	813-631-5500	631-5796
TF: 800-659-6090 ■ *Web:* www.achieveglobal.com					
ActionCOACH 5781 S Fort Apache Rd	Las Vegas	NV	89148	702-795-3188	795-3183
TF: 888-483-2828 ■ *Web:* www.actioncoach.com					
American Management Assn (AMA) 1601 Broadway	New York	NY	10019	212-586-8100	903-8168
TF: 800-262-9699 ■ *Web:* www.amanet.org					
American Management Assn International Keye Productivity Center Div 600 AMA Way	Saranac Lake	NY	12983	518-891-1500	891-0368
TF Cust Svc: 800-262-9699 ■ *Web:* www.amanet.org					
Avalar Network Inc 6430 Medical Ctr St # 100	Las Vegas	NV	89148	702-895-8988	895-8998
TF: 877-895-8988 ■ *Web:* www.avalar.biz					
Baker Communications Inc 10101 SW Fwy #630	Houston	TX	77074	713-627-7700	587-2051
Web: www.bakercommunications.com					
Breakthrough Learning Inc 17800 Woodland Ave	Morgan Hill	CA	95037	408-779-0701	779-5158
TF: 800-221-3637 ■ *Web:* www.blearning.com					
Canterbury Consulting Group Inc 352 Stokes Rd Suite 200	Medford	NJ	08055	609-953-0044	953-0062
TF: 800-873-2040					
Center for Creative Leadership 1 Leadership Pl PO Box 26300	Greensboro	NC	27438	336-545-2810	282-3284
Web: www.ccl.org					
Center for Professional Advancement 25 Kennedy Blvd # 400	East Brunswick	NJ	08816	732-238-1600	238-9113
Web: www.cfpa.com					

				Phone	Fax
Corpedia Corp 2020 N Central Ave Suite 1050	Phoenix	AZ	85004	602-712-9919	712-0019
TF: 877-629-8724 ■ Web: www.welcome.corpedia.com					
Creative Training Techniques International Inc 7620 W 78th St	Edina	MN	55439	952-829-1954	829-0260
TF: 800-383-9210 ■ Web: www.bobpikegroup.com					
Crestcom International Ltd 6900 E Belleview Ave Suite 300	Greenwood Village	CO	80111	303-267-8200	267-8207
TF: 888-273-7826 ■ Web: www.crestcom.com					
Dale Carnegie & Assoc Inc 290 Motor Pkwy	Hauppauge	NY	11788	800-231-5800	644-5532*
*Fax Area Code: 212 ■ TF: 800-231-5800 ■ Web: www.dale-carnegie.com					
Don Hutson Organization 516 Tennessee St Suite 219	Memphis	TN	38103	901-767-0000	767-5959
TF: 800-647-9166 ■ Web: www.donhutson.com					
Elite Business Services PO Box 9630	Rancho Santa Fe	CA	92067	800-204-3548	756-4781*
*Fax Area Code: 858 ■ TF: 800-204-3548 ■ Web: www.eliteworldwidestore.com					
Executive Enterprises Institute 2 Shaw's Cove Suite 205	New London	CT	06320	860-701-5900	250-3861*
*Fax Area Code: 800 ■ TF: 800-831-8333 ■ Web: www.eeiconferences.com					
Forum Corp 265 Franklin St 4th Fl	Boston	MA	02110	617-523-7300	371-3300
TF: 800-367-8611 ■ Web: www.forum.com					
Franklin Covey Co 2200 W PkwyBlvd	Salt Lake City	UT	84119	801-817-1776	817-6085
NYSE: FC ■ TF: 800-827-1776 ■ Web: www.franklincovey.com					
Fred Pryor Seminars 9757 Metcalf Ave	Overland Park	KS	66212	800-780-8476	967-8842*
*Fax Area Code: 913 ■ TF: 800-780-8476 ■ Web: www.pryor.com					
Frontline Group of Texas LLC 14550 Torrey Chase Blvd Suite 330	Houston	TX	77014	281-453-6000	453-8000
TF: 800-285-5512 ■ Web: www.frontline-group.com					
General Physics Corp 6095 Marshalee Dr Suite 300	Elkridge	MD	21075	410-379-3600	540-5311
TF: 800-727-6677 ■ Web: www.gpworldwide.com					
HealthStream Inc 209 10th Ave S Suite 450	Nashville	TN	37203	615-301-3100	301-3200
NASDAQ: HSTM ■ TF: 800-933-9293 ■ Web: www.healthstream.com					
Hinda Incentives Inc 2440 W 34th St	Chicago	IL	60608	773-890-5900	890-4606
TF: 800-621-4412 ■ Web: www.hinda.com					
Insight Information 214 King St W Suite 300	Toronto	ON	M5H3S6	416-777-2020	777-1292*
*Fax Area Code: 866 ■ TF: 888-777-1707 ■ Web: www.insightinfo.com					
ITC Learning Corp 1616 Anderson Rd Suite 109	McLean	VA	22102	703-286-0756	852-7174
TF: 800-638-3757 ■ Web: www.itclearning.com					
Jones Knowledge Group Inc 9697 E Mineral Ave	Centennial	CO	80112	303-792-3111	799-0966
TF: 800-350-6914 ■ Web: www.servicesknowledge.com					
Leadership Management Inc 4567 Lake Shore Dr	Waco	TX	76710	254-776-2060	772-9588
TF: 800-568-1241 ■ Web: www.lmi-usa.com					
Levinson Institute Inc 28 Main St Suite 100	Jaffrey	NH	03452	603-532-4700	532-4750
TF: 800-290-5735 ■ Web: www.levinsoninst.com					
Linkage Inc 16 New England Executive Pk Suite 205	Burlington	MA	01803	781-402-5400	402-5556
Web: www.linkageinc.com					
MSI/Canterbury Inc 200 Lanidex Plaza	Parsippany	NJ	07054	973-781-0428	781-9323
TF: 800-638-2252					
National Businesswomen's Leadership Assn PO Box 419107	Kansas City	MO	64141	913-432-7755	432-0824
TF: 800-258-7246 ■ Web: www.nationalseminarstraining.com					
National Seminars Group 6901 W 63rd St 3rd Fl	Overland Park	KS	66202	913-432-7755	432-0824
TF: 800-258-7246 ■ Web: www.nationalseminarstraining.com					
NTL Institute for Applied Behavioral Science 300 N Lee St Suite 300	Alexandria	VA	22314	703-548-8840	684-1256
TF: 800-777-5227 ■ Web: www.ntl.org					
Pacific Institute 1709 Harbor Ave SW	Seattle	WA	98126	206-628-4800	587-6007
TF: 800-426-3660 ■ Web: www.thepacificinstitute.com					
Priority Management Systems Inc 11160 Silversmith Pl	Richmond	BC	V7A5E4	604-214-7772	214-7773
Web: www.prioritymanagement.com					
Productivity Inc 4 Armstrong Rd 3rd Fl	Shelton	CT	06484	203-225-0451	225-0771
TF: 800-966-5423 ■ Web: www.productivityinc.com					
Rockhurst University Continuing Education Center Inc PO Box 419107	Kansas City	MO	64141	913-432-7755	432-0824
TF: 800-258-7246 ■ Web: www.nationalseminarstraining.com					
Sandler Sales Institute 10411 Stevenson Rd	Stevenson	MD	21153	410-653-1993	358-7858
TF: 800-638-5686 ■ Web: www.sandler.com					
Schiller Ctr 801 Duke St	Alexandria	VA	22314	703-684-4735	684-4738
Web: www.schiller.org					
SkillSoft PLC 107 Northeastern Blvd	Nashua	NH	03062	603-324-3000	
TF: 877-545-5763 ■ Web: www.skillsoft.com					
SmartPros Ltd 12 Skyline Dr	Hawthorne	NY	10532	914-345-2620	345-2603
NASDAQ: SPRO ■ Web: www.smartpros.com					
Speakeasy Inc 1180 W Peachtree St Suite 600	Atlanta	GA	30309	404-541-4800	541-4848
Web: www.speakeasyinc.com					
Toastmasters International 23182 Arroyo Vista	Rancho Santa Margarita	CA	92688	949-858-8255	858-1207
Web: www.toastmasters.org					
US Learning Inc 516 Tennessee St Suite 219	Memphis	TN	38103	901-767-5700	767-5959
TF: 800-647-9166 ■ Web: www.uslearning.com					
Wilson Learning Corp 8000 W 78th St Suite 200	Edina	MN	55439	952-944-2880	828-8835
TF: 800-328-7937 ■ Web: www.wilsonlearning.com					

769 TRAINING PROGRAMS (MISC)

SEE ALSO Children's Learning Centers p. 1604; Training & Certification Programs - Computer & Internet p. 2724; Training Programs - Corporate p. 2724

				Phone	Fax
Academy for Guided Imagery Inc 10780 Santa Monica Blvd Suite 290	Los Angeles	CA	90025	800-726-2070	727-2070
TF: 800-726-2070 ■ Web: www.acadgi.com					
American College of Orgonomy 4419 Rt 27 PO Box 490	Princeton	NJ	08542	732-821-1144	821-0174
Web: www.orgonomy.org					
Audio-Digest Foundation 1577 E Chevy Chase Dr	Glendale	CA	91206	818-240-7500	240-7379
TF: 800-423-2308 ■ Web: www.audio-digest.org					
Canter & Assoc LLC 12975 Coral Tree Pl	Los Angeles	CA	90066	310-578-4700	578-4710
TF Cust Svc: 800-733-1711 ■ Web: www.canter.net					
Ed Necco & Assoc 178 Private Rd 19423	South Point	OH	45680	866-627-7748	894-1132*
*Fax Area Code: 740 ■ TF: 877-506-3226 ■ Web: www.necco.org					
Executive Protection Institute 276 Journey's End Way PO Box 802	Berryville	VA	22611	540-554-2540	554-2558
Web: www.personalprotection.com					
Feng Shui Institute of America LLC 7547 Bruns Ct	Canal Winchester	OH	43110	614-837-8370	834-9760
Web: www.windwater.com					
Global University 1211 S Glenstone Ave	Springfield	MO	65804	417-862-9533	865-7167
TF: 800-443-1083 ■ Web: www.globaluniversity.edu					
Megatech Corp 525 Woburn St	Tewksbury	MA	01876	978-937-9600	453-9936
TF: 800-767-6342 ■ Web: www.megatechcorp.com					
Mission Essential Personnel LLC 4343 Easton Commons Suite 100	Columbus	OH	43219	614-416-2345	416-2346
TF: 888-542-3447 ■ Web: www.missionep.com					
National Tuberculosis Ctr 3180 18th St Suite 101	San Francisco	CA	94110	415-502-4600	502-4620
TF: 877-390-6682 ■ Web: www.nationaltbcenter.edu					
Outward Bound 910 Jackson St	Golden	CO	80401	845-424-4000	424-4121
TF: 800-243-8520 ■ Web: www.outwardbound.org					
Penland School of Crafts 67 Doras Trail PO Box 37	Penland	NC	28765	828-765-2359	765-7389
Web: www.penland.org					
Quilogy Services 117 S Main St	Saint Charles	MO	63301	636-947-9393	916-5448
Web: www.quilogy.com					
Sailboats Inc 250 Marina Dr	Superior	WI	54880	715-392-7131	395-6968
TF: 800-826-7010 ■ Web: www.sailboats-inc.com					
Smith & Wesson Academy 299 Page Blvd	Springfield	MA	01104	413-846-6461	736-0776
Web: www.smith-wesson.com					
Yamaha Music Education System 6600 Orangethorpe Ave	Buena Park	CA	90620	858-621-2222	
Web: www.yamaha.com/musiced/newmusiced/main.html					

770 TRANSFORMERS - POWER, DISTRIBUTION, SPECIALTY

				Phone	Fax
Active Power Inc 2128 W Breaker Ln	Austin	TX	78758	512-836-6464	836-4511
NASDAQ: ACPW ■ TF: 800-288-5081 ■ Web: www.activepower.com					
AFP Transformers Inc 206 Talmedge Rd	Edison	NJ	08817	732-248-0305	248-0542
TF: 800-843-1215 ■ Web: www.afp-transformers.com					
Bodine Co 236 S Mt Pleasant Rd	Collierville	TN	38027	901-853-7211	853-5009
TF: 800-223-5778 ■ Web: www.bodine.com					
Central Moloney Inc 2400 W 6th Ave	Pine Bluff	AR	71601	870-534-5332	536-4002
Web: www.centralmoloneyinc.com					
Controlled Power Co 1955 Stephenson Hwy Suite G	Troy	MI	48083	248-528-3700	528-0411
TF: 800-521-4792 ■ Web: www.controlledpwr.com					
Cooper Power Systems Inc 2300 Badger Dr	Waukesha	WI	53187	262-896-2400	896-2313
Web: www.cooperpower.com					
Daykin Electric Corp 34425 Schoolcraft Rd	Livonia	MI	48150	734-261-3310	261-3352
Web: www.daykin.com					
DC Group Inc 1977 W River Rd N	Minneapolis	MN	55411	612-529-9516	529-9518
TF: 800-838-7927 ■ Web: www.dc-group.com					
Delta Star Inc 270 Industrial Rd	San Carlos	CA	94070	650-508-2850	593-0658
TF: 800-892-8673 ■ Web: www.deltastar.com					
Electric Research & Mfg Co-op Inc PO Box 1228	Dyersburg	TN	38025	731-285-9121	287-4101
TF: 800-238-5587 ■ Web: www.ermco-eci.com					
Ensign Corp 201 Ensign Rd	Bellevue	IA	52031	563-872-3900	872-4575
Web: www.ensigncorp.com					
Federal Pacific PO Box 8200	Bristol	VA	24203	276-669-4084	669-1869
Web: www.federalpacific.com					
Hamilton Sundstrand Power Systems 4400 Ruffin Rd PO Box 85757	San Diego	CA	92186	858-627-6000	627-6601
Web: www.hsapps.utc.com					
Hitran Corp 362 SR- 31	Flemington	NJ	08822	908-782-5525	782-9733
Web: www.hitrancorp.com					
Howard Industries Inc 322 Pendorff Rd	Laurel	MS	39440	601-425-3151	649-8090
Web: www.howard-ind.com					
Hunterdon Transformer Co 75 Industrial Dr	Alpha	NJ	08865	908-454-2400	454-6266
Web: www.hunterdontransformer.com					
Johnson Electric Coil Co 821 Watson St	Antigo	WI	54409	715-627-4367	623-2812
TF: 800-826-9741 ■ Web: www.johnsoncoil.com					
Lamination Specialties Corp 235 N Artesian Ave	Chicago	IL	60612	312-243-2181	243-2873
Web: www.laminationspecialties.com					
MGM Transformer Co 5701 Smithway St	Commerce	CA	90040	323-726-0888	726-8224
TF: 800-423-4366 ■ Web: www.mgm-transformer.com					
MTE Corp PO Box 9013	Menomonee Falls	WI	53051	262-253-8200	253-8222
TF: 800-253-8210 ■ Web: www.mtecorp.com					
Neeltran Inc 71 Pickett District Rd	New Milford	CT	06776	860-350-5964	350-5024
Web: www.neeltran.com					
Niagara Transformer Corp 1747 Dale Rd	Buffalo	NY	14225	716-896-6500	896-8871
TF: 800-817-5652 ■ Web: www.niagaratransformer.com					
Norlake Mfg Co PO Box 215	Elyria	OH	44036	440-353-3200	353-3232
Web: www.norlakemfg.com					
Olsun Electrics Corp 10901 Commercial St	Richmond	IL	60071	815-678-2421	678-4909
TF: 800-336-5786 ■ Web: www.olsun.com					
Philips Advance 10275 W Higgins Rd	Rosemont	IL	60018	847-390-5000	423-1882*
*Fax Area Code: 888 ■ TF: 800-322-2086 ■ Web: www.advance.philips.com					
PWR LLC 6402 Deere Rd Suite 3	Syracuse	NY	13206	315-701-0210	701-0217
TF: 800-342-0878 ■ Web: www.pwrllc.com					
Quality Transformer & Electronics 963 Ames Ave	Milpitas	CA	95035	408-263-8444	263-8448
Web: www.qte.com					

Phone Fax

Raf Technologies Inc 200 Lexington Ave................Deland FL 32724 386-736-1698 736-7338
Web: www.raftech.com
RE Uptegraff Mfg Co
120 Uptegraff Dr PO Box 182........................Scottdale PA 15683 724-887-7700 887-4748
Web: www.uptegraff.com
Shape LLC 2105 Corporate Dr........................Addison IL 60101 630-620-8394 620-0784
TF: 800-367-5811 ■ *Web:* www.shapellc.com
T & R Electric Supply Co Inc PO Box 180.............Colman SD 57017 605-534-3555 534-3861
TF: 800-843-7994 ■ *Web:* www.t-r.com
Tech-Tran Corp 50 Indel Ave PO Box 232..............Rancocas NJ 08073 609-267-6750 267-6751
TF: 800-257-9420 ■ *Web:* www.tech-tran.com
Unique Lighting Systems Inc
1240 Simpson Way.............................Escondido CA 92029 760-489-1245 740-0977
TF: 800-955-4831 ■ *Web:* www.uniquelighting.com
VanTran Industries Inc 7711 Imperial Dr.................Waco TX 76712 254-772-9740 772-0016
TF: 800-433-3346 ■ *Web:* www.vantran.com
Victor Products USA PO Box 1980......... Cranberry Township PA 16066 724-776-4900 776-3855
Web: www.victorproductsusa.com
Virginia Transformer Corp 220 Glade View Dr......... Roanoke VA 24012 540-345-9892 342-7694
TF: 800-882-3944 ■ *Web:* www.vatransformer.com
Warner Power LLC 40 Depot St.......................Warner NH 03278 603-456-3111 456-3754
Web: www.warnerpower.com
Waukesha Electric Systems Inc
400 S Prairie Ave...............................Waukesha WI 53186 262-547-0121 521-0198
TF: 800-835-2732 ■ *Web:* www.waukeshaelectric.com

771 TRANSLATION SERVICES

SEE ALSO Language Schools p. 2143

Phone Fax

AltaVista Translation 701 1st Ave...................Sunnyvale CA 94089 408-349-3300 349-3301
Web: www.babelfish.altavista.com
Boston Language Institute Inc
648 Beacon St Kenmore Sq...........................Boston MA 02215 617-262-3500 262-3595
Web: www.bostonlanguage.com
Cosmopolitan Translation Bureau Inc
53 W Jackson Blvd Suite 1260.......................Chicago IL 60604 312-726-2610 427-8591
TF: 866-370-1439 ■ *Web:* www.cosmopolitantranslation.net
Kane Transport Inc
40925 403rd Ave PO Box 126......................Sauk Centre MN 56378 320-352-2762 352-6141
TF: 800-892-8557 ■ *Web:* www.kanetransport.com
Language Line Services
1 Lower Ragsdale Dr Bldg 2........................Monterey CA 93940 831-648-7541
TF: 877-886-3885 ■ *Web:* www.languageline.com
Linguistics Systems Inc 201 Broadway..............Cambridge MA 02139 617-864-3900 864-5186
TF: 800-654-5006 ■ *Web:* www.linguist.com
Lionbridge Technologies Inc
1050 Winter St Suite 2300.........................Waltham MA 02451 781-434-6000 434-6034
NASDAQ: LIOX
Master Translating Services Inc
10651 N Kendall Dr Suite 220.......................Miami FL 33176 305-279-2484 279-4016
Web: www.mastertranslating.com
OmniTranslations 41-29 41st St Suite 6A.............Sunnyside NY 11104 718-729-6115
Opies Transport Inc 21 Hwy FF PO Box 89...............Eldon MO 65026 573-392-6525 392-2284
Web: www.opiestransport.com
Professional Translating Services Inc
Douglas Rd..................................Coral Gables FL 33134 305-371-7887 381-9824
Web: www.protranslating.com
SDL International 5700 Granite Pkwy Suite 560............Plano TX 75024 214-387-8500 387-9120
Web: www.sdl.com
SimulTrans LLC 1804 N Shoreline Blvd........... Mountain View CA 94043 650-605-1300 605-1301
Web: www.simultrans.com
Spanish-American Translating
330 Eagle Ave...............................West Hempstead NY 11552 516-481-3339 481-7905
TransPerfect Translations Inc
3 Pk Ave 39th Fl................................New York NY 10016 212-689-5555 689-1059
Web: www.transperfect.com
TripleInk 60 S 6th St Suite 2800.................. Minneapolis MN 55402 612-342-9800 342-9745
TF: 800-632-1388 ■ *Web:* www.tripleink.com

772 TRANSPLANT CENTERS - BLOOD STEM CELL

Phone Fax

All Children's Hospital Bone Marrow Transplant Program
801 6th St S Dept 6630 .... Saint Petersburg FL 33701 727-767-6856 767-4803
Web: www.allkids.org
Arthur G James Cancer Hospital & Richard J Solove Research Institute
Bone Marrow Transplant Program
300 W 10th Ave Suite 114..........................Columbus OH 43210 614-293-3153 293-5919
TF: 800-293-5066 ■ *Web:* www.cancer.osu.edu
Barnes-Jewish Hospital Bone Marrow & Stem Cell Transplant Program
660 E Euclid Ave CB 8007 ....Saint Louis MO 63110 314-454-8304 454-5656
TF: 800-635-2371 ■ *Web:* www.barnesjewish.org
Baylor University Medical Center at Dallas
Blood & Marrow Transplant Services
3409 Worth St Suite 600..........................Dallas TX 75246 214-820-8764 820-7346
Web: www.baylorhealth.com/Locations/Hospitals/BUMC
Beth Israel Deaconess Medical Ctr Hematologic Malignancies/Bone Marrow Transplantation Program
330 Brookline Ave...............................Boston MA 02215 617-667-9920 667-9922
Web: www.bidmc.org
Blood & Marrow Transplant Group of Georgia (BMTGA)
5670 Peachtree Dunwoody Rd Suite 1000..............Atlanta GA 30342 404-255-1930 255-1939
Web: www.bmtga.com
Blood Donor Center at Presbyterian/St Luke's Medical Ctr
1719 E 19th Ave.................................Denver CO 80218 720-208-9678
TF: 877-268-9300 ■ *Web:* www.pslmc.com

Phone Fax

Cedars-Sinai Medical Ctr Blood & Marrow Transplant Program
8700 Beverly Blvd AC1060.........................Los Angeles CA 90048 310-423-2942 423-2320
TF: 800-265-4186 ■ *Web:* www.cedars-sinai.edu/bloodmarrow
Children's Healthcare of Atlanta at Egleston AFLAC Cancer Center & Blood Disorders Service
1405 Clifton Rd NE.................................Atlanta GA 30322 404-785-1200 785-6288
Web: www.choa.org/OurServices/Transplant/BMT
Children's Hospital & Research Center at Oakland Blood & Marrow Transplantation Program
747 52nd St.......................................Oakland CA 94609 510-428-3000 601-3916
Web: www.childrenshospitaloakland.org/t_healthcare.cfm?id=253
Children's Hospital Bone Marrow Transplant Program
LSU Health Science Ctr
200 Henry Clay Ave .... New Orleans LA 70118 504-896-9740 896-9758
Web: www.chnola.org
Children's Hospital Colorado
Anschutz Medical Campus 13123 E 16th Ave.............Aurora CO 80045 720-777-1234 777-6597
Web: www.thechildrenshospital.org
Children's Hospital of Los Angeles Research Immunology/Bone Marrow Transplant Div
4650 Sunset Blvd MS 62........................Los Angeles CA 90027 323-669-2546 906-8185
Web: www.chla.org
Children's Hospital of New York-Presbyterian
Pediatric Blood & Marrow Transplantation Program
3959 Broadway 11 Central.......................New York NY 10032 212-305-5593 305-8428
Web: www.childrensnyp.org
Children's Hospital of Orange County Blood & Donor Services
505 S Main St....................................Orange CA 92868 714-532-8339 532-8830
Web: www.choc.org
Children's Hospital of Philadelphia Stem Cell Transplant Program
3405 Civic Ctr Blvd Wood Bldg Rm 4324........... Philadelphia PA 19104 215-590-2141 590-4744
Web: www.chop.edu
Children's Hospital of Wisconsin Bone Marrow Transplant Clinic (CHW)
9000 W Wisconsin Ave PO Box 1997................Milwaukee WI 53226 414-266-2000 266-2426
TF: 877-266-8989 ■ *Web:* www.chw.org
Children's Medical Center of Dallas Center for Cancer & Blood Disorders (CMC)
1935 Medical District Dr............................. Dallas TX 75235 214-456-7000 456-6133
TF: 800-222-1222 ■ *Web:* www.childrens.com
Children's Memorial Hospital Stem Cell Transplant Program
2300 Children's Plaza PO Box 30.....................Chicago IL 60614 773-880-4562 880-3053
Web: www.childrensmemorial.org
Children's National Medical Ctr Hematology/Oncology Dept
111 Michigan Ave NW ....Washington DC 20010 202-884-2800
Web: www.childrensnational.org
Cincinnati Children's Hospital Medical Ctr Blood & Marrow Transplantation Program
3333 Burnet Ave.............................. Cincinnati OH 45229 513-636-7609
Web: www.cincinnatichildrens.org
City of Hope National Medical Ctr Hematology & Hematopoietic Cell Transplantation Div
1500 E Duarte Rd................................ Duarte CA 91010 626-256-4673 301-8888
TF: 800-535-7119 ■ *Web:* www.cityofhope.org/HCT
Cleveland Clinic Bone Marrow Transplantation Program
9500 Euclid Ave................................ Cleveland OH 44195 216-444-0261 445-7444
TF: 800-223-2273 ■ *Web:* www.clevelandclinic.org
Cook Children's Medical Ctr Bone Marrow Transplant Unit
801 7th Ave.....................................Fort Worth TX 76104 682-885-1405 885-7190
Web: www.cookchildrens.org
Dana-Farber Cancer Institute Stem Cell/Bone Marrow Transplant Program
44 Binney St Dana Bldg 1B Rm 30......................Boston MA 02115 617-632-2434 632-4139
Web: www.dana-farber.org
Duke Clinical Research & Treatment Ctr
Bone Marrow & Stem Cell Transplant Program
2400 Pratt St suite 7028 ....Durham NC 27710 919-668-1002 668-1091
Web: www.dukehealth.org
Fairfax PET Imaging Ctr
3060 Communications Pkwy Suite 120 ....Fairfax VA 22031 703-970-3200
TF: 800-358-8831 ■ *Web:* www.inova.org
Fairview University Medical Ctr
Blood & Marrow Transplant Clinic
420 Delaware St SE........................... Minneapolis MN 55455 612-273-2800 626-2664
Web: www.uofmmedicalcenter.org
Fox Chase Cancer Ctr Bone Marrow Transplant Program
7604 Central Ave
Friends Hall Physicians Bldg .... Philadelphia PA 19111 215-214-3122 214-3131
Web: www.fccc.edu
Froedtert Hospital Bone Marrow Transplant Program
9200 W Wisconsin Ave............................Milwaukee WI 53226 414-805-3666
TF: 800-272-3666 ■ *Web:* www.froedtert.com
H Lee Moffitt Cancer Center & Research Institute Blood & Marrow Transplantation Program
12902 Magnolia Dr.................................. Tampa FL 33612 888-663-3488
TF: 888-860-2778 ■ *Web:* www.moffitt.org
Hackensack University Medical Ctr Bone Marrow Transplantation Div
30 Prospect Ave................................Hackensack NJ 07601 201-996-5600
Web: www.humed.com/cancercenter/trans.shtml
Bone Marrow Transplant Program
230 N Broad St MS 451...................... Philadelphia PA 19102 215-762-7510 762-4406
Web: www.hahnemannhospital.com
Helen DeVos Children's Hospital Pediatric Hematology/Oncology Program
100 Michigan NE ....Grand Rapids MI 49503 616-391-9000 391-9430
TF: 866-989-7999 ■ *Web:* www.helendevoschildrens.org
Henry Ford Hospital Bone Marrow Transplant Program
2799 W Grand Blvd ....Detroit MI 48202 313-916-2767
Web: www.henryfordhealth.org
Hospital for Sick Children The
555 University Ave .... Toronto ON M5G1X8 416-813-6800 813-5327
Web: www.sickkids.ca/bonemarrowtransplant
Indiana Blood & Marrow Transplantation
Saint Francis Hospital 1600 Albany St
6th Tower .... Beech Grove IN 46107 317-782-7355 782-6316
TF: 800-361-0016 ■ *Web:* www.ibmtindy.com
Indiana University Cancer Center Bone Marrow & Stem Cell Transplant Team
550 N University Blvd Suite 5630.................Indianapolis IN 46202 317-948-9401 944-4243
TF: 877-814-7594 ■ *Web:* www.cancer.iu.edu/programs/bmt

	City	State	Zip	Phone	Fax
James Graham Brown Cancer Ctr					
529 S Jackson St	Louisville	KY	40202	502-562-4369	
TF: 866-530-5516 ■ *Web:* www.browncancercenter.org					
Jewish Hospital Blood & Marrow Transplant Program					
4777 E Galbraith Rd	Cincinnati	OH	45236	513-686-3000	686-5483
Web: www.jewishhospitalcincinnati.com					
Karmanos Cancer Institute Bone Marrow/Stem Cell Transplant Program					
4100 John R Rm 1308-A	Detroit	MI	48201	313-576-9096	576-8422
TF: 800-527-6266 ■ *Web:* www.karmanos.org					
Lombardi Comprehensive Cancer Center at Georgetown University Bone Marrow Transplantation Program					
3800 Reservoir Rd NW	Washington	DC	20057	202-444-7253	
Web: lombardi.georgetown.edu/clinicalcare					
Mayo Clinic Bone Marrow Transplant Program					
200 1st St SW	Rochester	MN	55905	507-284-4100	266-2855
Web: www.mayoclinic.org/bonemarrowtransplant					
MCV Hospital					
Bone Marrow Transplant Program					
1300 E Marshall St 10th Fl PO Box 980157	Richmond	VA	23298	804-828-9000	828-7825
Web: www.vcuhealth.org/programs.asp					
Medical City Hospital Transplant Ctr					
7777 Forest Ln Bldg A 12 S	Dallas	TX	75230	972-566-6547	566-3897
TF: 800-348-4318 ■ *Web:* www.medicalcityhospital.com					
Medical University of South Carolina Blood & Marrow Transplant Program					
86 Jonathan Lucas St					
3rd Fl Hollings Cancer Ctr	Charleston	SC	29425	843-792-9300	792-1407
Web: www.hcc.musc.edu/patient/multidisciplinary					
Memorial Sloan-Kettering Cancer Ctr Bone Marrow Transplant Service					
1275 York Ave	New York	NY	10065	212-639-6009	
TF: 877-836-2268 ■ *Web:* www.mskcc.org					
Miami Children's Hospital Bone Marrow Transplant Program					
3100 SW 62nd Ave	Miami	FL	33155	305-669-6466	663-8511
Web: www.mch.com					
Mount Sinai Hospital Bone Marrow Transplant Program					
19 E 98th St Suite 3-D	New York	NY	10029	212-241-6021	410-0978
Web: www.mountsinai.org					
New York Presbyterian Hospital Stem Cell Transplantation Program					
525 E 68th St Payson Rm 3	New York	NY	10021	212-746-2119	746-9853
Web: www.weillcornell.org					
North Shore-Long Island Jewish Health System					
Bone Marrow & Blood Cell Transplant Program					
300 Community Dr	Manhasset	NY	11030	516-562-8973	562-8924
Web: www.northshorelij.com					
Northwestern Memorial Hospital					
222 E Superior Rm 600	Chicago	IL	60611	312-926-5400	
Web: www.nmh.org					
OU Medical Ctr					
Bone Marrow Transplant Program					
920 SL Young Blvd WP-2040	Oklahoma City	OK	73104	405-271-6369	271-4221
Web: www.oumedcenter.com					
Penn State Milton S Hershey Medical Ctr Bone Marrow Transplantation Program					
500 University Dr	Hershey	PA	17033	717-531-1657	531-1656
Web: www.hmc.psu.edu					
Roper Cancer Ctr					
Bone Marrow Transplant Program					
316 Calhoun St	Charleston	SC	29401	843-724-2296	724-1977
Web: www.ropersaintfrancis.com/cancer					
Roswell Park Cancer Institute Blood & Marrow Transplantation Program					
Elm & Carlton Sts	Buffalo	NY	14263	716-845-3516	845-8564
TF: 800-685-6825 ■ *Web:* www.roswellpark.org					
Rush Cancer Institute Bone Marrow Transplant Ctr					
Rush University Medical Ctr					
1725 W Harrison St Suite 864	Chicago	IL	60612	312-942-3049	942-6863
Web: www.bone-marrow-transplant.org					
Saint Francis Medical Ctr Bone Marrow Transplant Program					
2228 Liliha St Suite 102-B	Honolulu	HI	96820	808-547-6154	547-6979
Web: www.stfrancishawaii.org					
Saint Joseph's Regional Medical Ctr Marrow & Stem Cell Transplant Ctr					
703 Main St	Paterson	NJ	07503	973-754-4360	
Web: www.stjosephshealth.org					
Saint Jude Children's Research Hospital Stem Cell Transplantation Div					
262 Danny Thomas Pl	Memphis	TN	38105	901-595-3300	
TF: 888-419-5833 ■ *Web:* www.stjude.org					
Saint Louis University Cancer Center Hematology & Oncology Div					
3655 Vista Ave	Saint Louis	MO	63110	314-977-4440	773-1167
TF: 866-977-4440 ■ *Web:* www.slu.edu/x24691.xml					
Scripps Green Hospital Blood & Marrow Transplant Ctr					
10666 N Torrey Pines Rd	La Jolla	CA	92037	858-554-8597	
Web: www.scripps.org/41_613.asp					
Seattle Cancer Care Alliance					
825 Eastlake Ave E PO Box 19023	Seattle	WA	98109	206-288-1024	288-1025
TF: 800-804-8824 ■ *Web:* www.seattlecca.org					
Shands Hospital at the University of Florida Blood & Bone Marrow Transplant Program					
1600 SW Archer Rd PO Box 100403	Gainesville	FL	32610	352-265-0062	265-0525
TF: 800-749-7424 ■ *Web:* www.shands.org					
Sidney Kimmel Comprehensive Cancer Center at Johns Hopkins Bone Marrow Transplant Program					
401 N Broadway Suite 1100	Baltimore	MD	21231	410-955-0432	502-1153
Web: www.hopkinsmedicine.org					
SSM Cardinal Glennon Children's Hospital Stem Cell Transplant Unit					
1465 S Grand Blvd	Saint Louis	MO	63104	314-577-5638	
Web: www.cardinalglennon.com					
Stanford University School of Medicine Blood & Marrow Transplant Program					
300 Pasteur Dr Rm H-3249 MC 5623	Stanford	CA	94305	650-723-0822	725-8950
Web: bmt.stanford.edu					
Stem Cell Transplantation Ctr					
601 Elmwood Ave PO Box 610	Rochester	NY	14642	585-275-1941	275-5590
Web: www.stronghealth.com					
Texas Children's Hospital Stem Cell & Bone Marrow Transplant Program					
6621 Fannin St MC3-3320	Houston	TX	77030	832-826-5059	
Web: www.texaschildrenshospital.org/carecenters					
Texas Transplant Institute					
7700 Floyd Curl Dr	San Antonio	TX	78229	210-575-3817	575-4113
TF: 800-298-7824 ■ *Web:* www.texastransplant.org					
Thomas Jefferson University Hospital Blood & Marrow Transplant Unit					
125 S 9th St Suite 801	Philadelphia	PA	19107	215-955-6612	935-9791
Web: www.jefferson.edu					
Trustees of the University of Pennsylvania					
Bone Marrow & Stem Cell Transplant Program					
3400 Spruce St	Philadelphia	PA	19003	215-662-4533	615-0071
Web: www.penncancer.com					
Tufts-New England Medical Ctr					
Bone Marrow Transplant Program					
800 Washington St PO Box 542	Boston	MA	02111	617-636-5000	636-2520
TF: 866-636-5001 ■ *Web:* www.tuftsmedicalcenter.org					
Tulane University Hospital & Clinic					
Allergy & Immunology Clinic					
1415 Tulane Ave 7th fl	New Orleans	LA	70112	504-988-6326	988-8860
Web: www.tulane.edu					
UCLA Bone Marrow/Stem Cell Transplant					
200 UCLA Medical Plaza	Los Angeles	CA	90095	310-206-5755	206-5511
Web: transplants.ucla.edu/body.cfm?id=30					
Bone Marrow Transplant Program					
55 Lake Ave N	Worcester	MA	01655	508-856-6255	334-7983
Web: www.umassmemorial.org					
UNC Lineberger Comprehensive Cancer Center Bone Marrow Transplant Program					
3009 Old Clinic Bldg CB 7305	Chapel Hill	NC	27599	919-966-0931	
Web: cancer.med.unc.edu					
University Hospitals of Cleveland Blood & Marrow Transplant Program					
11100 Euclid Ave	Cleveland	OH	44106	216-844-1000	
Web: www.uhhospitals.org					
University Medical Ctr Blood & Marrow Transplantation Program					
1501 N Campbell Ave PO Box 24-5176	Tucson	AZ	85724	520-694-9043	694-0230
TF: 800-831-9205 ■ *Web:* www.azumc.com					
University Medical Ctr Bone Marrow & Blood Stem Cell Transplant Program (UMC)					
602 Indiana Ave	Lubbock	TX	79415	806-743-3178	775-9981
Web: www.umchealthsystem.com					
University of California Davis Cancer Ctr					
Blood Marrow Transplant Program					
4501 X St Suite 3016	Sacramento	CA	95817	916-734-3771	734-7946
Web: www.ucdmc.ucdavis.edu					
University of California San Diego Medical Ctr Blood & Marrow Transplantation Program					
3855 Health Sciences Dr Suite 0960					
Moores UCSD Cancer Ctr	La Jolla	CA	92093	858-822-6842	822-6844
Web: health.ucsd.edu/transplant/bmt					
University of Chicago Medical Ctr Stem Cell Transplant Program					
5841 S Maryland Ave	Chicago	IL	60637	773-702-1000	
Web: www.uchospitals.edu					
University of Illinois Medical Ctr Stem Cell Transplant Unit					
1740 W Taylor St	Chicago	IL	60612	312-996-3900	996-7049
TF: 866-600-2273 ■ *Web:* uillinoismedcenter.org					
University of Iowa Hospitals & Clinics Blood & Marrow Transplantation Program					
200 Hawkins Dr C332 General Hospital	Iowa City	IA	52242	319-356-3337	353-6585
TF: 800-944-8220 ■ *Web:* www.int-med.uiowa.edu/clinical/BoneMarrow					
University of Kansas Medical Ctr					
Bone Marrow/Hematopoietic Stem Cell Transplant Program					
3901 Rainbow Blvd Rm 1417	Kansas City	KS	66160	913-588-5000	588-3996
Web: www.kumc.edu/stem-cell-101/stem-cell-research-resources.html					
University of Kentucky Chandler Medical Ctr Blood & Marrow Transplant Program					
800 Rose St Rm CC 301	Lexington	KY	40536	859-323-5768	323-8990
University of Maryland Greenebaum Cancer Center					
Univ of Maryland 22 S Greene St					
Gudelsky Bldg Rm N9E11	Baltimore	MD	21201	410-328-1299	328-1971
TF: 800-888-8823 ■ *Web:* www.umm.edu/cancer/canc_stem.html					
University of Miami Hospital & Clinics (UMHC)					
Sylvester Comprehensive Cancer Ctr					
1475 NW 12th Ave	Miami	FL	33136	305-243-1000	243-1129
TF: 800-545-2292 ■ *Web:* www.sylvester.org					
University of Michigan Cancer Center Blood & Marrow Transplantation Program					
1500 E Medical Ctr Dr B2-352 CCGC	Ann Arbor	MI	48109	734-936-8785	
Web: www.cancer.med.umich.edu					
University of Mississippi Medical Ctr Bone Marrow Transplant Program					
2500 N State St	Jackson	MS	39216	601-984-5617	984-5621
University of Nebraska Medical Ctr Bone Marrow & Stem Cell Transplantation Program (Adults)					
987400 Nebraska Medical Ctr	Omaha	NE	68198	402-559-2000	
TF: 800-922-0000 ■ *Web:* www.nebraskamed.com					
University of Texas MD Anderson Cancer Ctr The					
1515 Holcombe Blvd	Houston	TX	77030	713-792-2121	
TF: 877-632-6789 ■ *Web:* www.mdanderson.org					
University of Texas Southwestern Medical Center Dallas					
Hematopoietic Cell Transplant Program					
2201 Inwood Rd 2nd Fl	Dallas	TX	75390	214-645-4673	645-2661*
**Fax:* Hum Res ■ *Web:* www.utsouthwestern.edu					
University of Utah Hospital & Clinics Blood & Marrow Transplant Program (UUHSC)					
50 N Medical Dr	Salt Lake City	UT	84132	801-581-2121	585-5825
TF: 800-664-8268 ■ *Web:* www.healthcare.utah.edu/hospital					
Vanderbilt University Medical Ctr Stem Cell Transplant Program					
1301 22nd Ave S 2665 TVC	Nashville	TN	37232	615-936-1803	936-1812
Web: www.mc.vanderbilt.edu/transplant					
Veterans Affairs Puget Sound Medical Ctr Marrow Transplant Unit					
1660 S Columbian Way	Seattle	WA	98108	206-762-1010	
TF: 800-329-8387					
Wake Forest University Baptist Medical Ctr Comprehensive Cancer Ctr					
Medical Ctr Blvd	Winston-Salem	NC	27157	336-716-2011	716-5687
Web: www.wakehealth.edu					
West Virginia University Hospitals Blood & Marrow Transplant Program					
1 Medical Ctr Dr PO Box 9162	Morgantown	WV	26506	304-293-6859	293-2134
Web: www.hsc.wvu.edu/mbrcc/bmt					
Westchester Medical Center Advanced Imaging					
Bone Marrow/Stem Cell Program					
19 Bradhurst Ave Suite 2100	Hawthorne	NY	10532	914-493-1448	493-2428
Web: www.worldclassmedicine.com					

Western Pennsylvania Hospital Hematology/Oncology Patient Care Unit
4800 Friendship Ave Suite 2303 NT ... Pittsburgh PA 15224 412-578-4707 578-4391
TF: 866-680-0004 ■ *Web:* www.wpahs.org/wph
Winship Cancer Institute of Emory University
1365 Clifton Rd NE ... Atlanta GA 30322 404-778-4342 778-1930
TF: 888-946-7447 ■ *Web:* www.winshipcancer.emory.edu
Yale-New Haven Hospital Blood Stem Cell Transplant Unit
20 York St 8 W Pavilion ... New Haven CT 06510 203-688-7557
Web: www.ynhh.org

773 TRANSPORTATION EQUIPMENT & SUPPLIES - WHOL

A & K Railroad Materials Inc
1505 S Redwood Rd ... Salt Lake City UT 84104 801-974-5484 972-2041*
**Fax:* Sales ■ *TF Sales:* 800-453-8812 ■ *Web:* www.akrailroad.com
AAR Aircraft Turbine Ctr
1100 N Wood Dale Rd 1 AAR Pl ... Wood Dale IL 60191 630-227-2000 227-2329
TF General: 800-422-2213 ■ *Web:* www.aarcorp.com
AAR Corp 1100 N Wood Dale Rd 1 AAR Pl ... Wood Dale IL 60191 630-227-2000 227-2019
NYSE: AIR ■ *TF:* 800-422-2213 ■ *Web:* www.aarcorp.com
AAR Defense Systems & Logistics
1100 N Wood Dale Rd 1 AAR Pl ... Wood Dale IL 60191 630-227-2353 227-2929
Web: www.aarcorp.com/gov/gov_2_3.htm
AAR Distribution
1100 N Wood Dale Rd 1 AAR Pl ... Wood Dale IL 60191 630-227-2000
TF: 800-422-2213 ■ *Web:* www.aarcorp.com
Aero Hardware & Parts Co Inc
130 Business Pk Dr ... Armonk NY 10504 914-273-8550 273-8612
Web: www.aerohardwareparts.com
Aerotech World Trade Corp
11 New King St ... White Plains NY 10604 914-681-3000 428-3621
TF: 800-499-2982 ■ *Web:* www.aerotechworld.com
Africair Inc 13551 SW 132nd Ave # 1 ... Miami FL 33186 305-255-6973 255-4064
Web: www.africair.com
Aim Mro Holdings Inc
8500 Glendale Milford Rd ... Camp Dennison OH 45111 513-831-2938 831-3859
Web: www.aimmro.com
AIRCO Group 1853 S Eisenhower Ct ... Wichita KS 67209 316-945-0445 945-8014
TF: 800-835-2243 ■ *Web:* www.airco-ict.com
Aircraft Trading Center Inc
17885 SE Federal Hwy ... Tequesta FL 33469 561-747-3500 744-6000
Web: www.atcjets.com
AirLiance Materials LLC 450 Medinah Rd ... Roselle IL 60172 847-233-5800 233-5900
TF: 877-233-5800 ■ *Web:* www.airliance.com
Airline Spares America Inc (ASA)
1022 E Newport Ctr Dr ... Deerfield Beach FL 33442 954-429-8600 429-8388
Web: www.asaspares.com
Airparts Co Inc 2310 NW 55th Ct ... Fort Lauderdale FL 33309 954-739-3575 739-9514
TF: 800-392-4999 ■ *Web:* www.airpartsco.com
Alamo Aircraft Ltd
2538 SW 36th St PO Box 37343 ... San Antonio TX 78237 210-434-5577 434-1030
Web: www.alamoaircraft.com
Alexander/Ryan Marine & Safety Co of Louisiana
120 Pintail St ... Saint Rose LA 70087 504-496-0151 496-0160
TF: 800-496-0151 ■ *Web:* www.armsnola.com
Allied International Corp 7 Hill St ... Bedford Hills NY 10507 914-241-6900 241-6985
Web: www.alliedinter.com
American Equipment Co
4775 Technology way Suite 208 ... Boca Raton FL 33431 561-997-2080 997-2110
Web: www.ameco.net
American General Supplies Inc
7840 Airpark Rd ... Gaithersburg MD 20879 301-590-9200 590-3069
Web: www.agsusa.com
Argo International Corp 140 Franklin St ... New York NY 10013 212-431-1700 226-9072
TF: 877-274-6468 ■ *Web:* www.argointl.com
Arrow Trading Inc
5290 NW 20th Terr Hangar 57-101 ... Fort Lauderdale FL 33309 954-771-9366 771-8966
Web: www.arrowtrading.com
ASC Industries Inc 1227 Corporate Dr W ... Arlington TX 76006 817-640-1300 649-2685
TF: 800-733-1580 ■ *Web:* www.ascintl.com
Atlantic Track & Turnout Co
270 N Broad St ... Bloomfield NJ 07003 973-748-5885 748-4520
TF: 800-631-1274 ■ *Web:* www.atlantictrack.com
Aviation Power & Marine
3030 SW 13th Pl ... Boynton Beach FL 33426 561-732-6000 732-6562
Aviojet Corp 76 Brookside Dr ... Upper Saddle River NJ 07458 201-825-3111 825-6950
Web: www.aviojet.com
Banner Aerospace Inc
1750 Tysons Blvd Suite 1400 ... McLean VA 22102 703-478-5800 478-5767
Web: www.bannneraerospace.com
Birmingham Rail & Locomotive Co Inc
PO Box 530157 ... Birmingham AL 35253 205-424-7245 424-7436
TF: 800-241-2260 ■ *Web:* www.bhamrail.com
Centurion Investments Inc
18377 Edison Ave ... Chesterfield MO 63005 636-532-2674
Web: www.avmats.com
Chand LLC 157 Hwy 654 ... Mathews LA 70375 985-532-2512 532-2571
Web: www.chand.com
Core Inc 6590 W Rogers Cir Suites 1 & 2 ... Boca Raton FL 33487 561-241-4580 241-4582
Web: www.core-aerospace.com
DAC International Inc 6702 McNeil Dr ... Austin TX 78729 512-331-5323 331-4516
TF: 800-527-2531 ■ *Web:* www.dacint.com
Defender Industries Inc 42 Great Neck Rd ... Waterford CT 06385 860-701-3400 701-3424
TF: 800-628-8225 ■ *Web:* www.defender.com
Dodson Aviation Inc 2110 Montana Rd ... Ottawa KS 66067 785-242-4000 242-9227
TF: 800-255-0034 ■ *Web:* www.dodson.com
Donovan Marine Inc 6316 Humphreys St ... Harahan LA 70123 504-488-5731 486-3258
TF: 800-347-4464
Dreyfus-Cortney & Lowery Bros Rigging
4400 N Galvez St ... New Orleans LA 70117 504-944-3366 947-8557
TF: 800-228-7660 ■ *Web:* www.dcl-usa.com
Dutch Valley Supply Co Inc (DVS)
970 Progress Ctr Ave ... Lawrenceville GA 30043 770-513-0612 513-0716
Web: www.dutchvalley.com
East Air Corp 337 2nd St ... Hackensack NJ 07601 201-487-6060 487-5938
Web: www.eastair.com
Edmo Distributors Inc
12830 E Mirabeau Pkwy ... Spokane Valley WA 99216 509-535-8280 535-8266
TF: 800-235-3300 ■ *Web:* www.edmo.com
ERS Industries Inc 1005 Indian Church Rd ... West Seneca NY 14224 716-675-2040 675-0300
TF: 800-993-6446 ■ *Web:* www.ersindustries.com
Fatair Inc 17033 Evergreen Pl ... City of Industry CA 91745 626-839-7513 839-7523
First Aviation Services Inc
15 Riverside Ave ... Westport CT 06880 203-291-3300 291-3330
NASDAQ: FAVS ■ *Web:* www.firstaviation.com
Fisheries Supply Co 1900 N Northlake Way ... Seattle WA 98103 206-632-4462 634-4600
TF: 800-426-6930 ■ *Web:* www.fisheriessupply.com
Flight Director Inc 100 Michael Angelo Way ... Austin TX 78728 512-834-2000 833-6097
Web: www.flightdirector.com
Freundlich Supply Co Inc
2200 Arthur Kill Rd ... Staten Island NY 10309 718-356-1500 356-3661
TF: 800-221-0260 ■ *Web:* www.fresupco.com
GC Supply Inc 3587 Clover Ln ... New Castle PA 16105 724-658-1741 658-2940
TF: 800-248-4653 ■ *Web:* www.golfcarsupply.com
General Aviation Services LLC
1155 E Ensell Rd ... Lake Zurich IL 60047 847-726-5000 726-7668
TF: 800-382-3658 ■ *Web:* www.genav.com
Gulf Marine & Industrial Supplies Inc
5501 Jefferson Hwy # 116 ... New Orleans LA 70123 504-525-6252 525-4761
Web: www.gulfmarine.net
Heli-Mart Inc 3184 Airway Ave Suite E ... Costa Mesa CA 92626 714-755-2999 755-2995
TF: 800-826-6899 ■ *Web:* www.helimart.com
Helicopter Support Inc (HSI)
124 Quarry Rd PO Box 111068 ... Trumbull CT 06611 203-416-4000 416-4291
TF: 800-795-6051 ■ *Web:* www.hsius.com
IHI Inc 280 Pk Ave W Bldg 30th Fl ... New York NY 10017 212-599-8100 599-8111
Industry-Railway Suppliers Inc
811 Golf Ln ... Bensenville IL 60106 630-766-5708 766-0017
TF: 800-728-0029 ■ *Web:* www.industryrailway.com
Integrated Procurement Technologies Inc
320 Storke Rd Suite 100 ... Goleta CA 93117 805-682-0842
Web: www.iptsb.com
Intermountain Air LLC 301 N 2370 W ... Salt Lake City UT 84116 801-322-1645 521-6534
TF: 800-433-9617 ■ *Web:* www.intermountainair.com
Jerry's Marine Service
100 SW 16th St ... Fort Lauderdale FL 33315 954-525-0311 525-0361*
**Fax:* Sales ■ *TF:* 800-432-2231 ■ *Web:* www.jerrysmarine.com
Jet International Co LLC 1811 Elmdale Ave ... Glenview IL 60026 847-657-8666 657-9197
Web: www.jetinternational.com
Jet Turbine Service Inc 620 NW 35th St ... Boca Raton FL 33431 561-417-4537 417-0772
JMA Railroad Supply Co 381 S Main Pl ... Carol Stream IL 60188 630-653-9224 653-9040
TF: 800-874-0643 ■ *Web:* www.jmarail.com
Kampi Components Co Inc 88 Canal Rd ... Fairless Hills PA 19030 215-736-2000 736-9000
Web: www.kampi.com
KAPCO/VALTEC 3120 Enterprise St ... Brea CA 92821 714-223-5400 996-3490
TF: 800-825-8321 ■ *Web:* www.kapcousa.com
Kellogg Marine Supply Inc 5 Enterprise Dr ... Old Lyme CT 06371 860-434-6002 628-1304*
**Fax Area Code:* 800 ■ *TF:* 800-243-9303 ■ *Web:* www.kelloggmarine.com
Kellstrom Industries 3701 Flamingo Rd ... Miramar FL 33027 954-538-2000 538-6626
Web: www.kellstrom.com
Lewis Marine Supply Co Inc
220 SW 32nd St ... Fort Lauderdale FL 33315 954-523-4371 463-7715*
**Fax:* Sales ■ *TF Sales:* 800-327-3792 ■ *Web:* www.lewismarine.com
M & M Aerospace Hardware Inc
10000 NW 15th Terr ... Miami FL 33172 305-592-5155 507-7191
TF: 800-533-5155 ■ *Web:* www.mmaero.com
Macgregor (usa) Inc
14 Ridgedale Ave Suite 205 ... Cedar Knolls NJ 07927 973-285-7860 285-7861
Web: www.macgregor-group.com
Meridian Aerospace Group Ltd
3796 Vest Mill Rd ... Winston-Salem NC 27103 336-765-5454 765-5577
TF: 800-538-7767
National Salvage & Service Corp
6755 Old SR 37 S PO Box 300 ... Bloomington IN 47401 812-339-9000 331-8235
TF General: 800-769-8437 ■ *Web:* www.nssccorp.com
O'halloran International Inc PO Box 1804 ... Des Moines IA 50305 515-967-3300 967-0206
TF: 800-800-6503 ■ *Web:* www.ohallorans.com
Octagon Aerospace Inc 511 5th St Unit A ... San Fernando CA 91340 818-898-2200 898-2221
Web: www.octagonaero.com
Omni Jet Trading Ctr 9415 Jet Ln Hangar 3 ... Easton MD 21601 410-820-7300 820-5082
Web: www.omnijet.com
Ottosen Propeller & Accessories Inc
105 S 28th St ... Phoenix AZ 85034 602-275-8514 275-8594
TF: 800-528-7551
Pacific Meridian Group 222 Juana Ave ... San Leandro CA 94577 510-618-1600 618-1605
Web: www.melchers.com
Parker Hannifin Corp Aircraft Wheel & Brake Div
1160 Ctr Rd ... Avon OH 44011 440-937-6211 937-5409
TF: 800-272-5464
PartsBase Inc 905 Clint Moore Rd ... Boca Raton FL 33487 561-953-0700 953-0795
TF Cust Svc: 888-322-6896 ■ *Web:* www.partsbase.com
Paxton Co 1111 Ingleside Rd ... Norfolk VA 23502 757-853-6781 853-7709
TF: 800-234-7290 ■ *Web:* www.paxtonco.com
Rails Co 101 Newark Way ... Maplewood NJ 07040 973-763-4320 763-2585
TF: 800-217-2457 ■ *Web:* www.railsco.com
Relli Technology Inc 1200 S Rogers Cir ... Boca Raton FL 33487 561-886-0200 886-0201
Web: www.relli.com
Sabine Universal Products Inc PO Box 295 ... Port Arthur TX 77641 409-982-9446 982-0420
TF: 800-482-9446 ■ *Web:* www.sabineuniversalproducts.com
Satair USA Inc 3993 Trade Port Blvd Suite 100 ... Atlanta GA 30354 404-675-6333 675-6311
Web: www.satair.com

				Phone	Fax
SkyTech Inc 701 Wilson Pt Rd # 3	Baltimore	MD	21220	410-574-4144	687-2927
TF: 888-386-3596 ■ *Web:* www.skytechinc.com					
Spencer Industries Inc 19308 68th Ave S	Kent	WA	98032	253-796-1100	796-1101*
**Fax:* Sales ■ *TF:* 800-367-5646 ■ *Web:* www.spencer-ind.com					
Steiner Shipyard Inc 8640 Hemley St PO Box 742	Bayou La Batre	AL	36509	251-824-4143	824-4178
Web: www.steinershipyard.com					
Summit Aviation Supply 1008 Teaneck Rd	Teaneck	NJ	07666	201-837-3644	837-9464
Sun Aviation Inc 10010 E 87th St	Kansas City	MO	64138	816-358-4925	737-0658
Web: www.sunav.com					
Taos Industries Inc 480 Production Ave	Madison	AL	35758	256-772-7743	772-7789
Web: www.taos-inc.com					
TPS Aviation Inc 1515 Crocker Ave	Hayward	CA	94544	510-475-1010	475-8817
Tractor & Equipment Co 4001 River Dr N	Great Falls	MT	59405	406-761-7900	652-6865
TF: 800-332-2016 ■ *Web:* www.tractorandequipment.com					
Turbo Resources International Inc 5780 W Oakland St	Chandler	AZ	85226	480-961-3600	961-1775
Web: www.turboresources.com					
Unical Aviation Inc 680 S LemonAve	City of Industry	CA	91789	626-813-1901	813-1908
TF: 800-813-1901 ■ *Web:* www.unical.com					
Unirex Inc 9310 E 37th St N	Wichita	KS	67226	316-636-1228	636-5482
TF: 800-397-1257 ■ *Web:* www.unirexinc.com					
United Aerospace Corp 9800 Premier Pkwy	Miramar	FL	33025	954-364-0085	364-0089
Valley Power Systems Inc 425 S Hacienda Blvd	City of Industry	CA	91745	626-333-1243	369-7096
TF: 800-924-4265 ■ *Web:* www.valleypowersystems.com					
Van Bortel Aircraft Inc 4900 S Collins St	Arlington	TX	76018	817-468-7788	468-7886
TF: 800-759-4295 ■ *Web:* www.vanbortel.com					
Washington Chain & Supply Inc 2901 Utah Ave S PO Box 3645	Seattle	WA	98124	206-623-8500	621-9834
TF: 800-851-3429 ■ *Web:* www.wachain.com					
West Marine Inc 500 Westridge Dr	Watsonville	CA	95076	831-728-2700	728-4360
NASDAQ: WMAR ■ *TF:* 800-538-0775 ■ *Web:* www.westmarine.com					
Western Branch Diesel Inc 3504 Shipwright St	Portsmouth	VA	23703	757-673-7000	673-7190
Web: www.wbdiesel.com					
Yingling Aircraft Inc 2010 Airport Rd	Wichita	KS	67209	316-943-3246	943-2484
TF: 800-835-0083 ■ *Web:* www.yinglingaviation.com					
ZAP 501 4th St	Santa Rosa	CA	95401	707-525-8658	525-8692
TF Orders: 800-251-4555 ■ *Web:* www.zapworld.com					

774 TRAVEL AGENCIES

SEE ALSO Tour Operators p. 2720; Travel Agency Networks p. 2731

				Phone	Fax
A1SuperCruises.com 3380 Fairline Farms Rd Suite 7	West Palm Beach	FL	33414	561-204-2669	753-3141
TF: 866-878-8785 ■ *Web:* www.a1supercruises.com					
ABC Corporate Services 6400 Shafer Ct Suite 310	Rosemont	IL	60018	847-384-6868	318-1448
TF: 800-722-5179 ■ *Web:* www.abccst.com					
Abracadabra! Cruises 1735 Roswell Rd Suite 100	Marietta	GA	30062	770-509-8080	509-7229
TF: 800-474-5678 ■ *Web:* www.cruisemagic.com					
Adelman Travel Group 6980 N Port Washington Rd	Milwaukee	WI	53217	414-352-7600	352-3900
TF Cust Svc: 800-248-5562 ■ *Web:* www.adelmantravel.com					
ADTRAV Travel Management 4555 S Lake Pkwy	Birmingham	AL	35244	205-444-4800	444-4808
TF: 800-476-2952 ■ *Web:* www.adtrav.com					
AESU Travel Inc 3922 Hickory Ave	Baltimore	MD	21211	410-366-5494	366-6999
TF: 800-638-7640 ■ *Web:* www.aesu.com					
Alamo Travel Group Inc 8930 Wurzbach Rd # 100	San Antonio	TX	78240	210-593-0084	614-2448
TF: 800-692-5266 ■ *Web:* www.alamotravel.com					
Alaska Tour & Travel 9170 Jewel Lake Rd Suite 202 PO Box 221011	Anchorage	AK	99502	907-245-0200	245-0400
TF: 800-208-0200 ■ *Web:* www.alaskatravel.com					
Alaska Travel Adventures Inc 18384 Redmond Way	Redmond	WA	98052	425-497-1212	882-2479
TF: 800-323-5757 ■ *Web:* www.alaskarv.com					
Alaska Vacation Packages PO Box 622	Palmer	AK	99645	907-745-8872	745-8873
TF Cust Svc: 888-745-8872 ■ *Web:* www.alaskavacationpackages.com					
All Aboard Cruise Ctr PO Box 540685	Grand Prairie	TX	75054	972-262-4638	
TF: 866-510-8256 ■ *Web:* www.cruisingfun.com					
All Aboard Cruises Inc 11114 SW 127th Ct	Miami	FL	33186	305-385-8657	419-4873*
**Fax Area Code:* 786 ■ *TF:* 800-883-8657 ■ *Web:* www.allaboardcruises.com					
All Cruise Travel 1213 Lincoln Ave Suite 205	San Jose	CA	95125	408-295-1200	295-2254
TF: 800-227-8473 ■ *Web:* www.allcruise.com					
All-Inclusive Vacations Inc 1595 Iris St	Lakewood	CO	80215	303-980-6483	233-1597
TF: 866-980-6483 ■ *Web:* www.all-inclusivevacations.com					
All-Waves Cruise & Travel 20381 Lake Forest Dr Suite B-3	Lake Forest	CA	92630	949-829-8031	829-8394
TF: 800-449-0767					
American Express Travel Service Co 200 Vesey St American Express Tower C 3 World Financial Ctr	New York	NY	10285	212-640-2000	640-9365
Web: www134.americanexpress.com/travel					
Anchors Away Cruise Ctr 3702 Independence Pl	Rocklin	CA	95677	916-625-0722	625-0724
TF: 888-516-6306 ■ *Web:* www.mustcruise.com					
Anchors Away Cruise Outlet 3750 Caribou St PO Box 871723	Wasilla	AK	99687	907-373-3494	373-3498
TF Sales: 800-580-3494 ■ *Web:* www.1anchorsaway.com					
Andavo Travel Inc 5680 Greenwood Plaza Blvd # 400	Greenwood Village	CO	80111	303-694-3322	741-6329
TF: 800-685-0038 ■ *Web:* www.andavotravel.com					
Apple Vacations Inc 101 NW Pt Blvd	Elk Grove Village	IL	60007	847-640-1150	640-1950
TF: 800-365-2775 ■ *Web:* www.applevacations.com					
Austin Travel 265 Bethpage-Spagnoli Rd	Melville	NY	11747	516-465-1000	390-6940
TF: 800-645-7466 ■ *Web:* www.austintravel.com					
Avanti Destinations Inc 851 SW 6th St	Portland	OR	97204	503-295-1100	422-9505*
**Fax Area Code:* 800 ■ *TF:* 800-422-5053 ■ *Web:* www.avantidestinations.com					
Azumano Travel Service Inc 400 SW 4th Ave	Portland	OR	97204	503-294-2000	221-6349
TF: 800-777-2018 ■ *Web:* www.azumano.com					
Balboa Travel Management Inc 5414 Oberlin Dr Suite 300	San Diego	CA	92121	858-678-3700	678-3399
TF: 800-359-8773 ■ *Web:* www.balboa.com					
Best Travel Inc 8600 W Bryn Mawr Ave	Chicago	IL	60631	773-380-0150	693-1689
TF: 800-323-3015 ■ *Web:* www.besttravel.com					
Boeing Travel Management Co 325 JS McDonnell Blvd Bldg 303 M-S3069236	Hazelwood	MO	63042	314-551-4025	551-4098
TF: 800-243-8292 ■ *Web:* www.boeing.com					
Bon Voyage Travel 1640 E River Rd Suite 115	Tucson	AZ	85718	520-797-1110	797-2408
TF: 800-439-7963 ■ *Web:* www.bvtravel.com					
Branson Deals 152 Christie Ln	Walnut Shade	MO	65771	800-221-5692	334-8211*
**Fax Area Code:* 417 ■ *TF:* 800-221-5692 ■ *Web:* www.bdr-llc.com/bransondeals					
Brennco Travel Services Inc 6600 College Blvd Suite 130	Overland Park	KS	66211	913-660-0121	660-0160
TF: 800-955-1909 ■ *Web:* www.brennco.com					
Brownell World Travel 813 Shades Creek Pkwy Suite 100	Birmingham	AL	35209	205-802-6222	414-7167
TF: 800-999-3960 ■ *Web:* www.brownelltravel.com					
BTS Travel & Tours 323 Silvergrove Dr NW	Calgary	AB	T3B4M4	403-286-1205	547-3639
TF: 877-929-9019					
Burkhalter Travel Agency 6501 Mineral Pt Rd	Madison	WI	53705	608-833-5200	
TF: 800-556-9286 ■ *Web:* www.burkhaltertravel.com					
Carefree Vacations Inc 9710 Scranton Rd Suite 300	San Diego	CA	92121	858-450-4060	450-0628
TF: 800-800-8505 ■ *Web:* www.carefreevacations.com					
Cass Tours 109 N Maple St Suite B	Corona	CA	92880	951-371-3511	371-3530
TF: 800-593-6510 ■ *Web:* www.casstours.com					
Casto Travel Inc 900 Lafayette St Suite 105	Santa Clara	CA	95050	408-984-7000	984-7007
TF: 800-832-3445 ■ *Web:* www.casto.com					
Certified Vacations Group Inc 110 E Broward Blvd	Fort Lauderdale	FL	33301	954-522-1440	357-4604
TF: 800-233-7260					
City Escape Holidays 13470 Washington Blvd Suite 101	Marina del Rey	CA	90292	310-827-5031	827-5575
TF: 800-222-0022 ■ *Web:* www.cityescapeholidays.com					
Classic Custom Vacations 5893 Rue Ferrari	San Jose	CA	95138	408-287-4550	287-4550
TF: 800-635-1333 ■ *Web:* www.classiccustomvacations.com					
Clipper Navigation Inc 2701 Alaskan Way Pier 69	Seattle	WA	98121	206-443-2560	443-2583
Web: www.clippervacations.com					
Collette Vacations 162 Middle St	Pawtucket	RI	02860	401-727-9000	728-1380
TF: 800-340-5158 ■ *Web:* www.collettevacations.com					
Conlin Travel Inc 3270 Washtenaw Ave	Ann Arbor	MI	48104	734-677-0900	677-0901
TF: 800-426-6546 ■ *Web:* www.conlintravel.com					
Consolidated Cruises 300 Market St	Kingston	PA	18704	570-283-8480	288-3699
Corporate Travel Management Group 450 E 22nd St Suite 100	Lombard	IL	60148	630-691-9100	691-8136*
**Fax:* Mktg ■ *TF:* 800-323-3800 ■ *Web:* www.corptrav.com					
Cosmos 5301 S Federal Cir	Littleton	CO	80123	303-797-2800	798-5441
TF: 800-276-1241 ■ *Web:* www.cosmos.com					
Costamar Travel Inc 531 E Oakland Pk Blvd	Fort Lauderdale	FL	33334	954-630-0060	630-0703
TF: 800-444-7171 ■ *Web:* www.costamar.com					
Covington International Travel 4401 Dominion Blvd	Glen Allen	VA	23060	804-747-7077	273-0009
TF: 800-922-9238 ■ *Web:* www.covingtontravel.com					
Creative Leisure International 951 Transport Way	Petaluma	CA	94954	707-778-1800	778-1223
TF: 800-426-6367					
Crown Travel & Cruises 240 Newton Rd Suite 106	Raleigh	NC	27615	919-870-1986	870-1666
TF: 800-869-7447 ■ *Web:* www.crowncruise.com					
Cruise & Travel Inc 26212 Carmel St	Laguna Hills	CA	92656	949-360-8081	305-1774
TF: 888-484-3732 ■ *Web:* www.cruiseandtravel.com					
Cruise & Travel Shoppe 5809 NW 48th Ave	Coconut Creek	FL	33073	954-427-3216	
TF: 800-957-4477 ■ *Web:* www.cruiseandtravelshoppe.com					
Cruise Brokers 4802 Gunn Hwy Suite 141	Tampa	FL	33624	813-288-9597	264-5736
TF: 800-409-1919 ■ *Web:* www.cruisebrokers.com					
Cruise Concepts 34034 US Hwy 19 N	Palm Harbor	FL	34684	727-784-7245	789-5398
TF: 800-752-7963 ■ *Web:* www.cruiseconcepts.com					
Cruise Connection LLC 7932 N Oak Suite 210	Kansas City	MO	64118	816-420-8688	420-8667
TF: 800-572-0004 ■ *Web:* www.cruiseconnectionllc.com					
Cruise Connections Inc 1422 S Stratford Rd	Winston-Salem	NC	27103	336-659-9772	701-1156*
**Fax Area Code:* 215 ■ *TF:* 800-248-7447 ■ *Web:* www.cruiseconnections.com					
Cruise Holidays International Inc 3033 Campus Dr Suite 320	Plymouth	MN	55401	800-866-7245	212-5266*
**Fax Area Code:* 763 ■ *TF:* 800-866-7245 ■ *Web:* www.cruiseholidays.com					
Cruise People Inc 10191 W Sample Rd Suite 215	Coral Springs	FL	33065	954-753-0069	340-1968
TF: 800-642-2469 ■ *Web:* www.cruisepeople.com					
Cruise People Ltd 1252 Lawrence Ave E Suite 210	Don Mills	ON	M3A1C3	416-444-2410	447-2628
TF: 800-268-6523 ■ *Web:* www.thecruisepeople.ca					
Cruise Shop The 700 Pasquinelli Dr Suite C	Westmont	IL	60559	630-325-7447	321-1669
TF: 800-622-6456 ■ *Web:* www.cruise-shop.com					
Cruise Vacation Ctr 2042 Central Pk Ave	Yonkers	NY	10710	914-337-8500	337-8672
TF: 800-803-7245 ■ *Web:* www.cruisevacationcenter.com					
Cruise Vacation Inc 917 Chatterson Rd PO Box 12304	Huntsville	AL	35815	256-880-6700	880-6785
TF: 800-239-9997 ■ *Web:* www.cruisevacationinc.com					
Cruise Ventures 870 N Military Hwy Suite 200	Norfolk	VA	23510	757-461-0022	626-0536
TF: 888-461-0022 ■ *Web:* www.citravel.com					
Cruise Web Inc 8100 Corporate Dr Suite 300	Landover	MA	20785	240-487-0155	487-0154
TF: 800-377-9383 ■ *Web:* www.cruiseweb.com					

Name / Address	City	State	Zip	Phone	Fax
CruiseOne Inc 1415 NW 62nd St Suite 205 *TF:* 800-832-3592 ■ *Web:* www.cruiseone.com	Fort Lauderdale	FL	33309	954-958-3700	958-3703
Cruises by Kay 306 Shore Dr *TF:* 800-938-2602 ■ *Web:* www.cruisesbykay.com	Bremerton	WA	98310	360-782-9600	479-3025
Cruises Cruises 6606 W Mt Houston Rd *TF:* 800-245-9806 ■ *Web:* www.cruisescruises.net	Houston	TX	77091	713-681-9866	957-2076
Cruises Inc 1415 SW 62nd St *TF Cust Svc:* 800-854-0500 ■ *Web:* www.cruisesinc.com	Fort Lauderdale	FL	33309	954-958-3700	958-3703
CTS Corporate Travel Solutions 5900 Rowland Rd *Web:* www.ctsinc.com	Minnetonka	MN	55343	952-746-3500	746-3582
Delta Vacations 110 E Broward Blvd *TF:* 800-221-6666 ■ *Web:* www.deltavacations.com	Fort Lauderdale	FL	33301	800-221-6666	
Direct Travel 860 Wyckoff Ave *TF:* 800-343-8861 ■ *Web:* www.dt.com	Mahwah	NJ	07430	201-847-9000	847-2102
E Tour & Travel 3626 Quadrangle Blvd Suite 400 *TF Sales:* 866-912-9286 ■ *Web:* www.etourandtravel.com	Orlando	FL	32817	407-515-2400	658-1768
Elegant Voyages 6348 Skywalker Dr *TF:* 800-555-3534 ■ *Web:* www.elegantvoyages.com	San Jose	CA	95135	408-239-0300	239-0304
Euro Lloyd Travel Inc 1640 Hempstead Tpke *TF:* 800-334-2724 ■ *Web:* www.lcc-eurolloyd.com	East Meadow	NY	11554	516-228-4970	228-8258
Fantasy Holidays Inc 400 Jericho Tpke Suite 301 *TF:* 800-645-2555	Jericho	NY	11753	516-935-8500	932-4622
Freighter World Cruises Inc 180 S Lake Ave Suite 335 *TF:* 800-531-7774 ■ *Web:* www.freighterworld.com	Pasadena	CA	91101	626-449-3106	449-9573
Funjet Vacations 8907 N Port Washington Rd *TF:* 800-558-6654 ■ *Web:* www.funjet.com	Milwaukee	WI	53217	414-351-3553	351-1453
Future Vacations Inc 110 E Broward Blvd 11th Fl *TF:* 888-335-4657	Fort Lauderdale	FL	33301	888-335-4657	
Gant Travel Management 304 W Kirkwood Ave Suite 1 **Fax Area Code:* 812 ■ *TF Cust Svc:* 800-742-4198 ■ *Web:* www.ganttravel.com	Bloomington	IN	47404	800-742-4198	332-6263*
Gil Tours Travel Inc 1511 Walnut St Suite 200 *TF:* 800-223-3855 ■ *Web:* www.giltravel.com	Philadelphia	PA	19102	215-568-6655	568-0696
Giselle's Travel Inc 1300 Ethan Way Suite 100 *TF:* 800-782-5545 ■ *Web:* www.globaltrav.com	Sacramento	CA	95825	916-922-5500	679-3090
Global Travel 900 W Jefferson St *TF:* 800-584-8888 ■ *Web:* www.globaltrav.com	Boise	ID	83702	208-387-1000	338-6042
GOGO WorldWide Vacations 69 Spring St *TF:* 800-899-9800 ■ *Web:* www.gogowwv.com	Ramsey	NJ	07446	201-934-3500	934-3764
Golden Bear Travel Inc 16 Digital Dr *TF:* 800-551-1000	Novato	CA	94949	415-382-8900	382-9086
Golden Sports Tours 301 W Parker Rd Suite 206 *TF:* 800-966-8258 ■ *Web:* www.goldensports.com	Plano	TX	75023	972-578-1166	578-0786
Golf Packages of the Carolinas 218 Main St *TF:* 877-833-2255 ■ *Web:* www.golfvacationpackages.com	North Myrtle Beach	SC	29582	877-732-6999	
Gwin's Travel Planners Inc 212 N Kirkwood Rd *TF:* 800-325-1904 ■ *Web:* www.gwins.com	Kirkwood	MO	63122	314-822-1957	835-1107
HRG North America 16 E 34th St 3rd Fl *TF:* 800-622-6622 ■ *Web:* www.hrgworldwide.com	New York	NY	10016	212-689-9525	481-2933
InnovAsian Travel Inc 10 N Ln *TF:* 800-553-4665 ■ *Web:* www.innovasian.com	Armonk	NY	10504	914-273-6716	273-6719
International Cruise & Excursion Gallery 10030 N 25th Ave *TF:* 888-320-4234 ■ *Web:* www.icegallery.com	Phoenix	AZ	85021	602-395-1995	395-0030
Islands in the Sun Cruises & Tours 348 Thompson Creek Mall Suite 107 **Fax Area Code:* 443 ■ *TF:* 800-278-7786 ■ *Web:* www.crus-sun.com	Stevensville	MD	21666	410-827-3812	782-2371*
Japan Travel Bureau USA Inc 156 W 56th St 3rd Fl *TF:* 800-235-3523 ■ *Web:* www.jtbusa.com	New York	NY	10019	212-698-4900	586-9686
JourneyCorp 350 Madison Ave 15th Fl *TF:* 800-305-4911 ■ *Web:* www.journeycorp.com	New York	NY	10016	212-753-5511	644-8171
Kintetsu International 1290 Ave Suite 900 *Web:* www.kintetsu.com	New York	NY	10104	212-259-9600	259-9625
Lawyers' Travel Service 71 5th Ave 10th Fl *TF:* 800-431-1112 ■ *Web:* www.wtsg.com	New York	NY	10003	212-679-1166	679-4629
Liberty Travel Inc 69 Spring St *TF:* 800-899-9800 ■ *Web:* www.libertytravel.com	Ramsey	NJ	07446	201-934-3500	934-3651
Lorraine Travel BUREAU INC 377 Alhambra Cir **Fax:* Sales ■ *TF:* 800-666-8911 ■ *Web:* www.lorrainetravel.com	Coral Gables	FL	33134	305-446-4433	441-9444*
Maine Windjammer Assn 251 Jefferson St MS-06 *TF:* 800-807-9463 ■ *Web:* www.sailmainecoast.com	Waldoboro	ME	04572	800-807-9463	
Mark Travel Corp 8907 N Port Washington Rd *TF:* 800-558-3060 ■ *Web:* www.marktravel.com	Milwaukee	WI	53217	414-228-7472	351-5256
Marshall Field's Travel Service 700 Nicollet Mall *TF:* 800-316-6166	Minneapolis	MN	55402	612-375-2200	375-2200
Martz Travel 239 Old River Rd *TF:* 800-822-1727 ■ *Web:* www.martzlines.com	Wilkes-Barre	PA	18702	570-821-3860	821-3810
Maupin Travel Inc 2501 Blue Ridge Rd *TF:* 800-786-2738 ■ *Web:* www.maupintravel.com	Raleigh	NC	27607	919-821-2146	861-8340
MC & A Inc 615 Piikoi St Suite 1000 *TF:* 877-589-5500 ■ *Web:* www.mcahawaii.com	Honolulu	HI	96814	808-589-5500	589-5501
Merit Travel Group Inc 101 Peter St Suite 200 *TF:* 800-268-5940 ■ *Web:* www.merit.ca	Toronto	ON	M5V2H1	416-364-3775	364-9918
Miller Travel Services Inc 4380 W 12th St *TF:* 800-989-8747 ■ *Web:* www.millertravel.com	Erie	PA	16505	814-833-8888	838-0082
MLT Vacations 4660 W 77th St **Fax Area Code:* 651 ■ *TF:* 800-362-3520 ■ *Web:* www.worryfreevacations.com	Edina	MN	55435	952-474-2540	367-8420*
Montrose Travel 2355 Honolulu Ave *TF:* 800-766-4687 ■ *Web:* www.montrosetravel.com	Montrose	CA	91020	818-553-3210	248-7364
More Hawaii for Less Inc 1200 Quail St Suite 290 *TF:* 800-967-6687 ■ *Web:* www.hawaii4less.com	Newport Beach	CA	92660	949-724-5050	724-5046
National Discount Cruise Co 1401 N Cedar Crest Blvd Suite 56 *TF:* 800-788-8108 ■ *Web:* www.nationaldiscountcruise.com	Allentown	PA	18104	610-439-4883	439-8086
Navigant International Canada 2810 Matheson Blvd E 3rd FL *TF:* 800-668-1116 ■ *Web:* www.navigant.ca	Mississauga	ON	L4W4X7	905-629-9975	629-0361
Navigant Luxury Vacations 2810 Matheson Blvd E Suite 101 *Web:* www.navigantvacations.ca	Mississauga	ON	L4W4X7	905-206-8244	206-8286
Nippon Express Travel USA 8 California St 8th Fl *TF:* 800-654-8228 ■ *Web:* www.nipponexpresstravel.us	San Francisco	CA	94111	415-421-1822	421-1809
Northstar Cruises 80 Bloomfield Ave Suite 102 *TF:* 800-249-9360 ■ *Web:* www.northstarcruises.com	Caldwell	NJ	07006	973-228-5005	228-5014
Ocean One Cruise Outlet 3264 Marilynn St *TF:* 877-362-7770 ■ *Web:* www.oceanone.com	Lancaster	CA	93536	661-949-2873	949-3311
Omega World Travel Inc 3102 Omega Office Pk Dr Suite 100 *TF:* 800-756-6342 ■ *Web:* www.owt.net	Fairfax	VA	22031	703-359-8888	359-8887
Orvis International Travel 178 Conservation Way *TF:* 800-547-4322 ■ *Web:* www.orvis.com	Sunderland	VT	05250	802-362-8790	362-8795
Outdoor Connection Inc 424 Neosho *Web:* www.outdoor-connection.com	Burlington	KS	66839	620-364-5500	364-5563
Ovation Travel Group 71 5th Ave 11th Fl *TF:* 800-431-1112 ■ *Web:* www.ovationtravel.com	New York	NY	10003	212-679-1600	679-4629
Paradise Island Vacations 1000 S Pine Island Rd Suite 800 **Fax:* Cust Svc ■ *TF:* 800-722-7466 ■ *Web:* www.atlantis.com	Plantation	FL	33324	954-809-2000	713-2098*
Patterson TravelStore 855 Howe Ave Suite 5 *TF:* 800-283-2772 ■ *Web:* www.pattravel.com	Sacramento	CA	95825	916-929-5555	649-3633
Pleasant Holidays LLC 2404 Townsgate Rd **Fax Area Code:* 805 ■ *TF:* 800-242-9244 ■ *Web:* www.pleasantholidays.com	Westlake Village	CA	91361	818-991-3390	495-4972*
Premier Golf 4355 River Green Pkwy *TF:* 800-283-4653 ■ *Web:* www.premiergolf.com	Duluth	GA	30096	770-291-4100	291-5157
Prestige Travel & Cruises Inc 6175 Spring Mountain Rd *TF:* 800-553-0204 ■ *Web:* www.prestigecruises.com	Las Vegas	NV	89146	702-251-5552	253-6316
Pro Golf Travel 515 Madison Ave 10th Fl *TF:* 888-227-1059 ■ *Web:* www.protravelinc.com	New York	NY	10022	212-775-4550	593-4907
Professional Travel Inc 25000 Country Club Blvd Suite 170 *TF:* 800-247-0060 ■ *Web:* www.protrav.com	North Olmsted	OH	44070	440-734-8800	734-4528
Protravel International Inc 515 Madison Ave 10th Fl *TF:* 800-227-1059 ■ *Web:* www.protravelinc.com	New York	NY	10022	212-755-4550	593-4907
Qantas Vacations 300 Continental Blvd Suite 350 *TF:* 800-348-8145 ■ *Web:* www.qantasvacations.com	El Segundo	CA	90245	310-322-6359	535-1057
Regal Travel 720 Iwilei Rd Suite 101 *TF:* 800-817-9920 ■ *Web:* www.regaltravel.com	Honolulu	HI	96817	808-566-7000	566-7498
Rich Worldwide Travel Inc 500 Mamaroneck Ave *TF:* 800-431-1130 ■ *Web:* www.richtravel.com	Harrison	NY	10528	914-835-7600	835-1666
Rocky Mountain Escape PO Box 5029 *Web:* www.ecolodge.com	Hinton	AB	T7V1X3	780-865-0124	865-5029
Roeder Travel Ltd 9805 York Rd *TF:* 800-379-9887 ■ *Web:* www.roedertravel.com	Cockeysville	MD	21030	410-667-6090	
SeaEurope Holidays Inc 6801 Lake Worth Rd Suite 107 **Fax Area Code:* 561 ■ *TF:* 800-533-3755 ■ *Web:* www.seaeurope.com	Lake Worth	FL	33467	800-533-3755	491-5156*
SGH Golf Inc 9403 Kenwood Rd Suite C110 *TF:* 800-284-8884 ■ *Web:* www.sghgolf.com	Cincinnati	OH	45242	513-984-0414	984-9648
Ship N Shore 100 Sylvan Rd Suite 600 *TF Cust Svc:* 866-711-7447 ■ *Web:* www.cruisesonly.com	Woburn	MA	01801	800-892-5537	
Simply Cruises Inc 5344 Tholozan Ave *TF:* 888-367-9398 ■ *Web:* www.simplycruises.com	Saint Louis	MO	63109	314-832-8880	832-8182
Sita World Travel Inc 16250 Ventura Blvd *TF:* 800-421-5643 ■ *Web:* www.sitatours.com	Encino	CA	91436	818-990-9530	
Spartan Travel Inc 3032 E Lake Lansing Rd *TF:* 800-748-0406 ■ *Web:* www.pways.com	East Lansing	MI	48823	517-351-1080	351-8111
Sports Empire PO Box 6169 *TF:* 800-255-5258 ■ *Web:* www.sports-empire.com	Lakewood	CA	90714	562-920-2350	920-1828
Star Travel Services Inc 301 N Morton St	Bloomington	IN	47404	812-336-6811	331-6670
Sterling Cruises & Travel 8700 W Flagler St Suite 105 *TF:* 800-435-7967 ■ *Web:* www.cruisewin.com	Miami	FL	33174	305-592-2522	592-7442
Stevens Travel Management Inc 119 W 40th St 14th Fl *TF:* 800-275-7400 ■ *Web:* www.stevenstravel.com	New York	NY	10018	212-696-4300	679-5072
Stratton Travel Management 860 Wyckoff Ave *TF:* 800-223-0599 ■ *Web:* www.strattontravel.com	Mahwah	NJ	07430	201-405-1999	405-1199
Studentcity.com Inc 8 Essex Ctr Dr *TF:* 888-777-4642 ■ *Web:* www.studentcity.com	Peabody	MA	01960	978-531-3301	563-1852
Sun Holidays Inc 7208 Sand Lake Rd Suite 207 *TF:* 800-422-8000 ■ *Web:* www.sunholidaytours.com	Orlando	FL	32819	800-422-8000	
Sun Islands Hawaii Inc 2299 Kuhio Ave 1st Fl *TF:* 800-560-3338 ■ *Web:* www.sunislandshawaii.com	Honolulu	HI	96830	808-926-3888	922-6951
SunQuest Vacations 77-6435 Kuakini Hwy *TF:* 800-367-5168 ■ *Web:* www.sunquest-hawaii.com	Kailua-Kona	HI	96740	808-329-6438	329-5480
Sunsational Cruises 710 W Elliot Rd *TF:* 800-239-6252 ■ *Web:* www.sunsationalcruises.com	Tempe	AZ	85284	480-491-6248	491-6251
SunSpots International 1918 NE 181st Ave *TF:* 800-266-6115 ■ *Web:* www.sunspotsintl.com	Portland	OR	97230	503-666-3893	661-7771

	City	State	Zip	Phone	Fax
Tenenbaum's Vacation Stores Inc 300 Market St. TF: 800-545-7099 ■ Web: www.tenenbaums.com	Kingston	PA	18704	570-288-8747	283-0918
Teplis Travel 244 Perimeter Ctr Pkwy Suite 280 Web: www.teplis.com	Atlanta	GA	30346	404-843-7460	843-7490
Thomas Cook Canada 130 Merton St TF: 800-387-8438 ■ Web: www.thomascook.com	Toronto	ON	M4S1A4	416-485-1700	485-1700
TNT Vacations 2 Charlesgate W Web: www.tntvacations.com	Boston	MA	02215	617-262-9200	
Tower Travel Management 1 Tower Ln Suite 2520 TF: 800-542-9700 ■ Web: www.towertravel.com	Oakbrook Terrace	IL	60181	630-954-3000	954-3040
Tramex Travel Inc 4505 Spicewood Springs Rd Suite 200 TF: 800-527-3039 ■ Web: www.tramex.com	Austin	TX	78759	512-343-2201	343-0022
Transat AT Inc 300 Leo-Pariseau St Suite 600 TSE: TRZB ■ TF: 877-470-1011 ■ Web: www.transat.com	Montreal	QC	H2X4C2	514-987-1660	987-8035
Transat Holidays USA Inc 1211 Stirling Rd TF: 866-828-4872 ■ Web: www.transatusa.com	Dania Beach	FL	33004	954-920-0090	920-0190
Travel & Transport Inc 2120 S 72nd St *Fax: Hum Res ■ TF: 800-228-2545 ■ Web: www.tandt.com	Omaha	NE	68124	402-399-4500	398-9950*
Travel Advisors 7930 Lee Blvd TF: 800-745-6260	Leawood	KS	66206	913-649-6266	649-0179
Travel Authority Inc 702 N Shore Dr Suite 300 TF: 800-626-2717 ■ Web: www.thetravelauthority.com	Jeffersonville	IN	47130	812-206-5100	206-5400
Travel Destinations Management Group Inc 110 Painters Mill Rd Suite 36 TF: 800-635-7307 ■ Web: www.traveldest.com	Owings Mills	MD	21117	410-363-3111	363-1816
Travel focus First Class International 8111 LBJ Fwy Suite 900 TF: 800-222-9968 ■ Web: www.travelfocus.com	Dallas	tx	75251	949-829-5300	829-5333
Travel Holdings Inc 220 E Central Pkwy Suite 4000 Web: www.travelholdings.com	Altamonte Springs	FL	32701	407-667-8700	
Travel Impressions Ltd 465 Smith St TF: 800-284-0044 ■ Web: www.travimp.com	Farmingdale	NY	11735	631-845-8000	845-8095
Travel Inc 4355 River Green Pkwy *Fax: Hum Res ■ TF: 800-452-6575 ■ Web: www.travelinc.com	Duluth	GA	30096	770-291-4100	291-5232*
Travel Team Inc 2495 Main St TF: 800-633-6782 ■ Web: www.thetravelteam.com	Buffalo	NY	14214	716-862-7600	862-7650
Travel-Rite International 3000 Dundee Rd Suite 309 TF: 877-880-3033	North Brooke	IL	60062	847-412-1420	412-0438
TraveLeaders Group LLC 3033 Campus Dr Suite W320 TF: 800-335-8747 ■ Web: www.traveleaders.com	Plymouth	FL	55441	800-335-8747	
Travelennium Inc 556 Colonial Rd TF: 800-844-4924 ■ Web: www.travelennium.com	Memphis	TN	38117	901-767-0761	766-0126
Traveline Travel Agencies Inc 4074 Erie St TF: 888-700-8747 ■ Web: www.traveline.com	Willoughby	OH	44094	440-946-4040	946-3613
Travelmore 212 W Colfax Ave Web: www.travelleaders.com	South Bend	IN	46601	574-232-3061	251-3027
Travelong Inc 225 W 35th St Suite 1501 TF: 800-537-6043 ■ Web: www.travelong.com	New York	NY	10001	212-736-2166	736-6161
TravelStore Inc 11601 Wilshire Blvd TF: 800-343-9779 ■ Web: www.travelstoreusa.com	Los Angeles	CA	90025	310-575-5540	575-5541
TravelVisions 1000 Heritage Ctr Cir TF: 800-452-2256	Round Rock	TX	78664	512-238-3000	238-3001
Travizon Inc 275 Mishawum Rd 3rd Fl TF: 888-781-5200 ■ Web: www.travizon.com	Woburn	MA	01801	781-994-1200	343-6128
Tzell Travel Group 119 W 40th St 14th Fl Web: www.tzell.com	New York	NY	10018	212-944-2121	944-7100
Ultramar Travel Management International 14 E 47th St 5th Fl TF: 888-856-2929 ■ Web: www.ultramartravel.com	New York	NY	10017	212-856-5600	856-0129
United Vacations 8907 N Port Washington Rd *Fax: Cust Svc ■ TF: 800-377-1816 ■ Web: www.unitedvacations.com	Milwaukee	WI	53217	414-351-8470	351-2831*
Usa Hosts 3068 E Simset Rd Suite 9 TF: 800-634-6133 ■ Web: www.usahosts.com	Las Vegas	NV	89120	702-798-0000	798-5396
User-Friendly Group Inc 3081 S Sycamore Village Dr *Fax Area Code: 480 ■ TF: 800-842-1786 ■ Web: www.friendlycruises.com	Superstition Mountain	AZ	85118	888-842-1786	358-1498*
Valerie Wilson Travel Inc 475 Pk Ave S TF: 800-776-1116 ■ Web: www.vwti.com	New York	NY	10016	212-532-3400	779-7073
Virtuoso 505 Main St Suite 5 TF: 800-401-4274 ■ Web: www.virtuoso.com	Fort Worth	TX	76102	817-870-0300	870-1050
World Travel Bureau Inc 618 N Main St TF: 800-899-3370 ■ Web: www.wtbtvl.com	Santa Ana	CA	92701	714-835-8111	835-8124
World travel Holdings (WTH) 100 Sylvan Rd Bldg C TF: 800-278-4737 ■ Web: www.wth.com	Wilmington	MA	01887	617-424-7990	424-1943
World Travel Inc 1724 W Schuylkill Rd TF: 800-341-2014 ■ Web: www.worldtravelinc.com	Douglassville	PA	19518	610-327-9000	327-8222
Worldwide Holidays Inc 7800 SW 57th Ave # 112 TF: 800-327-9854 ■ Web: www.galapagoscruises.net	South Miami	FL	33143	305-665-0841	661-1457
Worldwide Travel & Cruise Assoc Inc 150 S University Dr Suite E TF: 800-881-8484 ■ Web: www.cruiseco.com	Plantation	FL	33324	954-452-8800	474-7629
Wright Travel Inc 2505 21st Ave S Fifth Fl TF: 800-577-0888 ■ Web: www.wrighttravel.net	Nashville	TN	37212	615-783-1111	783-1100
YMT Vacations 100 N Sepulveda Blvd Suite 1700 TF: 800-922-9000 ■ Web: www.ymtvacations.com	El Segundo	CA	90245	310-649-3820	649-2118

775 TRAVEL AGENCY NETWORKS

SEE ALSO Travel Agencies p. 2729

A Travel Agency Network Is A Consortium Of Travel Agencies In Which A Host Agency Provides Technology, Marketing, Distribution, Customer Support, And Other Services To The Network Member Agencies In Exchange For A Percentage Of The Member Agencies' Profits.

	City	State	Zip	Phone	Fax
Algonquin Travel Corp 130 Merton St TF Cust Svc: 888-599-0789 ■ Web: www.algonquintravel.com	Toronto	ON	M4S1A4	416-485-1700	482-5901
American Express Co Inc World Financial Ctr 200 Vesey St NYSE: AXP ■ TF: 800-666-1775 ■ Web: www.home.americanexpress.com	New York	NY	10285	212-640-2000	640-0128
BCD Travel USA LLC 2700 Patriot Blvd Suite 2002 Web: www.bcdtravel.us	Glenview	IL	60026	847-901-5035	901-5147
BTI Canada 370 King St W Suite 700	Toronto	ON	M5V1J9	416-593-8866	593-7158
Carlson Wagonlit Travel Inc 701 Carlson Pkwy TF: 800-335-8747 ■ Web: www.carlsonwagonlit.com	Minnetonka	MN	55305	763-212-5000	212-5458
CP Franchising LLC 3300 University Dr Suite 602 TF: 800-683-0206 ■ Web: www.cruiseplanners.com	Coral Springs	FL	33065	954-344-8060	344-4479
CruiseOne Inc 1415 NW 62nd St Suite 205 TF: 800-832-3592 ■ Web: www.cruiseone.com	Fort Lauderdale	FL	33309	954-958-3700	958-3703
CTS Cruise & Travel 5435 Scotts Valley Dr	Scotts Valley	CA	95066	831-438-8844	
Design Travel Management Group Inc (DTMGI) 2168 Lake Shore Cir TF: 800-773-7930 ■ Web: www.dtmgi.com	Arlington Heights	IL	60004	847-577-7930	577-7917
Ensemble Travel 29 W 36th St 8th Fl TF: 800-442-6871 ■ Web: www.ensembletravel.com	New York	NY	10018	212-545-7460	545-7428
eTravCo Inc 100 Oakwood Ave Suite 100	State College	PA	16803	814-238-2860	238-1204
Global Travel International 2600 Lake Lucien Dr Suite 201 TF: 800-715-4440 ■ Web: www.globaltravel.com	Maitland	FL	32751	407-660-7800	875-0711
GTM Travel Group 100 Executive Way Suite 202	Ponte Vedra	FL	32082	904-285-7100	285-4620
IT Group Inc 100 Executive Way Suite 202 TF: 888-482-4636 ■ Web: www.itgroupnetwork.com	Ponte Vedra Beach	FL	32082	904-285-9796	285-9794
MAST Vacation Partners Inc 635 Butterfield Rd Suite 150 Web: www.mvptravel.com	Oakbrook Terrace	IL	60181	630-889-9817	889-9832
Nexion 1 E Kirkwood Blvd Suite E TF: 800-747-6813 ■ Web: www.nexionnet.com	Southlake	TX	76092	408-280-6410	271-2039
RADIUS 4330 East-West Hwy Suite 1100 TF: 800-989-3059 ■ Web: www.radiustravel.com	Bethesda	MD	20814	301-718-9500	718-4290
Results Travel 701 Carlson Pkwy TF: 800-523-2200 ■ Web: www.resultstravel.com	Minnetonka	MN	55305	763-212-5000	212-2302
REZconnect Technologies Inc 560 Sylvan Ave TF: 800-669-9000	Englewood Cliffs	NJ	07632	201-567-8500	567-4405
Riverside Travel Group Inc 13343 SE Stark St Suite 200 TF: 800-772-2228 ■ Web: www.riversidetravel.com	Portland	OR	97233	503-255-2950	255-7268
Sabre Travel Network 3150 Sabre Dr Web: www.sabretravelnetwork.com/home	Southlake	TX	76092	682-605-1000	
Tix Travel & Ticket Agency Inc 201 Main St *Fax Area Code: 845 ■ TF: 800-269-6849 ■ Web: www.tixtravel.com	Nyack	NY	10960	800-269-6849	358-1266*
Travel Society Inc 600 S Cherry St Suite 100 Web: www.travelsociety.com	Denver	CO	80246	303-321-0900	321-0025
Travelex International Inc 2061 N Barrington Rd TF: 800-882-0499 ■ Web: www.excapes.com	Hoffman Estates	IL	60169	847-882-0400	882-1212
Travelsavers Inc 71 Audrey Ave Web: www.travelsavers.com	Oyster Bay	NY	11771	516-624-0500	624-0308
UNIGLOBE Travel USA LLC 18662 MacArthur Blvd Suite 100 TF: 800-863-1606 ■ Web: www.uniglobetravelusa.com	Irvine	CA	92612	949-623-9000	623-9008
Vacation.com Inc 1650 King St Suite 450 TF: 800-843-0733 ■ Web: www.vacation.com	Alexandria	VA	22314	703-535-5505	548-6815
Virtuoso 505 Main St Suite 5 TF: 800-401-4274 ■ Web: www.virtuoso.com	Fort Worth	TX	76102	817-870-0300	870-1050
Western Assn of Travel Agencies (WESTA) 5933 NE Win Sivers Dr TF: 800-288-8191	Portland	OR	97220	503-251-8170	251-8174
WorldClass Travel Network 4300 Marke Pointe Dr Suite 240 TF: 800-234-3576 ■ Web: www.worldclassnetwork.net	Bloomington	MN	55435	952-835-8636	835-2340
Worldtek Travel Inc 111 Water St TF: 800-243-1723 ■ Web: www.worldtek.com	New Haven	CT	06511	203-772-0470	865-2034

TRAVEL INFORMATION - CITY

SEE Convention & Visitors Bureaus p. 1753

776 TRAVEL SERVICES - ONLINE

SEE ALSO Hotel Reservations Services p. 2078

	City	State	Zip	Phone	Fax
11th Hour.com 1200 Lake Hearn Dr Suite 300 TF: 800-291-8968	Atlanta	GA	30319	404-256-6620	256-6679
4Deals.com 3102 Omega Office Pk Web: www.4deals.com	Fairfax	VA	22031	703-359-0200	359-8880
A & E Travel 3307 Northland Dr Suite 220 TF: 877-238-6877	Austin	TX	78731	512-244-9883	857-0077

				Phone	Fax
AirGorilla LLC 579 Orange Ave *Web:* www.airgorilla.com	Coronado	CA	92118	619-435-2147	
Away.com Inc 1001 G St NW *Web:* www.away.com	Washington	DC	20001	202-654-8000	654-8081
BedandBreakfast.com 700 Brazos St Suite B-700 *TF Sales:* 800-462-2632 ■ *Web:* www.bedandbreakfast.com	Austin	TX	78701	512-322-2700	320-0883
Car Rental Express 2817 138th St *TF:* 888-557-8188 ■ *Web:* www.carrentalexpress.com	Surrey	BC	V4P1T6	604-714-5911	731-5772
Cheap Tickets Inc 7 Sylvan Way *TF:* 888-922-8849 ■ *Web:* www.cheaptickets.com	Parsippany	NJ	07054	888-922-8849	
Cheapseats.com 11145 Tampa Ave Suite 17-B *TF:* 800-243-2773 ■ *Web:* www.cheapseats.com	Northridge	CA	91326	800-243-2773	
Cruise.com 1701 Eller Dr. *TF:* 888-333-3116 ■ *Web:* www.cruise.com	Fort Lauderdale	FL	33316	954-763-6828	
Cruises.com 100 Sylvan Rd Bldg C 2nd Fl *TF:* 800-288-6006 ■ *Web:* www.cruises.com	Wilmington	MA	01887	800-288-6006	
Elegant Small Hotels Lanier Publishing International PO Box 2240 *Web:* www.elegantsmallhotel.com	Petaluma	CA	94953	707-763-0271	763-5762
Flights.com 96 Engle St *Web:* www.flights.com	Englewood	NJ	07631	516-228-4972	228-8258
Fodors.com 1745 Broadway *TF:* 888-264-1745 ■ *Web:* www.fodors.com	New York	NY	10019	212-782-9000	940-7352
Frommer's Travel Guides 111 River St 5th Fl *Web:* www.frommers.com	Hoboken	NJ	07030	201-748-6000	748-5612
GetThere LP 3150 Sabre Dr *TF:* 800-850-3906 ■ *Web:* www.getthere.com	Southlake	TX	76092	682-605-1000	
Hidden America PO Box 4262 *Web:* www.hiddenamerica.com	River Edge	NJ	07661	201-487-1190	986-1373
Hotwire.com 655 Montgomery St # 600 *TF:* 877-468-9473 ■ *Web:* www.hotwire.com	San Francisco	CA	94111	415-343-8400	343-8401
iExplore Inc 833 W Jackson Blvd # 500 *TF:* 800-439-7567 ■ *Web:* www.iexplore.com	Chicago	IL	60607	312-492-9443	
Kayak.com 27 Ann St Suite 300 *Web:* www.kayak.com	Norwalk	CT	06854	203-899-3120	899-3125
Lanier TravelGuides Network Lanier Publishing International PO Box 2240 *Web:* www.travelguides.com	Petaluma	CA	94953	707-763-0271	763-5762
LastMinuteTravel.com Inc 220 E Central Pkwy Suite 4010 *TF:* 800-442-0568 ■ *Web:* www.lastminutetravel.com	Altamonte Springs	FL	32701	407-667-8700	667-8850
Lonely Planet Online 150 Linden St *TF:* 800-275-8555 ■ *Web:* www.lonelyplanet.com	Oakland	CA	94607	510-250-6400	893-8572
MapQuest Inc 3710 Hempland Rd PO Box 601 *Web:* www.mapquest.com	Mountville	PA	17554	717-285-8500	285-8411
Mobissimo 984 Folsom St *Web:* www.mobissimo.com	San Francisco	CA	94109	415-344-0838	348-1496
National Park Service Reservation Ctr 12501 Willowbrook Rd *Fax Area Code: 301 ■ *TF:* 800-365-2267 ■ *Web:* www.recreation.gov	Cumberland	MD	21502	800-365-2267	784-9079*
National Recreation Reservation Service (NRRS) PO Box 140 *TF:* 877-444-6777 ■ *Web:* www.recreation.gov	Ballston Spa	NY	12020	518-885-3639	
New Orleans Hospitality Cos 4220 Howard Ave *TF:* 866-899-1211 ■ *Web:* www.neworleanshc.com	New Orleans	LA	70125	866-899-1211	
OnlineCityGuide.com LLC 1940 Elm Hill Pike *TF:* 800-467-1218 ■ *Web:* www.onlinecityguide.com	Nashville	TN	37210	615-259-4500	777-5500
Orbitz LLC 200 S Wacker Dr Suite 1900 *TF:* 888-656-4546 ■ *Web:* www.orbitz.com	Chicago	IL	60606	312-894-5000	894-5001
Pamela Lanier's Bed & Breakfast Guide Lanier Publishing International PO Box 2240 *Web:* www.lanierbb.com	Petaluma	CA	94953	707-763-0271	763-5762
Pamela Lanier's Family Travel Guides Lanier Publishing International PO Box 2240 *Web:* www.familytravelguides.com	Petaluma	CA	94953	707-763-0271	763-5762
Priceline.com Inc 800 Connecticut Ave *NASDAQ: PCLN* ■ *Fax: Mktg ■ *TF:* 800-774-2354 ■ *Web:* www.priceline.com	Norwalk	CT	06854	203-299-8000	299-8955*
ReserveAmerica Holdings Inc 2480 Meadowvale Blvd Suite 120 *TF:* 800-695-4636 ■ *Web:* www.reserveamerica.com	Mississauga	ON	L5N8M6	905-286-6600	286-0371
Resorts OnLine 400 E 59th St Suite 12B *Web:* www.resortsonline.com	New York	NY	10022	212-744-6586	744-6823
Roadside America PO Box 324 *Web:* www.roadsideamerica.com	Novato	CA	94948	732-957-0080	957-0514
Spa Finder Inc 257 Pk Ave S 10th Fl *TF:* 800-255-7727 ■ *Web:* www.spafinder.com	New York	NY	10010	212-924-6800	924-7240
TravelNow.com Inc 318 Pk Central E Suite 418 *TF:* 800-568-1972 ■ *Web:* www.travelnow.com	Springfield	MO	65806	417-864-3600	864-8811
Travelzoo Inc 590 Madison Ave 37th Fl *NASDAQ: TZOO* ■ *TF:* 800-990-6397 ■ *Web:* www.travelzoo.com	New York	NY	10022	212-521-4200	521-4230
TripAdvisor LLC 464 Hillside Ave Suite 304 *Web:* www.tripadvisor.com	Needham	MA	02494	781-444-1113	444-1146
Vacation.com Inc 1650 King St Suite 450 *TF:* 800-843-0733 ■ *Web:* www.vacation.com	Alexandria	VA	22314	703-535-5505	548-6815
Yahoo! Maps 701 1st Ave *Web:* www.maps.yahoo.com	Sunnyvale	CA	94089	408-349-3300	349-3301
Yahoo! Travel 701 1st Ave *Web:* travel.yahoo.com	Sunnyvale	CA	94089	408-349-5080	349-7821

777 TRAVEL & TOURISM INFORMATION - CANADIAN

				Phone	Fax
Canadian Tourism Commission 1055 Dunsmuir St PO Box 49230 *Web:* www.fr-corporate.canada.travel	Vancouver	BC	V7X1L2	604-638-8300	
Newfoundland & Labrador Tourism PO Box 8700 *TF:* 800-563-6353 ■ *Web:* www.newfoundlandlabrador.com	Saint John's	NL	A1B4J6	709-729-2830	729-0870
Nova Scotia Dept of Tourism & Culture 1800 Argyle St PO Box 456 *TF:* 800-565-0000 ■ *Web:* www.NovaScotia.com	Halifax	NS	B3J2R5	902-425-5781	424-2668
NWT Tourism PO Box 610 *TF:* 800-661-0788 ■ *Web:* www.spectacularnwt.com	Yellowknife	NT	X1A2N5	867-873-7200	873-4059
Ontario Tourism Marketing Partnership Corp 10 Dundas St E Suite 900 *TF:* 800-668-2746 ■ *Web:* www.ontariotravel.net	Toronto	ON	M7A2A1	905-282-1721	282-7433
Prince Edward Island Tourism PO Box 2000 *TF:* 800-463-4734 ■ *Web:* www.gov.pe.ca	Charlottetown	PE	C1A7N8	902-368-4000	368-4438
Tourism New Brunswick 19 Aberdeen St PO Box 12345 *TF:* 800-561-0123 ■ *Web:* www.tourismnewbrunswick.ca	Campbellton	NB	E3N2J6	506-789-4982	789-2044
Tourism Saskatchewan 1621 Albert St *TF:* 877-237-2273 ■ *Web:* www.sasktourism.com	Regina	SK	S4P2S5	306-787-9600	787-0715
Tourism Yukon PO Box 2703 *TF:* 800-661-0494 ■ *Web:* www.travelyukon.com	Whitehorse	YT	Y1A2C6	867-667-5036	393-7005
Tourisme Quebec 1255 Peel St Suite 400 *TF:* 888-883-8801 ■ *Web:* www.tourisme.gouv.qc.ca/anglais/index.html	Montreal	QC	H3B4V4	514-873-7977	864-3838
Travel Manitoba 155 Carlton St 7th Fl *TF:* 800-665-0040 ■ *Web:* www.travelmanitoba.com	Winnipeg	MB	R3C3H8	204-927-7800	927-7828
Travel.bc.ca Online Inc 4708 Beaver Rd *TF:* 866-810-6645 ■ *Web:* www.travel.bc.ca	Victoria	BC	V9E2J7	866-810-6645	768-1899
York Region Tourism 17250 Young St 4th Fl PO Box 147 *TF:* 888-448-0000 ■ *Web:* www.yorktourism.com	Newmarket	ON	L3Y6Z1	905-883-3442	895-3482

778 TRAVEL & TOURISM INFORMATION - FOREIGN TRAVEL

SEE ALSO Embassies & Consulates - Foreign, in the US p. 1815

				Phone	Fax
Anguilla Tourist Marketing Office 246 Central Ave *TF:* 877-426-4845 ■ *Web:* www.anguilla-vacation.com	White Plains	NY	10606	914-287-2400	287-2404
Antigua & Barbuda Dept of Tourism & Trade 25 SE 2nd Ave Suite 300 *TF:* 888-268-4227 ■ *Web:* www.antigua-barbuda.org	Miami	FL	33131	305-381-6762	381-7908
Antigua & Barbuda Dept of Tourism & Trade 305 E 47th St 6th Fl *TF:* 888-268-4227 ■ *Web:* www.antigua-barbuda.org	New York	NY	10007	212-541-4117	541-4789
Argentina National Tourist Office 12 W 56th St	New York	NY	10019	212-603-0443	315-5545
Argentina National Tourist Office 1101 Brickell Ave S Tower Suite 901	Miami	FL	33131	305-577-3834	372-5167
Aruba Tourism Authority 1750 Powder Springs Rd Suite 190 *Web:* www.aruba.com	Marietta	GA	30064	404-892-7822	873-2193
Aruba Tourism Authority 1144 E State St Suite A-300 *TF:* 800-862-7822 ■ *Web:* www.aruba.com	Geneva	IL	60134	630-262-5580	262-5581
Aruba Tourism Authority 1 Financial Plaza Suite 2508 *TF:* 800-862-7822 ■ *Web:* www.aruba.com	Fort Lauderdale	FL	33394	954-767-6477	767-0432
Aruba Tourism Authority 10655 Six Pines Dr Suite 145 *TF:* 800-862-7822 ■ *Web:* www.aruba.com	The Woodlands	TX	77380	281-362-1616	362-1644
Austrian Tourist Office PO Box 1142 *Web:* www.austria.info/us	New York	NY	10108	212-944-6880	730-4568
Bahamas Tourism Office 1200 S Pine Island Rd Suite 750 *TF:* 800-224-3681 ■ *Web:* www.bahamas.com	Plantation	FL	33324	954-236-9292	236-9282
Bahamas Tourism Office 8600 W Bryn Mawr Ave Suite 580 N *Web:* www.bahamas.com	Chicago	IL	60631	773-693-1500	693-1114
Bahamas Tourism Office 11400 W Olympic Blvd Suite 204 *TF:* 800-439-6993 ■ *Web:* www.bahamas.com	Los Angeles	CA	90064	310-312-9544	445-8800
Bahamas Tourism Office 60 E 42nd St Suite 1850 *TF:* 800-823-3136 ■ *Web:* www.bahamas.com	New York	NY	10165	212-758-2777	753-6531
Barbados Tourism Authority 2121 Ponce De Leon Blvd # 1300 *TF:* 800-221-9831 ■ *Web:* www.barbados.org	Coral Gables	FL	33134	305-442-7471	774-9497
Barbados Tourism Authority 800 2nd Ave 2nd Fl *TF:* 800-221-9831 ■ *Web:* www.barbados.org	New York	NY	10017	212-986-6516	573-9850
Barbados Tourism Authority (BTA) 3440 Wilshire Blvd Suite 1215 *Web:* www.visitbarbados.org	Los Angeles	CA	90010	213-380-2198	384-2763
Belgian Tourist Office 220 E 42nd St Suite 3402 *Web:* www.visitbelgium.com	New York	NY	10017	212-758-8130	355-7675
Bermuda Dept of Tourism 675 Third Ave 20th Fl *TF:* 800-223-6106 ■ *Web:* www.gotobermuda.com	New York	NY	10017	212-818-9800	983-5289
Bonaire Government Tourist Office 80 Broad St Suite 3202 32nd Fl *TF:* 800-266-2473 ■ *Web:* www.infobonaire.com	New York	NY	10004	212-956-5912	956-5913
British Virgin Islands Tourist Board 1270 Broadway Suite 705 *TF:* 800-835-8530 ■ *Web:* www.bvitourism.com	New York	NY	10001	212-696-0400	563-2263
British Virgin Islands Tourist Board 1 W 34th St Suite 302 *TF:* 800-835-8530 ■ *Web:* www.bvitourism.com	New York	NY	10001	212-563-3117	563-2263
Caribbean Tourism Organization 80 Broad St 32nd Fl *Web:* www.doitcaribbean.com	New York	NY	10004	212-635-9530	635-9511
Cayman Islands Dept of Tourism 350 5th Ave *TF:* 877-422-9626 ■ *Web:* www.caymanislands.ky	New York	NY	10118	212-889-9009	889-9125

Organization / Address	City	State	Zip	Phone	Fax
Cayman Islands Dept of Tourism 18 W 140 Butterfield Rd Suite 920 *Web:* www.caymanislands.ky	Oakbrook Terrace	IL	60181	630-705-0650	705-1383
Cayman Islands Dept of Tourism 8300 NW 53rd St Suite 103 *Web:* www.caymanislands.ky	Miami	FL	33166	305-599-9033	599-3766
Cayman Islands Dept of Tourism 820 Gessner Rd Suite 1335 *Web:* www.caymanislands.ky	Houston	TX	77024	713-461-1317	461-7409
China National Tourist Office 370 Lexington Ave Suite 912 *TF:* 888-760-8218 ■ *Web:* www.cnto.org	New York	NY	10017	212-760-8218	760-8809
China National Tourist Office 550 N Brand Blvd Suite 910 *TF:* 800-670-2228 ■ *Web:* www.cnto.org	Glendale	CA	91203	818-545-7507	545-7506
Croatian National Tourist Office 350 5th Ave Suite 4003 *TF:* 800-829-4416 ■ *Web:* www.croatia.hr	New York	NY	10118	212-279-8672	279-8683
Curacao Tourist Board 3361 SW 3rd Ave Suite 102	Miami	FL	33145	954-370-5887	723-7949
Cyprus Tourism Organization 13 E 40th St. *Web:* www.visitcyprus.com	New York	NY	10016	212-683-5280	683-5282
Czech Center & Tourist Authority 1109 Madison Ave *Web:* www.czechcenter.com	New York	NY	10028	212-288-0830	288-0971
Danish Tourist Board 655 3rd Ave 18th Fl PO Box 4649 *Web:* www.visitdenmark.com	New York	NY	10017	212-885-9700	885-9710
Dominican Republic Tourist Board 136 E 57th St Suite 803 *TF:* 888-374-6361 ■ *Web:* www.dominicanrepublic.com	New York	NY	10022	212-588-1012	588-1015
Dominican Republic Tourist Board 848 Brickell Ave Suite 405 *Web:* www.dominicanrepublic.com	Miami	FL	33131	305-358-2899	358-4185
Egyptian Tourist Authority 45 Rockefeller Plaza # 2305 *TF:* 877-773-4978 ■ *Web:* www.egypttourism.org	New York	NY	10111	212-332-2570	956-6439
Fiji Visitors Bureau 5777 W Century Blvd Suite 220 *Web:* www.fijime.com	Los Angeles	CA	90045	310-568-1616	670-2318
Finnish Tourist Board 655 3rd Ave 18th Fl *Web:* www.gofinland.org	New York	NY	10017	212-885-9700	885-9710
French Government Tourist Office 825 3rd Ave *Web:* www.us.franceguide.com	New York	NY	10022	212-838-7800	838-7855
French Government Tourist Office 9454 Wilshire Blvd Suite 210 *Web:* www.franceguide.com	Beverly Hills	CA	90212	310-271-6665	276-2835
French Government Tourist Office 205 N Michigan Ave Suite 3770 *Web:* www.franceguide.com	Chicago	IL	60601	312-327-0290	
German National Tourist Office 122 E 42nd St 52nd Fl *Web:* www.germany.travel/en	New York	NY	10168	212-661-7176	687-4138
Greek National Tourist Organization 645 5th Ave Suite 903 *Web:* www.visitgreece.gr	New York	NY	10022	212-421-5777	826-6940
Grenada Board of Tourism PO Box 1668 *TF:* 800-927-9554 ■ *Web:* www.grenadagrenadines.com	Lake Worth	FL	33460	561-588-8176	588-7267
Guided Tours of Trois-Rivieres 1457 Rue Notre Dame *TF:* 800-313-1123 ■ *Web:* www.tourismetroisrivieres.com	Trois-Rivieres	QC	G9A4X4	819-375-1122	375-0022
Honduras Tourism Institute 299 Alhambra Cir Suite 226 *TF:* 800-410-9608 ■ *Web:* www.letsgohonduras.com	Coral Gables	FL	33134	305-461-0601	461-0602
Hong Kong Tourism Board 10940 Wilshire Blvd Suite 2050 *TF:* 800-282-4582 ■ *Web:* www.discoverhongkong.com	Los Angeles	CA	90024	310-208-4582	208-1869
Hong Kong Tourism Board 115 E 54th St 2nd Fl *Web:* www.discoverhongkong.com	New York	NY	10022	212-421-3382	421-8428
Hungarian National Tourist Office (HNTO) 447 Broadway 5th Fl *Web:* www.gotohungary.com	Manhattan	NY	10013	212-695-1221	695-0809
Icelandic Tourist Board PO Box 4649 *Web:* www.icelandtouristboard.com	Grand Central Station	NY	10163	212-885-9700	885-9710
India Tourist Office 3550 Wilshire Blvd Suite 204 *TF:* 800-422-4634 ■ *Web:* www.tourismofindia.com	Los Angeles	CA	90010	213-380-8855	380-6111
India Tourist Office 1270 Avenue of the Americas Suite 1808 *TF:* 800-953-9399 ■ *Web:* www.tourismofindia.com	New York	NY	10020	212-586-4901	582-3274
Irish Tourist Board 345 Pk Ave 17th Fl. *TF:* 800-669-9967 ■ *Web:* www.tourismireland.com	New York	NY	10154	212-418-0800	371-9052
Israel Government Tourist Office 800 2nd Ave 16th Fl *TF:* 888-774-7723 ■ *Web:* www.goisrael.com	New York	NY	10017	212-499-5660	499-5645
Israel Government Tourist Office 6380 Wilshire Blvd Suite 1700 *Web:* www.goisrael.com	Los Angeles	CA	90048	323-658-7463	658-6543
Italian Government Tourist Board 500 N Michigan Ave Suite 2240 *Web:* www.italiantourism.com	Chicago	IL	60611	312-644-0996	644-3019
Italian Government Tourist Board 12400 Wilshire Blvd Suite 550 *Web:* www.italiantourism.com	Los Angeles	CA	90025	310-820-1898	820-6357
Italian Government Tourist Board 45 Rockefeller Plaza # 1565 *Web:* www.italiantourism.com	New York	NY	10111	212-245-5618	586-9249
Jamaica Tourist Board 5201 Blue Lagoon Dr Suite 1101 *TF:* 800-233-4582 ■ *Web:* www.visitjamaica.com	Miami	FL	33126	305-665-0557	666-7239
Japan National Tourist Organization 515 S Figueroa St Suite 1470 *Web:* www.japantravelinfo.com	Los Angeles	CA	90071	213-623-1952	623-6301
Japan National Tourist Organization 11 W 42nd St *Web:* www.japantravelinfo.com	New York	NY	10110	212-757-5640	307-6754
Jordan Tourism Board 6867 Elm St Suite 102 *TF:* 877-733-5673 ■ *Web:* www.seejordan.org	McLean	VA	22101	703-243-7404	243-7406
Kenya Tourism Board c/o Custom Destination Marketing Services 6442 City West Pkwy **Fax Area Code:* 952 ■ *TF:* 866-445-3692 ■ *Web:* www.magicalkenya.com	Minneapolis	MN	55344	866-445-3692	914-6946*
Korea National Tourism Organization 2 Executive Dr Suite 750 *TF:* 800-868-7567 ■ *Web:* www.english.tour2korea.com	Fort Lee	NJ	07024	201-585-0909	585-9041
Korea National Tourism Organization 737 N Michigan Ave Suite 910 *TF:* 800-868-7567 ■ *Web:* www.english.tour2korea.com	Chicago	IL	60611	312-981-1717	981-1721
Luxembourg National Tourist Office 17 Beekman Pl *Web:* www.ont.lu	New York	NY	10022	212-935-8888	935-5896
Macau Government Tourist Office 1334 Parkview Ave Suite 300 *TF:* 866-656-2228 ■ *Web:* www.macautourism.gov.mo	Manhattan Beach	CA	90266	310-545-3464	545-4221
Martinique Promotion Bureau 444 Madison Ave 16th Fl *TF:* 800-391-4909 ■ *Web:* www.martinique.org	New York	NY	10022	800-391-4909	
Mexico Tourism Board 225 N Michigan Ave Suite 1850 *TF:* 800-446-3942 ■ *Web:* www.visitmexico.com	Chicago	IL	60601	312-228-0517	228-0515
Mexico Tourism Board 4507 San Jacinto Suite 308 *TF:* 800-446-3942 ■ *Web:* www.visitmexico.com	Houston	TX	77004	713-772-2581	772-6058
Mexico Tourism Board 5975 Sunset Dr Suite 305 *TF:* 800-446-3942 ■ *Web:* www.visitmexico.com	Miami	FL	33143	786-621-2909	621-2907
Mexico Tourism Board 152 Madison Ave Suite 1800 *TF:* 800-446-3942 ■ *Web:* www.visitmexico.com	New York	NY	10016	212-308-2110	308-9060
Monaco Government Tourist Office 565 5th Ave 23rd Fl *TF:* 800-753-9696 ■ *Web:* www.visitmonaco.com	New York	NY	10017	212-286-3330	286-9890
Moroccan National Tourist Office 7208 Sand Lake Rd Suite 204 *Web:* www.tourism-in-morocco.com	Orlando	FL	32819	407-264-0133	264-0134
Moroccan National Tourist Office 20 E 46th St Suite 1201 *Web:* www.tourism-in-morocco.com	New York	NY	10017	212-557-2520	949-8148
Netherlands Board of Tourism & Conventions 355 Pk Ave S Suite 2005 *Web:* www.holland.com	New York	NY	10003	212-370-7360	370-9507
New Zealand Tourism Board 501 Santa Monica Blvd Suite 300 *TF:* 866-639-9325 ■ *Web:* www.newzealand.com/travel	Santa Monica	CA	90401	310-395-7480	395-5453
Norwegian Tourist Board 655 3rd Ave 18th Ave *Web:* www.visitnorway.com	New York	NY	10017	212-885-9700	885-9710
Philippine Dept of Tourism 556 5th Ave 1st Fl Mezzanine *Web:* www.tourism.gov.ph	New York	NY	10036	212-575-7915	302-6759
Polish National Tourist Office 5 Marine View Plaza Suite 208 *Web:* www.poland.travel	Hoboken	NJ	07030	201-420-9910	584-9153
Portuguese Trade & Tourism Office 590 5th Ave 4th Fl **Fax Area Code:* 212 ■ *TF:* 800-767-8842 ■ *Web:* www.visitportugal.com	New York	NY	10036	646-723-0200	575-4737*
Puerto Rico Tourism Co 901 Ponce de Leon Blvd Suite 101 *TF:* 800-815-7391 ■ *Web:* www.prtourism.com	Coral Gables	FL	33134	305-445-9112	445-9450
Puerto Rico Tourism Co Paseo La Princesa PO Box 902-3960 *Web:* www.gotopuertorico.com	Old San Juan	PR	00902	787-721-2400	722-6238
Puerto Rico Tourism Co (PRTC) 666 5th Ave 15th Fl *TF:* 800-223-6530 ■ *Web:* www.prtourism.com	New York	NY	10103	212-586-6262	586-1212
Puerto Rico Tourism Co 3575 W Cahuenga Blvd Suite 620 *TF:* 800-874-1230	Los Angeles	CA	90068	323-874-5991	874-7257
Romanian National Tourist Office 355 Lexington Ave 19th Fl *Web:* www.romaniatourism.com	New York	NY	10017	212-545-8484	
Russian National Tourist Office 224 W 30th St Suite 701 *TF:* 877-221-7120 ■ *Web:* www.russia-travel.com	New York	NY	10001	646-473-2233	473-2205
Saint Barthelemy Tourist Office 444 Madison Ave 16th Fl *Web:* us.franceguide.com	New York	NY	10022	212-838-7800	838-7855
Saint Kitts Tourism Authority 414 E 75th St Suite 5 *TF:* 800-582-6208 ■ *Web:* www.stkittstourism.kn	New York	NY	10021	212-535-1234	734-6511
Saint Lucia Tourist Board 800 2nd Ave 9th Fl *TF:* 800-456-3984 ■ *Web:* www.stlucia.org	New York	NY	10017	212-867-2950	867-2795
Saint Maarten Tourist Office 675 3rd Ave Suite 1807 *TF:* 800-786-2278 ■ *Web:* www.st-maarten.com	New York	NY	10017	212-953-2084	953-2145
Saint Martin Tourist Office 675 3rd Ave Suite 1807 *TF:* 877-956-1234 ■ *Web:* www.st-martin.org	New York	NY	10017	646-227-9440	227-9448
Saint Vincent & the Grenadines Tourist Information Office 801 2nd Ave 21st Fl *TF:* 800-729-1726	New York	NY	10017	212-687-4981	949-5946
Scandinavian Tourist Boards 655 3rd Ave *Web:* www.goscandinavia.com	New York	NY	10017	212-885-9700	885-9710
Singapore Tourism Board 5670 Wilshire Blvd Suite 1550	Los Angeles	CA	90036	323-677-0808	677-0801

Name / Address	City	State	Zip	Phone	Fax
Singapore Tourism Board 1156 Avenue of Americas Suite 702	New York	NY	10036	212-302-4861	302-4801
South African Tourism Board 500 5th Ave 20th Fl Suite 2040 *TF:* 800-593-1318 ■ *Web:* www.southafrica.net	New York	NY	10110	212-730-2929	764-1980
Swedish Travel & Tourism Council Grand Central Stn PO Box 4649 *Web:* www.visitsweden.com	New York	NY	10163	212-885-9700	885-9710
Switzerland Tourism 608 5th Ave Suite 202 *TF:* 800-794-7795 ■ *Web:* www.myswitzerland.com	New York	NY	10020	212-757-5944	262-6116
Tahiti Tourism 300 Continental Blvd Suite 160 *Web:* www.tahiti-tourisme.com	El Segundo	CA	90245	310-414-8484	414-8490
Taiwan Tourism Bureau 3731 Wilshire Blvd Suite 780 *Web:* www.taiwan.net.tw	Los Angeles	CA	90010	213-389-1158	389-1094
Taiwan Visitors Assn 1 E 42nd St # 9 *Web:* www.taiwan.net.tw	New York	NY	10017	212-867-1632	867-1635
Taiwan Visitors Assn 555 Montgomery St Suite 505 *Web:* www.taiwan.net.tw	San Francisco	CA	94111	415-989-8677	989-7242
Tourism Australia 6100 Ctr Dr Suite 1150 *TF:* 800-369-6863 ■ *Web:* www.australia.com	Los Angeles	CA	90045	310-695-3200	695-3201
Tourism Authority of Thailand 611 N Larchmont Blvd 1st Fl *TF:* 800-842-4526 ■ *Web:* www.tourismthailand.org	Los Angeles	CA	90004	323-461-9814	461-9834
Tourism Authority of Thailand 61 Broadway Suite 2810 *TF:* 800-842-4526 ■ *Web:* www.tourismthailand.org	New York	NY	10006	212-432-0433	269-2588
Tourism Malaysia (MTPB) 120 E 56th St Suite 810 *TF:* 800-558-6787 ■ *Web:* www.tourismmalaysiany.com	New York	NY	10022	212-754-1113	754-1116
Tourism Malaysia 818 W 7th St Suite 970 *TF:* 800-336-6842 ■ *Web:* www.tourism.gov.my	Los Angeles	CA	90017	213-689-9702	689-1530
Tourist Office of Spain 1395 Brickell Ave Suite 1130 *Web:* www.spain.info	Miami	FL	33131	305-358-1992	358-8223
Tourist Office of Spain 845 N Michigan Ave Suite 915-E *Web:* www.spain.info	Chicago	IL	60611	312-642-1992	642-9817
Tourist Office of Spain 8383 Wilshire Blvd Suite 960 *Web:* www.spain.info	Beverly Hills	CA	90211	323-658-7188	658-1061
Tourist Office of Spain 666 5th Ave	New York	NY	10103	212-265-8822	265-8864
Turkish Tourist Office 821 UN Plaza 1st Fl *TF:* 877-367-8875 ■ *Web:* www.tourismturkey.org	New York	NY	10017	212-687-2194	599-7568
Turkish Tourist Office 5055 Wilshire Blvd Suite 850 *Web:* www.tourismturkey.org	Los Angeles	CA	90036	323-937-8066	937-1271
Turks & Caicos Islands Tourism Office 60 E 42nd St Suite 2817 *TF:* 800-241-0824 ■ *Web:* www.turksandcaicostourism.com	New York	NY	10165	646-375-8830	375-8835
US Virgin Islands Dept of Tourism 444 N Capitol St NW Suite 305 *TF:* 800-372-8784 ■ *Web:* www.visitusvi.com	Washington	DC	20001	202-624-3590	624-3594
US Virgin Islands Dept of Tourism 2655 S LeJeune Rd Suite 907 *TF:* 800-372-8784 ■ *Web:* www.usvitourism.vi	Coral Gables	FL	33134	305-442-7200	445-9044
US Virgin Islands Dept of Tourism PO Box 6400 *TF:* 800-372-8784 ■ *Web:* www.visitusvi.com	Saint Thomas	VI	00804	340-774-8784	774-4390
US Virgin Islands Dept of Tourism 245 Peachtree Ctr Ave Suite MB-05 *Web:* www.visitusvi.com	Atlanta	GA	30303	404-688-0906	525-1102
US Virgin Islands Dept of Tourism 500 N Michigan Ave Suite 2030 **Fax Area Code:* 312 ■ *TF:* 888-656-8784 ■ *Web:* www.visitusvi.com	Chicago	IL	60611	888-656-8784	670-8788*
US Virgin Islands Dept of Tourism 3460 Wilshire Blvd Suite 412 *Web:* www.visitusvi.com	Los Angeles	CA	90010	213-739-0138	739-2005
US Virgin Islands Dept of Tourism 1270 Avenue of the Americas Suite 2108 *Web:* www.visitusvi.com	New York	NY	10020	212-332-2222	332-2223
VisitBritain 551 5th Ave Suite 701 *TF:* 800-462-2748 ■ *Web:* www.visitbritain.com	New York	NY	10176	212-986-2266	986-1188

779 TREE SERVICES

SEE ALSO Landscape Design & Related Services p. 2143

Name / Address	City	State	Zip	Phone	Fax
Asplundh Tree Expert Co 708 Blair Mill Rd *TF:* 800-248-8733 ■ *Web:* www.asplundh.com	Willow Grove	PA	19090	215-784-4200	784-4405
Asplundh Tree Services 708 Blair Mill Rd *TF:* 800-248-8733	Willow Grove	PA	19090	215-784-4200	784-4493
Care of Trees Inc 2371 Foster Ave *Web:* www.thecareoftrees.com	Wheeling	IL	60090	847-394-4220	394-3376
Davey Tree Expert Co 1500 N Mantua St **Fax:* Hum Res ■ *TF:* 800-445-8733 ■ *Web:* www.davey.com	Kent	OH	44240	330-673-9511	673-1037*
FA Bartlett Tree Expert Co 1290 E Main St *TF:* 877-227-8538 ■ *Web:* www.bartlett.com	Stamford	CT	06902	203-323-1131	323-1129
Lewis Tree Service Inc 300 Lucius Gordon Dr *TF:* 800-333-1593 ■ *Web:* www.lewistree.com	West Henrietta	NY	14586	585-436-3208	235-5864
Nelson Tree Service Inc 3300 Office Pk Dr Suite 205 *TF:* 800-522-4311 ■ *Web:* www.nelsontree.com	Dayton	OH	45439	937-294-1313	294-8673
Shade Tree Service Co Inc 520 S Hwy Dr *Web:* www.stsco.net	Fenton	MO	63026	636-343-1212	343-5660
Townsend Corp The 101 S Main St PO Box 128 *TF:* 800-428-8128 ■ *Web:* www.thetownsendcorp.com	Parker City	IN	47368	765-468-3007	468-3131
Trees Inc 650 N Sam Houston Pkwy E Suite 209 *TF:* 800-260-0728 ■ *Web:* www.treesinc.com	Houston	TX	77060	281-447-1327	447-5045
West Tree Service Inc 6300 Forbing Rd *TF:* 800-779-2967 ■ *Web:* www.westtree.com	Little Rock	AR	72209	501-568-5111	562-9378
Wright Tree Service Inc PO Box 1718 *TF:* 800-882-1216 ■ *Web:* www.wrighttree.com	Des Moines	IA	50306	515-277-6291	274-3852

780 TROPHIES, PLAQUES, AWARDS

Name / Address	City	State	Zip	Phone	Fax
Architectural Bronze Aluminum Corp 655 Deerfield Rd Suite 100 *TF:* 800-339-6581 ■ *Web:* www.architecturalbronze.com	Deerfield	IL	60015	847-266-7300	266-7301
Au Sable Woodworking Co PO Box 108 *TF:* 800-248-9261	Frederic	MI	49733	989-348-7086	348-5246
Award Products Inc 4830 N Front St *Web:* www.amprostrophy.com	Philadelphia	PA	19120	215-324-0414	324-0417
Bruce Fox Inc 1909 McDonald Ln *TF:* 800-289-3699 ■ *Web:* www.brucefox.com	New Albany	IN	47150	812-945-3511	945-0275
Champion Awards Inc 3649 Winplace Rd *TF:* 800-242-6781 ■ *Web:* www.champion-awards.com	Memphis	TN	38118	901-365-4830	365-2796
Classic Medallics Inc 520 S Fulton Ave *TF:* 800-221-1348 ■ *Web:* www.classic-medallics.com	Mount Vernon	NY	10550	914-530-6259	530-6258
Crown Trophy 9 Skyline Dr **Fax Area Code:* 914 ■ *TF:* 800-583-8228 ■ *Web:* www.crowntrophy.com	Hawthorne	NY	10532	800-583-8228	347-0211*
F & H Ribbon Co Inc PO Box 1338 **Fax Area Code:* 800 ■ *TF:* 800-877-5775 ■ *Web:* www.fhribbon.com	Hurst	TX	76053	817-283-5891	344-3010*
Jostens Inc 3601 Minnesota Ave Suite 400 **Fax:* Hum Res ■ *TF:* 800-235-4774 ■ *Web:* www.jostens.com	Minneapolis	MN	55435	952-830-3300	830-3309*
Metallic Arts Inc 914 N Lake Rd *TF:* 800-541-3200 ■ *Web:* www.metallicarts.com	Spokane	WA	99212	509-489-7173	483-1759
Neff Athletic Lettering Co 645 Pine St PO Box 218 **Fax Area Code:* 800 ■ *TF Cust Svc:* 800-232-6333 ■ *Web:* www.neffco.com	Greenville	OH	45331	937-548-3194	544-9030*
Plastic Dress-Up Co 11077 Rush St *TF:* 800-800-7711 ■ *Web:* www.pdu.com	South El Monte	CA	91733	626-442-7711	442-1814
Regalia Mfg Co PO Box 4448 *TF:* 800-798-7471 ■ *Web:* www.regaliamfg.com	Rock Island	IL	61204	309-788-7471	788-0788
RS Owens & Co 5535 N Lynch Ave *TF:* 800-282-6200 ■ *Web:* www.rsowens.com	Chicago	IL	60630	773-282-6000	545-4501
Trophyland USA Inc 7001 W 20th Ave **Fax Area Code:* 305 ■ *TF:* 800-327-5820 ■ *Web:* www.trophyland.com	Hialeah	FL	33014	800-327-5820	823-4836*
Tuff-Weld Wood Specialties 7569 Woodman Pl *TF Cust Svc:* 800-223-2955	Van Nuys	CA	91405	818-988-0991	782-6697
US Bronze Sign Co 811 2nd Ave *TF:* 800-872-5155 ■ *Web:* www.usbronze.com	New Hyde Park	NY	11040	516-352-5155	352-1761
Western Badge & Trophy Co 831 Monterae Pass Rd *TF:* 800-367-4332 ■ *Web:* www.westernbadge.com	Los Angeles	CA	91754	323-735-1201	735-8571
Wilson Trophy Co 1724 Frienza Ave *TF:* 800-325-4911 ■ *Web:* www.wilsontrophy.com	Sacramento	CA	95815	916-927-9733	927-9955

TRUCK BODIES

781 TRUCK RENTAL & LEASING

Name / Address	City	State	Zip	Phone	Fax
Brody Transportation Co Inc 621 S Bentalou St	Baltimore	MD	21223	410-947-5800	947-5858
Carco National Lease Inc 2905 N 32nd St *TF:* 800-643-2596	Fort Smith	AR	72904	479-441-3200	441-3212
DeCarolis Truck Rental Inc 333 Colfax St *TF:* 800-666-1169 ■ *Web:* www.decarolis.com	Rochester	NY	14606	585-254-1169	458-4072
Enterprise Holdings Inc 600 Corporate Pk Dr *Web:* www.enterpriseholdings.com	St. Louis	MO	63105	314-512-1000	512-4706
GE Trailer Fleet Services 530 E Swedesford Rd *TF Cust Svc:* 800-333-2030 ■ *Web:* www.trailerservices.com	Wayne	PA	19087	484-254-0100	
Idealease Inc 430 N Rand Rd *Web:* www.idealease.com	North Barrington	IL	60010	847-304-6000	304-0076
Interstate NationaLease 2700 Palmyra Rd	Albany	GA	31702	229-883-7250	888-9251
Kris Way Truck Leasing Inc 43 Hemco Rd Suite 1 *Web:* www.kris-way.com	South Portland	ME	04106	207-799-8593	799-8657
Lily Transportation Corp 145 Rosemary St *Web:* www.lily.com	Needham	MA	02494	781-449-8811	449-7128
Mendon Leasing Corp 362 Kingsland Ave *Web:* www.mendonleasing.com	Brooklyn	NY	11222	718-391-5300	349-2514
MHC Kenworth 1524 N Corrington Ave *TF:* 888-259-4826 ■ *Web:* www.mhctruck.com	Kansas City	MO	64120	816-483-7035	483-4391
National Semi Trailer Corp 2300 E Landstreet Rd *Web:* www.nationalsemi.com	Orlando	FL	32824	407-351-8686	351-2304
National Truck Leasing System 1 S 450 Summit Ave Suite 300 *TF:* 800-729-6857 ■ *Web:* www.ntls.com	Oakbrook Terrace	IL	60181	630-953-8878	953-0040
PACCAR Leasing Corp 777 106th Ave NE *TF:* 800-426-1420 ■ *Web:* www.paclease.com	Bellevue	WA	98004	425-468-7877	468-8211
Penske Truck Leasing Co LP Rt 10 Green Hills PO Box 563 **Fax:* Acctg ■ *TF:* 800-222-0277 ■ *Web:* www.pensketruckleasing.com	Reading	PA	19603	610-775-6000	775-5064*
Rapid Ways Truck Leasing Inc 3900 Great Midwest Dr *TF:* 800-962-7322 ■ *Web:* www.rapidwaysleasing.com	Kansas City	MO	64161	816-455-7262	459-3221
Rush Enterprises Inc 555 IH 35 S Suite 500 *NASDAQ: RUSHA* ■ *TF:* 800-973-7874 ■ *Web:* www.rushenterprises.com	New Braunfels	TX	78130	830-626-5200	626-5310
Ryder System Inc 11690 NW 105th St *NYSE: R* ■ *TF:* 800-327-3399 ■ *Web:* www.ryder.com	Miami	FL	33178	305-500-3726	500-4599
Salem Leasing Corp PO Box 24788 *TF:* 800-877-2536 ■ *Web:* www.salemleasing.com	Winston-Salem	NC	27114	336-768-6800	760-9644
Stan Koch & Sons Trucking Inc 4200 Dahlberg Dr	Minneapolis	MN	55422	763-302-5400	302-5800

				Phone	Fax
Web: www.kochcompanies.com					
Star Leasing Co 4080 Business Pk Dr	Columbus	OH	43204	614-278-9999	340-3137
TF: 888-771-1004 ■ *Web:* www.starleasing.com					
Star Truck Rentals Inc 3940 Eastern Ave SE	Grand Rapids	MI	49508	616-243-7033	243-7498
TF: 800-748-0468 ■ *Web:* www.starlease.com					
U-Haul International Inc 2727 N Central Ave	Phoenix	AZ	85004	800-528-0361	263-6772*
**Fax Area Code:* 602 ■ *TF:* 800-528-0361 ■ *Web:* www.uhaul.com					

782 TRUCK TRAILERS

SEE ALSO Motor Vehicles - Commercial & Special Purpose p. 2260

				Phone	Fax
4-Star Trailers Inc 10000 NW 10th St	Oklahoma City	OK	73127	405-324-7827	324-8423
TF: 800-848-3095 ■ *Web:* www.4startrailers.com					
American Carrier Equipment Corp 2285 E Date Ave	Fresno	CA	93706	559-442-1500	442-3618
TF: 800-344-2174 ■ *Web:* www.trailer1.com					
Arkansas Trailer Mfg Co 3200 S Elm St	Little Rock	AR	72204	501-666-5417	666-1787
TF: 800-666-5417					
Austin-Westran LLC 602 E Blackhawk Dr PO Box 921	Byron	IL	61010	815-234-2811	234-3009
Web: www.austinwestran.com					
Barrett Trailers Inc 1831 Hardcastle Blvd	Purcell	OK	73080	405-527-5050	527-3206
TF: 888-405-4050 ■ *Web:* www.barrett-trailers.com					
Beall Corp 8801 N Vancouver Ave	Portland	OR	97217	503-735-2110	735-2601
Web: www.beallcorp.com					
Brenner Tank LLC 450 Arlington Ave	Fond du Lac	WI	54935	920-922-5020	922-3303
TF: 800-558-9750 ■ *Web:* www.brennertank.com					
Bri-Mar Mfg LLC 1080 S Main St	Chambersburg	PA	17201	717-263-6116	263-6479
TF: 800-732-5845 ■ *Web:* www.bri-mar.com					
Circle J Trailers 312 Simplot Blvd	Caldwell	ID	83605	208-459-0842	459-0106
TF: 800-247-2535 ■ *Web:* www.circlejtrailers.com					
Clement Industries Inc PO Box 914	Minden	LA	71058	318-377-2776	377-2776
TF Cust Svc: 800-562-5948 ■ *Web:* www.clementind.com					
CM Trailers Inc 200 County Rd PO Box 680	Madill	OK	73446	580-795-5536	795-7263
TF: 888-268-7577 ■ *Web:* www.cmtrailers.com					
Cottrell Inc 2125 Candler Rd	Gainesville	GA	30507	770-532-7251	535-2831
TF Sales: 800-827-0132 ■ *Web:* www.cottrelltrailers.com					
Dakota Mfg Co Inc 1909 S Rowley St	Mitchell	SD	57301	605-996-5571	996-5572
TF: 800-232-5682					
Delavan Industries 199 Lein Rd	West Seneca	NY	14224	716-677-4080	677-4085
TF Sales: 888-508-0700 ■ *Web:* www.delavan.net					
Dexter Chassis Group 501 Miller Dr	White Pigeon	MI	49099	269-483-7681	483-9089
TF: 800-669-7681 ■ *Web:* www.dexterchassisgroup.com					
Doonan Trailer Corp PO Box 1988	Great Bend	KS	67530	620-792-6222	792-3308
Web: www.doonan.com					
Eager Beaver 14893 Hwy 27	Lake Wales	FL	33853	863-638-1421	638-3705
TF Sales: 800-257-8163 ■ *Web:* www.eagerbeavertrailers.com					
East Mfg Corp 1871 State Rt 44 PO Box 277	Randolph	OH	44265	330-325-9921	325-7851
TF: 888-405-3278 ■ *Web:* www.eastmfg.com					
Everlite Inc 607 Fisher Rd	Longview	TX	75604	903-297-3444	295-1474*
**Fax:* Sales ■ *TF:* 800-600-3867					
Featherlite Trailers Hwy 63 & 9 PO Box 320	Cresco	IA	52136	563-547-6000	547-6100
TF: 800-800-1230 ■ *Web:* www.fthr.com					
Florig Equipment Inc 904 W Ridge Pike	Conshohocken	PA	19428	610-825-0900	825-0909
Web: www.florig.com					
Fontaine Trailer Co 430 Letson Rd PO Box 619	Haleyville	AL	35565	205-486-5251	486-7291
TF: 800-821-6535 ■ *Web:* www.fontainetrailer.com					
General Trailer Parts LLC 1420 S B St	Springfield	OR	97477	541-746-8218	726-4707
TF: 800-452-9532 ■ *Web:* www.generaltrailerparts.com					
Great Dane Trailers Inc 602 E Lathrop Ave	Savannah	GA	31415	912-644-2100	644-2166
Web: www.greatdanetrailers.com					
Heil Trailer International 5741 Cornelison Rd Bldg A	Chattanooga	TN	37411	423-499-1300	855-6389*
**Fax:* Sales ■ *TF:* 800-400-6913 ■ *Web:* www.heiltrailer.com					
Hesse Inc 6700 St John Ave	Kansas City	MO	64123	816-483-7808	241-9010
TF: 800-821-5562 ■ *Web:* www.grouphesse.com					
Hudson Bros Trailer Mfg Inc 1508 Hwy 218 W	Indian Trail	NC	28079	704-753-4393	753-2011
Web: www.hudsontrailers.com					
J & L's Cargo Express Inc 405 Kesco Dr	Bristol	IN	46507	574-848-7441	848-1407
Web: www.cargoexpress.com					
K-Dee Supply Inc 621 E Lake St	Lake Mills	WI	53551	920-648-8202	648-8138
TF: 800-221-6417					
Kalyn/Siebert LP 1505 W Main St PO Box 1078	Gatesville	TX	76528	254-865-7235	865-7234
Kentucky Trailer 7201 Logistics Dr	Louisville	KY	40258	502-637-2551	636-3675
TF: 888-598-7245 ■ *Web:* www.kytrailer.com					
Kentucky Trailer Technologies 1240 N Pontiac Trial	Walled Lake	MI	48390	248-960-9700	960-7775
TF: 800-521-9700 ■ *Web:* www.kytrailers.com					
Kiefer Built Inc 305 E 1st St	Kanawha	IA	50447	641-762-3201	762-3425
TF: 888-254-3337 ■ *Web:* www.kieferbuiltinc.com					
Lakes Enterprises Inc 1300 38th Ave W	Spencer	IA	51301	712-262-2992	262-1022
TF: 888-274-6010 ■ *Web:* www.maurermfg.com					
LBT Inc 11502 "I" St	Omaha	NE	68137	402-333-4900	333-0685
Ledwell & Son Enterprises 3300 Waco St	Texarkana	TX	75501	903-838-6531	831-2719*
**Fax:* Sales ■ *Web:* www.ledwell.com					
Liberty Industries Inc 162 E Cemetery Rd	Fillmore	IN	46128	765-246-4031	
Web: www.liberty-industries.com					

				Phone	Fax
Loadcraft Industries Inc 3811 N Bridge St PO Box 1429	Brady	TX	76825	325-597-2911	597-0781
Web: www.hri-rig.com					
Lufkin Industries Inc 601 S Raguet St	Lufkin	TX	75902	936-634-2211	637-5474
NASDAQ: LUFK ■ *Web:* www.lufkin.com					
Mac Trailer Mfg Inc 14599 Commerce St NE	Alliance	OH	44601	330-823-9900	823-0232
TF: 800-795-8454 ■ *Web:* www.mactrailer.com					
Magic Tilt Trailers Inc 2161 Lions Club Rd	Clearwater	FL	33764	727-535-5561	539-8472
TF: 800-998-8458 ■ *Web:* www.boattrailers.com					
MCT Industries Inc 7451 Pan American Fwy NE	Albuquerque	NM	87109	505-345-8651	345-8659
Web: www.mct-ind.com					
Merritt Equipment Co 9339 Hwy 85	Henderson	CO	80640	303-289-2286	288-6127
TF: 800-634-3036 ■ *Web:* www.merrittequipment.com					
Mickey Truck Bodies Inc 1305 Trinity Ave PO Box 2044	High Point	NC	27261	336-882-6806	882-6856
TF: 800-334-9061 ■ *Web:* www.mickeybody.com					
Midwest Systems 5911 Hall St	St. Louis	MO	63147	314-389-6280	389-9443
Web: www.mwsystems.com					
Nu Van Technology Inc 2155 Hwy 1187 PO Box 759	Mansfield	TX	76063	817-477-1734	473-3942*
**Fax:* Orders ■ *TF:* 800-487-1734 ■ *Web:* www.nuvan.com					
Pace American Inc 11550 Harter Dr	Middlebury	IN	46540	574-825-7223	825-7393
TF: 800-247-5767 ■ *Web:* www.paceamerican.com					
Parco-Hesse Corp 1060 Andre-Line St	Granby	QC	J2J1J9	450-378-4696	469-0341
TF: 800-363-5975 ■ *Web:* www.grouphesse.com					
Performance Co The 1263 US Hwy 59 N	Cleveland	TX	77327	281-593-8888	593-8918
Web: www.performancetruck.com					
Pines Trailer Corp 2555 S Blue Island Ave	Chicago	IL	60608	773-254-5533	254-7610
Polar Service Centers 7600 E Sam Houston Pkwy N	Houston	TX	77049	281-459-6400	459-5382
TF: 800-955-8558 ■ *Web:* www.polartank.com					
Polar Tank Trailer Inc 400 S Main St	Holdingford	MN	56340	320-746-2255	746-2937
TF: 800-826-6589 ■ *Web:* www.polartank.com					
Redneck Trailer Supplies 2100 N W By-Pass	Springfield	MO	65803	417-864-5210	864-7764
TF: 877-973-3632 ■ *Web:* www.redneck-trailer.com					
Road Systems Inc 2001 S Benton St	Searcy	AR	72143	501-279-0991	279-2644
Web: www.cnf.com/road_systems.asp					
Rogers Bros Corp 100 Orchard St	Albion	PA	16401	814-756-4121	756-4830
TF: 800-441-9880 ■ *Web:* www.rogerstrailers.com					
Schwend Inc 28945 Johnston Rd	Dade City	FL	33523	352-588-2220	588-2221
TF: 800-243-7757 ■ *Web:* www.schwendinc.com					
Steco Mfg PO Box 3127	Enid	OK	73702	580-237-7433	242-1635
TF: 800-627-8326 ■ *Web:* www.stecotrailers.com					
Stoughton Trailers LLC 416 S Academy St	Stoughton	WI	53589	608-873-2500	873-2575
Web: www.stoughton-trailers.com					
Summit Trailer Sales Inc 1 Summit Plaza	Summit Station	PA	17979	570-754-3511	754-7025
TF: 800-437-3729 ■ *Web:* www.summittrailer.com					
Timpte Inc 1827 Industrial Dr	David City	NE	68632	402-367-3056	367-4340
TF: 888-256-4884 ■ *Web:* www.timpte.com					
Towmaster Inc 61381 US Hwy 12	Litchfield	MN	55355	320-693-7900	693-7921
TF: 800-462-4517					
Trail King Industries Inc 147 Industrial Pk Rd	Brookville	PA	15825	814-849-2342	849-5063
TF: 800-545-1549 ■ *Web:* www.trailking.com					
Trailiner Corp PO Box 5270	Springfield	MO	65801	417-866-7258	866-4398
TF: 800-428-5500 ■ *Web:* www.trailiner.com					
Trailstar Mfg Corp 20700 Harrisburg-Westville Rd	Alliance	OH	44601	330-821-9900	821-6941
TF: 800-235-5635 ■ *Web:* www.trailstar-trailers.com					
Travis Body & Trailer Inc 13955 Furman Rd FM 529	Houston	TX	77041	713-466-5888	466-3238
TF: 800-535-4372 ■ *Web:* www.travistrailers.com					
Trinity Trailer Mfg Inc 8200 S Eisenman Rd	Boise	ID	83716	208-336-3666	336-3741
TF: 800-235-6577 ■ *Web:* www.trinitytrailer.com					
Truck Equipment Service Co 800 Oak St	Lincoln	NE	68521	402-476-3225	476-3726
TF: 800-869-0363 ■ *Web:* www.cornhusker800.com					
Utility Tool & Trailer Co 151 E 16th St	Clintonville	WI	54929	715-823-3167	823-5274
Web: www.utilitytoolandtrailer.com					
Utility Trailer Mfg Co 17295 E Railroad St	City of Industry	CA	91748	626-965-1541	965-2790
Web: www.utilitytrailer.com					
Utility-Peterbilt 4255 S Harding St	Indianapolis	IN	46217	317-788-0299	780-2889
TF: 800-201-2227 ■ *Web:* www.utility-peterbilt.com					
Vanco USA Trailer Mfg 1170 Florence Rd PO Box 430	Columbus	NJ	08022	609-499-4141	499-8865
Web: www.vancotrailers.com					
Vantage Trailers Inc 29335 Hwy 90	Katy	TX	77494	281-391-2664	391-2668
TF: 800-826-8245 ■ *Web:* www.vantagetrailer.com					
VE Enterprises Inc PO Box 369	Springer	OK	73458	580-653-2171	653-2773
Web: www.veenterprises.com					
Wabash National Corp 1000 Sagamore PkwyS PO Box 6129	Lafayette	IN	47903	765-771-5300	771-5474
NYSE: WNC ■ *TF Sales:* 800-937-4784 ■ *Web:* www.wabashnational.com					
Wells Cargo Inc 1503 W McNaughton St	Elkhart	IN	46514	574-264-9661	264-5938
TF: 800-348-7553 ■ *Web:* www.wellscargo.com					
Western Trailer Co 251 W Gowen Rd	Boise	ID	83716	208-344-2539	344-1521
TF: 888-344-2539 ■ *Web:* www.westerntrailer.com					
Wilson Trailer Co 4400 S Lewis Blvd	Sioux City	IA	51106	712-252-6500	252-6510
TF: 800-798-2002 ■ *Web:* www.wilsontrailer.com					
Witzco Trailers Inc 6101 McIntosh Rd	Sarasota	FL	34238	941-922-5301	924-2402
TF: 888-922-9900 ■ *Web:* www.witzco.com					
WW Trailer Mfg Inc PO Box 807	Madill	OK	73446	580-795-5571	

783 TRUCKING COMPANIES

SEE ALSO Logistics Services (Transportation & Warehousing) p. 2183; Moving Companies p. 2264

Company	City	State	Zip	Phone	Fax
A & A Express Inc PO Box 707 *TF:* 800-658-3549 ■ *Web:* www.aaexpressinc.com	Brandon	SD	57005	605-582-2402	582-6774
A-1 Fargo International 7700 SW 100th St *TF:* 800-944-0877 ■ *Web:* www.a1fargo.com	Miami	FL	33156	305-670-9501	670-1208
AAA Cooper Transportation 1751 Kinsey Rd *TF:* 800-633-7571 ■ *Web:* www.aaacooper.com	Dothan	AL	36303	334-793-2284	793-1063
Aaa Moving & Storage Inc 747 E Ship Creek Ave *TF:* 866-641-4446 ■ *Web:* www.aaa-moving.com	Anchorage	AK	99501	907-276-3506	258-3986
ABF Freight Systems Inc 3801 Old Greenwood Rd **Fax:* Cust Svc ■ *Web:* www.abfs.com	Fort Smith	AR	72903	479-785-8700	785-8800*
Ace Doran Hauling & Rigging Co Inc 1601 Blue Rock St *TF:* 800-829-0929 ■ *Web:* www.acedoran.com	Cincinnati	OH	45223	513-681-7900	853-3188
Ace Relocation Systems Inc 5608 Eastgate Dr *TF:* 800-453-0964 ■ *Web:* www.acerelocation.com	San Diego	CA	92121	858-677-5500	677-5587
Ace Transportation Inc PO Box 91714	Lafayette	LA	70509	337-837-4567	837-1423
Acme Truck Line Inc 121 Pailet Dr *TF:* 800-825-6246 ■ *Web:* www.acmetruck.com	Harvey	LA	70058	504-368-2510	368-2510
Action Carrier Inc 3902 N National Ave	Sioux Falls	SD	57104	605-335-5500	335-0789
Admiral-Merchants Motor Freight Inc 215 S 11th St *TF:* 800-972-8864 ■ *Web:* www.ammf.com	Minneapolis	MN	55403	612-332-4819	332-4765
Alabama Motor Express Inc 10720 E US Hwy 84 E *TF:* 800-633-7590 ■ *Web:* www.amxtrucking.com	Ashford	AL	36312	334-899-2101	899-2107
Alan Ritchey Inc 740 S I-35 E Frontage Rd *TF:* 800-877-0273 ■ *Web:* www.alanritchey.com	Valley View	TX	76272	940-726-3276	726-5335
All American Moving Group LLC PO Box 271277 *TF:* 800-467-2900 ■ *Web:* www.allamericanmoving.com	Memphis	TN	38167	901-353-3900	353-4113
All Freight Systems Inc PO Box 5279 *TF:* 800-377-7575 ■ *Web:* www.allfreightsystems.com	Kansas City	KS	66119	913-281-1203	281-5741
Allegheny Design Management Inc 1154 Parks Industrial Dr *TF:* 800-927-2611 ■ *Web:* www.alleghenydesignmgmt.com	Vandergrift	PA	15690	724-845-7336	845-9889
Allied Automotive Group 2302 ParkLake Dr Bldg 15 Suite 600 *Web:* www.aag1.com	Atlanta	GA	30345	404-370-4206	373-4285
Ameril-Co Carriers Inc 1702 E Overland PO Box 1649 *TF:* 800-806-1352 ■ *Web:* www.americo-carriers.com	Scottsbluff	NE	69361	308-635-3157	635-1447
Amstan Logistics 101 Knightsbridge Dr *Web:* www.amstan.com	Hamilton	OH	45011	513-863-4627	863-0866
Anderson Trucking Service Inc 725 Opportunity St PO Box 1377 *TF:* 800-328-2316 ■ *Web:* www.ats-inc.com	Saint Cloud	MN	56301	320-255-7400	255-7494
Anson County School District PO Box 719 *Web:* www.ansonschools.org	Wadesboro	NC	28170	704-694-4417	694-7479
Apgar Bros Inc PO Box 631	Bound Brook	NJ	08805	732-356-3900	356-2557
Ards Trucking Co Inc 1702 N Gov Williams Hwy *TF:* 800-845-7462 ■ *Web:* www.ardtrucking.com	Darlington	SC	29540	843-393-5101	393-6080
ARG Trucking Corp 369 Bostwick Rd **Fax:* Hum Res ■ *TF:* 800-334-1314 ■ *Web:* www.wadhams.com	Phelps	NY	14532	315-789-8871	789-8879*
Arkansas Best Corp (ABC) 3801 Old Greenwood Rd PO Box 10048 *NASDAQ:* ABFS ■ *Web:* www.arkbest.com	Fort Smith	AR	72903	479-785-6000	785-6009
Arlo G. Lott Trucking Inc PO Box 110 *TF:* 800-443-5688 ■ *Web:* www.agltrucking.com	Jerome	ID	83338	208-324-5053	324-8668
Armellini Express Lines Inc 3446 SW Armellini Ave **Fax:* Cust Svc ■ *TF:* 800-626-1815 ■ *Web:* www.armellini.com	Palm City	FL	34990	772-287-0575	221-3284*
Arnold Transportation Services Inc 9523 Florida Mining Blvd *TF:* 800-388-8320 ■ *Web:* www.arnoldtrans.com	Jacksonville	FL	32257	904-262-4285	260-0628
Associated Petroleum Carriers Inc PO Box 2808 *TF Cust Svc:* 800-573-9301 ■ *Web:* www.apccorporate.com	Spartanburg	SC	29304	864-573-9301	573-9305
Atkinson Freight Lines Co 2950 State Rd PO Box 984 *TF:* 800-345-8052 ■ *Web:* www.atkinsonfreight.com	Bensalem	PA	19020	215-638-1130	638-9375
Autolog Corp 1701 E Linden Ave *TF:* 800-526-6078 ■ *Web:* www.autolog.net	Linden	NJ	07036	908-587-9400	587-9685
Averitt Express Inc 1415 Neal St *TF:* 800-283-7488 ■ *Web:* www.averittexpress.com	Cookeville	TN	38501	931-526-3306	528-7804
B-D-R Transport Inc 7994 US Rt 5 *TF:* 800-421-0126 ■ *Web:* www.bdrtransport.com	Westminster	VT	05158	802-463-0606	463-0608
Baggett Transportation Co 2 S 32nd St *TF:* 800-633-8982 ■ *Web:* www.baggetttransport.com	Birmingham	AL	35233	205-322-6501	320-2329
Bailey's Express Inc 61 Industrial Pk Rd *TF:* 800-523-3758 ■ *Web:* www.baileysxpress.com	Middletown	CT	06457	860-632-0388	632-9089
Baraboo Bancorporation Inc The 101 3rd Ave PO Box 50 *OTC:* BAOB ■ *TF:* 800-559-0011 ■ *Web:* www.baraboobancorp.com	Baraboo	WI	53913	608-356-7703	355-3029
Barlow Truck Lines Inc 1305 Grand Dd SE *TF:* 800-688-1202 ■ *Web:* www.barlowtruckline.com	Faucett	MO	64448	816-238-3373	238-1481
Bastian Trucking Inc 440 S Main *TF:* 800-452-5126 ■ *Web:* www.bastiantrucking.com	Aurora	UT	84620	435-529-7453	529-7137
Baylor Trucking Inc 9269 E State Rd 48 *TF:* 800-322-9567 ■ *Web:* www.baylortrucking.com	Milan	IN	47031	812-623-2020	623-2026
Bayshore Transportation System Inc 901 Dawson Dr *TF:* 888-665-7342 ■ *Web:* www.bayshoreallied.com	Newark	DE	19713	302-366-0220	366-8085
Beam Mack Sales & Service Inc 2674 W Henrietta Rd *Web:* www.beammack.com	Rochester	NY	14623	585-424-4860	272-8851
Beaver Express Service LLC 4310 Oklahoma Ave PO Box 1147 *TF:* 800-593-2328 ■ *Web:* www.beaverexpress.com	Woodward	OK	73802	580-256-6460	256-6239
Bee Trucking Inc 9540 Ball St *TF:* 800-594-2040 ■ *Web:* www.beetrucking.com	San Antonio	TX	78217	210-646-7211	646-6218
Beelman Truck Co 1 Racehorse Dr *TF Sales:* 800-541-5918	East Saint Louis	IL	62205	618-646-5300	646-5400
Beeville Independent School District 201 N Saint Marys St *Web:* www.beevilleisd.net	Beeville	TX	78102	361-358-7111	358-7837
Benton Express Inc 1045 S River Industrial Blvd SE *TF:* 888-423-6866 ■ *Web:* www.benton-express.com	Atlanta	GA	30315	404-267-2200	267-2201
Besl Transfer Co 5700 Este Ave *TF:* 800-456-2375 ■ *Web:* www.besl.com	Cincinnati	OH	45232	513-242-3456	242-4013
Best Way Express Inc 2242 S Old Decker Rd PO Box 728 *TF:* 800-777-4668 ■ *Web:* www.bestwayexpress.com	Vincennes	IN	47591	812-828-6448	885-1542
Bestway Enterprises Inc 3877 Luker Rd *Web:* www.bestwaylumber.com	Cortland	NY	13045	607-753-8261	753-9948
Big G Express Inc PO Box 1650 *TF:* 800-955-9140 ■ *Web:* www.biggexpress.com	Shelbyville	TN	37162	931-684-9140	
Bilkays Express Co 400 S 2nd St *TF:* 800-526-4006 ■ *Web:* www.bilkays.com	Elizabeth	NJ	07206	908-289-2400	289-6364
BJJ Co Inc PO Box 30010 *TF:* 800-776-2551	Stockton	CA	95213	209-941-8361	941-0476
Bob's Transport & Storage Co Inc 7980 Tar Bay Dr PO Box 1305 *Web:* www.bobstransport.com	Jessup	MD	20794	410-799-0832	799-0951
Boyd Bros Transportation Inc 3275 Alabama 30 *TF:* 800-338-2693 ■ *Web:* www.boydbros.com	Clayton	AL	36016	334-775-1400	775-9310
Britt Trucking Co Inc PO Drawer 707 *TF Cust Svc:* 800-448-9098	Lamesa	TX	79331	806-872-3353	872-2673
Brooke County Schools 1201 Pleasant Ave *Web:* www.edline.net/pages/brookecountyschools	Wellsburg	WV	26070	304-737-3481	737-3480
Brph Cos Inc 5700 N US Hwy 1 *Web:* www.brph.com	Melbourne	FL	32940	321-254-7666	259-4703
Bryan Construction Co 1007 N Earl Rudder Fwy PO Box 4087 *Web:* www.bryan-construction-co.com	Bryan	TX	77805	979-776-6000	776-6008
Bryan Systems 14020 US 20A Hwy **Fax Area Code:* 419 ■ *Web:* www.bryansystems.com	Montpelier	OH	43543	800-745-2796	485-6653*
Buchanan Hauling & Rigging 4625 Industrial Rd *TF:* 888-544-4285 ■ *Web:* www.buchananhauling.com	Fort Wayne	IN	46825	260-471-1877	471-8878
Buddy Moore Trucking Inc PO Box 10047 *TF:* 866-704-1598 ■ *Web:* www.buddymooretrucking.com	Birmingham	AL	35202	205-949-2260	327-5178
Bulk Transit Corp 7177 Industrial Pkwy *Web:* www.bulktransit.com	Plain City	OH	43064	614-873-4632	873-3393
Bulkmatic Transport Co 2001 N Cline Ave *TF:* 800-535-8505 ■ *Web:* www.bulkmatic.com	Griffith	IN	46319	219-972-7630	972-7655
Bunning John Transfer Co Inc PO Box 128 *TF All:* 800-443-2753	Rock Springs	WY	82902	307-362-3791	362-9040
Burnet Consolidated Independent School District 208 E Brier Ln *Web:* www.burnet.txed.net	Burnet	TX	78611	512-756-2124	756-7498
Burns Motor Freight Inc 500 Seneca Trail N *TF:* 800-598-5674 ■ *Web:* www.burns-motor-freight.com	Marlinton	WV	24954	304-799-6106	799-4257
Butler & Co Inc 205 Butler Cir SW *TF:* 800-633-8988	Vernon	AL	35592	205-695-7132	695-9500
Butler Transport Inc 347 N James St *TF:* 800-345-8158 ■ *Web:* www.butlertransport.com	Kansas City	KS	66118	913-321-0047	342-5725
Butler Trucking Co PO Box 88 *TF Cust Svc:* 800-458-3777	Woodland	PA	16881	814-857-7644	857-5186
Cal-ark Inc PO Box 990 *Web:* www.calark.com	Mabelvale	AR	72103	501-455-3399	455-5962
Caldwell Freight Lines Inc PO Box 1950 *TF:* 800-438-8244 ■ *Web:* www.caldwellfreight.com	Lenoir	NC	28645	828-728-9231	728-7072
Calex Express Inc 58 Pittston Ave *TF:* 800-292-2539 ■ *Web:* www.calexlogistics.com	Pittston	PA	18640	570-603-0180	603-0940
California Cartage Co Inc 3545 Long Beach Blvd 5th Fl *TF:* 888-537-1432 ■ *Web:* www.calcartage.com	Long Beach	CA	90807	562-427-1143	427-6855
CAR Transportation Brokerage Co PO Box 712 *TF:* 800-648-6588	Springdale	AR	72765	479-751-8747	751-6921
Cardinal Transport Inc 7180 E Reed Rd *Web:* www.cardinaltransport.com	Coal City	IL	60416	815-634-4443	634-8267
Cargo Transporters Inc 3390 N Oxford St PO Box 850 *Web:* www.cargotransporters.com	Claremont	NC	28610	828-459-3282	459-3291
Carroll Fulmer Logistics Corp 8340 American Way **Fax:* Mktg ■ *TF:* 800-468-9400	Groveland	FL	34736	352-429-5000	429-0350*
Cassens Transport Co 145 N Kansas St *Web:* www.cassens.com/transport	Edwardsville	IL	62025	618-656-3006	692-7316
Cedar Rapids Truck Center Inc 9201 6th St SW *TF:* 866-602-1597 ■ *Web:* www.cedarrapidstruckcenter.com	Cedar Rapids	IA	52404	319-848-6230	848-4302
Celadon Trucking Services Inc 9503 E 33rd St *TF:* 800-235-2366 ■ *Web:* www.celadontrucking.com	Indianapolis	IN	46235	317-972-7000	890-1922
Centra Financial Holdings Inc 101 Venture Drá *Web:* www.centrabank.com	Morgantown	WV	26508	304-598-2000	
Central Freight Lines Inc PO Box 2638 **Fax Area Code:* 254 ■ *TF:* 800-782-5036 ■ *Web:* www.centralfreight.com	Waco	TX	76702	800-782-5036	741-5370*
Central Petroleum Transport Inc 6115 Mitchell St *TF:* 800-798-6357 ■ *Web:* www.cptrans.com	Sioux City	IA	51111	712-258-6357	258-8592
Central Refrigerated Service Inc 5175 W 2100 S *TF:* 800-777-0069 ■ *Web:* www.centralref.com	West Valley City	UT	84120	801-924-7000	924-7337

Company / Address	City	State	Zip	Phone	Fax
Central Trucking Inc (CTI) 11930 N Hartman Dr Suite A	Edinburgh	IN	46124	812-526-9737	526-2095
TF: 800-633-7766 ■ Web: www.ctitruck.com					
Chadderton Trucking Inc 40 Stewart Way	Sharon	PA	16146	724-981-5050	981-1615
TF: 800-942-8074 ■ Web: www.chaddertontrucking.com					
Charles G Lawson Trucking 7815 Mobile Hwy	Hope Hull	AL	36043	334-284-3220	281-4672
TF: 800-239-3877 ■ Web: www.lawsontrucking.com					
Chester Bross Construction Co 6739 CR 423	Palmyra	MO	63461	573-221-5958	221-1892
Web: www.cbrossgroup.com					
Christenson Transportation Inc PO Box 4267	Springfield	MO	65808	417-866-5993	866-5166
TF: 800-318-8200 ■ Web: www.christensontrans.com					
Cimarron Express Inc 21611 SR-51 PO Box 185	Genoa	OH	43430	419-855-7713	855-7510
TF: 800-759-8979 ■ Web: www.cimarronexpress.com					
Clipper Americas Inc 2500 City W Blvd Suite 500	Houston	TX	77042	713-953-2200	953-2201
Web: www.clipper-group.com					
Coastal Transport Co Inc 5714 Star Ln	Houston	TX	77057	713-784-1010	784-1302
TF: 800-256-8897 ■ Web: www.coastaltransport.net					
Coleman American Moving Services Inc PO Box 960	Midland City	AL	36350	334-983-6500	983-6700
TF: 877-693-7060 ■ Web: www.colemanallied.com					
Colonial Freight Systems Inc 10924 McBride Ln	Knoxville	TN	37932	865-966-9711	966-3649
TF: 800-826-1402 ■ Web: www.cfsi.com					
Colonial Truck Co 1833 Commerce Rd	Richmond	VA	23224	804-232-3492	230-1932
TF: 800-234-8782 ■ Web: www.colonialtruck.com					
Combined Transport Inc 5656 Crater Lake Ave	Central Point	OR	97502	541-734-7418	826-2001
TF: 800-547-2870 ■ Web: www.combinedtransport.com					
Comcar Industries Inc 502 E Bridgers Ave	Auburndale	FL	33823	863-967-1101	965-1023
TF Cust Svc: 800-524-1101 ■ Web: www.comcar.com					
Commercial Storage & Distribution Co 432 Richmond Rd	Texarkana	TX	75503	903-794-2202	793-4295
Con-Way Central Express Inc 4880 Venture Dr	Ann Arbor	MI	48108	734-994-6600	663-2966
TF: 800-421-4007 ■ Web: www.con-way.com/aboutcts/ccx.html					
Con-way Inc 2855 Campus Dr Suite 300	San Mateo	CA	94403	650-378-5200	357-9160
NYSE: CNW ■ TF: 800-755-2728 ■ Web: www.con-way.com					
Con-Way Southern Express 14500 Trinity Blvd Suite 118	Fort Worth	TX	76155	817-358-3600	358-3715
TF: 800-525-3117 ■ Web: www.con-way.com/aboutcts/cse.html					
Con-Way Transportation Services Inc 110 Parkland Plaza	Ann Arbor	MI	48103	734-769-0203	214-5650
Web: www.con-way.com					
Con-Way Western Express 6301 Beach Blvd Suite 300	Buena Park	CA	90621	714-562-0110	562-0761
TF: 800-545-9683 ■ Web: www.con-way.com/aboutcts/cwx.html					
Container Port Group 1340 Depot St Suite 103	Cleveland	OH	44116	440-333-1330	333-6898
Web: www.containerport.com					
Cooke Trucking Co Inc 1759 S Andy Griffith Pkwy	Mount Airy	NC	27030	336-786-5181	789-7132
TF: 800-888-9502 ■ Web: www.cooketrucking.com					
Corvallis School District 509 J 1555 SW 35th St PO Box 3509J	Corvallis	OR	97333	541-757-5811	
Web: www.csd509j.net					
Covenant Transport Inc 400 Birmingham Hwy	Chattanooga	TN	37419	423-821-1212	821-5442
NASDAQ: CVTI ■ TF: 800-334-9686 ■ Web: www.covenanttransport.com					
Cox Transportation Services Inc 10448 Dow Gil Rd	Ashland	VA	23005	804-798-1477	798-1299
TF: 800-288-8118 ■ Web: www.truckingforamerica.com					
CR England & Sons Inc 4701 W 2100 S	Salt Lake City	UT	84120	801-972-2712	
TF: 800-453-8826 ■ Web: www.crengland.com					
Craig Transportation Co 26699 Eckel Rd	Perrysburg	OH	43551	419-872-3333	874-9372
TF: 800-521-9119 ■ Web: www.craigtransport.com					
Cresco Lines Inc 15220 S Halsted St	Harvey	IL	60426	708-339-1186	596-9759
TF: 800-323-4476 ■ Web: www.crescolines.com					
Crete Carrier Corp 400 NW 56th St PO Box 81228	Lincoln	NE	68528	402-475-9521	479-2073*
*Fax: Mktg ■ TF Cust Svc: 800-998-4095 ■ Web: www.cretecarrier.com					
Crook County School District 1 108 N 4th St PO Box 830	Sundance	WY	82729	307-283-2299	283-1810
Web: www.crook1.com					
Crossett Inc PO Box 946	Warren	PA	16365	814-723-2200	723-4270
TF: 800-876-2778 ■ Web: www.crossettinc.com					
CRST International Inc 3930 16th Ave SW PO Box 68	Cedar Rapids	IA	52406	319-396-4400	390-2649*
*Fax: Sales ■ TF: 800-366-8460 ■ Web: www.crst.com					
CRST Malone Inc 1901 Floyd Bradford Rd	Trussville	AL	35173	205-951-1900	951-5957
TF: 800-366-6361 ■ Web: www.malonefreightlines.com					
Crysteel Truck Equipment Inc PO Box 733	Lake Crystal	MN	56055	507-726-6041	726-2984
TF: 800-722-0588 ■ Web: www.crysteeltruckequipment.com					
CS Henry Transfer Inc 2440 N Church St	Rocky Mount	NC	27804	252-446-5116	446-3468
TF: 800-849-6400 ■ Web: www.cshenry.com					
CTI Inc 11105 Norrth Casa Grande Hwy	Rillito	AZ	85654	520-624-2348	682-3509
TF: 800-362-4952 ■ Web: www.cti-az.com					
CTL Distribution Inc 4201 Bonnie Mine Rd	Mulberry	FL	33860	863-428-2373	428-1731
TF: 800-237-9088 ■ Web: www.drivectl.com					
Curtiss Arlin Trucking Inc 582 SW 1st St # 1	Montevideo	MN	56265	320-269-5581	269-9417
TF: 800-328-8940					
D M Bowman Inc 10228 Governor Ln Blvd Suite 3006	Williamsport	MD	21795	301-223-6900	223-5968
TF: 800-326-3274 ■ Web: www.dmbowman.com					
D&d Sexton Inc PO Box 156	Carthage	MO	64836	417-358-8727	358-5669
TF: 800-743-0265 ■ Web: www.ddsextoninc.com					
D. P. Curtis Trucking Inc 1450 S Hwy 118	Richfield	UT	84701	435-896-4417	896-6553
Web: www.dpcurtis.com					
Daggett Truck Line Inc 32717 County Rd 10	Frazee	MN	56544	218-334-3711	334-2566
TF: 800-262-9393					
Dahlsten Truck Line Inc 101 W Edgar PO Box 95	Clay Center	NE	68933	402-762-3511	762-3592
TF: 800-228-4313 ■ Web: www.dahlsten.com					
Daily Express Inc 1072 Harrisburg Pike	Carlisle	PA	17013	717-243-5757	240-2103
TF: 800-735-3136 ■ Web: www.dailyexp.com					
Dakota Line Inc PO Box 476	Vermillion	SD	57069	605-624-5228	624-5338
TF: 800-532-5682 ■ Web: www.dakotalines.com					
Dana Transport Inc 210 Essex Ave E	Avenel	NJ	07001	732-750-9100	636-7441
TF: 800-733-3262 ■ Web: www.danacompanies.com					
Dancor Transit Inc PO Box 849	Van Buren	AR	72957	479-474-9756	474-2140
TF: 866-677-4333 ■ Web: www.dancortransit.com					
Dart Transit Co Inc PO Box 64110	Saint Paul	MN	55164	651-688-2000	683-1600
TF: 800-366-9000 ■ Web: www.dartadvantage.com					
Davis Express Inc PO Box 1276	Starke	FL	32091	904-964-6619	964-2738
TF: 800-874-4270 ■ Web: www.davis-express.com					
Daylight Transport 1501 Hughes Way	Long Beach	CA	90810	310-507-8200	
TF: 800-468-9999 ■ Web: www.dylt.com					
Deboer Transportation Inc PO Box 145	Blenker	WI	54415	715-652-2911	652-2830
Web: www.deboertrans.com					
Decker Truck Line Inc 3584 5th Ave S	Fort Dodge	IA	50501	515-576-4141	576-4158
Web: www.deckercompanies.com/decker.htm					
Dejana Truck & Utility Equipment Co Inc 490 Pulaski Rd	Kings Park	NY	11754	631-544-9000	544-0942
TF: 877-335-2621 ■ Web: www.dejana.com					
Detroit Lakes Public Schools District 22 702 Lake Av	Detroit Lakes	MN	56501	218-847-9271	847-9273
Web: www.rschooltoday.com/se3bin/clientschool.cgi?schoolname=school478					
Devine Intermodal 3870 Ch Dr	West Sacramento	CA	95691	916-371-4430	371-0355
TF: 800-371-4430 ■ Web: www.devineintermodal.com					
Diamond Transportation System Inc 5021 21st St	Racine	WI	53406	262-554-5400	554-5412
TF: 800-927-5702 ■ Web: www.diamondtrans.net					
Dick Lavy Trucking Inc 8848 SR- 121	Bradford	OH	45308	937-448-2104	448-2312
TF: 800-345-5289 ■ Web: www.dicklavytrucking.com					
Dilmar Oil Co Inc 1951 W Darlington St PO Box 5629	Florence	SC	29501	800-922-5823	
TF: 800-922-5823 ■ Web: www.dilmar.com					
Dino's Trucking Inc 9615 Continental Indus Dr	Saint Louis	MO	63123	314-631-3001	638-3562
TF: 800-771-7805 ■ Web: www.dinoslogistics.com					
Dircks Moving Services Inc 4340 W Mohave St	Phoenix	AZ	85043	602-267-9401	267-8188
TF: 800-523-5038 ■ Web: www.dircks.com					
Distribution Technologies Inc 14841 Sperry Rd	Newbury	OH	44065	440-338-1010	338-1256
TF: 800-321-3143 ■ Web: www.disttech.com					
Don Hummer Trucking Corp 1486 Hwy 6 NW PO Box 310	Oxford	IA	52322	319-828-2000	828-2105
TF: 866-248-6637 ■ Web: www.donhummertrucking.com					
Doudell Trucking Co 555 E Capitol Ave	Milpitas	CA	95035	408-263-7300	263-2266
Dts Cos Inc 1640 Monad Rd	Billings	MT	59101	406-245-4695	245-5404
TF: 877-896-3420 ■ Web: www.dtsb.com					
Duffy Bros Inc PO Box 250	Columbus	WI	53925	920-623-4160	623-4199
TF: 800-242-1887					
Dun Transportation & Stringing Inc 304 Reynolds Ln	Sherman	TX	75092	903-891-9660	891-9660
Web: www.duntrans.com					
Duncan & Son Lines Inc 23860 W US Hwy 85	Buckeye	AZ	85326	623-386-4511	386-3656
TF: 800-528-4283 ■ Web: www.duncanandson.com					
Duncan Machinery Movers Inc 2004 Duncan Machinery Dr	Lexington	KY	40504	859-233-7333	233-7365
TF: 800-331-0116 ■ Web: www.dmmlex.com					
E & L Transport Co LLC 35005 W Michigan Ave	Wayne	MI	48184	734-729-9500	729-9500*
*Fax: Hum Res ■ TF: 800-833-8322					
Eagle Express Lines Inc 715 W 172nd St PO Box 348	South Holland	IL	60473	708-333-8401	333-4747
Web: www.eagleexpresslines.com					
Eagle Transport Corp 300 S Wesleyan Blvd Suite 202	Rocky Mount	NC	27804	252-937-2464	937-2198
TF: 800-776-9937 ■ Web: www.eagletransportcorp.com					
Earl L Henderson Trucking Inc 1 Industrial Pk	Salem	IL	62881	618-548-4667	548-6204
TF: 800-447-8084 ■ Web: www.hendersontrucking.com					
ECL Group of Cos Ltd 7100 44th St SE	Calgary	AB	T2C2V7	403-720-5000	720-5060
Web: www.eclgroup.com					
EL Farmer & Co 300 S Grant Ave	Odessa	TX	79761	432-332-1496	334-6057
TF: 800-592-4753					
Epes Carriers Inc 3400 Edgefield Ct	Greensboro	NC	27409	336-668-3358	668-7005
TF: 800-869-3737 ■ Web: www.epestransport.com					
Equity Transportation Co Inc 3685 Dykstra Dr NW	Grand Rapids	MI	49544	616-785-3800	785-0999
Web: www.equityinc.com					
Erickson Transport Corp 2255 N Packer Rd	Springfield	MO	65803	417-862-6741	862-4992
TF: 800-641-4595					
Esparza Enterprises Inc 7201 Schirra Ct Suite A	Bakersfield	CA	93313	661-323-3772	831-0040
Essex County Public Schools 109 Cross St PO Box 756	Tappahannock	VA	22560	804-443-4366	443-4498
Web: www.essex.k12.va.us					
Estes Express Lines Inc 3901 W Broad St PO Box 25612	Richmond	VA	23230	804-353-1900	353-8001*
*Fax: Sales ■ Web: www.estes-express.com					
Evans Dedicated Systems Inc PO Box 9	Maywood	CA	90270	323-725-2928	726-0796
Web: www.evansdedicated.com					
EW Wylie Corp 1520 2nd Ave NW	West Fargo	ND	58078	701-282-5550	281-0415
TF Cust Svc: 800-437-4132 ■ Web: www.wylietrucking.com					
Exchange Bancshares Inc 700 Front St PO Box 446	Natchitoches	LA	71458	318-352-8141	352-1647
Web: www.exchange-bank.com					
Falcon Express Inc 2250 E Church St PO Box 4897	Philadelphia	PA	19124	215-992-3140	992-3150
TF: 800-544-6566 ■ Web: www.falconexp.com					
Falcon Transport Inc PO Box 6147	Youngstown	OH	44501	330-793-1345	799-2305
Web: www.falcontransport.com					

				Phone	Fax
Fauquier County Public Schools 320 Hospital Dr Suite 40 *Web:* www.schoolcenter.fcps1.org	Warrenton	VA	20186	540-422-7000	
FedEx Freight East PO Box 840 *TF:* 800-874-4723 ■ *Web:* www.fedexfreight.fedex.com	Harrison	AR	72602	870-741-9000	741-3002
Fenix Constructors Inc 215 Drew St SW *Web:* www.fenixci.com	Ardmore	OK	73401	580-223-4313	223-4315
FFE Transportation Inc 1145 Empire Central Pl *TF:* 800-569-9200 ■ *Web:* www.ffeinc.com	Dallas	TX	75247	214-630-8090	819-5625
First Class Services Inc 9355 US Hwy 60 E *Web:* www.firstclassservices.com	Lewisport	KY	42351	270-295-3746	295-3270
Firstexpress Inc 1135 Freightliner Dr **Fax Area Code:* 615 ■ *TF:* 800-848-9203 ■ *Web:* www.firstexpress.net	Nashville	TN	37210	800-848-9203	244-1448*
Five Star Trucking Inc 4380 Glenbrook Rd *TF:* 800-321-3658 ■ *Web:* www.fivestartrucking.com	Willoughby	OH	44094	440-953-9300	953-1863
Florida Hardware Co PO Box 6759 *Web:* www.floridahardware.com	Jacksonville	FL	32236	904-783-1650	783-4556
Floyd & Beasley Transfer Co Inc 18060 Alabama Hwy 21 PO Box 8 *TF:* 800-952-7599 ■ *Web:* www.fbtcinc.com	Sycamore	AL	35149	256-245-4385	249-3002
Foothills Trucking Co Inc PO Box 192 *TF:* 800-562-7428 ■ *Web:* www.foothillstrucking.com	Conover	NC	28613	828-322-1380	322-3085
Fort Edward Express Co Inc PO Box 394 *TF:* 800-342-1233	Fort Edward	NY	12828	518-792-6571	792-6985
Forward Air Corp 420 Airport Rd PO Box 1058 *NASDAQ:* FWRD ■ *TF:* 800-726-6654 ■ *Web:* www.forwardair.com	Greeneville	TN	37744	423-636-7100	497-4625
Frank C. Alegre Trucking Inc PO Box 1508 *TF:* 800-769-2440 ■ *Web:* www.alegretrucking.com	Lodi	CA	95241	209-334-2112	367-0572
Fredericksen Tank Lines Inc 840 Delta Ln *TF:* 800-441-2109	West Sacramento	CA	95691	916-371-4655	371-7983
Fry-Wagner Moving & Storage Co 3700 Rider Trail S *TF:* 800-899-4035 ■ *Web:* www.fry-wagner.com	Earth City	MO	63045	314-291-4100	291-1263
Gabler Trucking Inc 5195 Technology Ave *Web:* www.hcgabler.com	Chambersburg	PA	17201	717-261-1492	264-8967
Godfrey Trucking Inc 6173 W 2100 S *TF:* 800-444-7669 ■ *Web:* www.godfreytrucking.com	West Valley City	UT	84128	801-972-0660	972-0709
Gordon Trucking Inc 151 Stewart Rd SW *TF:* 800-426-8486 ■ *Web:* www.gordontrucking.com	Pacific	WA	98047	253-863-7777	863-8497
Gra-Bell Truck Line Inc PO Box 1019 *TF:* 800-632-5300 ■ *Web:* www.gra-bell.com	Holland	MI	49422	616-396-1453	396-3882
Grammer Industries Inc 18375 E 345 S *TF:* 800-333-7410 ■ *Web:* www.grammerindustries.com	Grammer	IN	47236	812-579-5655	579-5643
Grayson Mitchell Inc 2462 Sussex Dr *TF:* 800-247-6321 ■ *Web:* www.graysonmitchell.com	Emporia	VA	23847	434-634-9159	634-2592
Great Lakes Cartage Co PO Box 4704 *TF Cust Svc:* 800-228-4274	Youngstown	OH	44515	330-793-9331	793-6505
Greatwide Logistics Services LLC 12404 Pk Central Dr Suite 300S *TF:* 800-283-9700 ■ *Web:* www.greatwide.com	Dallas	TX	75251	972-228-7300	228-7328
Green Transfer & Storage Co 10099 N Portland Rd	Portland	OR	97203	503-286-0673	286-0676
Groendyke Transport Inc 2510 Rock Island Blvd *TF:* 800-843-2103 ■ *Web:* www.groendyke.com	Enid	OK	73701	580-234-4663	234-1216
Gully Transportation Inc 3820 Wismann Ln *Web:* www.gullyicx.com	Quincy	IL	62305	217-224-0770	224-9885
Guy M Turner Inc 4514 S Holden Rd PO Box 7776 *TF:* 800-432-4859 ■ *Web:* www.guymturner.com	Greensboro	NC	27406	336-294-4660	294-6668
H & M International Transportation Inc 485B Rt 1 S *TF:* 800-446-4685 ■ *Web:* www.hmit.net	Iselin	NJ	08830	732-510-4640	510-4697
H & W Trucking Co Inc 1772 N Andy Griffith Pkwy PO Box 1545 *TF:* 800-334-9181 ■ *Web:* www.hwtrucking.com	Mount Airy	NC	27030	336-789-2188	789-7973
H. F. Campbell & Son PO Box 260 *TF:* 800-233-7112 ■ *Web:* www.camel-express.com	Millerstown	PA	17062	717-589-3194	589-3909
H. O. Wolding Inc PO Box 217 *TF:* 800-950-0054 ■ *Web:* www.howolding.com	Amherst	WI	54406	715-824-5513	824-5018
Hallamore Motor Transportation Inc 795 Plymouth St *TF:* 800-242-1300 ■ *Web:* www.hallamore.com	Holbrook	MA	02343	781-767-2000	767-0845
Harbor Express Inc 501 Quay Ave *Web:* www.harbor-express.com	Wilmington	CA	90744	310-513-6478	835-3794
Harrisonburg City Public Schools (HCPS) 317 S Main St *Web:* www.harrisonburg.k12.va.us	Harrisonburg	VA	22801	540-434-9916	434-5196
Hazen Transport Inc 27050 Wick Rd **Fax Area Code:* 734 ■ *TF:* 800-251-2120 ■ *Web:* www.hazentransport.com	Taylor	MI	48180	313-292-2120	946-4452*
Heartland Express Inc 1515 Ware Bottom Spring Rd *TF:* 800-444-4929 ■ *Web:* www.heartlandexpress.com	Chester	VA	23836	804-768-0016	768-4686
Heartland Express Inc 2777 Heartland Dr *NASDAQ:* HTLD ■ *TF:* 800-553-1201 ■ *Web:* www.heartlandexpress.com	Coralville	IA	52241	319-545-2728	545-1349
Higgins Erectors & Haulers Inc 7715 Lockport Rd	Niagara Falls	NY	14304	716-297-2600	205-0159
High Country Transportation Inc PO Box 700 *TF:* 800-635-7687 ■ *Web:* www.highcountrytrans.com	Cortez	CO	81321	970-565-6402	565-6338
Highway Transport Inc 1500 Amherst Rd *Web:* www.hytt.com	Knoxville	TN	37909	865-584-8631	584-2851
Hirschbach Motor Lines Inc 920 W 21st St PO Box 9 **Fax Area Code:* 800 ■ *TF:* 800-554-2969 ■ *Web:* www.hirschbach.com	South Sioux City	NE	68776	402-494-5000	772-2500*
Hnb Corp 126 S Summit St PO Box 1047	Arkansas City	KS	67005	620-442-4040	441-2121
Hodges Trucking Co LLC 4050 W I-40 *TF:* 800-733-7764 ■ *Web:* www.hodgestruckingcompany.com	Oklahoma City	OK	73108	405-947-7764	942-5636
Holman Transportation Services Inc 1010 Holman Ct *TF:* 800-375-2416 ■ *Web:* holmantransport.com	Caldwell	ID	83605	208-454-0779	454-2226

				Phone	Fax
Hot-Line Freight System Inc PO Box 205 *TF:* 800-468-4686 ■ *Web:* www.hotlinefreight.com	West Salem	WI	54669	608-486-1600	486-1601
Houff Transfer Inc 46 Houff Rd *TF:* 800-476-4683 ■ *Web:* www.houff.com	Weyers Cave	VA	24486	540-234-9233	234-9011
Howard F Baer Inc 1301 Foster Ave *TF:* 800-447-7430	Nashville	TN	37210	615-255-7351	726-1529
Howard Sheppard Inc PO Box 797 *Web:* www.howardsheppard.com	Sandersville	GA	31082	478-552-5127	552-6973
Howell's Motor Freight Inc PO Box 12308 *TF:* 800-444-0585 ■ *Web:* www.howellsmotor.com	Roanoke	VA	24024	540-966-3200	966-3202
HR Ewell Inc 4535 Division Hwy *TF:* 800-233-0161 ■ *Web:* www.hrewell.com	East Earl	PA	17519	717-354-4556	355-9184
Hribar Trucking Inc 1521 Waukesha Rd *Web:* www.hribarcompanies.com	Caledonia	WI	53108	262-835-4401	835-4043
Hvh Transportation Inc 181 E 56th Ave Suite 200 *TF:* 800-525-4844 ■ *Web:* www.hvhtransportation.com	Denver	CO	80216	303-292-3656	292-9713
Indian River Transport Co 2580 Executive Rd *TF:* 800-877-2430 ■ *Web:* www.indianrivertransport.com	Winter Haven	FL	33884	863-324-2430	326-9702
Interstate Distributor Co 11707 21st Ave S **Fax Area Code:* 800 ■ *TF:* 800-426-8560 ■ *Web:* www.intd.com	Tacoma	WA	98444	253-537-9455	795-1050*
Irvin Dick Inc 475 Wilson Ave *TF:* 800-332-5131	Shelby	MT	59474	406-434-5583	434-5505
J & J Motor Service Inc 2338 S Indiana Ave	Chicago	IL	60616	312-225-3323	225-9873
J & R Schugel Trucking Inc PO Box 278 **Fax Area Code:* 507 ■ *TF:* 800-359-2037 ■ *Web:* www.jrschugel.com	New Ulm	MN	56073	800-359-2037	354-4366*
J A T of Fort Wayne Inc 5031 Industrial Rd *TF:* 800-522-3306 ■ *Web:* www.jatoffortwayne.com	Fort Wayne	IN	46825	260-482-8447	482-9990
J M Turner & Co Inc 130 Church Ave PO Box 2140 *Web:* www.jmturner.com	Roanoke	VA	24011	540-343-6749	343-6031
J P Noonan Transportation Inc 415 W St PO Box 400 *TF:* 800-922-8026 ■ *Web:* www.jpnoonan.com	West Bridgewat	MA	02379	508-583-2880	559-0401
J R C Transportation Inc 47 Maple Ave PO Box 366 *TF:* 866-572-7297 ■ *Web:* www.jrctransportation.com	Thomaston	CT	06787	860-283-0207	283-2511
J-Mar Enterprises Inc PO Box 4143 *Web:* www.j-mar-enterprises.com	Bismarck	ND	58502	701-222-4518	255-7587
Jack B Kelley Inc 801 S Fillmore St # 500 *TF:* 800-225-5525 ■ *Web:* www.jackbkelley.com	Amarillo	TX	79101	806-353-3553	353-9611
Jack Cooper Transport Co Inc 2345 Grand Blvd Suite 400 *TF:* 866-449-6301 ■ *Web:* www.jackcooper.com	Kansas City	MO	64108	816-983-4000	983-5000
Jack Gray Transport Inc 4600 E 15th Ave *Web:* www.jackgray.com	Gary	IN	46403	219-938-7020	938-6866
Jaro Transportation Services Inc 975 Post Rd PO Box 1890 *TF:* 888-636-5276 ■ *Web:* www.jarotrans.com	Warren	OH	44483	330-393-5659	393-5906
Jerry Lipps Inc 3888 Nash Rd PO Drawer F *TF:* 800-325-3331 ■ *Web:* www.jerrylippsinc.com	Cape Girardeau	MO	63702	573-335-8204	335-4483
Jet Star Inc 10825 Andrade Dr *TF:* 877-538-7827 ■ *Web:* www.jetstarinc.com	Zionsville	IN	46077	317-873-4222	873-4361
Jevic Transportation Inc 700 Creek Rd **Fax Area Code:* 856 ■ **Fax:* Hum Res ■ *TF:* 800-257-0427 ■ *Web:* www.jevic.com	Delanco	NJ	08075	800-257-0427	764-6734*
JH Walker Trucking Co Inc 152 N Hollywood Rd *TF:* 800-535-5992 ■ *Web:* www.jhwalkertrucking.com	Houma	LA	70364	985-868-8330	873-5210
Jim Palmer Trucking Inc 9730 Derby Dr *TF:* 800-682-8605 ■ *Web:* www.jimpalmertrucking.com	Missoula	MT	59808	406-721-5151	728-7376
Jnj Express Inc 3935 Old Getwell Rd PO Box 30983 *TF:* 888-383-7157 ■ *Web:* www.jnjexpress.com	Memphis	TN	38130	901-362-3444	362-2331
Johnson Carlier Inc 738 S 52nd St **Fax Area Code:* 480 ■ *Web:* www.johnsoncarlier.com	Tempe	AZ	85281	602-275-2222	921-9255*
Jones Motor Co Inc 900 W Bridge St PO Box 137 *TF:* 800-825-6637 ■ *Web:* www.jonesmotor.com	Spring City	PA	19475	610-948-7900	948-5660
KAG West 4076 Seaport Blvd *TF:* 800-547-1587 ■ *Web:* www.kagwest.com	West Sacramento	CA	95691	916-371-8241	372-1760
Kahului Trucking & Storage Inc 140 Hobron Ave	Kahului	HI	96732	808-877-5001	877-0572
Kaplan Trucking Co 6600 Bessemer Ave *Web:* www.kaplantrucking.com	Cleveland	OH	44127	216-341-3322	341-3348
Karl R. Johnson Trucking Inc PO Box 1508 *TF:* 888-564-6767 ■ *Web:* www.karljohnsontrucking.com	Lyndonville	VT	05851	802-626-8769	626-5306
Kauai Commercial Co Inc 1811 Leleiona St	Lihue	HI	96766	808-245-1985	245-2079
Keith Titus Corp PO Box 920 *Web:* www.pagetrucking.com	Weedsport	NY	13166	315-834-6681	834-9687
Kenan Advantage Group Inc (KAG) 4366 Mt Pleasant St NW *TF:* 800-969-5419 ■ *Web:* www.thekag.com	North Canton	OH	44720	330-491-0474	491-1471
Kenan Transport Co 100 Europa Ctr Suite 320 *TF:* 800-768-8765	Chapel Hill	NC	27517	919-967-8221	929-5295
Kenworth Sales Co 2125 Constitution Blvd *TF:* 800-222-7831 ■ *Web:* www.kenworthsalesco.com	West Valley City	UT	84119	801-487-4161	467-3820
Kephart Trucking Co PO Box 386 *TF:* 800-637-9697 ■ *Web:* www.kephartrucking.com	Bigler	PA	16825	814-768-0300	768-0302
Key Energy 2210 W Broadway *TF:* 800-749-6613 ■ *Web:* www.keyenergy.com	Sweetwater	TX	79556	325-236-6611	236-6106
Kildeer Countryside Ccsd 96 1050 Ivy Hall Ln *Web:* www.district96.k12.il.us	Buffalo Grove	IL	60089	847-459-4260	
KLLM Inc 134 Riverview Dr *TF:* 800-925-5556 ■ *Web:* www.kllm.com	Richland	MS	39218	601-939-2545	
Knight Transportation Inc 5601 W Buckeye Rd *NYSE:* KNX ■ *TF:* 800-489-2000 ■ *Web:* www.knighttrans.com	Phoenix	AZ	85043	602-269-2000	269-8409
Kruepke Trucking Inc 2881 Hwy P *TF Cust Svc:* 800-798-5000	Jackson	WI	53037	262-677-3155	677-3206

Company / Address	City	State	Zip	Phone	Fax
Kuntzman Trucking Inc 13515 Oyster Rd	Alliance	OH	44601	330-821-9160	821-9163
TF: 800-362-9779 ■ *Web:* www.kmantrucking.com					
La Rosa Del Monte Express Inc 1133-35 Tiffany St	Bronx	NY	10459	718-991-3300	893-1948
TF: 800-452-7672 ■ *Web:* www.larosadelmonte.com					
Land Span Inc 1120 Griffin Rd	Lakeland	FL	33805	863-688-1102	683-2190
TF: 800-248-4847 ■ *Web:* www.landspan.com					
Landair Corp 1110 Myers St	Greeneville	TN	37743	423-783-1300	
TF: 888-526-3247 ■ *Web:* www.landair.com					
Landes Trucking Inc 31 Rigg Dr PO Box 1152	Jacksonville	IL	62651	217-245-9753	243-3726
TF: 800-747-0004 ■ *Web:* www.landestruckinginc.com					
Landmark Construction Group Inc 6100 N Robinson Ave Suite 101	Oklahoma City	OK	73118	405-843-8041	
Landmark International Trucks Inc 4550 Rutledge Pike	Knoxville	TN	37914	865-637-4881	522-0865
TF: 800-968-9999 ■ *Web:* www.landmarktrucks.com					
Landstar Express America Inc 13410 Sutton Pk Dr S	Jacksonville	FL	32224	800-872-3278	390-1216*
NASDAQ: LSTR ■ **Fax Area Code:* 904 ■ **Fax:* Hum Res ■ *TF:* 800-872-3278 ■ *Web:* www.Landstar.com					
Landstar Gemini Inc 13410 Sutton Pk Dr S	Jacksonville	FL	32224	800-862-9232	
TF: 800-862-9232					
Landstar Inway Inc 1000 Simpson Rd	Rockford	IL	61102	815-972-5000	972-5270*
**Fax:* Hum Res ■ *TF:* 800-435-4373					
Landstar Ligon Inc 13410 Sutton Pk Dr S	Jacksonville	FL	32224	904-306-2440	235-1991*
**Fax Area Code:* 800 ■ *TF:* 800-235-4466					
Landstar Ranger Inc 13410 Sutton Pk Dr S	Jacksonville	FL	32224	904-398-9400	872-1216*
**Fax Area Code:* 800 ■ **Fax:* Hum Res ■ *TF:* 800-872-9400					
Landstar System Inc 13410 Sutton Pk Dr S	Jacksonville	FL	32224	904-398-9400	390-1437
NASDAQ: LSTR ■ *TF:* 800-872-9400 ■ *Web:* www.landstar.com					
Lange Trucking Inc PO Box 1557	Pleasanton	CA	94566	510-836-1105	
Web: www.langetrucking.net					
Lanter Delivery Systems Inc 1 Caine Dr	Madison	IL	62060	618-452-5300	452-5931
TF: 800-966-6137 ■ *Web:* www.lanterdeliverysystems.com					
Lawrence Transportation Systems (LTS) 872 Lee Hwy PO Box 7667	Roanoke	VA	24019	540-966-4000	966-4555
TF: 800-336-9626 ■ *Web:* www.lawrencetransportation.com					
LCT Transportation Services 26444 County Rd 33	Okahumpka	FL	34762	352-326-8900	365-1181
TF: 800-874-3344					
Lee & Eastes Tank Lines Inc 2418 Airport Way S	Seattle	WA	98134	206-623-5403	623-3611
TF: 800-552-7496					
Lee's Trucking Inc PO Box 1552	El Dorado	AR	71731	870-862-5477	863-6963
TF: 800-826-3413 ■ *Web:* www.leestrucking.com					
Leonard's Express Inc PO Box 25130	Farmington	NY	14425	585-924-8140	924-0508
TF: 866-924-8140 ■ *Web:* www.leonardsexpress.com					
Liberty Moving & Storage Inc 350 Moreland Rd	Commack	NY	11725	631-234-3000	234-3639
Web: www.libertymoving.com					
Lightning Transportation Inc 16820 Blake Rd	Hagerstown	MD	21740	301-582-5700	582-5898
TF: 800-233-0624 ■ *Web:* www.lightningtrans.com					
Linden Bulk Transportation Co Inc 4200 Tremley Pt Rd	Linden	NJ	07036	908-862-3883	986-5090*
**Fax:* Sales ■ *TF:* 800-333-2855 ■ *Web:* www.lindenbulk.com					
Linden Warehouse & Distribution Co Inc 1300 Lower Rd	Linden	NJ	07036	908-862-1400	862-7539
Web: www.lindenmotorfreight.com					
Liquid Transport Corp 8470 Allison Pointe Blvd Suite 400	Indianapolis	IN	46250	317-841-4200	841-8259
TF: 800-942-3175 ■ *Web:* www.liquidtransport.com					
Lisa Motor Lines Inc PO Box 4529	Fort Worth	TX	76164	214-630-8090	336-2816*
**Fax Area Code:* 817 ■ *Web:* www.lisamtc.com					
LL Smith Trucking Inc PO Box 987	Riverton	WY	82501	307-856-2491	856-7432
Lockwood Bros Inc 220 Salters Creek Rd	Hampton	VA	23661	757-722-1946	722-3699
TF: 800-367-5295					
Lodi Truck Service Inc PO Box 1120	Lodi	CA	95241	209-334-4100	333-0609
TF Cust Svc: 800-967-8443 ■ *Web:* www.tigerlines.com					
Lotz Trucking Inc 807 E Dayton Rd	Ottawa	IL	61350	815-587-6090	587-6095
Web: www.lotztrucking.com					
Lynden Transport Inc 3027 Rampart Dr	Anchorage	AK	99501	907-276-4800	257-5155
TF: 800-327-9390 ■ *Web:* www.ltia.lynden.com					
Mail Contractors of America 3800 N Rodney Paraham Rd Suite 331	Little Rock	AR	72212	501-280-0500	280-0111
TF: 800-294-7743 ■ *Web:* www.mcalogistics.com					
Market Transport Ltd 110 N Marine Dr	Portland	OR	97217	503-283-2405	289-8453
TF: 800-547-0781 ■ *Web:* www.markettransportservices.com					
Marten Transport Ltd 129 Marten St	Mondovi	WI	54755	715-926-4216	926-5609
NASDAQ: MRTN ■ *TF:* 800-395-3000 ■ *Web:* www.marten.com					
Martin Howard Inc 4315 Meyer Rd	Fort Wayne	IN	46806	260-447-5591	447-4026
TF: 800-348-4759					
Martin Trucking Inc PO Box M	Hugoton	KS	67951	620-544-4920	544-4990
TF: 800-737-0047					
Mason City School District 211 N E St	Mason	OH	45040	513-398-0474	
Web: www.masonohioschools.com					
Matheson Trucking Inc 9785 Goethe Rd	Sacramento	CA	95827	916-685-2330	686-5358
TF: 800-455-7678 ■ *Web:* www.mathesoninc.com					
Maust Transportation 2200 140th Ave E Suite 200	Sumner	WA	98390	253-321-3196	321-3197
TF: 800-446-2878 ■ *Web:* www.maustcorp.com					
Maverick USA Inc PO Box 16173	Little Rock	AR	72231	501-955-1255	955-4670*
**Fax:* Hum Res ■ *TF:* 800-289-6600 ■ *Web:* www.maverickusa.com					
Mawson & Mawson Inc 1800 Old Lincoln Hwy PO Box 248	Langhorne	PA	19047	215-750-1100	750-0396
TF: 800-262-9766 ■ *Web:* www.mawsonandmawson.com					
May Trucking Co 4185 Brooklake Rd PO Box 9039	Salem	OR	97305	503-393-7030	642-0105*
**Fax Area Code:* 208 ■ *TF:* 800-547-9169 ■ *Web:* www.maytrucking.com					
Mayfield Transfer Co Inc 3200 W Lake St	Melrose Park	IL	60160	708-681-4440	681-4483
TF: 800-222-2959 ■ *Web:* www.mfld.net					
McC Construction Corp 5990 Greenwood Plaza Blvd Suite 205	Englewood	CO	80111	303-741-0404	741-0505
Web: www.mccconstruction.com					
McClendon Trucking Co PO Box 641	Lafayette	AL	36862	334-864-9311	864-0028
TF: 800-633-7710					
McDermott Inc PO Box 544	Enosburg Falls	VT	05450	802-933-2144	933-2867
McKenzie Tank Lines Inc 2778 W Tharpe St	Tallahassee	FL	32303	850-576-1221	574-2351
Web: www.mckenzietank.com					
McLeod Trucking & Rigging 3027 N Tryon St	Charlotte	NC	28206	704-372-3611	372-3611
TF: 800-438-0330					
MCT Transportation LLC 1600 E Benson Rd	Sioux Falls	SD	57104	605-339-8400	339-8407
TF Cust Svc: 800-843-9904 ■ *Web:* www.midwest-coast.com					
Melloul-Blamey Construction Ltd 55 Commerce Ctr	Greenville	SC	29615	864-627-0302	627-0804
Web: www.melloul.com					
Melton Truck Lines Inc 808 N 161 E Ave	Tulsa	OK	74116	918-234-8000	234-1004
TF: 800-545-6651 ■ *Web:* www.meltontruck.com					
Mercer County State Bancorp Inc 3279 S Main St	Sandy Lake	PA	16145	724-376-7015	376-7015
Web: www.mcsbank.net					
Mercer Transportation Co 1128 W Main St PO Box 35610	Louisville	KY	40232	502-584-2301	
TF: 800-626-5375 ■ *Web:* www.mercer-trans.com					
Mergenthaler Transfer & Storage 1414 N Montana Ave	Helena	MT	59601	406-442-9470	442-4340
TF: 888-225-1458 ■ *Web:* www.mergenthaler.net					
Mid Seven Transportation Co 2323 Delaware Ave	Des Moines	IA	50317	515-266-5181	266-1457
TF: 800-247-7448 ■ *Web:* www.mid7.com					
Middlesboro Independent School District 220 N 20th St PO Box 959	Middlesboro	KY	40965	606-242-8800	242-8805
Web: www.mboro.k12.ky.us					
Midwest Motor Express Inc 5015 E Main Ave	Bismarck	ND	58502	701-223-1880	224-1405
TF: 800-741-4097 ■ *Web:* www.mmeinc.com					
Milan Express Co Inc 1091 Kefauver Dr PO Box 699	Milan	TN	38358	731-686-7428	686-8829
TF: 800-231-7303 ■ *Web:* www.milanexpress.com					
Miller Transporters Inc 5500 Hwy 80 W	Jackson	MS	39209	601-922-8331	923-2535
TF Cust Svc: 800-645-5378 ■ *Web:* www.millert.com					
Milton Transportation Inc 5505 State Rt 405	Milton	PA	17847	570-742-8774	742-2856
TF: 800-776-1150 ■ *Web:* www.miltontrans.com					
Minuteman Trucks Inc 2181 Providence Hwy	Walpole	MA	02081	508-668-3112	668-8466
TF: 800-231-8458 ■ *Web:* www.minutemantrucks.com					
Morris School District 54 54 White Oak Dr	Morris	IL	60450	815-942-0056	942-0240
Web: www.dist54.mornet.org					
Morristown Drivers Service Inc PO Box 2158	Morristown	TN	37816	423-581-6048	581-9696
Web: www.mdstrucking.com					
Motor West Inc PO Box 1178	Caldwell	ID	83606	208-454-9238	454-9872
TF: 800-888-7001 ■ *Web:* www.motorwestinc.com					
Murrows Transfer Inc PO Box 4095	High Point	NC	27263	336-475-6101	475-1240
TF Cust Svc: 800-669-2928 ■ *Web:* www.murrows.com					
National Carriers Inc PO Box 1358	Liberal	KS	67905	620-624-1621	626-0627
TF: 800-835-9180 ■ *Web:* www.nationalcarriers.com					
National Highway Express Co 971 Old Henderson St PO Box 20262	Columbus	OH	43220	614-459-4900	459-4945
TF: 800-837-5700 ■ *Web:* www.nationalhighwayexpress.com					
Nationwide Express Inc PO Box 1800	Shelbyville	TN	37162	931-680-2400	684-3864
TF: 800-456-1553 ■ *Web:* www.nationwide-express.com					
Nationwide Transport Services Inc PO Box 42726	Cincinnati	OH	45242	513-389-4144	389-4156
TF: 800-901-1922 ■ *Web:* www.nationwidetransport.net					
Nationwide Truck Brokers Inc (NTB) 1240 84th St SW	Byron Center	MI	49315	616-878-5554	878-5569
TF: 800-224-4485 ■ *Web:* www.ntbtrk.com					
Navajo Express Inc PO Box 17880	Denver	CO	80217	303-287-3800	286-9661*
**Fax:* Sales ■ *TF:* 800-525-1969 ■ *Web:* www.navajo.com					
NE Finch Co 1925 S Darst St	Peoria	IL	61607	309-671-1433	671-1474
New England Motor Freight Inc 1-71 N Ave E	Elizabeth	NJ	07201	908-965-0100	965-1881
Web: www.nemf.com					
New Penn Motor Express Inc 625 S 5th Ave	Lebanon	PA	17042	717-274-2521	274-5593
TF Cust Svc: 800-285-5000 ■ *Web:* www.newpenn.com					
Newark School District 100 E Miller St 4th FL	Newark	NY	14513	315-332-3230	332-3517
Web: www.newark.k12.ny.us					
Newton Independent School District 414 Main St	Newton	TX	75966	409-379-8137	379-2189
Web: www.newtonisd.com					
Nick Strimbu Inc 3500 PkwyRd	Brookfield	OH	44403	330-448-4071	448-1672
TF: 800-446-8785 ■ *Web:* www.nickstrimbu.com					
North Park Transportation Co 5150 Columbine St	Denver	CO	80216	303-295-0300	295-6244
Web: www.nopk.com					
North Shore Central Illinois Freight Co 5101 S Lawndale Ave	Summit	IL	60501	708-496-8222	496-8449
Web: www.northshorelogistics.net					
Northland Trucking Inc 1515 S 22nd Ave	Phoenix	AZ	85009	602-254-0007	254-0455
TF: 800-214-5564 ■ *Web:* www.northlandtrucking.com					
Nussbaum Trucking Inc 2200 N Main St	Normal	IL	61761	309-452-4426	452-4431
TF: 800-322-7305 ■ *Web:* www.nussbaum.com					
O & S Trucking Inc 3769 E Evergreen St	Springfield	MO	65803	417-864-4780	831-7763
TF: 800-395-4780 ■ *Web:* www.oandstrucking.com					
Old Dominion Freight Line Inc 500 Old Dominion Way	Thomasville	NC	27360	336-889-5000	802-5229
NASDAQ: ODFL ■ *TF:* 800-432-6335 ■ *Web:* www.odfl.com					
Oliver Construction Co 1770 Executive Dr PO Box 65	Oconomowoc	WI	53066	262-567-6677	567-4676
Web: www.oliverconstruction.com					
Oliver Trucking Co Inc PO Box 53	Winchester	KY	40392	859-744-6373	744-6379
Web: www.oliverpipe.com					
Oliver Trucking Corp 1101 Harding Ct	Indianapolis	IN	46217	317-787-1101	787-1102
TF: 888-561-4449 ■ *Web:* www.oltg.com					

				Phone	Fax
Online Transport System Inc 6311 W Stoner Dr *TF:* 866-543-1235 ■ *Web:* www.onlinetransport.com	Greenfield	IN	46140	317-894-2159	894-2160
Orcutt Union School District 500 Dyer St *Web:* www.orcutt-schools.net	Orcutt	CA	93455	805-938-8900	938-8919
Ormsby Trucking Inc 888 W Railroad St PO Box 67 *TF:* 800-348-2089 ■ *Web:* www.ormtrk.com	Uniondale	IN	46791	260-543-2233	543-2842
Osborn Transportation Inc PO Box 1830 *Web:* www.osborntransportation.com	Gadsden	AL	35902	256-442-2514	413-0002
Otto Trucking Inc 4025 E Presidio St *Web:* www.ottotrucking.com	Mesa	AZ	85215	480-641-3500	641-3550
Overland Express Co 5539 Harvey Wilson PO Box 262322 *Web:* www.overlandexp.com	Houston	TX	77207	713-672-6161	672-5040
Ozark Motor Lines Inc 3934 Homewood Rd *TF:* 800-264-4100 ■ *Web:* www.ozark.com	Memphis	TN	38118	901-251-9711	251-0222
P J Hoerr Inc 107 Commerce Pl *Web:* www.pjhoerr.com	Peoria	IL	61604	309-688-9567	688-9556
Palmetto State Transportation Co Inc 1050 Pk W Blvd *TF:* 800-269-0175 ■ *Web:* www.palmettostatetrans.com	Greenville	SC	29611	864-672-3800	672-3810
PAM Transportation Services Inc 297 W Henri De Tonti Blvd PO Box 188 *NASDAQ: PTSI* ■ *TF:* 800-879-7261	Tontitown	AR	72770	479-361-9111	361-5335
Pan Western Corp 4910 Donovan Way Suite A *TF:* 800-443-1560 ■ *Web:* www.panwestern.com	North Las Vegas	NV	89081	702-632-2931	632-2956
Paper Transport Inc 2701 Executive Dr *Web:* www.papertransport.com	Green Bay	WI	54304	920-497-6222	497-0990
Patriot Transportation Holding Inc 501 Riverside Ave Suite 500 *NASDAQ: PATR* ■ *TF:* 877-704-1776 ■ *Web:* www.patriottrans.com	Jacksonville	FL	32202	904-396-5733	396-0258
Peet Frate Line Inc 650 S Eastwood Dr PO Box 1129 *TF:* 800-435-6909 ■ *Web:* www.peetfrateline.com	Woodstock	IL	60098	815-338-5500	338-1052
Penn's Best Inc PO Box 128 *TF:* 800-852-3243 ■ *Web:* www.pennsbest.net	Meshoppen	PA	18630	570-833-2583	833-5902
Peoples Bancshares-Pnt Coupee 805 Hospital Rd PO Box 747 *Web:* www.thefriendlybank.com/index_home.php	New Roads	LA	70760	225-638-3713	638-6772
Perkins Specialized Transportation Inc 14450 Getz Rd *TF:* 800-428-3762 ■ *Web:* www.perkinslogistics.com	Noblesville	IN	46060	317-297-3550	298-2071
Phoenix Transportation Services LLC 335 E Yusen Dr *TF:* 800-860-0889 ■ *Web:* www.phoenix-transportation.net	Georgetown	KY	40324	502-863-0108	863-0029
Pitt Ohio Express 15 27th St *TF Cust Svc:* 800-366-7488 ■ *Web:* www.works.pittohio.com	Pittsburgh	PA	15222	412-232-3015	232-0944
Pleasant Trucking Inc 2250 Industrial Dr PO Box 778 **Fax Area Code:* 724 ■ *TF:* 800-245-2402 ■ *Web:* www.pleasanttrucking.com	Connellsville	PA	15425	800-245-2402	628-5868*
Powers Transportation Systems Inc PO Box 103 *TF:* 888-673-1287 ■ *Web:* www.ptran.com	Savannah	GA	31402	912-966-2198	966-2791
Pozas Bros Trucking Co Inc 8130 Enterprise Dr *TF:* 800-874-8383	Newark	CA	94560	510-742-9939	742-9979
Predator Trucking Co 1775 N State St *TF:* 800-235-5624	Girard	OH	44420	330-545-9763	545-2276
Prestera Trucking PO Box 399 *TF:* 800-759-9555	South Point	OH	45680	740-894-4770	894-5051
Pride Transport Inc 5499 W 2455 S *TF:* 800-877-1320 ■ *Web:* www.pridetransport.com	Salt Lake City	UT	84120	801-972-8890	972-1450
Prime Inc PO Box 4208 **Fax:* Sales ■ *TF Cust Svc:* 800-848-4560 ■ *Web:* www.primeinc.com	Springfield	MO	65808	417-866-0001	521-6850*
Pritchett Trucking Inc 1050 SE 6th St PO Box 311 *TF:* 800-486-7504 ■ *Web:* www.pritchetttrucking.com	Lake Butler	FL	32054	386-496-2630	496-2883
Puget Sound Truck Lines Inc 3720 Airport Way S *TF:* 800-638-2254 ■ *Web:* www.psfl.com	Seattle	WA	98134	206-623-1600	621-7793
Q Carriers Inc 1415 Maras St *TF:* 800-800-4755 ■ *Web:* www.qcarriers.com	Shakopee	MN	55379	952-445-8718	445-8794
Quality Carriers Inc PO Box 580129	Pleasant Prairie	WI	53158	262-857-2341	857-7497
Quality Distribution Inc 4041 Pk Oaks Blvd Suite 200 *NASDAQ: QLTY* ■ **Fax Area Code:* 813 ■ *TF:* 800-282-2031 ■ *Web:* www.qualitydistribution.com	Tampa	FL	33610	800-282-2031	630-9637*
Queensboro Co 113 E Broad St PO Box 467 *TF:* 877-625-2030 ■ *Web:* www.qnbtrust.com	Louisville	GA	30434	478-625-2000	625-2008
R & R Trucking Inc 302 Thunder Rd PO Box 545 *TF:* 800-625-6885 ■ *Web:* www.randrtruck.com	Duenweg	MO	64841	417-623-6885	623-6479
Ralph Moyle Inc PO Box 248 *Web:* www.ralphmoyle.com	Mattawan	MI	49071	269-668-4531	668-4677
Ram Nationwide Inc 240 W N Bend Rd *TF:* 800-837-0110 ■ *Web:* www.ramnationwide.com	Cincinnati	OH	45216	513-821-0010	761-4632
Raven Transport Co Inc 6800 Broadway Ave *Web:* www.raventrans.com	Jacksonville	FL	32254	904-880-1515	880-1913
Rbx Inc PO Box 2118 *TF:* 877-450-2200 ■ *Web:* www.rbxinc.com	Springfield	MO	65801	417-862-7258	862-5428
Redwood Coast Trucking 2210 Peninsula Dr	Arcata	CA	95521	707-443-0857	
Refrigerated Food Express Inc 57 Littlefield St *TF:* 800-225-2350 ■ *Web:* www.rfxinc.com	Avon	MA	02322	508-587-4600	588-9655
Relco Systems Inc 7310 Chestnut Ridge Rd *TF:* 800-262-1020 ■ *Web:* www.relcosystems.com	Lockport	NY	14094	716-434-8100	434-7229
RFK Transportation 5650 6th St SW	Cedar Rapids	IA	52404	319-364-8102	364-8339
Riechmann Transport Inc 3328 W Chain of Rocks Rd *TF:* 800-844-4225 ■ *Web:* www.riechmanntransport.com	Granite City	IL	62040	618-797-6700	931-4246
River Forest Public Schools 90 7776 Lake St *Web:* www.district90.org	River Forest	IL	60305	708-771-8282	771-8291
Riverview Gardens School District (RGSD) 1370 Northumberland Dr *Web:* www.rgsd.org	Saint Louis	MO	63137	314-869-2505	869-6354
Roadtex Transportation Corp 13 Jensen Dr *TF:* 800-762-3839 ■ *Web:* www.roadtex.com	Somerset	NJ	08873	800-762-3839	
Robert Bearden Inc 2601 Industrial Pk Dr PO Box 870 *TF:* 888-298-6928 ■ *Web:* www.rbitrucking.com	Cairo	GA	39828	229-377-6928	377-2880
Robert Heath Trucking Inc 1201 E 40th St *Web:* www.robertheath.com	Lubbock	TX	79404	806-747-1651	747-0339
Roehl Transport Inc 1916 E 29th St PO Box 750 *TF:* 800-826-8367 ■ *Web:* www.roehl.net	Marshfield	WI	54449	715-591-3795	387-1942
Roger Ward Inc 17275 Green Mountain Rd *TF:* 800-915-6740 ■ *Web:* www.wardnorthamerican.com	San Antonio	TX	78247	210-655-8623	967-5420
Ross Neely Systems Inc 1500 2nd St *Web:* www.rossneely.com	Birmingham	AL	35214	205-798-1137	798-0751
Rountree Transport & Rigging Inc 2640 N Ln Ave *TF:* 800-342-5036 ■ *Web:* www.rountreetransport.com	Jacksonville	FL	32254	904-781-1033	786-6229
Roy Bros Inc 764 Boston Rd *TF Cust Svc:* 800-225-0830	Billerica	MA	01821	978-667-1921	667-5091
Royal Trucking Co 1323 Eshman Ave N PO Box 387 *TF:* 800-321-1293 ■ *Web:* www.royaltruck.com	West Point	MS	39773	662-494-1637	495-1066
Rwh Trucking Inc PO Box 968 *TF:* 800-256-8119 ■ *Web:* www.rwhtrucking.com	Oakwood	GA	30566	770-534-0095	287-7912
S & S Transport Inc PO Box 12579 *Web:* www.sstransport.com	Grand Forks	ND	58208	701-746-8484	746-5665
S T Bunn Construction 1904 University Blvd PO Box 20109 *TF:* 800-297-6302 ■ *Web:* www.stbunn.com	Tuscaloosa	AL	35401	205-752-8195	349-4288
S-j Transportation Co Inc PO Box 169 *Web:* www.sjtransportation.com	Woodstown	NJ	08098	856-769-2741	769-9811
Saia Inc 11465 Johns Creek Pkwy Suite 400 *TF:* 800-765-7242 ■ *Web:* www.scstransportation.com	Johns Creek	GA	30097	800-765-7242	
Saia Motor Freight Line Inc 11456 Johns Creek Pkwy Suite 400 **Fax:* Cust Svc ■ *TF:* 800-950-7242 ■ *Web:* www.saia.com	Duluth	GA	30097	770-232-4050	232-4055*
Salida Union School District 4801 Sisk Rd PO Box 1329 *Web:* www.salida.k12.ca.us	Salida	CA	95368	209-545-0339	545-2270
Sammons Trucking 3665 W Broadway *TF:* 800-548-9276 ■ *Web:* www.sammonstrucking.com	Missoula	MT	59808	406-728-2600	549-4989
Satterwhite Cos Inc 8405 US Hwy 259 *TF:* 800-777-7288 ■ *Web:* www.slh.net	Longview	TX	75605	903-663-1729	663-1721
Schilli Transportation Services Inc 6358 W US 24 *TF:* 800-759-2101 ■ *Web:* www.schilli.com	Remington	IN	47977	219-261-2101	261-2879
Security Van Lines LLC 100 W Airline Dr PO Box 830 *TF:* 800-794-5961 ■ *Web:* www.securityvanlines.net	Kenner	LA	70063	504-466-4449	464-1818
Selland Auto Transport Inc 615 S 96th St *Web:* www.sellandauto.com	Seattle	WA	98108	206-767-5960	767-0604
Seward Motor Freight Inc PO Box 126 *TF:* 800-786-4468 ■ *Web:* www.sewardmotor.com	Seward	NE	68434	402-643-4503	643-2693
Shaffer Trucking Inc 49 E Main St PO Box 418 *TF Cust Svc:* 800-742-3337 ■ *Web:* www.shaffertrucking.com	New Kingstown	PA	17072	717-766-4708	795-5550
Shaw Trucking Inc 7804 Belvedere Rd **Fax Area Code:* 954 ■ *TF:* 800-930-7263 ■ *Web:* www.shawtrucking.com	West Palm Beach	FL	33411	800-930-7263	731-7627*
Sheedy Drayage Co Inc 1215 Michigan St *TF:* 800-792-2984 ■ *Web:* www.sheedycrane.com	San Francisco	CA	94107	415-648-7171	648-1535
Shelba D. Johnson Trucking Inc PO Box 7287 *Web:* www.sdjtrucking.com	High Point	NC	27264	336-476-2000	476-0187
Shetler Moving & Storage Inc 1253 E Diamond Ave *TF:* 800-321-5069 ■ *Web:* www.shetlermoving.com	Evansville	IN	47711	812-421-7750	421-7759
Shippers Express Co 1651 Kerr Dr *TF:* 800-647-2480	Jackson	MS	39204	601-948-4251	948-5232
Short Freight Lines Inc 459 S River Rd *TF:* 800-248-0625	Bay City	MI	48708	989-893-3505	893-3151
Shuster's Transportation Inc 750 E Valley St	Willits	CA	95490	707-459-4131	459-1855
Simons Trucking Inc 920 Simon Dr PO Box 8 *TF:* 800-373-2580 ■ *Web:* www.simonstrucking.com	Farley	IA	52046	563-744-3304	744-3726
Skinner Transfer Corp PO Box 438 *Web:* www.skinnertransfer.com	Reedsburg	WI	53959	608-524-2326	524-9660
South Shore Transportation Inc 4010 Columbus Ave *TF:* 800-418-9726 ■ *Web:* www.sshoretrans.com	Sandusky	OH	44870	419-626-6267	626-9640
Southeastern Freight Lines Inc 420 Davega Rd **Fax:* Cust Svc ■ *TF:* 800-637-7335 ■ *Web:* www.sefl.com	Lexington	SC	29073	803-794-7300	939-3462*
Southern Pan Services Co (SPS) 2385 Lithonia Industrial Blvd PO Box 679 *TF:* 800-334-9145 ■ *Web:* www.southernpan.com	Lithonia	GA	30058	678-301-2400	301-2439
Southwest Freightlines 11991 Transpark Dr Horizon City *TF:* 800-776-5799 ■ *Web:* www.swflines.com	El Paso	TX	79927	915-860-8592	860-9606
Southwestern Motor Transport Inc 4600 Goldfield *TF:* 800-531-1071 ■ *Web:* www.smtlines.com	San Antonio	TX	78218	210-661-6791	662-3295
Spectraserv Inc 75 Jacobus Ave *TF:* 800-445-4436 ■ *Web:* www.spectraserv.com	South Kearny	NJ	07032	973-589-0277	589-0415
Stahly Cartage Co 119 S Main St *TF:* 800-851-5553	Edwardsville	IL	62025	618-656-5070	656-0293
Star Fleet Inc PO Box 769 *TF:* 877-805-9547 ■ *Web:* www.starfleettrucking.com	Goshen	IN	46527	574-534-9702	825-9700
Star Transportation Inc PO Box 100925 **Fax:* Cust Svc ■ *TF Cust Svc:* 800-333-3060 ■ *Web:* www.startransportation.com	Nashville	TN	37224	615-256-4336	255-9013*

	City	State	Zip	Phone	Fax
Steelman Transportation Inc 2160 N Burton Ave	Springfield	MO	65803	417-831-6300	831-6349
TF: 800-488-6287 ■ *Web:* www.steelmantransport.com					
Stevens Transport PO Box 279010	Dallas	TX	75227	214-647-3765	289-7002*
**Fax Area Code:* 972 ■ *TF:* 800-233-9369 ■ *Web:* www.stevenstransport.com					
Styer Transportation Co 7870 215th St W	Lakeville	MN	55044	952-469-4491	469-3422
TF: 800-548-9149 ■ *Web:* www.styertrans.com					
Suffolk Cement Products Inc PO Box 241	Calverton	NY	11933	631-727-2317	727-6211
Web: www.suffolkcement.com					
Sullivan RM Transportation 649 Cottage St	Springfield	MA	01104	413-739-2558	739-1955
TF: 800-628-1064 ■ *Web:* www.sulco.com					
Summitt Trucking LLC 1800 Progress Way	Clarksville	IN	47129	812-285-7777	285-8949
TF: 866-999-7799 ■ *Web:* www.summitttrucking.com					
Sunbelt Furniture Express Inc PO Box 487	Hickory	NC	28603	828-464-7240	465-3560
TF: 800-766-1117					
Sunco Carriers Inc 1025 N Chestnut Rd	Lakeland	FL	33805	863-688-1948	680-1759
TF: 800-237-8288 ■ *Web:* www.suncocarriers.com					
Superior Carriers Inc 711 Jory Blvd Suite 101-N	Oak Brook	IL	60523	630-573-2555	573-2570
TF: 800-654-7707 ■ *Web:* www.superior-carriers.com					
Sweetwater County School District 1 (SCSD) 3550 Foothill Blvd PO Box 1089	Rock Springs	WY	82901	307-352-3400	352-3411
Web: www.sweetwater1.org					
Swift Transportation Co Inc 2200 S 75th Ave	Phoenix	AZ	85043	602-269-9700	907-7380*
NASDAQ: SWFT ■ **Fax Area Code:* 623 ■ *TF:* 800-800-2200 ■ *Web:* www.swifttrans.com					
Swing Transport Inc 1405 N Salisbury Ave	Salisbury	NC	28144	704-633-3567	636-2160
Web: www.swingtransport.com					
T & T Trucking Inc 11396 N Hwy 99	Lodi	CA	95240	209-368-3629	931-6156
TF Cust Svc: 800-692-3457 ■ *Web:* www.tttrucking.com					
T S Keim Inc PO Box 226	Sabetha	KS	66534	785-284-2147	
T-w Transport Inc 7405 S Hayford Rd	Cheney	WA	99004	509-623-4000	623-4069
TF: 800-356-4070 ■ *Web:* www.twtrans.com					
Tankstar USA Inc PO Box 736	Milwaukee	WI	53201	414-671-1600	647-7947
TF: 800-338-5699 ■ *Web:* www.tankstar.com					
TanTara Transportation Corp 2420 Stewart Rd	Muscatine	IA	52761	563-262-8621	264-8998
TF: 800-650-0292 ■ *Web:* www.tantara.us					
Taylor Made Transportation Services Inc 2901 Druid Pk Dr Suite 206	Baltimore	MD	21215	410-728-1951	
Web: www.tmtransportation.com					
Taylor Truck Line Inc 31485 Northfield Blvd	Northfield	MN	55057	507-645-4531	645-9722
TF: 800-962-5994 ■ *Web:* www.taylortruckline.com					
Teal's Express Inc 22411 Teal Dr PO Box 6010	Watertown	NY	13601	315-788-6437	788-5060
TF: 800-836-0369 ■ *Web:* www.teals.com					
Telfer Oil Co 211 Foster St	Martinez	CA	94553	925-228-1515	229-3955
Web: www.telferoil.com					
Tennessee Steel Haulers Inc PO Box 78189	Nashville	TN	37207	615-271-2400	271-2450
TF: 800-776-4004 ■ *Web:* www.tenh.com					
Teresi Trucking Inc 900 1/2 Victor Rd	Lodi	CA	95240	209-368-2472	369-2830
Web: www.teresitrucking.com					
Texas Transeastern Inc PO Box 5339	Pasadena	TX	77508	281-604-3100	604-3102
TF: 800-866-8579 ■ *Web:* www.texastranseastern.com					
Thomas WS Transfer Inc 1854 Morgantown Ave	Fairmont	WV	26554	304-363-8050	363-8052
Tiona Truck Line Inc PO Box 90	Butler	MO	64730	660-679-4197	679-3616
TF: 800-821-3046					
Total Package Express Inc 5871 Cheviot Rd	Cincinnati	OH	45247	513-741-5500	741-5505
TF: 800-420-5505 ■ *Web:* tp-exp.com					
TP Trucking LLC 5630 Table Rock Rd	Central Point	OR	97502	541-664-4776	664-5070
TF: 800-777-1121 ■ *Web:* www.tptrucking.com					
Trailer Bridge Inc 10405 New Berlin Rd E	Jacksonville	FL	32226	904-751-7100	751-7444
NASDAQ: TRBR ■ *TF:* 800-554-1589 ■ *Web:* www.trailerbridge.com					
Trailer Transit Inc 1130 E US 20	Porter	IN	46304	219-926-2111	859-1191*
**Fax Area Code:* 877 ■ *TF:* 800-423-3647 ■ *Web:* www.trailertransit.com					
Trans-Carriers Inc 5135 US Hwy 78	Memphis	TN	38118	901-368-2900	368-0336
TF: 800-999-7383 ■ *Web:* www.transcarriers.com					
Trans-Phos Inc PO Box 9004	Bartow	FL	33831	863-534-1575	534-3200
TF: 800-940-1575 ■ *Web:* www.transphos.com					
TransAm Trucking Inc 15910 S 169th Hwy	Olathe	KS	66051	913-782-5300	324-7194
TF: 800-573-0588 ■ *Web:* www.transamtruck.com					
Transco Leasing Inc PO Box 1400	Russellville	AR	72811	479-967-5700	968-3373
TF: 800-276-5427 ■ *Web:* www.transcolines.com					
Transfreight LLC 4123 Olympic Blvd	Erlanger	KY	41018	859-372-5942	282-9028
TF: 888-890-0400 ■ *Web:* www.transfreight.com					
Transport Corp of America Inc 1715 Yankee Doodle Rd	Eagan	MN	55121	651-686-2500	686-2566
TF: 800-328-3927 ■ *Web:* www.transportamerica.com					
Transport Distribution Co PO Box 306	Joplin	MO	64802	417-624-3814	624-9767
TF: 800-866-7709 ■ *Web:* www.gotdc.com					
Transport Inc 2225 Main Ave SE	Moorhead	MN	56560	218-236-6300	236-0227
TF: 800-598-7267 ■ *Web:* www.transport-inc.com					
Transport Service Co 2001 Spring Rd Suite 400	Oak Brook	IL	60523	630-472-5900	920-6806
TF Sales: 800-323-5561 ■ *Web:* www.transportserviceco.com					
TransWood CarriersInc 2565 St Marys Ave PO Box 189	Omaha	NE	68101	402-346-8092	341-2112
Web: www.transwood.com					
Tri Star Freight System Inc 5407 Mesa Dr	Houston	TX	77028	713-631-1095	631-1099
Web: www.tristarfreightsys.com					
Tri-State Delivery Inc 3411 Summerhill Rd	Texarkana	TX	75503	903-794-1423	793-0771
Web: www.tsdinc.com					
Triad Transport Inc PO Box 818	McAlester	OK	74502	918-426-4751	426-4770
TF: 800-324-1139 ■ *Web:* www.triadtransport.com					
Trinity Logistics Group Inc 2525 N Stemmons Fwy	Dallas	TX	75207	214-631-4420	589-8501
Web: www.trinitytrucking.com					
Triple Crown Services 2720 Dupont Commerce Ct Suite 200	Fort Wayne	IN	46825	260-416-3600	416-3771
TF: 800-325-6510 ■ *Web:* www.triplecrownsvc.com					
Truck Transport Inc 2280 Cassens Dr	Fenton	MO	63026	636-343-1877	343-3042
TF: 800-274-5995					
Truline Corp 9390 Redwood St	Las Vegas	NV	89139	702-362-7495	362-3215
TF: 800-634-6489 ■ *Web:* www.trulinecorp.com					
Tryon Trucking Inc PO Box 68	Fairless Hills	PA	19030	215-295-6622	295-7168
TF: 800-523-5254 ■ *Web:* www.tryontrucking.com					
Underwood Transfer Co LLC 940 W Troy Ave	Indianapolis	IN	46225	317-783-9235	782-2769
TF: 800-428-2372 ■ *Web:* www.underwoodcompanies.com					
United Road Services Inc 10701 Middlebelt Rd	Romulus	MI	48174	734-947-7900	
TF: 888-730-7797 ■ *Web:* www.unitedroad.com					
Universal Truckload Services Inc 12755 E Nine Mile Rd	Warren	MI	48089	586-920-0100	920-0258
NASDAQ: UACL ■ *TF:* 800-233-9445 ■ *Web:* www.goutsi.com					
Upper Township School District 525 Perry Rd	Woodbine	NJ	08270	609-628-3500	628-2002
Web: www.upperschools.org					
US Xpress Enterprises Inc 4080 Jenkins Rd	Chattanooga	TN	37421	423-510-3000	510-4006
TF: 800-251-6291 ■ *Web:* www.usxpress.com					
USA Truck Inc 3200 Industrial Pk Rd	Van Buren	AR	72956	479-471-2500	471-2577
NASDAQ: USAK ■ *TF:* 800-872-8782 ■ *Web:* www.usa-truck.com					
USF Holland Inc 750 E 40th St	Holland	MI	49423	616-395-5000	392-3104
TF: 800-456-6322 ■ *Web:* www.yrcregional.com					
USF Reddaway Inc 16277 SE 130th Ave PO Box 1035	Clackamas	OR	97015	503-650-1286	650-3635
TF: 800-395-1360 ■ *Web:* www.yrcregional.com					
V & S Midwest Carriers Corp 2001 Hyland Ave PO Box 107	Kaukauna	WI	54130	920-766-9696	766-1772
TF: 800-876-4330 ■ *Web:* www.vsmidwest.com					
Valley Bulk Transport Inc 919 Western Ave	Washington	PA	15301	724-745-7702	745-7712
TF: 866-405-2855 ■ *Web:* www.valleybulk.com					
Van Eerden Foodservice Co 650 Ionia Ave SW	Grand Rapids	MI	49503	616-475-0900	475-0990
TF: 800-833-7374 ■ *Web:* www.vaneerden.com					
Van Wyk Freight Lines Inc PO Box 70	Grinnell	IA	50112	641-236-7551	236-4247
TF: 800-362-2595 ■ *Web:* www.middlewest.com					
Venezia Transport Service Inc PO Box 909	Royersford	PA	19468	610-495-5200	495-5086
Web: www.veneziainc.com					
Vitran Express Canada Inc 1201 Creditstone Rd	Concord	ON	L4K0C2	416-798-4965	798-4753
NASDAQ: VTNC ■ *TF:* 800-263-9588 ■ *Web:* www.vitran.com					
Vitran Express Inc 6500 E 30th St	Indianapolis	IN	46219	317-803-6400	543-1228
TF: 800-366-0150 ■ *Web:* www.vitranexpress.com					
Volume Transportation Inc 6575 Marshall Blvd	Lithonia	GA	30058	770-482-1400	482-4817
TF: 800-879-5565 ■ *Web:* www.volinc.com					
Waggoners Trucking 5220 Midland Rd	Billings	MT	59101	406-248-1919	248-7557
TF: 800-999-9097 ■ *Web:* www.waggonerstrucking.com					
Waller Truck Co Inc 400 S McCleary Rd	Excelsior Springs	MO	64024	816-629-3400	629-3460
TF: 800-821-2196 ■ *Web:* www.wallertruck.com					
Walpole Inc PO Box 1177	Okeechobee	FL	34973	863-763-5593	763-7874
TF: 800-741-6500 ■ *Web:* www.walpoleinc.com					
Ward Trucking Corp PO Box 1553	Altoona	PA	16603	814-944-0803	944-2369
TF: 800-458-3625 ■ *Web:* www.wardtrucking.com					
Warren Transport Inc 210 Beck Ave	Waterloo	IA	50701	319-233-6113	233-7459
TF: 800-553-2792 ■ *Web:* www.warrentransport.com					
Watsontown Trucking Co Inc 60 Belford Blvd	Milton	PA	17847	570-522-9820	538-0254
TF: 800-344-0313 ■ *Web:* www.watsontowntrucking.com					
WC McQuaide Inc 153 Macridge Rd	Johnstown	PA	15904	814-269-6000	269-6092
TF: 800-456-0292 ■ *Web:* www.mcquaide.com					
Weaver Bros Inc 2230 Spar Ave	Anchorage	AK	99501	907-278-4526	276-4316
TF: 800-478-4600 ■ *Web:* www.wbialaska.com					
Wel Cos Inc 1625 S Broadway PO Box 5610	De Pere	WI	54115	920-339-0110	983-2139
TF: 800-333-4415 ■ *Web:* www.welcompanies.com					
Werner Enterprises Inc 14507 Frontier Rd	Omaha	NE	68138	402-895-6640	894-3927*
NASDAQ: WERN ■ **Fax:* Hum Res ■ *TF:* 800-228-2240 ■ *Web:* www.werner.com					
West Bros Transportation Services Inc PO Box 21019	Durham	NC	27703	919-281-1151	281-1171
TF: 800-743-9378 ■ *Web:* www.westbros.com					
Western Co-op Transport Assn 4501 72nd St SW	Montevideo	MN	56265	320-269-5531	269-5532
TF: 800-992-8817 ■ *Web:* www.westernco-op.com					
Western Express Inc 7135 Centennial Pl	Nashville	TN	37209	615-259-9920	350-9957
TF: 800-316-7160 ■ *Web:* www.westernexp.com					
Westwood Contractors Inc 951 W 7th St	Fort Worth	TX	76102	817-877-3800	877-4731
Web: www.westwoodcontractors.com					
White Bros Trucking Co PO Box 82	Wasco	IL	60183	630-584-3810	584-3816
TF: 800-323-4762					
White River Paper Co 1118 Rt 14	Hartford	VT	05047	802-295-3188	295-5494
TF: 800-639-7226 ■ *Web:* www.wrpaper.com					
White Settlement Independent School District 401 S Cherry Ln Po Box 150187	Fort Worth	TX	76108	817-367-1300	367-1351
Web: www.wsisd.com					
Whitefish Bay Schools 1200 E Fairmount Ave	Whitefish Bay	WI	53217	414-963-3901	
Web: www.wfbschools.com					
Wildwood Express Trucking 12416 E Swanson Ave	Kingsburg	CA	93631	559-897-1035	897-1038
TF: 800-627-3115					
Wilhelm Trucking & Rigging Co 3250 NW St Helens Rd PO Box 10363	Portland	OR	97296	503-227-0561	241-4913
TF Cust Svc: 800-275-3974 ■ *Web:* www.wilhelmtruck.com					
Willis Shaw Express Inc 201 N Elm St	Elm Springs	AR	72728	479-248-7261	248-1967
TF: 800-643-3540 ■ *Web:* www.willisshaw.com					
Wilson Lines of Minnesota Inc 2131 2nd Ave	Newport	MN	55055	651-459-2384	769-3050
TF: 800-525-5555 ■ *Web:* www.wilsonlines.com					
Wilson Trucking Corp 137 Wilson Blvd	Fishersville	VA	22939	540-949-3200	949-3205
TF: 800-494-5766 ■ *Web:* www.wilsontrucking.com					
Wiseway Motor Freight Inc PO Box 838	Hudson	WI	54016	800-876-1660	381-3197*
**Fax Area Code:* 715 ■ *TF:* 800-876-1660 ■ *Web:* www.wiseway.com					
Woodruff Construction LLC 1890 Kountry Ln	Fort Dodge	IA	50501	515-576-1118	955-2170
Web: www.woodruffcompanies.com					

	Phone	Fax
Woody Bogler Trucking Co PO Box 229 .... Rosebud MO 63091 TF: 800-899-4120 ■ Web: www.woodybogler.com	573-764-3700	764-4200
Wragtime Air Freight Inc 2315 Nadeau St .... Huntington Park CA 90255 *Fax Area Code: 856 ■ TF: 800-586-9701 ■ Web: www.visionexpressltl.com	323-586-9700	854-8416*
Wright Transportation Inc PO Box 50317 .... Mobile AL 36605 TF: 800-342-4598 ■ Web: www.wrighttrans.com	251-432-6390	432-5845
Wyatt Transfer Inc 3035 Bells Rd PO Box 24326 .... Richmond VA 23224 *Fax: Administration ■ TF: 800-552-5708 ■ Web: www.wyatttransferinc.com	804-743-3800	271-9598*
Wynne Transport Service Inc 2222 N 11th St .... Omaha NE 68108 TF: 800-383-9330 ■ Web: www.wynnetr.com	402-342-4001	342-4608
Yanke Group of Cos 2815 Lorne Ave .... Saskatoon SK S7J0S5 TF: 800-667-7988 ■ Web: www.yanke.ca	306-955-4221	955-5663
Yeatts Transfer Co PO Box 687 .... Altavista VA 24517 TF: 800-446-0939	434-369-5695	369-5705
Yorkville Community Unit School District 115 602A Center Pkwy PO Box 579 .... Yorkville IL 60560 Web: www.yorkville.k12.il.us	630-553-4382	553-4398
Young's Commercial Transfer 2075 W Scranton Ave .... Porterville CA 93257 TF: 800-289-1639 ■ Web: www.yctinc.com	559-784-6651	784-5280
Yourga Trucking Inc 154 JH Yourga Pl .... Wheatland PA 16161 TF: 800-245-1722 ■ Web: www.yourga.com	724-981-3600	981-3603

784 TYPESETTING & RELATED SERVICES

SEE ALSO Graphic Design p. 1999; Printing Companies - Commercial Printers p. 2451

	Phone	Fax
Acitronics 746 E Main St .... Branford CT 06405	203-481-0308	481-5901
Ano-Coil Corp 60 E Main St .... Rockville CT 06066 TF: 800-492-7286 ■ Web: www.anocoil.com	860-871-1200	872-0534
Aptara Inc 3110 Fairview Pk Dr .... Falls Church VA 22042 Web: www.aptaracorp.com	703-352-0001	352-8862
Auto-Graphics Inc 3201 Temple Ave .... Pomona CA 91768 TF: 800-776-6939 ■ Web: www4.auto-graphics.com	909-595-7204	595-3506
BeaconPMG 1797 Seddon Ct .... Ashland OH 44805 Web: www.beacon.com	419-289-0558	289-8923
Blanks Printing & Imaging Inc 2343 N Beckley Ave .... Dallas TX 75208 TF: 800-325-7651 ■ Web: www.blanks.com	214-741-3905	741-6105
Carey Digital 1718 Central Pkwy .... Cincinnati OH 45214 TF: 800-767-6071 ■ Web: www.careydigital.com	513-241-5210	241-2205
Casablanca Printing Inc 2716 S Grand Ave .... Santa Ana CA 92705 Web: www.casablancaprinting.com	714-662-2250	662-2825
Cohber Press PO Box 93100 .... Rochester NY 14692 TF: 800-724-3032 ■ Web: www.cohber.com	585-475-9100	475-9406
Color Communication Inc 4000 W Fillmore St .... Chicago IL 60624 TF: 800-458-5743 ■ Web: www.ccicolor.com	773-638-1400	638-0887
Composing Room of Michigan Inc 678 Front Ave NW Suite 135 .... Grand Rapids MI 49504	616-776-7940	776-7940
Computer Composition Corp 1401 W Girard Ave .... Madison Heights MI 48071 Web: www.computercomposition.com	248-545-4330	544-1611
Container Graphics Corp 113 Edinburgh Dr S Suite 110 .... Cary NC 27511 Web: www.containergraphics.com	919-481-4200	469-4897
Continental Colorcraft 1166 W Garvey Ave .... Monterey Park CA 91754 Web: www.continentalcolorcraft.com	323-283-3000	283-3206
Dixie Graphics Co 636 Grassmere Pk .... Nashville TN 37211 Web: www.dixiegraphics.com	615-832-7000	832-7621
ET Lowe Publishing Co 2920 Sidco Dr .... Nashville TN 37204 Web: www.etlowe.com	615-254-8866	254-8867
G & S Typesetters Inc 410 Baylor St .... Austin TX 78703	512-478-5341	476-4756
GGS Technical Publications Services 3265 Farmtrail Rd .... York PA 17409 TF: 800-927-4474 ■ Web: www.ggs-techpubs.com	717-764-2222	767-0027
Graphics Group 2800 Taylor St .... Dallas TX 75226 Web: www.graphicsgroup.com	214-749-2222	749-2252
Imaging Technologies Services Inc 655 Lambert Dr NE .... Atlanta GA 30324 Web: www.itrepro.com	404-874-8400	872-1215
IPC Communications Services 2179 Maiden Ln .... Saint Joseph MI 49085 TF: 800-369-2646 ■ Web: www.ipc-world.com	269-983-7105	983-5736
IPP Lithoplate Corp 1313 W Randolph St 2nd Fl .... Chicago IL 60607 Web: www.ipplitho.com	312-243-0465	243-6318
Jackson Typesetting Co Inc 1820 W Ganson St .... Jackson MI 49202	517-784-0576	784-1200
KC Photo Engraving Co 2666 E Nina St .... Pasadena CA 91107 TF: 800-660-4127	323-681-0203	681-6506
Kreber Graphics Inc 2580 Westbelt Dr .... Columbus OH 43228 TF: 800-777-3501 ■ Web: www.kreber.com	614-529-5701	777-4890
Lake Shore Imaging Inc 815 25th Ave .... Bellwood IL 60104	312-427-8216	427-4949
Lasergraphics Inc 4 Squire Rd .... Revere MA 02151 Web: www.laserg.com	781-289-2022	289-2027
Ligature The 4909 Alcoa Ave .... Los Angeles CA 90058 TF: 800-944-5440 ■ Web: www.theligature.com	323-585-6000	585-1737
Mark Trece Inc 2001 Stockton Rd .... Joppa MD 21085 Web: www.marktrece.com	410-879-0060	879-3438
Maryland Composition Co 14880 Sweitzer Rd .... Laurel MD 20707 Web: www.marylandcomp.com	410-760-7900	760-5295
MATRIX Publishing Co 1920 Bank Ln .... York PA 17404 Web: www.matrixpublishing.com	717-764-9673	764-9672
Memphis Engraving Co (IMEC) 5120 Elmore Rd .... Memphis TN 38134 TF: 800-426-6803 ■ Web: www.goimec.com	901-388-8200	377-2739
New England Typographic Service Inc 206 W Newberry Rd .... Bloomfield CT 06002 Web: www.netype.com	860-242-2251	242-9350
Newtype Inc 447 Rt 10E Suite 14 .... Randolph NJ 07869 Web: www.newtypeinc.com	973-361-6000	361-6005
Pal Graphics Inc 2525 Braga Dr .... Broadview IL 60155 Web: www.palgraphics.com	708-344-8500	344-8503
Para Plate & Plastics Inc 15910 Shoemaker Ave .... Cerritos CA 90701 TF: 800-788-1556	562-404-3434	404-2496
Presstek Inc 55 Executive Dr .... Hudson NH 03051 NASDAQ: PRST ■ TF: 877-862-2227 ■ Web: www.presstek.com	603-595-7000	546-4234
Printing Prep Inc 12 E Tupper St .... Buffalo NY 14203 TF: 877-878-7114 ■ Web: www.printleader.us	716-852-5011	852-3150
Progressive Information Technologies 315 Busser Rd .... Emigsville PA 17318 TF: 800-673-2500 ■ Web: www.pit-magnus.com	717-764-5908	767-4092
Reed Technology & Information Services Inc 7 Walnut Grove Dr .... Horsham PA 19044 Web: www.reedtech.com	215-441-6400	
Regency Infographics Inc 2867 E Allegheny Ave .... Philadelphia PA 19134 TF: 800-829-0020 ■ Web: www.sed.com/desktop-publishing.html	215-425-8810	634-0780
Richards Graphic Communications Inc 2700 Van Buren St .... Bellwood IL 60104 Web: www.rgcnet.com	708-547-6000	547-6044
Ridgways Inc 6300 Gulfton St .... Houston TX 77081 Web: www.ridgways.com	713-782-8580	782-2862
Riverpoint Media Group 150 Eva St .... Saint Paul MN 55107	651-227-4037	227-7368
Schawk Inc 1600 Sherwin Ave .... Des Plaines IL 60018 TF: 800-621-1909 ■ Web: www.schawk.com	847-296-6000	296-9466
Southern Graphic Systems Inc 2823 S Floyd St .... Louisville KY 40209 TF: 800-228-3720	502-637-5443	624-5299
Southern Graphics Systems 7435 Empire Dr .... Florence KY 41042	859-525-1190	647-8205
Spectragraphic Inc 4 Brayton Ct .... Commack NY 11725 Web: www.spectragraphic.com	631-499-3100	499-5255
ST Assoc Inc One Teal Rd .... Wakefield MA 01880 Web: www.stassoc.com	781-246-4700	246-4218
Stevenson The Color Co Inc 535 Wilmer Ave .... Cincinnati OH 45226 Web: www.stevensoncolor.com	513-321-7500	321-7502
Stratford Textech 70 Landmark Hill Dr .... Brattleboro VT 05301 TF: 800-451-4328	802-254-6073	254-5240
T & R Graphic Imaging Inc 2535 17th St .... Denver CO 80211 TF: 800-525-2497 ■ Web: www.tandrinc.com	303-458-0626	455-8905
Texas Graphics Resource 1601 Prudential Dr .... Dallas TX 75235	214-630-2800	630-0713
Total Works Inc 2222 N Elston Ave .... Chicago IL 60614 TF: 866-489-4313 ■ Web: www.totalworks.net	773-489-4313	489-0482
Typesetting Inc 1144 S Robertson Blvd .... Los Angeles CA 90035 TF: 800-794-8973	310-273-3330	273-0733
VT Graphics Inc 465 Penn St PO Box 5334 .... Yeadon PA 19050 Web: www.vtgraph.com	610-259-4090	259-7235
West Essex Graphics Inc (WEG) 305 Fairfield Ave .... Fairfield NJ 07004 TF: 800-221-5859 ■ Web: www.westessexgraphics.com	973-227-2400	227-2906
Yaeger Graphics Inc 935 W 3rd Ave .... Columbus OH 43212	614-294-6326	294-7363

785 ULTRASONIC CLEANING EQUIPMENT

SEE ALSO Dental Equipment & Supplies - Mfr p. 1782

	Phone	Fax
Branson Ultrasonics Corp 41 Eagle Rd .... Danbury CT 06813 Web: www.branson-plasticsjoin.com	203-796-0400	796-9838
Crest Ultrasonics Corp PO Box 7266 .... Trenton NJ 08628 TF: 800-992-7378 ■ Web: www.crest-ultrasonics.com	609-883-4000	883-6452
L & R Mfg Co 577 Elm St .... Kearny NJ 07032 Web: www.lrultrasonics.com	201-991-5330	991-5870
Sonicor Instrument Corp 14 Connor Ln .... Deer Park NY 11729 TF: 800-864-5022 ■ Web: www.sonicor.com	631-842-3344	842-3389
Sonics & Materials Inc 53 Church Hill Rd .... Newtown CT 06470 TF: 800-745-1105 ■ Web: www.sonicsandmaterials.com	203-270-4600	270-4610
Sterigenics 2015 Spring Rd Suite 650 .... Oak Brook IL 60523 TF: 800-472-4508 ■ Web: www.sterigenics.com	630-928-1700	928-1701

786 UNITED NATIONS AGENCIES, ORGANIZATIONS, PROGRAMS

	Phone	Fax
United Nations UN Plaza Rm DC2-2220 .... New York NY 10017 *Fax: PR ■ Web: www.un.org	212-963-1234	963-4260*
Food & Agriculture Organization of the UN (FAO) 1 UN Plaza Suite DC1-1125 .... New York NY 10017 Web: www.fao.org	212-963-6036	963-5425
Inter-American Development Bank 1300 New York Ave NW .... Washington DC 20577 Web: www.iadb.org	202-623-1000	623-3096
International Atomic Energy Agency (IAEA) 1 UN Plaza Rm DC1-1155 .... New York NY 10017 *Fax Area Code: 917 ■ Web: www.iaea.org	212-963-6010	367-4046*
International Fund for Agricultural Development (IFAD) 1775 K St NW Suite 410 .... Washington DC 20006 Web: www.ifad.org	202-331-9099	331-9366
International Labour Organization (ILO) 220 E 42nd St Suite 3101 .... New York NY 10017 Web: www.ilo.org	212-697-0150	697-5218
International Monetary Fund (IMF) 700 19th St NW .... Washington DC 20431 Web: www.imf.org	202-623-7000	623-4661
International Tsunami Information Ctr 737 Bishop St Suite 2200 .... Honolulu HI 96813 Web: www.itic.ioc-unesco.org	808-532-6422	532-5576
United Nations Children's Fund (UNICEF) 3 United Nations Plaza .... New York NY 10017 TF: 800-553-1200 ■ Web: www.unicef.org	212-326-7000	888-7465
United Nations Development Programme 1 UN Plaza .... New York NY 10017 Web: www.undp.org	212-906-5000	906-5364

	City	State	Zip	Phone	Fax
United Nations Educational Scientific & Cultural Organization (UNESCO)					
2 UN Plaza Suite 900	New York	NY	10017	212-963-5995	963-8014
Web: www.unesco.org					
United Nations Environment Programme (UNEP)					
900 17th St NW Suite 506	Washington	DC	20006	202-785-0465	785-2096
Web: www.rona.unep.org					
United Nations Industrial Development Organization (UNIDO)					
1 UN Plaza Suite DC1-1110	New York	NY	10017	212-963-6890	963-7904
Web: www.unido.org					
World Bank Group The (WBG) 1818 H St NW	Washington	DC	20433	202-473-1000	477-6391
Web: www.worldbank.org					
World Food Programme North America					
2 UN Plaza DC-2 Rm 2500	New York	NY	10017	212-963-8364	963-8019
Web: www.wfp.org					
World Health Organization (WHO)					
2 UN Plaza Suite DC2-0970	New York	NY	10017	212-963-4388	963-8565
Web: www.who.int					
World Intellectual Property Organization (WIPO)					
2 UN Plaza Rm 2525	New York	NY	10017	212-963-6813	963-4801
Web: www.wipo.int					

787 UNITED NATIONS MISSIONS

SEE ALSO Embassies & Consulates - Foreign, in the US p. 1815

All Of The Missions Listed Here Are Permanent Missions Except The Holy See, Which Has The Status Of Permanent Observer Mission To The Un. Two Member States, Kiribati And Palau, Are Not Listed Because They Do Not Maintain Offices In New York. Another Member State, Guinea Bissau, Has A New York Office But Is Excluded From This List Because No Telephone Number Was Available For It.

	City	State	Zip	Phone	Fax
Afghanistan					
Permanent Mission of Islamic Republic of Afghanistan to the UN					
633 Third Ave 27A Fl	New York	NY	10017	212-972-1212	972-1216
Web: www.afghanistan-un.org					
Albania					
Permanent Mission to the UN 320 E 79th St	New York	NY	10075	212-249-2059	535-2917
Web: www.albania-un.org					
Algeria					
Permanent Mission to the UN 326 E 48th St	New York	NY	10017	212-750-1960	759-9538
Web: www.algeria-un.org					
Andorra					
Permanent Mission to the UN					
2 UN Plaza 27th Fl	New York	NY	10017	212-750-8064	750-6630
Angola					
Permanent Mission to the UN					
820 2nd Ave 12th Fl	New York	NY	10017	212-861-5656	861-9295
Web: www.un.int					
Antigua & Barbuda					
Permanent Mission to the UN					
305 E 47th St 6th Fl	New York	NY	10017	212-541-4117	757-1607
Web: www.un.int/antigua					
Argentina					
Permanent Mission to the UN					
1 UN Plaza 25th Fl	New York	NY	10017	212-688-6300	980-8395
Web: www.un.int/argentina					
Armenia					
Permanent Mission to the UN 119 E 36th St	New York	NY	10016	212-686-9079	686-3934
Web: www.un.int					
Australia					
Permanent Mission to the UN					
150 E 42nd St 33rd Fl	New York	NY	10017	212-351-6600	351-6610
Web: www.unny.mission.gov.au					
Austria					
Permanent Mission to the UN					
600 3rd Ave 31st Fl	New York	NY	10016	917-542-8400	949-1840*
**Fax Area Code:* 212 ■ *Web:* www.un.int/austria					
Azerbaijan					
Permanent Mission to the UN					
866 UN Plaza Suite 560	New York	NY	10017	212-371-2559	371-2784
Web: www.un.int					
Bahrain					
Permanent Mission to the UN					
866 2nd Ave 14th Fl	New York	NY	10017	212-223-6200	319-0687
Web: www.un.int/bahrain					
Bangladesh					
Permanent Mission to the UN					
227 E 45th St 14th Fl	New York	NY	10017	212-867-3434	972-4038
Web: www.un.int					
Belarus					
Permanent Mission to the UN					
136 E 67th St 4th Fl	New York	NY	10021	212-535-3420	734-4810
Web: www.un.int					
Belgium					
Permanent Mission to the UN					
885 2nd Ave 41st Fl	New York	NY	10017	212-378-6300	681-7618
Web: www.diplomatie.be/newyorkun					
Belize					
Permanent Mission to the UN					
675 3rd Ave Suite 1911	New York	NY	10017	212-593-0999	593-0932
Benin					
Permanent Mission to the UN 125 E 38th St	New York	NY	10016	212-684-1339	684-2058
Web: www.un.int					
Bolivia					
Permanent Mission to the UN					
211 E 43rd St Rm 802	New York	NY	10017	212-682-8132	687-4642
Bosnia & Herzegovina					
Permanent Mission to the UN					
420 Lexington Ave Suite 607	New York	NY	10017	212-751-9015	751-9019
Web: www.bhmisijaun.org					
Botswana					
Permanent Mission to the UN 154 E 46th St	New York	NY	10017	212-889-2277	725-5061
Brazil					
Permanent Mission to the UN					
747 3rd Ave 9th Fl	New York	NY	10017	212-372-2600	371-5716
Web: www.un.int					
Bulgaria					
Permanent Mission to the UN 11 E 84th St	New York	NY	10028	212-737-4790	472-9865
Web: www.un.int/bulgaria					
Burkina Faso					
Permanent Mission to the UN					
866 UN Plaza Suite 326	New York	NY	10017	212-308-4720	308-4690
Web: www.burkina-onu.org					
Burundi					
Permanent Mission to the UN					
336 E 45th St 12th Fl	New York	NY	10017	212-499-0001	499-0006
Cambodia					
Permanent Mission to the UN 327 E 58th St	New York	NY	10022	212-759-7129	759-7672
Web: www.un.int/cambodia					
Cameroon					
Permanent Mission to the UN 22 E 73rd St	New York	NY	10021	212-794-2296	249-0533
Web: www.delecam.us					
Canada					
Permanent Mission to the UN					
885 2nd Ave 14th Fl	New York	NY	10017	212-848-1100	848-1195
Web: www.canadainternational.gc.ca					
Cape Verde					
Permanent Mission to the UN 27 E 69th St	New York	NY	10021	212-472-0333	794-1398
Chad					
Permanent Mission to the UN 1329 E 36th St	New York	NY	10016	212-986-0980	986-0152
Chile					
Permanent Mission to the UN					
305 E 47th St 10th Fl	New York	NY	10017	212-832-3323	832-0236
China					
Permanent Mission to the UN 350 E 35th St	New York	NY	10016	212-655-6100	634-7626
Web: www.china-un.org					
Colombia					
Permanent Mission to the UN 140 E 57th St	New York	NY	10022	212-355-7776	355-7776
Web: www.colombiaun.org					
Comoros					
Permanent Mission to the UN					
866 UN Plaza Suite 418	New York	NY	10017	212-750-1637	750-1657
Web: www.un.int					
Congo Democratic Republic of					
Permanent Mission to the UN					
866 UN Plaza Suite 511	New York	NY	10017	212-319-8061	319-8232
Web: www.un.int					
Congo Republic of					
Permanent Mission to the UN 14 E 65th St	New York	NY	10021	212-744-7840	744-7975
Web: www.un.int					
Costa Rica					
Permanent Mission to the UN					
211 E 43rd St Rm 903	New York	NY	10017	212-986-6373	986-6373
Web: www.un.int/wcm/content/site/costarica					
Cote d'Ivoire					
Permanent Mission to the UN					
800 2nd Ave E 5th Fl	New York	NY	10017	646-649-5061	781-9974
Web: www.un.int/cotedivoire					
Croatia					
Permanent Mission to the UN					
820 2nd Ave 19th Fl	New York	NY	10017	212-986-1585	986-2011
Web: www.un.int/croatia					
Cuba					
Permanent Mission to the UN					
315 Lexington Ave	New York	NY	10016	212-689-7215	689-9073
Web: www.un.int/cuba					
Cyprus					
Permanent Mission to the UN 13 E 40th St	New York	NY	10016	212-481-6023	685-7316
Web: www.un.int					
Czech Republic					
Permanent Mission to the UN					
1109 Madison Ave	New York	NY	10028	212-717-5643	717-5064
Web: www.mzv.cz/un.newyork					
Dominican Republic					
Permanent Mission to the UN					
144 E 44th St 4th Fl	New York	NY	10017	212-867-0833	297-2509
Web: www.un.int					
Ecuador					
Permanent Mission to the UN					
866 UN Plaza Suite 516	New York	NY	10017	212-935-1680	935-1835

				Phone	Fax
Egypt					
Permanent Mission to the UN 304 E 44th St	New York	NY	10017	212-503-0300	949-5999
El Salvador					
Permanent Mission to the UN 46 Pk Ave 3rd Fl	New York	NY	10016	212-679-1616	725-3467
Eritrea					
Permanent Mission to the UN 800 2nd Ave 18th Fl. *Web:* www.eritrea-unmission.org	New York	NY	10017	212-687-3390	687-3138
Estonia					
Permanent Mission to the UN 305 E 47th St 6th Fl. **Fax Area Code: 646* ■ *Web:* www.un.estemb.org	New York	NY	10017	212-883-0640	514-0099*
Ethiopia					
Permanent Mission to the UN 866 2nd Ave 3rd Fl *Web:* www.un.int/ethiopia	New York	NY	10017	212-421-1830	754-0360
Fiji					
Permanent Mission to the UN 630 3rd Ave 7th Fl	New York	NY	10017	212-687-4130	687-3963
Finland					
Permanent Mission to the UN 866 UN Plaza Suite 222 *Web:* www.finlandun.org	New York	NY	10017	212-355-2100	759-6156
France					
Permanent Mission to the UN 1 Dag Hammarskjold Plaza # 36 *Web:* www.un.int	New York	NY	10017	212-308-5700	421-6889
Gabon					
Permanent Mission to the UN 18 E 41st St 9th Fl *Web:* www.un.int/gabon	New York	NY	10017	212-686-9720	689-5769
Gambia					
Permanent Mission to the UN 800 2nd Ave Rm 400F	New York	NY	10017	212-949-6640	856-9820
Permanent Mission to the UN 1 UN Plaza 26th Fl *Web:* www.un.int/georgia	New York	NY	10017	212-759-1949	759-1832
Germany					
Permanent Mission to the UN 871 UN Plaza *Web:* www.new-york-un.diplo.de	New York	NY	10017	212-940-0400	940-0402
Ghana					
Permanent Mission to the UN 19 E 47th St *Web:* www.un.int/ghana	New York	NY	10017	212-832-1300	751-6743
Greece					
Permanent Mission to the UN 866 2nd Ave 13th Fl. *Web:* www.greeceun.org	New York	NY	10017	212-888-6900	888-4440
Grenada					
Permanent Mission to the UN 800 2nd Ave Suite 400-K	New York	NY	10017	212-599-0301	599-1540
Guatemala					
Permanent Mission to the UN 57 Pk Ave *Web:* www.un.int	New York	NY	10016	212-679-4760	685-8741
Guinea					
Permanent Mission to the UN 140 E 39th St *Web:* www.un.int	New York	NY	10016	212-687-8115	687-8248
Guyana					
Permanent Mission to the UN 801 2nd Ave 5th Fl	New York	NY	10017	212-573-5828	573-6225
Haiti					
Permanent Mission to the UN 801 2nd Ave Rm 600	New York	NY	10017	212-370-4840	661-8698
Holy See					
Permanent Observer Mission to the UN 25 E 39th St *Web:* www.holyseemission.org	New York	NY	10016	212-370-7885	370-9622
Honduras					
Permanent Mission to the UN 866 UN Plaza Suite 417 *Web:* www.un.int	New York	NY	10017	212-752-3370	223-0498
Hungary					
Permanent Mission to the UN 223 E 52nd St *Web:* www.un.int	New York	NY	10022	212-752-0209	755-5395
Iceland					
Permanent Mission to the UN 800 3rd Ave 36th Fl *Web:* www.iceland.org/un/nyc	New York	NY	10022	212-593-2700	593-6269
India					
Permanent Mission to the UN 235 E 43rd St *Web:* www.un.int	New York	NY	10017	212-490-9660	490-9656
Indonesia					
Permanent Mission to the UN 325 E 38th St *Web:* www.indonesiamission-ny.org	New York	NY	10016	212-972-8333	972-9780
Iran					
Permanent Mission to the UN 622 3rd Ave 34th Fl *Web:* www.un.int	New York	NY	10017	212-687-2020	867-7086
Iraq					
Permanent Mission to the UN 14 E 79th St	New York	NY	10021	212-737-4433	772-1794
Ireland					
Permanent Mission to the UN 1 Dag Hammarskjold Plaza # 885 *Web:* www.un.int	New York	NY	10017	212-421-6934	752-4726
Israel					
Permanent Mission to the UN 800 2nd Ave *Web:* www.israel-un.org	New York	NY	10017	212-499-5510	499-5515
Italy					
Permanent Mission to the UN 885 Second Ave *Web:* www.italyun.org	New York	NY	10017	212-486-9191	486-1036
Jamaica					
Permanent Mission to the UN 767 3rd Ave 9th Fl *Web:* www.un.int	New York	NY	10017	212-935-7509	935-7607
Japan					
Permanent Mission to the UN 866 UN Plaza 2nd Fl *Web:* www.un.int	New York	NY	10017	212-223-4300	751-1966
Kazakhstan					
Permanent Mission to the UN 305 E 47th St 3rd Fl. *Web:* www.kazakhstanun.org	New York	NY	10017	212-230-1900	230-1172
Kenya					
Permanent Mission to the UN 866 UN Plaza Rm 304 *Web:* www.un.int/kenya	New York	NY	10017	212-421-4740	486-1985
Korea Democratic People's Republic of					
Permanent Mission to the UN 820 2nd Ave 13th Fl.	New York	NY	10017	212-972-3105	972-3154
Korea Republic of					
Permanent Mission to the UN 335 E 45th St *Web:* www.un.int	New York	NY	10017	212-439-4000	986-1083
Kuwait					
Permanent Mission to the UN 321 E 44th St *Web:* www.kuwaitmission.com	New York	NY	10017	212-973-4300	370-1733
Kyrgyzstan					
Permanent Mission to the UN 866 UN Plaza Suite 477	New York	NY	10017	212-486-4214	486-5259
Lao People's Democratic Republic					
Permanent Mission to the UN 317 E 51st St *Web:* www.un.int	New York	NY	10022	212-832-2734	750-0039
Latvia					
Permanent Mission to the UN 333 E 50th St	New York	NY	10022	212-838-8877	838-8920
Lebanon					
Permanent Mission to the UN 866 UN Plaza Rm 531-533 *Web:* www.un.int/wcm/content/site/lebanon	New York	NY	10017	212-355-5460	838-2819
Lesotho					
Permanent Mission to the UN 204 E 39th St *Web:* www.un.int	New York	NY	10016	212-661-1690	682-4388
Liberia					
Permanent Mission to the UN 866 UN Plaza Suite 480	New York	NY	10017	212-687-1033	687-1035
Libyan Arab Jamahiriya					
Permanent Mission to the UN 309-315 E 48th St	New York	NY	10017	212-752-5775	593-4787
Liechtenstein					
Permanent Mission to the UN 633 3rd Ave 27th Fl *Web:* www.newyork.liechtenstein.li	New York	NY	10017	212-599-0220	599-0064
Lithuania					
Permanent Mission to the UN 708 3rd Ave 10th Fl *Web:* www.un.int/lithuania/lithuania.html	New York	NY	10017	212-983-9474	983-9473
Luxembourg					
Permanent Mission to the UN 17 Beekman Pl *Web:* www.un.int/luxembourg	New York	NY	10022	212-935-3589	935-5896
Macedonia					
Permanent Mission to the UN 866 UN Plaza Suite 517 *Web:* www.macedonia-un.org	New York	NY	10017	212-308-8504	308-8724
Madagascar					
Permanent Mission to the UN 820 2nd Ave Suite 800	New York	NY	10017	212-986-9491	986-6271
Malawi					
Permanent Mission to the UN 866 UN Plaza Suite 486 *Web:* www.un.int/wcm/content/site/malawi	New York	NY	10017	212-317-8738	317-8729
Malaysia					
Permanent Mission to the UN 313 E 43rd St *Web:* www.un.int/malaysia	New York	NY	10017	212-986-6310	490-8576
Maldives					
Permanent Mission to the UN 800 2nd Ave Suite 400-E *Web:* www.un.int/maldives	New York	NY	10017	212-599-6194	661-6405
Mali					
Permanent Mission to the UN 111 E 69th St *Web:* www.un.int/mali	New York	NY	10021	212-737-4150	472-3778
Malta					
Permanent Mission to the UN 249 E 35th St *Web:* www.msa.gov.mt	New York	NY	10016	212-725-2345	779-7097
Marshall Islands					
Permanent Mission to the UN 800 2nd Ave 18th Fl.	New York	NY	10017	212-983-3040	983-3202

	City	State	ZIP	Phone	Fax
Mauritania					
Permanent Mission to the UN 116 E 38th St	New York	NY	10016	212-252-0113	252-0175
Mauritius					
Permanent Mission to the UN 211 E 43rd St 15th Fl	New York	NY	10017	212-949-0190	697-3829
Mexico					
Permanent Mission to the UN 2 UN Plaza 28th Fl	New York	NY	10017	212-752-0220	688-8862
Web: www.un.int/mexico					
Micronesia					
Permanent Mission to the UN 820 2nd Ave Suite 17A	New York	NY	10017	212-697-8370	697-8295
Web: www.fsmgov.org/fsmun					
Moldova					
Permanent Mission to the UN 35 E 29th St	New York	NY	10016	212-447-1867	447-4067
Web: www.un.int/moldova					
Monaco					
Permanent Mission to the UN 866 UN Plaza Suite 520	New York	NY	10017	212-832-0721	832-5358
Web: www.monaco-un.org					
Mongolia					
Permanent Mission to the UN 6 E 77th St	New York	NY	10075	212-861-9460	861-9464
Web: www.un.int/mongolia					
Morocco					
Permanent Mission to the UN 866 2nd Ave 6th & 7th Fl	New York	NY	10017	212-421-1580	980-1512
Web: www.un.int/morocco					
Mozambique					
Permanent Mission to the UN 420 E 50th St	New York	NY	10022	212-644-6800	644-5972
Web: www.un.int					
Myanmar					
Permanent Mission to the UN 10 E 77th St	New York	NY	10075	212-744-1271	744-1290
Web: www.myanmarmission.com					
Namibia					
Permanent Mission to the UN 360 Lexington Ave Suite 1502	New York	NY	10017	212-685-2003	685-1561
Web: www.un.int/namibia					
Nepal					
Permanent Mission to the UN 820 2nd Ave Suite 17B	New York	NY	10017	212-370-3988	953-2038
Web: www.un.int/nepal					
Netherlands					
Permanent Mission to the UN 235 E 45th St 16th Fl	New York	NY	10017	212-519-9500	370-1954
Web: www.netherlandsmission.org/homepage.asp					
Nicaragua					
Permanent Mission to the UN 820 2nd Ave Suite 801	New York	NY	10017	212-490-7997	286-0815
Web: www.un.int					
Niger					
Permanent Mission to the UN 417 E 50th St	New York	NY	10022	212-421-3260	753-6931
Web: www.un.int					
Nigeria					
Permanent Mission to the UN 828 2nd Ave	New York	NY	10017	212-953-9130	697-1970
Web: www.un.int/nigeria					
Norway					
Permanent Mission to the UN 825 3rd Ave 39th Fl	New York	NY	10022	212-421-0280	688-0554
Web: www.norway-un.org					
Oman					
Permanent Mission to the UN 305 E 47th St 12th Fl	New York	NY	10017	212-355-3505	644-0070
Pakistan					
Permanent Mission to the UN 8 E 65th St	New York	NY	10065	212-879-8600	744-7348
Web: www.pakun.org					
Panama					
Permanent Mission to the UN 866 UN Plaza Suite 4030	New York	NY	10017	212-421-5420	421-2694
Web: www.panama-un.org/en.html					
Papua New Guinea					
Permanent Mission to the UN 201 E 42nd St Suite 405	New York	NY	10017	212-557-5001	557-5009
Paraguay					
Permanent Mission to the UN 211 E 43rd St Suite 400	New York	NY	10017	212-687-3490	818-1282
Web: www.un.int/paraguay					
Permanent Mission of Solomon Islands to the United Nations					
800 2nd Ave Suite 400L	New York	NY	10017	212-599-6192	661-8925
Web: www.un.int/wcm/content/site/solomonislands					
Permanent Mission of Sweden to the United Nations					
885 2nd Ave Fl 46 1 Dag Hammarskjold Plaza	New York	NY	10017	212-583-2500	583-2549
Web: www.swedenabroad.com					
Permanent Mission of the Republic of Seychelles to the United Nations					
800 2nd Ave Suite 400C	New York	NY	10017	212-972-1785	972-1786
Web: www.un.int/wcm/content/site/seychelles					
Peru					
Permanent Mission to the UN 820 2nd Ave Suite 1600	New York	NY	10017	212-687-3336	972-6975
Philippines					
Permanent Mission to the UN 556 5th Ave 5th Fl	New York	NY	10036	212-764-1300	840-8602
Web: www.un.int					
Poland					
Permanent Mission to the UN 9 E 66th St	New York	NY	10065	212-744-2506	517-6771
Web: www.polandun.org					
Portugal					
Permanent Mission to the UN 866 2nd Ave 9th Fl	New York	NY	10017	212-759-9444	355-1124
Web: www.missionofportugal.org					
Qatar					
Permanent Mission to the UN 809 UN Plaza 4th Fl	New York	NY	10017	212-486-9335	758-4952
Romania					
Permanent Mission to the UN 200 E 38th St	New York	NY	10016	212-682-3274	682-9746
Web: www.un.int					
Russia					
Permanent Mission to the UN 136 E 67th St	New York	NY	10065	212-861-4900	628-0252
Web: www.un.int/russia					
Rwanda					
Permanent Mission to the UN 124 E 39th St	New York	NY	10016	212-679-9010	679-9133
Saint Kitts & Nevis					
Permanent Mission to the UN 414 E 75th St Suite 5	New York	NY	10021	212-535-1234	535-6854
Web: www.stkittsnevis.org					
Saint Lucia					
Permanent Mission to the UN 800 2nd Ave 9th Fl	New York	NY	10017	212-697-9360	697-4993
Web: www.un.int/stlucia					
Saint Vincent & the Grenadines					
Permanent Mission to the UN 800 2nd Ave 4th Fl	New York	NY	10017	212-599-0950	599-1020
Samoa					
Permanent Mission to the UN 800 2nd Ave Suite 400J	New York	NY	10017	212-599-6196	599-0797
San Marino					
Permanent Mission to the UN 327 E 50th St	New York	NY	10022	212-751-1234	751-1436
Senegal					
Permanent Mission to the UN 238 E 68th St	New York	NY	10065	212-517-9030	517-3032
Web: www.un.int					
Serbia					
Permanent Mission to the UN 854 5th Ave	New York	NY	10021	212-879-8700	879-8705
Web: www.un.int					
Sierra Leone					
Permanent Mission to the UN 245 E 49th St	New York	NY	10017	212-688-1656	688-4924
Web: www.un.int/sierraleone					
Singapore					
Permanent Mission to the UN 231 E 51st St	New York	NY	10022	212-223-3331	826-5028
Web: www.mfa.gov.sg/newyork					
Slovakia					
Permanent Mission to the UN 801 2nd Ave 12th Fl	New York	NY	10017	212-286-8418	286-8419
Web: www.unnewyork.mfa.sk					
Slovenia					
Permanent Mission to the UN 600 3rd Ave 24th Fl	New York	NY	10016	212-370-3007	370-1824
Web: www.un.int/slovenia					
Somalia					
Permanent Mission to the UN 425 E 61st St Suite 702	New York	NY	10065	212-688-9410	759-0651
South Africa					
Permanent Mission to the UN 333 E 38th St 9th Fl	New York	NY	10016	212-213-5583	692-2498
Web: www.southafrica-newyork.net					
Spain					
Permanent Mission to the UN 245 E 47th St 36th Fl	New York	NY	10017	212-661-1050	949-7247
Web: www.spainun.org					
Sudan					
Permanent Mission to the UN 305 E 47th St 4th Fl	New York	NY	10017	212-573-6033	573-6160
Suriname					
Permanent Mission to the UN 866 UN Plaza Suite 320	New York	NY	10017	212-826-0660	980-7029
Web: www.un.int					
Swaziland					
Permanent Mission to the UN 408 E 50th St	New York	NY	10022	212-371-8910	754-2755
Switzerland					
Permanent Mission to the UN 633 3rd Ave 29th Fl	New York	NY	10011	212-286-1540	286-1555
Web: www.eda.admin.ch					
Syria					
Permanent Mission to the UN 820 2nd Ave 15th Fl	New York	NY	10017	212-661-1313	983-4439
Tanzania					
Permanent Mission to the UN 201 E 42nd St Suite 1700	New York	NY	10017	212-972-9160	682-5232
Web: www.tanzania-un.org					
Thailand					
Permanent Mission to the UN 351 E 52nd St.	New York	NY	10022	212-754-2230	688-3029
Timor-Leste					
Permanent Mission to the UN 866 UN Plaza Suite 441	New York	NY	10017	212-759-3675	759-4196
Web: www.timor-leste-un.org					

	City	State	Zip	Phone	Fax
Togo					
Permanent Mission to the UN 112 E 40th St	New York	NY	10016	212-490-3455	983-6684
Trinidad & Tobago					
Permanent Mission to the UN 820 2nd Ave	New York	NY	10017	212-697-7620	682-3580
Tunisia					
Permanent Mission to the UN 31 Beekman Pl	New York	NY	10022	212-751-7503	751-0569
Turkey					
Permanent Mission to the UN 821 UN Plaza 10th Fl	New York	NY	10017	212-949-0150	949-0086
Web: www.un.int/turkey					
Tuvalu					
Permanent Mission to the UN 800 2nd Ave Suite 400-D	New York	NY	10017	212-490-0534	808-4975
Uganda					
Permanent Mission to the UN 336 E 45th St	New York	NY	10017	212-949-0110	687-4517
Ukraine					
Permanent Mission to the UN 220 E 51st St	New York	NY	10022	212-759-7003	355-9455
Web: www.un.int/ukraine					
United Arab Emirates					
Permanent Mission to the UN 305 E 47th St 7th Fl	New York	NY	10017	212-371-0480	371-4923
United Kingdom					
Permanent Mission to the UN 885 2nd Ave 28th Fl	New York	NY	10017	212-745-9200	745-9316
Web: www.ukun.org					
United States of America					
Permanent Mission to the UN 799 United Nations Plaza	New York	NY	10017	212-415-4000	415-4443
Web: www.un.int					
Uruguay					
Permanent Mission to the UN 866 UN Plaza Suite 322	New York	NY	10017	212-752-8240	593-0935
Web: www.un.int/uruguay					
Vanuatu					
Permanent Mission to the UN 800 E 2nd Ave	New York	NY	10017	212-661-4303	422-3427
Web: www.un.int					
Venezuela					
Permanent Mission to the UN 335 E 46th St	New York	NY	10017	212-557-2055	557-3528
Web: www.un.int					
Vietnam					
Permanent Mission to the UN 866 UN Plaza Suite 435	New York	NY	10017	212-644-0594	644-5732
Web: www.un.int					
Yemen					
Permanent Mission to the UN 413 E 51st St	New York	NY	10022	212-355-1730	750-9613
Zambia					
Permanent Mission to the UN 237 E 52nd St	New York	NY	10022	212-888-5770	888-5213
Web: www.un.int					
Zimbabwe					
Permanent Mission to the UN 128 E 56th St	New York	NY	10022	212-980-9511	308-6705

788 UNIVERSITIES - CANADIAN

	City	Prov	Postal Code	Phone	Fax
Acadia University 15 University Ave	Wolfville	NS	B4P2R6	902-542-2201	585-1081
TF: 877-585-1121 ■ *Web:* www2.acadiau.ca					
Alberta College of Art & Design 1407 14th Ave NW	Calgary	AB	T2N4R3	403-284-7600	289-6682
TF: 800-251-8290 ■ *Web:* www.acad.ab.ca					
Athabasca University 1 University Dr	Athabasca	AB	T9S3A3	780-675-6111	675-6174
TF: 800-788-9041 ■ *Web:* www.athabascau.ca					
Atlantic Baptist University 333 Gorge Rd	Moncton	NB	E1G3H9	506-858-8970	858-9694
TF: 888-968-6228 ■ *Web:* www.abu.nb.ca					
Bethany Bible College 26 Western St	Sussex	NB	E4E1E6	506-432-4400	432-4425
TF: 888-432-4444 ■ *Web:* www.bbc.ca					
Bishop's University 2600 College St	Sherbrooke	QC	J1M1V7	819-822-9600	822-9661
TF: 800-567-2792 ■ *Web:* www.ubishops.ca					
Brandon University 18th St Suite 270	Brandon	MB	R7A6A9	204-727-7337	728-7346
Web: www.brandonu.ca					
Brescia University College 1285 Western Rd	London	ON	N6G1H2	519-432-8353	858-5137
Web: www.brescia.uwo.ca					
Brock University 500 Glenridge Ave	Saint Catharines	ON	L2S3A1	905-688-5550	988-5488
Web: www.brocku.ca					
Campion College at the University of Regina 3737 Wascana Pkwy	Regina	SK	S4S0A2	306-586-4242	359-1200
TF: 800-667-7282 ■ *Web:* www.campioncollege.sk.ca					
Canadian College of Naturopathic Medicine 1255 Sheppard Ave E	Toronto	ON	M2K1E2	416-498-1255	498-1576
TF: 866-241-2266 ■ *Web:* www.ccnm.edu					
Canadian Memorial Chiropractic College 6100 Leslie St	Toronto	ON	M2H3J1	416-482-2340	482-9745
Web: www.cmcc.ca					
Cape Breton University 1250 Grand Lake Rd	Sydney	NS	B1P6L2	902-539-5300	562-0119
TF: 888-959-9995 ■ *Web:* www.cbu.ca					
Carleton University 1125 Colonel By Dr	Ottawa	ON	K1S5B6	613-520-7400	520-3847
TF: 888-354-4414 ■ *Web:* www.carleton.ca					
Columbia Bible College 2940 Clearbrook Rd	Abbotsford	BC	V2T2Z8	604-853-3358	853-3063
Web: www.columbiabc.edu					
Concordia University 1455 de Maisonneuve Blvd W	Montreal	QC	H3G1M8	514-848-2424	848-2621
Web: www.concordia.ca					
Concordia University College of Alberta 7128 Ada Blvd NW	Edmonton	AB	T5B4E4	780-479-9220	378-8460
TF: 866-479-5200 ■ *Web:* www.concordia.ab.ca					
Dalhousie University 6299 S St Rm 125 Henry Hicks A&A Bldg	Halifax	NS	B3H4R2	902-494-3998	494-2839
Web: www.dal.ca					
Dominican University College 96 Empress Ave	Ottawa	ON	K1R7G3	613-233-5696	233-6064
Web: www.collegedominicain.ca					
Emmanuel Bible College 100 Fergus Ave	Kitchener	ON	N2A2H2	519-894-8900	894-5331
Web: www.ebcollege.on.ca					
First Nations University of Canada					
Northern 1301 Central Ave	Prince Albert	SK	S6V4W1	306-763-0066	764-3511
Web: www.firstnationsuniversity.ca					
Regina 1 First Nations Way	Regina	SK	S4S7K2	306-790-5950	790-5999
Web: www.firstnationsuniversity.ca					
Saskatoon 710 Duke St	Saskatoon	SK	S7K0P8	306-931-1800	665-0175
TF: 800-267-6303 ■ *Web:* www.firstnationsuniversity.ca					
Heritage College & Seminary 175 Holiday Inn Dr	Cambridge	ON	N3C3T2	519-651-2869	651-2870
TF: 800-465-1961 ■ *Web:* www.heritage-theo.edu					
Huntington University 935 Ramsey Lake Rd	Sudbury	ON	P3E2C6	705-673-4126	673-6917
TF: 800-461-6366 ■ *Web:* www.huntington.laurentian.ca					
Huron University College 1349 Western Rd	London	ON	N6G1H3	519-438-7224	438-3938
Web: www.huronuc.on.ca					
King's University College 9125 50th St	Edmonton	AB	T6B2H3	780-465-3500	465-3534
TF: 800-661-8582 ■ *Web:* www.kingsu.ab.ca					
Lakehead University 955 Oliver Rd	Thunder Bay	ON	P7B5E1	807-343-8110	343-8023
Web: www.lakeheadu.ca					
Laurentian University 935 Ramsey Lake Rd	Sudbury	ON	P3E2C6	705-675-1151	675-4807
TF: 800-461-4030 ■ *Web:* www.laurentian.ca/Laurentian/Home/Laurentian+Homepage.htm?Laurentian_Lang=en-CA					
Laval University 2325 Rue University	Quebec	QC	G1V0A6	418-656-2131	656-5216
TF: 877-785-2825 ■ *Web:* www2.ulaval.ca					
McGill University 845 Sherbrooke St W	Montreal	QC	H3A2T5	514-398-4455	398-8939*
**Fax:* Admissions ■ *Web:* www.mcgill.ca					
McMaster University 1280 Main St W	Hamilton	ON	L8S4L8	905-525-9140	527-1105
Web: www.mcmaster.ca					
Memorial University of Newfoundland PO Box 4200	Saint John's	NL	A1C5S7	709-737-8000	737-4569
Web: www.mun.ca					
Mount Allison University 65 York St	Sackville	NB	E4L1E2	506-364-2269	364-2272
Web: www.mta.ca					
Mount Royal College 4825 Mt Royal Gate SW	Calgary	AB	T3E6K6	403-440-6111	440-6339
TF: 877-440-5001 ■ *Web:* www.mtroyal.ab.ca					
Mount Saint Vincent University 166 Bedford Hwy	Halifax	NS	B3M2J6	902-457-6117	457-6498
TF: 877-733-6788 ■ *Web:* www.msvu.ca					
Nipissing University 100 College Dr PO Box 5002	North Bay	ON	P1B8L7	705-474-3450	495-4421
Web: www.nipissingu.ca/Pages/default.aspx					
Brantford 67 Darling St	Brantford	ON	N3T2K6	519-756-8228	720-9996
Web: www.nipissingu.ca					
Muskoka 440 Ecclestone Dr	Bracebridge	ON	P1L1Z6	705-645-2921	645-2922
Web: www.nipissingu.ca					
NSCAD University 5163 Duke St	Halifax	NS	B3J3J6	902-444-9600	425-2420
Web: www.nscad.ca					
Ontario College of Art & Design 100 McCaul St	Toronto	ON	M5T1W1	416-977-6000	977-6006
Web: www.ocad.on.ca					
Prairie Bible Institute 330 6th Ave N PO Box 4000	Three Hills	AB	T0M2N0	403-443-5511	443-5540
TF: 800-661-2425 ■ *Web:* www.prairie.edu					
Queen's University 99 University Ave	Kingston	ON	K7L3N6	613-533-2000	533-2068
Web: www.queensu.ca					
Redeemer University College 777 Garner Rd E	Ancaster	ON	L9K1J4	905-648-2131	648-2134
TF: 877-779-0913 ■ *Web:* www.redeemer.on.ca					
Royal Military College of Canada Stn Forces PO Box 17000	Kingston	ON	K7K7B4	613-541-6000	541-6599
Web: www.rmc.ca					
Royal Roads University 2005 Sooke Rd	Victoria	BC	V9B5Y2	250-391-2550	391-2500
TF: 800-788-8028 ■ *Web:* www.royalroads.ca					
Ryerson University 350 Victoria St	Toronto	ON	M5B2K3	416-979-5000	979-5221
Web: www.ryerson.ca/home.html					
Saint Frances Xavier University PO Box 5000	Antigonish	NS	B2G2W5	902-863-3300	867-2329*
**Fax:* Admissions ■ *TF Admissions:* 877-867-7839 ■ *Web:* www.stfx.ca					
Saint Jerome's University 290 Westmount Rd N	Waterloo	ON	N2L3G3	519-884-8110	884-5759
Web: www.sju.ca					
Saint Mary's University 923 Robie St	Halifax	NS	B3H3C3	902-420-5756	420-5141
Web: www.smu.ca					
Saint Paul University 223 Main St	Ottawa	ON	K1S1C4	613-236-1393	782-3014
TF: 800-637-6859 ■ *Web:* www.ustpaul.ca					
Saint Thomas University 51 Dineen Dr	Fredericton	NB	E3B5G3	506-452-0640	450-9615
Web: www.w3.stu.ca					
Simon Fraser University					
Burnaby 8888 University Dr MBC 1150	Burnaby	BC	V5A1S6	778-782-2667	782-5496
Web: www.sfu.ca					
Harbour Centre 515 W Hastings St	Vancouver	BC	V6B5K3	778-782-6930	782-5219
Web: www.harbour.sfu.ca					
Surrey 2400 Central City 10153 King George Hwy	Surrey	BC	V3T2W1	604-268-7500	
Web: www.surrey.sfu.ca					
Taylor University College & Seminary 11525 23rd Ave	Edmonton	AB	T6J4T3	780-431-5200	436-9416
TF: 800-567-4988 ■ *Web:* www.taylor-edu.ca					
Thompson Rivers University 900 McGill Rd PO Box 3010	Kamloops	BC	V2C5N3	250-828-5000	371-5960*
**Fax:* Admissions ■ *TF:* 800-663-1663 ■ *Web:* www.tru.ca					
Thorneloe University 935 Ramsey Lake Rd	Sudbury	ON	P3E2C6	705-673-1730	673-4979
TF: 866-846-7635 ■ *Web:* thorneloe.laurentian.ca					
Toronto Baptist Seminary & Bible College 130 Gerrard St E	Toronto	ON	M5A3T4	416-925-3263	925-8305
Web: www.tbs.edu					
Toronto School of Theology 47 Queen's Pk Crescent E	Toronto	ON	M5S2C3	416-978-4039	978-7821
Web: www.tst.edu					
Trent University 1600 W Bank Dr	Peterborough	ON	K9J7B8	705-748-1011	748-1629
TF: 888-739-8885 ■ *Web:* www.trentu.ca					
Trinity Western University 7600 Glover Rd	Langley	BC	V2Y1Y1	604-888-7511	513-2064*
**Fax:* Admissions ■ *TF:* 888-468-6898 ■ *Web:* www.twu.ca					
Universite de Moncton					
Edmundston 165 Blvd Hebert	Edmundston	NB	E3V2S8	506-737-5051	737-5373
TF: 888-736-8623 ■ *Web:* www.umce.ca					
Shippagan 218 Blvd JD Gauthier	Shippagan	NB	E8S1P6	506-336-3400	336-3604
TF: 800-363-8336 ■ *Web:* www.umcs.ca					

Phone | Fax

Universite de Montreal
CP 6128 Succursale Centre Ville .... Montreal QC H3C3J7 514-343-6111 343-5788*
Fax: Admissions ■ *Web:* www.umontreal.ca
Universite de Sherbrooke
2500 boul de l'Universite .... Sherbrooke QC J1K2R1 819-821-8000 821-7966
Web: www.usherbrooke.ca
Longueil
1111 Rue St Charles O
Tour O 5 Etage Bureau 500 .... Longueil QC J4K5G4 450-463-1835 670-3689
Web: www.usherbrooke.ca
Universite du Quebec 475 Rue du Parvis .... Quebec QC G1K9A9 418-657-3551 657-2132
Web: www.uquebec.ca
Universite du Quebec a Montreal
CP 8888 Succursale Centre-Ville .... Montreal QC H3C3P8 514-987-3000 987-8932
Web: www.uqam.ca
Universite du Quebec a Trois-Rivieres
3351 Boul des Forges CP 500 .... Trois-Rivieres QC G9A5H7 819-376-5011 376-5210
Web: www.uqtr.ca
Universite Sainte Anne 1695 Rte1 .... Pointe-de-l'Eglise NS B0W1M0 902-769-2114 769-2930
Web: www.usainteanne.ca
University of Alberta
89th Ave & 114th St 201 Administration Bldg .... Edmonton AB T6G2M7 780-492-3111 492-7172
Web: www.ualberta.ca
Augustana 4901 46th Ave .... Camrose AB T4V2R3 780-679-1100 679-1129
TF: 800-661-8714 ■ *Web:* www.augustana.ab.ca
University of British Columbia
2016-1874 E Mall................................ Vancouver BC V6T1Z1 604-822-9836 822-3599
TF: 877-272-1422 ■ *Web:* www.ubc.ca
Okanagan 3333 University Way...................... Kelowna BC V1V1V7 250-491-6500
Web: www.web.ubc.ca
University of Calgary 2500 University Dr NW .... Calgary AB T2N1N4 403-220-5110 282-7298
Web: www.ucalgary.ca
University of Guelph 50 Stone Rd E.................... Guelph ON N1G2W1 519-824-4120 766-9481
Web: www.uoguelph.ca
University of Lethbridge
4401 University Dr .... Lethbridge AB T1K3M4 403-329-2111 329-5159*
Fax: Admissions ■ *Web:* www.uleth.ca
University of Manitoba
65 Chancellors Cir 424 University Ctr .... Winnipeg MB R3T2N2 204-474-8880 474-7554
TF Admissions: 800-224-7713 ■ *Web:* www.umanitoba.ca
University of Moncton
18 Ave Antonine-Maillet............................ Moncton NB E1A3E9 506-858-4000 858-4544
TF: 800-363-8336 ■ *Web:* www.umoncton.ca
University of New Brunswick
100 Tucker Park Rd PO Box 4400.................. Fredericton NB E2L4L5 506-453-4666 453-5016
Web: www.unb.ca
Saint John 100 Tucker Pk Rd PO Box 5050........... Saint John NB E2L4L5 506-648-5500 648-5528
Web: www.unbsj.ca
University of Northern British Columbia
3333 University Way.......................... Prince George BC V2N4Z9 250-960-5555 960-6330
Web: www.unbc.ca
University of Ottawa 550 Cumberland St .... Ottawa ON K1N6N5 613-562-5800 562-5323
TF: 877-868-8292 ■ *Web:* www.uottawa.ca
University of Prince Edward Island
550 University Ave .... Charlottetown PE C1A4P3 902-566-0400 628-4311
TF: 800-606-8734 ■ *Web:* www.home.upei.ca
University of Regina 3737 Wascana Pkwy.............. Regina SK S4S0A2 306-585-4111 337-2525
TF: 800-644-4756 ■ *Web:* www.uregina.ca
Luther College 3737 Wascana Pkwy .... Regina SK S4S0A2 306-585-5333 585-5267
Web: www.luthercollege.edu
University of Saskatchewan
105 Administration Pl............................ Saskatoon SK S7N5A2 306-966-8565 966-8676
Web: www.usask.ca
Saint Thomas More College 1437 College Dr .... Saskatoon SK S7N0W6 306-966-8900 966-8904
TF: 800-667-2019 ■ *Web:* www.stmcollege.ca
University of Sudbury 935 Ramsey Lake Rd .... Sudbury ON P3E2C6 705-673-5661 673-4912
Web: www.usudbury.com
University of Toronto 315 Bloor St W .... Toronto ON M5S1A3 416-978-2190 978-7022*
Fax: Admissions ■ *Web:* www.utoronto.ca
Mississauga 3359 Mississauga Rd N .... Mississauga ON L5L1C6 905-828-5399 569-4301
Web: www.utm.utoronto.ca
Scarborough 1265 Military Trail .... Toronto ON M1C1A4 416-287-8872 978-7022
Web: www.utsc.utoronto.ca
University of Trinity College 6 Hoskin Ave.............. Toronto ON M5S1H8 416-978-2522 978-2797
Web: www.trinity.utoronto.ca
Victoria University 140 Charles St.................... Toronto ON M5S1K9 416-585-4524 585-4524
Web: www.vicu.utoronto.ca
University of Victoria
3800 Finnerty Rd PO Box 1700 Stn CSC .... Victoria BC V8P5C2 250-472-5416 472-5477
Web: www.uvic.ca
University of Waterloo 200 University Ave W .... Waterloo ON N2L3G1 519-888-4567 746-3242
Web: uwaterloo.ca
University of Western Ontario
1393 Western Rd Suite 6100 .... London ON N6A3K7 519-661-2111 661-3630*
Fax: Purchasing ■ *Web:* www.uwo.ca
King's University College 266 Epworth Ave............. London ON N6A2M3 519-433-3491 433-2227
TF: 800-265-4406 ■ *Web:* www.uwo.ca
University of Windsor 401 Sunset Ave .... Windsor ON N9B3P4 519-253-3000 973-7070
Web: www.uwindsor.ca

University of Winnipeg 515 Portage Ave.............. Winnipeg MB R3B2E9 204-786-9914 783-8910
Web: www.uwinnipeg.ca
Victoria Motion Picture School Ltd
775 Topaz Ave Suite 101............................. Victoria BC V8T4Z7 250-381-3032
TF: 888-522-3456 ■ *Web:* www.vicfilm.com
Wilfrid Laurier University
75 University Ave W .... Waterloo ON N2L3C5 519-884-1970 886-9351
Web: www.wlu.ca
York University 4700 Keele St........................ Toronto ON M3J1P3 416-736-2100 736-5536
Web: www.yorku.ca/web/index.htm

789 UNIVERSITY SYSTEMS

Listings Are Organized By State Names.

Phone | Fax

Alabama Higher Education Commission
100 N Union St PO Box 302000.................. Montgomery AL 36130 334-242-1998 242-0268
Web: www.ache.state.al.us
University of Alabama System
401 Queen City Ave .... Tuscaloosa AL 35401 205-348-5861 348-9788
Web: www.uasystem.ua.edu
University of Alaska System
910 Yukon Dr PO Box 775000 .... Fairbanks AK 99775 907-450-8000 450-8012
Web: www.alaska.edu
Arakansas Higher Education Dept
114 E Capitol Ave.............................. Little Rock AR 72201 501-371-2000 371-2001
Web: www.arkansashighered.com
University of Arkansas System
2404 N University Ave .... Little Rock AR 72207 501-686-2500 686-2507
Web: www.uasys.edu
California State University
401 Golden Shore.............................. Long Beach CA 90802 562-951-4000 951-4899
Web: www.calstate.edu
University of California System
1111 Franklin St 12th Fl............................ Oakland CA 94607 510-987-9074 987-9086
Web: www.ucop.edu
Colorado State University System
410 17th St Suite 2440.............................. Denver CO 80202 303-534-6290 534-6298
Web: www.csusystem.edu
University of Colorado System
1800 Grant St Suite 800 .... Denver CO 80203 303-860-5600 860-5610
Web: www.cu.edu
Connecticut State University System
39 Woodland St .... Hartford CT 06105 860-493-0000 493-0085
Web: www.ctstateu.edu
Delaware Higher Education Commission
820 N French St 5th Fl .... Wilmington DE 19801 302-577-3240 577-6765
TF: 800-292-7935 ■ *Web:* www.doe.state.de.us
State University System of Florida
325 W Gaines St Suite 1614...................... Tallahassee FL 32399 850-245-0466 245-9685
University System of Georgia
270 Washington St SW.............................. Atlanta GA 30334 404-656-2250 657-6979
Web: www.usg.edu
University of Hawaii System 2500 Campus Rd .... Honolulu HI 96822 808-956-8111 956-3952
Web: www.hawaii.edu
Illinois Eastern Community Colleges District 529 (inc)
233 E Chestnut St.................................. Olney IL 62450 618-393-2982
TF: 866-582-4322 ■ *Web:* www.iecc.edu
Illinois Higher Education Board
431 E Adams St 2nd Fl.......................... Springfield IL 62701 217-782-2551 782-8548
Web: www.ibhe.org
University of Illinois System
506 S Wright St Suite 352 .... Urbana IL 61801 217-333-1920 244-2282
Web: www.uillinois.edu
Louisiana State University System
3810 W Lakeshore Dr......................... Baton Rouge LA 70808 225-578-2111 578-5524
Web: www.lsusystem.lsu.edu
Southern University System
JS Clark Administrative Bldg 4th Fl .... Baton Rouge LA 70813 225-771-4500 771-5522
Web: www.sus.edu
University of Louisiana System
1201 N 3rd St Suite 7-300 .... Baton Rouge LA 70802 225-342-6950 342-6473
Web: www.ulsystem.net
University of Maine System 16 Central St.............. Bangor ME 04401 207-973-3200 973-3296
Web: www.maine.edu
University System of Maryland
3300 Metzerott Rd .... Adelphi MD 20783 301-445-2740 445-1931
TF: 800-477-8437 ■ *Web:* www.ums.edu
Massachusetts Higher Education Board
1 Ashburton Pl Rm 1401 .... Boston MA 02108 617-994-6950 727-6397
Web: www.mass.edu
University of Massachusetts System
225 Franklin St 33rd Fl............................. Boston MA 02110 617-287-7050 287-7044
Web: www.massachusetts.edu
Minnesota State Colleges & Universities
Wells Fargo Pl 30 7th St E Suite 350 .... Saint Paul MN 55101 651-296-8012 297-5550
TF: 888-667-2848 ■ *Web:* www.mnscu.edu
University of Missouri System
321 University Hall............................ Columbia MO 65211 573-882-2011 882-2721
TF: 800-225-6075 ■ *Web:* www.umsystem.edu
Montana University System 2500 E Broadway St......... Helena MT 59601 406-444-6570 444-1469
Web: www.montana.edu
Nebraska State College System
1115 K St # 102 .... Lincoln NE 68508 402-471-2505 471-2669
Web: www.nscs.edu
University of Nebraska System
3835 Holdrege St Varner Hall........................ Lincoln NE 68583 402-472-2111 472-1237
TF: 800-542-1602 ■ *Web:* www.nebraska.edu
Nevada System of Higher Education
2601 Enterprise Rd.................................. Reno NV 89512 775-784-4905 784-1127
Web: system.nevada.edu

Phone | Fax

University System of New Hampshire
25 Concord Rd Dunlap Ctr Durham NH 03824 603-862-1800 862-0946
Web: www.usnh.edu

New Jersey Higher Education Commission
20 W State St PO Box 542 Trenton NJ 08625 609-292-4310 292-7225
Web: www.state.nj.us

New Mexico Higher Education Dept
1068 Cerrillos Rd Santa Fe NM 87505 505-476-1100 476-6511
TF: 800-279-9777 ■ *Web:* www.hed.state.nm.us

City University of New York (CUNY)
535 E 80th St New York NY 10075 212-794-5555 794-5397
TF: 800-286-9937 ■ *Web:* www.cuny.edu

New York State Education Dept
89 Washington Ave 5N EB Albany NY 12234 518-474-3901
Web: www.highered.nysed.gov

State University of New York The (SUNY)
State University Plaza Albany NY 12246 518-320-1888 443-5322
TF: 800-342-3811 ■ *Web:* www.suny.edu

North Carolina Community College System
200 W Jones St Raleigh NC 27603 919-807-7100 807-7164
Web: www.nccs.cc.nc.us

University of North Carolina
910 Raleigh Rd PO Box 2688 Chapel Hill NC 27515 919-962-1000 962-6725
Web: www.northcarolina.edu

North Dakota University System
600 E Blvd Ave Dept 215 10th Fl Bismarck ND 58505 701-328-2960 328-2961
Web: www.ndus.edu

Ohio State University System
190 N Oval Mall 205 Bricker Hall Columbus OH 43210 614-292-2424 292-1231
Web: www.osu.edu

Oklahoma State System of Higher Education
655 Research Pkwy Suite 200 Oklahoma City OK 73104 405-225-9120 225-9235
Web: www.okhighered.org

Pennsylvania State System of Higher Education
2986 N 2nd St Harrisburg PA 17110 717-720-4000 720-4011
TF: 800-457-7743 ■ *Web:* www.passhe.edu

South Carolina Commission on Higher Education
1333 Main St Suite 200 Columbia SC 29201 803-737-2260 737-2297
Web: www.che400.state.sc.us

University of South Dakota Foundation
1110 N Dakota St PO Box 5555 Vermillion SD 57069 605-677-6703 677-6717
TF: 800-521-3575 ■ *Web:* www.usdfoundation.com

Tennessee Higher Education Commission
404 James Robertson Pkwy Suite 1900 Nashville TN 37243 615-741-3605 741-6230
Web: www.state.tn.us

University of Tennessee System
800 Andy Holt Tower 8th Fl Knoxville TN 37996 865-974-2241 974-3753
Web: www.utk.edu/system

Texas A & M University System The
200 Technology Way Suite 2043 College Station TX 77845 979-458-6000 458-6044
Web: www.tamus.edu

Texas State University System (TSUS)
208 E 10th St Suite 600 Austin TX 78701 512-463-1808 463-1816
Web: www.tsus.edu

Texas Tech University System
124 Administration Bldg MS 42013 Lubbock TX 79409 806-742-0012 742-8050
Web: www.texastech.edu

University of Texas System 601 Colorado St Austin TX 78701 512-499-4200 499-4215
Web: www.utsystem.edu

Utah System of Higher Education
60 S 400 W Salt Lake City UT 84101 801-321-7101 366-8405
Web: www.higheredutah.org

Vermont State Colleges
1 Pk St Stanley Hall 3rd Fl PO Box 359 Waterbury VT 05676 802-241-2520 241-3369
Web: web.vsc.edu

Virginia Community College System
101 N 14th St 15th Fl Richmond VA 23219 804-819-4901 819-4766
Web: www.vccs.edu

Washington Higher Education Coordinating Board
917 Lakeridge Way PO Box 43430 Olympia WA 98504 360-753-7800 753-7808
Web: www.hecb.wa.gov

West Virginia Higher Education Policy Commission
1018 Kanawha Blvd E Suite 700 Charleston WV 25301 304-558-2101 558-5719
TF: 888-825-5707 ■ *Web:* www.wvhepcnew.wvnet.edu

University of Wisconsin System
1220 Linden Dr 1720 Van Hise Hall Madison WI 53706 608-262-2321 262-3985
Web: www.uwsa.edu

Wyoming Community College Commission
2020 Carey Ave 8th Fl Cheyenne WY 82002 307-777-7763 777-6567
Web: www.commission.wcc.edu

790 UTILITY COMPANIES

SEE ALSO Electric Companies - Cooperatives (Rural) p. 1792; Gas Transmission - Natural Gas p. 1903
Types Of Utilities Included Here Are Electric Companies, Water Supply Companies, And Natural Gas Companies.

Phone | Fax

AEP Public Service Co of Oklahoma
PO Box 24404 Canton OH 44701 888-216-3523
TF: 888-216-3523 ■ *Web:* www.psoklahoma.com

AEP Texas North Co 1 Riverside Plaza Columbus OH 43215 614-716-4020 716-1823
TF: 866-322-5563 ■ *Web:* www.aeptexas.com

AES Corp 4300 Wilson Blvd 11th Fl Arlington VA 22203 703-522-1315 528-4510
NYSE: AES ■ *Web:* www.aes.com

AGL Resources Inc 10 Peachtree Pl PO Box 4569 Atlanta GA 30309 404-584-4000 584-3945*
NYSE: AGL ■ **Fax:* Hum Res ■ *TF Cust Svc:* 800-427-5463 ■ *Web:* www.aglresources.com

Alabama Gas Corp (Alagasco)
605 Richard Arrington Jr Blvd N Birmingham AL 35203 205-326-8100 326-2617
TF: 800-292-4005 ■ *Web:* www.alagasco.com

Alabama Power Co PO Box 2641 Birmingham AL 35291 205-257-1000 226-1988*
**Fax:* Cust Svc ■ *TF:* 800-245-2244 ■ *Web:* www.southernco.com/site/alapower

Alameda County Water District
43885 S Grimmer Blvd Fremont CA 94537 510-668-4200 770-1793
Web: www.acwd.org

Alaska Power & Telephone Co
193 Otto St PO Box 3222 Port Townsend WA 98368 360-385-1733 385-5177
TF Cust Svc: 800-982-0136 ■ *Web:* www.aptalaska.com

Allegheny Power 800 Cabin Hill Dr Greensburg PA 15601 724-837-3000
TF Cust Svc: 800-255-3443 ■ *Web:* www.alleghenypower.com

Alliant Energy Corp
4902 N Biltmore Ln PO Box 77007 Madison WI 53707 608-458-3311 458-0100
NYSE: LNT ■ *TF Cust Svc:* 800-255-4268 ■ *Web:* www.alliantenergy.com

AmerenUE PO Box 66149 Saint Louis MO 63166 314-621-3222 554-4535*
**Fax:* Hum Res ■ *TF:* 800-552-7583

American Consumer Industries Inc
1105 N Market St Suite 1300 Wilmington DE 19801 303-471-4928 470-9956
Web: www.aciinc.net

American Electric Power (AEP)
1 Riverside Plaza Columbus OH 43215 614-716-1000 716-1823
Web: www.aep.com

American Municipal Power Inc
1111 Schrock Rd Suite 100 Columbus OH 43229 614-540-1111 540-1113
Web: www.amppartners.org

Aqua America Inc 762 W Lancaster Ave Bryn Mawr PA 19010 610-527-8000 645-1061
NYSE: WTR ■ *TF:* 877-987-2782

Aquarion Co 835 Main St Bridgeport CT 06604 203-336-7624 336-7775
TF: 800-732-9678 ■ *Web:* www.aquarion.com

AREVA Inc 4800 Hampden Ln Suite 1100 Bethesda MD 20814 301-652-9197 652-5691
Web: www.areva.com

Arizona Public Service Co (APS)
1 E Washington St ; Corporate Office Ctr Phoenix AZ 85004 602-250-1000 944-8208
TF: 800-253-9405 ■ *Web:* www.aps.com

Arkansas Western Gas Co 1083 E Sain St Fayetteville AR 72703 479-521-5400 582-4747
TF: 800-773-2113 ■ *Web:* www.awgonline.com

ATCO Ltd 1600, 909 - 11th Ave SW Calgary AB T2R1N6 403-292-7550 292-7532
TSE: ACO.X ■ *Web:* www.atco.com

Atlantic City Electric 800 King St Wilmington DE 19899 302-429-3011 429-3018
Web: www.atlanticcityelectric.com

Atmos Energy 5430 LBJ Fwy Suite 1800 Dallas TX 75240 972-934-9227 855-3040
TF: 888-363-7427 ■ *Web:* www.atmosenergy.com

Avista Corp 1411 E Mission St Spokane WA 99202 509-495-4817 495-8725
NYSE: AVA ■ *TF:* 800-727-9170 ■ *Web:* www.avistacorp.com

Avista Utilities 1411 E Mission St Spokane WA 99252 509-495-4817 495-4184
TF: 800-227-9187 ■ *Web:* www.avistautilities.com

Baltimore Gas & Electric Co
110 W Fayette St Baltimore MD 21201 410-234-5000 234-7406
TF: 800-685-0123 ■ *Web:* www.bge.com

Bangor Hydro Electric Co 21 Telcom Dr Bangor ME 04402 207-945-5621 990-6954
TF: 800-499-6600 ■ *Web:* www.bhe.com

Berkshire Gas Co Inc 115 Cheshire Rd Pittsfield MA 01201 413-442-1511 443-0546
TF: 800-292-5012 ■ *Web:* www.berkshiregas.com

Brownstown Electric Supply Co Inc
690 E State Rd 250 PO Box L Brownstown IN 47220 812-358-4555 358-2484
TF: 800-742-8492 ■ *Web:* www.brownstown.com

Cabot Oil & Gas Corp
840 Gessner Rd Suite 1200 Houston TX 77024 281-848-2799 589-4910*
NYSE: COG ■ **Fax:* Hum Res ■ *TF:* 800-434-3985 ■ *Web:* www.cabotog.com

Cadiz Inc 550 S Hope St Suite 2850 Los Angeles CA 90071 213-271-1600 271-1614
NASDAQ: CDZI ■ *Web:* www.cadizinc.com

Caithness Corp 565 5th Ave 29Fl New York NY 10017 212-921-9099 921-9239
Web: www.caithnessdevelopment.com

CalEnergy a MidAmerican Energy Holdings Co
302 S 36th St Suite 400 Omaha NE 68131 402-341-4500 398-7214
Web: www.calenergy.com

California ISO
151 Blue Ravine Rd PO Box 639014 Folsom CA 95630 916-351-4400 608-7222
Web: www.caiso.com

California Water Service Group
1720 N 1st St San Jose CA 95112 408-367-8200 367-8430
NYSE: CWT ■ *TF:* 800-750-8200 ■ *Web:* www.calwater.com

Calpine Corp 717 Texas Ave Suite 1000 Houston TX 77002 713-830-2000 830-2001
NYSE: CPN ■ *TF:* 800-359-5115 ■ *Web:* www.calpine.com

Canadian Utilities Ltd
909 11th Ave SW Suite 1600 Calgary AB T2R1N6 403-292-7500 292-7532
TSE: CU ■ *Web:* www.canadian-utilities.com

Carthage Water & Electric Plant PO Box 611 Carthage MO 64836 417-237-7300 237-7310
Web: www.cwepnet.com

Cascade Natural Gas Corp (CNGC)
8113 W Grandridge Blvd Kennewick WA 99336 206-624-3900 624-7215
NYSE: CGC ■ *TF:* 888-522-1130 ■ *Web:* www.cngc.com

Central Hudson Gas & Electric Corp
284 S Ave Poughkeepsie NY 12601 845-452-2700 486-5415*
**Fax:* Hum Res ■ *TF:* 800-527-2714 ■ *Web:* www.centralhudson.com

Central Maine Power Co 83 Edison Dr Augusta ME 04336 207-623-3521 623-5908
TF: 800-565-0121 ■ *Web:* www.cmpco.com

Central Vermont Public Service Corp
77 Grove St Rutland VT 05701 800-649-2877 747-2199*
NYSE: CV ■ **Fax Area Code:* 802 ■ *TF:* 800-649-2877 ■ *Web:* www.cvps.com

Chesapeake Utilities Corp 909 Silver Lake Blvd Dover DE 19904 302-734-6799 734-6750
NYSE: CPK ■ *Web:* www.chpk.com

Cheyenne Light Fuel & Power Co
108 W 18th St Cheyenne WY 82001 307-638-3361 778-2106
Web: www.cheyennelight.com

Chubu Electric Power Co Inc
900 17th St NW Suite 1220 Washington DC 20006 202-775-1960 331-9256
Web: www.chuden.co.jp/english/index.html

Citizens Gas & Coke Utility
2020 N Meridian St Indianapolis IN 46202 317-924-3311 927-4395
TF: 800-427-4217 ■ *Web:* www.citizensgas.com

City Public Service Board 145 Navarro St San Antonio TX 78296 210-353-2222 353-4633
TF: 800-773-3077 ■ *Web:* www.citypublicservice.com

Company	City	State	Zip	Phone	Fax
Cleco Power LLC 2030 Donahue Ferry Rd *Fax: Hum Res ■ TF Cust Svc: 800-622-6537 ■ Web: www.cleco.com	Pineville	LA	71361	318-484-7400	484-7488*
Colorado Springs Utilities 111 S Cascade Ave PO Box 1103 TF: 800-238-5434 ■ Web: www.csu.org	Colorado Springs	CO	80903	719-448-4800	668-3400
Columbia Gas of Kentucky Inc 2001 Mercer Rd TF: 800-432-9345 ■ Web: www.columbiagasky.com	Lexington	KY	40511	859-288-0210	288-6349
Columbia Gas of Ohio Inc 200 Civic Ctr Dr TF: 800-282-3044 ■ Web: www.columbiagasohio.com	Columbus	OH	43215	614-460-6000	460-4947
Columbia Gas of Pennsylvania Inc 501 Technology Dr *Fax: Mktg ■ TF Cust Svc: 888-460-4332	Canonsburg	PA	15317	724-416-6300	416-6383*
Columbia Gas of Virginia Inc 1809 Coyote Dr TF Cust Svc: 800-543-8911 ■ Web: www.columbiagasva.com	Chester	VA	23836	804-323-5300	323-5338
Commissioners of Public Works 121 W Ct Ave PO Box 549 Web: www.greenwoodcpw.com	Greenwood	SC	29649	864-942-8100	942-8111
Conergy Inc 2460 W 26th Ave Suite Suite 280C *Fax Area Code: 505 ■ TF: 888-396-6611 ■ Web: www.conergy.us	Denver	CO	80211	888-396-6611	473-3830*
Connecticut Light & Power Co 107 Selden St *Fax: PR ■ TF Cust Svc: 800-286-2000 ■ Web: www.cl-p.com	Berlin	CT	06037	860-665-5000	665-2032*
Connecticut Natural Gas Corp (CNG) PO Box 1500 *Fax: Mktg ■ Web: www.cngcorp.com	Hartford	CT	06144	860-727-3000	727-3326*
Consolidated Edison Co of New York 4 Irving Pl *Fax: Hum Res ■ TF: 800-752-6633 ■ Web: www.coned.com	New York	NY	10003	212-460-4600	260-8647*
Consumers Energy Co 1 Energy Plaza *Fax: Hum Res ■ TF Cust Svc: 800-477-5050 ■ Web: www.consumersenergy.com	Jackson	MI	49201	517-788-0550	788-2451*
Covanta Energy Corp 40 Ln Rd TF: 866-268-2682 ■ Web: www.covantaenergy.com	Fairfield	NJ	07004	973-882-9000	882-7234
CrossCountry Energy LLC 5444 Westheimer Rd	Houston	TX	77056	713-989-2000	
Dakota Gasification Co PO Box 5540 Web: www.dakotagas.com	Bismarck	ND	58506	701-221-4400	557-5336
Dayton Power & Light Co PO Box 1247 TF: 800-433-8500 ■ Web: www.dpandl.com	Dayton	OH	45401	937-331-3900	331-3900
Delmarva Power 800 King St Po Box 17000 TF: 800-375-7117 ■ Web: www.delmarva.com	Wilmington	DE	19886	800-898-8042	
Delta Natural Gas Co Inc 3617 Lexington Rd NASDAQ: DGAS ■ TF: 800-262-2012 ■ Web: www.deltagas.com	Winchester	KY	40391	859-744-6171	744-3623
Detroit Edison Co 2000 2nd Ave TF Cust Svc: 800-477-4747 ■ Web: www.dteenergy.com	Detroit	MI	48226	313-235-8000	235-8000
Direct Energy LP 2225 Sheppard Ave E 4th Fl Web: www.directenergy.com	Toronto	ON	M2J5C2	416-758-8700	
Dominion East Ohio PO Box 26785 TF Cust Svc: 800-573-1153 ■ Web: www.dom.com/about/companies/eohio/index.jsp	Richmond	VA	23261	800-362-7557	
Dominion Hope PO Box 26783 *Fax: Cust Svc ■ TF: 888-667-3000 ■ Web: www.dom.com/about/companies/hope	Richmond	VA	23261	304-623-8600	623-8603*
Dominion North Carolina Power 701 E Cary St TF: 888-667-3000 ■ Web: www.dom.com	Richmond	VA	23219	804-771-3000	
Dominion Peoples 625 Liberty Ave TF: 800-764-0111 ■ Web: www.dom.com/about/companies/peoples	Pittsburgh	PA	15222	412-244-2626	
Dominion Virginia Power 120 Tredegar St TF: 888-667-3000 ■ Web: www.dom.com	Richmond	VA	23219	804-771-3000	
Duke Energy Kentucky Inc 139 E 4th St *Fax: Cust Svc ■ TF Cust Svc: 800-544-6900 ■ Web: www.duke-energy.com	Cincinnati	OH	45202	513-421-9500	287-2376*
Duke Energy North America 5400 Westheimer Ct TF: 800-873-3853 ■ Web: www.dena.duke-energy.com	Houston	TX	77056	713-627-5400	627-6577
Duke Energy Services Group 5400 Westheimer Ct TF: 800-873-3853 ■ Web: www.duke-energy.com	Houston	TX	77056	713-627-5400	627-4145
Duke Energy Trading & Marketing 5400 Westheimer Ct TF: 800-873-3853 ■ Web: www.duke-energy.com	Houston	TX	77056	713-260-1800	627-4145
Duke Power Co Nantahala Power & Light Div 301 NP & L Loop Web: www.duke-energy.com/north-carolina	Franklin	NC	28734	828-524-2121	369-4608
Duquesne Light Co 411 7th Ave TF Cust Svc: 888-393-7000 ■ Web: www.duquesnelight.com	Pittsburgh	PA	15219	412-393-7000	393-7000
Eastern Shore Natural Gas Co 1110 Forest Ave Suite 201 NYSE: CBK ■ Web: www.esng.com	Dover	DE	19904	302-734-6720	734-6745
Edison Sault Electric Co 725 E Portage Ave TF: 800-562-4960 ■ Web: www.edisonsault.com	Sault Sainte Marie	MI	49783	906-632-2221	632-8444
El Paso Electric Co 100 N Stanton, Stanton Tower NYSE: EE ■ TF: 800-351-1621 ■ Web: www.epelectric.com	El Paso	TX	79901	915-543-5711	543-2299
Elizabethtown Gas Co 1 Elizabethtown Plaza TF: 800-242-5830 ■ Web: www.elizabethtowngas.com	Union	NJ	07083	908-289-5000	859-5307
Emerald Coast Utilities Authority (ECUA) 9255 Sturdevant St PO Box 15311 Web: www.ecua.org	Pensacola	FL	32514	850-476-0480	
Empire District Electric Co The 602 Joplin St PO Box 127 NYSE: EDE ■ *Fax: Hum Res ■ TF: 800-206-2300 ■ Web: www.empiredistrict.com	Joplin	MO	64802	417-625-5100	625-5146*
Energy West Inc 1 First Ave S NASDAQ: EWST ■ TF: 800-570-5688 ■ Web: www.ewst.com	Great Falls	MT	59401	406-791-7500	791-7560
EnergyUSA-TPC Corp 1500 165th St Cisc Bldg TF: 800-531-1193	Hammond	IN	46324	219-853-5929	853-5951
Enron Creditors Recovery Corp (ECRC) 1331 Lamar St Suite 1600 PO Box 1188 TF: 800-973-6766 ■ Web: www.enron.com	Houston	TX	77010	713-853-6161	853-3129
ENSTAR Natural Gas Co 401 E Intl Airport Rd Web: www.enstargas.com	Anchorage	AK	99518	907-277-5551	276-6696
Entergy Arkansas Inc 425 W Capitol Ave TF: 800-368-3749 ■ Web: www.entergy-arkansas.com	Little Rock	AR	72201	501-377-4000	
Entergy Louisiana Inc 639 Loyola Ave *Fax: Cust Svc ■ TF Cust Svc: 800-368-3749 ■ Web: www.entergy.com	New Orleans	LA	70113	504-529-5262	576-2509*
Entergy Mississippi Inc PO Box 1640 *Fax: Hum Res ■ Web: www.entergy-mississippi.com	Jackson	MS	39215	601-368-5000	351-4464*
Entergy New Orleans Inc 639 Loyola Ave *Fax: Cust Svc ■ TF Cust Svc: 800-368-3749 ■ Web: www.entergy-neworleans.com	New Orleans	LA	70113	504-529-5262	576-2509*
Entergy Texas Inc 350 Pine St TF: 800-368-3749 ■ Web: www.entergy-texas.com	Beaumont	TX	77701	409-838-6631	
Environmental Power Corp 1 Cate St 4th Fl AMEX: EPG ■ TF: 888-430-3082	Portsmouth	NH	03801	603-431-1780	431-2650
EQT Corp 625 Liberty Ave Suite 1700 NYSE: EQT ■ TF: 800-242-1776 ■ Web: www.eqt.com	Pittsburgh	PA	15222	412-553-5700	
Equitable Gas Co PO Box 6766 TF: 877-577-8735 ■ Web: www.equitablegas.com	Pittsburgh	PA	15212	800-654-6335	
Erie County Water Authority (ECWA) 295 Main St Rm 350 Web: www.ecwa.org	Buffalo	NY	14203	716-849-8484	849-8467
Florida City Gas (FCG) 955 E 25th St TF: 800-993-7546 ■ Web: www.floridacitygas.com	Hialeah	FL	33013	305-691-8710	
Florida Power & Light Co (FPL) 700 Universe Blvd Web: www.fpl.com	Juno Beach	FL	33408	561-691-7171	691-7177
Florida Public Utilities Co (FPUC) 401 S Dixie Hwy AMEX: FPU ■ TF: 800-427-7712 ■ Web: www.fpuc.com	West Palm Beach	FL	33401	561-832-0872	833-0151
FPL Energy Inc *NextEra Energy Resources LLC* 700 Universe Blvd PO Box 14000 TF: 888-867-3050 ■ Web: www.nexteraenergyresources.com	Juno Beach	FL	33408	561-691-7171	691-7177
Gas Co The 745 Fort St Mall # 1800 Web: www.hawaiigas.com	Honolulu	HI	96813	808-535-5933	535-5932
Gaz Metro LP 1717 Rue du Havre TSX: GZM.UN] ■ TF: 800-567-1313 ■ Web: www.gazmetro.com	Montreal	QC	H2K2X3	514-598-3444	598-3144
Georgia Power Co 241 Ralph McGill Blvd NE TF Cust Svc: 888-660-5890 ■ Web: www.southernco.com	Atlanta	GA	30308	404-506-6526	506-3771
Ges USA Inc 101 W Elm St Suite 550 Web: www.ges-usa.com	Conshohocken	PA	19428	610-940-6088	940-4771
Goleta Water District 4699 Hollister Ave Web: www.goletawater.com	Goleta	CA	93110	805-964-6761	879-4609
Green Mountain Energy Co 3815 Capital of Texas Hwy TF Cust Svc: 800-286-5856 ■ Web: www.greenmountain.com	Austin	TX	78704	512-691-6100	691-6151
Green Mountain Power Corp 163 Acorn Ln NYSE: GMP ■ TF: 888-835-4672 ■ Web: www.greenmountainpower.com	Colchester	VT	05446	802-864-5731	655-8419
GridPoint Inc 2801 Clarendon Blvd Suite 100 Web: www.gridpoint.com	Arlington	VA	22201	703-667-7000	667-7001
Gulf Power Co 1 Energy Pl *Fax: Hum Res ■ TF: 800-487-6937 ■ Web: www.southernco.com/gulfpower	Pensacola	FL	32520	850-444-6111	444-6238*
HaloSource Inc 1631 220th St SE Suite 100 Web: www.halosource.com	Bothell	WA	98021	425-881-6464	882-2476
Horizon Wind Energy LLC 808 Travis St Suite 700 Web: www.horizonwind.com	Houston	TX	77002	713-265-0350	265-0365
Hydro One Inc 483 Bay St 15th Fl TF: 888-664-9376 ■ Web: www.hydroone.com	Toronto	ON	M5G2P5	416-345-5000	345-6060
Idaho Power Co 1221 W Idaho St *Fax: Hum Res ■ TF: 800-488-6151 ■ Web: www.idahopower.com	Boise	ID	83702	208-388-2200	388-6695*
Illuminating Co 76 S Main St *Fax Area Code: 877 ■ *Fax: Cust Svc ■ TF: 800-646-0400 ■ Web: www.firstenergycorp.com	Akron	OH	44308	216-622-9800	289-3674*
Indianapolis Power & Light Co 1 Monument Cir TF: 888-261-8222 ■ Web: www.iplpower.com	Indianapolis	IN	46204	317-261-8261	
Intermountain Gas Co Inc 555 S Cole Rd TF Cust Svc: 800-548-3679 ■ Web: www.intgas.com	Boise	ID	83709	208-377-6839	377-6081
Jackson Energy Authority 119 E College St TF: 888-577-6427 ■ Web: www.jaxenergy.com	Jackson	TN	38301	731-422-7500	422-7307
Kansas City Power & Light Co 1200 Main Web: www.kcpl.com	Kansas City	MO	64141	816-556-2200	654-1125
Kansas Gas Service 7421 W 129th St TF: 800-794-4780 ■ Web: www.kansasgasservice.com	Overland Park	KS	66213	913-319-8600	
Kentucky Utilities Co 1 Quality St TF: 800-981-0600 ■ Web: www.eon-us.com/ku	Lexington	KY	40507	859-255-2100	
Kinder Morgan Inc 500 Dallas St Suite 1000 NYSE: KMI ■ TF: 800-525-3752 ■ Web: www.kne.com	Houston	TX	77002	713-369-9000	369-9100
Kinder Morgan Inc KN Energy Retail Div 370 Van Gordon St TF: 800-232-1627 ■ Web: www.kindermorgan.com	Lakewood	CO	80228	303-989-1740	
Kissimmee Utility Authority Inc (KUA) 1701 W Carroll St TF: 877-582-7700 ■ Web: www.kua.com	Kissimmee	FL	34741	407-933-7777	933-7715
Laclede Gas Co 720 Olive St *Fax: Hum Res ■ TF: 800-887-4173 ■ Web: www.lacledegas.com	Saint Louis	MO	63101	314-342-0500	588-0615*
Lake Haven Utility District 31627-1st Ave South PO Box 4249 Web: www.lakehaven.org	Federal Way	WA	98063	253-941-1516	
Lampton-Love Inc 2829 Lakeland Dr Suite 1505 Web: www.lamptonlove.com	Jackson	MS	39232	601-933-3400	933-3420
Laney's Inc 55 27 St S PO Box 2562 Web: www.laneysinc.com	Fargo	ND	58103	701-237-0543	
Lineage Power Corp 601 Shiloh Rd TF: 877-546-3243 ■ Web: www.lineagepower.com	Plano	TX	75074	972-244-9288	
Long Island Power Authority 333 Earle Ovington Blvd Suite 403 TF Cust Svc: 877-275-5472 ■ Web: www.lipower.org	Uniondale	NY	11553	516-222-7700	222-9137
Lord Electric Co Of Puerto Rico Inc 8 Simon Madera Web: www.lordelectric.com	San Juan	PR	00924	787-758-4040	763-3320
Louisville Gas & Electric Co 220 W Main St *Fax: Cust Svc ■ TF: 800-331-7370 ■ Web: www.lgeenergy.com	Louisville	KY	40202	502-627-2000	627-2690*
Madison Gas & Electric Co 133 S Blair St TF: 800-245-1125 ■ Web: www.mge.com	Madison	WI	53703	608-252-7000	252-7098
Marts & Lundy Inc 1200 Wall St W TF: 800-526-9005 ■ Web: www.martsandlundy.com	Lyndhurst	NJ	07071	201-460-1660	460-0680

Phone Fax

MEAG Power 1470 Riveredge Pkwy NW. . . . Atlanta GA 30328 770-563-0300 563-0004
TF: 800-333-6324 ■ *Web:* www.meagpower.org

Medley Communications Inc
560-6 Birch St . . . . Lake Elsinore CA 92530 951-245-5200 241-3539*
**Fax Area Code:* 866 ■ *TF:* 888-551-7208 ■ *Web:* www.medleycom.com

Meitec Inc 4625 Airline Dr. . . . Metairie LA 70001 504-455-2600 888-1428
Web: www.meitec.net

Mel-Kay Electric Co Inc 1511 N Garvin St . . . . Evansville IN 47711 812-423-1128 423-5117
Web: www.mel-kayelectric.com

Memphis Light Gas & Water (MLGW)
220 S Main St PO Box 430. . . . Memphis TN 38101 901-528-4011 528-4758
Web: www.mlgw.com

Menasha Utilities 321 Milwaukee St PO Box 340 . . . . Menasha WI 54952 920-967-3400 967-3441
Web: www.menashautilities.com

Merrill Lynch Commodities
20 Greenway Plaza # 700 . . . . Houston TX 77027 713-544-6222 544-4121
TF: 866-820-6000 ■ *Web:* www.entergykoch.com

Mesa Consolidated Water District
1965 Placentia Ave. . . . Costa Mesa CA 92627 949-574-1022 574-1035
Web: www.mesawater.org

Metromedia Energy Inc
6 Industrial Way W Suite F . . . . Eatontown NJ 07724 732-542-7575 542-8655
TF: 800-828-9427 ■ *Web:* www.metromediaenergy.com

Metropolitan Utilities District
1723 Harney St PO Box 3600. . . . Omaha NE 68102 402-449-8155 504-7020*
**Fax:* Cust Svc ■ *TF Cust Svc:* 800-732-5864 ■ *Web:* www.mudomaha.com

Michael W Middleton PC (MWMPC)
3330 Longmire Dr . . . . College Station TX 77845 979-695-2726 695-2754
Web: www.mwmpc.com

MidAmerican Energy Co 666 Grand Ave. . . . Des Moines IA 50309 515-242-4300 281-2981
TF: 800-338-8007 ■ *Web:* www.midamericanenergy.com

Middle Tennessee Natural Gas Utility District (MTNG)
1036 W Broad St PO Box 670. . . . Smithville TN 37166 615-597-4300 597-6331
TF: 800-880-6373 ■ *Web:* www.mtng.com

Middlesex County Utilities Authority Inc (MCUA)
2571 Main St PO Box 159 . . . . Sayreville NJ 08872 732-721-3800 721-0206
Web: www.mcua.com

Middlesex Water Co 1500 Ronson Rd. . . . Iselin NJ 08830 732-634-1500 750-5981
NASDAQ: MSEX ■ *TF:* 800-729-4030 ■ *Web:* www.middlesexwater.com

Miller-Eads Co inc
4125 N Keystone Ave PO Box 55234 . . . . Indianapolis IN 46205 317-545-7101 545-4660
TF: 800-530-0684 ■ *Web:* www.miller-eads.com

Minnesota Power 30 W Superior St. . . . Duluth MN 55802 218-722-2625 723-3944
TF: 800-228-4966 ■ *Web:* www.mnpower.com

Missouri Gas Energy 3420 Broadway. . . . Kansas City MO 64111 816-360-5500 360-5630
TF: 800-582-1234 ■ *Web:* www.missourigasenergy.com

Mobile Gas Service Corp 2828 Dauphin St. . . . Mobile AL 36606 251-476-2720 471-2588*
**Fax:* Mktg ■ *Web:* www.mobile-gas.com

Monroe County Water Authority
475 Norris Dr PO Box 10999 . . . . Rochester NY 14610 585-442-2000 442-0220
TF: 866-426-6292 ■ *Web:* www.mcwa.com

Montana-Dakota Utilities Co (MDU)
122 E Broadway . . . . Bismarck ND 58502 701-222-7900 222-4329
TF: 800-638-3278 ■ *Web:* www.montana-dakota.com

Morristown Utility Systems PO Box 667 . . . . Morristown TN 37815 423-586-4121 587-6590
Web: www.morristownutilities.org

Mount Carmel Public Utility Co
316 Market St PO Box 220. . . . Mount Carmel IL 62863 618-262-5151
TF: 877-262-7036 ■ *Web:* www.mtcpu.com

National Fuel Gas Distribution Corp
6363 Main St . . . . Williamsville NY 14221 716-857-7000 857-7310
TF: 800-365-3234 ■ *Web:* www.natfuel.com

National Fuel Gas Supply Corp
6363 Main St . . . . Williamsville NY 14226 716-857-7000 857-7206
TF Cust Svc: 800-365-3234 ■ *Web:* www.nfg.natfuel.com

National Fuel Resources Inc
165 Lawrence Bell Dr Suite 120. . . . Williamsville NY 14221 716-630-6786 630-6798
TF: 800-839-9993 ■ *Web:* www.nfrinc.com

Neal Electri Corp 13250 Kirkham Way . . . . Poway CA 92064 858-513-2525 513-9488
Web: www.nealelectric.com

Nevada Irrigation District (NID)
1036 W Main St . . . . Grass Valley CA 95945 530-273-6185 271-6838
TF: 800-222-4102 ■ *Web:* www.nid.dst.ca.us

Nevada Power Co 6226 W Sahara Ave . . . . Las Vegas NV 89146 702-367-5000 367-5535
NYSE: NVE ■ *TF Cust Svc:* 800-331-3103 ■
Web: www.investors.nvenergy.com/phoenix.zhtml?c=117698&p=irol-irhome

New England Gas Co 670 Allens Ave . . . . Providence RI 02905 401-272-5040 421-6760
TF: 800-227-8000 ■ *Web:* www.negasco.com

New York Power Authority
123 Main St Suite 10-H . . . . White Plains NY 10601 914-681-6200 681-6949
Web: www.nypa.gov

New York State Electric & Gas Corp
Corporate Dr PO Box 5240. . . . Binghamton NY 13902 800-572-1111
TF: 800-572-1111 ■ *Web:* www.nyseg.com

Nicor Gas 1844 Ferry Rd . . . . Naperville IL 60563 630-983-8888 983-4229
TF: 888-642-6748 ■ *Web:* www.nicor.com

North Shore Gas Co 3001 Grand Ave . . . . Waukegan IL 60085 866-556-6004 336-8815*
**Fax Area Code:* 847 ■ **Fax:* Mktg ■ *TF:* 866-556-6004

Northern Electric Inc 1275 W 124th Ave. . . . Denver CO 80234 303-428-6969 428-6669
Web: www.northernelec.com

Northern Indiana Fuel & Light Co Inc
220 E 7th St . . . . Auburn IN 46706 260-925-2700 925-5255

Northern Indiana Public Service Co (NIPSCO)
801 E 86th Ave . . . . Merrillville IN 46410 219-853-5200 647-5589*
**Fax:* Hum Res ■ *TF Cust Svc:* 800-464-7726

Northern Kentucky Water District
2835 Cresent Springs Rd PO Box 18640 . . . . Erlanger KY 41018 859-578-9898 578-5456
Web: www.nkywater.org

Northwest Natural Gas Co 220 NW 2nd Ave. . . . Portland OR 97209 503-226-4211 220-2584
NYSE: NWN ■ *TF:* 800-422-4012 ■ *Web:* www.nwnatural.com

NorthWestern Energy 600 Market St W . . . . Huron SD 57350 605-352-8411 353-8361
TF: 800-245-6977 ■ *Web:* www.northwesternonline.com

Phone Fax

Nova Scotia Power Inc PO Box 910 . . . . Halifax NS B3J2W5 902-428-6230 428-6108
TF: 800-428-6230 ■ *Web:* www.nspower.ca

NRG Energy Inc 211 Carnegie Ctr . . . . Princeton NJ 08540 609-524-4500 524-4501
NYSE: NRG ■ *TF:* 800-241-4674 ■ *Web:* www.nrgenergy.com

NRG Texas LLC PO Box 4710. . . . Houston TX 77210 713-795-6000 795-7431
Web: www.txgenco.com

NSTAR Electric 1 Nstar Way . . . . Westwood MA 02090 781-441-8000 441-8025
TF Cust Svc: 800-592-2000 ■ *Web:* www.nstaronline.com

NSTAR Gas 1 N Star Way . . . . Westwood MA 02090 800-592-2000
TF: 800-592-2000 ■ *Web:* www.nstaronline.com

OG & E Electric Services 3220 S High . . . . Oklahoma City OK 73124 405-553-3000 553-3165
TF: 800-272-9741 ■ *Web:* www.oge.com

Ohio Edison Co 76 S Main St PO Box 3637. . . . Akron OH 44309 800-646-0400 384-4796*
**Fax Area Code:* 330 ■ **Fax:* Cust Svc ■ *TF Cust Svc:* 800-633-4766

Oklahoma Natural Gas Co
401 N Harvey PO Box 401 . . . . Oklahoma City OK 73101 405-551-6500 551-6610
TF: 800-664-5463 ■ *Web:* www.oklahomanaturalgas.com

Oncor 1616 Woodall Rodgers Fwy Suite 6C-006 . . . . Dallas TX 75202 214-486-2000 486-2175
TF: 888-313-6862 ■ *Web:* www.txuelectricdelivery.com

Orange & Rockland Utilities Inc
1 Blue Hill Plaza. . . . Pearl River NY 10965 845-352-6000 577-2958
TF Cust Svc: 877-434-4100 ■ *Web:* www.oru.com

Orange Water & Sewer Authority (inc)
400 Jones Ferry Rd PO Box 366. . . . Carrboro NC 27510 919-968-4421 968-4464
Web: www.owasa.org

Osaka Gas Co Ltd 375 Pk Ave Suite 2109. . . . New York NY 10152 212-980-1666 832-0946
Web: www.osakagas.co.jp/indexe.htm

Otter Tail Power Co 215 S Cascade St. . . . Fergus Falls MN 56537 218-739-8200 739-8218
TF: 800-551-3593 ■ *Web:* www.otpco.com

Oxbow Power Corp
1601 Forum Pl Suite 1400 . . . . West Palm Beach FL 33401 561-697-4300 640-8847
Web: www.oxbow.com

Pacific Data Electric Inc (PDE)
9970 Bell Ranch Dr Suite 109. . . . Santa Fe Springs CA 90670 562-204-3550 204-0380
Web: www.pdeinc.com

Pacific Gas & Electric Co 77 Beale St . . . . San Francisco CA 94105 415-973-7000 543-0841*
**Fax:* Hum Res ■ *TF Cust Svc:* 800-743-5000 ■ *Web:* www.pge.com

Pacific Power & Light 825 NE Multnomah St. . . . Portland OR 97232 503-813-5000 800-2851*
**Fax Area Code:* 888 ■ **Fax:* Cust Svc ■ *TF Cust Svc:* 888-221-7070 ■ *Web:* www.pacificpower.net

PacifiCorp 825 NE Multnomah St . . . . Portland OR 97232 503-813-5000 813-5023*
**Fax:* Hum Res ■ *TF:* 877-722-5001 ■ *Web:* www.pacificorp.com

Paducah Power System 1500 Broadway PO Box 180. . . . Paducah KY 42002 270-575-4000 575-4027
Web: www.paducahpower.com

Park Water Co 9750 Washburn Rd . . . . Downey CA 90241 562-923-0711 861-5902
TF: 800-727-5987 ■ *Web:* www.parkwater.com

Parkway Electric Inc 11952 James St Suite A. . . . Holland MI 49424 616-392-2788 392-6880
TF: 800-574-9553 ■ *Web:* www.parkwayelectric.com

Passaic Valley Water Commission
1525 Main Ave . . . . Clifton NJ 07011 973-340-4300 340-5598
Web: www.pvwc.com

Pennichuck Corp 25 Manchester St . . . . Merrimack NH 03054 603-882-5191 913-2362
NASDAQ: PNNW ■ *TF:* 800-553-5191 ■ *Web:* www.pennichuck.com

Peoples Gas Light & Coke Co
130 E Randolph Dr . . . . Chicago IL 60601 312-240-4000 240-4120
TF Cust Svc: 866-556-6001

Pepco Energy Services Inc
1300 N 17th St Suite 1600 . . . . Arlington VA 22209 703-253-1800 253-1698
TF: 800-363-7499 ■ *Web:* www.pepco.com

Pepco Holdings Inc 701 Ninth St NW . . . . Washington DC 20068 202-872-2000 331-6874
NYSE: POM ■ *Web:* www.pepcoholdings.com

Philadelphia Gas Works (PGW)
800 W Montgomery Ave PO Box 3500. . . . Philadelphia PA 19122 215-236-0500 684-6500*
**Fax:* Hum Res ■ *Web:* www.pgworks.com

Piedmont Natural Gas
4720 Piedmont Row Dr PO Box 33068. . . . Charlotte NC 28210 704-364-3120 365-3849
NYSE: PNY ■ *TF:* 800-752-7504 ■ *Web:* www.piedmontng.com

Pinnacle Gas Resources Inc 1 E Aalger St. . . . Sheridan WY 82801 307-673-9710 673-9711
Web: www.pinnaclegas.com

Pinnacle West Energy Corp
400 N 5th St Suite 800 . . . . Phoenix AZ 85004 602-250-1000 250-3007
TF: 800-457-2983 ■ *Web:* www.pinnaclewest.com

Placer County Water Agency
144 Ferguson Rd PO Box 6570 . . . . Auburn CA 95604 530-823-4850
Web: www.pcwa.net

Portland General Electric 121 SW Salmon St . . . . Portland OR 97204 503-464-8000 464-2676*
**Fax:* Hum Res ■ *TF:* 800-542-8818 ■ *Web:* www.portlandgeneral.com

Portland Water District
225 Douglass St PO Box 3553. . . . Portland ME 04104 207-774-5961 761-8307
Web: www.pwd.org

Power Marketing Administrations
Bonneville Power Administration
905 NE 11th Ave . . . . Portland OR 97232 503-230-3000
Web: www.bpa.gov

PowerSecure International Inc
1609 Heritage Commerce Ct. . . . Wake Forest NC 27587 919-556-3056 556-3596
NASDAQ: POWR ■ *TF:* 866-347-5455 ■ *Web:* www.powersecure.com

PPL Electric Utilities Corp 2 N 9th St. . . . Allentown PA 18101 610-774-5151 774-5408*
**Fax:* Cust Svc ■ *TF Cust Svc:* 800-342-5775 ■ *Web:* www.pplweb.com

PPL EnergyPlus LLC 2 N 9th St . . . . Allentown PA 18101 610-774-5803 774-6523
TF Cust Svc: 800-281-2000 ■ *Web:* www.pplenergyplus.com

PPL Global LLC 2 N 9th St. . . . Allentown PA 18101 610-774-5151 774-6043
TF: 800-342-5775 ■ *Web:* www.pplweb.com/pplglobal/index.htm

Pratt Communications 2913 Tech Ctr . . . . Santa Ana CA 92705 714-540-6840 540-0506
TF: 800-980-2323 ■ *Web:* www.prattcommunications.com

Progress Energy Florida Inc
100 Central Ave . . . . Saint Petersburg FL 33701 727-820-5151

ProLiance Energy LLC
111 Monument Cir Suite 2200. . . . Indianapolis IN 46204 317-231-6800 231-6900
Web: www.proliance.com

PS Energy Group Inc
2987 Clairmont Rd Suite 500. . . . Atlanta GA 30329 404-321-5711 321-3938
TF: 800-334-7548 ■ *Web:* www.psenergy.com

Company	City	State	ZIP	Phone	Fax
PSEG Power LLC 80 Pk Plaza *TF:* 800-436-7734 ■ *Web:* www.pseg.com	Newark	NJ	07101	973-430-7000	824-5382
Public Service Electric & Gas Co 80 Pk Plaza **Fax:* Hum Res ■ *TF Cust Svc:* 800-436-7734 ■ *Web:* www.pseg.com/companies/pseandg	Newark	NJ	07102	973-430-7000	824-5382*
Public Service of New Hampshire 780 N Commercial St *TF:* 800-662-7764 ■ *Web:* www.psnh.com	Manchester	NH	03105	603-669-4000	
Public Works Commission of The City of Fayetteville North Carolina 955 Old Wilmington Rd PO Box 1089 *TF:* 877-687-7921 ■ *Web:* www.faypwc.com	Fayetteville	NC	28301	910-483-1382	
Puget Sound Energy Inc 10885 NE 4th St *TF:* 888-225-5773 ■ *Web:* www.pse.com	Bellevue	WA	98009	425-454-6363	424-6537
Questar Gas Co PO Box 45841 *TF:* 800-323-5517 ■ *Web:* www.questargas.com	Salt Lake City	UT	84139	801-324-5111	324-5483
Reliant Energy Retail Services LLC 1000 Main St *TF:* 866-872-6646 ■ *Web:* www.reliant.com	Houston	TX	77002	713-497-3000	488-5925
RF Fisher Electric Co LLC 1707 W 39th Ave PO Box 3110 *TF:* 800-385-3880 ■ *Web:* www.rffisher.com	Kansas City	KS	66103	913-384-1500	384-1503
Roanoke Gas Co 519 Kimball Rd *TF:* 800-552-6514 ■ *Web:* www.roanokegas.com	Roanoke	VA	24030	540-777-3800	777-3957
Rochester Gas & Electric Corp 89 E Ave **Fax Area Code:* 585 ■ *TF:* 888-253-8888 ■ *Web:* www.rge.com	Rochester	NY	14649	800-743-2110	771-2895*
Rockland Electric Co 1 Blue Hill Plaza *TF:* 877-434-4100 ■ *Web:* www.oru.com	Pearl River	NY	10965	845-352-6000	577-2958
Roland's Electric Inc 307 Suburban Ave Suite A *TF:* 800-981-8010 ■ *Web:* www.rolandselectric.com	Deer Park	NY	11729	631-242-8080	242-6392
S N Tannor Inc 222 02 Merrick Blvd *Web:* www.tannor.com	Springfield Gardens	NY	11413	718-276-6985	528-5694
S R Bray Corp 1210 N Red Gum *TF:* 800-863-2525 ■ *Web:* www.powerplus.com	Anaheim	CA	92806	714-764-0020	
S&W Contracting Co Inc 952 New Salem Rd *Web:* www.sandwcontracting.com	Murfreesboro	TN	37129	615-893-2511	895-2030
Salt River Project (SRP) 1521 N Project Dr *TF:* 800-258-4777 ■ *Web:* www.srpnet.com	Tempe	AZ	85281	602-236-5900	236-2442
San Diego Gas & Electric Co 101 Ash St **Fax Area Code:* 858 ■ **Fax:* Cust Svc ■ *TF:* 800-411-7343 ■ *Web:* www.sdge.com	San Diego	CA	92101	619-696-2000	654-1755*
San Jacinto River Authority 1577 Dam Site Rd *Web:* www.sanjacintoriverauthority.com	Conroe	TX	77304	936-588-1111	588-3043
SCANA Energy Marketing Inc 1426 Main St MC 092 *TF:* 800-472-1051 ■ *Web:* www.scana.com	Columbia	SC	29201	803-217-1300	217-1329
SemCanada Energy Co 530 8th Ave SW Suite 1000 *Web:* www.semcanadaenergy.com	Calgary	AB	T2P3S8	403-213-6000	213-6224
SEMCO Energy Gas Co 1411 3rd St Suite A *TF:* 800-624-2019 ■ *Web:* www.semcoenergy.com	Port Huron	MI	48060	810-987-2200	987-7286
Shell Trading 909 Fannin St Plaza Level 1 *TF:* 800-281-2824 ■ *Web:* www.shell.us	Houston	TX	77010	713-767-5400	
Sid Richardson Carbon & Energy Cos 201 Main St *Web:* www.sidrich.com	Fort Worth	TX	76102	817-390-8600	
Solar Power Inc 1115 Orlando Ave *Web:* www.solarpowerinc.net	Roseville	CA	95661	916-745-0900	745-0999
South Carolina Electric & Gas Co PO Box 100255 *TF:* 800-251-7234 ■ *Web:* www.sceg.com	Columbia	SC	29202	803-748-3000	
South Coast Water District 31592 W St *Web:* www.scwd.org	Laguna Niguel	CA	92651	949-499-4555	499-4256
South Florida Natural Gas 4090 S Ridgewood Ave *Web:* www.fpuc.com	Port Orange	FL	32121	386-428-5721	427-6663
South Jersey Gas Co 1 S Jersey Plaza Rt 54 *TF:* 888-766-9900 ■ *Web:* www.sjindustries.com/sjg.htm	Folsom	NJ	08037	609-561-9000	561-8225
Southeastern Telecom Inc 2525 Perimeter Pl Dr Suite 135 PO Box 292307 *TF:* 800-743-1340 ■ *Web:* www.setelecom.com	Nashville	TN	37214	615-874-6000	874-6319
Southern California Edison Co 2244 Walnut Grove Ave *TF:* 800-655-4555 ■ *Web:* www.sce.com	Rosemead	CA	91770	626-302-1212	302-8984
Southern California Gas Co 555 W 5th St *TF:* 800-427-2200 ■ *Web:* www.socalgas.com	Los Angeles	CA	90013	213-244-1200	244-8293
Southern California Public Power Authority (SCPPA) 225 S Lake Ave Suite 1250 *Web:* www.scppa.org	Pasadena	CA	91101	626-793-9364	793-9461
Southern Connecticut Gas Co (SCG) 77 Hartland St 4th Fl **Fax Area Code:* 860 ■ *TF:* 866-268-2887 ■ *Web:* www.soconngas.com	East Hartford	CT	06108	866-268-2887	727-3064*
Southern Union Co 5444 Westheimer Rd *NYSE:* SUG ■ *Web:* www.southernunionco.com	Houston	TX	77056	713-989-2000	
Southwest Gas Corp 5241 Spring Mountain Rd PO Box 98510 *NYSE:* SWX ■ *TF:* 800-748-5539 ■ *Web:* www.swgas.com	Las Vegas	NV	89193	702-876-7237	876-7037
Southwest Gas Corp Central Arizona Div 10851 N Black Canyon Hwy *TF Cust Svc:* 800-873-2440 ■ *Web:* www.swgas.com	Phoenix	AZ	85029	602-395-4080	861-3361
Southwest Gas Corp Northern Nevada Div 400 Eagle Stn Ln *TF:* 877-860-6020 ■ *Web:* www.swgas.com	Carson City	NV	89701	775-887-2706	884-3027
Southwest Gas Corp Southern Arizona Div 3401 E Gas Rd *TF:* 877-860-6020 ■ *Web:* www.swgas.com	Tucson	AZ	85714	520-794-6596	295-1991
Southwest Gas Corp Southern California Div 13471 Mariposa Rd *TF:* 877-860-6020 ■ *Web:* www.swgas.com	Victorville	CA	92395	760-241-8120	
Southwest Gas Corp Southern Nevada Div 5241 Spring Mountain Rd *TF:* 877-860-6020 ■ *Web:* www.swgas.com	Las Vegas	NV	89150	702-876-7011	
Southwest Water Co 1211 E Ctr Ct Dr *Web:* www.swwc.com	Covina	CA	91724	626-543-2500	331-4848
Southwestern Energy Co 2350 N Sam Houston Pkwy E Suite 300 *NYSE:* SWN ■ *TF:* 866-322-0801 ■ *Web:* www.swn.com	Houston	TX	77032	281-618-4700	618-4757
Stream Gas & Electric Ltd 1950 Stemmons Fwy Suite 3000 **Fax Area Code:* 214 ■ *TF:* 888-313-4747 ■ *Web:* www.streamenergy.net	Dallas	TX	75207	866-447-8732	800-4444*
SUEZ Energy North America Inc 1990 Post Oak Blvd Suite 1900 *Web:* www.suezenergyna.com	Houston	TX	77056	713-636-0000	636-1364
Superior Water Light & Power 2915 Hill Ave *TF:* 800-227-7957 ■ *Web:* www.mnpower.com/about_mp/swlp	Superior	WI	54880	715-394-2200	395-6300
Sweetwater Authority PO Box 2328 *Web:* www.sweetwater.org	Chula Vista	CA	91912	619-420-1413	425-7469
SWEPCo 1 Riverside Plaza *TF:* 888-216-3523 ■ *Web:* www.swepco.com	Columbus	OH	43215	888-216-3523	
System Engineering International Inc (SEI) 5115 Pegasus Ct Suite Q *TF:* 800-765-4734 ■ *Web:* www.seipower.com	Frederick	MD	21704	301-694-9601	694-9608
Tenaska Inc 1044 N 115th St Suite 400 *Web:* www.tenaska.com	Omaha	NE	68154	402-691-9500	691-9526
Texarkana Water Utilities 801 Wood St *Web:* secure.txkusa.org/twucontact	Texarkana	TX	75501	903-798-3800	791-0724
Texas-New Mexico Power Co (TNMP) 4100 International Plaza Tower 2 9th Fl *TF:* 800-435-2822 ■ *Web:* www.tnmp.com	Fort Worth	TX	76109	817-731-0099	737-1392
Thompson Electric Co (TEC) 721 14th St PO Box 207 *TF:* 800-832-2936 ■ *Web:* www.thompsonelectriccompany.com	Sioux City	IA	51105	712-252-4221	
Tokyo Electric Power Co Inc 1901 L St NW Suite 720 *Web:* www.tepco.co.jp/en/index-e.html	Washington	DC	20036	202-457-0790	457-0810
Toledo Edison Co 76 S Main St **Fax Area Code:* 419 ■ *TF:* 800-447-3333	Akron	OH	44308	800-447-3333	249-5345*
Trans-Tel Central Inc (TTC) 2805 Broce Dr *TF:* 800-729-4636 ■ *Web:* www.trans-tel.com	Norman	OK	73072	405-447-5025	447-5029
TransAlta Corp 110 12th Ave SW PO Box 1900 Stn M *NYSE:* TAC ■ *Web:* www.transalta.com	Calgary	AB	T2P2M1	403-267-7110	
Tricomm Services Corp 1247 N Church St Suite 8 *TF:* 800-872-2401 ■ *Web:* www.tricommcorp.com	Moorestown	NJ	08057	856-914-9001	914-9065
Tucker Technology Inc 300 Frank H Ogawa Plaza 2nd Fl *Web:* www.tuckertech.com	Oakland	CA	94612	510-836-0422	836-2625
Tucson Electric Power Co 1 S Church Ave # 100 *TF:* 800-328-8853 ■ *Web:* www.tucsonelectric.com	Tucson	AZ	85701	520-571-4000	770-2004
TXU Electric 1601 Bryan St *TF:* 800-242-9113 ■ *Web:* www.txu.com/us/ourbus/elecgas	Dallas	TX	75201	214-812-4600	812-5453
Underground Specialists Inc (USI) 570 SW 16th Ter Bldg 1500 *Web:* www.usicable.com	Pompano Beach	FL	33069	954-782-8740	782-1919
United Electric Supply Inc 10 Bellecor Dr *TF:* 800-322-3374 ■ *Web:* www.unitedelectric.com	New Castle	DE	19720	302-322-3333	324-3333
United Illuminating Co 157 Church St **Fax:* Hum Res ■ *TF Cust Svc:* 800-722-5584 ■ *Web:* www.uinet.com	New Haven	CT	06510	203-499-2000	499-5906*
United States Information Systems Inc (USIS) 35 W Jefferson Ave *TF:* 866-222-3778 ■ *Web:* www.usis.net	Pearl River	NY	10965	845-358-7755	358-7882
Upper Trinity Regional Water District 900 N Kealy St PO Box 305 *Web:* www.utrwd.com	Lewisville	TX	75067	972-219-1228	221-9896
Virginia American Water Co (VAWC) 2223 Duke St *Web:* www.amwater.com	Alexandria	VA	22314	703-549-7080	836-6652
Virginia Natural Gas Inc 3719 E Virginia Beach Blvd *TF:* 866-229-3578 ■ *Web:* www.vng.aglr.com	Norfolk	VA	23502	757-466-5400	466-5437
W Bradley Electric Inc 90 Hill Rd *Web:* www.wbeinc.com	Novato	CA	94945	415-898-1400	898-5991
Wachter Inc 16001 W 99th St *Web:* www.wachter.com	Lenexa	KS	66219	913-541-2500	541-2529
Wang Electric Inc 4107 E Winslow Ave Suite C *Web:* www.wangelectric.com	Phoenix	AZ	85040	602-324-5350	324-5360
Ward's Marine Electric Inc 617 SW 3rd Ave *TF:* 800-545-9273 ■ *Web:* www.wardsmarine.com	Fort Lauderdale	FL	33315	954-523-2815	523-1967
Washington Gas & Light Co 6801 Industrial Rd **Fax Area Code:* 202 ■ *TF:* 800-752-7520 ■ *Web:* www.washgas.com	Springfield	VA	22151	703-750-4440	624-6010*
Washington Gas Energy Services Inc (WGES) 13865 Sunrise Valley Dr Suite 200 *TF:* 888-884-9437 ■ *Web:* www.wges.com	Herndon	VA	20171	703-793-7500	
We Energies 231 W Michigan St PO Box 2046 **Fax:* Mktg ■ *TF:* 800-242-9137 ■ *Web:* www.we-energies.com	Milwaukee	WI	53203	414-221-2345	221-3853*
Weber Basin Water Conservancy District 2837 E Hwy 193 *Web:* www.weberbasin.com	Layton	UT	84040	801-771-1677	
Westar Energy PO Box 758500 *TF:* 800-794-4780 ■ *Web:* www.wr.com	Topeka	KS	66675	785-575-6300	575-1796
Western Massachusetts Electric Co 1 Federal St Bldg 111-4 PO Box 2010 *TF:* 800-286-2000 ■ *Web:* www.wmeco.com	Springfield	MA	01090	413-781-4300	787-9352
Western Water Co 705 Mission Ave Suite 200 *TF:* 877-928-9282 ■ *Web:* www.wwtr.com	San Rafael	CA	94901	415-256-8800	256-8803
Wisconsin Power & Light Co 4902 N Biltmore Ln PO Box 77007 **Fax Area Code:* 608 ■ *TF:* 800-862-6222 ■ *Web:* www.alliantenergy.com	Madison	WI	53718	800-255-4268	758-1466*
Wisconsin Public Service Corp PO Box 19001 **Fax Area Code:* 920 ■ **Fax:* Mktg ■ *TF:* 800-450-7260 ■ *Web:* www.wisconsinpublicservice.com	Green Bay	WI	54307	800-450-7260	433-1527*

Phone | Fax

Worldwide Energy & Mfg USA Inc
408 N Canal St Suite A&B South San Francisco CA 94080 650-794-9888 794-9878
PINK: WEMU ■ *Web:* www.wwmusa.com
Xcel Energy Inc 414 Nicollet Mall Minneapolis MN 55401 612-330-5500 330-2900
NYSE: XEL ■ *TF:* 800-328-8226 ■ *Web:* www.xcelenergy.com
Xcel Energy Inc PO Box 840 Denver CO 80201 303-571-7511 294-8533
TF: 800-772-7858 ■ *Web:* www.xcelenergy.com
Yankee Gas Services Co 107 Selden St Berlin CT 06037 800-989-0900 841-8684
TF: 800-989-0900 ■ *Web:* www.yankeegas.com
York Water Co The 130 E Market St PO Box 15089 York PA 17405 717-845-3601 845-3792
NASDAQ: YORW ■ *TF:* 800-750-5561 ■ *Web:* www.yorkwater.com
Yucaipa Valley Water District PO Box 730 Yucaipa CA 92399 909-797-5117 797-6381
Web: www.yvwd.dst.ca.us

791 VACUUM CLEANERS - HOUSEHOLD

SEE ALSO Appliances - Small - Mfr p. 1397

Phone | Fax

Beam Industries 1700 W 2nd St Webster City IA 50595 515-832-4620 832-6659
TF: 800-369-2326 ■ *Web:* www.beamvac.com
Bissell Inc 2345 Walker NW Grand Rapids MI 49544 616-453-4451 453-3485*
**Fax:* Hum Res ■ *Web:* www.bissell.com
CentralVac International Inc 1525 E 5th St Kimball NE 69145 308-235-4139 235-4687
TF: 800-666-3133 ■ *Web:* www.centralvac.com
Electrolux Home Care Products Inc PO Box 3900 Peoria IL 61612 309-828-2367 823-5203
TF Cust Svc: 800-282-2886 ■ *Web:* www.eureka.com
Electrolux LLC 5420 LBJ Fwy Suite 800 Dallas TX 75240 214-361-4300 378-7561
TF Cust Svc: 800-243-9078 ■ *Web:* www.electroluxusa.com
HMI Industries Inc
13325 Darice Pkwy Unit A Stongsville OH 44149 440-846-7800
TF Cust Svc: 800-344-1840 ■ *Web:* www.filterqueen.com
Hoover Co 7005 Cochran Rd Glenwillow OH 44139 800-944-9200 497-5845*
**Fax Area Code:* 330 ■ **Fax:* Mail Rm ■ *TF:* 800-944-9200 ■ *Web:* www.hoovercompany.com
Kirby Co 1920 W 114th St Cleveland OH 44102 216-228-2400 221-3162
TF: 800-437-7170 ■ *Web:* www.kirby.com
Lindsay Mfg Inc PO Box 1708 Ponca City OK 74602 580-762-2457 762-9547
TF: 800-546-3729 ■ *Web:* www.lindsaymfg.com
Metropolitan Vacuum Cleaner Co Inc
1 Ramapo Ave PO Box 149 Suffern NY 10901 845-357-1600 357-1640
TF: 800-822-1602 ■ *Web:* www.metrovacworld.com
Oreck Corp 1400 Salem Rd Cookeville TN 38506 800-289-5888
TF: 800-289-5888 ■ *Web:* www.oreck.com
Rexair Inc 50 W Big Beaver Rd Suite 350 Troy MI 48084 248-643-7222 643-7676
Web: www.rainbowsystem.com
Sanyo Fisher Co 21605 Plummer St Chatsworth CA 91311 818-998-7322 701-4194
Web: us.sanyo.com
Sequoia Vacuum Systems Inc
164 Jefferson Dr Menlo Park CA 94025 650-322-7281 322-8745
TF: 800-994-0494 ■ *Web:* www.sequoiavacuum.com

792 VALVES - INDUSTRIAL

Phone | Fax

American Cast Iron Pipe Co (ACIPCO)
1501 31st Ave N Birmingham AL 35207 205-325-7701 307-2747
TF: 800-442-2347 ■ *Web:* www.acipco.com
Anderson Brass Co 1629 W Bobo Newsome Hwy Hartsville SC 29550 843-332-4111 332-3752
TF: 800-476-9876 ■ *Web:* www.andersonbrass.com
Anderson Greenwood/Crosby Inc
43 Kendrick St Wrentham MA 02093 508-384-3121 384-3152
Web: www.andersongreenwood.com/SrvProd.asp
Armstrong International Inc
2081 SE Ocean Blvd 4th Fl Stuart FL 34996 772-286-7175 286-1001
Web: www.armstronginternational.com
Automatic Switch Co 50-60 Hanover Rd Florham Park NJ 07932 973-966-2000 966-2628
TF: 800-524-1023 ■ *Web:* www.asco.com
Automatic Valve Corp 41144 Vincenti Ct Novi MI 48375 248-474-6700 474-6732
Web: www.automaticvalve.com
Balon Corp 3245 S Hattie Ave Oklahoma City OK 73129 405-677-3321
Web: www.balon.com
Barksdale Inc 3211 Fruitland Ave Los Angeles CA 90058 323-589-6181 589-3463
TF: 800-835-1060 ■ *Web:* www.barksdale.com
Bonney Forge Corp US Rt 522 S Mount Union PA 17066 814-542-2545 542-9977
TF Cust Svc: 800-345-7546 ■ *Web:* www.bonneyforge.com
Circle Seal Controls Inc 2301 Wardlow Cir Corona CA 92880 951-270-6200 270-6201
Web: www.circle-seal.com
Clow Valve Co 902 S 2nd St Oskaloosa IA 52577 641-673-8611 673-8269
TF: 800-829-2569 ■ *Web:* www.clowvalve.com
Continental Disc Corp 3160 W Heartland Dr Liberty MO 64068 816-792-1500 792-2277
Web: www.contdisc.com
Control Components Inc
22591 Avenida Empresa Rancho Santa Margarita CA 92688 949-858-1877 858-1878
TF: 800-788-8762 ■ *Web:* www.ccivalve.com
Conval Inc 265 Field Rd Somers CT 06071 860-749-0761 763-3557
Web: www.conval.com
Cook Compression 12950 Royal Dr Stafford TX 77477 281-261-5700 403-1027
Web: www.cookcompression.com
Crane Co 100 1st Stamford Pl 4th Fl Stamford CT 06902 203-363-7300 363-7295
NYSE: CR ■ *Web:* www.craneco.com
Crane Co Stockham Div 2129 3rd Ave SE Cullman AL 35055 256-775-3800 775-3860
TF: 800-786-2542 ■ *Web:* www.stockham.com
Crane Valve Group North America
9200 New Trails Dr Suite 200 The Woodlands TX 77381 281-298-5463 298-1920
Web: www.cranevalve.com
Curtiss-Wright Flow Control Target Rock Div
1966 Broadhollow Rd Farmingdale NY 11735 631-293-3800 293-6144
Web: www.curtisswright.com
DeZurik Water Controls 250 Riverside Ave N Sartell MN 56377 320-259-2000 259-2227
TF: 800-788-0288 ■ *Web:* www.dezurik.com

Phone | Fax

Dresser Flow Solutions 16240 Port St NW Houston TX 77041 832-590-2300 590-2331
TF: 800-847-1099 ■ *Web:* www.dresser.com
Dynex Rivett Inc 770 Capitol Dr Pewaukee WI 53072 262-691-0300 691-0312
Web: www.dynexhydraulics.com
Engineered Controls International Inc (ECII)
100 Rego Dr PO Box 247 Elon NC 27244 336-449-7707 449-6594
Web: www.regoproducts.com
Fike Corp 704 SW 10th St Blue Springs MO 64015 816-229-3405 228-9277
TF: 877-342-3453 ■ *Web:* www.fike.com
Fisher Controls International Inc
205 S Ctr St PO Box 190 Marshalltown IA 50158 641-754-3011 754-2830
Web: www.emersonprocess.com/fisher
Fleck Controls Inc 20580 Enterprise Ave Brookfield WI 53045 262-784-4490 784-7794
TF Cust Svc: 888-784-9065 ■ *Web:* www.fleckcontrols.com
Flowserve Corp 5215 N O'Connor Blvd Suite 2300 Irving TX 75039 972-443-6500 443-6800
NYSE: FLS ■ *Web:* www.flowserve.com
FMC Technologies Inc 1803 Gears Rd Houston TX 77067 281-591-4000 591-4102
NYSE: FTI ■ *TF:* 800-869-6999 ■ *Web:* www.fmctechnologies.com
GA Industries Inc
9025 Marshall Rd Cranberry Township PA 16066 724-776-1020 776-1254
Web: www.gaindustries.com
Gemini Valve Inc 2 Gemini St Raymond NH 03077 603-895-4761 895-6785
TF: 800-370-0936 ■ *Web:* www.geminivalve.com
Gemu Valves Inc 3800 Camp Creek Pkwy SW Atlanta GA 30331 678-553-3400 344-9350*
**Fax Area Code:* 404 ■ *Web:* www.gemu.com
Goulds Pumps Inc Goulds Water Technologies Group
2881 E Bayard St Ext Seneca Falls NY 13148 315-568-2811 568-7973
TF: 800-327-7700
Groth Corp 13650 N Promenade Blvd Stafford TX 77477 281-295-6800 295-6999
TF: 800-531-3140 ■ *Web:* www.grothcorp.com
Halkey-Roberts Corp
2700 Halkey-Roberts Pl N Saint Petersburg FL 33716 727-471-4200 578-0450
TF Sales: 800-303-4384 ■ *Web:* www.halkeyroberts.com
High Vacuum Apparatus LLC (HVA) 12880 Moya Blvd Reno NV 89506 775-359-4442 359-1369
TF: 800-551-4422 ■ *Web:* www.highvac.com
Hilton Valve Inc 14520 NE 91st Ct Redmond WA 98052 425-883-7000 883-8080
Web: www.hiltonvalve.com
Hoerbiger Corp of America Inc
3350 Gateway Dr Pompano Beach FL 33069 954-974-5700 974-0964
TF: 800-327-8961
Hudson Valve Co Inc
5301 Office Pk Dr Suite 330 Bakersfield CA 93309 661-869-1126 607-8731*
**Fax Area Code:* 800 ■ *TF:* 800-748-6218 ■ *Web:* www.hudsonvalve.com
Humphrey Products Co
5070 E N Ave PO Box 2008 Kalamazoo MI 49048 269-381-5500 381-4113
TF: 800-477-8707 ■ *Web:* www.humphrey-products.com
Hunt Valve Co Inc 1913 E State St Salem OH 44460 330-337-9535 337-3754
TF: 800-321-2757 ■ *Web:* www.huntvalve.com
Hydroseal Valve Co Inc 1500 SE 89th St Oklahoma City OK 73149 405-631-1533 644-2575
TF: 800-654-4842 ■ *Web:* www.hydroseal.com
ITT Goulds Pumps Industries/Goulds Industrial Pumps Group
240 Fall St Seneca Falls NY 13148 315-568-2811 568-2418
TF: 800-327-7700 ■ *Web:* www.gouldspumps.com
ITT Industries Inc Engineered Valves Div
33 Centerville Rd Lancaster PA 17603 717-509-2200 509-2336
TF: 800-366-1111 ■ *Web:* www.engvalves.com
Jarecki Valves 6910 W Ridge Rd Fairview PA 16415 814-474-2666 474-3645
Kennedy Valve 1021 E Water St Elmira NY 14902 607-734-2211 734-3288
TF: 800-782-5831 ■ *Web:* www.kennedyvalve.com
Kerotest Mfg Corp 5500 2nd Ave Pittsburgh PA 15207 412-521-4200 521-5990
Web: www.kerotest.com
KF Industries Inc 1500 SE 89th St Oklahoma City OK 73149 405-631-1533 631-5034
TF: 800-654-4842 ■ *Web:* www.kfvalves.com
Kraft Fluid Systems Inc
14300 Foltz Pkwy Strongsville OH 44149 440-238-5545 238-5266
TF: 800-257-1155 ■ *Web:* www.kraftfluid.com
Lee Co 2 Pellitaug Rd PO Box 424 Westbrook CT 06498 860-399-6281 399-7058*
**Fax:* Sales ■ *Web:* www.theleeco.com
Leonard Valve Co 1360 Elmwood Ave Cranston RI 02910 401-461-1200 941-5310
TF: 888-797-4456 ■ *Web:* www.leonardvalve.com
Leslie Controls Inc 12501 Telecom Dr Tampa FL 33637 813-978-1000 978-0984
TF: 800-253-7543 ■ *Web:* www.lesliecontrols.com
Mac Valves Inc 30569 Beck Rd Wixom MI 48393 248-624-7700 624-0549
TF: 800-622-8587 ■ *Web:* www.macvalves.com
Marotta Controls Inc
78 Boonton Ave PO Box 427 Montville NJ 07045 973-334-7800 334-1219
TF: 888-627-6882 ■ *Web:* www.marotta.com
Marshall Gas Controls Inc
1000 Civic Ctr Loop San Marcos TX 78666 512-396-2257 396-2217
TF: 800-447-9513
Maxon Corp 201 E 18th St PO Box 2068 Muncie IN 47307 765-284-3304 286-8394
Web: www.maxoncorp.com
McKenzie Valve & Machining Co
145 Airport Rd McKenzie TN 38201 731-352-5027 352-3029
Web: www.mckenzievalve.com
McWane Inc 2900 Hwy 280 Suite 300 Birmingham AL 35223 205-414-3100 414-3170
Web: www.mcwane.com
Milwaukee Valve Co Inc
16550 W Stratton Dr New Berlin WI 53151 262-432-2800 432-2801
TF: 800-348-6544 ■ *Web:* www.milwaukeevalve.com
Mueller Co 500 W Eldorado St Decatur IL 62522 217-423-4471 425-7537*
**Fax:* Cust Svc ■ *Web:* www.muellerflo.com
Mueller Refrigeration Co Inc
121 Rogers St PO Box 239 Hartsville TN 37074 615-374-2124 374-2080
TF Cust Svc: 800-251-8983 ■ *Web:* www.muellerindustries.com
Newport News Industrial Corp
182 Enterprise Dr Newport News VA 23603 757-380-7053 688-3841
TF: 800-627-0353
NIBCO Inc 1516 Middlebury St Elkhart IN 46515 574-295-3000 295-3307
TF: 800-234-0227 ■ *Web:* www.nibco.com
Ogontz Corp 2835 Terwood Rd Willow Grove PA 19090 215-657-4770 657-0460
TF: 800-523-2478 ■ *Web:* www.ogontz.com

Company	City	State	ZIP	Phone	Fax
Parker Hannifin Corp 95 Edgewood Ave *TF:* 800-825-8305 ■ *Web:* www.parker.com/sc	New Britain	CT	06051	860-827-2300	827-2384
Parker Hannifin Corp Hydraulic Valve Div 520 Ternes Ave *Fax: Sales ■ *TF:* 800-272-7537 ■ *Web:* www.parker.com	Elyria	OH	44035	440-366-5200	366-5253*
Parker Hannifin Corp Sporlan Div 711 Industrial Ave	Washington	MO	63090	636-239-6524	239-5042
Parker Instrumentation Group 6035 Parkland Blvd *TF:* 800-272-7537 ■ *Web:* www.parker.com/instrumentation	Cleveland	OH	44124	216-896-3000	896-4022
Peter Paul Electronics Co Inc 480 John Downey Dr *Web:* www.peterpaul.com	New Britain	CT	06051	860-229-4884	223-1734
PGI International 16101 Vallen Dr *TF:* 800-231-0233 ■ *Web:* www.pgiint.com	Houston	TX	77041	713-466-0056	744-9892
Plast-O-Matic Valves Inc 1384 Pompton Ave *Web:* www.plastomatic.com	Cedar Grove	NJ	07009	973-256-3000	256-4745
Plattco Corp 7 White St *TF:* 800-352-1731 ■ *Web:* www.plattco.com	Plattsburgh	NY	12901	518-563-4640	563-4892
Primore Inc 2304 W Beecher Rd *Web:* www.primore.com	Adrian	MI	49221	517-265-6168	265-6160
Richards Industries Inc 3170 Wasson Rd *Fax: Sales ■ *TF Cust Svc:* 800-543-7311 ■ *Web:* www.richardsind.com	Cincinnati	OH	45209	513-533-5600	871-0105*
Robert H Wager Co 570 Montroyal Rd *TF:* 800-562-7024 ■ *Web:* www.wagerusa.com	Rural Hall	NC	27045	336-969-6909	969-6375
Sedco 2300 W Beecher Rd *Web:* www.sedco-prv.com	Adrian	MI	49221	517-263-2220	263-2546
Servotronics Inc 1110 Maple St PO Box 300 *AMEX: SVT* ■ *Web:* www.servotronics.com	Elma	NY	14059	716-655-5990	655-6012
Shan-Rod Inc 7308 Driver Rd PO Box 380 *Web:* www.shanrod.com	Berlin Heights	OH	44814	419-588-2066	588-3310
Sherwood 2111 Liberty Dr *TF:* 800-438-2916 ■ *Web:* www.sherwoodvalve.com	Niagara Falls	NY	14304	800-438-2916	
Snap-Tite Inc 8325 Hessinger Dr *Web:* www.snap-tite.com	Erie	PA	16509	814-838-5700	833-0145
Spence Engineering Co Inc 150 Coldenham Rd *Web:* www.spenceengineering.com	Walden	NY	12586	845-778-5566	778-1072
Standard Machine & Mfg Co Inc 10014 Big Bend Blvd	Saint Louis	MO	63122	314-966-4500	966-2532
Starflo Corp 2503 Spring roof Ave *Fax: Sales ■ *TF Sales:* 800-852-2000 ■ *Web:* www.powellvalves.com	Cincinnati	OH	45214	513-852-2000	852-2997*
Storm Mfg Group Inc 23201 Normandie Ave *TF:* 800-210-2525 ■ *Web:* www.storm-manufacturing.com	Torrance	CA	90501	310-326-8287	326-8310
Tapco International 11307 W Little York Rd *TF:* 866-827-2660 ■ *Web:* www.tapcointernational.com	Houston	TX	77041	713-466-0300	466-8425
Transtech Industries Inc 200 Centennial Ave Suite 202	Piscataway	NJ	08854	732-564-3122	981-1856
United Brass Works Inc 714 S Main St *TF:* 800-334-3035 ■ *Web:* www.ubw.com	Randleman	NC	27317	336-498-2661	498-4267
Valcor Engineering Corp 2 Lawrence Rd *Web:* www.valcor.com	Springfield	NJ	07081	973-467-8400	467-8382
Valvtechnologies Inc 5904 Bingle Rd *Web:* www.valv.com	Houston	TX	77092	713-860-0400	860-0499
Velan Inc 7007 Cote de Liesse *Web:* www.velan.com	Montreal	QC	H4T1G2	514-748-7743	748-8635
Watts Water Technologies Inc 815 Chestnut St *NYSE: WTS* ■ *Web:* www.wattswater.com	North Andover	MA	01845	978-688-1811	794-1848
William Powell Co 2503 Spring Grove Ave *TF:* 800-888-2583 ■ *Web:* www.powellvalves.com	Cincinnati	OH	45214	513-852-2000	852-2997
Zimmermann & Jansen Inc 620 N Houston Ave *Web:* www.zjinc.com	Humble	TX	77338	281-446-8000	446-8126

793 VALVES & HOSE FITTINGS - FLUID POWER

SEE ALSO Carburetors, Pistons, Piston Rings, Valves p. 1555

Company	City	State	ZIP	Phone	Fax
A-1 Components Corp 625 W 18th St *Fax Area Code: 800 ■ *TF:* 800-759-2872 ■ *Web:* www.a-1components.com	Hialeah	FL	33010	305-885-1911	759-9299*
Air-Way Mfg Co 586 N Main St *TF Cust Svc:* 800-253-1036 ■ *Web:* www.air-way.com	Olivet	MI	49076	269-749-2161	749-3161
Arkwin Industries Inc 686 Main St *Fax: Sales ■ *Web:* www.arkwin.com	Westbury	NY	11590	516-333-2640	334-6786*
Bosch Rexroth Corp 5150 Prairie Stone Pkwy *TF:* 800-860-1055 ■ *Web:* www.boschrexroth-us.com	Hoffman Estates	IL	60192	847-645-3600	645-6201
Bosch Rexroth Corp Mobile Hydraulics Div PO Box 394 *TF:* 866-230-2790 ■ *Web:* www.boschrexroth-us.com	Wooster	OH	44691	330-263-3300	263-3333
Cameron Valves & Measurement 3250 Briarpark Dr Suite 300 *Web:* www.c-a-m.com	Houston	TX	77042	281-499-8511	261-3588
Cashco Inc 607 W 15th St *Web:* www.cashco.com	Ellsworth	KS	67439	785-472-4461	472-3539
Civacon 4304 N Mattox Rd *TF Sales:* 888-526-5657 ■ *Web:* www.civacon.com	Kansas City	MO	64150	816-741-6600	741-1061
Clippard Instrument Lab 7390 Colerain Ave *TF:* 877-245-6247 ■ *Web:* www.clippard.com	Cincinnati	OH	45239	513-521-4261	521-4464
Continental Machines Inc Continental Hydraulics Div 12520 Quentin Ave S *Web:* www.continentalhydraulics.com	Savage	MN	55378	952-895-6400	895-6444
Control Flow Inc 9201 Fairbanks N Houston Rd *TF:* 800-231-9922 ■ *Web:* www.controlflow.com	Houston	TX	77064	281-890-8300	890-3947
Crissair Inc 38905 10th St E *Web:* www.crissair.com	Palmdale	CA	93550	661-273-5411	273-1280
Daman Products Co Inc 1811 N Home St *Web:* www.damanifolds.com	Mishawaka	IN	46545	574-259-7841	259-7665
Delta Power Co 4484 Boeing Dr *Web:* www.delta-power.com	Rockford	IL	61109	815-397-6628	397-2526
Deltrol Fluid Products 3001 Grant Ave *Fax: Sales ■ *Web:* www.deltrolfluid.com	Bellwood	IL	60104	708-547-0500	547-6881*
Dynaquip Controls 10 Harris Industrial Pk *TF:* 800-545-3636 ■ *Web:* www.dynaquip.com	Saint Clair	MO	63077	636-629-3700	629-5528
EA Patten Co 303 Wetherell St	Manchester	CT	06040	860-649-2851	649-6230
EKK Eagle America 33 Plan Way Bldg 5 *TF:* 800-314-9246 ■ *Web:* www.eagle-america.net	Warwick	RI	02886	401-732-0333	732-2201
Essex Mfg Inc 6 Sunnen Dr *Web:* www.essexind.com	Saint Louis	MO	63143	314-644-3000	644-3857
Faber Enterprises Inc 6606 Variel Ave *Web:* www.faberent.com	Canoga Park	CA	91303	818-999-1300	712-0512
Fresno Valves & Castings Inc 7736 E Springfield Ave PO Box 40 *TF:* 800-333-1658 ■ *Web:* www.fresnovalves.com	Selma	CA	93662	559-834-2511	834-2017
Gar-KenyonTechnologies 238 Water St PO Box 559 *Web:* www.garkenyon.com	Naugatuck	CT	06770	203-729-4900	729-4950
Hays Fluid Controls 114 Eason Rd *TF:* 800-354-4297 ■ *Web:* www.haysfluidcontrols.com	Dallas	NC	28034	704-922-9565	922-9595
Henry Pratt Co 401 S Highland Ave *TF:* 877-436-7728 ■ *Web:* www.henrypratt.com	Aurora	IL	60506	630-844-4000	844-4124
Hoke Inc 405 Centura Ct PO Box 4866 *Web:* www.hoke.com	Spartanburg	SC	29305	864-574-7966	574-0998
Hunt Valve Co Inc 1913 E State St *TF:* 800-321-2757 ■ *Web:* www.huntvalve.com	Salem	OH	44460	330-337-9535	337-3754
HUSCO International Inc 2239 Pewaukee Rd *Web:* www.huscointl.com	Waukesha	WI	53188	262-513-4200	513-4514
Hydraforce Inc 500 Barclay Blvd *TF:* 800-282-9125 ■ *Web:* www.hydraforce.com	Lincolnshire	IL	60069	847-793-2300	793-0087
Hyson Products 10367 Brecksville Rd *TF:* 800-876-4976 ■ *Web:* www.asbg.com/default_hyson.html	Brecksville	OH	44141	440-526-5900	838-7684
ITT Aerospace Controls 28150 Industry Dr *Web:* www.ittaerospace.com	Valencia	CA	91355	661-295-4000	294-1750
ITT Industries Inc 1133 Westchester Ave *NYSE: ITT* ■ *Web:* www.itt.com	White Plains	NY	10604	914-641-2000	696-2950
JD Gould Co Inc 4707 Massachusetts Ave *TF:* 800-634-6853 ■ *Web:* www.gouldvalve.com	Indianapolis	IN	46218	317-547-5289	547-5234
Jetstream of Houston LLP 4930 Cranswick *TF:* 800-231-8192 ■ *Web:* www.waterblast.com	Houston	TX	77041	713-462-7000	462-5387
Kepner Products Co 995 N Ellsworth Ave *Web:* www.kepner.com	Villa Park	IL	60181	630-279-1550	279-9669
Kimray Inc 52 NW 42nd St *Web:* www.kimray.com	Oklahoma City	OK	73118	405-525-6601	525-7520
LDI Industries Inc 1864 Nage Ave PO Box 1810 *Web:* www.ldi-industries.com	Manitowoc	WI	54221	920-682-6877	684-7210
Mead Fluid Dynamics Inc 4114 N Knox Ave *TF Cust Svc:* 877-632-3872 ■ *Web:* www.mead-usa.com	Chicago	IL	60641	773-685-6800	685-7002
Midland Mfg Corp 7733 Gross Pt Rd *Web:* www.midlandmfg.net	Skokie	IL	60077	847-677-0333	
Morrison Bros Co 570 E 7th St *TF:* 800-553-4840 ■ *Web:* www.morbros.com	Dubuque	IA	52001	563-583-5701	583-5028
Norgren 5400 S Delaware St *Fax: Mktg ■ *Web:* www.norgren.com/usa	Littleton	CO	80120	303-794-5000	795-9487*
Oilgear Co 2300 S 51st St PO Box 343924 *Web:* www.oilgear.com	Milwaukee	WI	53219	414-327-1700	327-0532
Omega Flex Inc 451 Creamery Way *NASDAQ: OFLX* ■ *TF:* 800-355-1039 ■ *Web:* www.omegaflex.com	Exton	PA	19341	610-524-7272	524-7282
Parker Climate & Industrial Controls Group 6035 Parkland Blvd *Web:* www.parker.com/cig	Cleveland	OH	44124	216-896-3000	896-4007
Parker Fluid Connectors Group 6035 Parkland Blvd *TF:* 800-272-7537 ■ *Web:* www.parker.com/fcg	Cleveland	OH	44124	216-896-3000	896-4000
Parker Hannifin Corp Brass Products Div 100 Parker Dr *TF:* 800-272-7537 ■ *Web:* www.parker.com	Otsego	MI	49078	269-694-9411	694-4614
Parker Hannifin Corp General Valve Div 26 Clinton Dr Unit 103 *TF:* 800-482-8258 ■ *Web:* www.parker.com	Hollis	NH	03049	603-545-1500	585-8080
Parker Hannifin Corp Hydraulics Valve Div 520 Ternes Ave *Web:* www.parker.com	Elyria	OH	44035	440-366-5100	366-5253
Parker Hannifin Corp Instrumentation Pneutronics Div 26 Clinton Dr Suite 103 *Web:* www.parker.com	Hollis	NH	03049	603-595-1500	595-8080
Parker Hannifin Corp Pneumatic Div 8676 E M 89	Richland	MI	49083	269-629-5000	629-5385
Parker Hannifin Corp Skinner Valve Div 95 Edgewood Ave *TF:* 800-825-8305 ■ *Web:* www.parker.com	New Britain	CT	06051	860-827-2300	827-2384
PBM Inc 1070 Sandy Hill Rd *TF:* 800-967-4726 ■ *Web:* www.pbmvalve.com	Irwin	PA	15642	724-863-0550	864-9255
PerkinElmer Inc 45 William St *NYSE: PKI* ■ *Web:* www.perkinelmer.com	Wellesley	MA	02481	781-237-5100	237-9386
Pima Valve Inc 6525 W Allison Rd *Web:* www.pimavalve.com	Chandler	AZ	85226	520-796-1095	796-4012
Plattco Corp 7 White St *TF:* 800-352-1731 ■ *Web:* www.plattco.com	Plattsburgh	NY	12901	518-563-4640	563-4892
Rexarc Inc PO Box 7 *Web:* www.rexarc.com	West Alexandria	OH	45381	937-839-4604	839-5897
Richards Industries Inc 3170 Wasson Rd *Fax: Sales ■ *TF Cust Svc:* 800-543-7311 ■ *Web:* www.richardsind.com	Cincinnati	OH	45209	513-533-5600	871-0105*
Ritter Technology LLC 100 Williams Dr *TF:* 800-374-8837 ■ *Web:* www.ritter1.com	Zelienople	PA	16063	724-452-6000	452-0766
Ross Controls 1250 Stephenson Hwy *TF:* 800-438-7677 ■ *Web:* www.rosscontrols.com	Troy	MI	48083	248-764-1800	764-1850
SafeWay Hydraulics Inc 4040 Norex Dr *TF Cust Svc:* 800-222-1169 ■ *Web:* www.safewayhyd.com	Chaska	MN	55318	952-448-2600	448-3466
Sedco 2300 W Beecher Rd *Web:* www.sedco-prv.com	Adrian	MI	49221	517-263-2220	263-2546

Company	City	State	Zip	Phone	Fax
SH Leggitt Co 1000 Civic Ctr Loop *TF:* 800-877-2495 ■ *Web:* www.marshallgas.com	San Marcos	TX	78666	512-396-0707	396-2619
SMC Pneumatics Inc 3011 N Franklin Rd PO Box 26646 *TF:* 800-762-7621 ■ *Web:* www.smcusa.com	Indianapolis	IN	46226	317-899-4440	899-3102
Specialty Mfg Co 5858 Centerville Rd *Web:* www.specialtymfg.com	Saint Paul	MN	55127	651-653-0599	653-0989
Sterling Hydraulics Inc 850 Arthur Ave *Web:* www.sterling-hydraulics.com	Elk Grove Village	IL	60007	847-690-1333	690-1334
Sun Hydraulics Corp 1500 W University Pkwy *NASDAQ: SNHY* ■ *Web:* www.sunhydraulics.com	Sarasota	FL	34243	941-362-1200	355-4497
Teleflex Fluid Systems Inc One Firestone Dr *TF:* 800-225-9077 ■ *Web:* www.teleflexhose.com	Suffield	CT	06078	860-668-1285	668-2353
Versa Products Co Inc 22 Spring Valley Rd *Web:* www.versavalves.com	Paramus	NJ	07652	201-843-2400	843-2931
Watts Fluidair Inc 9 Cutts Rd **Fax:* Cust Svc ■ *TF:* 877-467-4323 ■ *Web:* www.wattsfluidair.com	Kittery	ME	03904	207-439-9511	475-4010*
Watts Regulator Co 815 Chestnut St *Web:* www.watts.com	North Andover	MA	01845	978-688-1811	794-1848
Whitco Supply LLC 200 N Morgan Ave *Web:* www.whitcosupply.com	Broussard	LA	70518	337-837-2440	837-4450
Young & Franklin Inc (Y&F) 942 Old Liverpool Rd *Web:* www.yf.com	Liverpool	NY	13088	315-457-3110	457-9204

794 VARIETY STORES

Company	City	State	Zip	Phone	Fax
99 Cents Only Stores 4000 Union Pacific Ave *NYSE: NDN* ■ *TF:* 877-399-2368 ■ *Web:* www.99only.com	Commerce	CA	90023	323-980-8145	980-8160
Andersons Inc Retail Group 480 W Dussel Dr PO Box 119 *TF:* 800-537-3370 ■ *Web:* www.andersonsinc.com	Maumee	OH	43537	419-893-5050	891-6452
B & B Sales Inc 712 S Broadway	Oklahoma City	OK	73109	405-232-3578	232-2848
Ben Franklin Stores Promotions Unlimited Corp 7601 *TF:* 800-992-9307 ■ *Web:* www.benfranklinstores.com	Racine	WI	53408	262-681-7000	
Big Lots Inc (BLI) 300 Phillipi Rd *NYSE: BLI* ■ *TF:* 800-877-1253 ■ *Web:* www.biglots.com	Columbus	OH	43228	614-278-6800	278-6739
Bomgaars 300 Elliott Ave W *Web:* www.bomgaars.com	Sioux City	IA	51103	712-277-2000	277-1247
Building No 19 Inc 319 Lincoln St *TF:* 800-225-5061 ■ *Web:* www.building19.com	Hingham	MA	02043	781-749-6900	749-3691
Buy.com Inc 85 Enterprise St *TF:* 877-880-1030 ■ *Web:* www.buy.com	Aliso Viejo	CA	92656	949-389-2000	389-2800
Dollar Discount Stores of America Inc 1362 Naamans Creek Rd *TF:* 800-227-5314 ■ *Web:* www.dollardiscount.com	Boothwyn	PA	19061	610-497-1991	485-6439
Dollar General Corp 100 Mission Ridge *NYSE: DG* ■ *TF:* 877-855-8797 ■ *Web:* www.dollargeneral.com	Goodlettsville	TN	37072	615-855-4000	
Dollar Tree Stores Inc 500 Volvo Pkwy *NASDAQ: DLTR* ■ *TF:* 877-530-8733 ■ *Web:* www.dollartree.com	Chesapeake	VA	23320	757-321-5000	321-5292
Duckwall-ALCO Stores Inc 401 Cottage Ave *NASDAQ: DUCK* ■ *TF:* 800-334-2526 ■ *Web:* www.duckwall.com	Abilene	KS	67410	785-263-3350	263-7531
Dueber's Inc 300 Industrial Blvd	Norwood Young America	MN	55397	952-467-3085	467-3001
Exchange The 3911 S Walton Walker Blvd **Fax Area Code:* 800 ■ *TF:* 800-527-2345 ■ *Web:* www.shopmyexchange.com	Dallas	TX	75236	214-312-2011	446-0163*
Family Dollar Stores Inc 10401 Monroe Rd PO Box 1017 *NYSE: FDO* ■ *Web:* www.familydollar.com	Charlotte	NC	28201	704-847-6961	847-5534
JWT Stores Inc 1310 Long Beach Blvd *Web:* www.handstores.com	Beach Haven	NJ	08008	609-207-1755	
Marc Glassman Inc 5841 W 130th St *Web:* www.marcs.com	Parma	OH	44130	216-265-7700	267-0088
Marden's Inc 184 College Ave *TF:* 800-564-3337 ■ *Web:* www.mardenssurplus.com	Waterville	ME	04901	207-873-6111	873-6680
Mazel Co The 31000 Aurora Rd *TF:* 800-443-4789 ■ *Web:* www.themazelcompany.com	Solon	OH	44139	440-248-5200	349-1931
Navy Exchange Service Command (NEXCOM) 3280 Virginia Beach Blvd *TF:* 800-628-3924 ■ *Web:* www.mynavyexchange.com	Virginia Beach	VA	23452	757-463-6200	
Ocean State Jobbers Inc 375 Commerce Pk Rd *Web:* www.oceanstatejoblot.com	North Kingstown	RI	02852	401-295-2672	885-0359
Overstock.com Inc 6350 S 3000 E *NASDAQ: OSTK* ■ *TF Cust Svc:* 800-843-2446 ■ *Web:* www.overstock.com	Salt Lake City	UT	84121	801-947-3100	944-4629
Pride Products Corp 4333 Veterans Memorial Hwy **Fax Area Code:* 877 ■ *TF:* 800-898-5550 ■ *Web:* www.prideproducts.com	Ronkonkoma	NY	11779	631-737-4444	729-4749*
R J Schinner Co Inc 16950 W Lincoln Ave PO Box 510470 *TF:* 800-234-1460 ■ *Web:* www.rjschinner.com	New Berlin	WI	53151	262-797-7180	797-7190
Shoplet.com 39 Broadway 20th Fl *TF:* 800-757-3015 ■ *Web:* www.shoplet.com	New York	NY	10006	212-619-3353	619-3389
Swain's General Store Inc 602 E 1st St *Web:* www.swainsinc.com	Port Angeles	WA	98362	360-452-2357	452-7561
U-line Corp PO Box 245040 *TF:* 800-779-2547 ■ *Web:* www.u-line.com	Milwaukee	WI	53224	414-354-0300	354-0349
Unclaimed Baggage Ctr 509 W Willow St *Web:* www.unclaimedbaggage.com	Scottsboro	AL	35768	256-259-1525	259-0818

795 VENTURE CAPITAL FIRMS

Companies Listed Here Are Investors, Not Lenders.

Company	City	State	Zip	Phone	Fax
4C Ventures 21 E 94th St 3rd Fl *Web:* www.4cventures.com	New York	NY	10028	212-996-3133	996-4644
AAVIN Equity Partners LP 118 3rd Ave SE Suite 630 *Web:* www.aavin.com	Cedar Rapids	IA	52401	319-247-1072	363-9519
Abbott Capital Management LLC 1211 Avenue of the Americas Suite 4300 *Web:* www.abbottcapital.com	New York	NY	10036	212-757-2700	757-0835
Aberdare Ventures One Embarcadero Ctr Suite 4000 *Web:* www.aberdare.com	San Francisco	CA	94111	415-392-7442	392-4264
ABS Capital Partners 400 E Pratt St Suite 910 *Web:* www.abscapital.com	Baltimore	MD	21202	410-246-5600	246-5606
ABS Ventures 950 Winter St # 2600 *Web:* www.absventures.com	Waltham	MA	02451	781-250-0400	250-0345
Accel Partners 428 University Ave *Web:* www.accel.com	Palo Alto	CA	94301	650-614-4800	614-4880
Accuitive Medical Ventures LLC 2750 Premiere Pkwy Suite 200 *TF:* 888-935-4411 ■ *Web:* www.amvpartners.com	Duluth	GA	30097	678-812-1101	417-7325
Adams Capital Management Inc 500 Blackburn Ave *Web:* www.acm.com	Sewickley	PA	15143	412-749-9454	749-9459
Adams Harkness Techventures 60 State St *Web:* www.ahventures.com	Boston	MA	02109	617-788-1670	788-1663
Adams Street Partners LLC 1 N Wacker Dr Suite 2200 *Web:* www.adamsstreetpartners.com	Chicago	IL	60606	312-553-7890	553-7891
Adena Ventures 20 E Cir Dr *Web:* www.adenaventures.com	Athens	OH	45701	740-597-1470	597-1399
Adobe Ventures LP 345 Pk Ave *Web:* www.adobe.com	San Jose	CA	95110	408-536-6000	537-6000
Advanced Technology Ventures 1000 Winter St Suite 3700 *Web:* www.atvcapital.com	Waltham	MA	02451	781-290-0707	684-0045
Advanced Technology Ventures 485 Ramona St *Web:* www.atvcapital.com	Palo Alto	CA	94301	650-321-8601	321-0934
Advantage Capital Partners 16750 Gulf Blvd *Web:* www.advantagecap.com	North Redington Beach	FL	33708	813-261-5040	282-3381
Advent International Corp 75 State St 29th Fl *Web:* www.adventinternational.com	Boston	MA	02109	617-951-9400	951-0566
Agilent Technologies Inc 5301 Stevens Creek Blvd *NYSE: A* ■ **Fax Area Code:* 408 ■ *TF:* 877-424-4536 ■ *Web:* www.home.agilent.com	Santa Clara	CA	95051	877-424-4536	345-8474*
Alerion Partners 105 Rowayton Ave *Web:* www.alerionpartners.com	Rowayton	CT	06853	203-838-6700	838-6712
Alexander Hutton Venture Partners 1215 4th Ave Suite 900 *Web:* www.ahvp.com	Seattle	WA	98161	206-341-9800	341-9810
Allegis Capital 130 Lytton Ave Suite 210 *Web:* www.allegiscapital.com	Palo Alto	CA	94301	650-687-0500	687-0234
Allegra Partners 320 Pk Ave 18th Fl *Web:* www.allegrapartners.com	New York	NY	10022	212-277-1526	277-1533
Alloy Ventures 400 Hamilton Ave 4th Fl *Web:* www.alloyventures.com	Palo Alto	CA	94301	650-687-5000	687-5010
Allstate Insurance Co Private Equity Div 3075 Sanders Rd Suite Q5D	Northbrook	IL	60062	847-402-6029	402-4726
Alpha Capital Partners Ltd 122 S Michigan Ave Suite 1700 *Web:* www.alphacapital.com	Chicago	IL	60603	312-322-9800	322-9808
Alta Communications Inc 28 State St # 18A *Web:* www.altacomm.com	Boston	MA	02109	617-262-7770	262-9779
Alta Partners 1 Embarcadero Ctr 37th Fl *Web:* www.altapartners.com	San Francisco	CA	94111	415-362-4022	362-6178
Altira Group LLC 1675 Broadway Suite 2400 *Web:* www.altiragroup.com	Denver	CO	80202	303-592-5500	592-5519
Altos Ventures 2882 Sand Hill Rd Suite 100 *Web:* www.altosventures.com	Menlo Park	CA	94025	650-234-9771	233-9821
Altotech Ventures LLC 205 De Anza Blvd Suite 14 *Web:* www.altotechventures.com	San Mateo	CA	94402	650-574-1870	
AM Pappas & Assoc 2520 Meridian Pkwy *Web:* www.ampappas.com	Durham	NC	27713	919-998-3300	998-3301
American Capital Group Inc 175 Technology Dr Suite 100 *TF:* 800-305-0224 ■ *Web:* www.americancapitalgroup.com	Irvine	CA	92618	949-271-5800	271-5850
American River Ventures 2270 Douglas Blvd Suite 212 *Web:* www.arventures.com	Roseville	CA	95661	916-780-2828	780-5443
Ampersand Capital Partners 55 William St Suite 240 *Web:* www.ampersandcapital.com	Wellesley	MA	02481	781-239-0700	239-0824
Antares Capital Corp 9999 NE 2nd Ave Suite 306 *Web:* www.antarescapital.com	Miami Shores	FL	33138	305-894-2888	894-3227
Apax Partners Inc 153 E 53rd St 53rd Fl *TF:* 800-220-2526 ■ *Web:* www.apax.com	New York	NY	10022	212-753-6300	319-6155
Aperture Venture Partners 645 Madison Ave 20th Fl *Web:* www.aperturevp.com	New York	NY	10022	212-758-7325	319-8779
Apex Investment Partners 225 W Washington St Suite 1500 *Web:* www.apexvc.com	Chicago	IL	60606	312-857-2800	857-1800
Appian Ventures 1512 Larimer St Suite 200 *Web:* www.appianvc.com	Denver	CO	80202	303-830-2450	830-2449
Arbor Partners LLC 130 S 1st St *Web:* www.arborpartners.com	Ann Arbor	MI	48104	734-668-9000	669-4195
Arboretum Ventures 303 Detroit St *Web:* www.arboretumvc.com	Ann Arbor	MI	48104	734-998-3688	998-3689
ARCH Development Partners LLC 20 N Wacker Dr Suite 2000 *Web:* www.archdp.com	Chicago	IL	60606	312-442-4400	263-0724

Firm / Address	City	State	Zip	Phone	Fax
ARCH Venture Partners 8725 W Higgins Rd Suite 290	Chicago	IL	60631	773-380-6600	380-6606
Web: www.archventure.com					
Arete Corp PO Box 1299	Center Harbor	NH	03226	603-253-9797	253-9799
Web: www.arete-microgen.com					
Ascension Health Ventures LLC 11775 Borman Dr Suite 310	Saint Louis	MO	63146	314-733-8113	733-8678
Web: www.ascensionhealthventures.org					
Ascent Venture Partners 255 State St 5th Fl	Boston	MA	02109	617-720-9400	720-9401
Web: www.ascentvp.com					
Asset Management Co 2100 Geng Rd Suite 200	Palo Alto	CA	94303	650-494-7400	856-1826
Web: www.assetman.com					
Associated Venture Investors Management 130 Lytton Ave Suite 210	Palo Alto	CA	94301	650-687-0235	687-0234
ATA Ventures 203 Redwood Shores Pkwy Suite 550	Redwood City	CA	94065	650-594-0189	594-0257
Web: www.ataventures.com					
Atlas Venture 890 Winter St Suite 320	Waltham	MA	02451	781-622-1700	622-1701
Web: www.atlasventure.com					
August Capital 2480 Sand Hill Rd Suite 101	Menlo Park	CA	94025	650-234-9900	234-9910
Web: www.augustcap.com					
Aurora Funds 3100 Tower Blvd	Durham	NC	27707	919-484-0400	484-0444
Web: www.aurorafunds.com					
Austin Ventures 300 W 6th St Suite 2300	Austin	TX	78701	512-485-1900	476-3952
Web: www.austinventures.com					
Avansis Ventures LLC 12010 Sunset Hills Rd Suite 830	Reston	VA	20190	703-796-0222	935-0574
Web: www.avansis.com					
Axiom Venture Partners LP CityPlace II 17th Fl 185 Asylum St	Hartford	CT	06103	860-548-7799	548-7797
Web: www.axiomventures.com					
Bachow & Assoc Inc 3 Bala Plaza E 5th Fl	Bala Cynwyd	PA	19004	610-660-4900	660-4930
Web: www.bachow.com					
Bain Capital Inc 111 Huntington Ave	Boston	MA	02199	617-516-2000	516-2010
Web: www.baincap.com					
Battelle Ventures 103 Carnegie Ctr Suite 100	Princeton	NJ	08540	609-921-1456	921-8703
Web: www.battelleventures.com					
Battery Ventures 930 Winter St Suite 2500	Waltham	MA	02451	781-478-6600	478-6601
Web: www.battery.com					
Bay Partners 10600 N De Anza Blvd Suite 100	Cupertino	CA	95014	408-725-2444	446-4502
Web: www.baypartners.com					
BCM Technologies 1709 Dryden Rd # 1790	Houston	TX	77030	713-795-0105	795-4602
Web: www.bcmtechnologies.com					
Beecken Petty O'Keefe & Co 131 S Dearborn St Suite 2800	Chicago	IL	60603	312-435-0300	435-0371
Web: www.beeckenpetty.com					
Ben Franklin Technology Ctr 125 Goodman Dr	Bethlehem	PA	18015	610-865-6550	865-6427
Benchmark Capital 2480 Sand Hill Rd Suite 200	Menlo Park	CA	94025	650-854-8180	854-8183
Web: www.benchmark.com					
Beringea LLC 32330 W 12 Mile Rd	Farmington Hills	MI	48334	248-489-9000	489-8819
Web: www.beringea.com					
Berkeley International Capital Corp 650 California St 26th Fl	San Francisco	CA	94108	415-249-0450	249-0553
Web: www.berkeleyvc.com					
BioAdvance 3701 Market St	Philadelphia	PA	19104	215-966-6214	966-6215
Web: www.bioadvance.com					
Bioventures Investors 101 Main St Suite 1750	Cambridge	MA	02142	617-252-3443	621-7993
Web: www.bioventuresinvestors.com					
Blue Chip Venture Co 250 E 5th St 1100 Chiquita Ctr	Cincinnati	OH	45202	513-723-2300	723-2306
TF: 800-775-1812 ■ *Web:* www.bcvc.com					
Blueprint Ventures 601 Gateway Blvd Suite 1140	South San Francisco	CA	94080	415-901-4000	901-4035
Web: www.blueprintventures.com					
BlueRun Ventures 545 Middlefield Rd Suite 210	Menlo Park	CA	94025	650-462-7250	462-7252
Web: www.bluerunventures.com					
BNP Paribas Capital Funding LLC 787 7th Ave 33rd Fl	New York	NY	10019	212-841-2000	841-2146
Web: www.bnpparibas.com/en/home					
Boldcap Ventures LLC 750 Lexington Ave Sixth Fl	New York	NY	10022	212-730-5498	591-0880*
**Fax Area Code:* 917 ■ *Web:* www.boldcap.com					
Borealis Ventures 10 Allen St	Hanover	NH	03755	603-643-1500	643-7600
Web: www.borealisventures.com					
Boston Capital Ventures 84 State St # 320	Boston	MA	02109	617-227-6550	227-3847
Web: www.bcv.com					
Boston Millennia Partners 30 Rowes Wharf Suite 400	Boston	MA	02110	617-428-5150	428-5160
Web: www.bostonmillenniapartners.com					
Boston Ventures Management Inc 125 High St 17 Fl	Boston	MA	02110	617-350-1500	350-1509
Web: www.bostonventures.com					
Braemar Energy Ventures 340 Madison Ave 18th Fl	New York	NY	10017	212-697-0900	682-9439
Web: www.braemarenergy.com					
Brantley Partners 3550 Lander Rd Suite 300	Pepper Pike	OH	44124	216-464-8400	464-8405
Web: www.brantleypartners.com					
BTG International Inc 300 Barr Harbor Dr 7th Fl	West Conshohocken	PA	19428	610-278-1660	278-1605
Web: www.btgplc.com					
Burrill & Co 1 Embarcadero Ctr Suite 2700	San Francisco	CA	94111	415-591-5400	591-5401
Web: www.burrillandco.com					
BV Cornerstone Ventures LP 11001 W 120th Ave Suite 310	Broomfield	CO	80021	303-410-2500	466-9316
Web: www.bvcv.com					

Firm / Address	City	State	Zip	Phone	Fax
Cambridge Innovations Inc *Cambridge Innovation Ctr* 1 Broadway 14th Fl	Cambridge	MA	02142	617-758-4200	758-4101
Web: www.cictr.com					
Cambridge Light Partners 955 Massachusetts Ave Suite 304	Cambridge	MA	02139	617-497-6310	
Web: www.cambridgelight.com					
Camp Ventures LLC 280 Second St Suite 280	Los Altos	CA	94022	650-949-0804	618-1719
Web: www.campventures.com					
Capital Network Inc The PO Box 39	Groton	MA	01450	978-846-3972	
Web: www.thecapitalnetwork.org					
Capital Resource Partners 200 State St 13th Fl	Boston	MA	02109	617-478-9600	478-9605
Web: www.crp.com					
Capital Southwest Corp 12900 Preston Rd Suite 700	Dallas	TX	75230	972-233-8242	233-7362
NASDAQ: CSWC ■ *Web:* www.capitalsouthwest.com					
Cardinal Partners 600 Alexander Pk Suite 204	Princeton	NJ	08540	609-924-6452	683-0174
Web: www.cardinalpartners.com					
Cardinal Venture Capital 1010 El Camino Real Suite 325	Menlo Park	CA	94025	650-289-4700	614-4865
Web: www.cardinalvc.com					
Cargill Ventures 1200 Pk Pl Suite 300	San Mateo	CA	94403	650-356-7060	356-7077
Web: www.cargillventures.com					
Castile Ventures 930 Winter St Suite 500	Waltham	MA	02451	781-890-0060	890-0065
Web: www.castileventures.com					
Catamount Ventures 400 Pacific Ave 3rd Fl	San Francisco	CA	94133	415-277-0300	277-0301
Web: www.catamountventures.com					
Catterton Partners 599 W Putnam Ave Suite 200	Greenwich	CT	06830	203-629-4901	629-4903
Web: www.cpequity.com					
CB Health Ventures 360 Madison Ave 5th Fl	New York	NY	10017	212-869-5600	869-6418
Web: www.health-ventures.com					
CCG Venture Partners LLC 14405 Brown Rd	Tomball	TX	77375	281-290-8331	290-8332
Web: www.ccgvp.com					
CEI Ventures Inc 2 Portland Fish Pier Suite 206	Portland	ME	04021	207-772-5356	772-5503
Web: www.ceiventures.com					
CenterPoint Ventures 6300 Bridge Pt Pkwy Bldg 1 Suite 500	Austin	TX	78730	512-795-5800	795-5849
Web: www.cpventures.com					
Charles River Ventures 1000 Winter St Bay Colony Corporate Ctr Suite 3300	Waltham	MA	02451	781-768-6000	768-6100
TF: 866-278-3278 ■ *Web:* www.crv.com					
Charter Venture Capital 525 University Ave Suite 1400	Palo Alto	CA	94301	650-325-6953	325-4762
Web: www.charterventures.com					
Cherry Tree Investment Co 301 Carlson Pkwy Suite 103	Minnetonka	MN	55305	952-893-9012	893-9036
Web: www.cherrytree.com					
Chevron Texaco Technology Venture Investments LLC 3901 Briar Pk Rd	Houston	TX	77042	713-954-6974	954-6388
Web: www.chevron.com/technologyventures					
CHL Medical Partners 1055 Washington Blvd 6th Fl	Stamford	CT	06901	203-324-7700	324-3636
Web: www.chlmedical.com					
Chrysalis Ventures 101 S 5th St 1650 National City Tower	Louisville	KY	40202	502-583-7644	583-7648
Web: www.chrysalisventures.com					
Churchill Financial Group Inc 400 Pk Ave Suite 1510	New York	NY	10022	212-763-4600	763-4601
TF: 888-782-3328 ■ *Web:* www.churchillnet.com					
CIBC Wood Gundy Capital 425 Lexington Ave	New York	NY	10017	212-856-4000	
TF: 800-999-6726 ■ *Web:* www.cibcwm.com					
CID Capital Inc 201 W 103rd St Suite 200	Indianapolis	IN	46290	317-818-5030	644-2914
Web: www.cidcap.com					
CIVC Partners 191 N Wacker Dr Suite 1100	Chicago	IL	60606	312-873-7300	873-7300
Web: www.civc.com					
Clearstone Venture Partners 1351 4th St 4th Fl	Santa Monica	CA	90401	310-460-7900	460-7901
Web: www.clearstone.com					
CMEA Ventures 1 Embarcadero Ctr Suite 3250	San Francisco	CA	94111	415-352-1520	352-1524
Web: www.cmeaventures.com					
Code Hennessy & Simmons Inc 10 S Wacker Dr Suite 3175	Chicago	IL	60606	312-876-1840	876-3854
Web: www.chsonline.com					
Columbia Capital 201 N Union St Suite 300	Alexandria	VA	22314	703-519-2000	519-5870
TF: 800-247-7727 ■ *Web:* www.colcap.com					
Comcast Ventures 1701 John F Kennedy Blvd 1 Comcast Ctr 55th Fl	Philadelphia	PA	19103	215-981-8450	981-8429
Web: www.civentures.com					
Commons Capital LP 320 Washington St 4th Fl	Brookline	MA	02445	617-739-3500	
Web: www.commonscapital.com					
Commonwealth Capital Ventures 950 Winter St Suite 4100	Waltham	MA	02451	781-890-5554	890-3414
Web: www.commonwealthvc.com					
Compass Technology Partners LP 261 Hamilton Ave Suite 200	Palo Alto	CA	94301	650-322-7595	322-0588
Web: www.compasstechpartners.com					
Connecticut Innovations Inc 200 Corporate Pl 3rd Fl	Rocky Hill	CT	06067	860-563-5851	563-4877
TF: 888-337-5454 ■ *Web:* www.ctinnovations.com					
Cordova Ventures 4080 McGinnis Ferry Rd Suite 1201	Alpharetta	GA	30005	678-942-0300	942-0301
Web: www.cordovaventures.com					
Core Capital Partners 901 15th St NW Suite 950	Washington	DC	20005	202-589-0090	589-0091
Web: www.core-capital.com					

Firm	State	ZIP	Phone	Fax
Cornerstone Equity Investors LLC 281 Tresser Blvd 12th Fl, Stamford *Web:* www.cornerstone-equity.com	CT	06901	212-753-0901	826-6798
Court Square Ventures 455 2nd St SE Suite 401, Charlottesville *Web:* www.courtsquareventures.com	VA	22902	434-817-3300	817-3299
Cravey Green & Wahlen Inc 3060 Peachtree Rd Suite 895, Atlanta **Fax Area Code:* 678 ■ *TF:* 800-249-6669 ■ *Web:* www.cgwlp.com	GA	30305	404-841-3325	705-9940*
Crescendo Ventures 600 Hansen Way, Palo Alto *Web:* www.crescendoventures.com	CA	94304	650-470-1200	470-1201
Cross Atlantic Capital Partners 5 Radnor Corporate Ctr, 100 Matsonford Rd Suite 555, Radnor *Web:* www.xacp.com	PA	19087	610-995-2650	971-2062
Cross Atlantic Partners Inc 551 Madison Ave 7th Fl, New York *Web:* www.crossatlanticpartners.com	NY	10022	646-521-7500	497-0061
Crossbow Ventures 1 N Clematis St Suite 510, West Palm Beach *TF:* 866-831-3454 ■ *Web:* www.crossbowventures.com	FL	33401	561-838-9005	838-4105
Crosslink Capital Two Embarcadero Ctr Suite 2200, San Francisco *Web:* www.crosslinkcapital.com	CA	94111	415-617-1800	
Crosspoint Venture Partners 2925 Woodside Rd, Woodside *Web:* www.cpvp.com	CA	94062	650-851-7600	851-7600
Cutlass Capital LLC 229 Marlborough St, Boston *Web:* www.cutlasscapital.com	MA	02116	617-867-0820	624-9669
Cypress Ventures 525 Middlefield Rd Suite 140, Menlo Park *Web:* www.noventivc.com	CA	94025	650-325-6699	325-7799
Davis Tuttle Venture Partners LP 110 W 7th St Suite 1000, Tulsa *Web:* www.davistuttle.com	OK	74119	918-584-7272	582-3403
Defta Partners 111 Pine St Suite 1410, San Francisco *Web:* www.deftapartners.com	CA	94111	415-433-2262	433-2264
Delphi Ventures 3000 Sand Hill Rd Bldg 1 Suite 135, Menlo Park *Web:* www.delphiventures.com	CA	94025	650-854-9650	854-2961
DeMuth Folger & Wetherill 300 Frank W Burr Blvd 5th Fl Glenpointe Ctr E, Teaneck *Web:* www.dfwcapital.com	NJ	07666	201-836-6000	836-5666
Desai Capital Management Inc 410 Pk Ave, New York *TF:* 800-337-2484 ■ *Web:* www.desaicapital.com	NY	10022	212-838-9191	838-9807
Digital Power Capital 411 W Putnam Ave Suite 125, Greenwich *Web:* www.digitalpower.com	CT	06830	203-862-7096	862-7396
DoCoMo Capital 3240 Hillview Ave, Palo Alto *Web:* www.docomo-capital.com	CA	94304	650-493-9600	493-9664
Doll Capital Management 2420 Sand Hill Rd Suite 200, Menlo Park *Web:* www.dcm.com	CA	94025	650-233-1400	854-9159
Dolphin Equity Partners 750 Lexington Ave 16th Fl, New York *TF:* 800-838-1207 ■ *Web:* www.dolphinequity.com	NY	10022	212-446-1600	446-1638
Domain Assoc 1 Palmer Sq Suite 515, Princeton *TF:* 800-241-1901 ■ *Web:* www.domainvc.com	NJ	08542	609-683-5656	683-9789
Dominion Ventures Inc 1656 N California Blvd Suite 300, Walnut Creek *TF:* 800-875-4890 ■ *Web:* www.dominion.com	CA	94596	925-280-6300	280-6338
Draper Fisher Jurvetson (DFJ) 2882 Sand Hill Rd Suite 150, Menlo Park *Web:* www.dfj.com	CA	94025	650-233-9000	233-9233
Duchossois Technology Partners 845 Larch Ave, Elmhurst *Web:* www.duchtec.com	IL	60126	630-530-6105	993-8644
East Gate Capital Management 514 High St Suite 5, Palo Alto *Web:* www.eg-group.com	CA	94301	650-325-5077	325-5072
Edelson Technology Partners 300 Tice Blvd, Woodcliff Lake *Web:* www.edelsontech.com	NJ	07677	201-930-9898	930-8899
EDF Ventures 425 N Main St, Ann Arbor *Web:* www.edfvc.com	MI	48104	734-663-3213	663-7358
Edison Venture Fund 1009 Lenox Dr Bldg 4, Lawrenceville *Web:* www.edisonventure.com	NJ	08648	609-896-1900	896-0066
EGL Holdings 3495 Piedmont Rd 11 Piedmont Ctr Suite 412, Atlanta *Web:* www.eglholdings.com	GA	30305	404-949-8300	949-8311
El Dorado Ventures 2884 Sand Hill Rd, Menlo Park *Web:* www.eldorado.com	CA	94025	650-854-1200	854-1202
Empire Ventures 1020 SW Taylor St Suite 415, Portland	OR	97205	503-222-1556	222-1607
Endeavor Capital Management 49 Richmondville Ave Suite 215, Westport *Web:* www.endeavorcap.com	CT	06880	203-341-7788	341-7799
EnerTech Capital 625 W Ridge Pike Bldg D Suite 105, Conshohocken *Web:* www.enertechcapital.com	PA	19428	484-539-1860	539-1870
Enterprise Partners Venture Capital (EPVC) 2223 Avenida de la Playa Suite 300, La Jolla *Web:* www.epvc.com	CA	92037	858-731-0300	454-9069
Entrepia Ventures Inc 5201 Great American Pkwy Suite 456, Santa Clara *Web:* www.entrepia.com	CA	95054	408-492-9040	492-9540
Envest Ventures 2101 Parks Ave Suite 401, Virginia Beach *Web:* www.envestventures.com	VA	23451	757-437-3000	437-3884
Equus Capital Corp 8 Greenwood St # 930, Houston *TF:* 800-856-0901 ■ *Web:* www.equuscap.com	TX	77011	713-529-0900	529-9545

Firm	State	ZIP	Phone	Fax
Euclid SR Partners 45 Rockefeller Plaza Suite 3240, New York *Web:* www.euclidsr.com	NY	10111	212-218-6880	218-6877
Ferrer Freeman & Co LLC 10 Glenville St The Mill, Greenwich *Web:* www.ffandco.com	CT	06831	203-532-8011	532-8016
Fidelity Ventures 1 Federal St # 27, Boston *Web:* www.fidelityventures.com	MA	02110	617-392-2448	476-9023
Finaventures 3340 Ocean Pk Blvd # 1050, Santa Monica *Web:* www.finaventures.com	CA	90405	310-399-5011	452-5492
First Analysis Corp 1 S Wacker Dr Suite 3900, Chicago *Web:* www.facvc.com	IL	60606	312-258-1400	258-0334
Fisher Lynch Capital 2929 Campus Dr Suite 420, San Mateo *Web:* www.fisherlynch.com	CA	94403	650-287-2700	287-2701
FLAG Capital Management LLC 1266 E Main St 5th Fl, Stamford *Web:* www.flagcapital.com	CT	06902	203-352-0440	352-0441
Flagship Ventures 1 Memorial Dr 7th Fl, Cambridge *Web:* www.flagshipventures.com	MA	02142	617-868-1888	868-1115
Fletcher Spaght Inc 222 Berkeley St 20th Fl, Boston *Web:* www.fletcherspaght.com	MA	02116	617-247-6700	247-7757
Focus Ventures 525 University Ave Suite 1400, Palo Alto *Web:* www.focusventures.com	CA	94301	650-325-7400	325-8400
Formative Ventures 2061 Avy Ave, Menlo Park *Web:* www.formativeventures.com	CA	94025	650-461-8000	461-8010
Forward Ventures 9393 Towne Centre Dr Suite 200, San Diego *Web:* www.forwardventures.com	CA	92121	858-964-5013	964-5028
Foundation Capital 70 Willow Rd Suite 200, Menlo Park *Web:* www.foundationcapital.com	CA	94025	650-614-0500	614-0505
Foundation Medical Partners 105 Rowayton Ave, Rowayton *Web:* www.foundmed.com	CT	06853	203-851-3900	831-8289
Frazier & Co 601 Union St Suite 3200, Seattle *TF:* 800-411-4499 ■ *Web:* www.frazierco.com	WA	98101	206-621-7200	621-1848
Frontenac Co 135 S La Salle St Suite 3800, Chicago *TF:* 800-368-3681 ■ *Web:* www.frontenac.com	IL	60603	312-368-0044	368-9520
FTV Management Co LP 555 California St Suite 2900, San Francisco *Web:* www.ftvcapital.com	CA	94104	415-229-3000	229-3005
G-51 Capital Management 901 S Mo Pac Expy Bldg 3 Suite 410, Austin *Web:* www.g51.com	TX	78746	512-929-5151	732-0886
Gabriel Venture Partners 350 Marine Pkwy Suite 200, Redwood Shores *Web:* www.gabrielvp.com	CA	94065	650-551-5000	551-5001
Garage Technology Ventures 3300 Hillview Ave Suite 150, Palo Alto *Web:* www.garage.com	CA	94304	650-354-1800	354-1801
Gazelle Techventures 11611 N Meridian St Suite 310, Carmel *Web:* www.gazellevc.com	IN	46032	317-275-6800	275-1100
Gefinor Ventures Management Inc 375 Pk Ave Suite 2401, New York *Web:* www.gefinorventures.com	NY	10152	212-308-1111	308-1182
General Atlantic LLC 3 Pickwick Plaza Suite 200, Greenwich *Web:* www.generalatlantic.com	CT	06830	203-629-8600	622-8818
Geocapital Partners 1 Executive Dr Suite 160, Fort Lee *Web:* www.geocapital.com	NJ	07024	201-461-9292	461-7793
GFI Energy Ventures LLC 11611 San Vicente Blvd Suite 710, Los Angeles *Web:* www.gfienergy.com	CA	90049	310-442-0542	442-0540
GKM Ventures 11150 Santa Monica Blvd Suite 825, Los Angeles *Web:* www.gkmventures.com	CA	90025	310-268-2610	268-0870
Globespan Capital Partners 1 Boston Pl Suite 2810, Boston *Web:* www.globespancapital.com	MA	02108	617-305-2300	305-2301
GrandBanks Capital 10 Langley Rd Suite 403, Newton Center *Web:* www.grandbankscapital.com	MA	02459	617-928-9314	928-9305
Granite Global Ventures 2494 Sand Hill Rd Suite 100, Menlo Park *Web:* www.ggvc.com	CA	94025	650-475-2150	475-2151
Granite Ventures LLC 1 Bush St Suite 1350, San Francisco *Web:* www.granitevc.com	CA	94104	415-591-7700	591-7720
Great Hill Partners LLC 1 Liberty Sq, Boston *Web:* www.greathillpartners.com	MA	02109	617-790-9400	790-9401
Greer Capital Advisors LLC 2200 Woodcrest Pl Suite 309, Birmingham *Web:* www.greercap.com	AL	35209	205-445-0800	445-1013
Grosvenor Funds 57 Old Post Rd #2 2nd Fl, Greenwich *Web:* www.grosvenorfund.com	CT	06830	203-629-8337	629-8506
Grotech Ventures 8000 Towers Crescent Dr Suite 850, Vienna *Web:* www.grotech.com	VA	22182	703-637-9555	827-9088
Grove Street Advisors 20 William St Suite 230, Wellesley *Web:* www.grovestreetadvisors.com	MA	02481	781-263-6100	263-6101
GRP Partners 2121 Avenue of the Stars Suite 1630, Los Angeles *Web:* www.grpvc.com	CA	90067	310-785-5100	785-5111
GTCR Golder Rauner LLC 300 N Lasalle Suite 5600, Chicago *Web:* www.gtcr.com	IL	60654	312-382-2200	382-2201
Guide Ventures 12509 Bel-Red Rd Suite 201-B, Bellevue *Web:* www.guideventures.com	WA	98005	425-450-0062	
Hamilton BioVentures 12555 High Bluff Dr Suite 310, San Diego *Web:* www.hamiltonbioventures.com	CA	92130	858-314-2350	314-2355

Firm / Address	City	State	Zip	Phone	Fax
HarbourVest Partners LLC 1 Financial Ctr 44th Fl	Boston	MA	02111	617-348-3707	350-0305
Web: www.harbourvest.com					
Harvard Management Co Inc 600 Atlantic Ave 16th Fl	Boston	MA	02210	617-523-4400	367-1361*
**Fax:* Hum Res ■ *TF:* 800-723-0044					
Harvest Partners 280 Pk Ave 33rd Fl	New York	NY	10017	212-599-6300	812-0100
TF: 866-427-8727 ■ *Web:* www.harvpart.com					
HC Wainwright & Co Inc 52 Vanderbilt Ave 12th Fl	New York	NY	10017	212-856-5700	856-5753
Web: www.hcwainwright.com					
HealthCare Ventures LLC 44 Nassau St	Princeton	NJ	08542	609-430-3900	430-9525
Web: www.hcven.com					
Hercules Technology Growth Capital Inc 400 Hamilton Ave Suite 310	Palo Alto	CA	94301	650-289-3060	473-9194
NASDAQ: HTGC ■ *Web:* www.herculestech.com					
Hickory Venture Group 301 Washington St NW Suite 301	Huntsville	AL	45801	256-539-1931	539-5130
Web: www.hvcc.com					
Highland Capital Partners 92 Hayden Ave	Lexington	MA	02421	781-861-5500	861-5499
Web: www.hcp.com					
HLM Venture Partners 222 Berkeley St 21st Fl	Boston	MA	02116	617-266-0030	266-3619
Web: www.hlmvp.com					
HMS Hawaii 841 Bishop St Suite 860	Honolulu	HI	96813	808-545-3755	531-2611
Web: www.hmshawaii.com					
HO2 Partners 2 Galleria Tower Suite 1670	Dallas	TX	75240	972-702-1144	702-8234
Web: www.ho2.com					
Housatonic Partners 111 Huntington Ave Suite 2850	Boston	MA	02199	617-399-9200	267-5565
Web: www.housatonicpartners.com					
Hummer Winblad Venture Partners 1 Lombard St Suite 300	San Francisco	CA	94111	415-979-9600	979-9601
Web: www.humwin.com					
Hunt Ventures LP 1445 Ross at Field Suite 1400	Dallas	TX	75202	214-978-8200	
Web: www.huntventures.com					
Idanta Partners Ltd 12526 High Bluff Dr Suite 160	San Diego	CA	92130	858-356-0150	356-0152
Idealab 130 W Union St	Pasadena	CA	91103	626-585-6900	535-2701
TF: 888-433-3522 ■ *Web:* www.idealab.com					
IDG Ventures 1 Letterman Dr	San Francisco	CA	94129	415-439-4420	439-4428
Web: www.idgvsf.com					
IGNITE Group 255 Shoreline Dr Suite 510	Redwood City	CA	94065	650-622-2000	622-2015
Web: www.ignitegroup.com					
In-Q-Tel PO Box 749	Arlington	VA	22216	703-248-3000	248-3001
Web: www.iqt.org					
Inflection Point Ventures (IPV) 1 Innovation Way Suite 302	Newark	DE	19711	302-452-1120	452-1122
Web: www.inflectpoint.com					
InnoCal LP 650 Town Ctr Dr Suite 770	Costa Mesa	CA	92626	714-850-6784	850-6798
Web: www.innocal.com					
Innovation Works Inc 2000 Technology Dr Suite 250	Pittsburgh	PA	15219	412-681-1520	681-2625
Web: www.innovationworks.org					
Institutional Venture Partners 3000 Sand Hill Rd Bldg 2 Suite 250	Menlo Park	CA	94025	650-854-0132	854-2009
Web: www.ivp.com					
Intelligent Systems Corp 4355 Shackleford Rd	Norcross	GA	30093	770-381-2900	381-2808
AMEX: INS ■ *Web:* www.intelsys.com					
Internet Capital Group Inc 690 Lee Rd Suite 310	Wayne	PA	19087	610-727-6900	727-6901
NASDAQ: ICGE ■ *Web:* www.icg.com					
Intersouth Partners 406 Blackwell St Suite 200	Durham	NC	27701	919-493-6640	493-6649
Web: www.intersouth.com					
InterWest Partners 2710 Sand Hill Rd 2nd Fl	Menlo Park	CA	94025	650-854-8585	854-4706
Web: www.interwest.com					
INVESCO Private Capital Inc 1166 Avenue of the Americas 26th Fl	New York	NY	10036	212-278-9000	278-9822
Web: www.invesco.com					
Ironside Ventures 161 Worcester Rd Suite 602	Framingham	MA	01701	781-622-5800	622-5801
Web: www.ironsideventures.com					
iSherpa Capital LLC 6400 S Fiddlers Green Cir	Greenwood Village	CO	80111	303-645-0500	645-0501
Web: www.isherpa.com					
Jafco Ventures Inc 505 Hamilton Ave Suite 310	Palo Alto	CA	94301	650-463-8800	463-8801
Web: www.jafco.com					
JatoTech Ventures 6300 Bridgepoint Pkwy Bldg 1 Suite 500	Austin	TX	78730	512-795-5860	692-2868
Web: www.jatotech.com					
JEGI Capital LLC 150 E 52nd St 18th Fl	New York	NY	10022	212-754-0710	754-0337
Web: www.jegi.com					
JH Whitney & Co LLC 130 Main St	New Canaan	CT	06840	203-716-6100	716-6122
TF: 800-881-6085 ■ *Web:* www.jhwhitney.com					
JK&B Capital 180 N Stetson Ave Suite 4500	Chicago	IL	60601	312-946-1200	946-1103
Web: www.jkbcapital.com					
Johnson & Johnson Development Corp 410 George St	New Brunswick	NJ	08901	732-524-3218	247-5309
Web: www.jnj.com					
Johnston Assoc Inc 155 Lambert Dr	Princeton	NJ	08540	609-924-2575	924-3135
Web: www.jaivc.com					
KB Partners LLC 1101 Skokie Blvd Suite 260	Northbrook	IL	60062	847-714-0444	714-0445
Web: www.kbpartners.com					
KBL Healthcare Ventures 380 Lexington Ave # 31	New York	NY	10168	212-319-5555	319-5591
Web: www.kblvc.com					
Key Principal Partners 50 California St Suite 2424	San Francisco	CA	94111	415-692-4660	402-0472
Web: www.key.com					

Firm / Address	City	State	Zip	Phone	Fax
Kirtland Capital Partners 3201 Enterprise Pkwy Suite 200	Beachwood	OH	44122	216-593-0100	593-0240
Web: www.kirtlandcapital.com					
Kleiner Perkins Caufield & Byers (KPCB) 2750 Sand Hill Rd	Menlo Park	CA	94025	650-233-2750	233-0300
Web: www.kpcb.com					
Kodiak Venture Partners 1000 Winter St Suite 3800	Waltham	MA	02451	781-672-2500	672-2501
Web: www.kodiakvp.com					
L Capital Partners 10 E 53rd St 37th Fl	New York	NY	10022	212-675-7755	206-9156
Web: www.lcapital.us					
Labrador Ventures 101 University Ave 4th Fl	Palo Alto	CA	94301	650-366-6000	366-6430
Web: www.labrador.com					
Lancet Capital 100 Technology Dr Suite 200	Pittsburgh	PA	15219	412-471-7107	
Web: www.lancetcapital.com					
Latterell Venture Partners 1 Embarcadero Ctr Suite 4050	San Francisco	CA	94111	415-399-9880	399-9879
Web: www.lvpcapital.com					
Lee Munder Capital Group 200 Clarendon St 28th Fl	Boston	MA	02116	617-380-5600	380-5601
Web: www.leemunderpim.com					
Legacy Venture 180 Lytton Ave 2nd Fl	Palo Alto	CA	94301	650-324-5980	324-5982
Web: www.legacyventure.com					
Life Sciences Greenhouse 225 Market St 5th Fl	Harrisburgh	PA	17101	717-635-2100	635-2010
Web: www.lsgpa.com					
Lighthouse Capital Partners 500 Drake's Landing Rd	Greenbrae	CA	94904	415-464-5900	925-3387
Web: www.lcpartners.com					
Lightspeed Venture Partners 2200 Sand Hill Rd Suite 100	Menlo Park	CA	94025	650-234-8300	234-8333
Web: www.lightspeedvp.com					
Lilly BioVentures DC 1089 Lilly Corporate Ctr	Indianapolis	IN	46285	317-651-3050	651-3051
Web: www.lillyventures.com					
Lubar & Co 700 N Water St Suite 1200	Milwaukee	WI	53202	414-291-9000	291-9061
Web: www.lubar.com					
Madison Dearborn Partners LLC (MDP) 3 1st National Plaza Suite 4600	Chicago	IL	60602	312-895-1000	895-1001
Web: www.mdcp.com					
Markpoint Venture Partners 15770 Dallas Pkwy Suite 800	Dallas	TX	75248	972-490-1976	490-1980
Web: www.markpt.com					
Mason Wells Biomedical Fund 411 E Wisconsin Ave Suite 1280	Milwaukee	WI	53202	414-727-6400	727-6410
Web: www.masonwells.com					
Massachusetts Capital Resource Co 420 Boylston St 5th Fl	Boston	MA	02116	617-536-3900	536-7930
Web: www.masscapital.com					
Massachusetts Growth Capital Corp (MGCC) 529 Main St Schrafft Ctr Suite 1M10	Charlestown	MA	02129	617-523-6262	523-7676
Web: www.mcdfc.com					
Massachusetts Technology Development Corp (MTDC) 40 Broad St	Boston	MA	02109	617-723-4920	723-5983
Web: www.mtdc.com					
Matrix Partners 1000 Winter St Bay Colony Corporate Ctr Suite 4500	Waltham	MA	02451	781-890-2244	890-2288
Web: www.matrixpartners.com					
Maveron LLC 505 5th Ave S Suite 600	Seattle	WA	98104	206-288-1700	288-1777
Web: www.maveron.com					
Mayfield Fund 2800 Sand Hill Rd Suite 250	Menlo Park	CA	94025	650-854-5560	854-5712
Web: www.mayfield.com					
MCG Capital Corp 1100 Wilson Blvd Suite 3000	Arlington	VA	22209	703-247-7500	247-7505
NASDAQ: MCGC ■ *TF:* 877-624-2733 ■ *Web:* www.mcgcapital.com					
McKellar & Co 311 E Rose Ln	Phoenix	AZ	85012	602-277-1800	217-1512*
**Fax Area Code:* 503					
MDT Advisors Inc 125 High St Oliver St Tower Fl 21	Boston	MA	02110	617-235-7100	235-7199
Web: www.mdtai.com					
Mediphase Venture Partners 2150 Washington St # 200	Newton	MA	02462	617-332-3408	332-8463
Web: www.mediphaseventure.com					
Menlo Ventures 3000 Sand Hill Rd Bldg 4 Suite 100	Menlo Park	CA	94025	650-854-8540	854-7059
Web: www.menloventures.com					
Mesirow Financial Private Equity 350 N Clark St	Chicago	IL	60610	312-595-6000	595-4246
TF: 800-453-0600 ■ *Web:* www.mesirowfinancial.com					
MidCoast Capital 259 N Radnor-Chester Rd Suite 210	Radnor	PA	19087	610-687-8580	971-2154
Web: www.midcoastcapital.com					
Milestone Venture Partners 551 Madison Ave 7th Fl	New York	NY	10022	212-223-7400	223-0315
Web: www.milestonevp.com					
Mission Ventures 11455 El Camino Real Suite 450	San Diego	CA	92130	858-350-2100	350-2101
Web: www.missionventures.com					
Mohr Davidow Ventures 3000 Sand Hill Rd Bldg 3 Suite 290	Menlo Park	CA	94025	650-854-7236	854-7365
Web: www.mdv.com					
Montagu Newhall Assoc Inc 100 Painters Mill Rd Suite 700	Owings Mills	MD	21117	410-363-2725	356-9937
Web: www.montagunewhall.com					
Montlake Capital 1200 5th Ave Suite 1800	Seattle	WA	98101	206-956-0898	956-0863
Web: montlakecapital.com					
Montreux Equity Partners 3000 Sand Hill Rd Bldg 1 Suite 260	Menlo Park	CA	94025	650-234-1200	234-1250
Web: www.montreuxequity.com					
Monumental Venture Partners LLC 8201 Greensboro Dr Suite 216	McLean	VA	22102	703-821-0400	821-0281
Web: www.mvpfunds.com					

Firm	Address	City	State	ZIP	Phone	Fax
Morgan Stanley Venture Partners	1585 Broadway 38th Fl	New York	NY	10036	212-761-6003	761-9580
	TF: 800-419-2861 ■ *Web:* www.morganstanley.com/institutional/venturepar					
Morgenthaler	2710 Sand Hill Rd Suite 100	Menlo Park	CA	94025	650-388-7600	388-7601
	Web: www.morgenthaler.com					
Morgenthaler Ventures	50 Public Sq Suite 2700	Cleveland	OH	44113	216-416-7500	416-7501
	Web: www.morgenthaler.com					
Mountaineer Capital LP	107 Capital St Suite 300	Charleston	WV	25301	304-347-7519	347-0072
	Web: www.mtncap.com					
MPM Capital Offices	200 Clarendon St 54th Fl	Boston	MA	02116	617-425-9200	425-9201
	TF: 888-799-6245 ■ *Web:* www.mpmcapital.com					
MRV Communications Inc	20415 Nordhoff St	Chatsworth	CA	91311	818-773-0900	773-0906
	NASDAQ: MRVC ■ *TF Sales:* 800-858-7815 ■ *Web:* www.mrv.com					
MVC Capital Inc	287 Bowman Ave 2nd Fl	New York	NY	10577	914-510-9400	701-0315
	NYSE: MVC ■ *Web:* www.mvccapital.com					
National Healthcare Services	320 Golden Shore Ave Suite 120	Long Beach	CA	90802	562-432-0047	432-0091
	Web: www.nationalhealthcareservices.com					
Nautic Partners LLC	50 Kennedy Plaza 12th Fl	Providence	RI	02903	401-278-6770	278-6387
	Web: www.nautic.com					
Nazem & Co	570 Lexington Ave 15th Fl	New York	NY	10022	212-371-7900	371-2150
	Web: www.nazem.com					
Nca Partners Inc	1200 Westlake Ave N Suite 600	Seattle	WA	98109	206-689-5615	689-5614
	Web: www.nwcap.com					
NCIC Capital Fund	900 Kettering Tower	Dayton	OH	45423	937-222-4422	222-1323
	Web: www.ncicfund.com					
NCT Ventures	PO Box 2790	Westerville	OH	43086	614-794-2732	794-2738
	Web: www.nctventures.com					
Needham & Co	445 Pk Ave	New York	NY	10022	212-705-0385	371-2311
	TF: 866-691-8263 ■ *Web:* www.needhamcapital.com					
Neocarta Ventures Inc	45 Fairfield St 4th Fl	Boston	MA	02116	617-239-9000	266-4107
	Web: www.neocarta.com					
NeuroVentures Capital LLC	Zero Ct Sq	Charlottesville	VA	22902	434-297-1000	297-1001
	Web: www.neuroventures.com					
New Capital Partners	2900 1st Ave S # 200	Birmingham	AL	35233	205-939-8400	939-8402
	Web: www.newcapitalpartners.com					
New Venture Partners LLC	98 Floral Ave	Murray Hill	NJ	07974	908-464-0900	464-8131
	Web: www.newventurepartners.com					
New York Life Venture Capital	51 Madison Ave	New York	NY	10010	212-576-7000	
NewSpring Capital	555 E Lancaster Ave Suite 520	Radnor	PA	19087	610-567-2380	567-2388
	Web: www.newspringcapital.com					
Newtek Business Services Inc	1440 Broadway 17th Fl	New York	NY	10018	212-356-9500	273-8252
	NASDAQ: NKBS ■ *TF Sales:* 866-820-8902 ■ *Web:* www.thesba.com					
Newton Technology Partners	555 Bryant St Suite 584	Palo Alto	CA	94301	650-331-3990	745-1222
NGEN Partners LLC	1114 State St Suite 247	Santa Barbara	CA	93101	805-564-3156	564-1669
	Web: www.ngenpartners.com					
NJTC Venture Fund	1001 Briggs Rd Suite 280	Mount Laurel	NJ	08054	856-273-6800	273-0990
	Web: www.njtcvc.com					
Noro-Moseley Partners	4200 Northside Pkwy NW Bldg 9	Atlanta	GA	30327	404-233-1966	239-9280
	TF: 800-648-0520 ■ *Web:* www.noromoseley.com					
North Atlantic Capital	2 City Ctr 5th Fl	Portland	ME	04101	207-772-4470	772-3257
	Web: www.northatlanticcapital.com					
North Bridge Venture Partners	950 Winter St Suite 4600	Waltham	MA	02451	781-290-0004	290-0999
	Web: www.nbvp.com					
North Hill Ventures	10 Post Office Sq 11th Fl	Boston	MA	02109	617-788-2150	788-2152
	Web: www.northhillventures.com					
Northleaf Capital Partners	79 Wellington St W 6th Fl PO Box 120	Toronto	ON	M5K1N9	866-964-4141	304-0195*
	**Fax Area Code:* 416 ■ *TF:* 866-964-4141 ■ *Web:* www.northleafcapital.com					
Northwood Ventures	485 Underhill Blvd Suite 205	Syosset	NY	11791	516-364-5544	364-0879
	Web: www.northwoodventures.com					
Norwest Equity Partners	80 S 8th St Suite 3600	Minneapolis	MN	55402	612-215-1600	215-1601
	Web: www.nep.com					
Norwest Venture Partners	525 University Ave Suite 800	Palo Alto	CA	94301	650-321-8000	321-8010
	Web: www.nvp.com					
Novak Biddle Venture Partners	7501 Wisconsin Ave E Tower Suite 1380	Bethesda	MD	20814	240-497-1910	223-0255
	Web: www.novakbiddle.com					
NTH Power Technologies Inc	1 Embarcadero Ctr # 1550	San Francisco	CA	94111	415-983-9983	983-9984
	Web: www.nthpower.com					
Oak Investment Partners	1 Gorham Island 1st Fl	Westport	CT	06880	203-226-8346	227-0372
	Web: www.oakinv.com					
OCA Ventures LLC	505 N La Salle Dr # 500	Chicago	IL	60654	312-542-8954	542-8952
	Web: www.ocaventures.com					
Olympic Venture Partners	1010 Market St	Kirkland	WA	98033	425-889-9192	889-0152
	Web: www.ovp.com					
Olympus Partners	1 Station Pl Metro Ctr 4th Fl N	Stamford	CT	06902	203-353-5900	353-5910
	Web: www.olympuspartners.com					
ONCAP	161 Bay St 48th Fl	Toronto	ON	M5J2S1	416-214-4300	214-6106
	Web: www.oncap.com					
One Equity Partners	320 Pk Ave 18th Fl	New York	NY	10022	212-277-1500	277-1533
	Web: www.oneequity.com					
Onset Ventures	2490 Sand Hill Rd	Menlo Park	CA	94025	650-529-0700	529-0777
	Web: www.onset.com					
Oxford Bioscience Partners	650 Town Ctr Dr Suite 880	Costa Mesa	CA	92626	714-754-5719	754-6802
	Web: www.oxbio.com					
Pacific Horizon Ventures	701 5th Ave Suite 4970	Seattle	WA	98104	206-682-1181	682-8077
	Web: www.pacifichorizon.com					
Palo Alto Venture Partners	555 Bryant St Suite 558	Palo Alto	CA	94301	650-462-1221	462-1227
	Web: www.pavp.com					
Palomar Ventures	100 Wilshire Blvd Suite 1700	Santa Monica	CA	90401	310-260-6050	656-4150
	Web: www.palomarventures.com					
Pappajohn Capital Resources	2116 Financial Ctr	Des Moines	IA	50309	515-244-5746	244-2346
	Web: www.pappajohn.com					
Partech International	50 California St Suite 3200	San Francisco	CA	94111	415-788-2929	788-6763
	Web: www.partechventure.com					
Path4 Ventures	*Path 4 LLC* 4030 W Braker Ln Suite 360	Austin	TX	78759	512-344-3300	344-3350
	Web: www.path4.com					
Paul Capital Partners	50 California St Suite 3000	San Francisco	CA	94111	415-283-4300	283-4301
	Web: www.paulcapital.com					
Peck's Management Partners Ltd	1 Rockefeller Plaza Suite 1730	New York	NY	10020	212-332-1333	332-1334
	Web: www.pecks.com					
Pelion Venture Partners	2755 E Cottonwood Pkwy Suite 520	Salt Lake City	UT	84121	801-365-0262	365-0233
	Web: www.pelionvp.com					
Peninsula Equity Partners	*PeninsulaVentures*					
	3000 Sand Hill Rd Bldg 2 Suite 100	Menlo Park	CA	94025	650-854-0314	854-0670
	Web: www.peninsulaventures.com					
Pennell Venture Partners LLC (PVP)	332 Bleecker St Suite K-67	New York	NY	10014	718-855-7087	365-3195*
	**Fax Area Code:* 646 ■ *Web:* www.pennell.com					
Pfingsten Partners LLC	300 N LaSalle St Suite 5400	Chicago	IL	60654	312-222-8707	222-8708
	Web: www.pfingstenpartners.com					
Pitango Venture Capital	2929 Campus Dr Suite 410	San Mateo	CA	94403	650-357-9080	357-9088
	Web: www.pitango.com					
PNC Equity Partners	2 PNC Plaza 620 Liberty Ave 22nd Fl	Pittsburgh	PA	15222	412-705-3669	762-6233
	Web: www.pncequity.com					
Pomona Capital	780 3rd Ave 44th Fl	New York	NY	10017	212-593-3639	593-3987
	Web: www.pomonacapital.com					
Posco BioVentures	2121 Palomar Airport Rd Suite 300	Carlsbad	CA	92009	760-448-2848	448-2840
	Web: www.poscobioventures.com					
Primus Venture Partners	5900 Landerbrook Dr Suite 200	Cleveland	OH	44124	440-684-7300	684-7342
	Web: www.primuscapital.com					
Prince Ventures	6475 Bold Venture Tr	Tallahassee	FL	32309	850-321-3353	668-7223
	Web: www.princeventures.com					
Prism Venture Partners	100 Lowder Brook Dr Suite 2500	Westwood	MA	02098	781-302-4000	302-4040
	Web: www.prismventure.com					
Private Capital Management	8889 Pelican Bay Blvd Suite 500	Naples	FL	34108	239-254-2500	254-2557
	TF: 800-763-0337 ■ *Web:* www.private-cap.com					
Prolog Ventures LLC	7701 Forsyth Blvd # 1095	Saint Louis	MO	63105	314-743-2400	743-2403
	Web: www.prologventures.com					
Prospect Venture Partners	435 Tasso St Suite 200	Palo Alto	CA	94301	650-327-8800	324-8838
	Web: www.prospectventures.com					
Provco Group	795 E Lancaster Ave Suite 200	Villanova	PA	19085	610-520-2010	520-1905
	Web: www.provcogroup.com					
Providence Equity Partners LLC	50 Kennedy Plaza 18th Fl	Providence	RI	02903	401-751-1700	751-1790
	Web: www.provequity.com					
Psilos Group Managers LLC	140 Broadway 51st Fl	New York	NY	10005	212-242-8844	212-8855
	Web: www.psilos.com					
PureTech Ventures	500 Boylston St Suite 1600	Boston	MA	02116	617-482-2333	482-3337
	Web: www.puretechventures.com					
Quaker BioVentures	2929 Arch St Cira Centre	Philadelphia	PA	19104	215-988-6800	988-6801
	Web: www.quakerbio.com					
Quellos	601 Union St 56th Fl	Seattle	WA	98101	206-613-6700	613-6710
	Web: www.quellos.com					
R Chaney & Co Inc	6363 Woodway Dr Suite 960	Houston	TX	77057	713-356-7555	750-0021
Radius Ventures LLC	400 Madison Ave 8th Fl	New York	NY	10017	212-897-7778	397-2656
	Web: www.radiusventures.com					
RedShift Ventures	5425 Wisconsin Ave Suite 704	Chevy Chase	MD	20815	703-904-9800	904-0571
	Web: www.redshiftventures.com					
Rembrandt Venture Partners	2440 Sandhill Rd #100	Menlo Park	CA	94025	650-326-7070	326-3780
	Web: www.rembrandtvc.com					
Research Corp Technologies	101 N Wilmot Rd Suite 600	Tucson	AZ	85711	520-748-4400	748-0025
	Web: www.rctech.com					
Reynolds Dewitt & Co	300 Main St	Cincinnati	OH	45202	513-241-8716	421-3602
	TF: 800-877-3344					
Rho Capital Partners Inc	152 W 57th St 23rd Fl	New York	NY	10019	212-751-6677	751-3613
	Web: www.rhoventures.com					
Rice Sangalis Toole & Wilson	5847 San Felipe Rd Suite 2929	Houston	TX	77057	713-783-7770	783-9750

Firm	City	State	ZIP	Phone	Fax
Richland Ventures 1201 16th Ave S. *Web:* www.richlandventures.com	Nashville	TN	37212	615-383-8030	269-0463
Ridgewood Capital 14 Philips Pkwy. *TF:* 800-942-5550 ■ *Web:* www.ridgewoodcapital.com	Montvale	NJ	07645	201-447-9000	447-0474
Riordan Lewis & Haden 10900 Wilshire Blvd Suite 850 *Web:* www.rlhinvestors.com	Los Angeles	CA	90024	310-405-7200	405-7222
RiverVest Venture Partners 7733 Forsyth Blvd Suite 1650 *Web:* www.rivervest.com	Saint Louis	MO	63105	314-726-6700	726-6715
Rockport Capital Partners 160 Federal St 18th Fl *Web:* www.rockportcap.com	Boston	MA	02110	617-912-1420	912-1449
Rocky Mountain Capital Partners LLP 7887 E Belleville Ave Suite 1100	Englewood	CO	80111	303-297-1701	557-0677
Rosewood Capital 1 Maritime Plaza Suite 1575 *Web:* www.rosewoodcap.com	San Francisco	CA	94111	415-362-5526	362-1192
RRE Ventures LLC 130 E 59th St 17th Fl. *Web:* www.rre.com	New York	NY	10022	212-418-5100	
Rustic Canyon Partners 2425 Olympic Blvd Suite 6050 W. *Web:* www.rusticcanyon.com	Santa Monica	CA	90404	310-998-8000	998-8001
Safeguard Scientifics Inc 435 Devon Pk Dr Suite 800 *NYSE: SFE* ■ *TF:* 877-506-7371 ■ *Web:* www.safeguard.com	Wayne	PA	19087	610-293-0600	293-0601
Sail Venture Partners LP 3161 Michelson Dr Suite 750 *Web:* www.sailcapital.com	Irvine	CA	92612	949-398-5100	398-5101
Saints Ventures LLC 475 Sansome St Suite 1850 *Web:* www.saintsvc.com	San Francisco	CA	94111	415-773-2080	835-5970
Sanderling 400 S El Camino Real Suite 1200 *Web:* www.sanderling.com	San Mateo	CA	94402	650-401-2000	375-7077
SAP Ventures 3412 Hillview Ave *Web:* www.sapventures.com	Palo Alto	CA	94304	650-849-3996	687-9097
Sapient Capital Management LLC 4020 Lake Creek Dr N. *Web:* www.sapientcapital.com	Wilson	WY	83014	307-733-3806	733-4630
Saugatuck Capital Co 187 Danbury Rd *Web:* www.saugatuckcapital.com	Stamford	CT	06897	203-348-6669	324-6995
Scale Venture Partners 950 Tower Ln Suite 700 *Web:* www.scalevp.com	Foster City	CA	94404	650-378-6000	378-6040
Seaflower Ventures 1000 Winter St Suite 1000 *Web:* www.seaflower.com	Waltham	MA	02451	781-466-9552	466-9553
SeaPoint Ventures 719 2nd Ave Suite 1405 *Web:* www.seapointventures.com	Seattle	WA	98104	206-438-1880	438-1886
Selby Venture Partners 3500 Alameda de las Pulgas Suite 200 *Web:* www.selbyventures.com	Menlo Park	CA	94025	650-854-7399	854-7039
Select Capital Ventures (SCV) 4718 Old Gettysburg Rd Suite 405 *Web:* www.selectcapitalventures.com	Mechanicsburg	PA	17055	717-972-1314	
Sequel Venture Partners 4430 Arapahoe Ave Suite 220 *Web:* www.sequelvc.com	Boulder	CO	80303	303-546-0400	546-9728
Sequoia Capital 3000 Sand Hill Rd Bldg 4 Suite 180 *Web:* www.sequoiacap.com	Menlo Park	CA	94025	650-854-3927	854-2957
Sevin Rosen Funds 13455 Noel Rd Suite 1670 *Web:* www.srfunds.com	Dallas	TX	75240	972-702-1100	702-1103
Shasta Ventures 2440 Sand Hill Rd Suite 300 *Web:* www.shastaventures.com	Menlo Park	CA	94025	650-543-1700	543-1799
Shepherd Ventures 12250 El Camino Real Suite 116 *Web:* www.shepherdventures.com	San Diego	CA	92130	858-509-4744	509-3662
SI Ventures 12600 Gateway Blvd *Web:* www.siventures.com	Fort Meyers	FL	33913	239-561-4760	561-4916
Sierra Ventures 2884 Sand Hill Rd Suite 100 *TF:* 800-819-9665 ■ *Web:* www.sierraven.com	Menlo Park	CA	94025	650-854-1000	854-5593
Sigma Partners 1600 El Camino Real Suite 280 *Web:* www.sigmapartners.com	Menlo Park	CA	94025	650-853-1700	853-1717
Signature Capital LLC 100 Commercial St Suite 410 *Web:* www.signaturecapital.com	Portland	ME	04101	207-773-8123	773-8128
Siguler Guff & Co LLC 825 3rd Ave 10th Fl *Web:* www.sigulerguff.com	New York	NY	10022	212-332-5100	332-5130
SmartForest Ventures 319 SW Washington St Suite 720 *Web:* www.smartforest.com	Portland	OR	97204	503-222-2552	222-2834
Sofinnova Ventures 140 Geary St 10th Fl *Web:* www.sofinnova.com	San Francisco	CA	94108	415-228-3380	228-3390
SOFTBANK Inc 1188 Centre St *Web:* www.softbank.com	Newton Center	MA	02459	617-928-9300	928-9304
Solstice Capital 6245 E Broadway Blvd Suite 620 *Web:* www.solcap.com	Tucson	AZ	85711	520-514-8000	
South Atlantic Capital Inc 614 W Bay St *Web:* www.southatlantic.com	Tampa	FL	33606	813-253-2500	253-2360
Southeast Interactive Technology Funds 630 Davis Dr Suite 220 *Web:* www.seinteractive.com	Morrisville	NC	27560	919-558-8324	558-2025
Space Center Ventures Inc 2501 Rosegate *Web:* www.scvinc.com	Roseville	MN	55113	651-604-4201	
Spectrum Equity Investors LP 1 International Pl 29th Fl *Web:* www.spectrumequity.com	Boston	MA	02110	617-464-4600	464-4601
Split Rock Partners 1600 El Camino Real Suite 290 *Web:* www.splitrock.com	Menlo Park	CA	94025	650-617-1500	617-1510
Sprout Group 11 Madison Ave 13th Fl *Web:* www.sproutgroup.com	New York	NY	10010	212-538-3600	538-8245
SR One Ltd 200 Barr Harbor Dr 4 Tower Bridge Suite 250	West Conshohocken	PA	19428	610-567-1000	567-1039
Steamboat Ventures 3601 W Olive Ave Suite 650 *Web:* www.steamboatvc.disney.go.com	Burbank	CA	91505	818-566-7400	566-7490
Sterling Venture Partners 650 S Exeter St # 10 *Web:* www.sterlingpartners.us	Baltimore	MD	21202	443-703-1700	703-1750
Storm Ventures 2440 Sand Hill Rd Suite 301 *Web:* www.stormventures.com	Menlo Park	CA	94025	650-926-8800	926-8888
Strategic Investments & Holdings Inc (SIHI) 50 Fountain Plaza Suite 1350 *Web:* www.sihi.net	Buffalo	NY	14202	716-857-6000	857-6490
Summit Partners 222 Berkeley St 18th Fl *Web:* www.summitpartners.com	Boston	MA	02116	617-824-1000	824-1100
Sutter Hill Ventures 755 Page Mill Rd Suite A-200 *Web:* www.shv.com	Palo Alto	CA	94304	650-493-5600	858-1854
SV Life Sciences (SVLS) 201 Washington St Suite 3900 *Web:* www.svlsa.com	Boston	MA	02108	617-367-8100	367-1590
T Rowe Price 100 E Pratt St *TF:* 800-638-7890 ■ *Web:* corporate.troweprice.com	Baltimore	MD	21202	410-345-2000	345-3618
TA Assoc Inc 200 Clarendon St 56th Fl *TF:* 800-836-8873 ■ *Web:* www.ta.com	Boston	MA	02116	617-574-6700	574-6728
TAT Capital Partners Ltd PO Box 23326 *Web:* www.tatcapital.com	San Jose	CA	95153	408-270-9200	270-4140
Techfarm 2275 E Bayshore Rd Suite 150 *Web:* www.techfarm.com	Palo Alto	CA	94303	650-934-0900	934-0910
Technology Crossover Ventures 528 Ramona St *Web:* www.tcv.com	Palo Alto	CA	94301	650-614-8200	614-8222
Technology Funding Inc 460 St Michael's Dr Suite 1000 *TF:* 800-821-5323 ■ *Web:* www.techfunding.com	Santa Fe	NM	87505	505-982-2200	820-6900
Technology Partners 550 University Ave *Web:* www.technologypartners.com	Palo Alto	CA	94301	650-289-9000	289-9001
Techxas Ventures 4401 W Gate Blvd Suite 300 *Web:* www.techxas.com	Austin	TX	78745	512-334-3140	334-3121
Telecommunications Development Fund (TDF) 2 Wisconsin Cir Suite 920 **Fax Area Code: 301* ■ *Web:* www.tdfund.com	Chevy Chase	MD	20815	240-483-4286	907-8850*
TeleSoft Partners 950 Tower Ln Suite 1600 *Web:* www.telesoftvc.com	Foster	CA	94404	650-358-2500	358-2501
TEOCO Corp 12150 Monument Dr Suite 400 *TF:* 888-868-3626 ■ *Web:* www.teoco.com	Fairfax	VA	22033	703-322-9200	259-2131
Texas Growth Fund 111 Congress Ave Suite 2900 *Web:* www.tgfmanagement.com	Austin	TX	78701	512-322-3100	322-3101
TGap Ventures 259 E Michigan Ave Suite 208 *Web:* www.tgapventures.com	Kalamazoo	MI	49007	269-217-1999	381-5453
Thoma Cressey Bravo Inc 600 Montgomery St 32nd Fl *Web:* www.tcb.com	San Francisco	CA	94111	415-263-3660	392-6480
Thomas McNerney & Partners 263 Tresser Blvd 16th Fl *Web:* www.tm-partners.com	Stamford	CT	06901	203-978-2000	978-2005
Thomas Weisel Partners Group LLC 1 Montgomery St *TF:* 800-933-3445 ■ *Web:* www.tweisel.com	San Francisco	CA	94104	415-364-2500	364-2695
TL Ventures 435 Devon Pk Dr 700 Bldg *Web:* www.tlventures.com	Wayne	PA	19087	610-971-1515	975-9330
Topspin Partners LP 3 Expy Plaza *Web:* www.topspinpartners.com	Roslyn Heights	NY	11577	516-625-9400	625-9499
Tortoise Energy Capital Corp 11550 Ash St Suite 300 *NYSE: TYY* ■ *TF:* 866-362-9331 ■ *Web:* www.tortoiseadvisors.com	Leawood	KS	66211	913-981-1020	981-1021
Trellis Partners 2600 Via Fortuna Suite 150 *Web:* www.trellis.com	Austin	TX	78746	512-330-9200	330-9400
Trelys Funds LP PO Box 545 *Web:* www.trelys.com	Columbia	SC	29202	919-484-0400	484-0444
Triathlon Medical Ventures (TMVP) 250 E 5th St 1100 Chiquita Ctr. *Web:* www.tmvp.com	Cincinnati	OH	45202	513-723-2600	723-2615
Trident Capital 505 Hamilton Ave Suite 200 *Web:* www.tridentcap.com	Palo Alto	CA	94301	650-289-4400	289-4444
Trillium Group LLC 1221 Pittsford Victor Rd *Web:* www.trillium-group.com	Pittsford	NY	14534	585-383-5680	383-0042
Trinity Ventures 3000 Sand Hill Rd Bldg 4 Suite 160 *Web:* www.trinityventures.com	Menlo Park	CA	94025	650-854-9500	854-9501
Triton Ventures 6300 Bridge Pt Pkwy Bldg 1 Suite 500 *Web:* www.tritonventures.com	Austin	TX	78730	512-795-5820	795-5828
Tullis Dickerson & Co Inc 263 Tresser Blvd *Web:* www.thi-funds.com	Stamford	CT	06901	203-629-8700	629-9293
TVM Techno Venture Management LP 101 Arch St Suite 1950 *Web:* www.tvmvc.com	Boston	MA	02110	617-345-9320	345-9377
Union Square Ventures 915 Broadway Suite 1408 *Web:* www.unionsquareventures.com	New York	NY	10010	212-994-7880	994-7399
UPS Strategic Enterprise Fund 55 Glenlake Pkwy NE Bldg 1 4th Fl *Web:* www.ups.com/sef	Atlanta	GA	30328	404-828-8814	828-8088
US Venture Partners (USVP) 2735 Sand Hill Rd Suite 300 *TF:* 877-773-8787 ■ *Web:* www.usvp.com	Menlo Park	CA	94025	650-854-9080	854-3018

	City	State	Zip	Phone	Fax
Valhalla Partners 8000 Towers Crescent Dr Suite 1050 *Web:* www.valhallapartners.com	Vienna	VA	22182	703-448-1400	448-1441
Vanguard Venture Partners 505 Hamilton Ave Suite 300 *Web:* www.vanguardventures.com	Palo Alto	CA	94301	650-321-2900	321-2902
VantagePoint Venture Partners 1001 Bayhill Dr Suite 300 *Web:* www.vpcp.com	San Bruno	CA	94066	650-866-3100	869-6078
Vector Capital 456 Montgomery St 19th Fl *Web:* www.vectorcapital.com	San Francisco	CA	94104	415-293-5000	293-5100
Venrock Assoc 3340 Hillview Ave *Web:* www.venrock.com	Palo Alto	CA	94304	650-561-9580	561-9180
Ventana Capital Management LP 31473 Rancho Viejo Rd Suite 206 *Web:* www.ventanavc.com	San Juan Capistrano	CA	92675	949-481-4200	481-4440
Venture Capital Fund of America 509 Madison Ave Suite 1400 *Web:* www.vcfa.com	New York	NY	10022	212-838-5577	838-7614
Venture Investors LLC 505 S Rosa Rd Suite 201 *Web:* www.ventureinvestors.com	Madison	WI	53719	608-441-2700	441-2727
VentureVest Capital Corp 2530 W Long Cir *Web:* www.venturevest.com	Littleton	CO	80120	303-730-7939	730-7947
Vertical Group 25 DeForest Ave *Web:* www.vertical-group.com	Summit	NJ	07901	908-277-3737	273-9434
Vesbridge Partners LLC 1700 W Pk Dr *Web:* www.vesbridge.com	Westboro	MA	01581	508-475-2300	475-2399
Village Ventures Inc 430 Main St Suite 1 *Web:* www.villageventures.com	Williamstown	MA	01267	413-458-1100	458-0338
VIMAC Ventures LLC 177 Milk St *Web:* www.vimac.com	Boston	MA	02109	617-350-9800	350-9899
Vision Capital 1 Bayshore Plaza 700 Airport Blvd Suite 370 *Web:* www.visioncap.com	Burlingame	CA	94010	650-373-2720	373-2727
Vista Ventures 1011 Walnut St 4th Fl *Web:* www.vistavc.com	Boulder	CO	80302	303-543-5716	543-5717
VSP Capital 201 Post St Suite 1100 *Web:* www.vspcapital.com	San Francisco	CA	94118	415-558-8600	558-8686
vSpring Capital 2795 E Cottonwood Pkwy Suite 360 *Web:* www.vspring.com	Salt Lake City	UT	84121	801-942-8999	942-1636
Walden International 1 California St Suite 2800 *Web:* www.waldenintl.com	San Francisco	CA	94111	415-765-7100	765-7200
Walden Venture Capital 750 Battery St Suite 700 *Web:* www.waldenvc.com	San Francisco	CA	94111	415-391-7225	391-7262
Warburg Pincus Ventures Co Inc 450 Lexington Ave *Web:* www.warburgpincus.com	New York	NY	10017	212-878-0600	878-9351
Washington Research Foundation 2815 Eastlake Ave E Suite 300 *Web:* www.wrfcapital.com	Seattle	WA	98102	206-336-5600	336-5615
WayPoint Ventures (RPMVC) *RPM Ventures* 320 N Main St Suite 400 *Web:* www.rpmvc.com	Ann Arbor	MI	48104	734-332-1700	332-1900
Western Technology Investment (WTI) 2010 N 1st St Suite 310 *Web:* www.westerntech.com	San Jose	CA	95131	408-436-8577	436-8625
Wicks Group of Cos LLC 405 Pk Ave Suite 702 *Web:* www.wicksgroup.com	New York	NY	10022	212-838-2100	223-2109
Willowridge Partners Inc 25 E 86th St *Web:* www.willowridgeinc.com	New York	NY	10028	212-369-4700	369-5661
Wind Point Partners 676 N Michigan Ave Suite 3700 *Web:* www.wppartners.com	Chicago	IL	60611	312-255-4800	255-4820
Windjammer Capital Investors 610 Newport Ctr Dr Suite 1100 *TF:* 800-314-2644 ■ *Web:* www.windjammercapital.com	Newport Beach	CA	92660	949-721-9944	720-4222
Windspeed Ventures 52 Waltham St *Web:* www.windspeed.com	Lexington	MA	02421	781-860-8888	860-0493
Woodside Fund 350 Marine Pkwy Suite 300 *TF:* 888-368-5545 ■ *Web:* www.woodsidefund.com	Redwood Shores	CA	94065	650-610-8050	610-8051
Worldview Technology Partners 435 Tasso St Suite 120 *Web:* www.worldview.com	Palo Alto	CA	94301	650-322-3800	322-3880
Zanett Inc 635 Madison Ave 15th Fl *NASDAQ: ZANE* ■ *TF:* 866-611-3282 ■ *Web:* www.zanett.com	New York	NY	10022	212-583-0300	583-0221
Zon Capital Partners 5 Vaughn Dr Suite 302 *Web:* www.zoncapital.com	Princeton	NJ	08540	609-452-1653	452-1693
ZS Fund LP 1133 Avenue of the Americas *TF:* 888-386-3573 ■ *Web:* www.zsfundlp.com	New York	NY	10036	212-398-6200	398-1808

796 VETERANS NURSING HOMES - STATE

SEE ALSO Veterans Hospitals p. 2076

	City	State	Zip	Phone	Fax
Arizona State Veterans Home 4141 N 3rd St	Phoenix	AZ	85012	602-248-1550	222-6687
Arkansas State Veterans Home 4701 W 20th St	Little Rock	AR	72204	501-296-1885	296-1888
Baldomero Lopez State Veterans' Nursing Home 6919 Pkwy Blvd	Land O"Lakes	FL	34639	813-558-5000	558-5021
Barboursville Veterans Home 512 Water St	Barboursville	WV	25504	304-736-1027	736-1093
Charlotte Hall Veterans Home 29449 Charlotte Hall Rd	Charlotte Hall	MD	20622	301-884-8171	884-4964
Chelsea Soldiers Home 91 Crest Ave	Chelsea	MA	02150	617-884-5660	884-1162
Colorado State Veterans Nursing Home-Homelake 3749 Sherman Ave *TF:* 888-838-2687	Monte Vista	CO	81144	719-852-5118	852-3881
Colorado State Veterans Nursing Home-Rifle 851 E 5th St	Rifle	CO	81650	970-625-0842	625-3706
DJ Jacobetti Home for Veterans 425 Fisher St *TF:* 800-433-6760 ■ *Web:* www.michigan.org	Marquette	MI	49855	906-226-3576	226-2380
Eastern Nebraska Veterans Home 12505 S 40th St	Bellevue	NE	68123	402-595-2180	595-2234
Emory L Bennett Memorial Veterans' Nursing Home 1920 Mason Ave	Daytona Beach	FL	32117	386-274-3460	274-3487
Floyd E "Tut" Fann State Veterans Home 2701 Meridian St	Huntsville	AL	35811	256-851-2807	859-4115
Georgia War Veterans Nursing Home 1101 15th St	Augusta	GA	30901	706-721-2824	721-3892
Grand Island Veterans' Home 2300 W Capital Ave	Grand Island	NE	68803	308-385-6252	385-6257*
Grand Rapids Home for Veterans 3000 Monroe Ave NW **Fax:* Hum Res ■ *Web:* www.state.mi.us/bnva/home/grhv	Grand Rapids	MI	49505	616-364-5300	364-5397*
Hastings Veterans Home 1200 E 18th St *TF:* 877-838-3803 ■ *Web:* www.mvh.state.mn.us	Hastings	MN	55033	651-438-8504	437-2012
Hollidaysburg Veterans Home PO Box 319	Hollidaysburg	PA	16648	814-696-5201	696-5260
Holyoke Soldiers Home 110 Cherry St *Web:* www.mass.gov/hoy	Holyoke	MA	01040	413-532-9475	538-7968
Idaho State Veterans Home-Boise 320 Collins Rd	Boise	ID	83702	208-334-5000	334-4753
Idaho State Veterans Home-Lewiston 821 21st Ave	Lewiston	ID	83501	208-799-3422	799-3414
Idaho State Veterans Home-Pocatello 1957 Alvin Ricken Dr	Pocatello	ID	83201	208-236-6340	236-6343
Illinois Veterans Home-Anna 792 N Main St	Anna	IL	62906	618-833-6302	833-3603
Illinois Veterans Home-La Salle 1015 O'Connor Ave *Web:* www.idva.org	La Salle	IL	61301	815-223-0303	223-5815
Illinois Veterans Home-Manteno 1 Veterans Dr	Manteno	IL	60950	815-468-6581	468-7001
Illinois Veterans Home-Quincy 1707 N 12th St	Quincy	IL	62301	217-222-8641	222-9621
Indiana Veterans Home 3851 N River Rd	West Lafayette	IN	47906	765-463-1502	497-8568
Iowa Veterans Home 1301 Summit St *Web:* www.iowava.org	Marshalltown	IA	50158	641-752-1501	753-4278
Long Island State Veterans Home 100 Patriots Rd	Stony Brook	NY	11790	631-444-8500	444-8575
Louisiana War Veterans' Home 4739 Hwy 10	Jackson	LA	70748	225-634-5265	634-4057
Luverne Veterans Home 1300 N Kniss Ave *Web:* www.mvh.state.mn.us	Luverne	MN	56156	507-283-1100	283-1127
Maine Veterans Home-Augusta 310 Cony Rd *Web:* www.maineveteranshomes.org	Augusta	ME	04330	888-684-4664	
Maine Veterans Home-Bangor 44 Hogan Rd *TF:* 888-684-4665 ■ *Web:* www.maineveteranshomes.org	Bangor	ME	04401	207-942-2333	942-4810
Maine Veterans Home-Caribou 163 Van Buren Rd Suite 2 *TF:* 888-684-4667 ■ *Web:* www.maineveteranshomes.org	Caribou	ME	04736	207-498-6074	498-3037
Maine Veterans Home-Scarborough 290 US Rt 1 *TF:* 888-684-4666 ■ *Web:* www.maineveteranshomes.org	Scarborough	ME	04074	207-883-7184	883-7852
Maine Veterans Home-South Paris 477 High St *TF:* 888-684-4668 ■ *Web:* www.maineveteranshomes.org	South Paris	ME	04281	207-743-6300	743-7595
Menlo Park Veterans Memorial Home 132 Evergreen Rd PO Box 3013	Edison	NJ	08818	732-452-4100	603-3192
Minnesota Veterans Home-Fergus Falls 1821 N Pk St *Web:* www.mvh.state.mn.us	Fergus Falls	MN	56537	218-736-0400	739-7686
Minnesota Veterans Home-Minneapolis 5101 Minnehaha Ave S *TF:* 877-838-6757 ■ *Web:* www.mvh.state.mn.us	Minneapolis	MN	55407	612-721-0600	721-0604
Minnesota Veterans Home-Silver Bay 45 Banks Blvd *TF:* 877-729-8387 ■ *Web:* www.mvh.state.mn.us	Silver Bay	MN	55614	218-226-6300	226-6336
Mississippi State Veterans' Home Collins 3261 Hwy 49 S	Collins	MS	39428	601-765-0403	765-5045
Mississippi State Veterans' Home Jackson 4607 Lindbergh Dr	Jackson	MS	39209	601-353-6142	969-1386
Mississippi State Veterans' Home Kosciusko 310 Autumn Ridge Dr	Kosciusko	MS	39090	662-289-7769	289-7803
Mississippi State Veterans' Home Oxford 120 Veterans Dr	Oxford	MS	38655	662-236-7641	236-2129
Missouri Veterans Home-Cape Girardeau 2400 Veterans Memorial Dr *Web:* www.mo.gov	Cape Girardeau	MO	63701	573-290-5870	290-5909
Missouri Veterans Home-Mount Vernon 1600 S Hickory *Web:* mvc.dps.mo.gov	Mount Vernon	MO	65712	417-466-7103	466-4040
Missouri Veterans Home-Saint James 620 N Jefferson St	Saint James	MO	65559	573-265-3271	265-5771
Missouri Veterans Home-Saint Louis 10600 Lewis & Clark Blvd	Saint Louis	MO	63136	314-340-6389	340-6379
Montana Veterans Home PO Box 250	Columbia Falls	MT	59912	406-892-3256	892-0256
New Hampshire Veterans Home 139 Winter St *Web:* www.nh.gov/veterans	Tilton	NH	03276	603-527-4400	527-4402
New Jersey Veterans Paramus Home 1 Veterans Dr	Paramus	NJ	07652	201-634-8200	
New Mexico State Veterans Ctr 992 S Broadway St *TF:* 800-964-3976 ■ *Web:* www.nmstateveteranshome.org	Truth or Consequences	NM	87901	575-894-4200	894-4270
New York State Veterans Home at Batavia 220 Richmond Ave	Batavia	NY	14020	585-345-2000	345-9030
New York State Veterans Home at Oxford 4211 State Hwy 220	Oxford	NY	13830	607-843-3100	843-3194
New York State Veterans Home at Saint Albans 178-50 Linden Blvd	Jamaica	NY	11434	718-481-6268	481-6860

	City	State	Zip	Phone	Fax
Norfolk Veterans Home 600 E Benjamin Ave.	Norfolk	NE	68701	402-370-3330	370-3190
North Dakota State Veterans Home 1400 Rose St	Lisbon	ND	58054	701-683-6500	683-6550
Ohio Veterans Home 3416 Columbus Ave *Fax: Admitting ■ TF Admissions: 800-572-7934	Sandusky	OH	44870	419-625-2454	609-2544*
Oklahoma Veterans Center Ardmore 1015 S Commerce Web: www.odva.state.ok.us	Ardmore	OK	73401	580-223-2266	221-5606
Oklahoma Veterans Center Claremore PO Box 988 Web: www.odva.state.ok.us	Claremore	OK	74018	918-342-5432	342-0835
Oklahoma Veterans Center Clinton PO Box 1209 Web: www.odva.state.ok.us	Clinton	OK	73601	580-331-2200	323-4834
Oklahoma Veterans Center Sulphur 200 E Fairlane Web: www.odva.state.ok.us	Sulphur	OK	73086	580-622-2144	622-5881
Oklahoma Veterans Center Talihina Hwy 63 A PO Box 1168	Talihina	OK	74571	918-567-2251	567-2950
Oregon Veterans' Home 700 Veterans Dr TF: 800-846-8460	The Dalles	OR	97058	541-296-7190	296-7862
Rhode Island Veterans' Home 480 Metacom Ave	Bristol	RI	02809	401-253-8000	254-1340
Richard M Campbell State Nursing Home 4605 Belton Hwy	Anderson	SC	29621	864-261-6734	261-0453
Rocky Hill Veterans Home & Healthcare Ctr 287 W St Web: www.ct.gov/ctva/cwp/view.asp?a=2005&q=482380	Rocky Hill	CT	06067	860-721-5891	721-5904
Tennessee State Veterans Home-Humboldt 2865 Main St	Humboldt	TN	38343	731-784-8405	784-2448
Tennessee State Veterans Home-Murfreesboro 345 Compton Rd	Murfreesboro	TN	37130	615-895-8850	895-5091
Thomson-Hood Veterans Ctr 100 Veterans Dr TF: 800-928-4838 ■ Web: www.kdva.net	Wilmore	KY	40390	859-858-2814	858-4039
Vermont Veterans Home 325 N St Web: www.vvh.vermont.gov	Bennington	VT	05201	802-442-6353	447-6466
Veterans Care Ctr 4550 Shenandoah Ave. Web: www.vdva.vipnet.org/carecenter_main.htm	Roanoke	VA	24017	540-982-2860	982-8667
Veterans Home of California-Barstow 100 E Veterans Pkwy TF: 800-746-0606 ■ Web: www.calvet.ca.gov/VetHomes/Barstow.aspx	Barstow	CA	92311	760-252-6200	252-6333
Veterans Home of California-Chula Vista 700 E Naples Ct TF: 888-857-2146 ■ Web: www.cdva.ca.gov	Chula Vista	CA	91911	619-482-6010	205-1903
Veterans Home of California-Yountville 1227 O St TF: 800-952-5626 ■ Web: www.calvet.ca.gov/VetHomes/Yountville.aspx	Sacramento	CA	95814	707-944-4541	944-4542
Washington Veterans Home PO Box 698	Retsil	WA	98378	360-895-4700	895-4719
Wisconsin Veterans Home N2665 County Rd QQ	King	WI	54946	715-258-5586	258-5736
Oklahoma Veterans Center Norman 1776 E Robinson St PO Box 1668 Web: www.ok.gov/ODVA/Veterans_Centers/Norman.html	Norman	OK	73070	405-360-5600	364-8432

797 VETERINARY HOSPITALS

	City	State	Zip	Phone	Fax
Animal Hospital Inc 5001 N 12th Ave Web: www.petcarehospital.com	Pensacola	FL	32504	850-479-2900	479-3322
Banfield the Pet Hospital 8000 NE Tillamook St TF: 800-838-6738 ■ Web: www.banfield.net	Portland	OR	97213	503-256-7299	256-7636
Noah's Animal Hospitals 5510 Millersville Rd Web: www.noahshospitals.com	Indianapolis	IN	46226	317-253-1327	726-2404
Pet Vet Animal Hospitals 4543 Post Oak Pl Suite 110 Web: www.petvethospitals.com	Houston	TX	77027	713-629-7521	629-7737
Radiocat 32-A Mellor Ave TF: 800-323-9729 ■ Web: www.radiocat.com	Baltimore	MD	21228	410-788-5200	788-5201
VCA Antech Inc 12401 W Olympic Blvd NASDAQ: WOOF ■ TF: 800-966-1822 ■ Web: www.vcaantech.com	Los Angeles	CA	90064	310-571-6500	571-6700
Veterinary Specialists of the Southeast 3169 W Montague Ave Web: www.ccvsllc.com	North Charleston	SC	29418	843-566-0023	747-7920
VetSelect Animal Hospital 2150 Old Novi Rd Web: www.vetselect.com	Novi	MI	48377	248-624-1100	624-6542

798 VETERINARY MEDICAL ASSOCIATIONS - STATE

	City	State	Zip	Phone	Fax
Alabama Veterinary Medical Assn 8116 Old Federal Rd # C Web: www.alvma.com	Montgomery	AL	36117	334-395-0086	270-3399
Alaska State Veterinary Medical Assn 1731 Bragaw St Web: www.akvma.org	Anchorage	AK	99508	907-563-3701	
Arizona Veterinary Medical Assn 100 W Coolidge St Web: www.azvma.org	Phoenix	AZ	85013	602-242-7936	249-3828
Arkansas Veterinary Medical Assn PO Box 17687 Web: www.arkvetmed.org	Little Rock	AR	72222	501-868-3036	868-3034
California Veterinary Medical Assn 1400 River Pk Dr Suite 100 TF: 800-655-2862 ■ Web: www.cvma.net	Sacramento	CA	95815	916-649-0599	646-9156
Colorado Veterinary Medical Assn 191 Yuma St TF: 800-228-5429 ■ Web: www.colovma.com	Denver	CO	80223	303-318-0447	318-0450
Connecticut Veterinary Medical Assn 100 Roscommon Dr Suite 320 Web: www.ctvet.org	Middletown	CT	06457	860-635-7770	635-6400
Delaware Veterinary Medical Assn 937 Monroe Terr Web: www.devma.org	Dover	DE	19904	302-242-7014	674-8581
District of Columbia Academy of Veterinary Medicine PO Box 710477 Web: www.dcavm.org	Herndon	VA	20171	703-733-0556	742-8745
Florida Veterinary Medical Assn 7131 Lake Ellenor Dr TF: 800-992-3862 ■ Web: www.fvma.com	Orlando	FL	32809	407-851-3862	240-3710
Georgia Veterinary Medical Assn 233 Peachtree St NE # 2205 TF: 800-853-1625 ■ Web: www.gvma.net	Atlanta	GA	30303	678-309-9800	309-3361
Idaho Veterinary Medical Assn (IVMA) 1841 W Secluded Ct Web: www.ivma.org	Kuna	ID	83634	208-922-9431	922-9435
Illinois State Veterinary Medical Assn 1121 Chatham Rd Web: www.isvma.org	Springfield	IL	62704	217-546-8381	546-5633
Indiana Veterinary Medical Assn 201 S Capitol Ave Suite 405 Web: www.invma.org	Indianapolis	IN	46225	317-974-0888	974-0985
Iowa Veterinary Medical Assn 1605 N Ankeny Blvd Suite 110 Web: www.iowavma.org	Ankeny	IA	50023	515-965-9237	965-9239
Kansas Veterinary Medical Assn 816 SW Tyler St Suite 200 Web: www.ksvma.org	Topeka	KS	66612	785-233-4141	233-2534
Kentucky Veterinary Medical Assn 108 Consumer Ln Web: www.kvma.org	Frankfort	KY	40601	502-226-5862	226-6177
Louisiana Veterinary Medical Assn 8550 United Plaza Blvd Suite 1001 TF: 800-524-2996 ■ Web: www.lvma.org	Baton Rouge	LA	70809	225-928-5862	408-4422
Maine Veterinary Medical Assn 97-A Exchange St Suite 305 *Fax Area Code: 888 ■ Web: netforum.avectra.com	Portland	ME	04101	800-448-2772	612-0941*
Maryland Veterinary Medical Assn 8015 Corporate Dr Suite A TF: 888-884-6862 ■ Web: www.mdvma.org	Baltimore	MD	21236	410-931-3332	931-2060
Massachusetts Veterinary Medical Assn 163Lakeside Ave Web: www.massvet.org	Marlborough	MA	01752	508-460-9333	460-9969
Michigan Veterinary Medical Assn (MVMA) 2144 Commons Pkwy Web: www.michvma.org	Okemos	MI	48864	517-347-4710	347-4666
Minnesota Veterinary Medical Assn 101 Bridgepoint Way Suite 100 Web: www.mvma.org	South Saint Paul	MN	55075	651-645-7533	645-7539
Mississippi Veterinary Medical Assn 209 S Lafayette St Web: www.msvet.org	Starkville	MS	39759	662-324-9380	324-9380
Missouri Veterinary Medical Assn 2500 Country Club Dr Web: www.mvma.us	Jefferson City	MO	65109	573-636-8612	659-7175
Montana Veterinary Medical Assn PO Box 6322 Web: www.mtvma.org	Helena	MT	59604	406-447-4259	442-8018
Nebraska Veterinary Medical Assn 2727 W 2nd St Suite 227 Web: www.nvma.org	Hastings	NE	68901	402-463-4704	463-4705
Nevada Veterinary Medical Assn PO Box 34420 Web: www.nevadavma.org	Reno	NV	89533	775-324-5344	747-9170
New Jersey Veterinary Medical Assn 390 Amwell Rd Suite 402 Web: www.njvma.org	Hillsborough	NJ	08844	908-281-0918	450-1286
New Mexico Veterinary Medical Assn 60 Placitas Trails Rd Web: www.nmvma.org	Placitas	NM	87043	505-867-6373	771-8963
New York State Veterinary Medical Society 9 Highland Ave TF: 800-876-9867	Albany	NY	12205	518-437-0787	437-0957
North Carolina Veterinary Medical Assn (NCVMA) 1611 Jones Franklin Rd Suite 108 TF: 800-446-2862 ■ Web: www.ciclt.net	Raleigh	NC	27606	919-851-5850	851-5859
North Dakota Veterinary Medical Assn 921 S 9th St Suite 120 TF: 877-637-6386 ■ Web: www.ndvma.com	Bismarck	ND	58504	701-221-7740	258-9005
Ohio Veterinary Medical Assn (OVMA) 3168 Riverside Dr TF: 800-662-6862 ■ Web: www.ohiovma.org	Columbus	OH	43221	614-486-7253	486-1325
Oklahoma Veterinary Medical Assn PO Box 14521 Web: www.okvma.org	Oklahoma City	OK	73113	405-478-1002	478-7193
Oregon Veterinary Medical Assn 1880 Lancaster Dr NE Suite 118 TF: 800-235-3502 ■ Web: www.oregonvma.org	Salem	OR	97305	503-399-0311	363-4218
Pennsylvania Veterinary Medical Assn 12 Briarquest Sq TF: 888-550-7862 ■ Web: www.pavma.org	Hershey	PA	17033	717-533-7934	533-4761
Puerto Rico Veterinary Medical Assn 352 San Claudio Ave Suite 248 Web: www.cmvpr.org	San Juan	PR	00926	787-283-0565	761-3440
Rhode Island Veterinary Medical Assn 302 Pearl St Suite 108 Web: www.rivma.org	Providence	RI	02907	401-751-0944	780-0940
South Carolina Assn of Veterinarians PO Box 11766 TF: 800-441-7228 ■ Web: www.scav.org	Columbia	SC	29211	803-254-1027	254-3773
Tennessee Veterinary Medical Assn PO Box 803 TF: 800-697-3587 ■ Web: www.tvmanet.org	Fayetteville	TN	37334	931-438-0070	433-6289
Texas Veterinary Medical Assn 8104 Exchange Dr Web: www.tvma.org	Austin	TX	78754	512-452-4224	452-6633
Vermont Veterinary Medical Assn 88 Beech St Web: www.vtvets.org	Essex Junction	VT	05452	802-878-6888	878-2871

Company / Address	City	State	Zip	Phone	Fax
Virginia Veterinary Medical Assn 2314-C Commerce Ctr Dr. *TF:* 800-937-8862 ■ *Web:* www.vvma.org	Rockville	VA	23146	804-749-8058	749-8003
Washington State Veterinary Medical Assn PO Box 962 *TF:* 800-399-7862 ■ *Web:* www.wsvma.org	Bellevue	WA	98009	425-454-8381	454-8382
West Virginia Veterinary Medical Assn 201 Virginia St W *Web:* www.wvvma.org	Charleston	WV	25302	304-437-0497	346-0589
Wisconsin Veterinary Medical Assn 301 N Broom St *TF:* 888-254-5202 ■ *Web:* www.wvma.org	Madison	WI	53703	608-257-3665	257-8989
Wyoming Veterinary Medical Assn (WVMA) 1841 W Secluded Ct. *TF:* 800-272-1813 ■ *Web:* www.wyvma.org	Kuna	ID	83634	208-922-9431	922-9435

799 VIATICAL SETTLEMENT COMPANIES

A Viatical Settlement Is The Sale Of An Existing Life Insurance Policy By A Terminally Ill Person To A Third Party In Return For A Percentage Of The Face Value Of The Policy Paid Immediately.

Company / Address	City	State	Zip	Phone	Fax
AmeriFirst Funding Group Inc 2015-A Osborne Rd	Saint Marys	GA	31558	912-882-8851	882-9461
AMG/Neuma Inc 4709 W Golf Rd Suite 525 *TF:* 800-457-7828 ■ *Web:* www.neumainc.com	Skokie	IL	60076	847-674-1150	674-1165
CMG Surety LLC 1016 Collier Ctr Way Suite 100 *Web:* www.cmgsurety.com	Naples	FL	34110	239-597-0128	597-1977
Coventry First LLC 7111 Valley Green Rd. *TF:* 877-836-8300 ■ *Web:* www.coventry.com	Fort Washington	PA	19034	215-233-5100	233-3201
Habersham Funding LLC 415 E Paces Ferry Rd NE Terr Level *TF:* 888-874-2402 ■ *Web:* www.habershamfunding.com	Atlanta	GA	30305	404-233-8275	233-9394
Legacy Benefits Corp 350 5th Ave Suite 4320. *TF:* 800-875-1000 ■ *Web:* www.legacybenefits.com	New York	NY	10118	212-643-1190	643-1180
Life Equity LLC 5611 Hudson Dr # 100. *Web:* www.lifeequity.net	Hudson	OH	44236	330-342-7772	342-7782
Life Partners Inc (LPI) 204 Woodhew Dr. *NASDAQ: LPHI* ■ *TF:* 800-368-5569 ■ *Web:* www.lifepartnersinc.com	Waco	TX	76712	254-751-7797	751-1025
Life Settlement Providers LLC 6302A N Pt Rd *Web:* www.lifesettlementproviders.com	Baltimore	MD	21210	410-477-1976	477-1978
Life Settlement Solutions Inc 9201 Spectrum Ctr Blvd Suite 105. *Web:* www.lss-corp.com	San Diego	CA	92123	858-576-8067	576-9329
Life Trust LLC 330 Madison Ave 6th Fl *Web:* www.life-trust.net	New York	NY	10017	212-653-0840	653-0844
Page & Assoc Inc 1979 Lakeside Pkwy Suite 200 **Fax Area Code: 770* ■ *TF:* 800-572-4346 ■ *Web:* www.thelifeline.com	Tucker	GA	30084	800-252-5282	724-7373*
Peachtree Life Settlements 3301 Quantum Blvd 2nd Fl. *TF:* 866-730-4411 ■ *Web:* www.peachtreelifesettlements.com	Boynton Beach	FL	33436	561-962-3900	962-7205
Phoenix Rising Enterprises LLC 304 E 2nd Ave Suite A *Web:* www.phoenixfirerise.com	Rome	GA	30161	706-235-8530	
Secondary Life Capital LLC 1010 Wisconsin Ave Suite 620. **Fax Area Code: 202* ■ *TF:* 888-600-5433 ■ *Web:* www.secondarylifecapital.com	Washington	DC	20007	888-600-5433	464-1068*
Senior Settlements LLC 303 Harper Dr. *Web:* www.seniorsettlementsllc.com	Moorestown	NJ	08057	856-235-2133	235-1294
Vespers Financial Group 3210 Grace St Suite 150.	Washington	DC	20007	202-333-4100	333-4662

800 VIDEO STORES

SEE ALSO Book, Music, Video Clubs p. 1534

Company / Address	City	State	Zip	Phone	Fax
Amazon.com Inc 1200 12th Ave S Suite 1200 *NASDAQ: AMZN* ■ **Fax: Hum Res* ■ *TF Cust Svc:* 800-201-7575 ■ *Web:* www.amazon.com	Seattle	WA	98144	206-266-1000	266-7601*
Archambault Group Inc 500 Rue Sainte-Catherine E *TF:* 877-849-8589 ■ *Web:* www.archambault.ca	Montreal	QC	H2L2C6	514-849-6206	849-0764
Best Buy Co Inc 7601 Penn Ave S. *NYSE: BBY* ■ **Fax Area Code: 952* ■ **Fax: Cust Svc* ■ *TF:* 888-237-8289 ■ *Web:* www.bestbuy.com	Richfield	MN	55423	612-291-1000	238-3160*
Border Entertainment LLC 206 E Northern Lights Blvd.	Anchorage	AK	99503	907-277-8525	277-8532
DVD Empire 2140 Woodland Rd. *TF:* 888-383-1880 ■ *Web:* www.dvdempire.com	Warrendale	PA	15086	724-776-9090	625-6623
Facets Multimedia Inc 1517 W Fullerton Ave. *TF Cust Svc:* 800-331-6197 ■ *Web:* www.facets.org	Chicago	IL	60614	773-281-9075	929-5437
Family Video 2500 Lehigh Ave **Fax Area Code: 217* ■ *TF:* 888-332-6843 ■ *Web:* www.familyvideo.com	Glenview	IL	60026	847-904-9000	544-8416*
Gameznflix Inc 1535 Blackjack Rd. **Fax Area Code: 270* ■ *TF:* 888-542-6817 ■ *Web:* www.gameznflix.com	Franklin	KY	42134	888-542-6817	778-0025*
Half.com Inc PO Box 1469 **Fax Area Code: 877* ■ *TF:* 800-545-9857 ■ *Web:* www.half.ebay.com	Draper	UT	84020	800-545-9857	349-5782*
NetFlix Inc 100 Winchester Cir *NASDAQ: NFLX* ■ *TF:* 888-638-3549 ■ *Web:* www.netflix.com	Los Gatos	CA	95032	408-540-3700	540-3737
Suncoast Motion Picture Co 10400 Yellow Cir Dr *TF:* 800-538-3465	Minnetonka	MN	55343	952-931-8000	931-8300
Videoflicks Canada 1701 Ave Rd. *Web:* www.myvideoflicks.ca	Toronto	ON	M5M3Y3	416-782-1883	782-1265

801 VISION CORRECTION CENTERS

Company / Address	City	State	Zip	Phone	Fax
Barnet-Dulaney Eye Ctr 4800 N 22nd St. *TF:* 800-966-7000 ■ *Web:* www.goodeyes.com	Phoenix	AZ	85016	602-955-1000	508-4700
Carolina Eye Assoc PA 2170 Midland Rd *Web:* www.carolinaeye.com	Southern Pines	NC	28387	910-295-2100	295-5339
Center for Lasik Ophthalmology Consultants The 5800 Colonial Dr Suite 103 *TF:* 800-448-8770 ■ *Web:* www.bestvision.com	Margate	FL	33063	954-969-0090	977-8774
Chicago Cornea Consultants Ltd 806 S Central Ave Suite 300. *Web:* www.chicagocornea.com	Highland Park	IL	60035	847-882-5900	882-6028
Eye Centers of Florida (ECOF) 4101 Evans Ave *TF:* 888-393-2455 ■ *Web:* www.ecof.com	Fort Myers	FL	33901	239-939-3456	936-8776
Gordon Binder Vision Institute 8910 University Ctr Ln Suite 800	San Diego	CA	92122	858-455-6800	455-0244
Hunkeler Eye Institute 4321 Washington St Suite 6000 *Web:* www.hunkeler.com	Kansas City	MO	64111	816-931-4733	931-9498
John-Kenyon Eye Ctr 1305 Wall St Suite 200. *TF:* 800-342-5393 ■ *Web:* www.johnkenyon.com	Jeffersonville	IN	47130	812-288-9011	288-7479
Jones Eye Clinic 4405 Hamilton Blvd PO Box 3246 *TF:* 800-334-2015	Sioux City	IA	51104	712-239-3937	239-1305
LaserSight of Wisconsin 240 1st St *TF:* 888-774-3937	Neenah	WI	54956	920-776-0808	729-6603
LaserVue Eye Ctr 3540 Mendocino Ave Suite 200 *TF:* 888-527-3745 ■ *Web:* www.laservue.com	Santa Rosa	CA	95403	707-522-6200	522-6213
LCA-Vision Inc 7840 Montgomery Rd. *NASDAQ: LCAV* ■ *TF:* 800-688-4550 ■ *Web:* www.lasikplus.com	Cincinnati	OH	45236	513-792-9292	792-5620
Maryland Regional Eye Assoc 800 Prince Frederick Blvd. *Web:* www.marylandvision.com	Prince Frederick	MD	20678	410-535-2270	535-9549
Minnesota Eye Consultants PA 710 E 24th St Suite 100 *TF:* 800-526-7632 ■ *Web:* www.mneye.com	Minneapolis	MN	55404	612-813-3600	813-3601
Pacific Cataract & Laser Institute 2517 NE Kresky Ave *TF:* 800-888-9903 ■ *Web:* www.pcli.com	Chehalis	WA	98532	360-748-8632	748-3869
Prado Vision & Lasik Ctr 7522 N Himes Ave *TF:* 877-455-2745 ■ *Web:* www.pradovision.com	Tampa	FL	33614	813-931-0500	935-4055
South Penn Eye Care Surgeons (SPECS) 250 E Walnut St	Hanover	PA	17331	717-632-6063	632-8337
Southwestern Eye Ctr 2610 E University Dr *TF:* 800-425-8404 ■ *Web:* www.sweye.com	Mesa	AZ	85213	480-892-8400	833-6246
TLC Vision Corp 50 Burnhamthorpe Rd W Suite 101 *PINK: TLCV* ■ *TF:* 888-225-5852 ■ *Web:* www.lzr.com	Mississauga	ON	L5B3C2	905-602-2020	602-2025
Vista Alliance Eye Care Assoc 160 E 56th St 9th Fl *TF:* 888-695-2745 ■ *Web:* www.nylasik.com	New York	NY	10022	212-758-3838	758-4175
Will Vision & Laser Centers 8100 NE Pkwy Dr Suite 125 *TF:* 877-542-3937 ■ *Web:* www.willvision.com	Vancouver	WA	98662	360-885-1327	885-1333

802 VITAMINS & NUTRITIONAL SUPPLEMENTS

SEE ALSO Diet & Health Foods p. 1855; Medicinal Chemicals & Botanical Products p. 2231; Pharmaceutical Companies p. 2414; Pharmaceutical Companies - Generic Drugs p. 2416

Company / Address	City	State	Zip	Phone	Fax
ADM Natural Health & Nutrition *Archer Daniels Midland Co* 4666 E Faries Pkwy **Fax: PR* ■ *TF:* 800-637-5843 ■ *Web:* www.admworld.com	Decatur	IL	62526	217-424-5200	451-4510*
Afexa life sciences 9604 20th Ave *TSX: FXA* ■ *TF:* 888-280-0022 ■ *Web:* www.afexa.com	Edmonton	AB	T6N1G1	780-432-0022	432-7772
Amazon Herb Co 1002 Jupiter Pk Ln Suite 1. *TF:* 800-835-0850 ■ *Web:* www.amazonherb.net	Jupiter	FL	33458	561-575-7663	575-7935
American Sports Nutrition Inc 1800 Silas Deane Hwy Unit 224 *TF:* 888-462-5671 ■ *Web:* www.americanwhey.com	Rocky Hill	CT	06067	860-563-0300	563-0301
Aspen Group Inc 10325 N Rt 47 *TF:* 888-227-7361 ■ *Web:* www.aspennutrients.com	Hebron	IL	60034	815-648-2001	648-2095
AST Sports Science Inc 120 Capitol Dr. *TF:* 800-627-2788 ■ *Web:* www.ast-ss.com	Golden	CO	80401	303-278-1420	278-1417
Atkins Nutritionals Inc 1050 17th St Suite 1000. **Fax Area Code: 631* ■ *TF:* 800-628-5467 ■ *Web:* www.atkins.com	Denver	CO	80265	303-633-2840	953-4001*
Bactolac Pharmaceutical Inc 7 Oser Ave *Web:* www.bactolac.com	Hauppauge	NY	11788	631-951-4908	951-4749
Beehive Botanicals Inc 16297 W Nursery Rd. *TF:* 800-233-4483 ■ *Web:* www.beehivebotanicals.com	Hayward	WI	54843	715-634-4274	634-3523
Cc Pollen Co 3627 E Indian School Rd Suite 209 *TF:* 800-875-0096 ■ *Web:* www.ccpollen.com	Phoenix	AZ	85018	602-957-0096	381-3130
Celex Laboratories Inc #115-21600 Westminster Hwy *Web:* www.celexlaboratories.com	Richmond	BC	V6V0A2	604-231-6077	231-6078
Champion Nutrition 1301 Sawgrass Corp Pkwy. *TF:* 800-752-7873 ■ *Web:* www.champion-nutrition.com	Sunrise	FL	33323	954-233-3300	
Chattem Inc 1715 W 38th St PO Box 2219 *NASDAQ: CHTT* ■ *TF:* 800-366-6077 ■ *Web:* www.chattem.com	Chattanooga	TN	37409	423-821-4571	821-0395

				Phone	Fax
CytoSport Inc 4795 Industrial Way *Fax Area Code: 707 ■ TF: 888-298-6629 ■ Web: www.cytosport.com	Benicia	CA	94510	925-685-6600	748-5732*
Douglas Laboratories Inc 600 Boyce Rd TF: 800-245-4440 ■ Web: www.douglaslabs.com	Pittsburgh	PA	15205	412-494-0122	494-0155
EAS Inc 625 Cleveland Ave *Fax Area Code: 303 ■ TF: 800-297-9776 ■ Web: www.eas.com	Columbus	OH	43215	614-624-7677	279-7358*
Edom Laboratories Inc 100 E Jefryn Blvd # M Web: www.edomlaboratories.com	Deer Park	NY	11729	631-586-2266	
Enzymatic Therapy 825 Challenger Dr TF: 800-783-2286 ■ Web: www.enzymatictherapy.com	Green Bay	WI	54311	920-469-1313	469-4444
Foodscience Corp 20 New England Dr Suite 1000 TF: 800-451-5190 ■ Web: www.foodsciencecorp.com	Essex Junction	VT	05452	802-878-5508	878-0549
Fruitful Yield Inc 395 Glen Ellyn Rd Web: www.nowfoods.com	Bloomingdale	IL	60108	630-545-9098	790-8019
Futurebiotics LLC 70 Commerce Dr TF: 800-367-5433 ■ Web: www.futurebiotics.com	Hauppauge	NY	11788	631-273-6300	273-1165
Garden of Life Inc 5500 Zillage Blvd Suite 202 TF Orders: 888-622-8986 ■ Web: www.gardenoflifeusa.com	West Palm Beach	FL	33407	561-748-2477	472-9298
Garden State Nutritionals 8 Henderson Dr TF: 800-526-9095 ■ Web: www.gardenstatenutritionals.com	West Caldwell	NJ	07006	973-575-9200	575-6782
Ginco International 725 E Cochran St Unit C TF: 800-284-2598 ■ Web: www.ginsengcompany.com	Simi Valley	CA	93065	805-520-2592	520-7509
GNC Corp 300 6th Ave *Fax: Cust Svc ■ TF Cust Svc: 888-462-2548 ■ Web: www.gnc.com	Pittsburgh	PA	15222	412-288-4600	338-8905*
Great Earth Cos 200 Adams Blvd TF: 800-284-8243	Farmingdale	NY	11735	909-510-4780	
Hammer Nutrition Ltd 4952 Whitefish Stage Rd TF Cust Svc: 800-336-1977 ■ Web: www.hammernutrition.com	Whitefish	MT	59937	406-862-1877	862-4543
Health Products Corp 1060 Nepperhan Ave Web: www.hpc7.com	Yonkers	NY	10703	914-423-2900	963-6001
Health Valley Co Inc 16100 Foothill Blvd Web: www.healthvalley.com	Irwindale	CA	91706	626-334-3241	969-3687
Herbalist The 2106 NE 65th St TF: 800-694-3727 ■ Web: www.theherbalist.com	Seattle	WA	98115	206-523-2600	522-3253
Integrated BioPharma Inc 225 Long Ave TF: 888-319-6962 ■ Web: www.chemintl.com	Hillside	NJ	07205	973-926-0816	926-1735
Irwin Naturals 5310 Beethoven St TF: 800-841-8448 ■ Web: www.omninutra.com	Los Angeles	CA	90066	310-306-3636	301-1546
Jarrow Formulas Inc 1824 S Robertson Blvd Web: www.jarrow.com	Los Angeles	CA	90035	310-204-6936	204-2520
Jo Mar Laboratories 583 Division St # B TF: 800-538-4545 ■ Web: www.jomarlabs.com	Campbell	CA	95008	408-374-5920	374-5922
Labrada Nutrition 403 Century Plaza Dr Suite 440 TF: 800-832-9948 ■ Web: www.labrada.com	Houston	TX	77073	281-209-2137	209-2135
Maxam Nutraceutics 1020 Wasco St Suite D TF: 800-800-9119 ■ Web: www.maxamlabs.com	Hood River	OR	97031	541-387-4500	387-4503
Maximum Human Performance Inc (MHP Inc) 21 Dwight Pl TF: 888-783-8844 ■ Web: www.maxperformance.com	Fairfield	NJ	07004	973-785-9055	785-9159
Mega-Pro International Inc 251 W Hilton Dr TF: 800-541-9469 ■ Web: www.mega-pro.com	Saint George	UT	84770	435-673-1001	673-1007
MET-Rx International 2100 Smithtown Ave TF: 800-556-3879 ■ Web: www.metrx.com	Ronkonkoma	NY	11779	800-556-3879	303-6457
National Vitamin Co 1145 W Gila Bend Hwy TF: 800-682-9862 ■ Web: www.nationalvitamin.com	Casa Grande	AZ	85122	520-426-3100	426-3005
Natrol Inc 21411 Prairie St Web: www.natrol.com	Chatsworth	CA	91311	818-739-6000	
Naturade Products Inc 2099 S State College Blvd Suite 210 TF: 800-367-2880 ■ Web: www.naturade.com	Anaheim	CA	92806	714-860-7600	935-9837
Natural Alternatives International Inc 1185 Linda Vista Dr NASDAQ: NAII ■ TF: 800-848-2646 ■ Web: www.nai-online.com	San Marcos	CA	92078	760-744-7340	744-9589
Natural Factors Nutritional Products Ltd 1550 United Blvd *Fax Area Code: 800 ■ TF: 800-663-8900 ■ Web: www.naturalfactors.com	Coquitlam	BC	V3K6Y7	604-420-4229	663-2115*
Natural Factors Nutritional Products Ltd 1111 80th St SW Suite 100 TF: 800-322-8704 ■ Web: www.naturalfactors.com	Everett	WA	98203	425-513-8800	348-9050
Natural Organics Inc 548 Broadhollow Rd TF: 800-645-9500 ■ Web: www.naturesplus.com	Melville	NY	11747	631-293-0030	980-9612
Naturally Vitamins 4404 E Elwood St TF: 800-899-4499 ■ Web: www.naturally.com	Phoenix	AZ	85040	480-991-0200	991-0551
Nature's Life 900 Larkspur Landing Cir Suite 105 *Fax Area Code: 800 ■ TF: 800-247-6997 ■ Web: www.natlife.com	Larkspur	CA	94939	435-655-6790	643-7195*
Nature's Sunshine Products Inc 75 E 1700 S *Fax: Mail Rm ■ TF Cust Svc: 800-223-8225 ■ Web: www.naturessunshine.com	Provo	UT	84606	801-342-4300	342-4305*
Nature's Way 1375 Mountain Springs Pkwy TF: 800-962-8873 ■ Web: www.naturesway.com	Springville	UT	84663	801-489-1500	489-1700
NBTY Inc 2100 Smithtown Ave Web: www.nbty.com	Ronkonkoma	NY	11779	631-200-2000	
Next Proteins International 2283 Cosmos Ct TF: 800-468-6398 ■ Web: www.designerprotein.com	Carlsbad	CA	92009	760-431-8152	431-0323
Nickers International Ltd PO Box 50066 TF: 800-642-5377	Staten Island	NY	10305	718-448-6283	448-6298
Nutraceutical International Corp 1400 Kearns Blvd NASDAQ: NUTR ■ *Fax Area Code: 800 ■ TF: 800-669-8877 ■ Web: www.nutraceutical.com	Park City	UT	84060	435-655-6000	767-8541*
Nutrilite Products Inc 5600 Beach Blvd PO Box 5940 Web: www.nutrilite.com	Buena Park	CA	90621	714-562-6200	736-7610
Pacific Health Laboratories Inc 100 Matawan Rd Suite 420 TF: 800-397-7683 ■ Web: www.pacifichealthlabs.com	Matawan	NJ	07747	732-739-2900	739-4360
Paragon Laboratories 20433 Earl St TF: 800-231-3670 ■ Web: www.paralabs.com	Torrance	CA	90503	310-370-1563	370-7354
Peak Nutrition Inc 1097 11th St PO Box 87 TF Sales: 800-600-2069 ■ Web: www.peaknutrition.com	Syracuse	NE	68446	402-269-2825	269-2649
Perrigo Co 515 Eastern Ave NASDAQ: PRGO ■ TF: 800-253-3606 ■ Web: www.perrigo.com	Allegan	MI	49010	269-673-8451	673-9128
Phibro Animal Health Corp 65 Challenger Rd 3rd Fl TF: 800-223-0434 ■ Web: www.phibrochem.com	Ridgefield Park	NJ	07660	201-329-7300	329-7399
Power Organics 301 S Old Stage Rd TF: 800-327-1956 ■ Web: www.klamathbluegreen.com	Mount Shasta	CA	96067	530-926-6684	926-6685
Prolab Nutrition 21411 Prairie St TF: 800-776-5221 ■ Web: www.prolab.com	Chatsworth	CA	91311	818-739-6000	739-6001
Randal Nutritional Products Inc 1595 Hampston Way PO Box 7328 TF: 800-221-1697	Santa Rosa	CA	95407	707-528-1800	528-0924
Robinson Pharma Inc 3330 S Harbor Blvd Web: www.robinsonpharma.com	Santa Ana	CA	92704	714-241-0235	751-6066
Santa Cruz Nutritionals 2200 Delaware Ave *Fax: Sales ■ Web: www.santacruznutritionals.com	Santa Cruz	CA	95060	831-457-3200	460-0610*
Schiff Nutrition International Inc 2002 S 5070 W NYSE: WNI ■ TF: 800-453-9542 ■ Web: www.schiffnutrition.com	Salt Lake City	UT	84104	801-975-5000	972-2223
Solae Co 4300 Dunkin Ave *Fax: Cust Svc ■ TF: 800-325-7108 ■ Web: www.solae.com	Saint Louis	MO	63110	314-659-3000	659-5730*
Sportika Export Inc 83 White Oak Dr Web: www.sportika.com	Berlin	CT	06037	860-828-9000	828-5962
SportPharma Inc 2 Terminal Rd Web: www.sportpharma.com	New Brunswick	NJ	08901	732-545-3130	214-1210
Swanson Health Products Inc PO Box 2803 TF: 800-824-4491 ■ Web: www.swansonvitamins.com	Fargo	ND	58108	701-356-2700	356-2708
Synutra International Inc 2275 Research Blvd Suite 500 NASDAQ: SYUT ■ TF: 866-405-2350 ■ Web: www.synutra.com	Rockville	MD	20850	301-840-3888	
Thayers Natural Pharmaceuticals Inc 20 Catbrier Rd TF: 888-842-9371 ■ Web: www.thayers.com	Westport	CT	06883	203-226-0940	227-8183
Tishcon Corp 50 Sylvester St TF: 800-848-8442 ■ Web: www.tishcon.com	Westbury	NY	11590	516-333-3050	997-1052
TSN Labs Inc PO Box 38 TF: 800-769-7290 ■ Web: www.tsn2000.com	Midvale	UT	84047	801-261-2252	261-4774
Twinlab 600 E Quality Dr TF: 800-645-5626 ■ Web: www.twinlab.com	American Fork	UT	74003	801-763-0700	763-0789
Ultra-Lab Nutrition Inc 7491 N Federal Hwy Suite C5-148 TF: 800-800-0267 ■ Web: www.ultralab.com	Boca Raton	FL	33487	561-367-1474	367-1707
USANA Health Sciences Inc 3838 W PkwyBlvd NASDAQ: USNA ■ TF: 888-950-9595 ■ Web: www.usana.com	Salt Lake City	UT	84120	801-954-7100	954-7300
Vitamins Inc 200 E Randolph Dr Web: www.vitamins-inc.com	Chicago	IL	60601	312-861-0700	861-0708
Wachters' Organic Sea Products Corp 550 Sylvan St TF: 800-682-7100 ■ Web: www.wachters.com	Daly City	CA	94014	650-757-9851	757-9858
Wakunaga of America Co Ltd 23501 Madero TF: 800-421-2998 ■ Web: www.kyolic.com	Mission Viejo	CA	92691	949-855-2776	458-2764
Windmill Health Products 100 Lehigh Dr TF: 800-822-4320 ■ Web: www.windmillvitamins.com	Fairfield	NJ	07004	973-575-6591	882-3256
Young Living Essential Oils 3125 Executive Pkwy TF: 866-203-5666 ■ Web: www.youngliving.com	Lehi	UT	84043	801-418-8900	418-8800

803 VOCATIONAL & TECHNICAL SCHOOLS

SEE ALSO Children's Learning Centers p. 1604; Colleges - Community & Junior p. 1618; Colleges - Culinary Arts p. 1634; Colleges - Fine Arts p. 1634; Colleges & Universities - Four-Year p. 1638; Language Schools p. 2143; Military Service Academies p. 2248; Universities - Canadian p. 2746

Listings In This Category Are Organized Alphabetically By States.

				Phone	Fax
Enterprise-Ozark Community College 1975 Ave C	Mobile	AL	36615	251-438-2816	438-2816
Ozark Aviation 3405 S US Hwy 231	Ozark	AL	36360	334-774-5113	774-6399
H Councill Trenholm State Technical College 1225 Air Base Blvd Web: www.trenholmtech.cc.al.us	Montgomery	AL	36108	334-832-9000	420-4206
Patterson 3920 Troy Hwy PO Box 10048 TF: 866-753-4544 ■ Web: www.trenholmtech.cc.al.us	Montgomery	AL	36116	334-420-4200	420-4201
Herzing College Birmingham 280 W Valley Ave *Fax: Admissions ■ TF: 800-425-9432 ■ Web: www.herzing.edu/birmingham	Birmingham	AL	35209	205-916-2800	916-2807*
ITT Technical Institute Birmingham 6270 Pk S Dr TF: 800-488-7033 ■ Web: www.itt-tech.edu	Bessemer	AL	35022	205-497-5700	497-5799
JF Drake State Technical College 3421 Meridian St N TF: 888-413-7253 ■ Web: www.drakestate.edu	Huntsville	AL	35811	256-539-8161	551-3142
Lawson State Community College *Bessemer* 1100 9th Ave SW Web: www.lawsonstate.edu	Bessemer	AL	35022	205-925-2515	929-3598
Lurleen B Wallace Community College *MacAurthur* 1708 N Main St PO Drawer 910 Web: www.lbwcc.edu	Opp	AL	36467	334-493-3573	493-7003

Phone Fax

Virginia College
Birmingham 65 Bagby Dr Suite 100 . . . . Birmingham AL 35209 205-802-1200 943-3940
TF: 877-812-8428 ■ *Web:* www.vc.edu
Huntsville 2021 Drake Ave SW . . . . Huntsville AL 35801 256-533-7387 533-7785
TF: 866-314-5635 ■ *Web:* www.vc.edu

Wallace Community College Selma
3000 Earl Goodwin Pkwy . . . . Selma AL 36703 334-876-9227 876-9250
Web: www.wccs.edu
Calgary 2700 3rd Ave SE. . . . Calgary AB T2A7W4 403-235-3450 207-6225
TF: 800-363-5558 ■ *Web:* www.devry.edu/calgary

Brown Mackie College Tucson
4585 E Speedway Blvd Suite 204. . . . Tucson AZ 85712 520-319-3300
Web: www.brownmackie.edu

DeVry University Phoenix 2149 W Dunlap Ave. . . . Phoenix AZ 85021 602-870-9222 331-1494
TF Cust Svc: 800-528-0250 ■ *Web:* www.phx.devry.edu

ITT Technical Institute Tempe
5005 S Wendler Dr . . . . Tempe AZ 85282 602-437-7500 437-7505
TF: 800-879-4881 ■ *Web:* www.itt-tech.edu

ITT Technical Institute Tucson
1455 W River Rd. . . . Tucson AZ 85704 520-408-7488 292-9899
TF: 800-870-9730 ■ *Web:* www.itt-tech.edu

Lamson College 875 W Elliot Rd Suite 206. . . . Tempe AZ 85284 480-898-7000
TF: 800-915-2164 ■ *Web:* www.lamsoncollege.edu

Southwest Institute of Healing Arts
1100 E Apache Blvd . . . . Tempe AZ 85281 480-994-9244 994-3228
TF: 888-504-9106 ■ *Web:* www.swiha.edu

Remington College
Little Rock 19 Remington Rd . . . . Little Rock AR 72204 501-312-0007 225-3819
Web: www.remingtoncollege.edu

Argosy University Santa Monica
2950 31st St. . . . Santa Monica CA 90405 310-866-4000 399-1804
TF: 866-505-0332 ■ *Web:* www.argosy.edu

Bryan College of Court Reporting
3580 Wilshire Blvd Suite 400. . . . Los Angeles CA 90010 213-484-8850 483-3936
TF: 877-484-8850 ■ *Web:* www.bryancollege.edu

Concorde Career Colleges Inc
San Bernardino 201 E Airport Dr. . . . San Bernardino CA 92408 909-884-8891 384-1768
TF: 800-852-8434 ■ *Web:* www.concorde.edu
San Diego 4393 Imperial Ave Suite 100 . . . . San Diego CA 92113 619-688-0800 220-4177
Web: www.concorde.edu

DeVry University Fremont 6600 Dumbarton Cir . . . . Fremont CA 94555 510-574-1200 742-0866*
**Fax:* Admissions ■ *TF:* 888-201-9941 ■ *Web:* www.fre.devry.edu

DeVry University Long Beach
3880 Kilroy Airport Way . . . . Long Beach CA 90806 562-997-5300 997-5371*
**Fax:* Admissions ■ *TF:* 800-597-1333 ■ *Web:* www.lb.devry.edu

DeVry University Pomona 901 Corporate Ctr Dr. . . . Pomona CA 91768 909-622-8866
TF: 800-243-3660 ■ *Web:* www.pom.devry.edu

DeVry University Sherman Oaks
15301 Ventura Blvd Bldg D-100. . . . Sherman Oaks CA 91403 818-713-8111 713-8118
Web: www.devry.edu

Everest College Alhambra 2215 W Mission Rd . . . . Alhambra CA 91803 626-979-4940 979-4960
TF: 800-722-7337 ■ *Web:* www.everest.edu

Everest College Anaheim
511 N Brookhurst Suite 300. . . . Anaheim CA 92801 714-953-6500 953-4163
Web: www.everest.edu

Everest College City of Industry
12801 Crossroads PkwyS. . . . City of Industry CA 91746 562-908-2500 908-7656
Web: www.everest.edu

Everest College Los Angeles
3000 S Robertson Blvd Suite 300. . . . Los Angeles CA 90034 310-840-5777 287-2344
Web: www.everest.edu

Everest College San Bernardino
217 E Club Ctr Dr Suite A. . . . San Bernardino CA 92408 909-777-3300 777-3313
Web: www.everest.edu

Everest College San Jose
1245 S Winchester Blvd Suite 102 . . . . San Jose CA 95128 408-246-4171 557-9874
TF: 877-246-4124 ■ *Web:* www.everest.edu

Everest Institute Long Beach
2161 Technology Pl . . . . Long Beach CA 90810 562-624-9530 437-8111
Web: www.everest.edu

Golden Gate University
Roseville 7 Sierra Gate Plaza Suite 101. . . . Roseville CA 95678 916-648-1446 780-2797
Web: www.ggu.edu
San Francisco 536 Mission St. . . . San Francisco CA 94105 415-442-7000 442-7807*
**Fax:* Admissions ■ *TF:* 800-448-4968 ■ *Web:* www.ggu.edu

Heald College
Concord 5130 Commercial Cir . . . . Concord CA 94520 925-288-5800 288-5896
TF: 800-755-3550 ■ *Web:* www.heald.edu
Fresno 255 W Bullard Ave. . . . Fresno CA 93704 559-438-4222 437-4184*
**Fax:* Admissions ■ *TF:* 800-284-0844 ■ *Web:* www.heald.edu
Hayward 25500 Industrial Blvd . . . . Hayward CA 94545 510-783-2100 783-3287
TF: 800-884-3253 ■ *Web:* www.heald.edu
Rancho Cordova 2910 Prospect Pk Dr. . . . Rancho Cordova CA 95670 916-638-1616 853-8282
Web: www.heald.edu
Roseville 7 Sierra Gate Plaza. . . . Roseville CA 95678 916-789-8600
Web: www.heald.edu
Salinas 1450 N Main St. . . . Salinas CA 93906 831-443-1700 443-1050
TF: 800-755-3550 ■ *Web:* www.heald.edu
San Francisco 350 Mission St. . . . San Francisco CA 94102 415-808-3000 808-3005*
**Fax:* Admissions ■ *Web:* www.heald.edu
San Jose 341 Great Mall Pkwy . . . . Milpitas CA 95035 408-934-4900 934-7777
TF: 800-884-3253 ■ *Web:* www.heald.edu
Stockton 1605 E March Ln . . . . Stockton CA 95210 209-473-5200 477-2739
TF: 800-884-3253 ■ *Web:* www.heald.edu

ITT Technical Institute
Lathrop 16916 S Harlan Rd. . . . Lathrop CA 95330 209-858-0077 858-0277
TF: 800-346-1786 ■ *Web:* www.itt-tech.edu
Oxnard 2051 Solar Dr Suite 150. . . . Oxnard CA 93036 805-988-0143 988-1813
TF: 800-530-1582 ■ *Web:* www.itt-tech.edu
Rancho Cordova 10863 Gold Ctr Dr . . . . Rancho Cordova CA 95670 916-851-3900 851-9225
TF: 800-488-8466 ■ *Web:* www.itt-tech.edu
San Bernardino 670 Carnegie Dr. . . . San Bernardino CA 92408 909-806-4600 806-4699
TF: 800-888-3801 ■ *Web:* www.itt-tech.edu
San Diego 9680 Granite Ridge Dr . . . . San Diego CA 92123 858-571-8500 571-1277
TF: 800-883-0380 ■ *Web:* www.itt-tech.edu
San Dimas 650 W Cienega Ave. . . . San Dimas CA 91773 909-971-2300 971-2350
TF: 800-414-6522 ■ *Web:* www.itt-tech.edu
Sylmar 12669 Encinitas Ave . . . . Sylmar CA 91342 818-364-5151 364-5150
TF: 800-363-2086 ■ *Web:* www.itt-tech.edu
Torrance 2555 W 190th St Suite 125. . . . Torrance CA 90504 310-965-5900 380-1557
Web: www.itt-tech.edu

Shasta College
11555 Old Oregon Trail PO Box 496006. . . . Redding CA 96049 530-242-7500 225-4896
Web: www.shastacollege.edu

West Orange College
12541 Brookhurst St Suite 104. . . . Garden Grove CA 92840 714-530-5000 530-5003*
**Fax:* Admissions ■ *Web:* www.westorangecollege.com

Westwood College Inland Empire 20 W 7th St. . . . Upland CA 91786 909-931-7550 931-9195
TF: 866-221-5632 ■ *Web:* www.westwood.edu

Westwood College Los Angeles
3250 Wilshire Blvd Suite 400. . . . Los Angeles CA 90010 213-739-9999 382-2468*
**Fax:* Admissions ■ *TF:* 866-930-9256 ■ *Web:* www.westwood.edu

Wyotech Fremont 200 Whitney Pl . . . . Fremont CA 94539 510-490-6900 490-8599
Web: www.wyotech.com

Wyotech Sacramento
980 Riverside Pkwy . . . . West Sacramento CA 95605 916-376-8888 617-2059*
**Fax:* Admissions ■ *TF:* 877-433-8800 ■ *Web:* www.wyotech.edu

Bel-Rea Institute of Animal Technology
1681 S Dayton St . . . . Denver CO 80247 303-751-8700 751-9969
TF: 800-950-8001 ■ *Web:* www.bel-rea.com

Colorado Technical University Denver
1865 W 121st Ave Bldg C Suite 100. . . . Westminster CO 80234 303-362-2900
TF: 877-250-9372 ■ *Web:* www.coloradotech.edu/Denver

Concorde Career Colleges Inc Denver
111 N Havana St. . . . Aurora CO 80010 303-861-1151 839-5478
Web: www.concorde.edu

Denver Academy of Court Reporting
9051 Harlan St Suite 20 . . . . Westminster CO 80031 303-427-5292 427-5383
TF: 866-712-2425 ■ *Web:* www.denveracademy.edu

DeVry University
Colorado Springs
1175 Kelly Johnson Blvd. . . . Colorado Springs CO 80920 719-632-3000 866-6770
TF: 877-691-3002 ■ *Web:* www.devry.edu
Denver 6312 S Fiddlers Green Cir Suite 150E. . . . Englewood CO 80111 303-329-3000 329-4486
TF: 877-773-3879 ■ *Web:* www.devry.edu

Everest College Aurora
14280 E Jewell Ave Suite 100. . . . Aurora CO 80012 303-745-6244 745-6245
Web: www.everest.edu

Everest College Thornton 9065 Grant St . . . . Thornton CO 80229 303-457-2757 457-4030
TF: 800-611-2101 ■ *Web:* www.everest.edu

ITT Technical Institute Thornton
500 E 84th Ave Suite B-12 . . . . Thornton CO 80229 303-288-4488 288-8166
TF: 800-395-4488 ■ *Web:* www.itt-tech.edu

Jones International University Ltd
9697 E Mineral Ave. . . . Centennial CO 80112 303-784-8904 799-0966*
**Fax:* Admissions ■ *TF:* 800-811-5663 ■ *Web:* www.jiu.edu

Lincoln College of Technology 460 S Lipan St . . . . Denver CO 80223 303-722-5724 778-8264
TF: 800-347-3232 ■ *Web:* www.lincolnedu.com/campus/denver-co

Redstone College
Denver 10851 W 120th Ave. . . . Broomfield CO 80021 303-466-1714 469-3797
TF: 800-888-3995 ■ *Web:* www.redstone.edu

Westwood College
Denver 7350 N Broadway . . . . Denver CO 80221 303-650-5050 487-0214
TF: 800-992-5050 ■ *Web:* www.westwood.edu

Delaware Technical & Community College
Owens 547 S Bedford St . . . . Georgetown DE 19947 302-856-5400 855-5961
Web: www.dtcc.edu
Stanton 400 Stanton-Christiana Rd . . . . Newark DE 19713 302-454-3900 453-3084*
**Fax:* Admissions ■ *Web:* www.dtcc.edu
Terry 100 Campus Dr. . . . Dover DE 19904 302-857-1000 857-1004
Web: www.dtcc.edu/terry

Acupuncture & Massage College
10506 N Kendall Dr . . . . Miami FL 33176 305-595-9500 595-2622*
**Fax:* Admissions ■ *Web:* www.amcollege.edu

ATI Health Education Ctr
1395 NW 167th St Suite 200 . . . . Miami FL 33169 305-628-1000 628-1461
TF: 800-275-2725

Brown Mackie College Miami 1 Herald Plaza . . . . Miami FL 33132 305-341-6600 428-5836*
**Fax:* Admissions ■ *TF:* 866-505-0335 ■ *Web:* www.brownmackie.edu

Concorde Career Colleges inc Jacksonville
7960 Arlington Expy. . . . Jacksonville FL 32211 904-725-0525 721-9944
Web: www.concorde.edu

Concorde Career Colleges inc Miramar
10922 Marks Way. . . . Miramar FL 33025 954-731-8880 874-9497
Web: www.concorde.edu

Concorde Career Colleges Inc Tampa
4202 W Spruce St. . . . Tampa FL 33607 813-874-0094 872-6884
Web: www.concorde.edu

Crane Institute of America Inc
3880 St Johns Pkwy . . . . Sanford FL 32771 407-322-6800 330-0660
TF: 800-832-2726 ■ *Web:* www.craneinstitute.com

DeVry University Miramar 2300 SW 145th Ave . . . . Miramar FL 33027 954-499-9800 499-9730
Web: www.devry.edu

DeVry University Orlando 4000 Millenia Blvd. . . . Orlando FL 32839 407-345-2800 370-3198*
**Fax:* Admissions ■ *TF:* 888-857-5757 ■ *Web:* www.devry.edu

Everest University
Brandon 3924 Coconut Palm Dr . . . . Tampa FL 33619 813-621-0041 628-0919*
**Fax:* Admissions ■ *TF:* 877-338-0068 ■ *Web:* www.everest.edu

				Phone	Fax
Jacksonville 8226 Phillips Hwy	Jacksonville	FL	32256	904-731-4949	731-0599
TF: 800-611-2101 ■ *Web:* www.everest.edu					
Lakeland 995 E Memorial Blvd Suite 110	Lakeland	FL	33801	863-686-1444	682-1077
Web: www.everest.edu					
Largo 1199 E Bay Dr	Largo	FL	33770	727-725-2688	373-4412
TF: 800-353-3687 ■ *Web:* www.everest.edu					
Melbourne 2401 N Harbor City Blvd	Melbourne	FL	32935	321-253-2929	255-2017
Web: www.fmu.edu					
North Orlando 5421 Diplomat Cir	Orlando	FL	32810	407-628-5870	628-1344*
**Fax:* Admissions ■ *TF:* 800-628-5870 ■ *Web:* www.everest.edu					
Orange Park 805 Wells Rd	Orange Park	FL	32073	904-264-9122	264-9952
Web: www.everest.edu					
Pompano Beach 225 N Federal Hwy	Pompano Beach	FL	33062	954-783-7339	783-7964
TF: 800-468-0168 ■ *Web:* www.everest.edu					
South Orlando 9200 Southpark Ctr Loop	Orlando	FL	32819	407-851-2525	851-1477
TF: 800-611-2101 ■ *Web:* www.everest.edu					
Tampa 3319 W Hillsborough Ave	Tampa	FL	33614	813-879-6000	871-2483
TF: 877-225-0009 ■ *Web:* www.everest.edu					
Florida Technical College					
12689 Challenger Pkwy Suite 130	Orlando	FL	32826	407-447-7300	447-7301
TF: 888-678-2929 ■ *Web:* www.ftccollege.edu					
Full Sail University					
3300 University Blvd Suite 160	Winter Park	FL	32792	407-679-6333	678-0070
TF: 800-226-7625 ■ *Web:* www.fullsail.com					
Herzing College Winter Park					
1595 S Semoran Blvd Suite 1501	Winter Park	FL	32792	407-478-0500	478-0501
TF: 800-492-1664 ■ *Web:* www.herzing.edu					
ITT Technical Institute Fort Lauderdale					
3401 S University Dr	Fort Lauderdale	FL	33328	954-476-9300	476-6889
TF: 800-488-7797 ■ *Web:* www.itt-tech.edu					
ITT Technical Institute Jacksonville					
7011 AC Skinner Pkwy Suite 140	Jacksonville	FL	32256	904-573-9100	573-0512
TF: 800-318-1264 ■ *Web:* www.itt-tech.edu					
ITT Technical Institute Miami					
7955 NW 12th St Suite 119	Miami	FL	33126	305-477-3080	477-7561*
**Fax:* Admissions ■ *Web:* www.itt-tech.edu					
ITT Technical Institute Tampa					
4809 Memorial Hwy	Tampa	FL	33634	813-885-2244	888-8451
TF: 800-825-2831 ■ *Web:* www.itt-tech.edu					
Kaplan University					
6301 Kaplan University Ave	Fort Lauderdale	FL	33309	954-515-3000	243-9880*
**Fax Area Code:* 888 ■ *TF:* 866-527-5268 ■ *Web:* www.online.kaplanuniversity.edu					
Keiser College					
Melbourne 900 S Babcock St	Melbourne	FL	32901	321-409-4800	725-3766
Web: www.keiseruniversity.edu					
Keiser University					
Daytona Beach 1800 Business Pk Blvd	Daytona Beach	FL	32114	386-274-5060	274-2725
Web: www.keiseruniversity.edu					
Fort Lauderdale					
1500 W Commercial Blvd	Fort Lauderdale	FL	33309	954-776-4456	351-4043
TF: 800-749-4456 ■ *Web:* www.keiseruniversity.edu					
Sarasota 6151 Lake Osprey Dr	Sarasota	FL	34240	941-907-3900	907-2016
TF: 866-534-7372 ■ *Web:* www.keiseruniversity.edu					
Lincoln College of Technology					
2410 Metro Centre Blvd	West Palm Beach	FL	33407	561-842-8324	842-9503
TF: 800-826-9986 ■ *Web:* www.lincolnedu.com					
Remington College Largo					
8550 Ulmerton Rd Suite 100	Largo	FL	33771	727-532-1999	530-7710
TF: 888-900-2343 ■ *Web:* www.remingtoncollege.edu					
Remington College Tampa					
6302 E MLK Blvd Suite 400	Tampa	FL	33619	813-935-5700	935-7415
TF: 800-992-4850 ■ *Web:* www.remingtoncollege.edu					
Stenotype Institute of Jacksonville					
3563 Phillips Hwy Bldg E Suite 501	Jacksonville	FL	32207	904-398-4141	398-7878
TF: 800-273-5090 ■ *Web:* www.stenotype.edu					
Athens Technical College (ATC) 800 US Hwy 29 N	Athens	GA	30601	706-355-5000	369-5756
Web: www.athenstech.edu					
Augusta Technical College					
3116 Deans Bridge Rd	Augusta	GA	30906	706-771-4000	771-4034
Web: www.augustatech.edu					
Bauder College 384 N Yards Blvd NW Suite 190	Atlanta	GA	30313	404-237-7573	237-1619*
**Fax:* Admissions ■ *TF:* 800-986-9710 ■ *Web:* www.atlanta.bauder.edu					
Brown College of Court Reporting & Medical Transcription (BCCR)					
1900 Emery St NW Suite 200	Atlanta	GA	30318	404-876-1227	876-4415
TF: 800-849-0703 ■ *Web:* www.bccr.edu					
Brown Mackie College Atlanta					
4370 Peachtree Rd NE	Atlanta	GA	30319	404-799-4500	
TF: 877-479-8419 ■ *Web:* www.brownmackie.edu					
Central Georgia Technical College					
3300 Macon Tech Dr	Macon	GA	31206	478-757-3400	757-3454
TF: 866-430-0135					
Columbus Technical College					
928 Manchester Expy	Columbus	GA	31904	706-649-1800	649-1804
Web: www.columbustech.edu					
Gupton-Jones College of Funeral Service					
5141 Snapfinger Woods Dr	Decatur	GA	30035	770-593-2257	593-1891
TF: 800-848-5352 ■ *Web:* www.gupton-jones.edu					
Herzing College					
Atlanta 3393 Peachtree Rd Suite 1003	Atlanta	GA	30326	404-816-4533	816-5576
TF: 800-573-4533 ■ *Web:* www.herzing.edu/atlanta					
Imedex Inc 4325 Alexander Dr	Alpharetta	GA	30022	770-751-7332	751-7334
TF: 800-243-6969 ■ *Web:* www.imedex.com					
ITT Technical Institute Kennesaw					
2065 Baker Rd NW	Kennesaw	GA	30144	770-426-2300	426-2350
Web: www.itt-tech.edu					
Savannah Technical College					
5717 White Bluff Rd	Savannah	GA	31405	912-443-5700	443-5705
TF: 800-769-6362 ■ *Web:* www.savannahtech.edu					
Westwood College Atlanta Northlake					
2309 Parklake Dr NE	Atlanta	GA	30345	404-962-2999	934-9539*
**Fax Area Code:* 770 ■ *TF:* 866-821-6145 ■ *Web:* www.westwood.edu					
Argosy University Hawaii					
400 ASB Tower 1001 Bishop St	Honolulu	HI	96813	808-536-5555	536-5505
TF: 888-323-2777 ■ *Web:* www.argosy.edu					
Remington College Honolulu					
1111 Bishop St Suite 400	Honolulu	HI	96813	808-942-1000	533-3064
Web: www.remingtoncollege.edu					
Eastern Idaho Technical College					
1600 S 25th E	Idaho Falls	ID	83404	208-524-3000	525-7026
TF: 800-662-0261 ■ *Web:* www.eitc.edu					
ITT Technical Institute Boise					
12302 W Explorer Dr	Boise	ID	83713	208-322-8844	322-0173
TF: 800-666-4888 ■ *Web:* www.itt-tech.edu					
DeVry University Addison 1221 N Swift Rd	Addison	IL	60101	630-953-1300	543-2196
TF: 800-346-5420 ■ *Web:* www.devry.edu					
DeVry University Chicago 3300 N Campbell Ave	Chicago	IL	60618	773-929-8500	697-2710*
**Fax:* Admissions ■ *Web:* www.chi.devry.edu					
DeVry University Tinley Park					
18624 W Creek Dr	Tinley Park	IL	60477	708-342-3300	342-3505
Web: www.devry.edu					
Gem City College 700 State St	Quincy	IL	62301	217-222-0391	222-1557
Web: www.gemcitycollege.com					
ITT Technical Institute Burr Ridge					
7040 High Grove Blvd	Burr Ridge	IL	60527	630-455-6470	455-6476
Web: www.itt-tech.edu					
ITT Technical Institute Mount Prospect					
1401 Feehanville Dr	Mount Prospect	IL	60056	847-375-8800	375-9022
Web: www.itt-tech.edu					
ITT Technical Institute Orland Park					
11551 184th Pl	Orland Park	IL	60467	708-326-3200	326-3250
Web: www.itt-tech.edu					
Lexington College 310 S Peoria St Suite 512	Chicago	IL	60607	312-226-6294	226-6405*
**Fax:* Admissions ■ *Web:* www.lexingtoncollege.edu					
MacCormac College 29 E Madison St	Chicago	IL	60602	312-922-1884	922-4286
Web: www.maccormac.edu					
Midstate College 411 W Northmoor Rd	Peoria	IL	61614	309-692-4092	692-3893
TF: 800-251-4299 ■ *Web:* www.midstate.edu					
Morrison Institute of Technology					
701 Portland Ave	Morrison	IL	61270	815-772-7218	772-7584
Web: www.morrison.tec.il.us					
Northwestern College 4829 N Lipps Ave	Chicago	IL	60630	773-777-4220	
TF: 888-205-2283 ■ *Web:* www.northwesterncollege.edu					
Westwood College O'Hare Airport					
8501 W Higgins Rd Suite 100	Chicago	IL	60631	773-380-6800	714-0828
TF: 866-235-2457 ■ *Web:* www.westwood.edu					
Westwood College River Oaks					
80 River Oaks Ctr Suite 111	Calumet City	IL	60409	708-832-1988	832-9623
TF: 888-549-4960 ■ *Web:* www.westwood.edu					
Worsham College of Mortuary Science					
495 Northgate Pkwy	Wheeling	IL	60090	847-808-8444	808-8493
Web: www.worshamcollege.com					
Brown Mackie College					
Fort Wayne 3000 E Coliseum Blvd	Fort Wayne	IN	46805	260-484-4400	484-2678
TF: 866-433-2289 ■ *Web:* www.brownmackie.edu					
Merrillville 1000 E 80th Pl Suite 101N	Merrillville	IN	46410	219-769-3321	738-1076
TF: 800-258-3321 ■ *Web:* www.brownmackie.edu					
Michigan City 325 E US Hwy 20	Michigan City	IN	46360	219-877-3100	
TF: 800-519-2416 ■ *Web:* www.brownmackie.edu					
South Bend 3454 Douglas Rd	South Bend	IN	46617	574-237-0774	237-3585
TF: 800-743-2447 ■ *Web:* www.brownmackie.edu					
College of Court Reporting Inc					
111 W 10th St Suite 111	Hobart	IN	46342	219-942-1459	942-1631
TF: 866-294-3974 ■ *Web:* www.ccr.edu					
International Business College					
5699 Coventry Ln	Fort Wayne	IN	46804	260-459-4500	436-1896
TF: 800-589-6363 ■ *Web:* www.ibcfortwayne.edu					
ITT Technical Institute Fort Wayne					
2810 Dupont Commerce Ct	Fort Wayne	IN	46825	260-497-6200	497-6299
TF: 800-866-4488 ■ *Web:* www.itt-tech.edu					
ITT Technical Institute Indianapolis					
9511 Angola Ct	Indianapolis	IN	46268	317-875-8640	875-8641
TF: 800-937-4488 ■ *Web:* www.itt-tech.edu					
ITT Technical Institute Newburgh					
10999 Stahl Rd	Newburgh	IN	47630	812-858-1600	858-0646
TF: 800-832-4488 ■ *Web:* www.itt-tech.edu					
Ivy Tech Columbus College					
Columbus 4475 Central Ave	Columbus	IN	47203	812-372-9925	372-0311
TF: 800-922-4838 ■ *Web:* www.ivytech.edu/columbus					
Ivy Tech Community College					
Bloomington 200 Daniels Way	Bloomington	IN	47404	812-330-6137	330-6140
TF: 866-447-0700 ■ *Web:* www.ivytech.edu					
Central Indiana					
50 W Fall Creek Pkwy N Dr	Indianapolis	IN	46208	317-921-4800	921-4753
TF: 888-489-5463 ■ *Web:* www.ivytech.edu/Indianapolis					
Kokomo 1815 E Morgan St	Kokomo	IN	46901	765-459-0561	454-5111
TF: 800-459-0561 ■ *Web:* www.ivytech.edu/kokomo					
Muncie 4301 S Cowan Rd	Muncie	IN	47302	765-289-2291	289-2292
TF: 800-589-8324 ■ *Web:* www.ivytech.edu/eastcentral					
North Central 220 Dean Johnson Blvd	South Bend	IN	46601	574-289-7001	236-7177
TF: 888-489-3478 ■ *Web:* www.ivytech.edu					
Northwest 1440 E 35th Ave	Gary	IN	46409	219-981-1111	981-4415
Web: www.ivytech.edu					
Richmond 2357 Chester Blvd	Richmond	IN	47374	765-966-2656	962-8741
TF: 800-659-4562 ■ *Web:* www.ivytech.edu					
Southeast 590 Ivy Tech Dr	Madison	IN	47250	812-265-2580	265-4028
TF: 800-403-2190 ■ *Web:* www.ivytech.edu					
Southern Indiana 8204 Indiana 311	Sellersburg	IN	47172	812-246-3301	246-9905
TF: 800-321-9021 ■ *Web:* www.ivytech.edu					

Name / Address	City	State	ZIP	Phone	Fax
Southwest Indiana 3501 N 1st Ave Web: www.ivytech.edu	Evansville	IN	47710	812-426-2865	429-9878
Wabash Valley 8000 S Education Dr Web: www.ivytech.edu	Terre Haute	IN	47802	812-298-2293	298-2294
Lincoln College of Technology 7225 Winton Dr Bldg 128 TF: 800-554-4465 ■ Web: www.lincolnedu.com	Indianapolis	IN	46268	317-632-5553	687-0475
Mid-America College of Funeral Science (MACFS) 3111 Hamburg Pike TF: 800-221-6158 ■ Web: www.mid-america.edu	Jeffersonville	IN	47130	812-288-8878	288-5942
AIB College of Business 2500 Fleur Dr TF: 800-444-1921 ■ Web: www.aib.edu	Des Moines	IA	50321	515-244-4221	244-6773
Brown Mackie College Bettendorf 2119 E Kimberly Rd TF: 888-420-1652 ■ Web: www.brownmackie.edu	Bettendorf	IA	52722	563-344-1500	
Des Moines Unviersity 3200 Grand Ave Web: www.dmu.edu	Des Moines	IA	50312	515-271-1400	
Western Iowa Tech Community College 4647 Stone Ave TF: 800-352-4649 ■ Web: www.witcc.com	Sioux City	IA	51102	712-274-6400	274-6412
Brown Mackie College Lenexa 9705 Lenexa Dr TF: 800-635-9101 ■ Web: www.brownmackie.edu	Lenexa	KS	66215	913-768-1900	495-9555
Brown Mackie College Salina 2106 S 9th St TF: 800-365-0433 ■ Web: www.brownmackie.com	Salina	KS	67401	785-825-5422	827-7623
Concorde Career Colleges 5800 Foxridge Dr Suite 500 TF: 800-515-1007 ■ Web: www.concorde.edu	Mission	KS	66202	913-831-9977	831-6556
Wichita Area Technical College 301 S Grove St Bldg A TF: 866-296-4031 ■ Web: www.watc.edu	Wichita	KS	67211	316-677-9400	677-9555
Bowling Green Technical College 1845 Loop Dr Web: www.bowlinggreen.kctcs.edu	Bowling Green	KY	42101	270-901-1000	901-1144
Brown Mackie College Hopkinsville 4001 Ft Campbell Blvd TF: 800-359-4753 ■ Web: www.brownmackie.edu	Hopkinsville	KY	42240	270-886-1302	886-3544
Brown Mackie College Louisville 3605 Fern Valley Rd TF: 800-999-7387 ■ Web: www.brownmackie.edu	Louisville	KY	40219	502-968-7191	357-9956
Brown Mackie College Northern Kentucky 309 Buttermilk Pike TF: 800-888-1445 ■ Web: www.brownmackie.edu	Fort Mitchell	KY	41017	859-341-5627	341-6483
Daymar College 3361 Buckland Sq	Owensboro	KY	42301	270-926-4040	685-4090
Gateway Community & Technical College (GCTC) 1025 Amsterdam Rd Web: www.gateway.kctcs.edu	Dovington	KY	41011	859-441-4500	292-6415
ITT Technical Institute Lexington 2473 Fortune Dr Suite 180 Web: www.itt-tech.edu	Lexington	KY	40509	859-246-3300	246-3350
ITT Technical Institute Louisville 9500 Ormsby Stn Rd Suite 100 TF: 888-790-7427 ■ Web: www.itt-tech.edu	Louisville	KY	40223	502-327-7424	327-7624
Louisville Technical Institute *Sullivan College of Technology & Design* 3901 Atkinson Sq Dr TF: 800-844-6528 ■ Web: www.sctd.edu	Louisville	KY	40218	502-456-6509	456-2341
National College *Lexington* 2376 Sir Barton Way Web: www.ncbt.edu	Lexington	KY	40509	859-253-0621	254-7664
National College of Business & Technology Danville 115 E Lexington Ave Web: www.ncbt.edu	Danville	KY	40422	859-236-6991	236-1063
National College of Business & Technology Florence 7627 Ewing Blvd Web: www.ncbt.edu	Florence	KY	41042	859-525-6510	525-8961
National College of Business & Technology Louisville 4205 Dixie Hwy Web: www.ncbt.edu	Louisville	KY	40216	502-447-7634	447-2442
National College of Business & Technology Pikeville 50 National College Blvd TF: 800-664-1886 ■ Web: www.ncbt.edu	Pikeville	KY	41501	606-478-7200	478-7209
National College of Business & Technology Richmond 125 S Killarney Ln Web: www.ncbt.edu	Richmond	KY	40475	859-623-8956	624-5544
Owensboro Community & Technical College 4800 New Hartford Rd TF: 866-755-6282 ■ Web: www.octc.kctcs.edu	Owensboro	KY	42303	270-686-4400	686-4496
Remington College Lafayette 303 Rue Louis XIV Web: www.remingtoncollege.edu	Lafayette	LA	70508	337-981-4010	983-7130
Andover College 265 Western Ave TF: 800-639-3110	South Portland	ME	04106	207-774-6126	774-1715
Beal College 99 Farm Rd TF: 800-660-7351 ■ Web: www.bealcollege.edu	Bangor	ME	04401	207-947-4591	947-0208
Central Maine Community College 1250 Turner St *TF Admissions:* 800-891-2002 ■ Web: www.cmcc.edu	Auburn	ME	04210	207-755-5100	755-5493
Central Maine Medical Center School of Nursing 70 Middle St Web: www.cmmcson.org	Lewiston	ME	04240	207-795-2840	795-2849
Eastern Maine Community College 354 Hogan Rd Web: www.emcc.edu	Bangor	ME	04401	207-974-4600	974-4608
Northern Maine Community College (NMCC) 33 Edgemont Dr Web: www.nmcc.edu	Presque Isle	ME	04769	207-768-2700	768-2848
Southern Maine Community College (SMCC) 2 Fort Rd TF: 877-282-2182 ■ Web: www.smccme.edu	South Portland	ME	04106	207-741-5500	741-5760
Broadcasting Institute of Maryland 7200 Harford Rd TF: 800-942-9246 ■ Web: www.bim.org	Baltimore	MD	21234	410-254-2770	254-5357
ITT Technical Institute Owings Mills 11301 Red Run Blvd TF: 877-411-6782 ■ Web: www.itt-tech.edu	Owings Mills	MD	21117	443-394-7115	394-7715
Maryland Bartending Academy 209 New Jersey Ave NE Web: www.marylandbartending.com	Glen Burnie	MD	21060	410-787-0020	787-0402
National Labor College 10000 New Hampshire Ave TF: 866-863-7293 ■ Web: www.nlc.edu	Silver Spring	MD	20903	301-431-6400	431-5411
Bay State College 122 Commonwealth Ave TF: 800-815-3276 ■ Web: www.baystate.edu	Boston	MA	02116	617-217-9000	249-0400
Benjamin Franklin Institute of Technology 41 Berkeley St Web: www.bfit.edu	Boston	MA	02116	617-423-4630	482-3706
Boston Architectural College 320 Newbury St **Fax:* Admissions ■ TF: 877-585-0100 ■ Web: www.the-bac.edu	Boston	MA	02115	617-262-5000	585-0100*
Cambridge College Inc 1000 Mass Ave Suite 31 Web: www.cambridgecollege.edu	Cambridge	MA	02138	617-868-1000	349-3545
FINE Mortuary College LLC 150 Kerry Pl Web: www.fine-ne.com	Norwood	MA	02062	781-762-1211	762-7177
ITT Technical Institute Wilmington 200 Ballardvale St Suite 200 TF: 800-430-5097 ■ Web: www.itt-tech.edu	Woburn	MA	01887	978-658-2636	
Laboure College 2120 Dorchester Ave Web: www.caritaschristi.org	Boston	MA	02124	617-296-8300	296-7947
Merrimack Education Ctr 101 Mill Rd Web: www.mec.edu	Chelmsford	MA	01824	978-256-3985	256-6890
National Aviation Academy 150 Hanscom Dr TF: 800-659-2080 ■ Web: www.naa.edu	Bedford	MA	01730	781-274-8448	274-8490
New England College of Business & Finance 10 High St Suite 204 TF: 888-696-6323 ■ Web: www.necb.edu	Boston	MA	02110	617-951-2350	951-2533
Sanford-Brown College *Boston* 126 Newbury St TF: 888-309-0444 ■ Web: www.sanfordbrown.edu	Boston	MA	02116	617-578-7100	
Academy of Court Reporting *Clawson* 1055 W Maple Rd Web: www.acr.edu	Clawson	MI	48017	248-435-9030	435-8570
Cleary University 3601 Plymouth Rd TF: 800-589-1979 ■ Web: www.cleary.edu	Ann Arbor	MI	48105	734-332-4477	332-4646
Livingston 3750 Cleary Dr Web: www.cleary.edu	Howell	MI	48843	517-548-3670	552-7805
Everest Institute 21107 Lahser Rd **Fax:* Admissions ■ TF: 800-611-2101 ■ Web: www.everest-institute.com	Southfield	MI	48033	248-799-9933	799-2912*
ITT Technical Institute Canton 1905 S Haggerty Rd TF: 800-247-4477 ■ Web: www.itt-tech.edu	Canton	MI	48188	734-397-7800	397-1945
ITT Technical Institute Grand Rapids 1980 Metro Ct SW TF: 800-632-4676 ■ Web: www.itt-tech.edu	Wyoming	MI	49519	616-406-1200	406-1250
ITT Technical Institute Troy 1522 E Big Beaver Rd TF: 800-832-6817 ■ Web: www.itt-tech.edu	Troy	MI	48083	248-524-1800	524-1965
Lewis College of Business 17370 Meyers Rd **Fax:* Admissions ■ Web: www.lewiscollege.edu	Detroit	MI	48235	313-862-6300	862-1027*
Anoka Technical College 1355 W Hwy 10 **Fax:* Admissions ■ TF: 800-627-3529 ■ Web: www.anokatech.edu	Anoka	MN	55303	763-576-4700	576-4756*
Brown College 1440 Northland Dr TF: 800-574-3777 ■ Web: www.browncollege.edu	Mendota Heights	MN	55120	651-905-3400	905-3540
Dakota County Technical College 1300 E 145th St TF: 877-937-3282 ■ Web: www.dctc.edu	Rosemount	MN	55068	651-423-8301	423-8775
Duluth Business University (DBU) 4724 Mike Colalilo Dr TF: 800-777-8406 ■ Web: www.dbumn.edu	Duluth	MN	55807	218-722-4000	628-2127
Dunwoody College of Technology 818 Dunwoody Blvd TF: 800-292-4625 ■ Web: www.dunwoody.edu	Minneapolis	MN	55403	612-374-5800	374-4128
Hennepin Technical College 9000 Brooklyn Blvd **Fax Area Code:* 763 ■ TF: 800-345-4655 ■ Web: www.hennepintech.edu	Brooklyn Park	MN	55445	952-995-1300	488-2944*
Northwest Technical Institute 950 Blue Gentian Rd Suite 500 TF: 800-443-4223 ■ Web: www.nti.edu	Eagan	MN	55121	952-944-0080	944-9274
Ridgewater College *Hutchinson* 2 Century Ave SE **Fax:* Admissions ■ TF: 800-722-1151 ■ Web: www.ridgewater.edu	Hutchinson	MN	55350	320-234-8500	587-9019*
Willmar 2101 15th Ave NW PO Box 1097 **Fax:* Admissions ■ TF: 800-722-1151 ■ Web: www.ridgewater.edu	Willmar	MN	56201	320-222-5200	222-5216*
Saint Cloud Technical & Community College 1540 Northway Dr TF: 800-222-1009 ■ Web: www.sctcc.edu	Saint Cloud	MN	56303	320-308-5089	308-5981
Saint Paul College 235 Marshall Ave TF: 800-227-6029 ■ Web: www.saintpaul.edu	Saint Paul	MN	55102	651-846-1600	846-1703
Virginia College Gulf Coast 920 Cedar Lake Rd Suite C TF: 888-208-6932 ■ Web: www.vc.edu	Biloxi	MS	39532	228-392-2994	392-2039
Virginia College Jackson 4795 IH- 55 N Web: www.vc.edu	Jackson	MS	39206	601-977-0960	956-4325
Concorde Career Colleges inc Kansas City 3239 Broadway Web: www.concorde.edu	Kansas City	MO	64111	816-531-5223	756-3231
DeVry University Kansas City 11224 Holmes Rd TF: 800-821-3766 ■ Web: www.kc.devry.edu	Kansas City	MO	64131	816-941-0430	942-8169
Everest College 1010 W Sunshine St TF: 800-475-2669 ■ Web: www.everest.edu	Springfield	MO	65807	417-864-7220	864-5697
ITT Technical Institute Arnold 1930 Meyer Drury Dr TF: 888-488-1082 ■ Web: www.itt-tech.edu	Arnold	MO	63010	636-464-6600	464-6611

				Phone	Fax
ITT Technical Institute Earth City 3640 Corporate Trail Dr *TF*: 800-235-5488 ■ *Web*: www.itt-tech.edu	Earth City	MO	63045	314-298-7800	513-5750
ITT Technical Institute Kansas City 9150 E 41st Terr *TF*: 877-488-1442 ■ *Web*: www.itt-tech.edu	Kansas City	MO	64133	816-276-1400	276-1410
Vatterott College Berkeley 8580 Evans Ave *TF*: 877-201-4442 ■ *Web*: www.vatterott-college.edu	Berkeley	MO	63134	314-264-1000	522-6174
Vatterott College Joplin 809 Illinois Ave *Web*: www.vatterott-college.edu	Joplin	MO	64801	417-781-5633	781-6437
Vatterott College Kansas City 8955 E 38th Terr *Fax*: Admissions ■ *TF*: 800-466-3997 ■ *Web*: www.vatterott-college.edu	Kansas City	MO	64129	816-861-1000	861-1400*
Vatterott College Saint Joseph 3131 Frederick Ave *TF*: 800-282-5327 ■ *Web*: www.vatterott-college.edu	Saint Joseph	MO	64506	816-364-5399	364-1593
Vatterott College South County 12970 Maurer Industrial Dr *TF*: 866-312-8276 ■ *Web*: www.vatterott-college.edu	Saint Louis	MO	63127	314-843-4200	843-1709
Vatterott College Springfield 3850 S Campbell *Fax*: Admissions ■ *TF*: 866-314-6454 ■ *Web*: www.vatterott-college.edu	Springfield	MO	65807	417-831-8116	831-5099*
ITT Technical Institute Omaha 9814 M St *TF*: 800-677-9260 ■ *Web*: www.itt-tech.edu	Omaha	NE	68127	402-331-2900	452-3512
Kaplan University Lincoln 1821 K St *Web*: www.lincoln.kaplanuniversity.edu	Lincoln	NE	68508	402-474-5315	
Kaplan University Omaha 5425 N 103rd St *TF*: 800-987-7734 ■ *Web*: www.portal.kaplanuniversity.edu	Omaha	NE	68134	402-572-8500	573-6482
Nebraska College of Technical Agriculture 404 E 7th *TF*: 800-328-7847 ■ *Web*: www.ncta.unl.edu	Curtis	NE	69025	308-367-4124	367-5203
Vatterott College *Omaha* 11818 I St *TF*: 866-483-1823 ■ *Web*: www.vatterott-college.edu	Omaha	NE	68137	866-483-1823	
ITT Technical Institute Henderson 168 Gibson Rd *TF*: 800-488-8459 ■ *Web*: www.itt-tech.edu	Henderson	NV	89014	702-558-5404	558-5412
Berkeley College *Garrett Mountain* 44 Rifle Camp Rd *TF*: 800-446-5400 ■ *Web*: www.berkeleycollege.edu	Woodland Park	NJ	07424	973-278-5400	278-9141
Paramus 64 E Midland Ave *TF*: 800-446-5400 ■ *Web*: www.berkeleycollege.edu	Paramus	NJ	07652	201-967-9667	265-6446
Woodbridge 430 Rahway Ave *TF*: 800-446-5400 ■ *Web*: www.berkeleycollege.edu	Woodbridge	NJ	10601	732-750-1800	750-0652
DeVry University North Brunswick 630 US Hwy 1 *Fax*: Admissions ■ *TF*: 800-333-3879 ■ *Web*: www.nj.devry.edu	North Brunswick	NJ	08902	732-435-4880	729-3965*
Divers Academy International 1500 Liberty Pl *TF*: 800-238-3483 ■ *Web*: www.diversacademy.com	Erial	NJ	08081	856-404-6100	404-6104
Central New Mexico Community College 10549 Universe Blvd NW *Web*: www.cnm.edu	Albuquerque	NM	87114	505-224-3000	224-3237
ITT Technical Institute Albuquerque 5100 Masthead St NE *TF*: 800-636-1114 ■ *Web*: www.itt-tech.edu	Albuquerque	NM	87109	505-828-1114	828-1849
Navajo Technical College PO Box 849 *Web*: www.navajotech.edu	Crownpoint	NM	87313	505-786-4100	786-5644
Southwestern Indian Polytechnic Institute 9169 Coors Blvd NW PO Box 10146 *TF*: 800-586-7474 ■ *Web*: www.sipi.edu	Albuquerque	NM	87120	505-346-2306	346-2311
American Academy McAllister Institute of Funeral Service 619 W 54th St 2nd Fl *TF*: 866-932-2264 ■ *Web*: www.funeraleducation.org	New York	NY	10019	212-757-1190	765-5923
Berkeley College New York City 3 E 43rd St *TF*: 800-446-5400 ■ *Web*: www.berkeleycollege.edu	New York	NY	10017	212-986-4343	818-1079
Berkeley College White Plains 99 Church St *TF*: 800-446-5400 ■ *Web*: www.berkeleycollege.edu	White Plains	NY	10601	914-694-1122	328-9469
Bramson ORT College 69-30 Austin St *Web*: www.bramsonort.org	Forest Hills	NY	11375	718-261-5800	575-5119
Bryant & Stratton College Albany 1259 Central Ave *Web*: www.bryantstratton.edu	Albany	NY	12205	518-437-1802	437-1048
Bryant & Stratton College Amherst 3650 Millersport Hwy *Web*: www.bryantstratton.edu	Getzville	NY	14068	716-625-6300	691-6716
Bryant & Stratton College Buffalo 465 Main St Suite 400 *Web*: www.bryantstratton.edu	Buffalo	NY	14203	716-884-9120	884-0091
Bryant & Stratton College Greece 150 Bellwood Dr *Web*: www.bryantstratton.edu	Rochester	NY	14606	585-720-0660	585-9226
Bryant & Stratton College Henrietta 1225 Jefferson Rd *Web*: www.bryantstratton.edu	Rochester	NY	14623	585-292-5627	292-6015
Bryant & Stratton College Southtowns 200 Red Tail *Web*: www.bryantstratton.edu	Orchard Park	NY	14127	716-677-9500	677-9599
Bryant & Stratton College Syracuse 953 James St *Web*: www.bryantstratton.edu	Syracuse	NY	13203	315-472-6603	474-4383
Bryant & Stratton College Syracuse North 8687 Carling Rd *Web*: www.bryantstratton.edu	Liverpool	NY	13090	315-652-6500	652-5500
Champlain Valley Educational Services PO Box 455 *Web*: www.cves.org	Plattsburgh	NY	12901	518-561-0100	
Cochran School of Nursing 967 N Broadway *Web*: www.riversidehealth.org	Yonkers	NY	10701	914-964-4283	964-4796
College of Westchester (CW) 325 Central Ave *Fax*: Admissions ■ *TF*: 800-660-7093 ■ *Web*: www.cw.edu	White Plains	NY	10606	914-948-4442	948-5441*
Commercial Driver Training 600 Patton Ave *Web*: www.cdtschool.com	West Babylon	NY	11704	631-249-1330	249-0428
DeVry University Long Island City 3020 Thomson Ave *Fax*: Admissions ■ *TF*: 888-713-3879 ■ *Web*: www.devry.edu	Long Island City	NY	11101	718-472-2728	269-4432*
Eastern Suffolk Boces Inc 201 N Service Rd *Web*: www.esboces.org	Patchogue	NY	11772	631-289-2200	
Helene Fuld College of Nursing 24 E 120th St *Web*: www.helenefuld.edu	New York	NY	10035	212-616-7200	616-7299
Institute of Design & Construction (IDC) 141 Willoughby St *Web*: www.idc.edu	Brooklyn	NY	11201	718-855-3661	852-5889
ITT Technical Institute Albany 13 Airline Dr *TF*: 800-489-1191 ■ *Web*: www.itt-tech.edu	Albany	NY	12205	518-452-9300	452-9393
ITT Technical Institute Getzville 2295 Millersport Hwy *TF*: 800-469-7593 ■ *Web*: www.itt-tech.edu	Getzville	NY	14068	716-689-2200	689-2828
ITT Technical Institute Liverpool 235 Greenfield Pkwy *TF*: 877-488-0011 ■ *Web*: www.itt-tech.edu	Liverpool	NY	13088	315-461-8000	461-8008
Jamestown Business College 7 Fairmount Ave PO Box 429 *Web*: www.jamestownbusinesscollege.edu	Jamestown	NY	14702	716-664-5100	664-3144
Long Island College Hospital School of Nursing (LICHSON) 350 Henry St 7th Fl *Web*: www.futurenurselich.org	Brooklyn	NY	11201	718-780-1071	780-1936
Monroe College 2501 Jerome Ave *Fax*: Admissions ■ *TF*: 800-556-6676 ■ *Web*: www.monroecollege.edu	Bronx	NY	10468	718-933-6700	364-3552*
New York Career Institute 11 Pk Pl 4th Fl *Web*: www.nyci.edu	New York	NY	10007	212-962-0002	385-7574
Olean Business Institute 301 N Union St *Web*: www.obi.edu	Olean	NY	14760	716-372-7978	372-2120
Phillips Beth Israel School of Nursing 776 Avenue of the Americas 4th Fl *Web*: www.futurenursebi.org	New York	NY	10001	212-614-6110	614-6109
Plaza College 74-09 37th Ave *Web*: www.plazacollege.edu	Jackson Heights	NY	11372	718-779-1430	779-7423
SBI Campus *Melville* 320 S Service Rd *Fax Area Code*: 516 ■ *TF*: 888-615-3444 ■ *Web*: www.sbmelville.com	Melville	NY	11747	631-370-3300	293-1763*
Simmons Institute of Funeral Service 1828 S Ave *TF*: 800-727-3536 ■ *Web*: www.simmonsinstitute.com	Syracuse	NY	13207	315-475-5142	475-3817
TCI College of Technology 320 W 31st St *TF*: 800-878-8246 ■ *Web*: www.tcicollege.edu	New York	NY	10001	212-594-4000	330-0891
Utica School of Commerce 201 Bleecker St *TF*: 800-321-4872 ■ *Web*: www.uscny.edu	Utica	NY	13501	315-733-2307	733-9281
Wood Tobe-Coburn School 8 E 40th St *TF*: 800-394-9663 ■ *Web*: www.woodtobecoburn.edu	New York	NY	10016	212-686-9040	686-9171
Forsyth Technical Community College 2100 Silas Creek Pkwy *Web*: www.forsythtech.edu	Winston-Salem	NC	27103	336-723-0371	761-2399
ITT Technical Institute High Point 4050 Piedmont Pkwy *TF*: 877-536-5231 ■ *Web*: www.itt-tech.edu	High Point	NC	27265	336-819-5900	819-5950
South College - Asheville 29 Turtle Creek Dr *Web*: www.southcollegenc.com	Asheville	NC	28803	828-277-5521	277-6151
Stanly Community College 141 College Dr *Web*: www.stanly.edu	Albemarle	NC	28001	704-982-0121	982-0819
United Tribes Technical College 3315 University Dr *Web*: www.uttc.edu	Bismarck	ND	58504	701-255-3285	530-0640
Academy of Court Reporting Akron (ACR) 2930 W Market St *Web*: www.acr.edu	Akron	OH	44333	330-867-4030	867-3432
Academy of Court Reporting Cleveland 2044 Euclid Ave *TF*: 888-203-7265 ■ *Web*: www.acr.edu	Cleveland	OH	44115	216-861-3222	861-4517
Academy of Court Reporting Columbus 150 E Gay St *Web*: www.miamijacobs.edu	Columbus	OH	43215	614-221-7770	221-8429
Belmont Technical College 120 Fox Shannon Pl *Web*: www.btc.edu	Saint Clairsville	OH	43950	740-695-9500	695-2247
Bradford School 2469 Stelzer Rd *Fax*: Admissions ■ *TF*: 800-678-7981 ■ *Web*: www.bradfordschoolcolumbus.edu	Columbus	OH	43219	614-416-6200	416-6210*
Brown Mackie College Akron 755 White Pond Dr *Web*: www.brownmackie.edu	Akron	OH	44320	330-869-3600	869-3650
Brown Mackie College Canton 4300 Munson Ave NW *Web*: www.brownmackie.edu	North Canton	OH	44718	330-494-1214	494-8112
Brown Mackie College Cincinnati 1011 Glendale-Milford Rd *TF*: 800-888-1455 ■ *Web*: www.brownmackie.edu	Cincinnati	OH	45215	513-771-2424	771-3413
Brown Mackie College Findlay 1700 Fostoria Ave Suite 100 *TF*: 800-842-3687 ■ *Web*: www.brownmackie.edu	Findlay	OH	45840	419-423-2211	423-0725
Bryant & Stratton College *Cleveland* 3121 Euclid Ave *Web*: www.bryantstratton.edu	Cleveland	OH	44115	216-771-1700	771-7787
Eastlake 35350 Curtis Blvd *Web*: www.bryantstratton.edu	Eastlake	OH	44095	440-510-1112	306-2015
Parma 12955 Snow Rd *Web*: www.bryantstratton.edu	Parma	OH	44130	216-265-3151	265-0325
Central Ohio Technical College 1179 University Dr *Web*: www.cotc.edu	Newark	OH	43055	740-366-1351	364-9531

	City	State	Zip	Phone	Fax
Cincinnati College of Mortuary Science					
645 W N Bend Rd	Cincinnati	OH	45224	513-761-2020	761-3333
TF: 888-377-8433 ■ *Web:* www.ccms.edu					
Cleveland Institute of Electronics					
1776 E 17th St	Cleveland	OH	44114	216-781-9400	781-0331
TF: 800-243-6446 ■ *Web:* www.cie-wc.edu					
Davis College 4747 Monroe St	Toledo	OH	43623	419-473-2700	473-2472
TF: 800-477-7021 ■ *Web:* www.daviscollege.edu					
DeVry University Dayton					
3610 Pentagon Blvd Suite 100	Dayton	OH	45431	937-320-3200	320-9380
Web: www.devry.edu					
ETI Technical College of Niles					
2076 Youngstown-Warren Rd	Niles	OH	44446	330-652-9919	652-4399
Web: www.eticollege.edu					
Hocking College 3301 Hocking Pkwy	Nelsonville	OH	45764	740-753-3591	753-7065
TF: 877-462-5464 ■ *Web:* www.hocking.edu					
ITT Technical Institute Dayton					
3325 S- Eight Rd	Dayton	OH	45414	937-264-7700	264-7799
TF: 800-568-3241 ■ *Web:* www.itt-tech.edu					
ITT Technical Institute Norwood					
4750 Wesley Ave	Norwood	OH	45212	513-531-8300	531-8368
TF: 800-314-8324 ■ *Web:* www.itt-tech.edu					
ITT Technical Institute Strongsville					
14955 Sprague Rd	Strongsville	OH	44136	440-234-9091	234-7694
TF: 800-331-1488 ■ *Web:* www.itt-tech.edu					
ITT Technical Institute Warrensville Heights					
4700 Richmond Rd	Warrensville Heights	OH	44128	216-896-6500	896-6599
TF: 800-741-3494 ■ *Web:* www.itt-tech.edu					
ITT Technical Institute Youngstown					
1030 N Meridian Rd	Youngstown	OH	44509	330-270-1600	270-8333
TF: 800-832-5001 ■ *Web:* www.itt-tech.edu					
James A Rhodes State College 4240 Campus Dr	Lima	OH	45804	419-995-8320	995-8098*
**Fax:* Admissions ■ *Web:* www.rhodesstate.edu					
Jefferson Community College					
4000 Sunset Blvd	Steubenville	OH	43952	740-264-5591	264-1338
Marion Technical College 1467 Mt Vernon Ave	Marion	OH	43302	740-389-4636	389-6136
Web: www.mtc.edu					
North Central State College					
2441 Kenwood Cir	Mansfield	OH	44906	419-755-4800	755-4750
TF: 888-755-4899 ■ *Web:* www.ncstatecollege.edu					
Northwest State Community College					
22600 SR-34	Archbold	OH	43502	419-267-5511	267-3688
Web: www.northweststate.edu					
Remington College Cleveland					
14445 Broadway Ave	Cleveland	OH	44125	216-475-7520	475-6055
Web: www.remingtoncollege.edu					
Southwestern College Dayton 111 W 1st St	Dayton	OH	45402	937-224-0061	224-0065
Web: www.lincolnedu.com					
Southwestern College Franklin 201 E 2nd St	Franklin	OH	45005	937-746-6633	746-6754
Web: www.lincolnedu.com					
Stark State College of Technology					
6200 Frank Ave NW	North Canton	OH	44720	330-494-6170	497-6313
TF: 800-797-8275 ■ *Web:* www.starkstate.edu					
University of Northwestern Ohio 1441 N Cable Rd	Lima	OH	45805	419-998-3120	998-3139
Web: www.unoh.edu					
Zane State College 1555 Newark Rd	Zanesville	OH	43701	740-454-2501	454-0035
TF: 800-686-8324 ■ *Web:* www.zanestate.edu					
Indian Capital Technology Ctr					
2403 N 41st St E	Muskogee	OK	74403	918-687-6383	
TF: 800-757-0877 ■ *Web:* www.ictctech.com					
Spartan College of Aeronautics & Technology					
8820 E Pine St PO Box 582833	Tulsa	OK	74115	918-836-6886	831-5287
TF Admissions: 800-331-1204 ■ *Web:* www.spartan.edu					
Heald College Portland					
625 SW Broadway # 200	Portland	OR	97205	503-229-0492	505-5544
TF: 800-432-5344 ■ *Web:* www.heald.edu					
ITT Technical Institute Portland					
9500 NE Cascades Pkwy	Portland	OR	97220	503-255-6500	
TF: 800-234-5488 ■ *Web:* www.itt-tech.edu					
American College 270 S Bryn Mawr Ave	Bryn Mawr	PA	19010	610-526-1000	526-1300*
**Fax:* Admissions ■ *TF:* 888-263-7265 ■ *Web:* www.theamericancollege.edu					
Aviation Institute of Maintenance					
3001 Grant Ave	Philadelphia	PA	19114	215-676-7700	671-0566
Web: www.aviationmaintenance.edu					
Berean Institute 1901 W Girard Ave	Philadelphia	PA	19130	215-763-4833	236-6011
Cambria-Rowe Business College (CRBC)					
221 Central Ave	Johnstown	PA	15902	814-536-5168	536-5160
TF: 800-639-2273 ■ *Web:* www.crbc.net					
Central Pennsylvania College					
600 Valley Rd PO Box 309	Summerdale	PA	17093	717-732-0702	732-5254
TF: 800-759-2727 ■ *Web:* www.centralpenn.edu					
CHI Institute					
Broomall 1991 Sproul Rd Suite 42	Broomall	PA	19008	610-353-7630	359-1370
Web: www.chitraining.com					
Franklin Mills 177 Franklin Mills Blvd	Philadelphia	PA	19154	215-612-6600	612-6695
TF: 800-989-1014 ■ *Web:* www.franklin-mills.chitraining.com					
Dean Institute of Technology					
1501 W Liberty Ave	Pittsburgh	PA	15226	412-531-4433	531-4435
Web: www.deantech.edu					
DeVry University Fort Washington					
1140 Virginia Dr	Fort Washington	PA	19034	215-591-5700	591-5745
Web: www.devry.edu					
DuBois Business College 1 Beaver Dr	Du Bois	PA	15801	814-371-6920	371-3974
TF: 800-692-6213 ■ *Web:* www.dbcollege.com					
Education Direct 925 Oak St	Scranton	PA	18515	570-342-7701	
Erie Business Ctr					
Erie 246 W 9th St	Erie	PA	16501	814-456-7504	456-4882
TF: 800-352-3743 ■ *Web:* www.eriebc.com					
New Castle 170 Cascade Galleria	New Castle	PA	16101	724-658-9066	658-3083
TF: 800-722-6227 ■ *Web:* www.eriebc.com					
Everest Institute					
100 Forbes Ave Suite 1200	Pittsburgh	PA	15222	412-261-4520	261-4546
Web: www.everest.edu					
ITT Technical Institute Bensalem					
3330 Tillman Dr	Bensalem	PA	19020	215-244-8871	244-8872
TF: 866-488-8324 ■ *Web:* www.itt-tech.edu					
ITT Technical Institute Harrisburg					
449 Eisenhower Blvd Suite 100	Harrisburg	PA	17111	717-565-1700	565-1750
TF: 800-847-4756 ■ *Web:* www.itt-tech.edu					
ITT Technical Institute King of Prussia					
760 Moore Rd Suite 150	King of Prussia	PA	19406	610-491-8004	491-9047
TF: 866-902-8324 ■ *Web:* www.itt-tech.edu					
ITT Technical Institute Pittsburgh					
10 PkwyCtr	Pittsburgh	PA	15220	412-937-9150	937-9425
TF: 800-353-8324 ■ *Web:* www.itt-tech.edu					
Johnson College 3427 N Main Ave	Scranton	PA	18508	570-342-6404	348-2181*
**Fax:* Admissions ■ *TF:* 800-293-9675 ■ *Web:* www.johnson.edu					
Kaplan Career Institute 5650 Derry St	Harrisburg	PA	17111	717-558-1300	558-1348
TF: 800-272-4632					
ICM Campus 10 Wood St	Pittsburgh	PA	15222	800-989-2378	261-0998*
**Fax Area Code:* 412 ■ *TF:* 800-989-2378 ■ *Web:* www.pittsburgh.kaplancareerinstitute.com					
Lansdale School of Business					
290 Wissahickon Ave	North Wales	PA	19454	215-699-5700	699-8770
Web: www.lsb.edu					
Lincoln Technical Institute					
5151 Tilghman St	Allentown	PA	18104	610-398-5300	395-2706
Web: www.lincolntech.com/c_allentown_pa.php					
Lincoln Technical Institute					
9191 Torresdale Ave	Philadelphia	PA	19136	215-335-0800	335-1443
Web: www.lincolntech.com/c_philadelphia_pa.php					
Mixology Wine Institute 77 W Broad St	Bethlehem	PA	18018	610-814-2900	
Web: www.mixologywine.com					
Newport Business Institute					
Lower Burrell 945 Greensburg Rd	Lower Burrell	PA	15068	724-339-7542	339-2950
TF: 800-752-7695 ■ *Web:* www.nbi.edu					
Williamsport 941 W 3rd St	Williamsport	PA	17701	570-326-2869	326-2136
TF: 800-962-6971 ■ *Web:* www.newportbusiness.com					
Penn Commercial Inc 242 Oak Spring Rd	Washington	PA	15301	724-222-5330	222-4722
TF: 888-309-7484 ■ *Web:* www.penncommercial.edu					
Pennco Tech 3815 Otter St	Bristol	PA	19007	215-824-3200	785-1945
TF: 800-575-9399 ■ *Web:* www.penncotech.com					
Pennsylvania College of Technology					
1 College Ave	Williamsport	PA	17701	570-326-3761	321-5551
TF Admissions: 800-367-9222 ■ *Web:* www.pct.edu					
Pennsylvania Institute of Technology (PIT)					
800 Manchester Ave	Media	PA	19063	610-892-1500	892-1533*
**Fax:* Admissions ■ *TF Admissions:* 800-422-0025 ■ *Web:* www.pit.edu					
Philadelphia College of Osteopathic Medicine (PCOM)					
4170 City Ave	Philadelphia	PA	19131	215-871-6100	
TF Admissions: 800-999-6998 ■ *Web:* www.pcom.edu					
Pittsburgh Institute of Aeronautics					
PO Box 10897	Pittsburgh	PA	15236	412-346-2100	466-0513
TF: 800-444-1440 ■ *Web:* www.pia.edu/aviation					
Pittsburgh Institute of Mortuary Science Inc					
5808 Baum Blvd	Pittsburgh	PA	15206	412-362-8500	362-1684
TF: 800-933-5808 ■ *Web:* www.pims.edu					
Pittsburgh Technical Institute (PTI)					
1111 McKee Rd	Oakdale	PA	15071	412-809-5100	809-5121*
**Fax:* Admissions ■ *TF:* 800-784-9675 ■ *Web:* www.pti.edu					
Thaddeus Stevens College of Technology (TSCT)					
750 E King St	Lancaster	PA	17602	717-299-7701	391-6929
TF: 800-842-3832 ■ *Web:* www.stevenstech.org					
Triangle Tech Inc					
Du Bois PO Box 551	Du Bois	PA	15801	814-371-2090	371-9227
TF: 800-874-8324 ■ *Web:* www.triangle-tech.com					
Erie 2000 Liberty St	Erie	PA	16502	814-453-6016	454-2818
TF: 800-874-8324 ■ *Web:* www.triangle-tech.edu					
Greensburg 222 E Pittsburgh St	Greensburg	PA	15601	724-832-1050	834-0325
TF: 800-533-4224 ■ *Web:* www.triangle-tech.com					
Welder Training & Testing Institute					
1144 N Graham St	Allentown	PA	18109	610-820-9551	820-0271
TF: 800-223-9884 ■ *Web:* www.welderinstitute.com					
Williamson Free School of Mechanical Trades The					
106 S New Middletown Rd	Media	PA	19063	610-566-1776	566-6502
Web: www.williamson.edu					
Wyotech Blairsville 500 Innovation Dr	Blairsville	PA	15717	724-459-9500	459-6499
Web: www.wyotech.com					
New England Institute of Technology					
2500 Post Rd	Warwick	RI	02886	401-467-7744	738-5122
TF: 800-736-7744 ■ *Web:* www.neit.edu					
Central Carolina Technical College					
506 N Guignard Dr	Sumter	SC	29150	803-778-1961	778-6696
Web: www.sum.tec.sc.us					
Denmark Technical College					
1126 Solomon Blatt Blvd PO Box 327	Denmark	SC	29042	803-793-5149	793-5942*
**Fax:* Admissions ■ *Web:* www.denmarktech.edu					
Florence-Darlington Technical College					
2715 W Lucas St	Florence	SC	29502	843-661-8324	661-8041
TF: 800-228-5745 ■ *Web:* www.fdtc.edu					
Horry-Georgetown Technical College					
2050 E Hwy 501	Conway	SC	29526	843-347-3186	347-4207
Web: www.hgtc.edu					
Myrtle Beach 743 Hemlock Ave	Myrtle Beach	SC	29577	843-477-0808	477-0775
Web: www.hgtc.edu					
ITT Technical Institute Greenville					
6 Independence Pointe					
Independence Corporate Pk	Greenville	SC	29615	864-288-0777	297-0930
TF: 800-932-4488 ■ *Web:* www.itt-tech.edu					
Piedmont Technical College					
620 N Emerald Rd	Greenwood	SC	29646	864-941-8324	941-8555
TF: 800-868-5528 ■ *Web:* www.ptc.edu					

				Phone	Fax
Spartanburg Community College 800 Brisack Rd PO Box 4386 *TF:* 866-591-3700 ■ *Web:* www.sccsc.edu	Spartanburg	SC	29305	864-592-4800	592-4564
Tri-County Technical College 7900 Hwy 76 *Web:* www.tctc.edu	Pendleton	SC	29670	864-646-8361	646-1890
Trident Technical College (TTC) 7000 Rivers Ave PO Box 118067 **Fax:* Admissions ■ *TF:* 877-349-7184 ■ *Web:* www.tridenttech.edu	North Charleston	SC	29406	843-574-6111	574-6483*
Southeast Technical Institute 2320 N Career Ave **Fax:* Hum Res ■ *TF:* 800-247-0789 ■ *Web:* www.southeasttech.edu	Sioux Falls	SD	57107	605-367-8355	367-4372*
Concorde Career Colleges Inc Memphis 5100 Poplar Ave Suite 132 *TF:* 800-693-7010 ■ *Web:* www.concorde.edu	Memphis	TN	38137	901-761-9494	761-3293
Draughons Junior College 340 Plus Pk Blvd *TF:* 866-888-9070	Nashville	TN	37217	615-361-7555	367-2736
Fountainhead College of Technology 3203 Tazewell Pike *TF:* 888-218-7335 ■ *Web:* www.fountainheadcollege.edu	Knoxville	TN	37918	865-688-9422	688-2419
ITT Technical Institute Cordova 7260 Goodlett Farms Pkwy *TF:* 866-444-5141 ■ *Web:* www.itt-tech.edu	Cordova	TN	38016	901-381-0200	381-0299
ITT Technical Institute Knoxville 10208 Technology Dr *TF:* 800-671-2801 ■ *Web:* www.itt-tech.edu	Knoxville	TN	37932	865-671-2800	671-2811
ITT Technical Institute Nashville 2845 Elm Hill Pike *TF:* 800-331-8386 ■ *Web:* www.itt-tech.edu	Nashville	TN	37214	615-889-8700	872-7209
John A Gupton College 1616 Church St *Web:* www.guptoncollege.com	Nashville	TN	37203	615-327-3927	321-4518
Nashville State Community College (NSCC) 120 White Bridge Rd **Fax:* Admissions ■ *TF:* 800-272-7363 ■ *Web:* www.nscc.edu	Nashville	TN	37209	615-353-3333	353-3243*
National College of Business & Technology Bristol 1328 Hwy 11 W *Web:* www.national-college.edu	Bristol	TN	37620	423-878-4440	793-1060
National College of Business & Technology Nashville 1638 Bell Rd *TF:* 800-986-1800 ■ *Web:* www.ncbt.edu	Nashville	TN	37211	615-333-3344	333-3429
Northeast State Technical Community College 2425 Hwy 75 PO Box 246 *TF:* 800-836-7822 ■ *Web:* www.nstcc.cc.tn.us	Blountville	TN	37617	423-323-3191	279-7646
Remington College Memphis 2710 Nonconnah Blvd *Web:* www.remingtoncollege.edu	Memphis	TN	38132	901-345-1000	396-8310
South College 3904 Lonas Dr *Web:* www.southcollegetn.edu	Knoxville	TN	37909	865-251-1800	584-7339
Aviation Institute of Maintenance Houston 7651 Airport Blvd *TF:* 888-349-5387 ■ *Web:* www.aviationmaintenance.edu	Houston	TX	77061	713-644-7777	644-0902
Concorde Career Colleges 600 E Lamar Blvd Suite 200 *TF:* 800-693-7010 ■ *Web:* www.concorde.edu/campus/arlington	Arlington	TX	76011	817-261-1594	461-3443
Court Reporting Institute of Dallas 1341 W Mockingbird Ln Suite 200-E *TF:* 866-382-1284 ■ *Web:* www.crid.com	Dallas	TX	75247	214-350-9722	631-0143
Court Reporting Institute of Houston 13101 NW Fwy Suite 100 *TF:* 866-996-8300 ■ *Web:* www.crid.com	Houston	TX	77040	713-996-8300	996-8360
Dallas Institute of Funeral Service 3909 S Buckner Blvd *TF:* 800-235-5444 ■ *Web:* www.dallasinstitute.edu	Dallas	TX	75227	214-388-5466	388-0316
DeVry University Houston 11125 Equity Dr *TF:* 866-703-3879 ■ *Web:* www.devry.edu	Houston	TX	77041	713-973-3100	896-7650
DeVry University Irving 4800 Regent Blvd *TF:* 800-633-3879 ■ *Web:* www.dal.devry.edu	Irving	TX	75063	972-929-6777	929-6778
Everest Institute San Antonio 6550 First Pk Ten Blvd **Fax:* Admissions ■ *Web:* www.everest-institute.com	San Antonio	TX	78213	210-732-7800	731-9313*
ITT Technical Institute Arlington 551 Ryan Plaza Dr **Fax:* Admissions ■ *TF:* 888-288-4950 ■ *Web:* www.itt-tech.edu	Arlington	TX	76011	817-794-5100	275-8446*
ITT Technical Institute Austin 6330 Hwy 290 E Suite 150 *TF:* 800-431-0677 ■ *Web:* www.itt-tech.edu	Austin	TX	78723	512-467-6800	467-6677
ITT Technical Institute Houston 15651 N Fwy **Fax:* Admissions ■ *TF:* 800-879-6486 ■ *Web:* www.itt-tech.edu	Houston	TX	77090	281-873-0512	873-0518*
ITT Technical Institute Richardson 2101 Waterview Pkwy *TF:* 888-488-5761 ■ *Web:* www.itt-tech.edu	Richardson	TX	75080	972-690-9100	690-0853
ITT Technical Institute San Antonio 5700 NW Pkwy **Fax:* Admissions ■ *TF:* 800-880-0570 ■ *Web:* www.itt-tech.edu	San Antonio	TX	78249	210-694-4612	694-4651*
Iverson Business School & Court Reporting 1600 E Pioneer Pkwy Suite 200 *Web:* www.iversonschool.edu	Arlington	TX	76010	817-274-6465	548-7607
Remington College Dallas 1800 Eastgate Dr *Web:* www.remingtoncollege.edu	Garland	TX	75041	972-686-7878	686-5116
Remington College Fort Worth 300 E Loop 820 *TF:* 800-336-6668 ■ *Web:* www.remingtoncollege.edu	Fort Worth	TX	76112	817-451-0017	496-1257
Virginia College Austin 6301 E Hwy 290 *TF:* 888-420-2048 ■ *Web:* www.vc.edu	Austin	TX	78723	512-371-3500	371-3502
Wade College 1950 N Stemmons Fwy Suite 2026 *TF:* 800-624-4850 ■ *Web:* www.wadecollege.edu	Dallas	TX	75207	214-637-3530	637-0827
Westwood College Dallas 8390 LBJ Fwy Suite 100 Executive Ctr One **Fax:* Admissions ■ *TF:* 800-331-4879 ■ *Web:* www.westwood.edu	Dallas	TX	75243	214-570-0100	570-2229*
Westwood College Fort Worth 4232 N Fwy **Fax:* Admissions ■ *TF:* 866-533-9997 ■ *Web:* www.westwood.edu	Fort Worth	TX	76137	817-547-9600	547-9602*
ITT Technical Institute Murray 920 Levoy Dr *TF:* 800-365-2136 ■ *Web:* www.itt-tech.edu	Murray	UT	84123	801-263-3313	263-3497
Latter Day Saints Business College 95 N 300 W *TF:* 800-999-5767 ■ *Web:* www.ldsbc.edu	Salt Lake City	UT	84101	801-524-8100	524-1900
Sterling College PO Box 72 *TF:* 800-648-3591 ■ *Web:* www.sterlingcollege.edu	Craftsbury Common	VT	05827	802-586-7711	586-2596
Vermont Technical College PO Box 500 *TF:* 800-442-8821 ■ *Web:* www.vtc.vsc.edu	Randolph Center	VT	05061	802-728-1445	728-1321
AKS Massage School 462 Herndon Pkwy Suite 208 *Web:* www.aksmassageschool.com	Herndon	VA	20170	703-464-0333	
Bryant & Stratton College Richmond 8141 Hull St Rd *TF:* 800-735-2420 ■ *Web:* www.bryantstratton.edu	Richmond	VA	23235	804-745-2444	745-6884
Bryant & Stratton College Virginia Beach 301 Ctr Pt Dr *Web:* www.bryantstratton.edu	Virginia Beach	VA	23462	757-499-7900	499-9977
DeVry University Crystal City 2450 Crystal Dr *Web:* www.devry.edu	Arlington	VA	22202	703-414-4000	414-4040
Everest College 1430 Spring Hill Rd Suite 200 *Web:* www.everest.edu	McLean	VA	22102	703-288-3131	288-3757
ITT Technical Institute Norfolk 863 Glenrock Rd Suite 100 *TF:* 888-253-8324 ■ *Web:* www.itt-tech.edu	Norfolk	VA	23502	757-466-1260	466-7630
ITT Technical Institute Richmond 300 Gateway Centre Pkwy *TF:* 888-330-4888 ■ *Web:* www.itt-tech.edu	Richmond	VA	23235	804-330-4992	330-4993
ITT Technical Institute Springfield 7300 Boston Blvd *TF:* 866-817-8324 ■ *Web:* www.itt-tech.edu	Springfield	VA	22153	703-440-9535	440-9561
Jefferson College of Health Sciences 101 Elm Ave SE *TF:* 888-985-8483 ■ *Web:* www.jchs.edu	Roanoke	VA	24031	540-985-8483	224-6703
National College of Business & Technology					
Bluefield 100 Logan St *Web:* www.national-college.edu	Bluefield	VA	24605	276-326-3621	322-5731
Charlottesville 1819 Emmet St *Web:* www.ncbt.edu	Charlottesville	VA	22901	434-295-0136	979-8061
Danville 336 Old Riverside Dr *Web:* www.national-college.edu	Danville	VA	24541	434-793-6822	793-3634
Harrisonburg 1515 Country Club Rd *Web:* www.ncbt.edu	Harrisonburg	VA	22802	540-432-0943	432-1133
Lynchburg 104 Candlewood Ct *Web:* www.ncbt.edu	Lynchburg	VA	24502	434-239-3500	239-3948
Martinsville 905 N Memorial Blvd *Web:* www.national-college.edu	Martinsville	VA	24112	276-632-5621	632-7915
Roanoke Valley 1813 E Main St *TF:* 800-664-1886 ■ *Web:* www.national-college.edu	Salem	VA	24153	540-986-1800	
Westwood College Arlington Ballston 4300 Wilson Blvd Suite 200 *Web:* www.westwood.edu	Arlington	VA	22203	703-243-3900	243-3992
DeVry University Federal Way 3600 S 344th Way **Fax:* Admissions ■ *TF:* 877-923-3879 ■ *Web:* www.devry.edu	Federal Way	WA	98001	253-943-2800	943-3291*
Highline Community College 2400 S 240th St *Web:* www.highline.edu	Des Moines	WA	98198	206-878-3710	870-4855
ITT Technical Institute Seattle 12720 Gateway Dr Suite 100 *TF:* 800-422-2029 ■ *Web:* www.itt-tech.edu	Seattle	WA	98168	206-244-3300	246-7635
Everest Institute 5514 Big Tyler Rd *Web:* www.everest.edu	Cross Lanes	WV	25313	304-776-6290	776-6262
Huntington Junior College 900 5th Ave *TF:* 800-344-4522 ■ *Web:* www.huntingtonjuniorcollege.com	Huntington	WV	25701	304-697-7550	697-7554
West Virginia Junior College					
Charleston 1000 Virginia St E *TF:* 800-924-5208 ■ *Web:* www.wvjc.edu	Charleston	WV	25301	304-345-2820	345-1425
Morgantown 148 Willey St *Web:* www.wvjcmorgantown.edu	Morgantown	WV	26505	304-296-8282	581-6990
West Virginia Junior College - Bridgeport 176 Thompson Dr *TF:* 800-470-5627 ■ *Web:* www.wvjcinfo.net	Bridgeport	WV	26330	304-842-4007	842-8191
Blackhawk Technical College 6004 S County Rd G *Web:* www.blackhawk.edu	Janesville	WI	53546	608-758-6900	743-4407
Bryant & Stratton College Milwaukee 310 W Wisconsin Ave Suite 500-E *Web:* www.bryantstratton.edu	Milwaukee	WI	53203	414-276-5200	276-3930
Chippewa Valley Technical College 620 W Clairemont Ave *TF:* 800-547-2882 ■ *Web:* www.cvtc.edu	Eau Claire	WI	54701	715-833-6200	833-6470
Fox Valley Technical College 1825 N Bluemound Dr PO Box 2277 *TF:* 800-735-3882 ■ *Web:* www.fvtc.edu	Appleton	WI	54912	920-735-5600	735-2484
Gateway Technical College 3520 30th Ave *TF:* 800-247-7122 ■ *Web:* www.gtc.edu	Kenosha	WI	53144	262-564-2200	564-2201
Herzing College Madison 5218 E Terr Dr *TF:* 800-582-1227 ■ *Web:* www.herzing.edu	Madison	WI	53718	608-249-6611	249-8593
ITT Technical Institute Greenfield 6300 W Layton Ave *Web:* www.itt-tech.edu	Greenfield	WI	53220	414-282-9494	282-9698
Lakeshore Technical College 1290 N Ave *TF:* 888-468-6582 ■ *Web:* www.gotoltc.com	Cleveland	WI	53015	920-693-1000	693-3561
Madison Area Technical College 3550 Anderson St *TF:* 800-322-6282 ■ *Web:* www.matcmadison.edu	Madison	WI	53704	608-246-6100	243-4353
Milwaukee Area Technical College 700 W State St *TF:* 800-720-6282 ■ *Web:* www.matc.edu	Milwaukee	WI	53233	414-297-6600	297-7990

				Phone	Fax
Moraine Park Technical College					
235 N National Ave	Fond du Lac	WI	54935	920-922-8611	924-3421
TF: 800-472-4554 ■ *Web:* www.morainepark.edu					
Northcentral Technical College					
1000 W Campus Dr	Wausau	WI	54401	715-675-3331	675-9776
TF: 888-682-7144 ■ *Web:* www.ntc.edu					
Northeast Wisconsin Technical College					
PO Box 19042	Green Bay	WI	54307	920-498-5400	498-6882
TF: 800-422-6982 ■ *Web:* www.nwtc.edu					
Southwest Wisconsin Technical College (SWTC)					
1800 Bronson Blvd	Fennimore	WI	53809	608-822-3262	822-6019
TF: 800-362-3322 ■ *Web:* www.swtc.edu					
Waukesha County Technical College					
800 Main St	Pewaukee	WI	53072	262-691-5566	695-3460
Web: www.wctc.edu					
Western Technical College 400 7th St N	La Crosse	WI	54601	608-785-9200	785-9205
TF: 800-322-9982 ■ *Web:* www.westerntc.edu					
Wisconsin Indianhead Technical College					
New Richmond Campus 1019 S Knowles Ave	New Richmond	WI	54017	715-246-6561	246-2777
TF: 800-243-9482 ■ *Web:* www.witc.edu					
Rice Lake Campus 1900 College Dr	Rice Lake	WI	54868	715-234-7082	234-5172
TF: 800-243-9482 ■ *Web:* www.witc.edu					
Superior Campus 600 N 21 St	Superior	WI	54880	715-394-6677	394-3771
TF: 800-243-9482 ■ *Web:* www.witc.edu					
WyoTech 4373 N 3rd St	Laramie	WY	82072	307-742-3776	742-4354
TF: 800-521-7158 ■ *Web:* www.wyotech.com					

804 VOTING SYSTEMS & SOFTWARE

				Phone	Fax
Avante International Technology Inc (AIT)					
70 Washington Rd	Princeton Junction	NJ	08550	609-799-8896	799-9308
TF: 800-735-5040 ■ *Web:* www.aitechnology.com					
Diebold Inc 5995 Mayfair Rd	North Canton	OH	44720	330-490-4000	
NYSE: DBD ■ *TF:* 800-999-3600 ■ *Web:* www.diebold.com					
Election Data Corp 29751 Valley Ctr Rd	Valley Center	CA	92082	760-751-1131	751-1141
Web: www.electiondata.com					
Election Services Corp 70 Trade Zone Ct	Ronkonkoma	NY	11779	516-248-4200	248-4770
Election Systems & Software Inc					
11208 John Galt Blvd	Omaha	NE	68137	402-593-0101	593-8107
TF: 800-247-8683 ■ *Web:* www.essvote.com					
Election Works Inc 3N840 Trotter Ln	Saint Charles	IL	60175	630-377-1973	377-9268
TF: 888-619-0500 ■ *Web:* www.electionworks.com					
Elections USA Inc 1927 E Saw Mill Rd	Quakertown	PA	18951	215-538-0779	538-3283
TF: 800-789-8683 ■ *Web:* www.electionsusainc.com					
Fidlar Technologies 4450 48th Ave Ct	Rock Island	IL	61201	309-794-3283	794-3201
TF: 800-747-4600 ■ *Web:* www.fidlar.com					
Guardian Voting Systems 1675 Delany Rd	Gurnee	IL	60031	800-888-9527	662-6633*
**Fax Area Code:* 847 ■ *TF:* 800-888-9527 ■ *Web:* www.controls-online.com/gvs					
Hart InterCivic					
15500 Wells Port Dr PO Box 80649	Austin	TX	78708	512-252-6400	831-1485*
**Fax Area Code:* 800 ■ *TF:* 800-223-4278 ■ *Web:* www.hartintercivic.com					
MicroVote General Corp					
6366 Guilford Ave	Indianapolis	IN	46220	317-257-4900	254-3269
TF: 800-257-4901 ■ *Web:* www.microvote.com					
UniLect Corp PO Box 3026	Danville	CA	94526	925-833-8660	833-8874
TF: 888-864-5328 ■ *Web:* www.unilect.com					
Voter Contact Services PO Box 390817	MountView	CA	94039	808-384-2000	
TF: 800-827-3453 ■ *Web:* www.vcsnet.com					

805 WALLCOVERINGS

				Phone	Fax
Blonder Home Co 3950 Prospect Ave	Cleveland	OH	44115	216-431-3561	431-9359
TF: 800-321-4070 ■ *Web:* www.blonderhome.com					
Blue Mountain Wallcoverings Inc 15 Akron Rd	Toronto	ON	M8W1T2	416-251-1678	251-8968
TF: 800-219-2424 ■ *Web:* www.blmtn.com					
Butler Printing & Laminating Inc					
250 Hamburg Tpke PO Box 836	Butler	NJ	07405	973-838-8550	838-1767
TF: 800-524-0786 ■ *Web:* www.butlerprinting.com					
F Schumacher & Co 79 Madison Ave	New York	NY	10016	212-213-7900	213-7848
TF: 800-523-1200 ■ *Web:* www.fschumacher.com					
Fashion Wallcoverings 4005 Carnegie Ave	Cleveland	OH	44103	216-432-1600	432-0800
TF Orders: 800-362-9930 ■ *Web:* www.fashionwallcoverings.com					
Goldcrest Wallcoverings					
1526 New Scotland Rd	Slingerlands	NY	12159	518-478-7214	478-7216
TF: 800-535-9513 ■ *Web:* www.wallcovering.com					
Hunter & Co of North Carolina Inc					
1945 W Green Dr PO Box 2363	High Point	NC	27261	336-883-4161	889-3270
TF: 800-523-8387 ■ *Web:* www.hunterwallpaper.com					
J Josephson Inc 35 Horizon Blvd	South Hackensack	NJ	07606	201-440-7000	440-7109*
**Fax:* Cust Svc ■ *Web:* www.jjosephson.com					
Seabrook Wallcoverings Inc 1325 Farmville Rd	Memphis	TN	38122	901-320-3611	320-3673*
**Fax:* Cust Svc ■ *TF:* 800-238-9152 ■ *Web:* www.seabrookwallcoverings.com					
Sellers & Josephson Inc PO 186	waine	NJ	07470	201-567-1353	567-8179
TF: 800-274-3385 ■ *Web:* www.sjocovering.com					
Thibaut Inc 480 Frelinghuysen Ave	Newark	NJ	07114	973-643-1118	643-3050
TF: 800-223-0704 ■ *Web:* www.thibautdesign.com					
York Wallcoverings Inc					
750 Linden Ave PO Box 5166	York	PA	17405	717-846-4456	843-5624
TF: 800-453-9281 ■ *Web:* www.yorkwall.com					

806 WAREHOUSING & STORAGE

SEE ALSO Logistics Services (Transportation & Warehousing) p. 2183

806-1 Commercial Warehousing

				Phone	Fax
Acme Distribution Centers Inc 18101 E Colfax Ave	Aurora	CO	80011	303-340-2100	340-2424
TF: 800-444-3614 ■ *Web:* www.acmedistribution.com					
American Warehouses Inc					
1918 Collingsworth St	Houston	TX	77009	713-228-6381	228-5913
Web: www.americanwarehouses.com					
Americold Logistics LLC					
10 Glenlake Pkwy Suite 800 S Tower	Atlanta	GA	30328	678-441-1400	441-6824
Web: www.americoldrealty.com					
Bay Logistics Inc 1202 Pontaluna Rd	Spring Lake	MI	49456	231-799-1015	
Web: www.baylogistics.com					
Brundage Management Co Inc					
254 Spencer Ln	San Antonio	TX	78201	210-735-9393	735-2061
TF: 800-531-7652 ■ *Web:* www.brundagemgt.com					
Columbian Distribution Services Inc					
900 Hall St SW	Grand Rapids	MI	49503	616-514-6000	514-6000
TF: 888-609-8542 ■ *Web:* www.columbianlogistics.com					
D & D Distribution Services Inc 789 Kings Mill Rd	York	PA	17403	717-845-1646	846-0414
Web: www.dd-dist.com					
Dart Entities 1430 S Eastman Ave	Los Angeles	CA	90023	323-264-1011	264-6925
TF: 800-963-3278 ■ *Web:* www.dartentities.com					
Datalok Co 5990 Malburg Way	Los Angeles	CA	90058	323-582-6100	581-8285
Web: www.datalok.com					
DD Jones Transfer & Warehouse Co Inc					
2115 Portlock Rd	Chesapeake	VA	23324	757-494-0225	494-0204
TF: 800-335-4787 ■ *Web:* www.ddjones.com					
Dependable Distribution Services Inc					
1301 Union Ave	Pennsauken	NJ	08110	856-665-1700	488-6332
Derby Industries LLC 4451 Robards Ln	Louisville	KY	40218	502-451-7373	451-6330
TF: 800-569-4812 ■ *Web:* www.derbyllc.com					
Distribution Technology Inc 1701 Continental Blvd	Charlotte	NC	28273	704-587-5587	587-5591
Web: www.distributiontechnology.com					
E L Hamm Assoc Inc					
4801 Columbus St Suite 400	Virginia Beach	VA	23462	757-497-5000	497-5007
TF: 800-819-4015 ■ *Web:* www.elhamm.com					
Edler & Co Inc 3500 Oakton St	Skokie	IL	60076	847-675-1900	675-2042
Evans Distribution Systems 18765 Seaway Dr	Melvindale	MI	48122	313-388-3200	388-0136
TF: 888-361-9850 ■ *Web:* www.evansdist.com					
Federal Compress & Warehouse Co Inc (FCWI)					
6060 Primacy Pkwy Suite 400	Memphis	TN	38119	901-524-4000	524-4050
Web: www.federalcompress.com					
Gulf Compress 201 N 19th St	Corpus Christi	TX	78408	361-882-5489	882-8081
Web: www.gulfcompress.com					
Gulf Winds International Inc 411 Brisbane St	Houston	TX	77061	713-747-4909	747-5330
TF: 866-238-4909 ■ *Web:* www.gwii.com					
Hansen Storage Co 538 E Erie St	Milwaukee	WI	53202	414-476-9221	476-0646
Web: www.hansenstorage.com					
Holman Distribution Center of Oregon Inc					
2300 SE Beta St	Milwaukie	OR	97222	503-652-1912	652-1970
Web: www.holmandc.com					
Iron Mountain 745 Atlantic Ave	Boston	MA	02111	617-535-4766	350-7881
NYSE: IRM ■ *TF:* 800-899-4766 ■ *Web:* www.ironmountain.com					
Kenco Group Inc 2001 Riverside Dr	Chattanooga	TN	37406	423-756-5552	756-1529
TF: 800-758-3289 ■ *Web:* www.kencogroup.com					
Longistics Transportation Inc					
10900 World Trade Blvd	Raleigh	NC	27617	919-872-7626	872-2883
TF: 800-289-0082 ■ *Web:* www.longistics.com					
Mid-West Terminal Warehouse Co Inc					
1700 Universal Ave	Kansas City	MO	64120	816-231-8811	231-0020
Web: www.mwtco.com					
Monsoon Commerce Solutions Inc					
1250 45th St Suite 100	Emeryville	CA	94608	510-500-0856	652-2403
TF: 800-520-2294 ■ *Web:* www.monsooncommerce.com					
Msi General Corp PO Box 7	Oconomowoc	WI	53066	262-367-3661	367-7390
Web: www.msigeneral.com					
Murphy Warehouse Co 701 24th Ave SE	Minneapolis	MN	55414	612-623-1200	623-9108
Web: www.murphywarehouse.com					
National Terminals Corp					
250 S NW Hwy Suite 300	Park Ridge	IL	60068	847-655-7700	655-7701
Pacific Coast Warehouse Inc (PCWS)					
5125 Schaefer Ave	Chino	CA	91710	909-590-1743	
Web: www.pcwc.com					
Pacific Storage Co PO Box 334	Stockton	CA	95201	209-320-6600	465-9533
Web: www.pacificstorage.com					
Quality Logistics Systems Inc PO Box 5637	Meridian	MS	39302	601-483-0265	483-7928
Web: www.qualitylogistics.com					
Recall Inc 1 Recall Ctr 180 Technology Pkwy	Norcross	GA	30092	888-732-2556	
TF: 888-732-2556 ■ *Web:* www.recall.com					
Robinson Terminal Warehouse Corp					
2 Duke St PO Box 550	Alexandria	VA	22313	703-836-8300	836-8307
Web: www.robinsonterminal.com					
Security Storage Co 1701 Florida Ave NW	Washington	DC	20009	202-234-5600	234-3513
TF: 800-736-6825 ■ *Web:* www.sscw.com					
Smart Warehousing LLC 3131 Caruso Ct	Orlando	FL	32806	407-839-1058	839-3974
Web: www.smartwarehousing.com					
SOPAKCO Inc 118 S Cypress St	Mullins	SC	29574	843-464-7851	
Web: www.sopakco.com					
Southern Warehousing & Distribution LP					
3232 N Pan Am Expy	San Antonio	TX	78219	210-224-7771	226-9485
Web: www.southernwd.com					
Tejas Logistics System 324 Pleasant St	Waco	TX	76704	254-752-9241	752-8950
TF: 800-535-9786 ■ *Web:* www.tejaswarehouse.com					
Tri Union Express Inc 1939 N Lafayette Ct	Griffith	IN	46319	219-838-5400	838-1680
TF: 800-228-9098 ■ *Web:* www.triunion.com					
Triad Mfg Inc 4321 Semple Ave	Saint Louis	MO	63120	314-381-5280	381-7786
Web: www.triadmfg.com					

				Phone	Fax
W O W Logistics Co 3040 W Wisconsin Ave *TF:* 800-236-3565 ■ *Web:* www.wowlogistics.com	Appleton	WI	54914	920-734-9924	734-2697
Western Carriers Inc PO Box 925 *Web:* www.westerncarriers.com	Worcester	MA	01613	508-756-4181	753-2424
Willis Day Storage Co 4100 Bennett Rd PO Box 676	Toledo	OH	43697	419-476-8000	476-1087

806-2 Refrigerated Storage

				Phone	Fax
American Growers Cooling Co 1569 Abbott St PO Box 10100	Salinas	CA	93912	831-753-6555	757-3233
Berkshire Refrigerated Warehousing 4550 S Packers Ave	Chicago	IL	60609	773-254-2424	254-5141
Burris Logistics 501 SE 5th St PO Box 219 *TF:* 800-805-8135 ■ *Web:* www.burrislogistics.com	Milford	DE	19963	302-839-5157	839-5175
MTC Logistics 4851 Holabird Ave *Web:* mtccold.com	Baltimore	MD	21224	410-342-9300	522-1163
New Orleans Cold Storage & Warehouse Co Inc (NOCS) 3411 Jourdan Rd *TF:* 800-782-2653 ■ *Web:* www.nocs.com	New Orleans	LA	70126	504-944-4400	944-8539
Perley-Halladay Assn Inc 1037 Andrew Dr *TF:* 800-248-5800 ■ *Web:* www.perleyhalladay.com	West Chester	PA	19380	610-296-5800	647-1711
Richmond Cold Storage Co LLC (RCS) 4808 Radford Ave PO Box 6885 *Web:* www.richmondcold.com	Richmond	VA	23230	804-644-2671	225-1369
United Freezer & Storage Co 650 N Meridian Rd PO Box 2446 *TF:* 800-716-1416 ■ *Web:* www.unitedfreezer.com	Youngstown	OH	44509	330-792-1739	792-2299
US Cold Storage Inc 201 Laurel Rd Suite 400, 4 Echelon Plaza *Web:* www.uscoldstorage.com	Voorhees	NJ	08043	856-354-8181	772-1876
VersaCold Inc 1731 Morrow St PO Box 220 *Web:* www.versacold.com	Green Bay	WI	54305	920-468-8311	468-0210

806-3 Self-Storage Facilities

				Phone	Fax
A-American Self Storage Management Co Inc 11560 Tennessee Ave *TF:* 800-499-3524 ■ *Web:* www.aamericanselfstorage.com	Los Angeles	CA	90064	310-914-4022	914-4042
American Storage 945 E Main St *Web:* www.americanstoragerentalspaces.com	Spartanburg	SC	29302	864-585-6178	591-2299
Derrel's Mini Storage 3265 W Ashlan Ave *Web:* www.derrels.com	Fresno	CA	93722	559-224-9900	224-1884
Devon Self Storage Holdings LLC 2000 Powell St Suite 1240 *TF:* 800-995-4480 ■ *Web:* www.devonselfstorage.com	Emeryville	CA	94068	510-450-1300	450-1325
Executive Self Storage Assoc Inc 5353 W Dartmouth Ave Suite 401 *Web:* www.executiveselfstorage.com	Denver	CO	80227	303-703-1290	703-1289
Lock Up Self Storage The 800 Frontage Rd *Web:* www.thelockup.com	Northfield	IL	60093	847-441-7760	441-7732
Metro Storage LLC 13528 Boulton Blvd *TF Cust Svc:* 888-498-1660 ■ *Web:* www.metrostorage.com	Lake Forest	IL	60045	847-235-8900	235-8901
National Self Storage Management Inc 1610 E River Rd Suite 117 *TF:* 877-648-9512 ■ *Web:* www.nationalselfstorage.com	Tucson	AZ	85718	520-577-9777	577-0824
Private Mini Storage 10575 Westoffice Dr **Fax:* Cust Svc ■ *Web:* www.private-mini.com	Houston	TX	77042	713-464-6944	464-6313*
Public Storage Inc 701 Western Ave *NYSE: PSA* ■ **Fax:* Mail Rm ■ *TF Cust Svc:* 800-567-0759 ■ *Web:* www.publicstorage.com	Glendale	CA	91201	818-244-8080	291-1015*
Sentry-Tech Enterprises 12233 Folsom Blvd *Web:* www.sentrystorage.com	Rancho Cordova	CA	95742	916-458-4199	351-0442
Shader Bros Corp 6327 Edgewater Dr *Web:* www.personalministorage.com	Orlando	FL	32810	407-297-3683	578-0400
Sovran Self Storage Inc 6467 Main St *NYSE: SSS* ■ *TF:* 800-242-1715 ■ *Web:* www.unclebobs.com	Buffalo	NY	14221	716-633-1850	633-3397
Stor-All Storage 1375 W Hillsboro Blvd *TF:* 877-786-7255 ■ *Web:* www.stor-all.com	Deerfield Beach	FL	33442	954-421-7888	426-1108
Storage Inns Inc 9909 Clayton Rd Suite 205	Saint Louis	MO	63124	314-997-6603	997-0376
U-Store-It 460 E Swedesford Rd Suite 3000 *NYSE: YSI* ■ *TF:* 877-279-0721 ■ *Web:* www.ustoreit.com	Wayne	PA	19087	610-293-5700	293-5771

807 WASTE MANAGEMENT

SEE ALSO Recyclable Materials Recovery p. 2530; Remediation Services p. 2533

				Phone	Fax
Allied Waste Bettendorf 6449 Valley Dr *TF:* 800-233-9634 ■ *Web:* www.alliedwasteiowa.com	Bettendorf	IA	52722	563-332-0050	332-4464
ARC Disposal & Recycling Co Inc 2101 S Busse Rd *Web:* www.arcdisposal.com	Mount Prospect	IL	60056	847-981-0091	981-9180
Aspen Waste Systems Inc 2951 Weeks Ave SE *Web:* www.aspenwaste.com	Minneapolis	MN	55414	612-884-8000	884-8010
Athens Services 14048 Valley Blvd *TF:* 888-336-6100 ■ *Web:* www.athensservices.com	City of Industry	CA	91746	626-336-3636	330-4686
Atlantic Scrap & Processing LLC PO Box 608 *Web:* www.atlanticscrap.com	Kernersville	NC	27285	336-996-2350	996-0493
Automated Waste Disposal Inc 307 White St *Web:* www.automatedwaste.com	Danbury	CT	06810	203-743-0405	794-1631
Avalon Holdings Corp 1 American Way *AMEX: AWX* ■ *Web:* www.avalonholdings.com	Warren	OH	44484	330-856-8800	856-8480
B.I. Duke Inc 2235 W 74th St *Web:* www.blduke.com	Chicago	IL	60636	773-778-3000	
Basin Disposal Inc 2021 N Commercial Ave *TF:* 800-642-6447 ■ *Web:* www.basindisposal.com	Pasco	WA	99301	509-547-2476	547-8617
Bend Garbage & Recycling Inc 20835 NE Montana St PO Box 504 *Web:* www.bendgarbage.com	Bend	OR	97709	541-382-2263	383-3640
Bluebonnet Waste Control PO Box 223845 *Web:* www.bluebonnetwaste.com	Dallas	TX	75222	214-748-5221	748-6886
Burrtec Waste Industries Inc 9890 Cherry Ave *Web:* www.burrtec.com	Fontana	CA	92335	909-429-4200	429-4291
CalMet Services Inc 9821 Downey Norwalk Rd *Web:* www.calmetservices.com	Downey	CA	90241	562-869-0901	529-7688
CalMet Services Inc 7202 Peterson Ln **Fax Area Code:* 562 ■ *TF:* 800-990-6387 ■ *Web:* www.calmetservices.com	Paramount	CA	90723	323-721-8120	529-7688*
Casella Waste Systems Inc 25 Greens Hill Ln *NASDAQ: CWST* ■ *TF:* 800-227-3552 ■ *Web:* www.casella.com	Rutland	VT	05701	802-775-0325	
Community Waste Disposal Inc 2010 California Crossing *Web:* www.communitywastedisposal.com	Dallas	TX	75220	972-392-9300	392-9301
Consolidated Disposal Services Inc 12949 Telegraph Rd **Fax Area Code:* 562 ■ *TF:* 800-299-4898	Santa Fe Springs	CA	90670	800-299-4898	347-4051*
Crown Disposal Co Inc 9189 De Garmo Ave PO Box 1081 *Web:* www.crowndisposal.com	Sun Valley	CA	91352	818-767-0675	768-3930
Curtis Bay Energy 3200 Hawkins Pt Rd *Web:* www.curtisbayenergy.com	Baltimore	MD	21226	410-354-3228	354-3591
Deffenbaugh Industries Inc 2601 Midwest Dr PO Box 3220 *TF:* 800-631-3301 ■ *Web:* www.deffenbaughindustries.com	Kansas City	KS	66111	913-631-3300	248-0267
Duncan Disposal Co *Arlington* 1212 Harrison Ave *Web:* www.duncandisposal.com	Arlington	TX	76012	817-317-2000	860-0330
E J Harrison & Sons PO Box 4009 *TF:* 800-418-7274 ■ *Web:* www.ejharrison.com	Ventura	CA	93007	805-647-1414	644-7751
Edco Disposal Corp 6670 Federal Blvd *Web:* www.edcodisposal.com	Lemon Grove	CA	91945	619-287-7555	287-4073
EL Harvey & Sons Inc 68 Hopkinton Rd *TF:* 800-321-3002 ■ *Web:* www.elharvey.com	Westborough	MA	01581	508-836-3000	836-3040
EnergySolutions LLC 423 W Broadway # 200 *Web:* www.energysolutions.com	Salt Lake City	UT	84101	801-649-2000	321-0453
EnerTech Environmental Inc 621 N Ave NE Suite A-100 *Web:* www.enertech.com	Atlanta	GA	30308	404-355-3390	355-3292
EQ-The Environmental Quality Co 36255 Michigan Ave *TF:* 800-592-5489 ■ *Web:* www.eqonline.com	Wayne	MI	48184	734-329-8000	329-8140
Exp Pharmaceutical Services Corp 48021 Warm Springs Blvd *TF:* 800-350-0397 ■ *Web:* www.expworld.com	Fremont	CA	94539	510-476-0909	933-1470
Gilton Solid Waste Management 755 S Yosemite Ave *TF:* 800-894-8980 ■ *Web:* www.gilton.com	Oakdale	CA	95361	209-527-3781	527-0422
Harold LeMay Enterprises Inc 13502 Pacific Ave *TF:* 800-345-3629 ■ *Web:* www.lemayinc.com	Tacoma	WA	98444	253-537-8687	537-8689
Harris Waste Management Group Inc 12625 Wetmore Rd Suite 120 *Web:* www.harrisequip.com	San Antonio	TX	78247	210-403-2087	403-2051
Headwaters Inc 10653 Riverfront Pkwy Suite 300 *NYSE: HW* ■ *Web:* www.headwaters.com	South Jordan	UT	84095	801-984-9400	984-9407
Heritage Environmental Services Inc 7901 W Morris St *TF:* 877-436-8778 ■ *Web:* www.heritage-enviro.com	Indianapolis	IN	46231	317-243-0811	486-5085
Homewood Disposal Service Inc 1501 W 175th St *Web:* www.homewooddisposal.com	Homewood	IL	60430	708-798-1004	798-7193
Industrial Services of America Inc 7100 Grade Ln *NASDAQ: IDSA* ■ *TF:* 800-824-2144 ■ *Web:* www.isa-inc.com	Louisville	KY	40213	502-368-1661	368-1440
K B Recycling Inc PO Box 550 *Web:* www.kbrecycling.com	Canby	OR	97013	503-266-7903	263-6477
Kaiser Ventures LLC 3633 Inland Empire Blvd # 48 *TF:* 800-889-3652 ■ *Web:* www.kaiserventures.com	Ontario	CA	91764	909-483-8500	944-6605
Kimmins Corp 1501 2nd Ave E *Web:* www.kimmins.com	Tampa	FL	33605	813-248-3878	247-0183
Little Rock Wastewater 11 Clearwater Dr *Web:* www.lrwu.com	Little Rock	AR	72204	501-376-2903	688-1409
Metro Waste Authority 300 E Locust St Suite 100 *Web:* www.mwatoday.com	Des Moines	IA	50309	515-244-0021	244-9477
Modern Corp 4746 Model City Rd *TF:* 800-662-0012 ■ *Web:* www.moderncorporation.com	Model City	NY	14107	716-754-8226	754-8964
N-Viro International Corp 2254 Centennial Rd *TF:* 800-666-8476 ■ *Web:* www.nviro.com	Toledo	OH	43606	419-535-6374	535-7008
Napa Recycling & Waste Services (NRWS) 820 Levitin Way PO Box 239 *Web:* www.naparecycling.com	Napa	CA	94559	707-256-3500	256-3565
National Serv-All Inc 6231 McBeth Rd *TF:* 800-876-9001	Fort Wayne	IN	46809	260-747-4117	478-4903
Norcal Waste Systems Inc 50 California St 24th Fl *TF:* 800-652-1275 ■ *Web:* www.recology.com	San Francisco	CA	94111	415-875-1000	875-1124
Oakleaf Waste Management LLC 415 Day Hill Rd *TF:* 888-625-5323 ■ *Web:* www.oakleafwastemgmt.com	Windsor	CT	06095	860-290-1250	290-1251

	City	State	Zip	Phone	Fax
Op-tech Environmental Services Inc 6392 Deere Rd *OTC: OTES* ■ *Web:* www.op-tech.us	Syracuse	NY	13206	315-437-2065	463-9764
Palm Springs Disposal Services 4690 E Mesquite Ave *TF:* 800-973-3873 ■ *Web:* www.palmspringsdisposal.com	Palm Springs	CA	92264	760-327-1351	323-5132
Republic Services 1131 N Blue Gum St **Fax:* Hum Res ■ *Web:* www.disposalservices.net	Anaheim	CA	92806	714-238-3300	238-3304*
Republic Services Inc 18500 N Allied *NYSE: RSG* ■ **Fax Area Code:* 954 ■ *TF:* 877-241-8396 ■ *Web:* www.republicservices.com	Phoenix	AZ	85054	480-627-2700	769-2647*
Republix Services of Southern Nevada 770 E Sahara Ave *Web:* www.republicservices.com	Las Vegas	NV	89193	702-735-5151	599-5586
Rubatino Refuse Removal Inc 2812 Hoyt Ave *Web:* www.rubatino.com	Everett	WA	98201	425-259-0044	339-4196
Rumpke 10795 Hughes Rd *TF:* 800-582-3107 ■ *Web:* www.rumpke.com	Cincinnati	OH	45251	513-851-0122	385-9634
San Luis Garbage Co 2925 McMillan St Suite 202	San Luis Obispo	CA	93401	805-543-0875	543-0620
Sanitary Services Co Inc 21 Bellwether Way Suite 404 *Web:* www.ssc-inc.com	Bellingham	WA	98225	360-734-3490	671-0239
Shaw Environmental & Infrastructure Inc 4171 Essen Ln *TF:* 800-747-3322 ■ *Web:* www.shawgrp.com	Baton Rouge	LA	70809	225-932-2500	
South Tahoe Refuse Co 2140 Ruth Ave *Web:* www.southtahoerefuse.com	South Lake Tahoe	CA	96150	530-541-5105	544-2608
Southland Waste Systems 8619 Western Way *Web:* www.southlandwaste.com	Jacksonville	FL	32256	904-731-2456	
Spirit Lake Tribe (SLT) PO Box 359 *Web:* www.spiritlakenation.com	Fort Totten	ND	58335	701-766-4221	766-4126
Stericycle Inc 28161 N Keith Dr *NASDAQ: SRCL* ■ *TF:* 866-783-7422 ■ *Web:* www.stericycle.com	Lake Forest	IL	60045	847-367-5910	367-9493
Sunset Scavenger Co 250 Executive Pk Suite 2100 *Web:* www.sunsetscavenger.com	San Francisco	CA	94134	415-330-1300	330-1338
Synagro Technologies Inc 1800 Bering Dr Suite 1000 *TF:* 800-370-0035 ■ *Web:* www.synagro.com	Houston	TX	77057	713-369-1700	369-1750
Tahoe Truckee Disposal Co PO Box 6479	Tahoe City	CA	96145	530-583-0148	583-0804
Texas Disposal Systems Inc (TDS) 12200 Carl Rd *TF:* 800-375-8375 ■ *Web:* www.texasdisposal.com	Creedmoor	TX	78610	512-421-1300	243-4123
Triumvirate Environmental 61 Innerbelt Rd *TF:* 800-966-9282 ■ *Web:* www.triumvirate.com	Somerville	MA	02143	617-628-8098	628-8099
Union Sanitary District (USD) 5072 Benson Rd PO Box 5050 *Web:* www.unionsanitary.com	Union City	CA	94587	510-477-7500	477-7501
Urban Services Systems 212 Van Buren St NW *TF:* 800-766-0635 ■ *Web:* www.urbanssc.com	Washington	DC	20012	202-543-2000	547-0159
Veolia Environmental Services 200 E Randolph St Suite 7900 *Web:* www.veoliaes.com	Chicago	IL	60601	312-552-2800	552-2859
Veolia Industrial Services 1980 N Hwy 146 *TF:* 877-719-5086 ■ *Web:* www.veoliaes-is.com	La Porte	TX	77571	713-307-2100	307-7600
Waste Connections Inc 2295 Iron Pt Rd Suite 200 *NYSE: WCN* ■ *TF:* 877-288-8200 ■ *Web:* www.wcnx.org	Folsom	CA	95630	916-608-8200	608-8290
Waste Industries Inc 3301 Benson Dr Suite 601 **Fax:* Mktg ■ *TF:* 800-647-9946 ■ *Web:* www.waste-ind.com	Raleigh	NC	27609	919-325-3000	325-3013*
Waste Management Inc 1001 Fannin St Suite 4000 *NYSE: WMI* ■ *TF:* 800-633-7871 ■ *Web:* www.wm.com	Houston	TX	77002	713-512-6200	512-6299
Waste Services Inc 1122 International Blvd Suite 601 *Web:* www.wasteservicesinc.com	Burlington	ON	L7L6Z8	905-319-1237	319-9050
Waste Stream Environmental Inc 9289 Bonta Bridge Rd	Jordan	NY	13080	315-689-1380	689-1359
WCA Waste Corp One Riverway Suite 1400 *NASDAQ: WCAA* ■ *Web:* www.wcawaste.com	Houston	TX	77056	713-292-2400	292-2455
Wheelabrator Technologies Inc 4 Liberty Ln W *TF:* 800-682-0026 ■ *Web:* www.wheelabratortechnologies.com	Hampton	NH	03842	603-929-3000	929-3139
York Waste Disposal Inc 3730 Sandhurst Dr	York	PA	17406	717-845-1557	764-1944

808 WATER - BOTTLED

	City	State	Zip	Phone	Fax
Absopure Water Co 8835 General Dr **Fax:* Cust Svc ■ *TF:* 800-422-7678 ■ *Web:* www.absopure.com	Plymouth	MI	48170	734-459-8000	451-0055*
Aquarion Water Co of Connecticut 200 Monroe Tpke *TF:* 800-732-9678 ■ *Web:* www.aquarionwater.com	Monroe	CT	06468	203-445-7310	330-4613
Beverage Corp International 3505 NW 107th St *TF:* 800-226-5061 ■ *Web:* www.bcibeverages.com	Miami	FL	33167	305-714-7000	714-7134
Calistoga Mineral Water Co 777 W Putnam Ave *Web:* www.calistogawater.com	Greenwich	CT	06830	203-531-4100	863-0298
Canadian Springs Ltd 1200 Britannia Rd E *TF Cust Svc:* 877-442-7884 ■ *Web:* www.canadiansprings.com	Mississauga	ON	L4W4T5	905-795-6500	670-3628
Carolina Mountain Water Co 150 Central Ave *TF:* 800-643-1501 ■ *Web:* www.mountainvalleyspring.com	Hot Springs	AR	71901	501-623-6671	623-5135
Chester Water Authority PO Box 467 *TF:* 800-793-2323 ■ *Web:* www.chesterwater.com	Chester	PA	19016	610-876-8185	
Clearly Canadian Beverage Corp 220 Viceroy Rd Units 11/12 *TSE: CLV* ■ *TF:* 800-735-7180 ■ *Web:* www.clearly.ca	Vaughan	ON	L4K3C2	905-761-0597	
Coca-Cola Enterprises Inc 2500 Windy Ridge Pkwy *NYSE: CCE* ■ *Web:* www.cokecce.com	Atlanta	GA	30339	770-989-3000	989-3597
Crystal Geyser Water Co 501 Washington St *TF Cust Svc:* 800-443-9737 ■ *Web:* www.crystalgeyser.com	Calistoga	CA	94515	707-942-0500	942-0647
Culligan International Co 9399 W Higgins Rd Suite 1100 *TF:* 800-285-5442 ■ *Web:* www.culligan.com	Rosemont	IL	60018	847-430-2800	205-6030
Deep Rock Water Co 2640 California St *TF:* 800-695-2020 ■ *Web:* www.deeprockwater.com	Denver	CO	80205	303-292-2020	296-8812
Deer Park Spring Water 777 W Putnam Ave *Web:* www.deerparkwater.com	Greenwich	CT	06830	203-531-4100	863-0298
Distillata Co 1608 E 24th St *TF Cust Svc:* 800-999-2906 ■ *Web:* www.distillata.com	Cleveland	OH	44114	216-771-2900	771-1672
DS Waters of America Inc 5660 New Northside Dr Suite 500 **Fax Area Code:* 770 ■ *TF Cust Svc:* 800-728-5508 ■ *Web:* www.water.com	Atlanta	GA	30328	800-669-3450	965-5011*
Glacier Clear Enterprises Inc 3291 Thomas St *TF Cust Svc:* 800-668-5118 ■ *Web:* www.glacierclear.com	Innisfil	ON	L9S3W4	705-436-6363	436-4949
Klarbrunn Inc 860 W St *TF:* 800-910-2837 ■ *Web:* www.klarbrunn.com	Watertown	WI	53094	920-262-6300	262-9273
Miscoe Springs Inc 89 Northbridge Rd	Mendon	MA	01756	508-473-0550	473-3971
Mountain Valley Spring Co 150 Central Ave *TF:* 800-828-0836 ■ *Web:* www.mountainvalleyspring.com	Hot Springs	AR	71901	501-624-1635	623-5135
Natural Springs Water Group LLC 128 LP Auer Rd *Web:* www.naturalspringsllc.com	Johnson City	TN	37604	423-926-7905	926-8210
Nestle Waters North America 777 W Putnam Ave *Web:* www.polandspring.com	Greenwich	CT	06830	203-531-4100	863-0256
Nestle Waters North America 900 Long Ridge Rd Bldg 2 *TF:* 866-676-1672 ■ *Web:* www.nestle-watersna.com	Stamford	CT	06902	203-531-4100	863-0298
Nestle Waters North America Inc 777 W Putnam Ave PO Box 2313 **Fax Area Code:* 714 ■ *TF:* 800-950-9393 ■ *Web:* www.nestle-watersna.com	Greenwich	CT	06830	203-531-4100	792-2600*
Nicolet Forest Bottling Co Inc 561 Plate Dr Suite 1 *TF:* 888-928-3756 ■ *Web:* www.nicoletwater.com	East Dundee	IL	60118	847-382-2950	382-2959
Polar Beverages Inc 1001 Southbridge St *TF Cust Svc:* 800-225-7410 ■ *Web:* www.polarbev.com	Worcester	MA	01610	508-753-4300	793-0813
Pure-Flo Water Co 7737 Mission Gorge Rd *TF Cust Svc:* 800-787-3356 ■ *Web:* www.pureflo.com	Santee	CA	92071	619-448-5120	596-4154
Temple Bottling Co Ltd 3510 Pkwy Dr PO Box 308 *Web:* www.templebot.com	Temple	TX	76501	254-773-3376	778-5414
Universal Beverages PO Box 448 *TF:* 888-426-7936	Ponte Vedra Beach	FL	32004	904-280-7795	280-7794
Zephyrhills Natural Spring Water 777 W Putnam Ave *TF:* 800-950-9398 ■ *Web:* www.zephyrhillswater.com	Greenwich	CT	06830	203-531-4100	863-0298

809 WATER TREATMENT & FILTRATION PRODUCTS & EQUIPMENT

	City	State	Zip	Phone	Fax
Aqua-Aerobic Systems Inc 6306 N Alpine Rd *TF:* 800-940-5008 ■ *Web:* www.aqua-aerobic.com	Rockford	IL	61111	815-654-2501	654-2508
AquaCell Technologies Inc 10410 Trademark St *AMEX: AQA* ■ *TF:* 800-326-5222 ■ *Web:* www.aquacell.com	Rancho Cucamonga	CA	91730	909-987-0456	987-6306
Aquion Water Treatment Products LLC 2080 E Lunt Ave *Web:* www.aquionwater.com	Elk Grove Village	IL	60007	847-437-9400	437-1594
Aquion Water Treatment Products LLC Rainsoft Div 2080 E Lunt Ave *TF:* 800-860-7638 ■ *Web:* www.rainsoft.com	Elk Grove Village	IL	60007	847-437-9400	437-5539
Atlas Water Systems Inc 301 2nd Ave *TF:* 800-215-9966 ■ *Web:* www.atlaswatersystems.com	Waltham	MA	02451	781-373-4700	547-4049
Beaufort-Jasper Water & Sewer Authority 6 Snake Rd *Web:* www.bjwsa.org	Okatie	SC	29909	843-987-9200	
Brentwood Industries Inc Polychem Systems Div 621 Brentwood Dr *Web:* www.polychemsys.com	Reading	PA	19611	484-651-1300	651-1499
Brita Products Co 1221 Broadway PO Box 24305 *TF:* 800-242-7482 ■ *Web:* www.brita.com	Oakland	CA	94623	510-271-7000	832-1463
Bucks County Water & Sewer Authority (BCWSA) 1275 Almshouse Rd **Fax Area Code:* 267 ■ *TF:* 800-222-2068 ■ *Web:* www.bcwsa.net	Warrington	PA	18976	215-343-2538	200-0339*
Carolina Filters Inc 109 E Newberry Ave PO Box 716 *TF:* 800-849-5646 ■ *Web:* www.carolinafilters.com	Sumter	SC	29151	803-773-6842	775-6190
Clack Corp 4462 Duraform Ln *Web:* www.clackcorp.com	Windsor	WI	53598	608-846-3010	846-2586
ClearWater Tech Div Aquion Water Treatment Products LLC 850 Capitolio Way # E *TF:* 800-262-0203 ■ *Web:* www.cwtozone.com	San Luis Obispo	CA	93401	805-549-9724	
Court Thomas Wingert 11800 Monarch St PO Box 6207 *Web:* www.jlwingert.com	Garden Grove	CA	92841	714-379-5519	379-5549
Crane Environmental 730 Commerce Dr *TF:* 800-828-2447 ■ *Web:* www.cranenv.com	Venice	FL	34292	941-480-9101	
Culligan International Co 9399 W Higgins Rd Suite 1100 *TF:* 800-285-5442 ■ *Web:* www.culligan.com	Rosemont	IL	60018	847-430-2800	205-6030
Deepwater Chemicals Inc 1210 Airpark Rd *TF:* 800-854-4064 ■ *Web:* www.deepwaterchemicals.com	Woodward	OK	73801	580-256-0500	256-0575
Dow Liquid Separations PO Box 1206 *TF:* 800-447-4369 ■ *Web:* www.dow.com/liquidseps	Midland	MI	48642	989-832-1311	832-1465
East Valley Water District 3654 E Highland Ave Suite 18 *Web:* www.eastvalley.org	Highland	CA	92346	909-889-9501	889-5732

Company	City	State	Zip	Phone	Fax
EcoWater Systems LLC PO Box 64420	Saint Paul	MN	55164	651-739-5330	731-7420
TF Cust Svc: 800-808-9899 ■ *Web:* www.ecowater.com					
Energy Recovery Inc 1717 Doolittle Dr	San Leandro	CA	94577	510-483-7370	483-7371
NASDAQ: ERII ■ *Web:* www.energyrecovery.com					
Everpure LLC 1040 Muirfield Dr.	Hanover Park	IL	60133	630-307-3000	307-3030
TF: 800-323-7873 ■ *Web:* www.everpure.com					
Filterspun 624 N Fairfield St	Amarillo	TX	79107	806-383-3840	383-3842
TF: 800-432-0108 ■ *Web:* www.filterspun.com					
Filtra-Systems Co 23900 Haggerty Rd	Farmington Hills	MI	48335	248-427-9090	427-9895
Web: www.filtrasystems.com					
GE Water & Process Technologies 4636 Somerton Rd	Trevose	PA	19053	215-355-3300	
TF: 866-439-2837 ■ *Web:* www.gewater.com					
Graver Technologies LLC 200 Lake Dr	Glasgow	DE	19702	302-731-1700	731-1707
TF: 800-249-1990 ■ *Web:* www.gravertech.com					
Graver Water Systems 750 Walnut Ave	Cranford	NJ	07016	908-653-4200	653-4300
TF: 877-472-8379 ■ *Web:* www.graver.com					
Hungerford & Terry Inc 226 N Atlantic Ave	Clayton	NJ	08312	856-881-3200	881-6859
Web: www.hungerfordterry.com					
Industrial Filter & Pump Mfg Co 4915 W 67th St.	Chicago	IL	60638	708-656-7800	656-7806
Web: www.industrialfilter.com					
Infilco Degremont Inc 8007 Discovery Dr PO Box 71390	Richmond	VA	23255	804-756-7600	756-7643
Web: www.degremont-technologies.com					
Integrated Separation Solutions LLC (ISS) 6333 Odana Rd.	Madison	WI	53719	608-276-6850	276-6856
Web: www.isepsol.com					
ITT Advanced Water Treatment 14125 S Bridge Cir.	Charlotte	NC	28273	704-716-7600	295-9080
Web: www.ittadvancedwatertreatment.com					
ITT Advanced Water Treatment FB Leopold Co Inc 227 S Division St	Zelienople	PA	16063	724-452-6300	452-1377
Web: www.fbleopold.com					
Kinetico Inc 10845 Kinsman Rd	Newbury	OH	44065	800-944-9283	564-9541*
**Fax Area Code:* 440 ■ *Web:* www.kinetico.com					
KX Technologies LLC 55 Railroad Ave	West Haven	CT	06516	203-799-9000	799-7000
Web: www.kxtech.com					
Lancaster Pump Co 1340 Manheim Pike	Lancaster	PA	17601	717-397-3521	392-0266
Web: www.lancasterpump.com					
Macon Water Authority 790 Second St PO Box 108	Macon	GA	31202	478-464-5600	741-9146
Web: www.maconwater.org					
McNish Corp 840 N Russell Ave	Aurora	IL	60506	630-892-7921	892-7951
TF: 800-992-5537					
Met-Pro Corp Keystone Filter Div 2385 N Penn Rd	Hatfield	PA	19440	215-822-1963	997-1839
TF: 800-811-4424 ■ *Web:* www.met-pro.com/html/key.htm					
Met-Pro Corp Systems Div 160 Cassell Rd PO Box 144	Harleysville	PA	19438	215-732-9300	723-8501
Web: www.met-prosystems.com					
MSC Filtration Technologies 198 Freshwater Blvd	Enfield	CT	06082	860-745-7475	745-7477
TF Cust Svc: 800-237-7359 ■ *Web:* www.mscfiltertech.com					
National Water Purifiers Corp 1065 E 14th St.	Hialeah	FL	33010	305-887-7065	887-6209
Pall Corp 2200 Northern Blvd.	East Hills	NY	11548	516-484-5400	801-9754
NYSE: PLL ■ *TF:* 800-645-6532 ■ *Web:* www.pall.com					
Pentair Inc 5500 Wayzata Blvd Suite 800	Golden Valley	MN	55416	763-545-1730	656-5400
NYSE: PNR ■ *TF:* 800-328-9626 ■ *Web:* www.pentair.com					
PEP Filters Inc 322 Rolling Hill Rd	Mooresville	NC	28117	704-662-3133	662-3155
TF: 800-243-4586 ■ *Web:* www.pepfilters.com					
Polaris Pool Systems Inc 2620 Commerce Way	Vista	CA	92081	760-599-9600	597-1235
TF: 800-822-7933 ■ *Web:* www.polarispoolsystems.com					
Pristine Water Solutions Inc 1570 S Lakeside Dr	Waukegan	IL	60085	847-689-1100	689-9289
TF: 800-562-1537 ■ *Web:* www.pristinewatersolutions.com					
Pro Products LLC 7201 Engle Rd	Fort Wayne	IN	46804	260-490-5970	490-9431
TF: 866-357-5063 ■ *Web:* www.proproducts.com					
Pure & Secure LLC 4120 NW 44th St.	Lincoln	NE	68524	402-467-9300	659-2939*
**Fax Area Code:* 800 ■ *TF Cust Svc:* 800-875-5915 ■ *Web:* www.mypurewater.com					
Schreiber LLC 100 Schreiber Dr	Trussville	AL	35173	205-655-7466	655-7669
Web: www.schreiberwater.com					
Severn Trent Services 580 Virginia Dr Suite 300	Fort Washington	PA	19034	215-646-9201	283-6138
TF: 866-646-9201 ■ *Web:* www.severntrentservices.com					
Sharp Water Inc 1033 Fowler Ct.	Dover	DE	19901	800-439-3853	543-2222*
**Fax Area Code:* 410 ■ *TF:* 800-439-3853 ■ *Web:* www.sharpwater.com					
Siemens Water Technologies 181 Thorn Hill Rd.	Warrendale	PA	15086	724-772-0044	772-1300
TF: 800-424-9300 ■ *Web:* www.water.siemens.com					
Slickbar Products Corp 18 Beach St.	Seymour	CT	06483	203-888-7700	888-7720
TF: 800-322-2666 ■ *Web:* www.slickbar.com					
Sydnor Hydro Inc 2111 Magnolia St PO Box 27186	Richmond	VA	23261	804-643-2725	788-9058
TF: 800-552-7714 ■ *Web:* www.sydnorhydro.com					
Taylor Technologies Inc 31 Loveton Cir	Sparks	MD	21152	410-472-4340	771-4291
TF Cust Svc: 800-837-8548 ■ *Web:* www.taylortechnologies.com					
Tomco2 Equipment Co 3340 Rosebud Rd	Loganville	GA	30052	770-979-8000	985-9179
TF: 800-832-4262 ■ *Web:* www.tomcoequipment.com					
Walker Process Equipment 840 N Russell Ave	Aurora	IL	60506	630-892-7921	892-7951
TF: 800-992-5537 ■ *Web:* www.walker-process.com					
Waterco USA Inc 1864 Tobacco Rd.	Augusta	GA	30906	706-793-7291	790-5688
TF: 800-247-7291 ■ *Web:* www.waterco.com					
Westech Engineering Inc 3665 S W Temple	Salt Lake City	UT	84115	801-265-1000	265-1080
Web: www.westech-inc.com					
Zodiac Pool Systems Inc 2620 Commerce Way	Vista	CA	92081	800-822-7933	479-8324
TF: 800-822-7933 ■ *Web:* www.zodiacpoolsystems.com					

810 WEAPONS & ORDNANCE (MILITARY)

SEE ALSO Firearms & Ammunition (Non-Military) p. 1846; Missiles, Space Vehicles, Parts p. 2252; Simulation & Training Systems p. 2658

Company	City	State	Zip	Phone	Fax
Amron LLC 920 Amron Ave.	Antigo	WI	54409	715-623-4176	623-5231
Armtec Defense Products Co 85-901 Ave 53	Coachella	CA	92236	760-398-0143	398-3896
Colt Defense LLC 547 New Pk Ave	West Hartford	CT	06110	860-232-4489	244-1442
TF: 800-241-2485 ■ *Web:* www.colt.com					
Essex Industries Inc 7700 Gravois Ave	Saint Louis	MO	63123	314-832-4500	832-1633
Web: www.essexind.com					
General Dynamics Corp 2941 Fairview Pk Dr Suite 100	Falls Church	VA	22042	703-876-3000	876-3125
NYSE: GD ■ *Web:* www.generaldynamics.com					
General Dynamics Land Systems 38500 Mound Rd	Sterling Heights	MI	48310	586-825-4000	825-4013
Web: www.gdls.com					
Kaman Aerospace Corp Old Windsor Rd PO Box 2	Bloomfield	CT	06002	860-242-4461	243-7514
Web: www.kamanaero.com					
Marvin Engineering Co 261 W Beach Ave	Inglewood	CA	90302	310-674-5030	673-9472
Web: www.marvingroup.com/index.php/companies/mec					
NAPCO International Inc 11055 Excelsior Blvd.	Hopkins	MN	55343	952-931-2400	931-2402
Web: www.napcointl.com					
Textron Marine & Land Systems 19401 Chef Menteur Hwy	New Orleans	LA	70129	504-245-6600	254-8000
Web: www.systems.textron.com					
Textron Systems Corp 201 Lowell St	Wilmington	MA	01887	978-657-5111	657-1843
Web: www.systems.textron.com					

811 WEB HOSTING SERVICES

SEE ALSO Internet Service Providers (ISPs) p. 2128

Companies Listed Here Are Engaged Primarily In Hosting Web Sites For Companies And Individuals. Although Many Internet Service Providers (Isps) Also Provide Web Hosting Services, They Are Not Included Among These Listings.

Company	City	State	Zip	Phone	Fax
50megs.com 1253 N Research Way Suite Q-2500	Orem	UT	84097	585-295-0885	
TF: 800-396-1999 ■ *Web:* www.50megs.com					
Angelfire 100 5th Ave.	Waltham	MA	02451	781-370-2700	370-2600
Web: www.angelfire.lycos.com					
Baillio's Inc 5301 Menaul Blvd Ne.	Albuquerque	NM	87110	505-883-7511	338-3377
TF: 800-540-7511 ■ *Web:* baillios.com					
Broadspire Inc 19425 Soledad Canyon Rd Suite 341	Santa Clarita	CA	91351	213-986-1050	607-3487
TF: 888-262-6161 ■ *Web:* www.broadspire.com					
Catalog.com Inc 14000 Quail Springs Pkwy Suite 3600	Oklahoma City	OK	73134	405-753-9300	753-9353
TF: 888-932-4376 ■ *Web:* www.webhero.com					
Chapel Services Inc 1212 W Main St	Richmond	KY	40475	859-623-1500	624-3019
TF: 888-747-4949					
Classified Ventures LLC 175 W Jackson Blvd Suite 800 8th Fl	Chicago	IL	60604	312-601-5000	
Web: www.classifiedventures.com					
Constellate 7505 John Carpenter Fwy	Dallas	TX	75247	972-439-1880	951-0305*
**Fax Area Code:* 214 ■ *TF:* 888-987-2656 ■ *Web:* www.constellate.com					
Coronado Unified School District 201 6th St	Coronado	CA	92118	619-522-8900	
Web: www.edline.net					
Cuadra Assoc Inc 3415 S Sepulveda Blvd Suite 210	Los Angeles	CA	90034	310-591-2490	591-2488
Web: www.cuadra.com					
DataPipe 10 Exchange Pl	Jersey City	NJ	07302	201-792-4847	749-5821*
**Fax Area Code:* 888 ■ *TF:* 877-773-3306 ■ *Web:* www.datapipe.com					
DataRealm Internet Services LLC PO Box 1616	Hudson	WI	54016	602-850-4044	850-3660
TF: 877-227-3783 ■ *Web:* www.datarealm.com					
FASTNET 3864 Courtney St Suite 130	Bethlehem	PA	18017	610-266-6700	266-8653
TF: 888-321-3278 ■ *Web:* www.fast.net					
Fortress Integrated Technologies 100 Delawanna Ave.	Clifton	NJ	07014	973-572-1070	572-1061
TF: 888-734-9320 ■ *Web:* www.fortressitx.com					
FortuneCity Inc 322 8th Ave 11th Fl	New York	NY	10001	212-981-8600	981-8125
TF: 866-638-2489					
Freeservers.com 1253 N Research Way Suite Q-2500	Orem	UT	84097	801-437-6000	437-6020
TF: 800-396-1999 ■ *Web:* www.freeservers.com					
Global Knowledge Group Inc (GKG) 302 N Bryan Ave	Bryan	TX	77803	979-693-5447	694-7060
TF: 888-769-4805 ■ *Web:* www.gkg.net					
Homestead Technologies Inc 180 Jefferson Dr	Menlo Park	CA	94025	650-944-3100	364-7329
TF: 800-797-2958 ■ *Web:* www.homestead.com					
Host Depot Inc 12524 W Atlantic Blvd	Coral Springs	FL	33071	954-340-3527	340-3539
TF: 888-340-3527 ■ *Web:* www.hostdepot.com					
Hostcentric Inc 70 Blanchard Rd 3rd Fl	Burlington	MA	01803	602-716-5396	998-8277*
**Fax Area Code:* 781 ■ *TF:* 800-467-8669 ■ *Web:* www.hostcentric.com					
Hostedware Corp 16 Technology Dr Suite 116	Irvine	CA	92618	949-585-1500	585-0050
TF: 800-211-6967 ■ *Web:* www.hostedware.com					
Hosting.com 462 S 4th St	Louisville	KY	40202	502-214-4100	214-4141
TF: 800-446-7627 ■ *Web:* www.hosting.com					
Hostway Corp 100 N Riverside Plaza 8th Fl	Chicago	IL	60606	312-238-0125	236-1958
TF: 866-467-8929 ■ *Web:* www.hostway.com					
Hurricane Electric Internet Services 760 Mission Ct.	Fremont	CA	94539	510-580-4100	580-4151
Web: www.he.com					
INetU Inc 744 Roble Rd Suite 70	Allentown	PA	18109	610-266-7441	266-7434
TF: 888-664-6388 ■ *Web:* www.inetu.net					
Intercosmos Media Group Inc 650 Poydras St Suite 1150	New Orleans	LA	70130	504-679-5170	
Web: www.directnic.com					
LightEdge Solutions Inc 666 Walnut St Suite 1900	Des Moines	IA	50309	515-471-1000	471-1112
TF: 877-771-3343 ■ *Web:* www.lightedge.com					

	City	State	ZIP	Phone	Fax
Media3 Technologies LLC 33 Riverside Dr N River Commerce Pk *TF:* 800-903-7145 ■ *Web:* www.media3.net	Pembroke	MA	02359	781-826-1213	996-4971
Microserve Inc 276 5th Ave Suite 1011 *Web:* www.mserve.com	New York	NY	10001	212-683-2811	696-0123
Move Inc 30700 Russell Ranch Rd *TF Cust Svc:* 800-878-4166 ■ *Web:* www.move.com	Westlake Village	CA	91360	805-557-2300	557-2680
NetNation Communications Inc 550 Burrard St Suite 200 *TF:* 888-277-0000 ■ *Web:* www.netnation.com	Vancouver	BC	V6C2B5	604-688-8946	688-8934
OLM LLC 4 Trefoil Dr *TF:* 800-741-6813 ■ *Web:* www.olm.net	Trumbull	CT	06611	203-445-7700	
Opsource Inc 5201 Great America Pkwy Suite 120 *Web:* www.opsource.net	Santa Clara	CA	95054	408-567-2000	982-8902
Pacific Internet 105 W Clay St *TF:* 888-722-8638 ■ *Web:* www.pacific.net	Ukiah	CA	95482	707-468-1005	468-5822
Perimeter E-security 440 Wheelers Farms Rd Suite 202 *TF:* 800-234-2175 ■ *Web:* www.perimeterusa.com	Milford	CT	06461	203-541-3400	
Power Surge Web Solutions 2300 Swan Lake Blvd Suite 300 *TF:* 800-867-5055 ■ *Web:* www.powersurge.net	Independence	IA	50644	312-492-4053	224-8428
Radiant Communications Corp 1600-1050 W Pender St Suite 1600 *TF:* 888-219-2111 ■ *Web:* www.radiant.net	Vancouver	BC	V6E4T3	604-257-0500	608-0999
Salon Media Group Inc 101 Spear St Suite 203 *Web:* www.salon.com	San Francisco	CA	94105	415-645-9200	645-9204
ServInt Internet Services 6861 Elm St Suite 2-B **Fax Area Code:* 703 ■ *TF:* 800-573-7846 ■ *Web:* www.servint.net	McLean	VA	22101	571-766-1000	847-1383*
Superb Internet Corp 999 Bishop St Suite 1850 *TF:* 888-354-6128 ■ *Web:* www.superb.net	Honolulu	HI	96813	808-544-0387	441-0952
Telus 1000 Rue de Serigny Bureau 600 *TF:* 866-363-7447 ■ *Web:* www.telushealth.com	Longueuil	QC	J4K5B1	450-928-6000	928-6344
TierraNet Inc 14284 Dani Elson St *TF:* 877-843-7721 ■ *Web:* www.tierra.net	Poway	CA	92064	858-560-9416	560-9417
Verio Inc 8005 S Chester St Suite 200 *TF Sales:* 800-438-8374 ■ *Web:* www.verio.com	Centennial	CO	80112	561-912-2555	
VPOP Technologies Inc 1772J Avenida de los Arboles PMB 374 **Fax Area Code:* 213 ■ *TF Sales:* 888-811-8767 ■ *Web:* www.vpop.net	Thousand Oaks	CA	91362	805-529-9374	477-2113*
Walt Disney Internet Group (WDIG) 5161 Lankershim Blvd *Web:* www.corporate.disney.go.com/wdig	North Hollywood	CA	91601	818-623-3200	623-3577
WorldPost Technologies Inc 5886 De Zavala Rd Suite 102/535 *Web:* www.worldpost.com	San Antonio	TX	78249	210-212-5600	212-5800
ZDNet Inc 235 2nd St *Web:* www.zdnet.com	San Francisco	CA	94105	415-344-2000	
VLinteractive 52 Royal Rd Suite A *TF:* 888-248-4893 ■ *Web:* www.activeweb.net	Guelph	ON	N1H1G3	519-837-2711	821-1624
Web.com 12808 Grand Bay Pkwy W *Web:* www.web.com	Jacksonville	FL	32258	904-680-6600	880-0350

812 WEB SITE DESIGN SERVICES

SEE ALSO Advertising Agencies p. 1370; Advertising Services - Online p. 1374; Computer Systems Design Services p. 1694

	City	State	ZIP	Phone	Fax
415 Productions Inc 2507 Bryant St *Web:* www.415.com	San Francisco	CA	94110	415-642-4200	642-4210
Acro Media Inc 2303 Leckie Rd Suite 103 *TF:* 877-763-8844 ■ *Web:* www.acromediainc.com	Kelowna	BC	V1X6Y5	250-763-8884	763-6936
AKQA Inc 3299 K St NW *Web:* www.akqa.com	Washington	DC	20007	202-551-9900	551-9930
Aptinet Inc 130 W 42nd St 20th Fl *Web:* www.aptinet.com	New York	NY	10035	212-725-7255	730-2980
Ariesnet Inc 815A Brazos Suite 125 **Fax Area Code:* 512 ■ *TF:* 888-932-3375 ■ *Web:* www.ariesnet.com	Austin	TX	78701	214-932-3900	551-0352*
Bixler Inc 1600 Tysons Blvd Suite 800 *Web:* www.bixler.com	McLean	VA	22102	703-894-3000	894-3001
bx.com Inc 3 Davol Sq *TF:* 800-344-8487 ■ *Web:* www.bx.com	Providence	RI	02903	401-274-8991	274-8949
Cramer 425 University Ave *Web:* www.crameronline.com	Norwood	MA	02062	781-278-2300	278-8464
Digital West Media Inc PO Box 270219 **Fax Area Code:* 310 ■ *Web:* www.dwmi.com	San Diego	CA	92198	760-740-1787	257-0042*
Duffy & Partners 710 2nd St S Suite 602 *Web:* www.duffy.com	Minneapolis	MN	55401	612-321-2333	321-2334
Forum One Communications Corp 2200 Mt Vernon Ave *Web:* www.forumone.com	Alexandria	VA	22301	703-548-1855	995-4937
Fry Inc 650 Avis Dr *TF:* 800-379-6858 ■ *Web:* www.fry.com	Ann Arbor	MI	48108	734-741-0640	769-9918
Fusebox Inc 36 W 20th St 11th Fl *Web:* www.fusebox.com	New York	NY	10011	212-929-7644	929-7947
G2 Interactive 200 5th Ave *Web:* www.g2.com	New York	NY	10010	212-537-3700	
Genex Interactive 800 Corporate Pointe *Web:* www.genex.com	Culver City	CA	90230	424-672-9500	672-9501
GotData.com Inc 26895 Aliso Creek Rd Suite B606 *Web:* www.gotdata.com	Aliso Viejo	CA	92656	949-458-8602	269-9161
Grizzly Web Designers 154 Marina Bay Ct *Web:* www.grizzlywebdesigners.com	Sylvan Lake	AB	T4S1E9	403-304-7690	
Headquarters.Com Inc 625 Walnut Ridge Dr Suite 108 *TF:* 800-788-1298 ■ *Web:* www.headquarters.com	Hartland	WI	53029	262-369-0600	369-0800
IMC2 12404 Pk Central Suite 400 *Web:* www.imc2.com	Dallas	TX	75251	214-224-1000	224-1100
Intercosmos Media Group Inc 650 Poydras St Suite 1150 *Web:* www.directnic.com	New Orleans	LA	70130	504-679-5170	
ISITE Design Inc 115 NW 1st Ave Suite 500 *TF:* 888-269-9103 ■ *Web:* www.isitedesign.com	Portland	OR	97209	503-221-9860	212-0239
Paloma Systems Inc 11250 Waples Mill Rd *Web:* www.palomasys.com	Fairfax	VA	22030	703-563-2060	591-0985
Patel Consultants Corp 1525 Morris Ave *Web:* www.patelcorp.com	Union	NJ	07083	908-964-7575	964-3176
Sapient Corp 131 Dartmouth St 3rd Fl *NASDAQ: SAPE* ■ *Web:* www.sapient.com	Boston	MA	02116	617-621-0200	621-1300

813 WEIGHT LOSS CENTERS & SERVICES

SEE ALSO Health & Fitness Centers p. 2008; Spas - Health & Fitness p. 2659

	City	State	ZIP	Phone	Fax
American Laser Skincare 24555 Hallwood Ct *TF:* 877-252-2010 ■ *Web:* www.americanlaser.com	Farmington Hills	MI	48335	248-426-8250	426-8455
Barix Clinics 135 S Prospect St *TF:* 800-282-0066 ■ *Web:* www.barixclinics.com	Ypsilanti	MI	48198	734-547-4700	547-1281
Companions & Homemakers Inc 613 New Britain Ave *TF:* 800-348-4663 ■ *Web:* www.companionsandhomemakers.com	Farmington	CT	06032	860-677-4948	409-2930
Fit America MD 2201 Stirling Rd **Fax Area Code:* 954 ■ *TF:* 800-940-7546 ■ *Web:* www.fitamericamd.com	Fort Lauderdale	FL	33312	800-221-1186	783-5911*
Greenpath Inc 38505 Country Club Dr *TF:* 800-550-1961 ■ *Web:* www.greenpath.com	Farmington Hills	MI	48331	248-553-5400	699-1613
Jazzercise Inc 2460 Impala Dr *TF Cust Svc:* 800-348-4748 ■ *Web:* www.jazzercise.com	Carlsbad	CA	92010	760-476-1750	602-7180
Jenny Craig International Inc 5770 Fleet St *TF:* 800-443-2331 ■ *Web:* www.jennycraig.com	Carlsbad	CA	92008	760-696-4000	696-4506
LA Weight Loss Centers 747 Dresher Rd Suite 100 *TF:* 877-524-3571 ■ *Web:* www.laweightloss.com	Horsham	PA	19044	215-346-4300	
NutriSystem Inc 300 Welsh Rd Bldg 1 *NASDAQ: NTRI* ■ *TF:* 800-585-5483 ■ *Web:* www.nutrisystem.com	Horsham	PA	19044	215-706-5300	706-5388
Physicians Weight Loss Centers of America Inc 395 Springside Dr *TF:* 800-205-7887 ■ *Web:* www.pwlc.com	Akron	OH	44333	330-666-7952	666-2197
Primescape Solutions Inc 13221 Wdlnd Pk Dr Suite 300 *Web:* www.primescape.net	Herndon	VA	20171	703-650-1900	650-1901
Weight Management Centers 2605 W Swann Ave Suite 600 *Web:* www.weightmanagement.com	Tampa	FL	33609	813-876-7073	877-1277

814 WELDING & SOLDERING EQUIPMENT

	City	State	ZIP	Phone	Fax
Acro Automation Systems Inc 2900 W Green Tree Rd *Web:* www.acro.com	Milwaukee	WI	53209	414-352-4540	352-1609
AGM Industries Inc 16 Jonathan Dr *TF:* 800-225-9990 ■ *Web:* www.agmind.com	Brockton	MA	02301	508-587-3900	587-3283
Alliance Winding Equipment Inc 3939 Vanguard Dr *Web:* www.alliance-winding.com	Fort Wayne	IN	46809	260-478-2200	
American Ultraviolet Co 40 Morristown Rd Suite 2-B *Web:* www.americanultraviolet.com	Bernardsville	NJ	07924	908-696-1130	696-1131
Applied Fusion Inc 1915 Republic Ave	San Leandro	CA	94577	510-351-4511	351-0692
Arc Machines Inc 10500 Orbital Way *Web:* www.arcmachines.com	Pacoima	CA	91331	818-896-9556	890-3724
Arcos Industries 1 Arcos Dr *TF:* 800-233-8460 ■ *Web:* www.arcos.us	Mount Carmel	PA	17851	570-339-5200	339-5206
Argus International Ltd 108 Whispering Pines Dr Suite 110 *TF:* 800-862-7487 ■ *Web:* www.argusinternational.com	Scotts Valley	CA	95066	831-461-4700	461-4701
Aro Welding 48500 Structural Dr *Web:* www.arotechnologies.com	Chesterfield Township	MI	48051	586-949-9353	949-4493
Automation International Inc 1020 Bahls St *Web:* www.automation-intl.com	Danville	IL	61832	217-446-9500	446-6855
Banner Welder Inc N 117 W 18200 Fulton Dr **Fax:* Cust Svc ■ *Web:* www.bannerweld.com	Germantown	WI	53022	262-253-2900	253-2917*
BUG-O Systems Inc 161 Hillpointe Dr *TF:* 800-245-3186 ■ *Web:* www.bugo.com	Canonsburg	PA	15317	412-331-1776	331-0383
CK Worldwide Inc 3501 C St NE *TF:* 800-426-0877 ■ *Web:* www.ckworldwide.com	Auburn	WA	98002	253-854-5820	939-1746
Esab Welding & Cutting Products Inc 411 S Ebenezer Rd PO Box 100545 **Fax:* Hum Res ■ *TF:* 800-372-2123 ■ *Web:* www.esabna.com	Florence	SC	29501	843-669-4411	664-4258*
Eureka Welding Alloys Inc 2000 E Avis Dr *TF:* 800-962-8560 ■ *Web:* www.eurekaweldingalloys.com	Madison Heights	MI	48071	248-588-0001	585-7711
Eutectic Corp N 94 W 14355 Garwin Mace Dr *TF:* 800-558-8524 ■ *Web:* www.eutectic-na.com	Menomonee Falls	WI	53051	262-255-5520	255-5542
Forney Industries Inc 1830 LaPorte Ave PO Box 563 *TF:* 800-521-6038 ■ *Web:* www.forneyind.com	Fort Collins	CO	80522	970-482-7271	498-9505
Goss Inc 1511 William Flynn Hwy *TF:* 800-367-4677 ■ *Web:* www.gossonline.com	Glenshaw	PA	15116	412-486-6100	486-6844

	City	State	Zip	Phone	Fax
Grossel Tool Co 34190 Doreka *Web:* www.grosseltool.com	Fraser	MI	48026	586-294-3660	294-7134
Harris Products Group 4501 Quality Pl **Fax:* Sales ■ *TF:* 800-733-4043 ■ *Web:* www.harrisproductsgroup.com	Mason	OH	45040	513-754-2000	754-8778*
Hobart Bros Co 101 Trade Sq E *Web:* www.hobartbrothers.com	Troy	OH	45373	937-332-4000	332-5178
Industrial Welders & Machinists Inc PO Box 16720 *TF:* 800-689-9520	Duluth	MN	55806	218-628-1011	624-3319
Jetline Engineering 15 Goodyear St *Web:* www.jetline.com	Irvine	CA	92618	949-951-1515	951-9237
JWF Industries 84 Iron St PO Box 1286 *TF:* 800-225-9353 ■ *Web:* www.jwfi.com	Johnstown	PA	15907	814-539-6922	536-8093
Kuka Flexible Production Systems Corp 6600 Ctr Dr *Web:* www.kukausa.com	Sterling Heights	MI	48312	586-795-2000	978-0429
Lincoln Electric Co 22801 St Clair Ave *Web:* www.lincolnelectric.com	Cleveland	OH	44117	216-481-8100	486-1751
M K Products Inc 16882 Armstrong Ave *TF:* 800-787-9707 ■ *Web:* www.mkprod.com	Irvine	CA	92606	949-863-1234	474-1428
Maine Oxy 22 Albiston Way *TF:* 800-639-1108 ■ *Web:* www.maineoxy.com	Auburn	ME	04210	207-784-5788	784-5383
Manufacturing Technology Inc (MTI) 1702 W Washington St *Web:* www.mtiwelding.com	South Bend	IN	46628	574-233-9490	233-9489
Merrill Mfg Corp 236 S Genesee St *TF:* 800-826-5300 ■ *Web:* www.merrill-mfg.com	Merrill	WI	54452	715-536-5533	536-5590
Milco Mfg Co 2147 E 10-Mile Rd *TF:* 800-697-6452 ■ *Web:* www.milcomfg.com	Warren	MI	48091	586-755-7320	755-7442
Miller Electric Mfg Co 1635 W Spencer St **Fax:* Sales ■ *Web:* www.millerwelds.com	Appleton	WI	54914	920-734-9821	735-4134*
Nelson Stud Welding Inc 7900 W Ridge Rd PO Box 4019 *Web:* www.nelsonstud.com	Elyria	OH	44036	440-329-0484	329-0521
NLC Inc 100 Block S Oklahoma St PO Box 348 *TF:* 800-747-4743	Jackson	MO	63755	573-243-3141	243-7122
Northern Stamping Corp 6600 Chapek Pkwy	Cuyahoga Heights	OH	44125	216-883-8888	883-8237
Ogden Welding Systems Inc 372 Division St *Web:* www.ogdenwelding.com	Schererville	IN	46375	219-322-5252	865-1825
Palomar Technologies 2728 Loker Ave W *TF:* 800-854-3467 ■ *Web:* www.palomartechnologies.com	Carlsbad	CA	92010	760-931-3600	931-5191
Pandjiris Inc 5151 Northrup Ave *TF:* 800-237-2006 ■ *Web:* www.pandjiris.com	Saint Louis	MO	63110	314-776-6893	776-8763
Research Inc 7128 Shady Oak Rd *Web:* www.researchinc.com	Eden Prairie	MN	55344	952-941-3300	941-3628
RoMan Mfg Inc 861 47th St SW *Web:* www.romanmfg.com	Grand Rapids	MI	49509	616-530-8641	530-8953
RWC Inc 2105 S Euclid Ave *Web:* www.rwcinc.com	Bay City	MI	48706	989-684-4030	684-3960
Sciaky Inc 4915 W 67th St *Web:* www.sciaky.com	Chicago	IL	60638	708-594-3800	594-9213
Smith Equipment Mfg Co 2601 Lockheed Ave **Fax Area Code:* 800 ■ *TF Cust Svc:* 800-328-3363 ■ *Web:* www.smithequipment.com	Watertown	SD	57201	605-882-3200	685-3370*
Sonobond Ultrasonics Inc 1191 McDermott Dr *TF:* 800-323-1269 ■ *Web:* www.sonobondultrasonic.com	West Chester	PA	19380	610-696-4710	692-0674
Stulz-Sickles Steel Co 929 Julia St PO Box 273 *TF:* 800-351-1776 ■ *Web:* www.stulzsicklessteel.com	Elizabeth	NJ	07207	908-351-1776	351-8231
Systematics Inc 1025 Saunders Ln PO Box 2429 *TF:* 800-222-9353	West Chester	PA	19380	610-696-9040	430-8714
Taylor-Winfield Corp PO Box 500 *Web:* www.taylor-winfield.com	Brookfield	OH	44403	330-448-4464	448-3538
Thermadyne Holdings Corp 16052 Swingley Ridge Rd Suite 300 *Web:* www.thermadyne.com	Saint Louis	MO	63017	636-728-3000	
Thermatool Corp 31 Commerce St PO Box 120769 **Fax:* Cust Svc ■ *Web:* www.thermatool.com	East Haven	CT	06512	203-468-4100	468-4281*
Tuffaloy Products Inc 1400 S Batesville Rd *TF:* 800-521-3722 ■ *Web:* www.tuffaloy.com	Greer	SC	29650	864-879-0763	877-2212
Unitek Miyachi Corp 1820 S Myrtle Ave *TF:* 866-751-7378 ■ *Web:* www.miyachiunitek.com	Monrovia	CA	91017	626-303-5676	358-8048
Uniweld Products Inc 2850 Ravenswood Rd *TF:* 800-323-2111 ■ *Web:* www.uniweld.com	Fort Lauderdale	FL	33312	954-584-2000	587-0109
Vitronics Soltec Inc 2 Marin Way *Web:* www.vitronics-soltec.com	Stratham	NH	03885	603-772-7778	772-9340
Weld Mold Co 750 Rickett Rd *TF:* 800-521-9755 ■ *Web:* www.weldmold.com	Brighton	MI	48116	810-229-9521	229-9580
Weldmation Inc 31720 Stephenson Hwy *Web:* www.weldmation.com	Madison Heights	MI	48071	248-585-0010	585-0016
Western Enterprises Inc 875 Bassett Rd **Fax Area Code:* 440 ■ *TF:* 800-783-7890 ■ *Web:* www.westernenterprises.com	Westlake	OH	44145	800-783-7890	835-8283*

815 WHOLESALE CLUBS

	City	State	Zip	Phone	Fax
BJ's Wholesale Club 1 Mercer Rd *NYSE: BJ* ■ *TF:* 800-257-2582 ■ *Web:* www.bjs.com	Natick	MA	01760	508-651-7400	651-6251
Costco Wholesale Corp 999 Lake Dr *NASDAQ: COST* ■ *TF Cust Svc:* 800-774-2678 ■ *Web:* www.costco.com	Issaquah	WA	98027	425-313-8100	313-8103
Marukai Wholesale Mart 2310 Kamehameha Hwy *Web:* www.marukaihawaii.com	Honolulu	HI	96819	808-845-5051	841-2379
PriceSmart Inc 9740 Scranton Rd *NASDAQ: PSMT* ■ *Web:* www.pricesmart.com	San Diego	CA	92121	858-404-8800	
Wal-Mart Stores Inc Sam's Club Div 608 SW 8th St *TF:* 888-746-7726 ■ *Web:* www.samsclub.com	Bentonville	AR	72712	479-277-7000	

816 WIRE & CABLE

	City	State	Zip	Phone	Fax
Ace Wire & Cable Co Inc 7201 51st Ave *TF:* 800-225-2354 ■ *Web:* www.acewireco.com	Woodside	NY	11377	718-458-9200	458-6340
AFC Cable Systems Inc 272 Duchaine Blvd *TF:* 800-757-6996 ■ *Web:* www.afcweb.com	New Bedford	MA	02745	508-998-1131	998-1447
Alcan Cable 3 Ravinia Dr Suite 1600 *Web:* www.cable.alcan.com	Atlanta	GA	30346	770-394-9886	395-9053
Allwire Inc 16395 Ave 24 1/2 PO Box 1000 *TF:* 800-255-3828 ■ *Web:* www.allwire.com	Chowchilla	CA	93610	559-665-4893	665-7389
AmerCable Inc 350 Bailey Rd *TF:* 800-643-1516 ■ *Web:* www.amercable.com	El Dorado	AR	71730	870-862-4919	862-9613
Astro Industries Inc 4403 Dayton-Xenia Rd **Fax:* Sales ■ *TF:* 800-543-5810 ■ *Web:* www.astro-ind.com	Dayton	OH	45432	937-429-5900	429-4054*
Bekaert Corp 3200 W Market St Suite 303 *Web:* www.bekaert.com	Akron	OH	44333	330-867-3325	873-3424
Capro Inc 300 S Cochran St PO Box 588 *Web:* www.capro.com	Willis	TX	77378	936-856-2971	856-4328
Cerro Wire & Cable Co Inc 1099 Thompson Rd SE *TF:* 800-523-3869 ■ *Web:* www.cerrowire.com	Hartselle	AL	35640	256-773-2522	
Charter Wire 3700 W Milwaukee Rd *TF:* 800-436-9074 ■ *Web:* www.charterwire.com	Milwaukee	WI	53209	414-390-3000	390-3031
Coleman Cable Systems Inc 1430 12th St *TF:* 800-323-9355 ■ *Web:* www.colemancable.com	Waukegan	IL	60085	847-672-2300	689-1192
Cooner Wire Co 9265 Owensmouth Ave *Web:* www.coonerwire.com	Chatsworth	CA	91311	818-882-8311	709-8281
Cove Four-Slide & Stamping Corp 195 E Merrick Rd *Web:* www.covefour.com	Freeport	NY	11520	516-379-4232	379-4563
Dekko Technologies LLC 2505 Dekko Dr *TF:* 800-829-3101 ■ *Web:* www.dekko.com	Garrett	IN	46738	260-357-3621	357-3399
Draka Cableteq USA 22 Joseph E Warner Blvd *TF:* 888-520-1200 ■ *Web:* www.drakacableteqsa.com	North Dighton	MA	02764	508-822-5444	822-1944
Elektrisola Inc 126 High St *TF:* 800-325-2022 ■ *Web:* www.elektrisola.com	Boscawen	NH	03303	603-796-2114	796-2111
Encore Wire Corp 1329 Millwood Rd *NASDAQ: WIRE* ■ *TF:* 800-962-9473 ■ *Web:* www.encorewire.com	McKinney	TX	75069	972-562-9473	562-3644
Eubanks Engineering Co 3022 Inland Empire Blvd *Web:* www.eubanks.com	Ontario	CA	91764	909-483-2456	483-2498
Fiberwave Corp 140 58th St Bldg B - Unit 6E *TF:* 800-280-9011 ■ *Web:* www.fiberwave.com	Brooklyn	NY	11220	718-802-9011	802-0116
Foerster Instruments Inc 140 Industry Dr *Web:* www.foerstergroup.com	Pittsburgh	PA	15275	412-788-8976	788-8984
Gehr Industries 7400 E Slauson Ave *TF:* 800-688-6606 ■ *Web:* www.gehr.com/gehr	Los Angeles	CA	90040	323-728-5558	725-0864
Hendrix Wire & Cable Inc 53 Old Wilton Rd *Web:* www.hendrix-wc.com	Milford	NH	03055	603-673-2040	673-1497
Insteel Industries Inc 1373 Boggs Dr *NASDAQ: IIIN* ■ *TF:* 800-334-9504 ■ *Web:* www.insteel.com	Mount Airy	NC	27030	336-786-2141	786-2144
Inter-Wire Products (IWP) 355 Main St *Web:* www.interwiregroup.com	Armonk	NY	10504	914-273-6633	273-6848
International Wire Group Inc 12 Masonic Ave *Web:* www.mills-partners.com/operating/wire.htm	Camden	NY	13316	315-245-2000	245-1916
Kalas Mfg Inc 531 N 4th St *Web:* www.kalaswire.com	Denver	PA	17517	717-336-5575	336-4248
Kerite Co 49 Day St *TF:* 800-777-7483 ■ *Web:* www.kerite.com	Seymour	CT	06483	203-888-2591	888-1987
Keystone Consolidated Industries Inc 7000 SW Adams St *TF Sales:* 800-447-6444 ■ *Web:* www.redbrand.com	Peoria	IL	61641	309-697-7020	697-7120
Leggett Wire Co 1 Leggett Rd *TF:* 800-888-4569 ■ *Web:* www.leggett.com	Carthage	MO	64836	417-358-8131	358-6904
Leoni Wiring Systems Inc 2861 N Flowing Wells Rd Suite 121 *Web:* www.leoni.com	Tucson	AZ	85705	520-741-0895	741-0864
Major Custom Cable Inc 281 Lotus Dr *Web:* www.majorcustomcable.com	Jackson	MO	63755	573-204-1008	243-1365
Mercury Wire Products Inc 1 Mercury Dr *Web:* www.mercurywire.com	Spencer	MA	01562	508-885-6363	885-3316
Mid-South Wire Co Inc 1070 Visco Dr *TF:* 800-714-7800 ■ *Web:* www.midsouthwire.com	Nashville	TN	37210	615-244-5258	256-5836
Mount Joy Wire Corp 1000 E Main St *TF:* 800-321-2305 ■ *Web:* www.mjwire.com	Mount Joy	PA	17552	717-653-1461	653-0221
Nichols Wire 1547 Helton Dr *TF:* 800-633-3156 ■ *Web:* www.nicholswire.com	Florence	AL	35630	256-764-4271	767-5152
Okonite Co 102 Hilltop Rd *Web:* www.okonite.com	Ramsey	NJ	07446	201-825-0300	825-3524
Owl Wire & Cable Inc 3127 Seneca Tpke *TF:* 800-765-9473 ■ *Web:* www.owlwire.com	Canastota	NY	13032	315-697-2011	697-2123
Rea Magnet Wire Co Inc 3600 E Pontiac St *TF:* 800-732-9473 ■ *Web:* www.reawire.com	Fort Wayne	IN	46803	260-421-7321	422-4246
Ribbon Technology Corp 825 Taylor Stn Rd PO Box 30758 *TF:* 800-848-0477 ■ *Web:* www.ribtec.com	Gahanna	OH	43230	614-864-5444	864-5305
Rochester Corp 751 Old Brandy Rd *Web:* www.rochestercables.com	Culpeper	VA	22701	540-825-2111	825-2238
S & S Industries Inc 5 odell Plaza *Web:* www.sandsindustries.com	Yonkers	NY	10701	914-885-1500	885-1488
Santa Fe Textiles Inc 17370 Mt Herrmann St *Web:* www.barcel.com/link5.htm	Fountain Valley	CA	92708	949-251-1960	863-9788
Seneca Wire & Mfg Co 319 S Vine St *TF Sales:* 800-537-9537 ■ *Web:* www.senecawire.com	Fostoria	OH	44830	419-435-9261	435-9265

Company	City	State	ZIP	Phone	Fax
Shaped Wire Inc 30000 Solon Rd Web: www.shapedwire.com	Solon	OH	44139	440-248-7600	248-5491
Sivaco Wire Group 800 Rue Ouellette TF: 800-876-9473 ■ Web: www.sivaco.com	Marieville	QC	J3M1P5	450-658-8741	460-0310
Southwest Electronic Energy Corp PO Box 848 TF: 800-231-3612 ■ Web: www.swe.com	Stafford	TX	77497	281-240-4000	240-5672
Southwestern Wire Inc PO Box CC TF: 800-348-9473 ■ Web: www.southwesternwire.com	Norman	OK	73070	405-447-6900	447-2830
Southwire Co 1 Southwire Dr TF: 800-444-1700 ■ Web: www.southwire.com	Carrollton	GA	30119	770-832-4242	838-6462
Spotnails 1100 Hicks Rd TF: 800-873-2239 ■ Web: www.spotnails.com	Rolling Meadows	IL	60008	847-259-1620	259-9236
Sumitomo Electric USA Inc 21241 S Western Ave Suite 120 Web: www.sumitomoelectricusa.com	Torrance	CA	90501	310-782-0227	782-0211
Superior Essex Inc Magnet Wire/Winding Wire Div 1601 Wall St PO Box 1601 Web: www.superioressex.com	Fort Wayne	IN	46802	260-461-4550	461-4690
Tappan Wire & Cable Inc 100 Bradley Pkwy Web: www.tappanwire.com	Blauvelt	NY	10913	845-353-9000	353-9315
Techalloy Co Inc Baltimore Wire Div 2310 Chesapeake Ave TF: 800-638-1458 ■ Web: www.techalloy.com	Baltimore	MD	21222	410-633-9300	633-2033
TI Wire 12459 Arrow Rt TF: 800-255-6974 ■ Web: www.tiwire-usa.com	Rancho Cucamonga	CA	91739	909-594-7511	595-0439
Times Fiber Communications Inc 358 Hall Ave PO Box 384 TF: 800-677-2288 ■ Web: www.timesfiber.com	Wallingford	CT	06492	203-265-8500	265-8422
Tokusen USA Inc 1500 Amity Rd PO Box 1150 Web: www.tokusenusa.com	Conway	AR	72033	501-327-6800	327-0231
WireCo WorldGroup 12200 NW Ambassador Dr Web: www.wirecoworldgroup.com	Kansas City	MO	64163	816-270-4700	270-4707
Wirerope Works Inc 100 Maynard St TF Cust Svc: 800-541-7673 ■ Web: www.wwwrope.com	Williamsport	PA	17701	570-326-5146	327-4274
Wrap-On Co Inc 5550 W 70th Pl TF: 800-621-6947 ■ Web: www.wrapon.com	Bedford Park	IL	60638	708-496-2150	496-2154

817 WIRE & CABLE - ELECTRONIC

Company	City	State	ZIP	Phone	Fax
Alpha Wire Co 711 Lidgerwood Ave TF: 800-522-5742 ■ Web: www.alphawire.com	Elizabeth	NJ	07207	908-925-8000	925-5411
American Insulated Wire Corp 260 Forbes Blvd TF: 800-366-2492 ■ Web: www.aiwc.com	Mansfield	MA	02048	508-964-1200	964-1192
Belden Inc 7701 Forsyth Blvd Suite 800 NYSE: BDC ■ TF: 800-235-3361 ■ Web: www.belden.com	Saint Louis	MO	63105	314-854-8000	854-8001
Belden Inc Americas Div 2200 US Hwy 27 S PO Box 1980 TF: 800-235-3362 ■ Web: www.belden.com	Richmond	IN	47375	765-983-5200	983-5294
C & M Corp 51 S Walnut St PO Box 348 Web: www.cmcorporation.com	Wauregan	CT	06387	860-774-4812	774-7333
Cable USA Inc 2584 S Horseshoe Dr Web: www.cableusainc.com	Naples	FL	34104	239-643-6400	643-4230
Cables to Go Inc 3599 Dayton Pk Dr TF: 800-826-7904 ■ Web: www.cablestogo.com	Dayton	OH	45414	937-224-8646	496-2666
Champlain Cable Corp 175 Hercules Dr *Fax: Sales ■ TF: 800-451-5162 ■ Web: www.champcable.com	Colchester	VT	05446	802-654-4200	654-4224*
Cicoil Corp 24960 Ave Tibbitts Web: www.cicoil.com	Valencia	CA	91355	661-295-1295	295-0813
CommScope Inc 1100 Commscope Pl SE PO Box 339 NYSE: CTV ■ *Fax: Cust Svc ■ TF: 800-982-1708 ■ Web: www.commscope.com	Hickory	NC	28603	828-324-2200	328-3400*
Comprehensive Video Group 55 Ruta Ct TF: 800-526-0242 ■ Web: www.comprehensivecable.com	South Hackensack	NJ	07606	201-229-4270	814-0510
Compulink Inc 1205 Gandy Blvd N TF: 800-231-6685 ■ Web: www.compulink-usa.com	Saint Petersburg	FL	33702	727-579-1500	578-8420
Comtran Corp 1 Main St TF: 800-842-7809 ■ Web: www.comtrancorp.com	Whitinsville	MA	01588	508-234-6256	234-7132
Consolidated Electronic Wire & Cable Co 11044 King St TF: 800-621-4278 ■ Web: www.conwire.com	Franklin Park	IL	60131	847-455-8830	455-8837
Corning Cable Systems 800 17th St NW TF: 800-743-2671 ■ Web: www.corning.com	Hickory	NC	28603	828-901-5000	325-5060
CXtec 5404 S Bay Rd PO Box 4799 TF Orders: 800-913-9467 ■ Web: www.cxtec.com	Syracuse	NY	13212	315-476-3000	455-1800
Dc Electronics 1870 Little Orchard St Web: www.dcelectronics.com	San Jose	CA	95125	408-947-4500	947-4510
Dekoron Wire & Cable 1300 Industrial Blvd *Fax: Cust Svc ■ Web: www.dekoroncable.com	Mount Pleasant	TX	75455	903-572-3475	572-6153*
Draka Cableteq Holdings USA Inc 4440 Pga Blvd Suite 308 *Fax Area Code: 888 ■ Web: www.drakausa.com	Palm Beach Gardens	FL	33410	561-656-2550	201-8280*
Draka Comteq Americas 2512 Penny Rd PO Box 39 TF: 800-879-9862 ■ Web: www.communications.draka.com	Claremont	NC	28610	828-459-9821	459-8444
Fargo Assembly Co (FAC) 3300 7th Ave N PO Box 2340 Web: www.facnd.com	Fargo	ND	58108	701-298-3803	298-3806
Furukawa America Inc 200 Westpark Dr Suite 190 Web: www.furukawaamerica.com	Peachtree City	GA	30269	770-487-1234	487-9910
Gallant & Wein Corp 11-20 43rd Rd Web: www.galwein.com	Long Island City	NY	11101	718-784-5210	937-6426
General Cable Corp 4 Tesseneer Dr NYSE: BGC ■ TF: 800-572-8000 ■ Web: www.generalcable.com	Highland Heights	KY	41076	859-572-8000	547-8072
Harbour Industries Inc 4744 Shelburne Rd PO Box 188 TF: 800-659-4733 ■ Web: www.harbourind.com	Shelburne	VT	05482	802-985-3311	985-9534
Judd Wire Inc 124 Tpke Rd TF Cust Svc: 800-545-5833 ■ Web: www.juddwire.com	Turners Falls	MA	01376	413-863-4357	863-4362
Lynn Products Inc 2645 W 237th St Web: www.lynnprod.com	Torrance	CA	90505	310-530-5966	530-8426
Madison Cable Corp 125 Goddard Memorial Dr TF: 877-623-4766 ■ Web: www.madisoncable.com	Worcester	MA	01603	508-752-2884	752-4230
MNM Group Inc 3235 Sunset Ln TF: 800-645-3477 ■ Web: www.themnmgroup.com	Hatboro	PA	19040	215-672-9600	674-5380
Mohawk Div of Belden Inc 9 Mohawk Dr TF: 800-422-9961 ■ Web: www.mohawk-cable.com	Leominster	MA	01453	978-537-9961	537-4358
National Wire & Cable Corp 136 N San Fernando Rd Web: www.nationalwire.com	Los Angeles	CA	90031	323-225-5611	225-4630
Nehring Electric Works Inc 1005 E Locust St TF: 800-435-4481 ■ Web: www.nehringwire.com	DeKalb	IL	60115	815-756-2741	756-7048
Oleco Inc 18683 Trimble Ct PO Box 463	Spring Lake	MI	49456	616-842-6790	842-5886
Optical Cable Corp (OCC) 5290 Concourse Dr NASDAQ: OCC ■ TF: 800-622-7711 ■ Web: www.occfiber.com	Roanoke	VA	24019	540-265-0690	265-0724
Parlex Corp 1 Parlex Pl Web: www.parlex.com	Methuen	MA	01844	978-685-4341	685-8809
Pirelli Cables & Systems 700 Industrial Dr *Fax: Mktg ■ TF Cust Svc: 800-845-8507 ■ Web: www.pirelli.com/cables	Lexington	SC	29072	803-951-4800	951-4022*
Prestolite Wire Corp 200 Galleria Officentre Suite 212 TF: 800-498-3132 ■ Web: www.prestolitewire.com	Southfield	MI	48034	248-355-4422	386-4462
Rockbestos-Surprenant Cable Corp 20 Bradley Pk Rd Web: www.r-scc.com	East Granby	CT	06026	860-653-8300	653-8410
Siemon Co 101 Siemon Co Dr TF: 866-548-5814 ■ Web: www.siemon.com	Watertown	CT	06795	860-945-4200	945-4225
Superior Essex Inc 6120 Powers Ferry Rd Suite 150 NASDAQ: SPSX ■ TF: 800-551-8948 ■ Web: www.superioressex.com	Atlanta	GA	30339	770-657-6000	303-8883
Tensolite Co 100 Tensolite Dr TF: 800-458-9960 ■ Web: www.tensolite.com	Saint Augustine	FL	32092	904-829-5600	829-3447
Trilogy Communications Inc 2910 Hwy 80 E TF: 800-874-5649 ■ Web: www.trilogycoax.com	Pearl	MS	39208	601-932-4461	939-6637
Tyco Telecommunications 60 Columbia Rd Web: www.tycotelecom.com	Morristown	NJ	07960	973-656-8000	656-8990

818 WIRING DEVICES - CURRENT-CARRYING

Company	City	State	ZIP	Phone	Fax
Aerospace Optics Inc 3201 Sandy Ln TF: 888-848-4786 ■ Web: www.vivisun.com	Fort Worth	TX	76112	817-451-1141	654-3405
ALP Lighting Components Inc 6333 Gross Pt Rd TF: 877-257-5841 ■ Web: www.alplighting.com	Niles	IL	60714	773-774-9550	774-9331
AMI Doduco Inc 1003 Corporate Ln Web: www.amidoduco.com	Export	PA	15632	724-733-8332	733-2880
Amphenol Corp 358 Hall Ave NYSE: APH ■ TF: 877-267-4366 ■ Web: www.amphenol.com	Wallingford	CT	06492	203-265-8900	265-8628
Ark-Les Corp 95 Mill St TF: 800-342-6472 ■ Web: www.ark-les.com	Stoughton	MA	02072	781-297-6000	297-6160
Arlington Industries Inc 1 Stauffer Industrial Pk TF: 800-233-4717 ■ Web: www.aifittings.com	Scranton	PA	18517	570-562-0270	562-0646
AVA Electronics Corp 4000 Bridge St TF Sales: 800-331-8838	Drexel Hill	PA	19026	610-284-2500	259-8379
AVCON Corp 4640 Ironwood Dr TF: 877-423-8725 ■ Web: www.avconev.com	Franklin	WI	53132	414-817-6160	817-6161
Bizlink Technology Inc 3400 Gateway Blvd TF: 800-326-4193 ■ Web: www.bizlinktech.com	Fremont	CA	94538	510-252-0786	252-1178
Brainin Advance Industries Inc 48 Frank Mossberg Dr Web: www.brainin.com	Attleboro	MA	02703	508-226-1200	226-8703
Carling Technologies Inc 60 Johnson Ave TF: 800-243-8556 ■ Web: www.carlingtech.com	Plainville	CT	06062	860-793-9281	793-9231
Charles E Gillman Co 907 E Frontage Rd Web: www.gillman.com	Rio Rico	AZ	85648	520-281-1141	281-1372
Checon Corp 30 Larsen Way Web: www.checon.com	North Attleboro	MA	02763	508-809-5100	809-5163
Cherry Corp 11200 88th Ave TF: 800-898-3966 ■ Web: www.cherrycorp.com	Pleasant Prairie	WI	53158	262-942-6500	942-6577
Cinch Connectors Inc 1700 Findley Rd TF: 800-323-9612 ■ Web: www.cinch.com	Lombard	IL	60148	630-705-6000	705-6060
Cole Hersee Co 20 Old Colony Ave TF: 800-365-2653 ■ Web: www.colehersee.com	Boston	MA	02127	617-268-2100	268-9490
Component Enterprises Co 235-275 E Penn St	Norristown	PA	19401	610-272-7900	272-7040
Connector Mfg Co 3501 Symmes Rd Web: www.cmclugs.com	Hamilton	OH	45015	513-860-4455	860-6114
Cooper Bussmann Inc 114 Old State Rd *Fax: Cust Svc ■ Web: www.cooperindustries.com/content/public/en/bussmann.html	Ellisville	MO	63021	636-394-2877	394-2877*
Cooper Crouse-Hinds Wolf & 7th N St TF: 866-764-5454 ■ Web: www.cooperindustries.com	Syracuse	NY	13221	315-477-5531	477-5531
Cooper Industries 600 Travis St Suite 5800 NYSE: CBE ■ TF: 866-853-4293 ■ Web: www.cooperindustries.com	Houston	TX	77002	713-209-8400	209-8995
Cooper Wiring Devices Inc 203 Cooper Cir TF Cust Svc: 866-853-4293 ■ Web: www.cooperindustries.com	Peachtree City	GA	30269	770-631-2100	631-2100
Cord Sets Inc 1015 5th St N TF: 800-752-0580 ■ Web: www.cordsetsinc.com	Minneapolis	MN	55411	612-337-9700	337-0800
Cord Specialties Co 10632 Grand Ave Web: www.cordspecialties.com	Franklin Park	IL	60131	847-455-3503	455-0916
Cristek Interconnects Inc 5395 E Hunter Ave TF: 888-265-9162 ■ Web: www.cristek.com	Anaheim	CA	92807	714-696-5200	970-3711
Curtis Industries Inc 2400 S 43rd St PO Box 343925 TF: 800-657-0853 ■ Web: www.curtisind.com	Milwaukee	WI	53219	414-649-4200	649-4279
Ddh Enterprise Inc 2220 Oak Ridge Way Web: www.ddhent.com	Vista	CA	92081	760-599-0171	599-9397

Company	City	State	ZIP	Phone	Fax
Deutsch Engineered Connecting Devices 3850 Industrial Ave	Hemet	CA	92545	951-765-2250	765-2255
Web: www.deutschecd.com					
Edwin Gaynor Corp 200 Charles St	Stratford	CT	06615	203-378-5545	381-9019
TF: 800-342-9667 ■ Web: www.egaynor.com					
EECO Switch 880 Columbia St	Brea	CA	92821	714-835-6000	482-9429
TF: 800-854-3808 ■ Web: www.eecoswitch.com					
EFI Electronics Corp 1751 S 4800 W	Salt Lake City	UT	84104	801-977-9009	977-0200
TF: 800-877-1174 ■ Web: www.efinet.com					
Electri-Cord Mfg Co Inc 312 E Main St	Westfield	PA	16950	814-367-2265	367-2314
Web: www.electri-cord.com					
Electronic Systems Packaging LLC (ESP) 1175 W Victoria St	Rancho Dominguez	CA	90220	310-639-2535	632-6666
Web: www.espbus.com					
Electroswitch á 2010 Yonkers Rd	Raleigh	NC	27604	919-833-0707	833-8016
TF: 888-768-2797 ■ Web: www.electro-nc.com					
ERICO International Corp 31700 Holland Rd	Solon	OH	44139	440-349-2630	349-2996
TF: 800-800-9301 ■ Web: www.erico.com					
ERICO Products Inc 34600 Solon Rd	Solon	OH	44139	440-248-0100	248-0723
TF: 800-813-3378 ■ Web: www.erico.com					
ETCO Inc 25 Bellows St	Warwick	RI	02888	401-467-2400	467-9230
Web: www.etco.com					
Eureka Electrical Products Inc 79 Clay St	North East	PA	16428	814-725-9638	725-3670
FTZ Industries Inc 515 Palmetto Dr	Simpsonville	SC	29681	864-963-5000	963-5352
TF: 800-336-8989 ■ Web: www.ftzind.com					
G & W Electric Co 3500 Burr Oak Ave	Blue Island	IL	60406	708-388-5010	388-0755
Web: www.gwelec.com					
Glenair Inc 1211 Air Way	Glendale	CA	91201	818-247-6000	500-9912
Web: www.glenair.com					
Group Dekko Services LLC 2505 Dekko Dr	Garrett	IN	46738	260-357-3621	357-4293
TF: 800-829-3101 ■ Web: www.dekko.com					
Hi Rel Connectors Inc 760 Wharton Dr	Claremont	CA	91711	909-626-1820	399-0626
Web: www.hirelco.net					
Hi-Stat Mfg Co Inc 345 S Mill St	Lexington	OH	44904	419-884-1219	884-4196
Web: www.histat.com					
Hoffman Products 20700 Hubbell Ave	Oak Park	MI	48237	248-395-8462	908-1295*
*Fax Area Code: 800 ■ TF: 800-645-2014 ■ Web: www.hoffmanproducts.com					
Hoyt Corp 520 S Dean St	Englewood	NJ	07631	201-894-0707	894-0916
TF: 800-255-4698 ■ Web: www.hoyt-corp.com					
Hubbell Premise Wiring Inc 23 Clara Dr	Mystic	CT	06355	800-626-0005	535-8328*
*Fax Area Code: 860 ■ TF: 800-626-0005 ■ Web: www.hubbell-premise.com					
Hubbell Wiring Device-Kellems 40 Waterview Dr	Shelton	CT	06484	203-882-4800	882-4852*
*Fax: Tech Supp ■ TF Cust Svc: 800-288-6000 ■ Web: www.hubbell-wiring.com					
ILSCO 4730 Madison Rd	Cincinnati	OH	45227	513-533-6200	533-6226
TF Sales: 800-776-9775 ■ Web: www.ilsco.com					
Independent Protection Co Inc 1607 S Main St	Goshen	IN	46526	574-533-4116	534-3719
TF: 800-860-8388 ■ Web: www.ipclp.com					
ITT Neo-Dyn Industrial Switch 28150 Industry Dr	Valencia	CA	91355	661-295-4000	295-4181
Web: www.neodyn.com					
JB Nottingham & Co Inc Duraline Div 75 Hoffman Ln	Islandia	NY	11749	631-234-2002	234-2360
Web: www.store.jbn-duraline.com					
Joslyn High Voltage Corp 4000 E 116th St	Cleveland	OH	44105	216-271-6600	341-3615
TF: 800-621-5875 ■ Web: www.joslynhivoltage.com					
Kemlon Products & Development Co 1424 N Main St	Pearland	TX	77581	281-997-3300	997-1300
Web: www.kemlon.com					
Keystone Cable Corp 8200 Lynch Rd	Detroit	MI	48234	313-924-9720	924-0050
TF: 800-223-2996 ■ Web: www.keystonecable.net					
King Assoc Ltd 62 Industrial Cir	Lancaster	PA	17601	717-556-5673	
TF: 800-818-4916 ■ Web: www.kordking.com					
Lamcor Inc 2025 E Orangewood Ave	Anaheim	CA	92806	714-634-2950	634-4713
Lighting Concepts & Solutions Inc 11711 NW 39th St	Coral Springs	FL	33065	954-425-0123	
Web: www.lightingcomponents.com					
LL Rowe Co 66 Holton St	Woburn	MA	01801	781-729-7860	721-7264
Web: www.llrowe.com					
Marine Industries Co LLC 2655 Napa Valley Corp Dr	Napa	CA	94558	707-226-9600	226-9670
TF: 800-307-6702 ■ Web: www.marinco.com					
McGill Electrical Product Group 9377 W Higgins Rd	Rosemont	IL	60018	847-268-6000	356-4714*
*Fax Area Code: 800 ■ TF: 888-832-0660 ■ Web: www.mcgillelectrical.com					
Mill-Max Mfg Corp 190 Pine Hollow Rd	Oyster Bay	NY	11771	516-922-6000	922-9253
TF: 800-294-8027 ■ Web: www.mill-max.com					
Minnesota Wire & Cable Co 1835 Energy Pk Dr	Saint Paul	MN	55108	651-642-1800	642-9286
TF: 800-258-6922 ■ Web: www.mnwire.com					
Nexus Inc 50 Sunnyside Ave	Stamford	CT	06904	203-327-7300	324-7623
Web: www.nexus.com					
Ohio Associated Enterprises LLC 1382 W Jackson St	Painesville	OH	44077	440-354-3148	354-0687
TF: 800-863-9014 ■ Web: www.meritec.com					
Omnetics Connector Corp 7260 Commerce Cir E	Minneapolis	MN	55432	763-572-0656	572-3925
TF Cust Svc: 800-343-0025 ■ Web: www.omnetics.com					
Panduit Corp 17301 Ridgeland Ave	Tinley Park	IL	60477	708-532-1800	532-1811
TF: 888-506-5400 ■ Web: www.panduit.com					
Penn-Union Corp 229 Waterford St	Edinboro	PA	16412	814-734-1631	734-4946
Web: www.penn-union.com					
Philips Accessories 13895 Industrial Pk Blvd Suite 110	Plymouth	MN	55441	763-559-0841	
TF: 800-639-7646					
Phoenix Co of Chicago Inc 555 Pond Dr	Wood Dale	IL	60191	630-595-2300	595-6579
Web: www.phoenixofchicago.com					
Preformed Line Products 660 Beta Dr	Mayfield Village	OH	44143	440-461-5200	442-8816
NASDAQ: PLPC ■ TF: 888-773-3676 ■ Web: www.preformed.com					
Shape LLC 2105 Corporate Dr	Addison	IL	60101	630-620-8394	620-0784
TF: 800-367-5811 ■ Web: www.shapellc.com					
Special Mine Services Inc PO Box 188	West Frankfort	IL	62896	618-932-2151	937-2715
Web: www.smsconnectors.com					
Springfield Wire Inc 243 Cottage St	Springfield	MA	01104	413-781-6950	739-3809
Web: www.springfield-wire.com					
State Tool & Mfg Co 1650 E Empire Ave	Benton Harbor	MI	49022	269-927-3153	927-4230
Web: www.statetool.com					
Technology Research Corp 5250 140th Ave N	Clearwater	FL	33760	727-535-0572	530-7375
TF: 800-780-4324 ■ Web: www.trci.net					
Tower Mfg Corp 25 Reservoir Ave	Providence	RI	02907	401-467-7550	461-2710
Web: www.towermfg.com					
Transtector Systems Inc 10701 N Airport Rd	Hayden Lake	ID	83835	208-772-8515	762-6133*
*Fax: Sales ■ TF: 800-882-9110 ■ Web: www.protectiongroup.com/Transtector					
Tripp Lite Inc 1111 W 35th St	Chicago	IL	60609	773-869-1111	869-1329
Web: www.tripplite.com					
Veetronix Inc 1311 W Pacific Ave	Lexington	NE	68850	308-324-6661	324-4985
TF: 800-445-0007 ■ Web: www.veetronix.com					
Vitrus Inc 881 Main St	Pawtucket	RI	02860	401-724-9350	728-4620
Web: www.vitrus.com					
Volex Inc 915 Tate Blvd SE Suite 130	Hickory	NC	28602	828-485-4500	485-4501
Web: www.volex.com					
Weidmuller Inc 821 Southlake Blvd	Richmond	VA	23236	804-794-2877	379-2593
TF Cust Svc: 800-849-9343 ■ Web: www.weidmuller.com					
Wells-CTI Inc 1498 SE Tech Ctr Pl Suite 320	Vancouver	WA	98683	360-433-6230	433-6231
Web: www.wellscti.com					
Zierick Mfg Corp 131 Radio Cr	Mount Kisco	NY	10549	914-666-2911	666-0216
TF: 800-882-8020 ■ Web: www.zierick.com					

819 WIRING DEVICES - NONCURRENT-CARRYING

Company	City	State	ZIP	Phone	Fax
Adalet 4801 W 150th St	Cleveland	OH	44135	216-267-9000	267-1681*
*Fax: Sales ■ Web: www.adalet.com					
Allied Moulded Products Inc 222 N Union St	Bryan	OH	43506	419-636-4217	636-2450
Web: www.alliedmoulded.com					
Aluma-Form Inc 3625 Old Getwell Rd	Memphis	TN	38118	901-362-0100	794-9515
Web: www.alumaform.com					
Bedford Materials Co Inc 7676 Allegheny Rd	Manns Choice	PA	15550	800-773-4276	623-9199*
*Fax Area Code: 814 ■ TF: 800-773-4276 ■ Web: www.bedfordmaterials.com					
Bridgeport Fittings Inc 705 Lordship Blvd	Stratford	CT	06615	203-377-5944	381-3488
Web: www.bptfittings.com					
Chalfant Mfg Co 11525 Madison Ave	Cleveland	OH	44102	216-521-7922	521-6854
Web: www.chalfantcabletray.com					
Chase & Sons Inc 19 Highland Ave	Randolph	MA	02368	781-963-2601	963-9584
TF: 800-323-4182 ■ Web: www.chasecorp.com					
Conduit Pipe Products Co 1501 W Main St	West Jefferson	OH	43162	614-879-9114	879-5185
TF: 800-848-6125 ■ Web: www.conduitpipe.com					
Cooper B-Line Inc 509 W Monroe St	Highland	IL	62249	618-654-2184	356-1438*
*Fax Area Code: 800 ■ TF: 800-851-7415 ■ Web: www.cooperindustries.com					
Cottrell Paper Co Inc 1135 Rock City Rd PO Box 35	Rock City Falls	NY	12863	518-885-1702	885-1702
TF: 800-948-3559 ■ Web: www.cottrellpaper.com					
Durham Co 722 Durham Rd	Lebanon	MO	65536	417-532-7121	532-2366
Web: www.durhamcompany.com					
EGS Electrical Group LLC 9377 W Higgins Rd	Rosemont	IL	60018	847-268-6000	268-6060
TF: 800-621-1506 ■ Web: www.egseg.com					
Electri-Flex Co 222 Central Ave	Roselle	IL	60172	630-529-2920	529-0482
TF: 800-323-6174 ■ Web: www.electriflex.com					
Electric & Gas Technology Inc 3233 W Kingsley Rd	Garland	TX	75041	972-840-3223	271-8925*
Electro-Term/Hollingsworth 90 Memorial Dr	Springfield	MA	01104	413-734-6469	733-0827
TF: 800-638-8376 ■ Web: www.hollingsworth.com					
Flex-Cable 20 W Huron St	Pontiac	MI	48342	248-332-6900	332-4828
TF: 800-245-3539 ■ Web: www.flexcable.com					
Gaylord Mfg Co 1088 Montclaire Dr	Ceres	CA	95307	209-538-3313	
TF: 800-375-0091 ■ Web: www.gaylordmfg.com					
Gund Co 2121 Walton Rd	Saint Louis	MO	63114	314-423-5200	423-9009
Web: www.thegundcompany.com					
Hoffman Enclosures Inc 2100 Hoffman Way	Anoka	MN	55303	763-421-2240	422-2178
Web: www.hoffmanonline.com					
Hubbell Killark 3940 Martin Luther King Dr	Saint Louis	MO	63113	314-531-0460	531-7164
Web: www.hubbell-killark.com					
Hubbell Premise Wiring Inc 23 Clara Dr	Mystic	CT	06355	800-626-0005	535-8328*
*Fax Area Code: 860 ■ TF: 800-626-0005 ■ Web: www.hubbell-premise.com					
Hubbell RACO 3902 W Sample St	South Bend	IN	46619	574-234-7151	283-4244
TF: 800-722-6437 ■ Web: www.hubbell-raco.com					
Hubbell Wiegmann 501 W Apple St	Freeburg	IL	62243	618-539-3193	539-5794
Web: www.hubbell-wiegmann.com					
Hughes Bros Inc 210 N 13th St PO Box 159	Seward	NE	68434	402-643-2991	643-2149
Web: www.hughesbros.com					
ICO-RALLY Corp 2575 E Bayshore Rd	Palo Alto	CA	94303	650-856-9900	856-2006*
*Fax Area Code: 800 ■ Web: www.icorally.com					
Icore International Inc 3780 Flightline Dr	Santa Rosa	CA	95403	707-535-2700	521-2524
Web: www.icoregroup.com					
Ideal Industries Inc 1000 Pk Ave	Sycamore	IL	60178	815-895-5181	899-7712
TF: 800-435-0705 ■ Web: www.idealindustries.com					
Joslyn Sunbank Co LLC 1740 Commerce Way	Paso Robles	CA	93446	805-238-2840	238-0241*
*Fax: Cust Svc ■ TF: 800-275-8777 ■ Web: www.sunbankcorp.com					
Kortick Mfg Co 2230 Davis Ct	Hayward	CA	94545	510-856-3600	856-3606
Web: www.kortick.com					
LoDan Electronics Inc 3311 N Kennicott Ave	Arlington Heights	IL	60004	847-398-5311	398-5340
TF: 800-401-4995 ■ Web: www.lodanelec.com					
MacLean Power Systems 11411 Addison St	Franklin Park	IL	60131	847-455-0014	455-0029*
*Fax: Sales ■ Web: www.macleanpower.com					

Phone Fax

Monti Inc 333 W Seymour Ave...................... Cincinnati OH 45216 513-761-7775 948-6858
Web: www.monti-inc.com

MP Husky Corp
204 Old Piedmont Hwy PO Box 16749.............. Greenville SC 29605 864-234-4800 234-4822
TF: 800-277-4810 ■ Web: www.mphusky.com

Mulberry Metal Products Inc 2199 Stanley Terr .... Union NJ 07083 908-688-8850 688-7294
Web: www.mulberrymetal.com

Ngk-locke Polymer Insulators Inc
1609 Diamond Springs Rd.....................Virginia Beach VA 23455 757-460-3649 460-3550
Web: www.ngk-polymer.com

O-Z/Gedney 9377 W Higgins Rd.................... Rosemont IL 60018 847-268-6000 356-4714*
*Fax Area Code: 800 ■ TF: 800-621-1506 ■ Web: www.o-zgedney.com

Ohio Brass Co 1850 Richland Ave E ....Aiken SC 29801 803-648-8386 642-2959
Web: www.hubbellpowersystems.com

Opti-Com Mfg Network Co Inc 259 Plauche St ....Harahan LA 70123 504-736-0331 733-9046
TF: 800-345-8774 ■ Web: www.omni-opti.com

Rittal Corp 1 Rittal Pl.............................Springfield OH 45504 937-399-0500 390-5599
TF: 800-477-4000 ■ Web: www.rittal-corp.com

Robroy Industries Inc 10 River Rd.....................Verona PA 15147 412-828-2100 828-8934
TF: 800-500-0333 ■ Web: www.robroy.com

Saginaw Control & Engineering Inc
95 Midland Rd ....Saginaw MI 48638 989-799-6871 799-4524
TF: 800-234-6871 ■ Web: www.saginawcontrol.com

Thomas & Betts Corp 8155 T & B Blvd ....Memphis TN 38125 901-252-8000 252-1306
NYSE: TNB ■ TF: 800-858-6022 ■ Web: www.tnb.com

TJ Cope Inc 11500 Norcom Rd .... Philadelphia PA 19154 215-961-2570 961-2580
TF: 800-426-4293 ■ Web: www.tjcope.com

Varflex Corp 512 W Ct St PO Box 551....................Rome NY 13442 315-336-4400 336-0005
TF: 800-648-4014 ■ Web: www.varflex.com

Virginia Plastics Co Inc
3453 Aerial Way Dr PO Box 4577.................... Roanoke VA 24018 540-981-9700 981-2022
TF: 888-905-2225 ■ Web: www.vaplastics.com

Weidmann Electrical Technology
1 Gordon Mills Way PO Box 903 .... Saint Johnsbury VT 05819 802-748-8106 748-8029
TF: 800-242-6748 ■ Web: www.weidmann-electrical.com

820 WOOD MEMBERS - STRUCTURAL

Phone Fax

Alpine Engineered Products Inc
1200 Pk Central Blvd S PO Box 2225........... Pompano Beach FL 33061 954-781-3333 977-3149
TF: 800-735-8055 ■ Web: www.alpeng.com

American Laminators 600 Applegate St PO Box 297........ Drain OR 97435 541-836-2000 836-7144
Web: www.americanlaminators.com

Armstrong Lumber Co Inc 2709 Auburn Way N .... Auburn WA 98002 253-833-6666 833-5878
TF: 800-868-9066 ■ Web: www.armstrong-homes.com

Automated Bldg Components Inc
2359 Grant Rd ....North Baltimore OH 45872 419-257-2152 257-2779
TF: 800-837-2152 ■ Web: www.abctruss.com

Automated Products Inc 1812 Karau Dr.............Marshfield WI 54449 715-387-3426 387-6588

Bradco Supply Corp 13 Production Way ....Avenel NJ 07001 732-382-3400 382-6577
TF: 877-427-2320 ■ Web: www.bradcosupply.com

Buettner Bros Lumber Co 700 7th Ave SW.............Cullman AL 35055 256-734-4221 737-8102
TF: 800-500-0669

Burns Construction Inc 6676 S Old US Hwy 31 .... Macy IN 46951 574-382-2315 382-2522
TF Cust Svc: 800-552-3309

California Truss Co 23665 Cajalco Rd ....Perris CA 92570 951-657-7491 657-0486
Web: www.caltruss.com

Columbia Forest Products Inc
222 SW Columbia St Suite 1575 ....Portland OR 97201 503-224-5300 224-5294
TF: 800-547-4261 ■ Web: www.columbiaforestproducts.com

East Coast Lumber & Supply Co 308 Ave A..........Fort Pierce FL 34950 772-466-1700 465-8678
Web: www.eastcoastlumber.com

Engineered Bldg Component Co
146 Washington Ave S ....Hopkins MN 55343 952-935-4902 935-4902

Enwood Structures Inc
5724 McCrimmon Pkwy PO Box 2002...............Morrisville NC 27560 919-467-6155 469-2536
TF: 800-777-8648 ■ Web: www.enwood.com

Fullerton Bldg Systems Inc (FBS)
34620 250th St PO Box 308..................... Worthington MN 56187 507-376-3128 376-9530
TF: 800-450-9782 ■ Web: www.fullertonbuildingsystems.com

Gang Nail Truss Co of Visalia
1440 N Shirk Rd.....................................Visalia CA 93291 559-651-2121 651-1832

HM Stauffer & Sons Inc 33 Glenola Dr..................Leola PA 17540 717-656-2811 656-4392
Web: www.hmstauffeur.com

J C Snavely & Sons Inc 150 Main St................Landisville PA 17538 717-898-2241 898-5208
TF: 800-444-4663 ■ Web: www.jcsnavely.com

Laminate Technologies Inc 161 Maule Rd............... Tiffin OH 44883 419-448-0812 448-0811
Web: www.lamtech.net

Laminated Wood Systems Inc (LWS)
1327 285th Rd PO Box 386 .... Seward NE 68434 402-643-4708 643-4374
TF: 800-949-3526 ■ Web: www.lwsinc.com

Laminators Inc 3255 Penn St .... Hatfield PA 19440 215-723-8107 721-4669
TF: 877-663-4277 ■ Web: www.signboards.com

Lawrence R Mccoy & Co Inc
100 Front St Suite 800 .... Worcester MA 01608 508-368-7700 890-1199
TF: 800-346-2269 ■ Web: www.lrmccoy.com

Molpus Co The
502 Valley View Dr PO Box 59 .... Philadelphia MS 39350 601-656-3373 656-4947
TF: 800-535-5434 ■ Web: www.molpus.com

Montgomery Truss & Panel Inc
803 W Main St ....Grove City PA 16127 724-458-7500 458-0765
TF: 800-245-0334

Okaw Truss Inc 368 E St Rt 133 .... Arthur IL 61911 217-543-3371 543-3376
Web: www.okawtruss.com

Oso Lumber & Hardware Inc
21015 State Rd 9 NE..............................Arlington WA 98223 360-435-8397 435-6035

Powell Structural Systems Inc
130 Johnson Dr ....Delaware OH 43015 740-549-0465 549-0474
TF: 800-351-7176

Robbins Mfg Co
13001 N Nebraska Ave PO Box 17939 .... Tampa FL 33682 813-971-3030 972-3980
TF: 800-282-9336 ■ Web: www.robbinslumber.com

Roof Structures Inc 3333 Yale Way..................Fremont CA 94538 510-226-7171 226-8989
Web: www.roofstructures.com

Sentinel Structures Inc 477 S Peck Ave............. Peshtigo WI 54157 715-582-4544 582-4932
Web: www.sentinelstructures.com

Shelter Systems Ltd
1025 Meadow Branch Rd .... Westminster MD 21158 410-876-3900 857-5754
Web: www.sheltersystems.com

Shook Builder Supply Co 1400 16th St NE .... Hickory NC 28601 828-328-2051 328-2425
TF: 800-968-0758

Southern Components Inc
7360 Julie Frances Rd ....Shreveport LA 71129 318-687-3330 686-5159
TF: 800-256-2144 ■ Web: www.southerncomponents.com

Standard Structures Inc 5900 Pruitt Ave ....Windsor CA 95492 707-836-8100 836-8109
TF: 800-862-4936 ■ Web: www.standardstructures.com

Stark Truss Co Inc 109 Miles Ave SW ....Canton OH 44710 330-478-2100 478-9413
TF: 800-933-2258 ■ Web: www.starktruss.com

Stow Co The 3311 Windquest Dr..................... Holland MI 49424 616-399-3311 399-8784
TF: 800-562-4257 ■ Web: www.windquestco.com

Structural Wood Corp 4000 Labore Rd .... Saint Paul MN 55110 651-426-8111 426-6859
TF: 800-652-9058 ■ Web: www.structural-wood.com

Structural Wood Systems 321 Dohrimier St.......... Greenville AL 36037 334-382-6534 382-4260
Web: www.structuralwood.com

Tacoma Truss Systems Inc
20617 Mountain Hwy E .... Spanaway WA 98387 253-847-2204 847-2207
Web: www.tacomatruss.com

Timber Truss Housing Systems Inc
525 McClelland St PO Box 996 .... Salem VA 24153 540-387-0273 389-0849
TF: 800-766-9072 ■ Web: www.timbertruss.com

Trusco Inc 12527 Porr Rd .... Doylestown OH 44230 330-658-2027 658-4979
TF: 800-847-5841 ■ Web: www.truscoinc.com

Truss Mfg Co Inc 17317 Westfield Pk Rd .... Westfield IN 46074 317-896-2571 896-3776
TF: 800-467-4525

Trussway Ltd 9411 Alcorn Rd ....Houston TX 77093 713-691-6900 691-2064
Web: www.trussway.com

Valley Best-Way Bldg Supply 118 S Union Rd......... Spokane WA 99206 509-924-1250 922-5420
TF: 800-722-4491 ■ Web: www.valleybest-way.com

Villaume Industries Inc 2926 Lone Oak Cir .... Saint Paul MN 55121 651-454-3610 454-8556
TF Cust Svc: 800-488-3610 ■ Web: www.villaume.com

821 WOOD PRESERVING

Phone Fax

Appalachian Timber Services Inc
3939 Roswell Rd NE Suite 100.......................Marietta GA 30062 770-321-2500 321-2520
Web: www.atstimber.com

Atlantic Wood Industries Inc PO Box 1608...........Savannah GA 31402 912-964-1234 964-2633
Web: www.atlanticwood.com

Bell Lumber & Pole Co
778 1st St NW PO Box 120786..................New Brighton MN 55112 651-633-4334 633-8852
TF: 877-633-4334 ■ Web: www.bellpole.com

Brooks Mfg Co 2120 Pacific St PO Box 7 .... Bellingham WA 98227 360-733-1700 734-6668
Web: www.brooksmfg.com

Brown Wood Preserving Co Inc
6201 Camp Ground Rd...........................Louisville KY 40216 502-448-2337 448-9944
TF: 800-537-1765

Building Products Plus 12317 Almeda Rd ....Houston TX 77045 713-715-5506 433-7068
TF: 800-460-8627 ■ Web: www.buildingproductsplus.com

Burke-Parsons-Bowlby Corp Rt 21 S.................. Ripley WV 25271 304-372-2211 372-1211
TF: 800-272-8437 ■ Web: www.bpbcorp.com

Conrad Forest Products 68765 Wildwood Dr........ North Bend OR 97459 800-356-7146 756-0131*
*Fax Area Code: 541 ■ TF: 800-356-7146 ■ Web: www.conradfp.com

Cox Industries Inc
860 Cannon Bridge Rd PO Box 1124..............Orangeburg SC 29116 803-534-7467 534-1410
TF: 800-476-4401 ■ Web: www.coxwood.com

Elder Wood Preserving Co Inc
334 Elder Wood Rd............................... Mansura LA 71350 318-964-2196 964-5276
TF: 800-467-8018 ■ Web: www.elderwoodpreserving.com

Great Southern Wood Preserving Inc
1100 US Hwy 431 N...............................Abbeville AL 36310 334-585-2291 585-4353
TF: 800-633-7539 ■ Web: www.greatsouthernwood.com

Hoover Treated Wood Products Inc 154 Wire Rd......Thomson GA 30824 706-595-1264 595-8462
Web: www.frtw.com

Idaho Cedar Sales Inc 221 N Main St PO Box 399 ....Troy ID 83871 208-835-2161 835-2772

JH Baxter & Co 1700 S El Camino Real # 365..........San Mateo CA 94402 650-349-0201 570-6878
TF: 800-780-7073 ■ Web: www.jhbaxter.com

Koppers Inc 436 7th Ave .... Pittsburgh PA 15219 412-227-2001 227-2333
NYSE: KOP ■ TF: 800-321-9876 ■ Web: www.koppers.com

McFarland Cascade 1640 E Marc St PO Box 1496 .... Tacoma WA 98421 253-572-3033 627-0764
TF Cust Svc: 800-426-8430 ■ Web: www.ldm.com

Osmose Inc 980 Ellicott St...........................Buffalo NY 14209 716-882-5905 882-5139
TF: 800-877-7653 ■ Web: www.osmose.com

Pearson Lumber Co
1511 Hargrove Rd PO Box 1548.................... Tuscaloosa AL 35403 205-345-5516 345-5518

Perma Treat Corp 74 Airline Dr .... Durham CT 06422 860-349-1133 349-1365

Professional Coaters Inc
2148 Port of Tacoma Rd .... Tacoma WA 98421 253-627-1141 627-1150

Robbins Mfg Co
13001 N Nebraska Ave PO Box 17939 .... Tampa FL 33682 813-971-3030 972-3980
TF: 800-282-9336 ■ Web: www.robbinslumber.com

Rocky Top Bldg Products Inc
1050 N Main St ....Rocky Mount VA 24151 540-483-5264 483-1651
TF: 800-274-3443 ■ Web: www.rockytopwood.com

Seaman Timber Co Inc
1051 Hwy 25 S PO Box 372................. South Montevallo AL 35115 205-665-2536 665-2545
TF: 800-782-8155

Shenandoah Wood Preserving Co
PO Box 310 ....Scotland Neck NC 27874 252-826-4151 826-3369

Tolleson Lumber Co Inc 903 Jernigan St................ Perry GA 31069 478-988-3800 987-0160
TF: 800-768-2105 ■ Web: www.tollesonlumber.com

Company	City	State	ZIP	Phone	Fax
Western Wood Preserving Co 1310 Zehnder St PO Box 1250 *TF:* 800-472-7714 ■ *Web:* www.westernwoodpreserving.com	Sumner	WA	98390	253-863-8191	863-9129
Wood Preservers Inc 15939 Historyland Hwy PO Box 158 *TF:* 800-368-2536 ■ *Web:* www.woodpreservers.com	Warsaw	VA	22572	804-333-4022	333-9269

822 WOOD PRODUCTS - RECONSTITUTED

Company	City	State	ZIP	Phone	Fax
AinsworthßEngineered Canada LP 1055 Dunsmuir St PO Box 49307 *TF:* 877-661-3200 ■ *Web:* www.ainsworthengineered.com	Vancouver	BC	V7X1L3	604-661-3200	661-3201
Duraflame Inc 2894 Mt Diablo Ave PO Box 1230 *Web:* www.duraflame.com	Stockton	CA	95201	209-461-6600	462-9412
Forest Conex Products Inc PO Box 47256 *TF:* 888-811-8882 ■ *Web:* www.conexforestproducts.com	Jacksonville	FL	32247	904-399-4401	399-4403
Frontier Resources LLC 25310 Jeans Rd PO Box 876	Veneta	OR	97487	541-935-3626	431-1990
Homasote Co 932 Lower Ferry Rd PO Box 7240 *TF:* 800-257-9491 ■ *Web:* www.homasote.com	West Trenton	NJ	08628	609-883-3300	883-3497
Liberty Wood Products 874 Iotla Church Rd *Web:* www.libertywood.com	Franklin	NC	28734	828-524-7958	369-7652
Panel Processing Inc 120 N Industrial Hwy *TF:* 800-433-7142 ■ *Web:* www.panel.com	Alpena	MI	49707	989-356-9007	356-9000
Panolam Industries International Inc 20 Progress Dr *TF:* 800-672-6652 ■ *Web:* www.panolam.com	Shelton	CT	06484	203-925-1556	225-0051
Pasquier Panel Products Inc 1510 Puyallup St PO Box 1170 *Web:* www.pasquierpanel.com	Sumner	WA	98390	253-863-6323	891-7993
Potlatch Corp 601 W 1st Ave Suite 1600 *NASDAQ: PCH* ■ *Web:* www.potlatchcorp.com	Spokane	WA	99201	509-835-1500	835-1555
Potlatch Corp Wood Products Div 805 Mill Rd PO Box 1388 *Web:* www.potlatchcorp.com	Lewiston	ID	83501	208-799-0123	799-1918
Rex Lumber Co 840 Main St *TF:* 800-343-0567 ■ *Web:* www.rexlumber.com	Acton	MA	01720	978-263-0055	263-9806
Tectum Inc 105 S 6th St *TF:* 888-977-9691 ■ *Web:* www.tectum.com	Newark	OH	43055	740-345-9691	349-9305
Temple-Inland Inc 1300 S Mopac Expy *NYSE: TIN* ■ *TF:* 800-826-8807 ■ *Web:* www.temple-inland.com	Austin	TX	78746	512-434-5800	434-8723

823 WOOD PRODUCTS - SHAPED & TURNED

Company	City	State	ZIP	Phone	Fax
AinsworthßEngineered Canada LP 1055 Dunsmuir St PO Box 49307 *TF:* 877-661-3200 ■ *Web:* www.ainsworthengineered.com	Vancouver	BC	V7X1L3	604-661-3200	661-3201
Brown Wood Products Co 7040 N Lawndale Ave **Fax Area Code:* 800 ■ *TF:* 800-328-5858 ■ *Web:* www.brownwoodprod.com	Lincolnwood	IL	60712	847-673-4780	884-0423*
Burroughs-Ross-Colville Co 301 Depot St *Web:* www.brclumber.com	McMinnville	TN	37110	931-473-2111	473-5350
Chicago Dowel Co Inc 4700 W Grand Ave *TF:* 800-333-6935 ■ *Web:* www.chicagodowel.com	Chicago	IL	60639	773-622-2000	622-2047
Davidson Plyforms Inc 5505 33rd St SE *Web:* www.plyforms.com	Grand Rapids	MI	49512	616-956-0033	956-0041
Frank A Edmunds & Co 6111 S Sayre Ave *TF:* 800-447-3516	Chicago	IL	60638	773-586-2772	586-2783
Gateway Corp 100 E 5th St	Corinth	MS	38834	662-286-3351	
Indian Country Inc 791 Airport Rd	Deposit	NY	13754	607-467-3801	467-4559
Intermountain Wood Products Inc 1948 S W Temple *Web:* www.intermountainwood.com	Salt Lake City	UT	84115	801-486-5414	466-0428
Jarden Home Brands 345 S High St Suite 201 *TF Cust Svc:* 800-428-8150 ■ *Web:* www.jardenhomebrands.com	Mincie	IN	47305	765-281-5000	281-5450
Michigan Maple Block Co 1420 Standish Ave *Web:* www.mapleblock.com	Petoskey	MI	49770	231-347-4170	347-7975
Owens Handle Co Inc 4200 N Frazier St	Conroe	TX	77303	936-856-2981	856-2260
Saunders Bros Inc 170 Forest St *TF:* 800-343-0675 ■ *Web:* www.saundersbros.com	Westbrook	ME	04092	207-854-2551	854-1243
WJ Cowee LLC 28 Taylor Ave *TF:* 800-862-6933 ■ *Web:* www.cowee.com	Berlin	NY	12022	518-658-9000	658-2244

824 WOODWORKING MACHINERY

Company	City	State	ZIP	Phone	Fax
Acrowood Corp 4425 S 3rd Ave PO Box 1028 *Web:* www.acrowood.com	Everett	WA	98203	425-258-3555	252-7622
Baker Products Hwy 21 N PO Box 128 *TF:* 800-548-6914 ■ *Web:* www.baker-online.com	Ellington	MO	63638	573-663-7711	663-2787
Capital Machine Co Inc 2801 Roosevelt Ave *Web:* www.capitalmachineco.com	Indianapolis	IN	46218	317-638-6661	636-5122
Coe Mfg Inc 609 Bank St *Web:* www.coemfg.com	Painesville	OH	44077	440-352-9381	352-1487
Corley Mfg Co 2900 Crescent Cir PO Box 471 *Web:* www.corleymfg.com	Chattanooga	TN	37401	423-698-0284	622-3258
Diehl Machines 981 S Wabash St PO Box 465 *Web:* www.diehlmachines.com	Wabash	IN	46992	260-563-2102	563-0206
HMC Corp 284 Maple St *Web:* www.hmccorp.com	Contoocook	NH	03229	603-746-4691	746-4819
ITW Amp 888 Forest Edge Dr **Fax Area Code:* 800 ■ *TF:* 800-322-4204 ■ *Web:* www.itwamp.com	Vernon Hills	IL	60061	847-918-1970	426-7019*
James L. Taylor Mfg Co 108 Parker Ave *TF:* 800-952-1320 ■ *Web:* www.jamesltaylor.com	Poughkeepsie	NY	12601	845-452-3780	452-0764
Jenkins Systems LLC 4336 Gateway Dr *Web:* www.jenkins-systems.com	Sheboygan	WI	53081	920-452-2110	452-2338
Kimwood Corp 77684 Oregon 99 *TF:* 800-942-4401 ■ *Web:* www.kimwood.com	Cottage Grove	OR	97424	541-942-4401	942-0719
KVAL Inc 825 Petaluma Blvd S *TF:* 800-553-5825 ■ *Web:* www.kvalinc.com	Petaluma	CA	94952	707-762-7367	762-0621
McDonough Mfg Co 2320 Melby St PO Box 510 *Web:* www.mcdonough-mfg.com	Eau Claire	WI	54702	715-834-7755	834-3968
Memphis Machinery & Supply Co Inc 2881 Directors Cove *TF:* 800-388-4485 ■ *Web:* www.memphismachinery.com	Memphis	TN	38131	901-527-4443	529-9663
Mereen-Johnson Machine Co 4401 Lyndale Ave N *TF:* 888-465-7297 ■ *Web:* www.mereen-johnson.com	Minneapolis	MN	55412	612-529-7791	529-0120
Michael Weining Inc 124 Crosslake Pk Dr PO Box 3158 *Web:* www.weinigusa.com	Mooresville	NC	28117	704-799-0100	799-7400
Oliver Machinery Co 1210 Andover Pk E *TF:* 800-559-5065 ■ *Web:* www.olivermachinery.net	Tukwila	WA	98188	206-575-2722	575-2723
Pacific Hoe Co 2700 SE Tacoma St *TF:* 800-547-5537	Portland	OR	97202	503-234-9501	234-3506
Pendu Mfg Inc 718 N Shirk Rd *TF:* 800-233-0471 ■ *Web:* www.pendu.com	New Holland	PA	17557	717-354-4348	355-2148
Premier Gear & Machine Works Inc 1700 NW Thurman St *Web:* www.premier-gear.com	Portland	OR	97209	503-227-3514	227-1611
Safety Speed Cut Mfg Co Inc 13943 Lincoln St NE *TF:* 800-772-2327 ■ *Web:* www.safetyspeedcut.com	Ham Lake	MN	55304	763-755-1600	755-6080
Schutte Lumber Co 3001 SW Blvd *Web:* www.schuttelumber.com	Kansas City	MO	64108	816-753-6262	753-7935
Selway Corp PO Box 287 *Web:* www.selwaycorp.com	Stevensville	MT	59870	406-777-5471	777-5473
Thermwood Corp 904 Buffaloville Rd *TF Mktg:* 800-533-6901 ■ *Web:* www.thermwood.com	Dale	IN	47523	812-937-4476	937-2956
USNR Inc 558 Robinson Rd PO Box 310 *TF:* 800-289-8767 ■ *Web:* www.usnr.com	Woodland	WA	98674	360-225-8267	225-8017
Viking Engineering & Development Inc 5750 Main St NE *TF Sales:* 800-328-2403 ■ *Web:* www.vikingeng.com	Fridley	MN	55432	763-571-2400	586-1319
Voorwood Co 2350 Barney St PO Box 1127 *TF:* 800-826-0089 ■ *Web:* www.voorwood.com	Anderson	CA	96007	530-365-3311	365-3315
Yates-American Machine Co Inc 2880 Kennedy Dr *TF:* 800-752-6377 ■ *Web:* www.yatesamerican.com	Beloit	WI	53511	608-364-0333	364-0481

825 WORLD TRADE CENTERS

Company	City	State	ZIP	Phone	Fax
Atlantic Canada World Trade Centre 1800 Argyle St Suite 4126	Halifax	NS	B3J3N8	902-421-1302	420-8308
Bay Area World Trade Ctr 544 Water St *Web:* www.bawtc.com	Oakland	CA	94607	510-273-7350	273-7352
Greater Kansas City World Trade Ctr 911 Main St Suite 2600	Kansas City	MO	64105	816-374-5483	274-6483
Houston World Trade Ctr Greater Houston Partnership 1200 Smith St Suite 700 *Web:* www.houston.org	Houston	TX	77002	713-844-3639	844-0635
Kansas World Trade Ctr 125 N Market St Suite 1260 *Web:* www.kansaswtc.org	Wichita	KS	67202	316-264-5982	264-5983
Kentucky World Trade Ctr 333 W Vine St Suite 1600 *Web:* www.kwtc.org	Lexington	KY	40507	859-258-3139	233-0658
Messe Frankfurt Inc 1600 Parkwood Cir Suite 615 *Web:* www.usa.messefrankfurt.com	Atlanta	GA	30339	770-984-8016	984-8023
Minnesota World Trade Ctr 30 E 7th St E Suite 110	Saint Paul	MN	55101	651-297-4222	
Montana World Trade Ctr Gallagher Business Bldg University of Montana Suite 257 *TF:* 888-773-2703 ■ *Web:* www.mwtc.org	Missoula	MT	59812	406-243-6982	243-5259
Northern California World Trade Ctr 917 7th St *Web:* www.norcalwtc.org	Sacramento	CA	95814	916-319-4277	443-2672
Ronald Reagan Bldg & International Trade Ctr 1300 Pennsylvania Ave NW *TF:* 888-393-3306 ■ *Web:* www.itcdc.com	Washington	DC	20004	202-312-1300	312-1310
San Diego World Trade Ctr 2980 Pacific Hwy *Web:* www.wtcsd.org	San Diego	CA	92101	619-615-0868	615-0876
Seaport World Trade Center Boston 200 Seaport Blvd **Fax:* Sales ■ *Web:* www.seaportboston.com	Boston	MA	02210	617-385-4212	385-5090*
South Carolina World Trade Ctr 2750 Speissegger Dr Suite 100	North Charleston	SC	29405	843-852-9880	852-9890
State of Hawaii World Trade Ctr Business Development & Marketing Div 250 S Hotel St 5th Fl	Honolulu	HI	96813	808-587-2750	586-2589
Toronto Board of Trade 1 First Canadian Pl PO Box 60 *Web:* www.bot.com	Toronto	ON	M5X1C1	416-366-6811	366-8406
World Trade Center Alaska 431 W 7th Ave Suite 108 *Web:* www.wtcak.org	Anchorage	AK	99501	907-278-7233	278-2982
World Trade Center Assn Los Angeles-Long Beach 350 S Figueroa St Suite 272 *Web:* www.wtca-lalb.org	Los Angeles	CA	90071	213-680-1888	680-1878

	City	State	Zip	Phone	Fax
World Trade Center Atlanta 303 Peachtree St NE Lower Lobby 100 *Web:* www.wtcatlanta.com	Atlanta	GA	30308	404-880-9595	813-6674
World Trade Center Baltimore 401 E Pratt St Suite 232 *Web:* www.wtci.org	Baltimore	MD	21202	410-576-0022	576-0751
World Trade Center Delaware 702 N W St *Web:* www.wtcde.com	Wilmington	DE	19801	302-656-7905	656-7956
World Trade Center Denver 1625 Broadway Suite 680 *Web:* www.wtcdn.com	Denver	CO	80202	303-592-5760	592-5228
World Trade Center Detroit/Windsor 16630 Southfield Rd PO Box 637 *Web:* www.wtcdw.com	Allen Park	MI	48101	313-388-2345	388-9945
World Trade Center Illinois 200 E Randolph St Suite 2200	Chicago	IL	60601	312-467-0550	467-0615
World Trade Center Miami 1007 N America Way Suite 500 *Web:* www.worldtrade.org	Miami	FL	33132	305-871-7910	871-7904
World Trade Center Montreal 380 St Antoine St W Suite 6000 *Web:* www.ccmm.qc.ca	Montreal	QC	H2Y3X7	514-871-4000	871-1255
World Trade Center Norfolk 101 W Main St	Norfolk	VA	23510	757-627-9440	627-1548
World Trade Center North Carolina 10900 World Trade Blvd Suite 112 *Web:* www.wtcnc.org	Raleigh	NC	27617	919-281-2742	281-2741
World Trade Center of New Orleans 365 Canal St Suite 1120 *Web:* wtcno.org	New Orleans	LA	70130	504-529-1601	529-1691
World Trade Center Orlando 550 N Bumby Ave *Web:* www.worldtradecenterorlando.org	Orlando	FL	32803	407-649-1899	894-5740
World Trade Center Palm Beach 777 S Flagler Dr Suite 800-W *Web:* www.wtcpalmbeach.com	West Palm Beach	FL	33401	561-712-1443	712-1445
World Trade Center Portland 121 SW Salmon St Suite 1350 *Web:* www.wtcpd.com	Portland	OR	97204	503-464-8888	464-8880
World Trade Center Saint Louis 121 S Meramec Ave Suite 1111 *Web:* www.worldtradecenter-stl.com	Saint Louis	MO	63105	314-615-8141	615-8140
World Trade Center San Antonio 118 Broadway Suite 324	San Antonio	TX	78205	210-978-7600	978-7610
World Trade Center Seattle 2200 Alaskan Way Suite 410 *Web:* www.wtcseattle.com	Seattle	WA	98121	206-441-5144	770-7923
World Trade Center Tacoma 950 Pacific Ave Suite 310 *Web:* www.wtcta.org	Tacoma	WA	98402	253-396-1022	396-1033
World Trade Center Tampa Bay (WTC) 1101 Ch Side Dr 2nd Fl *Web:* www.wtctampa.com	Tampa	FL	33602	813-864-3000	864-4800
World Trade Center Wisconsin 750 N Lincoln Memorial Dr *Web:* www.wistrade.org	Milwaukee	WI	53202	414-274-3840	274-3846

826 ZOOS & WILDLIFE PARKS

SEE ALSO Aquariums - Public p. 1400; Botanical Gardens & Arboreta p. 1537

	City	State	Zip	Phone	Fax
Abilene Zoological Gardens 2070 Zoo Ln Nelson Pk *Web:* www.abilenetx.com	Abilene	TX	79602	325-676-6085	676-6084
Admiralty Island & Pack Creek Bear Preserve 8510 Mendenhall Loop Re	Juneau	AK	99801	907-586-8800	586-8808
African Lion Safari & Game Farm RR 1 *TF:* 800-461-9453 ■ *Web:* www.lionsafari.com	Cambridge	ON	N1R5S2	519-623-2620	623-9542
African Safari Wildlife Park 267 S Lightner Rd *TF:* 800-521-2660 ■ *Web:* www.africansafariwildlifepark.com	Port Clinton	OH	43452	419-732-3606	734-1919
Akron Zoological Park 500 Edgewood Ave *Web:* www.akronzoo.org	Akron	OH	44307	330-375-2550	375-2575
Alameda Park Zoo 1021 N White Sands Blvd *Web:* www.ci.alamogordo.nm.us	Alamogordo	NM	88310	575-439-4290	439-4103
Alaska Wildlife Conservation Ctr Milepost 79 Seward Hwy *TF:* 866-773-2025 ■ *Web:* www.alaskawildlife.org	Portage Glacier	AK	99587	907-783-2025	783-2370
Alaska Zoo 4731 O'Malley Rd *Web:* www.alaskazoo.org	Anchorage	AK	99507	907-346-3242	346-2673
Alexandria Zoological Park 3016 Masonic Dr *Web:* www.thealexandriazoo.com	Alexandria	LA	71301	318-441-6810	473-1149
Alligator Adventure 4604 Hwy 17 S Barefoot Landing *Web:* www.alligatoradventure.com	North Myrtle Beach	SC	29598	843-361-0789	361-0742
Amarillo Zoo NE 24 dumas Hwy Thompson Pk *Web:* www.amarillozoo.org	Amarillo	TX	79105	806-381-7911	381-7901
Animal Ark Wildlife Sanctuary & Nature Ctr 1265 Deerlodge Rd **Fax Area Code:* 866 ■ *Web:* www.animalark.org	Reno	NV	89508	775-970-3111	366-5771*
Arkansas Alligator Farm & Petting Zoo 847 Whittington Ave *TF:* 800-750-7891 ■ *Web:* www.arkansasalligatorfarm.com	Hot Springs	AR	71901	501-623-6172	
Assiniboine Park Zoo 460 Assiniboine Park Dr *Web:* www.zoosociety.com	Winnipeg	MB	R3P2N7	204-927-6001	832-5420
Audubon Zoo 6500 Magazine St *TF:* 800-774-7394 ■ *Web:* www.auduboninstitute.org	New Orleans	LA	70118	504-581-4629	861-2486
Austin Zoo 10807 Rawhide Trail *Web:* www.austinzoo.org	Austin	TX	78736	512-288-1490	
Beardsley Zoo 1875 Noble Ave *Web:* www.beardsleyzoo.org	Bridgeport	CT	06610	203-394-6565	394-6566
Bergen County Zoological Park 216 Forest Ave	Paramus	NJ	07652	201-262-3771	986-1788
Bever Park Zoo 2700 Bever Ave SE	Cedar Rapids	IA	52403	319-286-5761	286-5758
Binder Park Zoo 7400 Division Dr *Web:* www.binderparkzoo.org	Battle Creek	MI	49014	269-979-1351	979-8834
Binghampton Zoo at Ross Park 60 Morgan Rd *Web:* www.rossparkzoo.com	Binghamton	NY	13903	607-724-5461	724-5454
Birmingham Zoo 2630 Cahaba Rd *TF:* 888-966-2426 ■ *Web:* www.birminghamzoo.com	Birmingham	AL	35223	205-879-0409	879-9426
Blank Park Zoo 7401 SW 9th St *Web:* www.blankparkzoo.com	Des Moines	IA	50315	515-285-4722	323-8390
Bolsa Chica Ecological Reserve 3842 Warner Ave *Web:* www.bolsachica.org	Huntington Beach	CA	92649	714-846-1114	846-4065
Bowmanville Zoological Park Ltd 340 King St E *Web:* www.bowmanvillezoo.com	Bowmanville	ON	L1C3K5	905-623-5655	623-0957
Bramble Park Zoo 800 10th St NW PO Box 910 *Web:* www.brambleparkzoo.com	Watertown	SD	57201	605-882-6269	882-5232
Brandywine Zoo 1001 N Park Dr *Web:* www.brandywinezoo.org	Wilmington	DE	19802	302-571-7747	571-7787
BREC's Baton Rouge Zoo 3601 Thomas Rd *Web:* www.brzoo.org	Baton Rouge	LA	70807	225-775-3877	775-3931
Brevard Zoo 8225 N Wickham Rd *Web:* brevardzoo.org	Melbourne	FL	32940	321-254-9453	259-5966
British Columbia Wildlife Park 9077 Dallas Dr *Web:* www.bczoo.org	Kamloops	BC	V2C6V1	250-573-3242	573-2406
Bronx Zoo 2300 Southern Blvd *TF:* 800-234-5128 ■ *Web:* www.bronxzoo.com	Bronx	NY	10460	718-220-5100	
Brookfield Zoo 3300 Golf Rd *Web:* www.brookfieldzoo.org	Brookfield	IL	60513	708-485-2200	485-3532
Buffalo Zoological Gardens 300 Parkside Ave *Web:* www.buffalozoo.org	Buffalo	NY	14214	716-837-3900	837-0738
Busch Gardens Tampa Bay 10001 N McKinley Dr *TF:* 888-800-5447 ■ *Web:* www.buschgardens.com	Tampa	FL	33612	813-987-5082	987-5111
Busch Gardens Williamsburg 1 Busch Gardens Blvd **Fax Area Code:* 757 ■ **Fax:* Mktg ■ *TF:* 800-343-7946 ■ *Web:* www.buschgardens.com	Williamsburg	VA	23187	800-343-7946	253-3399*
Butterfly Pavilion & Insect Ctr 6252 W 104th Ave *Web:* www.butterflies.org	Westminster	CO	80020	303-469-5441	657-5944
Buttonwood Park Zoo 425 Hawthorn St *Web:* www.bpzoo.org	New Bedford	MA	02740	508-991-6178	979-1731
Caldwell Zoo 2203 ML King Blvd *Web:* www.caldwellzoo.org	Tyler	TX	75702	903-593-0121	595-5083
Calgary Zoo Botanical Garden & Prehistoric Park 1300 Zoo Rd NE *TF:* 800-588-9993 ■ *Web:* www.calgaryzoo.ab.ca	Calgary	AB	T2M4R8	403-232-9300	237-7582
Cameron Park Zoo 1701 N 4th St *Web:* www.cameronparkzoo.com	Waco	TX	76707	254-750-8400	750-8430
Cape May County Park & Zoo 707 Rt 9 N	Cape May Court House	NJ	08210	609-465-5271	465-5421
Capron Park Zoo 201 County St *Web:* www.capronparkzoo.com	Attleboro	MA	02703	508-222-3047	223-2208
Caribbean Gardens 1590 Goodlette-Frank Rd *TF:* 888-520-3756 ■ *Web:* www.caribbeangardens.com	Naples	FL	34102	239-262-5409	262-6866
Cat Tales Zoological Park N 17020 Newport Hwy *Web:* www.cattales.org	Mead	WA	99021	509-238-4126	238-4126
Central Florida Zoological Park 3755 NW Hwy 17-92 & I-4 PO Box 470309 *Web:* www.centralfloridazoo.org	Lake Monroe	FL	32747	407-323-4450	321-0900
Central Park Zoo 5th Ave & 64th St *Web:* www.centralparkzoo.org	New York	NY	10065	212-439-6500	988-0286
Chahinkapa Zoo & Prairie Rose Carousel 1004 RJ Hughes Dr *Web:* www.chahinkapazoo.com	Wahpeton	ND	58075	701-642-8709	642-9285
Charles Paddock Zoo 9305 Pismo Ave *Web:* www.charlespaddockzoo.org	Atascadero	CA	93422	805-461-5080	461-7625
Chattanooga Zoo 301 N Holltzclaw Ave *Web:* chattzoo.org	Chattanooga	TN	37404	423-697-1322	697-1329
Cherry Brook Zoo Inc 901 Foster Thurston Dr *Web:* www.cherrybrookzoo.com	Saint John	NB	E2K5H9	506-634-1440	634-0717
Cheyenne Mountain Zoological Park 4250 Cheyenne Mountain Zoo Rd *Web:* www.cmzoo.org	Colorado Springs	CO	80906	719-633-9925	633-2254
Cincinnati Zoo & Botanical Garden 3400 Vine St *TF:* 800-944-4776 ■ *Web:* www.cincinnatizoo.org	Cincinnati	OH	45220	513-281-4700	559-7790
Claws 'n' Paws Wild Animal Park 1475 Ledgedale Rd *Web:* www.clawsnpaws.com	Lake Ariel	PA	18436	570-698-6154	698-2957
Cleveland Metroparks Zoo 3900 Wildlife Way *Web:* www.clemetzoo.com	Cleveland	OH	44109	216-661-6500	
Clyde Peeling's Reptiland 18628 US Rt 15 *TF:* 800-737-8452 ■ *Web:* www.reptiland.com	Allenwood	PA	17810	570-538-1869	538-1714
Columbian Park Zoo 1915 Scott St *Web:* www.city.lafayette.in.us/zoo/division.php?fDD=34-38	Lafayette	IN	47904	765-807-1540	807-1547
Columbus Zoo & Aquarium 4850 W Powell Rd *TF:* 800-666-5397 ■ *Web:* www.colszoo.org	Powell	OH	43065	614-645-3400	645-3465
Como Zoo & Conservatory 1225 Estabrook Dr *Web:* www.ci.stpaul.mn.us/depts/parks/comopark	Saint Paul	MN	55103	651-487-8200	487-8254
Cosley Zoo 1356 N Gary Ave *Web:* www.cosleyzoo.org	Wheaton	IL	60187	630-665-5534	260-6408
Cougar Mountain Zoo 19525 SE 54th St *Web:* www.cougarmountainzoo.org	Issaquah	WA	98027	425-392-6278	392-1076
Dakota Zoo 602 Riverside Pk Rd *Web:* www.dakotazoo.org	Bismarck	ND	58504	701-223-7543	258-8350
Dallas Zoo 650 S RL Thornton Fwy *Web:* www.dallas-zoo.org	Dallas	TX	75203	214-670-6826	670-7450
David Traylor Zoo of Emporia 75 Soden Rd *Web:* www.emporiazoo.org	Emporia	KS	66801	620-341-4365	341-4367

Name / Address	City	State	Zip	Phone	Fax
Denver Zoo 2300 Steele St *Web:* www.denverzoo.org	Denver	CO	80205	303-376-4800	376-4801
Detroit Zoological Institute 8450 W Ten-Mile Rd *Web:* www.detroitzoo.org	Royal Oak	MI	48067	248-398-0903	541-0344
Dickerson Park Zoo 3043 N Fort *Web:* www.dickersonparkzoo.org	Springfield	MO	65803	417-833-1570	833-4459
Discovery Cove 6000 Discovery Cove Way Suite B *TF:* 877-434-7268 ■ *Web:* www.discoverycove.com	Orlando	FL	32821	407-370-1280	586-8046
Ecomuseum 21125 ch Sainte-Marie *Web:* www.ecomuseum.ca	Sainte-Anne-de-Bellevue	QC	H9X3Y7	514-457-9449	457-0769
El Paso Zoo 4001 E Paisano Dr *Web:* www.elpasozoo.org	El Paso	TX	79905	915-521-1850	
Ellen Trout Zoo 402 Zoo Cir *Web:* cityoflufkin.com/zoo	Lufkin	TX	75904	936-633-0399	633-0311
Elmwood Park Zoo 1661 Harding Blvd *Web:* www.elmwoodparkzoo.org	Norristown	PA	19401	610-277-3825	292-0332
Erie Zoo 423 W 38th St *Web:* www.eriezoo.org	Erie	PA	16508	814-864-4091	864-1140
Everglades Alligator Farm 40351 SW 192nd Ave *Web:* www.everglades.com	Homestead	FL	33034	305-247-2628	248-9711
Everglades Safari Park 26700 Tamiami Trail *Web:* www.evergladessafaripark.com	Miami	FL	33144	305-226-6923	554-5666
Felix Neck Wildlife Sanctuary 100 Felix Neck Dr	Edgartown	MA	02539	508-627-4850	627-6052
For-Mar Nature Preserve & Arboretum 2142 N Genesee Rd *Web:* www.geneseecountyparks.org	Burton	MI	48509	810-789-8567	743-0541
Fort Wayne Children's Zoo 3411 Sherman Blvd *Web:* www.kidszoo.org	Fort Wayne	IN	46808	260-427-6800	427-6820
Fort Worth Zoological Park 1989 Colonial Pkwy *Web:* www.fortworthzoo.com	Fort Worth	TX	76110	817-871-7000	759-7501
Fossil Rim Wildlife Ctr 2155 CR 2008 *Web:* www.fossilrim.com	Glen Rose	TX	76043	254-897-2960	897-3785
Franklin Park Zoo 1 Franklin Pk Rd *Web:* www.zoonewengland.com	Boston	MA	02121	617-541-5466	989-2025
Fresno Chaffee Zoo 894 W Belmont Ave *Web:* www.fresnochaffeezoo.com	Fresno	CA	93728	559-498-2671	264-9226
Gator Park 24050 SW 8th St *TF:* 800-559-2205 ■ *Web:* www.gatorpark.com	Miami	FL	33184	305-559-2255	559-2844
Gatorland 14501 S Orange Blossom Trail *TF:* 800-393-5297 ■ *Web:* www.gatorland.com	Orlando	FL	32837	407-855-5496	240-9389
Gibbon Conservation Ctr 19100 Esguerra Rd *Web:* www.gibboncenter.org	Santa Clarita	CA	91350	661-296-2737	296-1237
Gladys Porter Zoo 500 Ringgold St *Web:* www.gpz.org	Brownsville	TX	78520	956-546-7187	541-4940
Glen Oak Park 2218 N Prospect Rd *Web:* www.peoriazoo.org	Peoria	IL	61603	309-686-3365	685-6240
Global Wildlife Ctr 26389 Hwy 40 *Web:* www.globalwildlife.com	Folsom	LA	70437	985-796-3585	796-9487
Good Zoo & Benedum Planetarium Rt 88 N Oglebay Pk *TF:* 800-624-6988 ■ *Web:* www.oglebay-resort.com/goodzoo	Wheeling	WV	26003	304-243-4030	243-4110
Granby Zoo & Amazoo Water Park 525 St Hubert St *TF:* 877-472-6299 ■ *Web:* www.zoogranby.ca	Granby	QC	J2G5P3	450-372-9113	372-5531
Great Plains Zoo 805 S Kiwanis Ave *Web:* www.gpzoo.org	Sioux Falls	SD	57104	605-367-7059	367-8340
Greenville Zoo 150 Cleveland Pk Dr *Web:* www.greenvillezoo.com	Greenville	SC	29601	864-467-4300	467-4314
Grizzly & Wolf Discovery Ctr 201 S Canyon St *TF:* 800-257-2570 ■ *Web:* www.grizzlydiscoveryctr.com	West Yellowstone	MT	59758	406-646-7001	646-7004
Happy Hollow Park & Zoo 1300 Senter Rd Kelley Pk *Web:* www.hhpz.org	San Jose	CA	95112	408-794-6400	277-4470
Harmony Park Safari 431 Clouds Cove Rd *TF:* 877-726-4625	Huntsville	AL	35803	877-726-4625	
Hattiesburg Zoo 107 S 17th Ave Kamper Pk *Web:* www.hattiesburgms.com	Hattiesburg	MS	39401	601-545-4576	545-4653
Have Trunk Will Travel Inc 27575 Hwy 74 *Web:* www.havetrunkwilltravel.com	Perris	CA	92570	951-943-9227	943-9563
Henry Doorly Zoo 3701 S 10th St *Web:* www.omahazoo.com	Omaha	NE	68107	402-733-8401	733-7868
Henry Vilas Park Zoo 702 S Randall Ave *Web:* www.vilaszoo.org	Madison	WI	53715	608-266-4732	266-5923
Henson Robinson Zoo 1100 E Lake Dr *Web:* www.hensonrobinsonzoo.org	Springfield	IL	62707	217-753-6217	529-8748
Honolulu Zoo 151 Kapahulu Ave *Web:* www.honoluluzoo.org	Honolulu	HI	96815	808-971-7171	971-7173
Houston Zoo Inc 1513 N MacGregor Dr *Web:* www.houstonzoo.org	Houston	TX	77030	713-533-6500	533-6755
Hutchinson Zoo 6 Emerson Loop E Carey Pk	Hutchinson	KS	67501	620-694-2693	694-1980
Indianapolis Zoo 1200 W Washington St *Web:* www.indianapoliszoo.com	Indianapolis	IN	46222	317-630-2001	630-5153
International Exotic Feline Sanctuary PO Box 637 *Web:* www.bigcat.org	Boyd	TX	76023	940-433-5091	433-5092
Jackson Zoological Park 2918 W Capitol St *Web:* www.jacksonzoo.org	Jackson	MS	39209	601-352-2580	352-2594
Jacksonville Zoo & Gardens 370 Zoo Pkwy *Web:* www.jaxzoo.org	Jacksonville	FL	32218	904-757-4463	757-4315
John Ball Zoological Garden 1300 W Fulton St *Web:* www.johnballzoosociety.org	Grand Rapids	MI	49504	616-336-4301	336-3907
Jungle Adventures 26205 E Hwy 50 *TF:* 877-424-2867 ■ *Web:* www.jungleadventures.com	Christmas	FL	32709	407-568-1354	568-0038
Jungle Cat World Inc 3667 Concession Rd 6 *Web:* www.junglecatworld.com	Orono	ON	L0B1M0	905-983-5016	983-9858
Jungle Island 1111 Parrot Jungle Trail *Web:* www.jungleisland.com	Miami	FL	33132	305-400-7000	400-7290
Kangaroo Conservation Ctr 222 Bailey-Waters Rd *Web:* www.kangaroocenter.com	Dawsonville	GA	30534	706-265-6100	265-6261
Kansas City Zoo 6800 Zoo Dr *Web:* www.kansascityzoo.org	Kansas City	MO	64132	816-513-5700	513-5850
Kansas Wildlife Exhibit 700 N Nims St Central Riverside Pk *Web:* www.gpnc.org	Wichita	KS	67202	316-337-9211	
Kentucky Horse Park 4089 Iron Works Pkwy *TF:* 800-678-8813 ■ *Web:* www.kyhorsepark.com	Lexington	KY	40511	859-233-4303	254-0253
Kisma Preserve 446 Bar Harbor Rd	Trenton	ME	04605	207-667-3244	
Knoxville Zoological Gardens Inc 3500 Knoxville Zoo Dr PO Box 6040 *Web:* www.knoxville-zoo.org	Knoxville	TN	37914	865-637-5331	637-1943
Lake Superior Zoo 7210 Fremont St *Web:* www.lszoo.org	Duluth	MN	55807	218-730-4500	723-3750
Lee Richardson Zoo 312 E Finnup Dr *Web:* www.garden-city.org/zoo	Garden City	KS	67846	620-276-1250	276-1259
Lincoln Children's Zoo 1222 S 27th St *Web:* www.lincolnzoo.org	Lincoln	NE	68502	402-475-6741	475-6742
Lincoln Park Zoo 2001 N Clark St *Web:* www.lpzoo.com	Chicago	IL	60614	312-742-2000	742-2317
Lion Country Safari 2003 Lion Country Safari Rd *Web:* www.lioncountrysafari.com	Loxahatchee	FL	33470	561-793-1084	793-9603
Little Rock Zoo 1 Jonesboro Dr *Web:* www.littlerockzoo.com	Little Rock	AR	72205	501-666-2406	666-7040
Living Desert Zoo & Gardens 47900 Portola Ave *Web:* www.livingdesert.org	Palm Desert	CA	92260	760-346-5694	568-9685
Los Angeles Zoo & Botanical Gardens 5333 Zoo Dr *Web:* www.lazoo.org	Los Angeles	CA	90027	323-644-4200	662-9786
Louisville Zoo 1100 Trevilian Way *Web:* www.louisvillezoo.org	Louisville	KY	40213	502-459-2181	459-2196
Lowry Park Zoo 7530 N Blvd *Web:* www.lowryparkzoo.com	Tampa	FL	33604	813-935-8552	935-9486
Magnetic Hill Zoo 100 Worthington Ave	Moncton	NB	E1C9Z3	506-384-0303	853-3569
Maryland Zoo in Baltimore Druid Hill Pk *Web:* www.marylandzoo.org	Baltimore	MD	21217	410-396-7102	396-6464
Maymont 2201 Shields Dr *Web:* www.maymont.org	Richmond	VA	23219	804-358-7166	358-9994
Memphis Zoo 2000 Prentiss Pl *Web:* www.memphiszoo.org	Memphis	TN	38112	901-333-6500	333-6501
Mesker Park Zoo 1545 Mesker Pk Dr *Web:* www.meskerparkzoo.com	Evansville	IN	47720	812-435-6143	435-6140
Miami Metrozoo 12400 SW 152nd St *Web:* www.miamimetrozoo.com	Miami	FL	33177	305-251-0400	378-6381
Micke Grove Zoo 11793 N Micke Grove Rd *Web:* www.co.san-joaquin.ca.us/mgzoo	Lodi	CA	95240	209-953-8840	331-7271
Mill Mountain Zoo 2404 Prospect Rd Mill Mountain Pk *Web:* www.mmzoo.org	Roanoke	VA	24014	540-343-3241	343-8111
Miller Park Zoo 1020 S Morris Ave *Web:* www.millerparkzoo.org	Bloomington	IL	61701	309-434-2250	434-2823
Milwaukee County Zoo 10001 W Blue Mound Rd *Web:* www.milwaukeezoo.org	Milwaukee	WI	53226	414-771-3040	256-5410
Minnesota Zoo 13000 Zoo Blvd *TF:* 800-366-7811 ■ *Web:* www.mnzoo.com	Apple Valley	MN	55124	952-431-9200	431-9300
Mobile Zoo 15161 Ward Rd W *Web:* www.mobilezoo.cc	Wilmer	AL	36587	251-649-1845	649-0434
Monkey Jungle 14805 SW 216th St *Web:* www.monkeyjungle.com	Miami	FL	33170	305-235-1611	235-4253
Montgomery Zoo 2301 Coliseum Pkwy *Web:* www.montgomeryzoo.com	Montgomery	AL	36110	334-240-4900	240-4916
Nashville Zoo 3777 Nolensville Rd *Web:* www.nashvillezoo.org	Nashville	TN	37211	615-833-1534	333-0728
National Zoological Park (Smithsonian Institution) 3001 Connecticut Ave NW *Web:* www.nationalzoo.si.edu	Washington	DC	20008	202-633-4800	673-4836
Natural Bridge Wildlife Ranch 26515 Natural Bridge Caverns Rd *Web:* www.wildliferanchtexas.com	San Antonio	TX	78266	830-438-7400	438-3494
New York State Zoo 1 Thompson Pk *Web:* www.nyszoo.org	Watertown	NY	13601	315-782-6180	782-6192
North Carolina Zoological Park 4401 Zoo Pkwy *TF:* 800-488-0444 ■ *Web:* www.nczoo.org	Asheboro	NC	27205	336-879-7000	879-2891
Northeastern Wisconsin Zoo 4418 Reforestation Rd *Web:* www.co.brown.wi.us/parks/newzoo	Green Bay	WI	54313	920-448-4466	434-4162
Northwest Trek Wildlife Park 11610 Trek Dr E *Web:* www.nwtrek.org	Eatonville	WA	98328	360-832-6117	832-6118
Oakland Zoo 9777 Golf Links Rd *Web:* www.oaklandzoo.org	Oakland	CA	94605	510-632-9525	635-5719
Oklahoma City Zoological Park & Botanical Gardens 2101 NE 50th St *Web:* www.okczoo.com	Oklahoma City	OK	73111	405-424-3344	425-0297
Orange County Zoo 1 Irvine Pk Rd *Web:* www.ocparks.com	Orange	CA	92862	714-973-6847	
Oregon Zoo 4001 SW Canyon Rd *Web:* www.oregonzoo.org	Portland	OR	97221	503-226-1561	226-6836
Out of Africa Wildlife Park 4020 N Cherry Rd *Web:* www.outofafricapark.com	Camp Verde	AZ	86322	928-567-2840	567-2839

				Phone	Fax
Palm Beach Zoo at Dreher Park 1301 Summit Blvd *Web:* www.palmbeachzoo.org	West Palm Beach	FL	33405	561-533-0887	585-6085
Parc Safari 280 Rang Roxham *Web:* www.parcsafari.com	Saint-Bernard-de-Lacolle	QC	J0L1H0	450-247-2727	247-3563
Parks at Chehaw 105 Chehaw Pk Rd *Web:* www.parksatchehaw.org	Albany	GA	31701	229-430-5275	430-3035
Paul E Zollman Zoo 5731 County Rd 105 NW	Byron	MN	55920	507-775-2451	775-2544
Philadelphia Zoo 3400 W Girard Ave *Web:* www.phillyzoo.org	Philadelphia	PA	19104	215-243-1100	243-5385
Phoenix Zoo 455 N Galvin Pkwy *Web:* www.phoenixzoo.org	Phoenix	AZ	85008	602-273-1341	273-7078
Pittsburgh Zoo & PPG Aquarium 1 Wild Pl *TF:* 800-474-4966 ■ *Web:* www.pittsburghzoo.com	Pittsburgh	PA	15206	412-665-3639	665-3661
Pocatello Zoo 2900 S 2nd Ave *Web:* www.pocatellozoo.org	Pocatello	ID	83204	208-234-6264	234-6265
Point Defiance Zoo & Aquarium 5400 N Pearl St *Web:* www.pdza.org	Tacoma	WA	98407	253-591-5337	591-5448
Potter Park Zoo 1301 S Pennsylvania Ave *Web:* www.potterparkzoo.org	Lansing	MI	48912	517-483-4222	316-3894
Prospect Park Zoo 450 Flatbush Ave *Web:* www.nyzoosandaquarium.com	Brooklyn	NY	11225	718-399-7339	399-7337
Provincial Wildlife Park 149 Creighton Rd PO Box 299 *Web:* wildlifepark.gov.ns.ca	Shubenacadie	NS	B0N2H0	902-758-2040	758-7011
Pueblo Zoo 3455 Nuckolls Ave *Web:* www.pueblozoo.org	Pueblo	CO	81005	719-561-1452	561-8686
Queens Zoo 53-51 111th St *Web:* www.wcs.org	Flushing	NY	11368	718-271-1500	
Racine Zoo 200 Goold St *Web:* www.racinezoo.org	Racine	WI	53402	262-636-9189	636-9307
Red River Zoo 4255 23rd Ave S *Web:* www.redriverzoo.org	Fargo	ND	58104	701-277-9240	277-9238
Reid Park Zoo 1100 S Randolph Way *Web:* www.tucsonzoo.org	Tucson	AZ	85716	520-791-3204	791-5378
Rio Grande Zoo Albuquerque Biological Pk 903 10th St SW *Web:* www.cabq.gov/biopark/zoo	Albuquerque	NM	87102	505-764-6200	764-6281
Riverbanks Zoo & Botanical Garden 500 Wildlife Pkwy *Web:* www.riverbanks.org	Columbia	SC	29210	803-779-8717	253-6381
Riverside Zoo 1600 S Beltline Hwy W *Web:* www.riversidezoo.org	Scottsbluff	NE	69361	308-630-6236	632-2953
Riverview Park & Zoo 1230 Water St N *Web:* www.peterboroughutilities.ca/Park_and_Zoo.htm	Peterborough	ON	K9H7G4	705-748-9301	745-6866
Roger Williams Park Zoo 1000 Elmwood Ave *Web:* www.rogerwilliamsparkzoo.org	Providence	RI	02907	401-785-3510	941-3988
Rolling Hills Wildlife Adventure 625 N Hedville Rd *Web:* www.rhrwildlife.com	Salina	KS	67401	785-827-9488	827-3738
Roosevelt Park Zoo 1219 Burdick Expy *Web:* www.rpzoo.com	Minot	ND	58701	701-857-4166	857-4169
Rosamond Gifford Zoo at Burnet Park 1 Conservation Pl *Web:* rosamondgiffordzoo.com	Syracuse	NY	13204	315-435-8511	435-8517
Sacramento Zoo 3930 W Land Pk Dr *Web:* www.saczoo.com	Sacramento	CA	95822	916-808-5888	264-5887
Safari West Wildlife Preserve & Tent Camp 3115 Porter Creek Rd *TF:* 800-616-2695 ■ *Web:* www.safariwest.com	Santa Rosa	CA	95404	707-579-2551	579-8777
Saint Augustine Alligator Farm 999 Anastasia Blvd *Web:* www.alligatorfarm.com	Saint Augustine	FL	32084	904-824-3337	829-6677
Saint Louis Zoological Park 1 Government Dr *Web:* www.stlzoo.org	Saint Louis	MO	63110	314-781-0900	647-7969
Salisbury Zoological Park 755 S Pk Dr *Web:* www.salisburyzoo.org	Salisbury	MD	21804	410-548-3188	860-0919
Salmonier Nature Park PO Box 190 *Web:* www.gov.nf.ca/snp	Holyrood	NL	A0A2R0	709-229-3915	229-7078
San Antonio Zoological Gardens & Aquarium 3903 N St Mary's St *Web:* www.sazoo-aq.org	San Antonio	TX	78212	210-734-7184	734-7291
San Diego Zoo 2920 Zoo Dr *Web:* www.sandiegozoo.org	San Diego	CA	92101	619-231-1515	231-0249
San Diego Zoo Safari Park 15500 San Pasqual Valley Rd *TF Cust Svc:* 800-407-9534 ■ *Web:* www.sdzsafaripark.org	Escondido	CA	92027	760-747-8702	746-7081
San Francisco Zoo 1 Zoo Rd *Web:* www.sfzoo.org	San Francisco	CA	94132	415-753-7080	681-2039
Santa Ana Zoo 1801 E Chestnut Ave *Web:* www.santaanazoo.org	Santa Ana	CA	92701	714-835-7484	550-0346
Santa Barbara Zoological Gardens 500 Ninos Dr *Web:* www.santabarbarazoo.org	Santa Barbara	CA	93103	805-962-5339	962-1673
Santa Fe Community College Teaching Zoo 3000 NW 83rd St *Web:* inst.sfcc.edu/~zoo	Gainesville	FL	32606	352-395-5604	395-7365
Sarasota Jungle Gardens 3701 Bay Shore Rd *TF:* 877-861-6547 ■ *Web:* www.sarasotajunglegardens.com	Sarasota	FL	34234	941-355-5305	355-1222
Scovill Zoo 71 S Country Club Rd *Web:* www.decatur-parks.org	Decatur	IL	62521	217-421-7435	422-7330
Sedgwick County Zoo 5555 W Zoo Blvd *Web:* www.scz.org	Wichita	KS	67212	316-660-9453	942-3781
Seneca Park Zoo 2222 St Paul St *Web:* www.senecaparkzoo.org	Rochester	NY	14621	585-266-6846	342-1477
Sequoia Park Zoo 3414 W St *Web:* www.sequoiaparkzoo.net	Eureka	CA	95503	707-441-4263	442-5841
Sierra Safari Zoo 10200 N Virginia St *Web:* www.sierrasafarizoo.com	Reno	NV	89506	775-677-1101	677-7874
Silver Springs 5656 E Silver Springs Blvd *Web:* www.silversprings.com	Silver Springs	FL	34488	352-236-2121	236-1732
Southern Nevada Zoological-Botanical Park 1775 N Rancho Dr *Web:* www.lasvegaszoo.org	Las Vegas	NV	89106	702-648-5955	648-5955
Spring River Park & Zoo 1306 E College Blvd	Roswell	NM	88201	505-624-6760	624-6941
Staten Island Zoo 614 Broadway *Web:* www.statenislandzoo.org	Staten Island	NY	10310	718-442-3101	981-8711
Sunset Zoo 2333 Oak St *Web:* www.ci.manhattan.ks.us	Manhattan	KS	66502	785-587-2737	587-2730
Tautphaus Park Zoo 308 Constitution Way *Web:* www.idahofallszoo.org	Idaho Falls	ID	83402	208-612-8100	528-6256
Texas Zoo 110 Memorial Dr *Web:* www.texaszoo.org	Victoria	TX	77901	361-573-7681	576-1094
Toledo Zoo 2700 Broadway *Web:* www.toledozoo.org	Toledo	OH	43609	419-385-5721	389-8670
Topeka Zoological Park 635 SW Gage Blvd *Web:* www.topeka.org/zoo	Topeka	KS	66606	785-368-9180	368-9152
Toronto Zoo 361-A Old Finch Ave *Web:* www.torontozoo.com	Toronto	ON	M1B5K7	416-392-5900	392-5934
Tracy Aviary 600 E 900 S *Web:* www.tracyaviary.org	Salt Lake City	UT	84105	801-596-8500	596-7325
Trevor Zoo 131 Millbrook School Rd	Millbrook	NY	12545	845-677-3704	677-3774
Tulsa Zoo 6421 E 36th St N *Web:* www.tulsazoo.com	Tulsa	OK	74115	918-669-6600	669-6610
Tupelo Buffalo Park & Zoo 2272 N Coley Rd *TF:* 866-272-4766 ■ *Web:* www.tupelobuffalopark.com	Tupelo	MS	38803	662-844-8709	844-8850
Utah's Hogle Zoo 2600 E Sunnyside Ave *Web:* www.hoglezoo.org	Salt Lake City	UT	84108	801-582-1631	584-1770
Utica Zoo 99 Steele Hill Rd *Web:* www.uticazoo.org	Utica	NY	13501	315-738-0472	738-0475
Valley Zoo 13315 Buena Vista Rd	Edmonton	AB	T5R5R1	780-496-6912	944-7529
Virginia Zoological Park 3500 Granby St *Web:* www.virginiazoo.org	Norfolk	VA	23504	757-441-2374	441-5408
Waccatee Zoological Farm 8500 Enterprise Rd *Web:* www.waccateezoo.com	Myrtle Beach	SC	29588	843-650-8500	
Washington Park Zoological Gardens 115 Lakeshore Dr *Web:* www.washingtonparkzoo.com	Michigan City	IN	46360	219-873-1510	873-1539
West Virginia State Wildlife Ctr Rt 20 S	French Creek	WV	26218	304-924-6211	924-6781
Wild Animal Safari 1300 Oak Grove Rd *TF:* 800-367-2751 ■ *Web:* www.animalsafari.com	Pine Mountain	GA	31822	706-663-8744	663-8880
Wildlife Safari 16406 N 292nd St *Web:* www.omahazoo.org	Ashland	NE	68003	402-944-9453	944-3139
Wildlife Safari 1790 Safari Rd *Web:* www.wildlifesafari.org	Winston	OR	97496	541-679-6761	679-1148
Wildlife Sanctuary of Northwest Florida 105 N S St *Web:* www.pensacolawildlife.com	Pensacola	FL	32505	850-433-9453	438-6168
Wildlife West Nature Park 87 N Frontage Rd *Web:* www.wildlifewest.org	Edgewood	NM	87015	505-281-7655	281-7170
Wildlife World Zoo 16501 W Northern Ave *Web:* www.wildlifeworld.com	Litchfield Park	AZ	85340	623-935-9453	935-7499
Wilds The 14000 International Rd *Web:* www.thewilds.org	Cumberland	OH	43732	740-638-5030	638-2287
Wonders of Wildlife 500 W Sunshine St *Web:* www.wondersofwildlife.org	Springfield	MO	65807	417-890-9453	890-9278
Woodland Park Zoo 601 N 59th St *Web:* www.zoo.org	Seattle	WA	98103	206-548-2500	548-1536
World of Reptiles & Birds Park Edgartown-Vineyard Haven Rd *Web:* www.reptilesandbirds.com	Edgartown	MA	02539	508-627-5634	
Zoo Atlanta 800 Cherokee Ave SE *Web:* www.zooatlanta.org	Atlanta	GA	30315	404-624-5600	627-7514
Zoo Boise 355 N Julia Davis Dr *Web:* www.cityofboise.org/parks/zoo	Boise	ID	83702	208-384-4260	384-4194
Zoo in Forest Park The 302 Sumner Ave PO Box 80295 *Web:* www.forestparkzoo.org	Springfield	MA	01138	413-733-2251	733-2330
Zoo of Acadiana 5601 Hwy 90 E *Web:* www.zoofacadiana.org	Broussard	LA	70518	337-837-4325	837-4253
Zoo Sauvage de Saint-Felicien 2230 boul du Jardin *TF:* 800-667-5687 ■ *Web:* www.zoosauvage.qc.ca	Saint-Felicien	QC	G8K2P8	418-679-0543	679-3647
Zoo The 5701 Gulf Breeze Pkwy *Web:* www.the-zoo.com	Gulf Breeze	FL	32563	850-932-2229	932-3278
ZooAmerica North American Wildlife Park 100 W Hersheypark Dr *TF:* 800-437-7439 ■ *Web:* www.hersheypa.com/attractions/zooAmerica	Hershey	PA	17033	717-534-3860	534-3151
ZooMontana & Botanical Gardens 2100 S Shiloh Rd *Web:* www.zoomontana.org	Billings	MT	59106	406-652-8100	652-9281
ZooQuarium 674 Rt 28 *Web:* www.zooquariumcapecod.net	West Yarmouth	MA	02673	508-775-8883	

Area Code and Zip Code Guide

The information provided in this Guide is organized **alphabetically by city name,** with area code(s) and zip code(s) shown to the right of the city name.

A

City	Area Code(s)	Zip Code(s)
Abbeville, AL	334	36310
Abbeville, GA	229	31001
Abbeville, LA	337	70510-70511
Abbeville, SC	864	29620
Abbotsford, WI	715, 534	54405
Abbott Park, IL	224, 847	60064
Aberdeen, ID	208	83210
Aberdeen, MD	410	21001
Aberdeen, MS	662	39730
Aberdeen, NC	910	28315
Aberdeen, SD	605	57401-57402
Aberdeen, WA	360	98520
Aberdeen Proving Ground, MD	410	21005, 21010
Abernathy, TX	806	79311
Abilene, KS	785	67410
Abilene, TX	915	79601-79608, 79697-79699
Abingdon, VA	276	24210-24212
Abington, MA	339, 781	02351
Abington, PA	215, 267	19001
Accident, MD	301	21520
Accokeek, MD	301	20607
Accomac, VA	757	23301
Accord, NY	845	12404
Ackerman, MS	662	39735
Acme, MI	231	49610
Acton, MA	351, 978	01718-01720
Acworth, GA	470, 770	30101-30102
Ada, MI	616	49301, 49355-49357
Ada, MN	218	56510
Ada, OH	419, 567	45810
Ada, OK	580	74820-74821
Adairsville, GA	470, 770	30103
Adams, MA	413	01220
Adams, OR	541, 458	97810
Adamstown, MD	301	21710
Adamstown, PA	717	19501
Adamsville, TN	731	38310
Addison, AL	256	35540
Addison, IL	331, 630	60101
Addison, TX	469, 972	75001
Addison, VT	802	05491
Adel, GA	229	31620
Adel, IA	515	50003
Adelanto, CA	760, 442	92301
Adelphi, MD	301	20783, 20787
Adrian, GA	478	31002
Adrian, MI	517	49221
Advance, NC	336	27006
Affton, MO	314	63123
Afton, OK	918	74331
Afton, WY	307	83110
Agawam, MA	413	01001
Agoura Hills, CA	818	91301, 91376-91377
Aguadilla, PR	787, 939	00603-00605
Ahoskie, NC	252	27910
Aiea, HI	808	96701
Aiken, SC	803	29801-29808
Ainsworth, NE	402	69210
Airway Heights, WA	509	99001
Aitkin, MN	218	56431
Ajo, AZ	520	85321
Akron, CO	970	80720
Akron, IN	574	46910
Akron, NY	585	14001
Akron, OH	234, 330	44301-44328, 44333-44334*
Akron, PA	717	17501
Alabaster, AL	205	35007, 35144
Alachua, FL	386	32615-32616
Alamance, NC	336	27201
Alameda, CA	510	94501-94502
Alamo, CA	925	94507
Alamo, GA	912	30411
Alamo, TN	731	38001
Alamo, TX	956	78516
Alamogordo, NM	505	88310-88311
Alamosa, CO	719	81101-81102
Albany, CA	510	94706, 94710
Albany, GA	229	31701-31708
Albany, KY	606	42602
Albany, MN	320	56307
Albany, MO	660	64402
Albany, NY	518	12201-12214, 12220-12262*
Albany, OR	541, 458	97321
Albany, TX	915	76430
Albemarle, NC	704, 980	28001-28002
Albert Lea, MN	507	56007
Alberta, VA	434	23821
Albertson, NY	516	11507
Albertville, AL	256	35950-35951
Albia, IA	641	52531
Albion, IL	618	62806
Albion, IN	260	46701
Albion, MI	517	49224
Albion, NE	402	68620
Albion, NY	585	14411
Albion, PA	814	16401, 16475
Albuquerque, NM	505	87101-87125, 87131, 87153*
Alcoa, TN	865	37701
Alcorn State, MS	601, 769	39096
Alden, NY	585	14004
Alderson, WV	304	24910
Aledo, IL	309	61231
Alexander, AR	501	72002
Alexander, IA	641	50420
Alexander, NY	585	14005
Alexander City, AL	256	35010-35011
Alexandria, AL	256	36250
Alexandria, IN	765	46001
Alexandria, LA	318	71301-71309, 71315
Alexandria, MN	320	56308
Alexandria, SD	605	57311
Alexandria, TN	615	37012
Alexandria, VA	571, 703	22301-22315, 22320-22321*
Alexandria Bay, NY	315	13607
Alfred, ME	207	04002
Alfred, NY	607	14802
Algoma, WI	920	54201
Algona, IA	515	50511
Algona, WA	253	98001
Algonquin, IL	224, 847	60102, 60156
Alhambra, CA	626	91801-91804, 91841, 91896*
Alice, TX	361	78332-78333, 78342
Aliceville, AL	205	35442
Aliquippa, PA	724, 878	15001
Aliso Viejo, CA	949	92653-92656, 92698
Alledonia, OH	740	43902
Allegan, MI	616	49010
Allen, TX	469, 972	75002, 75013
Allen Park, MI	313	48101
Allendale, MI	616	49401
Allendale, NJ	201, 551	07401
Allendale, SC	803	29810
Allenhurst, NJ	732, 848	07709-07711
Allenstown, NH	603	03275
Allentown, NJ	609	08501
Allentown, PA	484, 610	18101-18109, 18175, 18195
Allenwood, NJ	732, 848	08720
Allenwood, PA	570	17810
Allgood, AL	205	35013
Alliance, NE	308	69301
Alliance, OH	234, 330	44601
Allison, IA	319	50602
Allison Park, PA	412, 878	15101
Allston, MA	617, 857	02134
Alma, GA	912	31510
Alma, KS	785	66401, 66501
Alma, MI	989	48801-48802
Alma, NE	308	68920
Alma, WI	608	54610
Almena, WI	715, 534	54805
Almo, ID	208	83312
Almont, MI	810	48003
Alpena, MI	989	49707
Alpha, NJ	908	08865
Alpharetta, GA	470, 678, 770	30004-30005, 30009, 30022*
Alpine, CA	619	91901-91903
Alpine, TX	915	79830-79832
Alpine, UT	801, 385	84004
Alsip, IL	708	60803
Alta, UT	801, 385	84092
Altadena, CA	626	91001-91003
Altamahaw, NC	336	27202
Altamont, KS	620	67330
Altamont, TN	931	37301
Altamonte Springs, FL	321, 407	32701, 32714-32716
Altavista, VA	434	24517
Alto, GA	706, 762	30510, 30596
Alton, IL	618	62002
Alton, MO	417	65606
Altona, NY	518	12910
Altoona, IA	515	50009
Altoona, PA	814	16601-16603
Alturas, CA	530	96101
Altus, OK	580	73521-73523
Altus AFB, OK	580	73523
Alva, OK	580	73717
Alvarado, TX	682, 817	76009
Alvin, TX	281, 832	77511-77512
Alviso, CA	408	95002
Amado, AZ	520	85640, 85645
Amana, IA	319	52203-52204
Amarillo, TX	806	79101-79124, 79159, 79163*
Ambler, PA	215, 267	19002
Amboy, IL	815	61310
Amboy, WA	360	98601
Ambridge, PA	724, 878	15003
Amelia Court House, VA	804	23002
Amelia Island, FL	904	32034
American Falls, ID	208	83211
American Fork, UT	801, 385	84003
Americus, GA	229	31709-31710
Ames, IA	515	50010-50014
Amesbury, MA	351, 978	01913
Amherst, MA	413	01002-01004, 01059
Amherst, NH	603	03031
Amherst, NY	716	14051, 14068, 14221, 14226*
Amherst, TX	806	79312
Amherst, VA	434	24521
Amidon, ND	701	58620
Amite, LA	985	70422
Amityville, NY	631	11701, 11708
Amlin, OH	614	43002
Amory, MS	662	38821
Amsterdam, NY	518	12010
Anaconda, MT	406	59711
Anacortes, WA	360	98221-98222
Anadarko, OK	405	73005
Anaheim, CA	714	92801-92817, 92825, 92850*
Anaheim Hills, CA	714	92807-92809, 92817
Anahuac, TX	409	77514
Analomink, PA	570	18320
Anamosa, IA	319	52205
Anchorage, AK	907	99501-99524, 99540, 99599*
Ancora, NJ	609	08037
Andalusia, AL	334	36420
Anderson, CA	530	96007
Anderson, IN	765	46011-46018
Anderson, MO	417	64831
Anderson, SC	864	29621-29626
Anderson, TX	936	77830, 77875
Andersonville, GA	229	31711
Andover, KS	316	67002
Andover, ME	207	04216
Andover, MA	351, 978	01810-01812, 01899, 05501*
Andover, NJ	862, 973	07821
Andover, OH	440	44003
Andrews, TX	915	79714
Andrews AFB, MD	240, 301	20762
Angel Fire, NM	505	87710
Angels Camp, CA	209	95221-95222
Angie, LA	985	70426, 70467

*Partial list of zip codes, including main range

City	Area Code(s)	Zip Code(s)
Angleton, TX	979	77515-77516
Angola, IN	260	46703
Angola, LA	225	70712
Angoon, AK	907	99820
Angwin, CA	707	94508, 94576
Ankeny, IA	515	50015, 50021
Ann Arbor, MI	734	48103-48109, 48113
Anna, IL	618	62906
Annandale, MN	320	55302
Annandale, NJ	908	08801
Annandale, VA	571, 703	22003
Annapolis, MD	410, 443	21401-21405, 21411-21412
Annapolis Junction, MD	301	20701
Anniston, AL	256	36201-36207
Annona, TX	903	75550
Annville, PA	717	17003
Anoka, MN	763	55303-55304
Anson, TX	915	79501
Ansonia, CT	203	06401
Ansonia, OH	937	45303
Ansted, WV	304	25812
Anthony, KS	620	67003
Anthony, TX	915	79821
Antigo, WI	715, 534	54409
Antioch, CA	925	94509, 94531
Antioch, IL	224, 847	60002
Antioch, TN	615	37011-37013
Antlers, OK	580	74523
Antonito, CO	719	81120
Antrim, NH	603	03440
Anza, CA	951	92539
Apache, OK	580	73006
Apache Junction, AZ	480	85217-85220, 85278, 85290
Apalachicola, FL	850	32320, 32329
Apex, NC	919	27502
Apopka, FL	321, 407	32703-32704, 32712
Apple Valley, CA	760, 442	92307-92308
Apple Valley, MN	952	55124
Appleton, WI	920	54911-54915, 54919
Appomattox, VA	434	24522
Aptos, CA	831	95001-95003
Aquebogue, NY	631	11931
Arab, AL	256	35016
Arapaho, OK	580	73620
Arbor Vitae, WI	715, 534	54568
Arbuckle, CA	530	95912
Arcade, NY	585	14009
Arcadia, CA	626	91006-91007, 91066, 91077
Arcadia, FL	863	34265-34269
Arcadia, LA	318	71001
Arcadia, SC	864	29320
Arcadia, WI	608	54612
Arcata, CA	707	95518-95521
Archbold, OH	419, 567	43502
Archdale, NC	336	27263
Archer, FL	352	32618
Archer City, TX	940	76351
Arco, ID	208	83213
Arcola, IL	217	61910
Arcola, TX	281, 832	77583
Arden, NC	828	28704
Arden Hills, MN	651	55112
Ardmore, OK	580	73401-73403
Ardmore, PA	484, 610	19003
Ardsley, NY	914	10502
Arecibo, PR	787, 939	00612-00614
Argonne, IL	331, 630	60439
Argyle, MN	218	56713
Arkadelphia, AR	870	71923, 71998-71999
Arkansas City, AR	870	71630
Arkansas City, KS	620	67005
Arlington, MA	339, 781	02474-02476
Arlington, MN	507	55307
Arlington, TN	901	38002
Arlington, TX	682, 817	76001-76019, 76094-76096
Arlington, VT	802	05250
Arlington, VA	571, 703	22201-22230, 22234, 22240*
Arlington, WA	360	98223
Arlington Heights, IL	224, 847	60004-60006
Armada, MI	586	48005
Armonk, NY	914	10504
Armour, SD	605	57313
Armstrong, IA	712	50514
Arnett, OK	580	73832
Arnold, MD	410	21012
Arnold, MO	636	63010
Arnold, PA	724, 878	15068
Arnold AFB, TN	931	37389
Aromas, CA	831	95004
Arroyo Grande, CA	805	93420-93421
Artesia, CA	562	90701-90703
Artesia, NM	505	88210-88211
Artesian, SD	605	57314
Arthur, IL	217	61911
Arthur, NE	308	69121
Arthurdale, WV	304	26520
Arvada, CO	303, 720	80001-80007, 80021, 80403
Arvilla, ND	701	58214
Arvin, CA	661	93203
Arvonia, VA	434	23004
Asbury, NJ	908	08802
Asbury Park, NJ	732, 848	07712
Ash Flat, AR	870	72513
Ashaway, RI	401	02804
Ashburn, GA	229	31714
Ashburn, VA	571, 703	20146-20149, 22093
Ashdown, AR	870	71822
Asheboro, NC	336	27203-27205
Asheville, NC	828	28801-28806, 28810-28816
Ashford, AL	334	36312
Ashford, WA	360	98304
Ashippun, WI	920	53003
Ashland, AL	256	36251
Ashland, KS	620	67831
Ashland, KY	606	41101-41105, 41114
Ashland, ME	207	04732, 04737, 04759
Ashland, MA	508, 774	01721
Ashland, MS	662	38603
Ashland, MT	406	59003-59004
Ashland, NE	402	68003
Ashland, NH	603	03217
Ashland, OH	419, 567	44805
Ashland, OR	541, 458	97520
Ashland, PA	570	17921
Ashland, VA	804	23005
Ashland, WI	715, 534	54806
Ashland City, TN	615	37015
Ashley, ND	701	58413
Ashtabula, OH	440	44004-44005
Ashton, ID	208	83420, 83447
Ashton, IL	815	61006
Ashville, AL	205	35953
Ashville, NY	716	14710
Ashville, OH	740	43103
Asotin, WA	509	99402
Aspen, CO	970	81611-81612
Aspermont, TX	940	79502
Assumption, IL	217	62510
Aston, PA	484, 610	19014
Astoria, NY	347, 718	11101-11106
Astoria, OR	503	97103
Atascadero, CA	805	93422-93423
Atchison, KS	913	66002
Atco, NJ	856	08004
Atglen, PA	484, 610	19310
Athens, AL	256	35611-35614
Athens, GA	706, 762	30601-30612
Athens, OH	740	45701
Athens, TN	423	37303, 37371
Athens, TX	903	75751-75752
Athens, WV	304	24712
Atherton, CA	650	94027
Athol, ID	208	83801
Athol, MA	351, 978	01331, 01368
Atkinson, NH	603	03811
Atlanta, GA	404, 470, 678	30301-30380, 30384-30399*
Atlanta, MI	989	49709
Atlanta, TX	903	75551
Atlantic, IA	712	50022
Atlantic, NC	252	28511
Atlantic Beach, FL	904	32224, 32233
Atlantic Beach, NC	252	28512
Atlantic City, NJ	609	08400-08406
Atmore, AL	251	36502-36504
Atoka, OK	580	74525, 74542
Attalla, AL	256	35954
Attica, IN	765	47918
Attica, NY	585	14011
Attica, OH	419, 567	44807
Attleboro, MA	508, 774	02703
Attleboro Falls, MA	508, 774	02763
Atwater, CA	209	95301, 95342
Atwood, KS	785	67730
Au Gres, MI	989	48703
Auburn, AL	334	36830-36832
Auburn, CA	530	95602-95604
Auburn, IL	217	62615
Auburn, IN	219	46706
Auburn, KY	270	42206
Auburn, ME	207	04210-04212
Auburn, MA	508, 774	01501
Auburn, NE	402	68305
Auburn, NY	315	13021-13024
Auburn, WA	253	98001-98003, 98023, 98047*
Auburn University, AL	334	36849
Auburndale, FL	863	33823
Auburndale, MA	617, 857	02466
Audubon, IA	712	50025
Audubon, PA	484, 610	19403, 19407
Augusta, AR	870	72006
Augusta, GA	706, 762	30901-30919, 30999
Augusta, KS	316	67010
Augusta, ME	207	04330-04338
Augusta, MI	616	49012
Augusta, MT	406	59410
Auke Bay, AK	907	99821
Aumsville, OR	503, 971	97325
Aurora, CO	303, 720	80002, 80010-80019, 80040*
Aurora, IL	331, 630	60504-60507, 60568, 60572*
Aurora, IN	812	47001
Aurora, MN	218	55705
Aurora, MO	417	65605
Aurora, NE	402	68818
Aurora, NY	315	13026
Aurora, OH	234, 330	44202
Aurora, OR	503, 971	97002
Austell, GA	470, 770	30106, 30168
Austin, IN	812	47102
Austin, MN	507	55912
Austin, PA	814	16720
Austin, TX	512	73301, 73344, 78701-78774*
Austinburg, OH	440	44010
Autaugaville, AL	334	36003
Ava, MO	417	65608
Avalon, CA	310, 424	90704
Avenal, CA	559	93204
Avenel, NJ	732, 848	07001
Aventura, FL	305, 786	33160, 33180, 33280
Avery Island, LA	337	70513
Avoca, PA	570	18641
Avon, CO	970	81620
Avon, CT	860	06001
Avon, MA	508, 774	02322
Avon, MN	320	56310
Avon, OH	440	44011
Avon Lake, OH	440	44012
Avon Park, FL	863	33825-33826
Avondale, AZ	623	85323
Avondale, PA	484, 610	19311
Axis, AL	251	36505
Axtell, KS	785	66403
Axtell, NE	308	68924
Ayer, MA	351, 978	01432
Azle, TX	682, 817	76020, 76098
Aztec, NM	505	87410
Azusa, CA	626	91702

B

City	Area Code(s)	Zip Code(s)
Babson Park, FL	863	33827
Babson Park, MA	339, 781	02457
Babylon, NY	631	11702-11707
Bad Axe, MI	989	48413
Bagdad, KY	502	40003
Bagley, MN	218	56621
Baileys Harbor, WI	920	54202
Bainbridge, GA	229	31717-31718
Bainbridge Island, WA	206	98110
Baird, TX	915	79504
Baker, LA	225	70704, 70714
Baker, MT	406	59313, 59354
Baker, NV	775	89311
Baker City, OR	541, 458	97814
Bakersfield, CA	661	93301-93313, 93380-93390
Bakerstown, PA	724, 878	15007
Bakersville, NC	828	28705
Bal Harbour, FL	305, 786	33154
Bala Cynwyd, PA	484, 610	19004
Baldwin, GA	706, 762	30511

*Partial list of zip codes, including main range

City	Area Code(s)	Zip Code(s)
Baldwin, LA	337	70514
Baldwin, MI	231	49304
Baldwin, NY	516	11510
Baldwin, WI	715, 534	54002
Baldwin City, KS	785	66006
Baldwin Park, CA	626	91706
Baldwinsville, NY	315	13027
Ball Ground, GA	470, 770	30107
Ballinger, TX	915	76821
Ballston Spa, NY	518	12020
Ballwin, MO	636	63011, 63021-63024
Bally, PA	484, 610	19503
Balsam Lake, WI	715, 534	54810
Baltimore, MD	410, 443	21075, 21201-21244, 21250*
Bamberg, SC	803	29003
Bandera, TX	830	78003
Bangor, ME	207	04401-04402
Bangor, PA	484, 610	18010-18013, 18050
Bangor, WI	608	54614
Banner Elk, NC	828	28604, 28691
Banning, CA	951	92220
Bannock, OH	740	43972
Bannockburn, IL	224, 847	60015
Bar Harbor, ME	207	04609
Baraboo, WI	608	53913
Baraga, MI	906	49908
Barberton, OH	234, 330	44203
Barboursville, WV	304	25504
Barbourville, KY	606	40906
Bardstown, KY	502	40004
Bardwell, KY	270	42023
Barker, NY	716	14012
Barksdale AFB, LA	318	71110
Barnard, VT	802	05031
Barnardsville, NC	828	28709
Barnesville, GA	470, 770	30204
Barneveld, NY	315	13304
Barnstable, MA	508, 774	02630, 02634
Barnwell, SC	803	29812-29813
Barre, MA	351, 978	01005
Barre, VT	802	05641
Barrington, IL	224, 847	60010-60011
Barrington, NH	603	03825
Barrington, NJ	856	08007
Barron, WI	715, 534	54812
Barrow, AK	907	99723, 99734, 99759, 99789*
Barstow, CA	760, 442	92310-92312
Bartlesville, OK	918	74003-74006
Bartlett, IL	331, 630	60103, 60108, 60133
Bartlett, NE	308	68622
Bartlett, TN	901	38133-38135, 38184
Bartlett, TX	254	76511
Bartow, FL	863	33830-33831
Basalt, CO	970	81621
Basin, WY	307	82410
Basking Ridge, NJ	908	07920, 07939
Bassett, NE	402	68714
Bassett, VA	276	24055
Bastrop, LA	318	71220-71221
Bastrop, TX	512	78602
Batavia, IL	331, 630	60510, 60539
Batavia, NY	585	14020-14021
Batavia, OH	513	45103
Batesburg, SC	803	29006
Batesville, AR	870	72501-72503
Batesville, IN	812	47006
Batesville, MS	662	38606
Bath, ME	207	04530
Bath, NY	607	14810
Bath, OH	234, 330	44210
Bath, PA	484, 610	18014
Bath, SD	605	57427
Baton Rouge, LA	225	70801-70827, 70831-70837*
Battle Creek, MI	616	49014-49018
Battle Creek, NE	402	68715
Battle Ground, WA	360	98604
Battle Mountain, NV	775	89820
Baudette, MN	218	56623
Baxley, GA	912	31513-31515
Bay City, MI	989	48706-48708
Bay City, TX	979	77404, 77414
Bay Harbor, MI	231	49770
Bay Harbor Islands, FL	305, 786	33154
Bay Minette, AL	251	36507
Bay Pines, FL	727	33744
Bay Saint Louis, MS	228	39520-39521, 39525
Bay Shore, NY	631	11706
Bay Springs, MS	601, 769	39422
Bay Village, OH	440	44140
Bayamon, PR	787, 939	00956-00961
Bayard, NE	308	69334
Bayboro, NC	252	28515
Bayfield, WI	715, 534	54814
Bayonne, NJ	201, 551	07002
Bayou La Batre, AL	251	36509
Bayport, MN	651	55003
Bayport, NY	631	11705
Bayside, NY	347, 718	11359-11361
Baytown, TX	281, 832	77520-77522
Bayville, NJ	732, 848	08721
Beach, ND	701	58621
Beach Lake, PA	570	18405
Beachwood, OH	216	44122
Beacon, NY	845	12508
Beale AFB, CA	530	95903
Bean Station, TN	865	37708
Bear Creek, WI	715, 534	54922
Bear Mountain, NY	845	10911
Bearden, AR	870	71720
Beatrice, NE	402	68310
Beattyville, KY	606	41311
Beaufort, NC	252	28516
Beaufort, SC	843	29901-29906
Beaumont, CA	951	92223
Beaumont, TX	409	77657, 77701-77713, 77720*
Beaumont, VA	804	23014
Beaver, OK	580	73932
Beaver, PA	724, 878	15009
Beaver, UT	435	84713
Beaver, WV	304	25813
Beaver City, NE	308	68926
Beaver Creek, CO	970	81620
Beaver Dam, KY	270	42320
Beaver Dam, WI	920	53916-53917
Beaver Dams, NY	607	14812
Beaver Falls, NY	315	13305
Beaver Falls, PA	724, 878	15010
Beavercreek, OH	937	45410, 45430-45434, 45440
Beaverton, OR	503, 971	97005-97008, 97075-97078
Bechtelsville, PA	484, 610	19505
Beckley, WV	304	25801-25802, 25926
Bedford, IN	812	47421
Bedford, IA	712	50833
Bedford, KY	502	40006
Bedford, MA	339, 781	01730-01731
Bedford, NH	603	03110
Bedford, OH	440	44146
Bedford, PA	814	15522
Bedford, TX	682, 817	76021-76022, 76095
Bedford, VA	540	24523
Bedford Heights, OH	216	44128, 44146
Bedford Hills, NY	914	10507
Bedford Park, IL	708	60455-60459, 60499-60501*
Bedminster, NJ	908	07921
Beebe, AR	501	72012
Beech Creek, PA	570	16822
Beech Grove, IN	317	46107
Beeville, TX	361	78102-78104
Bel Air, MD	410	21014-21015
Belcamp, MD	410	21017
Belcourt, ND	701	58316
Belding, MI	616	48809, 48887
Belfast, ME	207	04915
Belgrade, MT	406	59714
Belhaven, NC	252	27810
Bell, CA	323	90201-90202, 90270
Bell Gardens, CA	562	90201-90202
Bella Vista, AR	479	72714-72715
Bellaire, MI	231	49615
Bellaire, TX	713, 832	77401-77402
Belle Chasse, LA	504	70037
Belle Fourche, SD	605	57717
Belle Glade, FL	561	33430
Belle Mead, NJ	908	08502
Belle Plaine, MN	952	56011
Belle Vernon, PA	724, 878	15012
Bellefontaine, OH	937	43311
Bellefonte, PA	814	16823
Bellerose, NY	347, 718	11426
Belleview, FL	352	34420-34421
Belleville, IL	618	62220-62226
Belleville, KS	785	66935
Belleville, MI	734	48111-48112
Belleville, NJ	862, 973	07109
Belleville, PA	717	17004
Belleville, WI	608	53508
Bellevue, IA	563	52031
Bellevue, NE	402	68005, 68123, 68147, 68157
Bellevue, OH	419, 567	44811
Bellevue, WA	425	98004-98009, 98015
Bellflower, CA	562	90706-90707
Bellingham, MA	508, 774	02019
Bellingham, WA	360	98225-98228
Bellmawr, NJ	856	08031, 08099
Bellmore, NY	516	11710
Bellows Falls, VT	802	05101
Bellport, NY	631	11713
Bells, TN	731	38006
Bellville, OH	419, 567	44813
Bellville, TX	979	77418
Bellvue, CO	970	80512
Bellwood, IL	708	60104
Bellwood, PA	814	16617
Belmont, CA	650	94002-94003
Belmont, MA	617, 857	02478-02479
Belmont, MS	662	38827
Belmont, NH	603	03220
Belmont, NY	585	14813
Belmont, NC	704, 980	28012
Beloit, KS	785	67420
Beloit, WI	608	53511-53512
Belpre, OH	740	45714
Belton, SC	864	29627
Belton, TX	254	76513
Beltsville, MD	301	20704-20705
Belvidere, IL	815	61008
Belvidere, NJ	908	07823
Belzoni, MS	662	39038
Bemidji, MN	218	56601, 56619
Bend, OR	541, 458	97701-97702, 97707-97709
Benicia, CA	707	94510
Benjamin, TX	940	79505
Benkelman, NE	308	69021
Bennettsville, SC	843	29512
Bennington, NH	603	03442
Bennington, VT	802	05201
Bensalem, PA	215, 267	19020-19021
Bensenville, IL	331, 630	60105-60106, 60399
Benson, AZ	520	85602
Benson, MN	320	56215
Benson, NC	919	27504
Benton, AR	501	72015-72018, 72022, 72158
Benton, IL	618	62812
Benton, KY	270	42025
Benton, LA	318	71006
Benton, MO	573	63736
Benton, PA	570	17814
Benton, TN	423	37307
Benton Harbor, MI	616	49022-49023
Bentonville, AR	479	72712, 72716
Berea, KY	859	40403-40404
Berea, OH	440	44017
Bergenfield, NJ	201, 551	07621
Berkeley, CA	510	94701-94712, 94720
Berkeley, IL	708	60163
Berkeley, MO	314	63134, 63140
Berkeley Heights, NJ	908	07922
Berkeley Springs, WV	304	25411
Berlin, CT	860	06037
Berlin, MD	410	21811
Berlin, NH	603	03570
Berlin, NJ	856	08009
Berlin, NY	518	12022
Berlin, OH	234, 330	44610
Berlin, PA	814	15530
Berlin, WI	920	54923
Berlin Heights, OH	419, 567	44814
Bernalillo, NM	505	87004
Bernardsville, NJ	908	07924
Berne, IN	260	46711, 46769
Berrien Springs, MI	616	49103-49104
Berryville, AR	870	72616
Berryville, VA	540	22611
Berwick, PA	570	18603
Berwyn, IL	708	60402
Berwyn, PA	484, 610	19312
Beryl, UT	435	84714
Bessemer, AL	205	35020-35023
Bessemer, MI	906	49911
Bessemer City, NC	704, 980	28016
Bethany, CT	203	06524

*Partial list of zip codes, including main range

City	Area Code(s)	Zip Code(s)
Bethany, MO	660	64424
Bethany, OK	405	73008
Bethany, WV	304	26032
Bethany Beach, DE	302	19930
Bethel, AK	907	99559, 99637, 99679-99680*
Bethel, CT	203	06801
Bethel, ME	207	04217, 04286
Bethel, MN	763	55005
Bethel, VT	802	05032
Bethel Park, PA	412, 878	15102
Bethesda, MD	240, 301	20810-20817, 20824-20827*
Bethlehem, GA	470, 770	30620
Bethlehem, PA	484, 610	18015-18020, 18025
Bethpage, NY	516	11714
Bettendorf, IA	563	52722
Beulah, MI	231	49617
Beulah, ND	701	58523
Beverly, MA	351, 978	01915
Beverly, NJ	609	08010
Beverly, OH	740	45715, 45721
Beverly Hills, CA	310, 323, 424	90209-90213
Bexley, OH	614	43209
Biddeford, ME	207	04005-04007
Big Bear Lake, CA	909	92315
Big Bend National Park, TX	915	79834
Big Cabin, OK	918	74332
Big Island, VA	434	24526
Big Lake, AK	907	99652
Big Lake, MN	763	55309
Big Lake, TX	915	76932
Big Pine Key, FL	305, 786	33043
Big Rapids, MI	231	49307
Big Rock, IL	331, 630	60511
Big Sky, MT	406	59716
Big Spring, TX	915	79720-79721
Big Stone Gap, VA	276	24219
Big Sur, CA	831	93920
Big Timber, MT	406	59011
Bigfork, MN	218	56628, 56639
Bigfork, MT	406	59911
Biglerville, PA	717	17307
Billerica, MA	351, 978	01821-01822, 01862
Billings, MT	406	59101-59117
Billings, OK	580	74630
Biloxi, MS	228	39530-39535, 39540
Bingen, WA	509	98605
Binger, OK	405	73009
Bingham Farms, MI	248, 947	48025
Binghamton, NY	607	13901-13905
Bird-in-Hand, PA	717	17505
Birdsboro, PA	484, 610	19508
Birmingham, AL	205	35201-35249, 35253-35255*
Birmingham, MI	248, 947	48009-48012
Birmingham, NJ	609	08011
Bisbee, AZ	520	85603
Biscoe, NC	910	27209
Bishop, CA	760, 442	93512-93515
Bishopville, SC	803	29010
Bismarck, ND	701	58501-58507
Bison, SD	605	57620
Bixby, OK	918	74008
Black Butte Ranch, OR	541, 458	97759
Black Creek, NC	252	27813
Black Earth, WI	608	53515
Black Hawk, CO	303, 720	80403, 80422
Black Mountain, NC	828	28711
Black River Falls, WI	715, 534	54615
Blackfoot, ID	208	83221
Blacksburg, SC	864	29702
Blacksburg, VA	540	24060-24063
Blackshear, GA	912	31516
Blackwell, OK	580	74631
Blackwood, NJ	856	08012
Bladensburg, MD	301	20710
Blaine, MN	763	55014, 55434, 55449
Blaine, WA	360	98230-98231
Blair, NE	402	68008-68009
Blairsville, GA	706, 762	30512-30514
Blairsville, PA	724, 878	15717
Blakely, GA	229	31723
Blakeslee, PA	570	18610
Blanchester, OH	937	45107
Bland, VA	276	24315
Blanding, UT	435	84511
Blandon, PA	484, 610	19510
Blasdell, NY	716	14219
Blauvelt, NY	845	10913
Blissfield, MI	517	49228
Blomkest, MN	320	56216
Bloomfield, CT	860	06002
Bloomfield, IN	812	47424
Bloomfield, IA	641	52537-52538
Bloomfield, MO	573	63825
Bloomfield, NJ	862, 973	07003
Bloomfield Hills, MI	248, 947	48301-48304
Bloomingdale, IL	331, 630	60108, 60117
Bloomingdale, IN	765	47832
Bloomington, CA	909	92316
Bloomington, IL	309	61701-61704, 61709-61710*
Bloomington, IN	812	47401-47408, 47490
Bloomington, MN	952	55420, 55425, 55431, 55435*
Bloomsburg, PA	570	17815, 17839
Bloomsbury, NJ	908	08804
Blountstown, FL	850	32424
Blountville, TN	423	37617
Blowing Rock, NC	828	28605
Blue Anchor, NJ	609	08037
Blue Ash, OH	513	45242
Blue Ball, PA	717	17506
Blue Bell, PA	215	19422-19424
Blue Earth, MN	507	56013
Blue Hill, ME	207	04614
Blue Island, IL	708	60406, 60827
Blue Mounds, WI	608	53517
Blue Mountain, MS	662	38610
Blue Ridge, GA	706, 762	30513
Blue Springs, MO	816	64013-64015
Bluefield, VA	276	24605
Bluefield, WV	304	24701
Bluegrove, TX	940	76352
Bluffton, IN	260	46714
Bluffton, OH	419, 567	45817
Bluffton, SC	843	29910
Blunt, SD	605	57522
Blythe, CA	760, 442	92225-92226, 92280
Blytheville, AR	870	72315-72319
Blythewood, SC	803	29016
Boardman, OH	234, 330	44512-44513
Boardman, OR	541, 458	97818
Boaz, AL	256	35956-35957
Boca Raton, FL	561	33427-33434, 33464, 33481*
Bodega Bay, CA	707	94923
Boerne, TX	830	78006, 78015
Bogalusa, LA	985	70427-70429
Bogart, GA	706, 762	30622
Bogota, NJ	201, 551	07603
Bohemia, NY	631	11716
Boiling Springs, NC	704, 980	28017
Boise, ID	208	83701-83735, 83744, 83756*
Boise City, OK	580	73933
Boley, OK	918	74829
Bolingbrook, IL	331, 630	60439-60440, 60490
Bolivar, MO	417	65613, 65727
Bolivar, TN	731	38008, 38074
Bolivia, NC	910	28422
Bolton, CT	860	06043
Bolton, MA	351, 978	01740
Bolton Landing, NY	518	12814
Bon Air, VA	804	23235
Bon Secour, AL	251	36511
Bon Wier, TX	409	75928
Bonham, TX	903	75418
Bonifay, FL	850	32425
Bonita, CA	619	91902, 91908
Bonita Springs, FL	239	34133-34136
Bonner Springs, KS	913	66012
Bonners Ferry, ID	208	83805
Bono, AR	870	72416
Boone, IA	515	50036-50037
Boone, NC	828	28607-28608
Booneville, AR	479	72927
Booneville, KY	606	41314
Booneville, MS	662	38829
Boonton, NJ	862, 973	07005
Boonville, IN	812	47601
Boonville, MO	660	65233
Boothbay Harbor, ME	207	04536-04538, 04570
Boothwyn, PA	484, 610	19061
Borden, IN	812	47106
Bordentown, NJ	609	08505
Borger, TX	806	79007-79008
Boring, OR	503, 971	97009
Borrego Springs, CA	760, 442	92004
Boscawen, NH	603	03303
Boscobel, WI	608	53805
Bossier City, LA	318	71111-71113, 71171-71172
Boston, MA	617, 857	02101-02137, 02163, 02196*
Bothell, WA	425	98011-98012, 98021, 98028*
Botkins, OH	937	45306
Bottineau, ND	701	58318
Bouckville, NY	315	13310
Boulder, CO	303, 720	80301-80310, 80314, 80321*
Boulder, MT	406	59632
Boulder City, NV	702	89005-89006
Bound Brook, NJ	732, 848	08805
Bountiful, UT	801, 385	84010-84011
Bourbon, MO	573	65441
Bourbonnais, IL	815	60914
Bovey, MN	218	55709
Bow, NH	603	03304
Bow, WA	360	98232
Bowbells, ND	701	58721
Bowdon, GA	470, 770	30108
Bowerston, OH	740	44695
Bowie, AZ	520	85605
Bowie, MD	301	20715-20721
Bowie, TX	940	76230
Bowling Green, FL	863	33834
Bowling Green, KY	270	42101-42104
Bowling Green, MO	573	63334
Bowling Green, OH	419, 567	43402-43403
Bowling Green, VA	804	22427-22428
Bowman, ND	701	58623
Bowmansville, NY	716	14026
Box Elder, MT	406	59521
Boxborough, MA	351, 978	01719
Boyden, IA	712	51234
Boydton, VA	434	23917
Boyertown, PA	484, 610	19512
Boylston, MA	508, 774	01505
Boyne Falls, MI	231	49713
Boynton Beach, FL	561	33424-33426, 33435-33437*
Boys Town, NE	402	68010
Bozeman, MT	406	59715-59719, 59771-59773
Bozrah, CT	860	06334
Brackenridge, PA	724, 878	15014
Brackettville, TX	830	78832
Bradbury, CA	626	91010
Braddock, PA	412, 878	15104
Bradenton, FL	941	34201-34212, 34280-34282
Bradford, PA	814	16701
Bradford, VT	802	05033
Bradley, IL	815	60915
Bradley, ME	207	04411
Bradley, WV	304	25818
Brady, TX	915	76825
Braham, MN	320	55006
Braidwood, IL	815	60408
Brainard, NE	402	68626
Brainerd, MN	218	56401, 56425
Braintree, MA	339, 781	02184-02185
Braithwaite, LA	504	70040, 70046
Branchburg, NJ	908	08876
Branchville, NJ	862, 973	07826-07827, 07890
Brandenburg, KY	270	40108
Brandon, FL	813	33508-33511
Brandon, MS	601, 769	39042-39043, 39047, 39232
Brandon, VT	802	05733
Branford, CT	203	06405
Branson, MO	417	65615-65616
Braselton, GA	470, 678, 770	30517
Brattleboro, VT	802	05301-05304
Brawley, CA	760, 442	92227
Braymer, MO	660	64624
Brazil, IN	812	47834
Brea, CA	714	92821-92823
Breckenridge, CO	970	80424
Breckenridge, MN	218	56520
Breckenridge, TX	254	76424
Brecksville, OH	440	44141
Breese, IL	618	62230
Breezy Point, MN	218	56472
Bremen, GA	470, 770	30110
Bremen, IN	574	46506
Bremen, OH	740	43107
Bremerton, WA	360	98310-98314, 98337
Brenham, TX	979	77833-77834
Brent, AL	205	35034
Brentwood, NH	603	03833
Brentwood, NY	631	11717
Brentwood, TN	615	37024-37027

*Partial list of zip codes, including main range

City	Area Code(s)	Zip Code(s)
Bretton Woods, NH	603	03575
Brevard, NC	828	28712
Brewer, ME	207	04412
Brewerton, NY	315	13029
Brewster, MA	508, 774	02631
Brewster, NE	308	68821
Brewster, NY	845	10509
Brewster, OH	234, 330	44613
Brewster, WA	509	98812
Brewton, AL	251	36426-36427
Briarcliff Manor, NY	914	10510
Briarwood, NY	347, 718	11435
Brick, NJ	732, 848	08723-08724
Brickeys, AR	870	72320
Bridgeport, AL	256	35740
Bridgeport, CA	760, 442	93517
Bridgeport, CT	203	06601-06615, 06650, 06673*
Bridgeport, NE	308	69336
Bridgeport, NJ	856	08014
Bridgeport, PA	484, 610	19405
Bridgeport, WV	304	26330
Bridgeton, MO	314	63044-63045
Bridgeton, NJ	856	08302
Bridgeview, IL	708	60455
Bridgeville, PA	412, 878	15017
Bridgewater, MA	508, 774	02324-02325
Bridgewater, NJ	908	08807
Bridgewater, VA	540	22812
Bridgewater Corners, VT	802	05035
Bridgman, MI	616	49106
Bridgton, ME	207	04009
Brigantine, NJ	609	08203
Brigham City, UT	435	84302
Brighton, CO	303, 720	80601-80603
Brighton, MA	617, 857	02135
Brighton, MI	810	48114-48116
Brighton, UT	801, 385	84121
Brillion, WI	920	54110
Brimfield, IL	309	61517
Brinkley, AR	870	72021
Brinson, GA	229	31725
Brisbane, CA	415, 650	94005
Bristol, CT	860	06010-06011
Bristol, FL	850	32321
Bristol, IN	574	46507
Bristol, PA	215, 267	19007
Bristol, RI	401	02809
Bristol, TN	423	37620-37621, 37625
Bristol, VT	802	05443
Bristol, VA	276	24201-24203, 24209
Bristol, WI	262	53104
Britton, SD	605	57430
Broadalbin, NY	518	12025
Broadus, MT	406	59317
Broadview, IL	708	60153-60155
Broadview Heights, OH	440	44147
Broadway, VA	540	22815
Brockport, NY	585	14420
Brockton, MA	508, 774	02301-02305
Brockway, PA	814	15824
Brocton, NY	716	14716
Brodhead, WI	608	53520
Brodnax, VA	434	23920
Broken Arrow, OK	918	74011-74014
Broken Bow, NE	308	68822
Broken Bow, OK	580	74728
Bronson, FL	352	32621
Bronwood, GA	229	31726
Bronx, NY	347, 718	10451-10475, 10499
Bronxville, NY	914	10708
Brook Park, OH	216	44142
Brookfield, CT	203	06804
Brookfield, IL	708	60513
Brookfield, MO	660	64628
Brookfield, OH	234, 330	44403
Brookfield, WI	262	53005-53008, 53045
Brookhaven, MS	601, 769	39601-39603
Brookhaven, PA	484, 610	19015
Brookings, OR	541, 458	97415
Brookings, SD	605	57006-57007
Brookline, MA	617, 857	02445-02447
Brooklyn, CT	860	06234
Brooklyn, IA	641	52211
Brooklyn, MI	517	49230
Brooklyn, NY	347, 718	11201-11256
Brooklyn Center, MN	763	55428-55430, 55443-55444
Brooklyn Heights, OH	216	44109, 44131

City	Area Code(s)	Zip Code(s)
Brooklyn Park, MN	763	55428-55429, 55443-55445
Brooks AFB, TX	210	78235
Brookshire, TX	281, 832	77423
Brooksville, FL	352	34601-34614
Brooksville, KY	606	41004
Brookville, IN	765	47012
Brookville, OH	937	45309
Brookville, PA	814	15825
Brookwood, AL	205	35444
Broomall, PA	484, 610	19008
Broomfield, CO	303, 720	80020-80021, 80038, 80234
Broussard, LA	337	70518
Brown Deer, WI	414	53209, 53223
Brownfield, TX	806	79316, 79376
Browning, MT	406	59417
Browns Mills, NJ	609	08015
Brownsboro, AL	256	35741
Brownsburg, IN	317	46112
Brownstown, IN	812	47220
Brownsville, KY	270	42210
Brownsville, PA	724, 878	15417
Brownsville, TN	731	38012
Brownsville, TX	956	78520-78526
Brownsville, VT	802	05037
Brownsville, WI	920	53006
Brownville, NY	315	13615
Brownwood, TX	915	76801-76804
Bruce, SD	605	57220
Bruceton Mills, WV	304	26525
Brunswick, GA	912	31520-31527, 31561
Brunswick, ME	207	04011, 04053
Brunswick, NC	910	28424
Brunswick, OH	234, 330	44212
Brush, CO	970	80723
Brusly, LA	225	70719
Bryan, OH	419, 567	43506
Bryan, TX	979	77801-77808
Bryantown, MD	301	20617
Bryce Canyon, UT	435	84717
Bryn Athyn, PA	215, 267	19009
Bryn Mawr, PA	484, 610	19010
Bryson City, NC	828	28713
Buchanan, GA	470, 770	30113
Buchanan, MI	616	49107
Buchanan, VA	540	24066
Buckeye, AZ	623	85326
Buckhannon, WV	304	26201
Buckingham, VA	434	23921
Bucyrus, OH	419, 567	44820
Buda, TX	512	78610
Budd Lake, NJ	862, 973	07828
Buellton, CA	805	93427
Buena, NJ	856	08310
Buena Park, CA	714	90620-90624
Buena Vista, CO	719	81211
Buena Vista, GA	229	31803
Buena Vista, VA	540	24416
Buffalo, MN	763	55313
Buffalo, MO	417	65622
Buffalo, NY	716	14201-14233, 14240-14241*
Buffalo, OK	580	73834
Buffalo, SD	605	57720
Buffalo, WY	307	82834, 82840
Buffalo Gap, TX	915	79508
Buffalo Grove, IL	224, 847	60089
Buford, GA	470, 678, 770	30515-30519
Buhl, ID	208	83316
Buies Creek, NC	910	27506
Bullhead City, AZ	928	86426-86430, 86439-86442*
Bunker Hill, IN	765	46914
Bunker Hill, KS	785	67626
Bunn, NC	919	27508
Bunnell, FL	386	32110
Buras, LA	504	70041
Burbank, CA	818	91501-91510, 91521-91526
Burbank, IL	708	60459
Burgaw, NC	910	28425
Burgettstown, PA	724, 878	15021
Burien, WA	206	98146-98148, 98166-98168
Burke, SD	605	57523
Burke, VA	571, 703	22009, 22015
Burkesville, KY	270	42717
Burkeville, VA	434	23922
Burleigh, NJ	609	08210
Burleson, TX	682, 817	76028, 76097
Burley, ID	208	83318
Burlingame, CA	650	94010-94012

City	Area Code(s)	Zip Code(s)
Burlington, CO	719	80807
Burlington, IL	224, 847	60109
Burlington, IA	319	52601
Burlington, KS	620	66839
Burlington, KY	859	41005
Burlington, MA	339, 781	01803-01805
Burlington, NJ	609	08016
Burlington, NC	336	27215-27220
Burlington, VT	802	05401-05407
Burlington, WA	360	98233
Burlington, WI	262	53105
Burnet, TX	512	78611
Burnham, PA	717	17009
Burns, OR	541, 458	97710, 97720
Burnsville, MN	952	55306, 55337
Burnsville, NC	828	28714
Burr Ridge, IL	331, 630	60525-60527
Burton, MI	810	48509, 48519, 48529
Burton, OH	440	44021
Burtonsville, MD	301	20866
Burwell, NE	308	68823
Bushkill, PA	570	18324, 18371-18373
Bushnell, FL	352	33513
Bushnell, IL	309	61422
Butler, AL	205	36904
Butler, GA	478	31006
Butler, IN	260	46721
Butler, MD	410	21023
Butler, MO	660	64730
Butler, NJ	862, 973	07405
Butler, PA	724, 878	16001-16003
Butler, WI	262	53007
Butner, NC	919	27509
Butte, MT	406	59701-59703, 59707, 59750
Butte, NE	402	68722
Butterfield, MN	507	56120
Buxton, NC	252	27920
Buzzards Bay, MA	508, 774	02532, 02542
Byfield, MA	351, 978	01922
Byhalia, MS	662	38611
Byrdstown, TN	931	38549
Byron, IL	815	61010
Byron, MN	507	55920
Byron Center, MI	616	49315

C

City	Area Code(s)	Zip Code(s)
Cabazon, CA	951	92230, 92282
Cabot, AR	501	72023
Cabot, PA	724, 878	16023
Cadillac, MI	231	49601
Cadiz, KY	270	42211
Cadiz, OH	740	43907
Cahokia, IL	618	62206
Cairo, GA	229	31728
Cairo, IL	618	62914
Calabasas, CA	818	91301-91302, 91372
Calabasas Hills, CA	818	91301
Calais, ME	207	04619
Caldwell, ID	208	83605-83607
Caldwell, NJ	862, 973	07006-07007
Caldwell, OH	740	43724
Caldwell, TX	979	77836
Caledonia, MN	507	55921
Caledonia, NY	585	14423
Caledonia, WI	262	53108
Calexico, CA	760, 442	92231-92232
Calhoun, GA	706, 762	30701-30703
Calhoun, KY	270	42327
Calhoun, TN	423	37309
Calhoun City, MS	662	38916, 38955
Calico Rock, AR	870	72519
California, MD	301	20619
California, MO	573	65018, 65042
California, PA	724, 878	15419
Calipatria, CA	760, 442	92233
Calistoga, CA	707	94515
Callery, PA	724, 878	16024
Callicoon, NY	845	12723
Calmar, IA	563	52132
Calumet, MI	906	49913, 49918, 49942
Calumet City, IL	708	60409
Calumet Park, IL	708	60643, 60827
Camarillo, CA	805	93010-93012
Camas, WA	360	98607

*Partial list of zip codes, including main range

City	Area Code(s)	Zip Code(s)
Cambria, CA	805	93428
Cambridge, IL	309	61238
Cambridge, MD	410	21613
Cambridge, MA	617, 857	02138-02142, 02163, 02238*
Cambridge, MN	763	55008
Cambridge, NE	308	69022
Cambridge, OH	740	43725, 43750
Cambridge, WI	608	53523
Cambridge City, IN	765	47327
Cambridge Springs, PA	814	16403
Camden, AL	334	36726
Camden, AR	870	71701, 71711
Camden, DE	302	19934
Camden, IN	574	46917
Camden, ME	207	04843, 04847
Camden, MI	517	49232
Camden, NJ	856	08100-08110
Camden, NY	315	13316
Camden, NC	252	27921
Camden, SC	803	29020
Camden, TN	731	38320
Camdenton, MO	573	65020
Cameron, LA	337	70631
Cameron, MO	816	64429
Cameron, MT	760, 442	59720
Cameron, TX	254	76520
Cameron Park, CA	530	95682
Camilla, GA	229	31730
Camillus, NY	315	13031
Camp Douglas, WI	608	54618, 54637
Camp Hill, PA	717	17001, 17011-17012, 17089*
Camp Lejeune, NC	910	28542, 28547
Camp Pendleton, CA	760, 442	92054-92055
Camp Point, IL	217	62320
Camp Shelby, MS	601, 769	39401, 39407
Camp Springs, MD	301	20746-20748
Camp Verde, AZ	928	86322
Campbell, CA	408	95008-95011
Campbell Hall, NY	845	10916
Campbellsville, KY	270	42718-42719
Campton, KY	606	41301, 41342
Canadian, TX	806	79014
Canal Winchester, OH	614	43110
Canandaigua, NY	585	14424-14425
Canastota, NY	315	13032
Candler, NC	828	28715
Cando, ND	701	58324
Candor, NC	910	27229
Canfield, OH	234, 330	44406
Cannon AFB, NM	505	88101-88103
Cannon Beach, OR	503	97110
Cannon Falls, MN	507	55009
Canoga Park, CA	818	91303-91309, 91396
Canon City, CO	719	81212-81215, 81246
Canonsburg, PA	724, 878	15317
Canterbury, NH	603	03224
Canton, GA	470, 770	30114-30115
Canton, IL	309	61520
Canton, MA	339, 781	02021
Canton, MI	734	48187-48188
Canton, MS	601, 769	39046
Canton, MO	573	63435
Canton, NY	315	13617
Canton, OH	234, 330	44701-44714, 44718-44721*
Canton, PA	570	17724, 17743
Canton, SD	605	57013
Canton, TX	903	75103
Canyon, TX	806	79015-79016
Canyon City, OR	541, 458	97820
Canyonville, OR	541, 458	97417
Cape Canaveral, FL	321	32920
Cape Charles, VA	757	23310
Cape Coral, FL	239	33904, 33909-33910, 33914*
Cape Elizabeth, ME	207	04107
Cape Girardeau, MO	573	63701-63705
Cape May, NJ	609	08204
Cape May Court House, NJ	609	08210
Cape Vincent, NY	315	13618
Capitol Heights, MD	301	20731, 20743, 20753, 20790*
Capitola, CA	831	95010, 95062
Capron, VA	434	23829
Captain Cook, HI	808	96704
Captiva, FL	239	33924
Capulin, NM	505	88414
Carbondale, IL	618	62901-62903
Carbondale, PA	570	18407
Carefree, AZ	480	85377

City	Area Code(s)	Zip Code(s)
Carey, OH	419, 567	43316
Caribou, ME	207	04736
Carle Place, NY	516	11514
Carlinville, IL	217	62626
Carlisle, IN	812	47838
Carlisle, KY	859	40311, 40350
Carlisle, PA	717	17013
Carlisle, SC	864	29031
Carlsbad, CA	760, 442	92008-92009, 92013, 92018
Carlsbad, NM	505	88220-88221
Carlstadt, NJ	201, 551	07072
Carlton, MN	218	55718
Carlyle, IL	618	62231
Carmel, CA	831	93921-93923
Carmel, IN	317	46032-46033, 46082
Carmel, NY	845	10512
Carmel Valley, CA	831	93924
Carmi, IL	618	62821
Carmichael, CA	916	95608-95609
Carnegie, PA	412, 878	15106
Carnesville, GA	706, 762	30521
Carneys Point, NJ	856	08069
Caro, MI	989	48723
Carol Stream, IL	331, 630	60116, 60125-60128, 60132*
Carolina, PR	787, 939	00979-00988
Carpentersville, IL	224, 847	60110
Carpinteria, CA	805	93013-93014
Carrabassett Valley, ME	207	04947
Carrington, ND	701	58421
Carrizo Springs, TX	830	78834
Carrizozo, NM	505	88301
Carroll, IA	712	51401
Carroll Valley, PA	717	17320
Carrollton, AL	205	35447
Carrollton, GA	470, 770	30112, 30116-30119
Carrollton, IL	217	62016
Carrollton, KY	502	41008, 41045
Carrollton, MS	662	38917
Carrollton, MO	660	64633
Carrollton, OH	234, 330	44615
Carrollton, TX	469, 972	75006-75011
Carson, CA	310, 424	90745-90749, 90810
Carson, ND	701	58529
Carson City, MI	989	48811
Carson City, NV	775	89701-89706, 89711-89714*
Carter Lake, IA	712	51510
Carteret, NJ	732, 848	07008
Cartersville, GA	470, 770	30120-30121
Carterville, IL	618	62918
Carthage, IL	217	62321
Carthage, MS	601, 769	39051
Carthage, MO	417	64836
Carthage, NC	910	28327
Carthage, TN	615	37030
Carthage, TX	903	75633
Caruthersville, MO	573	63830
Carver, MA	508, 774	02330, 02355, 02366
Cary, IL	224, 847	60013
Cary, NC	919	27511-27513, 27518-27519
Casa Grande, AZ	520	85222, 85230
Cascade, ID	208	83611
Cascade Locks, OR	509	97014
Casey, IL	217	62420
Cashiers, NC	828	28717
Cashmere, WA	509	98815
Casper, WY	307	82601-82605, 82609, 82615*
Casselberry, FL	321, 407	32707-32708, 32718-32719*
Cassopolis, MI	616	49031
Cassville, MO	417	65623-65625
Castaic, CA	661	91310, 91384
Castine, ME	207	04420-04421
Castle Dale, UT	435	84513
Castle Point, NY	845	12511
Castle Rock, CO	303, 720	80104
Castleton, VT	802	05735
Castro Valley, CA	510	94546, 94552
Castroville, CA	831	95012
Catalina, AZ	520	85738-85739
Catasauqua, PA	484, 610	18032
Catawba, VA	540	24070
Catawissa, PA	570	17820
Cathedral City, CA	760, 442	92234-92235
Cathlamet, WA	360	98612
Catlettsburg, KY	606	41129
Catonsville, MD	410	21228
Catoosa, OK	918	74015
Catskill, NY	518	12414

City	Area Code(s)	Zip Code(s)
Cavalier, ND	701	58220
Cave Junction, OR	541, 458	97523, 97531
Cayce, SC	803	29033
Cazenovia, NY	315	13035
Cedar City, UT	435	84720-84721
Cedar Crest, NM	505	87008
Cedar Falls, IA	319	50613-50614
Cedar Falls, NC	336	27230
Cedar Grove, NJ	862, 973	07009
Cedar Grove, WI	920	53013
Cedar Hill, TX	469, 972	75104-75106
Cedar Knolls, NJ	862, 973	07927
Cedar Park, TX	512	78613, 78630
Cedar Rapids, IA	319	52401-52411, 52497-52499
Cedar Springs, GA	229	31732
Cedar Springs, MI	616	49319
Cedar Vale, KS	620	67024
Cedarburg, WI	262	53012
Cedartown, GA	470, 770	30125
Cedarville, OH	937	45314
Celebration, FL	321, 407	34747
Celina, OH	419, 567	45822, 45826
Celina, TN	931	38551
Centennial, CO	303, 720	80015-80016, 80111-80112*
Center, NE	402	68724
Center, ND	701	58530
Center, TX	936	75935
Center City, MN	651	55002, 55012
Center Hill, FL	352	33514
Center Line, MI	586	48015
Center Moriches, NY	631	11934
Center Point, TX	830	78010
Center Valley, PA	484, 610	18034
Centerburg, OH	740	43011
Centerport, NY	631	11721
Centerville, IA	641	52544
Centerville, MA	508, 774	02632-02636
Centerville, MO	573	63633
Centerville, OH	937	45458-45459
Centerville, TN	931	37033
Centerville, TX	903	75833
Centerville, UT	801, 385	84014
Central, SC	864	29630
Central City, CO	303, 720	80427
Central City, KY	270	42330
Central City, NE	308	68826
Central Falls, RI	401	02863
Central Islip, NY	631	11722, 11749, 11760
Central Point, OR	541, 458	97502
Centralia, IL	618	62801
Centralia, MO	573	65240
Centralia, WA	360	98531
Centre, AL	256	35960
Centre Hall, PA	814	16828
Centreville, AL	205	35042
Centreville, IL	618	62207
Centreville, MD	410	21617
Centreville, MI	616	49032
Centreville, MS	601, 769	39631
Centreville, VA	571, 703	20120-20122
Centuria, WI	715, 534	54824
Century, FL	850	32535
Ceres, CA	209	95307
Cerritos, CA	562	90701-90703
Chadds Ford, PA	484, 610	19317
Chadron, NE	308	69337
Chaffee, NY	585	14030
Chagrin Falls, OH	440	44022-44023
Chalfont, PA	215, 267	18914
Challis, ID	208	83226-83229
Chalmette, LA	504	70043-70044
Chama, NM	505	87520
Chamberlain, SD	605	57325-57326
Chambersburg, PA	717	17201
Chamblee, GA	470, 770	30341, 30366
Champaign, IL	217	61820-61826
Champion, PA	814	15622
Chandler, AZ	480	85224-85226, 85244-85249
Chandler, IN	812	47610
Chandler, OK	405	74834
Chandlerville, IL	217	62627
Chanhassen, MN	952	55317
Channahon, IL	815	60410
Channelview, TX	281, 832	77530
Channing, TX	806	79018, 79058
Chantilly, VA	571, 703	20151-20153
Chanute, KS	620	66720

Partial list of zip codes, including main range

City	Area Code(s)	Zip Code(s)
Chapel Hill, NC	919	27514-27517, 27599
Chapin, SC	803	29036
Chapmanville, WV	304	25508
Chappell, NE	308	69129
Chardon, OH	440	44024
Chariton, IA	641	50049
Charleroi, PA	724, 878	15022
Charles City, IA	641	50616, 50620
Charles City, VA	804	23030
Charles Town, WV	304	25414
Charleston, IL	217	61920
Charleston, ME	207	04422
Charleston, MS	662	38921, 38958
Charleston, MO	573	63834
Charleston, SC	843	29401-29425, 29492
Charleston, WV	304	25301-25339, 25350, 25356*
Charleston AFB, SC	843	29404
Charlestown, IN	812	47111
Charlestown, MA	617, 857	02129
Charlestown, NH	603	03603
Charlevoix, MI	231	49711, 49720
Charlotte, MI	517	48813
Charlotte, NC	704, 980	28201-28290, 28296-28299
Charlotte, TN	615	37036
Charlotte, VT	802	05445
Charlotte Court House, VA	434	23923
Charlotte Hall, MD	301	20622
Charlottesville, VA	434	22901-22911
Charlton City, MA	508, 774	01508
Chase City, VA	434	23924
Chaska, MN	952	55318
Chateaugay, NY	518	12920
Chatfield, MN	507	55923
Chatham, IL	217	62629
Chatham, MA	508, 774	02633
Chatham, NJ	862, 973	07928
Chatham, NY	518	12037
Chatham, VA	434	24531
Chatom, AL	251	36518
Chatsworth, CA	818	91311-91313
Chatsworth, GA	706, 762	30705
Chatsworth, IL	815	60921
Chattahoochee, FL	850	32324
Chattanooga, TN	423	37343, 37401-37424, 37450
Chautauqua, NY	716	14722
Chauvin, LA	985	70344
Cheboygan, MI	231	49721
Checotah, OK	918	74426
Cheektowaga, NY	716	14043, 14206, 14211-14215*
Chehalis, WA	360	98532
Chelan, WA	509	98816
Chelmsford, MA	351, 978	01824
Chelsea, MA	617, 857	02150
Chelsea, MI	734	48118
Chelsea, VT	802	05038
Cheltenham, PA	215, 267	19012
Cheney, KS	316	67025
Cheney, WA	509	99004
Cheraw, SC	843	29520
Cherokee, IA	712	51012
Cherokee, NC	828	28719
Cherokee, OK	580	73728
Cherry Hill, NJ	856	08002-08003, 08034
Cherry Point, NC	252	28533
Cherry Valley, IL	815	61016
Cherry Valley, MA	508, 774	01611
Cherryfield, ME	207	04622
Cherryville, NC	704, 980	28021
Chesapeake, VA	757	23320-23328
Chesapeake City, MD	410	21915
Cheshire, CT	203	06408-06411
Chester, CT	860	06412
Chester, GA	478	31012
Chester, IL	618	62233
Chester, MD	410	21619
Chester, MT	406	59522
Chester, NH	603	03036
Chester, NJ	908	07930
Chester, NY	845	10918
Chester, PA	484, 610	19013-19016, 19022
Chester, SC	803	29706
Chester, VA	804	23831, 23836
Chester, WV	304	26034
Chester Springs, PA	484, 610	19425
Chesterbrook, PA	484, 610	19087
Chesterfield, MI	586	48047, 48051
Chesterfield, MO	314, 636	63005-63006, 63017
Chesterfield, SC	843	29709
Chesterfield, VA	804	23832, 23838
Chesterfield Township, MI	586	48047, 48051
Chesterland, OH	440	44026
Chesterton, IN	219	46304
Chestertown, MD	410	21620, 21690
Chestertown, NY	518	12817
Chestnut Hill, MA	617, 857	02467
Chestnut Ridge, NY	845	10952, 10965, 10977
Cheswick, PA	724, 878	15024
Cheverly, MD	301	20781-20785
Chevy Chase, MD	301	20813-20815, 20825
Cheyenne, OK	580	73628
Cheyenne, WY	307	82001-82010
Cheyenne Wells, CO	719	80810
Cheyney, PA	484, 610	19319
Chicago, IL	312, 773	60601-60701, 60706-60707*
Chicago Heights, IL	708	60411-60412
Chickamauga, GA	706, 762	30707
Chickasaw, AL	251	36611
Chickasha, OK	405	73018, 73023
Chico, CA	530	95926-95929, 95973-95976
Chicopee, MA	413	01013-01014, 01020-01022
Chiefland, FL	352	32626, 32644
Childersburg, AL	256	35044
Childress, TX	940	79201
Chillicothe, IL	309	61523
Chillicothe, MO	660	64601
Chillicothe, OH	740	45601
Chilton, WI	920	53014
Chincoteague Island, VA	757	23336-23337
Chinle, AZ	928	86503, 86507, 86538, 86545*
Chino, CA	909	91708-91710
Chinook, MT	406	59523, 59535
Chipley, FL	850	32428
Chippewa Falls, WI	715, 534	54729, 54774
Chisholm, MN	218	55719
Chocorua, NH	603	03817
Choteau, MT	406	59422
Chowchilla, CA	559	93610
Christiana, PA	484, 610	17509
Christiansburg, VA	540	24068, 24073
Christmas, FL	321, 407	32709
Chuckey, TN	423	37641
Chula Vista, CA	619	91909-91915, 91921
Cicero, IL	708	60804
Cimarron, KS	620	67835
Cincinnati, OH	513	45201-45258, 45262-45280*
Cinnaminson, NJ	856	08077
Circle, MT	406	59215
Circle Pines, MN	763	55014
Circleville, OH	740	43113
Cisco, TX	254	76437
Citrus Heights, CA	916	95610-95611, 95621, 95662
City of Commerce, CA	323	90040, 90091
City of Industry, CA	626	90601, 91714-91716, 91732*
Clackamas, OR	503, 971	97015
Clairton, PA	412, 878	15025
Clallam Bay, WA	360	98326
Clanton, AL	205	35045-35046
Clare, MI	989	48617
Claremont, CA	909	91711
Claremont, NH	603	03743
Claremont, NC	828	28610
Claremore, OK	918	74017-74018
Clarence, NY	716	14031, 14221
Clarendon, AR	870	72029
Clarendon, TX	806	79226
Clarendon Hills, IL	331, 630	60514, 60527
Clarinda, IA	712	51632
Clarion, IA	515	50525-50526
Clarion, PA	814	16214
Clarissa, MN	218	56440
Clark, CO	970	80428
Clark, NJ	732, 848	07066
Clark, SD	605	57225
Clarkdale, AZ	928	86324
Clarkesville, GA	706, 762	30523
Clarks Summit, PA	570	18411
Clarksburg, MD	240, 301	20871
Clarksburg, WV	304	26301-26302, 26306, 26461
Clarksdale, MS	662	38614, 38669
Clarkston, MI	248, 947	48346-48348
Clarksville, AR	479	72830
Clarksville, IN	812	47129-47131
Clarksville, TN	931	37040-37044
Clarksville, TX	903	75426
Claude, TX	806	79019
Clawson, MI	248, 947	48017, 48398
Claxton, GA	912	30414-30417, 30438
Clay, WV	304	25043
Clay Center, KS	785	67432
Clay Center, NE	402	68933
Claymont, DE	302	19703
Clayton, AL	334	36016
Clayton, CA	925	94517
Clayton, DE	302	19938
Clayton, GA	706, 762	30525
Clayton, MO	314	63105, 63124
Clayton, NJ	856	08312
Clayton, NM	505	88415
Clayton, NC	919	27520
Clear Brook, VA	540	22624
Clear Creek, IN	812	47426
Clear Lake, IA	641	50428
Clear Lake, SD	605	57226
Clearfield, PA	814	16830
Clearfield, UT	801, 385	84015-84016, 84089
Clearwater, FL	727	33755-33769
Clearwater Beach, FL	727	33767
Cleburne, TX	682, 817	76031-76033
Cleghorn, IA	712	51014
Clementon, NJ	856	08021
Clements, CA	209	95227
Clements, MN	507	56224
Clemson, SC	864	29631-29634
Clermont, FL	352	34711-34713
Cleveland, GA	706, 762	30528
Cleveland, MS	662	38732-38733
Cleveland, OH	216, 440	44101-44149, 44177-44199
Cleveland, OK	918	74020
Cleveland, TN	423	37311-37312, 37320-37323*
Cleveland, TX	281, 832	77327-77328
Cleveland, WI	920	53015
Cleveland Heights, OH	216	44106, 44112, 44118-44121
Clewiston, FL	863	33440
Clifford, PA	570	18413
Cliffside, NC	828	28024
Cliffside Park, NJ	201, 551	07010
Cliffwood Beach, NJ	732, 848	07735
Clifton, AZ	928	85533
Clifton, KS	785	66937
Clifton, NJ	862, 973	07011-07015
Clifton, TN	931	38425
Clifton, TX	254	76634, 76644
Clifton Forge, VA	540	24422
Clifton Heights, PA	484, 610	19018
Clifton Park, NY	518	12065
Clifton Springs, NY	315	14432
Clines Corners, NM	505	87070
Clinton, AR	501	72031
Clinton, CT	860	06413
Clinton, IL	217	61727
Clinton, IN	765	47842
Clinton, IA	563	52732-52736, 52771
Clinton, KY	270	42031
Clinton, LA	225	70722
Clinton, ME	207	04927
Clinton, MD	301	20735
Clinton, MA	351, 978	01510
Clinton, MI	517	49236
Clinton, MN	320	56225
Clinton, MS	601, 769	39056-39060
Clinton, MO	660	64735
Clinton, NJ	908	08809
Clinton, NY	315	13323
Clinton, NC	910	28328-28329
Clinton, OK	580	73601
Clinton, SC	864	29325
Clinton, TN	865	37716-37717
Clinton Township, MI	586	48035-48038
Clintonville, WI	715, 534	54929
Clintwood, VA	276	24228
Clio, MI	810	48420
Clive, IA	515	50325
Cloquet, MN	218	55720
Closter, NJ	201, 551	07624
Cloudcroft, NM	505	88317, 88350
Clover, SC	803	29710
Clover, VA	434	24534
Cloverdale, VA	540	24077
Clovis, CA	559	93611-93613
Clovis, NM	505	88101-88103
Clute, TX	979	77531

*Partial list of zip codes, including main range

City	Area Code(s)	Zip Code(s)
Clyde, NY	315	14433
Clyde, NC	828	28721
Clyde Park, MT	406	59018
Coachella, CA	760, 442	92236
Coal Township, PA	570	17866
Coalgate, OK	580	74538
Coalinga, CA	559	93210
Coalmont, TN	931	37313
Coalville, UT	435	84017
Coatesville, PA	484, 610	19320
Cobleskill, NY	518	12043
Coburg, OR	541, 458	97408
Cochran, GA	478	31014
Cochranton, PA	814	16314
Cockeysville, MD	410	21030-21031
Cocoa, FL	321	32922-32927
Cocoa Beach, FL	321	32931-32932
Coconut Creek, FL	754, 954	33063-33066, 33073, 33097
Coconut Grove, FL	305, 786	33133-33134, 33146
Cody, WY	307	82414
Coeburn, VA	276	24230
Coeur d'Alene, ID	208	83814-83816
Coffeyville, KS	620	67337
Cogan Station, PA	570	17728
Cohasset, MA	339, 781	02025
Cohoes, NY	518	12047
Cokato, MN	320	55321
Coker, AL	205	35452
Colby, KS	785	67701
Colchester, CT	860	06415, 06420
Colchester, IL	309	62326
Colchester, VT	802	05439, 05446-05449
Cold Spring, KY	859	41076
Cold Spring, MN	320	56320
Cold Spring, NY	845	10516
Cold Spring Harbor, NY	516	11724
Cold Springs, NV	775	89506
Coldspring, TX	936	77331
Coldwater, KS	620	67029
Coldwater, MI	517	49036
Coldwater, OH	419, 567	45828
Coleman, FL	352	33521
Coleman, MI	989	48618
Coleman, OK	580	73432
Coleman, TX	915	76834
Colfax, IA	515	50054
Colfax, LA	318	71417
Colfax, WA	509	99111
College Corner, OH	513	45003
College Park, GA	404, 470	30337
College Park, MD	301	20740-20742
College Place, WA	509	99324
College Point, NY	347, 718	11356
College Station, TX	979	77840-77845
Collegedale, TN	423	37315
Collegeville, MN	320	56321
Collegeville, PA	484, 610	19426, 19473
Colleyville, TX	682, 817	76034
Collierville, TN	901	38017, 38027
Collingswood, NJ	856	08108
Collins, MS	601, 769	39428
Collins, NY	716	14034
Collinsville, IL	618	62234
Collinsville, OK	918	74021
Collinsville, VA	276	24078
Collinwood, TN	931	38450
Colman, SD	605	57017
Colmar, PA	215, 267	18915
Coloma, CA	530	95613
Coloma, MI	616	49038-49039
Colon, MI	616	49040
Colonial Heights, VA	804	23834
Colorado City, AZ	928	86021
Colorado City, TX	915	79512
Colorado Springs, CO	719	80901-80950, 80960-80962*
Colquitt, GA	229	31737
Colstrip, MT	406	59323
Colt, AR	870	72326
Colton, CA	909	92313, 92324
Columbia, IL	618	62236
Columbia, KY	270	42728, 42735
Columbia, LA	318	71418
Columbia, MD	410, 443	21044-21046
Columbia, MS	601, 769	39429
Columbia, MO	573	65201-65205, 65211-65218*
Columbia, NC	252	27925
Columbia, PA	717	17512
Columbia, SC	803	29201-29230, 29240, 29250*
Columbia, TN	931	38401-38402
Columbia City, IN	260	46725
Columbia Falls, MT	406	59912
Columbia Heights, MN	763	55421
Columbia Station, OH	440	44028
Columbiana, AL	205	35051
Columbiana, OH	234, 330	44408
Columbus, GA	706, 762	31829, 31901-31909, 31914*
Columbus, IN	812	47201-47203
Columbus, KS	620	66725
Columbus, MS	662	39701-39705, 39710
Columbus, MT	406	59019
Columbus, NE	402	68601-68602
Columbus, NC	828	28722
Columbus, ND	701	58727
Columbus, OH	614	43085, 43201-43236, 43240*
Columbus, TX	979	78934
Columbus, WI	920	53925
Columbus AFB, MS	662	39701
Columbus Grove, OH	419, 567	45830
Colusa, CA	530	95932
Colville, WA	509	99114
Comanche, TX	915	76442
Combined Locks, WI	920	54113
Commack, NY	631	11725
Commerce, CA	323	90040, 90091
Commerce, GA	706, 762	30529-30530, 30599
Commerce, TX	903	75428-75429
Commerce City, CO	303, 720	80022, 80037
Commerce Township, MI	248, 947	48382, 48390
Compton, CA	310, 424	90220-90224
Comstock, NY	518	12821
Comstock Park, MI	616	49321
Conception, MO	660	64433
Concord, CA	925	94518-94529
Concord, MA	351, 978	01742
Concord, NH	603	03301-03305
Concord, NC	704, 980	28025-28027
Concord, OH	440	44060, 44077
Concordia, KS	785	66901
Concordville, PA	484, 610	19331, 19339-19340
Condon, OR	541, 458	97823
Conejos, CO	719	81129
Conestoga, PA	717	17516
Congers, NY	845	10920
Conklin, NY	607	13748
Conneaut, OH	440	44030
Connell, WA	509	99326
Connellsville, PA	724, 878	15425
Connersville, IN	765	47331
Conover, NC	828	28613
Conrad, IA	641	50621
Conrad, MT	406	59425
Conroe, TX	936	77301-77306, 77384-77385
Conshohocken, PA	484, 610	19428-19429
Contoocook, NH	603	03229
Convent, LA	225	70723
Conway, AR	501	72032-72035
Conway, NH	603	03818
Conway, SC	843	29526-29528
Conyers, GA	470, 770	30012-30013, 30094
Cook, MN	218	55723
Cookeville, TN	931	38501-38506
Coolidge, AZ	520	85228
Coolidge, GA	229	31738
Coolidge, TX	254	76635
Coon Rapids, MN	763	55433, 55448
Cooper, TX	903	75432
Cooper City, FL	754, 954	33024-33026, 33328-33330
Coopersburg, PA	484, 610	18036
Cooperstown, NY	607	13326
Cooperstown, ND	701	58425
Coopersville, MI	616	49404
Coos Bay, OR	541, 458	97420
Copiague, NY	631	11726
Copley, OH	234, 330	44321
Coppell, TX	469, 972	75019, 75099
Copper Center, AK	907	99573
Copper Mountain, CO	970	80443
Copperas Cove, TX	254	76522
Coquille, OR	541, 458	97423
Cora, WY	307	82925
Coral Gables, FL	305, 786	33114, 33124, 33133-33134*
Coral Springs, FL	754, 954	33065-33067, 33071, 33075*
Coralville, IA	319	52241
Coraopolis, PA	412, 878	15108
Corbett, OR	503, 971	97019
Corbin, KY	606	40701-40702
Corcoran, CA	559	93212, 93282
Cordele, GA	229	31010, 31015
Cordell, OK	580	73632
Cordova, AK	907	99574, 99677
Cordova, TN	901	38016-38018, 38088
Core, WV	304	26529
Corinne, UT	435	84307
Corinth, MS	662	38834-38835
Corinth, TX	940	76208-76210
Cornelia, GA	706, 762	30531
Cornelius, NC	704, 980	28031
Cornelius, OR	503, 971	97113
Cornell, WI	715, 534	54732
Corning, AR	870	72422
Corning, CA	530	96021, 96029
Corning, IA	712	50841
Corning, NY	607	14830-14831
Cornish, NH	603	03745
Cornville, AZ	928	86325
Cornwall, NY	845	12518
Cornwall Bridge, CT	860	06754
Corona, CA	951	92877-92883
Corona, NY	347, 718	11368
Corona del Mar, CA	949	92625
Coronado, CA	619	92118, 92178
Corpus Christi, TX	361	78350, 78401-78419, 78426*
Corry, PA	814	16407
Corsicana, TX	903	75109-75110, 75151
Corte Madera, CA	415	94925, 94976
Cortez, CO	970	81321
Cortland, NY	607	13045
Cortlandt Manor, NY	845	10567
Corunna, MI	989	48817
Corvallis, MT	406	59828
Corvallis, OR	541, 458	97330-97333, 97339
Corydon, IN	812	47112
Corydon, IA	641	50060
Cos Cob, CT	203	06807
Coshocton, OH	740	43812
Costa Mesa, CA	714, 949	92626-92628
Cotati, CA	707	94926-94931
Cottage Grove, OR	541, 458	97424, 97472
Cottonport, LA	318	71327
Cottonwood, AZ	928	86326
Cottonwood, CA	530	96022
Cottonwood, ID	208	83522, 83533
Cottonwood, MN	507	56229
Cottonwood Falls, KS	620	66845
Cotuit, MA	508, 774	02635
Cotulla, TX	830	78001, 78014
Coudersport, PA	814	16915
Coulee City, WA	509	99115
Coulee Dam, WA	509	99116
Council, ID	208	83612
Council Bluffs, IA	712	51501-51503
Council Grove, KS	620	66846, 66873
Countryside, IL	708	60525
Coupeville, WA	360	98239
Courtland, VA	757	23837
Coushatta, LA	318	71019
Coventry, RI	401	02816
Covina, CA	626	91722-91724
Covington, GA	470, 770	30014-30016
Covington, IN	765	47932
Covington, KY	859	41011-41019
Covington, LA	985	70433-70435
Covington, TN	901	38019
Covington, VA	540	24426
Cowiche, WA	509	98923
Coxsackie, NY	518	12051, 12192
Cozad, NE	308	69130
Craftsbury Common, VT	802	05827
Craig, CO	970	81625-81626
Craigsville, VA	540	24430
Cranberry Township, PA	724, 878	16066
Cranbury, NJ	609	08512, 08570
Crandall, TX	469, 972	75114
Crandon, WI	715, 534	54520
Crane, TX	915	79731
Cranford, NJ	908	07016
Cranston, RI	401	02823, 02905-02910, 02920*
Craryville, NY	518	12521
Crater Lake, OR	541, 458	97604
Crawfordsville, IN	765	47933-47939
Crawfordville, FL	850	32326-32327

Partial list of zip codes, including main range

City	Area Code(s)	Zip Code(s)
Crawfordville, GA	706, 762	30631
Crazy Horse, SD	605	57730
Creede, CO	719	81130
Creedmoor, NC	919	27522, 27564
Creighton, NE	402	68729
Crescent City, CA	707	95531-95532, 95538
Crescent Springs, KY	859	41017
Cresco, IA	563	52136
Cresco, PA	570	18326
Cresskill, NJ	201, 551	07626
Cresson, PA	814	16630, 16699
Cresson, TX	682, 817	76035
Cressona, PA	570	17929
Creston, IA	641	50801
Crestview, FL	850	32536-32539
Crestview Hills, KY	859	41017
Creswell, OR	541, 458	97426
Crete, IL	708	60417
Crete, NE	402	68333
Creve Coeur, IL	309	61610
Creve Coeur, MO	314	63141
Crewe, VA	434	23930
Cripple Creek, CO	719	80813
Crisfield, MD	410	21817
Crockett, CA	510	94525
Crockett, TX	936	75835
Crofton, MD	410	21114
Cromwell, CT	860	06416
Crookston, MN	218	56716
Crosby, ND	701	58730
Crosbyton, TX	806	79322
Cross City, FL	352	32628
Cross Lanes, WV	304	25313, 25356
Cross Plains, WI	608	53528
Crossett, AR	870	71635
Crossville, TN	931	38555-38558, 38571-38572
Croswell, MI	810	48422
Crow Agency, MT	406	59022
Crowell, TX	940	79227
Crowley, CO	719	81033-81034
Crowley, LA	337	70526-70527
Crown Point, IN	219	46307-46308
Crownsville, MD	410	21032
Croydon, PA	215, 267	19021
Crum Lynne, PA	484, 610	19022
Crystal, MN	763	55422, 55427-55429
Crystal Bay, NV	775	89402
Crystal City, MO	636	63019
Crystal City, TX	830	78839
Crystal Falls, MI	906	49920
Crystal Lake, IL	815	60012-60014, 60039
Crystal River, FL	352	34423, 34428-34429
Crystal Springs, MS	601, 769	39059
Cuba, NY	585	14727
Cudahy, CA	323	90201
Cudahy, WI	414	53110
Cuddy, PA	412, 878	15031
Cuero, TX	361	77954
Cullman, AL	256	35055-35058
Cullowhee, NC	828	28723
Culpeper, VA	540	22701
Culver, OR	541, 458	97734
Culver City, CA	310, 424	90230-90233
Cumberland, KY	606	40823
Cumberland, MD	301	21501-21505
Cumberland, OH	740	43732
Cumberland, RI	401	02864
Cumberland, VA	804	23040
Cumberland Gap, TN	423	37724, 37752
Cumming, GA	470, 770	30028, 30040-30041
Cupertino, CA	408	95014-95015
Currie, NC	910	28435
Currituck, NC	252	27929
Curtis, NE	308	69025
Cushing, OK	918	74023
Cusick, WA	509	99119
Cusseta, GA	706, 762	31805
Custer, SD	605	57730
Cut Bank, MT	406	59427
Cuthbert, GA	229	31740
Cuyahoga Falls, OH	234, 330	44221-44224
Cuyahoga Heights, OH	216	44105, 44125-44127
Cynthiana, KY	859	41031
Cypress, CA	714	90630
Cypress, TX	281, 832	77410, 77429, 77433

D

City	Area Code(s)	Zip Code(s)
Dade City, FL	352	33523-33526
Dadeville, AL	256	36853
Dafter, MI	906	49724
Dahlgren, VA	540	22448
Dahlonega, GA	706, 762	30533, 30597
Daingerfield, TX	903	75638
Dakota, IL	815	61018
Dakota City, IA	515	50529
Dakota City, NE	402	68731
Dakota Dunes, SD	605	57049
Dale, IN	812	47523
Dalhart, TX	806	79022
Dallas, GA	470, 770	30132, 30157
Dallas, NC	704, 980	28034
Dallas, OR	503, 971	97338
Dallas, PA	570	18612, 18690
Dallas, TX	214, 469, 972	75201-75254, 75258-75270*
Dallastown, PA	717	17313
Dalton, GA	706, 762	30719-30722
Dalton, MA	413	01226-01227
Dalton, OH	234, 330	44618
Daly City, CA	650	94013-94017
Damariscotta, ME	207	04543
Dammeron Valley, UT	435	84783
Dana Point, CA	949	92624, 92629
Danboro, PA	215, 267	18916
Danbury, CT	203	06810-06817
Danbury, NC	336	27016
Dandridge, TN	865	37725
Dania Beach, FL	754, 954	33004, 33312
Daniel, WY	307	83115
Danielson, CT	860	06239
Danielsville, GA	706, 762	30633
Dannemora, NY	518	12929
Danube, MN	320	56230
Danvers, MA	351, 978	01923
Danville, AR	479	72833
Danville, CA	925	94506, 94526
Danville, IL	217	61832-61834
Danville, IN	317	46122
Danville, IA	319	52623
Danville, KY	859	40422-40423
Danville, PA	570	17821-17822
Danville, VA	434	24540-24544
Daphne, AL	251	36526
Darby, MT	406	59829
Dardanelle, AR	479	72834
Darien, CT	203	06820
Darien, GA	912	31305
Darien, IL	331, 630	60561
Darien Center, NY	585	14040
Darlington, SC	843	29532, 29540
Darlington, WI	608	53530
Darrow, LA	225	70725
Dartmouth, MA	508, 774	02714, 02747-02748
Dassel, MN	320	55325
Dauphin Island, AL	251	36528
Davenport, FL	863	33836-33837, 33896-33897
Davenport, IA	563	52801-52809
Davenport, WA	509	99122
David City, NE	402	68632
Davidson, NC	704, 980	28035-28036
Davie, FL	754, 954	33024, 33312-33317, 33324*
Davis, CA	530	95616-95618
Davis, WV	304	26260
Davison, MI	810	48423
Daviston, AL	256	36256
Davisville, WV	304	26142
Dawson, GA	229	31742
Dawsonville, GA	706, 762	30534
Dayton, IA	515	50530
Dayton, NV	775	89403
Dayton, NJ	732, 848	08810
Dayton, OH	937	45390, 45401-45441, 45448*
Dayton, TN	423	37321
Dayton, TX	936	77535
Dayton, WA	509	99328
Daytona Beach, FL	386	32114-32129, 32198
Daytona Beach Shores, FL	386	32116
Dayville, CT	860	06241
De Funiak Springs, FL	850	32433-32435
De Kalb, MS	601, 769	39328
De Pere, WI	920	54115
De Queen, AR	870	71832

City	Area Code(s)	Zip Code(s)
De Smet, SD	605	57231
De Witt, AR	870	72042
De Witt, IA	563	52742
Deadwood, SD	605	57732
Dearborn, MI	313	48120-48128
Dearborn Heights, MI	313	48125-48127
Death Valley, CA	760, 442	92328
Decatur, AL	256	35601-35603, 35609, 35699
Decatur, AR	479	72722
Decatur, GA	404, 470	30030-30037
Decatur, IL	217	62521-62527
Decatur, IN	260	46733
Decatur, MS	601, 769	39327
Decatur, TN	423	37322
Decatur, TX	940	76234
Decaturville, TN	731	38329
Deckerville, MI	810	48427
Declo, ID	208	83323
Decorah, IA	563	52101
Dedham, MA	339, 781	02026-02027
Deer Harbor, WA	360	98243
Deer Lodge, MT	406	59722
Deer Park, CA	707	94576
Deer Park, NY	631	11729
Deer Park, TX	281, 832	77536
Deer River, MN	218	56636
Deerfield, IL	224, 847	60015
Deerfield, MA	413	01342
Deerfield, WI	608	53531
Deerfield Beach, FL	754, 954	33064, 33441-33443
Deerwood, MN	218	56444
Defiance, OH	419, 567	43512
DeForest, WI	608	53532
DeGraff, OH	937	43318
DeKalb, IL	815	60115
Del City, OK	405	73115, 73135, 73165
Del Mar, CA	858	92014
Del Norte, CO	719	81132
Del Rey, CA	559	93616
Del Rio, TX	830	78840-78843, 78847
Delair, NJ	856	08110
Delanco, NJ	856	08075
DeLand, FL	386	32720-32724
Delano, CA	661	93215-93216
Delano, MN	763	55328
Delavan, MN	507	56023
Delavan, WI	262	53115
Delaware, OH	740	43015
Delaware City, DE	302	19706
Delaware Water Gap, PA	570	18327
Delbarton, WV	304	25670
DeLeon Springs, FL	386	32130
Delhi, NY	607	13753
Dellroy, OH	234, 330	44620
Delmar, MD	410	21875
Delmar, NY	518	12054
Delmont, NJ	856	08314
Delmont, PA	724, 878	15626
Delphi, IN	765	46923
Delphos, OH	419, 567	45833
Delray Beach, FL	561	33444-33448, 33482-33484
Delta, CO	970	81416
Delta, UT	435	84624
Deming, NM	505	88030-88031
Demopolis, AL	334	36732
Demorest, GA	706, 762	30535, 30544
Demotte, IN	219	46310
Denham Springs, LA	225	70706, 70726-70727
Denison, IA	712	51442
Denison, TX	903	75020-75021
Denmark, SC	803	29042
Denmark, WI	920	54208
Denton, MD	410	21629
Denton, NC	336	27239
Denton, TX	940	76201-76210
Denver, CO	303, 720	80002, 80010-80014, 80022*
Denver, IA	319	50622
Denver, NC	704, 980	28037
Denver, PA	717	17517
Denville, NJ	862, 973	07834
Depew, NY	716	14043
Depoe Bay, OR	541, 458	97341
Deposit, NY	607	13754
Dequincy, LA	337	70633
Derby, CT	203	06418
Derby, KS	316	67037
Derby, NY	716	14047

*Partial list of zip codes, including main range

City	Area Code(s)	Zip Code(s)
DeRidder, LA	337	70634
Dermott, AR	870	71638
Derry, NH	603	03038
Derwent, OH	740	43733
Des Allemands, LA	504	70030
Des Arc, AR	870	72040
Des Moines, IA	515	50301-50340, 50347-50350*
Des Moines, WA	206	98148, 98198
Des Plaines, IL	224, 847	60016-60019
Descanso, CA	760, 442	91916
Desert Hot Springs, CA	760, 442	92240-92241
Deshler, NE	402	68340
DeSoto, KS	913	66018
DeSoto, TX	469, 972	75115, 75123
Destin, FL	850	32540-32541, 32550
Destrehan, LA	985	70047
Detroit, MI	313, 734	48201-48244, 48255, 48260*
Detroit, OR	503, 971	97342
Detroit Lakes, MN	218	56501-56502
Devault, PA	484, 610	19432
Devens, MA	351, 978	01432
Devils Lake, ND	701	58301
Devils Tower, WY	307	82714
Devon, PA	484, 610	19333
Dewey, OK	918	74029
Dewey Beach, DE	302	19971
DeWitt, NY	315	13214
Dexter, MI	734	48130
Dexter, MO	573	63841
Diamond, MO	417	64840
Diamond Bar, CA	909	91765
Diamond Point, NY	518	12824
Diboll, TX	936	75941
Dickens, TX	806	79229
Dickinson, ND	701	58601-58602
Dickinson, TX	281, 832	77539
Dickson, TN	615	37055-37056
Dighton, KS	620	67839
Dighton, MA	508, 774	02715
Dillingham, AK	907	99576
Dillon, MT	406	59725
Dillon, SC	843	29536
Dillwyn, VA	434	23936
Dimmitt, TX	806	79027
Dinosaur, CO	970	81610, 81633
Dinuba, CA	559	93618
Dinwiddie, VA	804	23841
Dix Hills, NY	631	11746
Dixie, GA	229	31629
Dixmoor, IL	708	60406, 60426
Dixon, CA	707	95620
Dixon, IL	815	61021
Dixon, KY	270	42409
Dixon, MO	573	65459
Dobbs Ferry, NY	914	10522
Dobson, NC	336	27017
Dodge Center, MN	507	55927
Dodge City, KS	620	67801
Dodgeville, WI	608	53533, 53595
Dolgeville, NY	315	13329
Dolton, IL	708	60419
Donaldson, IN	574	46513
Donaldsonville, LA	225	70346
Donalsonville, GA	229	31745
Dongola, IL	618	62926
Doniphan, MO	573	63935
Dorado, PR	787, 939	00646
Doraville, GA	470, 770	30340, 30360-30362
Dorchester, MA	617, 857	02121-02125
Dorchester, NE	402	68343
Doswell, VA	804	23047
Dothan, AL	334	36301-36305
Double Springs, AL	205	35553
Douglas, AK	907	99824
Douglas, AZ	520	85607-85608, 85655
Douglas, GA	912	31533-31535
Douglas, MI	616	49406
Douglas, WY	307	82633
Douglassville, PA	484, 610	19518
Douglassville, TX	903	75560
Douglaston, NY	347, 718	11362-11363
Douglasville, GA	470, 770	30133-30135, 30154
Dove Creek, CO	970	81324
Dover, DE	302	19901-19906
Dover, FL	813	33527
Dover, NH	603	03820-03822
Dover, NJ	862, 973	07801-07806, 07869
Dover, OH	234, 330	44622
Dover, TN	931	37058
Dover AFB, DE	302	19902
Dover Plains, NY	845	12522
Dowagiac, MI	616	49047
Downers Grove, IL	331, 630	60515-60517
Downey, CA	562	90239-90242
Downieville, CA	530	95936
Downingtown, PA	484, 610	19335, 19372
Doylestown, OH	234, 330	44230
Doylestown, PA	215, 267	18901, 18933
Doyline, LA	318	71023
Dracut, MA	351, 978	01826
Dragoon, AZ	520	85609
Drain, OR	541, 458	97435
Draper, UT	801, 385	84020
Dravosburg, PA	412, 878	15034
Dresden, TN	731	38225
Dresher, PA	215, 267	19025
Dresser, WI	715, 534	54009
Drexel Hill, PA	484, 610	19026
Driggs, ID	208	83422
Drummond Island, MI	906	49726
Dry Ridge, KY	859	41035
Dryden, NY	607	13053
Du Bois, PA	814	15801
Duarte, CA	626	91009-91010
Dublin, CA	925	94568
Dublin, GA	478	31021, 31027, 31040
Dublin, NH	603	03444
Dublin, NC	910	28332
Dublin, OH	614	43016-43017
Dublin, VA	540	24084
Dubois, ID	208	83423, 83446
Dubois, WY	307	82513
Dubuque, IA	563	52001-52004, 52099
Duchesne, UT	435	84021
Duck, NC	252	27949
Duck Hill, MS	662	38925
Duck Key, FL	305, 786	33050
Dudley, GA	478	31022
Dudley, MA	508, 774	01571
Dudley, MO	573	63936
Dudley, NC	919	28333
Due West, SC	864	29639
Dugway, UT	435	84022
Dulles, VA	571, 703	20101-20104, 20163-20166*
Duluth, GA	470, 678, 770	30026-30029, 30095-30099
Duluth, MN	218	55701, 55801-55816
Dumas, TX	806	79029
Dunbar, PA	724, 878	15431
Dunbar, WV	304	25064
Dunbar, WI	715, 534	54119
Dunbridge, OH	419, 567	43414
Duncan, AZ	928	85534
Duncan, OK	580	73533-73536, 73575
Duncan, SC	864	29334, 29390-29391
Duncannon, PA	717	17020
Duncansville, PA	814	16635
Duncanville, TX	469, 972	75116, 75137-75138
Dundalk, MD	410	21222
Dundee, FL	863	33838
Dundee, IL	224, 847	60118
Dundee, NY	607	14837
Dundee, OR	503, 971	97115
Dunedin, FL	727	34697-34698
Dunkirk, IN	765	47336
Dunkirk, MD	301	20754
Dunkirk, NY	716	14048, 14166
Dunlap, IL	309	61525
Dunlap, TN	423	37327
Dunmore, PA	570	18509-18512
Dunn, NC	910	28334-28335
Dunnell, MN	507	56127
Dunnellon, FL	352	34430-34434
Dunning, NE	308	68833
Dunseith, ND	701	58329
Dupont, WA	253	98327
Dupree, SD	605	57623
DuQuoin, IL	618	62832
Durand, MI	989	48429
Durand, WI	715, 534	54736
Durango, CO	970	81301-81303
Durant, OK	580	74701-74702
Durham, CT	860	06422
Durham, NH	603	03824
Durham, NC	919	27701-27717, 27722
Duryea, PA	570	18642
Dushore, PA	570	18614
Duxbury, MA	339, 781	02331-02332
Dwight, IL	815	60420
Dyer, NV	760, 442	89010
Dyersburg, TN	731	38024-38025
Dyersville, IA	563	52040
Dyess AFB, TX	915	79607

E

City	Area Code(s)	Zip Code(s)
Eads, CO	719	81036
Eagan, MN	651	55120-55123
Eagle, CO	970	81631
Eagle, WI	262	53119
Eagle Creek, OR	503, 971	97022
Eagle Grove, IA	515	50533
Eagle Nest, NM	505	87710, 87718
Eagle Pass, TX	830	78852-78853
Eagle River, AK	907	99577
Eagle River, MI	906	49950
Eagle River, WI	715, 534	54521
Eagle Rock, CA	323	90041
Eagleville, PA	484, 610	19403, 19408, 19415
Earle, AR	870	72331
Earlville, IL	815	60518
Early Branch, SC	803	29916
Earth City, MO	314	63045
Easley, SC	864	29640-29642
East Alton, IL	618	62024
East Amherst, NY	716	14051
East Aurora, NY	585	14052
East Bend, NC	336	27018
East Berlin, CT	860	06023
East Bernstadt, KY	606	40729
East Bloomfield, NY	585	14443, 14469
East Boston, MA	617, 857	02128, 02228
East Brunswick, NJ	732, 848	08816
East Canton, OH	234, 330	44730
East Chicago, IN	219	46312
East Cleveland, OH	216	44110-44112, 44118
East Derry, NH	603	03041
East Dubuque, IL	815	61025
East Dundee, IL	224, 847	60118
East Durham, NY	518	12423
East Earl, PA	717	17519
East Elmhurst, NY	347, 718	11369-11371
East Falmouth, MA	508, 774	02536
East Farmingdale, NY	631	11735
East Granby, CT	860	06026
East Grand Forks, MN	218	56721
East Grand Rapids, MI	616	49506, 49546
East Greenville, PA	215, 267	18041
East Greenwich, RI	401	02818
East Haddam, CT	860	06423
East Hampstead, NH	603	03826
East Hampton, CT	860	06424, 06447
East Hampton, NY	631	11937
East Hanover, NJ	862, 973	07936
East Hartford, CT	860	06108, 06118, 06128, 06138
East Haven, CT	203	06512-06513
East Hazel Crest, IL	708	60429
East Hills, NY	516	11548, 11576-11577
East Jordan, MI	231	49727
East Lansing, MI	517	48823-48826
East Liberty, OH	937	43074, 43319
East Liverpool, OH	234, 330	43920
East Longmeadow, MA	413	01028, 01116
East Meadow, NY	516	11554
East Millstone, NJ	732, 848	08873-08875
East Moline, IL	309	61244
East Montpelier, VT	802	05651
East New Market, MD	410	21631
East Northport, NY	631	11731
East Norwalk, CT	203	06855
East Orange, NJ	862, 973	07017-07019
East Palatka, FL	386	32131
East Palestine, OH	234, 330	44413
East Palo Alto, CA	650	94303
East Pembroke, NY	585	14056
East Peoria, IL	309	61611
East Petersburg, PA	717	17520
East Point, GA	404, 470	30344, 30364
East Providence, RI	401	02914-02916
East Rochester, NH	603	03868

Partial list of zip codes, including main range

City	Area Code(s)	Zip Code(s)
East Rutherford, NJ	201, 551	07073
East Saint Louis, IL	618	62201-62208
East Stroudsburg, PA	570	18301
East Syracuse, NY	315	13057
East Taunton, MA	508, 774	02718
East Tawas, MI	989	48730
East Templeton, MA	351, 978	01438
East Texas, PA	484, 610	18046
East Troy, WI	262	53120
East Walpole, MA	508, 774	02032
East Weymouth, MA	339, 781	02189
East Windsor, CT	860	06016, 06088
East Windsor, NJ	609	08512, 08520
Eastaboga, AL	256	36260
Easthampton, MA	413	01027
Eastlake, MI	231	49626
Eastlake, OH	440	44095-44097
Eastland, TX	254	76448
Eastman, GA	478	31023
Easton, MD	410	21601, 21606
Easton, PA	484, 610	18040-18045
Eastpointe, MI	586	48021
Eastport, ME	207	04631
Eastsound, WA	360	98245
Eastville, VA	757	23347
Eaton, CO	970	80615
Eaton, IN	765	47338
Eaton, OH	937	45320
Eaton Rapids, MI	517	48827
Eatonton, GA	706, 762	31024
Eatontown, NJ	732, 848	07724, 07799
Eatonville, WA	360	98328
Eau Claire, WI	715, 534	54701-54703
Ebensburg, PA	814	15931
Edcouch, TX	956	78538
Eddyville, KY	270	42038
Eden, NC	336	27288-27289
Eden Prairie, MN	952	55343-55347
Edenton, NC	252	27932
Edgartown, MA	508, 774	02539
Edgefield, SC	803	29824
Edgeley, ND	701	58433
Edgerton, MN	507	56128
Edgerton, OH	419, 567	43517
Edgerton, WI	608	53534
Edgewater, FL	386	32132, 32141
Edgewater, MD	410, 443	21037
Edgewater, NJ	201, 551	07020
Edgewood, IA	563	52042-52044
Edgewood, MD	410	21040
Edgewood, NY	631	11717
Edgewood, WA	253	98371-98372, 98390
Edina, MN	952	55343, 55410, 55416, 55424*
Edina, MO	660	63537
Edinboro, PA	814	16412, 16444
Edinburg, TX	956	78539-78540
Edinburg, VA	540	22824
Edinburgh, IN	812	46124
Edison, CA	661	93220
Edison, NJ	732, 848	08817-08820, 08837, 08899
Edisto Beach, SC	843	29438
Edmeston, NY	607	13335
Edmond, OK	405	73003, 73013, 73034, 73083
Edmonds, WA	425	98020, 98026
Edmonton, KY	270	42129
Edmore, MI	989	48829
Edna, TX	361	77957
Edon, OH	419, 567	43518
Edwards, CA	661	93523-93524
Edwards, CO	970	81632
Edwardsburg, MI	616	49112, 49130
Edwardsville, IL	618	62025-62026
Edwardsville, KS	913	66111-66113
Edwardsville, PA	570	18704
Effingham, IL	217	62401
Egg Harbor, WI	920	54209
Egg Harbor City, NJ	609	08215
Egg Harbor Township, NJ	609	08234
Eglin AFB, FL	850	32542
Eielson AFB, AK	907	99702
Eighty Four, PA	724, 878	15330
Ekalaka, MT	406	59324
El Cajon, CA	619	92019-92022, 92090
El Campo, TX	979	77437
El Centro, CA	760, 442	92243-92244
El Cerrito, CA	510	94530
El Dorado, AR	870	71730-71731, 71768
El Dorado, KS	316	67042
El Dorado Hills, CA	916	95762
El Dorado Springs, MO	417	64744
El Monte, CA	626	91731-91735
El Paso, IL	309	61738
El Paso, TX	915	79821, 79901-79961, 79966*
El Reno, OK	405	73036
El Segundo, CA	310, 424	90245
El Sobrante, CA	510	94803, 94820
Elba, AL	334	36323
Elba, NY	585	14058
Elberfeld, IN	812	47613
Elberton, GA	706, 762	30635
Elbow Lake, MN	218	56531
Eldora, IA	641	50627
Eldorado, IL	618	62930
Eldorado, TX	915	76936
Eldorado Springs, CO	303, 720	80025
Eldridge, CA	707	95431
Eldridge, IA	563	52748
Eleele, HI	808	96705
Elephant Butte, NM	505	87935
Elgin, IL	224, 847	60120-60123
Elgin, SC	803	29045
Elizabeth, IL	815	61028
Elizabeth, IN	812	47117
Elizabeth, NJ	908	07201-07202, 07206-07208
Elizabeth, PA	412, 878	15037
Elizabeth, WV	304	26143
Elizabeth City, NC	252	27906-27909
Elizabethton, TN	423	37643-37644
Elizabethtown, IL	618	62931
Elizabethtown, KY	270	42701-42702
Elizabethtown, NY	518	12932
Elizabethtown, NC	910	28337
Elizabethtown, PA	717	17022
Elizabethville, PA	717	17023
Elk City, OK	580	73644, 73648
Elk Grove, CA	916	95624, 95758-95759
Elk Grove Village, IL	224, 847	60007-60009
Elk Point, SD	605	57025
Elk Rapids, MI	231	49629
Elk River, MN	763	55330
Elkader, IA	563	52043
Elkhart, IN	574	46514-46517
Elkhart, KS	620	67950
Elkhart Lake, WI	920	53020
Elkhorn, NE	402	68022
Elkhorn, WI	262	53121
Elkin, NC	336	28621
Elkins, WV	304	26241
Elkins Park, PA	215, 267	19027
Elkland, PA	814	16920
Elko, MN	952	55020
Elko, NV	775	89801-89803, 89815
Elkridge, MD	410	21075
Elkton, KY	270	42220
Elkton, MD	410	21921-21922
Elkton, OH	234, 330	44415
Ellaville, GA	229	31806
Ellendale, ND	701	58436
Ellensburg, WA	509	98926, 98950
Ellenville, NY	845	12428
Ellenwood, GA	404, 470	30294
Ellettsville, IN	812	47429
Ellicott City, MD	410	21041-21043
Ellicottville, NY	716	14731
Ellijay, GA	706, 762	30540
Ellington, CT	860	06029
Ellinwood, KS	620	67526
Ellis, KS	785	67637
Ellisville, MS	601, 769	39437
Ellisville, MO	636	63011, 63021, 63038
Ellsworth, KS	785	67439
Ellsworth, ME	207	04605
Ellsworth, WI	715, 534	54003, 54010-54011
Ellsworth AFB, SD	605	57706
Ellwood City, PA	724, 878	16117
Elm Grove, WI	262	53122
Elm Springs, AR	479	72728
Elma, NY	585	14059
Elma, WA	360	98541
Elmendorf AFB, AK	907	99505-99506
Elmer, NJ	856	08318
Elmhurst, IL	331, 630	60126
Elmhurst, NY	347, 718	11373, 11380
Elmira, NY	607	14901-14905, 14925
Elmira, OR	541, 458	97437
Elmira Heights, NY	607	14903
Elmont, NY	516	11003
Elmore, AL	334	36025
Elmore, OH	419, 567	43416
Elmsford, NY	914	10523
Elmwood, CT	860	06110, 06133
Elmwood Park, IL	708	60707
Elmwood Park, NJ	201, 551	07407
Elon, NC	336	27244
Elsah, IL	618	62028
Elsmere, KY	859	41018
Elverson, PA	484, 610	19520
Elwood, IN	765	46036
Elwood, NE	308	68937
Ely, MN	218	55731
Ely, NV	775	89301, 89315
Elyria, OH	440	44035-44039
Elysburg, PA	570	17824
Emerado, ND	701	58228
Emeryville, CA	510	94608, 94662
Emigrant, MT	406	59027
Emigsville, PA	717	17318
Eminence, KY	502	40019
Eminence, MO	573	65466
Emlenton, PA	724, 878	16373
Emmaus, PA	484, 610	18049, 18098-18099
Emmetsburg, IA	712	50536
Emmett, ID	208	83617
Emmitsburg, MD	301	21727
Emory, TX	903	75440
Emory, VA	276	24327
Empire, MI	231	49630
Emporia, KS	620	66801
Emporia, VA	434	23847
Emporium, PA	814	15834
Encinitas, CA	760, 442	92023-92024
Encino, CA	818	91316, 91335, 91416, 91426*
Endicott, NY	607	13760-13763
Enfield, CT	860	06082-06083
Enfield, NH	603	03748
Enfield, NC	252	27823
Engelhard, NC	252	27824
England, AR	501	72046
Englewood, CO	303, 720	80110-80112, 80150-80155*
Englewood, FL	941	34223-34224, 34295
Englewood, NJ	201, 551	07631-07632
Englewood, OH	937	45315, 45322
Englewood Cliffs, NJ	201, 551	07632
English, IN	812	47118
Englishtown, NJ	732, 848	07726
Enid, OK	580	73701-73706
Ennis, MT	406	59729
Ennis, TX	469, 972	75119-75120
Enola, PA	717	17025
Enon, OH	937	45323
Enoree, SC	864	29335
Enosburg Falls, VT	802	05450
Enterprise, AL	334	36330-36331
Enterprise, OR	541, 458	97828
Enumclaw, WA	360	98022
Ephraim, UT	435	84627
Ephrata, PA	717	17522
Ephrata, WA	509	98823
Epping, NH	603	03042
Epps, LA	318	71237
Epworth, IA	563	52045
Erdenheim, PA	215, 267	19038
Erie, CO	303, 720	80516
Erie, IL	309	61250
Erie, KS	620	66733
Erie, MI	734	48133
Erie, PA	814	16501-16515, 16522, 16530*
Erin, TN	931	37061
Erlanger, KY	859	41017-41018
Erving, MA	351, 978	01344
Erwin, TN	423	37650
Escalon, CA	209	95320
Escanaba, MI	906	49829
Escondido, CA	760, 442	92025-92033, 92046
Esopus, NY	845	12429
Espanola, NM	505	87532-87533
Essex, CT	860	06426
Essex, MD	410	21221
Essex Junction, VT	802	05451-05453
Essexville, MI	989	48732
Essington, PA	484, 610	19029

**Partial list of zip codes, including main range*

City	Area Code(s)	Zip Code(s)
Estancia, NM	505	87009, 87016
Estero, FL	239	33928
Estes Park, CO	970	80511, 80517
Estherville, IA	712	51334
Estill, SC	803	29918, 29939
Euclid, OH	216	44117-44119, 44123, 44132*
Eudora, AR	870	71640
Eufaula, AL	334	36027, 36072
Eufaula, OK	918	74432, 74461
Eugene, OR	541, 458	97401-97408, 97412, 97440*
Euless, TX	682, 817	76039-76040
Eunice, LA	337	70535
Eureka, CA	707	95501-95503, 95534
Eureka, IL	309	61530
Eureka, KS	620	67045
Eureka, MO	636	63025
Eureka, MT	406	59917
Eureka, NV	775	89316
Eureka Springs, AR	479	72631-72632
Eustis, FL	352	32726-32727, 32736
Eutaw, AL	205	35462
Evans, GA	706, 762	30809
Evans City, PA	724, 878	16033
Evanston, IL	224, 847	60201-60204, 60208-60209
Evanston, WY	307	82930-82931
Evansville, IN	812	47701-47750
Evansville, WI	608	53536
Evansville, WY	307	82636
Eveleth, MN	218	55734
Everett, MA	617, 857	02149
Everett, PA	814	15537
Everett, WA	425	98201-98208
Evergreen, AL	251	36401
Evergreen, CO	303, 720	80437-80439
Evergreen Park, IL	708	60805
Ewa Beach, HI	808	96706
Ewing, NJ	609	08618, 08628, 08638
Excelsior, MN	952	55331
Excelsior Springs, MO	816	64024
Exeter, CA	559	93221
Exeter, NH	603	03833
Exeter, PA	570	18643
Exeter, RI	401	02822
Export, PA	724, 878	15632
Exton, PA	484, 610	19341, 19353
Eynon, PA	570	18403

F

City	Area Code(s)	Zip Code(s)
Fabens, TX	915	79838
Fair Haven, VT	802	05731, 05743
Fair Lawn, NJ	201, 551	07410
Fair Oaks, CA	916	95628
Fairbanks, AK	907	99701-99716, 99767, 99775*
Fairborn, OH	937	45324, 45431
Fairburn, GA	470, 770	30213
Fairbury, NE	402	68352
Fairchild AFB, WA	509	99011
Fairfax, SC	803	29827
Fairfax, VA	571, 703	20151-20153, 22030-22039
Fairfax Station, VA	571, 703	22039
Fairfield, AL	205	35064
Fairfield, CA	707	94533-94535, 94585
Fairfield, CT	203	06430-06432
Fairfield, ID	208	83322, 83327
Fairfield, IL	618	62837
Fairfield, IA	641	52556-52557
Fairfield, ME	207	04937
Fairfield, MT	406	59436
Fairfield, NJ	862, 973	07004
Fairfield, OH	513	45011-45014, 45018
Fairfield, PA	717	17320
Fairfield, TX	903	75840
Fairfield, VT	802	05455
Fairfield Glade, TN	931	38555-38558
Fairgrove, MI	989	48733
Fairhaven, MA	508, 774	02719
Fairhope, AL	251	36532-36533
Fairlawn, OH	234, 330	44313, 44333-44334
Fairlee, VT	802	05045
Fairless Hills, PA	215, 267	19030
Fairmont, MN	507	56031, 56075
Fairmont, MT	406	59711
Fairmont, WV	304	26554-26555
Fairplay, CO	719	80432, 80440, 80456
Fairport, NY	585	14450
Fairport Harbor, OH	440	44077
Fairton, NJ	856	08320
Fairview, NJ	201, 551	07022
Fairview, OK	580	73737
Fairview, OR	503, 971	97024
Fairview, PA	814	16415
Fairview Heights, IL	618	62208, 62232
Fairview Park, OH	440	44126
Fairview Village, PA	484, 610	19409
Fajardo, PR	787, 939	00738
Falconer, NY	716	14733
Falfurrias, TX	361	78355
Fall Creek, WI	715, 534	54742
Fall River, MA	508, 774	02720-02726
Fall River, WI	920	53932
Fallbrook, CA	760, 442	92028, 92088
Fallon, NV	775	89406-89407, 89496
Falls Church, VA	571, 703	22040-22047
Falls City, NE	402	68355
Fallsburg, NY	845	12733
Fallston, MD	410	21047
Falmouth, KY	859	41040
Falmouth, ME	207	04105
Falmouth, MA	508, 774	02540-02543
Fanwood, NJ	908	07023
Far Hills, NJ	908	07931
Far Rockaway, NY	347, 718	11096, 11690-11697
Fargo, ND	701	58102-58109, 58121-58126
Faribault, MN	507	55021
Farina, IL	618	62838
Farmers Branch, TX	469, 972	75234, 75244
Farmerville, LA	318	71241
Farmingdale, NJ	732, 848	07727
Farmingdale, NY	631	11735-11737, 11774
Farmington, CT	860	06030-06034, 06085
Farmington, ME	207	04911, 04938
Farmington, MI	248, 947	48331-48336
Farmington, MN	651	55024
Farmington, MO	573	63640
Farmington, NH	603	03835
Farmington, NM	505	87401-87402, 87499
Farmington, NY	585	14425
Farmington, PA	724, 878	15437
Farmington, UT	801, 385	84025
Farmington Hills, MI	248, 947	48331-48336
Farmingville, NY	631	11738
Farmville, NC	252	27828
Farmville, VA	434	23901, 23909, 23943
Farnhamville, IA	515	50538
Farragut, TN	865	37922
Farwell, TX	806	79325
Faulkner, MD	301	20632
Faulkton, SD	605	57438
Fayette, AL	205	35555
Fayette, IA	563	52142
Fayette, MS	601, 769	39069, 39081
Fayette, MO	660	65248
Fayetteville, AR	479	72701-72704
Fayetteville, GA	470, 770	30214-30215, 30232
Fayetteville, NY	315	13066
Fayetteville, NC	910	28301-28314
Fayetteville, PA	717	17222
Fayetteville, TN	931	37334
Fayetteville, WV	304	25840
Feasterville, PA	215, 267	19053
Federal Way, WA	253	98001-98003, 98023, 98063*
Federalsburg, MD	410	21632
Feeding Hills, MA	413	01030
Felton, DE	302	19943
Fennimore, WI	608	53809
Fenton, MI	810	48430
Fenton, MO	636	63026, 63099
Fenwick, WV	304	26202
Ferdinand, IN	812	47532
Fergus Falls, MN	218	56537-56538
Ferguson, MO	314	63135-63136, 63145
Fernandina Beach, FL	904	32034-32035
Ferndale, CA	707	95536
Ferndale, MI	248, 947	48220
Ferndale, WA	360	98248
Ferriday, LA	318	71334
Ferrisburg, VT	802	05456
Ferrum, VA	540	24088
Ferrysburg, MI	616	49409
Fessenden, ND	701	58438
Festus, MO	636	63028
Fillmore, UT	435	84631
Fincastle, VA	540	24090
Findlay, OH	419, 567	45839-45840
Finksburg, MD	410	21048
Finley, ND	701	58230
Finleyville, PA	724, 878	15332
Firebaugh, CA	559	93622
Firth, ID	208	83236
Fisher Island, FL	305, 786	33109, 33139
Fishers, IN	317	46038
Fishersville, VA	540	22939
Fishkill, NY	845	12524
Fiskeville, RI	401	02823
Fitchburg, MA	351, 978	01420
Fitzgerald, GA	229	31750
Flagler Beach, FL	386	32136, 32151
Flagstaff, AZ	928	86001-86004, 86011, 86015*
Flanders, NJ	862, 973	07836
Flandreau, SD	605	57028
Flasher, ND	701	58535
Flat Rock, NC	828	28731
Flatonia, TX	361	78941
Fleetwood, PA	484, 610	19522
Flemingsburg, KY	606	41041
Flemington, NJ	908	08822
Fletcher, NC	828	28732
Fletcher, OH	937	45326
Flint, MI	810	48501-48509, 48519, 48529*
Flintstone, GA	706, 762	30725
Flippin, AR	870	72634
Flora, IL	618	62839
Flora, MS	601, 769	39071
Floral Park, NY	516	11001-11005
Florence, AL	256	35630-35634
Florence, AZ	520	85232, 85279
Florence, CO	719	81226, 81290
Florence, KY	859	41022, 41042
Florence, MA	413	01062
Florence, MS	601, 769	39073
Florence, NJ	609	08518
Florence, OR	541, 458	97439
Florence, SC	843	29501-29506
Florence, WI	715, 534	54121
Floresville, TX	830	78114
Florham Park, NJ	862, 973	07932
Florida, NY	845	10921
Florida City, FL	305, 786	33034
Florien, LA	318	71429
Florissant, CO	719	80816
Florissant, MO	314	63031-63034
Flourtown, PA	215, 267	19031
Flower Mound, TX	469, 972	75022, 75027-75028
Flowery Branch, GA	470, 770	30542
Flowood, MS	601, 769	39208, 39232
Floyd, VA	540	24091
Floydada, TX	806	79235
Flushing, MI	810	48433
Flushing, NY	347, 718	11351-11381, 11385-11386*
Fogelsville, PA	484, 610	18051
Folcroft, PA	484, 610	19032
Foley, AL	251	36535-36536
Foley, MN	320	56329, 56357
Folkston, GA	912	31537
Folsom, CA	916	95630, 95762-95763
Folsom, LA	985	70437
Folsom, NJ	609	08037
Fond du Lac, WI	920	54935-54937
Fonda, NY	518	12068
Fontana, CA	951	92334-92337
Fontana, WI	262	53125
Fontana Dam, NC	828	28733
Foothill Ranch, CA	949	92610
Ford, KS	620	67842
Fordland, MO	417	65652
Fords, NJ	732, 848	08863
Fordyce, AR	870	71742
Forest, MS	601, 769	39074
Forest, OH	419, 567	45843
Forest, VA	434	24551
Forest City, IA	641	50436
Forest City, NC	828	28043
Forest City, PA	570	18421
Forest Grove, OR	503, 971	97116
Forest Hill, MD	410	21050
Forest Hills, NY	347, 718	11375
Forest Lake, MN	651	55025
Forest Park, GA	404, 470	30297-30298

*Partial list of zip codes, including main range

City	Area Code(s)	Zip Code(s)
Forest Park, IL	708	60130
Forestville, CA	707	95436
Forestville, CT	860	06010
Forked River, NJ	609	08731
Forks, WA	360	98331
Forksville, PA	570	18616
Forman, ND	701	58032
Forrest City, AR	870	72335-72336
Forsyth, GA	478	31029
Forsyth, MO	417	65653
Forsyth, MT	406	59327
Fort Atkinson, WI	920	53538
Fort Belvoir, VA	571, 703	22060
Fort Benning, GA	706, 762	31905, 31995
Fort Benton, MT	406	59442
Fort Bliss, TX	915	79906-79908, 79916-79918
Fort Bragg, CA	707	95437, 95488
Fort Bragg, NC	910	28307-28310
Fort Buchanan, PR	787, 939	00920-00922, 00934-00936
Fort Calhoun, NE	402	68023
Fort Campbell, KY	270	42223
Fort Carson, CO	719	80913
Fort Collins, CO	970	80521-80528, 80553
Fort Davis, TX	915	79734
Fort Defiance, AZ	928	86504, 86549
Fort Deposit, AL	334	36032
Fort Dix, NJ	609	08640
Fort Dodge, IA	515	50501
Fort Dodge, KS	620	67801
Fort Drum, NY	315	13602-13603
Fort Edward, NY	518	12828
Fort Eustis, VA	757	23604
Fort Gaines, GA	229	31751
Fort Gibson, OK	918	74434
Fort Gordon, GA	706, 762	30905
Fort Harrison, MT	406	59636
Fort Hood, TX	254	76544
Fort Huachuca, AZ	520	85613, 85670
Fort Irwin, CA	760, 442	92310
Fort Jackson, SC	803	29207
Fort Jones, CA	530	96032
Fort Kent, ME	207	04741-04743
Fort Knox, KY	502	40121
Fort Laramie, WY	307	82212
Fort Lauderdale, FL	754, 954	33301-33340, 33345-33351*
Fort Leavenworth, KS	913	66027
Fort Lee, NJ	201, 551	07024
Fort Lee, VA	804	23801
Fort Leonard Wood, MO	573	65473
Fort Lewis, WA	253	98433
Fort Loramie, OH	937	45845
Fort Madison, IA	319	52627
Fort McPherson, GA	404, 470	30310, 30330
Fort Meade, MD	301	20755
Fort Meade, SD	605	57741
Fort Mill, SC	803	29708, 29715-29716
Fort Mitchell, KY	859	41017
Fort Monmouth, NJ	732, 848	07703
Fort Monroe, VA	757	23651
Fort Morgan, CO	970	80701, 80705, 80742
Fort Myer, VA	571, 703	22211
Fort Myers, FL	239	33901-33919, 33965, 33994
Fort Myers Beach, FL	239	33931-33932
Fort Oglethorpe, GA	706, 762	30742
Fort Payne, AL	256	35967-35968
Fort Pierce, FL	772	34945-34954, 34979-34988
Fort Pierre, SD	605	57532
Fort Polk, LA	337	71459
Fort Recovery, OH	419, 567	45846
Fort Richardson, AK	907	99504-99505
Fort Riley, KS	785	66442
Fort Rucker, AL	334	36362
Fort Sam Houston, TX	210	78234
Fort Scott, KS	620	66701
Fort Shafter, HI	808	96858
Fort Sill, OK	580	73503
Fort Smith, AR	479	72901-72908, 72913-72919
Fort Smith, MT	406	59035
Fort Snelling, MN	612	55111
Fort Stewart, GA	912	31313-31315
Fort Stockton, TX	915	79735
Fort Story, VA	757	23459
Fort Sumner, NM	505	88119
Fort Supply, OK	580	73841
Fort Thomas, KY	859	41075
Fort Totten, ND	701	58335
Fort Valley, GA	478	31030
Fort Wainwright, AK	907	99703
Fort Walton Beach, FL	850	32547-32549
Fort Washington, MD	301	20744, 20749-20750
Fort Washington, PA	215, 267	19034, 19048-19049
Fort Wayne, IN	260	46801-46809, 46814-46819*
Fort Worth, TX	682, 817	76101-76140, 76147-76150*
Fort Yates, ND	701	58538
Fortine, MT	406	59918
Fortuna, CA	707	95540
Forty Fort, PA	570	18704
Fossil, OR	541, 458	97830
Foster City, CA	650	94404
Fostoria, OH	419, 567	44830
Fountain Hills, AZ	480	85268-85269
Fountain Inn, SC	864	29644
Fountain Valley, CA	714	92708, 92728
Four Oaks, NC	919	27524
Fowler, CA	559	93625
Fowler, IN	765	47944, 47984-47986
Fowlerville, MI	517	48836
Fox Lake, WI	920	53933
Foxboro, MA	508, 774	02035
Foxborough, MA	508, 774	02035
Frackville, PA	570	17931-17932
Framingham, MA	508, 774	01701-01705
Francesville, IN	219	47946
Frankenmuth, MI	989	48734, 48787
Frankfort, IL	815	60423
Frankfort, IN	765	46041
Frankfort, KY	502	40601-40604, 40618-40622
Frankfort, MI	231	49635
Frankfort, NY	315	13340
Franklin, GA	706, 762	30217
Franklin, ID	208	83237
Franklin, IN	317	46131
Franklin, KY	270	42134-42135
Franklin, LA	337	70538
Franklin, MA	508, 774	02038
Franklin, NE	308	68939
Franklin, NH	603	03235
Franklin, NJ	862, 973	07416
Franklin, NC	828	28734, 28744
Franklin, OH	513	45005, 45342
Franklin, PA	814	16323
Franklin, TN	615	37064-37069
Franklin, TX	979	77856
Franklin, VA	757	23851
Franklin, WV	304	26807
Franklin, WI	414	53132
Franklin Furnace, OH	740	45629
Franklin Lakes, NJ	201, 551	07417
Franklin Park, IL	224, 847	60131, 60398
Franklin Springs, GA	706, 762	30639
Franklin Square, NY	516	11010
Franklinton, LA	985	70438
Franklinton, NC	919	27525
Franklinville, NY	585	14737
Franksville, WI	262	53126
Frankton, IN	765	46044
Franktown, CO	303, 720	80116
Fraser, MI	586	48026
Frazee, MN	218	56544
Frazer, PA	484, 610	19355
Frazeysburg, OH	740	43822
Frederic, MI	989	49733
Frederica, DE	302	19946
Frederick, CO	303, 720	80504, 80516, 80530
Frederick, MD	301	21701-21705, 21709
Frederick, OK	580	73542
Fredericksburg, PA	717	17026
Fredericksburg, TX	830	78624
Fredericksburg, VA	540	22401-22408, 22412
Fredericktown, MO	573	63645
Fredericktown, OH	740	43019
Fredonia, AZ	928	86022, 86052
Fredonia, KS	620	66736
Fredonia, NY	716	14063
Fredonia, WI	262	53021
Freeburg, IL	618	62243
Freeburg, MO	573	65035
Freedom, WY	307	83120
Freehold, NJ	732, 848	07728
Freeland, MI	989	48623
Freeland, PA	570	18224
Freeland, WA	360	98249
Freeport, IL	815	61032
Freeport, ME	207	04032-04034
Freeport, MI	616	49325
Freeport, NY	516	11520
Freeport, PA	724, 878	16229
Freeport, TX	979	77541-77542
Fremont, CA	510	94536-94539, 94555
Fremont, IN	260	46737
Fremont, MI	231	49412-49413
Fremont, NE	402	68025-68026
Fremont, OH	419, 567	43420
French Camp, CA	209	95231
French Creek, WV	304	26218-26219
French Lick, IN	812	47432
Frenchburg, KY	606	40322
Frenchtown, NJ	908	08825
Fresh Meadows, NY	347, 718	11365-11366
Fresno, CA	559	93650, 93701-93729, 93740*
Friday Harbor, WA	360	98250
Fridley, MN	763	55421, 55432
Friendship, WI	608	53927, 53934
Friendswood, TX	281, 832	77546-77549
Friona, TX	806	79035
Frisco, CO	970	80443
Frisco, TX	469, 972	75034-75035
Fritch, TX	806	79036
Front Royal, VA	540	22630
Frostburg, MD	301	21532
Frostproof, FL	863	33843
Fruita, CO	970	81521
Fruitland, ID	208	83619
Fruitport, MI	231	49415
Fullerton, CA	714	92831-92838
Fullerton, NE	308	68638
Fulton, AL	334	36446
Fulton, IL	815	61252
Fulton, MS	662	38843
Fulton, MO	573	65251
Fulton, NY	315	13069
Fultonville, NY	518	12016, 12072
Fuquay-Varina, NC	919	27526

G

City	Area Code(s)	Zip Code(s)
Gabriels, NY	518	12939
Gadsden, AL	256	35901-35907
Gaffney, SC	864	29340-29342
Gahanna, OH	614	43230
Gail, TX	806	79738
Gainesboro, TN	931	38562
Gainesville, FL	352	32601-32614, 32627, 32635*
Gainesville, GA	470, 678, 770	30501-30507
Gainesville, MO	417	65655
Gainesville, TX	940	76240-76241
Gaithersburg, MD	240, 301	20877-20886, 20898-20899
Galax, VA	276	24333
Galena, IL	815	61036
Galena, KS	620	66739
Galena, MD	410	21635
Galena, MO	417	65624, 65656
Galena Park, TX	713, 832	77547
Galesburg, IL	309	61401-61402
Galesburg, KS	620	66740
Galion, OH	419, 567	44833
Gallatin, MO	660	64640
Gallatin, TN	615	37066
Gallatin Gateway, MT	406	59730
Gallaway, TN	901	38036
Galliano, LA	985	70354
Gallipolis, OH	740	45631
Gallitzin, PA	814	16641
Galloway, NJ	609	08201, 08205
Gallup, NM	505	87301-87305, 87310, 87317*
Galt, CA	209	95632
Galveston, TX	409	77550-77555
Gambier, OH	740	43022
Ganado, AZ	928	86505, 86540
Gann Valley, SD	605	57341
Gap, PA	717	17527
Garden City, GA	912	31405-31408, 31415-31418
Garden City, KS	620	67846, 67868
Garden City, MI	734	48135-48136
Garden City, NY	516	11530-11531, 11535-11536*
Garden City, TX	915	79739
Garden City Park, NY	516	11040
Garden Grove, CA	714	92840-92846
Gardena, CA	310, 323, 424	90247-90249

*Partial list of zip codes, including main range

City	Area Code(s)	Zip Code(s)
Gardiner, ME	207	04345
Gardner, IL	815	60424
Gardner, KS	913	66030-66031
Gardner, MA	351, 978	01440
Gardners, PA	717	17324
Gardnerville, NV	775	89410
Garfield, NJ	862, 973	07026
Garfield Heights, OH	216	44105, 44125-44128
Garland, NC	910	28441
Garland, TX	469, 972	75040-75049
Garner, IA	641	50438
Garner, NC	919	27529
Garnett, KS	785	66032
Garretson, SD	605	57030
Garrett, IN	260	46738
Garrettsville, OH	234, 330	44231
Garrison, NY	845	10524
Garrison, ND	701	58540
Garwood, NJ	908	07027
Gary, IN	219	46401-46411
Garyville, LA	985	70051, 70076
Gaston, OR	503, 971	97119
Gastonia, NC	704, 980	28052-28056
Gate City, VA	276	24251
Gatesville, NC	252	27938
Gatesville, TX	254	76528, 76596-76599
Gatlinburg, TN	865	37738
Gautier, MS	228	39553
Gaylord, MI	989	49734-49735
Gaylord, MN	507	55334
Gearhart, OR	503, 971	97138
Geismar, LA	225	70734
Geneseo, IL	309	61254
Geneseo, NY	585	14454
Geneva, AL	334	36340
Geneva, IL	331, 630	60134
Geneva, NE	402	68361
Geneva, NY	315	14456
Geneva, OH	440	44041
Genoa, OH	419, 567	43430
Genoa City, WI	262	53128
Gentry, AR	479	72734
George, IA	712	51237
George West, TX	361	78022
Georgetown, CO	303, 720	80444
Georgetown, DE	302	19947
Georgetown, GA	229	31754
Georgetown, KY	502	40324
Georgetown, MA	351, 978	01833
Georgetown, NY	315	13072, 13129
Georgetown, OH	937	45121
Georgetown, SC	843	29440-29442
Georgetown, TX	512	78626-78628
Gering, NE	308	69341
Germantown, MD	301	20874-20876
Germantown, OH	937	45325-45327
Germantown, TN	901	38138-38139, 38183
Germantown, WI	262	53022
Gervais, OR	503, 971	97026
Gettysburg, PA	717	17325-17326
Gettysburg, SD	605	57442
Getzville, NY	716	14068
Geyserville, CA	707	95441
Gibbon, MN	507	55335
Gibbon, NE	308	68840
Gibbsboro, NJ	856	08026
Gibbstown, NJ	856	08027
Gibson, GA	706, 762	30810
Gibson City, IL	217	60936
Gibsonia, PA	724, 878	15044
Gibsonville, NC	336	27249
Giddings, TX	979	78942
Gig Harbor, WA	253	98329-98335
Gilbert, AZ	480	85233-85234, 85296-85299
Gilbertsville, KY	270	42044
Gilford, NH	603	03247-03249
Gillett, AR	870	72055
Gillette, WY	307	82716-82718, 82731-82732
Gilman, CT	860	06336
Gilmer, TX	903	75644-75645
Gilmore City, IA	515	50541
Gilroy, CA	408	95020-95021
Girard, KS	620	66743
Girard, OH	234, 330	44420
Girard, PA	814	16417
Girdwood, AK	907	99587, 99693
Gladstone, MI	906	49837

City	Area Code(s)	Zip Code(s)
Gladstone, MO	816	64116-64119, 64155-64156*
Gladstone, NJ	908	07934
Gladwin, MI	989	48624
Gladwyne, PA	484, 610	19035
Glasgow, KY	270	42141-42142, 42156
Glasgow, MT	406	59230-59231
Glassboro, NJ	856	08028
Glassport, PA	412, 878	15045
Glastonbury, CT	860	06033
Glen Allen, VA	804	23058-23060
Glen Arbor, MI	231	49636
Glen Arm, MD	410	21057
Glen Burnie, MD	410	21060-21062
Glen Cove, NY	516	11542
Glen Dale, WV	304	26038
Glen Echo, MD	301	20812
Glen Ellen, CA	707	95442
Glen Ellyn, IL	331, 630	60137-60138
Glen Gardner, NJ	908	08826
Glen Head, NY	516	11545
Glen Jean, WV	304	25846
Glen Lyn, VA	540	24093
Glen Raven, NC	336	27215
Glen Riddle, PA	484, 610	19037, 19063
Glen Ridge, NJ	862, 973	07028
Glen Rock, NJ	201, 551	07452
Glen Rock, PA	717	17327
Glen Rose, TX	254	76043
Glencoe, IL	224, 847	60022
Glencoe, MN	320	55336
Glendale, AZ	623	85301-85313, 85318
Glendale, CA	818	91201-91210, 91214, 91221*
Glendale, CO	303, 720	80246
Glendale, NY	347, 718	11385
Glendale, WI	414	53209-53212, 53217
Glendale Heights, IL	331, 630	60139
Glendive, MT	406	59330
Glendora, CA	626	91740-91741
Glendora, NJ	856	08029
Gleneden Beach, OR	541, 458	97388
Glenelg, MD	410	21737
Glenmont, OH	234, 330	44628
Glenmoore, PA	484, 610	19343
Glennallen, AK	907	99588
Glennville, GA	912	30427
Glens Falls, NY	518	12801-12804
Glenshaw, PA	412, 878	15116
Glenside, PA	215, 267	19038
Glenview, IL	224, 847	60025-60026
Glenville, NY	518	12302, 12325
Glenville, WV	304	26351
Glenwillow, OH	440	44139
Glenwood, IL	708	60425
Glenwood, IA	712	51534
Glenwood, MN	320	56334
Glenwood Springs, CO	970	81601-81602
Glidden, IA	712	51443
Glide, OR	541, 458	97443
Globe, AZ	928	85501-85502
Glorieta, NM	505	87535
Gloucester, MA	351, 978	01930-01931
Gloucester, NJ	856	08030-08031
Gloucester, VA	804	23061
Gloucester Point, VA	804	23062
Gloversville, NY	518	12078
Gnadenhutten, OH	740	44629
Godfrey, IL	618	62035
Godwin, NC	910	28344
Goffstown, NH	603	03045-03046
Golconda, IL	618	62938
Golconda, NV	480	89414
Gold Beach, OR	541, 458	97444
Gold Canyon, AZ	480	85218-85219
Gold Hill, NV	775	89440
Gold Hill, OR	541, 458	97525
Gold River, CA	916	95670
Golden, CO	303, 720	80401-80403, 80419
Golden, MS	662	38847
Golden Valley, MN	763	55416, 55422, 55426-55427
Goldendale, WA	509	98620
Goldfield, NV	775	89013
Goldsboro, NC	919	27530-27534
Goldthwaite, TX	915	76844
Goleta, CA	805	93110-93111, 93116-93118*
Golf, IL	224, 847	60029
Goliad, TX	361	77963
Gonzales, CA	831	93926

City	Area Code(s)	Zip Code(s)
Gonzales, LA	225	70707, 70737
Gonzales, TX	830	78629
Goochland, VA	804	23063
Goodfellow AFB, TX	915	76908
Goodfield, IL	309	61742
Gooding, ID	208	83330
Goodland, KS	785	67735
Goodlettsville, TN	615	37070-37072
Goodman, MS	662	39079
Goodrich, MI	810	48438
Goodwell, OK	580	73939
Goodyear, AZ	623	85338
Gordo, AL	205	35466
Gordon, NE	308	69343
Gordonsville, VA	540	22942
Gordonville, TX	903	76245
Gore, OK	918	74435
Gorham, ME	207	04038
Gorham, NH	603	03581
Goshen, IN	574	46526-46528
Goshen, NY	845	10924
Goulds, FL	305, 786	33170
Gouverneur, NY	315	13642
Gove, KS	785	67736
Gowanda, NY	716	14070
Grabill, IN	260	46741
Graceville, FL	850	32440
Gracewood, GA	706, 762	30812
Grady, AR	870	71644
Grafton, IL	618	62037
Grafton, MA	508, 774	01519
Grafton, ND	701	58237
Grafton, OH	440	44044
Grafton, WV	304	26354
Grafton, WI	262	53024
Graham, NC	336	27253
Graham, TX	940	76450
Grain Valley, MO	816	64029
Grambling, LA	318	71245
Gramercy, LA	225	70052
Gramling, SC	864	29348
Grampian, PA	814	16838
Granada Hills, CA	818	91344, 91394
Granbury, TX	682, 817	76048-76049
Granby, CO	970	80446
Granby, CT	860	06035, 06090
Grand Blanc, MI	810	48439
Grand Canyon, AZ	928	86023
Grand Chenier, LA	337	70643
Grand Forks, ND	701	58201-58208
Grand Forks AFB, ND	701	58204-58205
Grand Haven, MI	616	49417
Grand Island, NE	308	68801-68803
Grand Island, NY	716	14072
Grand Junction, CO	970	81501-81506
Grand Junction, MI	616	49056
Grand Ledge, MI	517	48837
Grand Marais, MN	218	55604
Grand Marsh, WI	608	53936
Grand Portage, MN	218	55605
Grand Prairie, TX	469, 972	75050-75054
Grand Rapids, MI	616	49501-49518, 49523-49525*
Grand Rapids, MN	218	55730, 55744-55745
Grand Rapids, OH	419, 567	43522
Grand Terrace, CA	909	92313, 92324
Grandview, MO	816	64030
Grandview, WA	509	98930
Grandville, MI	616	49418, 49468
Granger, IN	574	46530
Granger, WA	509	98932
Grangeville, ID	208	83530-83531
Granite, OK	580	73547
Granite City, IL	618	62040
Granite Falls, MN	320	56241
Granite Falls, NC	828	28630
Granite Quarry, NC	704, 980	28072
Graniteville, SC	803	29829
Graniteville, VT	802	05654
Grant, CO	303, 720	80448
Grant, MI	231	49327
Grant, NE	308	69140
Grant City, MO	660	64456
Grantham, PA	717	17027
Grants, NM	505	87020
Grants Pass, OR	541, 458	97526-97528, 97543
Grantsboro, NC	252	28529
Grantsburg, WI	715, 534	54840

*Partial list of zip codes, including main range

City	Area Code(s)	Zip Code(s)
Grantsville, MD	301	21536
Grantsville, WV	304	26147
Grantville, PA	717	17028
Granville, IL	815	61326
Granville, MA	413	01034
Granville, NY	518	12832
Granville, OH	740	43023
Grapevine, TX	682, 817	76051, 76092, 76099
Grass Valley, CA	530	95945, 95949
Graterford, PA	484, 610	19426
Gratz, PA	717	17030
Grawn, MI	231	49637
Gray, GA	478	31032
Gray, KY	606	40734
Gray, LA	985	70359
Grayling, MI	989	49738-49739
Grayslake, IL	224, 847	60030
Grayson, KY	606	41143
Grayville, IL	618	62844
Great Barrington, MA	413	01230
Great Bend, KS	620	67530
Great Falls, MT	406	59401-59406
Great Falls, VA	571, 703	22066
Great Lakes, IL	224, 847	60088
Great Neck, NY	516	11020-11027
Greeley, CO	970	80631-80634, 80638-80639
Greeley, NE	308	68842
Green Bay, WI	920	54301-54313, 54324, 54344
Green Brook, NJ	732, 848	08812
Green Cove Springs, FL	904	32043
Green Forest, AR	870	72638
Green Island, NY	518	12183
Green Lake, WI	920	54941
Green Lane, PA	215, 267	18054
Green Pond, AL	205	35074
Green River, UT	435	84515, 84525, 84540
Green River, WY	307	82935-82938
Green Springs, OH	419, 567	44836
Green Valley, AZ	520	85614, 85622
Greenbelt, MD	301	20768-20771
Greenbrae, CA	415	94904, 94914
Greencastle, IN	765	46135
Greencastle, PA	717	17225
Greendale, WI	414	53129
Greene, NY	607	13778
Greeneville, TN	423	37743-37745
Greenfield, IN	317	46140
Greenfield, IA	641	50849
Greenfield, MA	413	01301-01302
Greenfield, MO	417	65661
Greenfield, NH	603	03047
Greenfield, OH	937	45123, 45165
Greenfield, WI	414	53219-53221, 53227-53228
Greenland, NH	603	03840
Greenlawn, NY	631	11740
Greenport, NY	631	11944
Greens Farms, CT	203	06436
Greensboro, AL	334	36744
Greensboro, GA	706, 762	30642
Greensboro, NC	336	27401-27420, 27425-27429*
Greensburg, IN	812	47240
Greensburg, KS	620	67054
Greensburg, KY	270	42743
Greensburg, LA	225	70441
Greensburg, PA	724, 878	15601, 15605-15606
Greenup, KY	606	41144
Greenvale, NY	516	11548
Greenville, AL	334	36037
Greenville, DE	302	19807
Greenville, GA	706, 762	30222
Greenville, IL	618	62246
Greenville, KY	270	42345
Greenville, MI	616	48838
Greenville, MS	662	38701-38704, 38731
Greenville, MO	573	63944
Greenville, NC	252	27833-27836, 27858
Greenville, OH	937	45331
Greenville, PA	724, 878	16125
Greenville, RI	401	02828
Greenville, SC	864	29601-29617, 29698
Greenville, TX	903	75401-75404
Greenwell Springs, LA	225	70739
Greenwich, CT	203	06830-06832, 06836
Greenwood, AR	479	72936
Greenwood, DE	302	19950
Greenwood, IN	317	46142-46143
Greenwood, MS	662	38930, 38935
Greenwood, SC	864	29646-29649
Greenwood, WI	715, 534	54437
Greenwood Village, CO	303, 720	80110-80112, 80121, 80150*
Greer, SC	864	29650-29652
Gregory, SD	605	57533
Grenada, MS	662	38901-38902
Grenloch, NJ	856	08032
Gresham, OR	503, 971	97030, 97080
Gretna, LA	504	70053-70056
Gretna, NE	402	68028
Gretna, VA	434	24557
Greybull, WY	307	82426
Greystone Park, NJ	862, 973	07950
Griffin, GA	470, 770	30223-30224
Griffith, IN	219	46319
Griggsville, IL	217	62340
Grinnell, IA	641	50112, 50177
Groesbeck, TX	254	76642
Grosse Pointe, MI	313	48224, 48230, 48236
Grosse Pointe Farms, MI	313	48230, 48236
Grosse Pointe Park, MI	313	48215, 48224, 48230, 48236
Grosse Pointe Shores, MI	313	48230, 48236
Groton, CT	860	06340, 06349
Groton, MA	351, 978	01450, 01470-01471
Groton, VT	802	05046
Grove, OK	918	74344-74345
Grove City, OH	614	43123
Grove City, PA	724, 878	16127
Grove Hill, AL	251	36451
Groveland, FL	352	34736
Groveport, OH	614	43125, 43195-43199
Grover, NC	704, 980	28073
Grover Beach, CA	805	93433, 93483
Groves, TX	409	77619
Groveton, TX	936	75845
Grovetown, GA	706, 762	30813
Grundy, VA	276	24614
Grundy Center, IA	319	50638
Gruver, TX	806	79040
Guayama, PR	787, 939	00784-00785
Guerneville, CA	707	95446
Guilderland, NY	518	12084
Guildhall, VT	802	05905
Guilford, CT	203	06437
Guilford, ME	207	04443
Guin, AL	205	35563
Gulf Breeze, FL	850	32561-32566
Gulf Shores, AL	251	36542, 36547
Gulfport, FL	727	33707, 33711, 33737
Gulfport, MS	228	39501-39507
Gun Barrel City, TX	903	75147
Gunnison, CO	970	81230-81231, 81247
Gunnison, UT	435	84634
Guntersville, AL	256	35976
Guntown, MS	662	38849
Gurdon, AR	870	71743
Gurnee, IL	224, 847	60031
Gustavus, AK	907	99826
Guthrie, OK	405	73044
Guthrie, TX	806	79236
Guthrie Center, IA	641	50115
Guymon, OK	580	73942
Gwynedd, PA	215, 267	19436
Gwynedd Valley, PA	215, 267	19437

H

City	Area Code(s)	Zip Code(s)
Hackensack, NJ	201, 551	07601-07602
Hackettstown, NJ	908	07840
Haddam, CT	860	06438
Haddonfield, NJ	856	08033
Hadley, MA	413	01035
Hagerman, ID	208	83332
Hagerman, NM	505	88232
Hagerstown, MD	240, 301	21740-21742, 21746-21749
Hahnville, LA	985	70057
Hailey, ID	208	83333
Haines, AK	907	99827
Haines City, FL	863	33844-33845
Hainesport, NJ	609	08036
Haledon, NJ	862, 973	07508, 07538
Hales Corners, WI	414	53130-53132
Haleyville, AL	205	35565
Half Moon Bay, CA	650	94019
Halifax, MA	339, 781	02338
Halifax, NC	252	27839
Halifax, PA	717	17032
Halifax, VA	434	24558
Hall, NY	585	14463
Hallandale, FL	754, 954	33008-33009
Hallettsville, TX	361	77964
Hallock, MN	218	56728, 56740, 56755
Hallowell, ME	207	04347
Halls, TN	731	38040
Halstad, MN	218	56548
Halstead, KS	316	67056
Haltom City, TX	682, 817	76111, 76117, 76137, 76148*
Ham Lake, MN	763	55304
Hamburg, AR	870	71646
Hamburg, NJ	862, 973	07419
Hamburg, NY	716	14075, 14219
Hamburg, PA	484, 610	19526
Hamden, CT	203	06514-06518
Hamel, MN	763	55340
Hamer, ID	208	83425
Hamilton, AL	205	35570
Hamilton, GA	706, 762	31811
Hamilton, IL	217	62341
Hamilton, MT	406	59840
Hamilton, NJ	609	08609-08611, 08619-08620*
Hamilton, NY	315	13346
Hamilton, OH	513	45011-45026
Hamilton, TX	254	76531
Hamilton Square, NJ	609	08690
Hamlet, NC	910	28345
Hamlin, NY	585	14464
Hamlin, TX	915	79520
Hamlin, WV	304	25523
Hammond, IN	219	46320-46327
Hammond, LA	985	70401-70404
Hammond, WI	715, 534	54002, 54015
Hammondsport, NY	607	14840
Hammonton, NJ	609	08037
Hampden-Sydney, VA	434	23943
Hampshire, IL	224, 847	60140
Hampstead, MD	410	21074
Hampstead, NH	603	03841
Hampton, AR	870	71744
Hampton, GA	470, 770	30228
Hampton, IA	641	50441
Hampton, NH	603	03842-03843
Hampton, SC	803	29913, 29924
Hampton, VA	757	23605, 23630-23631, 23651*
Hampton Falls, NH	603	03844
Hamptonville, NC	336	27020
Hamtramck, MI	313	48211-48212
Hana, HI	808	96713
Hanahan, SC	843	29406, 29410
Hanceville, AL	256	35077
Hancock, MI	906	49930
Hancock, MN	320	56244
Hancock, WI	715, 534	54943
Hanford, CA	559	93230-93232
Hannibal, MO	573	63401
Hannibal, OH	740	43931
Hanover, IN	812	47243
Hanover, MD	410	21075-21076, 21098
Hanover, NH	603	03755
Hanover, PA	717	17331-17334
Hanover, VA	804	23069
Hanover Park, IL	331, 630	60108, 60133
Hanscom AFB, MA	339, 781	01731
Hanson, MA	339, 781	02341, 02350
Harahan, LA	504	70123
Harbor Beach, MI	989	48441
Harbor City, CA	310, 424	90710
Harbor Springs, MI	231	49737-49740
Harborcreek, PA	814	16421
Harcourt, IA	515	50544
Hardin, IL	618	62047
Hardin, MT	406	59034
Hardinsburg, KY	270	40143
Hardwick, GA	478	31034
Hardwick, VT	802	05843
Hardy, VA	540	24101
Harkers Island, NC	252	28531
Harlan, IA	712	51537, 51593
Harlan, KY	606	40831, 40840
Harlem, GA	706, 762	30814
Harlem, MT	406	59526
Harleysville, PA	215, 267	19438-19441
Harlingen, TX	956	78550-78553

*Partial list of zip codes, including main range

City	Area Code(s)	Zip Code(s)
Harlowton, MT	406	59036
Harpers Ferry, IA	563	52146
Harpers Ferry, WV	304	25425
Harrells, NC	910	28444
Harriman, NY	845	10926
Harriman, TN	865	37748
Harrington, DE	302	19952
Harrington Park, NJ	201, 551	07640
Harris, MN	651	55032
Harris, NY	845	12742
Harrisburg, AR	870	72432
Harrisburg, IL	618	62946
Harrisburg, NE	308	69345
Harrisburg, NC	704, 980	28075
Harrisburg, PA	717	17101-17113, 17120-17130*
Harrison, AR	870	72601-72602
Harrison, ID	208	83833, 83842
Harrison, MI	989	48625
Harrison, NE	308	69346
Harrison, NJ	862, 973	07029
Harrison, NY	914	10528
Harrison, OH	513	45030
Harrison Township, MI	586	48045
Harrisonburg, LA	318	71340
Harrisonburg, VA	540	22801-22803, 22807
Harrisonville, MO	816	64701
Harrisville, MI	989	48740
Harrisville, WV	304	26362
Harrodsburg, KY	859	40330
Harrogate, TN	423	37707, 37752
Hart, MI	231	49420
Hartford, AL	334	36344
Hartford, CT	860	06101-06156, 06160-06161*
Hartford, KY	270	42347
Hartford, WI	262	53027
Hartford City, IN	765	47348
Hartington, NE	402	68739
Hartland, ME	207	04943
Hartland, WI	262	53029
Hartsdale, NY	914	10530
Hartselle, AL	256	35640
Hartsville, SC	843	29550-29551
Hartsville, TN	615	37074
Hartville, MO	417	65667
Hartville, OH	234, 330	44632
Hartwell, GA	706, 762	30643
Hartwick, NY	607	13348
Harvard, IL	815	60033
Harvey, IL	708	60426
Harvey, LA	504	70058-70059
Harwich, MA	508, 774	02645
Harwood Heights, IL	708	60656, 60706
Hasbrouck Heights, NJ	201, 551	07604
Haskell, NJ	862, 973	07420
Haskell, TX	940	79521
Hastings, MI	616	49058
Hastings, MN	651	55033
Hastings, NE	402	68901-68902
Hastings-on-Hudson, NY	914	10706
Hatboro, PA	215, 267	19040
Hatfield, MA	413	01038
Hatfield, PA	215, 267	19440
Hato Rey, PR	787, 939	00917-00919
Hattiesburg, MS	601, 769	39401-39407
Haughton, LA	318	71037
Hauppauge, NY	631	11749, 11760, 11788
Havana, IL	309	62644
Haverford, PA	484, 610	19041
Haverhill, MA	351, 978	01830-01835
Haverstraw, NY	845	10927
Havertown, PA	484, 610	19083
Haviland, KS	620	67059
Havre, MT	406	59501
Havre de Grace, MD	410	21078
Haw River, NC	336	27258
Hawaii National Park, HI	808	96718
Hawaiian Gardens, CA	562	90716
Hawesville, KY	270	42348
Hawkins, TX	903	75765
Hawkins, WI	715, 534	54530
Hawkinsville, GA	478	31036
Hawthorn Woods, IL	224, 847	60047
Hawthorne, CA	310, 424	90250-90251
Hawthorne, NV	775	89415
Hawthorne, NJ	862, 973	07506-07507
Hawthorne, NY	914	10532
Hay Springs, NE	308	69347, 69367
Hayden, AZ	520	85235
Hayden, ID	208	83835
Hayden Lake, ID	208	83835
Hayes Center, NE	308	69032
Hayesville, NC	828	28904
Hayesville, OH	419, 567	44838
Haynesville, VA	804	22472
Hayneville, AL	334	36040
Hays, KS	785	67601, 67667
Haysville, KS	316	67060
Hayti, MO	573	63851
Hayti, SD	605	57241
Hayward, CA	510	94540-94546, 94552, 94557
Hayward, WI	715, 534	54843
Hazard, KY	606	41701-41702
Hazel Crest, IL	708	60429
Hazel Park, MI	248, 947	48030
Hazelwood, MO	314	63042-63045, 63135
Hazen, ND	701	58545
Hazlehurst, GA	912	31539
Hazlehurst, MS	601, 769	39083
Hazlet, NJ	732, 848	07730
Hazleton, PA	570	18201-18202
Healdsburg, CA	707	95448
Healy, AK	907	99743, 99755
Healy, KS	620	67850
Heartwell, NE	308	68945
Heath, OH	740	43056
Heathrow, FL	321, 407	32746
Heathsville, VA	804	22473
Hebbronville, TX	361	78361
Heber, CA	760, 442	92249
Heber City, UT	435	84032
Heber Springs, AR	501	72543-72545
Hebron, IL	815	60034
Hebron, KY	859	41048
Hebron, NE	402	68370
Hebron, OH	740	43025, 43098
Hector, MN	320	55342
Hedgesville, WV	304	25427
Heflin, AL	256	36264
Helen, GA	706, 762	30545
Helena, AL	205	35080
Helena, AR	870	72342
Helena, GA	229	31037
Helena, MT	406	59601-59604, 59620-59626
Helena, OK	580	73741
Helenwood, TN	423	37755
Hellertown, PA	484, 610	18055
Hemet, CA	951	92543-92546
Hemphill, TX	409	75948
Hempstead, NY	516	11549-11551
Hempstead, TX	979	77445
Henderson, CO	303, 720	80640
Henderson, KY	270	42419-42420
Henderson, NE	402	68371
Henderson, NV	702	89009-89016, 89052-89053*
Henderson, NC	252	27536-27537
Henderson, TN	731	38340
Henderson, TX	903	75652-75654, 75680
Hendersonville, NC	828	28739, 28791-28793
Hendersonville, TN	615	37075-37077
Hennepin, IL	815	61327
Henniker, NH	603	03242
Henning, TN	731	38041
Henrietta, NY	585	14467
Henrietta, TX	940	76365
Henry, TN	731	38231
Henryetta, OK	918	74437
Henryville, IN	812	47126
Heppner, OR	541, 458	97836
Hercules, CA	510	94547
Hereford, AZ	520	85615
Hereford, TX	806	79045
Herkimer, NY	315	13350
Hermann, MO	573	65041
Hermiston, OR	541, 458	97838
Hermitage, MO	417	65668
Hermitage, PA	724, 878	16148
Hermitage, TN	615	37076
Hermleigh, TX	915	79526
Hermon, ME	207	04401
Hermosa, SD	605	57744
Hernando, FL	352	34442
Hernando, MS	662	38632
Herndon, PA	570	17830
Herndon, VA	571, 703	20170-20172, 20190-20195*
Herrin, IL	618	62948
Hershey, PA	717	17033
Hertford, NC	252	27930, 27944
Hesperia, CA	760, 442	92340, 92345
Hesston, KS	620	67062
Hettinger, ND	701	58639
Heuvelton, NY	315	13654
Hewitt, NJ	862, 973	07421
Hewitt, TX	254	76643
Heyburn, ID	208	83336
Hialeah, FL	305, 786	33002, 33010-33018, 33054
Hialeah Gardens, FL	305, 786	33010, 33016-33018
Hiawassee, GA	706, 762	30546
Hiawatha, IA	319	52233
Hiawatha, KS	785	66434
Hibbing, MN	218	55746-55747
Hickam AFB, HI	808	96853
Hickman, KY	270	42050
Hickory, KY	270	42051
Hickory, NC	828	28601-28603
Hicksville, NY	516	11801-11804, 11815, 11819*
Hidden Valley, PA	814	15502
Higginsville, MO	660	64037
High Point, NC	336	27260-27265
High Ridge, MO	636	63049
High Shoals, GA	706, 762	30645
Highgate Springs, VT	802	05460
Highland, CA	909	92346
Highland, IL	618	62249
Highland, IN	219	46322, 47854
Highland, KS	785	66035
Highland, NY	845	12528
Highland Heights, KY	859	41076
Highland Heights, OH	440	44143
Highland Hills, OH	216	44122, 44128
Highland Park, IL	224, 847	60035-60037
Highland Park, MI	313	48203
Highland Springs, VA	804	23075
Highlands, NJ	732, 848	07732
Highlands Ranch, CO	303, 720	80124-80130, 80163
Highmore, SD	605	57345
Hightstown, NJ	609	08520
Hildebran, NC	828	28637
Hill AFB, UT	801, 385	84056
Hill City, KS	785	67642
Hill City, SD	605	57745
Hilliard, OH	614	43026
Hillsboro, IL	217	62049
Hillsboro, KS	620	67063
Hillsboro, MO	636	63050
Hillsboro, NH	603	03244
Hillsboro, ND	701	58045
Hillsboro, OH	937	45133
Hillsboro, OR	503, 971	97123-97124
Hillsboro, TX	254	76645
Hillsboro, WV	304	24946
Hillsboro, WI	608	54634
Hillsboro Beach, FL	754, 954	33062
Hillsborough, NJ	908	08844
Hillsborough, NC	919	27278
Hillsdale, MI	517	49242
Hillsdale, NJ	201, 551	07642, 07676
Hillsgrove, PA	570	18619
Hillside, IL	708	60162-60163
Hillside, NJ	973	07205
Hillsville, VA	276	24343
Hilmar, CA	209	95324
Hilo, HI	808	96720-96721
Hilton, NY	585	14468
Hilton Head Island, SC	843	29915, 29925-29928, 29938
Hinckley, MN	320	55037
Hinckley, OH	234, 330	44233
Hindman, KY	606	41822
Hines, IL	708	60141
Hinesville, GA	912	31310-31315
Hingham, MA	339, 781	02018, 02043-02044
Hinsdale, IL	331, 630	60521-60523, 60570
Hinsdale, NH	603	03451
Hinton, OK	405	73047
Hinton, WV	304	25951
Hiram, OH	234, 330	44234
Hixson, TN	423	37343
Hobart, IN	219	46342
Hobart, OK	580	73651
Hobbs, IN	765	46047
Hobbs, NM	505	88240-88244
Hobe Sound, FL	772	33455, 33475

Partial list of zip codes, including main range

City	Area Code(s)	Zip Code(s)
Hoboken, NJ	201, 551	07030
Hockessin, DE	302	19707
Hodgenville, KY	270	42748
Hodgkins, IL	708	60525
Hoffman, NC	910	28347
Hoffman Estates, IL	224, 847	60173, 60179, 60192-60195
Hohenwald, TN	931	38462
Hoisington, KS	620	67544
Holbrook, AZ	928	86025-86031
Holbrook, MA	339, 781	02343
Holbrook, NY	631	11741
Holden, MA	508, 774	01520
Holdenville, OK	405	74848
Holdingford, MN	320	56340
Holdrege, NE	308	68949, 68969
Holland, IN	812	47541
Holland, MI	616	49422-49424
Holland, NY	716	14080
Holland, OH	419, 567	43528
Hollandale, MS	662	38748
Hollidaysburg, PA	814	16648
Hollis, NH	603	03049
Hollis, OK	580	73550
Hollister, CA	831	95023-95024
Hollister, MO	417	65672-65673
Holliston, MA	508, 774	01746
Holloman AFB, NM	505	88330
Hollsopple, PA	814	15935
Holly, MI	248, 947	48442
Holly Hill, FL	386	32117
Holly Springs, MS	662	38634-38635, 38649
Hollywood, CA	323	90027-90028, 90038, 90068*
Hollywood, FL	754, 954	33019-33029, 33081-33084*
Holmdel, NJ	732, 848	07733, 07777
Holmen, WI	608	54636
Holstein, IA	712	51025
Holt, MI	517	48842
Holton, KS	785	66436
Holtsville, NY	631	00501, 00544, 11742
Holyoke, CO	970	80734
Holyoke, MA	413	01040-01041
Homer, AK	907	99603
Homer, GA	706, 762	30547
Homer, LA	318	71040
Homerville, GA	912	31634
Homestead, FL	305, 786	33030-33035, 33039, 33090*
Homestead, PA	412, 878	15120
Homewood, AL	205	35209, 35219, 35259
Homewood, IL	708	60430
Hominy, OK	918	74035
Homosassa Springs, FL	352	34447
Honaunau, HI	808	96726
Hondo, TX	830	78861
Honea Path, SC	864	29654
Honeoye, NY	585	14471
Honesdale, PA	570	18431
Honolulu, HI	808	96801-96830, 96835-96850
Hood River, OR	541, 458	97031
Hooker, OK	580	73945
Hooper, NE	402	68031
Hoosick Falls, NY	518	12090
Hoover, AL	205	35216, 35226, 35236, 35244
Hopatcong, NJ	862, 973	07843
Hope, AK	907	99605
Hope, AR	870	71801-71802
Hope Hull, AL	334	36043
Hope Valley, RI	401	02832
Hopedale, MA	508, 774	01747
Hopewell, VA	804	23860
Hopewell Junction, NY	845	12533
Hopkins, MI	616	49328
Hopkins, MN	952	55305, 55343-55345
Hopkins, SC	803	29061
Hopkinsville, KY	270	42240-42241
Hopkinton, MA	508, 774	01748
Hopkinton, NH	603	03229
Hopland, CA	707	95449
Hoquiam, WA	360	98550
Horn Lake, MS	662	38637
Hornell, NY	607	14843
Hornick, IA	712	51026
Horse Cave, KY	270	42749
Horseheads, NY	607	14844-14845
Horseshoe Bay, TX	830	78654-78657
Horsham, PA	215, 267	19044
Horton, KS	785	66439
Hot Springs, AR	501	71901-71903, 71909-71914
Hot Springs, SD	605	57747
Hot Springs, VA	540	24445
Hot Springs National Park, AR	501	71901-71903, 71909-71914*
Hot Sulphur Springs, CO	970	80451
Houghton, IA	319	52631
Houghton, MI	906	49921, 49931
Houghton, NY	585	14744
Houghton Lake, MI	989	48629
Houlka, MS	662	38850
Houlton, ME	207	04730, 04761
Houma, LA	985	70360-70364
Houston, MS	662	38851
Houston, MO	417	65483
Houston, TX	281, 713, 832	77001-77099, 77201-77293*
Houtzdale, PA	814	16651, 16698
Howard, KS	620	67349
Howard, SD	605	57349
Howard Lake, MN	320	55349, 55575
Howell, MI	517	48843-48844, 48863
Howell, NJ	732, 848	07731
Howes Cave, NY	518	12092
Howey in the Hills, FL	352	34737
Hoxie, KS	785	67740
Hubbard, OR	503, 971	97032
Huber Heights, OH	937	45424
Hudson, FL	727	34667-34669, 34674
Hudson, KS	620	67545
Hudson, MA	351, 978	01749
Hudson, MI	517	49247
Hudson, NH	603	03051
Hudson, NY	518	12534
Hudson, NC	828	28638
Hudson, OH	234, 330	44236-44238
Hudson, WI	715, 534	54016, 54082
Hudson Falls, NY	518	12839
Hueytown, AL	205	35022-35023
Hughesville, MD	301	20637
Hughson, CA	209	95326
Hugo, CO	719	80821
Hugo, MN	651	55038
Hugo, OK	580	74743
Hugoton, KS	620	67951
Hulbert, OK	918	74441
Hull, IA	712	51239
Hull, MA	339, 781	02045
Humacao, PR	787, 939	00791-00792
Humble, TX	281, 832	77325, 77338-77339, 77345*
Humboldt, IA	515	50548
Humboldt, KS	620	66748
Humboldt, TN	731	38343
Hummelstown, PA	717	17036
Hunlock Creek, PA	570	18621
Hunt, TX	830	78024
Hunt Valley, MD	410	21030-21031, 21065
Hunter, NY	518	12442
Huntersville, NC	704, 980	28070, 28078
Huntertown, IN	260	46748
Huntingburg, IN	812	47542
Huntingdon, PA	814	16652-16654
Huntingdon, TN	731	38344
Huntingdon Valley, PA	215, 267	19006
Huntington, IN	260	46750
Huntington, NY	631	11743
Huntington, UT	435	84528
Huntington, VT	802	05462
Huntington, WV	304	25701-25729, 25755, 25770*
Huntington Beach, CA	714	92605, 92615, 92646-92649
Huntington Park, CA	323	90255
Huntington Station, NY	631	11746-11750
Huntley, IL	224, 847	60142
Huntley, MT	406	59037
Huntsville, AL	256	35801-35816, 35824, 35893*
Huntsville, AR	479	72740
Huntsville, MO	660	65259
Huntsville, TN	423	37756
Huntsville, TX	936	77320, 77340-77344, 77348*
Hurley, WI	715, 534	54534, 54565
Huron, CA	559	93234
Huron, OH	419, 567	44839
Huron, SD	605	57350, 57399
Hurricane, WV	304	25526
Hurst, TX	682, 817	76053-76054
Hutchins, TX	469, 972	75141
Hutchinson, KS	620	67501-67505
Hutchinson, MN	320	55350
Huttonsville, WV	304	26273
Hyannis, MA	508, 774	02601
Hyannis, NE	308	69350
Hyattsville, MD	301	20781-20788
Hydaburg, AK	907	99922
Hyde Park, MA	617, 857	02136-02137
Hyde Park, NY	845	12538
Hyde Park, VT	802	05655
Hyden, KY	606	41749, 41762
Hyrum, UT	435	84319
Hysham, MT	406	59038, 59076

I

City	Area Code(s)	Zip Code(s)
Ida Grove, IA	712	51445
Idabel, OK	580	74745
Idaho City, ID	208	83631
Idaho Falls, ID	208	83401-83406, 83415
Idaho Springs, CO	303, 720	80452
Idyllwild, CA	951	92549
Imlay City, MI	810	48444
Immaculata, PA	484, 610	19345
Immokalee, FL	239	34142-34143
Imperial, CA	760, 442	92251
Imperial, MO	636	63052-63053
Imperial, NE	308	69033
Imperial Beach, CA	619	91932-91933
Ina, IL	618	62846
Incline Village, NV	775	89450-89452
Independence, CA	760, 442	93526
Independence, IA	319	50644
Independence, KS	620	67301
Independence, KY	859	41051
Independence, MO	816	64050-64058
Independence, OH	216	44131
Independence, OR	503, 971	97351
Independence, VA	276	24348
Indian, AK	907	99540
Indian Orchard, MA	413	01151
Indian Springs, NV	702	89018, 89070
Indian Trail, NC	704, 980	28079
Indian Wells, CA	760, 442	92210
Indiana, PA	724, 878	15701, 15705
Indianapolis, IN	317	46201-46260, 46266-46268*
Indianola, IA	515	50125
Indianola, MS	662	38749-38751
Indianola, PA	412, 878	15051
Indiantown, FL	772	34956
Indio, CA	760, 442	92201-92203
Inez, KY	606	41224
Ingalls, KS	620	67853
Inglewood, CA	310, 424	90301-90313, 90397-90398
Ingomar, PA	412, 878	15127
Inkster, MI	313	48141
Inman, SC	864	29349
Institute, WV	304	25112
Intercourse, PA	717	17534
Interior, SD	605	57750
Interlochen, MI	231	49643
International Falls, MN	218	56649
Inver Grove Heights, MN	651	55076-55077
Inverness, FL	352	34450-34453
Inwood, NY	516	11096
Iola, KS	620	66749
Iola, WI	715, 534	54945, 54990
Ione, CA	209	95640
Ionia, MI	616	48846
Iowa City, IA	319	52240-52246
Iowa Falls, IA	641	50126
Ipswich, MA	351, 978	01938
Ipswich, SD	605	57451
Irma, WI	715, 534	54442
Irmo, SC	803	29063
Iron Mountain, MI	906	49801-49802, 49831
Iron River, WI	715, 534	54847
Irondale, AL	205	35210
Ironton, MO	573	63650
Ironton, OH	740	45638
Ironwood, MI	906	49938
Irvine, CA	949	92602-92606, 92612-92623*
Irvine, KY	606	40336, 40472
Irvine, PA	814	16329
Irving, TX	214, 469, 972	75014-75017, 75037-75039*
Irvington, NJ	862, 973	07111
Irvington, NY	914	10533
Irvington, VA	804	22480
Irwin, PA	724, 878	15642

*Partial list of zip codes, including main range

City	Area Code(s)	Zip Code(s)
Irwindale, CA	626	91706
Irwinton, GA	478	31042
Iselin, NJ	732, 848	08830
Ishpeming, MI	906	49849, 49865
Islamorada, FL	305, 786	33036, 33070
Islandia, NY	631	11749, 11760
Isle of Palms, SC	843	29451
Isle of Wight, VA	757	23397
Islip, NY	631	11751
Isola, MS	662	38754
Issaquah, WA	425	98027-98029, 98075
Itasca, IL	331, 630	60143
Itasca, TX	254	76055
Ithaca, MI	989	48847
Ithaca, NY	607	14850-14853, 14882
Itta Bena, MS	662	38941
Iuka, MS	662	38852
Ivanhoe, CA	559	93235
Ivanhoe, MN	507	56142
Ivel, KY	606	41642
Ivins, UT	435	84738
Ivoryton, CT	860	06442
Ivyland, PA	215, 267	18974
Ixonia, WI	920	53036

J

City	Area Code(s)	Zip Code(s)
Jackman, ME	207	04945
Jackpot, NV	775	89825
Jacksboro, TN	423	37757
Jacksboro, TX	940	76458
Jackson, AL	251	36501, 36515, 36545
Jackson, CA	209	95642, 95654
Jackson, GA	470, 770	30233
Jackson, KY	606	41307, 41339
Jackson, LA	225	70748
Jackson, MI	517	49201-49204
Jackson, MN	507	56143
Jackson, MS	601, 769	39201-39218, 39225, 39232*
Jackson, MO	573	63755
Jackson, NH	603	03846
Jackson, NJ	732, 848	08527
Jackson, NC	252	27845
Jackson, OH	740	45640
Jackson, SC	803	29831
Jackson, TN	731	38301-38308, 38314
Jackson, WI	262	53037
Jackson, WY	307	83001-83002, 83025
Jackson Center, OH	937	45334
Jackson Heights, NY	347, 718	11372
Jackson Hole, WY	307	83001-83002
Jacksonville, AL	256	36265
Jacksonville, AR	501	72076-72078
Jacksonville, FL	904	32099, 32201-32250, 32254*
Jacksonville, IL	217	62650-62651
Jacksonville, NC	910	28540-28546
Jacksonville, TX	903	75766
Jacksonville Beach, FL	904	32227, 32240, 32250
Jaffrey, NH	603	03452
Jamaica, NY	347, 718	11405, 11411-11439, 11451*
Jamaica Plain, MA	617, 857	02130
Jamesburg, NJ	732, 848	08831
Jamestown, CA	209	95327
Jamestown, KY	270	42629
Jamestown, NY	716	14701-14704
Jamestown, NC	336	27282
Jamestown, ND	701	58401-58405
Jamestown, OH	937	45335
Jamestown, RI	401	02835
Jamestown, SC	843	29453
Jamestown, TN	931	38556
Janesville, IA	319	50647
Janesville, WI	608	53545-53547
Jarratt, VA	434	23867-23870
Jasper, AL	205	35501-35504
Jasper, AR	870	72641
Jasper, FL	386	32052
Jasper, GA	706, 762	30143
Jasper, IN	812	47546-47549
Jasper, MN	507	56144
Jasper, TN	423	37347
Jasper, TX	409	75951
Jay, FL	850	32565
Jay, ME	207	04239, 04262
Jay, OK	918	74346
Jay, VT	802	05859
Jayton, TX	806	79528
Jean, NV	702	89019, 89026
Jeanerette, LA	337	70544
Jeannette, PA	724, 878	15644
Jefferson, AR	870	72079
Jefferson, GA	706, 762	30549
Jefferson, IA	515	50129
Jefferson, LA	504	70121
Jefferson, NC	336	28640
Jefferson, OH	440	44047
Jefferson, OR	541, 458	97352
Jefferson, SD	605	57038
Jefferson, TX	903	75657
Jefferson, WI	920	53549
Jefferson City, MO	573	65101-65111
Jefferson City, TN	865	37760
Jefferson Valley, NY	914	10535
Jeffersontown, KY	502	40269, 40299
Jeffersonville, GA	478	31044
Jeffersonville, IN	812	47129-47134, 47144, 47199
Jeffersonville, NY	845	12748
Jeffersonville, OH	740	43128
Jekyll Island, GA	912	31527
Jelm, WY	970	82063, 82070-82072
Jena, LA	318	71342
Jenison, MI	616	49428-49429
Jenkintown, PA	215, 267	19046
Jenks, OK	918	74037
Jennerstown, PA	814	15547
Jennings, LA	337	70546
Jericho, NY	516	11753, 11853
Jermyn, PA	570	18433
Jerome, ID	208	83338
Jersey City, NJ	201, 551	07097, 07302-07311, 07399
Jerseyville, IL	618	62052
Jessup, MD	410, 443	20794
Jesup, GA	912	31545-31546, 31598-31599
Jetersville, VA	804	23083
Jetmore, KS	620	67854
Jewell, IA	515	50130
Jewett, TX	903	75846
Jim Thorpe, PA	570	18229
Johnson, KS	620	67855
Johnson, VT	802	05656
Johnson City, NY	607	13790
Johnson City, TN	423	37601-37605, 37614-37615
Johnson City, TX	830	78636
Johnston, IA	515	50131
Johnston, RI	401	02919
Johnston, SC	803	29832
Johnston City, IL	618	62951
Johnstown, NY	518	12095
Johnstown, OH	740	43031
Johnstown, PA	814	15901-15909, 15915, 15945
Joliet, IL	815	60431-60436
Jonesboro, AR	870	72401-72404
Jonesboro, GA	470, 770	30236-30238
Jonesboro, IL	618	62952
Jonesboro, LA	318	71251
Jonesborough, TN	423	37659
Jonesburg, MO	636	63351
Jonestown, MS	662	38639
Jonesville, LA	318	71343, 71377
Jonesville, VA	276	24263
Joplin, MO	417	64801-64804
Joppa, MD	410	21085
Jordan, MN	952	55352, 56071
Jordan, MT	406	59337
Jordan, NY	315	13080
Joshua Tree, CA	760, 442	92252
Jourdanton, TX	830	78026
Julesburg, CO	970	80737
Junction, TX	915	76849
Junction, UT	435	84740
Junction City, KS	785	66441-66442
Junction City, OR	541, 458	97448
Juneau, AK	907	99801-99803, 99811, 99821*
Juneau, WI	920	53039
Juno Beach, FL	561	33408
Jupiter, FL	561	33458, 33468-33469, 33477*

K

City	Area Code(s)	Zip Code(s)
Kadoka, SD	605	57543
Kahoka, MO	660	63445
Kahuku, HI	808	96731
Kahului, HI	808	96732-96733
Kailua, HI	808	96734
Kailua-Kona, HI	808	96739-96740, 96745
Kaiser, MO	573	65047
Kalaheo, HI	808	96741
Kalama, WA	360	98625
Kalamazoo, MI	616	49001-49009, 49019, 49024*
Kalaupapa, HI	808	96742
Kalida, OH	419, 567	45853
Kalispell, MT	406	59901-59904
Kalkaska, MI	231	49646
Kalona, IA	319	52247
Kamuela, HI	808	96743
Kanab, UT	435	84741
Kanawha, IA	641	50447
Kane, PA	814	16735
Kaneohe, HI	808	96744
Kankakee, IL	815	60901-60902
Kannapolis, NC	704, 980	28081-28083
Kansas City, KS	913	66101-66119, 66160
Kansas City, MO	816	64101-64173, 64179-64199*
Kapaa, HI	808	96746
Kapolei, HI	808	96707-96709
Karnes City, TX	830	78118
Karthaus, PA	814	16845
Kasson, MN	507	55944
Katonah, NY	914	10536
Katy, TX	281, 832	77449-77450, 77491-77494
Kaufman, TX	469, 972	75142
Kaukauna, WI	920	54130-54131
Kaumakani, HI	808	96747
Keaau, HI	808	96749
Kealakekua, HI	808	96750
Kearney, MO	816	64060
Kearney, NE	308	68845-68849
Kearneysville, WV	304	25429-25430
Kearny, NJ	201, 551	07032, 07099
Keene, CA	661	93531
Keene, NH	603	03431, 03435
Keene, TX	682, 817	76059
Keesler AFB, MS	228	39534
Keizer, OR	503, 971	97303, 97307
Keller, TX	682, 817	76244, 76248
Kellogg, ID	208	83837
Kelly, WY	307	83011
Kelseyville, CA	707	95451
Kelso, WA	360	98626
Kemmerer, WY	307	83101
Kenai, AK	907	99611, 99635
Kenansville, NC	910	28349
Kendall, FL	305, 786	33156-33158, 33173-33176*
Kendallville, IN	260	46720, 46755
Kenedy, TX	830	78119, 78125
Kenilworth, NJ	908	07033
Kenmare, ND	701	58746
Kenmore, NY	716	14217, 14223
Kenmore, WA	425	98028
Kennebec, SD	605	57544
Kennebunk, ME	207	04043
Kennebunkport, ME	207	04046
Kennedy Space Center, FL	321	32815
Kenner, LA	504	70062-70065
Kennesaw, GA	470, 770	30144, 30152, 30156, 30160
Kennett, MO	573	63857
Kennett Square, PA	484, 610	19348
Kennewick, WA	509	99336-99338
Kenosha, WI	262	53140-53144, 53158
Kenova, WV	304	25530
Kensington, CT	860	06037
Kensington, MD	301	20891, 20895
Kent, CT	860	06757
Kent, OH	234, 330	44240-44243
Kent, WA	253	98031-98035, 98042, 98064
Kentfield, CA	415	94904, 94914
Kentland, IN	219	47951
Kenton, OH	419, 567	43326
Kentwood, MI	616	49506-49508, 49512, 49518*
Kenwood, CA	707	95452
Kenyon, MN	507	55946
Keokuk, IA	319	52632
Keosauqua, IA	319	52565
Kermit, TX	915	79745
Kernersville, NC	336	27284-27285
Kernville, CA	760, 442	93238
Kerrville, TX	830	78028-78029

Partial list of zip codes, including main range

City	Area Code(s)	Zip Code(s)
Kershaw, SC	803	29067
Keshena, WI	715, 534	54135
Keswick, VA	434	22947
Ketchikan, AK	907	99901-99903, 99918-99919*
Ketchum, ID	208	83340
Kettering, OH	937	45409, 45419-45420, 45429*
Keuka Park, NY	315	14478
Kew Gardens, NY	347, 718	11415-11418
Kewanee, IL	309	61443
Kewanna, IN	574	46935, 46939
Kewaskum, WI	262	53040
Kewaunee, WI	920	54216
Key Biscayne, FL	305, 786	33149
Key Largo, FL	305, 786	33037
Key West, FL	305, 786	33040-33041, 33045
Keyser, WV	304	26726
Keystone, CO	970	80435
Keystone, SD	605	57751
Keystone Heights, FL	352	32656
Keytesville, MO	660	65261
Kiamesha Lake, NY	845	12751
Kiawah Island, SC	843	29455
Kidron, OH	234, 330	44636
Kiel, WI	920	53042
Kihei, HI	808	96753
Kilgore, TX	903	75662-75663
Kill Devil Hills, NC	252	27948
Killbuck, OH	234, 330	44637
Killeen, TX	254	76540-76549
Killington, VT	802	05751
Kimball, NE	308	69145
Kimberly, OR	541, 458	97848
Kimberly, WI	920	54136
Kincheloe, MI	906	49784-49788
Kinder, LA	337	70648
Kinderhook, NY	518	12106
Kindred, ND	701	58051
King, NC	336	27021
King, WI	715, 534	54946
King City, CA	831	93930
King Ferry, NY	315	13081
King George, VA	540	22485
King of Prussia, PA	484, 610	19406, 19487
King Salmon, AK	907	99549, 99613
King William, VA	804	23086
Kingfisher, OK	405	73750
Kingman, AZ	928	86401-86402, 86411-86413*
Kingman, KS	620	67068
Kings Bay, GA	912	31547
Kings Mountain, NC	704, 980	28086
Kings Point, NY	516	11024
Kingsburg, CA	559	93631
Kingsford, MI	906	49801-49802
Kingsport, TN	423	37660-37665, 37669
Kingston, MA	339, 781	02364
Kingston, MO	816	64650
Kingston, NJ	609	08528
Kingston, NY	845	12401-12402
Kingston, OK	580	73439
Kingston, PA	570	18704
Kingston, RI	401	02881
Kingston, TN	865	37763
Kingston, WA	360	98346
Kingstree, SC	843	29556
Kingsville, MD	410	21087
Kingsville, MO	816	64061
Kingsville, TX	361	78363-78364
Kingwood, TX	281, 832	77325, 77339, 77345-77346
Kingwood, WV	304	26519, 26537
Kinnelon, NJ	862, 973	07405
Kinsale, VA	804	22488
Kinsley, KS	620	67547
Kinsman, OH	234, 330	44428
Kinston, NC	252	28501-28504
Kiowa, CO	303, 720	80117
Kirbyville, TX	409	75956
Kirkland, WA	425	98033-98034, 98083
Kirksville, MO	660	63501
Kirkville, NY	315	13082
Kirkwood, MO	314	63122
Kirtland, OH	440	44094
Kirtland AFB, NM	505	87116-87118
Kissimmee, FL	321, 407	34741-34747, 34758-34759
Kittanning, PA	724, 878	16201, 16215
Kittery, ME	207	03904
Klamath Falls, OR	541, 458	97601-97603, 97625
Knights Landing, CA	530	95645
Knightstown, IN	765	46148
Knox, IN	574	46534
Knoxville, IA	641	50138, 50197-50198
Knoxville, TN	865	37901-37902, 37909-37933*
Kodiak, AK	907	99615, 99619, 99697
Kohler, WI	920	53044
Kokomo, IN	765	46901-46904
Koloa, HI	808	96756
Kosciusko, MS	662	39090
Koshkonong, MO	417	65692
Kotzebue, AK	907	99752
Kountze, TX	409	77625
Kreamer, PA	570	17833
Kula, HI	808	96790
Kulpsville, PA	215, 267	19443
Kuna, ID	208	83634
Kurten, TX	979	77862
Kutztown, PA	484, 610	19530

L

City	Area Code(s)	Zip Code(s)
La Belle, FL	863	33935
La Canada, CA	818	91011-91012
La Conner, WA	360	98257
La Crescenta, CA	818	91214, 91224
La Crosse, KS	785	67548, 67553
La Crosse, WI	608	54601-54603
La Fayette, GA	706, 762	30728
La Follette, TN	423	37729, 37766
La France, SC	864	29656
La Grande, OR	541, 458	97850
La Grange, IL	708	60525
La Grange, TX	979	78945
La Grange Park, IL	708	60526
La Habra, CA	562	90631-90633
La Jolla, CA	858	92037-92039, 92092-92093
La Junta, CO	719	81050
La Mesa, CA	619	91941-91944
La Mesa, NM	505	88044
La Mirada, CA	562, 714	90637-90639
La Moure, ND	701	58458
La Palma, CA	714	90623
La Pine, OR	541, 458	97739
La Plata, MD	301	20646
La Plume, PA	570	18440
La Porte, IN	574	46350-46352
La Porte, TX	281, 832	77571-77572
La Puente, CA	626	91744-91749
La Quinta, CA	760, 442	92253
La Rue, OH	740	43332
La Salle, IL	815	61301
La Union, NM	505	88021
La Vergne, TN	615	37086-37089
La Verne, CA	909	91750
La Veta, CO	719	81055
Lac du Flambeau, WI	715, 534	54538
Lacey, WA	360	98503-98509, 98513-98516
Lackawanna, NY	716	14218
Lackland AFB, TX	210	78236
Laclede, ID	208	83841
Lacon, IL	309	61540
Laconia, NH	603	03246-03249
Ladd, IL	815	61329
Ladysmith, WI	715, 534	54848
Lafayette, AL	334	36862
Lafayette, CA	925	94549, 94596
Lafayette, CO	303, 720	80026
Lafayette, IN	765	47901-47909, 47996
Lafayette, LA	337	70501-70509, 70593-70598
Lafayette, NJ	862, 973	07848
Lafayette, TN	615	37083
LaFox, IL	331, 630	60147
Lago Vista, TX	512	78645
LaGrange, GA	706, 762	30240-30241, 30261
LaGrange, IN	260	46761
LaGrange, KY	502	40031
Lagrangeville, NY	845	12540
Laguna Beach, CA	949	92607, 92637, 92651-92656*
Laguna Hills, CA	949	92637, 92653-92656
Laguna Niguel, CA	949	92607, 92677
Lahaina, HI	808	96761, 96767
Laie, HI	808	96762
Lake Alfred, FL	863	33850
Lake Andes, SD	605	57356
Lake Ariel, PA	570	18436
Lake Bluff, IL	224, 847	60044
Lake Buena Vista, FL	321, 407	32830
Lake Butler, FL	386	32054
Lake Charles, LA	337	70601-70616, 70629
Lake City, CO	970	81235
Lake City, FL	386	32024-32025, 32055-32056
Lake City, IA	712	51449
Lake City, MI	231	49651
Lake City, MN	651	55041
Lake City, PA	814	16423
Lake City, SC	843	29560
Lake Crystal, MN	507	56055
Lake Dallas, TX	940	75065
Lake Delton, WI	608	53940
Lake Elsinore, CA	951	92530-92532
Lake Forest, CA	949	92609, 92630
Lake Forest, IL	224, 847	60045
Lake Geneva, WI	262	53147
Lake George, CO	719	80827
Lake George, NY	518	12845
Lake Grove, NY	631	11755
Lake Harmony, PA	570	18624
Lake Havasu City, AZ	928	86403-86406
Lake Helen, FL	386	32744
Lake Hiawatha, NJ	862, 973	07034
Lake Isabella, CA	760, 442	93240
Lake Jackson, TX	979	77566
Lake Junaluska, NC	828	28745
Lake Lillian, MN	320	56253
Lake Lure, NC	828	28746
Lake Mary, FL	321, 407	32746, 32795
Lake Mills, WI	920	53551
Lake Monroe, FL	321, 407	32747
Lake Odessa, MI	616	48849
Lake Orion, MI	248, 947	48359-48362
Lake Oswego, OR	503, 971	97034-97035
Lake Ozark, MO	573	65049
Lake Park, GA	229	31636
Lake Placid, FL	863	33852, 33862
Lake Placid, NY	518	12946
Lake Pleasant, NY	518	12108
Lake Powell, UT	435	84533
Lake Providence, LA	318	71254
Lake Saint Louis, MO	636	63367
Lake Stevens, WA	425	98258
Lake Success, NY	516	11020, 11042
Lake Toxaway, NC	828	28747
Lake View, SC	843	29563
Lake Village, AR	870	71653
Lake Wales, FL	863	33853-33859, 33867, 33898
Lake Worth, FL	561	33454, 33460-33467
Lake Zurich, IL	224, 847	60047
Lakehurst, NJ	732, 848	08733, 08755, 08759
Lakeland, FL	863	33801-33815
Lakeland, GA	229	31635
Lakeland, LA	225	70752
Lakeport, CA	707	95453
Lakeside, AZ	928	85929
Lakeside, CA	619	92040
Laketon, IN	260	46943
Lakeview, AR	870	72642
Lakeview, CA	909	92567
Lakeview, OR	541, 458	97630
Lakeville, CT	860	06039
Lakeville, MN	952	55044
Lakeville, PA	570	18438
Lakeway, TX	512	78734, 78738
Lakewood, CA	562	90711-90716, 90805
Lakewood, CO	303, 720	80033, 80123, 80214-80215*
Lakewood, NJ	732, 848	08701
Lakewood, NY	716	14750
Lakewood, OH	216	44107
Lakewood, WA	253	98439, 98492, 98497-98499
Lakin, KS	620	67860
Lakota, ND	701	58344
Lamar, CO	719	81052
Lamar, MO	417	64759
Lamberton, MN	507	56152
Lambertville, NJ	609	08530
Lame Deer, MT	406	59043
Lamesa, TX	806	79331
Lamoni, IA	641	50140
Lamont, CA	661	93241
Lampasas, TX	512	76550
Lanai City, HI	808	96763
Lanark, IL	815	61046
Lancaster, CA	661	93534-93539, 93584-93586

**Partial list of zip codes, including main range*

City	Area Code(s)	Zip Code(s)
Lancaster, KY	859	40444-40446
Lancaster, MO	660	63548
Lancaster, NH	603	03584
Lancaster, NY	716	14043, 14086
Lancaster, OH	740	43130
Lancaster, PA	717	17601-17608, 17699
Lancaster, SC	803	29720-29722
Lancaster, TX	469, 972	75134, 75146
Lancaster, VA	804	22503
Lancaster, WI	608	53813
Lander, WY	307	82520
Landisburg, PA	717	17040
Landisville, PA	717	17538
Landover, MD	301	20785
Landrum, SC	864	29356
Lanett, AL	334	36863
Langdon, ND	701	58249
Langhorne, PA	215, 267	19047, 19053
Langley, WA	360	98260
Langley AFB, VA	757	23665
Langston, OK	405	73050
Lanham, MD	301	20703-20706, 20784
Lanham Seabrook, MD	301	20703-20706
Lansdale, PA	215, 267	19446
Lansdowne, PA	484, 610	19050
L'Anse, MI	906	49946
Lansford, PA	570	18232
Lansing, IL	708	60438
Lansing, KS	913	66043
Lansing, MI	517	48901, 48906-48924, 48929*
Lantana, FL	561	33460-33465
Lapeer, MI	810	48446
LaPlace, LA	985	70068-70069
Laporte, PA	570	18626
Laramie, WY	307	82051, 82063, 82070-82073
Larchmont, NY	914	10538
Laredo, TX	956	78040-78049
Largo, FL	727	33770-33779
Largo, MD	301	20774
Larkspur, CA	415	94939, 94977
Larned, KS	620	67550
Larose, LA	985	70373-70374
Las Animas, CO	719	81054
Las Cruces, NM	505	88001-88006, 88011-88012
Las Vegas, NV	702	89101-89164, 89170-89173*
Las Vegas, NM	505	87701, 87745
Latham, NY	518	12110-12111, 12128
Lathrop, CA	209	95330
Latrobe, PA	724, 878	15650
Latta, SC	843	29565
Latty, OH	419, 567	45855
Lauderdale-by-the-Sea, FL	754, 954	33062, 33308
Lauderhill, FL	754, 954	33311-33313, 33319-33321*
Laughlin, NV	702	89028-89029
Laughlin AFB, TX	830	78840-78843
Laurel, MD	240, 301	20707-20709, 20723-20726
Laurel, MS	601, 769	39440-39443
Laurel Hill, NC	910	28351
Laurelton, NY	347, 718	11413
Laurens, IA	712	50554
Laurens, SC	864	29360
Laurinburg, NC	910	28352-28353
Lava Hot Springs, ID	208	83246
LaVale, MD	301	21502-21504
Lawndale, CA	310, 424	90260-90261
Lawrence, KS	785	66044-66049
Lawrence, MA	351, 978	01840-01843
Lawrence, MI	616	49064
Lawrence, NY	516	11559
Lawrence, PA	724, 878	15055
Lawrenceburg, IN	812	47025
Lawrenceburg, KY	502	40342
Lawrenceburg, TN	931	38464
Lawrenceville, GA	470, 678, 770	30042-30049
Lawrenceville, IL	618	62439
Lawrenceville, NJ	609	08648
Lawrenceville, VA	434	23868
Lawton, MI	616	49065
Lawton, OK	580	73501-73507, 73558
Layton, NJ	862, 973	07851
Layton, UT	801, 385	84040-84041
Le Center, MN	507	56057
Le Grand, IA	641	50142
Le Mars, IA	712	51017, 51031
Le Roy, NY	585	14482
Le Sueur, MN	507	56058
Lead, SD	605	57754
Leadville, CO	719	80429, 80461
League City, TX	281, 832	77573-77574
Leakesville, MS	601, 769	39451
Leakey, TX	830	78873
Leander, TX	512	78641, 78645-78646
Leavenworth, KS	913	66043, 66048
Leavittsburg, OH	234, 330	44430
Leawood, KS	913	66206-66211, 66224
Lebanon, CT	860	06249
Lebanon, IL	618	62254
Lebanon, IN	765	46052
Lebanon, KY	270	40033
Lebanon, MO	417	65536
Lebanon, NH	603	03756, 03766
Lebanon, NJ	908	08833
Lebanon, OH	513	45036
Lebanon, OR	541, 458	97355
Lebanon, PA	717	17042, 17046
Lebanon, TN	615	37087-37090
Lebanon, VA	276	24266
Lebec, CA	661	93243
Lecanto, FL	352	34460-34461
Lee, MA	413	01238, 01264
Leechburg, PA	724, 878	15656
Leeds, AL	205	35094
Leeds, MA	413	01053
Lee's Summit, MO	816	64063-64065, 64081-64082*
Leesburg, FL	352	34748-34749, 34788-34789
Leesburg, GA	229	31763
Leesburg, NJ	856	08327
Leesburg, VA	571, 703	20175-20178
Leesville, LA	337	71446, 71459, 71496
Leesville, SC	803	29070
Lehi, UT	801, 385	84043
Lehigh Acres, FL	239	33936, 33970-33972
Lehigh Valley, PA	484, 610	18001-18003
Lehighton, PA	484, 610	18235
Lehman, PA	570	18627
Leicester, MA	508, 774	01524
Leicester, NY	585	14481
Leitchfield, KY	270	42754-42755
Leland, MI	231	49654
Leland, NC	910	28451
Lemmon, SD	605	57638
Lemon Grove, CA	619	91945-91946
Lemont, IL	331, 630	60439-60440, 60490
Lemoore, CA	559	93245-93246
Lemoyne, PA	717	17043
Lena, IL	815	61048
Lenexa, KS	913	66210-66220, 66227, 66285*
Lenni, PA	484, 610	19052
Lenoir, NC	828	28633, 28645
Lenoir City, TN	865	37771-37772
Lenox, MA	413	01240
Leola, PA	717	17540
Leola, SD	605	57456
Leominster, MA	351, 978	01453
Leon, IA	641	50144
Leonardtown, MD	301	20650
Leonia, NJ	201, 551	07605
Leoti, KS	620	67861
Lester, PA	484, 610	19029, 19113
Lester Prairie, MN	320	55354
Levelland, TX	806	79336-79338
Leverett, MA	413	01054
Levittown, NY	516	11756
Levittown, PA	215, 267	19054-19059
Lewes, DE	302	19958
Lewis Center, OH	740	43035
Lewis Run, PA	814	16738
Lewisberry, PA	717	17339
Lewisburg, PA	570	17837
Lewisburg, TN	931	37091
Lewisburg, WV	304	24901
Lewiston, ID	208	83501
Lewiston, ME	207	04240-04243
Lewiston, MI	989	49756
Lewiston, MN	507	55952
Lewiston, NY	716	14092
Lewiston, NC	252	27849
Lewistown, IL	309	61542
Lewistown, MO	573	63452
Lewistown, MT	406	59457
Lewistown, PA	717	17044
Lewisville, AR	870	71845
Lewisville, ID	208	83431
Lewisville, NC	336	27023
Lewisville, TX	469, 972	75022, 75027-75029, 75056*
Lexington, GA	706, 762	30648
Lexington, KY	859	40502-40517, 40522-40526*
Lexington, MA	339, 781	02420-02421
Lexington, MI	810	48450
Lexington, MS	662	39095
Lexington, MO	660	64067
Lexington, NE	308	68850
Lexington, NC	336	27292-27295
Lexington, OH	419, 567	44904
Lexington, OK	405	73051
Lexington, SC	803	29071-29073
Lexington, TN	731	38351
Lexington, VA	540	24450
Lexington Park, MD	301	20653
Libby, MT	406	59923
Liberal, KS	620	67901, 67905
Liberty, IN	765	47353
Liberty, KY	606	42539
Liberty, MS	601, 769	39645
Liberty, MO	816	64068-64069, 64087
Liberty, NC	336	27298
Liberty, SC	864	29657
Liberty, TX	936	77575
Liberty Corner, NJ	908	07938
Liberty Lake, WA	509	99019
Libertyville, IL	224, 847	60048, 60092
Licking, MO	573	65542
Lightfoot, VA	757	23090
Lighthouse Point, FL	754, 954	33064, 33074
Ligonier, PA	724, 878	15658
Lihue, HI	808	96766
Lilburn, GA	470, 770	30047-30048
Lillington, NC	910	27546
Lima, NY	585	14485
Lima, OH	419, 567	45801-45809, 45819, 45854
Lima, PA	484, 610	19037
Limerick, PA	484, 610	19468
Limon, CO	719	80826-80828
Lincoln, CA	916	95648
Lincoln, IL	217	62656
Lincoln, KS	785	67455
Lincoln, ME	207	04457
Lincoln, MA	339, 781	01773
Lincoln, MI	989	48742
Lincoln, NE	402	68501-68532, 68542, 68583*
Lincoln, RI	401	02802, 02865
Lincoln City, IN	812	47552
Lincoln City, OR	541, 458	97367
Lincoln Park, MI	313	48146
Lincoln Park, NJ	862, 973	07035
Lincoln University, PA	484, 610	19352
Lincolnshire, IL	224, 847	60069
Lincolnton, GA	706, 762	30817
Lincolnton, NC	704, 980	28092-28093
Lincolnwood, IL	224, 847	60645-60646, 60659, 60712
Lincroft, NJ	732, 848	07738
Linden, AL	334	36748
Linden, IN	765	47955
Linden, NJ	908	07036
Linden, TN	931	37096
Linden, TX	903	75563
Lindenhurst, NY	631	11757
Lindenwood, IL	815	61049
Lindon, UT	801, 385	84042
Lindsay, CA	559	93247
Lindsay, NE	402	68644
Lindsay, OK	405	73052
Lindsborg, KS	785	67456
Lindstrom, MN	651	55045
Linesville, PA	814	16424
Lingle, WY	307	82223
Linn, MO	573	65051
Linneus, MO	660	64653
Lino Lakes, MN	651	55014, 55038, 55110, 55126
Linthicum, MD	410	21090
Linthicum Heights, MD	410	21090
Linton, IN	812	47441
Linton, ND	701	58552
Linville, NC	828	28646
Linwood, KS	913	66052
Linwood, NJ	609	08221
Linwood, PA	484, 610	19061
Lionville, PA	484, 610	19353
Lipscomb, TX	806	79056
Lisbon, NH	603	03585
Lisbon, ND	701	58054

*Partial list of zip codes, including main range

City	Area Code(s)	Zip Code(s)
Lisbon, OH	234, 330	44432
Lisbon Falls, ME	207	04252
Lisle, IL	331, 630	60532
Litchfield, CT	860	06750, 06759
Litchfield, IL	217	62056
Litchfield, MI	517	49252
Litchfield, MN	320	55355
Litchfield Park, AZ	623	85340
Lithia, FL	813	33547
Lithia Springs, GA	470, 770	30122
Lithonia, GA	470, 770	30038-30039, 30058
Lititz, PA	717	17543
Little Chute, WI	920	54140
Little Compton, RI	401	02801, 02837
Little Elm, TX	469, 972	75068
Little Falls, MN	320	56345
Little Falls, NJ	862, 973	07424
Little Falls, NY	315	13365
Little Ferry, NJ	201, 551	07643
Little Neck, NY	347, 718	11362-11363
Little River, SC	843	29566
Little Rock, AR	501	72201-72227, 72231, 72260*
Little Rock AFB, AR	501	72076
Little Silver, NJ	732, 848	07739
Little Torch Key, FL	305, 786	33042
Little Valley, NY	716	14755
Littlefield, TX	806	79339
Littlerock, WA	360	98556
Littlestown, PA	717	17340
Littleton, CO	303, 720	80120-80130, 80160-80166
Littleton, MA	351, 978	01460
Live Oak, CA	530	95953
Live Oak, FL	386	32060, 32064
Livermore, CA	925	94550-94551
Livermore, CO	970	80536
Liverpool, NY	315	13088-13090
Livingston, AL	205	35470
Livingston, CA	209	95334
Livingston, LA	225	70754
Livingston, MT	406	59047
Livingston, NJ	862, 973	07039
Livingston, TN	931	38570
Livingston, TX	936	77351, 77399
Livingston Manor, NY	845	12758
Livonia, MI	734	48150-48154
Llano, TX	915	78643
Loa, UT	435	84747
Loch Sheldrake, NY	845	12759
Lock Haven, PA	570	17745
Lockhart, TX	512	78644
Lockport, IL	815	60441, 60446
Lockport, LA	985	70374
Lockport, NY	716	14094-14095
Locust Grove, VA	540	22508
Lodi, CA	209	95240-95242
Lodi, NJ	862, 973	07644
Logan, IA	712	51546, 51550
Logan, OH	740	43138
Logan, UT	435	84321-84323, 84341
Logan, WV	304	25601
Logansport, IN	574	46947
Loganville, GA	470, 770	30052
Loma Linda, CA	909	92350, 92354-92357
Lombard, IL	331, 630	60148
Lompoc, CA	805	93436-93438
London, KY	606	40741-40745
London, OH	740	43140
Londonderry, NH	603	03053
Lone Tree, CO	303, 720	80112, 80124
Lone Tree, IA	319	52755
Lone Wolf, OK	580	73655
Long Beach, CA	562	90745-90749, 90801-90815*
Long Beach, MS	228	39560
Long Beach, NY	516	11561
Long Beach, WA	360	98631
Long Branch, NJ	732, 848	07740
Long Grove, IL	224, 847	60047-60049
Long Island City, NY	347, 718	11101-11109, 11120
Long Pond, PA	570	18334
Long Prairie, MN	320	56347
Long Valley, NJ	908	07853
Longboat Key, FL	941	34228
Longmeadow, MA	413	01106, 01116
Longmont, CO	303, 720	80501-80504
Longview, TX	903	75601-75608, 75615
Longview, WA	360	98632
Longwood, FL	321, 407	32750-32752, 32779, 32791
Lonoke, AR	501	72086
Lookout Mountain, GA	706, 762	30750
Lookout Mountain, TN	423	37350
Loomis, CA	916	95650
Lorain, OH	440	44052-44055
Lordsburg, NM	505	88009, 88045, 88055
Lorenzo, TX	806	79343
Loretto, KY	270	40037
Loretto, PA	814	15940
Loretto, TN	931	38469
Loris, SC	843	29569
Lorman, MS	601, 769	39096
Lorton, VA	571, 703	22079, 22199
Los Alamitos, CA	562, 714	90720-90721
Los Alamos, NM	505	87544-87545
Los Altos, CA	650	94022-94024
Los Altos Hills, CA	650	94022-94024
Los Angeles, CA	213, 310, 323, 424	90001-90103, 90174, 90185*
Los Angeles AFB, CA	310, 424	90009
Los Banos, CA	209	93635
Los Gatos, CA	408	95030-95033
Los Lunas, NM	505	87031
Lostine, OR	541, 458	97857
Lotus, CA	530	95651
Loudon, NH	603	03307
Loudon, TN	865	37774
Loudonville, NY	518	12211
Loudonville, OH	419, 567	44842
Louisa, KY	606	41201, 41230
Louisa, VA	540	23093
Louisburg, NC	919	27549
Louisville, CO	303, 720	80027-80028
Louisville, GA	478	30434
Louisville, IL	618	62858
Louisville, KY	502	40201-40233, 40241-40245*
Louisville, MS	662	39339
Louisville, OH	234, 330	44641
Louisville, TN	865	37777
Loup City, NE	308	68853
Loveland, CO	970	80537-80539
Loveland, OH	513	45111, 45140
Lovell, WY	307	82431
Lovelock, NV	775	89419
Loves Park, IL	815	61111, 61130-61132
Lovingston, VA	434	22949
Lovington, NM	505	88260
Low Moor, VA	540	24457
Lowell, AR	479	72745
Lowell, FL	352	32663
Lowell, IN	219	46356
Lowell, MA	351, 978	01850-01854
Lowell, MI	616	49331
Lowellville, OH	234, 330	44436
Lower Burrell, PA	724, 878	15068
Lower Gwynedd, PA	215, 267	19002
Lower Waterford, VT	802	05848
Lowville, NY	315	13367
Loxahatchee, FL	561	33470
Loysville, PA	717	17047
Lubbock, TX	806	79401-79416, 79423-79424*
Lubec, ME	207	04652
Lucas, KY	270	42156
Lucasville, OH	740	45648, 45699
Lucedale, MS	601, 769	39452
Ludington, MI	231	49431
Ludlow, MA	413	01056
Ludlow, VT	802	05149
Ludowici, GA	912	31316
Lufkin, TX	936	75901-75904, 75915
Lugoff, SC	803	29078
Luke AFB, AZ	623	85307-85309
Lula, MS	662	38644
Luling, LA	985	70070
Lumber Bridge, NC	910	28357
Lumberton, NJ	856	08048
Lumberton, NC	910	28358-28360
Lumberton, TX	409	77657
Lumpkin, GA	229	31815
Lunenburg, MA	351, 978	01462
Lunenburg, VT	802	05906
Lunenburg, VA	434	23952
Luray, VA	540	22835
Lusk, WY	307	82225
Lutherville, MD	410	21093-21094
Lutsen, MN	218	55612
Luttrell, TN	865	37779
Luverne, AL	334	36049
Luverne, MN	507	56156
Luxemburg, WI	920	54217
Lykens, PA	717	17048
Lyman, SC	864	29365
Lyme, NH	603	03768
Lynbrook, NY	516	11563-11564
Lynchburg, TN	931	37352
Lynchburg, VA	434	24501-24506, 24512-24515
Lyndhurst, NJ	201, 551	07071
Lyndon, KS	785	66451
Lyndonville, NY	585	14098
Lyndonville, VT	802	05851
Lynn, IN	765	47355
Lynn, MA	339, 781	01901-01905, 01910
Lynn Haven, FL	850	32444
Lynnfield, MA	339, 781	01940
Lynnwood, WA	425	98036-98037, 98046
Lynwood, CA	310, 424	90262
Lyon, MS	662	38645
Lyon Mountain, NY	518	12952-12955
Lyon Station, PA	484, 610	19536
Lyons, CO	303, 720	80540
Lyons, GA	912	30436
Lyons, KS	620	67554
Lyons, NJ	908	07939
Lyons, NY	315	14489
Lyons, OR	503, 971	97358

M

City	Area Code(s)	Zip Code(s)
Mableton, GA	404, 470	30126
Macclenny, FL	386	32063
MacDill AFB, FL	813	33608
Macedon, NY	315	14502
Macedonia, OH	234, 330	44056
Machesney Park, IL	815	61115
Machias, ME	207	04654, 04686
Machiasport, ME	207	04655
Mackay, ID	208	83251
Mackinac Island, MI	906	49757
Mackinaw City, MI	231	49701
Macomb, IL	309	61455
Macomb, MI	586	48042-48044
Macomb Township, MI	586	48042-48044
Macon, GA	478	31201-31221, 31294-31299
Macon, MS	662	39341
Macon, MO	660	63552
Macungie, PA	484, 610	18062
Macy, IN	574	46951
Macy, NE	402	68039
Maddock, ND	701	58348
Madeira Beach, FL	727	33708, 33738
Madelia, MN	507	56062
Madera, CA	559	93637-93639
Madill, OK	580	73446
Madison, AL	256	35756-35758
Madison, CT	203	06443
Madison, FL	850	32340-32341
Madison, GA	706, 762	30650
Madison, IL	618	62060
Madison, IN	812	47250
Madison, ME	207	04950
Madison, MN	320	56256
Madison, MS	601, 769	39110, 39130
Madison, NE	402	68748
Madison, NJ	862, 973	07940
Madison, NC	336	27025
Madison, OH	440	44057
Madison, SD	605	57042
Madison, TN	615	37115-37116
Madison, VA	540	22719, 22727
Madison, WV	304	25130
Madison, WI	608	53562, 53593, 53701-53719*
Madison Heights, MI	248, 947	48071
Madisonville, KY	270	42431
Madisonville, LA	985	70447
Madisonville, TN	423	37354
Madisonville, TX	936	77864
Madras, OR	541, 458	97741
Maggie Valley, NC	828	28751
Magna, UT	801, 385	84044
Magnolia, AR	870	71753-71754
Magnolia, MS	601, 769	39652
Mahanoy City, PA	570	17948
Mahnomen, MN	218	56557

*Partial list of zip codes, including main range

City	Area Code(s)	Zip Code(s)
Mahomet, IL	217	61853
Mahopac, NY	845	10541
Mahwah, NJ	201, 551	07430, 07495-07498
Maiden, NC	828	28650
Maiden Rock, WI	715, 534	54750
Maitland, FL	321, 407	32751, 32794
Makanda, IL	618	62958
Makawao, HI	808	96768
Malad City, ID	208	83252
Malden, MA	339, 781	02148
Malden, MO	573	63863
Malibu, CA	310, 424	90263-90265
Malinta, OH	419, 567	43535
Malone, FL	850	32445
Malone, NY	518	12953
Malta, ID	208	83342
Malta, IL	815	60150
Malta, MT	406	59538
Malta, NY	518	12020
Malvern, AR	501	72104-72105
Malvern, OH	234, 330	44644
Malvern, PA	484, 610	19355
Malverne, NY	516	11565
Mamaroneck, NY	914	10543
Mammoth Cave, KY	270	42259
Mammoth Lakes, CA	760, 442	93546
Mamou, LA	337	70554
Manahawkin, NJ	609	08050
Manalapan, FL	561	33462
Manalapan, NJ	732, 848	07726
Manasquan, NJ	732, 848	08736
Manassas, VA	571, 703	20108-20113
Manassas Park, VA	571, 703	20111
Manawa, WI	920	54949
Manchester, CT	860	06040-06045
Manchester, IA	563	52057
Manchester, KY	606	40962
Manchester, ME	207	04351
Manchester, MI	734	48158
Manchester, NH	603	03101-03111
Manchester, TN	931	37349, 37355
Manchester, VT	802	05254
Manchester Center, VT	802	05255
Manchester Village, VT	802	05254
Mancos, CO	970	81328
Mandan, ND	701	58554
Mandeville, LA	985	70448, 70470-70471
Mangum, OK	580	73554
Manhasset, NY	516	11030
Manhattan, KS	785	66502-66506
Manhattan Beach, CA	310, 424	90266-90267
Manheim, PA	717	17545
Manila, UT	435	84046
Manistee, MI	231	49660
Manistique, MI	906	49854
Manitou, OK	580	73555
Manitou Springs, CO	719	80829
Manitowoc, WI	920	54220-54221
Mankato, KS	785	66956
Mankato, MN	507	56001-56006
Manlius, NY	315	13104
Manning, IA	712	51455
Manning, ND	701	58642
Manning, SC	803	29102
Manor, TX	512	78653
Mansfield, AR	479	72944
Mansfield, CT	860	06250, 06268
Mansfield, LA	318	71052
Mansfield, MA	508, 774	02031, 02048
Mansfield, MO	417	65704
Mansfield, OH	419, 567	44901-44907, 44999
Mansfield, PA	570	16933
Mansfield, TX	682, 817	76063
Manson, NC	252	27553
Manteca, CA	209	95336-95337
Manteno, IL	815	60950
Manteo, NC	252	27954
Manti, UT	435	84642
Mantorville, MN	507	55955
Mantua, NJ	856	08051
Mantua, OH	234, 330	44255
Many, LA	318	71449
Maple Glen, PA	215, 267	19002
Maple Grove, MN	763	55311, 55369, 55569
Maple Heights, OH	216	44137
Maple Park, IL	331, 630	60151
Maple Plain, MN	763	55348, 55359, 55393, 55570*
Maple Shade, NJ	856	08052
Maple Valley, WA	425	98038
Mapleton, OR	541, 458	97453
Mapleville, RI	401	02839
Maplewood, MN	651	55109, 55117-55119
Maplewood, NJ	862, 973	07040
Maplewood, NY	518	12189
Mappsville, VA	757	23407
Maquoketa, IA	563	52060
Marana, AZ	520	85653
Marathon, FL	305, 786	33050-33052
Marathon, WI	715, 534	54448
Marble City, OK	918	74945
Marble Falls, TX	830	78654-78657
Marblehead, MA	339, 781	01945
Marblehead, OH	419, 567	43440
Marceline, MO	660	64658
Marcellus, NY	315	13108
Marco Island, FL	239	34145-34146
Marcus, IA	712	51035
Marcy, NY	315	13403
Marengo, IL	815	60152
Marengo, IA	319	52301
Marfa, TX	915	79843
Margate, FL	754, 954	33063-33068, 33073, 33093
Marianna, AR	870	72360
Marianna, FL	850	32446-32448
Maricopa, AZ	520	85239
Marietta, GA	470, 678, 770	30006-30008, 30060-30069*
Marietta, OH	740	45750
Marietta, OK	580	73448
Marietta, PA	717	17547
Marina, CA	831	93933
Marina del Rey, CA	310, 424	90291-90295
Marine City, MI	810	48039
Marinette, WI	715, 534	54143
Marion, AL	334	36756
Marion, AR	870	72364
Marion, IL	618	62959
Marion, IN	765	46952-46953
Marion, IA	319	52302
Marion, KS	620	66861
Marion, KY	270	42064
Marion, MA	508, 774	02738
Marion, NY	315	14505
Marion, NC	828	28737, 28752
Marion, OH	740	43301-43302, 43306-43307
Marion, SC	843	29571
Marion, SD	605	57043
Marion, VA	276	24354
Marion, WI	715, 534	54950
Mariposa, CA	209	95338
Marissa, IL	618	62257
Marked Tree, AR	870	72365
Markham, IL	708	60426
Markle, IN	260	46770
Markleeville, CA	530	96120
Marks, MS	662	38646
Marksville, LA	318	71351
Marlboro, NJ	732, 848	07746
Marlboro, VT	802	05344
Marlborough, MA	508, 774	01752
Marlin, TX	254	76661
Marlinton, WV	304	24954
Marlow Heights, MD	301	20746-20748
Marlton, NJ	856	08053
Marquette, MI	906	49855
Marrero, LA	504	70072-70073
Marriottsville, MD	410	21104
Mars, PA	724, 878	16046
Mars Hill, NC	828	28754
Marshall, AR	870	72650
Marshall, IL	217	62441
Marshall, MI	616	49068-49069
Marshall, MN	507	56258
Marshall, MO	660	65340
Marshall, NC	828	28753
Marshall, TX	903	75670-75672
Marshall, WI	608	53559
Marshalls Creek, PA	570	18335
Marshalltown, IA	641	50158
Marshfield, MA	339, 781	02020, 02041, 02047-02051*
Marshfield, MO	417	65706
Marshfield, WI	715, 534	54404, 54441, 54449, 54472
Marshville, NC	704, 980	28103
Marstons Mills, MA	508, 774	02648
Martin, SD	605	57551
Martin, TN	731	38237-38238
Martinez, CA	925	94553
Martinez, GA	706, 762	30907
Martins Ferry, OH	740	43935
Martinsburg, WV	304	25401-25402
Martinsdale, MT	406	59053
Martinsville, IN	765	46151
Martinsville, VA	276	24112-24115
Maryland Heights, MO	314	63043
Marylhurst, OR	503, 971	97036
Marysville, CA	530	95901-95903
Marysville, KS	785	66508, 66555
Marysville, MI	810	48040
Marysville, OH	937	43040-43041
Marysville, PA	717	17053
Marysville, WA	360	98270-98271
Maryville, IL	618	62062
Maryville, MO	660	64468
Maryville, TN	865	37801-37804
Mascot, TN	865	37806
Mashantucket, CT	860	06339
Mashpee, MA	508, 774	02649
Mason, MI	517	48854
Mason, OH	513	45040
Mason, TX	915	76856
Mason City, IA	641	50401-50402, 50467
Maspeth, NY	347, 718	11378
Massapequa, NY	516	11758
Massena, IA	712	50853
Massena, NY	315	13662
Massillon, OH	234, 330	44646-44648
Matador, TX	806	79244
Matawan, NJ	732, 848	07747
Mather, CA	916	95655
Mathews, LA	985	70375
Mathews, VA	804	23109
Matteson, IL	708	60443
Matthews, NC	704, 980	28104-28106
Mattoon, IL	217	61938
Mattoon, WI	715, 534	54450
Mauldin, SC	864	29662
Maumee, OH	419, 567	43537
Maumelle, AR	501	72113, 72118
Maunaloa, HI	808	96770
Maury, NC	252	28554
Mauston, WI	608	53948
Maxton, NC	910	28364
Maxwell AFB, AL	334	36112-36113
Mayaguez, PR	787, 939	00680-00682
Maybrook, NY	845	12543
Mayersville, MS	662	39113
Mayetta, KS	785	66509
Mayfield, KY	270	42066
Mayfield, PA	570	18433
Mayfield Heights, OH	440	44124
Mayfield Village, OH	440	44143
Mayhill, NM	505	88339
Maynard, IA	563	50655
Maynard, MA	351, 978	01754
Maynardville, TN	865	37807
Mayo, FL	386	32066
Mayport, FL	904	32227-32228
Mays Landing, NJ	609	08330
Maysville, KY	606	41056
Maysville, MO	816	64469
Mayville, NY	716	14757
Mayville, ND	701	58257
Mayville, WI	920	53050
Maywood, CA	323	90270
Maywood, IL	708	60153-60155
Maywood, NE	308	69038
Maywood, NJ	201, 551	07607
Mazama, WA	509	98833
Mazomanie, WI	608	53560
McAdenville, NC	704, 980	28101
McAfee, NJ	862, 973	07428
McAlester, OK	918	74501-74502
McAllen, TX	956	78501-78505
McArthur, OH	740	45651
McBee, SC	843	29101
McCall, ID	208	83635-83638
McCalla, AL	205	35111
McCaysville, GA	706, 762	30555
McChord AFB, WA	253	98438-98439, 98499
McClelland, IA	712	51548
McCloud, CA	530	96057
McClusky, ND	701	58463

*Partial list of zip codes, including main range

City	Area Code(s)	Zip Code(s)
McComb, MS	601, 769	39648-39649
McComb, OH	419, 567	45858
McConnell AFB, KS	316	67221
McConnellsburg, PA	717	17233
McConnellsville, NY	315	13401
McConnelsville, OH	740	43756
McCook, IL	708	60525
McCook, NE	308	69001
McCordsville, IN	317	46055
McCormick, SC	864	29835
McDermott, OH	740	45652
McDonough, GA	470, 770	30252-30253
McEwen, TN	931	37101
McFarland, WI	608	53558
McGraw, NY	607	13101
McGregor, IA	563	52157
McGregor, MN	218	55760
McGregor, TX	254	76657
McGuire AFB, NJ	609	08641
McHenry, IL	815	60050-60051
McHenry, MD	301	21541
McIntosh, SD	605	57641
McKee, KY	606	40447
McKees Rocks, PA	412, 878	15136
McKeesport, PA	412, 878	15130
McKenzie, TN	731	38201
McKinleyville, CA	707	95519-95521
McKinney, TX	469, 972	75069-75071
McLean, TX	806	79057
McLean, VA	571, 703	22101-22106
McLeansboro, IL	618	62859
McLeansville, NC	336	27301
McLeod, MT	406	59052
McLoud, OK	405	74851
McLouth, KS	913	66054
McMinnville, OR	503, 971	97128
McMinnville, TN	931	37110-37111
McMurray, PA	724, 878	15317
McPherson, KS	620	67460
McRae, GA	229	31055
McShan, AL	205	35471
McSherrystown, PA	717	17344
Mead, WA	509	99021
Meade, KS	620	67864
Meadow Lands, PA	724, 878	15347
Meadowbrook, PA	215, 267	19046
Meadville, MS	601, 769	39653
Meadville, PA	814	16335, 16388
Mebane, NC	919	27302
Mechanicsburg, IL	217	62545
Mechanicsburg, PA	717	17050, 17055
Mechanicsville, VA	804	23111, 23116
Mechanicville, NY	518	12118
Medaryville, IN	219	47957
Medfield, MA	508, 774	02052
Medford, MA	339, 781	02153-02156
Medford, NJ	609	08055
Medford, NY	631	11763
Medford, OK	580	73759
Medford, OR	541, 458	97501-97504
Medford, WI	715, 534	54451
Media, PA	484, 610	19037, 19063-19065, 19086*
Medical Lake, WA	509	99022
Medicine Lake, MT	406	59247
Medicine Lodge, KS	620	67104
Medina, MN	763	55340, 55357-55359
Medina, NY	585	14103
Medina, OH	234, 330	44215, 44256-44258
Medley, FL	305, 786	33166, 33178
Medora, ND	701	58645
Medway, MA	508, 774	02053
Meeker, CO	970	81641
Mehoopany, PA	570	18629
Melba, ID	208	83641
Melbourne, AR	870	72556
Melbourne, FL	321	32901-32912, 32919, 32934*
Melbourne Beach, FL	321	32951
Melfa, VA	757	23410
Melrose, MA	339, 781	02176-02177
Melrose, MN	320	56352
Melrose Park, IL	708	60160-60165
Melrose Park, PA	215, 267	19027
Melville, NY	516, 631	11747, 11775
Melvin, IL	217	60952
Melvindale, MI	313	48122
Memphis, MO	660	63555
Memphis, TN	901	37501, 38101-38152, 38157*
Memphis, TX	806	79245
Mena, AR	479	71953
Menahga, MN	218	56464
Menan, ID	208	83434
Menard, IL	618	62259
Menard, TX	915	76859
Menasha, WI	920	54952
Mendenhall, MS	601, 769	39114
Mendham, NJ	862, 973	07945
Mendocino, CA	707	95460
Mendon, IL	217	62351
Mendon, MA	508, 774	01756
Mendota, CA	559	93640
Mendota, IL	815	61342
Mendota Heights, MN	651	55118-55120
Menlo, GA	706, 762	30731
Menlo Park, CA	650	94025-94029
Menominee, MI	906	49858
Menomonee Falls, WI	262	53051-53052
Menomonie, WI	715, 534	54751
Mentone, CA	909	92359
Mentone, IN	574	46539
Mentone, TX	915	79754
Mentor, OH	440	44060-44061
Mequon, WI	262	53092, 53097
Merced, CA	209	95340-95344, 95348
Mercedes, TX	956	78570
Mercer, PA	724, 878	16137
Mercer Island, WA	206	98040
Mercersburg, PA	717	17236
Mercerville, NJ	609	08619
Meredith, NH	603	03253
Meriden, CT	203	06450-06454
Meridian, GA	912	31319
Meridian, ID	208	83642, 83680
Meridian, MS	601, 769	39301-39309
Meridian, TX	254	76665
Merion, PA	484, 610	19066
Merkel, TX	915	79536
Merriam, KS	913	66202-66204
Merrick, NY	516	11566
Merrifield, VA	571, 703	22081-22082, 22116-22120
Merrill, MI	989	48637
Merrill, WI	715, 534	54452
Merrillville, IN	219	46410-46411
Merrimac, MA	351, 978	01860
Merrimac, WI	608	53561
Merrimack, NH	603	03054
Merritt Island, FL	321	32952-32954
Mertzon, TX	915	76941
Mertztown, PA	484, 610	19539
Mesa, AZ	480	85201-85216, 85274-85277
Mesa Verde National Park, CO	970	81330
Mesilla Park, NM	505	88047
Mesquite, NV	702	89024-89027
Mesquite, TX	469, 972	75149-75150, 75180-75187
Metairie, LA	504	70001-70011, 70033, 70055*
Metamora, IL	309	61548
Metcalf, GA	229	31792
Methuen, MA	351, 978	01844
Metlakatla, AK	907	99926
Metropolis, IL	618	62960
Metter, GA	912	30439
Metuchen, NJ	732, 848	08840
Mexia, TX	254	76667
Mexico, MO	573	65265
Mexico, NY	315	13114
Meyersdale, PA	814	15552
Miami, FL	305, 786	33010-33018, 33054-33056*
Miami, OK	918	74354-74355
Miami, TX	806	79059
Miami Beach, FL	305, 786	33109, 33119, 33139-33141*
Miami Lakes, FL	305, 786	33014-33018
Miami Shores, FL	305, 786	33138, 33150-33153, 33161*
Miami Springs, FL	305, 786	33166, 33266
Miamisburg, OH	937	45342-45343
Micanopy, FL	352	32667
Micaville, NC	828	28755
Michigan City, IN	219	46360-46361
Middle Granville, NY	518	12849
Middle Island, NY	631	11953
Middle River, MD	410	21220
Middle Village, NY	347, 718	11379
Middleboro, MA	508, 774	02344-02349
Middlebourne, WV	304	26149
Middleburg, PA	570	17842
Middleburg, VA	540	20117-20118
Middleburg Heights, OH	440	44130
Middlebury, CT	203	06762
Middlebury, IN	574	46540
Middlebury, VT	802	05753
Middlefield, CT	860	06455
Middlefield, OH	440	44062
Middleport, NY	585	14105
Middlesboro, KY	606	40965
Middlesex, NJ	732, 848	08846
Middleton, MA	351, 978	01949
Middleton, NH	603	03887
Middleton, WI	608	53562
Middletown, CA	707	95461
Middletown, CT	860	06457-06459
Middletown, DE	302	19709
Middletown, NJ	732, 848	07748
Middletown, NY	845	10940-10943
Middletown, OH	513	45042-45044
Middletown, PA	717	17057
Middletown, RI	401	02840-02842
Middletown, VA	540	22645, 22649
Midland, GA	706, 762	31820
Midland, MI	989	48640-48642, 48667-48670*
Midland, NC	704, 980	28107
Midland, TX	915	79701-79712
Midland, VA	540	22728
Midland Park, NJ	201, 551	07432
Midlothian, IL	708	60445
Midlothian, TX	469, 972	76065
Midlothian, VA	804	23112-23114
Midvale, UT	801, 385	84047
Midway, FL	850	32343
Midway, GA	912	31320
Midway, KY	859	40347
Midway, UT	435	84049
Midwest City, OK	405	73110, 73130, 73140, 73145
Mifflinburg, PA	570	17844
Mifflintown, PA	717	17059
Milaca, MN	320	56353
Milan, GA	229	31060
Milan, IL	309	61264
Milan, MI	734	48160
Milan, MO	660	63556
Milan, OH	419, 567	44846
Milan, TN	731	38358
Milbank, SD	605	57252-57253
Milbridge, ME	207	04658
Miles City, MT	406	59301
Milford, CT	203	06460
Milford, DE	302	19963
Milford, IN	574	46542
Milford, IA	712	51351
Milford, MA	508, 774	01757
Milford, MI	248, 947	48380-48381
Milford, NE	402	68405
Milford, NH	603	03055
Milford, OH	513	45150
Milford, PA	570	18337
Mililani, HI	808	96789
Mill City, OR	503, 971	97360
Mill Run, PA	724, 878	15464
Mill Valley, CA	415	94941-94942
Millboro, VA	540	24460
Millbrae, CA	650	94030-94031
Millbrook, NY	845	12545
Millburn, NJ	862, 973	07041
Millbury, MA	508, 774	01527, 01586
Millbury, OH	419, 567	43447
Milldale, CT	860	06467
Milledgeville, GA	478	31059-31062
Millen, GA	478	30442
Miller, SD	605	57362
Millersburg, OH	234, 330	44654
Millersburg, PA	717	17061
Millersville, MD	410	21108
Millersville, PA	717	17551
Millersville, TN	615	37072
Millerton, NY	518	12546
Milligan College, TN	423	37682
Millington, TN	901	38053-38055, 38083
Millinocket, ME	207	04462
Millis, MA	508, 774	02054
Mills, WY	307	82604, 82644
Millville, NJ	856	08332
Millwood, VA	540	22646
Milpitas, CA	408	95035-95036
Milroy, IN	765	46156

*Partial list of zip codes, including main range

City	Area Code(s)	Zip Code(s)
Milton, FL	850	32570-32572, 32583
Milton, MA	617, 857	02186
Milton, NY	845	12547
Milton, PA	570	17847
Milton, WV	304	25541
Milton, WI	608	53563
Milton-Freewater, OR	541, 458	97862
Milwaukee, WI	414	53201-53228, 53233-53237*
Milwaukie, OR	503, 971	97222, 97267-97269
Minden, LA	318	71055-71058
Minden, NE	308	68959
Minden, NV	775	89423
Mineola, NY	516	11501
Mineral, CA	530	96061-96063
Mineral Point, MO	573	63660
Mineral Wells, TX	940	76067-76068
Mineral Wells, WV	304	26120-26121, 26150
Minersville, PA	570	17954
Minerva, OH	234, 330	44657
Mineville, NY	518	12956
Mingo Junction, OH	740	43938
Minneapolis, KS	785	67467
Minneapolis, MN	612, 763, 952	55401-55450, 55454-55460*
Minnesota Lake, MN	507	56068
Minnetonka, MN	763, 952	55305, 55343-55345
Minnewaukan, ND	701	58351
Minonk, IL	309	61760
Minooka, IL	815	60447
Minot, ND	701	58701-58707, 58768
Minot AFB, ND	701	58704-58705
Minster, OH	419, 567	45865
Mio, MI	989	48647
Mira Loma, CA	951	91752
Miramar, FL	754, 954	33023-33029, 33083
Misenheimer, NC	704, 980	28109
Mishawaka, IN	574	46544-46546
Mishicot, WI	920	54228
Mission, KS	913	66201-66205, 66222
Mission, SD	605	57555
Mission, TX	956	78572-78573
Mission Hills, CA	818	91345-91346, 91395
Mission Viejo, CA	949	92675, 92690-92694
Mission Woods, KS	913	66205
Mississippi State, MS	662	39762
Missoula, MT	406	59801-59808, 59812
Missouri City, TX	281, 832	77459, 77489
Mitchell, IN	812	47446
Mitchell, NE	308	69357
Mitchell, SD	605	57301
Mitchells, VA	540	22729
Mitchellville, IA	515	50169
Mitchellville, MD	301	20716-20717, 20721
Moab, UT	435	84532
Moberly, MO	660	65270
Mobile, AL	251	36601-36633, 36640-36644*
Mocksville, NC	336	27028
Model City, NY	716	14107
Modesto, CA	209	95350-95358, 95397
Moffett Field, CA	650	94035
Mogadore, OH	234, 330	44260
Mohall, ND	701	58761
Mohawk, NY	315	13407
Mohnton, PA	484, 610	19540
Mojave, CA	661	93501-93502, 93519
Mokena, IL	708	60448
Molalla, OR	503, 971	97038
Moline, IL	309	61265-61266
Monaca, PA	724, 878	15061
Monahans, TX	915	79756
Monarch, CO	719	81227
Moncks Corner, SC	843	29430, 29461
Mondovi, WI	715, 534	54755, 54764
Monee, IL	708	60449
Monessen, PA	724, 878	15062
Monett, MO	417	65708
Monitor, WA	509	98836
Monmouth, IL	309	61462
Monmouth, OR	503, 971	97361
Monmouth Junction, NJ	732, 848	08852
Monona, IA	563	52159
Monongahela, PA	724, 878	15063
Monroe, CT	203	06468
Monroe, GA	470, 770	30655-30656
Monroe, IA	641	50170
Monroe, LA	318	71201-71203, 71207-71213
Monroe, MI	734	48161-48162
Monroe, NC	704, 980	28110-28112
Monroe, OH	513	45050, 45073, 45099
Monroe, WA	360	98272
Monroe, WI	608	53566
Monroe Township, NJ	609	08831
Monroeville, AL	251	36460-36462
Monroeville, PA	412, 878	15140, 15146
Monrovia, CA	626	91016-91017
Monsey, NY	845	10952
Mont Alto, PA	717	17237
Montague, MI	231	49437
Montague, TX	940	76251
Montauk, NY	631	11954
Montclair, CA	909	91763
Montclair, NJ	862, 973	07042-07043
Monte Vista, CO	719	81135, 81144
Montebello, CA	323	90640
Montebello, NY	845	10901
Montecito, CA	805	93108, 93150
Montello, WI	608	53949
Monterey, CA	831	93940-93944
Monterey, VA	540	24465
Monterey Park, CA	323, 626	91754-91756
Montesano, WA	360	98563
Montevallo, AL	205	35115
Montevideo, MN	320	56265
Montezuma, IA	641	50171
Montezuma, KS	620	67867
Montgomery, AL	334	36101-36125, 36130-36135*
Montgomery, IL	331, 630	60538
Montgomery, NY	845	12549
Montgomery, PA	570	17752
Montgomery, TX	936	77316, 77356
Montgomery, WV	304	25136
Montgomery City, MO	573	63361
Montgomery Village, MD	301	20877-20879, 20886
Montgomeryville, PA	215, 267	18936
Monticello, AR	870	71655-71657
Monticello, FL	850	32344-32345
Monticello, GA	706, 762	31064
Monticello, IL	217	61856
Monticello, IN	574	47960
Monticello, IA	319	52310
Monticello, KY	606	42633
Monticello, MN	763	55362-55365, 55561-55565*
Monticello, MS	601, 769	39654
Monticello, MO	573	63457
Monticello, NY	845	12701, 12777
Monticello, UT	435	84535
Montour Falls, NY	607	14865
Montoursville, PA	570	17754
Montpelier, IN	765	47359
Montpelier, OH	419, 567	43543
Montpelier, VT	802	05601-05604, 05609, 05620*
Montreat, NC	828	28757
Montrose, CA	818	91020-91021
Montrose, CO	970	81401-81402
Montrose, MI	810	48457
Montrose, NY	845	10548
Montrose, PA	570	18801
Montross, VA	804	22520
Montvale, NJ	201, 551	07645
Montville, NJ	862, 973	07045
Monument, OR	541, 458	97864
Moodus, CT	860	06469
Moody, AL	205	35004
Moon Township, PA	412, 878	15108
Moonachie, NJ	201, 551	07074
Moore, OK	405	73153, 73160, 73170
Moore Haven, FL	863	33471
Moorefield, WV	304	26836
Moorestown, NJ	856	08057
Mooresville, IN	317	46158
Mooresville, NC	704, 980	28115-28117
Moorhead, MN	218	56560-56563
Moorhead, MS	662	38761
Moorpark, CA	805	93020-93021
Moose, WY	307	83012
Moose Lake, MN	218	55767
Mooseheart, IL	331, 630	60539
Moosic, PA	570	18507
Moosup, CT	860	06354
Mora, MN	320	55051
Mora, NM	505	87732
Moraga, CA	925	94556, 94570, 94575
Moran, WY	307	83013
Moravia, NY	315	13118
Morehead, KY	606	40351
Morehead City, NC	252	28557
Morenci, AZ	928	85540
Morenci, MI	517	49256
Moreno Valley, CA	951	92551-92557
Morgan, GA	229	31766
Morgan, MN	507	56266
Morgan, UT	801, 385	84050
Morgan City, LA	985	70380-70381
Morgan Hill, CA	408	95037-95038
Morganfield, KY	270	42437
Morganton, NC	828	28655, 28680
Morgantown, KY	270	42261
Morgantown, PA	484, 610	19543
Morgantown, WV	304	26501-26508
Moro, OR	541, 458	97039
Moroni, UT	435	84646
Morrilton, AR	501	72110
Morris, AL	205	35116
Morris, IL	815	60450
Morris, MN	320	56267
Morris Plains, NJ	862, 973	07950
Morrison, CO	303, 720	80465
Morrison, IL	815	61270
Morristown, IN	765	46161
Morristown, NJ	862, 973	07960-07963
Morristown, OH	740	43759
Morristown, TN	423	37813-37816
Morrisville, NY	315	13408
Morrisville, NC	919	27560
Morrisville, PA	215, 267	19067
Morrisville, VT	802	05657, 05661
Morro Bay, CA	805	93442-93443
Morrow, GA	470, 770	30260, 30287
Morton, IL	309	61550
Morton, MN	507	56270
Morton, MS	601, 769	39117
Morton, TX	806	79346
Morton Grove, IL	224, 847	60053
Mosca, CO	719	81146
Moscow, ID	208	83843-83844
Moscow, TN	901	38057
Moselle, MS	601, 769	39459
Moses Lake, WA	509	98837
Mosinee, WI	715, 534	54455
Mosquero, NM	505	87733
Moss Beach, CA	650	94038
Moss Landing, CA	831	95039
Moss Point, MS	228	39562-39563, 39581
Motley, MN	218	56466
Mott, ND	701	58646
Moulton, AL	256	35650
Moultrie, GA	229	31768, 31776
Mound City, IL	618	62963
Mound City, KS	913	66056
Mound City, SD	605	57646
Moundridge, KS	620	67107
Mounds View, MN	763	55112
Moundsville, WV	304	26041
Mount Airy, NC	336	27030-27031
Mount Angel, OR	503, 971	97362
Mount Arlington, NJ	862, 973	07856
Mount Ayr, IA	641	50854
Mount Berry, GA	706, 762	30149
Mount Carmel, IL	618	62863
Mount Carmel, PA	570	17851
Mount Carroll, IL	815	61053
Mount Clemens, MI	586	48043-48046
Mount Crawford, VA	540	22841
Mount Crested Butte, CO	970	81225
Mount Dora, FL	352	32756-32757
Mount Freedom, NJ	862, 973	07970
Mount Gay, WV	304	25637
Mount Gilead, NC	910	27306
Mount Gilead, OH	419, 567	43338
Mount Holly, NJ	609	08060
Mount Holly, NC	704, 980	28120
Mount Hope, OH	234, 330	44660
Mount Ida, AR	870	71957
Mount Jackson, VA	540	22842
Mount Joy, PA	717	17552
Mount Juliet, TN	615	37121-37122
Mount Kisco, NY	914	10549
Mount Laurel, NJ	856	08054
Mount Lebanon, PA	412, 878	15228
Mount Marion, NY	845	12456
Mount Meigs, AL	334	36057
Mount Morris, IL	815	61054

**Partial list of zip codes, including main range*

City	Area Code(s)	Zip Code(s)
Mount Morris, NY	585	14510
Mount Olive, MS	601, 769	39119
Mount Olive, NJ	862, 973	07828
Mount Olive, NC	919	28365
Mount Olive, WV	304	25185
Mount Olivet, KY	606	41064
Mount Pleasant, IA	319	52641
Mount Pleasant, MI	989	48804, 48858-48859
Mount Pleasant, NC	704, 980	28124
Mount Pleasant, PA	724, 878	15666
Mount Pleasant, SC	843	29464-29466
Mount Pleasant, TN	931	38474
Mount Pleasant, TX	903	75455-75456
Mount Pocono, PA	570	18344
Mount Prospect, IL	224, 847	60056
Mount Pulaski, IL	217	62548
Mount Royal, NJ	856	08061
Mount Shasta, CA	530	96067
Mount Solon, VA	540	22843
Mount Sterling, IL	217	62353
Mount Sterling, KY	859	40353
Mount Sterling, OH	740	43143
Mount Vernon, AL	251	36560
Mount Vernon, GA	912	30445
Mount Vernon, IL	618	62864
Mount Vernon, IN	812	47620
Mount Vernon, IA	319	52314
Mount Vernon, KY	606	40456
Mount Vernon, MO	417	65712
Mount Vernon, NY	914	10550-10553, 10557-10558
Mount Vernon, OH	740	43050
Mount Vernon, TX	903	75457
Mount Vernon, VA	571, 703	22121
Mount Vernon, WA	360	98273-98274
Mount Washington, KY	502	40047
Mount Wolf, PA	717	17347
Mountain City, TN	423	37683
Mountain Grove, MO	417	65711
Mountain Home, AR	870	72653-72654
Mountain Home, ID	208	83647
Mountain Home, TN	423	37684
Mountain Home AFB, ID	208	83648
Mountain Lakes, NJ	862, 973	07046
Mountain Pass, CA	760, 442	92366
Mountain Pine, AR	501	71956
Mountain Top, PA	570	18707
Mountain View, AR	870	72533, 72560
Mountain View, CA	650	94035, 94039-94043
Mountain View, MO	417	65548
Mountain View, WY	307	82939
Mountainair, NM	505	87036
Mountainside, NJ	908	07092
Mountlake Terrace, WA	425	98043
Moville, IA	712	51039
Moxee, WA	509	98936
Muenster, TX	940	76252
Mukilteo, WA	425	98275
Mukwonago, WI	262	53149
Mulberry, FL	863	33860
Muleshoe, TX	806	79347
Mullen, NE	308	69152
Mullica Hill, NJ	856	08062
Muncie, IN	765	47302-47308
Muncy, PA	570	17756
Mundelein, IL	224, 847	60060
Munfordville, KY	270	42765
Munhall, PA	412, 878	15120
Munising, MI	906	49862
Munroe Falls, OH	234, 330	44262
Munster, IN	219	46321
Murdo, SD	605	57559
Murdock, NE	402	68407
Murfreesboro, AR	870	71958
Murfreesboro, NC	252	27855
Murfreesboro, TN	615	37127-37133
Murphy, ID	208	83650
Murphy, NC	828	28906
Murphysboro, IL	618	62966
Murray, KY	270	42071
Murray, UT	801, 385	84107, 84117, 84121-84123*
Murray Hill, NJ	908	07974
Murrells Inlet, SC	843	29576
Murrieta, CA	951	92562-92564
Murrysville, PA	724, 878	15668
Muscatine, IA	563	52761
Muscle Shoals, AL	256	35661-35662
Muskego, WI	262	53150
Muskegon, MI	231	49440-49445
Muskegon Heights, MI	231	49444
Muskogee, OK	918	74401-74403
Mustang, OK	405	73064
Myerstown, PA	717	17067
Myrtle Beach, SC	843	29572-29579, 29587-29588
Mystic, CT	860	06355, 06388

N

City	Area Code(s)	Zip Code(s)
Nacogdoches, TX	936	75961-75965
Nageezi, NM	505	87037
Nags Head, NC	252	27959
Nahunta, GA	912	31553
Naknek, AK	907	99633
Nampa, ID	208	83651-83653, 83686-83687
Nanticoke, MD	410	21840
Nanticoke, PA	570	18634
Nantucket, MA	508, 774	02554, 02564, 02584
Nanuet, NY	845	10954
Napa, CA	707	94558-94559, 94581
Napanoch, NY	845	12458
Naperville, IL	331, 630	60540, 60563-60567
Naples, FL	239	34101-34120
Naples, NY	585	14512
Napoleon, ND	701	58561
Napoleon, OH	419, 567	43545
Napoleonville, LA	985	70390
Nappanee, IN	574	46550
Narberth, PA	484, 610	19072
Narragansett, RI	401	02874, 02879-02882
Naselle, WA	360	98638
Nashotah, WI	262	53058
Nashua, NH	603	03060-03064
Nashville, AR	870	71852
Nashville, GA	229	31639
Nashville, IL	618	62263
Nashville, IN	812	47448
Nashville, NC	252	27856
Nashville, TN	615	37201-37250
Nassau, NY	518	12123
Nassau Bay, TX	281, 832	77058, 77258
Nassawadox, VA	757	23413
Natchez, MS	601, 769	39120-39122
Natchitoches, LA	318	71457-71458, 71497
Nathrop, CO	719	81236
Natick, MA	508, 774	01760
National City, CA	619	91950-91951
Natrona Heights, PA	724, 878	15065
Natural Bridge Station, VA	540	24579
Naugatuck, CT	203	06770
Navarre, MN	952	55392
Navarre, OH	234, 330	44662
Navasota, TX	936	77868-77869
Navesink, NJ	732, 848	07752
Nazareth, PA	484, 610	18064
Nebo, NC	828	28761
Nebraska City, NE	402	68410
Nederland, TX	409	77627
Nedrow, NY	315	13120
Needham, MA	339, 781	02492-02494
Needham Heights, MA	339, 781	02494
Neenah, WI	920	54956-54957
Neillsville, WI	715, 534	54456
Neligh, NE	402	68756
Nellis AFB, NV	702	89191
Nelson, NE	402	68961
Nelsonville, OH	740	45764
Neodesha, KS	620	66757
Neosho, MO	417	64850-64853
Nephi, UT	435	84648
Neponset, IL	309	61345
Neptune, NJ	732, 848	07753-07754
Neptune Beach, FL	904	32266
Nespelem, WA	509	99155
Nesquehoning, PA	570	18240
Ness City, KS	785	67560
Netcong, NJ	862, 973	07857
Nettleton, MS	662	38858
Nevada, IA	515	50201
Nevada, MO	417	64772
Nevada City, CA	530	95959
Neversink, NY	845	12765
New Albany, IN	812	47150-47151
New Albany, MS	662	38652
New Albany, OH	614	43054
New Augusta, MS	601, 769	39462
New Baltimore, MI	586	48047, 48051
New Bedford, MA	508, 774	02740-02746
New Berlin, NY	607	13411
New Berlin, WI	262	53146, 53151
New Bern, NC	252	28560-28564
New Bethlehem, PA	814	16242
New Bloomfield, PA	717	17068
New Boston, TX	903	75570
New Braunfels, TX	830	78130-78135
New Bremen, OH	419, 567	45869
New Brighton, MN	651	55112
New Brighton, PA	724, 878	15066
New Britain, CT	860	06050-06053
New Brunswick, NJ	732, 848	08901-08906, 08922, 08933*
New Canaan, CT	203	06840-06842
New Carlisle, IN	574	46552
New Carlisle, OH	937	45344
New Castle, CO	970	81647
New Castle, DE	302	19720-19721
New Castle, IN	765	47362
New Castle, KY	502	40050
New Castle, PA	724, 878	16101-16108
New Castle, VA	540	24127
New Century, KS	913	66031
New City, NY	845	10956
New Columbia, PA	570	17856
New Concord, OH	740	43762
New Cumberland, PA	717	17070
New Cumberland, WV	304	26047
New England, ND	701	58647
New Enterprise, PA	814	16664
New Era, MI	231	49446
New Fairfield, CT	203	06812
New Freedom, PA	717	17349
New Glarus, WI	608	53574
New Gretna, NJ	609	08224
New Hampton, IA	641	50659-50661
New Hampton, NY	845	10958
New Harbor, ME	207	04554, 04558
New Hartford, CT	860	06057
New Hartford, NY	315	13413
New Haven, CT	203	06501-06525, 06530-06540
New Haven, IN	260	46774
New Haven, MI	586	48048-48050
New Hill, NC	919	27562
New Holland, PA	717	17557
New Hope, MN	763	55427-55428
New Hope, PA	215, 267	18938
New Hyde Park, NY	516	11040-11044, 11099
New Iberia, LA	337	70560-70563
New Kensington, PA	724, 878	15068-15069
New Kent, VA	804	23124
New Kingstown, PA	717	17072
New Knoxville, OH	419, 567	45871
New Lebanon, NY	518	12125
New Lenox, IL	815	60451
New Lexington, OH	740	43764
New Lisbon, NJ	609	08064
New Lisbon, WI	608	53950
New London, CT	860	06320
New London, IA	319	52645
New London, MO	573	63459
New London, NH	603	03257
New London, OH	419, 567	44851
New London, WI	920	54961
New Madrid, MO	573	63869
New Market, VA	540	22844
New Martinsville, WV	304	26155
New Milford, CT	860	06776
New Milford, NJ	201, 551	07646
New Orleans, LA	504	70112-70131, 70139-70190*
New Oxford, PA	717	17350
New Paltz, NY	845	12561
New Paris, IN	574	46553
New Philadelphia, OH	234, 330	44663
New Port Richey, FL	727	34652-34656
New Providence, NJ	908	07974
New Richmond, OH	513	45157
New Richmond, WI	715, 534	54017
New Roads, LA	225	70760
New Rochelle, NY	914	10801-10805
New Rockford, ND	701	58356
New Sharon, IA	641	50207
New Smyrna Beach, FL	386	32168-32170
New Springfield, OH	234, 330	44443

*Partial list of zip codes, including main range

City	Area Code(s)	Zip Code(s)
New Tazewell, TN	423	37824-37825
New Town, ND	701	58763
New Ulm, MN	507	56073
New Wilmington, PA	724, 878	16142, 16172
New Windsor, MD	410	21776
New Windsor, NY	845	12553
New York, NY	212, 646, 917	10001-10048, 10055, 10060*
New York Mills, MN	218	56567
New York Mills, NY	315	13417
Newark, CA	510	94560
Newark, DE	302	19702, 19711-19718, 19725*
Newark, NJ	862, 973	07101-07108, 07112-07114*
Newark, NY	315	14513
Newark, OH	740	43055-43058, 43093
Newaygo, MI	231	49337
Newberg, OR	503, 971	97132
Newberry, MI	906	49868
Newberry, SC	803	29108
Newburg, WI	262	53060
Newburgh, IN	812	47629-47630
Newburgh, NY	845	12550-12555
Newbury, OH	440	44065
Newbury Park, CA	805	91319-91320
Newburyport, MA	351, 978	01950-01951
Newcastle, WY	307	82701, 82715
Newcomerstown, OH	740	43832
Newell, SD	605	57760
Newell, WV	304	26050
Newfane, VT	802	05345
Newhall, CA	661	91321-91322, 91381-91382
Newington, CT	860	06111, 06131
Newington, NH	603	03801
Newington, VA	571, 703	22122
Newkirk, OK	580	74647
Newland, NC	828	28657
Newman Grove, NE	402	68758
Newnan, GA	470, 678, 770	30263-30265, 30271
Newport, AR	870	72112
Newport, DE	302	19804
Newport, IN	765	47966
Newport, KY	859	41071-41076, 41099
Newport, MN	651	55055
Newport, NH	603	03773
Newport, NC	252	28570
Newport, OR	541, 458	97365-97366
Newport, RI	401	02840-02841
Newport, TN	423	37821-37822
Newport, VT	802	05855
Newport, WA	509	99156
Newport Beach, CA	949	92657-92663
Newport News, VA	757	23600-23612, 23628
Newton, GA	229	31770
Newton, IL	618	62448
Newton, IA	641	50208
Newton, KS	316	67114-67117
Newton, MA	617, 857	02456-02468, 02495
Newton, NJ	862, 973	07860
Newton, NC	828	28658
Newton, TX	409	75966
Newton Center, MA	617, 857	02459
Newton Falls, OH	234, 330	44444
Newton Grove, NC	910	28366
Newton Upper Falls, MA	617, 857	02464
Newtonville, NY	518	12110, 12128
Newtown, CT	203	06470
Newtown, PA	215, 267	18940
Newtown Square, PA	484, 610	19073
Nezperce, ID	208	83543
Niagara Falls, NY	716	14301-14305
Niagara University, NY	716	14109
Niantic, CT	860	06357
Niceville, FL	850	32578, 32588
Nicholasville, KY	859	40340, 40356
Niles, IL	224, 847	60714
Niles, MI	616	49120-49121
Niles, OH	234, 330	44446
Ninety Six, SC	864	29666
Niota, TN	423	37826
Nipomo, CA	805	93444
Niskayuna, NY	518	12309
Nisswa, MN	218	56468
Nixon, TX	830	78140
Noble, OK	405	73068
Noblesville, IN	317	46060-46061
Nocona, TX	940	76255
Nogales, AZ	520	85621, 85628, 85648, 85662
Nokomis, FL	941	34274-34275

City	Area Code(s)	Zip Code(s)
Nome, AK	907	99762
Norco, CA	951	92860
Norcross, GA	470, 678, 770	30003, 30010, 30071, 30091*
Norfolk, CT	860	06058
Norfolk, MA	508, 774	02056
Norfolk, NE	402	68701-68702
Norfolk, VA	757	23500-23523, 23529-23530*
Normal, AL	256	35762
Normal, IL	309	61761, 61790
Norman, OK	405	73019, 73026, 73069-73072
Norridge, IL	708	60634, 60656, 60706
Norristown, PA	484, 610	19401-19409, 19488-19489
North Adams, MA	413	01247
North Amityville, NY	631	11701
North Andover, MA	351, 978	01845
North Anson, ME	207	04958
North Attleboro, MA	508, 774	02760-02763
North Augusta, SC	803	29841-29842, 29860-29861
North Aurora, IL	331, 630	60542
North Babylon, NY	631	11703
North Baltimore, OH	419, 567	45872
North Barrington, IL	224, 847	60010
North Bay Village, FL	305, 786	33141
North Bend, OR	541, 458	97459
North Bend, WA	425	98045
North Bergen, NJ	201, 551	07047
North Berwick, ME	207	03906
North Billerica, MA	351, 978	01862
North Branch, MN	651	55056
North Branch, NJ	908	08876
North Branford, CT	203	06471
North Brookfield, MA	508, 774	01535
North Brunswick, NJ	732, 848	08902
North Canton, OH	234, 330	44709, 44720
North Charleston, SC	843	29405-29406, 29410, 29415*
North Chelmsford, MA	351, 978	01863
North Chicago, IL	224, 847	60064, 60086-60088
North Chili, NY	585	14514
North Clarendon, VT	802	05759
North Conway, NH	603	03860
North Dartmouth, MA	508, 774	02747
North Dighton, MA	508, 774	02764
North East, MD	410	21901
North East, PA	814	16428
North Easton, MA	508, 774	02356-02357
North Falmouth, MA	508, 774	02556, 02565
North Fort Myers, FL	239	33903, 33917-33918
North Grafton, MA	508, 774	01536
North Grosvenordale, CT	860	06255
North Haledon, NJ	862, 973	07508, 07538
North Haven, CT	203	06473
North Haverhill, NH	603	03774
North Hero, VT	802	05474
North Highlands, CA	916	95660
North Hills, CA	818	91343, 91393
North Hollywood, CA	818	91601-91618
North Huntingdon, PA	724, 878	15642
North Judson, IN	574	46366
North Kansas City, MO	816	64116
North Kingstown, RI	401	02852-02854, 02874
North Kingsville, OH	440	44068
North Lake, WI	262	53064
North Las Vegas, NV	702	89030-89036, 89084-89086
North Liberty, IA	319	52317
North Lima, OH	234, 330	44452
North Little Rock, AR	501	72113-72120, 72124, 72190*
North Logan, UT	435	84341
North Manchester, IN	260	46962
North Mankato, MN	507	56002-56003
North Miami, FL	305, 786	33161-33162, 33167-33169*
North Miami Beach, FL	305, 786	33160-33162, 33169, 33179*
North Monmouth, ME	207	04265
North Myrtle Beach, SC	843	29582, 29597-29598
North Newton, KS	316	67117
North Olmsted, OH	440	44070
North Palm Beach, FL	561	33403, 33408-33410
North Pekin, IL	309	61554
North Plains, OR	503, 971	97133
North Platte, NE	308	69101-69103
North Providence, RI	401	02904, 02908-02911
North Quincy, MA	617, 857	02171
North Redington Beach, FL	727	33708
North Richland Hills, TX	682, 817	76118, 76180-76182
North Ridgeville, OH	440	44035, 44039
North Riverside, IL	708	60546
North Royalton, OH	440	44133
North Saint Paul, MN	651	55109

City	Area Code(s)	Zip Code(s)
North Salt Lake, UT	801, 385	84054
North Scituate, RI	401	02857
North Sioux City, SD	605	57049
North Smithfield, RI	401	02824, 02896
North Springfield, VT	802	05150
North Stonington, CT	860	06359
North Syracuse, NY	315	13212
North Tonawanda, NY	716	14120
North Vernon, IN	812	47265
North Versailles, PA	412, 878	15137
North Wales, PA	215, 267	19436, 19454-19455, 19477
North Warren, PA	814	16365
North Webster, IN	574	46555
North White Plains, NY	914	10603
North Wilkesboro, NC	336	28656-28659, 28674
Northampton, MA	413	01060-01063
Northampton, PA	484, 610	18067
Northborough, MA	508, 774	01532
Northbrook, IL	224, 847	60062-60065
Northeast Harbor, ME	207	04662
Northfield, IL	224, 847	60093
Northfield, MN	507	55057
Northfield, NJ	609	08225
Northfield, OH	234, 330	44056, 44067
Northfield, VT	802	05663
Northford, CT	203	06472
Northlake, IL	708	60164
Northport, AL	205	35473-35476
Northport, NY	631	11768
Northridge, CA	818	91324-91330, 91343
Northumberland, PA	570	17857
Northvale, NJ	201, 551	07647
Northville, MI	248	48167
Northwood, IA	641	50459
Northwood, OH	419, 567	43605, 43619
Norton, KS	785	67654
Norton, MA	508, 774	02766
Norton, OH	234, 330	44203
Norton, VA	276	24273
Norton Shores, MI	231	49441
Norwalk, CA	562	90650-90652, 90659
Norwalk, CT	203	06850-06860
Norwalk, OH	419, 567	44857
Norway, IA	319	52318
Norwell, MA	339, 781	02018, 02061
Norwich, CT	860	06351, 06360, 06365
Norwich, KS	620	67118
Norwich, NY	607	13815
Norwich, OH	740	43767
Norwood, MA	339, 781	02062
Norwood, MN	952	55368, 55383, 55554, 55583
Norwood, NJ	201, 551	07648
Norwood, NC	704, 980	28128
Norwood, OH	513	45207, 45212
Notre Dame, IN	574	46556
Nottingham, PA	484, 610	19362
Nottoway, VA	434	23955
Novato, CA	415	94945-94949, 94998
Novi, MI	248, 947	48374-48377
Nowata, OK	918	74048
Nucla, CO	970	81424
Nuevo, CA	951	92567
Nutley, NJ	862, 973	07110
Nyack, NY	845	10960
Nyssa, OR	541, 458	97913

O

City	Area Code(s)	Zip Code(s)
Oak Brook, IL	331, 630	60521-60523, 60527, 60561
Oak Creek, WI	414	53154
Oak Forest, IL	708	60452
Oak Grove, LA	318	71263
Oak Grove, OR	503, 971	97222, 97267-97268
Oak Grove, VA	804	22443
Oak Harbor, WA	360	98277-98278
Oak Hill, WV	304	25901
Oak Lawn, IL	708	60453-60459
Oak Park, IL	708	60301-60304
Oak Park, MI	248, 947	48237
Oak Ridge, NJ	862, 973	07438
Oak Ridge, TN	865	37830-37831
Oakbrook Terrace, IL	331, 630	60181
Oakdale, CA	209	95361
Oakdale, LA	318	71463
Oakdale, MN	651	55042, 55128

Partial list of zip codes, including main range

City	Area Code(s)	Zip Code(s)
Oakdale, NY	631	11769
Oakdale, PA	412, 878	15071
Oakdale, WI	608	54649
Oakham, MA	508, 774	01068
Oakhurst, CA	559	93644
Oakhurst, NJ	732, 848	07755
Oakland, CA	510	94601-94627, 94643, 94649*
Oakland, MD	301	21550
Oakland, NJ	201, 551	07436
Oakland, TN	901	38060
Oakland City, IN	812	47660
Oakland Park, FL	754, 954	33304-33311, 33334
Oakley, CA	925	94513, 94561
Oakley, KS	785	67748
Oakmont, PA	412, 878	15139
Oaks, PA	484, 610	19456
Oakton, VA	571, 703	22124
Oakville, CA	707	94562
Oakville, IA	319	52646
Oakwood, GA	470, 770	30502, 30566
Oakwood, OH	419, 567	45409, 45419, 45873
Oakwood, VA	276	24631
Oakwood Village, OH	440	44146
Oberlin, KS	785	67749
Oberlin, LA	337	70655
Oberlin, OH	440	44074
Oblong, IL	618	62449
Ocala, FL	352	34470-34483
Ocean, NJ	732, 848	07712
Ocean City, MD	410	21842-21843
Ocean City, NJ	609	08226
Ocean Shores, WA	360	98569
Ocean Springs, MS	228	39564-39566
Oceano, CA	805	93445
Oceanport, NJ	732, 848	07757
Oceanside, CA	760, 442	92049-92058
Oceanside, NY	516	11572
Oceanville, NJ	609	08231
Ochopee, FL	239	34141
Ocilla, GA	229	31774
Ocoee, FL	321, 407	34761
Oconomowoc, WI	262	53066
Oconto, WI	920	54153
Oconto Falls, WI	920	54154
Odenton, MD	410	21113
Odessa, FL	813	33556
Odessa, MO	816	64076
Odessa, TX	915	79760-79769
Odessa, WA	509	99144, 99159
Odon, IN	812	47562
Odum, GA	912	31555
Oelwein, IA	319	50662
O'Fallon, MO	636	63366-63367
Offutt AFB, NE	402	68113
Ogallala, NE	308	69153
Ogden, UT	801, 385	84201, 84244, 84401-84415
Ogdensburg, NY	315	13669
Oglesby, IL	815	61348
Oglethorpe, GA	478	31068
Ogunquit, ME	207	03907
Oil City, PA	814	16301
Ojai, CA	805	93023-93024
Ojo Caliente, NM	505	87549
Ojus, FL	305, 786	33163, 33180
Okahumpka, FL	352	34762
Okanogan, WA	509	98840
Okarche, OK	405	73762
Okeechobee, FL	863	34972-34974
Okemah, OK	918	74859
Okemos, MI	517	48805, 48864
Oklahoma City, OK	405	73101-73173, 73177-73180*
Okmulgee, OK	918	74447
Olathe, KS	913	66051, 66061-66063
Old Bethpage, NY	631	11804
Old Bridge, NJ	732, 848	08857
Old Brookville, NY	516	11545-11548
Old Chatham, NY	518	12136
Old Forge, PA	570	18518
Old Fort, NC	828	28762
Old Greenwich, CT	203	06870
Old Hickory, TN	615	37138
Old Lyme, CT	860	06371
Old Orchard Beach, ME	207	04064
Old Saybrook, CT	860	06475
Old Town, ME	207	04468
Old Westbury, NY	516	11568
Oldwick, NJ	908	08858
Olean, NY	585	14760
Olive Branch, MS	662	38654
Olive Hill, KY	606	41164
Olivet, MI	616	49076
Olivet, SD	605	57052
Olivia, MN	320	56277
Olney, IL	618	62450
Olney, MD	301	20830-20832
Olney, TX	940	76374
Olustee, FL	386	32072
Olympia, WA	360	98501-98516, 98599
Olympia Fields, IL	708	60461
Olympic Valley, CA	530	96146
Olyphant, PA	570	18447-18448
Omaha, NE	402	68046, 68101-68147, 68152*
Omak, WA	509	98841
Onalaska, WI	608	54650
Onamia, MN	320	56359
Onawa, IA	712	51040
Onaway, MI	989	49765
Oneida, NY	315	13421
Oneida, TN	423	37841
Oneida, WI	920	54155
O'Neill, NE	402	68763
Oneonta, AL	205	35121
Oneonta, NY	607	13820
Onida, SD	605	57564
Onley, VA	757	23418
Only, TN	931	37140
Onsted, MI	517	49265
Ontario, CA	909	91758-91764, 91798
Ontario, NY	585	14519
Ontario, OR	541, 458	97914
Ontonagon, MI	906	49953
Ooltewah, TN	423	37363
Opa Locka, FL	305, 786	33014, 33054-33056
Opelika, AL	334	36801-36804
Opelousas, LA	337	70570-70571
Opheim, MT	406	59250
Opp, AL	334	36467
Oquawka, IL	309	61469
Oracle, AZ	520	85623
Oradell, NJ	201, 551	07649
Orange, CA	714	92856-92869
Orange, CT	203	06477
Orange, MA	351, 978	01355, 01364, 01378
Orange, NJ	862, 973	07050-07051
Orange, TX	409	77630-77632
Orange, VA	540	22960
Orange Beach, AL	251	36561
Orange City, IA	712	51041
Orange Cove, CA	559	93646, 93675
Orange Park, FL	904	32003-32006, 32065-32067*
Orange Village, OH	216	44022, 44122, 44128, 44146
Orangeburg, NY	845	10962
Orangeburg, SC	803	29115-29118
Orangevale, CA	916	95662
Orchard Lake, MI	248, 947	48323-48324
Orchard Park, NY	716	14127
Ord, NE	308	68862
Ordway, CO	719	81063
Orefield, PA	484, 610	18069
Oregon, IL	815	61061
Oregon, MO	660	64473
Oregon, OH	419, 567	43605, 43616-43618
Oregon, WI	608	53575
Oregon City, OR	503, 971	97045
Orem, UT	801, 385	84057-84059, 84097
Orestes, IN	765	46063
Orient, OH	614	43146
Oriental, NC	252	28571
Orinda, CA	925	94563
Orion, MI	248, 947	48359-48362
Oriskany, NY	315	13424
Orland, CA	530	95963
Orland Park, IL	708	60462, 60467
Orlando, FL	321, 407	32801-32839, 32853-32862*
Orleans, IN	812	47452
Orleans, MA	508, 774	02653
Ormond Beach, FL	386	32173-32176
Orofino, ID	208	83544
Orondo, WA	509	98843
Orono, ME	207	04469, 04473
Orosi, CA	559	93647
Oroville, CA	530	95915, 95940, 95965-95966*
Orrtanna, PA	717	17353
Orrville, OH	234, 330	44667
Ortonville, MI	248, 947	48462
Ortonville, MN	320	56278
Orwigsburg, PA	570	17961
Osage, IA	641	50454, 50461
Osage Beach, MO	573	65065
Osage City, KS	785	66523
Osawatomie, KS	913	66064
Osborne, KS	785	67473
Osceola, AR	870	72370
Osceola, IA	641	50213
Osceola, MO	417	64776
Osceola, NE	402	68651
Osceola, WI	715, 534	54020
Osceola Mills, PA	814	16666
Oscoda, MI	989	48750
Osgood, IN	812	47037
Osgood, OH	419, 567	45351
Oshkosh, NE	308	69154, 69190
Oshkosh, WI	920	54901-54906
Oskaloosa, IA	641	52577
Oskaloosa, KS	785	66066
Osseo, MN	763	55311, 55369, 55569
Ossining, NY	914	10562
Ossipee, NH	603	03864
Osterville, MA	508, 774	02655
Oswego, IL	331, 630	60543
Oswego, KS	620	67356
Oswego, NY	315	13126
Otisville, NY	845	10963
Otsego, MI	616	49078
Ottawa, IL	815	61350
Ottawa, KS	785	66067
Ottawa, OH	419, 567	45875
Ottawa Lake, MI	734	49267
Otter River, MA	351, 978	01436
Otter Rock, OR	541, 458	97369
Ottsville, PA	484, 610	18942
Ottumwa, IA	641	52501
Ouray, CO	970	81427
Overland Park, KS	913	66202-66215, 66221-66225*
Overton, NV	702	89040
Oviedo, FL	321, 407	32762-32766
Owasso, OK	918	74055, 74073
Owatonna, MN	507	55060
Owego, NY	607	13827
Owen, WI	715, 534	54460
Owensboro, KY	270	42301-42304
Owensville, MO	573	65066
Owenton, KY	502	40359
Owings Mills, MD	410	21117
Owingsville, KY	606	40360
Owosso, MI	989	48841, 48867
Oxford, AL	256	36203
Oxford, CT	203	06478
Oxford, GA	470, 770	30054
Oxford, ME	207	04270
Oxford, MI	248, 947	48370-48371
Oxford, MS	662	38655
Oxford, NY	607	13830
Oxford, NC	919	27565
Oxford, OH	513	45056
Oxford, PA	484, 610	19363
Oxford, WI	608	53952
Oxnard, CA	805	93030-93035
Oyster Bay, NY	516	11771
Ozark, AL	334	36360-36361
Ozark, AR	479	72949
Ozark, MO	417	65721
Ozawkie, KS	785	66070
Ozona, TX	915	76943
Ozone Park, NY	347, 718	11416-11417

P

City	Area Code(s)	Zip Code(s)
Pablo, MT	406	59855
Pace, FL	850	32571
Pacheco, CA	925	94553
Pacific, MO	636	63069
Pacific, WA	253	98047
Pacific Beach, CA	858	92109
Pacific Grove, CA	831	93950
Pacific Palisades, CA	310, 424	90272
Pacifica, CA	650	94044-94045
Packwood, IA	319	52580
Pacoima, CA	818	91331-91334

*Partial list of zip codes, including main range

City	Area Code(s)	Zip Code(s)
Paden City, WV	304	26159
Paducah, KY	270	42001-42003
Paducah, TX	806	79248
Page, AZ	928	86036, 86040
Pageland, SC	843	29728
Pagosa Springs, CO	970	81147, 81157
Pahoa, HI	808	96778
Pahokee, FL	561	33476
Pahrump, NV	775	89041, 89048, 89060-89061
Paicines, CA	831	95043
Paincourtville, LA	985	70391
Painesville, OH	440	44077
Paint Rock, TX	915	76866
Painted Post, NY	607	14870
Paintsville, KY	606	41240
Palatine, IL	224, 847	60038, 60055, 60067, 60074*
Palatine Bridge, NY	518	13428
Palatka, FL	386	32177-32178
Palestine, TX	903	75801-75803, 75882
Palisade, NE	308	69040
Palisades, NY	845	10964
Palisades Park, NJ	201, 551	07650
Palm Bay, FL	321	32905-32911
Palm Beach, FL	561	33480
Palm Beach Gardens, FL	561	33403, 33408-33412, 33418*
Palm Beach Shores, FL	561	33404
Palm City, FL	772	34990-34991
Palm Coast, FL	386	32135-32137, 32142, 32164
Palm Desert, CA	760, 442	92210-92211, 92255, 92260*
Palm Harbor, FL	727	34682-34685
Palm Springs, CA	760, 442	92262-92264, 92292
Palmdale, CA	661	93550-93552, 93590-93591*
Palmer, AK	907	99645
Palmer, MA	413	01069
Palmerton, PA	484, 610	18071
Palmetto, FL	941	34220-34221
Palmetto, GA	470, 770	30268
Palmyra, IN	812	47164
Palmyra, MO	573	63461
Palmyra, NJ	856	08065
Palmyra, NY	315	14522
Palmyra, PA	717	17078
Palmyra, VA	434	22963
Palmyra, WI	262	53156
Palo Alto, CA	650	94301-94310
Palo Pinto, TX	940	76484
Palos Heights, IL	708	60463
Palos Hills, IL	708	60465
Palos Verdes Peninsula, CA	310, 424	90274-90275
Pampa, TX	806	79065-79066
Pana, IL	217	62557
Panama City, FL	850	32401-32413, 32417, 32461
Panama City Beach, FL	850	32401, 32407-32408, 32413*
Panguitch, UT	435	84759
Panhandle, TX	806	79068
Panorama City, CA	818	91402, 91412
Pantego, NC	252	27860
Paola, KS	913	66071
Paoli, IN	812	47454
Paoli, PA	484, 610	19301
Paonia, CO	970	81428
Papaikou, HI	808	96781
Papillion, NE	402	68046, 68133, 68157
Paradise, CA	530	95967-95969
Paradise, PA	717	17562
Paragould, AR	870	72450-72451
Paramount, CA	562	90723
Paramus, NJ	201, 551	07652-07653
Parchman, MS	662	38738
Paris, ID	208	83261, 83287
Paris, IL	217	61944
Paris, KY	859	40361-40362
Paris, MO	660	65275
Paris, TN	731	38242
Paris, TX	903	75460-75462
Park City, KY	270	42160
Park City, UT	435	84060, 84068, 84098
Park Falls, WI	715, 534	54552
Park Forest, IL	708	60466
Park Hill, OK	918	74451
Park Hills, MO	573	63601, 63653
Park Rapids, MN	218	56470
Park Ridge, IL	224, 847	60068
Park Ridge, NJ	201, 551	07656
Parker, AZ	928	85344
Parker, CO	303, 720	80134, 80138
Parker, SD	605	57053
Parker, WA	509	98939
Parker City, IN	765	47368
Parker Ford, PA	484, 610	19457
Parkersburg, WV	304	26101-26106
Parksley, VA	757	23421
Parkville, MO	816	64151-64152
Parlier, CA	559	93648
Parlin, NJ	732, 848	08859
Parma, ID	208	83660
Parma, OH	216, 440	44129-44134
Parowan, UT	435	84761
Parshall, CO	970	80468
Parsippany, NJ	862, 973	07054
Parsons, KS	620	67357
Parsons, TN	731	38363
Parsons, WV	304	26287
Pasadena, CA	626	91050-91051, 91101-91110*
Pasadena, MD	410	21122-21123
Pasadena, TX	281, 713, 832	77501-77508
Pascagoula, MS	228	39562-39563, 39567-39569*
Pasco, WA	509	99301-99302
Pascoag, RI	401	02859
Paso Robles, CA	805	93446-93447
Passaic, NJ	862, 973	07055
Patagonia, AZ	520	85624
Patchogue, NY	631	11772
Paterson, NJ	862, 973	07501-07514, 07522-07524*
Paterson, WA	509	99345
Patrick AFB, FL	321	32925
Patterson, CA	209	95363
Patterson, GA	912	31557
Patterson, LA	985	70392
Patterson, NY	845	12563
Patton, CA	909	92369
Patuxent River, MD	301	20670
Paul, ID	208	83347
Paulding, OH	419, 567	45879
Pauls Valley, OK	405	73075
Paw Paw, MI	616	49079
Pawcatuck, CT	860	06379
Pawhuska, OK	918	74009, 74056
Pawleys Island, SC	843	29585
Pawling, NY	845	12564
Pawnee, OK	918	74058
Pawnee City, NE	402	68420
Pawtucket, RI	401	02860-02862
Paxton, IL	217	60957
Paxton, MA	508, 774	01612
Payette, ID	208	83661
Paynesville, MN	320	56362
Payson, AZ	928	85541, 85547
Payson, UT	801, 385	84651
Peabody, MA	351, 978	01960-01961
Peace Dale, RI	401	02879, 02883
Peach Glen, PA	717	17375
Peachtree City, GA	470, 770	30269
Peapack, NJ	908	07977
Pearce, AZ	520	85625
Pearisburg, VA	540	24134
Pearl, MS	601, 769	39208, 39218, 39232, 39288
Pearl City, HI	808	96782
Pearl Harbor, HI	808	96860
Pearl River, NY	845	10965
Pearland, TX	281, 832	77581-77584, 77588
Pearsall, TX	830	78061
Pearson, GA	912	31642
Pebble Beach, CA	831	93953
Pecos, NM	505	87552
Pecos, TX	915	79772
Peculiar, MO	816	64078
Peekskill, NY	845	10566
Pekin, IL	309	61554-61558
Pekin, IN	812	47165
Pelham, AL	205	35124
Pelham, GA	229	31779
Pelham, NH	603	03076
Pelham, NY	845	10803
Pelham Manor, NY	845	10803
Pelican Rapids, MN	218	56572
Pell City, AL	205	35125-35128
Pella, IA	641	50219
Pelzer, SC	864	29669
Pemberton, NJ	609	08068
Pembroke, GA	912	31321
Pembroke, MA	339, 781	02327, 02358-02359
Pembroke, NH	603	03275
Pembroke, NC	910	28372
Pembroke, VA	540	24136
Pembroke Park, FL	754, 954	33009, 33021-33023
Pembroke Pines, FL	754, 954	33019-33029, 33081-33084*
Pen Argyl, PA	484, 610	18072
Penacook, NH	603	03303
Penasco, NM	505	87553
Pender, NE	402	68047
Pendergrass, GA	706, 762	30567
Pendleton, IN	765	46064
Pendleton, OR	541, 458	97801
Pendleton, SC	864	29670
Penfield, NY	585	14526
Penfield, PA	814	15849
Peninsula, OH	234, 330	44264
Penland, NC	828	28765
Penn Yan, NY	315	14527
Penndel, PA	215, 267	19047
Pennington, NJ	609	08534
Pennsauken, NJ	856	08109-08110
Pennsburg, PA	215, 267	18073
Pennsville, NJ	856	08070
Penrose, CO	719	81240
Pensacola, FL	850	32501-32516, 32520-32526*
Pensacola Beach, FL	850	32561
Pentwater, MI	231	49449
Peoria, AZ	623	85345, 85380-85385
Peoria, IL	309	61601-61616, 61625-61644*
Peoria Heights, IL	309	61614-61616
Peosta, IA	563	52068
Peotone, IL	708	60468
Pepper Pike, OH	216	44122-44124
Pequannock, NJ	862, 973	07440
Perdue Hill, AL	251	36470
Perham, MN	218	56573
Perkasie, PA	215, 267	18944
Perkinston, MS	601, 769	39573
Perris, CA	951	92570-92572, 92599
Perry, FL	850	32347-32348
Perry, GA	478	31069
Perry, IA	515	50220
Perry, KS	785	66073
Perry, OH	440	44081
Perry, OK	580	73077
Perrysburg, OH	419, 567	43551-43552
Perrysville, OH	419, 567	44864
Perryton, TX	806	79070
Perryville, AR	501	72126
Perryville, MO	573	63747, 63775-63776, 63783
Perth Amboy, NJ	732, 848	08861-08863
Peru, IL	815	61354
Peru, IN	765	46970-46971
Peru, NE	402	68421
Pescadero, CA	650	94060
Peshastin, WA	509	98847
Peshtigo, WI	715, 534	54157
Petal, MS	601, 769	39465
Petaluma, CA	707	94952-94955, 94975, 94999
Peterborough, NH	603	03458
Petersburg, AK	907	99833
Petersburg, IL	217	62659, 62675
Petersburg, IN	812	47567
Petersburg, TX	806	79250
Petersburg, VA	804	23801-23806
Petersburg, WV	304	26847
Petersburgh, NY	518	12138
Peterson AFB, CO	719	80914
Petoskey, MI	231	49770
Pewaukee, WI	262	53072
Pewee Valley, KY	502	40056
Pflugerville, TX	512	78660, 78691
Pharr, TX	956	78577
Phelps, NY	315	14532
Phenix City, AL	334	36867-36870
Phil Campbell, AL	256	35581
Philadelphia, MS	601, 769	39350
Philadelphia, PA	215, 267	19019, 19092-19093, 19099*
Philip, SD	605	57567
Philippi, WV	304	26416
Philipsburg, MT	406	59858
Philipsburg, PA	814	16866
Phillips, WI	715, 534	54555
Phillipsburg, KS	785	67661
Phillipsburg, NJ	908	08865
Philmont, NY	518	12565
Philomath, OR	541, 458	97370
Philpot, KY	270	42366
Phoenix, AZ	480, 602	85001-85055, 85060-85087*

*Partial list of zip codes, including main range

City	Area Code(s)	Zip Code(s)
Phoenix, OR	541, 458	97535
Phoenixville, PA	484, 610	19453, 19460
Picayune, MS	601, 769	39466
Pickens, SC	864	29671
Pickerington, OH	614	43147
Pico Rivera, CA	562	90660-90665
Piedmont, AL	256	36272
Pierce, NE	402	68767
Pierre, SD	605	57501
Pierz, MN	320	56364
Piffard, NY	585	14533
Pigeon, MI	989	48755
Pigeon Forge, TN	865	37862-37864, 37868, 37876
Piggott, AR	870	72454
Pikesville, MD	410	21208, 21282
Pikeville, KY	606	41501-41502
Pikeville, TN	423	37367
Pilot Grove, IA	319	52648
Pima, AZ	928	85535, 85543
Pinckneyville, IL	618	62274
Pinconning, MI	989	48650
Pine Bluff, AR	870	71601-71603, 71611-71613
Pine Bluffs, WY	307	82082
Pine Brook, NJ	862, 973	07058
Pine City, MN	320	55063
Pine City, NY	607	14871
Pine Island, MN	507	55963
Pine Mountain, GA	706, 762	31822
Pine Plains, NY	518	12567
Pine River, MN	218	56456, 56474
Pinedale, WY	307	82941
Pinehurst, NC	910	28370, 28374
Pinellas Park, FL	727	33780-33782
Pinetops, NC	252	27864
Pineville, KY	606	40977
Pineville, LA	318	71359-71361
Pineville, MO	417	64856
Pineville, NC	704, 980	28134
Pineville, WV	304	24859, 24874
Piney Flats, TN	423	37686, 37699
Pinole, CA	510	94564
Pioche, NV	775	89043
Pioneer, OH	419, 567	43554
Pipersville, PA	215, 267	18947
Pipestem, WV	304	25979
Pipestone, MN	507	56164
Pippa Passes, KY	606	41844
Piqua, OH	937	45356
Piru, CA	805	93040
Piscataway, NJ	732, 848	08854-08855
Pismo Beach, CA	805	93420, 93433, 93448-93449
Pitman, NJ	856	08071
Pittsboro, MS	662	38951
Pittsboro, NC	919	27228, 27312
Pittsburg, CA	925	94565
Pittsburg, KS	620	66762-66763
Pittsburg, TX	903	75686
Pittsburgh, PA	412, 878	15122-15123, 15201-15244*
Pittsfield, IL	217	62363
Pittsfield, ME	207	04967
Pittsfield, MA	413	01201-01203
Pittsfield, NH	603	03263
Pittsford, NY	585	14534
Pittston, PA	570	18640-18644
Pittstown, NJ	908	08867
Pittsville, WI	715, 534	54466
Placentia, CA	714	92870-92871
Placerville, CA	530	95667
Plain, WI	608	53577
Plain City, OH	614	43064
Plainfield, IL	815	60544
Plainfield, IN	317	46168
Plainfield, NJ	908	07060-07063, 07069
Plainfield, VT	802	05667
Plainfield, WI	715, 534	54966
Plains, GA	229	31780
Plains, PA	570	18702-18705
Plains, TX	806	79355
Plainsboro, NJ	609	08536
Plainview, MN	507	55964
Plainview, NY	516	11803
Plainview, TX	806	79072-79073
Plainville, CT	860	06062
Plainville, KS	785	67663
Plainville, MA	508, 774	02762
Plainville, NY	315	13137
Plainwell, MI	616	49080
Plankinton, SD	605	57368
Plano, IL	331, 630	60545
Plano, TX	469, 972	75023-75026, 75074-75075*
Plant City, FL	813	33564-33567
Plantation, FL	754, 954	33311-33313, 33317-33318*
Plantsville, CT	860	06479
Plaquemine, LA	225	70764-70765
Plato, MN	320	55370
Platte City, MO	816	64079
Platteville, WI	608	53818
Plattsburg, MO	816	64477
Plattsburgh, NY	518	12901-12903
Plattsmouth, NE	402	68048
Pleasant Gap, PA	814	16823
Pleasant Grove, UT	801, 385	84062
Pleasant Hill, CA	925	94523
Pleasant Plains, IL	217	62677
Pleasant Prairie, WI	262	53142-53143, 53158
Pleasant Valley, NY	845	12569
Pleasanton, CA	925	94566-94568, 94588
Pleasanton, TX	830	78064
Pleasantville, NJ	609	08232-08234
Pleasantville, NY	914	10570-10572
Plentywood, MT	406	59254
Plover, WI	715, 534	54467
Plymouth, IN	574	46563
Plymouth, MA	508, 774	02345, 02360-02362
Plymouth, MI	734	48170
Plymouth, MN	763	55441-55442, 55447
Plymouth, NH	603	03264
Plymouth, NC	252	27962
Plymouth, VT	802	05056
Plymouth, WI	920	53073
Plymouth Meeting, PA	484, 610	19462
Pocahontas, AR	870	72455
Pocahontas, IA	712	50574
Pocatello, ID	208	83201-83209
Pocomoke City, MD	410	21851
Pocono Manor, PA	570	18349
Point Clear, AL	334	36564
Point Comfort, TX	361	77978
Point Lookout, MO	417	65726
Point Lookout, NY	516	11569
Point Marion, PA	724, 878	15474
Point of Rocks, MD	301	21777
Point Pleasant, WV	304	25550
Point Pleasant Beach, NJ	732, 848	08742
Point Richmond, CA	510	94801
Poland, OH	234, 330	44514
Polk City, FL	863	33868
Polk City, IA	515	50226
Polkton, NC	704, 980	28135
Pollocksville, NC	252	28573
Polson, MT	406	59860
Pomeroy, OH	740	45769
Pomeroy, WA	509	99347
Pomfret, CT	860	06258
Pomfret Center, CT	860	06259
Pomona, CA	909	91765-91769, 91797-91799
Pomona, NJ	609	08240
Pomona, NY	845	10970
Pompano Beach, FL	754, 954	33060-33077, 33093, 33097
Pompton Lakes, NJ	862, 973	07442
Pompton Plains, NJ	862, 973	07444
Ponca, NE	402	68770
Ponca City, OK	580	74601-74604
Ponce Inlet, FL	386	32127
Ponchatoula, LA	985	70454
Ponte Vedra Beach, FL	904	32004, 32082
Pontiac, IL	815	61764
Pontiac, MI	248, 947	48340-48343
Pontotoc, MS	662	38863
Pooler, GA	912	31322
Pope AFB, NC	910	28308
Poplar, MT	406	59255
Poplar Bluff, MO	573	63901-63902
Poplarville, MS	601, 769	39470
Poquoson, VA	757	23662
Port Allen, LA	225	70767
Port Angeles, WA	360	98362-98363
Port Aransas, TX	361	78373
Port Arthur, TX	409	77640-77643
Port Charlotte, FL	941	33948-33954, 33980-33983
Port Chester, NY	914	10573
Port Clinton, OH	419, 567	43452
Port Ewen, NY	845	12466
Port Gibson, MS	601, 769	39150
Port Hueneme, CA	805	93041-93044
Port Huron, MI	810	48060-48061
Port Isabel, TX	956	78578, 78597
Port Jefferson, NY	631	11777
Port Jefferson Station, NY	631	11776-11777
Port Jervis, NY	845	12771, 12785
Port Lavaca, TX	361	77972, 77979
Port Ludlow, WA	360	98365
Port Neches, TX	409	77651
Port Orange, FL	386	32118-32119, 32124-32129
Port Orchard, WA	360	98366-98367
Port Orford, OR	541, 458	97465
Port Saint Joe, FL	850	32410, 32456-32457
Port Saint Lucie, FL	772	34952-34953, 34983-34988
Port Sulphur, LA	504	70083
Port Tobacco, MD	301	20677
Port Townsend, WA	360	98368
Port Washington, NY	516	11050-11055
Port Washington, WI	262	53074
Portage, IN	219	46368
Portage, MI	616	49002, 49024, 49081
Portage, WI	608	53901
Portageville, MO	573	63873
Portales, NM	505	88123, 88130
Porter, IN	219	46304
Porterville, CA	559	93257-93258
Portland, AR	870	71663
Portland, CT	860	06480
Portland, IN	260	47371
Portland, ME	207	04101-04112, 04116, 04122*
Portland, MI	517	48875
Portland, OR	503, 971	97201-97242, 97251-97259*
Portland, TN	615	37148
Portola, CA	530	96122, 96129
Portola Valley, CA	650	94028
Portsmouth, NH	603	03801-03804
Portsmouth, OH	740	45662-45663
Portsmouth, RI	401	02871-02872
Portsmouth, VA	757	23701-23709
Portville, NY	585	14770
Post, TX	806	79356
Post Falls, ID	208	83854, 83877
Post Mills, VT	802	05058
Postville, IA	563	52162
Poteau, OK	918	74953
Potomac, MD	301	20854, 20859
Potosi, MO	573	63664
Potsdam, NY	315	13676, 13699
Pottsboro, TX	903	75076
Pottstown, PA	484, 610	19464-19465
Pottsville, PA	570	17901
Poughkeepsie, NY	845	12601-12604
Poughquag, NY	845	12570
Poulsbo, WA	360	98370
Poultney, VT	802	05741, 05764
Pound, VA	276	24279
Poway, CA	858	92064, 92074
Powderhorn, CO	970	81243
Powell, OH	614	43065
Powell, TN	865	37849
Powell, WY	307	82435
Powhatan, VA	804	23139
Prairie City, IL	309	61470
Prairie du Chien, WI	608	53821
Prairie du Sac, WI	608	53578
Prairie Grove, IL	815	60012, 60050
Prairie View, TX	936	77446
Prairie Village, KS	913	66202-66208
Prairieville, LA	225	70769
Pratt, KS	620	67124
Prattville, AL	334	36066-36068
Preble, IN	260	46782
Prentiss, MS	601, 769	39474
Prescott, AZ	928	86301-86305, 86313, 86330
Prescott, AR	870	71857
Prescott, WA	509	99348
Prescott, WI	715, 534	54021
Prescott Valley, AZ	928	86312-86314
Presidio of San Francisco, CA	415	94129
Presque Isle, ME	207	04769
Preston, GA	229	31824
Preston, ID	208	83263
Preston, MN	507	55965
Preston, WA	425	98050
Prestonsburg, KY	606	41653
Price, UT	435	84501
Prichard, AL	251	36610, 36617

Partial list of zip codes, including main range

City	Area Code(s)	Zip Code(s)
Prides Crossing, MA	617, 857	01965
Primghar, IA	712	51245
Primm, NV	702	89019
Primos, PA	484, 610	19018
Prince Frederick, MD	410	20678
Prince George, VA	804	23875
Prince William, VA	571, 703	22193
Princess Anne, MD	410	21853
Princeton, ID	208	83857
Princeton, IL	815	61356
Princeton, IN	812	47670
Princeton, KY	270	42445
Princeton, MN	763	55371
Princeton, MO	660	64673
Princeton, NJ	609	08540-08544
Princeton, WV	304	24740
Princeton Junction, NJ	609	08550
Princeville, HI	808	96714, 96722
Princeville, IL	309	61559
Prineville, OR	541, 458	97754
Prinsburg, MN	320	56281
Prior Lake, MN	952	55372
Proctor, MN	218	55810
Proctor, VT	802	05765
Prophetstown, IL	815	61277
Prospect, CT	203	06712
Prospect, ME	207	04981
Prospect Harbor, ME	207	04669
Prospect Heights, IL	224, 847	60070
Prospect Hill, NC	336	27314
Prosperity, SC	803	29127
Prosser, WA	509	99350
Providence, RI	401	02901-02912, 02918, 02940
Provincetown, MA	508, 774	02657
Provo, UT	801, 385	84601-84606
Pryor, OK	918	74361-74362
Pueblo, CO	719	81001-81015
Pueblo West, CO	719	81007
Puerto Nuevo, PR	787, 939	00920-00921
Pulaski, NY	315	13142
Pulaski, TN	931	38478
Pulaski, VA	540	24301
Pulaski, WI	920	54162
Pullman, WA	509	99163-99165
Punta Gorda, FL	941	33950-33951, 33955, 33980*
Punxsutawney, PA	814	15767
Purcell, OK	405	73080
Purcellville, VA	540	20132-20134, 20160
Purchase, NY	914	10577
Purvis, MS	601, 769	39475
Put-in-Bay, OH	419, 567	43456
Putnam, CT	860	06260
Putney, VT	802	05346
Puunene, HI	808	96784
Puyallup, WA	253	98371-98375
Pyote, TX	915	79777

Q

City	Area Code(s)	Zip Code(s)
Quakertown, PA	215, 267	18951
Quanah, TX	940	79252
Quantico, VA	571, 703	22134-22135
Quapaw, OK	918	74363
Quarryville, PA	717	17566
Queens Village, NY	347, 718	11427-11429
Queensbury, NY	518	12801-12804
Queenstown, MD	410	21658
Quimby, IA	712	51049
Quinault, WA	360	98575
Quincy, CA	530	95971
Quincy, FL	850	32351-32353
Quincy, IL	217	62301, 62305-62306
Quincy, MA	617, 857	02169-02171, 02269
Quincy, PA	717	17247
Quincy, WA	509	98848
Quinlan, TX	903	75474
Quinter, KS	785	67752
Quitman, GA	229	31643
Quitman, MS	601, 769	39355
Quitman, TX	903	75783

R

City	Area Code(s)	Zip Code(s)
Racine, WI	262	53401-53408, 53490
Radcliff, KY	270	40159-40160
Radcliffe, IA	515	50230
Radford, VA	540	24141-24143
Radisson, WI	715, 534	54867
Radnor, PA	484, 610	19087
Raeford, NC	910	28361, 28376
Rahway, NJ	732, 848	07065
Raiford, FL	386, 904	32026, 32083
Rainsville, AL	256	35986
Raleigh, MS	601, 769	39153
Raleigh, NC	919	27601-27629, 27634-27636*
Ralls, TX	806	79357
Ralston, IA	712	51459
Ralston, NE	402	68127
Ramah, NM	505	87321, 87357
Ramona, CA	760, 442	92065
Ramona, OK	918	74061
Ramseur, NC	336	27316
Ramsey, MN	763	55303
Ramsey, NJ	201, 551	07446
Rancho Cordova, CA	916	95670, 95741-95743
Rancho Cucamonga, CA	909	91701, 91729-91730, 91737*
Rancho Dominguez, CA	310, 424	90220, 90224
Rancho Mirage, CA	760, 442	92270
Rancho Palos Verdes, CA	310, 424	90275
Rancho Santa Fe, CA	858	92067, 92091
Rancho Santa Margarita, CA	949	92688
Rancho Viejo, TX	956	78575
Rancocas, NJ	609	08073
Randallstown, MD	410	21133
Randleman, NC	336	27317
Randolph, MA	339, 781	02368
Randolph, NJ	862, 973	07869
Randolph, UT	435	84064
Randolph, VT	802	05060
Randolph, WI	920	53956-53957
Randolph AFB, TX	210	78148-78150
Randolph Center, VT	802	05061
Random Lake, WI	920	53075
Rangely, CO	970	81648
Ranger, TX	254	76470
Rankin, PA	412, 878	15104
Rankin, TX	915	79778
Rantoul, IL	217	61866
Rapid City, SD	605	57701-57703, 57709
Rapidan, VA	540	22733
Raritan, NJ	908	08869, 08896
Raton, NM	505	87740
Ravenna, MI	231	49451
Ravenna, OH	234, 330	44266
Ravenswood, WV	304	26164
Rawlins, WY	307	82301, 82310
Ray Brook, NY	518	12977
Raymond, ME	207	04071
Raymond, MS	601, 769	39154
Raymond, NH	603	03077
Raymond, WA	360	98577
Raymondville, TX	956	78580, 78598
Raymore, MO	816	64083
Rayne, LA	337	70578
Raynham, MA	508, 774	02767
Raytown, MO	816	64129, 64133, 64138
Rayville, LA	318	71269
Readfield, ME	207	04355
Reading, MA	339, 781	01867
Reading, PA	484, 610	19601-19612, 19640
Readville, MA	617, 857	02136-02137
Reamstown, PA	717	17567
Red Bank, NJ	732, 848	07701-07704
Red Bay, AL	256	35582
Red Bluff, CA	530	96080
Red Bud, IL	618	62278
Red Cloud, NE	402	68970
Red Feather Lakes, CO	970	80536, 80545
Red Hill, PA	215, 267	18073-18076
Red Lake Falls, MN	218	56750
Red Lion, PA	717	17356
Red Lodge, MT	406	59068
Red Oak, IA	712	51566, 51591
Red River, NM	505	87558
Red Rock, AZ	520	85245
Red Springs, NC	910	28377
Red Wing, MN	651	55066
Redding, CA	530	96001-96003, 96049, 96099
Redding, CT	203	06896
Redfield, SD	605	57469
Redford, MI	313	48239-48240
Redlands, CA	909	92373-92375
Redmond, OR	541, 458	97756
Redmond, WA	425	98052-98053, 98073-98074
Redondo Beach, CA	310, 424	90277-90278
Redstone, CO	970	81623
Redstone Arsenal, AL	256	35808-35809
Redwood, NY	315	13679
Redwood City, CA	650	94059-94065
Redwood Falls, MN	507	56283
Reed City, MI	231	49677
Reedley, CA	559	93654
Reedsburg, WI	608	53958-53959
Refugio, TX	361	78377
Rego Park, NY	347, 718	11374
Rehoboth Beach, DE	302	19971
Reidsville, GA	912	30453, 30499
Reidsville, NC	336	27320-27323
Reinbeck, IA	319	50669
Reisterstown, MD	410	21071, 21136
Rembert, SC	803	29128
Remington, IN	219	47977
Remus, MI	989	49340
Renick, WV	304	24966
Reno, NV	775	89501-89515, 89520-89523*
Rensselaer, IN	219	47978
Rensselaer, NY	518	12144
Renton, WA	425	98055-98059
Renville, MN	320	56284
Represa, CA	916	95671
Republic, MO	417	65738
Republic, WA	509	99166
Research Triangle Park, NC	919	27709
Reseda, CA	818	91335-91337
Reserve, NM	505	87830
Reston, VA	571, 703	20190-20196, 22096
Retsil, WA	360	98378
Revere, MA	339, 781	02151
Rexburg, ID	208	83440-83441, 83460
Reynolds, GA	478	31076
Reynoldsburg, OH	614	43068
Rhinebeck, NY	845	12572
Rhinelander, WI	715, 534	54501
Rhodes, MI	989	48652
Rialto, CA	909	92376-92377
Rice Lake, WI	715, 534	54868
Riceboro, GA	912	31323
Rich Square, NC	252	27869
Richardson, TX	214, 469, 972	75080-75085
Richfield, MN	612	55423
Richfield, OH	234, 330	44286
Richfield, UT	435	84701
Richfield, WI	414	53076
Richland, MI	616	49083
Richland, MS	601, 769	39208, 39218, 39232
Richland, PA	717	17087
Richland, WA	509	99352-99353
Richland Center, WI	608	53581
Richland Hills, TX	682, 817	76118, 76180
Richlands, VA	276	24641
Richmond, CA	510	94801-94808, 94820, 94850
Richmond, IL	815	60071
Richmond, IN	765	47374-47375
Richmond, KY	859	40475-40476
Richmond, MO	816	64085
Richmond, TX	281, 832	77406, 77469
Richmond, VA	804	23173, 23218-23242, 23249*
Richmond Heights, MO	314	63117
Richmond Heights, OH	216	44143
Richmond Hill, NY	347, 718	11418
Richvale, CA	530	95974
Rickreall, OR	503, 971	97371
Riddle, OR	541, 458	97469
Riderwood, MD	410	21139
Ridge, NY	631	11961
Ridge Spring, SC	803	29129
Ridgecrest, CA	760, 442	93555-93556
Ridgedale, MO	417	65739
Ridgefield, CT	203	06877-06879
Ridgefield, NJ	201, 551	07657
Ridgefield Park, NJ	201, 551	07660
Ridgeland, MS	601, 769	39157-39158
Ridgeland, SC	843	29912, 29936
Ridgeville, SC	843	29472

Partial list of zip codes, including main range

City	Area Code(s)	Zip Code(s)
Ridgeway, SC	803	29130
Ridgeway, VA	276	24148
Ridgewood, NJ	201, 551	07450-07452
Ridgewood, NY	347, 718	11385-11386
Ridgway, CO	970	81432
Ridgway, PA	814	15853
Ridley Park, PA	484, 610	19078
Rifle, CO	970	81650
Rigby, ID	208	83442
Rillito, AZ	520	85654
Rindge, NH	603	03461
Ringgold, GA	706, 762	30736
Ringoes, NJ	908	08551
Ringwood, NJ	862, 973	07456
Rio, WI	920	53960
Rio Grande, NJ	609	08242
Rio Grande, OH	740	45674
Rio Grande City, TX	956	78582
Rio Rancho, NM	505	87124, 87174
Rio Rico, AZ	520	85648
Rio Verde, AZ	480	85263
Rio Vista, CA	707	94571
Ripley, MS	662	38663
Ripley, TN	731	38063
Ripley, WV	304	25271
Ripon, CA	209	95366
Ripon, WI	920	54971
Ririe, ID	208	83443
Rising Sun, IN	812	47040
Rising Sun, MD	410	21911
Rison, AR	870	71665
Ritzville, WA	509	99169
River Edge, NJ	201, 551	07661
River Falls, WI	715, 534	54022
River Forest, IL	708	60305
River Grove, IL	708	60171
River Rouge, MI	313	48218
Riverbank, CA	209	95367, 95390
Riverdale, GA	470, 770	30274, 30296
Riverdale, IL	708	60827
Riverdale, MD	301	20737-20738
Riverdale, NJ	862, 973	07457
Riverdale, NY	347, 718	10463, 10471
Riverdale, UT	801, 385	84405
Riverhead, NY	631	11901
Riverside, CA	951	92501-92509, 92513-92522
Riverside, MI	616	49084
Riverside, MO	816	64150-64151, 64168
Riverside, NJ	856	08075
Riverton, NJ	856	08076-08077
Riverton, UT	801, 385	84065, 84095
Riverton, WY	307	82501
Riverview, FL	813	33568-33569
Riverwoods, IL	224, 847	60015
Riviera Beach, FL	561	33403-33407, 33418-33419
Roanoke, IN	260	46783
Roanoke, VA	540	24001-24050
Roanoke Rapids, NC	252	27870
Roaring Spring, PA	814	16673
Robbins, NC	910	27325
Robbinsdale, MN	763	55422
Robbinsville, NJ	609	08691
Robbinsville, NC	828	28771
Robert Lee, TX	915	76945
Roberta, GA	478	31078
Roberts, IL	217	60962
Robertsdale, AL	251	36567, 36574
Robesonia, PA	484, 610	19551
Robins AFB, GA	478	31098
Robinson, IL	618	62454
Robinsonville, MS	662	38664
Robstown, TX	361	78380
Roby, TX	915	79543
Rochdale, MA	508, 774	01542
Rochelle, IL	815	61068
Rochelle Park, NJ	201, 551	07662
Rochester, IN	574	46975
Rochester, MI	248, 947	48306-48309
Rochester, MN	507	55901-55906
Rochester, NH	603	03839, 03866-03868
Rochester, NY	585	14601-14627, 14638-14653*
Rochester, PA	724, 878	15074
Rochester, VT	802	05767
Rochester, WA	360	98579
Rochester, WI	262	53167
Rochester Hills, MI	248, 947	48306-48309
Rock City Falls, NY	518	12863
Rock Creek, OH	440	44084
Rock Falls, IL	815	61071
Rock Hill, NY	845	12775
Rock Hill, SC	803	29730-29734
Rock Island, IL	309	61201-61204, 61299
Rock Port, MO	660	64482
Rock Rapids, IA	712	51246
Rock Spring, GA	706, 762	30739
Rock Springs, WY	307	82901-82902, 82942
Rockaway, NJ	862, 973	07866
Rockaway Beach, NY	347, 718	11693
Rockaway Park, NY	347, 718	11694
Rockford, AL	256	35136
Rockford, IL	815	61101-61114, 61125-61126
Rockford, MI	616	49341, 49351
Rockford, MN	763	55373
Rockford, TN	865	37853
Rockingham, NC	910	28379-28380
Rockland, ME	207	04841
Rockland, MA	339, 781	02370
Rockledge, FL	321	32955-32956
Rockleigh, NJ	201, 551	07647
Rocklin, CA	916	95677, 95765
Rockmart, GA	470, 770	30153
Rockport, IN	812	47635
Rockport, ME	207	04856
Rockport, MA	351, 978	01966
Rockport, TX	361	78381-78382
Rocksprings, TX	830	78880
Rockton, IL	815	61072
Rockville, CT	860	06066
Rockville, IN	765	47872
Rockville, MD	240, 301	20847-20859
Rockville Centre, NY	516	11570-11572, 11592
Rockwall, TX	469, 972	75032, 75087
Rockwell, NC	704, 980	28138
Rockwell City, IA	712	50579
Rockwood, MI	734	48173
Rocky Ford, CO	719	81067
Rocky Hill, CT	860	06067
Rocky Mount, NC	252	27801-27804
Rocky Mount, VA	540	24151
Roebuck, SC	864	29376
Rogers, AR	479	72756-72758
Rogers, CT	860	06263
Rogers City, MI	989	49779
Rogersville, AL	256	35652
Rogersville, TN	423	37857
Rogue River, OR	541, 458	97537
Rohnert Park, CA	707	94927-94928
Roland, AR	501	72135
Roland, IA	515	50236
Rolla, MO	573	65401-65402, 65409
Rolla, ND	701	58367
Rolling Fork, MS	662	39159
Rolling Hills Estates, CA	310, 424	90274-90275
Rolling Meadows, IL	224, 847	60008
Rome, GA	706, 762	30149, 30161-30165
Rome, NY	315	13440-13442, 13449
Romeo, MI	586	48065
Romeoville, IL	815	60441, 60446
Romney, WV	304	26757
Romulus, MI	734	48174
Romulus, NY	315	14541
Ronceverte, WV	304	24970
Ronkonkoma, NY	631	11749, 11779
Roodhouse, IL	217	62082
Roosevelt, AZ	928	85545
Roosevelt, UT	435	84066
Rootstown, OH	234, 330	44272
Rosamond, CA	661	93560
Roscoe, IL	815	61073
Roscoe, PA	412, 878	15477
Roscommon, MI	989	48653
Rose Hill, NC	910	28458
Roseau, MN	218	56751
Rosebud, TX	254	76570
Roseburg, OR	541, 458	97470
Rosedale, MS	662	38769
Roseland, NJ	862, 973	07068
Roselle, IL	331, 630	60172
Roselle, NJ	908	07203
Roselle Park, NJ	908	07204
Rosemead, CA	626	91770-91772
Rosemont, IL	224, 847	60018
Rosemont, PA	484, 610	19010
Rosemount, MN	651	55068
Rosenberg, TX	281, 832	77471
Rosendale, WI	920	54974
Rosenhayn, NJ	856	08352
Roseville, CA	916	95661, 95678, 95746-95747
Roseville, MI	586	48066
Roseville, MN	651	55112-55113, 55126
Roseville, OH	740	43777
Rosiclare, IL	618	62982
Roslindale, MA	617, 857	02131
Roslyn, NY	516	11576
Roslyn Heights, NY	516	11577
Rosman, NC	828	28772
Rosslyn, VA	571, 703	22209
Rossville, GA	706, 762	30741-30742
Roswell, GA	470, 678, 770	30075-30077
Roswell, NM	505	88201-88203
Rothschild, WI	715, 534	54474
Round Lake, IL	224, 847	60073
Round Rock, TX	512	78664, 78680-78683
Roundup, MT	406	59072-59073
Rouses Point, NY	518	12979
Rowayton, CT	203	06853
Rowe, MA	413	01367
Rowlett, TX	469, 972	75030, 75088-75089
Rowley, MA	351, 978	01969
Roxboro, NC	336	27573
Roxbury, MA	617, 857	02118-02120
Roxbury Crossing, MA	617, 857	02120
Roy, NM	505	87743
Roy, UT	801, 385	84067
Roy, WA	360	98580
Royal Oak, MI	248, 947	48067-48068, 48073
Royal Palm Beach, FL	561	33411-33412, 33421
Royersford, PA	484, 610	19468
Rugby, ND	701	58368
Ruidoso Downs, NM	505	88346
Rumford, RI	401	02916
Running Springs, CA	909	92382
Rupert, ID	208	83343, 83350
Rural Hall, NC	336	27045, 27094, 27098-27099
Rush, NY	585	14543
Rush City, MN	320	55067-55069
Rushford, MN	507	55971
Rushville, IL	217	62681
Rushville, IN	765	46173
Rushville, NE	308	69360
Rusk, TX	903	75785
Ruskin, FL	813	33570-33573
Russell, KS	785	67665
Russellville, AL	256	35653-35654
Russellville, AR	479	72801-72802, 72811-72812
Russellville, KY	270	42276
Russia, OH	937	45363
Rustburg, VA	434	24588
Ruston, LA	318	71270-71273
Rutherford, CA	707	94573
Rutherford, NJ	201, 551	07070
Rutherfordton, NC	828	28139
Rutland, MA	508, 774	01543
Rutland, VT	802	05701-05702
Rutledge, TN	865	37861
Rydal, PA	215, 267	19046
Rye, NY	914	10580
Rye Brook, NY	914	10573
Ryegate, MT	406	59074

S

City	Area Code(s)	Zip Code(s)
Sabetha, KS	785	66534
Sac City, IA	712	50583
Saco, ME	207	04072
Sacramento, CA	916	94203-94211, 94229-94263*
Saddle Brook, NJ	201, 551	07663
Saegertown, PA	814	16433
Safety Harbor, FL	727	34695
Safford, AZ	928	85546-85548
Sag Harbor, NY	631	11963
Saginaw, MI	989	48601-48609, 48663
Sagle, ID	208	83809, 83860
Saguache, CO	719	81149
Sahuarita, AZ	520	85629
Saint Albans, VT	802	05478-05479
Saint Albans, WV	304	25177
Saint Ann, MO	314	63074
Saint Ansgar, IA	641	50472, 50481

*Partial list of zip codes, including main range

City	Area Code(s)	Zip Code(s)
Saint Anthony, ID	208	83445
Saint Anthony, MN	612	55418-55421
Saint Augustine, FL	904	32080, 32084-32086, 32092*
Saint Bonaventure, NY	585	14778
Saint Bonifacius, MN	952	55375
Saint Catharine, KY	859	40061
Saint Charles, IL	331, 630	60174-60175
Saint Charles, MI	989	48655
Saint Charles, MO	636	63301-63304
Saint Clair, MI	810	48079
Saint Clair, MN	507	56080
Saint Clair, MO	636	63077
Saint Clair, PA	570	17970
Saint Clair Shores, MI	586	48080-48082
Saint Clairsville, OH	740	43950
Saint Cloud, FL	321, 407	34769-34773
Saint Cloud, MN	320	56301-56304, 56372, 56387*
Saint Croix Falls, WI	715, 534	54024
Saint Davids, PA	484, 610	19087
Saint Francis, KS	785	67756
Saint Francis, WI	414	53207, 53235
Saint Francisville, IL	618	62460
Saint Francisville, LA	225	70775
Saint Gabriel, LA	225	70776
Saint George, SC	843	29477
Saint George, UT	435	84770-84771, 84782-84783*
Saint Helena, CA	707	94574
Saint Helena Island, SC	843	29920
Saint Helens, OR	503, 971	97051
Saint Henry, OH	419, 567	45883
Saint Hilaire, MN	218	56754
Saint Ignace, MI	906	49781
Saint James, LA	225	70086
Saint James, MN	507	56081
Saint James, MO	573	65559
Saint James, NY	631	11780
Saint Joe, IN	260	46785
Saint John, KS	620	67576
Saint Johns, AZ	928	85936
Saint Johns, MI	989	48879
Saint Johnsbury, VT	802	05819
Saint Joseph, LA	318	71366
Saint Joseph, MI	616	49085
Saint Joseph, MN	320	56374-56375
Saint Joseph, MO	816	64501-64508
Saint Leo, FL	352	33574
Saint Louis, MI	989	48880
Saint Louis, MO	314	63101-63151, 63155-63171*
Saint Louis Park, MN	952	55416, 55424-55426, 55436
Saint Maries, ID	208	83861
Saint Martin, OH	513	45118
Saint Martinville, LA	337	70582
Saint Marys, GA	912	31558
Saint Marys, OH	419, 567	45885
Saint Marys, PA	814	15857
Saint Marys, WV	304	26170
Saint Matthews, SC	803	29135
Saint Meinrad, IN	812	47577
Saint Michael, MN	763	55376
Saint Michaels, MD	410	21624, 21647, 21663
Saint Nazianz, WI	920	54232
Saint Paul, MN	651	55101-55129, 55133, 55144*
Saint Paul, NE	308	68873
Saint Pauls, NC	910	28384
Saint Pete Beach, FL	727	33706, 33736
Saint Peter, MN	507	56082
Saint Peters, MO	636	63303-63304, 63376
Saint Petersburg, FL	727	33701-33716, 33728-33743*
Saint Rose, LA	504	70087
Saint Simons Island, GA	912	31522
Sainte Genevieve, MO	573	63670
Salamanca, NY	716	14779
Salem, AR	870	72576
Salem, IL	618	62881
Salem, IN	812	47167
Salem, MA	351, 978	01970-01971
Salem, MO	573	65560
Salem, NH	603	03079
Salem, NJ	856	08079
Salem, OH	234, 330	44460
Salem, OR	503, 971	97301-97314
Salem, SC	864	29676
Salem, SD	605	57058
Salem, VA	540	24153-24157
Salem, WV	304	26426
Salida, CA	209	95368
Salida, CO	719	81201, 81227-81228, 81237*

City	Area Code(s)	Zip Code(s)
Salina, KS	785	67401-67402
Salinas, CA	831	93901-93908, 93912-93915*
Saline, MI	734	48176
Salineville, OH	234, 330	43945
Salisbury, CT	860	06068, 06079
Salisbury, MD	410	21801-21804
Salisbury, MA	351, 978	01952
Salisbury, NC	704, 980	28144-28147
Sallisaw, OK	918	74955
Salmon, ID	208	83467
Salt Flat, TX	915	79847
Salt Lake City, UT	801, 385	84101-84153, 84157-84158*
Saltillo, MS	662	38866
Saltsburg, PA	724, 878	15681
Saluda, SC	864	29138
Saluda, VA	804	23149
Salyersville, KY	606	41465
San Andreas, CA	209	95249-95250
San Angelo, TX	915	76901-76909
San Anselmo, CA	415	94960, 94979
San Antonio, FL	352	33576
San Antonio, TX	210	78201-78270, 78275-78299
San Augustine, TX	936	75972
San Benito, TX	956	78586
San Bernardino, CA	909	92401-92427
San Bruno, CA	650	94066-94067, 94096-94098
San Carlos, CA	650	94070-94071
San Clemente, CA	949	92672-92674
San Diego, CA	619, 858	92101-92199
San Dimas, CA	909	91773
San Fernando, CA	818	91340-91346
San Francisco, CA	415	94101-94177, 94188
San Gabriel, CA	626	91775-91778
San Gregorio, CA	650	94074
San Jacinto, CA	951	92581-92583
San Joaquin, CA	559	93660
San Jose, CA	408	95101-95142, 95148-95164*
San Juan, PR	787, 939	00901-00902, 00906-00940*
San Juan Bautista, CA	831	95045
San Juan Capistrano, CA	949	92675, 92690-92694
San Leandro, CA	510	94577-94579
San Lorenzo, CA	510	94580
San Luis, CO	719	81134, 81152
San Luis Obispo, CA	805	93401-93412
San Marcos, CA	760, 442	92069, 92078-92079, 92096
San Marcos, TX	512	78666-78667
San Marino, CA	626	91108, 91118
San Mateo, CA	650	94401-94409, 94497
San Pablo, CA	510	94806
San Pedro, CA	310, 424	90731-90734
San Quentin, CA	415	94964, 94974
San Rafael, CA	415	94901-94904, 94912-94915
San Ramon, CA	925	94583
San Saba, TX	915	76877
San Ysidro, CA	619	92143, 92173
Sanborn, NY	716	14132
Sand Point, AK	907	99661
Sand Springs, OK	918	74063
Sanderson, FL	386	32087
Sanderson, TX	915	79848
Sandersville, GA	478	31082
Sandia Park, NM	505	87047
Sandpoint, ID	208	83862-83864, 83888
Sandston, VA	804	23150
Sandstone, MN	320	55072
Sandusky, MI	810	48471
Sandusky, OH	419, 567	44870-44871
Sandwich, MA	508, 774	02563, 02644
Sandy, UT	801, 385	84070, 84090-84094
Sandy Hook, CT	203	06482
Sandy Hook, KY	606	41171
Sandy Lake, PA	724, 878	16145
Sandy Spring, MD	301	20860
Sanford, FL	321, 407	32771-32773
Sanford, ME	207	04073
Sanford, NC	919	27237, 27330-27332
Sanger, CA	559	93657
Sangerfield, NY	315	13455
Sanibel, FL	239	33957
Santa Ana, CA	714, 949	92701-92712, 92725-92728*
Santa Ana Pueblo, NM	505	87004
Santa Barbara, CA	805	93101-93111, 93116-93121*
Santa Clara, CA	408	95050-95056
Santa Clarita, CA	661	91310, 91321-91322, 91350*
Santa Claus, IN	812	47579
Santa Cruz, CA	831	95060-95067
Santa Cruz, NM	505	87567

City	Area Code(s)	Zip Code(s)
Santa Fe, NM	505	87500-87509, 87592-87594
Santa Fe Springs, CA	562	90605, 90670-90671
Santa Maria, CA	805	93454-93458
Santa Monica, CA	310, 424	90401-90411
Santa Paula, CA	805	93060-93061
Santa Rosa, CA	707	95401-95409
Santa Rosa, NM	505	88435
Santa Rosa, TX	956	78593
Santa Rosa Beach, FL	850	32459
Santa Teresa, NM	505	88008, 88063
Santa Ynez, CA	805	93460
Santee, CA	619	92071-92072
Santurce, PR	787, 939	00907-00916, 00936, 00940
Sapulpa, OK	918	74066-74067
Saraland, AL	251	36571
Saranac Lake, NY	518	12983
Sarasota, FL	941	34230-34243, 34260, 34276*
Saratoga, CA	408	95070-95071
Saratoga, WY	307	82331
Saratoga Springs, NY	518	12866
Sardinia, OH	937	45171
Sardis, MS	662	38666
Sarita, TX	361	78385
Sartell, MN	320	56377
Sasabe, AZ	520	85633
Satanta, KS	620	67870
Satsuma, AL	251	36572
Saugerties, NY	845	12477
Sauget, IL	618	62201
Saugus, CA	661	91350, 91390
Saugus, MA	339, 781	01906
Sauk Centre, MN	320	56378, 56389
Sauk City, WI	608	53583
Sauk Rapids, MN	320	56379
Saukville, WI	262	53080
Sault Sainte Marie, MI	906	49783, 49788
Sausalito, CA	415	94965-94966
Savage, MD	410, 443	20763
Savage, MN	952	55378
Savanna, IL	815	61074
Savannah, GA	912	31401-31422, 31498-31499
Savannah, MO	816	64485
Savannah, TN	731	38372
Savoy, IL	217	61874
Saxonburg, PA	724, 878	16056
Sayre, OK	580	73662
Sayre, PA	570	18840
Sayreville, NJ	732, 848	08871-08872
Scandia, KS	785	66966
Scandinavia, WI	715, 534	54977
Scappoose, OR	503, 971	97056
Scarborough, ME	207	04070, 04074
Scarsdale, NY	914	10583
Schaefferstown, PA	717	17088
Schaumburg, IL	224, 847	60159, 60168, 60173, 60192*
Schenectady, NY	518	12008, 12301-12309, 12325*
Schererville, IN	219	46375
Schertz, TX	210	78154
Schiller Park, IL	224, 847	60176
Schnecksville, PA	484, 610	18078
Schofield, WI	715, 534	54476
Schoharie, NY	518	12157
Schoolcraft, MI	616	49087
Schuyler, NE	402	68661
Schuylkill Haven, PA	570	17972
Schwertner, TX	254	76573
Scituate, MA	339, 781	02040, 02055, 02060, 02066
Scobey, MT	406	59263
Scooba, MS	662	39358
Scotch Plains, NJ	908	07076
Scotia, CA	707	95565
Scotia, NY	518	12302
Scotland Neck, NC	252	27874
Scotrun, PA	570	18355
Scott, AR	501	72142
Scott, LA	337	70583
Scott, MS	662	38772
Scott AFB, IL	618	62225
Scott City, KS	620	67871
Scott City, MO	573	63780
Scott Depot, WV	304	25560
Scottdale, GA	404, 470	30079
Scottdale, PA	724, 878	15683
Scotts Valley, CA	831	95060, 95066-95067
Scottsbluff, NE	308	69361-69363
Scottsboro, AL	256	35768-35769
Scottsburg, IN	812	47170

*Partial list of zip codes, including main range

City	Area Code(s)	Zip Code(s)
Scottsdale, AZ	480	85250-85271
Scottsville, KY	270	42164
Scottsville, NY	585	14546
Scottsville, TX	903	75688
Scottville, MI	231	49454
Scranton, PA	570	18501-18522, 18540, 18577
Sea Island, GA	912	31561
Seabrook, NH	603	03874
Seabrook, NJ	856	08302
Seabrook, TX	281, 832	77586
Seabrook Island, SC	843	29455
Seaford, DE	302	19973
Seagoville, TX	469, 972	75159
Seal Beach, CA	562	90740
Seale, AL	334	36875
Searcy, AR	501	72143-72145, 72149
Searsmont, ME	207	04973
Searsport, ME	207	04974
Seaside, CA	831	93955
Seaside, OR	503	97138
Seaside Heights, NJ	732, 848	08751
Seattle, WA	206	98101-98138, 98144-98191*
Sebastian, FL	772	32958, 32976-32978
Sebastopol, CA	707	95472-95473
Sebastopol, MS	601, 769	39359
Sebring, FL	863	33870-33876
Sebring, OH	234, 330	44672
Secaucus, NJ	201, 551	07094-07096
Sedalia, CO	303, 720	80135
Sedalia, MO	660	65301-65302
Sedalia, NC	336	27342
Sedan, KS	620	67361
Sedona, AZ	928	86336-86341, 86351
Sedro Woolley, WA	360	98284
Seeley Lake, MT	406	59868
Seffner, FL	813	33583-33584
Seguin, TX	830	78155-78156
Selah, WA	509	98942
Selby, SD	605	57472
Selden, NY	631	11784
Selinsgrove, PA	570	17870
Selkirk, NY	518	12158
Sellersburg, IN	812	47172
Sellersville, PA	215, 267	18960
Sells, AZ	520	85634
Selma, AL	334	36701-36703
Selma, CA	559	93662
Selma, TX	210	78154
Selmer, TN	731	38375
Seminole, FL	727	33772-33778
Seminole, OK	405	74818, 74868
Seminole, TX	915	79360
Semmes, AL	251	36575
Senatobia, MS	662	38665-38668
Seneca, KS	785	66538
Seneca, SC	864	29672, 29678-29679
Seneca Falls, NY	315	13148
Sequatchie, TN	423	37374
Seven Hills, OH	216	44131
Severn, MD	410	21144
Severn, NC	252	27877
Severna Park, MD	410	21146
Sevierville, TN	865	37862-37864, 37868, 37876
Seville, OH	234, 330	44273
Sewanee, TN	931	37375, 37383
Seward, AK	907	99664
Seward, NE	402	68434
Sewell, NJ	856	08080
Sewickley, PA	412, 878	15143, 15189
Seymour, CT	203	06478, 06483
Seymour, IN	812	47274
Seymour, TX	940	76380
Seymour Johnson AFB, NC	919	27531
Shady Grove, PA	717	17256
Shadyside, OH	740	43947
Shafter, CA	661	93263
Shaftsbury, VT	802	05262
Shaker Heights, OH	216	44118-44122
Shakopee, MN	952	55379
Shallotte, NC	910	28459, 28467-28470
Shamokin, PA	570	17872
Shamokin Dam, PA	570	17876
Shannock, RI	401	02875
Sharon, CT	860	06069
Sharon, MA	339, 781	02067
Sharon, PA	724, 878	16146-16148
Sharon, WI	262	53585
Sharon Center, OH	234, 330	44274
Sharon Springs, KS	785	67758
Sharonville, OH	513	45241
Sharpsburg, MD	301	21782
Sharpsville, PA	724, 878	16150
Sharptown, MD	410	21861
Shavertown, PA	570	18708
Shaw AFB, SC	803	29152
Shawano, WI	715, 534	54166
Shawnee, CO	303, 720	80448, 80475
Shawnee, KS	913	66203, 66214-66220, 66226*
Shawnee, OK	405	74801-74804
Shawnee Mission, KS	913	66201-66227, 66250, 66276*
Shawnee on Delaware, PA	570	18356
Shawneetown, IL	618	62984
Sheboygan, WI	920	53081-53083
Sheboygan Falls, WI	920	53085
Sheffield, AL	256	35660
Sheffield, IA	641	50475
Sheffield, MA	413	01257
Sheffield, PA	814	16347
Sheffield, TX	915	79781
Shelbina, MO	573	63468
Shelburne, VT	802	05482
Shelburne Falls, MA	413	01370
Shelby, MI	231	49455
Shelby, MT	406	59474
Shelby, NE	402	68662
Shelby, NC	704, 980	28150-28152
Shelby, OH	419, 567	44875
Shelby Township, MI	586	48315-48318
Shelbyville, IL	217	62565
Shelbyville, IN	317	46176
Shelbyville, KY	502	40065-40066
Shelbyville, MO	573	63469
Shelbyville, TN	931	37160-37162
Sheldon, IA	712	51201
Shell, WY	307	82441
Shell Lake, WI	715, 534	54871
Shelley, ID	208	83274
Shellman, GA	229	31786
Shelocta, PA	724, 878	15774
Shelton, CT	203	06484
Shelton, NE	308	68876
Shelton, WA	360	98584
Shenandoah, IA	712	51601-51603
Shenandoah, PA	570	17976
Shepherdstown, WV	304	25443
Shepherdsville, KY	502	40165
Sheppard AFB, TX	940	76311
Sherburne, NY	607	13460
Sheridan, AR	870	72150
Sheridan, IN	317	46069
Sheridan, MI	989	48884
Sheridan, OR	503, 971	97378
Sheridan, WY	307	82801
Sherman, MS	662	38869
Sherman, TX	903	75090-75092
Sherman Oaks, CA	818	91401-91403, 91411-91413*
Sherwood, AR	501	72116-72120, 72124
Sherwood, OR	503, 971	97140
Shickshinny, PA	570	18655
Shillington, PA	484, 610	19607
Shiloh, OH	419, 567	44878
Shiloh, TN	731	38376
Shiner, TX	361	77984
Ship Bottom, NJ	609	08008
Shippensburg, PA	717	17257
Shippenville, PA	814	16254
Shiprock, NM	505	87420, 87461
Shipshewana, IN	260	46565
Shirley, MA	351, 978	01464
Shirley, NY	631	11967
Shoals, IN	812	47581
Shoemakersville, PA	484, 610	19555
Shoreline, WA	206	98133, 98155, 98177
Shoreview, MN	651	55126
Shorewood, IL	815	60431, 60435-60436
Short Hills, NJ	862, 973	07078
Shoshone, ID	208	83324, 83352
Show Low, AZ	928	85901-85902, 85911
Shreveport, LA	318	71101-71110, 71115-71120*
Shrewsbury, MA	508, 774	01545-01546
Shrewsbury, NJ	732, 848	07702
Shrub Oak, NY	914	10588
Sibley, IA	712	51249
Sibley, MO	816	64088
Sidney, IA	712	51652
Sidney, MI	989	48885
Sidney, MT	406	59270
Sidney, NE	308	69160-69162
Sidney, NY	607	13838
Sidney, OH	937	45365-45367
Sierra Blanca, TX	915	79851
Sierra Madre, CA	626	91024-91025
Sierra Vista, AZ	520	85613, 85635-85636, 85650*
Signal Hill, CA	562	90804-90807
Signal Mountain, TN	423	37377
Sigourney, IA	641	52591
Sikeston, MO	573	63801
Siler City, NC	919	27344
Siloam Springs, AR	479	72761
Silsbee, TX	409	77656
Silver Bay, MN	218	55614
Silver City, NM	505	88022, 88036, 88053, 88061*
Silver Creek, NE	308	68663
Silver Creek, NY	716	14136
Silver Lake, IN	260	46982
Silver Lake, NH	603	03875
Silver Spring, MD	301	20901-20918, 20997
Silver Spring, PA	717	17575
Silver Springs, FL	352	34488-34489
Silverdale, WA	360	98315, 98383
Silverton, CO	970	81433
Silverton, OH	513	45236
Silverton, OR	503, 971	97381
Silverton, TX	806	79257
Silvis, IL	309	61282
Simi Valley, CA	805	93062-93065, 93093-93094*
Simpson, PA	570	18407
Simpsonville, KY	502	40067
Simpsonville, SC	864	29680-29681
Simsbury, CT	860	06070, 06081, 06089-06092
Singer Island, FL	561	33404
Sinking Spring, PA	484, 610	19608
Sinton, TX	361	78387
Sioux Center, IA	712	51250
Sioux City, IA	712	51101-51111
Sioux Falls, SD	605	57101-57110, 57117-57118*
Siren, WI	715, 534	54872
Sisseton, SD	605	57262
Sisters, OR	541, 458	97759
Sitka, AK	907	99835-99836
Skagway, AK	907	99840
Skaneateles Falls, NY	315	13119, 13153
Skillman, NJ	908	08558
Skokie, IL	224, 847	60076-60077
Skowhegan, ME	207	04976
Sky Valley, GA	706, 762	30537
Skytop, PA	570	18357
Slater, CO	970	81653
Slater, IA	515	50244
Slatersville, RI	401	02876
Slaton, TX	806	79364
Slayton, MN	507	56172
Sleepy Eye, MN	507	56085
Slidell, LA	985	70458-70461, 70469
Slippery Rock, PA	724, 878	16057
Smackover, AR	870	71762
Smethport, PA	814	16749
Smith Center, KS	785	66967
Smithfield, NC	919	27577
Smithfield, RI	401	02828, 02917
Smithfield, VA	757	23430-23431
Smithland, KY	270	42081
Smithton, PA	724, 878	15479
Smithtown, NY	631	11745, 11787-11788
Smithville, MO	816	64089
Smithville, OH	234, 330	44677
Smithville, TN	615	37166
Smithville, TX	512	78957
Smyrna, DE	302	19977
Smyrna, GA	404, 770	30080-30082, 30339
Smyrna, TN	615	37167
Sneads, FL	850	32460
Sneedville, TN	423	37869
Snellville, GA	770	30039, 30078
Snohomish, WA	360	98290-98291, 98296
Snoqualmie, WA	425	98065-98068
Snow Hill, MD	410	21863
Snow Hill, NC	252	28580
Snowbird, UT	801, 385	84092
Snowflake, AZ	928	85937, 85942
Snowmass Village, CO	970	81615

*Partial list of zip codes, including main range

City	Area Code(s)	Zip Code(s)
Snowshoe, WV	304	26209
Snyder, NE	402	68664
Snyder, TX	915	79549-79550
Social Circle, GA	470, 770	30025
Socorro, NM	505	87801
Soda Springs, ID	208	83230, 83276, 83285
Sodus, NY	315	14551
Solana Beach, CA	858	92075
Soldotna, AK	907	99669
Soledad, CA	831	93960
Solitude, UT	801, 385	84121
Solomon, KS	785	67480
Solomons, MD	410	20688
Solon, OH	440	44139
Solvang, CA	805	93463-93464
Somers, CT	860	06071
Somers, NY	914	10589
Somers Point, NJ	609	08244
Somerset, KY	606	42501-42503, 42564
Somerset, MA	508, 774	02725-02726
Somerset, NJ	732, 848	08873-08875
Somerset, PA	814	15501, 15510
Somerton, AZ	928	85350
Somerville, MA	617, 857	02143-02145
Somerville, NJ	908	08876
Somerville, TN	901	38060, 38068
Sonoita, AZ	520	85637
Sonoma, CA	707	95476
Sonora, CA	209	95370-95373
Sonora, TX	915	76950
Sonyea, NY	585	14556
Soperton, GA	912	30457
Sorrento, LA	225	70778
Souderton, PA	215, 267	18964
South Attleboro, MA	508, 774	02703
South Barre, VT	802	05670
South Barrington, IL	224, 847	60010
South Bay, FL	561	33493
South Beloit, IL	815	61080
South Bend, IN	574	46601-46604, 46612-46620*
South Bend, WA	360	98586
South Boston, VA	434	24592
South Brunswick, NJ	732, 848	08810
South Burlington, VT	802	05401-05407
South Canaan, PA	570	18459
South Carver, MA	508, 774	02366
South Casco, ME	207	04077
South Charleston, WV	304	25303, 25309
South Chicago Heights, IL	708	60411
South Deerfield, MA	413	01373
South Easton, MA	508, 774	02375
South El Monte, CA	626	91733
South Elgin, IL	224, 847	60177
South Euclid, OH	216	44118-44121
South Fallsburg, NY	845	12779
South Fork, PA	814	15956
South Fulton, TN	731	38257
South Gate, CA	323, 562	90280
South Hackensack, NJ	201, 551	07606
South Hadley, MA	413	01075
South Haven, MI	616	49090
South Hill, VA	434	23970
South Holland, IL	708	60473
South Houston, TX	713, 832	77587
South Jordan, UT	801, 385	84065, 84095
South Kearny, NJ	862, 973	07032
South Laguna, CA	949	92651
South Lake Tahoe, CA	530	96150-96158
South Lancaster, MA	351, 978	01561
South Lee, MA	413	01260
South Lyon, MI	248, 947	48178
South Miami, FL	305, 786	33143-33146, 33155-33156*
South Milwaukee, WI	414	53172
South Mountain, PA	717	17261
South Natick, MA	508, 774	01760
South Norwalk, CT	203	06854
South Orange, NJ	862, 973	07079
South Otselic, NY	315	13155
South Padre Island, TX	956	78597
South Paris, ME	207	04281
South Pasadena, CA	626	91030-91031
South Pittsburg, TN	423	37380
South Plainfield, NJ	908	07080
South Plymouth, NY	607	13844
South Point, OH	740	45680
South Portland, ME	207	04106, 04116
South River, NJ	732, 848	08877, 08882
South Saint Paul, MN	651	55075-55077
South Salt Lake, UT	801, 385	84107, 84115, 84119, 84123*
South San Francisco, CA	650	94080-94083, 94099
South Sioux City, NE	402	68776
South Weymouth, MA	339, 781	02190
South Whitley, IN	260	46787
South Williamson, KY	606	41503
South Williamsport, PA	570	17702
South Windham, CT	860	06266
South Windham, ME	207	04082
South Windsor, CT	860	06074
South Yarmouth, MA	508, 774	02664, 02673
Southampton, NY	631	11968-11969
Southampton, PA	215, 267	18954, 18966
Southaven, MS	662	38671-38672
Southborough, MA	508, 774	01745, 01772
Southbridge, MA	508, 774	01550
Southbury, CT	203	06488
Southern Pines, NC	910	28387-28388
Southfield, MI	248, 947	48034-48037, 48075-48076*
Southgate, MI	734	48195
Southington, CT	860	06489
Southlake, TX	682, 817	76092
Southold, NY	631	11971
Southport, CT	203	06490
Southport, NC	910	28461, 28465
Southwest Harbor, ME	207	04656, 04679
Southwick, MA	413	01077
Spalding, ID	208	83540, 83551
Spanaway, WA	253	98387
Spanish Fort, AL	251	36527, 36577
Sparkill, NY	845	10976
Sparks, MD	410	21152
Sparks, NV	775	89431-89436
Sparta, GA	706, 762	31087
Sparta, MI	616	49345
Sparta, NJ	862, 973	07871
Sparta, NC	336	28675
Sparta, TN	931	38583
Sparta, WI	608	54656
Spartanburg, SC	864	29301-29307, 29316-29319
Spearfish, SD	605	57783, 57799
Spearman, TX	806	79081
Spearville, KS	620	67876
Speedway, IN	317	46224
Spencer, IN	812	47460
Spencer, IA	712	51301, 51343
Spencer, MA	508, 774	01562
Spencer, NY	607	14883
Spencer, NC	704, 980	28159
Spencer, TN	931	38585
Spencer, WV	304	25276
Spencerport, NY	585	14559
Spencerville, OH	419, 567	45887
Spiceland, IN	765	47385
Spindale, NC	828	28160
Spirit Lake, IA	712	51360
Spokane, WA	509	99201-99224, 99228, 99251*
Spotsylvania, VA	540	22553
Spring, TX	281, 832	77373, 77379-77393
Spring Arbor, MI	517	49283
Spring City, PA	484, 610	19475
Spring City, UT	435	84662
Spring Green, WI	608	53588
Spring Grove, IL	815	60081
Spring Hill, FL	352	34604-34611
Spring Hill, TN	931	37174
Spring Hope, NC	252	27882
Spring House, PA	215, 267	19477
Spring Lake, MI	231, 616	49456
Spring Lake, NJ	732, 848	07762
Spring Lake Park, MN	612, 763	55432
Spring Mills, PA	814	16875
Spring Valley, CA	619	91976-91979
Spring Valley, IL	815	61362
Spring Valley, MN	507	55975
Spring Valley, NY	845	10977
Spring Valley, WI	715, 534	54767
Springboro, OH	513	45066
Springdale, AR	479	72762-72766
Springdale, OH	513	45246
Springdale, PA	724, 878	15144
Springdale, UT	435	84767, 84779
Springer, NM	505	87729, 87747
Springer, OK	580	73458
Springfield, CO	719	81073
Springfield, GA	912	31329
Springfield, IL	217	62701-62709, 62713-62726*
Springfield, KY	859	40069
Springfield, MA	413	01101-01119, 01128-01129*
Springfield, MN	507	56087
Springfield, MO	417	65721, 65742, 65801-65810*
Springfield, NJ	862, 973	07081
Springfield, OH	937	45501-45506
Springfield, OR	541, 458	97477-97478, 97482
Springfield, PA	484, 610	19064, 19118
Springfield, SD	605	57062
Springfield, TN	615	37172
Springfield, VT	802	05156
Springfield, VA	571, 703	22009, 22015, 22150-22161
Springfield Gardens, NY	347, 718	11413
Springs, PA	814	15562
Springtown, TX	682, 817	76082
Springvale, ME	207	04083
Springview, NE	402	68778
Springville, AL	205	35146
Springville, UT	801, 385	84663
Spruce Pine, NC	828	28777
Stafford, TX	281, 832	77477, 77497
Stafford, VA	540	22554-22555
Stafford Springs, CT	860	06076
Stamford, CT	203	06901-06914, 06920-06928
Stamford, NY	607	12167
Stamps, AR	870	71860
Stanardsville, VA	434	22973
Stanberry, MO	660	64489
Standish, ME	207	04084
Standish, MI	989	48658
Stanfield, AZ	520	85272
Stanford, CA	650	94305, 94309
Stanford, KY	606	40484
Stanford, MT	406	59479
Stanhope, NJ	862, 973	07874
Stanley, NC	704, 980	28164
Stanley, ND	701	58784
Stanleytown, VA	276	24168
Stanton, CA	714	90680
Stanton, KY	606	40380
Stanton, MI	989	48888
Stanton, NE	402	68779
Stanton, ND	701	58571
Stanton, TX	915	79782
Stanwood, WA	360	98282, 98292
Staples, MN	218	56479
Stapleton, NE	308	69163
Star, NC	910	27356
Star City, AR	870	71667
Starbuck, MN	320	56381
Starke, FL	904	32091
Starkville, MS	662	39759-39760
State Center, IA	641	50247
State College, PA	814	16801-16805
State Farm, VA	804	23160
State University, AR	870	72467
Stateline, NV	775	89449
Staten Island, NY	347, 718	10301-10314
Statenville, GA	229	31648
Statesboro, GA	912	30458-30461
Statesville, NC	704, 980	28625, 28677, 28687
Staunton, VA	540	24401-24402, 24407
Stayton, OR	503, 971	97383
Steamboat Springs, CO	970	80477, 80487-80488
Stearns, KY	606	42647
Steele, ND	701	58482
Steeleville, IL	618	62288
Steelville, MO	573	65565-65566
Steilacoom, WA	253	98388
Stennis Space Center, MS	228	39522, 39529
Stephenville, TX	254	76401-76402
Sterling, CO	970	80751
Sterling, IL	815	61081
Sterling, KS	620	67579
Sterling, VA	571, 703	20163-20167
Sterling City, TX	915	76951
Sterling Heights, MI	586	48310-48314
Steubenville, OH	740	43952-43953
Stevens Point, WI	715, 534	54481, 54492
Stevensburg, VA	540	22741
Stevenson, AL	256	35772
Stevenson, CT	203	06491
Stevenson, MD	410	21153
Stevenson, WA	509	98648
Stevensville, MD	410	21666
Stevensville, MI	616	49127

*Partial list of zip codes, including main range

City	Area Code(s)	Zip Code(s)
Stewart, MN	320	55385
Stewartville, MN	507	55976
Stigler, OK	918	74462
Stillwater, ME	207	04489
Stillwater, MN	651	55082-55083
Stillwater, NY	518	12170
Stillwater, OK	405	74074-74078
Stilwell, OK	918	74960
Stinnett, TX	806	79083
Stirling, NJ	908	07980
Stockbridge, GA	470, 770	30281
Stockbridge, MA	413	01262-01263
Stockton, CA	209	95201-95215, 95219, 95267*
Stockton, KS	785	67669
Stockton, MO	417	65785
Stockville, NE	308	69042
Stone Creek, OH	234, 330	43840
Stone Mountain, GA	470, 770	30083-30088
Stone Ridge, NY	845	12484
Stoneham, MA	339, 781	02180
Stoneville, MS	662	38776
Stonington, CT	860	06378
Stony Brook, NY	631	11790, 11794
Stony Creek, VA	434	23882
Stony Point, NY	845	10980
Storm Lake, IA	712	50588
Stormville, NY	845	12582
Storrs, CT	860	06268
Stoughton, MA	339, 781	02072
Stoughton, WI	608	53589
Stow, OH	234, 330	44224
Stowe, PA	484, 610	19464
Stowe, VT	802	05672
Stoystown, PA	814	15563
Strafford, MO	417	65757
Strasburg, CO	303, 720	80136
Strasburg, OH	234, 330	44680
Strasburg, VA	540	22641, 22657
Stratford, CA	559	93266
Stratford, CT	203	06497, 06614-06615
Stratford, NJ	856	08084
Stratford, TX	806	79084
Stratford, WI	715, 534	54484
Stratham, NH	603	03885
Stratton, CO	719	80836
Stratton Mountain, VT	802	05155
Strausstown, PA	484, 610	19559
Strawberry Point, IA	563	52076
Streamwood, IL	331, 630	60107
Streator, IL	815	61364
Streetsboro, OH	234, 330	44241
Stringtown, OK	580	74569
Stromsburg, NE	402	68666
Strongsville, OH	440	44136, 44149
Stroudsburg, PA	570	18360
Stryker, OH	419, 567	43557
Stuart, FL	772	34994-34997
Stuart, VA	276	24171
Stuarts Draft, VA	540	24477
Studio City, CA	818	91602-91607, 91614
Sturbridge, MA	508, 774	01518, 01566
Sturgeon Bay, WI	920	54235
Sturgis, MI	616	49091
Sturgis, SD	605	57785
Sturtevant, WI	262	53177
Stuttgart, AR	870	72160
Subiaco, AR	479	72865
Sublette, KS	620	67877
Sublimity, OR	503, 971	97385
Succasunna, NJ	862, 973	07876
Sudbury, MA	351, 978	01776
Suffern, NY	845	10901
Suffield, CT	860	06078-06080, 06093
Suffolk, VA	757	23432-23439
Sugar Grove, IL	331, 630	60554
Sugar Land, TX	281, 832	77478-77479, 77487, 77496
Sugar Valley, GA	706, 762	30746
Sugarcreek, OH	234, 330	44681
Suitland, MD	301	20746, 20752
Sullivan, IL	217	61951
Sullivan, IN	812	47864, 47882
Sullivan, MO	573	63080
Sullivans Island, SC	843	29482
Sulphur, LA	337	70663-70665
Sulphur, OK	580	73086
Sulphur Springs, TX	903	75482-75483
Sultan, WA	360	98294
Summerdale, AL	251	36580
Summerdale, PA	717	17093
Summersville, WV	304	26651
Summerville, GA	706, 762	30747
Summerville, SC	843	29483-29485
Summit, IL	708	60501
Summit, MS	601, 769	39666
Summit, NJ	908	07901-07902
Summit, NY	518	12175
Summit Station, PA	570	17979
Summitville, OH	234, 330	43962
Sumner, WA	253	98352, 98390
Sumter, SC	803	29150-29154
Sumterville, FL	352	33585
Sun City, AZ	623	85351, 85372-85379, 85387
Sun City, CA	951	92584-92587
Sun City, FL	813	33586
Sun City Center, FL	813	33570-33573
Sun City West, AZ	623	85374-85379, 85387
Sun Lakes, AZ	480	85248
Sun Prairie, WI	608	53590-53591, 53596
Sun Valley, CA	818	91352-91353
Sun Valley, ID	208	83353-83354
Sunbury, OH	740	43074
Sunbury, PA	570	17801, 17877
Suncook, NH	603	03275
Sundance, WY	307	82729
Sunland, CA	818	91040-91041
Sunland Park, NM	505	88008, 88063
Sunman, IN	812	47041
Sunny Isles Beach, FL	305, 786	33160
Sunnyside, NY	347, 718	11104
Sunnyside, WA	509	98944
Sunnyvale, CA	408	94085-94090
Sunnyvale, TX	469, 972	75182
Sunrise, FL	754, 954	33304, 33313, 33319-33326*
Sunriver, OR	541, 458	97707
Superior, AZ	520	85273
Superior, MT	406	59872
Superior, WI	715, 534	54880
Supply, NC	910	28462
Surfside, FL	305, 786	33154
Surfside Beach, SC	843	29575, 29587
Surgoinsville, TN	423	37873
Surry, VA	757	23883
Susanville, CA	530	96127-96130
Sussex, NJ	862, 973	07461
Sussex, VA	434	23884
Sussex, WI	262	53089
Sutherlin, OR	541, 458	97479
Sutter, CA	530	95982
Sutton, MA	508, 774	01590
Sutton, WV	304	26601
Suttons Bay, MI	231	49682
Suwanee, GA	470, 678, 770	30024
Swainsboro, GA	478	30401
Swampscott, MA	339, 781	01907
Swannanoa, NC	828	28778
Swanquarter, NC	252	27885
Swansea, IL	618	62220-62226
Swansea, MA	508, 774	02777
Swanton, OH	419, 567	43558
Swanton, VT	802	05488
Swarthmore, PA	484, 610	19081
Swartz Creek, MI	810	48473
Swea City, IA	515	50590
Swedesboro, NJ	856	08085
Sweet Briar, VA	434	24595
Sweet Home, OR	541, 458	97386
Sweetwater, TN	423	37874
Sweetwater, TX	915	79556
Swepsonville, NC	336	27359
Swiftwater, PA	570	18370
Swissvale, PA	412, 878	15218
Swords Creek, VA	276	24649
Swoyersville, PA	570	18704
Sycamore, AL	256	35149
Sycamore, IL	815	60178
Sykesville, MD	410	21784
Sylacauga, AL	256	35150-35151
Sylmar, CA	818	91342, 91392
Sylva, NC	828	28779
Sylvania, GA	912	30467
Sylvania, OH	419, 567	43560
Sylvester, GA	229	31791
Syosset, NY	516	11773, 11791
Syracuse, IN	574	46567
Syracuse, KS	620	67878
Syracuse, NE	402	68446
Syracuse, NY	315	13201-13225, 13235, 13244*

T

City	Area Code(s)	Zip Code(s)
Tabor, SD	605	57063
Tabor City, NC	910	28463
Tacoma, WA	253	98401-98424, 98431-98433*
Taft, CA	661	93268
Taft, OK	918	74463
Taftville, CT	860	06380
Tahlequah, OK	918	74464-74465
Tahoe City, CA	530	96145-96146
Tahoka, TX	806	79373
Takoma Park, MD	301	20903, 20912-20913
Talbotton, GA	706, 762	31827
Talihina, OK	918	74571
Talladega, AL	256	35160-35161
Tallahassee, FL	850	32301-32318, 32395, 32399
Tallapoosa, GA	470, 770	30176
Tallassee, AL	334	36023, 36045, 36078
Tallevast, FL	941	34270
Tallmadge, OH	234, 330	44278
Tallulah, LA	318	71282-71284
Talmage, PA	717	17580
Taloga, OK	580	73667
Tama, IA	641	52339
Tamaqua, PA	570	18252
Tamarac, FL	754, 954	33309, 33319-33323, 33351*
Tamiment, PA	570	18371
Tamms, IL	618	62988, 62993
Tampa, FL	813	33601-33637, 33647-33651*
Taneytown, MD	410	21787
Tangent, OR	541, 458	97389
Tannersville, PA	570	18372
Taos, NM	505	87571
Tappahannock, VA	804	22560
Tarboro, NC	252	27886
Tarentum, PA	724, 878	15084
Tarpon Springs, FL	727	34688-34691
Tarrytown, NY	914	10591
Tarzana, CA	818	91335, 91356-91357
Taunton, MA	508, 774	02718, 02780-02783
Tavares, FL	352	32778
Tavernier, FL	305, 786	33070
Tawas City, MI	989	48763-48764
Taylor, MI	313, 734	48180
Taylor, NE	308	68879
Taylor, PA	570	18517
Taylor, TX	512	76574
Taylors, SC	864	29687
Taylorsville, KY	502	40071
Taylorsville, MS	601, 769	39168
Taylorsville, NC	828	28681
Taylorville, IL	217	62568
Tazewell, TN	423	37879
Tazewell, VA	276	24608, 24651
Teaneck, NJ	201, 551	07666
Teays, WV	304	25569
Tecumseh, MI	517	49286
Tecumseh, NE	402	68450
Tecumseh, OK	405	74873
Tehachapi, CA	661	93561, 93581
Tekamah, NE	402	68061
Telford, PA	215, 267	18969
Tell City, IN	812	47586
Telluride, CO	970	81435
Temecula, CA	951	92589-92593
Tempe, AZ	480, 602	85280-85289
Temperance, MI	734	48182
Temple, PA	484, 610	19560
Temple, TX	254	76501-76508
Temple City, CA	626	91780
Temple Hills, MD	301	20748, 20752, 20757, 20762
Temple Terrace, FL	813	33617, 33637, 33687
Templeton, CA	805	93465
Tenafly, NJ	201, 551	07670
Tenino, WA	360	98589
Tenstrike, MN	218	56683
Tequesta, FL	561	33469
Terminal Island, CA	310, 424	90731
Terra Bella, CA	559	93270
Terre Haute, IN	812	47801-47814
Terrell, TX	469, 972	75160-75161

*Partial list of zip codes, including main range

City	Area Code(s)	Zip Code(s)
Terry, MT	406	59349
Terryville, CT	860	06786
Teterboro, NJ	201, 551	07608
Teton Village, WY	307	83025
Teutopolis, IL	217	62467
Tewksbury, MA	351, 978	01876
Texarkana, AR	870	71854
Texarkana, TX	903	75501-75507, 75599
Texas City, TX	409	77590-77592
Thatcher, AZ	928	85552
The Colony, TX	469, 972	75034, 75056
The Dalles, OR	541, 458	97058
The Sea Ranch, CA	707	95445, 95497
The Villages, FL	352	32159-32162
The Woodlands, TX	281, 832	77380-77387, 77393
Thedford, NE	308	69166
Theodore, AL	251	36582, 36590, 36619
Thermopolis, WY	307	82443
Thibodaux, LA	985	70301-70302, 70310
Thief River Falls, MN	218	56701
Thiensville, WI	262	53092, 53097
Thomaston, CT	860	06778, 06787
Thomaston, GA	706, 762	30286
Thomaston, ME	207	04861
Thomasville, AL	334	36762, 36784
Thomasville, GA	229	31757-31758, 31792, 31799
Thomasville, NC	336	27360-27361
Thomasville, PA	717	17364
Thompson, CT	860	06277
Thompson, IA	641	50478
Thompson Falls, MT	406	59873
Thompsons Station, TN	615	37179
Thompsonville, MI	231	49683
Thomson, GA	706, 762	30824
Thorndale, PA	484, 610	19372
Thornton, CO	303, 720	80020, 80221, 80229, 80233*
Thornton, IL	708	60476
Thornville, OH	740	43076
Thornwood, NY	914	10594
Thorofare, NJ	856	08086
Thousand Oaks, CA	805	91319-91320, 91358-91362
Three Lakes, WI	715, 534	54562
Three Rivers, CA	559	93271
Three Rivers, MI	616	49093
Three Rivers, TX	361	78060, 78071
Throckmorton, TX	940	76483
Thurmont, MD	301	21788
Tiburon, CA	415	94920
Tie Siding, WY	307	82084
Tierra Amarilla, NM	505	87575
Tierra Verde, FL	727	33715
Tiffin, OH	419, 567	44883
Tifton, GA	229	31793-31794
Tigard, OR	503, 971	97223-97224, 97281
Tigerville, SC	864	29688
Tilden, TX	361	78072
Tillamook, OR	503	97141
Tillery, NC	252	27887
Tilton, NH	603	03276, 03298-03299
Timber Lake, SD	605	57656
Timberline Lodge, OR	503, 971	97028
Timmonsville, SC	843	29161
Timonium, MD	410	21093-21094
Tinker AFB, OK	405	73145
Tinley Park, IL	708	60477
Tinton Falls, NJ	732, 848	07724
Tionesta, PA	814	16353
Tipp City, OH	937	45371
Tipton, IN	765	46072
Tipton, IA	563	52772
Tipton, MO	660	65081
Tipton, OK	580	73570
Tipton, PA	814	16684
Tiptonville, TN	731	38079
Tishomingo, OK	580	73460
Titusville, FL	321	32780-32783, 32796
Titusville, NJ	609	08560
Titusville, PA	814	16354
Toa Baja, PR	787, 939	00949-00951
Toccoa, GA	706, 762	30577
Toccoa Falls, GA	706, 762	30598
Togo, MN	218	55723
Tok, AK	907	99776-99780
Tokeland, WA	360	98590
Toledo, IL	217	62468
Toledo, IA	641	52342
Toledo, OH	419, 567	43601-43624, 43635, 43652*
Tolland, CT	860	06084
Tolleson, AZ	623	85353
Tollhouse, CA	559	93667
Tolono, IL	217	61880
Toluca, IL	815	61369
Tomah, WI	608	54660
Tomball, TX	281, 832	77337, 77375-77377
Tombstone, AZ	520	85638
Tompkinsville, KY	270	42167
Toms River, NJ	732, 848	08753-08757
Tonalea, AZ	928	86044, 86053-86054
Tonawanda, NY	716	14150-14151, 14217, 14223
Tonkawa, OK	580	74653
Tonopah, NV	775	89049
Tontitown, AR	479	72770
Tooele, UT	435	84074
Topeka, IN	260	46571
Topeka, KS	785	66601-66629, 66634-66638*
Toppenish, WA	509	98948
Topsfield, MA	351, 978	01983
Topsham, ME	207	04086
Topton, PA	484, 610	19562
Torrance, CA	310, 424	90501-90510
Torrance, PA	724, 878	15779
Torrey, UT	435	84775
Torrington, CT	860	06790-06791
Torrington, WY	307	82240
Totowa, NJ	862, 973	07511-07512
Tougaloo, MS	601, 769	39174
Toulon, IL	309	61483
Toutle, WA	360	98645, 98649
Towaco, NJ	862, 973	07082
Towanda, PA	570	18848
Towner, ND	701	58788
Townsend, MA	351, 978	01469, 01474
Townsend, MT	406	59644
Townsend, TN	865	37882
Towson, MD	410	21204, 21284-21286
Tracy, CA	209	95304, 95376-95378, 95385*
Travelers Rest, SC	864	29690
Traverse City, MI	231	49684-49686, 49696
Travis AFB, CA	707	94535
Tremonton, UT	435	84337
Trenton, FL	352	32693
Trenton, GA	706, 762	30752
Trenton, ME	207	04605
Trenton, MI	734	48183
Trenton, MO	660	64683
Trenton, NE	308	69044
Trenton, NJ	609	08601-08611, 08618-08620*
Trenton, NC	252	28585
Trenton, OH	513	45067
Trenton, SC	803	29847
Trenton, TN	731	38382
Trevor, WI	262	53102, 53179
Trevose, PA	215, 267	19053
Triangle, VA	571, 703	22172
Tribune, KS	620	67879
Trinidad, CO	719	81074, 81082
Trinity, AL	256	35673
Trinity, NC	336	27370
Trinity Center, CA	530	96091
Trion, GA	706, 762	30753
Trotwood, OH	937	45406, 45415-45418, 45426*
Troutdale, OR	503, 971	97060
Troy, AL	334	36079-36082
Troy, ID	208	83871
Troy, IL	618	62294
Troy, KS	785	66087
Troy, MI	248, 947	48007, 48083-48085, 48098*
Troy, MO	636	63379
Troy, NY	518	12179-12183
Troy, NC	910	27371
Troy, OH	937	45373-45374
Troy, VA	434	22974
Truckee, CA	530	96160-96162
Truman, MN	507	56088
Trumann, AR	870	72472
Trumbauersville, PA	215, 267	18970
Trumbull, CT	203	06611
Trussville, AL	205	35173
Truth or Consequences, NM	505	87901
Tryon, NE	308	69167
Tryon, NC	828	28782
Tsaile, AZ	928	86556
Tualatin, OR	503, 971	97062
Tuba City, AZ	928	86045
Tuckahoe, NY	914	10707
Tucker, AR	501	72168
Tucker, GA	470, 678, 770	30084-30085
Tucson, AZ	520	85701-85754, 85775-85777
Tucumcari, NM	505	88401, 88416
Tukwila, WA	206, 425	98108, 98138, 98168, 98178*
Tulare, CA	559	93274-93275
Tulelake, CA	530	96134
Tulia, TX	806	79088
Tullahoma, TN	931	37388-37389
Tullytown, PA	215, 267	19007
Tulsa, OK	918	74101-74121, 74126-74137*
Tumacacori, AZ	520	85640, 85645-85646
Tumwater, WA	360	98501, 98511-98512
Tunica, MS	662	38676
Tunkhannock, PA	570	18657
Tupelo, MS	662	38801-38804
Turbeville, SC	843	29162
Turlock, CA	209	95380-95382
Turner, OR	503, 971	97359, 97392
Turners Falls, MA	413	01349, 01376
Turnersville, NJ	856	08012
Turpin, OK	580	73950
Turtle Creek, PA	412, 878	15145
Turtle Lake, WI	715, 534	54004, 54889
Tuscaloosa, AL	205	35401-35407, 35485-35487
Tuscola, IL	217	61953
Tuscola, TX	915	79562
Tuscumbia, AL	256	35674
Tuscumbia, MO	573	65082
Tuskegee, AL	334	36083
Tuskegee Institute, AL	334	36083, 36087-36088
Tustin, CA	714	92780-92782
Twentynine Palms, CA	760, 442	92277-92278
Twin Bridges, MT	406	59754
Twin Falls, ID	208	83301-83303
Twinsburg, OH	234, 330	44087
Two Harbors, MN	218	55616
Two Rivers, WI	920	54241
Tybee Island, GA	912	31328
Tyler, MN	507	56178
Tyler, TX	903	75701-75713, 75798-75799
Tylertown, MS	601, 769	39667
Tyndall, SD	605	57066
Tyndall AFB, FL	850	32403
Tyngsboro, MA	351, 978	01879
Tyrone, GA	470, 770	30290
Tyrone, PA	814	16686

U

City	Area Code(s)	Zip Code(s)
Ubly, MI	989	48475
Uhrichsville, OH	740	44683
Ukiah, CA	707	95418, 95482
Ullin, IL	618	62992
Ulm, MT	406	59485
Ulysses, KS	620	67880
Umatilla, OR	541, 458	97882
Una, SC	864	29378
Unadilla, GA	478	31091
Unadilla, NY	607	13849
Unalakleet, AK	907	99684
Unalaska, AK	907	99547, 99685, 99692
Uncasville, CT	860	06382
Union, IL	815	60180
Union, MO	636	63084
Union, NJ	908	07083
Union, SC	864	29379
Union, WA	360	98592
Union, WV	304	24983
Union City, CA	510	94587
Union City, GA	470, 770	30291
Union City, IN	765	47390
Union City, NJ	201, 551	07086-07087
Union City, PA	814	16438
Union City, TN	731	38261, 38281
Union Gap, WA	509	98901-98903
Union Grove, WI	262	53182
Union Lake, MI	248, 947	48387
Union Springs, AL	334	36089
Uniondale, NY	516	11553-11556, 11588
Uniontown, AL	334	36786
Uniontown, OH	234, 330	44685
Uniontown, PA	724, 878	15401
Unionville, MO	660	63565

*Partial list of zip codes, including main range

City	Area Code(s)	Zip Code(s)
Unity, ME	207	04988
Universal City, CA	818	91608, 91618
Universal City, TX	210	78148-78150
University, MS	662	38677
University Center, MI	989	48710
University City, MO	314	63124, 63130
University Heights, OH	216	44118, 44122
University of Richmond, VA	804	23173
University Park, IL	708	60466
University Park, IA	641	52595
University Park, PA	814	16802
Upland, CA	909	91784-91786
Upland, IN	765	46989
Upland, PA	484, 610	19013-19015
Upper Arlington, OH	614	43220-43221
Upper Black Eddy, PA	484, 610	18972
Upper Marlboro, MD	301	20772-20775, 20792
Upper Montclair, NJ	862, 973	07043
Upper Saddle River, NJ	201, 551	07458
Upper Saint Clair, PA	724, 878	15241
Upper Sandusky, OH	419, 567	43351
Upperville, VA	540	20184-20185
Upton, MA	508, 774	01568
Upton, NY	631	11973
Urbana, IL	217	61801-61803
Urbana, IN	260	46990
Urbana, IA	319	52345
Urbana, OH	937	43078
Urbandale, IA	515	50322-50323
Ursa, IL	217	62376
USAF Academy, CO	719	80841
Utica, MI	586	48315-48318
Utica, MS	601, 769	39175
Utica, NY	315	13501-13505, 13599
Uvalde, TX	830	78801-78802

V

City	Area Code(s)	Zip Code(s)
Vacaville, CA	707	95687-95688, 95696
Vail, CO	970	81657-81658
Valdese, NC	828	28690
Valdez, AK	907	99686
Valdosta, GA	229	31601-31606, 31698-31699
Vale, OR	541, 458	97918
Valencia, CA	661	91354-91355, 91380, 91385
Valencia, PA	724, 878	16059
Valentine, NE	402	69201
Valhalla, NY	914	10595
Vallejo, CA	707	94503, 94589-94592
Valley, AL	334	36854, 36872
Valley Center, CA	760, 442	92082
Valley Center, KS	316	67147
Valley City, ND	701	58072
Valley City, OH	234, 330	44280
Valley Cottage, NY	845	10989
Valley Falls, NY	518	12185
Valley Forge, PA	484, 610	19481-19485, 19493-19496
Valley Park, MO	636	63088
Valley Stream, NY	516	11580-11583
Valley View, OH	216	44125, 44131
Valley View, TX	940	76272
Valley Village, CA	818	91607, 91617
Valparaiso, IN	219	46383-46385
Valyermo, CA	661	93563
Van Alstyne, TX	903	75495
Van Buren, AR	479	72956-72957
Van Buren, MO	573	63965
Van Horn, TX	915	79855
Van Nuys, CA	818	91316, 91388, 91401-91416*
Van Wert, OH	419, 567	45891
Vanceburg, KY	606	41179
Vancouver, WA	360	98660-98668, 98682-98687
Vandalia, IL	618	62471
Vandalia, OH	937	45377
Vandenberg AFB, CA	805	93437
Vanderbilt, MI	989	49795
Vandergrift, PA	724, 878	15690
Vansant, VA	276	24656
Vashon, WA	206	98013, 98070
Vassar, MI	989	48768-48769
Vega, TX	806	79092
Vega Alta, PR	787, 939	00692
Velva, ND	701	58790
Venice, CA	310, 424	90291-90296
Venice, FL	941	34284-34293
Ventura, CA	805	93001-93009
Verdi, NV	775	89439
Vergennes, VT	802	05491
Vermillion, SD	605	57069
Vernal, UT	435	84078-84079
Vernon, AL	205	35592
Vernon, CA	323	90058
Vernon, CT	860	06066
Vernon, IN	812	47282
Vernon, NJ	862, 973	07462
Vernon, NY	315	13476
Vernon, TX	940	76384-76385
Vernon Hills, IL	224, 847	60061
Vernonia, OR	503, 971	97064
Vero Beach, FL	772	32960-32969
Verona, MS	662	38879
Verona, NY	315	13478
Verona, PA	412, 878	15147
Verona, VA	540	24482
Verona, WI	608	53593
Versailles, IN	812	47042
Versailles, KY	859	40383-40386
Versailles, MO	573	65084
Vesta, VA	276	24177
Vestal, NY	607	13850-13851
Vevay, IN	812	47043
Vicksburg, MI	616	49097
Vicksburg, MS	601, 769	39180-39183
Victor, ID	208	83455
Victor, NY	585	14564
Victoria, MN	952	55386
Victoria, TX	361	77901-77905
Victoria, VA	434	23974
Vidalia, GA	912	30474-30475
Vidalia, LA	318	71373
Vienna, GA	229	31092
Vienna, IL	618	62995
Vienna, MO	573	65582
Vienna, OH	234, 330	44473
Vienna, VA	571, 703	22027, 22124, 22180-22185
Vienna, WV	304	26101, 26105
Viera, FL	321	32940, 32955
Villa Park, IL	331, 630	60181
Villanova, PA	484, 610	19085
Ville Platte, LA	337	70586
Vinalhaven, ME	207	04863
Vincennes, IN	812	47591
Vincent, AL	205	35178
Vineland, NJ	856	08360-08362
Vineyard Haven, MA	508, 774	02568, 02573
Vinita, OK	918	74301
Vinton, IA	319	52349
Vinton, LA	337	70668
Vinton, VA	540	24179
Virginia, IL	217	62691
Virginia, MN	218	55777, 55792
Virginia Beach, VA	757	23450-23471, 23479
Virginia City, MT	406	59755
Virginia City, NV	775	89440
Viroqua, WI	608	54665
Visalia, CA	559	93277-93279, 93290-93292
Vista, CA	760, 442	92083-92085
Vivian, LA	318	71082
Vonore, TN	423	37885
Voorhees, NJ	856	08043
Voorheesville, NY	518	12186

W

City	Area Code(s)	Zip Code(s)
Wabash, IN	260	46992
Wabasha, MN	651	55981
Wabasso, FL	772	32970
Waco, TX	254	76701-76716, 76795-76799
Waconia, MN	952	55375, 55387
Waddington, NY	315	13694
Wadena, MN	218	56482
Wadesboro, NC	704, 980	28170
Wadley, AL	256	36276
Wadley, GA	478	30477
Wadsworth, OH	234, 330	44281-44282
Wagoner, OK	918	74467, 74477
Wahoo, NE	402	68066
Wahpeton, ND	701	58074-58076
Waianae, HI	808	96792
Waikoloa, HI	808	96738
Wailea, HI	808	96753
Wailuku, HI	808	96793
Waimanalo, HI	808	96795
Waipahu, HI	808	96797
Waite Park, MN	320	56387-56388
Wakarusa, IN	574	46573
Wake Forest, NC	919	27587-27588
WaKeeney, KS	785	67672
Wakefield, MA	339, 781	01880
Wakefield, MI	906	49968
Wakefield, RI	401	02879-02883
Wakulla Springs, FL	850	32327
Walbridge, OH	419, 567	43465
Walcott, IA	563	52773
Walden, CO	970	80430, 80480
Walden, NY	845	12586
Waldorf, MD	301	20601-20604
Waldron, AR	479	72924, 72958
Wales, WI	262	53183
Waleska, GA	470, 770	30183
Walhalla, SC	864	29691
Walker, MI	616	49544
Walker, MN	218	56484
Walkerton, IN	574	46574
Wall, NJ	732, 848	07719
Wall, SD	605	57790
Walla Walla, WA	509	99362
Wallace, ID	208	83873-83874
Wallace, NC	910	28466
Wallace, SC	843	29596
Walland, TN	865	37886
Walled Lake, MI	248, 947	48390-48391
Waller, TX	281, 832	77484
Wallingford, CT	203	06492-06495
Wallingford, PA	484, 610	19086
Wallington, NJ	862, 973	07057
Wallkill, NY	845	12589
Walls, MS	662	38680, 38686
Walnut, CA	909	91788-91789, 91795
Walnut, IL	815	61376
Walnut Creek, CA	925	94595-94598
Walnut Creek, OH	234, 330	44687
Walnut Ridge, AR	870	72476
Walpole, MA	508, 774	02032, 02071, 02081
Walpole, NH	603	03608
Walsenburg, CO	719	81089
Walstonburg, NC	252	27888
Walterboro, SC	843	29488
Walters, OK	580	73572
Walthall, MS	662	39771
Waltham, MA	339, 781	02451-02455
Walthourville, GA	912	31333
Walton, IN	574	46994
Walton Hills, OH	440	44146
Walworth, WI	262	53184
Wamego, KS	785	66547
Wampsville, NY	315	13163
Wanamingo, MN	507	55983
Wanatah, IN	219	46390
Wantagh, NY	516	11793
Wapakoneta, OH	419, 567	45819, 45895
Wapato, WA	509	98951
Wapello, IA	319	52653
Wapiti, WY	307	82450
Wappingers Falls, NY	845	12590
Ward, CO	303, 720	80481
Ward Hill, MA	351, 978	01835
Warden, WA	509	98857
Ware, MA	413	01082
Wareham, MA	508, 774	02571
Warfordsburg, PA	301	17267
Warm Springs, GA	706, 762	31830
Warm Springs, MT	406	59756
Warm Springs, OR	541, 458	97761
Warm Springs, VA	540	24484
Warminster, PA	215, 267	18974, 18991
Warner, NH	603	03278
Warner, OK	918	74469
Warner Robins, GA	478	31088, 31093-31099
Warren, AR	870	71671
Warren, MI	586	48088-48093, 48397
Warren, MN	218	56762
Warren, NJ	908	07059
Warren, OH	234, 330	44481-44488
Warren, PA	814	16365-16369
Warren, RI	401	02885
Warren, VT	802	05674

*Partial list of zip codes, including main range

City	Area Code(s)	Zip Code(s)
Warrendale, PA	724, 878	15086, 15095-15096
Warrensburg, MO	660	64093
Warrensville Heights, OH	216	44122, 44128
Warrenton, GA	706, 762	30828
Warrenton, MO	636	63383
Warrenton, NC	252	27589
Warrenton, OR	503	97146
Warrenton, VA	540	20186-20188
Warrenville, IL	331, 630	60555
Warrington, PA	215, 267	18976
Warrior, AL	205	35180
Warroad, MN	218	56741, 56763
Warsaw, IN	574	46580-46582
Warsaw, KY	859	41095
Warsaw, MO	660	65355
Warsaw, NY	585	14569
Warsaw, NC	910	28398
Warsaw, VA	804	22572
Wartburg, TN	423	37887
Warwick, NY	845	10990
Warwick, RI	401	02818, 02886-02889
Wasco, IL	331, 630	60183
Waseca, MN	507	56093
Washburn, MO	417	65772
Washburn, ND	701	58577
Washburn, WI	715, 534	54891
Washington, CT	860	06777, 06793-06794
Washington, DC	202	20001-20020, 20024-20082*
Washington, GA	706, 762	30673
Washington, IL	309	61571
Washington, IN	812	47501
Washington, IA	319	52353
Washington, KS	785	66968
Washington, MO	636	63090
Washington, NJ	908	07882
Washington, NC	252	27889
Washington, PA	724, 878	15301
Washington, VA	540	22747
Washington, WV	304	26181
Washington Court House, OH	740	43160
Washington Green, CT	860	06793
Washington Island, WI	920	54246
Washington Navy Yard, DC	202	20374-20376, 20388-20391*
Washingtonville, NY	845	10992
Washougal, WA	360	98671
Wasilla, AK	907	99652-99654, 99687, 99694
Wassaic, NY	845	12592
Watauga, TX	682, 817	76148
Water Valley, MS	662	38965
Waterbury, CT	203	06701-06712, 06716, 06720*
Waterbury, VT	802	05671, 05676
Waterbury Center, VT	802	05677
Waterford, CT	860	06385-06386
Waterford, MI	248, 947	48327-48330
Waterford, NY	518	12188
Waterford, PA	814	16441
Waterford, WI	262	53185
Waterloo, IL	618	62298
Waterloo, IN	260	46793
Waterloo, IA	319	50701-50707, 50799
Waterloo, NY	315	13165
Waterloo, WI	920	53594
Watertown, CT	860	06779, 06795
Watertown, MA	617, 857	02471-02472, 02477
Watertown, MN	952	55388
Watertown, NY	315	13601-13603
Watertown, SD	605	57201
Watertown, WI	920	53094, 53098
Waterville, ME	207	04901-04903
Waterville, OH	419, 567	43566
Waterville, WA	509	98858
Waterville Valley, NH	603	03215
Watervliet, NY	518	12189
Watford City, ND	701	58854
Watkins Glen, NY	607	14891
Watkinsville, GA	706, 762	30677
Watonga, OK	580	73772
Watrous, NM	505	87750-87753
Watseka, IL	815	60970
Watsonville, CA	831	95076-95077
Wauchula, FL	863	33873
Waucoma, IA	563	52171
Wauconda, IL	224, 847	60084
Waukegan, IL	224, 847	60079, 60085-60087
Waukesha, WI	262	53146, 53151, 53186-53189
Waukon, IA	563	52172
Waunakee, WI	608	53597

City	Area Code(s)	Zip Code(s)
Waupaca, WI	715, 534	54981
Waupun, WI	920	53963
Wauregan, CT	860	06387
Waurika, OK	580	73573
Wausau, WI	715, 534	54401-54403
Wauseon, OH	419, 567	43567
Wautoma, WI	920	54982
Wauwatosa, WI	414	53210-53213, 53222, 53226
Waverly, FL	863	33877
Waverly, IA	319	50677
Waverly, OH	740	45690
Waverly, TN	931	37185
Waverly, VA	804	23890-23891
Wawaka, IN	260	46794
Waxahachie, TX	469, 972	75165-75168
Waycross, GA	912	31501-31503
Wayland, MA	508, 774	01778
Wayland, MI	616	49348
Wayland, NY	585	14572
Waymart, PA	570	18472
Wayne, MI	734	48184
Wayne, NE	402	68787
Wayne, NJ	862, 973	07470, 07474-07477
Wayne, PA	484, 610	19080, 19087-19089
Wayne, WV	304	25570
Waynesboro, GA	706, 762	30830
Waynesboro, MS	601, 769	39367
Waynesboro, PA	717	17268
Waynesboro, TN	931	38485
Waynesboro, VA	540	22980
Waynesburg, PA	724, 878	15370
Waynesville, MO	573	65583
Waynesville, NC	828	28738, 28785-28786
Wayzata, MN	763, 952	55391
Weatherford, OK	580	73096
Weatherford, TX	682, 817	76085-76088
Weaverville, CA	530	96093
Weaverville, NC	828	28787
Webb City, MO	417	64870
Webberville, MI	517	48892
Webster, MA	508, 774	01570
Webster, NY	585	14580
Webster, SD	605	57274
Webster, TX	281, 832	77598
Webster City, IA	515	50595
Webster Groves, MO	314	63119
Webster Springs, WV	304	26288
Wedowee, AL	256	36278
Weed, CA	530	96094
Weehawken, NJ	201, 551	07086-07087
Weidman, MI	989	48893
Weimar, CA	530	95736
Weirsdale, FL	352	32195
Weirton, WV	304	26062
Weiser, ID	208	83672
Welch, WV	304	24801
Welches, OR	503, 971	97067
Weldon, NC	252	27890
Wellesley, MA	339, 781	02457, 02481-02482
Wellesley Hills, MA	339, 781	02481
Wellesley Island, NY	315	13640
Wellfleet, MA	508, 774	02667
Wellington, CO	970	80549
Wellington, FL	561	33414, 33421, 33467
Wellington, KS	620	67152
Wellington, OH	440	44090
Wellington, TX	806	79095
Wells, ME	207	04090
Wells, MN	507	56097
Wells, NV	775	89835
Wellsboro, PA	570	16901
Wellsburg, NY	570	14894
Wellsburg, WV	304	26070
Wellsville, NY	585	14895
Wellsville, OH	234, 330	43968
Wellton, AZ	928	85356
Wenatchee, WA	509	98801-98802, 98807
Wendell, NC	919	27591
Wenham, MA	351, 978	01984
Wentworth, NC	336	27375
Wernersville, PA	484, 610	19565
Weslaco, TX	956	78596-78599
Wesley Chapel, FL	813	33543-33544
Wessington Springs, SD	605	57382
Wesson, MS	601, 769	39191
West Alexandria, OH	937	45381
West Allis, WI	414	53214, 53219, 53227

City	Area Code(s)	Zip Code(s)
West Atlantic City, NJ	609	08232
West Babylon, NY	631	11704-11707
West Barnstable, MA	508, 774	02668
West Bath, ME	207	04530
West Belmar, NJ	732, 848	07719
West Bend, IA	515	50597
West Bend, WI	262	53090, 53095
West Bethesda, MD	301	20817, 20827
West Bloomfield, MI	248, 947	48322-48325
West Boylston, MA	508, 774	01583
West Branch, IA	319	52358
West Branch, MI	989	48661
West Brentwood, NY	631	11717
West Bridgewater, MA	508, 774	02379
West Burlington, IA	319	52655
West Caldwell, NJ	862, 973	07006-07007
West Carrollton, OH	937	45439, 45449
West Chester, OH	513	45069-45071
West Chester, PA	484, 610	19380-19383
West Chicago, IL	331, 630	60185-60186
West Columbia, SC	803	29033, 29169-29172
West Columbia, TX	979	77486
West Conshohocken, PA	484, 610	19428
West Covina, CA	626	91790-91793
West Deptford, NJ	856	08066
West Des Moines, IA	515	50265-50266, 50398
West Dover, VT	802	05351, 05356
West Dundee, IL	224, 847	60118
West Falmouth, MA	508, 774	02574
West Fargo, ND	701	58078
West Frankfort, IL	618	62896
West Franklin, NH	603	03235
West Glacier, MT	406	59921, 59936
West Greenwich, RI	401	02817
West Grove, PA	484, 610	19390
West Hartford, CT	860	06107-06110, 06117-06119*
West Haven, CT	203	06516
West Haverstraw, NY	845	10993
West Hazleton, PA	570	18202
West Helena, AR	870	72390
West Hempstead, NY	516	11552
West Henrietta, NY	585	14586
West Hills, CA	818	91304-91308
West Hollywood, CA	310, 323, 424	90038, 90046-90048, 90069
West Homestead, PA	412, 878	15120
West Hurley, NY	845	12491
West Islip, NY	631	11795
West Jefferson, OH	614	43162
West Jordan, UT	801, 385	84084, 84088
West Kennebunk, ME	207	04094
West Kingston, RI	401	02892
West Lafayette, IN	765	47906-47907, 47996
West Lafayette, OH	740	43845
West Lebanon, IN	765	47991
West Lebanon, NH	603	03784
West Liberty, IA	319	52776
West Liberty, KY	606	41472
West Liberty, WV	304	26074
West Long Branch, NJ	732, 848	07764
West Los Angeles, CA	310, 424	90025
West Mansfield, OH	937	43358
West Melbourne, FL	321	32904, 32912
West Memphis, AR	870	72301-72303
West Middlesex, PA	724, 878	16159
West Mifflin, PA	412, 878	15122-15123, 15236
West Milford, NJ	862, 973	07480
West Monroe, LA	318	71291-71294
West New York, NJ	201, 551	07093
West Nyack, NY	845	10994
West Olive, MI	616	49460
West Orange, NJ	862, 973	07052
West Palm Beach, FL	561	33401-33422
West Park, NY	845	12493
West Paterson, NJ	862, 973	07424
West Pittsburg, PA	724, 878	16160
West Plains, MO	417	65775-65776
West Point, GA	706, 762	31833
West Point, MS	662	39773
West Point, NE	402	68788
West Point, NY	845	10996-10997
West Point, PA	215, 267	19486
West Point, VA	804	23181
West Redding, CT	203	06896
West Roxbury, MA	617, 857	02132
West Sacramento, CA	916	95605, 95691, 95798-95799
West Saint Paul, MN	651	55107, 55118
West Salem, OH	419, 567	44287

*Partial list of zip codes, including main range

City	Area Code(s)	Zip Code(s)
West Salem, WI	608	54669
West Sayville, NY	631	11796
West Seneca, NY	716	14206, 14210, 14218-14220*
West Springfield, MA	413	01089-01090
West Tawakoni, TX	903	75474
West Terre Haute, IN	812	47885
West Trenton, NJ	609	08628
West Union, IA	563	52175
West Union, OH	937	45693
West Union, WV	304	26456
West Valley, NY	716	14171
West Valley City, UT	801, 385	84118-84120, 84128
West Warren, MA	413	01092
West Warwick, RI	401	02893
West Yellowstone, MT	406	59758
Westampton, NJ	609	08060
Westborough, MA	508, 774	01580-01582
Westbrook, CT	860	06498
Westbrook, ME	207	04092, 04098
Westbury, NY	516	11568, 11590-11597
Westby, WI	608	54667
Westchester, IL	708	60154
Westcliffe, CO	719	81252
Westerlo, NY	518	12055, 12193
Westerly, RI	401	02808, 02891
Westerville, OH	614	43081-43082, 43086
Westfield, IN	317	46074
Westfield, MA	413	01085-01086
Westfield, NJ	908	07090-07091
Westfield, NY	716	14787
Westfield, PA	814	16927, 16950
Westfield, VT	802	05874
Westfield Center, OH	234, 330	44251
Westford, MA	351, 978	01886
Westhampton Beach, NY	631	11978
Westlake, LA	337	70669
Westlake, OH	440	44145
Westlake, TX	682, 817	76262
Westlake Village, CA	805, 818	91359-91363
Westland, MI	734	48185-48186
Westminster, CA	714	92683-92685
Westminster, CO	303, 720	80003-80005, 80020-80021*
Westminster, MD	410	21157-21158
Westminster, MA	351, 978	01441, 01473
Westminster Station, VT	802	05159
Westmont, IL	331, 630	60559-60561
Westmont, NJ	856	08108
Westmoreland, KS	785	66426, 66549
Weston, CT	203	06883
Weston, FL	754, 954	33326-33327, 33331-33332
Weston, MA	339, 781	02493
Weston, MO	816	64098
Weston, WV	304	26452
Westover, MD	410	21871, 21890
Westport, CT	203	06880-06881, 06888-06889
Westport, MA	508, 774	02790
Westport, WA	360	98595
Westville, IN	574	46391
Westwego, LA	504	70094-70096
Westwood, KS	913	66205
Westwood, MA	339, 781	02090
Westwood, NJ	201, 551	07675-07677
Wethersfield, CT	860	06109, 06129
Wetumpka, AL	334	36092-36093
Wewahitchka, FL	850	32465
Wewoka, OK	405	74884
Wexford, PA	724, 878	15090
Weyers Cave, VA	540	24486
Weymouth, MA	339, 781	02188-02191
Wharton, TX	979	77488
Whately, MA	413	01093, 01373
Wheat Ridge, CO	303, 720	80002, 80033-80034, 80212*
Wheatland, IA	563	52777
Wheatland, PA	724, 878	16161
Wheatland, WY	307	82201
Wheaton, IL	331, 630	60187-60189
Wheaton, MD	301	20902, 20906, 20915
Wheaton, MN	320	56296
Wheeler, TX	806	79096
Wheeling, IL	224, 847	60090
Wheeling, WV	304	26003
Whippany, NJ	862, 973	07981-07983, 07999
Whiskeytown, CA	530	96095
White Bear Lake, MN	651	55110, 55115
White Castle, LA	225	70788
White City, OR	541, 458	97503
White Cloud, MI	231	49349
White Deer, PA	570	17887
White Haven, PA	570	18661
White Lake, MI	248, 947	48383-48386
White Oak, PA	412, 878	15131
White Oak, TX	903	75693
White Pigeon, MI	616	49099
White Plains, NY	914	10601-10610, 10650
White River, SD	605	57579
White River Junction, VT	802	05001, 05009
White Sands, NM	505	88002
White Sands Missile Range, NM	505	88002
White Stone, VA	804	22578
White Sulphur Springs, MT	406	59645
White Sulphur Springs, WV	304	24986
Whitefish, MT	406	59937
Whitehall, MI	231	49461-49463
Whitehall, PA	484, 610	18052
Whitehall, WI	715, 534	54773
Whitehouse, NJ	908	08888
Whitehouse, OH	419, 567	43571
Whitehouse Station, NJ	908	08889
Whitesburg, KY	606	41858
Whitestone, NY	347, 718	11357
Whiteville, NC	910	28472
Whiteville, TN	901	38075
Whitewater, WI	262	53190
Whitfield, MS	601, 769	39193
Whiting, IN	219	46394
Whiting, NJ	732, 848	08759
Whitinsville, MA	508, 774	01588
Whitley City, KY	606	42653
Whitsett, NC	336	27377
Whittier, AK	907	99693
Whittier, CA	562	90601-90612
Wibaux, MT	406	59353
Wichita, KS	316	67201-67236, 67251, 67256*
Wichita Falls, TX	940	76301-76311
Wickenburg, AZ	928	85358, 85390
Wickliffe, KY	270	42087
Wickliffe, OH	440	44092
Wiggins, MS	601, 769	39577
Wilber, NE	402	68465
Wilberforce, OH	937	45384
Wilbraham, MA	413	01095
Wilburton, OK	918	74578
Wilder, KY	859	41071, 41076
Wilder, VT	802	05088
Wildomar, CA	951	92595
Wildorado, TX	806	79098
Wildwood, FL	352	34785
Wildwood, NJ	609	08260
Wildwood Crest, NJ	609	08260
Wilkes-Barre, PA	570	18701-18711, 18761-18769*
Wilkesboro, NC	336	28697
Willard, OH	419, 567	44888-44890
Willard, UT	435	84340
Willcox, AZ	520	85643-85644
Williams Bay, WI	262	53191
Williamsburg, IA	319	52361
Williamsburg, KY	606	40769
Williamsburg, OH	513	45176
Williamsburg, PA	814	16693
Williamsburg, VA	757	23081, 23185-23188
Williamson, WV	304	25661
Williamsport, IN	765	47993
Williamsport, MD	301	21795
Williamsport, PA	570	17701-17705
Williamston, MI	517	48895
Williamston, NC	252	27892
Williamstown, KY	859	41097
Williamstown, MA	413	01267
Williamstown, NJ	856	08094
Williamstown, WV	304	26187
Williamsville, NY	716	14221, 14231
Willimantic, CT	860	06226
Willingboro, NJ	609	08046
Willis, TX	936	77318, 77378
Williston, FL	352	32696
Williston, ND	701	58801-58802
Williston, SC	803	29853
Williston, VT	802	05495
Willits, CA	707	95429, 95490
Willmar, MN	320	56201
Willoughby, OH	440	44094-44097
Willow Grove, PA	215, 267	19090
Willow Springs, MO	417	65793
Willow Street, PA	717	17584
Willowbrook, IL	331, 630	60527
Willows, CA	530	95988
Willsboro, NY	518	12996
Wilmerding, PA	412, 878	15148
Wilmette, IL	224, 847	60091
Wilmington, CA	310, 424	90744, 90748
Wilmington, DE	302	19801-19810, 19850, 19880*
Wilmington, MA	978	01887
Wilmington, NC	910	28401-28412
Wilmington, OH	937	45177
Wilmore, KY	859	40390
Wilson, NY	716	14172
Wilson, NC	252	27893-27896
Wilson, WY	307	83014
Wilsonville, OR	503, 971	97070
Wilton, CT	203	06897
Wilton, IA	563	52778
Wilton, ME	207	04294
Wilton, NH	603	03086
Wilton, NY	518	12831
Wimberley, TX	512	78676
Winamac, IN	574	46996
Winchester, IL	217	62694
Winchester, IN	765	47394
Winchester, KY	859	40391-40392
Winchester, MA	339, 781	01890
Winchester, NH	603	03470
Winchester, TN	931	37398
Winchester, VA	540	22601-22604, 22638
Wind Gap, PA	484, 610	18091
Windber, PA	814	15963
Winder, GA	470, 770	30680
Windermere, FL	321, 407	34786
Windham, NH	603	03087
Windom, MN	507	56101, 56118
Window Rock, AZ	928	86515
Windsor, CA	707	95492
Windsor, CT	860	06006, 06095
Windsor, NC	252	27983
Windsor, VT	802	05089
Windsor, VA	757	23487
Windsor, WI	608	53598
Windsor Locks, CT	860	06096
Winfield, AL	205	35594
Winfield, IL	331, 630	60190
Winfield, KS	620	67156
Winfield, WV	304	25213
Wingate, NC	704, 980	28174
Winlock, WA	360	98596
Winn, ME	207	04495
Winnebago, WI	920	54985
Winneconne, WI	920	54986
Winnemucca, NV	775	89445-89446
Winner, SD	605	57580
Winnetka, CA	818	91306, 91396
Winnett, MT	406	59084-59087
Winnfield, LA	318	71483
Winnsboro, LA	318	71295
Winnsboro, SC	803	29180
Winona, MN	507	55987-55988
Winona, MS	662	38967
Winona, MO	573	65588
Winona Lake, IN	219	46590
Winooski, VT	802	05404
Winslow, AZ	928	86047
Winslow, ME	207	04901
Winslow, NJ	609	08095
Winsted, CT	860	06063, 06094, 06098
Winston, OR	541, 458	97496
Winston-Salem, NC	336	27101-27109, 27113-27117*
Winter Garden, FL	321, 407	34777-34778, 34787
Winter Haven, FL	863	33880-33888
Winter Park, CO	970	80482
Winter Park, FL	321, 407	32789-32793
Winters, CA	530	95694
Winters, TX	915	79567
Winterset, IA	515	50273
Wintersville, OH	740	43952-43953
Winterthur, DE	302	19735
Winthrop, ME	207	04364
Winthrop, WA	509	98862
Winton, NC	252	27986
Wiscasset, ME	207	04578
Wisconsin Dells, WI	608	53965
Wisconsin Rapids, WI	715, 534	54494-54495
Wisdom, MT	406	59761
Wise, VA	276	24293

*Partial list of zip codes, including main range

City	Area Code(s)	Zip Code(s)
Wixom, MI	248, 947	48393
Woburn, MA	781	01801, 01806-01808, 01813*
Wolcott, CT	203	06716
Wolcott, IN	219	47995
Wolcott, NY	315	14590
Wolf, WY	307	82844
Wolf Point, MT	406	59201
Wolfe City, TX	903	75496
Wolfeboro, NH	603	03894
Womelsdorf, PA	484, 610	19567
Wood Dale, IL	331, 630	60191
Wood River, IL	618	62095
Woodbine, GA	912	31569
Woodbine, IA	712	51579
Woodbine, MD	301	21797
Woodbourne, NY	845	12788
Woodbridge, CT	203	06525
Woodbridge, NJ	732, 848	07095
Woodbridge, VA	571, 703	22191-22195
Woodburn, IN	260	46797
Woodburn, OR	503, 971	97071
Woodbury, CT	203	06798
Woodbury, MN	651	55125, 55129
Woodbury, NJ	856	08096-08097
Woodbury, NY	516	11797
Woodbury, TN	615	37190
Woodcliff Lake, NJ	201, 551	07677
Woodhaven, MI	734	48183
Woodhaven, NY	347, 718	11421
Woodinville, WA	425	98072
Woodland, CA	530	95695, 95776
Woodland, PA	814	16881
Woodland, WA	360	98674
Woodland Hills, CA	818	91302-91303, 91364-91367*
Woodridge, IL	331, 630	60517, 60540
Woodruff, SC	864	29388
Woodruff, WI	715, 534	54568
Woods Cross, UT	801, 385	84010, 84087
Woods Hole, MA	508, 774	02543
Woodsfield, OH	740	43793
Woodside, CA	650	94062
Woodside, NY	347, 718	11377
Woodstock, CT	860	06281
Woodstock, GA	470, 770	30188-30189
Woodstock, IL	815	60098
Woodstock, NY	845	12498
Woodstock, VT	802	05091
Woodstock, VA	540	22664
Woodstown, NJ	856	08098
Woodville, MS	601, 769	39669
Woodville, OH	419, 567	43469
Woodville, TX	409	75979, 75990
Woodville, WI	715, 534	54028
Woodward, IA	515	50276
Woodward, OK	580	73801-73802
Woolrich, PA	570	17779
Woonsocket, RI	401	02895
Woonsocket, SD	605	57385
Wooster, OH	234, 330	44691
Worcester, MA	508, 774	01601-01615, 01653-01655
Worcester, PA	484, 610	19490
Worland, WY	307	82401, 82430
Wormleysburg, PA	717	17043
Worth, IL	708	60482
Worthington, MN	507	56187
Worthington, OH	614	43085
Wrangell, AK	907	99929
Wray, CO	970	80758
Wrens, GA	706, 762	30818, 30833
Wrentham, MA	508, 774	02070, 02093
Wright, WY	307	82732
Wright City, MO	636	63390
Wright-Patterson AFB, OH	937	45433
Wrightstown, NJ	609	08562
Wrightsville, AR	501	72183
Wrightsville, GA	478	31096
Wrightsville, PA	717	17368
Wrightsville Beach, NC	910	28480
Wyalusing, PA	570	18853
Wyandanch, NY	631	11798
Wyandotte, MI	734	48192
Wyckoff, NJ	201, 551	07481
Wye Mills, MD	410	21679
Wylliesburg, VA	434	23976
Wyncote, PA	215, 267	19095
Wyndmoor, PA	215, 267	19038
Wynne, AR	870	72396
Wynnewood, PA	484, 610	19096
Wyoming, MI	616	49418, 49508-49509, 49548
Wyoming, MN	651	55092
Wyoming, PA	570	18644
Wyomissing, PA	484, 610	19610
Wysox, PA	570	18854
Wytheville, VA	276	24382

X

City	Area Code(s)	Zip Code(s)
Xenia, OH	937	45385

Y

City	Area Code(s)	Zip Code(s)
Yabucoa, PR	787, 939	00767
Yacolt, WA	360	98675
Yadkinville, NC	336	27055
Yakima, WA	509	98901-98909
Yakutat, AK	907	99689
Yale, IA	641	50277
Yanceyville, NC	336	27379
Yankton, SD	605	57078-57079
Yardley, PA	215, 267	19067
Yardville, NJ	609	08620
Yarmouth, ME	207	04096
Yates Center, KS	620	66783
Yazoo City, MS	662	39194
Yeadon, PA	484, 610	19050
Yellow Springs, OH	937	45387
Yellowstone National Park, WY	307	82190
Yellville, AR	870	72687
Yelm, WA	360	98597
Yerington, NV	775	89447
Yoakum, TX	361	77995
Yonkers, NY	914	10701-10710
Yorba Linda, CA	714	92885-92887
York, AL	205	36925
York, NE	402	68467
York, PA	717	17315, 17401-17407, 17415
York, SC	803	29745
York Harbor, ME	207	03910-03911
York Haven, PA	717	17370
York Springs, PA	717	17372
Yorktown, VA	757	23690-23693
Yorktown Heights, NY	914	10598
Yorkville, IL	331, 630	60560
Yorkville, NY	315	13495
Young America, MN	952	55394-55399, 55473, 55550*
Young Harris, GA	706, 762	30582
Youngstown, OH	234, 330	44501-44515, 44555, 44598*
Youngsville, LA	337	70592
Youngsville, NC	919	27596
Youngsville, PA	814	16371
Youngwood, PA	724, 878	15697
Yountville, CA	707	94599
Ypsilanti, MI	734	48197-48198
Yreka, CA	530	96097
Yuba City, CA	530	95991-95993
Yucaipa, CA	909	92399
Yucca Valley, CA	760, 442	92284-92286
Yukon, OK	405	73085, 73099
Yuma, AZ	928	85364-85369
Yuma, CO	970	80759

Z

City	Area Code(s)	Zip Code(s)
Zachary, LA	225	70791
Zachow, WI	715, 534	54182
Zanesville, OH	740	43701-43702
Zapata, TX	956	78076
Zebulon, GA	470, 770	30295
Zebulon, NC	919	27597
Zeeland, MI	616	49464
Zelienople, PA	724, 878	16063
Zellwood, FL	321, 407	32798
Zenda, WI	262	53195
Zephyrhills, FL	813	33539-33544
Zillah, WA	509	98953
Zion, IL	224, 847	60099
Zionsville, IN	317	46077
Zionsville, PA	484, 610	18092
Zolfo Springs, FL	863	33890
Zumbrota, MN	507	55992

**Partial list of zip codes, including main range*

Index to Classified Headings

Citations given in this index refer to the subject headings under which listings are organized in the Classified Section. The page numbers given for each citation refer to the page on which a particular subject category begins rather than to a specific company or organization name. "See" and "See also" references are included to help in the identification of appropriate subject categories.

A

B

D

E

Index citations refer to **page numbers.**

G

I

M

N

O

P

Q

R

S

T

U

X

Y

Z

How To Use This Directo

Illustrated here are the various symbols, terms, and other features typically found on the pages of this directory, t concise explanations of what those features represent. For more detailed information about what's included in t please refer to the introductory section also titled "How To Use This Directory."

PLEASE NOTE: Listing data printed here are sample purposes only. Consult directory for actual entries.

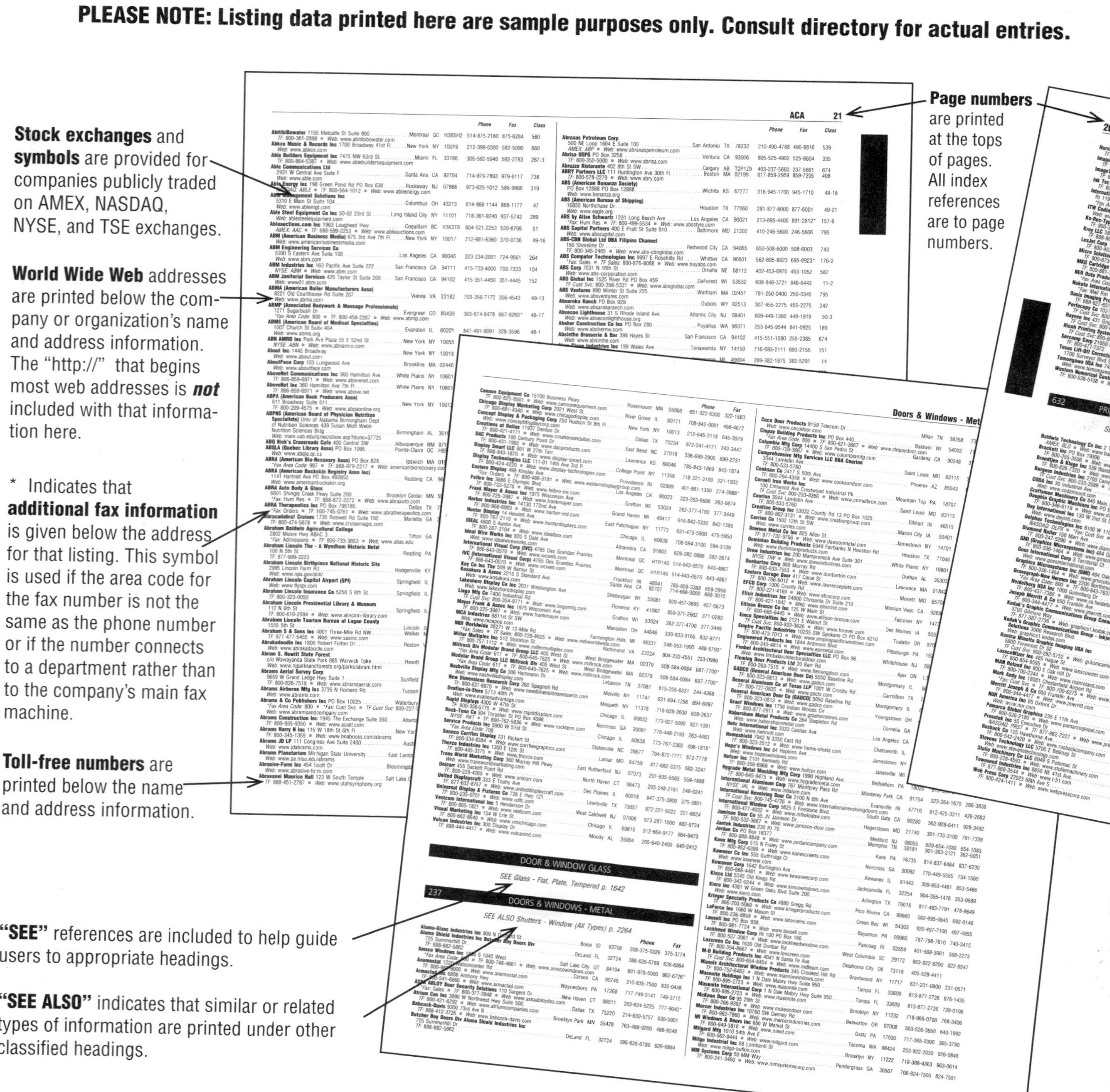
Stock exchanges and **symbols** are provided for companies publicly traded on AMEX, NASDAQ, NYSE, and TSE exchanges.
World Wide Web addresses are printed below the company or organization's name and address information. The "http://" that begins most web addresses is ***not*** included with that information here.
* Indicates that **additional fax information** is given below the address for that listing. This symbol is used if the area code for the fax number is not the same as the phone number or if the number connects to a department rather than to the company's main fax machine.
Toll-free numbers are printed below the name and address information.
"SEE" references are included to help guide users to appropriate headings.
"SEE ALSO" indicates that similar or related types of information are printed under other classified headings.
Page numbers are printed at the tops of pages. All index references are to page numbers.
ACA 21
Doors & Windows - Met
DOOR & WINDOW GLASS
SEE Glass - Flat, Plate, Tempered p. 1642
237 DOORS & WINDOWS - METAL
SEE ALSO Shutters - Window (All Types) p. 2264
632